2016 Higher Education Directory®

Published by

Higher Education Publications, Inc.

Edited by

Mary Pat Rodenhouse

Editor Emerita

Jeanne M. Burke

Reston, Virginia

2016

2016 Edition

Higher Education Publications, Inc.
1801 Robert Fulton Drive, Suite 555
Reston, VA 20191-5499
(888) 349-7715
(571) 313-0478
FAX (571) 313-0526
Email: info@hepinc.com
Internet address: www.hepinc.com

Carnegie classification codes with permission from The Carnegie Foundation for the Advancement of Teaching.

Internet addresses (URL's) were originally drawn from lists maintained by Washington and Lee University and the University of North Carolina-Chapel Hill and through the annual survey sent out by Higher Education Publications, Inc.

Printed in the United States of America

ISBN-10: 0-914927-75-2; ISBN-13: 978-0-914927-75-4
ISSN 0736-0797
Library of Congress Catalogue Card Number: 83-641119
Library of Congress Cataloging-in Publication Data

HEP. . . Higher Education Directory®
Reston, VA; Higher Education Publications.
V.: 28cm
Annual
Began with issue for 1983.

A directory of accredited postsecondary, degree-granting institutions in the U.S., its possessions and territories accredited by regional, national, professional and specialized agencies recognized as accrediting bodies by the U.S. Secretary of Education and the Council for Higher Education Accreditation (CHEA) which honors recognition provided by the former Council on Postsecondary Accreditation (COPA)/Commission on Recognition of Postsecondary Accreditation (CORPA)
Description based on 2015.
Cover title: 2016 Higher Education Directory®
Spine title: 2016 Higher Education Directory® Thirty-fourth Edition

ISSN 0736-0797 = The Higher Education Directory®.

1. Education, Higher—United States—Directories.
2. Recognized accrediting agencies and associations—United States—Directories.
3. Acronyms, explanatory notes and symbols—United States—Directories.
4. Institution changes (additions, deletions, mergers and name changes)—United States—Directories.
5. Administrative officers, titles and title codes—United States—Directories.
6. United States Department of Education offices, statewide agencies for higher education and educational associations (and consortia)—United States—Directories.
7. Religious affiliation by denomination.
8. Carnegie classification codes.
9. Statistics.
10. Universities and colleges—United States—Directories.
11. College administrators alphabetical listing, phone numbers—United States—Directories.
12. Regional, national, professional and specialized accreditation alphabetical listing—United States—Directories.
13. Institutional FICE & Unit ID Number listing—United States—Directories.
14. Institutional alphabetical listing—United States—Directories.

I. Higher Education Publications, Inc.
II. Title: Higher Education Directory®.

L901.E34 378.73-dc19 83-641119 AACR 2 MARC-S

Table of Contents

Acknowledgments

Thirty-three years ago, Higher Education Publications, Inc. was formed to produce a directory to succeed the Department of Education's *Education Directory: Colleges and Universities*.

When we undertook the *Higher Education Directory* project, we worked toward three main goals: To publish accurate data, to make the directory more usable, and to have the directory ready for distribution much earlier in the academic year.

We continue to meet these objectives and more, while keeping the changing landscape of reference publishing in mind. In 2014, we modified our definition of branch campuses to conform to the definition used by the United States Department of Education (34 CFR §600.2). As a result, we added or reclassified over 1,400 institutional listings. Due to space limitations in the printed directory, we list limited information on these additional branch campuses, but more detailed information is available online with HED-Connect.

Our thanks to the thousands of people who have supplied us the necessary data contained in the directory. Over this past year we have had a response/update rate of 99.5% from main campuses—truly outstanding! We are most appreciative of the many subscribers who have supported us in our efforts to bring you the most accurate and current information available. And, a special thanks to all of you who suggest improvements to our directory.

We continue to work on a tight schedule starting in mid-June to distribution in November—especially when you consider the complexity and increase in the size of the database.

The accuracy and completeness of the contents of the 2016 edition was assured by a group of editors, updating and proofing specialists including Mary Pat Rodenhouse, Jodi Mondragon, Emmy Brown, Jackie Hafner, Doris Jean, Ebony Neal and Fred Hafner. Barbara Herrman handled our typesetting. Mark Schreiber managed the HED-Connect update system and the database.

You may be familiar with our Website, but if you have not yet visited it, I encourage you to go to www.hepinc.com. The site features the latest news on higher education, accreditations and administrative changes along with many helpful resources. Also, please visit our new LinkedIn and Facebook pages. We feel that our increased Internet and social media presence will help us to continue to meet the goals we established for ourselves thirty-three years ago—to provide you with the most authoritative, timely and accurate information on the higher education community.

Frederick F. Hafner
Publisher

Reston, Virginia

Foreword

The 2016 edition of the *Higher Education Directory®* contains listings of accredited, degree-granting institutions of postsecondary education in the United States and its territories.

Criteria for Listing in this Directory

To be listed in this Directory, an institution must meet the following guidelines:

(1) They are degree-granting (legally authorized to offer and are offering a program of college-level studies leading toward a degree[1]);
(2) They have submitted the information required for listing; and
(3) They meet one of the following criteria for listing:
   - A. The institution is accredited at the college level by an accrediting agency that is recognized by the U.S. Secretary of Education;
   - B. The institution holds pre-accredited status with an accrediting agency recognized by the U.S. Secretary of Education whose recognition includes the pre-accreditation status;
   - C. The institution is accredited at the college level by an accrediting agency recognized by the Council for Higher Education Accreditation (CHEA).

"College level" means a postsecondary associate, baccalaureate, post-baccalaureate, or rabbinical education program.

Verification of Accreditations

Verification of each accreditation for all institutions was done by comparing the accreditation against the current Directory (and updated lists) for each respective regional, national, professional and specialized association or agency, along with telephone calls to numerous accrediting associations whenever there was a question of accuracy. Over 22,000 accreditations were verified through September 2015.

The reader is reminded that many institutions have programs which may not be recognized by a professional or specialized association, but are considered fine programs. The institutions may or may not have sought such recognition.

General Organization of the Directory

Our approach to the organization of the material is to make the desired information readable and easy to find. There are four indexes which are cross-referenced to the main institutional listing.

A. Prologue
   1. Accrediting agencies with addresses. Regional accrediting commissions are listed alphabetically while national, professional and specialized bodies are listed alphabetically under headings showing their specialties.
   2. Acronyms used in the Directory for accrediting bodies are listed alphabetically.
   3. Explanatory notes and symbols.
   4. U.S. postal abbreviations of states.
   5. Institution changes.
   6. Administrative officers' description and job codes.
   7. U.S. Department of Education offices.
   8. Statewide agencies of higher education.
   9. Higher education associations.
   10. Consortia of institutions of higher education.
   11. Association name index.
   12. Religious affiliation by denomination.
   13. Carnegie classification codes.
   14. Statistical data.

B. College and university listings by state with institutional characteristics and administrative officers.
   1. Institution Name. If an * appears before the institution's name, it is a part of a system. A line between institutions separates two systems.
   2. Alpha Code. The first institution listed on a page is coded (A), the second (B), etc. The Administrators' index is also coded to enable the reader to locate the desired institution quickly.
   3. Address.
   4. County.
   5. FICE Identification. This was the Federal Interagency Commission on Education number originally assigned by the Department of Education. We continue to use the term FICE. However, the Department of Education in their Office of Student Financial Assistance uses OPEID, Office of Postsecondary Education Identification. OPEID consists of the first six digits of the FICE plus two more digits indicating branch campuses. Numbers beginning with 66 are for accredited institutions for which we cannot locate a FICE or OPEID number. These are identification numbers only.
   6. Telephone Number.
   7. Unit ID Number. A unique number developed by the National Center for Education Statistics (NCES) for the Education Department's IPEDS Reports.
   8. Carnegie Classification Code. (see page **xlix**)
   9. Main FAX Number.
   10. School Calendar.
   11. URL (Universal Resource Locator).
   12. Date Established.
   13. Annual Tuition & Fees for 2015-16 school year.
   14. Fall 2014 Enrollment. Head count (not FTE) in degree programs as reported on the latest IPEDS survey.
   15. Type of Student Body.
   16. Affiliation or Control.
   17. IRS Status.
   18. Highest Degree Offered.
   19. Program. This is the general type of education offered.
   20. Accreditation (see page **vi**). **N.B. Institutional accreditation is in bold face.**
   21. Administrative and academic officers with job classification code (see page **xxvii** for descriptions).
   22. Non-system branch campuses. The names of these campuses are in italic type and their listings are shortened. Non-system branch campuses are listed if they are identified by the parent institutions' accrediting organization as a branch campus.

C. Index of administrators is an alphabetical listing of all the administrators with their most direct phone number and E-mail address. The page and reference letter indicate the page on which the administrator's institution listing begins.

D. Index of regional, national, professional and specialized accreditation alphabetically by state. This index standardizes and simplifies reviewing of the 142 accrediting classifications.

E. FICE number index. Numeric listing of FICE number and school.

F. Alphabetic index of institutions.

---

[1]The *Higher Education Directory®* lists degree-granting institutions approved by regional, national, professional or specialized accrediting agencies.

Accrediting Agencies

The following regional, national, professional and specialized accrediting agencies are recognized by the U.S. Secretary of Education or the Council for Higher Education Accreditation (CHEA). The U.S. Department of Education (USDE) dates specified are the date of initial listing as a U.S. Department of Education recognized agency, the date of the U.S. Secretary's most recent grant of renewed recognition based on the last full review of the agency by the National Advisory Committee on Institutional Quality and Integrity, and the date of the agency's next scheduled review for renewal of recognition.[1] The Council for Higher Education (CHEA) date reflects initial or continued recognition by CHEA.

Regional Accrediting Bodies

Delaware, District of Columbia, Maryland, New Jersey, New York, Pennsylvania, Puerto Rico, Virgin Islands

Middle States Commission on Higher Education M
USDE: 1952/2012/2017 CHEA: 2013
3624 Market Street, Second Floor West
Philadelphia, PA 19104
(267) 284-5000 Fax (215) 662-5501
Elizabeth H. Sibolski, President
E-mail: info@msche.org
URL: www.msche.org

Connecticut, Maine, Massachusetts, New Hampshire, Rhode Island, Vermont

Commission on Institutions of Higher Education
New England Association of Schools and Colleges EH
USDE: 1952/2015/2017 CHEA: 2013
3 Burlington Woods Drive, Suite 100
Burlington, MA 01803-4514
(781) 425-7700 Fax (781) 425-1001
Barbara E. Brittingham, Director
E-mail: cihe@neasc.org
URL: http://cihe.neasc.org

Arizona, Arkansas, Colorado, Illinois, Indiana, Iowa, Kansas, Michigan, Minnesota, Missouri, Nebraska, New Mexico, North Dakota, Ohio, Oklahoma, South Dakota, West Virginia, Wisconsin, Wyoming

Higher Learning Commission NH
USDE: 1952/2015/2017 CHEA: 2015
230 South LaSalle Street, Suite 7-500
Chicago, IL 60604-1411
(800) 621-7440 Fax (312) 263-7462
Barbara Gelman-Danley, President
E-mail: info@hlcommission.org
URL: www.hlcommission.org

Alaska, Idaho, Montana, Nevada, Oregon, Utah, Washington

Northwest Commission on Colleges and Universities NW
USDE: 1952/2013/2015
8060 165th Avenue, NE, Suite 100
Redmond, WA 98052
(425) 558-4224 Fax (425) 376-0596
Sandra E. Elman, President
E-mail: selman@nwccu.org
URL: www.nwccu.org

Alabama, Florida, Georgia, Kentucky, Louisiana, Mississippi, North Carolina, South Carolina, Tennessee, Texas, Virginia

Commission on Colleges
Southern Association of Colleges and Schools SC
USDE: 1952/2014/2017 CHEA: 2003
1866 Southern Lane
Decatur, GA 30033-4097
(404) 679-4500 Fax (404) 679-4558
Belle S. Wheelan, President
E-mail: questions@sacscoc.org
URL: www.sacscoc.org

California, Hawaii, American Samoa, Guam, Commonwealth of the Northern Marianas, Federated States of Micronesia, Republic of the Marshall Islands, Republic of Palau

Accrediting Commission for Senior Colleges and Universities
Western Association of Schools and Colleges WC
USDE: 1952/2012/2017 CHEA: 2014
985 Atlantic Avenue, Suite 100
Alameda, CA 94501
(510) 748-9001 Fax (510) 748-9797
Mary Ellen Petrisko, President
E-mail: wasc@wascsenior.org
URL: www.wascsenior.org

Accrediting Commission for Community and Junior Colleges
Western Association of Schools and Colleges WJ
USDE: 1952/2013/2015
10 Commercial Boulevard, Suite 204
Novato, CA 94949
(415) 506-0234 Fax (415) 506-0238
Barbara A. Beno, President
E-mail: accjc@accjc.org
URL: www.accjc.org

[1] U.S. Department of Education, Nationally Recognized Accrediting Agencies, www2.ed.gov/admins/finaid/accred/accreditation.html.

National, Professional and Specialized Accrediting Bodies

Acupuncture

Accreditation Commission for Acupuncture and Oriental Medicine (ACAOM)
USDE: 1988/2013/2016
8941 Aztec Drive
Eden Praire, MN 55347
(952) 212-2434 Fax (952) 657-7068
Mark S. McKenzie, Executive Director
E-mail: coordinator@acaom.org
URL: www.acaom.org

First-professional master's degree, professional master's level certificate and diploma programs and professional post-graduate doctoral programs in acupuncture and Oriental medicine, and free-standing institutions that offer such programs **ACUP**

Allied Health

Accrediting Bureau of Health Education Schools (ABHES)
USDE: 1969/2011/2016
7777 Leesburg Pike, Suite 314N
Falls Church, VA 22043
(703) 917-9503 Fax (703) 917-4109
Florence Tate, Executive Director
E-mail: info@abhes.org
URL: www.abhes.org

Institutions specializing in allied health education **ABHES**
Specialized programs for
Medical laboratory technician **MLTAB**
Medical assistant **MAAB**
Surgical technologist **SURTEC**

Commission on Accreditation of Allied Health Education Programs (CAAHEP)
CHEA: 2011
1361 Park Street
Clearwater, FL 33756
(727) 210-2350 Fax (727) 210-2354
Kathleen Megivern, Executive Director
E-mail: mail@caahep.org
URL: www.caahep.org

The Commission on Accreditation of Allied Health Education Programs (CAAHEP) is recognized as an accrediting agency for accreditation of education for the allied health occupations. In carrying out its accreditation activities, CAAHEP cooperates with the Committees on Accreditation sponsored by various allied health and medical specialty organizations. CAAHEP is the coordinating agency for accreditation of education for the following allied health occupations:
Anesthesiologist assistant **AA**
Blood bank technology **BBT**
Cardiovascular technologist **CVT**
Cytotechnologist **CYTO**
Diagnostic medical sonographer **DMS**
Emergency medical technician-paramedic **EMT**
Exercise science **EXSC**
Kinesiotherapy **KIN**
Medical assistant **MAC**
Medical illustrator **MIL**
Neurodiagnostic technologist **NDT**
Orthotist/prosthetist **OPE**
Perfusionist **PERF**
Polysomnographic technologist **POLYT**
Recreation therapist **RECTHP**
Surgical assistant **SURGA**
Surgical technologist **SURGT**

Anesthesiologist Assistant

Commission on Accreditation of Allied Health Education Programs (see listing under Allied Health)
Accreditation Review Committee for the Anesthesiologist Assistant
N84 W33137 Becker Lane
Merton, WI 53066
(612) 836-3311
Jennifer Anderson Warwick, Executive Director
E-mail: jennifer@arc-aa.org
URL: www.caahep.org/arc-aa

Post-baccalaureate programs for anesthesiologist assistant **AA**

Art

Commission on Accreditation
National Association of Schools of Art and Design (NASAD)
USDE: 1966/2014/2017
11250 Roger Bacon Drive, Suite 21
Reston, VA 20190
(703) 437-0700 Fax (703) 437-6312
Karen P. Moynahan, Executive Director
E-mail: info@arts-accredit.org
URL: www.arts-accredit.org

Institutions and departments within institutions offering degree and non-degree granting programs in art/design and art/design-related programs **ART**

Athletic Training

Commission on Accreditation of Athletic Training Education (CAATE)
CHEA: 2014
6850 Austin Center Boulevard, Suite 100
Austin, TX 78731-3184
(512) 733-9700
Micki Cuppett, Executive Director
E-mail: micki@caate.net
URL: www.caate.net

Programs for athletic training **CAATE**

Audiology

Accreditation Commission for Audiology Education
CHEA: 2012
1718 M Street, NW #297
Washington, DC 20036-4504
(202) 986-9500 Fax (202) 986-9550
Doris Gordon, Executive Director
E-mail: info@acaeaccred.org
URL: www.acaeaccred.org

Programs leading to the Doctor of Audiology degree **ACAE**

Council on Academic Accreditation in Audiology and Speech Language Pathology
American Speech-Language-Hearing Association (ASHA)
USDE: 1967/2010/2015 CHEA: 2014
2200 Research Boulevard
Rockville, MD 20850-3289
(301) 296-5700 Fax (301) 296-8570
Patrima L. Tice, Director of Accreditation
E-mail: accreditation@asha.org
URL: www.asha.org

Doctoral degree programs in audiology **AUD**

Aviation

Aviation Accreditation Board International
CHEA: 2013
3410 Skyway Drive
Auburn, AL 36830
(334) 844-2431 Fax (334) 844-2432
Gary J. Northam, President
E-mail: bavenva@auburn.edu
URL: www.aabi.aero

Non-engineering programs for aviation **AAB**

Bible College Education

Commission on Accreditation
Association for Biblical Higher Education (ABHE)
USDE: 1952/2014/2017 CHEA: 2011
5850 T. G. Lee Boulevard, Suite 130
Orlando, FL 32822
(407) 207-0808 Fax (407) 207-0840
Ron Kroll, Director
E-mail: info@abhe.org
URL: www.abhe.org

Bible colleges and programs offering undergraduate and graduate programs **BI**

Blood Bank Technology

Commission on Accreditation of Allied Health Education Programs (see listing under Allied Health)
American Association of Blood Banks (AABB) Committee on Accreditation of Specialists in Blood Bank Technology Schools
8101 Glenbrook Road
Bethesda, MD 20814-2749
(301) 907-6977 Fax (301) 907-6895
Anne Chenoweth, Deputy Director Accreditation and Quality Department
E-mail: aabb@aabb.org
URL: www.aabb.org

Programs for blood bank technologist **BBT**

Business

AACSB International-The Association to Advance Collegiate Schools of Business
CHEA: 2002
777 South Harbour Island Boulevard, Suite 750
Tampa, FL 33602
(813) 769-6500 Fax (813) 769-6559
Robert Reid, Executive Vice President and Chief Accreditation Officer
E-mail: accreditation@aacsb.edu
URL: www.aacsb.edu

Programs for:
Business administration education **BUS**
Accounting **BUSA**

Accrediting Council for Independent Colleges and Schools (ACICS)
USDE: 1956/2013/2016 CHEA: 2012
750 First Street NE, Suite 980
Washington, DC 20002-4223
(202) 336-6780 Fax (202) 842-2593
Albert C. Gray, Executive Director
E-mail: agray@acics.org
URL: www.acics.org

Institutions offering certificates/diplomas, associate, baccalaureate and master's degree programs to educate students for professional, technical, or occupational careers **ACICS**

Accreditation Council for Business Schools and Programs (ACBSP)
CHEA: 2011
11520 West 119th Street
Overland Park, KS 66213
(913) 339-9356 Fax (913) 339-6226
Douglas Viehland, Executive Director
E-mail: info@acbsp.org
URL: www.acbsp.org

Business administration, management, accounting and related business fields **ACBSP**

International Assembly for Collegiate Business Education
CHEA: 2011
11374 Strang Line Rd
Lenexa, KS 66215
(913) 631-3009 Fax (913) 631-9154

Dennis N. Gash, President
E-mail: iacbe@iacbe.org
URL: www.iacbe.org

Undergraduate and graduate level business programs in institutions that grant bachelor's and/or graduate degrees **IACBE**

Cardiovascular Technology

Commission on Accreditation of Allied Health Education Programs (see listing under Allied Health)
Joint Review Committee on Education in Cardiovascular Technology (JRC-CVT)
1449 Hill Street
Whitinsville, MA 01588-1032
(978) 456-5594
William W. Goding, Executive Director
E-mail: office@jrccvt.org
URL: www.jrccvt.org

Programs for cardiovascular technology **CVT**

Chiropractic

The Council on Chiropractic Education (CCE)
USDE: 1974/2013/2016 CHEA: 2015
8049 North 85th Way
Scottsdale, AZ 85258-4321
(480) 443-8877 Fax (480) 483-7333
Craig S. Little, President
E-mail: cce@cce-usa.org
URL: www.cce-usa.org

Programs leading to and institutions offering the Doctorate of Chiropractic (D.C.) degree **CHIRO**

Christian Studies Education

Accreditation Commission
Transnational Association of Christian Colleges and Schools (TRACS)
USDE: 1991/2013/2016 CHEA: 2011
15935 Forest Road
Forest, VA 24551
(434) 525-9539 Fax (434) 525-9538
Timothy Eaton, Interim President
E-mail: info@tracs.org
URL: www.tracs.org

Christian liberal arts institutions which offer certificates/diplomas and associate, baccalaureate and graduate degrees **TRACS**

Clinical Laboratory Sciences

National Accrediting Agency for Clinical Laboratory Sciences (NAACLS)
CHEA: 2013
5600 North River Road, Suite 720
Rosemont, IL 60018
(773) 714-8880 Fax (773) 714-8886
Dianne M. Cearlock, Chief Executive Officer
E-mail: info@naacls.org
URL: www.naacls.org

Programs for:
- clinical assistant **CA**
- cytogenetic technologist **CGTECH**
- diagnostic molecular scientist **DMOLS**
- histologic technician/technologist **HT**
- medical laboratory technician **MLTAD**
- medical technologist/laboratory scientist **MT**
- pathologists' assistant **PA**
- phlebotomy **PHLEB**

Clinical Pastoral Education

Accreditation Commission
Association for Clinical Pastoral Education, Inc. (ACPEI)
USDE: 1969/2013/2017
One West Court Square, Suite 325
Decatur, GA 30030
(404) 320-1472 Fax (404) 320-0849
Trace Haythorn, Executive Director
E-mail: acpe@acpe.edu
URL: www.acpe.edu

Basic, advanced and supervisory clinical pastoral education programs **PAST**

Construction Education

American Council for Construction Education (ACCE)
CHEA: 2011
1717 North Loop 1604 East, Suite 320
San Antonio, TX 78232-1570
(210) 495-6161 Fax (210) 495-6168
Michael Holland, President
E-mail: mholland@acce-hq.org
URL: www.acce-hq.org

Associate and baccalaureate degree programs **CONST**

Continuing Education

Accrediting Council for Continuing Education and Training (ACCET)
USDE: 1978/2013/2018
1722 N Street NW
Washington, DC 20036
(202) 955-1113 Fax (202) 955-1118
William V. Larkin, Executive Director
E-mail: wvlarkin@accet.org
URL: www.accet.org

Institutions offering noncollegiate continuing education and institutions offering occupational associate degree programs **CNCE**

Cosmetology

National Accrediting Commission of Career Arts and Sciences (NACCAS)
USDE: 1970/2010/2015
4401 Ford Avenue, Suite 1300
Alexandria, VA 22302-1432
(703) 600-7600 Fax (703) 379-2200
Anthony Mirando, Executive Director
E-mail: naccas@naccas.org
URL: www.naccas.org

Postsecondary schools and departments of cosmetology arts and sciences and massage therapy **COSME**

Counseling and Related Educational Programs

Council for Accreditation of Counseling and Related Educational Programs (CACREP)
CHEA: 2015
1001 North Fairfax Street, Suite 510
Alexandria, VA 22314
(703) 535-5990 Fax (703) 739-6209
Carol L. Bobby, Executive Director
E-mail: cacrep@cacrep.org
URL: www.cacrep.org

Master's degree programs in addiction counseling, career counseling, marriage, couple and family counseling, mental health counseling, school counseling, student affairs and college counseling and doctorate degree programs in counselor education and supervision **CACREP**

Culinary Arts

Accrediting Commission
American Culinary Federation
CHEA: 2004
180 Center Place Way
St. Augustine, FL 32095
(904) 824-4468 Fax (904) 940-0741
Heidi Cramb, Executive Director
E-mail: acf@acfchefs.net
URL: www.acfchefs.org

Programs in culinary arts which award certificates, diplomas or associate degrees and bachelor degree programs in culinary management **ACFEI**

Cytotechnology

Commission on Accreditation of Allied Health Education Programs (see listing under Allied Health)
Cytotechnology Programs Review Committee
American Society of Cytopathology
100 West 10th Street, Suite 605
Wilmington, DE 19801
(302) 543-6583 Fax (302) 543-6597
Elizabeth Jenkins, Executive Director
E-mail: asc@cytopathology.org
URL: www.cytopathology.org

Programs for the cytotechnologist **CYTO**

Dance

Commission on Accreditation
National Association of Schools of Dance (NASD)
USDE: 1983/2015/2019
11250 Roger Bacon Drive, Suite 21
Reston, VA 20190
(703) 437-0700 Fax (703) 437-6312
Karen P. Moynahan, Executive Director
E-mail: info@arts-accredit.org
URL: www.arts-accredit.org

Institutions and departments within institutions offering degree and non-degree-granting programs in dance and dance-related disciplines **DANCE**

Dental and Dental Auxiliary Programs

Commission on Dental Accreditation
American Dental Association (ADA)
USDE: 1952/2013/2017
211 East Chicago Avenue, Suite 1900
Chicago, IL 60611
(800) 621-8099 Fax (312) 440-2915
Sherin Tooks, Director
E-mail: tookss@ada.org
URL: www.ada.org

Programs leading to:
- D.D.S. or D.M.D. degree, advanced general dentistry and specialty programs **DENT**
- Dental hygiene **DH**
- Dental assisting **DA**
- Dental laboratory technology **DT**

Diagnostic Medical Sonography

Commission on Accreditation of Allied Health Education Programs (see listing under Allied Health)
Joint Review Committee on Education in Diagnostic Medical Sonography
6021 University Boulevard, Suite 500
Ellicot City, MD 21043-6090
(443) 973-3251 Fax (866) 738-3444
Cindy Weiland, Executive Director
E-mail: mail@jrcdms.org
URL: www.jrcdms.org

Programs for the diagnostic medical sonographer **DMS**

Dietetics

Accreditation Council for Education in Nutrition and Dietetics
Academy of Nutrition and Dietetics
USDE: 1974/2012/2017
120 South Riverside Plaza, Suite 2000

Chicago, IL 60606-6995
(312) 899-0040 Fax (312) 899-4817
Mary B. Gregoire, Executive Director
E-mail: acend@eatright.org
URL: www.eatright.org/cade

Coordinated programs in dietetics **DIETC**
Didactic programs **DIETD**
Post-baccalaureate internships **DIETI**
Dietetic technician programs **DIETT**

Distance Education and Training

Distance Education Accrediting Commission
USDE: 1959/2012/2017 CHEA: 2013
1101 17th Street NW, Suite 808
Washington, DC 20036
(202) 234-5100 Fax (202) 332-1386
Leah K. Matthews, Executive Director
E-mail: info@deac.org
URL: www.deac.org

Distance education institutions including associate, baccalaureate, master's, and doctoral degree-granting programs primarily through the distance learning method **DEAC** (formerly DETC)

Emergency Medical Services

Commission on Accreditation for Allied Health Programs (see listing under Allied Health)
Committee on Accreditation of Educational Programs for the Emergency Medical Services Professions
8301 Lakeview Parkway, Suite 111-312
Rowlett, TX 75088
(214) 703-8445 Fax (214) 703-8992
George Hatch, Executive Director
E-mail: george@coaemsp.org
URL: www.coaemsp.org

Programs for the emergency medical technician-paramedic **EMT**

Engineering

ABET, Inc.
CHEA: 2015
415 North Charles Street
Baltimore, MD 21201
(410) 347-7700 Fax (410) 625-2238
Michael Milligan, Executive Director
E-mail: accreditation@abet.org
URL: www.abet.org

Baccalaureate programs in computer science **CS**
Basic (baccalaureate) and advanced (master's) level programs in engineering **ENG**
Applied science programs at the associate, baccalaureate and master's level **ENGR**
Associate and baccalaureate degree programs in engineering technology **ENGT**

English Language

Commission on English Language Program Accreditation (CEA)
USDE: 2003/2013/2016
801 North Fairfax Drive, Suite 402A
Alexandria, VA 22314
(703) 665-3400 Fax (703) 519-2071
Mary Reeves, Executive Director
E-mail: info@cea-accredit.org
URL: www.cea-accredit.org

English language programs **CEA**

Exercise Sciences

Commission on Accreditation of Allied Health Education Programs (see listing under Allied Health)
Committee on Accreditation for the Exercise Sciences
401 West Michigan Street
Indianapolis, IN 46202
(317) 637-9200 Fax (317) 634-7817
Traci Sue Rush, Executive Director
E-mail: trush@acsm.org
URL: www.coaes.org

Programs for exercise science and related departments **EXSC**

Family and Consumer Sciences

Council for Accreditation
American Association of Family and Consumer Sciences (AAFCS)
CHEA: 2014
400 North Columbus Street, Suite 202
Alexandria, VA 22314
(703) 706-4600 Fax (703) 706-4663
Carolyn W. Jackson, Executive Director
E-mail: accreditation@aafcs.org
URL: www.aafcs.org

Baccalaureate programs in family and consumer sciences **AAFCS**

Fire and Emergency

International Fire Service Accreditation Congress
CHEA: 2011
1812 Tyler Avenue
Oklahoma State University
Stillwater, OK 74078
(405) 744-8303 Fax (405) 744-8802
Clayton Moorman, Director IFSAC Administration
E-mail: admin@ifsac.org
URL: www.ifsac.org

Undergraduate fire and emergency related programs **IFSAC**

Forensic Science

Forensic Science Educational Program Accreditation Commission
American Academy of Forensic Sciences (AAFS)
CHEA: 2012
410 North 21st Street
Colorado Springs, CO 80904
(719) 636-1100 Fax (719) 636-1993
Nancy J. Jackson, Director of Development and Accreditation
Email: njackson@aafs.org
URL: www.aafs.org

Bachelor or master's degree programs in forensic science **FEPAC**

Funeral Service Education

Committee on Accreditation
American Board of Funeral Service Education (ABFSE)
USDE: 1972/2010/2015 CHEA: 2012
3414 Ashland Avenue, Suite G
St. Joseph, MO 64506
(816) 233-3747 Fax (816) 233-3793
Robert C. Smith III, Executive Director
E-mail: exdir@abfse.org
URL: www.abfse.org

Institutions and programs awarding diplomas, associate and bachelor's degrees in funeral service or mortuary science **FUSER**

Health Informatics and Information Management

Commission on Accreditation for Health Informatics and Information Management Education (CAHIIM)
CHEA: 2012
233 North Michigan Avenue, 21st Floor
Chicago, IL 60601-5800
(312) 233-1100 Fax (312) 233-1948
Claire Dixon-Lee, Executive Director
Email: info@cahiim.org
URL: www.cahiim.org

Associate and baccalaureate degree programs in health information management and master's degree programs in health informatics and health information management **CAHIIM**

Healthcare Management

Commission on Accreditation of Healthcare Management Education (CAHME)
CHEA: 2014
1700 Rockville Pike, Suite 400
Rockville, MD 20852
(301) 998-6101
Margaret Schulte, President and CEO
E-mail: info@cahme.org
URL: www.cahme.org

Graduate programs in healthcare management **HSA**

Histologic Technology

See Clinical Laboratory Sciences

Home Study Education

See Distance Education and Training

Human Services

Council for Standards in Human Services Education (CSHSE)
CHEA: 2014
3337 Duke Street
Alexandria, VA 22314
(571) 257-3959
Elaine Green, President
E-mail: info@cshse.org
URL: www.cshse.org

Human services educational programs **CSHSE**

Industrial Technology

The Association of Technology, Management, and Applied Engineering
CHEA: 2013
275 North York Street, Suite 401
Elmhurst, IL 60126
(630) 433-4514 Fax (630) 563-9181
Kelly Schild, Director of Accreditation
E-mail: kelly@atmae.org
URL: www.atmae.org

Technology, applied technology, engineering technology and technology-related programs at the associate, baccalaureate and master's degree level **NAIT**

Interior Design

Council for Interior Design Accreditation (CIDA)
CHEA: 2013
206 Grandville Avenue, Suite 350
Grand Rapids, MI 49503
(616) 458-0400 Fax (616) 458-0460
Holly Mattson, Executive Director
E-mail: info@accredit-id.org
URL: www.accredit-id.org

First professional degree level programs (master's and baccalaureate degrees) **CIDA**

Journalism and Mass Communications

Accrediting Committee
Accrediting Council on Education in Journalism and Mass Communications (ACEJMC)
CHEA: 2014
University of Kansas School of Journalism
Stauffer-Flint Hall
1435 Jayhawk Boulevard
Lawrence, KS 66045-7575
(785) 864-3973 Fax (785) 864-5225
Susanne Shaw, Executive Director
E-mail: sshaw@ku.edu
URL: www2.ku.edu/~acejmc

Units within institutions offering professional baccalaureate and master's degree programs in journalism and mass communications **JOUR**

Kinesiotherapy

Commission on Accreditation of Allied Health Education Programs (see listing under Allied Health)
Committee on Accreditation of Education Programs for Kinesiotherapy
118 College Drive #5142
Hattiesburg, MS 39406-0002
(601) 266-5371 Fax (601) 266-4445
Jerry W. Purvis, Coord COPSKT
E-mail: jerry.purvis@usm.edu
URL: www.akta.org

Kinesiotherapy programs **KIN**

Landscape Architecture

Landscape Architectural Accreditation Board
American Society of Landscape Architects (ASLA)
CHEA: 2015
636 Eye Street, NW
Washington, DC 20001-3736
(202) 898-2444 Fax (202) 898-1185
Ron Leighton, Executive Director
E-mail: info@asla.org
URL: www.asla.org

Baccalaureate and master's programs leading to the first professional degree **LSAR**

Law

Council of the Section of Legal Education and Admissions to the Bar
American Bar Association (ABA)
USDE: 1952/2013/2016
321 North Clark Street, 21st Fl
Chicago, IL 60654-7598
(312) 988-6738 Fax (312) 988-5681
Barry A. Currier, Managing Director of Accreditation and Legal Education
E-mail: legaled@americanbar.org
URL: www.americanbar.org/groups/legal_education.html

Programs in legal education; professional schools of law **LAW**

Librarianship

Committee on Accreditation
American Library Association (ALA)
CHEA: 2012
50 East Huron Street
Chicago, IL 60611-2795
(312) 280-2432 Fax (312) 280-2433
Karen O'Brien, Director of Accreditation
E-mail: accred@ala.org
URL: www.ala.org/accreditation

Master's programs in library and information studies **LIB**

Marriage and Family Therapy

Commission on Accreditation for Marriage and Family Therapy Education
American Association for Marriage and Family Therapy (AAMFT)
CHEA: 2014
112 South Alfred Street
Alexandria, VA 22314-3061
(703) 838-9808 Fax (703) 838-9805
Tanya A. Tamarkin, Director of Accreditation
E-mail: coa@aamft.org
URL: www.aamft.org

Clinical training programs at the master's, doctorate and post-graduate levels **MFCD**

Massage Therapy

Commission on Massage Therapy Accreditation
USDE: 2002/2010/2015
5335 Wisconsin Avenue NW, Suite 440
Washington, DC 20015
(202) 888-6790 Fax (202) 888-6787
Kate Zulaski, Executive Director
E-mail: info@comta.org
URL: www.comta.org

Institutions that award postsecondary certificates, diplomas, and associate degrees in the practice of massage therapy, bodywork, aesthetics/esthetics and skin care **COMTA**

Medical Assistant Education

(see listing under Allied Health)
Accrediting Bureau of Health Education Schools (ABHES)

Medical assistant programs **MAAB**

Commission on Accreditation of Allied Health Education Programs (see listing under Allied Health)
Medical Assisting Education Review Board
20 North Wacker Drive, Suite 1575
Chicago, IL 60606-2963
(312) 899-1500 Fax (312) 899-1259
Sarah R. Marino, Executive Director
E-mail: maerb@maerb.org
URL: www.maerb.org

One and two year medical assistant programs **MAC**

Medical Illustrator Education

Commission on Accreditation of Allied Health Education Programs (see listing under Allied Health)
Accreditation Review Committee for the Medical Illustrator
Saint Luke's Hospital Instructional Resources
32531 Meadowlark Way
Pepper Pike, OH 44124
(216) 595-9363 Fax (216) 595-9360
Kathy Jung, Chair, ARC-MI
E-mail: kijung@aol.com
URL: www.ami.org

Programs for medical illustrator **MIL**

Medical Laboratory Technician Education

(see listing under Allied Health)
Accrediting Bureau of Health Education Schools (ABHES)

Schools and programs for the medical laboratory technician **MLTAB**

(see listing under Clinical Laboratory Sciences)
National Accrediting Agency for Clinical Laboratory Sciences (NAACLS)

Programs for medical laboratory technician **MLTAD**

Medical Technology

(see listing under Clinical Laboratory Sciences)
National Accrediting Agency for Clinical Laboratory Sciences (NAACLS)

Programs for medical technologist/laboratory scientist **MT**

Medicine

Liaison Committee on Medical Education (LCME) of the Council on Medical Education of the American Medical Association and the Association of American Medical Colleges
USDE: 1952/2014/2017
The LCME is administered in odd-numbered years, beginning each July 1, by:
Council on Medical Education of the American Medical Association (AMA)
330 North Wabash Avenue
Chicago, IL 60611
(312) 464-4690 Fax (312) 464-5830
Barbara Barzansky, LCME Co-Secretary
E-mail: barbara.barzansky@ama-assn.org
URL: www.ama-assn.org

The LCME is administered in even-numbered years, beginning each July 1, by:
Association of American Medical Colleges (AAMC)
655 K Street NW, Suite 100
Washington, DC 20001-2399
(202) 828-0596 Fax (202) 828-1125
Dan Hunt, LCME Co-Secretary
E-mail: dhunt@aamc.org
URL: www.aamc.org

Programs leading to the M.D. degree **MED**

Midwifery Education

Midwifery Education Accreditation Council (MEAC)
USDE: 2001/2012/2015
1935 Pauline Boulevard, Suite 100B
Ann Arbor, MI 48103
(360) 466-2080 Fax (480) 907-2936
Sandra Bitonti Stewart, Executive Director
E-mail: info@meacschools.org
URL: www.meacschools.org

Accreditation of direct-entry midwifery educational institutions and programs conferring degrees and certificates **MEAC**

Montessori Teacher Education

Montessori Accreditation Council for Teacher Education (MACTE)
USDE: 1995/2013/2015
108 Second Street, SW, Suite 7
Charlottesville, VA 22902
(434) 202-7793 Fax (888) 525-8838
Rebecca Pelton, Executive Director
E-mail: info@macte.org
URL: www.macte.org

Montessori teacher-education programs and institutions **MACTE**

Music

Commission on Accreditation
National Association of Schools of Music (NASM)
USDE: 1952/2015/2019
11250 Roger Bacon Drive, Suite 21
Reston, VA 20190
(703) 437-0700 Fax (703) 437-6312
Karen P. Moynahan, Executive Director

E-mail: info@arts-accredit.org
URL: www.arts-accredit.org

Institutions and departments within institutions offering degree and non-degree-granting programs in music and music-related disciplines **MUS**

Naturopathic Medical Education

Council on Naturopathic Medical Education (CNME)
USDE: 2003/2010/2015
PO Box 178
Great Barrington, MA 01230
(413) 528-8877 Fax (413) 528-8880
Daniel Seitz, Executive Director
E-mail: council@cnme.org
URL: www.cnme.org

Graduate-level, four-year naturopathic medical education programs **NATUR**

Neurodiagnostic Technology

Commission on Accreditation of Allied Health Education Programs (see listing under Allied Health)
Committee on Accreditation for Education in Neurodiagnostic Technology
1449 Hill Street
Whitinsville, MA 01588
(978) 338-6300 Fax (978) 832-2638
Jackie Long-Goding, Executive Director
E-mail: office@coa-ndt.org
URL: http://coa-ndt.org

Programs for the electroneurodiagnostic technologist **NDT**

Nuclear Medicine Technology

Joint Review Committee on Educational Programs in Nuclear Medicine Technology
CHEA: 2013
2000 West Danforth Road, Suite 130 #203
Edmund, OK 73003
(405) 285-0546 Fax (405) 285-0579
Jan M. Winn, Executive Director
E-mail: mail@jrcnmt.org
URL: www.jrcnmt.org

Programs for the nuclear medicine technologist **NMT**

Nurse Anesthetists

Council on Accreditation of Nurse Anesthesia Educational Programs
USDE: 1955/2013/2015 CHEA: 2014
222 South Prospect Avenue, Suite 304
Park Ridge, IL 60068-4001
(847) 655-1160 Fax (847) 692-7137
Francis Gerbasi, Executive Director
E-mail: accreditation@coa.us.com
URL: home.coa.us.com

Nurse anesthesia educational institutions and programs at the post-master's certificate, master's and doctoral degree levels **ANEST**

Nurse-Midwifery

Accreditation Commission for Midwifery Education
USDE: 1982/2014/2017
8403 Colesville Road, Suite 1550
Silver Spring, MD 20910
(240) 485-1800 Fax (240) 485-1818
Heather Maurer, Executive Director
E-mail: hmaurer@acnm.org
URL: www.midwife.org/accreditation

Pre-certification, basic certificate and master's degree nurse-midwifery educational programs **MIDWF**

Nursing

Commission on Collegiate Nursing Education (CCNE)
USDE: 2000/2014/2017
One Dupont Circle NW, Suite 530
Washington, DC 20036-1120
(202) 887-6791 Fax (202) 887-8476
Jennifer Butlin, Executive Director
E-mail: info@aacn.nche.edu
URL: www.aacn.nche.edu/ccne-accreditation

Baccalaureate and higher degree nursing education **NURSE**

Accreditation Commission for Education in Nursing
USDE: 1952/2014/2015 CHEA: 2011
3343 Peachtree Road NE, Suite 850
Atlanta, GA 30326
(404) 975-5000 Fax (404) 975-5020
Marsal P. Stoll, CEO
E-mail: info@acenursing.org
URL: www.acenursing.org

Programs in:
- Practical nursing (certificate) **PNUR**
- Diploma nurse education **DNUR**
- Associate degree **ADNUR**
- Baccalaureate and higher degree nurse education **NUR**

Occupational Education

Council on Occupational Education (COE)
USDE: 1969/2013/2016
7840 Roswell Road, Bldg 300, Suite 325
Atlanta, GA 30350
(770) 396-3898 Fax (770) 396-3790
Gary Puckett, Executive Director
E-mail: info@council.org
URL: www.council.org

Occupational/vocational institutions that grant certificates or diplomas and the applied associate degree in specific career and technical education **COE**

Occupational Therapy

Accreditation Council for Occupational Therapy Education
American Occupational Therapy Association
USDE: 1952/2012/2017 CHEA: 2013
4720 Montgomery Lane, Suite 200
Bethesda, MD 20814-3449
(301) 652-6611 Fax (301) 652-7711
Heather Stagliano, Director of Accreditation
E-mail: accred@aota.org
URL: www.aota.org

Occupational therapy programs **OT**
Occupational therapy assistant programs **OTA**

Opticianry

Commission on Opticianry Accreditation
CHEA: 2010
PO Box 592
Canton, NY 13617
(703) 468-0566
Debra White, Director of Accreditation
E-mail: director@COAccreditation.com
URL: www.coaccreditation.com

Two-year opticianry degree programs **OPD**
One year programs for opthalmic laboratory technician **OPLT**

Optometry

Accreditation Council on Optometric Education
American Optometric Association (AOA)
USDE: 1952/2015/2017 CHEA: 2012
243 North Lindbergh Boulevard
St. Louis, MO 63141
(314) 991-4100 Fax (314) 991-4101
Joyce L. Urbeck, Administrative Director
E-mail: accredit@aoa.org
URL: www.theacoe.org

Programs in:
- First professional **OPT**
- Optometric residency **OPTR**
- Optometric technology **OPTT**

Orthotic and Prosthetic Education

Commission on Accreditation of Allied Health Education Programs (see listing under Allied Health)
National Commission on Orthotic and Prosthetic Education (NCOPE)
330 John Carlyle Street, Suite 200
Alexandria, VA 22314
(703) 836-7114 Fax (703) 836-0838
Robin C. Seabrook, Executive Director
E-mail: info@ncope.org
URL: www.ncope.org

Programs for orthotic and prosthetic education **OPE**

Osteopathic Medicine

Commission on Osteopathic College Accreditation
American Osteopathic Association
USDE: 1952/2011/2016
Department of Education
142 East Ontario Street
Chicago, IL 60611-2864
(312) 202-8048 Fax (312) 202-8200
Alissa Craft, VP, Accreditation
E-mail: predoc@osteopathic.org
URL: www.aoacoca.org

Programs leading to and institutions offering the D.O. (Doctor of Osteopathy/Osteopathic Medicine) degree **OSTEO**

Perfusion

Commission on Accreditation of Allied Health Education Programs (see listing under Allied Health)
Accreditation Committee - Perfusion Education
6663 South Sycamore Street
Littleton, CO 80120
(303) 794-6283 Fax (206) 350-1651
Theresa Sisneros, Executive Director
E-mail: office@ac-pe.org
URL: www.ac-pe.org

Programs for the perfusionist **PERF**

Pharmacy

Accreditation Council for Pharmacy Education (ACPE)
USDE: 1952/2014/2017 CHEA: 2014
135 South LaSalle Street, Suite 4100
Chicago, IL 60603
(312) 664-3575 Fax (312) 664-4652
Peter H. Vlasses, Executive Director
E-mail: csinfo@acpe-accredit.org
URL: www.acpe-accredit.org

Professional degree programs in pharmacy **PHAR**

Physical Therapy

Commission on Accreditation in Physical Therapy Education
American Physical Therapy Association (APTA)
USDE: 1977/2014/2017 CHEA: 2012

Trans Potomac Plaza
1111 North Fairfax Street
Alexandria, VA 22314
(703) 706-3245 Fax (703) 684-7343
Sandra Wise, Senior Director
E-mail: accreditation@apta.org
URL: www.capteonline.org

Professional programs for the physical therapist **PTA**
Programs for the physical therapist assistant **PTAA**

Physician Assistant

Accreditation Review Commission on Education for the Physician Assistant (ARC-PA)
CHEA: 2015
12000 Findley Road, Suite 150
John's Creek, GA 30097
(770) 476-1224 Fax (770) 476-1738
John McCarty, Executive Director
E-mail: arc-pa@arc-pa.org
URL: www.arc-pa.org

Programs for the physician assistant **ARCPA**

Planning (City and Regional)

Planning Accreditation Board
CHEA: 2013
2334 West Lawrence Avenue, Suite 209
Chicago, IL 60625
(773) 334-7200
Shonagh Merits, Executive Director
E-mail: smerits@planningaccreditationboard.org
URL: www.planningaccreditationboard.org

Bachelor and master's level programs in planning **PLNG**

Podiatry

Council on Podiatric Medical Education
American Podiatric Medical Association (APMA)
USDE: 1952/2013/2016 CHEA: 2015
9312 Old Georgetown Road
Bethesda, MD 20814-1621
(301) 581-9200 Fax (301) 571-4903
Alan R. Tinkleman, Director
E-mail: artinkleman@apma.org
URL: www.cpme.org

Colleges and programs of podiatric medicine, including first professional and doctorate degree programs **POD**

Polysomnographic Technology

Commission on Accreditation of Allied Health Education Programs (see listing under Allied Health)
Committee on Accreditation for Polysomnographic Technologist Education
1711 Frank Avenue
New Bern, NC 28560
(252) 626-3238
Karen Monarchy Rowe, Executive Director
E-mail: office@coapsg.org
URL: www.coapsg.org

Programs for polysomnographic technology **POLYT**

Psychology

Psychological Clinical Science Accreditation System (PCSAS)
CHEA: 2012
1101 East Tenth Street
IU Psychology Building
Bloomington, IN 47405-7007
(812) 856-2570 Fax (812) 322-5545
Richard M. McFall, Executive Director
Email: mcfall@pcsas.org
URL: www.pcsas.org

Psychological clinical science doctoral training programs **PCSAS**

Commission on Accreditation
American Psychological Association (APA)
USDE: 1970/2013/2016 CHEA: 2013
750 First Street NE
Washington, DC 20002-4242
(202) 336-5979 Fax (202) 336-5978
Jacqueline Remondet Wall, Director Program Consultation and Accreditation
E-mail: apaaccred@apa.org
URL: www.apa.org

Doctoral programs in:
- Clinical psychology **CLPSY**
- Counseling psychology **COPSY**
- Combined professional-scientific psychology **PSPSY**
- School psychology **SCPSY**
- Pre-doctoral internship program in professional psychology **IPSY**
- Post-doctoral residency in professional psychology **PDPSY**

Public Affairs and Administration

Commission on Peer Review and Accreditation
Network of Schools of Public Policy, Affairs and Administration (NASPAA)
CHEA: 2014
1029 Vermont Avenue, NW, Suite 1100
Washington, DC 20005
(202) 628-8965 Fax (202) 626-4978
Crystal Calarusse, Chief Accreditation Officer
E-mail: copra@naspaa.org
URL: www.naspaa.org

Master's degree programs in public affairs, public policy and administration **SPAA**

Public Health

Council on Education for Public Health (CEPH)
USDE: 1974/2013/2018
1010 Wayne Avenue, Suite 220
Silver Spring, MD 20910-5600
(202) 789-1050 Fax (202) 789-1895
Laura Rasar King, Executive Director
E-mail: lking@ceph.org
URL: www.ceph.org

Baccalaureate and graduate level programs in schools of public health and public health programs outside of schools of public health **PH**

Rabbinical and Talmudic Education

Accreditation Commission
Association of Advanced Rabbinical and Talmudic Schools (AARTS)
USDE: 1974/2015/2017 CHEA: 2011
11 Broadway, Suite 405
New York, NY 10004
(212) 363-1991 Fax (212) 533-5335
Keith Sharfman, Director
E-mail: k.sharfman.aarts@gmail.com

Advanced rabbinical and Talmudic schools **RABN**

Radiologic Technology

Joint Review Committee on Education in Radiologic Technology
USDE: 1957/2013/2016 CHEA: 2014
20 North Wacker Drive, Suite 2850
Chicago, IL 60606-3182
(312) 704-5300 Fax (312) 704-5304
Leslie F. Winter, Chief Executive Officer
E-mail: mail@jrcert.org
URL: www.jrcert.org

Programs for:
- Magnetic resonance **RADMAG**
- Medical dosimetry **RADDOS**
- Radiographer **RAD**
- Radiation therapist technologist **RTT**

Recreation, Park and Leisure Studies

Council on Accreditation of Parks, Recreation, Tourism and Related Professions
National Recreation and Park Association
CHEA: 2014
22377 Belmont Ridge Road
Ashburn, VA 20148-4501
(703) 858-2195 Fax (703) 858-0794
Brenda Beales, Awards and Accreditation Manager
E-mail: coaprt@nrpa.org
URL: www.nrpa.org

Baccalaureate degree programs in recreation, park resources and leisure studies **NRPA**

Recreation Therapy

Commission on Accreditation of Allied Health Education Programs (see listing under Allied Health)
Committee on Accreditation of Recreational Therapy Education (CARTE)
East Carolina University, Mail Stop 540
Greenville, NC 27858
(252) 328-0018 Fax (252) 328-4642
Thomas K. Skalko, Chair
E-mail: cartecoa@gmail.com
URL: www.atra-online.com/education

Recreational therapy education programs **CARTE**

Rehabilitation Education

Commission on Standards and Accreditation
Council on Rehabilitation Education (CORE)
CHEA: 2012
1699 Woodfield Road, Suite 300
Schaumburg, IL 60173
(847) 944-1345 Fax (847) 944-1346
Frank Lane, CEO
E-mail: flane@core-rehab.org
URL: www.core-rehab.org

Rehabilitation counselor education programs at the master's level and rehabilitation services at the bachelor's level **CORE**

Respiratory Care

Commission on Accreditation for Respiratory Care (CoARC)
CHEA: 2012
1248 Harwood Road
Bedford, TX 76021-4244
(817) 283-2835 Fax (817) 354-8519
Thomas Smalling, Executive Director
Email: tom@coarc.com
URL: www.coarc.com
- Degree programs in respiratory care **COARC**
- Certificate programs in polysomnography **COARCP**

Social Work

Commission on Accreditation
Council on Social Work Education (CSWE)
CHEA: 2014
1701 Duke Street, Suite 200
Alexandria, VA 22314-3457
(703) 683-8080 Fax (703) 683-8099
Jo Ann Regan, Vice President of Accreditation
E-mail: info@cswe.org

URL: www.cswe.org

Master's and baccalaureate degree programs **SW**

Speech-Language Pathology

Council on Academic Accreditation in Audiology and Speech Language Pathology
American Speech-Language-Hearing Association (ASHA)
USDE: 1967/2010/2015 CHEA: 2014
2200 Research Boulevard
Rockville, MD 20850-3289
(301) 296-5700 Fax (301) 296-8570
Patrima L. Tice, Director of Accreditation
E-mail: accreditation@asha.org
URL: www.asha.org

Master's in speech-language pathology **SP**

Surgical Assisting and Technology

(see listing under Allied Health)
Accrediting Bureau of Health Education Schools (ABHES)

Surgical technologist programs **SURTEC**

Commission on Accreditation of Allied Health Education Programs (see listing under Allied Health)
Accreditation Review Council on Education in Surgical Technology and Surgical Assisting
6 West Dry Creek Circle, Suite 110
Littleton, CO 80120
(303) 694-9262 Fax (303) 741-3655
Keith Orloff, Executive Director
E-mail: info@arcstsa.org
URL: www.arcstsa.org

Programs for the surgical technologist **SURGT**
Programs for the surgical assistant **SURGA**

Teacher Education

Council for the Accreditation of Educator Preparation*
CHEA: 2014
1140 19th Street NW, Suite 400
Washington, DC 20036
(202) 223-0077
Christopher Koch, Interim President
Email: caep@caepnet.org
URL: caepnet.org

Educator preparation programs **CAEP**

*On July 1 2013, the National Council for Accreditation of Teacher Education (NCATE) and the Teacher Education Accreditation Council (TEAC) consolidated, making the Council for the Accreditation of Educator Preparation (CAEP) the new, sole specialized accreditor for educator preparation. Under the consolidation, NCATE and TEAC are subsidiaries of CAEP, maintaining their recognition by the U.S. Department of Education and the Council for Higher Education Accreditation for the purpose of maintaining the accreditation of educator preparation providers until such time as said providers come up for accreditation under CAEP.

National Council for Accreditation of Teacher Education (NCATE)
USDE: 1952/2006/2014 CHEA: 2013

Baccalaureate and graduate programs for the preparation of teachers and other professional personnel for elementary and secondary schools **TED**

Accreditation Committee
Teacher Education Accreditation Council (TEAC)
USDE: 2003/2005/2014 CHEA: 2012

Professional teacher education programs in institutions offering baccalaureate and graduate degrees for the preparation of K-12 teachers **TEAC**

Theatre

Commission on Accreditation
National Association of Schools of Theatre (NAST)
USDE: 1982/2015/2019
11250 Roger Bacon Drive, Suite 21
Reston, VA 20190
(703) 437-0700 Fax (703) 437-6312
Karen P. Moynahan, Executive Director
E-mail: info@arts-accredit.org
URL: www.arts-accredit.org

Institutions and departments within institutions offering degree granting and non-degree-granting programs in theatre and theatre-related disciplines **THEA**

Theology

Commission on Accrediting of the Association of Theological Schools (ATS)
USDE: 1952/2013/2016 CHEA: 2012
10 Summit Park Drive
Pittsburgh, PA 15275-1103
(412) 788-6505 Fax (412) 788-6510
Daniel O. Aleshire, Executive Director
E-mail: ats@ats.edu
URL: www.ats.edu

Freestanding schools, as well as schools or programs affiliated with larger institutions, offering graduate professional education for ministry and graduate study of theology **THEOL**

Trade and Technical Education

Accrediting Commission of Career Schools and Colleges (ACCSC)
USDE: 1967/2011/2016
2101 Wilson Boulevard, Suite 302
Arlington, VA 22201
(703) 247-4212 Fax (703) 247-4533
Michale McComis, Executive Director
E-mail: info@accsc.org
URL: www.accsc.org

Private, postsecondary degree-granting and non-degree-granting institutions that are predominantly organized to educate students for trade, occupational or technical careers **ACCSC**

Veterinary Medicine

Council on Education
American Veterinary Medical Association (AVMA)
USDE: 1952/2012/2016 CHEA: 2012
1931 North Meacham Road, Suite 100
Schaumburg, IL 60173
(800) 248-2862 Fax (847) 285-5732
Karen Martens Brandt, Director Education and Research
E-mail: avmainfo@avma.org
URL: www.avma.org

Colleges of veterinary medicine offering programs leading to a D.V.M./D.M.V. professional degree **VET**

Other

New York State Board of Regents Commission of Education
USDE: 1952/2012/2017
State Education Department
The University of the State of New York
89 Washington Avenue, Room 1106B
Albany, NY 12234
(518) 474-5844 Fax (518) 473-4909
Elizabeth Berlin, Acting Commissioner of Education
E-mail: beth.berlin@mail.nysed.gov
URL: www.nysed.gov

Degree-granting institutions of higher education in New York that designate the agency as their sole or primary nationally recognized accrediting agency for purposes of establishing eligibility to participate in Higher Education Act programs **NY**

Accrediting Agencies Recognized for their Pre-accreditation Categories[1]

Under the terms of the Higher Education Act and other Federal legislation providing funding assistance to postsecondary education, an institution or program is eligible to apply for participation in certain Federal programs if, in addition to meeting other statutory requirements, it is accredited by a nationally recognized accrediting agency—or if it is an institution with respect to which the U.S. Secretary of Education has determined that there is satisfactory assurance the institution or program will meet the accreditation standards of such agency or association within a reasonable time. An institution or program may establish satisfactory assurance of accreditation by acquiring pre-accreditation status with a nationally recognized accrediting agency which has been recognized by the U.S. Secretary of Education for the award of such status. According to the Criteria for Nationally Recognized Accrediting Agencies, if an accrediting agency has developed a pre-accreditation status, it must demonstrate that it applies criteria and follows procedures that are appropriately related to those used to award accreditation status. The criteria for recognition also requires an agency's standards for pre-accreditation to permit an institution or program to hold pre-accreditation no more than five years.

The following is a list of accrediting agencies recognized by the U.S. Secretary of Education for their pre-accreditation categories and the categories which are recognized.

Regional Institution Accrediting Bodies

Middle States Commission on Higher Education:
Candidate for Accreditation

New England Association of Schools and Colleges:
Commission on Institutions of Higher Education: *Candidate for Accreditation*

Higher Learning Commission: *Candidate for Accreditation*

Northwest Commission on Colleges and Universities:
Candidate for Accreditation

Southern Association of Colleges and Schools
Commission on Colleges: *Candidate for Accreditation*

Western Association of Schools and Colleges
Accrediting Commission for Community and Junior Colleges: *Candidate for Accreditation*

Western Association of Schools and Colleges
Accrediting Commission for Senior Colleges and Universities: *Candidate for Accreditation*

National, Institutional and Specialized Accrediting Bodies

Academy of Nutrition and Dietetics
Accreditation Council for Education in Nutrition and Dietetics: *Pre-accreditation*

Accreditation Commission for Acupuncture and Oriental Medicine: *Candidate for Accreditation*

Accreditation Commission for Midwifery Education: *Pre-accreditation*

Accreditation Council for Pharmacy Education: *Candidate, Pre-candidate*

American Optometric Association
Accreditation Council on Optometric Education: *Preliminary Approval* (for professional degree programs); *Candidacy Pending* (for optometric residency programs in Veterans Administration facilities)

American Osteopathic Association
Commission on Osteopathic College Accreditation: *Provisional Accreditation*

American Physical Therapy Association
Commission on Accreditation in Physical Therapy Education: *Candidate for Accreditation*

American Podiatric Medical Association
Council on Podiatric Medical Education: *Candidate for Accreditation*

American Speech-Language-Hearing Association
Council on Academic Accreditation: *Candidate for Accreditation*

American Veterinary Medical Association
Council on Education: *Reasonable Assurance of Accreditation*

Association for Biblical Higher Education
Commission on Accreditation: *Candidate for Accreditation*

Association of Advanced Rabbinical and Talmudic Schools
Accreditation Commission: *Correspondent, Candidate for Accreditation*

Commission on Accrediting of the Association of Theological Schools: *Candidate for Accredited Membership*

Council on Education for Public Health: *Pre-accreditation*

Council on Naturopathic Medical Education: *Pre-accreditation*

Council on Occupational Education: *Candidate for Accreditation*

Midwifery Education Accreditation Council: *Pre-accreditation*

Teacher Education Accreditation Council Accreditation Committee: *Pre-accreditation*

Transnational Association of Christian Colleges and Schools
Accreditation Commission: *Candidate for Accreditation*

[1]U.S. Department of Education, Nationally Recognized Accrediting Agencies and Associations, www2.ed.gov/admins/finaid/accred/accreditation_pg8.html.

Abbreviations, Explanatory Notes and Symbols

Abbreviations

Listed below are the abbreviations used in this Directory for the recognized regional accrediting commissions and the recognized national, professional and specialized accrediting bodies. Addresses for these associations can be found under our listing of Accrediting Agencies beginning on page viii.

The recognized regional accrediting commissions are indicated throughout this Directory by the following abbreviations:

EH New England Association of Schools and Colleges, Commission on Institutions of Higher Education

M Middle States Commission on Higher Education

NH Higher Learning Commission, North Central Association

NW Northwest Commission on Colleges and Universities

SC Southern Association of Colleges and Schools, Commission on Colleges

WC Western Association of Schools and Colleges, Accrediting Commission for Senior Colleges and Universities

WJ Western Association of Schools and Colleges, Accrediting Commission for Community and Junior Colleges

National, professional and specialized accrediting agencies and associations are listed below. Wherever possible, degree levels are shown by the following symbols: (C) diploma/certificate; (A) associate; (B) baccalaureate; (M) master's; (S) beyond master's but less than doctorate; (FP) first professional; (D) doctorate.

AA Commission on Accreditation of Allied Health Education Programs: anesthesiologist assistant (M)

AAB Aviation Accreditation Board International: aviation (A,B,M)

AAFCS American Association of Family and Consumer Sciences: family and consumer sciences (B)

ABHES Accrediting Bureau of Health Education Schools: allied health (C,A,B)

ACAE Accreditation Commission for Audiology Education: audiology (D)

ACBSP Accreditation Council for Business Schools and Programs: business administration, management, accounting and related business fields (A,B,M,D)

ACCSC Accrediting Commission of Career Schools and Colleges: occupational, trade and technical education (C,A,B,M)

ACFEI American Culinary Federation, Inc.: culinary arts and culinary management (C,A,B)

ACICS Accrediting Council for Independent Colleges and Schools: business and business-related programs (C,A,B,M)

ACUP Accreditation Commission for Acupuncture and Oriental Medicine: acupuncture (C,M,D)

ADNUR Accreditation Commission for Education in Nursing: nursing (A)

ANEST Council on Accreditation of Nurse Anesthesia Educational Programs: nurse anesthesia (C,M,D)

ARCPA Accreditation Review Commission on Education for the Physician Assistant: physician assisting programs (C,A,B,M)

ART National Association of Schools of Art and Design: art and design (C,A,B,M,D)

AUD American Speech-Language-Hearing Association: audiology (D)

BBT Commission on Accreditation of Allied Health Education Programs: blood bank technology (C,M)

BI Association for Biblical Higher Education: bible college education (C,A,B,M,FP,D)

BUS AACSB-The Association to Advance Collegiate Schools of Business: business and management (B,M,D)

BUSA AACSB-The Association to Advance Collegiate Schools of Business: accounting (B,M,D)

CA National Accrediting Agency for Clinical Laboratory Sciences: clinical assistant (C)

CAATE Commission on Accreditation of Athletic Training Education: athletic training (B,M)

CACREP Council for Accreditation of Counseling & Related Education programs: addiction counseling, career counseling, marriage, couple and family counseling, mental health counseling, school counseling, student affairs and college counseling (M) and counselor education and supervision (D)

CAEP Council for the Accreditation of Educator Preparation: teacher education (B,M,D)

CAHIIM Commission on Accreditation for Health Informatics and Information Management Education: health information management and health informatics (A,B,M)

CARTE Commission on Accreditation of Recreational Therapy Education: recreational therapy (B,M)

CEA Commission on English Language Program Accreditation: english language (C)

CGTECH National Accrediting Agency for Clinical Laboratory Sciences: cytogenetic technologist (B)

CHIRO Council on Chiropractic Education: chiropractic education (FP,D)

CIDA Council for Interior Design Accreditation: interior design (B,M)

CLPSY American Psychological Association: clinical psychology (D)

CNCE Accrediting Council for Continuing Education and Training: continuing education (C,A)

COARC Commission on Accreditation for Respiratory Care: respiratory care (A,B,M)

COARCP Commission on Accreditation for Respiratory Care: polysomnography (C)

COE Council on Occupational Education: occupational, trade, and technical education (C,A)

COMTA Commission on Massage Therapy Accreditation: massage therapy, bodywork, aesthetics/esthetics and skin care (C,A)

CONST American Council for Construction Education: construction education (A,B)

COPSY American Psychological Association: counseling psychology (D)

CORE Council on Rehabilitation Education: rehabilitation counseling and rehabilitation services (B,M)

COSME National Accrediting Commission of Career Arts and Sciences: cosmetology and massage therapy (C)

CS ABET, Inc.: computer science (B)

CSHSE Council for Standards in Human Services Education: human services (A,B,M)

CVT Commission on Accreditation of Allied Health Education Programs: cardiovascular technology (C,A,B)

CYTO Commission on Accreditation of Allied Health Education Programs: cytotechnology (C,B,M)

DA American Dental Association: dental assisting (C,A)

DANCE National Association of Schools of Dance: dance (C,A,B,M,D)

DEAC Distance Education and Accrediting Commission: home study schools (A,B,M,D)

DENT American Dental Association: dentistry (FP,D)

DH American Dental Association: dental hygiene (C,A,B,M)

DIETC Academy of Nutrition and Dietetics: coordinated dietetics programs (B,M)

DIETD Academy of Nutrition and Dietetics: didactic dietetics programs (B,M)

DIETI Academy of Nutrition and Dietetics: dietetic post-baccalaureate internships

DIETT Academy of Nutrition and Dietetics: dietetic technician (A)

DMOLS National Accrediting Agency for Clinical Laboratory Sciences: diagnostic molecular scientist (C,B,M)

DMS Commission on Accreditation of Allied Health Education Programs: diagnostic medical sonography (C,A,B,M)

DNUR Accreditation Commission for Education in Nursing: nursing (C)

DT American Dental Association: dental laboratory technology (C,A)

EMT Commission on Accreditation of Allied Health Education Programs: emergency medical technician-paramedic (C,A,B)

ENG ABET, Inc.: engineering (B,M)

ENGR ABET, Inc.: applied science (A,B,M)

ENGT ABET, Inc.: engineering technology (A,B)

EXSC Commission on Accreditation of Allied Health Education Programs: exercise science (C,B,M)

FEPAC American Academy of Forensic Sciences: forensic science (B,M)

FUSER American Board of Funeral Service Education: funeral service education (C,A,B)

HSA Commission on Accreditation of Healthcare Management Education: healthcare management (B,M)

HT National Accrediting Agency for Clinical Laboratory Sciences: histologic technology (C,A,B)

IACBE International Assembly for Collegiate Business Education: business programs in institutions that grant bachelor/graduate degrees (A,B,M,D)

IFSAC International Fire Service Accreditation Congress Degree Assembly: fire and emergency related degree (A,B)

IPSY American Psychological Association: pre-doctoral internships in professional psychology

JOUR Accrediting Council on Education for Journalism and Mass Communications: journalism and mass communications (B,M)

KIN Commission on Accreditation of Allied Health Education Programs: kinesiotherapy (B)

LAW American Bar Association: law (FP,D)

LIB American Library Association: librarianship (M)

LSAR American Society for Landscape Architects: landscape architecture (B,M)

MAAB Accrediting Bureau of Health Education Schools: medical assisting (C,A)

MAC Commission on Accreditation of Allied Health Education Programs: medical assisting (C,A)

MACTE Montessori Accreditation Council for Teacher Education: Montessori teacher education (C)

MEAC Midwifery Education Accreditation Council: midwifery education (C,A,B,M,D)

MED Liaison Committee on Medical Education: medicine (FP,D)

MFCD American Association for Marriage and Family Therapy: marriage and family therapy (M,D)

MIDWF Accreditation Commission for Midwifery Education: nurse midwifery (C,M,D)

MIL Commission on Accreditation of Allied Health Education Programs: medical illustrator (M)

MLTAB Accrediting Bureau of Health Education Schools: medical laboratory technician (C,A)

MLTAD National Accrediting Agency for Clinical Laboratory Sciences: medical laboratory technician (C,A)

MT National Accrediting Agency for Clinical Laboratory Sciences: medical technology/laboratory scientist (C,B)

MUS National Association of Schools of Music: music (C,A,B,M,D)

NAIT The Association of Technology, Management, and Applied Engineering: technology, applied technology, engineering technology and technology-related programs (A,B,M)

NATUR Council on Naturopathic Medical Education: naturopathic medical education (FP,D)

NDT Commission on Accreditation of Allied Health Education Programs: neurodiagnostic technology (C,A)

NMT Joint Review Committee on Educational Programs in Nuclear Medicine Technology: nuclear medicine technology (C,A,B)

NRPA National Recreation and Park Association: recreation, park resources, and leisure studies (B)

NUR Accreditation Commission for Education in Nursing: nursing (B, M,D)

NURSE Commission on Collegiate Nursing Education: nursing (B,M,D)

NY New York State Board of Regents:
Degree-granting institutions of higher education in New York that designate the agency as their sole or primary nationally recognized accrediting agency for purposes of establishing elibility to participate in Higher Education Act programs

OPD Commission on Opticianry Accreditation: opticianry (A)

OPE Commission on Accreditation of Allied Health Education Programs: orthotics and prosthetics (C,B,M)

OPLT Commission on Opticianry Accreditation: opthalmic laboratory technician (C)

OPT American Optometric Association: optometry (FP,D)

OPTR American Optometric Association: optometric residency programs

OPTT American Optometric Association: optometric technician (C,A)

OSTEO American Osteopathic Association, Office of Osteopathic Education: osteopathic medicine (FP,D)

OT American Occupational Therapy Association: occupational therapy (M,D)

OTA American Occupational Therapy Association: occupational therapy assistant (C,A)

PA National Accrediting Agency for Clinical Laboratory Sciences: pathologist's assistant (C,M)

PAST Association for Clinical Pastoral Education: clinical pastoral education

PCSAS Psychological Clinical Science Accreditation System: psychological clinical science (D)

PDPSY American Psychological Association: post-doctorate residency in professional psychology

PERF Commission on Accreditation of Allied Health Education Programs: perfusionist (C,B,M)

PH Council on Education for Public Health: public health (B,M,D)

PHAR Accreditation Council for Pharmaceutical Education: pharmacy (FP,D)

PHLEB National Accrediting Agency for Clinical Laboratory Sciences: phlebotomist (C)

PLNG Planning Accreditation Board: certified planning (B,M)

PNUR Accreditation Commission for Education in Nursing: practical nursing (C)

POD American Podiatric Medical Association: podiatry (FP,D)

POLYT Commission on Accreditation of Allied Health Education Programs: polysomnographic technologist education (C,A)

PSPSY American Psychological Association: combined professional-scientific psychology (D)

PTA American Physical Therapy Association: physical therapy (M,D)

PTAA American Physical Therapy Association: physical therapy assistant (A)

RABN Association of Advanced Rabbinical and Talmudic Schools: rabbinical and Talmudic education (B,M,D)

RAD Joint Review Committee on Education in Radiologic Technology: radiography (C,A,B)

RADDOS Joint Review Committee on Education in Radiologic Technology: medical dosimetry (C,B,M)

RADMAG Joint Review Committee on Education in Radiologic Technology: magnetic resonance (C,B)

RTT Joint Review Committee on Education in Radiologic Technology: radiation therapist/technologist (C,A,B)

SCPSY American Psychological Association: school psychology (D)

SP American Speech-Language-Hearing Association: speech-language pathology (M)

SPAA Network of Schools of Public Policy, Affairs and Administration: public affairs and administration (M)

SURGA Commission on Accreditation of Allied Health Education Programs: surgical assistant (C,A)

SURGT Commission on Accreditation of Allied Health Education Programs: surgical technology (C,A)

SURTEC Accrediting Bureau of Health Education Schools: surgical technologist (C,A)

SW Council on Social Work Education: social work (B,M)

TEAC Teacher Education Accreditation Council: teacher education (B,M,D)

TED National Council for Accreditation of Teacher Education: teacher education (B,M,S,D)

THEA National Association of Schools of Theatre: theatre (C,A,B,M,D)

THEOL Association of Theological Schools: theology (M,FP,D)

TRACS Transnational Association of Christian Colleges and Schools: christian studies education (C,A,B,M,D)

VET American Veterinary Medical Association: veterinary medicine (FP,D)

Explanatory Notes and Symbols

Associate degree: includes junior colleges, community colleges, technical institutes, and schools offering at least a two-year program of college-level studies, either leading to an associate degree wholly or principally creditable toward a baccalaureate degree.

Baccalaureate: includes those institutions offering programs of studies leading to the customary bachelor of arts or bachelor of science degrees.

First professional degree: includes those institutions that offer the academic requirements for selected professions based on programs that require at least two academic years of previous college work for entrance and a total of at least six years of college work for completion.

Master's: includes those institutions offering the customary first graduate degree, master of arts or master of science degree in the liberal arts and sciences, or the next degree in the same field after the first professional degree.

Beyond master's but less than doctorate: includes those institutions offering "postgraduate pre-doctoral degrees".

Graduate non-degree granting: includes institutions offering work beyond the bachelor's level but not conferring degrees. In some instances the degrees are conferred by cooperating institutions.

Doctorate: includes those institutions offering a Ph.D. or its equivalent in any field.

Postdoctoral research only: includes institutions operating solely for the purpose of research at the postdoctoral level.

First Talmudic degree: undergraduate degree granted by accredited Rabbinical schools. The schools in New York "using this designation do not imply that the 'First Talmudic Degree' is equivalent to any secular academic degree recognized by the Board of Regents".*

Second Talmudic degree: graduate degree granted by accredited Rabbinical schools. The schools in New York "using this designation do not imply that the 'Second Talmudic Degree' is equivalent to any secular academic degree recognized by the Board of Regents".*

*The University of the State of New York, The State Education Department, Albany, New York, letter August 17, 1983.

Type of Program

Occupational: refers to programs beyond high school designed to provide students with knowledge and skills necessary for immediate employment.

Two-year principally bachelor's creditable: refers to the first two years of college work.

Liberal arts and general: refers to four or five year baccalaureate or postbaccalaureate degree programs in the liberal arts and sciences.

Teacher preparatory programs: refers to programs of at least four years duration.

Professional programs: refers to separate programs of at least four years beyond high school and organized around a professionally oriented academic discipline.

Business, fine arts, music, nursing, religious, or technical emphasis: refers to programs that are organized around a specific discipline.

Symbols

* The institution is part of a system.

Used preceding any of the acronyms for the accrediting agencies the following symbols indicate that:

The accrediting agency has stated publicly that the institution or program is preliminary or provisionally accredited, accredited with some reservations, or approved on probation.

@ The institution or program has attained a pre-accredited status.

& The institution is covered under the regional accreditation of the parent institution.

U.S. Postal Abbreviation of States and Territories

Alabama .... AL
Alaska .... AK
American Samoa .... AS
Arizona .... AZ
Arkansas .... AR
California .... CA
Colorado .... CO
Connecticut .... CT
Delaware .... DE
District of Columbia .... DC
Florida .... FL
Georgia .... GA
Guam .... GU
Hawaii .... HI
Idaho .... ID
Illinois IL
Indiana .... IN
Iowa .... IA
Kansas .... KS
Kentucky .... KY
Louisiana .... LA
Maine .... ME
Maryland .... MD
Marshall Islands .... MH
Massachusetts .... MA
Michigan .... MI
Micronesia .... FM
Minnesota .... MN
Mississippi .... MS
Missouri .... MO
Montana .... MT
Nebraska .... NE
Nevada .... NV
New Hampshire .... NH
New Jersey .... NJ
New Mexico .... NM
New York .... NY
North Carolina .... NC
North Dakota .... ND
Northern Marianas .... MP
Ohio .... OH
Oklahoma .... OK
Oregon .... OR
Palau .... PW
Pennsylvania .... PA
Puerto Rico .... PR
Rhode Island .... RI
South Carolina .... SC
South Dakota .... SD
Tennessee .... TN
Texas .... TX
Utah .... UT
Vermont .... VT
Virgin Islands VI
Virginia .... VA
Washington .... WA
West Virginia .... WV
Wisconsin .... WI
Wyoming .... WY

Institution Changes

FICE/ID Number

Institutions and Offices Added

Alabama

Legacy Christian University 667251

Arkansas

Jefferson Regional Medical Center School of Nursing 023308

California

China Evangelical Seminary North America 667256
Christian Witness Theological Seminary 667255
Herguan University 667236
Kingston University 667237
Los Angeles Academy of Figurative Art 667231
National Polytechnic College 039104
The Broad Center for the Management of School Systems 667228
The Santa Barbara and Ventura Colleges of Law 667229
Zaytuna College 667230

Colorado

William Loveland College 667234

Delaware

Delaware Technical Community College, George Campus 770855

Florida

Advance Science Institute 037573
Atlantis University 042339
Bethesda College of Health Sciences 667258
Institute of Healthcare Professions 667238
Keiser University 770854
Taylor College 041166

Georgia

Pacific Institute of Technology 667239
Reformed University 667247

Hawaii

Hawaii Medical College 041822

Illinois

Northwest Suburban College 667240

Indiana

Faith Bible Seminary 667250
Union Bible College 667253

FICE/ID Number

Iowa

Simpson College 770849

Louisiana

NationsUniversity 667257
Southern University Law Center 667233

Michigan

Career Quest Learning Center 039153
Chamberlain College of Nursing-Troy 770851

Minnesota

Association Free Lutheran Bible School and Seminary 667235
Bethlehem College and Seminary 667249

Missouri

American Trade School 041748
Drury University Rolla Campus 770321
WellSpring School of Allied Health-Kansas City 039704

Montana

Yellowstone Christian College 667254

Nevada

Chamberlain College of Nursing-Las Vegas 770852

New Jersey

Bais Medrash Zicron Meir 667259
Chamberlain College of Nursing-North Brunswick 770850
Yeshiva Gedolah Shaarei Schmuel 667260

New Mexico

Burrell College of Osteopathic Medicine 667248
EC-Council University 667232

New York

Elim Bible Institute 667245

Oregon

Pacific Bible College 667252

Pennsylvania

Pittsburgh Career Institute 022023
Widener University Commonwealth Law School 667244

South Dakota

John Witherspoon College 667246

FICE/ID Number

Texas

Chamberlain College of Nursing-Irving 770853
School of Automotive Machinists 030323
Texas Tech University Health Sciences Center at El Paso 667243
Texas Tech University System 667242

Virginia

Danville Regional Medical Center School of Health Professions 021116
The Art Institute of Washington 770945
University of North America 667241

Wisconsin

Brensten Education 041379

Wyoming

Wyoming Catholic College 667227

Institutions and Offices Dropped

Alaska

Charter College 770626
(No longer separately accredited by ACICS)

Arizona

Everest College Phoenix 022950
(Closed)
Everest College Phoenix-Mesa 770010
(Closed)

California

Bryan College 033993
(Closed)
Charter College-Long Beach 770847
(Closed)
Chicago School of Professional Psychology-Westwood Campus 770491
(No longer listed as branch campus)
Everest College-Anaheim 011107
(Closed)
Everest College-City of Industry 030426
(Closed)
Everest College-Ontario Metro 666621
(Closed)
Everest College-Reseda 011109
(Closed)
Everest College-San Bernardino 004494
(Closed)
Everest College-Santa Ana 770610
(Closed)

FICE/ID Number

Everest College-West LA 666749
(Closed)
Four-D College 031623
(Closed)
Heald College, Central Office 666712
(Closed)
Heald College, Concord 020798
(Closed)
Heald College, Fresno 008093
(Closed)
Heald College, Hayward 025929
(Closed)
Heald College, Milpitas 025932
(Closed)
Heald College, Modesto 667043
(Closed)
Heald College, Rancho Cordova 007477
(Closed)
Heald College, Roseville 025931
(Closed)
Heald College, Salinas 030340
(Closed)
Heald College, San Francisco 007234
(Closed)
Heald College, Stockton 025933
(Closed)
Institute of Technology 770557
(Closed)
International Academy of Design and Technology 666740
(Closed)
ITT Technical Institute 022915
(Closed)
ITT Technical Institute 030874
(Closed)
United States University 770925
(Closed)
WyoTech-Fremont 007190
(Closed)
WyoTech-Long Beach 012873
(Closed)

Colorado

Yeshiva Toras Chaim Talmudical Seminary of Denver 667113
(No longer RABN accredited)

Connecticut

Lincoln College of New England Hartford College Campus 770130
(No longer degree granting)
University of Saint Joseph School of Pharmacy 770109
(no longer listed as a branch of University of Saint Joseph)

FICE/ID Number

Delaware

Delaware Technical Community College, Office of the President — 008074
(Closed)

Florida

American InterContinental University — 666336
(Closed)

Central Florida Institute — 034254
(Closed)

Central Florida Institute — 667022
(Closed)

Clearwater Christian College — 001473
(Closed)

Everest Institute — 021218
(Closed)

Everest Institute — 030032
(Closed)

Florida Career College — 025862
(Closed)

Florida College of Natural Health — 666830
(Closed)

Fortis College — 022455
(No longer degree granting)

Fortis College — 770564
(Branch of non-degree granting main campus)

Fortis College — 770565
(Branch of non-degree granting main campus)

International Academy of Design and Technology — 770686
(Closed)

ITT Technical Institute — 666536
(Closed)

Jones College — 770687
(Closed)

Kaplan College — 770688
(Closed)

Miami Ad School — 031256
(No longer degree granting)

Northwood University — 770279
(Closed)

Professional Golfers Career College — 666300
(Closed)

Sanford-Brown Institute — 666027
(Closed)

Sanford-Brown Institute — 770689
(Closed)

Georgia

Bauder College — 011574
(Closed)

Everest College — 770570
(Branch of non-degree granting main campus)

Hawaii

Heald College, Honolulu — 004546
(Closed)

FICE/ID Number

Illinois

Northwestern University Chicago Downtown Campus — 770090
(Closed)

Kentucky

Daymar College-Louisville — 666391
(Closed)

Daymar College-Paducah — 008425
(Closed)

Louisiana

Delta College of Arts & Technology — 025383
(No longer degree granting)

South Louisiana Community College Ardoin Campus — 022148
(Closed)

Maine

New England Bible College — 667135
(Withdrew accreditation)

Maryland

Sojourner-Douglass College — 021279
(Closed)

Massachusetts

Boston University Medical Campus — 770110
(No longer listed as branch of Boston University)

Marian Court College — 006873
(Closed)

Michigan

Davenport University Flint — 770265
(Closed)

International Academy of Design and Technology — 666632
(Closed)

Sanford-Brown College — 770694
(Closed)

Western Michigan University Cooley Law School Ann Arbor Campus — 770287
(Closed)

Mississippi

Blue Cliff College — 035253
(No longer degree granting)

Missouri

Everest College — 770618
(Closed)

Metro Business College — 770736
(Closed)

Sanford-Brown College — 022052
(Closed)

	FICE/ID Number
The School of Professional Psychology at Forest Institute *(Closed)*	021642

Nebraska

Vatterott College-Omaha *(Closed)*	007501

New Hampshire

University of New Hampshire at Manchester *(No longer listed as branch of University of New Hampshire)*	009009
University of New Hampshire School of Law *(No longer listed as branch of University of New Hampshire)*	020979

New York

Everest Institute *(Closed)*	004811
Institute of Design and Construction *(Withdrew accreditation)*	012107
Medaille College Amherst Branch Campus *(Closed)*	770139

Ohio

Cleveland Institute of Electronics *(No longer DETC accredited)*	005210
Daymar College-Chillicothe *(Closed)*	020568
Daymar College-Jackson *(Closed)*	666468
Daymar College-Lancaster *(Closed)*	666469
Daymar College-New Boston *(Closed)*	667082
Kaplan Career Institute *(Closed)*	025829
Ohio Mid-Western College (Formerly Temple Baptist College) *(Closed)*	037263
Sandford-Brown College *(Closed)*	770759

Oregon

Heald College, Portland *(Closed)*	037454
Oregon University System *(Closed)*	009190

Pennsylvania

Erie Business Center South *(Closed)*	003305
Erie Business Center, Main *(Closed)*	004894
Yorktowne Business Institute *(Closed)*	021208

	FICE/ID Number

Rhode Island

Mater Ecclesiae College *(Closed)*	041449

Tennessee

All Saints Bible College *(Denied accreditation)*	667014
International Academy of Design and Technology *(Closed)*	666347
West Tennessee Business College *(Closed)*	004947

Texas

Court Reporting Institute of Dallas *(Closed)*	021192
Everest College *(Closed)*	770789
Lighthouse College *(Closed)*	667106
Sanford-Brown College-Houston *(Closed)*	666382
Southwest Institute of Technology *(Closed)*	020936
The College of Saints John Fisher & Thomas More *(Closed)*	031894

Utah

Everest College *(Closed)*	022985

Virginia

Everest College *(Closed)*	770792
Sanford-Brown College-Tysons Corner *(Closed)*	009420

Washington

Charter College *(No longer separately accredited by ACICS)*	770820
Tacoma Bible College *(Closed)*	667139

West Virginia

Everest Institute *(Closed)*	010356

Wisconsin

ITT Technical Institute *(Closed)*	030875
Northland International University *(Closed)*	038725

FICE/ID Number

Merged Institutions

Arizona

Thunderbird School of Global Management *into* 001070
Arizona State University 001081

California

American College of Traditional Chinese Medicine *into* 030782
California Institute of Integral Studies 012154

Connecticut

Lyme Academy College of Fine Arts *into* 030794
University of New Haven *to become* 30794

Georgia

Moultrie Technical College *into* 005255
Merged with Southwest Georgia Technical College *to become*
Southern Regional Technical College 005615

Southern Polytechnic State University *into* 001570
Kennesaw State University 001577

Tennessee

Emmanuel Christian Seminary *into* 012547
Milligan College 003511

Tennessee Temple University *into* 003524
Piedmont International University 002956

Texas

The University of Texas at Brownsville and Texas Southmost College *into* 030646
University of Texas - Pan American *to become*
University of Texas Rio Grande Valley 003599

Name Changes

Alabama

from: Brown Mackie College 770625
to: Brown Mackie College - Birmingham

from: J.F. Drake State Technical College 005260
to: J.F. Drake State Community and Technical College

Arkansas

from: Mid-South Community College 023482
to: Arkansas State University-Mid-South

FICE/ID Number

California

from: Carrington College California - Administrative Office 666086
to: Carrington College - Administrative Office

from: Carrington College California - Citrus Heights 667042
to: Carrington College - Citrus Heights

from: Carrington College California - Pleasant Hill 666043
to: Carrington College - Pleasant Hill

from: Carrington College California - Pomona 770506
to: Carrington College - Pomona

from: Carrington College California - Sacramento 009748
to: Carrington College - Sacramento

from: Carrington College California - San Jose 666042
to: Carrington College - San Jose

from: Carrington College California - San Leandro 666751
to: Carrington College - San Leandro

from: Carrington College California - Stockton 666140
to: Carrington College - Stockton

from: Clovis Community College Center 667125
to: Clovis Community College

from: Empire College School of Business 009032
to: Empire College

from: Monterey Institute of International Studies 001241
to: Middlebury Institute of International Studies at Monterey

from: Mount St. Mary's College 001243
to: Mount Saint Mary's University

from: Sanford-Burnham Graduate School of Biomedical Sciences 667069
to: Sanford Burnham Prebys Medical Discovery Institute

Colorado

from: IntelliTec Medical Institute 008635
to: IBMC College

from: Mesa State College-Montrose Campus 770031
to: Colorado Mesa University-Montrose Campus

Delaware

from: Delaware Technical Community College, Stanton-Wilmington Campus 021449
to: Delaware Technical Community College, Stanton Campus

from: Widener University School of Law 012962
to: Widener University Delaware Law School

Florida

from: Chamberlain College of Nursing 770498
to: Chamberlain College of Nursing-Miramar

from: Med-Life Institute-Pompano Beach 667221
to: Med-Life Institute-Lauderdale Lakes

from: Southeastern College 666758
to: Keiser University at Clearwater

from: Southwest Florida College 770708
to: Southern Technical College-Tampa

	FICE/ID Number
from: Southwest Florida College *to:* Southern Technical College-Port Charlotte	770709

Georgia

	FICE/ID Number
from: Bainbridge College *to:* Bainbridge State College	011074
from: Georgia Regents University *to:* Augusta University	001579
from: Luther Rice University *to:* Luther Rice College and Seminary	031009
from: Middle Georgia State College *to:* Middle Georgia State University	007728
from: Southwest Georgia Technical College *to:* Southern Regional Technical College	005615

Hawaii

	FICE/ID Number
from: New Hope Christian College-Hawaii *to:* Pacific Rim Christian University	667010

Illinois

	FICE/ID Number
from: Adler School of Professional Psychology *to:* Adler University	020681
from: Chamberlain College of Nursing *to:* Chamberlain College of Nursing-Administrative Office	667149
from: Chamberlain College of Nursing *to:* Chamberlain College of Nursing-Chicago	770495
from: Chamberlain College of Nursing Tinley Park *to:* Chamberlain College of Nursing-Tinley Park	770496
from: John Hancock University *to:* Ellis University	041433
from: Southwestern Illinois College Granite City Campus *to:* Southwestern Illinois College Sam Wolf Granite City Campus	770095

Indiana

	FICE/ID Number
from: Chamberlain College of Nursing Indianapolis Campus *to:* Chamberlain College of Nursing-Indianapolis Campus	770503
from: National College *to:* American National University	010489
from: National College *to:* American National University	770695
from: National College *to:* American National University	770696

Iowa

	FICE/ID Number
from: Iowa Wesleyan College *to:* Iowa Wesleyan University	001871

Kansas

	FICE/ID Number
from: Hutchinson Community College and Area Vocational School *to:* Hutchinson Community College	001923
from: Kansas City College and Bible School *to:* Kansas Christian College	667134

Kentucky

	FICE/ID Number
from: Midway College *to:* Midway University	001975
from: National College *to:* American National University	666441
from: National College *to:* American National University	666442
from: National College *to:* American National University	666443
from: National College *to:* American National University	666444
from: National College *to:* American National University	666445
from: National College *to:* American National University	667202

Louisiana

	FICE/ID Number
from: Central Louisiana Technical College Huey P. Long Campus *to:* Central Louisiana Technical & Community College-Huey P. Long Campus	005480
from: Louisiana State University System Office *to:* Louisiana State University Administration	002009
from: South Central Louisiana Technical College River Parishes Campus *to:* South Central Louisiana Technical College Reserve Campus	023334

Maryland

	FICE/ID Number
from: Capitol College *to:* Capitol Technology University	001436

Massachusetts

	FICE/ID Number
from: Becker College-Worcester *to:* Becker College	002123
from: Massachusetts School of Professional Psychology *to:* William James College	021636
from: University of Massachusetts Central Office *to:* University of Massachusetts System Office	008017

Michigan

	FICE/ID Number
from: Bay Noc Community College *to:* Bay de Noc Community College	002240
from: Henry Ford Community College *to:* Henry Ford College	002270
from: University of Detroit Mercy Riverfront Campus *to:* University of Detroit Mercy School of Law	770292

Minnesota

	FICE/ID Number
from: Bethany College of Missions *to:* Bethany Global University	667136

FICE/ID Number

from: Brown College — 770733
to: Sanford-Brown College

from: Hazelden Graduate School of Addiction Studies — 040443
to: Hazelden Betty Ford Graduate School of Addiction Studies

from: Minnesota School of Business — 770717
to: Globe University

from: University of Minnesota-Twin Cities Rochester Campus — 770316
to: University of Minnesota-Rochester Campus

Missouri

from: Chamberlain College of Nursing-St. Louis — 770494
to: Chamberlain College of Nursing - St. Louis

from: City Vision College — 041191
to: City Vision University

from: Saint Louis Community College at Forest Park — 002471
to: Saint Louis Community College Center

from: Wentworth Military Academy and Junior College — 002522
to: Wentworth Military Academy and College

Nevada

from: Carrington College — 770742
to: Carrington College - Las Vegas

from: Carrington College — 770743
to: Carrington College - Reno

New Hampshire

from: The College of Saint Mary Magdalen — 022233
to: Northeast Catholic College

New Jersey

from: Burlington County College — 007730
to: Rowan College at Burlington County

from: The Richard Stockton College of New Jersey — 009345
to: Stockton University

New Mexico

from: Brown Mackie College — 770741
to: Brown Mackie College - Albuquerque

New York

from: City University of New York College of Staten Island — 002698
to: College of Staten Island CUNY

from: Crouse Hospital College of Nursing — 006445
to: Bill and Sandra Pomeroy College of Nursing at Crouse Hospital

from: State University of New York at Stony Brook — 002838
to: Stony Brook University

FICE/ID Number

North Carolina

from: New Life Theological Seminary — 038273
to: Charlotte Christian College and Theological Seminary

Ohio

from: National College — 770697
to: American National University

from: National College — 770698
to: American National University

from: National College — 770701
to: American National University

from: National College — 770699
to: American National University

from: National College — 770700
to: American National University

from: National College — 770702
to: American National University

from: National College — 770703
to: American National University

from: The Art Institute of Cincinnati — 021286
to: AIC College of Design

Oklahoma

from: Carl Albert State College Sallisaw Campus — 770366
to: Carl Albert State College

Pennsylvania

from: Baptist Bible College and Seminary — 002670
to: Summit University of Pennsylvania

from: Delaware Valley College — 003252
to: Delaware Valley University

from: Edinboro University of Pennsylvania — 003321
to: Edinboro University

from: Orleans Technical Institute — 021830
to: Orleans Technical College

from: The Penn State Dickinson School of Law — 003254
to: Dickinson Law

from: Valley Forge Christian College — 003306
to: University of Valley Forge

Puerto Rico

from: Bayamon Central University — 005022
to: Universidad Central de Bayamon

from: Columbia Centro Universitario — 008902
to: Columbia Central University

from: John Dewey College — 031121
to: Dewey University

from: John Dewey College-Bayamon — 770777
to: Dewey University-Bayamon

from: John Dewey College-Carolina — 770776
to: Dewey University-Carolina

from: John Dewey College-Fajardo — 770775
to: Dewey University-Fajardo

from: John Dewey College-Juana Diaz — 770774
to: Dewey University-Juana Diaz

FICE/ID Number

from: John Dewey College-Manati 770807
to: Dewey University-Manati

South Dakota

from: Augustana College 003458
to: Augustana University

Tennessee

from: National College of Business and Technology 004617
to: National College

from: National College of Business and Technology 666500
to: American National University

from: National College of Business and Technology 770783
to: National College

from: National College of Business and Technology 770784
to: National College

from: National College of Business and Technology 770785
to: National College

from: National College of Business and Technology 770786
to: American National University

Texas

from: Brown Mackie College 770798
to: Brown Mackie College - Dallas/Ft. Worth

from: Brown Mackie College 770799
to: Brown Mackie College - San Antonio

from: Chamberlain College of Nursing Pearland 770934
to: Chamberlain College of Nursing-Pearland Campus

from: Hallmark College of Technology 010509
to: Hallmark University

from: KD College-Conservatory of Film and Dramatic Arts 023182
to: KD Conservatory College of Film and Dramatic Arts

from: Remington College 030265
to: Remington College-Dallas Campus

from: Wade College Infomart 010130
to: Wade College

Vermont

from: Bread Loaf School of English in Vermont 770119
to: Middlebury Bread Loaf School of English

Virginia

from: Chamberlain College of Nursing 770497
to: Chamberlain College of Nursing - Arlington Campus

from: ECPI College of Technology 010198
to: ECPI University

from: Washington Baptist University 666234
to: Washington University of Virginia

FICE/ID Number

Washington

from: Bainbridge Graduate Institute 041612
to: Pinchot University

from: Cascadia Community College 034835
to: Cascadia College

from: Highline Community College 003781
to: Highline College

from: Seattle Central Community College 003787
to: Seattle Central College

West Virginia

from: West Virginia Junior College 770823
to: West Virginia Junior College-Bridgeport

Wisconsin

from: Herzing University Online Campus 770431
to: Herzing University Online

from: Maranatha Baptist Bible College & Seminary 023172
to: Maranatha Baptist University

from: Sacred Heart School of Theology 020780
to: Sacred Heart Seminary and School of Theology

Codes and Descriptions of Administrative Officers

(01) **Chief Executive Officer (President/Chancellor)** - Directs all affairs and operations of a higher education institution.

(02) **Chief Executive Officer Within a System (President/Chancellor)** - Directs all affairs and operations of a campus or an institution which is part of a university-wide system.

(03) **Executive Vice President** - Responsible for all or most functions and operations of an institution under the direction of the Chief Executive Officer.

(04) **Administrative Assistant to the President** - Senior administrative assistant to the Chief Executive Officer.

(05) **Chief Academic Officer** - Directs the academic program of the institution. Typically includes academic planning, teaching, research, extensions and coordination of interdepartmental affairs.

(06) **Registrar** - Responsible for student registration, scheduling of classes, examinations and classroom facilities, student records and related matters.

(07) **Director of Admissions** - Responsible for the recruitment, selection and admission of students.

(08) **Head Librarian** - Directs the activities of all institutional libraries.

(09) **Director of Institutional Research** - Conducts research and studies on the institution including design of studies, data collection, analysis and reporting.

(10) **Chief Financial/Business Officer** - Directs business and financial affairs including accounting, purchasing, investments, auxiliary enterprises and related business matters.

(11) **Chief of Operations/Administration** - Responsible for administrative functions that are generally non-academic and non-financial.

(12) **Director of Branch Campus** - Official who is in charge of a branch campus.

(13) **Director, Computing and Information Management** - Coordinates computing systems and the flow of information to and from computing operations.

(14) **Director, Computer Center** - Directs the institution's major data processing facilities and services.

(15) **Director, Personnel Services** - Administers the institution's personnel policies and programs for staff or faculty and staff.

(16) **Chief, Personnel** - Responsible for establishing and directing personnel policies including government related requirements.

(17) **Chief, Health Care Professions** - Senior administrator of academic health care programs, hospitals, clinic or affiliated healthcare programs.

(18) **Chief, Facilities/Physical Plant** - Responsible for the construction, rehabilitation and maintenance of buildings and grounds.

(19) **Director, Security/Safety** - Manages campus police. Responsible for security programs, training, traffic and parking regulations.

(20) **Associate Academic Officer** - Responsible for many of the functions and operations under the direction of the Chief Academic Officer.

(21) **Associate Business Officer** - Assists and reports to the Chief Business Officer.

(22) **Director, Affirmative Action/Equal Opportunity** - Responsible for the institution's program relating to affirmative action and equal opportunity.

(23) **Director, Health Services** - Directs the operation of clinics, medical staff and other programs which provide institutional health services.

(24) **Director, Educational Media** - Responsible for audio-visual services and multimedia learning devices.

(25) **Contract Administrator** - Conducts administrative activities in connection with contracts and grants.

(26) **Chief Public Relations Officer** - Directs public relations program. May include alumni relations, publication, marketing and development.

(27) **Chief Information Officer** - Provides information about the institution to students, faculty, staff and the public.

(28) **Director of Diversity** - Responsible for the institution's programs relating to diversity.

(29) **Director, Alumni Relations** - Coordinates alumni activities between the institution and the alumni.

(30) **Chief, Development** - Organizes and directs programs connected with the fund raising activities of the institution.

(31) **Chief Community Relations Officer** - Directs the educational (usually non-credit), cultural and recreational services to the community.

(32) **Chief Student Life Officer** - Responsible for the direction of student life programs including counseling and testing, housing, placement, student union, relationships with student organizations and related functions.

(33) **Dean of Men** - Directs student life activities solely concerned with male students.

(34) **Dean of Women** - Directs student life activities solely concerned with female students.

(35) **Director, Student Affairs** - Assists Chief Student Life Officer in the non-academic student life activities.

(36) **Director, Student Placement** - Directs the operation of the student placement office to provide career counseling and job placement services to undergraduates, graduates and alumni.

(37) **Director, Student Financial Aid** - Directs the administration of all forms of student aid.

(38) **Director, Student Counseling** - Directs non-academic counseling and testing for students including referral to outside agencies.

(39) **Director, Student Housing** - Manages student housing operations.

(40) **Director, Bookstore** - Responsible for the operation of the bookstore including purchasing, advertising, sales, employment, inventory and related functions.

(41) **Athletic Director** - Manages intramural and intercollegiate programs including employment, scheduling, promotion, maintenance and related functions.

(42) **Chaplain, Director Campus Ministry** - Plans, directs the pastoral ministry and religious activities.

(43) **Director, Legal Services (General Counsel)** - Salaried staff person responsible for advising on legal rights, obligations and related matters.

(44) **Director, Annual or Planned Giving** - Operates the annual giving from all supporters of the institutions.

(45) **Chief Planning Officer** - Directs the long-range planning and the allocation of the institution's resources.

(46) **Chief, Research and Development (not fundraising)** - Initiates and directs research in using the facilities and personnel in new areas of academic and scientific exploration.

Dean or Director. Serves as the principal administrator for the institutional program indicated:

- (47) **Agriculture**
- (48) **Architecture**
- (49) **Art and Sciences**
- (50) **Business**
- (51) **Continuing Education**
- (52) **Dentistry**
- (53) **Education**
- (54) **Engineering**
- (55) **Evening Division**
- (56) **Extension**
- (57) **Fine Arts**
- (58) **Graduate Programs**
- (59) **Home Economics**
- (60) **Journalism/Communications**
- (61) **Law**
- (62) **Library Services**
- (63) **Medicine**
- (64) **Music**
- (65) **Natural Resources**
- (66) **Nursing**
- (67) **Pharmacy**
- (68) **Physical Education**
- (69) **Public Health**
- (70) **Social Work**
- (71) **Special Session**
- (72) **Technology**
- (73) **Theology**
- (74) **Veterinary Medicine**
- (75) **Vocational/Occupational Education**
- (76) **Allied Health Sciences**
- (77) **Computer Science**
- (78) **Cooperative Education**
- (79) **Humanities**
- (80) **Government/Public Affairs**
- (81) **Mathematics/Sciences**
- (82) **Political Science/International Affairs**
- (83) **Social and Behavioral Sciences**
- (87) **Summer School/Session**
- (89) **Freshmen Studies**
- (92) **Honors Program**
- (93) **Minority Students**
- (94) **Women's Studies**
- (97) **General Studies**
- (106) **Online Education/E-learning**
- (107) **Professional Studies**

(84) **Director, Enrollment Management** - Plans, develops, and implements strategies to sustain enrollment. Supervises administration of all admissions and financial aid operations.

(85) **Director, Foreign Students** - Directs student life activities solely concerned with foreign students.

(86) **Director, Government Relations** - Coordinates institution's relations with local, state, and federal government.

(90) **Director, Academic Computing** - Responsible for operation and coordination of the institution's various academic computer facilities and labs.

(91) **Director, Administrative Computing** - Responsible for operation of the institution's administrative computing facility.

(96) **Director of Purchasing** - Coordinates purchasing of goods and services.

(100) **Chief of Staff** - Senior non-secretarial staff assistant to the President/Chancellor. Manages administration and operations of The Office of the President.

(101) **Secretary of the Institution/Board of Governors** - Responsible for liaison between the Board and the institution. Maintains governance and official Board records.

(102) **Director, Foundation/Corporate Relations** - Directs institution's efforts in the area of soliciting grants and gifts from foundations and corporations.

(103) **Director, Workforce Development** - Directs the institution's efforts in course development and instruction for students and the community in skills necessary to gain employment.

(104) **Director, Study Abroad** - Coordinates and advises students and faculty on academic studies conducted internationally.

(105) **Director, Web Services** - Directs the development, operations and content of the institution's web sites.

(108) **Director, Institutional Assessment** - Facilitates and directs institution-wide assessment activities for academic programs and non-academic departments.

(109) **Chief Auxiliary Services Officer** - Responsible for management and operations of college support services including food service, bookstore, vending, student union, and printing.

(88) Use this code for those titles that do not fit the above positions.

(00) **President Emeritus**

United States Department of Education Offices

Arne Duncan (A)
Secretary of Education
United States Department of Education
400 Maryland Avenue, SW
Washington, DC 20202
(202) 401-3000
FAX: (202) 260-7867
URL: www.ed.gov

Mr. Ted Mitchell (B)
Under Secretary of Education
United States Department of Education
400 Maryland Avenue, SW
Room 7E307
Washington, DC 20202
(202) 401-2616
URL: www.ed.gov

Lynn Mahaffie (C)
Assistant Secretary
Office of Postsecondary Education
United States Department of Education
1990 K Street, NW
Room 7115
Washington, DC 20006
(202) 502-7750
URL: www2.ed.gov/about/offices/list/ope/index.html

Jennifer Hong Ed.D. (D)
Executive Director
National Advisory Committee on Institutional Quality & Integrity
Office of Postsecondary Education
United States Department of Education
1990 K Street, NW
Room 8073
Washington, DC 20006
(202) 502-7696
FAX: (202) 219-7005
E-MAIL: jennifer.hong@ed.gov
URL: www.ed.gov/about/bdscomm/list/naciqi.html

Herman Bounds Jr., Ed.S. (E)
Director
Accreditation Group
Office of Postsecondary Education
U.S. Department of Education
1990 K Street, NW
Room 8074
Washington, DC 20006-8509
(202) 219-7011
URL: www2.ed.gov/admins/finaid/accred/index.html

Dr. Peggy G. Carr (F)
Acting Commissioner
National Center for Education Statistics
1990 K Street, NW
Room 8095
Washington, DC 20006
(202) 502-7448
URL: www.nces.ed.gov

Jennifer Hong Ed.D. (G)
Executive Director
National Committee on Foreign Medical Education
and Accreditation (NCFMEA)
U.S. Department of Education
1990 K Street, NW
Room 8073
Washington, DC 20006
(202) 502-7696
FAX: (202) 219-7005
E-MAIL: jennifer.hong@ed.gov
URL: www2.ed.gov/about/bdscomm/list/ncfmea.html

Statewide Agencies of Higher Education

ALABAMA

Alabama Commission on Higher Education (H)
PO Box 302000
Montgomery, AL 36130-2000
(334) 242-1998
FAX: (334) 242-0268
Dr. Gregory G. Fitch
Executive Director
E-MAIL: gregory.fitch@ache.alabama.gov
URL: www.ache.alabama.gov

Alabama Community College System (I)
135 South Union Street
PO Box 302130
Montgomery, AL 36130
(334) 293-4524
FAX: (334) 293-4526
Mark A. Heinrich Ph.D.
Chancellor
E-MAIL: mark.heinrich@accs.edu
URL: www.accs.edu

ALASKA

Alaska Commission on Postsecondary Education (J)
PO Box 110505
Juneau, AK 99811-0505
(907) 465-6740
FAX: (907) 465-3293
Ms. Diane Barrans
Executive Director
E-MAIL: ACPE.execdirector@alaska.gov
URL: www.acpe.alaska.gov

ARIZONA

Arizona Board of Regents (K)
2020 North Central Avenue
Suite 230
Phoenix, AZ 85004-4593
(602) 229-2500
FAX: (602) 229-2555
Eileen Klein
President
E-MAIL: eileen.klein@azregents.edu
URL: www.azregents.edu

Arizona Commission for Postsecondary Education (L)
2020 North Central Avenue
Suite 650
Phoenix, AZ 85004-4503
(602) 258-2435
FAX: (602) 258-2483
Dr. April L. Osborn
Executive Director
E-MAIL: acpe@azhighered.gov
URL: highered.az.gov

ARKANSAS

Arkansas Department of Higher Education (M)
423 Main Street
Suite 400
Little Rock, AR 72201
(501) 371-2030
FAX: (501) 371-2003
Dr. Brett Powell
Director of Higher Education
E-MAIL: brett.powell@adhe.edu
URL: www.adhe.edu

CALIFORNIA

California Community Colleges Chancellor's Office (N)
1102 Q Street
4th Floor
Sacramento, CA 95811
(916) 322-4005
FAX: (916) 322-4783
Dr. Brice W. Harris
Chancellor
E-MAIL: bharris@cccco.edu
URL: www.cccco.edu

COLORADO

Colorado Department of Higher Education (O)
1560 Broadway
Suite 1600
Denver, CO 80202
(303) 862-3001
FAX: (303) 996-1329
Lt.Gov. Joseph Garcia
Executive Director
E-MAIL: josephgarcia.executivedirector@dhe.state.co.us
URL: highered.colorado.gov

Colorado Community College System (P)
9101 East Lowry Boulevard
Denver, CO 80230-6011
(303) 595-1552
FAX: (303) 620-4043
Dr. Nancy J. McCallin
President
E-MAIL: president@cccs.edu
URL: www.cccs.edu

CONNECTICUT

Board of Regents for Higher Education (Q)
Connecticut State Colleges & Universities
39 Woodland Street
Hartford, CT 06105
(860) 723-0011
FAX: (860) 723-0009
Dr. Gregory W. Gray
President
E-MAIL: grayg@ct.edu
URL: www.ct.edu

Office of Higher Education (R)
61 Woodland Street
Hartford, CT 06105-2326
(860) 947-1801
FAX: (860) 947-1310
Jane A. Ciarleglio
Executive Director
E-MAIL: jciarleglio@ctohe.org
URL: www.ctohe.org

DELAWARE

Delaware Department of Education Higher Education Office (S)
Townsend Building
401 Federal Street
Suite 2
Dover, DE 19901
(302) 735-4120
FAX: (302) 739-5894
Shana Payne
Director
E-MAIL: dheo@doe.k12.de.us
URL: www.doe.k12.de.us

Delaware Technical Community College (T)
PO Box 897
Dover, DE 19903
(302) 857-1667
FAX: (302) 857-1647
Dr. Mark T. Brainard
President
E-MAIL: brainard@dtcc.edu
URL: www.dtcc.edu

DISTRICT OF COLUMBIA

Office of the State Superintendent of Education Government of the District of Columbia (U)
810 First Street, NE
3rd Floor
Washington, DC 20002
(202) 741-0471
FAX: (202) 727-2019
Antoinette S. Mitchell
Assistant Superintendent, Postsecondary Education
E-MAIL: antoinette.mitchell@dc.gov
URL: www.osse.dc.gov

District of Columbia Education Licensure Commission (V)
810 First Street, NE
2nd Floor
Washington, DC 20002
(202) 481-3951
FAX: (202) 741-0229
Ms. Angela Lee
Executive Director
E-MAIL: osse.elcmail@dc.gov
URL: osse.dc.gov/service/education-licensure-commission-elc

FLORIDA

Board of Governors State University System of Florida (W)
325 West Gaines Street
Suite 1614
Tallahassee, FL 32399-0400
(850) 245-0466
FAX: (850) 245-9685
Mr. Marshall M. Criser III
Chancellor
E-MAIL: chancellor@flbog.edu
URL: www.flbog.edu

Florida Department of Education Division of Florida Colleges (X)
325 West Gaines Street
1544 Turlington Building
Tallahassee, FL 32399-0400
(850) 245-0407
FAX: (850) 245-9525
Ms. Madeline M. Pumariega
Chancellor
E-MAIL: chancellorfcs@fldoe.org
URL: www.fldoe.org/schools/higher-ed/fl-college-system/

GEORGIA

Board of Regents of the University System of Georgia (Y)
270 Washington Street, SW
Atlanta, GA 30334
(404) 962-3000
FAX: (404) 962-3013
Mr. Henry Huckaby
Chancellor
E-MAIL: chancellor@usg.edu
URL: www.usg.edu

University System of Georgia (Z)
270 Washington Street, SW
Atlanta, GA 30334
(404) 962-3069
FAX: (404) 962-3094
Dr. Angela Bell
Sr. Executive Director Research & Policy Analysis
E-MAIL: angela.bell@usg.edu
URL: www.usg.edu

HAWAII

University of Hawaii Board of Regents (a)
2444 Dole Street
Bachman Hall, Room 209
Honolulu, HI 96822
(808) 956-8213
FAX: (808) 956-5156
Mr. Randolph G. Moore
Chair
E-MAIL: bor@hawaii.edu
URL: www.hawaii.edu/offices/bor/

IDAHO

Idaho State Board of Education (A)
PO Box 83720
Boise, ID 83720-0037
(208) 334-2270
FAX: (208) 334-2632
Mr. Matt Freeman
Executive Director
E-MAIL: matt.freeman@osbe.idaho.gov
URL: www.boardofed.idaho.gov

ILLINOIS

Illinois Board of Higher Education (B)
1 N. Old State Capitol Plaza
Suite 333
Springfield, IL 62701-1377
(217) 782-2551
FAX: (217) 782-8548
Dr. James L. Applegate
Executive Director
E-MAIL: applegate@ibhe.org
URL: www.ibhe.org

Illinois Community College Board (C)
401 East Capitol Avenue
Springfield, IL 62701-1874
(217) 785-0123
FAX: (217) 785-7495
Dr. Karen Hunter Anderson
Executive Director
E-MAIL: karen.h.anderson@illinois.gov
URL: www.iccb.org

INDIANA

Indiana Commission for Higher Education (D)
101 West Ohio Street
Suite 300
Indianapolis, IN 46204
(317) 464-4400
FAX: (317) 464-4410
Mrs. Teresa Lubbers
Commissioner for Higher Education
E-MAIL: tlubbers@che.in.gov
URL: www.che.in.gov

IOWA

Board of Regents, State of Iowa (E)
11260 Aurora Avenue
Urbandale, IA 50322-7905
(515) 281-3934
FAX: (515) 281-6420
Mr. Robert Donley
Executive Director
E-MAIL: bdonley@iastate.edu
URL: www.regents.iowa.gov

Iowa College Student Aid Commission (F)
430 East Grand Avenue
3rd Floor
Des Moines, IA 50309
(515) 725-3410
FAX: (515) 725-3401
Ms. Karen Misjak
Executive Director
E-MAIL: karen.misjak@iowa.gov
URL: www.iowacollegeaid.gov

Iowa Department of Education Division of Community Colleges (G)
400 East 14th Street
Grimes State Office Building
Des Moines, IA 50319-0146
(515) 281-8260
FAX: (515) 242-5988
Jeremy Varner
Administrator
E-MAIL: jeremy.varner@iowa.gov
URL: www.educateiowa.gov

KANSAS

Kansas Board of Regents (H)
1000 SW Jackson
Suite 520
Topeka, KS 66612-1368
(785) 296-3421
FAX: (785) 296-0983
Dr. Blake Flanders
President and CEO
E-MAIL: bflanders@ksbor.org
URL: www.kansasregents.org

Kansas Legislative Research Department (I)
Room 68 West, State Capitol Building
300 SW 10th Avenue
Topeka, KS 66612-1504
(785) 296-3181
FAX: (785) 296-3824
Mr. Raney L. Gilliland
Director
E-MAIL: kslegres@klrd.ks.gov
URL: www.kslegresearch.org

KENTUCKY

Kentucky Council on Postsecondary Education (J)
1024 Capital Center Drive
Suite 320
Frankfort, KY 40601
(502) 573-1555
FAX: (502) 573-1535
Mr. Robert L. King
President
E-MAIL: mary.allison@ky.gov
URL: cpe.ky.gov

Kentucky Community & Technical College System (K)
300 North Main Street
Versailles, KY 40383
(859) 256-3132
FAX: (859) 256-3116
Dr. Jay K. Box
President
E-MAIL: president@kctcs.edu
URL: www.kctcs.edu

LOUISIANA

Louisiana Board of Regents (L)
PO Box 3677
Baton Rouge, LA 70821-3677
(225) 342-4253
FAX: (225) 342-9318
Dr. Joseph C. Rallo
Commissioner of Higher Education
E-MAIL: joseph.rallo@la.gov
URL: regents.la.gov

Louisiana Department of Education (M)
PO Box 94064
Baton Rouge, LA 70804-9064
(225) 342-3607
FAX: (225) 342-7316
Mr. John White
State Superintendent of Education
E-MAIL: louisianabelieves@la.gov
URL: www.louisianabelieves.com

MAINE

Maine Department of Education Office of Higher Education (N)
23 State House Station
Augusta, ME 04333-0023
(207) 624-6600
FAX: (207) 624-6700
Mr. Thomas A. Desjardin
Acting Commissioner
E-MAIL: commish.doe@maine.gov
URL: www.maine.gov/doe/

MARYLAND

Maryland Higher Education Commission (O)
6 North Liberty Street, 10th Floor
Baltimore, MD 21201
(410) 767-3301
FAX: (410) 332-0270
Jennie C. Hunter-Cevera
Acting Secretary of Higher Education
E-MAIL: jennie.hunter-cevera@maryland.gov
URL: www.mhec.state.md.us

MASSACHUSETTS

Massachusetts Department of Higher Education (P)
One Ashburton Place
Room 1401
Boston, MA 02108
(617) 994-6901
FAX: (617) 727-6656
Mr. Carlos Santiago
Commissioner
E-MAIL: commissioner@bhe.mass.edu
URL: www.mass.edu

MICHIGAN

Department of Licensing and Regulatory Affairs Corporations, Securities & Commercial Licensing Bureau Licensing Division (Q)
PO Box 30714
Lansing, MI 48909-8214
(517) 241-1017
FAX: (517) 373-3085
Mr. Michael Beamish
Manager
E-MAIL: beamishm@michigan.gov
URL: www.michigan.gov/cscl

Workforce Development Agency, State of Michigan Division of Education and Career Success (R)
201 North Washington Square
Victor Building, 5th Floor
Lansing, MI 48913
(517) 335-5858
FAX: (517) 241-8217
Ms. Christine Quinn
Director
URL: www.michigan.gov/adulteducation

MINNESOTA

Minnesota Office of Higher Education (S)
1450 Energy Park Drive
Suite 350
St. Paul, MN 55108-5227
(651) 642-0567
FAX: (651) 642-0597
Mr. Larry Pogemiller
Commissioner
E-MAIL: info.ohe@state.mn.us
URL: www.ohe.state.mn.us

Minnesota State Colleges and Universities (T)
30 7th Street East
Suite 350
St. Paul, MN 55101-7804
(651) 201-1696
FAX: (651) 297-7465
Dr. Steven J. Rosenstone
Chancellor
E-MAIL: steven.rosenstone@so.mnscu.edu
URL: www.mnscu.edu

MISSISSIPPI

Board of Trustees of State Institutions of Higher Learning (U)
3825 Ridgewood Road
Jackson, MS 39211
(601) 432-6198
FAX: (601) 432-6972
Dr. Glenn Boyce
Commissioner of Higher Education
E-MAIL: gboyce@ihl.state.ms.us
URL: www.mississippi.edu

Mississippi Community College Board (V)
3825 Ridgewood Drive
Jackson, MS 39211
(601) 432-6684
FAX: (601) 432-6480
Mrs. Deborah Gilbert CPA
Interim Executive Director
E-MAIL: info@mccb.edu
URL: www.mccb.edu

MISSOURI

Coordinating Board for Higher Education Missouri Department of Higher Education (W)
205 Jefferson Street, 11th Floor
PO Box 1469
Jefferson City, MO 65102-1469
(573) 751-2361
FAX: (573) 751-6635
Dr. David R. Russell
Commissioner of Higher Education
E-MAIL: david.russell@dhe.mo.gov
URL: www.dhe.mo.gov/cbhe/

MONTANA

Office of the Commissioner of Higher Education (X)
PO Box 203201
Academic, Research & Student Affairs
Helena, MT 59620-3201
(406) 444-0316
FAX: (406) 444-1469
John Cech
Deputy Commissioner
E-MAIL: jcech@montana.edu
URL: www.mus.edu/che

NEBRASKA

Coordinating Commission for Postsecondary Education (Y)
PO Box 95005
Lincoln, NE 68509-5005
(402) 471-2847
FAX: (402) 471-2886
Dr. Michael Baumgartner
Executive Director
E-MAIL: mike.baumgartner@nebraska.gov
URL: www.ccpe.ne.gov

NEVADA

Nevada System of Higher Education (Z)
4300 S. Maryland Parkway
Las Vegas, NV 89119
(702) 889-8426
FAX: (702) 889-8495
Mr. Daniel J. Klaich
Chancellor
E-MAIL: chancellor@nevada.edu
URL: www.nevada.edu

Nevada System of Higher Education (a)
2601 Enterprise Road
Reno, NV 89512
(775) 784-3222
FAX: (775) 784-6520
Mr. Daniel J. Klaich
Chancellor
E-MAIL: chancellor@nevada.edu
URL: www.nevada.edu

NEW HAMPSHIRE

New Hampshire Department of Education Division of Higher Education Higher Education Commission (b)
101 Pleasant Street
Concord, NH 03301
(603) 271-0256
FAX: (603) 271-1953
Dr. Edward R. MacKay
Director
E-MAIL: patricia.edes@doe.nh.gov
URL: www.education.nh.gov/highered

Community College System of New Hampshire (c)
26 College Drive
Concord, NH 03301
(603) 230-3501
FAX: (603) 271-2725
Dr. Ross Gittell
Chancellor
E-MAIL: rgittell@ccsnh.edu
URL: www.ccsnh.edu

NEW JERSEY

Office of the Secretary of Higher Education (d)
20 West State Street, 4th Floor
PO Box 542
Trenton, NJ 08625-0542
(609) 292-4310
FAX: (609) 292-7225
E-MAIL: njhe@oshe.nj.gov
URL: www.state.nj.us/highereducation

NEW MEXICO

New Mexico Higher Education Department (e)
2044 Galisteo Street
Santa Fe, NM 87505
(505) 476-8404
FAX: (505) 476-8454
Dr. Barbara Damron
Cabinet Secretary
E-MAIL: exec.admin@state.nm.us
URL: www.hed.state.nm.us

NEW YORK

New York State Education Department (A)
89 Washington Avenue
Education Building, Room 111
Albany, NY 12234
(518) 474-5844
Fax: (518) 473-4909
MaryEllen Elia
Commissioner
E-mail: commissioner@nysed.gov

Community Colleges and the Education Pipeline (B)
The State University of New York
SUNY Plaza, 353 Broadway, Room T7
Albany, NY 12246
(518) 320-1276
Fax: (518) 320-1570
Johanna Duncan-Poitier
Senior Vice Chancellor
E-mail: johanna.duncan-poitier@suny.edu
URL: www.suny.edu

New York State Education Department Office of Higher Education (C)
Education Building Annex
Room 977
Albany, NY 12234
(518) 486-3633
Fax: (518) 486-2254
Mr. John D'Agati
Deputy Commissioner
E-mail: john.dagati@nysed.gov
URL: www.highered.nysed.gov

NORTH CAROLINA

The University of North Carolina (D)
910 Raleigh Road
Chapel Hill, NC 27514
(919) 962-9000
Fax: (919) 843-9695
Mr. Thomas W. Ross
President
E-mail: tomross@northcarolina.edu
URL: www.northcarolina.edu

North Carolina Community College System (E)
200 West Jones Street
Raleigh, NC 27603
(919) 807-6950
Fax: (919) 807-7166
Dr. Scott Ralls
President
E-mail: rallss@nccommunitycolleges.edu
URL: www.nccommunitycolleges.edu

NORTH DAKOTA

North Dakota State Board of Higher Education (F)
600 East Boulevard Avenue
State Capitol
10th Floor
Bismarck, ND 58505-0230
(701) 328-2960
Fax: (701) 328-2961
Dr. Kathleen Neset
Board Chair
E-mail: k.neset@ndus.edu
URL: www.ndus.edu/board

OHIO

Ohio Department of Higher Education (G)
25 South Front Street
Columbus, OH 43215
(614) 466-6000
Fax: (614) 466-5866
Mr. John Carey
Chancellor
E-mail: chancellor@regents.state.oh.us
URL: www.regents.ohio.gov

OKLAHOMA

Oklahoma State Regents for Higher Education (H)
655 Research Parkway
Suite 200
Oklahoma City, OK 73104
(405) 225-9100
Fax: (405) 225-9235
Dr. Glen D. Johnson
Chancellor
E-mail: gjohnson@osrhe.edu
URL: www.okhighered.org

OREGON

Higher Education Coordinating Commission (I)
775 Court Street NE
Salem, OR 97301
(503) 378-5690
Ben Cannon
Executive Director
E-mail: info.HECC@state.or.us
URL: www.oregon.gov/HigherEd

Oregon Department of Community Colleges and Workforce Development (J)
255 Capitol Street, NE
Salem, OR 97310
(503) 378-8648
Fax: (503) 378-3365
Mr. Jim Middleton
Commissioner
E-mail: jim.middleton@state.or.us
URL: www.oregon.gov/ccwd

PENNSYLVANIA

Pennsylvania Department of Education Postsecondary and Higher Education Institutions (K)
333 Market Street
12th Floor
Harrisburg, PA 17126-0333
(717) 772-3737
Fax: (717) 772-3622
Dr. Wil Del Pilar
Acting Deputy Secretary
E-mail: widelpilar@pa.gov
URL: www.education.state.pa.us

Pennsylvania Department of Education Liaison to Postsecondary and Higher Education Institutions (L)
333 Market Street
12th Floor
Harrisburg, PA 17126-0333
(717) 783-8228
Fax: (717) 772-3622
Ms. Patricia Landis
Division Chief - Higher and Career Education
E-mail: plandis@pa.gov
URL: www.education.pa.gov

RHODE ISLAND

Rhode Island Council on Postsecondary Education (M)
80 Washington Street
Suite 524
Providence, RI 02903
(401) 456-6000
Fax: (401) 456-6028
Commissioner of Postsecondary Education
URL: www.ribghe.org

Community College of Rhode Island (N)
400 East Avenue
Warwick, RI 02886
(401) 825-2188
Fax: (401) 825-2166
Mr. Ray M. Di Pasquale
President
E-mail: rmdipasquale@ccri.edu
URL: www.ccri.edu

SOUTH CAROLINA

South Carolina Commission on Higher Education (O)
1122 Lady Street
Suite 300
Columbia, SC 29201
(803) 737-2275
Fax: (803) 737-2297
Ms. Julie Carullo
Interim Executive Director
E-mail: jcarullo@che.sc.gov
URL: www.che.sc.gov

South Carolina State Board for Technical and Comprehensive Education (P)
111 Executive Center Drive
Columbia, SC 29210
(803) 896-5320
Fax: (803) 896-5281
Dr. James C. Williamson
System President
URL: www.sctechsystem.edu

SOUTH DAKOTA

South Dakota Board of Regents (Q)
306 East Capitol Avenue
Suite 200
Pierre, SD 57501
(605) 773-3455
Fax: (605) 773-5320
Dr. Michael G. Rush
Executive Director and Chief Executive Officer
E-mail: mike.rush@sdbor.edu
URL: www.sdbor.edu

South Dakota Department of Education (R)
Office of the Secretary
800 Governors Drive
Pierre, SD 57501-2291
(605) 773-5669
Fax: (605) 773-6139
Dr. Melody Schopp
Secretary
E-mail: melody.schopp@state.sd.us
URL: www.doe.sd.gov

TENNESSEE

Tennessee Higher Education Commission (S)
404 James Robertson Parkway
Suite 1900
Nashville, TN 37243
(615) 741-3605
Fax: (615) 741-6230
Mr. Russ Deaton
Interim Executive Director
E-mail: russ.deaton@tn.gov
URL: www.tn.gov/thec/

Tennessee Board of Regents (T)
1415 Murfreesboro Road
Suite 350
Nashville, TN 37217
(615) 366-4448
Fax: (615) 366-3903
Dr. Tristan Denley
Vice Chancellor for Academics
E-mail: tristan.denley@tbr.edu
URL: www.tbr.edu

University of Tennessee Board of Trustees (U)
719 Andy Holt Tower
Knoxville, TN 37996-0170
(865) 974-3245
Fax: (865) 974-3074
Ms. Catherine S. Mizell
General Counsel and Secretary
E-mail: cmizell@tennessee.edu
URL: bot.tennessee.edu

TEXAS

Texas Higher Education Coordinating Board (V)
PO Box 12788
Austin, TX 78711
(512) 427-6101
Fax: (512) 427-6127
Dr. Raymund A. Paredes
Commissioner of Higher Education
E-mail: raymund.paredes@thecb.state.tx.us
URL: www.thecb.state.tx.us

Texas Higher Education Coordinating Board Division of College Readiness and Success (W)
PO Box 12788
Austin, TX 78711-2788
(512) 427-6545
Fax: (512) 427-6444
Dr. Mary E. Smith
Interim Assistant Commissioner
E-mail: mary.smith@thecb.state.tx.us
URL: www.thecb.state.tx.us

UTAH

Utah System of Higher Education State Board of Regents (X)
60 South 400 West
Salt Lake City, UT 84101-1284
(801) 321-7101
Fax: (801) 321-7156
David L. Buhler
Commissioner of Higher Education
E-mail: dbuhler@ushe.edu
URL: higheredutah.org

VERMONT

Vermont Agency of Education (Y)
219 North Main Street
Suite 402
Barre, VT 05641
(802) 479-1043
Mr. Brad James
Education Finance Manager
E-mail: brad.james@vermont.gov
URL: www.education.vermont.gov

VIRGINIA

State Council of Higher Education for Virginia (Z)
101 North 14th Street
James Monroe Building
10th Floor
Richmond, VA 23219
(804) 225-2600
Fax: (804) 225-2604
Mr. Peter Blake
Director
E-mail: peterblake@schev.edu
URL: www.schev.edu

Virginia Community College System (a)
300 Arboretum Place
Suite 200
Richmond, VA 23236
(804) 819-4903
Fax: (804) 819-4760
Dr. Glenn DuBois
Chancellor
E-mail: gdubois@vccs.edu
URL: www.vccs.edu

WASHINGTON

Washington Student Achievement Council (b)
917 Lakeridge Way, SW
PO Box 43430
Olympia, WA 98504-3430
(360) 753-7800
Fax: (360) 753-7808
Dr. Gene Sharratt Ph.D.
Executive Director
E-mail: info@wsac.wa.gov
URL: www.wsac.wa.gov

Washington State Board for Community and Technical Colleges (c)
PO Box 42495
1300 Quince Street, SE
Olympia, WA 98504-2495
(360) 704-4355
Fax: (360) 704-4415
Mr. Marty Brown
Executive Director
URL: www.sbctc.edu

WEST VIRGINIA

West Virginia Higher Education Policy Commission (d)
1018 Kanawha Boulevard, East
Suite 700
Charleston, WV 25301-2800
(304) 558-0699
Fax: (304) 558-1011
Dr. Paul L. Hill
Chancellor
E-mail: paul.hill@hepc.wvnet.edu
URL: www.wvhepc.edu

WISCONSIN

State of Wisconsin Higher Educational Aids Board (e)
PO Box 7885
Madison, WI 53707-7885
(608) 267-2206
Fax: (608) 267-2808
Mr. John Reinemann
Executive Secretary
E-mail: heabmail@wisconsin.gov
URL: heab.wi.gov

Wisconsin Technical College System (f)
PO Box 7874
Madison, WI 53707-7874
(608) 267-9066
Fax: (608) 266-1285
Ms. Morna K. Foy
President
E-mail: president@wtcsystem.edu
URL: www.wtcsystem.edu

WYOMING

Wyoming Community College Commission (A)
2300 Capital Avenue
5th Floor, Suite B
Cheyenne, WY 82002
(307) 777-7763
FAX: (307) 777-6567
Dr. Jim Rose
Executive Director
E-MAIL: jim.rose@wyo.gov
URL: www.communitycolleges.wy.edu

AMERICAN SAMOA

Board of Higher Education (American Samoa) American Samoa Community College (B)
PO Box 2609
Pago Pago, AS 96799
(684) 699-9155
FAX: (684) 699-6259
E-MAIL: info@amsamoa.edu
URL: www.amsamoa.edu

FEDERATED STATES OF MICRONESIA

Board of Regents College of Micronesia-FSM (C)
PO Box 159
Kolonia Pohnpei, FM 96941
(691) 320-2480
FAX: (691) 320-2479
E-MAIL: national@comfsm.fm
URL: www.comfsm.fm

PUERTO RICO

Puerto Rico Council on Education (D)
PO Box 19900
San Juan, PR 00910-1900
(787) 641-7100, ext. 2045
FAX: (787) 641-2573
Mr. David Baez-Davila
Interim Executive Director
E-MAIL: dbaez@ce.pr.gov
URL: www.ce.pr.gov

Higher Education Associations

AACSB International-The Association to Advance Collegiate Schools of Business (A)
777 South Harbour Island Boulevard
Suite 750
Tampa, FL 33602-5730
(813) 769-6500
FAX: (813) 769-6559
Mr. Thomas R. Robinson
President and Chief Executive Officer
E-MAIL: mediarelations@aacsb.edu
URL: www.aacsb.edu

AASA The School Superintendents Association (B)
1615 Duke Street
Alexandria, VA 22314
(703) 528-0700
FAX: (703) 841-1543
Dr. Daniel A. Domenech
Executive Director
E-MAIL: ddomenech@aasa.org
URL: www.aasa.org

AAUW (C)
1111 Sixteenth Street, NW
Washington, DC 20036
(202) 785-7700
FAX: (202) 872-1425
Linda D. Hallman CAE
Chief Executive Officer
E-MAIL: connect@aauw.org
URL: www.aauw.org

ABET (D)
415 North Charles Street
Baltimore, MD 21201
(410) 347-7700
FAX: (410) 625-2238
Michael K. J. Milligan Ph.D., PE
Executive Director and CEO
E-MAIL: info@abet.org
URL: www.abet.org

Academy of Legal Studies in Business (E)
University of Florida
College of Business Administration
PO Box 117165
Gainesville, FL 32611
(352) 392-0136
Mr. Robert E. Thomas
Interim Secretary-Treasurer
E-MAIL: rethomas@ufl.edu
URL: www.alsb.org

Academy of Nutrition and Dietetics Accreditation Council for Education in Nutrition and Dietetics (ACEND) (F)
120 South Riverside Plaza
Suite 2000
Chicago, IL 60606-6995
(312) 899-0040, ext. 5400
FAX: (312) 899-4817
Dr. Mary B. Gregoire
Executive Director
E-MAIL: acend@eatright.org
URL: www.eatright.org/acend

Accreditation Commission for Acupuncture and Oriental Medicine (ACAOM) (G)
8941 Aztec Drive
Eden Prairie, MN 55347
(952) 212-2434
FAX: (952) 657-7068
Mr. Mark McKenzie
Executive Director
E-MAIL: mark.mckenzie@acaom.org
URL: www.acaom.org

Accreditation Commission for Education in Nursing (ACEN) (H)
3343 Peachtree Road, NE
Suite 850
Atlanta, GA 30326
(404) 975-5000
FAX: (404) 975-5020
Dr. Marsal Stoll
CEO
E-MAIL: mstoll@acenursing.org
URL: www.acenursing.org

Accreditation Commission for Midwifery Education (ACME) (I)
8403 Colesville Road
Suite 1550
Silver Spring, MD 20910
(240) 485-1803
FAX: (240) 485-1818
Heather L. Maurer MA
Executive Director
E-MAIL: hmaurer@acnm.org
URL: www.midwife.org/Accreditation

Accreditation Committee - Perfusion Education (J)
6663 South Sycamore Street
Littleton, CO 80120
(303) 794-6283
Ms. Theresa Sisneros
Executive Director
E-MAIL: office@ac-pe.org
URL: www.ac-pe.org

Accreditation Council for Business Schools and Programs (K)
11520 West 119th Street
Overland Park, KS 66213
(913) 339-9356
FAX: (913) 339-6226
Mr. Jeffrey Alderman
President & CEO
E-MAIL: info@acbsp.org
URL: www.acbsp.org

Accreditation Council for Pharmacy Education (L)
135 South LaSalle Street
Suite 4100
Chicago, IL 60603
(312) 664-3575
FAX: (312) 664-4652
Peter H. Vlasses, PharmD BCPS
Executive Director
E-MAIL: pvlasses@acpe-accredit.org
URL: www.acpe-accredit.org

Accreditation Review Commission on Education for the Physician Assistant (ARC-PA) (M)
12000 Findley Road
Suite 150
John's Creek, GA 30097
(770) 476-1224
FAX: (770) 476-1738
Mr. John McCarty
Executive Director
E-MAIL: arc-pa@arc-pa.org
URL: www.arc-pa.org

Accreditation Review Committee for the Anesthesiologist Assistant (N)
N84 W33137 Becker Lane
Oconomowoc, WI 53066
(612) 836-3311
Ms. Jennifer Anderson Warwick
Executive Director
E-MAIL: arc-aa@arc-aa.org
URL: www.caahep.org/arc-aa

Accreditation Review Committee for the Medical Illustrator (O)
32531 Meadowlark Way
Pepper Pike, OH 44124
(216) 595-9363
FAX: (216) 595-9360
Kathleen Jung
ARC-MI Chair
E-MAIL: kijung@aol.com
URL: www.caahep.org/arc-mi

Accreditation Review Council on Education in Surgical Technology and Surgical Assisting (P)
6 West Dry Creek Circle
Suite 110
Littleton, CO 80120
(303) 694-9262
FAX: (303) 741-3655
Mr. Keith Orloff
Executive Director
E-MAIL: info@arcstsa.org
URL: www.arcstsa.org

Accrediting Bureau of Health Education Schools (Q)
7777 Leesburg Pike
Suite 314 N
Falls Church, VA 22043
(703) 917-9503
FAX: (703) 917-4109
Florence Tate
Executive Director
E-MAIL: info@abhes.org
URL: www.abhes.org

Accrediting Commission for Community and Junior Colleges Western Association of Schools and Colleges (R)
10 Commercial Boulevard
Suite 204
Novato, CA 94949
(415) 506-0234
FAX: (415) 506-0238
Dr. Barbara A. Beno
President
E-MAIL: accjc@accjc.org
URL: www.accjc.org

Accrediting Commission of Career Schools and Colleges (S)
2101 Wilson Boulevard
Suite 302
Arlington, VA 22201
(703) 247-4212
FAX: (703) 247-4533
Dr. Michale McComis
Executive Director
E-MAIL: mccomis@accsc.org
URL: www.accsc.org

Accrediting Council for Continuing Education & Training (ACCET) (T)
1722 N Street, NW
Washington, DC 20036
(202) 955-1113
FAX: (202) 955-1118
Mr. Bill Larkin
Executive Director
E-MAIL: info@accet.org
URL: www.accet.org

Accrediting Council for Independent Colleges and Schools (U)
750 First Street, NE
Suite 980
Washington, DC 20002-4223
(202) 336-6780
FAX: (202) 842-2593
Dr. Albert Gray
President & CEO
E-MAIL: agray@acics.org
URL: www.acics.org

Accrediting Council on Education in Journalism and Mass Communications (V)
University of Kansas, School of Journalism
1435 Jayhawk Boulevard
Stauffer-Flint Hall
Lawrence, KS 66045-7515
(785) 864-3986
FAX: (785) 864-5225
Prof. Susanne Shaw
Executive Director
E-MAIL: sshaw@ku.edu
URL: www2.ku.edu/~acejmc

ACT, Inc. (W)
500 ACT Drive
Box 168
Iowa City, IA 52243-0168
(319) 337-1079
FAX: (319) 337-1059
Dr. Marten Roorda
CEO
E-MAIL: sandy.serbousek@act.org
URL: www.act.org

ACUTA: the Association for College and University Technology Advancement (X)
152 West Zandale Drive
Suite 200
Lexington, KY 40503
(859) 721-1654
FAX: (859) 278-3268
Ms. Corinne Hoch
CEO
E-MAIL: choch@acuta.org
URL: www.acuta.org

American Academy for Liberal Education (AALE) (Y)
127 S. Peyton Street
Suite 200
Alexandria, VA 22314
(703) 717-9719
Prof. Charles Butterworth
President
E-MAIL: aaleinfo@aale.org
URL: www.aale.org

American Anthropological Association (Z)
2300 Clarendon Boulevard
Suite 1301
Arlington, VA 22201
(703) 528-1902
FAX: (703) 528-3546
Mr. Edward Liebow
Executive Director
E-MAIL: eliebow@aaanet.org
URL: www.aaanet.org

American Association for Adult and Continuing Education (AAACE) (a)
10111 Martin Luther King, Jr. Highway
Suite 200C
Bowie, MD 20720
(301) 459-6261
FAX: (301) 459-6241
Jean Fleming
President
E-MAIL: aaace10@aol.com
URL: www.aaace.org

American Association for Employment in Education (b)
PO Box 173
Slippery Rock, PA 16057
(614) 485-1111
FAX: (360) 244-7802
Ms. Deb Snyder
Executive Director
E-MAIL: execdir@aaee.org
URL: www.aaee.org

American Association for Marriage and Family Therapy Commission on Accreditation for Marriage and Family Therapy Education (c)
112 South Alfred Street
Alexandria, VA 22314-3061
(703) 253-0517
FAX: (703) 253-0508
Ms. Tanya A. Tamarkin
Director of Education
E-MAIL: kpritchard@aamft.org
URL: www.aamft.org

American Association for Vocational Instructional Materials (d)
220 Smithonia Road
Winterville, GA 30683
(706) 742-5355
FAX: (706) 742-7005
Director
URL: www.aavim.com

American Association for Women in Community Colleges (AAWCC) (e)
PO Box 3098
Gaithersburg, MD 20855
(301) 442-3374
Dr. Beverly Walker-Griffea
President
E-MAIL: info@aawccnatl.org
URL: www.aawccnatl.org

American Association of Blood Banks Committee on Accreditation of Specialist in Blood Banking Technology Schools (f)
8101 Glenbrook Road
Bethesda, MD 20814-2749
(301) 215-6586
FAX: (301) 657-0957
Anne Chenoweth
Deputy Director Accreditation and Quality
E-MAIL: accreditation@aabb.org
URL: www.aabb.org

American Association of Colleges for Teacher Education (g)
1307 New York Avenue, NW
Suite 300
Washington, DC 20005-4701
(202) 293-2450
FAX: (202) 457-8095
Dr. Sharon P. Robinson
President & Chief Executive Officer
E-MAIL: smonroe@aacte.org
URL: www.aacte.org

American Association of Colleges of Nursing (h)
1 Dupont Circle, NW
Suite 530
Washington, DC 20036-1120
(202) 463-6930
FAX: (202) 785-8320
Dr. Deborah Trautman
Chief Executive Officer
E-MAIL: dtrautman@aacn.nche.edu
URL: www.aacn.nche.edu

American Association of Colleges of Osteopathic Medicine (A)
5550 Friendship Boulevard
Suite 310
Chevy Chase, MD 20815-7231
(301) 968-4142
Fax: (301) 968-4101
Stephen C. Shannon DO, MPH
President and CEO
E-mail: president@aacom.org
URL: www.aacom.org

American Association of Collegiate Registrars and Admissions Officers (AACRAO) (B)
1 Dupont Circle, NW
Suite 520
Washington, DC 20036-1135
(202) 293-9161
Fax: (202) 872-8857
Mr. Michael Reilly
Executive Director
E-mail: reillym@aacrao.org
URL: www.aacrao.org

American Association of Community Colleges (C)
1 Dupont Circle, NW
Suite 410
Washington, DC 20036
(202) 728-0200, ext. 235
Fax: (202) 452-1461
Dr. Walter G. Bumphus
President/CEO
E-mail: wbumphus@aacc.nche.edu
URL: www.aacc.nche.edu

American Association of Family and Consumer Sciences (AAFCS) (D)
400 North Columbus Street
Suite 202
Alexandria, VA 22314
(703) 706-4600
Fax: (703) 706-4663
Ms. Carolyn W. Jackson
Chief Executive Officer
E-mail: accreditation@aafcs.org
URL: www.aafcs.org

American Association of Medical Assistants (E)
20 North Wacker Drive
Suite 1575
Chicago, IL 60606
(312) 899-1500
Fax: (312) 899-1259
Mr. Donald A. Balasa J.D., MBA
Executive Director
E-mail: dbalasa@aama-ntl.org
URL: www.aama-ntl.org

American Association of Physics Teachers (F)
One Physics Ellipse
College Park, MD 20740-3845
(301) 209-3311
Fax: (301) 209-0845
Dr. Beth A. Cunningham
Executive Officer
E-mail: eo@aapt.org
URL: www.aapt.org

American Association of Presidents of Independent Colleges and Universities (G)
PO Box 7070
Provo, UT 84602-7070
(801) 422-2235
Fax: (801) 422-0265
Mr. Steven M. Sandberg
Executive Director
E-mail: aapicu@byu.edu
URL: www.aapicu.org

American Association of State Colleges and Universities (H)
1307 New York Avenue, NW
5th Floor
Washington, DC 20005-4701
(202) 293-7070
Fax: (202) 296-5819
Dr. Muriel A. Howard
President
E-mail: howardm@aascu.org
URL: www.aascu.org

American Association of Teachers of Slavic and East European Languages (I)
University of Southern California
3501 Trousdale Parkway
THH 255L
Los Angeles, CA 90089-4353
(213) 740-2734
Fax: (213) 740-8550
Dr. Elizabeth Durst
Executive Director
E-mail: aatseel@usc.edu
URL: www.aatseel.org

American Association of University Professors (J)
1133 19th Street, NW
Suite 200
Washington, DC 20036
(202) 737-5900
Fax: (202) 737-5526
Dr. Julie Schmid
Executive Director
E-mail: aaup@aaup.org
URL: www.aaup.org

American Bar Association Section of Legal Education and Admissions to the Bar (K)
321 North Clark Street
21st Floor
Chicago, IL 60654
(312) 988-6746
Fax: (312) 988-5681
Mr. Barry A. Currier
Managing Director Accreditation & Legal Education
E-mail: legaled@americanbar.org
URL: www.americanbar.org/groups/legal_education

American Board of Funeral Service Education Committee on Accreditation (L)
3414 Ashland Avenue
Suite G
St. Joseph, MO 64506
(816) 233-3747
Fax: (816) 233-3793
Dr. Robert C. Smith III
Executive Director
E-mail: exdir@abfse.org
URL: www.abfse.org

American Catholic Philosophical Association (M)
University of St. Thomas
3800 Montrose Boulevard
Houston, TX 77006
(713) 942-5062
Fax: (713) 942-3464
Dr. Mirela Oliva
National Secretary
E-mail: acpa@stthom.edu
URL: www.acpaweb.org

American Chemical Society Committee on Professional Training (N)
1155 Sixteenth Street, NW
Washington, DC 20036
(202) 872-4589
Fax: (202) 872-6066
Ms. Cathy A. Nelson
Assistant Director
E-mail: cpt@acs.org
URL: www.acs.org/cpt

American College of Microbiology Committee on Postgraduate Educational Programs (O)
1752 N Street, NW
Washington, DC 20036-2804
(202) 942-9225
Fax: (202) 942-9353
Ms. Peggy McNult
Director
E-mail: clinmicro@asmusa.org
URL: www.asm.org/cpep

American College of Nurse-Midwives (P)
8403 Colesville Road
Suite 1550
Silver Spring, MD 20910
(240) 485-1800
Fax: (240) 485-1818
Ms. Lorrie Kaplan
Executive Director
E-mail: info@acnm.org
URL: www.midwife.org

American College Personnel Association (ACPA) (Q)
1 Dupont Circle, NW
Suite 300
Washington, DC 20036-1188
(202) 835-2272
Fax: (202) 827-0601
Dr. Cindi Love
Executive Director
E-mail: info@acpa.nche.edu
URL: www.myacpa.org

American Collegiate Retailing Association (R)
Texas State University
School of Family and Consumer Sciences
101 FCS Building
San Marcos, TX 78666
(512) 245-2155
Dr. Rodney C. Runyan
Director
E-mail: rcr56@txstate.edu
URL: www.acraretail.org

American Conference of Academic Deans (ACAD) (S)
1818 R Street, NW
Washington, DC 20009
(202) 884-7419
Fax: (202) 265-9532
Mrs. Laura A. Rzepka
Executive Director
E-mail: info@acad.org
URL: www.acad.org

American Council for Construction Education (T)
1717 North Loop 1604 East
Suite 320
San Antonio, TX 78232-1570
(210) 495-6161
Fax: (210) 495-6168
Mr. Michael Holland
President
E-mail: acce@acce-hq.org
URL: www.acce-hq.org

American Council of Trustees and Alumni (U)
1730 M Street, NW
Suite 600
Washington, DC 20036-4511
(202) 467-6787
Fax: (202) 467-6784
Ms. Anne D. Neal
President
E-mail: info@goacta.org
URL: www.goacta.org

American Council on Education (V)
1 Dupont Circle, NW
Washington, DC 20036
(202) 939-9300
Fax: (202) 833-4760
Molly Corbett Broad
President
E-mail: president@acenet.edu
URL: www.acenet.edu

American Council on Education Center for Education Attainment and Innovation (W)
1 Dupont Circle, NW
Suite 250
Washington, DC 20036
(202) 939-9306
Fax: (202) 833-3005
Ms. Deborah Seymour
Asst Vice President
E-mail: dseymour@acenet.edu
URL: www.acenet.edu

American Council on Education Division of Leadership Programs (X)
1 Dupont Circle, NW
Suite 250-73A
Washington, DC 20036
(202) 939-9389
Fax: (202) 939-9302
Dr. Claire Van Ummersen
Senior Adviser
E-mail: cvanummersen@acenet.edu
URL: www.acenet.edu

American Counseling Association (Y)
6101 Stevenson Avenue
Alexandria, VA 22304
(800) 347-6647, ext. 231
Fax: (800) 473-2329
Mr. Richard Yep CAE, FASAE
Chief Executive Officer
E-mail: ryep@counseling.org
URL: www.counseling.org

American Culinary Federation Education Foundation Accrediting Commission (Z)
180 Center Place Way
St. Augustine, FL 32095
(904) 824-4468
Fax: (904) 825-4758
E-mail: lweber@acfchefs.net
URL: www.acfchefs.org

American Educational Research Association (a)
1430 K Street, NW
Suite 1200
Washington, DC 20005
(202) 238-3200
Fax: (202) 238-3250
Dr. Felice J. Levine
Executive Director
E-mail: flevine@aera.net
URL: www.aera.net

American Forensic Association (b)
Box 256
River Falls, WI 54022-0256
(800) 228-5424
Fax: (715) 425-9533
Dr. James W. Pratt
Executive Secretary
E-mail: amforensicassoc@aol.com
URL: www.americanforensics.org

American Institute of Architecture Students (c)
1735 New York Avenue, NW
Washington, DC 20006-5209
(202) 808-0075
Danielle Mitchell Assoc. AIA
2015-2016 AIAS President
E-mail: mailbox@aias.org
URL: www.aias.org

American Library Association Office for Accreditation (d)
50 East Huron Street
Chicago, IL 60611-2729
(312) 280-2432
Fax: (312) 280-2433
Karen O'Brien
Director, Office for Accreditation
E-mail: accred@ala.org
URL: www.ala.org/accreditation

American Mathematical Association of Two Year Colleges (e)
Southwest Tennessee Community College
5983 Macon Cove
Memphis, TN 38134
(901) 333-6243
Fax: (901) 333-6251
Wanda Garner
Executive Director
E-mail: amatyc@amatyc.org
URL: www.amatyc.org

American Occupational Therapy Association (f)
4720 Montgomery Lane
Suite 200
Bethesda, MD 20814-3449
(301) 652-6611 Ext. 2914
Fax: (240) -762-5140
Dr. Heather Stagliano
Director of Accreditation
E-mail: accred@aota.org
URL: www.aota.org

American Optometric Association Accreditation Council on Optometric Education (g)
243 North Lindbergh Boulevard
Floor 1
St. Louis, MO 63141
(314) 991-4100
Fax: (314) 991-4101
Ms. Joyce L. Urbeck
Director
E-mail: jlurbeck@aoa.org
URL: www.theacoe.org

American Osteopathic Association (h)
Commission on Osteopathic College Accreditation
142 East Ontario Street
Chicago, IL 60611-2864
(312) 202-8048
Fax: (312) 202-8209
Ms. Alissa Craft DO, MBA
Secretary
E-mail: acraftdo@osteopathic.org
URL: www.aoacoca.org

American Physical Therapy Association (A)
1111 North Fairfax Street
Alexandria, VA 22314
(703) 706-3253
Mr. Michael Bowers
Chief Executive Officer
E-MAIL: dorisellmore@apta.org
URL: www.apta.org

American Political Science Association (B)
1527 New Hampshire Avenue, NW
Washington, DC 20036
(202) 483-2512
FAX: (202) 483-2657
Dr. Steven Rathgeb Smith
Executive Director
E-MAIL: apsa@apsanet.org
URL: www.apsanet.org

American Psychological Association Program Consultation & Accreditation (C)
750 First Street, NE
Washington, DC 20002-4242
(202) 572-3037
Dr. Jacqueline Remondet Wall
Dir. Program Consultation & Accred
E-MAIL: apaaccred@apa.org
URL: www.apa.org/ed/accreditation/

American Real Estate and Urban Economics Association (D)
PO Box 3061110
Tallahassee, FL 32306-1110
(850) 644-7898
FAX: (850) 644-4077
Ms. Liz Laffitte
Executive Director
E-MAIL: elaffitte@fsu.edu
URL: www.areuea.org

American Society for Engineering Education (E)
1818 N Street, NW
Suite 600
Washington, DC 20036
(202) 331-3545
FAX: (202) 265-8504
Dr. Norman L. Fortenberry
Executive Director
E-MAIL: n.fortenberry@asee.org
URL: www.asee.org

American Society for Microbiology (F)
1752 N Street, NW
Washington, DC 20036
(202) 942-9264
FAX: (202) 942-9329
Ms. Amy Chang
Director, Education Department
E-MAIL: education@asmusa.org
URL: www.asm.org

American Society of Cytopathology Cytotechnology Programs Review Committee (CPRC) (G)
100 West 10th Street
Suite 605
Wilmington, DE 19801
(302) 543-6583
FAX: (302) 543-6597
Deborah M. Sheldon
Cytology Education Coordinator
E-MAIL: asc@cytopathology.org
URL: www.cytopathology.org

American Society of Landscape Architects Landscape Architectural Accreditation Board (H)
636 Eye Street, NW
Washington, DC 20001-3736
(202) 216-2359
FAX: (202) 898-1185
Mr. Kristopher Pritchard
Accred & Education Programs Manager
E-MAIL: kpritchard@asla.org
URL: www.asla.org

American Speech-Language-Hearing Association (I)
2200 Research Boulevard
Rockville, MD 20850
(301) 296-5700
Dr. Arlene L. Pietrantan
Chief Executive Officer
E-MAIL: accreditation@asha.org
URL: www.asha.org

American Student Government Association (J)
412 NW 16th Avenue
Gainesville, FL 32601-4203
(352) 373-6907
FAX: (352) 373-8120
Mr. W. H. Oxendine Jr.
Executive Director
E-MAIL: info@asgaonline.com
URL: www.asgaonline.com

American Veterinary Medical Association (K)
1931 North Meacham Road
Suite 100
Schaumburg, IL 60173
(800) 248-2862
FAX: (847) 285-5732
Dr. Karen Martens Brandt
Director Education and Research
E-MAIL: kbrandt@avma.org
URL: www.avma.org

APPA (L)
1643 Prince Street
Alexandria, VA 22314
(703) 684-1446
FAX: (703) 549-2772
E. Lander Medlin
Executive Vice President
E-MAIL: lander@appa.org
URL: www.appa.org

Association for Asian Studies (M)
825 Victors Way
Suite 310
Ann Arbor, MI 48108
(734) 665-2490
FAX: (734) 665-3801
Mr. Michael Paschal
Executive Director
E-MAIL: mpaschal@asian-studies.org
URL: www.asian-studies.org

Association for Biblical Higher Education Commission on Accreditation (N)
5850 T.G. Lee Boulevard
Suite 130
Orlando, FL 32822
(407) 207-0808
FAX: (407) 207-0840
Dr. Ronald C. Kroll
Director, Commission on Accreditation
E-MAIL: coa@abhe.org
URL: www.abhe.org

Association for Business Communication (O)
355 Shanks Hall (0112)
181 Turner Street, NW
Blacksburg, VA 24061
(540) 231-8460
FAX: (540) 231-1452
Dr. James Dubinsky
Executive Director
E-MAIL: exec_director@businesscommunication.org
URL: www.businesscommunication.org

Association for Business Simulation and Experiential Learning (P)
University of South Carolina Aiken
School of Business Administration
471 University Parkway
Aiken, SC 29801
(803) 641-3340
Dr. Mick Fekula
VP/Executive Director
E-MAIL: absel@email.com
URL: www.absel.org

The Association for Canadian Studies in the United States (ACSUS) (Q)
732 Clemens Hall
University of Buffalo - SUNY
Buffalo, NY 14260
(716) 645-0829
FAX: (716) 645-5976
Mr. Kenneth Holland
President
E-MAIL: info@acsus.org
URL: www.acsus.org

Association for Clinical Pastoral Education, Inc. (R)
One West Court Square
Suite 325
Decatur, GA 30030
(404) 320-1472
FAX: (404) 320-0849
RevDr. David Clark Johnson
President
E-MAIL: acpe@acpe.edu
URL: www.acpe.edu

Association for Collaborative Leadership (ACL) (S)
c/o NELLCO
80 New Scotland Avenue
Albany, NY 12208
(518) 772-3921
FAX: (518) 694-3027
E-MAIL: admin@national-acl.org
URL: www.national-acl.org

Association for Continuing Higher Education (T)
University of Oklahoma Outreach
OCCE Administration Building, Room 129C
1700 Asp Avenue
Norman, OK 73072-6400
(800) 807-2243
FAX: (405) 325-4888
Ynez Henningsen
Executive Secretary
E-MAIL: admin@acheinc.org
URL: www.acheinc.org

Association for Education in Journalism and Mass Communication (U)
234 Outlet Pointe Boulevard
Suite A
Columbia, SC 29210-5667
(803) 798-0271
FAX: (803) 772-3509
Ms. Jennifer H. McGill
Executive Director
E-MAIL: aejmchq@aol.com
URL: www.aejmc.org

Association for General and Liberal Studies (V)
445 Fifth Street
Columbus, IN 47201
(812) 376-7468
Ms. Joyce Lucke
Executive Director
E-MAIL: execdir@agls.org
URL: www.agls.org

Association for Institutional Research (W)
1435 East Piedmont Drive
Suite 211
Tallahassee, FL 32308
(850) 385-4155
FAX: (850) 385-5180
Dr. Randy L. Swing
Executive Director
E-MAIL: executivedirector@airweb.org
URL: www.airweb.org

Association for Library and Information Science Education (ALISE) (X)
2150 N. 107th Street
Suite 205
Seattle, WA 98133
(206) 209-5267
FAX: (206) 367-8777
Mr. Andrew Estep
Executive Director
E-MAIL: office@alise.org
URL: www.alise.org

Association for Prevention Teaching and Research (Y)
1001 Connecticut Avenue, NW
Suite 610
Washington, DC 20036
(202) 463-0550
FAX: (202) 463-0555
Ms. Allison L. Lewis
Executive Director
E-MAIL: info@aptrweb.org
URL: www.aptrweb.org

Association for the Study of Higher Education (ASHE) (Z)
UNLV
4505 South Maryland Parkway
Box 453068
Las Vegas, NV 89154-3068
(702) 895-2737
FAX: (702) 895-4269
Dr. Kimberly Nehls
Executive Director
E-MAIL: ASHE@unlv.edu
URL: www.ashe.ws

Association for Theatre in Higher Education (ATHE) (a)
9700 W. Bryn Mawr Avenue
Suite 210
Rosemont, IL 60028
(847) 447-1701
FAX: (847) 447-1150
Mr. Eric Ewald
Executive Director
E-MAIL: erice@athe.org
URL: www.athe.org

Association of Advanced Rabbinical and Talmudic Schools Accreditation Commission (b)
11 Broadway
Suite 405
New York, NY 10004
(212) 363-1991
FAX: (212) 533-5335
Prof. Keith Sharfman
Director

Association of American Colleges & Universities (c)
1818 R Street, NW
Washington, DC 20009
(202) 387-3760
Dr. Carol G. Schneider
President
E-MAIL: info@aacu.org
URL: www.aacu.org

Association of American Law Schools (d)
1614 20th Street, NW
Washington, DC 20009-1001
(202) 296-1526
FAX: (202) 296-8869
Ms. Judith Areen
Executive Director
E-MAIL: aals@aals.org
URL: www.aals.org

Association of American Medical Colleges (e)
655 K Street, NW
Suite 100
Washington, DC 20001-2399
(202) 828-0460
FAX: (202) 481-7801
Dr. Darrell G. Kirch
President/CEO
E-MAIL: aamcpresident@aamc.org
URL: www.aamc.org

Association of American Universities (f)
1200 New York Avenue, NW
Suite 550
Washington, DC 20005
(202) 408-7500
FAX: (202) 408-8184
Dr. Hunter R. Rawlings III
President
URL: www.aau.edu

Association of American University Presses (g)
28 West 36th Street
Suite 602
New York, NY 10018
(212) 989-1010, ext. 29
FAX: (212) 989-0275
Peter M. Berkery Jr.
Executive Director
E-MAIL: info@aaupnet.org
URL: www.aaupnet.org

Association of Catholic Colleges and Universities (h)
1 Dupont Circle, NW
Suite 650
Washington, DC 20036
(202) 457-0650
FAX: (202) 728-0977
Michael Galligan-Stierle Ph.D.
President/CEO
E-MAIL: accu@accunet.org
URL: www.accunet.org

Association of College and University Housing Officers-International (A)
1445 Summit Street
Columbus, OH 43201-2105
(614) 292-0099
FAX: (614) 292-3205
Ms. Mary DeNiro
Executive Director
E-MAIL: office@acuho-i.org
URL: www.acuho-i.org

Association of College and University Religious Affairs (B)
Vassar College
124 Raymond Avenue
Box 488
Poughkeepsie, NY 12604-0488
(845) 437-5550
Mr. Samuel H. Speers
President
E-MAIL: saspeers@vassar.edu
URL: www.acuraonline.net

Association of College Unions International (C)
One City Centre
Suite 200
120 West Seventh Street
Bloomington, IN 47404-3925
(812) 245-2284
FAX: (812) 245-6710
Mr. John Taylor
Chief Executive Officer
E-MAIL: acui@acui.org
URL: www.acui.org

Association of Collegiate Conference and Events Directors-International (D)
2900 South College Avenue
Suite 3B
Fort Collins, CO 80525
(970) 449-4960
FAX: (970) 449-4965
Ms. Karen Nedbal
Executive Director
E-MAIL: karen@acced-i.org
URL: www.acced-i.org

Association of Collegiate Schools of Architecture (E)
1735 New York Avenue, NW
Washington, DC 20006
(202) 785-2324
FAX: (202) 628-0448
Michael Monti Ph.D.
Executive Director
E-MAIL: info@acsa-arch.org
URL: www.acsa-arch.org

Association of Collegiate Schools of Planning (F)
c/o Donna Dodd, Association Manager
6311 Mallard Trace Drive
Tallahassee, FL 32312
(850) 385-2054
FAX: (850) 385-2084
Dr. Louis Takahashi
President
E-MAIL: ddodd@acsp.org
URL: www.acsp.org

Association of Community College Trustees (G)
1101 17th Street NW
Suite 300
Washington, DC 20036
(202) 775-4667
FAX: (202) 223-1297
Mr. J. Noah Brown
President and CEO
E-MAIL: nbrown@acct.org
URL: www.acct.org

Association of Departments of English (H)
85 Broad Street
Suite 500
New York, NY 10004-2434
(646) 576-5130
FAX: (646) 458-0033
Dr. David Laurence
Director
E-MAIL: ade@mla.org
URL: www.ade.org

Association of Departments of Foreign Languages (I)
85 Broad Street
Suite 500
New York, NY 10004-2434
(646) 576-5140
FAX: (646) 458-0033
Dr. Dennis Looney
Director
E-MAIL: adfl@mla.org
URL: www.adfl.org

Association of Governing Boards of Universities and Colleges (J)
1133 20th Street, NW
Suite 300
Washington, DC 20036
(202) 296-8400
FAX: (202) 223-7053
Mr. Richard Legon
President
E-MAIL: rlegon@agb.org
URL: www.agb.org

Association of Graduate Liberal Studies Programs (K)
c/o Duke University
Box 90095
Durham, NC 27708-0095
(919) 684-1987
FAX: (919) 681-8905
Ms. Marialana Weitzel
Administrative Manager
E-MAIL: info@aglsp.org
URL: www.aglsp.org

Association of International Education Administrators (L)
Campus Box 90404
Duke University
Durham, NC 27708-0404
(919) 668-1928
FAX: (919) 684-8749
Dr. Darla K. Deardorff
Executive Director
E-MAIL: aiea@duke.edu
URL: www.aieaworld.org

Association of Jesuit Colleges and Universities (M)
1 Dupont Circle, NW
Suite 405
Washington, DC 20036
(202) 862-9893
FAX: (202) 862-8523
Rev. Michael J. Sheeran S.J.
President
E-MAIL: msheeran@ajcunet.edu
URL: www.ajcunet.edu

Association of Military Colleges and Schools of the United States (N)
12332 Washington Brice Road
Fairfax, VA 22033
(703) 272-8406
Ray Rottman
Executive Director
E-MAIL: amcsus@cox.net
URL: www.amcsus.org

Association of Performing Arts Presenters (O)
1211 Connecticut Avenue, NW
Suite 200
Washington, DC 20036
(202) 833-2787
FAX: (202) 833-1543
Ms. Margaret Stevens
Director, Executive Affairs
E-MAIL: info@artspresenters.org
URL: www.apap365.org

Association of Practical Theology (P)
Fordham University
441 East Fordham Road
Keating Hall 303
Bronx, NY 10458
(718) 817-5965
FAX: (718) 817-3352
Prof. Thomas M. Beaudoin
President
E-MAIL: tbeaudoin@fordham.edu
URL: www.practicaltheology.org

Association of Presbyterian Colleges and Universities (Q)
100 Witherspoon Street
Louisville, KY 40202-1396
(502) 569-5509
FAX: (502) 569-8077
Mr. Jeff Arnold
Executive Director
E-MAIL: jeff.arnold@presbyteriancolleges.org
URL: www.presbyteriancolleges.org

Association of Private Sector Colleges and Universities (APSCU) (R)
1101 Connecticut Avenue, NW
Suite 900
Washington, DC 20036
(202) 336-6810
FAX: (202) 336-6828
Ms. Sally Stroup
Exec VP of Government Relations/General Counsel
URL: www.apscu.org

Association of Public and Land-Grant Universities (S)
1307 New York Avenue, NW
Suite 400
Washington, DC 20005-4722
(202) 478-6040
FAX: (202) 478-6046
M. Peter McPherson
President
E-MAIL: pmcpherson@aplu.org
URL: www.aplu.org

Association of Research Libraries (T)
21 Dupont Circle, NW
Suite 800
Washington, DC 20036
(202) 296-2296
FAX: (202) 872-0884
Dr. Elliott Shore
Executive Director
E-MAIL: elliott@arl.org
URL: www.arl.org

Association of Schools of Allied Health Professions (U)
122 C Street, NW
Suite 650
Washington, DC 20001-2151
(202) 237-6481
FAX: (202) 237-6485
Mr. John Colbert
Executive Director
E-MAIL: john@asahp.org
URL: www.asahp.org

Association of Specialized and Professional Accreditors (V)
3304 North Broadway Street
#214
Chicago, IL 60657
(773) 857-7900
Mr. Joseph Vibert
Executive Director
E-MAIL: aspa@aspa-usa.org
URL: www.aspa-usa.org

Association of Teacher Educators (W)
PO Box 793
Manassas, VA 20113
(703) 659-1708
FAX: (703) 595-4792
Dr. David Ritchey
Executive Director
E-MAIL: dritchey@ate1.org
URL: www.ate1.org

Association of Teachers of Technical Writing (X)
University of North Texas
Dept. of Technical Communication
1155 Union Circle, #305298
Denton, TX 76203-5017
(940) 565-4458
Dr. Brenda R. Sims
Secretary
E-MAIL: sims@unt.edu
URL: www.attw.org

The Association of Technology, Management, and Applied Engineering (ATMAE) (Y)
275 N. York Street
Suite 401
Elmhurst, IL 60126
(630) 433-4514
FAX: (630) 563-9181
Mr. John Hausoul
Executive Director
E-MAIL: john@atmae.org
URL: www.atmae.org

Association of Theological Schools in the United States and Canada The Commission on Accrediting (Z)
10 Summit Park Drive
Pittsburgh, PA 15275-1110
(412) 788-6505
FAX: (412) 788-6510
Dr. Daniel O. Aleshire
Executive Director
E-MAIL: ats@ats.edu
URL: www.ats.edu

Association of University Programs in Health Administration (a)
2000 14th Street North
Suite 780
Arlington, VA 22201-2543
(703) 894-0940
FAX: (703) 894-0941
Gerald L. Glandon Ph.D.
President & CEO
E-MAIL: gglandon@aupha.org
URL: www.aupha.org

Association of University Research Parks (b)
6262 North Swan Road
Suite 100
Tucson, AZ 85718
(520) 529-2521
FAX: (520) 529-2499
Ms. Eileen Walker
CEO
E-MAIL: info@aurp.net
URL: www.aurp.net

Aviation Accreditation Board International (c)
3410 Skyway Drive
Auburn, AL 36830
(334) 844-2431
FAX: (334) 844-2432
Mr. Gary J. Northam
President
E-MAIL: bayenva@auburn.edu
URL: www.aabi.aero

Broadcast Education Association (d)
1771 N Street, NW
Washington, DC 20036-2891
(202) 602-0584
FAX: (202) 609-9940
Ms. Heather Birks
Executive Director
E-MAIL: heather@beaweb.org
URL: www.beaweb.org

The Carnegie Foundation for the Advancement of Teaching (e)
51 Vista Lane
15th Floor
Stanford, CA 94305
(650) 566-5100
FAX: (650) 326-0278
Dr. Anthony S. Bryk
President
E-MAIL: ncole@carnegiefoundation.org
URL: www.carnegiefoundation.org

Center for Women Policy Studies (f)
4620 North Park Avenue
Suite 302W
Chevy Chase, MD 20815
(202) 872-1770
Leslie R. Wolfe
President
E-MAIL: lwolfe@centerwomenpolicy.org
URL: www.centerwomenpolicy.org

CETE (Center on Education and Training for Employment) (g)
The Ohio State University
1900 Kenny Road
Columbus, OH 43210-1016
(614) 292-9072
FAX: (614) 292-3742
Mr. Robert A. Mahlman
Director
E-MAIL: mahlman.1@osu.edu
URL: www.cete.org

College and University Professional Association for Human Resources (CUPA-HR) (h)
1811 Commons Point Drive
Knoxville, TN 37932
(877) 287-2474
FAX: (865) 637-7674
Mr. Andy Brantley
President and Chief Executive Officer
E-MAIL: memberservice@cupahr.org
URL: www.cupahr.org

Higher Education Associations

College Art Association (A)
50 Broadway
Floor 21
New York, NY 10004
(212) 691-1051
Fax: (212) 627-2381
Ms. Linda Downs
Executive Director
E-mail: nyoffice@collegeart.org
URL: www.collegeart.org

The College Board (B)
250 Vesey Street
New York, NY 10281
(212) 713-8000
David Coleman
President and CEO
URL: www.collegeboard.org

College English Association (C)
Borough of Manhattan Community College
Dept. of Academic Literacy and Linguistics
199 Chambers Street, N499L
New York, NY 10007
(212) 220-1406
Fax: (718) 783-3317
Dr. Juliet Emanuel
Executive Director
E-mail: jaemanuel@cs.com
URL: cea-web.org

College Media Association (D)
355 Lexington Avenue
15th Floor
New York, NY 10017
(212) 297-2195
Meredith Taylor
Executive Director
E-mail: mltaylor@kellencompany.com
URL: www.collegemedia.org

Columbia Scholastic Press Association (E)
Columbia University
Mail Code 5711
New York, NY 10027-6902
(212) 854-9400
Fax: (212) 854-9401
Mr. Edmund J. Sullivan
Executive Director
E-mail: cspa@columbia.edu
URL: www.columbia.edu/cu/cspa

Commission on Accreditation for Health Informatics and Information Management Education (CAHIIM) (F)
233 North Michigan Avenue
21st Floor
Chicago, IL 60601-5800
(312) 233-1100
Fax: (312) 233-1948
Dr. Claire Dixon-Lee
Executive Director CAHIIM
E-mail: info@cahiim.org
URL: www.cahiim.org

Commission on Accreditation of Allied Health Education Programs (G)
1361 Park Street
Clearwater, FL 33756
(727) 210-2350
Fax: (727) 210-2354
Dr. Kathleen Megivern J.D., CAE
Executive Director
E-mail: megivern@caahep.org
URL: www.caahep.org

Commission on Accreditation of Healthcare Management Education (CAHME) (H)
1700 Rockville Pike
Suite 400
Rockville, MD 20852
(301) 998-6101
Margaret Schulte
President & CEO
E-mail: mschulte@cahme.org
URL: www.cahme.org

Commission on Collegiate Nursing Education (CCNE) (I)
One Dupont Circle, NW
Suite 530
Washington, DC 20036-1120
(202) 887-6791
Fax: (202) 887-8476
Dr. Jennifer Butlin
Executive Director
E-mail: jbutlin@aacn.nche.edu
URL: www.aacn.nche.edu/ccne-accreditation

Commission on Dental Accreditation (J)
211 East Chicago Avenue
Suite 1900
Chicago, IL 60611
(312) 440-4653
Fax: (312) 587-5107
Dr. Sherin Tooks
Director
E-mail: tookss@ada.org
URL: www.ada.org/coda

Commission on English Language Program Accreditation (CEA) (K)
801 North Fairfax Street
Suite 402A
Alexandria, VA 22314
(703) 665-3400, x101
Dr. Mary Reeves
Executive Director
E-mail: mhreeves@cea-accredit.org
URL: www.cea-accredit.org

Commission on Independent Colleges and Universities (CICU) (L)
17 Elk Street
PO Box 7289
Albany, NY 12224
(518) 436-4781
Fax: (518) 436-0417
Ms. Laura L. Anglin
President
E-mail: info@cicu.org
URL: www.cicu.org

Commission on Massage Therapy Accreditation (M)
5335 Wisconsin Avenue, NW
Suite 440
Washington, DC 20015
(202) 888-6790
Fax: (202) 888-6787
Ms. Kate Ivane Henri Zulaski
Executive Director
E-mail: kzulaski@comta.org
URL: www.comta.org

Commission on Opticianry Accreditation (N)
PO Box 592
Canton, NY 13617
(703) 468-0566
Mrs. Debra White
Director of Accreditation
E-mail: director@coaccreditation.com
URL: www.coaccreditation.com

Committee on Accreditation for Education in Neurodiagnostic Technology (O)
1449 Hill Street
Whitinsville, MA 01588
(978) 338-6300
Fax: (978) 832-2638
Dr. Jackie Long-Goding RRT-NPS
Executive Director
E-mail: office@coa-ndt.org
URL: www.coa-ndt.org

Committee on Accreditation for Polysomnographic Technologist Education (P)
1711 Frank Avenue
New Bern, NC 28560
(252) 626-3238
Ms. Karen Monarchy Rowe
Executive Director
E-mail: office@coapsg.org
URL: www.coapsg.org

Committee on Accreditation for the Exercise Sciences (Q)
401 West Michigan Street
Indianapolis, IN 46202
(317) 637-9200
Fax: (317) 634-7817
E-mail: trush@acsm.org
URL: www.coaes.org

Committee on Accreditation of Education Programs for Kinesiotherapy (R)
University of Southern Mississippi
118 College Drive
#5142
Hattiesburg, MS 39406-0002
(601) 266-5371
Fax: (601) 266-4445
Jerry W. Purvis
E-mail: jerry.purvis@usm.edu
URL: www.akta.org

Committee on Accreditation of Educational Programs for the Emergency Medical Services Professions (S)
8301 Lakeview Parkway
Suite 111-312
Rowlett, TX 75088
(214) 703-8445, ext. 112
Fax: (214) 703-8992
Dr. George W. Hatch Jr.
Executive Director
E-mail: george@coaemsp.org
URL: www.coaemsp.org

Committee on Institutional Cooperation (T)
1819 South Neil Street
Suite D
Champaign, IL 61820
(217) 333-8475
Fax: (217) 244-7127
Ms. Barbara McFadden Allen
Executive Director
E-mail: cic@staff.cic.net
URL: www.cic.net

Conference on College Composition and Communication (U)
1111 West Kenyon Road
Urbana, IL 61801-1096
(877) 369-6283
Fax: (217) 328-0977
Dr. Jessie L. Moore
Secretary
E-mail: cccc@ncte.org
URL: www.ncte.org/cccc

Council for Accreditation of Counseling and Related Educational Programs (CACREP) (V)
1001 North Fairfax Street
Suite 510
Alexandria, VA 22314
(703) 535-5990
Fax: (703) 739-6209
Dr. Carol L. Bobby
President and CEO
E-mail: cacrep@cacrep.org
URL: www.cacrep.org

Council for Adult and Experiential Learning (W)
55 East Monroe Street
Suite 2710
Chicago, IL 60603
(312) 499-2600
Fax: (312) 499-2601
Ms. Pamela Tate
President & CEO
E-mail: ptate@cael.org
URL: www.cael.org

Council for Advancement and Support of Education (X)
1307 New York Avenue, NW
Suite 1000
Washington, DC 20005-4701
(202) 328-2273
Fax: (202) 387-4973
Ms. Sue Cunningham
President
E-mail: president@case.org
URL: www.case.org

Council for Agricultural Science and Technology (CAST) (Y)
4420 West Lincoln Way
Ames, IA 50014-3447
(515) 292-2125
Fax: (515) 292-4512
Mr. Kent G. Schescke
Executive Vice President
E-mail: cast@cast-science.org
URL: www.cast-science.org

Council for Aid to Education (Z)
215 Lexington Avenue
New York, NY 10016-6023
(212) 661-5800, x808
Fax: (212) 661-9766
Dr. Roger Benjamin
President & CEO
E-mail: roger@cae.org
URL: www.cae.org

Council for Christian Colleges & Universities (a)
321 8th Street, NE
Washington, DC 20002-6107
(202) 546-8713
Fax: (202) 546-8913
Shirley V. Hoogstra J.D.
President
E-mail: council@cccu.org
URL: www.cccu.org

Council for Economic Education (b)
122 East 42nd Street
Suite 2600
New York, NY 10168
(212) 730-7007 or (800) 338-1192
Fax: (212) 730-1793
Ms. Nan Morrison
President and CEO
E-mail: njmorrison@councilforeconed.org
URL: www.councilforeconed.org

Council for Higher Education Accreditation (c)
1 Dupont Circle, NW
Suite 510
Washington, DC 20036-1135
(202) 955-6126
Fax: (202) 955-6129
Dr. Judith Eaton
President
E-mail: chea@chea.org
URL: www.chea.org

Council for Interior Design Accreditation (CIDA) (formerly FIDER) (d)
206 Grandville Avenue
Suite 350
Grand Rapids, MI 49503
(616) 458-0400
Fax: (616) 458-0460
Ms. Holly Mattson
Executive Director
E-mail: info@accredit-id.org
URL: www.accredit-id.org

Council for Research in Music Education (e)
University of Illinois at Urbana-Champaign
1114 West Nevada
Urbana, IL 61801
(217) 244-6310
Dr. Janet R. Barrett
Editor
E-mail: crme@illinois.edu
URL: bcrme.press.illinois.edu

Council for the Accreditation of Educator Preparation (f)
1140 19th Street, NW
Suite 400
Washington, DC 20036
(202) 223-0077
Fax: (202) 296-6620
Mr. Christopher Koch
Interim President
E-mail: caep@caepnet.org
URL: www.caepnet.org

Council for the Advancement of Standards in Higher Education (g)
One Dupont Circle, NW
Suite 300
Washington, DC 20036-1188
(202) 862-1400
Fax: (202) 296-3286
Dr. Marybeth Drechsler Sharp
Executive Director
E-mail: executive_director@cas.edu
URL: www.cas.edu

Council of Colleges of Acupuncture and Oriental Medicine (CCAOM) (h)
PO Box 65120
Baltimore, MD 21209
(410) 464-6041
Fax: (410) 464-6042
Mr. David M. Sale J.D., LL.M
Executive Director
E-mail: executivedirector@ccaom.comcastbiz.net
URL: www.ccaom.org

Council of Colleges of Arts and Sciences (A)
c/o The College of William and Mary
PO Box 8795
Williamsburg, VA 23187-8795
(757) 221-1784
FAX: (757) 221-1776
Dr. Anne-Marie McCartan
Executive Director
E-MAIL: ccas@wm.edu
URL: www.ccas.net

Council of Graduate Schools (B)
1 Dupont Circle, NW
Suite 230
Washington, DC 20036-1173
(202) 223-3791
FAX: (202) 331-7157
Dr. Suzanne Ortega
President
E-MAIL: president@cgs.nche.edu
URL: www.cgsnet.org

Council of Independent Colleges (C)
1 Dupont Circle, NW
Suite 320
Washington, DC 20036-1142
(202) 466-7230
FAX: (202) 466-7238
Dr. Richard Ekman
President
E-MAIL: cic@cic.nche.edu
URL: www.cic.edu

The Council of Writing Program Administrators (D)
University of Delaware
Department of English
212 Memorial Hall
Newark, DE 19716
(302) 831-2612
Mr. Michael McCamley
Secretary
E-MAIL: mccamley@udel.edu
URL: www.wpacouncil.org

Council on Accreditation of Nurse Anesthesia Educational Programs (COA) (E)
222 South Prospect Avenue
Park Ridge, IL 60068-4001
(847) 655-1154
FAX: (847) 692-7137
Francis Gerbasi CRNA,Ph.D.
Executive Director/Chief Executive Officer
E-MAIL: fgerbasi@coa.us.com
URL: www.home.coa.us.com

Council on Chiropractic Education (F)
8049 North 85th Way
Scottsdale, AZ 85258-4321
(480) 443-8877
FAX: (480) 483-7333
Craig S. Little D.C., M.Ed
President
E-MAIL: cce@cce-usa.org
URL: www.cce-usa.org

Council on Education for Public Health (G)
1010 Wayne Avenue
Suite 220
Silver Spring, MD 20910-5660
(202) 789-1050
FAX: (202) 789-1895
Ms. Laura Rasar King
Executive Director
E-MAIL: lking@ceph.org
URL: www.ceph.org

Council on Governmental Relations (H)
1200 New York Avenue, NW
Suite 460
Washington, DC 20005
(202) 289-6655
FAX: (202) 289-6698
Mr. Anthony DeCrappeo
President
E-MAIL: tdecrappeo@cogr.edu
URL: www.cogr.edu

Council on Higher Education Solutions for Adults (I)
104 Johnson Street
Marshall, TX 75670
(903) 472-2762
FAX: (903) 935-3890
Dr. Tracy Andrus
President/CEO
E-MAIL: tandrus@chesa1.com
URL: www.chesa1.com

Council on Law in Higher Education (J)
9386 Via Classico West
Wellington, FL 33411
(561) 792-4440
FAX: (561) 792-4441
Mr. Daren Bakst
President
E-MAIL: info@clhe.org
URL: www.clhe.org

Council on Naturopathic Medical Education (K)
PO Box 178
Great Barrington, MA 01230
(413) 528-8877
Dr. Daniel Seitz J.D., Ed.D
Executive Director
E-MAIL: danseitz@cnme.org
URL: www.cnme.org

Council on Occupational Education (L)
7840 Roswell Road
Building 300
Suite 325
Atlanta, GA 30350
(800) 917-2081
FAX: (770) 396-3790
Dr. Gary Puckett
President/Executive Director
E-MAIL: puckettg@council.org
URL: www.council.org

Council on Podiatric Medical Education (M)
9312 Old Georgetown Road
Bethesda, MD 20814
(301) 581-9200
FAX: (301) 571-4903
Mr. Alan R. Tinkleman
Director
E-MAIL: artinkleman@apma.org
URL: www.cpme.org

Council on Rehabilitation Education (CORE) (N)
1699 E. Woodfield Road
Suite 300
Schaumburg, IL 60173
(847) 944-1345
FAX: (847) 944-1346
Dr. Frank Lane
Chief Executive Officer
E-MAIL: flane@iit.edu
URL: www.core-rehab.org

Council on Social Work Education (O)
1701 Duke Street
Suite 200
Alexandria, VA 22314-3457
(703) 519-2048
FAX: (703) 683-8099
Dr. Jo Ann Regan
VP of Education
E-MAIL: jregan@cswe.org
URL: www.cswe.org

Council on Undergraduate Research (P)
734 15th Street, NW
Suite 550
Washington, DC 20005
(202) 783-4810
FAX: (202) 783-4811
Dr. Elizabeth L. Ambos
Executive Officer
E-MAIL: cur@cur.org
URL: www.cur.org

CSAB, Inc. (Q)
417 Terrace Way
Towson, MD 21204-3725
(410) 339-5456
Ms. Liz Glazer
Executive Director
E-MAIL: lglazer@csab.org
URL: www.csab.org

Cultural Vistas (R)
440 Park Avenue South
2nd Floor
New York, NY 10016
(212) 497-3500
FAX: (212) 497-3535
Mr. Robert Fenstermacher
President & CEO
E-MAIL: info@culturalvistas.org
URL: www.culturalvistas.org

Decision Sciences Institute (S)
University of Houston
C.T. Bauer College of Business
334 Melcher Hall, Suite 325
Houston, TX 77204-6021
(713) 743-4815
FAX: (713) 743-8984
E-MAIL: info@decisionsciences.org
URL: www.decisionsciences.org

Direct Marketing Association, Inc. (T)
1120 Avenue of the Americas
13th Floor
New York, NY 10036-6700
(212) 768-7277
FAX: (212) 302-6714
Mr. Thomas J. Benton
CEO
E-MAIL: info@the-dma.org
URL: www.thedma.org

Distance Education Accrediting Commission (U)
1101 17th Street, NW
Suite 808
Washington, DC 20036
(202) 234-5100
FAX: (202) 332-1386
Dr. Leah K. Matthews
Executive Director
E-MAIL: info@deac.org
URL: www.deac.org

Education Commission of the States (V)
700 Broadway
Suite 810
Denver, CO 80203-3442
(303) 299-3600
FAX: (303) 296-8332
Mr. Jeremy Anderson
President
E-MAIL: janderson@ecs.org
URL: www.ecs.org

Education Development Center, Inc. (W)
43 Foundry Avenue
Waltham, MA 02453-8313
(617) 969-7100
FAX: (617) 969-5979
Mr. Marvin J. Suomi
Acting President and CEO
E-MAIL: contact@edc.org
URL: www.edc.org

EDUCAUSE (X)
1150 18th Street, NW
Suite 900
Washington, DC 20036-3816
(202) 872-4200
FAX: (202) 872-4318
John O'Brien Ph.D.
President and CEO
E-MAIL: jobrien@educause.edu
URL: www.educause.edu

FHI360 (Y)
1825 Connecticut Avenue, NW
Suite 800
Washington, DC 20009
(202) 884-8000
FAX: (202) 884-8400
Dr. Patrick C. Fine
Chief Executive Officer
E-MAIL: contact@fhi.org
URL: www.fhi360.org

Financial Management Association International (Z)
University of South Florida
College of Business Administration
4202 East Fowler Avenue, BSN 3416
Tampa, FL 33620-9951
(813) 974-2084
FAX: (813) 974-3318
Executive Director
E-MAIL: fma@coba.usf.edu
URL: www.fma.org

Friends Association for Higher Education (a)
1501 Cherry Street
Philadelphia, PA 19102
(215) 241-7116
FAX: (215) 241-7078
Ms. Kimberley Haas
FAHE Coordinator
E-MAIL: fahe@quaker.org
URL: www.quakerfahe.com

The George Washington University HEATH Resource Center at the National Youth Transitions Center Graduate School of Education & Human Development (b)
2134 G Street, NW
Washington, DC 20052-0001
E-MAIL: askheath@gwu.edu
URL: www.heath.gwu.edu

The Gerontological Society of America (c)
1220 L Street, NW
Suite 901
Washington, DC 20005-4001
(202) 587-2821
FAX: (202) 587-2850
Mr. James Appleby
Executive Director and CEO
E-MAIL: geron@geron.org
URL: www.geron.org

Graduate Record Examinations Board (d)
Educational Testing Service
Mail Stop 57L
660 Rosedale Road
Princeton, NJ 08541
(609) 683-2014
FAX: (609) 683-2040
Dr. David G. Payne
Vice President & COO of Global Education Division
E-MAIL: dpayne@ets.org
URL: www.ets.org/highered

H. Wiley Hitchcock Institute for Studies in American Music (e)
Brooklyn College/CUNY
2900 Bedford Avenue
Brooklyn, NY 11210-2889
(718) 951-5655
FAX: (718) 951-4502
Dr. Jeffrey J. Taylor
Co-Director
E-MAIL: isam@brooklyn.cuny.edu
URL: www.hisam.org

Higher Education Resource Services (HERS) (f)
University of Denver
1901 East Asbury Avenue
Denver, CO 80208
(303) 871-6866
FAX: (303) 871-6766
Dr. Judith White
President/Executive Director
E-MAIL: judith.white@du.edu
URL: www.hersnet.org

Higher Learning Commission (g)
230 South LaSalle Street
Suite 7-500
Chicago, IL 60604-1411
(312) 263-0456 / (800) 621-7440
FAX: (312) 263-7462
Dr. Barbara Gellman-Danley
President
E-MAIL: info@hlcommission.org
URL: hlcommission.org

Hispanic Association of Colleges and Universities (h)
8415 Datapoint Drive
Suite 400
San Antonio, TX 78229
(210) 692-3805
FAX: (210) 692-0823
Dr. Antonio R. Flores
President and CEO
E-MAIL: hacu@hacu.net
URL: www.hacu.net

IACLEA (International Association of Campus Law Enforcement Administrators) (i)
342 N. Main Street
West Hartford, CT 06117-2507
(860) 586-7517, x565
FAX: (860) 586-7550
Mr. Christopher Blake CAE
Executive Director
E-MAIL: cblake@iaclea.org
URL: www.iaclea.org

The Institute for Higher Education Policy (A)
1825 K Street, NW
Suite 720
Washington, DC 20006
(202) 861-8223
FAX: (202) 861-9307
Michelle A. Cooper Ph.D.
President
E-MAIL: institute@ihep.org
URL: www.ihep.org

Institute of International Education (B)
809 United Nations Plaza
New York, NY 10017-3580
(212) 883-8200
FAX: (212) 984-5496
E-MAIL: info@iie.org
URL: www.iie.org

Institute of International Education Council for International Exchange of Scholars (C)
1400 K Street, NW
Suite 700
Washington, DC 20005
(202) 686-4000
FAX: (202) 686-4029
Maria de los Angeles Crummet
Executive Director
E-MAIL: scholars@iie.org
URL: www.cies.org

Intercollegiate Broadcasting System, Inc. (D)
367 Windsor Highway
New Windsor, NY 12553-7900
(845) 565-0003
Mr. Fritz Kass
Director-Operations
E-MAIL: ibshq@aol.com
URL: www.collegeradio.tv

International Assembly for Collegiate Business Education (E)
11374 Strang Line Road
Lenexa, KS 66215
(913) 631-3009
FAX: (913) 631-9154
Mr. Dennis N. Gash
President
E-MAIL: iacbe@iacbe.org
URL: www.iacbe.org

International Association of Baptist Colleges and Universities (F)
Samford University
800 Lakeshore Drive
Birmingham, AL 35229
(205) 726-2036
Mrs. Ashley Hill
Executive Secretary
E-MAIL: ashleyhill@baptistschools.org
URL: www.baptistschools.org

International Communication Association (G)
1500 21st Street, NW
Washington, DC 20036
(202) 955-1444
FAX: (202) 955-1448
Dr. Michael L. Haley
Executive Director
E-MAIL: mhaley@icahdq.org
URL: www.icahdq.org

International Council on Education for Teaching (H)
National-Louis University
1000 Capitol Drive
Wheeling, IL 60090
(847) 947-5881
FAX: (847) 947-5881
James O'Meara
President
E-MAIL: president@icet4u.org
URL: www.icet4u.org

International Fire Service Accreditation Congress (I)
Oklahoma State University
1812 Tyler Avenue
Stillwater, OK 74078
(405) 744-8303
FAX: (405) 744-8802
Mr. Clayton Moorman
Director
E-MAIL: admin@ifsac.org
URL: www.ifsac.org

Joint Review Committee on Education in Cardiovascular Technology (JRC-CVT) (J)
1449 Hill Street
Whitinsville, MA 01588-1032
(978) 456-5594
Mr. William W. Goding
Executive Director
E-MAIL: office@jrccvt.org
URL: www.jrccvt.org

Joint Review Committee on Education in Diagnostic Medical Sonography (K)
6021 University Boulevard
Suite 500
Ellicott City, MD 21043-6090
(443) 973-3251
FAX: (866) 738-3444
Mr. Gerry Magat
Accreditation Specialist
E-MAIL: mail@jrcdms.org
URL: www.jrcdms.org

Joint Review Committee on Education in Radiologic Technology (L)
20 North Wacker Drive
Suite 2850
Chicago, IL 60606-3182
(312) 704-5300
FAX: (312) 704-5304
Leslie F. Winter
Chief Executive Officer
E-MAIL: mail@jrcert.org
URL: www.jrcert.org

Joint Review Committee on Educational Programs in Nuclear Medicine Technology (M)
2000 West Danforth Road
Suite 130, #203
Edmond, OK 73003
(405) 285-0546
FAX: (405) 285-0579
Ms. Jan M. Winn
Executive Director
E-MAIL: mail@jrcnmt.org
URL: www.jrcnmt.org

Journalism Association of Community Colleges (N)
c/o CNPA Services, Inc.
2701 K Street
Sacramento, CA 95816-5131
(916) 288-6021
FAX: (916) 288-6002
Mr. Joe Wirt
Administrator
E-MAIL: joe@cnpa.com
URL: www.jacconline.org

LASPAU: Academic and Professional Programs for the Americas (O)
25 Mount Auburn Street
Suite 300
Cambridge, MA 02138-6095
(617) 495-5255
FAX: (617) 495-8990
Ms. Angelica Natera
Executive Director
E-MAIL: support@laspau.desk-mail.com
URL: www.laspau.harvard.edu

Law School Admission Council (P)
662 Penn Street
Newtown, PA 18940
(215) 968-1001
FAX: (215) 968-1119
Mr. Daniel Bernstine
President
E-MAIL: lsacinfo@lsac.org
URL: www.lsac.org

Liaison Committee on Medical Education (LCME) American Medical Association (Q)
330 North Wabash
Suite 39300
Chicago, IL 60611-5885
(312) 464-4933
FAX: (312) 464-5830
Barbara Barzansky Ph.D.,MHPE
LCME Co-Secretary
E-MAIL: barbara.barzansky@ama-assn.org
URL: www.lcme.org

Linguistic Society of America (R)
522 21st Street, NW
Suite 120
Washington, DC 20006-5012
(202) 835-1714
FAX: (202) 835-1717
Ms. Alyson Reed
Executive Director
E-MAIL: lsa@lsadc.org
URL: www.linguisticsociety.org

Literacy Research Association, Inc. (S)
222 South Westmonte Drive
#101
Altamonte Springs, FL 32714
(407) 774-7880
FAX: (407) 774-6440
Lynn Hupp
Executive Director
E-MAIL: lhupp@kmgnet.com
URL: www.LiteracyResearchAssociation.org

Lutheran Educational Conference of North America (T)
PMB #377
2601 South Minnesota Avenue
Suite 105
Sioux Falls, SD 57105-4750
(605) 271-9894
FAX: (605) 271-9895
Ms. Laurie Brill
Director of Marketing
E-MAIL: brill@lutherancolleges.org
URL: www.lutherancolleges.org

Marketing EDGE (U)
1120 Avenue of the Americas
13th Floor
New York, NY 10036-6700
(212) 768-7277
FAX: (212) 790-1561
Terri L. Bartlett
President
E-MAIL: admin@marketingedge.org
URL: www.marketingedge.org

Medical Assisting Education Review Board (V)
20 N. Wacker Drive
Suite 1575
Chicago, IL 60606-2963
(800) 228-2262
FAX: (312) 899-1259
Mr. Jim Hardman
Assistant Director of Accreditation
E-MAIL: jhardman@maerb.org
URL: www.maerb.org

Middle States Commission on Higher Education (W)
3624 Market Street
2nd Floor West
Philadelphia, PA 19104-2680
(267) 284-5000
FAX: (215) 662-5501
E-MAIL: info@msche.org
URL: www.msche.org

Midwest Association of Colleges and Employers (X)
3601 East Joppa Road
Baltimore, MD 21234
(410) 931-8100
FAX: (410) 931-8111
Ms. Amanda Bolinsky
Executive Director
E-MAIL: admin@mwace.org
URL: www.mwace.org

Midwestern Higher Education Compact (MHEC) (Y)
105 Fifth Avenue South
Suite 450
Minneapolis, MN 55401
(612) 677-2777
FAX: (612) 767-3353
Mr. Larry A. Isaak
President
E-MAIL: mhec@mhec.org
URL: www.mhec.org

Midwifery Education Accreditation Council (MEAC) (Z)
1935 Pauline Boulevard
Suite 100B
Ann Arbor, MI 48103
(360) 466-2080, ext. 4
FAX: (480) 907-2936
Ms. Sandra Stewart
Executive Director
E-MAIL: info@meacschools.org
URL: www.meacschools.org

Modern Language Association (a)
85 Broad Street
Suite 500
New York, NY 10004-2434
(646) 576-5000
FAX: (646) 458-0030
Dr. Rosemary G. Feal
Executive Director
E-MAIL: execdirector@mla.org
URL: www.mla.org

Montessori Accreditation Council for Teacher Education (MACTE) (b)
108 Second Street, SW
Suite 7
Charlottesville, VA 22902
(434) 202-7793
FAX: (888) 525-8838
Dr. Rebecca Pelton
Executive Director/President
E-MAIL: rebecca@macte.org
URL: www.macte.org

NACAS (c)
3 Boar's Head Lane
Suite B
Charlottesville, VA 22903-4610
(434) 245-8425
FAX: (434) 245-8453
CEO
E-MAIL: info@nacas.org
URL: www.nacas.org

NASPA-Student Affairs Administrators in Higher Education (d)
111 K Street, NE
10th Floor
Washington, DC 20002-4409
(202) 265-7500
FAX: (202) 898-5737
Dr. Kevin Kruger
President
E-MAIL: office@naspa.org
URL: www.naspa.org

National Academic Advising Association (e)
2323 Anderson Avenue
Suite 225
Manhattan, KS 66502-2912
(785) 532-5717
FAX: (785) 532-7732
Dr. Charlie L. Nutt
Executive Director
E-MAIL: nacada@ksu.edu
URL: www.nacada.ksu.edu

The National Academy of Education (f)
500 5th Street, NW
Washington, DC 20001
(202) 334-2340
FAX: (202) 334-2350
Mr. Gregory White
Executive Director
E-MAIL: info@naeducation.org
URL: www.naeducation.org

National Academy of Kinesiology (g)
1607 North Market Street
Champaign, IL 61820
(217) 403-7545
FAX: (217) 351-2674
Ms. Kim Scott
Business Manager
E-MAIL: kims@hkusa.com
URL: www.nationalacademyofkinesiology.org

National Accreditation Council for Blind and Low Vision Services (h)
PO Box 15368
Chattanooga, TN 37415
(423) 875-2033
FAX: (423) 875-2220
Mr. William A. Robinson III
Executive Director
E-MAIL: bill@nacblvs.org
URL: www.nacblvs.org

National Accrediting Agency for Clinical Laboratory Sciences (i)
5600 North River Road
Suite 720
Rosemont, IL 60018
(773) 714-8880
FAX: (773) 714-8886
Dr. Dianne M. Cearlock Ph.D.
CEO
E-MAIL: dcearlock@naacls.org
URL: www.naacls.org

National Accrediting Commission of Career Arts & Sciences (A)
4401 Ford Avenue
Suite 1300
Alexandria, VA 22302-1432
(703) 600-7600
Fax: (703) 379-2200
Tony Mirando M.S., D.C.
Executive Director
E-mail: amirando@naccas.org
URL: www.naccas.org

National Association for College Admission Counseling (B)
1050 North Highland Street
Suite 400
Arlington, VA 22201
(703) 836-2222
Fax: (703) 836-8015
Ms. Joyce E. Smith
Chief Executive Officer
E-mail: jsmith@nacacnet.org
URL: www.nacacnet.org

National Association for Equal Opportunity in Higher Education (C)
209 Third Street, SE
Washington, DC 20003
(202) 552-3300
Fax: (202) 552-3330
Lezli Baskerville Esquire
President & CEO
E-mail: admin@nafeo.org
URL: www.nafeonation.org

National Association for Ethnic Studies, Inc. (D)
Mississippi State University
Department of Ethnic Studies
PO Box PC
Mississippi State, MS 39762
(662) 325-7862
Fax: (662) 325-2716
E-mail: naes@ethnicstudies.org
URL: www.ethnicstudies.org

National Association for Legal Support of Alternative Schools (E)
1 Alcedo Court
Moffat, CO 81143
(719) 429-2672
Fax: (719) 298-3020
Mr. Ed Nagel
Coordinator
E-mail: nalsas@msn.com
URL: www.nalsas.org

National Association for Practical Nurse Education and Service, Inc. (F)
2071 N. Bechtle Avenue
PMB 307
Springfield, OH 45504
(703) 933-1003
Fax: (703) 940-4089
Ann Bauer LPN
President
E-mail: president@napnes.org
URL: www.napnes.org

National Association of Agricultural Educators (G)
300 Garrigus Building
University of Kentucky
Lexington, KY 40546-0215
(859) 257-2224
Fax: (859) 323-3919
Dr. Wm. Jay Jackman
Executive Director
E-mail: jjackman.naae@uky.edu
URL: www.naae.org

National Association of College and University Attorneys (H)
1 Dupont Circle, NW
Suite 620
Washington, DC 20036
(202) 833-8390
Fax: (202) 296-8379
Ms. Kathleen Curry Santora Esq.
President & Chief Executive Officer
E-mail: ksantora@nacua.org
URL: www.nacua.org

National Association of College and University Business Officers (I)
1110 Vermont Avenue, NW
Suite 800
Washington, DC 20005
(202) 861-2500
Fax: (202) 861-2583
Mr. John D. Walda
President & Chief Executive Officer
E-mail: john.walda@nacubo.org
URL: www.nacubo.org

The National Association of College & University Food Services (J)
2525 Jolly Road
Suite 280
Okemos, MI 48864-3680
(517) 332-2494
Fax: (517) 332-8144
Gretchen M. Couraud CAE, CFRE
Executive Director
E-mail: gcouraud@nacufs.org
URL: www.nacufs.org

National Association of College Stores (K)
500 East Lorain Street
Oberlin, OH 44074-1294
(440) 775-7777
Fax: (440) 775-4769
Mr. Brian E. Cartier CAE
Chief Executive Officer
E-mail: info@nacs.org
URL: www.nacs.org

National Association of College Wind and Percussion Instructors (L)
Department of Music
South Dakota State University
Lincoln Music Hall (SLM) 205
Box 2212
Brookings, SD 57007
Mr. Michael Walsh
President
E-mail: michael.walsh@sdstate.edu
URL: www.nacwpi.org

National Association of Colleges and Employers (M)
62 Highland Avenue
Bethlehem, PA 18017-9481
(610) 868-1421
Fax: (610) 868-0208
Dr. Marilyn Mackes
Executive Director
E-mail: mmackes@naceweb.org
URL: www.naceweb.org

National Association of Educational Procurement (N)
8840 Stanford Boulevard
Suite 2000
Columbia, MD 21045
(443) 543-5540
Fax: (443) 219-9687
Mrs. Doreen Murner
CEO
E-mail: dmurner@naepnet.org
URL: www.naepnet.org

National Association of Independent Colleges and Universities (O)
1025 Connecticut Avenue, NW
Suite 700
Washington, DC 20036-5405
(202) 785-8866
Fax: (202) 835-0003
Dr. David L. Warren
President
E-mail: geninfo@naicu.edu
URL: www.naicu.edu

National Association of Schools of Art and Design (P)
11250 Roger Bacon Drive
Suite 21
Reston, VA 20190
(703) 437-0700
Fax: (703) 437-6312
Karen P. Moynahan
Executive Director
E-mail: info@arts-accredit.org
URL: www.arts-accredit.org

National Association of Schools of Dance (Q)
11250 Roger Bacon Drive
Suite 21
Reston, VA 20190
(703) 437-0700
Fax: (703) 437-6312
Karen P. Moynahan
Executive Director
E-mail: info@arts-accredit.org
URL: www.arts-accredit.org

National Association of Schools of Music (R)
11250 Roger Bacon Drive
Suite 21
Reston, VA 20190
(703) 437-0700
Fax: (703) 437-6312
Karen P. Moynahan
Executive Director
E-mail: info@arts-accredit.org
URL: www.arts-accredit.org

National Association of Schools of Theatre (S)
11250 Roger Bacon Drive
Suite 21
Reston, VA 20190
(703) 437-0700
Fax: (703) 437-6312
Karen P. Moynahan
Executive Director
E-mail: info@arts-accredit.org
URL: www.arts-accredit.org

National Association of State Directors of Teacher Education and Certification (T)
1629 K Street, NW
Suite 300
Washington, DC 20006
(202) 204-2208
Fax: (202) 204-2210
Dr. Phillip S. Rogers
Executive Director
E-mail: philrogers@nasdtec.com
URL: www.nasdtec.net

National Association of Student Financial Aid Administrators (U)
1101 Connecticut Avenue, NW
Suite 1100
Washington, DC 20036-4303
(202) 785-0453
Fax: (202) 785-1487
Mr. Justin Draeger
President
E-mail: info@nasfaa.org
URL: www.nasfaa.org

National Association of System Heads (V)
1307 New York Avenue, NW
Washington, DC 20005
(202) 478-3747
Rebecca Martin
Executive Director
E-mail: rebecca@nash-dc.org
URL: www.nashonline.org

National Catholic Educational Association (W)
1005 North Glebe Road
Suite 525
Arlington, VA 22201-5792
(800) 711-6232
Fax: (703) 243-0025
Br. Robert R. Bimonte FSC
President
E-mail: president@ncea.org
URL: www.ncea.org

National Coalition for Campus Childrens Centers (X)
2036 Larkhall Circle
Folsom, CA 95630
(916) 790-8261
Fax: (916) 790-8261
Ms. Tonya Palla
Executive Director
E-mail: info@campuschildren.org
URL: www.campuschildren.org

National Collegiate Athletic Association (Y)
PO Box 6222
Indianapolis, IN 46206-6222
(317) 917-6222
Fax: (317) 917-6888
Mr. Todd Petr
Managing Director of Research
E-mail: tpetr@ncaa.org
URL: www.ncaa.org

National Commission on Orthotic and Prosthetic Education (NCOPE) (Z)
330 John Carlyle Street
Suite 200
Alexandria, VA 22314
(703) 836-7114 x 225
Fax: (703) 836-0838
Ms. Robin Seabrook
Executive Director
E-mail: rseabrook@ncope.org
URL: www.ncope.org

National Communication Association (a)
1765 N Street, NW
Washington, DC 20036
(202) 464-4622
Fax: (202) 464-4600
Nancy Kidd Ph.D.
Executive Director
E-mail: nkidd@natcom.org
URL: www.natcom.org

National Council for Continuing Education and Training (b)
PO Box 2916
Columbus, OH 43216-2916
(888) 771-0179
Fax: (877) 835-5798
Jennifer Starkey
Executive Director
E-mail: nccetdirector@nccet.org
URL: www.nccet.org

National Council of Instructional Administrators (NCIA) Dept of Educational Administration (c)
141 Teachers College Hall
PO Box 880360
University of Nebraska - Lincoln
Lincoln, NE 68588-0360
(402) 472-8958
Fax: (402) 472-4300
Katherine Wesley
Executive Director
E-mail: ncia@unl.edu
URL: ncia.unl.edu

National Council of University Research Administrators (d)
1015 18th Street, NW
Suite 901
Washington, DC 20036
(202) 466-3894
Fax: (202) 223-5573
Mrs. Kathleen M. Larmett
Executive Director
E-mail: info@ncura.edu
URL: www.ncura.edu

National Education Association (e)
1201 Sixteenth Street, NW
Suite 310
Washington, DC 20036
(202) 833-4000
Fax: (202) 822-7974
Mr. John C. Stocks
Executive Director
URL: www.nea.org/he

National Forensic Association (f)
Illinois State University
School of Communication
Campus Box 4480
Normal, IL 61790-4480
(309) 438-8447
Fax: (309) 438-3048
Prof. Megan Koch
National Secretary-Treasurer
E-mail: mkoch@ilstu.edu
URL: www.nationalforensics.org

National Institute for Learning Outcomes Assessment (g)
University of Illinois at Urbana-Champaign
360 Education Building
Champaign, IL 61820
(217) 244-2155
Fax: (217) 244-5632
E-mail: njankow2@illinois.edu
URL: www.learningoutcomeassessment.org

National League for Nursing (A)
The Watergate Buliding, 8th Floor
2600 Virginia Avenue, NW
Washington, DC 20037
(800) 669-1656
Dr. Beverly Malone
Chief Executive Officer
E-MAIL: oceo@nln.org
URL: www.nln.org

National Recreation and Park Association Council on Accreditation for Parks, Recreation, Tourism and Related Professions (COAPRT) (B)
22377 Belmont Ridge Road
Ashburn, VA 20148-4501
(703) 858-2141
FAX: (703) 858-0794
Ms. Brenda Beales
Awards and Accreditation Manager
E-MAIL: coaprt@nrpa.org
URL: www.nrpa.org

National Rural Education Association (C)
Purdue University
Beering Hall of Liberal Arts & Education
100 North University Street
West Lafayette, IN 47907
(765) 494-0086
FAX: (765) 496-1228
Dr. John Hill
Executive Director
E-MAIL: jehill@purdue.edu
URL: www.nrea.net

National Society for Experiential Education (D)
c/o Talley Management Group, Inc.
19 Mantua Road
Mt. Royal, NJ 08061
(856) 423-3427
FAX: (856) 423-3420
Haley Brust
Executive Director
E-MAIL: nsee@talley.com
URL: www.nsee.org

National Writing Project (E)
2105 Bancroft Way
#1042
University of California
Berkeley, CA 94720-1042
(510) 642-0963
FAX: (510) 642-4545
Elyse Eidman-Aadahl
Executive Director
E-MAIL: nwp@nwp.org
URL: www.nwp.org

Network of Schools of Public Policy, Affairs, and Administration (F)
1029 Vermont Avenue, NW
Suite 1100
Washington, DC 20005
(202) 628-8965
FAX: (202) 626-4978
Laurel McFarland
Executive Director
E-MAIL: naspaa@naspaa.org
URL: www.naspaa.org

New England Association of Schools and Colleges, Inc. Commission on Institutions of Higher Education (G)
3 Burlington Woods Drive
#100
Burlington, MA 01803
(781) 425-7747
FAX: (781) 425-1001
Dr. Barbara Brittingham
President of the Commission
E-MAIL: cihe@neasc.org
URL: cihe.neasc.org

New England Board of Higher Education (H)
45 Temple Place
Boston, MA 02111
(617) 357-9620, ext. 128
FAX: (617) 338-1577
Dr. Michael K. Thomas
President and CEO
E-MAIL: mthomas@nebhe.org
URL: www.nebhe.org

North American Association of Summer Sessions (I)
1501 West Bradley Avenue
Peoria, IL 61625
(866) 880-9607
FAX: (309) 677-3321
Ms. Janet Lange
Executive Secretary
E-MAIL: lange@bradley.edu
URL: www.naass.org

North Central Conference on Summer Sessions (J)
Bradley University
Peoria, IL 61625
(309) 677-2374
FAX: (309) 677-3321
Ms. Janet M. Lange
Executive Secretary
E-MAIL: lange@bradley.edu
URL: www.nccss.org

Northwest Commission on Colleges and Universities (K)
8060 165th Avenue, NE
Suite 100
Redmond, WA 98052
(425) 558-4224
FAX: (425) 376-0596
Dr. Sandra E. Elman
President
E-MAIL: ruthb@nwccu.org
URL: www.nwccu.org

Organizational Systems Research Association (L)
Morehead State University
Department of Information Systems
150 University Boulevard, Box 2478
Morehead, KY 40351-1689
(606) 783-2718
FAX: (606) 783-5025
Dr. Donna R. Everett
Executive Director
E-MAIL: d.everett@moreheadstate.edu
URL: www.osra.org

Planning Accreditation Board (M)
2334 W. Lawrence Avenue
Suite 209
Chicago, IL 60625
(773) 334-7200
Ms. Shonagh Merits
Executive Director
E-MAIL: smerits@planningaccreditationboard.org
URL: www.planningaccreditationboard.org

Quality Education for Minorities (QEM) Network (N)
1818 N Street, NW
Suite 350
Washington, DC 20036
(202) 659-1818
FAX: (202) 659-5408
Dr. Shirley M. McBay
President
E-MAIL: qemnetwork@qem.org
URL: qemnetwork.qem.org

Society for College and University Planning (O)
1330 Eisenhower Place
Ann Arbor, MI 48108
(734) 669-3270
FAX: (734) 661-0157
Mike Moss CAE
President
E-MAIL: info@scup.org
URL: www.scup.org

Society for Slovene Studies (P)
381 Cathance Road
Topsham, ME 04086
Ms. Kristina Helena Reardon
Secretary
E-MAIL: kristina.reardon@gmail.com
URL: www.slovenestudies.com

Society for the Advancement of Scandinavian Study (Q)
Department of Scandanavian Studies
University of Wisconsin-Madison
1306 Van Hise Hall
1220 Linden Drive
Madison, WI 53706
(608) 262-2090
Ms. Susan Brantley
Managing Editor
E-MAIL: sbrantley@wisc.edu
URL: www.scandinavianstudy.org

Society for Values in Higher Education (R)
c/o Western Kentucky University
1906 College Heights Boulevard
#8020
Bowling Green, KY 42101
(270) 745-2907
FAX: (270) 745-5347
Mrs. Sandy McAllister
Director
E-MAIL: society@svhe.org
URL: www.svhe.org

Society of American Foresters (S)
5400 Grosvenor Lane
Bethesda, MD 20814-2198
(866) 897-8720
FAX: (301) 897-3690
Mr. Matt Menashes
Chief Executive Officer
URL: www.safnet.org

Society of Professors of Education (T)
University of West Georgia
Department of L & I
1600 Maple Street
Carrollton, GA 30118-5160
(678) 839-6132
FAX: (678) 839-6097
Dr. Robert C. Morris
Secretary-Treasurer
E-MAIL: rmorris@westga.edu

Southeastern Universities Research Association (U)
1201 New York Avenue, NW
Suite 430
Washington, DC 20005
(202) 408-7872
FAX: (202) 408-8250
Dr. Jerry Draayer
President & CEO
E-MAIL: draayer@sura.org
URL: www.sura.org

Southern Association for College Student Affairs (V)
Armstrong State University
11935 Abercorn Street
Savannah, GA 31419
(912) 344-2510
FAX: (912) 344-3468
Dr. Joe Buck
Executive Director
E-MAIL: joe.buck@armstrong.edu
URL: www.sacsa.org

Southern Association of Colleges and Schools Commission on Colleges (W)
1866 Southern Lane
Decatur, GA 30033-4097
(404) 679-4500
FAX: (404) 994-6592
Dr. Belle S. Wheelan
President
E-MAIL: bwheelan@sacscoc.org
URL: www.sacscoc.org

Southern States Communication Association (X)
College of Charleston
Office of the Dean
School of Humanities and Social Sciences
2 Green Way
Charleston, SC 29424
(843) 953-0760
FAX: (843) 953-0758
Mr. Jerold L. Hale
Executive Director
E-MAIL: director@ssca.net
URL: www.ssca.net

State Higher Education Executive Officers (Y)
3035 Center Green Drive
Suite 100
Boulder, CO 80301-2205
(303) 541-1600
FAX: (303) 541-1639
Mr. George Pernsteiner
President
E-MAIL: george@sheeo.org
URL: www.sheeo.org

Tennessee Independent Colleges and Universities Association (Z)
1031 17th Avenue South
Nashville, TN 37212
(615) 242-6400
FAX: (615) 242-8033
Dr. Claude O. Pressnell Jr.
President
E-MAIL: pressnell@ticua.org
URL: www.ticua.org

Transnational Association of Christian Colleges and Schools (TRACS) (a)
15935 Forest Road
Forest, VA 24551
(434) 525-9539
FAX: (434) 525-9538
Dr. Timothy Eaton
Interim President
E-MAIL: info@tracs.org
URL: www.tracs.org

The Tuition Exchange, Inc. (b)
3 Bethesda Metro Center
Suite 700
Bethesda, MD 20814
(301) 941-1827
FAX: (301) 657-9776
Mr. Robert D. Shorb
Executive Director/CEO
E-MAIL: rshorb@tuitionexchange.org
URL: www.tuitionexchange.org

UNCF (c)
1805 7th Street NW
Washington, DC 20001
(202) 810-0200
FAX: (202) 234-0222
Dr. Michael Lomax
President & CEO
URL: www.uncf.org

University Aviation Association (d)
2415 Moore's Mill Road
Suite 265-216
Auburn, AL 36830-6444
(334) 528-0300
Ms. Dawn Vinson
Executive Director
E-MAIL: uaamail@uaa.aero
URL: www.uaa.aero

University Film and Video Association (e)
UNLV Department of Film
4505 Maryland Parkway
Box 455015
Las Vegas, NV 89154-5015
(702) 235-7297
Mr. Francisco Menendez
President
E-MAIL: ufvahome@gmail.com
URL: www.ufva.org

University Photographers' Association of America (f)
Moraine Valley Community College
9000 W. College Parkway
Palos Hills, IL 60465
(708) 974-5495
Mr. Glenn Carpenter
UPAA President
E-MAIL: carpenter@morainevalley.edu
URL: www.upaa.org

University Professional & Continuing Education Association (UPCEA) (g)
One Dupont Circle, NW
Suite 615
Washington, DC 20036
(202) 659-3130
FAX: (202) 785-0374
Dr. Robert Hansen
CEO
E-MAIL: rhansen@upcea.edu
URL: www.upcea.edu

Urban Affairs Association (h)
c/o Urban Studies Program
University of Wisconsin-Milwaukee
PO Box 413
Milwaukee, WI 53201-0413
(414) 229-3025
Dr. Margaret Wilder
UAA Executive Director
E-MAIL: info@uaamail.org
URL: www.urbanaffairsassociation.org

WASC Senior College and University Commission (A)
985 Atlantic Avenue
Suite 100
Alameda, CA 94501
(510) 748-9001
FAX: (510) 748-9797
Mary Ellen Petrisko
President
URL: www.wascsenior.org

Western Interstate Commission for Higher Education (B)
3035 Center Green Drive
Suite 200
Boulder, CO 80301-2204
(303) 541-0201
FAX: (303) 541-0245
Dr. David A. Longanecker
President
E-MAIL: dlonganecker@wiche.edu
URL: www.wiche.edu

Consortia of Institutions of Higher Education

Alabama Association of Independent Colleges and Universities (A)
5950 Carmichael Place
Suite 213
Montgomery, AL 36117
(334) 356-2220
FAX: (334) 356-2202
Gen. Paul M. Hankins
President
E-MAIL: hankinsp@knology.net
URL: www.aaicu.net

Arkansas' Independent Colleges and Universities (B)
One Riverfront Place
Suite 610
North Little Rock, AR 72114
(501) 378-0843
FAX: (501) 374-1523
Dr. Rex M. Horne
President
E-MAIL: rhorne@arkindcolleges.org
URL: www.arkindcolleges.org

Associated Colleges of Central Kansas (C)
210 South Main Street
McPherson, KS 67460
(620) 241-5150
FAX: (620) 241-5153
Ms. Cindy Sutton
Director/Business Manager
E-MAIL: cindy@mail.acck.edu
URL: www.acck.edu

Associated Colleges of the Midwest (D)
11 East Adams Street
Suite 800
Chicago, IL 60603
(312) 263-5000
FAX: (312) 263-5879
Dr. Christopher Welna
President
E-MAIL: acm@acm.edu
URL: www.acm.edu

Associated Colleges of the Twin Cities (ACTC) (E)
1619 Dayton Avenue
Suite 105
Saint Paul, MN 55104
(651) 493-9162
Dr. Carole Chabries
Executive Director
E-MAIL: info@actc-mn.org
URL: www.actc-mn.org

Association of Independent California Colleges and Universities (F)
1100 Eleventh Street
Suite 10
Sacramento, CA 95814
(916) 446-7626
FAX: (916) 446-7948
Ms. Kristen F. Soares
President
E-MAIL: aiccu@aiccu.edu
URL: www.aiccu.edu

Association of Independent Colleges and Universities in Massachusetts (G)
11 Beacon Street
Suite 1224
Boston, MA 02108-3093
(617) 742-5147
FAX: (617) 742-3089
Mr. Richard Doherty
President
E-MAIL: richard.doherty@aicum.org
URL: www.masscolleges.org -or- www.aicum.org

Association of Independent Colleges and Universities in New Jersey (H)
797 Springfield Avenue
Summit, NJ 07901-1107
(908) 277-3738
FAX: (908) 277-3424
Mr. John B. Wilson
President and CEO
E-MAIL: jbwilson@njcolleges.org
URL: www.njcolleges.org

Association of Independent Colleges and Universities of Nebraska (I)
635 South 14th Street
Suite 310
Lincoln, NE 68508
(402) 434-2818
FAX: (402) 434-2825
Mr. Thomas O'Neill
President
E-MAIL: tiponeill2@aol.com

Association of Independent Colleges and Universities of Ohio (J)
41 South High Street
Suite 1690
Columbus, OH 43215
(614) 228-2196
FAX: (614) 228-8406
Mr. C. Todd Jones
President & General Counsel
E-MAIL: tjones@aicuo.edu
URL: www.aicuo.edu

Association of Independent Colleges and Universities of Pennsylvania (K)
101 North Front Street
Harrisburg, PA 17101-1405
(717) 232-8649
FAX: (717) 233-8574
Dr. Don L. Francis
President
E-MAIL: francis@aicup.org
URL: www.aicup.org

Association of Independent Colleges and Universities of Rhode Island (L)
50 Park Row West
Suite 100
Providence, RI 02903
(401) 272-8270
Mr. Daniel Egan
President
E-MAIL: degan@aicuri.org
URL: www.aicuri.org

Association of Independent Colleges of Art & Design (M)
236 Hope Street
Providence, RI 02906
(401) 270-5991
FAX: (401) 270-5993
Ms. Deborah Obalil
Executive Director
E-MAIL: deborah@aicad.org
URL: www.aicad.org

Association of Independent Kentucky Colleges and Universities (N)
484 Chenault Road
Frankfort, KY 40601
(502) 695-5007
FAX: (502) 695-5057
Dr. Gary S. Cox
President
E-MAIL: gary.cox@aikcu.org
URL: www.aikcu.org

Association of Vermont Independent Colleges (O)
PO Box 254
Montpelier, VT 05601
(802) 828-8826
Susan Stitely
President
E-MAIL: sstitely@vermont-icolleges.org
URL: www.vermont-icolleges.org

Atlanta Regional Council for Higher Education (P)
133 Peachtree Street, NE
Suite 4925
Atlanta, GA 30303-2923
(404) 651-2668
FAX: (404) 880-9816
Ms. Tracey Johnson
E-MAIL: arche@atlantahighered.org
URL: www.atlantahighered.org

Boston Theological Institute (Q)
PO Box 391395
Cambridge, MA 02139-0014
(617) 527-4880
FAX: (617) 527-1073
Dr. Ann McClenahan
Executive Director
E-MAIL: mcclenahan@bostontheological.org
URL: www.bostontheological.org

Central Pennsylvania Consortium (R)
c/o Franklin & Marshall College
PO Box 3003
Lancaster, PA 17604-3003
(717) 291-4282
FAX: (717) 358-4455
Ms. Kathryn Missildine
Executive Assistant
E-MAIL: kathy.missildine@fandm.edu
URL: www.centralpennsylvaniaconsortium.org

CHESLA (S)
10 Columbus Boulevard
Hartford, CT 06106-1978
(860) 761-8453
Ms. Jeanette W. Weldon
Executive Director
E-MAIL: jweldon@chefa.com
URL: www.chesla.org

Christian College Consortium (T)
255 Grapevine Road
Wenham, MA 01984-1813
(978) 867-4802
FAX: (978) 867-4650
Dr. Stan D. Gaede
President
E-MAIL: president@gordon.edu
URL: www.ccconsortium.org

Community College Futures Assembly (U)
University of Florida, College of Education
Box 117040
140 Norman Hall
Gainesville, FL 32611-7044
(352) 273-4293
Dr. Dale F. Campbell
Director
E-MAIL: futures@coe.ufl.edu
URL: www.education.ufl.edu/futures/

The Consortium for Graduate Study in Management (V)
229 Chesterfield Business Parkway
Chesterfield, MO 63005
(636) 681-5487
FAX: (636) 681-5497
Mr. Peter J. Aranda III
Executive Director and CEO
E-MAIL: recruiting@cgsm.org
URL: www.cgsm.org

Consortium of College & University Media Centers (W)
Indiana University
306 N. Union Street
Bloomington, IN 47405-3888
(812) 855-6049
Aileen Scales
Executive Director
E-MAIL: ccumc@ccumc.org
URL: www.ccumc.org

Consortium of Universities of the Washington Metropolitan Area (X)
1100 H Street, NW
Suite 500
Washington, DC 20005
(202) 331-8080
FAX: (202) 331-7925
Dr. John Cavanaugh
President & CEO
E-MAIL: jcavanaugh@consortium.org
URL: www.consortium.org

Consortium on Financing Higher Education (Y)
238 Main Street
Suite 402
Cambridge, MA 02142-1046
(617) 253-5030
FAX: (617) 258-8280
Dr. Kristine E. Dillon
President
E-MAIL: kedillon@mit.edu
URL: www.cofhe.org

Cooperating Raleigh Colleges (Z)
Meredith College
3800 Hillsborough Street
Raleigh, NC 27607-5298
(919) 760-8538
Ms. Jenny Spiker
Director
E-MAIL: crc@meredith.edu
URL: www.crcraleighcolleges.org

Council of Independent Colleges in Virginia (a)
PO Box 1005
Bedford, VA 24523
(540) 586-0606
FAX: (540) 586-2630
Mr. Robert B. Lambeth Jr.
President
E-MAIL: lambeth@cicv.org
URL: www.cicv.org

Council of North Central Two Year Colleges (b)
200 South 14th Street
Parsons, KS 67357
(620) 820-1223
FAX: (620) 421-0921
Dr. George Knox
Executive Director
E-MAIL: meganf@labette.edu
URL: www.labette.edu/cnctyc

Council of Presidents (c)
410 Eleventh Avenue, SE
Suite 101
Olympia, WA 98501
(360) 292-4100
FAX: (360) 292-4110
Mr. Paul Francis
Executive Director
E-MAIL: pfrancis@cop.wsu.edu
URL: www.councilofpresidents.org

Federation of Independent Illinois Colleges and Universities (d)
1123 South Second Street
Springfield, IL 62704
(217) 789-1400
FAX: (217) 789-6259
Mr. David W. Tretter
President
E-MAIL: davetretter@federationedu.org
URL: www.federationedu.org

Five Colleges, Incorporated (e)
97 Spring Street
Amherst, MA 01002
(413) 542-4009
FAX: (413) 542-4029
Dr. Neal B. Abraham
Executive Director
E-MAIL: nabraham@fivecolleges.edu
URL: www.fivecolleges.edu

Georgia Independent College Association (f)
600 West Peachtree Street, NW
Suite 1710
Atlanta, GA 30308
(404) 233-5433
FAX: (404) 233-6309
Dr. Susanna Baxter
President
E-MAIL: sbaxter@georgiacolleges.org
URL: www.georgiacolleges.org

Graduate Theological Foundation Oxford/Rome/Indiana Consortia (g)
Dodge House
415 Lincoln Way East
Mishawaka, IN 46544-2213
(800) 423-5983
FAX: (574) 255-7520
Bethany Morgan MBA
Registrar
E-MAIL: information@gtfeducation.org
URL: www.gtfeducation.org

Great Lakes Colleges Association (h)
535 West William
Suite 301
Ann Arbor, MI 48103
(734) 661-2350
FAX: (734) 661-2349
Dr. Richard A. Detweiler
President
E-MAIL: detweiler@glca.org
URL: www.glca.org

Greater Cincinnati Consortium of Colleges and Universities (i)
Northern Kentucky University
241 Campbell Hall
Highland Heights, KY 41099
(859) 392-2428
Ms. Janet Piccirillo
Executive Director
E-MAIL: gcccu@nku.edu
URL: www.gcccu.org

Hartford Consortium for Higher Education (A)
31 Pratt Street
5th Floor
Hartford, CT 06103
(860) 702-3800
FAX: (860) 241-1130
Dr. Martin Estey
Executive Director
E-MAIL: mestey@metrohartford.com
URL: www.hartfordconsortium.org

Higher Education Consortium for Urban Affairs, Inc. (HECUA) (B)
2233 University Avenue West
Suite 210
St. Paul, MN 55114
(651) 287-3300
FAX: (651) 659-9421
Dr. Jenny Keyser
Executive Director
E-MAIL: hecua@hecua.org
URL: www.hecua.org

Higher Education Consortium of Metropolitan St. Louis (C)
8420 Delmar Boulevard
Suite 504
St. Louis, MO 63124
(314) 991-2700
FAX: (314) 991-2874
Mr. Thomas George
Chair
E-MAIL: purchasing@heccstl.com
URL: www.heccstl.com

Higher Education Data Sharing (HEDS) Consortium (D)
Wabash College
410 West Wabash Avenue
Crawfordsville, IN 47933
(765) 361-6331
Charles Blaich
Director
E-MAIL: charles.blaich@gmail.com
URL: www.hedsconsortium.org

Independent Colleges and Universities of Missouri (E)
PO Box 1865
Jefferson City, MO 65102-1865
(573) 635-9160
FAX: (573) 635-6258
Mr. William A. Gamble
Executive Director
E-MAIL: bill@molobby.com
URL: www.icum.org

Independent Colleges and Universities of Texas, Inc. (F)
400 West 15th Street
Suite 850
Austin, TX 78701
(512) 472-9522
FAX: (512) 472-2371
Ray Martinez III
President
E-MAIL: info@icut.org
URL: www.icut.org

Independent Colleges of Indiana (G)
30 S. Meridian Street
Suite 800
Indianapolis, IN 46204
(317) 236-6090
FAX: (317) 236-6086
Dr. Richard L. Ludwick
President and CEO
E-MAIL: smartchoice@icindiana.org
URL: www.icindiana.org

Independent Colleges of Washington (H)
600 Stewart Street
Suite 600
Seattle, WA 98101
(206) 623-4494
FAX: (206) 625-9621
Ms. Violet A. Boyer
President & CEO
E-MAIL: info@icwashington.org
URL: www.icwashington.org

Inter-University Consortium for Political and Social Research (I)
The University of Michigan
Institute for Social Research
PO Box 1248
Ann Arbor, MI 48106-1248
(734) 615-8400
FAX: (734) 647-8200
Dr. George Alter
Director
E-MAIL: altergc@umich.edu
URL: www.icpsr.umich.edu

Inter-University Council of Ohio (IUC) (J)
10 West Broad Street
Suite 450
Columbus, OH 43215
(614) 464-1266
FAX: (614) 464-9281
Ms. Cindy McQuade
Vice President of Operations
E-MAIL: mcquade.2@osu.edu
URL: www.iuc-ohio.org

Iowa Association of Community College Trustees (K)
855 East Court Avenue
Des Moines, IA 50309
(515) 282-4692
FAX: (515) 282-3743
M. J. Dolan J.D.
Executive Director
E-MAIL: mjdolan@iacct.com
URL: www.iacct.com

Iowa Association of Independent Colleges and Universities (L)
505 Fifth Avenue
Suite 1030
Des Moines, IA 50309-2315
(515) 282-3175
FAX: (515) 282-8177
Mr. Gary W. Steinke
President
E-MAIL: president@iaicu.org
URL: www.iowaprivatecolleges.org

Kansas Independent College Association (M)
700 South Kansas Avenue
Suite 622
Topeka, KS 66603
(785) 235-9877
FAX: (785) 235-1437
Mr. Matthew E. Lindsey
President
E-MAIL: matt@kscolleges.org
URL: www.kscolleges.org

Lehigh Valley Association of Independent Colleges (N)
1309 Main Street
Bethlehem, PA 18018
(610) 625-7888
FAX: (610) 625-7891
Diane Dimitroff
Executive Director
E-MAIL: dimitroffd@lvaic.org
URL: www.lvaic.org

Louisiana Association of Independent Colleges and Universities (O)
320 Third Street
Suite 104
Baton Rouge, LA 70801
(225) 389-9885
FAX: (225) 389-0149
Ms. Mary Ann Coleman
President
E-MAIL: maryann@laicu.org
URL: www.laicu.org

Maine Independent Colleges Association (P)
c/o Preti Flaherty
PO Box 1058
Augusta, ME 04332-0158
(207) 623-5300
FAX: (207) 623-2914
Dr. Daniel Walker
President
E-MAIL: dwalker@preti.com

Maryland Independent College and University Association (Q)
140 South Street
Annapolis, MD 21401
(410) 269-0306
FAX: (410) 269-5905
Ms. Tina M. Bjarekull
President
E-MAIL: tbjarekull@micua.org
URL: www.micua.org

Massachusetts Education & Career Opportunities Inc (R)
484 Main Street
Suite 500
Worcester, MA 01608
(508) 754-6829
FAX: (508) 797-0069
Ms. Pamela Boisvert
CEO
E-MAIL: info@massedco.org
URL: www.massedco.org

Michigan Independent Colleges & Universities (S)
One Michigan Avenue
Suite 950
Lansing, MI 48933
(517) 372-9160
FAX: (517) 372-9165
Robert LeFevre
E-MAIL: rlefevre@micolleges.org
URL: www.micolleges.org

Midwest Universities Consortium for International Activities, Inc. (T)
4700 South Hagadorn Road
Suite 150
East Lansing, MI 48823-6808
(517) 432-0661
FAX: (517) 432-4457
Dr. Philip R. Smith
President & Executive Director
E-MAIL: mucia@msu.edu
URL: www.muciainc.org

Minnesota Private College Council, Inc. (U)
445 Minnesota Street
Suite 500
St. Paul, MN 55101-2903
(651) 228-9061
FAX: (651) 228-0379
E-MAIL: colleges@mnprivatecolleges.org
URL: www.mnprivatecolleges.org

Mississippi Association of Independent Colleges and Universities (V)
PO Box 2933
Ridgeland, MS 39158-2933
(601) 957-2052
FAX: (601) 977-0233
Dr. E. Harold Fisher
Executive Director
E-MAIL: ehfisher@bellsouth.net

National Student Exchange (W)
4656 West Jefferson
Suite 140
Fort Wayne, IN 46804
(260) 436-2634
FAX: (260) 436-5676
Ms. Bette Worley
President
E-MAIL: bworley@nse2.org
URL: www.nse.org

New England Faculty Development Consortium (X)
Mount Ida College
777 Dedham Street
Newton, MA 02459
(617) 928-7396
Dakin Burdick Ph.D.
President
E-MAIL: dburdick@mountida.edu
URL: www.nefdc.org

New Hampshire College & University Council (Y)
3 Barrell Court
Suite 100
Concord, NH 03301-8543
(603) 225-4199
FAX: (603) 225-8108
Thomas R. Horgan
President and CEO
E-MAIL: horgan@nhcuc.org
URL: www.nhcuc.org

New Jersey Association of State Colleges and Universities (Z)
150 West State Street
Trenton, NJ 08608
(609) 989-1100
Dr. Michael W. Klein
CEO
E-MAIL: crpipher@njascu.org
URL: www.njascu.org

New Jersey Council of County Colleges (a)
330 West State Street
Trenton, NJ 08618
(609) 392-3434
FAX: (609) 392-8158
Dr. Lawrence A. Nespoli
President
E-MAIL: info@njccc.org
URL: www.njccc.org

New Orleans Educational Telecommunications Consortium, Inc. (b)
5000 West Esplanade Avenue
#290
Metairie, LA 70006
(504) 524-0350
E-MAIL: noetc@noetc.org
URL: www.noetc.com

North Carolina Independent Colleges and Universities (c)
530 North Blount Street
Raleigh, NC 27604
(919) 832-5817
FAX: (919) 833-0794
Dr. A. Hope Williams
President
E-MAIL: williams@ncicu.org
URL: www.ncicu.org

North Dakota Independent College Fund (d)
University of Mary
7500 University Drive
Bismarck, ND 58504
(701) 355-8030
FAX: (701) 255-7687
Mr. Neal Kalberer
Executive Director
E-MAIL: kalberer@umary.edu

Northeast Consortium of Colleges and Universities in Massachusetts (NECCUM) (e)
Office of the President
Salem State University
552 Lafayette Street
Salem, MA 01970
(978) 542-6134
FAX: (978) 542-6126
Katie Sadowski
E-MAIL: ksadowski@salemstate.edu
URL: www.salemstate.edu/students/27600.php

Northeast Ohio Council on Higher Education (f)
1501 Euclid Avenue
Suite 423
Cleveland, OH 44115
(216) 420-9200
FAX: (216) 420-9292
Mr. Robert W. Briggs
President
E-MAIL: rbriggs@noche.org
URL: www.noche.org

Oak Ridge Associated Universities (g)
MC-100-22
PO Box 117
Oak Ridge, TN 37831-0117
(865) 576-3300
FAX: (865) 576-3816
Mr. Harry A. Page
President and CEO
E-MAIL: andy.page@orau.org
URL: www.orau.org

Oklahoma Independent Colleges and Universities (h)
PO Box 57148
Oklahoma City, OK 73157-7148
(405) 371-1780
Lesa Smaligo
Executive Director
E-MAIL: lesa@oicu.org
URL: www.oicu.org

Consortia of Institutions of Higher Education

Oregon Alliance of Independent Colleges & Universities (A)
16101 SW 72nd Avenue
Suite 100
Portland, OR 97224
(503) 639-4541
FAX: (503) 639-4851
Dr. Larry D. Large
President
E-MAIL: larry@oaicu.org
URL: www.oaicu.org

Pennsylvania Association of Colleges and Universities (B)
950 Walnut Bottom Road
Suite 15-214
Carlisle, PA 17015
(800) 687-9010
FAX: (717) 240-0673
URL: www.pacu.org

Pennsylvania State System of Higher Education Foundation, Inc. (C)
2986 North Second Street
Harrisburg, PA 17110
(717) 720-4056
FAX: (717) 720-7082
Ms. Jennifer S. Hartman
President/CEO
E-MAIL: jhartman@thepafoundation.org
URL: www.thepafoundation.org

Pittsburgh Council on Higher Education (D)
201 Wood Street
Pittsburgh, PA 15222
(412) 657-8105
Ms. Katrina Chavez
Executive Director
URL: www.pchepa.org

Quad-Cities Graduate Study Center (E)
WIU - QC Campus
3300 River Drive
Moline, IL 61265
(309) 762-9481
Shirley Moore
Administrative Assistant
E-MAIL: qc@gradcenter.org
URL: www.gradcenter.org

South Carolina Independent Colleges & Universities, Inc. (F)
PO Box 12007
Columbia, SC 29211
(803) 799-7122
FAX: (803) 254-7504
Mr. Michael G. LeFever
President & CEO
E-MAIL: mike@scicu.org
URL: www.scicu.org

South Metropolitan Higher Education Consortium (G)
One University Parkway
University Park, IL 60484
(708) 534-4984
FAX: (708) 534-8458
Ms. Genevieve F. Boesen
Executive Director
E-MAIL: gboesen@southmetroed.org
URL: www.southmetroed.org

Southern Regional Education Board (H)
592 Tenth Street, NW
Atlanta, GA 30318-5776
(404) 875-9211
FAX: (404) 872-1477
Dr. David S. Spence
President
E-MAIL: dave.spence@sreb.org
URL: www.sreb.org

Southwestern Ohio Council for Higher Education (SOCHE) (I)
3155 Research Boulevard
Suite 204
Dayton, OH 45420-4015
(937) 258-8890
FAX: (937) 258-8899
Dr. Sean Creighton
President
E-MAIL: soche@soche.org
URL: www.soche.org

Texas International Education Consortium (J)
1103 West 24th Street
Austin, TX 78705
(512) 477-9283, ext. 114
FAX: (512) 322-0592
Dr. Ronald Aqua
President & CEO
E-MAIL: ron.aqua@tiec.org
URL: www.tiec.org

Tuition Plan Consortium/Private College 529 Plan (K)
7425 Forsyth Boulevard
St. Louis, MO 63105
(314) 727-0900
FAX: (314) 727-0930
Ms. Nancy Farmer
President
E-MAIL: nancy@pc529.com
URL: www.tomorrowstuitiontoday.org

University City Science Center (L)
3711 Market Street
8th Floor
Philadelphia, PA 19104
(215) 966-6000
FAX: (215) 966-6002
Dr. Stephen Tang
President & CEO
E-MAIL: info@sciencecenter.org
URL: www.sciencecenter.org

The Virginia College Fund (M)
4900 Augusta Avenue
Suite 101
Richmond, VA 23230
(804) 355-3271
FAX: (804) 359-5765
Mr. James K. Dill
President
E-MAIL: jkdill@thevcf.org
URL: www.thevcf.org

Virginia Tidewater Consortium for Higher Education (N)
4900 Powhatan Avenue
Norfolk, VA 23508-1836
(757) 683-3183
FAX: (757) 683-4515
Dr. Lawrence G. Dotolo
President
E-MAIL: lgdotolo@aol.com
URL: www.vtc.odu.edu

Washington Theological Consortium (O)
3025 4th Street, NE
Suite 120
Washington, DC 20017-1103
(202) 832-2675
FAX: (202) 526-0818
Dr. Larry Golemon
Executive Director
E-MAIL: wtc@washtheocon.org
URL: washtheocon.org

West Virginia Independent Colleges & Universities, Inc. (P)
1 Stamm Lane
Wheeling, WV 26003
(304) 242-7223
FAX: (304) 242-7223
Mr. Ben Exley IV
Executive Director
E-MAIL: benexley@wvicu.org
URL: www.wvicu.org

Wisconsin Association of Independent Colleges and Universities (Q)
122 West Washington Avenue
Suite 700
Madison, WI 53703-2723
(608) 256-7761
FAX: (608) 256-7065
Dr. Rolf Wegenke
President
E-MAIL: mail@waicu.org
URL: www.waicu.org

The Work Colleges Consortium (R)
CPO 2163
Berea, KY 40404
(859) 985-3154
Ms. Robin Taffler
Executive Director
E-MAIL: robin@workcolleges.org
URL: www.workcolleges.org

NAME INDEX

US Department of Education Offices, Statewide Agencies of Higher Education, Higher Education Associations, Consortia of Institutions of Higher Education

Institutions By Religious Affiliation

African Methodist Episcopal
Allen University .... SC
Edward Waters College .... FL
Paul Quinn College .... TX
Payne Theological Seminary .... OH
Shorter College .... AR
Wilberforce University .... OH

African Methodist Episcopal Zion Church
Clinton College .... SC
Hood Theological Seminary .... NC
Livingstone College .... NC

Alabama Baptist State Convention
Judson College .... AL

American Baptist
Alderson Broaddus University .... WV
American Baptist Seminary of the West .. CA
Bacone College .... OK
Eastern University .... PA
Franklin College of Indiana .... IN
Judson University IL
Linfield College .... OR
Northern Seminary IL
Ottawa University .... KS
Palmer Theological Seminary of Eastern University .... PA
University of Sioux Falls .... SD

Assemblies Of God Church
American Indian College of the Assemblies of God .... AZ
Assemblies of God Theological Seminary MO
Bethel College .... VA
Evangel University .... MO
Global University .... MO
Native American Bible College .... NC
North Central University .... MN
Northpoint Bible College .... MA
Northwest University .... WA
Southeastern University .... FL
Southwestern Assemblies of God University .... TX
Trinity Bible College .... ND
University of Valley Forge .... PA
Vanguard University of Southern California .... CA

Baptist
American Baptist College .... TN
Arkansas Baptist College .... AR
Arlington Baptist College .... TX
Baptist Bible College .... MO
Baptist Missionary Association Theological Seminary .... TX
Baptist University of the Americas .... TX
Baylor University .... TX
Bethel University .... MN
Bluefield College .... VA
Boston Baptist College .... MA
Brewton-Parker College .... GA
Campbell University .... NC
Campbellsville University .... KY
Cedarville University .... OH
Central Baptist College .... AR
Central Baptist Theological Seminary ...... KS
Central Baptist Theological Seminary of Minneapolis .... MN
Chowan University .... NC
Dallas Baptist University .... TX
Gardner-Webb University .... NC
Georgetown College .... KY
Hardin-Simmons University .... TX
Howard Payne University .... TX
Huntsville Bible College .... AL
International Baptist College and Seminary .... AZ
Jacksonville College .... TX
Maple Springs Baptist Bible College & Seminary .... MD
Missouri Baptist University .... MO
Morris College .... SC
Oakland City University .... IN
Selma University .... AL
Shaw University .... NC
Shorter University .... GA
Simmons College of Kentucky .... KY
Southeastern Baptist College .... MS
Summit University of Pennsylvania .... PA
The Crown College of the Bible .... TN
The John Leland Center for Theological Studies .... VA
Trinity Baptist College .... FL
Truett McConnell College .... GA

University of the Cumberlands .... KY
Virginia Baptist College .... VA
Virginia Beach Theological Seminary ...... VA
Virginia Union University .... VA
Washington University of Virginia .... VA

Brethren Church
Ashland University .... OH

Christian Church (Disciples Of Christ)
Barton College .... NC
Bethany College .... WV
Chapman University .... CA
Christian Theological Seminary .... IN
Columbia College .... MO
Culver-Stockton College .... MO
Eureka College IL
Jarvis Christian College .... TX
Lexington Theological Seminary .... KY
Lynchburg College .... VA
Midway University .... KY
Northwest Christian University .... OR
Phillips Theological Seminary .... OK
Texas Christian University .... TX
Transylvania University .... KY
William Woods University .... MO

Christian Churches And Churches of Christ
Belmont University .... TN
Boise Bible College .... ID
Central Christian College of the Bible ...... MO
Cincinnati Christian University .... OH
Crossroads College .... MN
Dallas Christian College .... TX
Great Lakes Christian College .... MI
Johnson University .... TN
Kentucky Christian University .... KY
Lincoln Christian University IL
Manhattan Christian College .... KS
Nebraska Christian College .... NE
Point University .... GA

Christian Methodist Episcopal
Lane College .... TN
Miles College .... AL
Texas College .... TX

Christian Reformed Church
Calvin College .... MI
Calvin Theological Seminary .... MI
Dordt College .... IA

Church Of Christ
Pepperdine University .... CA

Church Of God
Anderson University .... IN
Lee University .... TN
Mid-America Christian University .... OK
Pentecostal Theological Seminary .... TN
The University of Findlay .... OH
Universidad Teologica Del Caribe .... PR
Warner Pacific College .... OR
Warner University .... FL

Church of New Jerusalem
Bryn Athyn College of the New Church ... PA

Church Of The Brethren
Bethany Theological Seminary .... IN
Bridgewater College .... VA
Elizabethtown College .... PA
Manchester University .... IN
McPherson College .... KS

Church Of The Nazarene
Eastern Nazarene College .... MA
MidAmerica Nazarene University .... KS
Mount Vernon Nazarene University .... OH
Nazarene Bible College .... CO
Nazarene Theological Seminary .... MO
Northwest Nazarene University .... ID
Olivet Nazarene University IL
Point Loma Nazarene University .... CA
Southern Nazarene University .... OK
Trevecca Nazarene University .... TN

Churches Of Christ
Abilene Christian University .... TX
Amridge University .... AL
Crowley's Ridge College .... AR
Faulkner University .... AL
Freed-Hardeman University .... TN
Harding University Main Campus .... AR

Heritage Christian University .... AL
Lipscomb University .... TN
Lubbock Christian University .... TX
Mid-Atlantic Christian University .... NC
Ohio Valley University .... WV
Southwestern Christian College .... TX
York College .... NE

Cumberland Presbyterian
Bethel University .... TN
Memphis Theological Seminary .... TN

Evangelical Congregational Church
Evangelical Theological Seminary .... PA

Evangelical Covenant Church Of America
North Park University IL

Evangelical Free Church Of America
Trinity International University IL

Evangelical Lutheran Church In America
Augsburg College .... MN
Augustana College IL
Augustana University .... SD
Bethany College .... KS
California Lutheran University .... CA
Capital University .... OH
Carthage College .... WI
Concordia College .... MN
Finlandia University .... MI
Gettysburg College .... PA
Grand View University .... IA
Gustavus Adolphus College .... MN
Lenoir-Rhyne University .... NC
Luther College .... IA
Luther Seminary .... MN
Lutheran School of Theology at Chicago IL
Lutheran Theological Seminary at Gettysburg .... PA
Lutheran Theological Seminary at Philadelphia .... PA
Midland University .... NE
Muhlenberg College .... PA
Newberry College .... SC
Pacific Lutheran University .... WA
Roanoke College .... VA
St. Olaf College .... MN
Susquehanna University .... PA
Texas Lutheran University .... TX
Thiel College .... PA
Trinity Lutheran Seminary .... OH
Wartburg College .... IA
Wartburg Theological Seminary .... IA
Wittenberg University .... OH

Evangelical Lutheran Synod
Bethany Lutheran College .... MN

Fellowship Of Grace Brethren Churches
Grace College and Seminary .... IN

Free Methodist
Central Christian College of Kansas .... KS
Greenville College IL
Seattle Pacific University .... WA
Spring Arbor University .... MI

Free Will Baptist
California Christian College .... CA
Hillsdale Free Will Baptist College .... OK
Welch College .... TN

Friends
Earlham College and Earlham School of Religion .... IN
George Fox University .... OR
Guilford College .... NC
Malone University .... OH
William Penn University .... IA
Wilmington College .... OH

Greek Orthodox
Hellenic College-Holy Cross Greek Orthodox School of Theology .... MA

Interdenominational
Bethany Global University .... MN
Carolina Graduate School of Divinity ...... NC
Christian Witness Theological Seminary . CA
Denver Seminary .... CO
Evangelical Seminary of Puerto Rico ...... PR
Faith Evangelical College & Seminary ..... WA

God's Bible School and College .... OH
Inste Bible College .... IA
Interdenominational Theological Center .. GA
Legacy Christian University .... AL
Messiah College .... PA
Oak Hills Christian College .... MN
Palm Beach Atlantic University .... FL
Phoenix Seminary .... AZ
Rocky Mountain College .... MT
Shepherd University School of Theology . CA
South Florida Bible College .... FL
Union Bible College .... IN
Wesley Biblical Seminary .... MS

Jewish
Academy for Jewish Religion .... CA
Hebrew Union College-Jewish Institute of Religion .... NY
New York Medical College .... NY
Rabbi Isaac Elchanan Theological Seminary .... NY
Reconstructionist Rabbinical College ...... PA

Latter-day Saints
Brigham Young University .... UT
Brigham Young University Hawaii .... HI
Brigham Young University-Idaho .... ID
LDS Business College .... UT

Lutheran
Valparaiso University .... IN

Lutheran Church - Missouri Synod
Concordia College .... NY
Concordia College Alabama .... AL
Concordia Seminary .... MO
Concordia Theological Seminary .... IN
Concordia University .... CA
Concordia University .... NE
Concordia University .... OR
Concordia University Ann Arbor .... MI
Concordia University Chicago IL
Concordia University Texas .... TX
Concordia University Wisconsin .... WI
Concordia University, St. Paul .... MN

Mennonite Brethren Church
Fresno Pacific University .... CA
Tabor College .... KS

Mennonite Church
Anabaptist Mennonite Biblical Seminary .. IN
Bethel College .... KS
Bluffton University .... OH
Eastern Mennonite University .... VA
Goshen College .... IN
Hesston College .... KS
Rosedale Bible College .... OH

Missionary Church
Bethel College .... IN

Moravian Church
Moravian College .... PA
Salem College .... NC

Multiple Protestant Denominations
Huston-Tillotson University .... TX
LeMoyne-Owen College .... TN
Paine College .... GA

Non-denominational
Carolina College of Biblical Studies .... NC
Cedar Crest College .... PA
China Evangelical Seminary North America .... CA
Faith Theological Seminary .... MD
Heartland Christian College .... MO
Manthano Christian College .... MI
Midwest University .... MO
Montreat College .... NC
North American University .... TX
Pacific Bible College .... OR
Providence Christian College .... CA
University of Fort Lauderdale .... FL
Williamson College .... TN

North American Baptist
Sioux Falls Seminary .... SD

Original Free Will Baptist Church
University of Mount Olive .... NC

Other Protestant
Beulah Heights University ... GA
Grace College of Divinity ... NC
Ohio Christian University ... OH
Saint Louis Christian College ... MO
Urshan Graduate School of Theology ... MO

Pentecostal Church of God
Messenger College ... TX
Universidad Pentecostal Mizpa ... PR

Pentecostal Holiness Church
Emmanuel College ... GA
Southwestern Christian University ... OK

Pentecostal/Charismatic Non-Denominational
Christian Life College ... IL

Presbyterian
Grove City College ... PA
Sterling College ... KS
Whitworth University ... WA

Presbyterian Church (U.S.A.)
Agnes Scott College ... GA
Austin College ... TX
Austin Presbyterian Theological Seminary ... TX
Belhaven University ... MS
Blackburn College ... IL
Bloomfield College ... NJ
Buena Vista University ... IA
Carroll University ... WI
Columbia Theological Seminary ... GA
Davidson College ... NC
Davis & Elkins College ... WV
Eckerd College ... FL
Hampden-Sydney College ... VA
Hanover College ... IN
Hastings College ... NE
King University ... TN
Lees-McRae College ... NC
Louisville Presbyterian Theological Seminary ... KY
Lyon College ... AR
Macalester College ... MN
Mary Baldwin College ... VA
Maryville College ... TN
McCormick Theological Seminary ... IL
Millikin University ... IL
Missouri Valley College ... MO
Monmouth College ... IL
Muskingum University ... OH
Pittsburgh Theological Seminary ... PA
Presbyterian College ... SC
Princeton Theological Seminary ... NJ
Queens University of Charlotte ... NC
Rhodes College ... TN
San Francisco Theological Seminary ... CA
Schreiner University ... TX
Stillman College ... AL
Tusculum College ... TN
Union Presbyterian Seminary ... VA
University of Dubuque ... IA
University of Jamestown ... ND
University of Pikeville ... KY
University of the Ozarks ... AR
Warren Wilson College ... NC
Waynesburg University ... PA
Westminster College ... PA
William Peace University ... NC
Wilson College ... PA

Presbyterian Church In America
Covenant College ... GA
Covenant Theological Seminary ... MO
Grace Mission University ... CA
Presbyterian Theological Seminary in America ... CA
Reformed University ... GA

Protestant Episcopal
Bexley Seabury ... IL
Church Divinity School of the Pacific ... CA
Episcopal Divinity School ... MA
General Theological Seminary ... NY
Nashotah House ... WI
Protestant Episcopal Theological Seminary in Virginia ... VA
Saint Augustine's University ... NC
Seminary of the Southwest ... TX
Sewanee: The University of the South ... TN
Trinity Episcopal School for Ministry ... PA
Voorhees College ... SC

Reformed Church In America
Central College ... IA
Hope College ... MI
New Brunswick Theological Seminary ... NJ
Northwestern College ... IA
Western Theological Seminary ... MI

Reformed Episcopal Church
Reformed Episcopal Seminary ... PA

Reformed Presbyterian Church
Evangelia University ... CA
Geneva College ... PA
Reformed Presbyterian Theological Seminary ... PA

Roman Catholic
Alvernia University ... PA
Ancilla College ... IN
Anna Maria College ... MA
Aquinas College ... MI
Aquinas College ... TN
Aquinas Institute of Theology ... MO
Assumption College ... MA
Assumption College for Sisters ... NJ
Athenaeum of Ohio ... OH
Augustine Institute ... CO
Ave Maria School of Law ... FL
Avila University ... MO
Barry University ... FL
Belmont Abbey College ... NC
Benedictine College ... KS
Benedictine University ... IL
Boston College ... MA
Brescia University ... KY
Briar Cliff University ... IA
Cabrini College ... PA
Caldwell University ... NJ
Calumet College of Saint Joseph ... IN
Canisius College ... NY
Cardinal Stritch University ... WI
Carlow University ... PA
Carroll College ... MT
Catholic Theological Union ... IL
Chestnut Hill College ... PA
Christ the King Seminary ... NY
Christendom College ... VA
Christian Brothers University ... TN
Clarke University ... IA
College of Our Lady of the Elms ... MA
College of Saint Benedict ... MN
College of Saint Elizabeth ... NJ
College of Saint Mary ... NE
College of St. Joseph ... VT
College of the Holy Cross ... MA
Conception Seminary College ... MO
Creighton University ... NE
DePaul University ... IL
DeSales University ... PA
Divine Word College ... IA
Dominican School of Philosophy and Theology ... CA
Dominican University ... IL
Donnelly College ... KS
Duquesne University ... PA
Edgewood College ... WI
Emmanuel College ... MA
Fairfield University ... CT
Felician College ... NJ
Fontbonne University ... MO
Franciscan University of Steubenville ... OH
Gannon University ... PA
Georgetown University ... DC
Georgian Court University ... NJ
Gonzaga University ... WA
Gwynedd Mercy University ... PA
Holy Apostles College and Seminary ... CT
Holy Cross College ... IN
Holy Family University ... PA
Immaculata University ... PA
John Carroll University ... OH
Kenrick-Glennon Seminary-Kenrick School of Theology ... MO
King's College ... PA
La Roche College ... PA
La Salle University ... PA
Laboure College ... MA
Lewis University ... IL
Loras College ... IA
Lourdes University ... OH
Loyola Marymount University ... CA
Loyola University Chicago ... IL
Loyola University Maryland ... MD
Loyola University New Orleans ... LA
Madonna University ... MI
Marian University ... IN
Marian University ... WI
Marquette University ... WI
Marygrove College ... MI
Marymount California University ... CA
Marymount University ... VA
Marywood University ... PA
Mercy College of Health Sciences ... IA
Mercy College of Ohio ... OH
Mercyhurst University ... PA
Merrimack College ... MA
Misericordia University ... PA
Mount Angel Seminary ... OR
Mount Carmel College of Nursing ... OH
Mount Marty College ... SD
Mount Mary University ... WI
Mount Mercy University ... IA
Mount Saint Mary's University ... CA
Mount St. Joseph University ... OH
Mount St. Mary's University ... MD
Neumann University ... PA
Newman University ... KS
Northeast Catholic College ... NH
Notre Dame College ... OH
Notre Dame of Maryland University ... MD
Notre Dame Seminary, Graduate School of Theology ... LA
Oblate School of Theology ... TX
Ohio Dominican University ... OH
Our Lady of Holy Cross College ... LA
Our Lady of the Lake College ... LA
Our Lady of the Lake University ... TX
Pontifical College Josephinum ... OH
Pontifical Faculty of the Immaculate Conception at the Dominican House of Studies ... DC
Pontifical John Paul II Institute for Studies on Marriage and Family ... DC
Pope St. John XXIII National Seminary ... MA
Presentation College ... SD
Providence College ... RI
Quincy University ... IL
Regis University ... CO
Rivier University ... NH
Rockhurst University ... MO
Rosemont College ... PA
Sacred Heart Major Seminary ... MI
Sacred Heart Seminary and School of Theology ... WI
Saint Anselm College ... NH
Saint Anthony College of Nursing ... IL
Saint Bernard's School of Theology & Ministry ... NY
Saint Charles Borromeo Seminary ... PA
Saint Francis Medical Center College of Nursing ... IL
Saint Francis University ... PA
Saint Gregory the Great Seminary ... NE
Saint John's Seminary ... CA
Saint John's Seminary ... MA
Saint John's University ... MN
Saint Joseph Seminary College ... LA
Saint Joseph's College ... IN
Saint Joseph's College of Maine ... ME
Saint Joseph's Seminary ... NY
Saint Joseph's University ... PA
Saint Leo University ... FL
Saint Louis University ... MO
Saint Martin's University ... WA
Saint Mary Seminary and Graduate School of Theology ... OH
Saint Mary's College ... IN
Saint Mary's College of California ... CA
Saint Mary's Seminary and University ... MD
Saint Mary's University of Minnesota ... MN
Saint Mary-of-the-Woods College ... IN
Saint Meinrad School of Theology ... IN
Saint Michael's College ... VT
Saint Norbert College ... WI
Saint Patrick's Seminary & University ... CA
Saint Peter's University ... NJ
Saint Vincent College ... PA
Saint Vincent Seminary ... PA
Saint Xavier University ... IL
Salve Regina University ... RI
Seattle University ... WA
Seton Hall University ... NJ
Seton Hill University ... PA
Siena Heights University ... MI
Silver Lake College of the Holy Family ... WI
Spring Hill College ... AL
SS. Cyril and Methodius Seminary ... MI
St. Ambrose University ... IA
St. Bonaventure University ... NY
St. Catharine College ... KY
St. Catherine University ... MN
St. Gregory's University ... OK
St. John Vianney College Seminary ... FL
St. John Vianney Theological Seminary ... CO
St. John's University ... NY
St. Mary's University ... TX
St. Thomas University ... FL
St. Vincent De Paul Regional Seminary ... FL
Stonehill College ... MA
The Catholic University of America ... DC
The College of Saint Scholastica ... MN
The Pontifical Catholic University of Puerto Rico ... PR
The University of Scranton ... PA
Thomas More College ... KY
Trinity Washington University ... DC
Universidad Central de Bayamon ... PR
University of Dallas ... TX
University of Dayton ... OH
University of Detroit Mercy ... MI
University of Great Falls ... MT
University of Mary ... ND
University of Notre Dame ... IN
University of Saint Francis ... IN
University of Saint Joseph ... CT
University of Saint Mary ... KS
University of Saint Mary of the Lake-Mundelein Seminary ... IL
University of Saint Thomas ... MN
University of San Diego ... CA
University of San Francisco ... CA
University of St. Francis ... IL
University of St. Thomas ... TX
University of the Incarnate Word ... TX
University of the Sacred Heart ... PR
Ursuline College ... OH
Villanova University ... PA
Viterbo University ... WI
Walsh University ... OH
Wheeling Jesuit University ... WV
Wyoming Catholic College ... WY
Xavier University ... OH
Xavier University of Louisiana ... LA

Russian Orthodox
Holy Trinity Orthodox Seminary ... NY

Seventh-day Adventist
Adventist University of Health Sciences ... FL
Andrews University ... MI
Kettering College ... OH
La Sierra University ... CA
Loma Linda University ... CA
Oakwood University ... AL
Pacific Union College ... CA
Southern Adventist University ... TN
Southwestern Adventist University ... TX
Union College ... NE
Universidad Adventista de las Antillas ... PR
Walla Walla University ... WA
Washington Adventist University ... MD

Southern Baptist
B.H. Carroll Theological Institute ... TX
Blue Mountain College ... MS
California Baptist University ... CA
Carson-Newman University ... TN
Charleston Southern University ... SC
Clear Creek Baptist Bible College ... KY
East Texas Baptist University ... TX
Golden Gate Baptist Theological Seminary ... CA
Hannibal-LaGrange University ... MO
Houston Baptist University ... TX
Louisiana College ... LA
Midwestern Baptist Theological Seminary ... MO
Mississippi College ... MS
New Orleans Baptist Theological Seminary ... LA
North Greenville University ... SC
Oklahoma Baptist University ... OK
Ouachita Baptist University ... AR
Samford University ... AL
Southeastern Baptist Theological Seminary ... NC
Southwest Baptist University ... MO
Southwestern Baptist Theological Seminary ... TX
The Baptist College of Florida ... FL
The Southern Baptist Theological Seminary ... KY
Union University ... TN
University of Mary Hardin-Baylor ... TX
University of Mobile ... AL
Wayland Baptist University ... TX
William Carey University ... MS
Williams Baptist College ... AR
Wingate University ... NC

The Christian And Missionary Alliance
Crown College ... MN
Nyack College ... NY
Simpson University ... CA
Toccoa Falls College ... GA

Unification Church
Unification Theological Seminary ... NY

Unitarian Universalist
Meadville Lombard Theological School ... IL
Starr King School for the Ministry ... CA

United Brethren Church
Huntington University ... IN

United Church Of Christ

- Catawba College ...... NC
- Chicago Theological Seminary IL
- Doane College ...... NE
- Eden Theological Seminary ...... MO
- Elmhurst College IL
- Heidelberg University ...... OH
- Lakeland College ...... WI
- Lancaster Theological Seminary ...... PA
- Northland College ...... WI
- Piedmont College ...... GA
- The Defiance College ...... OH
- Tougaloo College ...... MS
- United Theological Seminary of the Twin Cities ...... MN

United Methodist

- Adrian College ...... MI
- Albion College ...... MI
- Albright College ...... PA
- Allegheny College ...... PA
- American University ...... DC
- Andrew College ...... GA
- Baker University ...... KS
- Baldwin Wallace University ...... OH
- Bennett College ...... NC
- Bethune Cookman University ...... FL
- Birmingham-Southern College ...... AL
- Brevard College ...... NC
- Centenary College of Louisiana ...... LA
- Central Methodist University ...... MO
- Claflin University ...... SC
- Claremont School of Theology ...... CA
- Clark Atlanta University ...... GA
- Columbia College ...... SC
- Cornell College ...... IA
- Dakota Wesleyan University ...... SD
- DePauw University ...... IN
- Dillard University ...... LA
- Emory & Henry College ...... VA
- Emory University ...... GA
- Ferrum College ...... VA
- Florida Southern College ...... FL
- Garrett-Evangelical Theological Seminary IL
- Greensboro College ...... NC
- Hamline University ...... MN
- Hendrix College ...... AR
- High Point University ...... NC
- Hiwassee College ...... TN
- Huntingdon College ...... AL
- Iliff School of Theology ...... CO
- Iowa Wesleyan University ...... IA
- Kansas Wesleyan University ...... KS
- Kentucky Wesleyan College ...... KY
- LaGrange College ...... GA
- Lebanon Valley College ...... PA
- Lindsey Wilson College ...... KY
- Louisburg College ...... NC
- Lycoming College ...... PA
- MacMurray College IL
- Martin Methodist College ...... TN
- McKendree University IL
- McMurry University ...... TX
- Methodist Theological School in Ohio ...... OH
- Methodist University ...... NC
- Millsaps College ...... MS
- Morningside College ...... IA
- Nebraska Wesleyan University ...... NE
- North Carolina Wesleyan College ...... NC
- North Central College IL
- Ohio Northern University ...... OH
- Ohio Wesleyan University ...... OH
- Oklahoma City University ...... OK
- Otterbein University ...... OH
- Pfeiffer University ...... NC
- Philander Smith College ...... AR
- Randolph College ...... VA
- Randolph-Macon College ...... VA
- Reinhardt University ...... GA
- Rust College ...... MS
- Saint Paul School of Theology ...... KS
- Shenandoah University ...... VA
- Simpson College ...... IA
- Southern Methodist University ...... TX
- Southwestern College ...... KS
- Southwestern University ...... TX
- Spartanburg Methodist College ...... SC
- Tennessee Wesleyan College ...... TN
- Texas Wesleyan University ...... TX
- Union College ...... KY
- United Theological Seminary ...... OH
- University of Evansville ...... IN
- University of Indianapolis ...... IN
- University of Mount Union ...... OH
- Virginia Wesleyan College ...... VA
- Wesley College ...... DE
- Wesley Theological Seminary ...... DC
- Wesleyan College ...... GA
- West Virginia Wesleyan College ...... WV
- Wiley College ...... TX
- Wofford College ...... SC
- Young Harris College ...... GA

Wesleyan Church

- Allegheny Wesleyan College ...... OH
- Houghton College ...... NY
- Indiana Wesleyan University ...... IN
- Oklahoma Wesleyan University ...... OK
- Southern Wesleyan University ...... SC

Wisconsin Evangelical Lutheran Synod

- Martin Luther College ...... MN

Carnegie Classification Code Definitions*

This year, the Higher Education Directory lists the updated 2010 Carnegie Classifications. The 2010 Classification update retains the same structure of classifications initially adopted in 2005. Due to space limitation, the *Higher Education Directory* ® only lists the original classification framework—now called the basic classification—which was substantially revised in 2005. These new codes are listed below:

Associate's Colleges: Includes institutions where all degrees are at the associate's level, or where bachelor's degrees account for less than 10 percent of all undergraduate degrees. Excludes institutions eligible for classification as Tribal Colleges or Special Focus Institutions.

Assoc/Pub-R-S: Associate's — Public Rural-serving Small
Assoc/Pub-R-M: Associate's — Public Rural-serving Medium
Assoc/Pub-R-L: Associate's — Public Rural-serving Large
Assoc/Pub-S-SC: Associate's — Public Suburban-serving Single Campus
Assoc/Pub-S-MC: Associate's — Public Suburban-serving Multicampus
Assoc/Pub-U-SC: Associate's — Public Urban-serving Single Campus
Assoc/Pub-U-MC: Associate's — Public Urban-serving Multicampus
Assoc/Pub-Spec: Associate's — Public Special Use
Assoc/PrivNFP: Associate's — Private Not-for-profit
Assoc/PrivFP: Associate's — Private For-profit
Assoc/Pub2in4: Associate's — Public 2-year Colleges under Universities
Assoc/Pub4: Associate's — Public 4-year, Primarily Associate's
Assoc/PrivNFP4: Associate's — Private Not-for-profit 4-year, Primarily Associate's
Assoc/PrivFP4: Associate's — Private For-profit 4-year, Primarily Associate's

Doctorate-granting Universities. Includes institutions that award at least 20 doctoral degrees per year (excluding doctoral-level degrees that qualify recipients for entry into professional practice, such as the JD, MD, PharmD, DPT, etc.). Excludes Special Focus Institutions and Tribal Colleges.

RU/VH: Research Universities (very high research activity)
RU/H: Research Universities (high research activity)
DRU: Doctoral/Research Universities

Master's Colleges and Universities. Includes institutions that award at least 50 master's degrees per year. Excludes Special Focus Institutions and Tribal Colleges.

Master's/L: Master's Colleges and Universities (larger programs)
Master's/M: Master's Colleges and Universities (medium programs)
Master's/S: Master's Colleges and Universities (smaller programs)

Baccalaureate Colleges. Includes institutions where baccalaureate degrees represent at least 10 percent of all undergraduate degrees and that award fewer than 50 master's degrees or fewer than 20 doctoral degrees per year. Excludes Special Focus Institutions and Tribal Colleges.

Bac/A&S: Baccalaureate Colleges — Arts & Sciences
Bac/Diverse: Baccalaureate Colleges — Diverse Fields
Bac/Assoc: Baccalaureate/Associate's Colleges

Special Focus Institutions. Institutions awarding baccalaureate or higher-level degrees where a high concentration of degrees is in a single field or set of related fields. Excludes Tribal Colleges.

Spec/Faith: Theological seminaries, Bible colleges, and other faith-related institutions
Spec/Medical: Medical schools and medical centers
Spec/Health: Other health profession schools
Spec/Engg: Schools of engineering
Spec/Tech: Other technology-related schools
Spec/Bus: Schools of business and management
Spec/Arts: Schools of art, music, and design
Spec/Law: Schools of law
Spec/Other: Other special-focus institutions

Tribal Colleges. Colleges and universities that are members of the American Indian Higher Education Consortium, as identified in IPEDS Institutional Characteristics.

Tribal: Tribal Colleges

*All data provided by The Carnegie Foundation for the Advancement of Teaching. For more detailed information on the revised Carnegie Codes, please visit http://classifications.carnegiefoundation.org/

Statistics

Institutions of Higher Education by Control, Level and State

STATE	TWO YEAR		FOUR YEAR		TOTAL		SYSTEM	GRAND
	PRIVATE	PUBLIC	PRIVATE	PUBLIC	PRIVATE	PUBLIC	OFFICE	TOTAL
AL	2	26	23	15	25	41	2	68
AK	2	1	3	3	5	4	1	10
AZ	10	19	27	4	37	23	1	61
AR	2	22	12	11	14	33	2	49
CA	49	116	238	36	287	152	28	467
CO	19	13	29	16	48	29	3	80
CT	0	12	21	7	21	19	1	41
DE	1	1	4	2	5	3	0	8
DC	2	0	13	3	15	3	0	18
FL	42	4	73	37	115	41	1	157
GA	9	24	38	30	47	54	1	102
HI	2	6	7	4	9	10	2	21
ID	0	4	5	4	5	8	0	13
IL	16	47	96	12	112	59	6	177
IN	7	1	46	15	53	16	2	71
IA	1	18	40	3	41	21	3	65
KS	3	25	26	9	29	34	0	63
KY	1	16	35	8	36	24	1	61
LA	10	18	14	17	24	35	4	63
ME	3	7	11	8	14	15	2	31
MD	4	16	21	16	25	32	1	58
MA	3	16	83	14	86	30	2	118
MI	4	25	45	19	49	44	1	94
MN	4	30	47	11	51	41	3	95
MS	0	15	10	9	10	24	0	34
MO	12	17	63	13	75	30	3	108
MT	6	5	6	6	12	11	1	24
NE	6	7	18	7	24	14	2	40
NV	4	1	2	6	6	7	1	14
NH	1	7	12	4	13	11	2	26
NJ	4	19	32	13	36	32	1	69
NM	0	13	9	8	9	21	0	30
NY	31	36	192	44	223	80	5	308
NC	2	59	53	16	55	75	2	132
ND	1	4	7	7	8	11	1	20
OH	24	24	74	17	98	41	1	140
OK	5	12	16	15	21	27	0	48
OR	6	16	26	8	32	24	0	56
PA	56	16	114	20	170	36	1	207
RI	0	1	8	3	8	4	0	12
SC	2	19	23	14	25	33	0	58
SD	1	5	10	6	11	11	1	23
TN	9	13	52	10	61	23	2	86
TX	25	64	74	46	99	110	9	218
UT	2	4	13	6	15	10	1	26
VT	0	1	17	5	17	6	1	24
VA	17	24	59	17	76	41	1	118
WA	4	25	27	14	31	39	2	72
WV	7	8	11	11	18	19	2	39
WI	3	16	32	14	35	30	2	67
WY	1	7	1	1	2	8	0	10
AS	0	0	0	1	0	1	0	1
GU	0	1	1	1	1	2	0	3
MH	0	1	0	0	0	1	0	1
MP	0	0	0	1	0	1	0	1
PR	7	0	40	14	47	14	3	64
FM	0	1	0	0	0	1	0	1
PW	0	1	0	0	0	1	0	1
VI	0	0	0	1	0	1	0	1
Total	**432**	**909**	**1959**	**662**	**2391**	**1571**	**111**	**4073**

Figures do not include 1,391 additional branch campus listings.

50 Largest Universities by Fall 2014 Enrollment

Institution	Enrollment
1. Arizona State University	83301
2. Liberty University	81459
3. Texas A & M University	62392
4. Grand Canyon University	62304
5. University of Central Florida	60376
6. The Ohio State University Main Campus	58322
7. American Public University System	57539
8. Ashford University	54120
9. Western Governors University	53800
10. Air University	53102
11. Walden University	52188
12. Kaplan University	52018
13. University of Texas at Austin	51313
14. University of Minnesota-Twin Cities	51147
15. University of Florida	50350
16. Michigan State University	50081
17. Florida International University	49703
18. Ohio University (all campuses)	49277
19. New York University	49274
20. Rutgers the State University of New Jersey New Brunswick Campus	48378
21. University of Maryland University College	47906
22. Penn State University Park	46502
23. Indiana University Bloomington	46416
24. University of Washington	44784
25. Southern New Hampshire University	43743
26. University of Cincinnati Main Campus	43691
27. University of Michigan-Ann Arbor	43625
28. University of Illinois at Urbana-Champaign	43603
29. University of Southern California	43000
30. University of Wisconsin-Madison	42598
31. University of Arizona	42236
32. University of South Florida	42065
33. University of California-Los Angeles	41845
34. Florida State University	41226
35. University of Houston	40914
36. California State University-Northridge	40131
37. The University of Texas at Arlington	39740
38. Purdue University Main Campus	38770
39. Strayer University	38159
40. California State University-Fullerton	38128
41. Temple University	37788
42. University of California-Berkeley	37565
43. California State University-Long Beach	37492
44. Texas State University	36790
45. University of North Texas	36164
46. The University of Alabama	36155
47. University of Missouri - Columbia	35441
48. University of California-Davis	35415
49. University of Georgia	35197
50. Texas Tech University	35158

Institutions by Control and Tuition Range

Tuition	Public*	Private	Total
0 - 1,000	37	65	102
1,001 - 2,000	160	7	167
2,001 - 4,000	455	41	496
4,001 - 6,000	367	100	467
6,001 - 8,000	253	93	346
8,001 - 10,000	144	123	267
Over 10,000	155	1962	2117
Total	**1571**	**2391**	**3962**

* Figures for Public Institutions are In-State Tuitions

Universities, Colleges and Schools

by State*

*Includes the District of Columbia and, separately, U.S. Service Schools, American Samoa, Federated States of Micronesia, Guam, Marshall Islands, Northern Marianas, Palau, Puerto Rico, and Virgin Islands.

ALABAMA

Alabama Agricultural and Mechanical University (A)

4900 Meridian Street, Normal AL 35762-1357

County: Madison FICE Identification: 001002
Unit ID: 100654
Telephone: (256) 372-5230 Carnegie Class: Master's L
FAX Number: (256) 372-5244 Calendar System: Semester
URL: www.aamu.edu
Established: 1875 Annual Undergrad Tuition & Fees (In-State): $7,770
Enrollment: 5,333 Coed
Affiliation or Control: State IRS Status: 501(c)3
Highest Offering: Doctorate
Program: Liberal Arts And General; Teacher Preparatory; Professional
Accreditation: SC, AAFCS, CORE, CS, #DIETD, ENG, ENGT, PLNG, SP, SW, TED

01 President .... Dr. Andrew HUGINE, JR.
03 Executive VP/COO .... Dr. Kevin A. ROLLE
05 Provost/VP Academic Affairs .... Dr. Daniel K. WIMS
10 Vice Pres of Business & Finance .... Mr. Clayton GIBSON
26 Int VP Mktg/Comm/Advancement .... Mr. Archie TUCKER
32 Interim VP Student Affairs .... Dr. Bennie G. MCMORRIS
46 Interim VP Inst Rsrch/Spons Pgms .... Dr. Vann NEWKIRK
21 AVP Budget & Planning .... Mr. Gregory JACKSON
84 AVP of Enrollment Management .... Ms. Venita KING
13 Chief Information Officer .... Dr. Kimberly MARSHALL
21 AVP Finance/Comptroller .... Mr. Norman JONES
15 Director Human Resources .... Ms. Cassandra TARVER-ROSS
18 Int Director Facilities Services .... Mr. Vincent WEAVER
06 Registrar .... Ms. Brenda K. WILLIAMS
30 Int Director of Development .... Ms. Reba JASMIN
41 Director of Athletics .... Mr. Bryan HICKS
35 Director of Student Activities .... Ms. Jasmine BUXTON
37 Director of Financial Aid .... Mr. Darryl JACKSON
88 Director of Emergency Management .... Ms. Monica RAY
23 Dir Student Health & Counseling .... Dr. Jennifer PARKER-AYERS
36 Dir Career Development Services .... Ms. Yvette CLAYTON
09 Dir Institutional Research .... Dr. Thomas COAXUM
88 Director Marketing & PR .... Mr. Jerome SAINTJONES
39 Dir of Residential Housing .... Mr. Kenneth MADDOX
19 Chief of Police .... Ms. Monica RAY
08 Dean Learn Resources Center .... Dr. Annie PAYTON
96 Director of Purchasing .... Mr. Jeffrey ROBINSON
58 Dean Graduate School/AVP Acad Affs .... Dr. Vann NEWKIRK
47 Dean Col Agricultural/Life/Nat Sci .... Dr. Lloyd WALKER
53 Dean College of Education .... Dr. Curtis MARTIN
54 Dean College of Engineering .... Dr. Chance GLENN
50 Int Dean Col of Business/Pub Affs .... Dr. Barbara JONES
49 Interim Dean University College .... Dr. Juarine STEWART

Alabama College of Osteopathic Medicine (B)

445 Health Sciences Boulevard, Dothan AL 36303

County: Houston Identification: 667138
Telephone: (334) 699-2266 Carnegie Class: Not Classified
FAX Number: N/A Calendar System: Semester
URL: www.acomedu.org
Established: 2011 Annual Graduate Tuition & Fees: $42,580
Enrollment: 316 Coed
Affiliation or Control: Independent Non-Profit IRS Status: 501(c)3
Highest Offering: First Professional Degree; No Undergraduates
Program: Professional
Accreditation: @OSTEO

01 President .... Ronald S. OWEN
05 Dean/Senior Vice President .... Craig J. LENZ
32 Assoc Dean Student Services .... Philip REYNOLDS

Alabama Southern Community College (C)

PO Box 2000, Monroeville AL 36461-2000

County: Monroe FICE Identification: 001034
Unit ID: 101949
Telephone: (251) 575-3156 Carnegie Class: Assoc/Pub-R-S
FAX Number: (251) 575-5356 Calendar System: Semester
URL: www.ascc.edu
Established: 1965 Annual Undergrad Tuition & Fees (In-State): $4,260
Enrollment: 1,398 Coed
Affiliation or Control: State IRS Status: 501(c)3
Highest Offering: Associate Degree
Program: Occupational; 2-Year Principally Bachelor's Creditable
Accreditation: SC, ADNUR

01 President .... Dr. Reginald SYKES
11 VP Operations/Campus Director .... Mr. Roger CHANDLER
05 Dean of Instruction .... Mrs. Ann CLANTON
32 Dean of Students .... Dr. Melissa HAAB
08 Director of Library Services .... Ms. Alisha LINAM
06 Registrar .... Ms. Jana HORTON
37 Director of Financial Aid .... Ms. Amy ROWELL
26 Director of Public Information .... Ms. Maconica SAWYER
18 Director of Maintenance .... Mr. Tom REED
41 Athletic Director .... Mr. Daniel HEAD
15 Dir of Human Resources/Admin Svcs .... Mr. Rodney LORD

Alabama State University (D)

915 S Jackson Street, Montgomery AL 36101-0271

County: Montgomery FICE Identification: 001005
Unit ID: 100724
Telephone: (334) 229-4200 Carnegie Class: Master's L
FAX Number: (334) 834-6861 Calendar System: Semester
URL: www.alasu.edu
Established: 1867 Annual Undergrad Tuition & Fees (In-State): $8,720
Enrollment: 5,000 Coed
Affiliation or Control: State IRS Status: 501(c)3
Highest Offering: Doctorate
Program: Liberal Arts And General; Teacher Preparatory; Professional
Accreditation: SC, ACBSP, ART, CACREP, CAHIIM, CORE, MUS, OPE, OT, PTA, SW, TED, THEA

01 President .... Dr. Gwendolyn E. BOYD
100 Chief of Staff .... Mr. Bernard HOUSTON
05 Provost/Vice Pres Academic Affs .... Dr. Leon C. WILSON
10 Vice President Business & Finance .... Ms. Wanda SMITH
13 Vice President Technology Services .... Ms. Diane ALEXANDER
30 Vice Pres Institutional Advancement .... Ms. Zillah FLUKER
18 Director Physical Plant .... Mr. Brian THORNTON
15 Director Human Resources .... Mrs. Willie DIXON
04 Administrative Asst to President .... Mrs. Kathy GRANT
32 Vice Pres Student Affairs .... Dr. Davida HAYWOOD
84 Assistant Vice Pres Enrollment Mgmt .... Dr. Ronald BROWN
20 Assoc Provost Academic Affairs .... Dr. Karyn GUNN
45 Assoc Prov Institutional Effectiv .... Dr. Legand BURGE
35 Asst Vice Pres Student Affairs .... Mr. Rick DRAKE
21 Int Comt/Asst VP Business & Finance .... Mrs. Alondrea J. PRITCHETT
20 Assistant VP Academic Advisement .... Vacant
108 Dir Acad Planning & Evaluation .... Dr. Christine C. THOMAS
09 Director Institutional Research .... Dr. Yiyun JIE
88 Dir Quality Enhancement Plng .... Vacant
08 Dean Libraries/Learning Resource .... Dr. Janice FRANKLIN
07 Director Admissions/Recruitment .... Dr. William SMITH
37 Financial Aid Director .... Mr. Marcus BYRD
36 Dir Placement Svcs/Cooperative Educ .... Mr. Jeremy HODGE
50 Dean College Business Admin .... Dr. LaQuita BOOTH
89 Dean University College .... Dr. Evelyn HODGE
53 Int Dean College of Education .... Dr. Doris SCREWS
64 Dean Visual & Performing Arts .... Dr. Tommie T. STEWART
58 Dean Graduate Studies .... Dr. William PERSON
81 Dean College of Sci Math & Tech .... Dr. Kennedy WEKESA
49 Inter Dean Liberal Arts/Social Sci .... Dr. Anthony T. ADAMS
76 Dean College Health Sciences .... Dr. Steven B. CHESBRO
51 Int Dir Cont Education .... Mr. Olan L. WESLEY
29 Director Alumni Relations .... Mr. Cromwell HANDY
23 Director Student Health Services .... Ms. Gwendolyn MANN
19 Chief of Campus Police .... Mr. James GRAYBOYS
38 Dir Counseling & Development Svcs .... Vacant
39 Dir Housing/Residential Life .... Mr. Gourdine WADE
41 Acting Director of Athletics .... Mr. Melvin HINES
25 Director Grants Sponsored Pgms .... Mrs. Tamara LEE
96 Director of Purchasing .... Ms. Ann SMITH
101 Board Liaison .... Mrs. Kisha HOWARD
106 Dir Online Education/E-learning .... Vacant
43 General Counsel .... Mr. Kenneth THOMAS

Amridge University (E)

1200 Taylor Road, Montgomery AL 36117-3553

County: Montgomery FICE Identification: 025034
Unit ID: 100690
Telephone: (800) 351-4040 Carnegie Class: Bac/A&S
FAX Number: (334) 387-3878 Calendar System: Semester
URL: www.amridgeuniversity.edu
Established: 1967 Annual Undergrad Tuition & Fees: $6,000
Enrollment: 625 Coed
Affiliation or Control: Churches Of Christ IRS Status: 501(c)3
Highest Offering: Doctorate
Program: Liberal Arts And General; Professional; Religious Emphasis
Accreditation: SC

01 President .... Dr. Michael C. TURNER
05 Academic Vice President/Dean .... Dr. Lee TAYLOR
32 VP of Student Affairs .... Mrs. Laina T. COSTANZA
09 VP of Inst Research and IDD .... Vacant
06 Registrar .... Mrs. Elaine P. TARENCE
07 Admissions .... Vacant
08 Director of Library .... Ms. Kay S. NEWMAN
10 Chief Business Officer .... Mrs. B. P. TURNER
21 Chief Accountant .... Mrs. Anita L. CROSBY
37 Financial Aid Director .... Ms. Starr FAIN
42 Director of Church Relations .... Mr. Curtis SAMPLEY
88 Director of World Missions .... Mr. Demar ELAM
29 Director of Alumni Relations .... Vacant
13 System Admin Network Operations .... Mr. Jack TEMPLE
18 Chief Facilities/Physical Plant .... Mr. Robert SHIRLEY
24 Coordinator of Network Opers .... Mr. Thomas PATTERSON
38 Director of Student Counseling .... Vacant
26 Chief Public Relations Officer .... Mrs. Laina COSTANZA
42 Chaplain/Director Campus Ministry .... Vacant
73 Dean of School of Theology .... Dr. Rodney CLOUD
50 Dean of Col of Business & Ldrshp .... Dr. Kenyetta MCCURTY
97 Dean of College of General Studies .... Dr. Roger SHEPHERD
88 Dean of Sch of Human Svcs .... Dr. Jerry MARTIN
15 Director Personnel Services .... Vacant
08 Head Librarian .... Mr. Terence SHERIDAN
35 Student Affairs Coordinator .... Mr. Carl BYRD

Athens State University (F)

300 N Beaty Street, Athens AL 35611-1902

County: Limestone FICE Identification: 001008
Unit ID: 100812
Telephone: (256) 233-8100 Carnegie Class: Bac/Diverse
FAX Number: (256) 216-3324 Calendar System: Semester
URL: www.athens.edu
Established: 1822 Annual Undergrad Tuition & Fees (In-State): $6,270
Enrollment: 3,129 Coed
Affiliation or Control: State IRS Status: 501(c)3
Highest Offering: Baccalaureate
Program: Liberal Arts And General; Teacher Preparatory
Accreditation: SC, ACBSP, TED

01 President .... Dr. Robert K. GLENN
05 Provost & VP for Academic Affs .... Vacant
20 Associate VP for Academic Affairs .... Ms. Belinda KRIGEL
20 Asst VP for Academic Affairs .... Dr. Jackie SMITH
32 Vice Pres for Enroll & Student Supp .... Ms. Sarah MCABEE
35 Asst VP for Enrollment & Stdnt Svcs .... Ms. Crystal CREEKMORE
10 Vice President for Financial Aff .... Mr. Mike MCCOY
21 Associate Business Officer .... Mr. Evan THORNTON
26 Vice Pres for University Advance .... Vacant
08 Director of Libraries .... Vacant
50 Dean College of Business .... Dr. Kimberly LAFEVOR
53 Dean College of Education .... Dr. Patricia SIMS
49 Dean College of Arts & Sciences .... Dr. Ronald FRITZE
36 Dir of Career Services .... Ms. Saralyn MITCHELL
37 Dir of Student Financial Services .... Ms. Mary CHAMBLISS
06 Registrar .... Ms. Teresa SUIT
07 Director of Admissions & Records .... Ms. Necedah HENDERSON
35 Director of Student Activities .... Mr. Terry STEPP
29 Director of Alumni Affairs/Ann Giv .... Ms. Trish DI LULLO
30 Director of Development .... Vacant
88 Director of Printing & Public Rels .... Mr. Guy MCCLURE
09 Director of Institutional Research .... Ms. Sylvia CORREA
18 Director of Physical Plant .... Mr. Jerry BRADFORD
15 Director of Human Resources .... Ms. Suzanne SIMS
51 Director of Ctr for Lifelong Lrng .... Vacant
88 Dir of Transfer Stdnt Success Ctr .... Ms. Lisa PAYNE

Auburn University (G)

Auburn AL 36849

County: Lee FICE Identification: 001009
Unit ID: 100858
Telephone: (334) 844-4000 Carnegie Class: RU/H
FAX Number: N/A Calendar System: Semester
URL: www.auburn.edu
Established: 1856 Annual Undergrad Tuition & Fees (In-State): $10,424
Enrollment: 25,912 Coed
Affiliation or Control: State IRS Status: 501(c)3
Highest Offering: Doctorate
Program: Liberal Arts And General; Teacher Preparatory; Professional
Accreditation: SC, AAB, ART, AUD, BUS, BUSA, CACREP, CIDA, CLPSY, CONST, COPSY, CORE, CS, DIETD, ENG, JOUR, LSAR, MFCD, MUS, NURSE, PHAR, SP, SPAA, SW, TED, THEA, VET

01 President .... Dr. Jay GOGUE
03 Executive Vice President .... Dr. Donald L. LARGE, JR.
05 Provost/VP Acad Affairs .... Dr. Timothy R. BOOSINGER
29 VP Alumni Affairs .... Ms. Gretchen R. VANVALKENBURG
10 VP Business & Finance & CFO .... Ms. Marcie SMITH
30 VP Development .... Ms. Jane DIFOLCO PARKER
32 VP Student Affairs & Assoc Provost .... Dr. Bobby R. WOODARD
46 VP Research & Economic Development .... Dr. John M. MASON
101 Secretary to Board of Trustees .... Mr. C. Grant DAVIS, JR.
43 General Counsel .... Mr. Lee F. ARMSTRONG
13 Chief Information Officer .... Mr. Bliss BAILEY
84 Dean of Enrollment Services .... Dr. Charles W. ALDERMAN
56 Dir AL Cooperative Extension Syst .... Dr. Gary D. LEMME
41 Director of Athletics .... Mr. John O. JACOBS, JR.
86 Exec Director Governmental Affairs .... Ms. Sherri FULFORD
11 Director Public Affairs .... Mr. Brian C. KEETER
88 Exec Director Internal Audit .... Mr. M. Kevin ROBINSON
88 Exec Director Risk Mgmt & Safety .... Ms. Christine L. EICK
19 Exec Dir Security & Pub Safety .... Mr. Melvin OWENS
26 Director Univ Communications .... Mr. Mike CLARDY, JR.
88 Univ Ombudsperson .... Mr. Kevin COONROD
20 Associate Provost & Professor .... Dr. Emmett WINN
28 Assoc Provost Div & Multi Affairs .... Dr. Overtoun JENDA
46 Assoc VP Research & Assoc Provost .... Dr. Zhanjiang LIU
20 Assoc Provost Undergrad Studies .... Dr. Constance C. RELIHAN
25 Assistant VP Research .... Ms. Martha M. TAYLOR
35 Assistant VP Student Affairs .... Ms. Lady D. COX
56 Assistant VP Univ Outreach .... Dr. Royrickers COOK
92 Asst Provost & Dir Honors College .... Dr. Melissa J. BAUMANN
85 Asst Provost Intl Programs .... Dr. Andrew R. GILLESPIE
28 Asst Provost Women's Initiatives .... Dr. Donna L. SOLLIE
109 Associate VP Auxiliary Services .... Mr. Robert C. RITENBAUGH, III
18 Associate VP Facilities .... Mr. Daniel P. KING
15 Associate VP Human Resources .... Ms. Karla S. MCCORMICK
21 Controller .... Ms. Amy K. DOUGLAS
96 Exec Dir Procur & Paymnt Svcs .... Ms. Melissa M. MORRIS
37 Exec Dir Student Financial Svcs .... Mr. Michael C. REYNOLDS
108 Director Academic Assessment .... Dr. Megan R. GOOD
22 Director Affirmative Action/EEO .... Ms. Kelley G. TAYLOR
09 Director Institutional Research .... Dr. James A. CLARK
88 Director JCS Museum of Art .... Dr. Marilyn LAUFER
39 Director Residence Life .... Dr. Virginia A. KOCH
36 Director Student Career Services .... Mrs. Nancy M. BERNARD

38 Director Student Counseling Svcs ... Dr. Doug HANKES
14 Director IT ... Ms. Ellyn HIX
40 Director University Bookstore ... Ms. Catherine LEE
06 Univ Registrar ... Ms. Laura Ann FOREST
47 Acting Dean Agriculture & Dir AAES ... Dr. Paul M. PATTERSON
48 Dean Architecture/Design/Construct ... Dr. Vini NATHAN
50 Dean Business ... Dr. Bill HARDGRAVE
53 Dean Education ... Dr. Betty Lou WHITFORD
54 Dean Engineering ... Dr. Christopher B. ROBERTS
65 Dean Forestry/Wildlife Sci ... Dr. Janaki R. ALAVALAPATI
59 Dean Human Sciences ... Dr. June M. HENTON
49 Dean Liberal Arts ... Dr. Joe AISTRUP
66 Dean Nursing ... Dr. Gregg NEWSCHWANDER
67 Dean Pharmacy ... Dr. R. Lee EVANS, JR.
81 Dean Sciences & Mathematics ... Dr. Nicholas J. GIORDANO
74 Dean Veterinary Medicine ... Dr. Calvin M. JOHNSON
58 Dean Graduate School ... Dr. George FLOWERS
08 Dean University Libraries ... Dr. Bonnie MACEWAN
04 Administrative Asst to President ... Ms. Jolene M. PATTERSON

Auburn University at Montgomery (A)

PO Box 244023, Montgomery AL 36124-4023
County: Montgomery FICE Identification: 008310
Unit ID: 100830
Telephone: (334) 244-3000 Carnegie Class: Master's L
FAX Number: (334) 244-3762 Calendar System: Semester
URL: www.aum.edu
Established: 1967 Annual Undergrad Tuition & Fees (In-State): $8,700
Enrollment: 5,057 Coed
Affiliation or Control: State IRS Status: 501(c)3
Highest Offering: Doctorate
Program: Teacher Preparatory; Professional
Accreditation: SC, BUS, BUSA, CACREP, MT, NURSE, SPAA, TED

01 Chancellor ... Dr. John G. VERES, III
05 Provost ... Dr. Joe M. KING
30 Vice Chancellor Advancement ... Ms. Carolyn GOLDEN
10 Vice Chanc Financial/Admin Svcs ... Ms. Kathy MITCHELL
88 Vice Chanc Outreach/Strat Init ... Dr. Katherine JACKSON
32 Vice Chancellor of Student Affairs ... Ms. Janice LYN
28 Chief Diversity Officer ... Mr. Timothy SPRAGGINS
58 Assoc Provost Research/Grad Studies ... Dr. Matthew RAGLAND
20 Assoc Provost Undergraduate Studies ... Dr. Joy CLARK
09 Asst Provost IE & Accreditation ... Dr. Cara Mia BRASWELL
84 Assoc Prov of Enrollment Management ... Ms. Lisa KERR
41 Athletic Director ... Mr. Steve CROTZ
85 Director of International Affairs ... Mr. Gokhan ALKANAT
15 Chief Human Resources Officer ... Ms. Jeanine BODDIE-LAVAN
18 Sodexo ... Mr. Ken CORNELIUS
08 Dean of Library ... Mr. Phil JOHNSON
07 Director of Admissions/Recruiting ... Mr. Olivier CHARLES
37 Sr Director of Financial Aid ... Mr. Anthony RICHEY
109 Chief Campus Services Officer ... Mr. Daryl MORRIS
39 Dir Housing & Residence Life ... Mr. Iyisha HAMPTON
13 Chief Information Officer ... Dr. Jeffery ANDERSON
35 Associate Dean of Student Affairs ... Dr. Chaundra THOMPSON
19 Director of Police Operations ... Ms. Brenda MITCHELL
06 Registrar ... Ms. Elizabeth WARD
14 Asst Chief Information Officer ... Ms. Carolyn D. RAWL
14 Asst Chief Information Officer ... Mr. Jon FISHER
21 Chief Accounting Officer ... Ms. Kim DECKER
36 Director Career Development ... Mr. Bradley ROBBINS
40 Director of Bookstore ... Mr. Jeffrey P. VINZANT
26 Exec Dir Strategic Comm & Marketing ... Ms. Marla VICKERS
25 Director of Sponsored Programs ... Ms. Fariba S. DERAVI
35 Dir Stdnt Involvement/Leadership ... Mrs. Lakecia HARRIS
85 Coord Intl Student Admissions ... Mr. Ron BLAESING
49 Dean of College of Arts & Sciences ... Dr. Michael BURGER
50 Dean of Business ... Dr. Wanda Rhea INGRAM
53 Dean of Education ... Dr. Sheila AUSTIN
66 Int Dean of Nursing ... Dr. Ramona LAZENBY
51 Exec Dir of Continuing Education ... Ms. Kathy GUNTER
38 Director Student Counseling ... Ms. Jennifer BRADLEY
96 Dir of Procurement & Payment Svcs ... Ms. Lori NIELSEN

Bevill State Community College (B)

1411 Indiana Avenue, Jasper AL 35501
County: Walker FICE Identification: 005733
Unit ID: 102429
Telephone: (205) 387-0511 Carnegie Class: Assoc/Pub-R-M
FAX Number: (205) 387-5192 Calendar System: Semester
URL: www.bscc.edu
Established: 1965 Annual Undergrad Tuition & Fees (In-State): $4,350
Enrollment: 2,445 Coed
Affiliation or Control: State IRS Status: 501(c)3
Highest Offering: Associate Degree
Program: Occupational; 2-Year Principally Bachelor's Creditable
Accreditation: SC, ADNUR, EMT, PNUR, SURGT

01 Interim President ... Mr. Mark D. ELLARD
03 Executive Vice President ... Mr. Mark ELLARD
05 Dean of Instruction ... Dr. Leslie CUMMINGS
32 Dean of Students ... Dr. Kim ENNIS
26 Director of Public Relations ... Dr. Chris FRANKLIN
10 Director of Accounting & Finance ... Ms. Carolyn MORGAN
07 Asst Dean Admissions/Financial Aid ... Ms. Melissa STOWE
09 Dir Inst Effect/Plng/Grants/Rsrch ... Ms. Kristi BARNETT

Birmingham-Southern College (C)

900 Arkadelphia Road, Birmingham AL 35254-0001
County: Jefferson FICE Identification: 001012
Unit ID: 100937
Telephone: (205) 226-4600 Carnegie Class: Bac/A&S
FAX Number: (205) 226-4627 Calendar System: 4/1/4
URL: www.bsc.edu
Established: 1856 Annual Undergrad Tuition & Fees: $33,128
Enrollment: 1,185 Coed
Affiliation or Control: United Methodist IRS Status: 501(c)3
Highest Offering: Baccalaureate
Program: Liberal Arts And General; Teacher Preparatory; Professional
Accreditation: SC, MUS, TED

01 President ... Dr. Edward F. LEONARD
05 Provost ... Dr. Michelle BEHR
10 Vice President of Finance/CFO ... Mr. Eli H. PHILLIPS
11 Vice Pres Administration/Govt Rels ... Mr. Lane ESTES
30 VP Institutional Advancement ... Mr. Charles VINSON
26 Director of Communications ... Ms. Hannah WOLFSON
13 Vice Pres Information Technology ... Mr. Anthony HAMBEY
32 Vice Pres Student Development ... Dr. David EBERHARDT
07 Assoc Vice President of Admissions ... Ms. Sheri SALMON
88 Asst to the President Emeriti ... Mrs. Terri L. HICKS
20 Associate Provost Academic Affairs ... Dr. Susan HAGEN
20 Assistant Provost Academic Affairs ... Ms. Martha A. STEVENSON
06 Registrar ... Mr. Keith KARRIKER
42 Chaplain ... Rev. Jack HINNEN
29 Dir of Alumni Affairs/Stewardship ... Ms. Chris LAMBERT
23 Assoc Director of Health Services ... Ms. Yvette SPENCER
04 Exec Asst to the President ... Ms. Katie GLENN
08 Director of the Library ... Ms. Charlotte FORD
18 Director of Facilities & Events ... Ms. Anne CURRY
37 Director of Financial Planning ... Mr. Brian QUISENBERRY
15 Director of Human Resources ... Ms. Susan E. KINNEY
27 Director of Church Relations ... Ms. Laura SISSON
88 Director of New Media ... Mr. Mike HAMILTON
38 Director of Counseling/Health Svcs ... Ms. Sara HOOVER
41 Athletic Director ... Mr. Joe DEAN, JR.
19 Chief of Campus Police ... Mr. Randy YOUNGBLOOD
36 Director of Career Services ... Mr. Michael LEBEAU
30 Director Advancement Services ... Mr. Jeff SHERRELL
28 Director of Multi-Cultural Affairs ... Ms. Erica BROWN
108 Director of Inst Effective/Assess ... Dr. Noreen GAUBATZ
68 Dir Physical Fitness & Recreation ... Mr. Mike ROBINSON
88 Director of Leadership Studies ... Mr. Kent ANDERSEN
88 Director of Service Learning ... Ms. Kristin HARPER
88 Sports Information Director ... Ms. Sarah ERRECA
88 Assoc Dir of International Programs ... Ms. Anne LEDVINA
88 Manager of Printing Services ... Mr. Jerome DAVIS
40 Bookstore Manager ... Mr. William ALEXANDER
96 Purchasing Manager ... Vacant

Bishop State Community College (D)

351 N Broad Street, Mobile AL 36603-5898
County: Mobile FICE Identification: 001030
Unit ID: 102030
Telephone: (251) 405-7000 Carnegie Class: Assoc/Pub-U-MC
FAX Number: (251) 438-3249 Calendar System: Semester
URL: www.bishop.edu
Established: 1965 Annual Undergrad Tuition & Fees (In-State): $4,260
Enrollment: 3,320 Coed
Affiliation or Control: State IRS Status: 501(c)3
Highest Offering: Associate Degree
Program: Occupational; 2-Year Principally Bachelor's Creditable
Accreditation: SC, ACBSP, ACFEI, ADNUR, CAHIIM, FUSER, PNUR, PTAA

01 President ... Dr. James LOWE, JR.
05 Dean of Instructional Services ... Dr. Latitia MCCANE
12 Director of Carver Campus ... Dr. Betty LESLIE
12 Dir Baker-Gaines Central Campus ... Mrs. Madeline STOKES
72 Dean of Tech Educ/Workforce Dev ... Dr. Kathy THOMPSON
32 Dean of Students ... Dr. Terry HAZZARD
10 Dean of Business/Finance ... Mrs. Bonita ALLEN
35 Assistant to the Dean of Students ... Mrs. Wanda DANIELS
15 Director of Human Resources ... Mrs. Marcella SIMS
18 Director of Physical Plant ... Mr. Lorenzo GRAYSON
26 Director of Public Relations ... Mr. Herb JORDAN
12 SW Campus Dir/Tech Faculty Spvr ... Mr. Roderick MCSWAIN
37 Mgr Student Fin Aid/Veterans Svcs ... Dr. Samuel CHUKS

Brown Mackie College - Birmingham (E)

105 Vulcan Road, Birmingham AL 35209
Telephone: (205) 909-1500 Identification: 770625
Accreditation: &NH, OTA, SURTEC

† Regional accreditation is carried under the parent institution in Salina, KS.

Calhoun Community College (F)

PO Box 2216, Decatur AL 35609-2216
County: Limestone FICE Identification: 001013
Unit ID: 101514
Telephone: (256) 306-2500 Carnegie Class: Assoc/Pub-R-L
FAX Number: (256) 306-2877 Calendar System: Semester
URL: www.calhoun.edu
Established: 1963 Annual Undergrad Tuition & Fees (In-State): $3,456
Enrollment: 10,802 Coed
Affiliation or Control: State IRS Status: 501(c)3
Highest Offering: Associate Degree
Program: 2-Year Principally Bachelor's Creditable
Accreditation: SC, ACBSP, ADNUR, DA, EMT, MLTAD, PNUR, PTAA, SURGT

01 President ... Dr. James S. KLAUBER
05 Acting VP for Instruct/Student Succ ... Dr. Stephen CALATRELLO
32 Dean of Student Affairs ... Dr. Kermit CARTER
10 Vice Pres for Finance & Admin Svcs ... Mr. James B. HELMS
07 Actg Dir Admiss/Records/Registrar ... Ms. Heather PAGE
08 Interim Head Librarian ... Mr. James LOYD
13 Director Information Systems ... Mr. Nathan TYLER
30 Dean Inst Advancement ... Ms. Terri BRYSON
12 Dean Research Park Campus ... Vacant
55 Director Evening Program ... Dr. Vinetta WESLEY
29 Director of Alumni Relations .. Ms. Janet KINCHERLOW-MARTIN
18 Director of Physical Plant ... Mr. Bruce CAUSEY
09 Dean Planning/Research & Grants ... Dr. Debra HENDERSHOT
103 Dean Workforce Development ... Ms. Bethany SHOCKNEY
84 Coord Enrollment Management ... Mr. Brian GANN
26 Chief Public Relations Officer ... Ms. Janet KINCHERLOW-MARTIN
76 Dean Health Sciences ... Mr. Bret MCGILL
81 Dean Mathematics & Natural Science ... Dr. Kemba CHAMBERS
79 Dean Humanities & Social Sciences ... Dr. Donna ESTILL
15 Coordinator/Human Resources ... Mrs. Kim GAINES
19 Director Public Safety ... Mr. Kevin DAVENPORT
36 Coord Career Placement ... Mrs. Kelli MORRIS
37 Int Director Student Financial Aid ... Dr. Pat WILSON

Central Alabama Community College (G)

1675 Cherokee Road, Alexander City AL 35010
County: Tallapoosa FICE Identification: 001007
Unit ID: 100760
Telephone: (256) 234-6346 Carnegie Class: Assoc/Pub-R-M
FAX Number: (256) 234-0384 Calendar System: Semester
URL: www.cacc.edu
Established: 1963 Annual Undergrad Tuition & Fees (In-State): $4,176
Enrollment: 1,726 Coed
Affiliation or Control: State IRS Status: 501(c)3
Highest Offering: Associate Degree
Program: Occupational; 2-Year Principally Bachelor's Creditable
Accreditation: SC, ADNUR

01 Interim President ... Dr. Susan BURROW
10 Executive Vice President/CFO ... Mr. Richard HAWKSHEAD
05 Dean of Instruction ... Ms. Barbara Anne SPEARS
32 Dean of Students ... Dr. Sherri TAYLOR
35 Associate Dean of Student Services ... Ms. Glenda BLAND
09 Assoc Dn Instruct/Inst Effect/Compl ... Ms. Helen GALLAGHER
76 Associate Dean of Health Science ... Dr. Melanie BOLTON
08 Librarian ... Ms. Denita OLIVER
06 Registrar ... Vacant
26 Chief Public Relations Officer ... Mr. Brett PRITCHARD
37 Director Student Financial Aid ... Ms. Cindy ENTREKIN
30 Advancement Officer ... Mr. Michael LOVETT

Chattahoochee Valley Community College (H)

2602 College Drive, Phenix City AL 36869-7960
County: Russell FICE Identification: 012182
Unit ID: 101028
Telephone: (334) 291-4900 Carnegie Class: Assoc/Pub-R-M
FAX Number: (334) 291-4944 Calendar System: Semester
URL: www.cv.edu
Established: 1973 Annual Undergrad Tuition & Fees (In-State): $5,256
Enrollment: 1,795 Coed
Affiliation or Control: State IRS Status: 501(c)3
Highest Offering: Associate Degree
Program: Occupational; 2-Year Principally Bachelor's Creditable
Accreditation: SC, ADNUR, PNUR

01 Interim President ... Dr. Valerie RICHARDSON
05 Vice President/Dean of the College ... Dr. David HODGE
32 Dean of Student Services ... Dr. Joy HAMM
103 Assoc Dean of Workforce Development ... Vacant
50 Chair of Business & Social Sciences ... Dr. Bob DANSBY
81 Chair of Science ... Ms. Susan MCCOLLUM
57 Chair of Humanities ... Mr. Andy SCALES
76 Chair of Health Sciences ... Ms. Resa LORD
81 Chair of Mathematics ... Ms. Mary JOHNSON
88 Program Dir Public Safety Academy ... Mr. Kenneth HARRISON
77 Chair Computer & Information Tech ... Ms. Debra PLOTTS
08 Director Learning Resources Center ... Ms. Rachel COTNEY
37 Director of Financial Aid ... Mrs. Joan WATERS
18 Director Facilities & Maintenance ... Mr. Johann WELLS
30 Dean of Advancement/Inst Effect ... Dr. Joree JONES
41 Director of Athletics ... Mr. Adam THOMAS
38 Dir Counseling/Advising & Testing ... Ms. Cynthia FLOYD
13 Director of Information Systems ... Mr. Jody NOLES
88 Director of Student Development ... Mrs. Vickie WILLIAMS
51 Director of Adult Education ... Ms. Laodecea SEAY
15 Director of Human Resources ... Ms. Debbie BOONE
44 Director of Development ... Ms. Karen KELLY
10 Chief Financial Officer ... Ms. Brenda KELLEY
55 Evening Coordinator ... Mr. Reggie GORDY
07 Director of Admissions/Registrar ... Ms. Sanquita ALEXANDER
04 Administrative Asst to President ... Ms. Emily DYKES
19 Security/Safety ... Mr. Keith MANUEL
26 Marketing & Media Coordinator . Ms. Kelly WILLIAMS-SOWERS

Columbia Southern University (A)

21982 University Lane, Orange Beach AL 36561-3845

County: Baldwin | FICE Identification: 041215 | Unit ID: 450933
Telephone: (251) 981-3771 | Carnegie Class: Master's L
FAX Number: (251) 981-3815 | Calendar System: Other
URL: www.columbiasouthern.edu
Established: 1993 | Annual Undergrad Tuition & Fees: $5,135
Enrollment: 21,359 | Coed
Affiliation or Control: Proprietary | IRS Status: Proprietary
Highest Offering: Master's
Program: Occupational; 2-Year Principally Bachelor's Creditable; Liberal Arts And General; Professional; Business Emphasis
Accreditation: DEAC

01 President .... Mr. Robert G. MAYES, JR.
03 Senior Vice President .... Ms. Chantell COOLEY
05 Provost/CAO .... Dr. Jeffrey BARKSDALE
09 VP of IE and Accreditation .... Dr. Anna WAGGENER
26 VP of University Relations .... Mr. Billy HAYES
13 Chief Information Officer .... Mr. Ken STYRON
88 VP Business Development/Mil Init .... Mr. Rick COOPER
15 VP of Human Resources .... Ms. Sue BUTTS
20 Asst Provost of Academic Affairs .... Dr. John WEIDERT
05 Asst Prov/Dean of Faculty Services .... Dr. Elwin JONES
108 Asst Prov Inst Effect/Accreditation .... Ms. Khalilah BURTON
07 Director of Admissions .... Ms. Kelli GROS
10 Chief Financial Officer .... Mr. Pat TROUP
24 Dean of Instructional Design .... Dr. John HOPE
29 Dir Student & Alumni Engagement .... Ms. Amanda MANJONE
40 Director of Bookstore Operations .... Mr. David BARNES
09 Director of Institutional Research .... Ms. Megan BUNNELL
06 Registrar .... Ms. Rachel FARRIS
37 Director of Financial Aid .... Ms. Tammy COMALANDER
88 Director of Quality Assurance .... Ms. Mona MCPHERSON
08 Director of Learning Resources .... Ms. Marsha HINNEN
27 Director of Marketing .... Mr. Beau VIGNES
88 Director of State Authorization .... Ms. Alexis BANKS

Concordia College Alabama (B)

1712 Broad Street, Selma AL 36701

County: Dallas | FICE Identification: 010554 | Unit ID: 101073
Telephone: (334) 874-5700 | Carnegie Class: Bac/Diverse
FAX Number: (334) 874-5755 | Calendar System: Semester
URL: www.ccal.edu
Established: 1922 | Annual Undergrad Tuition & Fees: $10,420
Enrollment: 546 | Coed
Affiliation or Control: Lutheran Church - Missouri Synod | IRS Status: 501(c)3
Highest Offering: Baccalaureate
Program: 2-Year Principally Bachelor's Creditable; Liberal Arts And General; Teacher Preparatory; Business Emphasis
Accreditation: SC

01 President/Chief Executive Officer .... Dr. Tilahun M. MENDEDO
05 Vice Pres Academic Affairs .... Dr. Cheryl WASHINGTON
32 VP of Student Services .... Dr. Donald JEFFERSON
30 VP Institutional Advancement .... Mr. Daniel JENKINS
10 Vice Pres Business/Finance .... Mr. Dexter JACKSON
37 Director Financial Aid .... Mrs. Tharsteen BRIDGES
09 Effectiveness/Research and Plng .... Mrs. Ruthie J. ORSBORN
64 Director of Music .... Vacant
08 Library Director .... Mr. J. Scott WHITING
06 Registrar .... Mrs. Chinester GRAYSON
29 Director Alumni Affairs/Development .... Mrs. Minnie MCMILLAN
26 Director Public Relations .... Ms. Abigail CAMPBELL
36 Dir Student Placement/Counseling .... Ms. Sadie JARETT
15 Director of Human Resources .... Vacant
13 Chief Information Officer .... Mr. Wayne GREEN
41 Director of Athletics .... Mr. Frankie PEOPLES
35 Director Student Activities .... Mr. Coley C. CHESTNUT, SR.
85 Director of International Students .... Mr. Katiso ALEMU
42 Chaplain .... Rev. Lavaugn WIGGINS
21 Controller .... Mr. Aron EZAZ
07 Asst Director of Enrollment .... Ms. Theresa BROWN
84 Director Enrollment Management .... Ms. Meseret ALEMU

*Education Corporation of America (C)

3660 Grandview Parkway Suite 300, Birmingham AL 35243

County: Jefferson | Identification: 666006
Telephone: (205) 329-7900 | Carnegie Class: N/A
FAX Number: (205) 329-7906
URL: www.ecacolleges.com

01 Chief Executive Officer .... Mr. Stuart C. REED
05 Exec VP/Chf Compl Ofcr/Gen Counsel .... Mr. Roger L. SWARTZWELDER
26 Exec VP/Chief Marketing Officer .... Mr. Charles S. TRIERWEILER
10 Exec VP/Chief Financial Officer .... Mr. Christopher BOEHM
15 EVP Chief Human Resources Officer .... Mr. David KAHN
05 Exec VP Chief Academic Officer .... Dr. John WOODS
13 Exec VP Chief Information Officer .... Mr. Mark MULLISON
21 SVP Finance .... Mr. Ryan BREWER
37 SVP Student Finance .... Ms. Kathy CHEATHAM
26 SVP of Marketing .... Mr. Jason MANN
84 SVP of Student Enrollment .... Mr. Dean MAHAFFEY
20 SVP Academic Operations .... Ms. Rita CHUBICK
20 SVP Academic Compliance Curriculum .... Ms. Judy E. LIMA
43 SVP Associate General Counsel .... Mr. Benjamin J. DEGWECK
20 SVP Academics .... Ms. Sandra H. UGOL
88 Group President VC West .... Mr. John SCHUMAN
88 Group President VC East .... Mr. Jack CLARK
88 Group President Emerging Brands .... Mr. Geoffrey BAIRD
88 Group President of Operations .... Mr. Dominick FEDELE

*Virginia College (D)

488 Palisades Boulevard, Birmingham AL 35209

County: Jefferson | FICE Identification: 030106 | Unit ID: 420307
Telephone: (205) 802-1200 | Carnegie Class: Master's S
FAX Number: (205) 271-8225 | Calendar System: Quarter
URL: www.vc.edu
Established: 1993 | Annual Undergrad Tuition & Fees: $14,000
Enrollment: 4,676 | Coed
Affiliation or Control: Proprietary | IRS Status: Proprietary
Highest Offering: Master's
Program: Occupational; 2-Year Principally Bachelor's Creditable
Accreditation: ACICS, ACFEI, CIDA, #COARC, DMS, MAAB, SURGT

02 Campus President .... Mr. Khaled SAKALLA
07 Vice President of Enrollment .... Mr. Kenneth MACON
05 Academic Dean .... Mr. Keven W. ROBINSON

*Virginia College (E)

2021 Drake Avenue SW, Huntsville AL 35801

Telephone: (256) 533-7387 | Identification: 666400
Accreditation: ACICS, MAAB

† Branch campus of Virginia College, Birmingham, AL.

*Virginia College (F)

3725 Airport Boulevard, Suite 165, Mobile AL 36608

Telephone: (251) 343-7227 | Identification: 666069
Accreditation: ACICS, ACFEI, MAAB, SURGT

† Branch campus of Virginia College, Birmingham, AL.

*Virginia College (G)

6200 Atlanta Highway, Montgomery AL 36117-2802

Telephone: (334) 277-3390 | Identification: 666408
Accreditation: ACICS, MAAB

† Branch campus of Virginia College, Birmingham, AL.

Enterprise State Community College (H)

PO Box 1300, Enterprise AL 36331-1300

County: Coffee | FICE Identification: 001015 | Unit ID: 101143
Telephone: (334) 347-2623 | Carnegie Class: Assoc/Pub-R-M
FAX Number: (334) 393-6223 | Calendar System: Semester
URL: www.escc.edu
Established: 1963 | Annual Undergrad Tuition & Fees (In-State): $4,050
Enrollment: 1,957 | Coed
Affiliation or Control: State | IRS Status: 501(c)3
Highest Offering: Associate Degree
Program: Occupational; 2-Year Principally Bachelor's Creditable
Accreditation: SC

01 Interim President .... Dr. Cynthia ANTHONY
05 Dean of Instruction .... Vacant
32 Dean of Students .... Vacant
10 Dean Administration & Finance .... Ms. Alonzetta LANDRUM-SIMS
45 Dn Plng/Info Svcs/Inst Effective .... Ms. Veronica CROCK
35 Associate Dean of Students .... Mr. Kevin AMMONS
26 Dir Marketing & Media Relations .... Mr. Brandon PIERCE
37 Director Student Financial Aid .... Dr. Henry L. QUISENBERRY, JR.
55 Director Evening Division .... Mr. Carl HOLBROOK
06 Registrar .... Mr. Kevin AMMONS
04 Administrative Asst to President .... Ms. Jennifer ADAMS
07 Director of Admissions .... Mr. Joey HOLLEY

Faulkner University (I)

5345 Atlanta Highway, Montgomery AL 36109-3398

County: Montgomery | FICE Identification: 001003 | Unit ID: 101189
Telephone: (334) 272-5820 | Carnegie Class: Bac/Diverse
FAX Number: (334) 386-7107 | Calendar System: Semester
URL: www.faulkner.edu
Established: 1942 | Annual Undergrad Tuition & Fees: $19,300
Enrollment: 3,335 | Coed
Affiliation or Control: Churches Of Christ | IRS Status: 501(c)3
Highest Offering: Doctorate
Program: Liberal Arts And General; Teacher Preparatory; Professional
Accreditation: SC, LAW, TED, @THEOL

01 President .... Dr. Michael D. WILLIAMS
00 Chancellor .... Dr. Billy D. HILYER
05 Vice President Academic Affairs .... Dr. Marci JOHNS
10 Vice President Financial Services .... Mrs. Wilma D. PHILLIPS
32 Vice President Student Services .... Dr. Jean-Noel THOMPSON
84 Vice President Enrollment Mgmt .... Mr. Keith MOCK
18 Vice Pres Facilities & Risk Mgmt .... Mr. Jim SPRATLIN
30 Vice President Advancement .... Dr. Ben BRUCE
43 General Counsel .... Dr. Gerald JONES
61 Dean Jones School of Law .... Mr. Charles NELSON
49 Dean College Arts & Sciences .... Dr. Dave RAMPERSAD
50 Dean College Business/Exec Educ .... Dr. Dave KHADANGA
73 Dean College of Biblical Studies .... Dr. Scott GLEAVES
53 Dean College of Education .... Dr. Tammy BROWN
88 Assoc Dean Academics Jones Law .... Mr. Charles CAMPBELL
21 Associate Vice President of Finance .... Mr. Jamie HORN
44 Assoc Vice President Development .... Mr. Billy CAMP
88 Assoc Vice Pres Exec & Prof Enroll .... Mr. Mark HUNT
15 Asst VP Human Resources/Diversity .... Mrs. Renee DAVIS
06 Registrar .... Mr. Don REYNOLDS
37 Director Student Financial Aid .... Mr. Buddy JACKSON
12 Director Mobile Center .... Mrs. Diane NEWELL
12 Director Birmingham Center .... Mr. Tim PARKER
12 Director Huntsville Center .... Vacant
35 Associate Dean of Students .... Mr. Art ROUSSEAU
41 Acting Athletic Director .... Mr. Hal WYNN
08 Director of Libraries .... Mrs. Barbara KELLY
09 Director of Institutional Research .... Dr. Brenda TURNER
88 Director Quality Enhancement Plan .... Dr. Cindy WALKER
104 Director of Study Abroad .... Dr. Ed HICKS
26 Director of University Marketing .... Mr. Patrick GREGORY
07 Director of Admissions .... Mr. Neil SCOTT
88 Director Student Success .... Mrs. Michelle OTWELL
29 Director of Alumni Relations .... Mr. Adam DONALDSON
92 Director of Honors Program .... Mr. Andrew JACOBS
36 Director Career Services .... Mrs. Marie OTTINGER
38 Counselor .... Mrs. Michelle BOND
04 Exec Assistant to the President .... Mrs. Darlene GREGORY
19 Director Security/Safety .... Mr. Anthony DEAN

Fortis College (J)

7033 Airport Blvd, Mobile AL 36608

County: Mobile | FICE Identification: 023410 | Unit ID: 371052
Telephone: (251) 344-1203 | Carnegie Class: Assoc/PrivFP
FAX Number: (251) 344-1299 | Calendar System: Other
URL: www.fortiscollege.edu
Established: 1978 | Annual Undergrad Tuition & Fees: $15,035
Enrollment: 352 | Coed
Affiliation or Control: Proprietary | IRS Status: Proprietary
Highest Offering: Associate Degree
Program: Occupational; 2-Year Principally Bachelor's Creditable; Technical Emphasis
Accreditation: ABHES, DA

01 Campus President .... Joseph DALTO
05 Chief Academic Officer .... Jennifer WELCH
06 Registrar .... Katherine MCKINTYRE
07 Director of Admissions .... Aquila TORIAN
19 Director Security/Safety .... Darren DAIGLE
32 Chief Student Affairs/Student Life .... Nakita GABLE
36 Director Student Placement .... Laura PINION
37 Director Student Financial Aid .... Felicia WILLIAMS
10 Business Office .... Shantreese YOUNG

Fortis College-Montgomery (Atlanta Highway) (K)

3736 Atlanta Highway, Montgomery AL 36109

Telephone: (334) 272-3857 | Identification: 770511
Accreditation: ABHES

† Branch campus of Fortis College, Mobile, AL.

Fortis College-Montgomery (Eastdale Circle) (L)

3470 Eastdale Circle, Montgomery AL 36117

Telephone: (334) 244-1827 | Identification: 770512
Accreditation: ABHES

† Branch campus of Fortis College, Mobile, AL.

Fortis Institute (M)

100 London Parkway Suite 150, Birmingham AL 35211

Telephone: (205) 940-7800 | Identification: 666683
Accreditation: ACICS, DH

† Branch campus of Fortis Institute, Erie, PA.

Gadsden State Community College (N)

1001 George Wallace Dr, PO Box 227, Gadsden AL 35902-0227

County: Etowah | FICE Identification: 001017 | Unit ID: 101240
Telephone: (256) 549-8200 | Carnegie Class: Assoc/Pub-R-L
FAX Number: (256) 549-8288 | Calendar System: Semester
URL: www.gadsdenstate.edu
Established: 1925 | Annual Undergrad Tuition & Fees (In-State): $4,020
Enrollment: 5,289 | Coed
Affiliation or Control: State | IRS Status: 501(c)3
Highest Offering: Associate Degree
Program: Occupational; 2-Year Principally Bachelor's Creditable
Accreditation: SC, ACBSP, ADNUR, COMTA, EMT, MLTAD, PNUR, RAD

01 Interim President .... Dr. Martha G. LAVENDER
03 Vice President .... Dr. Valerie RICHARDSON
10 Dean Financial/Administrative Svcs .... Dr. James R. PRUCNAL
72 Dean Tech Educ/Workforce Develop .... Mr. Tim GREEN
05 Dean of Academic Programs/Services .Dr. Leslie WORTHINGTON
30 Assoc Dean Instnl Advance/Cmty Svc .... Ms. Pam JOHNSON
20 Assoc Dean Instructional Services .... Dr. Karen BLYTHE-SMITH
09 Asst to President for IE/IR/Plng .... Dr. Teresa C. RHEA
26 Director Public Relations/Marketing .... Ms. Jackie EDMONDSON
19 Director Physical Plant .... Mr. Stewart DAVIS
21 Director of Financial Services .... Ms. Jacqueline CLARK
88 Director of Legal Affairs/Title IX .... Ms. Michele BRADFORD
13 Director of Computer Services .... Mr. Tim SMITH
15 Director Human Resources .... Ms. Kim S. COBB
41 Athletic Director .... Mr. Mike CANCILLA
38 Assoc Dean Stdnt Svcs & Counse Svcs ... Dr. Cheryl C. VICKERS
51 Director Adult Education .... Mr. Johnny BAKER
37 Director of Financial Aid .... Ms. Kelly D'EATH
06 Registrar .... Mrs. Jennie P. DOBSON

George C. Wallace Community College - Dothan (A)

1141 Wallace Drive, Dothan AL 36303-9234

County: Dale | FICE Identification: 001018 | Unit ID: 101286
Telephone: (334) 983-3521 | Carnegie Class: Assoc/Pub-R-M
FAX Number: (334) 983-6066 | Calendar System: Semester
URL: www.wallace.edu
Established: 1947 | Annual Undergrad Tuition & Fees (In-State): $4,200
Enrollment: 4,695 | Coed
Affiliation or Control: State | IRS Status: 501(c)3
Highest Offering: Associate Degree
Program: Occupational; 2-Year Principally Bachelor's Creditable; Business Emphasis
Accreditation: SC, ADNUR, COARC, EMT, MAC, PNUR, PTAA, RAD

01 President .... Dr. Linda C. YOUNG
32 Dean of Student Affs/Sparks Campus .Ms. Jacqueline B. SCREWS
05 Dean of Instructional Affairs .... Mr. Tony HOLLAND
10 Dean of Business Affairs .... Mr. Lynn BELL
07 Director Enroll Svcs/Registrar .... Mr. Keith SAULSBERRY
08 Dir Learning Resources Ctrs System .... Mr. A. P. HOFFMAN
37 Director of Financial Aid .... Ms. Erma PERRY
13 AS-400 Progm/Sys Admin .... Mr. Bruce COLLINS
15 Director of Human Resources .... Ms. Brooke STRICKLAND
09 Dir Institutional Effectiveness .... Mr. Frank BAREFIELD
40 Bookstore Manager .... Mr. Jeremy JAMES
21 Director of Accounting & Finance .... Ms. Kay GAMBLE
26 Dir Public Relations & Marketing .... Ms. Barbara THOMPSON
30 Dean Institutional Svcs/Com Dev .... Dr. Ashli WILKINS
41 Athletic Director .... Mr. Mackey SASSER

George Corley Wallace State Community College - Selma (B)

PO Box 2530, 3000 Earl Goodwin Pkwy, Selma AL 36702-2530

County: Dallas | FICE Identification: 005699 | Unit ID: 101301
Telephone: (334) 876-9227 | Carnegie Class: Assoc/Pub-R-M
FAX Number: (334) 876-9250 | Calendar System: Semester
URL: www.wccs.edu
Established: 1963 | Annual Undergrad Tuition & Fees (In-State): $3,216
Enrollment: 1,627 | Coed
Affiliation or Control: State | IRS Status: 501(c)3
Highest Offering: Associate Degree
Program: Occupational; 2-Year Principally Bachelor's Creditable
Accreditation: SC, ACBSP, ADNUR, PNUR

01 President .... Dr. James M. MITCHELL
05 Acting Dean of Instruction .... Mrs. Donitha GRIFFIN
20 Instructional Administrator .... Mr. Raji GOURDINE
10 Dean of Business & Finance .... Mrs. Jacqueline SMITH
32 Dean of Students/Exec to President .... Mrs. Donitha GRIFFIN
08 Librarian .... Ms. Minnie CARSTARPHEN
66 Int Assoc Degree Nursing Coord .... Dr. Tracey SHANNON
37 Interim Financial Aid Director .... Ms. Anessa KIDD
38 Counselor College Division .... Mr. Lonzy CLIFTON
09 Director of Institutional Research .... Mrs. Earlene LARKIN
26 Coord College Rels/Instl Research .... Mrs. Rita LETT
19 Director Security/Safety .... Mr. Charles DYSART
41 Athletic Director .... Mr. Marcus HANNAH
18 Act Chief Facilities/Physical Plant .... Mr. Jimmie GOLDSBY
28 Director of Diversity .... Vacant
40 Bookstore Manager .... Ms. Marie JONES
15 Human Resource Generalist .... Vacant

Heritage Christian University (C)

PO Box HCU, Florence AL 35630-0050

County: Lauderdale | FICE Identification: 021997 | Unit ID: 101453
Telephone: (256) 766-6610 | Carnegie Class: Spec/Faith
FAX Number: N/A | Calendar System: Semester
URL: www.hcu.edu
Established: 1971 | Annual Undergrad Tuition & Fees: $9,792
Enrollment: 93 | Coed
Affiliation or Control: Churches Of Christ | IRS Status: 501(c)3
Highest Offering: Master's
Program: Religious Emphasis
Accreditation: BI

01 President .... Mr. Dennis H. JONES
05 Vice President of Academic Affairs .... Dr. Bill BAGENTS
10 VP Business/Finance/Operations .... Mr. Freddie P. MOON
30 Vice Pres University .... Mr. Philip GOAD
32 Dean of Students .... Mr. Brad MCKINNON
33 Dean of Men .... Dr. Ed GALLAGHER
34 Dean of Women .... Dr. Rosemary SNODGRASS
58 Director of Graduate Studies .... Dr. Jeremy BARRIER
06 Registrar .... Mrs. Charlotte ORR
08 Librarian .... Miss Jamie S. COX
42 Director of Christian Service .... Mr. Brad MCKINNON
84 Dir Enrollment Svcs/Stdnt Fin Aid .... Mr. Jim COLLINS

Herzing University (D)

280 W Valley Avenue, Birmingham AL 35209-4816

Telephone: (205) 916-2800 | FICE Identification: 010193
Accreditation: &NH, EMT

† Regional accreditation is carried under the parent institution in Madison, WI.

Huntingdon College (E)

1500 East Fairview Avenue, Montgomery AL 36106-2148

County: Montgomery | FICE Identification: 001019 | Unit ID: 101435
Telephone: (334) 833-4222 | Carnegie Class: Bac/Diverse
FAX Number: (334) 833-4486 | Calendar System: Semester
URL: www.huntingdon.edu
Established: 1854 | Annual Undergrad Tuition & Fees: $25,050
Enrollment: 1,160 | Coed
Affiliation or Control: United Methodist | IRS Status: 501(c)3
Highest Offering: Baccalaureate
Program: Liberal Arts And General
Accreditation: SC, MUS

01 President .... Rev. J. Cameron WEST
10 Treasurer & Sr VP for Plng & Admin .... Mr. Jay A. DORMAN
30 VP for College & Alumni Relations .... Mr. Anthony J. LEIGH
84 VP for Enrollment Management .... Ms. Laura H. DUNCAN
05 Provost & Dean of the College .... Dr. Sidney J. STUBBS
32 VP Student Life & Dean of Students .Dr. Frank R. PARSONS, JR.
20 Assoc Provost for Curr/Faculty Dev .Dr. Frank W. BUCKNER, JR.
108 Assoc Provost for Inst Assessment .... Dr. Cinzia BALIT-MOUSSALLI
50 Dean School for Bus & Prof Stds .... Dr. Samir R. MOUSSALLI
53 Dean School Teacher Ed/Sprt Science .... Dr. Lisa OLENIK-DORMAN
81 Dean School Natural Sciences & Math .... Dr. Erastus C. DUDLEY
55 Director Evening Studies Program .... Dr. Renee CULVERHOUSE
26 Assoc VP for Comm and Marketing .... Ms. Suellen S. OFE
35 Director of Student Activities .... Ms. Sallie FORRESTER
06 Registrar .... Ms. Maryann M. BECK
13 Dir of Institutional Technology .... Mr. Frank O. GRIER
36 Dir of the Center for Career & Voc .... Ms. Francis H. TAYLOR
37 Dir of Student Financial Aid .... Ms. Belinda G. DUETT
18 Director of Facilities and Grounds .... Mr. T. Michael DUNN
40 Manager Follett Bookstore .... Ms. Sharon HENDERSON
23 Director of Student Health .... Ms. Camilla IRVIN
04 Exec Asst to President/Corp Secy .... Ms. Sandra B. KELSER
08 Director Houghton Memorial Library .... Mr. Eric A. KIDWELL
21 Comptroller .... Ms. Jo-Ann M. HOLSTON
39 Director of Residence Life .... Ms. Christine SIMONE
41 Director of Athletics .... Mr. Mike TURK
42 Chaplain .... Rev. Woods B. LISENBY
19 Chief of Security .... Mr. Michael S. WARD
104 Director of Event Planning & Travel .... Ms. Tricia S. GRIER
88 Director of Academic Services .... Ms. Adrienne S. GAINES
88 Asst Provost for Learning Enrichmnt .... Dr. Chad EGGLESTON

Huntsville Bible College (F)

904 Oakwood Avenue NW, Huntsville AL 35811-1632

County: Madison | FICE Identification: 038943 | Unit ID: 449348
Telephone: (256) 539-0834 | Carnegie Class: Assoc/PrivNFP4
FAX Number: (256) 539-0854 | Calendar System: Semester
URL: www.hbc1.edu
Established: 1986 | Annual Undergrad Tuition & Fees: $5,250
Enrollment: 138 | Coed
Affiliation or Control: Baptist | IRS Status: 501(c)3
Highest Offering: Master's
Program: Liberal Arts And General; Religious Emphasis
Accreditation: BI

01 President .... Dr. John L. CLAY
05 Dean of Academics/Instruction .... Rev. David L. FAYLOR
07 Admissions Officer .... Ms. Jessica COPELAND
10 Chief Financial Officer .... Ms. Jacqueline ROBINSON
26 Public Relations Officer .... Rev. Earla LOCKHART

ITT Technical Institute (G)

6270 Park South Drive, Bessemer AL 35022-5655

Telephone: (205) 497-5700 | Identification: 666530
Accreditation: ACICS

† Branch campus of ITT Technical Institute, Indianapolis, IN.

ITT Technical Institute (H)

9238 Madison Boulevard, Suite 500, Madison AL 35758

Telephone: (256) 542-2900 | Identification: 666695
Accreditation: ACICS

† Branch campus of ITT Technical Institute, Indianapolis, IN.

ITT Technical Institute (I)

3100 Cottage Hill Road, Bldg 3, Mobile AL 36606-2913

Telephone: (251) 472-4760 | Identification: 666165
Accreditation: ACICS

† Branch campus of ITT Technical Institute, Indianapolis, IN.

J.F. Drake State Community and Technical College (J)

3421 Meridian Street N, Huntsville AL 35811-1584

County: Madison | FICE Identification: 005260 | Unit ID: 101462
Telephone: (256) 539-8161 | Carnegie Class: Assoc/Pub-R-S
FAX Number: (256) 539-6439 | Calendar System: Semester
URL: www.drakestate.edu
Established: 1961 | Annual Undergrad Tuition & Fees (In-State): $3,432
Enrollment: 1,062 | Coed
Affiliation or Control: State | IRS Status: 501(c)3
Highest Offering: Associate Degree
Program: Occupational; 2-Year Principally Bachelor's Creditable; Technical Emphasis
Accreditation: SC

01 President .... Dr. Helen T. MCALPINE
05 Dean of Instruction .... Mrs. Joyce L. RENTZ
10 Business Manager/Treasurer .... Ms. Teresa A. HILL
103 Dean of Workforce Development .... Dr. Mary J. CAYLOR
45 Dean of Planning & Research Dev .... Dr. John REUTTER
20 Associate Dean of Instruction .... Vacant
15 Human Resource Specialist .... Mrs. Katie CHANCE
13 Director Computer Services .... Vacant
08 Director of Library Services .... Ms. Carla CLIFT
07 Director of Admissions/Registrar .... Mr. Cedric ARRINGTON
37 Director Student Financial Aid .... Ms. Jennifer O'LINGER
26 Director of Public Relations .... Mrs. Amelia DAWKINS-FALTER
36 College Counselor .... Ms. Denise GAYMON
09 Dean of Institutional Effectiveness .... Dr. Alice RAYMOND
32 Dean of Student Support Services .... Dr. Nicole BARNETT
51 Director of Adult Education .... Mrs. Wendy ROBERTS
18 Dean of Operations .... Mr. Bruce BULLUCK
84 Enrolllment Services Manager .... Ms. Tiffany GREEN

J.F. Ingram State Technical College (K)

PO Box 220350, Deatsville AL 36022-0350

County: Elmore | FICE Identification: 030025 | Unit ID: 101471
Telephone: (334) 285-5177 | Carnegie Class: Assoc/Pub-R-S
FAX Number: (334) 285-5328 | Calendar System: Semester
URL: www.istc.edu
Established: 1965 | Annual Undergrad Tuition & Fees (In-State): $4,824
Enrollment: 479 | Coed
Affiliation or Control: State | IRS Status: 501(c)3
Highest Offering: Associate Degree
Program: Occupational; Technical Emphasis
Accreditation: COE

01 President .... Dr. Hank DASINGER
10 Dean of Administration .... Mr. Jon KLAAREN
05 Dean of Instruction .... Mr. Stanley CARTER
32 Dean Students/Support Services .... Mrs. Rosie EDWARDS
45 Dean of Strategic Planning and Eval .... Mr. Bill GRISWOLD
15 Human Resources Coordinator .... Ms. Erica PORTIS-TURNER
06 Registration & Admissions Director .... Ms. Bonita OWENSBY
36 Job Placement & Transition Coord .... Mrs. Mary KING

Jacksonville State University (L)

700 Pelham Road N, Jacksonville AL 36265-1602

County: Calhoun | FICE Identification: 001020 | Unit ID: 101480
Telephone: (256) 782-5781 | Carnegie Class: Master's L
FAX Number: (256) 782-5291 | Calendar System: Semester
URL: www.jsu.edu
Established: 1883 | Annual Undergrad Tuition & Fees (In-State): $7,500
Enrollment: 8,659 | Coed
Affiliation or Control: State | IRS Status: 501(c)3
Highest Offering: Doctorate
Program: Liberal Arts And General; Teacher Preparatory; Professional
Accreditation: SC, AAFCS, ART, BUS, CACREP, CS, DIETD, JOUR, MUS, NAIT, NURSE, SPAA, SW, TED, THEA

01 President .... Dr. John M. BEEHLER
05 Provost/VP Academic/Student Affairs .... Dr. Rebecca O. TURNER
10 Vice Pres Admin/Business Affs .... Ms. Allyson BARKER
30 Vice Pres University Advancement .... Dr. Charles R. LEWIS
13 Vice Pres Information Technology .... Mr. Vinson HOUSTON
84 Assoc VP Enrol Mgmt/Student Affairs .... Dr. Tim KING
58 Vice Prov/Dean Col Graduate Stds .... Dr. Joe DELAP

08 Dean of Library Services .... Mr. John-Bauer GRAHAM
49 Dean College Arts & Sciences .... Dr. James E. WADE
66 Dean College Nursing/Health Science .... Dr. Christie SHELTON
53 Dean College Education/Prof Studies .... Dr. John HAMMETT
50 Dean Col Commerce/Business Admin .... Dr. William FIELDING
21 University Controller .... Mr. Kevin MCFRY
07 Director of Enrollment Management .... Mr. Andy GREEN
109 Assoc VP Business/Auxiliary Svcs .... Mr. Joe WHITMORE
44 Director University Development .... Mr. Earl WARREN
39 Dir Univ Housing/Residence Life .... Mr. Kevin HOULT
88 Interim Dir International House .... Dr. Teresa REED
29 Director of Alumni Relations .... Ms. Kaci OGLE
15 Director of Human Resources .... Dr. Heidi LOUISY
37 Dir Student Financial Services .... Ms. Vickie ADAMS
72 Director Department of Technology .... Mr. Terry MARBUT
41 Interim Director Athletics .... Mr. Greg SEITZ
09 VP Research/Planning/Collaboration .... Dr. Alicia SIMMONS
06 Registrar .... Ms. Emily WHITE
18 Director Physical Plant .... Mr. David THOMPSON
36 Director Career Placement Services .... Ms. Rebecca E. TURNER
38 Dir Counseling/Disability Sppt Svcs .... Ms. Julie NIX
32 Director Student Life .... Mr. Terry CASEY
96 Director of Purchasing .... Ms. Pamela L. FINDLEY
26 Exec Dir Marketing/Communications .... Mr. Tim GARNER

James H. Faulkner State Community College (A)

1900 Highway 31 S, Bay Minette AL 36507-2698
County: Baldwin FICE Identification: 001060
Unit ID: 101161
Telephone: (251) 580-2100 Carnegie Class: Assoc/Pub-S-MC
FAX Number: (251) 580-2253 Calendar System: Semester
URL: www.faulknerstate.edu
Established: 1965 Annual Undergrad Tuition & Fees (In-State): $4,320
Enrollment: 4,481 Coed
Affiliation or Control: State IRS Status: 501(c)3
Highest Offering: Associate Degree
Program: Occupational; 2-Year Principally Bachelor's Creditable
Accreditation: SC, ACFEI, ADNUR, DA, EMT, PNUR, SURGT

01 President .... Dr. Gary L. BRANCH
32 VP of Inst Adv & Student Dev .... Dr. Brenda J. KENNEDY
05 Dean of Instruction .... Vacant
35 Dean of Student Services .... Mr. Michael NIKOLAKIS
86 Dean of Federal Programs .... Mrs. Lena DEXTER
11 Dean Administrative Services .... Mr. Jim FITZ-GERALD
103 Dean of Workforce Development .... Ms. Patty HUGHSTON
26 Director College Relations .... Vacant
06 Asst Registrar .... Ms. Beth BYARS
08 Dir Learning Resource .... Ms. Rheena ELMORE
37 Financial Aid Director .... Dr. Jim THEEUWES
88 Director High School Relations .... Ms. Carmelita MIKKELSEN
18 Director of Buildings & Ground .... Mr. Jim FITZ-GERALD
19 Chief of Police .... Mr. Chris JOHNSON
15 Director Human Resources .... Mrs. Laura BURKS
39 Dir of Housing and Special Events .... Ms. Linda CALDWELL
66 Director Nursing & Allied Health .... Ms. Jean GRAHAM
13 Technology Services Coordinator .... Mr. Brian STRICKLAND
07 Admissions Officer .... Ms. Theresa MCCLELLAND

Jefferson Davis Community College (B)

PO Box 958, Brewton AL 36427-0958
County: Escambia FICE Identification: 001021
Unit ID: 101499
Telephone: (251) 867-4832 Carnegie Class: Assoc/Pub-R-S
FAX Number: (251) 867-7399 Calendar System: Semester
URL: www.jdcc.edu
Established: 1965 Annual Undergrad Tuition & Fees (In-State): $3,224
Enrollment: 1,087 Coed
Affiliation or Control: State IRS Status: 501(c)3
Highest Offering: Associate Degree
Program: Occupational; 2-Year Principally Bachelor's Creditable
Accreditation: SC, ADNUR

01 Interim President .... Dr. William BLOW
05 Dean of Instruction .... Dr. Catherine PACKER-WILLIAMS
10 Dean of Business Affairs .... Dr. Donald KELLY
32 Dean of Student Affairs .... Mr. David JONES
20 Associate Dean of Instruction .... Vacant
15 Director of Human Resources .... Ms. Denise STEWART
06 Registrar .... Ms. Robin SESSIONS
13 Director of MIS .... Mr. Anthony HARDY
26 Director Mktg & Community Relations .... Vacant
08 Librarian .... Mr. Jeffrey FAUST
37 Financial Aid Director .... Ms. Vanessa M. KYLES
09 Dir Institutional Research/Testing .... Mr. Anthony HARDY
18 Chief Facilities/Physical Plant .... Mr. Richard LYNN
35 Dir Stdnt Support Svcs/Development .... Ms. Kina BURKETT
84 Dir of Stdnt Recruitment/Enrollment .... Mr. Lee BARRENTINE

Jefferson State Community College (C)

2601 Carson Road, Birmingham AL 35215-3098
County: Jefferson FICE Identification: 001022
Unit ID: 101505
Telephone: (205) 853-1200 Carnegie Class: Assoc/Pub-U-MC
FAX Number: (205) 853-8505 Calendar System: Semester
URL: www.jeffstateonline.com
Established: 1963 Annual Undergrad Tuition & Fees (In-State): $4,320
Enrollment: 8,518 Coed
Affiliation or Control: State IRS Status: 501(c)3
Highest Offering: Associate Degree
Program: Occupational; 2-Year Principally Bachelor's Creditable
Accreditation: SC, ACBSP, ACFEI, ADNUR, CONST, EMT, FUSER, MLTAD, PTAA, RAD

01 Interim President .... Mr. Keith A. BROWN
03 Vice President .... Vacant
05 Dean of Instruction .... Ms. Danielle COBURN
75 Dean Career & Technical Education .... Ms. Norma G. BELL
30 Dean Campus Development/Campus Svcs .... Mr. Keith A. BROWN
10 Director Financial Services .... Ms. Mary WATSON
32 Director of Student Services .... Dr. Linda J. HOOTON
97 Assoc Dean Transf Gen Stds Shelby .... Ms. Liesl W. HARRIS
97 Assoc Dean Transf Gen Stds Jeffrsn .... Dr. Aliakbar R. YAZDI
106 Associate Dean Distance Education .... Mr. Alan B. DAVIS
51 Director College/Cmty/Corp Educ .... Ms. Kay C. POTTER
13 Chief Information Officer .... Mr. Nader ZANDI
37 Director Financial Aid .... Ms. Tracy R. ADAMS
84 Dean of Enrollment Services .... Dr. Phillip M. HOBBS
18 Director Maintenance .... Mr. Bill MIXON
08 Director of Learning Resources .... Ms. Barbara GOSS
36 Director Career/Job Resource Center .... Dr. Tamara PAYNE
07 Director Admissions and Retention .... Ms. Lillian OWENS
15 Director Human Resources .... Mr. Shain WILSON
26 Director Media Relations .... Mr. David BOBO
96 Purchasing Coordinator .... Ms. Ann CIMALORE
19 Director Safety & Security .... Mr. Mark BAILEY
09 Assoc Dean Inst Effectiveness .... Ms. Amanda E. KIN

Judson College (D)

302 Bibb Street, Marion AL 36756-2504
County: Perry FICE Identification: 001023
Unit ID: 101541
Telephone: (334) 683-5100 Carnegie Class: Bac/A&S
FAX Number: (334) 683-5147 Calendar System: Semester
URL: www.judson.edu
Established: 1838 Annual Undergrad Tuition & Fees: $15,774
Enrollment: 381 Female
Affiliation or Control: Alabama Baptist State Convention
IRS Status: 501(c)3
Highest Offering: Baccalaureate
Program: Liberal Arts And General; Teacher Preparatory
Accreditation: SC, MUS, SW

01 President .... Dr. David E. POTTS
05 Sr Vice Pres & Academic Dean .... Dr. Scott W. BULLARD
32 Sr VP & Dean of Students .... Ms. Susan JONES
84 Exec Dir for Enrollment Services .... Mrs. Layne HOGGLE
10 Vice President Business Affairs .... Vacant
30 VP Institutional Advancement .... Dr. Terry SMITH MORGAN
43 VP and General Counsel .... Vacant
06 Registrar .... Ms. Eleanor DRAKE
106 Dir Online Education/E-learning .... Dr. Kathy CHEN
13 Chief Info Technology Officer (CIO) .... Mrs. Traci L. FOSTER
18 Chief Facilities/Physical Plant .... Mr. Robb LEAVELL
36 Director Student Placement .... Mrs. Kendel GILCHREST
37 Director Student Financial Aid .... Ms. Anita SMITH
26 Marketing/Web Communications Spec .... Ms. Mary A. TAYLOR

Lawson State Community College (E)

3060 Wilson Road, SW, Birmingham AL 35221-1798
County: Jefferson FICE Identification: 001059
Unit ID: 101569
Telephone: (205) 925-2515 Carnegie Class: Assoc/Pub-U-MC
FAX Number: (205) 925-8526 Calendar System: Semester
URL: www.lawsonstate.edu
Established: 1949 Annual Undergrad Tuition & Fees (In-State): $4,290
Enrollment: 3,092 Coed
Affiliation or Control: State IRS Status: 501(c)3
Highest Offering: Associate Degree
Program: Occupational; 2-Year Principally Bachelor's Creditable
Accreditation: SC, ACBSP, ADNUR, DA, PNUR

01 President .... Dr. Perry W. WARD
05 Vice Pres Instructional Services .... Dr. Bruce CRAWFORD
11 Vice President of Administration .... Mrs. Sharon CREWS
32 Interim Dean of Students .... Mr. Darren ALLEN
09 Coordinator of Data Management .... Mrs. Jamie GLASS
10 Director of Financial Services .... Mr. Craig D. LAWRENCE
20 Academic Dean .... Dr. Sherri DAVIS
75 Asc Dean Business/Information Tech .... Dr. Alice MILTON
49 Asc Dn Liberal Arts/Coll Trans Pgms .... Dr. Karl PRUITT
76 Assoc Dean of Health Occupations .... Dr. Shelia MARABLE
75 Asst Dean Career Technical Programs .... Mr. Donald SLEDGE
84 Asst Dean of Admissions/Records .... Mr. Darren ALLEN
07 Director of Admissions .... Dr. Jeff SHELLEY
08 Librarian .... Ms. Sandra HENDERSON
37 Director Student Financial Aid .... Ms. Cassandra MATTHEWS
15 Director of Personnel Services .... Mrs. Janice MCGEE
26 Chief Public Relations Officer .... Mrs. Geri ALBRIGHT
18 Chief Facilities/Physical Plant .... Mr. Chad YANCY
19 Director Safety/Security .... Mr. Robert TATE
13 Dir Computing and Information Mgmt .... Mr. James MANKOWICH
40 Director Bookstore .... Mr. Al YOUNG
109 Director Auxiliary Services .... Dr. Craig LAWRENCE
41 Athletic Director .... Mr. Carlton RICE
06 Registrar .... Ms. Lori CHISEM
39 Director Student Housing .... Mr. Robert SMITH
38 Coordinator Student Counseling .... Ms. Philana SUGGS

Legacy Christian University (F)

6806 Whitesburg Dr, Huntsville AL 35802
County: Madison Identification: 667251
Telephone: (256) 924-0511 Carnegie Class: Not Classified
FAX Number: N/A Calendar System: Semester
URL: www.legacyu.net
Established: 1981 Annual Undergrad Tuition & Fees: $1,740
Enrollment: 47 Coed
Affiliation or Control: Interdenominational IRS Status: 501(c)3
Highest Offering: Master's
Program: Religious Emphasis
Accreditation: @BI

01 President .... Dr. Lee BARNETT
05 Provost/VP for Academic Affairs .... Dr. Bobby BURT
32 Dean of Students .... Mr. Chris KENNEDY
42 Campus Pastor .... Rev. Tim PAYNE
108 Dir of Institutional Effectiveness .... Ms. L.A BREANDAU
30 Director of Develop & Alumni Rels .... Mr. Charles GARRETT
10 Chief Financial Officer .... Ms. Vicki HEREFORD
84 Dean of Enrollment Mgmt & Registrar .... Mrs. Trish BROWN

Lurleen B. Wallace Community College (G)

PO Drawer 1418, 1000 Dannelly Blvd, Andalusia AL 36420-1224
County: Covington FICE Identification: 008988
Unit ID: 101602
Telephone: (334) 222-6591 Carnegie Class: Assoc/Pub-R-S
FAX Number: (334) 881-2300 Calendar System: Semester
URL: www.lbwcc.edu
Established: 1969 Annual Undergrad Tuition & Fees (In-State): $4,320
Enrollment: 1,599 Coed
Affiliation or Control: State IRS Status: 501(c)3
Highest Offering: Associate Degree
Program: Occupational; 2-Year Principally Bachelor's Creditable; Technical Emphasis
Accreditation: SC, ADNUR, DMS, EMT

01 President .... Dr. Herbert H. RIEDEL
05 Dean of Instruction .... Ms. Peggy LINTON
32 Dean of Student Affairs .... Mr. Jason JESSIE
10 Director of Finance/Comptroller .... Ms. Lynne DAYTON
21 Director of Business Services .... Ms. Debra MOODY
12 Vice Pres/Greenville Campus Dir .... Dr. James D. KRUDOP
103 Assoc Dean Adult Educ/Workforce Dev .... Mr. Jimmy HUTTO
13 Assoc Dean Instr/Info Technology .... Mr. Greg APLIN
15 Director of Human Resources .... Ms. Peige JOSEY
09 Dir Inst Effectiveness & Quality .... Dr. Shannon LEVITZKE
18 Dir College Facilities/Maintenance .... Mr. Tim JONES
07 Director Admissions & Records .... Ms. Jan RILEY
41 Athletic Director .... Mr. Steve HELMS
08 Director of Learning Resources .... Mr. Hugh CARTER
88 Director Student Support Services .... Dr. Patricia POWELL
88 Dir Upward Bound/Andalusia Camp Dir .... Mr. Bridges ANDERSON
37 Director of Financial Aid .... Ms. Donna BASS
26 Public Info Officer/Dir Mktg & Dev .... Ms. Renee LEMAIRE

Marion Military Institute (H)

1101 Washington Street, Marion AL 36756-3213
County: Perry FICE Identification: 001026
Unit ID: 101648
Telephone: (800) 664-1842 Carnegie Class: Assoc/Pub-R-S
FAX Number: (334) 683-2380 Calendar System: Semester
URL: www.marionmilitary.edu
Established: 1842 Annual Undergrad Tuition & Fees (In-State): $8,570
Enrollment: 438 Coed
Affiliation or Control: State IRS Status: 501(c)3
Highest Offering: Associate Degree
Program: 2-Year Principally Bachelor's Creditable
Accreditation: SC

01 President .... Col. David J. MOLLAHAN
03 Executive Vice President .... Dr. Susan G. STEVENSON
10 VP for Finance & Business Affs .... Mrs. Jennifer C. BARNETTE
05 Chief Instructional Officer .... Mr. David TIPMORE
32 VP for Student Affairs & Commandant .... Col. Thomas L. TATE
30 VP for Institutional Advancement .... Mrs. Suzanne MCKEE
103 Dir Career/Leadership Initiatives .... Vacant
41 Director of Athletics .... Dr. Michelle IVEY
07 Director of Admissions .... Mrs. Brittany CRAWFORD
29 Director of Alumni and Comm Affairs .... Mrs. O'Neal HOLMES
88 ROTC Professor of Military Science .... Maj. Gregory WALL
09 Director of Institutional Research .... Mrs. Donna LEEMON
06 Registrar .... Mrs. Wanda CALAME
38 Director of Guidance .... Ms. Brenda A. COOK
37 Director of Financial Aid .... Ms. Jacqueline WILSON
08 Library Director .... Vacant
18 Supt of Buildings & Grounds .... Mr. Brian HALE
17 Director of Health Services .... Mrs. Rene SUMLIN

Miles College (I)

5500 Myron Massey Boulevard, Fairfield AL 35064-2621
County: Jefferson FICE Identification: 001028
Unit ID: 101675

Telephone: (205) 929-1000 Carnegie Class: Bac/Diverse
FAX Number: (205) 929-1453 Calendar System: Semester
URL: www.miles.edu
Established: 1898 Annual Undergrad Tuition & Fees: $11,604
Enrollment: 1,782 Coed
Affiliation or Control: Christian Methodist Episcopal IRS Status: 501(c)3
Highest Offering: Baccalaureate
Program: Liberal Arts And General; Teacher Preparatory
Accreditation: **SC**, ACBSP, SW, TED

01 President ... Dr. George T. FRENCH, JR.
05 Dean & VP Academic Affairs ... Dr. Emmanuel CHEKWA
10 Sr VP Finance/Business Admin ... Ms. Diana KNIGHTON
84 VP Enrollment Management ... Ms. Cherise PETERS
29 VP Alumni Affairs/Security ... Mr. Charles CROCKROM, SR.
42 VP/Dean Student Engagement/Chapel ... Rev. Larry BATIE
100 Special Asst/Chief of Staff ... Mr. Kenneth COACHMAN
07 Director Admissions & Recruitment ... Mr. Christopher ROBERTSON
08 Director Library ... Dr. Geraldine BELL
32 Director Student Activities ... Ms. Diane BROWN
20 Associate Dean ... Dr. Joyce DUGAN-WOOD
09 Director Strategic Iniatives ... Dr. Ba-Shen T. WELCH
37 Director Financial Aid ... Mr. Percy LANIER
18 Director Physical Plant ... Mr. Thomas BROWN
25 Director Sponsored Programs ... Vacant
38 Dir Counseling/Advising/Testing ... Ms. Keisha LEWIS
15 Director Human Resources ... Mrs. Verlanda TATE
13 Manager of Data Processing ... Ms. Jackie HUDSON

Northeast Alabama Community College (A)

PO Box 159, 138 Alabama Highway 35, Rainsville AL 35986-0159
County: DeKalb/Jackson FICE Identification: 001031
Unit ID: 101897
Telephone: (256) 638-4418 Carnegie Class: Assoc/Pub-R-M
FAX Number: (256) 638-3052 Calendar System: Semester
URL: www.nacc.edu
Established: 1963 Annual Undergrad Tuition & Fees (In-State): $4,320
Enrollment: 2,708 Coed
Affiliation or Control: State IRS Status: 501(c)3
Highest Offering: Associate Degree
Program: Occupational; 2-Year Principally Bachelor's Creditable; Business Emphasis
Accreditation: **SC**, ADNUR, EMT, PNUR

01 President ... Dr. J. David CAMPBELL
05 Vice Pres/Dean of Instruction ... Dr. Joseph D. BURKE
56 Dean of Extended Day Program ... Vacant
32 Dean of Student Services ... Ms. Sherie GRACE
11 Dean of Admin Services ... Mr. Larry D. GUFFEY
37 Director of Financial Aid ... Mr. Nixon WILLMON
103 Dir Workforce Devel/Skills Training ... Mr. Mike KENNAMER
26 Chief Public Relations Officer ... Mrs. Debra A. BARRENTINE
09 Dir Instl Planning & Assessment ... Mr. Brad FRICKS
18 Chief Facilities/Physical Plant ... Mr. Kent JONES
06 Registrar/Chief Bus Ofcr/Dir Purchg ... Mr. Larry D. GUFFEY
30 Director of Development ... Ms. Heather RICE
19 Director of Police/Security ... Mr. Norman SMITH
04 Administrative Asst to President ... Ms. Patricia WILDMAN
08 Dir Learning Resource Ctr/Library ... Mrs. Julia EVERETT
102 Dir Foundation/Corporate Relations ... Mrs. Heather RICE

Northwest - Shoals Community College (B)

800 George Wallace Boulevard, Muscle Shoals AL 35661-3205
County: Colbert FICE Identification: 005697
Unit ID: 101736
Telephone: (256) 331-5200 Carnegie Class: Assoc/Pub-R-M
FAX Number: (256) 331-5222 Calendar System: Semester
URL: www.nwscc.edu
Established: 1963 Annual Undergrad Tuition & Fees (In-State): $3,360
Enrollment: 3,923 Coed
Affiliation or Control: State IRS Status: 501(c)3
Highest Offering: Associate Degree
Program: Occupational; 2-Year Principally Bachelor's Creditable
Accreditation: **SC**, ADNUR, EMT

01 President ... Dr. Humphrey LEE
05 Vice President ... Dr. Glenda COLAGROSS
10 Chief Fiscal Officer ... Mr. Paul MERRILL
09 Assoc Dean Inst Effect/Dist Ed/Dev ... Mr. John MCINTOSH
20 Assoc Dean Instructional Programs ... Dr. Timmy JAMES
30 Director of Foundation/Advancement ... Vacant
37 Director of Financial Aid ... Ms. Shauna JAMES
07 Asst Dean Recruit/Adm/FA ... Mr. Tom CARTER
15 Human Resources Coordinator ... Ms. Tia STONE
29 Director of Alumni Relations ... Vacant
36 Director/Counselor ETS/YSP ... Vacant
13 Director of Management Info Systems ... Mr. Alan MITCHELL
19 Director of Safety and Security ... Mr. Doug HARGETT
06 Registrar ... Ms. Tracy WALDROP
07 Coordinator Admissions ... Vacant
103 Assoc Dean of Workforce Develop ... Ms. Rose JONES
21 Comptroller ... Ms. Janet JONES
88 Director of Adult Education ... Mr. Donnie SWEENEY
88 Dir College and Career Readiness ... Mr. Ed CARTER
88 Coordinator/Advisor RTW ... Ms. Tara BRANSCOME
04 Administrative Asst to President ... Ms. Teresa K. HARRISON
18 Chief Facilities/Physical Plant ... Mr. Joe HACKWORTH
26 Chief Public Relations/Marketing ... Mr. Trent RANDOLPH

Oakwood University (C)

7000 Adventist Boulevard, NW, Huntsville AL 35896-0003
County: Madison FICE Identification: 001033
Unit ID: 101912
Telephone: (256) 726-7000 Carnegie Class: Bac/Diverse
FAX Number: (256) 726-8335 Calendar System: Semester
URL: www.oakwood.edu
Established: 1896 Annual Undergrad Tuition & Fees: $16,720
Enrollment: 1,924 Coed
Affiliation or Control: Seventh-day Adventist IRS Status: 501(c)3
Highest Offering: Master's
Program: Occupational; Liberal Arts And General; Teacher Preparatory
Accreditation: **SC**, ACBSP, DIETD, DIETI, NUR, SW, TED

01 President ... Dr. Leslie POLLARD
03 Provost & Sr Vice President ... Dr. Tim MCDONALD
05 Vice Pres Academic Affairs ... Dr. Tricia PENNIECOOK
10 Vice President Financial Affairs ... Ms. Sabrina COTTON
32 Vice President Student Services ... Mr. David KNIGHT
30 Executive Director Advancement/Dev ... Ms. Kisha NORRIS
20 Asst VP Academic Affairs ... Dr. Finbar BENJAMIN
21 Asst VP Financial Affs/Controller ... Mrs. Gail CALDWELL
35 Asst Vice Pres Student Services ... Mr. Ryan SMITH
15 Director Human Resources ... Mrs. Sylvia GERMANY
25 Contracts ... Mrs. Evangeline RIVERS LANG
26 Director Public Relations ... Mr. George JOHNSON
07 Director Enrollment Management ... Mr. Malcolm TAYLOR
37 Director Financial Aid ... Mrs. Lynda BARTHOLOMEW
06 Interim Registrar ... Mr. John HILL
39 Residence Life Coordinator-Men ... Mr. Woodrow VAUGHN
88 Resident Life Coordinator-Women ... Ms. Linda ANDERSON
08 Director Library Services ... Mrs. Paulette JOHNSON
09 Director Inst Effectiveness ... Mrs. Janis NEWBORN
18 Director Physical Plant ... Mr. Colins ALEXANDER
19 Acting Director Security ... Mr. Melvin HARRIS
29 Director Alumni Relations ... Ms. Edith PRUITT
36 Director Career Services & Testing ... Vacant
38 Dir Counseling & Health Services ... Dr. Janice LEWIS-THOMAS
51 Dir Adult & Continuing Education ... Mrs. Ellengold GOODRIDGE
42 Chaplain ... Dr. Howard WEEMS
46 Dir Research & Faculty Dev ... Dr. Prudence L. POLLARD
89 Director Freshmen Studies ... Mrs. Regina JACOB
50 Chair Business & Info Systems ... Dr. Faye BRATHWAITE
53 Chair Education ... Dr. James MBYIRUKIRA
76 Chair Allied Health ... Vacant
60 Chair English & Foreign Languages ... Dr. Benson PRIGG
64 Chair Music ... Dr. Wayne BUCKNOR
65 Acting Chair Biological Sciences ... Dr. Juliett BAILEY PENROD
65 Chair Chemistry ... Dr. Kenneth LAI HING
66 Chair Nursing ... Mrs. Angerlita SMITH
68 Chair Health & Physical Education ... Dr. Howard SHAW
70 Chair Social Work ... Dr. Octavio RAMIREZ
73 Acting Chair Religion & Theology ... Dr. Finbar BENJAMIN
81 Chair Math & Computer Science ... Dr. Lisa JAMES
82 Chair History ... Dr. Samuel LONDON
83 Chair Psychology ... Dr. Martin HODNETT
60 Chair Communication ... Dr. Rennae ELLIOTT
96 Director Purchasing ... Mrs. Belita NEWBY

Reid State Technical College (D)

PO Box 588, Evergreen AL 36401-0588
County: Conecuh FICE Identification: 005692
Unit ID: 101994
Telephone: (251) 578-1313 Carnegie Class: Assoc/Pub-R-S
FAX Number: (251) 578-5355 Calendar System: Semester
URL: www.rstc.edu
Established: 1966 Annual Undergrad Tuition & Fees (In-State): $4,320
Enrollment: 549 Coed
Affiliation or Control: State IRS Status: 501(c)3
Highest Offering: Associate Degree
Program: Occupational; Technical Emphasis
Accreditation: **COE**

01 President ... Dr. Douglas M. LITTLES
05 Dean Students/Instructional Svcs ... Dr. Tangela PURIFOY
103 Assoc Dean Workforce Development ... Dr. Alesia K. STUART
09 Asst Dean for Institutional Effect ... Ms. Coretta BOYKIN
37 Director Financial Aid ... Ms. Christy GOODWIN
07 Dir of Recruiting/Retention/Rsrch ... Mrs. Brenda JACKSON
10 Business Manager ... Mr. David J. RHODES
06 Registration Services Coordinator ... Ms. Vickie NICHOLSON
38 Director of Counseling/ADA Coord ... Ms. Monica ROBINSON

Remington College, Mobile Campus (E)

828 Downtowner Loop W, Mobile AL 36609-5404
County: Mobile FICE Identification: 026055
Unit ID: 366535
Telephone: (251) 343-8200 Carnegie Class: Assoc/PrivFP4
FAX Number: (251) 343-0577 Calendar System: Quarter
URL: www.remingtoncollege.edu
Established: 1986 Annual Undergrad Tuition & Fees: $15,995
Enrollment: 518 Coed
Affiliation or Control: Independent Non-Profit IRS Status: 501(c)3
Highest Offering: Associate Degree
Program: Occupational; 2-Year Principally Bachelor's Creditable; Technical Emphasis
Accreditation: **ACCSC**

01 President ... Mr. Stephen M. BACKMAN

Samford University (F)

800 Lakeshore Drive, Birmingham AL 35229-0001
County: Jefferson FICE Identification: 001036
Unit ID: 102049
Telephone: (205) 726-2011 Carnegie Class: Master's M
FAX Number: (205) 726-2171 Calendar System: 4/1/4
URL: www.samford.edu
Established: 1841 Annual Undergrad Tuition & Fees: $28,370
Enrollment: 4,933 Coed
Affiliation or Control: Southern Baptist IRS Status: 501(c)3
Highest Offering: Doctorate
Program: Liberal Arts And General; Teacher Preparatory; Professional
Accreditation: **SC**, ANEST, BUS, CAATE, CIDA, DIETD, @DIETI, LAW, MUS, NURSE, PHAR, @PTA, @SP, @SW, TED, THEA, THEOL

01 President ... Dr. T. Andrew WESTMORELAND
03 Provost ... Dr. Michael HARDIN
32 Vice President for Student Affairs ... Dr. Phil KIMREY
30 Vice President of Advancement ... Mr. W. Randall PITTMAN
10 Exec VP Business & Fin Affairs ... Mr. Harry B. BROCK, III
31 Chief Marketing Officer ... Dr. Betsy B. HOLLOWAY
45 Chief Strategy Officer ... Mr. Colin M. COYNE
04 Assistant to the President ... Dr. Michael D. MORGAN
21 Controller ... Mr. Mike DARWIN
13 Chief Information Officer ... Mr. Doug RIGNEY
43 General Counsel ... Mr. W. Clark WATSON
11 Associate Provost Administration ... Dr. Nancy BIGGIO
108 Asst Provost Assess & Accred ... Dr. Katrina H. MINTZ
05 Associate Provost Academics ... Dr. Chris METRESS
41 Athletic Director ... Mr. Martin NEWTON
88 Dir of Ethics & Leadership ... Mr. Drayton NABERS, JR.
88 Director of Donor Relations ... Mrs. Judi F. AUCOIN
29 Director of Alumni ... Ms. Molly MCGUIRE
88 Dir Orientation/Parent Prgm ... Ms. Susan DOYLE
21 Director of Business Services ... Mr. Mike MCCORMACK
88 Director of Capital Planning & Imp ... Mr. David T. WHITT
88 Dir Event Management ... Ms. Allison TOLAR
18 Director of Facilities Management ... Mr. Mark FULLER
37 Director of Student Financial Svcs ... Mr. Lane M. SMITH
15 Director of Human Resources ... Mr. Fred R. ROGAN
09 Director Inst Effectiveness ... Mrs. Karen G. HAMBY
43 Assoc VP Business Affairs/Invest ... Ms. Lisa IMBRAGULIO
08 Dean of University Library ... Dr. Kimmetha D. HERNDON
30 Director of Univ Advancement ... Mr. Douglas WILSON
19 Director of Pub Safety & Emer Mgmt ... Mr. Wayne PITTMAN
39 Director Residence Life & Univ Svcs ... Ms. Lauren M. TAYLOR
88 Director of Risk Mmgt & Insurance ... Mr. James A. CLEMENT
10 Director of Budget & Financial Plng ... Mr. Matt DEFORE
102 Dir Development/Auxiliary ... Ms. Sharon SMITH
07 Dean of Admissions ... Mr. Jason BLACK
42 Assistant Dean for Spiritual Life ... Dr. Matthew S. KERLIN
35 Assistant Dean of Student Services ... Mr. Garry L. ATKINS
35 Assistant Dean for Campus Life ... Ms. Renie MOSS
26 Exec Dir University Communication ... Mr. Philip POOLE
88 Dir of University Fellows ... Mr. Bryan M. JOHNSON
53 Dean Education/Professional Studies ... Dr. Jean A. BOX
49 Dean Howard College Arts/Sciences ... Dr. David W. CHAPMAN
17 Vice Provost College of Health Sci ... Dr. Nena F. SANDERS
76 Dean of Health Professions ... Dr. Alan JUNG
67 Dean School of Pharmacy ... Dr. Michael A. CROUCH
73 Dean Beeson School of Divinity ... Dr. Timothy F. GEORGE
50 Dean Brock School of Business ... Dr. J. Howard FINCH
61 Dean Cumberland School of Law ... Mr. Henry C. STRICKLAND
66 Dean Ida Moffett School of Nursing ... Dr. Eleanor V. HOWELL
57 Dean School of the Arts ... Dr. Joseph HOPKINS
06 Registrar ... Mr. John FLYNN
44 Director of Annual Giving ... Ms. Kimberly CRIPPS
44 Director Gift and Estate Planning ... Mr. Stan DAVIS
28 Dir Diversity & Intercultural Ed ... Dr. Denise GREGORY
104 Director of International Education ... Dr. Angela FERGUSON

Selma University (G)

1501 Lapsley Street, Selma AL 36701-5232
County: Dallas FICE Identification: 001037
Unit ID: 102058
Telephone: (334) 872-2533 Carnegie Class: Spec/Faith
FAX Number: (334) 872-7746 Calendar System: Semester
URL: www.selmauniversity.edu
Established: 1878 Annual Undergrad Tuition & Fees: $6,680
Enrollment: 558 Coed
Affiliation or Control: Baptist IRS Status: 501(c)3
Highest Offering: Master's
Program: Liberal Arts And General; Religious Emphasis
Accreditation: **BI**

01 President ... Dr. Alvin A. CLEVELAND, SR.
05 Vice President Academic Affairs ... Dr. Rosa ASHMON
32 Vice Pres Student Affairs ... Rev. Frankie HUTCHINS
06 Registrar ... Mr. Terrence JACKSON
37 Director of Financial Aid ... Mr. Nareiko STEPHENS
07 Director of Admissions ... Mrs. Collette FIKES

Shelton State Community College (A)

9500 Old Greensboro Road, Tuscaloosa AL 35405-8522
County: Tuscaloosa FICE Identification: 005691
Unit ID: 102067
Telephone: (205) 391-2211 Carnegie Class: Assoc/Pub-R-L
FAX Number: (205) 391-2426 Calendar System: Semester
URL: www.sheltonstate.edu
Established: 1953 Annual Undergrad Tuition & Fees (In-State): $4,020
Enrollment: 4,989 Coed
Affiliation or Control: State IRS Status: 501(c)3
Highest Offering: Associate Degree
Program: Occupational; 2-Year Principally Bachelor's Creditable
Accreditation: SC, ADNUR, #COARC, PNUR

01 President ... Dr. Andrea MAYFIELD
05 Associate Dean of Academic Services ... Mr. Lee AMMONS
10 Comptroller ... Mrs. Ann BRACKNELL
32 Associate Dean of Student Services ... Dr. Fran TURNER
13 Dean Technology/Inst Research ... Dr. Michelle JARRELL
12 Dean Fredd Campus/Title III ... Mr. Ronald RANGE
88 Assoc Dean for Corporate Programs ... Mr. Jason MOORE
30 Assoc Dean of Advancement ... Mr. Byron ABSTON
76 Assistant Dean for Health Services ... Ms. Gladys HILL
37 Asst Dean Financial Aid ... Ms. Amanda HARBISON
88 Executive Asst to the President ... Ms. Channing H. MARLOWE
08 Director Library Services ... Mr. Glen JOHNSON
103 Dean of Instruct & Workforce Dev ... Ms. Joyce JONES
88 Director Adult Education ... Mr. Phillip JOHNSON
38 Director of Student Support ... Ms. Holly ELLIOTT
88 Dean of Technical Services ... Mr. Steve FAIR
109 Dean of Auxiliary Services ... Dr. Thomas TAYLOR
04 Administrative Asst to President ... Mrs. Betty PRUITT
09 Director of Institutional Research ... Mr. Louis SHEDD
106 Instructional Tech and eLearning ... Mr. John ALEXANDER
106 Instructional Tech and eLearning ... Ms. Molly BOOTH
18 Chief Facilities ... Mr. Tim HINTON
26 Director of Media Communication ... Ms. Jill SWINDLE

Snead State Community College (B)

PO Box 734, Boaz AL 35957-0734
County: Marshall FICE Identification: 001038
Unit ID: 102076
Telephone: (256) 593-5120 Carnegie Class: Assoc/Pub-R-M
FAX Number: (256) 593-7180 Calendar System: Semester
URL: www.snead.edu
Established: 1898 Annual Undergrad Tuition & Fees (In-State): $4,544
Enrollment: 2,258 Coed
Affiliation or Control: State IRS Status: Exempt
Highest Offering: Associate Degree
Program: Occupational; 2-Year Principally Bachelor's Creditable
Accreditation: SC, ADNUR

01 President ... Dr. Robert EXLEY
32 Vice President for Student Services ... Mr. Jason CANNON
10 Chief Financial Officer ... Mr. Mark RICHARD
05 Chief Academic Officer ... Dr. Jason WATTS
13 Chief IT Officer ... Mr. Randy MALTBIE
26 Director of PR/Marketing ... Ms. Shelley SMITH
38 Coordinator of Testing ... Ms. Tonya SHIELDS
09 Assoc Dean Acad Planning/Research ... Dr. Annette CEDERHOLM
81 Science Division Director ... Ms. Deborah RHODEN
79 Humanities Division Director ... Dr. Cynthia DENHAM
83 Social Science Division Director ... Mr. Alan BATES
81 Mathematics Division Director ... Mr. Blake LEETH
50 Business Division Director ... Mr. Vann SCOTT
75 Technology Division Director ... Mr. Greg RANDALL
103 Director Workforce Development ... Ms. Teresa WALKER
76 Director Health Sciences ... Ms. Amy LANGLEY
41 Athletic Director ... Mr. Mark RICHARD
08 Head Librarian ... Mr. John MILLER
15 Director of Human Resources ... Ms. Amanda GUNNELS
18 Director of Physical Plant ... Mr. Steve WILLIAMS
07 Director of Admissions ... Ms. Lesley KUBIK
106 Dir Online Education/E-learning ... Mr. John HANEY
19 Director Security/Safety ... Mr. Paul GORE
29 Director Alumni Relations ... Ms. Shelley SMITH
30 Development Coordinator ... Ms. Kelli CONLEY
37 Financial Aid Coordinator ... Ms. Amanda CHILDRESS

South University (C)

5355 Vaughn Road, Montgomery AL 36116-1120
Telephone: (334) 395-8800 FICE Identification: 004463
Accreditation: &SC, ACBSP, MAC, NURSE, PTAA

† Regional accreditation is carried under the parent institution in Savannah, GA.

Southeastern Bible College (D)

2545 Valleydale Road, Birmingham AL 35244-2083
County: Shelby FICE Identification: 022704
Unit ID: 102261
Telephone: (205) 970-9200 Carnegie Class: Spec/Faith
FAX Number: (205) 970-9207 Calendar System: Semester
URL: www.sebc.edu
Established: 1935 Annual Undergrad Tuition & Fees: $11,790
Enrollment: 173 Coed
Affiliation or Control: Independent Non-Profit IRS Status: 501(c)3
Highest Offering: Baccalaureate
Program: Liberal Arts And General; Religious Emphasis
Accreditation: BI

01 President ... Dr. Alexander GRANADOS
05 Provost ... Dr. Vicki WOLFE
32 Dean of Students ... Ms. Kristie HARRICK
42 Campus Pastor ... Mr. Micah SIMPSON
49 Chair Dept of Arts & Sciences ... Dr. Dwain WALDREP
53 Chair Dept of Education ... Dr. Lynn GANNETT-MALICK
73 Chair Dept of Biblical Studies ... Dr. Jason SNYDER
10 Business Manager ... Mrs. Carme PHILLIPS
04 Admin Asst to the President ... Mrs. Anita SCROGGINS
06 Dir of Inst Effect & Registrar ... Mr. Joel WOLFE
07 Associate Dir of Admissions ... Ms. Deidra WHITFIELD
08 Director of Library Services ... Mr. Paul ROBERTS
37 Director of Financial Aid ... Mrs. Joanne BELIN
55 Dir of ACHIEVE Adult Educ ... Dr. Steven CLECKLER

Southern Union State Community College (E)

PO Box 1000, Wadley AL 36276-1000
County: Randolph FICE Identification: 001040
Unit ID: 251260
Telephone: (256) 395-2211 Carnegie Class: Assoc/Pub-R-M
FAX Number: (256) 395-2215 Calendar System: Semester
URL: www.suscc.edu
Established: 1922 Annual Undergrad Tuition & Fees (In-State): $3,696
Enrollment: 4,727 Coed
Affiliation or Control: State IRS Status: 501(c)3
Highest Offering: Associate Degree
Program: Occupational; 2-Year Principally Bachelor's Creditable
Accreditation: SC, ADNUR, EMT, RAD, SURGT

01 Interim President ... Dr. Glenda COLAGROSS
05 Dean of Academics ... Dr. Linda NORTH
32 Dean of Students ... Ms. Tiffany SANDERS
20 Assoc Dean of Instruction ... Mr. Steve SPRATLIN
72 Dean of Technical Educ/Wrkfce Dev ... Mr. Darin BALDWIN
35 Dean Student Development ... Mr. Gary BRANCH
41 Athletic Director ... Mr. Ron RADFORD
06 Registrar ... Ms. Catherine STRINGFELLOW
10 Business Manager ... Mr. Ben JORDAN

Spring Hill College (F)

4000 Dauphin Street, Mobile AL 36608-1791
County: Mobile FICE Identification: 001041
Unit ID: 102234
Telephone: (251) 380-4000 Carnegie Class: Master's S
FAX Number: (251) 460-2182 Calendar System: Semester
URL: www.shc.edu
Established: 1830 Annual Undergrad Tuition & Fees: $32,468
Enrollment: 1,376 Coed
Affiliation or Control: Roman Catholic IRS Status: 501(c)3
Highest Offering: Master's
Program: Liberal Arts And General; Teacher Preparatory
Accreditation: SC, NURSE

01 President ... Dr. Christopher PUTO
05 Provost/Vice Pres Academic Affairs ... Dr. George E. SIMS
10 Vice President Finance/Accounting ... Ms. Rhonda SHIRAZI
30 Vice President Advancement ... Mr. Francis SALANCY
32 Vice Pres Student Affairs ... Ms. Rosalie CARPENTER
84 Vice Pres Enrollment Svcs ... Mr. Robert STEWART
11 Chief Operating Officer ... Mr. John BARTER
13 Chief Information Officer ... Dr. Margaret MASSEY
20 Assistant VP for Academic Affairs ... Vacant
20 Associate Provost ... Ms. Jennifer GOOD
35 Associate Dean of Students ... Ms. Margarita PEREZ
21 Controller ... Ms. Wendy BOUTWELL
37 Director of Financial Aid ... Mrs. Ellen FOSTER
06 Registrar ... Mr. Stuart MOORE
88 Director Student Development Center ... Ms. Josetta MULLOY
29 Director of Alumni & Parents ... Mrs. Monde DONALDSON
91 Director Administrative Computing ... Mr. Mac HORTON
15 Director of Personnel ... Ms. Patricia A. DAVIS
19 Director of Public Safety/Security ... Mr. Todd WARREN
23 Director of Health Services ... Mrs. Melissa MELTON
42 Director of Campus Ministry ... Ms. Maureen BERGAN
41 Director Athletics & Recreation ... Mr. James HALL
31 Dir Foley CommunityService Center ... Dr. Kathleen ORANGE
26 Dir Communications/Instl Mktng ... Vacant
27 Communications Officer ... Ms. Natasha MOORE
40 Bookstore Manager ... Ms. Genevieve MORRIS
36 Coordinator of Career Services ... Ms. Elizabeth DEXTER-WILSON
38 Counselor ... Ms. Lynda OLEN

Stillman College (G)

3601 Stillman Boulevard, POB 1430,
Tuscaloosa AL 35403-1430
County: Tuscaloosa FICE Identification: 001044
Unit ID: 102270
Telephone: (205) 349-4240 Carnegie Class: Bac/A&S
FAX Number: (205) 366-8996 Calendar System: Semester
URL: www.stillman.edu
Established: 1876 Annual Undergrad Tuition & Fees: $15,865
Enrollment: 1,056 Coed
Affiliation or Control: Presbyterian Church (U.S.A.) IRS Status: 501(c)3
Highest Offering: Baccalaureate
Program: Liberal Arts And General; Teacher Preparatory
Accreditation: SC, IACBE, MUS, TED

01 President ... Dr. Peter MILLET
05 Provost/VP Academic Affairs ... Vacant
10 Vice President Fiscal Affairs ... Mr. Sama MONDEH
84 Vice President Retention ... Dr. Charlotte CARTER
30 VP Institutional Advancement ... Mr. Anthony HOLLOMAN
32 Vice President for Students Affairs ... Dr. Sharon WHITTAKER-DAVIS
31 Vice Pres External Affairs ... Dr. Eddie B. THOMAS
44 Associate VP for Development ... Mr. Adrian L. SCOTT
26 Assoc Vice President/Marketing & PR ... Mrs. Daryka REEVES
21 Asst Vice Pres/Business Manager ... Vacant
29 Assoc Vice Pres Alumni Affairs ... Mr. Adrian SCOTT
18 Asst VP Logistics/Plant Operations ... Vacant
53 Dean of Professional Educ/Asst VP ... Dr. Linda BRADFORD
49 Dean of Arts & Sciences/Asst VP ... Dr. Mary Jane KROTZER
08 Dean of Library ... Mr. Robert HEATH
09 Director of Institutional Research ... Ms. Cynthia LEATHERWOOD
06 Registrar ... Mrs. Barbara SMITH
37 Director of Financial Aid ... Mrs. Jacqueline MORRIS
38 Dir Student Development/Health Svcs ... Ms. Jacqueline CURRIE
13 Director of Info Technology ... Mr. Dominic MURUAKO
07 Director of Admissions ... Mr. Joseph TINSLEY
19 Chief of Campus Police ... Mr. James TAGGART
41 Interim Athletic Director ... Ms. Cassandra MOORER
15 Human Resources Director ... Mrs. Patricia WILSON
42 College Chaplain ... Dr. Mark MCCORMICK

Talladega College (H)

627 W. Battle Street, Talladega AL 35160-2354
County: Talladega FICE Identification: 001046
Unit ID: 102298
Telephone: (256) 761-6100 Carnegie Class: Bac/A&S
FAX Number: (256) 761-9206 Calendar System: Semester
URL: www.talladega.edu
Established: 1867 Annual Undergrad Tuition & Fees: $12,510
Enrollment: 879 Coed
Affiliation or Control: Independent Non-Profit IRS Status: 501(c)3
Highest Offering: Baccalaureate
Program: Liberal Arts And General; Teacher Preparatory; Professional; Business Emphasis
Accreditation: SC, SW

01 President ... Dr. Billy C. HAWKINS
05 Int Provost/VP for Academic Affairs ... Dr. Lisa LONG
10 Vice Pres Finance & Administration ... Dr. Gerald WILLIAMS
32 Int Vice President Student Affairs ... Mr. Anthony M. JONES, JR.
30 Vice Pres Institutional Advancement ... Ms. Kimberly ALEXANDER
18 Director Facilities Management ... Mr. Gary LAWSON
37 Director Financial Aid ... Mrs. Russelle KEESE
07 Director of Admissions ... Mr. Brian GIPSON
09 Int Director Institutional Research ... Dr. Syed RAZA
35 Director of Student Activities ... Mr. Anthony M. JONES, JR.
41 Athletic Director ... Mr. Wilberto RAMOS
08 Librarian ... Dr. Joseph MCDONALD
13 Information Technology Director ... Mrs. LaRita BREWSTER
36 Director of Career Placement ... Ms. Delores TRAYLOR
15 Director of Human Resources ... Mrs. Brenda RHODEN
19 Chief Campus Police ... Mr. Kevin GILLILAN
50 Dean Div Administration & Business ... Ms. Charmaine BALFOUR
79 Dean Div Humanities/Fine Arts ... Dr. Isaac BRUNSON
81 Dean Div of Natural Sci/Math ... Dr. Charlie STINSON
83 Dean Div EWJ Social Sciences/Educ ... Dr. Susan VICKERSTAFF
51 Dean of Adult Degree Programs ... Vacant
23 Health Services on Campus ... Mrs. Valarie ALFRED
25 Title III Coor/Grants Administrator ... Ms. Peggy ROXBURY
29 Director Alumni Relations ... Ms. Kimberly ALEXANDER
06 Registrar ... Mr. Juan CARWELL
38 Director Student Counseling ... Ms. Delores TRAYLOR
04 Exec Admin Asst to President ... Vacant
104 Director Study Abroad ... Mr. John VERBURG
22 Dir Affirmative Action/EEO ... Mrs. Brenda RHODEN
96 Director of Purchasing ... Mr. Michael GARRIS

Trenholm State Technical College (I)

PO Box 10048, Montgomery AL 36108
County: Montgomery FICE Identification: 005734
Unit ID: 102313
Telephone: (334) 420-4200 Carnegie Class: Assoc/Pub-R-S
FAX Number: (334) 420-4206 Calendar System: Semester
URL: www.trenholmstate.edu
Established: 1963 Annual Undergrad Tuition & Fees (In-State): $5,076
Enrollment: 1,338 Coed
Affiliation or Control: State IRS Status: 501(c)3
Highest Offering: Associate Degree
Program: Occupational; 2-Year Principally Bachelor's Creditable; Technical Emphasis
Accreditation: SC, ACFEI, COE, DA, DMS, EMT, MAC, PNUR, RAD

01 President ... Mr. Sam MUNNERLYN
10 Dean of Finance/Admin Svcs ... Ms. Cathy WRIGHT
05 Dean of Instruction ... Dr. Tanjula PETTY
30 Dean of Development ... Dr. Suresh C. KAUSHIK
32 Dean of Students ... Ms. Beverly ROSS
103 Dean of Workforce Development ... Mr. Wilford HOLT
13 Assoc Dean of IT ... Mr. Charles HARRIS
09 Director of Institutional Research ... Dr. Mimi JOHNSON
18 Director Physical Plant ... Mr. Dennis MONROE
37 Director Student Financial Aid ... Ms. Betty EDWARDS
07 Director of Admissions/Registrar ... Mrs. Tennie S. MCBRYDE
26 Public Information Officer ... Mr. Michael EVANS

15 Director of Human Resources .... Ms. Pam ROLLINS
51 Dir Title III/Marketing/Cont Educ .... Ms. Arlinda KNIGHT
36 Coordinator Job Placement .... Ms. Maria RICHARDSON
04 Administrative Asst to President .... Ms. Angela W. CONE
08 Head Librarian .... Mr. Paul BLACKMON

Troy University (A)

University Avenue, Troy AL 36082-0001
County: Pike FICE Identification: 001047
Unit ID: 102368
Telephone: (334) 670-3100 Carnegie Class: Master's L
FAX Number: (334) 670-3774 Calendar System: Semester
URL: www.troy.edu
Established: 1887 Annual Undergrad Tuition & Fees (In-State): $9,880
Enrollment: 19,579 Coed
Affiliation or Control: State IRS Status: 501(c)3
Highest Offering: Doctorate
Program: Liberal Arts And General; Teacher Preparatory; Professional
Accreditation: SC, ACBSP, ADNUR, CAATE, CACREP, CORE, ENGR, MUS, NUR, SPAA, SW, TED

01 Chancellor .... Dr. Jack HAWKINS, JR.
05 Sr Vice Chanc for Academic Affairs .... Dr. Earl INGRAM
32 Sr Vice Chanc Student Svcs/Admin .... Dr. John R. DEW
30 Sr Vice Chanc Advance/External Affs .... Gen. Walter GIVHAN
10 Sr VC for Finance & Business Affs .... Dr. James BOOKOUT
15 Vice Chancellor/Dir Human Resources .... Dr. Ray WHITE
12 Vice Chancellor Troy Global Campus .... Dr. Don JEFFREY
12 Vice Chancellor Troy Dothan .... Dr. Skip AMES
12 Vice Chancellor Troy Phenix City .... Dr. David WHITE
35 Dean of Student Svcs Troy Dothan .... Vacant
49 Assoc Dean Col Arts/Sci Troy Dothan .... Dr. Robert SAUNDERS
50 Assoc Dean Col Bus Troy Dothan .... Dr. Skip AMES
53 Assoc Dean Col of Educ Troy Dothan .... Dr. Robin BYNUM
12 Vice Chanc Troy Montgomery .... Mr. Lance TATUM
49 Assoc Dean Arts/Sci Troy Montgomery .... Dr. Robert SAUNDERS
53 Assoc Dean Col Educ Troy Montgomery .... Dr. Pamela ARRINGTON
30 Assoc Vice Chanc for Development .... Dr. Jean LALIBERTE
37 Assoc Vice Chanc for Financial Aid .... Ms. Carol BALLARD
20 Associate Provost for Academics .... Dr. Lee VARDAMAN
26 Assoc VC for Mktg/Communication .... Mrs. Donna SCHUBERT
06 Registrar .... Mrs. Vickie MILES
84 Dean Enrollment Services .... Mr. Buddy STARLING
08 Dean Library Services .... Dr. Chris SHAFFER
13 Chief Technology Officer .... Mr. Greg PRICE
27 Director University Relations .... Mr. Andrew ELLIS
29 Director Alumni Affairs .... Ms. Faith W. WARD
36 Coordinator Career Services .... Ms. Lauren COLE
18 Director Facilities/Physical Plant .... Mr. Mark SALMON
60 Director of Journalism .... Dr. Jefferson SPURLOCK
04 Exec Assistant to the Chancellor .... Mr. Tom DAVIS
38 Director Student Counseling .... Ms. Teresa P. RODGERS
07 Director of Graduate Admissions .... Mrs. Jessica KIMBRO
88 Dir Not for Profit/Assoc Controller .... Mrs. Lauri DORRILL
106 eTROY Dir Educational Technology .... Mr. Ronnie CREEL
86 Director of Federal/State Govt Rels .... Mr. Marcus PARAMORE
86 Dir of Local Governmental Relations .... Mr. Alan BOOTHE
44 Director of Annual Giving .... Mrs. Bronda DENISON
25 Director Sponsored Programs .... Mrs. Judy FULMER
62 Dir of Library Svcs Troy Dothan .... Mr. Chris SHAFFER
62 Dir of Library Svcs Troy Montgomery .... Mr. Kent SNOWDEN
20 Dean Undergrad Pgms/Assoc Provost .... Dr. Hal FULMER
35 Dean of Student Svcs Troy Campus .... Mr. Herbert REEVES
49 Dean Arts & Sciences .... Vacant
49 Assoc Dean Col Arts/Sci .... Dr. Bill GRANTHAM
50 Dean Business .... Dr. Judson EDWARDS
53 Dean Education .... Dr. Kathryn HILDEBRAND
58 Dean Graduate Pgms/Assoc Provost .... Dr. Dianne BARRON
76 Int Dean Health/Human Services .... Dr. Mark TILLMAN
57 Dean Communication/Fine Arts .... Dr. Larry BLOCHER
35 Assoc Dean Student Svcs Troy Mont .... Dr. James SMITH
09 Director of Institutional Research .... Mrs. Kimberly B. JONES
39 Director Student Housing .... Mr. Herbert REEVES
41 Athletic Director .... Vacant

Tuskegee University (B)

1200 W. Montgomery Road, Tuskegee Inst. AL 36088
County: Macon FICE Identification: 001050
Unit ID: 102377
Telephone: (334) 727-8011 Carnegie Class: Bac/Diverse
FAX Number: (334) 727-5276 Calendar System: Semester
URL: www.tuskegee.edu
Established: 1881 Annual Undergrad Tuition & Fees: $19,060
Enrollment: 3,103 Coed
Affiliation or Control: Independent Non-Profit IRS Status: 501(c)3
Highest Offering: Doctorate
Program: Liberal Arts And General; Teacher Preparatory; Professional
Accreditation: SC, BUS, #DIETD, ENG, MT, NUR, #OT, SW, TED, #VET

01 President .... Dr. Brian L. JOHNSON
05 Provost/VP Academic Affairs .... Dr. Cesar D. FERMIN
10 Vice President Finance/CFO .... Mr. Rick KISNER
30 Vice Pres Dev & Advancement .... Mr. Robert BLAKELY
46 Vice Pres Research/Sponsored Pgms .... Dr. Shaik JEELANI
18 VP Capital Projects/Facility Svcs .... Mr. Harold TATE
84 VP Student Affairs/Enrollment Mgmt .... Ms. Regina BURTON
26 Sr Dir Comm/Public Rels/Mktg .... Mr. Jeremy R. ALPHORD
101 Exec Asst to Pres/Secy to the Board .... Mrs. Verna S. LITTLE
100 Chief of Staff .... Mr. Edward BROWN
13 Chief Information Officer .... Ms. Jenell SARGENT
45 Asst VP & Dir Budget & Planning .... Ms. Belinda HOGUE
20 Assoc Provost & Director Intl Pgms .... Dr. Eloise CARTER
47 Vice Provost/Dean of CAENS .... Dr. Walter A. HILL
49 Dean School of Education .... Dr. Carlton E. MORRIS
50 Dean Col Business/Information Sci .... Dr. Tejnder SARA
54 Dean College of Engineering .... Dr. Legand L. BURGE
74 Dean Col Vet Med/Nurs/Allied Health .... Dr. Tsegaye HABTEMARIAM
32 Interim Dean of Students .... Mr. Joe BROWN
42 Dean of the Chapel .... Dr. Gregory S. GRAY
08 Director of Library Services .... Mrs. Juanita ROBERTS
29 Alumni Affairs Director .... Vacant
86 Director Federal Relations .... Mrs. Willa HALL SMITH
51 Int Assoc Prov Cont Educ/Extension .... Dr. Ntam BAHARANYI
36 Assoc Dir Career Devel/Placement .... Ms. Sarah STRINGER
21 Bursar .... Ms. Barbara CHISHOLM
37 Director of Financial Aid .... Mr. A. D. JAMES
15 Director Human Resources .... Dr. Shantay BOLTON
18 Project Mgr Sodexho/Physical Plant .... Mr. Tony WARD
91 Director of Applications Support .... Mr. James E. COOPER
06 Acting Registrar .... Ms. Elaine BROMFIELD
38 Director Student Counseling .... Dr. Joyce RHODEN
09 Coordinator Institutional Research .... Dr. Courtney L. GRIFFIN
96 Director of Purchasing .... Vacant

United States Sports Academy (C)

One Academy Drive, Daphne AL 36526-7055
County: Baldwin FICE Identification: 021706
Unit ID: 102395
Telephone: (251) 626-3303 Carnegie Class: Spec/Other
FAX Number: (251) 626-3874 Calendar System: Semester
URL: www.ussa.edu
Established: 1972 Annual Undergrad Tuition & Fees: $9,440
Enrollment: 339 Coed
Affiliation or Control: Independent Non-Profit IRS Status: 501(c)3
Highest Offering: Doctorate
Program: Professional
Accreditation: SC

01 President .... Dr. Thomas P. ROSANDICH
11 Vice President & COO .... Dr. Thomas J. ROSANDICH
05 Dean of Academic Affairs .... Dr. Stephen L. BUTLER
10 Dean of Admin & Finance .... Ms. Holly H. MCLELLAN
51 Director Distance Learning .... Dr. Brandon SPRADLEY
32 Director of Student Services .... Vacant
26 Communications Assistant .... Ms. Erin BOSARGE
06 Registrar .... Ms. Sara LEE
08 Director of Library/Archivist .... Dr. Robert HUDSON
37 Director of Financial Aid .... Vacant
18 Building and Grounds .... Mr. Bob KLINE

*University of Alabama System Office (D)

500 University Boulevard East, Tuscaloosa AL 35401
County: Tuscaloosa FICE Identification: 008004
Unit ID: 100733
Telephone: (205) 348-5861 Carnegie Class: N/A
FAX Number: (205) 348-9788
URL: www.uasystem.ua.edu

01 Chancellor .... Dr. Robert E. WITT
101 Sec Board & Exec Asst to Chanc .... Mr. Michael A. BOWNES
05 Vice Chancellor Academic Affairs .... Dr. Charles R. NASH
10 Exec Vice Chanc Financial Affairs .... Mr. Ray HAYES
26 Vice Chancellor System Relations .... Mrs. Kellee C. REINHART
86 Vice Chanc Govt Rels/Economic Devel .... Mr. Jo BONNER
43 General Counsel .... Mr. R. Cooper SHATTUCK
21 General Auditor .... Ms. Sabrina B. HEARN

*The University of Alabama (E)

Tuscaloosa AL 35487-0100
County: Tuscaloosa FICE Identification: 001051
Unit ID: 100751
Telephone: (205) 348-6010 Carnegie Class: RU/H
FAX Number: (205) 348-9046 Calendar System: Semester
URL: www.ua.edu
Established: 1831 Annual Undergrad Tuition & Fees (In-State): $12,865
Enrollment: 36,155 Coed
Affiliation or Control: State IRS Status: 501(c)3
Highest Offering: Doctorate
Program: Liberal Arts And General; Teacher Preparatory; Professional
Accreditation: SC, ART, BUS, BUSA, CAATE, CACREP, CEA, CIDA, CLPSY, CORE, CS, DANCE, DIETC, DIETD, ENG, JOUR, LAW, LIB, MUS, NURSE, SP, SW, TED, THEA

02 President .... Dr. Stuart R. BELL
05 Interim Provost .... Dr. Kevin WHITAKER
10 Vice Pres for Financial Affairs .... Dr. Lynda GILBERT
30 Interim Vice Pres for Advancement .... Mr. Calvin BROWN
46 Vice President for Research .... Dr. Carl PINKERT
32 Vice Pres for Student Affairs .... Dr. David L. GRADY
31 Vice Pres for Community Affairs .... Dr. Samory T. PRUITT
13 Vice Provost/Chief Information Ofcr .... Dr. John MCGOWAN
18 Assistant VP University Facilities .... Mr. Duane LAMB
18 Ast VP Univ Facilities/Construction .... Mr. Tim LEOPARD
19 Asst Vice Pres Public Safety .... Mr. Steven TUCKER
20 Vice Provost Academic Affairs .... Vacant
11 Asst Provost for Administration .... Vacant
15 Interim Assoc VP Human Resources .. Ms. Nancy H. WHITTAKER
21 Assoc Vice President for Finance .... Ms. Julie SHELTON
21 Assoc Vice Pres Financial Affairs .... Ms. Dana S. KEITH
26 Asst VP University Relations .... Ms. Deborah LANE
29 Director of Alumni Affairs .... Mr. Calvin BROWN
85 Asst VP Internatl Ed/Global Affairs .... Dr. Teresa WISE
06 University Registrar .... Dr. Kenneth H. FOSHEE
09 Director Inst Research/Assessment .... Dr. Lorne KUFFEL
36 Exec Director of Career Center .... Mr. Travis RAILSBACK
07 Dir of Undergraduate Admissions .... Ms. Mary K. SPIEGEL
22 Dir & University Compliance Officer .... Ms. Gwendolyn D. HOOD
37 Director of Student Financial Aid .... Ms. Helen ALLEN
84 Director Enrollment Management .... Mrs. Teri TERRY
39 Director Dept of Housing/Res Cmty .... Dr. Steven HOOD
40 Director of University Supply Store .... Ms. Teresa SHREVE
41 Athletic Director .... Mr. Bill BATTLE
43 University Counsel .... Mr. Mike SPEARING
08 Dean of University Libraries .... Dr. Louis A. PITSCHMANN
49 Dean of Arts & Sciences .... Dr. Robert F. OLIN
50 Interim Dean College of C&BA .... Dr. Brian GRAY
51 Dean Col of Cont Studies .... Dr. Craig EDELBROCK
53 Dean College of Education .... Dr. Peter HLEBOWITSH
54 Dean College of Engineering .... Dr. Charles L. KARR
58 Dean Graduate School/Asst Acad VP .... Dr. David A. FRANCKO
59 Dean Human Environmental Sciences .... Dr. Milla BOSCHUNG
60 Dean Col of Communication/Info Sci .... Dr. Mark NELSON
61 Dean School of Law .... Dr. Mark E. BRANDON
62 Dir Sch of Library/Info Studies .... Dr. Heidi JULIEN
38 Manager Stdnt Support Svcs-Trio Pgm .. Ms. Wendy L. COGBURN
96 Asc Purchasing Mgr Genl Procurement .... Ms. Pollye HARDY
96 Asc Purchas Mgr Facil Procurement .... Mr. Lane COX
76 Dean Cmty Health Sciences .... Dr. Rick STREIFFER
66 Dean Capstone College of Nursing .... Dr. Suzanne S. PREVOST
70 Dean School of Social Work .... Dr. Vikki VANDIVER
92 Dean of Honors College .... Dr. Shane SHARPE
94 Chair of Women's Studies .... Ms. Lamea SHAABAN-MAGANA

*University of Alabama at Birmingham (F)

1720 2nd Avenue South, Birmingham AL 35294-0001
County: Jefferson FICE Identification: 001052
Unit ID: 100663
Telephone: (205) 934-4011 Carnegie Class: RU/VH
FAX Number: N/A Calendar System: Semester
URL: www.uab.edu
Established: 1969 Annual Undergrad Tuition & Fees (In-State): $7,766
Enrollment: 17,028 Coed
Affiliation or Control: State IRS Status: 501(c)3
Highest Offering: Doctorate
Program: Liberal Arts And General; Teacher Preparatory; Professional
Accreditation: SC, ANEST, ARCPA, ART, BUS, BUSA, CACREP, CAHIIM, CEA, CLPSY, COARC, CS, DENT, DIETI, ENG, FEPAC, HSA, IPSY, MED, MT, MUS, NMT, NURSE, OPT, OPTR, OT, PAST, PH, PTA, SPAA, SW, TED, THEA

02 President .... Dr. Ray L. WATTS
05 Provost .... Dr. Linda C. LUCAS
10 Vice Pres Financial Affairs/Admin .... Mr. G. Allen BOLTON
17 CEO UAB Health System .... Dr. Will FERNIANY
30 Sr VP Dev/Alumni/External Rels .... Dr. Shirley S. KAHN
13 Vice Pres Info Technology/CIO .... Dr. Curtis A. CARVER, JR.
28 Vice Pres for Equity and Diversity .... Dr. Louis DALE
46 Vice Pres for Research/Economic Dev .Dr. Richard B. MARCHASE
63 Sr VP/Dean School of Medicine .... Dr. Selwyn M. VICKERS
20 Sr VP Student/Faculty Success .... Dr. Suzanne E. AUSTIN
32 Vice Pres Student Affairs .... Dr. John R. JONES, III
43 University Counsel .... Mr. W. John DANIEL
49 Dean College of Arts & Sciences .... Dr. Robert PALAZZO
50 Dean School of Business .... Dr. Eric JACK
52 Dean School of Dentistry .... Dr. Michael S. REDDY
53 Dean School of Education .... Dr. Deborah L. VOLTZ
54 Dean School of Engineering .... Dr. Iwan ALEXANDER
76 Dean School of Health Professions .... Dr. Harold P. JONES
66 Dean School of Nursing .... Dr. Doreen C. HARPER
88 Dean School of Optometry .... Dr. Kelly NICHOLS
69 Dean School of Public Health .... Dr. Max MICHAEL, III
58 Interim Dean Graduate School .... Dr. Jeffrey A. ENGLER
18 Assoc Vice President Facilities .... Mr. Robert E. MCMAINS, III
109 Assoc VP Business/Auxillary Svcs .... Mr. Christopher CLIFFORD
29 Assoc VP Alumni/Annual Giving .... Ms. Rebecca WATSON
44 Asst Vice Pres Development .... Mr. Thomas I. BRANNAN
26 Assoc VP Public Relations & Mktg .... Ms. Anne BUCKLEY
84 Assoc Provost Enrollment Management .... Dr. Bradley BARNES
21 Assoc Vice Pres Financial Affairs .... Ms. Patricia A. RACZYNSKI
35 Asst Vice Pres for Student Life .... Mr. Andrew J. MARSCH, III
08 Dean of Libraries .... Mr. John M. MEADOR
08 Director Lister Hill Library .... Mr. Scott PLUTCHAK
41 Athletic Director .... Mr. Mark T. INGRAM
15 Chief Human Resources Officer .... Ms. Alesia M. JONES
09 Exec Dir Inst Effect & Analysis .... Mr. Lee SMITH
19 Assistant VP & Chief of Police .... Mr. Anthony B. PURCELL
07 Director Undergraduate Admissions .... Mr. Kirk KLUVER
37 Director of Financial Aid .... Ms. Helen M. MCINTYRE
06 University Registrar .... Ms. Tina DENEEN
39 Interim Director Student Housing .... Mr. Marc BOOKER
36 Executive Director Career Services .... Ms. Suzanne SCOTT-TRAMMELL
38 Dir Student Counseling & Wellness .... Mr. Jacob BAGGOTT
04 Executive Asst to President .... Ms. Jane K. LUCAS
106 Int Dir E-Learning & Prof Studies .... Dr. Elizabeth A. FISHER
96 Director of Purchasing .... Ms. Belinda MITCHELL

*University of Alabama in Huntsville (A)

301 Sparkman Drive, Huntsville AL 35899-1911
County: Madison FICE Identification: 001055
Unit ID: 100706
Telephone: (256) 824-1000 Carnegie Class: RU/VH
FAX Number: (256) 824-6073 Calendar System: Semester
URL: www.uah.edu
Established: 1950 Annual Undergrad Tuition & Fees (In-State): $9,128
Enrollment: 7,348 Coed
Affiliation or Control: State IRS Status: 501(c)3
Highest Offering: Doctorate
Program: Liberal Arts And General; Teacher Preparatory; Professional
Accreditation: SC, ART, BUS, CS, ENG, MUS, NURSE, TED

02 President ... Dr. Robert A. ALTENKIRCH
05 Provost & Exec VP Academic Affairs ... Dr. Christine CURTIS
10 Sr VP Finance & Administration ... Mr. Ray PINNER
41 Director Intercollegiate Athletics ... Dr. William E. BROPHY, JR.
43 University Counsel ... Mr. Robert W. RIEDER, JR.
46 VP Research & Econ Dev ... Dr. Ray VAUGHN
30 VP University Advancement ... Mr. Robert LYON
28 VP Diversity ... Ms. Delois SMITH
32 VP of Student Affairs ... Dr. Kristi MOTTER
86 Dir Govt Relations & Public Affairs ... Mr. Ray GARNER
30 Asst VP for Development ... Vacant
39 Asst VP for Student Affairs ... Mr. John MAXON
46 Assoc VP Research ... Dr. Thomas M. KOSHUT
46 Associate VP for Research ... Dr. Robert LINDQUIST
35 Interim Dean of Students ... Mr. TJ BRECCIAROLI
11 Assoc VP Finance & Business Svcs ... Mr. Robert LEONARD
13 CIO/Assoc Provost ... Ms. Dee CHILDS
18 Assoc VP Facilities & Operations ... Mr. Michael S. FINNEGAN
20 Assoc Provost UG Studies/Inst Effec ... Dr. Brent M. WREN
21 Associate VP Budgets & Fin Planning ... Mr. Chih LOO
26 Assoc VP of Marketing and Comm ... Mr. Joel C. LONERGAN
15 Assoc VP Human Resources ... Ms. Laurel LONG
09 Director Institutional Research ... Dr. Suzanne SIMPSON
88 Director Internal Audit ... Ms. Tharanee M. RAVINDRAN
85 Dir International Engagement ... Dr. Susan STEEN
36 Exec Dir Student Success Center ... Mr. Alan CONSTANT
25 Director Sponsored Programs ... Ms. Gloria GREENE
88 Director Institute for Science Educ ... Dr. James A. MILLER
08 Director Library ... Dr. David P. MOORE
79 Interim Dean of Liberal Arts ... Dr. Mitch BERBRIER
81 Dean College of Science ... Dr. Sundar CHRISTOPHER
50 Dean College Business Admin ... Dr. Caron ST. JOHN
51 Director of Prof & Cont Studies ... Dr. Karen CLANTON
54 Dean College of Engineering ... Dr. Shankar MAHALINGAM
58 Dean Graduate Studies ... Dr. David BERKOWITZ
66 Dean College of Nursing ... Dr. Marsha ADAMS
88 Dir of Cybersecurity Research ... Mr. Tommy MORRIS
40 Bookstore Manager ... Ms. Amber YOUNG
37 Director Financial Aid ... Mr. Patrick JAMES
38 Dir Counseling & Disability ... Mr. Parrish PAUL
23 Dir Faculty & Staff Clinic ... Ms. Louise O'KEEFE
19 Director Public Safety ... Mr. Michael R. SNELLGROVE
06 Registrar ... Ms. Janet WALLER
07 Director Admissions ... Ms. Peggy MASTERS
29 Director Alumni Relations ... Ms. Rachel V. OSBY
88 Director Advancement Services ... Ms. Marcie T. EPPLING
23 Director Student Health Services ... Ms. Kathleen S. RHODES
88 Director ITSC ... Dr. Sara J. GRAVES
88 Dir Small Business Develop Center ... Mr. Foster PERRY
102 Asst Dir Corp & Foundation Gifts ... Ms. Katie S. THURSTON
96 Director of Procurement ... Mr. Terence HALEY
88 Director Library Computer Systems ... Mr. Jack DROST
90 Manager Academic Technology ... Mr. John THYGERSON
88 Director Research Institute ... Dr. Steven MESSERVY
88 Director CMSA ... Dr. Mikel D. PETTY
88 Director SMAP Center ... Dr. Gary MADDUX
88 Director Rotocraft Center ... Mr. Dave ARTERBURN
27 Chief Public Relations Officer ... Mr. Ray GARNER
88 Director Ctr for Applied Optics ... Dr. Robert LINDQUIST
88 Dir Ctr Mgmt & Econ Research ... Mr. Nic LOYD
88 Director Propulsion Research Center ... Dr. Robert FREDERICK
88 Dir Center Space Plsm & Aeron Res ... Dr. Gary ZANK
88 Director Earth Systems Science Ctr ... Dr. John R. CHRISTY
88 Dir University Ctr & Charger Union ... Mr. William M. HALL
91 Director Enterprise Apps & IAM ... Mr. Malcolm RICE
104 Director Global Studies Program ... Dr. David JOHNSON
92 Dean of the Honors College ... Dr. William WILKERSON

University of Mobile (B)

5735 College Parkway, Mobile AL 36613-2842
County: Mobile FICE Identification: 001029
Unit ID: 101693
Telephone: (251) 675-5990 Carnegie Class: Bac/Diverse
FAX Number: (251) 675-6293 Calendar System: Semester
URL: www.umobile.edu
Established: 1961 Annual Undergrad Tuition & Fees: $19,970
Enrollment: 1,600 Coed
Affiliation or Control: Southern Baptist IRS Status: 501(c)3
Highest Offering: Master's
Program: 2-Year Principally Bachelor's Creditable; Liberal Arts And General; Teacher Preparatory; Professional
Accreditation: SC, ACBSP, ADNUR, CAATE, MUS, NURSE

01 President ... Dr. Mark R. FOLEY
05 Vice Pres for Academic Affairs ... Dr. Audrey C. EUBANKS
10 Vice President for Business Affairs ... Mr. Lindsey BONEY
30 VP Institutional Advancement ... Mr. Brian BOYLE
84 VP Enrollment/Student Life ... Mrs. Kim LEOUSIS
11 VP for Operations ... Mr. Kris NELSON
21 Associate VP for Business Affairs ... Ms. Carol CAMP
84 Assoc VP Enroll/Dir Financial Aid ... Ms. Marie BATSON
88 Assoc VP for Development ... Mr. Bill HART
04 Assistant to the President ... Dr. Fred G. LACKEY
26 Executive Director of Marketing ... Ms. Lesa MOORE
41 Athletic Director ... Mr. Joe NILAND
07 Director of Enrollment Services ... Mrs. Charity WITTNER
08 Director of Library Services ... Mr. Jeffrey D. CALAMETTI
27 Director of Media Relations ... Mrs. Kathy L. DEAN
50 Dean School of Business ... Dr. Jane FINLEY
49 Dean College of Arts & Sciences ... Dr. Lonnie BURNETT
53 Dean School of Education ... Dr. Joyce WOODBURN
66 Dean School of Nursing ... Dr. Jan WOOD
64 Dean School of Music ... Dr. Al MILLER
88 Dean Sch of Worship Leadership ... Dr. Al MILLER
88 Exec Dean Sch of Christian Ministry ... Dr. Joe SAVAGE
73 Dean School of Christian Ministries ... Dr. Doug WILSON
44 Director Annual Giving ... Mrs. Tonya GOLLETTE
102 Dev Officer for Corp/Govt Relations ... Mr. Claude BUMPERS
90 Director Academic Computing Lab ... Mr. Mitch DAVIS
32 Dir of Campus Life/Dean of Student ... Mr. Neal LEDBETTER
15 Director of Human Resources ... Mrs. Diane BLACK
13 Director of Information Technology ... Mr. Buck NORRED
18 Director of Campus Operations ... Mrs. Vicki BURGIN
38 Director Student Retention ... Mrs. Shirley SUTTERFIELD
88 VP for Project Development ... Dr. Roger BRELAND
06 Registrar ... Mr. Stuart MOORE
106 Director Adult/Online Programs ... Mr. Danny CHANCEY
108 Director of Inst Effectiveness ... Mrs. Debra H. CHANCEY
29 Director of Alumni ... Mr. David CAGLE
36 Director Career Services ... Mrs. Brenda DAVIS
88 Director Faculty Support and QEP ... Dr. Pamela B. MILLER

University of Montevallo (C)

Station 6001, Montevallo AL 35115-6001
County: Shelby FICE Identification: 001004
Unit ID: 101709
Telephone: (205) 665-6000 Carnegie Class: Master's M
FAX Number: (205) 665-6003 Calendar System: Semester
URL: www.montevallo.edu
Established: 1896 Annual Undergrad Tuition & Fees (In-State): $11,410
Enrollment: 3,073 Coed
Affiliation or Control: State IRS Status: 501(c)3
Highest Offering: Beyond Master's But Less Than Doctorate
Program: Liberal Arts And General; Teacher Preparatory; Professional
Accreditation: SC, AAFCS, ART, BUS, CACREP, DIETC, DIETD, MUS, SP, SW, TED

01 President ... Dr. John W. STEWART, III
05 Provost and VP Academic Affairs ... Dr. Suzanne OZMENT
32 Dean of Students ... Dr. Tammi DAHLE
30 VP for Enrollment Management ... Dr. Rick BARTH
10 VP Business Affairs ... Ms. DeAnna M. SMITH
18 Director Physical Plant ... Mr. Billy HUGHES
35 Director Student Life ... Ms. Jenny BELL
06 Registrar ... Mr. Daniel STRICKLAND
08 Director Libraries ... Ms. Kathy LOWE
07 Director Admissions ... Mr. Greg EMBRY
13 Chief Information Officer ... Mr. Craig GRAY
37 Dir of Student Financial Services ... Vacant
38 Director Counseling Services ... Mr. Joshua MILLER
19 Chief of Police ... Mr. Chadd ADAMS
39 Dir Housing & Residence Life ... Mr. John DENSON
41 Director Athletics ... Mr. Mark RICHARD
15 Director of HR and Risk Management ... Ms. Barbara FORREST
51 Dir of Regional Inservice Center ... Mr. Dwight JINRIGHT
58 Dir Graduate Admissions & Records ... Mr. Kevin THORNTHWAITE
49 Dean College Arts & Sciences ... Dr. Mary Beth ARMSTRONG
50 Dean College of Business ... Dr. Stephen CRAFT
53 Dean College of Education ... Dr. Anna E. MCEWAN
57 Dean College of Fine Arts ... Dr. Steven PETERS
09 Director of Institutional Research ... Ms. Kris MASCETTI

University of North Alabama (D)

One Harrison Plaza, Florence AL 35632-0001
County: Lauderdale FICE Identification: 001016
Unit ID: 101879
Telephone: (256) 765-4100 Carnegie Class: Master's L
FAX Number: (256) 765-4644 Calendar System: Semester
URL: www.una.edu
Established: 1830 Annual Undergrad Tuition & Fees (In-State): $7,774
Enrollment: 6,841 Coed
Affiliation or Control: State IRS Status: 501(c)3
Highest Offering: Beyond Master's But Less Than Doctorate
Program: Liberal Arts And General; Teacher Preparatory; Professional
Accreditation: SC, ACBSP, ART, CACREP, CIDA, CS, ENGR, JOUR, MUS, NURSE, SW, TED

01 President ... Dr. Kenneth KITTS
05 Vice Pres Acad Affairs & Provost ... Dr. John THORNELL
88 Senior Vice Provost Intl Affairs ... Dr. Chunsheng ZHANG
10 VP Business/Financial Affs ... Mr. Clinton P. CARTER
32 Vice President Student Affairs ... Mr. David P. SHIELDS, JR.
30 Vice President Advancement ... Dr. Daniel L. HENDRICKS
84 Vice Pres Enrollment Management ... Dr. Thomas C. CALHOUN, JR.
44 Assoc VP Advancement Services ... Dr. Judy T. JACKSON
49 Dean College of Arts & Sciences ... Dr. Carmen L. BURKHALTER
50 Dean College of Business ... Dr. Gregory A. CARNES
53 Dean Col Education/Human Sciences ... Dr. Donna P. LEFORT
66 Dean College of Nursing ... Dr. Vicki G. PIERCE
31 Director University Events ... Mr. Bret JENNINGS
41 Director of Athletics ... Mr. Mark LINDER
21 Controller ... Ms. Donna F. TIPPS
39 Director of Housing ... Ms. Audrey MITCHELL
37 Int Director Stdnt Financial Svcs ... Dr. Laura B. BOZOVIC
15 Asst VP for Human Resources ... Ms. Catherine D. WHITE
26 Dir Univ Communications ... Mr. Bryan RACHAL
18 Asst VP for Facilities ... Mr. Michael B. GAUTNEY
19 Chief of University Police ... Mr. Kevin L. GILLLILAN
23 Director University Health Services ... Dr. Kyrel L. BUCHANAN
35 Dir Judicial Affairs/Stdnt Aff Plng ... Dr. Kimberly GREENWAY
07 Director of Admissions ... Ms. Kim MAULDIN
09 Dir Inst Rsrch/Plng & Assessment ... Dr. Andrew L. LUNA
29 Director Alumni Relations ... Ms. Carol S. LYLES
96 Asst VP Business Services ... Ms. Cindy H. CONLON
28 Dir Diversity/Institutional Equity ... Ms. Joan J. WILLIAMS
36 Dir Career Planning & Development ... Ms. Melissa T. MEDLIN
06 Registrar ... Ms. Lisa E. BURTON
38 Director University Advising ... Dr. Amy CREWS
40 Manager University Bookstore ... Mr. Griffin HITE
107 Dir Prof/Interdiscip Studies ... Dr. Craig T. ROBERTSON
08 Dean Library/Educ Tech Svcs ... Dr. Melvin D. DAVIS
13 Chief Info Technology Officer (CIO) ... Mr. Stephen PUTMAN

University of Phoenix Birmingham Campus (E)

100 Corporate Parkway, Suite 250,
Birmingham AL 35242-2982
Telephone: (205) 747-1001 Identification: 770187
Accreditation: &NH, ACBSP

† No longer accepting campus-based students.

University of South Alabama (F)

307 University Boulevard, N, Mobile AL 36688-0002
County: Mobile FICE Identification: 001057
Unit ID: 102094
Telephone: (251) 460-6101 Carnegie Class: RU/H
FAX Number: (251) 461-1537 Calendar System: Semester
URL: www.southalabama.edu
Established: 1963 Annual Undergrad Tuition & Fees (In-State): $8,790
Enrollment: 16,055 Coed
Affiliation or Control: State IRS Status: 501(c)3
Highest Offering: Doctorate
Program: Liberal Arts And General; Teacher Preparatory; Professional
Accreditation: SC, ARCPA, AUD, BUS, BUSA, CACREP, COARC, CS, EMT, ENG, MED, MUS, NURSE, OT, PSPSY, PTA, RAD, RTT, SP, SW, TED

01 President ... Dr. Tony G. WALDROP
03 Executive Vice President ... Dr. John SMITH
05 Provost & Sr VP Academic Affairs ... Dr. G. David JOHNSON
23 Int Vice President Health Sciences ... Dr. Samuel STRADA
10 Int VP Financial Affairs & Admin ... Dr. John SMITH
30 Vice Pres Developmental/Alumni Rels ... Dr. Joseph F. BUSTA
46 VP for Research & Economic Devel ... Dr. Lynne CHRONISTER
43 Sr University Attorney ... Ms. Jean TUCKER
58 Assoc VP Acad Affs/Dean Grad Sch ... Dr. B. Keith HARRISON
84 Dir Enrollment Services ... Mr. Christopher LYNCH
13 Exec Director of Information Tech ... Mr. Chris CANNON
20 Assoc Vice Pres Academic Affairs ... Dr. Charles GUEST
15 Asst Vice President Human Resources . Ms. Pamela HENDERSON
17 Dean College of Medicine ... Dr. Samuel J. STRADA
86 Exec Dir Government Relations ... Mr. William J. FULFORD
32 VP Stdnt Affairs/Dean of Stdnt ... Dr. Michael MITCHELL
88 Dir Student Acad Success/Retention ... Dr. Nicole T. CARR
88 Director of Assessment ... Ms. Cecelia MARTIN
26 Exec Dir Marketing/Communication ... Mr. Michael HASKINS
41 Director of Athletics ... Dr. Joel ERDMANN
07 Director of Admissions ... Ms. Norma J. TANNER
85 Director Intl Student Services ... Ms. Brenda HINSON
07 Director New Student Recruitment ... Mr. Christopher LYNCH
09 Dir Inst Research/Plng & Analysis ... Dr. Gordon E. MILLS, JR.
06 Registrar ... Ms. Kelly OSTERBIND
29 Director Alumni Relations ... Ms. Karen EDWARDS
19 Chief of Police ... Mr. Zeke AULL, JR.
37 Director of Financial Aid ... Ms. Emily JOHNSTON
36 Director Career Services ... Ms. Bevley W. GREEN
12 Director USA Baldwin County ... Ms. Cynthia WILSON
18 Director Facilities Management ... Mr. Randy MOON
38 Dir Student Counseling/Test ... Dr. Robert HANKS
28 Director Multicultural Student Affs ... Dr. Carl G. CUNNINGHAM
96 Purchasing Agent ... Mr. Robert M. BROWN
54 Dean College of Engineering ... Dr. John STEADMAN
51 Int Dean Continuing Educ/Spec Pgms ... Dr. James (Jim) CONNORS
49 Dean of Arts and Sciences ... Dr. Andrzej WIERZBICKI
08 Dean of University Libraries ... Dr. Richard J. WOOD
50 Dean Mitchell College of Business ... Dr. Carl C. MOORE
53 Dean of Education ... Dr. Richard L. HAYES
66 Dean of College of Nursing ... Dr. Debra C. DAVIS
76 Dean of Allied Health Professions ... Dr. Richard TALBOTT
77 Dean Computer & Information Science ... Dr. Alec YASINSAC

The University of West Alabama (G)

205 N Washington Street, Livingston AL 35470-2099
County: Sumter FICE Identification: 001024
Unit ID: 101587
Telephone: (205) 652-3400 Carnegie Class: Master's L

FAX Number: (205) 652-3718 Calendar System: Semester
URL: www.uwa.edu
Established: 1835 Annual Undergrad Tuition & Fees (In-State): $8,326
Enrollment: 3,989 Coed
Affiliation or Control: State IRS Status: 501(c)3
Highest Offering: Beyond Master's But Less Than Doctorate
Program: Liberal Arts And General; Teacher Preparatory; Professional
Accreditation: SC, ACBSP, ADNUR, CAATE, TED

01 President Dr. Ken TUCKER
05 Provost Dr. Tim EDWARDS
10 Vice President Financial Affairs Mr. T. Raiford NOLAND
30 Vice Pres Institutional Advancement Mr. Clemit W. SPRUIELL
32 Vice President for Student Affairs Mr. Thomas D. BUCKALEW
49 Interim Dean of Liberal Arts Dr. Mark DAVIS
50 Interim Dean of Business Dr. Wayne BEDFORD
53 Interim Dean of Teacher Education Dr. B.J KIMBROUGH
81 Dean of Natural Science/Math Dr. John MCCALL
58 Interim Dean of Graduate Studies Dr. B.J KIMBROUGH
51 Dean Continuing Education Dr. Tina N. JONES
106 Dean Online Programs Dr. Jan MILLER
66 Chairperson of Nursing Mrs. Lynn LASHLEY
08 Director of Library Dr. Neil SNIDER
09 Dir Institutional Effectiveness Mrs. Angel JOWERS
41 Athletic Director Mr. Stan WILLIAMSON
35 Director of Student Life & Housing Mr. Luther GREMMELS
06 Registrar Mrs. Susan SPARKMAN
37 Director Student Financial Aid Mr. Don RAINER
13 Director Information Systems Mr. Michael PRATT
18 Director of Physical Plant Mr. Bobbty TRUELOVE
109 Director of Auxiliary Services Mr. Lee WALKER
36 Director Career Services/Placement Ms. Tammy S. WHITE
29 Director Alumni Relations Ms. Danielle BUCKALEW
38 Director Student Success Center Dr. Vicki P. SPRUIELL
86 Director Government Relations Mr. Clemit W. SPRUIELL
07 Dir of Undergraduate Recruiting Mr. Richard HESTER
96 Director of Purchasing Mr. Lawson C. EDMONDS
89 Director Freshmen Studies Dr. James GENTSCH
92 Director Honors Program Dr. Lesa SHAUL
15 Director Personnel Services Mrs. Jessie W. EGBERT
30 Director of Development Mr. Tom TARTT
20 Associate Academic Officer Mrs. Angel JOWERS
26 Chief Public Relations Officer Ms. Betsy COMPTON
19 Director of Security/Safety Mr. Jeff MANUEL
103 Director Workforce Development Mr. Kenneth WALKER
105 Director of Web Services Mrs. Christi GEORGE
101 Secretary Board of Trustees Mrs. Earlene LINDSEY
28 Director of Diversity Dr. Tim EDWARDS
85 Int Director of Foreign Students Ms. Sue Ann BALCH

Wallace State Community College - Hanceville (A)

PO Box 2000, 801 Main Street, NW,
Hanceville AL 35077-2000
County: Cullman FICE Identification: 007871
Unit ID: 101295
Telephone: (256) 352-8000 Carnegie Class: Assoc/Pub-R-M
FAX Number: (256) 352-8228 Calendar System: Semester
URL: www.wallacestate.edu
Established: 1966 Annual Undergrad Tuition & Fees (In-State): $5,184
Enrollment: 5,343 Coed
Affiliation or Control: State IRS Status: 501(c)3
Highest Offering: Associate Degree
Program: Occupational; 2-Year Principally Bachelor's Creditable
Accreditation: SC, ACBSP, ACFEI, ADNUR, CAHIIM, COARC, DA, DH, DMS, EMT, MAC, MLTAD, OTA, PNUR, POLYT, PTAA, RAD

01 President Dr. Vicki HAWSEY KAROLEWICS
03 Executive Vice President Dr. Tomesa SMITH
10 Dean of Finance & Admin Svcs Jason MORGAN
05 College Dean Johnny MCMOY
20 Dean of Applied Technologies Jimmy HODGES
26 Dean of Institutional Outreach Melinda EDWARDS
76 Dean of Health Sciences Lisa GERMAN
84 Asst Dean Enrollment Management Jennifer HILL
109 Auxiliary Director Mark BOLIN
08 Head Librarian Lisa HULLETT
07 Director Admissions & Registrar Vacant
37 Director of Financial Aid Becky GRAVES
56 Extended Day Program Director Wayne MANORD
15 Director of Human Resources Alyce FLANAGAN
30 Director of Advancement Suzanne HARBIN
18 Director of Physical Plant Billy ROSE
26 Director of Communication/Marketing Kristen HOLMES
06 Registrar Jennifer TWITTY

ALASKA

Alaska Bible College (B)

248 East Elmwood Avenue, Palmer AK 99645
County: Matanuska-Susitna FICE Identification: 008843
Unit ID: 102580
Telephone: (907) 745-3201 Carnegie Class: Not Classified
FAX Number: N/A Calendar System: Semester
URL: www.akbible.edu
Established: 1966 Annual Undergrad Tuition & Fees: $9,300
Enrollment: 46 Coed
Affiliation or Control: Independent Non-Profit IRS Status: 501(c)3
Highest Offering: Baccalaureate
Program: Religious Emphasis
Accreditation: BI

01 Interim President Mr. Bob LEE
05 Vice Pres Academic Affairs Mr. John FERCH
32 Vice Pres Student Development Mr. Jeff GAIL
11 Vice Pres Business Admin Mr. Chris GATES
88 Vice Pres of Broadcasting Mr. Scott YAHR
34 Dean of Women Ms. Katie FERCH
06 Registrar Mr. Ben OLSON
08 Library Director Ms. Harley BOWERMAN
07 Director of Admissions Ms. Becky OLSON
37 Director Financial Aid Ms. Sandy ANDERSON
88 Radio Program Director Ms. Michelle EASTTY

Alaska Career College (C)

1415 E. Tudor Road, Anchorage AK 99507-1033
County: Anchorage FICE Identification: 025410
Unit ID: 103501
Telephone: (907) 563-7575 Carnegie Class: Not Classified
FAX Number: (907) 563-8330 Calendar System: Other
URL: www.alaskacareercollege.edu
Established: 1985 Annual Undergrad Tuition & Fees: $14,290
Enrollment: 479 Coed
Affiliation or Control: Proprietary IRS Status: Proprietary
Highest Offering: Associate Degree
Program: Occupational; 2-Year Principally Bachelor's Creditable; Technical Emphasis
Accreditation: ACCSC

01 Director Ms. Linda STURE

Alaska Pacific University (D)

4101 University Drive, Anchorage AK 99508-4672
County: Anchorage FICE Identification: 001061
Unit ID: 102669
Telephone: (907) 561-1266 Carnegie Class: Master's S
FAX Number: (907) 562-4276 Calendar System: Semester
URL: www.alaskapacific.edu
Established: 1957 Annual Undergrad Tuition & Fees: $19,680
Enrollment: 579 Coed
Affiliation or Control: Independent Non-Profit IRS Status: 501(c)3
Highest Offering: Doctorate
Program: Liberal Arts And General; Teacher Preparatory
Accreditation: NW, IACBE, TED

01 President Dr. Don BANTZ
04 Assistant to the President Ms. Debbie ROLL
05 Academic Dean Ms. Tracy STEWART
10 Chief Financial Officer Ms. Deborah JOHNSTON
32 Dean of Students Mr. Ben HAHN
06 Registrar Ms. Michelle WHEELER
07 Asst Director of Admissions Mr. Brian MCDERMOTT
37 Director of Financial Aid Mr. Phong MOUA
18 Director Facilities Management Ms. Kathy MINCKS
13 Director Information Technology Mr. Michael BAKER
30 Chief Development Officer Vacant
42 Chaplain Ms. Karen DAMMAN-MCCRAE
15 Director Human Resources Ms. Kathleen WYRICK
40 Campus Store Manager Ms. Lydia HARVEY
29 Alumni Relations Coord Ms. Heather HANSEN
19 Director Security/Safety Mr. Tyler EGGEN
38 Dir of Career/Counseling & Disabil Vacant
39 Director Student Housing Mr. Ben HAHN

Charter College (E)

2221 E Northern Lights Blvd, #120,
Anchorage AK 99508-4157
County: Anchorage FICE Identification: 025769
Unit ID: 102845
Telephone: (907) 277-1000 Carnegie Class: Bac/Assoc
FAX Number: (907) 274-3342 Calendar System: Quarter
URL: www.chartercollege.edu
Established: 1985 Annual Undergrad Tuition & Fees: $19,532
Enrollment: 3,267 Coed
Affiliation or Control: Proprietary IRS Status: Proprietary
Highest Offering: Master's
Program: Occupational; 2-Year Principally Bachelor's Creditable
Accreditation: ACICS

01 President Ms. Brenda YOUNG
36 Director of Career Services Ms. Wendy NOVAK
07 Director of Admission Ms. Callie EASTMAN
32 Director of Student Success Ms. Kayla TAYLOR

Ilisagvik College (F)

PO Box 749, Barrow AK 99723
County: North Slope Borough FICE Identification: 034613
Unit ID: 434584
Telephone: (907) 852-3333 Carnegie Class: Tribal
FAX Number: (907) 862-2729 Calendar System: Semester
URL: www.ilisagvik.edu
Established: 1996 Annual Undergrad Tuition & Fees: $3,340
Enrollment: 243 Coed
Affiliation or Control: Independent Non-Profit IRS Status: 501(c)3
Highest Offering: Associate Degree
Program: Occupational; 2-Year Principally Bachelor's Creditable
Accreditation: NW

01 President Ms. Pearl K. BROWER
06 Registrar Ms. Amm CAHOON
05 Chief Academic Officer Ms. Birgit MEANY
15 Director Human Resources Mrs. Linda STANFORD
18 Chief Facilities/Physical Plant Mr. Tom CARAWAY
26 Chief Public Relations Officer Mrs. Sarah MARTINSEN
32 Dean of Students Mr. Joshua STEIN
37 Director Student Financial Aid Mr. Fred MILLER

*University of Alaska System (G)

910 Yukon Drive, Suite 202, Fairbanks AK 99775-5000
County: Fairbanks FICE Identification: 008005
Unit ID: 103529
Telephone: (907) 450-8000 Carnegie Class: N/A
FAX Number: (907) 450-8012
URL: www.alaska.edu

01 President Mr. Patrick K. GAMBLE
26 Vice President for Univ Relations Ms. Carla BEAM
05 VP for Academic Affairs & Research Dr. Daniel WHITE
10 Vice Pres for Finance & Admin/CFO Dr. Ashok ROY
102 VP Univ Rels/Pres UA Foundation Ms. Carla BEAM
46 Chief Strategy/Planning/Budget Ofcr Ms. Michelle RIZK
09 AVP Institutional Rsrch & Analysis Ms. Gwendolyn GRUENIG
84 Assoc VC Student/Enrollment Svcs Mr. Saichi OBA
43 General Counsel Mr. Michael HOSTINA
15 Chief HR Officer Mr. Erik SEASTEDT
13 Chief Information Technology Ofcr Mr. Karl KOWALSKI
06 Registrar & Director of Admissions Ms. Libby EDDY
27 Director of Public Affairs Vacant
16 Director Labor & Employee Relations Ms. Rhonda OOMS
88 Chief Risk Officer Ms. Nancy SPINK

*University of Alaska Anchorage (H)

3211 Providence Drive, Anchorage AK 99508-8000
County: Anchorage FICE Identification: 011462
Unit ID: 102553
Telephone: (907) 786-1800 Carnegie Class: Master's L
FAX Number: (907) 786-4888 Calendar System: Semester
URL: www.uaa.alaska.edu
Established: 1954 Annual Undergrad Tuition & Fees (In-State): $5,545
Enrollment: 18,649 Coed
Affiliation or Control: State IRS Status: 501(c)3
Highest Offering: Doctorate
Program: Occupational; 2-Year Principally Bachelor's Creditable; Liberal Arts And General; Teacher Preparatory; Professional
Accreditation: NW, ACFEI, ADNUR, ART, BUS, CLPSY, CONST, CS, CSHSE, DA, DH, DIETD, DIETI, EMT, ENG, ENGR, #JOUR, MAC, MT, MUS, NUR, PH, @PTAA, SW, TED

02 Chancellor Gen. Tom CASE
05 Provost & Exec VC Academic Affairs Dr. Sam GINGERICH
11 Vice Chancellor Administrative Svcs Dr. William SPINDLE
09 Sr Vice Provost Inst Effectiveness Ms. Renee M. CARTER-CHAPMAN
84 Assoc Vice Chanc Enrollment Svcs Mr. Eric R. PEDERSEN
30 Vice Chancellor Univ Advancement Ms. Megan OLSON
32 Vice Chancellor Student Affairs Dr. Bruce SCHULTZ
26 Asst Vice Chanc Univ Relations Ms. Kristin DESMITH
91 Assoc Vice Chanc Information Tech Mr. Pat SHIER
09 Assoc Vice Provost Inst Research Dr. Erin HOLMES
18 Assoc Vice Chanc Facilities Mr. Christopher TURLETES
96 Assoc Vice Chanc Financial Services Ms. Sandi CULVER
29 Asst Vice Chanc Alumni Relations Ms. Rachel MORSE
88 AVC Student Access/Advis/Transition Dr. Lacy KARPILO
88 Int Exec Dir Acad/Multicul Success Ms. Theresa LYONS
35 Dean of Students Dr. Dewain LEE
37 Dir Student Financial Assistance Ms. Sonya STEIN
85 Director Multicultural Center Mr. Andre THORN
35 Director Student Life & Leadership Ms. Annie ROUTE
07 Interim Director of Admissions Ms. Cathy EWING
28 Dir Campus Diversity & Compliance Ms. Marva WATSON
41 Director Athletics Mr. Keith HACKETT
06 University Registrar Ms. Lora VOLDEN
36 Director Career Services Center Ms. Diane KOZAK
15 Director Human Resources Mr. Ron KAMAHELE
08 Dean Consortium Library Mr. Stephen J. ROLLINS
63 Director Biomedical Program Dr. Jane SHELBY
88 Director Native Student Services Mr. William TEMPLETON
38 Director Student Health/Counseling Ms. Georgia DEKEYSER
50 Dean Col Business/Public Policy Dr. Rashmi PRASAD
51 Dean Community/Tech College Dr. Bonnie K. NYGARD
76 Dean College of Health Mr. William HOGAN
54 Interim Dean College of Engineering Dr. T. Bart QUIMBY
49 Dean College Arts & Sciences Dr. John STALVEY
53 Dean College of Education Dr. Paul DEPUTY
92 Interim Dean Honors College Dr. John MOURACADE
27 Senior Public Relations Specialist Ms. Jessica HAMLIN
106 Director Academic Innov E-learning Dr. Dave DANNENBERG
20 Vice Provost Undergrad Acad Affairs Dr. Susan KALINA
19 Chief University Police Mr. Rick SHELL
58 Vice Prov Research & Grad School Dr. Helena WISNIEWSKI
39 Director Univ Housing Dining & Conf Mr. David WEAVER
44 Annual Giving Director Mr. Jim SMITH

*University of Alaska Fairbanks (I)

505 South Chandlar Drive, Fairbanks AK 99775
County: Fairbanks North Star Borough FICE Identification: 001063
Unit ID: 102614
Telephone: (907) 474-7500 Carnegie Class: RU/H
FAX Number: (907) 474-5379 Calendar System: Semester

URL: www.uaf.edu
Established: 1917 Annual Undergrad Tuition & Fees (In-State): $6,800
Enrollment: 8,601 Coed
Affiliation or Control: State IRS Status: 501(c)3
Highest Offering: Doctorate
Program: Occupational; 2-Year Principally Bachelor's Creditable; Liberal Arts And General; Teacher Preparatory; Professional
Accreditation: NW, BUS, BUSA, CLPSY, CS, DH, EMT, ENG, JOUR, MAC, MUS, SW, TED

02 Interim Chancellor .... Mr. Michael K. POWERS
05 Provost .... Dr. Susan M. HENRICHS
11 Vice Chancellor Administrative Svcs .... Ms. Kari BURRELL
18 Assoc Vice Chancellor Facilities .... Mr. Scott BELL
32 VC University & Student Advancement .... Dr. Mike SFRAGA
45 Interim Vice Chancellor Research .... Mr. Larry HINZMAN
10 Assoc VC for Financial Services .... Mr. Raaj KURAPATI
84 Assoc VC for Enrollment Mgmt .... Mr. Eric PEDERSEN
30 Director of Development .... Ms. Emily DRYGAS
58 Dean Graduate School .... Dr. John EICHELBERGER
81 Dean Col of Natural Science/Math .... Dr. Paul LAYER
35 Assoc Vice Chanc for Student Life .... Vacant
31 VC Rural/Cmty & Native Educ .... Mr. Evon PETER
12 Dean UAF Comm & Tech College .... Ms. Michele STALDER
47 Interim Dean/Director SNRAS/AFES .... Dr. Stephen SPARROW
88 Dean Sch Fisheries & Ocean Sciences .... Ms. Joan BRADDOCK
50 Dean School of Management .... Dr. Mark HERRMANN
54 Dean Col of Engineering & Mines .... Dr. Doug GOERING
88 Dir Intl Arctic Research Center .... Dr. Larry HINZMAN
88 Dir Institute of Arctic Biology .... Dr. Brian M. BARNES
54 Int Dir Inst Northern Engineering .... Dr. William SCHNABEL
15 Director Human Resources .... Ms. Anita HARTMANN
19 Chief of Police .... Mr. Keith MALLARD
37 Director Financial Aid .... Ms. Deanna L. DIERINGER
41 Director Athletics .... Dr. Gary GRAY
39 Director Residence Life .... Ms. Laura L. MCCOLLOUGH
56 Vice Provost for Extension/Outreach .... Mr. Fred SCHLUTT
109 Director of Aux/Recharge/Cntrct Ops .... Vacant
85 Director International Programs .... Ms. Donna ANGER
88 Fire Chief .... Mr. Doug SCHRAGE
88 Dir Institute of Marine Science .... Dr. Terry WHITLEDGE
49 Dean College of Liberal Arts .... Mr. Todd SHERMAN
53 Dean School of Education .... Dr. Allan MOROTTI
12 Director Bristol Bay Campus .... Dr. Deborah MCLEAN
12 Director Chukchi Campus .... Mr. Pete PINNEY
12 Director Interior Aleutians Campus .... Ms. Teisha SIMMONS
12 Director Kuskokwim Campus .... Ms. Mary C. PETE
12 Director Northwest Campus .... Mr. Robert METCALF
28 Dir Diversity & Equal Opportunity .... Ms. Mae MARSH
23 Director Health and Counseling .... Dr. B.J ALDRICH
29 Exec Director Alumni Association .... Ms. Kate RIPLEY
06 Registrar .... Ms. Libby EDDY
88 Director Geophysical Institute .... Mr. Robert MCCOY
21 Director Business Operations .... Ms. Amanda WALL
36 Director Career Services .... Ms. Patti PICHA
38 Director Academic Advising Center .... Ms. Linda M. HAPSMITH
92 Director Honors Program .... Ms. Marsha SOUSA
94 Coordinator Women's Studies .... Dr. Sine ANAHITA
09 Dir Planning/Analysis/Inst Research .... Mr. Ian OLSON
26 Director Marketing/Communications .... Ms. Michelle RENFREW
08 Interim Dean of Libraries .... Ms. Suzan HAHN
88 Interim Dir UA Museum of the North .... Dr. Aldona JONAITIS
13 Chief Info Technology Officer .... Mr. Karl KOWALSKI
22 Director for Disability Services .... Ms. Mary MATTHEWS
96 Dir of Procurement & Contract Svcs .... Mr. John HEBARD
88 Director Wood Center Student Union .... Vacant
46 AVC Research .... Dr. John BLAKE
46 AVC Research .... Dr. Nettie LABELLE-HAMER
44 AVC for Univ & Student Advancement .... Ms. Kris RACINA
97 Vice Provost/Dean Gen Studies .... Dr. Alex FITTS

*University of Alaska Southeast (A)

11120 Glacier Highway, Juneau AK 99801-8681
County: Juneau FICE Identification: 001065
Unit ID: 102632
Telephone: (907) 796-6000 Carnegie Class: Master's S
FAX Number: N/A Calendar System: Semester
URL: www.uas.alaska.edu
Established: 1956 Annual Undergrad Tuition & Fees (In-State): $6,132
Enrollment: 3,055 Coed
Affiliation or Control: State IRS Status: 501(c)3
Highest Offering: Master's
Program: Occupational; 2-Year Principally Bachelor's Creditable; Liberal Arts And General; Teacher Preparatory; Professional
Accreditation: NW, CAHIIM, TED

02 Chancellor .... Dr. Richard CAULFIELD
05 Provost & Executive Dean SCE .... Dr. Richard CAULFIELD
75 Associate Dean Sch of Career Educ .... Mr. Pete TRAXLER
46 Vice Provost for Research .... Dr. Karen SCHMITT
11 Vice Chanc & Director Admin Svcs .... Mr. Michael CIRI
12 Sitka Campus Director .... Dr. Chris GILMER
12 Ketchikan Campus Director .... Dr. Priscilla SCHULTE
49 Dean of Arts & Sciences .... Dr. Karen SCHMITT
88 Dean of School of Management .... Ms. Vickie WILLIAMS
53 Dean Education & Graduate Studies .... Dr. Deborah LO
37 Acting Financial Aid Director .... Mr. Eric RAMAEKERS
26 Dir of Marketing/Public Relations .... Ms. Katie BAUSLER
06 Registrar .... Ms. Barbara HEGEL
84 VC Enrollment Mgmt & Stdnt Affs .... Mr. Joseph NELSON
09 Institutional Effectiveness Manager .... Mr. Brad EWING
10 Director Business Services .... Mr. Tom DIENST
15 Director Personnel Services .... Vacant
18 Director Facilities Services .... Mr. Keith GERKEN
08 Director Library Services .... Ms. Elise TOMLINSON
13 Director Information/Technology .... Mr. Michael CIRI
30 Dir Development/Alumni Relations .... Ms. Lynne JOHNSON
29 Alumni Relations/Annual Fund Mgr .... Ms. Heather MITCHELL
21 Chief Budget Officer .... Ms. Margaret REA
88 Director Learning Center .... Ms. Hildegard SELLNER
32 Director Stdnt Resource Services .... Ms. Lori KLEIN
39 Director of Campus Life .... Mr. Eric SCOTT
88 Director of PITAAS .... Ms. Ronalda CADIENTE-BROWN
75 Associate Dean Sch of Career Educ .... Dr. Jill DUMESNIL
88 Director of AK Coastal Rainforest .... Ms. Alison BIDLACK

*Prince William Sound Community College (B)

PO Box 97, Valdez AK 99686-0097
County: Valdez-Cordova-Glennallen Identification: 666659
Unit ID: 103361
Telephone: (907) 834-1600 Carnegie Class: Assoc/Pub-R-M
FAX Number: (907) 834-1611 Calendar System: Semester
URL: www.pwscc.edu
Established: 1978 Annual Undergrad Tuition & Fees (In-State): $4,745
Enrollment: 950 Coed
Affiliation or Control: State IRS Status: 501(c)3
Highest Offering: Associate Degree
Program: Occupational; 2-Year Principally Bachelor's Creditable; Fine Arts Emphasis
Accreditation: NW

02 President .... Mr. J. Daniel O'CONNOR
05 Director of Academic Affairs .... Ms. Denise RUNGE
10 Director Administrative Services .... Mr. Steve SHIELL
07 Int Asst Director Student Services .... Ms. Ana HINKLE
30 Inst Development/Advancement Ofcr .... Mr. Ryan BELNAP
26 Chief Public Relations Officer .... Ms. Wendy GOLDSTEIN
38 Director Student Counseling .... Vacant
88 Director of Training .... Mr. BJ WILLIAMS
06 Records/Registration Coordinator .... Ms. Shannon FOSTER

ARIZONA

Acacia University (C)

7665 South Research Drive, Tempe AZ 85284-1812
County: Maricopa Identification: 667017
Telephone: (480) 428-6034 Carnegie Class: Not Classified
FAX Number: (480) 428-6033 Calendar System: Other
URL: www.acacia.edu
Established: 2003 Annual Undergrad Tuition & Fees: $8,100
Enrollment: 200 Coed
Affiliation or Control: Proprietary IRS Status: Proprietary
Highest Offering: Master's
Program: Occupational; Teacher Preparatory; Professional; Technical Emphasis
Accreditation: DEAC

01 President .... Mr. Tim MOMAN
05 Provost/Executive Vice President .... Dr. Marilynn D. HENLEY
27 CIO .... Mr. Michael TURICO

American Indian College of the Assemblies of God (D)

10020 N 15th Avenue, Phoenix AZ 85021-2199
County: Maricopa FICE Identification: 021999
Unit ID: 103787
Telephone: (602) 944-3335 Carnegie Class: Bac/Diverse
FAX Number: (602) 943-8299 Calendar System: Semester
URL: www.aicag.edu
Established: 1957 Annual Undergrad Tuition & Fees: $12,000
Enrollment: 91 Coed
Affiliation or Control: Assemblies Of God Church IRS Status: 501(c)3
Highest Offering: Baccalaureate
Program: 2-Year Principally Bachelor's Creditable; Liberal Arts And General; Teacher Preparatory; Professional; Religious Emphasis
Accreditation: #NH

01 President & CFO .... Dr. David J. MOORE
03 Executive Vice Pres & Campus Pastor .... Rev. Jim H. LOPEZ
05 Vice President for Academic Affairs .... Dr. Joseph J. SAGGIO
10 Vice Pres Financial Services .... Mr. Steve CHANEY
37 VP Financial Aid/Enroll Mgmt .... Ms. Andrea AVALOS
09 Director of Institutional Research .... Dr. Lori P. KUBA
84 Director Enrollment Management .... Ms. Sandra M. GONZALES
38 Director of Student Counseling .... Rev. Blair SCHLEPP
06 Registrar .... Ms. Erica ZAMARANO
08 Library Director .... Rev. Debra RAMM
18 Chief Facilities Engineer .... Mr. Steve MORGAN
50 Business Chairperson .... Dr. Barry SHENNUM
73 Christian Ministry Chairperson .... Rev. Ron CLOUSE
53 Education Chairperson .... Dr. Lori P. KUBA
97 General Education Chairperson .... Ms. Karen BRAMBLE

Argosy University, Phoenix (E)

2233 W Dunlap Avenue, Phoenix AZ 85021
Telephone: (602) 216-2600 Identification: 666790
Accreditation: &WC, ACBSP, CLPSY

† Regional accreditation is carried under the parent institution in Orange, CA.

Arizona Christian University (F)

2625 E Cactus Road, Phoenix AZ 85032-7042
County: Maricopa FICE Identification: 007113
Unit ID: 105899
Telephone: (602) 489-5300 Carnegie Class: Bac/Diverse
FAX Number: (602) 404-2159 Calendar System: Semester
URL: www.arizonachristian.edu
Established: 1960 Annual Undergrad Tuition & Fees: $23,110
Enrollment: 737 Coed
Affiliation or Control: Independent Non-Profit IRS Status: 501(c)3
Highest Offering: Baccalaureate
Program: 2-Year Principally Bachelor's Creditable; Liberal Arts And General; Teacher Preparatory; Professional
Accreditation: NH

01 President .... Mr. Len MUNSIL
03 Executive Vice President/Provost .... Dr. Paul KREMER
10 Chief Financial Officer .... Vacant
84 VP for Enrollment .... Mr. Pete HAMSTRA
107 Director Profession/Adult Studies .... Dr. James ELLIS
21 Controller .... Mr. Rick SHARPE
09 Director of Institutional Research .... Ms. Theresa MILTON
06 Registrar & Asst Dir of Enroll Mgmt .... Mr. Lambert CRUZ
37 Director Financial Aid .... Mr. Steven YOUNG
13 Director of Information Technology .... Mr. Robert TERRY
08 Librarian .... Mr. Robert OLIVERIO
19 Director of Campus Security .... Mr. John HOEBEE
18 Director of Facilities .... Mr. David HOOK
41 Athletic Director .... Mr. Jeff RUTTER
39 Residence Director .... Ms. Wendy CLYDE
15 Human Resources Coordinator .... Ms. Nancy STOCKING
04 Executive Assistant to President .... Mrs. Barbara SMALL

Arizona College (G)

4425 W Olive Avenue, Suite 300,
Glendale AZ 85302-3851
County: Maricopa FICE Identification: 031150
Unit ID: 421708
Telephone: (602) 222-9300 Carnegie Class: Assoc/PrivFP
FAX Number: (602) 200-8726 Calendar System: Other
URL: www.arizonacollege.edu
Established: 1991 Annual Undergrad Tuition & Fees: $15,223
Enrollment: 630 Coed
Affiliation or Control: Proprietary IRS Status: Proprietary
Highest Offering: Associate Degree
Program: 2-Year Principally Bachelor's Creditable; Nursing Emphasis
Accreditation: ABHES

01 President .... Mr. Nick MANSOUR
10 Chief Financial Officer .... Mr. Matthew CALHOUN

Arizona College-Mesa (H)

163 N. Dobson Road, Mesa AZ 85201
Telephone: (480) 265-3600 Identification: 770514
Accreditation: ABHES

† Branch campus of Arizona College, Glendale, AZ.

Arizona School of Acupuncture and Oriental Medicine (I)

2856 E Fort Lowell Rd., Tucson AZ 85716
County: Pima FICE Identification: 036955
Unit ID: 446039
Telephone: (520) 795-0787 Carnegie Class: Spec/Health
FAX Number: (877) 222-4606 Calendar System: Quarter
URL: www.asaom.edu
Established: 1996 Annual Graduate Tuition & Fees: $17,827
Enrollment: 44 Coed
Affiliation or Control: Proprietary IRS Status: Proprietary
Highest Offering: Master's; No Undergraduates
Program: Professional
Accreditation: #ACUP

01 CEO/Owner .... Mr. Jonathan HU
05 Academic Dean .... Dr. Jane MEYERS
37 Financial Aid Advisor .... Ms. Susan WAGNER
07 Admissions Director .... Mr. Tim DUNN

Arizona State University (J)

300 E. University Drive, Tempe AZ 85281
County: Maricopa FICE Identification: 001081
Unit ID: 104151
Telephone: (855) 278-5080 Carnegie Class: RU/VH
FAX Number: N/A Calendar System: Semester
URL: www.asu.edu
Established: 1885 Annual Undergrad Tuition & Fees (In-State): $10,478
Enrollment: 83,301 Coed
Affiliation or Control: State IRS Status: 501(c)3
Highest Offering: Doctorate
Program: Liberal Arts And General; Professional
Accreditation: NH, AAB, ART, AUD, BUS, BUSA, CACREP, CIDA, CLPSY, CONST, COPSY, CS, DIETD, DIETI, ENG, ENGT, IPSY, JOUR, LAW, LSAR, MT, MUS, NRPA, NURSE, PCSAS, PLNG, SCPSY, SP, SPAA, SW

01 President .... Dr. Michael M. CROW

05 Interim University Provost .... Dr. Mark S. SEARLE
10 Exec Vice President/Treasurer & CFO .... Dr. Morgan R. OLSEN
03 Sr Vice Pres/Sec of the University ... Dr. Christine K. WILKINSON
102 CEO ASU Foundation .... Mr. Rick SHANGRAW
43 Sr Vice President & General Counsel ...... Mr. José A. CÁRDENAS
32 Sr VP Educ Outreach & Student Svcs .... Dr. James A. RUND
41 Vice President for Athletics .... Mr. Ray ANDERSON
13 Chief Information Officer .... Mr. Gordon D. WISHON
88 Sr VP Ofc of Knowledge Ent Dev .... Dr. Sethuraman PANCHANATHEN
15 VP & Chief Human Resources Ofc .... Mr. Kevin J. SALCIDO
100 Sr VP Univ Affairs/Chief of Staff .... Mr. Jim O'BRIEN
106 Exec Vice Provost/Dean EdPlus .... Dr. Philip R. REGIER
49 VP/Dean of Liberal Arts & Sciences .... Dr. Patrick KENNEY
84 Vice Provost Enrollment Managment .... Mr. Kent HOPKINS
50 Dean WP Carey School of Business .... Dr. Amy HILLMAN
54 Int Dean Ira A Fulton Sch Engr .... Dr. Kyle SQUIRES
53 Dean Mary Lou Fulton Teachers Col .... Dr. Mari E. KOERNER
58 Vice Provost Graduate Education .... Dr. Andrew WEBBER
92 Dean of Barrett Honors College .... Dr. Mark JACOBS
12 Dean New College of Int Arts & Sci .... Dr. Marlene TROMP
57 Dean Herberger Inst for Design/Arts .... Dr. Steven J. TEPPER
60 Dean Cronkite Sch Journal/Mass Comm .... Mr. Christopher CALLAHAN
61 Dean College of Law .... Mr. Douglas SYLVESTER
66 Dean College of Nursing & Health In .... Dr. Teri BRITT PIPE
47 Dean School of Sustainability .... Dr. Christopher G. BOONE
72 Vice Pres/Dean Entrepreneurship .... Dr. Mitzi M. MONTOYA
20 Vice Provost Undergrad Education .... Dr. Frederick C. COREY
76 Exec VP/Dean Health Solutions .... Dr. Keith D. LINDOR
88 Dean College of Public Svc & Comm .... Mr. Jonathan KOPPELL
07 Exec Director of Admissions .... Vacant
08 University Librarian .... Dr. James O'DONNELL
107 CEO/DirGen Thunderbird Sch Glbl Mgt .... Dr. Allen MORRISON
97 Dean Col Letters & Sci/Univ College .... Mr. Duane ROEN

Arizona Summit Law School (A)

One North Central 14th Floor, Phoenix AZ 85004
County: Maricopa — FICE Identification: 041314
Unit ID: 450942
Telephone: (602) 682-6800 — Carnegie Class: Spec/Law
FAX Number: (602) 682-6999 — Calendar System: Semester
URL: www.azsummitlaw.edu
Established: 2005 — Annual Graduate Tuition & Fees: $42,759
Enrollment: 752 — Coed
Affiliation or Control: Proprietary — IRS Status: Proprietary
Highest Offering: First Professional Degree; No Undergraduates
Program: Professional
Accreditation: LAW

01 Dean .... Ms. Shirley L. MAYS
05 Assoc Dean of Academic Affairs .... Ms. Penny L. WILLRICH
10 Senior Director Finance/Fin Aid .... Ms. Gail SAUERS
06 Dir Acad Svcs & Registration .... Mr. Tim DOWNING
07 Director of Admissions .... Ms. Maria HINDERLEIDER

Arizona Western College (B)

2020 Avenue 8E, Yuma AZ 85365
County: Yuma — FICE Identification: 001071
Unit ID: 104160
Telephone: (928) 317-6000 — Carnegie Class: Assoc/Pub-R-L
FAX Number: (928) 344-7730 — Calendar System: Semester
URL: www.azwestern.edu
Established: 1963 — Annual Undergrad Tuition & Fees (In-District): $2,290
Enrollment: 8,574 — Coed
Affiliation or Control: State/Local — IRS Status: Exempt
Highest Offering: Associate Degree
Program: Occupational; 2-Year Principally Bachelor's Creditable
Accreditation: NH, ADNUR, RAD

01 President .... Dr. Glenn MAYLE
10 Vice Pres Finance/Administration .... Mrs. Carole T. COLEMAN
26 Dean Public Relations & Marketing .... Mrs. Lori STOFFT
09 Dean Instnl Effect/Rsrch/Grants .... Dr. Mary SCHAAL
05 Vice President Learning Services ...... Dr. Linda ELLIOTT-NELSON
51 Assoc Dean of Continuing Educ .... Mrs. Maria E. AGUIRRE
07 Vice President for Student Services .... Mr. Bryan E. DOAK
75 Dean of Career & Technical Educ .... Mr. Daniel BARAJAS
30 Director Institutional Advancement .... Mrs. Renee L. SMITH
06 Interim Dir of Admissions/Registrar .... Mrs. Nicole D. HARRAL
21 Dir Financial Services/Controller .... Mrs. Diana G. DOUCETTE
15 Chief Human Resources Officer .... Dr. Ruth WHISLER
96 Director of Purchasing & Aux Svcs .... Ms. Margaret HAYES
18 Director of District Operations .... Mr. Steve ECKERT
13 Interim Dir Computer Info Services .... Mr. Chad COLEMAN
14 Dir Tech & Network Services .... Ms. Brenda WARNOCK
08 Director of Library Services .... Ms. Angie CREEL
41 Director of Athletics .... Mr. Jerry SMITH
19 Chief of Police .... Mr. John EDMUNDSON
32 Dean for Campus Life .... Ms. Mary Kay HARTON
12 Associate Dean La Paz County Svcs .... Ms. Kathy O'CAMPO
12 Assoc Dean for South Yuma County .... Mr. Everardo MARTINEZ
37 Director of Financial Aid .... Ms. Lisa SEALE
85 Director of International Program .... Mr. Ken KUNTZELMAN
106 Associate Dean for Distance Educ .... Mrs. Jana MOORE
88 Director of Testing Services .... Mrs. Leticia MARTINEZ
105 Webmaster II .... Mr. Damien BATES
04 Executive Asst to President & Board .... Ms. Rachel CALDWELL
36 Director Career/Advisement Services ... Mr. James R. HUTCHISON

The Art Institute of Phoenix (C)

2233 W Dunlap Avenue, Phoenix AZ 85021-2859
County: Maricopa — FICE Identification: 040513
Unit ID: 428444
Telephone: (602) 331-7500 — Carnegie Class: Spec/Arts
FAX Number: (602) 331-5301 — Calendar System: Quarter
URL: www.artinstitutes.edu/phoenix
Established: 1995 — Annual Undergrad Tuition & Fees: $17,416
Enrollment: 1,009 — Coed
Affiliation or Control: Proprietary — IRS Status: Proprietary
Highest Offering: Baccalaureate
Program: 2-Year Principally Bachelor's Creditable; Professional; Fine Arts Emphasis
Accreditation: ACICS, ACFEI, CIDA

01 President .... Mr. Chad WILLIAMS
05 Dean of Academic Affairs .... Mr. Gil MEJIA
07 Senior Director of Admissions .... Ms. Bree FULP
32 Dean of Student Affairs .... Ms. Tanisha FRASIER
36 Director of Career Services .... Ms. Jennifer BOHNSACK
15 Human Resources Generalist .... Mr. Daniel ALLEN
13 Technology Support Supervisor .... Mr. Nate YOUNG
37 Director of Student Financial Svcs .... Ms. Abigail GARCIA
06 Registrar .... Mr. Joseph SALINAS

The Art Institute of Tucson (D)

5099 East Grant Road, Suite 100, Tucson AZ 85712-2733
Telephone: (520) 318-2700 — FICE Identification: 037405
Accreditation: ACICS

† Branch campus of The Art Institute of Phoenix, Phoenix, AZ.

Aventis College (E)

1414 W. Broadway Road, Suite 117, Tempe AZ 85282
County: Maricopa — Identification: 667225
Telephone: (602) 492-9223 — Carnegie Class: Not Classified
FAX Number: (480) 621-8857 — Calendar System: Semester
URL: aventis.edu
Established: 2011 — Annual Undergrad Tuition & Fees: N/A
Enrollment: N/A — Coed
Affiliation or Control: Proprietary — IRS Status: Proprietary
Highest Offering: Associate Degree
Program: Occupational
Accreditation: COE

01 Director .... Mr. Dennis WILLIS

Benedictine University at Mesa (F)

51 E Main Street, Suite 105, Mesa AZ 85201
Telephone: (602) 888-5000 — Identification: 770068
Accreditation: &NH

† Branch campus of Benedictine University, Lisle, IL.

Brighton College (G)

8777 E. Via de Ventura, Scottsdale AZ 85258
County: Maricopa — Identification: 666710
Telephone: (800) 231-3803 — Carnegie Class: Not Classified
FAX Number: (602) 212-0502 — Calendar System: Other
URL: www.brightoncollege.edu
Established: 1961 — Annual Undergrad Tuition & Fees: $2,000
Enrollment: 530 — Coed
Affiliation or Control: Proprietary — IRS Status: Proprietary
Highest Offering: Associate Degree
Program: Occupational; 2-Year Principally Bachelor's Creditable; Technical Emphasis
Accreditation: DEAC

01 Vice President .... Matthew TIDWELL
26 Vice President Marketing Operations .... Chris CARAWAY
84 Vice Pres Enrollment Management .... Robert BLAKELY
10 Dir of Financial Operations .... Patricia MCCOY
32 Director of Student Management .... Kayla HOBBIEBRUNKEN

Brookline College (H)

2445 West Dunlap Avenue, Suite 100, Phoenix AZ 85021
County: Maricopa — FICE Identification: 022188
Unit ID: 104090
Telephone: (602) 242-6265 — Carnegie Class: Bac/Assoc
FAX Number: (602) 973-2572 — Calendar System: Other
URL: www.brooklinecollege.edu
Established: 1979 — Annual Undergrad Tuition & Fees: $21,000
Enrollment: 1,468 — Coed
Affiliation or Control: Proprietary — IRS Status: Proprietary
Highest Offering: Baccalaureate
Program: Occupational
Accreditation: ACICS, MLTAD, NUR, NURSE, #PTAA

01 Campus Director .... Ms. Valentina CREWSE

Brookline College (I)

1140 South Priest Drive, Tempe AZ 85281
Telephone: (480) 545-8755 — Identification: 666403
Accreditation: ACICS, SURTEC

† Branch campus of Brookline College, Phoenix, AZ.

Brookline College (J)

5441 E 22nd Street, Suite 125, Tucson AZ 85711-5444
Telephone: (520) 748-9799 — Identification: 666402
Accreditation: ACICS

† Branch campus of Brookline College, Phoeniz, AZ.

Brown Mackie College-Phoenix (K)

13430 North Black Canyon Highway, Phoenix AZ 85029
Telephone: (602) 337-3044 — Identification: 666782
Accreditation: ACICS, OTA, SURTEC

† Branch campus of Brown Mackie College-Tucson, Tucson, AZ.

Brown Mackie College-Tucson (L)

4585 E Speedway Boulevard, Tucson AZ 85712-5300
Telephone: (520) 319-3300 — FICE Identification: 009451
Accreditation: ACICS, OTA, SURTEC

† Branch campus of The Art Institute of Phoenix, Phoenix, AZ.

Bryan University (M)

350 West Washington Street, Ste 100, Tempe AZ 85281
Telephone: (602) 384-2555 — Identification: 770627
Accreditation: ACICS

† Branch campus of Bryan University, Springfield, MO.

Carrington College - Mesa (N)

1001 W Southern Avenue, Suite 130, Mesa AZ 85210
Telephone: (480) 212-1600 — FICE Identification: 023352
Accreditation: &WJ, DH, MAAB, PTAA

† Regional accreditation is carried under the parent institution in Sacramento, CA.

Carrington College - Phoenix (O)

8503 N 27th Avenue, Phoenix AZ 85051-4096
Telephone: (602) 393-5900 — FICE Identification: 021006
Accreditation: &WJ, ADNUR, MAAB

† Regional accreditation is carried under the parent institution in Sacramento, CA.

Carrington College - Tucson (P)

201 N. Bonita Ave., Ste. 101, Tucson AZ 85745
Telephone: (520) 888-5885 — FICE Identification: 030898
Accreditation: &WJ, MAAB

† Regional accreditation is carried under the parent institution in Sacramento, CA.

Carrington College - Westside (Q)

2701 W Bethany Home Road, Phoenix AZ 85017-1705
Telephone: (602) 433-1333 — Identification: 666248
Accreditation: &WJ, COARC, #RAD

† Regional accreditation is carried under the parent institution in Sacramento, CA.

Central Arizona College (R)

8470 N Overfield Road, Coolidge AZ 85128-9779
County: Pinal — FICE Identification: 007283
Unit ID: 104346
Telephone: (520) 494-5444 — Carnegie Class: Assoc/Pub-S-MC
FAX Number: (520) 494-5008 — Calendar System: Semester
URL: www.centralaz.edu
Established: 1962 — Annual Undergrad Tuition & Fees (In-District): $2,550
Enrollment: 5,937 — Coed
Affiliation or Control: Local — IRS Status: 501(c)3
Highest Offering: Associate Degree
Program: Occupational; 2-Year Principally Bachelor's Creditable
Accreditation: NH, ADNUR, CAHIIM, DIETT, EMT, IFSAC, MAC, RAD

01 President .... Dr. Doris HELMICH
05 VP College Affairs .... Dr. James MOORE
20 VP Academic Affairs .... Dr. Mary K. GILLILAND
76 Academic Dean .... Mr. Julian EASTER
107 Academic Dean .... Dr. Janice PRATT
49 Academic Dean .... Ms. Terri ACKLAND
10 Vice President Business Affairs .... Mr. Chris WODKA
15 Executive Director Human Resources .... Ms. Brandi CLARK
09 Exec Dir II Institutional Research .... Mr. William BROWN
08 Director Library Services .... Ms. Adrianna SAAVEDRA
37 Director of Financial Aid .... Ms. Elisa JUAREZ
41 Athletic Director .... Mr. Chuck SCHNOOR
39 Director of Residence Life .... Mr. Nev KRAGULJEVIC
18 Exec Director of Facilities .... Mr. Ernesto VALENZUELA
96 Director of Purchasing .... Mr. Mark SALAZ
06 Registrar .... Ms. Veronica DURAN
07 Director of Admissions/Recruitment .... Mr. Luis SANCHEZ
21 Exec Dir Accounting Svc/Comptroller .... Ms. Luisa OTT
30 Chief Development/Advancement .... Ms. Margaret DOOLEY
32 Dean Student Affairs .... Ms. Jenni GONZALES
35 Asst Dean Student Affairs .... Ms. Ashlei TOBIN

Chamberlain College of Nursing-Phoenix Campus (A)

2149 West Dunlap Avenue, Phoenix AZ 85021

Telephone: (602) 331-2720 Identification: 770502

Accreditation: &NH, NURSE

† Branch campus of Chamberlain College of Nursing-Addison, Addison, IL.

Cochise College (B)

4190 West Highway 80, Douglas AZ 85607-6190

County: Cochise FICE Identification: 001072

Unit ID: 104425

Telephone: (800) 966-7943 Carnegie Class: Not Classified

FAX Number: N/A Calendar System: Semester

URL: www.cochise.edu

Established: 1964 Annual Undergrad Tuition & Fees (In-District): $2,310

Enrollment: 4,482 Coed

Affiliation or Control: State/Local IRS Status: 170(c)1

Highest Offering: Associate Degree

Program: Occupational; 2-Year Principally Bachelor's Creditable

Accreditation: NH, #COARC

01 Chief Executive Officer (President) ..... Dr. James D. ROTTWEILER
04 Administrative Asst to President .... Ms. Loretta MOUNTJOY
05 VP for Instruction/Provost ....Dr. Verlyn FICK
10 VP Administration .... Mr. LaMont SCHIERS
15 VP Human Resources .... Ms. Wendy DAVIS
13 VP for Information Technology .... Mr. Carlos CARTAGENA
102 Exec Dir Foundation & Ext Affairs .... Ms. Denise HOYOS
18 Exec Dir Fac Mgt Planning .... Mr. Frank DYKSTRA
07 Registrar/Dir of Admissions .... Ms. Debra QUICK
06 Assistant Registrar .... Ms. Heather AUGENSTEIN
49 Dean Liberal Arts .... Mr. Chuck HOYACK
81 Dean Math and Science ....Dr. Beth KRUEGER
76 Dean Nursing/Allied Health ....Ms. Jennifer LAKOSIL
50 Dean Business and Technology ....Mr. Bruce RICHARDSON
56 Dean Extended Learning ....Mr. George SELF
32 Dean Student Services/Athl Director ....Dr. James HALL
35 Asst Dean Student Svc ....Mr. Mark BOGGIE
09 Dean Institutional Effectiveness ....Ms. Sandy BRYAN
08 Director Library Services ....Dr. John WALSH
96 Director Procurement Svc .... Ms. Lourdes ESTRADA
39 Director Student Housing .... Ms. Marisol ARENIVAS
88 Director Occ Health Safety ....Mr. Randy DENNEY
37 Director Student Financial Aid .... Ms. Karen EMMER
38 Director Counseling and Advising .... Ms. Nanette ROMO
88 Dir TRIO Student Support Services .... Ms. Gabriela AMAVIZCA
88 Director Disability Support Service ....Ms. Carla BOYD
26 Director Mktg and Communication ....Ms. Robyn MARTIN
88 Director Continuous Improvement ....Ms. Karen DALE
66 Director Nursing ....Ms. Polly GOSA
88 Director Aviation Programs .... Ms. Belinda BURNETT
88 Director Adult Education ....Ms. Susan MORSS
88 Director Small Business Dev Center ....Mr. Mark SCHMITT
51 Director Ctr for Lifelong Learning .... Ms. Sharon GILMAN
12 Director Fort Huachuca ....Mr. Mark DOTTLE
12 Director Willcox Center .... Ms. Barbara RICHARDSON
12 Director Santa Cruz Center ....Mr. Gabriel GALINDO
12 Director Benson Center .... Ms. Barbara RICHARDSON
106 Director Virtual Campus .... Ms. Tasneem ASHRAF
88 Assistant Director Virtual Campus ....Mr. Adam WOODROW

Cochise College (C)

901 N. Colombo Ave., Sierra Vista AZ 85635-2317

Telephone: (800) 966-7943 Identification: 770004

Accreditation: &NH, ADNUR, EMT

† Branch campus of Cochise College, Douglas, AZ.

Coconino Community College (D)

2800 S Lone Tree Road, Flagstaff AZ 86005

County: Coconino FICE Identification: 031004

Unit ID: 404426

Telephone: (928) 527-1222 Carnegie Class: Assoc/Pub-R-M

FAX Number: (928) 226-4106 Calendar System: Semester

URL: www.coconino.edu

Established: 1991 Annual Undergrad Tuition & Fees (In-State): $2,328

Enrollment: 3,607 Coed

Affiliation or Control: State IRS Status: 501(c)3

Highest Offering: Associate Degree

Program: 2-Year Principally Bachelor's Creditable

Accreditation: NH

01 President ....Vacant
05 Vice President for Academic Affairs .... Dr. Russ ROTHAMER
10 VP for Business & Administration ....Ms. Jami VAN ESS
32 Dean of Student Services .... Ms. Veronica HIPOLITO
12 Page Campus Director ....Mr. Jim HUNTER
49 Dean of Art & Sciences ....Vacant
15 Director for Human Resources .... Ms. Gayle BENTON
09 Dir Institutional Research/Assess ....Mr. Michael MERICA
37 Director for Financial Aid ....Mr. Robert VOYTEK
06 Registrar/Dir Enrollment Services ....Ms. Kimmi GRULKE
75 Dean of Career & Tech Education .... Dr. Monica BAKER
18 Director Facilities ....Mr. Mark EASTON
13 Chief Technical Officer .... Mr. Joe TRAINO
96 Director Purchasing/Auxiliary Svcs ....Mr. Robert SEDILLO
21 Director of Accounting & Finance .... Ms. Siri MULLANEY
30 Director Institutional Advancement .... Mr. Scott TALBOOM
04 Exec Assistant to the President .... Ms. April SANDOVAL

Coconino County Community College Flagstaff Fourth Street Campus (E)

3000 N Fourth Street, Flagstaff AZ 86004

Telephone: (928) 526-7600 Identification: 770005

Accreditation: &NH

† Branch campus of Coconino Community College, Flagstaff, AZ.

Coconino County Community College Page/ Lake Powell Campus (F)

475 S Lake Powell Blvd., PO Box 728,
Page AZ 86040-0728

Telephone: (928) 645-3987 Identification: 770006

Accreditation: &NH

† Branch campus of Coconino Community College, Flagstaff, AZ.

CollegeAmerica-Flagstaff (G)

399 S. Malpais, 2nd Floor, Flagstaff AZ 86001

County: Coconino FICE Identification: 031203

Unit ID: 103945

Telephone: (928) 213-6060 Carnegie Class: Assoc/PrivFP

FAX Number: (928) 526-3468 Calendar System: Other

URL: www.collegeamerica.edu

Established: 1964 Annual Undergrad Tuition & Fees: $16,968

Enrollment: 569 Coed

Affiliation or Control: Independent Non-Profit IRS Status: 501(c)3

Highest Offering: Baccalaureate

Program: Occupational

Accreditation: ACCSC

01 Executive Director ....Dr. Kathy A. TURNER

CollegeAmerica-Phoenix (H)

9801 N. Metro Parkway East, Phoenix AZ 85051

Telephone: (602) 589-9860 Identification: 666017

Accreditation: ACCSC

† Branch campus of CollegeAmerica-Flagstaff, Flagstaff, AZ

DeVry University - Phoenix Campus (I)

2149 W Dunlap Avenue, Phoenix AZ 85021-2995

Telephone: (602) 749-7301 FICE Identification: 008322

Accreditation: &NH, ENGT, MT

† Regional accreditation is carried under the parent institution in Downers Grove, IL.

Diné College (J)

One Circle Drive, Tsaile AZ 86556-9998

County: Apache FICE Identification: 008246

Unit ID: 105297

Telephone: (928) 724-6671 Carnegie Class: Tribal

FAX Number: (928) 724-3327 Calendar System: Semester

URL: www.dinecollege.edu

Established: 1968 Annual Undergrad Tuition & Fees (In-District): $720

Enrollment: 1,555 Coed

Affiliation or Control: Local IRS Status: 501(c)3

Highest Offering: Baccalaureate

Program: Occupational; 2-Year Principally Bachelor's Creditable

Accreditation: NH

01 President ....Dr. Maggie GEORGE
10 Vice President for Finance .... Ms. Cheryl THOMPSON
32 Int Vice Pres of Student Success ....Mr. Abe BITOK
05 Vice President of Academics .... Mr. Martin AHUMADA
30 Director of Development ....Mr. Cameron DAINES
06 Registrar .... Ms. Louise LITZIN
20 Dean ....Vacant
37 Director Student Financial Aid ....Mr. Formon THOMPSON
15 Dir Department of Human Resources ....Mrs. Perphelia FOWLER
18 Supt Maintenance Operations .... Mr. Delbert PAQUIN
21 Controller ....Vacant
26 Public Relations Director .... Mr. Ed MCCOMBS
46 Dir Inst Grants/Sponsored Projects .... Ms. Amanda MCNEIL

Dunlap-Stone University (K)

19820 North 7th Street, Suite 100, Phoenix AZ 85024

County: Maricopa Identification: 666315

Telephone: (602) 648-5750 Carnegie Class: Not Classified

FAX Number: (602) 648-5755 Calendar System: Other

URL: www.dunlap-stone.edu

Established: 1995 Annual Undergrad Tuition & Fees: $8,490

Enrollment: 390 Coed

Affiliation or Control: Proprietary IRS Status: Proprietary

Highest Offering: Master's

Program: Professional; Business Emphasis

Accreditation: DEAC

01 President ....Dr. Donald N. BURTON
106 Vice Pres Online Programs/Registrar .... Mrs. Caulyne BARRON

Eastern Arizona College (L)

615 N Stadium Avenue, Thatcher AZ 85552-0769

County: Graham FICE Identification: 001073

Unit ID: 104577

Telephone: (928) 428-8233 Carnegie Class: Assoc/Pub-R-L

FAX Number: (928) 428-2578 Calendar System: Semester

URL: www.eac.edu

Established: 1888 Annual Undergrad Tuition & Fees (In-District): $1,040

Enrollment: 8,847 Coed

Affiliation or Control: State/Local IRS Status: 501(c)3

Highest Offering: Associate Degree

Program: Occupational; 2-Year Principally Bachelor's Creditable

Accreditation: NH

01 President ....Mr. Mark BRYCE
03 Executive Vice President ....Mr. Brent MCEUEN
10 Chief Business Officer ....Mr. Timothy CURTIS
05 Provost ....Mrs. Jeanne BRYCE
20 Dean of Instruction ....Mr. Michael CROCKETT
20 Dean of Instruction ....Dr. Phil MCBRIDE
20 Dean of Curriculum and Instruction .... Dr. Janice LAWHORN
32 Dean of Students ....Dr. Gary SORENSEN
06 Associate Dean/Registrar .... Dr. Randall SKINNER
38 Assistant Dean of Counseling .... Ms. Sharon ALLEN
12 Director of Discovery Park Campus ....Mr. Paul ANGER
21 Director Fiscal Control/Controller ....Mr. Darwin WEECH
37 Director of Financial Aid ....Mr. William OSBORN
13 Director of Information Resources ....Mr. Thomas THOMPSON
09 Director of Institutional Research ....Mr. Glen SNIDER
08 Director of Library Services ....Mrs. Karen JAGGERS
26 Dir of Marketing & Public Relations ....Mr. Todd HAYNIE
18 Director of Physical Resources ....Mr. Dan WELKER
102 Executive Director EAC Foundation ....Mr. David UDALL
35 Director of Student Life .... Mr. Danny BATTRAW
41 Athletic Director .... Mr. James BAGNALL
15 Assoc Director Admin Support EEO Co ....Ms. Lauri AVILA
04 Exec Asst to the President and DGB ....Mrs. Laurie PENNINGTON

Eastern Arizona College Gila Pueblo Campus (M)

8274 Six Shooter Canyon PO Box 2656, Globe AZ 85502

Telephone: (928) 425-8481 Identification: 770008

Accreditation: &NH

† Branch campus of Eastern Arizona College, Thatcher, AZ.

Eastern Arizona College Payson Campus (N)

201 N Mud Springs Rd., PO Box 359, Payson AZ 85547

Telephone: (928) 468-8039 Identification: 770009

Accreditation: &NH

† Branch campus of Eastern Arizona College, Thatcher, AZ.

Embry-Riddle Aeronautical University-Prescott (O)

3700 Willow Creek Road, Prescott AZ 86301-3270

Telephone: (800) 888-3728 FICE Identification: 021047

Accreditation: &SC, AAB, ENG

† Regional accreditation is carried under the parent institution in Daytona Beach, FL.

Fortis College, Phoenix (P)

555 N 18th Street, Suite 110, Phoenix AZ 85006

Telephone: (602) 254-3099 Identification: 666761

Accreditation: ACCSC, DH

† Branch campus of Fortis College, Centerville, OH. Tuition varies by degree program.

Frank Lloyd Wright School of Architecture (Q)

PO Box 4430, Scottsdale AZ 85261-4430

County: Maricopa FICE Identification: 025332

Unit ID: 104665

Telephone: (480) 860-2700 Carnegie Class: Spec/Arts

FAX Number: N/A Calendar System: Other

URL: www.taliesin.edu

Established: 1932 Annual Undergrad Tuition & Fees: $40,500

Enrollment: 5 Coed

Affiliation or Control: Independent Non-Profit IRS Status: 501(c)3

Highest Offering: Master's

Program: Professional; Music Emphasis

Accreditation: NH

01 Head of School and Dean ....Mr. Aaron BETSKEY
05 Director of Academic Affairs ....Dr. Stephanie Grace SCHULL
08 Director of Libraries .... Ms. Elizabeth AL-HAZZAM DAWASARI
07 Dir Admissions/Student Services ....Mr. Gerasimos (Jerry) KAVALIERATOS
10 COO and Vice President Finance ....Ms. Lisa MURPHY
30 Vice President of Development ....Ms. Dottie O'ÇARROLL

Golf Academy of America (R)

2031 N. Arizona Ave Suite 2, Chandler AZ 85225

Telephone: (800) 342-7342 Identification: 666023

Accreditation: ACICS

† Branch campus of Virginia College, Birmingham, AL.

Grand Canyon University (A)

3300 W Camelback Road, Phoenix AZ 85017-3030
County: Maricopa FICE Identification: 001074
Unit ID: 104717
Telephone: (602) 639-7500 Carnegie Class: Master's L
FAX Number: N/A Calendar System: Semester
URL: www.gcu.edu
Established: 1949 Annual Undergrad Tuition & Fees: $17,000
Enrollment: 62,304 Coed
Affiliation or Control: Proprietary IRS Status: Proprietary
Highest Offering: Doctorate
Program: Liberal Arts And General; Teacher Preparatory; Professional
Accreditation: NH, ACBSP, CAATE, NURSE

01 President/Chief Executive Officer .... Mr. Brian MUELLER
10 Chief Financial Officer .... Mr. Dan BACHUS
11 Chief Operations Officer .... Mr. Stan MEYER
05 Provost .... Dr. Hank RADDA
15 Vice President Human Resources .... Mr. Scott RALEIGH
32 VP Student Svcs/Dean of Students .... Pastor Tim GRIFFIN
50 Dean Ken Blanchard Col Business .... Dr. Randy GIBB
53 Dean College of Education .... Dr. Kimberly LAPRADE
66 Dean College Nursing/Hlth Care Prof .... Dr. Melanie LOGUE
49 Dean College Sci/Engineering/Tech .... Dr. K. Mark WOODEN
58 Dean College Doctoral Studies .... Dr. Michael BERGER
57 Dean of Fine Arts and Production .... Mr. Claude PENSIS
73 Dean College of Theology .... Dr. Jason HILES
79 Dean College Human/Social Science .... Dr. Sherman ELLIOTT

Han University of Traditional Medicine (B)

2856 E. Fort Lowell Road, Tucson AZ 85716
County: Pima FICE Identification: 041193
Telephone: (520) 322-6330 Carnegie Class: Not Classified
FAX Number: (520) 322-5661 Calendar System: Quarter
URL: www.hanuniversity.edu
Established: 2000 Annual Undergrad Tuition & Fees: $51,780
Enrollment: 4 Coed
Affiliation or Control: Proprietary IRS Status: Proprietary
Highest Offering: Master's
Program: Professional
Accreditation: ACUP

01 President .... Mr. Alex HOLLAND
07 Admissions Director .... Mrs. Jamie SZYBALA
06 Registrar .... Mr. Alex HOLLAND

Harrison Middleton University (C)

1105 East Broadway Road, Tempe AZ 85282-1505
County: Maricopa Identification: 666169
Telephone: (877) 248-6724 Carnegie Class: Not Classified
FAX Number: (800) 762-1622 Calendar System: Other
URL: www.hmu.edu
Established: 1998 Annual Undergrad Tuition & Fees: $7,900
Enrollment: 400 Coed
Affiliation or Control: Proprietary IRS Status: Proprietary
Highest Offering: Doctorate
Program: Liberal Arts And General
Accreditation: DEAC

01 President .... Mr. David CURD
05 Director of Education .... Mr. Michael CURD
06 Registrar .... Ms. Lauren GUTHRIE
51 Director of Continuing Education .... Ms. Rebecca FISHER

International Baptist College and Seminary (D)

2211 W Germann Road, Chandler AZ 85286
County: Maricopa FICE Identification: 033473
Unit ID: 436614
Telephone: (480) 245-7903 Carnegie Class: Spec/Faith
FAX Number: (480) 245-7909 Calendar System: 4/1/4
URL: www.ibcs.edu
Established: 1980 Annual Undergrad Tuition & Fees: $10,500
Enrollment: 69 Coed
Affiliation or Control: Baptist IRS Status: 501(c)3
Highest Offering: Doctorate
Program: Occupational; 2-Year Principally Bachelor's Creditable; Teacher Preparatory; Religious Emphasis
Accreditation: TRACS

00 Chancellor .... Dr. Jerry C. TETREAU
01 President .... Rev. Kenneth M. ENDEAN
32 Dean of Students .... Mr. Nathan M. MESTLER
05 Chief Academic Officer .... Dr. Michael A. BRYSON
10 Chief Financial Officer .... Mr. Matt EBERLE
07 Director of Enrollment .... Mrs. Lauren BRADY
09 Director of Inst Effectiveness .... Mrs. Lauren BRADY
20 Undergraduate Academic Officer .... Mr. Jeffrey G. CAUPP
20 Graduate Academic Officer .... Dr. David SHUMATE
88 Teaching Site Liaison .... Dr. Keith HUHTA
08 Media Center Director .... Mr. Lee WILL
34 Dean of Women .... Ms. Marcia L. GAMMON
06 Registrar .... Mr. Stephen M. PENA
37 Financial Aid Administrator .... Mrs. Jane L. BUSHEY
04 Administrative Asst to President .. Mrs. Rebecca M. STERTZBACH
30 Chief Development/Advancement .... Dr. Jerry C. TETREAU

ITT Technical Institute (E)

10220 North 25th Avenue, Suite 100, Phoenix AZ 85021
Telephone: (602) 749-7900 Identification: 666696
Accreditation: ACICS

† Branch campus of ITT Technical Institute, Indianapolis, IN.

ITT Technical Institute (F)

1840 N 95th Avenue, Suite 132, Phoenix AZ 85037
Telephone: (623) 474-7900 Identification: 667190
Accreditation: ACICS

† Branch campus of ITT Technical Institute, Indianapolis, IN.

ITT Technical Institute (G)

5005 S Wendler Drive, Tempe AZ 85282-6321
Telephone: (602) 437-7500 FICE Identification: 020652
Accreditation: ACICS

† Branch campus of ITT Technical Institute, Indianapolis, IN.

ITT Technical Institute (H)

1455 W River Road, Tucson AZ 85704-5829
Telephone: (520) 408-7488 FICE Identification: 023611
Accreditation: ACICS

† Branch campus of ITT Technical Institute, Indianapolis, IN.

Le Cordon Bleu College of Culinary Arts in Scottsdale (I)

8100 E Camelback Road, Ste 1001,
Scottsdale AZ 85251-3940
County: Maricopa FICE Identification: 026167
Unit ID: 262332
Telephone: (480) 990-3773 Carnegie Class: Spec/Other
FAX Number: (480) 990-0351 Calendar System: Other
URL: www.chefs.edu/scottsdale
Established: 1986 Annual Undergrad Tuition & Fees: $12,944
Enrollment: 1,567 Coed
Affiliation or Control: Proprietary IRS Status: Proprietary
Highest Offering: Baccalaureate
Program: Occupational
Accreditation: ACCSC, ACFEI, ACICS

01 President .... Mr. Craig BARTHOLOMEW
37 Vice Pres/Director of Financial Aid .... Ms. Saundra ASCHENDRENER
11 Director Administration .... Mr. Jason KIMMELL
36 Director Career Services .... Ms. Kathleen DOELLER
06 Registrar .... Ms. Polly GIBSON
07 Director of Admission .... Mr. Jason KIMMELL

*Maricopa County Community College District Office (J)

2411 W 14th Street, Tempe AZ 85281-6941
County: Maricopa FICE Identification: 001075
Unit ID: 105136
Telephone: (480) 731-8000 Carnegie Class: N/A
FAX Number: (480) 731-8850
URL: www.maricopa.edu

01 Chancellor .... Dr. Rufus GLASPER
05 Executive Vice Chancellor/ Provost .... Dr. Maria HARPER-MARINICK
26 VC Resource Devel/Community Rels .... Dr. Steven HELFGOT
10 Vice Chanc Business Services .... Ms. Debra THOMPSON
15 Vice Chancellor Human Resources .... Ms. LaCoya SHELTON-JOHNSON
13 Chief Information Officer .... Mr. Ed KELTY
21 Assoc Vice Chanc Business Services .... Ms. Gaye MURPHY
103 Dir Center Workforce Development .... Dr. Randy KIMMENS
30 Exec Director Resource Development .... Ms. Mary O'CONNOR
09 Assoc VC Inst Strategy/Rsrch/Effect .... Vacant
18 Assoc Vice Chanc Cap Plng/Spec Proj .... Mr. Arlen SOLOCHEK
04 Special Assistant to the Chancellor .... Dr. Sue KATER

*Chandler-Gilbert Community College (K)

2626 E Pecos Road, Chandler AZ 85225-2499
County: Maricopa FICE Identification: 030722
Unit ID: 364025
Telephone: (480) 732-7000 Carnegie Class: Assoc/Pub-U-MC
FAX Number: (480) 732-7090 Calendar System: Semester
URL: www.cgc.maricopa.edu
Established: 1992 Annual Undergrad Tuition & Fees (In-District): $2,550
Enrollment: 14,500 Coed
Affiliation or Control: State/Local IRS Status: 501(c)3
Highest Offering: Associate Degree
Program: 2-Year Principally Bachelor's Creditable
Accreditation: NH, ADNUR, DIETT

02 President .... Dr. Linda LUJAN
04 Administrative Asst to President .... Ms. Susan D. AROZ
05 Vice President Academic Affairs .... Dr. William GUERRIERO
32 Vice President Student Affairs .... Dr. William H. CRAWFORD, III
11 Vice Pres Administrative Services .... Mr. Bradley S. KENDREX
49 Dean of Arts and Sciences .... Vacant
31 Dean of Community Affairs .... Dr. Cindy BARNES PHARR
75 Dean of Career & Technical Educ .... Ms. Maria A. REYES
32 Dean of Student Affairs .... Mr. Daniel HERBST
10 Assoc Dean Finance/Business Svcs .... Vacant
07 Dir Admissions/Registr & Records .... Ms. Linda SHAW
13 Vice President of IT & Media Svcs .... Dr. Charles NWANKWO
09 Dir Research/Planning/Development .... Ms. Theresa WONG
36 Dir Career/Education Planning Svcs .... Vacant
85 Director International Educ Program .... Ms. Anna A. JIMENEZ
32 Director College Student Services .... Ms. Dawn GRUICHICH
18 Director Col Facilities Plng & Dev .... Mr. Charles POURE
35 Director Student Life & Leadership .... Mr. Mike GREENE
41 Director Athletics .... Mr. Ed YEAGER
19 Public Safety Commander .... Mr. Robert EVERETT
37 Director Financial Aid .... Mr. Timothy WOLSEY
26 Director Marketing/Public Relations .... Vacant
88 Director Learning Center .... Ms. Eva R. FALLETTA
88 Director Early Outreach Programs .... Ms. Laura MATYAS
88 Director Instr Tech & Course Prod .... Ms. Juliane M. ROYBAL
66 Director Nursing & Health Sciences .... Ms. Jill A. ANDERSON
14 Director Computer Labs/Instr Svcs .... Ms. Joni M. BRUMMER
21 Manager College Cashier Services .... Vacant
15 Senior Manager Human Resources .... Ms. Bernadette LA MAZZA

*Estrella Mountain Community College (L)

3000 N Dysart Road, Avondale AZ 85392
County: Maricopa FICE Identification: 031563
Unit ID: 384333
Telephone: (623) 935-8000 Carnegie Class: Assoc/Pub-U-MC
FAX Number: (623) 935-8008 Calendar System: Semester
URL: www.estrellamountain.edu
Established: 1990 Annual Undergrad Tuition & Fees (In-District): $2,520
Enrollment: 9,164 Coed
Affiliation or Control: State/Local IRS Status: 501(c)3
Highest Offering: Associate Degree
Program: Occupational; 2-Year Principally Bachelor's Creditable
Accreditation: NH, ADNUR

02 President .... Dr. Ernest LARA
11 Vice President Admin Services .... Ms. Sue TAVAKOLI
32 Vice President Student Affairs .... Dr. Patricia CARDENAS-ADAME
05 Vice President of Learning .... Dr. Clay GOODMAN
20 Dean of Academic Affairs .... Dr. Kathleen IUDICELLO
20 Dean of Academic Affairs .... Dr. Sylvia ORR
13 Director Information Technology .... Mr. Chad GALLIGAN
35 Dean of Student Services .... Ms. Laura DULGAR
08 Division Chair Information Resource .... Ms. Nikol PRICE
09 Dean Planning/Rsrch/Effectiveness .... Dr. Rene G. WILLEKENS
18 Director Facilities Planning/Devel .... Mr. Randy NAUGHTON
07 Director of Enrollment Services .... Mr. Frank AMPARO
10 Manager College Fiscal Services .... Ms. Leda JOHNSON
29 Director Alumni/Corp Relations .... Mr. Jonathan ROBLES
37 Director Student Financial Aid .... Ms. Rosanna SHORT
21 Manager College Budget .... Ms. Maggie CASTILLO

*Gateway Community College (M)

108 N 40th Street, Phoenix AZ 85034-1795
County: Maricopa FICE Identification: 008303
Unit ID: 105145
Telephone: (602) 286-8000 Carnegie Class: Assoc/Pub-U-MC
FAX Number: (602) 286-8072 Calendar System: Semester
URL: www.gatewaycc.edu/
Established: 1968 Annual Undergrad Tuition & Fees (In-District): $2,016
Enrollment: 5,651 Coed
Affiliation or Control: State/Local IRS Status: 501(c)3
Highest Offering: Associate Degree
Program: Occupational; 2-Year Principally Bachelor's Creditable
Accreditation: NH, ADNUR, COARC, DMS, NDT, NMT, POLYT, PTAA, RAD, RTT, SURGT

02 President .... Dr. Steven GONZALEZ
05 Vice President Academic Affairs .... Dr. Maria WISE
32 Vice President Student Affairs .... Dr. Joni GROVER
11 Vice President Administrative Svcs .... Mr. Tony ASTI
07 Director Enrollment Services .... Ms. Kristie FOK
09 Dir Research Planning & Development ... Ms. Cathy HERNANDEZ
88 College Budget Analyst .... Ms. Janet BOSE
10 Manager College Fiscal Services .... Ms. Cecilia SOTO
18 Chief Facilities/Physical Plant .... Vacant
26 Director Marketing/Public Relations .... Ms. Christine LAMBRAKIS
30 Director Inst Advance & Entrep Pgm .... Vacant
37 Director Student Financial Aid .... Ms. Suzanne RINGLE
84 Coordinator Enrollment Services .... Ms. Kelly MCPHEE
15 Manager College Employee Services .... Ms. Chantal LUGO

*Glendale Community College (N)

6000 W Olive Avenue, Glendale AZ 85302-3006
County: Maricopa FICE Identification: 001076
Unit ID: 104708
Telephone: (623) 845-3000 Carnegie Class: Assoc/Pub-U-MC
FAX Number: (623) 845-3329 Calendar System: Semester
URL: www.gccaz.edu

Established: 1965 Annual Undergrad Tuition & Fees (In-District): $2,520
Enrollment: 20,506 Coed
Affiliation or Control: State/Local IRS Status: 170(c)1
Highest Offering: Associate Degree
Program: Occupational; 2-Year Principally Bachelor's Creditable
Accreditation: NH, ADNUR, EMT

02 President .... Dr. Irene H. KOVALA
05 VP Academic Affairs .... Dr. Janet LANGLEY
11 VP Admin Services & CIO .... Mr. Greg ROGERS
20 Dean of Academic Affairs .... Dr. Fernando CAMOU
20 Dean of Academic Affairs .... Mr. Scott SCHULZ
20 Dean of Academic Affairs .... Mr. Eric LESHINSKIE
84 Dean Enrollment Services .... Ms. Mary D. BLACKWELL
32 Dean Student Life .... Ms. Monica CASTANEDA
12 Dean GCC North .... Mr. Charles F. JEFFERY
37 Director Financial Aid .... Ms. Ellen NEEL
18 Director Facilities .... Mr. Al GONZALES
10 Dir Col Business Services .... Ms. Augustine ERPELDING
26 Dir Sales Mktg & Public Rels .... Ms. Tressa JUMPS
45 Dean of Strat/Plng & Accountability .... Dr. Alka ARORA SINGH
15 Manager College Employee Svcs .... Ms. June S. FESSENDEN
30 Director of Development .... Ms. Frances MATEO
38 Dept Chair Counseling .... Ms. Marjane MATON
08 Dept Chair Librarian .... Mr. Frank TORRES
19 Director College Safety .... Ms. Debra PALOK
04 Admin Assistant I to College Pres .... Ms. Esmeralda M. ACOSTA

*Mesa Community College (A)

1833 W Southern Avenue, Mesa AZ 85202-4866
County: Maricopa FICE Identification: 001077
Unit ID: 105154
Telephone: (480) 461-7000 Carnegie Class: Assoc/Pub-U-MC
FAX Number: (480) 461-7805 Calendar System: Semester
URL: www.mesacc.edu/
Established: 1965 Annual Undergrad Tuition & Fees (In-District): $2,520
Enrollment: 22,711 Coed
Affiliation or Control: State/Local IRS Status: 501(c)3
Highest Offering: Associate Degree
Program: Occupational; 2-Year Principally Bachelor's Creditable
Accreditation: NH, ADNUR, DH, FUSER

02 President .... Dr. Shouan PAN
05 Interim Vice Pres Academic Affairs .... Dr. Roger YOHE
32 Vice Pres Student Affairs .... Dr. Sonya PEARSON
10 Vice Pres Admin Services .... Mr. Jeff DARBUT
13 Vice Pres Information Technology .... Mr. Sasan POUREETEZADI
12 Provost Red Mountain/Downtown Ctr .... Mr. Patrick BURKHART
09 Dean of Inst Planning & Analysis .... Mr. Matthew ASHCRAFT
35 Dean of Student Affairs .... Ms. Meredith WARNER
20 Dean Instruction .... Dr. Rodney HOLMES
20 Dean Instruction .... Ms. Carol ACHS
20 Interim Dean Instruction .... Dr. Nora REYES
06 Registrar .... Dr. Barbara BOROS
18 Director Facilities .... Mr. Richard CLUFF
26 Director of Institutional Advance .... Ms. Sonia FILAN
30 Director of Development .... Mr. Jared LANGKILDE
37 Dir Fin Aid/Scholarships .... Ms. Patricia PEPPIN
38 Dept Chair Counseling .... Dr. Karen HARDIN
19 Director Security/Safety .... Mr. John S. CORICH
25 Chief Contracts/Grants Admin .... Mr. Kenichi MARUYAMA
29 Director Alumni Relations .... Ms. Marcy SNITZER
41 Athletic Director .... Mr. John MULHERN

*Paradise Valley Community College (B)

18401 N 32nd Street, Phoenix AZ 85032-1210
County: Maricopa FICE Identification: 026236
Unit ID: 364016
Telephone: (602) 787-6500 Carnegie Class: Assoc/Pub-U-MC
FAX Number: (602) 787-6625 Calendar System: Semester
URL: www.paradisevalley.edu
Established: 1985 Annual Undergrad Tuition & Fees (In-District): $2,460
Enrollment: 8,909 Coed
Affiliation or Control: State/Local IRS Status: 501(c)3
Highest Offering: Associate Degree
Program: Occupational; 2-Year Principally Bachelor's Creditable
Accreditation: NH, ADNUR, DIETT, EMT

02 President .... Dr. Paul DALE
05 Vice President of Academic Affairs .... Dr. Mary Lou MOSLEY
11 VP Administrative Services .... Mr. Herman GONZALEZ
32 Vice President of Student Affairs .... Ms. Veronica GARCIA
20 Dean of Academic Affairs .... Dr. Denise DIGIANFILIPPO
35 Dean of Students .... Dr. Shirley GREEN
13 Dean of Information Technology .... Mr. Paul GOLISCH
07 Supervisor of Admissions .... Ms. Stella NAPOLES
84 Dean Admin Affs/Enrollment Services .... Ms. Sandy MCDILL
15 Director Personnel Services .... Ms. Lori LINDSETH
18 Chief Facilities/Physical Plant .... Mr. David MATUS
37 Director Student Financial Aid .... Ms. Katharine JOHNSON
38 Director Student Counseling .... Dr. James RUBIN
06 Registrar .... Ms. Stella NAPOLES
36 Director Student Placement .... Ms. Norma CHANDLER
26 Dir of Marketing/Public Relations .... Ms. Candace OEHLER
09 Dir Institutional Research/Effect .... Mr. John SNELLING
19 Director Security/Safety .... Mr. Scott MEEK
41 Athletic Director .... Mr. Greg SILCOX
30 Dir Development/Community Relations .... Dr. Julia MOORE

*Phoenix College (C)

1202 W Thomas Road, Phoenix AZ 85013-4234
County: Maricopa FICE Identification: 001078
Unit ID: 105428
Telephone: (602) 285-7800 Carnegie Class: Assoc/Pub-U-MC
FAX Number: (602) 285-7700 Calendar System: Semester
URL: www.pc.maricopa.edu
Established: 1920 Annual Undergrad Tuition & Fees (In-District): $2,050
Enrollment: 11,929 Coed
Affiliation or Control: State/Local IRS Status: 501(c)3
Highest Offering: Associate Degree
Program: Occupational; 2-Year Principally Bachelor's Creditable; Technical Emphasis
Accreditation: NH, ADNUR, CAHIIM, DA, DH, HT, MLTAD

02 Interim President .... Ms. Christina HAINES
05 VP of Academic Affairs .... Dr. Casandra KAKAR
11 VP Administrative Services .... Mr. Paul DEROSE
32 Vice Pres of Student Affairs .... Vacant
35 Dean of Student Affairs .... Dr. Heather KRUSE
20 Dean of Academic Affairs .... Mr. Wilbert NELSON
88 Dean of Industry & Public Service .... Dr. Sharon HALFORD
13 Dean of Technology .... Dr. Mark KOAN
08 Department Chair Library .... Ms. Linda SOLAND
38 Department Chair Counseling .... Ms. Nancy NAVARRETE
06 Dir Admissions/Registration/Records .... Ms. Brenda STARCK
07 Director of Enrollment Services .... Ms. Carmen NEWLAND
41 Athletic Director .... Ms. Samantha EZELL
37 Director Financial Aid .... Ms. Cynthia RAMOS
88 Director Student Leadership .... Vacant
84 Director Advisement Enrollment .... Ms. Julie VOLLER
09 Dir Instl Plng/Rsrch/Effectiveness .... Ms. Jan BINDER
19 Director of College Safety .... Mr. Doug SPARKS
30 Director Institutional Advancement .... Ms. Michelle KLINGER
18 Director of Facilities .... Mr. Douglas MCCARTHY
10 Manager Business Services .... Ms. Angela GENNA
15 Supv College Employee Services .... Ms. Martha ANDERSON
29 Coord Alumni/Community Relations .... Vacant
04 Assistant to the President .... Ms. Renee HOLGUIN
26 Chief Public Relations/Marketing .... Vacant

*Rio Salado College (D)

2323 W 14th Street, Tempe AZ 85281-6950
County: Maricopa FICE Identification: 021775
Unit ID: 105668
Telephone: (480) 517-8000 Carnegie Class: Assoc/Pub-U-MC
FAX Number: (480) 377-4719 Calendar System: Semester
URL: www.riosalado.edu
Established: 1978 Annual Undergrad Tuition & Fees (In-District): $2,046
Enrollment: 20,215 Coed
Affiliation or Control: State/Local IRS Status: 501(c)3
Highest Offering: Associate Degree
Program: Occupational; 2-Year Principally Bachelor's Creditable; Business Emphasis
Accreditation: NH, DA, DH

02 President .... Dr. Chris BUSTAMANTE
05 Acting Vice Pres Teaching & Lrng .... Dr. Dana REID
10 Vice Pres Business & Employee Svcs .... Mr. Todd SIMMONS
32 Vice President Student Affairs .... Dr. LeRodrick TERRY
13 Chief Information Officer .... Mr. David O'SHEA
20 Dean of Instruction .... Mr. Rick KEMP
105 Dean of Instruction .... Ms. Shannon MCCARTY
20 Dean of Instruction .... Dr. Jo JORGENSON
07 Dean of Enrollment Services .... Mr. Kevin BILDER
07 Dean of Enrollment Services .... Ms. Rachelle CLARKE
37 Director of Financial Aid .... Ms. Nanci REGEHR
09 Dir Research Planning & Development .... Mr. Daniel HUSTON
18 Director of Facilities .... Mr. Ernest ADKINS
19 Director College Safety .... Ms. Margaret TURNER-SAMPLE
21 Director College Business Services .... Mr. Anthony DISCALA
15 Manager College Employee Services .... Ms. Anna FLORES
28 Director of Diversity .... Dr. Sharon KOBERNA
08 Faculty Chair Library .... Ms. Hazel DAVIS

*Scottsdale Community College (E)

9000 E Chaparral, Scottsdale AZ 85256-2626
County: Maricopa FICE Identification: 008304
Unit ID: 105747
Telephone: (480) 423-6000 Carnegie Class: Assoc/Pub-U-SC
FAX Number: (480) 423-6200 Calendar System: Semester
URL: www.scottsdalecc.edu
Established: 1969 Annual Undergrad Tuition & Fees (In-District): $2,046
Enrollment: 9,863 Coed
Affiliation or Control: State/Local IRS Status: 501(c)3
Highest Offering: Associate Degree
Program: Occupational; 2-Year Principally Bachelor's Creditable
Accreditation: NH, ACFEI, ADNUR

02 President .... Dr. Jan L. GEHLER
05 Vice Pres Academic/Student Affairs .... Dr. Daniel P. CORR
11 Vice Pres Administrative Services .... Mr. Carl COUCH
13 Dir ITS/College CTO .... Mr. Grant GAGNON
20 Dean of Instruction .... Dr. Stephanie FUJI
32 Dean of Student Affairs .... Dr. Donna YOUNG
84 Dean of Student Enrollment .... Ms. Gia TAYLOR
07 Director of Admissions .... Ms. Fran VITALE
09 Director of Institutional Research .... Dr. Laurie COHEN

30 Exec Dir Instl Advance/Cmty Eng .... Ms. Nancy NEFF
08 Director of Library Services .... Dr. Pat LOKEY
37 Director Financial Aid/Placement .... Ms. Stacie BECK
18 Director Buildings/Grounds .... Mr. Samuel J. VAN CLEAVE
19 Director of College Safety .... Mr. Les STRICKLAND
41 Athletic Director .... Mr. Vernon MUMMERT
88 Dir of Southwest Studies Program .... Mr. Marshall TRIMBLE
38 Director Student Advisement .... Mr. Michael CORNELIUS

*South Mountain Community College (F)

7050 S 24th Street, Phoenix AZ 85042-5806
County: Maricopa FICE Identification: 021466
Unit ID: 105792
Telephone: (602) 243-8000 Carnegie Class: Assoc/Pub-U-MC
FAX Number: (602) 243-8329 Calendar System: Semester
URL: www.southmountaincc.edu
Established: 1979 Annual Undergrad Tuition & Fees (In-District): $2,050
Enrollment: 4,287 Coed
Affiliation or Control: State/Local IRS Status: 501(c)3
Highest Offering: Associate Degree
Program: Occupational; 2-Year Principally Bachelor's Creditable
Accreditation: NH, MACTE

02 President .... Dr. Shari L. OLSON
05 Vice Pres Academic Affairs .... Dr. Rey RIVERA
11 Vice Pres Administrative Svcs .... Dr. Janet ORTEGA
32 Vice Pres Student Affairs .... Dr. Osaro IGHODARO
09 Dean Research/Plng & Development .... Ms. Damita KALOOSTIAN
20 Dean Academic Affairs .... Ms. Matilda CHAVEZ
84 Dean Enrollment Services .... Mr. Guy GOODMAN
37 Director Financial Aid .... Ms. Inez MORENO-WEINERT
07 Director of Admission & Records .... Ms. Jean WATERMOLEN
10 Director College Business Services .... Mr. John MOLL
18 Director of Facilities .... Mr. Robert HOLMES
26 Director Marketing/Public Relations .... Ms. Jennifer GRENTZ
21 Manager Fiscal Services .... Ms. Jeanette CERNETIC
15 Coordinator Human Resources .... Ms. Margie MESANKO
07 Coordinator Advisement/Recruitment .... Ms. Christine NEILL
36 Coordinator Job Placement .... Ms. Suzanne HIPPS

*Chandler-Gilbert Community College-Williams Campus (G)

7360 E Tahoe Avenue, Mesa AZ 85212-0908
Telephone: (480) 988-8000 Identification: 770178
Accreditation: &NH

† Branch campus of Chandler-Gilbert Community College, Chandler, AZ.

*Glendale Community College North (H)

5727 W Happy Valley Road, Phoenix AZ 85310
Telephone: (623) 845-4000 Identification: 770179
Accreditation: &NH

† Branch campus of Glendale Community College, Glendale, AZ.

*Mesa Community College at Red Mountain (I)

7110 East McKellips Road, Mesa AZ 85207
Telephone: (480) 654-7200 Identification: 770180
Accreditation: &NH

† Branch campus of Mesa Community College, Mesa, AZ.

Midwestern University (J)

19555 N 59th Avenue, Glendale AZ 85308
Telephone: (623) 572-3215 Identification: 666001
Accreditation: &NH, ANEST, ARCPA, CLPSY, DENT, OPT, OSTEO, OT, PERF, PHAR, POD, PTA, @VET

† Regional accreditation is carried under the parent institution in Downers Grove, IL.

Mohave Community College (K)

1971 E. Jagerson Avenue, Kingman AZ 86409-1238
County: Mohave FICE Identification: 011864
Unit ID: 105206
Telephone: (928) 757-0879 Carnegie Class: Assoc/Pub-S-MC
FAX Number: (928) 757-0836 Calendar System: Semester
URL: www.mohave.edu
Established: 1971 Annual Undergrad Tuition & Fees (In-District): $2,112
Enrollment: 3,647 Coed
Affiliation or Control: State/Local IRS Status: 501(c)3
Highest Offering: Associate Degree
Program: Occupational; 2-Year Principally Bachelor's Creditable; Technical Emphasis
Accreditation: NH, ADNUR, DH, EMT, PTAA, RAD, SURGT

01 President .... Dr. Michael KEARNS
03 Executive Vice President .... Dr. Diana STITHEM
05 Dean of Instruction .... Ms. Jill LOVELESS
32 Dean of Student Services .... Ms. Ana MASTERSON
10 Dean of Business Services .... Mr. Jess JACOBS
30 Assoc Dean College Advancement .... Mr. Dan LARA
13 Chief Information Officer .... Mr. Will FARMER
26 Chief Public Relations Officer .... Mr. Ted KERSHNER
12 Campus Dean Bullhead City .... Mr. Shawn BRISTLE

12 Campus Dean Lake Havasu ... Dr. Paula NORBY
12 Campus Dean Neal Kingman ... Dr. Fred GILBERT
12 Campus Dean North Mohave ... Ms. Carolyn HAMBLIN
21 Bursar ... Ms. Camille HOLDEN
37 Financial Aid Director ... Ms. Shannon SHEAFF
09 Dir of Institutional Research ... Mr. Bob FAUBERT
15 Director Personnel Services ... Ms. Jenny DIXON
84 Enrollment Services Manager ... Ms. Sharon HANKS
06 Registrar ... Mr. Brian ZOLL

National Paralegal College (A)

717 East Maryland Avenue, Phoenix AZ 85014-1561
County: Maricopa — FICE Identification: 041574 — Unit ID: 461023
Telephone: (800) 371-6105 — Carnegie Class: Not Classified
FAX Number: (866) 347-2744 — Calendar System: Other
URL: nationalparalegal.edu
Established: 2003 — Annual Undergrad Tuition & Fees: $8,070
Enrollment: 780 — Coed
Affiliation or Control: Proprietary — IRS Status: Proprietary
Highest Offering: Master's
Program: Occupational; 2-Year Principally Bachelor's Creditable; Professional; Business Emphasis
Accreditation: DEAC

01 President ... Avi KATZ
05 Dean/Director ... Mark GELLER
88 Technical Director ... David COHEN
20 Educational Director ... Stephen HAAS
07 Director of Admissions ... Danielle BACKMAN
37 Director Student Financial Aid ... Lisa PIMBER

Northcentral University (B)

10000 E University Drive, Prescott Valley AZ 86314-2336
County: Yavapai — FICE Identification: 038133 — Unit ID: 444130
Telephone: (928) 541-7777 — Carnegie Class: DRU
FAX Number: (928) 541-7817 — Calendar System: Other
URL: www.ncu.edu
Established: 1996 — Annual Undergrad Tuition & Fees: $8,800
Enrollment: 11,160 — Coed
Affiliation or Control: Proprietary — IRS Status: Proprietary
Highest Offering: Doctorate
Program: Teacher Preparatory; Professional; Business Emphasis
Accreditation: NH, ACBSP, MFCD, TEAC

01 President ... Dr. George A. BURNETT
05 Provost/Chief Academic Officer ... Dr. Scott BURRUS
20 Sr Vice Pres Academic Affairs ... Dr. John LA NEAR
10 Chief Financial Officer ... Ms. Karen WHITNEY
100 Chief of Staff ... Mr. Eric STODDARD
43 Gen Counsel/Chf Comp/Hum Res Ofcr ... Mr. David HARPOOL
04 Director Office of the President ... Ms. Stephnie HOPPLE
50 Dean School of Business & Tech Mgmt ... Dr. Peter BEMSKI
53 Dean School of Education ... Dr. Cindy GUILLAUME
83 Dean School of Psychology ... Dr. Robert HAUSSMANN
83 Dean Sch of Marriage & Family Sci ... Dr. James BILLINGS
97 Chair of General Education ... Ms. Melinda LYONS
21 Controller ... Ms. Shannyn STERN
06 Registrar ... Ms. Barbara HICKS
13 Chief Information Officer ... Mr. Patrick PENDLETON
37 Dir of Learner Financial Services ... Ms. Valerie STEINBOCK
08 Director of Library Services ... Mr. Ed SALAZAR
26 Director of Marketing ... Mr. Kevin LUSTIG
50 Director of Strategic Business Know ... Vacant
84 Enrollment Manager ... Mr. Bob HANKS

Northern Arizona University (C)

South San Francisco Street, Flagstaff AZ 86011-0001
County: Coconino — FICE Identification: 001082 — Unit ID: 105330
Telephone: (928) 523-9011 — Carnegie Class: RU/H
FAX Number: (928) 523-1848 — Calendar System: Semester
URL: www.nau.edu
Established: 1899 — Annual Undergrad Tuition & Fees (In-State): $10,358
Enrollment: 27,715 — Coed
Affiliation or Control: State — IRS Status: 501(c)3
Highest Offering: Doctorate
Program: Liberal Arts And General; Teacher Preparatory; Professional
Accreditation: NH, ACBSP, #ARCPA, BUS, CAATE, CACREP, CONST, CS, DH, ENG, MUS, NRPA, NURSE, PTA, SP, SW, TED

01 President ... Dr. Rita CHENG
03 Executive VP and Chief of Staff ... Ms. Joanne KEENE
05 Interim Provost/VP Academic Affairs ... Dr. Daniel KAIN
30 Interim VP University Advancement ... Dr. Betsy MENNELL
84 VP Enrollment Mgmt/Student Affs ... Ms. Sheila Jane KUHN
09 VP Planning/Budget/Inst Research ... Mr. Bjorn FLUGSTAD
10 VP Finance and Administration ... Dr. Jennus L. BURTON
46 Vice President Research ... Dr. William GRABE
56 Sr VP Extended Campuses ... Dr. Fred HURST
86 VP Govt Affairs/Business Ptnr ... Ms. Christy FARLEY
41 VP Intercollegiate Athletics ... Ms. Lisa CAMPOS
43 VP and General Counsel ... Mr. Mark NEUMAYR
88 Vice Provost Academic Personnel ... Dr. Daniel KAIN
13 Interim Chief Information Tech Ofc ... Mr. Ricky ROBERTS
32 Interim Assoc VP Student Affairs ... Ms. Erin GRISHAM
28 Associate VP of Diversity ... Dr. David E. CAMACHO
12 Assoc VP/Campus Executive Officer ... Dr. Michael SABATH
15 Associate VP Human Resources ... Ms. Diane VERKEST
18 Assoc VP Facility Services ... Mr. John MORRIS
21 Interim Assoc VP Financial Services ... Ms. Wendy SWARTZ
20 Vice Provost Academic Affairs ... Dr. Pauline ENTIN
85 Interim Vice Provost Ctr Intl Educ ... Dr. Liz GROBSMITH
08 Dean/University Librarian ... Ms. Cynthia A. CHILDREY
53 Dean College of Education ... Dr. Ramona MELLOTT
54 Dean College Eng/Forestry/Nat Sci ... Dr. Paul JAGODZINSKI
50 Dean WA Franke College of Business ... Dr. Craig VAN SLYKE
49 Dean College of Arts & Letters ... Dr. Michael VINCENT
83 Dean Col Social/Behavioral Sciences ... Dr. Karen L. PUGLIESI
17 Exec Dean Col of Health/Human Svcs ... Dr. Debera THOMAS
06 University Registrar ... Ms. Pamela L. ANASTASSIOU
19 Director University Police ... Mr. Gregory T. FOWLER
22 Director Affirmative Action ... Ms. Priscilla L. MILLS
23 Interim Exec Dir Campus Health Svcs ... Ms. Jamie AXELROD
39 Exec Dir Housing/Residence Life ... Mr. Rich PAYNE
29 Director Alumni Relations ... Ms. Georgette VIGIL
36 Dir Gateway Student Success Center ... Ms. Monica BAI
07 Director of Admissions ... Ms. Anika OLSEN
26 Director of Public Affairs ... Mr. Thomas BAUER
35 Dean of Students ... Ms. Cynthia ANDERSON
38 Dir Counseling & Testing Center ... Ms. Carol O'SABEN
96 Director of Purchasing ... Ms. Becky E. MCGAUGH
04 Assistant to the President ... Ms. Dianna GRIMALDI
102 Dir Foundation/Corporate Relations ... Ms. Elizabeth WILKINSON
104 Director Study Abroad ... Dr. Eric DESCHAMPS
25 Assistant VP Grant & Contracts ... Ms. Wilma ENNENGA
37 Director Student Financial Aid ... Ms. Nydia NITTMANN
27 Director of Marketing ... Ms. Sandra KOWALSKI
40 Bookstore Manager ... Ms. Diana WHITE
16 Director Human Resource Programs ... Ms. Cynthia A. CHILCOAT
64 Director School of Music ... Mr. Todd SULLIVAN
92 Director Honors Program ... Dr. George GUMERMAN
94 Director Women and Gender Studies ... Ms. Sheila NAIR
88 Dean University College ... Dr. Cyndi BANKS
58 Dean Graduate College ... Dr. Maribeth WATWOOD

Northern Arizona University Yuma Branch Campus (D)

2020 S Avenue 8E, Yuma AZ 85365
Telephone: (928) 317-6400 — Identification: 770011
Accreditation: &NH

† Branch campus of Northern Arizona University, Flagstaff, AZ.

Northland Pioneer College (E)

PO Box 610, Holbrook AZ 86025-0610
County: Navajo — FICE Identification: 011862 — Unit ID: 105349
Telephone: (928) 524-7311 — Carnegie Class: Assoc/Pub-R-L
FAX Number: (928) 524-7312 — Calendar System: Semester
URL: www.npc.edu
Established: 1973 — Annual Undergrad Tuition & Fees (In-State): $2,112
Enrollment: 3,211 — Coed
Affiliation or Control: State — IRS Status: 501(c)3
Highest Offering: Associate Degree
Program: Occupational; 2-Year Principally Bachelor's Creditable
Accreditation: NH, ADNUR

01 President ... Dr. Jeanne SWARTHOUT
05 Vice Pres Learning/Student Services ... Mr. Mark H. VEST
11 Vice Pres Administrative Services ... Mr. Blaine HATCH
13 Director of Information Services ... Vacant
32 Director of Student Services ... Mr. Josh ROGERS
04 Assistant to the President ... Ms. Lisa JAYNE
10 Director of Financial Services ... Ms. Maderia ELLISON
21 Controller ... Ms. Amber HILL
15 Director of Human Resources ... Ms. Sharon HOKANSON
37 Director of Financial Aid ... Ms. Beaulah BOB-PENNYPACKER
88 Director of Developmental Services ... Mr. Rickey JACKSON
103 Dean of Career/Technical Education ... Ms. Peggy BELKNAP
49 Dean of Arts & Sciences ... Dr. Eric HENDERSON
66 Dean of Nursing and Allied Health ... Ms. Peg ERDMAN
18 Director of Facilities and Vehicles ... Mr. David HUISH
26 Dir of Marketing/Public Relations ... Ms. Ann HESS
09 Director of Institutional Effective ... Vacant
14 Network and Systems Administrator ... Vacant
88 Director Small Business Development ... Ms. Tracy MANCUSO
08 Head Librarian ... Mr. Stan PIROG
19 Director of Public Safety ... Mr. Stuart BISHOP
84 Director of Enrollment Services ... Mr. Jeremy RAISOR

Northland Pioneer College Little Colorado Campus (F)

1400 E. Third Street, Winslow AZ 86047
Telephone: (928) 289-6511 — Identification: 770015
Accreditation: &NH

† Branch campus of Northland Pioneer College, Holbrook, AZ.

Northland Pioneer College Painted Desert Campus (G)

2251 E Navajo Boulevard, Holbrook AZ 86025
Telephone: (928) 524-7311 — Identification: 770012
Accreditation: &NH

† Branch campus of Northland Pioneer College, Holbrook, AZ.

Northland Pioneer College Silver Creek Campus (H)

1611 S Main Street, Snowflake AZ 85937
Telephone: (928) 536-6211 — Identification: 770014
Accreditation: &NH

† Branch campus of Northland Pioneer College, Holbrook, AZ.

Northland Pioneer College White Mountain Campus (I)

1001 W Deuce of Clubs, Show Low AZ 85901
Telephone: (928) 532-6111 — Identification: 770013
Accreditation: &NH

† Branch campus of Northland Pioneer College, Holbrook, AZ.

Ottawa University Arizona (J)

9414 North 25th Avenue, Phoenix AZ 85021
Telephone: (602) 371-1188 — Identification: 666066
Accreditation: &NH

† Regional accreditation is carried under the parent institution in Ottawa, KS.

The Paralegal Institute at Brighton College (K)

7332 E Butherus Drive, Suite 102, Scottsdale AZ 85260
County: Maricopa — FICE Identification: 030737 — Unit ID: 105385
Telephone: (800) 354-1254 — Carnegie Class: Not Classified
FAX Number: (602) 212-0502 — Calendar System: Other
URL: www.theparalegalinstitute.edu
Established: 1974 — Annual Undergrad Tuition & Fees: $9,000
Enrollment: 360 — Coed
Affiliation or Control: Proprietary — IRS Status: Proprietary
Highest Offering: Associate Degree
Program: Occupational; 2-Year Principally Bachelor's Creditable; Business Emphasis
Accreditation: DEAC

01 President/CAO ... Kathleen MIRABILE
03 Vice President ... Matthew TIDWELL
26 Vice President Marketing ... Chris CARAWAY
10 Director Financial Operations ... Patricia MCCOY
32 Director of Student Management ... Kayla HOBBIEBRUNKEN

Penn Foster College (L)

14300 N Northsight Blvd, Suite 125, Scottsdale AZ 85260-3673
County: Maricopa — FICE Identification: 004049 — Unit ID: 211486
Telephone: (480) 947-6644 — Carnegie Class: Not Classified
FAX Number: (480) 951-6030 — Calendar System: Other
URL: www.pennfostercollege.edu
Established: 1974 — Annual Undergrad Tuition & Fees: $4,341
Enrollment: 25,716 — Coed
Affiliation or Control: Proprietary — IRS Status: Proprietary
Highest Offering: Baccalaureate
Program: 2-Year Principally Bachelor's Creditable; Business Emphasis
Accreditation: DEAC, MAAB

01 Chief Executive Officer ... Mr. Frank BRITT
05 Chief Certification/Licensing Ofcr ... Ms. Connie DEMPSEY
06 Registrar ... Ms. Stephanie SCHROEDER
10 Chief Financial Officer ... Mr. William HOLLYER
26 Chief Marketing Offier ... Ms. Dara WARN

Phoenix Institute of Herbal Medicine and Acupuncture (M)

301 E Bethany Home Road, Ste A-100, Phoenix AZ 85012-1275
County: Maricopa — FICE Identification: 036175 — Unit ID: 447698
Telephone: (602) 274-1885 — Carnegie Class: Spec/Health
FAX Number: (602) 274-1895 — Calendar System: Semester
URL: www.pihma.edu
Established: 1996 — Annual Graduate Tuition & Fees: $13,574
Enrollment: 73 — Coed
Affiliation or Control: Proprietary — IRS Status: Proprietary
Highest Offering: Master's; No Undergraduates
Program: Professional
Accreditation: ACUP

01 President ... Ms. Catherine NIEMIEC
05 Dean for Academic Affairs ... Mr. David MYRICK
07 Admissions ... Ms. Yvette MORAN

Phoenix Seminary (N)

4222 E Thomas Road, Suite 400, Phoenix AZ 85018-7607
County: Maricopa — FICE Identification: 034784 — Unit ID: 381459
Telephone: (602) 850-8000 — Carnegie Class: Spec/Faith
FAX Number: (602) 850-8080 — Calendar System: Semester
URL: www.phoenixseminary.edu

Established: 1988 Annual Graduate Tuition & Fees: $11,662
Enrollment: 187 Coed
Affiliation or Control: Interdenominational IRS Status: 501(c)3
Highest Offering: Doctorate; No Undergraduates
Program: Religious Emphasis
Accreditation: NH, THEOL

01 President .... Dr. Darryl L. DELHOUSAYE
05 Executive Vice President/Provost .... Dr. W. Bingham HUNTER
32 Vice President Student Development .... Dr. Chip MOODY
20 Dir Acad Services/Admiss/Assess .... Ms. Roma ROYER
06 Registrar .... Mrs. Merry STENSON
84 Director of Enrollment .... Mr. Jonathan GRIFFIN
08 Director of Library Services .... Mr. Doug OLBERT
10 Director of Finance .... Mr. Dave HESTON
37 Financial Aid Officer .... Mrs. Lynn GORDON
26 Director of Communications .... Mr. Don BALTZER

Pima Community College (A)

4905 East Broadway Boulevard, Tucson AZ 85709-1005
County: Pima FICE Identification: 007266
Unit ID: 105525
Telephone: (520) 206-4500 Carnegie Class: Assoc/Pub-U-MC
FAX Number: (520) 206-4535 Calendar System: Semester
URL: www.pima.edu
Established: 1966 Annual Undergrad Tuition & Fees (In-District): $1,959
Enrollment: 24,937 Coed
Affiliation or Control: State/Local IRS Status: 501(c)3
Highest Offering: Associate Degree
Program: Occupational; 2-Year Principally Bachelor's Creditable
Accreditation: NH, ADNUR, COARC, DA, DH, DT, EMT, MAC, MLTAD, RAD, SURGT

01 Chancellor .... Mr. Lee D. LAMBERT
05 Provost/Exec Vice Chancellor .... Dr. Erica HOLMES
10 Exec Vice Chanc for Finance/Admin .... Dr. David BEA
15 Vice Chanc for Human Resources .... Mr. Daniel BERRYMAN
13 Interim Vice Chanc Information Tech .... Ms. Cindy DOOLING
100 Interim Vice Chanc Operation .... Dr. Stella PEREZ
18 Vice Chancellor Facilities .... Mr. Bill WARD
12 President Northwest Campus .... Dr. David DORE
12 President East Campus .... Dr. Lorraine MORALES
12 President Downtown Campus .... Dr. David DORE
12 President Community Campus .... Dr. Lorraine MORALES
12 President West Campus .... Dr. Morgan PHILLIPS
12 President Desert Vista Campus .... Dr. Morgan PHILLIPS
43 College General Counsel .... Mr. Jeffrey SILVYN
04 Assistant Vice Chancellor .... Ms. Deborah YOKLIC
20 AVC Academic Services .... Vacant
09 AVC Planning & Inst Research .... Dr. Nicola RICHMOND
32 Asst Vice Chanc for Student Dev .... Dr. Karrie MITCHELL
26 Exec Dir Public Info & Media Rels .... Ms. Elizabeth HOWELL
41 Executive Director of Athletics .... Mr. Edgar SOTO
19 Exec Director Dept of Public Safety .... Vacant
102 Executive Director Foundation .... Vacant
103 VP Workforce Development .... Dr. Ian ROARK
76 Dean of Health Related Prof .... Mr. James CRAIG
07 Director Admissions/Registrar .... Ms. Yolanda ESPINOZA
37 Director of Financial Aid .Ms. Norma NAVARRO-CASTELLANOS
96 Director of Purchasing .... Mr. Mark DWORSCHAK

Pima Community College Community Campus (B)

401 North Bonita Avenue, Tucson AZ 85709
Telephone: (520) 206-3933 Identification: 770016
Accreditation: &NH

† Branch campus of Pima Community College, Tucson, AZ.

Pima Community College Desert Vista Campus (C)

5901 South Calle Santa Cruz, Tucson AZ 85709
Telephone: (520) 206-5000 Identification: 770017
Accreditation: &NH

† Branch campus of Pima Community College, Tucson, AZ.

Pima Community College Downtown Campus (D)

1255 North Stone Avenue, Tucson AZ 85709-3000
Telephone: (520) 206-7171 Identification: 770018
Accreditation: &NH

† Branch campus of Pima Community College, Tucson, AZ.

Pima Community College East Campus (E)

8181 East Arrington Road, Tucson AZ 85709-4000
Telephone: (520) 206-7000 Identification: 770019
Accreditation: &NH

† Branch campus of Pima Community College, Tucson, AZ.

Pima Community College Northwest Campus (F)

7600 North Shannon Road, Tucson AZ 85709-7200
Telephone: (520) 206-2200 Identification: 770020
Accreditation: &NH

† Branch campus of Pima Community College, Tucson, AZ.

Pima Community College West Campus (G)

2202 West Alklam Road, Tucson AZ 85709-0001
Telephone: (520) 206-3210 Identification: 770021
Accreditation: &NH

† Branch campus of Pima Community College, Tucson, AZ.

Pima Medical Institute-East Valley (H)

2160 S Power Road, Mesa AZ 85209
Telephone: (480) 898-9898 Identification: 770515
Accreditation: ABHES

† Branch campus of Pima Medical Institute-Tucson, Tucson, AZ.

Pima Medical Institute-Mesa (I)

957 S Dobson Road, Mesa AZ 85202-2903
Telephone: (480) 644-0267 FICE Identification: 011570
Accreditation: ABHES, COARC, OTA, PTAA, RAD

† Branch campus of Pima Medical Institute-Tucson, Tucson, AZ.

Pima Medical Institute-Tucson (J)

3350 E Grant Road, Suite 200, Tucson AZ 85716-2932
County: Pima FICE Identification: 022171
Unit ID: 105534
Telephone: (520) 326-1600 Carnegie Class: Assoc/PrivFP
FAX Number: (520) 326-4125 Calendar System: Other
URL: www.pmi.edu
Established: 1972 Annual Undergrad Tuition & Fees: $11,830
Enrollment: 1,948 Coed
Affiliation or Control: Proprietary IRS Status: Proprietary
Highest Offering: Baccalaureate
Program: Occupational
Accreditation: ABHES, COARC, OTA, PTAA, RAD

01 Director .... Mr. Dale BERG

Prescott College (K)

220 Grove Avenue, Prescott AZ 86301-2912
County: Yavapai FICE Identification: 020653
Unit ID: 105589
Telephone: (928) 350-2100 Carnegie Class: Master's S
FAX Number: (928) 776-5137 Calendar System: Semester
URL: www.prescott.edu
Established: 1966 Annual Undergrad Tuition & Fees: $28,965
Enrollment: 848 Coed
Affiliation or Control: Independent Non-Profit IRS Status: 501(c)3
Highest Offering: Doctorate
Program: Liberal Arts And General; Teacher Preparatory
Accreditation: NH

01 President .... Mr. John FLICKER
05 Exec VP of Academic Affairs/Provost .... Dr. Paul BURKHARDT
10 Chief Financial Officer .... Ms. Anne LABRUZZO
30 Chief Advancement Officer .... Mr. Richard ACH
84 Dean of Enrollment Management .... Ms. Jerri BROWN
06 Registrar .... Ms. Bobbie DAVIDSON
88 Assoc Dean Enrollment Management ..Ms. Mary Frances CAUSEY
04 Executive Assistant .... Ms. Cathy CHURCH
39 Dean Resident Programs .... Mr. Steven PACE
106 Dean of Limited-Residency Prorams .... Dr. Bev SANTO
18 Director of Facilities .... Mr. Greg LAZZELL
08 Director of Library .... Mr. Richard LEWIS
13 Dir Information Technology Services .... Mr. Jonah VAN TUYL
29 Director of Alumni Relations .... Ms. Marie SMITH
20 Academic Operations Coordinator .... Ms. Karyn FINNELL
26 Integrated Mktg/Communications Ofcr .... Mr. Brian SAJKO

The Refrigeration School (L)

4210 E Washington Street, Phoenix AZ 85034-1816
County: Maricopa FICE Identification: 011689
Unit ID: 105659
Telephone: (602) 275-7133 Carnegie Class: Assoc/PrivFP
FAX Number: (602) 267-4805 Calendar System: Other
URL: www.refrigerationschool.com
Established: 1965 Annual Undergrad Tuition & Fees: $31,950
Enrollment: 695 Coed
Affiliation or Control: Proprietary IRS Status: Proprietary
Highest Offering: Associate Degree
Program: Occupational; Technical Emphasis
Accreditation: ACCSC

01 Campus President .... Mr. Stephen M. MALUTICH
37 Director of Financial Aid .... Ms. Melanie ZUVERINK
07 Director of Admissions .... Mr. John PALUMBO
32 Director of Student Operations .... Mr. Eric ROBIDOUX
53 Director of Education .... Mr. Greg HARRIS
06 Registrar .... Ms. Tara BOURLOTOS

Sessions College for Professional Design (M)

350 S. Mill Avenue, Suite B-104, Tempe AZ 85281-2863
County: Maricopa FICE Identification: 042176
Unit ID: 475839
Telephone: (480) 212-1704 Carnegie Class: Not Classified
FAX Number: (480) 212-1705 Calendar System: Semester
URL: www.sessions.edu
Established: 1997 Annual Undergrad Tuition & Fees: $11,700
Enrollment: 99 Coed
Affiliation or Control: Proprietary IRS Status: Proprietary
Highest Offering: Associate Degree
Program: Occupational; 2-Year Principally Bachelor's Creditable
Accreditation: DEAC

00 CEO .... Ms. Doris GRANATOWSKI
01 President .... Mr. Gordon DRUMMOND
03 Executive Vice President .... Mr. Louis J. SCHILT
11 Chief Operating Officer .... Mr. Robert TIMM
10 Chief Financial Officer/Bursar .... Ms. Carole Anne BAILO
32 Dir Student Services/Acad Pgms .... Mr. Jared ELIZARES

Sonoran Desert Institute (N)

8767 E. Via de Ventura, Suite 126, Scottsdale AZ 85258-3376
County: Maricopa Identification: 667057
Telephone: (480) 314-2102 Carnegie Class: Not Classified
FAX Number: (480) 314-2138 Calendar System: Semester
URL: www.sdi.edu
Established: 2000 Annual Undergrad Tuition & Fees: $15,000
Enrollment: 900 Coed
Affiliation or Control: Proprietary IRS Status: Proprietary
Highest Offering: Associate Degree
Program: Occupational
Accreditation: DEAC

01 President .... Paul L. ZAGNONI

Southwest College of Naturopathic Medicine & Health Sciences (O)

2140 E Broadway Road, Tempe AZ 85282-1751
County: Maricopa FICE Identification: 031070
Unit ID: 420246
Telephone: (480) 858-9100 Carnegie Class: Spec/Health
FAX Number: (480) 858-9116 Calendar System: Quarter
URL: www.scnm.edu
Established: 1993 Annual Graduate Tuition & Fees: $30,990
Enrollment: 403 Coed
Affiliation or Control: Independent Non-Profit IRS Status: 501(c)3
Highest Offering: First Professional Degree; No Undergraduates
Program: Professional
Accreditation: NH, NATUR

01 President/Chief Executive Officer .... Paul A. MITTMAN
03 Executive Vice President .... Christine L. GIRARD
10 Vice Pres Finance & Administration .... Dawn RECTOR
32 Vice President Student Affairs .... Melissa WINQUIST
13 Chief IT Officer .... Mark LIERLEY

Southwest Institute of Healing Arts (P)

1100 E Apache Boulevard, Tempe AZ 85281-5822
County: Maricopa FICE Identification: 035933
Unit ID: 442879
Telephone: (480) 994-9244 Carnegie Class: Assoc/PrivFP
FAX Number: (480) 994-3228 Calendar System: Other
URL: www.swiha.edu
Established: 1992 Annual Undergrad Tuition & Fees: $17,625
Enrollment: 986 Coed
Affiliation or Control: Proprietary IRS Status: Proprietary
Highest Offering: Associate Degree
Program: Occupational
Accreditation: CNCE

01 President/Owner .... Mrs. K. C. MILLER
05 Exec Director of Online Faculty .... Mr. Michael DYE
10 Dir Finance & Human Res/Controller .... Ms. Salisha TAMANDL
32 Director Student Support/Analytics .... Mr. Matt BILACH
35 Director Student Services .... Ms. Maria HUNTER
20 Assoc Director of Education .... Ms. Janell ERICKSON
37 Financial Aid Manager .... Ms. Joy KLEIN
06 Registrar .... Ms. Frannie WALSH

Southwest University of Visual Arts (Q)

2525 N Country Club Road, Tucson AZ 85716-2505
County: Pima FICE Identification: 024915
Unit ID: 104188
Telephone: (520) 325-0123 Carnegie Class: Spec/Arts
FAX Number: (520) 325-5535 Calendar System: Semester
URL: www.suva.edu
Established: 1983 Annual Undergrad Tuition & Fees: $34,541
Enrollment: 277 Coed
Affiliation or Control: Proprietary IRS Status: Proprietary
Highest Offering: Master's
Program: Fine Arts Emphasis
Accreditation: NH, CIDA

01 President .... Mrs. Sharmon WOODS
07 Director of Admissions .... Mr. Steve DIETZMAN
32 Director of Student Services .... Mr. Rob MAIR
12 Director of Albuquerque Campus .... Ms. Cindy WHITAKER
06 Registrar .... Vacant

Tohono O'odham Community College (A)

PO Box 3129, Sells AZ 85634-3129

County: Pima FICE Identification: 037844
Unit ID: 442781
Telephone: (520) 383-8401 Carnegie Class: Tribal
FAX Number: (520) 383-0029 Calendar System: Semester
URL: www.tocc.edu
Established: 1998 Annual Undergrad Tuition & Fees: $1,604
Enrollment: 225 Coed
Affiliation or Control: Tribal Control IRS Status: 501(c)3
Highest Offering: Associate Degree
Program: Occupational; 2-Year Principally Bachelor's Creditable
Accreditation: NH

01 President Dr. James VANDER HOOVEN
05 Vice President for Education Ms. Juana Clare JOSE
10 Vice Pres Admin Services/Finance Ms. Karla VOLPI
32 Vice Pres of Student Services Ms. Sylvia HENDRICKS
46 Vice Pres Inst Research/Development Ms. Jane LATANE
75 Acad Chair Occupational Pgms Mr. George MIGUEL
97 Acad Chair for General Education Dr. Maria MONTES-HELU
07 Director of Admissions/Records Mr. Leslie LUNA
08 College Librarian Ms. Elaine CUBBINS
37 Director of Financial Aid Mr. Al RIVERA
88 Director Project NATIVE Ms. Camille MARTINEZ-YADEN
88 Director Project NATIVE Dr. Sandra LUCAS
30 Director of Fundraising Ms. Andrea AHMED
15 Human Resources Director Ms. Stacy OWSLEY
25 Sponsored Projects Manager Mr. Antonio BENAVIDEZ

Tohono O'odham Community College West Campus (B)

PO Box 3129, Sells AZ 85634-3129

Telephone: (520) 383-8401 Identification: 770022
Accreditation: &NH

† Branch campus of Tohono O'odham Community College, Sells, AZ.

Universal Technical Institute (C)

10695 W Pierce Street, Avondale AZ 85323-7946

County: Maricopa FICE Identification: 008221
Unit ID: 106041
Telephone: (623) 245-4600 Carnegie Class: Assoc/PrivFP
FAX Number: (623) 245-4601 Calendar System: Other
URL: www.uti.edu
Established: 1965 Annual Undergrad Tuition & Fees: $41,900
Enrollment: 2,340 Coed
Affiliation or Control: Proprietary IRS Status: Proprietary
Highest Offering: Associate Degree
Program: Occupational
Accreditation: ACCSC

01 Campus President Mr. Michael ROMANO
05 Director of Education Mr. Gary STARK
32 Director of Student Services Mr. Patrick BENNETT
10 Director of Campus Accounting Mrs. Gayle PARSONS
07 Admissions Director Mr. Adam HELLER
36 Director of Graduate Employment Ms. Cheryl RADKE
37 Director of Financial Aid Ms. Terri MEIXSEL-CORDERO
18 Maintenance Director Mr. George MICKENS

University of Advancing Technology (D)

2625 W Baseline Road, Tempe AZ 85283-1056

County: Maricopa FICE Identification: 025590
Unit ID: 363934
Telephone: (602) 383-8228 Carnegie Class: Bac/Diverse
FAX Number: (602) 383-8250 Calendar System: Other
URL: www.uat.edu
Established: 1983 Annual Undergrad Tuition & Fees: $23,150
Enrollment: 819 Coed
Affiliation or Control: Proprietary IRS Status: Proprietary
Highest Offering: Master's
Program: Technical Emphasis
Accreditation: NH

01 President Mr. Jason PISTILLO
05 Provost/Dean & Secretary Mr. Dave BOLMAN
11 Chief Administrative Officer Vacant
07 Vice President Admissions Ms. Shawn ALEXANDER
10 Senior Controller Ms. Erika GARNEY

University of Arizona (E)

1401 E University Blvd, Tucson AZ 85721-0001

County: Pima FICE Identification: 001083
Unit ID: 104179
Telephone: (520) 621-2211 Carnegie Class: RU/VH
FAX Number: (520) 621-9323 Calendar System: Semester
URL: www.arizona.edu
Established: 1885 Annual Undergrad Tuition & Fees (In-State): $9,576
Enrollment: 42,236 Coed
Affiliation or Control: State IRS Status: 501(c)3
Highest Offering: Doctorate
Program: Liberal Arts And General; Teacher Preparatory; Professional
Accreditation: NH, ANEST, ART, AUD, BUS, BUSA, CEA, CLPSY, CORE, DANCE, DIETD, ENG, ENGR, IPSY, JOUR, LAW, LIB, LSAR, MED, MUS, NURSE, PCSAS, PERF, PH, PHAR, PLNG, SCPSY, SP, SPAA, THEA

01 President Dr. Ann WEAVER HART
05 Sr VP for Acad Affairs & Provost Dr. Andrew C. COMRIE
10 Sr VP and CFO/Business Affairs Mr. Gregg GOLDMAN
26 Sr VP University Relations Dr. Teresa THOMPSON
17 Sr VP Health Sciences Dr. Joe GARCIA
32 Sr VP Student Affairs & Enroll Mgmt Dr. Melissa VITO
46 Sr VP for Research Dr. Kimberly A. ESPY
41 VP and Director Athletics Mr. Gregory K. BYRNE
88 VP for Strategic Planning & Anal Dr. Barbara BRYSON
43 VP Legal Affs/General Counsel Dr. Laura T. JOHNSON
88 VP Global Initiatives Dr. Michael A. PROCTOR
49 VP Innovation & Strategy Dr. Joaquin RUIZ
21 VP Business Affairs Mr. Robert R. SMITH
29 VP Alumni Relations Ms. Melinda W. BURKE
15 VP Institutional Effectiveness & HR Dr. Allison M. VAILLANCOURT
88 VP Tech Launch AZ Dr. David N. ALLEN
20 Sr Vice Provost Academic Affairs Dr. Gail D. BURD
86 Sr Assoc VP Legis & Comm Relations Mr. Timothy S. BEE
88 Sr Assoc VP University Relations Mr. Chris W. SIGURDSON
88 Sr Assoc VP Health Sciences Mr. Mike JONEN
88 Sr Assoc to the Pres/Secretary Univ Dr. Jon DUDAS
47 V Provost/Dean Agri/Life Sci Dr. Shane C. BURGESS
88 Vice Provost Faculty Affairs Dr. Thomas P. MILLER
88 Assoc VP Research Ms. Caroline M. GARCIA
88 Assoc VP for Research Dr. Jennifer K. BARTON
88 Assoc VP External Relations-Phoenix Ms. Judith A. BERNAS
07 Assoc VP/Std Aff/Enr Mgmt/Dean Adm Dr. Kasandra K. URQUIDEZ
88 Assoc VP Health Sci - Interprof Ed Dr. Sally J. REEL
88 Assoc VP Clinical Affairs Mr. Steven GOLDSCHMID
88 Assoc VP Precision Health Sciences Mr. Kenneth RAMOS
108 Assoc Vice Provost Instruc/Assess Dr. Debra J. TOMANEK
88 Assoc VP Institutional Analysis Mr. James S. FLORIAN
88 Assoc VP Tech Parks Arizona Mr. Bruce A. WRIGHT
27 Assoc VP External Communications Ms. Andrea C. SMILEY
88 Assoc VP Marketing/Brand Mgmt Mr. Michael A. PROUDFOOT
88 Sr Asst VP Student Affairs Dr. Jeffrey M. ORGERA
13 CIO/Exec Director UITS Ms. Michele L. NORIN
88 Sr Asst VP Finance Administration Ms. Marilyn TAYLOR
88 Asst VP Dean of Students Ms. Kendal H. WASHINGTON WHITE
88 Asst VP Budget Ms. Kathryn E. WHISMAN
88 Asst VP Program Innovation Dr. Randy M. BURD
09 Asst Provost Inst Research Dr. Angela Y. BALDASARE
88 Asst VP Student Affairs/Fin & Admin Mr. Joel S. HAUFF
18 Asst VP Plng/Design & Construction Mr. Peter DOURLEIN
31 Asst VP Community Relations Ms. Tannya R. GAXIOLA GAXIOLA
88 Asst VP Tribal Relations Ms. Karen F. BEGAY
88 Asst VP Health Sciences/Pub Affairs Mr. George D. HUMPHREY
06 Registrar/Enrollment Management Dr. Elizabeth A. ACREE
18 Asst VP Facilities Management Mr. Christopher M. KOPACH
88 Asst VP Finance & Admin Ms. Karen L. TUMLINSON
19 Asst VP Risk Management/Safety Mr. Steven C. HOLLAND
63 Dean College of Medicine Dr. Charles B. CAIRNS
63 Dean College of Med-Phoenix Campus Dr. Stuart D. FLYNN
54 Dean College of Engineering Dr. Jeffrey B. GOLDBERG
69 Dean Public Health Dr. Iman A. HAKIM
57 Dean Fine Arts Dr. Jory L. HANCOCK
50 Dean Eller College of Management Dr. Jeffrey W. SCHATZBERG
67 Dean Pharmacy Dr. J. L. BOOTMAN
83 Dean Social/Behav Science Dr. John P. JONES
81 Dean College of Optical Sciences Dr. Thomas L. KOCH
92 Dean Honors College Dr. Patricia MACCORQUODALE
48 Dean Col Arch & Landscape Arch Dr. Janice A. CERVELLI
53 Dean Education Dr. Ronald W. MARX
58 Dean Graduate College Dr. Andrew H. CARNIE
61 Dean James E Rogers College of Law Dr. Marc L. MILLER
66 Dean College of Nursing Dr. Joan L. SHAVER
12 Dean UA South Dr. James W. SHOCKEY
08 Dean of Libraries Ms. Karen A. WILLIAMS
79 Dean College of Humanities Dr. Mary E. WILDNER-BASSETT
23 Exec Director Campus Health Dr. Harry MCDERMOTT
88 Exec Dir Analytics & Inst Research Mr. Henry A. CHILDERS
85 Director International Admissions Dr. Rachel A. BEECH
36 Director Career Services Ms. Eileen M. MCGARRY
96 Director Procurement & Contract Svs Mr. Edward D. NASSER
25 Director Sponsored Proj/Services Ms. Sherry L. ESHAM
40 Director Univ of Arizona Bookstores Ms. Debby L. SHIVELY
22 Dir Office of Institutional Equity Ms. Mary E. TUCKER

University of Arizona Phoenix Biomedical Campus (F)

550 E Van Buren Street, Phoenix AZ 85004

Telephone: (602) 827-2001 Identification: 770023
Accreditation: &NH, #MED

† Branch campus of University of Arizona, Tucson, AZ.

University of Arizona South (G)

1140 N Colombo Avenue, Sierra Vista AZ 85635

Telephone: (520) 458-8278 Identification: 770024
Accreditation: &NH

† Branch campus of University of Arizona, Tucson, AZ.

University of Phoenix (H)

1625 W. Fountainhead Parkway, Tempe AZ 85282

County: Maricopa FICE Identification: 020988
Unit ID: 105516
Telephone: (480) 557-2000 Carnegie Class: Master's L
FAX Number: N/A Calendar System: Other
URL: www.phoenix.edu
Established: 1976 Annual Undergrad Tuition & Fees: N/A
Enrollment: 206,900 Coed
Affiliation or Control: Proprietary IRS Status: Proprietary
Highest Offering: Doctorate
Program: Liberal Arts And General; Teacher Preparatory; Professional
Accreditation: NH, ACBSP, CACREP, NURSE

01 President University of Phoenix Mr. Timothy SLOTTOW
04 Assistant to the President Ms. Cindy WHIPPO
05 Provost Dr. Meredith CURLEY
03 Chief Operating Officer Mr. Jerrad TAUSZ
88 Vice Provost Inst Tech & Learning Dr. Becky LODEWYCK
09 Vice Provost Inst Effectiveness Dr. Kathleen SCHNIER
20 Associate Provost Dr. Len KELPSH
53 Exec Dean College of Education Vacant
50 Exec Dean School of Business Ms. Ruth VELORIA
88 Exec Dean Sch of Advanced Studies Dr. Hinrich EYLERS
88 Exec Dean Col of Security & CJ Mr. Spider MARKS
76 Exec Dean Col of Health Prof Dr. Tamara ROZHON
72 Exec Dean IS&T Mr. Dennis BONILLA
79 Exec Dean Col of Humanities & Sci Dr. Constance ST. GERMAIN
83 Exec Dean Col of Social Sciences Dr. Constance ST. GERMAIN
10 Chief Financial Officer Mr. Byron JONES
15 SVP Human Resources Ms. Cheryl NAUMANN
88 SVP Academic Operations Dr. Russ PADEN
37 SVP Student Administrative Services Mr. Jeff SONNENBERG
88 SVP Campus Services Mr. Matt JOHNSTON
84 SVP Enrollment Services Vacant
88 VP Financial Services Mr. Bronson LEDBETTER
06 Registrar Ms. Audra MCQUARIE

University of Phoenix Southern Arizona Campus (I)

300 S Craycroft Road, Tucson AZ 85711-4574

Telephone: (520) 881-6512 Identification: 770236
Accreditation: &NH, ACBSP

† Branch campus of University of Phoenix, Tempe, AZ.

West Coast Ultrasound Institute (J)

4250 E Camelback Road, #K158, Phoenix AZ 85018

Telephone: (602) 954-3834 Identification: 770550
Accreditation: ACCSC

† Branch campus of West Coast Ultrasound Institute, Beverly Hills, CA.

Western International University (K)

1601 W. Fountainhead Parkway, Tempe AZ 85282

County: Maricopa FICE Identification: 021715
Unit ID: 106102
Telephone: (602) 943-2311 Carnegie Class: Master's M
FAX Number: (602) 371-8637 Calendar System: Other
URL: www.west.edu
Established: 1978 Annual Undergrad Tuition & Fees: $6,000
Enrollment: 1,374 Coed
Affiliation or Control: Proprietary IRS Status: Proprietary
Highest Offering: Master's
Program: Professional; Business Emphasis
Accreditation: NH

01 President Ms. Tracy LORENZ
03 Senior Vice Pres & Provost Dr. Benjamin PRYOR
05 VP of Academic Affairs Dr. Christopher DAVIS
11 Sr VP University Operations Mr. Kris MCCALL
13 VP InformationTechnology Ms. Stephanie LEACH
10 CFO Ms. Heidi PHIPPS
26 Senior Director of Marketing Mr. Chris HEWITT
15 Manager Human Resources Ms. Jena MURRAY
88 Senior Director of University Ms. Hue HASLIM
88 Sr Dir of Operations & Analysis Mr. Ken COSTELLO
06 Sr Dir Student Admin Svcs/Registrar Ms. Beth CARLISLE

Yavapai College (L)

1100 E Sheldon Street, Prescott AZ 86301-3297

County: Yavapai FICE Identification: 001079
Unit ID: 106148
Telephone: (928) 445-7300 Carnegie Class: Assoc/Pub-R-L
FAX Number: (928) 776-2109 Calendar System: Semester
URL: www.yc.edu
Established: 1966 Annual Undergrad Tuition & Fees (In-District): $2,064
Enrollment: 7,842 Coed
Affiliation or Control: Local IRS Status: 501(c)3
Highest Offering: Associate Degree
Program: Occupational; 2-Year Principally Bachelor's Creditable
Accreditation: NH, ADNUR, EMT, IFSAC, RAD

01 President Dr. Penelope WILLS
05 Provost & VP Instruction/Stdnt Dev Dr. Stuart BLACKLAW

10 Vice Pres Finance/Admin Svcs ..... Dr. Clint EWELL
30 VP College Development/Foundation ..... Mr. Steve WALKER
20 Dean for Comp Tech & Instr Support ..... Ms. Stacey HILTON
12 Exec Dean Verde Valley Campus ..... Dr. James PEREY
75 Dean Career Technical Education ..... Mr. John MORGAN
66 Dean Sci/Health/Public Safety ..... Mr. Scott FARNSWORTH
79 Dean Arts & Humanities ..... Dr. Craig RALSTON
32 Dean for Student Development ..... Ms. Tania SHELDAHL
26 Director of Marketing/Public Info ..... Mr. Mike LANGE
37 Assoc Dean Stdnt Dev & Dir Fin Aid ..... Ms. Terri ECKEL
09 Dir Inst Effectiveness & Research ..... Mr. Tom HUGHES
15 Director for Human Resources ..... Dr. Monica BELKNAP
19 Chief of Police ..... Mr. Frank LOPEZ
21 Dir of Business Svcs & Controller ..... Mr. Frank D'ANGELO
07 Recruitment Officer ..... Vacant
18 Director for Facilities ..... Mr. David LAURENCE
13 Chief Information Officer ..... Mr. Patrick BURNS
06 Registrar ..... Ms. Sheila JARRELL
96 Director of Purchasing ..... Mr. Ryan BOUWHUIS

Yavapai College Verde Valley Campus (A)

601 Black Hills Drive, Clarkdale AZ 86324
Telephone: (928) 634-7501 Identification: 770029
Accreditation: &NH

† Branch campus of Yavapai College, Prescott, AZ.

ARKANSAS

Arkansas Baptist College (B)

1621 Martin Luther King Drive, Little Rock AR 72202-6099
County: Pulaski FICE Identification: 001087
Unit ID: 106306
Telephone: (501) 370-4000 Carnegie Class: Bac/Assoc
FAX Number: (501) 372-7992 Calendar System: Semester
URL: www.arkansasbaptist.edu
Established: 1884 Annual Undergrad Tuition & Fees: $8,760
Enrollment: 899 Coed
Affiliation or Control: Baptist IRS Status: 501(c)3
Highest Offering: Baccalaureate
Program: 2-Year Principally Bachelor's Creditable; Liberal Arts And General
Accreditation: NH

01 President ..... Dr. Fitz HILL
04 President's Executive Assistant ..... Ms. Patsy BIGGS
10 Chief Financial Officer ..... Ms. Charlotte COMER
100 Chief of Staff ..... Mrs. LaCresha NEWTON
05 VP of Academic Affairs ..... Dr. Joyce O. JENKINS
32 VP of Student Affairs ..... Dr. Vicki WILLIAMS
09 Director of Inst Research/Registrar ..... Dr. Jerelyn L. DUNCAN
103 Dir of Adult Ed & Workforce Dev ..... Vacant
07 Director of Admissions/Recruitment ..... Mr. Willie HICKS
84 Dean of Enrollment Management ..... Dr. Yvette WIMBERLY
37 Director of Financial Aid ..... Mr. Phillip RODGERS
08 Director of Library/Media Services ..... Dr. Wille HARDIN
26 College Relations/Marketing ..... Mrs. Linda GILLAM WEIR
34 Dean of Women ..... Vacant
35 Asst Dean of Student Affairs ..... Mr. Brian MILLER
33 Dean of Men ..... Vacant
19 Chief of Campus Safety ..... Mr. Curtis JOHNSON
18 Facilities Director ..... Vacant

Arkansas Northeastern College (C)

2501 S Division Street, Blytheville AR 72315-5111
County: Mississippi FICE Identification: 012860
Unit ID: 107327
Telephone: (870) 762-1020 Carnegie Class: Assoc/Pub-R-M
FAX Number: (870) 763-3704 Calendar System: Semester
URL: www.anc.edu
Established: 1974 Annual Undergrad Tuition & Fees (In-District): $1,170
Enrollment: 1,425 Coed
Affiliation or Control: State/Local IRS Status: 501(c)3
Highest Offering: Associate Degree
Program: Occupational; 2-Year Principally Bachelor's Creditable
Accreditation: NH, ADNUR, DA, EMT

01 President ..... Dr. James SHEMWELL
05 Executive Vice President/CAO ..... Mrs. June WALTERS
10 Vice President for Finance ..... Ms. Pacey BOWENS
32 Vice Pres Student Services ..... Mrs. Laura YARBROUGH
30 Vice President for Advancement ..... Mrs. Sherri BENNETT
09 Vice President MITS/Human Resources ..... Mr. James W. MCCLAIN
26 Assoc VP for Dev/College Relations ..... Ms. Rachel GIFFORD
72 Dean Tech Programs & Training ..... Mrs. Robin SINGLETON
20 Assistant CAO ..... Mrs. Deborah PARKER
88 Dean for Economic Development ..... Mr. Gene BENNETT
66 Dean Nursing/Allied Hlth/PE/Rec ..... Mrs. Brenda HOLIFIELD
49 Dean for Arts and Sciences ..... Mrs. Deanita HICKS
88 Coordinator University Center ..... Mrs. Candice BLANKENSHIP
31 Community Education Specialist ..... Ms. Mary Ann GARREN
08 Director of College Library ..... Mrs. Bronwyn MORGAN
07 Director of Admissions ..... Vacant
36 Coordinator of Placement Services ..... Dr. Bridget SHEMWELL
37 Director Financial Aid ..... Mrs. Melinda WALKER
72 Dean MITS ..... Mrs. Ruby MEADOR
21 Controller ..... Vacant
15 Human Resources & ADA Coordinator ..... Mrs. Carol WILF
90 Director Academic Tech Services ..... Mr. James ODOM

18 Director Physical Plant and Grounds ..... Mr. Scott CREECY
88 Director Talent Search/Educ Opp Ctr ..... Mrs. Tonya HARRIS
35 Director Student Support Services ..... Ms. Lisa MCGHEE
04 Assistant to Board/President ..... Mrs. Courtney FISHER
06 Registrar ..... Mrs. Laura YARBROUGH
19 Director Security/Safety ..... Mr. Jim LOWE
27 Information/Marketing Specialist ..... Ms. Sheiron BEARDON

*Arkansas State University System (D)

501 Woodlane Drive, Suite 600, Little Rock AR 72201
County: Pulaski Identification: 666187
Telephone: (501) 660-1000 Carnegie Class: N/A
FAX Number: (501) 660-1010
URL: www.asusystem.edu

01 President ..... Dr. Charles L. WELCH
04 Exec Assistant to the President ..... Ms. Pam KAIL
10 Executive Vice President ..... Ms. Julie BATES
86 Vice Pres Governmental Relations ..... Mr. Shane BROADWAY
45 Vice Pres Strategic Comm/Econ Dev ..... Mr. Jeff HANKINS
102 Interim President ASU Foundation ..... Mr. Philip JACKSON
43 Legal Counsel ..... Ms. Lucinda MCDANIEL
88 Internal Auditor ..... Ms. Jo LUNBECK

*Arkansas State University-Beebe (E)

PO Box 1000, Beebe AR 72012-1000
County: White FICE Identification: 001091
Unit ID: 106449
Telephone: (501) 882-3600 Carnegie Class: Assoc/Pub2in4
FAX Number: (501) 882-8970 Calendar System: Semester
URL: www.asub.edu
Established: 1927 Annual Undergrad Tuition & Fees (In-State): $4,071
Enrollment: 4,140 Coed
Affiliation or Control: State IRS Status: 501(c)3
Highest Offering: Associate Degree
Program: Occupational; 2-Year Principally Bachelor's Creditable
Accreditation: NH, EMT, MLTAD, NAIT

02 Chancellor ..... Dr. Eugene MCKAY
100 Executive Assistant to Chancellor ..... Mr. Joe BERRY
12 Vice Chancellor ASU-Heber Springs ..... Dr. James C. BOYETT
12 Vice Chancellor of ASU-Searcy ..... Mr. Barry FARRIS
05 Vice Chancellor Academic Affairs ..... Dr. Theodore J. KALTHOFF
32 Vice Chancellor Student Services ..... Dr. Deborah A. GARRETT
10 Vice Chanc Finance & Administration ..... Mr. Jerry H. CARLISLE
30 Vice Chanc Inst Advancement ..... Dr. Keith PINCHBACK
26 Director of Marketing/PR ..... Ms. Nancy MEADOR
06 Registrar ..... Ms. Amy J. MAHAN
08 Head Librarian ..... Ms. Tracy D. SMITH
15 Director of Human Resources ..... Ms. Susan A. COLLIE
19 Chief of Police ..... Mr. James J. MARTIN
18 Director of Physical Plant ..... Mr. Jerry L. THOMPSON
37 Director Student Financial Aid ..... Ms. Louise DRIVER
09 Director of Institutional Research ..... Ms. Bonnie SMYTH-MCGAHA
13 Chief Information Technology Office ..... Mr. Chris LEE
21 Business Manager ..... Ms. Charlette MOORE
21 Controller ..... Ms. Sharon A. BEEN
84 Director of Enrollment Management ..... Mr. David M. MAYES
38 Dir Student Success and Retention ..... Mr. Roger MOORE
36 Career Service/Transfer Coord ..... Ms. Heather GARCIA
39 Director of Student Life ..... Vacant
24 Director of Learning Center ..... Ms. Rebecca E. WOLF
72 Director Advanced Tech/Allied Hlth ..... Dr. Keith MCCLANAHAN
106 Director of Distance Learning ..... Ms. Rhonda DURHAM
96 Dir Administrative Support Services ..... Ms. Robin LANCASTER
12 Dir ASU-Beebe Degree Ctr at LRAFB ..... Ms. Nancy A. SHEFFLETTE
07 Director of Admissions ..... Ms. Robin A. HAYES
35 Coordinator of Campus Life ..... Mr. Andy ISOM
105 Website Coordinator ..... Mr. Rikky L. FREE

*Arkansas State University-Jonesboro (F)

PO Box 600, State University AR 72467
County: Craighead FICE Identification: 001090
Unit ID: 106458
Telephone: (870) 972-2100 Carnegie Class: Master's L
FAX Number: (870) 972-3465 Calendar System: Semester
URL: www.astate.edu
Established: 1909 Annual Undergrad Tuition & Fees (In-State): $8,050
Enrollment: 13,144 Coed
Affiliation or Control: State IRS Status: 501(c)3
Highest Offering: Doctorate
Program: Liberal Arts And General; Teacher Preparatory; Professional
Accreditation: NH, ADNUR, ANEST, ART, BUS, CAATE, CACREP, CEA, CORE, @DIETC, DMS, ENG, JOUR, MLTAD, MT, MUS, NUR, PTA, PTAA, RAD, RADMAG, RTT, SP, SPAA, SW, TED, THEA

02 Chancellor ..... Dr. Tim HUDSON
100 Chief of Staff ..... Ms. Shawnie CARRIER
05 Provost & VC Acad Affair & Research ..... Dr. Lynita COOKSEY
10 VC Finance & Administration ..... Dr. Len T. FREY
32 Vice Chancellor Student Affairs ..... Dr. William R. STRIPLING
30 Vice Chancellor Univ Advancement ..... Dr. Jason PENRY
28 Asst Vice Chancellor Diversity ..... Dr. Maurice GIPSON
41 Director of Athletics ..... Mr. Terry MOHAJIR
20 Assoc Vice Chanc Academic Svcs ..... Dr. Gina HOGUE
21 Assoc Vice Chancellor Finance ..... Dr. Russ HANNAH
21 Asst Vice Chanc Budget ..... Ms. Donna MCMILLIN
15 Asst VC Human Resources ..... Ms. Lori WINN
35 Assoc Vice Chanc Student Affairs ..... Dr. Lonnie R. WILLIAMS
46 Vice Provost Resrch & Grad Studies ..... Dr. Andrew SUSTICH
35 Asst Vice Chanc Student Affairs ..... Dr. Craig JOHNSON
13 Asst Vice Chanc/CIO ..... Mr. Henry TORRES
18 Asst Vice Chancellor Facilities ..... Mr. Al STOVERINK
37 Dir of Financial Aid & Scholarship ..... Mr. Terry FINNEY
09 Dir Inst Research/Plng/Assessment ..... Dr. Kathryn C. JONES
06 Dir Admissions/Records/Registration ..... Ms. Tracy FINCH
07 Director of Recruitment ..... Dr. Tammy L. FOWLER
39 Director of Residence Life ..... Mr. Patrick DIXON
88 Director of Leadership Center ..... Ms. Martha SPACK
19 Chief University Police ..... Mr. Randy MARTIN
28 Director of Disability Services ..... Dr. Jenifer RICE-MASON
36 Director Career Services ..... Vacant
38 Director Counseling Center ..... Dr. Phil HESTAND
23 Director Student Health Center ..... Ms. Victoria WILLIAMS
29 Exec Dir Alumni Relations ..... Ms. Beth SMITH
26 Exec Dir Mktg & Communications ..... Dr. Bill SMITH
26 Director of Media Relations ..... Ms. Gina BOWMAN
88 Director Pub & Creative Services ..... Mr. Mark REEVES
96 Dir Procurement & Travel Svcs ..... Ms. Carol BARNHILL
62 Dir Library ..... Mr. Jeff BAILEY
47 Dean College Agri/Technology ..... Dr. Timothy BURCHAM
81 Dean College Sciences & Math ..... Dr. John PRATTE
50 Dean College of Business ..... Dr. Shane HUNT
53 Dean Col of Educ & Behavioral Sci ..... Dr. Gina HOGUE
60 Dean Humanities/Soc Sci/Media/Comm ..... Dr. Brad RAWLINS
66 Dean College of Nursing Health Prof ..... Dr. Susan N. HANRAHAN
88 Dean University College ..... Dr. Jill SIMONS
57 Dean Fine Arts ..... Dr. Donald BOWYER
92 Director of The Honors College ..... Ms. Rebecca OLIVER
54 Interim Dean College of Engineering ..... Dr. Paul MIXON

*Arkansas State University-Mid-South (G)

2000 W Broadway, West Memphis AR 72301-3829
County: Crittenden FICE Identification: 023482
Unit ID: 107318
Telephone: (870) 733-6722 Carnegie Class: Assoc/Pub-S-SC
FAX Number: (870) 733-6799 Calendar System: Semester
URL: www.midsouthcc.edu
Established: 1992 Annual Undergrad Tuition & Fees (In-District): $2,554
Enrollment: 1,895 Coed
Affiliation or Control: State/Local IRS Status: 501(c)3
Highest Offering: Associate Degree
Program: Occupational; 2-Year Principally Bachelor's Creditable
Accreditation: NH, #COARC

02 Chancellor ..... Dr. Debra WEST
03 Executive Vice President ..... Vacant
05 Sr Vice Pres Learning/Instruction ..... Dr. Cliff JONES
10 Vice Pres Finance & Administration ..... Mrs. Susan MARSHALL
30 Vice Pres Institutional Advancement ..... Ms. Diane HAMPTON
32 Vice Chanc Student Affairs ..... Mr. Jeremy REECE
88 AVP Secondary Technical Education ..... Vacant
103 Associate VP Workforce Programs ..... Mr. Pete SELDEN
21 Associate Vice Pres Finance ..... Ms. Karyn WEAVER
20 Assoc VP Learning/Instruction ..... Ms. Roshell COLEMAN
37 Director of Financial Aid ..... Ms. Carol MCHANN
08 Director of Library/Media Center ..... Ms. Rene JONES
06 Registrar ..... Ms. Leslie ANDERSON
15 Director of Human Resources ..... Ms. Jackie BRUBAKER
18 Director Facilities/Physical Plant ..... Mr. Randy WEBB
07 Director of Admissions ..... Mr. Jeremy REECE

*Arkansas State University-Mountain Home (H)

1600 S College Street, Mountain Home AR 72653-5326
County: Baxter Identification: 666311
Unit ID: 420538
Telephone: (870) 508-6100 Carnegie Class: Assoc/Pub2in4
FAX Number: (870) 508-6287 Calendar System: Semester
URL: www.asumh.edu
Established: 1995 Annual Undergrad Tuition & Fees (In-District): $3,420
Enrollment: 1,309 Coed
Affiliation or Control: State/Local IRS Status: 501(c)3
Highest Offering: Associate Degree
Program: 2-Year Principally Bachelor's Creditable; Business Emphasis
Accreditation: NH, #COARC, EMT, FUSER

02 Chancellor ..... Dr. Robin MYERS
05 Vice Chanc Academic Affairs ..... Dr. Martin EGGENSPERGER
10 Vice Chanc Administrative Affairs ..... Mr. John DAVIDSON
32 Vice Chancellor for Student Affairs ..... Mrs. Rosalyn BLAGG
30 Vice Chancellor Development ..... Vacant
88 Assoc VC Special Projects ..... Mrs. Karen S. HOPPER
06 Registrar ..... Vacant
18 Chief Facilities/Physical Plant ..... Mr. Nickey L. ROBBINS
26 Director of Communications ..... Mrs. Christy C. KEIRN
35 Director Student Affairs ..... Mr. Mason CAMPBELL
37 Director Student Financial Aid ..... Mr. Clay BERRY
08 Head Librarian ..... Ms. Tina BRADLEY
09 Dir of Inst Research/Effectiveness ..... Mr. David CULLIPHER

*Arkansas State University-Newport (I)

7648 Victory Boulevard, Newport AR 72112-8912
County: Jackson Identification: 666153
Unit ID: 440402
Telephone: (870) 512-7800 Carnegie Class: Assoc/Pub2in4
FAX Number: (870) 512-7807 Calendar System: Semester

URL: www.asun.edu
Established: 1991 Annual Undergrad Tuition & Fees (In-State): $3,270
Enrollment: 2,477 Coed
Affiliation or Control: State IRS Status: 501(c)3
Highest Offering: Associate Degree
Program: Occupational; 2-Year Principally Bachelor's Creditable
Accreditation: NH, SURGT

02 Chancellor ... Dr. Sandra MASSEY
04 Assistant to the Chancellor ... Ms. Laura KING
05 Int Vice Chanc Academic Affairs ... Dr. Martha S. SHULL
10 Vice Chanc Finance/Administration ... Mr. Adam ADAIR
32 Vice Chancellor Student Affairs ... Ms. Jacqueline A. FAULKNER
12 Vice Chancellor Jonesboro Campus ... Mr. Charley APPLEBY
12 Vice Chancellor Marked Tree Campus ... Mr. Jeff BOOKOUT
88 Division Chair ... Mr. Ike WHEELER
88 Division Chair ... Dr. Allen MOONEYHAN
88 Division Chair ... Mr. Robert SUMMERS
88 Division Chair ... Mr. Joeseph CAMPBELL
07 Dean of Enrollment Services ... Ms. Candace GROSS
13 Director of IT Services ... Ms. Tamya STALLINGS
15 Director Human Resources ... Mr. Charles WALKER
18 Director of Physical Plant ... Mr. David WINSTON
21 Controller ... Ms. Melissa WATSON
25 Dir Budget/Grants Management ... Ms. Monika PHILLIPS
37 Director Financial Aid ... Ms. Bonnie BURGOYNE
35 Dean of Students ... Ms. Kimberly LONG
38 Counselor ... Ms. Amber GRADY
08 Librarian ... Ms. Jennifer BALLARD
24 Director of Learning Resource Ctr ... Ms. Christy MANN
19 Public Safety Officer ... Mr. Jeff GRIZZLE
96 Director of Procurement ... Ms. Lee WEBB
66 Director of Nursing/Allied Health ... Ms. Nancy WEAVER
108 Director of Career Pathways ... Ms. Penny LOGAN
75 Adult Education Coordinator ... Ms. Martha TAUSSIG

* *Arkansas State University-Heber Springs* (A)

101 River Crest Drive, Heber Springs AR 72543
Telephone: (501) 362-1100 Identification: 770001
Accreditation: &NH

† Branch campus of Arkansas State University-Beebe, Beebe, AR.

* *Arkansas State University-Searcy* (B)

1800 East Monroe Avenue, Searcy AR 72143
Telephone: (501) 207-6200 Identification: 770002
Accreditation: &NH

† Branch campus of Arkansas State University-Beebe, Beebe, AR.

Arkansas Tech University (C)

1509 North Boulder Avenue, Russellville AR 72801-2222
County: Pope FICE Identification: 001089
Unit ID: 106467
Telephone: (479) 968-0389 Carnegie Class: Master's L
FAX Number: (479) 964-0522 Calendar System: Semester
URL: www.atu.edu
Established: 1909 Annual Undergrad Tuition & Fees (In-State): $6,192
Enrollment: 12,002 Coed
Affiliation or Control: State IRS Status: 501(c)3
Highest Offering: Doctorate
Program: Liberal Arts And General; Teacher Preparatory; Professional
Accreditation: NH, BUS, CAHIIM, CORE, CS, EMT, ENG, MAC, MUS, NRPA, NUR, PTAA, TED

01 President ... Dr. Robin E. BOWEN
10 Sr Vice Pres Administration/Finance ... Mr. David MOSELEY
05 Interim Vice Pres Academic Affairs ... Dr. AJ ANGLIN
32 VP Student Services/Univ Rels ... Ms. Susie S. NICHOLSON
30 Vice President for Development ... Ms. Jayne W. JONES
12 Chancellor Ozark Campus ... Mr. Bruce SIKES
20 Assoc Vice Pres Academic Affairs ... Dr. David UNDERWOOD
43 Associate VP & Counsel to President . Mr. Thomas PENNINGTON
20 Assistant VP for Academic Affairs ... Dr. Hanna NORTON
84 Assistant VP Enrollment Management ... Ms. Shauna H. DONNELL
35 Chief Student Officer Ozark Campus ... Mr. Richard HARRIS
10 Chief Fiscal Officer Ozark Campus ... Ms. Sandra CHEFFER
06 Registrar ... Ms. Tammy WEAVER
88 Controller ... Ms. Donna RANKIN
08 Librarian ... Mr. Brent ETZEL
09 Director of Institutional Research ... Mr. Wyatt WATSON
13 Director Information Systems ... Mr. Ken WESTER
37 Director of Student Accounts ... Ms. Angela CROW
15 Director Human Resources ... Ms. Angela REYNOLDS
37 Director Student Financial Aid ... Ms. Shirley M. GOINES
29 Director Alumni Relations ... Mr. Kelly DAVIS
85 Director of International Students ... Mr. Yasushi ONODERA
18 Director of Physical Plant Services ... Mr. Brian LASEY
96 Director of Purchasing ... Ms. Jessica HOLLOWAY
92 Director of Honors Program ... Dr. Jan JENKINS
22 Director of Affirmative Action ... Ms. Jennifer FLEMING
108 Dir Assessment/Inst Effectiveness ... Dr. Christine AUSTIN
58 Dean of Graduate College ... Dr. Mary GUNTER
53 Dean of College of Education ... Dr. Sherry FIELD
49 Dean College of Arts & Humanities ... Dr. Jeffrey WOODS
50 Dean of College of Business ... Dr. Edward BASHAW
77 Dn Col Engineering & Applied Sci ... Dr. William HOEFLER
81 Dean College of Natural & Health Sc ... Dr. Jeff ROBERTSON
102 Dir Foundation/Corporate Relations ... Ms. Debra FITHEN
105 Director Web Strategies/Operations ... Mr. Michael STOKER
19 Director Public Safety ... Mr. Josh MCMILLIAN
26 Director of University Relations ... Mr. Sam STRASNER
28 Assoc Dean Diversity & Inclusion ... Dr. MarTeze HAMMONDS
36 Director of Career Services ... Mr. Brandon WRIGHT
38 Assoc Dean Student Student Wellness ... Ms. Kristy DAVIS
39 Associate Dean Residence Life ... Mr. Aaron HOGAN
41 Athletic Director ... Mr. Steve MULLINS

Arkansas Tech University-Ozark Campus (D)

1700 Helberg Lane, Ozark AR 72949
Telephone: (866) 225-2884 Identification: 770003
Accreditation: &NH, CVT, OTA

† Branch campus of Arkansas Tech University, Russellville, AR.

Black River Technical College (E)

PO Box 468, Pocahontas AR 72455-0468
County: Randolph FICE Identification: 020522
Unit ID: 106625
Telephone: (870) 248-4000 Carnegie Class: Assoc/Pub-R-M
FAX Number: (870) 248-4100 Calendar System: Semester
URL: www.blackrivertech.org
Established: 1991 Annual Undergrad Tuition & Fees (In-State): $3,060
Enrollment: 1,966 Coed
Affiliation or Control: State IRS Status: 501(c)3
Highest Offering: Associate Degree
Program: Occupational; 2-Year Principally Bachelor's Creditable
Accreditation: NH, #COARC, DIETT, EMT

01 President ... Dr. Eric TURNER
05 Vice President General Education ... Dr. Roger JOHNSON
72 Vice President Technical Education ... Mrs. Angela CALDWELL
10 Vice President of Administration ... Mrs. Brenda GILLOGLY
32 Vice President Student Affairs ... Mrs. Martha NELSON
30 VP of Institutional Advancement ... Mrs. Karen LIEBHABER
37 Director of Financial Aid ... Mrs. Brandi CHESTER
06 Registrar ... Mrs. Kimberly BIGGER
04 Administrative Asst to President ... Mrs. Vickie FRENCH
08 Head Librarian ... Mrs. Anne SIMPSON
106 Dir Online Education/E-learning ... Mrs. Regina MOORE
15 Director Personnel Services ... Mrs. Julie EDINGTON
19 Director Security/Safety ... Mr. Tony SAYLORS
26 Chief Public Relations/Marketing ... Ms. Ann SAVAGE
96 Director of Purchasing ... Mrs. Angie FRENCH
13 Chief Info Technology Officer (CIO) ... Mr. Michael GREENE
18 Chief Facilities/Physical Plant ... Mr. Trent INGRAM

Bryan University (F)

3704 West Walnut, Rogers AR 72756-1825
Telephone: (479) 899-6644 Identification: 666252
Accreditation: ACICS

† Branch campus of Bryan University, Springfield, MO.

Central Baptist College (G)

1501 College Avenue, Conway AR 72034-6470
County: Faulkner FICE Identification: 001093
Unit ID: 106713
Telephone: (501) 329-6872 Carnegie Class: Bac/Diverse
FAX Number: (501) 329-2941 Calendar System: Semester
URL: www.cbc.edu
Established: 1952 Annual Undergrad Tuition & Fees: $14,400
Enrollment: 858 Coed
Affiliation or Control: Baptist IRS Status: 501(c)3
Highest Offering: Baccalaureate
Program: Liberal Arts And General; Teacher Preparatory; Religious Emphasis
Accreditation: NH

01 President ... Mr. Terry KIMBROW
04 Admin Asst to President ... Mrs. Peggy PILLOW
05 Vice President Academic Affairs ... Dr. Gary MCALLISTER
10 Vice President for Finance ... Mr. Paul CHERRY
30 VP for Advancement ... Mrs. Sancy FAULK
84 VP for Enrollment Mgmt ... Mr. Ryan JOHNSON
07 Director of Admissions ... Mr. Jonathan WILSON
06 Registrar ... Mrs. Stacy JORDAN
19 Dean of Students/Campus Security ... Mr. Chris MITCHELL
08 Library Director ... Mrs. Rachel WHITTINGHAM
26 Director of Public Relations ... Mrs. Deanna OTT
37 Director of Financial Aid ... Mrs. Tonya HAMMONTREE
88 Director of Special Events ... Mrs. Jessica FAULKNER
13 Director of Information Technology ... Mr. Doug BIBLE
41 Athletic Director ... Mr. Lyle MIDDLETON
32 Director of Student Services ... Mrs. Rachel STEELE
39 Director of Student Housing ... Mr. Michael MAYO
15 Director of Human Resources ... Ms. Pam TEAGUE
29 Alumni & Communications Officer ... Ms. Meagan LOWRY
88 Director of Military Relations ... Ms. Robin STEPHENS
108 Director Institutional Assessment ... Mr. Dwain EAST
18 Director of Physical Plant ... Mr. Jerry CLIFTON
09 Institutional Research Analyst ... Ms. Michelle COLLINS
106 Director of Online Studies ... Mr. Chad LINN

College of the Ouachitas (H)

One College Circle, Malvern AR 72104-0816
County: Hot Spring FICE Identification: 009976
Unit ID: 107521
Telephone: (501) 337-5000 Carnegie Class: Assoc/Pub-R-S
FAX Number: (501) 337-9382 Calendar System: Semester
URL: www.coto.edu
Established: 1991 Annual Undergrad Tuition & Fees (In-State): $3,620
Enrollment: 1,444 Coed
Affiliation or Control: State IRS Status: 501(c)3
Highest Offering: Associate Degree
Program: Occupational; 2-Year Principally Bachelor's Creditable; Technical Emphasis
Accreditation: NH

01 President ... Dr. Stephen SCHOONMAKER
04 Administrative Asst to President ... Mrs. Jill HOULIHAN
05 Vice President of Instruction ... Mr. Pat SIMMS
32 Vice President Student Affairs ... Dr. Kim ARMSTRONG
10 Vice Pres Admin & Operations ... Mr. David SEE
30 Exec Dir College Advancement ... Ms. Amber CHILDERS
108 Exec Dir Planning & Assessment ... Ms. Carla CRUTCHFIELD
20 Dean of Learning ... Dr. Casey ROCKWELL
103 Dean of Workforce Education & Trng .. Mrs. Lynda RICHARDSON
76 Dean of Health Sciences ... Ms. Debbie FREYMAN
88 Interim Director Adult Education ... Mrs. Brenda KEISLER
08 Director Learning Resources ... Ms. Mary Ann HARPER
75 Director Career & Technical Studies ... Mr. Mike DINGLER
92 Director Honors College ... Mrs. Tricia BAAR
60 Director Concurrent Enrollment ... Mrs. Terri COLANANNI
37 Director of Financial Aid ... Ms. Vickie YOUNG
36 Director Career Pathways ... Ms. Johnnie MITCHELL
88 Dir TRIO Student Support Services ... Ms. Vergina SMITH
35 Interim Director Student Success ... Ms. Janet HUNT
06 Director of Admissions/Registrar ... Ms. Keesha JOHNSON
21 Controller ... Ms. Jackie HOLLOWAY
15 Human Resources ... Mrs. Kori CLAYTON
16 Interim Director IT ... Mr. Kee KRATZ

Crowley's Ridge College (I)

100 College Drive, Paragould AR 72450-9775
County: Greene FICE Identification: 001095
Unit ID: 106810
Telephone: (870) 236-6901 Carnegie Class: Assoc/PrivNFP4
FAX Number: (870) 236-7748 Calendar System: Semester
URL: www.crc.edu
Established: 1964 Annual Undergrad Tuition & Fees: $11,900
Enrollment: 223 Coed
Affiliation or Control: Churches Of Christ IRS Status: 501(c)3
Highest Offering: Baccalaureate
Program: Liberal Arts And General
Accreditation: NH

01 President ... Mr. Ken HOPPE
05 Vice President for Academic Affairs ... Dr. Rob WILLIAMS
32 Vice President for Student Affairs ... Mr. Art SMITH
30 Vice President for Advancement ... Mr. Richard JOHNSON
06 Registrar ... Mr. Paul MCFADDEN
37 Director Student Financial Services ... Mr. David W. GOFF
26 Director Public Information ... Mrs. Andrea JOHNSON
07 Director Admissions/Student Life ... Mrs. Nancy JONESHILL
41 Athletic Director/Campus Minister ... Mr. Paul MCFADDEN
08 Director Learning Center ... Mr. Mark WARNICK
10 Business Office Manager ... Mrs. Sonia JOHNSON
13 Director of Information Services ... Mr. Larry JOHNSON

East Arkansas Community College (J)

1700 Newcastle Road, Forrest City AR 72335-2204
County: Saint Francis FICE Identification: 012260
Unit ID: 106883
Telephone: (870) 633-4480 Carnegie Class: Assoc/Pub-R-S
FAX Number: (870) 633-7222 Calendar System: Semester
URL: www.eacc.edu
Established: 1974 Annual Undergrad Tuition & Fees (In-District): $2,790
Enrollment: 1,270 Coed
Affiliation or Control: State/Local IRS Status: 501(c)3
Highest Offering: Associate Degree
Program: Occupational; 2-Year Principally Bachelor's Creditable
Accreditation: NH, ADNUR, EMT

01 President ... Dr. Coy F. GRACE
05 Vice President Academic Affairs ... Dr. Janie BAILEY
10 Vice President Business Affairs ... Mr. Richard STIPE
32 Vice President Student Affairs ... Mrs. Catherine T. COLEMAN
37 Director Student Financial Aid ... Mr. Alvin COLEMAN
88 Assoc VP for Applied Sciences ... Mrs. Joanne LAWSON
88 AVP for Community/Business Outreach ... Mrs. Tiffany BILLINGSLEY
97 Assoc VP for General Studies ... Dr. Cathie CLINE
08 Director Library Services ... Mrs. Paige LAWS
84 Director Enrollment Management ... Mrs. Sharon COLLIER
26 Director of Public Relations/Mktg ... Mrs. Lindsay MIDKIFF
15 Director Personnel Management ... Mrs. Yvonne RUCKER-FRANKLIN
18 Director Physical Plant ... Mr. Glenn FORD
35 Assoc VP for Student Affairs ... Mrs. Michelle WILSON
96 Purchasing Specialist ... Mrs. Susan GUEST
88 Title III Project Manager ... Mr. Christopher A. HEIGLE
51 Director of Continuing Education ... Mrs. Kara DOSS

Ecclesia College (K)

9653 Nations Drive, Springdale AR 72762-8159
County: Benton FICE Identification: 038553
Unit ID: 446233
Telephone: (479) 248-7236 Carnegie Class: Spec/Faith

FAX Number: (479) 248-1455　Calendar System: Semester
URL: www.ecollege.edu
Established: 1975　Annual Undergrad Tuition & Fees: $15,140
Enrollment: 161　Coed
Affiliation or Control: Independent Non-Profit　IRS Status: 501(c)3
Highest Offering: Master's
Program: Liberal Arts And General; Religious Emphasis
Accreditation: BI

01 President ... Mr. Oren PARIS, III
05 Academic Dean ... Dr. Robert HEADRICK
10 Business Office Manager ... Ms. Shannon NEWMAN
32 Dean of Students ... Mr. Jesse E. WADKINS
30 Director of Financial Development ... Mr. Mike NOVAK
26 Director of Communications ... Ms. Angie P. SNYDER
37 Director Student Financial Aid ... Mr. Tommy STRINGFELLOW
41 Athletic Director ... Mr. Dean SKINNER
06 Registrar ... Mrs. Donna BROWN
08 Head Librarian ... Mrs. Joanne CAMPBELL
103 Director Work/Learning/Service Pgms ... Mr. Jesse E. WADKINS
07 Director of Admissions ... Mr. Chad HOWARD
04 Administrative Asst to President ... Mrs. Elizabeth NEWLUN
18 Chief Facilities/Physical Plant ... Mr. Dennis HAGGARD
106 Director Distance Education ... Mr. Paul SNYDER
39 Director Student Housing ... Ms. Kathrynn FINK

Harding University Main Campus (A)

915 E. Market Avenue, Searcy AR 72149-5615
County: White　FICE Identification: 001097
Unit ID: 107044
Telephone: (501) 279-4000　Carnegie Class: Master's L
FAX Number: (501) 279-4600　Calendar System: Semester
URL: www.harding.edu
Established: 1924　Annual Undergrad Tuition & Fees: $17,805
Enrollment: 6,075　Coed
Affiliation or Control: Churches Of Christ　IRS Status: 501(c)3
Highest Offering: Doctorate
Program: Occupational; Liberal Arts And General; Teacher Preparatory; Professional
Accreditation: NH, ACBSP, ARCPA, CAATE, CACREP, CIDA, DIETD, ENG, MUS, NUR, PHAR, PTA, SP, SW, TED

01 President ... Dr. Bruce D. MCLARTY
03 Executive Vice President ... Dr. David COLLINS
05 Provost ... Dr. Larry LONG
88 Senior Vice President ... Dr. James W. CARR
10 Vice President Finance ... Dr. Mel SANSOM
30 Vice President Advancement ... Dr. Bryan BURKS
42 Vice President of Church Relations ... Dr. Dan WILLIAMS
13 VP Information Systems & Technology ... Mr. Keith CRONK
41 Athletic Director ... Mr. Greg HARNDEN
29 VP of Alumni Relations ... Mrs. Liz HOWELL
20 Associate Provost Undergraduate ... Dr. Marty SPEARS
20 Assistant Provost Graduate ... Dr. Cheri YECKE
20 Assistant Provost Health Sciences ... Dr. Julie HIXSON-WALLACE
88 Dean College of Bible & Ministry ... Dr. Monte COX
92 Dean of Honors College ... Dr. Mike JAMES
50 Dean College of Business ... Dr. Al FRAZIER
53 Dean College of Education ... Dr. Donny LEE
66 Dean College of Nursing ... Dr. Susan KEHL
79 Dean College of Arts & Humanities ... Dr. Warren CASEY
81 Dean College of Sciences ... Dr. Travis THOMPSON
76 Dean College of Allied Health ... Dr. Beckie WEAVER
88 Dean of International Programs ... Dr. Jeffry HOPPER
84 Asst VP Enrollment Management ... Mr. Glenn DILLARD
21 Asst VP Finance ... Mrs. Tammy HALL
32 Asst VP Student Life/Dean Students ... Mr. Zach NEAL
88 Asst VP of IS&T ... Mr. Mike CHALENBURG
06 Registrar ... Mr. Tod MARTIN
38 Director of Counseling ... Dr. Lew MOORE
19 Director Security/Safety ... Mr. Craig RUSSELL
26 Director of Public Relations ... Mr. David CROUCH
37 Director Student Financial Aid ... Dr. Jonathan ROBERTS
58 Director of Graduate Studies ... Vacant
08 Librarian ... Mrs. Jean WALDROP
18 Chief Facilities/Physical Plant ... Mr. Danny DERAMUS
15 Director Personnel Services ... Mr. David ROSS
36 Director Student Placement ... Mr. Butch GARDNER
09 Director of Institutional Research ... Mr. Dustin HOWELL
96 Director of Purchasing ... Vacant
35 Assistant Dean of Students ... Mr. Brandon TITTLE
35 Assistant Dean of Students ... Mrs. Kara ABSTON
35 Assistant Dean of Students ... Mrs. Ranan HESTER
35 Assistant Dean of Students ... Mr. Chad JOICE
28 Director of Diversity ... Mrs. Tiffany BYERS
39 Director Student Housing ... Mrs. Kathy ALLEN

Henderson State University (B)

1100 Henderson Street, Arkadelphia AR 71999-0001
County: Clark　FICE Identification: 001098
Unit ID: 107071
Telephone: (870) 230-5000　Carnegie Class: Master's M
FAX Number: (870) 230-5144　Calendar System: Semester
URL: www.hsu.edu
Established: 1890　Annual Undergrad Tuition & Fees (In-State): $7,809
Enrollment: 3,627　Coed
Affiliation or Control: State　IRS Status: 501(c)3
Highest Offering: Beyond Master's But Less Than Doctorate
Program: Liberal Arts And General; Teacher Preparatory; Professional
Accreditation: NH, BUS, CAATE, CACREP, DIETD, MUS, NURSE, TED

01 President ... Dr. Glendell JONES
05 Provost/VPAA ... Dr. Steve ADKISON
10 Vice Pres Finance & Administration ... Mr. Bobby G. JONES
32 VP Student Services/External Affair ... Dr. Lewis A. SHEPHERD, JR.
30 VP Advancement/Exec Dir Found ... Ms. Jennifer BOYETT
43 General Counsel ... Ms. Elaine KNEEBONE
35 Asst VP/Dean of Students ... Mr. Chad FIELDING
39 Asst VP/Director of Residence Life ... Mr. Dan MABERY
13 Director Computer/Communication Svc ... Mr. David H. EPPERHART
29 Director of Development & Alumni ... Ms. Carrie ROBERSON
41 Director Athletics ... Mr. Shawn JONES
26 Exec Director of Marketing/Comm ... Ms. Tonya OAKS SMITH
49 Dean Ellis Col Arts/Sciences ... Dr. John HARDEE
50 Dean of School of Business ... Dr. Brenda PONSFORD
53 Dean Teachers College Henderson ... Dr. Judy HARRISON
58 Dean of Graduate School ... Dr. Kenneth TAYLOR
06 Registrar ... Mr. Tom GATTIN
08 Director Huie Library ... Mr. Robert F. YEHL
15 Director of Human Resources ... Ms. Kathy TAYLOR
19 Director of University Police ... Mr. Jonathan CAMPBELL
38 Dir Student Health/Counseling Ctr ... Ms. Deborah COLLINS
07 Director Univ Relations/Admissions ... Ms. Vikita B. HARDWRICK
37 Director of Financial Aid ... Ms. Vicki TAYLOR
92 Director of Honors College ... Dr. David T. THOMSON
88 Director of Student Research ... Dr. Martin CAMPBELL
96 Director of Purchasing ... Mr. Tim JONES
24 Dir Multi Media Learning Center ... Ms. Jennifer HOLBROOK
85 Director International Students ... Dr. Drew SMITH

Hendrix College (C)

1600 Washington Avenue, Conway AR 72032-3080
County: Faulkner　FICE Identification: 001099
Unit ID: 107080
Telephone: (501) 329-6811　Carnegie Class: Bac/A&S
FAX Number: (501) 450-1200　Calendar System: Semester
URL: www.hendrix.edu
Established: 1876　Annual Undergrad Tuition & Fees: $52,114
Enrollment: 1,358　Coed
Affiliation or Control: United Methodist　IRS Status: 501(c)3
Highest Offering: Master's
Program: Liberal Arts And General
Accreditation: NH, MUS, TED

01 President ... Dr. William M. TSUTSUI
04 Executive Assistant to President ... Ms. Donna PLEMMONS
88 VP for Strategic Initiatives/Chief ... Ms. Courtney Lee CORWIN
30 Sr Exec Vice Pres/Dean Inst Advance ... Mr. W. Ellis ARNOLD, III
05 Provost ... Dr. Terri BONEBRIGHT
26 Vice Pres Marketing Communications ... Ms. Helen PLOTKIN
10 Executive Vice President and CFO ... Mr. Tom SIEBENMORGEN
84 Vice Pres for Enrollment ... Ms. Karen R. FOUST
15 Vice Pres for Human Resources ... Ms. Vicki LYNN
18 Int Assoc VP Operations/Facilities ... Mr. Nate COWDEN
32 Exec VP Student Affs/Dean of Stdnts ... Mr. Jim WILTGEN, JR.
27 Assoc VP Marketing Communications ... Mr. Rob O'CONNOR
06 Registrar ... Ms. Brenda ADAMS
08 Director of Libraries ... Ms. Britt Anne MURPHY
13 VP Technology/Chief Info Officer ... Mr. Sam NICHOLS
29 Director Alumni Relations ... Ms. Pamela OWEN
37 Director of Financial Aid ... Ms. Kristina BURFORD
40 Bookstore Manager ... Ms. Dee Dee ALLEN
79 Area Head/Humanities ... Dr. Alex VERNON
81 Area Head/Natural Sciences ... Dr. Matt MORAN
83 Area Head/Social Sciences ... Dr. Leslie TEMPLETON
42 Interim Chaplain ... Rev. J.J WHITNEY
07 Director of Admission ... Mr. Fred BAKER
20 Associate Academic Officer ... Dr. David SUTHERLAND
21 Associate Business Officer ... Mr. Shawn MATHIS
36 Assistant Director Career Services ... Ms. Jamie FOTIOO
38 Director Student Counseling ... Ms. Mary Anne SIEBERT

ITT Technical Institute (D)

12200 Westhaven Drive, Little Rock AR 72211
Telephone: (501) 565-5550　Identification: 666531
Accreditation: ACICS

† Branch campus of ITT Technical Institute, Indianapolis, IN.

Jefferson Regional Medical Center School of Nursing (E)

1600 W. 40th Avenue, Pine Bluff AR 71603
County: Jefferson　FICE Identification: 023308
Telephone: (870) 541-7850　Carnegie Class: Not Classified
FAX Number: N/A　Calendar System: Semester
URL: www.jrmc.org
Established: 1981　Annual Undergrad Tuition & Fees: $12,650
Enrollment: 73　Coed
Affiliation or Control: Independent Non-Profit　IRS Status: 501(c)3
Highest Offering: Associate Degree
Program: Occupational; Nursing Emphasis
Accreditation: ABHES, DNUR, PAST

01 Director ... Ms. Kathy PIERCE

John Brown University (F)

2000 W University Street, Siloam Springs AR 72761-2121
County: Benton　FICE Identification: 001100
Unit ID: 107141
Telephone: (479) 524-9500　Carnegie Class: Bac/Diverse
FAX Number: (479) 524-9548　Calendar System: Semester
URL: www.jbu.edu
Established: 1919　Annual Undergrad Tuition & Fees: $24,468
Enrollment: 2,850　Coed
Affiliation or Control: Independent Non-Profit　IRS Status: 501(c)3
Highest Offering: Master's
Program: Liberal Arts And General; Teacher Preparatory
Accreditation: NH, ACBSP, CONST, ENG, TED

01 President ... Dr. Charles POLLARD
10 Vice Pres Finance & Administration ... Mrs. Kim HADLEY
84 Vice Pres Enrollment Management ... Mr. Donald W. CRANDALL
30 Vice Pres of University Advancement ... Dr. Jim KRALL
32 Vice Pres for Student Development ... Dr. Stephen T. BEERS
05 VP Academic Affairs/Dean of Faculty ... Dr. Ed ERICSON, III
88 Dean Degree Completion Program ... Vacant
42 Campus Pastor/Assoc Dean of Stdnts ... Mr. Rod REED
06 Registrar ... Mrs. Rebecca LAMBERT
21 Controller ... Mr. Tom PERRY
13 Chief Information Systems Ofcr ... Mr. Paul NAST
18 Director of Facilities Services ... Mr. Steve BRANKLE
44 Director of Planned Giving ... Mr. Eric GREENHAW
08 Director of Library ... Mrs. Mary HABERMAS
85 Director International Programs ... Mr. Bill STEVENSON
29 Director of Alumni/Parent Relations ... Mr. Jerry ROLLENE
37 Director of Financial Aid ... Mr. Kim ELDRIDGE
07 Director of Admissions ... Mr. Kent SHAFFER
41 Athletic Director ... Ms. Robyn DAUGHERTY
38 Director of Counseling ... Dr. Tim DINGER
04 Administrative Asst to President ... Ms. Kory J. DALE

Lyon College (G)

PO Box 2317, Batesville AR 72503-2317
County: Independence　FICE Identification: 001088
Unit ID: 106342
Telephone: (870) 307-7000　Carnegie Class: Bac/A&S
FAX Number: (870) 307-7001　Calendar System: Semester
URL: www.lyon.edu
Established: 1872　Annual Undergrad Tuition & Fees: $33,390
Enrollment: 713　Coed
Affiliation or Control: Presbyterian Church (U.S.A.)　IRS Status: 501(c)3
Highest Offering: Baccalaureate
Program: Liberal Arts And General; Teacher Preparatory; Fine Arts Emphasis
Accreditation: NH, TED

01 President ... Dr. Donald V. WEATHERMAN
05 VP Academic Svcs/Dean of Faculty ... Dr. Philip CAVALIER
10 Vice President Business & Finance ... Mr. John D. JONES
11 Vice Pres for Administration ... Mr. Jim SCHLIMMER
32 Vice President Student Life ... Dr. Patrick MULICK
30 VP Institutional Advancement ... Mr. Jon VESTAL
06 Director of Admissions/Registrar ... Mr. Donald R. TAYLOR
08 Director Library ... Mr. Dean COVINGTON
26 Dir of Marketing and Communications ... Vacant
29 Executive Dir of Advancement ... Mrs. Gina GARRETT
15 Director of Administration and HR ... Mrs. Clarinda L. FOOTE
37 Director of Financial Assistance ... Mr. Tommy TUCKER
36 Director Career Development ... Ms. Vicki WEBB
13 Director Information Services ... Mr. Josh KEMP
41 Director of Athletics ... Mr. Kevin JENKINS
42 Chaplain ... Rev. Ray MCCALLA
53 Int Director of Teacher Education ... Ms. Kim CROSBY
38 Director Student Counseling ... Ms. Diane ELLIS
18 Director Security ... Mr. Kyle HAYS
40 Director Bookstore ... Mrs. Donna GLASCOCK
08 Head Librarian ... Ms. Kathy WHITTENTON
23 Director of Health Services ... Mrs. LuAnn BAKER
18 Chief Facilities/Physical Plant ... Mr. Layne SESSIONS
20 Associate Academic Officer ... Dr. Anthony GRAFTON

National Park Community College (H)

101 College Drive,
Hot Springs National Park AR 71913-9174
County: Garland　FICE Identification: 012105
Unit ID: 106980
Telephone: (501) 760-4222　Carnegie Class: Assoc/Pub-R-M
FAX Number: (501) 760-4100　Calendar System: Semester
URL: www.npcc.edu
Established: 1973　Annual Undergrad Tuition & Fees (In-District): $3,538
Enrollment: 3,001　Coed
Affiliation or Control: State/Local　IRS Status: 501(c)3
Highest Offering: Associate Degree
Program: Occupational; 2-Year Principally Bachelor's Creditable; Technical Emphasis
Accreditation: NH, ADNUR, CAHIIM, #COARC, EMT, MLTAD, RAD

01 President ... Dr. John HOGAN
05 Vice Pres Academic Affairs ... Dr. Wade DERDEN
10 Vice President Financial Affairs ... Ms. Janis SAWYER
32 Exec Vice President Student Svcs ... Dr. Gordon WATTS
72 Assoc Vice Pres Technical Education ... Mr. David HUGHES
31 Assoc VP External Affairs ... Mr. Jeff WEAVER
20 Assoc Dean for Academic Affairs ... Dr. Brad MOODY
35 Director of Student Affairs ... Ms. Holly GARRETT-MILLER
15 Director of Human Resources ... Ms. Janet BREWER
08 Director of the Library ... Ms. Sara SEAMAN
37 Director of Financial Aid ... Ms. Lisa HOPPER

26 Director Marketing/Public Relations ....Dr. Susan ALDRIDGE
30 Chief Development ....Ms. Sara BROWN
38 Director Student Counseling ....Mr. Ron CHESSER
06 Registrar ....Dr. Brad MOODY
103 Director Workforce Development ....Ms. Kelli ALBRECHT

North Arkansas College (A)

1515 Pioneer Drive, Harrison AR 72601-5599
County: Boone FICE Identification: 012261
Unit ID: 107460
Telephone: (870) 743-3000 Carnegie Class: Assoc/Pub-R-M
FAX Number: (870) 391-3250 Calendar System: Semester
URL: www.northark.edu
Established: 1974 Annual Undergrad Tuition & Fees (In-District): $2,550
Enrollment: 1,705 Coed
Affiliation or Control: State/Local IRS Status: 501(c)3
Highest Offering: Associate Degree
Program: Occupational; 2-Year Principally Bachelor's Creditable; Nursing Emphasis
Accreditation: NH, ACBSP, ADNUR, EMT, MLTAD, RAD, SURGT

01 President ....Dr. Jacquelyn ELLIOTT
05 Exec Vice President of Learning ....Dr. Michael WIGGINS
10 Vice Pres Finance & Administration ....Mr. Donald SUGG
30 Vice Pres Institutional Advancement ....Dr. Rodney ARNOLD
04 Executive Assistant to President ....Mrs. Trish VILLINES
49 Dean Arts & Science/Business & IT ....Dr. Laura BERRY
66 Dean Nursing/Allied Hlth/Tech Pgms ....Mrs. Cindy MAYO
31 Dean of Outreach ....Mrs. Nell BONDS
08 Interim Director of Libraries ....Mrs. Michelle PALMER
44 Dir Institutional Effectiveness ....Mrs. Katherine VAUGHN
32 Director of Student Success ....Mrs. Tavonda BROWN
41 Athletic Director ....Mrs. Stacie KLOTT
15 Director Human Resources ....Mrs. Kris GREENING
18 Chief Facilities/Physical Plant ....Mr. Kevin SOMERS
96 Director of Purchasing ....Mrs. Shari HOLT
37 Director Student Financial Aid ....Mrs. Jennifer HADDOCK
06 Registrar ....Mrs. Charla JENNINGS
07 Director of Admissions ....Mr. Randy SCAGGS
26 Director of Public Relations ....Mrs. Micki SOMERS
90 Director Academic Computing ....Mr. Rick WILLIAMS
91 Director Administrative Computing ....Mr. Glenn COLMAN
31 Director of Community Education ....Mrs. Amy BELL

NorthWest Arkansas Community College (B)

1 College Drive, Bentonville AR 72712-5091
County: Benton FICE Identification: 030633
Unit ID: 367459
Telephone: (479) 636-9222 Carnegie Class: Assoc/Pub-R-L
FAX Number: (479) 619-4335 Calendar System: Semester
URL: www.nwacc.edu
Established: 1989 Annual Undergrad Tuition & Fees (In-District): $3,208
Enrollment: 8,098 Coed
Affiliation or Control: State/Local IRS Status: 501(c)3
Highest Offering: Associate Degree
Program: Occupational; 2-Year Principally Bachelor's Creditable
Accreditation: NH, ACBSP, ACFEI, COARC, EMT, IFSAC, PTAA

01 President ....Dr. Evelyn E. JORGENSON
10 VP of Finance & Administration ....Ms. Debi BUCKLEY
05 Vice Pres for Learning ....Dr. Ricky TOMPKINS
32 VP of Student Services ....Dr. Todd KITCHEN
36 VP of Career & Workforce Education ....Mr. Tim CORNELIUS
103 Dean of Workforce Development ....Mr. Keith PETERSON
13 AVP IT/Chief Information Officer ....Mr. Jason DEGN
88 Dir Retail & Supplier Education ....Ms. Teresa WARREN
11 Executive Director of Operations ....Mr. Jack THOMPSON
51 Dean of Adult Education ....Mr. Ben ALDAMA
35 Dean of Students ....Mr. Dale MONTGOMERY
06 Dean of Learner Success & Registrar ....Ms. Brooke HOLT
30 Executive Director of Development ....Dr. Meredith BRUNEN
84 Executive Director of Enrollment ....Ms. Diana JOHNSON
26 Exec Director of Public Relations ....Mr. Steven HINDS
86 Exec Dir Community/Government Rels ....Mr. Jim HALL
21 Accountant/General Ledger ....Mr. John HIXSON
21 Dir Budget/Fin Analysis/Reporting ....Ms. Gulizar BAGGSON
15 Exec Director of Human Resources ....Ms. Wendi CADLE
106 Director of Distance Learning ....Dr. Kate BURKES
50 Exec Dir of Business Development ....Ms. Teresa WHITMIRE
88 Coordinator of Building Sciences ....Mr. Mike DEWBERRY
88 Director of Learning Resources ....Ms. Gwen DOBBS
25 Exec Dir Grants & Effectiveness Res ....Dr. Shauna STERLING
88 Associate Dean Student Success ....Ms. Tay Sha CARTER
07 Director of Admissions/Advising ....Mr. Zach PHARR
37 Director Student Financial Aid ....Ms. Michelle CORDELL
88 Director Academic Success Center ....Mr. Eric VEST
28 Director of Diversity & Inclusion ....Ms. Kathryn BIRKHEAD
109 Dir Food Services/Event Management ....Ms. Diane BOSS
09 Director of Institutional Research ....Dr. Lisa ANDERSON
18 Director of Physical Plant ....Mr. Jim NELSON
88 Coordinator Culinary & Hospitality ....Ms. Dede HAMM
77 Dean for Bus Computer Information ....Dr. Christine DAVIS
76 Dean of Health Professions ....Ms. Mary ROSS
04 Administrative Asst to President ....Ms. Miranda SMITH
19 Exec Director Policy/Risk & Comp ....Mr. Ethan BECKCOM
44 Planned Giving Officer ....Ms. Jean ANDERSON

Ouachita Baptist University (C)

410 Ouachita Street, Arkadelphia AR 71998-0001
County: Clark FICE Identification: 001102
Unit ID: 107512
Telephone: (870) 245-5000 Carnegie Class: Bac/A&S
FAX Number: (870) 245-5500 Calendar System: Semester
URL: www.obu.edu
Established: 1886 Annual Undergrad Tuition & Fees: $24,120
Enrollment: 1,501 Coed
Affiliation or Control: Southern Baptist IRS Status: 501(c)3
Highest Offering: Baccalaureate
Program: Liberal Arts And General; Teacher Preparatory
Accreditation: NH, BUS, DIETD, MUS, TED

01 President ....Vacant
44 Vice Pres Institutional Advancement ....Dr. Keldon HENLEY
05 Vice President Academic Affairs ....Dr. Stan POOLE
10 Chief Financial Officer ....Mr. Jason TOLBERT
32 Vice President for Student Services ....Dr. Wesley KLUCK
30 Vice President for Development ....Mrs. Terry G. PEEPLES
26 Vice Pres for Communications ....Mr. Trennis HENDERSON
04 Asst to President/Administration ....Mr. Philip W. HARDIN
07 Director of Admissions Counseling ....Mrs. Lori MOTL
09 Director of Institutional Research ....Mr. Phil HARDIN
15 Director of Human Resources ....Mrs. Sherri PHELPS
18 Chief Facilities/Physical Plant ....Mr. John HARDMAN
29 Director of Alumni Relations ....Mr. Jon MERRYMAN
35 Dean of Students ....Dr. Scott HAYNES
20 Assoc Vice Pres Academic Affairs ....Dr. Doug REED
36 Director of Career Services ....Mrs. Rachel ROBERTS
38 University Counselor ....Mr. Dan JARBOE
08 Librarian ....Dr. Ray GRANADE
06 Registrar/Director of Admissions ....Vacant
37 Director Student Financial Svcs ....Mrs. Susan HURST
96 Director of Purchasing ....Ms. Rachel MARTINEZ
92 Director Honors Program ....Dr. Barbara PEMBERTON
13 Asst to Pres for Info Tech Svcs ....Mr. Bill PHELPS
39 Director of Housing ....Ms. Stacey PERRY
41 Athletic Director ....Mr. David SHARP
43 General Counsel ....Mr. Bryan MCKINNEY
21 Director of Financial Services ....Mrs. Debbie CADDELL
40 Bookstore Manager ....Ms. Beverly DICKERSON
57 Dean of School of Fine Arts ....Dr. Gary GERBER
50 Dean of the School of Business ....Mr. Bryan MCKINNEY
53 Dean Sch of Interdisciplinary Stds ....Dr. Stan POOLE
73 Dean School of Christian Studies ....Dr. Danny HAYS
53 Dean School of Education ....Dr. Merribeth BRUNING
79 Dean School of Humanities ....Dr. Jeff ROOT
81 Dean School of Natural Sciences ....Dr. Tim KNIGHT
83 Dean School of Social Sciences ....Dr. Randall WIGHT

Ozarka College (D)

PO Box 10, Melbourne AR 72556-0010
County: Izard FICE Identification: 020870
Unit ID: 107549
Telephone: (870) 368-7371 Carnegie Class: Assoc/Pub-R-S
FAX Number: (870) 368-2091 Calendar System: Semester
URL: www.ozarka.edu
Established: 1991 Annual Undergrad Tuition & Fees (In-State): $2,776
Enrollment: 1,326 Coed
Affiliation or Control: State IRS Status: 501(c)3
Highest Offering: Associate Degree
Program: Occupational; 2-Year Principally Bachelor's Creditable
Accreditation: NH

01 President ....Dr. Richard L. DAWE
05 Executive Vice Pres & Provost ....Vacant
10 Vice President of Finance ....Ms. Tina WHEELIS
11 Vice President of Administration ....Mr. Jason LAWRENCE
32 Vice President of Student Services ....Mr. Ron C. HELM
45 Assoc Vice President of Planning/IR ....Mr. Josh WILSON
13 Chief Information Officer ....Mr. Scott PINKSTON
04 Executive Asst to the President ....Ms. Tess WEATHERFORD
30 Director of College Advancement ....Ms. Suellen DAVIDSON
29 Development Officer/Dir Alumni Rels ....Vacant
37 Director of Financial Aid ....Ms. Laura LAWRENCE
07 Director of Admissions ....Mr. Dylan MOWERY
06 Registrar ....Mrs. Zeda WILKERSON
26 Dir Public Relations/Marketing ....Ms. Manda JACKSON
21 Business Manager ....Ms. Amber RUSH

Philander Smith College (E)

900 W. Daisy L. Gatson Bates Drive,
Little Rock AR 72202-3799
County: Pulaski FICE Identification: 001103
Unit ID: 107600
Telephone: (501) 375-9845 Carnegie Class: Bac/Diverse
FAX Number: (501) 370-5277 Calendar System: Semester
URL: www.philander.edu
Established: 1877 Annual Undergrad Tuition & Fees: $12,564
Enrollment: 553 Coed
Affiliation or Control: United Methodist IRS Status: 501(c)3
Highest Offering: Baccalaureate
Program: Liberal Arts And General; Teacher Preparatory
Accreditation: NH, ACBSP, SW, TED

01 President ....Dr. Roderick L. SMOTHERS, SR.
04 Admin Assistant to the President ....Mrs. Anita HATLEY
05 VP of Academic Affairs ....Dr. Hazel ERVIN
10 Vice President for Fiscal Affairs ....Mr. Terry WALLACE
32 VP of Student Affairs ....Mr. Kevin HAMILTON
30 Vice Pres Inst Advancement ....Mr. C. J DUVALL
108 VP of Institutional Effectiveness ....Dr. Annie WILLIAMS
20 Assoc VP Academic Affairs ....Dr. Zollie STEPHENSON
100 Sr Executive Assistant to President ....Dr. Darnell WILLIAMS
06 Registrar ....Ms. Bertha OWENS
21 Controller ....Ms. LaTonya HAYES
42 Chaplain/Dir Ofc Religious Life ....Rev. Ronnie MILLER-YOW
35 Dean of Students/Residential Life ....Mr. Kevin HAMILTON
15 Exec Director of Human Resources ....Mr. Christopher NEWTON
37 Director of Financial Aid ....Ms. Kisa HINTON
18 Director of Physical Plant ....Mr. Robert YOUNG
26 Director Marketing/Public Relations ...Mr. Michael HUTCHINSON
07 Director of Admissions ....Mr. Maurice OSBORNE
08 Director of the Library ....Ms. Teresa OJEZUA
84 VP of Enrollment Management ....Vacant
29 Director of Alumni Relations ....Ms. Yvonne ALEXANDER
41 Athletic Director ....Mr. Sam WEAVER
13 Int Dir Computer Information Sys ....Mr. Brian CLAY
09 Director of Institutional Research ....Ms. Kayla SAPKOTA
19 Chief of Security ....Ms. Anita PHILLIPS
51 Dir of Continuing Education (PSMI) ....Mr. Bruce JAMES
88 Kendall Mission Center Director ....Dr. Cynthia BURROUGHS
40 Bookstore Manager ....Mr. Alvin HARRIS
17 Campus Nurse ....Ms. Martie SAVAGE
88 Director Integrated Campus Center ....Ms. Rhonda LOVELACE
49 Div Chair Natural/Physical Sciences ....Dr. Samar SWAID
50 Div Chair of Business/Economics ....Dr. Bruce JAMES
53 Int Division Chair of Education ....Dr. Betty DICKSON
70 Director of Social Work ....Ms. Angela SANDERS
79 Div Chair Humanities ....Dr. Lia STEELE-MARCELL
83 Div Chair Social Sciences ....Dr. Daniel EGBE

Pulaski Technical College (F)

3000 W Scenic Drive, North Little Rock AR 72118-3399
County: Pulaski FICE Identification: 020753
Unit ID: 107664
Telephone: (501) 812-2200 Carnegie Class: Assoc/Pub-U-SC
FAX Number: (501) 771-2844 Calendar System: Semester
URL: www.pulaskitech.edu
Established: 1991 Annual Undergrad Tuition & Fees (In-State): $4,055
Enrollment: 9,241 Coed
Affiliation or Control: State IRS Status: 501(c)3
Highest Offering: Associate Degree
Program: Occupational; 2-Year Principally Bachelor's Creditable; Technical Emphasis
Accreditation: NH, ACFEI, COARC, DA, OTA

01 President ....Dr. Margaret ELLIBEE
05 Executive Vice President/Provost ....Mr. Michael DELONG
20 Vice President for Learning ....Ms. Mary Ann SHOPE
32 Vice President for Student Services ....Vacant
10 Vice President for Finance ....Ms. Patricia PALMER
30 VP for Economic Development ....Mr. Bentley WALLACE
20 Associate Vice President/Learning ....Dr. Pam CICIRELLO
44 Chief Development Officer ....Ms. Shannon BOSHEARS
84 Dean Enrollment Svcs ....Vacant
07 Director of Admissions ....Vacant
08 Library Director ....Ms. Wendy DAVIS
18 Director of Physical Plant ....Mr. David KROAMER
09 Assoc VP for Institutional Research ....Ms. Jasmine RAY
21 Assoc Vice President for Finance ....Ms. Stacey HOGUE
96 Director of Purchasing ....Mr. Tim WALBERT
13 Assoc VP for Information Services ....Mr. David GLOVER
15 Interim Assoc VP of Human Resources ....Ms. Gloria MADDOX POWELL
04 Assistant to the President ....Ms. Tena CARRIGAN
37 Director of Financial Aid ....Ms. Lavonne JUHL
26 Assoc VP Public Relations/Marketing ....Mr. Tim JONES
72 Dean Technical Education Division ....Mr. Dick BURCHETT
81 Dean Mathematics/Nat Social Scis ....Mr. Ben RAINS
50 Dean Business/IT Division ....Ms. Christy SHERRILL
57 Dean Fine Arts & Humanities ....Mr. Joey COLE
06 Registrar ....Ms. Catherine DIVITO
76 Dean Allied Health/Human Services ....Ms. Jeanne WILLIAMS

Remington College-Little Rock (G)

19 Remington Drive, Little Rock AR 72204-8202
Telephone: (501) 312-0007 Identification: 666286
Accreditation: ACCSC

† Branch campus of Remington College, Dallas, TX.

Rich Mountain Community College (H)

1100 College Drive, Mena AR 71953-2500
County: Polk FICE Identification: 021111
Unit ID: 107743
Telephone: (479) 394-7622 Carnegie Class: Assoc/Pub-R-S
FAX Number: (479) 394-7295 Calendar System: Semester
URL: www.rmcc.edu
Established: 1983 Annual Undergrad Tuition & Fees (In-District): $1,530
Enrollment: 1,005 Coed
Affiliation or Control: State/Local IRS Status: 501(c)3
Highest Offering: Associate Degree
Program: Occupational; 2-Year Principally Bachelor's Creditable; Liberal Arts And General
Accreditation: NH

01 President ... Dr. Phillip WILSON
05 Vice Pres Academic Affairs ... Dr. Steve ROOK
32 Vice Pres Student Affairs/Registrar ... Dr. Steve ROOK
10 VP Administration/CFO ... Mr. Morris BOYDSTUN
13 Dir of Information Technology ... Mr. J. Mark BARTON
08 Interim Director Library Services ... Ms. Brenda MINER
37 Financial Aid Director ... Ms. Mary STANDERFER
30 Director of Development ... Ms. Tammy YOUNG
18 Director of Physical Plant ... Mr. Dennis HILL
53 Director of Adult Basic Education ... Ms. Shannon ROGERS
15 Director of Human Resources ... Ms. Amy LUDWIG
07 Director of Admissions ... Ms. Wendy MCDANIEL
21 Controller ... Ms. Patricia HALL
26 Chief Public Relations Officer ... Ms. Tammy YOUNG
40 Bookstore Manager ... Mr. Jason WOOD
09 Coordinator Institutional Research ... Ms. Tammy ODOM
21 Fiscal Project Coordinator ... Ms. Amy LUDWIG

Shorter College (A)

604 Locust Street, North Little Rock AR 72114
County: Pulaski   FICE Identification: 001105
Unit ID: 107840
Telephone: (501) 374-6305   Carnegie Class: Not Classified
FAX Number: (501) 374-9333   Calendar System: Semester
URL: www.shortercollege.edu
Established: 1886   Annual Undergrad Tuition & Fees: $4,200
Enrollment: 403   Coed
Affiliation or Control: African Methodist Episcopal   IRS Status: 501(c)3
Highest Offering: Associate Degree
Program: 2-Year Principally Bachelor's Creditable
Accreditation: TRACS

01 President ... Dr. O. Jerome GREEN
05 Dean of Academic Affairs ... Dr. Jean MANNING
32 Dean of Student Services ... Mr. Kenneth JONES
10 Director of Fiscal Affairs ... Mr. Richard DENNY

South Arkansas Community College (B)

300 S West Avenue, PO Box 7010,
El Dorado AR 71731-7010
County: Union   FICE Identification: 020746
Unit ID: 107974
Telephone: (870) 862-8131   Carnegie Class: Assoc/Pub-R-S
FAX Number: (870) 864-7190   Calendar System: Semester
URL: www.southark.edu
Established: 1992   Annual Undergrad Tuition & Fees (In-State): $2,642
Enrollment: 1,693   Coed
Affiliation or Control: State   IRS Status: 501(c)3
Highest Offering: Associate Degree
Program: Occupational; 2-Year Principally Bachelor's Creditable
Accreditation: NH, COARC, EMT, MLTAD, OTA, PHLEB, PTAA, RAD, SURGT

01 President ... Dr. Barbara JONES
05 VP of Academic Learning ... Mr. Mickey BEST
32 Vice Pres of Student Services ... Dr. Jim BULLOCK
11 Int Chief Admin Svc Ofcr ... Mr. Michael CHIKELEGE
13 Chief Information Officer ... Dr. Tim KIRK
26 Public Information Officer ... Mr. Heath WALDROP
84 Dean of Enrollment Services ... Mr. Dean INMAN
08 Director Library Media Center ... Mrs. Francis KUYKENDALL
31 Dean of Community Education ... Ms. Jamie MCCONATHY
37 Director of Financial Aid ... Ms. Veronda TATUM
04 Executive Asst to the President ... Ms. Susan JORDAN
15 Director Personnel Services ... Mrs. Becky RIGGS
18 Director of Physical Plant ... Mr. Graham PETERSON
30 Dir of Foundation/External Funding ... Ms. Cynthia REYNA
09 CIEAO ... Dr. Stephanie TULLY-DARTEZ
96 Director of Purchasing ... Ms. Ann SOUTHALL
07 Student Recruitment & Activities ... Ms. Sarah PASTERNIAK
49 Dean of Liberal Arts ... Mr. Phillip BALLARD
76 Dean Health/Natural Sciences ... Mr. Arthur BROWN
50 Dean Business/Inform Tech ... Mr. Jim ROOMSBURG

Southeast Arkansas College (C)

1900 Hazel Street, Pine Bluff AR 71603-3900
County: Jefferson   FICE Identification: 005707
Unit ID: 107637
Telephone: (870) 543-5900   Carnegie Class: Assoc/Pub-R-M
FAX Number: (870) 850-8636   Calendar System: Semester
URL: www.seark.edu
Established: 1991   Annual Undergrad Tuition & Fees (In-State): $3,070
Enrollment: 1,432   Coed
Affiliation or Control: State   IRS Status: 501(c)3
Highest Offering: Associate Degree
Program: Occupational; 2-Year Principally Bachelor's Creditable; Technical Emphasis
Accreditation: NH, ADNUR, COARC, EMT, PHLEB, RAD, SURGT

01 President ... Dr. Stephen HILTERBRAN
05 Vice President Academic Affairs ... Dr. Kaleybra MOREHEAD
32 Vice President Student Affairs ... Dr. Michael GUNTER
10 Vice President Financial Affairs ... Ms. Debbie WALLACE
21 Controller ... Mr. Steve BALLARD
13 Director of Technology Services ... Ms. JoAnn DUPRA
06 Registrar/Director of Admissions ... Ms. Lozanne CALHOUN
15 Director of Human Resources ... Ms. Kristi CAMPBELL
18 Chief Facilities/Physical Plant ... Mr. Joel BARBAREE
37 Director Student Financial Aid ... Ms. Donna COX
04 Administrative Asst to President ... Ms. Karen BOGARD
08 Head Librarian ... Ms. Kim WILLIAMS
103 Dir Workforce/Career Development ... Ms. Wanda LINDSAY
105 Director Web Services ... Mr. Terry CLAUSEN
53 Dean or Director Education ... Dr. Mark SHANLEY
96 Director of Purchasing ... Ms. Alice WEATHERLY

Southern Arkansas University (D)

100 E University Street, Magnolia AR 71753-5000
County: Columbia   FICE Identification: 001107
Unit ID: 107983
Telephone: (870) 235-4000   Carnegie Class: Master's M
FAX Number: (870) 235-5005   Calendar System: Semester
URL: www.saumag.edu
Established: 1909   Annual Undergrad Tuition & Fees (In-State): $6,510
Enrollment: 3,545   Coed
Affiliation or Control: State   IRS Status: 501(c)3
Highest Offering: Master's
Program: Liberal Arts And General; Teacher Preparatory; Professional
Accreditation: NH, ADNUR, BUS, CAATE, MUS, NUR, SW, TED

01 President ... Dr. Trey BERRY
05 Provost/Vice Pres Academic Affairs ... Dr. Ben JOHNSON
11 VP Administration/General Counsel ... Mr. Roger W. GILES
32 Vice President Student Affairs ... Dr. Donna Y. ALLEN
18 Vice President of Facilities ... Mr. C. Jasper LEWIS
10 Vice President for Finance ... Vacant
30 Asst Vice President for Development ... Mr. Josh KEE
49 Dean Col Liberal/Perform Arts ... Dr. Helmut LANGERBEIN
50 Dean College of Business ... Dr. Lisa C. TOMS
53 Dean College of Education ... Dr. Zaidy MOHDZAIN
72 Dean College of Sci & Technology ... Dr. Scott MCKAY
58 Dean School of Graduate Studies ... Dr. Kim K. BLOSS
06 Registrar ... Mrs. Sandra WALKER
84 Dean Enrollment Services ... Ms. Sarah E. JENNINGS
35 Associate Deans of Students ... Mr. Carey BAKER
08 Director of Library ... Mr. Del G. DUKE
13 Director Info Technology Services ... Mr. Mike A. ARGO
38 Director Counsel/Testing Center ... Ms. Paula WASHINGTON-WOODS
35 Dean of Students ... Ms. Sandra E. SMITH
29 Director of Alumni Affairs ... Ms. Ceil L. BRIDGES
44 Director of Development ... Ms. Jeanie BISMARK
37 Director of Financial Aid ... Ms. Marcela C. MCRAE-BRUNSON
51 Director of Continuing Education ... Vacant
41 Director of Athletics ... Mr. Steve BROWNING
88 Director Student Support Services ... Ms. Eunice E. WALKER
36 Director of Placement Services ... Vacant
26 Asst Dean Integrated Marketing ... Mr. Aaron J. STREET
28 Assoc Dean Multicultural Affairs ... Mr. Cledis D. STUART
21 Coordinator of Fringe Benefits ... Mr. Alan DAVIS
27 Assoc Dir Communications Center ... Ms. Vicki BUTLER

Southern Arkansas University Tech (E)

Post Office Box 3499, Camden AR 71711
County: Calhoun   FICE Identification: 007738
Unit ID: 107992
Telephone: (870) 574-4500   Carnegie Class: Assoc/Pub2in4
FAX Number: (870) 574-4520   Calendar System: Semester
URL: www.sautech.edu
Established: 1967   Annual Undergrad Tuition & Fees (In-State): $4,050
Enrollment: 1,561   Coed
Affiliation or Control: State   IRS Status: 501(c)3
Highest Offering: Associate Degree
Program: Occupational; 2-Year Principally Bachelor's Creditable; Technical Emphasis
Accreditation: NH

01 Chancellor ... Dr. Corbet J. LAMKIN
10 VC for Finance & Administration ... Mrs. Gaye MANNING
05 Executive Vice Chancellor ... Mr. Robert GUNNELS
32 VC for Student Services ... Mr. David MCLEANE
13 VC for Information Technology ... Mrs. Valerie WILSON
26 Director of Communications ... Mrs. Kim COKER
09 Director of Research ... Mr. Lee SANDERS
84 Director of Enrollment Services ... Mrs. Patricia SINDLE
103 Director of Career Pathways ... Ms. LaTonya REED
31 Director of Special Programs ... Mr. Robert WHITE
75 Director of B & I Training ... Vacant
88 Director of Career Academy ... Mr. James UTSEY
88 Director of AETA ... Mr. Randy HARPER
88 Director of AFTA ... Mrs. Rachel NIX
14 Director of ITS ... Mrs. Laura JOHNSON
37 Director of Financial Aid ... Ms. Jennifer WILLIAMS
18 Director of Physical Plant ... Mr. Gerald MANNING
35 Director of Student Life ... Vacant
06 Registrar ... Mr. Wayne BANKS
08 Director of LRC ... Ms. Allison MALONE
04 Assistant to the Chancellor ... Mrs. Paula BERGSTROM
15 Human Resources Director ... Mrs. Olivia CLACK
21 Controller ... Mr. Dale TOMMEY
45 Vice Chancellor for PAD ... Dr. Diane BETTS
39 Residential Advisor ... Mrs. LaDonna FUSILIER
96 Buyer ... Mrs. Angela FRY
51 Director of Adult Education ... Mrs. Barbara HAMILTON
19 Director Security/Safety ... Mr. John FERGUSON

*University of Arkansas System Office (F)

2404 N University Avenue, Little Rock AR 72207-3608
County: Pulaski   FICE Identification: 008008
Unit ID: 108056
Telephone: (501) 686-2500   Carnegie Class: N/A
FAX Number: (501) 686-2507
URL: www.uasys.edu

01 President ... Dr. Donald R. BOBBITT
04 Assistant to the President ... Ms. Angela HUDSON
05 Vice President Academic Affairs ... Dr. Michael K. MOORE
10 Vice President for Finance & CFO ... Ms. Barbara GOSWICK
11 Vice President for Administration ... Ms. Ann KEMP
26 Vice President University Relations ... Ms. Melissa RUST
47 Vice President Agriculture ... Dr. Mark J. COCHRAN
43 General Counsel ... Mr. Fred H. HARRISON
88 Director Internal Audit ... Mr. Jacob W. FLOURNOY
21 Assoc Vice President for Finance ... Ms. Rita FLEMING

*University of Arkansas Main Campus (G)

Fayetteville AR 72701-1201
County: Washington   FICE Identification: 001108
Unit ID: 106397
Telephone: (479) 575-2000   Carnegie Class: RU/VH
FAX Number: (479) 575-2361   Calendar System: Semester
URL: www.uark.edu
Established: 1871   Annual Undergrad Tuition & Fees (In-State): $8,522
Enrollment: 26,237   Coed
Affiliation or Control: State   IRS Status: 501(c)3
Highest Offering: Doctorate
Program: Liberal Arts And General; Teacher Preparatory; Professional
Accreditation: NH, AAFCS, BUS, BUSA, CAATE, CACREP, CIDA, CLPSY, CORE, CS, DIETD, ENG, JOUR, LAW, LSAR, MUS, NURSE, #SP, SW, TED

02 Interim Chancellor ... Dr. Daniel E. FERRITOR
04 Executive Asst to the Chancellor ... Vacant
05 Provost & Vice Chanc Academic Affs ... Dr. Ashok SAXENA
10 Interim Vice Chanc Finance & Admin ... Mr. Tim O'DONNELL
30 Vice Chanc University Advancement ... Mr. Chris WYRICK
86 Vice Chanc Governmental Relations ... Mr. Randy MASSANELLI
09 Vice Provost Planning/Dir Inst Res ... Dr. Kathy M. VAN LANINGHAM
46 Vice Provost Research/Econ Dev ... Dr. James M. RANKIN
32 Vice Prov Stdnt Affs/Dean Students ... Vacant
28 Vice Chanc Diversity & Community ... Mr. Charles ROBINSON
84 Vice Prov Enrol Mgt/Dean Admissions ... Dr. Suzanne MCCRAY
26 Assoc Vice Chanc Univ Relations ... Ms. Laura JACOBS
15 Assoc Vice Chanc Human Resources ... Ms. Barbara A. ABERCROMBIE
18 Assoc Vice Chanc Facilities Mgmt ... Mr. Mike JOHNSON
21 Assoc Vice Chanc Business Affairs ... Ms. Colleen M. BRINEY
08 Dean of Libraries ... Ms. Carolyn H. ALLEN
49 Dean of Arts & Sciences ... Dr. Todd G. SHIELDS
50 Dean Sam Walton College of Business ... Dr. Eli JONES
47 Dean of Agriculture ... Dr. Michael E. VAYDA
53 Dean Education/Health Professions ... Dr. Tom SMITH
48 Dean of Architecture ... Mr. Peter MACKEITH
51 Interim Dean of Graduate School ... Dr. Kim NEEDY
54 Dean of Engineering ... Dr. John ENGLISH
92 Dean Honors College ... Vacant
61 Dean of the Law School ... Ms. Stacy LEEDS
29 Assoc Vice Chanc for Alumni ... Ms. Brandy A. COX
22 Director of Equal Opportunity ... Ms. Danielle L. WOOD
37 Exec Director Financial Aid ... Ms. Wendy D. STOUFFER
38 Dir of Counseling/Psych Services ... Dr. Jonathan C. PERRY
25 Director Research & Sponsored Pgms ... Ms. Rosemary H. RUFF
19 Director University Police ... Mr. Steve GAHAGANS
36 Dir of Career Development Center ... Ms. Angela S. WILLIAMS
13 Assoc VC for Info Technology ... Dr. Dennis BREWER
06 Registrar ... Mr. Dave DAWSON
96 Director of Purchasing ... Ms. Linda FAST
58 Director Graduate & Intl Admissions ... Ms. Lynn MOSESSO

*University of Arkansas at Fort Smith (H)

PO Box 3649, Fort Smith AR 72913-3649
County: Sebastian   FICE Identification: 001110
Unit ID: 108092
Telephone: (479) 788-7000   Carnegie Class: Bac/Assoc
FAX Number: (479) 788-7003   Calendar System: Semester
URL: www.uafs.edu
Established: 1928   Annual Undergrad Tuition & Fees (In-District): $6,322
Enrollment: 6,823   Coed
Affiliation or Control: State/Local   IRS Status: 501(c)3
Highest Offering: Master's
Program: Occupational; Liberal Arts And General; Teacher Preparatory
Accreditation: NH, BUS, DH, DMS, MUS, NAIT, NUR, RAD, SURGT, TED

02 Chancellor ... Dr. Paul B. BERAN
05 Provost/Vice Chanc Academic Affairs ... Dr. Georgia HALE
30 Vice Chancellor Univ Advancement ... Dr. Mary LACKIE
10 Vice Chanc Finance & Administration ... Vacant
32 Vice Chancellor Student Affairs ... Dr. Lee KREHBIEL
07 VC for Enrollment Management ... Ms. Julie BURDICK
31 Assoc VC Campus/Cmty Events ... Mr. Stacey JONES
86 Assoc VC Govt & Univ Relations ... Dr. Elizabeth UNDERWOOD

20 Asst to Provost ... Ms. Diana ROWDEN
20 Asst to Provost ... Ms. Penny PENDLETON
76 Dean College of Health Sciences ... Dr. Carolyn MOSLEY
50 Interim Dean College of Business ... Dr. Margaret TANNER
72 Dean Col Applied Science/Tech ... Dr. Ken WARDEN
72 Dean Col Sci/Tech/Engineering/Math ... Dr. Ron DARBEAU
60 Dean Col of Comm/Lang/Arts & Soc ... Vacant
15 Dir Human Resources/EEO Officer ... Ms. Bev MCCLENDON
12 Dir Western Arkansas Tech Ctr ... Dr. Darrell C. RINK
88 Dir of Student Professional Dev Ctr ... Mr. Ron ORICK
45 Dir Institutional Effectiveness ... Dr. Fnu MIHIR
88 Director of Instructional Support ... Dr. Tara MISHRA
08 Director of Library Services ... Mr. Robert FRIZZELL
39 Director of Student Housing ... Ms. Beth EPPINGER
37 Int Director of Financial Aid ... Ms. Rhonda BOYD
07 Director of Admissions ... Ms. Kelly WESTEEN
88 Int Director of Advisement ... Ms. Anna LAYNE
06 Registrar ... Mr. Wayne WOMACK
88 Exec Dir of International Relations ... Mr. Takeo SUZUKI
26 Act Dir Marketing & Communications ... Mr. Carl HULSEY
41 Director of Athletics ... Dr. Dustin SMITH
96 Director of Procurement Services ... Ms. Rhonda CATON
26 Director of Public Information ... Mr. John POST
18 Director of Plant Operations ... Mr. Bill PIERCE
103 Dir CBPD/Family Enterprise Ctr ... Mr. Dave ROBERTSON
13 Director of Technology ... Mr. Curtis SPEARS
19 Dir Chief of University Police ... Mr. Ray OTTMAN
29 Director of Alumni Affairs ... Mr. Rick GOINS
44 Director of Planned Giving ... Ms. Anne THOMAS
36 Asst Director Career Services ... Ms. Danielle JOLIE
25 Coordinator Grants ... Mr. Edward SERNA

*University of Arkansas at Little Rock (A)

2801 S University Avenue, Little Rock AR 72204-1099
County: Pulaski FICE Identification: 001101
Unit ID: 106245
Telephone: (501) 569-3000 Carnegie Class: DRU
FAX Number: (501) 569-8915 Calendar System: Semester
URL: www.ualr.edu
Established: 1927 Annual Undergrad Tuition & Fees (In-State): $8,108
Enrollment: 11,645 Coed
Affiliation or Control: State IRS Status: 501(c)3
Highest Offering: Doctorate
Program: Occupational; Liberal Arts And General; Teacher Preparatory; Professional
Accreditation: NH, ADNUR, ART, BUS, CONST, CORE, CS, DENT, ENG, ENGT, LAW, MUS, NUR, SPAA, SW, TED, THEA

02 Chancellor ... Dr. Joel E. ANDERSON
05 Executive Vice Chancellor & Provost ... Dr. Zulma R. TORO
32 Int Vice Chanc Educ Student Svcs ... Dr. Randall B. PATTERSON
10 Vice Chanc Finance & Administration ... Dr. Charles L. CANSLER
30 Vice Chancellor Advancement ... Mr. Bob G. DENMAN
13 Vice Chanc IT Services ... Mr. John M. RATHJE
84 Vice Chanc Enrollment Management ... Dr. Dean R. KAHLER
06 Int Registrar ... Ms. Malissa MATHIS
15 Director of Human Resource Devel ... Dr. Ignatius C. AZEBEOKHAI
26 Director of Communications ... Ms. Judy G. WILLIAMS
09 Director Inst Research ... Dr. William C. DECKER
37 Director Financial Aid ... Ms. Carlia G. SMITH
29 Director of Alumni Relations ... Mr. Christian O'NEAL
07 Director of Admissions ... Ms. Katie YOUNG
08 Head Librarian ... Dr. Deborah J. BALDWIN
19 Director Security/Safety ... Ms. Regina W. CARTER
25 Int Chief Contracts/Grants Admin ... Ms. Tammie L. CASH
41 Athletic Director ... Mr. Chasse S. CONQUE

*University of Arkansas for Medical Sciences (B)

4301 W Markham, Little Rock AR 72205-7199
County: Pulaski FICE Identification: 001109
Unit ID: 106263
Telephone: (501) 686-7000 Carnegie Class: Spec/Med
FAX Number: (501) 686-5905 Calendar System: Semester
URL: www.uams.edu
Established: 1879 Annual Undergrad Tuition & Fees (In-State): $8,468
Enrollment: 2,890 Coed
Affiliation or Control: State IRS Status: 501(c)3
Highest Offering: Doctorate
Program: Occupational; 2-Year Principally Bachelor's Creditable; Liberal Arts And General; Professional
Accreditation: NH, #ARCPA, AUD, CAHIIM, COARC, CYTO, DH, DIETI, DMS, EMT, HSA, IPSY, MED, MT, NMT, NURSE, PH, PHAR, @PTA, RAD, SP, SURGT

02 Chancellor ... Dr. Daniel RAHN
05 Provost and CAO ... Dr. Stephanie F. GARDNER
10 Vice Chancellor Finance & CEO ... Mr. Bill BOWES
26 Vice Chancellor Communications ... Ms. Leslie W. TAYLOR
30 Vice Chancellor Development ... Mr. Lance E. BURCHETT
11 Vice Chancellor Campus Operations ... Mr. Mark A. KENNEDAY
28 Vice Chancellor for Diversity ... Dr. Billy R. THOMAS
08 Assoc Provost Library/Stdnt Svcs ... Dr. Jan HART
13 Chief Information Officer ... Ms. Rhonda JORDEN
15 Assoc Vice Chancellor for HR ... Mr. Jeff A. RISINGER
20 Assoc ProvostTeaching Lrng Support ... Dr. Steve E. BOONE
07 Assoc Provost Enroll Svcs Admin ... Ms. Elizabeth BARD
37 Director Financial Services ... Ms. Gloria KEMP
63 Dean College of Medicine ... Dr. Pope H. MOSELEY
76 Dean Col Health Professions ... Dr. Douglas L. MURPHY
66 Interim Dean College of Nursing ... Dr. Jean MCSWEENEY
67 Dean College of Pharmacy ... Dr. Stephanie F. GARDNER
58 Dean of the Graduate School ... Dr. Robert E. MCGEHEE, JR.
88 Dean College of Public Health ... Dr. James M. RACZYNSKI
06 Chief Registrar ... Mr. Clinton D. EVERHART
39 Dir Campus Life/Stdnt Support Svcs ... Ms. Cheri D. GOFORTH

† Tuition figure is for Medical School. Other school's tuitions vary widely.

*University of Arkansas at Monticello (C)

346 University Drive, Monticello AR 71656-3596
County: Drew FICE Identification: 001085
Unit ID: 106485
Telephone: (870) 367-1020 Carnegie Class: Master's S
FAX Number: (870) 460-1321 Calendar System: Semester
URL: www.uamont.edu
Established: 1909 Annual Undergrad Tuition & Fees (In-State): $6,446
Enrollment: 3,854 Coed
Affiliation or Control: State IRS Status: 501(c)3
Highest Offering: Master's
Program: Occupational; 2-Year Principally Bachelor's Creditable; Liberal Arts And General; Teacher Preparatory
Accreditation: NH, EMT, MUS, NUR, SW, TED

02 Interim Chancellor ... Mr. Jay JONES
05 Provost/VC for Acad Affairs ... Dr. Jimmie YEISER
10 Vice Chanc Finance & Administration ... Mr. Jay JONES
30 Vice Chanc Advancement/Univ Rels ... Ms. Linda YEISER
32 Vice Chanc Student Affairs ... Mr. Jay HUGHES
12 Vice Chanc UAM Col of Tech Crossett ... Ms. Linda RUSHING
12 Vice Chanc UAM Col of Tech McGehee ... Mr. Bob WARE
21 Assoc VC for Finance and Admin ... Ms. Debbie GASAWAY
06 Registrar ... Ms. Carol DOLBERRY
07 Director of Admissions ... Ms. Mary WHITING
84 Director of Enrollment Mgmt ... Ms. Mary WHITING
41 Director of Athletics ... Mr. Chris RATCLIFF
35 Dean of Students ... Mr. Scott KUTTENKULER
13 Director Information Technology ... Ms. Anissa ROSS
08 Director of Library ... Vacant
26 Director of Media Services ... Mr. Jim L. BREWER
37 Director of Financial Aid ... Ms. Susan BREWER
09 Director of Institutional Research ... Ms. Christy PACE
04 Assistant to the Chancellor ... Ms. Christy PACE
18 Chief Facilities/Physical Plant ... Mr. Chester ASHCRAFT
38 Dir Counseling/Testing Services ... Ms. Laura HUGHES
96 Director of Purchasing ... Ms. Gay PACE
29 Director of Alumni Affairs ... Vacant
86 Director Government Relations ... Mr. Scott KUTTENKULER
19 Director of Public Safety ... Mr. John KIDWELL

*University of Arkansas at Pine Bluff (D)

1200 N University Drive, Pine Bluff AR 71601-2799
County: Jefferson FICE Identification: 001086
Unit ID: 106412
Telephone: (870) 575-8000 Carnegie Class: Bac/Diverse
FAX Number: (870) 543-8009 Calendar System: Semester
URL: www.uapb.edu
Established: 1873 Annual Undergrad Tuition & Fees (In-State): $6,271
Enrollment: 2,513 Coed
Affiliation or Control: State IRS Status: 501(c)3
Highest Offering: Doctorate
Program: Liberal Arts And General; Teacher Preparatory; Professional
Accreditation: NH, AAFCS, ACBSP, ART, @DIETD, MUS, NAIT, SW, TED

02 Chancellor ... Dr. Laurence B. ALEXANDER
05 Int Vice Chanc Academic Affairs ... Dr. Jacquelyn MCCRAY
10 Vice Chanc Finance & Admin ... Dr. Carla M. MARTIN
32 Vice Chancellor Student Affairs ... Mr. Elbert BENNETT
45 Vice Chanc Reserach/Innovation ... Dr. Mary E. BENJAMIN
30 Vice Chanc Institutional Advancemnt ... Mr. James B. TYSON
100 Chief of Staff ... Mrs. Janet BROILES
41 Athletics Director ... Mr. Lonza HARDY
15 Director of Human Resources ... Mrs. Gladys BENFORD
13 Director of Technical Services ... Mrs. Willette TOTTEN
09 Director of Institutional Research ... Mrs. Margaret TAYLOR
06 Registrar ... Mrs. Erica FULTON
29 Director of Alumni Affairs ... Mr. John KUYKENDALL
08 Head Librarian ... Mr. Edward FONTENETTE
103 Dir Workforce/Career Development ... Mrs. Shirley CHERRY
108 Director Institutional Assessment ... Dr. Steve LOCHMANN
37 Director Student Financial Aid ... Mrs. Janice KEARNEY

*Cossatot Community College of the University of Arkansas (E)

183 College Drive, De Queen AR 71832
County: Sevier FICE Identification: 022209
Unit ID: 106795
Telephone: (870) 584-4471 Carnegie Class: Assoc/Pub2in4
FAX Number: (870) 642-3320 Calendar System: Semester
URL: www.cccua.edu
Established: 1991 Annual Undergrad Tuition & Fees (In-District): $1,920
Enrollment: 1,584 Coed
Affiliation or Control: State/Local IRS Status: 501(c)3
Highest Offering: Associate Degree
Program: Occupational; 2-Year Principally Bachelor's Creditable
Accreditation: NH, ACBSP, OTA

02 Chancellor ... Dr. Steve COLE
05 Vice Chancellor of Academics ... Dr. Maria PARKER
45 VC of Planning and Facilities ... Mr. Mike KINKADE
10 Vice Chancellor Business/Finance ... Mrs. Charlotte JOHNSON
32 Director of Student Services ... Mr. Justin WHITE
37 Director Student Financial Aid ... Mrs. Denise HAMMOND
26 Director of Marketing ... Ms. Alisha LEWIS
09 Director of Inst Research/Registrar ... Mrs. Brenda MORRIS
103 Dir of Public Svc/Workforce Dev ... Mrs. Tammy COLEMAN
12 Director of Ashdown Campus ... Mr. Barrett REED
15 Director of Human Resources ... Ms. Kelly PLUNK
13 Information Manager ... Mr. Tony HARGROVE
102 Executive Director of Foundation ... Mr. Dustin ROBERTS

*Phillips Community College of the University of Arkansas (F)

PO Box 785, Helena AR 72342-0785
County: Phillips FICE Identification: 001104
Unit ID: 107619
Telephone: (870) 338-6474 Carnegie Class: Assoc/Pub2in4
FAX Number: (870) 338-7542 Calendar System: Semester
URL: www.pccua.edu
Established: 1965 Annual Undergrad Tuition & Fees (In-District): $2,592
Enrollment: 1,799 Coed
Affiliation or Control: State/Local IRS Status: 501(c)3
Highest Offering: Associate Degree
Program: Occupational; 2-Year Principally Bachelor's Creditable
Accreditation: NH, ACBSP, ADNUR, MLTAD, PHLEB

02 Chancellor ... Dr. G. Keith PINCHBACK
05 Vice Chancellor for Instruction ... Dr. Deborah KING
10 Vice Chanc Finance & Administration ... Mr. Stan SULLIVANT
32 Vice Chanc Student Svcs/Registrar ... Mr. Scott POST
30 Vice Chanc Col Advancement/Bus Dev ... Mrs. Rhonda ST. COLUMBIA
12 Int Vice Chanc Stuttgart Campus ... Ms. Kim KIRBY
12 Vice Chancellor DeWitt Campus ... Mrs. Carolyn TURNER

*University of Arkansas Community College at Batesville (G)

2005 White Drive, PO Box 3350,
Batesville AR 72503-3350
County: Independence FICE Identification: 020735
Unit ID: 106999
Telephone: (870) 612-2000 Carnegie Class: Assoc/Pub2in4
FAX Number: (870) 793-4988 Calendar System: Semester
URL: www.uaccb.edu
Established: 1975 Annual Undergrad Tuition & Fees (In-District): $2,820
Enrollment: 1,317 Coed
Affiliation or Control: State/Local IRS Status: 501(c)3
Highest Offering: Associate Degree
Program: Occupational; 2-Year Principally Bachelor's Creditable
Accreditation: NH, ADNUR, EMT

02 Chancellor ... Ms. Deborah J. FRAZIER
04 Assistant to the Chancellor ... Vacant
05 Vice Chancellor for Academics ... Dr. Brian SHONK
32 Vice Chanc Student Affairs ... Mr. Greg THORNBURG
10 Vice Chancellor Finance and Admin ... Mr. Gayle COOPER
09 VC Research/Planning/Assessment ... Dr. Anne AUSTIN
49 Chair Div of Arts & Humanities ... Ms. Susan TRIPP
50 Chair Div Business/Tech/Public Svc ... Dr. Tamara GRIFFIN
76 Int Chair Div Nursing/Allied Health ... Ms. Marietta CANDLER
81 Chair Div of Math and Science ... Mr. Douglas MUSE
103 Dir of Workforce Development ... Dr. Gene TULBERG
09 Dir of Institutional Research ... Ms. Beth BRUCE
07 Director of Admissions ... Ms. Amy FOREE
13 Director Information Services ... Mr. Steve COLLINS
06 Dir Student Information/Registrar ... Ms. Shelly MOSER
37 Director of Financial Aid ... Ms. Kristen CROSS
30 Director of Development ... Ms. Tina PAUL
18 Director of Maintenance ... Mr. Heath WOOLDRIDGE
36 Director Student Development ... Ms. Louise HUGHES
38 Career/Disabilities Coordinator ... Ms. Becky WARREN
08 Director Library ... Mr. Jay STRICKLAND
21 Controller ... Ms. Waynna DOCKINS
15 Personnel Officer ... Ms. Alexa SMITH
96 Purchasing Agent ... Ms. Peggy JACKSON
40 Bookstore Manager ... Ms. Luanne BARBER

*University of Arkansas Community College at Hope (H)

PO Box 140, 2500 S Main Street, Hope AR 71802-0140
County: Hempstead FICE Identification: 005732
Unit ID: 107725
Telephone: (870) 777-5722 Carnegie Class: Assoc/Pub2in4
FAX Number: (870) 777-5957 Calendar System: Semester
URL: www.uacch.edu
Established: 1991 Annual Undergrad Tuition & Fees (In-State): $2,670
Enrollment: 1,360 Coed
Affiliation or Control: State IRS Status: 501(c)3
Highest Offering: Associate Degree
Program: Occupational; 2-Year Principally Bachelor's Creditable
Accreditation: NH, EMT, FUSER

02 Chancellor ... Mr. Chris THOMASON
05 Vice Chancellor for Academics ... Ms. Laura CLARK
32 Vice Chancellor Student Services ... Mr. Brian BERRY
10 Vice Chancellor for Finance ... Dr. Belinda AARON
08 Librarian ... Ms. Marielle MCFARLAND
51 Director of Cont Educ/Ind Relations ... Mr. Shaun CLARK
26 Communications Coordinator ... Mr. Brent TALLEY
24 Director of Telecommunications ... Mr. Dave PHILLIPS
15 Human Resources Officer ... Ms. Kathryn HOPKINS
06 Registrar ... Ms. Diana SYATA
12 Texarkana Campus Director ... Ms. Jolane COOK

*University of Arkansas Community College at Morrilton (A)

1537 University Boulevard, Morrilton AR 72110-9601

County: Conway FICE Identification: 005245
Unit ID: 107585
Telephone: (501) 354-2465 Carnegie Class: Assoc/Pub2in4
FAX Number: (501) 977-2134 Calendar System: Semester
URL: www.uaccm.edu
Established: 1961 Annual Undergrad Tuition & Fees (In-State): $3,785
Enrollment: 1,996 Coed
Affiliation or Control: State IRS Status: 501(c)3
Highest Offering: Associate Degree
Program: Occupational; 2-Year Principally Bachelor's Creditable
Accreditation: NH

02 Chancellor ... Dr. Larry D. DAVIS
05 Vice Chancellor Academic Services ... Ms. Diana ARN
10 Vice Chancellor for Finance ... Ms. Lisa WILLENBERG
11 Vice Chancellor for Administration ... Dr. Linda M. BIRKNER
32 Vice Chancellor Student Services ... Mr. Darren JONES
09 Director of Institutional Research ... Ms. Beth HAWKINS
08 Librarian ... Ms. Rebecka EMBRY
06 Registrar ... Ms. Linda HOLLAND
37 Financial Aid Director ... Mrs. Teresa Y. CASH
13 Chief Information Officer ... Ms. Mary CLARK
14 Director of Computer Services ... Mr. Richard O. GROWNS
18 Director of the Physical Plant ... Mr. C. Allen HOLLOWAY
07 Director of Admissions ... Ms. Rachel MULLINS
103 Coord Workforce Develop/Cmty Educ ... Ms. Kim DARLING
15 Director Personnel Services ... Ms. Judy SANDERS
26 Chief Public Relations Officer ... Ms. Mary CLARK
30 Chief Development ... Ms. Morgan ZIMMERMAN
38 Director Student Counseling ... Ms. Staci DUVALL
96 Director of Purchasing ... Ms. Anna HALBROOK

**Phillips Community College of the University of Arkansas-DeWitt* (B)

1210 Rice Belt Avenue, DeWitt AR 72042

Telephone: (870) 946-3506 Identification: 770174
Accreditation: &NH

† Branch campus of Phillips Community College of the University of Arkansas, Helena, AR.

**Phillips Community College of the University of Arkansas-Stuttgart* (C)

2807 Hwy 165 South, Stuttgart AR 72160-2408

Telephone: (870) 338-6474 Identification: 770175
Accreditation: &NH

† Branch campus of Phillips Community College of the University of Arkansas, Helena, AR.

**University of Arkansas at Monticello College of Technology-Crossett* (D)

1326 Highway 52 W, Crossett AR 71635

Telephone: (870) 364-6414 Identification: 770176
Accreditation: &NH

† Branch campus of University of Arkansas at Monticello, Monticello, AR.

**University of Arkansas at Monticello College of Technology-McGehee* (E)

PO Box 747, McGehee AR 71654

Telephone: (870) 222-5360 Identification: 770177
Accreditation: &NH

† Branch campus of University of Arkansas at Monticello, Monticello, AR.

University of Central Arkansas (F)

201 Donaghey Avenue, Conway AR 72035-0001

County: Faulkner FICE Identification: 001092
Unit ID: 106704
Telephone: (501) 450-5000 Carnegie Class: Master's L
FAX Number: (501) 450-5003 Calendar System: Semester
URL: www.uca.edu
Established: 1907 Annual Undergrad Tuition & Fees (In-State): $7,888
Enrollment: 11,698 Coed
Affiliation or Control: State IRS Status: 501(c)3
Highest Offering: Doctorate
Program: Occupational; Liberal Arts And General; Teacher Preparatory; Professional
Accreditation: NH, ART, BUS, CAATE, CIDA, CS, DIETD, DIETI, MUS, NURSE, OT, PTA, SCPSY, SP, TED, THEA

01 President ... Mr. Tom COURTWAY
05 Provost/Exec VP Academic Affairs ... Dr. Steve RUNGE
10 VP Finance/Administration ... Ms. Diane D. NEWTON
32 VP Student Services/Inst Diversity ... Mr. Ronnie D. WILLIAMS
43 General Counsel ... Mr. Warren READNOUR
30 VP for UCA Advancement ... Vacant
41 Athletics Director ... Dr. Brad TEAGUE
15 Assoc Vice Pres for Human Resources ... Dr. Graham GILLIS
85 AVP International Engagement ... Ms. Jane Ann WILLIAMS
20 Assoc Provost Finance & Admin ... Ms. Laura YOUNG
20 Assoc Provost/Academic Services ... Dr. Jonathan A. GLENN
20 Assoc Provost/Instructional Support ... Dr. Kurt BONIECKI
26 Assoc VP Comm/PR/Marketing ... Ms. Christina MADSEN
100 Chief of Staff ... Mr. Kelley ERSTINE
21 Controller ... Mr. Jeremy BRUNER
58 Dean of Graduate School ... Dr. Stephanie BELLAR
50 Dean of Col Business Admin ... Dr. Michael HARGIS
53 Dean of College of Education ... Dr. Victoria GROVES-SCOTT
76 Dean Col Health/Applied Science ... Dr. Jimmy ISHEE
49 Dean of Liberal Arts ... Dr. Maurice A. LEE
81 Dean Col Natural Sci/Math ... Dr. Steve ADDISON
57 Dean Fine Arts & Communication ... Mr. Terry WRIGHT
35 Dean of Students ... Dr. Gary A. ROBERTS
92 Dean of Honors College ... Dr. Richard I. SCOTT
07 Director Admissions ... Ms. Courtney MULLEN
08 Library Director ... Mr. Art LICHTENSTEIN
06 Registrar ... Ms. Becky D. RASNICK
09 Dir Institutional Research ... Ms. Amber L. HALL
13 Chief Technology Officer ... Dr. Chris DAVIS
37 Director Student Financial Aid ... Ms. Cheryl C. LYONS
36 Dir Career Svcs/Cooperative Educ ... Dr. Kathy RICE-CLAYBORN
19 Chief University Police ... Mr. Larry K. JAMES
38 Director Counseling Center ... Dr. Susan SOBEL
39 Asst VP for Housing & Contract Svcs ... Mr. Rick L. MCCOLLUM
29 Director of Alumni Services ... Mr. Jesse THILL
21 Director Internal Audits ... Ms. Pamela L. MASSEY
18 Director Physical Plant ... Mr. Larry D. LAWRENCE
24 Director Creative Services ... Mr. Richard R. HANCOCK
96 Director of Purchasing ... Ms. Cassandra MCCUIEN-SMITH
21 Director Student Accounts ... Mr. Chad HEARNE

University of Phoenix Little Rock Campus (G)

10800 Financial Ctr Pkwy, Suite 125,
Little Rock AR 72211-3552

Telephone: (501) 225-9337 Identification: 770188
Accreditation: &NH, ACBSP

† No longer accepting campus-based students.

University of the Ozarks (H)

415 College Avenue, Clarksville AR 72830-2880

County: Johnson FICE Identification: 001094
Unit ID: 107558
Telephone: (479) 979-1000 Carnegie Class: Bac/Diverse
FAX Number: (479) 979-1355 Calendar System: Semester
URL: www.ozarks.edu
Established: 1834 Annual Undergrad Tuition & Fees: $31,440
Enrollment: 587 Coed
Affiliation or Control: Presbyterian Church (U.S.A.) IRS Status: 501(c)3
Highest Offering: Baccalaureate
Program: Liberal Arts And General; Teacher Preparatory; Professional
Accreditation: NH, IACBE, TED

01 President ... Mr. Richard L. DUNSWORTH
05 Provost ... Mr. Travis FEEZELL
10 VP for Finance & Administration ... Mr. Jeff SCACCIA
84 Vice President for Enrollment ... Vacant
07 Assistant Director of Admission ... Mr. Joseph HUGHES
07 Dean of Admissions & Financial Aid ... Ms. Jana D. HART
42 Chaplain ... Rev. Elizabeth GABBARD
06 Registrar ... Ms. Wilma K. HARRIS
08 Librarian ... Mr. Stuart P. STELZER
36 Director Student Placement ... Ms. Kim A. SPICER
29 Director Alumni Affairs ... Ms. Ashley A. SENTER
41 Athletic Director ... Mr. Jimmy CLARK
26 Dir University/Public Relations ... Mr. Larry A. ISCH
30 Director of Development ... Ms. Lori A. MCBEE
18 Chief Facilities/Physical Plant ... Mr. Mike QUALLS
88 Director Jones Learning Center ... Ms. Julia H. FROST
09 Director of Institutional Research ... Mr. Rick OTTO
96 Director of Purchasing ... Mr. Darrell W. WILLIAMS
89 Director of Freshmen Studies ... Vacant
13 Director of Information Technology ... Ms. Vickie ALSTON
32 Dean of Students ... Mr. Steven WEAVER
81 Chair Division Sciences/Mathematics ... Mr. Stacy KEY
50 Chair Division of Business ... Vacant
53 Chair Division of Education ... Ms. Janie CHAPPELL
79 Chair Division Humanities/Fine Arts ... Vacant
37 Student Financial Aid Counselor ... Vacant
105 Director Web Services ... Ms. Cara FLINN
15 Director Personnel Services ... Ms. Karen SCHLUTERMAN
19 Director Security/Safety ... Ms. Jeannett WILLIS

Williams Baptist College (I)

60 W. Fulbright Avenue, Walnut Ridge AR 72476

County: Lawrence FICE Identification: 001106
Unit ID: 107877
Telephone: (870) 886-6741 Carnegie Class: Bac/Diverse
FAX Number: (870) 886-3924 Calendar System: Semester
URL: www.wbcoll.edu
Established: 1941 Annual Undergrad Tuition & Fees: $14,360
Enrollment: 560 Coed
Affiliation or Control: Southern Baptist IRS Status: 501(c)3
Highest Offering: Baccalaureate
Program: Liberal Arts And General; Religious Emphasis
Accreditation: NH, TED

01 President ... Dr. Tom O. JONES
05 Vice Pres Academic Affairs ... Dr. Kenneth M. STARTUP
10 Vice President for Business Affairs ... Mr. W. Dale LEATHERMAN
30 Vice Pres Institutional Advancement ... Dr. Brett COOPER
84 VP for Enrollment Mgmt/Student Svcs ... Dr. Jeremy D. DUTSCHKE
32 Dean of Students ... Ms. Amber N. GRADY
06 Registrar ... Mrs. Tonya D. BOLTON
04 Administrative Asst to President ... Mrs. Jo C. PHILLIPS
08 Librarian ... Mrs. Pamela MERIDITH
37 Director Student Financial Aid ... Mrs. Barbara J. TURNER
38 Director of Counseling ... Ms. Aneita COOPER
42 Campus Minister ... Mr. Josh MCCARTY
18 Director Physical Plant ... Mr. Tony CONLEY
44 Dir of Annual Giving & Alumni Rels ... Mr. Aaron ANDREWS
13 Director Information Technology ... Mr. Blake MCGINNIS
41 Athletic Director ... Mr. Jeff RIDER
106 Dean of Adult Education ... Dr. Eric TURNER
85 Director of International Programs ... Mr. Adam ADAMS
07 Director of Admissions ... Mr. Andrew WATSON

CALIFORNIA

Abraham Lincoln University (J)

3530 Wilshire Blvd, Ste 1430, Los Angeles CA 90010

County: Los Angeles Identification: 667049
Unit ID: 480444
Telephone: (213) 252-5100 Carnegie Class: Not Classified
FAX Number: (213) 252-5112 Calendar System: Other
URL: www.alu.edu
Established: 1996 Annual Undergrad Tuition & Fees: $8,000
Enrollment: 144 Coed
Affiliation or Control: Proprietary IRS Status: Proprietary
Highest Offering: First Professional Degree
Program: 2-Year Principally Bachelor's Creditable; Liberal Arts And General; Professional
Accreditation: DEAC

01 President & CEO/Dean School of Law ... Mr. Hyung PARK
61 CIO & Dir of School of Law ... Ms. Jessica PARK
11 Director of Univ Programs ... Dr. Susan LOMELI
13 Technology Coordinator ... Mr. Daniel JUNG
06 Registrar ... Ms. Elizabeth GOMEZ
14 Software Engineer ... Mr. Tae KIM
07 Coordinator of Enrollment ... Ms. Malana JONES

Academy for Jewish Religion (K)

574 Hilgard Avenue, Los Angeles CA 90024-3234

County: Los Angeles FICE Identification: 041555
Unit ID: 457271
Telephone: (310) 824-1586 Carnegie Class: Not Classified
FAX Number: (310) 824-1614 Calendar System: Trimester
URL: www.ajrca.org
Established: 2001 Annual Graduate Tuition & Fees: $22,550
Enrollment: 65 Coed
Affiliation or Control: Jewish IRS Status: 501(c)3
Highest Offering: Master's; No Undergraduates
Program: Professional; Religious Emphasis
Accreditation: WC

01 President ... Dr. Tamar FRANKIEL
10 Chief Financial Officer ... Dr. Alvin MARTIN
11 Director Administration ... Ms. Lauren GOLDNER
06 Registrar/Operations Manager ... Ms. Reesa ROTMAN
07 Director of Admissions/Recruitment ... Ms. Robin FEDERMAN
26 Chief Public Relations Officer ... Ms. Cheryl AZAIR
36 Director of Placement ... Rabbi Faith TESSLER
88 Dean of Cantorial School ... Cantor Nathan LAM
73 Dean of Rabbinical School ... Rabbi Michael MENITOFF
88 Associate Dean of Cantorial School ... Cantor Perryne ANKER

Academy of Art University (L)

79 New Montgomery Street,
San Francisco CA 94105-3410

County: San Francisco FICE Identification: 007531
Unit ID: 108232
Telephone: (415) 274-2200 Carnegie Class: Spec/Arts
FAX Number: (415) 274-8665 Calendar System: Semester
URL: www.academyart.edu
Established: 1929 Annual Undergrad Tuition & Fees: $23,550
Enrollment: 15,212 Coed
Affiliation or Control: Proprietary IRS Status: Proprietary
Highest Offering: Master's
Program: Fine Arts Emphasis
Accreditation: WC, ART, #CIDA

01 President ... Ms. Elisa STEPHENS

Academy of Chinese Culture and Health Sciences (A)

1600 Broadway Street, Suite 200, Oakland CA 94612
County: Alameda FICE Identification: 032883
Unit ID: 108269
Telephone: (510) 763-7787 Carnegie Class: Spec/Health
FAX Number: (510) 834-8646 Calendar System: Other
URL: www.acchs.edu
Established: 1982 Annual Undergrad Tuition & Fees: $17,920
Enrollment: 146 Coed
Affiliation or Control: Independent Non-Profit IRS Status: 501(c)3
Highest Offering: Master's; No Lower Division
Program: Professional
Accreditation: ACUP

01 President .... Dr. Jun WANG
03 Vice President .... Mr. Phillip TOU
11 Dean of Administration .... Ms. Jane ZHANG

Academy of Couture Art (B)

8484 Wilshire Boulevard, Suite 730,
Beverly Hills CA 90211-3235
County: Los Angeles FICE Identification: 041855
Unit ID: 475635
Telephone: (310) 360-8888 Carnegie Class: Not Classified
FAX Number: (310) 857-6974 Calendar System: Quarter
URL: www.academyofcoutureart.edu
Established: 2005 Annual Undergrad Tuition & Fees: $19,998
Enrollment: 55 Coed
Affiliation or Control: Proprietary IRS Status: Proprietary
Highest Offering: Baccalaureate
Program: Occupational; 2-Year Principally Bachelor's Creditable; Professional; Fine Arts Emphasis
Accreditation: ACICS

01 CEO .... Sonia ETE
05 Chief Academic Officer .... Sarey TORRES
11 Chief Operating Officer .... Thierry ETE
07 Director of Admissions .... Jennifer PARK ZERBEL

Acupuncture and Integrative Medicine College-Berkeley (C)

2550 Shattuck Avenue, Berkeley CA 94704-2724
County: Alameda FICE Identification: 033274
Unit ID: 384306
Telephone: (510) 666-8248 Carnegie Class: Spec/Health
FAX Number: (510) 666-0111 Calendar System: Trimester
URL: www.aimc.edu
Established: 1990 Annual Undergrad Tuition & Fees: $17,000
Enrollment: 138 Coed
Affiliation or Control: Independent Non-Profit IRS Status: 501(c)3
Highest Offering: Master's; No Lower Division
Program: Professional
Accreditation: ACUP

01 President .... Mr. Yasuo TANAKA
05 Academic Dean .... Ms. Megan HAUNGS
05 Clinic Dean .... Mr. Mike MORGAN
07 Director of Admissions .... Ms. Julie SCHEFF
06 Registrar .... Mr. Brian LIESKE
20 Student Advisor .... Mr. Peter BLACKMAN
08 Head Librarian .... Ms. Patricia WARD
37 Director Student Financial Aid .... Ms. Victoria LABRADOR

Advanced College (D)

13180 Paramount Boulevard, South Gate CA 90280-7956
County: Los Angeles FICE Identification: 037863
Unit ID: 444343
Telephone: (562) 408-6969 Carnegie Class: Assoc/PrivFP
FAX Number: (562) 408-0471 Calendar System: Other
URL: www.advancedcollege.edu
Established: 1999 Annual Undergrad Tuition & Fees: $30,053
Enrollment: 125 Coed
Affiliation or Control: Proprietary IRS Status: Proprietary
Highest Offering: Associate Degree
Program: Occupational
Accreditation: COE

01 Chief Executive Officer .... Dr. Mehdi KARIMPOR
66 Director Vocational Nursing .... Dr. Minnie L. DOUGLAS
11 Director of Operations .... Dr. Mehdi KARIMPOUR

Advanced Computing Institute (E)

3470 Wilshire Blvd #1100, Los Angeles CA 90010
County: Los Angeles Identification: 667142
Unit ID: 481234
Telephone: (213) 383-8999 Carnegie Class: Not Classified
FAX Number: (213) 383-5765 Calendar System: Semester
URL: www.advancedcomputinginstitute.com
Established: 1992 Annual Undergrad Tuition & Fees: N/A
Enrollment: 211 Coed
Affiliation or Control: Proprietary IRS Status: Proprietary
Highest Offering: Associate Degree
Program: Occupational
Accreditation: COE

01 School Director/CEO .... Mr. Daniel MAINCA
05 Exec Vice Pres/Academic Dean .... Dr. Michael RAHNI

Advanced Training Associates (F)

1810 Gillespie Way, Suite 104, El Cajon CA 92020-1234
County: San Diego FICE Identification: 035324
Unit ID: 444361
Telephone: (619) 596-2766 Carnegie Class: Not Classified
FAX Number: (619) 596-4526 Calendar System: Other
URL: www.advancedtraining.edu
Established: 2000 Annual Undergrad Tuition & Fees: $11,990
Enrollment: 85 Coed
Affiliation or Control: Proprietary IRS Status: Proprietary
Highest Offering: Associate Degree
Program: Occupational; Technical Emphasis
Accreditation: COE

01 President/CEO .... Henry MARENTES
11 Senior Director of Operations .... Valerie PHILLIPS

Alhambra Medical University (G)

25 S. Raymond Ave., Suite 201, Alhambra CA 91801
County: Los Angeles Identification: 667052
Telephone: (626) 289-7719 Carnegie Class: Not Classified
FAX Number: (626) 289-8641 Calendar System: Quarter
URL: www.amuedu.com
Established: 2005 Annual Graduate Tuition & Fees: $13,282
Enrollment: N/A Coed
Affiliation or Control: Proprietary IRS Status: Proprietary
Highest Offering: Master's; No Undergraduates
Program: Professional
Accreditation: ACUP

01 President .... Dr. Jonathan WU
05 Academic Dean .... Jerome JIANG
23 Director of University Clinic .... Yue LU
07 Director of Admissions .... Qing MA
06 Registrar .... Alan LIU
08 Librarian .... Dr. Luke CHEN

Allan Hancock College (H)

800 S College Drive, Santa Maria CA 93454-6399
County: Santa Barbara FICE Identification: 001111
Unit ID: 108807
Telephone: (805) 922-6966 Carnegie Class: Assoc/Pub-R-L
FAX Number: (805) 928-7905 Calendar System: Semester
URL: www.hancockcollege.edu
Established: 1920 Annual Undergrad Tuition & Fees (In-District): $1,418
Enrollment: 11,047 Coed
Affiliation or Control: State/Local IRS Status: 501(c)3
Highest Offering: Associate Degree
Program: Occupational; 2-Year Principally Bachelor's Creditable
Accreditation: WJ

01 Superintendent/President .... Dr. Kevin G. WALTHERS
10 Assoc Supt/VP Finance/Admin .... Dr. Michael R. BLACK
05 Assoc Supt/VP Academic Affairs .... Dr. George RAILEY
32 VP Student Services .... Ms. Nohemy ORNELAS
18 Vice Pres Facilities & Operations .... Mr. Felix HERNANDEZ
35 Dean Student Services .... Mr. Rob PARISI
38 Dean Counseling & Matriculation .... Vacant
20 Dean Academic Affairs .... Ms. Nancy MEDDINGS
20 Dean Acad Afrs/Dir HSI STEM .... Dr. Paul MURPHY
12 Dean The Extended Campus .... Mr. Rick RANTZ
41 Assoc Dean Athletics/Kinesiology .... Ms. Kim ENSING
102 Executive Director AHC Foundation .... Vacant
88 Artistic Director PCPA .... Mr. Mark BOOHER
13 Director Information Technology .... Ms. Carol MOORE
21 Director Business Services .... Mr. Richard CARMODY
07 Director Admissions & Records .... Ms. Marian QUAID-MALTAGLIATI
37 Director Student Financial Aid .... Mr. Robert PARISI
26 Int Dir Public Affairs/Publications .... Mr. Andrew MASUDA
40 Int Director Bookstore Services .... Ms. Tammy YORK
88 Director EOPS & Special Outreach .... Mr. Will BRUCE
18 Director Plant .... Mr. Rex VANDENBERG
09 Director Inst Research & Planning .... Dr. Susanne VALERY
19 Int Dir Public Safety/Chf of Police .... Mr. John STAUGAARD
88 Director Cal-SOAP .... Ms. Diana PEREZ
25 Director Institutional Grants .... Dr. Suzanne VALERY
81 Counselor/Coordinator MESA .... Ms. Christine REED
88 Managing Director PCPA .... Mr. Michael BLACK

*Alliant International University President's Office (I)

One Beach Street, Suite 100,
San Francisco CA 94133-1221
County: San Francisco Identification: 666132
Unit ID: 110431
Telephone: (415) 955-2100 Carnegie Class: N/A
FAX Number: (414) 955-2062
URL: www.alliant.edu

01 President .... Dr. Geoffrey COX
05 Provost/Vice Pres Academic Affairs .... Dr. Russ NEWMAN
11 Interim Director Administration .... Ms. Betsy GOMEZ
32 VP Student Services .... Dr. Mary OLING-SISAY
10 Vice Pres Finance & Administration .... Ms. Nellis PARTS
53 Int Dean Grad School of Education .... Dr. Rhonda BRINKLEY-KENNEDY
06 Registrar .... Mr. Paul WELCH
15 Chief Human Resources Officer .... Ms. Lesa HAMMOND
07 Director of Admissions .... Ms. Melanie SCHWARTZ

*Alliant International University-San Diego (J)

10455 Pomerado Road, San Diego CA 92131-1799
County: San Diego FICE Identification: 011117
Unit ID: 110468
Telephone: (858) 635-4772 Carnegie Class: DRU
FAX Number: (858) 693-8562 Calendar System: Semester
URL: www.alliant.edu
Established: 1952 Annual Undergrad Tuition & Fees: $16,350
Enrollment: 3,957 Coed
Affiliation or Control: Independent Non-Profit IRS Status: 501(c)3
Highest Offering: Doctorate
Program: Liberal Arts And General; Teacher Preparatory; Professional
Accreditation: WC, CLPSY, MFCD

02 President .... Dr. Geoffrey COX
05 Provost/Vice Pres Academic Affairs .... Dr. Russ NEWMAN

*_Alliant International University-Fresno_ (K)

5130 E Clinton Way, Fresno CA 93727-2014
Telephone: (559) 456-2777 FICE Identification: 001158
Accreditation: &WC, CLPSY, MFCD

† Branch campus of Alliant International University-San Diego, San Diego, CA.

*_Alliant International University-Irvine_ (L)

2855 Michelle Drive, Suite 300, Irvine CA 92606
Telephone: (949) 812-7440 Identification: 666157
Accreditation: &WC, MFCD

† Branch campus of Alliant International University-San Diego, San Diego, CA.

*_Alliant International University-Los Angeles_ (M)

1000 S Fremont Avenue, Unit 5,
Alhambra CA 91803-1360
Telephone: (626) 284-2777 FICE Identification: 010013
Accreditation: &WC, CLPSY, MFCD

† Branch campus of Alliant International University-San Diego, San Diego, CA.

*_Alliant International University-San Francisco_ (N)

One Beach Street, San Francisco CA 94133-1221
Telephone: (415) 955-2100 FICE Identification: 011881
Accreditation: &WC, CLPSY, MFCD

† Branch campus of Alliant International University-San Diego, San Diego, CA.

Allied American University (O)

22952 Alcalde Drive, Laguna Hills CA 92653-1337
County: Orange FICE Identification: 041893
Unit ID: 460729
Telephone: (888) 384-0849 Carnegie Class: Not Classified
FAX Number: (949) 707-2978 Calendar System: Other
URL: www.allied.edu
Established: 2008 Annual Undergrad Tuition & Fees: $9,334
Enrollment: 2,244 Coed
Affiliation or Control: Proprietary IRS Status: Proprietary
Highest Offering: Baccalaureate
Program: Liberal Arts And General
Accreditation: @WC, DEAC

01 President .... Bill LUTON
05 Provost .... Dr. Chelsea HANSEN
20 Chief Innovation/Outcomes Officer .... Eric SHARKEY
11 Chief Operating Officer .... Christopher BISHOP
06 Registrar .... Abby DOLAN
84 Chief Enrollment Mgmt Officer .... Lindsay OGLESBY
09 Institutional Research Officer .... Sasha HEARD
100 Chief of Staff .... Frank VAZQUEZ

AMDA College and Conservatory of the Performing Arts (P)

6305 Yucca Street, Los Angeles CA 90028
County: Los Angeles Identification: 666721
Telephone: (323) 469-3300 Carnegie Class: Not Classified
FAX Number: (323) 469-1448 Calendar System: Semester
URL: www.amda.edu
Established: 1964 Annual Undergrad Tuition & Fees: $33,920
Enrollment: 1,241 Coed
Affiliation or Control: Independent Non-Profit IRS Status: 501(c)3
Highest Offering: Baccalaureate

Program: Liberal Arts And General; Fine Arts Emphasis
Accreditation: THEA

01 President/Artistic Director .... David MARTIN
05 Executive Director/Vice President .... Jan RUGGAR MARTIN
07 Natl Dir of Admissions/Career Svcs .... Karen JACKSON
37 Associate Director of Financial Aid .... Jillian DOYLE
26 Associate Marketing Manager .... Jenny YU

American Academy of Dramatic Arts, Los Angeles Campus (A)

1336 N La Brea Avenue, Hollywood CA 90028-7504
Telephone: (323) 464-2777 FICE Identification: 021069
Accreditation: &M, THEA

† Regional accreditation is carried under the parent institution in New York, NY.

American Baptist Seminary of the West (B)

2606 Dwight Way, Berkeley CA 94704-3097
County: Alameda FICE Identification: 001120
Unit ID: 108861
Telephone: (510) 841-1905 Carnegie Class: Spec/Faith
FAX Number: (510) 841-2446 Calendar System: Semester
URL: www.absw.edu
Established: 1871 Annual Graduate Tuition & Fees: $17,550
Enrollment: 53 Coed
Affiliation or Control: American Baptist IRS Status: 501(c)3
Highest Offering: Doctorate; No Undergraduates
Program: Professional; Religious Emphasis
Accreditation: THEOL

01 President .... Dr. Paul MARTIN
03 Vice President .... Rev. Michelle M. HOLMES
05 Academic Dean .... Dr. LeAnn SNOW FLESHER
10 Chief Financial Officer .... Rev. Michelle M. HOLMES
06 Registrar/Dir Academic Admin .... Ms. Nancy SVENSSON
07 Director of Admissions .... Ms. Marie ONWUBUARIRI
32 Director of Student Services .... Ms. Valerie MILES-TRIBBLE

American Career College-Los Angeles (C)

4021 Rosewood Avenue, Los Angeles CA 90004
County: Los Angeles FICE Identification: 022418
Unit ID: 109040
Telephone: (323) 668-7555 Carnegie Class: Assoc/PrivFP
FAX Number: (322) 953-3654 Calendar System: Other
URL: www.americancareercollege.edu
Established: 1978 Annual Undergrad Tuition & Fees: $17,521
Enrollment: 1,613 Coed
Affiliation or Control: Proprietary IRS Status: Proprietary
Highest Offering: Associate Degree
Program: Occupational
Accreditation: ABHES, SURTEC

01 Director .... Ms. Rita TOTTEN

American Career College-Ontario (D)

3130 East Sedona Court, Ontario CA 91764
County: San Bernardino FICE Identification: 039713
Unit ID: 447768
Telephone: (909) 218-3253 Carnegie Class: Assoc/PrivFP
FAX Number: (909) 218-3340 Calendar System: Other
URL: www.americancareercollege.edu
Established: 2006 Annual Undergrad Tuition & Fees: $18,200
Enrollment: 1,483 Coed
Affiliation or Control: Proprietary IRS Status: Proprietary
Highest Offering: Associate Degree
Program: Occupational
Accreditation: ABHES, COARC, SURTEC

01 Campus President .... Mr. Scott WARDALL

American Career College-Orange County (E)

1200 North Magnolia Avenue, Anaheim CA 92801-2607
Telephone: (714) 952-9066 Identification: 667073
Accreditation: ABHES, CAHIIM, COARC, @PTAA, SURTEC

† Branch campus of American Career College-Los Angeles, Los Angeles, CA.

American Conservatory Theater (F)

30 Grant Avenue, 6th floor, San Francisco CA 94108-5800
County: San Francisco FICE Identification: 020992
Unit ID: 109086
Telephone: (415) 439-2350 Carnegie Class: Spec/Arts
FAX Number: (415) 834-3210 Calendar System: Semester
URL: www.act-sf.org
Established: 1969 Annual Graduate Tuition & Fees: $26,750
Enrollment: 32 Coed
Affiliation or Control: Independent Non-Profit IRS Status: 501(c)3
Highest Offering: Master's; No Undergraduates
Program: Professional; Fine Arts Emphasis
Accreditation: WC

01 Conservatory Director .... Melissa SMITH
88 Artistic Director .... Carey PERLOFF
05 Director of Academic Affairs .... Jack SHARRAR
10 Finance Director .... Jason SEIFER
30 Director Development .... Amber Jo MANUEL
37 Director of Financial Aid .... Jerry LOPEZ
26 Marketing Manager .... Christine MILLER

American Evangelical University (G)

1818 S. Western Avenue #409, Los Angeles CA 90006
County: Los Angeles Identification: 667090
Telephone: (323) 643-0301 Carnegie Class: Not Classified
FAX Number: (323) 643-0302 Calendar System: Semester
URL: www.aeui.us
Established: 2001 Annual Undergrad Tuition & Fees: $4,800
Enrollment: N/A Coed
Affiliation or Control: Independent Non-Profit IRS Status: 501(c)3
Highest Offering: Doctorate
Program: Technical Emphasis
Accreditation: BI

01 President .... Dr. Jong KIL RYU
05 Academic Dean .... Dr. Mark SUKKIL YOON
32 Dean of Student Affairs .... Rev. Choong LEE
10 CFO .... Rev. Timothy LEE
30 Chief Development Officer .... Dr. Yo Han CYEON
08 Director of Library .... Dr. Duk YOUNG WON

American Film Institute Conservatory (H)

2021 N Western Avenue, Los Angeles CA 90027-1657
County: Los Angeles FICE Identification: 022220
Unit ID: 108870
Telephone: (323) 856-7600 Carnegie Class: Spec/Arts
FAX Number: (323) 467-4578 Calendar System: Semester
URL: www.afi.com
Established: 1969 Annual Graduate Tuition & Fees: $48,676
Enrollment: 324 Coed
Affiliation or Control: Independent Non-Profit IRS Status: 501(c)3
Highest Offering: Master's; No Undergraduates
Program: Professional; Fine Arts Emphasis
Accreditation: WC, ART

01 Director American Film Institute .... Mr. Bob GAZZALE
11 Chief Operating Officer .... Ms. Nancy HARRIS
30 Sr Vice President Advancement .... Mr. Tom WEST
05 Exec Vice Dean of Conservatory .... Mr. Joe PETRICCA
20 Vice Dean for Production/Post Prod .... Mr. Phil LINSON
84 Vice Dean of Enrollment Services .... Ms. Sheryl REINSCHMIDT
20 Dean of Conservatory .... Ms. Jan SCHUETTE
32 Vice Dean Fellow Affairs .... Ms. Carolyn BROOKS
57 Artistic Director .... Mr. James L. BROOKS
06 Registrar .... Ms. Carmela CHANEY
15 Manager Human Resources .... Ms. Roschoune FRANKLIN
37 Financial Aid Director .... Ms. Trina RODLER
08 Librarian .... Mr. Robert VAUGHN
13 Chief Information Officer .... Mr. Paul JACQUES

American Graduate University (I)

733 N Dodsworth Avenue, Covina CA 91724-2408
County: Los Angeles Identification: 666982
Unit ID: 109095
Telephone: (626) 966-4576 Carnegie Class: Not Classified
FAX Number: (626) 915-1709 Calendar System: Other
URL: www.agu.edu
Established: 1969 Annual Graduate Tuition & Fees: $2,925
Enrollment: 981 Coed
Affiliation or Control: Proprietary IRS Status: Proprietary
Highest Offering: Master's; No Undergraduates
Program: Professional; Business Emphasis
Accreditation: DEAC

01 President .... Mr. Paul R. MCDONALD
05 Director Academic Affairs .... Mr. Paul R. MCDONALD
11 Dir of Administration/Admissios .... Ms. Laurie MEJIA
32 Director of Student Services .... Ms. Sherrie ANGSTER
06 Registrar .... Ms. Debbie MCDONALD
26 Director of Marketing .... Ms. Barbara YOUNG

American Jewish University (J)

15600 Mulholland Drive, Los Angeles CA 90077-1599
County: Los Angeles FICE Identification: 002741
Unit ID: 116846
Telephone: (310) 476-9777 Carnegie Class: Bac/A&S
FAX Number: (310) 471-1278 Calendar System: Semester
URL: www.ajula.edu
Established: 1947 Annual Undergrad Tuition & Fees: $29,708
Enrollment: 204 Coed
Affiliation or Control: Independent Non-Profit IRS Status: 501(c)3
Highest Offering: Master's
Program: Liberal Arts And General; Teacher Preparatory; Professional
Accreditation: WC

01 President .... Dr. Robert WEXLER

American University of Armenia (K)

300 Lakeside Drive, 7th Floor, Oakland CA 94612
County: Alameda Identification: 666013
Telephone: (510) 987-9452 Carnegie Class: Not Classified
FAX Number: (510) 208-3576 Calendar System: Semester
URL: www.aua.am
Established: 1991 Annual Graduate Tuition & Fees: $6,400
Enrollment: 302 Coed
Affiliation or Control: Independent Non-Profit IRS Status: 501(c)3
Highest Offering: Master's; No Undergraduates
Program: Professional
Accreditation: WC

01 President .... Dr. Armen DER KIUREGHIAN
05 Provost .... Dr. N. Dennis LEAVENS
11 Vice President Operations .... Ashot GHAZARYAN
10 Vice President of Finance .... Gevorg GOYUNYAN
06 Associate Registrar .... Chaghig ARZROUNI-CHAHINIAN
26 Public Relations Coordinator .... Diana MANUKYAN
07 Dir Admissions/Recruit/Intl Stdnts .... Perouz TASLAKIAN
09 Institutional Research Manager .... Anush BEZHANYAN

American University of Health Sciences (L)

1600 E Hill St Building #1, Signal Hill CA 90755
County: Los Angeles FICE Identification: 032253
Unit ID: 433004
Telephone: (562) 988-2278 Carnegie Class: Assoc/PrivFP4
FAX Number: (562) 988-1791 Calendar System: Quarter
URL: www.auhs.edu
Established: 1994 Annual Undergrad Tuition & Fees: $23,162
Enrollment: 282 Coed
Affiliation or Control: Proprietary IRS Status: Proprietary
Highest Offering: Master's
Program: Professional
Accreditation: ACICS, NURSE

01 President .... Dr. Joyce Newman GIGER
11 Chief Operating Officer .... Pastor Gregory A. JOHNSON

Anaheim University (M)

1240 S State College Blvd, Ste 110,
Anaheim CA 92806-5152
County: Orange Identification: 666651
Telephone: (714) 772-3330 Carnegie Class: Not Classified
FAX Number: (714) 772-3331 Calendar System: Other
URL: www.anaheim.edu
Established: 1996 Annual Graduate Tuition & Fees: N/A
Enrollment: 350 Coed
Affiliation or Control: Proprietary IRS Status: Proprietary
Highest Offering: Doctorate; No Undergraduates
Program: Professional; Business Emphasis
Accreditation: DEAC

07 Director of Admissions .... Ms. Kate STRAUSS

Angeles College (N)

3440 Wilshire Boulevard, Suite 310,
Los Angeles CA 90010
County: Los Angeles FICE Identification: 041604
Unit ID: 457299
Telephone: (213) 487-2211 Carnegie Class: Not Classified
FAX Number: (213) 487-2299 Calendar System: Semester
URL: www.angelescollege.edu
Established: 2004 Annual Undergrad Tuition & Fees: $27,389
Enrollment: 94 Coed
Affiliation or Control: Proprietary IRS Status: Proprietary
Highest Offering: Baccalaureate
Program: Occupational; 2-Year Principally Bachelor's Creditable
Accreditation: ABHES

01 Chief Operating Officer .... Ms. Teresa KRAUSE

Angeles College-Garden Grove (O)

17595 Almahurst Street, Suite 101-3,
City of Industry CA 91748
Telephone: (626) 965-5566 Identification: 770518
Accreditation: ABHES

† Branch campus of Angeles College, Los Angeles, CA.

Antelope Valley College (P)

3041 W Avenue K, Lancaster CA 93536-5426
County: Los Angeles FICE Identification: 001113
Unit ID: 109350
Telephone: (661) 722-6300 Carnegie Class: Assoc/Pub-S-SC
FAX Number: (661) 722-6333 Calendar System: Semester
URL: www.avc.edu
Established: 1929 Annual Undergrad Tuition & Fees (In-District): $1,380
Enrollment: 15,112 Coed
Affiliation or Control: State/Local IRS Status: 501(c)3
Highest Offering: Associate Degree
Program: Occupational; 2-Year Principally Bachelor's Creditable
Accreditation: WJ, COARC, RAD

01 President/Superintendent .... Mr. Edward T. KNUDSON
05 VP Academic Affairs .... Dr. Bonnie SUDERMAN
32 VP Student Services .... Dr. Erin E. VINES
15 Vice President Human Resources .... Mr. Mark BRYANT
84 Dean Enrollment Services .... Ms. LaDonna TRIMBLE
35 Dean of Student Services .... Dr. Jill ZIMMERMAN
88 Director Disabled Students .... Dr. Louis LUCERO
26 Exec Dir Marketing/Public Info .... Ms. Elizabeth DIACHUN
18 Dir Facilities Services .... Mr. Doug JENSEN
13 Director Information Technology .... Mr. Rick SHAW
30 Dir Inst Advancement & Foundation .... Ms. Bridget RAZO
09 Director Inst Research & Planning .... Dr. Meeta GOEL
37 Director Financial Aid .... Ms. Nichelle WILLIAMS
68 Dean PE/Athlet/Visual and Perf Arts .... Mr. Newton CHELETTE
79 Dean Language Arts/Academic Dev .... Dr. Charlotte FORTE-PARNELL
83 Dean Soc & Beh Sci/Bus/Comp Stds .... Dr. Tom O'NEIL
38 Dean Counseling & Matriculation .... Mr. Gary ROGGENSTEIN
76 Dean Health Sciences/Tech Ed .... Dr. Karen COWELL
81 Dean of Math/Science & Engineering .... Dr. Les UHAZY

Antioch University Los Angeles (A)

400 Corporate Pointe, Culver City CA 90230
Telephone: (310) 578-1080 Identification: 666236
Accreditation: &NH

† Regional accreditation is carried under the parent institution in Yellow Springs, OH.

Antioch University Santa Barbara (B)

602 Anacapa Street, Santa Barbara CA 93101
Telephone: (805) 962-8179 Identification: 666231
Accreditation: &NH

† Regional accreditation is carried under the parent institution in Yellow Springs, OH.

Apollos University (C)

17011 Beach Boulevard, Ste 900,
Huntington Beach CA 92647
County: Orange Identification: 667096
Telephone: (714) 841-6252 Carnegie Class: Not Classified
FAX Number: (866) 287-1938 Calendar System: Quarter
URL: www.apollos-university.edu
Established: 2005 Annual Undergrad Tuition & Fees: $5,570
Enrollment: N/A Coed
Affiliation or Control: Proprietary IRS Status: Proprietary
Highest Offering: Doctorate
Program: Liberal Arts And General; Business Emphasis
Accreditation: DEAC

01 President & CEO .... Dr. Paul EIDSON

APT College (D)

1939 Palomar Oaks Way, Suite A,
Carlsbad CA 92011-1311
County: San Diego Identification: 666245
Telephone: (800) 431-8488 Carnegie Class: Not Classified
FAX Number: (888) 431-8588 Calendar System: Semester
URL: www.aptc.edu
Established: 1993 Annual Undergrad Tuition & Fees: $5,500
Enrollment: 1,500 Coed
Affiliation or Control: Proprietary IRS Status: Proprietary
Highest Offering: Associate Degree
Program: Occupational; 2-Year Principally Bachelor's Creditable
Accreditation: DEAC

01 President/Chief Executive Officer .... Mr. Anthony MORENO
05 Director of Academics .... Dr. Gabriella MAIELLO
06 Registrar .... Ms. Julie B. LOVE
10 Dir of Accounting & Administration .... Ms. Cheryl DODDS

Argosy University, Inland Empire (E)

3401 Centre Lake Drive, Suite 200, Ontario CA 91761
Telephone: (909) 472-0800 Identification: 666007
Accreditation: &WC, ACBSP

† Regional accreditation is carried under the parent institution in Orange, CA.

Argosy University, Los Angeles (F)

5230 Pacific Concourse Drive, Los Angeles CA 90045
Telephone: (310) 531-9700 Identification: 666011
Accreditation: &WC, ACBSP

† Regional accreditation is carried under the parent institution in Orange, CA.

Argosy University, Orange County (G)

601 South Lewis Street, Orange CA 92868
County: Orange FICE Identification: 021799
Unit ID: 436438
Telephone: (714) 620-3700 Carnegie Class: DRU
FAX Number: (714) 620-3802 Calendar System: Semester
URL: www.argosy.edu/orangecounty
Established: 1999 Annual Undergrad Tuition & Fees: $13,836
Enrollment: 606 Coed
Affiliation or Control: Proprietary IRS Status: Proprietary
Highest Offering: Doctorate
Program: Professional
Accreditation: WC, ACBSP, CLPSY, #TED

01 University President .... Dr. Craig D. SWENSON
05 Vice President of Academic Affairs .... Vacant
32 GVP West .... Mr. Michael FALOTICO
32 GVP East .... Dr. William BROWN
03 Executive Vice President .... Mr. Eric EVENSON
07 VP Admissions .... Mr. Jeff CROSS
26 VP of Marketing .... Mr. Daron RODRIGUEZ
15 Vice President Human Resources .... Ms. Sheri NESHIEM
35 VP Academic Ops & Student Services .... Ms. Julie JOHNSON
106 VP for Online & Distance Learning .... Ms. Kate NOONE
10 Vice President of Finance .... Mr. Ken STEVENS
50 Dean College of Business .... Ms. Cynthia LARSON
83 Dean Psychology and Behav Sciences .... Vacant
76 Dean College of Health Sciences .... Ms. Kristin BENSON
53 Dean College of Education .... Vacant
97 Dean Undergraduate Studies .... Ms. Ruki JAYARAMAN
12 Campus President Twin Cities .... Mr. Scott TJADEN
12 Campus President Atlanta .... Dr. Ronald SWANSON
12 Campus President Dallas .... Mr. Ronald HYSON
12 Campus President Hawaii .... Dr. Warren EVANS
12 Campus President Washington DC .... Mr. David EREKSON
12 Campus President Seattle .... Mr. Tom DYER
12 Campus President Sarasota .... Vacant
12 Campus Pres Orange Cty/Inland Emp .... Dr. James COX
12 Campus President Schaumburg .... Mr. James CHITWOOD
12 Campus President Tampa .... Dr. Patricia MEREDITH
12 Campus President Phoenix .... Mr. Bart LERNER
12 Campus Pres San Francisco Bay Area .... Dr. Lucille SANSING
12 Campus President Nashville .... Dr. Sandra WISE
12 Int Campus President San Diego .... Dr. James COX
12 Campus President Los Angeles .... Dr. James COX
12 Campus President Salt Lake City .... Vacant
12 Campus President Denver .... Dr. Marcia BANKIRER

† Main Campus and HQ moved from Chicago, IL to Orange, CA

Argosy University, San Diego (H)

1615 Murray Canyon Rd, Suite 100,
San Diego CA 92108-4423
Telephone: (619) 321-3000 Identification: 666034
Accreditation: &WC, ACBSP

† Regional accreditation is carried under the parent institution in Orange, CA.

Argosy University, San Francisco Bay Area (I)

1005 Atlantic Avenue, Alameda CA 94501-1148
Telephone: (510) 217-4700 Identification: 666081
Accreditation: &WC, ACBSP, CLPSY

† Regional accreditation is carried under the parent institution in Orange, CA.

Art Center College of Design (J)

1700 Lida Street, Pasadena CA 91103-1999
County: Los Angeles FICE Identification: 001116
Unit ID: 109651
Telephone: (626) 396-2200 Carnegie Class: Spec/Arts
FAX Number: N/A Calendar System: Semester
URL: www.artcenter.edu
Established: 1930 Annual Undergrad Tuition & Fees: $39,230
Enrollment: 2,045 Coed
Affiliation or Control: Independent Non-Profit IRS Status: 501(c)3
Highest Offering: Master's
Program: Professional
Accreditation: WC, ART

01 President .... Dr. Lorne M. BUCHMAN
10 Sr VP/Chief Financial Officer .... Mr. Rich HALUSCHAK
05 Provost .... Mr. Fred FEHLAU
30 Sr Vice Pres Development .... Ms. Emily LASKIN
18 Senior Vice President Operations .... Mr. George FALARDEAU
07 Sr VP Admissions/Enrollment Mgmt .... Ms. Kit BARON
88 VP Exhibitions .... Mr. Steve NOWLIN
13 VP Information Technology .... Ms. Theresa ZIX
26 VP Marketing & Communication .... Mr. Jered GOLD
15 Vice Pres Human Resources .... Ms. Lisa M. SANCHEZ
32 Associate Provost Student Affairs .... Mr. Ray QUIROLGICO
08 College Librarian & Managing Dir .... Mr. Mario ASCENCIO
21 Controller .... Ms. Diane WITTENBERG
37 Managing Director Financial Aid .... Ms. Victoria AMEZCUA
29 Director of Alumni Affairs .... Ms. Kristine BOWNE
06 Director of Enrollment & Registrar .... Mr. William GARTRELL
09 Director of Institutional Research .... Ms. Esmeralda NAVA
19 Dir Environmental Health & Safety .... Ms. Vicky MCCORMICK
102 Sr Dir Foundation/Govt Relations .... Mr. Darryl MORI
36 Director of Career Development .... Vacant
18 Director of Facilities .... Mr. Jess RIVAS
96 Director of Purchasing .... Ms. Monica MATSUO

The Art Institute of California, A College of Argosy University - Hollywood (K)

5250 Lankershim Boulevard, North Hollywood CA 91601
Telephone: (213) 251-3636 FICE Identification: 031254
Accreditation: &WC, CIDA

† Regional accreditation is carried under the parent institution, Argosy University in Orange, CA.

The Art Institute of California, A College of Argosy University - Inland Empire (L)

674 East Brier Drive, San Bernardino CA 92408-2800
Telephone: (909) 915-2100 FICE Identification: 016471
Accreditation: &WC

† Regional accreditation is carried under the parent institution, Argosy University in Orange, CA.

The Art Institute of California, A College of Argosy University - Los Angeles (M)

2900 31st Street, Santa Monica CA 90405-3035
Telephone: (310) 752-4700 Identification: 666045
Accreditation: &WC, ACFEI, CIDA

† Regional accreditation is carried under the parent institution, Argosy University in Orange, CA.

The Art Institute of California, A College of Argosy University - Orange County (N)

3601 W Sunflower Avenue, Santa Ana CA 92704-7931
Telephone: (714) 830-0200 Identification: 666182
Accreditation: &WC, ACFEI, CIDA

† Regional accreditation is carried under the parent institution, Argosy University in Orange, CA.

The Art Institute of California, A College of Argosy University - Sacramento (O)

2850 Gateway Oaks Drive, Suite 100,
Sacramento CA 95833-4348
Telephone: (916) 830-6320 Identification: 666619
Accreditation: &WC

† Regional accreditation is carried under the parent institution, Argosy University in Orange, CA.

The Art Institute of California, A College of Argosy University - San Diego (P)

7650 Mission Valley Road, San Diego CA 92108-4423
Telephone: (858) 598-1200 FICE Identification: 023276
Accreditation: &WC, ACFEI, CIDA

† Regional accreditation is carried under the parent institution, Argosy University in Orange, CA.

The Art Institute of California - San Francisco, a campus of Argosy University (Q)

1170 Market Street, San Francisco CA 94102-4908
Telephone: (888) 493-3261 FICE Identification: 007236
Accreditation: &WC

† Regional accreditation is carried under the parent institution, Argosy University in Orange, CA.

The Art Institute of California, A College of Argosy University - Sunnyvale (R)

1120 Kifer Road, Sunnyvale CA 94086-5303
Telephone: (408) 962-6400 Identification: 666620
Accreditation: &WC

† Regional accreditation is carried under the parent institution, Argosy University in Orange, CA. Campus is in teach-out plan.

Ashdown College of Health Sciences (S)

101 E. Redlands Boulevard, Ste 285, Redlands CA 92373
County: San Bernardino FICE Identification: 041789
Unit ID: 461777
Telephone: (909) 793-4263 Carnegie Class: Not Classified
FAX Number: (909) 793-5763 Calendar System: Semester
URL: www.ashdowncollege.edu
Established: 2003 Annual Undergrad Tuition & Fees: $11,186
Enrollment: 31 Coed
Affiliation or Control: Proprietary IRS Status: Proprietary
Highest Offering: Associate Degree
Program: Occupational; Technical Emphasis
Accreditation: COE

01 CEO/Director .... Mr. William HERKELRATH
05 School Director .... Ms. Tamika HARRIS
32 Director Student Services .... Ms. Jolene LITTLE
10 Chief Business Officer .... Mr. William HERKELRATH
37 Director Student Financial Aid .... Mr. David LITTLE
06 Registrar .... Ms. Keelin MCCOLLOM

Asher College (T)

1215 Howe St., Ste 101, Sacramento CA 95825
County: Sacramento FICE Identification: 040573
Unit ID: 447777
Telephone: (916) 649-9600 Carnegie Class: Not Classified
FAX Number: N/A Calendar System: Other
URL: www.asher.edu
Established: 1998 Annual Undergrad Tuition & Fees: $17,656

Enrollment: 640 Coed
Affiliation or Control: Proprietary IRS Status: Proprietary
Highest Offering: Associate Degree
Program: Occupational; Technical Emphasis
Accreditation: CNCE

01 President .... David VICE

Ashford University (A)

8620 Spectrum Center Blvd, San Diego CA 92123
County: San Diego FICE Identification: 001881
Unit ID: 154022
Telephone: (866) 974-5700 Carnegie Class: Master's L
FAX Number: (866) 685-4091 Calendar System: Semester
URL: www.ashford.edu
Established: 1918 Annual Undergrad Tuition & Fees: $14,400
Enrollment: 54,120 Coed
Affiliation or Control: Proprietary IRS Status: Proprietary
Highest Offering: Master's
Program: Liberal Arts And General; Teacher Preparatory; Professional
Accreditation: WC, IACBE

01 University President/CEO .... Dr. Richard PATTENAUDE
05 Provost .... Dr. Lorraine WILLIAMS
10 Chief Finance Officer .... Mr. Stephen QUATTROCIOCCHI
108 VP Assessment & Academic Quality .... Dr. Elna VAN HEERDEN
11 Sr VP University Svcs & Strat Plng .... Ms. Sheri JONES
07 Sr VP Enrollment Services .... Mr. Bill NESS
37 Sr VP of Financial Aid & Svcs .... Ms. Bridget MCGUIRE
32 VP of Student Affairs & Retention .... Ms. Amber ECKERT
35 VP Student Services .... Ms. Nancy CERVASIO
49 Dean Division of General Education .... Dr. Justin HARRISON
50 Dean Forbes School of Business .... Dr. Patricia RYAN
53 Dean College of Education .... Dr. Courtney FARRELL
76 Dean College Health .... Dr. Mihaela TANASESCU
06 University Registrar .... Mr. Kirk MORRISON
41 Director of Athletics .... Mr. Andy EBERHART

Azusa Pacific University (B)

901 E Alosta Avenue, Azusa CA 91702-7000
County: Los Angeles FICE Identification: 001117
Unit ID: 109785
Telephone: (626) 969-3434 Carnegie Class: DRU
FAX Number: (626) 969-7180 Calendar System: Semester
URL: www.apu.edu
Established: 1899 Annual Undergrad Tuition & Fees: $42,734
Enrollment: 10,325 Coed
Affiliation or Control: Independent Non-Profit IRS Status: 501(c)3
Highest Offering: Doctorate
Program: Liberal Arts And General; Teacher Preparatory; Professional
Accreditation: WC, ART, CAATE, CLPSY, IACBE, MUS, NURSE, PTA, SW, TED, THEOL

01 President .... Dr. Jon R. WALLACE
05 Provost .... Dr. Mark STANTON
26 Exec Vice Pres External Affairs .... Mr. David E. BIXBY
11 Exec Vice President Administration .... Mr. John C. REYNOLDS
32 Senior Vice Pres for Student Life .... Dr. Terry FRANSON
10 Vice President Business Affairs/CFO .... Mr. Bob L. JOHANSEN
43 VP Legal Affs/Cmty Rels/Gen Counsel .... Mr. Mark DICKERSON
13 Vice President/CIO .... Mr. Don DAVIS
84 VP Grad/Nontrdtnl Enroll/Stdnt Svc .... Mrs. Heather PETRIDIS
84 VP for Enrollment Mangement .... Mr. David DUFAULT-HUNTER
58 Vice Provost Graduate Programs .... Dr. Diane GUIDO
20 Vice Provost Undergraduate Programs .... Dr. Vicky BOWDEN
35 AVP Student Life/Chief Judicial Ofc .... Mr. Willie HAMLETT
88 Assoc VP University Services .... Mr. Roger HODSDON
26 VP University Relations .... Mr. David PECK
49 Dean College Liberal Arts/Sci .... Dr. Jennifer WALSH
83 Dean School Behav/Applied Sciences .... Dr. Robert WELSH
50 Dean School of Business Mgmt .... Dr. Robert ROLLER
53 Dean School of Education .... Dr. Anita HENCK
73 Int Dean Haggard Sch of Theology .... Dr. Robert DUKE
64 Dean College of Music and the Arts .... Dr. Stephen JOHNSON
66 Dean School of Nursing .... Dr. Aja LESH
88 Dean Honors College .... Dr. David WEEKS
35 Assoc Dean Students/Dir Student Act .... Mrs. Shino SIMONS
15 Exec Director Human Resources .... Mr. John BAUGUS
30 VP University Advancement .... Mr. Corbin HOORNBEEK
21 Executive Director Finance .... Vacant
42 Campus Pastor .... Mr. Woody MOORWOOD
37 Dir Graduate Student Financial Svcs .... Mrs. Michelle JOHNSON
06 Registrar-Graduate .... Mrs. Norma MOCABEE
06 Associate Registrar-Undergraduate .... Ms. Mona MIKHAIL
29 Director Alumni Relations .... Vacant
09 Director Acad Info Mgmt Analysis .... Vacant
41 Director Athletics .... Mr. Gary PINE
38 Director Counseling Center .... Dr. Bill FIALA
37 Exec Dir UG Acad/Student Fin Svcs .... Mr. Todd ROSS
18 Associate VP Facilities Management .... Mr. Thomas HUNT
07 Director Undergraduate Admissions .... Mr. David BURKE
36 Director Career Services .... Ms. Lynn PEARSON
28 Exec Dir Diversity Planning/Assess .... Mr. Richard MARTINEZ
96 Purchasing Manager .... Mrs. Jo Ann BENGEL

Barstow Community College District (C)

2700 Barstow Road, Barstow CA 92311-6699
County: San Bernardino FICE Identification: 001119
Unit ID: 109907
Telephone: (760) 252-2411 Carnegie Class: Assoc/Pub-S-SC
FAX Number: (760) 252-1875 Calendar System: Semester
URL: www.barstow.edu
Established: 1959 Annual Undergrad Tuition & Fees (In-District): $1,104
Enrollment: 3,606 Coed
Affiliation or Control: State/Local IRS Status: 170(c)1
Highest Offering: Associate Degree
Program: Occupational; 2-Year Principally Bachelor's Creditable
Accreditation: WJ

01 Superintendent/President .... Dr. Deborah DITHOMAS
04 Exec Assistant to the President .... Ms. Michelle HENDERSON
10 Vice President Admin Services .... Mr. George WALTERS
05 Vice President Academic Affairs .... Mr. Stephen B. EATON
32 Vice President Student Services .... Dr. Khushnur Z. DADABHOY
15 Assoc Vice President of HR .... Mr. Clint DOUGHERTY
09 Dean Research Dev & Planning .... Vacant
49 Dean of Instruction .... Ms. Penny SHREVE
103 Dean Workforce & Econ Dev .... Ms. Sandi THOMAS
26 Dir of Public Rels/Comm & Marketing .... Mr. Chris CLARKE
18 Director Maintenance & Operations .... Mr. Richard HERNANDEZ
21 Director Fiscal Services .... Ms. Shawna L. ROBBINS
84 Director Enrollment Services .... Ms. Heather MINEHART
88 Civic Center & Event Manager .... Ms. Sherry SIMBURGER
41 Assoc Dean of Students & Athletics .... Mr. Thomas ARMSTRONG
35 Director Student Life & Dev .... Ms. Joann GARCIA
88 Director CTE Grants .... Mr. Dirk BROLSMA
88 Director Military Programs .... Mr. Jerry PETERS
88 Director Special Pgms & Svcs .... Ms. Megan FREELAND
22 Director Student Success & Equity .... Ms. Kimberly YOUNG
21 Budget Analyst .... Ms. Maureen DAVIS

Bergin University of Canine Studies (D)

5860 Labath Avenue, Rohnert Park CA 94928
County: Sonoma FICE Identification: 041763
Unit ID: 461643
Telephone: (707) 545-3647 Carnegie Class: Not Classified
FAX Number: (707) 545-0800 Calendar System: Semester
URL: www.berginu.edu
Established: 1991 Annual Undergrad Tuition & Fees: $9,400
Enrollment: 61 Coed
Affiliation or Control: Independent Non-Profit IRS Status: 501(c)3
Highest Offering: Master's
Program: Occupational; Technical Emphasis
Accreditation: ACICS

01 President .... Dr. Bonita M. BERGIN
06 Registrar .... Denise GREGERSEN
07 Director of Admissions .... Rebecca RICHARDSON
11 Chief of Administration .... Dennis KOHKE

Bethesda University of California (E)

730 N Euclid Street, Anaheim CA 92801-4115
County: Orange FICE Identification: 032663
Unit ID: 110060
Telephone: (714) 517-1945 Carnegie Class: Spec/Faith
FAX Number: (714) 683-1440 Calendar System: Semester
URL: www.buc.edu
Established: 1976 Annual Undergrad Tuition & Fees: $9,120
Enrollment: 331 Coed
Affiliation or Control: Independent Non-Profit IRS Status: 501(c)3
Highest Offering: Doctorate
Program: Religious Emphasis
Accreditation: BI, TRACS

01 President .... Dr. Young Joon SONG
03 Vice President .... Mr. Young Gull LEE
05 Chief Academic Officer .... Ms. Hyunhye KIM
10 Chief Financial Officer .... Mr. Myung Hee KIM
32 Dean of Student Affairs .... Dr. Estee SONG
08 Librarian .... Ms. Ho Kyung WOO
07 Admissions Director .... Ms. Helen CHUN
37 Financial Aid Officer .... Ms. William MIN

Biola University (F)

13800 Biola Avenue, La Mirada CA 90639-0001
County: Los Angeles FICE Identification: 001122
Unit ID: 110097
Telephone: (562) 903-6000 Carnegie Class: DRU
FAX Number: (562) 903-4748 Calendar System: 4/1/4
URL: www.biola.edu
Established: 1908 Annual Undergrad Tuition & Fees: $34,498
Enrollment: 6,358 Coed
Affiliation or Control: Independent Non-Profit IRS Status: 501(c)3
Highest Offering: Doctorate
Program: Liberal Arts And General; Teacher Preparatory; Professional
Accreditation: WC, ACBSP, ART, CLPSY, MUS, NURSE, THEOL

01 President .... Dr. Barry H. COREY
05 Interim Provost/Sr Vice President .... Dr. Deborah TAYLOR
10 Vice Pres Business/Financial Affs .... Mr. Michael PIERCE
30 Vice President Advancement .... Dr. Adam MORRIS
11 Vice President University Services .... Mr. Gregory R. BALSANO
84 Vice Pres Enrollment Management .... Mr. Greg VAUGHAN
26 VP Univ Communications & Marketing .... Mr. Lee WILHITE
20 Vice Provost/Academic Admin .... Dr. Patricia PIKE
28 Vice Prov Incl/Cross Cultural Eng .... Dr. Pamela CHRISTIAN
07 Assoc VP University Admissions .... Mr. Andre STEPHENS
73 Dean Talbot School Theology .... Dr. Clinton E. ARNOLD
83 Dean Rosemead School Psychology .... Dr. Clark D. CAMPBELL
88 Dean Cook Sch Intercultural Studies .... Dr. Bulus GALADIMA
53 Dean School of Education .... Dr. June HETZEL
50 Dean Crowell School of Business .... Dr. Gary LINDBALD
81 Dean of Science and Health .... Dr. Walt STANGL
57 Dean of Fine Arts and Communication .... Dr. Douglas TARPLEY
08 Dean of the Library .... Dr. Gregg GEARY
42 Dean of Spiritual Development .... Dr. Todd PICKETT
32 Dean of Students .... Mr. Danny PASCHALL
06 Dean Academic Records/Inst Research .... Mr. Ken GILSON
79 Assoc Dean of Humanities/Soc Sci .... Ms. Jamie CAMPBELL
57 Assoc Dean Fine Arts & Comm .... Mr. Jonathan PULS
15 Sr Director Human Resources .... Mr. Ronald G. MOORADIAN
45 Sr Dir Financial Plng/Operations .... Ms. Sandie WEAVER
29 Sr Dir Alumni & Parent Relations .... Dr. Richard BEE
37 Sr Director Financial Aid .... Mr. Geoff MARSH
21 Director Financial Mgmt/Reporting .... Mr. David KOONTZ
19 Chief Campus Safety .... Mr. John O. OJEISEKHOBA
90 Sr Director Information Technology .... Mr. Steven R. EARLE
36 Director Career Dev & Success .... Mr. Mark MATTHES
41 Athletics Director .... Dr. David HOLMQUIST
40 Manager Bookstore .... Mr. Harry EDWARDS
24 Supervisor Media Services .... Ms. Jill WATSON
18 Sr Director Facilities Management .... Mr. Brian PHILLIPS
38 Director Counseling Center .... Dr. Melanie TAYLOR
96 Purchasing Manager .... Mrs. Breanna KLETT
13 Chief Education Technology Officer .... Mrs. Susan ISHII
07 Sr Director Graduate Admissions .... Mr. Roy ALLINSON
106 Dir Digital Learning and Pgm Devel .... Dr. Ron G. HANNAFORD
108 Director of University Assessment .... Dr. Rebecca HONG

Brandman University (G)

16355 Laguna Canyon Road, Irvine CA 92618
County: Orange FICE Identification: 041618
Unit ID: 262086
Telephone: (949) 753-4774 Carnegie Class: Master's L
FAX Number: (714) 753-7875 Calendar System: Other
URL: www.brandman.edu
Established: 1958 Annual Undergrad Tuition & Fees: $12,000
Enrollment: 7,795 Coed
Affiliation or Control: Independent Non-Profit IRS Status: 501(c)3
Highest Offering: Doctorate
Program: Liberal Arts And General
Accreditation: WC, NURSE, @SW

01 Chancellor .... Dr. Gary BRAHM
12 Campus Director .... Mr. Jan HARTZ
05 Associate Dean of Education .... Ms. Patricia CLARK-WHITE
07 Director of Admissions .... Ms. Leticia TORRES

† A member of the Chapman University System.

Bristol University (H)

2390 E Orangewood Avenue, Suite 485, Anaheim CA 92806
County: Orange FICE Identification: 033083
Unit ID: 397270
Telephone: (714) 542-8086 Carnegie Class: Not Classified
FAX Number: (714) 245-2425 Calendar System: Semester
URL: www.bristoluniversity.edu
Established: 1991 Annual Undergrad Tuition & Fees: $10,795
Enrollment: 62 Coed
Affiliation or Control: Proprietary IRS Status: Proprietary
Highest Offering: Master's
Program: Occupational; 2-Year Principally Bachelor's Creditable; Business Emphasis
Accreditation: ACICS

01 President .... Dr. Gene RALTZ
03 Vice President Compliance .... Ms. Lourdes CRUZ
05 Chief Academic Officer .... Mrs. Fathiah INSERTO
37 Financial Aid Dir/Human Resources .... Ms. Lourdes CRUZ
06 Registrar .... Ms. Gina BORELLI

The Broad Center for the Management of School Systems (I)

2121 Avenue of the Stars, Ste 3000, Los Angeles CA 90067
County: Los Angeles Identification: 667228
Telephone: (310) 954-5080 Carnegie Class: Not Classified
FAX Number: N/A Calendar System: Other
URL: www.broadcenter.org
Established: Annual Graduate Tuition & Fees: N/A
Enrollment: 92 Coed
Affiliation or Control: Independent Non-Profit IRS Status: 501(c)3
Highest Offering: Master's; No Undergraduates
Program: Professional
Accreditation: WC

01 Executive Director .... Becca BRACY KNIGHT
13 Asst Director Information Systems .... Eulogio GALLO
26 Senior Director Communications .... Stephanie GERMERAAD

Brooks Institute (J)

5301 Ventura Ave, Ventura CA 93101
County: Ventura FICE Identification: 001123
Unit ID: 110185

Telephone: (888) 304-3456 Carnegie Class: Spec/Arts
FAX Number: (805) 585-8001 Calendar System: Semester
URL: www.brooks.edu
Established: 1945 Annual Undergrad Tuition & Fees: $20,112
Enrollment: 441 Coed
Affiliation or Control: Proprietary IRS Status: Proprietary
Highest Offering: Master's
Program: Professional; Technical Emphasis
Accreditation: @WC, ACICS

01 President Dr. Tim GRAMLING
05 Director of Academic Affairs Toni JOHNSON
10 Director of Finance and Operations Steve HAMAKER
07 Vice President Admissions Maggie BALDERAS
36 Dir Career Services Laura NIELSEN
06 Registrar April REYES
08 Librarian Donna BURR

Bryan University (A)

3580 Wilshire Boulevard, Suite 400,
Los Angeles CA 90010
County: Los Angeles FICE Identification: 007164
Unit ID: 110219
Telephone: (213) 484-8850 Carnegie Class: Assoc/PrivFP
FAX Number: (213) 483-3936 Calendar System: Semester
URL: www.bryancollege.edu
Established: 1940 Annual Undergrad Tuition & Fees: $11,850
Enrollment: 1,358 Coed
Affiliation or Control: Proprietary IRS Status: Proprietary
Highest Offering: Master's
Program: Occupational; 2-Year Principally Bachelor's Creditable
Accreditation: ACICS

01 President Mr. John KOLACINSKI

Butte College (B)

3536 Butte Campus Drive, Oroville CA 95965-8399
County: Butte FICE Identification: 008073
Unit ID: 110246
Telephone: (530) 895-2511 Carnegie Class: Assoc/Pub-R-L
FAX Number: (530) 895-2345 Calendar System: Semester
URL: www.butte.edu
Established: 1966 Annual Undergrad Tuition & Fees (In-District): $1,916
Enrollment: 12,161 Coed
Affiliation or Control: State/Local IRS Status: 501(c)3
Highest Offering: Associate Degree
Program: Occupational; 2-Year Principally Bachelor's Creditable
Accreditation: WJ, COARC, EMT

01 Int Superintendent/President Dr. Samia YAQUB
05 Int Vice Pres Student Learning Mr. David DANIELSON
10 VP Administrative Service/CBO Mr. Andrew SULESKI
45 Vice President Planning & Info Mr. Les JAURON
32 Vice President Student Services Mr. Allen RENVILLE
20 Dean Student Learning Mr. David DANIELSON
20 Dean Student Learning Ms. Kam BULL
20 Dean Student Learning Ms. Donna WEAVER
20 Dean Student Learning Ms. Denise ADAMS
20 Dean Student Learning Dr. Luozhu CEN
37 Director Financial Aid/Vet Svcs Ms. Carolyn STEPHEN
15 Director Human Resources Ms. Kelly BARRON
18 Dir Facilities Planning/Management Mr. Ken ALBRIGHT
09 Director of Institutional Research Dr. Baba ADAM
07 Director Admissions/Records Mr. Clinton SLAUGHTER
103 Exec Dir Econ Workforce Development Ms. Linda ZORN
30 Director Institutional Advancement Ms. Lisa DELABY
41 Dir Physical Education/Athletics Mr. Craig RIGSBEE
13 Director Information Services Mr. Tom ONWILER
08 Director of Library Services Dr. Luozhu CEN
21 Director Business Services Mr. Trevor STEWART
38 Coordinator of Counseling Ms. Susan CAREY

Cabrillo College (C)

6500 Soquel Drive, Aptos CA 95003-3194
County: Santa Cruz FICE Identification: 001124
Unit ID: 110334
Telephone: (831) 479-6100 Carnegie Class: Assoc/Pub-R-L
FAX Number: (831) 479-6425 Calendar System: Semester
URL: www.cabrillo.edu
Established: 1959 Annual Undergrad Tuition & Fees (In-District): $1,415
Enrollment: 13,594 Coed
Affiliation or Control: State/Local IRS Status: 501(c)3
Highest Offering: Associate Degree
Program: Occupational; 2-Year Principally Bachelor's Creditable; Business Emphasis
Accreditation: WJ, DH, MAC, RAD

01 Superintendent/President Dr. Laurel JONES
05 Asst Supt/Vice Pres Instruction Dr. Kathleen WELCH
10 Asst Supt/VP Administrative Svcs Ms. Victoria LEWIS
32 Asst Supt/Vice Pres Student Svcs Mr. Dennis BAILEY-FOUGNIER
35 Dean Student Services Ms. Michelle DONOHUE
13 Int Information Technology Director Ms. Spring ANDREWS
08 Library Director Mr. Georg ROMERO
26 Director Marketing & Communications Ms. Kristin FABOS
15 Director Personnel/Human Resources Ms. Loree MCCAWLEY
21 Director Business Services Mr. Graciano MENDOZA

07 Director of Enrollment Services Ms. Tama BOLTON
09 Dir Planning/Research/Knowledge Sys Mr. Terrence WILLETT
18 Dir Facilities Planning/Plant Ops Mr. Joe NUGENT
40 Bookstore Manager Ms. Linda CULLENS
102 Executive Director Foundation Ms. Melinda SILVERSTEIN
37 Asst Dir Financial Aid/Scholarships Ms. Tootie TZIMBAL
38 Dn Stdnt Counseling/Educ Spprt Svcs Ms. Margery REGALADO RODRIGUEZ
96 Dir Purchasing/Contracts/Risk Mgmt Mr. Michael ROBINS
04 Administrative Asst to President Ms. Cheryl ROMER

California Baptist University (D)

8432 Magnolia Avenue, Riverside CA 92504-3297
County: Riverside FICE Identification: 001125
Unit ID: 110361
Telephone: (951) 689-5771 Carnegie Class: Master's L
FAX Number: (951) 351-1808 Calendar System: Semester
URL: www.calbaptist.edu
Established: 1950 Annual Undergrad Tuition & Fees: $30,384
Enrollment: 7,957 Coed
Affiliation or Control: Southern Baptist IRS Status: 501(c)3
Highest Offering: Doctorate
Program: Liberal Arts And General; Teacher Preparatory; Professional
Accreditation: WC, ACBSP, CAATE, CONST, ENG, MUS, NURSE

01 President Dr. Ronald L. ELLIS
04 Admin Asst to the President Ms. Nancy ATAYDE
10 Vice President for Finance & Admin Mr. Mark HOWE
15 Director of Human Resources Ms. Julie FRESQUEZ
18 Director Facilities/Physical Plant Mr. Steve SMITH
21 Director of Financial Services Mr. Calvin SPARKMAN
21 Director of Accounting Ms. Jackie STILWELL
37 Director Financial Aid Ms. Rebecca SANCHEZ
40 Director of University Campus Store Ms. Carol BRACEY
26 Vice Pres Marketing & Communication Dr. Mark A. WYATT
88 Director of Conferences & Events Mr. Coreylon POLK
27 Director of Marketing Mr. Jeremy ZIMMERMAN
27 Director of Communications Vacant
105 Web Site Manager Mr. Waylon BAUMGARDNER
32 VP Enrollment & Student Services Mr. Kent DACUS
35 Dean of Students Mr. Anthony LAMMONS
07 Dean of Admissions Mr. Allen JOHNSON
41 Director of Athletics Dr. Micah PARKER
42 Dean Spiritual Life/Campus Minister Mr. John MONTGOMERY
19 Director of Public Safety Mr. Jim WALTERS
39 Director of Residence Life Mr. Daron HUBBERT
36 Director Career Services Mr. Mike BISHOP
30 Vice Pres University Advancement Dr. Arthur CLEVELAND
88 Assoc VP University Advancement Mr. Michael MEYER
44 Director of Annual Giving Mr. Brian BUNNELL
102 Grants Administrator Mr. Sam LIVELY
29 Director Alumni & Parent Relations Ms. Gail RONVEAUX
88 Vice Pres for Global Initiatives Dr. Larry LINAMEN
07 Dir of International Admissions Mr. Bryant KONG
85 Dean of International Programs Mr. Bryan DAVIS
106 Vice Pres for Online & Prof Studies Dr. David POOLE
13 Assoc Vice Pres of Technology Dr. Tran HONG
106 Dean for Online and Prof Studies Dr. Dirk DAVIS
43 Vice Pres and General Counsel Mr. Adam BURTON
05 VP of Academic Affairs/Provost Dr. Charles SANDS
20 Assoc Provost Administration Dr. Tracy WARD
20 Vice Provost & Accreditation Liason Dr. Dawn Ellen JACOBS
45 Assoc Provost Institution Planning Dr. Neal MCBRIDE
06 University Registrar Ms. Shawnn KONING
08 Director of Library Dr. Steve EMERSON
108 Director of Assessment Mr. Phil MARTINEZ
90 Dir of Instructional Technology Mr. Keith CASTILLO
20 Dean of Academic Services Dr. Jeffrey BARNES
09 Director of Institutional Research Ms. Vicki CLEVELAND
48 Dean College of Architecture Mr. Mark A. ROBERSON
49 Dean College of Arts & Sciences Dr. Gayne ANACKER
50 Interim Dean School of Business Dr. Steve STROMBECK
53 Dean School of Education Dr. John SHOUP
54 Dean College of Engineering Dr. Anthony DONALDSON
64 Dean School of Music Dr. Judd BONNER
66 Dean School of Nursing Dr. Geneva OAKS
73 Dean School of Christian Ministries Dr. Chris MORGAN
83 Dean School Behavioral Sciences Dr. Jacqueline GUSTAFSON
76 Interim Dean College Allied Health Dr. David PEARSON

California Christian College (E)

4881 E University Avenue, Fresno CA 93703-3599
County: Fresno FICE Identification: 008844
Unit ID: 110918
Telephone: (559) 251-4215 Carnegie Class: Spec/Faith
FAX Number: (559) 251-4231 Calendar System: Semester
URL: www.calchristiancollege.edu
Established: 1955 Annual Undergrad Tuition & Fees: $8,750
Enrollment: 18 Coed
Affiliation or Control: Free Will Baptist IRS Status: 501(c)3
Highest Offering: Baccalaureate
Program: 2-Year Principally Bachelor's Creditable; Liberal Arts And General; Religious Emphasis
Accreditation: TRACS

01 President Mr. Wendell L. WALLEY
05 VP of Academic Affairs Dr. Timothy M. POWELL
06 Registrar Mrs. Makenzie ZUERCHER
10 Chief Business Officer Mrs. Anna-Jean WALLEY
09 Dir Institutional Effectiveness Ms. Ingrid VOSS

08 Head Librarian Mrs. Nancy SINGH
37 Coordinator Financial Aid Ms. Melinda SCROGGINS
07 Director of Admissions Mr. Trent WALLEY
39 Director Student Housing Ms. Jennifer WALLEY

California Coast University (F)

925 N. Spurgeon Street, Santa Ana CA 92701-3515
County: Orange FICE Identification: 041276
Unit ID: 110936
Telephone: (714) 547-9625 Carnegie Class: Not Classified
FAX Number: (714) 547-5777 Calendar System: Other
URL: www.calcoast.edu
Established: 1973 Annual Undergrad Tuition & Fees: $3,600
Enrollment: 7,500 Coed
Affiliation or Control: Proprietary IRS Status: Proprietary
Highest Offering: Doctorate
Program: Professional; Business Emphasis
Accreditation: DEAC

01 President Dr. Thomas M. NEAL
03 Executive Vice President Ms. Shelly MARQUARDT
05 Academic Vice President Dr. Patricia INSLEY
32 Vice President of Student Affairs Dr. Murl TUCKER
20 Director of Academic Affairs Mr. Douglas PETRIKAT
06 Registrar Ms. Angela CENINA

California College of the Arts (G)

1111 Eighth Street, San Francisco CA 94107-2247
County: San Francisco FICE Identification: 001127
Unit ID: 110370
Telephone: (415) 703-9500 Carnegie Class: Spec/Arts
FAX Number: (510) 655-3541 Calendar System: Semester
URL: www.cca.edu
Established: 1907 Annual Undergrad Tuition & Fees: $43,708
Enrollment: 1,968 Coed
Affiliation or Control: Independent Non-Profit IRS Status: 501(c)3
Highest Offering: Master's
Program: Professional
Accreditation: WC, ART, CIDA

01 President Mr. Stephen BEAL
05 Provost Ms. Melanie CORN
10 Sr VP Finance & Administration Mrs. Laura HAZLETT
30 Sr Vice President of Advancement Ms. Susan AVILA
11 Vice President of Operations Ms. Jennifer STEIN
84 Sr Vice Pres of Enrollment Mgmt Ms. Sheri MCKENZIE
26 Vice President for Communications Ms. Chris BLISS
32 Vice President Student Affairs Mr. George SEDANO
15 Assoc Vice Pres Human Resources Ms. Leslie GRAY
21 Assoc Vice Pres Financial Services Mr. Ken TANZER
20 Associate Provost Dr. Thomas O. HAAKENSON
36 Director Career Development Ms. Kate DEY
06 Registrar Mr. Jerry ALLEN
37 Director Financial Aid Mr. Scott CLINE
29 Director Alumni Relations Vacant
13 Chief Information Officer Ms. Mara HANCOCK
07 Director Undergrad Admissions Ms. Robynne ROYSTER
38 Director Student Counseling Dr. Tara RECH
45 Director Research and Planning Mr. David MECKEL
18 Chief Facilities/Physical Plant Mr. Noah BARTLETT
07 Director Graduate Admissions Mr. Noel DAHL
09 Director of Institutional Research Ms. Brianna MOORE
96 Manager of Purchasing Ms. Jackie CRADDOCK

California College San Diego (H)

6602 Convoy Court Suite 100, San Diego CA 92111
County: San Diego FICE Identification: 021108
Unit ID: 110945
Telephone: (619) 680-4430 Carnegie Class: Spec/Health
FAX Number: (619) 295-5985 Calendar System: Other
URL: www.cc-sd.edu
Established: 1978 Annual Undergrad Tuition & Fees: $18,480
Enrollment: 688 Coed
Affiliation or Control: Independent Non-Profit IRS Status: 501(c)3
Highest Offering: Baccalaureate
Program: Occupational; 2-Year Principally Bachelor's Creditable; Business Emphasis
Accreditation: ACCSC, COARC

01 Executive Director Dr. Ken WEBB
03 Executive Vice President Mr. Eric JUHLIN
05 Chief Academic Officer Dr. Jason KART
06 Registrar Ms. Lashanna BOYKIN
07 Director of Admissions Mr. Baris YUCELT
08 Head Librarian Ms. Patricia BERMEL
36 Director Student Placement Ms. Betty NAVARETTE

California College San Diego (I)

277 Rancheros Drive, Suite 200, San Marcos CA 92069
Telephone: (619) 680-4430 Identification: 770551
Accreditation: ACCSC, COARC

† Branch campus of California College San Diego, San Diego, CA.

California Health Sciences University (A)

120 N. Clovis Ave, Clovis CA 93612

County: Fresno — Identification: 667218
Telephone: (559) 325-3600 — Carnegie Class: Not Classified
FAX Number: N/A — Calendar System: Semester
URL: chsu.org
Established: 2012 — Annual Graduate Tuition & Fees: $42,630
Enrollment: 84 — Coed
Affiliation or Control: Proprietary — IRS Status: Proprietary
Highest Offering: Doctorate; No Undergraduates
Program: Professional
Accreditation: @PHAR

01 President ... Florence DUNN
03 Sr VP Academic Affairs/Provost ... Wendy DUNCAN
10 Vice President of Finance ... Derek HAYASKI
05 VP Academic Affs/Dean Of Pharmacy ... David HAWKINS
26 VP Marketing/Communications ... Richele KLEISER
20 Assoc Dean Acad Affs/Assessment ... John MARTIN
32 Assoc Dean Professional Devel ... Patty HAVARD
07 Director Admissions ... Leslie WILLIAMS

California Institute of the Arts (B)

24700 McBean Parkway, Valencia CA 91355-2397

County: Los Angeles — FICE Identification: 001132
Unit ID: 111081
Telephone: (661) 255-1050 — Carnegie Class: Spec/Arts
FAX Number: (661) 254-8352 — Calendar System: Semester
URL: www.calarts.edu
Established: 1961 — Annual Undergrad Tuition & Fees: $43,400
Enrollment: 1,471 — Coed
Affiliation or Control: Independent Non-Profit — IRS Status: 501(c)3
Highest Offering: Doctorate
Program: Professional; Fine Arts Emphasis
Accreditation: WC, ART, DANCE

01 President ... Dr. Steven D. LAVINE
05 Provost ... Dr. Jeannene PRZYBLYSKI
10 Vice Pres/Chief Financial Officer ... Donald MATTHEWSON
11 Vice President/Operations & COO ... Michael CARTER
26 Vice President/Communication ... Jason CARDUCCI
30 Vice Pres/Advancement ... Elizabeth ROBISON
21 Assoc Vice President and Controller ... Karla TALAVERA
15 Assoc Vice Pres Human Resources ... Charmagne SHEARRILL
18 Assoc Vice Pres Facilities ... Jesse SMITH
88 Asst VP Special Projects ... Patricia GONZALEZ
09 Assoc Provost Inst Rsrch/Effectiv ... Brian HARLAN
28 Assoc Provost Equity and Diversity ... Vacant
20 Associate Provost Academic Affairs ... Kim RUSSO
08 Dean Div of Library & Info Resource ... Jeffrey GATTEN
32 Dean of Students ... Travis GREENE
57 Dean School of Art ... Thomas LAWSON
64 Dean Herb Alpert School of Music ... David ROSENBOOM
88 Dean School of Critical Studies ... Amanda BEECH
88 Dean Sharon D Lund School of Dance ... Stephan KOPLOWITZ
88 Dean School Film & Video ... Leighton PIERCE
88 Dean School of Theater ... Travis PRESTON
06 Registrar ... Anna JABLONSKI
07 Executive Director of Admissions ... Molly RYAN
37 Director of Financial Aid ... Robin BAILEY-CHEN
29 Director Alumni & Parent Relations ... Nicole STARK LANE
88 Artistic Director Community Arts ... Glenna AVILA
88 Director Community Arts Partnership ... Nadine RAMBEAU
39 Director of Residence Life ... Vacant
88 Director of Recruitment ... Claire JOY
87 Director of Summer Session ... Hilary DARLING
19 Campus Safety Supervisor ... Mark FARLEY
88 Director of Leadership Gifts ... Sally BICKERTON
88 Director of Institute Partnerships ... Claudia BLOOM
44 Director of Development/Major Gift ... Aaron CAMPBELL
88 Director Print & Electronic Comm ... Stuart FROLICK
23 Director Health Services ... Audrey HAMPTON
88 Director Advancement Services ... Korey JANSE
88 Director Prospect Strategy ... Natalie LARMON
13 Director Information Technology ... Sean MURPHY
102 Director Corp/Foundation/Govt ... Sarah NELSON
27 Director Office of Communications ... Denise NELSON
88 Director Special Events ... Lindsey SCHIFF-ABRAMS
36 Director Career Services ... Rita SOLTANIAN
18 Director Facilities Management ... John THOMAS
04 Sr Administrative Asst to President ... Judy MCGINNIS
104 Asst Dir Intl Students & Programs ... Penelope WESTON
105 Director Web Communications ... Christine ZIEMBA

California Institute of Integral Studies (C)

1453 Mission Street, 4th Floor,
San Francisco CA 94103-2557

County: San Francisco — FICE Identification: 012154
Unit ID: 110316
Telephone: (415) 575-6100 — Carnegie Class: DRU
FAX Number: (415) 575-1264 — Calendar System: Semester
URL: www.ciis.edu
Established: 1968 — Annual Undergrad Tuition & Fees: $19,585
Enrollment: 1,251 — Coed
Affiliation or Control: Independent Non-Profit — IRS Status: 501(c)3
Highest Offering: Doctorate
Program: Professional
Accreditation: WC, ACUP

01 President ... Mr. Joseph L. SUBBIONDO
05 Academic Vice President ... Dr. Judie WEXLER
30 Vice President of Development ... Ms. Dorotea REYNA
32 Int Director of Student Affairs ... Ms. Lauren SELFRIDGE
29 Dean of Alumni/Dir of Travel Pgms ... Dr. Richard BUGGS
20 Dean Academic Plng/Administration ... Mr. Chip B. GOLDSTEIN
10 Controller/Director Finance ... Mr. David BLOHM
15 Director of Human Resources ... Ms. S. Michelle COLEMAN
07 Director of Admissions ... Mr. Wendell TULL
13 Director Information Technology ... Ms. Janet CRAGIN
08 Library Director ... Mr. Noah LOWENSTEIN
06 Registrar ... Mr. Dan GURLER
26 Director of Communications ... Mr. Jim David MARTIN
37 Director of Financial Aid ... Ms. I. CHEN
51 Dir Public Programs/Performances ... Mr. Karim BAER
18 Director Facilities & Operations ... Mr. Jonathan MILLS
40 Bookstore Manager ... Mr. Steven SWANSON
85 International Student Advisor ... Ms. Jody O'CONNOR

California Institute of Technology (D)

1200 E California Boulevard, Pasadena CA 91125-0001

County: Los Angeles — FICE Identification: 001131
Unit ID: 110404
Telephone: (626) 395-6811 — Carnegie Class: RU/VH
FAX Number: (626) 795-1547 — Calendar System: Trimester
URL: www.caltech.edu
Established: 1891 — Annual Undergrad Tuition & Fees: $45,390
Enrollment: 2,241 — Coed
Affiliation or Control: Independent Non-Profit — IRS Status: 501(c)3
Highest Offering: Doctorate
Program: Professional; Technical Emphasis
Accreditation: WC, ENG

01 President ... Dr. Thomas F. ROSENBAUM
04 Secretary to the BOT/Exec Asst ... Mrs. Mary L. WEBSTER
05 Provost ... Dr. Edward M. STOLPER
88 Vice President/Director JPL ... Dr. Charles ELACHI
10 Vice President Business & Finance ... Mr. Dean W. CURRIE
30 Vice Pres Dev/Institute Relations ... Mr. Brian K. LEE
88 VP for Strategy Implementation ... Dr. Diana JERGOVIC
32 Vice President Student Affairs ... Dr. Anneila I. SARGENT
43 General Counsel ... Ms. Victoria D. STRATMAN
39 Asst VP Housing & Dining ... Vacant
20 Vice Provost ... Dr. Cindy A. WEINSTEIN
20 Vice Provost ... Dr. Morteza GHARIB
15 Assoc Vice Pres HR/Campus Svcs ... Ms. Julia M. MCCALLIN
44 Assoc Vice President Development ... Ms. Valerie A. OTTEN
31 Asst VP Campus & Cmty Relations ... Ms. Diane M. BINNEY
86 Director Govt Rels ... Mr. Hall P. DAILY
35 Senior Dir for Student Activities ... Mr. Tom N. MANNION
26 Asst VP for Strategic Comm ... Ms. Kristen BROWN
81 Chair Biology & Biological Engr Div ... Dr. Stephen L. MAYO
81 Chair Chemistry & Chemical Engr Div . Dr. Jacqueline K. BARTON
54 Chair Engr & Applied Science Div ... Dr. Ares J. ROSAKIS
65 Chair Geology/Planet Science Div ... Dr. John P. GROTZINGER
79 Chair Humanities/Social Science Div ... Dr. Jean-Laurent ROSENTHAL
81 Chair Physics/Math/Astro Division ... Dr. Fiona HARRISON
06 Registrar ... Mrs. Mary N. MORLEY
07 Director of Admissions ... Mr. Jarrid WHITNEY
08 University Librarian ... Ms. Kristin ANTELMAN
13 Chief Information Officer ... Mr. Rich E. FAGEN
18 Assoc Vice Pres for Facilities ... Mr. James W. COWELL, JR.
18 Sr Director Facilities Management ... Mr. William R. TAYLOR
19 Manager Security Office ... Mr. Gregg HENDERSON
16 Exec Director of HR ... Ms. April WHITE CASTENADA
23 Director Health Services ... Dr. Stuart C. MILLER
25 Director Sponsored Research ... Dr. Richard P. SELIGMAN
29 Executive Director Alumni Assoc ... Ms. Alexandra C. TOBEK
37 Director Financial Aid ... Mr. Don CREWELL
36 Director Career Development ... Ms. Lauren B. STOLPER
40 Manager Bookstore ... Ms. Karyn SEIXAS
41 Director Athletics & Physical Ed ... Ms. Betsy MITCHELL
58 Dean of Graduate Studies ... Dr. Doug C. REES
88 Associate Dean of Students ... Dr. Barbara C. GREEN
85 Assoc Dir International Student Pgm ... Ms. Laura FLOWER KIM
96 Dir of Purchasing & Payment Svcs ... Ms. Tina LOWENTHAL
101 Secretary of the Board ... Mrs. Mary L. WEBSTER
102 Dir Foundation Relations ... Ms. Marjorie A. BEALE
104 Dir Fellowshp Advising/Study Abroad ... Ms. Lauren B. STOLPER
38 Sr Dir Health/Counseling ... Mr. Kevin P. AUSTIN

California Intercontinental University (E)

17310 Red Hill Ave, Ste 200, Irvine CA 91765-3954

County: Orange — Identification: 666670
Unit ID: 455451
Telephone: (866) 687-2258 — Carnegie Class: Not Classified
FAX Number: (909) 804-5151 — Calendar System: Other
URL: www.caluniversity.edu
Established: 2003 — Annual Undergrad Tuition & Fees: $13,800
Enrollment: 400 — Coed
Affiliation or Control: Proprietary — IRS Status: Proprietary
Highest Offering: Doctorate
Program: Professional; Business Emphasis
Accreditation: DEAC

01 Executive Chairman ... Dr. Finian TAN
05 Chief Academic Ofcr/Dean Acad Affs ... Dr. Leslie GARGIULO
32 Dean of Student Success ... Dr. Steve HESS
10 Director of Finance ... Vacant
06 Senior Registrar ... Ms. Odeta AYVAZYAN

California International Business University (F)

520 West Ash Street, Ste. 300, San Diego CA 92101

County: San Diego — Identification: 666711
Telephone: (619) 702-9400 — Carnegie Class: Not Classified
FAX Number: (619) 702-9476 — Calendar System: Quarter
URL: www.cibu.edu
Established: 1994 — Annual Undergrad Tuition & Fees: $15,000
Enrollment: 200 — Coed
Affiliation or Control: Independent Non-Profit — IRS Status: 501(c)3
Highest Offering: Master's
Program: Occupational; Teacher Preparatory; Professional; Business Emphasis
Accreditation: ACICS

01 President ... Dr. Phillip BABB
05 Dean of Academic Affairs ... Dr. William HOWE
07 Director of Admissions/Registrar ... Ms. Susi HAUGH
30 Dir Inst Development/Compliance ... Dr. Marcus BENNIEFIELD

California Jazz Conservatory (G)

2087 Addison Street, Berkeley CA 94704

County: Alameda — Identification: 667217
Telephone: (510) 845-5373 — Carnegie Class: Not Classified
FAX Number: (510) 841-5373 — Calendar System: Semester
URL: www.cjc.edu
Established: 2008 — Annual Undergrad Tuition & Fees: $13,200
Enrollment: N/A — Coed
Affiliation or Control: Independent Non-Profit — IRS Status: 501(c)3
Highest Offering: Baccalaureate
Program: Music Emphasis
Accreditation: MUS

01 Executive Director ... Susan MUSCARELLA

California Lutheran University (H)

60 W Olsen Road, Thousand Oaks CA 91360-2787

County: Ventura — FICE Identification: 001133
Unit ID: 110413
Telephone: (805) 492-2411 — Carnegie Class: Master's L
FAX Number: (805) 493-3513 — Calendar System: Semester
URL: www.callutheran.edu
Established: 1959 — Annual Undergrad Tuition & Fees: $57,641
Enrollment: 4,160 — Coed
Affiliation or Control: Evangelical Lutheran Church In America
IRS Status: 501(c)3
Highest Offering: Doctorate
Program: Liberal Arts And General; Teacher Preparatory; Professional
Accreditation: WC, CLPSY, TED, THEOL

01 President ... Dr. Christopher KIMBALL
05 Provost/Vice Pres Academic Affairs ... Dr. Leanne NEILSON
30 Vice Pres University Advancement ... Mr. Stephen WHEATLY
10 Vice Pres Admin/Finance/Treasurer ... Ms. Karen DAVIS
32 Vice Pres Stdnt Life/Dean of Stdnts ... Ms. Melinda ROPER
84 VP Enrollment Mgmt & Marketing ... Dr. Matthew WARD
08 Int Assoc Provost Information Svcs ... Mr. Zareh MARSELIAN
18 Assoc Vice Pres Facilities ... Mr. Ryan VAN OMMEREN
26 Assoc VP University Relations ... Ms. Lynda FULFORD
49 Dean College Arts & Sciences ... Dr. Joan GRIFFIN
53 Dean of School of Education ... Dr. Michael HILLIS
50 Dean of School of Management ... Dr. Gerhard APFELTHALER
15 Director of Human Resources ... Ms. Patricia PARHAM
06 Director Academic Svcs/Registrar ... Ms. Maria KOHNKE
42 University Pastor ... Rev. Scott MAXWELL-DOHERTY
42 University Pastor ... Rev. Melissa MAXWELL-DOHERTY
44 Director Major Planned Giving ... Mr. Richard HOLMES, IV
41 Director Athletics ... Mr. Daniel KUNTZ
107 Director Professionals ... Dr. Lisa BUONO
36 Director of Career Services ... Ms. Cindy LEWIS
35 Director Multicultural/Intl Pgm ... Dr. Juanita HALL
21 Dir of Budget/Management Analysis ... Ms. Barbara REX
29 Director Alumni Relations ... Ms. Rachel RONNING LINDGREN
38 Director Counseling Services ... Dr. Alan GOODWIN
19 Director Security/Safety ... Vacant
07 Director of Undergrad Admissions ... Mr. Michael ELGARICO
09 Director of Institutional Research ... Dr. Rodney REYNOLDS
37 Director of Financial Aid ... Mr. Jerry MCKEEN

California Miramar University (I)

9750 Miramar Road Suite 180, San Diego CA 92126-7501

County: San Diego — Identification: 666713
Unit ID: 480781
Telephone: (858) 653-3000 — Carnegie Class: Not Classified
FAX Number: (858) 653-6786 — Calendar System: Other
URL: www.calmu.edu
Established: 2005 — Annual Undergrad Tuition & Fees: $8,050
Enrollment: 324 — Coed
Affiliation or Control: Proprietary — IRS Status: Proprietary
Highest Offering: Doctorate
Program: Professional
Accreditation: ACICS

01 President ... Dr. Jeanie FOSTER
07 Admissions Director ... Ms. Kelly ACKERSON

California National University for Advanced Studies (A)

18520 Hawthorne Blvd 1st Floor, Torrance CA 90504
County: Los Angeles — Identification: 666786
Telephone: (800) 782-2422 — Carnegie Class: Not Classified
FAX Number: (310) 370-7072 — Calendar System: Trimester
URL: www.cnuas.edu
Established: 1993 — Annual Undergrad Tuition & Fees: $5,400
Enrollment: 250 — Coed
Affiliation or Control: Proprietary — IRS Status: Proprietary
Highest Offering: Master's
Program: Professional; Business Emphasis
Accreditation: DEAC

01 President ... Mr. Carlton G. BRYANT
32 Vice Pres Student Affs/Registrar ... Ms. Stephanie M. SMITH
07 Admissions ... Ms. Cynthia SPEED
05 Director of Instruction ... Dr. Carol BACKER
50 Dean Business Administration ... Dr. Philip CHONG
54 Associate CNU Col of Engineering ... Dr. Robert RYAN
13 MIS Director ... Mr. Charles NG
06 Registrar ... Ms. Stephanie M. SMITH

California Northstate University College of Pharmacy (B)

9700 West Taron Dr, Elk Grove CA 95757
County: Sacramento — Identification: 667020
Telephone: (916) 686-7400 — Carnegie Class: Not Classified
FAX Number: (916) 686-8143 — Calendar System: Semester
URL: pharmacy.cnsu.edu
Established: 2008 — Annual Undergrad Tuition & Fees: $45,100
Enrollment: N/A — Coed
Affiliation or Control: Independent Non-Profit — IRS Status: 501(c)3
Highest Offering: Doctorate
Program: Professional
Accreditation: WC, #MED, PHAR

01 President ... Dr. Alvin CHEUNG
03 Vice President ... Mr. Norman FONG
05 Dean ... Dr. Karen HASSELL
32 Assoc Dean Student Affs/Admissions ... Ms. Cyndi PORTER
11 Operation Resource Officer ... Vacant
108 VP of Inst Effect/Assessment ... Ms. Karen MCCLENDON
43 Legal Counsel ... Mr. Paul WAGSTAFFE
08 Director of Library Resources ... Mr. Scott MINOR
06 Registrar ... Ms. Melissa DEAN

California Southern University (C)

930 Roosevelt, Irvine CA 92620
County: Orange — Identification: 666770
Telephone: (714) 882-7800 — Carnegie Class: Not Classified
FAX Number: (714) 480-0834 — Calendar System: Semester
URL: www.calsouthern.edu
Established: 1978 — Annual Undergrad Tuition & Fees: $6,000
Enrollment: N/A — Coed
Affiliation or Control: Independent Non-Profit — IRS Status: 501(c)3
Highest Offering: Doctorate
Program: Liberal Arts And General; Professional
Accreditation: DEAC

01 President ... Dr. Caroll RYAN

*The California State University System Office (D)

401 Golden Shore, Long Beach CA 90802-4210
County: Los Angeles — FICE Identification: 001136
Unit ID: 110501
Telephone: (562) 951-4000 — Carnegie Class: N/A
FAX Number: (562) 951-4986
URL: www.calstate.edu

01 Chancellor ... Dr. Timothy P. WHITE
03 Executive Vice Chancellor & CAO ... Dr. Loren J. BLANCHARD
10 Executive Vice Chancellor & CFO ... Mr. Steve RELYEA
15 Vice Chancellor Human Resources ... Ms. Lori LAMB
30 Vice Chanc Univ Rels/Advancement ... Mr. Garrett P. ASHLEY
43 Exec Vice Chanc/General Counsel ... Mr. Framroze M. VIRJEE
88 Vice Chancellor/Chief Audit Officer ... Mr. Larry MANDEL
100 Chief of Staff ... Dr. Lars WALTON
88 Deputy Chief of Staff ... Ms. Jessica DARIN

*California Polytechnic State University-San Luis Obispo (E)

1 Grand Avenue, San Luis Obispo CA 93407-9000
County: San Luis Obispo — FICE Identification: 001143
Unit ID: 110422
Telephone: (805) 756-1111 — Carnegie Class: Master's L
FAX Number: (805) 756-5400 — Calendar System: Quarter
URL: www.calpoly.edu
Established: 1901 — Annual Undergrad Tuition & Fees (In-State): $9,004
Enrollment: 20,186 — Coed
Affiliation or Control: State — IRS Status: 501(c)3
Highest Offering: Master's
Program: Liberal Arts And General; Teacher Preparatory; Professional; Technical Emphasis
Accreditation: WC, ART, BUS, CONST, CS, DIETD, DIETI, ENG, LSAR, MUS, NAIT, NRPA, PLNG, TED

02 President ... Dr. Jeffrey D. ARMSTRONG
100 Chief of Staff ... Ms. Betsy KINSLEY
05 Provost ... Dr. Kathleen ENZ FINKEN
32 Vice President Student Affairs ... Dr. Keith HUMPHREY
30 Vice Pres Univ Advance/CEO Found ... Ms. Deborah READ
10 Int Vice Pres Admin & Finance ... Ms. Karen WEBB
20 Vice Provost Intl/Grad & Ext Educ ... Dr. Brian TIETJE
41 Athletic Director ... Mr. Don OBERHELMAN
13 Vice Provost Info Services/CIO ... Dr. Michael D. MILLER
88 Exec Dir CalPoly Corporation ... Ms. Lorlie LEETHAM
46 Int VP Research & Economic Dev ... Mr. Bradford ANDERSON
21 Associate Vice Pres Admin & Finance ... Vacant
44 Assoc Vice Pres Advancement Ops ... Mr. Grant TREXLER
44 Interim Assoc VP Development ... Ms. Tanya KIANI
26 Director of Media Relations ... Mr. Matt LAZIER
18 Associate Vice Pres Facilities ... Vacant
39 Exec Dir Univ Housing & Assoc VP/SA ... Mr. Preston C. ALLEN
15 Assoc Vice Prov Academic Personnel ... Dr. Al LIDDICOAT
20 Vice Provost Academic Pgms/Planning ... Dr. Mary E. PEDERSEN
88 Assoc Vice Prov Systems & Resources ... Ms. Kimi M. IKEDA
84 Assoc Vice Prov Mktg & Enrollment ... Mr. James L. MARAVIGLIA
88 Director Center Teach Learn & Tech ... Mr. Patrick O'SULLIVAN
29 Int Asst Vice Pres Alumni Relations ... Ms. Ellen COHUNE
19 University Police Department ... Chief George HUGHES
06 University Registrar ... Mr. Cem SUNATA
28 Director Diversity & Inclusivity ... Dr. Annie HOLMES
22 Dir Employment Equity ... Ms. Martha CODY
45 Dir Facil Planning/Capital Projects ... Mr. Joel NEEL
23 Exec Dir Health/Counseling Services ... Dr. David HARRIS
38 Director of Counseling Services ... Dr. Geneva ABIKO
35 ASI Executive Director ... Ms. Marcy MALONEY
24 Technology Strategist ... Mr. Ryan MATTESON
40 Director University Bookstore ... Mr. William HOCKENSMITH
35 Dean of Students ... Dr. Jean DECOSTA
46 Dean of Research ... Dr. Dean WENDT
102 Industry Outreach/Applied Research ... Mr. Jim DUNNING
47 Dean Agriculture/Food & Env Sci ... Dr. Andrew THULIN
48 Dean Architect/Environmental Design ... Ms. Christine THEODOROPOULOS
50 Dean College of Business ... Dr. Scott DAWSON
54 Dean College of Engineering ... Dr. Debra LARSON
49 Dean College of Liberal Arts ... Dr. Douglas EPPERSON
81 Dean Science & Mathematics ... Dr. Philip S. BAILEY, JR.
53 Dean School of Education ... Dr. Jon MARGERUM-LEYS
16 Executive Director Human Resources ... Ms. Beth E. GALLAGHER
96 Dir Contract & Procrurement Svcs ... Mr. Dru ZACHMEYER
37 Director Financial Aid ... Ms. Lois M. KELLY
36 Director Career Services ... Mr. Martin C. SHIBATA
09 Director Institutional Research ... Mr. Mauricio SAAVEDRA
104 Director of International Center ... Ms. Caroline MOORE
92 Director Honors Program ... Dr. Gregg FIEGEL
04 Administrative Asst to President ... Ms. Diane HAUPT
07 Director Admissions Operations ... Mr. Terrance HARRIS
08 Dean of Library Services ... Ms. Anna GOLD
25 Director Grants Development ... Ms. Amy VELASCO
43 Dir Legal Services/General Counsel ... Ms. Dawn S. THEODORA
14 Assoc Vice Provost IT Services ... Ms. Johanna MADJEDI
91 Director Administrative Computing ... Ms. Sharon ANDERSON
86 Director Government Relations ... Mr. Justin WELLNER

*California State Polytechnic University-Pomona (F)

3801 W Temple Avenue, Pomona CA 91768-2557
County: Los Angeles — FICE Identification: 001144
Unit ID: 110529
Telephone: (909) 869-7659 — Carnegie Class: Master's L
FAX Number: (909) 869-4535 — Calendar System: Quarter
URL: www.cpp.edu
Established: 1938 — Annual Undergrad Tuition & Fees (In-State): $7,330
Enrollment: 23,966 — Coed
Affiliation or Control: State — IRS Status: 501(c)3
Highest Offering: Master's
Program: Liberal Arts And General; Teacher Preparatory; Professional; Business Emphasis
Accreditation: WC, ART, BUS, CEA, CIDA, CS, DIETD, DIETI, ENG, ENGT, LSAR, MUS, PLNG, SPAA

02 President ... Dr. Soraya M. COLEY
05 Provost/VP Academic Affairs ... Dr. Sylvia A. ALVA
32 Acting Vice Pres Student Affairs ... Dr. Rebecca GUTIERREZ KEETON
11 Vice Pres Administrative Affairs ... Dr. Steve GARCIA
30 Vice Pres University Advancement ... Mr. Bedford MCINTOSH
102 Exec Dir Cal Poly Pomona Found Inc ... Mr. G. Paul STOREY
20 Assoc Provost Academic Affairs ... Dr. Claudia L. PINTER-LUCKE
18 Assoc VP Facilities Planning & Mgmt ... Dr. Walter MARQUEZ
35 Acting Assoc VP & Dean of Students ... Dr. Byron E. HOWLETT
84 Assoc VP Enroll Management & Svcs ... Ms. Kathleen A. STREET
88 Exec Asst to the Provost ... Ms. Marissa M. MARTINEZ
46 Assoc VP Research ... Dr. Frank W. EWERS
20 AVP Acad Planning & Faculty Affairs ... Dr. Shanthi A. SRINIVAS
26 Assoc Vice Pres for Univ Relations ... Vacant
10 Assoc VP Finance/Admin Svcs ... Mr. Darwin LABORDO
35 Assoc VP Student Services ... Dr. Kevin T. COLANER
35 AVP Student Affairs Administration ... Ms. Christi R. CHISLER
13 Vice President & CIO ... Mr. John W. MCGUTHRY
15 AVP for Human Resources ... Ms. Sharon L. REITER

100 Chief of Staff ... Mr. Gary A. HAMILTON
04 Exec Assistant to the President ... Vacant
47 Dean College of Agriculture ... Dr. Mary HOLZ-CLAUSE
49 Dean Col Letters/Arts/Soc Sci ... Dr. Sharon HILLES
50 Interim Dean Col of Business Admin ... Dr. Cheryl WYRICK
54 Dean College of Engineering ... Dr. Mahyar AMOUZEGAR
48 Dean Col Environmental Design ... Mr. Michael WOO
88 Dean Collins College of Hosp Mgmt ... Dr. Lea R. DOPSON
81 Dean College of Science ... Dr. Brian JERSKY
53 Interim Dean Col Educ/Integrat Stds ... Dr. Nancy HURLBUT
44 Assoc VP for Development ... Vacant
08 Dean University Library ... Dr. Ray WANG
41 Director of Athletics ... Mr. Brian R. SWANSON
86 Dir of Government/External Affairs ... Mr. Doug P. GLAESER
19 Interim Chief of Police ... Mr. W. Bruce WILSON
09 Exec Dir Inst Rsrch & Acad Resource ... Ms. Lisa M. ROTUNNI
37 Dir Financial Aid & Scholarships ... Ms. Diana Y. MINOR
06 Registrar/Academic Records Svcs ... Ms. Maria L. MARTINEZ
96 Director of Procurement ... Ms. Kathleen A. PRUNTY
07 Exec Dir Admissions & Outreach ... Ms. Deborah L. BRANDON

*California State University-Bakersfield (G)

9001 Stockdale Highway, Bakersfield CA 93311-1022
County: Kern — FICE Identification: 007993
Unit ID: 110486
Telephone: (661) 654-2011 — Carnegie Class: Master's L
FAX Number: (661) 654-3194 — Calendar System: Quarter
URL: www.csub.edu
Established: 1965 — Annual Undergrad Tuition & Fees (In-State): $6,811
Enrollment: 8,720 — Coed
Affiliation or Control: State — IRS Status: 501(c)3
Highest Offering: Master's
Program: Occupational; Liberal Arts And General; Teacher Preparatory; Professional; Nursing Emphasis
Accreditation: WC, BUS, NURSE, SPAA, SW, TED

02 President ... Dr. Horace MITCHELL
100 Executive Asst to the President ... Ms. Evelyn YOUNG
04 Admin Asst to the President ... Ms. Tina GIBLIN
05 Provost/Vice Pres Academic Affairs ... Dr. Jenny ZORN
10 Vice Pres Business/Admin Services ... Mr. Thom DAVIS
32 Vice President Student Affairs ... Dr. Thomas WALLACE
30 Vice Pres University Advancement ... Dr. Jim DRNEK
84 Assoc VP for Enrollment Management ... Dr. Jacqueline MIMMS
12 Int Assoc VP Antelope Valley Center ... Dr. Craig KELSEY
20 Assoc VP for Academic Programs ... Dr. Carl KEMNITZ
20 Assoc VP Faculty Affairs ... Dr. David SCHECTER
15 AVP Human Res/Administrative Svcs ... Ms. Kellie GARCIA
88 Int AVP Information Tech Services ... Mr. Kallya SHENOY
88 Spec Asst to Provost Academic Aff ... Vacant
21 Asst Vice Pres Fiscal Services ... Mr. Douglas WADE
13 Asst Vice Pres Info Technology Svcs ... Mr. Kallya SHENOY
18 Asst VP Facilities Management/Dev ... Mr. Pat JACOBS
09 Asst VP Inst Rsrch/Planning/Assess ... Dr. Kris KRISNAN
25 Assoc Vice Pres Grants/Resources ... Dr. Imeh EBONG
35 Assoc VP Student Affairs ... Dr. Jim DRNEK
50 Dean Business/Public Administration ... Dr. John EMERY
53 Dean Social Sciences and Education ... Dr. Kathleen KNUTZEN
79 Dean Arts & Humanities ... Dr. Richard COLLINS
81 Dean Natural Sciences/Math/Eng ... Dr. Anne HOUTMAN
56 Dean Extended University ... Dr. Mark NOVAK
58 Dir of Academic Operation & Support ... Dr. John DIRKSE
08 Dean University Library ... Dr. Curt ASHER
06 Registrar ... Vacant
88 Director Academic Advising ... Vacant
91 Dir Admn Computing Svcs/CMS Pgm Dir ... Mr. Kallya SHENOY
07 Asst Director Admissions & Records ... Mrs. Debbie BLOWERS
29 Director Alumni Relations ... Ms. Sarah HENDRICK
41 Director Athletics ... Mr. Kenneth (Ziggy) SIEGFRIED
36 Dir for Cmty Engagement/Career Edu ... Dr. Markel QUARLES
88 Director Children's Center ... Ms. Gladys GARCIA
96 Dir Contract Services/Procurement ... Mr. Michael CHAVEZ
38 Admin Supervisor Counseling Center ... Dr. Janet MILLAR
106 Director E-Learning Services ... Vacant
37 Director Financial Aid/Scholarships ... Dr. Ron RADNEY
92 Int Director CSUB Honors Program ... Dr. Jacquelyn KEGLEY
39 Director Housing & Residential Life ... Ms. Crystal BECKS
88 Director Safety & Risk Management ... Mr. Tim RIDLEY
88 Dir Svcs Students w/Disabilities ... Ms. Janice CLAUSEN
17 Director Student Health Services ... Dr. Oscar RICO
30 Director of Development ... Mr. Victor MARTIN
88 Director Outreach Services ... Mr. Darius RIGGINS
19 Chief University Police ... Chief Marty WILLIAMSON
88 Director of Food Services ... Mr. Matt MORRIS
18 Manager Facilities Operations ... Mr. Tom VELASQUEZ
40 Bookstore Manager ... Ms. Lori FULLER
26 Public Affairs/Communications Coord ... Ms. Elizabeth FERGON
28 Asst to the President for EIC ... Ms. Claudia CATOTA

*California State University-Channel Islands (H)

One University Drive, Camarillo CA 93012-8599
County: Ventura — FICE Identification: 039803
Unit ID: 441937
Telephone: (805) 437-8400 — Carnegie Class: Master's S
FAX Number: (805) 437-8414 — Calendar System: Semester
URL: www.csuci.edu
Established: 2002 — Annual Undergrad Tuition & Fees (In-District): $6,532
Enrollment: 5,788 — Coed
Affiliation or Control: State/Local — IRS Status: 501(c)3

Highest Offering: Master's
Program: Liberal Arts And General
Accreditation: WC, NURSE

02 President .... Dr. Richard R. RUSH
05 Provost/VP Academic Affairs .... Dr. Gayle HUTCHINSON
10 VP Business & Financial Affairs .... Ms. Ysabel TRINIDAD
32 VP Student Affairs .... Dr. Wm. Gregory SAWYER
13 VP Technology & Communication .... Dr. Michael BERMAN
30 VP University Advancement .... Ms. Nichole IPACH
100 Chief of Staff .... Dr. Genevieve EVANS TAYLOR
20 Associate Provost .... Dr. Dan WAKELEE
20 Assistant Provost .... Dr. Elizabeth HARTUNG
56 Associate VP Extended University .... Dr. Gary BERG
49 Associate VP Arts & Sciences .... Dr. Karen CAREY
50 Associate VP MVS School of Bus/Econ .... Dr. William CORDEIRO
84 Associate VP Enrollment Management .... Mr. Hung DANG
53 Int Assoc VP & Dir School of Educ .... Dr. Merilyn BUCHANAN
46 Senior Research Officer .... Dr. Jason MILLER
08 Associate VP University Library .... Ms. Amy WALLACE
35 Associate VP Dean of Students .... Mr. Damien PEÑA
88 Associate VP Wellness & Athletics .... Mr. Ed LEBIODA
21 Associate VP Financial Services .... Ms. Missy JARNAGIN
15 Associate VP Human Resources .... Ms. Anna PAVIN
88 Dir Special Projects & Operations .... Ms. Melissa REMOTTI
09 Dir Inst Rsrch/Plng & Effectiveness .... Dr. Michael BOURGEOIS
86 Dir Community & Govt Relations .... Ms. Celina ZACARIAS
88 Title IX Inclusion Officer .... Ms. Brittany GRICE
30 Dir Advancement Operations .... Mr. Christopher ABE
44 Dir Major Gifts .... Mr. Carrick DEHART
29 Dir Dev/Alumni Relations .... Ms. Tania GARCIA
44 Dir Planned & Major Gifts .... Ms. Grace G. ROBINSON
44 Dir Annual Giving & Special Gifts .... Ms. Eva C. GOMEZ
19 Dir Public Safety & Chief of Police .... Mr. John REID
19 Dir Transportation & Parking Svcs .... Mr. Ray PORRAS
39 Exec Dir Housing & Residential Ed .... Ms. Cindy DERRICO
06 Assoc Dir Records & Registration .... Ms. Gina R. FARRAR
07 Dir Admissions & Records .... Ms. Ginger REYES
108 Dir Assessment/Research/Staff Dev .... Dr. Jennifer MILLER
104 Dir Intl Pgms/AD Ctr Intl Affairs .... Ms. Mayumi KOWTA
27 Dir Communication & Marketing .... Ms. Nancy GILL
37 Dir Financial Aid & Scholarships .... Ms. Sunshine GARCIA
88 Dir Special Projects for F&A .... Ms. Caroline DOLL
96 Dir Procurement & Contract Services ..... Ms. Valerie PATSCHECK
04 Presidential Aide .... Ms. Alanna TREJO

*California State University-Chico (A)

400 W First Street, Chico CA 95929-0001
County: Butte   FICE Identification: 001146
Unit ID: 110538
Telephone: (530) 898-6116   Carnegie Class: Master's L
FAX Number: (530) 898-6824   Calendar System: Semester
URL: www.csuchico.edu
Established: 1887   Annual Undergrad Tuition & Fees (In-State): $7,022
Enrollment: 17,287   Coed
Affiliation or Control: State   IRS Status: 501(c)3
Highest Offering: Master's
Program: Liberal Arts And General; Teacher Preparatory; Professional
Accreditation: WC, ART, BUS, CONST, CS, DIETD, DIETI, ENG, JOUR, MUS, NAIT, NRPA, NURSE, SP, SPAA, SW, TED, THEA

02 President .... Dr. Paul J. ZINGG
100 Chief of Staff/Dir of Govt Rels .... Ms. Karla J. ZIMMERLEE
05 Interim Provost .... Dr. Susan L. ELROD
10 Vice President Business/Finance .... Ms. Lorraine B. HOFFMAN
32 Vice President Student Affairs .... Mr. Drew CALANDRELLA
30 Vice Pres University Advancement .... Mr. Ahmad BOURA
45 Vice Prov Planning/Res Allocation .... Vacant
46 Vice Provost for Reseach .... Vacant
84 Vice Provost Enrollment Management .... Ms. Barbara FORTIN
13 Vice Prov Information Resources/CIO ...... Mr. Michael SCHILLING
21 Assoc VP Financial Svcs/Univ Budget .... Ms. Stacie CORONA
15 Asst Vice Pres Faculty Affairs .... Ms. Wenshu LEE
47 Int Dean College of Agriculture .... Dr. David DALEY
51 Dean Continuing Education .... Ms. Debra E. BARGER
72 Dean Col Engr/Comp Sci/Const Mgmt .... Dr. Ricardo JACQUEZ
83 Dean Col Behavior & Social Sci .... Dr. Eddie VELA
50 Dean College of Business .... Dr. Judith HENNESSEY
79 Dean College Humanities/Fine Arts .... Dr. Robert KNIGHT
81 Dean College Natural Sciences .... Dr. David M. HASSENZAHL
60 Dean Coll Communication & Educ .... Ms. Angela TRETHEWEY
26 Director Public Affairs .... Mr. Joe WILLS
29 Director Alumni Relations .... Ms. Susan M. ANDERSON
09 Director Institutional Research .... Mr. William R. ALLEN
06 Registrar .... Ms. Jean H. IRVING
07 Director of Admissions .... Mr. Adam STOLTZ
36 Interim Director Student Placement .... Ms. Megan ODOM
37 Director Financial Aid/Scholarships .... Mr. Dan REED
18 Int Dir Facilities Management Svcs .... Mr. Kevin DOYLE
96 Director of Procurement .... Ms. Sara RUMIANO
92 Director Univ Honors Program .... Mr. John MAHONEY
35 Director Student Judicial Affairs .... Ms. Lisa ROOT
28 Director of Diversity and Inclusion .... Mr. Tray ROBINSON

*California State University-Dominguez Hills (B)

1000 E Victoria Street, Carson CA 90747-0005
County: Los Angeles   FICE Identification: 001141
Unit ID: 110547
Telephone: (310) 243-3696   Carnegie Class: Master's L
FAX Number: N/A   Calendar System: Semester
URL: www.csudh.edu
Established: 1960   Annual Undergrad Tuition & Fees (In-State): $6,252
Enrollment: 13,733   Coed
Affiliation or Control: State   IRS Status: 501(c)3
Highest Offering: Master's
Program: Liberal Arts And General; Teacher Preparatory; Professional
Accreditation: WC, CS, MT, MUS, NURSE, OPE, OT, SPAA, SW, TED, THEA

02 President .... Dr. Willie J. HAGAN
05 Provost/Vice Pres Academic Affairs .... Dr. Ellen JUNN
10 Vice Pres Administration/Finance .... Mr. Robert FENNING
32 Vice President Student Affairs .... Dr. William FRANKLIN
30 VP Univ Advancement .... Ms. Carrie E. STEWART
11 Assoc VP Administration/Finance .... Mr. Stephen MASTRO
44 Assoc Vice President Development .... Mr. Jeff POLTORAK
13 VP/Chief Information Officer .... Mr. Chris MANRIQUEZ
35 Assoc VP Student Affs/Dean Students .... Dr. Sonja DANIELS
37 Director of Financial Aid .... Ms. Delores LEE
06 Dir Stdnt Rec/Info Svcs/Registrar .... Ms. Brandy MCLELLAND
09 Assoc Director Institutional Rsrch ... Mr. Pete VAN HAMERSVELD

*California State University-East Bay (C)

25800 Carlos Bee Boulevard, Hayward CA 94542-3001
County: Alameda   FICE Identification: 001138
Unit ID: 110574
Telephone: (510) 885-3000   Carnegie Class: Master's L
FAX Number: (510) 885-3808   Calendar System: Quarter
URL: www.csueastbay.edu
Established: 1957   Annual Undergrad Tuition & Fees (In-State): $6,564
Enrollment: 14,823   Coed
Affiliation or Control: State   IRS Status: 501(c)3
Highest Offering: Doctorate
Program: Liberal Arts And General; Teacher Preparatory; Professional
Accreditation: WC, BUS, ENG, MUS, NURSE, SP, SW, TED

02 President .... Dr. Leroy M. MORISHITA
05 Interim Provost/VP Academic Affairs .... Dr. Carolyn NELSON
10 Interim Vice Pres Admin & Finance .... Ms. Debbie CHAW
30 Vice President Univ Advancement .... Ms. Tanya HAUCK
32 Vice President Student Affs .... Dr. Julie WONG
28 University Diversity Officer .... Dr. Dianne RUSH WOODS
100 Chief of Staff .... Mr. Derek AITKEN
49 Dean Col of Ltrs/Arts/Soc Sci .... Dr. Kathleen ROUNTREE
50 Dean Col of Business/Economics .... Dr. Jagdish AGRAWAL
53 Dean Col of Educ/Allied Studies .... Dr. Carolyn NELSON
81 Dean College of Science .... Dr. Michael LEUNG
08 Dean of Libraries .... Dr. John WENZLER
13 Chief Info Technology Officer (CIO) .... Mr. Borre ULRICHSEN
06 Registrar .... Ms. Angela SCHNEIDER

*California State University-Fresno (D)

5200 N. Barton Avenue, Fresno CA 93740-8027
County: Fresno   FICE Identification: 001147
Unit ID: 110556
Telephone: (559) 278-4240   Carnegie Class: Master's L
FAX Number: (559) 278-4715   Calendar System: Semester
URL: www.csufresno.edu
Established: 1911   Annual Undergrad Tuition & Fees (In-State): $5,472
Enrollment: 23,179   Coed
Affiliation or Control: State   IRS Status: 501(c)3
Highest Offering: Doctorate
Program: Liberal Arts And General; Teacher Preparatory; Professional
Accreditation: WC, BUS, CAATE, CACREP, CIDA, CONST, CORE, DIETD, DIETI, ENG, MUS, NRPA, NURSE, PH, PTA, SP, SPAA, SW, TED, THEA

02 President .... Dr. Joseph I. CASTRO
05 Provost/Vice Pres Academic Affs .... Dr. Lynnette ZELEZNY
10 VP Administration/Chief Fin Ofcr .... Dr. Cynthia TENIENTE-MATSON
30 Vice Pres University Advancement .... Ms. Paula CASTADIO
32 Vice Pres Student Affairs .... Dr. Frank LAMAS
15 Assoc VP Academic Personnel .... Dr. Michael CALDWELL
26 Assoc VP University Communications .... Ms. Shirley ARMBRUSTER
20 Assoc VP/Dean Undergrad Students .... Dr. Dennis L. NEF
45 Assoc Vice President Research .... Dr. Thomas H. MCCLANAHAN
44 Assoc Vice Pres Univ Development .... Vacant
21 Assoc VP for Financial Services .... Mr. Clinton MOFFITT
18 Associate Vice President Facilities .... Mr. Robert BOYD
84 Assoc Vice Pres Enrollment Services .... Mr. Bernie VINOVRSKI
51 Int Dean/AVP Continuing/Global Ed .... Dr. Scott MOORE
47 Dean Agricultural Science/Tech .... Vacant
79 Dean of Arts & Humanities .... Vacant
50 Dean Craig School of Business .... Dr. Robert HARPER
53 Dean of Kremen School of Education .... Dr. Paul BEARE
54 Dean of Engineering .... Dr. Ramakrishna NUNNA
76 Int Dean of Health/Human Services .... Dr. Jody HIRONAKA-JUTEAU
83 Dean of Social Sciences .... Dr. Luz GONZALEZ
81 Dean of Science & Mathematics .... Dr. Susan ELROD
08 Dean of Library Services .... Mr. Peter MCDONALD
58 Dean of Graduate Studies .... Dr. Sandra WITTE
23 Dir Univ Health/Psyc Svcs Oper .... Ms. Maria MADRIGAL-SHAFFER
19 Director of Public Safety .... Mr. David HUERTA
41 Director of Athletics .... Mr. Thomas BOEH
16 Director of Human Resources .... Ms. Janice PARTEN
13 Exec Director Technology Services .... Mr. Jim MICHAEL
09 Dir of Inst Research/Assessment .... Dr. Angel SANCHEZ
37 Director of Financial Aid .... Mr. Bernie OGDEN
06 Registrar .... Ms. Tina BEDDALL
27 Director of Publications .... Mr. Bruce WHITWORTH
29 Executive Director Alumni Relations ..... Ms. Jacquelyn GLASENER
36 Director of Career Services .... Ms. Rita BOCCHINFUSO-COHEN
39 Director Univ Courtyard (Housing) .... Ms. Erin BOELE
96 Dir Procurement & Support Services .... Mr. Brian COTHAM
07 Director of Admissions .... Ms. Tina BEDDALL
35 Director of Student Involvement .... Ms. Melissa GINOTTI
40 Bookstore Manager .... Mr. Curt PARKINSON

*California State University-Fullerton (E)

PO Box 34080, 800 N State Col Blvd, Fullerton CA 92831-3547
County: Orange   FICE Identification: 001137
Unit ID: 110565
Telephone: (657) 278-2011   Carnegie Class: Master's L
FAX Number: (657) 278-2649   Calendar System: Semester
URL: www.fullerton.edu
Established: 1957   Annual Undergrad Tuition & Fees (In-State): $6,440
Enrollment: 38,128   Coed
Affiliation or Control: State   IRS Status: 501(c)3
Highest Offering: Doctorate
Program: Liberal Arts And General; Teacher Preparatory; Professional
Accreditation: WC, ANEST, ART, BUS, BUSA, CAATE, CACREP, CS, CSHSE, DANCE, ENG, JOUR, MIDWF, MUS, NURSE, PH, SP, SPAA, SW, TED, THEA

02 President .... Dr. Mildred GARCIA
100 Chief of Staff .... Ms. Ann CAMP
05 Provost & VP Academic Affairs .... Dr. Josè CRUZ
10 VP Admin & Finance/CFO .... Mr. Danny C. KIM
32 Vice President of Student Affairs .... Dr. Berenecea J. EANES
30 VP University Advancement .... Mr. Greg SAKS
13 VP Info Tech/Chief Info Ofcr .... Mr. Amir DABIRIAN
15 VP of Hum Res/Diversity & Inclusion .... Ms. Lori GENTLES
102 Executive Director/CFO Foundation .... Ms. Tara GARCIA
44 Assoc VP University Advancement .... Mrs. Michele CESCA
58 AVP Academic Programs .... Dr. Peter NWOSU
26 Assoc VP Strategic Communications .... Mr. Jeffrey COOK
20 Deputy Provost & AVP Acad Affs .... Dr. Shari MCMAHAN
88 AVP Rsrch/Creative/Tech .... Dr. Patrick PELLICANE
88 AVP South County Ops & Initiatives ...... Dr. Marteza RAHMATIAN
21 Associate VP of Financial Services .... Vacant
86 Assc VP Public Affs/Government Rels .... Mr. Owen HOLMES
44 Assoc VP Advancement .... Ms. Theresa DAVIS
45 Dir Budget Planning & Admin .... Ms. Laleh GRAYLEE
35 AVP Student Affairs .... Dr. Lea JARNAGIN
35 AVP Student Affairs .... Dr. Vijay PENDAKUR
35 Int AVP Student Affairs .... Mr. Darren BUSH
11 Chief of Operations .... Vacant
18 Int AVP Facilities Planning/Mgmt .... Mr. Willem VAN DER POL
84 Asst Vice Pres Enrollment Services .... Ms. Nancy DORITY
09 Int Dir Inst Res/Analytical Stds .... Dr. Sunny MOON
16 Assoc VP of Hum Res/Diversity & Inc .... Vacant
14 Asst VP for Information Technology .... Mr. Rommel HIDALGO
29 Exec Director Alumni Relations .... Ms. Dianna L. FISHER
88 Exec Director/CEO Aux Services Corp .... Mr. Frank MUMFORD
06 University Registrar .... Ms. Melissa WHATLEY
08 Interim University Librarian .... Dr. Scott HEWITT
07 Director of Admissions .... Ms. Jessica WAGONER
36 Director Career Center .... Mr. Jim CASE
40 Director Titan Shops .... Ms. Kimberly BALL
23 Director Health Center .... Ms. Kathy SPOFFORD
19 Chief University Police .... Mr. Dennis DEMAIO
28 Director Diversity/Equity Programs .... Vacant
37 Director Financial Aid .... Ms. Cecilia SCHOUWE
41 Director of Athletics .... Mr. James DONOVAN
96 Director of Contracts & Procurement .... Mr. Don GREEN
35 Dean of Students .... Dr. Tonantzin OSEGUERA
88 Dir Intl Admissions & Outreach .... Mr. Joseph SAÑOSA
85 Dir Intl Students & Scholars ..... Ms. Christine PIRCHER-BARNES
88 Director Women's Center/Re-Entry .... Ms. Mary BECERRA
88 Dir Educational Partnerships .... Ms. Melba CASTRO
39 Director Housing .... Mr. Larry MARTIN
88 Int Dir Univ Outreach/New Stdnt Pgm .... Ms. Deanna MERINO
88 Dir Athletic Academic Services .... Ms. Meredith BASIL
88 Dir Center for Internship/Com Eng .... Ms. Dawn MACY
88 Dir Student Academic Services .... Dr. Rochelle WOODS
88 Dir Veteran Student Services .... Mr. Lui AMADOR
38 Dir Counseling/Psychological Svcs .... Dr. Leticia GUTIERREZ-LOPEZ
14 Int AVP IT/Infrastructure Services .... Mr. Berhanu TADESSE
90 AVP IT/Academic Technology Svcs .... Dr. Kenneth KASS
51 Int Dean Extend Ed & AVP Intl Pgm .... Dr. Kari KNUTSON-MILLER
79 Dean Humanities/Social Sciences .... Dr. Sheryl FONTAINE
81 Int Dean Natural Sciences & Math .... Dr. David BOWMAN
50 Dean Mihaylo Col Business/Economics .... Dr. Anil PURI
83 Int Dean Health/Human Development .... Dr. Jessie JONES
57 Dean College of the Arts .... Mr. Dale MERRILL
53 Dean College of Education .... Dr. Claire CAVALLARO
54 Dean Col Engineering & Computer Sci .... Dr. Raman UNNIKRISHNAN
60 Int Dean College of Communications .... Dr. Irene MATZ
12 Dean Irvine Campus .... Dr. Susan COOPER

*California State University-Long Beach (F)

1250 Bellflower Boulevard, Long Beach CA 90840-0115
County: Los Angeles   FICE Identification: 001139
Unit ID: 110583
Telephone: (562) 985-4111   Carnegie Class: Master's L

FAX Number: (562) 985-5419 Calendar System: Semester
URL: www.csulb.edu
Established: 1949 Annual Undergrad Tuition & Fees (In-State): $6,452
Enrollment: 37,492 Coed
Affiliation or Control: State IRS Status: 501(c)3
Highest Offering: Doctorate
Program: Liberal Arts And General; Teacher Preparatory; Professional
Accreditation: WC, AAFCS, ART, BUS, CAATE, CEA, CONST, CS, DANCE, DIETD, DIETI, ENG, HSA, IPSY, JOUR, MUS, NRPA, NURSE, PH, PTA, SP, SPAA, SW, TED, THEA

02 President ....Dr. Jane C. CONOLEY
05 Provost/Sr Vice Pres Academic Affs ....Dr. David DOWELL
11 Vice Pres Administration/Finance ....Ms. Mary E. STEPHENS
32 Vice President Student Affairs ....Dr. Carmen TILLERY TAYLOR
30 Vice Pres University Rels/Devel ....Ms. Andrea TAYLOR
100 Chief of Staff ....Dr. Karen NAKAI
10 Assoc VP Financial Management ....Ms. Sharon TAYLOR
20 Assoc VP Undergraduate Studies ....Dr. Nele HEMPEL-LAMER
35 Assoc Vice Pres Student Affairs ....Dr. Mary Ann TAKEMOTO
82 Assoc VP Intl Educ/Global Engagemnt ....Dr. Jeet JOSHEE
18 Vice Pres Phys Plng/Facilities Mgt ....Mr. David SALAZAR
20 Vice Provost/Dean Undergrad Studies ....Dr. Cecile LINDSAY
46 Assoc Vice Pres University Research ....Dr. Simon KIM
15 Assoc VP Budget/Human Resource Mgmt ....Mr. Scott APEL
91 Int Assoc VP Academic Technology ....Dr. Shawna DARK
26 Asst Vice Pres Public Affairs ....Ms. Terri CARBAUGH
29 Assoc VP Alumni and Univ Relations ....Ms. Janice HATANAKA
09 Director Institutional Research ....Mahmoud ALBAWANEH
84 Assoc Vice Pres Enrollment Services ....Mr. Thomas ENDERS
13 Assoc VP Information Technology ....Ms. Janet FOSTER
76 Dean College Health/Human Svcs ....Dr. James KOVAL
50 Dean College of Business Admin ....Dr. Michael SOLT
53 Dean College of Education ....Dr. Marquita GRENOT-SCHEYER
54 Dean College of Engineering ....Dr. Forouzan GOLSHANI
57 Dean College of the Arts ....Cyrus PARKER-JEANNETTE
81 Dean College Natural Science/Math ....Dr. Laura KINGSFORD
49 Dean College of Liberal Arts ....Dr. David WALLACE
51 Dean Col Continuing & Profess Educ ....Dr. Jeet JOSHEE
08 Dean Library/Learning Resources ....Mr. Roman KOCHAN
06 Dir of Registration/Records/Evals ....Ms. Donna GREEN
39 Director Housing Administration ....Ms. Carol ROBERTS-CORB
16 Director Staff Personnel Services ....Ms. Nancy TORRES
41 Director Athletics ....Mr. Victor CEGLES
07 Interim Director of Admissions ....Ms. Janice MILLER
36 Director Career Plng & Placement ....Mr. Manuel PEREZ
23 Interim Director Health Services ....Dr. Mary Ann TAKEMOTO
19 Chief University Police ....Mr. Fernando SOLORZANO
38 Director Counseling/Psych Services ....Dr. Brad COMPLIMENT
37 Director Financial Aid/Admissions ....Mr. Nicolas VALDIVIA
25 Director Foundation Grants/Contract ....Ms. Sandra SHEREMAN
102 Chief Operating Officer/Foundation ....Dr. Brian NOWLIN
28 Director of Equity & Diversity ....Ms. Larisa HAMADA
96 Director Procurement & Contracts ....Ms. Malia KINIMAKA
109 General Manager/49'er Shops ....Mr. Donald PENROD
104 Director Education Abroad ....Ms. Sharon OLSON
44 Dir Leadership Annual Giving ....Ms. Kendra KOMAR
86 AVP Legislative & External Rels ....Ms. Terri CARBAUGH

*California State University-Los Angeles (A)

5151 State University Drive, Los Angeles CA 90032-8530
County: Los Angeles FICE Identification: 001140
Unit ID: 110592
Telephone: (323) 343-3000 Carnegie Class: Master's L
FAX Number: (323) 343-2670 Calendar System: Quarter
URL: www.calstatela.edu
Established: 1947 Annual Undergrad Tuition & Fees (In-State): $6,344
Enrollment: 24,488 Coed
Affiliation or Control: State IRS Status: 501(c)3
Highest Offering: Doctorate
Program: Liberal Arts And General; Teacher Preparatory; Professional
Accreditation: WC, ART, BUS, CACREP, CORE, CS, DIETC, DIETD, ENG, FEPAC, MUS, NAIT, NURSE, SP, SPAA, SW, TED

02 President ....Dr. William A. COVINO
03 Sr VP and Chief Operating Officer ....Dr. Jose GOMEZ
05 Provost/Vice Pres Academic Affs ....Dr. Lynn MAHONEY
10 VP Administration & CFO ....Ms. Lisa M. CHAVEZ
32 Vice President Student Affairs ....Vacant
13 Vice Pres/Chief Technology Officer ....Mr. Peter QUAN
44 Vice Pres Institutional Advancement ....Dr. Janet DIAL
20 Int Vice Provost Academic Affairs ....Dr. Ron VOGEL
21 Assoc VP Admin & Finance/Budget ....Ms. Mae SANTOS
84 Sr AVP for Enrollment Mgmt ....Dr. Nancy WADA-MCKEE
30 Assoc VP University Advancement ....Mr. Mario PEREZ
20 AVP for Research & Acad Personnel ....Dr. Philip LAPOLT
29 Exec Director Alumni Relations ....Ms. Maria UBAGO
26 AVP Communications & Public Affairs ....Ms. Elena STERN
41 Director Intercollegiate Athletics ....Dr. Daniel BRIDGES
83 Int Dean Natural & Social Sciences ....Dr. Scott R. BOWMAN
08 Int University Librarian ....Ms. Marla PEPPERS
06 University Registrar ....Mr. Christopher COBB
58 Interim Dean Grad Studies ....Dr. Karin A. ELLIOT BROWN
88 Assoc Dean Graduate Studies ....Vacant
09 Director Institutional Research ....Dr. Mark PAVELCHAK
36 Director Career Placement & Plng ....Mr. Christopher LENZ
37 Director Student Financial Services ....Ms. Tamie NGUYEN
23 Director Health Center ....Dr. Monica JAZZABI
39 Director Housing Svc/Residence Life ....Mr. Stephen FLEISCHER
22 Director Equal Opportunity Pgm ....Ms. Becky HOPKINS

18 AVP Fac/Plng/Design & Construct ....Mr. Warren JACOBS
19 Chief of Police ....Mr. Rick WALL
15 AVP Human Resources Management ....Ms. Susie VARELA
85 Director Intl Programs & Services ....Ms. Amy WANG
43 University Counsel ....Mr. Victor I. KING
07 Director Admissions & Recruitment ....Mr. Vince LOPEZ
96 Director Procurement & Contracts ....Mr. Thomas JOHNSON
09 Asst Dir Institutional Research ....Ms. Vivien KO
28 Dir Equity/Diversity/Inclusion ....Ms. Mariel MULET
40 Manager Bookstore ....Mr. Todd MURPHY
88 Int Assoc Dean Undergrad Studies ....Dr. Margaret GARCIA
49 Dean Arts & Letters ....Dr. Peter MCALLISTER
54 Dean Engr/Computer Science/Tech ....Dr. Emily ALLEN
107 Dean Col of Profess/Global Studies ....Dr. Eric A. BULLARD
76 Dean Health & Human Services ....Dr. Beatrice YORKER
53 Int Dean Charter Col of Education ....Dr. Cheryl NEY
50 Dean Business & Economics ....Dr. James A. GOODRICH
97 Dean Undergraduate Studies ....Dr. Michelle HAWLEY
92 Director Honors College ....Dr. Trinh PHAM

† Grants Joint Doctoral degree in cooperation with the University of California-Los Angeles.

*California State University Maritime Academy (B)

200 Maritime Academy Drive, Vallejo CA 94590-0644
County: Solano FICE Identification: 001134
Unit ID: 111188
Telephone: (707) 654-1000 Carnegie Class: Bac/Diverse
FAX Number: (707) 654-1001 Calendar System: Semester
URL: www.csum.edu
Established: 1929 Annual Undergrad Tuition & Fees (In-State): $6,563
Enrollment: 1,048 Coed
Affiliation or Control: State IRS Status: 501(c)3
Highest Offering: Master's
Program: Occupational; Professional; Business Emphasis
Accreditation: WC, ENG, ENGT, IACBE

02 President ....RADM. Thomas A. CROPPER, USMS
05 Provost/VP Academic Affairs ....Dr. Susan OPP
10 VP of Administration/Finance ....Mr. Franz LOZANO
44 VP Univ Advancement/Exec Dir Found ....Mr. Robert ARP
32 VP Student Affairs ....Mr. Steve KRETA
13 Chief Information Officer ....Mr. Daman GREWAL
20 Academic Dean ....Vacant
88 Master of Training Ship ....Capt. Harry BOLTON
30 Senior Development Officer ....Ms. Melissa COHEA
21 Budget Officer ....Ms. Sarah SONG
26 Director of University Affairs ....Mr. Brigham TIMPSON
06 Registrar ....Ms. Evelyn ANDREWS
08 Dean of Library ....Ms. Michele VAN HOECK
07 Dir Admissions/Enrollment Services ....Mr. Marc MCGEE
37 Director of Financial Aid ....Mr. Howard YAMAMOTO
109 Exec Director Auxiliary Services ....Ms. Diane RAWICZ
88 Director Ctr Excellence & Learning ....Ms. Vineeta DHILLON
36 Dean of Student Development ....Mr. James DALSKE
18 Director Facilities Planning ....Mr. Isidro FARIAS
19 Chief Security Officer ....Chief Roseann RICHARD
15 Exec Director of Human Resources ....Dr. Ingrid WILLIAMS
41 Director of Athletics ....Mr. Marv CHRISTOPHER
26 Director Public Relations ....Mr. Bobby KING
40 Bookstore Manager ....Mr. Andre JIMENEZ
96 Purchasing Manager ....Vacant
04 Administrative Asst to President ....Ms. Lisa RAQUEL
09 Director of Institutional Research ....Mr. Gary MOSER
29 Director of Alumni Relations ....Ms. Kathy BAIRD

*California State University-Monterey Bay (C)

100 Campus Center, Seaside CA 93955-8000
County: Monterey FICE Identification: 032603
Unit ID: 409698
Telephone: (831) 582-3000 Carnegie Class: Master's S
FAX Number: (831) 582-3783 Calendar System: Semester
URL: www.csumb.edu
Established: 1994 Annual Undergrad Tuition & Fees (In-State): $5,795
Enrollment: 6,631 Coed
Affiliation or Control: State IRS Status: 501(c)3
Highest Offering: Master's
Program: Liberal Arts And General
Accreditation: WC, SW, TED

02 President ....Dr. Eduardo M. OCHOA
05 Provost ....Dr. Bonnie IRWIN
10 Vice Pres Admin & Finance/CFO ....Mr. Kevin SAUNDERS
30 Vice Pres University Development ....Ms. Barbara ZAPPAS
32 VP Student Affairs & Enroll Service ....Dr. Ronnie HIGGS
26 Assoc VP for University Affairs ....Mr. Andre LEWIS
35 Dean of Student Life ....Dr. Christine ERICKSON
21 Assoc Vice President for Finance ....Mr. John FITZGIBBON
28 Assoc VP Inclusive Excellence ....Dr. Patti HIRAMOTO
108 AVP Institutional Effect/Acad Plng ....Ms. Fran HORVATH
06 Registrar ....Ms. Sheila HERNANDEZ
22 Director Employee Rels/EEO & ADA ....Ms. Tamberly PETROVICH
37 Director Financial Aid ....Ms. Angeles FUENTES
15 Assoc VP for Human Resources ....Ms. Natalie KING
19 Chief of Police ....Chief Earl LAWSON
18 Chief Facilities/Physical Plant ....Mr. John MARKER
07 Dir for Admissions & Recruitment ....Mr. David LINNEVERS
29 Director Alumni Relations ....Ms. Pilar GOSE

41 Athletic Director ....Mr. Kirby GARRY
96 Director of Purchasing ....Mr. Art EVJEN

*California State University-Northridge (D)

18111 Nordhoff Street, Northridge CA 91330-0001
County: Los Angeles FICE Identification: 001153
Unit ID: 110608
Telephone: (818) 677-1200 Carnegie Class: Master's L
FAX Number: N/A Calendar System: Semester
URL: www.csun.edu
Established: 1958 Annual Undergrad Tuition & Fees (In-State): $6,564
Enrollment: 40,131 Coed
Affiliation or Control: State IRS Status: 501(c)3
Highest Offering: Doctorate
Program: Liberal Arts And General; Teacher Preparatory; Professional
Accreditation: WC, AAFCS, ART, BUS, CAATE, CACREP, CIDA, CONST, CS, DIETD, DIETI, ENG, IPSY, JOUR, MUS, NRPA, NURSE, PH, PTA, RAD, SP, SW, TED, THEA

02 President ....Dr. Dianne F. HARRISON
05 Provost/Vice Pres Academic Affairs ....Dr. Harry HELLENBRAND
10 Vice President Admin/Finance ....Mr. Colin DONAHUE
32 VP Student Affairs/Dean of Students ....Dr. William WATKINS
30 Vice Pres University Advancement ....Dr. Robert GUNSALUS
13 Vice President IT/CIO ....Ms. Hilary BAKER
88 Exec Director University Corp ....Mr. Rick EVANS
20 Vice Provost Academic Affairs ....Dr. Michael NEUBAUER
100 Chief of Staff ....Ms. Jill SMITH
18 Assoc VP Facilities Dev/Operations ....Mr. Ken ROSENTHAL
58 Assoc VP Grad Studies/Intl Pgms ....Dr. Crist KHACHIKIAN
21 Associate VP Financial Services ....Ms. Deborah WALLACE
15 Interim Assoc VP of Human Resources ....Ms. Kristina DE LA VEGA
29 Asst Vice Pres Alumni Relations ....Vacant
26 Assoc VP of Mktg/Comm ....Mr. Jeffrey NOBLITT
20 Assoc VP of Undergraduate Studies ....Dr. Elizabeth T. ADAMS
91 Assoc VP of Academic Resources ....Ms. Diane S. STEPHENS
07 Director of Admissions and Records ....Ms. Patty R. LORD
08 Dean University Library ....Dr. Mark STOVER
51 Dean College of Extended Learning ....Dr. Joyce A. FEUCHT-HAVIAR
79 Dean College of Humanities ....Dr. Elizabeth A. SAY
50 Dean College Business/Economics ....Dr. Kenneth R. LORD
53 Dean College of Education ....Dr. Michael E. SPAGNA
57 Dean College Arts/Media/Commun ....Mr. Jay KVAPIL
83 Dean Col Social/Behavioral Sci ....Dr. Stella Z. THEODOULOU
76 Dean Col Health/Human Development ....Dr. Sylvia A. ALVA
81 Dean College Science & Math ....Dr. Jerry STINNER
54 Dean College Engr/Computer Science ....Dr. S. K. RAMESH
09 Director Institutional Research ....Dr. Bettina HUBER
37 Director Financial Aid/Scholarships ....Mrs. Lili C. VIDAL
38 Director Univ Counseling Services ....Dr. Mark STEVENS
36 Director Career Center ....Ms. Ann N. MOREY
25 Dir Research/Sponsored Projects ....Mr. Scott L. PEREZ
18 Senior Dir Physical Plant Mgmt ....Mr. Jason WANG
19 Director of Police Services ....Ms. Anne P. GLAVIN
28 Director of Equity and Diversity ....Ms. Susan HUA
86 Dir Government/Community Relations ....Ms. Francesca VEGA
23 Director Student Health Center ....Dr. Linda REID-CHASSIAKOS
39 Dir Student Housing/Conf Services ....Mr. Timothy J. TREVAN
40 Director Matador Bookstore ....Ms. Amy C. BERGER
41 Director of Athletics ....Dr. Brandon MARTIN
88 Director Student Involvement & Dev ....Mr. Patrick BAILEY
92 Dir General Education Honors Pgm ....Dr. Beth A. WIGHTMAN
96 Manager Purchasing ....Ms. Deborah FLUGUM
84 Director Enrollment Management ....Dr. William WATKINS
06 Registrar ....Mr. Todd WOLFE

*California State University-Sacramento (E)

6000 J Street, Sacramento CA 95819-2694
County: Sacramento FICE Identification: 001150
Unit ID: 110617
Telephone: (916) 278-6011 Carnegie Class: Master's L
FAX Number: (916) 278-6664 Calendar System: Semester
URL: www.csus.edu
Established: 1947 Annual Undergrad Tuition & Fees (In-State): $6,872
Enrollment: 26,648 Coed
Affiliation or Control: State IRS Status: 501(c)3
Highest Offering: Doctorate
Program: Liberal Arts And General; Teacher Preparatory; Professional
Accreditation: WC, ART, BUS, CAATE, CACREP, CIDA, CONST, CORE, CS, DIETD, DIETI, EMT, ENG, MUS, NRPA, NURSE, PTA, SP, SW

02 President ....Dr. Robert S. NELSEN
05 Provost/Vice Pres Acad Affairs ....Dr. Frederika HARMSEN
10 Vice President Administration & CFO ....Dr. Ming-Tung (Mike) LEE
30 Vice Pres University Advancement ....Mr. Vince SALES
32 VP Student Affairs ....Dr. Edward MILLS
13 VP & Chief Information Officer ....Dr. Larry GILBERT
15 Vice President for Human Resources ....Ms. Christine D. LOVELY
26 Vice Pres Public Affairs/Advocacy ....Dr. Phil GARCIA
46 Asst VP Research Affairs ....Mr. David EARWICKER
20 Vice Provost ....Dr. James PRINCE
18 Assoc Vice Pres Facilities Mgmt ....Dr. Ali IZADIAN
27 Assoc VP University Communications ....Ms. Jeannie WONG
35 AVP Student Engagement & Success ....Dr. Beth LESEN
21 Interim Assoc VP Financial Svcs ....Ms. Gina CURRY
43 University Counsel ....Ms. Jill PETERSON

09 Director Institutional Research .... Dr. Jing WANG
07 Director Outreach & Admissions .... Mr. Emiliano DIAZ
08 Library Dean .... Ms. Amy KAUTZMAN
29 Director Alumni Relations .... Ms. Jennifer BARBER
19 Director Public Safety .... Mr. Mark IWASA
39 Dir Housing and Residential Life .... Mr. Michael SPEROS
41 Interim Director Intercol Athletics .... Dr. Bill MACRISS
37 Director Financial Aid .... Ms. Anita KERMES
22 Director of Employment Equity .... Mr. William BISHOP
40 Bookstore Director .... Ms. Julia MILARDOVICH
100 Chief of Staff .... Ms. Carol ENSLEY
06 University Registrar .... Mr. Dennis GEYER
85 Dir Intl Pgm/Global Engagement .... Dr. Frank LI
23 Dir Student Health Ctr & Psych Svcs . Dr. Joy STEWART-JAMES
96 Mgr Procurement/Contract Services .... Mr. John GUION
49 Dean College of Arts & Letters .... Dr. Edward INCH
50 Dean Col of Business Admin .... Dr. Pierre BALTHAZARD
53 Dean College of Education .... Dr. Vanessa SHEARED
54 Dean College of Engr/Computer Sci .... Dr. Lorenzo SMITH
76 Dean College of Health/Human Svcs .... Dr. Fred BALDINI
81 Dean College of Natural Sci/Math .... Dr. Jill TRAINER
51 Dean College Continuing Education .... Dr. Guido KRICKX
83 Dean College Soc Sci/Interdisc Stds .... Dr. Orn BODVARSSON
58 Dean Graduate Studies .... Dr. Chevelle NEWSOME

*California State University-San Bernardino (A)

5500 University Parkway, San Bernardino CA 92407-2393
County: San Bernardino FICE Identification: 001142
Unit ID: 110510
Telephone: (909) 537-5000 Carnegie Class: Master's L
FAX Number: N/A Calendar System: Quarter
URL: www.csusb.edu
Established: 1960 Annual Undergrad Tuition & Fees (In-State): $6,596
Enrollment: 18,952 Coed
Affiliation or Control: State IRS Status: 501(c)3
Highest Offering: Doctorate
Program: Liberal Arts And General; Teacher Preparatory; Professional
Accreditation: WC, ART, BUS, CORE, CS, DIETD, ENG, MUS, NURSE, SPAA, SW, TED, THEA

02 President .... Dr. Tomas MORALES
05 Provost/Vice Pres Academic Affairs .... Vacant
10 Vice Pres Administration/Finance .... Dr. Doug FREER
32 Vice Pres Student Affairs .... Dr. Brian L. HAYNES
30 Vice Pres University Advancement .... Dr. Ronald FREMONT
13 Vice Pres ITS/CIO .... Dr. Samuel SUDHAKAR
28 Co-Chief Diversity Officer .... Mr. Cesar PORTILLO
28 Co-Chief Diversity Officer .... Dr. Jacqueline HUGHES
88 Director Executive Affairs .... Ms. Pamela LANGFORD
20 Int Assoc Provost Acad Programs .... Dr. Rong CHEN
88 Assoc Provost Research .... Dr. Jeffrey M. THOMPSON
16 Assoc Provost Academic Personnel .... Dr. Jacqueline HUGHES
20 Assoc VP & Dean Undergrad Studies .... Dr. William VANDERBURGH
21 Assoc VP Finance .... Mr. M. Monir AHMED
15 Assoc VP Human Resources .... Mr. Cesar PORTILLO
84 Assoc VP Enrollment Mgmt .... Ms. Olivia ROSAS
35 Assoc VP and Dean of Students .... Dr. Alysson M. SATTERLUND
88 Assoc VP ITS .... Mr. Gerard AU
88 Assoc VP Development .... Ms. Beth BRENNER
26 Assoc VP Strategic Communications .... Mr. Dave JOHNSON
09 AVP Inst Effectiveness & Dir IR .... Dr. Muriel LOPEZ-WAGNER
88 Director Title IX & Gender Equity .... Ms. Cristina MARTIN
36 Director Career Center .... Ms. Christina RODRIGUEZ
06 Director/University Registrar .... Ms. Grace KING
07 Director Admissions .... Ms. Arlene REED
23 Director Health & Counseling Center .... Dr. Patricia SMITH
08 University Librarian .... Mr. Cesar CABALLERO
37 Director Financial Aid .... Ms. Roseanna RUIZ
39 Director Housing & Residential Life .... Dr. John YAUN
45 Director Plng Design/Construction .... Mr. Hamid U. AZHAND
18 Sr Director Facilities Services .... Vacant
41 Asst VP and Director Athletics .... Dr. Kevin L. HATCHER
29 Director Alumni Affairs .... Ms. Doreen HATCHER
96 Director Purchasing .... Ms. Kathy HANSEN
40 Director Bookstore .... Mr. David WATTS
94 Director Gender & Sexuality Studies .... Dr. Todd JENNINGS
92 Director University Honors Program . Dr. William VANDERBURGH
56 Dean Col of Extended Learning .... Dr. Tatiana KARMANOVA
49 Dean College of Arts & Letters .... Dr. Terry BALLMAN
81 Dean Col Natural Sciences .... Dr. Kirsten FLEMING
83 Dean Col Social/Behavioral Sciences .... Dr. Rafik MOHAMED
53 Dean College of Education .... Dr. Jay FIENE
50 Dean College of Business .... Dr. Lawrence D. ROSE
58 Dean Graduate Studies .... Dr. Jeffrey M. THOMPSON
12 Dean CSUSB Palm Desert .... Dr. Sharon BROWN-WELTY
100 Chief of Staff .... Ms. Tracy L. WISE

*California State University-San Marcos (B)

333 S Twin Oaks Valley Road, San Marcos CA 92096-0001
County: San Diego FICE Identification: 030113
Unit ID: 366711
Telephone: (760) 750-4000 Carnegie Class: Master's M
FAX Number: (760) 750-4030 Calendar System: Semester
URL: www.csusm.edu
Established: 1989 Annual Undergrad Tuition & Fees (In-State): $7,264
Enrollment: 12,154 Coed
Affiliation or Control: State IRS Status: 501(c)3
Highest Offering: Doctorate
Program: Liberal Arts And General; Teacher Preparatory
Accreditation: WC, NURSE, SP, @SW, TED

02 President .... Dr. Karen S. HAYNES
04 Presidential Aide .... Ms. Viviana GARCIA
10 Vice President Finance/Admin Svcs .... Dr. Linda HAWK
05 Vice President Academic Affairs .... Dr. Graham OBEREM
32 Vice President of Student Affairs .... Dr. Lorena MEZA
30 Vice Pres University Advancement .... Mr. Neal HOSS
20 Assoc Vice Pres Academic Affairs .... Dr. Regina EISENBACH
88 Assoc VP Planning/Acad Resources .... Dr. Kamel HADDAD
84 Assoc Vice Pres Enrollment Mgmt .... Mr. Scott HAGG
15 Assoc VP Human Resource/Equal Oppty .... Mr. Travis GREGORY
22 Assoc VP Diversity & Educ Equity .... Mr. Arturo OCAMPO
49 Dean Col Hum Arts/Behav & Soc Sci .... Dr. Adam SHAPIRO
50 Dean Col Business Administration .... Dr. Jim HAMERLY
53 Dean Col Educ/Health & Human Svcs .... Dr. Janet POWELL
08 Dean of Library Services .... Dr. Jennifer FABBI
81 Dean Col of Science & Mathematics .... Dr. Katherine KANTARDJIEFF
56 Dean of Extended Studies .... Mr. Michael SCHRODER
72 Dean Instructional/Info Technology .... Mr. Kevin MORNINGSTAR
37 Director Financial Aid .... Ms. Vonda GARCIA
06 Registrar .... Mr. Thomas SWANGER
07 Dir of Admissions & Recruitment .... Ms. Carol MCALLISTER
100 Chief of Staff/Dir Inst Plng & Anal .... Mr. Matthew CEPPI
18 Director Facility Services .... Mr. Gary CINNAMON
21 Associate Business Officer .... Mrs. Mary HINCHMAN
29 Director Alumni/Parent Relations .... Ms. Lori BROCKETT
96 Director Procurment/Support Svcs .... Ms. Bella NEWBERG
38 Director Undergraduate Advising .... Mr. Andres FAVELA

† Grants Joint Doctoral degree in cooperation with the University of California-San Diego.

*California State University-Stanislaus (C)

1 University Circle, Turlock CA 95382-0299
County: Stanislaus FICE Identification: 001157
Unit ID: 110495
Telephone: (209) 667-3122 Carnegie Class: Master's L
FAX Number: N/A Calendar System: Semester
URL: www.csustan.edu
Established: 1957 Annual Undergrad Tuition & Fees (In-State): $6,708
Enrollment: 9,045 Coed
Affiliation or Control: State IRS Status: 170(c)1
Highest Offering: Doctorate
Program: Liberal Arts And General; Teacher Preparatory; Professional
Accreditation: WC, ART, BUS, MUS, NURSE, SPAA, SW, TED, THEA

02 President .... Dr. Joseph F. SHELEY
05 Provost/VP Academic Affairs .... Dr. James T. STRONG
10 VP Business/Finance .... Mr. Douglas DAWES
84 VP Enrollment/Student Affairs .... Dr. Suzanne M. ESPINOZA
30 VP University Advancement .... Ms. Shirley M. POK
15 VP Faculty Affairs/HR .... Mr. Dennis W. SHIMEK
32 AVP Student Services .... Dr. J. Martyn GUNN
100 Exec Assistant to the President .... Ms. Carrie M. RASMUSSEN
79 Dean College Arts/Humanities & SS .... Dr. James A. TUEDIO
50 Dean College of Business Admin .... Dr. Nael ALY
53 Dean College of Education .... Dr. Oddmund R. MYHRE
81 Dean College of Science .... Vacant
08 Dean Library Services .... Mr. Ron RODRIGUEZ
106 Interim Dean Stockton Center .... Dr. Ashour BADAL
51 Dean Extended Education .... Dr. Helene CAUDILL
20 Int AVP Academic Planning/Analysis .... Dr. Marjorie A. JAASMA
41 Director Athletics .... Mr. Michael MATOSO
35 AVP Student Affairs/Dean of Student .... Mr. Ronald J. NOBLE
21 Assoc VP Financial Services .... Ms. Julie K. BENEVEDES
13 Int Assoc VP Information Technology .... Mr. Stan TREVENA
18 Assoc VP Facilities Services .... Ms. Melody MAFFEI
26 AVP Communications & Public Affairs .... Mr. Tim LYNCH
44 Assoc VP University Advancement .... Ms. Michele LAHTI
19 Interim Police Chief .... Mr. Andy ROY
22 Campus Compliance Officer .... Ms. Julie A. JOHNSON
06 Registrar .... Ms. Lisa M. BERNARDO

*Humboldt State University (D)

1 Harpst Street, Arcata CA 95521-8222
County: Humboldt FICE Identification: 001149
Unit ID: 115755
Telephone: (707) 826-3011 Carnegie Class: Master's M
FAX Number: (707) 826-5555 Calendar System: Semester
URL: www.humboldt.edu
Established: 1913 Annual Undergrad Tuition & Fees (In-State): $7,190
Enrollment: 8,485 Coed
Affiliation or Control: State IRS Status: 501(c)3
Highest Offering: Master's
Program: Liberal Arts And General; Teacher Preparatory; Professional
Accreditation: WC, ART, ENG, IACBE, MUS, SW

02 President .... Dr. Lisa ROSSBACHER
100 Chief of Staff .... Ms. Denice HELWIG
05 Provost .... Vacant
20 Vice Prov Acad Pgms/Undergrad Stds .... Dr. Jena BURGES
32 VP Student Affairs & Enroll Mgmt .... Dr. Peg BLAKE
11 Vice Pres Administrative Affairs .... Ms. Joyce LOPES
30 Vice President of Advancement .... Mr. Craig WRUCK
15 Sr AVP Faculty Affairs and HR .... Dr. Colleen MULLERY
10 Assoc Vice Pres Business Services .... Ms. Carol LORENTZEN
84 Assoc VP Enrollment Management .... Mr. Vikash LAKHANI
88 Executive Director Development .... Ms. Kimberley PITTMAN-SCHULZ
106 Assoc VP eLearning & Ext Educ .... Dr. Alex HWU
26 Assoc VP for Mktg & Communications .... Mr. Frank WHITLATCH
18 Assoc Vice President Facilities .... Ms. Traci FERDOLAGE
88 Director University Budget Office .... Ms. Amber BLAKESLEE
88 Director of Academic Resources .... Mr. Volga KOVAL
06 Registrar .... Mr. Clint REBIK
07 Director of Admissions .... Mr. Steven LADWIG
08 Dean of Library .... Dr. Cyril OBERLANDER
44 Director of Annual Giving .... Mr. Travis WILLIAMS
19 Chief of University Police .... Chief Donn PETERSON
41 Athletic Director .... Mr. Dan COLLEN
39 Director of Housing .... Mr. Stephen ST. ONGE
13 Chief Information Officer .... Ms. Anna KIRCHER
36 Director Career Devel Center .... Ms. Kathy THORNHILL
28 Director Diversity & Inclusion .... Ms. Radha WEBLEY
46 Dean of Research & Sponsored Prgms .... Dr. Rhea WILLIAMSON
85 Director International Programs .... Ms. Rebecca BROWN
104 Study Abroad Advisor .... Ms. Penelope SHAW
35 Dean Student Affairs .... Ms. Randi DARNALL BURKE
37 Director Student Financial Aid .... Ms. Peggy METZGER
09 Dir Institutional Research & Plng .... Dr. Lisa CASTELLINO
96 Director of Contracts & Procurement .... Mr. Michael BURGHART
90 Director ITS User Support .... Ms. Jeanne WIELGUS
14 Director ITS Enterprise Data .... Ms. Bethany RIZZARDI
23 Dir Health/Counseling/Psych Svcs ... Ms. Mary Grooms VANCOTT
38 Director Counseling & Psy Svc .... Dr. Jennifer SANFORD
56 Dean of eLearning & Ext Education .... Mr. Carl F. HANSEN
79 Dean Col Arts/Humanities/Soc Sci .... Dr. Kenneth AYOOB
107 Dean College Professional Studies .... Dr. John LEE
81 Dean Col Natural Resources/Science .... Dr. Steven SMITH
21 Director Financial Services .... Mr. Brian MITCHELL
06 Registrar eLearning & Ext Educ .... Ms. Terri GEORGOPOULOS
105 Web Manager .... Mr. Matt HODGSON
04 Administrative Asst to President .... Ms. Mary HACKETT

*San Diego State University (E)

5500 Campanile Drive, San Diego CA 92182-8000
County: San Diego FICE Identification: 001151
Unit ID: 122409
Telephone: (619) 594-5200 Carnegie Class: RU/H
FAX Number: (619) 594-8894 Calendar System: Semester
URL: www.sdsu.edu
Established: 1897 Annual Undergrad Tuition & Fees (In-State): $6,976
Enrollment: 33,483 Coed
Affiliation or Control: State IRS Status: 501(c)3
Highest Offering: Doctorate
Program: Teacher Preparatory; Professional
Accreditation: WC, ART, AUD, BUS, BUSA, CAATE, #CIDA, CLPSY, CORE, DIETD, ENG, HSA, JOUR, MFCD, MIDWF, NURSE, PH, PTA, SP, SPAA, SW, TED, THEA

02 President .... Dr. Elliot HIRSHMAN
05 Provost and Senior Vice President ... Dr. Chukuka S. ENWEMEKA
10 Vice President/CFO Business Affairs .... Mr. Tom MCCARRON
32 Vice President for Student Affairs .... Mr. Eric RIVERA
30 VP University Relations/Development .. Ms. Mary Ruth CARLETON
46 VP for Research & Graduate Dean .... Dr. Stephen WELTER
20 Assoc Vice Pres Academic Affairs .... Dr. Kathryn LAMASTER
88 Assoc VP Real Estate Planning & Dev .... Mr. Robert SCHULZ
88 Assoc Vice Pres Faculty Affairs .... Dr. Joanna BROOKS
21 Assoc VP for Financial Operations .... Dr. Agnes WONG NICKERSON
15 Associate VP Administration .... Ms. Jessica RENTTO
85 Asst Vice President Intl Programs .... Dr. Alan R. SWEEDLER
26 Chief Communications Officer .... Mr. Greg BLOCK
35 Assoc VP for Student Affairs .... Mr. Tony CHUNG
35 Assoc VP for Student Affairs .... Dr. Vitaliano FIGUEROA
35 Assoc VP for Student Affairs .... Dr. Antionette MARBRAY
35 Assoc VP for Student Affairs .... Ms. Christy SAMARKOS
29 Assistant VP for Alumni Engagement .... Mr. James S. HERRICK
100 Chief of Staff President's Office .... Ms. Megan COLLINS
23 Dir Student Health Services .... Dr. Gregg LICHTENSTEIN
84 Assoc VP Enrollment Management .... Dr. Sandra COOK
38 Director Counseling/Psych Services .... Dr. Jennifer RIKARD
08 Dean Library/Information Access .... Dr. Gale ETSCHMAIER
44 Associate VP for Development .... Ms. Leslie SCHIBSTED
45 Exec Dir Research Foundation .... Mr. Bob E. WOLFSON
51 Dean of Extended Studies .... Dr. Joe SHAPIRO
58 Assoc Dean of Graduate Affairs .... Dr. Edmund BALSDON
49 Dean of Div Undergraduate Studies .... Dr. Geoffrey W. CHASE
79 Dean of College Arts & Letters .... Dr. Norma BOUCHARD
81 Dean of College of Sciences .... Dr. Stanley MALOY
54 Dean of College of Engineering .... Dr. Monte MEHRABADI
50 Dean College of Business Admin .... Dr. J. Dennis CRADIT
76 Dean of Col Health/Human Services .... Dr. Marilyn NEWHOFF
53 Dean of College of Education .... Dr. Joseph JOHNSON, JR.
12 Dean Imperial Valley Campus .... Dr. David PEARSON
57 Dean of Profess Studies/Fine Arts .... Dr. Joyce M. GATTAS
84 Assoc Exec Dir Enrollment Services .... Ms. Sandra TEMORES-VALDEZ
19 Director Public Safety .... Mr. Lamine SECKA
28 Chief Diversity Officer .... Dr. Aaron I. BRUCE
06 Registrar .... Ms. Rayanne WILLIAMS
07 Director of Admissions .... Ms. Sabrina CORTELL
36 Executive Director Career Services .... Dr. James TARBOX
39 Director Office of Housing Admin .... Dr. Eric HANSEN
40 CEO Aztec Shops .... Mrs. Donna TUSACK
41 Director Intercollegiate Athletics .... Mr. Jim STERK

85 Dir International Student Center .... Mr. Noah HANSEN
88 Director Environ Health & Safety .... Mr. Terry GEE
13 Assoc Vice President & CIO .... Mr. Christopher XANTHOS
09 Dir Univ Analytic Stds/Instnl Rsrch .... Ms. Jeanne STRONACH
31 Dir Government/Community Relations .... Ms. Megan COLLINS
96 Mgr Contract/Procurement Mgmt .... Vacant
21 University Controller .... Mr. Chris BRONSDON
18 Director of Facilities Services .... Mr. John FERRIS
88 Director of Communications ... Ms. Kimberly LAMKE-CALDERON
22 Dir Educ Opportunity Pgms .... Dr. Beverly WARREN
37 Dir Financial Aid & Scholarships .... Ms. Rose PASENELLI
88 Ombudsman .... Ms. Marit BESSESEN
88 Director of Residential Education .... Ms. Kara BAUER
88 Director Student Disability Svcs .... Dr. Pamela STARR
88 Director Technology Services .... Mr. Ananth PADMANABHAM

*San Francisco State University (A)

1600 Holloway Avenue, San Francisco CA 94132-1740
County: San Francisco FICE Identification: 001154
Unit ID: 122597
Telephone: (415) 338-1111 Carnegie Class: Master's L
FAX Number: (415) 338-2514 Calendar System: Semester
URL: www.sfsu.edu
Established: 1899 Annual Undergrad Tuition & Fees (In-State): $6,476
Enrollment: 29,465 Coed
Affiliation or Control: State IRS Status: 501(c)3
Highest Offering: Doctorate
Program: Liberal Arts And General
Accreditation: **WC**, AAFCS, ART, BUS, CACREP, CORE, DIETD, DIETI, ENG, JOUR, MT, MUS, NRPA, NURSE, PH, PTA, SP, SPAA, SW, TED, THEA

02 President .... Dr. Leslie E. WONG
05 Provost & VP Academic Affairs .... Dr. Sue V. ROSSER
30 Vice Pres University Advancement .... Mr. Robert J. NAVA
10 VP & CFO Administration and Finance ...... Mr. Ronald S. CORTEZ
32 VP Student Affairs/Enroll Mgmt .... Dr. Luoluo HONG
43 University Counsel .... Ms. Patricia B. BARTSCHER
20 Assoc VP Academic Resources .... Dr. John J. KIM
46 Interim AVP Research Sponsored Pgms .... Ms. Allison SANDERS
20 Assoc VP Academic Affairs Operation .... Dr. Brian BEATTY
85 Assoc VP International Education .... Dr. Yenbo WU
45 Assoc VP Capital Plan Design Const .... Mr. Simon Y. LAM
13 Interim AVP Info Tech Services .... Mr. Robert MOULTON
84 Senior AVP Enrollment Management .... Dr. Jo VOLKERT
18 Sr Assoc VP Physical Plng & Develop .... Mr. Thomas LOLLINI
21 Assoc VP Fiscal Affairs .... Ms. Agnes WONG-NICKERSON
15 Sr Assoc VP Human Resources .... Ms. Ann M. SHERMAN
35 Assoc VP Student Affairs .... Mr. Gene CHELBERG
88 AVP University Property Management .... Mr. Mark GOODRICH
100 Chief of Staff .... Mr. Shawn WHALEN
50 Dean College Business .... Ms. Linda OUBRE
53 Dean College Education .... Dr. Judith MUNTER
88 Dean College Ethnic Studies .... Dr. Kenneth P. MONTEIRO
51 Interim AVP/Dean of CELIA .... Dr. Angela JONES
69 Int Dean Col Health & Soc Science .... Dr. Alvin ALVAREZ
79 Int Dean Col Lib & Creative Arts .... Dr. Daniel BERNARDI
81 Dean College Science & Engineering .... Dr. Sheldon AXLER
88 Dean Faculty Affairs & Prof Dev .... Dr. Sacha BUNGE
58 Dean Graduate Studies .... Dr. Ann HALLUM
88 Dean Undergraduate Studies .... Dr. Jennifer SUMMIT
102 SF State President Foundation .... Mr. Robert J. NAVA
08 University Librarian .... Ms. Deborah C. MASTERS
24 Director Academic Technology .... Dr. Maggie BEERS
85 Director International Programs .... Ms. Hildy HEATH
30 Associate Vice Pres Development .... Ms. Anne HARRIS
86 Director Government & Community Rel ..... Ms. Lisbet SUNSHINE
26 AVP University Communications .... Ms. Ellen GRIFFIN
88 Dir Env/Health & Safety .... Mr. Lawrence WONG
39 Interim Director Resident Life .... Mr. Kevin J. KINNEY
37 Director Student Financial Aid .... Ms. Barbara HUBLER
88 Director Student Outreach Services .... Ms. Ree'shema THORNTON
07 Interim Dir Undergrad Admissions .... Mr. Edward CARRIGAN
21 Director Univ Budget Planning .... Mr. Andrew SOM
06 Registrar .... Ms. Renee MONTE
41 Director Athletics .... Mr. Charles GUTHRIE
38 Director Counseling & Psych Svcs .... Dr. Derethia DUVAL
88 Director Disability Pgms/Res Ctr .... Ms. Nicole BOHN
88 Dir Education Opportunity Program .... Mr. Oscar M. GARDEA
19 Int Chief Police/Dir Public Safety .... Chief Reginald PARSON
23 Medical Dir Student Health Svcs .... Dr. Alastair SMITH
35 Interim Dean of Students .... Dr. Mary Ann BEGLEY
96 Director Procurement Department .... Mr. Stephen C. SMITH
29 Director Alumni Relations .... Mr. Doug HUPKE
88 Budget Officer .... Vacant
36 Dir Student Involvement .... Vacant
44 Chief of Operations Advancement .... Ms. Venesia THOMPSON
88 Dir Internal Audit/Audit & Adv Svcs .... Ms. Helen STORRS
36 Interim Director Career Center .... Ms. Mariko HINGSTON
88 Exec Dir Budget Adm & Oper .... Mr. Jay ORENDORFF
88 Dir Environmental Health & Safety .... Mr. Marc MAJEWSKI
88 Sr Dir Facilities & Services Enter .... Mr. Charles MEYER

† Grants additional Doctoral degrees in cooperation with the UC-Berkeley and UC-San Francisco.

*San Jose State University (B)

One Washington Square, San Jose CA 95192-0001
County: Santa Clara FICE Identification: 001155
Unit ID: 122755
Telephone: (408) 924-1000 Carnegie Class: Master's L
FAX Number: (408) 924-1018 Calendar System: Semester
URL: www.sjsu.edu
Established: 1857 Annual Undergrad Tuition & Fees (In-State): $7,378
Enrollment: 32,713 Coed
Affiliation or Control: State IRS Status: 501(c)3
Highest Offering: Doctorate
Program: Liberal Arts And General; Teacher Preparatory; Professional; Business Emphasis
Accreditation: **WC**, ART, BUS, CAATE, CEA, CS, DANCE, DIETD, DIETI, ENG, IPSY, #JOUR, LIB, MT, MUS, NAIT, NRPA, NURSE, OT, PH, PLNG, SP, SPAA, SW, TED, THEA

02 Interim President .... Dr. Susan W. MARTIN
05 Provost/Vice Pres Acad Affairs .... Dr. Andrew FEINSTEIN
10 Vice Pres Administration & Finance .... Ms. Josee LAROCHELLE
32 Vice President Student Affairs .... Mr. Reginald BLAYLOCK
30 VP University Advancement .... Mr. Paul LANNING
13 Deputy CIO .... Ms. Terry VAHEY
45 Vice Provost Academic Budgets/Plng .... Ms. Marna GENES
14 Int Assoc VP Univ Computing/Telecom .... Mr. Don BAKER
09 Assoc VP Institutional Research .... Vacant
100 Interim Chief of Staff .... Ms. Stacy GLEIXNER
20 Associate Vice Pres Faculty Affairs .... Dr. Elna GREEN
58 Assoc VP Graduate Studies/Research .... Dr. Pamela STACKS
20 Assoc VP Undergrad Studies .... Dr. Dennis JAEHNE
21 VP Assoc Admin Systems/Finance .... Ms. Josee LAROCHELLE
18 Assoc VP for Facilities/Operations .... Mr. Chris BROWN
15 Associate VP Human Resources .... Ms. Beth PUGLIESE
26 Assoc VP Public Affairs .... Vacant
29 Assoc VP Devel/Exec Dir Alumni Rels .... Mr. Brian BATES
51 Assoc VP/Dean Intl/Extended Stds .... Ms. Karen HAWORTH
84 Int Assoc VP Enroll/Academic Svcs .... Ms. Sharon WILLEY
08 Dean of the University Library .... Dr. Ruth KIFER
28 Dir Equal Opportunity & Emp Rel .... Ms. Julie PAISANT
27 AVP Marketing Communications .... Mr. Barry SHILLER
06 Registrar .... Ms. Marian SOFISH
41 Director Intercollegiate Athletics .... Mr. Gene BLEYMAIER
96 Director Procurement Services .... Vacant
40 Director Spartan Bookstore .... Mr. Ryland METZINGER
19 Chief of Police .... Mr. Peter DECENA
36 Interim Director Career Center .... Ms. Susan ROCKWELL
38 Director Counseling Services .... Ms. Ellen LIN
37 Director Fin Aid/Schlarship Ofc .... Ms. Coleetta MCELROY
39 Dir University Housing Svcs .... Mr. Victor CULATTA
23 Dir Student Health Center .... Dr. Roger ELROD
49 Dean College of Applied Sci & Art .... Dr. Mary SCHUTTEN
50 Dean College of Business .... Dr. David STEELE
53 Dean College of Education .... Dr. Elaine CHIN
54 Dean College of Engineering .... Dr. Andrew HSU
79 Dean College of Humanities/Arts .... Dr. Lisa VOLLENDORF
81 Dean College of Science .... Dr. J. Michael PARRISH
83 Dean College Social Sciences .... Ms. Jan ENGLISH-LUECK

*Sonoma State University (C)

1801 E Cotati Avenue, Rohnert Park CA 94928-3609
County: Sonoma FICE Identification: 001156
Unit ID: 123572
Telephone: (707) 664-2880 Carnegie Class: Master's L
FAX Number: (707) 664-2505 Calendar System: Semester
URL: www.sonoma.edu
Established: 1960 Annual Undergrad Tuition & Fees (In-State): $7,330
Enrollment: 9,290 Coed
Affiliation or Control: State IRS Status: 501(c)3
Highest Offering: Master's
Program: Liberal Arts And General; Teacher Preparatory; Professional
Accreditation: **WC**, ART, BUS, CACREP, MUS, NUR, TED

02 President .... Dr. Ruben ARMIÑANA
05 Provost & Vice Pres Academic Affs .... Dr. Andrew ROGERSON
10 Vice Pres Administration & Finance .... Mr. Laurence FURUKAWA-SCHLERETH
26 Vice President University Affairs .... Mr. Dan CONDRON
30 Vice President Development .... Mr. Erik GREENY
32 VP of Student Affairs .... Mr. Matthew LOPEZ-PHILLIPS
20 Assoc VP for Faculty Affairs .... Dr. Melinda BARNARD
09 Director Institutional Research .... Mr. Sean JOHNSON
13 Assoc VP CIO/Information Technology .... Mr. Jason WENRICK
08 Dean of Library .... Ms. Karen SCHNEIDER
79 Dean School of Arts & Humanities .... Dr. Thaine STEARNS
50 Dean Sch of Business/Economic .... Dr. William SILVER
53 Dean School of Education .... Dr. Carlos AYALA
81 Dean School Science & Tech .... Dr. Lynn STAUFFER
83 Interim Dean of Social Sciences .... Dr. John D. WINGARD
56 Dean School of Extended Education .... Dr. Robert EYLER
38 Dir of Counseling/Psych Services .... Dr. Laura WILLIAMS
37 Director of Financial Aid .... Mrs. Susan GUTIERREZ
18 Assoc VP Facilities Services/CPDC .... Mr. Christopher DINNO
27 Assoc VP for Communications & Mktg .... Ms. Susan KASHACK
41 Director Athletics .... Mr. William J. FUSCO
19 Chief Police Services .... Mr. Nathan JOHNSON
21 Director Seawolf Services .... Ms. Elizabeth O'BRIEN
88 Assoc VP Entrepreneurial Srvcs .... Mr. Neil MARKLEY
06 Registrar .... Ms. Lisa NOTO
07 Interim Director of Admissions .... Ms. Natalie KALOGIANNIS
84 Director of Enrollment Management .... Mr. Gustavo FLORES
29 Dir Alumni Relations/Annual Giving .... Ms. Laurie OGG
28 Mg Dir Employee Rel/Comp Svcs .... Ms. Joyce SUZUKI
15 Sr Director Human Resources .... Ms. Tammy KENBER
96 Managing Dir for Purchasing .... Ms. Jenifer BARNETT

California University of Management and Sciences (D)

721 North Euclid Street, Anaheim CA 92801
County: Orange FICE Identification: 041331
Unit ID: 460075
Telephone: (714) 533-3946 Carnegie Class: Not Classified
FAX Number: (714) 533-7778 Calendar System: Quarter
URL: www.calums.edu
Established: 1998 Annual Undergrad Tuition & Fees: $13,000
Enrollment: 510 Coed
Affiliation or Control: Independent Non-Profit IRS Status: 501(c)3
Highest Offering: Master's
Program: 2-Year Principally Bachelor's Creditable; Professional; Business Emphasis
Accreditation: **ACICS**

01 President .... David PARK
03 Vice President .... Jason SHIN
10 Director of Finance .... Hong Jun AHN
05 Academic Dean .... Silvio VELOVICI
20 Program Director .... Woo Jin HAN
11 Director Administration .... Velina LIM
07 Admissions Officer .... Lisa LEE
32 Director of Student Services .... Andrew PRESS
08 Library Director .... Edwin FOLLICK
90 Academic Computing/Network Support .... Donghyun SUNG
88 Taekwondo Instructor & Dept Chair .... Andrew CHOI

California Western School of Law (E)

225 Cedar Street, San Diego CA 92101-3090
County: San Diego FICE Identification: 013103
Unit ID: 111391
Telephone: (619) 239-0391 Carnegie Class: Spec/Law
FAX Number: (619) 525-7092 Calendar System: Trimester
URL: www.cwsl.edu
Established: 1924 Annual Graduate Tuition & Fees: $47,260
Enrollment: 643 Coed
Affiliation or Control: Independent Non-Profit IRS Status: 501(c)3
Highest Offering: First Professional Degree; No Undergraduates
Program: Professional
Accreditation: **LAW**

01 President & Dean .... Dean Neils SCHAUMANN
05 Vice Dean Academic Affairs .... Prof. Barbara J. COX
46 Associate Dean Research & Fac Devel .... Prof. Joanna SAX
88 Assoc Dean of Exper Learning .... Prof. Linda MORTON
32 Asst Dean Students/Diversity Svcs .... Ms. Susan GARRETT FINSTER
36 Assistant Dean Career Services .... Ms. Courtney MIKLUSAK
88 Asst Dean Mission Development .... Mr. James M. COOPER
37 Exec Director Financial Aid .... Mr. William KAHLER
13 Exec Director Computer Services .... Ms. Mary Lou MITCHELL
18 Exec Dir Facilities Management .... Ms. Jolie L. CARTIER
88 Ex Dir Inst for Criminal Def Advoc .... Prof. Justin P. BROOKS
88 Dir Inst of Health Law Studies .... Prof. Susan A. CHANNICK
08 Assoc Dean Law Library/Info Res .... Prof. Phyllis C. MARION
10 Chief Financial Officer .... Ms. Pamela A. DUFFY
07 Assistant Dean Admissions .... Ms. Traci D. HOWARD
06 Registrar .... Ms. Sandra E. MOREAU
88 Director MCL/LLM Program .... Prof. Jacquelyn H. SLOTKIN
26 Chief Public Relations Officer .... Ms. Pamela HARDY
29 Director Alumni Relations .... Ms. Lori BOYLE
15 VP Human Resources .... Ms. Rikklyn S. UEDA
28 Director Diversity .... Ms. Marion E. CLOETE
21 Director Business Office .... Ms. Ruth GOULDING
04 Administrative Asst to President .... Ms. Marilyn L. JORDAN
43 Dir Legal Services/General Counsel .... Ms. Lisa JORDAN
44 Director Annual or Planned Giving .... Ms. Melissa WELLS
30 Director of Development .... Mr. Brian DALY

Cambridge Junior College (F)

990-A Klamath Lane, Yuba City CA 95993-8978
County: Sutter FICE Identification: 038743
Unit ID: 446093
Telephone: (530) 674-9199 Carnegie Class: Assoc/PrivFP
FAX Number: (530) 671-7319 Calendar System: Other
URL: www.cambridge.edu
Established: 2010 Annual Undergrad Tuition & Fees: $15,408
Enrollment: 159 Coed
Affiliation or Control: Proprietary IRS Status: Proprietary
Highest Offering: Associate Degree
Program: Occupational
Accreditation: **ACICS**

01 Director .... Ms. Sandy FOWLER

Carnegie Mellon University Silicon Valley Campus (G)

NASA Research Pk, Bld 23 MS 23-11,
Moffett Field CA 94035
Telephone: (650) 335-2810 Identification: 770149
Accreditation: **&M**

† Branch campus of Carnegie Mellon University, Pittsburgh, PA.

*Carrington College - Administrative Office (H)

7801 Folsom Boulevard, Suite 210,
Sacramento CA 95826-2620
County: Sacramento Identification: 666086
Telephone: (916) 388-2800 Carnegie Class: N/A
FAX Number: (916) 381-1609
URL: www.carrington.edu

01 President Carrington Colleges .... Dr. Jeff AKENS
05 VP Academic Affairs .... Dr. Danika BOWEN
11 Senior Director Operations .... Mr. Jim MURPHY
07 Vice President Enrollment Services .... Mr. Mitch CHARLES

*Carrington College - Sacramento (A)

8909 Folsom Boulevard, Sacramento CA 95826-9823

County: Sacramento FICE Identification: 009748
Unit ID: 125532
Telephone: (916) 361-1660 Carnegie Class: Assoc/PrivFP
FAX Number: (916) 361-6666 Calendar System: Other
URL: www.carrington.edu
Established: 1983 Annual Undergrad Tuition & Fees: $19,329
Enrollment: 1,385 Coed
Affiliation or Control: Proprietary IRS Status: Proprietary
Highest Offering: Associate Degree
Program: Occupational; 2-Year Principally Bachelor's Creditable
Accreditation: WJ, DH, MAC

02 Executive Director .... Ms. Sue SMITH
06 Registrar .... Ms. Ryanne GREEN
07 Director Enrollment Services .... Mr. Vance KLINKE
05 Dean of Academic Affairs .... Mr. James CRAIG

*Carrington College - Citrus Heights (B)

7301 Greenback Lane, Suite A, Citrus Heights CA 95621
Telephone: (916) 722-8200 Identification: 667042
Accreditation: &WJ, MAC, SURGT

† Regional accreditation is carried under the parent institution in Sacramento, CA.

*Carrington College - Pleasant Hill (C)

380 Civic Drive, Suite 300, Pleasant Hill CA 94523-1984
Telephone: (925) 609-6650 Identification: 666043
Accreditation: &WJ, COARC, MAC, PTAA

† Regional accreditation is carried under the parent institution in Sacramento, CA.

*Carrington College - Pomona (D)

901 Corporate Center Drive, #300, Pomona CA 91768
Telephone: (909) 868-5800 Identification: 770506
Accreditation: &WJ

† Regional accreditation is carried under the parent institution in Sacramento, CA.

*Carrington College - San Jose (E)

6201 San Ignacio Avenue, San Jose CA 95119-1325
Telephone: (408) 960-0162 Identification: 666042
Accreditation: &WJ, DH, MAC, SURGT

† Regional accreditation is carried under the parent institution in Sacramento, CA.

*Carrington College - San Leandro (F)

15555 E 14th Street, Suite 500,
San Leandro CA 94578-9930
Telephone: (510) 276-3888 Identification: 666751
Accreditation: &WJ, MAC

† Regional accreditation is carried under the parent institution in Sacramento, CA.

*Carrington College - Stockton (G)

1313 W Robinhood Drive, Suite B,
Stockton CA 95207-5509
Telephone: (209) 956-1240 Identification: 666140
Accreditation: &WJ, MAC

† Regional accreditation is carried under the parent institution in Sacramento, CA.

Casa Loma College-Anaheim (H)

2641 W LaPalma Avenue, Anaheim CA 92801
Telephone: (818) 785-2726 Identification: 770519
Accreditation: ABHES

† Branch campus of Casa Loma College-Van Nuys, Van Nuys, CA.

Casa Loma College-Van Nuys (I)

6725 Kester Avenue, Van Nuys CA 91405

County: Los Angeles FICE Identification: 006731
Unit ID: 111638
Telephone: (818) 785-2726 Carnegie Class: Assoc/PrivNFP
FAX Number: (818) 785-2191 Calendar System: Other
URL: www.casalomacollege.edu
Established: 1966 Annual Undergrad Tuition & Fees: $31,125
Enrollment: 780 Coed
Affiliation or Control: Independent Non-Profit IRS Status: 501(c)3
Highest Offering: Associate Degree
Program: 2-Year Principally Bachelor's Creditable
Accreditation: ABHES, PTAA

01 Campus Director/Controller .... Ms. Veronica PANTOJA
05 Dean of Education .... Dr. Stephanie SHELBURNE
66 Director of Nursing .... Ms. Brenda BEALL
06 Registrar .... Ms. Vicki KIM
07 Director of Admissions .... Ms. Deanna BERNAL
86 Director of Compliance .... Ms. Sharon DUGAN
37 Director Studend Financial Aid .... Ms. Rosleen AURORA
08 Head Librarian .... Ms. Deborah FARBER
106 Dir Online Education/E-learning .... Ms. Stephanie SHELBURNE
13 Chief Info Technology Officer .... Mr. James P. DUGAN
18 Chief Facilities/Physical Plant .... Ms. Veronica PANTOJA
36 Director Student Placement .... Ms. Sharon M. DUGAN

CBD College (J)

3699 Wilshire Boulevard, 4th Floor,
Los Angeles CA 90010

County: Los Angeles FICE Identification: 032503
Unit ID: 439367
Telephone: (213) 427-2200 Carnegie Class: Assoc/PrivNFP
FAX Number: (213) 427-9278 Calendar System: Other
URL: www.cbd.edu
Established: 1982 Annual Undergrad Tuition & Fees: $23,700
Enrollment: 411 Coed
Affiliation or Control: Independent Non-Profit IRS Status: 501(c)3
Highest Offering: Associate Degree
Program: Occupational
Accreditation: ABHES, @PTAA, SURTEC

01 President .... Mr. Alan HESHEL

Cedars-Sinai Medical Center Graduate Program in Biomedical Sciences and Translational Medicine (K)

8700 Beverly Boulevard, Los Angeles CA 90048

County: Los Angeles Identification: 667071
Telephone: (310) 423-6252 Carnegie Class: Not Classified
FAX Number: (310) 423-0120 Calendar System: Trimester
URL: www.cedars-sinai.edu
Established: Annual Graduate Tuition & Fees: N/A
Enrollment: 10 Coed
Affiliation or Control: Independent Non-Profit IRS Status: 501(c)3
Highest Offering: Doctorate; No Undergraduates
Program: Professional
Accreditation: WC

01 President .... Mr. Thomas PRISELAC
05 Sr Vice President Academic Affairs .... Dr. Shlomo MELMED

Cerritos College (L)

11110 Alondra Boulevard, Norwalk CA 90650-6298

County: Los Angeles FICE Identification: 001161
Unit ID: 111887
Telephone: (562) 860-2451 Carnegie Class: Assoc/Pub-S-SC
FAX Number: (562) 467-5005 Calendar System: Semester
URL: www.cerritos.edu
Established: 1955 Annual Undergrad Tuition & Fees (In-District): $1,162
Enrollment: 25,212 Coed
Affiliation or Control: State/Local IRS Status: 501(c)3
Highest Offering: Associate Degree
Program: Occupational; 2-Year Principally Bachelor's Creditable
Accreditation: WJ, ADNUR, DA, DH, PTAA

01 President .... Dr. Jose L. FIERRO
05 Vice President Academic Affairs .... Dr. JoAnna SCHILLING
10 Vice President Business Services .... Dr. David EL FATTAL
32 Vice President Student Services .... Dr. Stephen JOHNSON
15 Vice President Human Resources .... Dr. Mary Anne GULARTE
20 Dean of Academic Affairs .... Mr. Edmund (Rick) MIRANDA
07 Dean of Admissions/Records & Svcs ..... Ms. Stephanie MURGUIA
38 Dean of Counseling Services .... Dr. Renee DeLong CHOMIAK
86 Dir College/Govt Rels & Pub Affs .... Ms. Miya WALKER
88 Dean Disabled Student Pgms & Svcs .... Dr. Lucinda ABORN
88 Dean of Student Support Services .... Ms. Kim WESTBY
50 Instr Dean Business/Humanities/SS .... Ms. Rachel MASON
57 Instr Dean Fine Arts/Communications .... Dr. Gary PRITCHARD
76 Instr Dean Health Occupations .... Ms. Sandra MARKS
83 Dean Academic Success .... Ms. Shawna BASKETTE
49 Instr Dean Liberal Arts .... Mr. David FABISH
68 Instr Dean Health/PE/Dance/Athletic .... Dr. Daniel SMITH
54 Instr Dean Science/Engineering/Math ...... Dr. Connie BOARDMAN
73 Instr Dean Technology .... Dr. Yannick REAL
14 Acting Dir Information Technology .... Mr. Patrick O'DONNELL
21 Director of Fiscal Services .... Mr. Noorali DELAWALLA
35 Dean of Student Services .... Dr. Gilbert J. CONTRERAS
36 Dir of Career/Assessment Services .... Ms. Theresa LOPEZ
18 Director Physical Plant & Const Svc .... Mr. David C. MOORE
102 Executive Director Foundation .... Mr. Steven RICHARDSON
88 Director Community Advancement .... Ms. Bellegran GOMEZ
96 Dir Purchasing/Contract Admin .... Mr. Mark LOGAN
16 Director Human Resources/Risk Mgmt .... Dr. Adriana FLORES-CHURCH
105 Web Administrator .... Mr. Ty BOWMAN
19 Acting Chief of Campus Police .... Mr. Thomas GALLIVAN
28 Assoc Dn Adult Educ/Diversity Pgms .... Ms. Graciela VASQUEZ
31 Director Community Education .... Dr. Patricia ROBBINS SMITH
88 Director Child Development Center .... Ms. Debra WARD

88 Operations Manager .... Mr. Thomas RICHEY
88 Payroll Manager .... Ms. Deanna HART
88 Budget Manager .... Mr. Conrad SELORIO
13 Acting Mgr Information Technology .... Mr. Vince ORTON
23 Assoc Dean Student Health Wellness .... Dr. Hillary MENNELLA
88 Director of Student Program Svcs .... Ms. Norma RODRIGUEZ
09 Dir Inst Effec Research & Planning .... Dr. Kristi BLACKBURN
88 Director Adv Trans Tech Projects .... Ms. Jannet MALIG
22 Director Emp/Diversity/Compliance .... Vacant
88 EOPS Assistant Director .... Ms. Yvette TAFOYA
19 Dir Educational Partnerships .... Ms. Sue PARSONS
88 Accounting Manager .... Ms. Kathy BURGOS
88 Facilities Manager .... Mr. Shannon KAVENEY

*Chabot-Las Positas Community College District (M)

7600 Dublin Blvd., 3rd Flr., Dublin CA 94568

County: Alameda Identification: 666925
Telephone: (925) 485-5208 Carnegie Class: N/A
FAX Number: (925) 485-5256
URL: www.clpccd.org

01 Chancellor .... Dr. Jannett N. JACKSON
10 Vice Chanc Business Svcs .... Mr. Lorenzo LEGASPI
05 Vice Chanc Educational Svcs .... Vacant
15 Vice Chanc Human Resource Svcs .... Mr. Wyman FONG

*Chabot College (N)

25555 Hesperian Boulevard, Hayward CA 94545-2400

County: Alameda FICE Identification: 001162
Unit ID: 111920
Telephone: (510) 723-6600 Carnegie Class: Assoc/Pub-S-MC
FAX Number: (510) 782-9315 Calendar System: Semester
URL: www.chabotcollege.edu
Established: 1961 Annual Undergrad Tuition & Fees (In-District): $1,414
Enrollment: 13,047 Coed
Affiliation or Control: State/Local IRS Status: 501(c)3
Highest Offering: Associate Degree
Program: Occupational; 2-Year Principally Bachelor's Creditable
Accreditation: WJ, DH, #MAC

02 President .... Dr. Susan S. SPERLING
05 VP Academic Services .... Ms. Stacy THOMPSON
32 Vice President Student Services .... Dr. Matthew KRITSCHER
11 Vice Pres Administrative Services .... Ms. Connie WILLIS
04 Exec Asst to the College President .... Ms. Kirti REDDY
08 Librarian .... Ms. Kim MORRISON
38 Dean Counseling/Guidance .... Dr. Matt KRITSCHER
41 Dean Health/PE/Athletics .... Mr. Jeff DROUIN
07 Dir Admissions & Records/Registrar .... Mrs. Paulette LINO
37 Director of Financial Aid .... Ms. Kathryn LINZMEYER
19 Director Safety & Security .... Sgt. Bobbie KOLLER
09 Director of Institutional Research .... Dr. Carolyn ARNOLD
15 Director Human Resources .... Dr. Wyman FONG
18 Chief Facilities/Physical Plant .... Mr. Tim NELSON
30 Exec Dir Devel/Foundation .... Dr. Maria OCHOA
35 Dir Student Life/Student Services .... Mr. Arnold PAGUIO
96 Manager Purchasing/Warehouse Svcs .... Ms. Victoria LAMICA

*Las Positas College (O)

3000 Campus Hill Drive, Livermore CA 94551-7623

County: Alameda FICE Identification: 030357
Unit ID: 366401
Telephone: (925) 424-1000 Carnegie Class: Assoc/Pub-S-MC
FAX Number: (925) 443-0742 Calendar System: Semester
URL: www.laspositascollege.edu
Established: 1975 Annual Undergrad Tuition & Fees (In-District): $1,138
Enrollment: 8,835 Coed
Affiliation or Control: State/Local IRS Status: 501(c)3
Highest Offering: Associate Degree
Program: Occupational; 2-Year Principally Bachelor's Creditable; Business Emphasis
Accreditation: WJ

02 President .... Dr. Barry A. RUSSELL
05 Vice President Academic Svcs .... Roanna BENNIE
32 Vice President Student Svcs .... Ms. Diana RODRIGUEZ
11 Vice Pres Administrative Services .... Mr. Jeffrey KINGSTON
04 Exec Assistant to the President .... Ms. Kelly ABAD
35 Dean of Student Services .... Vacant
49 Dean Arts/Letters/Social Sciences .... Dr. Donald MILLER
81 Dean Sci/Tech/Engr/Math/Pub Safety .... Dr. Lisa EVERETT
83 Dean Behav Sci/Business/Athletics .... Ms. Dyan MILLER
07 Dean of Admissions/Records .... Ms. Sylvia RODRIGUEZ
45 Director of Research & Planning .... Mr. Rajinder SAMRA
37 Financial Aid/Veterans Assistance .... Ms. Andi SCHREIBMAN
19 Campus Safety Supervisor .... Mr. Sean PRATHER
26 Exec Dir Public Info & Marketing .... Vacant
08 Head Librarian .... Dr. Tina INZERILLA
102 LPC Foundation CEO .... Dr. Ted KAYE
41 Athletic Director .... Ms. Dyan MILLER
21 Associate Business Officer .... Ms. Natasha LANG
18 Project Planner/Manager Facilities .... Mr. Jeffrey KINGSTON
06 Registrar .... Ms. Sylvia RODRIGUEZ
88 Project Manager CTE .... Ms. Vicki SHIPMAN
88 Director Child Development Center .... Ms. Corinna CALICA

Chaffey College (A)

5885 Haven Avenue, Rancho Cucamonga CA 91737-3002
County: San Bernardino FICE Identification: 001163
Unit ID: 111939
Telephone: (909) 652-6000 Carnegie Class: Assoc/Pub-S-MC
FAX Number: (909) 652-6006 Calendar System: Semester
URL: www.chaffey.edu
Established: 1883 Annual Undergrad Tuition & Fees (In-District): $1,153
Enrollment: 21,721 Coed
Affiliation or Control: State/Local IRS Status: 501(c)3
Highest Offering: Associate Degree
Program: Occupational; 2-Year Principally Bachelor's Creditable
Accreditation: WJ, ADNUR, DA, RAD

01 Superintendent/President ... Dr. Henry D. SHANNON
11 Vice Pres Administrative Affairs ... Ms. Melanie SIDDIQI
10 Assoc Supt Bus Svcs/Econ Dev ... Ms. Lisa BAILEY
05 Assoc Supt Instruction/Inst Effect ... Dr. Sherrie L. GUERRERO
09 Dean Inst Research/Research Dev ... Mr. Jim FILLPOT
29 Director Alumni Relations ... Ms. Janeth RODRIGUEZ
85 Director Transfer Center/Intl Pgms ... Vacant
32 Director Student Activities ... Vacant
07 Admin Admissions/Records ... Ms. Kathy LUCERO
21 Exec Director Business Services ... Ms. Kim ERICKSON
88 Director Technical Services ... Mr. Michael FINK
88 Director Childrens Center ... Ms. Birgit MONKS
23 Director Student Health Services ... Ms. Katherine PEEK
37 Director Financial Aid ... Ms. Patricia BOPKO
109 Director Auxiliary Services ... Vacant
26 Director Marketing/Public Relations ... Vacant
21 Exec Dir Budgeting & Fiscal Svc ... Ms. Anita UNDERCOFFER
88 Director Museum Gallery ... Ms. Rebecca TRAWICK
18 Manager Facilities Development ... Ms. Sarah RILEY
12 Dean Chino Campus/Int Dn Font Camp ... Dr. Teresa HULL
88 Dean Visual Performing Arts ... Dr. Jason CHEVALIER
50 Dean Bus & Applied Tech ... Ms. Joy HAERENS
81 Dean Mathematics & Science ... Mr. Theodore YOUNGLOVE
83 Dean Social & Behav Sci & PE ... Dr. Corene SCHWARTZ
88 Dean Language Arts & Health Science ... Mr. Anthony DISALVO
38 Dean Counseling & Matricula ... Ms. Amy NEVAREZ
12 Int Dean Fontana Campus ... Ms. Leona FISHER
08 Dean Instruct Support/Library Svcs ... Ms. Laura HOPE
04 Exec Assistant Supt/Pres Office ... Ms. Kathy NAPOLI
84 Dean Discipline & Enroll Mgmt ... Mr. Len CROW
41 Interim Director Athletics ... Mr. Jeff KLEIN
86 Manager Government Relations ... Ms. Lorena CORONA

Chapman University (B)

One University Drive, Orange CA 92866-1099
County: Orange FICE Identification: 001164
Unit ID: 111948
Telephone: (714) 997-6815 Carnegie Class: Master's L
FAX Number: (714) 997-6713 Calendar System: 4/1/4
URL: www.chapman.edu
Established: 1861 Annual Undergrad Tuition & Fees: $47,260
Enrollment: 8,132 Coed
Affiliation or Control: Christian Church (Disciples Of Christ)
IRS Status: 501(c)3
Highest Offering: Doctorate
Program: Liberal Arts And General; Teacher Preparatory; Professional
Accreditation: WC, BUS, CAATE, DANCE, LAW, MFCD, MUS, @PHAR, PTA, SP, TEAC, THEA

01 President ... Dr. James L. DOTI
05 Chancellor ... Dr. Daniele C. STRUPPA
03 Executive Vice President & COO ... Mr. Harold W. HEWITT, JR.
30 Exec VP University Advancement ... Ms. Sheryl BOURGEOIS
32 Vice Chancellor & Dean of Students ... Dr. Jerry PRICE
84 Vice Chancellor/Dean Enrollment Mgt ... Mr. Michael PELLY
20 Vice Chancellor for Academic Admin ... Dr. Glenn PFEIFFER
09 Vice Chan Inst Eff & Fac Affairs ... Mr. Joseph SLOWENSKY
49 Dean Wilkinson Col Hum/Soc Sci ... Dr. Patrick FUERY
61 Dean School of Law ... Dr. Tom CAMPBELL
50 Dean School Business/Economics ... Mr. Reginald GILYARD
67 Dean School of Pharmacy ... Dr. Ronald JORDAN
53 Dean College of Educational Studies ... Dr. Margaret GROGAN
88 Dean College of Film & Media Arts ... Mr. Robert BASSETT
88 Dean College of Performing Arts ... Guilio ONGARO
81 Dean Col of Science/Tech ... Dr. Janeen HILL
88 Dean/Artistic Dir Center for Arts ... Dr. William HALL
88 Director Ctr for Global Education ... Dr. James COYLE
97 Vice Chancellor Undergrad Education ... Nina LENOIR
45 Vice President Campus Planning ... Mr. Kris OLSEN
15 Vice President of Human Resources ... Ms. Becky CAMPOS
43 Assoc Vice Pres of Legal Affairs ... Ms. Janine DUMONTELLE
10 Assoc Vice President & Controller ... Mr. Behzad BINESH
07 Dir UG Admission ... Ms. Marcela MEJIA MARTINEZ
88 Assistant Chancellor ... Ms. Iris GERBASI
18 Assoc VP Facilities ... Mr. Rick TURNER
26 Director Public Relations ... Ms. Mary PLATT
08 Dean of Library ... Ms. Charlene BALDWIN
29 Asst VP Strategic Engagement/Dev ... Ms. Delite TRAVIS
13 Chief Information Officer ... Ms. Helen NORRIS
09 Director of Institutional Research ... Dr. Marisol ARREDONDO
06 Registrar ... Ms. Jan MCCUEN
46 Director Sponsored Research ... Ms. Yolanda UZZELL
37 Director Financial Aid ... Mr. Jack MILLIS
85 Director Intl Student Services ... Ms. Susan SAMS
19 Chief of Public Safety ... Mr. Randy BURBA
39 Assoc Dean/Director Residence Life ... Ms. Deborah MILLER
41 Athletic Director ... Mr. Terry BOESEL
42 Dean of the Chapel ... Dr. Gail STEARNS
04 Associate to the President ... Ms. Ann CAMERON
88 Exec Assistant to the Chancellor ... Ms. Christina ZERMENO
23 Director Student Health Services ... Ms. Jacqueline DEATS
35 Director of Student Engagement ... Mr. Chris HUTCHISON
36 Asst Dir Career Education ... Ms. Sally JAFARI
38 Assoc Dean/Dir Student Psych Couns ... Ms. Jeannie WALKER
96 Purchasing Coordinator ... Ms. Wendy SEIRUP
04 Assistant to the President ... Ms. Dorothy FAROL
58 Vice Chancellor for Graduate Educ ... Dr. Richard REDDING
102 Dir Corporate/Foundation Relations ... Mr. Mike STRINGER
44 Dir Legacy Planning ... Mr. David MOORE
90 Dir Academic Tech/Digital Media ... Dr. Mary LITCH

Charles R. Drew University of Medicine & Science (C)

1731 E 120th Street, Los Angeles CA 90059-3025
County: Los Angeles FICE Identification: 010365
Unit ID: 111966
Telephone: (323) 563-4800 Carnegie Class: Spec/Health
FAX Number: (323) 563-5987 Calendar System: Semester
URL: www.cdrewu.edu
Established: 1966 Annual Undergrad Tuition & Fees: $16,150
Enrollment: 482 Coed
Affiliation or Control: Independent Non-Profit IRS Status: 501(c)3
Highest Offering: Master's
Program: Occupational; 2-Year Principally Bachelor's Creditable; Professional
Accreditation: WC, NURSE, PH, RAD

01 President & CEO ... Dr. David M. CARLISLE
05 EVP Academic Affairs/Provost ... Dr. Steve O. MICHAEL
100 Chief of Staff ... Ms. Jackie BROWN
45 VP Research & Health Affairs ... Dr. Jadutt VADGAMA
30 VP for Strategic Advancement ... Ms. Angela L. MINNIEFIELD
15 Chief Human Resources Officer ... Dr. Toni C. ELBOUSHI
11 University Auditor ... Mr. Nathaniel CLARK
63 Interim Dean College of Medicine ... Dr. Daphne CALMES
66 Dean School of Nursing ... Dr. Sheldon FIELDS
76 Int Dean Col of Science & Health ... Dr. Ronald EDELSTEIN
20 Asst Provost Faculty Affairs ... Dr. William SHAY
32 Asst Provost Student Services ... Dr. Rita GLORIA SAWYER
58 Interim Assoc Dean GME ... Dr. Jimmy HARA
20 Sr Assoc Dean Academic Affairs ... Dr. Ronald A. EDELSTEIN
09 Director Inst Research & Effectiv ... Mr. Richard W. LINDSTROM
37 Interim Chief Financial Officer ... Mr. John GERAGHTY
13 Chief Technology Officer ... Mr. Anthony WILLIAMS
08 Director Health Sciences Library ... Ms. Darlene PARKER-KELLY
06 Registrar ... Ms. Stephanie SANTORO
07 Director of Admissions ... Mr. Amin MAGHSOODI

Charter College-Canyon Country (D)

19034 Soledad Canyon Road, Santa Clarita CA 91351
County: Los Angeles FICE Identification: 032783
Unit ID: 434317
Telephone: (661) 252-1864 Carnegie Class: Not Classified
FAX Number: (661) 252-2153 Calendar System: Other
URL: chartercollege.edu
Established: 1998 Annual Undergrad Tuition & Fees: $18,313
Enrollment: 1,062 Coed
Affiliation or Control: Proprietary IRS Status: Proprietary
Highest Offering: Associate Degree
Program: Occupational
Accreditation: ACICS

01 Campus Manager ... Ms. Jamila KINDLE

Charter College-Lancaster Campus (E)

43141 Business Center Pkwy, Ste 102, Lancaster CA 93535
Telephone: (661) 341-3500 Identification: 770846
Accreditation: ACICS

† Branch campus of Charter College-Canyon Country, Santa Clarita, CA.

Charter College-Oxnard (F)

2000 Outlet Center Drive, Suite 150, Oxnard CA 93036
Telephone: (805) 973-1240 Identification: 666675
Accreditation: ACICS

† Branch campus of Charter College, Anchorage, AK.

Chicago School of Professional Psychology Los Angeles Campus (G)

617 West 7th Street, Los Angeles CA 90017
County: Los Angeles FICE Identification: 021553
Unit ID: 455664
Telephone: (213) 615-2700 Carnegie Class: Not Classified
FAX Number: (213) 615-7274 Calendar System: Semester
URL: www.the chicagoschool.edu
Established: 2008 Annual Graduate Tuition & Fees: N/A
Enrollment: 1,877 Coed
Affiliation or Control: Independent Non-Profit IRS Status: 501(c)3
Highest Offering: Doctorate; No Undergraduates
Program: Professional
Accreditation: WC

01 National President ... Dr. Michele NEALON-WOODS
05 Provost/Chief Academic Officer ... Dr. Joseph STEVENSON
10 Chief Financal Officer ... Mr. Darryl LYCETT
32 Vice Pres Student Affairs ... Ms. Jennifer STRIPE PORTILLO
15 Vice Pres Human Resources ... Dr. David IWANE
106 Dean Online Programs ... Dr. Cindy LARSON
07 Assoc Vice Pres Admissions ... Ms. Katie CURRAN
30 Chief Development Officer ... Dr. Orlando TAYLOR
27 National Director of Communications ... Ms. Elinor GILBERT

Chicago School of Professional Psychology-Irvine Campus (H)

4199 Campus Drive, Irvine CA 92612
Telephone: (949) 769-7700 Identification: 770492
Accreditation: &WC

† Branch campus of Chicago School of Professional Psychology Los Angeles Campus, Los Angeles, CA.

China Evangelical Seminary North America (I)

1520 W. Cameron Avenue Ste 275, West Covina CA 91790
County: Los Angeles Identification: 667256
Telephone: (626) 917-9482 Carnegie Class: Not Classified
FAX Number: (626) 851-1371 Calendar System: Semester
URL: www.cesnac.org
Established: 2007 Annual Graduate Tuition & Fees: $10,000
Enrollment: 60 Coed
Affiliation or Control: Non-denominational IRS Status: 501(c)3
Highest Offering: Doctorate; No Undergraduates
Program: Religious Emphasis
Accreditation: THEOL

01 President ... Katheryn LEUNG
05 Academic Dean ... Gee LOWE

Christian Witness Theological Seminary (J)

1975 Concourse Drive, San Jose CA 95131
County: Santa Clara Identification: 667255
Telephone: (408) 433-2280 Carnegie Class: Not Classified
FAX Number: (408) 433-9855 Calendar System: Other
URL: www.cwts.edu
Established: 1978 Annual Graduate Tuition & Fees: $7,040
Enrollment: 78 Coed
Affiliation or Control: Interdenominational IRS Status: 501(c)3
Highest Offering: Doctorate; No Undergraduates
Program: Religious Emphasis
Accreditation: @THEOL

01 President ... Rev. Jeffrey LU

Church Divinity School of the Pacific (K)

2451 Ridge Road, Berkeley CA 94709-1217
County: Alameda FICE Identification: 001165
Unit ID: 112127
Telephone: (510) 204-0700 Carnegie Class: Spec/Faith
FAX Number: (510) 644-0712 Calendar System: Semester
URL: www.cdsp.edu
Established: 1893 Annual Graduate Tuition & Fees: $16,800
Enrollment: 71 Coed
Affiliation or Control: Protestant Episcopal IRS Status: 501(c)3
Highest Offering: Doctorate; No Undergraduates
Program: Professional; Religious Emphasis
Accreditation: THEOL

01 President & Dean ... Dr. W. Mark RICHARDSON
05 Dean Academic Affairs ... Dr. Ruth MEYERS
10 Director of Operations & Personnel ... Mr. Bob RYBICKI
30 Dir of Institutional Advancement ... Mr. Patrick DELAHUNT
32 Dean of Students ... Rev. L. Ann HALLISEY
06 Registrar ... Ms. Elly RHEE
07 Director of Recruitment/Admissions ... Rev. Andrew HYBL
88 Program Manager ... Ms. Alissa FENCSIK
37 Director of Financial Aid ... Ms. Elly RHEE
04 Administrative Asst to President ... Ms. Elsbeth WETHERILL
29 Director Alumni Relations ... Ms. Laurel JOHNSTON

Citrus College (L)

1000 W Foothill Boulevard, Glendora CA 91741-1899
County: Los Angeles FICE Identification: 001166
Unit ID: 112172
Telephone: (626) 963-0323 Carnegie Class: Assoc/Pub-S-SC
FAX Number: (626) 914-8618 Calendar System: Semester
URL: www.citruscollege.edu
Established: 1915 Annual Undergrad Tuition & Fees (In-District): $1,174
Enrollment: 13,101 Coed
Affiliation or Control: State/Local IRS Status: 501(c)3
Highest Offering: Associate Degree
Program: Occupational; 2-Year Principally Bachelor's Creditable; Business Emphasis

Accreditation: WJ, DA

01 Superintendent/President ... Dr. Geraldine M. PERRI
05 Vice President Academic Affairs ... Dr. Arvid SPOR
32 Vice President Student Services ... Vacant
10 Vice Pres Finance/Admin Services ... Ms. Claudette E. DAIN
07 Dean Admissions & Records ... Dr. Gerald SEQUEIRA
51 Dean Career/Technical/Continuing Ed ... Dr. James LANCASTER
38 Dean of Counseling ... Dr. Lucinda OVER
15 Director Human Resources ... Dr. Robert L. SAMMIS
102 Director Foundation ... Ms. Christina M. GARCIA
35 Executive Dean ... Dr. Martha MCDONALD
18 Director Facilities & Construction ... Mr. Fred DIAMOND
09 Director of Institutional Research ... Dr. Lan HAO
06 Registrar ... Ms. Kristina HANNON
37 Director Financial Aid ... Ms. Carol THOMAS
96 Director of Purchasing ... Mr. Robert IVERSON
21 Director of Fiscal Services ... Ms. Rosalinda BUCHWALD
26 Director of Communication ... Ms. Paula GREEN
23 Director of Health Sciences ... Vacant
28 Staff Diversity Officer ... Mrs. Brenda FINK
13 Chief Information Services Officer ... Ms. Linda WELZ
19 Campus Security Supervisor ... Mr. Benjamin MACIAS
83 Dean Social/Behavioral Sciences/DE ... Dr. Dana HESTER
41 Dean of Kinesiology & Athletics ... Ms. Jody WISE
79 Dean of Lang Arts & Enrollment Mgt ... Dr. Samuel LEE
65 Dean Library/Natural & Physical Sci ... Dr. Eric RABITOY
57 Dean of Fine & Performing Arts ... Mr. Robert SLACK
81 Dean Math/Business/Health Sciences ... Mr. James MCCLAIN
88 Dir EOPS CARE CalWORKS ... Ms. Sarah GONZALES-TAPIA
88 Project Dir RACE to STEM ... Ms. Marianne SMITH

City College of San Francisco (A)

33 Gough Street, San Francisco CA 94103-1292

County: San Francisco FICE Identification: 001167
Unit ID: 112190
Telephone: (415) 239-3000 Carnegie Class: Assoc/Pub-U-MC
FAX Number: (415) 239-3919 Calendar System: Semester
URL: www.ccsf.edu
Established: 1935 Annual Undergrad Tuition & Fees (In-District): $720
Enrollment: 25,575 Coed
Affiliation or Control: State/Local IRS Status: 501(c)3
Highest Offering: Associate Degree
Program: Occupational; 2-Year Principally Bachelor's Creditable
Accreditation: WJ, ACFEI, CAHIIM, DA, EMT, MAC, RAD, RTT

01 Chancellor ... Ms. Susan E. LAMB
10 Vice Chanc Finance/Administration ... Dr. Mark ZACOVIC
05 Vice Chancellor Academic Affairs ... Vacant
46 Dean of Institutional Effectiveness ... Dr. Pam MERY
12 Dean Civic Center Campus ... Mr. Carl JEW
12 Dean Southeast Campus ... Mr. Torrance BYNUM
12 Dean Mission Campus ... Mr. Jorge BELL
12 Dean Downtown/Business School ... Dr. Geisce LY
26 Dir of Communications/Marketing ... Vacant
32 Vice President Student Services ... Mr. Samuel SANTOS
37 Dean Financial Aid & Scholarships ... Ms. Elizabeth CORIA
07 Dean Admissions & Records ... Ms. Marylou LEYBA
20 Assoc Vice Chanc of Instruction ... Mr. Tom BOEGEL
103 Assoc Vice Chanc Workforce Dev ... Vacant
15 Assoc Vice Chanc Human Resources ... Ms. Clara STARR
38 Dean/Dir Counseling/Student Support ... Vacant
108 Assoc Dean Matriculation/Assessment ... Ms. Margaret SANCHEZ
85 Dean Chinatown/Intl Educ/ESL ... Dr. Minh-Hoa TA
88 Dean School of Visual & Performing ... Vacant
83 Dean Behavioral/Social Sciences ... Mr. Raymond GAMBA
81 Dean Science & Math ... Mr. David YEE
68 Dean J Adams Campus/Sch Hlth Educ ... Mr. Terry HALL
30 Assoc Vice Chanc Institutional Dev ... Ms. Kristin CHARLES
13 Director Information Services ... Mr. Doug RE
16 Director Employee Relations ... Mr. Mickey BRANCA
18 Superintendent Buildings/Grounds ... Mr. Scott CLINE
27 Chief Information Technology Office ... Mr. Jay FIELD
96 Director of Purchasing ... Ms. Kathy HENNIG
19 Chief of Police ... Mr. Andre BARNES
88 ADA Compliance Officer ... Dr. Leilani BATTISTE
21 Assoc Vice Chanc/CFO ... Mr. David MARTING
25 Dean Grants & Resource Dev ... Ms. Kristin CHARLES
06 Assoc Dean Admission & Records ... Ms. Monika LIU
88 Dean Faculty Support Svcs ... Dr. Minh-Hoa TA
23 Director Student Health ... Dr. Elizabeth PERELLI
101 Liason to the Board of Trustees ... Ms. Linda SHAW
41 Athletic Director ... Mr. Harold BROWN
43 Dir Legal Services/General Counsel ... Mr. Steve BRUCKMAN
86 Director Government Relations ... Mr. Jeff HAMILTON

City of Hope (B)

1500 East Duarte Road, Duarte CA 91010-3000

County: Los Angeles FICE Identification: 035924
Unit ID: 441238
Telephone: (626) 256-4673 Carnegie Class: Spec/Med
FAX Number: (626) 301-8105 Calendar System: Semester
URL: www.cityofhope.org
Established: 1994 Annual Graduate Tuition & Fees: N/A
Enrollment: 75 Coed
Affiliation or Control: Independent Non-Profit IRS Status: 501(c)3
Highest Offering: Doctorate; No Undergraduates
Program: Professional
Accreditation: WC

01 President/CEO ... Robert STONE
05 Provost/Chief Scientific Officer ... Dr. Steven T. ROSEN
58 Dean of Graduate School ... Dr. John J. ROSSI
06 Registrar ... Queenie DU
07 Director of Admissions ... Dr. Kate M. SLEETH
08 Head Librarian ... Andrea LYNCH

Claremont Lincoln University (C)

250 West First Street Ste 330, Claremont CA 91711

County: Los Angeles Identification: 667215
Telephone: (909) 468-4400 Carnegie Class: Not Classified
FAX Number: N/A Calendar System: Quarter
URL: claremontlincoln.org
Established: 2011 Annual Graduate Tuition & Fees: $15,000
Enrollment: N/A Coed
Affiliation or Control: Independent Non-Profit IRS Status: 501(c)3
Highest Offering: Master's; No Undergraduates
Program: Professional
Accreditation: @WC

01 President ... Dr. Eileen ARANDA
03 Exec Vice President ... Dr. Laura BURGIS
10 Chief Financial Officer ... Ms. Linda RABITOY
27 Sr Vice Pres & Chief Info Officer ... Dr. Jay SAMPLE
07 Director of Admission & Recruitment ... Ms. Natalie DYMCHENKO
32 Director of Student Services ... Ms. Heather CASE PRYOR
09 Director of Institutional Research ... Dr. Terri ROSETT

*Claremont University Consortium (D)

101 South Mills Avenue, Claremont CA 91711-5053

County: Los Angeles Identification: 666003
Telephone: (909) 621-8026 Carnegie Class: N/A
FAX Number: (909) 621-8517
URL: www.cuc.claremont.edu

01 Chief Executive Officer ... Mr. Stig LANESSKOG
10 Vice Pres for Bus Admin/Treasurer ... Ms. Lori HUSEIN
32 Vice President of Student Affairs ... Dr. Denise HAYES
26 Director of Communications ... Ms. Kim LANE
19 Director Campus Safety ... Mr. Stan SKIPWORTH
101 Sec to Brd of Overseers/Asst to CEO ... Dr. Bonnie CLEMENS
08 Dean Library ... Dr. Kevin MULROY
15 Director Human Resources ... Ms. Stephanie DORNES

*Claremont Graduate University (E)

150 E 10th Street, Claremont CA 91711-5909

County: Los Angeles FICE Identification: 001169
Unit ID: 112251
Telephone: (909) 621-8000 Carnegie Class: RU/H
FAX Number: (909) 621-8390 Calendar System: Semester
URL: www.cgu.edu
Established: 1925 Annual Graduate Tuition & Fees: $43,632
Enrollment: 2,160 Coed
Affiliation or Control: Independent Non-Profit IRS Status: 501(c)3
Highest Offering: Doctorate; No Undergraduates
Program: Liberal Arts And General; Teacher Preparatory; Professional
Accreditation: WC, BUS, PH

02 President ... Mr. Robert W. SCHULT
04 Exec Asst to the President ... Ms. Donna STANDLEA
05 Exec Vice President and Provost ... Dr. Jacob ADAMS
10 VP for Finance and Admin/Treasurer ... Mr. Dean CALVO
30 Vice President for Advancement ... Vacant
84 Vice Pres Enroll/Student Services ... Dr. Patricia EASTON
46 Vice Provost/Research ... Dr. Dean GERSTEIN
88 Vice Provost/Transdisciplin Studies ... Dr. Patrick MASON
108 Director Institutional Effectivenes ... Ms. Alana OLSCHWANG
15 Assoc VP for Human Resources ... Ms. Brenda LESWICK
47 Botany Center ... Dr. Lucinda MCDADE
50 Drucker-Ito Grad School of Mgt ... Mr. Thomas HORAN
83 Behavioral & Organizational Sci ... Dr. Stewart DONALDSON
69 Community & Global Health ... Dr. Stewart DONALDSON
53 Educational Studies ... Dr. Scott THOMAS
77 Center for Information Science ... Dr. Thomas HORAN
81 Institute for Math Sciences ... Dr. Allon PERCUS
82 Politics & Economics ... Dr. Stewart DONALDSON
73 Arts and Humanities ... Dr. Tammi SCHNEIDER
09 Institutional Research Officer ... Ms. Jeannette GURROLA
44 Senior Director of Development ... Mr. Eric EWING
44 Director of Development ... Ms. Teresa WILMOTT
21 Assoc VP Finance/Admin ... Ms. Leslie NEGRITTO
29 Director of Alumni Engagement ... Mr. Jason BARQUERO
26 Ex Dir Mktg & Communications ... Ms. Andrea GUTIERREZ
06 Dir of Records/Enrollment Mgmt ... Ms. Lindsay STADLER
37 Director Student Financial Aid ... Ms. Beverly GREEN
85 International Student Coordinator ... Ms. Marianna PANOSSI
07 Assoc Director of Admissions ... Ms. Edlyn DELANO
32 Assoc Dean of Student Services ... Ms. Lisa FLORES GRIFFITH
18 Interim Director of Facilities ... Mr. Sam LEON
39 Housing Manager ... Mr. Chris BASS
13 Asst VP/Tech & Info Systems ... Mr. Manoj CHITRE
91 Director of Enterprise Infras ... Mr. Robert FORD
101 Secretary to the Board ... Ms. Louise WEBBER

*Claremont McKenna College (F)

500 E 9th Street, Claremont CA 91711-6400

County: Los Angeles FICE Identification: 001170
Unit ID: 112260
Telephone: (909) 621-8000 Carnegie Class: Bac/A&S
FAX Number: (909) 621-8790 Calendar System: Semester
URL: www.claremontmckenna.edu
Established: 1946 Annual Undergrad Tuition & Fees: $49,045
Enrollment: 1,324 Coed
Affiliation or Control: Independent Non-Profit IRS Status: 501(c)3
Highest Offering: Master's
Program: Liberal Arts And General
Accreditation: WC

02 President and CEO ... Hiram E. CHODOSH
05 VP Academic Affs/Dean Faculty ... Peter UVIN
30 Vice President for Development ... Ernie ISEMINGER
10 Vice Pres Business Admin/Treasurer ... Robin J. ASPINALL
11 VP for Planning and Administration ... Matthew G. BIBBENS
32 VP Student Affs/Admissions/Fin Aid ... Jefferson HUANG
21 VP and Chief Investment Officer ... James J. FLOYD
29 Vice President for Alumni Relations ... Evan RUTTER
35 Dean of Students ... Mary SPELLMAN
07 AVP & Dean Admission/Financial Aid ... Georgette DEVERES
26 Assoc VP Public Affs/Communications ... Max BENAVIDEZ
13 Assoc VP/Chief Technology Officer ... Cynthia HUMES
36 Assoc Dean/Dir Career Services ... Diana SEDER
18 Dir Facilities and Campus Services ... Brian WORLEY
06 Registrar/Dir Institutional Rsrch ... Elizabeth MORGAN
15 Director of Human Resources ... Andrea GALE
104 Director of Off-Campus Study ... Kristen MALLORY
41 Athletic Director ... Michael SUTTON
04 Special Assistant to the President ... Cheryl M. AGUILAR

*Claremont School of Theology (G)

1325 N College Avenue, Claremont CA 91711-3199

County: Los Angeles FICE Identification: 001288
Unit ID: 124283
Telephone: (909) 447-2500 Carnegie Class: Spec/Faith
FAX Number: (909) 626-7062 Calendar System: Semester
URL: www.cst.edu
Established: 1885 Annual Graduate Tuition & Fees: $18,300
Enrollment: 327 Coed
Affiliation or Control: United Methodist IRS Status: 501(c)3
Highest Offering: Doctorate; No Undergraduates
Program: Professional; Religious Emphasis
Accreditation: WC, THEOL

02 President ... Dr. Jeffrey KUAN
04 Exec Assistant to the President ... Ms. Maria Lise IANNUZZI
10 Vice Pres for Business Affairs/CFO ... Mr. Gamward QUAN
05 Vice Pres Academic Affairs & Dean ... Dr. Sheryl KUJAWA-HOLBROOK
20 Associate Dean/Vice President ... Rev. Belva Brown JORDAN
08 Dean of Library & Info Services ... Dr. Tom PHILLIPS
18 Director of Facilities ... Mr. Charles BRYANT
32 Assoc Dean Student & Community Life ... Ms. Lea APPLETON
30 VP Advancement & Communications ... Ms. Wendy LEE
26 Director of Communications ... Mr. Nathaniel KATZ
29 Director of Alumni/ae Relations ... Ms. Noemi ORTEGA
21 Controller ... Mr. Haroon AHMED
07 Sr Dir Admissions/Enrollment Svcs ... Mr. Murad DUBBINI
37 Director Student Financial Services ... Ms. Brenda NIEVES
06 Registrar ... Ms. Jennie ALLEN
42 Director of Field Education ... RevDr. Karen DALTON
22 Affirmative Action Officer ... Ms. Elaine WALKER

*Keck Graduate Institute (H)

535 Watson Drive, Claremont CA 91711-4817

County: Los Angeles FICE Identification: 038533
Unit ID: 440031
Telephone: (909) 607-7855 Carnegie Class: Assoc/PrivNFP4
FAX Number: (909) 607-8086 Calendar System: Semester
URL: www.kgi.edu
Established: 1997 Annual Graduate Tuition & Fees: $37,900
Enrollment: 286 Coed
Affiliation or Control: Independent Non-Profit IRS Status: 501(c)3
Highest Offering: Doctorate; No Undergraduates
Program: Professional; Technical Emphasis
Accreditation: WC, @PHAR

02 President ... Dr. Sheldon M. SCHUSTER
05 Vice President Academic Affairs ... Vacant
10 Vice Pres for Finance & Operations ... Michael JONES
06 Registrar ... Melissa S. BROWN
84 Dean of Stdnt Engagement/Enrol Svcs ... Sofia TORO
07 Director of Admissions ... Marcia PARKER

CNI College (I)

702 West Town and Country Road, Orange CA 92868

County: Orange FICE Identification: 032423
Unit ID: 433013
Telephone: (714) 437-9697 Carnegie Class: Not Classified
FAX Number: (714) 437-9356 Calendar System: Other
URL: www.cnicollege.edu
Established: 1994 Annual Undergrad Tuition & Fees: N/A
Enrollment: 561 Coed
Affiliation or Control: Proprietary IRS Status: Proprietary
Highest Offering: Baccalaureate
Program: Occupational
Accreditation: ABHES, SURTEC

01 President ... Mr. James BUFFINGTON

*Coast Community College District Administration Offices (A)

1370 Adams Avenue, Costa Mesa CA 92626-5429

County: Orange FICE Identification: 008711
Unit ID: 112376
Telephone: (714) 438-4600 Carnegie Class: N/A
FAX Number: (714) 438-4882
URL: www.cccd.edu

01 Chancellor .... Mr. Gene FARRELL
10 Vice Chancellor Finance & Adm Svcs .... Dr. Andrew DUNN
05 Vice Chanc Educ Svcs & Technology .... Dr. Andreea SERBAN
15 Vice Chanc Human Resources .... Dr. Cindy VYSKOCIL
26 Dir Public Affairs/Mktg/Govt .... Ms. Letitia CLARK
96 Director of Purchasing .... Mr. John ERIKSEN

*Coastline Community College (B)

11460 Warner Avenue, Fountain Valley CA 92708-2597

County: Orange FICE Identification: 020635
Unit ID: 112385
Telephone: (714) 546-7600 Carnegie Class: Assoc/Pub-S-MC
FAX Number: (714) 241-6277 Calendar System: Semester
URL: www.coastline.edu
Established: 1976 Annual Undergrad Tuition & Fees (In-District): $1,136
Enrollment: 11,313 Coed
Affiliation or Control: State/Local IRS Status: 501(c)3
Highest Offering: Associate Degree
Program: Occupational; 2-Year Principally Bachelor's Creditable
Accreditation: WJ

02 President .... Dr. Loretta P. ADRIAN
05 Vice Pres of Instruction .... Mr. Vince RODRIGUEZ
10 VP of Administrative Services .... Ms. Christine NGUYEN
32 Vice Pres Student Services .... Mr. Ross MIYASHIRO
84 Dean of Enrollment Services .... Ms. Lois WILKERSON
46 Admin Dean Instr Systems Devel .... Vacant
38 Dean Counseling/Matriculation .... Ms. Christine LEON
106 Assoc Dean of Distance Learning .... Mr. Bob NASH
12 Dean of Instruction Newport Beach .... Ms. Michelle PRIEST
12 Dean Instruct Tech Ed Garden Grove .... Ms. Nancy JONES
12 Dean Instruction Westminster .... Dr. Vinicio LOPEZ
88 Dean Military Programs/Contract Ed .... Ms. Joycelyn GROOT
26 Director of Mktg/Public Relations .... Ms. Nhadira JOHNSON
07 Director of Admissions/Records .... Ms. Jennifer MCDONALD
37 Director of Financial Aid .... Mr. Steve WOODYARD
18 Director Maintenance & Operations .... Mr. David CANT
21 Director Fiscal Services .... Ms. Helen ROTHGEB
102 Exec Director College Foundation .... Ms. Mariam KHOSRAVANI
40 Director Bookstore .... Mr. Matthew IRBY
09 Director Research/Planning/Develop .... Dr. Jorge R. SANCHEZ
88 Mgr Contract Education Program Dev .... Mr. Peter MAHARAJ
24 Director of Electronic Media .... Ms. Judy GARVEY
15 Int Director of Personnel Services .... Ms. Helen ROTHGEB
88 Director of EBUS program .... Ms. Laurie MELBY
13 Exec Dean eLearning Research/IT .... Mr. Dan JONES
103 Interim Dir Workforce & Econ Dev .... Ms. Sallie SALINAS

*Golden West College (C)

15744 Golden West Street,
Huntington Beach CA 92647-2748

County: Orange FICE Identification: 001206
Unit ID: 115126
Telephone: (714) 892-7711 Carnegie Class: Assoc/Pub-S-MC
FAX Number: (714) 895-8243 Calendar System: Semester
URL: www.gwc.info
Established: 1966 Annual Undergrad Tuition & Fees (In-District): $1,176
Enrollment: 12,516 Coed
Affiliation or Control: State/Local IRS Status: Exempt
Highest Offering: Associate Degree
Program: Occupational; 2-Year Principally Bachelor's Creditable
Accreditation: WJ, ADNUR

02 President .... Mr. Wes BRYAN
05 Vice Pres Instruc & Stdnt Learning .... Mr. Omid POURZANJANI
32 Vice Pres Student Life & Admin Supp .... Ms. Janet M. HOULIHAN
38 Dean Counseling & Social Sciences .... Ms. Robyn BRAMMER
72 Interim Dean Business & CTE .... Ms. Angela ALLISON
81 Dean Math & Science .... Mr. Jeff COURCHAINE
49 Dean Arts & Letters .... Dr. David D. HUDSON
66 Associate Dean School of Nursing .... Ms. Beverley BROWNELL
23 Assoc Dean/Dir Student Health Svcs .... Mr. Robin BACHMANN
09 Admin Dir Research/Plan/Inst Effect .... Dr. Kay NGUYEN
88 Dean Criminal Justice .... Mr. Ron LOWENBERG
35 Dean Student Life .... Ms. Carla MARTINEZ
84 Dean Enrollment Management .... Dr. Claudia LEE-SADDUL
88 Interim Dean Learning Res .... Mr. Alex MIRANDA
15 Director Personnel Services .... Vacant
10 Director Fiscal Services .... Mr. Paul WISNER
102 Director Foundation/Community Rels .... Mr. Bruce BERMAN
88 Director Scholarships & Spec Events .... Ms. Valerie A. VENEGAS
07 Director of Admissions .... Ms. Jennifer L. ORTBERG
37 Director of Financial Aid .... Ms. Adrienne BURTON
18 Chief Facilities/Physical Plant .... Mr. Joseph B. DOWLING
68 Dean Health PE & Athleics .... Mr. Albert GASPARIAN
04 Executive Asst to President .... Ms. Christina OJA
19 Dir Public Safety/Emerg Prep .... Mr. Jon ARNOLD

*Orange Coast College (D)

2701 Fairview Road, POB 5005,
Costa Mesa CA 92628-5005

County: Orange FICE Identification: 001250
Unit ID: 120342
Telephone: (714) 432-0202 Carnegie Class: Assoc/Pub-S-MC
FAX Number: (714) 432-5609 Calendar System: Semester
URL: www.orangecoastcollege.edu
Established: 1947 Annual Undergrad Tuition & Fees (In-District): $1,450
Enrollment: 20,473 Coed
Affiliation or Control: State/Local IRS Status: 501(c)3
Highest Offering: Associate Degree
Program: Occupational; 2-Year Principally Bachelor's Creditable
Accreditation: WJ, ACFEI, COARC, CVT, DA, DIETT, DMS, NDT, POLYT, RAD

02 President .... Dr. Dennis HARKINS
05 Vice President Instruction .... Mr. Kevin M. BALLINGER
32 Vice President Student Services .... Dr. Kristin CLARK
10 Director of Fiscal Services .... Ms. Rachel KUBIK
11 Vice Pres Administrative Services .... Dr. Richard PAGEL
84 Dean Enrollment Services .... Mr. Madjid NIROUMAND
38 Dean of Counseling .... Dr. Hue PHAM
35 Dean Student Services .... Mr. Michael MORVICE
26 Director Community Relations .... Mr. Juan GUTIERREZ
30 Exec Dir Institutional Advancement .... Mr. Douglas BENNETT
09 Director of IR/Planning and IE .... Ms. Sheri STERNER
07 Director Admiss/Records/Enroll Tech .... Mr. Efren GALVAN
15 Interim Director Personnel Services .... Mr. William BENJAMIN
06 Associate Registrar .... Mr. James K. WEST
18 Director M & O .... Mr. Mark GOODE
37 Director Student Financial Aid .... Vacant
13 Director Information Technology .... Ms. Rupa SARAN
23 Associate Dean Health Services .... Ms. Sylvia WORDEN
88 Manager Child Care Center .... Ms. Sue BIERLICH
41 Athletic Director .... Dr. Michael SUTLIFF
88 Interim Dean Consmr & Hlth Sciences .... Ms. Susan COLEMAN
68 Dean of Kiniseology & Athletics .... Dr. Michael SUTLIFF
72 Dean of Technology .... Dr. Daniel SHRADER
50 Dean of Business & Computer Science .... Dr. Ronald JOHNSON
83 Dean of Social & Behavioral Science .... Dr. Kevin HENSON
88 Dean of Literature & Languages .... Dr. Michael MANDELKERN
81 Dean of Math & Sciences .... Dr. Tara GIBLIN
57 Dean of Visual & Performing Arts .... Mr. Joe POSHEK
62 Dean of Library and Media Services .... Mr. Joe POSHEK
51 Director Career & Cmty Education .... Vacant
19 Director Security/Safety .... Mr. John FARMER
40 Manager Bookstore .... Mr. Todd MURPHY

Cogswell Polytechnical College (E)

1175 Bordeaux Drive, Sunnyvale CA 94089-1299

County: Santa Clara FICE Identification: 001177
Unit ID: 112394
Telephone: (408) 498-5100 Carnegie Class: Bac/Diverse
FAX Number: (408) 877-7373 Calendar System: Semester
URL: www.cogswell.edu
Established: 1887 Annual Undergrad Tuition & Fees: $16,640
Enrollment: 611 Coed
Affiliation or Control: Proprietary IRS Status: Proprietary
Highest Offering: Baccalaureate
Program: Liberal Arts And General; Professional; Technical Emphasis
Accreditation: WC

01 President .... Dr. Deborah SNYDER
05 Dean of the College .... Mr. Jerome SOLOMON
10 Chief Financial Officer .... Mr. Kenneth BANKS
26 VP of Admissions and Marketing .... Mr. Abraham CHACKO
06 Registrar .... Mr. David NORIEGA
08 Librarian & Resource Manager .... Ms. Lauren MIKLOVIC
07 Director of Admissions .... Mr. Aaron KARK
04 Executive Assistant to President .... Ms. Barbara GURNARI
09 Executive Director of IR and QA .... Ms. Milla ZLATANOV
13 VP of Information Technology .... Dr. Andrey FEDIN
32 Interim Dean of Students .... Ms. Brittany BOGLE
36 Director of Career Services .... Mr. Nando GAPASIN
37 Financial Aid Manager .... Ms. Yariela PEREZ-GONZALEZ
88 Director of Compliance .... Ms. Nikki LOVE

The Colburn School (F)

200 S Grand Avenue, Los Angeles CA 90012-3007

County: Los Angeles Identification: 666233
Telephone: (213) 621-2200 Carnegie Class: Not Classified
FAX Number: (213) 621-2110 Calendar System: Semester
URL: www.colburnschool.edu
Established: 2003 Annual Undergrad Tuition & Fees: $112
Enrollment: 115 Coed
Affiliation or Control: Independent Non-Profit IRS Status: 501(c)3
Highest Offering: Master's
Program: Music Emphasis
Accreditation: MUS

01 President & CEO .... Mr. Sel KARDAN
30 Sr VP Advancement/External Affairs .... Ms. Allison SAMPSON
26 Vice President Communications .... Mr. Mark A. BERRY
10 Chief Financial Officer .... Mr. Seth WEINTRAUB

† Full room, board, and tuition are provided to accepted students through the school's endowment.

Coleman University (G)

8888 Balboa Avenue, San Diego CA 92123-1506

County: San Diego FICE Identification: 007296
Unit ID: 112446
Telephone: (858) 499-0202 Carnegie Class: Bac/Assoc
FAX Number: (858) 499-0233 Calendar System: Quarter
URL: www.coleman.edu
Established: 1963 Annual Undergrad Tuition & Fees: $21,200
Enrollment: 688 Coed
Affiliation or Control: Independent Non-Profit IRS Status: 501(c)3
Highest Offering: Master's
Program: Occupational; Professional; Technical Emphasis
Accreditation: @WC, ACICS

01 President/CEO .... Mr. Norbert J. KUBILUS
05 Vice President Academics .... Dr. Kim LOBERA
07 Director of Admissions .... Ms. Bobbie A. STROHM
32 Director of Student Services .... Mr. Jason KRANZ
10 Chief Financial Officer .... Mr. Ron D. KLINGENSMITH
13 Chief Technology Officer .... Mr. Jason T. ABEL
09 Director of Institutional Research .... Mr. Bruce F. GILDEN
15 Director Human Resource .... Ms. Maria HAMZAVI
06 Registrar .... Mr. Alex WISSMAN
37 Director of Financial Aid .... Mr. Axel N. HERNANDEZ
36 Director Career Services .... Mr. Bob SWEIGART
21 Business Manager .... Ms. Laura SALES
08 Librarian .... Mr. Manuel A. BERNAD
29 Alumni Relations Coordinator .... Ms. Julia V. KATAWAZI
14 Network Administrator .... Mr. Brian J. MORGAN
105 Web Master .... Mr. Chris J. CAREY
30 Chief Development Officer .... Mr. Rod P. WEISS
18 Facilities Manager .... Mr. Terry S. GLYNN

College of the Canyons (H)

26455 Rockwell Canyon Road,
Santa Clarita CA 91355-1899

County: Los Angeles FICE Identification: 008903
Unit ID: 111461
Telephone: (661) 259-7800 Carnegie Class: Assoc/Pub-S-SC
FAX Number: (661) 259-8302 Calendar System: Semester
URL: www.canyons.edu
Established: 1967 Annual Undergrad Tuition & Fees (In-District): $1,154
Enrollment: 19,995 Coed
Affiliation or Control: State/Local IRS Status: 501(c)3
Highest Offering: Associate Degree
Program: Occupational; 2-Year Principally Bachelor's Creditable
Accreditation: WJ, ADNUR

01 Chancellor SCCCD & President COC .... Dr. Dianne G. VAN HOOK
10 Asst Supt/VP Business Services .... Ms. Sharlene COLEAL
15 Asst Supt/Vice Pres Human Resources .... Dr. Diane FIERO
18 Asst Supt/VP Facil Plan Op/Const .... Mr. Jim SCHRAGE
32 Asst Superintendent/VP Student Svcs .... Dr. Michael WILDING
05 Asst Supt/Vice Pres Instruction .... Dr. Jerry BUCKLEY
26 VP Public Info/Advoc/Ext Relations .... Mr. Eric HARNISH
20 Assoc Vice Pres Academic Affairs .... Ms. Audrey GREEN
13 Vice President Technology .... Dr. James TEMPLE
03 Deputy Chancellor .... Dr. Barry GRIBBONS
03 Deputy Superintendent .... Vacant
57 Div Dean Fine & Performing Arts .... Dr. Carmen DOMINGUEZ
79 Division Dean Humanities .... Dr. Jennifer BREZINA
68 Division Dean PE/Athletics .... Mr. Len MOHNEY
83 Div Dean Social Sci & Business .... Dr. Patricia ROBINSON
81 Int Div Dean Math Sciences Engineer .... Mr. Joseph GERDA
106 Dean Educ Tech/Lrng Resrc/Dist Educ .... Mr. James GLAPA-GROSSKLAG
50 Dean School of Business .... Vacant
75 Dean Career Technical Education .... Ms. Kristin HOUSER
35 Dean Student Services .... Mr. Mike JOSLIN
88 Dean Instr Support & Student Succ .... Ms. Denee PESCARMONA
06 Dean Enrollment Services .... Ms. Deborah RIO
31 Dean ECE/TeachTraining/CommEd/Noncr .... Ms. Diane STEWART
12 VP Canyon Country Campus and Grants .... Mr. Ryan THEULE
103 Interim Dean Economic Development .... Mr. Joe KLOCKO
46 Dean Inst Research/Plng/Inst Effect .... Dr. Daylene MEUSCHKE
72 Dean School of Applied Tech .... Vacant
21 Assoc VP Business Services .... Ms. Cynthia GRANDGEORGE
102 COO COC Foundation/Int Dir UC .... Ms. Cathy RITZ
44 Chief Devel Officer COC Foundation .... Mr. Murray WOOD
04 Special Assistant to the Chancellor .... Ms. Claudia DUNN-MARTINTEZ
27 Managing Director District Comm .... Mr. John GREEN
88 Exec Dir Small Business Dev Ctr .... Mr. John HOSKINSON
88 Exec Dir Performing Arts Center .... Ms. Evelyn WARSHAWSKI
88 DSN Advanced Manuc/Dir CACT .... Mr. Larry MCLAUGHLIN
88 Interim Dep Sector Nav ICT/DM .... Ms. Paula HODGE
07 Dir Admissions/Records/Online Svcs .... Dr. Jasmine RUYS
88 Director Art Gallery .... Mr. Larry HURST
19 Director Campus Safety .... Ms. Tammy CASTOR
36 Act Dean Campus Ops CCC/Career Svs .... Mr. Anthony MICHAELIDES
88 Dir Central Energy Syst/Reg Comp .... Mr. Carl EBAUGH
88 Director Civic Center .... Mr. Robin WILLIAMS
30 Director Development .... Ms. Michele EDMONSON
96 Director Contracts Proc & Risk Mgmt .... Ms. April GRAHAM
105 Dir Distance & Accelerated Learning .... Vacant
88 Director Employee Training Inst .... Mr. John MILBURN
88 Director Facilities Projects .... Mr. William KARRAT
37 Director Financial Aid .... Mr. Tom BILBRUCK
88 Director Fiscal Services .... Ms. Balbir CHANDI

88 Director Grant & Categorical Acct Ms. Jennifer LIGHTFOOD
25 Director Grants Development Ms. Theresa ZUZEVICH
16 Director Human Resources Ms. Christina CHUNG
88 Act Asst Dean Inter/Job Dev/Cr Ctr Ms. Gina BOGNA
85 Director International Students Pgm Dr. Jia-Yi CHENG-LEVINE
88 Dir Outreach & School Relations Ms. Kari SOFFA
88 Director Professional Development Ms. Leslie CARR
88 Dir Reentry Pgm & Veterans Affair Mr. Renard THOMAS
88 Director Student Business Office Ms. Kathleen BENZ
23 Director Student Health & Wellness Ms. Mary MANUEL
88 Technical Director Performing Arts Mr. Brodie STEELE
88 Art Dir/Mgr Graphic Design Svcs Mr. Nick PAVICK
88 Theater Manager Ms. Tami TOON

College of the Desert (A)

43-500 Monterey Avenue, Palm Desert CA 92260-9399
County: Riverside FICE Identification: 001182
Unit ID: 113573
Telephone: (760) 346-8041 Carnegie Class: Assoc/Pub-S-MC
FAX Number: (760) 341-8678 Calendar System: Semester
URL: www.collegeofthedesert.edu
Established: 1958 Annual Undergrad Tuition & Fees (In-District): $1,327
Enrollment: 10,782 Coed
Affiliation or Control: State/Local IRS Status: 501(c)3
Highest Offering: Associate Degree
Program: Occupational; 2-Year Principally Bachelor's Creditable
Accreditation: WJ

01 Superintendent/President Dr. Joel L. KINNAMON
05 Executive Vice Pres SS/SL Vacant
10 Vice President Admin Services Ms. Lisa HOWELL
15 Interim Vice Pres Human Resources Ms. Diane WIRTH
30 Exec Dir Institutional Advancement Ms. Pam HUNTER
09 Exec Dean Inst Effectiveness Dr. Annebelle NERY
38 Dean Student Success/Learning Mr. Scott COOPER
102 Exec Dir of Foundation Mr. Jim HUMMER
13 Exec Dir Educational Technology Ms. Sherilyn WILLIS
18 Director of Maintenance/Operations Mr. Jason AREBALOS
29 Exec Director Alumni Relations Ms. Cindy STILLMAN
37 Director Financial Aid Ms. Deanna MURRELL
21 Director of Fiscal Services Mr. John RAMONT
06 Registrar/Director of Admissions Mr. Curt LUTTRELL

College of Marin (B)

835 College Avenue, Kentfield CA 94904-2590
County: Marin FICE Identification: 001178
Unit ID: 118347
Telephone: (415) 457-8811 Carnegie Class: Assoc/Pub-S-MC
FAX Number: (415) 456-6017 Calendar System: Semester
URL: www.marin.edu
Established: 1926 Annual Undergrad Tuition & Fees (In-District): $1,488
Enrollment: 5,737 Coed
Affiliation or Control: State/Local IRS Status: 501(c)3
Highest Offering: Associate Degree
Program: Occupational; 2-Year Principally Bachelor's Creditable
Accreditation: WJ, ADNUR, DA

01 Superintendent/President Dr. David W. COON
05 VP Student Svcs & Learning Mr. Jonathan ELDRIDGE
20 Asst VP Instructional Support Ms. Cari TORRES
32 Vice President Student Services Mr. Jonathan ELDRIDGE
10 Vice President Finance & Oper Mr. Greg NELSON
15 Exec Dir Human Res/Labor Relations Ms. Kristina A. COMBS
84 Dean Enrollment Services Ms. Diane TRAVERSI
49 Dean Arts & Humanities Dr. David SNYDER
103 Dean Career & Tech Education Ms. Elizabeth PRATT
81 Dean Math/Sciences Dr. Carol HERNANDEZ
21 Director Fiscal Services Ms. Peggy ISOZAKI
09 Exec Dir Plng/Research/Inst Plng Dr. Christina LEIMER
37 Asst Dean Enroll/Financial Aid Ms. Emily SILLCOCKS
18 Dir Facil Planning & M&O Ms. Heidi RANK
13 CIO & Director of IT Mr. Patrick EKOUE-TOTOU
35 Dir Student Activities/Advocacy Ms. Sadika SULAIMAN HARA
19 Chief of Police/Director of Safety Mr. Mitch LEMAY
68 Dir Kinesiolgy/Athletics Mr. Matt MARKOVICH
76 Dean Health Sciences Dr. Marshall ALAMEIDA
31 Dir Cmty/Lifelong/Intl Education Ms. Carol HILDEBRAND
30 Exec Director of Development Dr. Linda FRANK
08 Director of Library Services Vacant
04 Exec Asst to Pres/Board Ms. Kathy JOYNER

College of the Redwoods Community College District (C)

7351 Tompkins Hill Road, Eureka CA 95501-9300
County: Humboldt FICE Identification: 001185
Unit ID: 121707
Telephone: (707) 476-4100 Carnegie Class: Assoc/Pub-R-L
FAX Number: (707) 476-4400 Calendar System: Semester
URL: www.redwoods.edu
Established: 1964 Annual Undergrad Tuition & Fees (In-District): $1,182
Enrollment: 4,965 Coed
Affiliation or Control: State/Local IRS Status: 501(c)3
Highest Offering: Associate Degree
Program: Occupational; 2-Year Principally Bachelor's Creditable
Accreditation: WJ, DA, EMT, NAIT

01 President/Superintendent Ms. Kathryn G. SMITH
05 Vice President Instruction Mr. Keith SNOW-FLAMER
04 Assistant to the President Ms. Michelle ANDERSON
10 VP Administrative Services Mr. Lee LINDSEY
32 VP Student Development Dr. Keith SNOW-FLAMER
31 Exec Dir Cmty/Economic Development Ms. Ahn FIELDING
15 Director Human Resources Ms. Ahn FIELDING
12 Director Del Norte Center Mr. Rory JOHNSON
12 Manager Mendocino Coast Center Ms. Kathrine WYLIE
68 Dean PE/Athletics/Health Occup Mr. Joseph HASH
37 Director Financial Aid Ms. Lynn THIESEN
88 Dir Special Pgms/Academic Support Ms. Cheryl TUCKER
88 Director Disabled Student Pgm Svcs Ms. Patricia BLAIR
18 Director Maintenance & Operations Mr. Garry PATRICK
26 Public Information Officer Mr. Paul DEMARK
08 Dir Learning Resource Ctr/Library Ms. Ruth MOON
09 Director of Institutional Research Dr. Angeline HILL
07 Mgr Admissions/Records Ms. Rianne CONNOR
19 Lead Public Safety Officer Mr. George KAPITAN
88 Director Administration of Justice Mr. Ron WATERS

College of the Sequoias (D)

915 S Mooney Boulevard, Visalia CA 93277-2234
County: Tulare FICE Identification: 001186
Unit ID: 123217
Telephone: (559) 730-3700 Carnegie Class: Assoc/Pub-R-L
FAX Number: (559) 730-3894 Calendar System: Semester
URL: www.cos.edu
Established: 1925 Annual Undergrad Tuition & Fees (In-District): $1,362
Enrollment: 10,303 Coed
Affiliation or Control: State/Local IRS Status: 501(c)3
Highest Offering: Associate Degree
Program: Occupational; 2-Year Principally Bachelor's Creditable
Accreditation: WJ, PTAA

01 Superintendent/President Mr. Stan A. CARRIZOSA
05 Vice President Academic Services Dr. Jennifer VEGA-LA SERNA
11 Vice President Administrative Svcs Ms. Christine STATTON
10 Dir Budgets & Categorical Accts Ms. Leangela MILLER-HERNANDEZ
32 Vice President Student Services Mr. Brent CALVIN
37 Dean Student Svcs/Financial Aid Ms. Jessica FIGALLO
88 Provost Tulare Center Dr. Louann WALDNER
88 Provost Hanford Center Dr. Kristin ROBINSON
81 Dean Science/Math/Eng Dr. Robert URTECHO
76 Dean Allied Health/Phys Education Ms. Cindy DELAIN
49 Dean Arts & Letters Ms. Stephanie COLLIER
15 Dean Human Resources/Legal Affairs Mr. John BRATSCH
18 Dean Facilities Mr. Byron WOODS
102 Director Foundation Mr. Tim FOSTER
66 Dir Nursing/Allied Health Ms. Belen KERSTEN
08 Dir Library/Instructional Tech Ms. Mary-Catherine OXFORD
09 Director of Research Dr. Mehmet OZTURK
06 Registrar/Record Technician Ms. Velia RODRIGUEZ
41 Associate Dean/Athletic Director Mr. Brent DAVIS
19 Chief District Police Mr. Robert MASTERSON
40 Bookstore Manager Ms. Dorianna MENDIETTA
23 Coord Health Center Ms. Patricia ALVAREZ
35 Dir Student Activities/Affairs Ms. Debbie DOUGLASS
103 Dean CTE/Voc Ed Vacant
88 Coord Welcome/Transfer Center Ms. Catherine MCGUIRE
26 Coord Mktg/Public Info Ms. Kristen FOSTER
04 Executive Asst to President Ms. Meghan TIERCE
13 Dean Info Technology Mr. Tim HOLLABAUGH

College of the Siskiyous (E)

800 College Avenue, Weed CA 96094-2899
County: Siskiyou FICE Identification: 001187
Unit ID: 123484
Telephone: (530) 938-5200 Carnegie Class: Assoc/Pub-R-M
FAX Number: (530) 938-5506 Calendar System: Semester
URL: www.siskiyous.edu
Established: 1957 Annual Undergrad Tuition & Fees (In-District): $1,410
Enrollment: 2,060 Coed
Affiliation or Control: State/Local IRS Status: 501(c)3
Highest Offering: Associate Degree
Program: Occupational; 2-Year Principally Bachelor's Creditable
Accreditation: WJ

01 Superintendent/President Mr. Scotty THOMASON
04 Exec Assistant President & Board Ms. Sheila GRIMES
10 Vice President Administrative Svcs Ms. Nancy FUNK
05 Vice President Instruction Vacant
32 Vice President Student Services Ms. Melissa GREEN
08 Assoc Dean Learn Resources & Tech Ms. Nancy SHEPARD
35 Director Student Life Mr. Doug HAUGEN
09 Director Research & Evaluation Mr. Bart SCOTT
41 Asst Dean KinesiologyAthletics Mr. Dennis ROBERTS
20 Dean Student Learning Dr. Gregory SOUTH
103 Dean Career & Technical Education Dr. Robert TAYLOR
07 Director Enrollment Services Ms. Meghan WITHERELL
15 Executive Director Personnel Ms. Nancy MILLER
37 Director Financial Aid Ms. Janette HARRIS
18 Interim Asst Director MOT Mr. Phil ALVARADO
30 Dir of Institutional Advancement Vacant
28 Director of Diversity Ms. Nancy MILLER

Columbia College Hollywood (F)

18618 Oxnard Street, Tarzana CA 91356-1411
County: Los Angeles FICE Identification: 021102
Unit ID: 112570
Telephone: (800) 785-0585 Carnegie Class: Spec/Arts
FAX Number: (818) 345-9053 Calendar System: Quarter
URL: www.columbiacollege.edu
Established: 1952 Annual Undergrad Tuition & Fees: $20,600
Enrollment: 344 Coed
Affiliation or Control: Independent Non-Profit IRS Status: 501(c)3
Highest Offering: Baccalaureate
Program: Liberal Arts And General; Fine Arts Emphasis
Accreditation: WC, ART

01 President/CEO Mr. Richard KOBRITZ
05 Dean of the College Mr. Alan L. GANSBERG
101 Board Secretary Mr. Theodore O'KARMA
22 Sr Compliance/Accreditation Manager Mr. Jan HASTINGS
10 Sr Director of Finance/Comptroller Mr. Richard CROWE
32 Dean of Student Services Dr. Yolanda DAWSON
13 Director of IT and Production Svcs Mr. Ronald REEVES
07 Director of Admissions Ms. Carmen MUNOZ
37 Financial Aid Manager Mr. James BURGESS
36 Student Placement Ms. Kate MCARDLE
06 Registrar Ms. LaVona THOMAS

Community Christian College (G)

1849 N. Wabash, Redlands CA 92374
County: San Bernardino FICE Identification: 038744
Unit ID: 446163
Telephone: (909) 794-1084 Carnegie Class: Assoc/PrivNFP
FAX Number: (909) 794-1093 Calendar System: Quarter
URL: www.communitychristiancollege.com
Established: 1995 Annual Undergrad Tuition & Fees: $6,485
Enrollment: 104 Coed
Affiliation or Control: Independent Non-Profit IRS Status: 501(c)3
Highest Offering: Associate Degree
Program: 2-Year Principally Bachelor's Creditable
Accreditation: #TRACS

01 President Mr. Josh TURNSKY
05 Vice Pres Academic Affs/Registrar Dr. Steve AVALOS
08 Director Information Services Ms. Marilyn HOPE

Concord Law School of Kaplan University (H)

10866 Wilshire Blvd, Suite 1200,
Los Angeles CA 90024-4356
Telephone: (310) 689-3200 FICE Identification: 041259
Accreditation: &NH, DEAC

† Regional accreditation is carried under the parent institution in Davenport, IA.

Concorde Career College (I)

12951 Euclid Street, Suite 101,
Garden Grove CA 92840-1451
County: Orange FICE Identification: 008071
Unit ID: 123679
Telephone: (714) 703-1900 Carnegie Class: Assoc/PrivFP
FAX Number: (714) 530-8421 Calendar System: Semester
URL: www.concorde.edu
Established: 1960 Annual Undergrad Tuition & Fees: $27,220
Enrollment: 974 Coed
Affiliation or Control: Proprietary IRS Status: Proprietary
Highest Offering: Associate Degree
Program: Occupational; Nursing Emphasis
Accreditation: ACCSC, COARC, DH, PTAA

01 Campus President Mr. Mark LUCERO

Concorde Career College (J)

12412 Victory Boulevard, North Hollywood CA 91606-3134
County: Los Angeles FICE Identification: 007607
Unit ID: 124937
Telephone: (818) 766-8151 Carnegie Class: Assoc/PrivFP
FAX Number: (818) 766-1587 Calendar System: Quarter
URL: www.concordecareercolleges.com
Established: 1955 Annual Undergrad Tuition & Fees: $14,993
Enrollment: 620 Coed
Affiliation or Control: Proprietary IRS Status: Proprietary
Highest Offering: Associate Degree
Program: Occupational
Accreditation: ACCSC, COARC, PTAA, SURGT

01 Campus President Carmen BOWEN

Concorde Career College (K)

201 E Airport Drive, San Bernadino CA 92408
County: San Bernardino FICE Identification: 008537
Unit ID: 124706
Telephone: (909) 884-8891 Carnegie Class: Assoc/PrivFP
FAX Number: (909) 884-1831 Calendar System: Semester
URL: www.concorde.edu
Established: 1970 Annual Undergrad Tuition & Fees: $15,401
Enrollment: 668 Coed
Affiliation or Control: Proprietary IRS Status: Proprietary
Highest Offering: Associate Degree
Program: Occupational
Accreditation: ACCSC, COARC, DH, NDT, SURGT

01 Campus President Ken GUERRERO

Concorde Career College (A)

4393 Imperial Avenue, Suite 100,
San Diego CA 92113-1962

County: San Diego FICE Identification: 007930
Unit ID: 120661
Telephone: (619) 688-0800 Carnegie Class: Assoc/PrivFP
FAX Number: (619) 220-4177 Calendar System: Semester
URL: www.concorde.edu
Established: 1966 Annual Undergrad Tuition & Fees: $15,542
Enrollment: 967 Coed
Affiliation or Control: Proprietary IRS Status: Proprietary
Highest Offering: Associate Degree
Program: Occupational
Accreditation: ACCSC, COARC, DH, PTAA, SURGT

01 Campus President .... Ms. Rachel SASSEL

Concordia University (B)

1530 Concordia W, Irvine CA 92612-3299

County: Orange FICE Identification: 020705
Unit ID: 112075
Telephone: (949) 854-8002 Carnegie Class: Master's L
FAX Number: (949) 214-3520 Calendar System: Semester
URL: www.cui.edu
Established: 1972 Annual Undergrad Tuition & Fees: $31,985
Enrollment: 4,311 Coed
Affiliation or Control: Lutheran Church - Missouri Synod
IRS Status: 501(c)3
Highest Offering: Doctorate
Program: Liberal Arts And General; Teacher Preparatory
Accreditation: WC, CAATE, NURSE

01 President .... Dr. Kurt J. KRUEGER
05 Provost/Exec VP .... Dr. Mary K. SCOTT
84 Exec VP Student & Enroll Services .... Dr. Gary R. MCDANIEL
30 Exec VP Advancement .... Mr. Timothy J. JAEGER
10 Exec VP/Chief Finance Officer .... Mr. Kevin TILDEN
20 Assoc Provost/VP Acad Affs .... Dr. Peter SENKBEIL
20 Asst Provost Adult/Grad/Online .... Dr. Doug GROVE
49 Dean School of Arts and Sciences .... Dr. Timothy PREUSS
50 EVP Ext Rels/Dean Sch of Business .. Mr. Stephen CHRISTENSEN
107 Dean School of Professional Studies .... Dr. Timothy C. PETERS
53 Dean School of Education .... Dr. Janice NELSON
73 Dean Christ College .... Dr. Steven P. MUELLER
06 Dean of Academic Records/Registrar .... Prof. Kenneth R. CLAVIR
32 Dean of Students .... Dr. Gilbert FUGITT
07 Director of Undergrad Admissions .... Mr. Doug WIBLE
07 Director of Graduate Admissions .... Mrs. Rina CAMPBELL
37 Director of Financial Aid .... Ms. Lori MCDONALD
21 Bursar .... Mr. Edgar LOPEZ
43 General Counsel .... Mr. Ronald VAN BLARCOM
15 Director of Human Resources .... Mrs. Pamela CLAVIR
08 Director of Library Services .... Prof. Carolina BARTON
41 Athletic Director .... Prof. David BIRELINE
39 Director Residence Life .... Mr. Scott KEITH
19 Director Security/Safety .... Mr. Steven RODRIGUEZ
29 Exec Director of Alumni Relations .... Mr. Michael BERGLER
24 Director Educational Media .... Prof. John RANDALL
36 Director of Career Services .... Mrs. Victoria JAFFEE
44 Director Major Gift Planning .... Mr. Dennis COX
85 Exec Director Global Programs .... Dr. Dan WAITE
13 Director of IT Services .... Mr. Chris HARRIS
09 Director of Institutional Research .... Ms. Deborah LEE

*Contra Costa Community College District Office (C)

500 Court Street, Martinez CA 94553-1278

County: Contra Costa FICE Identification: 001189
Unit ID: 112817
Telephone: (925) 229-1000 Carnegie Class: N/A
FAX Number: (925) 370-2019
URL: www.4cd.edu

01 Chancellor .... Dr. Helen BENJAMIN
05 Int Exec VC Education & Technology .... Dr. Andrew JONES
11 Exec VC Administrative Services .... Mr. Eugene C. HUFF
18 Chief Facilities Planner .... Mr. Ray PYLE

*Contra Costa College (D)

2600 Mission Bell Drive, San Pablo CA 94806-3195

County: Contra Costa FICE Identification: 001190
Unit ID: 112826
Telephone: (510) 235-7800 Carnegie Class: Assoc/Pub-S-MC
FAX Number: (510) 236-6768 Calendar System: Semester
URL: www.contracosta.edu
Established: 1948 Annual Undergrad Tuition & Fees (In-District): $1,125
Enrollment: 6,892 Coed
Affiliation or Control: State/Local IRS Status: 501(c)3
Highest Offering: Associate Degree
Program: Occupational; 2-Year Principally Bachelor's Creditable
Accreditation: WJ

02 Interim President .... Ms. Mojdeh MEHDIZADEH
03 Vice President .... Ms. Tammeil GILKERSON
05 Senior Dean of Instruction .... Dr. Donna FLOYD
32 Dean of Student Services .... Ms. Vicki FERGUSON
103 Int Sr Acad/Stdnt Svcs Mgr Wkf Dev .... Ms. Kelly SCHELIN
07 Director Admissions & Records .... Ms. Catherine FROST
10 Director Business Services .... Ms. Mariles MAGALONG
09 Director of Institutional Research .... Vacant
37 Financial Aid Supervisor .... Ms. Monica RODRIGUEZ
18 Manager Buildings & Grounds .... Mr. Bruce KING

*Diablo Valley College (E)

321 Golf Club Road, Pleasant Hill CA 94523-1544

County: Contra Costa FICE Identification: 001191
Unit ID: 113634
Telephone: (925) 685-1230 Carnegie Class: Assoc/Pub-S-MC
FAX Number: (925) 685-1551 Calendar System: Semester
URL: www.dvc.edu
Established: 1949 Annual Undergrad Tuition & Fees (In-District): $1,380
Enrollment: 18,904 Coed
Affiliation or Control: State/Local IRS Status: 501(c)3
Highest Offering: Associate Degree
Program: Occupational; 2-Year Principally Bachelor's Creditable
Accreditation: WJ, ACFEI, CEA, DA, DH

02 President .... Mr. Peter GARCIA
05 Interim Vice President Instruction .... Ms. Rachel WESTLAKE
32 Vice President Student Services .... Dr. Newin ORANTE
10 Interim Vice Pres Bus & Admin Svcs .... Mr. John NAHLEN
20 Senior Dean of Curriculum & Instr .... Ms. Kimberely SCHENK
84 Dean Outreach/Enroll Mgt/
Matric .... Ms. Elizabeth HAUSCARRIAGUE
12 Dean San Ramon Campus .... Ms. Kathleen COSTA
41 Dean of PE/Athl/Dance/Athletic Dir .... Ms. Christine WORSLEY
62 Dean Library/Ed Tech & Learn Sup .... Mr. Rick ROBISON
26 Dir of Marketing & Communications .... Ms. Chrisanne KNOX
57 Dean Applied & Fine Arts .... Mr. Michael ALMAGUER
54 Dean Physical Sci/Engr/Bio Sci .... Dr. Patricia YOUNG
83 Dean English & Social Science .... Mr. Obed VAZQUEZ
50 Int Dean Business Ed/Math/Comp
Sci .... Ms. Despina PRAPAVESSI
06 Registrar .... Ms. Stephanie ALVES
35 Dean Student Support Services .... Ms. Emily STONE

*Los Medanos College (F)

2700 E Leland Road, Pittsburg CA 94565-5197

County: Contra Costa FICE Identification: 010340
Unit ID: 117894
Telephone: (925) 439-2181 Carnegie Class: Assoc/Pub-S-MC
FAX Number: (925) 427-1599 Calendar System: Semester
URL: www.losmedanos.edu
Established: 1973 Annual Undergrad Tuition & Fees (In-District): $1,380
Enrollment: 8,695 Coed
Affiliation or Control: State/Local IRS Status: 501(c)3
Highest Offering: Associate Degree
Program: Occupational; 2-Year Principally Bachelor's Creditable
Accreditation: WJ

02 President .... Mr. Bob KRATOCHVIL
04 Senior Executive Assistant .... Ms. Jennifer ADAMS
05 Vice Pres Instruction & Stdnt Svcs .... Dr. Kevin HORAN
10 Director of Business Services .... Ms. Aderonke OLATUNJI
45 Sr Dean Plng & Inst Effectiveness .... Ms. Kiran KAMATH
32 Sr Dean Stdnt Svcs & Brentwood Ctr .... Ms. Gail NEWMAN
35 Dean of Student Success .... Mr. David BELMAN
102 Senior Foundation Director .... Ms. Ruth GOODIN
07 Director of Admissions .... Ms. Robin ARMOUR
37 Financial Aid Supervisor .... Ms. Jennifer MA
88 Dir Student Life & Transfer Pgms .... Ms. Carla ROSAS
88 Outreach Director .... Mr. Jorge CEA
40 Bookstore Manager .... Mr. Robert ESTRADA
103 Program Mgr Workforce Dev Projects .... Mr. David WAHL
88 Director Early Childhood Lab School .... Ms. Kathryn NIELSEN
26 Director of Mktg & Media Design .... Ms. Barbara CELLA
13 Technology Systems Manager .... Mr. Mike BECKER
18 Buildings & Grounds Manager .... Mr. Russ HOLT
88 Custodial Manager .... Mr. Barry EDWARDS
88 Office of Instruction Supervisor .... Ms. Eileen VALENZUELA
19 Police Services Lieutenant .... Mr. Ryan HUDDLESTON
81 Dean of Math & Sciences .... Dr. A'kilah MOORE
75 Dean of Career Tech Ed & Social Sci .... Ms. Natalie HANNUM
79 Dean of Liberal Arts .... Ms. Nancy YBARRA
38 Dean of Counseling & Stdnt Support .... Mr. Jeffrey BENFORD

Copper Mountain College (G)

6162 Rotary Way, Box 1398, Joshua Tree CA 92252-6102

County: San Bernardino FICE Identification: 035424
Unit ID: 395362
Telephone: (760) 366-3791 Carnegie Class: Assoc/Pub-S-SC
FAX Number: (760) 366-5255 Calendar System: Semester
URL: www.cmccd.edu
Established: 1999 Annual Undergrad Tuition & Fees (In-District): $1,380
Enrollment: 2,702 Coed
Affiliation or Control: State/Local IRS Status: 501(c)3
Highest Offering: Associate Degree
Program: Occupational; 2-Year Principally Bachelor's Creditable
Accreditation: WJ

01 Superintendent/President .... Mr. Jeff CUMMINGS
05 Dean of Instruction/CIO .... Dr. Pam KERSEY
32 Exec VP for Academic & Student Affs .... Mr. Greg BROWN
15 Manager of Human Resources .... Ms. Andrea RIESGO
18 Director of Facilities & Operations .... Mr. Jerry PHIPPS
56 Coordinator of Base Programs .... Mr. Zachary GINDER
102 Executive Director of Foundation .... Ms. Sandy SMITH
10 Chief Business Officer .... Ms. Meredith PLUMMER
37 Director of Financial Aid .... Mr. Brian HEINEMANN
76 Dir Hlth Science-Registered Nursing .... Ms. Christi BLAUWKAMP
13 Director of Information Systems .... Mr. Steve KEMP
26 Public Relations & Event Specialist .... Ms. Jolie ALPIN

Cuesta College (H)

PO Box 8106, San Luis Obispo CA 93403-8106

County: San Luis Obispo FICE Identification: 001192
Unit ID: 113193
Telephone: (805) 546-3100 Carnegie Class: Assoc/Pub-R-L
FAX Number: (805) 546-3904 Calendar System: Semester
URL: www.cuesta.edu
Established: 1963 Annual Undergrad Tuition & Fees (In-District): $1,400
Enrollment: 9,211 Coed
Affiliation or Control: State/Local IRS Status: 501(c)3
Highest Offering: Associate Degree
Program: Occupational; 2-Year Principally Bachelor's Creditable
Accreditation: WJ, EMT

01 Superintendent/President .... Dr. Gilbert H. STORK
05 VP/Asst Supt Academic Affairs .... Dr. Deborah WULFF
10 VP/Asst Supt Administrative Svcs .... Mr. Chris GREEN
32 VP/Asst Supt Student Svcs Col Ctrs .... Ms. Sandee MCLAUGHLIN
12 Dean North Co Campus/S Co Ctr .... Dr. Maria ESCOBEDO
35 Dean of Student Services .... Ms. Catherine RIEDSTRA
30 Exec Dir Foundation/Inst Adv .... Ms. Shannon HILL
08 Director Library/Lrng Resources/DE .... Mr. Mark STENGEL
35 Coordinator Student Life/Leadership .... Dr. Anthony GUTIERREZ
13 Exec Director Info Sys and Tech .... Mr. Keith STEARNS
66 Director of Nursing .... Ms. Marcia SCOTT
15 Exec Dir Human Res Labor Rels .... Ms. Melissa RICHERSON
19 Director of Public Safety .... Mr. Joseph ARTEAGA
40 Director of Bookstore .... Ms. Trudy BELL
41 Director of Athletics .... Mr. Robert MARIUCCI
18 Dir Maintenance/Operations/Grounds .... Mr. Terry REECE
38 Director Counseling Services .... Mr. Candelario MUNOZ
103 Dir Workforce Econ Devel Cmty Pgm .... Dr. Matthew GREEN
23 Coordinator of Health Services .... Ms. Joan DUFFY
81 Dean Acad Affs Sciences & Math .... Dr. Jason CURTIS
79 Dean Ac Aff Arts/Humanities/Soc Sci .... Dr. Pamela RALSTON
103 Dean Ac Aff Workforce Econ Dev .... Dr. John CASCAMO
76 Associate Director of Allied Health .... Vacant
07 Director of Admissions & Records .... Ms. Kristin PIMENTEL
09 Director of Institutional Research .... Dr. Ryan CARTNAL
21 Director Fiscal Services .... Vacant
102 Director Foundation Programs .... Ms. Karen TACKET

The Culinary Institute of America at Greystone (I)

2555 Main Street, Saint Helena CA 94574-9504

Telephone: (707) 967-1100 Identification: 666260
Accreditation: &M

† Regional accreditation is carried under the parent institution in Hyde Park, NY.

Deep Springs College (J)

HC 72 Box 45001, Via Dyer, NV 89010-9803

County: Inyo FICE Identification: 001194
Unit ID: 113528
Telephone: (760) 872-2000 Carnegie Class: Not Classified
FAX Number: (760) 874-7077 Calendar System: Other
URL: www.deepsprings.edu
Established: 1917 Annual Undergrad Tuition & Fees: $0
Enrollment: 27 Male
Affiliation or Control: Independent Non-Profit IRS Status: 501(c)3
Highest Offering: Associate Degree
Program: Occupational
Accreditation: WJ

01 President .... Mr. David NEIDORF
05 Academic Dean .... Ms. Amity WILCZEK
88 Ranch Manager .... Ms. Janice HUNTER
10 Director of Operations .... Mr. Padraic MACLEISH
06 Registrar/Librarian .... Ms. Gwen VON KLAN
21 Office Manager .... Ms. Niki FRISHMAN
88 Chef/BH Manager .... Mr. Marc MORA
88 Farm Manager/Maintenance .... Mr. Noah BEYELER

Dell'Arte International School of Physical Theatre (K)

P.O. Box 816, 131 H Street, Blue Lake CA 95525

County: Humboldt FICE Identification: 030256
Unit ID: 113537
Telephone: (707) 668-5663 Carnegie Class: Spec/Arts
FAX Number: (707) 668-5665 Calendar System: Other
URL: www.dellarte.com
Established: 1975 Annual Graduate Tuition & Fees: $12,750
Enrollment: 42 Coed
Affiliation or Control: Independent Non-Profit IRS Status: 501(c)3
Highest Offering: Master's; No Undergraduates
Program: Professional; Fine Arts Emphasis
Accreditation: THEA

01 Executive Director ... Ms. Stephanie THOMPSON
05 Producing Artistic Director ... Mr. Michael FIELDS
10 Chief Financial Officer ... Ms. Stephanie WITZEL
30 Development/Community Coordinator ... Ms. Meghan FRANK
06 School Administrator/Registrar ... Ms. Sarah PETERS
07 Director of Admissions ... Mr. Matt CHAPMAN

Design Institute of San Diego (A)

8555 Commerce Avenue, San Diego CA 92121-2685
County: San Diego FICE Identification: 022980
Unit ID: 113582
Telephone: (858) 566-1200 Carnegie Class: Spec/Arts
FAX Number: (858) 566-2711 Calendar System: Semester
URL: www.disd.edu
Established: 1977 Annual Undergrad Tuition & Fees: $17,547
Enrollment: 171 Coed
Affiliation or Control: Proprietary IRS Status: Proprietary
Highest Offering: Baccalaureate
Program: Professional; Fine Arts Emphasis
Accreditation: **ACICS**, CIDA

01 President ... Mr. Arthur ROSENSTEIN
05 Vice President ... Ms. Gloria ROSENSTEIN
11 Campus Director/COO ... Ms. Margot DOUCETTE
07 Director of Admissions ... Ms. Kairyn HAINES
37 Director Financial Aid ... Ms. Jackie GLORIA
32 Director of Student Services ... Ms. Tena MOIOLA
08 Librarian ... Ms. Lisa SCHATTMAN
06 Registrar ... Ms. Tracy GULINO
07 Outreach & Admissions ... Ms. Amelie RACICOT
07 Admissions ... Ms. Elizabeth BARRY

DeVry University - Pomona Campus (B)

901 Corporate Center Drive, Pomona CA 91768-2642
Telephone: (909) 622-8866 FICE Identification: 023329
Accreditation: **&NH**, CAHIIM, ENGT

† Regional accreditation is carried under the parent institution in Downers Grove, IL.

Dominican School of Philosophy and Theology (C)

2301 Vine Street, Berkeley CA 94708-1816
County: Alameda FICE Identification: 001296
Unit ID: 113704
Telephone: (510) 849-2030 Carnegie Class: Spec/Faith
FAX Number: (510) 849-1372 Calendar System: Semester
URL: www.dspt.edu
Established: 1932 Annual Undergrad Tuition & Fees: $16,680
Enrollment: 92 Coed
Affiliation or Control: Roman Catholic IRS Status: 501(c)3
Highest Offering: Master's
Program: Professional; Religious Emphasis
Accreditation: **WC**, THEOL

01 President ... Rev. Michael SWEENEY
05 Academic Dean ... Rev. Christopher M. RENZ
10 COO/CFO ... Mr. Ian BROOKS
07 Director of Admissions ... Ms. Jamie D. MARTOS
06 Registrar ... Sr. Francis Marie SEALE
26 Director of Communications ... Ms. Heidi MCKENNA
84 Recruitment/Development Officer ... Ms. Justyna KRUKOWSKA

Dominican University of California (D)

50 Acacia Avenue, San Rafael CA 94901-2298
County: Marin FICE Identification: 001196
Unit ID: 113698
Telephone: (415) 457-4440 Carnegie Class: Master's M
FAX Number: (415) 485-3205 Calendar System: Semester
URL: www.dominican.edu
Established: 1890 Annual Undergrad Tuition & Fees: $42,100
Enrollment: 2,108 Coed
Affiliation or Control: Independent Non-Profit IRS Status: 501(c)3
Highest Offering: Master's
Program: Liberal Arts And General; Teacher Preparatory; Professional
Accreditation: **WC**, ART, NURSE, OT

01 President ... Dr. Mary B. MARCY
05 Vice President Academic Affairs ... Dr. Nicola PITCHFORD
10 Vice President Business & Finance ... Ms. Michele HINKEN
32 Dean of Students ... Dr. Paul RACCANELLO
84 Vice President Enrollment Mgmt ... Mr. Peter JOHNSON
20 Associate VP Academic Affairs ... Dr. Mojgan BEHMAND
26 Director Marketing ... Ms. Nancy BULETTE
27 Director Comm & Media Relations ... Ms. Sarah GARDNER
04 Exec Assistant to the President ... Mrs. Sarita PURECE
100 Dir Board Relations/Special Events ... Ms. Jackie GENTILE
79 Dean Sch Arts/Humanities/Soc Sci ... Dr. Laura STIVERS
76 Dean Sch Health/Natural Sci ... Dr. Ching-Hua WANG
53 Dean Sch Educ/Counsel Psych ... Dr. Robin GAYLE
50 Dean Barowsky Sch Business ... Dr. Sam BELDONA
18 Exec Dir Facilities/Physical Plant ... Mr. Jacques CHARTON
08 University Librarian ... Mr. Gary GORKA
09 Director Institutional Research ... Mr. Christopher ANTONS
37 Director Financial Aid ... Ms. Shanon LITTLE
07 Director Undergrad Admissions ... Vacant
06 AVP Academic Services & Registrar ... Ms. Marianne STICKEL
29 Director Alumni Relations ... Ms. Katherine KUNZ
15 Director Human Resources ... Ms. Wendy LEE
36 Director Career Services ... Ms. Vanessa IOANNIDES
28 Dean Diversity and Equity ... Dr. Suresh APPAVOO
92 Director Honors Program ... Vacant
38 Director Counseling Center ... Dr. Charles BILLINGS
85 Director Global Education ... Dr. Kati BELL
30 VP Advancement/Alumni Engagement ... Ms. Kathleen KRUEGER PARK
11 Chief of Administration ... Ms. Michele HINKEN
41 Athletic Director ... Ms. Amy HENKELMAN
45 Sr Advisor Strategy & Planning ... Dr. Hanna RODRIGUEZ-FARRAR
102 Director Foundation ... Ms. Cyndi WEINGARD
108 Director of Assessment ... Dr. Matthew BRONSON

Dongguk University (E)

440 Shatto Place, Los Angeles CA 90020-1704
County: Los Angeles FICE Identification: 031095
Unit ID: 122117
Telephone: (213) 487-0110 Carnegie Class: Spec/Health
FAX Number: (213) 487-0527 Calendar System: Quarter
URL: www.dula.edu
Established: 1979 Annual Undergrad Tuition & Fees: $11,900
Enrollment: 171 Coed
Affiliation or Control: Independent Non-Profit IRS Status: 501(c)3
Highest Offering: Master's; No Lower Division
Program: Professional
Accreditation: **ACUP**

01 President ... Dr. Min Sub HWANG
05 Dean of Academic Affairs ... Mr. David LEE
10 Director of Finance ... Mr. Albert KIM
37 Financial Aid Officer ... Ms. Julia PARK
06 Registrar ... Mr. Hoon SEO
63 Director of Oriental Medical Center ... Ms. Kay JOO
18 Director of Facilities ... Mr. Arturo AGUIRRE
21 Office Manager ... Ms. Min PARK
85 International Student Advisor ... Mr. Phillip YEW

East San Gabriel Valley Regional Occupational Program and Technical Center (F)

1501 W. Del Norte Street, West Covina CA 91790
County: Los Angeles FICE Identification: 031166
Unit ID: 413802
Telephone: (626) 472-5121 Carnegie Class: Not Classified
FAX Number: (626) 472-5125 Calendar System: Semester
URL: www.esgvrop.org
Established: Annual Undergrad Tuition & Fees (In-District): $6,615
Enrollment: 581 Coed
Affiliation or Control: State/Local IRS Status: 501(c)3
Highest Offering: Associate Degree
Program: Occupational
Accreditation: **COE**, MAC

01 Superintendent ... Dr. Laurel ADLER
10 Chief Financial Officer ... Ms. Josephine QUACH

El Camino College (G)

16007 Crenshaw Boulevard, Torrance CA 90506-0002
County: Los Angeles FICE Identification: 001197
Unit ID: 113980
Telephone: (310) 660-3670 Carnegie Class: Assoc/Pub-S-SC
FAX Number: (310) 660-7798 Calendar System: Semester
URL: www.elcamino.edu
Established: 1947 Annual Undergrad Tuition & Fees (In-District): $1,140
Enrollment: 24,263 Coed
Affiliation or Control: State/Local IRS Status: 501(c)3
Highest Offering: Associate Degree
Program: Occupational; 2-Year Principally Bachelor's Creditable
Accreditation: **WJ**, COARC, RAD

01 President ... Dr. Thomas M. FALLO
05 Vice President Academic Affairs ... Dr. Jean SHANKWEILER
11 Vice Pres Administrative Services ... Dr. Jo Ann HIGDON
32 Vice Pres Student/Community Advance ... Dr. Jeanie NISHIME
15 Vice Pres of Human Resources ... Ms. Linda BEAM
30 Dean Community Advancement ... Mr. Jose ANAYA
45 Director Research Planning ... Ms. Irene GRAFF
72 Dean Industry & Technology ... Dr. Stephanie RODRIGUEZ
81 Dean Math ... Ms. Jacquelyn SIMS
50 Dean of Business ... Dr. Virginia RAPP
83 Dean Behavioral & Social Science ... Dr. Gloria MIRANDA
68 Dean Health/Exer/Science/Sport ... Mr. Rory NATIVIDAD
57 Dean Fine Arts ... Dr. Connie FITZSIMONS
76 Interim Dean Natural Sciences ... Dr. Amy GRANT
79 Dean Humanities ... Mr. Tom LEW
38 Dean Counseling Matriculation Svcs ... Dr. Dipte PALEL
84 Dean of Enrollment Services ... Mr. William GARCIA
13 Director of Information Systems ... Vacant
31 Director of Community Relations ... Ms. Ann GARTEN
66 Interim Director of Nursing ... Ms. Wanda MORRIS
07 Dir Admissions/Records/Registrar ... Mr. Bill MULROONEY
10 Chief Business Officer ... Dr. Jo Ann HIGDON
26 Chief Public Relations Officer ... Ms. Ann M. GARTEN
102 Executive Director Foundation ... Ms. Andrea SALA
96 Director of Purchasing ... Mr. Rocky BONURA
40 Director of Bookstore ... Ms. Julie BOURLIER
19 Chief of Campus Police ... Mr. Michael TREVIS
18 Director of Facilities Plng/Svcs ... Mr. Tom BROWN
35 Acting Director of Student Affairs ... Ms. Michelle ARTHUR
37 Director Student Financial Aid ... Ms. Melissa GUESS
06 Registrar ... Mr. Bill MULROONEY
29 Director Alumni Relations ... Ms. Andrea SALA
09 Director Institutional Research ... Ms. Irene GRAFF
28 Director of Diversity ... Ms. Jayne ISHIKAWA
21 Business Manager ... Ms. Janice ELY
25 Resource Devel/Grants Coordinator ... Ms. Andrea SALA

El Camino College Compton Center (H)

1111 E Artesia Boulevard, Compton CA 90221-5393
Telephone: (310) 900-1600 FICE Identification: 001188
Accreditation: **&WJ**

† Regional accreditation is carried under the parent institution in Torrance, CA.

Emperor's College of Traditional Oriental Medicine (I)

1807-B Wilshire Boulevard, Santa Monica CA 90403-5678
County: Los Angeles FICE Identification: 026090
Unit ID: 114114
Telephone: (310) 453-8300 Carnegie Class: Spec/Health
FAX Number: (310) 829-3838 Calendar System: Quarter
URL: www.emperors.edu
Established: 1983 Annual Undergrad Tuition & Fees: $15,500
Enrollment: 222 Coed
Affiliation or Control: Proprietary IRS Status: Proprietary
Highest Offering: Doctorate
Program: Professional
Accreditation: **ACUP**

01 Chief Executive Officer/President ... Yun KIM
05 Academic Dean ... Jacques MORAMARCO
07 Admissions Director ... Nicole WETHERINGTON
37 Financial Aid Officer ... Farida LUGEMBE
11 COO/Administrator ... George PARK
58 Dean Doctoral Programs ... John FANG

Empire College (J)

3035 Cleveland Avenue, Santa Rosa CA 95403-2100
County: Sonoma FICE Identification: 009032
Unit ID: 114123
Telephone: (707) 546-4000 Carnegie Class: Assoc/PrivFP
FAX Number: (707) 546-4058 Calendar System: Other
URL: www.empcol.edu
Established: 1961 Annual Undergrad Tuition & Fees: $18,450
Enrollment: 417 Coed
Affiliation or Control: Proprietary IRS Status: Proprietary
Highest Offering: Master's
Program: Occupational; Technical Emphasis
Accreditation: **ACICS**

01 President ... Mr. Roy HURD
26 Vice Pres Marketing/Administration ... Mrs. Sherie HURD
05 Director of Education ... Mr. Mark KALAGORGEVICH
61 Dean Law School ... Mr. Michael MULLINS
07 Director of Admissions ... Ms. Dahnja STRAUB
37 Director Student Financial Aid ... Mrs. Mary O'BRIEN
11 Administrative Services Manager ... Ms. Karina NUNO
10 Director of Accounting ... Mr. David YARBROUGH
36 Co-Advisor Career Placement ... Ms. Tammy SAMS
36 Co-Advisor Career Placement ... Ms. Jennifer SEDNA
40 Bookstore Manager ... Ms. Kass VON DER MEHDEN
06 Registrar ... Ms. Renee DIXON
38 Student Success Advisor ... Ms. Nora SONGSTER

Epic Bible College & Graduate School (K)

4330 Auburn Boulevard, Sacramento CA 95841
County: Sacramento FICE Identification: 034033
Unit ID: 124487
Telephone: (916) 348-4689 Carnegie Class: Spec/Faith
FAX Number: (916) 468-0866 Calendar System: Trimester
URL: www.EPIC.edu
Established: 1974 Annual Undergrad Tuition & Fees: $9,166
Enrollment: 164 Coed
Affiliation or Control: Independent Non-Profit IRS Status: 501(c)3
Highest Offering: Master's
Program: Liberal Arts And General; Religious Emphasis
Accreditation: **TRACS**

01 President ... Dr. Ronald W. HARDEN
05 Vice President of Academics ... Dr. Greg L. HARTLEY
88 Director MA in Ethical Leadership ... Dr. Ed FUNK
88 Director MA In Biblical Studies ... Dr. Gene MAYNARD
108 Director of Assessment ... Ms. Rosemarie HOWELL
08 Director Learning Resource ... Rev. Dave SOLBERG
10 Chief Financial Officer ... Mr. C. Steven CHANEY
37 Director of Financial Services ... Mr. David PINESCHI
06 Director of Records ... Ms. Kathy CLARKE
106 Director of Online Program ... Rev. John GALLEGOS
26 Director of Marketing ... Rev. Daniel HARDEN

Eternity Bible College (A)

2136 Winifred Street, Simi Valley CA 93063
County: Ventura Identification: 667045
Telephone: (805) 581-1233 Carnegie Class: Not Classified
FAX Number: (805) 581-1245 Calendar System: Semester
URL: www.eternitybiblecollege.com
Established: 2004 Annual Undergrad Tuition & Fees: $5,000
Enrollment: 183 Coed
Affiliation or Control: Independent Non-Profit IRS Status: 501(c)3
Highest Offering: Baccalaureate
Program: Religious Emphasis
Accreditation: @BI

01 President .... Joshua WALKER
05 Academic Dean .... Spencer MACCUISH
07 Director of Admissions .... Mary Beth DRAGOUN
06 Registrar/Finance Manager .... Ryan MCGLADDERY
32 Dir Student Life/Exec Asst .... Nicole MCGLADDERY

Evangelia University (B)

2660 West Woodland Drive, Suite 200,
Anaheim CA 92801-2650
County: Orange Identification: 666640
Telephone: (714) 527-0691 Carnegie Class: Not Classified
FAX Number: (714) 527-0693 Calendar System: Other
URL: www.evangelia.edu
Established: 1999 Annual Undergrad Tuition & Fees: $3,650
Enrollment: 50 Coed
Affiliation or Control: Reformed Presbyterian Church IRS Status: 501(c)3
Highest Offering: Doctorate
Program: Liberal Arts And General; Religious Emphasis
Accreditation: TRACS

01 President .... Dr. David H. SHIN
05 Academic Dean .... Dr. Soo Young LEE
11 Dean Admin/Chief Operating Officer .... Ki Won HAN
06 Registrar/Foreign Student Advisor .... Charley LEE
57 Chair Masters of Arts Program .... Cha Hi WON
32 Dean of Students .... Ki Won HAN

Ex'pression College (C)

6601 Shellmound Street, Emeryville CA 94608-1021
County: Alameda FICE Identification: 039733
Unit ID: 447458
Telephone: (510) 654-2934 Carnegie Class: Spec/Arts
FAX Number: (510) 658-3414 Calendar System: Quarter
URL: www.expression.edu
Established: 1999 Annual Undergrad Tuition & Fees: $23,600
Enrollment: 500 Coed
Affiliation or Control: Proprietary IRS Status: Proprietary
Highest Offering: Baccalaureate
Program: Professional; Fine Arts Emphasis
Accreditation: ACCSC

01 Executive Director & CEO .... Mr. Fred FARIDIAN
05 Director of Education .... Mr. Drew WATERS

Ex'pression College - San Jose (D)

1751 Fox Drive, San Jose CA 95131
Telephone: (408) 620-3300 Identification: 770552
Accreditation: ACCSC

† Branch campus of Ex'pression College, Emeryville, CA.

Fashion Institute of Design and Merchandising-Orange County (E)

17590 Gillette Avenue, Irvine CA 92614-5610
Telephone: (888) 974-3436 Identification: 666004
Accreditation: &WC, ART

† Regional accreditation is carried under the parent institution in Los Angeles, CA.

Fashion Institute of Design and Merchandising-San Diego (F)

350 10th Avenue, 3rd Floor, San Diego CA 92101
Telephone: (619) 235-2049 Identification: 666005
Accreditation: &WC, ART

† Regional accreditation is carried under the parent institution in Los Angeles, CA.

Fashion Institute of Design and Merchandising-San Francisco (G)

55 Stockton Street, San Francisco CA 94108-5829
Telephone: (415) 675-5200 FICE Identification: 013041
Accreditation: &WC, ART

† Regional accreditation is carried under the parent institution in Los Angeles, CA.

Feather River College (H)

570 Golden Eagle Avenue, Quincy CA 95971-9124
County: Plumas FICE Identification: 008597
Unit ID: 114433
Telephone: (530) 283-0202 Carnegie Class: Assoc/Pub-R-M
FAX Number: (530) 283-3757 Calendar System: Semester
URL: www.frc.edu
Established: 1968 Annual Undergrad Tuition & Fees (In-District): $1,461
Enrollment: 1,623 Coed
Affiliation or Control: State/Local IRS Status: 501(c)3
Highest Offering: Associate Degree
Program: 2-Year Principally Bachelor's Creditable
Accreditation: WJ

01 Superintendent/President .... Dr. Kevin TRUTNA
10 Chief Financial Officer .... Mr. Jim SCOUBES
05 Chief Instructional Officer .... Dr. Derek LERCH
32 Chief Student Services Officer .... Dr. Karen PIERSON
15 Director Human Resources/EEO .... Mr. David BURRIS
18 Director of Facilities/CTO .... Mr. Nick BOYD
06 Registrar/Dir of Admissions .... Ms. Leslie MIKESELL
37 Director Student Financial Aid .... Mr. Andre VAN DER VELDEN
96 Purchasing Agent .... Ms. Tamara CLINE
04 Administrative Asst to President .... Ms. Cynthia HALL
09 Director of Institutional Research .... Dr. Agnes KOOS

FIDM/Fashion Institute of Design and Merchandising-Los Angeles (I)

919 S Grand Avenue, Los Angeles CA 90015-1421
County: Los Angeles FICE Identification: 011112
Unit ID: 114354
Telephone: (213) 624-1200 Carnegie Class: Spec/Arts
FAX Number: (213) 624-9354 Calendar System: Quarter
URL: www.fidm.edu
Established: 1969 Annual Undergrad Tuition & Fees: $29,930
Enrollment: 3,142 Coed
Affiliation or Control: Proprietary IRS Status: Proprietary
Highest Offering: Baccalaureate
Program: 2-Year Principally Bachelor's Creditable; Business Emphasis
Accreditation: WC, ART

01 President .... Mrs. Tonian HOHBERG
10 Vice President Finance .... Ms. Annie JOHNSON
45 Vice President Planning .... Mrs. Vivien LOWY
05 Vice President Education .... Mrs. Barbara BUNDY
20 Dean of Academic Development .... Dr. Carol ROOKSTOOL
12 Director Orange County Campus .... Ms. Dorothy METCALFE
12 Director San Francisco Campus .... Ms. Barbara CUPPER
27 Exec Director Industry Relations .... Ms. Sharon RYAN
08 Director Library .... Ms. Kathy BAILON
06 Registrar .... Mr. Michael GILBERT
37 Director Financial Aid .... Ms. Norine FULLER
26 Director Public Relations .... Ms. Shirley WILSON
88 Director Adv Fashion Design .... Ms. Mary STEPHENS
09 Director Institutional Research .... Dr. Andrea HELEKAR
38 Articulation Officer .... Mr. Ben WEINBERG
21 Director Student Financial Services .... Mr. Chris JENNINGS
96 Director of Purchasing .... Mrs. Darlene LATINVILLE
97 Chair General Educ/Dean Education .... Ms. Sheryl RABINOVICH
72 Chair Apparel Manufacturing Mgmt .... Ms. Roni MILLER START
07 Director of Admissions .... Ms. Susan ARONSON
108 Director Institutional Assessment .... Dr. Andrea D. HELEKAR
13 Chief Info Technology Officer (CIO) .... Ms. Roxanne REYNOLDS-LAIR
15 Director Personnel Services .... Ms. Julie Ann OTTESON

Fielding Graduate University (J)

2020 De La Vina Street, Santa Barbara CA 93105-3538
County: Santa Barbara FICE Identification: 020961
Unit ID: 114549
Telephone: (805) 687-1099 Carnegie Class: DRU
FAX Number: (805) 687-4590 Calendar System: Trimester
URL: www.fielding.edu
Established: 1974 Annual Graduate Tuition & Fees: $25,650
Enrollment: 1,201 Coed
Affiliation or Control: Independent Non-Profit IRS Status: 501(c)3
Highest Offering: Doctorate; No Undergraduates
Program: Professional
Accreditation: WC, CLPSY

01 President .... Dr. Katrina ROGERS
101 Exec Asst to President & Provost .... Ms. Maisee THAO
05 Provost .... Vacant
09 VP Strategic Initiative/Research .... Mr. Orlando TAYLOR
10 VP and Chief Financial Officer .... Ms. Lisa LEWIS
30 VP Univ Advancement & Development .... Mr. David EDELMAN
20 VP Academic Services .... Dr. Monique L. SNOWDEN
15 Director Human Resources .... Ms. Amy RAMOS
06 Registrar/Dir Enrollment Services .... Ms. Bridget BRADY

Five Branches University, Graduate School of Traditional Chinese Medicine (K)

3031 Tisch Way, Ste 507, San Jose CA 95128
County: Santa Clara Identification: 667008
Telephone: (408) 260-0208 Carnegie Class: Not Classified
FAX Number: (408) 261-3166 Calendar System: Semester
URL: www.fivebranches.edu
Established: 2005 Annual Undergrad Tuition & Fees: $12,210
Enrollment: 300 Coed
Affiliation or Control: Proprietary IRS Status: Proprietary
Highest Offering: Doctorate; No Lower Division
Program: Professional
Accreditation: ACUP

01 President/CEO .... Ron ZAIDMAN
05 VP Academic Affairs .... Joanna ZHAO
06 Registrar .... Gina HUANG
88 Director of Doctoral Program .... Fei-Ing TZENG
10 Chief Financial Officer .... Liana CHEN
88 Associate Director Doctoral .... Nan WANG
88 Associate Director Doctoral .... E-Sing HONG
88 Director of Chinese Masters of TCM .... Jasmine HUANG
88 Director of Korean Masters of TCM .... Heerei PARK
56 Director of Extension Program .... Sumedha GOH
88 Clinic Manager .... Yi-Chia LEE

Five Branches University, Graduate School of Traditional Chinese Medicine (L)

200 7th Avenue, Santa Cruz CA 95062-4669
County: Santa Cruz FICE Identification: 031313
Unit ID: 114585
Telephone: (831) 476-9424 Carnegie Class: Spec/Health
FAX Number: (831) 476-8928 Calendar System: Semester
URL: www.fivebranches.edu
Established: 1984 Annual Undergrad Tuition & Fees: $14,286
Enrollment: 371 Coed
Affiliation or Control: Proprietary IRS Status: Proprietary
Highest Offering: Master's; No Lower Division
Program: Professional
Accreditation: ACUP

01 President & CEO .... Ron ZAIDMAN
05 Vice President of Academic Affairs .... Joanna ZHAO
11 Director of Operations .... Gina HUANG
10 Chief Accounting Officer .... Liana CHEN
26 Dir of Marketing & Public Relations .... Ali POLK
08 Librarian .... Jim EMDY
17 Clinic Quality Control Director .... Sally LEWIS
06 Registrar .... Ling ZHANG
07 Admissions Director .... Eleonor MENDELSON
37 Director Student Financial Aid .... Mecca MATILDA
32 Director of Student Services .... Ana LOBATO
56 Director of Extension Programs .... Sumheda GOH
88 Student Accounts Manager .... Kayoko YAMAMOTO

*Foothill-De Anza Community College District System Office (M)

12345 El Monte Road, Los Altos Hills CA 94022-4597
County: Santa Clara FICE Identification: 009020
Unit ID: 114831
Telephone: (650) 949-6100 Carnegie Class: N/A
FAX Number: (650) 941-6289
URL: www.fhda.edu

01 Chancellor .... Dr. Judy C. MINER
10 Vice Chancellor Business Services .... Mr. Kevin MCELROY
15 Vice Chancellor Human Resources .... Ms. Dorene NOVOTNY
13 Vice Chancellor Technology .... Mr. Joseph MOREAU
18 Exec Dir Facilities/Operations .... Mr. Steve KITCHEN

*De Anza College (N)

21250 Stevens Creek Boulevard,
Cupertino CA 95014-5793
County: Santa Clara FICE Identification: 004480
Unit ID: 113333
Telephone: (408) 864-5678 Carnegie Class: Assoc/Pub-S-MC
FAX Number: (408) 864-5698 Calendar System: Quarter
URL: www.deanza.edu
Established: 1967 Annual Undergrad Tuition & Fees (In-District): $1,500
Enrollment: 23,230 Coed
Affiliation or Control: State/Local IRS Status: 501(c)3
Highest Offering: Associate Degree
Program: Occupational; 2-Year Principally Bachelor's Creditable
Accreditation: WJ, MLTAD

02 President .... Dr. Brian MURPHY
05 Vice Pres of Instruction .... Ms. Christina ESPINOSA-PIEB
32 Vice Pres of Student Services .... Dr. Stacey A. COOK
10 VP Finance/College Operations .... Ms. Susan CHEU
20 Assoc Vice Pres Instruction .... Ms. Rowena TOMANENG
35 Dean Student Development/EOPS .... Ms. Michele LEBLEU BURNS
38 Dean Counseling & Matriculation .... Dr. Angela CABALLERO DE CORDERO
07 Dean Admissions & Records .... Vacant
37 Director Student Financial Aid .... Ms. Lisa MANDY
15 Director Personnel Services .... Mr. Bret WATSON
18 Assoc Vice Pres College Operations .... Ms. Donna JONES-DULIN
21 Director Budget .... Mr. Bret WATSON
26 Director Marketing/Communications .... Ms. Marisa SPATAFORE
102 Int Exec Director Foundation .... Ms. Robin LYSSENKO
84 Director Enrollment Management .... Ms. Christina ESPINOSA PIEB
28 Director of Diversity .... Dr. Veronica NEAL
96 Director of Purchasing .... Ms. Pam GREY
36 Director Student Placement .... Dr. Stephen FLETCHER
09 Institutional Research Specialist .... Dr. Mallory NEWELL
06 Supervisor Admissions and Records .... Mr. Barry JOHNSON

*Foothill College (A)

12345 El Monte Road, Los Altos Hills CA 94022-4599
County: Santa Clara FICE Identification: 001199
Unit ID: 114716
Telephone: (650) 949-7777 Carnegie Class: Assoc/Pub-S-MC
FAX Number: (650) 949-7375 Calendar System: Quarter
URL: www.foothill.edu
Established: 1957 Annual Undergrad Tuition & Fees (In-District): $1,116
Enrollment: 13,277 Coed
Affiliation or Control: State/Local IRS Status: 501(c)3
Highest Offering: Associate Degree
Program: Occupational; 2-Year Principally Bachelor's Creditable
Accreditation: WJ, COARC, DA, DH, DMS, EMT, RAD

02 Interim President Dr. Kimberlee S. MESSINA
04 Executive Asst to the President Ms. Casie WHEAT
45 VP Institutional Resources Ms. Bernata SLATER
05 VP Instruction & Inst Research Vacant
32 VP Student Services Dr. Denise SWETT
103 VP Workforce Development/Instr Advc Vacant
20 Associate VP Instruction Dr. Andrew LAMANQUE
35 Dean Student Affairs & Activities Vacant
85 Dean International Education Dr. Vinita BALI
38 Dean Counseling & Special Programs Ms. Lan TRUONG
12 Dean FHDA Education Center Ms. Dawn GIRADELLI
88 Dean Disb Student Svcs & Vet Pgms Ms. Teresa ONG
35 Dir Student Activities & Affairs Ms. Daphne SMALL
08 Librarian Vacant
40 Director Bookstore Mr. Romeo PAULE
84 Dean Enrollment Services Ms. Nazy GALOYAN
37 Director Financial Aid Mr. Kevin HARRAL
26 Director of Marketing Ms. Andrea HANSTEIN
23 Coordinator Student Health Services Ms. Naomi KITAJIMA
76 Dean Biology/Health Science Dr. Nanette SOLVASON
50 Dean Business/Social Science Mr. Kurt HUEG
88 Dean Foothill Global Access Dr. Judy BAKER
57 Dean Fine Arts/Communications Mr. Mark ANDERSON
88 Dean Language Arts & LRC Mr. Paul STARER
68 Dean Kinesiology & Athletics Mr. Mark ANDERSON
81 Dean Physical Science/Math/Engr Dr. Victor TAM

Franciscan School of Theology (B)

4050 Mission Avenue, Oceanside CA 92057
County: San Diego FICE Identification: 011792
Unit ID: 114734
Telephone: (760) 547-1800 Carnegie Class: Spec/Faith
FAX Number: (760) 547-1806 Calendar System: Semester
URL: www.fst.edu
Established: 1968 Annual Graduate Tuition & Fees: $17,500
Enrollment: 42 Coed
Affiliation or Control: Independent Non-Profit IRS Status: 501(c)3
Highest Offering: Master's; No Undergraduates
Program: Professional; Religious Emphasis
Accreditation: WC, THEOL

01 President and Rector Fr. Joseph CHINNICI, OFM
05 Vice President for Academic Affairs Fr. Michael J. HIGGINS, TOR
06 Registrar Ms. Jackie GAMBLE
07 Co-Director of Recruitment Ms. Jeanette GONZALEZ
07 Co-Director of Recruitment Ms. Gabriela HEINTSCHEL
30 Associate Development Director Ms. Randi QUAID
10 Chief Financial Officer Ms. Kimberly RENNA

Fremont College (C)

18000 Studebaker Road, 9th Floor, Cerritos CA 90703
County: Los Angeles FICE Identification: 030399
Unit ID: 372073
Telephone: (562) 809-5100 Carnegie Class: Assoc/PrivFP
FAX Number: (562) 809-7100 Calendar System: Other
URL: www.fremont.edu
Established: 1985 Annual Undergrad Tuition & Fees: $33,802
Enrollment: 387 Coed
Affiliation or Control: Proprietary IRS Status: Proprietary
Highest Offering: Baccalaureate
Program: Occupational; 2-Year Principally Bachelor's Creditable
Accreditation: ACCSC

01 Chancellor/CEO Dr. Sabrina KAY

Fremont College (D)

3440 Wilshire Blvd, 6th Floor, Los Angeles CA 90010
Telephone: (213) 355-7777 Identification: 770553
Accreditation: ACCSC

† Branch campus of Fremont College, Cerritos, CA.

Fresno Pacific University (E)

1717 S Chestnut Avenue, Fresno CA 93702-4798
County: Fresno FICE Identification: 001253
Unit ID: 114813
Telephone: (559) 453-2000 Carnegie Class: Master's M
FAX Number: (559) 453-2007 Calendar System: Semester
URL: www.fresno.edu
Established: 1944 Annual Undergrad Tuition & Fees: $27,430
Enrollment: 3,718 Coed
Affiliation or Control: Mennonite Brethren Church IRS Status: 501(c)3
Highest Offering: Master's
Program: Liberal Arts And General; Teacher Preparatory
Accreditation: WC, NURSE, THEOL

01 President Dr. Richard KRIEGBAUM
05 Provost Dr. Stephen VARVIS
10 Vice President Finance Mr. Robert LIPPERT
30 Vice Pres Communications/Univ Rels Mrs. Diana BATES MOCK
11 Vice Pres of Operations Vacant
84 Vice Pres Enrollment Mgmt Mr. Jon ENDICOTT
50 Dean School of Business Dr. John KILROY
79 Int Dean Sch of Human/Rel/Soc Sci Dr. Ron HERMS
53 Dean School of Education Dr. Gary GRAMENZ
78 Dean School of Natural Sciences Dr. Karen CIANCI
42 Dean of Spiritual Formation Rev. Angulus WILSON
32 Dean of Student Life Dr. Randy WORDEN
06 Registrar Mr. Michael ALLEN
08 Director of Library Mr. Kevin ENNS-REMPEL
36 Director of Career Resource Center Ms. Alicia ANDRADE
15 Human Resources Director Mrs. Marylou MILLER
25 Director of Grants & Research Vacant
27 Publications Director Mr. Wayne STEFFEN
29 Director Alumni Development Ms. Ali SENA
37 Director of Financial Aid Mr. Gary NICHOLES
41 Athletic Director Vacant
19 Director of Security Vacant
26 Chief Public Relations Officer Ms. Diana MOCK
104 Dir International Pgms/Svcs Ofc Mr. Arnie PRIEB
07 Director of Admissions Vacant
18 Facilities Manager Mr. Gary METCALF
40 Bookstore Manager Ms. Erin NOEL
04 Administrative Asst to President Ms. Gwenevera E. BURKS
88 Seminary President Dr. Terry BRENSINGER
101 Secretary of the Institution/Board Ms. Arlene MACK
102 Dir Foundation/Corporate Relations Mr. Mark DEFFENBACHER
44 Director Major Gifts Mrs. Karin CHAO-BUSHOVEN
21 Controller Mr. Orren WANG

Fuller Theological Seminary (F)

135 N Oakland, Pasadena CA 91182-1780
County: Los Angeles FICE Identification: 001200
Unit ID: 114840
Telephone: (626) 584-5200 Carnegie Class: Spec/Faith
FAX Number: (626) 795-8767 Calendar System: Quarter
URL: www.fuller.edu
Established: 1947 Annual Graduate Tuition & Fees: $18,384
Enrollment: 2,305 Coed
Affiliation or Control: Independent Non-Profit IRS Status: 501(c)3
Highest Offering: Doctorate; No Undergraduates
Program: Professional; Religious Emphasis
Accreditation: WC, CLPSY, THEOL

01 President Dr. Mark A. LABBERTON
05 Provost & Sr Vice President Dr. C. Douglas MCCONNELL
28 Vice Provost Dr. Juan MARTINEZ
10 Vice President for Finance Mr. John WARD
30 Vice President Development Mr. Jon YASUDA
26 Vice President Comm/Mktg & Admiss Mrs. Irene NELLER
88 Vice President Vocation & Formation Dr. Tod BOLSINGER
73 Dean School of Theology Dr. Joel B. GREEN
88 Dean School of Psychology Dr. Mari CLEMENTS
88 Dean School Intercultural Studies Dr. Scott W. SUNQUIST
32 Dean of Students Dr. Steve YAMAGUCHI
71 Dean of the Chapel and Spirit Form Dr. Laura HARBERT
13 Assoc Provost Information Svc/CIO Dr. Kevin OSBORN
108 Assoc Prov Accreditation & Educ Eff Dr. Mignon R. JACOBS
88 Assoc Dean Doctor of Ministry Pgm Dr. Kurt FREDRICKSON
06 Registrar Mr. David E. KIEFER
15 Exec Director of HR & Org Dev Ms. Bernadette (BJ) BARBER
35 Assistant Dean of Students Mr. Sam BANG
07 Exec Dir Admiss & Stdnt Fin Svcs Mr. Steve SMITH
39 Director of Housing Services Ms. Inge-Lise TITHERADGE
04 Assistant to President Mr. Len TANG
18 Facilities Director Mr. Nathan MERRITT
109 Director of Auxiliary Services Mrs. Jeanne HANDOJO
43 General Counsel Ms. Rita K. ROWLAND
85 Dir Student Affs/International Svcs Mr. Sam BANG
37 Director Student Financial Services Mr. David RICHARDS
106 Dir Online Education/E-learning Mr. Tommy LISTER

Gavilan College (G)

5055 Santa Teresa Boulevard, Gilroy CA 95020-9599
County: Santa Clara FICE Identification: 001202
Unit ID: 114938
Telephone: (408) 848-4800 Carnegie Class: Assoc/Pub-S-SC
FAX Number: (408) 848-4801 Calendar System: Semester
URL: www.gavilan.edu
Established: 1919 Annual Undergrad Tuition & Fees (In-District): $2,171
Enrollment: 6,298 Coed
Affiliation or Control: State/Local IRS Status: 501(c)3
Highest Offering: Associate Degree
Program: Occupational; 2-Year Principally Bachelor's Creditable
Accreditation: WJ

01 Superintendent/President Dr. Steven M. KINSELLA
05 Exec Vice Pres Instructional Svcs Dr. Kathleen A. ROSE
11 Vice Pres Administrative Services Mr. Fred HARRIS
32 Vice President Student Services Ms. Kathleen MOBERG
06 Registrar Ms. Candice WHITNEY
08 Head Librarian Dr. Douglas ACHTERMAN
37 Director Student Financial Aid Ms. Veronica MARTINEZ
09 Director of Institutional Research Dr. Randy BROWN
15 Director Personnel Services Mr. Eric RAMONES
18 Chief Facilities/Physical Plant Mr. Jeff GOPP
13 Dir Computing & Information Mgmt Ms. Mimi ARVIZU
19 Director Security/Safety Ms. Ana GARCIA
26 Director Public Information Ms. Jan CHARGIN
23 Director Health Services Ms. Alice DUFRESNE-REYES
41 Athletic Director Mr. Ron HANNON
40 Director Bookstore Ms. Alexis BOLIN
49 Dean Liberal Arts/Sci/Dir Cont Educ Ms. Fran LOZANO
72 Dean Career Technical Education Ms. Sherrean CARR
07 Director of Admissions Ms. Candice WHITNEY
10 Chief Business Officer Ms. Susan CHEU
96 Director of Purchasing Ms. Connie CAMPOS
03 Executive Vice President Dr. Kathleen ROSE

Glendale Career College (H)

240 N. Brand Blvd, Lower Level, Glendale CA 91203
County: Los Angeles FICE Identification: 023385
Unit ID: 115010
Telephone: (818) 243-1131 Carnegie Class: Not Classified
FAX Number: (818) 243-6028 Calendar System: Semester
URL: www.glendalecareer.com
Established: 1946 Annual Undergrad Tuition & Fees: $11,394
Enrollment: 346 Coed
Affiliation or Control: Proprietary IRS Status: Proprietary
Highest Offering: Associate Degree
Program: Occupational
Accreditation: ABHES, SURGT, SURTEC

01 Campus Director Ms. Connie BELL

Glendale Community College (I)

1500 N Verdugo Road, Glendale CA 91208-2894
County: Los Angeles FICE Identification: 001203
Unit ID: 115001
Telephone: (818) 240-1000 Carnegie Class: Assoc/Pub-S-SC
FAX Number: (818) 549-9436 Calendar System: Semester
URL: www.glendale.edu
Established: 1927 Annual Undergrad Tuition & Fees (In-District): $1,175
Enrollment: 15,112 Coed
Affiliation or Control: State/Local IRS Status: 501(c)3
Highest Offering: Associate Degree
Program: Occupational; 2-Year Principally Bachelor's Creditable
Accreditation: WJ

01 Superintendent/President Dr. David VIAR
11 Exec Vice Pres Administrative Svcs Mr. Ron NAKASONE
05 Vice Pres Instructional Services Dr. Mary MIRCH
32 Vice President Student Services Dr. Ricardo PEREZ
51 Admn Dn Workforce Dev Cont/Cmty Ed Mr. Alfred RAMIREZ
15 Assoc VP Human Resources Ms. Teyanna WILLIAMS
45 Dean Research/Planning/Grants Dr. Edward KARPP
07 Director Admissions & Records Ms. Michelle MORA
20 Dean Instructional Services Mr. Michael RITTERBROWN
103 Dean Workforce Development Ms. Jan SWINTON
32 Dean Student Affairs Dr. Paul SCHLOSSMAN
35 Dean of Student Services Dr. Jeanette STIRDIVANT
37 Assoc Dean Stdnt Financial Aid Svcs Dr. Patricia HURLEY
10 Director Business Services Ms. Susan COURTEY
102 Exec Director College Foundation Ms. Lisa BROOKS

Golden Gate Baptist Theological Seminary (J)

201 Seminary Drive, Mill Valley CA 94941-3197
County: Marin FICE Identification: 001204
Unit ID: 115047
Telephone: (415) 380-1300 Carnegie Class: Not Classified
FAX Number: (415) 383-1302 Calendar System: Semester
URL: www.ggbts.edu
Established: 1944 Annual Graduate Tuition & Fees: $5,712
Enrollment: 1,297 Coed
Affiliation or Control: Southern Baptist IRS Status: 501(c)3
Highest Offering: Doctorate; No Undergraduates
Program: Professional; Religious Emphasis
Accreditation: WC, THEOL

00 President Emeritus Dr. William O. CREWS
01 President/Chairman of the Faculty Dr. Jeff IORG
30 Vice Pres Institutional Advancement Dr. Ben SKAUG
10 Vice Pres Strategic Services/CFO Mr. Gary GROAT
05 Vice President Academic Affairs Dr. D. Michael MARTIN
84 VP Enrollment/Student Svcs/Dn Stdts Dr. Adam GROZA
21 Controller Mr. Harry WEAVER
06 Registrar Ms. Jennifer PEACH
08 Director of Library Services Dr. Bob PHILLIPS
12 Director SC Campus Dr. Earl WAGGONER
12 Director PNW Campus Dr. Mark BRADLEY
12 Director Arizona Campus Dr. Dallas BIVINS
12 Director Rocky Mountain Campus Dr. Steve VETETO
13 Director Information Technology Mr. Jeff COLBERT
15 Director Personnel Services Vacant
18 Chief Facilities/Physical Plant Mr. Robert DVORAK
40 Director Bookstore Mrs. Amanda MCCORMICK
07 Director Admissions Ms. Karen ROBINSON
44 Director of Development Mr. Jay BADRY
84 Director Enrollment Management Ms. Karen ROBINSON
39 Resident Life Manager Mr. Shane TANIGAWA

Golden Gate University (A)

536 Mission Street, San Francisco CA 94105-2968
County: San Francisco FICE Identification: 001205
Unit ID: 115083
Telephone: (415) 442-7000 Carnegie Class: Master's L
FAX Number: (415) 495-2671 Calendar System: Trimester
URL: www.ggu.edu
Established: 1901 Annual Undergrad Tuition & Fees: $18,720
Enrollment: 3,016 Coed
Affiliation or Control: Independent Non-Profit IRS Status: 501(c)3
Highest Offering: Doctorate
Program: Professional; Business Emphasis
Accreditation: WC, LAW

01 President ..... Dr. David J. FIKE
05 VP of Academic Affairs ..... Ms. Barbara H. KARLIN
10 VP of Business Affairs & CFO ..... Mr. Robert D. HITE
30 VP of University Advancement ..... Ms. Tasia NEEVE
15 VP Human Resources/EEO ..... Ms. Terri SHULTIS
61 Dean School of Law ..... Ms. Rachel VAN CLEAVE
50 Dean Ageno School of Business ..... Dr. Paul FOUTS
88 Dean School of Taxation & Acctng ..... Mr. Fred SROKA
49 Dean Undergraduate Programs ..... Dr. Nate HINERMAN
100 Executive Director Ofc of President ..... Dr. John FYFE
106 Director E-Learning ..... Mr. Doug GEIER
32 Dean of Students & Student Affairs ..... Ms. Kayla KRUPNICK
08 Director University Library ..... Mr. James KRUSLING
08 Associate Dean Law Library ..... Mr. Michael DAW
84 Director Enrollment Services ..... Mr. Louis D. RICCARDI, JR.
06 University Registrar ..... Ms. Amy BARRON CHUNG
27 Chief Information Officer ..... Vacant
26 Director Marketing & Communications ..... Ms. Sandra HENAO
88 Director PLUS Program ..... Dr. Karen MCROBIE
09 Dir Planning/Resources/Analysis ..... Dr. Mercy LIM
18 Director Business Svcs/Facilities ..... Mr. Mike KOPERSKI
21 Controller ..... Mr. Altaf RAJAN
37 Director Student Financial Aid ..... Ms. Kathi KELLEY
38 Clinical Director/Counseling Svcs ..... Ms. Michael Anne CONLEY
108 Director Institutional Assessment ..... Ms. Lisa KRAMER

Golf Academy of America (B)

1950 Camino Vida Roble, Suite 125, Carlsbad CA 92008
Telephone: (800) 342-7342 FICE Identification: 015609
Accreditation: ACICS

† Branch campus of Virginia College, Birmingham, AL.

Grace Communion Seminary (C)

2011 E. Financial Way, PO Box 5005,
Glendora CA 91740-0730
County: Los Angeles Identification: 667115
Telephone: (626) 650-2306 Carnegie Class: Not Classified
FAX Number: (626) 650-2307 Calendar System: Semester
URL: www.gcs.edu
Established: 2008 Annual Graduate Tuition & Fees: $3,020
Enrollment: 43 Coed
Affiliation or Control: Independent Non-Profit IRS Status: 501(c)3
Highest Offering: Master's; No Undergraduates
Program: Religious Emphasis
Accreditation: DEAC

01 President/CEO ..... Dr. Gary DEDDO
05 Dean of Faculty ..... Dr. Michael MORRISON
06 Registrar ..... Ms. Susan WILLIAMS
10 CFO/Liaison Officer ..... Dr. Russell DUKE

Grace Mission University (D)

1645 West Valencia Drive, Fullerton CA 92833-3860
County: Orange Identification: 666642
Unit ID: 481058
Telephone: (714) 525-0088 Carnegie Class: Not Classified
FAX Number: (714) 525-0089 Calendar System: Semester
URL: www.gm.edu
Established: 1995 Annual Undergrad Tuition & Fees: $6,800
Enrollment: 88 Coed
Affiliation or Control: Presbyterian Church In America IRS Status: 501(c)3
Highest Offering: Doctorate
Program: Professional; Religious Emphasis
Accreditation: BI, @THEOL, TRACS

01 President ..... Kwangsin KIM
03 Executive Vice President & CEO ..... Dr. Kyunam CHOI
05 Academic Dean ..... Dr. Hyun Wan KIM
10 Chief Financial Officer ..... Mr. Chong Won CHOI
32 Dean of Students ..... Mr. Dong Hyun HUH
11 Dir Administration/Financial Aid ..... Mr. James KOO
06 Registrar ..... Ms. JungMo YOOK
08 Librarian ..... Mr. Brian SONG

Graduate Theological Union (E)

2400 Ridge Road, Berkeley CA 94709-1212
County: Alameda FICE Identification: 001207
Unit ID: 115214
Telephone: (510) 649-2400 Carnegie Class: Spec/Faith
FAX Number: (510) 649-1417 Calendar System: Semester
URL: www.gtu.edu
Established: 1962 Annual Graduate Tuition & Fees: $29,000
Enrollment: 237 Coed
Affiliation or Control: Independent Non-Profit IRS Status: 501(c)3
Highest Offering: Doctorate; No Undergraduates
Program: Professional; Religious Emphasis
Accreditation: WC, THEOL

01 President ..... Dr. Riess POTTERVELD
05 Dean/Vice Pres Academic Affairs ..... Dr. Arthur HOLDER
10 Vice Pres Administration/Finance ..... Mr. Steven G. ARGYRIS
30 Vice President for Advancement ..... Mr. Alan KELCHNER
32 VP Student Affairs/Dean Students ..... Dr. Kathleen KOOK
07 Director of Admissions ..... Dr. Andrea SHEAFFER
37 Director of Financial Aid ..... Ms. Kathleen ANTOKHIN
08 Library Director ..... Mr. Robert BENEDETTO
06 Consortial Registrar ..... Mr. John SEAL
13 Chief Information Officer ..... Mr. Jeffrey DIGREORIO
26 Director of Marketing & Comm ..... Mr. Jake STAFFORD
18 Building & Grounds Engineer ..... Mr. Curtis OSBORNE
15 Personnel Officer ..... Ms. Debi WALKER
04 Executive Assistant to President ..... Ms. Teresa JOYE

*Grossmont-Cuyamaca Community College District (F)

8800 Grossmont College Drive, El Cajon CA 92020-1799
County: San Diego FICE Identification: 007006
Unit ID: 115287
Telephone: (619) 644-7010 Carnegie Class: N/A
FAX Number: (619) 644-7936
URL: www.gcccd.edu

01 Chancellor ..... Dr. Cindy MILES
10 Vice Chanc Business Services ..... Ms. Sue REARIC
15 Vice Chanc Human Resources ..... Mr. Tim CORCORAN

*Cuyamaca College (G)

900 Rancho San Diego Parkway, El Cajon CA 92019-4304
County: San Diego FICE Identification: 021113
Unit ID: 113218
Telephone: (619) 660-4000 Carnegie Class: Assoc/Pub-S-MC
FAX Number: (619) 660-4399 Calendar System: Quarter
URL: www.cuyamaca.edu
Established: 1978 Annual Undergrad Tuition & Fees (In-District): $1,152
Enrollment: 8,774 Coed
Affiliation or Control: State/Local IRS Status: 501(c)3
Highest Offering: Associate Degree
Program: Occupational; 2-Year Principally Bachelor's Creditable
Accreditation: WJ

02 Interim President ..... Dr. Wei ZHOU
05 Interim Vice President Instruction ..... Dr. Scott HERRIN
32 Vice Pres Student Services ..... Dr. Scott THAYER
11 Vice Pres Admin Services ..... Ms. Sahar ABUSHABAN
81 Int Dean of Math/Sci/Engineering ..... Dr. Donna RILEY
79 Dean of Arts/Humanities/Social Sci ..... Mr. Pat SETZER
72 Dean of Career Technical Education ..... Dr. Kate ALDER
51 Dean Cont Educ/Workforce Training ..... Ms. Jennifer LEWIS
08 Dean Learning/Technology Resources ..... Ms. Kerry KILBER REBMAN
88 Assistant Dean EOPS ..... Dr. Wendy CRAIG
41 Interim Assoc Dean Athletics ..... Mr. Ryan SHUMAKER
35 Assoc Dean Student Affairs ..... Dr. Lauren VAKNIN
38 Dean Counseling & Enrollment Svc ..... Dr. Marsha GABLE
37 Director of Financial Aid ..... Mr. Ray REYES
07 Supervisor Admissions & Records ..... Vacant
18 Facilities Director ..... Mr. Bruce FARNHAM
04 Administrative Asst to President ..... Ms. Valeri WILSON

*Grossmont College (H)

8800 Grossmont College Drive, El Cajon CA 92020-1799
County: San Diego FICE Identification: 001208
Unit ID: 115296
Telephone: (619) 644-7000 Carnegie Class: Assoc/Pub-S-MC
FAX Number: (619) 644-7922 Calendar System: Semester
URL: www.grossmont.edu
Established: 1961 Annual Undergrad Tuition & Fees (In-District): $1,123
Enrollment: 16,269 Coed
Affiliation or Control: State/Local IRS Status: 501(c)3
Highest Offering: Associate Degree
Program: Occupational; 2-Year Principally Bachelor's Creditable
Accreditation: WJ, ADNUR, CEA, COARC, CVT, OTA

02 President ..... Dr. Nabil ABU-GHAZALEH
05 Vice Pres of Academic Affairs ..... Dr. Katrina VANDERWOUDE
32 Int Vice Pres of Student Services ..... Dr. Chris HILL
38 Dean Counseling Svcs ..... Ms. Martha CLAVELLE
72 Dean Career & Technical Workforce ..... Mr. Jim CUSTEAU
81 Dean Math/Natural Sci/Phys Educ ..... Dr. Mike REESE
60 Dean Arts/Languages/Communication ..... Mr. Steve BAKER
79 Dean English/Social & Behav Sci ..... Mr. Agustin ALBARRAN
08 Dean of Learning Resources ..... Dr. Taylor RUHL
35 Associate Dean Student Affairs ..... Ms. Victoria KERBA MILLER
09 Director of Institutional Research ..... Mr. Christopher TARMAN
10 Chief Business Officer ..... Mr. Tim FLOOD
15 Director Personnel Services ..... Vacant
18 Chief Facilities/Physical Plant ..... Mr. Ken EMMONS
26 Chief Public Relations Officer ..... Vacant
36 Director Student Placement ..... Ms. Nancy DAVIS
37 Director Student Financial Aid ..... Mr. Michael COPENHAVER
96 Director of Purchasing ..... Ms. Linda BERTOLUCCI

Gurnick Academy of Medical Arts (I)

2121 S. El Camino Real Bldg C200, San Mateo CA 94403
County: San Mateo FICE Identification: 041698
Unit ID: 459213
Telephone: (650) 685-6616 Carnegie Class: Not Classified
FAX Number: (650) 685-6640 Calendar System: Other
URL: www.gurnick.edu
Established: 2004 Annual Undergrad Tuition & Fees: $28,480
Enrollment: 873 Coed
Affiliation or Control: Proprietary IRS Status: Proprietary
Highest Offering: Associate Degree
Program: Occupational
Accreditation: ABHES, PTAA, RAD

01 CEO ..... Konstantin GOURJI
12 Campus Director ..... Debra FERRARI
11 Chief Operating Officer ..... Burke MALIN
05 Chief Academic Officer ..... Larisa REVZINA

Hartnell College (J)

411 Central Avenue, Salinas CA 93901-1697
County: Monterey FICE Identification: 001209
Unit ID: 115393
Telephone: (831) 755-6700 Carnegie Class: Assoc/Pub-R-L
FAX Number: (831) 755-6751 Calendar System: Semester
URL: www.hartnell.edu
Established: 1920 Annual Undergrad Tuition & Fees (In-District): $552
Enrollment: 17,133 Coed
Affiliation or Control: State/Local IRS Status: 501(c)3
Highest Offering: Associate Degree
Program: Occupational; 2-Year Principally Bachelor's Creditable
Accreditation: WJ, #COARC

01 Superintendent/President ..... Dr. Willard LEWALLEN
32 VP Student Affairs ..... Dr. Romero JALOMO
10 VP Administrative Services ..... Vacant
13 VP Information & Tech Systems ..... Vacant
05 VP Academic Affairs ..... Ms. Lori KILDAL
30 Exec Dir of Advancement ..... Ms. Jackie CRUZ
15 Assoc VP Human Resources/EEO ..... Ms. Terri PYER
21 Controller ..... Ms. Tracey RICHARDSON
18 Director of Facilities ..... Mr. Joseph REYES
20 Dean Academic Aff Programs/Support ..... Ms. Kathy MENDELSOHN
81 Dean Academic Affs Math/Science ..... Ms. Shannon BLISS
35 Director of Student Life ..... Mr. Augustine NEVAREZ
26 Director of Communications ..... Ms. Esmeralda OWENS
88 Dir of Student Affairs EOPS/DSPS ..... Mr. Paul CASEY
66 Dean Academic Affairs/Nursing ..... Ms. Debra KACZMAR
72 Dean Academic Affs Adv Tech ..... Dr. Zahi ATALLAH
83 Dean Acad Affs Soc/Fine Lang Arts ..... Dr. Celine PINET
88 Dean South County Educ Programs ..... Ms. Renata FUNKE
04 Senior Executive Assistant ..... Ms. Lucille SERRANO
35 Dean of Student Affairs ..... Ms. Mary DOMINGUEZ
09 Director of Institutional Research ..... Dr. Brian LOFMAN
101 Secretary of the Institution/Board ..... Ms. Lucille SERRANO
35 Dean of Student Affairs ..... Dr. Mark SANCHEZ
41 Director Athletics ..... Mr. Daniel TERESA
45 Dean Inst Planning and Effective ..... Dr. Brian LOFMAN

Harvey Mudd College (K)

301 Platt Boulevard, Claremont CA 91711-5990
County: Los Angeles FICE Identification: 001171
Unit ID: 115409
Telephone: (909) 621-8000 Carnegie Class: Bac/A&S
FAX Number: (909) 621-8360 Calendar System: Semester
URL: www.hmc.edu
Established: 1955 Annual Undergrad Tuition & Fees: $50,649
Enrollment: 804 Coed
Affiliation or Control: Independent Non-Profit IRS Status: 501(c)3
Highest Offering: Baccalaureate
Program: Liberal Arts And General; Professional; Technical Emphasis
Accreditation: WC, ENG

01 President ..... Dr. Maria M. KLAWE
30 Vice President Advancement ..... Mr. Daniel MACALUSO
10 Vice President/Treasurer ..... Mr. Andrew R. DORANTES
05 Dean of the Faculty ..... Dr. Jeffrey GROVES
07 Vice Pres/Dean of Admissions ..... Ms. Thyra BRIGGS
32 Vice Pres/Dean of Students ..... Dr. Marguerite BROWNING
13 VP/CIO ..... Mr. Joseph VAUGHAN
09 Asst VP Institutional Research ..... Vacant
15 AVP of Human Resources ..... Ms. Cynthia A. BECKWITH
18 AVP Facilities/Physical Plant ..... Ms. Theresa LAUER
28 Assoc Dean Institutional Diversity ..... Ms. Sumun (Sumi) PENDAKUR
06 Registrar ..... Mr. Mark ASHLEY
26 Director of College Relations ..... Ms. Stephanie GRAHAM
29 Director of Alumni Relations ..... Ms. Jennifer GREEN
37 Director of Student Financial Aid ..... Ms. Gilma LOPEZ
101 Exec Asst to the Pres/Secy to Board ..... Ms. Karen ANGEMI
100 Chief of Staff ..... Ms. Karen ANGEMI

Henley-Putnam University (L)

2804 Mission College Blvd #240, Santa Clara CA 95054
County: Santa Clara Identification: 666120
Telephone: (408) 453-9900 Carnegie Class: Not Classified
FAX Number: (408) 453-9700 Calendar System: Quarter
URL: www.henley-putnam.edu
Established: 2001 Annual Undergrad Tuition & Fees: $12,200

Enrollment: N/A　Coed
Affiliation or Control: Proprietary　IRS Status: Proprietary
Highest Offering: Doctorate
Program: Professional; Technical Emphasis
Accreditation: DEAC

01 President .... Jim P. KILLIN
05 Provost of Academics .... Dr. Amy DIMAIO
88 Provost of Co-Curricular Activites .... Amanda MORROW-JENSEN
10 Director of Finance .... Marlys YOSHIMURA
07 Director of Admissions .... Nancy REGGIO

Herguan University (A)

595 Lawrence Expressway, Sunnyvale CA 94085
County: Santa Clara　Identification: 667236
Telephone: (408) 481-9988　Carnegie Class: Not Classified
FAX Number: (408) 749-1111　Calendar System: Semester
URL: www.herguanuniversity.edu
Established: 2005　Annual Graduate Tuition & Fees: $5,823
Enrollment: N/A　Coed
Affiliation or Control: Proprietary　IRS Status: Proprietary
Highest Offering: Master's; No Undergraduates
Program: Professional
Accreditation: ACICS

01 Acting President .... Dr. D. Kandy SIMMONS
07 Director of Admissions .... Kalpana WUNNAVA

High Tech High Graduate School of Education (B)

2861 Womble Road, San Diego CA 92106-6025
County: San Diego　Identification: 667118
Telephone: (619) 398-4902　Carnegie Class: Not Classified
FAX Number: (619) 758-1960　Calendar System: Other
URL: gse.hightechhigh.org
Established: 2007　Annual Graduate Tuition & Fees: $12,500
Enrollment: N/A　Coed
Affiliation or Control: Independent Non-Profit　IRS Status: 501(c)3
Highest Offering: Master's; No Undergraduates
Program: Teacher Preparatory
Accreditation: @WC

01 President .... Rob RIORDAN
05 Dean .... Larry ROSENSTOCK
11 Chief Admin Officer/General Counsel .... Maria HEREDIA
12 Director of Clinical Sites .... Ben DALEY

Holy Names University (C)

3500 Mountain Boulevard, Oakland CA 94619-1699
County: Alameda　FICE Identification: 001183
Unit ID: 115728
Telephone: (510) 436-1000　Carnegie Class: Master's M
FAX Number: (510) 436-1199　Calendar System: Semester
URL: www.hnu.edu
Established: 1868　Annual Undergrad Tuition & Fees: $35,166
Enrollment: 1,353　Coed
Affiliation or Control: Independent Non-Profit　IRS Status: 501(c)3
Highest Offering: Master's
Program: Liberal Arts And General; Teacher Preparatory; Professional
Accreditation: WC, NURSE

01 President .... Dr. William J. HYNES
05 Vice President for Academic Affairs .... Dr. Lizbeth J. MARTIN
10 Vice President for Finance/Admin .... Mr. Karl SOLIBAKKE
32 Vice President for Student Affairs .... Mr. Michael S. MILLER
30 Vice President University Advance .... Mr. Richard ORTEGA
84 Asst Dean Enrollment Mgmt .... Mr. Matt SLAVIN
06 Registrar .... Mr. Steven LIND
08 Director of Library Services .... Vacant
37 Dir Student Financial Assistance .... Ms. Tam LEE-OPERARIO
31 Director Campus Services .... Mr. Luis GUERRA
42 Co-Director of Campus Ministry ...... Ms. Jenny GIRARD-MALLEY
42 Co-Director of Campus Ministry .... Fr. Sal RAGUSA
41 Director of Athletics .... Mr. Greg SAMPADIAN
26 Director Marketing/Communications .... Ms. Lesley SIMS
29 Director of Alumni Relations .... Ms. Frances WILLIAMS
13 Director Information Technology .... Ms. Elena OLKHOVSKAYA
19 Director Campus Safety .... Ms. Dana KIRKPATRICK
15 Director Human Resources .... Ms. Patricia BARTON

Hope International University (D)

2500 E Nutwood Avenue, Fullerton CA 92831-3104
County: Orange　FICE Identification: 001252
Unit ID: 120537
Telephone: (714) 879-3901　Carnegie Class: Bac/Diverse
FAX Number: (714) 681-7451　Calendar System: 4/1/4
URL: www.hiu.edu
Established: 1928　Annual Undergrad Tuition & Fees: $27,900
Enrollment: 1,842　Coed
Affiliation or Control: Independent Non-Profit　IRS Status: 501(c)3
Highest Offering: Master's
Program: 2-Year Principally Bachelor's Creditable; Liberal Arts And General; Teacher Preparatory; Professional; Religious Emphasis
Accreditation: WC, BI, #MFCD

01 President .... Dr. John L. DERRY
04 Exec Asst to the President .... Mrs. Sharon L. CARTER
05 Vice President for Academic Affairs .... Dr. Paul H. ALEXANDER
49 Dean College of Arts and Sciences .... Dr. Steve EDGINGTON
50 Dean College of Business & Mgmt .... Vacant
53 Dean College of Education .... Dr. George E. WEST
88 Dean College of Ministry & Bib Stds .... Dr. Joe GRANA
83 Dean College of Psych & Counseling .... Dr. Laura L. STEELE
09 Assc VP for Education Effectiveness .... Dr. Tamsen MURRAY
08 Librarian .... Mrs. Robin HARTMAN
06 Registrar .... Mr. Ron ARCHER
10 Vice President for Business/Finance .... Mr. Frank SCOTTI
37 Director Student Financial Services ...... Mrs. Shannon O'SHIELDS
15 Director of Human Resources .... Mrs. Wende HOLTZEN
13 Director of Information Systems .... Mr. Mike CARTER
18 Director of Campus Facilities .... Mr. Steve MULLINS
30 Vice Pres Institutional Advancement .... Mr. Michael MULRYAN
26 Chief Public Relations Officer .... Mr. Michael MULRYAN
32 Vice President for Student Affairs .... Dr. Mark COMEAUX
36 Dean of Students .... Mr. Reid W. MCCORMICK
41 Athletic Director .... Mr. John G. TUREK
42 Chaplain/Director Campus Ministry .... Mr. Bryan A. SANDS
85 Director of International Students .... Ms. Judy E. KIM
38 Director Student Counseling .... Dr. Laura L. STEELE
36 Dir Student Career Services .... Mrs. Kirsten M. MCCORMICK
84 Vice Pres for Enrollment Management .... Mrs. Teresa L. SMITH
07 Director Undergraduate Admissions .. Mrs. Dionne K. GUTIERREZ

Horizon University (E)

5331 Mt Alifan Drive, San Diego CA 92111
County: San Diego　FICE Identification: 041405
Unit ID: 457226
Telephone: (858) 695-8587　Carnegie Class: Not Classified
FAX Number: (858) 695-9527　Calendar System: Semester
URL: www.horizonuniversity.edu
Established: 1993　Annual Undergrad Tuition & Fees: $13,600
Enrollment: 37　Coed
Affiliation or Control: Independent Non-Profit　IRS Status: 501(c)3
Highest Offering: Baccalaureate
Program: Liberal Arts And General; Religious Emphasis
Accreditation: BI

01 President .... Mr. Bill GOODRICH
05 Dean of Academics .... Mr. Dave KOSOBUCKI
08 Head Librarian .... Vacant
11 Dean of Administration .... Ms. Becky KIRSININKAS
84 Dir Enrollment & Student Services .... Vacant
10 Chief Financial Officer .... Mr. Scott ELLMAN
38 Director Student Counseling .... Mr. Tracy GRAY

Humphreys College (F)

6650 Inglewood Street, Stockton CA 95207-3896
County: San Joaquin　FICE Identification: 001212
Unit ID: 115773
Telephone: (209) 478-0800　Carnegie Class: Bac/Diverse
FAX Number: (209) 478-8721　Calendar System: Quarter
URL: www.humphreys.edu
Established: 1896　Annual Undergrad Tuition & Fees: $15,174
Enrollment: 856　Coed
Affiliation or Control: Independent Non-Profit　IRS Status: 501(c)3
Highest Offering: First Professional Degree
Program: Liberal Arts And General; Professional
Accreditation: WC

01 President .... Dr. Robert G. HUMPHREYS, JR.
05 Dn Instruction/Dir Arts & Sciences .... Ms. Cynthia BECERRA
11 Dean Administration/Ofc Admin Pgm .... Ms. Wilma OKAMOTO-VAUGHN
09 Dean of Institutional Research .... Dr. Jess BONDS
61 Dean Law School .... Mr. Patrick L. PIGGOTT
20 Associate Dean of Instruction .... Dr. Lisa KOOREN
06 Registrar .... Ms. Maria GARCIA-MILLER
07 Director of Admissions .... Ms. Santa E. LOPEZ
26 Chief Public Relations Officer .... Vacant
08 Head Librarian .... Dr. Stanislav PERKNER
88 Director Court Reporting Program .... Mrs. Kay REINDL
10 Chief Business Officer .... Ms. Carol KRAMLICH
37 Director Student Financial Aid .... Ms. Rita FRANCO
13 Director of Information Services .... Mr. Fred WHITE

Imperial Valley College (G)

380 E Aten Road, Imperial CA 92251-0158
County: Imperial　FICE Identification: 001214
Unit ID: 115861
Telephone: (760) 352-8320　Carnegie Class: Assoc/Pub-R-L
FAX Number: (760) 355-2663　Calendar System: Semester
URL: www.imperial.edu
Established: 1922　Annual Undergrad Tuition & Fees (In-District): $1,327
Enrollment: 7,879　Coed
Affiliation or Control: Local　IRS Status: 501(c)3
Highest Offering: Associate Degree
Program: Occupational; 2-Year Principally Bachelor's Creditable
Accreditation: WJ, EMT

01 Superintendent/President .... Dr. Victor JAIME
05 Vice President Academic Services .... Dr. Nicholas AKINKUOYE
32 Acting Vice Pres Student Services .... Mr. Sergio LOPEZ
10 VP Administrative Services .... Mr. John LAU
15 Chief Human Resources Officer .... Dr. Shawn LARRY
103 Dean Economic & Worforce Develop .... Mr. Efrain SILVA
76 Dean of Health & Sciences .... Mrs. Tina AGUIRRE
49 Dean Arts/Letters/Learning Svc .... Mr. David ZIELINSKI
38 Dean of Counseling .... Mr. Ted CEASAR
35 Dean Student Affs/Enrollment Svcs .... Mr. Sergio LOPEZ
07 Director of Admissions and Records ...... Ms. Gloria HOISINGTON
37 Director of Financial Aid .... Ms. Lisa SEALS
09 Dir Institutional Research .... Mr. Jose CARRILLO
59 Dir Child/Family/Consumer Sciences .... Ms. Rebecca GREEN
26 Chief Public Relations Officer .... Mr. Bill GAY
13 Interim Chief Technology Officer .... Mr. Jeff ENZ

Institute of Technology (H)

564 West Herndon Avenue, Clovis CA 93612
County: Fresno　FICE Identification: 030675
Unit ID: 431141
Telephone: (559) 297-4500　Carnegie Class: Assoc/PrivFP
FAX Number: (559) 297-5822　Calendar System: Semester
URL: www.iot.edu
Established:　Annual Undergrad Tuition & Fees: $22,000
Enrollment: 685　Coed
Affiliation or Control: Proprietary　IRS Status: Proprietary
Highest Offering: Associate Degree
Program: Occupational; 2-Year Principally Bachelor's Creditable; Technical Emphasis
Accreditation: ACCSC, ACFEI

01 President .... Timothy VOGELEY

Institute of Technology (I)

5737 Stoddard Road, Modesto CA 95356
Telephone: (209) 545-3100　Identification: 770554
Accreditation: ACCSC, ACFEI

† Branch campus of Institute of Technology, Clovis, CA.

Institute of Technology (J)

1755 Hilltop Drive, Redding CA 96002
Telephone: (530) 224-1000　Identification: 770555
Accreditation: ACCSC

† Branch campus of Institute of Technology, Clovis, CA.

Intercoast College (K)

3745 W. Chapman Avenue, Orange CA 92868
County: Orange　FICE Identification: 025594
Unit ID: 366289
Telephone: (714) 712-7900　Carnegie Class: Not Classified
FAX Number: N/A　Calendar System: Other
URL: www.intercoast.edu
Established: 1985　Annual Undergrad Tuition & Fees: $20,115
Enrollment: 357　Coed
Affiliation or Control: Proprietary　IRS Status: Proprietary
Highest Offering: Associate Degree
Program: Occupational
Accreditation: CNCE

01 President .... Geeta A. BROWN

Interior Designers Institute (L)

1061 Camelback Road, Newport Beach CA 92660-3228
County: Orange　FICE Identification: 025203
Unit ID: 116226
Telephone: (949) 675-4451　Carnegie Class: Spec/Arts
FAX Number: (949) 759-0667　Calendar System: Quarter
URL: www.idi.edu
Established: 1984　Annual Undergrad Tuition & Fees: $17,950
Enrollment: 380　Coed
Affiliation or Control: Proprietary　IRS Status: Proprietary
Highest Offering: Master's
Program: Professional
Accreditation: ACCSC, CIDA

01 Executive Director .... Ms. Judy DEATON
37 Financial Aid Director .... Ms. Shanen FOYE

International Professional School of Bodywork (M)

9025 Balboa Avenue, Suite 130, San Diego CA 92123
County: San Diego　FICE Identification: 041347
Unit ID: 454740
Telephone: (858) 505-1100　Carnegie Class: Not Classified
FAX Number: (858) 565-4118　Calendar System: Quarter
URL: www.ipsb.edu
Established: 1977　Annual Undergrad Tuition & Fees: $12,361
Enrollment: 169　Coed
Affiliation or Control: Proprietary　IRS Status: Proprietary
Highest Offering: Associate Degree
Program: Occupational
Accreditation: #COMTA

01 Chief Executive Officer (President) .... Karen HOBSON
05 Chief Academic Officer .... Shari GRAYSON
06 Registrar .... Abigail ALVAREZ
10 Chief Business Officer .... Cindy NAUTA

International Reformed University and Seminary (A)

125 S. Vermont Avenue, Los Angeles CA 90004
County: Los Angeles Identification: 667132
Telephone: (213) 381-0081 Carnegie Class: Not Classified
FAX Number: (213) 381-0010 Calendar System: Semester
URL: www.irus.edu
Established: 1977 Annual Undergrad Tuition & Fees: $4,000
Enrollment: 100 Coed
Affiliation or Control: Independent Non-Profit IRS Status: 501(c)3
Highest Offering: Doctorate
Program: Religious Emphasis
Accreditation: **BI**

01 President .... Dr. Hun Sung PARK
11 Dean of College .... Dr. Young Chong OH
05 Academic Dean .... Dr. Kwang Hoon LEE
32 Dean of Students .... Dr. Sung Hwan JUNG
10 Business Manager .... Dr. Joha OH
108 Director for Assessment & Planning .... Dr. Yumee RAH
88 Accreditation Liaison .... Dr. Grace KOOK
08 Librarian .... Ms. Hyun KIM
88 Secretary .... Ms. Jung Ae KAM

International Technological University (B)

355 W. San Fernando Street, San Jose CA 95113
County: Santa Clara Identification: 667070
Unit ID: 443128
Telephone: (888) 488-4968 Carnegie Class: Not Classified
FAX Number: (408) 331-1026 Calendar System: Trimester
URL: www.itu.edu
Established: 1994 Annual Graduate Tuition & Fees: $11,870
Enrollment: 1,866 Coed
Affiliation or Control: Independent Non-Profit IRS Status: 501(c)3
Highest Offering: Doctorate; No Undergraduates
Program: Professional; Technical Emphasis
Accreditation: **WC**

01 President and CEO .... Dr. Gregary O'BRIEN
05 Provost .... Dr. Karl WANG
10 CFO .... Edward LAM
06 Registrar .... Sophia GU
08 Head Librarian .... Christa BAILEY
101 Secretary of the Institution/Board .... Angie LO
26 Chief Public Relations/Marketing .... Sameer BHASIN

International Theological Seminary (C)

3215-3225 Tyler Avenue, El Monte CA 91731-3355
County: Los Angeles Identification: 666360
Unit ID: 396985
Telephone: (626) 448-0023 Carnegie Class: Not Classified
FAX Number: (626) 350-6343 Calendar System: Quarter
URL: www.itsla.edu
Established: 1982 Annual Undergrad Tuition & Fees: $11,280
Enrollment: 73 Coed
Affiliation or Control: Independent Non-Profit IRS Status: 501(c)3
Highest Offering: Doctorate
Program: Religious Emphasis
Accreditation: **THEOL**

01 President .... Dr. James S. LEE
05 Vice President for Academics .... Dr. Jaretha Joy PALMER
11 Vice President for Administration .... Ms. Monica KAO
32 Vice Pres Student Affairs .... Dr. David MCKINLEY
06 Registrar .... Mrs. Zenda Gay P. EUSEBIO
07 Director of Admissions .... Mr. Paul YANG

ITT Technical Institute (D)

362 N Clovis Avenue, Clovis CA 93612-0300
Telephone: (559) 325-5400 Identification: 666144
Accreditation: **ACICS**

† Branch campus of ITT Technical Institute, Indianapolis, IN.

ITT Technical Institute (E)

1140 Galaxy Way, Suite 400, Concord CA 94520
Telephone: (925) 674-8200 Identification: 666697
Accreditation: **ACICS**

† Branch campus of ITT Technical Institute, Indianapolis, IN.

ITT Technical Institute (F)

4160 Temescal Canyon Rd, Suite 100, Corona CA 92883
Telephone: (951) 277-5400 Identification: 667194
Accreditation: **ACICS**

† Branch campus of ITT Technical Institute, Indianapolis, IN.

ITT Technical Institute (G)

6101 W Centinela Avenue, Suite 180,
Culver City CA 90230
Telephone: (310) 417-5800 Identification: 667192
Accreditation: **ACICS**

† Branch campus of ITT Technical Institute, Indianapolis, IN.

ITT Technical Institute (H)

16916 S Harlan Road, Lathrop CA 95330-8737
Telephone: (209) 858-0077 Identification: 666533
Accreditation: **ACICS**

† Branch campus of ITT Technical Institute, Indianapolis, IN.

ITT Technical Institute (I)

401 Mile of Cars Way, Suite 100, National City CA 91950
Telephone: (619) 327-1800 Identification: 667193
Accreditation: **ACICS**

† Branch campus of ITT Technical Institute, Indianapolis, IN.

ITT Technical Institute (J)

7901 Oakport Street, Suite 3000, Oakland CA 94621
Telephone: (510) 553-2800 Identification: 667195
Accreditation: **ACICS**

† Branch campus of ITT Technical Institute, Indianapolis, IN.

ITT Technical Institute (K)

4000 West Metropolitan Dr, Ste. 100, Orange CA 92868
Telephone: (714) 941-2400 FICE Identification: 023219
Accreditation: **ACICS**, CAHIIM

† Branch campus of ITT Technical Institute, Indianapolis, IN.

ITT Technical Institute (L)

2051 Solar Drive, Suite 150, Oxnard CA 93036-0641
Telephone: (805) 988-0143 Identification: 666534
Accreditation: **ACICS**

† Branch campus of ITT Technical Institute, Indianapolis, IN.

ITT Technical Institute (M)

10863 Gold Center Drive,
Rancho Cordova CA 95670-6034
Telephone: (916) 851-3900 FICE Identification: 021209
Accreditation: **ACICS**

† Branch campus of ITT Technical Institute, Indianapolis, IN.

ITT Technical Institute (N)

670 E Carnegie Drive, San Bernardino CA 92408-3519
Telephone: (909) 806-4600 FICE Identification: 030704
Accreditation: **ACICS**, CAHIIM

† Branch campus of ITT Technical Institute, Indianapolis, IN.

ITT Technical Institute (O)

12669 Encinitas Avenue, Sylmar CA 91342-3664
Telephone: (818) 364-5151 FICE Identification: 023218
Accreditation: **ACICS**, CAHIIM

† Branch campus of ITT Technical Institute, Indianapolis, IN.

John F. Kennedy University (P)

100 Ellinwood Way, Pleasant Hill CA 94523-4817
County: Contra Costa FICE Identification: 004484
Unit ID: 116712
Telephone: (925) 969-3300 Carnegie Class: Master's M
FAX Number: (925) 969-3399 Calendar System: Quarter
URL: www.jfku.edu
Established: 1964 Annual Undergrad Tuition & Fees: N/A
Enrollment: 1,230 Coed
Affiliation or Control: Independent Non-Profit IRS Status: 501(c)3
Highest Offering: Doctorate
Program: Liberal Arts And General; Professional
Accreditation: **WC**, CLPSY, IACBE

01 Interim President .... Ms. Debra DEAN

John Paul the Great Catholic University (Q)

220 West Grand Avenue, Escondido CA 92025
County: San Diego FICE Identification: 041937
Unit ID: 462354
Telephone: (858) 653-6740 Carnegie Class: Not Classified
FAX Number: (858) 653-3791 Calendar System: Quarter
URL: www.jpcatholic.com
Established: 2003 Annual Undergrad Tuition & Fees: $24,000
Enrollment: 284 Coed
Affiliation or Control: Independent Non-Profit IRS Status: 501(c)3
Highest Offering: Master's
Program: Professional
Accreditation: **WC**

01 President .... Dr. Derry CONNOLLY
05 Provost & Academic Dean .... Dr. James MONAGHAN
10 VP for Finance .... Vlad BOLSAKOV
11 VP for Administration .... Lidy CONNOLLY
07 VP of Admissions .... Martin HAROLD
32 Dean of Students .... Julia CARRANO
13 VP for Technology & Real Estate .... Kevin MEZIERE
37 Director of Financial Aid .... Lisa WILLIAMS
06 Registrar .... Nick HEYE
42 Chaplain .... Fr. Richard HUSTON
09 Institutional Research Analyst .... Clare OVEN
39 Director Student Life .... Joe CROSS

Kaiser Permanente School of Allied Health Sciences (R)

938 Marina Way South, Richmond CA 94804
County: Contra Costa Identification: 667152
Telephone: (510) 231-5000 Carnegie Class: Not Classified
FAX Number: (510) 231-5001 Calendar System: Quarter
URL: www.kpsahs.org
Established: 1989 Annual Undergrad Tuition & Fees: $7,590
Enrollment: N/A Coed
Affiliation or Control: Proprietary IRS Status: Proprietary
Highest Offering: Baccalaureate
Program: Occupational
Accreditation: **WC**, DMS, NMT, RAD

01 Medical Director .... Dr. Darryl JONES
05 Director of Academic Affairs .... Kristina LOPEZ
10 Assoc Director of Finance .... Pamela PRESSLEY
11 Regional School Administrator .... James FITZGIBBONS
32 Student Services Administrator .... Candra RAYNOR

Kaplan College (S)

1914 Wible Road, Bakersfield CA 93304
Telephone: (661) 836-6300 Identification: 666291
Accreditation: **ACICS**

† Branch campus of Kaplan College, Sacramento, CA.

Kaplan College (T)

555 Broadway, Suite 144, Chula Vista CA 91910-5342
Telephone: (619) 498-4100 Identification: 770560
Accreditation: **ACICS**

† Branch campus of Kaplan College, San Diego, CA.

Kaplan College (U)

44 Shaw Avenue, Clovis CA 93612
Telephone: (559) 325-5100 Identification: 770559
Accreditation: **ACICS**

† Branch campus of Kaplan College, Salida, CA.

Kaplan College (V)

6180 Laurel Canyon Blvd., Ste 101,
North Hollywood CA 91606
County: Los Angeles FICE Identification: 025391
Unit ID: 118967
Telephone: (818) 763-2563 Carnegie Class: Not Classified
FAX Number: (818) 763-1623 Calendar System: Other
URL: www.kaplancollege.com
Established: 1982 Annual Undergrad Tuition & Fees: $19,760
Enrollment: 789 Coed
Affiliation or Control: Proprietary IRS Status: Proprietary
Highest Offering: Associate Degree
Program: Occupational
Accreditation: **ACICS**, RAD

01 Campus President .... Mr. Josh LEVENSON

Kaplan College (W)

2475 E Tahquitz Canyon Way, Palm Springs CA 92262
Telephone: (760) 778-3540 Identification: 770558
Accreditation: **ACICS**

† Branch campus of Kaplan College, Vista, CA.

Kaplan College (X)

4330 Watt Avenue, Suite 400,
Sacramento CA 95821-7000
County: Sacramento FICE Identification: 023519
Unit ID: 118259
Telephone: (916) 649-8168 Carnegie Class: Assoc/PrivFP
FAX Number: (916) 649-8344 Calendar System: Quarter
URL: www.kaplancollege.edu
Established: 1982 Annual Undergrad Tuition & Fees: $14,268
Enrollment: 429 Coed
Affiliation or Control: Proprietary IRS Status: Proprietary
Highest Offering: Associate Degree
Program: Occupational
Accreditation: **ACICS**

01 Executive Director .... Jackie RUPE
05 Director of Education .... Jeff GRAVES
37 Director of Student Financial Aid .... Ryan SMITH
07 Director of Admissions .... Queena FULLER
36 Director of Career Services .... Julie MUIR

Kaplan College (A)

5172 Kiernan Court, Salida CA 95368

County: Stanislaus FICE Identification: 023063
Unit ID: 366960
Telephone: (209) 543-7000 Carnegie Class: Assoc/PrivFP
FAX Number: (209) 543-1755 Calendar System: Other
URL: www.kaplancollege.com
Established: 1986 Annual Undergrad Tuition & Fees: $16,452
Enrollment: 429 Coed
Affiliation or Control: Proprietary IRS Status: Proprietary
Highest Offering: Associate Degree
Program: Occupational
Accreditation: ACICS, COARC

01 Campus President Mr. Bill JONES

Kaplan College (B)

9055 Balboa Avenue, San Diego CA 92123-1509

County: San Diego FICE Identification: 020917
Unit ID: 118277
Telephone: (858) 279-4500 Carnegie Class: Assoc/PrivFP
FAX Number: (858) 279-4885 Calendar System: Other
URL: www.kaplancollege.com
Established: 1976 Annual Undergrad Tuition & Fees: $32,992
Enrollment: 1,025 Coed
Affiliation or Control: Proprietary IRS Status: Proprietary
Highest Offering: Associate Degree
Program: Occupational; 2-Year Principally Bachelor's Creditable; Nursing Emphasis
Accreditation: ACICS, CAHIIM, MAAB

01 Executive Director Mr. David MOVSESIAN
05 Director of Education Ms. Tammy ESQUIVEL
07 Director of Admissions Ms. Serica ERVIN

Kaplan College (C)

2022 University Drive, Vista CA 92083-7736

County: San Diego FICE Identification: 025490
Unit ID: 118286
Telephone: (760) 630-1555 Carnegie Class: Assoc/PrivFP
FAX Number: (760) 630-1656 Calendar System: Other
URL: www.kaplancollege.com
Established: 1976 Annual Undergrad Tuition & Fees: $14,987
Enrollment: 812 Coed
Affiliation or Control: Proprietary IRS Status: Proprietary
Highest Offering: Associate Degree
Program: Occupational; Technical Emphasis
Accreditation: ACICS, MAAB

01 Executive Director Ms. Laura STINSON
05 Director of Education Mr. Destry LIEVANOS
07 Director of Admissions Ms. Renee CODNER
36 Director of Career Services Ms. Sipel TAHA
37 Director of Financial Aid Ms. Elizabeth LLAMAS
66 Director of Nursing Ms. Beth BUNYI

*Kern Community College District (D)

2100 Chester Avenue, Bakersfield CA 93301-4099

County: Kern FICE Identification: 006994
Unit ID: 436313
Telephone: (661) 336-5100 Carnegie Class: N/A
FAX Number: (661) 336-5134
URL: www.kccd.edu

01 Chancellor Ms. Sandra V. SERRANO
05 Vice Chanc Educational Services Vacant
11 Vice Chanc Operations Management Mr. Sean P. JAMES
15 Vice Chanc Human Resources Mr. Abe ALI
30 Assoc Vice Chanc Govt/External Rels Ms. Michele BRESSO
10 Chief Financial Officer Mr. Tom J. BURKE
13 Asst Dir Information Technology Mr. David W. PALINSKY
91 Asst Dir Information Technology Mr. Eddie D. ALVARADO
43 General Counsel Mr. Christopher HINE

*Bakersfield College (E)

1801 Panorama Drive, Bakersfield CA 93305-1299

County: Kern FICE Identification: 001118
Unit ID: 109819
Telephone: (661) 395-4011 Carnegie Class: Assoc/Pub-U-MC
FAX Number: (661) 395-4241 Calendar System: Semester
URL: www.bakersfieldcollege.edu
Established: 1913 Annual Undergrad Tuition & Fees (In-District): $1,416
Enrollment: 18,698 Coed
Affiliation or Control: State/Local IRS Status: 501(c)3
Highest Offering: Associate Degree
Program: Occupational; 2-Year Principally Bachelor's Creditable
Accreditation: WJ, EMT, RAD

02 President Dr. Sonya CHRISTIAN
05 Exec VP Academic Affairs/Stdnt Svcs Ms. Nan GOMEZ-HEITZEBERG
10 VP Finance & Administrative Svcs Dr. Anthony CULPEPPER
32 Vice Pres Student Affairs Dr. Zavareh DADABHOY
72 Dean Learning Resources/Info Tech Dr. Todd COSTON
30 Director Foundation & Development Mr. Tom GELDER
11 Exec Dir Admin Svc/Maint/Operations Mr. Sean JAMES
12 Director Delano Center Mr. Rich MCCROW
37 Financial Aid Director Ms. Primavera ARVIZU
07 Director Enrollment Services Mrs. Suzanne A. VAUGHN
26 Dir Marketing & Public Relations Mrs. Amber CHIANG
04 Admin Assistant to the President Ms. Jennifer MARDEN
13 Director Information Technology Mr. Todd COSTON
20 Int Assoc Dean of Instruction Ms. Michelle BRESSO
66 Dir of Nursing & Allied Health Ms. Cindy COLLIER
41 Director of Athletics Mr. Andi TAYLOR
20 Dean of Instruction/Engr/Ind Tech Ms. Liz ROZELL
20 Dean of Instruction Dr. Emmanuel MOURTZANOS

*Cerro Coso Community College (F)

College Heights Boulevard, Ridgecrest CA 93555-7777

County: Kern FICE Identification: 010111
Unit ID: 111896
Telephone: (760) 384-6100 Carnegie Class: Assoc/Pub-U-MC
FAX Number: (760) 375-4776 Calendar System: Semester
URL: www.cerrocoso.edu
Established: 1973 Annual Undergrad Tuition & Fees (In-District): $1,380
Enrollment: 4,845 Coed
Affiliation or Control: State/Local IRS Status: 501(c)3
Highest Offering: Associate Degree
Program: Occupational; 2-Year Principally Bachelor's Creditable
Accreditation: WJ

02 President Ms. A. Jill BOARD
05 Vice President Academic Affairs Dr. Corey MARVIN
32 Vice President of Student Services Ms. Heather OSTASH
12 Dir Eastern Sierra College Center Ms. Deanna CAMPBELL
12 Campus Manager Kern River Valley Ms. Lisa STEPHENS
75 Dean Career Technical Education Mr. Mike MCNAIR
21 Director of Admin Services Ms. Gale LEBSOCK
38 Dir of Students & Counseling Svcs Ms. Paula SUOREZ
07 Dir Admiss/Records/VA/Fin Aid Ms. Jennifer SAN NICOLAS
10 Accounting Manager Ms. Lisa COUCH
15 Human Resources Manager Ms. Resa HESS
88 Child Development Coordinator Vacant
26 Public Rel/Marketing & Dev Mgr Ms. Natalie DORRELL
13 Information Technology Manager Mr. Michael CAMPBELL
41 Dir Student Programs & Athletics Vacant
106 Director Distance Education Ms. Rebecca PANG
04 Administrative Asst to President Ms. Jennifer CURTIS

*Porterville College (G)

100 E College Avenue, Porterville CA 93257-6058

County: Tulare FICE Identification: 001268
Unit ID: 121363
Telephone: (559) 791-2200 Carnegie Class: Assoc/Pub-U-MC
FAX Number: (559) 784-4779 Calendar System: Semester
URL: www.portervillecollege.edu
Established: 1927 Annual Undergrad Tuition & Fees (In-District): $1,178
Enrollment: 3,853 Coed
Affiliation or Control: State/Local IRS Status: 501(c)3
Highest Offering: Associate Degree
Program: Occupational; 2-Year Principally Bachelor's Creditable
Accreditation: WJ

02 President Dr. Rosa F. CARLSON
05 Vice President Instruction Mr. Bill HENRY
32 Vice President Student Services Mr. Valentin GARCIA
04 Administrative Asst to President Ms. Carol BROWN
20 Dean Instruction Vacant
23 Assoc Dean Health Careers Ms. Kim BEHRENS
18 Maintenance & Operations Manager Mr. John WORD
07 Director Admissions/Records Ms. Erin CRUZ
10 Director Finance & Admin Services Ms. Arlitha WILLIAMS-HARMON
15 Human Resources Manager Ms. Andreia CUEVAS
37 Director Financial Aid Ms. Erin CRUZ
09 Institutional Researcher Mr. Michael CARLEY
13 Director Information Technology Mr. Jay NAVARRETTE
35 Director Student Services Ms. Diane THOMPSON
21 Accounting Manager Ms. Sonia HUCKABAY
88 Program Manager Child Dev Center Ms. Karen BALL
08 Interim Director Library Ms. Lorie BARKER
35 Student Programs/Athletics Vacant
26 Pub Relations/Mkting/Outreach Mgr Ms. Maureen MONTGOMERY
105 Website Coordinator Mrs. Randy MORGAN

Kingston University (H)

12100 Imperial Hwy, Ste 101, Norwalk CA 90650

County: Los Angeles Identification: 667237
Telephone: (562) 868-6488 Carnegie Class: Not Classified
FAX Number: (562) 868-6378 Calendar System: Other
URL: www.kingston-edu.org
Established: 2002 Annual Undergrad Tuition & Fees: N/A
Enrollment: N/A Coed
Affiliation or Control: Proprietary IRS Status: Proprietary
Highest Offering: Master's
Program: Business Emphasis
Accreditation: ACICS

01 President Stephen ATCHLEY
05 Dean of Academics Gilbert SANCHEZ
11 Administrator Rosalia HSIEH

La Sierra University (I)

4500 Riverwalk Parkway, Riverside CA 92515-8247

County: Riverside FICE Identification: 001215
Unit ID: 117627
Telephone: (951) 785-2000 Carnegie Class: Master's M
FAX Number: (951) 785-2901 Calendar System: Quarter
URL: www.lasierra.edu
Established: 1922 Annual Undergrad Tuition & Fees: $29,895
Enrollment: 2,510 Coed
Affiliation or Control: Seventh-day Adventist IRS Status: 501(c)3
Highest Offering: Doctorate
Program: Liberal Arts And General; Teacher Preparatory; Professional; Business Emphasis
Accreditation: WC, MUS, SW, THEOL

01 President Dr. Randal R. WISBEY
05 Provost Dr. Steve PAWLUK
10 Vice President for Finance Mr. David GERIGUIS
32 Vice President for Student Life Ms. Yamilet BAZAN
30 Vice Pres Advancement/Univ Rels Mr. Norman YERGEN
84 Vice Pres Enrollment Services Mr. David R. LOFTHOUSE
26 VP Communication/Integrated Mktg Dr. Marilyn THOMSEN
21 Associate Vice President Finance Ms. Pamela CHRISPENS
20 Associate Provost Dr. Barbara FAVORITO
49 Dean College Arts/Sciences Dr. Adeny SCHMIDT
50 Dean School of Business Dr. John THOMAS
53 Dean School of Education Dr. Ginger KETTING-WELLER
73 Dean School of Divinity Dr. Bailey GILLIESPIE
35 Dean of Students Ms. Marjorie ROBINSON
26 Exec Director University Relations Mr. Larry BECKER
55 Director Adult Evening Program Ms. Nancy DITTEMORE
29 Director Alumni Relations Ms. Julie NARDUCCI
15 Director Human Resources Ms. Dell Jean VAN FOSSEN
08 Director Library Ms. Kitty SIMMONS
37 Director Student Financial Services Ms. Esther KINZER
42 Director Campus Ministries Mr. Samuel E. LEONOR, JR.
13 Director Information Technology Mr. Geoff INGRAM
09 Director of Institutional Research Mr. Guru UPPALA
18 Director Physical Plant Mr. Al VALDEZ
38 Director Counseling Center Ms. Debra WRIGHT
92 Director Honors Program Dr. Douglas R. CLARK
07 Director of Admissions/Registrar Mr. Issmael NZAMUTUNA
36 Director Career Services Mr. Natan VIGNA
41 Athletic Director Mr. Javier KRUMM

LACM, Los Angeles College of Music (J)

300 South Fair Oaks Avenue, Pasadena CA 91105

County: Los Angeles FICE Identification: 038684
Unit ID: 446385
Telephone: (626) 568-8850 Carnegie Class: Assoc/PrivFP
FAX Number: (626) 568-8854 Calendar System: Quarter
URL: www.lacm.edu
Established: 1996 Annual Undergrad Tuition & Fees: $22,575
Enrollment: 148 Coed
Affiliation or Control: Proprietary IRS Status: Proprietary
Highest Offering: Associate Degree
Program: Occupational; 2-Year Principally Bachelor's Creditable; Music Emphasis
Accreditation: MUS

01 President Tom AYLESBURY
05 EVP Academic Operations Mike PACKER
84 Vice Pres Enrollment Management Vacant
06 Registrar Jorge OJEDA
32 Dean of Students & Faculty Dave POZZI
37 Director of Financial Aid Mary OLMOS

Laguna College of Art & Design (K)

2222 Laguna Canyon Road, Laguna Beach CA 92651-1136

County: Orange FICE Identification: 023305
Unit ID: 117168
Telephone: (949) 376-6000 Carnegie Class: Spec/Arts
FAX Number: (949) 376-6009 Calendar System: Semester
URL: www.lcad.edu
Established: 1961 Annual Undergrad Tuition & Fees: $28,100
Enrollment: 566 Coed
Affiliation or Control: Independent Non-Profit IRS Status: 501(c)3
Highest Offering: Master's
Program: Professional; Fine Arts Emphasis
Accreditation: WC, ART

01 President Dr. Jonathan BURKE
05 Vice President Academic Affairs Dr. Helene GARRISON
30 Vice Pres of Development Mr. Kevin CARTWRIGHT
07 Dean of Admissions Mr. Christopher BROWN
10 Chief Financial Officer Mr. Jim GODEK
06 Registrar Ms. Laura PATRICK
08 Library Director Ms. Jennifer WORMSER
04 Assistant to the President Ms. Jeni RICHARDS
37 Director Financial Aid Mr. Christopher BROWN
09 Director of Institutional Research Ms. Laura PATRICK
13 Chief Info Technology Officer (CIO) Mr. Matt MORTON
18 Chief Facilities/Physical Plant Mr. John EERTWEGH
26 Chief Public Relations/Marketing Mr. Mike STICE
32 Chief Student Affairs/Student Life Mr. Doug DAVEE

Lake Tahoe Community College (A)

1 College Drive, South Lake Tahoe CA 96150-4524
County: El Dorado FICE Identification: 012907
Unit ID: 117195
Telephone: (530) 541-4660 Carnegie Class: Assoc/Pub-S-SC
FAX Number: (530) 541-7852 Calendar System: Quarter
URL: www.ltcc.edu
Established: 1975 Annual Undergrad Tuition & Fees (In-District): $1,397
Enrollment: 2,426 Coed
Affiliation or Control: State/Local IRS Status: 501(c)3
Highest Offering: Associate Degree
Program: 2-Year Principally Bachelor's Creditable
Accreditation: WJ

01 Superintendent/President ..... Dr. Kindred MURILLO
04 Executive Assistant to President ..... Ms. Lisa SHAFER
05 Interim VP Academic Affairs ..... Dr. Michelle RISDON
10 Vice Pres Administrative Svcs ..... Mr. Jeff DEFRANCO
20 Dean of Instruction & CTE ..... Dr. Virginia BERRY
32 Executive Dean of Student Success ..... Ms. Sue GOCHIS
20 Dean of Instruction ..... Ms. Michelle SOWER
08 Director of Library ..... Ms. Lisa FOLEY
13 Director Tech & Education Svcs ..... Mr. Dave BURBA
84 Director Enrollment Services ..... Ms. Alysa BORELLI
21 Director of Fiscal Services ..... Ms. Andrea SALAZAR
15 Director of Human Resources ..... Ms. Shelley HANSEN
18 Director of Facilities ..... Mr. Randy JOSLIN
88 Director Child Development Center ..... Vacant
37 Director Financial Aid ..... Ms. Julie CATHIE
09 Director of Institutional Research ..... Vacant
26 Public Information Officer ..... Ms. Diane LEWIS
102 Foundation Director ..... Ms. Nancy HARRISON
40 Bookstore Manager ..... Mr. Trevor OSTENDORF
96 Purchasing Agent ..... Ms. Heather CADE

Lassen Community College (B)

PO Box 3000, 478-200 Highway 139,
Susanville CA 96130-3000
County: Lassen FICE Identification: 001217
Unit ID: 117274
Telephone: (530) 257-6181 Carnegie Class: Assoc/Pub-R-M
FAX Number: (530) 251-8872 Calendar System: Semester
URL: www.lassencollege.edu
Established: 1925 Annual Undergrad Tuition & Fees (In-District): $647
Enrollment: 2,291 Coed
Affiliation or Control: State/Local IRS Status: 501(c)3
Highest Offering: Associate Degree
Program: Occupational; 2-Year Principally Bachelor's Creditable
Accreditation: WJ

01 District Superintendent/President ..... Dr. Marlon R. HALL
04 Assistant to President ..... Ms. Julie L. JOHNSTON
05 Exec Vice Pres of Academic Services ... Dr. Terri A. ARMSTRONG
11 Vice Pres Administrative Services ..... Mr. Dave CLAUSEN
32 Dean of Student Services ..... Mr. Patrick WALTON
08 Librarian ..... Dr. John TAYLOR
09 Assoc Dean Inst Effectiveness/Rsrch ..... Mr. Brian MURPHY
37 Director Financial Aid ..... Mr. Matt LEVINE
35 Director Student Life ..... Mr. Francis BEAUJON
41 Athletic Director ..... Dr. Terri A. ARMSTRONG
18 Chief Facilities/Physical Plant ..... Mr. Gregory COLLINS
15 Director Human Resources ..... Ms. Vickie RAMSEY
13 Director of Information Technology ..... Mr. David CORLEY

Laurus College (C)

81 Higuera Street, Ste 110, San Luis Obispo CA 93401
County: San Luis Obispo FICE Identification: 041414
Unit ID: 454786
Telephone: (805) 267-1690 Carnegie Class: Not Classified
FAX Number: (805) 352-1307 Calendar System: Quarter
URL: www.lauruscollege.com
Established: 2006 Annual Undergrad Tuition & Fees: $11,400
Enrollment: 897 Coed
Affiliation or Control: Proprietary IRS Status: Proprietary
Highest Offering: Associate Degree
Program: Occupational
Accreditation: ACICS

01 President ..... Mr. Steve JOHNSON

Le Cordon Bleu College of Culinary Arts (D)

350 Rhode Island Street, San Francisco CA 94103
County: San Francisco FICE Identification: 022202
Unit ID: 111009
Telephone: (888) 897-3222 Carnegie Class: Assoc/PrivFP
FAX Number: (415) 771-2194 Calendar System: Other
URL: www.chefs.edu/san-francisco
Established: 1977 Annual Undergrad Tuition & Fees: $18,500
Enrollment: 442 Coed
Affiliation or Control: Proprietary IRS Status: Proprietary
Highest Offering: Associate Degree
Program: Occupational
Accreditation: ACCSC, ACICS, ACFEI

01 President ..... Mr. Marvin SABIBO

Le Cordon Bleu College of Culinary Arts in Los Angeles (E)

530 East Colorado Boulevard, Pasadena CA 91101
County: Los Angeles FICE Identification: 032103
Unit ID: 423980
Telephone: (626) 229-1300 Carnegie Class: Assoc/PrivFP
FAX Number: (626) 204-3907 Calendar System: Quarter
URL: www.chefs.edu/los-angeles
Established: 1994 Annual Undergrad Tuition & Fees: $18,534
Enrollment: 1,792 Coed
Affiliation or Control: Proprietary IRS Status: Proprietary
Highest Offering: Associate Degree
Program: Occupational
Accreditation: ACICS, ACFEI

01 President ..... Mr. Michael GIACOMINI

Learnet Academy (F)

3251 W. 6th Street, 2nd Floor, Los Angeles CA 90020
County: Los Angeles Identification: 667223
Telephone: (213) 387-4242 Carnegie Class: Not Classified
FAX Number: (213) 387-5365 Calendar System: Other
URL: www.learnet.edu
Established: 1993 Annual Undergrad Tuition & Fees: $3,625
Enrollment: 157 Coed
Affiliation or Control: Proprietary IRS Status: Proprietary
Highest Offering: Associate Degree
Program: Occupational; Business Emphasis
Accreditation: ACICS

01 Executive Director ..... Ms. Tia SHIN

Life Chiropractic College West (G)

25001 Industrial Boulevard, Hayward CA 94545-2801
County: Alameda FICE Identification: 022285
Unit ID: 117520
Telephone: (510) 780-4500 Carnegie Class: Spec/Health
FAX Number: (510) 780-4525 Calendar System: Quarter
URL: www.lifewest.edu
Established: 1976 Annual Undergrad Tuition & Fees: $33,520
Enrollment: 499 Coed
Affiliation or Control: Independent Non-Profit IRS Status: 501(c)3
Highest Offering: First Professional Degree; No Lower Division
Program: Professional
Accreditation: CHIRO

01 President ..... Dr. Brian KELLY
03 Executive Vice President ..... Dr. Anatole BOGATSKI
05 Vice President of Academic Affairs ..... Dr. Scott DONALDSON
17 Vice President of the Health Center ..... Dr. Tim GAY
09 Director of Institutional Research ..... Dr. Dale JOHNSON
71 Director of Special Projects ..... Dr. George CASEY
10 Director of Finance ..... Mr. Victor MADAMBA
07 Dean of Admissions ..... Dr. Mary FLANNERY
108 Dir of Assessment & Educ Effectiv ..... Dr. Kristen GATES
46 Director of Research ..... Dr. Monica SMITH
30 Director Institutional Advancement ..... Mr. David HOHL
51 Director of Continuing Education ..... Mr. Jacob COVERSTONE
26 Chief Communications Officer ..... Ms. Diana LAVIGNE-ROHINI
24 Director of Educational Technology ..... Mr. Garet MARLING
08 Director Learning Resource Center ..... Ms. Annette OSENGA
76 Chair Clinical Education ..... Vacant
29 Ambassador of Alumni Relations ..... Dr. James HAWKINS
37 Director Financial Aid ..... Ms. Brenda JOHNSON
06 Registrar ..... Ms. Michelle MONTOYA
18 Manager Campus Enhancement ..... Mr. Baldomero FLORES
15 Manager Human Resources ..... Ms. Joanne GAPUZ
32 Director of Student Life ..... Mrs. Jackie BIRON
105 Webmaster ..... Mr. Steve SARMIENTO
38 Academic Counselor ..... Ms. Lori PINO
40 Bookstore Manager ..... Ms. Kandice PODLONE
04 Executive Assistant to President ..... Mr. Michael HURSCHMANN
41 Athletic Director ..... Mr. Adriann FERRIS
84 Director Enrollment ..... Mr. Marc MARTIN

Life Pacific College (H)

1100 W. Covina Boulevard, San Dimas CA 91773-3298
County: Los Angeles FICE Identification: 022706
Unit ID: 117104
Telephone: (909) 599-5433 Carnegie Class: Spec/Faith
FAX Number: (909) 599-6690 Calendar System: Semester
URL: www.lifepacific.edu
Established: 1923 Annual Undergrad Tuition & Fees: $13,320
Enrollment: 584 Coed
Affiliation or Control: Other IRS Status: 501(c)3
Highest Offering: Master's
Program: 2-Year Principally Bachelor's Creditable; Liberal Arts And General; Professional; Religious Emphasis
Accreditation: WC, BI

01 President ..... Dr. Jim J. ADAMS
04 Exec Assistant to the President ..... Ms. Karli ALBANESE
05 Vice President Academic Affairs ..... Dr. Michael SALMEIER
84 Vice President Enrollment Mgt ..... Rev. Angie RICHEY
32 Director Student Development ..... Mr. Joshua ARNOLD
10 CFO ..... Mr. Todd ESKES
08 Librarian ..... Mr. Gary MERRIMAN
06 Registrar ..... Mr. Bruce PRIMROSE
18 Director of Facilities ..... Mr. Rick MEYER
37 Director of Financial Aid ..... Mrs. Luci PEREZ
09 Dean Institutional Effectiveness ..... Rev. Brian TOMHAVE
30 Director of Development ..... Mr. Tom SASSER
40 Bookstore Director ..... Mr. Jared BJUR
13 Chair IT Committee ..... Mr. Jeff GABLE
15 Director Personnel Services ..... Mr. Todd ESKES
39 Director Residence Life ..... Mr. George BOSTANIC
41 Athletic Director ..... Mr. Rick MEYER

Lincoln University (I)

401 15th Street, Oakland CA 94612-2801
County: Alameda FICE Identification: 006975
Unit ID: 117557
Telephone: (510) 628-8010 Carnegie Class: Master's S
FAX Number: (510) 628-8012 Calendar System: Semester
URL: www.lincolnuca.edu
Established: 1919 Annual Undergrad Tuition & Fees: $10,105
Enrollment: 603 Coed
Affiliation or Control: Independent Non-Profit IRS Status: 501(c)3
Highest Offering: Master's
Program: Professional; Business Emphasis
Accreditation: ACICS

01 President/Rector ..... Dr. Mikhail BRODSKY
05 Dean of Faculty ..... Dr. Michael GUERRA
32 Dean of Students ..... Mr. William HESS
07 Director of Admissions & Records ..... Ms. Peggy AU
58 Director of Graduate Programs ..... Dr. Marshall J. BURAK
08 Head Librarian ..... Ms. Nicole Y. MARSH
35 Director of Student Services ..... Ms. Annique DALLEY
13 Computer & Information System Dir ..... Mr. Abhishek VAIDYA
37 Chief Financial Aid Director ..... Mr. James PETERSON
06 Registrar ..... Ms. Maggie HUA
10 Controller ..... Ms. Sherry LIANG
20 Assistant Dean of Academic Affairs ..... Ms. Mariya ORSHANSKY

Logos Evangelical Seminary (J)

9358 Telstar Avenue, El Monte CA 91731-2816
County: Los Angeles FICE Identification: 039454
Unit ID: 397553
Telephone: (626) 571-5110 Carnegie Class: Not Classified
FAX Number: (626) 571-5119 Calendar System: Semester
URL: www.logos-seminary.edu
Established: 1989 Annual Graduate Tuition & Fees: $9,856
Enrollment: 170 Coed
Affiliation or Control: Other IRS Status: 501(c)3
Highest Offering: Doctorate; No Undergraduates
Program: Religious Emphasis
Accreditation: WC, THEOL

01 President ..... Dr. Kuoliang LIN
05 Academic Dean ..... Dr. Ekron CHEN
10 Director of Advancement ..... Mr. Steven WU
32 Dean of Students ..... Dr. James HWANG
04 Executive Asst to President ..... Ms. Kathleen LIN
08 Head Librarian ..... Mr. Sheng-Chung CHANG
09 Institutional Research Specialist ..... Ms. Teresa KAO
13 Chief Info Technology Officer (CIO) ..... Mr. Alex HUNG

Loma Linda University (K)

Loma Linda CA 92350-0001
County: San Bernardino FICE Identification: 001218
Unit ID: 117636
Telephone: (909) 558-1000 Carnegie Class: Spec/Med
FAX Number: (909) 558-0242 Calendar System: Quarter
URL: www.llu.edu
Established: 1905 Annual Undergrad Tuition & Fees: $23,370
Enrollment: 4,629 Coed
Affiliation or Control: Seventh-day Adventist IRS Status: 501(c)3
Highest Offering: Doctorate
Program: Occupational; Liberal Arts And General; Professional
Accreditation: WC, ANEST, ARCPA, CAHIIM, CLPSY, COARC, CVT, CYTO, DENT, DH, DIETC, DMS, IPSY, MED, MFCD, MT, NURSE, OPE, OT, PAST, PH, PHAR, PTA, PTAA, RAD, RADDOS, RTT, SP, SW

01 President ..... Dr. Richard H. HART
05 Provost ..... Dr. Ronald L. CARTER
10 Sr Vice President Financial Affairs ..... Mr. Rodney NEAL
30 Sr Vice President Advancement ..... Mrs. Rachelle BUSSELL
13 Vice President Information Systems ..... Dr. David P. HARRIS
84 VP Enrollment Mgmt/Student Services ..... Dr. Rick E. WILLIAMS
63 Dean of Medicine ..... Dr. H. Roger HADLEY
52 Dean of Dentistry ..... Dr. Ronald DAILEY
69 Dean of Public Health ..... Dr. Helen Hopp MARSHAK
66 Dean of Nursing ..... Dr. Elizabeth (Becky) BOSSERT
76 Dean of Allied Health Professions ..... Dr. Craig R. JACKSON
67 Dean School of Pharmacy ..... Dr. W. William HUGHES
83 Dean School of Behavioral Health ..... Dr. Beverly J. BUCKLES
73 Dean of School of Religion ..... Dr. Jon PAULIEN
58 Dean Faculty of Graduate Studies ..... Dr. Anthony J. ZUCCARELLI
06 Director of Records ..... Ms. Erin SEHEULT
08 Director of University Libraries ..... Ms. Carlene DRAKE
38 Director of Counseling ..... Dr. William G. MURDOCH
43 General Legal Counsel ..... Mr. Kent A. HANSEN
33 Dean of Men ..... Mr. John NAFIE

34 Dean of Women ... Ms. Lynette BATES
37 Director Student Financial Aid ... Ms. Verdell SCHAEFER
09 Dir Educational Effectiveness ... Dr. Marilyn EGGERS
15 Exec Director Human Services ... Ms. Charlene WILSON
18 Director Campus Engineering ... Mr. Randy STEVENS
96 Director of Purchasing ... Mr. Tim HICKMAN
40 Campus Bookstore Manager ... Ms. Michelle GURA
42 Campus Chaplain ... Pastor Terry SWENSON

Long Beach City College (A)

4901 E Carson Street, Long Beach CA 90808-1780
County: Los Angeles FICE Identification: 001219
Unit ID: 117645
Telephone: (562) 938-4111 Carnegie Class: Assoc/Pub-U-MC
FAX Number: (562) 938-4118 Calendar System: Other
URL: www.lbcc.edu
Established: 1927 Annual Undergrad Tuition & Fees (In-District): $1,182
Enrollment: 24,889 Coed
Affiliation or Control: State/Local IRS Status: 501(c)3
Highest Offering: Associate Degree
Program: Occupational; 2-Year Principally Bachelor's Creditable
Accreditation: WJ, ADNUR

01 Superintendent-President ... Mr. Eloy OAKLEY
25 Executive Vice Pres Econ & Res Dev ... Ms. Lou Anne BYNUM
05 Vice Pres Academic Affairs ... Dr. Terri LONG
10 Vice Pres Administrative Services ... Ms. Ann-Marie GABEL
15 Vice President Human Resources ... Ms. Rose DELGAUDIO
32 Vice Pres Student Support Services ... Dr. Greg PETERSON
12 Assoc Vice President PCC Campus ... Dr. Meena SINGHAL
16 Interim Assoc VP Human Resources ... Ms. Diane BANGS
13 Chief Information Systems Officer ... Ms. Sylvia LYNCH
07 Director Admissions/Records ... Ms. Lillian JUSTICE
09 Dean Academic Services ... Vacant
38 Dean Counseling/Stdnt Supp Svcs ... Ms. Nohel CORRAL
83 Dean Social Sciences & Arts ... Mrs. Dina HUMBLE
79 Dean of Language Arts ... Dr. Jennifer RODDEN
35 Dean Student Affs/Kinesiology/Athl ... Ms. Connie SEARS
76 Dean School Health & Science ... Mr. Paul CREASON
45 Assoc Dean Inst Effectiveness ... Dr. Eva BAGG
26 Dir Communications/College Adv ... Mr. John POPE
102 Exec Director Foundation ... Dr. Ginny BAXTER
96 Director Business Support Services ... Mrs. Margie PADRON
18 Director of Facilities/Maint/Oper ... Mr. Tim WOOTTON
21 Director Fiscal Services & Payroll ... Mr. John THOMPSON
37 Dep Dir Enrollment Svcs/Fin Aid ... Mr. Juan MENJIVAR

Los Angeles Academy of Figurative Art (B)

16926 Saticoy Street, Van Nuys CA 91406
County: Los Angeles Identification: 667231
Telephone: (818) 708-9232 Carnegie Class: Not Classified
FAX Number: (818) 474-8679 Calendar System: Quarter
URL: www.laafa.org
Established: 2002 Annual Undergrad Tuition & Fees: $20,400
Enrollment: N/A Coed
Affiliation or Control: Independent Non-Profit IRS Status: 501(c)3
Highest Offering: Baccalaureate
Program: Fine Arts Emphasis
Accreditation: ART

01 President ... Maryam STORM

*Los Angeles Community College District Office (C)

770 Wilshire Boulevard, Los Angeles CA 90017
County: Los Angeles FICE Identification: 001221
Unit ID: 117681
Telephone: (213) 891-2000 Carnegie Class: N/A
FAX Number: N/A
URL: www.laccd.edu

01 Chancellor ... Dr. Francisco C. RODRIGUEZ
43 General Counsel ... Ms. Camille A. GOULET
03 Deputy Chancellor ... Dr. Adriana D. BARRERA
05 Interim VC Educ Pgms/Inst Effective ... Ms. Bobbi KIMBLE
103 Vice Chanc Econ Workforce Devel ... Dr. Felicito CAJAYON

*East Los Angeles College (D)

1301 Avenida Cesar Chavez,
Monterey Park CA 91754-6001
County: Los Angeles FICE Identification: 022260
Unit ID: 113856
Telephone: (323) 265-8650 Carnegie Class: Assoc/Pub-U-MC
FAX Number: (323) 265-8763 Calendar System: Semester
URL: www.elac.edu
Established: 1945 Annual Undergrad Tuition & Fees (In-District): $1,700
Enrollment: 36,012 Coed
Affiliation or Control: State/Local IRS Status: 501(c)3
Highest Offering: Associate Degree
Program: Occupational; 2-Year Principally Bachelor's Creditable
Accreditation: WJ, CAHIIM, COARC

02 President ... Mr. Marvin MARTINEZ
05 VP Academic Affairs ... Dr. Richard MOYER
103 VP Workforce & Economic Development . Ms. Laura M. RAMIREZ
32 VP Student Services/Special Pgms ... Mr. Oscar VALERIANO
10 Interim VP Administrative Services ... Ms. Erlinda DEOCAMPO
75 Dean Acad Affs/Career & Tech Educ ... Mr. Laureano FLORES
49 Dean Academic Affairs/Liberal Arts ... Ms. Carol KOZERACKI
49 Dean Academic Affairs Liberal Arts ... Ms. Kerrin MCMAHAN
49 Dean Academic Affairs Liberal Arts ... Ms. Vi LY
07 Dean Admissions & Records ... Mr. Jeremy P. ALLRED
12 Dean Academic Affairs Southgate Ctr ... Mr. Alfonso RIOS
30 Dean Resource & Inst Development ... Ms. Selina CHI
09 Dean Institutional Effectiveness ... Dr. Ryan CORNNER
51 Dean Continuing Education ... Ms. Adrienne A. MULLEN
35 Dean Student Activities ... Ms. Sonia LOPEZ
88 Dean EOP&S/CARE ... Ms. Danelle FALLERT
88 Dean CFES ... Ms. Angelica TOLEDO
25 Assoc Dean Resource Development ... Dr. John RUDE
25 Assistant Dean Grants Management ... Ms. Martha ERMIAS
26 Chief Public Relations Officer ... Vacant
22 Affirmative Action Officer ... Ms. Maria E. YEPES
37 Financial Aid Manager ... Ms. Lindy FONG
40 Director Student Store ... Ms. Joyce GARCIA
41 Athletic Director (Men/Women) ... Mr. Allen J. CONE
28 Director of Diversity ... Ms. Maria Elena YEPES
88 Child Development Director ... Ms. Marcia CAGIGAS
38 Department Chair Counseling ... Mr. Daniel ORNELAS
21 College Fiscal Administrator ... Ms. Erlinda N. DEOCAMPO
08 Library Coordinator ... Ms. Choonhee L. RHIM
85 Foreign Student Advisement ... Ms. Nancy C. WONG
88 Director Vincent Price Art Museum ... Ms. Karen RAPP

*Los Angeles City College (E)

855 N Vermont Avenue, Los Angeles CA 90029-9990
County: Los Angeles FICE Identification: 001223
Unit ID: 117788
Telephone: (323) 953-4000 Carnegie Class: Assoc/Pub-U-MC
FAX Number: (323) 953-4013 Calendar System: Semester
URL: www.lacitycollege.edu
Established: 1929 Annual Undergrad Tuition & Fees (In-District): $959
Enrollment: 21,345 Coed
Affiliation or Control: Local IRS Status: 501(c)3
Highest Offering: Associate Degree
Program: Occupational; 2-Year Principally Bachelor's Creditable
Accreditation: WJ, #DIETT, DT, RAD

02 President ... Mrs. Renee D. MARTINEZ
05 Vice President Academic Affairs ... Dr. Dan WALDEN
10 Vice President Administrative Svcs ... Dr. John AL-AMIN
32 Vice President of Student Services ... Dr. Regina SMITH
21 Asst Vice Pres Administrative Svcs ... Mr. Anil JAIN
20 Dean of Academic Affairs ... Dr. Thelma DAY
20 Dean of Academic Affairs ... Ms. Allison JONES
20 Dean of Academic Affairs ... Dr. Todd SCOTT
103 Dean Workforce Development ... Dr. A. Alex DAVIS
09 Dean of Institutional Effectiveness ... Vacant
84 Dean of Enrollment Services ... Mr. William MARMOLEJO
35 Dean Student Svcs Special Programs ... Dr. Randy ANDERSON
35 Assoc Dean of EOPS ... Ms. Jeannette MAGEE
37 Assoc Dean Financial Aid ... Dr. Jeremy VILLAR
35 Assoc Dean Office of Student Life ... Mr. Alen ANDRIASSIAN
40 Bookstore Manager ... Ms. Christi O'CONNOR
85 Director International Students ... Vacant
15 Human Resources Manager ... Vacant
66 Nursing Department Chair ... Vacant
38 Counseling Chairperson ... Vacant
18 Facilities Director ... Mr. Bob GARCIA

*Los Angeles Harbor College (F)

1111 Figueroa Place, Wilmington CA 90744-2397
County: Los Angeles FICE Identification: 001224
Unit ID: 117690
Telephone: (310) 233-4000 Carnegie Class: Assoc/Pub-U-MC
FAX Number: (310) 233-4223 Calendar System: Semester
URL: www.lahc.edu
Established: 1949 Annual Undergrad Tuition & Fees (In-District): $1,128
Enrollment: 10,059 Coed
Affiliation or Control: State/Local IRS Status: 501(c)3
Highest Offering: Associate Degree
Program: Occupational; 2-Year Principally Bachelor's Creditable
Accreditation: WJ, ADNUR

02 President ... Dr. Otto LEE
04 Executive Assistant to President ... Ms. Danielle JACK
05 Int Vice Pres Academic Affairs ... Dr. Bobbi VILLALOBOS
10 Vice Pres Administrative Services ... Mr. Robert E. SUPPELSA
32 Int Vice Pres Student Services ... Ms. Phyllis D. BRAXTON
21 Assoc Vice Pres Administrative Svcs ... Mr. Nestor TAN
09 Dean of Institutional Effectiveness ... Dr. Edward PAI
20 Dean of Academic Affairs ... Vacant
07 Dean Enrollment/Eve Ops ... Mr. Corey RODGERS
35 Dean of Student Services ... Ms. Mercedes YANEZ
20 Dean of Academic Affairs ... Dr. Stephanie ATKINSON-ALSTON
25 Assoc Dean Grants Mgmt ... Ms. Susan RHI-KLEINERT
88 Assoc Dean EWD ... Ms. Priscilla LOPEZ
103 Dean of Economic/Workforce Devel ... Ms. Sandra SANCHEZ
88 Assistant Dean Title V ... Mr. Andrew SANCHEZ
83 Div Chair Behavioral/Social Sci ... Mr. Bradley J. YOUNG
50 Division Chairperson Business ... Mr. Stanley C. SANDELL
60 Div Chairperson Communications ... Ms. Carmen CARRILLO
57 Div Chair Humanities/Fine Arts ... Mr. Juan BAEZ
81 Div Chairperson Math/Phys Science ... Ms. Farah SADDIGH
76 Div Chairperson Health Sciences ... Mrs. Lynn YAMAKAWA
68 Div Chairperson Physical Education ... Mr. Nabeel M. BARAKAT
88 Div Chrp Sci & Fam/Consum Stds ... Mrs. Joyce E. PARKER
08 Division Chairperson Library ... Mr. Jonathan LEE
38 Division Chairperson Counseling ... Ms. Joy FISHER
41 Athletic Director ... Mr. Nabeel BARAKAT
37 Director Student Financial Aid ... Ms. Peggy LOEWY-WELLISCH
18 Facilities Manager ... Mr. William C. ENGLERT
13 Manager Information Technology ... Mr. Ivan CLARKE
31 Community Services Manager .. Ms. Carla R. MUSSA-MULDOON
85 Foreign Student Advisor ... Vacant

*Los Angeles Mission College (G)

13356 Eldridge Avenue, Sylmar CA 91342-3244
County: Los Angeles FICE Identification: 012550
Unit ID: 117867
Telephone: (818) 364-7600 Carnegie Class: Assoc/Pub-U-MC
FAX Number: (818) 364-7826 Calendar System: Semester
URL: www.lamission.edu
Established: 1975 Annual Undergrad Tuition & Fees (In-District): $1,220
Enrollment: 11,150 Coed
Affiliation or Control: State/Local IRS Status: 501(c)3
Highest Offering: Associate Degree
Program: Occupational; 2-Year Principally Bachelor's Creditable
Accreditation: WJ

02 President ... Dr. Monte E. PEREZ
05 Vice President Academic Affairs ... Mr. Michael K. ALLEN
11 Vice President Administrative Svcs .... Mr. Daniel G. VILLANUEVA
32 Vice President of Student Services ... Vacant
20 Dean of Academic Affairs ... Vacant
35 Dean of Student Services ... Ms. Ludi VILLEGAS-VIDAL
88 Associate Dean of Academic Affairs ... Ms. Cathy BRINKMAN
88 Director Title V HSI ... Mr. Carlos R. GONZALEZ
09 Dean of Institutional Effectiveness ... Dr. Sarah L. MASTER
20 Dean of Academic Affairs ... Ms. Madelline HERNANDEZ
26 Chief Public Relations Officer ... Vacant
88 Director Child Development Center ... Ms. Diane STEIN
41 Athletic Director ... Mr. Steve RUYS
08 Head Librarian ... Ms. Donna AYERS
38 Counseling Chairperson ... Ms. Park MICHONG
37 Financial Aid Manager ... Mr. Dennis J. SCHROEDER
31 Community Services Manager ... Mr. Dennis SOLARES
18 Facilities/Physical Plant Manager ... Mr. Walter J. BORTMAN
88 EOP & S/Care Director ... Ms. Ludi VILLEGAS-VIDAL
06 Sr Admissions & Records Supervisor ... Ms. Rosalie S. TORRES
04 Administrative Asst to President ... Mrs. Oliva AYALA
10 Chief Business Officer ... Mr. Jerry HUANG
102 Dir Foundation/Corporate Relations ... Mr. Albert ALVAREZ
15 Director Personnel Services ... Ms. Alice YEE
07 Director of Admissions ... Ms. Rosalie TORRES
36 Director Student Placement ... Ms. Wendy RIVERA
84 Director Enrollment Management ... Mr. Michael ALLEN
96 Director of Purchasing ... Ms. Josefina BLANCO

*Los Angeles Pierce College (H)

6201 Winnetka Avenue, Woodland Hills CA 91371-0001
County: Los Angeles FICE Identification: 001226
Unit ID: 117706
Telephone: (818) 710-4100 Carnegie Class: Assoc/Pub-U-MC
FAX Number: (818) 710-4300 Calendar System: Semester
URL: www.piercecollege.edu
Established: 1947 Annual Undergrad Tuition & Fees (In-District): $1,104
Enrollment: 21,143 Coed
Affiliation or Control: State/Local IRS Status: 501(c)3
Highest Offering: Associate Degree
Program: Occupational; 2-Year Principally Bachelor's Creditable
Accreditation: WJ

02 President ... Dr. Kathleen F. BURKE
05 Vice President Academic Affairs ... Ms. Sheri BERGER
11 Vice President Administrative Svcs ... Mr. Rolf SCHLEICHER
32 Vice President Student Services ... Dr. Earic PETERS
10 Assoc Vice President Admin Services ... Mr. Bruce ROSKY
10 Assoc Vice President Admin Services ... Mr. Larry KRAUS
08 Chairman Library Services ... Ms. Paula PAGGI
38 Chair Student Counseling ... Mr. Rudy DOMPE
20 Dean of Academic Affairs ... Dr. Donna-Mae VILLANUEVA
20 Dean of Academic Affairs ... Ms. Mary Anne GAVARRA-OH
20 Dean of Academic Affairs ... Ms. Barbara ANDERSON
20 Dean of Academic Affairs ... Mr. Jose Luis FERNANDEZ
07 Dean Admissions/Records ... Vacant
37 Director of Financial Aid ... Ms. Anafe ROBINSON
09 Dean Institutional Effectiveness ... Mr. Oleg BESPALOV
26 Public Information Officer ... Ms. Doreen CLAY
31 Director Community Services ... Ms. Cindy CHANG
102 Director of Foundation ... Vacant
18 Director of College Facilities ... Mr. Paul NIEMAN
41 Athletic Director ... Mr. Bob LOFRANO
106 Dir Online Education/E-learning ... Ms. Wendy BASS KEER
35 Dean Student Services ... Dr. Kalynda WEBBER MCLEAN
35 Associate Dean Student Services ... Ms. Stephanie SCHLATTER
06 Registrar ... Ms. Lorena LOPEZ

*Los Angeles Southwest College (I)

1600 W Imperial Highway, Los Angeles CA 90047-4899
County: Los Angeles FICE Identification: 007047
Unit ID: 117715
Telephone: (323) 241-5225 Carnegie Class: Assoc/Pub-U-MC
FAX Number: (323) 241-5220 Calendar System: Semester
URL: www.lasc.edu
Established: 1967 Annual Undergrad Tuition & Fees (In-District): $2,520

Enrollment: 6,937 Coed
Affiliation or Control: State/Local IRS Status: 501(c)3
Highest Offering: Associate Degree
Program: Occupational; 2-Year Principally Bachelor's Creditable
Accreditation: WJ

02 President Dr. Linda ROSE
05 Vice President Academic Affairs Dr. Lawrence BRADFORD
32 Vice President Student Services Vacant
10 Vice President Admin Services Mr. Ferris E. TRIMBLE
46 Dean Resource Development Ms. Felicia DUENAS
09 Dean Institutional Effectiveness Vacant
103 Dean Career/Technical Education Mr. Rick HODGE
20 Dean Academic Affairs Dr. Tangelia ALFRED
20 Dean Academic Affairs Ms. Stephanie L. BRASLEY
38 Chairperson Counseling Mr. Reggie MORRIS
08 Chairperson Library Ms. Shelley WERTS
06 Registrar Ms. Kimberly CARPENTER
18 Director of Facilities Mr. Al MAH
37 Manager Student Financial Aid Ms. Lynda HALL
35 Dean Student Services Vacant

*Los Angeles Trade-Technical College (A)

400 W Washington Boulevard,
Los Angeles CA 90015-4108
County: Los Angeles FICE Identification: 001227
Unit ID: 117724
Telephone: (213) 763-7000 Carnegie Class: Assoc/Pub-U-MC
FAX Number: (213) 763-5393 Calendar System: Semester
URL: www.lattc.edu
Established: 1925 Annual Undergrad Tuition & Fees (In-District): $1,220
Enrollment: 14,688 Coed
Affiliation or Control: State/Local IRS Status: 501(c)3
Highest Offering: Associate Degree
Program: Occupational; 2-Year Principally Bachelor's Creditable
Accreditation: WJ, ACFEI

02 President Mr. Larry FRANK
11 VP Administrative Services Dr. Mary GALLAGHER
05 VP Academic Affs & Workforce Devel Ms. Leticia BARAJAS
32 VP President Student Services Dr. Kaneesha TARRANT
21 Assoc Vice Pres Administrative Svcs Mr. William GASPER
20 Dean Academic Affairs & Workforce Mr. Vincent JACKSON
20 Dean Academic Affairs & Workforce Ms. Cynthia MORLEY-MOWER
20 Dean Academic Affairs & Workforce Mr. Joe GUERRIERI
20 Dean Academic Affairs & Workforce Ms. Nicole ALBO-LOPEZ
37 Supervisor Financial Aid Ms. Ruth BLEDSOE
09 Dean Inst Effectiveness Dr. Anna BADALYAN
35 Dean Student Services Ms. Dorothy SMITH
35 Dean Student Services Dr. Luis DORADO
18 Chief Facilities/Physical Plant Mr. Bill SMITH
06 Supervisor Admission & Records Ms. Mai LE
10 Chief Business Officer Ms. Mary GALLAGHER
38 Chair Student Counseling Mr. Tom DAWKINS
96 Director of Purchasing Vacant
102 Director Foundation/Corporate Rels Vacant
26 Public Relations Manager Mr. David YSAIS
13 Manager IT Mr. Sang BAIK

*Los Angeles Valley College (B)

5800 Fulton Avenue, Valley Glen CA 91401-4096
County: Los Angeles FICE Identification: 001228
Unit ID: 117733
Telephone: (818) 947-2600 Carnegie Class: Assoc/Pub-U-MC
FAX Number: N/A Calendar System: Semester
URL: www.lavc.edu
Established: 1949 Annual Undergrad Tuition & Fees (In-District): $1,128
Enrollment: 18,230 Coed
Affiliation or Control: State/Local IRS Status: 501(c)3
Highest Offering: Associate Degree
Program: Occupational; 2-Year Principally Bachelor's Creditable
Accreditation: WJ, ADNUR, COARC

02 President Ms. Erika A. ENDRIJONAS
05 Vice President Academic Affairs Ms. Karen DAAR
10 Vice Pres Administrative Services Mr. Mike C. LEE
32 Vice Pres Student Services Mr. Florentino MANZANO
11 Assoc Vice Pres Administrative Svcs Mr. Raul D. GONZALEZ
45 Chief Financial Anaylist Ms. Violet AMRIKHAS
20 Dean Academic Affairs Dr. Laurie NALEPA
20 Dean Academic Affairs Mr. Rudolph J. BESIKOF
20 Dean of Academic Affairs Dr. Deborah A. DICESARE
08 Chairperson of Library Service Ms. Dora E. ESTEN
37 Financial Aid Manager Mr. Vernon D. BRIDGES
09 Dean Research & Planning Ms. Michelle R. FOWLES
35 Associate Dean Student Services Dr. Elizabeth NEGRETE
88 Associate Dean of EOPS Dr. Sherri RODRIGUEZ
88 Associate Dean DSPS Mr. David M. GREEN
35 Assoc Dean of Student Services Ms. Annie G. REED
102 Director Foundation/Alumni Rels Mr. Raul V. CASTILLO
26 Public Relations Manager Ms. Jennifer C. FONG
18 Director of College Facilities Mr. Tom LOPEZ
40 Bookstore Manager Vacant
13 Manager College Info Svcs Ms. Hanh TRAN
31 Community Services Manager Mr. Michael B. ATKIN
38 Director Student Counseling Ms. Lynn BROWER
41 Athletic Director Mr. Jim FENWICK
06 Registrar Ms. Ashley DUNN
29 Director Alumni Relations Mr. Raul V. CASTILLO

*West Los Angeles College (C)

9000 Overland Avenue, Culver City CA 90230-5002
County: Los Angeles FICE Identification: 008596
Unit ID: 125471
Telephone: (310) 287-4200 Carnegie Class: Assoc/Pub-U-MC
FAX Number: (310) 841-0396 Calendar System: Semester
URL: www.wlac.edu
Established: 1969 Annual Undergrad Tuition & Fees (In-District): $1,030
Enrollment: 10,032 Coed
Affiliation or Control: State/Local IRS Status: 501(c)3
Highest Offering: Associate Degree
Program: Occupational; 2-Year Principally Bachelor's Creditable
Accreditation: WJ, DH

02 Interim President Mr. Robert SPRAGUE
11 Vice President Administrative Svcs Ms. Iris INGRAM
05 Vice President Academic Affairs Mr. Robert L. SPRAGUE
32 Vice President Student Services Ms. Phyllis BRAXTON
84 Dean Student Svcs Enrollment Mr. John M. GOLTERMANN
97 Dean General Education/Transfer Dr. Walter JONES
20 Dean Advance Program Development Mr. Mark PRACHER
75 Dean Career/Technology Education Ms. Aracely AGUIAR
35 Dean of Student Support Services Dr. Shalamon DUKE
09 Dean of Research and Planning Ms. Rebecca TILLBERG
56 Dean Distance Learning/Inst Tech Mr. Eric ICHON
20 Dean of Academic Affairs Ms. Kathy S. WALTON
11 Associate Dean Contract Ed Mr. Barry SLOAN
35 Interim Dean Student Svcs Dr. Celena ALCALA
88 Academic Senate President Dr. Adrienne FOSTER
10 Chief Financial Administrator Ms. Rasel MENENDEZ
102 Development Specialist Foundation Vacant
26 Dir Advtg/Marketing/Public Rels Ms. Michelle LONG-COFFEE
41 Athletic Director Mr. Ricardo HOOPER
18 Facilities Manager Vacant
19 Sheriff/Deputy Mr. Leander DAVIS
37 Financial Aid Manager Mr. Glenn SCHENK
40 College Enterprise Manager Mr. Larry PACKHAM
88 Operations Manager Mr. Bruce HICKS
22 Compliance Officer Vacant

Los Angeles County College of Nursing and Allied Health (D)

1237 N Mission Road, Los Angeles CA 90033-1083
County: Los Angeles FICE Identification: 006165
Unit ID: 117803
Telephone: (323) 226-4911 Carnegie Class: Assoc/Pub-Spec
FAX Number: (323) 226-6343 Calendar System: Semester
URL: dhs.lacounty.gov/wps/portal/dhs/conah/
Established: 1895 Annual Undergrad Tuition & Fees (In-District): $4,925
Enrollment: 204 Coed
Affiliation or Control: Local IRS Status: 501(c)3
Highest Offering: Associate Degree
Program: Occupational; 2-Year Principally Bachelor's Creditable
Accreditation: WJ

01 Interim Provost Ms. Barbara COLLIER
05 Dean of Nursing Programs Ms. Barbara COLLIER
32 Dean Administrative/Student Svcs Ms. Maria C. CABALLERO
53 Dean Education/Consulting Services Ms. Tammy BLASS
37 Director of Financial Aid Ms. Doris DEHART

Los Angeles Film School (E)

6363 Sunset Boulevard, Hollywood CA 90028
County: Los Angeles FICE Identification: 040373
Unit ID: 436429
Telephone: (323) 860-0789 Carnegie Class: Assoc/PrivFP
FAX Number: (323) 646-0770 Calendar System: Other
URL: www.lafilm.edu
Established: 1999 Annual Undergrad Tuition & Fees: $29,500
Enrollment: 2,284 Coed
Affiliation or Control: Proprietary IRS Status: Proprietary
Highest Offering: Baccalaureate
Program: 2-Year Principally Bachelor's Creditable; Fine Arts Emphasis
Accreditation: ACCSC

01 President/CEO Ms. Diana DERYCZ-KESSLER

Los Angeles ORT College (F)

6435 Wilshire Boulevard, Los Angeles CA 90048
County: Los Angeles FICE Identification: 025703
Unit ID: 368780
Telephone: (323) 966-5444 Carnegie Class: Assoc/PrivNFP
FAX Number: (323) 966-5455 Calendar System: Other
URL: www.laort.edu
Established: 1985 Annual Undergrad Tuition & Fees: $19,460
Enrollment: 306 Coed
Affiliation or Control: Independent Non-Profit IRS Status: 501(c)3
Highest Offering: Associate Degree
Program: Occupational; Technical Emphasis
Accreditation: CNCE

01 Director Mr. Joseph NEMAN

Los Angeles Pacific College (G)

3325 Wilshire Boulevard, Ste 550, Los Angeles CA 90010
County: Los Angeles Identification: 667143
Telephone: (213) 384-2318 Carnegie Class: Not Classified
FAX Number: (213) 384-0419 Calendar System: Semester
URL: www.lapacific.net
Established: 1989 Annual Undergrad Tuition & Fees: $13,200
Enrollment: N/A Coed
Affiliation or Control: Proprietary IRS Status: Proprietary
Highest Offering: Associate Degree
Program: Occupational; 2-Year Principally Bachelor's Creditable
Accreditation: COE, CEA

01 President Ms. Mary YOON

*Los Rios Community College District Office (H)

1919 Spanos Court, Sacramento CA 95825-3981
County: Sacramento FICE Identification: 001231
Unit ID: 117900
Telephone: (916) 568-3021 Carnegie Class: N/A
FAX Number: (916) 568-3023
URL: www.losrios.edu

01 Chancellor Dr. Brian KING
04 Chancellor's Executive Assistant Ms. Jennifer DELUCCHI
10 Vice Chancellor Finance/Admin Ms. Theresa MATISTA
05 Vice Chancellor Education/Tech Dr. Susan L. LORIMER
30 Vice Chanc Resource/Economic Dev Dr. Beverly A. SANDEEN
26 Assoc Vice Chanc Comm/Media Rels Mr. Mitchel BENSON
18 Assoc Vice Chanc Facilities Mgmt Mr. Pablo MANZO
15 Assoc Vice Chanc Human Resouces Mr. Ryan COX
13 Assoc Vice Chanc Information Tech Mr. Douglas MELINE
20 Assoc Vice Chanc Instruction Mr. Jamey NYE
32 Assoc Vice Chanc Student Services Dr. Victoria ROSARIO
43 General Counsel Mr. J.P SHERRY
37 Director Financial Aid Mr. Roy BECKHORN
96 Director General Services Mr. Jon AASTED
09 Director Institutional Research Ms. Betty GLYER-CULVER

*American River College (I)

4700 College Oak Drive, Sacramento CA 95841-4286
County: Sacramento FICE Identification: 001232
Unit ID: 109208
Telephone: (916) 484-8011 Carnegie Class: Assoc/Pub-U-MC
FAX Number: (916) 484-8674 Calendar System: Semester
URL: www.arc.losrios.edu
Established: 1955 Annual Undergrad Tuition & Fees (In-District): $1,200
Enrollment: 30,192 Coed
Affiliation or Control: State/Local IRS Status: 501(c)3
Highest Offering: Associate Degree
Program: Occupational; 2-Year Principally Bachelor's Creditable
Accreditation: WJ, COARC, EMT, FUSER

02 President Dr. Thomas G. GREENE
05 Vice President of Instruction Ms. Colleen H. OWINGS
32 Interim VP of Student Services Dr. Lisa LAWRENSON
10 Vice President of Admin Services Mr. Raymond DI GUILIO
20 Interim AVP of Instruction Dr. Stephen BOYD
62 Assoc VP of Instruction/Lrng Res Dr. Tammy MONTGOMERY
103 Assoc VP Workforce Development Mr. Jerome COUNTEE
09 Dean Plng/Research/Tech Dr. Adam KARP
26 Public Information Officer Mr. Scott CROW
30 Director of College Advancement Ms. Kirsten DUBRAY
37 Financial Aid Supervisor Mr. Chad FUNK
07 Dean of Enrollment Services Dr. Robin NEAL
57 Interim Dean Fine & Applied Arts Dr. Kale BRADEN
83 Dean Behavioral Social/Science Mr. Carlos REYES
79 Dean Humanities Ms. Kate JAQUES
38 Int Dean Counseling & Student Svcs Dr. Judy MAYS
88 Dean of English Mr. Doug HERNDON
81 Interim Dean of Mathematics Ms. Nancy REITZ
68 InteriDean of Kinesiology/Athletics Dr. Bruce WERNER
81 Dean Science/Engineering Dr. Rina ROY
75 Dean of Technical Educ Dr. Trish CALDWELL
56 Dean McClellan Center Mr. Steve SEGURA
35 Dean Student Services Ms. Kolleen OSTGAARD
66 Dean Health & Education Vacant
56 Dean Natomas Center Mr. Frank KOBAYASHI
35 Dean Student Development Mr. Manuel PEREZ
50 Dean Business/Computer Science Dr. Derrick BOOTH
04 Administrative Asst to President Ms. Sue MCCOY
11 Director Admin Services Mr. Dan MCKECHNIE
28 Interim Dean Equity & Ed Pathways Dr. Jeff STEPHENSON

*Cosumnes River College (J)

8401 Center Parkway, Sacramento CA 95823-5799
County: Sacramento FICE Identification: 007536
Unit ID: 113096
Telephone: (916) 691-7344 Carnegie Class: Assoc/Pub-U-MC
FAX Number: (916) 691-7375 Calendar System: Semester
URL: www.crc.losrios.edu
Established: 1970 Annual Undergrad Tuition & Fees (In-District): $1,104
Enrollment: 14,807 Coed
Affiliation or Control: State/Local IRS Status: 501(c)3
Highest Offering: Associate Degree
Program: Occupational; 2-Year Principally Bachelor's Creditable
Accreditation: WJ, CAHIIM, MAC

02 President Dr. Deborah J. TRAVIS
05 VP Instruction & Student Learning Mr. Whitney YAMAMURA
11 VP Admin Svcs & Student Support Mr. Cory WATHEN

32 VP Student Svcs/Enrollment Mgmt ... Dr. Kimberly MCDANIEL
84 Dean Student Svcs/Enrollment Mgmt ... Ms. Christine THOMAS
20 Assoc VP Instruction/Student Lrng ... Vacant
08 Dean Learning Res/College Tech ... Mr. Stephen MCGLOUGHLIN
38 Dean Counseling & Student Services ... Dr. Shannon DICKSON
50 Dean Business & Family Science ... Dr. Brian BEDFORD
79 Dean Humanities & Social Science ... Dr. Alexander CASARENO
41 Dean Kinesiology & Athletics ... Ms. Elizabeth BELYEA
81 Dean Science/Math/Engineering ... Dr. Robert MONTANEZ
72 Dean Careers & Technology ... Mr. Robert JOHNSON
60 Dean Comm/Visual/Performing Arts ... Mr. Torence POWELL
45 Dean of College Planning & Research ... Ms. Katherine MCLAIN
06 Registrar/Admissions & Records ... Mr. Richard ANDREWS
18 Chief Facilities/Physical Plant ... Mr. Augustine CHAVEZ
26 Public Information Officer ... Ms. Kristie WEST

*Folsom Lake College (A)

10 College Parkway, Folsom CA 95630-6798
County: Sacramento | FICE Identification: 038713
Unit ID: 444219
Telephone: (916) 608-6500 | Carnegie Class: Assoc/Pub-U-MC
FAX Number: (916) 608-6584 | Calendar System: Semester
URL: www.flc.losrios.edu
Established: 2004 | Annual Undergrad Tuition & Fees (In-District): $1,380
Enrollment: 7,942 | Coed
Affiliation or Control: State/Local | IRS Status: 501(c)3
Highest Offering: Associate Degree
Program: 2-Year Principally Bachelor's Creditable
Accreditation: WJ

02 President ... Dr. Rachel ROSENTHAL
11 Vice President Administration ... Kathleen KIRKLIN
05 Vice President Instruction ... Dr. Monica PACTOL
32 Int Vice President Student Services ... Melanie DIXON
35 Dean Student Success ... Parrish GEARY
20 Dean of Instruction & Technology ... Gary HARTLEY
68 Dean Kinesiology/Athletics ... Dr. Kim HARRELL
20 Dean of Instruction/EDC ... Dale VAN DAM
20 Dean of Instruction/OIR & VAPA ... David WILLIAMS
35 Dean of Student Services ... Bernard GIBSON
88 Executive Director VAPAC ... David PIER
30 Director College Advancement ... Sally HOWARD
07 Admissions & Records Supervisor ... Christine WURZER
40 College Store Manager ... Rob MULLIGAN
10 Business Services Supervisor ... Joany HARMAN
18 Campus Operations Supervisor ... Colleen JOHNSON
12 Educational Center Supervisor ... Adrienne ANDREWS
37 Financial Aid Supervisor ... Ali PADASH
26 Comm & Public Information Officer ... Kristy HART
04 Assistant to the President ... Sandra LEE

*Sacramento City College (B)

3835 Freeport Boulevard, Sacramento CA 95822-1386
County: Sacramento | FICE Identification: 001233
Unit ID: 122180
Telephone: (916) 558-2111 | Carnegie Class: Assoc/Pub-U-MC
FAX Number: (916) 558-2449 | Calendar System: Semester
URL: www.scc.losrios.edu
Established: 1916 | Annual Undergrad Tuition & Fees (In-State): $1,209
Enrollment: 22,054 | Coed
Affiliation or Control: State Related | IRS Status: 501(c)3
Highest Offering: Associate Degree
Program: Occupational; 2-Year Principally Bachelor's Creditable
Accreditation: WJ, DA, DH, OTA, PTAA

02 President ... Dr. Kathryn JEFFERY
05 Vice Pres Instructional Services ... Dr. Mary TURNER
10 Vice Pres Administrative Services ... Mr. Laduan SMEDLEY
32 Vice Pres Student Svcs ... Mr. Michael POINDEXTER
20 Associate Vice Pres Instruction ... Ms. Gabriel MEEHAN
20 Associate Vice Pres Instruction ... Ms. Julia A. JOLLY
35 Associate Vice Pres Student Svcs ... Dr. Debra LUFF
13 Dean Information Technology ... Dr. Elaine ADER
07 Dean Financial Aid/Enrollment ... Ms. Christine HERNANDEZ
46 Dean Planning/Research/Development ... Dr. Marybeth BUECHNER
08 Dean Learning Resources ... Mr. Kevin FLASH
36 Interim Dean Coun/Student Success ... Mr. Richard YANG
88 Interim Dean Student Equity/Success ... Mr. Aiden ELY
40 Director College Store ... Mr. Randy CLEM
66 Director Nursing ... Ms. Dale S. COHEN
18 Director College Operations ... Mr. Gregory HAYMAN
30 Director College Advancement ... Ms. Mary LELAND
26 Public Information Officer ... Mr. Rick BREWER
76 Dean Science & Allied Health ... Mr. James COLLINS
50 Dean Business ... Dr. Deborah SAKS
79 Dean Humanities/Fine Arts ... Mr. Chris IWATA
88 Dean Languages/Literature ... Dr. Albert GARCIA
72 Dean Advanced Technology ... Ms. Donnetta WEBB
41 Dean PE/Health/Athletics ... Mr. Mitchell L. CAMPBELL
81 Dean Statistics/Math/Engineering ... Mr. Daniel STYER
83 Dean Behavorial & Social Science ... Dr. Frank MALARET
56 Dean Davis Center ... Mr. Don PALM
56 Dean West Sacramento Ctr ... Mr. Art PIMENTEL
06 Records & Admissions Officer ... Ms. Kim GOFF
04 Administrative Asst to President ... Ms. Pamela MORRISON

Loyola Marymount University (C)

1 LMU Drive, Los Angeles CA 90045-2659
County: Los Angeles | FICE Identification: 011649
Unit ID: 117946
Telephone: (310) 338-2700 | Carnegie Class: Master's L
FAX Number: N/A | Calendar System: Semester
URL: www.lmu.edu
Established: 1911 | Annual Undergrad Tuition & Fees: $42,576
Enrollment: 9,515 | Coed
Affiliation or Control: Roman Catholic | IRS Status: 501(c)3
Highest Offering: Doctorate
Program: Liberal Arts And General; Teacher Preparatory; Professional
Accreditation: WC, ART, BUS, DANCE, ENG, LAW, MUS, TED, THEA, THEOL

01 President ... Dr. Timothy L. SNYDER
00 Chancellor ... Rev. Patrick J. CAHALAN, SJ
05 Exec Vice President & Provost ... Dr. Joseph B. HELLIGE
20 Vice Provost for Academic Affairs ... Dr. Michael J. O'SULLIVAN
84 Vice Provost Enrollment Management ... Dr. Maureen WEATHERALL
10 Sr Vice Pres/Chief Financial Ofcr ... Mr. Tom O. FLEMING
30 Sr Vice Pres University Relations ... Mr. Dennis SLON
32 Sr Vice Pres for Student Affairs ... Dr. Elena M. BOVE
11 Sr Vice Pres for Administration ... Ms. Lynne B. SCARBORO
13 VP for Information Technology Svcs ... Mr. Patrick FRONTIERA
15 VP for Human Resources ... Ms. Rebecca CHANDLER
18 VP for Facilities Management ... Mr. Timothy HAWORTH
28 Vice Pres for Intercultural Affs ... Dr. Abbie ROBINSON-ARMSTRONG
46 Assoc Provost Inst Effectiveness ... Dr. Margaret KASIMATIS
36 Assoc Provost Career & Professional ... Mr. Branden GRIMMETT
109 Assoc VP Auxiliary Mgmt & Business ... Mr. Raymond DENNIS
100 Chief of Staff ... Dr. Joseph LABRIE
08 Dean of University Library ... Ms. Kristine BRANCOLINI
06 University Registrar ... Ms. Kathy REED
61 Dean Loyola Law School/Sr VP ... Mr. Paul T. HAYDEN
49 Dean College Liberal Arts ... Dr. Robbin D. CRABTREE
53 Dean Sch of Educ/Dean Graduate Ed ... Dr. Shane P. MARTIN
50 Dean College of Business Admin ... Dr. Dennis DRAPER
57 Dean Communication & Fine Arts ... Dr. Bryant ALEXANDER
54 Dean College of Science & Engineer ... Dr. Tina CHOE
44 Ex Dir Dev Plnd Gvng/Princpal Gifts ... Ms. Joanie POHAS
07 Director of Admissions ... Mr. Matthew X. FISSINGER
37 Director of Financial Aid ... Ms. Catherine GRAHAM
41 Athletic Director ... Dr. William HUSAK
27 Assistant Director of Marketing ... Mr. Benjamin ALKALY
09 Director of Institutional Research ... Dr. Francisco HERRERA
108 Director of Assessment ... Dr. Laura MASSA
26 Executive Dir of Comm & Marketing ... Mr. John KIRALLA
29 Executive Director of Alumni Rels ... Ms. Lisa FARLAND
23 Director of Student Health Services ... Ms. Katherine ARCE
104 Interim Director Study Abroad ... Mr. Adrian DOYLE
25 Director Research & Sponsored Proj ... Dr. Joseph MCNICHOLAS
90 Director of Academic Technology ... Ms. Crista COPP
04 Executive Asst to President ... Ms. Maria G. MANCERA
102 Exec Dir Corp/Foundation Relations ... Mr. David A. TILLIPMAN
19 Chief of Public Safety ... Mr. Hampton CANTRELL
22 EEO Officer and Title IX Coordinato ... Ms. Sara TRIVEDI
39 Director Student Housing ... Mr. Steven NYGAARD
43 General Counsel ... Mr. Harold A. BRIDGES

Marshall B. Ketchum University (D)

2575 Yorba Linda Boulevard, Fullerton CA 92831-1699
County: Orange | FICE Identification: 001230
Unit ID: 123943
Telephone: (714) 870-7226 | Carnegie Class: Spec/Health
FAX Number: (714) 879-9834 | Calendar System: Quarter
URL: www.ketchum.edu
Established: 1904 | Annual Graduate Tuition & Fees: $37,910
Enrollment: 427 | Coed
Affiliation or Control: Independent Non-Profit | IRS Status: 501(c)3
Highest Offering: Doctorate; No Undergraduates
Program: Professional
Accreditation: WC, #ARCPA, OPT, OPTR

01 President ... Dr. Kevin L. ALEXANDER
05 Provost ... Dr. Morris S. BERMAN
30 Vice Pres University Advancement ... Mr. Paul A. STOVER
17 Vice Pres for Clinical Affairs ... Dr. Julie A. SCHORNACK
32 Vice President for Student Affairs ... Dr. Lorraine I. VOORHEES
15 Vice Pres Human Resources ... Ms. Gail S. DEUTSCH
10 Controller ... Ms. Andrea DUBOIS
46 Associate Dean for Research ... Dr. Jerry PAUGH
18 Director Campus Operations ... Mr. Gregory SMITH
51 Director Continuing Education ... Ms. Susan J. ATKINSON
13 Director of Information Technology ... Mr. Gary W. GRAY
84 Sr Dir Enroll Mgmt & Financial Aid ... Ms. Tami A. SATO
37 Director Financial Aid ... Ms. Barbara BREFFLE
07 Asst Dean for Optometry Admissions ... Dr. Jane Ann MUNROE
29 Dir Development/Alumni Affairs ... Ms. Erika BERNAL
08 Director of Library Services ... Ms. Donnajean MATTHEWS
23 Dir Special Clinic Programs ... Ms. Michele WHITECAVAGE
26 Dir Marketing/Communications ... Mrs. Katie SANTOS-COY
40 Manager Campus Store ... Ms. Debra WOODS
88 Dean for Optometry ... Dr. Stanley WOO
67 Dean for Pharmacy ... Dr. Robert ROSENOW
76 Dean for Health Sciences ... Ms. Judy ORTIZ
03 Executive Vice President ... Vacant
108 Dir Institutional Effectiveness ... Dr. Ajoy KOOMER

Marymount California University (E)

30800 Palos Verdes Drive E,
Rancho Palos Verdes CA 90275-6299
County: Los Angeles | FICE Identification: 010474
Unit ID: 118541
Telephone: (310) 377-5501 | Carnegie Class: Assoc/PrivNFP
FAX Number: (310) 377-6223 | Calendar System: Semester
URL: www.marymountcalifornia.edu
Established: 1932 | Annual Undergrad Tuition & Fees: $34,680
Enrollment: 1,107 | Coed
Affiliation or Control: Roman Catholic | IRS Status: 501(c)3
Highest Offering: Master's
Program: Occupational; 2-Year Principally Bachelor's Creditable; Liberal Arts And General; Professional; Business Emphasis
Accreditation: WC

01 President ... Dr. Michael S. BROPHY
10 Vice President of Finance ... Mr. James REEVES
05 Dean of Academic Affairs ... Dr. Ariane SCHAUER
30 Dean Institutional Development ... Ms. Kristi BIEBER
84 Vice President Enrollment Mgmt ... Mr. Alan LIEBRECHT
32 Dean of Students ... Mr. Ryan ALCANTARA
20 Associate Academic Officer ... Ms. Susie MARTIN
08 Librarian ... Mr. Gary MEDINA
37 Director Student Financial Aid ... Ms. Alexis GONZALEZ
15 Director Personnel Services ... Ms. Karen THORDARSON
18 Chief Facilities/Physical Plant ... Mr. Richard SCHULT
26 Chief Public Relations Officer ... Ms. Kelly CURTIS
29 Director Alumni Relations ... Ms. Megan MCCORMICK
36 Director Student Placement ... Dr. Virginia WADE
38 Director Student Counseling ... Dr. David DRAPER
96 Director of Purchasing ... Ms. Denise FESSENBECKER
06 Registrar ... Ms. Paula AVERY
35 Dir Student Life & Engagement ... Ms. Kelly KRUSEE
09 Director of Institutional Research ... Mr. Michael SEMENOFF
21 Associate Business Officer ... Ms. Kathleen RUIZ
04 Administrative Asst to President ... Ms. Kimberly RAMSEY
19 Director Security/Safety ... Mr. Michael MACMENAMIE
39 Director Student Housing ... Ms. Laura DORFMAN
41 Athletic Director ... Mr. Gary WHITE
104 Director Study Abroad ... Dr. David DRAPER
105 Director Web Services ... Mr. Maury HILLSTROM
11 Chief of Administration ... Mr. Jim REEVES
13 Chief Info Technology Officer (CIO) ... Mr. Monte SCHMEISER

The Master's College and Seminary (F)

21726 Placerita Canyon Road,
Santa Clarita CA 91321-1200
County: Los Angeles | FICE Identification: 001220
Unit ID: 117751
Telephone: (661) 259-3540 | Carnegie Class: Bac/Diverse
FAX Number: N/A | Calendar System: Semester
URL: www.masters.edu
Established: 1927 | Annual Undergrad Tuition & Fees: $30,920
Enrollment: 1,118 | Coed
Affiliation or Control: Independent Non-Profit | IRS Status: 501(c)3
Highest Offering: Doctorate
Program: Liberal Arts And General; Teacher Preparatory
Accreditation: WC, MUS

01 President ... Dr. John MACARTHUR
03 Exec Vice President ... Dr. Lee DUNCAN
05 Vice President Academic Affairs ... Dr. John STEAD
32 Dean of Student Life ... Mr. Joe KELLER
58 Vice President Graduate School ... Mr. Rich GREGORY
11 Vice President of Operations ... Vacant
30 Director of Development ... Mr. Luke CHERRY
46 Vice Pres Institutional Research ... Dr. John HUGHES
10 Chief Financial Officer ... Mr. Jason HARTUNG
18 Chief of Operations ... Mr. Jason HARTUNG
06 Registrar ... Mr. Don GILMORE
08 Director Library Services ... Mr. John STONE
20 Associate Dean of Students ... Mr. David HULET
84 Director Enrollment ... Mr. John MELCON
41 Athletic Director ... Mr. Steve WALDECK
37 Director Financial Aid ... Mr. Gary EDWARDS
35 Director Campus Activities ... Mr. Peter BARGAS
29 Director Alumni Affairs ... Ms. Shayna ANDERSON
09 Director of Institutional Research ... Mr. John M. WALTER
36 Director Student Placement ... Miss Elise AYDELOTTE
85 International Students Advisor ... Miss Lisa LAGEORGE
04 Administrative Asst to President ... Ms. Sharon STAATS
13 Chief Info Technology Officer (CIO) ... Mr. Nate PRINCE
15 Director Personnel Services ... Mr. Kent HANEY
19 Director Security/Safety ... Mr. Chris POWELL

† The Master's Seminary is located at 13248 Roscoe Boulevard, Sun Valley, CA 91352.

Mayfield College (G)

35-325 Date Palm Drive, Suite 101,
Cathedral City CA 92234
County: Riverside | FICE Identification: 041156
Unit ID: 454698
Telephone: (760) 328-5554 | Carnegie Class: Not Classified
FAX Number: (760) 328-5357 | Calendar System: Semester
URL: mayfieldcollege.org
Established: 1997 | Annual Undergrad Tuition & Fees: $12,874
Enrollment: 509 | Coed
Affiliation or Control: Proprietary | IRS Status: Proprietary
Highest Offering: Associate Degree
Program: Occupational
Accreditation: COE

01 Campus President ... Kevin HA

Mendocino College (A)

1000 Hensley Creek Road, Ukiah CA 95482-7821
County: Mendocino FICE Identification: 011672
Unit ID: 118684
Telephone: (707) 468-3000 Carnegie Class: Assoc/Pub-R-L
FAX Number: (707) 468-3120 Calendar System: Semester
URL: www.mendocino.edu
Established: 1973 Annual Undergrad Tuition & Fees (In-District): $1,422
Enrollment: 3,830 Coed
Affiliation or Control: State/Local IRS Status: 501(c)3
Highest Offering: Associate Degree
Program: Occupational; 2-Year Principally Bachelor's Creditable
Accreditation: WJ

01 Superintendent/President .... Mr. Arturo REYES
05 VP of Education & Student Services .... Ms. Virginia GULEFF
10 Vice Pres Administrative Services .... Ms. Eileen CICHOCKI
08 Head Librarian .... Mr. John KOETZNER
20 Dean of Instruction .... Ms. Debra POLAK
32 Dean of Student Services .... Dr. Ketmani KOUANCHAO
75 Dean Career and Technical Education .... Mr. Steve HIXENBAUGH
15 Director Human Resources .... Ms. Sabrina MEYER
18 Director Maintenance and Operations .... Mr. Steve OLIVERIA
26 Director Public Info & Marketing .... Ms. Jessica SILVA
41 Director of Athletics .... Mr. Matthew GORDON
21 Director Fiscal Services .... Mr. Joe ATHERTON
13 Director Information Technology .. Ms. Karen CHRISTOPHERSON
09 Director of Institutional Research .... Ms. Minerva FLORES
07 Director Admissions/Registrar .... Ms. Anastasia SIMPSON-LOGG
37 Director of Financial Aid .... Mr. Ulises VELASCO
04 Administrative Asst to President .... Ms. Mary LAMB
102 Dir Foundation/Corporate Relations .... Ms. Katie FAIRBAIRN

Menlo College (B)

1000 El Camino Real, Atherton CA 94027-4301
County: San Mateo FICE Identification: 001236
Unit ID: 118693
Telephone: (800) 556-3656 Carnegie Class: Bac/Diverse
FAX Number: (650) 543-4085 Calendar System: Semester
URL: www.menlo.edu
Established: 1927 Annual Undergrad Tuition & Fees: $38,100
Enrollment: 794 Coed
Affiliation or Control: Independent Non-Profit IRS Status: 501(c)3
Highest Offering: Baccalaureate
Program: Liberal Arts And General; Business Emphasis
Accreditation: WC, BUS

01 President .... Dr. Richard A. MORAN
05 Provost .... Dr. Terri GIVENS
03 Executive Vice President .... Mr. Steven WEINER
10 Director of Business and Financial .... Ms. Raagini ALI
30 VP for Institutional Advancement .... Mr. Bill HOPKINS
20 Dean for Academic/Prof Success .... Ms. Angela SCHMIEDE
84 Dean of Enrollment Management .... Ms. Holly DALTON
107 Dean of Professional Studies Pgm .... Dr. James WOOLEVER
08 Dean Library Services .... Ms. Linda SMITH
32 Dean of Student Affairs .... Ms. Yasmin LAMBIE-SIMPSON
35 Associate Dean of Student Affairs .... Ms. Sharyn MOORE
108 Assoc Director IR & Assessment .... Ms. Ivana IZVONAR
15 Director of Human Resources .... Mr. Jay NAIDU
18 Director Facilities & Operations .... Mr. Robert TALBOTT
41 Director of Athletics .... Mr. Keith SPATARO
37 Director Office of Financial Aid .... Ms. Jessica AYRES
36 Internship Program Director .... Dr. Angela SCHMIEDE
26 Director of Commun/PR & Marketing .... Ms. Darcy BLAKE
07 Director Office of Admissions .... Ms. Priscila DE SOUZA
06 Registrar .... Ms. Cristine RABAGO
29 Dir Alumni/Cmty Rels/Advancement .... Ms. Tina FAIRBAIRN

Merced College (C)

3600 M Street, Merced CA 95348-2898
County: Merced FICE Identification: 001237
Unit ID: 118718
Telephone: (209) 384-6000 Carnegie Class: Assoc/Pub-R-L
FAX Number: (209) 384-6043 Calendar System: Semester
URL: www.mccd.edu
Established: 1962 Annual Undergrad Tuition & Fees (In-District): $902
Enrollment: 9,753 Coed
Affiliation or Control: State/Local IRS Status: 501(c)3
Highest Offering: Associate Degree
Program: Occupational; 2-Year Principally Bachelor's Creditable; Business Emphasis
Accreditation: WJ, DMS, RAD

01 President .... Dr. Ron TAYLOR
04 Executive Assistant to President .... Mrs. Stacey MARTINEZ
05 Interim Vice President Instruction .... Dr. Susan WALSH
32 Vice President Student Services .... Mr. Chris VITELLI
12 Dean Los Banos Campus .... Dr. Brenda LATHAM
81 Dean Instructional Services .... Dr. Douglas KAIN
71 Dean Instructional Services .... Dr. Kevin KISTLER
47 Dean Instructional Services .... Mr. Jim ANDERSEN
50 Dean Instructional Services .... Dr. Bobby ANDERSON
83 Dean Instructional Services .... Mr. John ALBANO
103 Dean Instructional Services .... Mrs. Shelley CONNER
35 Dean of Student Services .... Ms. Angela TOS
35 Dean of Student Equity & Success .... Mr. Michael MCCANDLESS
26 Chief Public Relations Officer .... Mr. Robin SHEPARD
06 Registrar & Dir Financial Aid .... Mrs. Sharon REINHARDT
08 Director Learning Resources Center .... Dr. Susan WALSH
09 Director of Institutional Research .... Ms. Cherie DAVIS
15 Director of Human Resources .... Ms. Tracie GREEN

Methodist Theological Seminary in America (D)

2525 James M Wood Blvd, Los Angeles CA 90006
County: Los Angeles Identification: 667133
Telephone: (213) 386-0080 Carnegie Class: Not Classified
FAX Number: (213) 386-5229 Calendar System: Semester
URL: www.mtsamerica.com
Established: 1880 Annual Undergrad Tuition & Fees: N/A
Enrollment: N/A Coed
Affiliation or Control: Independent Non-Profit IRS Status: 501(c)3
Highest Offering: Master's
Program: Religious Emphasis
Accreditation: @BI

01 Chancellor .... Dr. Eisung CHAE
05 Dean .... Dr. Sung Do KANG

Middlebury Institute of International Studies at Monterey (E)

460 Pierce Street, Monterey CA 93940-2691
Telephone: (831) 647-4100 FICE Identification: 001241
Accreditation: &EH, BUS, CEA

† Regional accreditation is carried under parent institution Middlebury College, VT.

Mills College (F)

5000 MacArthur Boulevard, Oakland CA 94613-1301
County: Alameda FICE Identification: 001238
Unit ID: 118888
Telephone: (510) 430-2255 Carnegie Class: Master's M
FAX Number: (510) 430-2256 Calendar System: Semester
URL: www.mills.edu
Established: 1852 Annual Undergrad Tuition & Fees: $44,002
Enrollment: 1,548 Female
Affiliation or Control: Independent Non-Profit IRS Status: 501(c)3
Highest Offering: Doctorate
Program: Liberal Arts And General; Teacher Preparatory
Accreditation: WC

01 President .... Ms. Alecia A. DECOUDREAUX
05 Interim Provost & Dean of Faculty .... Dr. Sharon WASHINGTON
10 VP Finance & Administration .... Ms. Maria CAMMARATA
26 VP Communications/Chief of Staff .... Ms. Renee JADUSHLEVER
30 VP for Inst Advancement .... Vacant
20 Associate Provost .... Dr. Chinyere OPARAH
15 Chief HR Officer & Career Svcs Dir .... Ms. Aurora REZAPOUR
84 VP for Enrollment Management .... Mr. Brian O'ROURKE
32 VP Student Life/Dean of Students .... Dr. Chicora MARTIN
07 Director of Undergraduate Admission .... Vacant
09 Dir Acad Assess/Inst Research/Plng .... Dr. Alice B. KNUDSEN
101 Secretary of Board of Trustees .... Dr. Marianne SHELDON
06 Registrar .... Ms. Karen SIVERSON
18 Associate VP for Operations .... Ms. Linda ZITZNER
38 Assoc Dean/Dir Counsel/Psych Svcs .... Vacant
41 Director of Athletics .... Ms. Themy ADACHI
29 Exec Director of Alumnae Relations .... Vacant

MiraCosta College (G)

One Barnard Drive, Oceanside CA 92056-3899
County: San Diego FICE Identification: 001239
Unit ID: 118912
Telephone: (760) 757-2121 Carnegie Class: Assoc/Pub-S-MC
FAX Number: (760) 795-6609 Calendar System: Semester
URL: www.miracosta.edu
Established: 1934 Annual Undergrad Tuition & Fees (In-District): $1,336
Enrollment: 14,715 Coed
Affiliation or Control: State/Local IRS Status: 501(c)3
Highest Offering: Associate Degree
Program: Occupational; 2-Year Principally Bachelor's Creditable
Accreditation: WJ, SURGT

01 Superintendent/President .... Dr. Sunita COOKE
04 Exec Assistant to Supt/President .... Ms. Evelyn CROGAN
04 Exec Assistant to Supt/President .... Ms. Jeanne SWANSON
05 Vice President Instructional Svcs .... Dr. Mary BENARD
32 Vice President Student Svcs .... Dr. Richard ROBERTSON
10 Vice President Business/Admin Svcs .... Mr. Charles NG
12 Dean San Elijo Campus-Letters/Comm .... Ms. Dana SMITH
20 Dean Academic Information Svcs .... Dr. Mario VALENTE
38 Dean Counseling/Student Devel .... Dr. Wendy STEWART
07 Dean Admissions/Student Support .... Dr. Alketa WOJCIK
88 Int Associate Dean San Elijo Campus .... Ms. Cynthia RICE-CARROLL
51 Interim Dean Community Education .... Dr. Nikki SCHAPER
49 Dean Arts/Intl Languages .... Mr. Jonathan FOHRMAN
81 Dean Math/Sciences .... Dr. Carlos LOPEZ
75 Dean Career/Technical Education .... Dr. Al TACCONE
88 Director Small Business Dev Ctr .... Mr. Sudershan SHAUNAK
31 Director Community Services .... Ms. Linda KUROKAWA
06 Interim Registrar .... Ms. Jane SPARKS
09 Dean Institutional Research .... Dr. Robert PACHECO
26 Director Marketing/Communications .... Ms. Cheryl BROOM
102 Director Foundation/Fund Devel .... Ms. Linda FOGERSON
18 Director Facilities .... Mr. Tom MACIAS
37 Interim Director Financial Aid .... Mr. John BENEFIELD
88 Director Risk Management .... Mr. Joseph MAZZA
88 Director Cashiering Services .... Ms. Jo FERRIS
15 Director Human Resources .... Ms. Sheri WRIGHT
36 Director Career Center .... Ms. Donna DAVIS
88 Director Transfer Center .... Ms. Lise FLOCKEN
96 Director Purchasing/Material Mgmt .... Ms. Susan ASATO
88 Director Retention Services .... Dr. Edward POEHLERT
21 Director Fiscal Services .... Ms. Katie WHITE
19 Director Campus Police .... Chief Robert NORCROSS
106 Director Online Education .... Dr. James JULIUS

Monterey Peninsula College (H)

980 Fremont Street, Monterey CA 93940-4799
County: Monterey FICE Identification: 001242
Unit ID: 119067
Telephone: (831) 646-4000 Carnegie Class: Assoc/Pub-R-L
FAX Number: (831) 655-2627 Calendar System: Semester
URL: www.mpc.edu
Established: 1947 Annual Undergrad Tuition & Fees (In-District): $1,264
Enrollment: 4,684 Coed
Affiliation or Control: State/Local IRS Status: 501(c)3
Highest Offering: Associate Degree
Program: Occupational; 2-Year Principally Bachelor's Creditable
Accreditation: WJ, ADNUR

01 Superintendent/President .... Dr. Walter TRIBLEY
05 Vice President Academic Affairs .... Ms. Kiran KAMATH
11 Vice Pres Administrative Services .... Vacant
32 Interim Vice Pres Student Services .... Mr. Laurence E. WALKER
20 Dean Instruction .... Ms. Laura FRANKLIN
45 Dean Instructional Planning .... Mr. Michael GILMARTIN
15 Associate Dean of Human Resources .... Ms. Susan KITAGAWA
35 Dean of Student Services .... Mr. Larry WALKER
09 Director of Institutional Research .... Dr. Rosaleen RYAN
06 Director of Admissions & Records .... Ms. Nicole DUNNE
08 Librarian .... Ms. Deborah RUIZ
37 Student Financial Services Director .... Mr. Francisco TOSTADO
41 Athletic Director .... Mr. Lyndon SCHUTZLER
18 Facilities Operations Supervisor .... Mr. Pete OLSEN
26 Public Relations Officer .... Vacant
96 Purchasing Agent .... Ms. Mary WEBER
19 Director of Security .... Mr. Arthur ST. LAURENT

Mount Saint Mary's University (I)

12001 Chalon Road, Los Angeles CA 90049-1599
County: Los Angeles FICE Identification: 001243
Unit ID: 119173
Telephone: (310) 954-4000 Carnegie Class: Master's S
FAX Number: (310) 954-4379 Calendar System: Semester
URL: www.msmu.edu
Established: 1925 Annual Undergrad Tuition & Fees: $34,934
Enrollment: 3,361 Female
Affiliation or Control: Roman Catholic IRS Status: 501(c)3
Highest Offering: Doctorate
Program: Occupational; 2-Year Principally Bachelor's Creditable; Liberal Arts And General; Teacher Preparatory; Professional
Accreditation: WC, NURSE, PTA

01 President .... Dr. Ann MCELANEY-JOHNSON
05 Interim Provost .... Dr. George ARNOLD
30 Vice Pres Institutional Advancement .... Dr. Stephanie CUBBA
10 Vice Pres Administration & Finance .... Mr. Chris MCALARY
13 VP Info Support Svcs/Enroll Mgmt .... Mr. Larry SMITH
32 Vice President Student Affairs .... Dr. Jane LINGUA
20 Assistant Provost .... Dr. Michele STARKEY
09 Asst VP Inst Planning & Research .... Dr. Heather BROWN
35 Asst VP Student Affairs .... Ms. Bernadette ROBERT
58 Graduate Dean .... Dr. Linda MOODY
55 Dean of Weekend College .... Ms. Suzanne WILLIAMS
84 Director Enrollment Management .... Mr. Dean KILGOUR
06 Registrar .... Ms. Rocio DELEON
26 Director of Public Relations .... Ms. Debbie REAM
15 Director of Human Resources .... Ms. Dana LOPEZ
18 Director of Facilities Mgmt .... Mr. Rick TORKELSON
37 Director of Student Financing .... Ms. La Royce HOUSLEY
08 Director of MSMC Libraries .... Ms. Claudia REED
28 Director of Diversity .... Dr. Pam HALDEMAN
29 Director Alumni Relations .... Ms. Elizabeth ROBLES
38 Director Student Counseling .... Dr. Susan SALEM
07 Assoc Director of Admissions .... Ms. Renee ROUZAN-KAY
36 Director Career Services .... Ms. Marlene SIMON
04 Administrative Asst to President .... Ms. Lucille VILLEGAS
19 Director Security/Safety .... Mr. Michael MCFATRIDGE
39 Director Residence Life .... Ms. Jessica CUEVAS
44 Director Individual Giving .... Ms. Maria SOLANO

Mt. San Antonio College (J)

1100 N Grand, Walnut CA 91789-1399
County: Los Angeles FICE Identification: 001245
Unit ID: 119164
Telephone: (909) 594-5611 Carnegie Class: Assoc/Pub-S-SC
FAX Number: (909) 598-2303 Calendar System: Semester
URL: www.mtsac.edu
Established: 1946 Annual Undergrad Tuition & Fees (In-District): $1,348
Enrollment: 29,326 Coed
Affiliation or Control: State/Local IRS Status: 501(c)3

Highest Offering: Associate Degree
Program: Occupational; 2-Year Principally Bachelor's Creditable; Fine Arts Emphasis
Accreditation: WJ, COARC, EMT, HT, RAD

01 President/CEO ... Dr. William T. SCROGGINS
05 Vice President Instruction ... Dr. Irene M. MALMGREN
10 Vice President Administrative Svcs ... Mr. Michael D. GREGORYK
88 Director Risk Management ... Ms. Karen SALDANA
32 Vice President Student Services ... Dr. Audrey YAMAGATA-NOJI
15 Vice President Human Resources ... Mr. James P. CZAJA
20 Exec Dean Instructional Services ... Dr. Joumana MCGOWAN
35 Dean Student Services ... Ms. Carolyn KEYS
08 Dean Library/Learning Resources ... Ms. Meghan CHEN
38 Dean Counseling ... Mr. Tom MAUCH
13 Chief Technology Officer/Info Tech ... Mr. Victor BELINSKI
84 Dean Enrollment Management ... Dr. George BRADSHAW
21 Assoc Vice Pres Fiscal Services ... Ms. Rosa ROYCE
102 Executive Director of Foundation ... Mr. Bill LAMBERT
37 Director Financial Aid ... Ms. Chau DAO
46 Director Grants ... Ms. Adrienne PRICE
26 Director Marketing & Public Affairs ... Ms. Uyen MAI
09 Dir Research & Inst Effectiveness ... Ms. Barbara MCNEICE-STALLARD
18 Director Facilities Planning & Mgmt ... Mr. Gary NELLESEN
35 Director Student Life ... Ms. Andrea SIMA
36 Director Career & Transfer Services ... Vacant
96 Purchasing Manager ... Ms. Teresa PATTERSON
50 Dean Business Division ... Ms. Jennifer GALBRAITH
68 Dean Physical Education ... Mr. Joe JENNUM
79 Dean Humanities & Social Science ... Mr. Jim JENKINS
72 Dean Tech/Health Science ... Ms. Jemma BLAKE-JUDD
65 Assoc Dean Natural Sciences ... Mr. Matthew JUDD
57 Dean Arts ... Dr. Susan LONG
51 Dean Continuing Education ... Vacant
04 Exec Asst to President & BOT ... Ms. Denise LINDHOLM

Mt. San Jacinto College (A)

1499 N State Street, San Jacinto CA 92583-2399
County: Riverside FICE Identification: 001246
Unit ID: 119216
Telephone: (951) 487-6752 Carnegie Class: Assoc/Pub-S-MC
FAX Number: (951) 654-9712 Calendar System: Semester
URL: www.msjc.edu
Established: 1962 Annual Undergrad Tuition & Fees (In-District): $1,100
Enrollment: 14,685 Coed
Affiliation or Control: State/Local IRS Status: 501(c)3
Highest Offering: Associate Degree
Program: Occupational; 2-Year Principally Bachelor's Creditable
Accreditation: WJ, DMS

01 Superintendent/President ... Dr. Roger W. SCHULTZ
100 Director President's Office ... Ms. Kathy S. DONNELL
05 Int Vice Pres Instructional Svcs ... Dr. Patrick SCHWERDTFEGER
32 Vice President Student Services ... Dr. William K. VINCENT
38 Dean Student Services ... Ms. Susan LOOMIS
10 Vice President Business Svcs ... Ms. Becky ELAM
15 Int Vice Pres of Human Resources ... Dr. Jack MIYAMOTO
18 Director Maint & Operations ... Mr. Brian TWITTY
19 Chief of Police ... Vacant
20 Dean of Academic Programs ... Mr. Brandon MOORE
20 Int Dean of Academic Programs ... Dr. Jeremy BROWN
20 Dean of Academic Programs - SJC ... Dr. Carlos TOVARES
21 Dean of Business Services ... Ms. Julie VENABLE
72 Dean Instruct Acad Success/Tech ... Mr. Micah ORLOFF
13 Dean of Information Tech ... Mr. Brian ORLAUSKI
41 Dean of Athletics ... Mr. Patrick SPRINGER
35 Dean Student Support Svcs ... Mr. Tom SPILLMAN
56 Dean of Off-Site Programs ... Vacant
103 Dean Career Education ... Ms. Joyce JOHNSON
26 Public Information Officer ... Ms. Karin MARRIOTT
09 Interim Director of Research ... Mr. Nikilos 'Nik' MESARIS
16 Int Assoc Dean of Human Resources ... Ms. Jeannine STOKES
37 Assoc Dean Financial Aid ... Ms. Dolores SMITH
84 Assoc Dean Enrollment Mgmt ... Vacant
88 Assoc Dean Institutional Planning ... Ms. Rebecca TEAGUE
66 Dean of Nursing and Allied Health ... Dr. Kathleen WINSTON
96 Assoc Dean Purchasing ... Ms. Teri SISCO

Mount Sierra College (B)

101 E Huntington Drive, Monrovia CA 91016-3414
County: Los Angeles FICE Identification: 031287
Unit ID: 398130
Telephone: (626) 873-2144 Carnegie Class: Bac/Diverse
FAX Number: (626) 359-5961 Calendar System: Quarter
URL: www.mtsierra.edu
Established: 1991 Annual Undergrad Tuition & Fees: $20,328
Enrollment: 469 Coed
Affiliation or Control: Proprietary IRS Status: Proprietary
Highest Offering: Baccalaureate
Program: Occupational; Professional
Accreditation: ACCSC

01 President ... Dr. William J. KAKISH
10 Chief Financial Officer ... Mr. John DAVIS
07 Director of Admissions ... Mr. Herman WHITAKER
04 Administrative Asst to President ... Ms. Katrin EBRAHAMIAN
05 Chief Academic Officer ... Dr. Jon PERSAVICH
32 Dean of Career and Student Services ... Ms. Patricia HOLLEY
37 Director Student Financial Aid ... Ms. Lida CASTILLO

MTI College (C)

5221 Madison Avenue, Sacramento CA 95841-3037
County: Sacramento FICE Identification: 012912
Unit ID: 118198
Telephone: (916) 339-1500 Carnegie Class: Assoc/PrivFP
FAX Number: (916) 339-0305 Calendar System: Quarter
URL: www.mticollege.edu
Established: 1965 Annual Undergrad Tuition & Fees: $26,265
Enrollment: 594 Coed
Affiliation or Control: Proprietary IRS Status: Proprietary
Highest Offering: Associate Degree
Program: Occupational
Accreditation: WJ

01 President ... Mr. John A. ZIMMERMAN
10 Vice Pres/Chief Financial Officer ... Mr. David W. ALLEN
12 Campus Director ... Mr. Malcolm CARLING SMITH
11 Director of Operations ... Mr. Michael ZIMMERMAN

Musicians Institute (D)

6752 Hollywood Boulevard, Hollywood CA 90028
County: Los Angeles FICE Identification: 021618
Unit ID: 119270
Telephone: (323) 462-1384 Carnegie Class: Spec/Arts
FAX Number: (323) 462-1575 Calendar System: Quarter
URL: www.mi.edu
Established: 1977 Annual Undergrad Tuition & Fees: $23,985
Enrollment: 1,162 Coed
Affiliation or Control: Proprietary IRS Status: Proprietary
Highest Offering: Baccalaureate
Program: Occupational; 2-Year Principally Bachelor's Creditable; Professional; Music Emphasis
Accreditation: MUS

01 President ... Mr. Hisatake SHIBUYA
03 Executive Vice President ... Vacant
05 VP Academic Affairs ... Mr. Donny GRUENDLER
108 Dean Compliance and Assessment ... Mr. Tom ENGFER

Napa Valley College (E)

2277 Napa-Vallejo Highway, Napa CA 94558-6236
County: Napa FICE Identification: 001247
Unit ID: 119331
Telephone: (707) 256-7000 Carnegie Class: Assoc/Pub-U-MC
FAX Number: (707) 253-3015 Calendar System: Semester
URL: www.napavalley.edu
Established: 1942 Annual Undergrad Tuition & Fees (In-District): $1,172
Enrollment: 6,348 Coed
Affiliation or Control: State/Local IRS Status: 501(c)3
Highest Offering: Associate Degree
Program: Occupational; 2-Year Principally Bachelor's Creditable
Accreditation: WJ, COARC, EMT

01 Superintendent/President ... Dr. Ronald D. KRAFT
10 Int Vice Pres Business & Finance ... Ms. Jeanine HAWK
05 Vice President Instruction ... Dr. Terry GIUGNI
32 Vice President Student Services ... Mr. Oscar DE HARO
15 Dean Human Resources ... Ms. Laura ECKLIN
38 Dean Counseling ... Mr. Howard WILLIS
103 Interim Dean of Instruction ... Ms. Diane WHITE
08 Dean Library/Learning Resource Ctr ... Ms. Rebecca SCOTT
37 Dean Fin Aid/EOPS/Pre-Col TRIO Pgms ... Ms. Patricia MORGAN
103 Dean Workforce Devel/Career ... Mr. Gregory MIRAGLIA
13 Dean Institutional Technology ... Mr. Robert BUTLER
12 Assoc Dean Upper Valley Campus ... Ms. Mechele MANNO
07 Assoc Dean Admissions/Records ... Ms. Jessica MILLIKAN
26 Chief Public Relations Officer ... Ms. Lissa GIBBS
18 Dir Camp Plng/Constr/Risk Mgmt Svcs . Mr. Matt CHRISTENSEN
102 Exec Director NVC Foundation ... Ms. Lissa GIBBS
19 Director College Police ... Mr. Kenneth L. ARNOLD
09 Director Institutional Research ... Dr. Robyn WORNALL
84 Enrollment Management ... Dr. Terry GUIGNI
88 Counselor/Coord Trans Center ... Mr. Jose HURTADO
36 Counselor/Coordinator WA III ... Vacant

National Career College (F)

14355 Roscoe Boulevard, Panorama City CA 91402
County: Los Angeles FICE Identification: 041460
Unit ID: 455868
Telephone: (818) 988-2300 Carnegie Class: Not Classified
FAX Number: (818) 988-9944 Calendar System: Semester
URL: www.nccusa.edu
Established: 2005 Annual Undergrad Tuition & Fees: $11,106
Enrollment: 147 Coed
Affiliation or Control: Proprietary IRS Status: Proprietary
Highest Offering: Associate Degree
Program: Occupational
Accreditation: ABHES

01 President ... Gayane KHANOYAN

The National Hispanic University (G)

14271 Story Road, San Jose CA 95127-3823
County: Santa Clara FICE Identification: 025184
Unit ID: 119544
Telephone: (408) 254-6900 Carnegie Class: Bac/A&S
FAX Number: (408) 254-1369 Calendar System: 4/1/4
URL: www.nhu.edu
Established: 1981 Annual Undergrad Tuition & Fees: $8,196
Enrollment: 120 Coed
Affiliation or Control: Proprietary IRS Status: Proprietary
Highest Offering: Master's
Program: 2-Year Principally Bachelor's Creditable; Liberal Arts And General; Teacher Preparatory; Business Emphasis
Accreditation: WC

01 President ... Dr. Gladys ATO
05 Provost ... Dr. Gladys ATO
03 Vice President Campus Operations ... Mr. Jorge ESCOBAR
10 Vice President/Gen Mgr/Bus Operat ... Dr. Gary BURKHOLDER
06 Registrar ... Ms. Pamela BUSTILLO
84 Director of Enrollment ... Mr. Augustin CERVANTES
77 Int Program Dir Computer Science ... Dr. Cynthia MARKOVA
09 Director Institutional Research ... Dr. Isabel VALLEJO
37 Director Student Financial Aid ... Mr. Diondrae COLLIER
07 Manager Admissions ... Mr. Jesus MORALES
81 Int Pgm Dir Mathematics & Science ... Dr. Cynthia MARKOVA
88 Int Chair Childhood Development ... Dr. Gladys ATO
97 Chair Liberal Studies ... Dr. Carlos NAVARRO
53 Int Chair of Teacher Education ... Dr. Cynthia MARKOVA
50 Int Chair Business Administration ... Dr. Cynthia MARKOVA

† School is in teach-out plan.

National Polytechnic College (H)

6630 Telegraph Rd., Ste 200, Commerce CA 90040
County: Los Angeles FICE Identification: 039104
Unit ID: 447759
Telephone: (323) 728-9636 Carnegie Class: Not Classified
FAX Number: (323) 728-0952 Calendar System: Semester
URL: www.npcollege.edu
Established: 1996 Annual Undergrad Tuition & Fees: $35,547
Enrollment: 198 Coed
Affiliation or Control: Proprietary IRS Status: Proprietary
Highest Offering: Associate Degree
Program: Occupational; 2-Year Principally Bachelor's Creditable
Accreditation: ACCSC, CEA

01 CEO and President ... Dariush (David) MADDAHI

National Test Pilot School (I)

PO Box 658, Mojave CA 93502-0658
County: Kern Identification: 667009
Telephone: (661) 824-2977 Carnegie Class: Not Classified
FAX Number: (661) 824-2943 Calendar System: Semester
URL: www.ntps.edu
Established: 1981 Annual Graduate Tuition & Fees: $46,000
Enrollment: 17 Coed
Affiliation or Control: Independent Non-Profit IRS Status: 501(c)3
Highest Offering: Master's; No Undergraduates
Program: Professional; Technical Emphasis
Accreditation: ENG

01 President/CEO ... Dr. Al L. PETERSON
05 Director NTPS ... Mr. Gregory V. LEWIS
54 Director NFTI ... Dr. Lester A. INGHAM
88 Deputy Director Systems ... Mr. Bob MC SHEA
88 Deputy Director P&FQ ... Mr. Ed SOLSKI
11 Chief of Operations ... Mr. Nicola PECILE
06 Assistant Registrar ... Ms. Sindy STANTON
21 Business Manager ... Ms. Lynda MATOS

National University (J)

11255 N Torrey Pines Road, La Jolla CA 92037-1011
County: San Diego FICE Identification: 011460
Unit ID: 119605
Telephone: (858) 642-8000 Carnegie Class: Master's L
FAX Number: (858) 642-8714 Calendar System: Other
URL: www.nu.edu
Established: 1971 Annual Undergrad Tuition & Fees: $12,744
Enrollment: 17,608 Coed
Affiliation or Control: Independent Non-Profit IRS Status: 501(c)3
Highest Offering: Master's
Program: 2-Year Principally Bachelor's Creditable; Liberal Arts And General; Teacher Preparatory; Professional
Accreditation: WC, ANEST, IACBE, NURSE, PH, RTT, TED

01 University President ... Dr. Michael R. CUNNINGHAM
05 Interim Provost ... Dr. Gangaram SINGH
10 Vice Chancellor Business & Admin ... Mr. Randy C. FRISCH
20 Interim Associate Provost ... Dr. Jo BIRDSELL
32 Vice President for Student Services ... Dr. Joseph ZAVALA
13 Vice President of Info Technology ... Mr. Christopher KRUG
07 Vice Chancellor of Marketing ... Mr. Gary KLEINMAN
30 VP Alumni Relations & Outreach ... Mr. Chris GRAHAM
84 Interim VP Enrollment Managment ... Dr. Brandon JOUGANATOS
12 AVP Regional Oper LAX Region ... Dr. Mahvash YADEGAR
15 AVP Human Resources ... Ms. Jane SAWYER
12 AVP Regional Oper Northern Region .. Dr. Brandon JOUGANATOS
88 AVP Military and VA Programs ... Mr. Vernon TAYLOR
50 Dean School Business & Management ... Dr. Steven J. LORENZET
53 Dean School of Education ... Dr. Judy MANTLE
54 Dean School Engineering & Computing ... Dr. John CICERO
49 Dean College of Letters & Sciences ... Dr. Carol RICHARDSON
76 Dean Health and Human Services ... Dr. Gloria J. MCNEAL

06 Registrar .... Ms. Veronica GARCIA
08 Director Library Services .... Ms. Anne-Marie SECORD
37 Director Financial Aid .... Ms. Valerie RYAN
18 Director of Facilities .... Mr. Craig CROSBY
88 Director of Credentials .... Mr. Brad DAMON

New York Film Academy, Los Angeles (A)

3300 Riverside Drive, Burbank CA 91505
County: Burbank FICE Identification: 041188
Unit ID: 470269
Telephone: (818) 333-3558 Carnegie Class: Not Classified
FAX Number: (818) 333-3557 Calendar System: Semester
URL: www.nyfa.edu
Established: 2006 Annual Undergrad Tuition & Fees: $42,000
Enrollment: 1,907 Coed
Affiliation or Control: Proprietary IRS Status: Proprietary
Highest Offering: Master's
Program: 2-Year Principally Bachelor's Creditable; Fine Arts Emphasis
Accreditation: ART

01 President .... Mr. Jerry SHERLOCK
05 Provost .... Mr. Michael YOUNG
20 Dean of College .... Mr. Sonny CALDERON
11 Senior Director .... Mr. Jean SHERLOCK
06 Registrar .... Mr. Vince VOSKANIAN
07 Director of Admissions .... Mrs. Amy ELLENBERGER
08 Head Librarian .... Mr. Josh MOORMON
39 Director Student Housing .... Mr. Brennan DILLION

NewSchool of Architecture and Design (B)

1249 F Street, San Diego CA 92101-6634
County: San Diego FICE Identification: 030439
Unit ID: 119775
Telephone: (619) 684-8800 Carnegie Class: Spec/Arts
FAX Number: (619) 684-8880 Calendar System: Quarter
URL: www.newschoolarch.edu
Established: 1980 Annual Undergrad Tuition & Fees: $25,938
Enrollment: 498 Coed
Affiliation or Control: Proprietary IRS Status: Proprietary
Highest Offering: Master's
Program: Professional
Accreditation: WC

01 Interim President .... Ms. Vivian SANCHEZ
05 Interim Provost .... Dr. Karen GERSTEN
88 Director Design .... Dr. Elena PACENTI
58 Chair Graduate Architecture .... Mr. Kurt HUNKER
48 Chair Undergraduate Architecture .... Mr. Len ZEGARSKI
88 Chair Construction Management .... Mr. George WELCH
88 Director Digital Arts .... Ms. Linda SELLHEIM
97 Director General Education .... Mr. Bruce MATTHES
20 Chief Academic Officer .... Ms. Fionna SCOTT
09 Director of Institutional Research .... Ms. Nga PHAN
10 Finance Manager .... Mr. Minh NGUYEN
06 Registrar .... Ms. Maureen QUINLAN
84 Director of Enrollment .... Ms. Julie GONICK
37 Director of Financial Aid .... Mr. Diondrae COLLIER
36 Director of Career Services .... Ms. Lisa GANEM
15 Director of Human Resources .... Ms. Marcy MADIX
26 Interim Director of Marketing .... Ms. Niki DOMINGUEZ
07 Admissions Manager .... Ms. La'Shea ENGLISH
21 Business Office Manager .... Ms. Terre CORTEZ-FARAH
32 Student Life Manager .... Ms. Ashley WAGNER
08 Librarian .... Ms. Lucy CAMPBELL
88 Faculty Coordinator .... Mr. Robin BRISEBOIS
27 Public Relations Manager .... Ms. Anna CEARLEY
35 Student Success Manager .... Ms. Virginia PHILLIPS
13 IT Specialist .... Mr. Joe SOSA
88 Materials Lab Manager .... Mr. Erik LUHTALA

Nine Star University of Health Sciences (C)

441 De Guigne Drive #201, Sunnyvale CA 94085
County: Santa Clara Identification: 667207
Telephone: (408) 532-5567 Carnegie Class: Not Classified
FAX Number: (408) 733-3610 Calendar System: Trimester
URL: www.nsuhs.org
Established: Annual Graduate Tuition & Fees: N/A
Enrollment: N/A Coed
Affiliation or Control: Independent Non-Profit IRS Status: 501(c)3
Highest Offering: Master's; No Undergraduates
Program: Professional
Accreditation: @ACUP

01 President .... Philip YANG
07 Director of Admission .... Vacant

*North Orange County Community College District (D)

1830 W Romneya Drive, Anaheim CA 92801-1819
County: Orange FICE Identification: 009742
Unit ID: 120023
Telephone: (714) 808-4500 Carnegie Class: N/A
FAX Number: (714) 808-4791
URL: www.nocccd.edu

01 Interim Chancellor .... Mr. Fred WILLIAMS
10 Int Vice Chanc Finance/Facilities .... Mr. Brian FAHNESTOCK
15 Vice Chancellor Human Resources .... Ms. Irma RAMOS
32 Int Vice Chanc Student Services .... Dr. Denise NOLDON
05 Vice Chanc Educational Svcs/Tech .... Dr. W. Cherry LI-BUGG
26 Vice Chanc Public/Govt Affairs .... Mr. Vincent W. STEWART
13 Dir Management Information Svcs .... Mr. Todd HOIG
04 Exec Admin Aide to Chancellor .... Ms. Violet R. AYON
22 Dist Director Equity & Diversity .... Mr. Kenneth I. ROBINSON

*Cypress College (E)

9200 Valley View, Cypress CA 90630-5897
County: Orange FICE Identification: 001193
Unit ID: 113236
Telephone: (714) 484-7000 Carnegie Class: Assoc/Pub-S-MC
FAX Number: (714) 527-8238 Calendar System: Semester
URL: www.cypresscollege.edu
Established: 1966 Annual Undergrad Tuition & Fees (In-District): $1,414
Enrollment: 16,067 Coed
Affiliation or Control: State/Local IRS Status: 501(c)3
Highest Offering: Associate Degree
Program: Occupational; 2-Year Principally Bachelor's Creditable
Accreditation: WJ, ADNUR, CAHIIM, DA, DH, DMS, FUSER, RAD

02 President .... Dr. Robert G. SIMPSON
05 Exec Vice Pres Ed Pgms/Student Svcs .... Dr. Santanu BANDYOPADHYAY
11 Vice Pres of Administrative Svcs .... Ms. Karen CANT
08 Dean Library/Lrng Res Ctr .... Dr. Treisa CASSENS
88 Dean Language Arts .... Mr. Eldon YOUNG
07 Dean Counseling/Admiss & Records .... Dr. Paul DEDIOS
06 Registrar .... Mr. David BOOZE
26 Director Campus Communications .... Mr. Marc POSNER
102 Exec Dir Foundation/Community Rels .... Mr. Raul ALVAREZ
32 Dean Student Support Services .... Dr. Richard RAMS
88 Director Disabled Student Services .... Ms. Celeste PHELPS
90 Manager Systems Technology Svcs .... Mr. Michael KAVANAUGH
37 Director Financial Aid .... Mr. Keith COBB
09 Dir Institutional Research/Planning .... Mr. Philip DYKSTRA
18 Director Physical Plant/Facilities .... Mr. Albert MIRANDA
19 Director Campus Safety .... Dr. Shirley SMITH
04 Executive Assistant to President .... Ms. Ty VOLCY
68 Dean Physical Education .... Dr. Richard RAMS
57 Dean Fine Arts .... Ms. Joyce CARRIGAN
50 Dean Business/CIS .... Mr. Dave WASSENAAR
83 Dean Social Sciences .... Ms. Nina DEMARKEY
53 Dean Science Engineering & Math .... Dr. Richard FEE
76 Dean Health Sciences .... Dr. John SCIACCA

*Fullerton College (F)

321 E Chapman Avenue, Fullerton CA 92832-2095
County: Orange FICE Identification: 001201
Unit ID: 114859
Telephone: (714) 992-7000 Carnegie Class: Assoc/Pub-S-MC
FAX Number: (714) 992-9930 Calendar System: Semester
URL: www.fullcoll.edu
Established: 1913 Annual Undergrad Tuition & Fees (In-District): $1,138
Enrollment: 24,829 Coed
Affiliation or Control: State/Local IRS Status: 501(c)3
Highest Offering: Associate Degree
Program: Occupational; 2-Year Principally Bachelor's Creditable; Liberal Arts And General
Accreditation: WJ

02 Interim President .... Dr. Greg SCHULZ
05 Vice President Instruction .... Dr. Jose Ramon NUNEZ
32 Int Vice Pres Student Services .... Dr. Savannah JONES
11 Vice Pres Administrative Svcs .... Mr. Richard STORTI
50 Dean Business & CIS .... Dr. Doug BENOIT
57 Interim Dean Fine Arts .... Mr. John TEBAY
79 Dean Humanities .... Mr. Dan WILLOUGHBY
81 Dean Math/Computer Science .... Mr. Mark GREENHALGH
88 Dean Natural Sciences .... Dr. Richard HARTMANN
68 Dean Physical Education .... Dr. David GROSSMAN
83 Dean Social Sciences .... Dr. Kathy BENOIT
72 Dean Technology & Engr .... Mr. Kenneth STARKMAN
37 Director of Financial Aid .... Mr. Greg RYAN
23 Director Health Services .... Dr. Vanessa MILLER
18 Dir Facilities/Physical Plant .... Mr. Larry LARA
40 Director of Bookstore .... Mr. Nick KARVIA
35 Director Student Affairs .... Vacant
06 Registrar .... Ms. Rena MARTINEZ STLUKA
19 Director Campus Safety .... Mr. Steve SELBY
38 Dean Counseling/Student Development .... Ms. Lisa CAMPBELL
08 Dean Library (LLR & ISPS) .... Ms. Dani WILSON
07 Dean Admissions & Records .... Mr. Albert ABUTIN
90 Academic Computing Technologies .... Mr. Co HO
09 Director Inst Research & Planning .... Mr. Carlos AYON
88 Director Transfer Center .... Ms. Cecilia ARRIAZA
26 Director Campus Communications .... Ms. Lisa MCPHERON
04 Exec Assistant to the President .... Ms. Melinda TAYLOR

Northwestern Polytechnic University (G)

47671 Westinghouse Drive, Fremont CA 94539-7474
County: Alameda Identification: 666759
Unit ID: 120166
Telephone: (510) 592-9688 Carnegie Class: Spec/Engg
FAX Number: (510) 657-8975 Calendar System: Trimester
URL: www.npu.edu
Established: 1984 Annual Undergrad Tuition & Fees: $8,720
Enrollment: 6,800 Coed
Affiliation or Control: Independent Non-Profit IRS Status: 501(c)3
Highest Offering: Master's
Program: Technical Emphasis
Accreditation: ACICS

01 President .... Dr. George HSIEH
03 Executive Vice President .... Mr. Peter HSIEH
108 Chief Institutional Assessment Ofcr .... Mr. Paul CHOI
43 Legal Counsel & Director of HR .... Mr. Gerald WONG

† ACICS scope of recognition as approved by US Dept of Education and CHEA includes diploma programs and degree programs through the Master's degree. However, NPU offers an ACICS accredited Doctorate of Computer Science and a Doctorate of Business.

Notre Dame de Namur University (H)

1500 Ralston Avenue, Belmont CA 94002-1908
County: San Mateo FICE Identification: 001179
Unit ID: 120184
Telephone: (650) 508-3500 Carnegie Class: Master's M
FAX Number: (000) 000-0000 Calendar System: Semester
URL: www.ndnu.edu
Established: 1851 Annual Undergrad Tuition & Fees: $32,208
Enrollment: 1,982 Coed
Affiliation or Control: Independent Non-Profit IRS Status: 501(c)3
Highest Offering: Master's
Program: Liberal Arts And General; Teacher Preparatory; Professional
Accreditation: WC, ACBSP

01 President .... Dr. Judith M. GREIG
05 Provost .... Dr. Paul EWALD
10 Vice Pres Finance & Administration .... Mr. Henry ROTH
32 Dean of Students .... Ms. Jean CONDE
84 Vice President of Enrollment Mgmt .... Mr. Jason MURRAY
30 VP Advancement .... Mr. Dino HERNANDEZ
04 Exec Assistant to the President .... Ms. Alison LYON
49 Dean Arts & Sciences .... Dr. John LEMMON
50 Dean Business & Management .... Dr. Craig BREWER
53 Dean Education & Leadership .... Dr. Caryl HODGES
06 Registrar .... Ms. Sandra LEE
36 Director Career Development .... Ms. Carrie MCKNIGHT
37 Director Financial Aid .... Mr. Charles WALZ
38 Director Student Counseling .... Ms. Karin SPONHOLZ
41 Athletic Director .... Mr. Josh DOODY
42 Director Spirituality .... Ms. Amy JOBIN
19 Director of Public Safety .... Mr. Kenneth BLACKWELL
29 Director Events/Alumni Relations .... Ms. Elizabeth VALENTE
26 Director Communications .... Vacant
15 Executive Director Human Resources .... Ms. Mary HAESLOOP
08 Library Director .... Ms. Mary WEGMANN
13 Director Office of Information Tech .... Mr. Merle MASON
18 Director Facilities .... Mr. Ryan MARTINI
20 Associate Provost .... Mr. Greg WHITE
21 Controller .... Ms. Emiko YAMADA
35 Int Dir Student Life & Leadership .... Ms. Gillian WALLACE
09 Director of Institutional Research .... Mr. John HOFMANN
102 Dir Foundation/Corporate Relations .... Mr. Reginald DUHE

Occidental College (I)

1600 Campus Road, Los Angeles CA 90041-3314
County: Los Angeles FICE Identification: 001249
Unit ID: 120254
Telephone: (323) 259-2500 Carnegie Class: Bac/A&S
FAX Number: (323) 259-2958 Calendar System: Semester
URL: www.oxy.edu
Established: 1887 Annual Undergrad Tuition & Fees: $48,690
Enrollment: 2,040 Coed
Affiliation or Control: Independent Non-Profit IRS Status: 501(c)3
Highest Offering: Master's
Program: Liberal Arts And General
Accreditation: WC

01 President .... Dr. Jonathan VEITCH
05 Dean of the College/VP Acad Affs .... Dr. Jorge GONZALEZ
30 Vice Pres Institutional Advancement .... Ms. Shelby RADCLIFFE
32 Vice Pres Stdnt Life/Dean of Stdnts .... Dr. Barbara AVERY
07 Vice Pres Admission & Financial Aid .... Mr. Vincent CUSEO
43 General Counsel .... Ms. Leora FRIEDMAN
10 Vice Pres for Finance & Planning .... Mr. Amos HIMMELSTEIN
41 Assoc Vice Pres/Dir Athletics .... Ms. Jaime HOFFMAN
18 Assoc VP for Facilities Management .... Mr. Thomas POLANSKY
29 Assoc VP Alumni/Parent Engagement .... Mr. Tyler REICH
04 Int Exec Assistant to President .... Ms. Teresa KVISLER
06 Registrar .... Mr. Victor T. EGITTO
08 Librarian .... Vacant
37 Director of Financial Aid .... Ms. Maureen MCRAE
36 Director Career Development Center .... Ms. Valerie SAVIOR
15 Director of Human Resources .... Ms. Danita MAXWELL
26 Director of Communications .... Mr. Jim TRANQUADA
09 Director of Institutional Research .... Ms. Teresa KALDOR
44 Director Advancement Services .... Ms. Sarah RAMAGE
39 Assoc Dean Students/Dir Res Life .... Mr. Tim CHANG
19 Chief of Campus Safety .... Mr. Victor CLAY

Ohlone College (J)

43600 Mission Boulevard, Fremont CA 94539-0390
County: Alameda FICE Identification: 004481
Unit ID: 120290
Telephone: (510) 659-6000 Carnegie Class: Assoc/Pub-S-SC

FAX Number: N/A Calendar System: Semester
URL: www.ohlone.edu
Established: 1966 Annual Undergrad Tuition & Fees (In-District): $1,508
Enrollment: 11,065 Coed
Affiliation or Control: State/Local IRS Status: 501(c)3
Highest Offering: Associate Degree
Program: Occupational; 2-Year Principally Bachelor's Creditable
Accreditation: WJ, ADNUR, COARC, PTAA

01 President/Superintendent .... Dr. Gari BROWNING
05 Vice President Academic Affairs .... Dr. Leta STAGNARO
10 Vice Pres Administrative Services .... Vacant
32 Vice President Student Services .... Dr. Ron TRAVENICK
13 Assoc Vice Pres Information Tech .... Dr. Chris DELA ROSA
15 Assoc Vice Pres Human Resources .... Ms. Shairon ZINGSHEIM
08 Dean Learning Resource/Instruc Tech .... Ms. Lesley BUEHLER
38 Dean Counseling .... Dr. Susan GUTKIND
09 Dean Institutional Research .... Mr. Michael BOWMAN
57 Dean Arts and Social Science .... Mr. Walter BIRKEDAHL
76 Dean Health Sciences & Env Studies .... Dr. Gale CARLI
83 Dean Language & Communication .... Mr. Mark LIEU
81 Dean Science/Engineering & Math .... Dr. Mike HOLTZCLAW
88 Associate Dean Deaf Studies .... Ms. Darline GUNSAULS
102 Executive Director Foundation .... Mr. Paul IANNACCONE
35 Director EOPS/Student Services .... Ms. Debra TRIGG
21 Director Business Services .... Mr. Farhad SABIT
30 Director College Advancement .... Ms. Patrice BIRKEDAHL
19 Chief Safety & Security .... Mr. John WORLEY
18 Director of Facilities .... Mr. David ORIAS
37 Director Financial Aid .... Ms. Deborah GRIFFIN
96 Director of Purchasing .... Mr. Alex LEBEDEFF
104 Director International Programs .... Mr. Bill SHARAR
84 Director Enrollment Mgmt .... Ms. Kimberly ROBBIE
04 Administrative Asst to President .... Ms. Shelby FOSTER
07 Dean Enrollment Services .... Ms. Laura WEAVER
41 Dean Kinesiology & Athletics .... Mr. Chris WARDEN

Oikos University (A)

7850 Edgewater Drive, Oakland CA 94621
County: Alameda Identification: 667212
Telephone: (510) 639-7879 Carnegie Class: Not Classified
FAX Number: (510) 639-7810 Calendar System: Semester
URL: www.oikosuniversity.org
Established: 2004 Annual Undergrad Tuition & Fees: $4,900
Enrollment: N/A Coed
Affiliation or Control: Independent Non-Profit IRS Status: 501(c)3
Highest Offering: Doctorate
Program: Religious Emphasis
Accreditation: @TRACS

01 President .... Dr. Jongin KIM

Olivet University (B)

1025 Howard Street, San Francisco CA 94103
County: San Francisco Identification: 666176
Telephone: (415) 371-0002 Carnegie Class: Not Classified
FAX Number: (415) 371-0003 Calendar System: Quarter
URL: www.olivetuniversity.edu
Established: 1992 Annual Undergrad Tuition & Fees: $28,440
Enrollment: 1,079 Coed
Affiliation or Control: Independent Non-Profit IRS Status: 501(c)3
Highest Offering: Doctorate
Program: Liberal Arts And General; Professional; Religious Emphasis
Accreditation: BI

01 University President .... Dr. Tracy DAVIS
03 Vice President .... Mr. Nathanael TRAN
05 Academic Dean .... Dr. Christy TRAN
10 Chief Financial Officer .... Mr. Barnabas JUNG
11 Chief Operating Officer .... Dr. Walker TZENG

Otis College of Art and Design (C)

9045 Lincoln Boulevard, Westchester CA 90045-3550
County: Los Angeles FICE Identification: 001251
Unit ID: 120403
Telephone: (310) 665-6800 Carnegie Class: Spec/Arts
FAX Number: (310) 665-6805 Calendar System: Semester
URL: www.otis.edu
Established: 1918 Annual Undergrad Tuition & Fees: $42,314
Enrollment: 1,146 Coed
Affiliation or Control: Independent Non-Profit IRS Status: 501(c)3
Highest Offering: Master's
Program: Professional
Accreditation: WC, ART

01 Interim President .... Dr. Bruce FERGUSON
05 Acting Provost .... Dr. Randall LAVENDER
10 VP of Administration & Finance Svcs .... Vacant
84 VP Enrollment Management .... Vacant
30 VP Institutional Advancement .... Ms. Carrie STEWART
15 Vice Pres Human Resources/Devel .... Ms. Jane MIYASHIRO
32 Dean of Students .... Dr. Laura KIRALLA
51 Dean of Continuing Education .... Ms. Amy GANTMAN
07 Director of Admissions .... Ms. Brooke RANDOLPH
06 Registrar .... Ms. Anna MANZANO
08 Director of Library .... Ms. Sue MABERRY
37 Director of Financial Aid .... Ms. Jessika HUERTA
36 Director Career Services .... Ms. Donna Lee ODA
13 Chief Information Officer .... Ms. Megan CLARK
18 Chief Facilities/Operation Ofcr .... Mr. Claude NICA
26 Dir Communications & Marketing .... Mr. John AXTELL
29 Director Alumni Relations .... Ms. Laura DAROCA

Pacific College (D)

3160 Redhill Avenue, Costa Mesa CA 92626-3402
County: Orange FICE Identification: 032993
Unit ID: 422695
Telephone: (800) 867-2243 Carnegie Class: Assoc/PrivFP
FAX Number: (714) 662-1702 Calendar System: Semester
URL: www.pacific-college.edu
Established: 1993 Annual Undergrad Tuition & Fees: $28,245
Enrollment: 274 Coed
Affiliation or Control: Proprietary IRS Status: Proprietary
Highest Offering: Baccalaureate
Program: Occupational; 2-Year Principally Bachelor's Creditable; Nursing Emphasis
Accreditation: ACCSC, NURSE

01 President .... Mr. William L. NELSON
05 Director of Education .... Mr. Brian CHILSTRON

Pacific College of Oriental Medicine (E)

7445 Mission Valley Road, #105,
San Diego CA 92108-4408
County: San Diego FICE Identification: 030277
Unit ID: 378576
Telephone: (619) 574-6909 Carnegie Class: Spec/Health
FAX Number: (619) 574-6641 Calendar System: Trimester
URL: www.pacificcollege.edu
Established: 1986 Annual Undergrad Tuition & Fees: $8,544
Enrollment: 459 Coed
Affiliation or Control: Proprietary IRS Status: Proprietary
Highest Offering: Doctorate
Program: Professional; Business Emphasis
Accreditation: WC, ACCSC, ACUP

01 President .... Mr. Jack MILLER
05 Vice Pres of Academic Affairs .... Ms. Stacy GOMES
10 Vice President Operations .... Ms. Elaine GATES-MILINER
37 Vice Pres of Financial Aid .... Mr. Kyle POSTON
12 Campus Director NY Campus .... Mr. Malcolm YOUNGREN
12 Campus Director CH Campus .... Mr. Edward LAMADRID
07 Director Admissions .... Mr. Reza GARAJEEAGHI
06 Registrar .... Mr. Nayeli CORONA
20 Academic Dean .... Ms. Teri POWERS
26 Director of Adv and Marketing .... Ms. Gail VOGT
23 Director of Clinical Services .... Mr. Greg LANE
08 Head Librarian .... Ms. Naomi BROERING
13 Director of Information Technology .... Mr. Roland ZAKARIA
88 Office Manager .... Ms. Cindy FLOYD
40 Bookstore Manager .... Ms. Patti HINES
21 Bursar .... Ms. Patti HINES
27 Pacific Symposium & Events Coord .... Ms. Tiffany MCCORT

Pacific Oaks College (F)

55 Eureka Street, Pasadena CA 91103
County: Los Angeles FICE Identification: 001255
Unit ID: 120768
Telephone: (626) 529-8500 Carnegie Class: Spec/Other
FAX Number: N/A Calendar System: Semester
URL: www.pacificoaks.edu
Established: 1945 Annual Undergrad Tuition & Fees: $30,750
Enrollment: 1,287 Coed
Affiliation or Control: Independent Non-Profit IRS Status: 501(c)3
Highest Offering: Master's
Program: Teacher Preparatory; Professional
Accreditation: WC

01 President .... Dr. Patricia A. BREEN
05 Dean Academic Affairs .... Dr. Carol RINKOFF
84 Vice Pres Enrollment Management .... Ms. Crystal CZUBERNAT
32 Assoc Vice Pres Student Services .... Mr. Frank FRIAS
88 Exec Director Children's School .... Ms. Pam MCCOMAS
15 Director of Human Resources .... Ms. Carolyn MATHIS
10 Director of Finance .... Ms. Yug Fon CHIQUITO
08 Campus Librarian .... Ms. Kelsey VUKIC
35 Dir Ctr Stdnt Achievmt/Res/Enrich .... Ms. Pat MEDA
06 Registrar .... Ms. Anne DELFIN-SCHNIRCH
13 IT Director .... Mr. Carlos BONILLA
04 Dir Pres Office & Board Affairs .... Ms. Amy SEYERLE
88 Dir Northern CA Instructional Site .... Dr. Marian BROWNING
88 Assoc Dean School of CFP .... Dr. Bree DAVIS
88 Assoc Dean School of HD .... Dr. Donald GRANT
30 Director Advancement .... Vacant

Pacific School of Religion (G)

1798 Scenic Avenue, Berkeley CA 94709-1323
County: Alameda FICE Identification: 001256
Unit ID: 120795
Telephone: (510) 849-8200 Carnegie Class: Spec/Faith
FAX Number: (510) 845-8948 Calendar System: Semester
URL: www.psr.edu
Established: 1866 Annual Graduate Tuition & Fees: $16,992
Enrollment: 175 Coed
Affiliation or Control: Independent Non-Profit IRS Status: 501(c)3
Highest Offering: Doctorate; No Undergraduates
Program: Professional; Religious Emphasis
Accreditation: WC, THEOL

01 President .... Rev. David VASQUEZ-LEVY
05 VP Academic Affairs/Dean Faculty .... Dr. Bernard SCHLAGER
10 Chief Business Officer .... Mr. Patrick O'LEARY
30 Chief Advancement Officer .... Ms. Julie CLEMENS
06 Asst Dean Academic Pgms/Registrar .... Ms. Delphine HWANG
07 Dir of Recruitment & Admissions .... Ms. Nicole NAFFAA
15 Personnel Director .... Ms. Deborah WALKER
04 Executive Asst to President .... Ms. Jen GALL
26 Marketing/Communications Manager .... Ms. Erin BURNS

Pacific States University (H)

3450 Wilshire Boulevard, 5th Floor,
Los Angeles CA 90010
County: Los Angeles FICE Identification: 031633
Unit ID: 120838
Telephone: (323) 731-2383 Carnegie Class: Spec/Bus
FAX Number: (323) 731-7276 Calendar System: Quarter
URL: www.psuca.edu
Established: 1928 Annual Undergrad Tuition & Fees: $16,036
Enrollment: 172 Coed
Affiliation or Control: Independent Non-Profit IRS Status: 501(c)3
Highest Offering: Master's
Program: Liberal Arts And General; Professional; Business Emphasis
Accreditation: ACICS

01 President .... Mr. Hee Young AHN
04 Special Assistant to President .... Mr. Jin Song KIM
101 Chief Secretary .... Mr. Jae Young CHUNG
88 Asst Dean General Affairs .... Mr. Keith KIM
10 Assoc Dean Strategy/Finance .... Mr. Keith K. KIM
05 Associate Dean Academic Affairs .... Dr. Min Sang KIM
32 Associate Dean Student Affairs .... Mr. Moonsik KIM
50 Director College of Business .... Dr. Kamol SOMVICHIAN
26 Dir Public Rels/International Affs .... Ms. Sarah MIN
72 Dir General & Technology Services .... Mr. Kuang Kai LU
88 Director ESL Program .... Ms. Karen CHEN
08 University Librarian .... Ms. Deborah HULL
06 Registrar .... Ms. Zolzaya ENKHBAYAR

Pacific Union College (I)

One Angwin Avenue, Angwin CA 94508-9797
County: Napa FICE Identification: 001258
Unit ID: 120865
Telephone: (707) 965-6311 Carnegie Class: Bac/A&S
FAX Number: (707) 965-6390 Calendar System: Quarter
URL: www.puc.edu
Established: 1882 Annual Undergrad Tuition & Fees: $27,999
Enrollment: 1,644 Coed
Affiliation or Control: Seventh-day Adventist IRS Status: 501(c)3
Highest Offering: Master's
Program: 2-Year Principally Bachelor's Creditable; Liberal Arts And General; Teacher Preparatory; Professional
Accreditation: WC, ADNUR, IACBE, MUS, NUR, SW

01 President .... Dr. Heather J. KNIGHT
05 Academic Dean/Vice Pres Admin .... Dr. Nancy LECOURT
10 VP Financial Administration/CFO .... Dr. Dave LAWRENCE
88 Vice President for Asset Management .... Dr. John COLLINS
32 Vice President Student Services .... Dr. Lisa BISSELL PAULSON
30 Vice President Advancement .... Mr. Walter COLLINS
84 Vice Pres Enrollment Mgt/Pub Rels .... Ms. Jennifer TYNER
33 Dean of Men .... Mr. James I. BOYD, JR.
34 Dean of Women .... Miss Janice R. WOOD
08 Director Library Services .... Mr. Adu WORKU
37 Director Student Financial Services .... Ms. Laurie WHEELER
13 Director Information Technology .... Mrs. Maria VANCE
06 Director Registration & Records .... Mrs. Marlo WATERS
15 Director Human Resources .... Ms. Iris CHUAH
21 Director Budgets & Fiscal Services .... Mrs. Joy L. HIRDLER
38 Director Counseling Center .... Mr. Michael JEFFERSON
18 Chief Facilities/Facil Management .... Mr. Dale WITHERS
20 Associate Academic Officer .... Mr. Edwin MOORE
07 Admissions Counselor .... Ms. Jordan THORNBURGH
09 Director of Institutional Research .... Mr. Serhii KALYNOVSKYI

Pacifica Graduate Institute (J)

249 Lambert Road, Carpinteria CA 93013-3019
County: Carpinteria FICE Identification: 031268
Unit ID: 115746
Telephone: (805) 969-3626 Carnegie Class: DRU
FAX Number: (805) 565-1932 Calendar System: Quarter
URL: www.pacifica.edu
Established: 1974 Annual Graduate Tuition & Fees: $28,100
Enrollment: 970 Coed
Affiliation or Control: Proprietary IRS Status: Proprietary
Highest Offering: Doctorate; No Undergraduates
Program: Professional
Accreditation: WC

01 Chancellor/Chief Executive Officer .... Dr. Stephen AIZENSTAT
05 Vice President/Provost .... Dr. Patricia KATSKY
10 Vice President/CFO .... Mr. David HENKEL
43 General Counsel .... Mr. Frank MICHAELSON
37 Director of Financial Aid .... Ms. Tracie TEAGUE

06 Registrar ... Ms. Francine MATAS
30 Dir of Institutional Advancement ... Mr. Erik DAVIS
15 Director of Human Resources ... Ms. Cynthia BATASTINI
39 Director of Guest Services ... Mr. Jeffrey ABRAHAM
29 Director of Alumni Relations ... Ms. Dianne TRAVIS-TEAGUE

Palmer College of Chiropractic, West Campus (A)

90 E Tasman Drive, San Jose CA 95134-1617
Telephone: (408) 944-6000 FICE Identification: 021849
Accreditation: &NH, &CHIRO

† Regional accreditation is carried under the parent institution in Davenport, IA.

Palo Alto University (B)

1791 Arastradero Road, Palo Alto CA 94304
County: San Mateo FICE Identification: 021383
Unit ID: 120698
Telephone: (800) 818-6136 Carnegie Class: Spec/Health
FAX Number: (650) 433-3888 Calendar System: Quarter
URL: www.paloaltou.edu
Established: 1975 Annual Undergrad Tuition & Fees: $20,428
Enrollment: 1,081 Coed
Affiliation or Control: Independent Non-Profit IRS Status: 501(c)3
Highest Offering: Doctorate
Program: Professional
Accreditation: WC, CLPSY

01 President ... Dr. Allen CALVIN
05 Provost/Academic Vice President ... Dr. William FROMING
32 Vice President Student Services ... Ms. Elizabeth HILT
31 Vice President for Community Devel ... Ms. Helen TING
88 Vice President for Prof Development ... Dr. Luli EMMONS
10 Vice Pres Business Affairs/CFO ... Ms. June KLEIN
20 Dean of Academic Admin/Oper ... Dr. James BRECKENRIDGE
17 Dir of Clinical Training-PhD Pgm ... Dr. Robert RUSSELL
17 Dir of Clinical Training-PsyD Pgm ... Dr. Shelly HOWELL
23 Director of Clinic ... Dr. Sandy MACIAS
06 Registrar ... Ms. Nora MARQUEZ
37 Financial Aid Director ... Ms. America BRYANT
42 Chaplain ... Rev. Byron BLAND
08 University Librarian/Dir Acad Tech ... Mr. Scott HINES
30 Director of Advancement ... Ms. Megan O'MAHONEY
07 Director of Admissions ... Ms. Eirian WILLIAMS
13 Director Information Technology ... Mr. David LEAVITT
29 Director of Alumni Relations ... Ms. Kemper MITCHELL
09 Institutional Research Admin ... Ms. Kristen GUY

Palo Verde College (C)

One College Drive, Blythe CA 92225-9561
County: Riverside FICE Identification: 001259
Unit ID: 120953
Telephone: (760) 921-5500 Carnegie Class: Assoc/Pub-S-MC
FAX Number: (760) 921-5590 Calendar System: Semester
URL: www.paloverde.edu
Established: 1947 Annual Undergrad Tuition & Fees (In-District): $1,380
Enrollment: 4,050 Coed
Affiliation or Control: State/Local IRS Status: 501(c)3
Highest Offering: Associate Degree
Program: Occupational; 2-Year Principally Bachelor's Creditable
Accreditation: WJ

01 Superintendent/President ... Dr. Donald WALLACE
05 Vice Pres Instructional/Stdnt Svcs ... Dr. Sean HANCOCK
04 Admin Asst to Supt/President ... Ms. Denise HUNT
66 Nursing & Allied Health Coord ... Vacant
08 Librarian ... Ms. June TURNER
07 Director of Admissions and Records ... Ms. Shelley HAMILTON
88 Site Supervsr Child Dev/Teacher Ctr ... Ms. Maria KEHL
09 Institutional Research/Professor ... Mr. Adam HOUSTON
18 Facilities & Operations Director ... Mr. Shad LEE
13 Director of Information Technology ... Mr. Eric EGAN
26 Outreach & Events Coordinator ... Ms. Staci LEE
15 Director of Human Resources ... Ms. Cecilia GARCIA
10 Chief Business Officer ... Ms. Russi EGAN
20 Instructional Service Manager ... Ms. Denise TAYLOR
37 Director Student Financial Aid ... Ms. Diana MENDEZ
04 Admin Asst to Supt/President/Board ... Ms. Carrie MULLION

Palomar College (D)

1140 W Mission Road, San Marcos CA 92069-1487
County: San Diego FICE Identification: 001260
Unit ID: 120971
Telephone: (760) 744-1150 Carnegie Class: Assoc/Pub-S-MC
FAX Number: (760) 744-8123 Calendar System: Semester
URL: www.palomar.edu
Established: 1946 Annual Undergrad Tuition & Fees (In-District): $1,328
Enrollment: 25,989 Coed
Affiliation or Control: State/Local IRS Status: 501(c)3
Highest Offering: Associate Degree
Program: Occupational; 2-Year Principally Bachelor's Creditable
Accreditation: WJ, ADNUR, DA, EMT

01 Interim Superintendent/President ... Mr. Adrian GONZALES
05 Int Asst Supt/Vice Pres Instruction ... Mr. Daniel SOURBEER
32 Asst Supt/VP Student Services ... Mr. Adrian GONZALES
10 Asst Supt/VP Finance/Admin Svcs ... Mr. Ron PEREZ
15 Int Asst Supt/VP Human Resources ... Mr. Michael POPIELSKI
04 Exec Assistant to the President ... Ms. Cheryl ASHOUR
79 Dean Languages & Literature ... Ms. Shayla SIVERT
81 Dean Math/Natural & Health Sciences ... Mr. Dan SOURBEER
38 Dean Counseling Services ... Mr. Brian STOCKERT
75 Int Dean Career/Tech/Extended Educ ... Mr. Paul KELLY
50 Dean Arts/Media/Bus & Computer Sci ... Vacant
83 Dean Social/Behavioral Sciences ... Mr. Jack HAHN
13 Director Info Systems & Services ... Vacant
84 Director Enrollment Svcs/Admissions ... Mr. Kendyl MAGNUSON
09 Sr Director Institutional Research ... Ms. Michelle BARTON
18 Director of Facilities ... Mr. Chris MILLER
35 Director Student Affairs ... Ms. Sherry TITUS
37 Director Student Financial Aid ... Vacant
21 Associate Business Officer ... Vacant
26 Dir Comm/Marketing/Public Affairs ... Ms. Laura GROPEN
102 Executive Director for Foundation ... Mr. Richard TALMO
51 Director Extended Education ... Vacant
19 Chief of Police ... Mr. Mark DIMAGGIO
23 Director Health Services ... Ms. Judy HARRIS
41 Director Athletics ... Mr. Scott CATHCART
24 Supervisor Media Equipment ... Vacant

Pardee RAND Graduate School of Policy Studies (E)

1776 Main Street, Santa Monica CA 90407-2138
County: Los Angeles FICE Identification: 010441
Unit ID: 121628
Telephone: (310) 393-0411 Carnegie Class: Spec/Other
FAX Number: (310) 451-6978 Calendar System: Quarter
URL: www.prgs.edu
Established: 1970 Annual Graduate Tuition & Fees: $26,500
Enrollment: 102 Coed
Affiliation or Control: Independent Non-Profit IRS Status: 501(c)3
Highest Offering: Doctorate; No Undergraduates
Program: Professional
Accreditation: WC

01 Dean ... Dr. Susan MARQUIS
05 Associate Dean ... Ms. Rachel SWANGER
06 Registrar ... Ms. Mary PARKER
10 Financial Aid/Budget Administrator ... Ms. Maggie CLAY

Pasadena City College (F)

1570 E Colorado Boulevard, Pasadena CA 91106-2041
County: Los Angeles FICE Identification: 001261
Unit ID: 121044
Telephone: (626) 585-7123 Carnegie Class: Assoc/Pub-S-SC
FAX Number: (626) 585-7910 Calendar System: Semester
URL: www.pasadena.edu
Established: 1924 Annual Undergrad Tuition & Fees (In-District): $1,152
Enrollment: 25,886 Coed
Affiliation or Control: State/Local IRS Status: 501(c)3
Highest Offering: Associate Degree
Program: Occupational; 2-Year Principally Bachelor's Creditable
Accreditation: #WJ, DA, DH, DT, MAC, RAD

01 Superintendent/President ... Dr. Rajen VURDIEN
05 Senior VP Academic & Student Affs ... Dr. Robert H. BELL
10 Senior VP Business & College Svcs ... Dr. Robert B. MILLER
21 Exec Dir Business & College Svcs ... Mr. Joseph W. SIMONESCHI
15 Exec Dir Human Resources ... Ms. Terri HAMPTON
43 General Counsel ... Ms. Gail S. COOPER
09 Dir Inst Planning/Research ... Ms. Crystal KOLLROSS
31 Director Extension ... Ms. Elaine CHAPMAN
38 Int Assoc Dean Counseling ... Mr. Armando DURAN
88 Assistant Dean Special Services ... Dr. Kent YAMAUCHI
07 Dean Admissions/Records ... Ms. Susan BRICKER
37 Director Financial Aid ... Mr. Vincent NGO
13 Director Technical Svcs ... Mr. Matthew KIAMAN
26 Public Relations ... Mr. Gilbert RIVERA
18 Exec Dir Facilities/Physical Plant ... Mr. Rueben SMITH
04 Administrative Asst to President ... Ms. Mary THOMPSON
19 Acting Director Security/Safety ... Mr. Steven MATCHAN
32 Chief Student Affairs/Student Life ... Ms. Rebecca COBB
96 Director of Purchasing ... Mr. George CHIDIAC

Patten University (G)

2433 Coolidge Avenue, Oakland CA 94601-2699
County: Alameda FICE Identification: 004490
Unit ID: 121071
Telephone: (510) 535-9394 Carnegie Class: Bac/Diverse
FAX Number: (510) 534-8696 Calendar System: Semester
URL: www.patten.edu
Established: 1944 Annual Undergrad Tuition & Fees: $5,592
Enrollment: 963 Coed
Affiliation or Control: Proprietary IRS Status: Proprietary
Highest Offering: Master's
Program: 2-Year Principally Bachelor's Creditable; Liberal Arts And General; Teacher Preparatory
Accreditation: WC

01 President ... Dr. Thomas STEWART
05 Int Chief Academic Officer ... Dr. Abraham RUELAS
10 Asst VP Finance/Administration ... Mr. Eric WAGENSONNER
32 Director of Student Experience ... Vacant
06 Registrar ... Ms. Cindi HOGEBOOM
85 Director of International Students ... Ms. Sharon BARTA
08 Director of Learning Commons ... Ms. Lisa HUBBELL
19 Manager of Operations and Security ... Mrs. Patricia RUELAS
37 Director of Financial Operations ... Ms. La'Vetta JOSEPH
100 Chief of Staff ... Ms. Stacy CHIANG
106 Dean of Online Learning ... Dr. Tana MONACO

Pepperdine University (H)

24255 Pacific Coast Highway, Malibu CA 90263-0001
County: Los Angeles FICE Identification: 010149
Unit ID: 121150
Telephone: (310) 506-4000 Carnegie Class: DRU
FAX Number: (310) 506-4861 Calendar System: Semester
URL: www.pepperdine.edu
Established: 1937 Annual Undergrad Tuition & Fees: $48,090
Enrollment: 7,417 Coed
Affiliation or Control: Church Of Christ IRS Status: 501(c)3
Highest Offering: Doctorate
Program: Liberal Arts And General; Teacher Preparatory; Professional
Accreditation: WC, BUS, CLPSY, DIETD, LAW, MUS

01 President ... Dr. Andrew K. BENTON
100 Chief of Staff ... Ms. Marnie D. MITZE
03 Executive Vice President ... Mr. Gary A. HANSON
04 Exec Assistant to the President ... Ms. Beverly GANDY
05 Provost ... Dr. Rick MARRS
00 Chancellor Emeritus ... Dr. Charles B. RUNNELS
30 Sr VP Advancement & Public Affairs ... Mr. Keith HINKLE
10 Senior Vice President Investments ... Mr. Jeff PIPPIN
43 General Counsel ... Mr. Marc P. GOODMAN
11 Vice President Administration ... Mr. Phil E. PHILLIPS
10 Chief Business Officer ... Mrs. Edna POWELL
13 Chief Information Officer ... Mr. Jonathan SEE
26 Chief Marketing Officer ... Mr. Rick GIBSON
10 VP and Chief Financial Officer ... Mr. Paul B. LASITER
21 Assoc VP Campus Ops/Business Svcs ... Mr. Alex PANG
06 Assoc VP & University Registrar ... Mr. Hung V. LE
104 Dean of International Programs ... Dr. Charles F. HALL
84 Dean of Admission/Enrollment Mgmt ... Dr. Kristy COLLINS
32 Dean of Student Affairs ... Dr. Mark DAVIS
08 Dean of Libraries ... Mr. Mark S. ROOSA
61 Dean of the School of Law ... Dr. Deanell TACHA
50 Dean of GSBM ... Dr. David M. SMITH
53 Dean of Graduate School Educ/Psych ... Dr. Helen E. WILLIAMS
49 Dean of Seaver College ... Dr. Michael E. FELTNER
80 Dean of School of Public Policy ... Dr. James R. WILBURN
42 University Chaplain ... Ms. Sara BARTON
46 Vice Provost for Research and Strat ... Dr. Lee KATS
108 Asst Provost Inst Effectiveness ... Dr. Lisa BORTMAN
29 Exec Director for Alumni Affairs ... Mr. Bob CLARK
15 Chief Human Resources Officer ... Mrs. Lauren COSENTINO
10 University Controller ... Mr. Brian THOMASON
10 Assistant Controller ... Mr. David BRANT
88 Director of Ministry Outreach ... Mr. Michael COPE
46 Director Research & Sponsored Pgm ... Mrs. Alexandra ROOSA
39 Assoc Dean of Students/Housing ... Mr. Jon MATHIS
88 Managing Dir Center for the Arts ... Ms. Rebecca CARSON
88 Director of Special Programs ... Ms. Kanet THOMAS
85 Sr Assoc Dir Intl Student Services ... Ms. Brooke CUTLER
27 Assoc VP IM Communications ... Mr. Matthew MIDURA
23 Director of Student Health Services ... Ms. Nancy SAFINICK
36 Assoc Dean of Students/Career Ctr ... Mr. Brad D. DUDLEY
41 Director of Athletics ... Dr. Steven POTTS
19 Assoc VP & Dir of Public Safety ... Mr. Lance BRIDGESMITH
18 Director Facilities Services ... Ms. Carly MISCHKE
86 Assoc VP Govt & Regulatory Affairs ... Ms. Rhiannon BAILARD
37 Director of Financial Assistance ... Mrs. Janet LOCKHART
38 Assoc VP & Dir Student Counseling ... Dr. Connie HORTON
09 Director of Institutional Research ... Ms. Lily PANG
44 Exec Dir Estate and Gift Planning ... Mr. Curt PORTZEL
88 Director Disability Services ... Ms. Sandra HARRISON
88 Director of Auditing Services ... Ms. Norma IADEVAIA

*Peralta Community Colleges District Office (I)

333 E Eighth Street, Oakland CA 94606-2889
County: Alameda FICE Identification: 001265
Unit ID: 121178
Telephone: (510) 466-7200 Carnegie Class: N/A
FAX Number: (510) 835-4078
URL: www.peralta.edu

01 Chancellor ... Dr. Jose M. ORTIZ
13 Assoc VC Information Technology ... Mr. Calvin MADLOCK
26 Exec Dir Public Info/Commun & Media ... Mr. Jeffrey HEYMAN

*Berkeley City College (J)

2050 Center Street, Berkeley CA 94704-1183
County: Alameda FICE Identification: 022427
Unit ID: 125170
Telephone: (510) 981-2800 Carnegie Class: Assoc/Pub-U-MC
FAX Number: (510) 841-7333 Calendar System: Semester
URL: www.berkeleycitycollege.edu
Established: 1974 Annual Undergrad Tuition & Fees (In-District): $1,293
Enrollment: 7,258 Coed
Affiliation or Control: State/Local IRS Status: 501(c)3
Highest Offering: Associate Degree
Program: 2-Year Principally Bachelor's Creditable
Accreditation: WJ

02 President .... Dr. Deborah BUDD
05 Vice President Instruction .... Ms. Tram VO-KUMAMOTO
32 Vice President Student Services .... Dr. May K. CHEN
20 Int Dean Acad Pathways/Wkforce Dev ...... Mr. Antonio BARREIRO
88 Dean Student Support Services .... Ms. Brenda JOHNSON
10 Director Business Services & Admin ...... Ms. Shirley SLAUGHTER
51 Dir Program Adult College Education .... Thomas KIES
35 Director of Campus and Student Life .... Mr. Mostafa GHOUS
71 Dean of Special Programs and Grants .... Ms. Maeve Katherine BERGMAN
27 Public Information Officer .... Ms. Shirley FOGARINO
06 Registrar .... Ms. Adela ESQUIVEL-SWINSON
07 Director of Admissions .... Ms. Adela ESQUIVEL-SWINSON
09 Director of Institutional Research .... Dr. Mike ORKIN
15 Director Personnel Services .... Ms. Trudy LARGENT
18 Chief Facilities/Physical Plant .... Dr. Sadiq IKHARO
21 Associate Business Officer .... Mr. John PANG
26 Chief Public Relations Officer .... Mr. Jeffrey HEYMAN
28 Director of Diversity .... Ms. Trudy LARGENT
29 Interim Director Alumni Relations .... Ms. Kaia BURKETT
04 Executive Assistant to President .... Ms. Cynthia REESE
36 Director Student Placement .... Ms. Gail PENDLETON
37 Director Student Financial Aid .... Ms. Loan NGUYEN
38 Director Student Counseling .... Ms. Allene YOUNG
38 Director Student Counseling .... Ms. Susan TRUONG
96 Director of Purchasing .... Mr. John PANG

*College of Alameda (A)

555 Ralph Appezzato Memorial Pkwy,
Alameda CA 94501-2109

County: Alameda — FICE Identification: 006720
Unit ID: 108667
Telephone: (510) 522-7221 — Carnegie Class: Assoc/Pub-U-MC
FAX Number: (510) 337-0619 — Calendar System: Semester
URL: www.alameda.peralta.edu
Established: 1968 — Annual Undergrad Tuition & Fees (In-District): $1,144
Enrollment: 5,712 — Coed
Affiliation or Control: State/Local — IRS Status: 501(c)3
Highest Offering: Associate Degree
Program: Occupational; 2-Year Principally Bachelor's Creditable
Accreditation: #WJ, DA

02 President .... Dr. Joi Lin BLAKE
05 Vice President of Instruction .... Mr. Tim KARAS
32 Int Vice President of Student Svcs .... Dr. William WATSON
88 Dean Special Programs .... Ms. Toni COOK
26 Chief Public Relations Officer .... Vacant
84 Dean Enrollment Services .... Ms. Amy LEE
88 Int Dn Acad Pathways/Stdnt Success .... Mr. Myron JORDAN
103 Dean Workforce Development .... Ms. Char PERLAS
10 Business & Administrative Svcs Mgr .... Ms. Mary Beth BENVENUTTI

*Laney College (B)

900 Fallon Street, Oakland CA 94607-4893

County: Alameda — FICE Identification: 001266
Unit ID: 117247
Telephone: (510) 834-5740 — Carnegie Class: Assoc/Pub-U-MC
FAX Number: (510) 464-3528 — Calendar System: Semester
URL: www.laney.edu
Established: 1953 — Annual Undergrad Tuition & Fees (In-District): $1,160
Enrollment: 10,548 — Coed
Affiliation or Control: State/Local — IRS Status: 501(c)3
Highest Offering: Associate Degree
Program: Occupational; 2-Year Principally Bachelor's Creditable
Accreditation: WJ

02 President .... Dr. Elnora T. WEBB
05 Vice President of Instruction .... Ms. Lilia CELHAY
32 Vice President of Student Services .... Ms. Trudy WALTON
10 Director Business/Admin Services .... Ms. Phyllis CARTER
49 Div Dean Liberal Arts .... Dr. Chuen CHAN
81 Div Dean Mathematics and Science .... Ms. Denise RICHARDSON
75 Div Dean Career & Technical Educ .... Mr. Peter CRABTREE
23 Director Peralta Wellness Center .... Ms. Indra THADANI
31 Dean Cmty Leadership & Civic Engag .... Dr. Mildred LEWIS
79 Div Dean Hum/Soc Sci & App Tech .... Dr. Phoumy SAYAVONG
04 Executive Assistant to President .... Ms. Maisha JAMESON
37 Financial Aid Supervisor .... Mr. Joseph KOROMA
41 Director Athletics .... Mr. John BEAM
88 Director Gateway to College Pgm .... Dr. Rogeair PURNELL
88 Director TRIO Supp Services Pgm .... Dr. Roxanne RIVAS
08 Head Librarian .... Ms. Evelyn LORD
35 Dir Student Activities/Campus Life ...... Ms. Tomoko ROUDEBUSH
43 District General Counsel .... Ms. Thuy T. NGUYEN

*Merritt College (C)

12500 Campus Drive, Oakland CA 94619-3196

County: Alameda — FICE Identification: 001267
Unit ID: 118772
Telephone: (510) 531-4911 — Carnegie Class: Assoc/Pub-U-MC
FAX Number: (510) 436-2405 — Calendar System: Semester
URL: www.merritt.edu
Established: 1953 — Annual Undergrad Tuition & Fees (In-District): $1,144
Enrollment: 5,989 — Coed
Affiliation or Control: State/Local — IRS Status: 501(c)3
Highest Offering: Associate Degree
Program: Occupational; 2-Year Principally Bachelor's Creditable
Accreditation: #WJ, DIETT, RAD

00 Chancellor .... Dr. Jowel LAGUERRE
02 President .... Dr. Norma AMBRIZ-GALAVIZ
05 Vice President of Instruction .... Dr. Elmer BUGG
32 Vice President of Student Services .... Dr. Arnulfo CEDILLO
96 Vice Chancellor of General Services .... Dr. Sadiq IKHARO
35 Assoc VC of Student Services .... Dr. Adela ESQUIVEL-SWINSON
15 Vice Chancellor for Human Resources .... Ms. Trudy LARGENT
20 Vice Chanc Educational Services .... Dr. Michael ORKIN
26 Exec Dir Marketing/Public Rels/Comm .... Mr. Jeffrey HEYMAN
08 Head Librarian .... Mr. Timothy HACKETT
06 Registrar .... Ms. Susana DE LA TORRE
10 Director of Business/Admin Services .... Ms. Dativa DEL ROSARIO
04 Administrative Asst to President .... Vacant
09 Director of Institutional Research .... Mr. Nathan PELLEGRIN
101 Board Clerk .... Ms. Brenda MARTINEZ
102 Interim Exec Dir Foundation .... Ms. Kaia BURKETT
13 Assoc VC of Information Technology .... Mr. Calvin MADLOCK
18 Facilities Dir/Physical Plant .... Mr. Brian ADAIR
37 Director Student Financial Aid .... Mr. Dave NGUYEN

Phillips Graduate Institute (D)

19900 Plummer Street, Chatsworth CA 91311

County: Los Angeles — FICE Identification: 022372
Unit ID: 110307
Telephone: (818) 386-5600 — Carnegie Class: Spec/Health
FAX Number: (818) 386-5636 — Calendar System: Semester
URL: www.pgi.edu
Established: 1971 — Annual Graduate Tuition & Fees: $36,139
Enrollment: 220 — Coed
Affiliation or Control: Independent Non-Profit — IRS Status: 501(c)3
Highest Offering: Doctorate; No Undergraduates
Program: Professional
Accreditation: WC

01 President .... Dr. Yolanda J. GORMAN
03 Vice President Administration ..... Dr. Karen L. SEMIEN-MCBRIDE
10 VP Finance & Business Affairs - CFO .... Ms. Tanya PONTEP
05 Vice President Academic Affairs .... Ms. Deborah BUTTITTA
07 Director of Admissions & Enrollment .... Ms. Teresa M. MOORE
08 Director Library .... Ms. Caroline SISNEROS
37 Assistant Director of Financial Aid .... Ms. Lavetta ANDERSON
13 IT/Operations Director .... Vacant
06 Registration & Records Coordinator .... Ms. Kacey GUILFOIL
09 Dir Institutional Rsrch/Assess/Plng .... Vacant
15 Director Human Resources .... Ms. Theresa WRAY

Pima Medical Institute-Chula Vista (E)

780 Bay Boulevard, Suite 101,
Chula Vista CA 91910-5261

Telephone: (619) 425-3200 — Identification: 666272
Accreditation: ABHES, COARC, RAD

† Branch campus of Pima Medical Institute, Tucson, AZ.

Pitzer College (F)

1050 N Mills Avenue, Claremont CA 91711-6110

County: Los Angeles — FICE Identification: 001172
Unit ID: 121257
Telephone: (909) 621-8129 — Carnegie Class: Bac/A&S
FAX Number: (909) 621-8770 — Calendar System: Semester
URL: www.pitzer.edu
Established: 1963 — Annual Undergrad Tuition & Fees: $48,670
Enrollment: 1,076 — Coed
Affiliation or Control: Independent Non-Profit — IRS Status: 501(c)3
Highest Offering: Baccalaureate
Program: Liberal Arts And General
Accreditation: WC

01 Interim President .... Dr. Thomas POON
03 Executive Vice President .... Dr. Jennifer BERKLEY
05 Vice Pres Acad Affs/Dean of Faculty .... Dr. Muriel POSTON
10 Treasurer/Vice Pres Administration .... Mr. Yuet LEE
30 Vice Pres College Advancement .... Dr. Adrian STEVENS
07 Interim VP Admissions/Financial Aid .... Ms. Jamila EVERETT
32 Vice Pres Student Affairs .... Mr. Brian CARLISLE
26 VP Marketing/Public Relations .... Mr. Mark BAILEY
44 Associate Vice Pres of Development .... Ms. Holly PREBLE
20 Associate Dean of Faculty .... Ms. Kathleen PURVIS-ROBERTS
88 Assistant Dean of Faculty .... Mrs. Barbara JUNISBAI
06 Registrar .... Ms. Eva PETERS
37 Director Financial Aid .... Ms. Robin THOMPSON
09 Director of Institutional Research .... Mr. Jason RIVERA
15 Director Human Resources .... Ms. Marni BOBICH
18 Director Facilities .... Mr. Larry BURIK
21 Associate Treasurer .... Ms. Lori YOSHINO
36 Director Career Services .... Mr. Brad THARPE
29 Director Alumni Relations .... Ms. Nancy TRESER-OSGOOD
38 Director Student Counseling .... Dr. Rebecca KORNBLUH
04 Administrative Asst to President .... Ms. Melanie LACY

Platt College (G)

1000 S Fremont Avenue, Building A10,
Alhambra CA 91803-8845

County: Los Angeles — FICE Identification: 030627
Unit ID: 260789
Telephone: (626) 300-5444 — Carnegie Class: Bac/Assoc
FAX Number: (626) 457-8295 — Calendar System: Other
URL: www.plattcollege.edu
Established: 1987 — Annual Undergrad Tuition & Fees: $19,950
Enrollment: 661 — Coed
Affiliation or Control: Proprietary — IRS Status: Proprietary
Highest Offering: Baccalaureate
Program: Occupational
Accreditation: ACCSC, #COARC, DMS

01 President .... Mr. Arnulfo RUNAS

Platt College (H)

3700 Inland Empire Blvd, Ste 400, Ontario CA 91764-4906

Telephone: (909) 941-9410 — Identification: 666056
Accreditation: ACCSC, #COARC

† Branch campus of Platt College, Ahambra, CA.

Platt College (I)

6465 Sycamore Canyon Boulevard, Riverside CA 95207

Telephone: (626) 300-5444 — Identification: 770561
Accreditation: ACCSC

† Branch campus of Platt College, Alhambra, CA.

Platt College (J)

6250 El Cajon Boulevard, San Diego CA 92115-3919

County: San Diego — FICE Identification: 023043
Unit ID: 121275
Telephone: (619) 265-0107 — Carnegie Class: Spec/Arts
FAX Number: (619) 265-8655 — Calendar System: Semester
URL: www.platt.edu
Established: 1980 — Annual Undergrad Tuition & Fees: $24,607
Enrollment: 300 — Coed
Affiliation or Control: Proprietary — IRS Status: Proprietary
Highest Offering: Baccalaureate
Program: Occupational; Professional; Technical Emphasis
Accreditation: ACCSC

00 Chairman .... Mr. Robert D. LEIKER
01 President .... Mrs. Meg LEIKER
03 Vice President .... Mr. Alfred MEDRO

Point Loma Nazarene University (K)

3900 Lomaland Drive, San Diego CA 92106-2899

County: San Diego — FICE Identification: 001262
Unit ID: 121309
Telephone: (619) 849-2200 — Carnegie Class: Master's L
FAX Number: (619) 849-2579 — Calendar System: Semester
URL: www.pointloma.edu
Established: 1902 — Annual Undergrad Tuition & Fees: $32,400
Enrollment: 3,374 — Coed
Affiliation or Control: Church Of The Nazarene — IRS Status: 501(c)3
Highest Offering: Beyond Master's But Less Than Doctorate
Program: Liberal Arts And General; Teacher Preparatory; Professional
Accreditation: WC, ACBSP, CAATE, DIETD, EMT, MUS, NURSE, SW, TED

01 President .... Dr. Bob BROWER
05 Provost/Chief Academic Officer .... Dr. Kerry FULCHER
10 VP Finance/Administrative Svcs .... Mr. George LATTER
26 Vice President External Relations .... Dr. Joe WATKINS
32 Vice Pres for Student Development .... Dr. Caye SMITH
88 Vice Pres Spiritual Development .... Dr. Mary PAUL
15 Assoc VP for Human Resources .... Mr. Jeffrey HERMAN
37 Assoc Vice President for Finance .... Mrs. Cindy CHAPPELL
35 Assc VP Stdnt Dev/Chf Diversity Ofc .... Dr. Jeffrey CARR
30 Assoc VP University Advancement .... Vacant
21 Assoc VP for Budget/Accounting .... Ms. Sonia CHIN
84 Assoc VP Enrollment .... Dr. Scott SHOEMAKER
20 Vice Prov Academic Administration .... Dr. Mark PITTS
88 Vice Prov Program Dev and Accred .... Dr. Maggie BAILEY
35 Dean of Students .... Dr. Jeff BOLSTER
13 Chief Information Officer .... Mr. Corey FLING
09 Dir Inst Effectiveness & Assessment .... Mr. Brent GOODMAN
12 Director of Wesleyan Center .... Dr. Mark MANN
18 Director of Campus Facilities .... Mr. Bruce KUNKEL
36 Executive Dir Strengths & Vocation .... Vacant
88 Dir Corp Comm Education .... Ms. Jeanne COCHRAN
86 Dir Public Affairs .... Ms. Jill MONROE
88 Director Center Pastoral Leadship .... Dr. John CALHOUN
42 Ld Con for Mission Res & Pst Rel .... Dr. Ron BENEFIEL
88 Director of Outreach Ministries .... Ms. Dana HOJSACK
88 Director of Worship Ministries .... Mr. George WILLIAMSON
49 Dean College of Arts & Sciences .... Dr. Kathy MCCONNELL
83 Dean College of Social Sciences .... Dr. Holly IRWIN
07 Grad & Prof Adms Marketing Spec .... Ms. Laura LEINWEBER
07 Director Undergraduate Admissions .... Ms. Shannon HUTCHISON
08 Director of Ryan Library .... Dr. Frank QUINN
56 Dean Extended Learning .... Dr. Dave PHILLIPS
06 Dir Records/Institutional Research .... Ms. Cheryl GAUGHAN
26 Director Marketing/Creative Svcs .... Ms. Michele CORBETT
88 Assoc Dean Stdnt Success/Wellness .... Dr. Kim BOGAN
19 Director of Public Safety .... Mr. Mark GALBRAITH
29 Director of Alumni Relations .... Ms. Sheryl SMEE
40 Bookstore Manager .... Ms. Jillian RICHMOND
28 Dir Multicultural/Intl Stdnt Svcs .... Mr. Sam KWAPONG
41 Athletic Director .... Mr. Ethan HAMILTON
88 Director of Nicholson Commons .... Mr. Milton KARAHADIAN
94 Dir Stevenson Ctr for Women's Stds .... Dr. Linda BEAIL
104 Director Study Abroad .... Ms. Sandy SOOHOO-REFAEI
88 Dir of Programs & Operations .... Mr. Nick WOLF

04 Exec Asst to President .... Ms. Myra FISHER
103 Dir Workforce/Career Development .... Vacant
105 Director Web Services .... Mr. Dave BRUNO
106 Dir Online Education/E-learning .... Dr. Dave PHILLIPS
39 Asst Dir Student Housing .... Ms. Molly PETERSEN
44 Director Annual or Planned Giving .... Vacant
50 Dean of Business .... Mr. Dan BOTHE
53 Dean of Education .... Ms. Deb ERICKSON
101 Secretary of the Institution/Board .... Dr. Joe WATKINS

Pomona College (A)

550 N College Avenue, #206, Claremont CA 91711-6301
County: Los Angeles FICE Identification: 001173
Unit ID: 121345
Telephone: (909) 621-8000 Carnegie Class: Bac/A&S
FAX Number: (909) 621-8403 Calendar System: Semester
URL: www.pomona.edu
Established: 1887 Annual Undergrad Tuition & Fees: $47,620
Enrollment: 1,635 Coed
Affiliation or Control: Independent Non-Profit IRS Status: 501(c)3
Highest Offering: Baccalaureate
Program: Liberal Arts And General
Accreditation: WC

01 President .... Dr. David W. OXTOBY
05 Vice President/Dean of College .... Dr. Betsy CRIGHTON
45 Vice President Planning .... Dr. Richard A. FASS
10 Vice President/Treasurer .... Dr. Karen SISSON
30 VP for Institutional Advancement .... Ms. Pamela BESNARD
32 Vice President/Dean of Students .... Mrs. Miriam FELDBLUM
07 VP of Admissions & Financial Aid .... Mr. Seth ALLEN
26 VP & Chief Communications Ofcr .... Ms. Marylou FERRY
04 Special Assistant to President .... Dr. Teresa SHAW
06 Registrar .... Ms. Margaret ADORNO
27 Director Public Relations .... Mr. Mark WOOD
29 Assistant VP Alumni & Parent Engage .... Mr. Craig ARTEAGA-JOHNSON
37 Director Financial Aid .... Ms. Mary BOOKER
36 Director Career Development .... Ms. Mary RAYMOND
15 Director Human Resources .... Ms. Brenda RUSHFORTH
41 Director Physical Education .... Ms. Lesley IRVINE
44 Director Annual Giving .... Mr. Michael SPICER
21 Assoc Treasurer/Controller .... Ms. Mary Lou WOODS
09 Director of Institutional Research .... Dr. Jennifer RACHFORD
18 Chief Facilities/Physical Plant .... Mr. Robert ROBINSON

Presbyterian Theological Seminary in America (B)

15605 Carmenita Rd., Santa Fe Springs CA 90670
County: Los Angeles FICE Identification: 041228
Telephone: (562) 926-1023 Carnegie Class: Not Classified
FAX Number: (562) 926-1025 Calendar System: Semester
URL: www.ptsa.edu
Established: 1977 Annual Undergrad Tuition & Fees: $6,080
Enrollment: 166 Coed
Affiliation or Control: Presbyterian Church In America IRS Status: 501(c)3
Highest Offering: First Professional Degree
Program: Professional; Religious Emphasis
Accreditation: BI

01 President .... Dr. Sang Meyng LEE
05 Academic Dean .... Rev. Kyungmo KOO
11 Dean of Administration .... Vacant
32 Dean of Students/Student Ministry .... Rev. Choong Gi PARK
85 Dean/Dir of Intl Students/Fin Aid .... Mr. Mankyung SUNG
08 Head Librarian .... Mrs. Young Sook CHOI
10 Managing Treasurer .... Mrs. Mi PARK
06 Registrar .... Mrs. Michelle YOON
106 Dir Online Education/E-learning .... Mr. Woo Joong KANG
13 IT Director .... Mr. Eliot LEE

Presidio Graduate School (C)

36 Lincoln Boulevard, Suite 120, San Francisco CA 94129
County: San Francisco Identification: 667150
Telephone: (415) 561-6555 Carnegie Class: Not Classified
FAX Number: (415) 561-6483 Calendar System: Semester
URL: www.presidioedu.org
Established: 2003 Annual Graduate Tuition & Fees: $31,200
Enrollment: N/A Coed
Affiliation or Control: Independent Non-Profit IRS Status: 501(c)3
Highest Offering: Master's; No Undergraduates
Program: Professional
Accreditation: WC

01 President .... William SHUTKIN
05 Associate Dean .... Ryan CABINTE
05 Associate Dean .... Dwight COLLINS
10 Chief Financial Officer .... Santhi PERUMAL
32 Assoc Dir Student/Alumni Affairs .... Dawn MOKUAU
07 Director of Admissions .... Kari DORTH

Professional Golfers Career College (D)

26109 Ynez Road, Temecula CA 92591-6013
County: Riverside FICE Identification: 033673
Unit ID: 437750
Telephone: (951) 719-2994 Carnegie Class: Assoc/PrivFP
FAX Number: (951) 719-1643 Calendar System: Semester
URL: www.golfcollege.edu
Established: 1990 Annual Undergrad Tuition & Fees: $15,400
Enrollment: 248 Coed
Affiliation or Control: Proprietary IRS Status: Proprietary
Highest Offering: Associate Degree
Program: Occupational; 2-Year Principally Bachelor's Creditable; Business Emphasis
Accreditation: ACICS

01 President .... Dr. Tim SOMERVILLE

Providence Christian College (E)

1539 E. Howard Street, Pasadena CA 91104
County: Los Angeles FICE Identification: 041539
Unit ID: 455770
Telephone: (866) 323-0233 Carnegie Class: Bac/A&S
FAX Number: (626) 696-4040 Calendar System: Semester
URL: www.providencecc.edu
Established: 2002 Annual Undergrad Tuition & Fees: $27,224
Enrollment: 102 Coed
Affiliation or Control: Non-denominational IRS Status: 501(c)3
Highest Offering: Baccalaureate
Program: Liberal Arts And General
Accreditation: WC

01 President .... Dr. Jim BELCHER
05 VP Academic & Student Affairs .... John MILTON
10 VP Finance & Operations .... Dawn DIRKSEN
30 VP Advancement .... Michael KILEDJIAN
06 Registrar .... Patty TSAI
84 Director of Enrollment Management .... Larissa KAMPS
32 Director of Student Life .... Mark RIPPETOE
04 Administrative Asst to President .... Ruby BLEEKER

*Rancho Santiago Community College District (F)

2323 N. Broadway, Santa Ana CA 92706-1640
County: Orange FICE Identification: 006991
Unit ID: 438665
Telephone: (714) 480-7300 Carnegie Class: N/A
FAX Number: (714) 796-3915
URL: www.rsccd.edu

01 Chancellor .... Dr. Raul RODRIGUEZ
15 Exec Vice Chanc HR & Educ Services .... Mr. John DIDION
10 Vice Chanc Business & Fiscal Svcs .... Mr. Peter HARDASH
05 Asst Vice Chanc Educational Svcs .... Mr. Enrique PEREZ
19 Director Security/Safety .... Mr. Alistair WINTER
04 Exec Asst to the Chancellor .... Ms. Debra GERARD

*Santa Ana College (G)

1530 W 17th Street, Santa Ana CA 92706-3398
County: Orange FICE Identification: 001284
Unit ID: 121619
Telephone: (714) 564-6000 Carnegie Class: Assoc/Pub-S-MC
FAX Number: (714) 564-6379 Calendar System: Semester
URL: www.sac.edu
Established: 1915 Annual Undergrad Tuition & Fees (In-District): $1,434
Enrollment: 27,660 Coed
Affiliation or Control: State/Local IRS Status: 501(c)3
Highest Offering: Associate Degree
Program: Occupational; 2-Year Principally Bachelor's Creditable
Accreditation: WJ, ADNUR, OTA

02 President .... Dr. Erlinda J. MARTINEZ
05 Vice President Academic Affairs .... Vacant
32 Vice President Student Services .... Dr. Sara LUNDQUIST
10 Vice Chanc Bus Ops/Fiscal Svcs .... Mr. Peter HARDASH
51 Vice President Continuing Educ .... James KENNEDY
35 Dean Student Affairs .... Dr. Lilia TANAKEYOWMA
11 Vice Pres Administrative Svcs .... Dr. Michael COLLINS
07 Dean Enrollment Services .... Mark LIANG
06 Registrar .... Chris TRUONG
50 Interim Dean Business Division .... Madeline GRANT
35 Assoc Dean Student Development .... Vacant
38 Dean Counseling .... Dr. Micki BRYANT
37 Director of Financial Aid .... Robert MANSON
41 Dean KinesiologyAthletics .... Avie BRIDGES
57 Dean Fine & Performing Arts .... Eve KIKAWA
30 Exec Director College Advancement .... Christina ROMERO
18 Facilities Manager .... Mark WHEELER
79 Dean Humanities & Social Siences .... Shelly JAFFRAY
81 Dean Science/Math/Hlth Sci .... Cheryl CARRERA
103 Dean Career Educ/Workforce Develop .... Bart HOFFMAN
56 Associate Dean EOPS .... Christine LEON
88 Associate Dean DSPS .... Sherry DEROSA
04 Assistant to the President .... Kennethia J. VEGA
26 Dir of Public Affs/Communications .... Judy IANNACCONE

*Santiago Canyon College (H)

8045 E Chapman Avenue, Orange CA 92869-4512
County: Orange FICE Identification: 036957
Unit ID: 399212
Telephone: (714) 628-4900 Carnegie Class: Assoc/Pub-S-MC
FAX Number: (714) 628-4723 Calendar System: Semester
URL: www.sccollege.edu
Established: 1997 Annual Undergrad Tuition & Fees (In-District): $1,229
Enrollment: 10,996 Coed
Affiliation or Control: State/Local IRS Status: 501(c)3
Highest Offering: Associate Degree
Program: Occupational; 2-Year Principally Bachelor's Creditable
Accreditation: WJ

02 President .... Dr. John WEISPFENNING
04 Assistant to the President .... Ms. Lynn MANZANO
32 Vice President Student Services .... Dr. John HERNANDEZ
05 Vice President Academic Affairs .... Dr. Aracely MORA
51 Vice President Continuing Educ .... Mr. Jose VARGAS
11 Vice Pres Administrative Services .... Ms. Arleen SATELE
38 Dean Counseling .... Ms. Ruth BABESHOFF
41 Dean Math and Sciences .... Mr. Martin STRINGER
79 Dean Arts/Humanities/Social Science .... Ms. Marilyn FLORES
36 Dean Business/Career Tech Educ .... Mr. Von LAWSON
108 Dean Institutional Effectiveness .... Mr. Aaron VOELCKER
20 Dean Instruction/Student Services .... Ms. Lori FASBINDER
37 Dean Enrollment and Support Svcs .... Mr. Syed RIZVI
20 Int Dean Instruction/Student Svcs .... Ms. Mary WALKER
35 Assoc Dean Student Development .... Ms. Loretta JORDAN
07 Asst Dean of Admissions & Records .... Mr. Tuyen NGUYEN
37 Int Asst Dean Fin Aid/Scholarships .... Ms. Denise DONN
18 Physical Plant Manager .... Vacant

Rio Hondo College (I)

3600 Workman Mill Road, Whittier CA 90601-1699
County: Los Angeles FICE Identification: 001269
Unit ID: 121886
Telephone: (562) 692-0921 Carnegie Class: Assoc/Pub-S-SC
FAX Number: (562) 699-7386 Calendar System: Semester
URL: www.riohondo.edu
Established: 1960 Annual Undergrad Tuition & Fees (In-District): $1,356
Enrollment: 16,263 Coed
Affiliation or Control: State/Local IRS Status: 501(c)3
Highest Offering: Associate Degree
Program: Occupational; 2-Year Principally Bachelor's Creditable
Accreditation: WJ

01 Superintendent/President .... Ms. Teresa DREYFUSS
05 Vice President Academic Svcs .... Dr. Kenn PIERSON
10 Vice President Finance/Business .... Ms. Myeshia ARMSTRONG
32 Vice President Student Services .... Mr. Henry GEE
86 Dir Govt & Community Relations .... Mr. Russell CASTANEDA-CALLEROS
15 Director Human Resources .... Ms. Yolanda EMERSON
26 Dir Marketing & Communications .... Ms. Ruthie RETANA
35 Dir Student Life & Leadership .... Ms. Shaina PHILLIPS
06 Dir Admin & Records/Registrar .... Ms. Leigh UNGER
38 Dean Counseling & Student Succes .... Dr. Mike MUNOZ
102 Int Exec Director RHC Foundation .... Mr. Howard KUMMERMAN
37 Director Financial Aid & Veteran's .... Ms. Yvonne GUTIERREZ-SANDOVAL
18 Director Facilities Services .... Mr. James POPER
96 Director of Purchasing .... Mr. Timothy CONNELL
04 Admin Assistant to President .... Ms. Sandy SANDELLO
09 Director of Institutional Research .... Mr. Howard KUMMERMAN

*Riverside Community College District (J)

450 E Alessandro Blvd, Riverside CA 92508
County: Riverside Identification: 667039
Telephone: (951) 222-8000 Carnegie Class: N/A
FAX Number: (951) 222-8036
URL: www.rccd.edu

01 Chancellor .... Dr. Michael L. BURKE
05 Int VC Educ Svcs/Wrkforce Dev/Plng .... Dr. Michael REINER
10 VC Business & Financial Svcs .... Mr. Aaron BROWN
15 Int VC Div & Human Resources .... Ms. Sylvia THOMAS
100 Chief of Staff & Facilities Devel .... Ms. Chris CARLSON
12 President Moreno Valley College .... Dr. Sandra MAYO
12 President Norco College .... Dr. Paul PARNELL
12 President Riverside City Col .... Dr. Wolde-Ab ISAAC
84 Dean for Enrollment Services .... Ms. Dawn VALENCIA

*Moreno Valley College (K)

16130 Lasselle Street, Moreno Valley CA 92551
County: Riverside FICE Identification: 041735
Unit ID: 460394
Telephone: (951) 571-6100 Carnegie Class: Not Classified
FAX Number: N/A Calendar System: Semester
URL: www.mvc.edu
Established: 2010 Annual Undergrad Tuition & Fees (In-District): $1,418
Enrollment: 8,731 Coed
Affiliation or Control: State/Local IRS Status: 501(c)3
Highest Offering: Associate Degree
Program: Occupational; 2-Year Principally Bachelor's Creditable; Technical Emphasis
Accreditation: WJ, DA, DH, EMT

02 President .... Dr. Sandra MAYO
05 Vice Pres Academic Affairs .... Dr. Robin STEINBECK
10 Vice Pres Business Services .... Mr. Norm GODIN
32 Vice Pres of Student Services .... Mr. Dyrell FOSTER
20 Dean of Instruction .... Mr. David VAKIL
06 Director Enrollment Services .... Ms. Jamie CLIFTON
37 Director Student Financial Services .... Ms. Linda PRATT

*Norco College (A)

2001 Third Street, Norco CA 92860
County: Riverside FICE Identification: 041761
Unit ID: 460464
Telephone: (951) 372-7000 Carnegie Class: Not Classified
FAX Number: N/A Calendar System: Semester
URL: www.norcocollege.edu
Established: 2010 Annual Undergrad Tuition & Fees (In-District): $1,571
Enrollment: 9,947 Coed
Affiliation or Control: State/Local IRS Status: 501(c)3
Highest Offering: Associate Degree
Program: 2-Year Principally Bachelor's Creditable
Accreditation: WJ

02 President .... Dr. Paul PARNELL
05 Vice President Academic Affairs .... Dr. Diane DIECKMEYER
32 Vice President Student Services .... Dr. Monica GREEN
04 Executive Asst to President .... Ms. Debra CRESWELL
07 Dean Admissions & Records .... Mr. Mark DEASIS
09 Dean Institutional Effectiveness .... Dr. Greg AYCOCK
11 Vice President Business Services .... Ms. Beth GOMEZ
13 Dean Technology/Learning Resources .... Mr. Damon NANCE
18 Director Facilities .... Mr. Steve MONSANTO
25 Assistant Dean Grants .... Dr. Gustavo OCEGUERA
37 Director Student Financial Services .... Ms. Maria GONZALEZ
20 Dean Instruction .... Dr. Sheryl TSCHETTER
75 Dean Instruction/CTE .... Dr. Kevin FLEMING
35 Dean Student Services .... Dr. Koji UESUGI

*Riverside City College (B)

4800 Magnolia Avenue, Riverside CA 92506
County: Riverside FICE Identification: 001270
Unit ID: 121901
Telephone: (951) 222-8000 Carnegie Class: Assoc/Pub-U-MC
FAX Number: (951) 222-8036 Calendar System: Semester
URL: www.rcc.edu
Established: 1916 Annual Undergrad Tuition & Fees (In-District): $35,000
Enrollment: 18,259 Coed
Affiliation or Control: State/Local IRS Status: 501(c)3
Highest Offering: Associate Degree
Program: Occupational; 2-Year Principally Bachelor's Creditable
Accreditation: WJ, ADNUR, #ARCPA

02 President .... Dr. Wolde-Ab ISAAC
10 Vice Pres Business Services .... Ms. Mazie L. BREWINGTON
103 VP Workforce & Resource Development .... Vacant
05 Acting Vice Pres Academic Affairs .... Ms. Virginia MCKEE-LEONE
32 Int Vice President Student Services .... Ms. Cecilia ALVARADO
20 Dean of Instruction .... Vacant
66 Dean School of Nursing .... Dr. Sandy BAKER
08 Dean Instruction Library/Lrng Res ..... Dr. Fabienne CHAUDERLOT
57 Dean of Instr Fine & Perform Arts .... Dr. Scott BAUER
75 Dean Instruction Career/Tech Educ .... Ms. Patricia AVILA
88 Assoc Dean Academic Support .... Ms. Debbie WHITAKER
07 Dean Enrollment Services .... Ms. Dawn VALENCIA
35 Dean Student Services .... Vacant
06 Dean Records & Admissions .... Vacant
41 Interim Director Athletics .... Mr. James WOOLDRIDGE
23 Director Health Services .... Ms. Deborah CLOAN
19 Sergeant Safety & Police .... Mr. Robert KLEVENO

Rudolf Steiner College (C)

9200 Fair Oaks Boulevard, Fair Oaks CA 95628
County: Sacramento Identification: 667088
Telephone: (916) 961-8727 Carnegie Class: Not Classified
FAX Number: (877) 782-1884 Calendar System: Other
URL: www.rudolfsteinercollege.edu
Established: 1976 Annual Graduate Tuition & Fees: N/A
Enrollment: N/A Coed
Affiliation or Control: Independent Non-Profit IRS Status: 501(c)3
Highest Offering: Master's; No Undergraduates
Program: Teacher Preparatory
Accreditation: @WC

01 President .... Ms. Elizabeth BEAVEN

Sage College (D)

12125 Day Street, Building L,
Moreno Valley CA 92557-6720
County: Riverside FICE Identification: 030695
Unit ID: 410520
Telephone: (951) 781-2727 Carnegie Class: Assoc/PrivFP
FAX Number: (951) 781-0570 Calendar System: Semester
URL: www.sagecollege.edu
Established: 1973 Annual Undergrad Tuition & Fees: $12,550
Enrollment: 407 Coed
Affiliation or Control: Proprietary IRS Status: Proprietary
Highest Offering: Associate Degree
Program: Occupational; 2-Year Principally Bachelor's Creditable
Accreditation: ACICS

01 Executive Director .... Ms. Lauren SOMMA
03 Assistant Director .... Ms. Sharon GOUPIL

Sage College (E)

2820 Camino Del Rio South Ste 100,
San Diego CA 92108-3821
Telephone: (619) 683-2727 Identification: 666304
Accreditation: ACICS

† Branch campus of Sage College, Moreno Valley, CA.

Saint John's Seminary (F)

5012 Seminary Road, Camarillo CA 93012-2500
County: Ventura FICE Identification: 001299
Unit ID: 123855
Telephone: (805) 482-2755 Carnegie Class: Spec/Faith
FAX Number: (805) 482-3470 Calendar System: Semester
URL: www.stjohnsem.edu
Established: 1939 Annual Graduate Tuition & Fees: $35,000
Enrollment: 112 Male
Affiliation or Control: Roman Catholic IRS Status: 501(c)3
Highest Offering: Master's; No Undergraduates
Program: Professional; Religious Emphasis
Accreditation: WC, THEOL

01 Rector .... Msgr. Marc V. TRUDEAU
05 Academic Dean .... Dr. Anthony LILLES
07 Director of Admissions .... Dr. Anthony LILLES
06 Registrar .... Mr. Kevin GODFREY
04 Administrative Asst to President .... Ms. Maria GAETA
10 Director of Finance .... Ms. Jackie ROTTER
15 Director Personnel Services .... Ms. Mary BISSINGER
18 Chief Facilities/Physical Plant .... Mr. Greg JULIUS
30 Chief Development/Advancement .... Ms. Kim CABRAL
32 Chief Student Affairs/Student Life .... Fr. Gregory SEMENIUK
96 Director of Purchasing .... Ms. Julie ALLYN

Saint Mary's College of California (G)

1928 Saint Mary's Road, Moraga CA 94556-2744
County: Contra Costa FICE Identification: 001302
Unit ID: 123554
Telephone: (925) 631-4000 Carnegie Class: Master's L
FAX Number: (925) 376-8497 Calendar System: 4/1/4
URL: www.stmarys-ca.edu
Established: 1863 Annual Undergrad Tuition & Fees: $42,780
Enrollment: 3,909 Coed
Affiliation or Control: Roman Catholic IRS Status: 501(c)3
Highest Offering: Doctorate
Program: Liberal Arts And General; Teacher Preparatory; Professional
Accreditation: WC, BUS, MACTE

01 President .... Dr. James A. DONAHUE
05 Provost/Vice President Acad Affairs .... Dr. Bethami DOBKIN
32 Vice Provost Student Affairs .... Dr. Jane CAMARILLO
20 Vice Provost Undergrad Academics .... Dr. Richard M. CARP
10 Vice President for Finance/CFO .... Mr. Peter MICHELL
30 Vice President for Advancement .... Ms. Lisa MOORE
26 Asst VP College Communication .... Ms. Elizabeth SMITH
88 Vice President for Mission .... Dr. Carole SWAIN
84 Vice Provost Enrollment Services .... Mr. Hernan BUCHELI
107 Vice Prov Graduate/Professnl Stds .... Dr. Christopher SINDT
43 General Counsel .... Mr. Larry NUTI
53 Dean School of Education .... Dr. Christopher SINDT
50 Dean School Econ & Business Admin .... Dr. Zhan LI
81 Dean School of Science .... Dr. Roy WENSLEY
49 Dean School Liberal Arts .... Dr. Sheila HUGHES
35 Dean of Students .... Dr. Evette CASTILLO CLARK
08 Dean Academic Resources .... Ms. Patricia KREITZ
42 Director Mission & Ministry .... Ms. Karin MCCLELLAND
07 Dean of Admissions .... Mr. Michael MCKEON
15 Director Human Resources .... Mr. Eduardo SALAZ
58 Interim Assoc Dean Graduate Pgms .... Dr. Yung Jae LEE
06 Registrar .... Ms. Julia ODOM
20 Assistant Dean of Students .... Mr. Jim SCIUTO
37 Director of Financial Aid .... Ms. Priscilla MUHA
88 Director of Kinesiology .... Dr. Stephen MILLER
57 Director MFA in Creative Writing .... Ms. Brenda HILLMAN
29 Sr Director Alumni Engagement .... Ms. Courtney LOHMANN
14 Deputy CTO .... Mr. Lance HOURANY
13 Chief Technology Officer .... Mr. Peter GRECO
19 Director of Public Safety .... Mr. Adan TEJADA
38 Director of Counseling Center .... Ms. Dai L. TO
41 Dir of Athletic & Recreation Sports .... Mr. Mark C. ORR
88 Director Saint Mary's Art Museum .... Ms. Carrie BREWSTER
71 Director of January Term Program .... Dr. Sue FALLIS
18 Exec Director of Physical Plant .... Mr. Joseph KEHOE
102 Director of Foundation & Corp Rels .... Ms. Elizabeth GALLAGHER
30 Director of Development .... Mr. Daniel G. LEWIS
36 Interim Dir of Career Devel Center .... Ms. Jennifer BILLECI
23 Medical Director Health & Wellness .... Dr. Ali REZAPOUR
27 Media Relations Officer .... Mr. Michael MCALPIN
86 Director Community & Govt Relations .... Mr. Tim FARLEY
94 Director Women's Resource Ctr .... Ms. Sharon SOBOTTA
88 Director of CILSA .... Dr. Jennifer PIGZA
88 Associate Director of CILSA .... Vacant
21 Director of Finance/Controller .... Ms. Jeanne DEMATTEO
88 Director Ctr International Programs . Ms. M. Susan MILLER-REID
88 Director of Food Services .... Mr. Matt CARROLL
88 Director Conference Services .... Dr. Jessica PARK
92 Dir Student Engagement & Academic ...... Ms. Tracy PASCUA DEA
28 Dir of Delphine Intercultural Ctr .... Vacant
09 Director of Institutional Research .... Mr. Gregg THOMSON

88 Dir New Student/Family Programs .... Ms. Jennifer HERZOG
96 Purchasing/Buyer .... Ms. Janie KLEIN

Saint Patrick's Seminary & University (H)

320 Middlefield Road, Menlo Park CA 94025-3596
County: San Mateo FICE Identification: 010074
Unit ID: 122250
Telephone: (650) 325-5621 Carnegie Class: Not Classified
FAX Number: (650) 322-0997 Calendar System: Semester
URL: www.stpatricksseminary.org
Established: 1894 Annual Undergrad Tuition & Fees: $15,382
Enrollment: 92 Male
Affiliation or Control: Roman Catholic IRS Status: 501(c)3
Highest Offering: Master's
Program: Professional; Religious Emphasis
Accreditation: WC, THEOL

01 President/Rector .... Rev. Gladstone H. STEVENS
03 Exec Vice President/Academic Dean ...... Rev. Anthony POGORELC
05 Provost .... Dr. Melanie MOREY
11 VP Administration/Interim Dean Men .... Rev. Daniel DONOHOO
26 Vice President for External Affairs .... Rev. James MYERS
42 Dean of Spiritual Life .... Rev. Vincent BUI
08 Library Manager .... Mr. David KRIEGH
06 Registrar .... Ms. Nuria ORTIZ

The Salvation Army College for Officer Training at Crestmont (I)

30840 Hawthorne Boulevard,
Rancho Palos Verdes CA 90275-5301
County: Los Angeles FICE Identification: 036954
Unit ID: 122269
Telephone: (310) 377-0481 Carnegie Class: Not Classified
FAX Number: (310) 541-1697 Calendar System: Quarter
URL: www.crestmont.edu
Established: 1878 Annual Undergrad Tuition & Fees: $4,750
Enrollment: 92 Coed
Affiliation or Control: Other IRS Status: 501(c)3
Highest Offering: Associate Degree
Program: 2-Year Principally Bachelor's Creditable; Religious Emphasis
Accreditation: WJ

01 Training Principal .... Major Brian SAUNDERS
03 Assistant Training Principal .... Major Robert BIRKS
05 Director of Curriculum .... Major Brian JONES
10 Director of Business Administration .... Capt. Kelly NOLAN
32 Director of Campus Services .... Major Stacy BIRKS
04 Exec Secretary to Trng Principal .... Ms. Celeste SKINNER

Samuel Merritt University (J)

3100 Telegraph Avenue, Oakland CA 94609
County: Alameda FICE Identification: 007012
Unit ID: 122296
Telephone: (510) 869-6511 Carnegie Class: Spec/Health
FAX Number: (510) 869-6525 Calendar System: Semester
URL: www.samuelmerritt.edu
Established: 1909 Annual Undergrad Tuition & Fees: $41,330
Enrollment: 1,580 Coed
Affiliation or Control: Independent Non-Profit IRS Status: 501(c)3
Highest Offering: Doctorate
Program: Professional
Accreditation: WC, ANEST, ARCPA, NURSE, OT, POD, PTA

01 President .... Dr. Sharon C. DIAZ
05 Academic Vice President/Provost .... Dr. Scot FOSTER
10 Vice Pres Finance/Admin/CFO .... Mr. Gregory GINGRAS
84 Vice President Enrollment Services .... Vacant
20 Assistant Academic Vice President .... Dr. Penny BAMFORD
20 Asst Academic Vice President .... Dr. Terry NORDSTROM
32 Asst Vice President Student Affairs .... Mr. Craig ELLIOTT
21 Asst VP Finance & Admin/Controller .... Vacant
04 Assistant to the President .... Ms. Margrette PETERSON
66 Dean & Professor of Nursing .... Dr. Audrey BERMAN
63 Dean Podiatric Medicine .... Dr. John VENSON
88 Chair Dept Physical Therapy .... Dr. Nicole CHRISTENSEN
88 Chair Dept Occupational Therapy .... Dr. Kate HAYNER
66 Chair ABSN .... Dr. Nancy HAUGEN
66 Chairperson Undergraduate Nursing .... Dr. Margaret EARLY
07 Dean Admission .... Mr. Timothy CRANFORD
15 Exec Director Human Resources .... Ms. Elaine LEMAY
45 Exec Dir Planning/Business Dev .... Ms. Cynthia ULMAN
26 Exec Dir Communications/Ext Rels .... Ms. Stephanie BANGERT
30 Exec Dir of Development/Alumni Affs .... Ms. Susan VALENCIA
09 Director Institutional Research .... Ms. Nandini DASGUPTA
06 Registrar .... Ms. Anne SCHER
08 Library Director .... Mr. Marcus BANKS
37 Director Financial Aid .... Ms. Tanya GRIGGS
88 Dir Family Nurse Practitioner Pgm .... Ms. Suzanne AUGUST-SCHWARTZ
29 Director of Alumni Relations .... Ms. Carla ROSS
18 Director Facilities Management .... Ms. Lillian HARVIN
88 Director Physician Assistant Pgm .... Dr. Michael DEROSA
12 Site Manager Sacramento .... Ms. Rene ENGELHART
12 Site Manager San Mateo .... Dr. Mileva LEWIS SAULO
13 Dir of Information Technology Svcs .... Mr. Blair SIMMONS
28 Chief Diversity Officer .... Ms. Shirley STRONG

*San Bernardino Community College District (A)

114 S. Del Rosa Drive, San Bernardino CA 92401
County: San Bernardino Identification: 667040
Telephone: (909) 382-4091 Carnegie Class: N/A
FAX Number: (909) 382-0153
URL: www.sbccd.edu

01 Chancellor ... Bruce BARON
10 Int Vice Chancellor Fiscal Services ... Jose TORRES
15 Vice Chanc Human Resources ... Dr. Lisa NORMAN

*Crafton Hills College (B)

11711 Sand Canyon Road, Yucaipa CA 92399-1799
County: San Bernardino FICE Identification: 009272
Unit ID: 113111
Telephone: (909) 794-2161 Carnegie Class: Assoc/Pub-U-MC
FAX Number: (909) 794-0423 Calendar System: Semester
URL: www.craftonhills.edu
Established: 1972 Annual Undergrad Tuition & Fees (In-District): $1,338
Enrollment: 5,850 Coed
Affiliation or Control: State/Local IRS Status: 501(c)3
Highest Offering: Associate Degree
Program: Occupational; 2-Year Principally Bachelor's Creditable
Accreditation: WJ, COARC, EMT

02 President ... Dr. Cheryl A. MARSHALL
05 Vice President of Instruction ... Dr. Bryan REECE
11 Vice President Administrative Svcs ... Mr. Mike STRONG
32 Vice President Student Services ... Dr. Rebeccah WARREN-MARLATT
88 Dean Stdnt Svcs/Stdnt Development ... Mr. Joe CABRALES
49 Dean of Arts & Sciences ... Mr. Richard HOGREFE
81 Dean Math/English/Reading/Inst Supp ... Mr. Mark SNOWHITE
36 Dean Career Educ & Human Devel ... Ms. June Y. YAMAMOTO
38 Dean Student Services/Counseling ... Ms. Kirsten S. COLVEY
09 Dean Instl Effect/Research/Planning ... Dr. Keith WURTZ
30 Director Resource Development ... Ms. Michelle RIGGS
40 Director Bookstore ... Ms. Gloriann CHAVEZ
88 Director EOPS/CARE ... Dr. Rejoice CHAVIRA
37 Director Financial Aid ... Mr. John W. MUSKAVITCH
35 Director Student Life ... Dr. Ericka PADDOCK
18 Director Facilities ... Mr. Larry COOK
13 Director Technology Services ... Mr. Wayne BOGH
26 Director Marketing/Public Relations ... Ms. Donna HOFFMANN
08 Librarian ... Ms. Laura WINNINGHAM
06 Admissions and Records Coordinator ... Mr. Larry K. AYCOCK
04 Administrative Asst to President ... Mrs. Cyndie ST. JEAN

*San Bernardino Valley College (C)

701 S Mt. Vernon Avenue,
San Bernardino CA 92410-2798
County: San Bernardino FICE Identification: 001272
Unit ID: 123527
Telephone: (909) 384-4400 Carnegie Class: Assoc/Pub-U-MC
FAX Number: N/A Calendar System: Semester
URL: www.valleycollege.edu
Established: 1926 Annual Undergrad Tuition & Fees (In-District): $1,545
Enrollment: 12,643 Coed
Affiliation or Control: State/Local IRS Status: 501(c)3
Highest Offering: Associate Degree
Program: Occupational; 2-Year Principally Bachelor's Creditable
Accreditation: WJ, ADNUR

02 President ... Dr. Gloria M. FISHER
05 Vice President Instruction ... Dr. Haragewen KINDE
11 VP Administrative Services ... Mr. Scott STARK
32 VP Student Services ... Dr. Ricky SHABAZZ
72 Dean AT/TRANS/CULA ... Mr. Albert MANIAOL
79 Dean Arts & Humanities ... Dr. Kay WEISS
38 Dean Counseling/Matriculation ... Mr. Marco COTA
50 Dean Math/Bus/Computer Tech ... Mr. Henry HUA
09 Dean Research/Planning/Inst Effect ... Dr. James SMITH
81 Dean Sciences ... Dr. Susan BANGASSER
83 Dean SS/Human Development & PE ... Dr. Wallace JOHNSON
07 Director Admissions/Records ... Ms. April DALE-CARTER
40 Director Bookstores ... Ms. Gloriann CHAVEZ
88 Director Child Development Ctr ... Mr. Mark MERJIL
31 Dir Dev Community Relations ... Ms. Karen CHILDERS
88 Director EOP&S/CARE ... Ms. Carmen RODRIGUEZ
37 Director Financial Aid ... Ms. Amber GALLAGHER
25 Dir Grant Development/Management ... Dr. Kathleen ROWLEY
08 Dir Library/Learning Support Svcs ... Mr. Ron HASTINGS
26 Director Marketing/PR ... Mr. Paul BRATULIN
35 Int Director Student Life ... Ms. Joseph NGUYEN
13 Director Technology Services ... Mr. Rick HRDLICKA
88 Int Mgr Cafeteria & Snack Bar ... Ms. Valerie ALEX-SCHIEL
103 Mgr CalWORKS/Workforce Dev ... Ms. Shalita TILLMAN
88 Project Dir HSI STEM PASS GO ... Mr. Marc DONNHAUSER
66 Assoc Dean & Nursing Director ... Ms. Carol WELLS
68 Director Athletics ... Mr. Dave RUBIO
88 Interim Director Police Academies ... Mr. Jeff KLUG
18 Dir Facilities M&O ... Mr. Robert JENKINS
89 Int Dir First Year Experience ... Mr. Johnny CONLEY
88 Director DSP&S ... Mr. Marty MILLIGAN

San Diego Christian College (D)

200 Riverview Parkway, Santee CA 92071
County: San Diego FICE Identification: 012031
Unit ID: 112084
Telephone: (619) 201-8700 Carnegie Class: Bac/A&S
FAX Number: (619) 201-8749 Calendar System: Semester
URL: www.sdcc.edu
Established: 1970 Annual Undergrad Tuition & Fees: $28,550
Enrollment: 966 Coed
Affiliation or Control: Independent Non-Profit IRS Status: 501(c)3
Highest Offering: Master's
Program: Liberal Arts And General; Teacher Preparatory
Accreditation: WC

01 President ... Dr. Paul E. AGUE
04 Exec Assistant to the President ... Mrs. Kelly BUCHANAN
10 VP for Finance ... Mr. Steve CHANEY
05 VP for Academic Affairs ... Dr. Jon DEPRIEST
32 VP for Student Services ... Mr. David MADDOX
06 Registrar ... Mrs. Heather MILLER
37 Director of Financial Aid ... Mr. Daniel REED
07 Director of Admissions ... Ms. Christine ROBERTS
42 Director of Spiritual Life ... Mr. Steve JENKINS
30 VP for Advancement & Administration ... Mr. Robert JENSEN
15 VP for Human Resources ... Mr. Robert JENSEN
08 Director of Library Services ... Ms. Ruth MARTIN
29 Manager of Alumni/Donor Relations ... Ms. Stephanie EDWARDS
09 Dean of Assessment and Planning ... Mrs. Lundie CARSTENSEN
41 Athletic Director ... Mr. Kyle FERGUSON
23 Director of Health Services ... Mrs. Malia JENKINS
28 Director of Diversity ... Mr. Carl CALDERSON
18 Chief Facilities/Physical Plant ... Mr. Pete GOODMAN
36 Director Student Placement ... Ms. Sara AGUILAR

*San Diego Community College District Administrative Offices (E)

3375 Camino Del Rio South, San Diego CA 92108-3883
County: San Diego FICE Identification: 008895
Unit ID: 122339
Telephone: (619) 388-6500 Carnegie Class: N/A
FAX Number: (619) 388-6913
URL: www.sdccd.edu

01 Chancellor ... Dr. Constance M. CARROLL
10 Exec Vice Chanc Business Tech Svcs ... Dr. Bonnie Ann DOWD
32 Vice Chancellor Student Services ... Dr. Lynn C. NEAULT
15 Vice Chancellor Human Resources ... Mr. Will SURBROOK
18 Vice Chanc Facilities Management ... Mr. Christopher MANIS
05 Vice Chanc Instructional Svcs ... Dr. Stepahnie BULGER
26 Director Comm & Public Relations ... Mr. Jack BERESFORD
43 Director Legal Services & EEO ... Ms. Mary ROGERS
04 Exec Assistant to the Chancellor ... Ms. Margaret LAMB
13 Chief Info Technology Officer (CIO) ... Mr. Kent KEYSER
19 Chief of Police ... Mr. Raymund AGUIRRE

*San Diego City College (F)

1313 Park Boulevard, San Diego CA 92101-4787
County: San Diego FICE Identification: 001273
Unit ID: 122320
Telephone: (619) 388-3400 Carnegie Class: Not Classified
FAX Number: (619) 388-3063 Calendar System: Semester
URL: www.sdcity.edu
Established: 1914 Annual Undergrad Tuition & Fees (In-District): $2,868
Enrollment: 9,373 Coed
Affiliation or Control: State/Local IRS Status: 501(c)3
Highest Offering: Associate Degree
Program: Occupational; 2-Year Principally Bachelor's Creditable
Accreditation: WJ, ADNUR

02 President ... Dr. Anthony BEEBE
05 Vice President Instruction ... Vacant
32 Vice President Student Services ... Mrs. Denise WHISENHUNT
11 Vice President of Admin Services ... Ms. Seher AWAN
08 Dean Information/Learning Tech ... Mr. Robbi EWELL
79 Dean School of Arts/Humanities ... Ms. Trudy GERALD
50 Dean Sch Business/Info Tech ... Ms. Rose LAMURAGLIA
88 Dean Student Develop/Matriculation ... Vacant
88 Dean Engr & Tech/Math/Sci/Nurs ... Dr. Minou SPRADLEY
56 Director Off-Campus Programs ... Ms. Jeanie TYLER
18 Chief Facilities/Physical Plant ... Mr. Derrall CHANDLER
92 Director Honors Program ... Dr. Kelly MAYHEW
07 Admissions & Records Supervisor ... Ms. Megan SOTO
22 Affirmative Action Officer ... Mr. Edwin HIEL
40 Bookstore Supervisor ... Ms. DeeDee PORTER
26 Public Information Officer ... Ms. Heidi BUNKOWSKE
88 PgmMgr Disabled Student Services ... Ms. Julie PLUDOW
37 Financial Aid Supervisor ... Mr. Gregory SANCHEZ
88 Acting Director EOPS ... Ms. Bernice LORENZO
83 Dean Behav & Soc Sci/Consumer Stds ... Ms. Lori ERRECA
68 ADean Health/Exercise Sci/Athletics ... Mr. Randy BARNES
04 Administrative Asst to President ... Ms. Erin FLANAGAN

*San Diego Mesa College (G)

7250 Mesa College Drive, San Diego CA 92111-4998
County: San Diego FICE Identification: 001275
Unit ID: 122375
Telephone: (619) 388-2721 Carnegie Class: Assoc/Pub-U-MC
FAX Number: (619) 388-2929 Calendar System: Semester
URL: www.sdmesa.edu
Established: 1962 Annual Undergrad Tuition & Fees (In-District): $1,142
Enrollment: 24,159 Coed
Affiliation or Control: State/Local IRS Status: 501(c)3
Highest Offering: Associate Degree
Program: Occupational; 2-Year Principally Bachelor's Creditable
Accreditation: WJ, CAHIIM, DA, PTAA, RAD

02 President ... Dr. Pamela T. LUSTER
05 Vice President Instruction ... Dr. Tim MCGRATH
32 Vice Pres Student Services ... Dr. Juiliana BARNES
11 Vice Pres Administrative Services ... Ms. Rachelle AGATHA
88 Dean Student Development ... Ms. Susan TOPHAM
79 Dean Arts & Languages ... Ms. Leslie SHIMAZAKI
76 Dean Health Sciences/Public Svc ... Ms. Margie FRITCH
81 Dean School Math/Natural Sciences ... Dr. Saeid EIDGAHY
50 Dean Sch Business Technology ... Dr. Danene BROWN
62 Actg Dean Lrng Res/Educational Tech ... Mr. Paul GOMEZ
68 Dean PE/Health Educ & Athletics ... Mr. Dave EVANS
79 Dean of Humanities ... Mr. Andrew J. MACNEILL
83 Dean Social/Behav Sci/Mult Stds ... Dr. Charles ZAPPIA
35 Dean Student Affairs ... Ms. Ashanti HANDS
09 Actg Dean Inst Effectiveness ... Dr. Madeleine HINKES
26 Public Information Officer ... Ms. Lina HEIL
37 Financial Aid Officer ... Ms. Gilda MALDONADO
07 Student Svcs Supervisor Admission ... Ms. Ivonne ALVAREZ
04 Exec Asst to the President ... Ms. Sara Beth CAIN

*San Diego Miramar College (H)

10440 Black Mountain Road, San Diego CA 92126-2999
County: San Diego FICE Identification: 011820
Unit ID: 122384
Telephone: (619) 388-7800 Carnegie Class: Assoc/Pub-U-MC
FAX Number: (619) 388-7901 Calendar System: Semester
URL: www.sdmiramar.edu
Established: 1969 Annual Undergrad Tuition & Fees (In-District): $1,380
Enrollment: 11,876 Coed
Affiliation or Control: State/Local IRS Status: 501(c)3
Highest Offering: Associate Degree
Program: 2-Year Principally Bachelor's Creditable
Accreditation: WJ

02 President ... Dr. Patricia HSIEH
05 Int Vice President Instruction ... Ms. Paulette HOPKINS
32 Vice President Student Services ... Mr. Gerald RAMSEY
10 Vice President Admin Services ... Mr. Brett BELL
49 Dean of Liberal Arts ... Dr. Lou ASCIONE
50 Dean Business/Tech/Workforce Init ... Ms. Lynne ORNELAS
81 Actg Dean Math and Science ... Dr. Fred GARCES
88 Dean of Public Safety ... Mr. George BEITEY
88 Chair Physical Sciences ... Dr. Linda WOODS
27 Information Officer ... Mr. Stephen QUIS
37 Financial Aid Officer ... Ms. Teresa VILABOY
18 Chief Facilities/Physical Plant ... Mr. Dane LINDSAY
88 Child Development ... Ms. Dawn DIMARZO
35 Dean of Student Affairs ... Ms. Adela JACOBSON
08 Library Chair ... Ms. Mary HART
07 Admissions & Records Officer ... Ms. Dana STACK
88 Chair Admin Justice/Police Acad ... Mr. Steve LICKISS
50 Chair Business ... Mr. Wahid HAMIDY
72 Chair Fire Science ... Ms. Mary KJARTANSON
79 Chair Arts & Humanities ... Mr. Robert FRITSCH
81 Chair Math ... Mr. Francois BEREAUD
83 Chair Social Sciences ... Mr. Thomas SCHILZ
88 Chair Trade/Ind/Aviation Mtn Tech ... Mr. Larry PINK
88 Associate Dean ATTE Center Director ... Mr. Greg NEWHOUSE
88 Chair Diesel Technology ... Mr. Dan WILLKIE
38 Chair Counseling ... Mr. David NAVARRO
76 Chair Dept of Natural Sciences ... Dr. Marie MCMAHON
68 Chair Exercise Science ... Mr. Nick GEHLER
60 Chair Comm/English & World Language ... Ms. Sheryl GOBBLE
88 Co-Chair Automotive ... Mr. Joseph YOUNG
108 Dean PRIE/Library & Technology ... Dr. Daniel MIRAMONTEZ

San Francisco Art Institute (I)

800 Chestnut Street, San Francisco CA 94133-2206
County: San Francisco FICE Identification: 003948
Unit ID: 122454
Telephone: (415) 771-7020 Carnegie Class: Spec/Arts
FAX Number: (415) 749-4590 Calendar System: Semester
URL: www.sfai.edu
Established: 1871 Annual Undergrad Tuition & Fees: $40,402
Enrollment: 699 Coed
Affiliation or Control: Independent Non-Profit IRS Status: 501(c)3
Highest Offering: Master's
Program: Professional; Fine Arts Emphasis
Accreditation: WC, ART

00 Chair of the Board ... Cynthia PLEVIN
01 President ... Charles DESMARAIS
05 VP and Dean for Academic Affairs ... Rachel SCHREIBER
31 VP Exhibitions and Public Programs ... Hesse MCGRAW
10 Chief Operating Officer ... Espi SANJANA
30 Director of Development ... Maureen KEEFE
84 Vice President for Enrollment ... Elizabeth O'BRIEN
26 Dir of Marketing & Inst Messaging ... Vacant
04 Sr Admin Asst to the President ... Anne SHULOCK
06 Registrar ... Thomas CHAMPION
07 Sr Assoc Dir of Grad Admissions ... Nicole CRESCENZI
07 Sr Assoc Dir of Undergrad Admiss ... Colleen MULVEY
08 Director Library Services/Librarian ... Jeff GUNDERSON

09 Inst Research & Acad Planning Assoc .... Jose DE LOS REYES
11 Director of Operations .... Heather HICKMAN
13 AVP for Information Technology .... Bruce GRIFFIN
15 Sr Human Resources Administrator .... Rita SULLIVAN
18 Assistant Director of Facilities .... John SEDEN
20 Assoc Dean of Academic Affairs/ALO .... Jennifer RISSLER
21 Interim Controller .... Adrian TRUJILLO
24 Assoc Director of Media Services .... Vacant
25 Director of Academic Administration .... Vacant
29 Mgr of Alum Relations & Gala .... Lindsey LYONS
32 Dean of Students .... Megann SEPT
35 Assistant Dean of Students .... Anthony MOLINAR
37 Director of Financial Aid .... Annita ALLDREDGE
38 Director of Counseling Services .... Deb SCHNEIDER
39 Residence Director .... Nicholas ROUGELY
44 Manager of Institutional Giving .... Vacant
88 Director of Public Education .... Barbara GARBER
57 Chair of BFA Programs .... Paul KLEIN
57 Chair of BA Programs .... Nicole ARCHER
58 Chair of MFA Programs .... Tony LABAT
58 Chair of MA Programs .... Claire DAIGLE
58 Director of Graduate Administration .... Zeina BARAKEH
85 Global Programs Advisor/DSO .... Jill TOLFA
88 Asst Dean for Academic Success .... Susan MARTIN
88 Director of Admissions Operations .... Jeremy SIMMONS
88 Admin Dir School of Studio Prac .... Sherry KNUTSON
88 Director of City Studio .... JD BELTRAN
90 Academic Computing Manager .... Jeremy HOBBS
91 Director of Information Technology .... Andrew SIMAS
105 Content Mktg & Social Media Manager .... Vacant

San Francisco Conservatory of Music (A)

50 Oak Street, San Francisco CA 94102-6011

County: San Francisco — FICE Identification: 001278
Unit ID: 122506
Telephone: (415) 864-7326 — Carnegie Class: Spec/Arts
FAX Number: (415) 503-6299 — Calendar System: Semester
URL: www.sfcm.edu
Established: 1917 — Annual Undergrad Tuition & Fees: $42,210
Enrollment: 389 — Coed
Affiliation or Control: Independent Non-Profit — IRS Status: 501(c)3
Highest Offering: Beyond Master's But Less Than Doctorate
Program: Liberal Arts And General; Music Emphasis
Accreditation: WC, MUS

01 President .... David STULL
05 Provost and Dean .... Kate SHEERAN
10 Vice Pres Finance & Administration .... Kathryn WITTENMYER
30 Vice Pres of Advancement .... Stacy CULLISON
45 Vice Pres of Strategic Initiatives .... Susan MCCONKEY
32 Associate Dean of Student Life .... Jason SMITH
64 Asc Dean for New Media & Music Tech .... MaryClare BRZYTWA
06 Asst Dean Acad Affairs & Registrar .... Jonas WRIGHT
15 Human Resources Manager .... Michael PATTERSON
07 Director of Admission .... Melissa COCCO-MITTEN
37 Director of Financial Aid .... Doris HOWARD
56 Director Preparatory/Extension .... Joan GORDON
26 Director of Communications .... Sam SMITH
09 Director of Institutional Research .... Rebecca SORELL
08 Head Librarian .... Kevin MCLAUGHLIN
31 Performance Outreach Manager .... Elisabeth LOWRY
18 Chief Facilities Engineer .... David MITCHELL
27 Marketing Manager .... John BISCHOFF
04 Executive Assistant to President .... Jennifer SEAMAN
20 Assistant to the Dean .... Carissa IBERT

San Francisco Theological Seminary (B)

105 Seminary Road, San Anselmo CA 94960-2997

County: Marin — FICE Identification: 001279
Unit ID: 122603
Telephone: (415) 451-2800 — Carnegie Class: Spec/Faith
FAX Number: (415) 451-2852 — Calendar System: Semester
URL: www.sfts.edu
Established: 1871 — Annual Graduate Tuition & Fees: $12,700
Enrollment: 155 — Coed
Affiliation or Control: Presbyterian Church (U.S.A.) — IRS Status: 501(c)3
Highest Offering: Doctorate; No Undergraduates
Program: Professional; Religious Emphasis
Accreditation: WC, THEOL

01 President .... Dr. James L. MCDONALD
05 Dean Seminary/VP Academic Affs .... Dr. Jana CHILDERS
30 VP Inst Advance & External Comm .... Mr. Jack KIRKHAM
10 Vice Pres Finance/Operations .... Mr. Mike CAIRNS
32 Assoc Dean Student Svcs/Chaplain .... Rev. Scott CLARK
75 Assoc Dean for Vocations .... Ms. Elizabeth MCCORD
29 Dir Alumni/Church Relations .... Mr. Dan CHRISTIAN
04 Exec Administrator to President .... Ms. Anne LUESING
06 Registrar .... Ms. Susan LAWLOR
21 Interim Controller .... Mr. Marcel DEJIO
18 Director of Facilities .... Mr. Gary MILLER
91 Director of IT .... Mr. Larry PICKARD
35 Director Student Services .... Ms. Stephanie LAMONACA
15 Dir Human Resources .... Ms. Kathleen WATERS
44 Director of Annual Giving .... Mr. James SHARPE
27 Director of Communications .... Ms. Rachel HOWARD

San Joaquin College of Law (C)

901 Fifth Street, Clovis CA 93612-1312

County: Fresno — FICE Identification: 025000
Unit ID: 122649
Telephone: (559) 323-2100 — Carnegie Class: Spec/Law
FAX Number: (559) 323-5566 — Calendar System: Semester
URL: www.sjcl.edu
Established: 1969 — Annual Graduate Tuition & Fees: $20,425
Enrollment: 185 — Coed
Affiliation or Control: Independent Non-Profit — IRS Status: 501(c)3
Highest Offering: Doctorate; No Undergraduates
Program: Professional
Accreditation: WC

01 Dean .... Janice L. PEARSON
05 Dean Academic Affairs .... Justin ATKINSON
18 Facilities Manager .... Richard RODRIGUEZ
10 Chief Financial Officer .... Jill A. RANDLES
32 Director of Student Services .... Joyce K. MORODOMI
37 Financial Aid Administrator .... Jeannie M. LEWIS
08 Library Director .... Vacant
26 Public Relations Director .... Missy M. CARTIER
15 Chief of Personnel .... Beth PITCOCK
30 Chief Development .... Janice L. PEARSON
84 Director Enrollment Management .... Diane M. STEEL
61 Law Program Coordinator .... Pat A. SMITH

San Joaquin Delta College (D)

5151 Pacific Avenue, Stockton CA 95207-6370

County: San Joaquin — FICE Identification: 001280
Unit ID: 122658
Telephone: (209) 954-5151 — Carnegie Class: Assoc/Pub-U-MC
FAX Number: (209) 954-7001 — Calendar System: Semester
URL: www.deltacollege.edu
Established: 1935 — Annual Undergrad Tuition & Fees (In-District): $1,104
Enrollment: 19,650 — Coed
Affiliation or Control: State/Local — IRS Status: 501(c)3
Highest Offering: Associate Degree
Program: Occupational; 2-Year Principally Bachelor's Creditable
Accreditation: WJ, ADNUR

01 Superintendent/President .... Dr. Kathleen HART
05 Asst Supt/VP of Instruction .... Dr. Matt WETSTEIN
32 Asst Supt/VP of Student Svc .... Mr. Michael KERNS
10 Vice Pres of Administrative Svcs .... Vacant
15 Director of Human Resources .... Ms. Dianna GONZALES
13 Vice Pres Information Technology .... Vacant
38 Dean Counseling & Special Svcs .... Mrs. Delecia NUNNALLY
09 Dean Plng Research/Regional Educ .... Vacant
103 Dean Workforce/Economic Development .... Vacant
108 Dean Student Learning & Assessment .... Dr. Charles JENNINGS
08 Div Dean Library/Learning Res/Lang .... Mr. Joe GONZALES
12 Associate Dean of Tracy Center .... Dr. Jessie GARZA-RODERICK
27 Dir Public Information/Marketing .... Vacant
21 Controller .... Ms. Raquel PUENTES-GRIFFITH
18 Director Facilities Management .... Mr. Michael GARR
07 Director of Admissions & Records .... Ms. Amy COURTRIGHT
37 Director of Financial Aid/Vet Svcs .... Ms. Denise C. DONN
96 Director of Purchasing .... Ms. Maria BERNARDINO
06 Registrar .... Ms. Karen SEA

San Joaquin Valley College, Inc. - Visalia (E)

8344 West Mineral King Avenue, Visalia CA 93291-9283

County: Tulare — FICE Identification: 021207
Unit ID: 122685
Telephone: (559) 651-2500 — Carnegie Class: Assoc/PrivFP
FAX Number: (559) 651-0574 — Calendar System: Quarter
URL: www.sjvc.edu/campuses/central-california/visalia
Established: 1977 — Annual Undergrad Tuition & Fees: $18,855
Enrollment: 1,382 — Coed
Affiliation or Control: Proprietary — IRS Status: Proprietary
Highest Offering: Associate Degree
Program: Occupational; 2-Year Principally Bachelor's Creditable
Accreditation: WJ, #ARCPA, COARC, DH

01 President .... Mr. Mark PERRY
00 Chief Executive Officer .... Mr. Michael PERRY
05 College Director .... Mr. Donn RITTER
11 Vice President of Administration .... Ms. Wendy MENDES
84 Vice Pres of Enrollment Services .... Mr. Joseph HOLT
10 Chief Financial Officer .... Mr. Russ LEBO
37 Vice Pres of Student Financial Aid .... Mr. Kevin ROBINSON
96 Director of Purchasing .... Mr. Ralph ORTIZ

San Joaquin Valley College-Bakersfield (F)

201 New Stine Road, Bakersfield CA 93309-2668

Telephone: (661) 834-0126 — FICE Identification: 023135
Accreditation: &WJ, COARC, SURGT

† Regional accreditation is carried under the parent institution in Visalia, CA.

San Joaquin Valley College-Fresno (G)

295 East Sierra Avenue, Fresno CA 93710-3616

Telephone: (559) 448-8282 — Identification: 666008
Accreditation: &WJ, SURGT

† Regional accreditation is carried under the parent institution in Visalia, CA.

San Joaquin Valley College-Fresno Aviation Campus (H)

4985 East Andersen Avenue, Fresno CA 93727

Telephone: (559) 453-0123 — Identification: 666009
Accreditation: &WJ

† Regional accreditation is carried under the parent institution in Visalia, CA.

San Joaquin Valley College-Hanford (I)

215 West 7th Street, Hanford CA 93230-4523

Telephone: (559) 584-8840 — Identification: 770508
Accreditation: &WJ

† Branch campus of San Joaquin Valley College, Inc. - Visalia, Visalia, CA.

San Joaquin Valley College-Modesto (J)

5380 Pirrone Road, Salida CA 95368-9090

Telephone: (209) 543-8800 — Identification: 666128
Accreditation: &WJ

† Regional accreditation is carried under the parent institution in Visalia, CA.

San Joaquin Valley College-Ontario (K)

4580 Ontario Mills Parkway, Ontario CA 91764

Telephone: (909) 948-7582 — Identification: 666096
Accreditation: &WJ, COARC

† Regional accreditation is carried under the parent institution in Visalia, CA.

San Joaquin Valley College-Rancho Cordova (L)

11050 Olson Drive, Suite 210,
Rancho Cordova CA 95670-5600

Telephone: (916) 638-7582 — Identification: 666133
Accreditation: &WJ, COARC

† Regional accreditation is carried under the parent institution in Visalia, CA.

San Joaquin Valley College-Temecula (M)

27270 Madison Avenue, Suite 305, Temecula CA 92590

Telephone: (951) 296-6015 — Identification: 770507
Accreditation: &WJ, #COARC

† Branch campus of San Joaquin Valley College, Inc. - Visalia, Visalia, CA.

San Joaquin Valley College-Victor Valley (Hesperia) (N)

9331 Mariposa Road, Hesperia CA 92344-8000

Telephone: (760) 948-1947 — Identification: 667044
Accreditation: &WJ

† Regional accreditation is carried under the parent institution in Visalia, CA.

*San Jose/Evergreen Community College District (O)

4750 San Felipe Road, San Jose CA 95135-1599

County: Santa Clara — FICE Identification: 029042
Unit ID: 122737
Telephone: (408) 274-6700 — Carnegie Class: N/A
FAX Number: (408) 531-8722
URL: www.sjeccd.edu

01 Interim Chancellor .... Mr. John HENDRICKSON
11 Vice Chanc Administrative Services .... Mr. Douglas SMITH
15 Vice Chanc Human Resources .... Ms. Kim L. GARCIA
13 Vice Chanc Information Tech Svcs .... Dr. Ben SEABERRY
103 Vice Chanc Workfrce/Econ/Res Dev .... Ms. Carol COEN
09 Int VC Instl Effect/Student Success .... Ms. Tamela HAWLEY
86 Exec Dir Government/External Affs .... Ms. Rosalie LEDESMA
18 Dir Facilities/Const Mgmt/Operation .... Mr. Robert DIAS
07 Director Admiss/Records San Jose .... Mr. Carlo SANTOS
10 Director of Fiscal Services .... Mr. Peter FITZSIMMONS
28 Dir of Employment Svcs/Diversity .... Mr. Sam HO

*Evergreen Valley College (P)

3095 Yerba Buena Road, San Jose CA 95135-1598

County: Santa Clara — FICE Identification: 012452
Unit ID: 114266
Telephone: (408) 274-7900 — Carnegie Class: Assoc/Pub-U-MC
FAX Number: (408) 238-3179 — Calendar System: Semester
URL: www.evc.edu
Established: 1975 — Annual Undergrad Tuition & Fees (In-District): $1,338
Enrollment: 9,133 — Coed
Affiliation or Control: State/Local — IRS Status: 501(c)3
Highest Offering: Associate Degree
Program: Occupational; 2-Year Principally Bachelor's Creditable
Accreditation: WJ, ADNUR

02 President .... Mr. Henry C. YONG
05 VP Academic Affairs .... Mr. Keith AYTCH
32 Vice Pres Student Services .... Ms. Irma ARCHULETA
10 VP Administrarive Services .... Mr. Henry GEE
50 Dean Business & Workforce .... Dr. Lena TRAN
66 Dean Nursing & Allied Health .... Dr. Antoinette HERRERA
62 Dean Library/Lrng Res .... Dr. Merryl KRAVITZ
81 Dean Math/Science/Engineering .... Mr. Michael HIGHERS
83 Dean Soc Sci/PE/Arts/Humanities .... Mr. Mark GONZALES
84 Dean Enrollment Services .... Mr. Octavio CRUZ
38 Dean of Counseling .... Ms. Alexandra DURAN
35 Director Student Life & EOPS .... Dr. Victor GARZA, JR.
37 Director Financial Aid .... Ms. Alma TANON
88 Director Student Services Pgm .... Vacant
88 Director CalWorks/WIN .... Ms. Elizabeth TYRRELL
11 Supervisor Administrative Services .... Ms. Lauren MCKEE
79 Dean Language Arts .... Dr. Merryl KRAVITZ
13 Supervisor Campus Tech Svcs .... Mr. Eugenio CANOY

*San Jose City College (A)

2100 Moorpark Avenue, San Jose CA 95128-2799
County: Santa Clara FICE Identification: 001282
Unit ID: 122746
Telephone: (408) 298-2181 Carnegie Class: Assoc/Pub-U-MC
FAX Number: (408) 298-1935 Calendar System: Semester
URL: www.sjcc.edu
Established: 1921 Annual Undergrad Tuition & Fees (In-District): $6,048
Enrollment: 9,072 Coed
Affiliation or Control: State/Local IRS Status: 501(c)3
Highest Offering: Associate Degree
Program: Occupational; 2-Year Principally Bachelor's Creditable
Accreditation: WJ, DA

02 President .... Dr. Byron BRELAND
05 Vice President Academic Affairs .... Mr. Duncan GRAHAM
11 Vice President Administrative Svcs .... Mr. Jorge ESCOBAR
32 Vice President Student Services .... Dr. Marie-Elaine BURNS
84 Dean of Enrollment Services .... Mr. Takeo KUBO
88 Executive Director WIN Program .... Ms. Marilyn BRODIE
92 Director Honors Program .... Mr. Sean ABEL
41 Director of Athletics & Kinesiology .... Mr. Lamel HARRIS
04 Assistant to the President .... Ms. Judy WESSLER
50 Dean Business/Workforce Development .... Ms. Ingrid THOMPSON
79 Dean Humanities/Social Science .... Mr. Sean ABEL
38 Dean Couns/Retention/Spec Pgms .... Mr. Roland MONTEMAYOR
88 Dean Language Arts .... Dr. Keiko KIMURA
81 Dean Mathematics/Sciences Division .... Mr. Jamie ALONZO

*San Mateo County Community College District Office (B)

3401 CSM Drive, San Mateo CA 94402-3651
County: San Mateo FICE Identification: 004697
Unit ID: 122782
Telephone: (650) 574-6500 Carnegie Class: N/A
FAX Number: (650) 574-6566
URL: www.smccd.edu

01 Chancellor .... Mr. Ron D. GALATOLO
03 Executive Vice Chancellor .... Ms. Kathy BLACKWOOD
11 Deputy Chancellor .... Mr. James W. KELLER
15 Vice Chanc Employee Rels/Human Res .... Mr. Eugene WHITLOCK
05 Vice Chanc Educational Svcs/Plng .... Dr. Jing LUAN
18 Vice Chanc Facil Plng/Maint/Oper .... Mr. Jose NUNEZ
109 Vice Chanc Auxiliary Services .... Mr. Tom BAUER
31 Dir Community/Government Relations .... Ms. Barbara W. CHRISTENSEN
10 Chief Financial Officer .... Mr. Raymond CHOW
13 Chief Technology Officer .... Mr. Frank M. VASKELIS

*Cañada College (C)

4200 Farm Hill Boulevard, Redwood City CA 94061-1099
County: San Mateo FICE Identification: 006973
Unit ID: 111434
Telephone: (650) 306-3100 Carnegie Class: Assoc/Pub-S-MC
FAX Number: (650) 306-3457 Calendar System: Semester
URL: www.canadacollege.edu
Established: 1968 Annual Undergrad Tuition & Fees (In-District): $1,380
Enrollment: 6,498 Coed
Affiliation or Control: State/Local IRS Status: 501(c)3
Highest Offering: Associate Degree
Program: Occupational; 2-Year Principally Bachelor's Creditable
Accreditation: WJ, RAD

02 President .... Dr. Lawrence BUCKLEY
32 Vice President of Student Services .... Ms. Robin RICHARDS
05 Vice President of Instruction .... Mr. Gregory ANDERSON
38 Dean Counseling Services .... Ms. Kim LOPEZ
06 Registrar .... Ms. Ruth MILLER
10 Chief Business Officer .... Ms. Victoria NUNES
26 Director of Marketing .... Vacant
45 Dir Plng/Research/Student Success .... Ms. Chialin HSIEH
37 Director Financial Aid .... Ms. Margie CARRINGTON
18 Facilities Manager .... Mr. John HASHIZUME
103 Dean Business/Design & Workforce .... Ms. Linda HAYES
79 Dean of Humanities & Social Science .... Mr. David JOHNSON
81 Dean Science & Technology .... Dr. Janet STRINGER
41 Dean Athletics/Kinesiology .... Ms. Anniqua RANA

*College of San Mateo (D)

1700 W Hillsdale Boulevard, San Mateo CA 94402-3795
County: San Mateo FICE Identification: 001181
Unit ID: 122791
Telephone: (650) 574-6161 Carnegie Class: Assoc/Pub-S-MC
FAX Number: (650) 574-6680 Calendar System: Semester
URL: www.collegeofsanmateo.edu
Established: 1922 Annual Undergrad Tuition & Fees (In-District): $1,418
Enrollment: 8,935 Coed
Affiliation or Control: State/Local IRS Status: 501(c)3
Highest Offering: Associate Degree
Program: Occupational; 2-Year Principally Bachelor's Creditable
Accreditation: WJ, DA

02 President .... Mr. Michael CLAIRE
05 Vice President Instruction .... Dr. Sandra Stefani COMERFORD
32 Vice President Student Services .... Ms. Jennifer HUGHES
07 Dean Admissions & Records .... Dr. Henry VILLAREAL
38 Dean Counsel/Advis/Matriculation .... Ms. Marsha RAMEZANE
09 Dean Plng/Rsrch/Inst Effectiveness .... Dr. John J. SEWART
35 Dean Student Services/Counseling .... Ms. Marsha RAMEZANE
79 Dean Language Arts Division .... Dr. James CARRANZA
68 Dean Kinesiology/Athletics Division .... Mr. Andreas WOLF
81 Dean Math/Science Division .... Dr. Charlene FRONTIERA
83 Dean Creative Arts/Social Sci Div .... Dr. Kevin HENSON
50 Dean Business & Technology Division .... Ms. Kathleen ROSS
18 Exec Dir Facilities Plng/Operations .... Ms. Karen POWELL
06 Registrar .... Ms. Niruba SRINIVASAN
37 Director Financial Aid Services .... Ms. Claudia I. MENJIVAR
30 Dir College Development & Marketing .... Ms. Beverly MADDEN
26 Dir Marketing/Comm/Public Relations .... Ms. Cherie COLIN

*Skyline College (E)

3300 College Drive, San Bruno CA 94066-1698
County: San Mateo FICE Identification: 007713
Unit ID: 123509
Telephone: (650) 738-4100 Carnegie Class: Assoc/Pub-S-MC
FAX Number: (650) 738-4338 Calendar System: Semester
URL: www.skylinecollege.edu
Established: 1969 Annual Undergrad Tuition & Fees (In-District): $1,447
Enrollment: 9,820 Coed
Affiliation or Control: State/Local IRS Status: 501(c)3
Highest Offering: Associate Degree
Program: Occupational; 2-Year Principally Bachelor's Creditable
Accreditation: WJ, ACBSP, COARC, SURGT

02 President .... Dr. Regina STANBACK STROUD
05 Vice President Instruction .... Dr. Sarah F. PERKINS
32 Vice President Student Services .... Dr. Angelica GARCIA
84 Dean Enrollment Svcs/Financial Aid .... Mr. William MINNICH
09 Dean Plng/Rsrch/Inst Effective .... Mr. Aaron MCVEAN
10 Vice President Business Service .... Ms. Eloisa M. BRIONES
83 Dean Social Science/Creative Arts .... Ms. Donna J. BESTOCK
50 Dean Business/Ed/Prof Pgm .... Ms. Christine ROUMBANIS
60 Dean Language Arts/Learning Res .... Ms. Mary GUTIERREZ
68 Dean Kinesiology/Athletics/Dance .... Mr. Joseph MORELLO
81 Dean Science/Math/Technology .... Mr. Raymond HERNANDEZ
38 Dean Counsel/Advis/Matric .... Vacant
103 Director SparkPoint at Skyline Col .... Dr. Chad THOMPSON
26 Director Marketing/Comm/PR .... Ms. Cherie COLIN
08 Director Library Services .... Vacant
103 Director Workforce Development .... Dr. Rajesh LATHIGARA
85 Dean Global Learning Programs .... Dr. Tammy ROBINSON
88 Dean Acad Support & Learning Tech .... Dr. Jonathan PAVER
06 Registrar .... Ms. Susan LORENZO

Sanford Burnham Prebys Medical Discovery Institute (F)

10901 North Torrey Pines Road, La Jolla CA 92037
County: San Diego Identification: 667069
Unit ID: 481535
Telephone: (858) 646-3100 Carnegie Class: Not Classified
FAX Number: (858) 646-3199 Calendar System: Quarter
URL: www.shpdiscovery.org
Established: 2005 Annual Graduate Tuition & Fees: N/A
Enrollment: 32 Coed
Affiliation or Control: Independent Non-Profit IRS Status: 501(c)3
Highest Offering: Doctorate; No Undergraduates
Program: Professional
Accreditation: @WC

01 President .... Dr. Kristiina VUORI
10 Exec VP/Chief Admin Officer/CFO .... Dr. Gary RAISL
05 Dean .... Dr. Guy SALVESEN
15 Vice Pres Human Res/Org Effect .... Mr. John SCHIERER
26 Vice Pres for Communications .... Ms. Deborah ROBISON
30 Vice President Inst Advancement .... Mr. Philip GRAHAM
21 Vice President Finance/Controller .... Ms. Robin RYAN

The Santa Barbara and Ventura Colleges of Law (G)

4475 Market Street, Ventura CA 93003
County: Ventura Identification: 667229
Unit ID: 125037
Telephone: (805) 765-9300 Carnegie Class: Not Classified
FAX Number: (805) 658-0529 Calendar System: Semester
URL: www.collegesoflaw.edu
Established: 1969 Annual Graduate Tuition & Fees: $14,250
Enrollment: 93 Coed
Affiliation or Control: Independent Non-Profit IRS Status: 501(c)3
Highest Offering: Doctorate; No Undergraduates
Program: Professional
Accreditation: WC

01 President .... Dr. Charles MCCLINTOCK
05 Dean .... Ms. Heather GEORGAKIS
10 VP Finance & Administration .... Mr. David RISTIG
13 Director of Information Management .... Ms. Diane MCREYNOLDS
07 Director of Admissions .... Dr. Jason BECK
32 Director of Student Services .... Ms. Michelle WISE
06 Asst Dean & Registrar .... Ms. Barbara DOYLE
18 Facilities Manager .... Mr. Pete LOPEZ

Santa Barbara Business College (H)

5300 California Ave, Bakersfield CA 93309-2139
County: Kern FICE Identification: 025779
Unit ID: 122834
Telephone: (661) 835-1100 Carnegie Class: Assoc/PrivFP
FAX Number: (661) 835-0242 Calendar System: Semester
URL: www.sbbcollege.edu
Established: 1982 Annual Undergrad Tuition & Fees: N/A
Enrollment: 66 Coed
Affiliation or Control: Proprietary IRS Status: Proprietary
Highest Offering: Baccalaureate
Program: Occupational; 2-Year Principally Bachelor's Creditable
Accreditation: ACICS

01 President .... Matthew JOHNSTON
26 Marketing Coordinator .... Monica RAYMOND

Santa Barbara Business College (I)

34275 Monterey Ave, Rancho Mirage CA 92270
Telephone: (760) 341-7602 Identification: 666582
Accreditation: ACICS

† Branch campus of Santa Barbara Business College, Bakersfield, CA.

Santa Barbara Business College (J)

506 Chapala Street, Santa Barbara CA 93101-3412
Telephone: (805) 967-9677 Identification: 666099
Accreditation: ACICS

† Branch campus of Santa Barbara Business College, Ventura, CA.

Santa Barbara Business College (K)

303 E Plaza Drive, Santa Maria CA 93454
County: Santa Barbara FICE Identification: 025780
Unit ID: 122852
Telephone: (805) 922-8256 Carnegie Class: Assoc/PrivFP
FAX Number: (805) 346-1857 Calendar System: Semester
URL: www.sbbcollege.edu
Established: 1980 Annual Undergrad Tuition & Fees: N/A
Enrollment: 33 Coed
Affiliation or Control: Proprietary IRS Status: Proprietary
Highest Offering: Baccalaureate
Program: Occupational; 2-Year Principally Bachelor's Creditable
Accreditation: ACICS

01 President .... Matthew JOHNSTON
26 Marketing Coordinator .... Monica RAYMOND

Santa Barbara Business College (L)

4839 Market Street, Ventura CA 93003
County: Ventura FICE Identification: 009989
Unit ID: 433420
Telephone: (805) 339-2999 Carnegie Class: Assoc/PrivFP
FAX Number: (805) 339-2994 Calendar System: Other
URL: www.sbbcollege.edu
Established: 2003 Annual Undergrad Tuition & Fees: $13,663
Enrollment: 420 Coed
Affiliation or Control: Proprietary IRS Status: Proprietary
Highest Offering: Baccalaureate
Program: Occupational; 2-Year Principally Bachelor's Creditable
Accreditation: ACICS

01 President .... Matthew JOHNSTON
26 Marketing Coordinator .... Monica RAYMOND

Santa Barbara Business College-Online (M)

5777 Olivas Park Drive, Suite A, Ventura CA 93003
Telephone: (877) 305-7222 Identification: 770628
Accreditation: ACICS

† Branch campus of Santa Barbara Business College, Ventura, CA.

Santa Barbara City College (N)

721 Cliff Drive, Santa Barbara CA 93109-2394
County: Santa Barbara FICE Identification: 001285
Unit ID: 122889
Telephone: (805) 965-0581 Carnegie Class: Assoc/Pub-R-L
FAX Number: (805) 963-7222 Calendar System: Semester
URL: www.sbcc.edu
Established: 1909 Annual Undergrad Tuition & Fees (In-District): $1,378
Enrollment: 19,932 Coed

Affiliation or Control: State/Local IRS Status: 501(c)3
Highest Offering: Associate Degree
Program: Occupational; 2-Year Principally Bachelor's Creditable
Accreditation: WJ, ADNUR, CAHIIM, DMS, RAD

01 Superintendent/President .... Dr. Lori GASKIN
05 Exec Vice Pres Educational Programs ..... Dr. Jack FRIEDLANDER
10 Vice President Business Services .... Mr. Joseph SULLIVAN
15 Vice Pres Human Resources .... Ms. Patricia ENGLISH
13 Vice President Info Technology .... Dr. Paul BISHOP
72 Dean Educational Programs .... Dr. Ben PARTEE
76 Dean Educational Programs .... Dr. Alan PRICE
81 Dean Educational Programs .... Ms. Marilynn SPAVENTA
57 Dean Educational Programs .... Dr. Alice PEREZ
53 Dean Educational Programs .... Ms. Melissa MORENO
72 Dean Educational Programs .... Mr. Kenley NEUFELD
07 Associate Dean Admissions .... Ms. Allison CANNING
08 Librarian .... Ms. Elizabeth BOWMAN
102 Exec Dir Foundation for SBCC .... Mr. Geoff GREEN
09 Sr Director Institutional Research .... Mr. Robert ELSE
26 College Information Officer .... Ms. Joan GALVAN
37 Director of Student Financial Aid .... Mr. Brad HARDISON
18 Sr Dir of Facilities & Operations .... Ms. Julie HENDRICKS
85 Director International Students .... Ms. Carola SMITH
06 Director of Records .... Mr. Michael MEDEL
96 Manager of Purchasing .... Mr. Robert MORALES
04 Administrative Asst to President .... Ms. Angie ESQUEDA
19 Director Security/Safety .... Mr. Erik FRICKE
41 Athletic Director .... Mr. Ryan BYRNE
27 Director of Marketing/Publications .... Ms. Karen SOPHIEA
84 Coordinator for Enrollment Services .... Ms. Vanessa PELTON

Santa Clara University (A)

500 El Camino Real, Santa Clara CA 95053-0001
County: Santa Clara FICE Identification: 001326
Unit ID: 122931
Telephone: (408) 554-4000 Carnegie Class: Master's L
FAX Number: (408) 554-2700 Calendar System: Quarter
URL: www.scu.edu
Established: 1851 Annual Undergrad Tuition & Fees: $45,300
Enrollment: 9,015 Coed
Affiliation or Control: Independent Non-Profit IRS Status: 501(c)3
Highest Offering: Doctorate
Program: Liberal Arts And General; Teacher Preparatory; Professional
Accreditation: WC, BUS, BUSA, CS, ENG, LAW, THEOL

01 President .... Rev. Michael E. ENGH, SJ
05 Provost .... Dr. Dennis JACOBS
10 Vice President Finance and Admin .... Mr. Michael HINDERY
43 General Counsel .... Mr. John OTTOBONI
26 Vice President University Relations .... Mr. James LYONS
100 Chief of Staff to the President .... Ms. Molly MC DONALD
49 Dean of Arts & Sciences .... Dr. Debbie TAHMASSEBI
50 Dean of Business .... Ms. Caryn BECK-DUDLEY
53 Interim Dean Educ & Counseling Psyc .... Dr. Carol A. GITTENS
54 Dean of Engineering .... Dr. Godfrey MUNGAL
61 Dean of Law .... Ms. Lisa KLOPPENBERG
73 Dean Jesuit School of Theology .... Rev. Thomas MASSARO, SJ
88 Dean Academic Support Services .... Ms. Kathryn PALMIERI
88 Presidential Prof Global Outreach .... Dr. Don C. DODSON
20 Sr Vice Provost Academic Affairs .... Dr. Diane E. JONTE-PACE
32 Vice Provost and Dean Student Life . Ms. Jeanne ROSENBERGER
84 Vice President for Enrollment Mgmt .... Mr. Mike B. SEXTON
45 Vice Prov Inst Effectiveness .... Mr. Ed RYAN
13 CIO/Vice Provost Info Services .... Dr. Robert OWEN
20 Assoc Vice Prov Undergrad Studies .... Dr. Philip R. KESTEN
20 Assoc Provost Undergraduate Studies .... Mr. Jim BENNETT
88 Sr Assoc Provost Rsrch Faculty Affr .... Dr. Amy M. SHACHTER
88 Assoc Vice Provost Faculty Develop .... Dr. Eileen R. ELROD
07 Dean Undergraduate Admission .... Ms. Sandra L. HAYES
37 Dean University Financial Aid Svcs .... Dr. Richard TOOMEY
27 Assoc Vice President Mktg/Comm .... Mr. Richard GIACCHETTI
21 Assoc Vice President Finance .... Mr. Harry M. FONG
15 Asst Vice President Human Resources ..... Mr. Charlie AMBELANG
30 Assoc Vice President Development .... Mr. Mike J. WALLACE
109 Asst Vice Pres Auxiliary Services .... Ms. Jane BARRANTES
35 Assoc Dean for Student Life .... Mr. Matthew DUNCAN
06 University Registrar .... Ms. Monica L. AUGUSTIN
29 Asst Vice President Alumni Rels .... Ms. Kathy KALE
41 Director Athletics and Recreation .... Dr. Renee BAUMGARTNER
08 University Librarian .... Ms. Jennifer NUTEFALL
90 Director Academic Technology .... Ms. Nancy CUTLER
36 Director Career Center .... Ms. Elspeth ROSSETTI
09 Director Institutional Research .... Ms. Barbara A. STEWART
25 Director Sponsored Projects .... Ms. Mary-Ellen FORTINI
38 Director Health & Counseling Svcs .... Dr. Jill ROVARIS
85 Int Exec Dir International Programs .... Ms. Susan POPKO
21 University Director Budget .... Ms. Robin REYNOLDS
88 Chief Investment Officer .... Mr. John E. KERRIGAN
21 Controller .... Ms. Ramona SAUTER
18 Director of Facilities .... Mr. Jeffrey R. CHARLES
96 Director University Support Service .... Mr. Ed MERRYMAN
19 Director Campus Safety Services .... Mr. Philip BELTRAN
42 General Manager Bookstore .... Ms. Deborah KENDALL
42 Director of Campus Ministry .... Ms. Lulu SANTANA
22 EEO & Title IX Coordinator .... Ms. Belinda GUTHRIE
88 Director de Saisset Museum .... Ms. Rebecca M. SCHAPP
88 Exec Dir Ignatian Ctr Jesuit Educ ... Rev. Michael MCCARTHY, SJ
88 Executive Dir Ctr Sci/Tech/Society .... Dr. Thane KREINER
88 Exec Dir Markkula Ctr Applied Ethic .... Mr. Kirk O. HANSON
30 Assoc Vice President Development .... Ms. Nancy T. CALDERON
28 Assoc Provost Diversity & Inclusion .... Mr. Aldo BILLINGSLEA

44 Assoc Vice President Advance Svcs .... Ms. Caroline CHANG
92 Director University Honors Program .... Dr. Leilani M. MILLER
94 Director Womens & Gender Studies ..... Dr. Laura L. ELLINGSTON
93 Director Ethnic Studies .... Dr. James S. LAI
21 Director of Finance & Admin .... Mr. Dale LUXFORD

Santa Monica College (B)

1900 Pico Boulevard, Santa Monica CA 90405-1628
County: Los Angeles FICE Identification: 001286
Unit ID: 122977
Telephone: (310) 434-4000 Carnegie Class: Assoc/Pub-S-MC
FAX Number: (310) 434-4386 Calendar System: Semester
URL: www.smc.edu
Established: 1929 Annual Undergrad Tuition & Fees (In-District): $1,207
Enrollment: 33,616 Coed
Affiliation or Control: State/Local IRS Status: 501(c)3
Highest Offering: Associate Degree
Program: Occupational; 2-Year Principally Bachelor's Creditable
Accreditation: WJ, ADNUR

01 Interim Superintendent/President .... Mr. Jeffery SHIMIZU
03 Executive Vice President .... Vacant
10 Vice President Business/Admin .... Mr. Robert G. ISOMOTO
15 Vice President Human Resources .... Ms. Marcia WADE
05 Vice President Academic Affairs .... Dr. Georgia LORENZ
84 Vice Pres Enrollment Development .... Dr. Teresita RODRIGUEZ
32 Vice President Student Affairs .... Mr. Michael TUITASI
20 Dean Academic Affairs .... Ms. Erica LEBLANC
16 Dean Human Resources .... Ms. Sherri LEE-LEWIS
08 Dean Learning Resources .... Vacant
85 Dean International Education .... Ms. Kelley BRAYTON
56 Dean External Programs .... Vacant
38 Dean Counseling/Retention .... Ms. Brenda BENSON
13 Dean Information Technology .... Vacant
88 Interim Dean Education Enterprise .... Mr. Mitch HESKEL
43 Campus Counsel .... Mr. Robert MYERS
106 Assoc Dean Online Svcs & Support .... Ms. Julie YARRISH
51 Assoc Dean Emeritus College .... Ms. Gita RUNKLE
35 Dean Students .... Ms. Deyna HEARN
17 Associate Dean of Health Sciences .... Dr. Ida DANZEY
26 Public Information Officer .... Ms. Grace SMITH
31 Dean Community & Academic Relations ..... Ms. Kiersten ELLIOTT
86 Sr Director Government Relations .... Mr. Don GIRARD
37 Assoc Dean Financial Aid/Scholarshp .... Mr. Steve MYROW
18 Chief Dir Facilities Management .... Mr. Bruce WYBAN
21 Budget Manager .... Ms. Veronica DIAZ
09 Dean Institutional Research .... Ms. Hannah LAWLER
104 Assoc Dean International Education .... Ms. Denise KINSELLA
41 Asst Director Athletics .... Mr. Reggie ELLIS
102 Associate Dean Grants .... Ms. Laurel MCQUAY-PENINGER
88 Dir Performing Arts Center .... Vacant
88 Director of Classified Personnel .... Ms. Carol LONG
88 Director Network Services .... Mr. Bob DAMMER
25 Director of Contracts .... Mr. Charlie YEN
96 Director of Purchasing .... Ms. Cynthia MOORE
19 Dean Camp Security Stdnt Hlth/Safe .... Dr. Albert VASQUEZ
04 Admin Asst to the President .... Ms. Letty KILIAN
14 Director Management Info Systems .... Mr. Lee JOHNSTON
24 Mgr Media & Reprographic Services .... Mr. Albert DESALLES
40 Bookstore Manager .... Mr. David DEVER
103 Dean Workforce Development .... Dr. Patricia RAMOS
101 Coordinator Board of Trustees .... Ms. Lisa ROSE
88 Interim Assoc Dean Student Life .. Ms. Nancy GRASS-HEMMERT
88 Director Radio Station (KCRW) .... Ms. Jennifer FERRO
88 Director Facilities Programming .... Ms. Linda SULLIVAN
88 Dean Student Success Initiatives .... Dr. Roberto GONZALEZ
88 Dir Sustainability Coordination .... Mr. Ferris KAWAR
75 Dir Career & Contract Education .... Ms. Michelle KING
88 Assoc Dir Dual Enroll/Instr Svcs .... Ms. Maral HYELER
88 Dir Supplemental Instruct/Tutoring .... Dr. Tony PRESTBY
88 Director STEM Initiatives .... Ms. Melanie BOCANEGRA
88 Acting Dir Small Business Dev Ctr .... Ms. Sasha KING
88 Assoc Dean Instruct/Stdnt Pgm .... Mr. Frank DAWSON
29 Dir Student and Alumni Rels .... Ms. Deirdre WEAVER
88 Special Assistant to the President .... Ms. Katharine MULLER

Santa Rosa Junior College (C)

1501 Mendocino Avenue, Santa Rosa CA 95401-4395
County: Sonoma FICE Identification: 001287
Unit ID: 123013
Telephone: (707) 527-4011 Carnegie Class: Assoc/Pub-R-L
FAX Number: (707) 527-4816 Calendar System: Semester
URL: www.santarosa.edu
Established: 1918 Annual Undergrad Tuition & Fees (In-District): $1,144
Enrollment: 28,256 Coed
Affiliation or Control: State/Local IRS Status: 501(c)3
Highest Offering: Associate Degree
Program: Occupational; 2-Year Principally Bachelor's Creditable
Accreditation: WJ, DA, DH, DIETT, EMT, RAD

01 Superintendent/President .... Dr. Frank CHONG
12 Vice President Petaluma Campus ..... Dr. Jane SALDANA-TALLEY
05 VP Acad Affs/Asst Superintendent .... Dr. Mary Kay RUDOLPH
10 Vice President Business Services .... Mr. Doug ROBERTS
32 VP Student Svcs/Asst Superintendent . Mr. Ricardo NAVARRETTE
15 VP Human Resources .... Ms. Karen FURUKAWA
04 Executive Assistant to CEO/BOT .... Ms. Erin MAGEE
75 Dean Career/Tech Ed/Economic Dev .... Mr. Jerry MILLER
11 Dean Facilities Planning/Operations .... Mr. Tony ICHSAN
88 Dean Curriculum/Education Support .... Dr. Abraham FARKAS

49 Dean Liberal Arts & Sciences .... Dr. Kris ABRAHAMSON
08 Dean Learning Res/Educ Tech .... Ms. Alicia VIRTUE
88 Dean Counseling/Support Services .... Vacant
88 Dean Public Safety .... Ms. April CHAPMAN
81 Dean Sci/Tech/Engr/Math .... Mr. Stephen LEWIS
17 Dean Health Sciences .... Ms. Deborah CHIGAZOLA
50 Dean Business/Professional Studies .... Mr. Joshua ADAMS
79 Dean Arts & Humanities .... Ms. Anna SZABADOS
88 Dean Language Arts/Acad Foundation .... Mr. Victor CUMMINGS
41 Dean Kinesiology/Dance/Athletic Dir . Mr. Matthew MARKOVITCH
88 Dean Disabled Students Pgm & Svcs .... Ms. Patie WEGMAN
72 Dean Instruction & Enrollment Svcs ...... Ms. Catherine WILLIAMS
35 Dean Student Services Petaluma .... Ms. Vanessa SHANNON
88 Dean Child Dev & Teacher Education .... Ms. Yolanda GARCIA
88 Dean Student Success & Retention .... Ms. Li COLLIER
47 Dean Agriculture/Natural Resources .... Mr. Ganesan SRINIVASAN
19 Interim Chief of Police .... Mr. Robert BROWNLEE
13 Director Information Technology .... Mr. Scott CONRAD
103 Director Workforce Development .... Ms. Eve NIGHSWONGER
21 Director of Fiscal Services .... Ms. Kate JOLLEY
37 Director Student Financial Services .... Ms. Jana COX
18 Director Facilities Operations .... Mr. Paul BIELEN
23 Director Student Health Services .... Ms. Susan QUINN
09 Director Institutional Research .... Dr. KC GREANEY
35 Dir Student Affs/New Student Pgm .... Mr. Robert ETHINGTON
96 Director Purchasing & Graphics .... Ms. Laura RIVERA
40 Director Bookstore .... Mr. Anthony MARTINEZ
102 Executive Director Foundation .... Ms. Kate MCCLINTOCK
66 Interim Director Nursing Program .... Ms. Anna VALDEZ
06 Dean Acad Records/Intl Admissions .... Ms. Freyja PEREIRA
07 Director Admissions/Enrollment Svcs .... Ms. Vayta SMITH
31 Director Community Education .... Vacant
16 Director Human Resources .... Vacant
26 Director Public Relations Manager .... Ms. Ellen MAREMONT-SILVER
90 Manager Instructional Computing .... Mr. Michael ROTH
24 Manager Media Services .... Mr. Russ BOWDEN
24 Manager Media Services Petaluma .... Mr. Matt PEARSON

Saybrook University (D)

475 14th Street, Oakland CA 94612
County: Alameda FICE Identification: 021206
Unit ID: 123095
Telephone: (510) 593-2900 Carnegie Class: Spec/Health
FAX Number: N/A Calendar System: Semester
URL: www.saybrook.edu
Established: 1971 Annual Graduate Tuition & Fees: $24,760
Enrollment: 567 Coed
Affiliation or Control: Independent Non-Profit IRS Status: 501(c)3
Highest Offering: Doctorate; No Undergraduates
Program: Professional
Accreditation: WC

01 President .... Dr. Nathan LONG
05 VP Academics/Student Affs (CAO) .... Dr. Carol R. HUMPHREYS
06 Registrar .... Mr. Aaron HIATT
08 Director of Library Services .... Ms. Lorelette KNOWLES
100 Chief of Staff .... Mr. Tony TRAVERS
07 Director of Admissions .... Ms. Stacy KLEIN
15 Director College Operations .... Ms. Connie SHULMAN
13 IT Manager .... Mr. Alex SALTZBERG

Scripps College (E)

1030 Columbia, Claremont CA 91711-3948
County: Los Angeles FICE Identification: 001174
Unit ID: 123165
Telephone: (909) 621-8000 Carnegie Class: Bac/A&S
FAX Number: (909) 621-8323 Calendar System: Semester
URL: www.scrippscollege.edu
Established: 1926 Annual Undergrad Tuition & Fees: $49,146
Enrollment: 988 Female
Affiliation or Control: Independent Non-Profit IRS Status: 501(c)3
Highest Offering: Baccalaureate
Program: Liberal Arts And General
Accreditation: WC

01 President .... Dr. Lori BETTISON-VARGA
05 Vice Pres/Dean of the Faculty .... Dr. Amy MARCUS-NEWHALL
30 VP for Institutional Advancement .... Mr. Michael ARCHIBALD
10 VP for Business Affairs/Treasurer .... Vacant
32 Vice President of Student Affairs .... Ms. Charlotte JOHNSON
07 Vice President for Enrollment .... Ms. Victoria ROMERO
26 VP for Communications & Marketing .... Ms. Binti HARVEY
29 Asst VP Alumnae & Parent Engagement .... Ms. Nikki KHURANA
101 VP/Secretary of Board of Trustees ...... Ms. Denise NELSON NASH
04 Executive Asst to the President .... Ms. Christine COSTANZA
20 Associate Dean of Faculty .... Dr. Gretchen EDWALDS-GILBERT
15 Director of Human Resources .... Ms. Jennifer L. BERKLAS
09 Dir of Assessment/Inst Research .... Ms. Junelyn PEEPLES
08 Librarian .... Ms. Judy B. HARVEY-SAHAK
06 Registrar .... Ms. Kelly HOGENCAMP
37 Associate Director of Financial Aid .... Ms. Susan CHADWICK
36 Director of Career Planning .... Ms. Vicki P. KLOPSCH
13 Director of Information Technology .... Mr. Jeff SESSLER
18 Director of Facilities .... Mr. Josh REEDER
104 Director of Off-Campus Study .... Ms. Neva BARKER

The Scripps Research Institute (A)

10550 N Torrey Pines Road, TPC19,
La Jolla CA 92037-1000

County: San Diego FICE Identification: 033213
Unit ID: 435338
Telephone: (858) 784-8469 Carnegie Class: Not Classified
FAX Number: (858) 784-2802 Calendar System: Quarter
URL: www.scripps.edu
Established: 1989 Annual Graduate Tuition & Fees: $5,000
Enrollment: 239 Coed
Affiliation or Control: Independent Non-Profit IRS Status: 501(c)3
Highest Offering: Doctorate; No Undergraduates
Program: Professional
Accreditation: WC

01 Director .... Dr. Dawn L. EASTMOND
05 Dean Graduate Studies .... Dr. James R. WILLIAMSON

Shasta Bible College and Graduate School (B)

2951 Goodwater Avenue, Redding CA 96002-1544

County: Shasta FICE Identification: 023593
Unit ID: 123280
Telephone: (530) 221-4275 Carnegie Class: Spec/Faith
FAX Number: (530) 221-6929 Calendar System: Semester
URL: www.shasta.edu
Established: 1972 Annual Undergrad Tuition & Fees: $11,800
Enrollment: 51 Coed
Affiliation or Control: Independent Non-Profit IRS Status: 501(c)3
Highest Offering: Master's
Program: Religious Emphasis
Accreditation: TRACS

01 President .... Dr. David R. NICHOLAS
04 Exec Assistant to the President .... Mrs. Barbara WELLOCK
05 Academic Dean .... Dr. Stephen G. BROWN
07 Dean of Admissions & Records .... Mr. George A. GUNN
18 Coordinator Grounds & Maintenance .... Mr. Gary KELLOGG
06 Registrar .... Mrs. Faith MCCARTHY
10 Asst Dir Business Affs/Controller .... Mrs. Mary MCENTIRE
37 Financial Aid Officer .... Ms. Linda ILES
56 Director External Studies .... Mrs. Faith MCCARTHY
08 Head Librarian .... Mrs. Virginia M. WILLIAMS
39 Director Student Housing .... Mrs. Donna R. NICHOLAS

Shasta College (C)

PO Box 496006, 11555 Old Oregon Tr,
Redding CA 96049-6006

County: Shasta FICE Identification: 001289
Unit ID: 123299
Telephone: (530) 242-7500 Carnegie Class: Assoc/Pub-R-L
FAX Number: (530) 225-4990 Calendar System: Semester
URL: www.shastacollege.edu
Established: 1950 Annual Undergrad Tuition & Fees (In-District): $1,182
Enrollment: 8,479 Coed
Affiliation or Control: State/Local IRS Status: Exempt
Highest Offering: Associate Degree
Program: Occupational; 2-Year Principally Bachelor's Creditable
Accreditation: WJ, DH

01 Superintendent/President .... Dr. Joe WYSE
04 Asst to Superintendent/President .... Ms. Theresa MARKWORD
102 Executive Director SC Foundation .... Mr. Scott THOMPSON
05 VP Instruction .... Ms. Meridith RANDALL
10 VP Administrative Services .... Mr. Morris RODRIGUE
32 VP of Student Services .... Dr. Kevin O'RORKE
15 Assoc VP of Human Resources .... Ms. Laura CYPHERS BENSON
13 Director of Information Technology .... Mr. James CRANDALL
21 Comptroller .... Ms. Jill AULT
84 Dean Enrollment Services .... Mr. Timothy JOHNSTON
57 Dean Arts/Communication/Soc Science .... Dr. Ralph PERRIN
50 Dean Business/Ag/Ind/Tech/Safety .... Mr. Michael SLOAN
50 Dean EWD .... Ms. Eva JIMENEZ
76 Dean Health Sciences .... Ms. Kathy ROYCE
81 Dean Science/Language Arts/Math .... Dr. Frank NIGRO
56 Dean Extended Education .... Mr. Andy FIELDS
62 Dean Library Services/Educ Tech .... Mr. William BREITBACH
68 Dean Phys Ed and Athletics .... Mr. Mike MARI
35 Assoc Dean Student Services .... Ms. Sandra HAMILTON SLANE
28 Assoc Dean Access and Equity .... Dr. Sharon BRISOLARA
88 Assoc Dean Found Skills/Adult Ed .... Dr. Kate MAHAR
19 Director of Campus Safety .... Mr. Lonnie SEAY
37 Director Financial Aid/Veteran Svcs .... Ms. Becky MCCALL
109 Director Food Services .... Ms. Denise AXTELL
25 Director Grant Development .... Ms. Amy SCHUTTER
18 Director Physical Plant .... Mr. George ESTRADA
06 Chief Records Technician .... Ms. Sheree WHALEY
88 Supervisor HazMat Compliance Pgm .... Mr. Dave FREEMAN
39 Director Residence Life .... Mr. Stevan CROSS

Shepherd University School of Theology (D)

3200 N. Fernando Road, Los Angeles CA 90065

County: Los Angeles Identification: 667056
Telephone: (323) 550-8888 Carnegie Class: Not Classified
FAX Number: N/A Calendar System: Semester
URL: shepherduniversity.edu
Established: 1999 Annual Undergrad Tuition & Fees: $8,200
Enrollment: 51 Coed
Affiliation or Control: Interdenominational IRS Status: 501(c)3
Highest Offering: Doctorate
Program: Religious Emphasis
Accreditation: @WC, ACICS, THEOL

05 Vice Pres & Academic Dean .... Shalom Y. KIM

Sierra College (E)

5000 Rocklin Road, Rocklin CA 95677-3397

County: Placer FICE Identification: 001290
Unit ID: 123341
Telephone: (916) 624-3333 Carnegie Class: Assoc/Pub-S-MC
FAX Number: N/A Calendar System: Semester
URL: www.sierracollege.edu
Established: 1914 Annual Undergrad Tuition & Fees (In-District): $1,390
Enrollment: 18,565 Coed
Affiliation or Control: State/Local IRS Status: 501(c)3
Highest Offering: Associate Degree
Program: Occupational; 2-Year Principally Bachelor's Creditable
Accreditation: WJ

01 Superintendent/President .... Mr. William H. DUNCAN
05 Supt/Vice President Instruction .... Dr. Debra SUTPHEN
10 Vice Pres Administrative Services .... Mr. Chris YATOOMA
32 Vice Pres Student Services .... Ms. Mandy DAVIES
04 Exec Assistant Presidents Office .... Ms. Jeannette BISCHOFF
08 Dean Library/Learning Resource Ctr .... Ms. Sabrina PAPE
50 Dean Business & Technology .... Ms. Sonja LOLLAND
81 Dean Science & Mathematics .... Ms. Heather ROBERTS
49 Dean Liberal Arts .... Dr. Rebecca BOCCHICCHIO
68 Dean Phys Educ/Athletics Director .... Mr. Lucas MOOSMAN
09 Dean Planning/Research/Res Devel .... Mr. Erik COOPER
66 Dean Nursing .... Ms. Nancy SCHWAB
21 Director of Finance .... Vacant
15 Director Human Resources .... Mr. Cameron ABBOTT
18 Dir of Facilities & Construction .... Ms. Laura DOTY
88 Director Economic Development .... Vacant
37 Manager Financial Aid .... Dr. Linda WILLIAMS
31 Community Education Pgm Manager .... Ms. Jill ALCORN
22 EEO Program Manager .... Mr. Cameron ABBOTT
26 Manager Marketing/Public Relations .... Ms. Sue MICHAELS
39 Residence Life Supervisor .... Vacant
07 Manager of Admissions & Records .... Ms. Gail MODDER

Silicon Valley University (F)

2010 Fortune Drive, San Jose CA 95131

County: Santa Clara FICE Identification: 038103
Unit ID: 444848
Telephone: (408) 435-8989 Carnegie Class: Master's S
FAX Number: (408) 955-0887 Calendar System: Trimester
URL: www.svuca.edu
Established: 1997 Annual Undergrad Tuition & Fees: $11,700
Enrollment: 725 Coed
Affiliation or Control: Independent Non-Profit IRS Status: 501(c)3
Highest Offering: Master's
Program: Professional
Accreditation: ACICS

01 President .... Mr. Jerry SHIAO
05 Associate Academic Dean .... Mr. Simon AU
06 Registrar .... Mr. Kevin CHENG

Simpson University (G)

2211 College View Drive, Redding CA 96003-8606

County: Shasta FICE Identification: 001291
Unit ID: 123457
Telephone: (530) 224-5600 Carnegie Class: Bac/A&S
FAX Number: (530) 226-4860 Calendar System: Other
URL: www.simpsonu.edu
Established: 1921 Annual Undergrad Tuition & Fees: $25,200
Enrollment: 1,267 Coed
Affiliation or Control: The Christian And Missionary Alliance
IRS Status: 501(c)3
Highest Offering: Master's
Program: 2-Year Principally Bachelor's Creditable; Liberal Arts And General; Teacher Preparatory; Professional; Nursing Emphasis
Accreditation: WC

01 President .... Dr. Robin K. DUMMER
03 Executive Vice President .... Mr. Bradley E. WILLIAMS
05 Provost .... Dr. Gayle COPELAND
102 VP of Advancement/Marketing .... Vacant
32 Associate VP Student Development .... Dr. Michael LOOMIS
84 VP Enrollment Management .... Dr. Thomas SHAW
20 Associate Provost .... Dr. Ann S. MILLER
10 Controller .... Ms. Natalie E. MCKENZIE
18 Director of Facilities .... Mr. Merlin D. WEBER
04 Exec Assistant to the President .... Mrs. Regina ERICKSON
08 Dir Lib Svcs/Ast Prof Librarianship .... Mr. Larry L. HAIGHT
06 Registrar .... Mr. Harold E. LUND
88 Assoc Registrar for Records/Advis .... Ms. Cassandra A. HEATH
13 Director of IT .... Mr. Michael SUMPTION
41 Director of Athletics .... Mr. Thomas GALBRAITH
35 Director of Residence Life .... Mr. Mark ENDRASKE
38 Director of Wellness Center .... Ms. Beverly G. KLAIBER
09 Dir Institutional Research/Assess .... Ms. Jennifer FOX
39 Bookstore Manager .... Mrs. Kaitlin EVANS
15 Director of Human Resources .... Mrs. Kori D. OECHSLI
109 Director of Auxiliary Services .... Mr. Paul R. DAVIS
26 Director of Marketing .... Mr. Mark U. WOOD
42 Campus Pastor .... Vacant
23 Health Center Coordinator .... Mrs. Connie C. ECHOLS
36 Career Services Manager .... Ms. Karin STRUBE
51 Dean Adult Studies/Online Programs .... Dr. John BURLISON
73 Dean AW Tozer Seminary .... Dr. Patrick A. BLEWETT
54 Dean Educ/Assoc Prof Education .... Dr. Glee R. BROOKS
37 Director Student Financial Services .... Mrs. Melissa A. HUDSON
66 Dean School of Nursing .... Mrs. Kristie STEPHENS
107 Dean School Graduate Prof Studies .... Dr. Addie R. JACKSON
88 Director of Retention .... Mr. Adam PORCELLA
35 Director of Student Engagement .... Ms. Amber WELLS-KELLY

Sofia University (formerly Institute of Transpersonal Psychology) (H)

1069 E Meadow Circle, Palo Alto CA 94303-4231

County: Santa Clara FICE Identification: 022676
Unit ID: 110778
Telephone: (650) 493-4430 Carnegie Class: Spec/Health
FAX Number: (650) 493-6835 Calendar System: Quarter
URL: www.sofia.edu
Established: 1975 Annual Graduate Tuition & Fees: $31,025
Enrollment: 314 Coed
Affiliation or Control: Independent Non-Profit IRS Status: 501(c)3
Highest Offering: Doctorate; No Undergraduates
Program: Professional
Accreditation: WC

01 President & CEO .... Dr. Qiaoyun (Liz) LI
05 Dean of Faculty .... Dr. Barbara HECKER
10 Accounting Manager .... Ms. Linyan LIU
30 Vice President for Advancement .... Ms. Tracy BYARS
45 Vice Pres Strategic Planning .... Ms. Sara JAVID
09 Director of Institutional Research .... Dr. John HOFMANN
32 Dean Student Services .... Ms. Rosalie COOK
15 Director of Human Resources .... Mr. Mark DUNAWAY
37 Director Student Financial Aid .... Ms. Eufemia AQUINO
18 Facilities Manager .... Mr. Jorge ALEMAN
26 Director of Public Relations .... Ms. Liane LOUIE-BADUA

Soka University of America (I)

1 University Drive, Aliso Viejo CA 92656-8081

County: Orange FICE Identification: 038144
Unit ID: 399911
Telephone: (949) 480-4000 Carnegie Class: Bac/A&S
FAX Number: (949) 480-4001 Calendar System: Semester
URL: www.soka.edu
Established: 2001 Annual Undergrad Tuition & Fees: $28,938
Enrollment: 417 Coed
Affiliation or Control: Independent Non-Profit IRS Status: 501(c)3
Highest Offering: Master's
Program: Liberal Arts And General
Accreditation: WC

01 President/Professor of Economics .... Dr. Daniel Y. HABUKI
04 Exec Asst to the President .... Mr. Hiro SAKAI
05 Provost/Vice Pres Academic Affairs .... Dr. Edward M. FEASEL
10 Vice President Finance & Admin/CFO .... Mr. Archibald E. ASAWA
09 VP Inst Rsch/Dean of Graduate Sch .... Dr. Tomoko TAKAHASHI
20 Dean of Faculty/CAO .... Dr. Edward M. FEASEL
84 Dean of Enrollment Services .... Mr. Andrew WOOLSEY
32 Dean of Students .... Dr. John M. HEFFRON
19 Director Safety/Security/Events .... Mr. Clifford MOSHER
31 Director of Community Relations .... Ms. Wendy WETZEL HARDER
41 Director of Athletics & Recreation .... Mr. Mike MOORE
35 Director of Student Services .... Dr. Hyon MOON
39 Dir Stdnt Activities/Resident Life .... Ms. Michelle HOBBY-MEARS
30 Director of Philanthropy .... Ms. Linda KENNEDY
13 Director Information Technology .... Mr. John MIN
44 Dir of International Development .... Ms. Toshiko SATO
15 Director of Human Resources .... Ms. Katherine KING
104 Dir Study Abroad & Intl Internships .... Mr. Alex H. OKUDA
06 Registrar .... Ms. Nancy YOSHIMURA
18 Chief of Operations .... Mr. Tom HARKENRIDER
84 Mgr Student Recruitment Programs .... Ms. Marilyn GOVE
08 Director of Library .... Mr. Hiroko TONONO

Solano Community College (J)

4000 Suisun Valley Road, Fairfield CA 94534-3197

County: Solano FICE Identification: 001292
Unit ID: 123563
Telephone: (707) 864-7000 Carnegie Class: Assoc/Pub-S-SC
FAX Number: (707) 864-0361 Calendar System: Semester
URL: www.solano.edu
Established: 1945 Annual Undergrad Tuition & Fees (In-District): $1,380
Enrollment: 9,718 Coed
Affiliation or Control: State/Local IRS Status: 501(c)3
Highest Offering: Associate Degree
Program: Occupational; 2-Year Principally Bachelor's Creditable
Accreditation: WJ

01 Superintendent/President .... Mr. Stan R. ARTERBERRY
05 VP Academic Affairs .... Ms. Leslie MINOR
10 Vice President Finance & Admin .... Mr. Yulian LIGIOSO
13 Chief Technology Officer .... Mr. Roger CLAGUE
32 Vice President Student Services .... Dr. Gregory BROWN

38 Interim Dean Counseling ... Ms. Jocelyn MOUTON
37 Associate Dean Financial Aid ... Ms. Robin DARCANGELO
09 Dean Research and Planning ... Mr. Peter CAMMISH
21 Director of Fiscal Services ... Mr. Patrick KILLINGSWORTH
07 Associate Dean Admissions/Records ... Vacant
84 Director Enrollment Management ... Vacant
15 Associate VP Human Resources ... Dr. Wade LARSON
18 Director Facilities ... Mr. Dwight CALLOWAY
35 Dir Student Development/Mesa ... Dr. Jose BALLESTEROS
06 Registrar ... Vacant
13 Director Technology Services ... Vacant
88 Director Children's Programs ... Ms. Christie SPECK
88 Director Small Bus Development Ctr ... Ms. Kelly PENWELL
88 Director Theater Operations ... Vacant
26 Outreach/Public Relations Manager ... Ms. Shemila JOHNSON
96 Purchasing Tech/Buyer ... Ms. Laura SCOTT
36 Career & Job Placement Coordinator ... Ms. Patricia YOUNG
49 Dean School of Liberal Arts ... Mr. Neil GLINES
83 Int Dean Sch of Social & Behav Sci ... Dr. Keydron GUINN
81 Dean School Math/Science ... Dr. John YU
76 Dn Sch Career Tech Ed/Bus/Vcvl/TAFB ... Mrs. Maire MORINEC
12 Center Dean Vallejo ... Dr. Shirley LEWIS
100 Chief of Staff ... Dr. Yashica CRAWFORD
76 Dean Health Sciences ... Dr. Robert GABRIEL
41 Director of Athletics ... Mr. Erik VISSER

South Baylo University (A)

1126 N Brookhurst Street, Anaheim CA 92801-1702
County: Orange FICE Identification: 025973
Unit ID: 123633
Telephone: (714) 533-1495 Carnegie Class: Spec/Health
FAX Number: (714) 533-6040 Calendar System: Quarter
URL: www.southbaylo.edu
Established: 1977 Annual Undergrad Tuition & Fees: $12,104
Enrollment: 690 Coed
Affiliation or Control: Independent Non-Profit IRS Status: 501(c)3
Highest Offering: Doctorate
Program: Professional
Accreditation: ACUP

01 President ... Dr. Jason SHIN
05 Academic Dean ... Dr. Pia MELEN
11 Vice President Administration ... Dr. David KWON
07 Director of Admission ... Dr. Young Jin AHN
06 Registrar ... Ms. Christina PARK
10 Director of Finance ... Ms. Michelle JANG
15 Operations/Personnel Director ... Dr. Sohila MOHIYEDDINI
36 Program Student Advisor ... Dr. Henry CHOI
08 Director of Libraries ... Dr. Edwin FOLLICK
13 Dir Computer Information System ... Mr. James KIM
88 Director of Clinics ... Dr. Sang Jo KIM
37 Financial Aid Officer ... Ms. Mimi PARK
32 Stdnt/Alumni/English LG Coordinator ... Vacant
85 International Student Advisor ... Ms. Sue LEE
88 Doctoral Clerkship Coordinator ... Dr. Sheng LI
88 Doctoral Program Director ... Dr. Wayne CHENG
88 Master Program Director ... Dr. Hanjik KIM
18 Chief Facilities/Physical Plant ... Mr. Yong Hee PARK

South Baylo University (B)

2727 West 6th Street, Los Angeles CA 90057
Telephone: (213) 738-0712 Identification: 770911
Accreditation: ACUP

† Branch campus of South Baylo University, Anaheim, CA.

South Coast College (C)

2011 W Chapman Avenue, Orange CA 92868-2609
County: Orange FICE Identification: 022774
Unit ID: 123642
Telephone: (714) 867-5009 Carnegie Class: Assoc/PrivFP
FAX Number: (714) 867-5026 Calendar System: Quarter
URL: www.southcoastcollege.com
Established: 1961 Annual Undergrad Tuition & Fees: $42,750
Enrollment: 342 Coed
Affiliation or Control: Proprietary IRS Status: Proprietary
Highest Offering: Associate Degree
Program: Occupational
Accreditation: ACICS

01 President ... Ms. Jean GONZALEZ
03 Vice President ... Ms. Lonnie SKELTON
10 Dean Finance & Operations ... Ms. Jila ANDELIBI
11 Director of Operations ... Mr. Kevin MAGNER
37 Director of Financial Aid ... Mr. Michael LY
06 Registrar ... Ms. Yoshiko IZUMI

*South Orange County Community College District (D)

28000 Marguerite Parkway, Mission Viejo CA 92692-3697
County: Orange FICE Identification: 033433
Unit ID: 432144
Telephone: (949) 582-4500 Carnegie Class: N/A
FAX Number: (949) 364-2726
URL: www.socccd.edu

01 Chancellor ... Mr. Gary POERTNER
05 Vice Chanc Technology/Learning Svcs .. Dr. Robert S. BRAMUCCI
15 Vice Chancellor Human Resources ... Dr. David P. BUGAY
10 Vice Chancellor Business Services ... Ms. Debra FITZSIMONS
26 Dir Public Affairs/Government Rels ... Ms. Tere FLUEGEMAN
84 Dean for Enrollment Services ... Ms. Arleen ELSEROAD

*Irvine Valley College (E)

5500 Irvine Center Drive, Irvine CA 92618-4399
County: Orange FICE Identification: 025395
Unit ID: 116439
Telephone: (949) 451-5100 Carnegie Class: Assoc/Pub-S-MC
FAX Number: (949) 451-5270 Calendar System: Semester
URL: www.ivc.edu
Established: 1979 Annual Undergrad Tuition & Fees (In-District): $1,438
Enrollment: 13,157 Coed
Affiliation or Control: State/Local IRS Status: 501(c)3
Highest Offering: Associate Degree
Program: Occupational; 2-Year Principally Bachelor's Creditable
Accreditation: WJ

02 President ... Dr. Glenn R. ROQUEMORE
05 Vice President Instruction ... Dr. Stephen C. JUSTICE
32 Vice President Student Services ... Dr. Linda FONTANILLA
10 Vice President Admin Services ... Mr. Davit KHACHATRYAN
20 Dean Instruction/EWD ... Dr. Corine DOUGHTY
38 Dean Sch Guidance/Counseling ... Dr. Elizabeth CIPRES
79 Dean School Humanities ... Dr. Karima FELDHUS
54 Dean Sch Math/Computer Sci/Engrng ... Dr. Lianna ZHAO
50 Dean School Business Sciences ... Dr. Cathleen GREINER
76 Dean Kinesiology/Health/Athletics ... Mr. Keith SHACKLEFORD
72 Dean Life Sciences/Technologies ... Dr. Lianna ZHAO
57 Dean Fine Arts/Business Services ... Dr. David GATEWOOD
84 Dean of Enrollment Services ... Ms. Arleen ELSEROAD
102 Exec Director IVC Foundation ... Mr. Richard H. MORLEY
18 Dir Facilities & Maintenance ... Mr. John EDWARDS
19 Chief of Police ... Mr. Will GLEN
37 Director Financial Aid ... Vacant
35 Director Student Life ... Ms. Anissa HEARD
13 Director Technology Services ... Mr. Bruce HAGAN
09 Dir Research/Planning/Accreditation ... Dr. Craig HAYWARD
26 Director of Public Info & Marketing ... Ms. Diane G. OAKS
88 Child Development Center Manager ... Ms. Becky THOMAS
06 Registrar/Admissions/Records ... Mr. Ruben GUZMAN

*Saddleback College (F)

28000 Marguerite Parkway, Mission Viejo CA 92692-3635
County: Orange FICE Identification: 008918
Unit ID: 122205
Telephone: (949) 582-4500 Carnegie Class: Assoc/Pub-S-MC
FAX Number: (949) 347-0438 Calendar System: Semester
URL: www.saddleback.edu
Established: 1968 Annual Undergrad Tuition & Fees (In-District): $1,142
Enrollment: 25,594 Coed
Affiliation or Control: State/Local IRS Status: 501(c)3
Highest Offering: Associate Degree
Program: Occupational; 2-Year Principally Bachelor's Creditable
Accreditation: WJ, ADNUR, EMT

02 President ... Dr. Tod A. BURNETT
05 Vice President of Instruction ... Dr. Kathy WERLE
32 Vice President of Student Services ... Dr. Juan AVALOS
84 Int Dean of Enrollment Services ... Mr. Christian ALVARADO
45 Director Planning/Research/Grants ... Ms. Nicole ORTEGA
06 Registrar ... Ms. Joyce SEMANIK
19 Chief Of Police ... Mr. Pat HIGA
26 Director Public Information ... Ms. Jennie MCCUE
102 Director College Foundation ... Mr. Donald RICKNER
35 Director Student Development ... Ms. Audra DIPADOVA
31 Dean Cmty Educ/El & K-12 Partnership ... Ms. Estella GARRISON
88 Director of Emeritus Institute ... Mr. Dan PREDOEHL
66 Director of Nursing ... Ms. Tammy RICE
10 VP College Administrative Services ... Ms. Carol HILTON
15 Director Human Resources ... Ms. Teddi LORCH
18 Dir Facilities/Maint/Operation ... Mr. John OZUROVICH
37 Director Financial Assistance ... Mr. Christian ALVARADO
96 Director of Purchasing ... Ms. Brandye D'LENA
85 Intl Student Program Specialist ... Ms. Monika CONNOLLY
92 Honors Program ... Ms. Alannah ROSENBERG
38 Dean Counseling Svcs/Special Pgms ... Ms. Jerilyn CHUMAN
57 Dean Fine Arts ... Mr. Bart MCHENRY
50 Dean Bus/Science/Economic/Workforce ... Mr. John JARAMILLO
76 Dean Hlth Sci/Human Svcs & Emeritus ... Dr. Donna RANE-SZOSTAK
81 Dean Math/Science & Engineering ... Dr. Christopher MCDONALD
79 Dean Liberal Arts/Learning Res ... Dr. Kevin O'CONNOR
106 Dean Online Education/Learning Res ... Dr. Marina AMINY
72 Dean Advance Tech Appl Science ... Dr. Anthony TENG
68 Dean Kinesiology/Athletic Director ... Mr. Tony LIPOLD
83 Dean Social & Behavioral Sciences ... Dr. Cadence WYNTER
35 Asst Dean Couns Svcs/Spec Pgms ... Mr. Terence NELSON
103 Dir Economic/Workforce Development ... Mr. Israel DOMINGUEZ

Southern California Institute of Architecture (G)

960 E 3rd Street, Los Angeles CA 90013-1822
County: Los Angeles FICE Identification: 020758
Unit ID: 123952
Telephone: (213) 613-2200 Carnegie Class: Spec/Arts
FAX Number: (213) 613-2260 Calendar System: Semester
URL: www.sciarc.edu
Established: 1972 Annual Undergrad Tuition & Fees: $42,220
Enrollment: 523 Coed
Affiliation or Control: Independent Non-Profit IRS Status: 501(c)3
Highest Offering: Master's
Program: Professional
Accreditation: WC

01 Director ... Mr. Eric O. MOSS
04 Director's Assistant ... Ms. Jessica WHEELER
05 Director Academic Affairs ... Ms. Hsin-Ming FUNG
11 Chief Operating Officer ... Mr. Jamie BENNETT
13 Chief Information Officer ... Mr. Vic JABRASSIAN
30 Assoc Director Development ... Ms. Maria ROBINSON GLOVER
58 Graduate Program Chair ... Mr. Hernan DIAZ-ALONSO
88 Undergraduate Program Chair ... Mr. John ENRIGHT
05 Academic Affairs Manager ... Mr. Paul HOLLIDAY
20 Admin/Academic Affairs Assistant ... Ms. Nicole FISHER
10 Finance Director ... Mr. Christopher BANKS
07 Admissions Director ... Ms. Sandy FRIGO
37 Financial Aid Manager ... Mr. Pierre FLOOD
08 Library Manager ... Mr. Kevin MCMAHON
88 Wood & Metal Shop Manager ... Mr. Rodney ROJAS
88 Wood & Metal Shopmaster ... Mr. Katsumi MOROI
20 Academic Counselor ... Mr. Peter DUNG
06 Registrar/International Advisor ... Ms. Lisa RUSSO
18 Facilities Manager ... Mr. Andrew WERNER

Southern California Institute of Technology (H)

525 North Muller Street, Anaheim CA 92805-3758
County: Orange FICE Identification: 031136
Unit ID: 399869
Telephone: (714) 300-0300 Carnegie Class: Bac/Diverse
FAX Number: (714) 300-0311 Calendar System: Quarter
URL: www.scitech.edu
Established: 1987 Annual Undergrad Tuition & Fees: $16,000
Enrollment: 470 Coed
Affiliation or Control: Proprietary IRS Status: Proprietary
Highest Offering: Baccalaureate
Program: Technical Emphasis
Accreditation: ACCSC

01 President ... Dr. Parviz SHAMS
03 Vice President ... Mrs. Nazila SHAMS
05 Dean of Education ... Mr. Saravana RAMAN
13 MIS ... Mr. Arian SHAMS

Southern California Seminary (I)

2075 E Madison Avenue, El Cajon CA 92019-1108
County: San Diego FICE Identification: 033323
Unit ID: 117575
Telephone: (619) 201-8999 Carnegie Class: Spec/Faith
FAX Number: (619) 201-8975 Calendar System: Trimester
URL: www.socalsem.edu
Established: 1946 Annual Undergrad Tuition & Fees: $14,244
Enrollment: 201 Coed
Affiliation or Control: Independent Non-Profit IRS Status: 501(c)3
Highest Offering: Doctorate
Program: Religious Emphasis
Accreditation: TRACS

00 Chancellor ... Dr. Chuck EMERT
01 President ... Dr. Gary F. COOMBS
05 Vice President for Academics (CAO) ... Dr. Christopher CONE
32 Vice President of Student Services ... Dr. Gino PASQUARIELLO
58 Dean Graduate Biblical Studies ... Dr. Christopher CONE
83 Dean Grad Sch Behavioral Science ... Dr. Julie M. HAYDEN
73 Dean of Biblical Studies/Theology ... Mr. James I. FAZIO
06 Registrar ... Mrs. Cheryl OBST
37 Director of Financial Aid ... Mrs. Yuli MARTINEZ
08 Seminary Librarian ... Miss Jennifer EWING
07 Director of Admissions ... Mr. Bill GEORGE

Southern California University of Health Sciences (J)

16200 E Amber Valley Drive, Whittier CA 90604-4051
County: Los Angeles FICE Identification: 001229
Unit ID: 117672
Telephone: (562) 947-8755 Carnegie Class: Spec/Health
FAX Number: (562) 947-5724 Calendar System: Trimester
URL: www.scuhs.edu
Established: 1911 Annual Undergrad Tuition & Fees: $23,190
Enrollment: 876 Coed
Affiliation or Control: Independent Non-Profit IRS Status: 501(c)3
Highest Offering: First Professional Degree
Program: Professional
Accreditation: WC, ACUP, CHIRO

01 President ... Dr. John SCARINGE
05 Vice President of Academic Affs ... Dr. J. Todd KNUDSEN
30 VP Inst Advance/Enrol Mgt/Sdnt Aff ... Mrs. Debra MITCHELL BENAVENTE
11 VP Admin & Finance/CFO ... Mr. Thomas K. ARENDT
17 AVP of SCU Health Systems ... Dr. Melissa KIMURA
20 Int CSIH Dean ... Dr. Heidi CROCKER
06 Registrar ... Mrs. Debra MITCHELL BENAVENTE
84 Dir of Enroll Svcs/Fin Aid ... Ms. Kate MCCUNE
04 Exec Asst to President/BOR ... Mrs. Regina TORRES-ELLIS

20 AVPAA Teaching/Learning/Leadership .... Dr. Noni THREINEN
07 Dir of Admissions .... Mr. Jeff CORRAL
88 Dean of Chiropractic .... Dr. Mike SACKETT
88 Int Dean College of Eastern Med .... Dr. Bob DAMONE
13 Executive Director IT .... Ms. Theresa EGGLESTON
21 Controller .... Mrs. Kelly GALLO
10 Director of Auxillary Services .... Mr. Joseph EGGLESTON
09 Dean OSIE .... Dr. Heather VANVOLKINBURG
32 Director of Student Affairs .... Dr. Steven R. JAFFE
26 Director of Marketing .... Ms. Carolyn MATTHIES
08 Exec Dir of Seabury Learning Center .... Ms. Kathleen E. SMITH
96 Accounts Payable/Purchasing Coord .... Mrs. Catherine MCBRIDE
37 Asst Financial Aid Director .... Ms. Nida LABAO

Southern California University School of Oriental Medicine & Acupuncture (A)

3460 Wilshire Boulevard, Los Angeles CA 90010
County: Los Angeles FICE Identification: 041720
Unit ID: 459222
Telephone: (213) 413-9500 Carnegie Class: Spec/Health
FAX Number: (213) 413-5400 Calendar System: Quarter
URL: www.scusoma.edu
Established: Annual Undergrad Tuition & Fees: $12,000
Enrollment: 119 Coed
Affiliation or Control: Proprietary IRS Status: Proprietary
Highest Offering: Master's
Program: Professional
Accreditation: ACUP

01 President .... Ms. Judy OH
05 Academic Dean .... Dr. Katherine H S. CHO
06 Registrar/Student Services .... Ms. Sung Uk PARK
37 Director of Financial Aid .... Mr. Roberto QUINONES
07 Director of Admissions .... Ms. Sung Uk PARK

Southern States University (B)

1601 Dove Street, Suite 105, Newport Beach CA 92660
Telephone: (949) 833-8868 Identification: 770629
Accreditation: ACICS

† Branch campus of Southern States University, San Diego, CA.

Southern States University (C)

123 Camino de la Reina Ste 100 East, San Diego CA 92108
County: San Diego Identification: 667108
Telephone: (619) 298-1829 Carnegie Class: Not Classified
FAX Number: (619) 704-0175 Calendar System: Quarter
URL: www.ssu.edu
Established: 1985 Annual Undergrad Tuition & Fees: $6,000
Enrollment: 1,000 Coed
Affiliation or Control: Proprietary IRS Status: Proprietary
Highest Offering: Master's
Program: Business Emphasis
Accreditation: ACICS

01 Chancellor .... John D. TUCKER
05 Vice Chanc Academic Affairs/CAO .... Dr. Claudia ARAIZA
06 University Registrar .... Luke MARTIN
32 Dean of Students & Admissions .... William AMOKE
08 University Librarian .... Mary Kate DURKEE
10 Finance & Human Resources Manager .... Ruby WANG

Southwestern College (D)

900 Otay Lakes Road, Chula Vista CA 91910-7299
County: San Diego FICE Identification: 001294
Unit ID: 123800
Telephone: (619) 421-6700 Carnegie Class: Assoc/Pub-S-SC
FAX Number: (619) 482-6413 Calendar System: Semester
URL: www.swccd.edu
Established: 1961 Annual Undergrad Tuition & Fees (In-District): $1,336
Enrollment: 18,409 Coed
Affiliation or Control: State/Local IRS Status: 501(c)3
Highest Offering: Associate Degree
Program: Occupational; 2-Year Principally Bachelor's Creditable
Accreditation: WJ, ADNUR, DH, EMT, MLTAD, SURGT

01 Superintendent/President .... Dr. Melinda NISH
05 Vice President Academic Affairs .... Ms. Kathy TYNER
10 VP Business & Financial Affairs .... Mr. Steven CROW
32 Vice President Student Affairs .... Dr. Angelica SUAREZ
15 Vice Pres Employee Services .... Mr. John D R. CLARK
12 Dn High Ed Ctr Otay Mesa/San Ysidro .... Ms. Silvia CORNEJO
12 Dean HEC Natl City/Crown Cove .... Ms. Christine PERRI
79 Dean Language & Literature .... Dr. Joel LEVINE
81 Dean Math/Science Engineering .... Ms. Janet MAZZARELLA
30 Dean Inst Effect/Dir of Foundation .... Ms. Linda GILSTRAP
35 Dean Student Svcs/Student Develop .... Ms. Mia C. MCCLELLAN
83 Dean Social Sci/Business/Humanities .... Dr. Mark MEADOWS
38 Dean Couns/Student Support Pgms .... Ms. Beatrice ZAMORA-AGUILAR
68 Dean Hlth/Exer Sci/Athltc/App Tech .... Mr. Terry DAVIS
88 Dean Instructional Support Services .... Dr. Mink STAVENGA
26 Chief Comm Cmty & Gov Rels Officer .... Ms. Lillian LEOPOLD
16 Director Human Resources .... Mr. Marvin CASTILLO
88 Director Payroll Services .... Ms. Desiree KLAAR
09 Dir Inst Rsrch Grants & Planning .... Ms. Linda HENSLEY
40 Director Food Services/Bookstore .... Mr. Joe FIGHERA
88 Dir Center Ops San Ysidro .... Ms. Cynthia K. NAGURA
88 Director Crown Cove Aq Ctr .... Ms. Patrice MILKOVICH
37 Director Financial Aid .... Ms. Patti LARKIN
07 Director Admissions/Records .... Mr. Nicholas MONTEZ
96 Dir Procurement/Cntrl Svc/Risk Mgt .... Ms. Priya JEROME
54 Dir Math/Engr/Sci Achieve/Mesa Pgm .... Ms. Raga BAKHIET
88 Director Police Academy .... Mr. James DAVIS
88 Director Disability Support Svcs .... Dr. Malia FLOOD
52 Director Dental Hygiene Program .... Ms. Vickie KIMBROUGH-WALLS
66 Director Nursing & Health Occup .... Ms. Cathy MCJANNET
88 Int Director EOPS .... Mr. Omar ORIHUELA
51 Director Cont Educ/Special Projects .... Mr. Steve TADLOCK
21 Director of Finance .... Mr. Wayne YANDA
88 Director Child Development Center .... Ms. Patricia BARTOW
04 Exec Asst to Supt & President .... Ms. Mary GANIO
19 Director Security/Safety .... Mr. Michael CASH
13 Chief Info Technology Officer (CIO) .... Mr. Daniel BORGES
60 Int Dean Arts & Comm .... Ms. Cynthia MCGREGOR

Southwestern Law School (E)

3050 Wilshire Boulevard, Los Angeles CA 90010-1106
County: Los Angeles FICE Identification: 001295
Unit ID: 123970
Telephone: (213) 738-6700 Carnegie Class: Spec/Law
FAX Number: (213) 383-1688 Calendar System: Semester
URL: www.swlaw.edu
Established: 1911 Annual Graduate Tuition & Fees: $48,080
Enrollment: 1,109 Coed
Affiliation or Control: Independent Non-Profit IRS Status: 501(c)3
Highest Offering: Master's; No Undergraduates
Program: Professional
Accreditation: DEAC, LAW

01 Dean/Chief Executive Officer .... Ms. Susan WESTERBERG PRAGER
10 Chief Financial Officer .... Mr. Paul KALUSH
04 Corporate Secretary .... Ms. Janis K. YOKOYAMA
03 Vice Dean .... Ms. Catherine CARPENTER
05 Vice Dean for Academic Affairs .... Ms. Anahid GHARAKHANIAN
32 Dean of Students & Div Aff .... Ms. Nydia DUENEZ
20 Sr Assoc Dean for Academic Admin .... Ms. Doreen E. HEYER
30 Assoc Dean for Institutional Advanc .... Ms. Debra L. LEATHERS
07 Asst Dean of Admissions .... Ms. Lisa L. GEAR
35 Assoc Dean of Student Affairs .... Dr. Robert MENA
37 Director of Financial Aid .... Mr. Matt WAKEMAN
11 Director of Administrative Services .... Ms. Marcie CANAL
13 Chief Information Systems Officer .... Ms. Bo SUZOW

Stanbridge College (F)

2041 Business Center Dr., Suite 107, Irvine CA 92612
County: Orange FICE Identification: 038893
Unit ID: 446561
Telephone: (949) 794-9090 Carnegie Class: Assoc/PrivFP
FAX Number: (949) 794-9098 Calendar System: Other
URL: www.stanbridge.edu
Established: 1996 Annual Undergrad Tuition & Fees: $34,995
Enrollment: 1,660 Coed
Affiliation or Control: Proprietary IRS Status: Proprietary
Highest Offering: Master's
Program: Occupational; 2-Year Principally Bachelor's Creditable; Professional; Nursing Emphasis
Accreditation: ACCSC, NURSE, OTA, PTAA

01 Chief Executive Officer .... Yasith WEERASURIYA
10 Chief Financial Officer .... Nazi MASOUM
37 Director of Financial Aid .... Brian SILVANO
07 Director of Admissions .... Edward RIEPMA
05 VP of Instruction .... Dr. Everett PROCTER
66 Director of Nursing .... Kim MARTIN
66 RN-BSN & MSN Program Director .... Dr. Judith MCLEOD
75 Director of Occupational Therapy .... Satch PURCELL
75 MSOT Program Director .... Dr. Janis DAVIS
88 Director of Physical Therapy .... Elizabeth PEYTON
106 Asst Director of Online Programs .... Jered MADRID
20 Dean of Instruction .... Tim POWERS
32 Dean of Students .... Susan DUNN
36 Director of Career Services .... Vacant
105 VP of Internet and Media Technology .... Monir BOKTOR
74 Asst Program Director ASVT .... Emma CUSACK
74 Asst Program Director ASVT .... Karen HARTMAN
06 Registrar .... Stephanie ISNALI
08 Librarian .... Kate ARAS
29 Alumni & Community Service Coord .... Nataly MCBRIDE

Stanford University (G)

450 Serra Mall, Stanford CA 94305-2004
County: Santa Clara FICE Identification: 001305
Unit ID: 243744
Telephone: (650) 723-2300 Carnegie Class: RU/VH
FAX Number: (650) 725-6847 Calendar System: Quarter
URL: www.stanford.edu
Established: 1885 Annual Undergrad Tuition & Fees: $45,729
Enrollment: 16,795 Coed
Affiliation or Control: Independent Non-Profit IRS Status: 501(c)3
Highest Offering: Doctorate
Program: Liberal Arts And General; Professional
Accreditation: WC, ARCPA, BUS, ENG, IPSY, LAW, MED, PDPSY, TED

01 President .... Mr. John L. HENNESSY
43 Vice President & General Counsel .... Ms. Debra L. ZUMWALT
05 Provost .... Mr. John W. ETCHEMENDY
30 Vice President for Development .... Mr. Martin SHELL
10 Vice President Business Affairs/CFO .... Mr. Randy LIVINGSTON
26 Vice President for Public Affairs .... Mr. David F. DEMAREST
29 President of Alumni Associaton .... Mr. Howard E. WOLF
46 Vice Provost/Dean of Research .... Dr. Ann ARVIN
20 Vice Provost for Academic Affairs .... Dr. Stephanie KALFAYAN
88 Vice Provost Faculty Development .... Ms. Karen COOK
20 Vice Provost Undergrad Education .... Mr. Harry J. ELAM
18 Vice Provost for Land & Buildings .... Mr. Robert C. REIDY
109 Vice Provost Budget & Auxiliaries .... Mr. Timothy R. WARNER
32 Vice Provost Student Affairs .... Mr. Gregory E. BOARDMAN
04 Sr Assistant to the President .... Mr. Jeffrey H. WACHTEL
63 Dean School of Medicine .... Dr. Lloyd MINOR
50 Dean Graduate School Business .... Dr. Garth SALONER
65 Dean School of Earth Sciences .... Dr. Pamela A. MATSON
53 Dean School of Education .... Dr. Deborah STIPEK
54 Dean School of Engineering .... Dr. Persis DRELL
49 Dean School Humanities & Sciences .... Mr. Richard P. SALLER
61 Dean School of Law .... Ms. M. Elizabeth MAGILL
87 Dean Summer Session/Cont Stds .... Dr. Charles L. JUNKERMAN
42 Dean for Religious Life .... Rev. Jane SHAW
88 Director Hoover Institution .... Dr. John RAISIAN
88 Director Stanford Lin Accelerator .... Mr. Chi-Chang KAO
13 Executive Director IT Services .... Mr. Bill CLEBSCH
08 University Librarian .... Mr. Michael A. KELLER
41 Athletic Director .... Mr. Bernard MUIR
07 Director of Admission .... Ms. Colleen LIM
88 CEO Stanford Management Company .... Mr. John POWERS
15 Director of Compensation .... Ms. Linda S. LEE
21 Director of Business Development .... Ms. Susan L. WEINSTEIN
06 Registrar .... Mr. Thomas BLACK
36 Director Career Development Center .... Mr. Farouk DEY
09 Dir Inst Research/Assessment .... Ms. Kathleen DETTMAN
37 Director of Student Financial Aid .... Ms. Karen S. COOPER
27 Director Stanford News Service .... Mr. Dan STOBER
19 Director Public Safety .... Ms. Laura L. WILSON
96 Chief Procurement Officer .... Mr. Ben MORENO
35 Director of Student Activities .... Ms. Nanci HOWE
38 Director Student Counseling .... Dr. Ronald ALBURCHER
101 Secretary of the Board of Trustees .... Mr. Phil TAUBMAN
102 Dir Foundation/Corporate Relations .... Ms. Kathy VEIT
104 Director Study Abroad .... Ms. Irene KENNEDY
105 Director Web Services .... Mr. Scott STOCKER
39 Director Student Housing .... Mr. Roger WHITNEY

Stanton University (H)

9618 Garden Grove Boulevard, 2nd Fl, Garden Grove CA 92844
County: Orange Identification: 667053
Telephone: (714) 539-6561 Carnegie Class: Not Classified
FAX Number: (714) 539-6542 Calendar System: Quarter
URL: www.stantonuniversity.com
Established: Annual Undergrad Tuition & Fees: N/A
Enrollment: N/A Coed
Affiliation or Control: Proprietary IRS Status: Proprietary
Highest Offering: Master's
Program: Professional
Accreditation: @ACUP

01 President .... Dr. Franklin R. TURNER

Starr King School for the Ministry (I)

2441 Le Conte Avenue, Berkeley CA 94709-1299
County: Alameda FICE Identification: 004080
Unit ID: 123916
Telephone: (510) 845-6232 Carnegie Class: Spec/Faith
FAX Number: (510) 845-6273 Calendar System: Semester
URL: www.sksm.edu
Established: 1904 Annual Graduate Tuition & Fees: $20,058
Enrollment: 89 Coed
Affiliation or Control: Unitarian Universalist IRS Status: 501(c)3
Highest Offering: Master's; No Undergraduates
Program: Professional
Accreditation: THEOL

01 President .... Rev. Rosemary BRAY MCNATT
05 Provost .... Mr. Ibrahim ABDURRAHMAN FARAJAJE
30 Vice President Advancement .... Ms. Jessica CLOUD
20 Dean of the Faculty .... Dr. Gabriella LETTINI
06 Registrar .... Ms. Katrina CROSWELL
07 Director of Admissions/Recruitment .... Mr. Jeremiah KALENDAE
10 Acting Director Finance .... Mr. Massoud KHALEGHIRAD
106 Director Online Education .... Dr. Hugo CORDOVA QUERO
26 Communications Officer .... Mr. Matt VIOLET

*State Center Community College District (J)

1525 E Weldon Avenue, Fresno CA 93704-6398
County: Fresno FICE Identification: 001306
Unit ID: 123925
Telephone: (559) 226-0720 Carnegie Class: N/A
FAX Number: (559) 229-7039
URL: www.scccd.edu

01 Interim Chancellor ....Dr. Bill F. STEWART
05 Vice President of Instruction ....Dr. Timothy WOODS
10 Vice Chancellor Finance & Admin ....Mr. Edwin ENG
20 Int VC Educ Svcs/Instl Effective ....Dr. Barbara HIOCO
15 Vice Chanc Human Resources ....Ms. Diane CLEROU
11 Assc Vice Chanc Business/Operations .Ms. Christine MIKTARIAN
07 AVC Enroll Mgmt/Admiss & Records/IS ....Mr. Pedro AVILA
16 Director Human Resources ....Ms. Samerah CAMPBELL
26 Int Exec Dir Pub/Legislative Rels ....Ms. Lucy RUIZ
102 Int Executive Director Foundation ....Mr. James MEINERT
25 Int Dir Grants/External Funding ....Ms. Marilyn BEHRINGER
96 Director of Purchasing ....Mr. Randy VOGT
21 Director of Finance ....Mr. William SCHOFIELD
13 Director of Information Systems ....Mr. Scott OLDS
88 Director of Classified Personnel ....Ms. Elba GOMEZ
18 Director Maintenance/Operations ....Mr. Carl SIMMS
43 General Counsel ....Mr. Gregory TAYLOR
19 Chief of Police ....Chief Bruce HARTMAN

*Clovis Community College (A)

10309 N. Willow Avenue, Fresno CA 93730

County: Fresno Identification: 667125
Telephone: (559) 325-5200 Carnegie Class: Not Classified
FAX Number: (559) 499-6065 Calendar System: Semester
URL: www.cloviscenter.com
Established: 2007 Annual Undergrad Tuition & Fees (In-District): $10,300
Enrollment: 6,300 Coed
Affiliation or Control: State/Local IRS Status: 501(c)3
Highest Offering: Associate Degree
Program: Occupational; 2-Year Principally Bachelor's Creditable
Accreditation: WJ

02 President ....Ms. Deborah J. IKEDA
05 VP Instruction & Student Services ....Ms. Kelly FOWLER
10 VP Administrative Services ....Ms. Lorrie HOPPER
20 Dean of Instruction ....Mr. Lee BROWN
32 Dean of Student Services ....Ms. Doris GRIFFIN
13 Director of Technology ....Mr. Gary SAKAGUCHI
37 Financial Aid Manager ....Ms. Candy CANNON
12 Director of Herndon Campus ....Mr. Charles FRANCIS
88 Dir Student Success/Equity/Outrch ....Ms. Gurdeep HEBERT
04 Secretary to the President ....Ms. Linda LITTLE

*Fresno City College (B)

1101 E University Avenue, Fresno CA 93741-0002

County: Fresno FICE Identification: 001307
Unit ID: 114789
Telephone: (559) 442-4600 Carnegie Class: Assoc/Pub-U-MC
FAX Number: (559) 489-2281 Calendar System: Semester
URL: www.fresnocitycollege.edu
Established: 1910 Annual Undergrad Tuition & Fees (In-District): $1,104
Enrollment: 22,701 Coed
Affiliation or Control: State/Local IRS Status: 501(c)3
Highest Offering: Associate Degree
Program: Occupational; 2-Year Principally Bachelor's Creditable
Accreditation: WJ, CAHIIM, COARC, DH, EMT, RAD

02 Interim President ....Dr. Cynthia E. AZARI
05 Vice President of Instruction ....Dr. Timothy WOODS
32 Vice President of Student Services ....Dr. Christopher M. VILLA
10 Vice Pres Administrative Services ....Ms. Cheryl SULLIVAN
07 Dist Dean Admissions/Records ....Mr. Pedro AVILA
08 Dean Student Success/Learning ....Ms. Renee CRAIG-MARIUS
50 Dean Business Division ....Mr. Rojelio VASQUEZ
57 Dean Fine Perform Commun Arts ....Mr. Neil VANDERPOOL
79 Dean Humanities Division ....Dr. Jennifer JOHNSON
54 Dean Math/Science/Engineering Div ....Ms. Shirley MCMANUS
83 Dean Social Sciences Division ....Dr. Margaret E. MERICLE
76 Dean Health Sciences Division ....Ms. Lorraine SMITH
72 Dean Applied Technology Div ....Mr. Jacob JACKSON
38 Dean Counseling-Guidance ....Ms. Monica CUEVAS
35 Dean of Student Services ....Dr. Lee FARLEY
103 Dean Workforce Development & CTC ....Dr. Natalie C. DOCKINS
75 Director FCC Training Institute ....Mr. Charles FRANCIS
88 Director Disabled Stdnt Pgms & Svcs ....Dr. Janice EMERZIAN
09 Director Institutional Research ....Dr. Lijuan ZHAI
88 Director Police Academy ....Mr. Richard LINDSTROM
35 Director of Student Activities ....Mr. Sean HENDERSON
26 Director Marketing/Communications ....Ms. Cris M. BREMER
37 Director Financial Aid ....Ms. Kira TIPPINS
27 Public Information Officer ....Ms. Kathleen BONILLA
41 Athletic Director ....Mr. Eric SWAIN
38 Dir Distance Education/Inst Tech ....Ms. Autumn BELL
72 Director of Technology ....Mr. Don LOPEZ
36 Dir College Relations & Outreach ....Vacant
66 Director of Nursing ....Ms. Stephanie R. ROBINSON
88 Director CalWORKs Program ....Ms. Anne WATTS
06 Director Admissions & Records ....Ms. Frances LIPPMANN
88 Director TRIO Programs ....Mr. Perry ANGLE
88 Director EOPS/CARE ....Mr. Thomas GAXIOLA

*Reedley College (C)

995 N Reed Avenue, Reedley CA 93654-2099

County: Fresno FICE Identification: 001308
Unit ID: 117052
Telephone: (559) 638-3641 Carnegie Class: Assoc/Pub-U-MC
FAX Number: (559) 638-5040 Calendar System: Semester
URL: www.reedleycollege.edu
Established: 1926 Annual Undergrad Tuition & Fees (In-District): $1,198
Enrollment: 14,633 Coed
Affiliation or Control: State/Local IRS Status: 501(c)3
Highest Offering: Associate Degree
Program: Occupational; 2-Year Principally Bachelor's Creditable
Accreditation: WJ

02 President ....Dr. Sandra CALDWELL
05 Vice President of Instruction ....Mr. Jan DEKKER
11 Vice Pres Administrative Svcs ....Ms. Donna BERRY
32 Vice Pres of Student Services ....Dr. Claudia HABIB
12 Vice Pres Madera/Oakhurst Centers ....Dr. John FITZER
20 Dean of Instruction/Agri/Nat Res ....Dr. David CLARK
79 Dean of Instruction/Humanities ....Dr. Chris SPOMER
81 Dean Instruct/Math/Sci/Tech/PE/Hlth ....Dr. Marie BYRD-HARRIS
88 Dean Instruct/Madera/Oakhurst Ctrs ....Dr. Jim CHIN
26 Public Information Officer ....Ms. Lucy RUIZ
88 Director Disabled Stdnt Prgms/Svcs ....Dr. Janice EMERZIAN
22 Director EOPS ....Mr. Mario GONZALES
13 Director of Technology ....Mr. Gary SAKAGUCHI
37 Financial Aid Manager ....Ms. Chris CORTES
07 Admissions & Records Mgr/Registrar ....Ms. Leticia ALVAREZ
08 Librarian ....Ms. Kari JOHNSON

SUM Bible College and Theological Seminary (D)

735 105th Avenue, Oakland CA 94603-3603

County: Alameda FICE Identification: 037524
Unit ID: 447953
Telephone: (510) 567-6174 Carnegie Class: Spec/Faith
FAX Number: (510) 568-1024 Calendar System: Trimester
URL: www.sum.edu
Established: 1999 Annual Undergrad Tuition & Fees: $9,320
Enrollment: 536 Coed
Affiliation or Control: Independent Non-Profit IRS Status: 501(c)3
Highest Offering: Master's
Program: Occupational; Liberal Arts And General; Professional; Religious Emphasis
Accreditation: BI

01 President/Chancellor ....Rev. George NEAU
11 Vice President Operations ....Dr. Elsie COOK
05 Chief Academic Officer ....Dr. Bruce COATS
10 Vice President Finance ....Mr. Robert HORNICK
30 Director Marketing and Recruitment ....Ms. Aronne HAUKI
42 Dean of Student Ministry ....Rev. Rondale TERRY
08 Director of the Library ....Ms. Catherine DIETERLY
32 Dean of Student Life ....Vacant
20 Assistant Academic Dean ....Mr. Joey Alan LE
06 Institutional Research/Registrar ....Ms. D'Lonika JENKINS
37 Financial Aid Director ....Mrs. Kathryn MANGAN
88 US Cohort Director ....Rev. Dave WALLACE
21 Business Administrator ....Mr. Don DIETERLY
07 Admissions Administrator ....Ms. Vieneese KELLY

† Affiliated with School of Urban Missions-New Orleans, Gretna, LA.

Taft College (E)

29 Cougar Court, Taft CA 93268-2329

County: Kern FICE Identification: 001309
Unit ID: 124113
Telephone: (661) 763-7700 Carnegie Class: Assoc/Pub-S-SC
FAX Number: (661) 763-7703 Calendar System: Semester
URL: www.taftcollege.edu
Established: 1922 Annual Undergrad Tuition & Fees (In-District): $1,380
Enrollment: 5,051 Coed
Affiliation or Control: State/Local IRS Status: 501(c)3
Highest Offering: Associate Degree
Program: Occupational; 2-Year Principally Bachelor's Creditable; Liberal Arts And General
Accreditation: WJ, DH

01 Superintendent/President ....Dr. Dena MALONEY
10 Exec Vice Pres/Administrative Svcs ....Mr. Brock MCMURRAY
05 Vice President of Instruction ....Mr. Mark WILLIAMS
32 Vice Pres of Student Services ....Ms. Darcy BOGLE
04 Assistant to the President ....Ms. Shelley KLEIN
30 Director Foundation & Development ....Ms. Sheri HORN BUNK
13 Director Information Services ....Mr. Adrian AGUNDEZ
20 Dean of Instruction-Grants ....Ms. Agnes JOSE-EGUARAS
38 Lead Counselor ....Vacant
08 Research and Instruction Librarian ....Ms. Terri SMITH
46 Coord Inst Research/Assessment/Plng ....Dr. Eric BERUBE
41 Director Athletics ....Ms. Kanoe BANDY
15 Director Human Resources ....Vacant
21 Director of Fiscal Services ....Mr. Jim NICHOLAS
07 Director of Admissions & Records ....Ms. Amber ANDERSON
18 Supervisor Maintenance/Operations ....Mr. Michael CAPELA
37 Director Student Financial Aid ....Ms. Barbara AMERIO

Taft Law School (F)

3700 South Susan Street, Office 200, Santa Ana CA 92704-6954

County: Orange Identification: 666398
Unit ID: 454689
Telephone: (714) 850-4800 Carnegie Class: Spec/Law
FAX Number: (714) 708-2082 Calendar System: Other
URL: www.taftu.edu
Established: 1976 Annual Undergrad Tuition & Fees: $7,400
Enrollment: 666 Coed
Affiliation or Control: Proprietary IRS Status: Proprietary
Highest Offering: Doctorate
Program: Professional
Accreditation: DEAC

01 Chancellor ....Mr. David L. BOYD
05 Dean ....Mr. Robert K. STROUSE
86 VP of Governmental Relations ....Ms. Joan L. SLAVIN
20 Associate Dean ....Ms. Melody JOLLY
37 Director of Financial Aid ....Ms. Tina M. SAXON

Teachers College of San Joaquin (G)

2857 Transworld Dr, Stockton CA 95206

County: San Joaquin Identification: 667087
Telephone: (209) 468-4926 Carnegie Class: Not Classified
FAX Number: (209) 468-9124 Calendar System: Semester
URL: teacherscollegesj.edu
Established: 2009 Annual Graduate Tuition & Fees: $13,440
Enrollment: 480 Coed
Affiliation or Control: State IRS Status: 501(c)3
Highest Offering: Master's; No Undergraduates
Program: Teacher Preparatory
Accreditation: WC

01 President ....Dr. Diane CARNAHAN
06 Registrar/Admissions ....Ms. Lisa NEUGEBAUER
58 Director Graduate Studies ....Dr. Sylvia TURNER
04 Administrative Asst to President ....Ms. Victoria L. DE PRATER
10 Chief Business Officer ....Mr. Jim THOMAS

Theatre of Arts (H)

1536 N Highland Avenue, Hollywood CA 90028

County: Los Angeles Identification: 667098
Telephone: (323) 463-2500 Carnegie Class: Not Classified
FAX Number: (323) 463-2500 Calendar System: Trimester
URL: www.toa.edu
Established: 1927 Annual Undergrad Tuition & Fees: $19,800
Enrollment: 17 Coed
Affiliation or Control: Proprietary IRS Status: Proprietary
Highest Offering: Associate Degree
Program: Occupational; 2-Year Principally Bachelor's Creditable; Fine Arts Emphasis
Accreditation: THEA

01 President ....Amir KORANGY
07 Director of Admissions ....Leslie DELMORO
11 Chief of Administration ....Elizabeth INIGUEZ

Thomas Aquinas College (I)

10,000 Ojai Road, Santa Paula CA 93060-9621

County: Ventura FICE Identification: 023580
Unit ID: 124292
Telephone: (805) 525-4417 Carnegie Class: Bac/A&S
FAX Number: (805) 525-9342 Calendar System: Semester
URL: www.thomasaquinas.edu
Established: 1971 Annual Undergrad Tuition & Fees: $24,500
Enrollment: 378 Coed
Affiliation or Control: Independent Non-Profit IRS Status: 501(c)3
Highest Offering: Baccalaureate
Program: Liberal Arts And General
Accreditation: WC

01 President ....Dr. Michael F. MCLEAN
04 Secretary to the President ....Ms. Sarah KAISER
26 Asst to Pres/Dir College Relations ....Mrs. Anne S. FORSYTH
30 Vice President for Development ....Dr. Paul J. O'REILLY
43 General Counsel ....Mr. John Q. MASTELLER
10 Vice President for Admn & Finance ....Mr. Peter L. DELUCA
05 Academic Dean ....Dr. Brian KELLY
46 Director of Development ....Mr. Robert A. BAGDAZIAN
44 Director of Gift Planning ....Mr. Thomas J. SUSANKA
07 Director of Admissions ....Mr. Jonathan P. DALY
21 Supervisor Business/Finance ....Mr. Michael COLLINS
37 Director of Financial Aid ....Mr. Gregory J. BECHER
32 Asst Dean for Student Affairs ....Mr. Steven R. CAIN
06 Registrar ....Mr. Mark KRETSCHMER
36 Director of Student Placement ....Mr. Mark R. KRETSCHMER
08 Librarian ....Mrs. Viltis A. JATULIS
42 Chaplain ....Fr. Hildebrand GARCEAU
27 Communications Manager ....Mr. Christopher WEINKOPF
13 Development Database Manager ....Mr. Aaron DUNKEL

Thomas Jefferson School of Law (J)

1155 Island Avenue, San Diego CA 92101

County: San Diego FICE Identification: 010854
Unit ID: 126049
Telephone: (619) 297-9700 Carnegie Class: Spec/Law
FAX Number: (619) 961-4370 Calendar System: Semester
URL: www.tjsl.edu
Established: 1969 Annual Graduate Tuition & Fees: $46,200
Enrollment: 849 Coed
Affiliation or Control: Independent Non-Profit IRS Status: 501(c)3
Highest Offering: Doctorate; No Undergraduates
Program: Professional
Accreditation: LAW

01 President and Dean ....Thomas F. GUERNSEY
05 Assoc Dean Academic Affairs ....Linda KELLER
10 Chief Financial Officer ....Nancy VU
32 Assoc Dean for Student Affairs ....Vacant

35	Assistant Dean for Student Affairs	Lisa FERREIRA
36	Assistant Dean for Career Services	Vacant
84	Asst Dean for Enrollment Mgmnt	Tim SPEARMAN
08	Library Director	Leigh INMAN
37	Director Financial Assistance	Marc BERMAN
06	Registrar	Carrie KAZYAKA
21	Business Office Manager	Madeleine CARRASCO
88	Dir Clin/Judicial Educ & Acad Cnslr	Judybeth TROPP
15	Director of Personnel Services	Lisa CHIGOS
29	Director Alumni Relations	Stephanie MARQUEZ
43	Dir Legal Services/General Counsel	Karin K. SHERR
04	Exec Asst to the President/Dean	Jan DAUSS
13	Director of IT	Gil SUSANA

Touro College Los Angeles (A)

1317 N Crescent Heights Blvd,
West Hollywood CA 90046-4506
County: Los Angeles Identification: 770944
Unit ID: 459727
Telephone: (323) 822-9700 Carnegie Class: Not Classified
FAX Number: (310) 654-2086 Calendar System: Semester
URL: www.touro.edu/losangeles/
Established: 2005 Annual Undergrad Tuition & Fees: $16,900
Enrollment: 363 Coed
Affiliation or Control: Independent Non-Profit IRS Status: 501(c)3
Highest Offering: Baccalaureate
Program: Liberal Arts And General; Business Emphasis
Accreditation: WC

01	President	Dr. Alan KADISH
11	CEO	Dr. Yoram NEUMANN
03	Provost	Dr. Edith NEUMANN
05	Dean	Dr. Michael D. HAMLIN
07	Director of Admissions	Ms. Leah MIZRAHI
09	Dir Inst Research/Assessment	Dr. Aaron BROWNSTEIN
10	Chief Business Officer/Bursar	Mr. Kamran MANUEL
06	Registrar & Fin Aid Coordinator	Ms. Rivka WEINBERG

† Branch campus of Touro University Worldwide, Los Alamitos, CA.

Touro University California (B)

1310 Club Drive, Vallejo CA 94592
County: Solano FICE Identification: 041426
Unit ID: 459736
Telephone: (707) 638-5200 Carnegie Class: Not Classified
FAX Number: (707) 638-5255 Calendar System: Trimester
URL: www.tu.edu
Established: 1997 Annual Undergrad Tuition & Fees: $45,000
Enrollment: 1,378 Coed
Affiliation or Control: Independent Non-Profit IRS Status: 501(c)3
Highest Offering: Doctorate
Program: Teacher Preparatory; Professional
Accreditation: WC, ARCPA, OSTEO, PH, PHAR

01	President & CEO Univ System	Dr. Alan KADISH
03	Sr Provost/CEO Touro Western Div	Hon. Shelley BERKLEY
05	Provost & COO	Dr. Marilyn HOPKINS
32	Dean of Students	Dr. Lisa WAITS
35	Associate Dean of Students	Dr. James BINKERD
06	Registrar	Vacant
07	Director of Admissions	Mr. Steven DAVIS
09	Dir of Institutional Effectiveness	Dr. Meiling TANG
10	Director of Fiscal Affairs and Acct	Ms. Jonalee ADRIANO
15	Director Human Resources	Ms. Kathy LOWE
11	Associate VP of Administration	Mr. Jay RITCHIE
08	Director University Library	Ms. Tamara TRUJILLO
63	Dean College of Osteopathic Med	Dr. Michael CLEARFIELD
67	Dean College of Pharmacy	Dr. Rae MATSUMOTO
53	Dean Col of Education & Health Sci	Dr. Jim O'CONNOR
13	Director of Information Technology	Ms. Julia WELCH
26	Dir of University Communication	Ms. Andrea GARCIA
37	Director of Student Financial Aid	Ms. Lynne MOSELEY
30	Chief Officer of Advancement	Vacant
35	Director of Student Activities	Rabbi Elchonon TENENBAUM
23	Director of Student Health Center	Ms. Laura SCHWARTZ

Touro University Worldwide (C)

10601 Calle Lee Ste 179, Los Alamitos CA 90720
County: Orange FICE Identification: 041425
Unit ID: 459727
Telephone: (818) 575-6800 Carnegie Class: Not Classified
FAX Number: (818) 707-0316 Calendar System: Semester
URL: www.tuw.edu
Established: 2005 Annual Undergrad Tuition & Fees: $12,000
Enrollment: 541 Coed
Affiliation or Control: Independent Non-Profit IRS Status: 501(c)3
Highest Offering: Doctorate
Program: Liberal Arts And General
Accreditation: WC

01	CEO	Dr. Yoram NEUMANN
05	Provost & Chief Academic Officer	Dr. Edith NEUMANN
10	CFO	Mr. Jayson CAPUTO

Trident University International (D)

5757 Plaza Drive, Suite 100, Cypress CA 90630
County: Orange FICE Identification: 041279
Unit ID: 450979
Telephone: (714) 816-0366 Carnegie Class: DRU
FAX Number: (714) 816-0367 Calendar System: Semester
URL: www.trident.edu
Established: 1998 Annual Undergrad Tuition & Fees: $11,200
Enrollment: 11,404 Coed
Affiliation or Control: Proprietary IRS Status: Proprietary
Highest Offering: Doctorate
Program: Liberal Arts And General; Professional; Business Emphasis
Accreditation: WC

01	President/COO	Mr. Travis J. ALLEN
10	Chief Financial Officer	Mr. David BARRETT
05	Exec Vice President/Provost	Dr. Michael MAHONEY
13	Exec Vice President/CIO	Mr. Vahid SHARIAT
86	VP/Chief Compliance Officer	Dr. Afshin AFROOKHTEH
20	Vice Provost	Dr. Scott AMUNDSEN
50	Dean Business/Information Systems	Dr. Simcha POLLARD
04	Executive Assistant	Ms. Patricia PARKS
15	Director Human Resources	Ms. Melissa ROTHMEYER
06	Registrar	Mr. Mark MCKELLIP
37	Director Student Financial Aid	Ms. Taisha AZLIN WRIGHT
09	Director of Institutional Research	Dr. Heidi SATO
08	Librarian	Ms. Leslie ANDERSEN
21	Director of Financial Operation	Mr. Scott PAK
76	Dean Educ/Health Sciences	Dr. Holly OROZCO
07	Director of Admissions	Ms. Jameela FRIERSON
18	Facilities Manager	Mr. Fred WILSON
101	Board of Trustees Secretary	Mr. Brian VAN KLOMPENBERG
108	Interim Assessment Director	Dr. Belarmina RICHARDS

Trinity Law School (E)

2200 N Grand Avenue, Santa Ana CA 92705
Telephone: (714) 836-7500 Identification: 770098
Accreditation: &NH

† Branch campus of Trinity International University, Deerfield, IL.

United Education Institute (F)

6055 Pacific Boulevard, Huntington Park CA 90255
County: Los Angeles FICE Identification: 025593
Unit ID: 124681
Telephone: (323) 319-9500 Carnegie Class: Not Classified
FAX Number: (949) 788-2505 Calendar System: Other
URL: www.uei.edu
Established: 1986 Annual Undergrad Tuition & Fees: $19,500
Enrollment: 3,564 Coed
Affiliation or Control: Proprietary IRS Status: Proprietary
Highest Offering: Associate Degree
Program: Occupational
Accreditation: CNCE

01	Executive Area President	Mr. Louis ARNENDARIC

United States University (G)

830 Bay Boulevard, Chula Vista CA 91911
County: San Diego FICE Identification: 040053
Unit ID: 447050
Telephone: (619) 477-6310 Carnegie Class: Bac/A&S
FAX Number: (619) 477-7340 Calendar System: Semester
URL: www.usuniversity.edu
Established: 1997 Annual Undergrad Tuition & Fees: $12,380
Enrollment: 414 Coed
Affiliation or Control: Proprietary IRS Status: Proprietary
Highest Offering: Master's
Program: Professional; Business Emphasis
Accreditation: #WC, NURSE

01	President and CEO	Dr. Barry T. RYAN
05	Provost/Chief Academic Officer	Dr. Steven A. STARGARDTER
11	Chief Operating Officer	Dawn WERLING
10	Chief Financial Officer	Will TITERA
25	VP Compliance/Regulatory Aff	Robyn BURRELL
26	VP Marketing	Jennifer MARTINEZ
07	Director of Admissions	Vacant
88	Director of International Affairs	Arti MARTINEZ
106	Associate Provost Online Learning	Dr. Elizabeth ARCHER
09	Asst Provost Research & Assessment	Nga PHAN
53	Dean College of Education	Dr. Roberta MASO-FLEISHMAN
49	Dean College of Arts & Sciences	Dr. Rosalinda MILLA
50	Dean College of Business	Vacant
66	Dean College of Nursing	Dr. Renee MCLEOD

Unitek College (H)

4670 Auto Mall Parkway, Fremont CA 94538
County: Alameda FICE Identification: 041697
Unit ID: 459204
Telephone: (888) 775-1514 Carnegie Class: Not Classified
FAX Number: (510) 249-9125 Calendar System: Other
URL: www.unitekcollege.edu
Established: 1992 Annual Undergrad Tuition & Fees: $22,256
Enrollment: 1,017 Coed
Affiliation or Control: Proprietary IRS Status: Proprietary
Highest Offering: Baccalaureate
Program: Occupational; 2-Year Principally Bachelor's Creditable; Nursing Emphasis
Accreditation: ACCSC, NURSE

01	School President	Mr. Navraj BAWA

University of Antelope Valley (I)

44055 Sierra Hwy, Lancaster CA 93534
County: Los Angeles FICE Identification: 034275
Unit ID: 442930
Telephone: (661) 726-1911 Carnegie Class: Assoc/PrivFP
FAX Number: (661) 726-5158 Calendar System: Other
URL: www.uav.edu
Established: Annual Undergrad Tuition & Fees: $12,500
Enrollment: 772 Coed
Affiliation or Control: Proprietary IRS Status: Proprietary
Highest Offering: Master's
Program: Occupational; 2-Year Principally Bachelor's Creditable
Accreditation: ACICS, EMT

01	President	Mr. Marco JOHNSON
03	Vice President/CEO	Ms. Sandra JOHNSON
05	Dean of Academic Affairs	Ms. Melea FIELDS
32	Dean of Student Affairs	Mr. Ronald FELTS
06	Registrar/Dir Institutional Rsch	Mrs. Jaime MORRIS
37	Director of Financial Aid	Mr. Araceli JIMENEZ
11	Director of Operations	Ms. Crystal STEPHENS
13	Director Information Technology	Mr. Noel SANCHEZ
36	Director Career Services	Ms. Mirna TURCIOS

*University of California Office of the President (J)

1111 Franklin Street, Oakland CA 94607-5200
County: Alameda FICE Identification: 001311
Unit ID: 124557
Telephone: (510) 987-0700 Carnegie Class: N/A
FAX Number: (510) 987-0328
URL: www.ucop.edu

01	President	Janet NAPOLITANO
05	Provost/EVP Acad Affairs	Aimee DORR
10	EVP/Chief Financial Officer	Nathan E. BROSTROM
11	EVP/Chief Operating Officer	Rachael NAVA
17	Exec Vice Pres UC Health	John D. STOBO
26	Sr Vice Pres External Relations	Julie HENDERSON
86	SVP Government Relations	Nelson PEACOCK
108	Sr Vice Pres Compliance/Audit	Sheryl S. VACCA
47	Vice Pres Agriculture/Nat Resources	Barbara H. ALLEN-DIAZ
45	VP Budget & Capital Resources	Patrick J. LENZ
44	Vice President of Investments	Jagdeep S. BACHHER
09	Vice Pres Inst Rsrch/Acad Planning	Pamela BROWN
88	VP Office of National Laboratories	Kimberly S. BUDIL
15	Vice Pres Human Resources	Dwaine B. DUCKETT
43	General Counsel/VP Legal Affairs	Charles F. ROBINSON
32	Vice President Student Affairs	Judy K. SAKAKI
46	Interim VP Innovation Alliance Svcs	William TUCKER
13	CIO Information Technology Svcs	Tom ANDRIOLA
20	Vice Provost Ed Partnerships	Yvette GULLATT
20	Vice Provost Academic Personnel	Susan CARLSON
21	Assoc VP Budget Analysis & Planning	Debora OBLEY

*University of California-Berkeley (K)

Berkeley CA 94720-0001
County: Alameda FICE Identification: 001312
Unit ID: 110635
Telephone: (510) 642-6000 Carnegie Class: RU/VH
FAX Number: (510) 643-5499 Calendar System: Semester
URL: www.berkeley.edu
Established: 1868 Annual Undergrad Tuition & Fees (In-State): $10,361
Enrollment: 37,565 Coed
Affiliation or Control: State IRS Status: 501(c)3
Highest Offering: Doctorate
Program: Liberal Arts And General; Professional; Technical Emphasis
Accreditation: WC, BUS, CLPSY, CS, DIETD, ENG, IPSY, JOUR, LAW, LSAR, OPT, OPTR, PCSAS, PH, PLNG, SCPSY, SW

02	Chancellor	Nicholas B. DIRKS
05	Exec Vice Chancellor & Provost	Claude M. STEELE
11	Vice Chanc Administration & Finance	John WILTON
32	Vice Chancellor Student Affairs	Harry LE GRANDE
26	Vice Chanc University Relations	Scott BIDDY
18	Vice Chancellor Real Estate	Bob LALANNE
22	Vice Chanc Equity & Inclusion	Gibor BASRI
100	Assoc Chancellor/Chief of Staff	Vacant
25	Asst VC Research Admin & Compliance	Patrick SCHLESINGER
13	Asst Vice Chanc Info Technology	Lyle NEVELS
10	Assoc Vice Chancellor/CFO	Rosemarie RAE
84	Assc Vice Chanc Admiss & Enrollment	Anne DE LUCA
43	Chief Campus Counsel	Christopher M. PATTI
27	Assoc Vice Chanc Public Affairs	Claire HOLMES
88	Asst Vice Chanc Finance/Controller	Delphine REGALIA
07	Asst VC & Dir Undergrad Admissions	Amy JARICH
35	Assc Vice Chanc/Dean of Students	Joseph D. GREENWELL
37	Asst VC & Dir Fin Aid & Scholarship	Rachelle FELDMAN
08	University Librarian	Thomas C. LEONARD
06	Associate Registrar	Johanna METZGAR
38	Dir Counseling & Psychological Svcs	Jeff PRINCE
36	Director Career Center	Thomas C. DEVLIN
87	Dean Sum Sess/Study Abr/Life Lrng	Richard RUSSO
41	Int Director of Athletics	Michael WILLIAMS
58	Dean of the Graduate Division	Fiona M. DOYLE
61	Acting Dean of Law	Gillian LESTER
88	Dean of Optometry	John FLANAGAN
54	Dean School of Engineering	S. Shankar SASTRY
88	Dean of Environmental Design	Jennifer WOLCH

65 Dean of Natural Resources ... J. Keith GILLESS
50 Dean of Haas School of Business ... Richard K. LYONS
70 Dean of Social Welfare ... Jeffrey EDELSON
88 Dean School of Information ... AnnaLee SAXENIAN
69 Dean of Public Health ... Stefano BERTOZZI
53 Dean of Education ... Judith W. LITTLE
60 Dean of Journalism ... Ed WASSERMAN
88 Dean of Chemistry ... Douglas S. CLARK
80 Dean Graduate School/Public Policy ... Henry E. BRADY
79 Dean of Arts and Humanities ... Anthony CASCARDI
88 Dean of Biological Sciences ... G. Steven MARTIN
81 Dean Mathematical/Physical Sciences ... Mark RICHARDS
83 Dean of Social Sciences ... Carla HESSE
97 Int Dean of the Undergrad Division ... Bob JACOBSON
56 Dean of University Extension ... Diana WU

*University of California-Davis (A)

One Shields Avenue, Davis CA 95616-5270
County: Yolo FICE Identification: 001313
Unit ID: 110644
Telephone: (530) 752-1011 Carnegie Class: RU/VH
FAX Number: N/A Calendar System: Quarter
URL: www.ucdavis.edu
Established: 1905 Annual Undergrad Tuition & Fees (In-State): $14,534
Enrollment: 35,415 Coed
Affiliation or Control: State IRS Status: 501(c)3
Highest Offering: Doctorate
Program: Liberal Arts And General; Teacher Preparatory; Professional
Accreditation: WC, ARCPA, BUS, CS, DIETD, DIETI, ENG, IPSY, LAW, LSAR, MED, MT, NURSE, PAST, PH, VET

02 Chancellor ... Dr. Linda P. KATEHI
05 Provost & Exec Vice Chancellor ... Dr. Ralph J. HEXTER
100 Associate Chancellor ... Mr. Karl M. ENGELBACH
26 Assoc Chanc Strategic Commun ... Ms. Luanne M. LAWRENCE
88 Assoc Chancellor Admin Reorg ... Dr. Prasant MOHAPATRA
46 Vice Chancellor Research ... Dr. Harris A. LEWIN
30 Vice Chanc Dev/Alumni Relations ... Dr. Shaun B. KEISTER
32 Vice Chancellor Student Affairs ... Dr. Adela I. DE LATORRE
10 VC & CFO Finance & Res Mngmnt ... Mr. Dave LAWLOR
63 VC Human Health Sci/Dean Sch of Med ... Dr. Julie FREISCHLAG
17 CEO UCD Medical Center ... Ms. Ann M. RICE
66 Assoc VC/Dean Sch of Nursing ... Dr. Heather M. YOUNG
22 Assoc Exec VC Campus Cmty Relations ... Mr. Rahim REED
21 Sr Assoc VC Finance ... Ms. Kelly RATLIFF
11 Acting Sr AVC Plng/Fac/Safety ... Mr. Dave LAWLOR
88 Exec Assoc VC Research ... Dr. Cindy M. KIEL
88 Assoc VC Research ... Dr. Paul DODD
88 Assoc VC Research ... Dr. Dushyant PATHAK
15 Assoc VC Human Resources ... Ms. Susan M. GILBERT
88 Assoc VC Accounting/Financial Svcs ... Mr. J. Michael ALLRED
88 Assoc VC Development ... Mr. Jason L. WOHLMAN
88 Assoc VC Development ... Mr. Paul PROKOP
88 Assoc VC Development Health Sci ... Ms. Chong U. PORTER
39 Assoc VC Student Affairs ... Ms. Emily GALINDO
84 Assoc VC Student Affairs ... Ms. Lora J. BOSSIO
35 Assoc VC Student Affairs ... Dr. Milton LANG
07 Assoc VC Undergrad Admissions ... Mr. Walter A. ROBINSON
88 Assoc VC Safety Services ... Ms. Jill PARKER
86 Asst Chanc Govt & Comm Relations ... Ms. Marjorie M. DICKINSON
88 Asst Executive Vice Chancellor ... Mr. Karl MOHR
45 Asst VC Campus Planning ... Mr. Robert B. SEGAR
88 Asst VC Environmental Stewardship ... Dr. Sid ENGLAND
88 Assoc VC Design & Construct ... Mr. Clayton HALLIDAY
18 Asst VC Facilities Management ... Mr. Allen TOLLEFSON
29 AVC/Exec Director Alumni Relations ... Mr. Richard R. ENGEL
13 CIO & VP Info/Educ Tech ... Ms. Viji MURALI
88 VP & Dean Undergraduate Educ ... Dr. Carolyn THOMAS
58 VP Grad Education/Dean Grad Studies ... Dr. Jeffery C. GIBELING
20 Vice Provost Academic Affairs ... Dr. Maureen L. STANTON
104 Int Vice Prov Global Affairs ... Dr. Adrienne L. MARTIN
88 Assoc Vice Provost Global Affairs ... Dr. Jan W. HOPMANS
47 Dean Agricultural/Environ Sci ... Dr. Helene DILLARD
88 Int Dean Biological Sciences ... Dr. Peter C. WAINWRIGHT
54 Int Dean Engineering ... Dr. Jean VANDERGHEYNST
83 Int Dean Social Sciences ... Dr. Li ZHANG
81 Int Dean Math & Physical Sciences ... Dr. Alexandra NAVROTSKY
79 Int Dean Humanities/Arts & Culture ... Dr. Susan B. KAISER
61 Dean School of Law ... Dr. Kevin R. JOHNSON
50 Int Dean Grad School of Management ... Dr. Ann STEVENS
74 Dean Veterinary Medicine ... Dr. Michael D. LAIRMORE
53 Dean School of Education ... Dr. Harold G. LEVINE
56 Dean University Extension ... Dr. Paul M. MCNEIL
88 Exec Director Mondavi Center ... Dr. Don F. ROTH
23 Exec Dir Student Health Services ... Dr. Michelle S. FAMULA
37 Director Financial Aid ... Ms. Deborah G. AGEE
38 Director Counseling & Psych Svcs ... Dr. Sarah HAHN
36 Director Internship & Career Center ... Ms. Marcie KIRK-HOLLAND
40 Director Bookstore ... Mr. Jason LORGAN
41 Int Dir Intercollegiate Athletics ... Ms. Teresa GOULD
88 Director Internal Audit Services ... Mr. Jeremiah J. MAHER
88 Director World Food Center ... Dr. Roger BEACHY
19 Chief of Police ... Chief Matt CARMICHAEL
43 Chief Campus Counsel ... Mr. Jacob A. APPELSMITH
06 Registrar ... Dr. Elias S. LOPEZ
08 University Librarian ... Ms. MacKenzie SMITH

*University of California-Hastings College of the Law (B)

200 McAllister Street, San Francisco CA 94102-4978
County: San Francisco FICE Identification: 003947
Unit ID: 110398
Telephone: (415) 565-4600 Carnegie Class: Spec/Law
FAX Number: (415) 565-4865 Calendar System: Semester
URL: www.uchastings.edu
Established: 1878 Annual Graduate Tuition & Fees: $48,638
Enrollment: 933 Coed
Affiliation or Control: State IRS Status: 501(c)3
Highest Offering: First Professional Degree; No Undergraduates
Program: Professional
Accreditation: WC, LAW

02 Chancellor and Dean ... Mr. Frank H. WU
05 Provost & Academic Dean ... Ms. Elizabeth L. HILLMAN
43 General Counsel ... Ms. Elise TRAYNUM
10 Chief Financial Officer ... Mr. David SEWARD
20 Associate Academic Dean ... Ms. Heather M. FIELD
19 Acting Chief Public Safety ... Mr. Scott HALLAHAN
06 Registrar ... Ms. Gina BARNETT
07 Director of Admissions ... Mr. Bryan ZERBE
32 Director Student Services ... Ms. Rupa BHANDARI
13 Chief Information Officer ... Mr. Jake HORNSBY
36 Asst Dean Career & Profess Devel ... Ms. Sari ZIMMERMAN
26 Dir Communications/Public Affairs ... Mr. Alex A G. SHAPIRO
22 Director LEOP ... Ms. Jan JEMISON
23 Student Health Manager/Admin Nurse ... Ms. Laurie BROOKNER
21 Controller ... Ms. Deborah TRAN
37 Director Financial Aid ... Mr. Victor HO
18 Property Manager ... Ms. Pansy MAR
96 Director of Purchasing ... Mr. Darryl SWEET
30 Chief Development Officer ... Mr. Eric DUMBLETON
108 Director of Accreditation & Assess ... Ms. Andrea BING
84 Sr Assistant Dean of Enrollment Mgm ... Ms. June SAKAMOTO

*University of California-Irvine (C)

Campus Drive, Irvine CA 92697-0001
County: Orange FICE Identification: 001314
Unit ID: 110653
Telephone: (949) 824-5011 Carnegie Class: RU/VH
FAX Number: N/A Calendar System: Quarter
URL: www.uci.edu
Established: 1965 Annual Undergrad Tuition & Fees (In-State): $14,749
Enrollment: 30,757 Coed
Affiliation or Control: State IRS Status: 501(c)3
Highest Offering: Doctorate
Program: Liberal Arts And General; Teacher Preparatory
Accreditation: WC, BUS, CEA, CS, ENG, IPSY, LAW, MED, MT, NURSE, PH, PLNG

02 Chancellor ... Howard GILLMAN
05 Int Provost & Exec Vice Chancellor ... Michael P. CLARK
10 Vice Chanc Admin/Business Services ... Wendell C. BRASE
46 Vice Chancellor for Research ... John C. HEMMINGER
32 Vice Chanc Student Affairs ... Thomas A. PARHAM
30 Vice Chanc Univ Advancement ... Gregory R. LEET
45 Vice Chanc Planning & Budget ... Meredith MICHAELS
20 Senior Vice Provost for Acad Plng ... Michael P. CLARK
15 Vice Provost for Academic Personnel ... Herbert KILLACKEY
29 Asst Vice Chanc Alumni Relations ... Vacant
35 Assoc Vice Chancellor Stdnt Affairs ... Daniel J. DOOROS
22 Asst Executive Vice Chancellor OEOD ... Kirsten K. QUANBECK
100 Associate Chancellor/Chief of Staff ... Ramona AGRELA
20 Associate Exec Vice Chancellor ... Michael R. ARIAS
35 Asst Vice Chanc/Dean of Students ... Rameen A. TALESH
84 Asst Vice Chanc Enrollment Services ... Brent W. YUNEK
06 University Registrar ... Elizabeth C. BENNETT
43 Chief Campus Counsel ... Diane F. GEOCARIS
51 Dean Continuing Educ/Summer Session ... Gary W. MATKIN
08 University Librarian ... Lorelei A. TANJI
37 Interim Director Financial Aid ... Brice K. KIKUCHI
36 Director Career Center ... Suzanne C. HELBIG
41 Director Intercollegiate Athletics ... Michael A. IZZI
09 Asst Vice Chanc Inst Research ... Ryan M. CHERLAND
58 Dean Graduate Division ... Frances M. LESLIE
20 Dean Undergraduate Education ... Sharon V. SALINGER
63 Interim Dean School of Medicine ... Roger F. STEINERT
61 Dean of Law School ... Erwin CHEMERINSKY
81 Dean Biological Sciences ... Frank LAFERLA
81 Dean Physical Sciences ... Kenneth C. JANDA
83 Dean School of Social Sciences ... William M. MAURER
50 Dean Paul Merage School of Business ... Eric SPANGENBERG
79 Dean Humanities ... Georges VAN DEN ABBEELE
49 Dean Arts ... Joseph S. LEWIS
83 Dean Social Ecology ... Valerie JENNESS
54 Dean School of Engineering ... Gregory WASHINGTON
77 Dean Bren Sch of Info & Comp Sci ... Hal S. STERN
88 Chair Academic Senate ... Peter KRAPP
53 Dean School of Education ... Deborah L. VANDELL
13 CIO and Asst Vice Chancellor IT ... Dana F. ROODE
96 Director Materiel & Risk Management ... Richard COULON
26 Assoc Vice Chanc Communications ... Ria M. CARLSON
28 Director ADVANCE Program ... Douglas M. HAYNES
07 Director of Admissions ... Patricia MORALES

*University of California-Los Angeles (D)

405 Hilgard Avenue, Los Angeles CA 90095-1405
County: Los Angeles FICE Identification: 001315
Unit ID: 110662
Telephone: (310) 825-4321 Carnegie Class: RU/VH
FAX Number: N/A Calendar System: Quarter
URL: www.ucla.edu
Established: 1919 Annual Undergrad Tuition & Fees (In-State): $13,806
Enrollment: 41,845 Coed
Affiliation or Control: State IRS Status: 501(c)3
Highest Offering: Doctorate
Program: Liberal Arts And General; Professional
Accreditation: WC, BUS, CLPSY, CS, CYTO, DENT, DIETI, EMT, ENG, ENGR, HSA, IPSY, LAW, LIB, MED, NURSE, PAST, PCSAS, PH, PLNG, RAD, SW, THEA

02 Chancellor ... Gene D. BLOCK
05 Exec Vice Chancellor and Provost ... Scott WAUGH
11 Actg Administrative Vice Chancellor ... Steve OLSEN
32 Vice Chancellor Student Affairs ... Janina MONTERO
26 Vice Chancellor External Affairs ... Rhea TURTELTAUB
10 VC and Chief Financial Officer ... Steven A. OLSEN
23 Vice Chancellor Health Sciences ... John MAZZIOTTA
46 Vice Chancellor Research ... James S. ECONOMOU
58 Vice Provost Graduate Educ & Dean ... Robin L. GARRELL
15 Vice Chancellor Academic Personnel ... Carole E. GOLDBERG
43 Vice Chancellor Legal Affairs ... Kevin REED
82 Int Vice Prov International Studies ... C. Cindy FAN
97 Vice Provost/Dean Undergrad Educ ... Patricia A. TURNER
28 Vice Chanc Diversity/Equity/Incl ... Jerry KANG
13 Vice Provost Information Technology ... James DAVIS
88 Vice Prov New Collaborative Initiat ... Kathryn ATCHISON
17 Assoc VC and CEO Hospital Systems ... Vacant
24 AVP Instructional Development ... Larry L. LOEHER
20 Asst Provost ... Margaret LEAL-SOTELO
20 Assistant Provost ... Maryann J. GRAY
88 Assoc Vice Chanc Acad Plng/Budget ... Glyn DAVIES
27 Assoc Vice Chanc Univ Communication ... Lawrence H. LOKMAN
18 Assoc Vice Chanc General Services ... Jack POWAZEK
30 Vice President Development ... Nick GOLDSBOROUGH
21 Assoc Vice Chancellor/Controller ... Vacant
16 Assoc Vice Chanc Campus Human Res ... Lubbe LEVIN
35 Assoc VC Dean Student & Campus Life ... Vacant
29 Asst Vice Chanc/Exec Dir Alumni Rel ... Vacant
86 Asst Vice Chanc Govt/Cmty Rels ... Keith S. PARKER
91 Asst Vice Chanc Adm Info Systems ... Andrew WISSMILLER
39 Asst VC Housing & Hospitality Svcs ... Peter ANGELIS
88 Executive Director Volunteer Center ... Antoinette MONGELLI
84 Assoc Vice Chanc Enrollment Mgmt ... Youlonda COPELAND-MORGAN
25 Asst VC Res Policy & Compliance ... Ann M. POLLACK
06 Registrar ... Frank Y. WADA
87 Asst Prov Academic Program Dev ... David UNRUH
09 Dir Analysis/Information Management ... Caroline S. WEST
08 University Librarian ... Virginia STEEL
19 Chief of Police ... James HERREN
07 Dir Undergrad Admiss/Rels w/Schools ... Vacant
36 Director Career Center ... Kathy L. SIMS
37 Director Financial Aid Office ... Ronald W. JOHNSON
38 Dir Student Psychological Services ... Elizabeth GONG-GUY
85 Dir Ctr for Intl Students/Scholars ... Robert B. ERICKSEN
41 Director Intercollegiate Athletics ... Daniel G. GUERRERO
22 Director Staff Affirmative Action ... Linda C. AVILA
96 Director of Purchasing ... William S. PROPST
88 Executive Director ASUCLA ... Robert WILLIAMS
51 Int Dean Cont Educ/UCLA Extension ... Cathy SANDEEN
53 Dean Grad Sch Educ/Info Studies ... Marcelo M. SUAREZ-OROZCO
54 Dean Sch of Engr & Applied Sci ... Vijay K. DHIR
61 Dean School of Law ... Rachel MORAN
50 Dean Anderson Grad Sch Management ... Judy D. OLIAN
52 Dean School of Dentistry ... No Hee PARK
66 Dean School of Nursing ... Courtney LYDER
48 Dean Sch of the Arts/Architecture ... Christopher WATERMAN
88 Dean School of Theater/Film/TV ... Teri SCHWARTZ
69 Dean School of Public Health ... Jody HEYMANN
63 Dean D Geffen School of Medicine ... A. Eugene WASHINGTON
80 Dean School of Public Affairs ... Franklin D. GILLIAM, JR.
79 Dean Division of Humanities ... David SCHABERG
88 Dean of Life Sciences ... Victoria SORK
88 Dean of Physical Sciences ... Joseph RUDNICK
83 Dean of Social Sciences ... Alessandro DURANTI
90 Director Academic Tech Svcs ... William LABATE
40 Divisional Manager Textbooks ... Anne COLLUM

*University of California-Merced (E)

5200 North Lake Road, Merced CA 95343
County: Merced FICE Identification: 041271
Unit ID: 445188
Telephone: (209) 228-4400 Carnegie Class: Not Classified
FAX Number: (209) 228-4424 Calendar System: Semester
URL: www.ucmerced.edu
Established: 2005 Annual Undergrad Tuition & Fees (In-District): $13,772
Enrollment: 6,268 Coed
Affiliation or Control: State/Local IRS Status: 501(c)3
Highest Offering: Doctorate
Program: Liberal Arts And General; Teacher Preparatory; Professional
Accreditation: WC, ENG

02 Chancellor ... Dr. Dorothy LELAND

88 Assoc Chancellor & Senior Advisor .... Luanna PUTNEY
05 Provost & Exec Vice Chancellor .... Dr. Tom PETERSON
11 Vice Chancellor Admin Svcs .... Michael REESE
30 Vice Chancellor Develop/Alumni Rels .... Kyle D. HOFFMAN
32 Int Vice Chancellor Student Affairs .... Dr. Charles NIES
10 Vice Chancellor Budget/Planning .... Daniel FEITELBERG
46 Vice Chancellor Research .... Dr. Samuel TRAINA
84 Assoc Vice Chanc Enrollment Mgmt .... Jill ORCUTT
26 Asst Vice Chanc University Communications .... Patti W. WAID
58 Vice Provost/Dean of Graduate Educ .... Marjorie ZATZ
20 Vice Provost UG Education .... Elizabeth WHITT
86 Exec Director of Govt Relations .... Cori LUCERO
100 Asst Chancellor & Chief of Staff .... Vacant
04 Exec Assistant to the Chancellor .... Kim GARNER
13 Chief Information Officer .... Ann KOVALCHICK
65 Dean Natural Sciences .... Dr. Juan MEZA
79 Dean School of SSHA .... Dr. Mark S. ALDENDERFER
54 Dean Engineering .... Dr. Mark MATSUMOTO
07 Director of Admissions .... Encarnacion RUIZ
06 University Registrar .... Dr. Laurie HERBRAND
37 Director of Financial Aid .... Diana RALLS
41 Director of Campus Athletics & Rec .... David DUNHAM
23 Assoc Vice Chanc Health & Wellness .... Dr. Fuji COLLINS
85 Director of International Programs .... Rebecca SWEELEY
19 Int Chief of Police .... Chou HER
08 University Librarian .... Haipeng LI
39 Director of Housing and Residence .... Martin REED
43 Campus Counsel .... Elisabeth GUNTHER

*University of California-Riverside (A)

900 University Avenue, Riverside CA 92521
County: Riverside FICE Identification: 001316
Unit ID: 110671
Telephone: (951) 827-1012 Carnegie Class: RU/VH
FAX Number: (951) 827-3800 Calendar System: Quarter
URL: www.ucr.edu
Established: 1954 Annual Undergrad Tuition & Fees (In-State): $15,180
Enrollment: 21,669 Coed
Affiliation or Control: State IRS Status: 501(c)3
Highest Offering: Doctorate
Program: Liberal Arts And General; Teacher Preparatory; Professional
Accreditation: WC, BUS, CS, ENG, IPSY, #MED, SCPSY

02 Chancellor .... Dr. Kim A. WILCOX
100 Associate Chancellor .... Ms. Cynthia R. GIORGIO
05 Exec Vice Chancellor/Provost .... Dr. Paul D'ANIERI
45 Vice Chanc Planning & Budget .... Ms. Maria ANGUIANO
32 Vice Chancellor Student Affairs .... Mr. James W. SANDOVAL
10 Vice Chanc Business & Admin Svcs .... Mr. Ron T. COLEY
26 Vice Chanc University Advancement .... Mr. Peter A. HAYASHIDA
46 Vice Chancellor Research .... Dr. Michael J. PAZZANI
17 VC Hlth Affs/Dean School of Med .... Vacant
20 Vice Provost Academic Personnel .... Dr. Ameae WALKER
18 Assoc Vice Chanc Facil Plant Admin .... Vacant
84 Assoc Vice Chanc Enrollment .... Ms. LaRae LUNDGREN
30 Int Assoc Vice Chanc Development .... Mr. Hieu NGUYEN
09 Asst Vice Chanc Strat Acad Rsrch An .... Vacant
28 Asst Vice Chanc Affirm Action .... Ms. Gladys BROWN
58 Dean Graduate Division .... Dr. Joseph CHILDERS
50 Dean School of Business Admin .... Dr. Yungzeng WANG
53 Dean Grad School of Educ .... Dr. Thomas SMITH
54 Dean Bourns College of Engineering .... Dr. Reza ABBASCHIAN
79 Dean College of Humanities Arts SS .... Dr. Milagros PEÑA
81 Dean Col of Nat and Agr Sciences .... Dr. Cynthia LARIVE
06 Registrar .... Ms. Bracken J. DAILEY
80 Dean School of Public Policy .... Dr. Anil DEOLALIKAR
36 Director Career Center .... Mr. Sean GILL
37 Director Financial Aid .... Mr. Jose A. AGUILAR
38 Director Counseling Center .... Vacant
07 Director of Admissions .... Ms. Emily D. ENGELSCHALL
96 Director Material Management .... Mr. Russ LEWIS
08 Head Librarian .... Mr. Steve MANDEVILLE-GAMBLE

*University of California-San Diego (B)

9500 Gilman Drive, La Jolla CA 92093-0014
County: San Diego FICE Identification: 001317
Unit ID: 110680
Telephone: (858) 534-2230 Carnegie Class: RU/VH
FAX Number: (858) 534-6523 Calendar System: Quarter
URL: www.ucsd.edu
Established: 1960 Annual Undergrad Tuition & Fees (In-State): $15,088
Enrollment: 31,502 Coed
Affiliation or Control: State IRS Status: 501(c)3
Highest Offering: Doctorate
Program: Liberal Arts And General; Professional; Technical Emphasis
Accreditation: WC, AUD, BUS, CEA, CLPSY, DIETI, DMS, ENG, IPSY, MED, MT, PDPSY, PHAR

02 Chancellor .... Dr. Pradeep K. KHOSLA
05 Executive VC Academic Affairs .... Dr. Suresh SUBRAMANI
10 VC and Chief Financial Officer .... Mr. Pierre-Yves OUILLET
32 VC Student Affairs .... Dr. Juan GONZALEZ
11 Vice Chanc Resource Mgmt/Planning .... Mr. Gary C. MATTHEWS
65 Vice Chancellor Marine Sciences .... Dr. Margaret LEINEN
63 VC Health Science/Dean Sch Med .... Dr. David A. BRENNER
46 Vice Chancellor Research .... Dr. Sandra BROWN
28 VC for Equity Diversity & Inclusion .... Dr. Becky R. PETITT
30 Vice Chancellor Advancement .... Mr. Steve GAMER
100 Associate Chancellor/Chief of Staff .... Ms. Clare M. KRISTOFCO
56 Assoc VC Public Pgms/Dean Univ Ext .... Dr. Mary L. WALSHOK
43 Chief Campus Counsel .... Mr. Daniel W. PARK
21 AVC Business Fin Svcs/Controller .... Ms. Cheryl ROSS
88 Director Policy Admin .... Ms. Paula J. JOHNSON, CRM
23 AVC Student Health/Wellness .... Ms. Karen J. CALFAS
26 University Communications .... Ms. Clare M. KRISTOFCO
20 Asst Vice Chanc Academic Affairs .... Vacant
35 Assoc Vice Chanc Student Affairs .... Vacant
15 Int Asst VC Human Resources .... Ms. Catherine M. LEDFORD
88 Associate Vice Chancellor Research .... Dr. Miroslav KRSTIC
84 Asst Vice Chanc Admiss/Enroll Svcs .... Ms. Mae W. BROWN
13 Asst VC Admin Computing/Teleco .... Mr. Min YAO
08 University Librarian .... Mr. Brian E C. SCHOTTLAENDER
06 University Registrar .... Mr. William R. HAID
23 CEO UCSD Medical Center .... Mr. Paul VIVIANO
29 Assistant Vice Chancellor .... Vacant
96 Assoc Controller/Chief Procurement .... Mr. Ted JOHNSON
54 Dean Jacobs Sch of Engineering .... Dr. Albert P. PISANO
49 Dean Arts & Humanities .... Dr. Cristina DELLA COLETTA
81 Dean Div of Biological Sciences .... Dr. William MCGINNIS
83 Dean of Social Sciences .... Dr. Carol A. PADDEN
88 Dean Rady School of Management .... Mr. Robert S. SULLIVAN
81 Dean Physical Science .... Dr. Mark H. THIEMENS
82 Dean Sch Intl Rels/Pacific Stds .... Dr. Peter F. COWHEY
58 Dean Graduate Studies .... Dr. Kim E. BARRETT
12 Provost John Muir College .... Dr. John C. MOORE
12 Prov Thurgood Marshall Coll .... Mr. Allan HAVIS
12 Provost Earl Warren College .... Mr. Steven ADLER
12 Provost Revelle College .... Dr. Paul K. YU
12 Provost Eleanor Roosevelt College .... Dr. Richard P. MADSEN
12 Provost Sixth College .... Dr. Daniel J. DONOGHUE
38 Director Stdt Psych/Counseling Svcs .... Dr. Reina JUAREZ
18 AVC EH&S and Facilities Management .... Mr. Garry L. MAC PHERSON
41 Athletic Director .... Mr. Earl W. EDWARDS

*University of California-San Francisco (C)

513 Parnassus Avenue, Box 0402,
San Francisco CA 94143
County: San Francisco FICE Identification: 001319
Unit ID: 110699
Telephone: (415) 476-9000 Carnegie Class: Spec/Med
FAX Number: (415) 476-9634 Calendar System: Quarter
URL: www.ucsf.edu
Established: 1864 Annual Graduate Tuition & Fees: N/A
Enrollment: 3,079 Coed
Affiliation or Control: State IRS Status: 501(c)3
Highest Offering: Doctorate; No Undergraduates
Program: Professional
Accreditation: WC, DENT, DIETI, IPSY, MED, MIDWF, NURSE, PAST, PHAR, PTA

02 Chancellor .... Dr. Samuel HAWGOOD
03 Executive Vice Chancellor & Provost .... Dr. Daniel H. LOWENSTEIN
100 Associate Chancellor .... Dr. Theresa O'BRIEN
10 Interim Sr VC Finance & Admin .... Ms. Teresa COSTANTINIDIS
05 Vice Provost Academic Affairs .... Dr. Brian ALLDREDGE
63 Dean School of Medicine/VC Med Affs .... Dr. Talmadge E. KING, JR.
20 Vice Chanc Student Academic Affairs .... Dr. Elizabeth WATKINS
30 Vice Chanc Univ Develop & Alum Rels .... Mr. John FORD
26 VC Strat Communications & Univ Rels .... Ms. Barbara FRENCH
13 Assoc VC & Chief Info Officer - ITS .... Mr. Joseph BENGFORT
28 VC Diversity & Outreach .... Dr. Renee NAVARRO
32 Assoc VC Campus Life Services .... Ms. Clare SHINNERL
15 Assoc VC Human Resources .... Mr. David ODATO
18 Assoc VC Cap Pgms/Campus Architect .... Mr. Michael BADE
20 Vice Dean Academic Affairs .... Dr. Elena FUENTES-AFFLICK
37 Interim Dir Student Financial Svcs .... Mr. Ronald JAMES
43 Chief Campus Counsel .... Ms. Greta SCHNETZLER
08 University Librarian/AVC .... Ms. Karen BUTTER
19 Chief of Police .... Vacant
22 Director Affirmative Action .... Ms. Cristina PEREZ
66 Dean School of Nursing .... Dr. David VLAHOV
52 Dean School of Dentistry .... Dr. John FEATHERSTONE
67 Dean School of Pharmacy .... Dr. B. Joseph GUGLIELMO
35 Exec Director Student Life .... Dr. Carol TAKAO
39 Exec Director Campus Life Svcs .... Dr. Gary FORMAN
96 Assoc VC/Chief Procurement Officer .... Mr. James HINE
07 Registrar .... Mr. Douglas CARLSON
06 Associate Registrar .... Ms. Jina SHAMIM
36 Exec Dir Career/Prof Development .... Mr. William LINDSTAEDT
23 Exec Dir Student Health Services .... Ms. Susan ROSEN
09 Director Institutional Research .... Dr. Ning WANG

*University of California-Santa Barbara (D)

552 University Road, Santa Barbara CA 93106-0001
County: Santa Barbara FICE Identification: 001320
Unit ID: 110705
Telephone: (805) 893-8000 Carnegie Class: RU/VH
FAX Number: N/A Calendar System: Quarter
URL: www.ucsb.edu
Established: 1909 Annual Undergrad Tuition & Fees (In-State): $14,477
Enrollment: 23,051 Coed
Affiliation or Control: State IRS Status: 501(c)3
Highest Offering: Doctorate
Program: Liberal Arts And General; Teacher Preparatory
Accreditation: WC, CS, DANCE, ENG, IPSY, PSPSY

02 Chancellor .... Dr. Henry T. YANG
04 Exec Assistant to the Chancellor .... Ms. Diane O'BRIEN
05 Executive Vice Chancellor .... Dr. David B. MARSHALL
10 Dir/Controller Business & Fin Svc .... Mr. Jim R. CORKILL
46 Vice Chancellor Research .... Dr. Michael S. WITHERELL
11 Vice Chancellor Admin Services .... Mr. Marc FISHER
88 Acting AVC Admin Services .... Ms. Pam LOMBARDO
32 Acting Vice Chanc Student Affairs .... Dr. Mary J. JACOB
45 Asst Chanc Budget & Planning .... Mr. Todd G. LEE
15 Assoc Vice Chanc Acad Personnel .... Dr. John E. TALBOTT
28 AVC Diversity/Equity/Acad Policy .... Dr. Maria HERRERA-SOBEK
20 AVC Academic Programs .... Vacant
30 Assoc Vice Chancellor Development .... Ms. Beverly COLGATE
27 AVC Public Affairs & Communications .... Mr. John LONGBRAKE
84 Acting Assoc Dean Enrollment Svcs .... Dr. Michael MILLER
88 Assoc Dean Student Acad Support Svc .... Ms. Lupe GARCIA
29 Asst Vice Chanc Alumni Affairs .... Mr. George THURLOW, III
88 Dean College Creative Studies .... Dr. Bruce H. TIFFNEY
54 Dean College of Engineering .... Dr. Rod ALFERNESS
58 Dean Graduate Division .... Dr. Carol GENETTI
53 Acting Dean Gevirtz Grad Sch Educ .... Dr. Merith COSDEN
65 Dean Bren School of Env Sci & Mgmt .... Dr. Steven D. GAINES
56 Dean UC Santa Barbara Extension .... Dr. Michael T. BROWN
35 Sr Assoc Dean of Student Life .... Ms. Debbie FLEMING
79 Interim Dean Humanities/Fine Arts .... Dr. John MAJEWSKI
81 Dean Math/Life & Physical Sciences .... Dr. Pierre WILTZIUS
87 Director Summer Sessions .... Dr. Cindy BUMGARNER
83 Dean Social Sciences .... Dr. Melvin L. OLIVER
85 Director Intl Students/Scholars .... Dr. Simran SINGH
06 Registrar .... Ms. Leesa BECK
16 Acting Director Human Resources .... Ms. Cynthia SENERIZ
37 Director Financial Aid .... Dr. Michael MILLER
88 Director Audit & Advisory Service .... Mr. Robert TARSIA
07 Director Admissions .... Ms. Lisa PRZEKOP
09 Director Institutional Research .... Dr. Steven C. VELASCO
23 Exec Director Student Health Svcs .... Dr. Mary FERRIS
39 Exec Dir Housing Residential Svcs .... Mr. Wilfred E. BROWN
40 Director of UCSB Bookstore .... Mr. Mark BEISECKER
19 Chief of Police .... Mr. Dustin OLSON
41 Director Intercollegiate Athletics .... Mr. John MCCUTCHEON
86 Dir Governmental Relations .... Ms. Kirsten DESHLER
88 Director Finance/Administration .... Mr. Eric J. SONQUIST
08 University Librarian .... Ms. Denise STEPHENS
88 Director Orientation Programs .... Ms. Tricia RASCON
44 Director Capital Development .... Mr. Chuck HAINES
46 Director Campus Planning & Design .... Ms. Alissa HUMMER
31 Director Arts & Lectures .... Ms. Celesta BILLECI
88 Director Disabled Students Pgm .... Mr. Gary R. WHITE
104 Dir Campus Education Abroad Program .... Dr. Juan E. CAMPO
88 Acting Dir Env Health & Safety .... Mr. Ali AGHAYAN
88 Director MultiCultural Center .... Ms. Zaveeni KHAN-MARCUS
38 Director Counseling Services .... Dr. Jeanne STANFORD
94 Acting Director Women's Center .... Ms. Kim EQUINOA
88 Ombuds .... Ms. Kirsi AULIN
88 Exec Dir Instructional Devel .... Mr. George H. MICHAELS
36 Director Career Services .... Mr. Ignacio GALLARDO
13 Chief Information Officer .... Ms. Denise STEPHENS
43 UCSB Legal Counsel .... Ms. Nancy G. HAMILL
88 Equal Opport Sexual Harras/Title IX .... Mr. Ricardo ALCAINO
18 Director Design & Construction .... Mr. Jack WOLEVER
88 Director Univ Center/Events Center .... Mr. Gary LAWRENCE
68 Interim Director of Recreation .... Ms. Cathy CZULEGER
92 Honors Coord/Academic Advisor .... Ms. Summer HOWATT-NAB

*University of California-Santa Cruz (E)

1156 High Street, Santa Cruz CA 95064-1077
County: Santa Cruz FICE Identification: 001321
Unit ID: 110714
Telephone: (831) 459-0111 Carnegie Class: RU/VH
FAX Number: (831) 459-0146 Calendar System: Quarter
URL: www.ucsc.edu
Established: 1962 Annual Undergrad Tuition & Fees (In-State): $26,922
Enrollment: 17,866 Coed
Affiliation or Control: State IRS Status: 501(c)3
Highest Offering: Doctorate
Program: Liberal Arts And General; Professional
Accreditation: WC, ENG, IPSY

02 Chancellor .... Dr. George R. BLUMENTHAL
05 Campus Provost/Exec Vice Chancellor .... Dr. Alison GALLOWAY
10 Vice Chanc Business/Admin Services .... Dr. Sarah LATHAM
45 Vice Chancellor Planning/Budget .... Dr. Peggy DELANEY
46 Vice Chancellor Research .... Dr. Scott BRANDT
30 Vice Chanc of University Relations .... Mr. Keith BRANT
13 Vice Chanc Information Technology .... Dr. Mary DOYLE
20 Vice Prov/Dean Undergrad Educ .... Dr. Richard HUGHEY
20 Vice Provost Academic Affairs .... Dr. Herbert LEE
88 Sr Dir Silicon Valley Initiative .... Dr. Gordon RINGOLD
84 Assoc VC Enrollment Mgmt .... Ms. Michelle WHITTINGHAM
16 Asst VC Academic Personnel .... Dr. Pamela PETERSON
18 Assoc VC & Campus Architect .... Mr. John BARNES
15 Int Asst VC Staff Human Resources .... Ms. Lori CASTRO
32 AVC Student Affairs/Dn of Students .... Ms. Alma SIFUENTES
08 University Librarian .... Ms. Elizabeth COWELL
79 Dean of Humanities .... Dr. William LADUSAW
81 Dean Physical & Biological Sci .... Dr. Paul KOCH
49 Dean of the Arts .... Dr. David YAGER
83 Dean of Social Sciences .... Dr. Sheldon KAMIENIECKI
54 Dean of Engineering .... Dr. Arthur RAMIREZ
58 Asst Dean of Graduate Studies .... Dr. Jim MOORE
65 Director Institute Marine Sciences .... Dr. Gary B. GRIGGS
81 Director Institute Particle Physics .... Dr. Steven RITZ

88 Director UCO/Lick Observatory ... Dr. Michael BOLTE
12 Provost Stevenson College ... Dr. Alice YANG
12 Provost Cowell College ... Dr. Faye CROSBY
12 Interim Provost Crown College ... Dr. Manel CAMPS
12 Provost Merrill College ... Dr. Elizabeth ABRAMS
12 Provost Porter College ... Dr. Sean KEILEN
12 Provost Kresge College ... Dr. Mary FOLEY
12 Provost College Eight ... Dr. Ronnie LIPSCHUTZ
06 Registrar ... Mr. Tchad SANGER
09 Director Institutional Research ... Dr. Julian L. FERNALD
29 Director of Alumni Relations ... Ms. Shayna KENT
37 Assoc Dir Financial Aid/Operations ... Mr. Patrick REGISTER
22 Staff Dir EEO/Affirmative Action ... Mr. Ashish SAHNI
86 Director Government Relations ... Ms. Donna M. BLITZER
26 Dir Marketing/Communications ... Ms. Lisa NIELSEN
38 Assoc Director Student Counseling ... Dr. Maryjan MURPHY
96 Director of Purchasing ... Mr. John BONO

University of East-West Medicine (A)

595 Lawrence Expressway, Sunnyvale CA 94085
County: Santa Clara FICE Identification: 039953
Unit ID: 447801
Telephone: (408) 733-1878 Carnegie Class: Spec/Health
FAX Number: (408) 636-7705 Calendar System: Trimester
URL: www.uewm.edu
Established: 1997 Annual Undergrad Tuition & Fees: $33,660
Enrollment: 234 Coed
Affiliation or Control: Proprietary IRS Status: Proprietary
Highest Offering: Master's
Program: Professional
Accreditation: ACUP

01 President ... Dr. Ying Qiu WANG
11 COO ... Doreen SIMMONS

† Granted candidacy at the Doctorate level.

University of La Verne (B)

1950 Third Street, La Verne CA 91750-4443
County: Los Angeles FICE Identification: 001216
Unit ID: 117140
Telephone: (909) 593-3511 Carnegie Class: DRU
FAX Number: (909) 593-0965 Calendar System: Semester
URL: www.laverne.edu
Established: 1891 Annual Undergrad Tuition & Fees: $38,560
Enrollment: 8,517 Coed
Affiliation or Control: Independent Non-Profit IRS Status: 501(c)3
Highest Offering: Doctorate
Program: Liberal Arts And General; Teacher Preparatory; Professional
Accreditation: WC, CAATE, CLPSY, #LAW, SPAA, TED

01 President ... Dr. Devorah A. LIEBERMAN
05 Provost & Vice President ... Dr. Jonathan REED
88 Special Assistant to Provost ... Dr. Mark GOOR
10 Chief Financial Officer ... Mr. Avedis (Avo) KECHICHIAN
30 Vice President Univ Advancement ... Ms. Myra GARCIA
84 Vice Pres Strategic Enroll & Comm ... Dr. Homa SHABAHANG
50 Dean College Business/Public Mgmt ... Dr. Ibrahim (Abe) HELOU
53 Int Dean College Educ/Org Ldrship ... Dr. Barbara POLING
61 Dean College of Law ... Mr. Gilbert HOLMES
32 Dean Student Affairs ... Dr. Loretta RAHMANI
12 Dean Regional & Online Programs ... Dr. Stephen L. LESNIAK
07 Dean of Admissions ... Mr. Chris KRZAK
88 Assoc VP Academic Sppt/Retent Svcs ... Ms. Adeline CARDENAS-CLAGUE
21 Associate Vice President of Finance . Ms. Lori K. GORDIEN CASE
15 Chief Human Resources Officer ... Ms. Jody L. BOMBA
18 Vice President of Facilities/ Tech ... Dr. Clive K. HOUSTON-BROWN
35 Associate Dean Student Affairs ... Mrs. Ruby S. MONTANO-CORDOVA
88 Asst Dean Grad Acad Supp/Ret Svcs ... Ms. Jo Nell BAKER
84 Assoc VP & Chief Marketing Officer ... Mr. Fred A. CHYR
85 Director International Student Svcs ... Dr. Jeffrey NONEMAKER
18 Sr Dir Physical Plant Oper & Svcs ... Mr. Robert D. BEEBE
07 Director Admin & Operation ... Mr. Jason NEAL
26 Director of Public Relations ... Mrs. Alisha ROSAS
29 Sr Dir Advancement Oper & Services ... Ms. Bianca ROMERO
38 Dir Counseling & Psych Services ... Dr. Elleni R. KOULOS
88 Director Student Accounts ... Ms. Xochitl E. MARTINEZ
104 Study Abroad Advisor ... Dr. Alfred CLARK
96 Director Purchasing & Procurement ... Mrs. Deborah S. DEACY
28 Director Multicultural Affairs ... Dr. Daniel L. LOERA
23 Dir Health Svcs/Svcs for Stds-Disab ... Ms. Cynthia K. DENNE
39 Assoc Dean of Stdnts/Dir Stdnt Hous ... Mr. Juan REGALADO
36 Asst Dean Student Career Support ... Ms. Mindy BAGGISH
88 Dir Center for Adv/Teaching & Lrng ... Dr. Sammy ELZARKA
88 Director Graduate Success Center ... Dr. Linda DELONG
41 Athletic Director ... Ms. Julie KLINE
06 Registrar ... Ms. Marilyn S. DAVIES
08 University Librarian ... Dr. Vinaya L. TRIPURANENI
28 Chief Diversity/Inclusivity Officer ... Dr. Joy LEI
09 Director of Institutional Research ... Dr. Leeshawn MOORE
42 Chaplain/Dir of Campus Ministry ... Dr. Zandra L. WAGONER
88 Director of La Verne Experience ... Dr. Kathleen WEAVER
90 Sr Dir Admission Oper/Tech Svcs ... Mrs. Loreto D'MONTE
88 Director High Desert ... Ms. Juli ROBERTS
88 Director Inland Empire ... Mr. Allen STOUT
88 Director Kern County ... Dr. Nora DOMINGUEZ
88 Director Orange County ... Dr. Todd ECKEL
88 Director Point Mugu NAWC ... Mr. Jamie DEMPSEY
88 Sr Ex Dir San Fernando Valley ... Dr. Nelly KAZMAN
88 Director Vandenberg AFB ... Ms. Kitt VINCENT
88 Director Ventura County ... Mr. Kevin LAACK
88 Director International Admission ... Mr. Adam WU
20 Associate Provost ... Dr. Beatriz GONZALEZ
88 Director of Civic Engagement ... Ms. Marisol MORALES

University of the Pacific (C)

3601 Pacific Avenue, Stockton CA 95211-0197
County: San Joaquin FICE Identification: 001329
Unit ID: 120883
Telephone: (209) 946-2011 Carnegie Class: DRU
FAX Number: (209) 946-2845 Calendar System: Semester
URL: www.pacific.edu
Established: 1851 Annual Undergrad Tuition & Fees: $42,414
Enrollment: 6,304 Coed
Affiliation or Control: Independent Non-Profit IRS Status: 501(c)3
Highest Offering: Doctorate
Program: Liberal Arts And General; Teacher Preparatory; Professional
Accreditation: WC, ART, @AUD, BUS, CAATE, CS, DENT, DH, ENG, IPSY, LAW, MUS, PHAR, PTA, SP, TED

01 President ... Pamela A. EIBECK
05 Provost ... Maria G. PALLAVICINI
10 Vice President Business & Finance ... Ken MULLEN
32 Vice President Student Life ... Patrick DAY
30 VP Development & Alumni Relations ... G. Burnham 'Burnie' ATTERBURY
101 VP & Secretary to Board of Regents ... Mary Lou LACKEY
13 VP Technology/CIO ... Art SPRECHER
21 Associate VP Business/Finance ... Ron ELLISON
84 Vice Provost for Enrollment Svcs ... J. Michael THOMPSON
88 Vice Provost for Distrib Learning ... Vernon SMITH
26 Interim Assoc VP Communications ... Stacy MCAFEE
51 Asst Provost Ctr Prof & Cont Educ ... Barbara L. SHAW
86 AVP External Relations ... Stacy MCAFEE
45 Assoc VP Planning ... Linda BUCKLEY
49 Dean College of the Pacific ... Rena FRADEN
50 Dean Eberhardt School Business ... Lewis GALE
52 Int Dean Dugoni School of Dentistry ... Nader NADERSHAHI
53 Int Dean Benerd School of Education ... Linda WEBSTER
54 Dean Sch of Eng/Comp Science ... Steven HOWELL
61 Dean McGeorge School of Law ... Jay MOOTZ
64 Interim Dean Conservatory of Music ... Daniel EBBERS
67 Dean Long Sch Pharm/Hlth Sciences ... Phillip R. OPPENHEIMER
36 Assoc VP for Career Development ... Tom VECCHIONE
08 Dean of the Library ... Vacant
58 Dean Research/Graduate Studies ... Bhaskara JASTI
25 Sponsored Pgms Administrator ... Vacant
29 Exec Dir of Alumni Relations ... Kelli PAGE
37 Director of Financial Aid ... Lynn FOX
07 Director of Admissions ... Rich TOLEDO
06 Registrar ... Ann GILLEN
09 Director Institutional Research ... Mike ROGERS
35 Director Student Activities ... Vacant
96 Director of Purchasing ... Ronda MARR
92 Director Honors Program ... Balint SZATARAY
93 Director Multicultural Affairs ... Ines RUIZ-HUSTON
94 Director Gender Studies ... Traci ROBERTS-CAMPS
38 Director of Counseling Services ... Stacie TURKS
39 Director of Housing ... Torry BROUILLARD-BRUCE
41 Director of Athletics ... Ted LELAND
42 University Chaplain ... Joel LOHR
15 Asst VP Human Resources ... Jane L. LEWIS
40 Director of Bookstore ... Nicole CASTILLO
19 Director of Public Safety ... Michael BELCHER
18 Director of Physical Plant ... Scott HEATON
82 Director Sch International Studies ... William HERRIN
04 Administrative Asst to President ... Julie LALONDE
102 AVP Foundation/Corporate Relations ... Scott BIEDERMANN
44 AVP Development ... Bill JOHNSON
100 Chief of Staff ... Bett SCHUMACHER
104 Dir International Programs Services ... Ryan GRIFFITH
43 Dir Legal Services/General Counsel ... Kevin MILLS

University of the People (D)

225 S. Lake Ave, Ste300, Pasadena CA 91101
County: Los Angeles Identification: 667160
Telephone: (626) 264-8880 Carnegie Class: Not Classified
FAX Number: N/A Calendar System: Other
URL: www.uopeople.edu
Established: 2009 Annual Undergrad Tuition & Fees: N/A
Enrollment: 560 Coed
Affiliation or Control: Independent Non-Profit IRS Status: 501(c)3
Highest Offering: Baccalaureate
Program: Occupational; 2-Year Principally Bachelor's Creditable
Accreditation: DEAC

01 President & Founder ... Mr. Shai RESHEF
05 Provost ... Dr. David HARRIS COHEN
45 VP for Strategy & Planning ... Mr. Yoav VENTURA
13 Vice President of Technology ... Ms. Hadass ADMON
10 CFO ... Mr. Paul AFFUSO
20 Vice Provost ... Dr. Roxie SMITH

University of Philosophical Research (E)

3910 Los Feliz Boulevard, Los Angeles CA 90027
County: Los Angeles Identification: 666373
Telephone: (323) 663-2167 Carnegie Class: Not Classified
FAX Number: (323) 663-9443 Calendar System: Quarter
URL: www.uprs.edu
Established: 1998 Annual Undergrad Tuition & Fees: $6,700
Enrollment: 205 Coed
Affiliation or Control: Independent Non-Profit IRS Status: 501(c)3
Highest Offering: Master's
Program: Liberal Arts And General
Accreditation: DEAC

01 President/Chief Executive Officer ... Dr. Obadiah HARRIS
05 Dean of Academic Affairs ... Dr. Debashish BANERJI
06 Registrar ... Mr. John CHASE
10 Chief Financial Officer ... Mr. Gregory WILLIS

University of Phoenix Bay Area Campus (F)

3590 N First Street, San Jose CA 95134-1805
Telephone: (800) 266-2107 Identification: 770193
Accreditation: &NH, ACBSP

† Branch campus of University of Phoenix, Tempe, AZ.

University of Phoenix Central Valley Campus (G)

45 River Park Place West, Fresno CA 93720-1552
Telephone: (800) 266-2107 Identification: 770190
Accreditation: &NH, ACBSP

† Branch campus of University of Phoenix, Tempe, AZ.

University of Phoenix Sacramento Valley Campus (H)

2860 Gateway Oaks Drive, Sacramento CA 95833-4334
Telephone: (800) 266-2107 Identification: 770191
Accreditation: &NH, ACBSP

† Branch campus of University of Phoenix, Tempe, AZ.

University of Phoenix San Diego Campus (I)

9645 Granite Ridge Dr, Suite 200, San Diego CA 92123-2658
Telephone: (800) 473-4346 Identification: 770192
Accreditation: &NH, ACBSP

† Branch campus of University of Phoenix, Tempe, AZ.

University of Phoenix Southern California Campus (J)

3100 Bristol Street, Costa Mesa CA 92626-3099
Telephone: (800) 888-1968 Identification: 770189
Accreditation: &NH, ACBSP

† Branch campus of University of Phoenix, Tempe, AZ.

University of Redlands (K)

PO Box 3080, Redlands CA 92373-0999
County: San Bernardino FICE Identification: 001322
Unit ID: 121691
Telephone: (909) 793-2121 Carnegie Class: Master's L
FAX Number: (909) 793-2029 Calendar System: Semester
URL: www.redlands.edu
Established: 1907 Annual Undergrad Tuition & Fees: $20,500
Enrollment: 5,333 Coed
Affiliation or Control: Independent Non-Profit IRS Status: 501(c)3
Highest Offering: Doctorate
Program: Liberal Arts And General; Teacher Preparatory; Professional
Accreditation: WC, MUS, SP

01 President ... Dr. Ralph W. KUNCL
05 Provost ... Dr. Kathy OGREN
10 Vice Pres Finance/Administration ... Mr. Cory NOMURA
26 Vice President University Relations ... Ms. Anita A. WEST
32 Vice President/Dean Student Life ... Ms. Charlotte G. BURGESS
84 Vice Pres of Enrollment Management ... Mr. Kevin DYERLY
30 Vice Pres for Advancement ... Ms. Anita WEST
100 Chief of Staff ... Ms. Michelle ROGERS
44 Assoc Vice Pres Development ... Mr. Ray WATTS
21 Director Financial Ops & Controller ... Ms. Patricia M. CAUDLE
50 Int Dean School of Business ... Dr. Keith ROBERTS
53 Dean School of Education ... Dr. Andrew WALL
49 Int Dean Arts & Sciences ... Dr. Fred RABINOWITZ
64 Dean School of Music ... Dr. Andrew GLENDENING
28 Asc Dean Campus Diversity/Inclusion .. Ms. Leela MADHAVARAU
42 Chaplain ... Rev. John T. WALSH
06 Registrar ... Ms. Maria JOHNSON
104 Director Study Abroad ... Ms. Sarah N. FALKENSTIEN
37 Director of Financial Aid ... Ms. Alisha AGUILAR
90 Director Academic Computing ... Mr. Shariq AHMED
81 Director Center of Sciences & Math ... Dr. Barbara M. MURRAY
88 Director of Environmental Programs ... Dr. Lamont C. HEMPEL
08 Director of Library Services ... Ms. Gabriela SONNTAG
15 Director of Human Resources ... Ms. Roberta G. DELLHIME
22 EEO & Employee Relations Manager ... Vacant
09 Director of Institutional Research ... Ms. Wendy MCEWEN
19 Director of Public Safety ... Mr. Jeffrey TALBOTT
18 Director of Facilities Management ... Mr. Roger CELLINI
29 Director of Alumni Relations ... Mr. John G. SERBEIN
20 Asst Dean of Academic/Student Life ... Ms. Amy WILMS

38 Director Student Counseling Ctr .... Dr. Lorraine YOUNG
41 Director of Athletics .... Mr. Jeffrey MARTINEZ
96 Director of Purchasing .... Ms. Sandi TAYLOR
36 Director Student Placement .... Ms. Kathryn WOOD

University of St. Augustine for Health Sciences (A)

700 Windy Point Drive, San Marcos CA 92069

County: San Diego FICE Identification: 031713
Unit ID: 367954

Telephone: (706) 591-3012 Carnegie Class: Spec/Health
FAX Number: (706) 591-3068 Calendar System: Trimester
URL: www.usa.edu
Established: 1979 Annual Graduate Tuition & Fees: $43,107
Enrollment: 1,913 Coed
Affiliation or Control: Proprietary IRS Status: Proprietary
Highest Offering: Doctorate; No Undergraduates
Program: Professional
Accreditation: WC, DEAC, OT, PTA

00 Interim CEO .... Dr. Susan SAXTON
01 President/Chief Academic Officer .... Dr. Wanda NITSCH
05 Vice President Academic Operations .... Dr. Cindy MATHENA
32 Vice Pres Student Admin .... Dr. Jeremy WELLS
10 Executive Director of Finance .... Ms. Jennifer BRIAR
75 Dir Inst of Occupational Therapy .... Dr. Karen HOWELL
75 Program Dir Occupational Therapy-CA .... Dr. Judith OLSON
88 Chair Institute of Physical Therapy .... Dr. Ellen LOWE
88 Program Dir Physical Therapy-FL .... Dr. Jeffrey ROT
88 Program Dir Physical Therapy-TX .... Dr. Manuel A. DOMENECH
88 Dir Trans Doctor Physical Therapy .... Dr. Jodi LIPHART
75 Director Trans Doctor Occup Therapy .... Dr. Anne HULL
88 Director of DHSc/EdD Programs .... Dr. Dan LOFALD
06 Registrar .... Ms. Diane RONDINELLI
07 Director of Admissions .... Ms. Adrianne JONES
51 Director of Continuing Education .... Ms. Lori HANKINS
08 Head Librarian .... Ms. Julie EVENER

University of San Diego (B)

5998 Alcala Park, San Diego CA 92110-2492

County: San Diego FICE Identification: 010395
Unit ID: 122436

Telephone: (619) 260-4600 Carnegie Class: DRU
FAX Number: (619) 260-6833 Calendar System: 4/1/4
URL: www.sandiego.edu
Established: 1949 Annual Undergrad Tuition & Fees: $44,586
Enrollment: 8,349 Coed
Affiliation or Control: Roman Catholic IRS Status: 501(c)3
Highest Offering: Doctorate
Program: Liberal Arts And General; Teacher Preparatory; Professional
Accreditation: WC, BUS, BUSA, CACREP, ENG, IPSY, LAW, MFCD, NURSE, TED

01 President .... Dr. James T. HARRIS
04 Special Assistant to the President .... Ms. Elaine ATENCIO
05 Vice President & Provost .... Dr. Andrew T. ALLEN
10 VP Finance/Chief Financial Officer .... Ms. Terry KALFAYAN
42 Vice President Mission & Ministry .... Msgr. Daniel J. DILLABOUGH
32 Vice President Student Affairs .... Ms. Carmen M. VAZQUEZ
30 Vice President Univ Relations .... Dr. Timothy L. O'MALLEY
41 Vice President for Athletics .... Mr. Ky L. SNYDER
49 Dean College of Arts & Sciences .... Dr. Noelle NORTON
50 Dean School of Business Admin .... Vacant
54 Dean Shiley-Marcos School of Engr .... Dr. Chell ROBERTS
61 Dean School of Law .... Mr. Stephen C. FERRUOLO
53 Dean Sch Leadership/Educ Sciences .... Dr. Nicholas LADANY
66 Dean School Nursing/Health Science .... Dr. Sally B. HARDIN
88 Dean School of Peace Studies .... Dr. Patricia MARQUEZ
51 Dean Prof & Continuing Education .... Dr. Jason LEMON
08 Dean University Library .... Dr. Theresa BYRD
43 General Counsel .... Ms. Kelly C. DOUGLAS
20 Vice Provost .... Dr. Thomas R. HERRINTON
13 Vice Provost & Chief Info Officer .... Mr. Christopher W. WESSELLS
06 University Registrar .... Ms. Susan H. BUGBEE
20 Associate Provost Academic Planning .... Dr. Carole HUSTON
28 Assoc Provost for Incl & Diversity .... Dr. Esteban DEL RIO
20 Assoc Provost International Affairs .... Dr. Denise DIMON
21 Assoc Vice Pres & Controller .... Ms. Katy ROIG
84 Asst VP Enrollment Management .... Mr. Stephen F. PULTZ
15 AVP & Chief Human Resources Officer .... Ms. Karen BRIGGS
18 Asst VP Facilities Management .... Mr. Roger MANION
26 Asst Vice Pres Univ Communications .... Mr. Peter MARLOW
26 Asst Vice Pres Media Communications .... Ms. Pamela GRAY PAYTON
19 Asst Vice President Public Safety .... Mr. Larry E. BARNETT
35 Asst VP & Dean of Students .... Dr. Donald R. GODWIN
109 Asst VP Auxiliary Services .... Mr. Andre MALLIE
07 Director of Admissions .... Ms. Minh-Ha HOANG
09 Dir Inst Research & Planning .... Dr. Paula S. KRIST
90 Sr Director Academic Tech Services .... Ms. Shahra MESHKATY
91 Senior Director EASS .... Mr. Avi BADWAL
102 Sr Director Foundation Relations .... Ms. Annette KETNER
86 Sr Dir Community/Govt Relations .... Mr. Thomas R. CLEARY
44 Senior Director Planned Giving .... Mr. John A. PHILLIPS
29 Senior Director Alumni Relations .... Mr. Charles BASS
44 Director Annual Giving .... Mr. Philip GARLAND
36 Director Career Services .... Ms. Robin DARMON
38 Director Counseling Center .... Dr. Stephen D. SPRINKLE
37 Director Financial Aid Services .... Ms. Judith LEWIS LOGUE
92 Director Honors Program .... Dr. James O. GUMP
39 Director Housing .... Vacant
85 Dir International Students/Scholars .... Ms. Chia-Yen LIN
104 Dir International Studies Abroad .... Dr. Kira A. ESPIRITU
93 Director Multicultural Center .... Dr. Mayte PEREZ-FRANCO
27 Director News Bureau .... Ms. Elizabeth HARMAN
96 Director Procurement Services .... Ms. Dawn L. ANDERSON
25 Director Sponsored Programs .... Ms. Traci MERRILL
23 Director Student Health Center .... Ms. Pamela J. SIKES
106 Dir Online Education/E-learning .... Ms. Roxanne MORRISON

University of San Francisco (C)

2130 Fulton Street, San Francisco CA 94117-1080

County: San Francisco FICE Identification: 001325
Unit ID: 122612

Telephone: (415) 422-5555 Carnegie Class: DRU
FAX Number: (415) 422-2303 Calendar System: 4/1/4
URL: www.usfca.edu
Established: 1855 Annual Undergrad Tuition & Fees: $42,180
Enrollment: 10,701 Coed
Affiliation or Control: Roman Catholic IRS Status: 501(c)3
Highest Offering: Doctorate
Program: Liberal Arts And General; Teacher Preparatory; Professional
Accreditation: WC, BUS, IPSY, LAW, NURSE, PH, SPAA

01 President .... Rev. Paul J. FITZGERALD, SJ
05 Interim Provost .... Dr. James WISER
00 Chancellor .... Vacant
10 Vice President Business & Finance .... Mr. Charles E. CROSS
26 Vice Pres Communication & Marketing .... Mr. David F. MACMILLAN
88 Vice Pres International Relations .... Dr. Stanley D. NEL
30 Vice President Development .... Mr. Peter J. WILCH
32 Vice Provost Student Life .... Dr. Peter J. NOVAK
43 University Counsel .... Ms. Donna J. DAVIS
13 Chief Information Officer .... Mr. Opinder BAWA
20 Senior Vice Provost Acad Affairs .... Dr. Gerardo MARIN
45 Vice Prov Ctr Inst Planning/Effect .... Dr. Jeff HAMRICK
84 Vice Provost Strategic Enrollment .... Mr. J. Robert SPATIG
88 Assoc Vice Prov Planning and Budget .... Mr. Michael J. HARRINGTON
12 Vice Prov Branch Campus .... Dr. Michael J. WEBBER
15 Asst Vice Pres Human Resources ... Ms. Martha A. PEUGH-WADE
21 Assoc Vice Pres Account & Bus Svcs .... Mr. Frank M. WASILEWSKI
26 Assoc VP Public Affairs/Univ Comm .... Mr. Gary MCDONALD
18 Asst Vice Pres Facilities Mgmt .... Mr. Michael LONDON
28 Assoc Vice Prov Diversity/ Community .... Dr. Mary J. WARDELL-GHIRARDUZZI
88 Assoc Vice Prov Acad Affs/Historian .... Dr. Alan L. ZIAJKA
61 Dean of the School of Law .... Mr. John D. TRASVINA
49 Dean College Arts & Sciences .... Dr. Marcelo F. CAMPERI
08 Dean of Libraries .... Dr. Tyrone H. CANNON
53 Dean School of Education .... Dr. Kevin K. KUMASHIRO
50 Dean School of Management .... Dr. Elizabeth B. DAVIS
66 Dean School of Nursing .... Dr. Judith KARSHMER
04 Exec Asst to President/Sec BOT .... Ms. Jaci E. NEESAM
37 Senior Assoc Dean Acad/Dir Fin Aid .... Ms. Susan L. MURPHY
07 Assoc Dean & Director of Admissions .... Mr. Michael HUGHES
06 Assoc Dean University Registrar .... Mr. Robert L. BROMFIELD
96 Exec Dir Purchasing & Ancillary Svc .... Ms. Janet L. TEYMOURTASH
38 Senior Director Counseling Center .... Dr. Barbara J. THOMAS
36 Senior Dir of Career Services .... Mr. James CATIGGAY
19 Senior Director of Public Safety .... Dr. Daniel LAWSON
42 Director University Ministry .... Ms. Julia A. DOWD
85 Director Ctr for Global Education .... Ms. Sharon F. LI
85 Dir International Student Services .... Ms. Laura GERTH
41 Director of Athletics .... Mr. Scott A. SIDWELL
09 Director Institutional Research .... Mr. Theodore M. LYDON, JR.
29 Asst VP Alumni Engage/Annual Giving .... Ms. Jessica JORDAN
16 Dir Employment & Employee Relations .... Ms. Diane L. NELSON
39 Int Dir Student Housing/Res Educ ..... Mr. Golden T. VENTERS, III
24 Dir Ctr Learning Tech & Instruct .... Dr. John BANSAVICH
102 Assoc Vice Pres Found/Corp Rel .... Ms. Marly A. NORRIS
105 Sr Director Web Communications .... Ms. Marlene K. TOM
108 Director Institutional Assessment .... Vacant
25 Director Contracts/Grants Admin .... Ms. Laurie TRELEVEN
91 Senior Director Admin Computing .... Mr. Way LEON
106 Vice Provost Online Education .... Cr. Carol BATKER

University of Southern California (D)

University Park, Los Angeles CA 90089-0012

County: Los Angeles FICE Identification: 001328
Unit ID: 123961

Telephone: (213) 740-2311 Carnegie Class: RU/VH
FAX Number: (213) 740-8502 Calendar System: Semester
URL: www.usc.edu
Established: 1880 Annual Undergrad Tuition & Fees: $49,464
Enrollment: 43,000 Coed
Affiliation or Control: Independent Non-Profit IRS Status: 501(c)3
Highest Offering: Doctorate
Program: Occupational; Liberal Arts And General; Teacher Preparatory; Professional
Accreditation: WC, ANEST, ARCPA, BUS, BUSA, CLPSY, CS, DENT, DH, @DIETC, ENG, HSA, IPSY, JOUR, LAW, LSAR, MED, OT, PCSAS, PDPSY, PH, PHAR, PLNG, PTA, SPAA, SW, TED

01 President .... Dr. C. L M. NIKIAS
05 Provost and Sr VP Academic Affairs .... Dr. Michael QUICK
11 Sr VP Administration .... Mr. Todd R. DICKEY
10 Sr VP Finance & CFO .... Mr. Robert ABELES
26 Sr VP University Relations .... Mr. Thomas SAYLES
30 Sr VP University Advancement .... Mr. Albert R. CHECCIO
23 Sr VP & CEO for USC Health .... Mr. Thomas E. JACKIEWICZ
88 Chief Investment Officer .... Ms. Lisa MAZZOCCO
43 General Counsel/Secretary of Univ .... Ms. Carol MAUCH AMIR
32 Vice Provost for Student Affairs .... Dr. Ainsley CARRY
07 VP Admissions and Planning .... Dr. L. Katharine HARRINGTON
46 VP for Research .... Dr. Randolph W. HALL
88 VP for Real Estate Dev & Asset .... Vacant
88 VP for Athletic Compliance .... Mr. David M. ROBERTS
88 VP Capital Construction/Facilities .... Mr. Lloyd SILBERSTEIN
21 VP for Finance .... Ms. Margo STEURBAUT
88 VP for Health Sciences Development .... Mr. Dave CARRERA
27 VP Public Relations & Marketing .... Ms. Brenda K. MACEO
41 Athletic Director .... Mr. Patrick C. HADEN
100 Chief of Staff/Dir of Protocol .... Mr. Dennis CORNELL
00 President Emeritus .... Dr. Steven B. SAMPLE
60 Dean Annenberg School Communication .... Dr. Ernest J. WILSON, III
48 Dean School of Architecture .... Mr. Qingyun MA
50 Dean Marshall School of Business .... Mr. James G. ELLIS
88 Dean School of Cinematic Arts .... Dr. Elizabeth M. DALEY
66 Dean Kaufman School of Dance .... Dr. Robert A. CUTIETTA
52 Dean Ostrow School of Dentistry .... Dr. Avishai SADAN
53 Dean Rossier School of Education .... Dr. Karen S. GALLAGHER
54 Dean Viterbi School of Engineering .... Dr. Yannis C. YORTSOS
57 Dean Roski School of Fine Arts .... Dr. Erica MUHL
88 Dean Davis School of Gerontology .... Dr. Pinchas COHEN
61 Dean Gould School of Law .... Mr. Andrew GUZMAN
63 Dean Keck School of Medicine .... Dr. Carmen A. PULIAFITO
64 Dean Thornton School of Music .... Dr. Robert A. CUTIETTA
67 Dean School of Pharmacy .... Dr. Glenn STIMMEL
70 Dean School of Social Work .... Dr. Marilyn L. FLYNN
88 Dean School of Dramatic Arts .... Mr. David BRIDEL
88 Dean Price School of Public Policy .... Dr. Jack H. KNOTT
49 Dean Dornsife Col Ltrs Arts & Sci .... Dr. Steve A. KAY
42 Dean Religious Life .... Mr. Varun SONI
06 Dean Academic Records & Registrar .... Dr. Douglas SHOOK
08 Dean University Libraries .... Ms. Catherine QUINLAN
07 Dean of Admission .... Mr. Timothy BRUNOLD
37 Dean of Financial Aid .... Mr. Thomas MCWHORTER
88 Assoc Sr VP Admin Operations .... Mr. David W. WRIGHT
29 Assoc Sr VP and Campaign Director .... Mr. Scott M. MORY
88 Asst VP Talent & Org Effectiveness .... Dr. Mary K. CAMPBELL
28 Exec Dir Office of Equity/Diversity .... Ms. Jody SHIPPER
38 Dir Counseling & Psychological Svcs .... Dr. Ilene ROSENSTEIN
88 Vice Provost and Senior Advisor .... Dr. Martin L. LEVINE
20 Vice Prov for Graduate Programs .... Dr. Sarah PRATT
20 Vice Prov for Undergraduate Program ...... Dr. Eugene N. BICKERS
13 Vice Prov for Info Tech Svcs/CIO .... Mr. Douglas SHOOK
88 Vice Prov Acad Ops & Strategy .... Mr. Mark TODD
88 Exec Dir USC Stevens Ctr for Innov .... Ms. Jennifer DYER
88 Vice Prov Global Initiatives .... Dr. Anthony BAILEY
20 Vice Provost for Faculty Affairs .... Dr. Beth E. MEYEROWITZ

University of the West (E)

1409 Walnut Grove Avenue, Rosemead CA 91770-3709

County: Los Angeles FICE Identification: 036963
Unit ID: 449870

Telephone: (626) 571-8811 Carnegie Class: Bac/Diverse
FAX Number: (626) 571-1413 Calendar System: Semester
URL: www.uwest.edu
Established: 1991 Annual Undergrad Tuition & Fees: $10,411
Enrollment: 368 Coed
Affiliation or Control: Independent Non-Profit IRS Status: 501(c)3
Highest Offering: Doctorate
Program: Liberal Arts And General
Accreditation: WC

01 President .... Dr. Stephen MORGAN
05 Chief Academic Officer .... Dr. Peter ROJCEWICZ
32 Dean of Student Affairs .... Ms. Vanessa KARAM
84 Dean of Enrollment .... Ms. Maria AYON
10 Chief Financial Officer .... Dr. Bill CHEN
08 Director of Library .... Ms. Ling Ling KUO
06 Registrar .... Ms. Jeanette ANDERSON
35 Student Life Coordinator .... Mr. Eddie ESCALANTE
73 Chair of Religious Studies .... Dr. Jane IWAMURA
50 Chair of Business Admin .... Dr. Victor KANE
97 Chair of General Education .... Dr. Janice GORE
83 Chair of Psychology .... Dr. Hiroshi SASASKI
88 Chair of English/ESL .... Mr. Michael GROSSO

Valley College of Medical Careers (F)

8399 Topanga Canyon Blvd Ste 200, West Hills CA 91304

County: Los Angeles FICE Identification: 041145
Unit ID: 449445

Telephone: (818) 883-9002 Carnegie Class: Not Classified
FAX Number: (818) 883-9003 Calendar System: Semester
URL: www.vcmc.edu
Established: Annual Undergrad Tuition & Fees: $13,550
Enrollment: 94 Coed
Affiliation or Control: Proprietary IRS Status: Proprietary
Highest Offering: Associate Degree
Program: Occupational
Accreditation: ABHES, SURTEC

01 Assistant Campus Director .... Mr. Tony PINA

Vanguard University of Southern California (A)

55 Fair Drive, Costa Mesa CA 92626-6597

County: Orange FICE Identification: 001293
Unit ID: 123651
Telephone: (714) 556-3610 Carnegie Class: Bac/Diverse
FAX Number: (714) 957-9317 Calendar System: Semester
URL: www.vanguard.edu
Established: 1920 Annual Undergrad Tuition & Fees: $30,050
Enrollment: 2,255 Coed
Affiliation or Control: Assemblies Of God Church IRS Status: 501(c)3
Highest Offering: Master's
Program: 2-Year Principally Bachelor's Creditable; Liberal Arts And General; Teacher Preparatory; Professional
Accreditation: WC, MUS, NURSE, THEA

01 President .... Dr. Michael J. BEALS
04 Exec Assistant to the President .... Ms. Shree CARTER
05 Provost/Vice President Acad Affairs .... Dr. Doretha O'QUINN
20 Assoc Provost/Dean Col Arts & Sci .... Dr. Michael D. WILSON
58 Dean Grad and Professional Studies .... Dr. Andrew STENHOUSE
73 Director for Graduate Religion .... Dr. Richard ISRAEL
53 Director for Graduate Education .... Dr. Jerry TERNES
83 Director for Graduate Psychology .... Dr. Jerre WHITE
06 Registrar .... Ms. Judy HAMILTON
09 Director of Institutional Research .... Dr. Ludmilla PRASLOVA
08 Head Librarian .... Ms. Alison ENGLISH
41 Athletic Director .... Mr. Bob WILSON
10 Chief Financial Officer .... Mr. Jeremy MOSER
21 Controller .... Ms. Jill ROBINSON
21 Asst Dir of Accounting Operations .... Ms. Krystal GOWENS
96 Asst Dir of Fiscal Management .... Ms. Katy BENITO
19 Director of Campus Safety Services .... Mr. Paul TURGEON
13 Chief Information Officer .... Mr. Derek DENSBERGER
15 Director of Human Resources .... Mr. Joe BAFFA
18 Director of Facility Services .... Mr. Bruce CROUCH
40 Bookstore Manager .... Mr. Matt ACUNA
101 Board Professional .... Ms. Shree CARTER
42 University Campus Pastor .... Rev. Jonathan ALLBAUGH
32 Vice President of Student Life .... Dr. Tim YOUNG
39 Student Housing Coordinator .... Ms. Susan PARK
24 Director of Learning Skills .... Ms. Barbi ROUSE
38 Director of Counseling Services .... Dr. Doug HUTCHINSON
36 Career Planning Coordinator .... Ms. Kimberly GREENE
28 Director of Diversity .... Vacant
84 VP for Enrollment Management .... Ms. Kim JOHNSON
07 Director of Undergrad Admissions .... Ms. Susan PARKS
07 Dir of Grad/Prof Studies Admissions .... Mrs. Kristy STARKEY
37 Director of Student Financial Aid .... Ms. Denise PENA
30 VP University Advancement .... Mr. Justin MCINTEE
44 Director of Annual Fund .... Ms. Erin MCHENRY
29 Director of Alumni Relations .... Mr. Joel GACKLE
26 Chief Communications Officer .... Ms. Erin HALES
86 Director of Veteran/Government Rels .... Mr. Brent THEOBALD

*Ventura County Community College District (B)

255 W Stanley Avenue, Suite 150, Ventura CA 93001-1348

County: Ventura FICE Identification: 006863
Unit ID: 125019
Telephone: (805) 652-5500 Carnegie Class: N/A
FAX Number: (805) 652-7700
URL: www.vcccd.edu

01 Chancellor .... Dr. Bernard LUSKIN
10 Int Vice Chanc Bus Svcs/Fin Mgmt .... Mr. Dave KEEBLER
15 Vice Chanc of Human Resources .... Mr. Michael SHANAHAN
13 Assoc Vice Chanc of IT .... Mr. Dave FUHRMANN
11 Director of Admin Relations .... Ms. Clare GEISEN
96 Director of General Services .... Ms. Terry COBOS
21 District Budget Officer .... Vacant
16 Director of HR/Operations .... Mr. Gary MAEHERA

*Moorpark College (C)

7075 Campus Road, Moorpark CA 93021-1695

County: Ventura FICE Identification: 007115
Unit ID: 119137
Telephone: (805) 378-1400 Carnegie Class: Assoc/Pub-U-MC
FAX Number: (805) 378-1499 Calendar System: Semester
URL: www.moorparkcollege.edu
Established: 1967 Annual Undergrad Tuition & Fees (In-State): $1,380
Enrollment: 13,880 Coed
Affiliation or Control: State IRS Status: 501(c)3
Highest Offering: Associate Degree
Program: Occupational; 2-Year Principally Bachelor's Creditable
Accreditation: WJ, ADNUR, RAD

02 President .... Mr. Luis P. SANCHEZ
05 Exec Vice Pres Student Learning .... Dr. Lori BENNETT
10 Vice President Business Services .... Ms. Sylvia BARAJAS
04 Executive Assistant to President .... Ms. Andrea RAMBO
18 Director Maintainence/Operations .... Mr. John SINUTKO
109 College Business Services Manager .... Ms. Darlene MELBY
06 Registrar .... Mr. David ANTER
37 Student Financial Aid Officer .... Ms. Kim KORINKE

*Oxnard College (D)

4000 S Rose Avenue, Oxnard CA 93033-6699

County: Ventura FICE Identification: 012842
Unit ID: 120421
Telephone: (805) 986-5800 Carnegie Class: Assoc/Pub-U-MC
FAX Number: (805) 986-5908 Calendar System: Semester
URL: www.oxnardcollege.edu
Established: 1975 Annual Undergrad Tuition & Fees (In-District): $1,338
Enrollment: 7,103 Coed
Affiliation or Control: State/Local IRS Status: 501(c)3
Highest Offering: Associate Degree
Program: Occupational; 2-Year Principally Bachelor's Creditable
Accreditation: WJ, DH, IFSAC

02 Interim President .... Dr. James LIMBAUGH
05 VP Acad Affairs/Student Learning .... Kenneth SHERWOOD
10 Vice President of Business Services .... Dr. Michael BUSH
32 Vice Pres Student Development .... Dr. Oscar COBIAN
79 Dean Liberal Studies .... Vacant
41 Director of Athletics .... Mr. Jonas CRAWFORD
88 Dean Career & Technical Education .... Dr. Christina TAFOYA
81 Dean Math Science/Health .... Dr. Carolyn INOUYE
18 Director Maintenance/Operations .... Mr. Bob SUBE
06 Registrar .... Mr. Joel DIAZ
88 Director STEM .... Dr. Cynthia HERRERA
37 Financial Aid Officer .... Ms. Linda FAASUA
40 Bookstore Manager .... Mr. Christopher RENBARGER

*Ventura College (E)

4667 Telegraph Road, Ventura CA 93003-3899

County: Ventura FICE Identification: 001334
Unit ID: 125028
Telephone: (805) 289-6000 Carnegie Class: Assoc/Pub-U-MC
FAX Number: (805) 289-6466 Calendar System: Semester
URL: www.venturacollege.edu
Established: 1925 Annual Undergrad Tuition & Fees (In-District): $1,380
Enrollment: 12,928 Coed
Affiliation or Control: State/Local IRS Status: 501(c)3
Highest Offering: Associate Degree
Program: Occupational; 2-Year Principally Bachelor's Creditable
Accreditation: WJ, ADNUR, EMT

02 President .... Dr. Greg GILLESPIE
05 VP Academic Affs/Student Learning .... Ms. Kim HOFFMANS
32 Vice Pres Student Development .... Dr. Patrick JEFFERSON
10 Vice President Business Services .... Mr. Tim HARRISON
04 Exec Assistant to the President .... Ms. Laura BROWER
75 Dean Career & Tech Education .... Dr. Kathleen SCHRADER
88 Dean Institutional Effectiveness .... Mr. Phillip BRIGGS
81 Dean Mathematics & Sciences .... Mr. Dan KUMPF
60 Dean Comm/Kinesiology/Athl/OS Pgm .... Vacant
83 Dean Dist Ed/Prof Dev/Soc Sci/Hum .... Ms. Gwen HUDDLESTON
32 Dean Student Services .... Ms. Victoria LUGO
35 Asst Dean Student Services/Support .... Ms. Karen ENGELSEN
102 Executive Director Foundation .... Mr. Norbert N. TAN
06 Registrar .... Vacant
18 Director Maintenance/Operations .... Mr. Jay MOORE
35 Coordinator Student Activities .... Mr. Rick TREVINO
37 Financial Aid Officer .... Ms. Alma RODRIGUEZ
09 Institutional Research .... Mr. Michael CALLAHAN
85 International Students .... Ms. Rosie STUTTS
103 Dir Center of Excellence .... Ms. Sharon DWYER
84 Enrollment Management .... Ms. Connie BAKER
23 Director Student Health Center .... Ms. Mary JONES
19 Campus Police .... Sgt. Mike PALLOTO

Veritas Evangelical Seminary (F)

3000 W. MacArthur Blvd, Santa Ana CA 92704

County: Orange Identification: 667103
Telephone: (714) 966-8500 Carnegie Class: Not Classified
FAX Number: (714) 966-8500 Calendar System: Semester
URL: www.ves.edu
Established: 2008 Annual Graduate Tuition & Fees: $7,740
Enrollment: 110 Coed
Affiliation or Control: Independent Non-Profit IRS Status: 501(c)3
Highest Offering: Master's; No Undergraduates
Program: Professional; Religious Emphasis
Accreditation: TRACS

00 Chancellor .... Norman L. GEISLER
01 President .... Joseph M. HOLDEN
06 Registrar/Dir of Admissions .... Vanessa ACOSTA
05 Chief Academic Officer .... Joel L. WINGO
08 Head Librarian .... Joe MCELROY
10 Chief Business Officer .... Deborah DELARGY
88 Director External Studies .... Scott MATSCHERZ
09 Dir Inst Effectiveness/Assessment .... Frank CORREA
32 Director Student Services .... Deborah DELARGY

Victor Valley College (G)

18422 Bear Valley Road, Victorville CA 92395-5850

County: San Bernardino FICE Identification: 001335
Unit ID: 125091
Telephone: (760) 245-4271 Carnegie Class: Assoc/Pub-S-SC
FAX Number: (760) 245-9019 Calendar System: Semester
URL: www.vvc.edu
Established: 1961 Annual Undergrad Tuition & Fees (In-District): $1,114
Enrollment: 11,635 Coed
Affiliation or Control: State/Local IRS Status: 501(c)3
Highest Offering: Associate Degree
Program: Occupational; 2-Year Principally Bachelor's Creditable
Accreditation: WJ, COARC, EMT

01 Superintendent/President .... Dr. Roger W. WAGNER
05 Exec VP Instruction/Stdnt Svcs .... Dr. Peter MAPHUMULO
10 Vice President Admin Services .... Vacant
15 Director Human Resources .... Ms. Trinda BEST
76 Dean Health Science & Public Safety .... Vacant
20 Dean Academic Programs .... Mr. Rolando REGINO
79 Dean Acad Pgms Humanities/Soc Sci .... Vacant
75 Dean Vocational Education .... Vacant
21 Director Fiscal Services .... Ms. Karen HARDY
07 Director of Admissions .... Mrs. Greta MOON
26 Director Public Info/Marketing .... Mr. Robert SEWELL
41 Director Athletics/Athletic Trainer .... Mrs. Jaye TASHIMA
18 Director Maintenance/Operations .... Mr. William B. BROWN
37 Director Financial Aid .... Mr. Jason JUDKINS
13 Director MIS .... Mr. Sergio OKLANDER
109 Director Auxiliary Services/ASB Adv .... Vacant
32 Dean Student Services .... Mr. Arthur LOPEZ
18 Director Facilities Construction .... Mr. Steve GARCIA
19 Chief Campus Police .... Mr. Leonard KNIGHT
72 Exec Dean Technology/Info Resource .... Mr. Frank SMITH
22 Dir Disabled Student/ADA Compl Ofcr .... Vacant
88 Director Child Development Center .... Mrs. Kelley JOHNSON
88 Dir Extended Optnty Pgms/Svcs/CARE .... Mr. Carl SMITH
09 Exec Dean Inst Effectiveness .... Ms. Virginia MORAN
55 Dir Evening Opers/Inst Support Pgm .... Vacant

West Coast Ultrasound Institute (H)

291 S. La Cienega Blvd, Ste 500, Beverly Hills CA 90211

County: Los Angeles FICE Identification: 036393
Unit ID: 441229
Telephone: (310) 289-5123 Carnegie Class: Not Classified
FAX Number: (310) 289-5136 Calendar System: Quarter
URL: www.wcui.edu
Established: 1998 Annual Undergrad Tuition & Fees: $32,900
Enrollment: 800 Coed
Affiliation or Control: Proprietary IRS Status: Proprietary
Highest Offering: Associate Degree
Program: Occupational
Accreditation: ACCSC

01 Campus Director .... Ms. Myra CHASON

West Coast Ultrasound Institute (I)

3700 E. Inland Empire Blvd, Ste 235, Ontario CA 91764
Telephone: (310) 280-5123 Identification: 770942
Accreditation: ACCSC

† Main campus is West Coast Ultrasound Institute in Los Angeles, CA.

West Coast University (J)

1477 South Manchester Avenue, Anaheim CA 92802
Telephone: (949) 783-4841 Identification: 770480
Accreditation: &WC, DH

† Branch campus of West Coast University, North Hollywood, CA.

West Coast University (K)

12215 Victory Boulevard, North Hollywood CA 91606-3206

County: Los Angeles FICE Identification: 036983
Unit ID: 443331
Telephone: (818) 299-5500 Carnegie Class: Spec/Health
FAX Number: (818) 299-5545 Calendar System: Semester
URL: www.westcoastuniversity.edu
Established: 1909 Annual Undergrad Tuition & Fees: $33,175
Enrollment: 1,659 Coed
Affiliation or Control: Proprietary IRS Status: Proprietary
Highest Offering: Doctorate
Program: Professional; Nursing Emphasis
Accreditation: WC, NURSE, OT, @PHAR, @PTA

01 President .... Dr. William C. CLOHAN
03 Executive Director .... Mr. Ladd GRAHAM
05 Provost .... Dr. Jeb EGBERT
66 Dean of Nursing Los Angeles Campus . Dr. Rosanne SILBERLING
20 Academic Dean .... Dr. Miriam KAHAN
76 Founding Dean Occupational Therapy .... Dr. Nicolaas VAN DEN HEEVER
67 Associate Dean School of Pharmacy .... Dr. Reza TAHERI
07 Director of Admissions .... Ms. Julie CHIN
37 Senior Director of Financial Aid .... Ms. Tracy CABUCO
75 Founding Dean of Physical Therapy .... Dr. Stan HARTGRAVES
81 Chair Science Department .... Dr. Evan PEPPER
32 Director of Student Affairs .... Mr. Gerry VANBOOVEN
08 Librarian .... Ms. Kathleen STUART
06 Registrar .... Ms. Felicia LOCKHART
09 Director of Institutional Research .... Mr. Mahmoud ALBAWANEH

West Coast University (L)

2855 E Guasti Road, Ontario CA 91761
Telephone: (909) 467-6100 Identification: 770484
Accreditation: &WC

† Branch campus of West Coast University, North Hollywood, CA.

*West Hills Community College District (A)

9900 Cody Street, Coalinga CA 93210
County: Fresno Identification: 667041
Telephone: (559) 934-2180 Carnegie Class: N/A
FAX Number: (559) 934-2810
URL: www.westhillscollege.com

01 Chancellor .... Dr. Frank P. GORNICK
10 Deputy Chancellor .... Mr. Ken STOPPENBRINK
05 VC Educ Svcs/Workforce Development .... Dr. Stuart VAN HORN
90 Assoc VC Enr Mgmt & Inst Eff .... Ms. Rita GROGAN
13 Assoc VC Educ Svcs/Info Technology . Ms. Michelle KOZLOWSKI
21 Assoc VC of Business Services .... Ms. Tammy WEATHERMAN
46 Assoc VC of Connected Learning .... Dr. Richard WU
15 Director of Human Resources .... Ms. Rebecca CAZARES
102 Exec Director WHCC Foundation .... Ms. Frances SQUIRE
26 Director of Marketing/PIO .... Mr. Tom WIXON
25 Director of Grants .... Ms. Anita WRIGHT
66 Interim Dist Dir of Health Careers .... Ms. Kathryn DEFEDE
88 Director of Child Dev Centers .... Ms. Conne CLEVELAND
103 Dir of Special Grant Programs .... Mr. David CASTILLO
04 Executive Assistant to Chancellor .... Ms. Donna ISAAC

*West Hills College Coalinga (B)

300 Cherry Lane, Coalinga CA 93210-1399
County: Fresno FICE Identification: 001176
Unit ID: 125462
Telephone: (559) 934-2000 Carnegie Class: Assoc/Pub-S-MC
FAX Number: N/A Calendar System: Semester
URL: www.westhillscollege.com/coalinga
Established: 1932 Annual Undergrad Tuition & Fees (In-District): $1,380
Enrollment: 2,516 Coed
Affiliation or Control: State/Local IRS Status: 501(c)3
Highest Offering: Associate Degree
Program: Occupational; 2-Year Principally Bachelor's Creditable
Accreditation: WJ

02 President .... Dr. Carole GOLDSMITH
05 Vice President of Educ Services .... Ms. Stephanie DROKER
32 Vice Pres of Student Services .... Ms. Sandy MCGLOTHLIN
35 Assoc Dean of Student Services .... Mr. Mark GRITTON
20 Assoc Dean of Educational Services .... Mr. Robert PIMENTEL
47 Director of Farm of the Future .... Mr. Clint COWDEN
85 Dir of International Student Svcs .... Mr. Daniel TAMAYO
88 Director of Title IV Projects .... Ms. Raquel RODRIGUEZ
88 Director of North District Center .... Ms. Bertha FELIX-MATA
37 Director of Financial Aid .... Ms. Mary MELLO
04 Administrative Asst to President .... Ms. Lorna DAVIS
08 Head Librarian .... Mr. Matthew MAGNUSON
18 Chief Facilities/Physical Plant .... Mr. Shaun BAILEY
39 Director Student Housing .... Mr. Alex VILLALOBOS

*West Hills College Lemoore (C)

555 College Avenue, Lemoore CA 93245-9248
County: Kings FICE Identification: 041113
Unit ID: 448594
Telephone: (559) 925-3000 Carnegie Class: Assoc/Pub-R-M
FAX Number: (559) 924-1243 Calendar System: Semester
URL: www.westhillscollege.com/lemoore
Established: 2002 Annual Undergrad Tuition & Fees (In-District): $1,380
Enrollment: 4,056 Coed
Affiliation or Control: State/Local IRS Status: 501(c)3
Highest Offering: Associate Degree
Program: Occupational; 2-Year Principally Bachelor's Creditable; Business Emphasis
Accreditation: WJ

02 President .... Mr. Don WARKENTIN
05 Vice President of Educational Svcs .... Mr. Dave BOLT
32 Vice President of Student Services .... Ms. Sylvia DORSEY-ROBINSON
20 Dean of Educational Svcs .... Mr. James PRESTON
35 Dean of Student Services .... Mr. Joel RUBLE
88 Director of Upward Bound .... Mr. Oscar VILLARREAL
37 Director of Financial Aid .... Ms. Deborah SORIA
88 Assoc Dean of Categorical Programs .... Ms. Lataria HALL
04 Administrative Asst to President .... Ms. Amber AVITIA
08 Head Librarian .... Mr. Ron OXFORD
18 Chief Facilities/Physical Plant .... Mr. Johnathan BERNAL
41 Athletic Director .... Mr. Allen FORTUNE

*West Valley-Mission Community College District (D)

14000 Fruitvale Avenue, Saratoga CA 95070-5698
County: Santa Clara FICE Identification: 029139
Unit ID: 125222
Telephone: (408) 741-2011 Carnegie Class: N/A
FAX Number: (408) 867-8273
URL: www.wvm.edu

01 Chancellor .... Dr. Patrick SCHMITT
11 Vice Chancellor Admin Services .... Mr. Ed MADULI
15 Vice Chanc Human Resources .... Mr. Albert MOORE
30 Dean Advancement .... Ms. Cynthia SCHELCHER
13 Director Information Systems .... Mr. Ron SMITH
18 Director of Facilities .... Mr. Javier CASTRUITA
19 Chief of Police .... Mr. Kenneth TANAKA

*Mission College (E)

3000 Mission College Boulevard,
Santa Clara CA 95054-1897
County: Santa Clara FICE Identification: 021191
Unit ID: 118930
Telephone: (408) 988-2200 Carnegie Class: Assoc/Pub-S-MC
FAX Number: (408) 496-0462 Calendar System: Semester
URL: www.missioncollege.org
Established: 1976 Annual Undergrad Tuition & Fees (In-District): $1,174
Enrollment: 8,435 Coed
Affiliation or Control: State/Local IRS Status: 501(c)3
Highest Offering: Associate Degree
Program: Occupational; 2-Year Principally Bachelor's Creditable
Accreditation: WJ

02 President .... Mr. Daniel A. PECK
05 Vice Pres of Instruction .... Dr. Leandra MARTIN
32 Vice President Student Services .... Dr. John MOSBY
11 Vice Pres Administrative Services .... Mr. Rick BENNETT
35 Dean of Student Support Services .... Mr. Daniel SANIDAD
20 Dean of Instruction .... Mr. Danny NGUYEN
27 Dir of Public Info & Graphic Design .... Vacant
20 Dean of Instruction .... Mr. Carl JONES
81 Dean Applied Science .... Ms. Mina JAHAN
19 Chief of Police .... Lt. Kenneth TANAKA
18 Manager of Facilities .... Mr. Don HOUSTON
07 Director of Admissions .... Mr. Asmare TADESSE
09 Director of Institutional Research .... Ms. Inge BOND
37 Dir Student Enroll & Financial Aid .... Ms. Rita GROGAN
04 Exec Assistant to the President .... Ms. Linda ANGELOTTI
88 Language Arts Division .... Ms. Kathy HENDERSON
60 Communications Dept .... Mr. Rob DEWIS
81 Mathematics and Science Division .... Mr. Rick HOBBS
83 Liberal Studies Division .... Mr. Keith JOHNSON
35 Student Services Division .... Ms. Thuy TRANG

*West Valley College (F)

14000 Fruitvale Avenue, Saratoga CA 95070-5698
County: Santa Clara FICE Identification: 001338
Unit ID: 125499
Telephone: (408) 867-2200 Carnegie Class: Assoc/Pub-S-MC
FAX Number: (408) 867-5033 Calendar System: Semester
URL: www.westvalley.edu
Established: 1963 Annual Undergrad Tuition & Fees (In-District): $1,186
Enrollment: 8,729 Coed
Affiliation or Control: State/Local IRS Status: 501(c)3
Highest Offering: Associate Degree
Program: Occupational; 2-Year Principally Bachelor's Creditable
Accreditation: WJ

02 President .... Mr. Bradley DAVIS
05 VP Instruction .... Ms. Kuni HAY
32 VP Student Services .... Dr. Victoria HINDES
11 VP Administrative Services .... Mr. Patrick FENTON
20 Dean Instruction .... Ms. Stephanie KASHIMA
30 Dean Advancement .... Ms. Cindy SCHELCHER
36 Dean Career Pgm/Wrkforce Dev .... Mr. Bradley WEISBERG
26 Director Marketing/Commun .... Mr. Scott LUDWIG
35 Dean of Student Services .... Dr. Matais POUNCIL
100 Interim Associate Vice Chancellor .... Mr. Albert MOORE
88 Director of Student Equity & Succes .... Ms. Herlisa HAMP
18 Chief Facilities/Physical Plant .... Mr. Bill TAYLOR
37 Dir Student Financial Aid/Admiss .... Ms. Maritza CANTARERO
09 Research Analyst .... Mr. Miqueas DIAL
35 Director Student Development .... Dr. Sean PEPIN
29 Director Alumni Relations .... Ms. Cindy SCHELCHER
106 Coord Instruct Tech/Distance Lrng .... Ms. Lisa KAAZ
04 Administrative Asst to President .... Vacant
41 Athletic Director .... Mr. John VLAHOS

Westcliff University (G)

4199 Campus Drive #650, Irvine CA 92612
County: Orange Identification: 667203
Telephone: (888) 491-8686 Carnegie Class: Not Classified
FAX Number: (888) 409-7306 Calendar System: Trimester
URL: www.westcliff.edu
Established: 1993 Annual Undergrad Tuition & Fees: $8,205
Enrollment: N/A Coed
Affiliation or Control: Proprietary IRS Status: Proprietary
Highest Offering: Master's
Program: Business Emphasis
Accreditation: DEAC

00 CEO .... Dr. Anthony LEE
01 President .... Dr. David MCKINNEY

Western State University College of Law (H)

1111 N State College Boulevard, Fullerton CA 92831-3014
Telephone: (714) 459-1000 FICE Identification: 010832
Accreditation: &WC, LAW

† Regional accreditation is carried under the parent institution, Argosy University in Orange, CA.

Western University of Health Sciences (I)

309 E 2nd Street, Pomona CA 91766-1854
County: Los Angeles FICE Identification: 024827
Unit ID: 112525
Telephone: (909) 623-6116 Carnegie Class: Spec/Med
FAX Number: N/A Calendar System: Semester
URL: www.westernu.edu
Established: 1977 Annual Graduate Tuition & Fees: N/A
Enrollment: 3,862 Coed
Affiliation or Control: Independent Non-Profit IRS Status: 501(c)3
Highest Offering: Doctorate; No Undergraduates
Program: Professional
Accreditation: WC, ARCPA, DENT, NURSE, OPT, OSTEO, PHAR, POD, PTA, VET

01 President .... Dr. Philip PUMERANTZ
05 Provost/COO .... Dr. Gary GUGELCHUK
10 Treasurer/Chief Financial Officer .... Mr. Kevin SHAW
46 Exec Vice Provost for Academic Dev .... Dr. Elizabeth REGA
03 Senior Vice President .... Dr. Thomas FOX
20 Vice Provost .... Dr. Sheree ASTON
32 Vice Pres Student Affs/Enroll Mgt .... Dr. Beverly SANKS GUIDRY
25 Asst VP Spnsrd Pgms/Contract Mgt .... Mr. Matthew KATZ
84 Asst VP Enroll Mgmt/Registrar .... Ms. Kimberly DEKRUIF
15 Executive Director Human Resources .... Ms. Linda EMILIO
18 Exec Dir Facilities/Physical Plant .... Mr. Todd CLARK
07 Director Admiss COP/CGN .... Ms. Kathy FORD
07 Director Admissions COMP/MSHS .... Ms. Susan HANSON
07 Director Admissions CO/CPM/CDM .... Ms. Marie ANDERSON
07 Director Admissions CVM/PT/PA .... Ms. Karen HUTTON-LOPEZ
11 Chief Administrative Officer .... Mr. Steve JASPERSON
08 Director of University Library .... Ms. Patricia VADER
37 Director Financial Aid .... Mr. Otto REYER
88 Dir Ctr Disability Issues/Hlth Prof .... Ms. Brenda PREMO
13 Exec Director Information Tech .... Ms. Denise WILCOX
96 Director of Procurement Services .... Mr. Michael BUTLER
26 Exec Director of Public Affs/Mrktg .... Mr. Jeff KEATING
88 Dir Learning Enhancement/Acad Devel .... Ms. Dagmar COFER
09 Director of Institutional Research .... Dr. Juan RAMIREZ
40 Bookstore Director .... Ms. Elizabeth GUERRA
52 Dean College of Dental Medicine ..Dr. Steven W. FRIEDRICHSEN
67 Dean College of Pharmacy .... Dr. Daniel C. ROBINSON
88 Founding Dean College of Optometry .... Dr. Elizabeth HOPPE
88 Founding Dean College of Podiatry .... Dr. Lawrence HARKLESS
76 Dean College Allied Health Profess .... Dr. Stephanie BOWLIN
66 Dean College of Graduate Nursing .... Dr. Karen HANFORD
58 Dean Grad Col Biomedical Sciences .... Dr. Michel BAUDRY
74 Dean College of Veterinary Medicine .... Dr. Phil NELSON
63 Chr Dept Osteopath Manipulative Med .....Dr. Michael SEFFINGER
88 Chair Dept of Physical Therapy .... Dr. Denise SCHILLING
76 Chair Dept of Health Sciences .... Dr. Tina MEYER
88 Chair Physician Assistant Program .... Mr. Roy GUIZADO
63 Chair Department Family Medicine .... Dr. Alan CUNDARI

Westminster Theological Seminary in California (J)

1725 Bear Valley Parkway, Escondido CA 92027-4128
County: San Diego FICE Identification: 022768
Unit ID: 125718
Telephone: (760) 480-8474 Carnegie Class: Spec/Faith
FAX Number: (760) 480-0252 Calendar System: Semester
URL: www.wscal.edu
Established: 1979 Annual Graduate Tuition & Fees: $12,915
Enrollment: 149 Coed
Affiliation or Control: Independent Non-Profit IRS Status: 501(c)3
Highest Offering: Master's; No Undergraduates
Program: Professional
Accreditation: WC, THEOL

01 President .... Dr. W. Robert GODFREY
11 Vice President for Administration .... Dr. Marcus MCARTHUR
05 Academic Dean .... Dr. John FESKO
84 VP for Enrollment Management .... Mr. Mark MACVEY
10 Vice President for Finance .... Mr. Dan TER HORST
30 Vice President for Advancement .... Ms. Dawn DOORN
32 Dean of Students .... Dr. Julius KIM
08 Library Director .... Mr. James LUND
06 Registrar .... Mr. Danny MARRIOTT

Westmont College (K)

955 La Paz Road, Santa Barbara CA 93108-1089
County: Santa Barbara FICE Identification: 001341
Unit ID: 125727
Telephone: (805) 565-6000 Carnegie Class: Bac/A&S
FAX Number: (805) 565-7006 Calendar System: Semester
URL: www.westmont.edu
Established: 1937 Annual Undergrad Tuition & Fees: $39,990
Enrollment: 1,300 Coed
Affiliation or Control: Independent Non-Profit IRS Status: 501(c)3
Highest Offering: Baccalaureate
Program: Liberal Arts And General; Teacher Preparatory
Accreditation: WC, MUS

01 President .... Dr. Gayle D. BEEBE
05 Provost/Dean of Faculty .... Dr. Mark L. SARGENT
10 Vice President Finance .... Mr. Douglas W. JONES

11 Vice President for Administration ... Mr. Christopher D. CALL
32 VP Student Life/Dean of Students ... Mrs. Edee SCHULZE
30 Vice President for Advancement ... Dr. Reed SHEARD
88 Vice President External Relations ... Mr. Cliff LUNDBERG
13 VP Information Technology & CIO ... Dr. Reed SHEARD
07 Dean of Admissions ... Mr. Silvio VAZQUEZ
35 Associate Dean of Students ... Mr. Timothy B. WILSON
88 Assoc Dean of Students for Res Life ... Mr. Stu CLEEK
06 Registrar ... Mrs. Michelle M. HARDLEY
08 Director Library/Information Svcs ... Mrs. Debra QUAST
09 Assoc Provost/Dir of Inst Research ... Dr. William A. WRIGHT
15 Director of Human Resources ... Ms. Beth CAUWELS
18 Director of Physical Plant ... Mr. Thomas BEVERIDGE
21 Controller ... Mr. Paul V. LARSON
23 Director of Student Health Services ... Dr. David HERNANDEZ
19 Public Safety Director ... Mr. Thomas G. BAUER
26 Director of Public Affairs ... Mrs. Nancy L. PHINNEY
29 Exec Director Alumni & Parent Rels ... Mrs. Teri BRADFORD ROUSE
36 Int Director of Career/Development ... Ms. Celia HOWEN
44 Senior Director of Planned Giving ... Mrs. Kati BUEHLER
88 Director of Campus Life ... Ms. Angela L. D'AMOUR
88 Director of Internships/Practica ... Mrs. Jennifer TAYLOR
37 Director of Financial Aid ... Mr. Sean SMITH
38 Director Counseling Services ... Mr. Eric NELSON
39 Director of Housing/Parking ... Mr. David W. KING
40 Bookstore Manager ... Mrs. Joanne GISH
41 Athletic Director ... Mr. David ODELL
42 Campus Pastor ... Rev. Ben PATTERSON
45 Director of Campus Planning ... Mr. Randy JONES
96 Assc Dir Procurement/Auxiliary Svcs ... Mr. Bill GROENEVELD
28 Director of Intercultural Programs ... Mr. Jason CHA
43 College Counsel ... Ms. Toya COOPER
20 Associate Academic Officer ... Dr. Tatiana NAZARENKO
24 Coord Media Services/Asst Librarian ... Ms. Mary LOGUE

Westwood College-Anaheim (A)

1551 S Douglass Road, Anaheim CA 92806-5949
Telephone: (714) 704-2720 — Identification: 666047
Accreditation: ACICS

† Branch campus of Westwood College-Denver North. Denver, CO.

Westwood College-Inland Empire (B)

20 W Seventh Street, Upland CA 91786-7148
Telephone: (909) 931-7550 — Identification: 666104
Accreditation: ACICS

† Branch campus of Westwood College-Denver North, Denver, CO.

Westwood College-Los Angeles Campus (C)

3250 Wilshire Boulevard, Suite 400, Los Angeles CA 90010-1437
County: Los Angeles — FICE Identification: 030727
Unit ID: 122843
Telephone: (213) 739-9999 — Carnegie Class: Bac/Diverse
FAX Number: (213) 382-2468 — Calendar System: Quarter
URL: www.westwood.edu
Established: 1997 — Annual Undergrad Tuition & Fees: $5,754
Enrollment: 450 — Coed
Affiliation or Control: Proprietary — IRS Status: Proprietary
Highest Offering: Master's
Program: Occupational
Accreditation: ACICS

01 Campus President ... Mr. DeWayne JOHNSON
07 Director of Admissions ... Mr. Carlos LANESE

Westwood College-South Bay (D)

19700 S Vermont Avenue, #100, Torrance CA 90502-1148
County: Los Angeles — FICE Identification: 011626
Unit ID: 121381
Telephone: (310) 965-0888 — Carnegie Class: Bac/Diverse
FAX Number: (310) 516-8232 — Calendar System: Other
URL: www.westwood.edu
Established: 2002 — Annual Undergrad Tuition & Fees: $24,900
Enrollment: 600 — Coed
Affiliation or Control: Proprietary — IRS Status: Proprietary
Highest Offering: Baccalaureate
Program: Occupational; Technical Emphasis
Accreditation: ACICS

01 Campus President ... Mr. Christopher TUREN

Whittier College (E)

13406 E Philadelphia St, PO Box 634, Whittier CA 90608-4413
County: Los Angeles — FICE Identification: 001342
Unit ID: 125763
Telephone: (562) 907-4200 — Carnegie Class: Bac/A&S
FAX Number: (562) 907-4242 — Calendar System: 4/1/4
URL: www.whittier.edu
Established: 1887 — Annual Undergrad Tuition & Fees: $44,848
Enrollment: 2,289 — Coed
Affiliation or Control: Independent Non-Profit — IRS Status: 501(c)3
Highest Offering: Doctorate
Program: Liberal Arts And General; Teacher Preparatory; Professional
Accreditation: WC, LAW, SW

01 President ... Dr. Sharon D. HERZBERGER
10 Vice Pres Finance & Administration ... Mr. James DUNKELMAN
05 VP Academic Affs/Dean of Faculty ... Dr. Darrin GOOD
61 VP Legal Education/Dean Sch of Law ... Ms. Penelope BRYAN
30 VP for Advancement ... Mr. Steve DELGADO
84 Vice President Dean of Enrollment ... Mr. Fred PFURSICH
32 Dean of Students ... Dr. Joel JOEL PEREZ
37 Director of Student Financial Aid ... Mr. David CARNEVALE
06 Registrar ... Vacant
08 Library Director ... Mrs. Laurel CRUMP
20 Dir Whtr Scholar Pgm/Assc Acad Dean ... Ms. Doreen O'CONNOR-GOMEZ
26 Dir Public Relations/Communications ... Ms. Ana Lilia BARRAZA
13 Director of Computing Services ... Mr. Troy GREENUP
09 Director of Institutional Research ... Mr. Fritz SMITH
41 Director of Athletics ... Mr. Rob COLEMAN
53 Dir Lib Educ Pgm/Assoc Acad Dean ... Dr. Fritz SMITH
07 Director of Admissions ... Mr. Kieron MILLER
15 Director of Human Resources ... Ms. Cynthia JOSEPH
21 Exec Director Finance/Business Svcs ... Vacant
35 Director Student Activies ... Ms. Shauna YOUNG
18 Director Facilities/Physical Plant ... Mr. Bill WEINMANN
19 Director of Campus Safety ... Mr. Jose PADILLA

William Jessup University (F)

333 Sunset Boulevard, Rocklin CA 95765-3707
County: Placer — FICE Identification: 001281
Unit ID: 122728
Telephone: (916) 577-2200 — Carnegie Class: Spec/Faith
FAX Number: (916) 577-2203 — Calendar System: Semester
URL: www.jessup.edu
Established: 1939 — Annual Undergrad Tuition & Fees: $26,480
Enrollment: 1,212 — Coed
Affiliation or Control: Independent Non-Profit — IRS Status: 501(c)3
Highest Offering: Master's
Program: 2-Year Principally Bachelor's Creditable; Liberal Arts And General; Teacher Preparatory
Accreditation: WC, BI

01 President ... Dr. John JACKSON
05 Provost/Chief Academic Officer ... Dr. Dennis JAMESON
11 Chief Financial Officer ... Mr. David PUNT
30 Chief Development Officer ... Mr. Eric HOGUE
13 Chief Information Officer ... Mrs. Judy RENTZ
88 Accreditation Liason Officer ... Dr. Kay LLOVIO
107 School of Professional Studies Dir ... Ms. Nancy THOMPSON
15 Director of Human Resources ... Ms. Wendy WEBSTER
10 Controller ... Ms. Diane KIM
08 Library Director ... Mr. Kevin PISCHKE
88 Director of Church Relations ... Mr. Jim JESSUP
32 Dean of Students ... Mr. Jonathan SAMPSON
06 Registrar ... Mrs. Tina PETERSEN
07 Director of Admission and Fin Aid ... Mr. Vance PASCUA
09 Institutional Research Director ... Mrs. Karen LAMBRECHTSEN
42 Campus Pasor ... Mr. Ryan HAYNES
41 Athletic Director ... Mr. Farnum SMITH
18 Facilities Director ... Mr. Ben NEWMAN
84 Associate Provost Enrollment Mgmt ... Dr. Todd ERICKSON
12 Academic Director Bay Area Center ... Dr. Daniel ALBRECHT
04 Administrative Asst to President ... Ms. Janice NEWMAN
19 Director Security/Safety ... Mr. Dean CROSS
28 Director of Diversity ... Dr. Henry GARDNER
36 Director Student Placement ... Ms. Christy JEWELL
106 Dir Online Education/E-learning ... Ms. Sandra WOODSON
37 Director Student Financial Aid ... Mr. John SWAN

Woodbury University (G)

7500 North Glenoaks Boulevard, Burbank CA 91504-7520
County: Los Angeles — FICE Identification: 001343
Unit ID: 125897
Telephone: (818) 767-0888 — Carnegie Class: Master's M
FAX Number: (818) 767-3470 — Calendar System: Semester
URL: www.woodbury.edu
Established: 1884 — Annual Undergrad Tuition & Fees: $35,808
Enrollment: 1,607 — Coed
Affiliation or Control: Independent Non-Profit — IRS Status: 501(c)3
Highest Offering: Master's
Program: Professional; Business Emphasis
Accreditation: WC, ACBSP, ART, BUS, CIDA

01 Interim President ... David DAUWALDER
101 Secretary of the Institution/Board ... Seta JAVOR
05 Provost & Exec Vice President ... Randy STAUFFER
10 Vice Pres Finance & Administration ... Ken JONES
84 Interim VP Enrollment Management ... Mauro DIAZ
30 Interim VP University Relations ... Andre VAN NIEKERK
13 Interim VP Information Technology ... Aida ARTENIAN
32 Vice Pres Student Development ... Phyllis A. CREMER
35 Dean of Students ... Anne R. EHRLICH
50 Dean School of Business ... Andre VAN NIEKERK
48 Dean School of Architecture ... Norman MILLAR
88 Interim Graduate Admission Director ... Paul W. DECKER
06 Assistant Registrar ... Tamara L. BLOK
07 Director of Enrollment Services ... Celeastia WILLIAMS
20 Dean of Faculty ... Nedra PETERSON
15 Director of Human Resources ... Natalie AVALOS
36 Director of Career Services ... Liana JINDARYAN
18 Director of Facilities ... Alfred W. VALDEZ
07 Director of Admissions ... Ashraf ZAWAIDEH
88 Dean Institute of Transdisciplinary ... Douglas CREMER
26 Chief Marketing Officer ... Shari GIBBONS
09 Director of Institutional Research ... Bruce FEINSTEIN
29 Director of University Relations ... Michael SEYMOUR

World Mission University (H)

500 Shatto Place, Suite 600, Los Angeles CA 90020-1789
County: Los Angeles — FICE Identification: 038683
Unit ID: 401223
Telephone: (213) 385-2322 — Carnegie Class: Spec/Faith
FAX Number: (213) 385-2332 — Calendar System: Semester
URL: www.wmu.edu
Established: 1989 — Annual Undergrad Tuition & Fees: $5,749
Enrollment: 301 — Coed
Affiliation or Control: Independent Non-Profit — IRS Status: 501(c)3
Highest Offering: First Professional Degree
Program: Religious Emphasis
Accreditation: BI, THEOL, TRACS

01 President ... Dr. John M. SONG
05 Exec Vice Pres/Chief Acad Officer ... Dr. Sung Jin LIM
32 Dean of Student Svcs/Financial Aid ... Mrs. Karen AHN
30 Director of Development ... Ms. Keum Hee LEE
10 Director of Business ... Mr. Paul LIM
06 Registrar ... Mrs. Jin Joo NAM

The Wright Institute (I)

2728 Durant Avenue, Berkeley CA 94704-1796
County: Alameda — FICE Identification: 008846
Unit ID: 126012
Telephone: (510) 841-9230 — Carnegie Class: Spec/Health
FAX Number: (510) 841-0167 — Calendar System: Trimester
URL: www.wi.edu
Established: 1969 — Annual Graduate Tuition & Fees: $31,100
Enrollment: 445 — Coed
Affiliation or Control: Independent Non-Profit — IRS Status: 501(c)3
Highest Offering: Doctorate; No Undergraduates
Program: Professional
Accreditation: WC, CLPSY

01 President ... Mr. Peter DYBWAD
05 Dean ... Dr. Gilbert NEWMAN
10 VP of Finance & Administrative Affs ... Ms. Tricia O'REILLY
32 Dean of Students/Registrar ... Ms. Ginny MORGAN
07 Dir of Admissions/Student Services ... Mr. John PITTS
08 Library Director ... Mr. Jason STRAUSS
37 Director of Financial Aid ... Ms. Julia KALYAYEVA

Yeshiva Ohr Elchonon Chabad/ West Coast Talmudical Seminary (J)

7215 Waring Avenue, Los Angeles CA 90046-7660
County: Los Angeles — FICE Identification: 022624
Unit ID: 126076
Telephone: (323) 937-3763 — Carnegie Class: Spec/Faith
FAX Number: (323) 937-9456 — Calendar System: Semester
URL: www.yoec.edu
Established: 1953 — Annual Undergrad Tuition & Fees: $13,900
Enrollment: 165 — Male
Affiliation or Control: Independent Non-Profit — IRS Status: 501(c)3
Highest Offering: Baccalaureate
Program: Professional
Accreditation: RABN

01 Chief Executive Officer ... Rabbi Ezra B. SCHOCHET
03 Executive Vice President ... Rabbi Mendel SPALTER
05 Curriculum Suprv/Education Counsel ... Rabbi Shimon RAICHIK
37 Director Student Financial Aid ... Mrs. Hendy TAUBER
06 Registrar ... Rabbi Chaim CITRON
38 Director Student Counseling ... Rabbi Mendel SCHAPIRO
08 Head Librarian ... Rabbi Ben Zion OSTER

Yo San University of Traditional Chinese Medicine (K)

13315 W Washington Boulevard, Los Angeles CA 90066
County: Los Angeles — FICE Identification: 030982
Unit ID: 401250
Telephone: (310) 577-3000 — Carnegie Class: Spec/Health
FAX Number: (310) 577-3033 — Calendar System: Trimester
URL: www.yosan.edu
Established: 1989 — Annual Undergrad Tuition & Fees: $15,614
Enrollment: 199 — Coed
Affiliation or Control: Independent Non-Profit — IRS Status: 501(c)3
Highest Offering: Doctorate; No Lower Division
Program: Professional
Accreditation: ACUP

01 President ... Lois GREEN
05 Vice Pres Academic & Clinical Educ ... Lawrence LAU
06 Director Operations & Registrar ... Tora FLINT
10 Chief Fin Ofcr/VP Admin/Finance/COO ... Tracy WANG
30 VP Advance/Stdnt Affs/Chf Dev Ofcr ... Scott SIVLEY
20 Assistant Academic Dean ... J. Matthew BRAND
84 Director of Enrollment ... Christina ANDRICK
37 Financial Aid ... Ed MERVINE
21 Controller/Bursar ... Mariani MAY
88 Dean of Doctoral Program ... Andrea MURCHISON

*Yosemite Community College District (A)

PO Box 4065, Modesto CA 95352-4065
County: Stanislaus FICE Identification: 009146
Unit ID: 126100
Telephone: (209) 575-6509 Carnegie Class: N/A
FAX Number: (209) 575-6565
URL: www.yosemite.edu

01 Chancellor ..... Dr. Joan E. SMITH
10 Exec Vice Chancellor Fiscal Service ..... Ms. Teresa M. SCOTT
15 Vice Chancellor Human Resources ..... Ms. Gina LEGURIA
13 Assistant Vice Chancellor Info Tech ..... Mr. Martin (Marty) GANG
09 Associate VC Institutional Research ..... Mr. Marc BEAM

*Columbia College (B)

11600 Columbia College Drive, Sonora CA 95370-8580
County: Tuolumne FICE Identification: 007707
Unit ID: 112561
Telephone: (209) 588-5100 Carnegie Class: Assoc/Pub-R-M
FAX Number: (209) 588-5104 Calendar System: Semester
URL: www.gocolumbia.edu
Established: 1968 Annual Undergrad Tuition & Fees (In-District): $1,162
Enrollment: 2,760 Coed
Affiliation or Control: State/Local IRS Status: 501(c)3
Highest Offering: Associate Degree
Program: Occupational; 2-Year Principally Bachelor's Creditable
Accreditation: WJ, ACFEI

02 President ..... Dr. Angela FAIRCHILDS
05 Vice Pres Student Learning ..... Dr. Leslie BUCKALEW
11 VP College & Administrative Svcs ..... Mr. Gary WHITFIELD
20 Dean Instruct Svcs/Career Tech Edu ..... Dr. Klaus TENBERGEN
49 Dean of Instruction/Arts & Sciences ..... Vacant
24 Director of Info Tech & Media Svcs ..... Mrs. Margo GUZMAN
41 Athletic Director ..... Mr. Nate RIEN
37 Financial Aid Manager ..... Ms. Marnie SHIVELY
27 Public Information Officer ..... Vacant
31 Director Community Services ..... Vacant
30 Director of Development ..... Ms. Amy NILSON
09 Dir of Institutional Rsrch & Plng ..... Ms. Diana SUNDAY
40 Bookstore Manager ..... Mr. Jeff WHALEN
18 Manager Facilities/Operations ..... Mr. Dave KEENER

*Modesto Junior College (C)

435 College Avenue, Modesto CA 95350-9977
County: Stanislaus FICE Identification: 001240
Unit ID: 118976
Telephone: (209) 575-6498 Carnegie Class: Assoc/Pub-R-L
FAX Number: (209) 575-6630 Calendar System: Semester
URL: www.mjc.edu
Established: 1921 Annual Undergrad Tuition & Fees (In-District): $1,004
Enrollment: 17,456 Coed
Affiliation or Control: State/Local IRS Status: 501(c)3
Highest Offering: Associate Degree
Program: Occupational; 2-Year Principally Bachelor's Creditable
Accreditation: WJ, COARC, MAC

02 President ..... Ms. Jill STEARNS
05 Vice President for Instruction ..... Ms. Brenda THAMES
32 Int Vice Pres for Student Services ..... Dr. James TODD
11 Vice President Administrative Svcs ..... Dr. Al ALT
57 Div Dean Arts/Humanites/Comm ..... Mr. Mike SUNDQUIST
83 Div Dean Business/Behav/Social Sci ..... Dr. Jennifer HAMILTON
76 Div Dean Inst/All Hlth/Fam/Con Sci ... Mr. Patrick BETTENCOURT
79 Div Dean Literature/Language Arts ..... Ms. Jillian DALY
54 Div Dean Science/Math/Engineering ..... Dr. Brian SANDERS
47 Dean Agri/Envir Science/Tech Ed ..... Vacant
31 Dean of Community & Economic Devel ..... Mr. Pedro MENDEZ
68 Dean Phys/Rec/Health Educ/Athl Dir ..... Vacant
84 Director Matriculation/Enroll Svcs ..... Vacant
09 Director of Institutional Research ..... Vacant
37 Director Student Financial Aid ..... Ms. Peggy FIKSE
40 Manager College Bookstore ..... Ms. Arbella SOLHKHAH

*Yuba Community College District (D)

2088 North Beale Road, Marysville CA 95901
County: Yuba Identification: 666478
Unit ID: 126119
Telephone: (530) 741-6700 Carnegie Class: N/A
FAX Number: (530) 634-7704
URL: www.yccd.edu

01 Chancellor ..... Dr. Douglas B. HOUSTON
05 VC Educ Planning & Services ..... Vacant
13 Director Information Technologies ..... Karen TRIMBLE
102 Ex Dir Foundation/Grants/Instnl Dev ..... Vacant
15 Chief Human Resources Officer ..... Mr. Jacques WHITFIELD
10 Chief Business Officer ..... Mrs. Kuldeep KAUR

*Woodland Community College (E)

2300 East Gibson Road, Woodland CA 95776-5156
County: Yolo FICE Identification: 041438
Unit ID: 455512
Telephone: (530) 661-5700 Carnegie Class: Assoc/Pub-R-M
FAX Number: (530) 666-9028 Calendar System: Semester
URL: www.yccd.edu/woodland/
Established: 2008 Annual Undergrad Tuition & Fees (In-District): $1,124
Enrollment: 2,638 Coed
Affiliation or Control: State/Local IRS Status: 501(c)3
Highest Offering: Associate Degree
Program: Occupational; 2-Year Principally Bachelor's Creditable
Accreditation: WJ

02 President ..... Dr. Michael WHITE
03 Vice President ..... Dr. Alfred B. KONUWA
04 Administrative Asst to President ..... Ms. Ana L. VILLAGRANA

*Yuba College (F)

2088 N Beale Road, Marysville CA 95901-7699
County: Yuba FICE Identification: 001344
Unit ID: 126119
Telephone: (530) 741-6700 Carnegie Class: Assoc/Pub-R-L
FAX Number: (530) 741-3541 Calendar System: Semester
URL: www.yccd.edu
Established: 1927 Annual Undergrad Tuition & Fees (In-District): $1,124
Enrollment: 6,640 Coed
Affiliation or Control: State/Local IRS Status: 501(c)3
Highest Offering: Associate Degree
Program: Occupational; 2-Year Principally Bachelor's Creditable
Accreditation: WJ, #RAD

02 President ..... Dr. G. H JAVAHERIPOUR
10 Chief Business Officer ..... Ms. Kuldeep KAUR
05 Int VP Academic/Student Services ..... Mr. Brian JUKES
32 Interim Dean Student Services ..... Ms. Delmy SPENCER
88 Interim Director TRIO Programs ..... Mr. Julio DELGADO
50 Dean Applied Academics ..... Dr. Daren OTTEN
88 Int Dir Child Dev Ctr/Foster Care ..... Ms. Karen STANIS
66 Director Nursing/Allied Health ..... Dr. Tom MCKAY
19 Director Public Safety ..... Mr. Pete VILLARREAL
79 Dean of Humanities & Education ..... Mr. Walter MASUDA
07 Int Dir Admissions/Records/Fin Aid ..... Mr. Martin GUTIERREZ
15 Chief Human Resources Officer ..... Mr. Jacques WHITFIELD
68 Director Athletics/Health/PE ..... Mr. Erick BURNS
81 Dean STEM & Outreach Centers ..... Mr. Karsten STEMMANN
88 Director Academic Excellence ..... Ms. Kristina VANNUCCI

Zaytuna College (G)

2401 Le Conte Avenue, Berkeley CA 94709
County: Alameda Identification: 667230
Telephone: (510) 356-4760 Carnegie Class: Not Classified
FAX Number: (510) 327-2688 Calendar System: Semester
URL: www.zaytunacollege.org
Established: 2009 Annual Undergrad Tuition & Fees: $15,000
Enrollment: 49 Coed
Affiliation or Control: Independent Non-Profit IRS Status: 501(c)3
Highest Offering: Baccalaureate
Program: Liberal Arts And General
Accreditation: WC

01 President ..... Hamza YUSUF
05 Vice Pres Academics & Student Affs ..... Dr. Colleen KEYES
10 Vice Pres Finance & Admin Services ..... Waheed RASHEED
108 Dir of Assessment & Accreditation ..... Sumaira AKHATAR

COLORADO

Academy of Natural Therapy (H)

625 8th Avenue, Greeley CO 80631
County: Weld FICE Identification: 040933
Unit ID: 449454
Telephone: (970) 352-1181 Carnegie Class: Not Classified
FAX Number: (970) 352-1906 Calendar System: Quarter
URL: www.natural-therapy.com
Established: 1989 Annual Undergrad Tuition & Fees: $17,500
Enrollment: 54 Coed
Affiliation or Control: Proprietary IRS Status: Proprietary
Highest Offering: Associate Degree
Program: Occupational
Accreditation: #COMTA

01 President ..... Mr. Jeremiah James MONGAN

Adams State University (I)

208 Edgemont Boulevard, Alamosa CO 81101-2320
County: Alamosa FICE Identification: 001345
Unit ID: 126182
Telephone: (719) 587-7011 Carnegie Class: Master's M
FAX Number: (719) 587-7522 Calendar System: Semester
URL: www.adams.edu
Established: 1921 Annual Undergrad Tuition & Fees (In-State): $8,574
Enrollment: 3,154 Coed
Affiliation or Control: State IRS Status: 501(c)3
Highest Offering: Doctorate
Program: 2-Year Principally Bachelor's Creditable; Liberal Arts And General; Teacher Preparatory
Accreditation: NH, CACREP, MUS, NURSE

01 President ..... Dr. Beverlee J. MCCLURE
05 Vice President for Academic Affairs ..... Dr. Frank J. NOVOTNY
10 VP Finance/Governmental Relations ..... Mr. Bill MANSHEIM
84 Sr VP Enrollment Mgmt/Program Devel ..... Vacant
30 VP Institutional Advancement ..... Vacant
18 Asst VP Facil Plng/Design/Construct ..... Vacant
56 Asst VP Extended Campus - Academics ..... Mr. Walter ROYBAL
21 Asst VP Budget & Technology ..... Ms. Heather HEERSINK
20 Asst VP for Academic Affairs ..... Ms. Margaret DOELL
32 VP for Student Affairs ..... Mr. Kenneth L. MARQUEZ
09 Senior Analyst Inst Research ..... Mrs. Andrea BENTON-MESTAS
08 Director Library ..... Ms. Carol SMITH
37 Director Student Financial Aid ..... Mr. Philip SCHROEDER
07 Director of Admissions ..... Mr. Eric CARPIO
06 Registrar ..... Ms. Belen MAESTAS
31 Exec Dir Community Partnerships ..... Ms. Mary HOFFMAN
13 Chief Information Officer ..... Mr. Kevin S. DANIEL
41 Athletic Director ..... Mr. Larry MORTENSEN
26 Asst to President Communications ..... Ms. Julie WAECHTER
109 Director of Auxiliary Services ..... Mr. Bruce DEL TONDO
38 Director Counseling/Career Services ..... Mr. Gregg ELLIOTT
15 Director Human Resources ..... Ms. Tracy ROGERS
102 Executive Director ASU Foundation ..... Ms. Tammy L. LOPEZ
29 Director Alumni Relations ..... Ms. Lori L. LASKE
96 Director of Purchasing ..... Ms. Renee VIGIL
19 Dir Adams State Univ Police Dept ..... Vacant
40 Director Bookstore ..... Mr. Darrell MEIS
27 Director of Communications ..... Mr. Mark SCHOENECKER
57 Chair English/Theatre/Communication ..... Dr. David MAZEL
50 Chair Business & Economics ..... Dr. Michael TOMLIN
53 Chair Education ..... Dr. Edward CROWTHER
77 Chair Chemistry/Computer Sci/Math ..... Dr. Matthew S. NEHRING
81 Chair Biology/Earth Science ..... Dr. Benita BRINK

Aims Community College (J)

Box 69, Greeley CO 80632-0069
County: Weld FICE Identification: 007582
Unit ID: 126207
Telephone: (970) 330-8008 Carnegie Class: Assoc/Pub-R-M
FAX Number: (970) 330-5705 Calendar System: Semester
URL: www.aims.edu
Established: 1967 Annual Undergrad Tuition & Fees (In-District): $2,280
Enrollment: 5,087 Coed
Affiliation or Control: Local IRS Status: 501(c)3
Highest Offering: Associate Degree
Program: Occupational; 2-Year Principally Bachelor's Creditable
Accreditation: NH, ADNUR, EMT, IFSAC, SURGT

01 President ..... Dr. Leah L. BORNSTEIN
100 Chief of Staff to the President ..... Ms. Ann GROTNESS
88 Special Asst to Pres External Affs ..... Dr. Geri ANDERSON
10 Chief Administrative Officer ..... Mr. Bob COX
13 Chief Information Officer ..... Mr. Bill WAGGONER
05 Provost/Chief Academic Officer ..... Ms. Donna NORWOOD
20 Academic Dean ..... Mr. Jeff SMITH
32 Dean for Student Services ..... Dr. Patricia MATIJEVIC
35 Associate Dean Student Services ..... Ms. Shannon MCCASLAND
43 Chief Legal Officer ..... Ms. Sandra OWENS
30 Dir Inst Advancement/Foundation ..... Ms. Julie BUDERUS
15 Director Human Resources ..... Ms. Dee SHULTZ
21 Budget Director ..... Vacant
18 Chief Facilities Management Officer ..... Mr. Michael MILLSAPPS
37 Director Student Financial Assist ..... Ms. Nancy GRAY
06 Registrar ..... Mr. Stuart THOMAS
38 Director Student Success Center ..... Ms. Paula YANISH
09 Assoc Dean Inst Effect & Assessment ..... Ms. Lee Ann SAPPINGTON
14 Director Information Technology ..... Ms. Andria ROGERS
31 Director College/Community Rel ..... Vacant
35 Director Student Leadership & Dev ..... Dr. Ryan BARONE
12 Director Loveland Campus ..... Ms. Heather LELCHOOK
88 Director Windsor Auto/Tech Ctr ..... Mr. Fred BROWN
12 Assoc Dean Ft Lupton Campus ..... Ms. Brenda RASK
75 Associate Dean Career & Tech Ed ..... Ms. Brenda RASK
96 Director of Purchasing ..... Mr. Jim DWYER
08 Academic Dean Extended Studies ..... Mr. Rob UMBAUGH
66 Interim Associate Dean Nursing ..... Ms. Erika GREENBERG
20 Academic Dean ..... Ms. Deborah JOHANSEN
88 Associate Dean Academic Pathways ..... Mr. Gene MEIER
88 Assoc Dean Early College ..... Ms. Libby KLINGSMITH
83 Academic Dean ..... Dr. Richard HANKS
88 Assistant Dean Academics ..... Vacant
106 Dir Online Education/E-learning ..... Ms. Cheryl COMSTOCK
19 Director Security/Safety ..... Mr. Todd DEPORTER
101 Secretary of the Institution/Board ..... Ms. Katelyn ELLIOTT
45 Chief Institutional Planning ..... Mr. Damion CORDOVA

American Sentinel University (K)

2260 South Xanadu Way, Ste 310, Aurora CO 80014
County: Arapahoe FICE Identification: 041277
Unit ID: 41277
Telephone: (303) 991-1575 Carnegie Class: Not Classified
FAX Number: (303) 991-1577 Calendar System: Other
URL: www.americansentinel.edu
Established: 2000 Annual Undergrad Tuition & Fees: $11,250
Enrollment: 3,173 Coed
Affiliation or Control: Proprietary IRS Status: Proprietary
Highest Offering: Doctorate
Program: Professional; Nursing Emphasis
Accreditation: DEAC, NUR, NURSE

01 President ..... Ms. Mary A. ADAMS
84 Sr Vice Pres Enrollment/Retention ..... Mr. Jeff CAPLAN

66 Dean of Nursing .... Dr. Judy BURCKHARDT
07 Director of Admissions .... Ms. Natalie NIXON
06 Registrar .... Mr. Thomas HARTMAN

Arapahoe Community College (A)

5900 S Santa Fe Drive, PO Box 9002,
Littleton CO 80160-9002
County: Arapahoe FICE Identification: 001346
Unit ID: 126289
Telephone: (303) 797-4222 Carnegie Class: Assoc/Pub-S-MC
FAX Number: (303) 797-5935 Calendar System: Semester
URL: www.arapahoe.edu
Established: 1965 Annual Undergrad Tuition & Fees (In-State): $5,134
Enrollment: 9,728 Coed
Affiliation or Control: State IRS Status: 501(c)3
Highest Offering: Associate Degree
Program: Occupational; 2-Year Principally Bachelor's Creditable
Accreditation: NH, ADNUR, CAHIIM, EMT, FUSER, MLTAD, PTAA

01 President .... Dr. Diana M. DOYLE
11 Vice President Admin Services .... Dr. Cindy SOMERS
05 Vice President Instruction .... Dr. Diane HEGEMAN
10 Chief Financial Officer .... Mr. Joseph LORENZO, JR.
103 Dean Community/Workforce Partnershp .... Mr. Matt MCKEEVER
32 Vice President of Student Services ... Dr. Lisa MATYE-EDWARDS
38 Director of Advising and Retention .... Mr. Michael MCMANUS
07 Director Admissions & Records .... Ms. Darcy BRIGGS
37 Dir of Student Financial Services .... Ms. Gail MCKINNEY
31 Exec Dir of Community/Workforce Pgm .... Ms. Kim LARSON-COONEY
83 Dean Legal/Comm/Soc & Behav Sci .... Dr. Vanessa ANDERSON
81 Dean Health/Math & Science .... Dr. Samuel DEVRIES
49 Dean Arts/Human/Business & Tech .... Ms. Rebecca WOULFE
102 Executive Director Foundation .... Ms. Courtney LOEHFELM
21 Controller .... Ms. Xochil QUIJANO
19 Chief of Police .... Mr. Joseph MORRIS
09 Director Institutional Research .... Mr. Jon PROCTOR
08 Director Learning Resource Center .... Ms. Lisa GRABOWSKI
26 Dir of Marketing/Public Relations .... Ms. Tina GRIESHEIMER
35 Assoc Dean of Judicial Affairs .... Ms. Heather WILCOX
96 Purchasing Coordinator .... Vacant
18 Facilities Director .... Mr. David CRAWFORD
13 Chief Info Technology Officer (CIO) .... Mr. Joseph MCCORMICK
15 Director Personnel Services .... Ms. Angela WILLIAMS

Argosy University, Denver (B)

7600 East Eastman Avenue, Denver CO 80231
Telephone: (303) 923-4110 Identification: 666654
Accreditation: &WC, ACBSP, CACREP

† Regional accreditation is carried under the parent institution in Orange, CA.

The Art Institute of Colorado (C)

1200 Lincoln Street, Denver CO 80203-2172
County: Denver FICE Identification: 020789
Unit ID: 126702
Telephone: (303) 837-0825 Carnegie Class: Spec/Arts
FAX Number: (303) 860-8520 Calendar System: Quarter
URL: www.artinstitutes.edu/denver
Established: 1952 Annual Undergrad Tuition & Fees: $17,632
Enrollment: 1,414 Coed
Affiliation or Control: Proprietary IRS Status: Proprietary
Highest Offering: Baccalaureate
Program: Occupational
Accreditation: NH, ACFEI, CIDA

01 President .... Mr. Benjamin C. VALDEZ
05 Vice President/Dean Academic Affs .... Dr. Janet TACKETT
07 Senior Director of Admissions .... Ms. Judith JOCHEMS
32 Director of Student Services .... Mr. John RICHARDSON
10 Director Admin & Financial Services .... Ms. Tanya TAMIM
37 Director of Financial Aid .... Ms. Debra SARTAIN
06 Registrar .... Mr. David WESSLER

Aspen University (D)

720 S Colorado Blvd, Suite 1150N, Denver CO 80246
County: Denver FICE Identification: 040803
Unit ID: 454829
Telephone: (800) 441-4746 Carnegie Class: Master's M
FAX Number: (303) 336-1144 Calendar System: Other
URL: www.aspen.edu
Established: 1987 Annual Undergrad Tuition & Fees: $6,150
Enrollment: 1,488 Coed
Affiliation or Control: Proprietary IRS Status: Proprietary
Highest Offering: Doctorate
Program: Business Emphasis
Accreditation: DEAC, NURSE

01 Chairman & CEO .... Mr. Michael MATTHEWS
05 Chief Academic Officer .... Dr. Cheri ST. ARNAULD
11 Vice Pres of Operations .... Ms. Barbara MAX
10 EVP Finance/Interim CFO .... Ms. Janet GILL
06 Registrar .... Ms. Ashley MOSS

Augustine Institute (E)

6160 S. Syracuse Way #310,
Greenwood Village CO 80111
County: Arapahoe Identification: 667219
Telephone: (303) 937-4420 Carnegie Class: Not Classified
FAX Number: (303) 468-2933 Calendar System: Semester
URL: augustineinstitute.org
Established: 2005 Annual Graduate Tuition & Fees: $9,500
Enrollment: 109 Coed
Affiliation or Control: Roman Catholic IRS Status: 501(c)3
Highest Offering: Master's; No Undergraduates
Program: Religious Emphasis
Accreditation: @THEOL

01 President .... Mr. Tim GRAY
05 Academic Dean .... Dr. Christopher BLUM

Bel-Rea Institute of Animal Technology (F)

1681 S Dayton Street, Denver CO 80247-3048
County: Arapahoe FICE Identification: 012670
Unit ID: 126359
Telephone: (800) 950-8001 Carnegie Class: Assoc/PrivFP
FAX Number: (303) 751-9969 Calendar System: Quarter
URL: www.bel-rea.com
Established: 1971 Annual Undergrad Tuition & Fees: $15,450
Enrollment: 500 Coed
Affiliation or Control: Proprietary IRS Status: Proprietary
Highest Offering: Associate Degree
Program: Occupational
Accreditation: ACCSC

01 Director .... Paulette KAUFMAN
05 Dean of Education .... Nolan RUCKER
37 Director Student Financial Aid .... Stasi BONTINELLI
32 Director Student Services .... Cynthia MEDINA

College for Financial Planning (G)

9000 E. Nichols Avenue #200, Centennial CO 80112
County: Denver Identification: 666809
Unit ID: 126526
Telephone: (303) 220-1200 Carnegie Class: Not Classified
FAX Number: (303) 220-4940 Calendar System: Other
URL: www.cffp.edu
Established: 1972 Annual Graduate Tuition & Fees: $6,300
Enrollment: 7,229 Coed
Affiliation or Control: Proprietary IRS Status: Proprietary
Highest Offering: Master's; No Undergraduates
Program: Professional
Accreditation: NH

01 President .... Mr. John SEARS
05 Vice President Academic Affairs .... Mr. Jim PASZTOR
10 Vice President Business Development .... Mr. Dirk PANTONE
84 Director of Enrollment .... Ms. Alicia MEAD
06 Registrar .... Ms. Viviane PRICE
38 Director Student Service Center .... Vacant

CollegeAmerica Colorado Springs (H)

2020 N Academy Boulevard, Ste 100,
Colorado Springs CO 80909
Telephone: (719) 637-0600 Identification: 666293
Accreditation: ACCSC

† Branch campus of CollegeAmerica Denver, Denver, CO.

CollegeAmerica Denver (I)

1385 S Colorado Blvd, 5th Floor, Denver CO 80222
County: Denver FICE Identification: 025943
Unit ID: 126872
Telephone: (303) 300-8740 Carnegie Class: Bac/Assoc
FAX Number: (303) 692-9156 Calendar System: Other
URL: www.collegeamerica.edu
Established: 1964 Annual Undergrad Tuition & Fees: $23,062
Enrollment: 407 Coed
Affiliation or Control: Independent Non-Profit IRS Status: 501(c)3
Highest Offering: Baccalaureate
Program: Occupational
Accreditation: #ACCSC

01 Executive Director .... Ms. Suzanne SCALES
05 Academic Director .... Ms. Kacey JECHURA
37 Director of Financial Aid .... Ms. Sonia MARTINEZ
07 Director of Admissions .... Ms. Mary GORDY
06 Registrar .... Ms. Lauren ELI

CollegeAmerica Fort Collins (J)

4601 S Mason, Fort Collins CO 80525-3740
Telephone: (970) 225-4860 Identification: 666362
Accreditation: #ACCSC

† Branch campus of CollegeAmerica Denver, Denver, CO.

Colorado Academy of Veterinary Technology (K)

2766 Janitell Road, Colorado Springs CO 80906
County: El Paso FICE Identification: 041850
Unit ID: 461953
Telephone: (719) 219-9636 Carnegie Class: Not Classified
FAX Number: (719) 302-5577 Calendar System: Quarter
URL: www.cavt.edu
Established: 2007 Annual Undergrad Tuition & Fees: $15,223
Enrollment: 75 Coed
Affiliation or Control: Proprietary IRS Status: Proprietary
Highest Offering: Associate Degree
Program: Occupational
Accreditation: COE

01 Site Director/Admissions .... Dr. Steve RUBIN
05 Chief Academic Officer .... Mrs. Ramona CRANE
38 Dir Student Counseling/Fin Aid .... Mrs. Traci THOMPSON

Colorado Christian University (L)

8787 W Alameda Avenue, Lakewood CO 80226-7499
County: Jefferson FICE Identification: 009401
Unit ID: 126669
Telephone: (303) 963-3000 Carnegie Class: Master's M
FAX Number: (303) 963-3001 Calendar System: Semester
URL: www.ccu.edu
Established: 1914 Annual Undergrad Tuition & Fees: $27,986
Enrollment: 4,235 Coed
Affiliation or Control: Independent Non-Profit IRS Status: 501(c)3
Highest Offering: Master's
Program: 2-Year Principally Bachelor's Creditable; Liberal Arts And General; Teacher Preparatory; Professional
Accreditation: NH, CACREP, MUS, NURSE

01 President .... Mr. William L. ARMSTRONG
10 VP for Business Affairs & CFO .... Mr. Daniel COHRS
05 VP Acad Affairs College UG Studies .... Dr. Cherri S. PARKS
30 VP for Development .... Mr. Paul ELDRIDGE
32 VP for Student Development .... Mr. Jim S. MCCORMICK
20 VP of Acad Affairs/Dean CAGS .... Dr. Sarah SCHERLING
35 Asst VP Stdnt Pgm/Dean of Students .... Ms. Sharon M. FELKER
42 Asst VP of Student Life/Ministry .... Vacant
07 VP Enrollment & Marketing for CAGS .... Mr. Matthew HANUSA
88 VP of Student Success .... Mr. Roger CHANDLER
50 Dean School of Business .... Dr. Gary EWEN
72 Dean of Business and Technology .... Dr. Mellani J. DAY
53 Dean School of Education .... Dr. Debora SCHEFFEL
53 Dean of Ed/Curriculum & Instruction .... Dr. Wendy WENDOVER
79 Dean Sch Humanities & Sciences .... Dr. William R. SAXBY
64 Dean School of Music .... Mr. Steven T. TAYLOR
73 Dean School of Theology .... Vacant
66 Dean of Nursing & Sciences .... Dr. Barbara WHITE
73 Dean of Biblical Studies & Theology .... Dr. Richard V. YOHN
07 Director of Admissions .... Ms. Jo Leda MARTIN
43 University Counsel .... Mr. Steven MILLER
21 Controller .... Mr. Wendell GEARY
06 Registrar .... Ms. Linda K. PERCIANTE
41 Athletic Director .... Mr. Darren A. RICHIE
38 Director of Counseling Services .... Dr. Joannie L. DEBRITO
44 Director of Development .... Ms. Kathy PETTIT
18 Director of Facilities .... Mr. Mathew J. GOTHARD
37 Director of Financial Aid .... Mr. Steve M. WOODBURN
23 Director of Health Services .... Ms. Mandy WILLIAMS
15 Director of Human Resources .... Mr. Rick GARRIS
13 Dir of Information Systems/Tech .... Mr. Bryan SHOLTEN
08 Library Director .... Ms. Gayle C. GUNDERSON
36 Director of Life Directions Center .... Ms. Joy STRICKLAND
39 Director of Residence Life .... Mr. Joseph BROOKS
19 Director of Security .... Mr. Harry G. CAROTHERS
26 Dir of University Communications .... Ms. Lisa L. ZELLER
29 Director Alumni Relations .... Ms. Missy SMITH
105 Director of Web Development .... Ms. Chris FRANZ
04 Executive Assistant to President .... Ms. Kerry BLEIKAMP

Colorado College (M)

14 E Cache La Poudre St.,
Colorado Springs CO 80903-3294
County: El Paso FICE Identification: 001347
Unit ID: 126678
Telephone: (719) 389-6000 Carnegie Class: Bac/A&S
FAX Number: (719) 634-4180 Calendar System: Other
URL: www.coloradocollege.edu
Established: 1874 Annual Undergrad Tuition & Fees: $49,000
Enrollment: 2,067 Coed
Affiliation or Control: Independent Non-Profit IRS Status: 501(c)3
Highest Offering: Master's
Program: Liberal Arts And General; Teacher Preparatory
Accreditation: NH

01 President .... Dr. Jill TIEFENTHALER
05 Dean of College & Faculty .... Dr. Sandra WONG
100 Chief of Staff .... Ms. Mary Frances KERR
10 Sr VP Business/Finance & Treas .... Mr. Robert G. MOORE
30 Vice Pres for Advancement .... Mr. Sean PIERI
84 Sr Vice Pres Enrollment Management .... Mr. Mark HATCH
32 VP Student Life/Dean of Students .... Mr. Mike EDMONDS
13 VP for Information Management/CTO .... Mr. Brian YOUNG
45 Asst VP for Institutional Planning .... Ms. Lyrae WILLIAMS

88 Assoc Dean of Academic Programs ....Dr. Emily CHAN
44 Asst VP Advancement Operations ....Ms. Molly BODNAR
39 Sr Assc Dn Stdnts/Dir Resident Life ....Mr. John LAUER
20 Associate Dean of the College ....Dr. Regula M. EVITT
20 Assoc Dean of the Faculty ....Dr. Mike SIDDOWAY
35 Associate Dean of Students ....Ms. Rochelle MASON
37 Director of Financial Aid ....Mr. Jim M. SWANSON
06 Registrar ....Mr. Phillip C. APODACA
26 Vice President for Communications ....Ms. Jane TURNIS
41 Director of Athletics ....Mr. Ken RALPH
104 Director International Programs ....Dr. Inger BULL
15 Director Human Resources ....Ms. Barbara WILSON
18 Director of Facilities ....Mr. Chris COULTER
19 Director Campus Safety ....Vacant
08 Library Director ....Mr. Ivan GAETZ
96 Director Administrative Svcs ....Mr. Don DAVIDSON
36 Director Career Center ....Ms. Megan NICKLAUS
28 Asst VP/Director of Butler Ctr ....Mr. Paul BUCKLEY
29 Director Alumni & Parent Relations ....Ms. Anita PARISEAU
91 Director Enterprise Info Svcs ....Mr. Vishvas PARADKAR
09 Dir Assessment/Program Review .....Ms. Amanda UDIS-KESSLER
21 Controller/Asst Treasurer ....Ms. Stacy LUTZ-DAVIDSON
24 Director of Enterprise Technology ....Mr. Vish PARADKAR
105 Director Web Communications ....Ms. Karen TO
21 Senior Budget Analyst ....Ms. Enid RUIZ-MATTEI
38 Counseling Sup/Clin Psychologist ....Mr. Bill DOVE
38 Dir Disability Services ....Ms. Jan EDWARDS
27 College News Director ....Ms. Leslie WEDDELL
90 Director Educational Tech Svcs ....Mr. Chad SCHOENWILL
88 Director of Innovative Technology ....Vacant
88 Dir Collab Cmty Engagement ....Mr. David HARKER
46 College Research Professor ....Dr. Kevin RASK
42 Chaplain ....Dr. Bruce CORIELL
101 Special Assistant Board of Trustees ....Ms. Caitlin APIGIAN
04 Executive Asst to the President ....Ms. Michelle BECKMANN

Colorado Heights University (A)

3001 S Federal Boulevard, Denver CO 80236-2711
County: Denver FICE Identification: 032893
Unit ID: 367839
Telephone: (303) 937-4225 Carnegie Class: Spec/Bus
FAX Number: (303) 937-4224 Calendar System: Other
URL: www.chu.edu
Established: 1990 Annual Undergrad Tuition & Fees: $6,546
Enrollment: 154 Coed
Affiliation or Control: Independent Non-Profit IRS Status: 501(c)3
Highest Offering: Master's
Program: Professional; Business Emphasis
Accreditation: ACICS

01 President ....Mr. Fred VAN LIEW
05 Dean of Academic Affairs ....Dr. Tracey TERNAM
10 VP of Finance & Administration ....Mr. Dave BOYLL
32 Dean of Student Affs/Enrollment Mgt ....Mr. Bryan CICERO
50 Dir of MBA and BA Intl Business ....Mr. Jon WILKERSON
06 Registrar ....Ms. Julie GORDON
15 Director of Human Resources ....Ms. Debra POWELL
37 Director of Financial Aid ....Ms. Beba PREDIC
39 Director of Public Safety ....Mr. Daniil YUSUFOV
13 Director Information Technology ....Mr. Mayer SALFITI
18 Director of Facilities ....Mr. Jose GALLEGOS

Colorado Mesa University (B)

1100 North Avenue, Grand Junction CO 81501-3122
County: Mesa FICE Identification: 001358
Unit ID: 127556
Telephone: (970) 248-1020 Carnegie Class: Bac/A&S
FAX Number: (970) 248-1076 Calendar System: Semester
URL: www.coloradomesa.edu
Established: 1925 Annual Undergrad Tuition & Fees (In-State): $6,406
Enrollment: 9,116 Coed
Affiliation or Control: State IRS Status: 501(c)3
Highest Offering: Doctorate
Program: Occupational; 2-Year Principally Bachelor's Creditable; Liberal Arts And General; Teacher Preparatory; Professional
Accreditation: NH, ADNUR, CAATE, MLTAD, MUS, NURSE, PNUR, RAD, @SW

01 President ....Mr. Tim FOSTER
05 Vice Pres Academic Affairs ....Dr. Carol FUTHEY
10 Vice President Financial/Admin Svcs ....Mr. Patrick DOYLE
31 Vice Pres Community College Affairs ....Ms. Brigitte SUNDERMANN
109 Asst Vice Pres Auxiliary Services ....Mr. Andy RODRIGUEZ
32 Vice Pres Student Services ....Mr. John MARSHALL
13 Exec Dir InformationTechnology/Comm ....Mr. Jeremy BROWN
08 Library Director ....Ms. Sylvia RAEL
30 Director of Development ....Ms. Peggy LAMM
37 Director Financial Aid ....Mr. Curt MARTIN
26 Director of Media Relations ....Ms. Dana NUNN
06 Registrar ....Ms. Holly TEAL
09 Dir of Inst Research/Assessment ....Ms. Sonia BRANDON
18 Chief Facilities/Physical Plant ....Mr. Kent MARSH
29 Director Alumni Relations ....Ms. Rebecca MCKENNA
84 Director Enrollment Management ....Mr. Michael POLL

Colorado Mesa University-Montrose Campus (C)

245 South Cascade Avenue, Montrose CO 81401
Telephone: (970) 249-7009 Identification: 770031
Accreditation: &NH

† Branch campus of Colorado Mesa University, Grand Junction, CO.

Colorado Mountain College (D)

802 Grand Avenue, Glenwood Springs CO 81602-3961
County: Garfield FICE Identification: 004506
Unit ID: 126711
Telephone: (970) 945-8691 Carnegie Class: Assoc/Pub-R-L
FAX Number: (970) 947-8385 Calendar System: Semester
URL: www.coloradomtn.edu
Established: 1965 Annual Undergrad Tuition & Fees (In-District): $1,710
Enrollment: 6,410 Coed
Affiliation or Control: Local IRS Status: 501(c)3
Highest Offering: Baccalaureate
Program: Occupational; 2-Year Principally Bachelor's Creditable
Accreditation: NH, ADNUR, EMT

01 President ....Dr. Carrie HAUSER
05 VP Academic Affairs ....Vacant
10 CFO ....Ms. Linda ENGLISH
09 VP Institutional Effectiveness ....Dr. Debra LOPER
12 Vice Pres Vail/Eagle Valley Campus ....Dr. Kathryn REGJO
32 VP Student Affairs ....Ms. Lin STICKLER
15 Vice President of Human Resources ....Ms. Jan ASPELUND
26 Public Relations Officer ....Ms. Debbie CRAWFORD
13 Chief Information Officer ....Vacant
07 Dir Pre-Enrollment Svcs/Registrar ....Mr. Shane LARSON
37 Director of Financial Aid ....Mr. Thomas VALLER
18 Director of College Facilities ....Mr. Peter WALLER
27 Director of Marketing/Publications ....Mr. Doug STEWART
96 Director of Purchasing ....Mr. Steve BOYD
20 Developmental Education Coordinator ....Ms. Karen A. ARMITANO
04 Administrative Asst to President ....Ms. Debbie NOVAK
100 Chief of Staff ....Mr. Matt GIANNESCHI
43 Dir Legal Services/General Counsel ....Mr. Richard GONZALES

Colorado Mountain College Alpine Campus (E)

1275 Crawford Avenue, Steamboat Springs CO 80487
Telephone: (970) 870-4444 Identification: 770038
Accreditation: &NH

† Branch campus of Colorado Mountain College, Glenwood Springs, CO.

Colorado Mountain College Aspen Campus (F)

0255 Sage Way, Aspen CO 81611
Telephone: (970) 925-7740 Identification: 770032
Accreditation: &NH

† Branch campus of Colorado Mountain College, Glenwood Springs, CO.

Colorado Mountain College Roaring Fork Campus-Spring Valley (G)

690 Colorado Avenue, Carbondale CO 81623
Telephone: (970) 963-2172 Identification: 770035
Accreditation: &NH

† Branch campus of Colorado Mountain College, Glenwood Springs, CO.

Colorado Mountain College Summit Campus-Breckinridge Campus (H)

PO Box 2208, Breckinridge CO 80424
Telephone: (970) 453-6757 Identification: 770033
Accreditation: &NH

† Branch campus of Colorado Mountain College, Glenwood Springs, CO.

Colorado Mountain College Timberline Campus (I)

27900 County Road 319, PO Box 897,
Buena Vista CO 81211
Telephone: (719) 395-8419 Identification: 770036
Accreditation: &NH

† Branch campus of Colorado Mountain College, Glenwood Springs, CO.

Colorado Mountain College Vail/Eagle Valley Campus (J)

150 Miller Ranch Road, Edwards CO 81632
Telephone: (970) 569-2900 Identification: 770034
Accreditation: &NH

† Branch campus of Colorado Mountain College, Glenwood Springs, CO.

Colorado Mountain College West Garfield Campus (K)

3695 Airport Road, Rifle CO 81650
Telephone: (970) 625-1871 Identification: 770037
Accreditation: &NH

† Branch campus of Colorado Mountain College, Glenwood Springs, CO.

Colorado Northwestern Community College (L)

500 Kennedy Drive, Rangely CO 81648-3598
County: Rio Blanco FICE Identification: 001359
Unit ID: 126748
Telephone: (970) 675-2261 Carnegie Class: Assoc/Pub-R-M
FAX Number: (970) 675-5046 Calendar System: Semester
URL: www.cncc.edu
Established: 1962 Annual Undergrad Tuition & Fees (In-District): $6,429
Enrollment: 1,145 Coed
Affiliation or Control: State/Local IRS Status: 170(c)1
Highest Offering: Associate Degree
Program: Occupational; 2-Year Principally Bachelor's Creditable
Accreditation: NH, ADNUR, DH

01 President ....Mr. Russell GEORGE
12 Vice Pres Craig Campus ....Ms. Janell OBERLANDER
05 Vice Pres Instruction/Student Svcs ....Mr. David SMITH
10 Vice Pres Business/Administration ....Mr. Christopher BISHOP
84 Dean of Enrollment Svcs/Registrar ....Ms. Tresa ENGLAND
08 Library Director ....Ms. Leana COX
15 Human Resource Specialist ....Ms. Kim TUCKER
26 Marketing Director ....Ms. Tresa ENGLAND
18 Facilities Director ....Mr. John BOTTELBERGHE
09 Director of Institutional Research ....Ms. Susan BOLES
38 Director Student Counseling ....Ms. Caitlan MOORE
96 Director of Purchasing ....Mr. Roger HANNA
37 Financial Aid Technician ....Ms. Merrie BYERS
20 Dean of Instruction in Rangely ....Ms. Judy ALLRED
20 Dean of Instruction in Craig ....Ms. Donna THEIMER

Colorado Northwestern Community College Craig (M)

2801 W 9th Street, Craig CO 81625
Telephone: (970) 824-1101 Identification: 770039
Accreditation: &NH

† Branch campus of Colorado Northwestern Community College, Rangely, CO.

Colorado School of Healing Arts (N)

7655 W Mississippi, Suite 100, Lakewood CO 80226-4332
County: Jefferson FICE Identification: 035844
Unit ID: 381732
Telephone: (303) 986-2320 Carnegie Class: Assoc/PrivFP
FAX Number: (303) 980-6594 Calendar System: Quarter
URL: www.csha.net
Established: 1986 Annual Undergrad Tuition & Fees: $13,200
Enrollment: 177 Coed
Affiliation or Control: Proprietary IRS Status: Proprietary
Highest Offering: Associate Degree
Program: Occupational; 2-Year Principally Bachelor's Creditable; Technical Emphasis
Accreditation: ACCSC

01 Executive Director & Owner ....Mr. Dennis SIMPSON
03 Director ....Ms. Gina SIMPSON
13 Director IT Dept ....Mr. Dan GOLDEN
06 Registrar ....Ms. Bryn HERSHBERGER
53 Director of Education Cert Pgm ....Ms. Chris SMITH
08 Head Librarian ....Ms. Kris WILL
11 Office Manager ....Ms. Tiffany LAYNE
40 Bookstore Manager ....Mr. Greg SENICH
36 Career Advisor/Placement ....Ms. Rebekah TREAT
37 Financial Aid Advisor ....Ms. Andrea NIECE
07 Admissions Representative ....Ms. Rosa TORRES

Colorado School of Mines (O)

1500 Illinois Street, Golden CO 80401-1843
County: Jefferson FICE Identification: 001348
Unit ID: 126775
Telephone: (303) 273-3000 Carnegie Class: RU/H
FAX Number: (303) 273-3278 Calendar System: Semester
URL: www.mines.edu
Established: 1874 Annual Undergrad Tuition & Fees (In-State): $17,353
Enrollment: 5,795 Coed
Affiliation or Control: State IRS Status: 501(c)3
Highest Offering: Doctorate
Program: Professional; Technical Emphasis
Accreditation: NH, ENG

01 President ....Dr. Paul C. JOHNSON
05 Provost ....Dr. Terry PARKER
10 Executive Vice Pres Finance & Admin ....Ms. Kirsten VOLPI
88 Sr Vice Pres Strat Enterprises ....Dr. Nigel T. MIDDLETON
32 Vice Pres Student Life ....Dr. Dan FOX
30 VP for Institutional Advancement ....Mr. Brian WINKELBAUER
100 Chief of Staff ....Mr. Peter HAN
06 Registrar ....Ms. Lara MEDLEY
07 Director of Admissions ....Mr. Bruce P. GOETZ
08 Librarian ....Ms. Joanne V. LERUD-HECK
13 Chief Information Officer ....Mr. Michael ERICKSON
26 Director Integrated Marketing Comm ....Ms. Karen GILBERT
37 Director of Financial Aid ....Ms. Jill ROBERTSON
51 Director of Special Programs ....Dr. Barry MARTIN
20 Associate Provost ....Dr. Thomas BOYD
18 Director of Plant Facilities ....Mr. Gary BOWERSOCK
22 Affirmative Action Officer ....Mr. Michael DOUGHERTY
39 Director of Student Housing ....Ms. Rebecca FLINTOFT
38 Director Student Counseling ....Ms. Sandra SIMMS
41 Athletic Director ....Mr. David HANSBURG
04 Spec Assistant to the President ....Ms. Kristi GITKIND
09 Director of Institutional Research ....Ms. Tricia DOUTHIT
15 Director Personnel Services ....Mr. Michael DOUGHERTY
84 Director Enrollment Management ....Ms. Heather BOYD
35 Director Student Affairs ....Mr. Derek MORGAN

36 Director Student Placement .... Ms. Jean MANNING-CLARK
19 Director Public Safety .... Mr. Greg BOHLEN
94 Exec Dir Women in Sci Eng & Math .... Ms. Deb LASICH
92 Director Honors Program .... Dr. Ken OSGOOD
45 Dir Financial Planning & Budget .... Ms. Vicki NICHOL
93 Director Minority Engineering Pgm .... Ms. Andrea MORGAN
91 Director Enterprise Systems .... Mr. David LEE
29 Director Alumni Relations .... Ms. Nancy BLANK
104 Director of International Programs .... Ms. Kay GODEL-GENGENBACH
108 Director of Assessment .... Ms. Kay SCHNEIDER
43 Dir Legal Services/General Counsel .... Ms. Anne WALKER
88 Sr VP Research & Tech Transfer .... Dr. Tony DEAN
88 Dean Earth Resource Sci & Engr .... Dr. Romana GRAVES
54 Dean Engr & Computer Science .... Dr. Kevin MOORE
88 Dean Applied Sci & Engineering .... Dr. Michael KAUFMAN

Colorado School of Trades (A)

1575 Hoyt Street, Lakewood CO 80215-2996
County: Jefferson　FICE Identification: 011572
Unit ID: 126784
Telephone: (800) 234-4594　Carnegie Class: Assoc/PrivFP
FAX Number: (303) 233-4723　Calendar System: Other
URL: www.schooloftrades.edu
Established: 1947　Annual Undergrad Tuition & Fees: $20,520
Enrollment: 196　Coed
Affiliation or Control: Proprietary　IRS Status: Proprietary
Highest Offering: Associate Degree
Program: Occupational
Accreditation: ACCSC

01 President .... Mr. Robert E. MARTIN

Colorado School of Traditional Chinese Medicine (B)

1441 York Street, Suite 202, Denver CO 80206-2127
County: Denver　FICE Identification: 036863
Unit ID: 381352
Telephone: (303) 329-6355　Carnegie Class: Spec/Health
FAX Number: (303) 388-8165　Calendar System: Trimester
URL: www.cstcm.edu
Established: 1989　Annual Undergrad Tuition & Fees: $16,700
Enrollment: 134　Coed
Affiliation or Control: Proprietary　IRS Status: Proprietary
Highest Offering: Master's
Program: Occupational; Professional
Accreditation: ACUP

01 Administrative Director .... Vladimir DIBRIGIDA
07 Recruiting Director .... Chris DUXBURY-EDWARDS
05 Academic Dean .... Camille RODRIQUEZ
05 Academic Dean .... Edie NEWALL
20 Assistant Academic Dean .... Robbin AJILO
06 Registrar .... William WALLIN
08 Head Librarian .... Edie NEWALL
88 Clinic Director .... Parago JONES
88 Receptionist .... Kirsten WEEKS
37 Financial Aid Administrator .... Joel SPENCER

*Colorado State University System Office (C)

410 17th Street, Suite 2440, Denver CO 80202-4426
County: Denver　FICE Identification: 033437
Telephone: (303) 534-6290　Carnegie Class: N/A
FAX Number: (303) 534-6298
URL: www.csusystem.edu

01 Chancellor .... Dr. Tony FRANK
05 Chief Academic Officer .... Dr. Rick MIRANDA
43 General Counsel .... Mr. Michael D. NOLSER
10 Chief Financial Officer .... Mr. Rich SCHWEIGERT
26 Director of Public Relations .... Mr. Kyle HENLEY
86 Government Relations Coordinator .... Mr. Rich SCHWEIGERT
04 Executive Asst to Chancellor .... Ms. Melanie GEARY

*Colorado State University (D)

200 W. Lake Street, Fort Collins CO 80523-0015
County: Larimer　FICE Identification: 001350
Unit ID: 126818
Telephone: (970) 491-1101　Carnegie Class: RU/VH
FAX Number: (970) 491-0501　Calendar System: Semester
URL: www.colostate.edu
Established: 1870　Annual Undergrad Tuition & Fees (In-State): $9,897
Enrollment: 31,354　Coed
Affiliation or Control: State　IRS Status: 501(c)3
Highest Offering: Doctorate
Program: Liberal Arts And General; Teacher Preparatory; Professional
Accreditation: NH, BUS, CACREP, CEA, CIDA, CONST, COPSY, DIETC, DIETD, ENG, ENGR, IPSY, JOUR, LSAR, MFCD, MUS, OT, PH, SW, TEAC, VET

02 President .... Dr. Anthony A. FRANK
05 Senior Executive VP/Provost .... Dr. Rick MIRANDA
46 Vice President for Research .... Dr. Alan S. RUDOLPH
10 Assoc VP for Finance and Budgets .... Ms. Lynn JOHNSON
11 VP for University Operations .... Ms. Lynn JOHNSON
30 VP Advancement/Strategic Initiative .... Mr. Brett B. ANDERSON
84 Vice Pres for Enrollment/Access .... Dr. Robin C. BROWN
20 Vice Prov for Undergraduate Affairs .... Dr. Kathleen A. PICKERING
58 Dean Graduate School .... Dr. Jodie R. HANZLIK
26 VP for External Relations .... Mr. Tom MILLIGAN
91 Director of Acad Comp/Network Svc .... Mr. Scott BAILY
15 Dir Human Resource Svcs .... Ms. Diana PRIETO
36 Director Career Services .... Mr. Jeremy PODANY
08 Exec Assoc Dean of Libraries .... Vacant
07 Assoc VP Enroll/VP for Diversity .... Ms. Mary R. ONTIVEROS
29 Exec Director Alumni Relations .... Ms. Kristi BOHLENDER
41 Athletic Director .... Mr. Joe PARKER
43 Deputy General Counsel .... Mr. Jason L. JOHNSON
47 Dean Agriculture Sciences .... Dr. Ajay MENON
88 Dean Applied Human Sciences .... Dr. Jeff MCCUBBIN
50 Dean of Business .... Dr. Beth WALKER
54 Dean of Engineering .... Dr. David MCLEAN
49 Dean of Liberal Arts .... Dr. Ann M. GILL
62 VP for IT/Dean of Libraries .... Dr. Patrick BURNS
65 Dean of Natural Resources .... Dr. John HAYES
81 Dean of Natural Sciences .... Dr. Janice L. NERGER
74 Dean of Veterinary Med & Biomed Sci .... Dr. Mark STETTER
56 Director Cooperative Extension Svcs .... Dr. Louis SWANSON
06 Registrar .... Mr. Chris SENG
18 Chief Facilities/Physical Plant .... Mr. Steve R. HULTIN
22 Dir of Equal Opportunity .... Ms. Diana PRIETO
37 Director of Student Financial Aid .... Mr. Thomas BIEDSCHEID
39 Exec Dir Housing & Dining Services .... Dr. James DOLAK
40 Director of Bookstore .... Mr. John PARRY
96 Director of Purchasing .... Mr. Frank KRAPPES
92 Director University Honors Program .... Dr. Donald MYKLES
94 Dir Women & Gender Advocacy Center .... Ms. Kathy SISNEROS
09 Director of Institutional Research .... Dr. Laura JENSEN
100 Chief of Staff - Office of the Pres .... Mr. Mark GILL

*Colorado State University-Global Campus (E)

7800 E Orchard Road, Suite 200, Greenwood Village CO 80111
County: Arapahoe　FICE Identification: 042087
Unit ID: 476975
Telephone: (800) 462-7845　Carnegie Class: Not Classified
FAX Number: N/A　Calendar System: Semester
URL: www.csuglobal.edu
Established: 2008　Annual Undergrad Tuition & Fees (In-State): $8,400
Enrollment: 9,529　Coed
Affiliation or Control: State　IRS Status: 501(c)3
Highest Offering: Master's
Program: Professional; Business Emphasis
Accreditation: NH

02 President & CEO .... Dr. Becky TAKEDA-TINKER

*Colorado State University-Pueblo (F)

2200 Bonforte Boulevard, Pueblo CO 81001-4901
County: Pueblo　FICE Identification: 001365
Unit ID: 128106
Telephone: (719) 549-2100　Carnegie Class: Master's S
FAX Number: (719) 549-2650　Calendar System: Semester
URL: www.csupueblo.edu
Established: 1933　Annual Undergrad Tuition & Fees (In-State): $8,281
Enrollment: 7,256　Coed
Affiliation or Control: State　IRS Status: 501(c)3
Highest Offering: Master's
Program: Liberal Arts And General; Teacher Preparatory; Professional
Accreditation: NH, BUS, CAATE, ENG, ENGT, MUS, NUR, SW, TEAC

02 President .... Dr. Lesley DI MARE
05 Provost/Exec VP for Academic Affs .... Dr. Rick KREMINSKI
10 VP Finance & Administration .... Mr. Karl SPIECKER
84 VP Student Svcs and Enrollment Mgmt .... Dr. Paul ORSCHELN
20 Asst Provost Assess/Student Lrng .... Dr. Helen CAPRIOGLIO
08 Dean Library .... Ms. Rhonda GONZALES
50 Dean Hasan School of Business .... Dr. Bruce RAYMOND
79 Int Dean Col of Humanities/Soc Sci .... Dr. William FOLKESTAD
54 Int Dean Engr/Educ/Profess Studies .... Dr. Sylvester KALEVELA
81 Int Dean Science/Math .... Dr. David LEHMPUHL
102 Executive Director Foundation .... Mr. Todd KELLY
26 Exec Director External Affairs .... Ms. Cora ZALETEL
09 Interim Dir Inst Research/Analysis .... Sixian YANG
21 Controller .... Mr. Robert GONZALES
37 Director Student Financial Services .... Mr. Sean MCGIVNEY
06 Registrar .... Ms. Amy ROBERTSHAW
36 Director Career Center .... Mrs. Michelle B. GJERDE
13 Dir Info Tech Svcs/Chief Tech Ofcr .... Mr. Erich MATOLA
41 Director Athletics .... Mr. Joe FOLDA
18 Dir Facilities/Construction/Plng .... Mr. Craig CASON
15 Director Human Resources .... Mr. Ralph JACOBS
39 Dir Residence Life & Housing .... Ms. Jamie HINSHAW
109 Int Director Auxiliary Services .... Mr. Chris FENDRICH
23 Student Health Services Nurse .... Ms. Carolyn DAUGHERTY
29 Director Alumni Relations .... Ms. Tracy SAMORA
38 Director Student Counseling .... Vacant
89 Director First Year Programs .... Dr. Derek LOPEZ
22 Director Affirmative Action .... Mr. Roosevelt WILSON
85 Assoc Dir International Programs .... Ms. Annie WILLIAMS
04 Executive Asst to the President .... Ms. Trisha MACIAS
07 Director of Admissions .... Ms. Chrissy HOLLIDAY
28 Director of Diversity .... Ms. Jennifer DELUNA
32 Dean of Students & ResidenceLife .... Dr. Marie HUMPHREY

Colorado Technical University (G)

3151 South Vaughn Way, Suite 400, Aurora CO 80014
Telephone: (303) 632-2300　Identification: 666732
Accreditation: &NH, ACBSP

† Regional accreditation is carried under the parent institution in Colorado Springs, CO.

Colorado Technical University (H)

4435 N Chestnut Street, Colorado Springs CO 80907-3896
County: El Paso　FICE Identification: 010148
Unit ID: 126827
Telephone: (719) 598-0200　Carnegie Class: DRU
FAX Number: (719) 598-3740　Calendar System: Quarter
URL: www.coloradotech.edu
Established: 1965　Annual Undergrad Tuition & Fees: $11,517
Enrollment: 1,566　Coed
Affiliation or Control: Proprietary　IRS Status: Proprietary
Highest Offering: Doctorate
Program: Occupational; 2-Year Principally Bachelor's Creditable; Professional; Technical Emphasis
Accreditation: NH, ACBSP, ENG

00 Interim CEO .... Mr. Jack KOEHN
01 Campus President .... Mr. Andrew HURST
05 Chief Academic Officer/Provost .... Dr. Connie JOHNSON
07 Vice President of Admissions .... Mr. Keith ARMSTRONG
09 VP Institutional Effectiveness .... Mr. Steve WHITTEN
20 Vice Provost .... Dr. Douglas STEIN
10 Regional Director of Operations .... Ms. Toni JOHNSON
36 Director of Career Services .... Ms. Belinda NICHOLS-ZONNO
08 Library Manager .... Ms. Nicole HULT
13 Manager of Information Systems .... Mr. Thomas LEIGH
77 Chair of Computer Science .... Dr. Yanzhen QU

Community College of Aurora (I)

16000 E Centre Tech Parkway, Aurora CO 80011-9036
County: Arapahoe　FICE Identification: 022769
Unit ID: 126863
Telephone: (303) 360-4700　Carnegie Class: Assoc/Pub-S-MC
FAX Number: (303) 360-4761　Calendar System: Semester
URL: www.ccaurora.edu
Established: 1983　Annual Undergrad Tuition & Fees (In-State): $4,767
Enrollment: 7,617　Coed
Affiliation or Control: State　IRS Status: 501(c)3
Highest Offering: Associate Degree
Program: Occupational; 2-Year Principally Bachelor's Creditable
Accreditation: NH, EMT

01 President .... Dr. Elizabeth OUDENHOVEN
05 Vice President of Academic Affairs .... Ms. Janet BRANDAU
10 VP of Administrative Services .... Mr. Duane RISSE
32 Vice President of Student Affairs .... Dr. Elena SANDOVAL-LUCERO
45 VP of Institutional Effectiveness .... Dr. Chris WARD
15 Director of Human Resources .... Ms. Cindy HESSE
21 Controller .... Ms. Lisa LEFEVRE
35 Dean of Students .... Ms. Tamara WHITE
20 Dean Academic Affairs .... Mr. Victor VIALPANDO
20 Dean Academic Affairs .... Dr. Ted SNOW
19 Director of Security .... Mr. Jeff SIMPSON
36 Director of Career Services .... Ms. Barbara LINDSAY
13 Director Information Technology .... Mr. Sam THOMAS
18 Facilities Director .... Mr. Mike DAVIS
26 Director of Marketing .... Mr. Ethan RUZZANO
37 Director Financial Aid .... Mr. John YOUNG
06 Director Admissions & Registrar .... Ms. Kristen CUSACK
08 Director Library Services .... Ms. Joanna PRIMUS
09 Director of Institutional Research .... Ms. Catherine TROUTH
84 Dean of Retention & Student Success .... Dr. Derrick HAYNES
27 Director Public & Media Relations .... Mr. Lee RASIZER
102 Exec Dir CCA Foundation .... Mr. Gene SOBCZAK

Community College of Denver (J)

Campus Box 250, PO Box 173363, Denver CO 80217-3363
County: Denver　FICE Identification: 009542
Unit ID: 126942
Telephone: (303) 556-2400　Carnegie Class: Assoc/Pub-U-MC
FAX Number: (303) 556-8555　Calendar System: Semester
URL: www.ccd.edu
Established: 1967　Annual Undergrad Tuition & Fees (In-State): $3,725
Enrollment: 5,700　Coed
Affiliation or Control: State　IRS Status: 501(c)3
Highest Offering: Associate Degree
Program: Occupational; 2-Year Principally Bachelor's Creditable
Accreditation: NH, CSHSE, DH, NDT, RAD

01 President .... Dr. Everette FREEMAN
05 Provost/Chief Academic Officer .... Vacant
10 Vice Pres Finance & Admin/CFO .... Mr. Duane RISSE
32 Vice Pres Student Affairs .... Ms. Judi DIAZ BONACQUISTI
75 Dean Career/Technical Education .... Dr. Chris BUDDEN
49 Dean Language/Arts/Behavioral Sci .... Ms. Ruthanne ORIHUELA
35 Dean Student Development/Retention .... Dr. Ryan ROSS
84 Dean of Enrollment Services .... Ms. Lori KESTER
35 Dean of Student Life .... Ms. Meloni RUDOLPH
37 Director Financial Aid .... Mr. Thad SPAULDING

07 Director Recruit/Student Outreach .... Mr. Nahum KISNER
15 Director Human Resources .... Ms. Patty DAVIES
13 Director IT Services .... Mr. Chris ARCARESE
09 Director Inst Research & Planning .... Ms. Margaret PURYEAR
04 Executive Asst to President .... Ms. Emily WILLAN
06 Registrar .... Mr. Tan BUI
18 Chief Facilities/Physical Plant .... Mr. Kevin SEILER

Concorde Career College (A)

111 N Havana Street, Aurora CO 80010-4314
County: Arapahoe FICE Identification: 008871
Unit ID: 126687
Telephone: (303) 861-1151 Carnegie Class: Assoc/PrivFP
FAX Number: (303) 839-5478 Calendar System: Other
URL: www.concorde.edu
Established: 1969 Annual Undergrad Tuition & Fees: $15,598
Enrollment: 761 Coed
Affiliation or Control: Proprietary IRS Status: Proprietary
Highest Offering: Associate Degree
Program: Occupational
Accreditation: ACCSC, COARC, DH, PTAA, RAD, SURGT

01 Campus President .... Ms. Staci HEGERTY
05 Academic Dean .... Ms. Cindy COBB
37 Director of Financial Aid .... Ms. Nancy DISATE
07 Director of Admissions .... Mr. Nick HRUBY

Denver School of Nursing (B)

1401 19th Street, Denver CO 80202
County: Denver FICE Identification: 041483
Unit ID: 454856
Telephone: (303) 292-0015 Carnegie Class: Spec/Health
FAX Number: (720) 974-0290 Calendar System: Quarter
URL: www.denverschoolofnursing.edu
Established: 2003 Annual Undergrad Tuition & Fees: $54,923
Enrollment: 790 Coed
Affiliation or Control: Proprietary IRS Status: Proprietary
Highest Offering: Master's
Program: Professional; Nursing Emphasis
Accreditation: NH, ADNUR, NUR

01 President .... Dr. Marcia BANKIRER
10 Director of Business Operations .... Ms. Renee MCMILLIN
32 Director of Student Services .... Mr. Michael RUSCHIVAL
05 Dean/Dir of Nursing Education Pgms ... Dr. Diana KOSTRZEWSKI

Denver Seminary (C)

6399 S Santa Fe Drive, Littleton CO 80120-2912
County: Arapahoe FICE Identification: 001352
Unit ID: 126979
Telephone: (303) 761-2482 Carnegie Class: Spec/Faith
FAX Number: (303) 761-8060 Calendar System: Semester
URL: www.denverseminary.edu
Established: 1950 Annual Graduate Tuition & Fees: $13,860
Enrollment: 952 Coed
Affiliation or Control: Interdenominational IRS Status: 501(c)3
Highest Offering: Doctorate; No Undergraduates
Program: Professional; Religious Emphasis
Accreditation: NH, CACREP, PAST, THEOL

01 President .... Dr. Mark S. YOUNG
00 Chancellor .... Dr. Gordon MACDONALD
05 Provost/Dean .... Dr. Randolph M. MACFARLAND
10 Vice President of Finance .... Ms. Deborah KELLAR
30 Vice President of Advancement .... Mr. Ron GASCHO
32 Vice President of Student Services .... Mr. Robert JONES
20 Associate Academic Dean .... Dr. W. David BUSCHART
06 Interim Associate Registrar .... Mrs. Sara RIESE
35 Dean of Student Services .... Mr. Rob FOLEY
07 Director of Admissions .... Mrs. Christine DE ZEEUW
44 Director of Development .... Mr. Chris JOHNSON
109 Director of Auxiliary Services .... Mr. Kent B. QUACKENBUSH
13 Director of Information Systems .... Mr. Jason ADAMS
26 Director of Communications .... Mrs. Katie LARIC
88 Dir Educational Technology .... Mr. Aaron JOHNSON
88 Dir Educational Projects .... Mrs. Lisa LINHART
18 Director of Physical Plant .... Mr. Rob BACHMAN
37 Director of Financial Aid .... Mr. Michael MURPHY
08 Director of Library .... Dr. Keith P. WELLS
73 Director of DMin Program .... Dr. Tim DOLAN
21 Director of Financial Services .... Ms. Diana SMITH
15 Director of Human Resources .... Ms. Zandy WENNERSTROM

DeVry University - Westminster Campus (D)

1870 W 122nd Avenue, Westminster CO 80234-2010
Telephone: (303) 280-7400 Identification: 666227
Accreditation: &NH, ENGT

† Regional accreditation is carried under the parent institution in Downers Grove, IL.

Ecotech Institute (E)

1400 South Abilene Street, Aurora CO 80012
Telephone: (303) 586-5290 Identification: 770840
Accreditation: ACICS

† Branch campus of Virginia College, Birmingham, AL.

Everest College (F)

14280 E Jewell Avenue, Suite 100, Aurora CO 80012
Telephone: (303) 745-6244 Identification: 666412
Accreditation: ACICS, MAC

† Branch campus of Everest College, Denver, CO. School is in teach-out plan.

Everest College (G)

1815 Jet Wing Drive, Colorado Springs CO 80916
County: El Paso FICE Identification: 004503
Unit ID: 126401
Telephone: (719) 638-6580 Carnegie Class: Assoc/PrivFP
FAX Number: (719) 638-6818 Calendar System: Quarter
URL: www.everest.edu
Established: 1897 Annual Undergrad Tuition & Fees: $14,400
Enrollment: 330 Coed
Affiliation or Control: Proprietary IRS Status: Proprietary
Highest Offering: Associate Degree
Program: Occupational; 2-Year Principally Bachelor's Creditable
Accreditation: ACICS, MAC

01 President .... Mr. Robert LANTZY
05 Dean of Education .... Ms. Ronda EVANS
07 Director Admissions .... Mr. Dan NOEL
37 Director Student Finance .... Vacant
36 Director Career Services .... Vacant

Everest College (H)

9065 Grant Street, Denver CO 80229-4339
County: Adams FICE Identification: 004507
Unit ID: 127787
Telephone: (303) 457-2757 Carnegie Class: Assoc/PrivFP
FAX Number: (303) 457-4030 Calendar System: Other
URL: www.everest.edu
Established: 1895 Annual Undergrad Tuition & Fees: $12,000
Enrollment: 243 Coed
Affiliation or Control: Independent Non-Profit IRS Status: 501(c)3
Highest Offering: Associate Degree
Program: Occupational; Technical Emphasis
Accreditation: ACICS, MAC, SURGT

01 President .... Ms. Pat SCHLOTTER
05 Academic Dean .... Mr. William WHITE
07 Director of Admissions .... Ms. Heather JACQUES
37 Director of Student Finance .... Ms. Kim MARTINEZ
36 Director of Career Services .... Ms. Diane BOOREN
06 Registrar .... Ms. Rochelle OWENS

Fort Lewis College (I)

1000 Rim Drive, Durango CO 81301-3999
County: La Plata FICE Identification: 001353
Unit ID: 127185
Telephone: (970) 247-7010 Carnegie Class: Bac/A&S
FAX Number: (970) 247-7175 Calendar System: Semester
URL: www.fortlewis.edu
Established: 1911 Annual Undergrad Tuition & Fees (In-State): $7,601
Enrollment: 3,776 Coed
Affiliation or Control: State IRS Status: 170(c)1
Highest Offering: Master's
Program: Liberal Arts And General; Teacher Preparatory
Accreditation: NH, BUS, CAATE, ENG, MUS, TEAC

01 President .... Dr. Dene Kay THOMAS
05 Provost/Vice Pres Academic Affairs .... Dr. Barbara MORRIS
10 Vice Pres Finance & Administration .... Mr. Steven J. SCHWARTZ
30 Vice President for Advancement .... Mr. Mark A. JASTORFF
84 Assoc Vice Pres Enrollment Mgmt .... Dr. Carol SMITH
32 Vice President Student Affairs .... Dr. Glenna W. SEXTON
20 Assoc Vice Pres Academic Affairs .... Dr. Kenneth PEPION
09 Asst Dir of Institutional Research .... Ms. Orien S. MCGLAMERY
21 Director Budget .... Ms. Michele PETERSON
06 Registrar .... Ms. Kathy KENDALL
21 Controller .... Ms. Cheryl WIESCAMP
25 Director of Grants Management .... Ms. Angela ROCHAT
37 Director Financial Aid .... Ms. Tracey PICCOLI
07 Director of Admission .... Mr. Andrew BURNS
38 Int Dir Counseling/Student Dev Ctr .... Ms. Karen NAKAYAMA
08 Director of the Library .... Ms. Martha A. TALMAN
18 Dir Physical Plant/College Engr .... Mr. Bob SMITH
15 Dir Human Resources/Equal Opptnty .... Mr. Darren MATHEWS
39 Dir Stdnt Housing/Conferences Svcs .... Ms. Julie N. LOVE
41 Athletic Director .... Mr. Gary HUNTER
13 Director Computing & Telecomm .... Mr. Matt MCGLAMERY
29 Director Alumni Relations .... Mr. David KERNS
96 Director of Purchasing .... Mr. Wayne J. HERMES
26 Chief Public Relations Officer .... Mr. Mitch DAVIS
40 Bookstore Manager .... Ms. Brooke INGLE
28 Coord Equal Opport/Judicial Affs .... Dr. Haeryon KIM
83 Dean Sch Natural & Behavioral Sci .... Dr. Maureen BRANDON
50 Interim Dean Sch of Business Admin .... Dr. Paul MCGURR
49 Assoc Dean Arts & Sciences .... Ms. Kimberly HANNULA
49 Assoc Dean Arts & Sciences .... Dr. Peter MCCORMICK
106 Dir Online Education/E-learning .... Ms. Kelly M. STANLEY
108 Director Institutional Assessment .... Dr. Lisa M. SNYDER
53 Director of Teacher Education .... Dr. Richard FULTON

Front Range Community College (J)

3645 W 112th Avenue, Westminster CO 80031-2105
County: Adams FICE Identification: 007933
Unit ID: 127200
Telephone: (303) 404-5000 Carnegie Class: Assoc/Pub-S-MC
FAX Number: (303) 466-1623 Calendar System: Semester
URL: www.frontrange.edu
Established: 1968 Annual Undergrad Tuition & Fees (In-State): $3,747
Enrollment: 18,763 Coed
Affiliation or Control: State IRS Status: 501(c)3
Highest Offering: Associate Degree
Program: Occupational; 2-Year Principally Bachelor's Creditable
Accreditation: NH, ADNUR, CAHIIM, DA, MAC, PNUR

01 President .... Mr. Andrew R. DORSEY
04 Asst to the President .... Ms. Kimberly STEFANSKI
10 Vice Pres Finance & Administration .... Mr. Joseph HARBOUK
05 Chief Academic Officer .... Dr. Sandra VELTRI
12 Vice Pres Westminster Camp .... Ms. Therese BROWN
12 Vice Pres Larimer Campus .... Dr. Jean RUNYON
12 Vice Pres Boulder County Campus .... Dr. Linda CURRAN
84 Assoc VP Enroll Mgmt & Student Svcs .... Dr. Kris BINARD
20 Dean of Instruction Larimer .... Dr. Shashi UNNITHAN
106 Dean of Online Learning .... Ms. Tammy VERCAUTEREN
20 Dean of Instruction Larimer .... Ms. Lauren SMITH
20 Dean of Instruction Larimer .... Dr. Kim DALE
20 Dean of Instruction Boulder County .... Mr. Matt JAMISON
20 Dean of Instruction Westminster .... Ms. Catherine PELLISH
32 Dean of Student Svcs Boulder County .... Ms. Carla STEIN
32 Dean of Student Svcs Westminster .... Mr. Aaron PRESTWICH
15 Exec Director of Human Resources .... Mr. Paul MEESE
09 Director of Institutional Research .... Ms. Kim WALLACE
21 Director of Budget & Auxiliary Svcs .... Ms. Patti ARROYO
06 Registrar .... Vacant
37 Dir of Financial Aid College Wide .... Ms. Carolee GOLDSMITH
08 Director of Library Services .... Vacant
18 Director of Facilities Westminster .... Mr. Patrick O'NEILL
18 Director of Facilities Larimer .... Mr. Dennis DEREMER
35 Director Student Life Westminster .... Ms. Julie BEGGS
35 Director Student Life Larimer .... Ms. Mary BRANTON-HOUSLEY
35 Dir Student Life Boulder County .... Ms. Amanda CLANCY
102 Director of Foundation .... Mr. Ryan MCCOY
26 Dir of Marketing & Communications .... Ms. Marian MAHARAS
27 Public Information Officer .... Mr. John FEELEY
13 Director of Information Technology .... Ms. Jeannine MENEFEE
19 Director Security/Preparedness .... Mr. Gordon GOLDSMITH

Front Range Community College-Boulder County Campus (K)

2190 Miller Drive, Longmont CO 80501
Telephone: (303) 678-3722 Identification: 770041
Accreditation: &NH

† Branch campus of Front Range Community College, Westminster, CO.

Front Range Community College Larimer Campus (L)

4616 S Shields Street, Fort Collins CO 80526
Telephone: (970) 226-2500 Identification: 770040
Accreditation: &NH, PHLEB

† Branch campus of Front Range Community College, Westminster, CO.

Heritage College (M)

4704 Harlan Street, Suite 100, Denver CO 80212
County: Jefferson FICE Identification: 026110
Unit ID: 262509
Telephone: (303) 477-7240 Carnegie Class: Assoc/PrivFP
FAX Number: (303) 477-7276 Calendar System: Other
URL: www.heritage-education.com
Established: 1986 Annual Undergrad Tuition & Fees: $25,999
Enrollment: 401 Coed
Affiliation or Control: Proprietary IRS Status: Proprietary
Highest Offering: Associate Degree
Program: Occupational
Accreditation: ABHES

01 College Director Denver .... Nathan LARSON
00 CEO .... Eric K. CHUSOLO
03 COO .... Stephen BREWSTER
05 Director of Education .... Kai HILLBERRY
07 Director of Admissions .... Vacant
06 Registrar .... Gwen ESTRIDGE
36 Director of Career Services .... Michelle TYMOCZKO
37 Director of Financial Aid .... Amanda MASELBAS
22 Director of Compliance .... Bill PASCHALL

Holmes Institute of Consciousness Studies (N)

573 Park Point Drive, Golden CO 80401
County: Jefferson Identification: 666255
Telephone: (720) 496-1370 Carnegie Class: Not Classified
FAX Number: (303) 526-0913 Calendar System: Quarter
URL: www.holmesinstitute.org
Established: 1972 Annual Graduate Tuition & Fees: $22,000
Enrollment: 80 Coed
Affiliation or Control: Other IRS Status: 501(c)3
Highest Offering: Master's; No Undergraduates

Program: Professional; Religious Emphasis
Accreditation: DEAC

01 Dir of HICS/Dir of Education .... Rev Dr. Robert DEEN
06 Registrar .... Ms. Maureen THURSTON

IBMC College (A)

6805 Corporate Drive, Suite 100,
Colorado Springs CO 80919
County: El Paso FICE Identification: 008635
Unit ID: 127839
Telephone: (719) 596-7400 Carnegie Class: Assoc/PrivFP
FAX Number: (719) 596-2464 Calendar System: Other
URL: www.ibmc.edu
Established: 1966 Annual Undergrad Tuition & Fees: $22,964
Enrollment: 357 Coed
Affiliation or Control: Proprietary IRS Status: Proprietary
Highest Offering: Associate Degree
Program: Occupational
Accreditation: ABHES, DA

01 Campus Director .... Mr. Sam PEDREGON

IBMC College (B)

3842 South Mason Street, Fort Collins CO 80526
County: Larimer FICE Identification: 030063
Unit ID: 372329
Telephone: (970) 223-2669 Carnegie Class: Assoc/PrivFP
FAX Number: (970) 223-2796 Calendar System: Quarter
URL: www.ibmc.edu
Established: 1987 Annual Undergrad Tuition & Fees: $12,240
Enrollment: 256 Coed
Affiliation or Control: Proprietary IRS Status: Proprietary
Highest Offering: Associate Degree
Program: Occupational
Accreditation: ACICS

00 CEO .... Mr. Steven STEELE
01 President .... Ms. Melissa MELTZER

Iliff School of Theology (C)

2323 E. Iliff Ave, Denver CO 80210-4798
County: Denver FICE Identification: 001354
Unit ID: 127273
Telephone: (303) 744-1287 Carnegie Class: Spec/Faith
FAX Number: (303) 777-3387 Calendar System: Quarter
URL: www.iliff.edu
Established: 1892 Annual Graduate Tuition & Fees: $20,169
Enrollment: 333 Coed
Affiliation or Control: United Methodist IRS Status: 501(c)3
Highest Offering: Doctorate; No Undergraduates
Program: Professional; Religious Emphasis
Accreditation: NH, THEOL

01 President .... Dr. Thomas V. WOLFE
05 Vice Pres/Dean Academic Affairs .... Dr. Albert HERNANDEZ
10 Vice President for Business Affairs ...... Ms. Kelly L. MCCORMICK
30 VP Inst Advancement/Enrollment .... Mr. David WORLEY
26 VP of Marketing Communications .... Ms. Greta GLOVEN
06 Registrar .... Ms. Carmen E. BACA-DOSTER
13 Dir of Academic and Info Technology ... Mr. Michael HEMENWAY
07 Director Admission/Financial Aid .... Ms. Peggy J. BLOCKER
28 Associate Dean of Diversities .... Dr. Edward ANTONIO
04 Executive Asst to President .... Mrs. Alisha ENO
18 Dir of Facilities Management .... Mr. Jerry ENO
29 Donor and Alumni Relations Director .. Ms. Caran WARE JOSEPH

Institute of Business and Medical Careers (D)

2863 35th Avenue, Greeley CO 80634-9421
Telephone: (970) 356-4733 Identification: 770631
Accreditation: ACICS

† Branch campus of IBMC College, Fort Collins, CO.

Institute of Business and Medical Careers (E)

2315 North Main Street, Longmont CO 80501
Telephone: (303) 651-6819 Identification: 770630
Accreditation: ACICS

† Branch campus of IBMC College, Fort Collins, CO.

Institute of Taoist Education and Acupuncture (F)

317 West South Boulder Road, Ste 5, Louisville CO 80027
County: Boulder FICE Identification: 041212
Unit ID: 454838
Telephone: (720) 890-8922 Carnegie Class: Spec/Health
FAX Number: (720) 890-7719 Calendar System: Other
URL: www.itea.edu
Established: 1996 Annual Graduate Tuition & Fees: $18,500
Enrollment: 31 Coed
Affiliation or Control: Independent Non-Profit IRS Status: 501(c)3
Highest Offering: Master's; No Undergraduates
Program: Professional
Accreditation: ACUP

01 President .... Sandra LILLIE
05 Director .... Hilary SKELLON
06 Registrar .... Claudia O'NIELL
10 Financial Administrator .... Angela SMITH

IntelliTec College (G)

2315 E Pikes Peak Avenue,
Colorado Springs CO 80909-6096
County: El Paso FICE Identification: 022537
Unit ID: 128179
Telephone: (719) 632-7626 Carnegie Class: Assoc/PrivFP
FAX Number: (719) 632-7451 Calendar System: Quarter
URL: www.intellitec.edu
Established: 1965 Annual Undergrad Tuition & Fees: $29,864
Enrollment: 623 Coed
Affiliation or Control: Proprietary IRS Status: Proprietary
Highest Offering: Associate Degree
Program: Occupational; Technical Emphasis
Accreditation: ACCSC

IntelliTec College (H)

772 Horizon Drive, Grand Junction CO 81506-3994
County: Mesa FICE Identification: 030669
Unit ID: 128188
Telephone: (970) 245-8101 Carnegie Class: Assoc/PrivFP
FAX Number: (970) 243-8074 Calendar System: Quarter
URL: www.intelliteccollege.com
Established: 1984 Annual Undergrad Tuition & Fees: $26,000
Enrollment: 600 Coed
Affiliation or Control: Proprietary IRS Status: Proprietary
Highest Offering: Associate Degree
Program: Occupational
Accreditation: ACCSC

01 President .... Mr. Michael SCHRANZ
05 Director .... Dr. Dave SCOTT

IntelliTec College (I)

3673 Parker Boulevard, Pueblo CO 81008-2211
Telephone: (719) 542-3181 Identification: 666366
Accreditation: ACCSC

† Branch campus of IntelliTec College, Grand Junction, CO.

ITT Technical Institute (J)

12500 E Iliff Avenue, Suite 100, Aurora CO 80014
Telephone: (303) 695-6317 Identification: 770636
Accreditation: ACICS

† Branch campus of ITT Technical Institute, Indianapolis, IN.

ITT Technical Institute (K)

8620 Wolff Court, Suite 100, Westminster CO 80031
Telephone: (303) 288-4488 Identification: 667189
Accreditation: ACICS

† Branch campus of ITT Technical Institute, Indianapolis, IN.

Johnson & Wales University - Denver Campus (L)

7150 Montview Boulevard, Denver CO 80220-1866
Telephone: (303) 256-9300 Identification: 666411
Accreditation: &EH, DIETD

† Regional accreditation is carried under the parent institution in Providence, RI.

Jones International University (M)

9697 E Mineral Avenue, Centennial CO 80112-3408
County: Arapahoe FICE Identification: 035343
Unit ID: 444723
Telephone: (800) 811-5663 Carnegie Class: Master's L
FAX Number: (303) 799-0966 Calendar System: Other
URL: www.jiu.edu
Established: 1993 Annual Undergrad Tuition & Fees: $12,720
Enrollment: 1,851 Coed
Affiliation or Control: Proprietary IRS Status: Proprietary
Highest Offering: Doctorate
Program: Teacher Preparatory; Professional; Business Emphasis
Accreditation: NH

01 Chancellor .... Dr. Milton GOLDBERG
05 Chief Academic Officer .... Dr. Lisa BRAVERMAN
10 Chief Financial Officer .... Ms. Christine SPATH
11 Chief Operating Officer .... Mr. Bryan WALLACE

† School is on teach-out plan.

Lamar Community College (N)

2401 S Main, Lamar CO 81052-3999
County: Prowers FICE Identification: 001355
Unit ID: 127389
Telephone: (719) 336-2248 Carnegie Class: Assoc/Pub-R-S
FAX Number: (719) 336-2448 Calendar System: Semester
URL: www.lamarcc.edu
Established: 1937 Annual Undergrad Tuition & Fees (In-State): $5,295
Enrollment: 839 Coed
Affiliation or Control: State IRS Status: 501(c)3
Highest Offering: Associate Degree
Program: Occupational; 2-Year Principally Bachelor's Creditable
Accreditation: NH, ADNUR

01 President .... Mr. John MARRIN
05 VP Academic Services/Student Svcs .... Mrs. Cheryl SANCHEZ
11 VP Admin Svcs/Institutional Rsrch .... Mr. Chad DE BONO
20 Dean of Academic Services .... Vacant
26 Director of Communication .... Mrs. Anne-Marie CRAMPTON
06 Registrar .... Mrs. Amber THOMPSON
08 Library Tech .... Ms. Ellen LOVELL
18 Director of Facilities .... Mr. Sean LIRLEY
15 Director Personnel Services .... Ms. Jennifer MORTIMEYER
39 Director Student Housing .... Mr. Chad DEBONO
27 Director of Marketing .... Ms. Kristin LUBBERS
38 Director Student Counseling .... Ms. Deanna SIEMSEN
96 Director of Purchasing .... Mrs. Ava BAIR
41 Athletic Director .... Mr. Chad DEBONO
37 Director Financial Aid .... Mrs. Teale HEMPHILL
07 Director of Admissions .... Mrs. Jenna DAVIS
09 Coordinator Institutional Research .... Mrs. Kim WALLACE
84 Coord for Concurrent Enrollment .... Ms. Del CHASE

Lincoln College of Technology (O)

11194 East 45th Avenue, Denver CO 80239
County: Denver FICE Identification: 007547
Unit ID: 126951
Telephone: (303) 722-5724 Carnegie Class: Assoc/PrivFP
FAX Number: (303) 778-8264 Calendar System: Other
URL: www.lincolnedu.com
Established: 1963 Annual Undergrad Tuition & Fees: N/A
Enrollment: 1,457 Coed
Affiliation or Control: Proprietary IRS Status: Proprietary
Highest Offering: Associate Degree
Program: Occupational; Technical Emphasis
Accreditation: ACCSC

01 Campus President .... Mr. Al SHORT
07 Senior Director Admissions .... Ms. Jennifer HASH
05 Director of Education .... Mr. Randy BOBZIEN

McKinley College (P)

2001 Lowe Street, Fort Collins CO 80525-3474
County: Larimer Identification: 666237
Telephone: (970) 207-4550 Carnegie Class: Not Classified
FAX Number: (877) 599-5863 Calendar System: Other
URL: www.mckinleycollege.edu
Established: 2004 Annual Undergrad Tuition & Fees: $7,400
Enrollment: N/A Coed
Affiliation or Control: Proprietary IRS Status: Proprietary
Highest Offering: Associate Degree
Program: Occupational; 2-Year Principally Bachelor's Creditable
Accreditation: DEAC

01 President .... Ann ROHR
32 Vice President of Student Affairs .... Joyce LINDQUIST
05 Dean of Faculty .... Nancy HAMPSON
09 Director of Compliance & Retention .... Janet PERRY

Metropolitan State University of Denver (Q)

PO Box 173362, Denver CO 80217-3362
County: Denver FICE Identification: 001360
Unit ID: 127565
Telephone: (303) 556-2400 Carnegie Class: Bac/Diverse
FAX Number: (303) 556-3912 Calendar System: Semester
URL: www.msudenver.edu
Established: 1963 Annual Undergrad Tuition & Fees (In-State): $6,420
Enrollment: 21,179 Coed
Affiliation or Control: State IRS Status: 501(c)3
Highest Offering: Master's
Program: Liberal Arts And General; Teacher Preparatory; Professional
Accreditation: NH, ART, CAATE, CS, CSHSE, DIETD, ENGT, EXSC, MT, MUS, NRPA, NUR, SW, TED, THEA

01 President .... Dr. Stephen M. JORDAN
05 Vice President Academic Affairs .... Dr. Vicki GOLICH
10 Vice Pres Admin/Finance/Facilities .... Mr. Steve KRIEDLER
30 VP Univ Advancement .... Mr. John BURTNESS
43 Gen Counsel/Sec to Board .... Ms. Loretta P. MARTINEZ
13 Assoc VP/CIO .... Dr. James LYALL
15 Director Human Resources .... Ms. Nicole TEFFT
84 Interim Assoc VP Enrollment Svcs .... Mr. Vaughn TOLAND
26 Chief of Staff/Marketing & Comm .... Ms. Catherine LUCAS
29 Director of Alumni Relations .... Ms. Jamie HURST
50 Dean School Business .... Dr. Ann B. MURPHY
107 Dean School Professional Studies .... Dr. Sandra HAYNES
32 Dean Student Life .... Ms. Braelin PANTEL
06 Registrar .... Ms. Paula MARTINEZ
37 Director Financial Aid .... Ms. Cindy HEJL
41 Athletic Director .... Vacant
35 Director Student Activities .... Ms. Angela LEVALLEY
36 Director Career Services .... Ms. Bridgette COBLE
28 Assoc to Pres Inst Diversity .... Dr. Myron ANDERSON

Morgan Community College (A)

920 Barlow Road, Fort Morgan CO 80701-4399
County: Morgan FICE Identification: 009981
Unit ID: 127617
Telephone: (970) 542-3100 Carnegie Class: Assoc/Pub-R-M
FAX Number: (970) 542-3115 Calendar System: Semester
URL: www.morgancc.edu
Established: 1967 Annual Undergrad Tuition & Fees (In-State): $3,394
Enrollment: 1,837 Coed
Affiliation or Control: State IRS Status: Exempt
Highest Offering: Associate Degree
Program: Occupational; 2-Year Principally Bachelor's Creditable
Accreditation: NH, ADNUR

01 President .... Dr. Kerry HART
10 Vice Pres Finance/Admin Services .... Ms. Susan CLOUGH
05 Vice President of Instruction .... Ms. Monica RAMIREZ
84 Vice President of Student Success .... Mr. Kent BAUER
04 Assistant to the President .... Ms. Jane FRIES
12 Center Director .... Ms. Mary ANDERSEN
12 Center Director .... Ms. Jessica FOURNIER
12 Center Director .... Ms. Kellie OVERTURF
12 Center Director .... Ms. Valerie RHOADES
09 Dir of Institutional Effectiveness .... Mr. Derek GRUBB
26 Dir of Communications & Marketing .... Ms. Katie BARRON
30 Dir Community Relations/Development .... Vacant
37 Director of Financial Aid .... Ms. Sally SHAWCROFT
07 Director of Admissions .... Ms. Kim MAXWELL
15 Director of Human Resources .... Ms. Andria KOPPELS
08 Director of Learning Resources .... Ms. April AMACK
96 Director of Purchasing .... Ms. Julie BEYDLER
40 Director of Bookstore .... Ms. Debbie CASTENEDA
18 Coordinator of M & O .... Mr. Seth NOBLE
36 Voc Guidance/Placement Counselor .... Mr. Dan MARLER
13 Director Information Technology .... Mr. Michael SHRIVER
66 Div Chr Hlth Occup/Dir Nursing Educ .... Ms. Kathy FRISBIE
49 Division Chair Arts & Sciences .... Mr. Todd SCHNEIDER
50 Division Chair Business .... Ms. Jaylene EVANS

Naropa University (B)

2130 Arapahoe Avenue, Boulder CO 80302-6697
County: Boulder FICE Identification: 021175
Unit ID: 127653
Telephone: (303) 444-0202 Carnegie Class: Master's L
FAX Number: (303) 444-0410 Calendar System: Semester
URL: www.naropa.edu
Established: 1974 Annual Undergrad Tuition & Fees: $30,570
Enrollment: 945 Coed
Affiliation or Control: Independent Non-Profit IRS Status: 501(c)3
Highest Offering: Master's
Program: Liberal Arts And General
Accreditation: NH

01 President .... Mr. Charles G. LIEF
04 Assistant to the President .... Ms. Rachel SOLUM
10 Vice President Business Affs/CFO .... Mr. Todd KILBURN
05 Provost/Vice Pres Academic Affs .... Dr. Janet CRAMER
20 Assistant Provost .... Ms. Judith SUMNER
26 Director of University Relations .... Mr. Bill RIGLER
30 Director of Development .... Ms. Andrea AUGUISTE
84 VP Student Affairs/Enrollment Mgmt .... Ms. Cheryl BARBOUR
13 Director of IT .... Mr. David EDMINSTER
07 Dean of Admissions .... Ms. Janet ERICKSON
97 Dean Undergrad Educ .... Ms. Carole CLEMENTS
58 Dean Graduate Education .... Vacant
32 Dean of Students .... Mr. Robert CILLO
35 Director of Student Life .... Mr. Matthew PETERSON
36 Dir Career & Community Eng .... Ms. Sarah STEWARD
38 Director Counseling Center .... Ms. Anne COWARDIN
39 Resident Hall Manager .... Mr. Derrick JONES
06 Registrar .... Ms. Keely PRESTON
08 Library Director .... Mr. Nicolas WEISS
18 Director of Facilities & Ops .... Mr. Aaron COOK
37 Dir Student Financial Services .... Ms. Nancy MORRELL
15 Director of Human Resources .... Ms. Angie GOSSETT
106 Director of Online Education .... Mr. Jirka HLADIS
29 Director of Alumni Relations .... Ms. Melissa HOLLAND
19 Safety & Security Manager .... Vacant
28 Director of Diversity .... Mr. Tommy WOON

National American University-Centennial (C)

8242 S University Blvd, Suite 100, Centennial CO 80122
Telephone: (303) 542-7000 Identification: 770389
Accreditation: &NH

† Branch campus of National American University, Rapid City, SD.

National American University-Colorado Springs (D)

1915 Jamboree Drive, Suite 185,
Colorado Springs CO 80920
Telephone: (719) 590-8300 Identification: 770390
Accreditation: &NH, MAC

† Branch campus of National American University, Rapid City, SD.

National American University-Colorado Springs South (E)

1079 Space Center Drive, Unit 140,
Colorado Springs CO 80915
Telephone: (719) 208-3800 Identification: 770391
Accreditation: &NH

† Branch campus of National American University, Rapid City, SD.

National American University-Denver (F)

1325 South Colorado Blvd, Suite 100, Denver CO 80222
Telephone: (303) 876-7100 Identification: 770392
Accreditation: &NH, MAC, OTA

† Branch campus of National American University, Rapid City, SD.

Nazarene Bible College (G)

1111 Academy Park Loop,
Colorado Springs CO 80910-3704
County: El Paso FICE Identification: 013007
Unit ID: 127714
Telephone: (719) 884-5000 Carnegie Class: Spec/Faith
FAX Number: (719) 884-5199 Calendar System: Trimester
URL: www.nbc.edu
Established: 1964 Annual Undergrad Tuition & Fees: $12,825
Enrollment: 792 Coed
Affiliation or Control: Church Of The Nazarene IRS Status: 501(c)3
Highest Offering: Baccalaureate
Program: Professional; Religious Emphasis
Accreditation: NH, BI

01 President .... Dr. Harold B. GRAVES
05 Vice President for Academic Affairs .... Dr. Alan D. LYKE
32 Director for Student Success .... Mrs. Tari D. COFIELD
10 Vice President for Finance .... Mrs. Shirley A. CADLE
84 VP for Enrollment Management .... Dr. David M. CHURCH
08 Library Director .... Prof. Ann M. ATTIG
37 Financial Aid Officer .... Ms. Jenny S. MADSEN
06 Registrar .... Ms. Meg K. FRANCIS
07 Director of Admissions .... Mr. Scott E. MCCONNAUGHEY

Northeastern Junior College (H)

100 College Avenue, Sterling CO 80751-2399
County: Logan FICE Identification: 001361
Unit ID: 127732
Telephone: (970) 521-6600 Carnegie Class: Assoc/Pub-R-M
FAX Number: (970) 522-4945 Calendar System: Semester
URL: www.njc.edu
Established: 1941 Annual Undergrad Tuition & Fees (In-State): $3,707
Enrollment: 1,762 Coed
Affiliation or Control: State IRS Status: 501(c)3
Highest Offering: Associate Degree
Program: Occupational; 2-Year Principally Bachelor's Creditable
Accreditation: NH, ADNUR, PNUR

01 President .... Mr. Jay LEE
05 Vice President Academic Services .... Mr. Stanton GARTIN
10 Vice Pres Finance & Administration .... Mr. Tyler KELSCH
32 Vice President Student Services .... Mr. Steven SMITH
84 Dean New Student Enroll/Admissions .... Vacant
29 Alumni Director .... Mr. Jack ANNAN
102 Executive Director NJC Foundation .... Vacant
06 Director Records/Admission Process .... Ms. Lisa SCHAEFER
37 Director of Financial Aid .... Ms. Alice WEINGARDT
35 Dir Resident Life & Student Activit .... Ms. Courtney WILKINS
18 Physical Plant Director .... Mr. Tracey KNOX
15 Human Resources Director .... Ms. Angela ANDERSON
41 Athletic Director .... Ms. Marci HENRY
96 Director of Purchasing .... Ms. Erin WAITLEY
09 Dir of Inst Research/Plng/Devel .... Mr. Derek HERBERT
26 Director of Marketing .... Ms. Barbara BAKER
21 Controller .... Ms. Judy MCFADDEN
13 Director Information Technology .... Ms. Cherie BRUNGARDT
40 Bookstore Director .... Ms. Heather BRUNGARDT
04 Executive Asst to President .... Ms. Shawn ROSE
07 Director of Admissions .... Mr. Terry RUCH
106 Dir Online Education/E-learning .... Ms. Cyndi VANDENBARK
108 Director Institutional Assessment .... Ms. Misti PIERCE
25 Chief Contracts/Grants Admin .... Ms. Rebecca ROMERO

Otero Junior College (I)

1802 Colorado Avenue, La Junta CO 81050-3346
County: Otero FICE Identification: 001362
Unit ID: 127778
Telephone: (719) 384-6831 Carnegie Class: Assoc/Pub-R-S
FAX Number: (719) 384-6933 Calendar System: Semester
URL: www.ojc.edu
Established: 1941 Annual Undergrad Tuition & Fees (In-State): $4,478
Enrollment: 1,436 Coed
Affiliation or Control: State IRS Status: 501(c)3
Highest Offering: Associate Degree
Program: Occupational; 2-Year Principally Bachelor's Creditable
Accreditation: NH, ADNUR, PHLEB

01 President .... Mr. James T. RIZZUTO
11 Vice Pres Administrative Services .... Mr. Pat MALOTT
05 Vice Pres Instructional Services .... Ms. Kim GRIMSLEY
32 Vice President Student Services .... Mr. Jeff PAOLUCCI
20 Assoc VP Instructional Services .... Vacant
08 Director Learning Resources .... Ms. Sue KEEFER
41 Athletic Director .... Mr. Gary ADDINGTON
15 Director of Human Resources .... Mrs. Marlene F. BOETTCHER
18 Director of Physical Plant .... Mr. John CANADAY
40 Bookstore Manager .... Mrs. Jenn JOHNSTON
37 Director of Financial Aid .... Ms. Angela BENFATTI
109 Director of Auxilliary Services .... Ms. Genia SHORT
26 Dir of Communications/PR/Foundation .... Mrs. Sue SAMANIEGO
13 Director of Computer Services .... Mr. Mark ALLEN
09 Director of Institutional Research .... Ms. Rebecca GRANTHAM
30 Resource Development & Director .... Ms. Audrey DEHDOUH-BERG
84 Assoc VP Enrollment Management .... Mrs. Almabeth KAESS

Pikes Peak Community College (J)

5675 S Academy Boulevard,
Colorado Springs CO 80906-5498
County: El Paso FICE Identification: 008896
Unit ID: 127820
Telephone: (719) 502-2000 Carnegie Class: Assoc/Pub-U-MC
FAX Number: (719) 502-2201 Calendar System: Semester
URL: www.ppcc.edu
Established: 1968 Annual Undergrad Tuition & Fees (In-State): $30,840
Enrollment: 19,950 Coed
Affiliation or Control: State IRS Status: 501(c)3
Highest Offering: Associate Degree
Program: Occupational; 2-Year Principally Bachelor's Creditable
Accreditation: NH, ACFEI, ADNUR, DA, EMT

01 President .... Dr. Lance BOLTON
04 Exec Assistant to the President .... Ms. Kimberly BARNETT
05 Vice Pres Instructional Services .... Dr. Lisa DONALDSON
88 Vice President Student Success .... Mr. Felix M. LOPEZ
10 Vice Pres Administrative Services .... Ms. Brenda LAUER
20 Director of Instructional Support .... Ms. Julie HAZEL
84 Director Enrollment Services .... Mr. Jeff HORNER
37 Director of Financial Aid .... Mr. Ronald SWARTWOOD
08 Director of Libraries .... Ms. Carole OLDS
15 Exec Dir of Human Resource Services .... Mr. Carlton BROOKS
26 Exec Dir Marketing/Communications .... Ms. Allison CORTEZ
21 Director of Business Svcs .... Ms. Eileen HOGUE
06 Registrar/Coordinator of Records .... Ms. Twila HUMPHREY
102 Exec Dir Found/Res/Cmty Development .... Ms. Sue FENSKE
18 Dir Facilities and Operations .... Mr. Bob LUND
13 Director of IT Support Services .... Mr. Cyrille PARENT
19 Dir Public Safety/Emergency Mgmt .... Mr. Jim BARRENTINE
88 Project Dir of Stdnt Spprt Svcs/Adj .... Mr. Edmond QUESADA
88 Dir Military & Veteran Programs .... Ms. Cheri ARFSTEN
76 Dean Health and Science .... Dr. Evan MCHUGH
81 Dean Mathematics & English .... Ms. Jacquelyn GAITERS-JORDAN
50 Dean Business//Public Service/SS .... Mr. Rob HUDSON
60 Dean Comm/Humanities/Tech Studies .... Ms. Fran HETRICK
36 Dir of Career Planning & Advising .... Mr. Lincoln WULF
32 Dean of Students .... Ms. Jennifer SENGENBERGER
96 Director of Purchasing .... Ms. Rockie HURRELL
38 Dir Stdnt Counseling/Resource Ctr .... Ms. Yolanda HARRIS
88 Dean of High School Programs .... Ms. Chelsy HARRIS
09 Exec Dir of Inst Effectiveness .... Dr. Patrica DIWARA
103 Vice Pres of Workforce Development .... Ms. Debbie SAGEN

Pima Medical Institute (K)

13750 E. Mississippi Avenue, Aurora CO 80012
County: Arapahoe FICE Identification: 041771
Unit ID: 461689
Telephone: (303) 368-7462 Carnegie Class: Not Classified
FAX Number: N/A Calendar System: Other
URL: pmi.edu
Established: 2012 Annual Undergrad Tuition & Fees: $11,734
Enrollment: 315 Coed
Affiliation or Control: Proprietary IRS Status: Proprietary
Highest Offering: Associate Degree
Program: Occupational
Accreditation: ABHES

01 Campus Director .... Mr. Michael BEATY

Pima Medical Institute-Colorado Springs (L)

3770 Citadel Drive North, Colorado Springs CO 80909
Telephone: (719) 482-7462 Identification: 770516
Accreditation: ABHES

† Branch campus of Pima Medical Institute-Tucson, Tucson, AZ.

Pima Medical Institute-Denver (M)

7475 Dakin Street, Westminster CO 80221
Telephone: (303) 426-1800 Identification: 666171
Accreditation: ABHES, COARC, OTA, PTAA, RAD

† Branch campus of Pima Medical Institute, Tucson, AZ.

Platt College (N)

3100 S Parker Road, Suite 200, Aurora CO 80014-3141
County: Arapahoe FICE Identification: 030149
Unit ID: 260813
Telephone: (303) 369-5151 Carnegie Class: Bac/Diverse
FAX Number: (303) 745-1433 Calendar System: Quarter
URL: www.plattcolorado.edu

Established: 1986 Annual Undergrad Tuition & Fees: $19,286
Enrollment: 210 Coed
Affiliation or Control: Proprietary IRS Status: Proprietary
Highest Offering: Baccalaureate
Program: Nursing Emphasis
Accreditation: **ACCSC**, NUR

01 President/CEO Mr. Jerald B. SIRBU
05 Vice President of Academic Affairs Dr. Julie BASLER
10 Director of Financial Services Mr. Robert CRAVER
37 Director of Financial Aid/Registrar Ms. Margie ROSE
08 Head Librarian Ms. Laura CULLERTON
66 Dean College of Nursing Ms. Hollie CALDWELL
06 Registrar Ms. Katie DAHL
07 Admissions Representative Ms. Rachael HORNBOSTEL

Pueblo Community College (A)

900 W Orman Avenue, Pueblo CO 81004-1499
County: Pueblo FICE Identification: 021163
Unit ID: 127884
Telephone: (719) 549-3200 Carnegie Class: Assoc/Pub-R-L
FAX Number: (719) 544-1179 Calendar System: Semester
URL: www.pueblocc.edu
Established: 1933 Annual Undergrad Tuition & Fees (In-State): $3,588
Enrollment: 6,209 Coed
Affiliation or Control: State IRS Status: 501(c)3
Highest Offering: Associate Degree
Program: Occupational; 2-Year Principally Bachelor's Creditable; Business Emphasis
Accreditation: **NH**, ACFEI, ADNUR, COARC, DA, DH, EMT, OTA

01 President Dr. Patricia ERJAVEC
10 Chief Business Officer Mr. Jon BRUDE
05 Chief Academic Officer Dr. Deborah SCHMITT
32 Dean of Student Success Mr. Keith WILDER
12 Exec Dean SWCCC Campus Mr. Norm JONES
12 Dean Fremont Campus Dr. Lana CARTER
76 Dean Health & Public Safety Ms. Mary CHAVEZ
49 Dean of Arts & Science Dr. Jeff ALEXANDER
50 Dean Business/Advance Technology Dr. Jennifer SHERMAN
31 Exec Dir Community Educ & Training Ms. Juanita FUENTES
102 Director of PCC Foundation Ms. Martha SIMMONS
07 Dir Admissions & Records/Registrar Ms. Barbara BENEDICT
21 Controller Ms. Emma ALCALA
37 Director Financial Aid Ms. Monica HARDWICK
15 Director Human Resources Mr. Ken NUFER
13 Director Information Technology Mr. Bryan CRAWFORD
18 Director Facility Svcs/Capital Plng Mr. Clifford KITCHEN
38 Director Learning Center Mr. Ross BARNHART
08 Director Library Services Ms. Jeanne W. GARDNER
27 Director Marketing/Communications Ms. Erin HERGERT
35 Dir Student & Judicial Affairs Mr. Dennis JOHNSON
84 Director of Recruitment Ms. Carriann MARTINEZ
09 Dir Institutional Effectiveness Mr. Corey SHILLING
96 Director of Purchasing Mr. Edmond INIGUEZ
103 Dir Econ & Workforce Dev Ops Ms. Amanda CORUM
88 Director of Academic Advising Mr. Gage MICHAEL
04 Administrative Asst to President Ms. Julie JIMENEZ
106 Multimedia Tech Specialist Mr. Robin LEACH

Pueblo Community College Fremont Campus (B)

51320 W Highway 50, Canon City CO 81212
Telephone: (719) 296-6100 Identification: 770042
Accreditation: **&NH**

† Branch campus of Pueblo Community College, Pueblo, CO.

Red Rocks Community College (C)

13300 W Sixth Avenue, Lakewood CO 80228-1255
County: Jefferson FICE Identification: 009543
Unit ID: 127909
Telephone: (303) 914-6600 Carnegie Class: Assoc/Pub-S-MC
FAX Number: (303) 914-6666 Calendar System: Semester
URL: www.rrcc.edu
Established: 1969 Annual Undergrad Tuition & Fees (In-State): $3,301
Enrollment: 8,112 Coed
Affiliation or Control: State IRS Status: 501(c)3
Highest Offering: Master's
Program: Occupational; 2-Year Principally Bachelor's Creditable
Accreditation: **NH**, ARCPA, MAC, RAD

01 President Dr. Michele HANEY
04 Exec Assistant to the President Ms. Kathy SCHISSLER
10 Vice Pres Administrative Services Ms. Peggy MORGAN
05 Vice President Instruction Ms. Linda COMEAUX
32 Vice Pres Stdnt Svc/Enrollment Mgt Vacant
35 Vice Pres Student Success Dr. Lisa FOWLER
103 Vice Pres Workforce/Community Devel Vacant
20 Dean Academic Services Ms. Kelly CIRCLE
20 Dean Instructional Services Mr. Rick REEVES
20 Dean Instructional Services Mr. Mike COSTE
13 Dean Technology CTE Mr. Bill MCGREEVY
88 Dean of Instruct/Exec Dir RMEC-OSHA Ms. Joan SMITH
85 Director International Education Ms. Linda YAZDANI
07 Dir Student Recruit/Advising/Admiss Ms. Nancy CARLSON
21 Controller Ms. Kathy KAOUDIS
37 Director Financial Aid Ms. Linda CROOK
06 Registrar/Dir Enrollment Services Dr. Dean RATHE
18 Director Facilities Mr. Mark BANA
15 Director Human Resources Mr. Bill DIAL
102 Exec Director RRCC Foundation Mr. Ron SLINGER
26 Director Marketing/Communications Ms. Kim REIN
35 Director Student Activities Ms. Carolyn MATTERN
88 Dir Childhood Ed & Support Svcs Vacant
09 Director Institutional Research Mr. Charles DUELL
28 Director of Diversity & Inclusion Ms. Jennifer MACKEN
96 Coordinator Purchasing Ms. Renee ARCHULETA
36 Director Student Outreach Mr. Andrew STEVENS
46 Exec Dir Planning/Rsrch/Inst Effect Dr. Tim GRIFFIN

Red Rocks Community College Arvada Campus (D)

5420 Miller Street, Arvada CO 80002
Telephone: (303) 914-6010 Identification: 770045
Accreditation: **&NH**

† Branch campus of Red Rocks Community College, Lakewood, CO.

Redstone College (E)

10851 W 120th Avenue, Broomfield CO 80021-3401
County: Broomfield FICE Identification: 007297
Unit ID: 126605
Telephone: (303) 466-1714 Carnegie Class: Assoc/PrivFP
FAX Number: (303) 469-3797 Calendar System: Other
URL: www.redstone.edu
Established: 1965 Annual Undergrad Tuition & Fees: $15,266
Enrollment: 552 Coed
Affiliation or Control: Proprietary IRS Status: Proprietary
Highest Offering: Associate Degree
Program: Occupational
Accreditation: **ACICS**

01 Campus President Mr. Glen WILSON
05 Campus Academic Dean Mr. Tim GUERRERO
07 Director of Admissions Mr. Rick EINSTEIN
11 Director of Campus Operations Ms. Kim VANDERWALL
06 Senior Registrar Ms. Vicki MIDDEKER

Redstone College-Denver East (F)

7350 N Broadway, Denver CO 80221
Telephone: (303) 426-7000 Identification: 770611
Accreditation: **ACICS**

† Branch campus of Redstone College, Broomfield, CO.

Regis University (G)

3333 Regis Boulevard, Denver CO 80221-1099
County: Denver FICE Identification: 001363
Unit ID: 127918
Telephone: (303) 458-4100 Carnegie Class: Master's L
FAX Number: (303) 964-5449 Calendar System: Semester
URL: www.regis.edu
Established: 1877 Annual Undergrad Tuition & Fees: $33,710
Enrollment: 9,208 Coed
Affiliation or Control: Roman Catholic IRS Status: 501(c)3
Highest Offering: Doctorate
Program: Liberal Arts And General; Teacher Preparatory; Professional
Accreditation: **NH**, CACREP, CAHIIM, CS, MFCD, NURSE, PHAR, PTA, TEAC

01 President Rev. John P. FITZGIBBONS, SJ
43 Legal Counsel Ms. Erika M. HOLLIS
05 Provost Dr. Patricia A. LADEWIG
30 Vice President Advancement Mr. Jason J. CANIGLIA
100 VP Mission//Chief of Staff Dr. Thomas E. REYNOLDS
10 Sr Vice President/CFO Dr. Salvador D. ACEVES
84 VP Enrollment Management Mr. Robert BLUST
84 Assoc VP Enrollment Services Mr. Bill HATHAWAY-CLARK
109 Assoc VP Aux and Business Services Ms. Susan LAYTON
15 Assoc VP Human Resources Mr. Tony L. CROW
18 Assoc VP Physical Plant Mr. Michael J. REDMOND
20 Assistant Provost Mr. Steve JACOBS
29 Asst VP Alumni Engagement Pgms Ms. Sarah BEHUNEK
13 Chief Information Officer Mr. Jaganmohan GUDUR
107 Dean Professional Studies Dr. Elisa ROBYN
77 Dean Computer & Info Sciences Dr. Shari PLANTZ-MASTERS
76 Dean Health Professions Dr. Janet HOUSER
49 Dean of Regis College Dr. Thomas BOWIE
08 Dean of Libraries Dr. Janet LEE
32 Dean of Students Ms. Diane M. MCSHEEHY
07 Dean of Admissions Ms. Kim FRISCH
37 Director Financial Aid Ms. Elinor MILLER
06 Director Registration Ms. Cathy GORRELL
06 Director Academic Records Ms. Terry GAURMER
38 Director Counseling Personal Dev Dr. Chaney GIVENS
19 Director of Campus Safety Mr. Manuel AMADO
25 Director Academic Grants Mr. Donald BRIDGER
42 Director of University Ministry Ms. Kristi GONSALVES-MCCABE
36 Director of Career Services Mr. Richard DELLIVENERI
41 Director Athletics Ms. Ann MARTIN
04 Administrative Asst to President Ms. Patti SCHOENINGER
09 Director of Institutional Research Ms. Cathy GORRELL
102 Dir Foundation/Corporate Relations Ms. Mary BROZOVICH
39 Director Student Housing Ms. Njal LUNDBERG
50 Dean of Business Dr. Timothy KEANE
90 Director Academic Computing Mr. Jeffrey GETCHELL
26 Chief Public Relations/Marketing Ms. Tara MOBERLY
44 Director Planned Giving Mr. Kurt BARTLEY

Rocky Mountain College of Art & Design (H)

1600 Pierce Street, Lakewood CO 80214-1433
County: Denver FICE Identification: 007649
Unit ID: 127945
Telephone: (303) 753-6046 Carnegie Class: Spec/Arts
FAX Number: (303) 759-4970 Calendar System: Semester
URL: www.rmcad.edu
Established: 1963 Annual Undergrad Tuition & Fees: $19,000
Enrollment: 1,045 Coed
Affiliation or Control: Proprietary IRS Status: Proprietary
Highest Offering: Master's
Program: Fine Arts Emphasis
Accreditation: **NH**, ART, CIDA

01 President/Provost Dr. Sage A. SCHEER
11 Chief Operating Officer Mr. Christopher MARCONI
10 Vice President of Operations Mr. Chris MINCHEFF
07 Director of Admissions Mr. Dave HOBLICK
15 Director of Human Resources Ms. Carrie BRANCHEAU
32 Director of Student Affairs Mr. Yves NAVANT
08 Library Director Mr. Hugh THURLOW
21 Senior Director of Finance Mr. Deepak KUMAR
06 Registrar Ms. Rebecca CORBIN

Rocky Vista University (I)

8401 South Chambers Road, Parker CO 80134
County: Douglas Identification: 667002
Unit ID: 480790
Telephone: (303) 373-2008 Carnegie Class: Not Classified
FAX Number: N/A Calendar System: Other
URL: www.rvu.edu
Established: 2006 Annual Graduate Tuition & Fees: $50,030
Enrollment: 633 Coed
Affiliation or Control: Proprietary IRS Status: Proprietary
Highest Offering: Doctorate; No Undergraduates
Program: Professional
Accreditation: **NH**, OSTEO

01 President Dr. Cheryl LOVELL
04 Executive Administrative Assistant Ms. Linda TERPENNING
09 Exec Dir Inst Plng & Assessment Dr. Jennifer WILLIAMS
09 Asst Dir Compliance & Quality Assur Dr. Terence BRENNAN
05 Dean Dr. Thomas TOLD
10 Chief Operating Officer/CFO Mr. Peter FREYTAG
37 Asst Dir Student Financial Svc Ms. Fran LATA
07 Exec Dir Admissions & Marketing Ms. Julie ROSENTHAL
32 Assoc Dean Student Affairs Ms. Amy SCHLUETER
06 Registrar Ms. Linda CAIRNS
08 Director of Library Services Dr. Frank AMES
19 Director Security/Safety Mr. Dan HAVENS

St. John Vianney Theological Seminary (J)

1300 S Steele Street, Denver CO 80210-2526
County: Denver Identification: 666127
Telephone: (303) 282-3427 Carnegie Class: Not Classified
FAX Number: (303) 282-3453 Calendar System: Semester
URL: www.sjvdenver.edu
Established: 1999 Annual Graduate Tuition & Fees: $28,567
Enrollment: 108 Male
Affiliation or Control: Roman Catholic IRS Status: 501(c)3
Highest Offering: Master's; No Undergraduates
Program: Professional; Religious Emphasis
Accreditation: **THEOL**

01 Rector V.Rev. Scott TRAYNOR
03 Vice Rector Rev. Jason WALLACE
05 Academic Dean Rev. Andreas HOECK
10 Director of Finance Mr. Paul VILLAMARIA
08 Library Director Mr. Stephen SWEENEY
06 Registrar Dr. Richard NEYENS

Southwest Acupuncture College (K)

6630 Gunpark Drive Suite 200, Boulder CO 80301-3339
Telephone: (303) 581-9955 Identification: 666618
Accreditation: **ACUP**

† Branch campus of Southwest Acupuncture College, Santa Fe, NM.

Southwest Colorado Community College-East (L)

701 Camino del Rio, Durango CO 81301
Telephone: (970) 247-2929 Identification: 770043
Accreditation: **&NH**

† Branch campus of Pueblo Community College, Pueblo, CO.

Southwest Colorado Community College-West (M)

33057 Highway 160, Mancos CO 81328
Telephone: (970) 564-6200 Identification: 770044
Accreditation: **&NH**

† Branch campus of Pueblo Community College, Pueblo, CO.

Trinidad State Junior College (A)

600 Prospect, Trinidad CO 81082-2396
County: Las Animas FICE Identification: 001368
Unit ID: 128258
Telephone: (719) 846-5011 Carnegie Class: Assoc/Pub-R-M
FAX Number: (719) 846-5667 Calendar System: Semester
URL: www.trinidadstate.edu
Established: 1925 Annual Undergrad Tuition & Fees (In-State): $4,500
Enrollment: 1,783 Coed
Affiliation or Control: State IRS Status: 501(c)3
Highest Offering: Associate Degree
Program: Occupational; 2-Year Principally Bachelor's Creditable
Accreditation: NH, ENGR

01 President .... Dr. Carmen M. SIMONE
05 Vice President of Academic Affairs .... Ms. Lynette BATES
32 VP Stdnt Affairs & Sponsored Pgm .... Ms. Kerry GABRIELSON
10 Exec Dir Admin Services/CFO .... Mr. Bryan BRYANT
49 Dean Arts & Sciences .... Ms. Debbie ULIBARRI
35 Dean Student Services .... Mr. Robert MARTINEZ
15 Human Resources Director .... Ms. Lorrie VELASQUEZ
37 Director Financial Aid .... Ms. Wilma ATENCIO
06 Registrar/Institutional Research .... Ms. Annette LUJAN
18 Director Facilities/Physical Plant .... Mr. Louis MANTELLI
21 Controller .... Ms. Alana BEST
106 Distance Lrng/Audio Visual Coord .... Mr. Doug BAK
04 Administrative Asst to President .... Ms. Donna HADDOW
26 Director of Marketing .... Mr. Greg BOYCE
41 Athletic Director .... Mr. Mike SALBATO

Trinidad State Junior College San Luis Valley Campus (B)

1011 Main Street, Alamosa CO 81101
Telephone: (719) 589-7000 Identification: 770047
Accreditation: &NH

† Branch campus of Trinidad State Junior College, Trinidad, CO.

UCH Memorial Hospital School Of Radiologic Technology (C)

1400 East Boulder Street, Colorado Springs CO 80909
County: El Paso Identification: 667097
Telephone: (719) 365-8291 Carnegie Class: Not Classified
FAX Number: (719) 365-5374 Calendar System: Semester
URL: www.uchealth.org
Established: 1969 Annual Undergrad Tuition & Fees: $10,000
Enrollment: 50 Coed
Affiliation or Control: Independent Non-Profit IRS Status: 501(c)3
Highest Offering: Associate Degree
Program: 2-Year Principally Bachelor's Creditable; Technical Emphasis
Accreditation: RAD

01 Director .... Elaine R. IVAN
88 Clinical Coordinator .... Lyle S. SMITH
05 Dean of Education .... Theresa TAYLOR
06 Registrar .... Scott SMITH
07 Director of Admissions .... Elaine R. IVAN

*University of Colorado System Office (D)

1800 Grant Street, Suite 800, Denver CO 80203
County: Denver FICE Identification: 007996
Unit ID: 128300
Telephone: (303) 860-5600 Carnegie Class: N/A
FAX Number: (303) 860-5610
URL: www.cu.edu

01 President .... Mr. Bruce D. BENSON
05 Assoc VP & Academic Affairs Officer .... Dr. Kathleen BOLLARD
100 Senior VP & Chief of Staff .... Mr. Leonard DINEGAR
10 VP & Chief Financial Officer .... Mr. Todd SALIMAN
43 VP University Counsel/Secy Board .... Mr. Pat O'ROURKE
15 Sr AVP/Chief Human Resource Ofcr .... Ms. Kathy NESBITT
86 VP Government Relations .... Ms. Tanya KELLY-BOWRY
26 Assoc VP University Relations .... Mr. Ken MCCONNELLOGUE
21 Asst VP & University Controller .... Mr. Robert KUEHLER
13 Asst VP & Chief Information Ofcr .... Mr. Robert WEIR
31 Dir Business & Community Relations .... Ms. Elizabeth COLLINS
26 Assistant VP External Relations .... Ms. Michele MCKINNEY

*University of Colorado Boulder (E)

Boulder CO 80309-0001
County: Boulder FICE Identification: 001370
Unit ID: 126614
Telephone: (303) 492-1411 Carnegie Class: RU/VH
FAX Number: N/A Calendar System: Semester
URL: www.colorado.edu
Established: 1876 Annual Undergrad Tuition & Fees (In-State): $11,091
Enrollment: 29,772 Coed
Affiliation or Control: State IRS Status: 501(c)3
Highest Offering: Doctorate
Program: Liberal Arts And General; Teacher Preparatory; Professional
Accreditation: NH, AUD, BUS, CEA, CLPSY, CS, ENG, IPSY, JOUR, LAW, MUS, SP, TED

02 Chancellor .... Dr. Phillip P. DISTEFANO
05 Provost & Exec VC for Acad Affairs .... Dr. Russell MOORE
10 Sr Vice Chanc & Chief Finan Officer .... Ms. Kelly L. FOX
46 Vice Chancellor for Research .... Dr. Stein STURE
11 Vice Chanc Administration .... Mr. Steven THWEATT
32 Vice Chanc Student Affairs .... Ms. Deborah J. COFFIN
28 Vice Chanc for Diversity/Equity .... Dr. Robert BOSWELL
26 Vice Chanc for Strategic Relations .... Ms. Frances DRAPER
21 Assc VC Budget & Finance/Controller .... Vacant
13 Assoc VC & Chief Information Offcr .... Dr. Lawrence M. LEVINE
100 Chief of Staff .... Ms. Catherine SHEA
30 Vice Chanc for Advancement .... Mr. Aaron CONLEY
29 Asst Vice Chanc Alumni Relations .... Mr. Ryan CHREIST
58 Dean of the Graduate School .... Dr. John A. STEVENSON
61 Dean of Law .... Dr. Philip J. WEISER
49 Dean of Arts & Science .... Dr. Steven R. LEIGH
54 Dean of Engineering .... Dr. Robert H. DAVIS
50 Dean of Business .... Dr. David L. IKENBERRY
53 Dean of Education .... Dr. Lorrie SHEPARD
64 Dean of Music .... Dr. Robert S. SHAY
60 Dean Media/Communica/Info .... Dr. Lori BERGEN
51 Dean of Division of Continuing Educ .... Dr. Sara THOMPSON
62 Dean of Libraries .... Mr. James F. WILLIAMS
35 Dean of Students .... Ms. Christina GONZALES
37 Director of Financial Aid .... Ms. Gwen E. POMPER
07 Director of Admissions .... Mr. Kevin L. MACLENNAN
06 Registrar .... Dr. Kristi WOLD-MCCORMICK
09 Dir of Institutional Research .... Mr. Robert STUBBS
25 Dir of Contracts and Grants .... Ms. Denitta D. WARD
15 Chief Human Resources Officer .... Mr. Scott MORRIS
41 Athletic Director .... Mr. Rick GEORGE
19 Director of Public Safety .... Ms. Melissa A. ZAK
23 Director of Student Health Center .... Dr. Donald MISCH
36 Director of Career Services .... Dr. Lisa E. SEVERY
88 Director of Museum .... Dr. Patrick KOCIOLEK
104 Director Study Abroad .... Ms. Mary DANDO

*University of Colorado Colorado Springs (F)

1420 Austin Bluffs Parkway, Colorado Springs CO 80918
County: El Paso FICE Identification: 004509
Unit ID: 126580
Telephone: (719) 255-8227 Carnegie Class: Master's L
FAX Number: (719) 255-3362 Calendar System: Semester
URL: www.uccs.edu
Established: 1965 Annual Undergrad Tuition & Fees (In-State): $9,428
Enrollment: 11,761 Coed
Affiliation or Control: State IRS Status: 501(c)3
Highest Offering: Doctorate
Program: Liberal Arts And General; Teacher Preparatory; Professional
Accreditation: NH, BUS, CACREP, #CAEP, CLPSY, CS, DIETD, ENG, NURSE, SPAA, TED

02 Chancellor .... Dr. Pam SHOCKLEY-ZALABAK
05 Provost .... Dr. Mary COUSSONS-READ
11 Vice Chanc Admin & Finance .... Susan SZPYRKA
32 Vice Chanc Student Success .... Dr. Homer A. WESLEY, III
30 Vice Chanc Univ Advancement .... Martin WOOD
20 Sr Vice Chanc Academic Affairs .... Dr. David MOON
43 Legal Counsel .... Jennifer GEORGE
25 Director of Sponsored Programs .... Gwen GENNARO
08 Dean of Library .... Vacant
84 Dir of Enrollment Mgmt/Registrar .... Matthew COX
09 Director of Institutional Research .... Dr. Robyn MARSCHKE
15 Human Resources .... Jeanne DURR
19 Director of Public Safety .... Brian MCPIKE
29 Director Alumni & Community Rels .... Jennifer HANE
37 Director Finan Aid/Stdnt Employment .... Jevita ROGERS
40 Manager of Bookstore .... Paul DENISTON
18 Chief Facilities/Physical Plant .... Gary REYNOLDS
26 Director Media Relations .... Tom HUTTON
38 Director Student Counseling .... Dr. Z. Benek ALTAYLI
41 Director of Athletics .... Stephen W. KIRKHAM
13 Director of Information Technology .... Jerry WILSON
21 Director Resource Management .... Gayanne SCOTT
49 Dean of Letters/Arts/Science .... Dr. Peter BRAZA
50 Dean of Business .... Dr. Venkateshwar REDDY
53 Dean of Education .... Dr. Valerie CONLEY
54 Dean of Engineering/Applied Science .... Dr. Ramaswami DANDAPANI
80 Assoc Dean of Public Affairs .... Dr. George REED
66 Dean Nursing/Health Sciences .... Dr. Nancy SMITH
58 Dean of Graduate School .... Dr. Kelli KLEBE
28 Assoc Vice Chancellor Diversity .... Dr. Kee WARNER
39 Director Campus Housing .... Ralph GIESE
88 Director of Sustainability .... Linda KOGAN
06 Registrar .... Tracy BARBER
04 Executive Asst to the Chancellor .... Brenda BONN
105 Director Web Services .... Craig DECKER
106 Dir Online Education/E-learning .... Venkateshwar REDDY

*University of Colorado Denver|Anschutz Medical Campus (G)

1250 14th Street, Denver CO 80204
County: Denver FICE Identification: 004508
Unit ID: 126562
Telephone: (303) 556-2400 Carnegie Class: RU/H
FAX Number: N/A Calendar System: Semester
URL: www.ucdenver.edu
Established: 1912 Annual Undergrad Tuition & Fees (In-State): $9,090
Enrollment: 18,345 Coed
Affiliation or Control: State IRS Status: 501(c)3
Highest Offering: Doctorate
Program: Liberal Arts And General; Teacher Preparatory; Professional
Accreditation: NH, AA, ARCPA, BUS, BUSA, CACREP, CLPSY, CS, DENT, DMS, ENG, HSA, IPSY, LSAR, MED, MIDWF, MUS, NURSE, PAST, PH, PHAR, PLNG, PTA, SPAA, TED

02 Chancellor .... Dr. Don ELLIMAN
03 VP Health Affairs/Exec VC AMC .... Ms. Lilly MARKS
10 Vice Chancellor Admin/Finance .... Mr. Jeffrey PARKER
46 Vice Chancellor for Research .... Dr. Richard TRAYSTMAN
17 VC Health Affairs/Dean of Medicine .... Dr. John REILLY
26 Vice Chanc of Univ Communications .... Ms. Leanna CLARK
05 Provost & VC Academic/Student Affs .... Dr. Roderick NAIRN
30 Vice Chanc of Development Anschutz .... Mr. Scott ARTHUR
30 Vice Chanc of Development Denver .... Mr. Matthew WASSERMAN
52 Dean School of Dental Medicine .... Dr. Denise KASSEBAUM
66 Dean College of Nursing .... Dr. Sarah THOMPSON
67 Dean School of Pharmacy .... Dr. Ralph ALTIERE
69 Dean CO School of Public Health .... Dr. David GOFF
58 Interim Dean Graduate School .... Dr. Terry POTTER
64 Dean College of Arts/Media .... Dr. Laurence KAPTAIN
80 Dean School of Pubilc Affairs .... Dr. Paul TESKE
49 Dean College Liberal Arts & Sci .... Dr. Pamela JANSMA
48 Dean College of Arch/Planning .... Mr. Mark GELERNTER
50 Dean Business School .... Ms. Sueann AMBRON
53 Dean School of Education .... Dr. Rebecca KANTOR
54 Dean College of Engineering .... Dr. Marc INGBER
46 Assoc VC for Research .... Dr. Robert DAMRAUER
20 Assoc VC Academic Affairs .... Dr. Laura GOODWIN
32 Assoc VC Student Affairs .... Dr. Raul CARDENAS
28 Assoc VC Diversity/Inclusion .... Dr. Brenda ALLEN
21 Assoc VC Budget/Finance/VC CU South .... Ms. Lisa DOUGLAS
18 Assoc VC Facilities Management .... Mr. David C. TURNQUIST
88 Assoc VC of Academic Planning .... Dr. Terry POTTER
15 Asst VC Human Resources .... Mr. Kevin JACOBS
13 Asst VC Information Technology Svcs .... Mr. Russell POOLE
88 Asst VC Academic Tech/Extd Learning .... Mr. Robert TOLSMA
84 Asst VC UG Admissions/K-12 Outreach .... Mr. Chris DOWEN
09 Asst VC Institutional Research .... Dr. Christine STROUP-BENHAM
88 Asst VC Student Success .... Ms. Peggy LORE
88 Interim Asst VC Univ Life .... Mr. Sam KIM
06 Registrar .... Ms. Ingrid ESCHHOLZ
08 Director Auraria Library .... Dr. Mary SOMERVILLE
08 Interim Dir Health Sciences Library .... Ms. Melissa DESANTIS
27 Director PR/Media Relations .... Vacant
37 Interim Director Financial Aid Svcs .... Mr. Justin JARAMILLO
19 Chief of Police .... Mr. Doug ABRAHAM
29 Director Alumni Relations .... Ms. Joy FRENCH
43 Assistant University Counsel .... Mr. Christopher PUCKETT
35 Interim Dean of Students .... Dr. Kristin KUSHMIDER
104 Director International Education .... Mr. John SUNNYGARD
45 Chief Institutional Planning .... Mr. Michale DEL GIUDICE

University of Denver (H)

2199 S. University Blvd., Denver CO 80208-0001
County: Denver FICE Identification: 001371
Unit ID: 127060
Telephone: (303) 871-2000 Carnegie Class: RU/H
FAX Number: (303) 871-3301 Calendar System: Quarter
URL: www.du.edu
Established: 1864 Annual Undergrad Tuition & Fees: $43,164
Enrollment: 11,806 Coed
Affiliation or Control: Independent Non-Profit IRS Status: 501(c)3
Highest Offering: Doctorate
Program: Liberal Arts And General; Teacher Preparatory; Professional
Accreditation: NH, ART, BUS, BUSA, CEA, CLPSY, COPSY, ENG, IPSY, LAW, LIB, MUS, SW

01 Chancellor .... Dr. Rebecca CHOPP
05 Provost .... Dr. Gregg O. KVISTAD
43 Vice Chanc Legal Affairs/Gen Couns .... Mr. Paul H. CHAN
32 Vice Chanc Campus Life/Inclus Excel .... Dr. Liliana RODRIGUEZ
10 Vice Chanc Business/Financial Affs .... Mr. Craig WOODY
41 Vice Chanc Athletics and Recreation .... Ms. Peg BRADLEY-DOPPES
30 Vice Chanc University Advancement .... Mr. Armin AFSAHI
26 Vice Chancellor Communications .... Mr. Kevin CARROLL
13 Assoc VC Tech/Chief Tech Officer .... Ms. Nancy ALLEN
84 Vice Chancellor for Enrollment .... Mr. Thomas WILLOUGHBY
37 Asst Vice Chanc Enroll/Dir Fin Aid .... Mr. John E. GUDVANGEN
04 Exec Assistant to the Chancellor .... Ms. Allison RIOLA
20 Associate Provost Academic Program .... Dr. Jennifer KARAS
35 Assoc Vice Chanc Campus Life .... Dr. Patti HELTON
88 Assoc Vice Chanc IE/Exec Dir CME .... Ms. Johanna LEYBA
28 Sr Advisor to Chancellor/Provost .... Dr. Frank TUITT
58 Assoc Provost Graduate Studies .... Dr. Barbara WILCOTS
08 Interim Dean Libraries .... Mr. Michael LEVINE-CLARK
34 Interim Dean CO Women's College .... Dr. Linda OLSON
45 Sr Assoc Provost Planning/Budget .... Ms. Julia MCGAHEY
102 Assc Vice Chanc Annual Giving/Found .... Ms. Kristine CECIL
44 Assoc Vice Chanc Major Gifts .... Mr. Mike MCCALL
06 Registrar .... Mr. Dennis M. BECKER
21 Controller/Assistant Treasurer .... Ms. Margaret HENRY
36 Exec Director Career Services .... Ms. Sue HINKIN
22 EO/ADA Compliance Director .... Vacant
18 Director Facilities Management .... Mr. Jeff BEMELEN
09 Interim Dir Institutional Research .... Mr. Mike FURNO
15 Vice Chancellor Human Resources .... Ms. Amy KING
19 Director Campus Safety .... Mr. Donald ENLOE
88 Dir Student Financial Services .... Ms. Janet BURKHARDT
88 Asst Vice Chanc Enterprise Services .... Ms. Susan LUTZ

23 Exec Dir of Univ Health Services .... Mr. Alan KENT
54 Dean Engr/Computer Science .... Mr. J.B HOLSTON
79 Dean Arts/Hum/Soc Science .... Dr. Daniel MCINTOSH
81 Dean Natural Science/Math .... Dr. Andrei KUTATELADZE
50 Dean College of Business ....Dr. Brent CHRITE
61 Dean College of Law .... Mr. Martin J. KATZ
82 Dean Graduate Sch Intl Studies .... Mr. Christopher R. HILL
70 Dean Graduate Sch Social Work .... Dr. James WILLIAMS
55 Dean University College ....Mr. Michael MCGUIRE
53 Dean College of Education ....Dr. Karen RILEY
64 Director Lamont School of Music .... Ms. Nancy COCHRAN
31 Exec Dir Special Community Programs .... Dr. Cathy GRIEVE
57 Director School of Art/Art History ....Dr. Sarah GJERTSON
07 Director of Enrollment Services .... Ms. Anne GROSS
35 Exec Director of Campus Life .... Mr. Carl JOHNSON
101 Secretary of the Institution/Board .... Ms. Claire BROWNELL
104 Study Abroad Assistant Director .... Ms. Michelle REMBOLT
105 Senior Digital Design and Architect ....Mr. Matt ESCHENBAUM
106 Director of Web-based Learning .... Ms. Kathy KEAIRNS
108 Director of Assessment .... Dr. Rob FLAHERTY
29 Exec Director Alumni Relations .... Ms. Deborah FOWLKES
38 Exec Director Health and Counseling ....Dr. Alan KENT
39 Exec Director Housing and Res Ed ....Mr. Patrick CALL
96 Director of Business Services .... Mr. Bob MCVEIGH

University of Northern Colorado (A)

501 20th Street, Greeley CO 80639-6900

County: Weld | FICE Identification: 001349 | Unit ID: 127741
Telephone: (970) 351-1890 | Carnegie Class: DRU
FAX Number: (970) 351-1880 | Calendar System: Semester
URL: www.unco.edu
Established: 1889 | Annual Undergrad Tuition & Fees (In-State): $7,906
Enrollment: 11,784 | Coed
Affiliation or Control: State | IRS Status: 501(c)3
Highest Offering: Doctorate
Program: Liberal Arts And General; Teacher Preparatory; Professional
Accreditation: NH, ART, AUD, BUS, BUSA, CAATE, CACREP, CEA, COPSY, CORE, DIETD, DIETI, IPSY, MUS, NURSE, PH, SCPSY, SP, TED, THEA

01 President ....Ms. Kay NORTON
05 Provost/Vice Pres Academic Affairs .... Ms. Robbyn WACKER
11 Vice President Administration ....Ms. Michelle QUINN
43 Vice President & University Counsel ....Mr. Dan SATRIANA
26 VP External & University Relations ....Mr. Dan WEAVER
30 Vice Pres Development/Alumni Rels .... Mr. Wayne WEBSTER
58 Dean Grad School ....Ms. Linda BLACK
20 Ast VP Undergrad Stds/Dean Univ Col ....Dr. Thomas SMITH
10 Asst Vice President Budgets/Analysi .... Ms. Susan SIMMERS
13 Asst Vice President Info Technology ....Mr. Bret NABER
84 Asst Vice Pres for Enrollment Mgmt ....Mr. Tobias GUZMAN
79 Dean Humanities/Social Sciences .... Dr. Laura CONNOLLY
50 Acting Dean Business ....Dr. Karen TURNER
53 Dean Education/Behavorial Sciences .... Dr. Eugene SHEEHAN
76 Dean Natural & Health Sciences ....Dr. Ellen GREGG
57 Dean Performing Visual Arts ....Dr. Leo WELCH
08 Dean University Libraries ....Ms. Helen REED
32 Dean of Students .... Dr. Katrina RODRIGUEZ
102 President University Foundation ....Mr. Rod ESCH
06 Registrar .... Mr. Charlie COUCH
07 Director of Admissions .... Dr. Sean M. BROGHAMMER
25 Actg AVP Sponsored Pgms/Research ....Dr. Robert HOUSER
37 Dir Student Financial Resources .... Mr. Marty SOMERO
36 Director of Career Services ....Ms. Renee WELCH
15 Director of Human Resources .... Mr. Marshall PARKS
29 Asst VP Alumni Relations ....Ms. Lyndsey CRUM
18 Director Facilities Management ....Mr. Kirk LEICHLITER
41 Director of NCAA Athletics ....Mr. Darren DUNN
39 Director of Residential Education .... Mr. Montez BUTTS
38 Director Student Counseling .... Ms. Kim WILCOX
19 Chief of University Police .... Mr. Dennis PUMPHREY
44 Director of Annual Giving .... Ms. Christina NICHOLS
27 Dir News & Public Relations ....Mr. Nate HAAS
96 Director of Purchasing .... Ms. Cristal SWAIN
104 Director Study Abroad .... Mr. Brent SPENCER
108 Director Institutional Assessment ....Ms. Kim BLACK

University of Phoenix Colorado Main Campus (B)

1000H Park Meadows Drive, Lone Tree CO 80124-5453

Telephone: (303) 755-9090 | Identification: 770195
Accreditation: &NH, ACBSP

† Branch campus of University of Phoenix, Tempe, AZ.

University of the Rockies (C)

555 E Pikes Peak Ave, Suite 108, Colorado Springs CO 80903-3612

County: El Paso | FICE Identification: 035453 | Unit ID: 441308
Telephone: (719) 442-0505 | Carnegie Class: Spec/Health
FAX Number: (719) 389-0359 | Calendar System: Other
URL: www.rockies.edu
Established: 1998 | Annual Graduate Tuition & Fees: $15,758
Enrollment: 1,639 | Coed
Affiliation or Control: Proprietary | IRS Status: Proprietary
Highest Offering: Doctorate; No Undergraduates
Program: Professional
Accreditation: NH

01 Interim President ....Dr. Craig SWENSON
05 Provost .... Dr. Amy KAHN
10 Vice President of Finance .... Mr. Chris JACKSON
11 Vice President of Operations ....Mr. Adam FORREST
58 Dean School of Prof Psychology ....Dr. David STEPHENS
106 Dean Sch Organizational Leadership ....Dr. Douglas GILBERT
21 Director of Financial Services ....Ms. Jamie ESQUIBEL
15 Director of Human Resources ....Ms. Barbara HENRY-QUINN
06 University Registrar ....Ms. Katina JORDAN
28 Director of Diversity .... Ms. Francesca GALARRAGA

U.S. Career Institute (D)

2001 Lowe Street, Fort Collins CO 80525

County: Larimer | Identification: 666776
Telephone: (970) 207-4500 | Carnegie Class: Not Classified
FAX Number: (970) 223-1678 | Calendar System: Other
URL: www.uscareerinstitute.edu
Established: 1981 | Annual Undergrad Tuition & Fees: $4,000
Enrollment: N/A | Coed
Affiliation or Control: Proprietary | IRS Status: Proprietary
Highest Offering: Associate Degree
Program: Occupational; 2-Year Principally Bachelor's Creditable; Business Emphasis
Accreditation: DEAC

01 President ....Ann ROHR
32 Vice President Student Affairs .... Joyce LINDQUIST
10 Vice President Finance .... Jason STANSBERRY
13 Vice President Information Tech ....Scott LYNCH
108 Director of Compliance & Retention ....Janet PERRY

Western Colorado Community College-Tilman M. Bishop Campus (E)

2508 Blichmann Avenue, Grand Junction CO 81505

Telephone: (970) 255-2600 | Identification: 770030
Accreditation: &NH

† Branch campus of Colorado Mesa University, Grand Junction, CO.

Western State Colorado University (F)

600 North Adams, Gunnison CO 81231-0001

County: Gunnison | FICE Identification: 001372 | Unit ID: 128391
Telephone: (970) 943-0120 | Carnegie Class: Bac/A&S
FAX Number: (970) 943-7069 | Calendar System: Semester
URL: www.western.edu
Established: 1911 | Annual Undergrad Tuition & Fees (In-State): $8,451
Enrollment: 2,584 | Coed
Affiliation or Control: State | IRS Status: 501(c)3
Highest Offering: Master's
Program: Liberal Arts And General; Teacher Preparatory; Professional
Accreditation: NH, MUS, @TEAC

01 President .... Dr. Greg SALSBURY
11 Exec Vice Pres and COO ....Mr. Brad BACA
05 Interim Vice Pres Academic Affairs ....Dr. Bill NIEMI
10 Chief Financial Officer .... Ms. Julie FEIER
32 Vice President of Student Affairs ....Mr. Gary PIERSON
30 VP Marketing/Inst Advancement ....Mr. John KAWAUCHI
20 Assoc Vice Pres Academic Affairs ....Dr. Kathleen KINKEMA
07 Director of Recruitment ....Mr. Paul FITZGERALD
35 Assoc Vice Pres Student Affairs .... Mr. Chris LUEKENGA
06 Registrar ....Ms. Ginny HAYES
37 Director Student Financial Aid ....Vacant
104 Dir Intl Student Pgms/Study Abroad ....Ms. Jessica VOGAN
41 Interim Athletic Director ....Mr. Jason CARMICHAEL
15 Director of Human Resources ....Ms. Kim GAILEY
40 Director Retail Operations .... Ms. Teri HAUS
91 Director Administrative Computing ....Mr. Chad ROBINSON
08 Director Library Services ....Ms. Nancy GAUSS
51 Director Extended Studies .... Ms. Erica BOUCHER
39 Director of Residence Life .... Ms. Shelley JANSEN
36 Career Services Coordinator ....Ms. Mariah GREEN
26 Director of Public Relations .... Mr. Brian BARKER
29 Director of Alumni Relations ....Ms. Tonya VANHEE
44 Director Annual & Special Gifts ....Ms. Deb HOSKINS
09 Director Institutional Research ....Mr. Doug DRIVER
28 Director of Multicultural Center ....Ms. Sally ROMERO
96 Business Services Manager ....Ms. Sherry FORD

*Westwood College (G)

7604 Technology Way Suite 400, Denver CO 80237

County: Denver | Identification: 667029
Telephone: (303) 846-1700 | Carnegie Class: N/A
FAX Number: N/A
URL: www.westwood.edu

01 Chief Executive Officer ....Mr. Dean GOUIN

*Westwood College-Denver North (H)

7350 N Broadway, Denver CO 80221-3653

County: Adams | FICE Identification: 007548 | Unit ID: 127024
Telephone: (303) 426-7000 | Carnegie Class: Bac/Diverse
FAX Number: (303) 429-5534 | Calendar System: Other
URL: www.westwood.edu
Established: 1953 | Annual Undergrad Tuition & Fees: $15,207
Enrollment: 342 | Coed
Affiliation or Control: Proprietary | IRS Status: Proprietary
Highest Offering: Baccalaureate
Program: Occupational; Technical Emphasis
Accreditation: ACICS

02 Campus President ....Dr. Thomas WICKE

Westwood College-Denver South (I)

350 Blackhawk Street, Aurora CO 80011

Telephone: (303) 934-1122 | Identification: 666512
Accreditation: ACICS

† Branch campus of Westwood College-Denver North, Denver, CO.

Westwood College-Online (J)

10249 Church Ranch Way, Broomfield CO 80021

Telephone: (720) 887-8888 | Identification: 770673
Accreditation: ACICS

† Branch campus of Westwood College-Los Angeles Campus, Los Angeles, CA.

William Howard Taft University (K)

600 South Cherry Street, Suite 525, Denver CO 80246

County: Denver | FICE Identification: 041004
Telephone: (303) 867-1155 | Carnegie Class: Not Classified
FAX Number: (303) 867-1156 | Calendar System: Other
URL: www.taft.edu
Established: 1976 | Annual Undergrad Tuition & Fees: N/A
Enrollment: 817 | Coed
Affiliation or Control: Proprietary | IRS Status: Proprietary
Highest Offering: Doctorate
Program: Professional
Accreditation: DEAC

01 President ....Mr. Jerome ALLEY
03 Chief Operating Officer .... Mr. Robert K. STROUSE
11 Director of Administration ....Ms. Christine A. BALDWIN
05 Chief Academic Officer .... Dr. Neil JOHNSON

† Tuition varies by degree program.

William Loveland College (L)

441 East 4th St., #101, Loveland CO 80537

County: Larimer | Identification: 667234
Telephone: (970) 410-0456 | Carnegie Class: Not Classified
FAX Number: (719) 452-3684 | Calendar System: Semester
URL: wlcollege.ilm.edu
Established: 1973 | Annual Graduate Tuition & Fees: $2,250
Enrollment: N/A | Coed
Affiliation or Control: Independent Non-Profit | IRS Status: 501(c)3
Highest Offering: Master's; No Undergraduates
Program: Professional
Accreditation: DEAC

01 Executive Director & Provost ....Mr. David E. LADY
05 Chief Academic Officer ....Dr. Randell ORNER
11 Vice Pres of Operations ....Mr. Jerry BOYLE

CONNECTICUT

Albertus Magnus College (M)

700 Prospect Street, New Haven CT 06511-1189

County: New Haven | FICE Identification: 001374 | Unit ID: 128498
Telephone: (203) 773-8550 | Carnegie Class: Master's L
FAX Number: (203) 773-9539 | Calendar System: Semester
URL: www.albertus.edu
Established: 1925 | Annual Undergrad Tuition & Fees: $43,258
Enrollment: 1,543 | Coed
Affiliation or Control: Independent Non-Profit | IRS Status: 501(c)3
Highest Offering: Master's
Program: Liberal Arts And General; Business Emphasis
Accreditation: EH, IACBE

01 President ....Dr. Julia M. MCNAMARA
05 Vice Pres Academic Affairs ....Dr. Sean O'CONNELL
10 Vice President Finance/Treasurer .... Mrs. Jeanne E. MANN
13 VP Information Technology Services .... Mr. Steven GSTALDER
29 VP Development/Alumni Relations .... Ms. Carolyn A. BEHAN KRAUS
32 Vice President for Student Services ....Mr. Andrew FOSTER
35 Asst Dean Campus Activities/Orien ....Ms. Erin MORRELL
06 Registrar .... Mrs. Angela HAGGERTY
08 Director Library/Information Svcs .... Ms. Anne LEENEY-PANAGROSSI
09 Inst Research & Assessment Analyst ....Ms. Viola SIMPSON
37 Director Financial Aid .... Mrs. Michelle COCHRAN
90 Director Academic Computing .... Mr. Robert HUBBARD
41 Director of Athletics .... Mr. James ABROMAITIS
58 Director MALS Program ....Ms. Julia COASH
89 Director of Freshmen Advising ....Mrs. Corey BRUSHETT
92 Director of Honors Program ....Dr. Christine ATKINS
96 Dir Purchas/Pub Sfty/Spec Projects .....Mr. James A. SCHAFRICK
15 Director Human Resources .... Ms. Renee SULLIVAN
26 Dir Communications/Community Rels .....Ms. Rosanne ZUDEKOFF

36 Interim Director Career Services Ms. Karyn STOKES
42 Coord of Dominican Ministries Mr. H. John HOFFMAN
18 Supervisor of Facilities Services Mr. Edward J. THOMASI, SR.

Beth Benjamin Academy of Connecticut (A)

132 Prospect Street, Stamford CT 06901-1202

County: Fairfield FICE Identification: 029120
Unit ID: 414975
Telephone: (203) 325-4351 Carnegie Class: Not Classified
FAX Number: (203) 323-6073 Calendar System: Trimester
Established: 1976 Annual Undergrad Tuition & Fees: $5,945
Enrollment: 61 Male
Affiliation or Control: Independent Non-Profit IRS Status: 501(c)3
Highest Offering: First Talmudic Degree
Program: Teacher Preparatory; Professional
Accreditation: RABN

01 Rosh Hayeshiva Rabbi M. HERSHKOWITZ
04 Associate Rosh Hayeshiva Rabbi Yeruchom ZEILBERGER
05 Dean Rabbi Michael BENDER

Charter Oak State College (B)

55 Paul Manafort Drive, New Britain CT 06053-2142

County: Hartford FICE Identification: 029171
Unit ID: 128780
Telephone: (860) 515-3800 Carnegie Class: Bac/A&S
FAX Number: (860) 606-9615 Calendar System: Other
URL: www.charteroak.edu
Established: 1973 Annual Undergrad Tuition & Fees (In-State): $7,114
Enrollment: 2,570 Coed
Affiliation or Control: State IRS Status: 501(c)3
Highest Offering: Baccalaureate
Program: Liberal Arts And General
Accreditation: EH

01 President Mr. Edward KLONOSKI
05 Provost Dr. Shirley M. ADAMS
20 Academic Dean Undergrad Programs Dr. Emily G. LEWIS
10 Chief Financial/Administrative Ofcr Mr. Clifford S. WILLIAMS
13 Chief Information Officer Mr. George F. CLAFFEY, JR.
09 Dir Institutional Effectiveness Mr. Michael BRODERICK
06 Registrar Ms. Jennifer WASHINGTON
37 Dir Financial Aid/Veterans Benefits Ms. Deborah FLINN
20 Director Academic Services Ms. Linda LARKIN
07 Director Admissions Ms. Lori GAGNE PENDLETON
88 Coord Prior Learning Assessment Pgm Ms. Linda WILDER
26 Director Marketing/Public Relations Ms. Carolyn HEBERT
04 Administrative Asst to President Ms. Angela CHAPMAN
102 Dir Foundation/Corporate Relations Ms. Angela CHAPMAN
105 Director Web Services Mr. Daniel RUSSELL
15 Director Personnel Services Ms. Rowena MCGOLDRICK
29 Director Alumni Relations Ms. Nancy TAYLOR

*Connecticut Board of Regents for Higher Education (C)

39 Woodland Street, Hartford CT 06105-2337

County: Hartford Identification: 666656
Unit ID: 129011
Telephone: (860) 723-0000 Carnegie Class: N/A
FAX Number: (860) 723-0009
URL: www.ct.ed

01 President Dr. Gregory W. GRAY
88 Vice President for CSU Dr. Elsa NUNEZ
88 Vice President for CCC Dr. David LEVINSON
15 Interim VP for Human Resources Ms. Laurie DUNN
26 Director PR & Mktg Mr. Michael KOZLOWSKI
10 Chief Financial Officer Ms. Erika STEINER
13 Chief Information Officer Mr. Joseph TOLISANO
101 Assoc Board Affairs/Secy to BOT Ms. Erin FITZGERALD
04 Administrative Assistant Ms. Judith S. NOSAL
100 Chief of Staff Ms. Liz CASWELL
05 Interim Provost Dr. Estela LOPEZ
09 Director of Institutional Research Dr. William GAMMELL
18 Chief Facilities/Physical Plant Mr. Keith EPSTEIN
43 Dir Legal Services/General Counsel Ms. Ernestine WEAVER

*Central Connecticut State University (D)

1615 Stanley Street, New Britain CT 06050-4010

County: Hartford FICE Identification: 001378
Unit ID: 128771
Telephone: (860) 832-3200 Carnegie Class: Master's L
FAX Number: (860) 832-2522 Calendar System: Semester
URL: www.ccsu.edu
Established: 1849 Annual Undergrad Tuition & Fees (In-State): $9,300
Enrollment: 12,037 Coed
Affiliation or Control: State IRS Status: 501(c)3
Highest Offering: Doctorate
Program: Liberal Arts And General; Teacher Preparatory; Professional
Accreditation: EH, BUS, CAATE, CACREP, CONST, CORE, CS, ENG, ENGT, EXSC, MFCD, MUS, NAIT, NURSE, SW, TED

02 President Dr. John W. MILLER
04 Assistant to the President Ms. Courtney MCDAVID
05 Provost/Vice Pres Academic Affs Dr. Carl R. LOVITT
30 Vice Pres Institutional Advancement Mr. Chris GALLIGAN
32 Vice President Student Affairs Dr. Laura TORDENTI
35 Asst Vice Pres/Dean of Students Vacant
20 Associate VP Academic Affairs Dr. Joseph P. PAIGE
44 Assoc VP Institutional Advancement Mr. Nicholas PETTINICO, JR.
58 Associate VP Graduate Studies Dr. Glynis A. FITZGERALD
26 Assoc VP Marketing/ Communications Dr. Mark W. MCLAUGHLIN
88 Special Assistant to the President Ms. Carolyn MAGNAN
11 Chief Administrative Officer Dr. Richard R. BACHOO
10 Chief Financial Officer Mrs. Charlene CASAMENTO
15 Chief Human Resources Officer Mrs. Anna SUSKI-LENCZEWSKI
13 Interim Chief Information Officer Ms. Jacquelynn BONESIO-PETERSON
28 Interim Chief Diversity Officer Ms. Rosa RODRIGUEZ
49 Dean School Arts & Sciences Dr. Susan PEASE
50 Dean School of Business Dr. Ken COLWELL
53 Dean School Educ & Prof Studies Dr. Michael P. ALFANO
54 Dean School Engineering/Technology Dr. Faris MALHUS
82 Dir Center International Education Dr. Momar NDIAYE
51 Dir Continuing Educ/Cmty Engagement Ms. Christa STERLING
07 Director Admissions & Recruitment Mr. Lawrence HALL
41 Director Athletics Mr. Paul SCHLICKMANN
39 Director Residence Life Ms. Jean ALICANDRO
19 Director Public Safety Mr. Gregory SNEED
37 Director Student Financial Aid Mr. Richard BISHOP
44 Director Institutional Advancement Ms. Cynthia B. CAYER
27 Media Relations Officer Ms. Janice PALMER
08 Interim Director Library Services Mr. Carl ANTONUCCI
36 Dir Ctr Advising/Career Exploration Mr. Kenneth POPPE
23 Director Health Services Dr. Christopher R. DIAMOND
24 Director Academic Technology Vacant
06 Registrar Mr. Patrick TUCKER
38 Int Assoc Dir Counseling & Wellness Mr. Jonathan POHL
18 Asst Chief Admin Ofcr/Dir Facil Mgt Mr. Salvatore CINTORINO
21 Director of Business Services Vacant
96 Purchasing Manager Mr. Thomas BRODEUR
09 Director of Institutional Research Ms. Yvonne KIRBY

*Eastern Connecticut State University (E)

83 Windham Street, Willimantic CT 06226-2295

County: Windham FICE Identification: 001425
Unit ID: 129215
Telephone: (860) 465-5000 Carnegie Class: Master's S
FAX Number: (860) 465-4485 Calendar System: Semester
URL: www.easternct.edu
Established: 1889 Annual Undergrad Tuition & Fees (In-State): $10,016
Enrollment: 5,300 Coed
Affiliation or Control: State IRS Status: 501(c)3
Highest Offering: Master's
Program: 2-Year Principally Bachelor's Creditable; Liberal Arts And General; Teacher Preparatory; Professional
Accreditation: EH, SW, TED

02 President Dr. Elsa M. NUNEZ
05 Provost Dr. Dimitrios C. PACHIS
10 VP Finance/Administration Mr. James R. HOWARTH
32 Vice Pres Student Affairs Mr. Ken BEDINI
30 Vice Pres Institutional Advance Mr. Kenneth J. DELISA
28 Assoc VP Equity & Diversity Dr. Stacey CLOSE
35 Dean of Students Mr. Walter DIAZ
09 Asst Dir of Institutional Research Dr. Brian R. LASHLEY
41 Director of Athletics Ms. Lori RUNKSMEIER
08 Director of Library Services Ms. Patricia S. BANACH
84 Dir of Enrollment Mgmt/Fin Aid Dr. Jennifer HORNER
36 Director of Career Services Mr. Clifford MARRETT
29 Director of Alumni Affairs Mr. Michael STENKO
06 Registrar Ms. Jennifer HUOPPI
19 Director of Public Safety Mr. Jeffrey A. GAREWSKI
39 Director Housing/Residence Life Mr. Lamar COLEMAN
40 Director of Bookstore Ms. Allyson HALL
42 Director of Campus Ministry Rev. Laurence LAPOINTE
18 Dir of Facilities Mgmt/Planning Ms. Renee KEECH
26 Director University Relations Mr. Edward H. OSBORN
49 Dean of Arts & Sciences Dr. Carmen R. CID
51 Assoc Dean Continuing Education Dr. Indira PETOSKEY
58 Dean Educ/Prof Studies/Grad Pgm Dr. Jacob EASLEY
96 Assoc Dir Fiscal Affs/Acquisition Ms. Terry O'BRIEN
38 Director Counseling/Psych Svcs Vacant
15 Int Vice Pres for Human Resources Mr. Steven WEINBERGER
07 Director of Admissions Mr. Christopher DORSEY

*Southern Connecticut State University (F)

501 Crescent Street, New Haven CT 06515-0901

County: New Haven FICE Identification: 001406
Unit ID: 130493
Telephone: (203) 392-7278 Carnegie Class: Master's L
FAX Number: N/A Calendar System: Semester
URL: www.southernct.edu
Established: 1893 Annual Undergrad Tuition & Fees (In-State): $9,600
Enrollment: 10,825 Coed
Affiliation or Control: State IRS Status: 501(c)3
Highest Offering: Doctorate
Program: Liberal Arts And General; Teacher Preparatory; Professional
Accreditation: EH, CAATE, CACREP, CS, EXSC, MFCD, NURSE, PH, SP, SW, TED

02 President Dr. Mary A. PAPAZIAN
04 Admin Assistant to the President Ms. Beth Ann H. JOHNSON
100 Chief of Staff Ms. Jaye BAILEY
05 Provost/Vice Pres Acad Affairs Dr. Bette BERGERON
10 EVP for Finance & Administration Mr. Mark ROZEWSKI
32 Vice Pres Student Affairs Dr. Tracy TYREE
30 Vice President Inst Advancement Mr. Robert L. STAMP
84 Assoc VP for Enrollment Management Dr. Terricita E. SASS
15 Chief Human Resources Officer Ms. Diane MAZZA
20 Associate VP for Academic Affairs Vacant
18 Assoc VP Capitol Budgeting/Fac Ops Mr. Robert G. SHEELEY
13 Chief Info Tech Officer Dr. Robert RENNIE
49 Dean School Arts & Sciences Mr. Steven BREESE
50 Dean School of Business Dr. Ellen DURNIN
53 Dean School Education Dr. Stephen HEGEDUS
58 Dean School Graduate Studies Dr. Gregory PAVEZA
70 Interim Dean School Health/Human Sv Dr. Sandra BULMER
41 Director of Athletics Mr. Jay MORAN
26 Director of Public Affairs Mr. Patrick DILGER
29 Director Alumni Affairs Ms. Michelle JOHNSTON
07 Director Admissions Ms. Alexis HAAKONSEN
06 Registrar Ms. Siham DOUGHMAN
08 Director of Library Services Dr. Christina BAUM
91 Director Computer Svcs/Admin Vacant
19 Director of Public Safety Mr. Joseph M. DOOLEY
25 Director of Sponsored Research Ms. Patricia M. ZIBLUK
37 Director of Financial Aid Ms. Gloria LEE
23 Director of Health Services Dr. Diane S. MORGENTHALER
35 Dean of Student Affairs Dr. Jules TETREAULT
46 AVP for Institutional Effectiveness Dr. Richard RICCARDI
38 Director of Counseling Services Dr. Jeffrey VANLONE
21 University Controller Ms. Lise M. BRULE
92 Director of Honors Program Dr. Terese GEMME
94 Director of Women's Studies Dr. Yi-Chun Tricia LIN
88 Dir of Academic & Career Advising Mr. Frank LADORE
39 Director of Residence Life Mr. Robert C. DEMEZZO

*Western Connecticut State University (G)

181 White Street, Danbury CT 06810-6885

County: Fairfield FICE Identification: 001380
Unit ID: 130776
Telephone: (203) 837-8200 Carnegie Class: Master's M
FAX Number: (203) 837-8276 Calendar System: Semester
URL: www.wcsu.edu
Established: 1903 Annual Undergrad Tuition & Fees (In-State): $9,516
Enrollment: 5,952 Coed
Affiliation or Control: State IRS Status: 501(c)3
Highest Offering: Doctorate
Program: Liberal Arts And General; Teacher Preparatory; Professional
Accreditation: EH, CACREP, MUS, NURSE, SW, TED

02 President Dr. John B. CLARK
05 Provost/Vice Pres Academic Affairs Dr. Jane MCBRIDE GATES
10 Assoc VP Finance & Administration Mr. Sean LOUGHRAN
30 VP Inst Advancement Mr. Robert A. SCHLESINGER
32 Vice Pres Student Affs/Ext Affs Dr. Keith BETTS
88 Int Dean of Visual/Performing Arts Mr. Jamie BEGIAN
35 Dean of Student Affairs Dr. Walter CRAMER
49 Dean of Macricostas Arts & Sciences Dr. Mary STEWART ALEXANDER
50 Dean of Ancell Business Dr. David MARTIN
107 Dean of Professional Studies Dr. Jess HOUSE
15 Assoc VP Human Resources Mr. Frederic W. CRATTY
13 Chief Information Officer Mr. Thomas DECHIARO
21 Director Fiscal Affairs/Controller Mr. Peter ROSA
44 Director of Development Ms. Lynne LEBARRON
22 Ex Asst to Pres/Chief Diversity Ofc Ms. Carolyn LANIER
06 Registrar Mr. Keith R. GAUVIN
08 Director of Library Services Ms. Veronica KENAUSIS
09 Director Inst Research/Assessment Dr. Jerry WILCOX
25 Director of Grant/Programs Ms. Gabrielle E. JAZWIECKI
38 Director of Counseling Svcs Dr. Rée GUNTER
37 Director of Financial Services Ms. Melissa STEPHENS
36 Director Career Development Center Ms. Maureen C. GERNERT
26 Director University Relations Mr. Paul STEINMETZ
39 Director Housing & Residence Life Mr. Ron MASON
35 Director Student Life Dr. Paul M. SIMON
41 Director of Athletics Mr. Edward FARRINGTON
29 Int Director of Alumni Affairs Mr. Thomas CURCITTI
07 Director of Admissions Mr. Jay MURRAY
45 Dir of Facilities Plng & Engr Mr. Peter VISENTIN
11 Director of Administrative Services Mr. Mark R. CASE
18 Assoc VP Facilities Mr. Luigi MARCONE
88 Dir Facil Utilization & Promotion Mr. John MURPHY
21 Director of Fin Planning & Budgets Ms. Mary Ann DEASE
27 Int Assoc Dir of Public Relations Ms. Sherri HILL
88 Police Captain Mr. Roger CONNOR
04 Administrative Asst to President Ms. Janet MCKAY
84 Assoc VP Enrollment Services Mr. Charles SPIRIDON

*Asnuntuck Community College (H)

170 Elm Street, Enfield CT 06082-3800

County: Hartford FICE Identification: 011150
Unit ID: 128577
Telephone: (860) 253-3000 Carnegie Class: Assoc/Pub-S-SC
FAX Number: (860) 253-3014 Calendar System: Semester
URL: www.asnuntuck.edu
Established: 1972 Annual Undergrad Tuition & Fees (In-State): $4,072
Enrollment: 1,603 Coed
Affiliation or Control: State IRS Status: 501(c)3
Highest Offering: Associate Degree

Program: Occupational; 2-Year Principally Bachelor's Creditable
Accreditation: EH

02 President .... Mr. James P. LOMBELLA
05 Dean of Academic Affairs .... Mr. Michael STEFANOWICZ
10 Dean of Administration .... Vacant
32 Dean Student Services .... Ms. Kathleen KELLEY
15 Director of Human Resources .... Mr. Joe BLEICHER
84 Director of Enrollment Management .... Mr. Tim ST. JAMES
06 Registrar .... Ms. Diane CLOKEY
37 Director of Financial Aid .... Mr. Gennaro DEANGELIS
09 Director Institutional Research .... Ms. Qing L. MACK
30 Director Institutional Advancement .... Mr. Keith MADORE
103 Dean Workforce Dev/Cont Educ .... Ms. Eileen PELTIER
18 Bldg Superintendent II/Phys Plant .... Mr. Joseph MULLER
26 Dir of Marketing/Business/Industry .... Mr. Gary CARRA
04 Executive Asst to President .... Ms. Susan L. BEAUDOIN

*Capital Community College (A)

950 Main Street, Hartford CT 06103-1207
County: Hartford FICE Identification: 007635
Unit ID: 129367
Telephone: (860) 906-5000 Carnegie Class: Assoc/Pub-U-SC
FAX Number: (860) 520-7906 Calendar System: Semester
URL: www.ccc.commnet.edu
Established: 1967 Annual Undergrad Tuition & Fees (In-State): $4,100
Enrollment: 4,083 Coed
Affiliation or Control: State IRS Status: 501(c)3
Highest Offering: Associate Degree
Program: Occupational; 2-Year Principally Bachelor's Creditable; Business Emphasis
Accreditation: EH, ADNUR, EMT, MAC, RAD

02 President .... Dr. Wilfredo NIEVES
05 Academic Dean .... Dr. Debbie THOMAS
32 Dean of Student Services .... Ms. Doris B. ARRINGTON
11 Dean of Administration .... Mr. Lester PRIMUS
51 Dean Continuing Educ/Community Svcs .... Ms. Linda GUZZO
09 Director of Institutional Research .... Ms. Jenny WANG
10 Director Finance/Administration .... Mr. Ted HALE
06 Registrar .... Mr. Argelio MARRERO
08 Director of Library Services .... Ms. Elaine IPPOLITO
07 Director of Admissions .... Mr. Gregg GORNEAULT
37 Director of Financial Aid .... Ms. Margaret MALASPINA
13 Director of Computer Services .... Mr. Roger FERRARO
66 Dir Cont Educ Nurse/Allied Health .... Ms. Ruth KREMS
36 Dir of Career Planning/Development .... Ms. Linda DOMENITZ
26 Director of Information/Marketing .... Ms. Jane BRONFMAN
15 Director of Human Resources .... Ms. Josephine AGNELLO-VELEY
20 Associate Academic Officer .... Mr. C. Raymond HUGHES
30 Director Institutional Advancement .... Mr. John MCNAMARA

*Gateway Community College (B)

20 Church St., New Haven CT 06510-5970
County: New Haven FICE Identification: 008037
Unit ID: 130396
Telephone: (203) 285-2000 Carnegie Class: Assoc/Pub-U-MC
FAX Number: (203) 285-2018 Calendar System: Semester
URL: www.gwcc.commnet.edu
Established: 1968 Annual Undergrad Tuition & Fees (In-State): $12,096
Enrollment: 11,207 Coed
Affiliation or Control: State IRS Status: 501(c)3
Highest Offering: Associate Degree
Program: Occupational; 2-Year Principally Bachelor's Creditable
Accreditation: EH, ADNUR, DIETT, NMT, RAD, RTT

02 President .... Dr. Dorsey L. KENDRICK
11 Dean of Administrative Services .... Mr. Louis S. D'ANTONIO
46 Dean of Research & Development .... Ms. Mary Ellen CODY
05 Dean of Academics .... Dr. Mark KOSINSKI
31 Dean Community Services .... Ms. Victoria BOZZUTO
15 Director Personnel/Contract Admin .... Ms. Lucille BROWN
04 Executive Assistant to President .... Vacant
09 Director Institutional Research .... Dr. Vincent P. TONG
26 Director Public Info & Marketing .... Ms. Evelyn GARD
10 Director Finance & Admin Svcs .... Ms. Jill MCDOWELL
30 Director Institutional Advancement .... Vacant
08 Director Library .... Ms. Clara OGBAA
84 Director of Enrollment Management .... Mr. Joseph CARBERRY
36 Director Career Development Center ..... Ms. Kellie BYRD-DANSO
37 Director Financial Aid .... Mr. Raymond ZEEK
38 Director Student Counseling .... Mr. Michael BUCCILLI
32 Director of College Life .... Ms. Roberta PRIOR
24 Director Educational Technologies .... Ms. Wendy SAMBERG
25 Grants Facilitator .... Vacant
13 Director Computer Services .... Mr. Lawrence SALAY
24 Director Early Learning Center .... Ms. Marjorie WEINER
88 Coord Center for Education Svcs .... Ms. Clara MENA
50 Chair Business Department .... Mr. Richard REES
79 Chair Humanities Department .... Mr. Chester H. SCHNEPF
83 Chair Social Sciences Department .... Ms. Susan LONGSTON
88 Coord Early Childhood Education .... Ms. Carmelita E. VALENCIA-DAYE
88 Coord Drug/Alcohol Rehab Counseling .... Mr. Jonah COHEN
67 Coordinator Pharmacy Tech Program ...... Ms. Louise A. PETROKA
81 Chair Math/Natural Sci Department .... Mr. Rocky TREMBLAY
50 Director Business & Industry Svcs .... Mr. John VINCZE
88 Director Dietetic Technician Pgm .... Ms. Elaine LICKTIEG
76 Director Allied Health .... Ms. Sheila SOLERNOU
20 Associate Dean of Learning .... Vacant
54 Dir Engineering/Applied Technology .... Mr. Eric F. FLYNN

18 Chief Facilities/Physical Plant .... Mr. Lucian SIMONE
06 Registrar .... Ms. Maribel LOPEZ

*Housatonic Community College (C)

900 Lafayette Boulevard, Bridgeport CT 06604-4704
County: Fairfield FICE Identification: 004513
Unit ID: 129543
Telephone: (203) 332-5000 Carnegie Class: Assoc/Pub-R-M
FAX Number: (203) 332-5123 Calendar System: Semester
URL: www.housatonic.edu
Established: 1966 Annual Undergrad Tuition & Fees (In-State): $4,052
Enrollment: 5,286 Coed
Affiliation or Control: State IRS Status: 501(c)3
Highest Offering: Associate Degree
Program: Occupational; 2-Year Principally Bachelor's Creditable
Accreditation: EH, OTA

02 President .... Dr. Paul BROADIE, II
05 Acting Academic Dean .... Dr. William Terry BROWN
11 Dean of Administration .... Mr. Ralph TYLER
32 Acting Dean of Students .... Mr. James D. CONNOLLY
20 Associate Dean Academics .... Vacant
88 Dean of Outreach Services .... Ms. Denise BUKOVAN
06 Registrar .... Mr. James CONNOLLY
07 Director of Admissions .... Mr. Earl GRAHAM
08 Librarian .... Ms. Shelly STROHM
37 Director of Financial Aid .... Ms. Barbara SUROWIEC
26 Public Relations Associate .... Vacant
19 Director of Security .... Mr. Christopher GOUGH
09 Director Institutional Research .... Ms. Jan SCHAEFFLER
13 Director of Computer Services .... Mr. Anthony VITOLA
15 Director Personnel/Labor Relations .... Ms. Theresa EISENBACH
30 Director University Advancement .... Mr. Chris CAROLLO
35 Director of Student Life .... Ms. Kelly HOPE
10 Director of Finance/Admin Svcs .... Ms. Teresa ORAVETZ
18 Coordinator of Facilities .... Mr. Richard HENNESSEY
04 Administrative Asst to President .... Ms. Camilla COSTANTINI
38 Director Student Counseling .... Mr. Hernan YEPES

*Manchester Community College (D)

PO Box 1046, Great Path, Manchester CT 06045-1046
County: Hartford FICE Identification: 001392
Unit ID: 129695
Telephone: (860) 512-3000 Carnegie Class: Assoc/Pub-S-SC
FAX Number: (860) 512-3631 Calendar System: Semester
URL: www.manchestercc.edu
Established: 1963 Annual Undergrad Tuition & Fees (In-State): $4,052
Enrollment: 7,300 Coed
Affiliation or Control: State IRS Status: 501(c)3
Highest Offering: Associate Degree
Program: Occupational; 2-Year Principally Bachelor's Creditable
Accreditation: EH, ACFEI, COARC, OTA, RAD, RTT, SURGT

02 President .... Dr. Gena GLICKMAN
05 Provost/Chief Academic Officer .... Dr. Sandra PALMER
32 Dean of Student Affairs .... Dr. G. Duncan HARRIS
11 Dean of Administrative Affairs .... Mr. James MCDOWELL
30 Dean of Advancement .... Ms. Endia DECORDOVA
51 Dean of Continuing Education .... Ms. Melanie HABER
20 Associate Dean of Academic Affairs .... Dr. Pamela MITCHELL-CRUMP
10 Director Finance & Admin Services .... Ms. Regina FERRANTE
07 Assoc Director of Admissions .... Ms. Cynthia ZELDNER
06 Registrar .... Ms. Anita SPARROW
08 Dir Library Svcs/Educational Tech .... Ms. Deborah HERMAN
13 Director of Information Technology .... Mr. Barry GRANT
09 Director Plng/Research & Assessment .... Mr. David NIELSEN
15 Interim Director of Human Resources .... Ms. Patricia LINDO
18 Dir Facilities Management/ Planning .... Ms. Darlene MANCINI-BROWN
26 Dir Marketing and Public Relations .... Ms. Charlene TAPPAN
37 Director of Financial Aid .... Ms. Ivette RIVERA-DREYER
72 Director Business/Engineering/Tech .... Ms. Catherine SEAVER
83 Director Social Science/Hospitality .... Dr. Christopher PAULIN
81 Dir Math/Science/Health Careers .... Ms. Marcia JEHNINGS
79 Interim Director of Liberal Arts .... Dr. Deborah SIMMONS
35 Director of Student Life .... Mr. Trent J. BARBER
44 Development Associate .... Ms. Diana REID
38 Dir Counseling and Career Svcs .... Ms. Julia GREENE
84 Director of Enrollment Management .... Mr. Peter HARRIS
04 Executive Assistant to President .... Ms. Sara VINCENT
103 Director of Business & Industry .... Ms. Janet ALAMPI
90 Director of Academic Support Ctr .... Mr. Brian CLEARY
85 Dir Multicultural/Intl Affairs .... Mr. Joseph MESQUITA
28 Director of Diversity .... Ms. Leah GLENDE
96 Assoc Director of Purchasing .... Mr. Paul MOUNDS

*Middlesex Community College (E)

100 Training Hill Road, Middletown CT 06457-4889
County: Middlesex FICE Identification: 008038
Unit ID: 129756
Telephone: (860) 343-5800 Carnegie Class: Assoc/Pub-S-SC
FAX Number: (860) 344-7488 Calendar System: Semester
URL: www.mxcc.commnet.edu
Established: 1966 Annual Undergrad Tuition & Fees (In-State): $4,072
Enrollment: 3,014 Coed
Affiliation or Control: State IRS Status: 501(c)3
Highest Offering: Associate Degree
Program: Occupational; 2-Year Principally Bachelor's Creditable

Accreditation: EH, OPD, RAD

02 President .... Dr. Anna WASESCHA
05 Dean of Academics .... Dr. Steven MINKLER
11 Interim Dean of Administration .... Ms. Kimberly HOGAN
32 Dean of Students .... Dr. Adrienne MASLIN
51 Dean Continuing Education .... Vacant
06 Registrar .... Ms. Susan SALOWITZ
08 Director Library Services .... Ms. Lan LIU
37 Director Financial Aid .... Ms. Irene MARTIN
30 Associate Dean of Development .... Vacant
07 Director of Admissions .... Ms. Gail BARRETT
09 Director of Institutional Research .... Dr. Paul CARMICHAEL
13 Director Information Technology .... Ms. Annie SCOTT
18 Chief Facilities/Physical Plant .... Mr. Steven CHESTER
103 Director of Business & Industry .... Vacant
15 Director Personnel Services .... Ms. Mary Lou PHILLIPS
88 Retention Specialist .... Ms. Judy MAZGULSKI
88 Disability Services Coordinator .... Ms. Hilary PHELPS
26 Chief Public Relations Officer .... Vacant
81 Division Director Math .... Vacant
79 Division Director Humanities .... Mr. Jaime FLORES

*Naugatuck Valley Community College (F)

750 Chase Parkway, Waterbury CT 06708-3089
County: New Haven FICE Identification: 006982
Unit ID: 129729
Telephone: (203) 575-8044 Carnegie Class: Assoc/Pub-R-L
FAX Number: (203) 575-8096 Calendar System: Semester
URL: www.nv.edu
Established: 1964 Annual Undergrad Tuition & Fees (In-State): $4,072
Enrollment: 7,110 Coed
Affiliation or Control: State IRS Status: 501(c)3
Highest Offering: Associate Degree
Program: Occupational; 2-Year Principally Bachelor's Creditable
Accreditation: EH, ADNUR, COARC, ENGT, PTAA, RAD

02 President .... Dr. Daisy Cocco DE FILIPPIS
05 Provost/Senior Dean Administration .... Mr. James TROUP
31 Director of Community Development .... Ms. Gina MARCANTONIO
32 Dean of Student Services .... Ms. Sarah GAGER
30 Dean of Community Engagement .... Mr. Waldemar KOSTRZEWA
13 Assoc Dean Information Technology .... Mr. Conal LARKIN
20 Dean of Academic Affairs .... Ms. Irene RIOS-KNAUF
06 Registrar .... Ms. Joan ARBUSTO
37 Director of Financial Aid .... Ms. Catherine HARDY
07 Director of Admissions .... Ms. Linda STANGO
22 Affirmative Action Officer .... Mr. Ron CLYMER
08 Director Learning Resource Ctr .... Ms. Jamie HAMMOND
10 Director of Finance/Admin Services .... Ms. Lisa PALEN
35 Director of Student Activities .... Ms. Karen BLAKE
18 Chief Facilities/Physical Plant .... Mr. Robert DIVJAK
09 Int Dir of Institutional Research .... Ms. Lisa RODRIGUES-DOOLABH
38 Director Student Development Svcs .... Mr. Bernd MATTHEIS
15 Director of Human Resources .... Ms. Kimberly CAROLINA
26 Director of Marketing .... Ms. Sydney VOGHEL-OCHS
27 Public Relations Associate .... Mr. Aaron KUPEC

*Northwestern Connecticut Community-Technical College (G)

Park Place E, Winsted CT 06098-1798
County: Litchfield FICE Identification: 001398
Unit ID: 130040
Telephone: (860) 738-6300 Carnegie Class: Assoc/Pub-S-SC
FAX Number: (860) 738-6488 Calendar System: Semester
URL: www.nwctc.commnet.edu
Established: 1965 Annual Undergrad Tuition & Fees (In-State): $3,942
Enrollment: 1,550 Coed
Affiliation or Control: State IRS Status: 501(c)3
Highest Offering: Associate Degree
Program: Occupational; 2-Year Principally Bachelor's Creditable
Accreditation: EH, ADNUR, MAC

02 President .... Dr. Barbara DOUGLASS
11 Dean of Administration .... Dr. Steven R. FRAZIER
05 Dean of Academic & Student Affairs .... Dr. Patricia A. BOUFFARD
07 Director of Admissions .... Ms. Joanne NARDI
08 Director of Library Services .... Mr. James PATTERSON
06 Registrar .... Ms. Debra REYNOLDS
15 Director of Human Resources .... Vacant
37 Financial Aid Officer .... Mr. Louis BRISTOL
13 Director of Computer Services .... Mr. Joseph DANAJOVITS
38 Dir of Student Development .... Ms. Ruth GONZALEZ
09 Director of Institutional Research ... Ms. Caitlin BOGER-HAWKINS
26 Director Marketing/Public Relations .... Mr. Grantley ADAMS
10 Director Financial/Admin Services .... Ms. Kimberly DRAGAN

*Norwalk Community College (H)

188 Richards Avenue, Norwalk CT 06854-1655
County: Fairfield FICE Identification: 001399
Unit ID: 130004
Telephone: (203) 857-7000 Carnegie Class: Assoc/Pub-R-L
FAX Number: (203) 857-7287 Calendar System: Semester
URL: www.norwalk.edu
Established: 1961 Annual Undergrad Tuition & Fees (In-State): $4,052
Enrollment: 6,482 Coed
Affiliation or Control: State IRS Status: 501(c)3
Highest Offering: Associate Degree

Program: Occupational; 2-Year Principally Bachelor's Creditable
Accreditation: EH, ADNUR, COARC, MAC, PTAA

02 President Dr. David L. LEVINSON
11 Dean of Administration Dr. Rose R. ELLIS
32 Dean of Students Vacant
09 Interim Dean of Academics Dr. Vanessa MOREST
30 Executive Director of Development Ms. Ann ROGERS
51 Director of Continuing Education Vacant
08 Director of Library Services Ms. Linda LERMAN
37 Financial Aid Officer Vacant
66 Int Director of Nursing Education Ms. Katherine FRIES
06 Registrar Ms. Danita BROWN
15 Director Human Resources Ms. Therese MARROCCO
26 Director of Public Relations Ms. Madeline K. BARILLO
38 Director Student Counseling Ms. Catherine MILLER
07 Acting Director of Admissions Mr. William CHAGNON
10 Director Finance/Administration Ms. Carrie MCGEE-YUROF
18 Chief Facilities/Physical Plant Mr. Anthony (Tony) CENTOPANTI

*Quinebaug Valley Community College (A)

742 Upper Maple Street, Danielson CT 06239-1440
County: Windham FICE Identification: 010530
Unit ID: 130217
Telephone: (860) 932-4000 Carnegie Class: Assoc/Pub-R-M
FAX Number: (860) 932-4306 Calendar System: Semester
URL: www.qvcc.commnet.edu
Established: 1971 Annual Undergrad Tuition & Fees (In-State): $4,062
Enrollment: 1,824 Coed
Affiliation or Control: State IRS Status: 501(c)3
Highest Offering: Associate Degree
Program: Occupational; 2-Year Principally Bachelor's Creditable
Accreditation: EH, MAC

02 President Dr. Carlee DRUMMER
05 Dean Academic Affs & Student Svcs Mr. Alfred WILLIAMS
11 Dean of Administrative Services Mr. Paul MARTLAND
08 Director of Library Services Ms. Sharon MOORE
37 Director of Student Financial Aid Ms. Kim RICH
09 Director of Institutional Research Dr. Donna SOHAN
10 Dir Finance/Administrative Svcs Ms. Kathleen CRAIG
18 Chief Facilities/Physical Plant Mr. David STIFEL
26 Chief Public Relations Officer Ms. Susan BREAULT
30 Dir of Institutional Advancement Ms. Monique WOLANIN
06 Registrar Ms. Amy KACERIK
27 Coordinator of Marketing Ms. Margie HUOPPI
07 Associate Director of Admissions Ms. Sarah HENDRICK

*Three Rivers Community College (B)

574 New London Turnpike, Norwich CT 06360
County: New London FICE Identification: 009765
Unit ID: 129808
Telephone: (860) 215-9000 Carnegie Class: Assoc/Pub-R-M
FAX Number: (860) 215-9901 Calendar System: Semester
URL: www.trcc.commnet.edu
Established: 1963 Annual Undergrad Tuition & Fees (In-State): $3,866
Enrollment: 4,530 Coed
Affiliation or Control: State IRS Status: 501(c)3
Highest Offering: Associate Degree
Program: Occupational; 2-Year Principally Bachelor's Creditable
Accreditation: EH, ACBSP, ADNUR, ENGT

02 President Dr. Mary Ellen JUKOSKI
05 Academic Dean Dr. Ann Z. BRANCHINI
11 Dean of Administration Mr. Michael LOPEZ
32 Dn Student Svcs/Enrol Mgt/Wrkf Dev Mr. Steve FINTON
13 Dean Admin Svcs Inform Technology Mr. Stephen GOETCHIUS
30 Dir Institutional Advancement Ms. Betty BAILLARGEON
06 Interim Registrar Ms. Betty WILLIAMSON
38 Director of Counseling Mrs. Jacqueline PHILLIPS
08 Director Learning Resources Ms. Mildred HODGE
15 Director Human Resources Ms. Louise J. SUMMA
37 Actg Dir Student Financial Aid Mr. Kenneth BRIGGS
18 Director of Facilities Mr. Arnie DE LA ROSSA
09 Office of Institutional Research Ms. Laura QIN
26 Public Relations Associate Ms. Tracy ROSIENE

*Tunxis Community College (C)

271 Scott Swamp Road, Farmington CT 06032-3187
County: Hartford FICE Identification: 009764
Unit ID: 130606
Telephone: (860) 255-3500 Carnegie Class: Assoc/Pub-S-SC
FAX Number: N/A Calendar System: Semester
URL: www.tunxis.edu/
Established: 1969 Annual Undergrad Tuition & Fees (In-State): $3,866
Enrollment: 4,193 Coed
Affiliation or Control: State IRS Status: 501(c)3
Highest Offering: Associate Degree
Program: Occupational; 2-Year Principally Bachelor's Creditable
Accreditation: EH, ACBSP, DA, DH

02 President Dr. Cathryn L. ADDY
05 Dean of Academic Affairs Dr. Michael ROOKE
32 Dean of Student Affairs Dr. Kirk PETERS
103 Dean of Workforce Development Mr. David ENGLAND
11 Dean of Administration Mr. Charles CLEARY
45 Dean of Institutional Effectiveness Dr. David C. ENGLAND
10 Dir Finance/Administrative Services Ms. Nancy ESCHENBRENNER
30 Dir of Institutional Advancement Ms. Leigh E. KNOPF
15 Director Human Resources Ms. Pamela KOWAR
08 Director Library Services Dr. Lisa LAVOIE
13 Director Information Technology Mr. Robert WAHL
07 Director of Admissions Ms. Tamika DAVIS
06 Registrar Ms. Susan WINN
35 Director Academic Support Center Ms. Kathleen SCHWAGER
09 Director of Institutional Research Vacant
37 Director Financial Aid Services Mr. David WELSH
18 Director of Facilities Mr. John LODOVICO
90 Coord Academic Info Technology Mr. Steven MEAD
91 Coord Admin Information Technology Mrs. Mary Ann DIORIO
26 Public Relations Associate Ms. Melissa LAMAR

Connecticut College (D)

270 Mohegan Avenue, New London CT 06320-4125
County: New London FICE Identification: 001379
Unit ID: 128902
Telephone: (860) 447-1911 Carnegie Class: Bac/A&S
FAX Number: (860) 439-2700 Calendar System: Semester
URL: www.conncoll.edu
Established: 1911 Annual Undergrad Tuition & Fees: $49,350
Enrollment: 1,900 Coed
Affiliation or Control: Independent Non-Profit IRS Status: 501(c)3
Highest Offering: Master's
Program: Liberal Arts And General; Teacher Preparatory
Accreditation: EH

01 President Ms. Katherine BERGERON
05 Dean of the Faculty Ms. Abigail A. VANSLYCK
10 Vice President for Finance Mr. Paul L. MARONI
30 Vice President College Advancement Ms. Ann GOODWIN
08 Vice Pres of Info Svcs/Librarian Dr. W. Lee HISLE
11 Vice President for Administration Mr. Ulyssess B. HAMMOND
26 VP College Communications Ms. Pamela DUMAS-SERFES
07 VP of Admission & Financial Aid Mr. Andrew STRICKLER
15 Asst VP HR/Professional Development Ms. Cheryl L. MILLER
20 Dean of the College Jefferson SINGER
32 Dean of Student Life Dr. Victor J. ARCELUS
28 Dean of Multicultural Affairs Vacant
20 Associate Dean of Faculty Prof. Jeffrey COLE
06 Registrar Ms. Elisabeth S. LABRIOLA
09 Director of Institutional Research Dr. John D. NUGENT
21 Controller Ms. Amanda B. MAYFIELD
37 Director of Financial Aid Mr. Sean MARTIN
41 Director of Athletics Mr. Francis SHIELDS
29 Director of Alumni Relations Ms. Bridget MCSHANE
38 Director Student Counseling Dr. Janet D. SPOLTORE
84 Director Enrollment Management Vacant
18 Chief Facilities/Physical Plant Mr. James NORTON
96 Director of Purchasing Mr. Steven M. JAGIELO
88 Secretary of the College Ms. Bonnie WELLS

Fairfield University (E)

1073 N Benson Road, Fairfield CT 06824-5195
County: Fairfield FICE Identification: 001385
Unit ID: 129242
Telephone: (203) 254-4000 Carnegie Class: Master's L
FAX Number: (203) 254-4101 Calendar System: Semester
URL: www.fairfield.edu
Established: 1942 Annual Undergrad Tuition & Fees: $44,875
Enrollment: 4,949 Coed
Affiliation or Control: Roman Catholic IRS Status: 501(c)3
Highest Offering: Doctorate
Program: 2-Year Principally Bachelor's Creditable; Liberal Arts And General; Teacher Preparatory; Professional; Business Emphasis
Accreditation: EH, ANEST, BUS, CACREP, ENG, MFCD, NURSE, TED

01 President Rev. Jeffrey P. VON ARX, SJ
42 Univ Chaplain/Special Asst to Pres Rev. Charles H. ALLEN, SJ
03 Exec VP & Chief Operating Officer Mr. Kevin P. LAWLOR
05 Provost/Sr Vice Pres Academic Affs Ms. Lynn BABINGTON
100 Exec Asst to Pres/Chief of Staff Mr. Michael TORTORA
10 Vice Pres Finance/Treasurer/CFO Mr. Michael TRAFECANTE
30 Vice Pres Univ Advancement Mr. Wally HALAS
15 Vice President of Human Resources Mr. Scott ESPOSITO
32 Sr Vice President Student Affairs Dr. Thomas C. PELLEGRINO
88 Vice Pres for Mission and Identity Dr. Nancy DALLAVALLE
27 AVP Marketing and Communications Ms. Jennifer ANDERSON
20 Assoc Vice Pres Academic Affairs Dr. Mary Frances MALONE
20 Assoc Vice Pres Academic Affairs Dr. Christine SIEGEL
18 Assoc Vice Pres Facilities Mgmt Mr. David W. FRASSINELLI
38 Asst Vice Pres/Dir Counseling Svcs Dr. Susan N. BIRGE
21 Asst VP of Finance/Controller Mr. Kenneth FONTAINE
35 Asst Vice Pres Student Affairs Mr. James D. FITZPATRICK
09 Dir Institutional Research/Plng Ms. Amy BOCZER
84 AVP Ugrad/Grad/CS Admiss/Dean Enr Ms. Karen A. PELLEGRINO
07 Director of Graduate Admission Ms. Marianne L. GUMPPER
06 University Registrar Mr. Robert C. RUSSO
13 Chief Information Officer Ms. Paige FRANCIS
37 Director of Financial Aid Ms. Diana M. DRAPER
36 Director of Career Planning Center Ms. Cathleen M. BORGMAN
29 Asst Vice Pres of Alumni Relations Ms. Janet A. CANEPA
42 Director of Campus Ministry Rev. Mark SCALESE
19 Director of Public Safety Mr. Todd A. PELAZZA
41 Director of Athletics Mr. Eugene P. DORIS
49 Dean College Arts & Science Dr. Yohuru WILLLIAMS
50 Dean Charles F Dolan Sch of Bus Dr. Donald E. GIBSON
54 Dean School of Engineering Dr. Bruce BERDANIER
66 Dean School of Nursing Dr. Meredith W. KAZER
53 Dean Grad Sch Educ/Allied Prof Dr. Robert HANNAFIN
35 AVP Student Affs/Dean of Students Ms. Karen A. DONOGHUE
88 Dir of Conference/Event Management Mr. Matthew A. DINNAN
28 Assoc Dn Stdnts/Dir Stdnt Div Pgm Mr. William H. JOHNSON
104 Director of Study Abroad Vacant
92 Director of Honors Program Dr. John E. THIEL
08 Univ Librarian/Dir of Library Svcs Ms. Joan T. OVERFIELD
23 Director of Student Health Center Ms. Julia A. DUFFY
16 Director Human Resources Mr. Mark J. GUGLIELMONI
96 Purchasing Manager Mr. Peter PEREZ

Goodwin College (F)

One Riverside Drive, East Hartford CT 06118-2777
County: Hartford FICE Identification: 022449
Unit ID: 129154
Telephone: (860) 528-4111 Carnegie Class: Assoc/PrivNFP
FAX Number: (860) 291-9550 Calendar System: Semester
URL: www.goodwin.edu
Established: 1999 Annual Undergrad Tuition & Fees: $19,450
Enrollment: 3,440 Coed
Affiliation or Control: Independent Non-Profit IRS Status: 501(c)3
Highest Offering: Baccalaureate
Program: 2-Year Principally Bachelor's Creditable
Accreditation: EH, ADNUR, #COARC, DA, DH, EMT, HT, MAAB, MAC, OTA

01 President Mr. Mark E. SCHEINBERG
03 Executive Vice President/Provost Ms. Ann B. CLARK
05 VP Academic Affs/Dean Faculty Ms. Danielle WILKEN
10 Vice President for Finance/CFO Mr. Jerry D. EMLET
45 Vice Pres for Inst Effectiveness Ms. Janet L. JEFFORD
30 Vice Pres Economic/Strategic Dev Mr. Todd J. ANDREWS
18 Vice Pres Facilities/Technology Mr. Bryant L. HARRELL
84 Vice Pres Enrollment/Mrktg/Comm Mr. Daniel NOONAN
30 Vice President for Advancement Ms. Brooke PENDERS
20 Asst Vice Pres Academic Affairs Ms. Danielle S. WILKEN
13 Asst VP Information Technology Mr. Dan REGO
32 AVP Stdnt Affs/Dean of Students Dr. Sandy WIRTH
09 Asst VP Institutional Effectiveness Dr. Henriette M. PRANGER
08 Director of Library Services Ms. Marilyn L. NOWLAN
88 Asst VP Strategy/Business Devel Dr. Clifford THERMER
88 Dean of Magnet Schools Mr. Alan KRAMER
07 Director of Admissions Mr. Nicholas LENTINO
36 Director of Career Services Mr. Lee HAMEROFF
26 Director of Communications Mr. Phil MOORE
44 Assoc Dir of Developmnt/Annual Fund Ms. Leia BELL
21 Director of Finance & Business Svcs Ms. Sharon N. DADDONA
37 Director of Financial Aid Mr. William MANGINI
09 Dir Inst Research/Educ Assessment Dr. Alan J. STURTZ
106 Director of Online Learning Dr. Mark FAZIOLI
06 Registrar Ms. Allison MISKY
29 Alumni Relations Coordinator Ms. Vanessa PERGOLIZZI
04 Executive Assistant to President Ms. Ann ZAJCHOWSKI
66 Dept Chair/Director Nursing Ms. Janice COSTELLO

Hartford Seminary (G)

77 Sherman Street, Hartford CT 06105-2260
County: Hartford FICE Identification: 001387
Unit ID: 129491
Telephone: (860) 509-9500 Carnegie Class: Spec/Faith
FAX Number: (860) 509-9509 Calendar System: Semester
URL: www.hartsem.edu
Established: 1834 Annual Graduate Tuition & Fees: $12,294
Enrollment: 162 Coed
Affiliation or Control: Independent Non-Profit IRS Status: 501(c)3
Highest Offering: Doctorate; No Undergraduates
Program: Professional; Religious Emphasis
Accreditation: EH, THEOL

01 President Dr. Heidi HADSELL
05 Academic Dean Dr. Uriah KIM
11 Director of Admin and Facilities Ms. Roseann LEZAK JANOW
30 Chief Development Officer Mr. Samuel LOCKE
07 Director of Recruitment/Admissions Ms. Tina DEMO
88 Director Religion Research Inst Dr. Scott THUMMA
88 Director Doctor of Ministry Program Dr. Scott THUMMA
88 Director of Islamic Center Vacant
08 Library Director Dr. Steven BLACKBURN
44 Comm & Development Associate Mr. Patrick BYRNE
10 Chief Business Officer Mr. Michael SANDNER
06 Registrar Ms. Danielle LAVINE
04 Exec Assistant to the President Ms. Heather HOLDA
26 Director of Communications Ms. Susan SCHOENEERGER

Holy Apostles College and Seminary (H)

33 Prospect Hill Road, Cromwell CT 06416-2027
County: Middlesex FICE Identification: 001389
Unit ID: 129534
Telephone: (860) 632-3010 Carnegie Class: Spec/Faith
FAX Number: (860) 632-3030 Calendar System: Semester
URL: www.holyapostles.edu
Established: 1956 Annual Undergrad Tuition & Fees: $10,870
Enrollment: 378 Coed
Affiliation or Control: Roman Catholic IRS Status: 501(c)3
Highest Offering: Beyond Master's But Less Than Doctorate
Program: Liberal Arts And General; Professional

Accreditation: EH

01 President & Rector .... V.Rev. Douglas L. MOSEY
11 Vice President Administration .... Dr. Sebastian MAHFOOD
05 Academic Dean/Chief Academic Ofcr .... Rev. Peter KUCER
32 Director of Student Services .... Mrs. Laura BROWN
10 Chief Financial Officer .... Mr. William RUSSELL
08 Director of Library Services .... Ms. Clare ADAMO
06 Registrar .... Dr. Cynthia TOOLIN

Lincoln College of New England (A)

2279 Mount Vernon Road, Southington CT 06489-1057
County: Hartford FICE Identification: 009407
Unit ID: 128683
Telephone: (860) 628-4751 Carnegie Class: Bac/Assoc
FAX Number: (860) 628-6444 Calendar System: Semester
URL: www.lincolncollegene.edu
Established: 1966 Annual Undergrad Tuition & Fees: $19,940
Enrollment: 715 Coed
Affiliation or Control: Proprietary IRS Status: Proprietary
Highest Offering: Baccalaureate
Program: Occupational; 2-Year Principally Bachelor's Creditable
Accreditation: EH, CAHIIM, DA, DH, DIETT, FUSER, MAC, #OTA

01 President .... Ms. Denise LEWICKI
04 Executive Assistant to President .... Mrs. Barbara PARE
05 VP Academic Affairs .... Dr. Vincent BEACH
11 VP Operations & Student Affairs .... Mr. Spencer MCNIVEN
10 VP of Finance & Admin Services .... Mrs. Denise LEWICKI
36 VP of Career Services .... Mr. Bob MCNAMARA
32 Associate Dean of Student Life .... Mr. Dwayne CAMERON
35 Assoc Dean of Student Services .... Mrs. Cynthia A. CLARK
20 Associate Dean of Academic Affairs .... Mr. Mark ANDERSON
06 Registrar .... Mr. Christopher DISTISO
07 Director of Admissions .... Mr. John ALONSO
08 Director of Library Services .... Mr. Shawn FIELDS
37 Director of Financial Aid .... Mrs. Gina D. SWENTON
09 Director of Institutional Research .... Mr. Jon DALY
19 Director Campus Safety & Security .... Mr. David C. ALLING
41 Athletic Director .... Mr. Preston BEVERLY
13 IT Administrator-Southington .... Mr. Edward D. CONNELLY

Mitchell College (B)

437 Pequot Avenue, New London CT 06320-4498
County: New London FICE Identification: 001393
Unit ID: 129774
Telephone: (860) 701-5000 Carnegie Class: Bac/Diverse
FAX Number: (860) 701-5090 Calendar System: Semester
URL: www.mitchell.edu
Established: 1938 Annual Undergrad Tuition & Fees: $31,000
Enrollment: 778 Coed
Affiliation or Control: Independent Non-Profit IRS Status: 501(c)3
Highest Offering: Baccalaureate
Program: Liberal Arts And General; Teacher Preparatory
Accreditation: EH

01 President .... Ms. Janet STEINMAYER
05 VP Acad Affs/Dean of the College .... Dr. Catherine WRIGHT
10 Vice Pres Administration & Finance .... Ms. Dyann J. BAKER
32 Vice Pres Student Affs/Dean Stdnts .... Mr. Jason EBBELING
41 Director Of Athletics .... Ms. Dana FULMER-GARFIELD
06 Registrar .... Ms. Amy VAN OOT
88 Director of Thames Academy .... Ms. Jacqueline JEWETT
08 Director of Library Services .... Ms. Elizabeth DAVIDSON
15 Director of Human Resources .... Mr. Jonathan HOWELL
13 Director of Academic Technologies .... Mr. Rich WALL
09 Dir Institutional Rsrch & Assesment .... Mr. David HEMENWAY
37 Director of Financial Aid .... Ms. Jacklyn C. STOLTZ
89 Director First Year Experience .... Ms. Jennifer R. WELSH
30 VP Advancement & Communications .... Vacant
36 Director of Career Services .... Ms. Amanda LJUBICIC
96 Purchasing Manager .... Ms. Jill RAKOFF
26 Director Marketing & Communications .... Ms. Kathryn GAFFNEY
39 Director of Residence Life .... Ms. Jamia DANZY
18 Director of Facilities .... Mr. Joseph PARDEE
88 Bursar .... Ms. Leah BRENNAN
07 Director of Admissions .... Mr. Bob MARTIN
04 Executive Assistant to President .... Ms. April HODSON
38 Director Health & Wellness .... Ms. Stacey TORPEY

Paier College of Art (C)

20 Gorham Avenue, Hamden CT 06514-3902
County: New Haven FICE Identification: 007459
Unit ID: 130110
Telephone: (203) 287-3031 Carnegie Class: Spec/Arts
FAX Number: (203) 287-3021 Calendar System: Semester
URL: www.paiercollegeofart.edu
Established: 1946 Annual Undergrad Tuition & Fees: $15,450
Enrollment: 126 Coed
Affiliation or Control: Proprietary IRS Status: Proprietary
Highest Offering: Baccalaureate
Program: Liberal Arts And General
Accreditation: ACCSC

01 President .... Mr. Jonathan E. PAIER
03 Vice President .... Mr. Daniel L. PAIER
05 Dean of the College .... Mr. Francis COOLEY
10 Director Finance .... Mrs. Maureen E. PAIER
57 Director Design/Graphics .... Mr. Peter MISERENDINO
102 Director Foundation/Arts .... Mr. Robert E. ZAPPALORTI
08 Librarian .... Ms. Beth HARRIS
37 Director Student Financial Aid .... Mr. John DE ROSE
32 Director of Student Services .... Mrs. Angela DEROSE
20 Assistant to the Dean .... Ms. Angela DEROSE
88 Director Interior Design .... Mr. Pierre STRAUCH
88 Director Photography .... Mr. Peter BENSON
07 Admissions Secretary .... Ms. Lynn PASCALE

Post University (D)

800 Country Club Road, Waterbury CT 06723-2540
County: New Haven FICE Identification: 001401
Unit ID: 130183
Telephone: (203) 596-4500 Carnegie Class: Bac/Diverse
FAX Number: (203) 756-5810 Calendar System: Semester
URL: www.post.edu
Established: 1890 Annual Undergrad Tuition & Fees: $27,450
Enrollment: 8,638 Coed
Affiliation or Control: Proprietary IRS Status: Proprietary
Highest Offering: Master's
Program: Occupational; 2-Year Principally Bachelor's Creditable; Liberal Arts And General; Professional
Accreditation: EH, ACBSP

00 Chief Executive Officer .... Dr. Thomas SAMPH
01 President .... Dr. Donald W. MROZ
84 Sr VP OEI Enrollment .... Ms. Veronica MONTALVO
05 Provost .... Dr. Jane BAILEY
10 Chief Financial Officer .... Mr. Scott T. ALLEN
15 VP of Human Resources .... Mr. Donald KELLY
06 Interim Registrar .... Mr. Adam CLYMER
41 Director of Athletics .... Mr. Ronnie PALMER
16 Human Resources Director .... Ms. Madelaine KELSEY
08 Library Director .... Ms. Tracy RALSTON
13 Chief Information Officer .... Mr. Michael STATMORE
36 Director Career Services .... Dr. Mary RIGALI
32 Dean of Students .... Ms. Erica PERYGA
40 Campus Store Manager .... Mrs. Frances R. KAMINSKY
19 Director of Campus Safety .... Mr. Robert TANSLEY
38 Director Student Counseling .... Ms. Lisa ANTEL
37 Interim Director Financial Aid .... Ms. Michelle GAMBACINI
27 Chief Marketing Officer .... Mr. David HIGLEY
88 Dir of Military Field Enrollment .... Mr. Charles YOUNG
50 Acting Dean of School of Business . Mr. Christopher SZPRYNGEL
53 Dean of School of Education .... Dr. Bonnie RABE
49 Dean of School of Arts & Sciences .... Dr. Elizabeth JOHNSON
80 Dean John P Burke Sch Pub Service .... Dr. Richard STROMPF
88 Executive Asst to the CEO .... Ms. Melissah KOCHERA
04 Executive Asst to the President .... Ms. Patti JENNINGS
20 Asst Provost Research/Innovation .... Dr. Jill BUBAN

Quinnipiac University (E)

275 Mount Carmel Avenue, Hamden CT 06518-1908
County: New Haven FICE Identification: 001402
Unit ID: 130226
Telephone: (203) 582-8200 Carnegie Class: Master's L
FAX Number: (203) 582-4703 Calendar System: Semester
URL: www.quinnipiac.edu
Established: 1929 Annual Undergrad Tuition & Fees: $42,270
Enrollment: 9,035 Coed
Affiliation or Control: Independent Non-Profit IRS Status: 501(c)3
Highest Offering: First Professional Degree
Program: Liberal Arts And General; Professional
Accreditation: EH, AA, ANEST, ARCPA, BUS, CAATE, CS, LAW, #MED, NURSE, OT, PA, PERF, PTA, RAD, @SW, TED

01 President .... Dr. John L. LAHEY
04 Vice President/Exec Assoc to Pres .... Ms. Jean L. HUSTED
03 Executive Vice President/Provost .... Dr. Mark A. THOMPSON
10 VP Finance/Chief Financial Ofcr .... Mr. Mark VARHOLAK
26 Vice President for Public Affairs .... Ms. Lynn M. BUSHNELL
18 Vice Pres Facilities & Capital Plng .... Mr. Salvatore FILARDI
15 Int VP for Human Resources .... Ms. Jean L. HUSTED
07 Vice Pres for Admissions & Fin Aid .... Ms. Joan I. MOHR
21 Assoc VP Budget & Fin Planning .... Vacant
30 Vice Pres Devel & Alumni Affairs .... Mr. Donald J. WEINBACH
32 Vice President & Dean of Students .... Dr. Monique DRUCKER
05 Vice President of Academic Affairs .... Dr. Paul TIYAMBE ZELEZA
13 VP/Chief Info & Tech Officer .... Mr. Fred E. TARCA
20 Assoc VP of Faculty Affairs .... Vacant
20 Assoc VP Academic & Strategic Plng .... Dr. Annalisa ZINN
27 VP & Chief Digital Comm Officer .... Mr. Keith RHODES
27 Assoc VP for Public Relations .... Mr. John MORGAN
06 Registrar .... Mr. Joshua BERRY
106 VP & COO for QU Online .... Ms. Cynthia GALLATIN
28 AVP Acad Affs/Chief Diversity Ofcr .... Dr. Diane M. ARIZA
35 Assoc VP Student Affairs .... Vacant
35 Assoc VP Student Affairs .... Ms. Cindy LONG PORTER
39 Director of Resident Life .... Ms. Jennifer CRANE
35 Asst Dean & Director Student Center .... Mr. Daniel W. BROWN
23 Dir of Student Health Services .... Ms. Christy CHASE
38 Director of Health & Wellness .... Ms. Kerry PATTON
19 Interim Chief of Public Safety .... Mr. Edgar RODRIGUEZ
08 Director of Arnold Bernhard Library .... Mr. Robert JOVEN
41 Director of Athletics & Recreation .... Mr. Greg AMODIO
40 Campus Store Manager .... Ms. Margaret SAMUL
104 Director for Global Education .... Ms. Andrea HOGAN
21 Assoc VP for Finance/Controller .... Mr. Daniel R. JOHNSON
96 Director of Shared Services ....Ms. Maria BIMONTE-YERGANIAN
109 Assoc VP for Auxiliary Services .... Mr. John MERIANO
29 Sr Dir Parent/Family Development .... Ms. Melinda FORMICA
44 Assoc VP Devel & Alumni Affairs .... Ms. Dianna PATEGAS
37 Assoc VP & Univ Director of Fin Aid .... Mr. Dominic YOIA
108 Dir Academic Assessment & Research .... Vacant
90 Director of Academic Technology .... Ms. Lauren ERARDI
66 Dean School of Nursing .... Dr. Jean LANGE
50 Dean School of Business .... Dr. Matthew L. O'CONNOR
49 Dean College of Arts & Sciences .... Dr. Robert SMART
76 Dean School of Health Sciences .... Dr. William C. KOHLHEPP
61 Dean School of Law .... Ms. Jennifer BROWN
61 Associate Dean School of Law .... Mr. David S. KING
60 Dean School of Communications .... Mr. Lee KAMLET
53 Dean School of Education .... Dr. Kevin BASMADJIAN
63 Dean School of Med & VP Health Affs .... Dr. Bruce KOEPPEN
94 Director of Women's Studies .... Ms. Michele HOFFNUNG

Rensselaer at Hartford (F)

275 Windsor Street, Hartford CT 06120-2991
Telephone: (860) 548-2400 FICE Identification: 002804
Accreditation: &M

† Regional accreditation is carried under the parent institution, Rensselaer Polytechnic Institute, NY.

Sacred Heart University (G)

5151 Park Avenue, Fairfield CT 06825-1000
County: Fairfield FICE Identification: 001403
Unit ID: 130253
Telephone: (203) 371-7999 Carnegie Class: Master's L
FAX Number: (203) 365-7652 Calendar System: Semester
URL: www.sacredheart.edu
Established: 1963 Annual Undergrad Tuition & Fees: $37,170
Enrollment: 7,781 Coed
Affiliation or Control: Independent Non-Profit IRS Status: 501(c)3
Highest Offering: Doctorate
Program: Liberal Arts And General; Teacher Preparatory; Professional
Accreditation: EH, BUS, CAATE, CEA, NURSE, OT, PTA, @SP, SW, TED

01 President .... Dr. John J. PETILLO
11 Sr VP for Finance & Administration .... Mr. Michael J. KINNEY
05 Provost/Vice Pres Academic Affairs .... Dr. Laura NIESEN DE ABRUNA
32 Sr VP Student Affairs & Athletics .... Mr. James M. BARQUINERO
15 Vice President for Human Resources .... Mr. Robert M. HARDY
26 VP Marketing & Communication .... Mr. Michael L. IANNAZZI
88 VP for Mission & Catholic Identity .... Dr. Michael J. HIGGINS
10 Vice President for Finance .... Mr. Philip J. MCCABE
13 VP for Information Tech & Security .... Mr. Michael D. TRIMBLE
30 Vice Pres University Advancement .... Mr. William REIDY
20 Vice Provost for Special Acad Pgms .... Ms. Mary Lou DEROSA
43 University General Counsel .... Mr. Michael D. LAROBINA
49 Dean College of Arts & Sciences .... Mrs. Robin CAUTIN
50 Dean College of Business .... Dr. John CHALYKOFF
76 Dean College of Health Professions .... Dr. Patricia W. WALKER
53 Dean College of Education .... Dr. James C. CARL
66 Dean College of Nursing .... Ms. Mary Alice DONIUS
100 Special Assistant to the President .... Dr. Rupendra PALIWAL
108 Pres University Academic Assessment .... Dr. Beau KJERULF GREER

St. Vincent's College (H)

2800 Main Street, Bridgeport CT 06606-4292
County: Fairfield FICE Identification: 006191
Unit ID: 130448
Telephone: (203) 576-5235 Carnegie Class: Assoc/PrivNFP
FAX Number: (203) 576-5893 Calendar System: Semester
URL: www.stvincentscollege.edu
Established: 1991 Annual Undergrad Tuition & Fees: $17,850
Enrollment: 751 Coed
Affiliation or Control: Independent Non-Profit IRS Status: 501(c)3
Highest Offering: Baccalaureate
Program: Occupational; 2-Year Principally Bachelor's Creditable; Nursing Emphasis
Accreditation: EH, ADNUR, MAC, NUR, RAD

01 Interim President/CEO .... Ms. Anita K. GLINIECKI
10 Chief Financial Officer .... Mr. Christopher GIVEN
32 VP Enrollment Svcs/Dean of Students .. Dr. L. Christie BORONICO
05 VP Academic Affairs/Dean of Faculty .... Dr. Susan CAPASSO
13 Director Information Technology .... Mrs. Anet SURRRUSCO
09 Institutional Researcher .... Mrs. Sandra SHARP
11 Director of Administrative Services .... Mrs. Janice N. FAYE
29 Director Alumni Relations .... Mrs. Sharon BEASLEY
15 Human Resources Officer/Title IX .... Ms. Nancy M. MUSANTE
37 Director of Financial Aid .... Vacant
06 Registrar .... Mr. Vincent B. CATAUDELLA
07 Director of Admissions .... Mr. Joseph MARRONE
51 Director of Continuing Education .... Ms. Tatiana RAMPINO
08 Librarian .... Ms. Vicky JACOBSON
66 Dean of Nursing .... Dr. Karen L. BARNETTT
66 Chair of Nursing-ADN .... Mrs. Margo M. MCCARTHY
66 Chair of Nursing-BSN .... Dr. Sharon MAKOWSKI
88 Chair of Radiography .... Ms. Terry HINE
97 Chair of General Education .... Dr. Susan CAPASSO
88 Chair of Medical Assisting .... Ms. Holly MULRENAN
21 Director Student Accounts .... Mr. Rogen MILLER

Trinity College (A)

300 Summit Street, Hartford CT 06106-3100
County: Hartford FICE Identification: 001414
Unit ID: 130590
Telephone: (860) 297-2000 Carnegie Class: Bac/A&S
FAX Number: (860) 297-2257 Calendar System: Semester
URL: www.trincoll.edu
Established: 1823 Annual Undergrad Tuition & Fees: $50,826
Enrollment: 2,408 Coed
Affiliation or Control: Independent Non-Profit IRS Status: 501(c)3
Highest Offering: Master's
Program: Liberal Arts And General
Accreditation: EH, ENG

01 President .... Dr. Joanne BERGER-SWEENEY
05 Dean of the Faculty/VP Acad Affairs .... Dr. Thomas MITZEL
10 Vice Pres Finance & Ops/Treasurer .... Mr. Paul MUTONE
13 Vice Pres Information Svcs/CIO .... Ms. Suzanne ABER
30 Vice Pres College Advancement .... Mr. Jack FRACASSO
32 Vice Pres Stdnt Affs/Dean Stdnts .... Mr. Joseph DICHRISTINA
84 Vice Pres Enrollment/Stdnt Success .... Dr. Angel B. PEREZ
101 Secretary of the College .... Mrs. MaryJo KEATING
07 Dean Admissions/Financial Aid .... Mr. Larry DOW
20 Associate Academic Dean .... Dr. Sonia CARDENA
20 Associate Academic Dean .... Dr. Melanie STEIN
27 Director of Media Relations .... Vacant
31 Director of Community Relations .... Mr. Jason ROJAS
37 Director of Financial Aid .... Ms. Kelly O'BRIEN
06 Registrar .... Ms. Patricia MCGREGOR
18 Dir of Facilities Mgmt/Plng & Svcs .... Mr. Gary BRICHER
15 Director of Human Resources .... Ms. Beth IACAMPO
21 Director of Business Operations .... Mr. Alan R. SAUER
21 Budget Director .... Ms. Marcia PHELAN JOHNSON
19 Director of Campus Safety .... Mr. Francisco ORTIZ
44 Director of Development .... Mr. Christopher FRENCH
44 Director of Annual Giving .... Mr. William KNAPP
36 Director of Career Development .... Ms. Violet GANNON
21 Comptroller .... Mr. Guy DRAPEAU
41 Director of Athletics .... Mr. Michael D. RENWICK
09 Director of Institutional Research .... Dr. James J. HUGHES
35 Director of Campus Life .... Ms. Amy DEBAUN
42 College Chaplain .... Rev. Allison READ
28 Dean Multicultural Affs/Sr Div Ofcr .... Ms. Karla SPURLOCK-EVANS
38 Director Student Counseling .... Dr. Randolph LEE
96 Director of Purchasing .... Mr. Michael S. ELLIOTT
88 Dean of Urban and Global Studies .... Dr. Xiangming CHEN
29 Acting Director of Alumni Relations .... Ms. Aliza FINN-WELCH
08 Head Librarian .... Dr. Richard S. ROSS
26 Director of Communications .... Ms. Jenny HOLLAND
04 Administrative Asst to President .... Ms. Carla PEREIRA

University of Bridgeport (B)

126 Park Avenue, Bridgeport CT 06604-5620
County: Fairfield FICE Identification: 001416
Unit ID: 128744
Telephone: (203) 576-4000 Carnegie Class: Master's L
FAX Number: (203) 576-4653 Calendar System: Semester
URL: www.bridgeport.edu
Established: 1927 Annual Undergrad Tuition & Fees: $30,850
Enrollment: 5,191 Coed
Affiliation or Control: Independent Non-Profit IRS Status: 501(c)3
Highest Offering: Doctorate
Program: Occupational; Liberal Arts And General; Teacher Preparatory; Professional; Business Emphasis
Accreditation: EH, ACBSP, ACUP, ARCPA, ART, CHIRO, DH, ENG, MT, NATUR

01 President .... Mr. Neil Albert SALONEN
04 Executive Assistant to President .... Ms. Joan E. FLORCZAK
05 Provost & VP for Academic Affairs .... Dr. Hans VAN DER GIESSEN
10 VP Administration & Finance .... Dr. Susan D. WILLIAMS
88 Vice Pres International Programs .... Dr. Thomas J. WARD
30 Vice Pres for University Relations .... Ms. Mary Jane FOSTER
18 VP of Facilities .... Mr. George ESTRADA
09 Exec Asst Pres Plng/Inst Research .... Ms. Barbara A. GABIANELLI
07 Dean of Admissions .... Ms. Karissa L. PECKHAM
32 Dean of Students .... Ms. Edina R. OESTREICHER
08 University Librarian .... Ms. Deborah L. DULEPSKI
15 Dir Human Resources/Affirm Act Ofcr .... Dr. Melitha R. PRZYGODA
21 Controller .... Mr. Thomas A. DEBRIZZI, JR.
13 Systems Architect & Interim CIO .... Mr. Matanya ELCHANANI
37 Director of Financial Aid .... Ms. Christine E. FALZERANO
90 Director of Academic Computing .... Mr. Abdelshakour A. ABUZNEID
19 Exec Director of Campus Security .... Ms. April J. VOURNELIS
38 Director of Counseling Services .... Vacant
06 University Registrar .... Mr. Christian HANSEN
85 Director of Intl Student Affairs .... Ms. Yumin WANG
39 Dir Residential Life/Stdnt Conduct .... Mr. Robert VASS
96 Director of Purchasing .... Ms. Jacqueline A. REEVES
35 Dir Campus Activity & Cmty Service .... Mr. Craig LENNON
12 Director of Waterbury Center .... Ms. Karen K. RINGWOOD
12 Director of Stamford Center .... Ms. Maureen L. MALONEY
29 Director Alumni Relations .... Ms. Aimee MARCELLA
26 Dir Public Info & Media Affairs .... Ms. Leslie H. GEARY
43 University Counsel .... Ms. Carolyn R. LINSEY
41 Athletic Director .... Mr. Anthony VITTI
51 Dean Continuing/Profess Studies .... Mr. Michael J. GIAMPAOLI
23 Director of Health Center .... Ms. Melissa H. LOPEZ
88 Director of Acupuncture Institute .... Dr. Jennifer BRETT

40 Manager of the Bookstore .... Ms. Jessica RALLIS
36 Director of Career Services .... Mr. Keith HASSELL
54 VP Grad Stds/Research & Dean Engr .... Dr. Tarek M. SOBH
49 Dean Arts & Sciences .... Dr. Manyul IM
53 Dean School of Education .... Dr. Allen P. COOK
88 Dean College of Chiropractic .... Dr. Michael A. CIOLFI
88 Dean College Naturopathic Medicine .... Dr. Marcia A. PRENGUBER
50 Dean School of Business .... Dr. Lloyd G. GIBSON
17 Vice Provost Div of Health Science .... Dr. David M. BRADY
97 Director Div of General Studies .... Dr. Edward V. GEIST
89 Director First Year Studies .... Ms. Roxie L. RAY
52 Dean Fones Sch of Dental Hygiene .... Dr. Marcia H. LORENTZEN
56 Director for Distance Learning .... Mr. Kris BICKELL
24 Media Services Coordinator .... Ms. Lynn DORSEY
57 Dir Shintaro Akatsu Sch of Design .... Mr. Richard W. YELLE
88 Dir Physician Assistant Institute .... Dr. Daniel CERVONKA
44 Director Annual Giving .... Ms. Emily BRADY

University of Connecticut (C)

352 Mansfield Road, Storrs CT 06269
County: Tolland FICE Identification: 001417
Unit ID: 129020
Telephone: (860) 486-2000 Carnegie Class: RU/VH
FAX Number: (860) 486-2627 Calendar System: Semester
URL: www.uconn.edu
Established: 1881 Annual Undergrad Tuition & Fees (In-State): $13,250
Enrollment: 31,119 Coed
Affiliation or Control: State IRS Status: 501(c)3
Highest Offering: Doctorate
Program: Liberal Arts And General; Teacher Preparatory; Professional
Accreditation: EH, ART, AUD, BUS, BUSA, CAATE, CACREP, CEA, CGTECH, CLPSY, CS, DIETC, DIETD, DIETI, DMOLS, ENG, IPSY, JOUR, LAW, LSAR, MFCD, MT, MUS, NURSE, PHAR, PTA, SCPSY, SP, SPAA, SW, TED

01 President .... Susan HERBST
100 Chief of Staff .... Rachel RUBIN
05 Provost/Exec VP Academic Affairs .... Mun CHOI
17 Interim Exec VP for Health Affairs .... Andrew AGWUNOBI
10 Exec VP for Admin and CFO .... Scott JORDAN
32 Vice President for Student Affairs .... Michael GILBERT
46 Vice President for Research .... Jeffrey SEEMANN
101 Executive Secretary to the Board .... Rachel RUBIN
26 Vice Pres for Communications .... P. Tysen KENDIG
41 Director of Athletics .... Warde J. MANUEL
43 Asst Attorney General .... Holly BRAY
43 Vice President and General Counsel .... Richard ORR
13 Vice Provost & Chief Info Officer .... Michael MUNDRANE
21 Assoc VP for Budget & Finance .... Vacant
19 Dir Public Safety/Chief of Police .... Barbara O'CONNOR
28 Assoc VP for Diversity & Equity .... Elizabeth CONKLIN
45 Asst VProv for Inst Rsrch & Effect .... Thulasi KUMAR
102 Pres Univ of Connecticut Foundation .... Joshua NEWTON
20 Vice Provost for Academic Affairs .... Sally REIS
20 Vice Provost fr Academic Operations .... Amy DONAHUE
84 VP Enrollment Planning & Mgmt .... Wayne LOCUST
08 Vice Prov for University Libraries .... Martha BEDARD
12 Director Stamford Campus .... Sharon WHITE
12 Director Avery Point Campus .... Joseph MADAUS
12 Director Waterbury Campus .... William J. PIZZUTO
12 Director Hartford Campus .... Michael MENARD
12 Interim Director Torrington Campus .... William J. PIZZUTO
92 AVProv Enrich Pgms/Dir Honors Pgms .... Jennifer LEASE BUTTS
25 AVP Research/Sponsored Pgms Svcs .... Michael GLASGOW
86 Director Government Relations .... Gail GARBER
86 Dir Govt Relations/Health Affairs .... Andrea KEILTY
06 Registrar .... Lauren DIGRAZIA
07 Director Undergrad Admissions .... Nathan FUERST
37 Director Student Financial Aid .... Mona LUCAS
29 Exec Director Alumni Assoc .... Montique COTTON KELLY
23 Int Director Student Health Svcs .... Elizabeth CRACCO
15 Director of Human Resources .... Aliza WILDER
96 Dir Procurement/Logistical Svcs .... Matthew LARSON
47 Dean Col of Agric/Natural Resources .... Gregory WEIDEMANN
50 Dean School of Business .... John ELLIOT
53 Dean Neag School of Education .... Richard SCHWAB
54 Dean of Engineering .... Kazem KAZEROUNIAN
88 Assoc Vice Prov Excell Teach/Lrng .... Peter DIPLOCK
57 Dean of Fine Arts .... Anne D'ALLEVA
58 Vice Prov Grad Ed/Dean Grad Sch .... Kent HOLSINGER
61 Dean School of Law .... Timothy FISHER
49 Dean College of Lib Arts/Sciences .... Jeremy TEITELBAUM
66 Dean School of Nursing .... Regina CUSSON
67 Dean School of Pharmacy .... James HALPERT
70 Interim Dean School of Social Work .... Nina ROVINELLI HELLER
52 Dean of Dental Medicine .... R. Lamont MACNEIL
63 Dean School of Medicine .... Bruce LIANG
38 Dir Student Counslg/Mental Hlth Svc .... Elizabeth CRACCO
39 Executive Director Residential Life .... Pamela SCHIPANI
88 Deputy Chief of Staff .... Michael KIRK
88 Master Planner/Chief Architect .... Laura CRUICKSHANK
88 Vice Provost for Global Affairs .... Daniel WEINER
36 Asst VProv/Exec Dir Career Services .... James R. LOWE
88 Asst VProvost for Student Success .... Maria D. MARTINEZ
88 Director Marketing Communications .... Patricia FAZIO
88 Ombuds .... James WOHL
20 Asst VProvost Acad Affs & Diversity .... Dana WILDER
88 Dir Institute for Materials Science .... Steven L. SUIB
04 Administrative Asst to President .... Debra MERRITT
104 Director Study Abroad .... Kevin BRENNAN
18 Assoc VP Facilities Ops & Bldg Svcs .... P. Michael JEDNAK
30 Vice President for Development .... Brian OTIS
44 Director of Planned Giving .... Gregory KNOTT
106 Dir Online Education/E-learning .... Peter DIPLOCK

University of Connecticut Health Center (D)

263 Farmington Avenue, Farmington CT 06030-1827
Telephone: (860) 679-2000 FICE Identification: 009867
Accreditation: &EH, DENT, MED, PAST, PH

† Regional accreditation is carried under the parent institution in Storrs, CT.

University of Connecticut School of Law (E)

55 Elizabeth Street, Hartford CT 06105-2290
Telephone: (860) 570-5000 Identification: 770108
Accreditation: &EH, LAW

† Branch campus of University of Connecticut, Storrs, CT.

University of Hartford (F)

200 Bloomfield Avenue, West Hartford CT 06117-1599
County: Hartford FICE Identification: 001422
Unit ID: 129525
Telephone: (860) 768-4100 Carnegie Class: Master's L
FAX Number: (860) 768-4070 Calendar System: Semester
URL: www.hartford.edu
Established: 1877 Annual Undergrad Tuition & Fees: $36,460
Enrollment: 6,866 Coed
Affiliation or Control: Independent Non-Profit IRS Status: 501(c)3
Highest Offering: Doctorate
Program: Liberal Arts And General; Teacher Preparatory; Professional
Accreditation: EH, ART, BUS, CLPSY, COARC, DANCE, ENG, ENGT, MUS, NURSE, OPE, PTA, RAD, TED, THEA

01 President .... Dr. Walter HARRISON
05 Provost .... Ms. Sharon VASQUEZ
10 Vice Pres Finance & Administration .... Mr. Arosha JAYAWICKREMA
30 Vice Pres Institutional Advancement .... Ms. Christine M. PINA
32 Vice Pres Student Affs/Dean Stdnts .... Dr. J. Lee PETERS
26 Vice Pres of Univ Relations .... Mr. John J. CARSON
21 Asst Vice Pres Finance/Controller .... Ms. Laura WHITNEY
35 Asst Vice Pres Student Development .... Ms. DeLois LINDSEY
04 Senior Advisor to the President .... Ms. Susan FITZGERALD
35 Assoc Vice Pres for Student Life .... Mr. Irwin NUSSBAUM
21 Assoc Vice Pres/Treasurer .... Mr. Brett CARROLL
43 Vice Pres/Gen Counsel & Secretary .... Mr. Thomas DORER
20 Sr Assoc Provost/Dean Enroll Mgmt .... Dr. Guy C. COLARULLI
20 Assoc Provost/Dean of Grad Studies .... Dr. Frederick SWEITZER
07 Dean of Admission .... Mr. Richard A. ZEISER
04 Exec Assistant to the President .... Ms. Ilena ROSENSTEIN
15 Exec Dir Human Resources & Devel .... Ms. Lisa BELANGER
08 Director University Libraries .... Ms. Randi L. ASHTON-PRITTING
37 Director Student Financial Aid .... Ms. Jennifer HORNER
06 Registrar .... Ms. Natalie DURANT
38 Dir Counsel & Personal Development .... Mr. Nick PINKERTON
36 Director Career Center .... Mr. John KNIERING
13 Interim Exec Dir Info Tech Svcs .... Mr. Richard LA FLAMME
19 Director Public Safety .... Mr. John SCHMALTZ
23 Director Health Services .... Ms. Mary NORRIS
24 Director Media Technology Services .... Mr. Sebastian SORRENTINO
25 Dir Inst Prtnrshp/Sponsored Rsrch .... Dr. Peter LISI
29 Director Alumni Relations .... Ms. Heather CORBETT
18 Assoc Vice Pres for Facilities/Mgmt .... Mr. Norman YOUNG
41 Director Athletics .... Mr. Anton GOFF
104 Director International Studies .... Ms. Sarah O'LEARY
09 Dir Institutional Effectiveness .... Ms. Nichole PETERSON
94 Director of Women's Center .... Ms. Kenna GRANT
88 Director of Judicial Process .... Ms. Kristy SEVERINO
96 Director of Purchasing .... Ms. Lisa CONDON
92 Director of University Honors .... Dr. Donald JONES
106 Asst Prov Online Lrng/Dean Univ Pgm .... Dr. R. J. MCGIVNEY
57 Dean Hartford Art School .... Dr. Nancy M. STUART
72 Dean College Engineer/Tech/Arch .... Dr. Louis MANZIONE
49 Dean College Arts & Science .... Dr. Katherine BLACK
50 Dean Barney School of Business .... Dr. Martin ROTH
12 Dean Hillyer Col/Int Dean Ungrd St .... Dr. David H. GOLDENBERG
53 Dean College of Education .... Dr. Ralph MUELLER
88 Dean Hartt School .... Dr. T. Clark SAUNDERS
39 Asst Vice Pres for Residential Life .... Mr. Michael MALONE
27 Dir of Marketing/Communications .... Mr. Jonathan EASTERBROOK
101 Secretary of the Institution/Board .... Mr. Thomas DORER
102 Dir Foundation/Corporate Relations .... Ms. Keeley PATRICK
103 Dir Workforce/Career Development .... Ms. Linda SCHULTZ
44 Director Annual or Planned Giving .... Mr. Clayton JASON

University of New Haven (G)

300 Boston Post Road, West Haven CT 06516-1916
County: New Haven FICE Identification: 001397
Unit ID: 129941
Telephone: (203) 932-7000 Carnegie Class: Master's L
FAX Number: (203) 931-6060 Calendar System: 4/1/4
URL: www.newhaven.edu
Established: 1920 Annual Undergrad Tuition & Fees: $35,650
Enrollment: 6,811 Coed
Affiliation or Control: Independent Non-Profit IRS Status: 501(c)3
Highest Offering: Doctorate
Program: Liberal Arts And General; Professional
Accreditation: EH, ART, BUS, CS, DH, DIETD, ENG, FEPAC, TED

01 President .... Dr. Steven H. KAPLAN

05 Provost/Vice Pres Academic Affs .... Dr. Daniel MAY
10 Vice Pres Finance/Treasurer of Univ .... Mr. George S. SYNODI
30 Vice President Univ Advancement .... Mr. Stephen J. MORIN
84 Vice Pres Enrollment Management .... Mr. Walter F. CAFFEY
15 Vice President Human Resources .... Ms. Caroline KOZIATEK
100 Chief of Staff & Univ Secretary .... Ms. Gayle S. TAGLIATELA
18 Assoc Vice President for Facilities .... Mr. Louis ANNINO
20 Assoc Provost Strategic Initiatives .... Dr. Stuart SIDLE
21 Assoc Vice Pres for Finance .... Mr. Patrick TORRE
13 Assoc VP Institutional Technology .... Mr. Vincent P. MANGIACAPRA
32 Assc VP Stdnt Affs/Dean of Students .. Ms. Rebecca D. JOHNSON
07 Assoc VP Enrollment Management .... Mr. Kevin J. PHILLIPS
41 Assc Vice Pres Athletics/Recreation .... Ms. Deborah CHIN
37 Assoc Vice Pres Financial Aid .... Ms. Karen FLYNN
88 Asst Provost Undergrad Stds/Assess .... Dr. Gordon SIMERSON
08 University Librarian .... Ms. Hanko H. DOBI
44 Assoc VP for Development .... Ms. Roslyn REABACK
06 University Registrar .... Ms. Lynn KOHRN
30 Exec Dir of Advancement Operations .... Mr. Carl PITRUZZELLO
07 Associate VP of Graduate Enrollment .... Mr. Sean-Michael GREEN
28 Director of Intercultural Relations .... Ms. Wanda TYLER
29 Director of Alumni Events .... Ms. Jennifer PJATAK
38 Associate Director of Counseling .... Dr. Deborah EVERHART
09 Director Institutional Research .... Ms. Susan TURNER
19 Chief of University Police .... Chief Mark DELIETO
85 Director of Intl Student Services .... Ms. Karima JACKSON
35 Director Student Activities .... Mr. Gregory OVEREND
96 Director of Procurement Services .... Mr. Robert STEVENS
85 Director International Admissions .... Mr. Joseph SPELLMAN
88 Dir Student Accounts/Risk Manager .... Mr. Marc MANIATIS
26 Assoc VP Communications/Pub Affairs ... Mr. Dean GOLEMBESKI
49 Dean College Arts & Sciences .... Dr. Lourdes ALVAREZ
50 Dean College Business .... Dr. Brian KENCH
54 Dean Tagliatela Col Engineering ...... Dr. Ronald HARICHANDRAN
88 Dean Col Crim Justice/Forensic Sci .... Dr. Mario GABOURY
103 Exec Director of Career Development ...... Mr. Matthew CAPORALE
104 Director International Study .... Ms. Jennie BROWN
39 Associate Dean of Residential Life .... Ms. Nicole MCGRATH
108 Director of Academic Assessment .... Dr. Kristy HUNTLEY

University of Saint Joseph (A)

1678 Asylum Avenue, West Hartford CT 06117-2791

County: Hartford | FICE Identification: 001409 | Unit ID: 130314
Telephone: (860) 232-4571 | Carnegie Class: Master's L
FAX Number: (860) 232-6927 | Calendar System: Semester
URL: www.usj.edu
Established: 1932 | Annual Undergrad Tuition & Fees: $36,140
Enrollment: 2,565 | Female
Affiliation or Control: Roman Catholic | IRS Status: 501(c)3
Highest Offering: Doctorate
Program: Liberal Arts And General; Teacher Preparatory; Professional
Accreditation: EH, CACREP, DIETD, DIETI, MFCD, NURSE, PHAR, SW, TED

01 President .... Dr. Rhona C. FREE
05 Provost .... Dr. Michelle KALIS
10 Sr VP Finance and Strategy .... Mr. Shawn M. HARRINGTON
30 VP Inst Advancement .... Ms. Marjorie PINNEY
84 Interim VP Enrollment Management .... Mr. Ned HARRIS
32 VP Student Affairs/Dean of Students .... Dr. Cheryl A. BARNARD
21 Assoc VP of Finance/Controller .... Mr. William HAWKINS
15 Director of Human Resources .... Ms. Deborah SPENCER
58 Dean Sch of Grad & Prof Studies .... Dr. Daniel NUSSBAUM
67 Dean School of Pharmacy .... Dr. Joseph OFOSU
53 Dean School of Education .... Dr. Ann MONROE-BAILLARGEON
76 Dean School of Health/Nat Sci .... Dr. Raouf BOULES
79 Dean School of Humanities/Soc Sci .... Dr. Wayne STEELY
08 Librarian .... Ms. Linda O. GEFFNER
06 Registrar .... Mr. Patrick MARTIN
41 Dir of Athletics/AVP Student Affair .... Mr. William CARDARELLI
26 AVP Marketing & Communications .... Ms. Laura SHEEHAN
18 Director of Facilities .... Mr. Kevin COCHRAN
29 Dir of Alumni Rels/Annual Giving .... Vacant
37 Director of Financial Aid .... Ms. Ashley DUTTON
36 Director of Career Services .... Mr. Stephen SEWARD
39 Director of Residential Life .... Mr. Frank KUSTER
35 Asst Dean Student Leadership .... Ms. Tracy LAKE
09 Director of Institutional Research .... Ms. Kathleen NEAL
13 Director of Info Tech (CIO) .... Mr. Joe GLEASON
19 Director of Public Safety .... Mr. Paul LOMBARDO
38 Director of Counseling & Wellness .... Dr. Meredith YUHAS
23 Director of Health Services .... Ms. Elizabeth COCOLA

Wesleyan University (B)

45 Wyllys Avenue, Middletown CT 06459

County: Middlesex | FICE Identification: 001424 | Unit ID: 130697
Telephone: (860) 685-2000 | Carnegie Class: Bac/A&S
FAX Number: (860) 685-2001 | Calendar System: Semester
URL: www.wesleyan.edu
Established: 1831 | Annual Undergrad Tuition & Fees: $48,974
Enrollment: 3,224 | Coed
Affiliation or Control: Independent Non-Profit | IRS Status: 501(c)3
Highest Offering: Doctorate
Program: Liberal Arts And General
Accreditation: EH

01 President .... Dr. Michael S. ROTH
05 Provost/Vice Pres Academic Affairs .... Dr. Joyce JACOBSEN
10 Vice President/Treasurer .... Dr. John MEERTS
26 Vice President University Relations .... Ms. Barbara-Jan WILSON
28 Vice President for Equity and Incl .... Mr. Antonio FARIAS
32 Vice Pres of Student Affairs .... Mr. Michael J. WHALEY
29 Assoc VP External Relations .... Ms. Gemma F. EBSTEIN
30 Assoc Asst Vice Pres Development .... Vacant
20 Senior Associate Provost .... Dr. Mark HOVEY
18 Asst Vice President for Facilities .... Ms. Joyce TOPSHE
35 Asst Vice Pres/Dean of Students .... Mr. Richard CULLITON
07 Dean of Admissions & Financial Aid .... Ms. Nancy HARGRAVE MEISLAHN
58 Dir Cont Stds/Graduate Liberal Stds .... Ms. Jennifer CURRAN
06 Registrar .... Ms. Anna VAN DER BURG
08 Interim University Librarian .... Ms. Diane KLARE
09 Director of Institutional Research .... Mr. Michael E. WHITCOMB
37 Director Financial Aid .... Mr. John GUDVANGEN
36 Director Career Development .... Ms. Sharon CASTONGUAY
15 Director Human Resources .... Ms. Julia HICKS
19 Director Public Safety .... Mr. Scott ROHDE
31 Dir Community Svcs/Volunteerism .... Ms. Catherine CRIMMINS LECHOWICZ
41 Director of Athletics .... Mr. Michael WHALEN
45 Director of Strategic Initiatives .... Dr. Charles G. SALAS
13 Chief Info Technology Officer (CIO) .... Dr. David BAIRD

Yale University (C)

New Haven CT 06520

County: New Haven | FICE Identification: 001426 | Unit ID: 130794
Telephone: (203) 432-4771 | Carnegie Class: RU/VH
FAX Number: N/A | Calendar System: Semester
URL: www.yale.edu
Established: 1701 | Annual Undergrad Tuition & Fees: $64,302
Enrollment: 12,336 | Coed
Affiliation or Control: Independent Non-Profit | IRS Status: 501(c)3
Highest Offering: Doctorate
Program: Liberal Arts And General; Professional
Accreditation: EH, ARCPA, BUS, CLPSY, ENG, IPSY, LAW, MED, MIDWF, NURSE, PAST, PH, THEOL

01 President .... Peter SALOVEY
05 Provost .... Benjamin POLAK
86 Vice Pres & Dir New Haven/State Aff .... Bruce D. ALEXANDER
32 Secretary & VP Student Affairs .... Kimberly GOFF-CREWS
10 Vice Pres Finance & CFO .... Stephen MURPHY
30 Vice President Development .... Joan E. O'NEILL
43 Vice President & General Counsel .... Alexander DREIER
15 Vice Pres/Chief HR Officer .... Michael A. PEEL
20 Deputy Provost Science & Tech .... Steven M. GIRVIN
20 Deputy Provost Arts and Humanities .... Emily P. BAKEMEIER
20 Deputy Prov Health Affairs .... Stephanie SPANGLER
20 Deputy Provost Academic Resources .... J. Lloyd SUTTLE
11 Deputy VP of HR & Admin .... Janet E. LINDNER
18 Assoc VP Facilities .... John H. BOLLIER
21 Assoc VP Finance .... Vacant
26 Chief Comm Ofcr/Dir Ofc Public Affs .... Vacant
96 Assoc VP & Chief Procurement Ofcr .... John A. MAYES
102 Assoc VP/Dir Corp & Found Rels .... Patricia E. PEDERSEN
08 Univ Librarian & Deputy Provost .... Susan GIBBONS
09 Acting Dir Institutional Research .... Russell K. ADAIR
13 Chief Information Officer .... Leonard PETERS
19 Chief University Police .... Ronnell A. HIGGINS
06 University Registrar .... Gabriel G. OLSZEWSKI
07 Dean Undergraduate Admissions .... Jeremiah QUINLAN
20 Dean Undergraduate Education .... Joseph W. GORDON
35 Dean Student Affairs .... Vacant
29 Exec Director Assoc of Yale Alumni .... Vacant
37 Director University Financial Aid .... Caesar T. STORLAZZI
22 Dir Ofc Equal Opportunities .... Valarie J. STANLEY
23 Director University Health Services .... Dr. Paul GENECIN
90 Deputy CIO Academic IT .... Gary KIDNEY
25 Interim Dir Grants & Contract Admn .. Alice TANGREDI-HANNON
36 Director Career Services .... Jeanine DAMES
44 Univ Director Planned Giving .... Eileen B. DONAHUE
39 Dir Grad & Prof Student Housing ...... George E. LONGYEAR, JR.
41 Director Athletics .... Thomas A. BECKETT
42 University Chaplain .... Sharon KUGLER
85 Director Intl Students & Scholars .... Ann KUHLMAN
84 Director of Enrollment Management .... Danielle CURTIS
48 Dean of the School of Architecture .... Robert A M. STERN
49 Dean of Yale College .... Jonathan HOLLOWAY
50 Dean School of Management .... Edward A. SNYDER
54 Dean School of Engineering .... Ms. T. Kyle VANDERLICK
57 Dean of the School of Art .... Robert STORR
58 Dean of Grad Sch Arts & Science .... Lynn COOLEY
57 Dean of the School of Drama .... James A. BUNDY
61 Dean of the Law School .... Robert C. POST
64 Dean of the School of Music .... Robert L. BLOCKER
65 Dean Sch of Forestry & Environ Stds .... Sir Peter CRANE
73 Dean of the Divinity School .... Gregory E. STERLING
88 Director Inst of Sacred Music .... Martin D. JEAN
63 Dean of School of Medicine .... Dr. Robert J. ALPERN
66 Dean of the School of Nursing .... Margaret GREY
69 Dean of Public Health .... Paul C. CLEARY
28 Chief Diversity Officer .... Deborah STANLEY-MCAULAY
104 Dean Intl & Professional Experience .... Jane EDWARDS

DELAWARE

Delaware College of Art and Design (D)

600 N Market Street, Wilmington DE 19801-3007

County: New Castle | FICE Identification: 041398 | Unit ID: 432524
Telephone: (302) 622-8000 | Carnegie Class: Assoc/PrivNFP
FAX Number: (302) 622-8870 | Calendar System: Semester
URL: www.dcad.edu
Established: 1997 | Annual Undergrad Tuition & Fees: $23,990
Enrollment: 188 | Coed
Affiliation or Control: Independent Non-Profit | IRS Status: 501(c)3
Highest Offering: Associate Degree
Program: 2-Year Principally Bachelor's Creditable; Fine Arts Emphasis
Accreditation: M, ART

01 President .... Mr. Stuart BARON
06 Registrar .... Ms. Krista ROTHWELL
07 Director of Admissions .... Ms. Tracy STEPHANSKI
08 Head Librarian .... Ms. Helena RICHARDSON
13 Information Technology Coordinator .... Mr. Bates CARTER
30 Director of Development .... Ms. Sara GANTER
37 Director Student Financial Aid .... Ms. Nicole LITTLE
32 Director of Student Services .... Mr. Jason MOKAR
26 Director of Communications .... Ms. Amanda CURRY
11 Chief Administrative Officer .... Ms. Traci PARMAN

Delaware State University (E)

1200 N DuPont Highway, Dover DE 19901-2275

County: Kent | FICE Identification: 001428 | Unit ID: 130934
Telephone: (302) 857-6060 | Carnegie Class: Master's M
FAX Number: (302) 857-6069 | Calendar System: Semester
URL: www.desu.edu
Established: 1891 | Annual Undergrad Tuition & Fees (In-State): $7,532
Enrollment: 4,644 | Coed
Affiliation or Control: State | IRS Status: 501(c)3
Highest Offering: Doctorate
Program: Liberal Arts And General; Teacher Preparatory; Professional
Accreditation: M, BUS, DIETD, NUR, SW, TED

01 President .... Dr. Harry L. WILLIAMS
04 Executive Asst to the President .... Mrs. Henrietta A. SAVAGE
05 Provost/Vice Pres Academic Affs .... Dr. Alton THOMPSON
10 Sr VP & Chief Operating Officer .... Dr. Teresa HARDEE
30 VP Inst Advancement/Chief of Staff .... Vacant
32 Vice Pres Student Affairs .... Dr. Stacy L. DOWNING
46 Vice President for Research .... Dr. Noureddine MELIKECHI
13 Assoc VP Information Technology .... Mr. Arthur LEIBLE
09 AVP Inst Research/Planning/Analysis ...... Dr. Kimberly R. SUDLER
15 Sr Assoc Vice Pres Human Resources .... Ms. Irene HAWKINS
43 General Counsel .... Mr. Thomas PRESTON
18 Director of Facilities .... Mr. Randy JONES
06 Registrar .... Mr. Terrell HOLMES
07 Director of Admissions .... Ms. Erin HILL
62 Dean of Library Services .... Ms. Rebecca BATSON
37 Director of Financial Aid .... Ms. Lynn IOCANO
29 Assistant VP Alumni Relations .... Ms. Lisa DUNNING
36 Director Career Services .... Ms. Lisa MOODY
19 Director of Public Safety .... Mr. Harry W. DOWNES
38 Director of Student Counseling .... Mr. Ralph ROBINSON
26 News Director .... Mr. Carlos HOLMES
41 Director of Athletics .... Mr. Louis PERKINS
101 Secretary of the Institution/Board .... Ms. Eleanor WILSON
102 Sr AVP for Development .... Ms. Vita PICKRUM
44 Director Annual Giving .... Mr. LaShawne PRYOR
86 Director Government Relations .... Mr. Victor SANTOS

Delaware Technical Community College, George Campus (F)

300 N. Orange Street, Wilmington DE 19801

Telephone: (302) 571-5300 | Identification: 770855
Accreditation: &M

† Branch campus of Delaware Technical Community College, Terry Campus, Dover, DE.

Delaware Technical Community College, Owens Campus (G)

21179 College Drive, Georgetown DE 19947-0610

Telephone: (302) 259-6000 | FICE Identification: 007053
Accreditation: &M, ACBSP, ADNUR, COARC, CSHSE, DMS, ENGT, MLTAD, OTA, PTAA, RAD

† Branch campus of Delaware Technical Community College, Terry Campus, Dover, DE.

Delaware Technical Community College, Stanton Campus (H)

400 Stanton-Christiana Road, Newark DE 19713-2197

Telephone: (302) 454-3900 | FICE Identification: 021449
Accreditation: &M, ACFEI, ADNUR, CAHIIM, CSHSE, ENGT, HT, NMT, RAD

† Branch campus of Delaware Technical Community College, Terry Campus, Dover, DE.

Delaware Technical Community College, Terry Campus (A)

100 Campus Drive, Dover DE 19904-1383
County: Kent FICE Identification: 011727
Unit ID: 130907
Telephone: (302) 857-1000 Carnegie Class: Assoc/Pub-R-M
FAX Number: (302) 857-1096 Calendar System: Semester
URL: www.dtcc.edu/terry
Established: 1972 Annual Undergrad Tuition & Fees (In-State): $3,700
Enrollment: 3,051 Coed
Affiliation or Control: State IRS Status: 501(c)3
Highest Offering: Associate Degree
Program: Occupational; 2-Year Principally Bachelor's Creditable; Technical Emphasis
Accreditation: M, ACBSP, ACFEI, ADNUR, CSHSE, EMT, PNUR, SURGT

01 Vice President & Campus Director .... Dr. June S. TURANSKY
05 Dean Instruction .... Mr. John M. BUCKLEY
32 Dean Student Affairs .... Ms. Jennifer P. PIRES
04 Director Communication and Planning .... Ms. Dana L. SAWYER
103 Director Workforce Development .... Dr. Lisa S. STRUSOWSKI
15 Director of Human Resources .... Ms. Charlotte T. LISTER
11 Director of Administrative Services .... Mr. William J. AYERS
37 Director Student Financial Aid .... Ms. Jennifer J. GRUNDEN
08 Head Librarian .... Dr. Margaret R. PROUSE
10 Director Business Services .... Ms. Christina C. SWEENEY
06 Registrar/Admissions Coordinator .... Ms. Nauleen A. PERRY
88 Asst Director of Admin Services .... Mr. Ray B. PARSONS
20 Assistant Dean of Instruction .... Mr. Bill J. MORROW

Goldey-Beacom College (B)

4701 Limestone Road, Wilmington DE 19808-0551
County: New Castle FICE Identification: 001429
Unit ID: 130989
Telephone: (302) 998-8814 Carnegie Class: Spec/Bus
FAX Number: (302) 998-8631 Calendar System: Semester
URL: www.gbc.edu
Established: 1886 Annual Undergrad Tuition & Fees: $22,950
Enrollment: 2,012 Coed
Affiliation or Control: Independent Non-Profit IRS Status: 501(c)3
Highest Offering: Master's
Program: Liberal Arts And General; Professional; Business Emphasis
Accreditation: M, ACBSP, IACBE

01 President .... Dr. Gary L. WIRT
03 Executive Vice President .... Ms. Kristine M. SANTOMAURO
10 Controller .... Ms. Susan M. MANNERING
05 Dean of Academic Affairs .... Ms. Alison Boord WHITE
32 Dean of Students .... Ms. Bernadette H. WIMBERLEY
07 Director of Admissions .... Mr. Larry EBY
84 Dean Enrollment Mgmt/Registrar .... Ms. Jane H. LYSLE
13 Dean of Information Technology/ACC .... Ms. Emily S. JACKSON
39 Director of Housing/Residence Life .... Mr. Kevin MARTIN
36 Career Service Specialist .... Ms. Elizabeth KIRKER
36 Career Service Specialist .... Ms. Bethann HIGLEY
18 Director of Facilities .... Mr. Meezie FOSTER
41 Athletic Director .... Mr. Charles A. HAMMOND
08 Head Librarian .... Mr. Russell MICHALAK

Irish American University (C)

404 East Savannah Road, Lewes DE 19958
County: Sussex Identification: 667120
Telephone: (302) 793-1101 Carnegie Class: Not Classified
FAX Number: (808) 334-0443 Calendar System: Semester
URL: www.acd.ie
Established: Annual Undergrad Tuition & Fees: $8,400
Enrollment: N/A Coed
Affiliation or Control: Independent Non-Profit IRS Status: 501(c)3
Highest Offering: Master's
Program: Liberal Arts And General
Accreditation: M

01 President/CEO .... Dr. Donald E. ROSS
03 Executive Vice President .... Mr. Christopher SARAFIAN
05 Academic Dean .... Dr. Rory MCENTERGART
30 Provost Institutional Advancement .... Mr. Joseph A. ROONEY

University of Delaware (D)

104 Hullihen Hall, Newark DE 19716
County: New Castle FICE Identification: 001431
Unit ID: 130943
Telephone: (302) 831-2000 Carnegie Class: RU/VH
FAX Number: (302) 831-8000 Calendar System: 4/1/4
URL: www.udel.edu
Established: 1743 Annual Undergrad Tuition & Fees (In-State): $12,520
Enrollment: 22,680 Coed
Affiliation or Control: State Related IRS Status: 501(c)3
Highest Offering: Doctorate
Program: 2-Year Principally Bachelor's Creditable; Liberal Arts And General; Teacher Preparatory; Professional
Accreditation: M, BUS, BUSA, CAATE, CEA, CLPSY, CSHSE, DIETC, DIETD, DIETI, ENG, IPSY, MT, MUS, NURSE, PCSAS, PTA, SPAA, TED

01 Acting President .... Dr. Nancy M. TARGETT
05 Provost .... Dr. Domenico GRASSO
03 Exec Vice President & Univ Treas .... Mr. Scott R. DOUGLASS
30 Vice Pres Development & Alum Rels .... Ms. Monica TAYLOR LOTTY
26 Vice Pres Communications & Mktg .... Ms. Deborah L. HAYES
13 Vice Pres Information Technologies .... Mr. Carl JACOBSON
43 Vice Pres and General Counsel .... Mr. Lawrence WHITE
100 Acting Vice Pres & Chief of Staff .... Dr. Franklin NEWTON
18 Vice Pres Fac/Real Estate & Aux Svc .... Mr. Alan BRANGMAN
46 Dpty Vice Prov Research & Schlrship .... Dr. Charles RIORDAN
58 Interim Vice Prov Grad & Prof Educ .... Dr. Ann ARDIS
88 Vice Provost for Faculty Affairs .... Dr. Matt KINSERVIK
28 Vice Provost for Diversity .... Dr. Carol E. HENDERSON
20 Int Deputy Prov Academic Affs .... Dr. Lynn OKAGAKI
101 Vice Pres & Univ Secretary .... Mr. Jeffrey W. GARLAND
86 Director of Government Relations .. Mr. Derrick DEADWYLER, JR.
51 Asst Provost Prof Cont Studies .... Dr. James K. BROOMALL
88 Assoc Provost & Chief of Staff .... Ms. Margaret B. BOTTORFF
32 Vice Pres for Student Life .... Ms. Dawn M. THOMPSON
84 Vice Pres Enrollment Management .... Mr. Chris LUCIER
88 Assoc Prov Inst Research & Effec .... Dr. John E. SAWYER
09 Director Institutional Research .... Dr. Heather A. KELLY
108 Director Educational Assessment .... Ms. Kathleen L. PUSECKER
29 Sr Assoc Director Alumni Relations .... Ms. Justine TALLEY-BECK
08 Vice Provost/Director Libraries .... Ms. Susan BRYNTESON
104 Assoc Provost Intl Programs .... Dr. Nancy GUERRA
37 Director Student Financial Services .... Ms. Melissa STONE
36 Interim Director Career Services .... Ms. Lynn SYDNOR-EPPS
19 Exec Dir Campus & Public Safety .... Mr. Albert J. HOMIAK, JR.
47 Dean Agric & Natural Resources .... Dr. Mark RIEGER
49 Dean Arts & Sciences .... Dr. George H. WATSON
50 Dean Lerner Col Business & Econ .... Dr. Bruce W. WEBER
54 Dean Engineering .... Dr. Babatunde A. OGUNNAIKE
65 Actg Dean Earth Ocean & Environment .... Dr. Mohsen BADIEY
76 Dean Health Sciences .... Dr. Kathleen S. MATT
53 Interim Dean Educ & Human Develop .... Dr. Carol VUKELICH
92 Director University Honors Program .... Dr. Michael A. ARNOLD
07 Director Undergraduate Admissions .... Dr. William D. ZANDER
88 Director of Graduate Admissions .... Mr. Michael ALEXO
15 Chief Human Resources Officer .... Mr. Thomas LAPENTA
96 Director Procurement Services .... Ms. Debra C. REESE
06 University Registrar .... Mr. Jeffrey L. PALMER
10 Chief Budget Officer .... Ms. Kathy L. DETTLOFF
22 Director Inst Equity and Inclusion .... Dr. Susan L. GROFF
35 Dean of Students .... Dr. José-Luis RIERA
38 Director Ctr for Couns/Student Dev .... Dr. Charles L. BEALE
39 Exec Director Res Life & Housing .... Dr. Kathleen G. KERR
85 Director Intl Students & Scholars .... Mr. Ravi AMMIGAN
41 Director Athletics & Recreation .... Mr. Eric ZIADY
23 Director Student Health Services .... Dr. Timothy F. DOWLING
04 Assistant to the President .... Ms. Susan L. WILLIAMS

Wesley College (E)

120 N State Street, Dover DE 19901-3876
County: Kent FICE Identification: 001433
Unit ID: 131098
Telephone: (302) 736-2300 Carnegie Class: Bac/Diverse
FAX Number: (302) 736-2301 Calendar System: Semester
URL: www.wesley.edu
Established: 1873 Annual Undergrad Tuition & Fees: $25,020
Enrollment: 1,590 Coed
Affiliation or Control: United Methodist IRS Status: 501(c)3
Highest Offering: Master's
Program: Liberal Arts And General; Teacher Preparatory; Professional
Accreditation: M, NUR, TED

01 President .... Mr. Robert E. CLARK, II
05 Vice President for Academic Affairs .... Dr. Jeffrey GIBSON
10 VP Finance .... Ms. Christine GIBSON
30 Vice Pres Institutional Advancement .... Mr. Chris WOOD
32 Dean of Students .... Ms. Wanda ANDERSON
84 Dean of Enrollment Management .... Mr. Greg POTTS
42 Dir Spiritual Life and Comm Involv .... Rev. Scot CLYMONT
21 CPA/Controller .... Ms. Adele FOLTZ
43 General Counsel .... Mr. David WILKS
06 Registrar .... Ms. Erin ELSBERRY
12 Part-time Admin Coord DAFB .... Ms. Tracey LUNDBLAD
08 Director of the Parker Library .... Ms. Jessica OLIN
35 Director Student Success/Retention .... Ms. Charlene STEPHENS
88 Asst Dir Academic Support Services . Ms. Christine MCDERMOTT
26 Director of Marketing .... Ms. Jessica COOK
09 Director of Institutional Research .... Ms. Jessica HANSEN
46 Dir Data Analy & Inst Assessment .... Vacant
07 Assoc Director of Admissions .... Mr. Christopher JESTER
41 Exec Dir of Sports & Recreation .... Mr. Mike DRASS
18 Director of the Physical Plant .... Mr. Rick RICHARDSON
40 Director of the Bookstore .... Mr. Kris MCGLOTHIN
19 Director of Safety/Security .... Mr. Walter BEAUPRE
23 Director Student Health Services .... Ms. Jill MASER
44 Dir of the Annual Wesley Fund .... Ms. Cathy NOSEL
88 Dir of The Wesley Society .... Ms. Cathy ANDERSON
39 Director of Residence Life .... Ms. Laura BLAZEWICZ
35 Director of Student Activities .... Ms. Baukman ELANA
37 Dir of Student Financial Planning .... Mr. Michael HALL
38 Director of Counseling .... Ms. Ann ROGGE
85 Director of Global Initiatives .... Mr. Kevin CULLEN
29 Director Alumni Affairs .... Ms. Cathy NOSEL
41 Assoc Dir of Sports & Rec .... Vacant
04 Assistant to the President .... Ms. Ellen COLEMAN
88 Supervisor Business Operations .... Ms. Adele FLAMM
103 Dir Workforce/Career Development .... Mr. Nicholas LANTZ
13 Chief Info Technology Officer (CIO) .... Mr. Paul COPELAND
15 Director Personnel Services .... Vacant

Widener University Delaware Law School (F)

PO Box 7474, Wilmington DE 19803-0474
Telephone: (302) 477-2100 FICE Identification: 012962
Accreditation: &M, LAW

† Branch campus of Widener University in Pennsylvania. This listing reflects the administrators for the school of law for the Harrisburg (PA) and Delaware campuses.

Wilmington University (G)

320 N Dupont Highway, New Castle DE 19720-6491
County: New Castle FICE Identification: 007948
Unit ID: 131113
Telephone: (302) 356-4636 Carnegie Class: DRU
FAX Number: (302) 328-5902 Calendar System: Trimester
URL: www.wilmu.edu
Established: 1967 Annual Undergrad Tuition & Fees: $10,430
Enrollment: 14,938 Coed
Affiliation or Control: Independent Non-Profit IRS Status: 501(c)3
Highest Offering: Doctorate
Program: Liberal Arts And General; Professional
Accreditation: M, CACREP, IACBE, NURSE, TED

01 President .... Dr. Jack P. VARSALONA
04 Executive Asst to President .... Ms. Donna M. QUINN
101 Secretary of the Institution/Board .... Ms. Donna M. QUINN
03 Executive Vice President .... Dr. LaVerne T. HARMON
10 Senior VP/CFO Financial Affs .... Ms. Heather A. O'CONNELL
88 Senior Vice President .... Dr. Erin DIMARCO
88 University Vice Pres .... Ms. Carole D. PITCHER
88 Vice President External Affairs .... Dr. Peter A. BAILEY
05 Vice President Academic Affairs .... Dr. James D. WILSON, JR.
11 VP as Admin & Legas Affairs .... Dr. Christian A. TROWBRIDGE
88 Asst Vice Pres/Dean of Locations ..... Dr. Richard D. GOCHNAUER
21 Asst Vice President/Controller .... Mr. David R. LEWIS
43 Asst VP of Admin & Legal Affairs .... Mr. P. Donald HAGERMANN
26 Asst Vice Pres Public Relations .... Mr. Christopher G. PITCHER
108 Asst Vice President .... Dr. Angela C. SUCHANIC
106 Asst VP Admin Affs/Dean Online .... Dr. Eileen G. DONNELLY
32 Asst VP Student Affairs/Alumni Rel .... Dr. Tina M. BARKSDALE
20 Asst VP Academic Affairs .... Dr. Sheila M. SHARBAUGH
19 Asst VP/University Safety/Athletic .... Dr. Jack L. CUNNINGHAM
88 Asst VP Univ Relations/Admission .... Jacque R. VARSALONA
88 Asst VP Academic Support Services .... Ms. Peg P. MITCHELL
15 Chief Human Resources Officer .... Mrs. Nicole ROMANO
105 Sr Director of Web Communications .... Mr. Kevin G. BARRY
18 Sr Director Buildings/Maintenance .... Mr. William P. QUINN
36 Sr Dir Career Svcs/Student Life .... Dr. Regina C. ALLEN-SHARPE
37 Sr Dir Student Financial Services .... Ms. Trudy E. HITE
106 Sr Dir Online Learning & Ed Tech .... Dr. Sallie A. REISSMAN
06 Registrar .... Ms. Elizabeth P. JORDAN
08 Director Library .... Mr. James M. MCCLOSKEY
88 Dir Administrative Services .... Mr. Bryan E. STEINBERG
41 Director Athletics .... Ms. Linda M. ANDRZJEWSKI
07 Director of Admissions .... Ms. Laura M. MORRIS
29 Director Alumni Relations .... Ms. Patricia L. JENNINGS
78 Director Cooperative Learning .... Mr. David C. CAFFO
09 Director of Institutional Research .... Ms. Dana S. EGGLESTON
86 Director Government Relations .... Ms. Simone M. GEORGE
96 Purchasing Specialist .... Mr. Mark S. PARIS
50 Dean College of Business .... Dr. Donald W. DURANDETTA
53 Dean College of Education .... Dr. John C. GRAY
76 Dean College of Health Professions . Ms. Denise Z. WESTBROOK
49 Dean College of Arts and Sciences .... Dr. Doreen B. TURNBO
83 Dean College of Soc & Beh .... Dr. Edward L. GUTHRIE

DISTRICT OF COLUMBIA

American University (H)

4400 Massachusetts Avenue, NW, Washington DC 20016
FICE Identification: 001434
Unit ID: 131159
Telephone: (202) 885-1000 Carnegie Class: DRU
FAX Number: N/A Calendar System: Semester
URL: www.american.edu
Established: 1893 Annual Undergrad Tuition & Fees: $43,103
Enrollment: 13,061 Coed
Affiliation or Control: United Methodist IRS Status: 501(c)3
Highest Offering: Doctorate
Program: Liberal Arts And General; Teacher Preparatory; Professional
Accreditation: M, BUS, CLPSY, IPSY, JOUR, LAW, MUS, SPAA, TED

01 President .... Dr. Cornelius M. KERWIN
05 Provost .... Dr. Scott A. BASS
30 Interim Vice President Development .... Ms. Raina LENNEY
10 Vice President Finance & Treasurer ..... Mr. Douglas KUDRAVETZ
32 Vice President Campus Life .... Dr. Gail S. HANSON
43 Vice President General Counsel .... Ms. Mary E. KENNARD
11 Vice Provost for Academic Admin .... Ms. Violeta ETTLE
18 Asst VP Facilities Management .... Mr. Vincent HARKINS
35 Asst Vice Pres and Dean of Students .... Dr. Robert HRADSKY
35 Asst Vice President Campus Life .... Dr. Fanta AW
29 Asst Vice Pres of Alumni Relations .... Ms. Raina LENNEY
21 Asst Vice President of Treasury .... Ms. Laura MCANDREW
84 Vice Provost Undergrad Enrollment .... Dr. Sharon ALSTON
13 Chief Information Officer .... Mr. David L. SWARTZ
100 Chief of Staff President's Office .... Mr. David E. TAYLOR
20 Dean Acad Affs/Sr Vice Provost .... Dr. Mary CLARK
58 Vice Provost Grad Studies & Rsrch ...... Dr. Jonathan G. TUBMAN

20 Vice Provost Undergrad Studies .....Dr. Virginia (Lyn) STALLINGS
49 Dean College Arts & Sciences ....Dr. Peter STARR
60 Dean Sch of Communication ....Dr. Jeffrey RUTENBECK
50 Interim Dean Kogod Sch of Business ....Dr. Erran CARMEL
61 Dean Washington College of Law ....Dr. Claudio GROSSMAN
82 Dean School of Intl Service ....Dr. James GOLDGEIER
107 Dean School of Prof & Extended Stds ....Dr. Carola WEIL
80 Dean School of Public Affairs ....Dr. Barbara ROMZEK
15 Asst VP of Human Resources ....Ms. Beth MUHA
36 Exec Director Career Center ....Mr. Gihan FERNANDO
88 Assoc Provost for Acad Admin ....Ms. Prita PATEL
09 Asst Provost Inst Res/ Assessment ....Ms. Karen L. FROSLID JONES
26 Vice President of Communication ....Dr. Teresa (Terry) FLANNERY
06 University Registrar ....Mr. Charles (Doug) MCKENNA
08 University Librarian ....Ms. Nancy DAVENPORT
21 Controller ....Mr. John R. SMIELL
88 Dir Student Accounts Operations ....Mr. Darrell COOK
21 Asst VP Budget & Finance Res Ctr ....Ms. Nana AN
88 Asst VP Risk Mgmt/Safety Svcs ....Vacant
42 University Chaplain ....Dr. Joseph T. ELDRIDGE
30 Asst Vice President Development ....Mr. Seth SPEYER
19 Exec Dir Risk/Safety/Transportation ....Mr. Daniel NICHOLS
37 Asst Vice Provost Financial Aid ....Mr. Brian LEE SANG
38 Director of Counseling Center ....Dr. Traci CALLANDRILLO
25 Director Contracting & Procurement ....Mr. Brian BLAIR
07 Asst Vice Provost UG Admissions ....Mr. Gregory GRAUMAN
85 Director Intl Student/Scholar Svcs ....Ms. Senem BAKAR
92 Dir Univ Honors Program ....Dr. David PIKE
41 Director Athletics & Recreation ....Dr. William (Billy) WALKER
28 Sr Dir Ctr Diversity & Inclusion ....Ms. Tiffany SPEAKS
104 Director AU Abroad ....Ms. Sara E. DUMONT
45 Asst VP Planning/Project Mgmt ....Mr. David DOWER
88 Asst VP Strategic Partnerships ....Ms. Roberta COHEN
88 Asst VP Campaigns and Planning ....Mr. Peter EDELMAN
88 Asst VP Univ Programs Develop ....Ms. Lee HOLSOPPLE
39 Asst VP Housing and Dining Programs ....Mr. Chris MOODY
07 Asst Vice Provost Admissions Ops ....Mr. Robert LINSON
04 Special Asst to President ....Ms. Margaret CLEMMER
22 Sr Dir Employee Relations/Recruitr ....Ms. Deadre JOHNSON
90 Assoc Chief Info Officer ....Ms. Kamalika SANDELL
88 Dir Office of Sponsored Programs ....Mr. James CASEY
88 Dir Univ Col & Learning Communities ..Prof. Sarah MENKE-FISH

The Catholic University of America (A)

620 Michigan Avenue, NE, Washington DC 20064-0002

FICE Identification: 001437
Unit ID: 131283
Telephone: (202) 319-5000 Carnegie Class: RU/H
FAX Number: (202) 319-4441 Calendar System: Semester
URL: www.cua.edu
Established: 1887 Annual Undergrad Tuition & Fees: $40,400
Enrollment: 6,699 Coed
Affiliation or Control: Roman Catholic IRS Status: 501(c)3
Highest Offering: Doctorate
Program: Liberal Arts And General; Teacher Preparatory; Professional
Accreditation: M, CLPSY, CS, ENG, IPSY, LAW, LIB, MUS, NURSE, SW, TED, THEOL

01 President ....Mr. John H. GARVEY
100 VP University Rels/Chief of Staff ....Mr. Frank G. PERSICO
05 Provost ....Dr. Andrew V. ABELA
10 Vice Pres Finance & Treasurer ....Vacant
32 Vice President Student Affairs ....Dr. Michael S. ALLEN
84 Vice Pres Enroll Mgmt/Marketing ....Mr. Christopher P. LYDON
35 Assoc VP Student Life/Dean Students ...Mr. Jonathan C. SAWYER
26 Assoc Vice Pres for Public Affairs ....Mr. Victor B. NAKAS
43 University Counsel ....Mr. Lawrence J. MORRIS
15 Assoc VP/Chief Human Resources .....Ms. Maureen BROOKBANK
18 Assoc VP Facilities Operations ....Mr. Jerry CONRAD
41 Assoc VP & Director Athletics ....Mr. Sean M. SULLIVAN
88 Assoc VP for Campus Services ....Mr. Timothy CARNEY
30 Vice Pres for Univ Advancement ....Mr. Scott REMBOLD
30 Int Assoc VP Univ Advancement ....Ms. Nancy MURRAY
25 Assoc Prov Sponsored Research ....Mr. Ralph ALBANO
58 Dean Graduate Studies ....Dr. James GREENE
48 Dean of Architecture ....Mr. Randall OTT
49 Acting Dean of Arts & Sciences ....Dr. Claudia BORNHOLDT
50 Int Dean Sch of Business/Economics ....Dr. Brian ENGELLAND
54 Dean of Engineering ....Dr. Charles C. NGUYEN
61 Dean of Law ....Mr. Daniel F. ATTRIDGE
64 Dean of Music ....Dr. Grayson WAGSTAFF
70 Dean Natl Catholic Sch Social Svcs ....Dr. William RAINFORD
66 Dean of Nursing ....Dr. Patricia MCMULLEN
73 Acting Dean Theology/Religious Stds ....Dr. William MATTISON
55 Acting Dean Metro Sch Profess Stds ....Dr. William RAINFORD
79 Dean of Philosophy ....Dr. John C. MCCARTHY
88 Dean of Canon Law ....Rev. Robert J. KASLYN, SJ
07 Acting Dir of Undergrad Admissions ....Mr. Andrew COX
13 Chief Information Officer ....Mr. Matthew MCNALLY
08 Director of Libraries ....Mr. Stephen CONNAGHAN
06 Registrar ....Ms. Julie ISHA
36 Director of Career Services ....Mr. Anthony CHIAPPETTA
29 Asst VP Alumni Relations & Univ Adv ....Ms. Kyra A. LYONS
19 Director of Public Safety ....Ms. Thomasine JOHNSON
38 Director of Counseling Center ....Dr. T. Monroe RAYBURN
23 Medical Director of Health Center ....Dr. Loretta STAUDT
37 Dir Student Financial Assistance ....Mr. Joe DOBROTA
39 Director of Housing Services ....Ms. Heidi E. ZEICH
44 Director of the CUA Fund ....Mr. Patrick DAVEY
42 Dir Univ Campus Ministry ....Rev. Jude DEANGELO, OFM CONV
09 Assoc VP Fin Plng/Inst Res/Assess ....Mr. Brian A. JOHNSTON

92 Director Univ Honors Program ....Dr. Peter SHOEMAKER
96 Sr Director of Procurement Services ....Ms. Debbie JACKSON
22 Dir of Employee Relations & EOO ....Ms. Lisa WOOD
88 Compliance and Ethics Officer ....Mr. Vincent A. LACOVARA
40 Manager Bookstore ....Mr. Jonathan HOWARD

Chicago School of Professional Psychology-Washington DC (B)

901 15th Street NW, Washington DC 20005
Telephone: (202) 706-5000 Identification: 770493
Accreditation: &WC

† Branch campus of Chicago School of Professional Psychology Los Angeles Campus, Los Angeles, CA.

Gallaudet University (C)

800 Florida Avenue, NE, Washington DC 20002-3695

FICE Identification: 001443
Unit ID: 131450
Telephone: (202) 651-5000 Carnegie Class: Master's S
FAX Number: (202) 651-5508 Calendar System: Semester
URL: www.gallaudet.edu
Established: 1864 Annual Undergrad Tuition & Fees: $15,625
Enrollment: 1,609 Coed
Affiliation or Control: Independent Non-Profit IRS Status: 501(c)3
Highest Offering: Doctorate
Program: Liberal Arts And General; Teacher Preparatory; Professional
Accreditation: M, ACBSP, AUD, CACREP, CEA, CLPSY, SP, SW, TED

01 President ....Dr. T. Alan HURWITZ
05 Provost ....Dr. Carol J. ERTING
10 Vice Pres Admin & Finance ....Mr. Paul KELLY
30 Vice Pres Dev & Alumni Relations ....Mr. Paul JULIN
88 VP Laurent Clerc Nat Deaf Ed Ctr ....Mr. Edward H. BOSSO
101 Spec Asst to Pres/Board Liaison ....Ms. Rita JENOURE
84 Chief Enrollment Mgmt Officer ....Vacant
28 Chief Diversity Officer ....Vacant
53 Int Dean Sch Educ/Bus/Human Svcs ....Dr. Isaac AGBOOLA
58 Int Dean Graduate School ....Dr. Guarav MATHUR
32 Dean Student Affs/Academic Support ....Mr. Dwight BENEDICT
49 Dean College Arts & Sciences ....Dr. Genie GERTZ
88 Exec Dir Academic Quality ....Dr. Patricia HULSEBOSCH
21 Executive Director Finance ....Ms. Jean CIBUZAR
45 Director University Budget ....Vacant
96 Exec Dir Business Support Services ....Mr. Gary ALLER
18 Director Facilities ....Mr. Amon BROWN
11 Asst Vice Pres Administration ....Mr. Fred WEINER
102 Dir Corp and Foundations Relations ....Vacant
26 Exec Dir Comm & Public Relations ....Ms. Catherine MURPHY
09 Dir Research & Info Services ....Ms. Sarah DUCRAY
29 Director Alumni Relations ....Mr. Samuel SONNENSTRAHL
15 Director Human Resources Svcs ....Ms. Elaine VANCE
14 Exec Dir Technology Services ....Mr. Earl PARKS
88 Dir Technology Servcies Enterprise ......Mr. Harvey GROSSINGER
13 Info Security Officer/Network Dir ....Vacant
88 Director Library Public Services ....Ms. Sarah HAMRICK
88 University Ombuds ....Ms. Elizabeth STONE
88 Dir Library Deaf Collection/Archive ....Mr. Michael OLSON
22 Director Equal Opportunity Programs ....Ms. Sharrell MCCASKILL
06 Registrar ....Ms. Elice PATTERSON

George Washington University (D)

2121 I Street, NW, Washington DC 20052-0002

FICE Identification: 001444
Unit ID: 131469
Telephone: (202) 994-1000 Carnegie Class: RU/VH
FAX Number: (202) 994-0458 Calendar System: Semester
URL: www.gwu.edu
Established: 1821 Annual Undergrad Tuition & Fees: $50,435
Enrollment: 25,613 Coed
Affiliation or Control: Independent Non-Profit IRS Status: 501(c)3
Highest Offering: Doctorate
Program: 2-Year Principally Bachelor's Creditable; Liberal Arts And General; Teacher Preparatory; Professional
Accreditation: M, ARCPA, ART, BUS, BUSA, CACREP, CIDA, CLPSY, CORE, CS, ENG, FEPAC, HSA, LAW, MED, MT, MUS, NURSE, PH, PTA, SP, SPAA, TED

01 President ....Dr. Steven KNAPP
100 Chief of Staff President's Office ....Ms. Barbara A. PORTER
05 Provost & Exec VP Academic Affairs ....Dr. Steven LERMAN
30 Vice Pres for Dev/Alumni Relations ....Mr. Aristide J. COLLINS
10 Exec Vice President & Treasurer ....Mr. Louis H. KATZ
43 Senior Vice Pres & General Counsel ....Ms. Beth NOLAN
26 Vice President External Relations ....Ms. Lorraine A. VOLES
20 Sr Vice Provost Academic Affairs ....Dr. Forrest MALTZMAN
20 Vice Provost of Budget and Finance ....Ms. Rene S. O'NEAL
28 Vice Provost Diversity & Inclusion ....Dr. Terri Harris REED
15 Chief Human Resources Officer ....Ms. Sabrina ELLIS
13 Chief Information Officer ....Mr. David STEINOUR
20 Vice Provost Faculty Affairs ....Dr. Diane C. MARTIN
11 Senior Assoc VP of Operations .....Ms. Alicia M. O'NEIL KNIGHT
32 Senior Assoc VP & Dean of Students ...Dr. Peter A. KONWERSKI
89 Assoc VP & Dean of Freshmen .Ms. Helen CANNADAY SAULNY
90 Assoc VP for Acad Technologies ....Ms. P. B. GARRETT
88 Assoc VP of Acad Plang & Assessment ....Dr. Cheryl BEIL
46 Vice President for Research ....Dr. Leo M. CHALUPA
21 Chief Budget Officer ....Mr. David GREER
21 University Comptroller ....Ms. Sharon HEINLE
09 Director Inst Research & Planning ....Mr. Joachim W. KNOP

86 Assistant Vice President DC Affairs ....Mr. Bernard DEMCZUK
87 Associate VP for International Pgms ....Dr. Donna SCARBORO
08 University Librarian ....Ms. Geneva HENRY
27 Asst VP for Communications ...Ms. Sarah GEGENHEIMER BALDASSARO
27 Exec Director of Media Relations ....Ms. Candace E. SMITH
29 Sr Associate VP Development ....Mr. David B. ANDERSON
06 Registrar ....Ms. Elizabeth A. AMUNDSON
07 Director of Undergrad Admissions ....Ms. Karen S. FELTON
38 Director Counseling Center ....Dr. Silvestro WEISNER
37 Assoc VP & Director Financial Aid ....Mr. Daniel E. SMALL
36 Asst Provost Career Center ....Ms. Rachel A. BROWN
18 Exec Director Facilities ....Mr. James D. SCHROTE
85 Director International Services ....Mr. Joseph G. LEONARD
19 Sr Assoc VP Safety & Security ....Mr. Darrell L. DARNELL
22 Dir EEO & Affirmative Action ....Ms. Vickie FAIR
23 Director Student Health Services ....Dr. Isabel GOLDENBERG
40 Director GW Bookstore ....Mr. Robert C. BLAKE
107 Dean Col of Professional Studies ....Dr. Ali ESKANDARIAN
49 Dean Columbian Col Arts/Sciences ....Dr. Ben VINSON
63 Interim Dean Medicine & Health Sci ....Dr. Jeffrey S. AKMAN
69 Dean School of Public Health ....Dr. Lynn R. GOLDMAN
61 Dean Law School ....Dr. Blake D. MORANT
54 Dean Engineer/Applied Science ....Dr. David DOLLING
53 Dean Education/Human Development ....Dr. Michael J. FEUER
50 Dean School of Business ....Dr. Linda A. LIVINGSTONE
82 Dean Elliott School Intl Affairs ....Dr. Michael E. BROWN
66 Dean School of Nursing ....Dr. Jean JOHNSON
12 Dean GW Virginia Sci/Tech Campus ....Dr. Ali ESKANDARIAN
88 Sen Assoc Dean Military & Veterans ....VAdm. Melvin G. WILLIAMS
41 Director Athletics/Recreation ....Mr. Patrick NERO
84 Asst VP Grad Student Enroll Mgmt ....Dr. Kristin WILLIAMS
92 Director University Honors Program ....Dr. Maria H. FRAWLEY
93 Director Multicultural Student Svc ....Mr. Michael R. TAPSCOTT
101 VP and Secretary of the University ....Mr. Aristide J. COLLINS
104 Director Study Abroad ....Mr. Robert HALLWORTH
39 Director Student Housing ....Mr. Seth D. WEINSHEL

Georgetown University (E)

37th & O Streets, NW, Washington DC 20057-1947

FICE Identification: 001445
Unit ID: 131496
Telephone: (202) 687-0100 Carnegie Class: RU/VH
FAX Number: N/A Calendar System: Semester
URL: www.georgetown.edu
Established: 1789 Annual Undergrad Tuition & Fees: $48,048
Enrollment: 17,858 Coed
Affiliation or Control: Roman Catholic IRS Status: 501(c)3
Highest Offering: Doctorate
Program: Liberal Arts And General; Professional
Accreditation: M, ANEST, BUS, CEA, HSA, LAW, MED, MIDWF, NURSE, PAST

01 President ....Dr. John (Jack) J. DEGIOIA
46 Sr VP Research/Chief Technology Off .....Dr. Spiros DIMOLITSAS
101 Secretary of the University ....Mr. Edward M. QUINN
100 Chief of Staff ....Mr. Joseph FERRARA
05 Provost ....Dr. Robert M. GROVES
17 Exec Vice Pres Health Sciences ....Dr. Howard J. FEDEROFF
61 Exec Vice Pres/Dean of Law School ......Dr. William M. TREANOR
30 Vice Pres for Advancement ....Mr. R. Bartley MOORE
42 Vice Pres for Mission and Ministry ....Rev. Kevin O'BRIEN, SJ
11 Sr Vice Pres and COO ....Mr. Christopher L. AUGOSTINI
10 Vice Pres Finance & Univ Treasurer ....Mr. David RUBENSTEIN
13 Interim Vice Pres/CIO ....Mr. Judd NICHOLSON
15 VP/Chief HR Officer ....Ms. Brenda R. MALONE
26 VP Public Affairs & Strategic Dev ....Mr. Erik SMULSON
27 Assoc VP Communications ....Ms. Stacy KERR
18 VP Planning & Facilities Mgmt ....Mr. Robin MOREY
32 Vice President for Student Affairs ....Dr. Todd OLSON
28 VP for Inst Diversity & Equity ....Ms. Rosemary KILKENNY
19 Chief of Police Dept Public Safety ....Mr. Jay GRUBER
43 VP & General Counsel ....Ms. Lisa M. BROWN
88 VP for Global Engagement ....Dr. Thomas BANCHOFF
29 Associate VP Alumni Relations ....Mr. William G. REYNOLDS
109 Assoc VP for Auxiliary Services ....Ms. Joelle D. WIESE
88 Assc VP Benefits/Chief Benefits Off ....Mr. Charles E. DESANTIS
14 Associate VP & Deputy CIO ....Mr. Judd L. NICHOLSON
91 Assoc VP Enterprise Apps ....Ms. Kelly P. DONEY
20 Vice Provost Education ....Dr. Randall BASS
20 Vice Provost Research ....Dr. Janet MANN
20 Vice Provost Faculty ....Dr. Adriana KUGLER
21 VP Fin Acctg & Systems ....Ms. Pim THUKRAL
21 Assoc VP Fin Ops ....Mr. Lennie M. CARTER
21 Asst VP Fin Planning & Budget ....Mr. Matthew C. GREAVES
06 Registrar ....Mr. John Q. PIERCE, IV
21 VP & COO Main Campus ....Mr. Darryl E. CHRISTMON
07 Dean Undergraduate Admissions ....Mr. Charles A. DEACON
90 AVP University Information Sys ....Ms. Ardoth HASSLER
35 Assoc VP Student Affairs ....Dr. Jeanne F. LORD
23 Asst VP for Student Health ....Dr. James C. WELSH
08 University Librarian ....Ms. Artemis G. KIRK
88 Ex Dir Ctr New Designs Lrng/Schlrs ....Dr. Edward J. MALONEY
37 Dean Student Financial Svcs ....Ms. Patricia A. MCWADE
25 Director of Sponsored Programs ....Ms. Mary E. SCHMIEDEL
49 Dean Georgetown College ....Dr. Chester GILLIS
82 Dean School Foreign Service ....Dr. Joel HELLMAN
50 Dean School of Business ....Dr. David A. THOMAS
63 Dean Medical School ....Dr. Stephen R. MITCHELL
66 Int Dean Sch of Nurs/Health Stds ....Dr. Patricia CLOONAN
51 Dean Continuing Studies ....Dr. Kelly OTTER
58 Dean of Grad School ....Dr. Norberto M. GRZYWACZ

80 Dean McCourt School Public Policy Dr. Edward B. MONTGOMERY
86 Asst to President Federal Relations Mr. Scott S. FLEMING
31 Interim AVP Community Engagement/ SI Ms. Brenda ATKINSON-WILLOUGHBY
96 Asst VP Purch/Contracts & AP Mr. Curt TOPPER
85 Director of Global Services Ms. Vanessa MEYERS
104 Director of Global Education Mr. Craig RINKER
36 Exec Director Career Center Dr. J. Michael SCHAUB
22 Director Affirmative Action Pgm Mr. Michael W. SMITH
24 Exec Dir Classroom Educ/Tech Svcs Mr. Mark J. COHEN
38 Director Counseling Center Dr. Philip W. MEILMAN
41 Director Athletics Mr. Lee REED
39 Director of Residence Life Ms. Stephanie J. LYNCH
108 Asst Dir CNDLS/Assessment Ms. Mindy MCWILLIAMS
25 Dir Spons Projects Financial Ops Vacant
102 Dir Found & Corp Relations Ms. Carma FAUNTLEROY
44 Exec Director Gift Planning Mr. Stephen LINK

Graduate School USA (A)

600 Maryland Ave, SW Ste 330, Washington DC 20024

Identification: 667121

Telephone: (202) 314-3300 Carnegie Class: Not Classified
FAX Number: (202) 479-2502 Calendar System: Semester
URL: www.graduateschool.edu
Established: Annual Undergrad Tuition & Fees: $6,550
Enrollment: 22 Coed
Affiliation or Control: Independent Non-Profit IRS Status: 501(c)3
Highest Offering: Associate Degree
Program: Occupational
Accreditation: @M

01 Interim CEO & President Dr. Elaine RYAN

Howard University (B)

2400 Sixth Street, NW, Washington DC 20059-0001

FICE Identification: 001448
Unit ID: 131520

Telephone: (202) 806-6100 Carnegie Class: RU/H
FAX Number: (202) 806-5934 Calendar System: Semester
URL: www.howard.edu
Established: 1867 Annual Undergrad Tuition & Fees: $23,970
Enrollment: 10,672 Coed
Affiliation or Control: Independent Non-Profit IRS Status: 501(c)3
Highest Offering: Doctorate
Program: Occupational; Liberal Arts And General; Teacher Preparatory; Professional
Accreditation: M, ARCPA, ART, BUS, BUSA, CLPSY, COPSY, CS, DENT, DH, DIETC, ENG, IPSY, JOUR, LAW, MED, MT, MUS, NURSE, OT, PHAR, #PTA, RTT, SP, SW, TED, THEA, THEOL

01 President Dr. Wayne FREDERICK
05 Provost/Chief Acad Officer Dr. Anthony K. WUTOH
101 Interim Secretary of Univ Ms. Florence PRIOLEAU
43 General Counsel Ms. Florence PRIOLEAU
10 Chief Financial Officer Mr. Michael MASCH
26 Vice President for External Affairs Ms. Gracia HILLMAN
11 Chief Operating Officer Mr. Tony BANSAL
30 Vice President Development Ms. Nesta BERNARD
17 CEO University Hospital Mr. James EDWARDS
46 Assoc Provost Research & Graduates Dr. Gary L. HARRIS
20 Assistant Provost Dr. Mary HILL
20 Assoc Provost Undergraduate Studies Dr. Melanie CARTER
32 Vice President Student Affairs Dr. Constance M. ELLISON
88 AVP Regulatory/Research Compliance Dr. Thomas O. OBISESAN
88 AVP for Research Health Sciences Dr. Kristy F. WOODS
13 Chief Information Officer Mr. Carlos DE LA ROSA
100 Chief of Staff Ms. LaRue BARKWELL
58 Dean Graduate School Dr. Gary L. HARRIS
49 Dean College Arts/Sciences Dr. Bernard A. MAIR
50 Dean School of Business Dr. Barron H. HARVEY
61 Dean School of Law Ms. Danielle R. HOLLEY-WALKER
63 Dean Medicine/VP Clinical Affairs Dr. Hugh E. MIGHTY
52 Dean College of Dentistry Dr. Leo E. ROUSE
54 Interim Dean Col Engr/Arch/Comp Sc Dr. Lorraine FLEMING
53 Dean School of Education Dr. Leslie T. FENWICK
60 Dean School Communications Dr. Gracie LAWSON-BORDERS
88 Dean Nursing/Allied Hlth Sc Dr. Gina S. BROWN
70 Dean School of Social Work Dr. Sandra CREWE
73 Dean School of Divinity Dr. Alton B. POLLARD, III
67 Dean School of Pharmacy Dr. Anthony WUTOH
48 Director School of Architecture Prof. Victor DZIDZIENYO
76 Assoc Dean/Div Allied Health Sci Dr. Shirley J. JACKSON
66 Assoc Dean/Div of Nursing Ms. Tammi L. DAMAS
57 Assoc Dean/Division of Fine Arts Dr. Gwendolyn H. EVERETT
81 Assoc Dean/Div Natural Sciences Dr. Robert CATCHINGS
83 Interim Assoc Dean/Social Sciences Dr. Terri ADAMS
23 Associate VP for Clinical Affairs Dr. Feseha WOLDU
06 Registrar Ms. LaTrice BYAM
37 Director Financial Aid Mr. Derek KINDLE
07 Director of Admissions Ms. Latrice BYAM
42 Dean Andrew Rankin Chapel Dr. Bernard L. RICHARDSON
35 Dean Student Life & Activities Ms. Tonya L. GUILLORY
39 Dean of Residence Life Mr. Lamar J. WHITE
36 Director Career Services Office Dr. Joan M. BROWNE
08 Director University Libraries Mr. Howard DODSON, JR.
88 Director Health Sciences Library Ms. Cynthia L. HENDERSON
88 Director Law Library Ms. Rhea BALLARD-THROWER
24 Dir Teaching Learning & Assmnt Ctr Dr. Theresa M. REDD
26 VP Communications & Marketing Mr. William WHITMAN, JR.
15 VP for Human Resources Ms. Carrolyn J. BOSTICK
16 Senior Director Human Resources Mr. Michael MCFADDEN
22 Dir Equal Employment Opportunity Mr. Antwan LOFTON
30 Director for Advancement Services Mr. Jeremy C. RANDALL
29 Senior Director Alumni Relations Mr. Charles GIBBS
44 Senior Director of Annual Giving Mr. Keith D. MILES
19 Chief of Campus Police Mr. Brian K. JORDAN
31 Director HU Community Association Ms. Maybelle T. BENNETT
109 Interim Asst VP Auxil Enterprises Mr. Antwan D. CLINTON
92 Director of Honors Program Dr. Daniel A. WILLIAMS, III
41 Interim Athletics Director Ms. Shelley DAVIS
23 Director Student Health Center Dr. Evelyn TREAKLE-MOORE
40 Gen Manager Barnes & Noble at HU Mr. Alex BAMFO
94 Director of Women's Studies Vacant
18 Director Physical Facilities Mr. Victor MCNAUGHTON
108 Director Institutional Assessment Dr. Gerunda B. HUGHES

The Institute of World Politics (C)

1521 16th Street, NW, Washington DC 20036-1464

FICE Identification: 041144
Unit ID: 455804

Telephone: (202) 462-2101 Carnegie Class: Spec/Other
FAX Number: (202) 464-0335 Calendar System: Semester
URL: www.iwp.edu
Established: 1990 Annual Graduate Tuition & Fees: $28,600
Enrollment: 144 Coed
Affiliation or Control: Independent Non-Profit IRS Status: 501(c)3
Highest Offering: Master's; No Undergraduates
Program: Professional
Accreditation: M

01 President Dr. John LENCZOWSKI
03 Executive Vice President Noah RUDOLPH
05 Academic Dean Dr. John TIERNEY
10 Director Financial Operations Elaine PINDER
30 VP Institutional Advancement Tom ATWOOD
32 VP Student Affairs and Admissions Jason JOHNSRUD
06 Registrar & Institutional Research Hasanna BENSON-TYUS
88 Director Professional Affiliations Dr. Tania MASTRAPA
84 Director Student Recruitment Tim STEBBINS
29 Director Alumni Relations Katie BRIDGES
36 Director Student Placement Derrick DORTCH
37 Director Financial Aid Thelbert SNOWDEN
26 Director Marketing and Comm MaryAnne GARNER
08 Director Libraries/Info Svcs Dmitry KULIK
04 Asst to President/Development Ofcr Kathy CARROLL

Medtech College (D)

529 14th Street, NW, Washington DC 20045

Telephone: (202) 872-4700 Identification: 666591
Accreditation: COE

† National accreditation is carried under parent institution in Falls Church, VA.

Pontifical Faculty of the Immaculate Conception at the Dominican House of Studies (E)

487 Michigan Avenue, NE, Washington DC 20017-1585

FICE Identification: 012803
Unit ID: 131405

Telephone: (202) 495-3820 Carnegie Class: Spec/Faith
FAX Number: (202) 495-3873 Calendar System: Semester
URL: www.dhs.edu
Established: 1902 Annual Graduate Tuition & Fees: $16,080
Enrollment: 95 Coed
Affiliation or Control: Roman Catholic IRS Status: 501(c)3
Highest Offering: Master's; No Undergraduates
Program: Professional; Religious Emphasis
Accreditation: M, THEOL

01 President Fr. John LANGLOIS, OP
05 Vice President/Academic Dean Fr. Thomas PETRI, OP
20 Secretary of Studies Fr. Brian CHRZASTEK, OP
08 Librarian Fr. John Martin RUIZ, OP
18 Director of Facilities Ms. Shauna ROYE
42 Chaplain to Commuter Students Fr. John Martin RUIZ, OP
06 Registrar Fr. Albert TRUDEL, OP
10 Treasurer/Director of Financial Aid Ms. Shauna ROYE
30 Assistant Director of Advancement Mr. George CERVANTES
13 IT Director Mr. Carlos MOLINA
36 Director of Career Placement Dr. Jem SULLIVAN
04 Executive Assistant Mrs. Patricia WORK
88 Administrative Secretary Ms. Sharon SMITH

Pontifical John Paul II Institute for Studies on Marriage and Family (F)

620 Michigan Ave, NE, McGivney Hall, Washington DC 20064

FICE Identification: 041427
Unit ID: 455813

Telephone: (202) 526-3799 Carnegie Class: Spec/Other
FAX Number: (202) 269-6090 Calendar System: Other
URL: www.johnpaulii.edu
Established: 1988 Annual Graduate Tuition & Fees: $17,460
Enrollment: 64 Coed
Affiliation or Control: Roman Catholic IRS Status: 501(c)3
Highest Offering: Doctorate; No Undergraduates
Program: Professional; Religious Emphasis
Accreditation: M

01 President Rev. Livio MELINA
03 Vice President Carl A. ANDERSON
05 Provost/Dean Fr. Antonio LOPEZ
20 Associate Dean for Academic Affairs David S. CRAWFORD
11 Assoc Dean Progams & Administration Nick J. BAGILEO
06 Registrar Joseph C. ATKINSON
07 Director of Admissions Sara L. TRUDEAU

† Affiliated with The Catholic University of America, DC.

Radians College (G)

1025 Vermont Avenue, Suite 200, Washington DC 20005

Identification: 667005
Unit ID: 481119

Telephone: (202) 291-9020 Carnegie Class: Not Classified
FAX Number: (202) 291-8013 Calendar System: Trimester
URL: www.radianscollege.edu
Established: 2005 Annual Undergrad Tuition & Fees: $47,037
Enrollment: 215 Coed
Affiliation or Control: Proprietary IRS Status: Proprietary
Highest Offering: Associate Degree
Program: Occupational; 2-Year Principally Bachelor's Creditable; Nursing Emphasis
Accreditation: ACICS

01 President Stephanie JACKSON
05 VP Academic Administration Vacant

Strayer University (H)

1133 15th Street, NW, Washington DC 20005-2710

FICE Identification: 001459
Unit ID: 131803

Telephone: (202) 408-2400 Carnegie Class: Master's L
FAX Number: (202) 419-1423 Calendar System: Quarter
URL: www.strayer.edu
Established: 1892 Annual Undergrad Tuition & Fees: $12,975
Enrollment: 38,159 Coed
Affiliation or Control: Proprietary IRS Status: Proprietary
Highest Offering: Master's
Program: Occupational; Liberal Arts And General; Professional
Accreditation: M, ACBSP, TEAC

01 President Dr. Michael PLATER
05 Provost/Chief Academic Ofcr Vacant
20 Sr Vice Provost of Academic Admin Vacant
32 Senior Vice Provost Student Affairs Ms. Chandra QUAYE
08 University Librarian Mr. David A. MOULTON
06 University Registrar Ms. Laurie KOHSMANN
20 Chamblee Campus Dean Dr. Charles SMITH, JR.
12 Chamblee Campus Director Mr. Rick WYLIE
20 Chesterfield Campus Dean Ms. Carol WILLIAMS
12 Chesterfield Campus Director Ms. Cheryl VAUGHAN
20 Christiana Campus Dean Dr. G. Mick SMITH
12 Christiana Campus Director Ms. Amy CESTONE
20 Charleston Campus Dean Dr. Andrea BRVENIK
12 Charleston Campus Director Ms. Colette REID
20 Cobb County Campus Dean Ms. Andrea BANTO
12 Cobb County Campus Director Ms. Jenna BAILEY
20 Columbia Campus Dean Dr. Vincent OSISEK
12 Columbia Campus Director Ms. Marcia JOHNSON
20 Delaware County Campus Dean Dr. Paul HINKSMAN
12 Delaware County Campus Director Ms. Tammy EVANS-COLQUITT
20 Fredericksburg Campus Dean Dr. Wesley PHILLIPS
12 Fredericksburg Campus Director Mr. Duan BUTLER
20 Greensboro Campus Dean Dr. Teresa GREENWOOD
12 Greensboro Campus Director Mr. David GORA
20 Asst Henrico Campus Dean Mr. Nate SMITH
12 Henrico Campus Director Ms. Amy BREEDEN
20 Lower Bucks Campus Dean Dr. John CRAIG
12 Lower Bucks Campus Director Ms. Lauren PLINER
20 Greenville Campus Dean Dr. Ingrid WRIGHT
12 Greenville Campus Director Ms. Ashley MILLS
20 Interim King of Prussia Campus Dean Dr. Tammy EVANS-COLQUITT
12 King of Prussia Campus Director Mr. Marvin HARRIS
20 Loudoun Campus Dean Mr. Hammad ELBEDOUR
12 Loudoun Campus Director Shirin SAGHAFI
20 Manassas Campus Dean Mr. Brian ABDUL-KARIM
12 Manassas Campus Director Mr. Nathan BEREZAN
20 North Raleigh Campus Dean Dr. Pang-Jen CRAIG KUNG
12 North Raleigh Campus Director Ms. Amy MISKO
20 Morrow Campus Dean Dr. Stephanie HAWKINS
12 Morrow Campus Director Mr. Cleveland (Tony) JACKSON
20 Nashville Campus Dean Dr. Carla HERYHAND
12 Nashville Campus Director Ms. Marilyn MAYE
20 Newport News Campus Dean Dr. Damita GOODS
12 Newport News Campus Director Mr. Ryan ALLEN
20 North Charlotte Campus Dean Dr. Jeffrey ROMANCZUK
12 North Charlotte Campus Director Ms. Christine VITO
20 Owings Mills Campus Dean Talil A. THOMAS
12 Owings Mills Campus Director Oleida WILLIAMS
20 Roswell Campus Dean Dr. Charles SMITH, JR.
12 Roswell Campus Director Mr. Paul LAWSON
20 Shelby Oaks Campus Dean Dr. Clinton MILLER
12 Shelby Oaks Campus Director Mr. Shawn COOK
20 Penn Center West Campus Dean Vacant
12 Penn Center West Campus Director Vacant

20 Prince Georges Campus Dean .... Dr. Tressa SHAVERS
12 Prince Georges Campus Director .... Ms. Chinneta COLLINS
20 Research Triangle Park Campus Dean .... Dr. Lila JORDAN
12 Research Triangle Park Campus Dir .... Pashuan ARMOND
20 Rockville Campus Dean .... Dr. Japheth KALUYU
12 Rockville Campus Director .... Ms. Tara VENTURA
20 South Charlotte Campus Dean .....Dr. Miranda CARLTON-CAREW
12 South Charlotte Campus Director .... Ms. Janet BEAMER
20 Virginia Beach Campus Dean ....Ms. Angela BARCLIFT-MCGEE
12 Virginia Beach Campus Director .... Mr. Tom LOTITO
12 Takoma Park Campus Director .... Mr. D'Andre WILSON
20 Takoma Park Campus Dean .... Dr. Yohannes ABATE
20 Tampa East Campus Dean .... Dr. Saul IVY
12 Tampa East Campus Director .... Mr. Jeffrey KEITH
20 Tampa Westshore Campus Dean .... Dr. Andrea BRVENIK
12 Tampa Westshore Campus Director .... Mr. Jeffrey KEITH
20 Woodbridge Campus Dean .... Dr. Doris MARTIN
12 Woodbridge Campus Director .... Mr. Haroon MOKEL
12 Thousand Oaks Campus Director .... Ms. Ginia RABB
20 Thousand Oaks Campus Dean ....Dr. Melody PRINCESS-KELLY
20 Washington Campus Dean .... Dr. Trenace RICHARDSON
12 Washington Campus Director .... Mr. Edmund BRIETLING
20 White Marsh Campus Dean .... Shadrack KOROS
12 White Marsh Campus Director .... Leator KNUCKLES
20 Arlington Campus Dean .... Ms. Shanee MAJOR-KELLY
12 Arlington Campus Director .... Ms. Breanna WINTER
20 Alexandria Campus Dean ....Dr. Angela AGBOLI-ESEDEBE
12 Alexandria Campus Director .... Ms. Ashley COLLINS
20 Center City Campus Dean .... Dr. Wanda ALLEN
12 Center City Campus Director .... Mr. Isaac WALTERS
20 Anne Arundel Campus Dean .... Dr. Twila LINDSAY
12 Anne Arundel Campus Director .... Ms. Cristen JONES
20 Birmingham Campus Dean .... Dr. Vidal ADADEVOH
12 Birmingham Campus Director .... Mr. Keith JOHNSON
20 Chesapeake Campus Dean .... Dr. Leslie KKAYANAN
12 Chesapeake Campus Director .... Ms. Jeanne POINDEXTER

Trinity Washington University (A)

125 Michigan Avenue, NE, Washington DC 20017-1090
FICE Identification: 001460
Unit ID: 131876
Telephone: (202) 884-9000 Carnegie Class: Master's L
FAX Number: (202) 884-9229 Calendar System: Semester
URL: www.trinitydc.edu
Established: 1897 Annual Undergrad Tuition & Fees: $22,686
Enrollment: 2,267 Female
Affiliation or Control: Roman Catholic IRS Status: 501(c)3
Highest Offering: Master's
Program: Liberal Arts And General; Teacher Preparatory; Professional
Accreditation: M, NURSE, TED

01 President .... Ms. Patricia A. MCGUIRE
04 Special Assistant to the President .... Ms. Kim MORTON
05 Vice President Academic Affairs .... Dr. Carlotta OCAMPO
84 Vice Pres Enrollment Development .... Dr. Stephanie L. KRUSEMARK
30 Vice Pres Institutional Advancement ....Ms. Ann PAULEY
11 Vice President Administration ....Mr. Michael MALEWICKI
32 Vice President for Student Affairs .... Dr. Karen GERLACH
44 Vice President of Development .... Ms. Kathleen ZEIFANG
15 Vice President for Human Resources .... Ms. Carole KING
49 Dean College of Arts & Science .... Dr. Pamela BARNETT
53 Dean School of Education .... Dr. Janet STOCKS
107 Dean School of Professional Studies .... Ms. Nevada WINROW
66 Dean Sch Nursing/Health Professions .... Dr. Mary ROMANELLO
35 Dean of Student Services .... Ms. Michelle BOWIE
41 Athletic Director .... Ms. Tracy RENKEN
42 Director of Campus Ministry .... Ms. Lynn MYRICK
18 Exec Director Facilities Services .... Mr. Tim KNIGHT
29 Director Alumnae Affairs .... Ms. Margy REAGAN

University of the District of Columbia (B)

4200 Connecticut Avenue, NW,
Washington DC 20008-1174
FICE Identification: 001441
Unit ID: 131399
Telephone: (202) 274-5000 Carnegie Class: Master's S
FAX Number: (202) 274-5304 Calendar System: Semester
URL: www.udc.edu
Established: 1976 Annual Undergrad Tuition & Fees (In-District): $7,420
Enrollment: 4,803 Coed
Affiliation or Control: Local IRS Status: 501(c)3
Highest Offering: Master's
Program: Occupational; 2-Year Principally Bachelor's Creditable; Liberal Arts And General; Teacher Preparatory; Professional
Accreditation: M, ACBSP, ADNUR, CACREP, COARC, CS, DIETD, ENG, FUSER, LAW, NUR, SP, SW, TED

01 President .... Mr. Ronald MASON, JR.
05 Provost/Vice Pres Academic Affairs .... Dr. Rachel PETTY
32 Vice President for Student Affairs .... Dr. Valerie EPPS
15 Vice President Human Resources .... Ms. Myrtho BLANCHARD
18 Acting VP Facilities & Real Estate .... Mr. Erik THOMPSON
30 Vice Pres University Advancement ....Mr. Michael C. ROGERS
20 Executive Asst to the Provost .... Mr. Herman PRESCOTT
10 Chief Financial Officer .... Mr. Donald RICKFORD
49 Dean Arts & Sciences .... Dr. April MASSEY
50 Dean Sch Business & Public Admin .... Dr. Sandra YATES
61 Dean School of Law .... Ms. Shelley BRODERICK
54 Dean Engineering/Applied Scis .... Dr. Devdas SHETTY
56 Dean Agric/Urban Sustainabilty .... Dr. Sabine O'HARA
06 University Registrar .... Ms. LaVerne M. HILL-FLANAGAN
37 Director Student Financial Aid .... Mr. James CONTRERAS
26 Dir Marketing & Communications .... Mr. Michael C. ROGERS
08 Interim Dean Learning Resources .... Ms. Melba BROOME
25 Director Grants Administration .... Ms. Cassandra PARKER
41 Athletic Director .... Ms. Patricia A. THOMAS
43 Acting General Counsel .... Mr. Smruti RADKAR
88 General Manager UDC Cable TV .... Mr. Edward JONES, JR.
18 Dir of Operations and Maintenance .... Mr. Alvin VENSON
30 Exec Director of Development .... Ms. Felicia BRANT
09 Director of Institutional Research .... Mrs. Jackie XU
38 Director Student Counseling .... Dr. Sislena LEDBETTER
96 Director of Procurement .... Ms. Mary A. HARRIS
27 Director of Communications .... Mr. John GORDON
88 Dean Student Achievement .... Ms. Hermina P. PETERS
103 Dean Workforce Development .... Ms. Kim R. FORD
19 Dir Public Safety/Chief of Police .... Mr. Larry E. VOLTZ
36 Director Career Services .... Mr. Jared E. MOFFETT
86 Director State & Local Affairs .... Mr. Thomas E. REDMOND
21 Director Financial Operations .... Mr. David FRANKLIN
88 Director STEM .... Ms. Barbara J. HOLMES
29 Director Alumni Affairs .... Mr. Joseph LIBERTELLI
89 Director of Advising and Retention .... Ms. Kimberly CREWS
102 Director Sponsored Programs .... Ms. Jovita WELLS
13 Dir Information Technology .... Mr. Michael ROGERS
07 Director Admissions/TRIO Programs .... Ms. Saundra CARTER
101 Exec Secretary Office the Board .... Ms. Beverly FRANKLIN
28 Director of Labor & Employee Rels .... Ms. Jennifer MATTHEWS
84 Director Office of Retention .... Mr. Timothy L. HATCHETT

University of Phoenix Washington DC Campus (C)

25 Massachusetts Avenue, NW,
Washington DC 20001-1431
Telephone: (202) 423-2520 Identification: 770196
Accreditation: &NH, ACBSP

† Branch campus of University of Phoenix, Tempe, AZ.

University of the Potomac (D)

1401 H Street NW, Suite 100, Washington DC 20005
FICE Identification: 032183
Unit ID: 384412
Telephone: (202) 274-2303 Carnegie Class: Spec/Bus
FAX Number: N/A Calendar System: Semester
URL: www.potomac.edu
Established: 1991 Annual Undergrad Tuition & Fees: $13,433
Enrollment: 264 Coed
Affiliation or Control: Proprietary IRS Status: Proprietary
Highest Offering: Master's
Program: Business Emphasis
Accreditation: #M

01 President/Chief Executive Officer .... Dr. Clinton GARDNER
108 VP Assessment/Inst Effectiveness .... Walter PERSON
08 Director of Learning Resource Ctr .... Edward ROBINSON
07 Director of Admissions .... Nerissa CONN-KULLING
26 Dir Marketing/Public Relations .... Danijel LOZIC

Wesley Theological Seminary (E)

4500 Massachusetts Avenue, NW,
Washington DC 20016-5690
FICE Identification: 001464
Unit ID: 131973
Telephone: (202) 885-8600 Carnegie Class: Spec/Faith
FAX Number: (202) 885-8605 Calendar System: Semester
URL: www.wesleyseminary.edu
Established: 1882 Annual Graduate Tuition & Fees: $18,662
Enrollment: 561 Coed
Affiliation or Control: United Methodist IRS Status: 501(c)3
Highest Offering: Doctorate; No Undergraduates
Program: Professional; Religious Emphasis
Accreditation: M, THEOL

01 President .... Dr. David MCALLISTER-WILSON
10 Vice Pres Finance/CFO .... Mr. Jeffrey STRAITS
11 Vice President for Administration .... Rev. Terry BRADFIELD
04 Exec Assistant to the President .... Ms. Elizabeth MATHIS
05 Dean .... Dr. Robert MARTIN
32 Assoc Dean for Community Life .... Rev. Asa LEE
07 Director of Admissions .... Rev. William D. ALDRIDGE
06 Registrar .... Ms. Eleanor GEASE
08 Director of Library .... Mr. James ESTES
15 Director Human Resources .... Ms. Yasmin LEWIS-WHITE
18 Chief Facilities/Physical Plant .... Mr. Randall ADAMS
37 Director Student Financial Aid .... Ms. Mary VIBERT
29 Director Alumni Relations .... Ms. Kristin SCHOL
26 Director of Marketing/Communication .... Ms. Amy SHELTON
84 Enrollment Counselor .... Mr. Patrick BARRETT

FLORIDA

Academy for Five Element Acupuncture (F)

305 SE Second Avenue, Gainesville FL 32601-6811
County: Alachua FICE Identification: 035243
Unit ID: 451079
Telephone: (352) 335-2332 Carnegie Class: Spec/Health
FAX Number: (352) 337-2535 Calendar System: Trimester
URL: www.acupuncturist.edu
Established: 1998 Annual Graduate Tuition & Fees: $4,770
Enrollment: 71 Coed
Affiliation or Control: Independent Non-Profit IRS Status: 501(c)3
Highest Offering: Master's; No Undergraduates
Program: Professional
Accreditation: ACUP

01 President .... Ms. Misti OXFORD-PICKERAL
11 Vice President Administration .... Ms. Joanne EPSTEIN
05 Academic Dean .... Mr. Chuck GRAHAM
10 Finance Director .... Ms. Odalis CRUZ
37 Financial Aid Administrator .... Mr. Glenn MORRIS
06 Registrar .... Ms. Rachel SIMS
07 Admissions Counselor .... Mr. Jim BROOKS

Academy for Nursing and Health Occupations (G)

5154 Okeechobee Blvd #201, West Palm Beach FL 33417
County: Palm Beach FICE Identification: 033463
Unit ID: 412173
Telephone: (561) 683-1400 Carnegie Class: Not Classified
FAX Number: (561) 683-6773 Calendar System: Other
URL: www.anho.edu
Established: 1978 Annual Undergrad Tuition & Fees: $26,113
Enrollment: 424 Coed
Affiliation or Control: Independent Non-Profit IRS Status: 501(c)3
Highest Offering: Associate Degree
Program: Occupational; 2-Year Principally Bachelor's Creditable; Nursing Emphasis
Accreditation: COE

01 President .... Lois M. GACKENHEIMER
05 Interim Academic Dean .... Dr. Rene WERNER
06 Registrar .... Elizabeth RODRIGUEZ
07 Admissions Specialist .... Angela STILES

Acupuncture & Massage College (H)

10506 N Kendall Drive, Miami FL 33176-1509
County: Miami-Dade FICE Identification: 034145
Unit ID: 439969
Telephone: (305) 595-9500 Carnegie Class: Spec/Health
FAX Number: (305) 595-2622 Calendar System: Semester
URL: www.amcollege.edu
Established: 1983 Annual Undergrad Tuition & Fees: $45,000
Enrollment: 148 Coed
Affiliation or Control: Proprietary IRS Status: Proprietary
Highest Offering: Master's
Program: Professional; Technical Emphasis
Accreditation: ACCSC, ACUP

01 President .... Dr. Richard M. BROWNE
05 Academic Dean .... Dr. Sylvia SANTANA
17 Clinic Director .... Dr. Wel LU
37 Financial Aid Director .... Ms. Christy WOOD
07 Admissions Director .... Mr. Joe CALARESO
06 Registrar/Student Services .... Ms. Maria GARCIA

Advance Science Institute (I)

3750 West 12 Avenue, Hialeah FL 33012
County: Miami-Dade FICE Identification: 037573
Unit ID: 444334
Telephone: (305) 827-5452 Carnegie Class: Not Classified
FAX Number: (305) 557-2268 Calendar System: Semester
URL: asimedschool.com
Established: 1997 Annual Undergrad Tuition & Fees: $15,660
Enrollment: 34 Coed
Affiliation or Control: Proprietary IRS Status: Proprietary
Highest Offering: Associate Degree
Program: Occupational; 2-Year Principally Bachelor's Creditable
Accreditation: ACCSC

01 President .... Pablo PEREZ

Adventist University of Health Sciences (J)

671 Winyah Drive, Orlando FL 32803-1204
County: Orange FICE Identification: 031155
Unit ID: 133872
Telephone: (407) 303-9798 Carnegie Class: Spec/Health
FAX Number: (407) 303-9408 Calendar System: Trimester
URL: www.adu.edu
Established: 1992 Annual Undergrad Tuition & Fees: $13,030
Enrollment: 2,090 Coed
Affiliation or Control: Seventh-day Adventist IRS Status: 501(c)3

Highest Offering: Master's
Program: Occupational; Professional
Accreditation: SC, ADNUR, ANEST, #ARCPA, DMS, NMT, NUR, OT, OTA, RAD

01 President ... Dr. David E. GREENLAW
05 Provost ... Dr. Edwin HERNANDEZ
10 Sr VP for Finance/CFO ... Mr. Ruben O. MARTINEZ
32 VP for Student Services ... Mr. Stephen H. ROCHE
26 VP Marketing & Public Relations ... Mr. Lonnie MIXON
106 VP for Educational Tech/Distance Ed ... Dr. Dan LIM
20 Associate VP for Academic Admin ... Dr. Len ARCHER
09 Dir of Institutional Effec & Accred ... Dr. Roy LUKMAN
37 Director of Financial Aid ... Ms. Rebecca VALENCIA
06 Registrar ... Dr. Janet CALDERON
45 Dir of Grant Management ... Ms. Stefanie JOHNSON
88 Director Ctr for Acad Achievement ... Ms. Yvette C. SALIBA
08 Library Director ... Ms. Deanna L. FLORES
42 Campus Chaplain ... Mr. Reynold ACOSTA
07 Director of Enrollment Services ... Mrs. Katie R. SHAW
21 Chief Accountant ... Mr. Grayson GOODMAN
39 Director of Residence Hall ... Mr. David A. BRYANT
30 Development Officer ... Dr. Carol BRADFIELD
15 Director of Human Resources ... Mr. Fred W. STEPHENS
13 Director of Information Technology ... Mr. Travis WOOLEY
04 Executive Asst to the President ... Mrs. Dawn H. CREFT
88 Chief Compliance Officer ... Ms. Starr S. BENDER

Allied Health Institute (A)

51 North State Road 7, Plantation FL 33317
County: Broward FICE Identification: 041359
Unit ID: 454883
Telephone: (866) 251-3244 Carnegie Class: Not Classified
FAX Number: (877) 493-7416 Calendar System: Other
URL: www.alliedhealthinstitute.edu
Established: 2004 Annual Undergrad Tuition & Fees: $13,375
Enrollment: 441 Coed
Affiliation or Control: Proprietary IRS Status: Proprietary
Highest Offering: Associate Degree
Program: Occupational; 2-Year Principally Bachelor's Creditable
Accreditation: ABHES

01 President ... Jennifer ANGLIN
03 Vice President ... Sondra GERHOFF

American College for Medical Careers (B)

5959 Lake Ellenor Drive, Orlando FL 32809
Telephone: (407) 738-4488 Identification: 770842
Accreditation: ACICS, #COARC, DMS

† Branch campus of Salter College, West Boylston, MA.

American Medical Academy (C)

12215 SW 112th Street, Miami FL 33186
County: Miami-Dade FICE Identification: 041921
Unit ID: 475714
Telephone: (305) 271-6555 Carnegie Class: Not Classified
FAX Number: (305) 271-6556 Calendar System: Semester
URL: www.ama.edu
Established: 2006 Annual Undergrad Tuition & Fees: $10,450
Enrollment: 247 Coed
Affiliation or Control: Proprietary IRS Status: Proprietary
Highest Offering: Associate Degree
Program: Occupational
Accreditation: ABHES

01 Chief Executive Officer ... Mr. Eduardo GUTIERREZ

Ana G. Mendez University System Metro Orlando Campus (D)

5601 S Semoran Boulevard, #55, Orlando FL 32822
Telephone: (407) 207-3363 Identification: 770921
Accreditation: &M

† Branch campus of Sistema Universitario Ana G. Mendez, Rio Piedras, PR.

Ana G. Mendez University System South Florida Campus (E)

3520 Enterprise Way, Miramar FL 33025
Telephone: (954) 885-5595 Identification: 770922
Accreditation: &M

† Branch campus of Sistema Universitario Ana G. Mendez, Rio Piedras, PR.

Ana G. Mendez University System Tampa Bay Campus (F)

3655 West Waters Avenue, Tampa FL 33614
Telephone: (813) 932-7500 Identification: 770923
Accreditation: &M

† Branch campus of Sistema Universitario Ana G. Mendez, Rio Piedras, PR.

Argosy University, Sarasota (G)

5250 17th Street, Sarasota FL 34235-8246
Telephone: (941) 379-0404 FICE Identification: 025906
Accreditation: &WC, ACBSP, CACREP

† Regional accreditation is carried under the parent institution in Orange, CA.

Argosy University, Tampa (H)

1403 N. Howard Avenue, Tampa FL 33607
Telephone: (813) 393-5290 Identification: 666082
Accreditation: &WC, ACBSP, CLPSY

† Regional accreditation is carried under the parent institution in Orange, CA.

The Art Institute of Fort Lauderdale (I)

1799 SE 17th Street, Fort Lauderdale FL 33316-3000
County: Broward FICE Identification: 010195
Unit ID: 132338
Telephone: (954) 463-3000 Carnegie Class: Spec/Arts
FAX Number: (954) 523-7676 Calendar System: Quarter
URL: www.aifl.edu
Established: 1968 Annual Undergrad Tuition & Fees: $17,704
Enrollment: 1,515 Coed
Affiliation or Control: Proprietary IRS Status: Proprietary
Highest Offering: Baccalaureate
Program: Occupational; Liberal Arts And General
Accreditation: ACICS, ACFEI, CIDA

01 President ... Carolyn PIERCE
32 Dean of Student Affairs ... Vacant
05 Dean of Academic Affairs ... Eric WATSON
10 Director of Accounting ... Maria V. BARRON
06 Registrar ... Monique P. DAVIS
07 Senior Director of Admissions ... Debra BARTKOWSKI
37 Director Student Financial Services ... Joyce CUMMINGS
36 Director of Career Services ... Wendy WAGNER-LIND
15 Human Resources Generalist ... Samantha GORDON

The Art Institute of Tampa (J)

4401 North Himes Avenue, Suite 150, Tampa FL 33614
Telephone: (813) 873-2112 Identification: 770935
Accreditation: &SC, ACFEI

† Branch campus of Miami International University of Art & Design, Miami, FL.

ATA Career Education-Spring Hill (K)

7351 Spring Hill Drive, Suite 11, Spring Hill FL 34606
Telephone: (352) 684-3007 Identification: 770521
Accreditation: ABHES

† Branch campus of ATA College, Louisville, KY.

Atlantic Institute of Oriental Medicine (L)

100 E Broward Boulevard, Suite 100,
Fort Lauderdale FL 33301-3510
County: Broward FICE Identification: 034296
Unit ID: 439446
Telephone: (954) 763-9840 Carnegie Class: Spec/Health
FAX Number: (954) 763-9844 Calendar System: Trimester
URL: www.atom.edu
Established: 1994 Annual Graduate Tuition & Fees: $17,000
Enrollment: 160 Coed
Affiliation or Control: Independent Non-Profit IRS Status: 501(c)3
Highest Offering: Doctorate; No Undergraduates
Program: Professional
Accreditation: ACUP

01 President ... Johanna C. YEN
11 Executive Director ... Dort BIGG
05 Academic Dean ... Yan CHENG
03 Executive Vice President ... Di FU
10 Financial Officer ... Celia MUNOZ
06 Registrar ... Milagros FERREIRA
08 Head Librarian ... Jeanne THOMAS

† Granted candidacy at the Doctorate level.

Atlantis University (M)

1442 Biscayne Blvd, Miami FL 33132
County: Miami-Dade FICE Identification: 042339
Telephone: (305) 377-8817 Carnegie Class: Not Classified
FAX Number: (305) 377-9557 Calendar System: Semester
URL: www.atlantisuniversity.edu
Established: 1975 Annual Undergrad Tuition & Fees: $9,856
Enrollment: N/A Coed
Affiliation or Control: Proprietary IRS Status: Proprietary
Highest Offering: Associate Degree
Program: Occupational; 2-Year Principally Bachelor's Creditable
Accreditation: ACCSC

Ave Maria School of Law (N)

1025 Commons Circle, Naples FL 34119
County: Collier FICE Identification: 036914
Unit ID: 442295
Telephone: (239) 687-5300 Carnegie Class: Spec/Law
FAX Number: (239) 353-3173 Calendar System: Semester
URL: www.avemarialaw.edu
Established: 2000 Annual Graduate Tuition & Fees: $40,300
Enrollment: 269 Coed
Affiliation or Control: Roman Catholic IRS Status: 501(c)3
Highest Offering: First Professional Degree; No Undergraduates
Program: Professional
Accreditation: LAW

01 President and Dean ... Mr. Kevin CIEPLY
04 Executive Assistant to the Dean ... Ms. Pamela KRAMER
05 Assoc Dean Academic Affairs ... Mr. W. Edward AFIELD
08 Director of the Law Library ... Mr. Ulysses JAEN
42 Chaplain ... Msgr. Frank MCGRATH
06 Registrar ... Ms. Dairys WHITE
37 Director of Financial Aid ... Mr. Kevin MCGOWAN
30 Chief Advancement/Comm Officer ... Ms. Donna HEISER
07 Director of Admissions ... Ms. Claire O'KEEFE
36 Director of Career Services ... Ms. Jennifer LUCAS-ROSS
10 Assoc Dean Student/Admin Affairs ... Ms. Kaye CASTRO
40 Bookstore Manager ... Ms. Kathryn LOVE

Ave Maria University (O)

5050 Ave Maria Boulevard, Ave Maria FL 34142-9505
County: Collier FICE Identification: 039413
Unit ID: 446048
Telephone: (239) 280-2500 Carnegie Class: Bac/A&S
FAX Number: (239) 352-2392 Calendar System: Semester
URL: www.avemaria.edu
Established: 2003 Annual Undergrad Tuition & Fees: $18,479
Enrollment: 1,019 Coed
Affiliation or Control: Independent Non-Profit IRS Status: 501(c)3
Highest Offering: Doctorate
Program: Liberal Arts And General; Teacher Preparatory; Religious Emphasis
Accreditation: SC

00 Chancellor ... Mr. Thomas S. MONAGHAN
01 President/CEO ... Mr. James TOWEY
03 Executive Vice President ... Mr. Dennis GRACE
05 VP Academic Affairs ... Dr. Seana SUGRUE
13 Chief Information Officer ... Mr. Eddie DEJTHAI
30 VP Institutional Advancement ... Mr. Kevin JOYCE
32 VP Student Affairs ... Ms. Julie COSDEN
10 Chief Financial Officer ... Mr. Robert FARNHAM
84 VP Enrollment and Marketing ... Vacant
07 Director of Admissions ... Ms. Billee SILVA
06 Registrar ... Ms. Stephanie E. NEGIP
09 Coordinator Institutional Research ... Mrs. Helen N. ALTOMARI
37 Managing Financial Aid Director ... Mrs. Anne HART
41 Athletic Director ... Mrs. Kimberly KING
42 Director of Campus Ministry ... Fr. Robert GARRITY
44 Director Planned Giving ... Mr. Jeffrey MCMANUS
35 Director of Student Life ... Ms. Julie COSDEN
88 Director of Mission/Outreach ... Ms. Grace CHEFFERS
08 Director of Library Services ... Ms. Jennifer NODES
15 Human Resources & Privacy Ofcr ... Ms. Kathy PHELPS
18 Director Physical Plant & Security ... Mr. Jason SYLVESTER
21 Controller ... Vacant
38 Mental Health Counselor ... Ms. Sharon O'REILLY
39 Director Resident Life ... Mrs. Erin VANDEVOORDE
29 Phoneathon Manager ... Mr. Gary HUBER
19 Director Security/Safety ... Mr. Peter VAN DE VOORDE
43 General Counsel ... Mr. William KIRK

Aviator College of Aeronautical Science & Technology (P)

3800 St. Lucie Boulevard, Fort Pierce FL 34946
County: Saint Lucie FICE Identification: 039863
Unit ID: 447847
Telephone: (772) 466-4822 Carnegie Class: Not Classified
FAX Number: (772) 462-4886 Calendar System: Semester
URL: www.aviator.edu
Established: 1984 Annual Undergrad Tuition & Fees: $74,787
Enrollment: 176 Coed
Affiliation or Control: Proprietary IRS Status: Proprietary
Highest Offering: Associate Degree
Program: Occupational; 2-Year Principally Bachelor's Creditable; Technical Emphasis
Accreditation: ACCSC

01 President ... Mr. Michael E. COHEN
10 Vice Pres & Chief Financial Officer ... Ms. T.J METE
05 Director of Education ... Mr. Pierre LAVIAL
06 Registrar ... Ms. Lisa KREAMER
07 Admission Director ... Ms. Michelle MILLER

Azure College (Q)

1525 NW 167th Street, Miami Gardens FL 33169
County: Miami-Dade Identification: 667116
Telephone: (305) 751-0001 Carnegie Class: Not Classified
FAX Number: (305) 751-9991 Calendar System: Quarter
URL: www.azure.edu

Established: 2004 Annual Undergrad Tuition & Fees: $35,500
Enrollment: 397 Coed
Affiliation or Control: Proprietary IRS Status: Proprietary
Highest Offering: Associate Degree
Program: Occupational
Accreditation: ABHES

01 CEO ... Mr. Jhonson NAPOLEON

The Baptist College of Florida (A)

5400 College Drive, Graceville FL 32440-3306
County: Jackson FICE Identification: 021596
Unit ID: 132408
Telephone: (850) 263-3261 Carnegie Class: Spec/Faith
FAX Number: (850) 263-9026 Calendar System: Semester
URL: www.baptistcollege.edu
Established: 1943 Annual Undergrad Tuition & Fees: $10,000
Enrollment: 486 Coed
Affiliation or Control: Southern Baptist IRS Status: 501(c)3
Highest Offering: Master's
Program: 2-Year Principally Bachelor's Creditable; Teacher Preparatory; Professional; Religious Emphasis
Accreditation: SC, MUS

01 President ... Dr. Thomas A. KINCHEN
30 Vice President for Development ... Mr. Charles R. PARKER
05 Dean of Faculty ... Dr. G. Robin JUMPER
06 Registrar ... Ms. Stephanie W. ORR
26 Director of Marketing ... Mrs. Sandra K. RICHARDS
09 Director of Institutional Research ... Dr. Ed SCOTT
37 Director of Financial Aid & VA ... Mrs. Stephanie E. POWELL
32 Dean of Students ... Dr. Roger C. RICHARDS
07 Director of Admissions ... Mrs. Sandra K. RICHARDS
18 Maintenance Director ... Mr. Huie G. WILSON
21 Associate Business Officer ... Ms. Polly K. FLOYD
30 Director of Development ... Vacant
04 Administrative Asst to President ... Ms. Laura L. TICE
08 Head Librarian ... Mr. John E. SHAFFETT
84 Director Enrollment Management ... Ms. Sandra K. RICHARDS

Barry University (B)

11300 NE Second Avenue, Miami Shores FL 33161-6695
County: Dade FICE Identification: 001466
Unit ID: 132471
Telephone: (305) 899-3000 Carnegie Class: DRU
FAX Number: (305) 899-3054 Calendar System: Semester
URL: www.barry.edu
Established: 1940 Annual Undergrad Tuition & Fees: $28,800
Enrollment: 8,518 Coed
Affiliation or Control: Roman Catholic IRS Status: 501(c)3
Highest Offering: Doctorate
Program: Liberal Arts And General; Teacher Preparatory; Professional
Accreditation: SC, ANEST, ARCPA, BUS, CAATE, CACREP, HT, LAW, MACTE, MT, NURSE, OT, PERF, POD, SW, THEOL

01 President ... Sr. Linda BEVILACQUA
04 Executive Asst to the President ... Ms. Mary Ellen LETSCHE
00 President Emerita ... Sr. Jeanne O'LAUGHLIN
05 Provost ... Vacant
10 Vice Pres Business & Finance ... Mrs. Susan ROSENTHAL
15 Vice Pres Human Resources ... Mrs. Jennifer N. BOYD-PUGH
30 VP Inst Adv & External Affairs ... Mrs. Sara B. HERALD
88 VP Mission & Inst Effectiveness ... Dr. Christopher STARRATT
32 Vice President Student Affairs ... Dr. Scott F. SMITH
13 VP Technology/CIO ... Ms. Yvette BROWN
43 General Counsel ... Mr. David DUDGEON
49 Dean College of Arts/Sciences ... Dr. Karen A. CALLAGHAN
50 Dean School of Business ... Dr. Tomislav MANDAKOVIC
53 Interim Dean School of Education ... Dr. Jill FARRELL
76 Dean College of Health Sciences ... Dr. John MCFADDEN
88 Dean Human Perf/Leisure Sci ... Dr. Darlene KLUKA
61 Dean School of Law ... Dr. Leticia M. DIAZ
63 Interim Dean School of Pod Med ... Dr. Albert ARMSTRONG
51 Dean School of Prof & Career Educ ... Dr. Andrea KEENER
70 Dean School of Social Work ... Dr. Phyllis SCOTT
35 Assoc VP Student Affs/Dean Students ... Dr. Maria L. ALVAREZ
35 Assoc Vice Pres Student Affairs ... Dr. Eileen MCDONOUGH
18 Director Fac Planning & Development ... Mr. Julian ANGEL
29 Assoc VP Alum Rels & Annual Giving ... Mr. Matthew BLAIR
84 Assoc Vice Pres Enrollment Services ... Ms. Angela SCOTT
105 Assoc VP Enrollment Mkt Strategy ... Mr. Michel SILY
19 Director Public Safety & Emerg Mgt ... Mr. John BUHRMASTER
08 Interim Dir Library Svcs/Libr Dir ... Mr. Rodrigo CASTRO
42 Chaplain ... Fr. Cristobal TORRES
44 Assoc VP Major Gifts Develop ... Ms. Margaret HUBBARD
44 Director Annual Giving ... Mrs. Kristy HENRY
06 University Registrar ... Ms. Cynthia A. CHRUSZCZYK
39 Director Housing and Residence Life ... Mr. Matthew R. CAMERON
36 Director Career Services ... Mr. John MORIARTY
37 Director Financial Aid ... Mr. Howard D. HUMESTON
92 Director Honors Program ... Dr. Pawena SIRIMANGKALA
38 Director Student Counseling Center ... Dr. James SCOTT
26 Assoc VP Brand Mkt & Communications ... Ms. Kim COX
07 Director of Undergraduate Admission ... Ms. Sarah RILEY
09 Director Institutional Research ... Ms. Shaunette GRANT
14 Associate CIO ... Mr. Hernan LONDONO
41 Director of Athletics ... Mr. Michael COVONE
86 Director External & Gov Affairs ... Mrs. Elizabeth BESADE
102 Director Foundation Relations ... Ms. Shannon BROWN
105 Director Digital Media Strat & Dev ... Mr. Miguel RAMIREZ
109 Dir Student Union & Food Services ... Mr. Mickie VOUTSINAS
25 Director Grant & Sponsored Programs ... Mrs. Sandra L. MANCUSO
40 Manager Bookstore ... Ms. Claudia HADJEZ

Bay Medical Center (C)

615 N Bonita Avenue, Panama City FL 32401-3600
County: Bay FICE Identification: 011127
Unit ID: 439464
Telephone: (800) 422-2418 Carnegie Class: Not Classified
FAX Number: (850) 747-6115 Calendar System: Semester
URL: www.baymedical.org/Career-Center.aspx
Established: 1969 Annual Graduate Tuition & Fees: $21,825
Enrollment: 52 Coed
Affiliation or Control: Independent Non-Profit IRS Status: 501(c)3
Highest Offering: Master's; No Undergraduates
Program: Occupational; Professional; Business Emphasis
Accreditation: ANEST

01 Interim CEO ... Mr. Mark GREGSON
10 Chief Financial Officer ... Mr. Ron PATRICK
05 Chief Nursing Officer ... Ms. Jan THORNTON

Beacon College (D)

105 E Main Street, Leesburg FL 34748-5162
County: Lake FICE Identification: 033733
Unit ID: 384254
Telephone: (352) 787-7660 Carnegie Class: Bac/A&S
FAX Number: (352) 787-0721 Calendar System: Semester
URL: www.beaconcollege.edu
Established: 1989 Annual Undergrad Tuition & Fees: $34,680
Enrollment: 223 Coed
Affiliation or Control: Independent Non-Profit IRS Status: 501(c)3
Highest Offering: Baccalaureate
Program: Liberal Arts And General
Accreditation: SC

01 President ... Dr. George J. HAGERTY
05 Vice President of Academic Affairs ... Dr. Shelly CHANDLER
32 Executive Vice President ... Dr. Robert BRIDGEMAN
30 VP of Institutional Development ... Mr. Stephen MULLER
10 VP of Finance & Administration ... Mr. Calvin SANSON
09 VP Institutional Effectiveness ... Dr. Shelly CHANDLER
06 Registrar ... Mr. David BROWN
18 Director of Facilities ... Mr. Chris HALL
37 Director of Financial Aid ... Ms. Shawna WELLS-BOOTH
08 Director of Library Resources ... Ms. Tiffany REITZ
13 Director of Information Technology ... Mr. Tim PAIGE
04 Exec Assistant to the President ... Ms. Tamara SYNDER
15 Director of Human Resources ... Mr. Tom BROWN
07 Dean of Admissions Enrollment Mgmt ... Ms. Dale HEROLD
101 Admin Asst to the Board ... Ms. Donna MARTIN
103 Dir Workforce/Career Development ... Dr. Andrea BRODE
29 Director Alumni Relations ... Ms. Chelsea EUBANK
38 Director Student Counseling ... Mr. Josh GROVER
19 Chief of Campus Security ... Mr. James ASHWORTH
39 Director Student Housing ... Ms. Carrie SANTAW

Bethesda College of Health Sciences (E)

3800 South Congress Ave Ste 9,
Boynton Beach FL 33426
County: Palm Beach Identification: 667258
Telephone: (561) 364-3064 Carnegie Class: Not Classified
FAX Number: N/A Calendar System: Semester
URL: www.BethesdaCollege.net
Established: 2011 Annual Undergrad Tuition & Fees: $4,218
Enrollment: N/A Coed
Affiliation or Control: Independent Non-Profit IRS Status: 501(c)3
Highest Offering: Associate Degree
Program: Occupational
Accreditation: RAD

01 Dean ... Jeanette KAMCIYAN

Bethune Cookman University (F)

640 Dr. Mary McLeod Bethune Blvd,
Daytona Beach FL 32114-3099
County: Volusia FICE Identification: 001467
Unit ID: 132602
Telephone: (386) 481-2000 Carnegie Class: Bac/Diverse
FAX Number: (386) 481-2010 Calendar System: Semester
URL: www.cookman.edu
Established: 1904 Annual Undergrad Tuition & Fees: $14,410
Enrollment: 4,045 Coed
Affiliation or Control: United Methodist IRS Status: 501(c)3
Highest Offering: Master's
Program: Liberal Arts And General; Technical Emphasis
Accreditation: SC, NUR, TED

01 President ... Dr. Edison O. JACKSON
10 Vice President Fiscal Affairs ... Ms. Shelly RICE
05 VP Student Development and Academic ... Dr. Michelle THOMPSON
30 Vice Pres Institutional Advancement ... Dr. Hakim J. LUCAS
09 VP Institutional Effectiveness ... Dr. Helena MARIELLA-WALROND
43 VP/General Counsel ... Ms. Darlene BELL-ALEXANDER
13 VP Info Tech/Chief Info Officer ... Mr. Franklin PATTERSON
20 Provost for Academic Affairs ... Dr. Makala M. ABDULLAH
21 Assoc Vice Pres Finance/Budget ... Vacant
84 Associate VP Enrollment Management ... Mr. Warren HEUSNER
100 Chief of Staff ... Mr. Fontaine DAVIS
39 Asst VP Resident Education and Comm ... Mr. Noel FEGUMPS
30 Director of Advancement ... Ms. Sophia HUGER
26 Director of Communications ... Mrs. Keisha BOYD
36 Dir Academic and Career Development ... Ms. Davita BONNER
08 Chief Librarian Dean of Library/LRC ... Dr. Tasha LUCAS-YOUMANS
06 Registrar ... Ms. Patricia KRESL
07 Director Admissions ... Vacant
37 Director Financial Aid ... Vacant
23 Director Health Services ... Vacant
41 Athletics Director ... Mr. Lynn THOMPSON
42 Chaplain/Dir of Religious Life ... Rev. David ALLEN
19 Director of Security ... Chief Melvin WILLIAMS
18 VP Capital Assets and Planning ... Mr. Graham GILCHRIST
66 Dean School of Nursing ... Dr. Sandra TUCKER
50 Dean School of Business ... Dr. Ida WRIGHT
53 Dean School of Education ... Dr. Willis WALTER
49 Dean School of Liberal Arts ... Dr. Janice ALLEN-KELSEY
81 Dean Sch Science/Engineering/Math ... Dr. Herbert THOMPSON
107 Dean School of Professional Studies ... Dr. Darryl FRASIER
58 Dean of Graduate Studies ... Dr. Hiram POWELL
97 Dean of Undergrad Studies ... Dr. Alexis BROOKS-WALTER
04 Executive Asst to President ... Mrs. Valerie WILT
90 Director Academic Computing ... Ms. Anna HEIN
76 Exec Dean/School of Health Sci ... Dr. Deanna WATHINGTON
88 Dean of Chapel ... Rev. David ALLEN, JR.
31 VP Business & Community Development ... Dr. Aubrey LONG
31 VP Community Affairs/K-16 Initiat ... Dr. Willis WALTER
15 Vice President Human Resources ... Dr. Nan FISHER-WILLIAMS
20 Associate Provost ... Dr. Adrienne COOPER
20 Associate Provost ... Dr. Annie REDD
32 Asst Vice Pres for Student Life ... Dr. Clyde WILSON, JR.
38 Asst VP Counseling & Disability Svc ... Ms. Nadine HEUSNER
88 Director of Testing ... Mr. James LAI
108 Director of Assessment ... Mr. Cory POTTER

Broward College (G)

111 E Las Olas Boulevard,
Fort Lauderdale FL 33301-2298
County: Broward FICE Identification: 001500
Unit ID: 132709
Telephone: (954) 201-6500 Carnegie Class: Assoc/Pub-U-MC
FAX Number: (954) 201-7576 Calendar System: Trimester
URL: www.broward.edu
Established: 1959 Annual Undergrad Tuition & Fees (In-State): $3,405
Enrollment: 44,119 Coed
Affiliation or Control: State IRS Status: 501(c)3
Highest Offering: Baccalaureate
Program: Occupational; 2-Year Principally Bachelor's Creditable; Liberal Arts And General; Teacher Preparatory; Professional
Accreditation: SC, ADNUR, CAHIIM, COARC, DA, DH, DMS, EMT, MAC, MUS, NUR, OPD, PTAA

01 President ... Mr. J. David ARMSTRONG, JR.
05 Sr Vice Pres Acad Affairs/Provost ... Dr. Linda HOWDYSHELL
10 Sr Vice Pres Finance/Administration ... Mr. Thomas OLLIFF
32 Vice Pres Student Affs/Enroll Mgmt ... Dr. Marielena DESANCTIS
26 VP Public Affairs and Marketing ... Vacant
11 Vice President of Operations ... Mr. John DUNNUCK
102 VP Advanc/Exec Dir BC Foundation ... Ms. Nancy BOTERO
13 Vice President Info Technology ... Ms. Patti BARNEY
86 VP Govt Policy/Regulatory Affairs ... Mr. Gregory A. HAILE
88 Assoc Vice President Economic Dev ... Mr. Norm SEAVERS
100 Chief of Staff ... Ms. Adriana FAZZANO
12 Campus President BC Online ... Dr. David SHULMAN
12 Campus President Central Campus ... Dr. Mercedes A. QUIROGA
12 Campus President North Campus ... Dr. Avis PROCTOR
12 Int Campus President South Campus ... Dr. Rolando GARCIA
21 Chief Financial Officer ... Mr. Jayson IROFF
18 Chief Facilities/Physical Plant ... Mr. Sean DEVANEY
09 Dean Institutional Research ... Ms. Pauline ANDERSON
45 Dean Inst Planning/Effectiveness ... Dr. Deborah POSNER
08 Dean of Libraries/Learning Res ... Ms. Sarah WIGGINS
37 Director of Student Financial Svcs ... Ms. Theresa COWAN
15 Exec Director Human Res & Equity ... Dr. Denese EDSALL
06 Registrar ... Mr. Willie ALEXANDER
29 Director Alumni Relations ... Ms. Danielle SYLVESTER
04 Sr Exec Asst to the President ... Mrs. Avis M. MCCOY
19 Director Security/Safety ... Mr. Peter AGNESI
25 Int Chief Contracts/Grants Admin ... Ms. Kareen TORRES
96 Director of Purchasing ... Dr. Judy SCHMELZER
07 Supervisor Admissions ... Mr. Willie ALEXANDER

Brown Mackie College-Miami (H)

3700 Lakeside Drive, Miramar FL 33027
Telephone: (305) 341-6600 Identification: 666110
Accreditation: ACICS

† Branch campus of Brown Mackie College, Cincinnati, OH.

Cambridge Institute of Allied Health & Technology (I)

5150 Linton Boulevard, Suite 340, Delray Beach FL 33484
County: Palm Beach FICE Identification: 040834
Unit ID: 454865
Telephone: (561) 381-4990 Carnegie Class: Assoc/PrivFP

FAX Number: (561) 381-4992 Calendar System: Other
URL: www.cambridgehealth.edu
Established: Annual Undergrad Tuition & Fees: $16,959
Enrollment: 210 Coed
Affiliation or Control: Proprietary IRS Status: Proprietary
Highest Offering: Associate Degree
Program: Occupational
Accreditation: ABHES, DMS

01 President Mr. Terry LAPIER

Carlos Albizu University Miami Campus (A)

2173 NW 99th Avenue, Miami FL 33172-2209
Telephone: (305) 593-1223 Identification: 666814
Accreditation: &M, CLPSY, SP

† Regional accreditation is carried under the parent institution in San Juan, PR.

Center of Cinematography, Art & Television (B)

1637 NW 27th Avenue, Miami FL 33125
Telephone: (305) 634-0550 Identification: 770562
Accreditation: ACCSC

† Branch campus of Colegio de Cinematografia, Artes y Television, Bayamon, PR.

Chamberlain College of Nursing-Jacksonville Campus (C)

5200 Belfort Road, Jacksonville FL 32256
Telephone: (904) 251-8100 Identification: 770501
Accreditation: &NH, NURSE

† Branch campus of Chamberlain College of Nursing-Addison, Addison, IL.

Chamberlain College of Nursing-Miramar (D)

2300 SW 145th Avenue, Miramar FL 33027
Telephone: (954) 885-3510 Identification: 770498
Accreditation: &NH, NURSE

† Branch campus of Chamberlain College of Nursing-Addison, Addison, IL.

Chipola College (E)

3094 Indian Circle, Marianna FL 32446-3065
County: Jackson FICE Identification: 001472
Unit ID: 133021
Telephone: (850) 526-2761 Carnegie Class: Assoc/Pub4
FAX Number: (850) 718-2388 Calendar System: Semester
URL: www.chipola.edu
Established: 1947 Annual Undergrad Tuition & Fees (In-District): $3,060
Enrollment: 2,080 Coed
Affiliation or Control: State/Local IRS Status: 501(c)3
Highest Offering: Baccalaureate
Program: Occupational; 2-Year Principally Bachelor's Creditable
Accreditation: SC, ADNUR, NUR

01 President Dr. Jason HURST
05 Sr VP Instructional/Student Svcs Dr. Sarah CLEMMONS
10 Vice Pres of Admin & Business Svcs Mr. Steve YOUNG
32 Vice Pres of Student Affairs Dr. Jayne ROBERTS
15 Assoc VP of HR & Equity Mrs. Karan P. DAVIS
13 Associate VP Information Systems Mr. Dennis F. EVERETT
108 Dean Assessment/Compliance & Grant Dr. Matthew HUGHES
18 Dir Facilities & Capital Projects Mr. Nolan BAKER
26 Director Public Relations Dr. Bryan C. CRAVEN
37 Director of Financial Aid Ms. Beverly HAMBRIGHT
41 Director of Athletics Mr. Jeffrey JOHNSON
40 Bookstore Manager Vacant
06 Registrar Ms. Kathy REHBERG

City College (F)

177 Montgomery Road, Altamonte Springs FL 32714
County: Seminole FICE Identification: 030799
Unit ID: 417327
Telephone: (407) 831-9816 Carnegie Class: Assoc/PrivNFP
FAX Number: (407) 831-1147 Calendar System: Quarter
URL: www.citycollegeorlando.edu
Established: 1997 Annual Undergrad Tuition & Fees: $15,840
Enrollment: 410 Coed
Affiliation or Control: Independent Non-Profit IRS Status: 501(c)3
Highest Offering: Associate Degree
Program: Occupational
Accreditation: ACICS, EMT, SURTEC

01 President Mrs. Esther FIKE
05 Executive Director Mr. Paul CASTELLANO
06 Registrar Ms. Jane STINIS

City College (G)

2000 W Commercial Boulevard,
Fort Lauderdale FL 33309-1916
County: Broward FICE Identification: 025154
Unit ID: 244233
Telephone: (954) 492-5353 Carnegie Class: Bac/Assoc
FAX Number: (954) 491-1965 Calendar System: Quarter
URL: www.citycollege.edu
Established: 1983 Annual Undergrad Tuition & Fees: $14,941
Enrollment: 575 Coed
Affiliation or Control: Independent Non-Profit IRS Status: 501(c)3
Highest Offering: Baccalaureate
Program: Occupational; 2-Year Principally Bachelor's Creditable; Business Emphasis
Accreditation: ACICS, EMT, SURTEC

01 President Esther FIKE
03 Executive Director Doug GOODWIN
36 Director of Career Development Traci ACKERMAN
05 Director of Education Anie BONILLA
07 Director of Admissions Marcy PRATT
13 Director of Technologies Jeffrey CLAYTON
08 Director of Library Sharon NEUBAUER
06 Registrar Sanchia WILLIAMS
15 Human Resources Generalist Patricia BURKHART
37 Director Student Financial Aid Carmen MONTEL

City College (H)

7001 NW Fourth Boulevard, Gainesville FL 32607
Telephone: (352) 335-4000 Identification: 666413
Accreditation: ACICS, EMT

† Branch campus of City College, Fort Lauderdale, FL.

City College (I)

6565 Taft Street, Hollywood FL 33024
Telephone: (954) 744-1777 Identification: 770674
Accreditation: ACICS

† Branch campus of City College, Fort Lauderdale, FL.

City College (J)

9300 S Dadeland Blvd, Suite PH, Miami FL 33156
Telephone: (305) 666-9242 Identification: 666414
Accreditation: ACICS, EMT, SURTEC

† Branch campus of City College, Fort Lauderdale, FL.

College of Business and Technology (K)

8991 SW 107th Avenue, Suite 200, Miami FL 33176-1412
County: Miami-Dade FICE Identification: 030716
Unit ID: 417318
Telephone: (305) 273-4499 Carnegie Class: Assoc/PrivFP
FAX Number: (305) 270-0779 Calendar System: Semester
URL: www.cbt.edu
Established: 1988 Annual Undergrad Tuition & Fees: $13,600
Enrollment: 63 Coed
Affiliation or Control: Proprietary IRS Status: Proprietary
Highest Offering: Associate Degree
Program: Occupational; 2-Year Principally Bachelor's Creditable; Technical Emphasis
Accreditation: ACICS

01 President Monica LLERENA
00 CEO Mr. Fernando N. LLERENA
03 Executive Director Mr. Luis E. LLERENA
05 Regional Director of Education Mrs. Gladys P. LLERENA
37 Financial Aid Director Mrs. Yazmin PALMA
36 Career Services Director Mr. Christian CONTRERAS
06 Registrar Ms. Shantal NATAL
84 Regional Director of Enrollment Op Mr. Armando ALVAREZ
50 Program Director Ms. Carolyn SMITH
10 Finance Director Ms. Maricel SPEZZACATENA
20 Director of Academic Operations Ms. Audra KINNEY
12 Acting Campus Director Ms. Audra KINNEY
08 Head Librarian Ms. Jennifer ROMA

College of Business and Technology - Cutler Bay (L)

19151 South Dixie Highway, Cutler Bay FL 33157
Telephone: (305) 273-4499 Identification: 770677
Accreditation: ACICS, CAHIIM

† Branch campus of College of Business and Technology, Miami, FL.

College of Business and Technology - Flagler (M)

8230 W Flagler Street, Miami FL 33144
Telephone: (305) 273-4499 Identification: 770676
Accreditation: ACICS

† Branch campus of College of Business and Technology, Miami, FL.

College of Business and Technology - Hialeah Campus (N)

935 West 49th Street, Hialeah FL 33012
Telephone: (305) 273-4499 Identification: 770675
Accreditation: ACICS

† Branch campus of College of Business and Technology, Miami, FL.

College of Business and Technology - Miami Gardens (O)

5190 NW 167 Street, Suite 200, Miami Gardens FL 33014
Telephone: (786) 693-8801 Identification: 770612
Accreditation: ACICS

† Branch campus of College of Business and Technology, Miami, FL.

College of Central Florida (P)

3001 S.W. College Road, Ocala FL 34474
County: Marion FICE Identification: 001471
Unit ID: 132851
Telephone: (352) 237-2111 Carnegie Class: Assoc/Pub-R-L
FAX Number: (352) 291-4450 Calendar System: Semester
URL: www.cf.edu
Established: 1957 Annual Undergrad Tuition & Fees (In-District): $3,213
Enrollment: 8,223 Coed
Affiliation or Control: Local IRS Status: 501(c)3
Highest Offering: Baccalaureate
Program: Occupational; 2-Year Principally Bachelor's Creditable; Liberal Arts And General; Teacher Preparatory; Professional
Accreditation: SC, ADNUR, CAHIIM, DA, EMT, PTAA, SURGT

01 President Dr. James D. HENNINGSEN
10 Vice President Adm & Fin Mr. Francis J. MAZUR, III
05 Vice President Academic Affairs Dr. Mark PAUGH
32 Vice President Student Affairs Dr. Saul REYES
12 Citrus Campus Vice President Dr. Vernon LAWTER, JR.
12 Provost Levy Center Mrs. Marilyn LADNER
09 VP Inst Effectiveness/College Rels Dr. Jillian RAMSAMMY
21 Assistant VP for Finance Mr. Steven ASH
75 Dean Bus Tech Careers & Tech Educ Ms. Shelia RIOS
49 Dean Liberal Arts & Sciences Mr. Allan DANUFF
88 Dean Public Service/Criminal Just Mr. Charles MCINTOSH
35 Dean Student Services Dr. Henri BENLOLO
88 Dean Academic Foundations Dr. Rayanne GIDDIS
53 Dean Teacher Education Ms. Debbie BOWE
84 Dean Enrollment Management Ms. Lyn POWELL
76 Dean Health Sciences Dr. Barbara LANGE
106 Associate Dean E-learning Dr. Tamara VIVIANO-BRODERICK
102 Executive Director Foundation Mr. Christopher KNIFE
37 Director Financial Aid Ms. Maureen ANDERSON
09 Director Inst Effectiveness Dr. Lawrence J. KUSZYNSKI
07 Director Admissions/Records Mrs. Teri LITTLE-BERRY
18 Director Facilities Mr. Tommy MORELOCK
15 Director Human Resources Ms. Tonya KELLY
35 Director Student Life Ms. Marjorie MCGEE
88 Director Student Support Services Ms. Lisa SMITH
41 Director Athletics/Wellness Mr. Bob ZELINSKI
88 Director Access and Counsel Service Ms. Maria GEORGO
26 Director Marketing/Public Relations Ms. Lois BRAUCKMULLER
88 Director Appleton Museum of Art Ms. Cindi MORRISON
25 Director Grants Funding Mr. Matt MATTHEWS
08 Library Director Ms. Teresa FAUST
19 Manager Public Safety Vacant
88 Manager Printing & Postal Service Ms. Katharine WADE
88 Manager Conference & Food Service Ms. Cheryl CROSBY
13 Associate VP Information Technology Vacant
06 Registrar Ms. Devona SEWELL
29 Annual Fund/Alumni Devel Coord Ms. Traci MASON

Concorde Career Institute (Q)

7259 Salisbury Road, Jacksonville FL 32256
County: Duval FICE Identification: 020896
Unit ID: 133845
Telephone: (904) 725-0525 Carnegie Class: Assoc/PrivFP
FAX Number: (904) 721-9944 Calendar System: Semester
URL: www.concorde.edu
Established: 1988 Annual Undergrad Tuition & Fees: $24,900
Enrollment: 652 Coed
Affiliation or Control: Proprietary IRS Status: Proprietary
Highest Offering: Associate Degree
Program: Occupational
Accreditation: ACCSC, COARC, PTAA, SURGT

01 Campus Director Melissa RYAN

Concorde Career Institute (R)

10933 Marks Way, Miramar FL 33025
County: Broward FICE Identification: 022751
Unit ID: 133854
Telephone: (954) 731-8880 Carnegie Class: Not Classified
FAX Number: (954) 484-2961 Calendar System: Other
URL: www.concorde.edu
Established: 1989 Annual Undergrad Tuition & Fees: $15,125
Enrollment: 640 Coed
Affiliation or Control: Proprietary IRS Status: Proprietary
Highest Offering: Associate Degree
Program: Occupational; 2-Year Principally Bachelor's Creditable
Accreditation: ACCSC, #COARC, OTA, PTAA, SURGT

01 Campus President Virginia CARPENTER

Concorde Career Institute (S)

3444 McCrory Place, Orlando FL 32803
Telephone: (407) 812-3060 Identification: 770563
Accreditation: ACCSC, #COARC, SURGT

† Branch campus of Concorde Career Institute, Jacksonville, FL.

Concorde Career Institute (A)

4202 West Spruce Street, Tampa FL 33607-4127

County: Hillsborough FICE Identification: 021727
Unit ID: 133863
Telephone: (813) 874-0094 Carnegie Class: Not Classified
FAX Number: (813) 872-6884 Calendar System: Other
URL: www.concorde.edu
Established: 1978 Annual Undergrad Tuition & Fees: $15,108
Enrollment: 411 Coed
Affiliation or Control: Proprietary IRS Status: Proprietary
Highest Offering: Associate Degree
Program: Occupational
Accreditation: **ACCSC**, COARC, SURGT

01 Campus President Mr. Rod KIRKWOOD

Dade Medical College (B)

3721 NW 7th Street, Miami FL 33126

County: Miami-Dade FICE Identification: 038323
Unit ID: 444574
Telephone: (786) 363-4910 Carnegie Class: Assoc/PrivFP
FAX Number: (786) 363-4924 Calendar System: Other
URL: www.dademedical.edu
Established: 1999 Annual Undergrad Tuition & Fees: $47,813
Enrollment: 1,037 Coed
Affiliation or Control: Proprietary IRS Status: Proprietary
Highest Offering: Baccalaureate
Program: 2-Year Principally Bachelor's Creditable; Nursing Emphasis
Accreditation: **ABHES**, DMS, RAD

01 Chief Executive Officer Mr. Raul MENDEZ
10 Chief Financial Officer Mr. Chris GRESSETT
11 Exec Vice President of Operations Ms. Elizabeth LAGARON

Dade Medical College-Hollywood (C)

6837 Taft Street, Hollywood FL 33024

Telephone: (954) 843-7930 Identification: 770522
Accreditation: **ABHES**, RAD

† Branch campus of Dade Medical College, Miami, FL.

Dade Medical College-Homestead (D)

381 N Krome Avenue, Homestead FL 33030

Telephone: (786) 454-9070 Identification: 770523
Accreditation: **ABHES**

† Branch campus of Dade Medical College, Miami, FL.

Dade Medical College-Jacksonville (E)

9550 Regency Square Blvd, S-1200,
Jacksonville FL 32225

Telephone: (904) 345-5678 Identification: 770524
Accreditation: **ABHES**

† Branch campus of Dade Medical College, Miami, FL.

Dade Medical College-Miami (F)

5875 NW 163rd Street, Suite 101, Miami Lakes FL 33014

Telephone: (786) 363-3340 Identification: 770525
Accreditation: **ABHES**

† Branch campus of Dade Medical College, Miami, FL.

Dade Medical College-West Palm Beach (G)

2601 South Military Trail, Bay 1-18,
West Palm Beach FL 33415

Telephone: (561) 965-7044 Identification: 770526
Accreditation: **ABHES**

† Branch campus of Dade Medical College, Miami, FL.

Daytona College (H)

425 South Nova Road, Ormond Beach FL 32174-8449

County: Volusia FICE Identification: 039396
Unit ID: 447014
Telephone: (386) 267-0565 Carnegie Class: Assoc/PrivFP
FAX Number: (386) 267-0567 Calendar System: Semester
URL: www.daytonacollege.edu
Established: 1996 Annual Undergrad Tuition & Fees: $13,950
Enrollment: 315 Coed
Affiliation or Control: Proprietary IRS Status: Proprietary
Highest Offering: Associate Degree
Program: Occupational
Accreditation: **ACCSC**

01 President Mr. Roger BRADLEY
05 Director Mr. Justin BERKOWITZ

Daytona State College (I)

PO Box 2811, Daytona Beach FL 32120-2811

County: Volusia FICE Identification: 001475
Unit ID: 133386
Telephone: (386) 506-3000 Carnegie Class: Assoc/Pub4
FAX Number: (386) 506-4440 Calendar System: Semester
URL: www.DaytonaState.edu
Established: 1958 Annual Undergrad Tuition & Fees (In-District): $3,134
Enrollment: 15,190 Coed
Affiliation or Control: State/Local IRS Status: 501(c)3
Highest Offering: Baccalaureate
Program: Occupational; 2-Year Principally Bachelor's Creditable
Accreditation: **SC**, ADNUR, CAHIIM, COARC, DA, DH, EMT, MAC, OTA, PNUR, PTAA, SURGT

01 President Dr. Thomas LOBASSO
03 Executive Vice President Mr. Brian T. BABB
05 Chief Academic Officer Dr. Amy LOCKLEAR
10 Chief Business Officer Ms. Isalene MONTGOMERY
13 VP Information Technology Mr. Roberto LOMBARDO
15 AVP Human Resources Ms. Robin BARR
103 AVP College of Workforce & CE Mrs. Mary BRUNO
84 Int VP Enrollment/Stdnt Development Dr. Richard PASTOR
46 AVP Institutional Effectiveness Dr. Nancy MORGAN
08 Head Librarian Ms. Mercedes CLEMENT
108 Director Assessment Ms. Janet SLEDGE
69 AVP Col Health and Pub Svc Dr. James GREENE
72 AVP College of Technology Dr. Ron EAGLIN
53 AVP College of Education Ms. Kristy PRESSWOOD
106 Exec Director Instructional Resourc Dr. Rob SAUM
88 Director Center for Women & Men Ms. Veronica OXFORD
35 Dean Student Development Mr. Keith KENNEDY
18 Exec Director Facilities Planning Mr. Steven ECKMAN
09 Dean Institutional Research Ms. Susan ANTILLON
37 Dean Financial Aid Mr. Kevin MCCRARY
88 Dean School of Health & Wellness Mr. Will DUNNE
19 Director Campus Safety Mr. Bill TILLARD
12 Dean DeLand Campus Mr. Bill WETHERELL
12 Dean Flagler/Palm Coast Campus Mr. Kent RYAN
12 Dean New Smryna Beach Campus Mr. Clarence MCCLOUD
12 Dean Deltona Campus Ms. Suzette CAMERON
43 College Counsel Mr. Brian BABB
51 Director Ctr for Business/Industry Mr. Frank MERCER
32 Asst Dean Student Activities Mr. Bruce COOK
38 Director Academic Advising Ms. LeeAnn DAVIS
07 Director Admissions/Recruitment Ms. Karen SANDERS
22 Director of Equity & Inclusion Mr. Lonnie THOMPSON
21 AVP Accounting Ms. Tina MYERS
06 Director Student Accounts Ms. Amy IVERSON
26 Director of Marketing Ms. Laurie WHITE
09 Dean Institutional Effectiveness Dr. Karla MOORE
88 Dean Adult Education Dr. Katrina BELL
102 Executive Director Foundation Ms. Kay BURNISTON

DeVry University - Miramar Campus (J)

2300 SW 145th Avenue, Miramar FL 33027-4150

Telephone: (954) 499-9775 Identification: 666196
Accreditation: **&NH**, ENGT

† Regional accreditation is carried under the parent institution in Downers Grove, IL.

DeVry University - Orlando Campus (K)

4000 Millenia Boulevard, Orlando FL 32839-2426

Telephone: (407) 345-2800 Identification: 666112
Accreditation: **&NH**, ENGT

† Regional accreditation is carried under the parent institution in Downers Grove, IL.

Digital Media Arts College (L)

5400 Broken Sound Blvd, Suite 100,
Boca Raton FL 33487

County: Palm Beach FICE Identification: 041274
Unit ID: 451060
Telephone: (561) 391-1148 Carnegie Class: Bac/Diverse
FAX Number: (561) 998-3430 Calendar System: Semester
URL: www.dmac.edu
Established: 2002 Annual Undergrad Tuition & Fees: $13,968
Enrollment: 317 Coed
Affiliation or Control: Proprietary IRS Status: Proprietary
Highest Offering: Master's
Program: Professional; Fine Arts Emphasis
Accreditation: **ACICS**

01 President Mr. Sunny SHARMA
10 Director Accounting & Finance Ms. Angela NOVATON

Dragon Rises College of Oriental Medicine (M)

1000 NE 16th Ave., Building F, Gainesville FL 32601-4557

County: Alachua FICE Identification: 038883
Unit ID: 449481
Telephone: (352) 371-2833 Carnegie Class: Spec/Health
FAX Number: (352) 244-0003 Calendar System: Semester
URL: www.dragonrises.edu
Established: 2001 Annual Undergrad Tuition & Fees: $16,000
Enrollment: 56 Coed
Affiliation or Control: Proprietary IRS Status: Proprietary
Highest Offering: Master's
Program: Professional
Accreditation: **ACUP**

01 Director/CEO Mr. George VALCOURT
05 Academic Dean Mr. George VALCOURT
23 Clinic Director Ms. Laisha CANNER-WARD
32 Dean of Student Services Ms. Ruth HAYES-MORRISON
37 Financial Aid Administrator Ms. Karen MARTIN-BROWN

East West College of Natural Medicine (N)

3808 N Tamiami Trail, Sarasota FL 34234-5362

County: Sarasota FICE Identification: 034297
Unit ID: 439394
Telephone: (941) 355-9080 Carnegie Class: Spec/Health
FAX Number: (941) 355-3243 Calendar System: Trimester
URL: www.ewcollege.edu
Established: 1994 Annual Undergrad Tuition & Fees: $53,220
Enrollment: 128 Coed
Affiliation or Control: Proprietary IRS Status: Proprietary
Highest Offering: Master's
Program: Professional
Accreditation: **ACICS**, ACUP

01 President/CEO Dr. Misha PAYANT
05 Academic Dean Mr. Misha PAYANT
07 Director of Admissions Mr. Russ EATTIATA

Eastern Florida State College (O)

1519 Clearlake Road, Cocoa FL 32922-6597

County: Brevard FICE Identification: 001470
Unit ID: 132693
Telephone: (321) 632-1111 Carnegie Class: Assoc/Pub-R-L
FAX Number: (321) 633-4565 Calendar System: Semester
URL: www.easternflorida.edu
Established: 1960 Annual Undergrad Tuition & Fees (In-District): $3,120
Enrollment: 15,931 Coed
Affiliation or Control: Local IRS Status: 501(c)3
Highest Offering: Baccalaureate
Program: Occupational; 2-Year Principally Bachelor's Creditable
Accreditation: **SC**, DA, DH, EMT, MLTAD, RAD, SURGT

01 President Dr. James H. RICHEY
10 Chief Financial Officer Mr. Mark CHERRY
13 VP Financial & Technology Services Mr. Richard LAIRD
05 VP Academic Affairs/CLO Dr. Linda L. MIEDEMA
04 Exec Advisor to the President Dr. Joe L. SMITH
20 Assoc Vice Pres Academic Programs Dr. Kathy COBB
41 Assoc Vice Pres of Athletics Mr. Jeffrey CARR
18 Assoc Vice Pres Facilities Dr. Richard PARADISE
15 AVP/Exec Dir Human Resources Ms. Darla FERGUSON
19 AVP Public Safety Inst/Security Mr. Jack PARKER
31 AVP Communications Mr. John GLISCH
12 Provost Palm Bay Campus Dr. Beverly SLAUGHTER
12 Provost Melbourne Campus Ms. Sandy HANDFIELD
12 Provost Cocoa Campus Dr. Ethel NEWMAN
12 Provost Titusville Campus Dr. Philip SIMPSON
12 Provost eBrevard Dr. Kathy COBB
103 Dean/Workforce Trng & Devel Mr. Frank MARGIOTTA
37 Director Student Financial Aid Ms. Eileen BRZOZOWSKI
07 Dir Collegewide Admiss/Advsmnt/Test Ms. Michelle LOUFER
102 Executive Director Foundation Vacant
04 Executive Asst to the President Ms. Gina CLINE
06 Registrar Ms. Stephanie BURNETTE
08 Dean Learning Sources Dr. Mem STAHLEY

Eckerd College (P)

4200 54th Avenue S, Saint Petersburg FL 33711-4700

County: Pinellas FICE Identification: 001487
Unit ID: 133492
Telephone: (727) 867-1166 Carnegie Class: Bac/A&S
FAX Number: (727) 864-1877 Calendar System: 4/1/4
URL: www.eckerd.edu
Established: 1958 Annual Undergrad Tuition & Fees: $40,020
Enrollment: 2,083 Coed
Affiliation or Control: Presbyterian Church (U.S.A.) IRS Status: 501(c)3
Highest Offering: Baccalaureate
Program: Liberal Arts And General
Accreditation: **SC**

01 President Dr. Donald R. EASTMAN, III
05 Exec Vice Pres/Provost/Dean Faculty Dr. Suzan HARRISON
10 VP Business and Finance Mr. Christopher P. BRENNAN
03 VP and Secretary of the College Dr. Lisa A. METS
30 Vice President Advancement Mr. Matthew S. BISSET
51 Vice Pres/Dean of Executive Ed Mr. Kelly KIRSCHNER
32 Vice Pres/Dean for Student Life Dr. James J. ANNARELLI
84 VP Enrollment Management Mr. John SULLIVAN
20 Assoc Dean Faculty Development Dr. Kathryn J. WATSON
26 VP Marketing and Communications Ms. Valerie GLIEM
21 Associate VP Business and Finance Ms. Luz ARCILA
30 Assoc VP Advancement Mr. Tom SCHNEIDER
88 Academic Director of PEL Dr. Margret SKAFTADOTTIR
105 Dir Web/Marketing/Communication Mr. Michel FOUGERES
27 Director Media and Public Relations Mr. Tom SCHERBERGER
88 Director of ASPEC Mr. Ken WOLFE
88 Director of CALA Dr. Norman SMITH
104 Director of International Education Ms. Diane L. FERRIS
85 Dir International Student Programs Mr. Olivier DEBURE
13 Dir of Information Tech Dr. John A. DUFF
09 Exec Dir Institutional Effectivenes Ms. Jacqueline MACNEIL

06 Registrar .... Ms. Linda SWINDALL
06 Student Enrollment Manager PEL .... Ms. Lin JORGENSEN
08 Director of Library .... Ms. Jamie W. GILL
38 Director Counseling Services .... Dr. Scott C. STRADER
29 Director Alumni Relations .... Ms. Jessica FUGATE
19 Director Campus Safety .... Mr. Adam COLBY
36 Assoc Dean Career Planning .... Mr. Andrew BLACK
37 Director Financial Aid .... Dr. Pat E. WATKINS
41 Athletic Director .... Dr. Robert FORTOSIS
07 Director of Admission .... Mr. Jacob BROWNE
42 Chaplain .... Rev. Doug MCMAHON
46 Director of Sponsored Research .... Vacant
21 Controller .... Ms. Robin SMALLEY
35 Assistant Dean of Student Affairs .... Ms. Lorisa LORENZO
88 Asst Dean Students for Campus Act .... Mr. Fred SABOTA
88 Assoc Dean Students Cmty Initiative .... Ms. Martie NEWBOLD
87 Dir Conferences and Summer School .... Ms. Cheryl GOLD
04 Administrative Asst to President .... Ms. JoAnn TOWNSEND

Edward Waters College (A)

1658 Kings Road, Jacksonville FL 32209-6199
County: Duval FICE Identification: 001478
Unit ID: 133526
Telephone: (904) 470-8000 Carnegie Class: Bac/Diverse
FAX Number: (904) 470-8039 Calendar System: Semester
URL: www.ewc.edu
Established: 1866 Annual Undergrad Tuition & Fees: $12,325
Enrollment: 929 Coed
Affiliation or Control: African Methodist Episcopal IRS Status: 501(c)3
Highest Offering: Baccalaureate
Program: Liberal Arts And General
Accreditation: SC, IACBE

01 President .... Dr. Nathaniel GLOVER
03 Executive Vice President/COO .... Dr. Anna HAMMOND
88 Special Asistant to the President .... Mr. George DANDELAKE
10 VP Business & Finance .... Mr. Randolph MITCHELL
32 VP Student Affairs/Enrollment Mgmt .... Dr. Eric JACKSON
05 VP Academic Affairs .... Dr. Marvin GRANT
30 VP Institutional Advancement .... Mr. Joseph MURGO
21 Assoc VP/Business and Finance .... Ms. Jacqueline DOWDY
15 Director Human Resources .... Ms. Ernestine ROBINSON
88 Accreditation Coordinator .... Dr. Phyllis WALKER
25 Dir Title III & Sponsored Pgms .... Mrs. Lisa WILLIAMS
06 Registrar .... Ms. Maretta LATIMER
20 Asst VP Academic Affairs .... Dr. Stephanie CAMPBELL
37 Dir Financial Aid .... Ms. Janice NOWAK
09 Dir Inst Research & Assessment .... Ms. Bernice PARKER-BELL
88 Dir Upward Bound .... Dr. Delacy SANFORD
36 Career Services Director .... Mr. Antonio STARKE
36 Dir Counseling Center .... Ms. Ragan SUMMERS
07 Dir of Admissions .... Mr. Joel WALKER
88 Dir of TRIO .... Mr. Selah BISHOP
31 Dir Community Resource Center .... Mrs. Marie HEATH
88 Dir of CTL .... Dr. Kenesha BRACELY
88 Dir of FAME .... Mrs. Gladys CLAY
41 Dir of Athletics .... Mr. Willie JACKSON
13 Dir IT .... Mr. David SIMFUKWE
08 Library Director .... Ms. Carmella MARTIN
101 Secy of the College/Clerk of Board .... Mrs. Linda FOSTER
26 Coordinator of Public Relations .... Ms. Dee REGISTRE
29 Director Devel & Alumni Affairs .... Ms. Anita WALTON
38 Director Counseling Cener .... Ms. Ragan SUMMERS
39 Dean of Students/Residence Life .... Dr. Karen BUCKMAN
96 Purchasing Clerk .... Ms. Susie MATTISON

Embry-Riddle Aeronautical University (B)

600 S Clyde Morris Boulevard,
Daytona Beach FL 32114-3900
County: Volusia FICE Identification: 001479
Unit ID: 133553
Telephone: (386) 226-6000 Carnegie Class: Master's M
FAX Number: (386) 226-6459 Calendar System: Semester
URL: www.erau.edu
Established: 1926 Annual Undergrad Tuition & Fees: $33,218
Enrollment: 5,538 Coed
Affiliation or Control: Independent Non-Profit IRS Status: 501(c)3
Highest Offering: Doctorate
Program: Occupational; Liberal Arts And General; Professional; Technical Emphasis
Accreditation: SC, AAB, ACBSP, ENG

01 Interim President .... Dr. John R. WATRET
05 Sr VP Academic Affairs & Research .... Dr. Richard HEIST
10 Sr VP for Finance and CFO .... Mr. Randy HOWARD
15 VP/Chief Human Resources Officer .... Mr. Brandon L. YOUNG
26 Sr VP External Relations .... Mr. William HAMPTON
13 Chief Information Officer .... Ms. Becky VASQUEZ
104 Director Study Abroad .... Mrs. Sue A. MACCHIARELLA

Embry-Riddle Aeronautical University-Worldwide (C)

600 S Clyde Morris Boulevard,
Daytona Beach FL 32114-3900
Telephone: (800) 522-6787 Identification: 666089
Accreditation: &SC, AAB, ACBSP

† Regional accreditation is carried under the parent institution in Daytona Beach, FL.

Everest University-Brandon Campus (D)

3924 Coconut Palm Drive, Tampa FL 33619-1354
Telephone: (813) 621-0041 Identification: 666416
Accreditation: ACICS, ADNUR, MAC, SURTEC

† Branch campus of Everest University-North Orlando Campus, Orlando, FL.

Everest University-Jacksonville Campus (E)

8226 Phillips Highway, Jacksonville FL 32256-1240
Telephone: (904) 731-4949 Identification: 666994
Accreditation: ACICS

† Branch campus of Everest University-North Orlando Campus, Orlando, FL.

Everest University-Lakeland Campus (F)

995 E Memorial Boulevard, Suite 110,
Lakeland FL 33801-1919
Telephone: (863) 686-1444 Identification: 666415
Accreditation: ACICS, MAC

† Branch campus of Everest University-North Orlando Campus, Orlando, FL.

Everest University-Largo (G)

1199 East Bay Drive, Largo FL 33770-2556
Telephone: (727) 725-2688 FICE Identification: 025998
Accreditation: ACICS, MAC

† Branch campus of Everest University-North Orlando Campus, Orlando, FL.

Everest University-Melbourne Campus (H)

2190 Sarno Road, Melbourne FL 32935
Telephone: (321) 253-2929 Identification: 666417
Accreditation: ACICS, MAC

† Branch campus of Everest University-North Orlando Campus, Orlando, FL.

Everest University-North Orlando Campus (I)

5421 Diplomat Circle, Orlando FL 32810-5674
County: Orange FICE Identification: 001499
Unit ID: 136288
Telephone: (407) 628-5870 Carnegie Class: Bac/Assoc
FAX Number: (407) 628-1344 Calendar System: Quarter
URL: www.everest.edu
Established: 1918 Annual Undergrad Tuition & Fees: $13,968
Enrollment: 634 Coed
Affiliation or Control: Proprietary IRS Status: Proprietary
Highest Offering: Master's
Program: Business Emphasis
Accreditation: ACICS, MAC

01 President .... Louise STEINKEOWAY
12 President of Branch Campus .... Thomas SCHEER
12 President of Melbourne Branch .... Mark JUDGE
05 Academic Dean .... Heidi POLLPETER
07 Director of Admissions .... Kenny ANDERSON
08 Librarian .... Tamara DUJARDIAN
37 Financial Aid Supervisor .... Linda KAISRLIK
06 Registrar .... Jasmine RIVIERA
36 Director Student Placement .... Danielle THORNTON

Everest University-Orange Park (J)

805 Wells Road, Orange Park FL 32073-2301
Telephone: (904) 264-9122 Identification: 666590
Accreditation: ACICS, MAAB

† Branch campus of Everest University-North Orlando Campus, Orlando, FL.

Everest University-Pompano Beach Campus (K)

225 N Federal Highway, Pompano Beach FL 33062
Telephone: (954) 783-7339 FICE Identification: 008146
Accreditation: ACICS, MAAB

† Branch campus of Everest University, Orlando, FL.Branch campus of Everest University-North Orlando Campus, Orlando, FL.

Everest University-South Orlando Campus (L)

9200 Southpark Center Loop, Orlando FL 32819-8606
Telephone: (407) 851-2525 Identification: 666418
Accreditation: ACICS, MAC

† Branch campus of Everest University-North Orlando Campus, Orlando, FL.

Everest University-Tampa Campus (M)

3319 W Hillsborough Avenue, Tampa FL 33614-5801
Telephone: (813) 879-6000 FICE Identification: 001534
Accreditation: ACICS, MAC

† Branch campus of Everest University-North Orlando Campus, Orlando, FL.

Everglades University (N)

5002 T-Rex Avenue, Suite 100,
Boca Raton FL 33431-4493
County: Palm Beach FICE Identification: 031085
Unit ID: 385619
Telephone: (888) 772-6077 Carnegie Class: Bac/Diverse
FAX Number: (561) 912-1191 Calendar System: Semester
URL: www.evergladesuniversity.edu
Established: 1990 Annual Undergrad Tuition & Fees: $28,800
Enrollment: 1,378 Coed
Affiliation or Control: Independent Non-Profit IRS Status: 501(c)3
Highest Offering: Master's
Program: Professional
Accreditation: SC

01 President/CEO .... Ms. Kristi L. MOLLIS
05 Vice President of Academic Affairs .... Dr. Jayne MOSCHELLA
37 Regional Director of Financial Aid .... Mrs. Seeta SINGH MOONILALL
84 Regional Dir of Enrollment Mgmt .... Ms. Cindy CHALOVICH
26 Marketing Coordinator .... Mrs. Shay LAWRENCE
09 Director Inst Effectiveness .... Dr. Chee PIONG
08 Director of Library Services .... Ms. Karen GELOVER
12 Vice President Boca Raton Campus .... Dr. Arlette PETERSSON
107 Vice President Online Division .... Mr. David SHELPMAN, JR.
12 Vice President Sarasota Campus .... Ms. Caroline KING
12 Vice President of Orlando Campus .... Ms. Elisabeth SAUTNER
20 Dean of Academics Online .... Dr. Ernest BURT
20 Dean of Academics Sarasota .... Dr. Melanie YERK
20 Dean of Academics Orlando .... Dr. Rosemarie BRANCIFORTE
20 Dean of Academics Boca Raton .... Dr. Jason ALVIENE
07 Director of Admissions Boca .... Mrs. Debra RODRIGUES
07 Director of Admissions Online .... Vacant
07 Director of Admissions Orlando .... Vacant
07 Director of Admission Sarasota .... Ms. Barbara BEASLEY
04 Executive Asst to the President .... Mrs. Christina OAKLEY
37 Financial Aid Director Online .... Ms. Emily HERRON
37 Financial Aid Director Sarasota .... Mrs. Courtney ROBERTSON
37 Financial Aid Director Orlando .... Mr. Anthony CHAMBERS
37 Asst Financial Aid Director Boca .... Ms. Anne RODNE
06 Head Registrar .... Mr. Adrian KACZOR
06 Asst Registrar Online Division .... Ms. Dana NGUYEN
06 Registrar Boca .... Mrs. Pamela QUINTANA
06 Registrar Orlando .... Mrs. Jane STINIS
06 Registrar Sarasota .... Ms. Donna BARANOWSKI
50 Business Department .... Mr. David SMITH
88 Program Dir of Construction Mgmt .... Dr. Cristian PENCIU
88 Associate Dean .... Mr. Michael VAN DUSEN
76 Program Dir of Allied Health .... Dr. Katia CHAMBERLAIN
76 Program Dir of Allied Health Online .... Dr. Lori KAUFMAN
08 Librarian Boca Raton .... Vacant
08 Librarian Sarasota .... Ms. Anisa HITT
08 Librarian Orlando .... Ms. Chemera IVORY
32 Dir of Student Services Online .... Mr. Adam CLUM
32 Dir of Student Services Boca Raton .... Mr. Ruben VALBUENA
32 Dir of Student Services Sarasota .... Ms. Melinda WALLER
32 Dir of Student Services Orlando .... Ms. Janie DICKEY
88 Bursar Online Division .... Ms. Cassandra GORDON
88 Bursar Online Division .... Ms. Deana Kaye RUSSELL
40 Bursar/Bookstore Manager Boca .... Ms. Kiesha PAUL
40 Bookstore Manager Online Division .... Ms. Pamela PETERSON
40 Bursar/Bookstore Manager Sarasota .... Ms. Anita WENDZEL
40 Bursar/Bookstore Manager Orlando .... Ms. Yara CARASAS
88 Online Trainer .... Mr. Ronnie ABUKHALAF
88 Dir of Teaching & Learning .... Dr. Ellen SCALESE

FCC-Anthem College (O)

989 N Semoran Boulevard, Orlando FL 32807
Telephone: (888) 852-7272 Identification: 770613
Accreditation: ACICS

† Branch campus of Florida Career College, Miami, FL.

Flagler College (P)

74 King Street, Saint Augustine FL 32084-4342
County: Saint Johns FICE Identification: 007893
Unit ID: 133711
Telephone: (904) 829-6481 Carnegie Class: Bac/Diverse
FAX Number: (904) 824-6017 Calendar System: Semester
URL: www.flagler.edu
Established: 1968 Annual Undergrad Tuition & Fees: $16,180
Enrollment: 3,240 Coed
Affiliation or Control: Independent Non-Profit IRS Status: 501(c)3
Highest Offering: Baccalaureate
Program: Liberal Arts And General; Teacher Preparatory; Business Emphasis
Accreditation: SC, @TEAC

01 President .... Dr. William T. ABARE, JR.
00 Chancellor .... Dr. William L. PROCTOR
10 Vice President Business Services .... Mr. David L. CARSON
30 Vice President Inst Advancement .... Dr. Beverly C. CARMICHAEL
05 Vice President Academic Affairs .... Dr. Alan WOOLFOLK
26 Exec Director College Relations .... Ms. Donna DELORENZO
21 Executive Director of Finance .... Mr. Jeff KNIGHT
09 Director Inst Research & Planning .... Dr. Will MILLER
27 Director of News and Information .... Mr. Brian L. THOMPSON
84 Vice Pres for Enrollment Mgmt .... Ms. Deborah L. THOMPSON
32 Vice President of Student Services .... Mr. Daniel P. STEWART

20 Associate Dean of Academic Affairs .... Mr. Yvan J. KELLY
35 Assistant Dean of Student Services .... Dr. Dirk HIBLER
38 Associate Dean of Counseling .... Dr. Amy FALVO
06 Registrar .... Mrs. Miriam C. ROBERSON
37 Director of Financial Aid .... Ms. Sheia I. PLEASANT-DOINE
36 Director of Career Services .... Ms. Tara STEVENSON
08 Director of Library Services .... Mr. Brian NESSELRODE
41 Director Intercollegiate Athletics .... Mr. Jud DAMON
19 Director of Safety & Security .... Mr. Kerry DAVIS
40 Bookstore Manager .... Mr. Bob SMITH
24 Director Educational Media Services .... Mr. Steven I. SKIPP
13 Director Technology Services .... Mr. Joseph S. PROVENZA
39 Director of Residence Life .... Ms. Michelle HOLLAND
35 Director of Student Activities .... Vacant
12 Dean Flagler College - Tallahassee .... Dr. Donald K. PARKS
88 Dir of Disability Services .... Ms. Eva Lynn FRANCISCO
18 Superintendent of Plant & Grounds .... Mr. Victor CHENEY
04 Assistant to the President .... Ms. Mary Jane DILLON
21 Director of Business Services .... Mr. Larry D. WEEKS
29 Director Alumni Relations .... Ms. Margo BROWN
44 Director Annual Fund .... Mr. Jeffrey DAVITT
15 HR Generalist/Benefits Specialist .... Ms. Tricia KRISTOFF
31 Director of College Relations .... Ms. Laura STEVENSON
88 Senior Woman Admin Athletic Dept .... Ms. Caryn SAVITZ
07 Director of Admissions .... Ms. Rachel U. BRANCH
101 Secretary of the Institution/Board .... Ms. Mary Jane DILLON
104 Director Study Abroad .... Ms. Barbara OTTAVIANI-JONES
105 Director Web Services .... Ms. Holly L. HILL

Florida Career College (A)

1743 N Congress Avenue, Boynton Beach FL 33426
Telephone: (561) 634-7400　Identification: 770678
Accreditation: ACICS

† Branch campus of Florida Career College, Miami, FL.

Florida Career College (B)

3750 West 18th Avenue, Hialeah FL 33012-7028
Telephone: (786) 534-0940　Identification: 666624
Accreditation: ACICS

† Branch campus of Florida Career College, Miami, FL.

Florida Career College (C)

6600 Youngerman Circle, Jacksonville FL 32244
Telephone: (904) 573-1900　Identification: 770679
Accreditation: ACICS

† Branch campus of Florida Career College, Miami, FL.

Florida Career College (D)

3383 North State Road 7,
Lauderdale Lakes FL 33319-5617
Telephone: (954) 908-4700　Identification: 666622
Accreditation: ACICS

† Branch campus of Florida Career College, Miami, FL.

Florida Career College - Margate Campus (E)

3271 North State Road 7, Margate FL 33063
Telephone: (954) 915-7701　Identification: 770681
Accreditation: ACICS

† Branch campus of Florida Career College, Miami, FL.

Florida Career College (F)

1321 SW 107th Avenue, Suite 201B,
Miami FL 33174-2521
County: Miami-Dade　FICE Identification: 023058
Unit ID: 133997
Telephone: (786) 534-0500　Carnegie Class: Assoc/PrivFP4
FAX Number: N/A　Calendar System: Quarter
URL: www.careercollege.edu
Established: 1982　Annual Undergrad Tuition & Fees: $18,184
Enrollment: 6,227　Coed
Affiliation or Control: Proprietary　IRS Status: Proprietary
Highest Offering: Associate Degree
Program: Occupational; 2-Year Principally Bachelor's Creditable; Technical Emphasis
Accreditation: ACICS

01 President/CEO .... Mr. David KNOBEL
03 Executive Director .... Mr. Jeff DAY
06 Registrar .... Ms. Evelyn DIEPA

Florida Career College (G)

11731 Mills Drive, Bldg #2, Miami FL 33183
Telephone: (305) 384-7900　Identification: 770680
Accreditation: ACICS

† Branch campus of Florida Career College, Miami, FL.

Florida Career College (H)

7891 Pines Boulevard, Pembroke Pines FL 33024-6916
Telephone: (954) 399-4800　Identification: 666025
Accreditation: ACICS

† Branch campus of Florida Career College, Miami, FL.

Florida Career College (I)

9950 Princess Palm Ave, Suite 100, Tampa FL 33619
Telephone: (813) 621-5775　Identification: 770682
Accreditation: ACICS

† Branch campus of Florida Career College, Miami, FL.

Florida Career College (J)

6058 Okeechobee Boulevard, West Palm Beach FL 33417
Telephone: (561) 689-0550　Identification: 770683
Accreditation: ACICS

† Branch campus of Florida Career College, Miami, FL.

Florida Coastal School of Law (K)

8787 Baypine, Jacksonville FL 32256-8528
County: Duval　FICE Identification: 033743
Unit ID: 434715
Telephone: (904) 680-7700　Carnegie Class: Spec/Law
FAX Number: (904) 680-7777　Calendar System: Semester
URL: www.fcsl.edu
Established: 1995　Annual Graduate Tuition & Fees: $43,001
Enrollment: 1,070　Coed
Affiliation or Control: Proprietary　IRS Status: Proprietary
Highest Offering: First Professional Degree; No Undergraduates
Program: Professional
Accreditation: LAW

01 President .... Mr. Dennis STONE
05 Dean .... Mr. Scott DEVITO
10 Vice Pres Finance & Administration .... Mr. Bruce WILSON
07 Director of Admissions .... Mr. Tony CARDENAS
30 Dir of Institutional Advancement .... Ms. Alicia EDWARDS
32 Associate Dean of Student Affairs .... Mr. Thomas TAGGART
62 Assoc Dean of Library & Technology .. Ms. Korin MUNSTERMAN
36 Dir for Professional Development .... Mrs. Jocelyn DONAHUE
20 Associate Dean of Academic Affairs .... Mrs. Cynthia IRVIN
106 Assoc Dean of Strategy & Innovation .... Ms. Margaret IOANNIDES
88 Dir of Academic Success .... Ms. Missy DAVENPORT
15 Sr Director of Human Resources .... Mrs. Susie PONTIFF STRINGER
09 Dir of Institutional Effectiveness .... Ms. Claire TORRES-LUGO
20 Assistant Dean of Academic Affairs .... Ms. Danielle NOE
37 Asst Dir of Financial Aid .... Ms. Leslie TIGNOR
06 Registrar .... Ms. Bridgette WAINES
18 Dir of Security & Facilities .... Mr. Bill BREEN
88 Process Partner .... Mr. Clay ROBERTSON
04 Assistant to the Dean & President .... Ms. Karen EUBANKS

Florida College (L)

119 N Glen Arven Avenue,
Temple Terrace FL 33617-5578
County: Hillsborough　FICE Identification: 001482
Unit ID: 133809
Telephone: (813) 988-5131　Carnegie Class: Bac/Assoc
FAX Number: (813) 899-6772　Calendar System: Semester
URL: www.floridacollege.edu
Established: 1944　Annual Undergrad Tuition & Fees: $16,074
Enrollment: 542　Coed
Affiliation or Control: Independent Non-Profit　IRS Status: 501(c)3
Highest Offering: Baccalaureate
Program: Liberal Arts And General; Religious Emphasis
Accreditation: SC, MUS

01 President .... Dr. Harry E. PAYNE, JR.
05 Vice Pres of Acad & Student Affairs .... Dr. Daniel W. PETTY
20 Dean of Academics .... Dr. Brian L. CRISPELL
32 Dean of Student Services .... Dr. Jason S. LONGSTRETH
10 Chief Business Officer .... Mr. Ronnie STACKPOLE
37 Director Student Financial Aid .... Mr. Stephen BLAYLOCK
07 Dir of Admissions & Retention Svcs .... Mr. Paul CASEBOLT
09 Director of Institutional Research .... Dr. M. Thaxter DICKEY
88 Director of Advising .... Mrs. Shannon MCKINNEY
06 Registrar .... Ms. Beth A. GRANT
08 Director of Library .... Mrs. Wanda DICKEY
90 Director of Academic Computing .... Mr. M. Ray HINDS
91 Director of Information Technology .... Mr. Jon RAE
30 Director of Development .... Mr. David L. CURRY
29 Director of Alumni Relations .... Mr. Adam J. OLSON
26 Director of Marketing/Info Officer .... Mr. Jared M. BARR
40 Manager of Bookstore .... Mrs. Amy CASEBOLT
88 Events Coordinator .... Mrs. Sharon L. CLARK

Florida College of Integrative Medicine (M)

7100 Lake Ellenor Drive, Orlando FL 32809-5721
County: Orange　FICE Identification: 032383
Unit ID: 434441
Telephone: (407) 888-8689　Carnegie Class: Spec/Health
FAX Number: (407) 888-8211　Calendar System: Semester
URL: www.fcim.edu
Established: 1990　Annual Undergrad Tuition & Fees: $15,125
Enrollment: 116　Coed
Affiliation or Control: Proprietary　IRS Status: Proprietary
Highest Offering: Master's; No Lower Division
Program: Professional
Accreditation: ACUP

01 President .... Mr. Larry L. HAN
108 Chief Quality Officer .... Ms. Yuan-Yuan HAN
05 Academic Dean .... Dr. Lin CHAI
11 Chief Administrative Officer .... Mr. Robert P. LYNCH
10 Director of Finance .... Ms. Susan HOEH
07 Admissions Advisor .... Ms. Michelle COLON
37 Director of Financial Aid .... Ms. Mary SIMMONS

Florida College of Natural Health (N)

2600 Lake Lucien Drive, Suite 240,
Maitland FL 32751-7253
Telephone: (407) 261-0319　Identification: 666513
Accreditation: ACCSC

† Branch campus of Florida College of Natural Health, Pompano Beach, FL.

Florida College of Natural Health (O)

7925 NW 12th Street, #201, Miami FL 33126-1821
Telephone: (305) 597-9599　Identification: 666514
Accreditation: ACCSC

† Branch campus of Florida College of Natural Health, Pompano Beach, FL.

Florida College of Natural Health (P)

2001 W Sample Road, #100,
Pompano Beach FL 33064-1342
County: Broward　FICE Identification: 030086
Unit ID: 387925
Telephone: (954) 975-6400　Carnegie Class: Assoc/PrivFP
FAX Number: (954) 975-9633　Calendar System: Other
URL: www.fcnh.com
Established: 1986　Annual Undergrad Tuition & Fees: $13,532
Enrollment: 284　Coed
Affiliation or Control: Proprietary　IRS Status: Proprietary
Highest Offering: Associate Degree
Program: Occupational
Accreditation: ACCSC

01 President .... Mr. Stephen LAZARUS
10 Controller .... Ms. Barbara KRANE
22 Vice President of Compliance .... Ms. Melissa WADE
05 Vice President of Education .... Ms. Dawnette CABALUNA

Florida Gateway College (Q)

149 SE College Place, Lake City FL 32025-2007
County: Columbia　FICE Identification: 001501
Unit ID: 135160
Telephone: (386) 752-1822　Carnegie Class: Assoc/Pub-R-M
FAX Number: (386) 755-1521　Calendar System: Semester
URL: www.fgc.edu
Established: 1947　Annual Undergrad Tuition & Fees (In-State): $3,127
Enrollment: 2,912　Coed
Affiliation or Control: State　IRS Status: 501(c)3
Highest Offering: Baccalaureate
Program: Occupational; 2-Year Principally Bachelor's Creditable; Liberal Arts And General; Teacher Preparatory
Accreditation: SC, ADNUR, EMT, PTAA

01 President .... Dr. Lawrence BARRETT
10 Vice President Business Services .... Mr. Stephen BENSON
04 Assistant to the President .... Ms. Karyn CONGRESSI
05 Vice President for Academic Pgms .... Dr. Brian DOPSON
75 Vice President Occupational Pgms .... Dr. Tracy HICKMAN
32 Vice President for Student Services .... Dr. Linda CROLEY
13 Exec Dir Info Technology/CIO .... Mr. Mike DAVIS
47 Exec Dir of Industrial & Agricult .... Mr. John PIERSOL
15 Executive Director Human Resources .... Ms. Sharon BEST
53 Exec Dir Ctr for Excell in Teaching .... Ms. Pamela CARSWELL
102 Executive Director Foundation .... Mr. Mike LEE
26 Exec Dir Media & Community Info .... Mr. Mike MCKEE
37 Director Financial Aid .... Mrs. Becky WESTBERRY
84 Director Enrollment Management .... Ms. Sandra JOHNSTON
06 Registrar .... Ms. Gayle HUNTER
21 Director Business Services .... Ms. Michelle HOLLOWAY
25 Director of Grants .... Mr. Daniel CRONRATH
09 Director of Research/Institutional .... Ms. Patty ANDERSON
66 Exec Director Nursing .... Ms. Melody CORSO
18 Director Facilities .... Mr. Ed D'AVI
96 Director of Purchasing .... Vacant
36 Director Advising/Student Dev .... Dr. Margaret MCLAUGHLIN
88 Director for Water Resources .... Ms. Pam MURAWSKI
88 Director for Criminal Justice .... Mr. John JEWETT
62 Director Library Services .... Ms. Christine BOATRIGHT

Florida Institute of Technology (R)

150 W University Boulevard, Melbourne FL 32901-6975
County: Brevard　FICE Identification: 001469
Unit ID: 133881
Telephone: (321) 674-8000　Carnegie Class: DRU
FAX Number: (321) 984-8461　Calendar System: Semester
URL: www.fit.edu
Established: 1958　Annual Undergrad Tuition & Fees: $38,540
Enrollment: 9,575　Coed
Affiliation or Control: Independent Non-Profit　IRS Status: 501(c)3
Highest Offering: Doctorate
Program: Liberal Arts And General; Teacher Preparatory; Professional; Technical Emphasis

Accreditation: SC, AAB, CLPSY, CS, ENG, IACBE

01 President .... Dr. Anthony J. CATANESE
04 Exec Asst to Pres & Ombudsman .... Mrs. Suzee S. LOUCHE
03 Executive Vice Pres & COO .... Dr. T. Dwayne MCCAY
10 Sr Vice Pres Financial Affairs/CFO .... Ms. Cathy WOOD
86 Sr VP Ext Relations/Economic Dev .... Capt. Winston SCOTT
30 Sr Vice Pres/Chief Development Ofcr .... Dr. Susan ST. ONGE
11 Deputy COO .... Dr. Donn MILLER-KERMANI
05 VP Acad Affairs/Dean Grad Programs .... Dr. Semen KOKSAL
88 Dean College of Aeronautics .... Dr. Korhan OYMAN
50 Dean College of Business .... Dr. S. Ann BECKER
54 Dean College of Engineering .... Dr. Martin GLICKSMAN
83 Dean Col of Psychology/Liberal Arts .... Dr. Mary Beth KENKEL
81 Dean College of Science .... Dr. Hamid RASSOUL
08 Dean of Libraries .... Dr. Sohair WASTAWY
29 VP Alum Rel/Exec Dir Alum Assn .... Mr. Albino P. CAMPANINI
88 Vice Pres for External Relations .... Dr. Kenneth STACKPOOLE
30 Vice President Development .... Mr. Michael SEELEY
18 Vice Pres Facilities Ops/Architect .... Mr. Gregory TSARK
13 Vice Pres IT/CIO .... Mr. Eric KLEDZIK
26 Vice Pres Marketing & Communication .. Mr. Wesley D. SUMNER
88 Vice President Orlando Center .... Ms. Leslie HIELEMA
46 Vice President Research .... Mr. Frank KINNEY
32 Vice President Student Affairs .... Dr. Randall L. ALFORD
88 Vice Pres Support Services .... Dr. Joni OGLESBY
21 Vice Pres Financial Planning .... Mr. Randy LIVINGSTON
108 VP Inst Effectiveness & Intl Pgms .... Dr. Monica BALOGA
84 Assoc Vice Pres Enrollment Mgmt .... Mr. Gary HAMME
35 Assoc VP Student Affs/Dean of Stdnt .... Mr. Rodney BOWERS
106 Assoc Vice Pres/Dir Online Learning .... Mr. Brian EHRLICH
109 Asst VP Business & Ret Operation .... Mr. Greg GRAHAM
25 Asst VP Research/Dir Sponsored Pgm ...... Mr. John P. POLITANO
06 Registrar .... Mr. David MICUS
88 Director Academic Support Services .... Mr. Rodd NEWCOMBE
41 Director Athletics .... Mr. William K. JURGENS
19 Director Campus Security .... Mr. Kevin GRAHAM
36 Director Career Services .... Ms. Dona E. GAYNOR
38 Dir Counseling/Psychological Svcs .... Dr. Robyn TAPLEY
88 Director Creative Services .... Ms. Judith E. TINTERA
88 Dir Environ & Regulatory Compliance .... Mr. Henry PEEBLES
18 Director Facilities Operations .... Mr. John M. MILBOURNE
37 Director Financial Aid .... Mr. Jay LALLY
07 Director Grad Adm Online Learning .... Ms. Carolyn P. FARRIOR
58 Director Graduate Programs .... Dr. Rosemary LAYNE
15 Director Human Resources .... Ms. Karen GATHERCOLE
09 Director Institutional Research .... Ms. Leslie L. SAVOIE
85 Director Intl Students/Scholar Svcs .... Ms. Judith BROOKE
96 Director Purchasing & AP .... Mr. Timothy KENEFICK
104 Director Study Abroad .... Ms. Heather EMMERT
07 Director Undergraduate Admission .... Mr. Michael PERRY
88 Director University Museums .... Ms. Carla FUNK
105 Director Web Services .... Mr. Joshua CULVER
07 Director Intl & Graduate Admissions .... Ms. Cheryl-Ann BROWN
102 Assoc VP Corp Sponsored Programs .... Gretchen SAUERMAN
90 Executive Director Ellucian .... Rebecca ARCHER

Florida Keys Community College (A)

5901 College Road, Key West FL 33040-4397

County: Monroe FICE Identification: 001485

Unit ID: 133960

Telephone: (305) 296-9081 Carnegie Class: Assoc/Pub-R-S

FAX Number: (305) 292-5155 Calendar System: Trimester

URL: www.fkcc.edu

Established: 1963 Annual Undergrad Tuition & Fees (In-District): $3,276

Enrollment: 1,200 Coed

Affiliation or Control: State/Local IRS Status: 501(c)3

Highest Offering: Associate Degree

Program: Occupational; 2-Year Principally Bachelor's Creditable; Fine Arts Emphasis

Accreditation: SC

01 President .... Dr. Jonathan GUEUERRA
05 Provost .... Mrs. Brittany SYNDER
10 Vice Pres Business & Admin Svcs .... Mrs. Jean MAUK
35 Dean Student Affairs .... Mrs. Erika MACWILLIAMS
32 Director Student Services .... Mrs. Michelle CHERRY
51 Dir Cont Ed/Workforce/Testing .... Mrs. Cathy TORRES
04 Director President's Office .... Mrs. Debbie LEONARD
26 Dir College and Public Relations .. Mrs. Amber ERNST-LEONARD
06 Registrar .... Mrs. Cheryl MALSHEIMER
08 Director Learning Resources .... Ms. Lori KELLY
37 Dir Student Fin Aid/Enrollment Svcs .... Mrs. Joyce LUBECK SONENBERG
18 Dir Purchasing & Plant Operations .... Mr. Douglas PRYOR
13 Director of IT .... Mrs. Michelle ADAM
15 Director Human Resources .... Vacant
25 Director Sponsored Research .... Mr. Samuel PETERSON
30 VP Advancement .... Dr. Frank WOOD
21 Controller .... Mrs. Jean MAUK
09 Director Institutional Research .... Ms. Linda MACMINN
30 Director Development/Alumni Rels .... Vacant
76 Director Allied Health & Nursing .... Mr. Mark ROBY
103 Dean Career Tech & Workforce .... Dr. Patrick RICE
49 Dean Arts & Sciences .... Mr. Michael MCPHERSON
39 Coord Residence Life .... Mr. Christopher DELISLE

Florida Memorial University (B)

15800 NW 42nd Avenue, Miami Gardens FL 33054-6199

County: Miami-Dade FICE Identification: 001486

Unit ID: 133979

Telephone: (305) 626-3600 Carnegie Class: Master's S

FAX Number: (305) 626-3769 Calendar System: Semester

URL: www.fmuniv.edu

Established: 1879 Annual Undergrad Tuition & Fees: $15,280

Enrollment: 1,528 Coed

Affiliation or Control: Independent Non-Profit IRS Status: 501(c)3

Highest Offering: Master's

Program: Liberal Arts And General; Teacher Preparatory

Accreditation: SC, AAB, ACBSP, CS, MUS, SW

01 President .... Dr. Roslyn CLARK ARTIS
05 Executive VP and Provost .... Vacant
20 Associate Provost .... Dr. Denise CALLWOOD-BRATHWAITE
04 Assistant to President .... Ms. Rachel TURNER
49 Dean of Arts and Sciences .... Dr. Keshia N. ABRAHAMN
10 Exec VP Finance/Administration .... Ms. Cynthia CURRY
84 Asst VP of Enrollment Mgmt .... Ms. Danneal JONES
30 Vice Pres University Advancement .... Mr. Marcus BURGESS
45 Assc VP Institutional Effectiveness .... Dr. William E. HOPPER
88 Chair Aviation and Safety .... Dr. Arnold J. TOLBERT
50 Dean School of Business .... Dr. Abbass ENTESSARI
53 Dean School of Education .... Dr. Idriss ABDOULAYE
81 Chair Health and Natural Sciences .... Dr. Rose Mary STIFFIN
83 Interim Chair Social Sciences .... Dr. Tameka HOBBS
64 Interim Chair Visual/Perf Arts .... Mr. Melvin WHITE
77 Chair Comp Science/Math & Tech .... Dr. Ben WONGSAROJ
79 Chair Humanities .... Dr. Keshia N. ABRAHAM
88 Int Dir Ctrs Acad Support & Reten .... Mr. Jae JACKSON
08 Director of Library Services .... Mr. Otis ALEXANDER
37 Director Financial Aid/Scholarships .... Mr. Calvin DAVIS
06 Registrar .... Mrs. Lelia A. EFFORD
09 Director of Institutional Research .... Dr. Carlos CANAS
15 Director Human Resources Management .... Vacant
41 Director Intercollegiate Athletics .... Mr. Robert SMITH
36 Director Career Development .... Ms. Athena JACKSON
39 Director Residential Life .... Mrs. Jacklan ALEXANDER
07 Interim Director of Admissions .... Ms. Zefonic DOBYNES
19 Chief of Campus Safety .... Chief Larry COLEMAN
18 Dir Facility Mgmt/Plant Operations .... Mr. David JACCARINO
42 Dean of Campus Ministry .... Dr. Jeffrey D. SWAIN
29 Director Alumni Affairs .... Mrs. Sheila POWELL-COHEN
35 Director Student Activities .... Mr. C. Vernon MARTIN, JR.
85 International Student Advisor .... Mr. Trevor LEWIS
13 Interim CIO .... Mr. Christopher BROMFIELD
32 Dean of Students .... Mrs. Valerie HALL
108 Director Institutional Assessment .... Dr. Richard YAKLICH

Florida National University Hialeah Campus (C)

4425 W. Jose Regueiro (20th) Ave, Hialeah FL 33012-4108

County: Dade FICE Identification: 025476

Unit ID: 408844

Telephone: (305) 821-3333 Carnegie Class: Assoc/PrivFP4

FAX Number: (305) 362-0595 Calendar System: Semester

URL: www.fnu.edu

Established: 1982 Annual Undergrad Tuition & Fees: $13,250

Enrollment: 1,710 Coed

Affiliation or Control: Proprietary IRS Status: Proprietary

Highest Offering: Master's

Program: 2-Year Principally Bachelor's Creditable; Business Emphasis

Accreditation: SC, #COARC, NURSE, @PTAA

01 President/CEO .... Dr. Maria C. REGUEIRO
09 VP of Assessment & Research/FA Dir .... Mr. Omar SANCHEZ
11 Vice President of Operations .... Mr. Frank ANDREU
05 Vice President of Academic Affairs .... Dr. Caridad HERNANDEZ
10 Controller .... Dr. Lourdes NIEVES
88 Accreditation Liaison .... Dr. Barbara J. RODRIGUEZ
07 Director of Admissions .... Mr. Robert LOPEZ
06 University Registrar .... Mr. Jose L. VALDES
32 Student Services Officer .... Ms. Cassandra FERRERA
106 Director of Distance Learning .... Mrs. Sandra LOMENA
12 Campus Dean .... Dr. Jorge ALFONSO
36 Job Placement Officer .... Mr. Candido AVEILLE
50 Business & Economics Division Head .... Dr. James BULLEN
76 Allied Health Division Head .... Dr. Loreto ALMONTE
66 RN Program Nursing Division Dir .... Mrs. Maida BURGOS
79 Humanities and Fine Arts Division .... Dr. Barbara RODRIGUEZ
88 ESL Division Head .... Mr. Oscar PEREZ
15 Human Resources Director .... Mr. Edward ZALDIVAR
41 Athletic Director .... Mr. Scott J. SCHMIDT
88 Assistant Campus Dean .... Mrs. Olga RODRIGUEZ
88 Assistant Campus Dean .... Mrs. Silvia BORGES
07 Admissions Supervisor Distance .... Mrs. Yolanda NAVARRO
07 Admissions Supervisor .... Mrs. Virginia RABELO
88 Academic Advisor .... Mrs. Carol ROMERO
88 Academic Advisor .... Mrs. Hazel RIVERA
31 Director Community Relations .... Mrs. Rachel TOURGEMAN
36 Job Placement Officer .... Mrs. Vanessa PEREZ

Florida National University South Campus (D)

11865 SW 26th Street Unit H-3, Miami FL 33175

Telephone: (305) 226-9999 Identification: 666691

Accreditation: &SC

† Regional accreditation is carried under the parent institution Florida National College, Hialeah, FL.

Florida National University Training Center (E)

4206 West 12th Avenue, Hialeah FL 33012

Telephone: (305) 231-3326 Identification: 666690

Accreditation: &SC

† Regional accreditation is carried under the parent institution Florida National College, Hialeah, FL.

Florida Southern College (F)

111 Lake Hollingsworth Drive, Lakeland FL 33801-5698

County: Polk FICE Identification: 001488

Unit ID: 134079

Telephone: (863) 680-4111 Carnegie Class: Bac/Diverse

FAX Number: (863) 680-4112 Calendar System: Semester

URL: www.flsouthern.edu

Established: 1883 Annual Undergrad Tuition & Fees: $31,460

Enrollment: 2,670 Coed

Affiliation or Control: United Methodist IRS Status: 501(c)3

Highest Offering: Doctorate

Program: Liberal Arts And General; Teacher Preparatory; Professional

Accreditation: SC, BUS, CAATE, MUS, NURSE

01 President .... Dr. Anne B. KERR
05 Provost .... Dr. Kyle FEDLER
10 Vice President Finance & Admin .... Mr. Terry DENNIS
84 Vice Pres/Dean Enrollment Mgmt .... Mr. John GRUNDIG
30 Vice President Advancement .... Dr. Robert H. TATE
41 Athletic Director .... Mr. Peter E. MEYER
13 Chief Information Officer .... Mr. John L. THOMAS
20 Assoc Provost Experiential Educ .... Dr. Mary L. CROWE
32 Dean of Student Development .... Mr. Bill C. LANGSTON, II
49 Dean Art and Sciences .... Dr. Brad E. HOLLINGSHEAD
50 Dean Business .... Dr. William RHEY
53 Dean Education .... Dr. Tracey D. TEDDER
66 Dean Nursing and Health Science .... Dr. Loretta REINHART
55 Dean Adult and Graduate Education .... Dr. Craig N. STORY
71 Dean of Student Success .... Dr. Susan FREEMAN
07 Director of Admissions .... Ms. Erin ERVIN
08 Director of the Library .... Mr. Randall M. MACDONALD
06 Registrar .... Ms. Sally L. THISSEN
09 Dir Inst Research/Effectiveness .... Dr. Kenneth M. REAVES
36 Director of Career Development .... Ms. Cara CIMA
37 Director of Student Financial Aid .... Mr. William L. HEALY
104 Coordinator Student Travel .... Ms. Bridgette MCARTHUR
42 Chaplain Director Campus Ministry .... Rev. Timothy S. WRIGHT
35 Asst Dean of Student Development .... Mr. Mike CRAWFORD
39 Director of Community Living .... Mr. Marc A. TUSCHEN
38 Director Student Counseling .... Dr. Carol BALLARD
28 Director Life and Cultural Center .... Ms. Brenda LEWIS
44 Asst VP for Advancement .... Ms. Kathy ELLIS
102 Director of Major Gifts .... Ms. Heather PHARRIS
21 Assoc Business Officer/Controller .... Ms. Judy ROBINSON
15 Director of Human Resources .... Ms. Katherine PAWLAK
26 Director of Marketing and Comm .... Ms. Katherine WHITAKER
105 Director Web Services .... Mr. James JARRETT
29 Coordinator of Alumni Services .... Ms. Betty MILLER
18 Director Operations .... Mr. William A. PHARRIS
19 Director Security/Safety .... Mr. William CAREW
40 Manager Bookstore .... Ms. Ashley LORD
04 Executive Asst to President .... Ms. Lynn M. DENNIS

Florida SouthWestern State College (G)

8099 College Parkway, SW, Fort Myers FL 33919-5566

County: Lee FICE Identification: 001477

Unit ID: 133508

Telephone: (239) 489-9300 Carnegie Class: Assoc/Pub4

FAX Number: (239) 489-9103 Calendar System: Semester

URL: www.fsw.edu

Established: 1961 Annual Undergrad Tuition & Fees (In-State): $3,711

Enrollment: 15,705 Coed

Affiliation or Control: State IRS Status: 501(c)3

Highest Offering: Baccalaureate

Program: Occupational; 2-Year Principally Bachelor's Creditable; Liberal Arts And General; Teacher Preparatory; Professional

Accreditation: SC, ADNUR, CAHIIM, COARC, CVT, DH, EMT, NUR, RAD

01 President .... Dr. Jeffery ALLBRITTEN
05 Provost & VP of Academic Affairs .... Dr. Denis WRIGHT
10 VP Administrative Services .... Dr. Gina DOEBLE
46 VP Research/Tech & Accountability .... Dr. Jeff STEWART
32 VP Student Affairs & Enroll Mgmt .... Dr. Christine DAVIS
30 VP Institutional Advancement .... Dr. Louis TRAINA
12 Regional VP/Pres Charlotte Campus .... Dr. Patricia LAND
12 Regional VP/Pres Collier Campus .... Dr. Robert JONES
100 Chief of Staff .... Dr. Henry PEEL
43 General Counsel .... Mr. Mark LUPE
26 Dir Comm & Public Info Officer .... Ms. Teresa MORGENSTERN
86 Dir Govermental Relations .... Mr. Matthew HOLLIDAY
49 Dean Arts/Humanities & Social Sci .... Dr. Emery ALFORD
49 Dean Pure & Applied Sciences .... Dr. Martin MCCLINTON
50 Dean Business & Technology .... Dr. John MEYER
53 Dean Education and Charter Schools .... Dr. Lawrence MILLER
76 Dean Health Professions .... Dr. Marie COLLINS
106 Dean Teach Innov/Fac Dev & Online .... Dr. Mary MYERS
20 Associate VP Academic Affairs .... Dr. Eileen DELUCA
20 Asst VP Academic Affairs .... Dr. Laura WEIR
08 Dean Learning Resources .... Vacant
06 Registrar .... Mr. Garnett SALMON
88 Assoc Dean Bacc Pgm & Acad Svcs .... Ms. Michelle FANSLAU
12 Director Hendry/Glades Center .... Mr. Jeffery GIBBS
88 Bursar .... Mr. Dwain KEDDO
18 Director Facilities Planning & Dev .... Mr. Steve NICE

15 Director Human Resources .... Ms. Susan BRONSTEIN
21 Asst VP Budget & Financial Svcs .... Mr. Tobias DISCENZA
96 Director of Procurement Services .... Ms. Lisa TUDOR
37 Director of Financial Aid .... Ms. Catherine MORGAN
19 Director Public Safety .... Mr. Richard PARFITT
109 Director Auxiliary Services .... Ms. Judith PULTRO
108 Dir Effectiveness & Accountability .... Dr. Susan HIBBARD
09 Director of Institutional Research .... Ms. Abby WILLCOX
13 Chief Information Officer .... Mr. Jason DUDLEY
84 Asst VP Enrollment & Student Succes .... Ms. Laura ANTCZAK
35 Assoc Dean Stdnt Life & Orientation .... Dr. Linda RICKMAN
35 Associate Dean of Students .... Mr. Mark BUKOWSKI
07 Director of Admissions .... Ms. Amber MCCOWN
88 Director of Testing Services .... Ms. Denise SWAFFORD
88 Director of Adaptive Services .... Ms. Angela HARTSELL
88 Director Student Support Services .... Ms. Sarah LIEKWEG
102 Sr Director Admin & Dev/Foundation .... Mr. Kevin MILLER
44 Senior Director Development .... Mr. Paul BOVA
88 Campus Dean Stdnt Affs & Acad Svcs .... Dr. Christy GILFERT
88 Campus Dean Stdnt Affs & Acad Svcs .... Dr. Gail MURPHY
39 Director Student Housing .... Mr. Justin LONG
41 Athletic Director .... Mr. Carl MCALOOSE

Florida State College at Jacksonville (A)

501 W State Street, Jacksonville FL 32202-4097
County: Duval FICE Identification: 001484
Unit ID: 133702
Telephone: (904) 646-2300 Carnegie Class: Assoc/Pub4
FAX Number: N/A Calendar System: Semester
URL: www.fscj.edu
Established: 1965 Annual Undergrad Tuition & Fees (In-District): $4,388
Enrollment: 25,514 Coed
Affiliation or Control: Local IRS Status: Exempt
Highest Offering: Baccalaureate
Program: Occupational; 2-Year Principally Bachelor's Creditable
Accreditation: SC, ACBSP, ACFEI, ADNUR, CAHIIM, COARC, CVT, DA, DH, DIETT, EMT, FUSER, HT, MLTAD, NUR, OTA, PTAA, SURGT

01 College President .... Dr. Cynthia A. BIOTEAU
05 Vice Pres of the College/Provost .... Dr. Judith BILSKY
32 Vice President Student Services .... Dr. Christopher HOLLAND
30 VP Inst Advance/Exec Dir FSCJ Found .... Dr. Eric BECHER
10 Vice Pres of Business Services .... Mr. Albert LITTLE
86 Dir Government/Cmty Engagement .... Ms. Jennifer SILVA
49 AVP Liberal Arts and Sciences .... Dr. Nancy K. WEBSTER
20 Associate Provost .... Dr. Margo MARTIN
35 AVP Student Success .... Ms. Melanie MILLER
103 AVP Workforce Educ/Econ Development ..... Ms. Linda WOODARD
12 Campus President North .... Dr. Sandy ROBINSON
12 Campus President Downtown .... Dr. Marie F. GNAGE
12 Campus President South .... Dr. Margarita A. CABRAL-MALY
12 Campus President Open/Deerwood .... Ms. Jana KOOI
12 Campus President Kent .... Dr. Ian NEUHARD
43 College General Counsel .... Dr. Colin C. MAILLOUX
13 Actg Chief Information Officer .... Mr. Christopher MARKHAM
21 Chief Financial Officer .... Mr. Cleve E. WARREN
15 Chief Human Resources Officer .... Mr. Mark LACEY
21 Chief Business Affairs Officer .... Mr. Laurence I. SNELL
19 Exec Dir Public Safety/Security .... Mr. James E. STEVENSON
18 Exec Dir Facilities & Const Mgmt .. Mr. Charles M. STRATMANN
88 Director of Security .... Mr. Gordon BASS
88 Exec Dean Student Success .... Dr. Roland BULLARD
22 Ex Dir Employee Rels/Col Equity Ofr .... Ms. Lisa J. MOORE
102 Exec Director Foundation .... Dr. Eric BECHER
26 Dir of Marketing & Communications .... Ms. Jill K. JOHNSON
88 Executive Director Artist Series .... Dr. Milton A. RUSSOS
06 Registrar .... Vacant
25 Director of Grants .... Vacant
37 Director Financial Aid .... Mr. Rodrick ANDREWS
41 Director of Athletics .... Mr. John MCGRAW
84 Dean of Enrollment Management .... Mr. Rick TURNER
09 Director Student Analytics/Research .... Mr. Greg MICHALSKI
88 Director of Students W/Disabilities ..... Ms. Denise J. GIARRUSSO
88 Executive Director of Nassau Center .... Ms. Donna MARTIN

Florida Technical College (B)

1199 S Woodland Boulevard, Deland FL 32720-7415
Telephone: (386) 734-3303 Identification: 666419
Accreditation: ACICS, MAAB

† Branch campus of Florida Technical College, Orlando, FL.

Florida Technical College (C)

3837 West Vine Street, Kissimmee FL 34741
Telephone: (407) 483-5700 Identification: 770684
Accreditation: ACICS, MAAB

† Branch campus of Florida Technical College, Orlando, FL.

Florida Technical College (D)

4715 South Florida Avenue, Suite 4, Lakeland FL 33813-2101
Telephone: (866) 967-8822 FICE Identification: 025981
Accreditation: ACICS, MAAB

† Branch campus of Florida Technical College, Orlando, FL.

Florida Technical College (E)

12900 Challenger Parkway, Orlando FL 32826
County: Orange FICE Identification: 022187
Unit ID: 134112
Telephone: (407) 447-7300 Carnegie Class: Assoc/PrivFP
FAX Number: (407) 447-7301 Calendar System: Quarter
URL: www.ftccollege.edu
Established: 1982 Annual Undergrad Tuition & Fees: $24,750
Enrollment: 4,300 Coed
Affiliation or Control: Proprietary IRS Status: Proprietary
Highest Offering: Baccalaureate
Program: Occupational; 2-Year Principally Bachelor's Creditable; Liberal Arts And General; Technical Emphasis
Accreditation: ACICS, MAAB

00 President/CEO .... Mr. David RUGGIERI
01 Executive Director .... Mr. John BUCK
05 Director of Education .... Dr. David PENN
07 Director of Admissions .... Ms. Ashley WALKER
37 Director of Financial Aid .... Ms. Ivette LUGO

Florida Technical College (F)

12520 Pines Boulevard, Pembroke Pines FL 33027
Telephone: (954) 556-1900 Identification: 770685
Accreditation: ACICS, MAAB

† Branch campus of Florida Technical College, Orlando, FL.

Fortis College (G)

700 Blanding Boulevard, Suite 16, Orange Park FL 32065
County: Clay FICE Identification: 034343
Unit ID: 439792
Telephone: (904) 269-7086 Carnegie Class: Assoc/PrivFP
FAX Number: (904) 269-6664 Calendar System: Semester
URL: www.fortis.edu
Established: 1985 Annual Undergrad Tuition & Fees: $14,975
Enrollment: 312 Coed
Affiliation or Control: Proprietary IRS Status: Proprietary
Highest Offering: Associate Degree
Program: Occupational; 2-Year Principally Bachelor's Creditable
Accreditation: ACICS, SURGT

01 Campus President .... Mr. Wyman DICKEY

Fortis Institute (H)

9035 Sunset Drive, Suite 200, Miami FL 33173-3431
Telephone: (305) 596-5553 Identification: 770542
Accreditation: COE

† Branch campus of Fortis Institute, Cookeville, TN.

Fortis Institute (I)

1630 South Congress Avenue, Ste 300, Palm Springs FL 33461-2171
Telephone: (561) 304-3466 Identification: 770541
Accreditation: COE, RAD

† Branch campus of Fortis Institute, Cookeville, TN.

Fortis Institute-Fort Lauderdale (J)

4850 W Oakland Park Blvd, Suite 224, Lauderdale Lakes FL 33313-7261
Telephone: (954) 587-7100 Identification: 666269
Accreditation: ABHES, #RAD, SURGT, SURTEC

† Branch campus Fortis Colleg, Baton Rouge, LA.

Fortis Institute-Pensacola (K)

4081 East Olive Road, Suite B, Pensacola FL 32514
Telephone: (850) 476-7607 Identification: 770513
Accreditation: ABHES

† Branch campus of Fortis College, Mobile, AL.

Fortis Institute-Port St. Lucie (L)

9022 South Federal Highway/US-1, Port St. Lucie FL 34952
Telephone: (772) 221-9799 Identification: 770527
Accreditation: ABHES

† Branch campus of Fortis Institute, Baton Rouge, LA.

Full Sail University (M)

3300 University Boulevard, Winter Park FL 32792
County: Orange FICE Identification: 023621
Unit ID: 134237
Telephone: (407) 679-0100 Carnegie Class: Master's L
FAX Number: (407) 679-9685 Calendar System: Other
URL: www.fullsail.edu
Established: 1979 Annual Undergrad Tuition & Fees: $22,400
Enrollment: 19,285 Coed
Affiliation or Control: Proprietary IRS Status: Proprietary
Highest Offering: Master's
Program: Occupational; 2-Year Principally Bachelor's Creditable
Accreditation: ACCSC

01 President .... Mr. Garry JONES
07 Vice President of Admissions .... Mr. Matt PENGRA

Galen College of Nursing (N)

11101 Roosevelt Blvd N, Suite 100, St. Petersburg FL 33716
Telephone: (727) 577-1497 Identification: 770539
Accreditation: &SC

† Branch campus of Galen College of Nursing, Louisville, KY.

Golf Academy of America (O)

510 South Hunt Club Blvd., Apopka FL 32703
Telephone: (800) 342-7342 Identification: 666186
Accreditation: ACICS

† Branch campus of Virginia College, Birmingham, AL.

Gordon-Conwell Theological Seminary-Jacksonville (P)

118 East Monroe Street, Jacksonville FL 32202-3214
Telephone: (904) 354-4800 Identification: 770111
Accreditation: &EH, THEOL

† Branch campus of Gordon-Conwell Theological Seminary, South Hamilton, MA.

Gulf Coast State College (Q)

5230 W Highway 98, Panama City FL 32401-1058
County: Bay FICE Identification: 001490
Unit ID: 134343
Telephone: (850) 769-1551 Carnegie Class: Assoc/Pub-R-L
FAX Number: (850) 913-3319 Calendar System: Semester
URL: www.gulfcoast.edu
Established: 1957 Annual Undergrad Tuition & Fees (In-State): $2,370
Enrollment: 6,441 Coed
Affiliation or Control: State Related IRS Status: 501(c)3
Highest Offering: Baccalaureate
Program: Occupational; 2-Year Principally Bachelor's Creditable; Teacher Preparatory
Accreditation: SC, ACFEI, ADNUR, COARC, DA, DH, EMT, NURSE, PTAA, RAD, SURGA, SURGT

01 President .... Dr. John R. HOLDNAK
10 Vice Pres Administration & Finance .... Mr. John D. MERCER
05 VP Academic Affairs & Learn Support .... Dr. George BISHOP
32 VP Student Affairs .... Dr. Melissa LAVENDER
45 VP Institutional Effect/Stratg Plng ...... Dr. Cheryl L. FLAX-HYMAN
13 Chief Information Officer .... Ms. Rhonda BARKER
08 Director of Library .... Ms. Lori DRISCOLL
84 Director of Enrollment Services .... Ms. Sharon O. TODD
15 Exec Director of Human Resources .... Ms. Roberta MACKEY
28 Assoc Dir Retention/Stdnt Diversity .... Dr. Carrie B. BAKER
26 Exec Director Media & Community Rel .... Mr. Christopher P. THOMES
96 Coordinator of Purchasing .... Mr. Fred BROWN
37 Exec Director Student Financial Svc .... Mr. Christopher J. WESTLAKE
09 Coordinator Institutional Research .... Ms. Dee NIELSEN
04 Executive Asst to President .... Ms. Eileen WILKES

Health Career Institute (R)

1764 N. Congress Avenue, West Palm Beach FL 33409
County: Palm Beach Identification: 667104
Telephone: (561) 586-0121 Carnegie Class: Not Classified
FAX Number: (561) 471-4010 Calendar System: Semester
URL: www.hci.edu
Established: 1993 Annual Undergrad Tuition & Fees: N/A
Enrollment: N/A Coed
Affiliation or Control: Proprietary IRS Status: Proprietary
Highest Offering: Associate Degree
Program: Occupational
Accreditation: ACCSC

01 President .... Brenda GREEN
10 Financial Director .... Elizabeth VAZQUEZ

Heritage Institute-Fort Myers (S)

6630 Orion Drive, Suite 200, Fort Meyers FL 33912-7130
County: Lee FICE Identification: 025971
Unit ID: 135124
Telephone: (239) 936-5822 Carnegie Class: Assoc/PrivFP
FAX Number: (239) 225-9117 Calendar System: Other
URL: www.heritage-education.com
Established: 2001 Annual Undergrad Tuition & Fees: $25,650
Enrollment: 738 Coed
Affiliation or Control: Proprietary IRS Status: Proprietary
Highest Offering: Associate Degree
Program: Occupational
Accreditation: ABHES

01 Director .... Ms. Eva HUTSON

Heritage Institute-Jacksonville (A)

4130 Salisbury Road, Suite 1100, Jacksonville FL 32216
County: Duval FICE Identification: 030358
Unit ID: 372772
Telephone: (904) 332-0910 Carnegie Class: Assoc/PrivFP
FAX Number: (904) 332-0920 Calendar System: Other
URL: www.heritage-education.com/campus_jacksonville.htm
Established: 2001 Annual Undergrad Tuition & Fees: $23,751
Enrollment: 285 Coed
Affiliation or Control: Proprietary IRS Status: Proprietary
Highest Offering: Associate Degree
Program: Occupational
Accreditation: ABHES

01 Director ... Ms. Jamie VALENCIA

Herzing University (B)

1865 SR 436, Winter Park FL 32792
Telephone: (407) 478-0500 Identification: 666422
Accreditation: &NH, ADNUR, NURSE, PTAA

† Regional accreditation is carried under the parent institution in Madison, WI.

Hillsborough Community College (C)

PO Box 31127, 39 Columbia Drive, Tampa FL 33631-3127
County: Hillsborough FICE Identification: 007870
Unit ID: 134495
Telephone: (813) 253-7000 Carnegie Class: Assoc/Pub-U-MC
FAX Number: (813) 253-7183 Calendar System: Semester
URL: www.hccfl.edu
Established: 1968 Annual Undergrad Tuition & Fees (In-State): $2,505
Enrollment: 27,298 Coed
Affiliation or Control: State IRS Status: 501(c)3
Highest Offering: Associate Degree
Program: Occupational; 2-Year Principally Bachelor's Creditable
Accreditation: SC, ACFEI, ADNUR, COARC, CSHSE, DA, DH, DIETT, DMS, EMT, MUS, NMT, OPD, RAD, RTT

01 President ... Dr. Ken ATWATER
10 VP Administration/CFO ... Mr. Al ERDMAN
05 VP for Academic Affairs ... Mr. Craig JOHNSON
13 VP Information Technology ... Mr. Daya PENDHARKAR
32 VP Student Services/Enrollment Mgt ... Dr. Ken RAY
12 Campus President Dale Mabry ... Dr. Robert CHUNN
12 Campus President Ybor City Campus ... Dr. Shawn ROBINSON
12 Campus President Plant City Campus ... Dr. Martyn CLAY
12 Campus President Brandon Campus ... Dr. Nancee SORENSON
12 Campus President South Shore Campus ... Dr. Allen WITT
22 Asst to Pres Equity/Special Pgms ... Dr. Joan HOLMES
26 Exec Dir Marketing/Public Relations ... Ms. Ashley CARL
09 Spc Asst to Pres Strat Plng & Analy ... Dr. Paul NAGY
102 Exec Director HCC Foundation ... Mr. Stephen SHEAR
43 College Attorney ... Ms. Martha Kaye KOEHLER
15 Interim Exec Dir Human Resources ... Ms. Kristin SMUDER
21 Controller ... Ms. Kimberly MCMILLON
103 VP of Workforce Trainining ... Dr. Ginger CLARK
75 Director Technical Programs ... Dr. Brian MANN
88 Director Assoc in Arts Programs ... Dr. Karen GRIFFIN
90 Director of Academic Technology ... Mr. Mark LEWIS
20 Interim Dean of Academic Affairs ... Dr. Keith BERRY
75 Associate Dean of Technical Pgms ... Vacant
88 Dean of AS Programs - Brandon ... Dr. Sabrina PEACOCK
88 Dean of Arts & Sciences-Dale Mabry ... Dr. Mary BENDICKSON
88 Dean of AS Programs - Dale Mabry ... Dr. Elizabeth JOHNSON
81 Dean AA Math/Science - Dale Mabry ... Dr. James WYSONG
76 Dean Health/Wellness & Sports Tech ... Mr. Leif PENROSE
37 Financial Aid Director ... Ms. Tierra SMITH
06 Registrar ... Ms. Jennifer WILLIAMS
18 Director Facilities/Physical Plant ... Mr. Ben MARSHALL
96 Director of Purchasing ... Ms. Vonda MELCHIOR
31 Dir of Community & Govt Relations ... Mr. Eric JOHNSON
19 Director Security/Safety ... Mr. Jeff COPELAND

Hobe Sound Bible College (D)

PO Box 1065, Hobe Sound FL 33475-1065
County: Martin FICE Identification: 021889
Unit ID: 134510
Telephone: (772) 546-5534 Carnegie Class: Spec/Faith
FAX Number: (772) 545-1422 Calendar System: Semester
URL: www.hsbc.edu
Established: 1960 Annual Undergrad Tuition & Fees: $5,645
Enrollment: 251 Coed
Affiliation or Control: Independent Non-Profit IRS Status: 501(c)3
Highest Offering: Baccalaureate
Program: Liberal Arts And General; Religious Emphasis
Accreditation: BI

01 President ... Mr. P. Daniel STETLER
05 Academic Dean ... Dr. Clifford W. CHURCHILL
10 Director of Finances ... Mr. Rick HUFF
11 Director of Administration ... Mr. Wesley HOLDEN
32 Dean of Students ... Mr. John S. JONES
33 Dean of Men ... Mr. Jonathan STRATTON
08 Librarian ... Mr. Phil JONES
26 Public Relations Director ... Mr. Paul STETLER
06 Registrar ... Mr. Lucas RYDER
07 Director of Admissions ... Ms. Pam DAVIS
51 Dean of External Studies ... Mr. Dalbert N. WALKER

Hodges University (E)

2655 Northbrooke Drive, Naples FL 34119-7932
County: Collier FICE Identification: 030375
Unit ID: 367884
Telephone: (239) 513-1122 Carnegie Class: Master's S
FAX Number: (239) 598-6253 Calendar System: Trimester
URL: www.hodges.edu
Established: 1990 Annual Undergrad Tuition & Fees: $15,900
Enrollment: 1,802 Coed
Affiliation or Control: Independent Non-Profit IRS Status: 501(c)3
Highest Offering: Master's
Program: Professional; Business Emphasis
Accreditation: SC, CACREP, CAHIIM, IACBE, MAC, PTAA

01 President ... Dr. David BOROFSKY
32 Senior Vice Pres of Student Svcs ... Ms. Carol MORRISON
11 Exec Vice Pres of Operations ... Ms. Erica TILLERY
35 Dean of Students ... Dr. Marcia TURNER
37 VP of Student Financial Services ... Mr. Joseph GILCHRIST
30 Vice Pres University Advancement ... Mr. Phil MEMOLI
38 Director Student Counseling ... Ms. April BROWN
26 Chief Marketing Officer ... Ms. Karen GREBING
09 Dir Institutional Effective/Rsrch ... Dr. Diane BALL
28 Director of Diversity ... Ms. Gail WILLIAMS
29 Director of Alumni Affairs ... Mr. Brian HAWKINS

Indian River State College (F)

3209 Virginia Avenue, Fort Pierce FL 34981-5596
County: Saint Lucie FICE Identification: 001493
Unit ID: 134608
Telephone: (772) 462-4772 Carnegie Class: Assoc/Pub4
FAX Number: (772) 462-4796 Calendar System: Semester
URL: www.irsc.edu
Established: 1960 Annual Undergrad Tuition & Fees (In-District): $2,810
Enrollment: 17,665 Coed
Affiliation or Control: Local IRS Status: 501(c)3
Highest Offering: Baccalaureate
Program: Occupational; 2-Year Principally Bachelor's Creditable; Liberal Arts And General; Teacher Preparatory
Accreditation: SC, ADNUR, CAHIIM, COARC, DA, DH, DT, EMT, MAC, MLTAD, NUR, PTAA, RAD, SURGT

01 President ... Dr. Edwin R. MASSEY
32 Vice President Student Affairs ... Mr. Frank WATKINS
05 Vice President Academic Affairs ... Dr. Anthony IACONO
10 Actg VP Administration/Finance ... Ms. Sheryl S. VITTITOE
88 Vice Pres Applied Science & Tech ... Dr. Alan L. ROBERTS
45 Associate VP Institutional Effectiv ... Dr. Christina HART
04 Exec Assistant to the President ... Mr. Andrew TREADWELL
12 Vice Pres/Provost-Fort Pierce ... Dr. Mary G. LOCKE
12 Provost Pt St Lucie/St Lucie W ... Dr. Harvey E. ARNOLD
12 Provost Okeechobee ... Mr. Russ BROWN
12 Provost Martin County ... Ms. Elizabeth GASKIN
12 Provost Indian River County ... Mr. Casey LUNCEFORD
12 Dean Northwest Center ... Mr. Andre HAWKINS
18 Assistant Dean Facilities ... Mr. Sean DONAHUE
72 Dean Institutional Tech ... Mr. Paul R. O'BRIEN
80 Asst Dean of Public Services Educ ... Mr. Evan BERRY
72 Dean Advanced Technology ... Mr. Jose L. FARINOS
93 Dean Minority Affairs ... Ms. Adriene JEFFERSON
08 Dean Learning Resources ... Ms. Patricia C. PROFETA
49 Dean of Arts & Sciences ... Mr. Paul HORTON
53 Admin Director School of Education ... Dr. Marta CRONIN
13 Assistant Dean Data Processing ... Mr. Anthony VIA
11 Assoc Dean Administrative Services ... Ms. Jan PAGANO
75 Associate Dean Industrial Education ... Ms. Donna RIVETT
76 Associate Dean of Health Science ... Ms. Jane P. CEBELAK
09 Associate Dean Research/Reports ... Mr. Gerald L. MOCK
20 Asst Dean Educational Services ... Ms. Eileen STORCK
50 Assistant Dean Business Technology ... Mr. Cedric GIBSON
15 Assistant Dean Human Resources ... Ms. Nancy CUNNINGHAM
21 Assistant Dean Finance ... Ms. Edith PACACHA
66 Administrative Director of Nursing ... Ms. Ann HUBBARD
102 Executive Director Foundation ... Ms. Ann DECKER
30 Director Institutional Advancement ... Ms. Michelle ABALDO
41 Director Athletics ... Mr. Scott KIMMELMAN
36 Director Student Success Services ... Ms. Flossie JACKSON
84 Director Enrollment Management ... Mr. Douglas DORAN
37 Director Student Financial Aid ... Ms. Mary LEWIS
38 Director Student Counseling ... Ms. Dale HAYES
35 Director Student Affairs ... Ms. Sharon LOWE
06 Registrar/Dir Student Affs/Admiss ... Ms. Karen CHAPDELAINE
96 Purchasing Agent ... Mr. Don WINDHAM

Institute of Healthcare Professions (G)

2100 45th St., Ste A-2A, West Palm Beach FL 33407
County: Palm Beach Identification: 667238
Telephone: (561) 202-6333 Carnegie Class: Not Classified
FAX Number: (561) 296-9647 Calendar System: Semester
URL: www.ihpedu.com
Established: Annual Undergrad Tuition & Fees: N/A
Enrollment: N/A Coed
Affiliation or Control: Proprietary IRS Status: Proprietary
Highest Offering: Associate Degree
Program: Occupational
Accreditation: ACICS

01 Campus President ... Karyn VIDAL

Institute of Technical Arts (H)

493 Semoran Blvd, Casselberry FL 32707
County: Seminole FICE Identification: 036183
Unit ID: 441441
Telephone: (407) 869-7387 Carnegie Class: Not Classified
FAX Number: (407) 678-3422 Calendar System: Other
URL: www.myita.edu
Established: 1999 Annual Undergrad Tuition & Fees: $15,300
Enrollment: 202 Coed
Affiliation or Control: Proprietary IRS Status: Proprietary
Highest Offering: Associate Degree
Program: Occupational
Accreditation: ACCSC

01 Chief Executive Officer ... Ms. Laura LUNDBERG
11 Executive Director ... Mr. Steve DICK

ITT Technical Institute (I)

13500 Powers Court, Suite 100, Fort Myers FL 33912
Telephone: (239) 603-8700 Identification: 666669
Accreditation: ACICS

† Branch campus of ITT Technical Institute, Indianapolis, IN.

ITT Technical Institute (J)

7011 A.C. Skinner Parkway, Ste. 140,
Jacksonville FL 32256-6954
Telephone: (904) 573-9100 Identification: 666537
Accreditation: ACICS

† Branch campus of ITT Technical Institute, Indianapolis, IN.

ITT Technical Institute (K)

1400 International Parkway South,
Lake Mary FL 32746-1607
Telephone: (407) 936-0600 FICE Identification: 030876
Accreditation: ACICS

† Branch campus of ITT Technical Institute, Indianapolis, IN.

ITT Technical Institute (L)

7955 NW 12th Street, Suite 119, Miami FL 33126-1823
Telephone: (305) 477-3080 Identification: 666026
Accreditation: ACICS

† Branch campus of ITT Technical Institute, Indianapolis, IN.

ITT Technical Institute (M)

877 Executive Ctr. Dr. W, Ste. 100,
St. Petersburg FL 33702
Telephone: (727) 209-4700 Identification: 666163
Accreditation: ACICS

† Branch campus of ITT Technical Institute, Indianapolis, IN.

ITT Technical Institute (N)

2639 N Monroe St, Bldg A, Suite 100,
Tallahassee FL 32303
Telephone: (850) 422-6300 Identification: 770638
Accreditation: ACICS

† Branch campus of ITT Technical Institute, Indianapolis, IN.

ITT Technical Institute (O)

4809 Memorial Highway, Tampa FL 33634-7350
Telephone: (813) 885-2244 FICE Identification: 022865
Accreditation: ACICS

† Branch campus of ITT Technical Institute, Indianapolis, IN.

ITT Technical Institute (P)

1756 N Congress Avenue, West Palm Beach FL 33409
Telephone: (561) 233-4900 Identification: 770641
Accreditation: ACICS

† Branch campus of ITT Technical Institute, Indianapolis, IN.

Jacksonville University (Q)

2800 University Boulevard N, Jacksonville FL 32211-3394
County: Duval FICE Identification: 001495
Unit ID: 134945
Telephone: (904) 256-8000 Carnegie Class: Master's M
FAX Number: N/A Calendar System: Semester
URL: www.ju.edu
Established: 1934 Annual Undergrad Tuition & Fees: $32,620
Enrollment: 4,085 Coed
Affiliation or Control: Independent Non-Profit IRS Status: 501(c)3
Highest Offering: Doctorate
Program: Liberal Arts And General; Teacher Preparatory; Professional; Business Emphasis
Accreditation: SC, AAB, BUS, DANCE, DENT, MUS, NURSE, @SP

01 President .... Mr. Timothy P. COST
05 Provost & Chief Academic Officer .... Dr. Wenying XU
10 Chief Financial Officer .... Mr. David HEALY
07 Chief Admissions Officer .... Ms. Marisol PRESTON
32 Chief Student Affairs Officer .... Dr. Kristie GOVER
30 Chief Advancement Officer .... Ms. Kimberly JONES
26 Chief Communications & Mktg Office .... Ms. Margaret DEES
13 Chief Information Officer .... Mr. Tom HALL
04 Exec Assistant to the President .... Ms. Dolores STARR
41 Chief Athletics Officer .... Dr. Donnie HORNER
06 Registrar .... Ms. Carolyn BARRETT
09 Director of Institutional Research .... Dr. Logan CROSS
08 Director of the Library .... Ms. Jessica COLLOGAN
35 Associate Dean of Students .... Mr. Luke MORRILL
36 Director of Career Development .... Ms. Toni HIGGS
37 Financial Aid Director .... Ms. Karen LAVERDIERE
21 Controller .... Ms. Liza MULLINS
11 Exec Dir Budgets/Business Opers .... Ms. Ellen M. PAIGE
96 Director of Purchasing .... Mr. Michael J. BOBBIN
40 Director of the Bookstore .... Mr. Patrick JONES
42 Campus Minister .... Mr. Lance BEAUCHAMP
15 Director of Human Resources .... Mr. James V. WILLIAMS
57 Dean of Col of Fine Arts .... Dr. Henry RINNE
49 Dean Col of Arts & Sciences .... Dr. Douglas HAZZARD
50 Dean College of Business .... Dr. Don CAPENER
76 Brooks Col of HealthCare Sciences .... Dr. Christine SAPIENZA
51 Assoc Dean of Continuing Studies .... Vacant
53 Dean School of Education .... Dr. Douglas HAZZARD
64 Chairman Division of Music .... Dr. Thomas HARRISON
79 Chair Div of Humanitites .... Dr. Scott KIMBROUGH
81 Chair Division of Science & Math .... Dr. Lee Ann J. CLEMENTS
38 Director Student Counseling .... Ms. Kristin R. ALBERTS
83 Chair Division of Social Science .... Dr. Sherry JACKSON
88 Chair Division of Naval Science .... Capt. Herbert HADLEY
88 Chair Div of Theatre Arts & Dance .... Mr. Brian PALMER
57 Chair Division Art/Art History .... Ms. Dana L. CHAPMAN
18 Chief Facilities/Physical Plant .... Mr. Samuel WISE
19 Director Security/Safety .... Mr. Kevin BENNETT
102 Dir Foundation/Corporate Relations .... Ms. Michele QUERRY
29 Director Alumni Relations .... Ms. Kim GRANT
39 Director of Residential Life .... Mr. Luke MORRILL
44 Director Annual or Planned Giving .... Ms. Maria YOKITIS

Johnson & Wales University (A)

1701 NE 127th Street, North Miami FL 33181-2518
Telephone: (305) 892-7000 Identification: 666423
Accreditation: &EH

† Regional accreditation is carried under the parent institution in Providence, RI.

Johnson University Florida (B)

1011 Bill Beck Boulevard, Kissimmee FL 34744-5301
Telephone: (407) 847-8966 FICE Identification: 021567
Accreditation: &SC, &BI

† Branch campus of Johnson University, Knoxville, TN.

Jones College (C)

1195 Edgewood Ave., South, Jacksonville FL 32205
County: Duval FICE Identification: 001497
Unit ID: 135063
Telephone: (904) 743-1122 Carnegie Class: Bac/Diverse
FAX Number: (904) 743-4446 Calendar System: Trimester
URL: www.jones.edu
Established: 1918 Annual Undergrad Tuition & Fees: $7,650
Enrollment: 448 Coed
Affiliation or Control: Independent Non-Profit IRS Status: 501(c)3
Highest Offering: Baccalaureate
Program: Business Emphasis
Accreditation: ACICS

01 Corporate President & CEO .... Dorothy D. JONES
05 President of the College .... Everett SMITH
07 Director of Admissions .... Dalia KENNEDY
36 Director Student Placement .... Angela MEALER
08 Librarian .... Marie LANIER

Jose Maria Vargas University (D)

10131 Pines Boulevard, Pembroke Pines FL 33026
County: Broward FICE Identification: 041620
Unit ID: 461281
Telephone: (954) 322-4460 Carnegie Class: Not Classified
FAX Number: (954) 322-4131 Calendar System: Semester
URL: www.jmvu.edu
Established: 2003 Annual Undergrad Tuition & Fees: $10,040
Enrollment: 159 Coed
Affiliation or Control: Proprietary IRS Status: Proprietary
Highest Offering: Master's
Program: Occupational; 2-Year Principally Bachelor's Creditable; Teacher Preparatory; Professional
Accreditation: ACICS, @TEAC

01 President .... Dr. Alicia F. PARRA

Keiser University (E)

1800 Business Park Blvd, Daytona Beach FL 32114
Telephone: (386) 274-5060 Identification: 770900
Accreditation: &SC, ACBSP, DIETC, DMS, MAC, OTA, RAD

† Branch campus of Keiser University, Fort Lauderdale, FL.

Keiser University (F)

1500 NW 49th Street, Fort Lauderdale FL 33309-3700
County: Broward FICE Identification: 021519
Unit ID: 135081
Telephone: (954) 776-4476 Carnegie Class: Bac/Assoc
FAX Number: N/A Calendar System: Semester
URL: www.keiseruniversity.edu
Established: 1977 Annual Undergrad Tuition & Fees: $17,664
Enrollment: 19,041 Coed
Affiliation or Control: Independent Non-Profit IRS Status: 501(c)3
Highest Offering: Doctorate
Program: Occupational
Accreditation: SC, ACBSP, ADNUR, ARCPA, CAHIIM, COARC, DMS, MLTAD, NURSE, OTA, PTAA, RAD

01 Chancellor .... Dr. Arthur KEISER
03 Executive Vice Chancellor .... Mr. Peter CROCITTO
05 Vice Chancellor of Academic Affairs .... Dr. John SITES
31 Vice Chancellor of Community Rels .... Ms. Belinda KEISER
84 Vice Chancellor of Enrollment Mgmt .... Mr. Brian WOODS
10 Vice Chancellor of Finance .... Mr. Joseph BERARDINELLI
85 Vice Chancellor International Affs .... Mr. Zhanjun YANG
26 Reg Dir Media & Public Relations .... Ms. Kimberly DALE

Keiser University (G)

9100 Forum Corporate Pkwy, Fort Myers FL 33905
Telephone: (239) 277-1336 Identification: 770901
Accreditation: &SC, ACBSP, DMS, OTA

† Branch campus of Keiser University, Fort Lauderdale, FL.

Keiser University (H)

6430 Southpoint Pkwy, Jacksonville FL 33216
Telephone: (904) 296-3440 Identification: 770902
Accreditation: &SC, ACBSP, ADNUR, OTA, PTAA, RAD

† Branch campus of Keiser University, Fort Lauderdale, FL.

Keiser University (I)

2400 Interstate Drive, Lakeland FL 33805
Telephone: (863) 682-6020 Identification: 770903
Accreditation: &SC, ACBSP, ADNUR, DIETC, PTAA, RAD

† Branch campus of Keiser University, Fort Lauderdale, FL.

Keiser University (J)

900 South Babcock Street, Melbourne FL 32901
Telephone: (321) 409-4800 Identification: 770904
Accreditation: &SC, ACBSP, ACFEI, ADNUR, DMS, OTA, RAD

† Branch campus of Keiser University, Fort Lauderdale, FL.

Keiser University (K)

2101 NW 117th Avenue, Miami FL 33172
Telephone: (305) 596-2226 Identification: 770905
Accreditation: &SC, ACBSP, ADNUR, OTA, @PTAA, RAD

† Branch campus of Keiser University, Fort Lauderdale, FL.

Keiser University (L)

6014 US Hwy 19 North, Ste 250,
New Port Richey FL 34652
Telephone: (727) 484-3110 Identification: 770854
Accreditation: &SC, DMS

† Branch campus of Keiser University, Fort Lauderdale, FL.

Keiser University (M)

5600 Lake Underhill Road, Orlando FL 32807
Telephone: (407) 381-1233 Identification: 770906
Accreditation: &SC, ACBSP, ADNUR, HT, OTA

† Branch campus of Keiser University, Fort Lauderdale, FL.

Keiser University (N)

1640 SW 145th Avenue, Pembroke Pines FL 33027
Telephone: (954) 431-4300 Identification: 770907
Accreditation: &SC, ACBSP, DIETC, HT, OTA

† Branch campus of Keiser University, Fort Lauderdale, FL.

Keiser University (O)

10330 S Federal Highway,
Port Saint Lucie FL 34952-5605
Telephone: (772) 398-9990 Identification: 666289
Accreditation: &SC, ACBSP

† Regional accreditation is carried under the parent institution Keiser University, Fort Lauderdale, FL.

Keiser University (P)

6151 Lake Osprey Drive, Sarasota FL 34240
Telephone: (941) 907-3900 Identification: 770908
Accreditation: &SC, ACBSP, ACFEI, ADNUR, PTAA, RAD

† Branch campus of Keiser University, Fort Lauderdale, FL.

Keiser University (Q)

1700 Halstead Blvd, Bldg 2, Tallahassee FL 32309
Telephone: (850) 906-9494 Identification: 770909
Accreditation: &SC, ACBSP, ACFEI, ADNUR, OTA

† Branch campus of Keiser University, Fort Lauderdale, FL.

Keiser University (R)

5002 West Waters Ave, Tampa FL 33634
Telephone: (813) 885-4900 Identification: 770910
Accreditation: &SC, ACBSP, ADNUR, OTA, SURGT

† Branch campus of Keiser University, Fort Lauderdale, FL.

Keiser University (S)

2085 Vista Parkway, West Palm Beach FL 33411-2719
Telephone: (561) 471-6000 Identification: 667032
Accreditation: &SC, ACBSP, ADNUR, OTA, @PTAA

† Regional accreditation is carried under the parent institution Keiser University, Fort Lauderdale, FL.

Keiser University at Clearwater (T)

16120 US Hwy 19 N, Clearwater FL 33764
Telephone: (727) 576-6500 Identification: 666758
Accreditation: ACCSC, SURGT

† Branch campus of Southeastern College, Greenacres, FL.

Key College (U)

225 E Dania Beach Blvd, Suite 130,
Dania Beach FL 33004-3042
County: Broward FICE Identification: 023251
Unit ID: 134422
Telephone: (954) 923-4440 Carnegie Class: Assoc/PrivFP
FAX Number: (954) 923-9226 Calendar System: Quarter
URL: www.keycollege.edu
Established: 1982 Annual Undergrad Tuition & Fees: $10,785
Enrollment: 89 Coed
Affiliation or Control: Proprietary IRS Status: Proprietary
Highest Offering: Associate Degree
Program: 2-Year Principally Bachelor's Creditable; Business Emphasis
Accreditation: ACICS

01 President .... Mr. Ronald DOOLEY
05 Director of Academic Affairs .... Ms. Marella DOOLEY
07 Director of Admissions .... Mr. Ron DOOLEY
37 Director of Financial Aid .... Ms. Traci ANDREWS
06 Registrar .... Mr. Rashad BENNETT

Knox Theological Seminary (V)

5554 N Federal Highway, Fort Lauderdale FL 33308-3209
County: Broward FICE Identification: 039923
Telephone: (954) 771-0376 Carnegie Class: Not Classified
FAX Number: (954) 351-3343 Calendar System: Semester
URL: www.knoxseminary.edu
Established: 1989 Annual Undergrad Tuition & Fees: $9,480
Enrollment: 287 Coed
Affiliation or Control: Independent Non-Profit IRS Status: 501(c)3
Highest Offering: Doctorate
Program: Religious Emphasis
Accreditation: THEOL

01 President & CEO .... Dr. Samuel LAMERSON
11 Vice President of Administration .... Dr. Timothy SANSBURY
106 Director of Distance Education .... Mr. Steve JECK
05 Dean of Faculty .... Dr. Michael ALLEN
32 Dir Student Svcs/Dean of Students .... Mr. Jonathan LINEBAUGH
06 Registrar .... Ms. Lori GOTTSHALL
08 Head Librarian .... Mr. Alan WIBBELS

Lake Erie College of Osteopathic Medicine Bradenton (W)

5000 Lakewood Rance Boulevard, Bradenton FL 34211
Telephone: (941) 756-0690 Identification: 770160
Accreditation: &M, DENT, OSTEO

† Branch campus of Lake Erie College of Osteopathic Medicine, Erie, PA.

Lake-Sumter State College (X)

9501 US Highway 441, Leesburg FL 34788-8751
County: Lake FICE Identification: 001502
Unit ID: 135188
Telephone: (352) 787-3747 Carnegie Class: Assoc/Pub-S-MC
FAX Number: (352) 365-3548 Calendar System: Semester
URL: www.lssc.edu
Established: 1962 Annual Undergrad Tuition & Fees (In-District): $3,172
Enrollment: 4,461 Coed

Affiliation or Control: State/Local IRS Status: 501(c)3
Highest Offering: Baccalaureate
Program: Occupational; 2-Year Principally Bachelor's Creditable
Accreditation: SC, ADNUR, CAHIIM

01 President ..... Dr. Charles R. MOJOCK
10 Sr VP Business Affairs ..... Mr. Richard M. SCOTT
05 Interim Academic Affairs ..... Dr. Mary Jo ROAGER
84 Int Enrollment & Student Affairs ..... Ms. Claire BRADY
21 Assoc VP for Business Affairs ..... Ms. Vicki WARD
53 Dean General Ed & Transfer Programs ..... Dr. Gary SLIGH
15 Exec Director Human Resources ..... Ms. Fran PISTILLI
13 Chief Information Officer ..... Mr. Douglas GUILER
09 Exec Dir Planning & IE ..... Mr. Dave WEBER
30 Exec Dir Inst Advance & Foundation ..... Ms. Rosanne BRANDEBURG
18 Director College Facilities ..... Mr. David MARTIN
08 Director Libraries ..... Ms. Denise K. ENGLISH
32 Interim Dir Student Development ..... Ms. Carolyn SCOTT
21 Director Accounting ..... Ms. Diana BILLINGHAM
66 Director Nursing ..... Ms. Cindy GRIFFIN
08 Director Learning Center ..... Ms. Marion J. KANE
26 Director College Relations ..... Ms. Sasheika TOMLINSON
37 Director Financial Aid ..... Ms. Audrey WILLIAMS
06 Registrar ..... Ms. Alba RODRIGUEZ
41 Athletic Director ..... Mr. Michael K. MATULIA
88 Director Youth Outreach Programs ..... Mr. Reinaldo CORTES
106 Director Distance Learning ..... Mr. Mike NATHANSON
07 Director Admissions ..... Mr. Bryan ANDERSON
28 Equity Officer ..... Ms. Chris HAMILTON
96 Asst Director of Purchasing ..... Mr. Bill PONKO
102 Coord Foundation/Alumni Scholarship ..... Ms. Claudia MORRIS
12 Assoc Dean South Lake ..... Mr. Thom KIEFT
103 Assoc Dean Workforce Programs ..... Dr. Eugene JONES

Le Cordon Bleu College of Culinary Arts in Miami (A)

3221 Enterprise Way, Miramar FL 33025-3929
Telephone: (954) 438-8882 Identification: 666369
Accreditation: ACCSC, ACICS, ACFEI

† Branch campus of Le Cordon Bleu Institute of Culinary Arts, Pittsburgh, PA.

Le Cordon Bleu College of Culinary Arts in Orlando (B)

8511 Commodity Circle, Orlando FL 32819-9002
Telephone: (407) 888-4000 Identification: 666064
Accreditation: ACCSC, ACICS, ACFEI

† Branch campus of International Academy of Design & Technology, Tampa, FL.

Lincoln College of Technology (C)

2410 Metrocentre Boulevard,
West Palm Beach FL 33407-3155
County: Palm Beach FICE Identification: 022808
Unit ID: 136066
Telephone: (561) 842-8324 Carnegie Class: Assoc/PrivFP
FAX Number: (561) 842-9503 Calendar System: Other
URL: www.lincolncollegeoftechnology.com
Established: 1982 Annual Undergrad Tuition & Fees: $15,580
Enrollment: 713 Coed
Affiliation or Control: Proprietary IRS Status: Proprietary
Highest Offering: Baccalaureate
Program: Occupational; Technical Emphasis
Accreditation: ACICS, ACFEI

01 President ..... Ms. Mike CLULING

Lincoln Tech Fern Park Orlando Campus (D)

7275 Estapona Circle, Fern Park FL 32730-2351
County: Seminole FICE Identification: 033903
Unit ID: 439437
Telephone: (407) 673-7406 Carnegie Class: Assoc/PrivFP
FAX Number: (407) 339-0295 Calendar System: Quarter
URL: www.lincolntech.com
Established: 1991 Annual Undergrad Tuition & Fees: $17,613
Enrollment: 242 Coed
Affiliation or Control: Proprietary IRS Status: Proprietary
Highest Offering: Associate Degree
Program: Occupational; 2-Year Principally Bachelor's Creditable; Nursing Emphasis
Accreditation: ABHES, DA, SURTEC

01 Executive Director ..... Dr. James VERNON
05 Director of Education ..... Ms. Maria-Ana SIERRA

† School is in teach-out plan through March 2016.

Lynn University (E)

3601 N Military Trail, Boca Raton FL 33431-5598
County: Palm Beach FICE Identification: 001505
Unit ID: 132657
Telephone: (561) 237-7000 Carnegie Class: DRU
FAX Number: (561) 237-7100 Calendar System: Semester
URL: www.lynn.edu
Established: 1962 Annual Undergrad Tuition & Fees: $35,200
Enrollment: 2,613 Coed
Affiliation or Control: Independent Non-Profit IRS Status: 501(c)3
Highest Offering: Doctorate
Program: Liberal Arts And General; Business Emphasis
Accreditation: SC, IACBE, MUS

01 President ..... Dr. Kevin M. ROSS
00 President Emeritus ..... Dr. Donald E. ROSS
11 Sr Vice President Administration ..... Mr. Gregory J. MALFITANO
05 Vice President Academic Affairs ..... Dr. Gregg COX
84 Vice Pres Enrollment Management ..... Dr. Gareth FOWLES
10 Vice President Business & Finance ..... Ms. Laurie LEVINE
32 Vice President for Student Life ..... Dr. Phil RIORDAN
30 Vice Pres Development/Alumni Affs .. Mr. Gregory J. MALFITANO
13 Chief Information Officer ..... Mr. Chris G. BONIFORTI
26 Chief Marketing Officer ..... Mrs. Sherrie WELDON
88 Dean of Administration ..... Mr. Thomas J. HEFFERNAN
35 Dean of Students ..... Mr. Gary MARTIN
43 General Counsel ..... Mr. Michael ANTONELLO
88 Exec Dir Stdnt Administrative Svcs ..... Ms. Evelyn C. NELSON
39 Director Housing & Residence Life ..... Ms. Meagan ELSBERRY
36 Executive Director Career Develop ..... Ms. Barbara CAMBIA
41 Director of Athletics ..... Dr. Kristen L. MORAZ
109 Director Auxiliary Services ..... Mr. Matthew P. CHALOUX
23 Director Health Center ..... Ms. Rita ALBERT
27 Director of Marketing and Comm ..... Ms. Stephanie BROWN
44 Director of Major Gifts ..... Mr. Jay J. BRANDT
29 Director Alumni Affairs ..... Mr. Matthew R. ROOS
42 Chaplain ..... Fr. Martin C. DEVEREAUX
07 Dir Undergraduate Admissions ..... Mr. Stefano PAPALEO
37 Dir Student Financial Assistance ..... Mrs. Chan J. PARK
38 Director of the Counseling Center ..... Ms. Nicole R. OVEDIA
96 Director of Purchasing ..... Mr. Alfredo H. BONIFORTI
06 Registrar ..... Ms. Jenifer MOSLEY
21 Director of Accounting ..... Mr. Michael C. BOLDUC
07 Dir Graduate & UG Evening Admiss ..... Mr. Steven PRUITT
09 Director of Institutional Research ..... Mrs. Lara MARTIN
15 Director of Employee Services ..... Vacant
40 Bookstore Manager ..... Ms. Rita D. LOUREIRO
50 Dean College Business & Management ..... Vacant
49 Dean College of Arts & Sciences ..... Dr. Katrina CARTER-TELLISON
88 Dean School of Aeronautics ..... Dr. Jeffrey C. JOHNSON
53 Dean Ross College of Education ..... Dr. Kathleen WEIGEL
60 Dean College Intl Communications ..... Dr. David L. JAFFE
64 Dean Conservatory of Music ..... Dr. Jon H. ROBERTSON
88 Exe Dir Inst Achievement Learning ..... Mr. Shaun EXSTEEN
08 Director of the Library ..... Ms. Amy FILIATREAU
104 Director Center for Learning Abroad ..... Mr. Brian PIRTTIMA
105 Director Web Strategy & Operations ..... Vacant
19 Chief ..... Mr. Larry RICKARD

Mattia College (F)

13926 SW 47th Street, Miami FL 33175-4404
County: Miami-Dade FICE Identification: 033484
Unit ID: 436702
Telephone: (305) 220-4120 Carnegie Class: Assoc/PrivFP
FAX Number: (305) 220-2889 Calendar System: Other
URL: www.mattiacollege.edu
Established: 1994 Annual Undergrad Tuition & Fees: $45,000
Enrollment: 965 Coed
Affiliation or Control: Proprietary IRS Status: Proprietary
Highest Offering: Baccalaureate
Program: Occupational; 2-Year Principally Bachelor's Creditable; Professional
Accreditation: ACICS, DMS, RAD

01 Chief Executive Officer ..... Mr. Antonio MATTIA
05 Dean of Academics ..... Ms. Maria CARRILLO
06 Academic Registrar ..... Mr. John KRAMER
07 Director of Admissions ..... Mr. Andrew ABREU
15 Human Resources Director ..... Ms. Alex SENSAT
37 Student Finance Director ..... Mr. Christopher GUITIERREZ
88 Director of Compliance ..... Mrs. Lisa EDWARDS
08 Librarian ..... Ms. Ofelia WILTZ
51 Continuing Education Dept Director ..... Mr. Jose ULACIA

Management Resources College (G)

550 NW 42nd Avenue, Miami FL 33126
County: Miami-Dade FICE Identification: 041284
Unit ID: 451103
Telephone: (305) 442-9223 Carnegie Class: Not Classified
FAX Number: (305) 442-8723 Calendar System: Other
URL: www.mrc.edu
Established: 1996 Annual Undergrad Tuition & Fees: $39,546
Enrollment: 708 Coed
Affiliation or Control: Proprietary IRS Status: Proprietary
Highest Offering: Baccalaureate
Program: Occupational; 2-Year Principally Bachelor's Creditable; Nursing Emphasis
Accreditation: ACICS

01 President & CEO ..... Ophelia SANCHEZ
03 Executive Vice President ..... Ophelia VALLS
05 Chief Academic Officer ..... Jay OBER
07 Director of Admissions ..... Lisa HYLTOM
08 Head Librarian ..... Yudit LAM
10 Chief Business Officer ..... Henry BABANI
15 Director Personnel Services ..... Mitsy SOUSA
36 Director Student Placement ..... Randy BREITER
37 Director Student Financial Aid ..... Marcie SILVA

Med-Life Institute-Lauderdale Lakes (H)

4000 N. State Road 7, Suite 301,
Lauderdale Lakes FL 33319
County: Broward Identification: 667221
Telephone: (954) 943-8667 Carnegie Class: Not Classified
FAX Number: (954) 943-0984 Calendar System: Quarter
URL: www.medlifeinstitute.com
Established: 2003 Annual Undergrad Tuition & Fees: N/A
Enrollment: N/A Coed
Affiliation or Control: Proprietary IRS Status: Proprietary
Highest Offering: Associate Degree
Program: Occupational
Accreditation: ABHES

01 CEO ..... Mr. Claude RIVETTE

Med-Life Institute-Naples (I)

4103 East Tamiami Trail, Naples FL 34112
County: Collier Identification: 667220
Telephone: (239) 732-1300 Carnegie Class: Not Classified
FAX Number: (239) 417-5110 Calendar System: Quarter
URL: www.medlifeinstitute.com
Established: 2003 Annual Undergrad Tuition & Fees: N/A
Enrollment: 43 Coed
Affiliation or Control: Proprietary IRS Status: Proprietary
Highest Offering: Associate Degree
Program: Occupational
Accreditation: ABHES

01 President ..... Mr. Cheophat TANIS

Mercy Hospital College of Nursing (J)

3663 South Miami Ave Ste 1500, Miami FL 33133
County: Miami-Dade Identification: 667222
Unit ID: 419217
Telephone: (305) 285-2777 Carnegie Class: Not Classified
FAX Number: (305) 285-2671 Calendar System: Semester
URL: www.mercymiami.com/professionals/college-of-nursing
Established: Annual Undergrad Tuition & Fees: $8,490
Enrollment: 122 Coed
Affiliation or Control: Proprietary IRS Status: Proprietary
Highest Offering: Associate Degree
Program: Nursing Emphasis
Accreditation: ABHES

66 Dean ..... Ms. Elizabeth HERNANDEZ

Meridian College (K)

7020 Professional Pkwy E, Sarasota FL 34240
County: Sarasota FICE Identification: 023268
Unit ID: 244279
Telephone: (941) 377-4880 Carnegie Class: Not Classified
FAX Number: (941) 378-2842 Calendar System: Other
URL: www.meridian.edu
Established: 1982 Annual Undergrad Tuition & Fees: $16,900
Enrollment: 182 Coed
Affiliation or Control: Proprietary IRS Status: Proprietary
Highest Offering: Associate Degree
Program: Occupational
Accreditation: ACCSC

01 Campus Director ..... Mr. Patrick MCDERMOTT

Miami Dade College (L)

300 NE Second Avenue, Miami FL 33132-2204
County: Miami-Dade County FICE Identification: 001506
Unit ID: 135717
Telephone: (305) 237-8888 Carnegie Class: Assoc/Pub4
FAX Number: (305) 237-7913 Calendar System: Semester
URL: www.mdc.edu/main/
Established: 1960 Annual Undergrad Tuition & Fees (In-State): $2,837
Enrollment: 61,470 Coed
Affiliation or Control: State IRS Status: 501(c)3
Highest Offering: Baccalaureate
Program: Occupational; 2-Year Principally Bachelor's Creditable; Liberal Arts And General; Teacher Preparatory
Accreditation: SC, ADNUR, ARCPA, ART, CAHIIM, COARC, DANCE, DH, DMS, EMT, FUSER, HT, MLTAD, MUS, NUR, OPD, PTAA, RAD, THEA

01 College President ..... Dr. Eduardo J. PADRON
05 Provost Academic & Student Affairs ..... Dr. Lenore RODICIO
11 Provost Operations ..... Dr. Rolando MONTOYA
10 Sr Vice Provost Business Affairs ..... Mr. E. H. LEVERING
13 Vice Provost Information Technology ..... Dr. Wendy CHANG
18 Interim Vice Provost Facilities ..... Ms. Neyda OTERO
15 Vice Provost Human Resources ..... Ms. Iliana CASTILLO-FRICK
09 Vice Provost Inst Effectiveness ..... Dr. Archieval CUBARRUBIA
12 Campus President Hialeah ..... Vacant
12 Campus President Kendall ..... Dr. Beverly MOORE-GARCIA
12 Campus President Medical ..... Dr. Armando FERRER

12	Campus President Wolfson	Dr. Jose VICENTE
12	Campus President North	Ms. Malou HARRISON
12	Campus President Homestead	Dr. Jeanne JACOBS
12	Campus President InterAmerican	Dr. Joanne BASHFORD
21	Assoc Vice Prov Business Affs	Ms. Delilah ALMEDA
35	Vice Provost Student Services	Dr. Kathy MAALOUF
102	Executive Dir MDC Foundation	Mr. Mark COLE
37	Assoc VP Student Financial Services	Ms. Mercedes AMAYA
93	Director Employee Relations/EOP/ADA	Dr. Joy C. RUFF
07	Interim Collegewide Dir Admissions	Ms. Ferne CREARY
26	Chief Public Rels Officer/Dir Comm	Mr. Juan MENDIETA
29	Director Annual Giving/Alumni Rels	Ms. Nairobi ABRAMS
32	Director Student Life	Ms. Nicole BRYANT
36	Dir Testing Admin/Pgm Evaluation	Mr. Silvio RODRIGUEZ
28	Director of Diversity	Dr. Joy C. RUFF
38	Director Student Advisement	Mr. Jose RODRIGUEZ
84	Director Enrollment Management	Dr. Rene GARCIA
96	Director of Purchasing	Mr. Roman MARTINEZ
41	Director Athletics & Student Life	Mr. Anthony FIORENZA
09	Director of Institutional Research	Dr. Silvio RODRIGUEZ
43	Legal Counsel	Ms. Carmen DOMINGUEZ
86	Director Governmental Affairs	Ms. Victoria HERNANDEZ
100	Chief of Staff	Mr. George ANDREWS
103	Exec Dir Workforce Educ & Partnrshp	Vacant
104	Interim Pgm Manager Study Abroad	Ms. Joanne MICHAUD
105	College Webmaster	Mr. Andrew SEAGA
08	Head Librarian/Dir Learning Resourc	Mr. Erick DOMINICIS
85	Director Intl Student Services	Ms. Anoush MCNAMEE
22	Dir Affirmative Action/EEO	Dr. Joy C. RUFF

Miami International University of Art & Design (A)

1501 Biscayne Boulevard, Suite 100,
Miami FL 33132-1418

County: Miami-Dade — FICE Identification: 008878 — Unit ID: 134811
Telephone: (305) 428-5700 — Carnegie Class: Spec/Arts
FAX Number: (305) 374-7946 — Calendar System: Quarter
URL: www.aimiu.aii.edu
Established: 1965 — Annual Undergrad Tuition & Fees: $17,714
Enrollment: 2,846 — Coed
Affiliation or Control: Proprietary — IRS Status: Proprietary
Highest Offering: Master's
Program: Fine Arts Emphasis
Accreditation: SC, CIDA

01	President	Ms. Erika FLEMING
05	Dean of Academic Affairs	Dr. Paul COX
10	Dir Admin & Financial Services	Mr. Joseph GIANNATTASIO
32	Dean of Student Affairs	Mr. John OSBORNE
07	Senior Director of Admissions	Mr. Kevin RYAN
08	Librarian	Ms. Tammie OLIVERA

Millennia Atlantic University (B)

3801 NW 97th Avenue, Doral FL 33178

County: Miami-Dade — FICE Identification: 041825 — Unit ID: 461883
Telephone: (786) 331-1000 — Carnegie Class: Not Classified
FAX Number: (305) 503-9680 — Calendar System: Semester
URL: www.maufl.edu
Established: — Annual Undergrad Tuition & Fees: $10,532
Enrollment: 239 — Coed
Affiliation or Control: Proprietary — IRS Status: Proprietary
Highest Offering: Master's
Program: Business Emphasis
Accreditation: ACICS

01	President	Dr. Aristides MAZA-DUERTO
10	CFO	Mrs. Orianna MAZA-MOSS
05	Director of Academic Program	Ms. Teresa FITZGERALD
06	Registrar	Ms. Natasha ALEONG
26	Marketing Coordinator	Ms. Maria BOLIVAR
07	Director of Admissions	Ms. Anna HERNANDEZ

North Florida Community College (C)

325 NW Turner Davis Drive, Madison FL 32340-1610

County: Madison — FICE Identification: 001508 — Unit ID: 136145
Telephone: (850) 973-2288 — Carnegie Class: Assoc/Pub-R-S
FAX Number: (850) 973-1696 — Calendar System: Semester
URL: www.nfcc.edu
Established: 1958 — Annual Undergrad Tuition & Fees (In-State): $2,994
Enrollment: 1,455 — Coed
Affiliation or Control: State — IRS Status: 501(c)3
Highest Offering: Associate Degree
Program: Occupational; 2-Year Principally Bachelor's Creditable
Accreditation: SC

01	President	Mr. John GROSSKOPF
05	Dean of Academic Affairs/CAO	Ms. Frances ADLEBURG
10	Dean Administrative Svcs & CBO	Ms. Amelia MULKEY
07	Dean of Enrollment/Student Services	Ms. Kay HOGAN
09	Manager of Networking Systems	Mr. John SIRMON
15	Director of Personnel Services	Mr. Bill HUNTER
08	Head Librarian	Ms. Lynn WYCHE
88	SSS and Disability Coordinator	Dr. Suzie CASHWELL
88	Director of Public Safety Academy	Mr. Rick DAVIS
06	Registrar	Ms. Lori PLEASANT
18	Chief Facilities/Physical Plant	Mr. Dale HACKLE
21	Controller	Vacant
26	Public Information Officer	Ms. Kim SCARBORO
29	Dir Foundation Alumni Relations	Dr. Cheryl JAMES
37	Director Student Financial Aid	Ms. Peggy HARRIS
28	Director of Diversity	Ms. Denise BELL
32	Director Student Services	Vacant
96	Director of Purchasing	Ms. Sarah NEWSOME
04	Executive Asst to President	Ms. Cindy M. GAYLARD

Northwest Florida State College (D)

100 College Boulevard, Niceville FL 32578-1295

County: Okaloosa — FICE Identification: 001510 — Unit ID: 136233
Telephone: (850) 678-5111 — Carnegie Class: Assoc/Pub4
FAX Number: (850) 729-5215 — Calendar System: Semester
URL: www.nwfsc.edu
Established: 1963 — Annual Undergrad Tuition & Fees (In-State): $3,120
Enrollment: 6,295 — Coed
Affiliation or Control: State — IRS Status: 501(c)3
Highest Offering: Baccalaureate
Program: Occupational; 2-Year Principally Bachelor's Creditable; Liberal Arts And General; Teacher Preparatory; Professional
Accreditation: SC, ADNUR, DA, EMT, NURSE

01	President	Dr. Ty HANDY
05	Vice Pres for Instruction	Dr. Sasha JARRELL
11	Vice Pres Administrative Services	Mr. Randy WHITE
30	Vice Pres College Advancement	Mrs. Cristie KEDROSKI
13	Chief Information Officer	Mr. Greg ELLER
09	Director of Institutional Research	Dr. Diane W. HODGINS
15	Director Human Resources/Diversity	Ms. Nancy MURPHY
07	Director of Admissions	Ms. Karyn COOPER
29	Assoc Director for Resource/Alumni	Ms. Carla REINLIE
41	Athletic Director	Mr. Ramsey ROSS
37	Director Financial Aid/Veteran Affs	Ms. Patricia BENNETT
18	Facilities Director	Mr. Sam JONES
36	Director Advising and Testing	Ms. Marlayna GOOSBY
08	Director Learning Resources Center	Ms. Janice HENDERSON
26	Director Marketing/Public Relations	Ms. Stephanie PETTIS
96	Coordinator of Purchasing	Ms. Dedria LUNDERMAN
32	Interim Dean of Students	Dr. Aimee WATTS
04	Admin Assistant to President	Ms. Carolyne LAUX
06	Registrar	Ms. Bree DURHAM
106	Dir Online Education/Online Ed	Dr. Melynda FITT
75	Dean of Career & Technical Educ	Mr. Dennis SHERWOOD
97	Dean of Education	Dr. Anne SOUTHARD
84	Assoc Dean for Enrollment Services	Ms. Olivia LITTLE
19	Director Security/Safety	Mr. William LOOPER
25	Grants Admin	Dr. Anne SOUTHARD

Nova Southeastern University (E)

3301 College Avenue, Fort Lauderdale FL 33314-7796

County: Broward — FICE Identification: 001509 — Unit ID: 136215
Telephone: (954) 262-7300 — Carnegie Class: RU/H
FAX Number: (954) 262-3800 — Calendar System: Trimester
URL: www.nova.edu
Established: 1964 — Annual Undergrad Tuition & Fees: $26,910
Enrollment: 24,148 — Coed
Affiliation or Control: Independent Non-Profit — IRS Status: 501(c)3
Highest Offering: Doctorate
Program: 2-Year Principally Bachelor's Creditable; Liberal Arts And General; Teacher Preparatory; Professional
Accreditation: SC, AA, ACAE, ARCPA, AUD, CAATE, CLPSY, #COARC, DENT, DMS, IACBE, IPSY, LAW, MFCD, NURSE, OPT, OPTR, OSTEO, OT, PH, PHAR, PTA, SP, SPAA, TED

01	President & CEO	Dr. George L. HANBURY, II
05	Provost & Exec VP Academic Affairs	Dr. Ralph V. ROGERS
11	Exec Vice President/COO	Ms. Jacqueline A. TRAVISANO
10	VP Finance/CFO	Ms. Alyson SILVA
00	Chancellor Nova Southeastern Univ	Mr. Ray FERRERO, JR.
00	University President Emeritus	Dr. Abraham FISCHLER
17	Chancellor Health Professions Div	Dr. Fred LIPPMAN
20	Exec Dean for Administration	Dr. Irving ROSENBAUM
88	SVP Transitional Rsrch & Econ Dev	Dr. H. Thomas TEMPLE
08	VP Info Svcs/Univ Librarian	Ms. Lydia M. ACOSTA
43	VP Legal Affairs	Mr. Joel BERMAN
46	VP Research Tech Transfer	Dr. Gary S. MARGULES
32	VP Student Affairs/Dean UG Studies	Dr. Brad WILLIAMS
30	VP Inst Advancement	Dr. Jennifer O'FLANNERY ANDERSON
13	VP Info Tech/Chief Info Ofcr	Mr. Tom WEST
15	VP Human Resources	Mr. Robert J. PIETRYKOWSKI
37	VP Enrollment and Stdnt Svcs	Dr. Stephanie BROWN
21	VP Business Services	Mr. Marc CROCQUET
26	Int Exec Director Univ Relations	Mr. Brandon HENSLER
19	Director Public Safety	Mr. James EWING
09	VP Institutional Effectiveness	Dr. Donald J. RUDAWSKY
88	Director Accreditation	Ms. Jane DUNCAN
24	Exec Dir Ed Tech/Digital Media Prod	Ms. Diane LIPPE
25	Director Sponsored Programs	Ms. Cathy HARLAN
86	Exec Dir Licensure/State Relations	Dr. Greg F. STIBER
12	Headmaster University School	Mr. William KOPAS
27	Director University Publications	Mr. Ron RYAN
27	Director Public Affairs	Ms. Julie SPECHLER
36	Director of Career Development	Ms. Shari SAPERSTEIN
29	Director of Alumni Relations	Mr. R.J STAMPER
06	Dir University Registrar's Office	Ms. G. Elaine N. POFF
41	Director Athletics	Mr. Michael MOMINEY
39	Dir Residential Life & Housing	Ms. Aarika CAMP
96	Director Office of Procurement Mgmt	Mr. Mike COROMINAS
88	Director Campus Recreation	Mr. Tom VITUCCI
88	VP Regional Campus Network/Online	Dr. Richard DAVIS
88	Executive Dir Internal Auditing	Mr. Ron MIDEI
31	Exec Dir Inst & Comm Engagement	Dr. Barbara PACKER-MUTI
88	VP Compliance/Chief Integrity Ofcr	Ms. Robin SUPLER
88	Dir Museum of Art	Ms. Bonnie CLEARWATER
63	Dean College Osteopathic Medicine	Ms. Elaine WALLACE
67	Dean College Pharmacy	Dr. Lisa DEZIEL
23	Vice Pres Clinical Operations	Mr. Kelly GREGG
88	Dean College Optometry	Dr. David LOSHIN
76	Dean College of Hlth Care Sciences	Dr. Stanley WILSON
77	Dean Grad Sch Computer/Info Sci	Dr. Amon SEAGULL
61	Dean Shepard Broad Law Center	Mr. Jon GARON
65	Dean Oceanographic Center	Dr. Richard DODGE
66	Dean College of Nursing	Dr. Marcella M. RUTHERFORD
50	Dn W Huizenga Grad Sch Bus/Entr	Dr. J. Preston JONES
92	Dean Farquhar Honors College	Dr. Donald ROSENBLUM
88	Dean Center Psychological Stds	Dr. Karen GROSBY
83	Dean Grad Sch Humanities/Social Sci	Dr. Honggang YANG
88	Dean Mailman Ctr for Human Devel	Dr. Roni LEIDERMAN
63	Dean College of Medical Sciences	Dr. Harold LAUBAUCH
83	Dean Inst Study Hum Svcs/Hlth/Just	Dr. Kimberly DURHAM
52	Dean of Dental Medicine	Dr. Linda NIESSEN

Orlando Medical Institute (F)

6220 S. Orange Blossom Tr, Ste 509, Orlando FL 32809

County: Orange — Identification: 667127
Telephone: (407) 251-0007 — Carnegie Class: Not Classified
FAX Number: (407) 251-0352 — Calendar System: Semester
URL: www.orlandomedicalinstitute.com
Established: 2004 — Annual Undergrad Tuition & Fees: $4,000
Enrollment: N/A — Coed
Affiliation or Control: Proprietary — IRS Status: Proprietary
Highest Offering: Associate Degree
Program: Occupational
Accreditation: ABHES

01	President	Felix J. MARQUEZ, JR.

Palm Beach Atlantic University (G)

901 S. Flagler Drive, West Palm Beach FL 33401

County: Palm Beach — FICE Identification: 008849 — Unit ID: 136330
Telephone: (561) 803-2000 — Carnegie Class: Master's M
FAX Number: (561) 803-2186 — Calendar System: Semester
URL: www.pba.edu
Established: 1968 — Annual Undergrad Tuition & Fees: $26,750
Enrollment: 3,865 — Coed
Affiliation or Control: Interdenominational — IRS Status: 501(c)3
Highest Offering: Doctorate
Program: Occupational; Liberal Arts And General; Teacher Preparatory; Professional
Accreditation: SC, CAATE, IACBE, MUS, NURSE, PHAR

01	President	Mr. William M. FLEMING
05	Provost	Dr. Gene FANT, JR.
10	Sr VP for Finance Admin & Plng	Mr. John KAUTZ, III
04	Executive Asst to President	Mr. Tim WORLEY
30	Vice President Development	Mrs. Vicki PUGH
32	Vice President Student Development	Vacant
09	Asst Vice Pres Rsrch/Effectiveness	Mrs. Carolanne BROWN
13	Assoc VP Campus Information Svcs	Mr. Phillip MAJOR
26	Assoc VP Univ Relations & Marketing	Mrs. Rebecca PEELING
51	Dean MacArthur School of Leadership	Dr. Craig DOMECK
49	Dean School of Arts & Sciences	Vacant
50	Dean School of Business	Dr. Leslie TURNER
53	Dean School of Education	Dr. Gene SALE
57	Dean School of Music/Fine Arts	Dr. Lloyd MIMS
66	Dean School of Nursing	Dr. Joanne MASELLA
67	Dean Gregory School of Pharmacy	Dr. Mary FERRILL
60	Dean School Communication/Media	Dr. J. Duane MEEKS
73	Dean School of Ministry	Dr. Randy RICHARDS
06	Registrar	Ms. Audrey SCHOFIELD
08	Dean of the Library	Mr. Steven BAKER
20	Dean of Faculty	Vacant
15	Assoc VP of Human Resources	Ms. Mona L. HICKS
18	Director of Physical Plant	Mr. Matt STEVENS
21	Controller	Mrs. Carla CROW
29	AVP Alumni Relations/Annual Fund	Mrs. Delesa MORRIS
31	Coordinator Community Services	Mrs. Cindy LAMERSON
38	Director of Student Success Center	Mrs. Vanetta BRATCHER
37	Director of Financial Aid	Mr. Joseph BRYAN
35	Dean of Students	Mr. Kevin ABEL
40	Director of Campus Store	Mrs. Abbie ROSEMEYER
41	Director of Athletics	Mrs. Carolyn STONE
42	Director of Campus Ministries	Mr. Mark KAPRIVE
92	Director of Supper Honors Program	Dr. Tom ST. ANTOINE
07	Dean of Admissions	Mr. Joe SHARP

Palm Beach State College (H)

4200 Congress Avenue, Lake Worth FL 33461-4796

County: Palm Beach — FICE Identification: 001512 — Unit ID: 136358
Telephone: (561) 967-7222 — Carnegie Class: Assoc/Pub-S-MC
FAX Number: (561) 868-3504 — Calendar System: Semester
URL: www.palmbeachstate.edu
Established: 1933 — Annual Undergrad Tuition & Fees (In-District): $3,686
Enrollment: 28,517 — Coed
Affiliation or Control: Local — IRS Status: 501(c)3

Highest Offering: Baccalaureate
Program: Occupational; 2-Year Principally Bachelor's Creditable
Accreditation: SC, ADNUR, CAHIIM, COARC, DA, DH, DMS, EMT, MAC, NUR, RAD, SURGT

01 President ... Dr. Dennis P. GALLON
05 Vice President for Academic Affairs ... Dr. Sharon A. SASS
10 Vice President Admin/Business Svcs ... Mr. Richard A. BECKER
32 Vice President for Student Services ... Dr. Peter BARBATIS
102 Exec Director/CEO Foundation ... Ms. Suellen MANN
12 Provost Glades Center ... Dr. Holly L. BENNETT
12 Provost South Campus ... Dr. Bernadette MENDONEZ RUSSELL
12 Provost Eissey Campus ... Dr. Jean WIHBEY
12 Provost Central Campus ... Dr. Maria M. VALLEJO
35 Dean Student Services/Central ... Ms. Penny J. MCISAAC
35 Dean Student Services/Boca Raton ... Ms. Nicole P. BANKS
35 Dean Student Services/Eissey ... Mr. Scott MACLACHLAN
35 Dean Educational Services/Glades ... Dr. Barry L. MOORE
84 Dean Enrollment Management ... Mr. Chuck H. ZETTLER
103 Dean Workforce ... Ms. Patricia V. RICHIE
37 Director Financial Aid ... Mr. Thomas VO
41 Dir Student Activities/Athletics ... Dr. David HOLSTEIN
09 Dir Inst Research/Effectiveness ... Dr. Jennifer D. CAMPBELL
86 Director Government Relations ... Ms. Erin S. MCCOLSKEY
18 Director Facilities ... Mr. John T. WASUKANIS
15 Exec Director Human Resources ... Ms. Barbara MATIAS
26 Dir College Relations & Marketing ... Dr. Grace H. TRUMAN
21 Controller ... Mr. James E. DUFFIE
06 Registrar/Director Admissions ... Mr. Edward MUELLER
96 Director of Purchasing ... Ms. Jodi HART
13 Chief Information Officer ... Mr. Anthony PARZIALE
14 Director Information Technology ... Vacant
29 Director Alumni Relations ... Ms. Suellen MANN
25 Manager Grant Development ... Ms. Maureen CAPP
88 Project Reports Coordinator ... Ms. Karen M. LIPPE

Palmer College of Chiropractic, Florida Campus (A)

4777 City Center Parkway, Port Orange FL 32129-4153
Telephone: (386) 763-2709 Identification: 666330
Accreditation: &NH, &CHIRO

† Regional accreditation is carried under the parent institution in Davenport, IA.

Pasco-Hernando State College (B)

10230 Ridge Road, New Port Richey FL 34654-5199
County: Pasco FICE Identification: 010652
Unit ID: 136400
Telephone: (727) 847-2727 Carnegie Class: Assoc/Pub-S-MC
FAX Number: (727) 816-1815 Calendar System: Semester
URL: www.phsc.edu
Established: 1972 Annual Undergrad Tuition & Fees (In-District): $3,155
Enrollment: 12,344 Coed
Affiliation or Control: State/Local IRS Status: 501(c)3
Highest Offering: Baccalaureate
Program: Occupational; 2-Year Principally Bachelor's Creditable
Accreditation: SC, ADNUR, DH, EMT

01 President ... Dr. Timothy L. BEARD
05 VP Instruction/Provost West Campus ... Dr. Bonnie M. CLARK
32 VP Stdnt Devel/Enrollment Mgmt ... Mr. Robert E. BADE
10 Vice Pres Administration & Finance ... Mr. Kenneth R. BURDZINSKI
12 Provost of the East Campus ... Dr. Lisa A. RICHARDSON
12 Provost North Campus ... Dr. Donna R. BURDZINSKI
12 Provost Spring Hill Campus ... Dr. Amy ANDERSON
12 Provost Porter Campus at Wiregrass ... Dr. Stanley M. GIANNET
103 Dean of Workforce Development ... Mr. Edwin G. GOOLSBY
24 Dean of Institutional Technology ... Dr. Melissa L. HARTS
35 Assoc Dean Stdnt Dev & Enroll Mgmt ... Ms. Chiquita A. HENDERSON
20 Assoc Dean of Dev Educ & Inst Svcs ... Mr. Kevin F. O'FARRELL
17 Dean Health Occupations ... Ms. Jayme S. ROTHBERG
49 Dean Arts and Sciences ... Dr. John L. WHITLOCK
21 Asst VP Admin/Finance/Comptroller ... Mr. Brian S. HORN
09 Dean Institutional Effectiveness ... Dr. Gerardine K. COCHRAN
13 Exec Dir Management Info Svcs ... Ms. Janice L. SCOTT
30 Asst VP Inst Advance/Exec Dir Fnd ... Dr. William J. SHUSTOWSKI, JR.
66 Associate Dean of Nursing .. Dr. Barbara SOUTHWORTH-FISHER
07 Dir Admissions & Student Records ... Mr. Chris BIBBO
37 Dean Financial Aid ... Ms. Rebecca SHANAFELT
43 Asst VP of Policy/General Counsel . Mr. Stephen C. SCHROEDER
08 Director of Libraries ... Mr. Raymond J. CALVERT
41 Athletics Director/Instructor ... Mr. Stephen A. WINTERLING
26 Exec Dir Marketing/Public Relation ... Ms. Lucy T. MILLER
18 Director of Facilities ... Mr. Keith V. BRAUN
15 Exec Director of Human Resources ... Ms. Vivian M. FRIEND
109 Auxiliary Services Manager ... Mr. John D. COLLINS
35 Asst Dean Stdnt Dev & Enroll Mgmt ... Dr. Katie M. BOWMAN
22 Dir of Global & Multi Aware & Spec ... Mr. Imani D. ASUKILE
96 Purchasing Agent ... Mr. Richard BORAGINE
04 Executive Asst to President & DBOT ... Ms. Rhonda M. DODGE
29 Director Alumni & Donor Relations ... Ms. Michelle L. BULLWINKEL

Pensacola Christian College (C)

250 Brent Lane, Pensacola FL 32503
County: Escambia Identification: 667101
Telephone: (850) 478-8496 Carnegie Class: Not Classified
FAX Number: (850) 479-6577 Calendar System: Semester
URL: www.pcci.edu
Established: 1974 Annual Undergrad Tuition & Fees: $5,486
Enrollment: 4,100 Coed
Affiliation or Control: Independent Non-Profit IRS Status: 501(c)3
Highest Offering: Doctorate
Program: Religious Emphasis
Accreditation: TRACS

01 President ... Dr. Troy SHOEMAKER
03 Vice President/Exec Asst to Pres ... Dr. Joel MULLENIX
05 Academic Vice President ... Dr. Raylene COCHRAN
30 Vice Pres Student Life ... Dr. Paul OHMAN
06 Registrar ... Ms. Linda TROUTMAN

Pensacola State College (D)

1000 College Boulevard, Pensacola FL 32504-8998
County: Escambia FICE Identification: 001513
Unit ID: 136473
Telephone: (850) 484-1000 Carnegie Class: Assoc/Pub-R-L
FAX Number: (850) 484-1826 Calendar System: Semester
URL: www.pensacolastate.edu
Established: 1948 Annual Undergrad Tuition & Fees (In-District): $2,902
Enrollment: 9,026 Coed
Affiliation or Control: Local IRS Status: 501(c)3
Highest Offering: Baccalaureate
Program: Occupational; 2-Year Principally Bachelor's Creditable; Liberal Arts And General
Accreditation: SC, ACFEI, ADNUR, CAHIIM, DH, EMT, MAC, PTAA, RAD, SURGT

01 President ... Dr. Ed MEADOWS
05 Vice Pres for Academic Affairs ... Dr. Erin SPICER
32 Vice President Student Affairs ... Mr. Tom GILLIAM
10 Vice President for Business ... Mrs. Gean Ann EMOND
103 Dean Workforce Educ/Vocational Supp ... Mr. Dan BUSSE
12 Dean Milton Campus ... Ms. Anthea AMOS
12 Dean Warrington Campus ... Ms. Frances DUNCAN
28 Assoc Vice Pres Inst Diversity ... Dr. Gael FRAZER
102 Exec Director College Foundation ... Mr. Aaron WEST
13 Executive Director ITS ... Mr. Bert MERRITT
86 Director of Govt Relations ... Ms. Sandy RAY
26 Director Marketing & College Info ... Ms. Sheila NICHOLS
06 Registrar ... Ms. Martha CAUGHEY
09 Dean Inst Research & Grants ... Dr. Debbie DOUMA
18 Director Physical Plant ... Mr. Walt WINTER
14 Director Computer Svcs/Telecommun ... Vacant
15 Director Human Resources/EA/EO ... Ms. Tammy HENDERSON
37 Dir Fin Aid/Veteran Affairs/Scholar ... Ms. Karen KESSLER
36 Coordinator Student Job Services ... Ms. Sherry DUFFEY
19 Public Safety Director ... Mr. Hank SHIRAH
43 General Counsel ... Mr. Thomas J. GILLIAM
08 District Dept Head Libraries ... Ms. Lisa Marie BARTUSIK
96 Director of Purchasing ... Ms. Cassie BOATWRIGHT
21 Associate Business Officer ... Ms. Jackie PADILLA
29 Exec Director Alumni Affairs ... Ms. Patrice WHITTEN
07 Director of Admissions ... Ms. Martha CAUGHEY
38 Director Student Counseling ... Ms. Monique COLLINS
41 Director Athletics ... Mr. Bill HAMILTON
84 Dean Enrollment Services ... Ms. Kathy DUTREMBLE
12 Director South Santa Rosa Center ... Ms. Michele HORTON
12 Director Century Center ... Ms. Paula BYRD
31 Coordinator Community Education ... Ms. Frances YEO
04 Executive Asst to President ... Ms. Patricia S. CREWS
106 Dir Online Education/E-learning ... Dr. Bill WATERS

Polk State College (E)

999 Avenue H, NE, Winter Haven FL 33881-4299
County: Polk FICE Identification: 001514
Unit ID: 136516
Telephone: (863) 297-1000 Carnegie Class: Assoc/Pub-R-L
FAX Number: (863) 297-1065 Calendar System: Trimester
URL: www.polk.edu
Established: 1964 Annual Undergrad Tuition & Fees (In-District): $3,366
Enrollment: 11,060 Coed
Affiliation or Control: Local IRS Status: 501(c)3
Highest Offering: Baccalaureate
Program: Occupational; 2-Year Principally Bachelor's Creditable; Technical Emphasis
Accreditation: SC, ADNUR, COARC, CVT, DMS, EMT, NUR, OTA, PTAA, RAD

01 President ... Dr. Eileen HOLDEN
10 Vice Pres Administrative Svcs/CFO ... Mr. Peter ELLIOTT
05 Vice Pres Academic Affairs ... Dr. Ken ROSS
32 Vice Pres Student Services ... Mr. Reginal WEBB
30 Vice Pres Inst Adv/Exec Dir PSCF ... Ms. Tracy PORTER
12 Campus Provost-LK ... Mr. Stephen HULL
12 Campus Provost-WH ... Dr. Martha SANTIAGO
88 AVP Strategic Initiatives ... Dr. Naomi BOYER
26 AVP Communications & Public Affs ... Ms. Tamara SAKAGAWA
20 District Dean Academic Affairs ... Dr. Patricia JONES
15 Director Human Resources ... Ms. Jill HALL
35 Dean Student Services-WH ... Mr. Lawrence PAKOWSKI
35 Dean Student Services-LK ... Mr. Sylvester LITTLE
20 Dean Academic Affairs-WH ... Ms. April ROBINSON
20 Dean Academic Affairs-LK ... Mr. Donald PAINTER
21 Controller ... Ms. Teresa VOROUS
06 Director Stdnt Enrollment/Registrar ... Ms. Kathy BUCKLEW
37 Director Student Financial Svcs ... Ms. Marcia CONLIFFE
66 Director Nursing ... Dr. Annette HUTCHERSON
102 Director Financial Affs/PSC Found ... Mr. Lynn WILSON
18 Director Facilities ... Mr. George URBANO
22 Director Equity & Diversity ... Ms. Valparisa BAKER
103 Director Corporate College ... Mr. Robert CLANCEY
88 Principal Chain of Lakes CHS ... Ms. Bridget FETTER
88 Principal Lakeland Collegiate HS ... Ms. Sallie BRISBANE
88 Center Director JDA ... Ms. Cheryl GARNETT
88 Associate Dean Student Svcs-LK ... Ms. Michelle SAMS
88 Associate Dean Student Svcs-WH ... Ms. Yulonda BELL
88 Associate Dean Academic Affs-LK ... Ms. Gerene THOMPSON
88 Associate Dean Academic Affs-WH ... Dr. Carole BYRD
41 Athletic Director ... Mr. Bing TYUS
96 Director Purchasing ... Mr. Mark LILLQUIST
86 Director Government Relations ... Ms. Ana Maria SANCHEZ
09 Director Strategic Plng & Assess ... Vacant

Polytechnic University of Puerto Rico (F)

8180 NW 36th Street, Suite 401, Miami FL 33166-6674
Telephone: (305) 418-4220 Identification: 666238
Accreditation: &M

† Regional accreditation is carried under the parent institution, Universidad Politecnica de Puerto Rico, San Juan, PR.

Polytechnic University of Puerto Rico-Orlando Campus (G)

550 N Econlockhatchee Trail, Orlando FL 32825
Telephone: (407) 677-7000 Identification: 770172
Accreditation: &M

† Branch campus of Universidad Politecnica De Puerto Rico, San Juan, PR.

The Praxis Institute (H)

1850 SW 8th Street, 4th Floor, Miami FL 33135
County: Miami-Dade FICE Identification: 031147
Unit ID: 430582
Telephone: (305) 642-4104 Carnegie Class: Not Classified
FAX Number: N/A Calendar System: Semester
URL: the-praxisinstitute.com
Established: 1988 Annual Undergrad Tuition & Fees: $7,500
Enrollment: 365 Coed
Affiliation or Control: Proprietary IRS Status: Proprietary
Highest Offering: Associate Degree
Program: Occupational
Accreditation: COE, PTAA

01 Executive Director ... Rebeca ALFIE

Professional Hands Institute (I)

3383 NW 7th Street, Suite 200, Miami FL 33125
County: Miami-Dade FICE Identification: 041431
Unit ID: 454908
Telephone: (305) 442-6011 Carnegie Class: Not Classified
FAX Number: (305) 442-6013 Calendar System: Semester
URL: www.prohands.edu
Established: 2004 Annual Undergrad Tuition & Fees: $9,950
Enrollment: 37 Coed
Affiliation or Control: Proprietary IRS Status: Proprietary
Highest Offering: Associate Degree
Program: Occupational
Accreditation: COE

12 Campus Director ... Ms. Caridad TRIANA

Rasmussen College - Fort Myers (J)

9160 Forum Corporate Parkway, Fort Myers FL 33905
Telephone: (239) 477-2100 Identification: 667062
Accreditation: &NH, MAAB

† Regional accreditation is carried under the parent institution in Saint Cloud, MN. The tuition figure is an average, actual tuition may vary.

Rasmussen College - Land O'Lakes (K)

18600 Fernview Street, Land O'Lakes FL 34638
Telephone: (813) 435-3601 Identification: 770488
Accreditation: &NH

† Regional accreditation carried under the parent institution in Saint Cloud, MN. The tuition figure is an average, actual tuition may vary.

Rasmussen College - New Port Richey (L)

8661 Citizens Drive, Suite 300, New Port Richey FL 34654
Telephone: (727) 942-0069 Identification: 666425
Accreditation: &NH, MAAB

† Regional accreditation is carried under parent institution in Saint Cloud, MN. The tuition figure is an average, actual tuition may vary.

Rasmussen College - Ocala (M)

4755 SW 46th Court, Ocala FL 34474
Telephone: (352) 629-1941 FICE Identification: 008501
Accreditation: &NH, ADNUR, MAAB

† Regional accreditation carried under the parent institution in Saint Cloud, MN. The tuition figure is an average, actual tuition may vary.

Rasmussen College - Tampa/Brandon (A)

4042 Park Oaks Boulevard, Tampa FL 33610
Telephone: (813) 246-7600 Identification: 667067
Accreditation: &NH, MAAB

† Regional accreditation is carried under the parent institution in Saint Cloud, MN. The tuition figure is an average, actual tuition may vary.

Reformed Theological Seminary (B)

1231 Reformation Drive, Oviedo FL 32765-7197
Telephone: (407) 366-9493 Identification: 666628
Accreditation: &SC, THEOL

† Regional accreditation is carried under the parent institution in Jackson, MS.

Remington College of Nursing (C)

660 Century Point, Lake Mary FL 32746
Telephone: (407) 562-9100 Identification: 770566
Accreditation: ACCSC, NURSE

† Branch campus of Remington College-Tampa Campus, Tampa, FL.

Remington College Online (D)

500 International Pkwy, Suite 200,
Heathrow FL 33612-5627
Telephone: (407) 562-5671 Identification: 770567
Accreditation: ACCSC, OTA

† Branch campus of Remington College-Tampa Campus, Tampa, FL.

Remington College-Tampa Campus (E)

6302 E Martin Luther King Dr, #400, Tampa FL 33619
County: Hillsborough FICE Identification: 007586
Unit ID: 135939
Telephone: (813) 935-5700 Carnegie Class: Bac/Assoc
FAX Number: (813) 935-7415 Calendar System: Quarter
URL: www.remingtoncollege.edu
Established: 1948 Annual Undergrad Tuition & Fees: $15,995
Enrollment: 151 Coed
Affiliation or Control: Independent Non-Profit IRS Status: 501(c)3
Highest Offering: Baccalaureate
Program: Occupational; 2-Year Principally Bachelor's Creditable; Technical Emphasis
Accreditation: ACCSC, NURSE

01 President ... Dr. Michael SELTZER
06 Registrar ... Ms. Luigidge GUSTIN
36 Director Student Placement ... Ms. Deborah HOFFMAN
37 Director Student Financial Aid ... Ms. Brittany SCHAUERMANN

Ringling College of Art and Design (F)

2700 N Tamiami Trail, Sarasota FL 34234-5895
County: Sarasota FICE Identification: 012574
Unit ID: 136774
Telephone: (941) 351-5100 Carnegie Class: Spec/Arts
FAX Number: (941) 359-7517 Calendar System: Semester
URL: www.ringling.edu
Established: 1931 Annual Undergrad Tuition & Fees: $40,040
Enrollment: 1,219 Coed
Affiliation or Control: Independent Non-Profit IRS Status: 501(c)3
Highest Offering: Baccalaureate
Program: Professional; Fine Arts Emphasis
Accreditation: SC, ART, CIDA

01 President ... Dr. Larry R. THOMPSON
04 Exec Assistant to President ... Ms. Cathy GAGLIARDI
05 Vice President Academic Affairs ... Mr. Jeff BELLANTONI
30 Vice Pres Advancement ... Mr. Michael MOORE
10 Vice President for Finance & Admin ... Ms. Tracy A. WAGNER
15 VP Human/Organizational Development ... Ms. Christine C. DEGEORGE
32 Vice Pres Student Life/Dean Stdnts ... Dr. Tammy S. WALSH
20 Assoc VP Academics/Faculty Affairs ... Mr. David H. JACKSON
21 Asst VP for Fin & Admn/Controller ... Ms. Monica K. WAID
18 Asst VP/Dir Facilities Operations ... Mr. Jeffrey A. POLESHEK
07 Dean of Admissions ... Mr. James H. DEAN
51 Assoc Dir Operation/Continuing Stds ... Ms. Diane ZORN
06 Registrar ... Mr. Justin SELPH
90 Director Institutional Technology ... Dr. Mahmoud PEGAH
36 Director Career Services ... Mr. Charles KOVACS
19 Director of Public Safety ... Mr. Richard E. TUBBS

The Robert E. Webber Institute for Worship Studies (G)

151 Kingsley Avenue, Orange Park FL 32073-5640
County: Clay Identification: 666616
Telephone: (904) 264-2172 Carnegie Class: Not Classified
FAX Number: (904) 278-2878 Calendar System: Semester
URL: www.iws.edu
Established: 1998 Annual Graduate Tuition & Fees: $5,517
Enrollment: 164 Coed
Affiliation or Control: Independent Non-Profit IRS Status: 501(c)3
Highest Offering: Doctorate; No Undergraduates
Program: Professional; Religious Emphasis
Accreditation: BI

01 Chief Executive Officer ... Dr. James R. HART
05 Chief Academic Officer ... Dr. Eric H. OHLMANN
10 Chief Financial Officer ... Ms. Christi G. MATTESON
06 Registrar ... Vacant
84 Director of Enrollment Management ... Mr. Mark J. MURRAY
08 Library Director ... Ms. Susan A. MASSEY
29 Director Alumni Relations ... Dr. Kent L. WALTERS
42 Dean of the Chapel ... Dr. Darrell A. HARRIS
88 Dir of Technical Services ... Mr. Samuel L. HOROWITZ
04 Asst to the President ... Ms. Dianna L. ANDREWS
32 Dir Student Services/Office Admin ... Ms. Sandy E. DINKINS
45 Dir Strategic Plng/Accreditation ... Dr. Steve E. HUNTLEY
13 Coordinator of Info Technology ... Dr. James Kenneth RUSHING
26 Dir of Missional Relations ... Dr. Frank FORTUNATO
30 Coordinator of Advancement ... Ms. Jessica COLEMAN

Rollins College (H)

1000 Holt Avenue, Winter Park FL 32789-4499
County: Orange FICE Identification: 001515
Unit ID: 136950
Telephone: (407) 646-2000 Carnegie Class: Master's L
FAX Number: (407) 646-2600 Calendar System: Semester
URL: www.rollins.edu
Established: 1885 Annual Undergrad Tuition & Fees: $44,760
Enrollment: 3,207 Coed
Affiliation or Control: Independent Non-Profit IRS Status: 501(c)3
Highest Offering: Doctorate
Program: Liberal Arts And General; Teacher Preparatory; Professional
Accreditation: SC, BUS, CACREP, MUS

01 Acting President ... Dr. Craig MCALLASTER
05 Vice President Acad Affairs/Provost ... Dr. Carol BRESNAHAN
32 Vice President Student Affairs ... Dr. Mamta ACCAPADI
10 Vice President Business/Finance ... Mr. Jeffrey EISENBARTH
30 VP for Institutional Advancement ... Dr. Ronald KORVAS
13 Chief Information Officer ... Dr. Pat SCHOKNECHT
49 Dean of Arts & Sciences ... Dr. Robert SMITHER
107 Dean of Professional Studies ... Dr. Debra WELLMAN
51 Dean of Hamilton Holt School ... Dr. David RICHARD
35 Asst VP Stdnt Affs & Dean of Stdnts ... Ms. Meghan HARTE WEYANT
84 Interim Dean of Enrollment Mgmt ... Mr. Steve BOOKER
50 Int Dean Crummer Grad Sch of Bus ... Mr. Thomas MCEVOY
42 Dean of the Chapel ... Vacant
21 Assoc VP Finance/Asst Treasurer ... Mr. William SHORT
26 Assoc VP Marketing & Communications ... Mr. Thomas HOPE
15 Asst VP Human Res/Risk Management ... Ms. Maria MARTINEZ
108 Asst Provost Inst Effectiveness ... Dr. Toni STROLLO HOLBROOK
08 Director of Olin Library ... Dr. Jonathan MILLER
41 Athletic Director ... Ms. Pennie PARKER
37 Director of Financial Aid ... Mr. Steve BOOKER
09 Director of Institutional Research ... Mr. Udeth LUGO
104 Director of International Programs ... Ms. Giselda BEAUDIN
07 Director of Admission ... Ms. Holly POHLIG
39 Sr Dir Res Life & Explorations ... Mr. Leon HAYNER
36 Asst VP of Career & Life Planning ... Ms. Lisa JOHNSON
18 Director of Facilities Management ... Mr. Scott BITIKOFER
96 Assistant VP of Business Services ... Dr. Pat SCHOKNECHT
19 Director of Campus Safety ... Mr. Ken MILLER
29 Senior Director of Alumni Relations ... Ms. Caitlin HACKENBERG
44 Assistant VP of Development ... Ms. Amanda HOPKINS
102 Director of Foundation Relations ... Mr. Joseph MONTI
06 Director of Student Records ... Ms. Robin MATEO
40 Manager of Bookstore ... Ms. Mary VITELLI
04 Exec Assistant to the President ... Dr. Lorrie KYLE
23 Director of Wellness ... Ms. Connie BRISCOE
25 Director Contracts/Grants Admin ... Ms. Devon MASSOT
35 Asst VP Student Affairs/Community ... Ms. Michele MEYER

Saber College (I)

3990 West Flagler Street, Ste 103, Miami FL 33134
County: Miami-Dade FICE Identification: 036964
Unit ID: 449506
Telephone: (305) 443-9170 Carnegie Class: Not Classified
FAX Number: (305) 443-8441 Calendar System: Other
URL: www.sabercollege.com
Established: 1972 Annual Undergrad Tuition & Fees: $42,475
Enrollment: 600 Coed
Affiliation or Control: Independent Non-Profit IRS Status: 501(c)3
Highest Offering: Associate Degree
Program: Occupational
Accreditation: COE, @PTAA

01 Director ... Ms. Angela GAUD

St. John Vianney College Seminary (J)

2900 SW 87th Avenue, Miami FL 33165-3244
County: Miami-Dade FICE Identification: 008075
Unit ID: 137272
Telephone: (305) 223-4561 Carnegie Class: Spec/Faith
FAX Number: (305) 223-0650 Calendar System: Semester
URL: www.sjvcs.edu
Established: 1959 Annual Undergrad Tuition & Fees: $21,000
Enrollment: 110 Male
Affiliation or Control: Roman Catholic IRS Status: 501(c)3
Highest Offering: Baccalaureate
Program: Liberal Arts And General
Accreditation: SC

01 Rector & President ... RevMsg. Roberto GARZA
32 Vice Rector/Dean of Students ... Rev. Scott CIRCE
05 Academic Dean ... Dr. Ramon SANTOS
06 Registrar ... Mrs. Bonnie DE ANGULO
10 Controller ... Mr. Carlos CALMET
08 Head Librarian ... Mrs. Maria RODRIGUEZ
38 Director of Counseling ... Vacant
09 Institutional Research Director ... Dr. Jose ORTA
42 Spiritual Director ... Rev. Joseph KOTTOYIL

St. Johns River State College (K)

5001 St. Johns Avenue, Palatka FL 32177-3897
County: Putnam FICE Identification: 001523
Unit ID: 137281
Telephone: (386) 312-4200 Carnegie Class: Assoc/Pub-R-L
FAX Number: (386) 312-4229 Calendar System: Semester
URL: www.sjrstate.edu
Established: 1958 Annual Undergrad Tuition & Fees (In-District): $3,240
Enrollment: 7,114 Coed
Affiliation or Control: State/Local IRS Status: 501(c)3
Highest Offering: Baccalaureate
Program: Occupational; 2-Year Principally Bachelor's Creditable; Teacher Preparatory
Accreditation: SC, ADNUR, CAHIIM, COARC, NUR

01 President ... Mr. Joe PICKENS
03 Exec Vice President/General Counsel ... Dr. Melissa C. MILLER
32 Vice President Student Affairs ... Dr. Gilbert L. EVANS, JR.
05 VP & CAO/Exec Dir St Augustine ... Dr. Melanie A. BROWN
10 Vice President Finance & Admin/CFO ... Dr. Lynn POWERS
30 Vice Pres Develop/External Affairs ... Mrs. Caroline D. TINGLE
108 VP for Research & Inst Effective ... Dr. Rosalind M. HUMERICK
103 VP Workforce/Exec Dir Orange Park ... Dr. Anna M. LEBESCH
13 Chief Information Officer ... Mr. Paul M. HAWKINS
49 Dean of Arts & Sciences ... Dr. Laura L. BOILINI
88 Dean of Crim Justice/Public Safety ... Mr. Gary A. KILLAM
57 Dean of Florida School of the Arts ... Mr. Alain R. HENTSCHEL
08 Dean of Library Services ... Mrs. Carmen M. CUMMINGS
66 Dean Nursing ... Dr. Mary A. LANEY
88 Dean of Adult & Secondary Education ... Dr. Edward K. JORDAN
53 Dean of Teacher Education ... Dr. Myrna L. ALLEN
76 Associate Dean of Allied Health ... Dr. Holly COULLIETTE
88 Exec Director TH Center for the Art ... Mr. Denton J. YOCKEY
88 Director of Business Education ... Mr. Joel C. ABO
84 Director of Dual Enrollment ... Dr. Melissa PERRY
103 Director of Workforce Services ... Mrs. Melissa E. O'CONNELL
51 Dir of Cont/Community Education ... Mrs. Meghan DEPUTY
26 Director of Public Relations ... Mrs. Susan B. KESSLER
37 Dir of Financial Aid/Veterans' Affs ... Mr. Daniel BARKOWITZ
38 Dir of Counsel/Acad Advising ... Ms. Sara J. MYERS
88 Director of Testing & Stdnt Support ... Mr. Todd DIXON
07 Director of Admissions and Records ... Mrs. Susanne B. LINEBERGER
15 Dir of Benefits/Employee Relations ... Mrs. Ginger C. STOKES
21 Controller ... Mr. Randall PETERSON

Saint Leo University (L)

33701 State Road 52 W, Saint Leo FL 33574-6665
County: Pasco FICE Identification: 001526
Unit ID: 137032
Telephone: (352) 588-8200 Carnegie Class: Master's L
FAX Number: (352) 588-8654 Calendar System: Semester
URL: www.saintleo.edu
Established: 1889 Annual Undergrad Tuition & Fees: $20,520
Enrollment: 16,349 Coed
Affiliation or Control: Roman Catholic IRS Status: 501(c)3
Highest Offering: Doctorate
Program: Liberal Arts And General; Teacher Preparatory; Professional
Accreditation: SC, ACBSP, IACBE, SW

01 President ... Dr. William J. LENNOX, JR.
05 VP Academic Affairs ... Dr. Michael NASTANSKI
51 VP Continuing Ed/Student Services ... Dr. Edward DADEZ
84 VP Enrollment & Online Services ... Ms. Kathryn MCFARLAND
10 VP Business Affairs ... Mr. Eric WEEKES
30 VP University Advancement ... Mr. Denny MOLLER
04 Assistant to the President ... Ms. Molly-Dodd ADAMS
13 Assoc VP/CIO Univ Technology Svcs ... Mr. Steven CARROLL
20 Associate VP Academic Affairs ... Dr. Jeffrey ANDERSON
20 Assoc VP Learning & Innovation ... Dr. Jeff BORDEN
20 Asst VP SACSCOC Liaison Acad Affs ... Dr. Patricia PARRISH
108 Director Academic Assessment ... Dr. Robert LUCIO
51 Associate VP Continuing Education ... Dr. Beth CARTER
43 Assoc VP/Gen Counsel Business Affs ... Ms. Kelly HILL
84 Assistant VP Enrollment ... Mr. Reggie HILL
42 Asst to the Pres for Univ Ministry ... Fr. Stephan BROWN
32 Associate VP Student Affairs ... Mr. Kenneth POSNER
38 Director Counseling Services ... Mr. Lawson JOLLY
49 Dean School of Arts & Sciences ... Dr. Mary SPOTO
75 Dean School of Educ/Social Svcs ... Dr. Carol WALKER
50 Dean School of Business ... Dr. Balbir BAL
58 Asst Dean Grad Studies in Business ... Dr. Lorrie MCGOVERN
58 Dir Grad Studies in Crim Justice ... Dr. Robert DIEMER
58 Dir Grad Studies in Education ... Dr. Fern AEFSKY
58 Dir Grad Studies in Social Work ... Dr. Cindy LEE
58 Dir Graduate Studies in Theology ... Dr. Randall WOODARD
06 Registrar ... Mrs. Karen HATFIELD
08 Director Library Services ... Mr. Brent SHORT
07 Assoc VP of Enrollment/Support Svcs ... Mr. Jeffrey WALSH

88 Asst VP Instructional Technology .... Vacant
88 Dir Academic Student Support Svcs .... Dr. Joanne MACEACHRAN
39 Director of Residence Life .... Mr. Sean VAN GUILDER
11 Director Academic Administration .... Mr. Joseph TADEO
41 Director Athletics .... Mr. Francis REIDY
26 Assoc VP Marketing .... Mr. Edward AUSTIN
18 Director Plant Operations .... Mr. Jose CABAN
19 Director Campus Security & Safety ...... Mr. Vincent D'AMBROSIO
23 Director Health Services .... Ms. Teresa DADEZ
88 Asst Director Disability Services .... Ms. Christine GEORGALLIS
35 Asst VP for Student Affairs .... Ms. Ana DI DONATO
29 Director Alumni & Parent Relations .... Mr. Edmond KENNY
44 Exec Director Development .... Ms. Dawn PARISI
102 Grant & Stewardship Officer .... Ms. Victoria REECE
85 Director International Svcs .... Ms. Paige RAMSEY-HAMACHER
88 Interim Dir Veteran Services .... Mr. Tedd WEISER
15 Human Resources Director .... Vacant
36 Director of Career Planning .... Mr. Robert LIDDELL
21 Assoc VP Finance .... Mr. James DETUCCIO
96 Mgr Accounts Payable/Procurement .... Ms. Laura SOLBERG
12 Asst VP Continuing Ed Virginia .... Ms. Susan PAULSON
12 Asst VP Continuing Ed Central Reg .... Mr. Jack NUSSEN
12 Asst VP Continuing Ed Florida .... Mr. Stephen HESS
103 Director Professional Development .... Mr. Joseph ARNER
88 Director Dining Services .... Mr. Rich VOGEL
101 Senior Executive Assistant .... Ms. Marcia MALIA
37 Asst VP of Financial Aid .... Ms. Melinda CLARK
27 Director University Communication .... Ms. Lucia RAATMA

St. Petersburg College (A)

PO Box 13489, Saint Petersburg FL 33733-3489
County: Pinellas FICE Identification: 001528
Unit ID: 137078
Telephone: (727) 341-4772 Carnegie Class: Bac/Assoc
FAX Number: (727) 341-3318 Calendar System: Semester
URL: www.spcollege.edu
Established: 1927 Annual Undergrad Tuition & Fees (In-District): $3,353
Enrollment: 33,177 Coed
Affiliation or Control: Local IRS Status: 501(c)3
Highest Offering: Baccalaureate
Program: Occupational; 2-Year Principally Bachelor's Creditable; Teacher Preparatory; Professional
Accreditation: SC, ADNUR, CAHIIM, COARC, DH, EMT, FUSER, NURSE, OPE, PTAA, RAD

01 President .... Dr. William D. LAW
05 Sr VP Instruction/Academic Pgm .... Dr. Anne M. COOPER
32 Sr Vice Pres Student Affairs .... Dr. Tonjua L. WILLIAMS
10 Sr VP Admin/Bus Svcs & Info Tech .... Dr. Douglas S. DUNCAN
18 Assoc VP Facilities Plng/Inst Svcs .... James WAECHTER
15 Human Resources/Dir of Operations .... Desiree WORONER
30 VP Inst Advance/Exec Dir Foundation .... Frances NEU
45 Assoc VP Strategic Exec & Sys Sup .... Vacant
84 Assoc VP Enrollment Services .... Dr. Pat RINARD
37 Assoc VP Financial Asst Svcs .... Michael J. BENNETT
20 Assoc VP Academic Affs/Partnership .... Catherine C. KENNEDY
20 Assoc Provost .... Heather DISLER
26 Exec Dir Marketing/Public Info .... Diana SABINO
103 Director Workforce Services .... Dr. Jason KRUPP
43 Acting General Counsel .... Suzanne GARDNER
12 Provost Allstate Center .... Dr. Scott FRONRATH
12 Provost Clearwater Campus .... Dr. Stanley VITTETOE
12 Provost/Health Education Center .... Dr. Eric CARVER
12 Provost St Petersburg Campus .... Jamelle CONNER
12 Provost Seminole Campus/eCampus .... Mark STRICKLAND
12 Provost Tarpon Springs Campus .... Dr. Marvin BRIGHT
12 Provost Downtown Center .... Dr. Kevin GORDON
22 Dir Equal Access/Equal Opp/Title IX .... Pam SMITH
96 Dir Procurement & Asset Mgmt .... Paul SPINELLI
38 Dir Student Success .... Joe DVORACSEK
88 Dean College of Public Safety Admin .... Brian FRANK
88 Dean Col of Policy Ethics/Leg Stds .... Dr. Susan S. DEMERS
83 Dean Social & Behavioral Sciences .... Dr. Joseph SMILEY
88 Principal St Pete Collegiate High .... Starla METZ
88 President Faculty Senate .... Dr. Richard MERCADANTE
50 Dean College of Business .... Dr. Greg NENSTIEL
81 Dean Mathematics .... Mr. Jimmy CHANG
65 Dean Natural Science .... Dr. John CHAPIN
79 Dean Humanities/Fine Arts .... Dr. Jonathan STEELE
53 Dean College of Education .... Dr. Kimberly HARTMAN
60 Dean Communications .... Dr. Martha CAMPBELL
76 Dean College of Health Sciences .... Dr. Rebecca LUDWIG
74 Dean Sch of Veterinary Technology .... Dr. Richard FLORA
72 Dean College of Comp & Info Tech .... Dr. Sharon SETTERLIND
66 Dean College of Nursing .... Dr. Susan BAKER
08 Director Learning Resources .... Joseph LEOPOLD
04 Executive Admin Svcs Specialist .... Rebecca TURNER
07 Director of Admissions and Records .... Eva CHRISTENSEN
09 Director of Institutional Research .... Vacant
100 Chief of Staff .... Deborah BOYLE
104 Director International Programs .... Ramona KIRSCH
106 Associate VP Online Learning/Svcs .... Dr. Susan COLARIC
108 Director Assessment .... Magaly TYMMS
13 Senior Director Enterprise Systems .... Zoran STANISIC
19 Director College Security Services .... Daniel BARTO
25 Exec Dir of Grants Development .... Jackie SKRYD
86 Director Government Relations .... Edward W. WOODRUFF, JR.

St. Thomas University (B)

16401 NW 37th Avenue, Miami Gardens FL 33054-6498
County: Miami-Dade FICE Identification: 001468
Unit ID: 137476
Telephone: (305) 625-6000 Carnegie Class: Master's L
FAX Number: (305) 628-6510 Calendar System: Semester
URL: www.stu.edu
Established: 1961 Annual Undergrad Tuition & Fees: $28,710
Enrollment: 2,220 Coed
Affiliation or Control: Roman Catholic IRS Status: 501(c)3
Highest Offering: Doctorate
Program: Liberal Arts And General; Teacher Preparatory; Professional
Accreditation: SC, LAW

01 President .... Msgr. Franklyn M. CASALE
05 Provost & Chief Academic Officer .... Dr. Irma BECERRA
10 VP Administration/Chief Exec Ofcr ..... Mr. Terrence L. O'CONNER
61 Dean of Law School .... Mr. Alfredo GARCIA
30 Vice Pres University Advancement .... Ms. Hilda FERNANDEZ
45 Vice Pres for Planning & Enrollment .... Vacant
20 Associate Provost .... Dr. Susan ANGULO
84 Dean Enrollment .... Mr. Celso ALVAREZ
26 Chief Marketing Officer .... Ms. Marivi PRADO
06 Executive Associate Registrar .... Mrs. Maria ABDEL
37 Assoc Director Financial Aid .... Ms. Yaidany RIVERO
08 University Librarian .... Mr. Lawrence TREADWELL, IV
21 Controller .... Mrs. Maribel SMITH
18 Director Facilities/Physical Plant .... Mr. Juan M. ZAMORA
09 Director Institutional Research .... Dr. Jerry WEINBERG
88 Assoc Dir Emergency/Risk Management .. Ms. Monique BRIJBASI
41 Athletic Director .... Mrs. Laura J. COURTLEY-TODD
07 Director of Admissions .... Mr. Celso J. ALVAREZ
32 Dean of Students .... Vacant
15 Assoc Director Human Resources .... Ms. Lenore M. PRADO
25 Director for Prospect Research .... Ms. Jacqueline HOUSE
38 Assoc Director Health & Wellness .... Vacant
73 Dean School of Theology .... RevMsg. Terrance E. HOGAN
12 Dean Biscayne College .... Vacant
13 Chief Information Officer .... Mr. Rudy IBARRA
29 Director Alumni Affairs .... Ms. Yisel CABRERA
44 Director Annual Giving .... Vacant
11 Director for Administration .... Mrs. Sylvia L. RODRIGUEZ

St. Vincent De Paul Regional Seminary (C)

10701 S Military Trail, Boynton Beach FL 33436-4899
County: Palm Beach FICE Identification: 008223
Unit ID: 136701
Telephone: (561) 732-4424 Carnegie Class: Spec/Faith
FAX Number: (561) 737-2205 Calendar System: Semester
URL: www.svdp.edu
Established: 1963 Annual Graduate Tuition & Fees: $32,000
Enrollment: 131 Coed
Affiliation or Control: Roman Catholic IRS Status: 501(c)3
Highest Offering: Master's; No Undergraduates
Program: Religious Emphasis
Accreditation: SC, THEOL

01 Rector/President .... Rev. David L. TOUPS
03 Vice Rector .... Rev. Remek BLASZKOWSKI
05 Academic Dean .... Rev. Alfredo HERNANDEZ
10 Treasurer .... Mr. Keith PARKER
08 Director of the Library .... Mr. Arthur QUINN
04 Administrative Asst to President .... Mrs. Herminia C. GARCIA
09 Dir Inst Research/Assessment .... Dr. Mary FROEHLE
30 Chief Development/Advancement .... Ms. Daniella COY
06 Registrar .... Mrs. Alicia RUEFF

San Ignacio College (D)

10395 NW 41st St, Ste 125, Doral FL 33178
County: Miami-Dade Identification: 667130
Telephone: (305) 629-2929 Carnegie Class: Not Classified
FAX Number: (305) 629-2910 Calendar System: Semester
URL: www.sanignaciocollege.edu
Established: 2007 Annual Undergrad Tuition & Fees: $10,300
Enrollment: 12 Coed
Affiliation or Control: Proprietary IRS Status: Proprietary
Highest Offering: Baccalaureate
Program: Occupational; 2-Year Principally Bachelor's Creditable
Accreditation: ACICS

01 President .... Luciana DE LA FUENTE
03 Executive Vice President .... Ezer TOSSAS
05 Chief Academic Officer .... Michael FLORES
06 Registrar .... Oscar CABRERA
08 Head Librarian .... Silvia LOPEZ
15 Human Resources Director .... Ligia BARROS
37 Director Student Financial Aid .... Elba CASTANOS

Sanford-Brown College Tampa (E)

3725 West Grace Street, Tampa FL 33607
County: Hillsborough FICE Identification: 030314
Unit ID: 134680
Telephone: (813) 881-0007 Carnegie Class: Spec/Arts
FAX Number: (813) 884-9327 Calendar System: Quarter
URL: www.sanfordbrown.edu/tampa
Established: 1984 Annual Undergrad Tuition & Fees: $13,736
Enrollment: 426 Coed
Affiliation or Control: Proprietary IRS Status: Proprietary
Highest Offering: Baccalaureate
Program: Fine Arts Emphasis
Accreditation: ACICS, CIDA, CVT

01 President .... Dr. Robert SWAIN
05 Dean .... Phil BULONE
36 Director of Career Services .... Matchez CHERSILS
08 Learning Resource Center Coord .... Vashba GREEN

† School is in teach-out plan through late 2016.

Sanford-Brown Institute (F)

1201 W Cypress Creek Road, Ste 101,
Fort Lauderdale FL 33309
Telephone: (954) 308-7400 Identification: 667031
Accreditation: ACICS, CVT, DH

† Branch campus of Sanford-Brown College, Atlanta, GA. School is in teach-out plan.

Sanford-Brown Institute (G)

10255 Fortune Parkway, Suite #501,
Jacksonville FL 32256-0757
County: Duval FICE Identification: 026164
Unit ID: 404505
Telephone: (904) 363-6221 Carnegie Class: Assoc/PrivFP
FAX Number: (904) 363-6824 Calendar System: Other
URL: www.sanfordbrown.edu/Jacksonville
Established: 1977 Annual Undergrad Tuition & Fees: $15,111
Enrollment: 340 Coed
Affiliation or Control: Proprietary IRS Status: Proprietary
Highest Offering: Associate Degree
Program: Occupational
Accreditation: ACICS, CVT, DH

01 President .... Mr. Ben SEDRINE
05 Director of Education .... Ms. Jennifer MULLINGS

† School is in teach-out plan.

Santa Fe College (H)

3000 NW 83rd Street, Gainesville FL 32606-6200
County: Alachua FICE Identification: 001519
Unit ID: 137096
Telephone: (352) 395-5000 Carnegie Class: Assoc/Pub-R-L
FAX Number: (352) 395-5581 Calendar System: Semester
URL: www.sfcollege.edu
Established: 1965 Annual Undergrad Tuition & Fees (In-District): $3,174
Enrollment: 16,273 Coed
Affiliation or Control: Local IRS Status: 501(c)3
Highest Offering: Baccalaureate
Program: Occupational; 2-Year Principally Bachelor's Creditable
Accreditation: SC, ADNUR, CAHIIM, COARC, CONST, CVT, DA, DH, DMS, EMT, MT, NMT, NURSE, POLYT, RAD, SURGT

01 President .... Dr. Jackson N. SASSER
05 Provost/Vice Pres Academic Affairs .... Dr. Edward BONAHUE
10 Chief Financial Ofcr/VP Admin Affs .... Ms. Ginger GIBSON
32 Vice President Student Affairs .... Dr. Naima BROWN
30 Vice President Development .... Mr. Chuck CLEMONS
108 VP Assessment/Research/Technology .... Dr. Lisa ARMOUR
04 Assistant to the President .... Ms. Cathy KEEN
20 Associate VP Academic Affairs .... Dr. Jodi LONG
13 Assoc VP Information Tech Services .... Mr. Bill PENNEY
18 Assoc VP Facilities Services .... Vacant
35 Assoc VP Student Affs/Financial Aid .... Dr. Dan RODKIN
88 Assoc Vice Pres Educational Centers .... Dr. Cheryl CALHOUN
25 Asst VP/Development/Grants/Projects .... Vacant
20 Assoc Vice Pres Academic Affairs .... Dr. Stefanie WASCHULL
35 Asst Vice Pres Student Affairs .... Dr. Beatrice AWONIYI
43 Legal Counsel .... Ms. Patti P. LOCASCIO
06 College Registrar .... Mr. Mike HUTLEY
88 Dir High Sch Dual Enrollment Pgm .... Ms. Jennifer HOMARD
88 Director Advisement Center ...... Ms. Kimberly FUGATE-ROBERTS
41 Athletic Director .... Mr. Jim KEITES
08 Director Library Service .... Ms. Myra STERRETT
19 Director Institute of Public Safety .... Mr. Tom ACKERMAN
35 Director of Student Life .... Dr. Tracey REEVES
96 Director of Purchasing .... Mr. David SHLAFER
28 Director of Diversity .... Ms. Elizabeth O'REGGIO
37 Int Director Student Financial Aid .... Ms. Kamia MWANGO
15 Director Human Resources .... Ms. Lela FRYE
09 Director of Institutional Research .... Mr. Gary HARTGE
07 Coordinator for Admissions .... Ms. Gayle JONES
26 Chief Public Relations/Marketing .... Mr. John CARMEAN

Schiller International University (I)

8560 Ulmerton Road, Largo FL 33771
County: Pinellas FICE Identification: 023141
Unit ID: 404338
Telephone: (727) 736-5082 Carnegie Class: Spec/Bus
FAX Number: (727) 734-0359 Calendar System: Semester
URL: www.schiller.edu
Established: 1964 Annual Undergrad Tuition & Fees: $21,540
Enrollment: 50 Coed
Affiliation or Control: Proprietary IRS Status: Proprietary
Highest Offering: Master's
Program: Occupational; Liberal Arts And General; Business Emphasis
Accreditation: ACICS

01 Campus Director .... Mr. Fabian FERNANDEZ
05 Provost .... Dr. Andrea BRZENIK
07 Director of Admissions .... Mr. Keith TOMLINSON

Seminole State College of Florida (A)

100 Weldon Boulevard, Sanford FL 32773-6199
County: Seminole FICE Identification: 001520
Unit ID: 137209
Telephone: (407) 708-4722 Carnegie Class: Assoc/Pub-S-SC
FAX Number: (407) 708-2139 Calendar System: Semester
URL: www.seminolestate.edu
Established: 1965 Annual Undergrad Tuition & Fees (In-District): $3,131
Enrollment: 18,411 Coed
Affiliation or Control: Local IRS Status: 501(c)3
Highest Offering: Baccalaureate
Program: Occupational; 2-Year Principally Bachelor's Creditable; Professional
Accreditation: SC, ADNUR, CAHIIM, COARC, EMT, PTAA

01 President .... Dr. E. Ann MCGEE
10 Executive VP/CFO .... Dr. Joseph SARNOVSKY
05 VP Academic Affairs/CAO .... Dr. Laura ROSS
32 VP Student Affairs/CSAO .... Vacant
13 VP Information Resources/CIO .... Dr. Dick T. HAMANN
102 Executive Director Foundation .... Dr. John GYLLIN
21 AVP Finance & Budget .... Ms. Judi COOPER
30 AVP Student Development .... Dr. Jan LLOYD
12 Dean of Students Altamonte Springs .... Ms. Lynn GARRETT
12 Dean of Students Oviedo Campus .... Mr. Randy PAWLOWSKI
08 Dean Learning Resources .... Dr. Erika WAYNE
36 AVP Career Programs .... Dr. Angela M. KERSENBROCK
54 Dean Engineering and Design .... Mr. Michael STALEY
51 Dean Academic Foundations .... Dr. Terri DANIELS
26 Dir College & Community Relations .... Ms. Deborah RICHARD
86 Director Government Relations .... Vacant
91 Director Networks .... Mr. Julio VALENTIN
38 Director Counseling and Advising .... Ms. Deborah LYNCH
20 Director Curriculum .... Ms. Carlene MCNEIL
15 AVP Human Resources .... Ms. Mae KLINE
07 Dir Enrollment Svcs/Registrar .... Ms. Kathy VOUDRY
37 Director Student Financial Aid .... Ms. Roseann AMATO
09 AVP Institutional Effectiveness .... Dr. Mark MORGAN
41 Director Intercollegiate Athletics .... Mr. John SCARPINO
84 AVP Student Recruitment .... Mrs. Pamela MENNECHEY
36 Director Career Development .... Ms. Heather ENGELKING
14 AVP Information Technology .... Ms. Pilar ACOSTA
106 Dir Online Education/E-learning .... Dr. Christine BROEKER
28 Director of Diversity .... Ms. Janet BALANOFF

South Florida Bible College (B)

1100 South Federal Highway, Deerfield Beach FL 33441
County: Broward FICE Identification: 032643
Unit ID: 366003
Telephone: (954) 545-4500 Carnegie Class: Spec/Faith
FAX Number: (954) 719-3780 Calendar System: Semester
URL: www.sfbc.edu
Established: 1985 Annual Undergrad Tuition & Fees: $6,300
Enrollment: 145 Coed
Affiliation or Control: Interdenominational IRS Status: 501(c)3
Highest Offering: Master's
Program: Professional; Religious Emphasis
Accreditation: BI

01 President .... Dr. Joseph GUADAGNINO
03 Senior Vice President .... Mary A. DRABIK
05 Chief Academic Officer .... Dr. John STEVENSON
10 Chief Financial Officer .... Zil WENCESLAU
06 Registrar .... Tom DRABIK
08 Librarian .... Paula STEVENSON
20 Dean of Faculty .... Dr. Esa AUTERO
32 Dean of Students .... Carol RICHARDSON
29 Director Alumni Relations .... George T. SHARP
84 Director Enrollment Management .... John MEZZACAPPA
108 Director Institutional Assessment .... Josiah STEPHAN
13 Chief Info Technology Officer (CIO) .... Joshua DRABIK
30 Chief Development/Advancement .... Wayne RICHARDSON

South Florida State College (C)

600 W College Drive, Avon Park FL 33825-9399
County: Highlands FICE Identification: 001522
Unit ID: 137315
Telephone: (863) 453-6661 Carnegie Class: Assoc/Pub-R-M
FAX Number: (863) 453-0165 Calendar System: Trimester
URL: www.southflorida.edu
Established: 1965 Annual Undergrad Tuition & Fees (In-District): $2,958
Enrollment: 2,799 Coed
Affiliation or Control: Local IRS Status: 501(c)3
Highest Offering: Baccalaureate
Program: Occupational; 2-Year Principally Bachelor's Creditable
Accreditation: SC, ADNUR, DA, DH, EMT, RAD

01 President .... Dr. Thomas C. LEITZEL
05 Vice Pres Educational/Stdnt Svcs .... Dr. Sidney VALENTINE
10 Controller .... Mrs. Anita A. KOVACS
11 Vice Pres Administrative Services .... Mr. Glenn W. LITTLE
20 Dean Academic Support .... Dr. Michael MCLEOD
75 Dean Applied Science & Tech .... Mr. J. Kevin BROWN
49 Dean Arts & Sciences .... Dr. Kimberly BATTY-HERBERT
88 Director Cultural Programs .... Ms. Cynthia GARREN
45 Dean Resource Development .... Mrs. Jamie BATEMAN
32 Dean Student Services .... Dr. Timothy WISE
12 Director DeSoto Campus .... Mrs. Suzanne DEMERS
12 Director Hardee Campus .... Ms. Teresa CRAWFORD
12 Director Lake Placid Center .... Mr. Randall K. PAEPLOW
26 Director Community Relations .... Ms. Deborah LATTER
106 Director eLearning .... Mrs. Melanie M. JACKSON
15 Director Human Res/EA-EO & ADA Ofcr .... Mrs. Susie HALE
18 Dir Remodeling/Reno & Maint .... Mr. Robert E. FLORES
06 Registrar .... Dr. Deborah M. FUSCHETTI
41 Athletic Director .... Mr. Richard J. HITT
36 Director Career Development Center .... Mrs. Colleen RAFATTI
37 Director Financial Aid .... Mr. Jerry DONNA
13 Chief Information Officer .... Dr. Christopher VAN DER KAAY
38 Chair Counseling .... Mrs. Charla ELLERKER
08 Library Services .... Ms. Lena PHELPS
96 Coordinator Purchasing .... Mrs. Deborah OLSON
07 Director of Admissions .... Ms. Lynn HINTZ
76 Dean Division of Health Services .... Mrs. Rebecca SRODA

South University (D)

9801 Belevedere Road, Royal Palm Beach FL 33411
Telephone: (561) 273-6500 Identification: 666117
Accreditation: &SC, ACBSP, CACREP, NURSE, OTA, PTAA

† Regional accreditation is carried under the parent institution in Savannah, GA.

South University (E)

4401 North Himes Ave Ste 175, Tampa FL 33614-7095
Telephone: (813) 393-3800 Identification: 770913
Accreditation: &SC, ACBSP, ARCPA, NURSE, OTA, PTAA

† Branch campus of South University, Savannah, GA.

Southeastern College (F)

6700 South Point Pkwy, Ste 400, Jacksonville FL 32216
County: Duval FICE Identification: 035533
Unit ID: 443270
Telephone: (904) 448-9499 Carnegie Class: Assoc/PrivFP
FAX Number: (904) 448-9270 Calendar System: Other
URL: www.sec.edu
Established: 1988 Annual Undergrad Tuition & Fees: $16,856
Enrollment: 173 Coed
Affiliation or Control: Proprietary IRS Status: Proprietary
Highest Offering: Associate Degree
Program: Occupational
Accreditation: ACCSC, SURTEC

01 Campus Vice President .... Mr. Shawn HUMPHREY

Southeastern College (G)

17395 NW 59th Avenue, Miami Lakes FL 33015-5111
Telephone: (305) 820-5003 Identification: 666290
Accreditation: ACCSC, MAAB, SURGT

† Branch campus of Southeastern College, Greenacres, FL.

Southeastern College (H)

6014 Hwy 19 North, Suite 250, New Port Richey FL 34652
Telephone: (727) 487-6855 Identification: 770568
Accreditation: ACCSC, DMS

† Branch campus of Southeastern College, West Palm Beach, FL.

Southeastern College (I)

5225 Memorial Highway, Tampa FL 33634
Telephone: (813) 961-2837 Identification: 770569
Accreditation: ACCSC

† Branch campus of Southeastern College, West Palm Beach, FL.

Southeastern College (J)

2081 Vista Parkway, Suite 100B, West Palm Beach FL 33411
County: Palm Beach FICE Identification: 031239
Unit ID: 428170
Telephone: (561) 433-2330 Carnegie Class: Not Classified
FAX Number: (561) 433-9025 Calendar System: Other
URL: www.sec.edu
Established: 1988 Annual Undergrad Tuition & Fees: $16,204
Enrollment: 1,157 Coed
Affiliation or Control: Proprietary IRS Status: Proprietary
Highest Offering: Associate Degree
Program: Occupational
Accreditation: ACCSC, MAAB, SURGT

01 Vice President .... Mr. Robert KEISER

Southeastern University (K)

1000 Longfellow Boulevard, Lakeland FL 33801-6099
County: Polk FICE Identification: 001521
Unit ID: 137564
Telephone: (863) 667-5000 Carnegie Class: Bac/Diverse
FAX Number: (863) 667-5200 Calendar System: Semester
URL: www.seu.edu
Established: 1935 Annual Undergrad Tuition & Fees: $22,840
Enrollment: 3,834 Coed
Affiliation or Control: Assemblies Of God Church IRS Status: 501(c)3
Highest Offering: Doctorate
Program: Liberal Arts And General; Teacher Preparatory; Religious Emphasis
Accreditation: SC, ACBSP, SW

01 President .... Dr. Kent INGLE
03 Executive Vice President .... Dr. Brian CARROLL
05 Provost .... Dr. William C. HACKET, JR.
32 VP for Student Development .... Mr. James (Chris) OWEN
84 VP for Enrollment Management .... Mr. Roy ROWLAND, IV
09 VP for Institutional Research & EE .... Dr. Andrew H. PERMENTER
08 Dean of Library Services .... Mrs. Grace VEACH
06 Dir Student Records/Registrar .... Mrs. Linda M. KELSO
37 Exec Dir Student Financial Services .... Ms. Rebekah BURDICK
88 Director of Hispanic Learning Ctr .... Ms. Betania TORRES
07 Director of Admissions .... Mrs. Sarah E. CLARK
15 Director Human Resources .... Ms. Betty KELLEY
26 Director External Relations .... Mr. Edward L. MANER
18 Exec Dir Facilities/Physical Plant .... Mr. Norman M. ALDERMAN
20 Director of Academic Services .... Mrs. Ramona CARROLL
36 Director of Career Services .... Mrs. Pamela CROSBY
10 Exec Director of Finance .... Mr. Frederick S. GORE
84 Director Enrollment Marketing .... Mr. Brandt MERRITT
38 Director Student Counseling .... Mr. Donald ENGLISH
88 Exec Dir of Inst Effectiveness .... Mr. Andrew MILLER
13 Chief Info Technology Officer (CIO) .... Mr. Jerry RAINS
19 Director Security/Safety .... Mr. Richard DAVIS

Southern Technical College (L)

1685 Medical Lane, Fort Myers FL 33907-1158
County: Lee FICE Identification: 022788
Unit ID: 366553
Telephone: (239) 939-4766 Carnegie Class: Bac/Assoc
FAX Number: (239) 790-2118 Calendar System: Quarter
URL: www.southerntech.edu
Established: 1974 Annual Undergrad Tuition & Fees: $13,860
Enrollment: 1,259 Coed
Affiliation or Control: Proprietary IRS Status: Proprietary
Highest Offering: Baccalaureate
Program: Occupational; 2-Year Principally Bachelor's Creditable; Teacher Preparatory; Professional; Business Emphasis
Accreditation: ACICS, CAHIIM, MAAB, SURTEC

01 President .... Mr. Pedro DEGUZMAN
05 VP of Academic Affairs .... Ms. Ilia MATOS

Southern Technical College (M)

2910 South Orlando Drive, Sanford FL 32773
County: Seminole FICE Identification: 039035
Unit ID: 446552
Telephone: (407) 323-4141 Carnegie Class: Assoc/PrivFP
FAX Number: (407) 323-4221 Calendar System: Semester
URL: www.southerntech.edu
Established: 1956 Annual Undergrad Tuition & Fees: $32,910
Enrollment: 1,404 Coed
Affiliation or Control: Proprietary IRS Status: Proprietary
Highest Offering: Associate Degree
Program: Occupational
Accreditation: ACICS

01 Dean .... Mr. David BRAME

Southern Technical College-Auburndale (N)

298 Havendale Boulevard, Auburndale FL 33823
Telephone: (407) 438-6000 Identification: 770705
Accreditation: ACICS

† Branch campus of Southern Technical College, Sanford, FL.

Southern Technical College-Brandon (O)

608 E Bloomingdale Avenue, Brandon FL 33511
Telephone: (813) 654-8800 Identification: 770707
Accreditation: ACICS

† Branch campus of Southern Technical College, Sanford, FL.

Southern Technical College-Mount Dora (P)

2799 W Old US Highway 441, Mount Dora FL 32757
Telephone: (352) 383-4242 Identification: 770706
Accreditation: ACICS

† Branch campus of Southern Technical College, Sanford, FL.

Southern Technical College-Orlando (Q)

1485 Florida Mall Avenue, Orlando FL 32809
Telephone: (407) 438-6000 Identification: 770704
Accreditation: ACICS

† Branch campus of Southern Technical College, Sanford, FL.

Southern Technical College-Port Charlotte (R)

950 Tamiami Trail, Unit 109, Port Charlotte FL 33953
Telephone: (239) 274-5860 Identification: 770709
Accreditation: ACICS, MAAB, SURTEC

† Branch campus of Southern Technical College, Fort Myers, FL.

Southern Technical College-Tampa (A)

3910 RIGA Boulevard, Tampa FL 33619-1269
Telephone: (813) 630-4401 Identification: 770708
Accreditation: ACICS, MAAB, SURTEC

† Branch campus of Southern Technical College, Fort Myers, FL.

State College of Florida, Manatee-Sarasota (B)

PO Box 1849, Bradenton FL 34206-7046
County: Manatee FICE Identification: 001504
Unit ID: 135391
Telephone: (941) 752-5000 Carnegie Class: Assoc/Pub-U-MC
FAX Number: (941) 758-6830 Calendar System: Semester
URL: www.scf.edu
Established: 1957 Annual Undergrad Tuition & Fees (In-District): $3,074
Enrollment: 10,314 Coed
Affiliation or Control: Local IRS Status: 501(c)3
Highest Offering: Baccalaureate
Program: Occupational; 2-Year Principally Bachelor's Creditable
Accreditation: SC, ADNUR, DH, NUR, OTA, PTAA, RAD

01 President ...... Dr. Carol F. PROBSTFELD
04 Exec Assistant to President ...... Ms. Susan MARROCCO
10 VP Business/Admin Services ...... Ms. Julie JAKWAY
05 VP Academic Affairs ...... Mr. Gary T. RUSSELL
32 VP Student Affairs ...... Dr. Donald R. BOWMAN
46 VP Strategic Initiatives ...... Dr. Michael J. MEARS
12 Venice Campus Executive Officer ...... Ms. Darlene WEDLER-JOHNSON
102 Executive Director SCF Foundation ...... Ms. Cassandra HOLMES
21 Assoc VP Finance ...... Ms. Karen A. KESTER
38 Assoc VP Student Development ...... Ms. Lynn DREES
35 Assoc VP Student Services ...... Ms. MariLynn J. LEWY
31 Assoc VP Corporate & Community Dev ...... Ms. Daisy VULOVICH
45 Assoc VP Planning & Inst Effect ...... Mr. Bradley W. DAVIS
18 Director Facilities Manager ...... Mr. Chris WELLMAN
103 Director Workforce Services ...... Ms. Lee KOTWICKI
21 Director Business Services ...... Mr. Josef RILL
22 Equity Officer ...... Ms. Gloria TRACY
08 Director Library Services ...... Ms. Tracy ELLIOTT
09 Director Institutional Research ...... Ms. Su-hua MEN
13 Chief Information Officer ...... Mr. Feng HOU
37 Director Financial Aid ...... Ms. Sandra SHIMP
07 Director of Admissions ...... Ms. Stacey SHARPLES
36 Director Career Resource Center ...... Ms. Denise D. GATCH
41 Director Athletics ...... Mr. Matt ENNIS
88 Director Academic Resource Center ...... Ms. Jaquelyn MCNEIL
43 General Counsel ...... Mr. Steve PROUTY
88 Head of SCF Collegiate School ...... Ms. Kelly MONOD
106 Director Online Learning ...... Mr. Gary BAKER

*State University System of Florida, Board of Governors (C)

325 W Gaines Street, Suite 1614, Tallahassee FL 32399-0400
County: Leon FICE Identification: 008068
Unit ID: 137449
Telephone: (850) 245-0466 Carnegie Class: N/A
FAX Number: (850) 245-9685
URL: www.flbog.edu

01 Chancellor ...... Mr. Marshall M. CRISER, III
05 Vice Chanc Academic/Student Affairs ...... Dr. Jan IGNASH
10 Vice Chanc Budget & Finance ...... Mr. Tim JONES
43 General Counsel ...... Ms. Vikki SHIRLEY
22 Inspector General & Compliance ...... Mr. Joseph MALESZEWSKI
101 Corporate Secretary ...... Ms. Vikki SHIRLEY
86 Assoc Vice Chanc Govt Relations ...... Vacant
04 Assistant to the Chancellor ...... Ms. Shannon M. MCDERMOTT
26 Director of Communications ...... Ms. Brittany DAVIS
13 Chief Info Technology Officer (CIO) ...... Mr. Gene KOVACS
15 Director Personnel Services ...... Ms. Sandy RADULSKI
18 Chief Facilities/Physical Plant ...... Mr. Chris KINSLEY

*Florida Agricultural and Mechanical University (D)

1601 S. Martin Luther King Jr. Blvd, Tallahassee FL 32307
County: Leon FICE Identification: 001480
Unit ID: 133650
Telephone: (850) 599-3000 Carnegie Class: DRU
FAX Number: (850) 599-3952 Calendar System: Semester
URL: www.famu.edu
Established: 1887 Annual Undergrad Tuition & Fees (In-State): $5,785
Enrollment: 10,241 Coed
Affiliation or Control: State IRS Status: 501(c)3
Highest Offering: Doctorate
Program: Occupational; Liberal Arts And General; Teacher Preparatory; Professional; Technical Emphasis
Accreditation: SC, ACBSP, CAHIIM, COARC, CS, ENG, ENGT, JOUR, LAW, NUR, OT, PH, PHAR, PTA, SW, TED

02 President (Chief Executive Officer) ...... Dr. Elmira MANGUM
05 Provost/Vice Pres Academic Affs ...... Ms. Marcella DAVID
10 Vice Pres Finance & Administration ...... Mr. Dale CASSIDY
32 Vice Pres Student Affairs ...... Dr. William HUDSON, JR.
30 Vice Pres University Advancement ...... Mr. George COTTON
25 Vice Pres for Research ...... Dr. Timothy E. MOORE
88 VP Audit and Compliance ...... Mr. Richard GIVENS
13 Assoc Vice Pres/CIO Enterprise Tech ...... Mr. David CANTRELL
35 Assoc Vice Pres Student Affairs ...... Dr. Angela COLEMAN
44 Assoc VP for University Development ...... Ms. Angela POOLE
06 University Registrar ...... Dr. Agatha ONWUNLI
43 VP for Legal Affs & General Counsel ...... Atty. Avery MCKNIGHT
07 Director of Admissions ...... Ms. Barbara COX
08 Director of University Libraries ...... Ms. Faye WATKINS
37 Director of Financial Aid ...... Ms. Lisa STEWART
36 Director of The Career Center ...... Dr. Delores DEAN
09 Director of Institutional Research ...... Dr. Kwadwo OWUSU-ADUEMIRI
28 Director of EEO ...... Ms. Carrie GAVIN
26 VP Communications and External Rels ...... Mr. Jimmy MILLER
21 University Controller ...... Vacant
15 Assistant VP for Human Resources ...... Ms. Joyce A. INGRAM
29 Director of Alumni Affairs ...... Ms. Carmen CUMMINGS
51 Director of Continuing Education ...... Ms. Phyllis WATSON
50 Dean of Business and Industry ...... Dr. Shawnta FRIDAY-STROUD
66 Dean of Nursing ...... Dr. Ruena NORMAN
67 Dean of Pharmacy ...... Dr. Michael THOMPSON
53 Interim Dean of Education ...... Dr. Patricia GREEN POWELL
72 Dean College of Science & Tech ...... Dr. Maurice EDINGTON
48 Dean of Architecture ...... Mr. Rodner WRIGHT
60 Dean of Journalism ...... Dr. Ann KIMBROUGH
58 Interim Dean of Graduate Studies ...... Dr. Verian THOMAS
76 Dean of Allied Health Sciences ...... Dr. Cynthia HUGHES HARRIS
54 Interim Dean FAMU/FSU Engineering ...... Dr. Bruce LOCKE
61 Interim Dean College of Law ...... Mr. Darryll JONES
83 Dean Soc Sci/Arts/Humanities ...... Dr. Valencia E. MATTHEWS
19 Chief of Police/Dir Public Safety ...... Mr. Terence CALLOWAY
23 Director of Student Health Services ...... Ms. Tanya TATUM
41 Director of Athletics ...... Mr. Milton OVERTON
38 Director Counseling Services ...... Dr. Yolanda BOGAN
96 Director of Purchasing ...... Ms. Stephany FALL
04 Assistant to the President ...... Ms. Jacqueline HIGHTOWER
88 Dean of School of the Environment ...... Dr. Victor IBEANUSI
86 Director of Governmental Relations ...... Mr. Tola THOMPSON
47 Dean College of Agri/Food Science ...... Dr. Robert TAYLOR
100 Special Assistant to the President ...... Mr. Funmi OJETAYO
102 Dir Foundation/Corporate Relations ...... Mr. George COTTON
39 Director Student Housing ...... Mr. Oscar CRUMITY

*Florida Atlantic University (E)

PO Box 3091, 777 Glades Road, Boca Raton FL 33431-0991
County: Palm Beach FICE Identification: 001481
Unit ID: 133669
Telephone: (561) 297-3000 Carnegie Class: RU/H
FAX Number: (561) 297-3942 Calendar System: Semester
URL: www.fau.edu
Established: 1961 Annual Undergrad Tuition & Fees (In-State): $5,432
Enrollment: 30,381 Coed
Affiliation or Control: State IRS Status: 501(c)3
Highest Offering: Doctorate
Program: Liberal Arts And General; Teacher Preparatory; Professional
Accreditation: SC, BUS, CACREP, CORE, CS, ENG, MED, MUS, NURSE, PLNG, SP, SPAA, SW, TED

02 President ...... Dr. John KELLY
05 Provost/VP Academic Affairs ...... Dr. Gary W. PERRY
10 VP Finance/Chief Fiscal Officer ...... Ms. Dororthy RUSSELL
32 Vice Pres Student Affairs ...... Dr. Corey KING
46 Vice President Research ...... Dr. Daniel FLYNN
11 VP Admin Affairs ...... Ms. Stacy VOLNICK
102 Int VP Cmty Engag/Exec Dir FAU Fdn ...... Ms. Joanne DAVIS
13 Assoc Provost IT/CIO ...... Mr. Jason BALL
29 Asst Vice Pres Alumni Relations ...... Mr. Bradford W. CREWS
35 Assoc Dean Student Affairs ...... Mr. Terry MENA
43 General Counsel ...... Mr. David KIAN
22 Exec Dir Equity/Inclusion/Compl ...... Mr. Ande DUROJAIYE
84 Asst Provost Enrollment Mgmt ...... Ms. Tracy BOULUKOS
63 Dean C E Schmidt Col of Medicine ...... Dr. David J. BJORKMAN
20 Vice Provost ...... Dr. Diane ALPERIN
80 Int Dean of Design/Social Inquiry ...... Dr. Wesley E. HAWKINS
49 Dean of Arts & Letters ...... Dr. Heather COLTMAN
50 Dean of Business ...... Dr. Daniel GROPPER
53 Dean of Education ...... Dr. Valerie BRISTOR
54 Dean of Engineering/Comp Sci ...... Dr. Mohammad ILYAS
66 Dean of Nursing ...... Dr. Marlaine SMITH
92 Dean of Honors College ...... Dr. Jeff BULLER
20 Dean Undergraduate Studies ...... Dr. Edward E. PRATT
81 Int Dean College of Science ...... Dr. Janet BLANKS
58 Dean of Graduate Studies ...... Dr. Deborah FLOYD
88 Asst Dean/PK-12 Sch/Educational Pgm ...... Mr. Joel HERBST
90 Director Enterprise Computing Svcs ...... Mr. Mehran BASIRATMAND
91 Dir Univ Administrative Systems ...... Ms. Kay RECKTENWALD
25 Int Dir Sponsored Programs ...... Ms. Camille COLEY
09 Director Inst Effective/Analysis ...... Vacant
06 Interim Registrar ...... Mr. Jeffrey HENDRICKS
08 Dean University Libraries ...... Ms. Carol HIXSON
15 Asst Vice Pres Human Resources ...... Mr. David TOMANIO
41 Vice Pres for Athletics ...... Mr. Patrick CHUN
39 Exec Director Student Housing ...... Dr. Larry FAERMAN
36 Dir Career Devel Ctr/Student Place ...... Ms. Sandra JAKUBOW
85 Director Intl Students/Scholar Svcs ...... Dr. Mihaela METIANU
37 Director Student Financial Aid ...... Ms. Tracy BOULUKOS

*Florida Gulf Coast University (F)

10501 FGCU Boulevard S, Fort Myers FL 33965-6565
County: Lee FICE Identification: 032553
Unit ID: 433660
Telephone: (239) 590-1000 Carnegie Class: Master's L
FAX Number: (239) 590-1166 Calendar System: Semester
URL: www.fgcu.edu
Established: 1991 Annual Undergrad Tuition & Fees (In-State): $6,172
Enrollment: 14,463 Coed
Affiliation or Control: State IRS Status: 501(c)3
Highest Offering: Doctorate
Program: Liberal Arts And General; Teacher Preparatory; Professional
Accreditation: SC, ANEST, BUS, CAATE, CACREP, ENG, MT, MUS, NURSE, OT, PTA, SPAA, SW, TED

02 President ...... Dr. Wilson G. BRADSHAW
05 Provost & VP Academic Affairs ...... Dr. Ronald B. TOLL
10 Vice Pres Admin Services/Finance ...... Mr. Steve L. MAGIERA
30 VP Univ Advance/Exec Dir Foundation ...... Mr. Christopher (Chris) J. SIMONEAU
32 Vice President Student Affairs ...... Dr. J. Michael ROLLO
100 Vice President & Chief of Staff ...... Ms. Susan EVANS
43 Vice President & General Counsel ...... Ms. Vee LEONARD
20 Assoc VP Academic/Curriculum Sppt ...... Dr. Cathy DUFF
45 Sr Asc Prov/Asc VP Plng & Inst Perf ...... Dr. Paul SNYDER
58 Assoc VP Research/Dean Grad Studies ...... Dr. T C YIH
26 AVP Communications & Marketing ...... Ms. Deborah WILTROUT
04 Asst to Pres/University Ombudsman ...... Dr. Helen MAMARCHEV
88 Asst Vice Pres Business Services ...... Mr. Joseph MCDONALD
13 Asst VP Business Technology Svcs ...... Ms. Mary BANKS
15 Asst Vice Pres Human Resources ...... Ms. Christine LLOYD
21 Controller ...... Ms. June GUTKNECHT
35 Dean Student Affairs ...... Dr. Michele YOVANOVICH
49 Dean College Arts & Sciences ...... Dr. Robert (Bob) GREGERSON
20 Int Dean of Undergraduate Studies ...... Dr. Sean KELLY
50 Dean Lutgert College of Business ...... Dr. Robert BEATTY
53 Int Dean College of Education ...... Dr. Ivan BANKS
76 Dean College Health Professions ...... Dr. Mitchell CORDOVA
54 Dean U.A. Whitaker Col Engineering ...... Dr. Richard A. BEHR
62 Dean Library Services ...... Dr. Kathleen MILLER
45 Asst Dir Planning/Inst Performance ...... Ms. Kristen VANSELOW
38 Asst Dir Counselng/Stdnt Hlth Svcs ...... Dr. Jon L. BRUNNER
43 Asst Dean Judicial Affairs ...... Ms. Cindy LYONS
07 Director of Admissions ...... Mr. Marc LAVIOLETTE
96 Director of Procurement Services ...... Ms. Maryan EGAN
19 Director Campus Police & Safety ...... Chief Steven C. MOORE
18 Director Facilities Planning ...... Mr. Tom MAYO
37 Director Student Financial Aid ...... Mr. Jorge LOPEZ-ROSADO
06 University Registrar ...... Ms. Susan BYARS
23 Dir Student Health Services/Med Dir ...... Dr. Kevin COLLINS
41 Director Intercollegiate Athletics ...... Mr. Kenneth KAVANAGH
28 Director Title IX Compliance ...... Mr. Brandon WASHINGTON
85 Director International Services ...... Ms. Elaine HOZDIK
106 Dir Web/E-learning/Publication Svcs ...... Mr. David JAEGER
72 Director Academic & Event Tech ...... Ms. Pat O'CONNOR-BENSON
36 Director Career Development Svcs ...... Mr. Reid LENNERTZ
31 Dir Cmty Engagement/Svc Learning ...... Ms. Jessica RHEA
29 Director Alumni Relations ...... Ms. Kimberly WALLACE
92 Director Honors Program ...... Dr. Clay MOTLEY
09 Director Inst Research/Analysis ...... Dr. Robert VINES
21 Director University Budgets ...... Mr. David VAZQUEZ
39 Director University Housing ...... Dr. Brian FISHER
86 Director Government Relations ...... Ms. Jennifer GOEN
88 Dir Environmental Health/Safety ...... Ms. Rhonda HOLTZCLAW
51 Exec Dir Cont Educ/Off-Campus Pgms ...... Dr. Paul THORNTON
88 General Manager/WGCU ...... Mr. Rick JOHNSON
40 Manager The University Store ...... Ms. Laura JENSEN

*Florida International University (G)

University Park, 11200 SW 8 Street, Miami FL 33199-0001
County: Miami-Dade FICE Identification: 009635
Unit ID: 133951
Telephone: (305) 348-2000 Carnegie Class: RU/H
FAX Number: N/A Calendar System: Semester
URL: www.fiu.edu
Established: 1965 Annual Undergrad Tuition & Fees (In-State): $6,556
Enrollment: 49,703 Coed
Affiliation or Control: State IRS Status: 501(c)3
Highest Offering: Doctorate
Program: Liberal Arts And General; Teacher Preparatory; Professional
Accreditation: SC, ANEST, #ARCPA, ART, BUS, BUSA, CAATE, CACREP, CIDA, CONST, CS, DIETC, DIETD, ENG, FEPAC, HSA, IPSY, JOUR, LAW, LSAR, MED, MUS, NURSE, OT, PH, PTA, SP, SPAA, SW, TED, THEA

02 President ...... Dr. Mark ROSENBERG
100 Chief of Staff ...... Mr. Javier MARQUES
03 Executive VP & COO ...... Dr. Kenneth FURTON
88 VP for Engagement ...... Dr. Irma BECERRA-FERNANDEZ
05 Vice Provost Academic Affairs ...... Dr. Elizabeth BEJAR
10 CFO & Sr VP for Administration ...... Dr. Kenneth JESSELL
30 Vice President for Advancement ...... Mr. Howard LIPMAN
32 VP Student Affairs ...... Dr. Larry LUNSFORD
09 Int Vice Planning/Inst Research ...... Dr. Joyce ELAM
46 VP for Research ...... Dr. Andres GIL
13 Vice President/CIO ...... Mr. Robert GRILLO
12 Vice Prov Biscayne Bay Campus ...... Mr. Stephen MOLL
84 VP Enrollment Management ...... Dr. Luisa HAVENS
35 Assoc VP and Dean of Students ...... Dr. Cathy AKENS
15 Assoc Vice Pres Human Resources ...... Dr. Jaffus HARDRICK
18 Assoc VP Facilities Operations ...... Mr. John CAL

07 Dir Undergraduate Admissions .... Ms. Jody GLASSMAN
20 Assoc VP Academic Affairs .... Ms. Tonja MOORE
49 Dean College Arts & Sciences .... Dr. Michael HEITHAUS
50 Int Dean College Business Admin .... Dr. Jose ALDRICH
54 Dean Col Engineering/Computing .... Dr. Amir MIRMIRAN
53 Dean College of Education .... Dr. Delia GARCIA
88 Dean Sch Hospitality Management .... Dr. Mike HAMPTON
60 Dean School Journ/Mass Communic .... Dr. Raul REIS
66 Dean Col Nursing/Health Science .... Dr. Ora STRICKLAND
69 Dean College of Public Health .... Dr. Michele CICCAZZO
61 Dean College of Law .... Mr. R. Alexander ACOSTA
63 Dean College of Medicine .... Dr. John ROCK
88 Dean Undergraduate Education .... Dr. Douglas ROBERTSON
58 Dean University Graduate School .... Dr. Lakshmi REDDI
92 Dean Honors College .... Dr. Lesley NORTHUP
48 Dean Col Architecture & the Arts .... Dr. Brian SCHRINER
77 Dir Sch Computing/Info Sciences .... Dr. Sundararaj IYENGAR
64 Director School of Music .... Mr. Orlando GARCIA
38 AVP Counseling/Psych Svcs .... Dr. Cheryl NOWELL
22 Director Equal Opportunity
Program .... Ms. Shirlyon J. MCWHORTER
88 Director School Accounting .... Dr. Ruth MCEWEN
88 Director Multicultural Programs .... Dr. Dorret SAWYERS
62 Dean of Libraries .... Dr. Anne PRESTAMO
25 Assoc VP Sponsored Research .... Dr. Joseph BARABINO
41 Athletics Director .... Mr. Pete GARCIA
86 Asst VP for Government Affairs .... Ms. Michelle PALACIO
06 University Registrar .... Dr. Kevin COUGHLIN
86 VP for Government Relations .... Mr. Steve SAULS
88 Dir Community Rel/Special Events .... Ms. Lynda RODRIGUEZ
37 Director Student Financial Aid .... Mr. Francisco VALINES
36 Director Career Services .... Dr. Fernando FIGUEREDO
23 Director Univ Health Services .... Dr. Oscar LOYNAZ
39 Executive Director Student Housing ... Ms. Lynn HENDRICKS, JR.
85 Director Intl Student/Scholar Svcs .... Ms. Ana M. SIPPIN
88 Director Disability Student Svcs .... Ms. Amanda NIGUIDULA
88 Director Internal Audit .... Mr. Allen VANN
24 Director Media & Technology Support .... Mr. Matthew HAGOOD
21 Associate VP and Univ Controller .... Ms. Cecilia HAMILTON
88 Dir Environmentl Health/Safety .... Mr. Roger RIDDLEMOSER
19 Chief of Police .... Chief Alexander CASAS
29 Assoc Vice Pres Alumni Affairs .... Mr. Bill DRAUGHON
26 Director Media Relations .... Ms. Maydel SANTANA-BRAVO
43 General Counsel .... Ms. Kristina RAATTAMA

*Florida State University (A)

600 W. College Avenue, Tallahassee FL 32306

County: Leon — FICE Identification: 001489
Unit ID: 134097
Telephone: (850) 644-2525 — Carnegie Class: RU/VH
FAX Number: (850) 644-9936 — Calendar System: Semester
URL: www.fsu.edu
Established: 1851 — Annual Undergrad Tuition & Fees (In-State): $6,507
Enrollment: 41,226 — Coed
Affiliation or Control: State — IRS Status: 501(c)3
Highest Offering: Doctorate
Program: Liberal Arts And General; Teacher Preparatory; Professional
Accreditation: SC, AAFCS, ANEST, ART, BUS, BUSA, CAATE, CACREP, CIDA, CLPSY, CS, DANCE, DIETD, DIETI, ENG, IPSY, LAW, LIB, MED, MFCD, MUS, NURSE, PH, PLNG, PSPSY, SP, SPAA, SW, TED, THEA

02 President .... Mr. John E. THRASHER
05 Int Prov/Exec VP Academic Affairs .... Dr. Sally E. MCRORIE
10 Vice Pres Finance & Admin .... Mr. Kyle CLARK
32 Vice President Student Affairs .... Dr. Mary B. COBURN
46 Vice President Research .... Dr. Gary K. OSTRANDER
26 Int Vice Pres University Relations .... Ms. Kathleen DALY
45 VP Planning and Programs .... Vacant
30 VP University Advancement .... Mr. Thomas W. JENNINGS
102 Exec VP FSU Foundation .... Mr. Andy A. JHANJI
20 Int Vice Pres Faculty Development .... Dr. Janet KISTNER
100 Chief of Staff to President .... Vacant
88 Assoc Vice President for Research .... Dr. Ross ELLINGTON
18 Associate VP for Facilities .... Mr. Dennis A. BAILEY
21 Assoc VP Budget/Planning/Fin Svcs .... Vacant
20 Associate VP for Academic Affairs .... Ms. Anne BLANKENSHIP
15 Asst Vice Pres for Human Resources .... Ms. Renisha L. GIBBS
11 Asst VP for Administrative Services .... Dr. Perry CROWELL
84 Asst VP Enrollment Mgmt .... Mr. John BARNHILL
27 Asst VP of University Communication .... Ms. Browning BROOKS
88 Dir Academic Pgm Professional Svcs .... Mr. Bill LINDNER
49 Dean Arts & Sciences .... Dr. Sam HUCKABA
50 Int Dean Business .... Dr. Michael HARTLINE
53 Dean Education .... Dr. Marcy P. DRISCOLL
59 Dean Human Sciences .... Dr. Michael DELP
88 Dean Communication & Information .... Dr. Larry DENNIS
66 Dean Nursing .... Dr. Judith MCFETRIDGE-DURDLE
88 Dean Criminology .... Dr. Thomas BLOMBERG
61 Dean Law .... Mr. Donald WEIDNER
83 Dean Social Sciences .... Dr. David W. RASMUSSEN
70 Dean Social Work .... Dr. Nicholas MAZZA
88 Dean Motion Picture Arts .... Mr. Frank PATTERSON
64 Dean Music .... Dr. Patricia J. FLOWERS
57 Dean Fine Arts .... Mr. Peter WEISHAR
54 Dean Engineering .... Dr. Yaw YEBOAH
63 Dean Medicine .... Dr. John FOGARTY
58 Dean Graduate Studies .... Dr. Nancy MARCUS
88 Dean Undergraduate Studies .... Dr. Karen L. LAUGHLIN
35 Dean of Students .... Dr. Jeanine WARD-ROOF
12 Int Dean Panama City Branch Campus .... Dr. Steve LEACH
06 University Registrar .... Dr. Kimberly BARBER
07 Director Admissions .... Ms. Janice FINNEY

92 Int Dir University Honors Program .... Ms. Allen PEGGY
37 Director Student Financial Aid .... Mr. Darryl MARSHALL
08 Director Libraries .... Ms. Julia ZIMMERMAN
13 Chief Information Officer .... Mr. Michael BARRETT
90 Dir University Computing Services .... Mr. Byron MENCHION
43 General Counsel .... Ms. Carolyn EGAN
104 Director International Programs .... Dr. James E. PITTS
88 Chief Budget Officer .... Mr. Michael P. LAKE
09 Director Institutional Research .... Dr. Richard BURNETTE
86 Director Governmental Relations .... Ms. Kathleen M. DALY
41 Athletic Director .... Mr. Stan WILCOX
38 Director Student Counseling .... Dr. Carlos J. GOMEZ
19 Director Public Safety .... Mr. David L. PERRY
23 Director Student Health Services .... Dr. Lesley SACHER
36 Director Career Center .... Ms. Myrna HOOVER
29 President Alumni Association .... Mr. Scott ATWELL
88 Chief Audit Officer .... Mr. Sam MCCALL
28 Dir Diversity/Equal Opportunity .... Vacant
96 Director of Purchasing .... Mr. Ian ROBBINS
39 Director Student Housing .... Vacant
88 Director Business Services .... Mr. Harvey BUCHANAN
106 Director Distance Learning .... Dr. Susann RUDASILL
25 Director Sponsored Research .... Ms. Pamela RAY
88 Director Information Technology .... Mr. Kenneth JOHNSON

*New College of Florida (B)

5800 Bay Shore Road, Sarasota FL 34243-2109

County: Sarasota — FICE Identification: 001507
Unit ID: 262129
Telephone: (941) 487-4100 — Carnegie Class: Bac/A&S
FAX Number: (941) 487-4101 — Calendar System: 4/1/4
URL: www.ncf.edu
Established: 1960 — Annual Undergrad Tuition & Fees (In-State): $6,968
Enrollment: 835 — Coed
Affiliation or Control: State — IRS Status: 501(c)3
Highest Offering: Baccalaureate
Program: Liberal Arts And General
Accreditation: SC

02 President .... Dr. Donal E. O'SHEA
05 Provost .... Dr. Stephen MILES
10 Vice Pres Finance & Administration .... Mr. John U. MARTIN
79 Chair of Humanities .... Dr. Alberto PORTUGAL
81 Chair of Natural Sciences .... Dr. Katherine WALSTROM
83 Chair of Social Sciences .... Dr. David HARVEY
08 Dean Cook Library .... Dr. Brian DOHERTY
84 Dean of Enrollment & Info Tech .... Ms. Kathleen KILLION
32 Dean of Students .... Mr. Tracy MURRY
07 Associate Dean of Admissions .... Ms. Sonia WU
20 Associate Academic Officer .... Dr. Robert ZAMSKY
21 Associate Business Officer .... Ms. Kimberly BENDICKSON
13 Chief Information Officer .... Mr. Ben FOSS
14 Director of Information Support .... Mr. Jeff SMITH
29 Director Alumnae/i Association .... Ms. Jessica ROGERS
06 Registrar .... Ms. Marta MORENO
26 Director Public Affairs .... Ms. Jessica ROOD
38 Director Counseling .... Dr. Anne E. FISHER
09 Director of Institutional Research .... Ms. Hui-Men WEN
15 Director Personnel Services .... Ms. Tonia SUBER
18 Chief Facilities/Physical Plant .... Mr. Alan BURR
28 Director of Diversity .... Vacant
96 Director of Purchasing .... Ms. Jean HARRIS
37 Director Student Financial Aid .... Ms. Tara KARAS
43 Director Legal Svcs/General Counsel .... Mr. Mark ST. LOUIS
25 Contract Administrator .... Ms. Lee Ann RODRIGUEZ
72 Director of Technology Support .... Mr. Jeff SMITH
30 Chief Development .... Ms. MaryAnne YOUNG
19 Chief of Police .... Sgt. Michael KESSIE
39 Director Student Housing .... Dr. Mark STIER
41 Athletic Director .... Mr. Colin JORDAN
86 Director Government Relations .... Ms. Suzanne JANNEY
04 Administrative Asst to President .... Ms. Shelley WILBUR

*University of Central Florida (C)

PO Box 160000, Orlando FL 32816-0001

County: Orange — FICE Identification: 003954
Unit ID: 132903
Telephone: (407) 823-2000 — Carnegie Class: RU/VH
FAX Number: N/A — Calendar System: Semester
URL: www.ucf.edu
Established: 1963 — Annual Undergrad Tuition & Fees (In-State): $6,368
Enrollment: 60,376 — Coed
Affiliation or Control: State — IRS Status: 501(c)3
Highest Offering: Doctorate
Program: Occupational; Liberal Arts And General; Teacher Preparatory; Professional
Accreditation: SC, BUS, BUSA, CAATE, CACREP, CAHIIM, CEA, CLPSY, CS, ENG, HSA, IPSY, MED, MT, MUS, NURSE, PTA, SP, SPAA, SW, TED

02 President .... Dr. John C. HITT
05 Provost/Executive Vice President .... Dr. A. Dale WHITTAKER
100 Vice President and Chief of Staff .... Dr. John SCHELL
10 Vice Pres Admin & Finance/CFO .... Mr. William F. MERCK, II
26 Vice President University Relations .... Dr. Daniel HOLSENBECK
43 Vice President/General Counsel .... Mr. W. Scott COLE
46 VP Research and Commercialization .... Dr. M. J. SOILEAU
32 VP Student Dev/Enrollment Svcs .... Dr. Maribeth EHASZ
30 VP Dev/Alum Rels/Foundation
CEO .... Mr. Michael J. MORSBERGER
31 Vice President Emerita Comm Rels .... Ms. Helen DONEGAN

63 VP Medical Affairs/Dean Med College .... Dr. Deborah GERMAN
49 Dean College of Arts & Humanities .... Dr. Jose B. FERNANDEZ
50 Dean College of Business Admin .... Dr. Paul JARLEY
53 Interim Dean College of Education .... Dr. Grant HAYES
54 Dean College of Engr/Comp Sci .. Dr. Michael GEORGIOPOULOS
76 Dean College of Hlth/Pub Affs .... Dr. Michael FRUMKIN
88 Dean Rosen College Hospitality Mgt .... Dr. Abraham PIZAM
66 Interim Dean College of Nursing .... Dr. Mary L. SOLE
88 Dean/Dir Col of Optics & Photonics .... Dr. Bahaa SALEH
81 Dean College of Sciences .... Dr. Michael D. JOHNSON
92 Dean Burnett Honors College .... Dr. Alvin WANG
20 Vice Provost Academic Pgm Quality .... Dr. Diane CHASE
13 Vice Provost & CIO Info Tech/Res .... Dr. Joel L. HARTMAN
88 Dir Space Plng/Analysis Admin .... Vacant
12 Vice Provost Regional Campuses .... Dr. Jeff JONES
58 Vice Provost/Dean Graduate Studies .... Dr. Mubarak SHAH
88 Interim Vice Provost/Dean Undergrad .... Dr. Manoj CHOPRA
18 Assoc VP Facilities and Safety .... Ms. Lee KERNEK
29 Assoc Vice Pres Alumni Relations .... Mr. Tom MESSINA
86 Assoc VP for University Relations .... Mr. Fred KITTINGER
88 Assoc VP Rsrch & Commercialization .... Mr. Tom O'NEAL
07 Assoc VP Enrollment Services .... Dr. Gordon CHAVIS
27 VP Communications & Marketing .... Mr. Grant HESTON
88 Assoc Vice Provost Fac Relation .... Dr. Lyman BRODIE
88 Asst VP Inst Knowledge Mgmt .... Dr. M. Paige BORDEN
37 Dir Student Financial Asst .... Ms. Alicia KEATON
06 University Registrar .... Mr. Brian BOYD
08 Director Libraries .... Mr. Barry BAKER
15 Int Assoc VP HR/Chief HR Officer .... Ms. Shelia DANIELS
19 Assoc VP Safety & Chief of Police .... Mr. Richard BEARY
93 Director Multicul Acad Suppt Svcs .... Mr. Wayne JACKSON
14 Chief Technology Officer .... Mr. Robert YANCKELLO
38 Director Counseling Center .... Dr. Karen HOFMANN
41 Int Vice Pres & Dir of Athletics .... Mr. George O'LEARY
22 Director EEO Affirmative Action .... Ms. Maria BECKMAN
23 Director Health Services .... Dr. Michael G. DEICHEN
39 Exec Dir Housing and Residence Life ...... Mrs. Christi HARTZLER
28 Chief Diversity Officer .... Ms. Karen MORRISON
96 Director of Purchasing .... Mr. Gregory ROBINSON
36 Exec Director Career Services .... Ms. Lynn HANSEN

*University of Florida (D)

235 Tigert Hall, Gainesville FL 32611-9500

County: Alachua — FICE Identification: 001535
Unit ID: 134130
Telephone: (352) 392-3261 — Carnegie Class: RU/VH
FAX Number: (352) 392-8735 — Calendar System: Semester
URL: www.ufl.edu
Established: 1853 — Annual Undergrad Tuition & Fees (In-State): $6,313
Enrollment: 50,350 — Coed
Affiliation or Control: State — IRS Status: 501(c)3
Highest Offering: Doctorate
Program: Liberal Arts And General; Teacher Preparatory; Professional
Accreditation: SC, ARCPA, ART, AUD, BUS, BUSA, CAATE, CACREP, CEA, CIDA, CLPSY, CONST, COPSY, DANCE, DENT, DIETD, DIETI, ENG, ENGR, HSA, IPSY, JOUR, LAW, LSAR, MED, MIDWF, MUS, NURSE, OT, PH, PHAR, PLNG, PTA, SCPSY, SP, TED, THEA, VET

02 President .... Dr. W. Kent FUCHS
05 Provost & Senior Vice President .... Dr. Joseph GLOVER
47 Sr Vice Pres Agric/Natural Res .... Dr. Jack M. PAYNE
17 Sr Vice Pres Health Affairs .... Dr. David S. GUZICK
10 Int VP/Chief Financial Ofcr .... Mr. Michael MCKEE
11 Sr Vice Pres/Chief Operating Ofcr .... Dr. Charles E. LANE
30 Vice President Dev/Alumni Affairs .... Mr. Thomas J. MITCHELL
21 Vice President Business Affairs .... Mr. Curtis REYNOLDS
32 Vice President Student Affairs .... Mr. David KRATZER
26 Vice President Univ Relations .... Ms. Jane A. ADAMS
15 Vice Pres Human Resources .... Ms. Paula V. FUSSELL
46 Vice President Research .... Dr. David P. NORTON
43 Vice President/General Counsel .... Ms. Jamie L. KEITH
13 Vice President & CIO .... Mr. Elias G. ELDAYRIE
84 Vice Pres Enroll Mgmt/Assoc Provost .... Dr. Zina EVANS
86 Assoc VP Government Relations .... Ms. Marion S. HOFFMAN
88 Associate Provost Teaching &
Tech .... Dr. William A. MCCOLLOUGH
27 Asst Vice Pres Marketing .... Mr. Dan WILLIAMS
27 Asst VP Media Rels/Public Affairs .... Ms. Janine SIKES
27 Senior Director Media Relations .... Mr. Stephen F. ORLANDO
16 Asst Vice Pres Human Resources .... Ms. Jodi D. GENTRY
21 Business Affs/Finance/Admin AVP .... Mr. Robert MILLER
18 AVP of Facilities/Plng/Construction .... Vacant
20 Associate Provost Academic
Affairs .... Dr. Angel KWOLEK-FOLLAND
92 Assoc Provost Undergrad Affairs .... Vacant
09 Asst Provost/Dir Inst Research/Plng .... Dr. Marie ZEGLEN
35 Dean Students/Assoc VP Student Affs .... Dr. Jen D. SHAW
08 Dean University Libraries .... Ms. Judith RUSSELL
50 Dean of Business Administration .... Dr. John KRAFT
49 Dean of Liberal Arts & Science .... Mr. David E. RICHARDSON
68 Dean of Health/Human Performance .... Dr. Michael B. REID
61 Dean of Law .... Ms. Laura A. ROSENBURY
66 Dean of Nursing .... Dr. Anna M. MCDANIEL
67 Dean of Pharmacy .... Dr. Julie A. JOHNSON
54 Dean of Engineering .... Dr. Cammy ABERNATHY
47 Dean Agricultural/Life Sciences .... Dr. R. Elaine TURNER
60 Dean of Journalism/Communications ..... Ms. Diane H. MCFARLIN
76 Dean Pub Health/Health Professions .... Dr. Michael PERRI
53 Dean of Education .... Dr. Glenn GOOD
47 Dean IFAS Extension .... Dr. Nick T. PLACE
74 Dean of Veterinary Medicine .... Dr. James W. LLOYD
57 Dean of Fine Arts .... Ms. Lucinda LAVELLI

48 Dean Design Construction Planning ....Dr. Christopher SILVER
63 Dean of Medicine ....Dr. Michael L. GOOD
46 Dean of IFAS Research ....Dr. Jacqueline BURNS
52 Dean of Dentistry ....Dr. Isabel GARCIA
58 Dean Graduate School ....Dr. Henry T. FRIERSON
65 Int Dir School Natural Res/Envir ....Dr. Thomas K. FRAZER
06 University Registrar ....Mr. Stephen J. PRITZ
23 Director of Student Health ....Dr. Guy NICOLETTE
38 Director of Counseling Center ....Dr. Sherry BENTON
37 Director Student Financial Aid ....Mr. Richard D. WILDER
36 Director of Career Resource Center ....Ms. Heather B. WHITE
14 Director of Computer Center ....Mr. Timothy J. FITZPATRICK
19 Director of University Police ....Ms. Linda J. STUMP
24 Director of Academic Technology ....Dr. Fedro S. ZAZUETA
65 Director of Forestry ....Dr. Timothy L. WHITE
39 Director of Housing ....Mr. Norbert W. DUNKEL
41 Athletic Director ....Mr. Jeremy N. FOLEY
29 Exec Director Alumni Affairs ....Ms. Danita NIAS
28 Director of Diversity ....Ms. Tamara COHEN
96 Director of Purchasing ....Ms. Lisa DEAL
07 Director of Admissions ....Mr. Patrick C. HERRING

*University of North Florida (A)

1 UNF Drive, Jacksonville FL 32224-7699
County: Duval FICE Identification: 009841
Unit ID: 136172
Telephone: (904) 620-1000 Carnegie Class: Master's L
FAX Number: (904) 620-2414 Calendar System: Semester
URL: www.unf.edu
Established: 1965 Annual Undergrad Tuition & Fees (In-State): $6,394
Enrollment: 16,187 Coed
Affiliation or Control: State IRS Status: 501(c)3
Highest Offering: Doctorate
Program: Liberal Arts And General; Teacher Preparatory; Professional
Accreditation: SC, ANEST, BUS, BUSA, CAATE, CACREP, CONST, CS, DIETD, DIETI, ENG, EXSC, HSA, MT, MUS, NURSE, PH, PTA, SPAA, @SW, TED

02 President ....Mr. John A. DELANEY
05 Provost ....Dr. Earle C. TRAYNHAM
20 Associate Provost ....Dr. Bob J. COLEMAN
100 VP/Chief of Staff ....Dr. Thomas S. SERWATKA
86 VP Governmental Affairs ....Ms. Janet D. OWEN
43 VP/General Counsel ....Ms. Karen J. STONE
15 VP Human Resources ....Ms. Rachelle GOTTLIEB
10 VP Administration/Finance ....Ms. Shari A. SHUMAN
30 VP Development Alumni Aff ....Mr. Joshua D. MERCHANT
32 VP Student & International Affairs ....Dr. Mauricio GONZALEZ
88 Assoc VP Enrollment Svs ....Dr. Alberto N. COLOM
84 Asst VP for Enrollment Svcs ....Ms. Karen LUCAS
88 Assoc VP/Compliance Officer ....Dr. Joann N. CAMPBELL
21 Assoc VP Admin & Finance ....Mr. Scott BENNETT
13 Assoc VP Chief Info Officer ....Mr. Reggie BRINSON
44 Dir for Major Gifts ....Ms. Christina LEVINE
35 Assoc VP Student Affairs ....Mr. Everett J. MALCOLM, III
45 Asst VP Research ....Dr. John KANTNER
88 Asst VP Development ....Ms. Ann S. MCCULLEN
26 VP Public Relations ....Ms. Sharon ASHTON
88 Asst VP Student Affairs ....Dr. Lucy S. CROFT
89 Dean of Undergraduate Studies ....Dr. Daniel C. MOON
58 Dean of the Graduate School ....Dr. John KANTNER
08 Dean of the Library ....Dr. Elizabeth A. CURRY
49 Dean College of Arts & Sciences ....Dr. Barbara HETRICK
50 Dean Coggin College of Business ....Dr. Mark DAWKINS
53 Interim Dean College of Education ....Dr. Marsha LUPI
76 Dean Brooks College of Health ....Dr. Pam CHALLY
77 Dean Computing Engineering & Constr ....Dr. Mark A. TUMEO
51 Dean Continuing Education ....Mr. Robert WOOD
16 Dir Human Resources ....Mr. Greg CATRON
88 Dir Internal Auditing ....Mr. Robert L. BERRY
22 Dir Equal Oppty Programs ....Ms. Cheryl N. GONZALEZ
88 Dir Professional Dev Training ....Ms. Kelly G. HARRISON
21 Chief Budget Officer ....Mr. Ricky B. ARJUNE
21 Controller ....Ms. Valerie O. STEVENSON
88 Dir of Compliance ....Ms. Donna R. KIRK
88 Dir Environment Health/Safety ....Mr. Daniel D. ENDICOTT
88 Dir ADA Compliance ....Ms. Rocelia T. GONZALEZ
88 Dir IT Networking ....Mr. Jeffrey A. DURFEE
88 Treasurer ....Mr. Michael S. NEGLIA
18 Dir Univ Facilities Planning ....Mr. Zak OVADIA
88 Dir University Center ....Mr. George ANDROUIN
29 Asst VP Alumni Engagement ....Mr. Christopher M. DECENT
19 Dir Safety Security ....Mr. Francis J. MACKESY
36 Dir Career Development Services ....Mr. Rick ROBERTS
85 Dir Intercultural Ctr for Peace ....Dr. Oupa SEANE
88 Dir Child Development Research Ctr ....Ms. Pam BELL
23 Chief Medical Officer ....Dr. Lisa DYNAN-DOBBERTIEN
38 Dir Univ Counseling Center ....Dr. Andrew B. KING
88 Dir Women's Center ....Ms. Sheila D. SPIVEY
85 Dir The International Center ....Dr. Timothy ROBINSON
39 Dir Housing Residence Life ....Mr. Robert J. BOYLE
41 Athletic Director ....Mr. Lee L. MOON
88 Dir Faculty Enhancement ....Dr. Dan RICHARD
108 Exec Dir of Assessment ....Dr. Judith E. MILLER
92 Dir Honors Program ....Dr. Jeff MICHELMAN
37 Dir Student Financial Aid ....Mrs. Anissa AGNE
06 Registrar ....Mrs. Megan R. KUEHNER
44 Director Annual Giving ....Vacant
09 Interim Dir Institutional Research ....Dr. Fen YU
88 Exec Dir FL Inst of Education ....Dr. Cheryl A. FOUNTAIN
88 Dir Small Business Dev Ctr ....Ms. Janice W. DONALDSON
88 Dir Disability Resource Center ....Dr. Russell G. DUBBERLY
96 Dir Purchasing ....Ms. Kathy RITTER

103 Dir Continuing Education ....Mr. Timothy W. GILES
106 Dir Center for Instr & Res Tech ....Ms. Deb MILLER
90 Director Academic Technology ....Dr. Gordon F. RAKITA

*University of South Florida (B)

4202 E Fowler Avenue, Tampa FL 33620-6100
County: Hillsborough FICE Identification: 001537
Unit ID: 137351
Telephone: (813) 974-2011 Carnegie Class: RU/VH
FAX Number: (813) 974-5530 Calendar System: Semester
URL: www.usf.edu
Established: 1956 Annual Undergrad Tuition & Fees (In-State): $6,410
Enrollment: 42,065 Coed
Affiliation or Control: State IRS Status: 501(c)3
Highest Offering: Doctorate
Program: Liberal Arts And General; Teacher Preparatory; Professional; Nursing Emphasis
Accreditation: SC, ANEST, ART, AUD, BUS, BUSA, CAATE, CACREP, CEA, CLPSY, CORE, CS, DANCE, ENG, ENGR, HSA, IPSY, LIB, MED, MUS, NURSE, PCSAS, PH, PHAR, PTA, SCPSY, SP, SPAA, SW, TED, THEA

02 President ....Dr. Judy L. GENSHAFT
100 Chief of Staff/President's Office ....Dr. Cynthia S. VISOT
05 Prov/Exec Vice Pres Academic Affs ....Dr. Ralph WILCOX
20 AVP USF World/Vice Prov Acad Affs ....Dr. Roger BRINDLEY
46 Sr Vice Pres Research & Innovation ....Dr. Paul SANBERG
17 Sr Vice Pres USF Health ....Dr. Charles LOCKWOOD
58 Sr Vice Provost/Dean Grad School ....Dr. Dwayne SMITH
10 Vice Pres Business & Finance ....Mr. Nick TRIVUNOVICH
11 Vice Pres Administrative Services ....Vacant
30 Sr Vice Pres University Advancement ....Mr. Joel MOMBERG
32 Int Vice President Student Affairs ....Dr. Thomas E. MILLER
13 Vice Pres Information Technology ....Mr. Sidney FERNANDES
26 Chief Marketing Officer ....Mr. Tom HOOF
29 Assoc Vice Pres Alumni Affairs ....Mr. Bill MCCAUSLAND
44 Assoc Vice Pres Development ....Vacant
14 Assoc Vice Pres Info Technologies ....Mr. George W. ELLIS
22 Assoc VP for Diversity/Equal Oppty ....Dr. Jose HERNANDEZ
84 Assoc VP Enrollment Planning & Mgmt ....Dr. Paul J. DOSAL
15 Assoc Vice Pres Personnel Services ....Ms. Theresea DRYE
86 Asst Vice Pres Government Rels ....Mr. Mark WALSH
35 Asst Vice Pres/Dean of Students ....Dr. Danielle MCDONALD
35 Asst Vice Pres Student Affairs ....Mr. Guy CONWAY
109 Asst VP Auxiliary Services ....Mr. Jeffrey A. MACK
43 General Counsel ....Mr. Steven D. PREVAUX
39 Asst VP Housing/Residential Educ ....Ms. Ana HERNANDEZ
83 Dean Behavioral/Community Sci ....Dr. Julianne SEROVICH
50 Dean Business Administration ....Dr. Moez LIMAYEM
53 Dean Education ....Dr. Vasti TORRES
54 Dean Engineering ....Dr. Robert H. BISHOP
57 Dean College of the Arts ....Dr. James S. MOY
49 Dean Arts & Sciences ....Dr. Eric EISENBERG
66 Dean Nursing ....Dr. Dianne MORRISON-BEEDY
69 Dean Public Health ....Dr. Donna PETERSEN
89 Dean of Undergraduate Studies ....Dr. W. Robert SULLINS
106 Asst Vice Provost Innovative Educ ....Dr. Cynthia A. DELUCA
48 Dir Sch of Architecture/Cmty Design ....Mr. Robert MACLEOD
12 Regional Chanc Sarasota-Manatee ....Dr. Sandra STONE
12 Regional Chanc USF St Petersburg ....Dr. Sophia WISNIEWSKA
21 Controller ....Ms. Jennifer CONDON
27 Director of News ....Ms. Lara WADE
06 Int University Registrar ....Ms. Carrie GARCIA
07 Director Admissions ....Mr. David HENRY
18 Associate Director Physical Plant ....Mr. Siva PRAKASH
21 University Budget Officer ....Ms. Nell PETERSON
37 Director Financial Aid ....Ms. Billie Jo HAMILTON
38 Director Counseling Center ....Dr. Ann JARONSKI
36 Asst Vice President Career Services ....Mr. Russ COUGHENAIR
19 Director University Police ....Mr. Thomas F. LONGO
08 USF Libraries Dean ....Dr. William GARRISON
41 Director of Athletics ....Mr. Mark HARLAN
28 Director of Diversity & Inclusion ....Ms. Patsy FELICIANO
96 Director Purchasing & Property Svcs ....Mr. Michael ABERNETHY
09 Asst VP Office of Decision Support ....Dr. Valeria GARCIA

*University of South Florida St. Petersburg (C)

140 7th Avenue S, Saint Petersburg FL 33701-5016
County: Pinellas FICE Identification: 009016
Unit ID: 448840
Telephone: (727) 873-4873 Carnegie Class: Master's M
FAX Number: (727) 873-4131 Calendar System: Semester
URL: www.usfsp.edu
Established: 1956 Annual Undergrad Tuition & Fees (In-District): $5,821
Enrollment: 4,491 Coed
Affiliation or Control: State/Local IRS Status: 501(c)3
Highest Offering: Master's
Program: Liberal Arts And General; Teacher Preparatory; Professional
Accreditation: SC, BUS, BUSA, JOUR, TED

02 Regional Chancellor ....Dr. Sophia T. WISNIEWSKA
04 Special Asst to Regional Chancellor ....Dr. Vivian FUEYO
05 Int Reg Vice Chanc Academic Affairs ....Dr. V. Mark DURAND
10 Reg Vice Chanc Admin/Financial Svcs ....Dr. Joseph TRUBACZ
44 Reg Vice Chanc Univ Advancement ....Dr. Helen LEVINE
32 Int Reg Assoc Vice Chanc Stdnt Affs ....Dr. Gardiner (Tuck) TUCKER
11 Reg Asst Vice Chanc Administration ....Dr. Chitra IYER
49 Dean College of Arts & Sciences ....Dr. Frank BIAFORA
50 Interim Dean College of Business ....Dr. Gary PATTERSON

53 Dean College of Education ....Dr. William HELLER
08 Dean of the Library ....Ms. Carol HIXSON
19 Chief of Police ....Dr. David HENDRY
13 Director of Campus Computing ....Mr. Jeff REISBERG
15 Director Human Resources ....Dr. Chitra IYER
37 Director of Financial Aid ....Ms. Erin DUNN
06 Director Records and Registration ....Ms. Linda CROSSMAN
07 Director Admissions & Marketing ....Ms. Holly KICKLITER
18 Dir Facil Plng/Construction Svcs ....Mr. John DICKSON
96 Purchasing Manager ....Mr. Bill BENJAMIN
21 Budget Director ....Mr. David EVERINGHAM
31 Communications Director ....Ms. Jessica BLAIS
30 Asst Director Development ....Ms. Sheree WYSOCKI
30 Asst Director Development ....Ms. Alexis SEARFOSS
105 Director Web Services ....Mr. Edgardo DANGOND

*University of South Florida Sarasota-Manatee (D)

8350 Tamiami Trail, Sarasota FL 34243-2049
County: Manatee Identification: 667058
Unit ID: 451671
Telephone: (941) 359-4200 Carnegie Class: Master's M
FAX Number: N/A Calendar System: Semester
URL: www.usfsm.edu
Established: 1956 Annual Undergrad Tuition & Fees (In-State): $5,587
Enrollment: 1,917 Coed
Affiliation or Control: State IRS Status: 501(c)3
Highest Offering: Master's; No Lower Division
Program: Liberal Arts And General; Teacher Preparatory; Professional
Accreditation: SC, TED

02 Regional Chancellor ....Dr. Sandra STONE
10 Vice Chancellor Business & Finance ....Mr. Ben ELLINOR
05 Vice Chancellor Academic Affairs ....Dr. Terry OSBORN
30 Vice Chancellor Advancement ....Mr. Dennis L. STOVER
32 AVP Enrollment & Student Services ....Ms. Mary Beth WALLACE
09 AVP Institutional Research ....Dr. Bonnie J. JONES
49 Dean College of Arts & Sciences ....Dr. Jane ROSE
50 Int Dean College of Business ....Dr. James CURRAN
53 Dean College of Education ....Dr. Pat WILSON
88 Int Dean Sch Hotel & Restaurant Mgt ....Dr. James CURRAN
06 Registrar ....Ms. Lynn LYNCH
09 Director of Institutional Research ....Ms. Laura HOFFMAN
13 Chief Info Technology Officer (CIO) ....Mr. Bryan MUDD
07 Director of Admissions ....Mr. Andrew TELATOVICH
105 Director Web Services ....Mr. Christopher FLANNIGAN
96 Director of Purchasing ....Ms. Michelle KRUEGER

*University of West Florida (E)

11000 University Parkway, Pensacola FL 32514-5750
County: Escambia FICE Identification: 003955
Unit ID: 138354
Telephone: (850) 474-2000 Carnegie Class: DRU
FAX Number: (850) 474-3131 Calendar System: Semester
URL: uwf.edu
Established: 1963 Annual Undergrad Tuition & Fees (In-State): $6,360
Enrollment: 12,602 Coed
Affiliation or Control: State IRS Status: 501(c)3
Highest Offering: Doctorate
Program: Occupational; Liberal Arts And General; Teacher Preparatory; Professional; Business Emphasis
Accreditation: SC, BUS, CAATE, ENG, MT, MUS, NURSE, PH, SW, TED

02 President ....Dr. Judith A. BENSE
05 Provost & Executive VP ....Dr. Martha SAUNDERS
32 Vice President Student Affairs ....Dr. Kevin BAILEY
30 Vice Pres University Advancement ....Dr. Brendan KELLY
20 Vice Provost ....Dr. George B. ELLENBERG
35 Sr Assoc Vice Pres Student Affairs ....Dr. James R. HURD
84 Asst Vice Pres Enrollment Mgt ....Dr. Joffery GAYMON
18 Assoc VP Facilities Dev/Operations ....Dr. James R. BARNETT
21 Asc VP Internal Audit/Mgmt Consultg ....Ms. J. Betsy BOWERS
15 Associate Vice Pres Human Resources ....Vacant
88 Assoc VP Business & Property Dev ....Mr. David J. O'BRIEN
104 Assoc VP International Educ/Pgms ....Dr. Angela E. MCCORVEY
43 General Counsel ....Ms. Patricia D. LOTT
35 Assistant VP/Dean of Students ....Dr. Brandon FRYE
50 Dean of Business ....Dr. Timothy O'KEEFE
49 Dean Arts/Social Sci/Humanities ....Dr. Steven BROWN
107 Dean Education & Prof Studies ....Dr. William CRAWLEY
08 Dean University Libraries ....Mr. Robert DUGAN
35 Associate Dean of Students ....Dr. LuSharon WILEY
10 Vice President and CFO ....Dr. Steven CUNNINGHAM
21 Asst VP Financial Services ....Ms. Colleen M. ASMUS
13 Executive Director ITS ....Mrs. Melanie J. HAVEARD
07 Director of Admissions ....Ms. Katherine CONDON
92 Director of Honors Program ....Vacant
37 Director of Financial Aid ....Ms. Shana GORE
19 Director of University Police ....Mr. John S. WARREN
39 Director of Housing/Residence Life ....Dr. Ruth L. DAVISON
38 Assistant VP Counseling Center ....Dr. Rebecca E. KENNEDY
29 Director of Alumni Relations ....Ms. Melissa H. GRACE
41 Athletic Director ....Mr. David L. SCOTT
81 Dean Science/Engineering/Health ....Dr. Michael HUGGINS
27 Director University Communication ....Ms. Megan GONZALEZ
26 Director Mktg & Creative Services ....Ms. Sabrina MCLAUGHLIN
44 Asst Vice Pres of Development ....Ms. Martha Lee BLODGETT
21 AVP Budget/Financial Planning ....Ms. Valerie Z. MONEYHAM
109 Director Business/Auxiliary Svcs ....Ms. Ellen P. TILL
57 Director Ctr Fine Performing Arts ....Mr. Jerre BRISKY

06 Registrar ... Ms. Ann DZIADON
86 Director Government Relations ... Ms. Janice GILLEY

Stetson University (A)

421 N Woodland Boulevard, DeLand FL 32723-0001
County: Volusia | FICE Identification: 001531
Unit ID: 137546
Telephone: (386) 822-7000 | Carnegie Class: Master's L
FAX Number: (386) 822-8832 | Calendar System: 4/1/4
URL: www.stetson.edu
Established: 1883 | Annual Undergrad Tuition & Fees: $41,590
Enrollment: 4,137 | Coed
Affiliation or Control: Independent Non-Profit | IRS Status: 501(c)3
Highest Offering: Doctorate
Program: Liberal Arts And General; Teacher Preparatory; Professional
Accreditation: **SC**, BUS, BUSA, CACREP, LAW, MUS, TED

01 President ... Dr. Wendy B. LIBBY
05 Exec Vice Pres & Provost ... Dr. Beth PAUL
10 Exec Vice Pres & CFO ... Mr. F. Robert HUTH
30 VP for Devel & Alumni Engagement ... Mr. Jeffrey ULMER
84 VP Enrollment Management ... Mr. Joel BAUMAN
26 VP for University Marketing ... Mr. Gregory CARROLL
32 Vice Provost Student Success ... Dr. Lua HANCOCK
61 Dean College of Law ... Mr. Christopher PIETRUSZKIEWICZ
49 Dean of College of Arts & Sciences ... Dr. Karen RYAN
50 Dean of School of Business Admin ... Vacant
64 Dean of School of Music ... Dr. Thomas G. MASSE
08 Dean of duPont-Ball Library ... Ms. Susan RYAN
20 Assoc Provost for Faculty Devlpmnt ... Dr. Rosalie RICHARDS
20 Assoc VP Academic Affairs ... Dr. John PEARSON
06 Registrar ... Mr. Robert BERWICK
41 Director of Athletics ... Mr. Jeffrey P. ALTIER
13 Assoc VP & CIO ... Dr. Jose BERNIER
15 Assoc VP for Human Resources ... Ms. Drew MACAN
18 Assoc Vice Pres Facilities Mgmt ... Mr. Al ALLEN
21 Assoc Vice Pres for Finance ... Mr. Jeffrey MARGHEIM
21 Assoc VP Budget ... Ms. Melissa PETERS
51 Assoc VP Boundless Learning ... Dr. Joy MCGUIRL-HADLEY
88 Spec Advsr to Pres for Philanthropy ... Ms. Linda P. DAVIS
35 Dean of Students ... Ms. Lynn SCHOENBERG
36 Exec Dir Career Dev & Advising ... Mr. Timothy STILES
42 University Chaplain ... Rev. Michael R. FRONK
09 Dir Institutional Research ... Dr. Resche HINES
104 Director of International Learning ... Vacant
44 Assoc VP Development ... Dr. Paul GLEASON
44 Asst VP Development ... Ms. Katheryn P. PEARCE
44 Asst VP for Development ... Ms. Rina TOVAR
44 Asst VP Dev & Communications ... Ms. Amy GIPSON
29 Exec Dir Alumni Engagement ... Mr. Woody O'CAIN
07 Director of Admissions ... Mr. Robert ANDREWS
37 Director Student Financial Aid ... Ms. Susan MERCHANT
39 Dir of Res Educ & Housing ... Dr. Larry CORRELL-HUGHES
25 Dir Ofc of Grants/Sponsored Rsrch ... Ms. Carol BUCKELS
16 Director Human Resources ... Ms. Betty WHITEMAN
96 Director of Purchasing ... Ms. Valinda WIMER
19 Chief Pubic Safety ... Mr. Robert MATUSICK
04 Executive Asst to President ... Ms. Joan BEASLEY

Tallahassee Community College (B)

444 Appleyard Drive, Tallahassee FL 32304-2895
County: Leon | FICE Identification: 001533
Unit ID: 137759
Telephone: (850) 201-6200 | Carnegie Class: Assoc/Pub-R-L
FAX Number: (850) 201-8682 | Calendar System: Semester
URL: www.tcc.fl.edu
Established: 1966 | Annual Undergrad Tuition & Fees (In-District): $2,570
Enrollment: 12,960 | Coed
Affiliation or Control: Local | IRS Status: 501(c)3
Highest Offering: Associate Degree
Program: Occupational; 2-Year Principally Bachelor's Creditable; Nursing Emphasis
Accreditation: **SC**, ADNUR, COARC, DA, DH, EMT, SURGT

01 President ... Dr. Jim MURDAUGH
10 Vice Pres Administrative Svcs/CFO ... Dr. Barbara WILLS
13 VP Information Technology ... Mr. Bret INGERMAN
05 Provost and VP for Academic Affairs ... Dr. Feleccia MOORE-DAVIS
32 Vice President for Student Affs ... Dr. Sally SEARCH
103 Vice Pres Workforce Development ... Ms. Kimberly MOORE
88 Assoc VP Inst Effectiveness ... Dr. Lei WANG
100 Chief of Staff ... Mr. Scott BALOG
57 Dean Communications & Humanities ... Dr. Marge BANOCY-PAYNE
83 Dean History & Social Sciences ... Dr. Monte FINKELSTEIN
81 Associate Dean Mathematics ... Dr. Kalynda HOLTON
72 Dean Technology & Professional Pgms ... Ms. Kate STEWART
88 Assoc Dean Dev Comm & Col Success ... Ms. Sharisse TURNER
88 Associate Dean Developmental Math ... Mr. David DELROSSI
88 Associate Dean Natural Sciences ... Mr. Anthony JONES
08 Director of Library Services ... Ms. Deborah P. ROBINSON
76 Dean Health Care Professions ... Dr. Alice NIED
37 Director of Financial Aid ... Mr. William SPIERS
84 Dir of Student Success & Retention ... Dr. Shanna AUTRY
15 Interim Director of Human Resources ... Ms. Jackie CHAIRES-LACEY
102 Director of TCC Foundation ... Ms. Heather MITCHELL
41 Director of Athletics ... Mr. Rob CHANEY
35 Dir of Campus & Civic Engagement ... Mr. Mike COLEMAN
26 Director of Communications ... Mr. Al MORAN
88 Exec Dir Florida Public Safety Inst ... Mr. E. E. EUNICE
18 Dir Facilities/Construction/Plng ... Mr. David WILDES
21 Controller ... Ms. Patricia MANNING
45 Director of Educational Research ... Dr. Barbara J. GILL
09 Director of Institutional Research ... Ms. Margaret WINGATE
106 Dir Center for Distance Learning ... Dr. Marilyn DICKEY
88 Dir Ctr for Teach/Learn/Ldrshp ... Dr. Karinda BARRETT
18 Construction Coordinator ... Mr. Bill HUNTER
85 International Students Coordinator ... Ms. Betty JENSEN
14 Director of User Services ... Mr. Chip SINGLETARY
14 Director of Enterprise Systems ... Mr. Mike ROBECK
25 Contracts and Grants Manager ... Ms. Vanessa WRIGHT
88 Director Grants & Special Projects ... Mr. Steven SOLOMON
96 Purchasing Manager ... Mr. Bobby HINSON
19 Chief of Police ... Mr. Christopher SUMMERS
06 Registrar ... Ms. Renee R. GREEN
20 Dean of Curriculum and Instruction ... Mrs. Calandra STRINGER
36 Director of Career Services ... Ms. Catie GOODMAN
04 Administrative Asst to President ... Ms. Lenda KLING
43 Dir Legal Services/General Counsel ... Mr. Craig KNOX

Talmudic College of Florida (C)

4000 Alton Road, Miami Beach FL 33140
County: Dade | FICE Identification: 025089
Unit ID: 137777
Telephone: (305) 534-7050 | Carnegie Class: Spec/Faith
FAX Number: (305) 534-8444 | Calendar System: Semester
URL: www.talmudicu.edu
Established: 1974 | Annual Undergrad Tuition & Fees: $13,000
Enrollment: 63 | Male
Affiliation or Control: Independent Non-Profit | IRS Status: 501(c)3
Highest Offering: Doctorate
Program: Teacher Preparatory; Professional; Religious Emphasis
Accreditation: **RABN**

01 President ... Rabbi Yitzchak ZWEIG
05 Dean/Vice President ... Rabbi Yochanan ZWEIG
06 Registrar ... Rabbi Yitzchak WINKLER
37 Director Student Financial Aid ... Ms. Sharon BRECHER
20 Director Educational Programs ... Rabbi Yeshaya GREENBERG
07 Director of Admissions ... Rabbi Yaakov BURSTYN

Taylor College (D)

5190 SE 125th Street, Belleview FL 34420
County: Marion | FICE Identification: 041166
Unit ID: 449524
Telephone: (352) 245-4119 | Carnegie Class: Not Classified
FAX Number: (352) 245-0276 | Calendar System: Other
URL: taylorcollege.edu
Established: 1999 | Annual Undergrad Tuition & Fees: $14,224
Enrollment: 150 | Coed
Affiliation or Control: Proprietary | IRS Status: Proprietary
Highest Offering: Associate Degree
Program: Occupational
Accreditation: **COE**, PTAA

01 President ... Dianne HAMMOND

Thomas M. Cooley Law School Tampa Bay Campus (E)

9445 Camden Field Parkway, Riverview FL 33578
Telephone: (813) 419-5100 | Identification: 770290
Accreditation: **&NH**

† Branch campus of Western Michigan University Cooley Law School, Lansing, MI.

Touro College South (F)

1701 Washington Avenue, Miami Beach FL 33139
Telephone: (305) 535-1066 | Identification: 770147
Accreditation: **&M**

† Branch campus of Touro College, New York, NY.

Trinity Baptist College (G)

800 Hammond Boulevard, Jacksonville FL 32221-1398
County: Duval | FICE Identification: 031019
Unit ID: 137953
Telephone: (904) 596-2400 | Carnegie Class: Spec/Faith
FAX Number: (904) 596-2532 | Calendar System: Semester
URL: www.tbc.edu
Established: 1974 | Annual Undergrad Tuition & Fees: $17,310
Enrollment: 376 | Coed
Affiliation or Control: Baptist | IRS Status: 501(c)3
Highest Offering: Master's
Program: Liberal Arts And General; Teacher Preparatory; Religious Emphasis
Accreditation: **TRACS**

00 Chancellor ... Dr. Thomas C. MESSER
01 President/CEO ... Mr. Mac HEAVENER
03 Senior Vice President ... Dr. Matthew BEEMER
32 Dean of Students ... Mr. Jeremiah STANLEY
84 Director of Enrollment Management ... Mrs. Melissa GIBSON
37 Director of Financial Aid ... Mr. Mark ELKINS
04 Administrative Asst to President ... Mrs. Sherry LENTZ
06 Registrar ... Dr. John CASH
08 Head Librarian ... Dr. John LUCY
10 Chief Business Officer ... Mr. Mike AKINS
41 Athletic Director ... Mr. John JONES
18 Chief Facilities/Physical Plant ... Mr. Roger CHASTAIN
19 Director Security/Safety ... Mr. John CASH, JR.
29 Director Alumni Relations ... Mrs. Jenny STANLEY
30 Chief Development/Advancement ... Mr. Matthew HEAVENER

Trinity College of Florida (H)

2430 Welbilt Boulevard, Trinity FL 34655-4401
County: Pasco | FICE Identification: 030282
Unit ID: 137962
Telephone: (727) 376-6911 | Carnegie Class: Spec/Faith
FAX Number: (727) 376-0781 | Calendar System: Semester
URL: www.trinitycollege.edu
Established: 1932 | Annual Undergrad Tuition & Fees: $13,670
Enrollment: 229 | Coed
Affiliation or Control: Independent Non-Profit | IRS Status: 501(c)3
Highest Offering: Baccalaureate
Program: Religious Emphasis
Accreditation: **BI**

01 President ... Dr. Mark T. O'FARRELL
32 Vice President Student Affairs ... Rev. Al DEPOUTOT
05 Vice President Academic Affairs ... Dr. Dennis COX
30 Vice President for Advancement ... Dr. Charlie MARTIN
10 Vice Pres for Business & Finance ... Mr. Paul S. WILLARD
06 Registrar ... Mrs. Shannon T. RANES
26 Asst VP Marketing/Communications ... Vacant
07 Director of Admissions ... Mr. Timothy P. BETTELLI

Trinity International University, Florida Regional Center (I)

8190 W State Road 84, Davie FL 33324-4611
Telephone: (954) 382-6400 | FICE Identification: 012314
Accreditation: **&NH**

† Regional accreditation is carried under the parent institution in Deerfield, IL.

Ultimate Medical Academy-Clearwater (J)

1255 Cleveland Street, Clearwater FL 33756
County: Pinellas | FICE Identification: 035493
Unit ID: 441371
Telephone: (727) 298-8685 | Carnegie Class: Not Classified
FAX Number: (727) 446-2489 | Calendar System: Semester
URL: www.ultimatemedical.edu
Established: 1998 | Annual Undergrad Tuition & Fees: $15,500
Enrollment: 332 | Coed
Affiliation or Control: Proprietary | IRS Status: Proprietary
Highest Offering: Associate Degree
Program: Occupational
Accreditation: **ABHES**, ACICS

01 Campus Director ... Ms. Silvina LANOUREUX

Ultimate Medical Academy Online-Tampa (K)

3101 W Martin Luther King Boulevard, Tampa FL 33607
Telephone: (813) 386-6350 | Identification: 770528
Accreditation: **ABHES**, ACICS, CAHIIM

† Branch campus of Ultimate Medical Academy-Clearwater, Clearwater, FL.

Unilatina International College (L)

3130 Commerce Pkwy, Miramar FL 33025
County: Broward | Identification: 667155
Telephone: (954) 607-4344 | Carnegie Class: Not Classified
FAX Number: (954) 357-1766 | Calendar System: Quarter
URL: www.unilatina.edu
Established: 2001 | Annual Undergrad Tuition & Fees: $17,575
Enrollment: 65 | Coed
Affiliation or Control: Proprietary | IRS Status: Proprietary
Highest Offering: Associate Degree
Program: 2-Year Principally Bachelor's Creditable; Business Emphasis
Accreditation: **ACICS**

01 President ... Lydia B. BAUTISTA MOLLER
05 Academic Director ... Angelica MOYANO

University of Fort Lauderdale (M)

4069 NW 16th Street, Lauderhill FL 33313-5809
County: Broward | FICE Identification: 041563
Unit ID: 457402
Telephone: (954) 486-7728 | Carnegie Class: Not Classified
FAX Number: (954) 486-7667 | Calendar System: Other
URL: www.uftl.edu
Established: | Annual Undergrad Tuition & Fees: $7,410
Enrollment: 43 | Coed
Affiliation or Control: Non-denominational | IRS Status: 501(c)3
Highest Offering: Doctorate
Program: Professional; Religious Emphasis

Accreditation: **TRACS**

01 Chancellor and CEO .... Dr. Henry B. FERNANDEZ
11 Chief Operating Officer .... Mr. Maurice HERRING
10 Chief Financial Officer .... Mr. Brian HANKERSON
32 Vice Pres for Academic Affairs .... Dr. C. Racquel CAREW
06 Registrar .... Ms. Lenice BARNETT
07 Director of Admissions .... Toneita BROWN

University of Miami (A)

1252 Memorial Drive, Coral Gables FL 33124
County: Miami-Dade FICE Identification: 001536
Unit ID: 135726
Telephone: (305) 284-2211 Carnegie Class: RU/VH
FAX Number: N/A Calendar System: Semester
URL: www.miami.edu
Established: 1925 Annual Undergrad Tuition & Fees: $45,724
Enrollment: 16,774 Coed
Affiliation or Control: Independent Non-Profit IRS Status: 501(c)3
Highest Offering: Doctorate
Program: Liberal Arts And General; Teacher Preparatory; Professional
Accreditation: **SC**, ANEST, BUS, BUSA, CAATE, CEA, CLPSY, COPSY, DENT, ENG, HSA, IPSY, LAW, MED, MUS, NURSE, PH, PTA, @TEAC

01 President .... Dr. Julio FRENK
05 Executive Vice President & Provost .... Dr. Thomas J. LEBLANC
10 Senior VP Business & Finance .... Mr. Joseph T. NATOLI
63 Senior VP & Dean School of Med . Dr. Pascal J. GOLDSCHMIDT
30 Sr VP Advancement/External Affairs ..... Mr. Sergio M. GONZALEZ
21 Vice President Finance & Treasurer .... Mr. Geoffrey E. KIRLES
43 Vice President & General Counsel .... Ms. Aileen M. UGALDE
32 Vice President Student Affairs .... Dr. Patricia A. WHITELY
17 VP Medical Administration .... Mr. Joseph T. NATOLI
15 Vice President Human Resources .... Ms. Nerissa E. MORRIS
13 VP Information Technology & CIO .... Mr. Steve CAWLEY
21 Vice President Budget & Planning .... Mr. Mark DIAZ
18 VP Real Estate & Facilities .... Mr. Larry D. MARBERT
26 VP University Communications ..... Ms. Jacqueline R. MENENDEZ
86 VP Government Affairs .... Mr. Rodolfo J. FERNANDEZ
84 VP Enrollment Management .... Mr. John G. HALLER
00 Chairman Board of Trustees .... Mr. Stuart A. MILLER
100 President's Chief of Staff .... Vacant
20 Sr Vice Provost/Dean Undergrad Educ .... Dr. William S. GREEN
46 Vice Provost Research .... Dr. John L. BIXBY
20 Vice Provost Faculty Affairs .... Dr. David J. BIRNBACH
41 Director Athletics .... Mr. Blake JAMES
29 Associate VP Alumni Relations .... Ms. Donna A. ARBIDE
31 AVP Community Relations .... Ms. Sarah N. ARTECONA
105 AVP Communications and Marketing ... Mr. Todd M. ELLENBERG
16 Associate Vice President/Med HR .... Ms. Oona A. JORGENSEN
27 Executive Director Media Relations .... Mrs. Elizabeth AMORE
19 Chief of Police .... Major David A. RIVERO
49 Dean College of Arts & Sciences .... Dr. Leonidas G. BACHAS
48 Dean School of Architecture .... Dr. Rodolphe EL-KOURY
50 Dean Business Administration .... Dr. Eugene ANDERSON
60 Dean School Communication .... Dr. Gregory J. SHEPHERD
53 Dean Education/Human Development . Dr. Isaac PRILLELTENSKY
54 Dean College of Engineering .... Dr. James M. TIEN
61 Dean School of Law .... Ms. Patricia WHITE
64 Dean School of Music .... Dr. Shelton G. BERG
65 Dean Marine & Atmospheric Science .... Dr. Roni AVISSAR
66 Dean Nursing & Health Studies .... Dr. Nilda P. PERAGALLO
58 Dean Graduate School .... Vacant
35 AVP Stdnt Affs & Dean of Students .... Dr. Ricardo D. HALL
07 Associate Dean Enrollment .... Mr. Mark REID
38 Director Student Counseling .... Dr. Rene MONTEAGUDO
85 Director Intl Student/Scholar Svc .Ms. Teresa S. DE LA GUARDIA
39 Director Student Housing .... Mr. James G. SMART
96 Chief Purchasing Officer .... Ms. Susan R. MONTES
14 Associate VP Enterprise App .... Mr. Jack J. GEORGE
14 Associate VP Technical Infrastruct .... Mr. Timothy C. RAMSAY
109 Executive Director Auxiliary Svcs .... Ms. Sandra REDWAY
51 Dean Continuing Education .... Dr. Rebecca MACMILLAN FOX
40 Director Bookstore .... Ms. Wendy SMITH
06 Registrar .... Ms. Karen J. BECKETT
08 Dean Libraries .... Dr. Charles ECKMAN
101 Assistant University Secretary .... Ms. Leslie DELLINGER ACEITUNO
102 Sr Director Foundation Relations .... Ms. Joanna DE VELASCO
36 Executive Director Career Services .... Mr. Christian GARCIA
104 Director Study Abroad .... Ms. Devika M. MILNER
22 AVP Workplace Equity .... Ms. Beverly PRUITT
25 AVP Business Services .... Mr. Humberto M. SPEZIANI
37 Executive Director Financial Aid .... Mr. Raymon E. NAULT-HIX
44 Executive Director Annual Giving .... Mr. Troy ODOM

University of Phoenix Central Florida Main Campus (B)

8325 South Park Circle Ste 100, Orlando FL 32819
Telephone: (407) 345-8868 Identification: 770932
Accreditation: **&NH**, ACBSP

† Branch campus of University of Phoenix, Tempe, AZ.

University of Phoenix North Florida Campus (C)

4500 Salisbury Road, Jacksonville FL 32216-0959
Telephone: (904) 636-6645 Identification: 770197
Accreditation: **&NH**, ACBSP

† Branch campus of University of Phoenix, Tempe, AZ.

University of Phoenix South Florida Main Campus (D)

2400 SW 145th Avenue, Miramar FL 33207-4145
Telephone: (954) 382-5303 Identification: 770237
Accreditation: **&NH**, ACBSP

† Branch campus of University of Phoenix, Tempe, AZ.

University of St. Augustine for Health Sciences (E)

One University Boulevard, St. Augustine FL 32086
Telephone: (904) 826-0084 Identification: 770939
Accreditation: **&WC**, DEAC, OT, PTA

† Branch campus of University of St. Augustine for Health Sciences, San Marcos, CA.

University of Southernmost Florida (F)

9550 Regency Square Blvd.Suite 1100, Jacksonville FL 32225
County: Duval FICE Identification: 025982
Unit ID: 134121
Telephone: (904) 724-2229 Carnegie Class: Assoc/PrivFP
FAX Number: (904) 520-7295 Calendar System: Quarter
URL: www.usmf.edu
Established: 1960 Annual Undergrad Tuition & Fees: $12,165
Enrollment: 173 Coed
Affiliation or Control: Proprietary IRS Status: Proprietary
Highest Offering: Associate Degree
Program: Occupational; 2-Year Principally Bachelor's Creditable; Nursing Emphasis
Accreditation: **ACICS**

01 Campus Director .... Mr. Orlando CASARIEGO
05 Director of Education .... Ms. Katrina BROOKS

University of Southernmost Florida-Coral Gables Campus (G)

178 Giralda Avenue, Coral Gables FL 33134
Telephone: (305) 644-1171 Identification: 770614
Accreditation: **ACICS**

† Branch campus of University of Southernmost Florida, Jacksonville, FL.

University of Tampa (H)

401 W Kennedy Boulevard, Tampa FL 33606-1490
County: Hillsborough FICE Identification: 001538
Unit ID: 137847
Telephone: (813) 253-3333 Carnegie Class: Master's L
FAX Number: (813) 258-7207 Calendar System: Other
URL: www.ut.edu
Established: 1931 Annual Undergrad Tuition & Fees: $27,044
Enrollment: 7,752 Coed
Affiliation or Control: Independent Non-Profit IRS Status: 501(c)3
Highest Offering: Master's
Program: Liberal Arts And General; Teacher Preparatory; Professional
Accreditation: **SC**, BUS, CAATE, CS, FEPAC, MUS, NUR

01 President .... Dr. Ronald L. VAUGHN
05 Provost/Vice Pres Academic Affairs .... Dr. David STERN
10 Vice Pres Administration/Finance .... Mr. Richard W. OGOREK
84 Vice President Enrollment .... Mr. Dennis L. NOSTRAND
30 Vice Pres Develop & Univ Relations .... Mr. Gary B. GRANT
44 Vice Pres Capital Campaign .... Mr. Daniel T. GURA
45 Vice Pres Operations & Planning .... Dr. Linda W. DEVINE
13 Chief Info Officer Info Technology .... Mr. Thomas WEEKS
88 Chief Information Security Officer .... Ms. Tammy L. CLARK
21 Assistant Vice Pres Admin/Finance .... Mr. T. Kevin LAFFERTY
32 Dean of Students .... Ms. Stephanie R. KREBS
20 Assoc Provost & Dean of Acad Svcs .... Dr. Katharine H. COLE
06 Registrar .... Ms. Michelle PELAEZ
08 Director of the Library .... Ms. Marlyn PETHE-COOK
29 Director of Alumni Relations .... Mr. James HARDWICK
37 Director of Financial Aid .... Ms. Jacqueline LATORELLA
26 Director of Public Information .... Mr. Eric D. CARDENAS
18 Director of Facilities Management .... Mr. David RAMSEY
15 Exec Director of Human Resources .... Ms. Donna B. POPOVICH
07 Sr Associate Director of Admissions .... Mr. Brent W. BENNER
41 Athletic Director .... Mr. Larry J. MARFISE
40 Manager Campus Store .... Ms. Angela M. O'CONNOR
39 Director of Residence Life .... Vacant
22 Affirmative Action Officer .... Ms. Donna B. POPOVICH
19 Director Safety & Security .... Mr. Kevin A. HOWELL
23 Dir Health Center/Stdnt Counseling .... Ms. Sharon P. SCHAEFER
38 Director Student Counseling .... Ms. Sharon P. SCHAEFER
96 Director of Procurement .... Ms. Cyn D. EZELL
09 Dir Institutional Effectiveness .... Dr. Jeanne M. ROBERTS
92 Director of Honors Program .... Dr. Gary S. LUTER
50 Dean College of Business .... Dr. F. Frank GHANNADIAN
83 Dean Social Science/Math Education .... Dr. Jack M. GELLER
81 Dean College Natural/Health Sci .... Dr. James A. GORE
57 Dean College of Arts/Letters .... Dr. Haig MARDIROSIAN
51 Assoc Dean Graduate/Continuing Stds .... Dr. Donald D. MORRILL
88 Assoc Dean Baccalaureate Experience .... Ms. Catherine CHASTAIN-ELLIOTT
36 Assoc Dean Career Dev & Engagement ..... Mr. Timothy HARDING
104 Assoc Dean International Programs .... Dr. Marca BEAR
04 Executive Asst to President .... Ms. Madelyn CASTRO

Valencia College (I)

PO Box 3028, Orlando FL 32802-3028
County: Orange FICE Identification: 006750
Unit ID: 138187
Telephone: (407) 299-5000 Carnegie Class: Assoc/Pub-U-MC
FAX Number: (407) 426-8970 Calendar System: Semester
URL: www.valenciacollege.edu
Established: 1967 Annual Undergrad Tuition & Fees (In-State): $3,092
Enrollment: 43,219 Coed
Affiliation or Control: State IRS Status: 501(c)3
Highest Offering: Baccalaureate
Program: Occupational; 2-Year Principally Bachelor's Creditable
Accreditation: **SC**, ADNUR, CEA, COARC, COARCP, CVT, DH, DMS, EMT, RAD

01 President .... Dr. Sanford C. SHUGART
05 VP Academic Affairs & Planning .... Dr. Susan E. LEDLOW
32 Vice President Student Affairs .... Dr. Joyce C. ROMANO
10 Vice Pres Business Ops & Finance .... Mr. Loren J. BENDER
30 Vice Pres Institutional Advancement .... Vacant
43 Vice Pres Policy & General Counsel .... Dr. William J. MULLOWNEY
15 VP Org Dev & Human Resources .... Dr. Amy N. BOSLEY
26 VP Public Affairs & Marketing .... Mr. James R. GALBRAITH
12 Campus President East Campus .... Dr. Stacey R. JOHNSON
12 Campus President Osceola Campus .... Dr. Kathleen A. PLINSKE
12 Campus President West Campus .... Dr. Falecia D. WILLIAMS
13 Chief Information Officer .... Mr. William A. WHITE
102 Foundation President and CEO . Ms. Geraldine M P. GALLAGHER
16 Asst VP Human Resources .... Mr. Joe A. LIVINGSTON
18 Asst VP Facilities & Sustain .... Mr. Eugene A. BOTTORFF
103 Asst VP Career & Workforce Ed .... Dr. Nasser HEDAYAT
21 Asst VP Financial Svcs .... Ms. Jacqueline D. LASCH
35 Asst VP Student Affairs .... Dr. Sonya F. JOSEPH
88 Asst VP College Transition .... Ms. Amy KLEEMAN
07 Asst VP Admissions & Records .... Dr. Renee K. SIMPSON
28 Asst VP Diversity & Inclusion .... Vacant
19 Asst VP Safety/Security Risk Mgmt .... Mr. Paul ROONEY
09 Asst VP IE & Planning .... Mr. Kurt E. EWEN
108 Asst VP Curric & Assessment .... Dr. Karen M. BORGLUM
109 Asst VP Budget/Aux Services .... Ms. Sherri L. DIXON
103 Foundation VP & COO .... Ms. Michelle D. MATIS
25 Asst VP Resource Development .... Ms. Kristeen R. CHRISTIAN
88 Asst VP Teaching & Learning .... Ms. Wendi M. DEW
35 Dean of Students East .... Mr. Joseph M. SARRUBBO
35 Dean of Students West .... Ms. Linda K. HERLOCKER
35 Dean of Students Osceola .... Ms. Jillian M. SZENTMIKLOSI
35 Dean of Students Winter Park .... Vacant
40 Director College Bookstore .... Mr. Todd A. HUNT
92 Director Honors Program .... Dr. Cheryl ROBINSON
105 Director Web and Portal Services .... Vacant
04 Senior Executive Assistant .... Ms. Barbara HALSTEAD
08 Campus Dir Library W .... Ms. Ruth S. SMITH
104 Director Study Abroad & Global Exp .... Ms. Jennifer ROBERTSON
37 Director Financial Aid .... Mr. Christen L. CHRISTENSEN
84 Director Enrollment Services .... Ms. Jacquelyn F. THOMPSON
14 Assistant Chief Info Officer .... Ms. Patricia T. SMITH
27 Director Public Relations .... Ms. Carol E. TRAYNOR
96 Managing Director Procurement .... Ms. Rholda S. ULMER
08 Campus Dir Library E .... Dr. Dennis F. WEEKS
08 Campus Dir Library WP .... Ms. Katherine A. MILLER
106 Assoc Dir Online Teach/Learn .... Ms. Page A. JERZAK

Virginia College (J)

5940 Beach Boulevard, Jacksonville FL 32207
Telephone: (904) 520-7400 Identification: 770839
Accreditation: **ACICS**, ACFEI, MAAB

† Branch campus of Virginia College, Birmingham, AL.

Virginia College (K)

312 East Nine Mile Road, Suite 34, Pensacola FL 32514-1475
Telephone: (850) 436-8444 FICE Identification: 031005
Accreditation: **ACICS**, MAAB, SURGT

† Branch campus of Virginia College, Birmingham, AL.

Warner University (L)

13895 Highway 27, Lake Wales FL 33859-2549
County: Polk FICE Identification: 008848
Unit ID: 138275
Telephone: (863) 638-1426 Carnegie Class: Master's S
FAX Number: (863) 638-1472 Calendar System: Semester
URL: www.warner.edu
Established: 1968 Annual Undergrad Tuition & Fees: $26,834
Enrollment: 1,162 Coed
Affiliation or Control: Church Of God IRS Status: 501(c)3
Highest Offering: Master's
Program: Liberal Arts And General; Teacher Preparatory
Accreditation: **SC**, SW

01 President .... Dr. Gregory V. HALL
88 Asst to the President/SACS Liaison .... Dr. James G. MOYER
10 Vice Pres for Finance & Business .... Mr. Greg A. RODDEN
30 Vice President for Advancement .... Mrs. Doris B. GUKICH
84 VP for Enrollment Mgmt & Marketing .... Mrs. Dawn M. RAFOOL
32 Dean of Students .... Rev. Dawn MEADOWS
43 General Counsel .... Dr. Norman WHITE

05 VP and Chief Academic Officer ....Dr. Steven DARR
06 Registrar ....Mrs. Sara F. KANE
07 Director of Admissions ....Mr. Bob MOBLEY
37 Director Student Financial Aid ....Mrs. Lorrie STEEDLEY
21 Controller ....Mr. Dean MEADOWS
08 Librarian ....Mrs. Sherill HARRIGER
29 Director Alumni Relations ....Miss Kareen PICKETT
09 Director of Institutional Research ....Mrs. Lisa B. MURPHY
18 Chief Facilities/Physical Plant ....Mr. Bill BROWN
97 Director of General Studies ....Mrs. Kelly MILLS
88 Chair Ministry ....Dr. Michael SANDERS
40 Director Bookstore ....Ms. Monica HAMILTON
13 Director of Institutional Tech ....Mr. Mark THOMAS
19 Director Campus Security ....Mr. Brian ROWLES
36 Director Career Counseling ....Mrs. Dawn MEADOWS
88 Director Academic Skills Ctr ....Mrs. Kelly MORGAN
106 Director Online Services ....Mr. Shawn TAYLOR
107 Dean Adult Prof Division ....Mr. Thomas MALCOLM
88 Dean Adult Ministry Division ....Mr. Thomas MALCOLM
04 Administrative Asst to President ....Mrs. Alane RICHARDVILLE
41 Athletic Director ....Mr. Kevin JONES

Webber International University (A)

1201 Scenic Highway N/P.O. Box 96,
Babson Park FL 33827-0096

County: Polk FICE Identification: 001540
Unit ID: 138293
Telephone: (863) 638-1431 Carnegie Class: Bac/Diverse
FAX Number: (863) 638-2823 Calendar System: Semester
URL: www.webber.edu
Established: 1927 Annual Undergrad Tuition & Fees: $47,368
Enrollment: 731 Coed
Affiliation or Control: Independent Non-Profit IRS Status: 501(c)3
Highest Offering: Master's
Program: Business Emphasis
Accreditation: SC, IACBE

01 President ....Dr. H. Keith WADE
05 Academic Dean ....Dr. Charles SHIEH
10 Vice President Finance ....Ms. Christina JORDON
32 Dean of Student Life ....Ms. Christina PATTERSON
06 Registrar/Dir of Financial Aid ....Mrs. Kathy A. WILSON
31 Director Cmty Rels & Marketing ....Mrs. Stephanie LEONE
08 Head Librarian ....Ms. Sue DUNNING
26 Dir Public Relations/Athletic Dir ....Mr. Bill HEATH
13 Director Information Technology ....Mr. Bob M. WEIS
18 Director of Campus Svcs/Maintenance ....Mr. Matt YENTES
40 Director of Bookstore ....Mr. Jay CULVER
07 Director of Admissions ....Mr. Ryan PICARD
09 Director of Institutional Effectiv ....Dr. Nelson MARQUEZ
50 Chair of Business Education ....Dr. Jeanette EBERLE
53 Chair of General Education Division ....Dr. Charles WUNKER
04 Executive Asst to President ....Ms. Gerlinde DANCY
19 Director Security/Safety ....Mr. Michael RITTER
29 Dir Annual Fund/Alumni Relations ....Ms. Jennifer MUELLER

West Coast University - Miami (B)

9250 NW 36th Street, Doral FL 33178

Telephone: (786) 501-7070 Identification: 770936
Accreditation: &WC

† Branch campus of West Coast University, North Hollywood, CA.

Wolford College (C)

1336 Creekside Boulevard, Suite 2,
Naples FL 34108-1931

County: Collier FICE Identification: 039393
Unit ID: 451130
Telephone: (239) 513-1135 Carnegie Class: Spec/Health
FAX Number: (239) 513-1368 Calendar System: Semester
URL: www.wolford.edu
Established: 2004 Annual Graduate Tuition & Fees: N/A
Enrollment: 208 Coed
Affiliation or Control: Independent Non-Profit IRS Status: 501(c)3
Highest Offering: Master's; No Undergraduates
Program: Professional
Accreditation: ANEST

01 President ....Dr. Norman R. WOLFORD
00 Chancellor ....Dr. Thomas COOK
37 Director of Financial Aid Services ....Mr. Gilbert CHANG
84 Dir Enrollment & Student Services ....Ms. Lori ELLISON
04 Administrative Asst/Accred Coord ....Ms. Jessica GARCIA

WyoTech (D)

470 Destination Daytona Lane, Ormond Beach FL 32174

County: Volusia FICE Identification: 023462
Unit ID: 132268
Telephone: (386) 255-0295 Carnegie Class: Not Classified
FAX Number: (386) 252-3523 Calendar System: Quarter
URL: www.wyotech.edu
Established: Annual Undergrad Tuition & Fees: $26,500
Enrollment: 400 Coed
Affiliation or Control: Proprietary IRS Status: Proprietary
Highest Offering: Associate Degree
Program: Occupational
Accreditation: ACCSC

01 Campus President ....Ms. Kareena SALTER

Yeshiva Gedolah Rabbinical College (E)

1140 Alton Road, Miami Beach FL 33139-4708

County: Dade FICE Identification: 032563
Unit ID: 363712
Telephone: (305) 653-8770 Carnegie Class: Spec/Faith
FAX Number: (305) 653-6790 Calendar System: Semester
Established: 1973 Annual Undergrad Tuition & Fees: $8,400
Enrollment: 51 Male
Affiliation or Control: Independent Non-Profit IRS Status: 501(c)3
Highest Offering: Master's
Program: Teacher Preparatory; Professional
Accreditation: @RABN

01 Executive Vice President ....Rabbi Benzion KORF
05 Dean ....Rabbi Abraham KORF
06 Registrar ....Ayelet BORTUNK

GEORGIA

Abraham Baldwin Agricultural College (F)

ABAC 1 - 2802 Moore Highway, Tifton GA 31793-2601

County: Tift FICE Identification: 001541
Unit ID: 138558
Telephone: (229) 391-5001 Carnegie Class: Assoc/Pub4
FAX Number: N/A Calendar System: Semester
URL: www.abac.edu
Established: 1908 Annual Undergrad Tuition & Fees (In-State): $3,453
Enrollment: 3,458 Coed
Affiliation or Control: State IRS Status: 501(c)3
Highest Offering: Baccalaureate
Program: 2-Year Principally Bachelor's Creditable; Liberal Arts And General; Professional; Business Emphasis
Accreditation: SC, ADNUR

01 President ....Dr. David BRIDGES
05 Interim VP for Academic Affairs ....Dr. Gail DILLARD
10 VP for Fiscal Affairs & Opers ....Mr. Paul WILLIS
30 Interim VP Ext Affairs/Advancement ....Mr. Paul WILLIAMS
08 Director of Library Services ....Ms. Marie DAVIS
32 Dean of Students ....Ms. Bernice HUGHES
41 Athletic Director ....Mr. Alan KRAMER
06 Registrar ....Dr. Amy WILLIS
38 Director of Student Development ....Dr. Maggie MARTIN
37 Director of Student Financial Svcs ....Mr. Michael WRIGHT
15 Director of Human Resources ....Mr. Richard SPANCAKE
26 Director of Public Relations ....Vacant
108 Director of Assessment ....Vacant
84 Director Enrollment Management ....Ms. Donna WEBB
96 Director of Procurement ....Ms. Teri MATHIS
19 Chief of Police ....Mr. Bryan A. GOLDEN
04 Administrative Asst to President ....Ms. Pam LEONARD
39 Director of Student Housing ....Dr. Chris S. KINSEY
13 Chief Info Technology Officer ....Mr. Robert GERHART

† Part of the University System of Georgia.

Agnes Scott College (G)

141 E. College Avenue, Decatur GA 30030-3770

County: DeKalb FICE Identification: 001542
Unit ID: 138600
Telephone: (404) 471-6000 Carnegie Class: Bac/A&S
FAX Number: (404) 471-6067 Calendar System: Semester
URL: www.agnesscott.edu
Established: 1889 Annual Undergrad Tuition & Fees: $37,236
Enrollment: 882 Female
Affiliation or Control: Presbyterian Church (U.S.A.) IRS Status: 501(c)3
Highest Offering: Baccalaureate
Program: Liberal Arts And General
Accreditation: SC

01 President ....Dr. Elizabeth KISS
05 Interim VP for Academic Affairs ....Dr. Kerry E. PANNELL
32 VP Student Life & Dean of Students ....Ms. Donna A. LEE
10 VP Business & Finance ....Mr. John P. HEGMAN
30 Interim VP for College Advancement ....Ms. Elizabeth K. WILSON
84 VP Enrollment & Dean of Admission ....Ms. Laura MARTIN
26 Senior Director of Communications ....Mr. J.D FITE
04 Director Office of the President ....Ms. Lea Ann HUDSON
13 Assoc VP Technology ....Ms. LaNeta COUNTS
20 Interim Assoc Dean of the College ....Dr. Lilia HARVEY
56 Associate VP Extended Programs ....Dr. Patricia SZYMURSKI
35 Associate Dean of Students ....Dr. Kijua SANDERS-MCMURTRY
06 Registrar ....Ms. Gail N. MEIS
08 Director of Library Services ....Ms. Elizabeth BAGLEY
29 Senior Director Alumnae Relations ....Ms. Kimberly VICKERS
18 Director of Facilities ....Mr. Tim BLANKENSHIP
15 Director of Human Resources ....Ms. Karen GILBERT
41 Director of Athletics ....Ms. Joeleen AKIN
42 Chaplain ....Rev. Kate COLUSSY-ESTES
37 Director of Student Financial Aid ....Mr. Patrick BONONES
09 Director of Institutional Research ....Ms. Corey DUNN
07 Director of Admissions ....Ms. Alexa GAETA
23 Executive Director Wellness Center ....Ms. Juanita G. MOTTLEY
19 Director Public Safety ....Mr. Henry HOPE

Albany State University (H)

504 College Drive, Albany GA 31705-2796

County: Dougherty FICE Identification: 001544
Unit ID: 138716
Telephone: (229) 430-4600 Carnegie Class: Master's M
FAX Number: (229) 430-4830 Calendar System: Semester
URL: www.asurams.edu
Established: 1903 Annual Undergrad Tuition & Fees (In-State): $4,858
Enrollment: 3,910 Coed
Affiliation or Control: State IRS Status: 501(c)3
Highest Offering: Beyond Master's But Less Than Doctorate
Program: Liberal Arts And General; Teacher Preparatory; Professional
Accreditation: SC, ACBSP, CACREP, FEPAC, NUR, SPAA, SW, TED

01 Interim President ....Dr. Arthur N. DUNNING
04 Senior Advisor/Spec Asst to Pres ....Ms. Cynthia HOKE
86 Exec to Pres Govt/Comm Relations ....Mr. Clifford PORTER
43 University Counsel ....Ms. Sharon (Nyota) TUCKER
05 Provost/VP Academic Affairs ....Dr. Abiodun OJEMAKINDE
20 Asst VP for Academic Affairs ....Dr. Linda GRIMSLEY
10 Vice President Fiscal Affairs ....Mr. Larry WAKEFIELD
13 VP & CIO ....Mr. Del KIMBROUGH
30 VP Inst Advancement ....Dr. Chanta HAYWOOD
32 Interim Vice Pres Student Affairs ... Dr. Stephanie HARRIS-JOLLY
46 Interim Assoc Provost Sponsored Prg ....Dr. Louise WRENSFORD
84 Assoc Prov Enrollment Mgmt ....Dr. Paul BRYANT
06 Registrar ....Ms. Victoria EILAND
19 Chief of Police ....Mr. John FIELDS
21 Controller ....Ms. Dorothy MARTIN
83 Dean Arts & Humanities ....Dr. Marcia HOOD
50 Interim Dean College of Business ....Dr. Michael ROGERS
53 Interim Dean College of Education ....Dr. Thomas THOMPSON
81 Dean Sciences & Health Professions ....Dr. Joyce JOHNSON
41 Director of Athletics ....Dr. Richard WILLIAMS
88 Director Internal Audits ....Ms. Katherine LASTER
88 Director Title III ....Mrs. Connie LEGGETT
88 Director Budgets and Contracts ....Mrs. Marion RYANT
96 Director Business Services ....Ms. Lori W. BURNETT
18 Interim Dir Facilities Management ....Mr. Robert LAWSON
15 Director Human Resources Mgmt ....Mr. Steve GRANT
39 Director Housing & Residence Life ....Mrs. Bonisha PORTER
88 Director Infrastructure Svcs ....Mr. Lonnie WORMLEY
88 Director Application Svcs ....Mr. Amitabh SINGH
106 Dir Academic On-Line Instruction ....Ms. LaQuata SUMTER
92 Dir Honors Program ....Dr. Melvin SHELTON
104 Director Global Programs ....Dr. Nneka-Nora OSAKWE
26 Director University Communic ....Ms. Landera CARROLL
29 Director Alumni Affairs ....Ms. Sue POLITE-SOLOMON
36 Director Career Services ....Ms. Tracy S. WILLIAMS
88 Director Sports Information ....Mr. Stanley MCCORMICK
35 Dir Student Life/Judicial Affairs ....Ms. Gwinetta L. TRICE
38 Director Counseling/Disability Svcs ....Dr. Stephanie HARRIS-JOLLY
23 Director Student Health Services ....Dr. Vicki PHILLIPS
88 Exec Asst Ctr African American Male ....Mr. Antonio LEROY
07 Director of Admissions ....Mrs. Leslie CHARLES
37 Director Financial Aid ....Mr. Thomas HARRIS, JR.
88 Dir of Academic Advising/Retention ....Dr. Kimberly BURGESS
25 Director Sponsored Programs ....Mrs. Melissa WIDNER
88 Undergrad Research Ctr Asst Dir ....Ms. Vanessa MCRAE
08 Director Library Services ....Dr. LaVerne MCLAUGHLIN
88 Director Academic Success Unit ....Mrs. Flo HILL
88 Director Quality Enhancement Plan ....Dr. Clancy THOMAS
88 Director Water Policy Center ....Mr. Mark MASTERS
09 Director Institutional Research ....Dr. Frank ARCHER, III
44 Director of Development ....Mr. Andrew FLOYD

† Part of the University System of Georgia.

Albany Technical College (I)

1704 S Slappey Boulevard, Albany GA 31701-3587

County: Dougherty FICE Identification: 005601
Unit ID: 138682
Telephone: (229) 430-3500 Carnegie Class: Assoc/Pub-R-M
FAX Number: (229) 430-3594 Calendar System: Semester
URL: www.albanytech.edu
Established: 1961 Annual Undergrad Tuition & Fees (In-State): $4,773
Enrollment: 3,439 Coed
Affiliation or Control: State IRS Status: 501(c)3
Highest Offering: Associate Degree
Program: Occupational; 2-Year Principally Bachelor's Creditable; Technical Emphasis
Accreditation: SC, DA, MAC, RAD, SURGT

01 President ....Dr. Anthony O. PARKER
05 Exec Vice Pres Academic Affairs ....Dr. Shirley ARMSTRONG
32 VP Student Affairs/Enrollment Mgmt ....Dr. Lisa DEJESUS
46 Vice President Economic Development ....Mr. Matt TRICE
10 Vice Pres Administrative Services ....Mrs. Kathy SKATES
45 Vice Pres of Inst Effectiveness ....Dr. Kimberly LEE
55 Vice Pres of Adult Education ....Mrs. Linda COSTON
04 Special Assistant to the President ....Mr. Joe NAJJAR
06 Registrar ....Ms. Suzann CULPEPPER
37 Director of Financial Aid ....Ms. Helen CATT
36 Dir of Job Placement/Career Svcs ....Ms. Judy JIMMERSON
21 Director of Accounting Services ....Ms. Janet HAYES
20 Dean of Academic Affairs ....Dr. Debra JONES
20 Dean of Academic Affairs ....Ms. Joy KNIGHTON
20 Dean of Academic Affairs ....Dr. Emmett GRISWOLD
55 Dean of Evening Administration ....Dr. Ed COOPER
88 Director of Business & Industry Svc ....Vacant

51 Director of Continuing Education ... Ms. Valerie WILLIAMS
09 Director of Institutional Research ... Mr. Joe NAJJAR
26 Director of Public Relations ... Ms. Wendy HOWELL
13 Director of Computer/Info Systems ... Mr. Bruce HOPKINS
88 Director of Special Programs ... Vacant
18 Director of Facilities ... Mr. Lavon ACKLEY
56 Dir Spec Proj/Tech in Curriculum ... Ms. Troycia WEBB
35 Director Student Activities ... Dr. Mary RICHARDSON
07 Director of Admissions ... Ms. Drenda DAVIS-JACKSON

American InterContinental University (A)

6600 Pchtree-Dunwdy Rd, 500 Embassy,
Atlanta GA 30328
Telephone: (404) 965-6500 Identification: 666723
Accreditation: &NH, ACBSP, CIDA

† Regional accreditation is carried under the parent institution in Hoffman Estates, IL.

Andrew College (B)

501 College Street, Cuthbert GA 39840-5550
County: Randolph FICE Identification: 001545
Unit ID: 138761
Telephone: (229) 732-2171 Carnegie Class: Assoc/PrivNFP
FAX Number: (229) 732-2176 Calendar System: Semester
URL: www.andrewcollege.edu
Established: 1854 Annual Undergrad Tuition & Fees: $14,924
Enrollment: 303 Coed
Affiliation or Control: United Methodist IRS Status: 501(c)3
Highest Offering: Associate Degree
Program: 2-Year Principally Bachelor's Creditable; Fine Arts Emphasis
Accreditation: SC

01 President ... Dr. Linda R. BUCHANAN
04 Executive Asst to President ... Mrs. Sandra SPIVEY
05 Int Dean of Academic Affairs ... Dr. Richard MCCALLUM
10 Vice President for Finance ... Mr. Bobby MOYE
11 Vice President for Administration ... Mr. Andy BRUBAKER
07 Director of Admission ... Mr. Andy JETER
21 Controller ... Mrs. Julie CADLE
32 Dean of Student Affairs ... Ms. Whitney MOSLEY
41 Athletic Director ... Dr. Edith SMITH
42 Chaplain ... Rev. Peter BERMUELLEN
08 Director of Library Services ... Mrs. Karan PITTMAN
40 Director of Bookstore ... Ms. McKenzie LANGFORD
88 Dir of Student Support Services ... Ms. Santee ARCHER
06 Registrar ... Ms. Tekesha JACKSON
18 Director of Maintenance ... Mr. Andrew LOWERY
19 Chief of Police ... Mr. Freddie JENKINS
39 Director of Residence Life ... Ms. Shaqualyn DAVIS
105 Web Services ... Mr. Brice HERRIN
88 FOCUS Director ... Mrs. Bennie MATTOX
09 Director of Student Success Ctr/IR ... Ms. Terri CRAFT
37 Director of Financial Aid ... Ms. Daquiri TYSON
15 Bursar/Human Resources ... Ms. Lola MOSES

Argosy University, Atlanta (C)

980 Hammond Drive, Suite 100, Atlanta GA 30328-6162
Telephone: (770) 671-1200 Identification: 666735
Accreditation: &WC, ACBSP, CACREP, CLPSY

† Regional accreditation is carried under the parent institution in Orange, CA.

Armstrong State University (D)

11935 Abercorn Street, Savannah GA 31419-1997
County: Chatham FICE Identification: 001546
Unit ID: 138789
Telephone: (912) 344-2576 Carnegie Class: Master's L
FAX Number: N/A Calendar System: Semester
URL: www.armstrong.edu
Established: 1935 Annual Undergrad Tuition & Fees (In-State): $6,332
Enrollment: 7,094 Coed
Affiliation or Control: State IRS Status: 501(c)3
Highest Offering: Doctorate
Program: 2-Year Principally Bachelor's Creditable; Liberal Arts And General; Teacher Preparatory; Professional
Accreditation: SC, COARC, CS, DMS, HSA, MT, MUS, NMT, NURSE, PH, PTA, RAD, RTT, SP, TED

01 President ... Dr. Linda M. BLEICKEN
05 Provost & VP Academic Affairs ... Dr. Robert SMITH
10 Vice President Business & Finance ... Mr. Christopher CORRIGAN
32 Vice President Student Affairs ... Dr. Georj LEWIS
30 Vice President for Advancement ... Mr. William KELSO
100 Chief of Staff ... Dr. Amy HEASTON
43 University Counsel ... Mr. Lee DAVIS
13 Chief Information Officer ... Mr. Robert P. HOWARD
90 Associate CIO ... Ms. Pamela CULBERSON
91 Associate CIO ... Mr. Timothy MOODY
21 Associate VP Business & Finance ... Mr. Cam REAGIN
20 Dean College of Health Professions ... Dr. David WARD
53 Dean College of Education ... Dr. Janet BUCKENMEYER
76 Interim Dean Health Professions ... Dr. Anne THOMPSON
49 Int Dean College of Liberal Arts ... Dr. David WHEELER
72 Interim Dean Science and Technology ... Dr. Jane WONG
08 University Librarian ... Mr. Doug FRAZIER
06 Registrar ... Mr. Rock MCCASKILL
19 Chief Campus Police ... Mr. Wayne WILLCOX
41 Athletic Director ... Ms. Lisa SWEANY
07 Director of Admissions ... Ms. Joanne LANDERS
88 Director Faculty Development ... Dr. Becky DA CRUZ
37 Director Financial Aid ... Ms. Kaye O'NEAL
89 Director First Year Experience ... Mr. Gregory ANDERSON
92 Director Honors Program ... Dr. Jonathan ROBERTS
36 Director of Career Services ... Mr. George LANTZOUNIS
09 Director Institutional Research ... Ms. Laura J. MILLS
85 Assistant to the VP Int Education ... Dr. James ANDERSON
104 Asst Director International Educ ... Dr. Kristin KASTING
35 Dean of Students ... Dr. Yvette UPTON
12 Director Liberty Center ... Mr. Peter HOFFMAN
106 Director Online & Blended Learning ... Vacant
15 Director of Human Resources ... Ms. Rebecca CARROLL
18 Director Facility Services ... Ms. Katie TWINING
38 Director Counseling Services ... Vacant
39 Director Housing & Residence Life ... Mr. Nick SHRADER
28 Director Multicultural Affairs ... Ms. Nashia WHITTENBURG
35 Assistant Dean of Students ... Ms. Kate STEINER
29 Director Alumni Development ... Ms. Cheryl ANDERSON
44 Assistant Vice President of Develop ... Ms. Julie GERBSCH
26 Director Marketing & Communications ... Dr. Allison HERSH
105 Manager of Web Communications ... Ms. Janice STANFORD
04 Executive Asst to President ... Ms. Trina SMITH
108 Director Assessment ... Ms. Angeles EAMES
22 Dir Affirmative Action/EEO ... Ms. Deidra DENNIE
25 Dir Grants & Sponsored Research ... Ms. Susan ARSHACK

† Part of the University System of Georgia.

The Art Institute of Atlanta (E)

6600 Peachtree Dunwoody Road, Atlanta GA 30328-1635
County: Fulton FICE Identification: 009270
Unit ID: 138813
Telephone: (770) 394-8300 Carnegie Class: Spec/Arts
FAX Number: (770) 394-0008 Calendar System: Quarter
URL: www.artinstitutes.edu/atlanta/
Established: 1949 Annual Undergrad Tuition & Fees: $17,596
Enrollment: 1,871 Coed
Affiliation or Control: Proprietary IRS Status: Proprietary
Highest Offering: Baccalaureate
Program: Fine Arts Emphasis
Accreditation: SC, ACFEI, CIDA

01 President ... Mr. Newton MYVETT
10 Director of Accounting ... Mr. Shane PATILLA
15 Director of Human Resources ... Ms. Michele DAVIS
07 Senior Director of Admissions ... Mr. Doug LOCHBAUM
05 Dean of Academic Affairs ... Dr. Ameeta JADAV
32 Dean of Student Affairs ... Mr. Michael DIXON
37 Director of Student Financial Svcs ... Ms. Kimberly PANCHANA
09 Dir of Inst Effectiveness/Research ... Vacant
08 Librarian ... Ms. Clara WILLIAMS
13 Director of Technology ... Mr. Patrick SLUDER
06 Registrar ... Ms. Diana HILL
36 Director of Career Services ... Ms. Sharon CLAY
26 Director of Communications ... Ms. Devra PRANSKY
18 Director of Facilities ... Ms. Stacey CARMICHAEL
39 Director of Residence Life/Housing ... Ms. Dominique CONTEH
04 Exec Assistant to the President ... Ms. Precious PRENDERGAST

Ashworth College (F)

6625 The Corners Parkway, Norcross GA 30092-3406
County: Gwinnett Identification: 666106
Telephone: (770) 729-8400 Carnegie Class: Not Classified
FAX Number: (770) 729-9296 Calendar System: Semester
URL: www.ashworthcollege.edu
Established: 2000 Annual Undergrad Tuition & Fees: $4,153
Enrollment: 12,000 Coed
Affiliation or Control: Proprietary IRS Status: Proprietary
Highest Offering: Master's
Program: Occupational; 2-Year Principally Bachelor's Creditable; Professional
Accreditation: DEAC

01 President ... Mr. Robert KLAPPER
05 Vice President of Education ... Ms. Lisa RUTSKY

Athens Technical College (G)

800 US Highway 29 N, Athens GA 30601-1500
County: Clarke FICE Identification: 005600
Unit ID: 246813
Telephone: (706) 355-5000 Carnegie Class: Assoc/Pub-R-M
FAX Number: (706) 369-5753 Calendar System: Semester
URL: www.athenstech.edu
Established: 1958 Annual Undergrad Tuition & Fees (In-State): $2,684
Enrollment: 4,336 Coed
Affiliation or Control: State IRS Status: 501(c)3
Highest Offering: Associate Degree
Program: Occupational; 2-Year Principally Bachelor's Creditable; Technical Emphasis
Accreditation: SC, ACBSP, ADNUR, CAHIIM, DA, DH, EMT, PTAA, RAD, SURGT

01 Interim President ... Dr. Gail THAXTON
05 Executive VP/Chief Academic Officer ... Dr. Daniel J. SMITH
32 Interim VP Student Affairs ... Ms. Jennifer BENSON
10 Vice Pres Administrative Services ... Ms. Kathryn S. THOMAS
45 Vice Pres Economic Devel Services ... Dr. Andrea DANIEL
12 Vice President of Off Campus Sites ... Vacant
13 Vice Pres Information Technology ... Mr. Dennis ASHWORTH
09 Vice President Adult Education ... Ms. Stephanie G. BENSON
72 Dean Technology/Engineering/Math ... Dr. Margaret MORGAN
76 Dean Life Sciences/Public Safety ... Mr. Glenn HENRY
50 Dean Business/Educ/Humanities ... Ms. Diane CAMPBELL
06 Director Registration & Records ... Ms. Kala MCNAIR
07 Director Admissions ... Ms. Jennifer BENSON
08 Director Library Services ... Ms. Carol STANLEY
08 Distance Educ & Outreach Librarian ... Ms. Beth THORNTON
36 Director Student Support/Career Dev ... Ms. Keli FEWOX
37 Director Financial Aid ... Ms. Wanda HICKS
12 Exec Dir Walton County Campus ... Mr. Lenzy REID, III
12 Director Greene County Campus ... Mr. Sibley BRYAN
35 Student Activities Director ... Mr. Alvie COLES
15 Director Human Resources ... Ms. Becky BURTON
18 Facilities Director ... Mr. Jim WALTER
30 Director Institutional Advancement ... Vacant
21 Director of Accounting ... Mr. Ryan STANLEY
106 Dean Academic Technology ... Dr. Mary Clare DIGIACOMO
19 Director Security/Safety ... Mr. Jeff STRICKLAND

Atlanta Metropolitan State College (H)

1630 Metropolitan Parkway, SW, Atlanta GA 30310-4498
County: Fulton FICE Identification: 012165
Unit ID: 138901
Telephone: (404) 756-4000 Carnegie Class: Assoc/Pub-U-SC
FAX Number: (404) 756-4460 Calendar System: Semester
URL: www.atlm.edu
Established: 1974 Annual Undergrad Tuition & Fees (In-State): $3,830
Enrollment: 3,033 Coed
Affiliation or Control: State IRS Status: 501(c)3
Highest Offering: Baccalaureate
Program: Occupational; 2-Year Principally Bachelor's Creditable
Accreditation: SC, ACBSP

01 President ... Dr. Gary A. MCGAHA, SR.
05 Vice Pres Academic Affairs ... Dr. Michael HEARD
10 Vice President Fiscal Affairs ... Mr. Freddie JOHNSON
32 Vice President Student Affairs ... Dr. Cynthia EVERS
30 Vice Pres Institutional Advancement ... Mr. Larion WILLIAMS
21 Assoc VP Fiscal Affairs ... Mrs. Michelle ALSTON-BROWN
50 Dean Div Business/Computer Sci ... Dr. Kristen BROADY
79 Dean Div Humanities/Fine Arts ... Dr. Frank JOHNSON
81 Dean Div of Sci/Math/Health Profess ... Dr. Marjorie CAMPBELL
83 Dean Div of Social Sciences ... Dr. Vance GRAY
06 Dir Enrollment Services/Registrar ... Mrs. Candace PERRY
15 Director of Human Resources ... Ms. Regina Ray SIMMONS
08 Director of the Library ... Mr. Robert QUARLES
35 Director of Student Activities ... Ms. Iris SHANKLIN
37 Director of Financial Aid ... Dr. Michelle CHAPMAN
38 Director Counseling/Disability Svcs ... Ms. Dorothy WILLIAMS
13 Chief Information Officer ... Mr. Antonio TRAVIS
09 Director Inst Effectiveness ... Dr. Mark CUNNINGHAM
19 Director of Campus Safety ... Mr. Antonio LONG
35 Dir of Student Outreach & Access ... Mr. Stephen WOODALL
18 Dir Plant Operations/Facilities ... Mr. E. Keith WILLIAMS
40 Bookstore Manager ... Ms. Gloria MCCLAIN
26 Media Relations Director/Marketing ... Ms. Sheila TENNEY
41 Athletic Director ... Mr. Robert PRICHETT

† Part of the University System of Georgia.

Atlanta Technical College (I)

1560 Metropolitan Parkway, SW, Atlanta GA 30310-4446
County: Fulton FICE Identification: 008543
Unit ID: 138840
Telephone: (404) 225-4400 Carnegie Class: Assoc/Pub-U-SC
FAX Number: (404) 225-4445 Calendar System: Semester
URL: www.atlantatech.edu
Established: 1967 Annual Undergrad Tuition & Fees (In-State): $4,920
Enrollment: 4,282 Coed
Affiliation or Control: State IRS Status: 501(c)3
Highest Offering: Associate Degree
Program: Occupational; 2-Year Principally Bachelor's Creditable; Technical Emphasis
Accreditation: SC, ACFEI, CAHIIM, DA, DH, DT, EMT, MAC, PTAA, RAD, SURGT

01 President ... Dr. Alvetta P. THOMAS
05 Vice President Academic Affairs ... Dr. Murray WILLIAMS
11 Vice Pres Administrative Services ... Mrs. Teresa BROWN
32 Vice President Student Affairs ... Dr. Rushton JOHNSON
30 Vice President Economic Development ... Mr. Harold CRAIG
04 Assistant to the President ... Dr. Joni WILLIAMS
26 Director Communications & Marketing ... Mrs. Terreta RODGERS
37 Director of Financial Aid ... Ms. Shawn THOMAS
84 Director of Enrollment Management ... Mr. Vory BILLUPS
20 Assoc Vice Pres Academic Affairs ... Dr. Kimberly FRAZIER
88 Dean Industrial and Transportation ... Vacant
51 Director of Continuing Education ... Dr. Deborah JOHNSON-BLAKE
36 Director Career Placement ... Mr. Michael BURNSIDE
50 Dean Business and Public Services ... Mrs. Phoebe COQUEREL
88 Dean Health and Public Safety ... Dr. Queenston THORPE
06 Registrar ... Mrs. Niya EADY
15 Director Human Resources ... Ms. Marilyn SMITH-ROBINSON
18 Director of Facilities ... Mr. Isaac VINING
09 Director of Institutional Research ... Ms. Jocelyn PETERSON
49 Interim Dean Arts and Sciences ... Mrs. Sonya MCCOY-WILSON

Atlanta's John Marshall Law School (A)

1422 West Peachtree Street NW, Atlanta GA 30309
County: Fulton | FICE Identification: 031733
Unit ID: 138929
Telephone: (404) 872-3593 | Carnegie Class: Spec/Law
FAX Number: (404) 873-3802 | Calendar System: Semester
URL: www.johnmarshall.edu
Established: 1933 | Annual Graduate Tuition & Fees: $39,460
Enrollment: 588 | Coed
Affiliation or Control: Proprietary | IRS Status: Proprietary
Highest Offering: First Professional Degree; No Undergraduates
Program: Professional
Accreditation: LAW

01 Dean/CEO ... Mr. Malcolm L. MORRIS
32 Assoc Dean of Students ... Ms. Sheryl E. HARRISON
10 Assoc Dean of Finance ... Mr. Allan BREZEL
06 Registrar ... Ms. Cheryl FEREBEE
26 Marketing Specialist ... Ms. Hilary WALDO
07 Director of Admissions ... Mrs. Rebecca MILTER
04 Executive Assistant to the Dean/CEO ... Ms. Farrah E. FISHER
37 Director of Financial Aid ... Mr. Montre EVERETT
29 Alumni Director ... Mrs. Virginia ARNOLD
36 Asst Dean of Career Development ... Mrs. Ivonne BETANCOURT
05 Assoc Dean for Academic Program ... Mr. M. Scott BOONE
20 Assoc Dean of Academic Admin ... Ms. Browning JEFFRIES
08 Director of Law Library ... Mr. Michael LYNCH

Augusta Technical College (B)

3200 Augusta Tech Drive, Augusta GA 30906-3399
County: Richmond | FICE Identification: 005599
Unit ID: 138956
Telephone: (706) 771-4000 | Carnegie Class: Assoc/Pub-R-M
FAX Number: (706) 771-4016 | Calendar System: Semester
URL: www.augustatech.edu
Established: 1961 | Annual Undergrad Tuition & Fees (In-District): $3,178
Enrollment: 4,269 | Coed
Affiliation or Control: State/Local | IRS Status: 501(c)3
Highest Offering: Associate Degree
Program: Occupational; Technical Emphasis
Accreditation: SC, COARC, CVT, DA, ENGT, MAC, OTA, PNUR, SURGT

01 President ... Mr. Terry D. ELAM
05 Sr Vice President Academic Affairs ... Dr. C. Rick HALL
10 Vice Pres Administrative Services ... Ms. Sheila M. HILL
32 Vice Pres Student Affairs ... Dr. Nicole KENNEDY
88 Vice President Economic Development ... Dr. Lisa PALMER
12 Dean/Director Waynesboro Campus ... Ms. Johnica MITCHELL
35 Dean Student Services ... Vacant
37 Director Financial Aid ... Ms. Beverly SMYRE HINES
07 Director Admissions ... Ms. Christine BALL
30 Director Institutional Advancement ... Ms. Beverly PELTIER
06 Registrar ... Mr. Mike VIOLETTE
45 Sr Vice Pres Inst Effectiveness ... Dr. Melissa F. ALSTON
21 Director Accounting ... Ms. Sherrick L. JOHNSON
26 Dir Marketing/Public Relations ... Ms. Kimberly HOLDEN
15 Director Human Resources ... Ms. Shannon PATTERSON
12 Dean Director Thomson Campus ... Ms. Julie LANGHAM
84 Enrollment Manager ... Ms. Jeanette LOWE
36 Director Career Services ... Ms. Donna WENDT
88 High School Coordinator ... Mrs. Evett DAVIS
76 Dean Allied Health Science ... Dr. Gwen TAYLOR
72 Dean Industrial Technology ... Mr. James PRICE
50 Dean Business/Public Safety ... Ms. Elizabeth A. JULIAN
97 Dean Gen Educ & Learning Support ... Mr. John RICHARDSON
54 Dean Information & Engineering Tech ... Mr. John ARENA

Augusta University (C)

1120 Fifteenth Street, Augusta GA 30912-0004
County: Richmond | FICE Identification: 001579
Unit ID: 140401
Telephone: (706) 721-0211 | Carnegie Class: Spec/Med
FAX Number: N/A | Calendar System: Semester
URL: www.gru.edu
Established: 1828 | Annual Undergrad Tuition & Fees (In-State): $8,282
Enrollment: 7,988 | Coed
Affiliation or Control: State | IRS Status: 501(c)3
Highest Offering: Doctorate
Program: Occupational; 2-Year Principally Bachelor's Creditable; Liberal Arts And General; Teacher Preparatory; Professional
Accreditation: SC, ANEST, ARCPA, ART, BUS, CACREP, CAHIIM, COARC, DENT, DH, IPSY, MED, MIL, MT, MUS, NMT, NURSE, OT, PH, PTA, RTT, SPAA, SW, TED

01 President ... Dr. Brooks A. KEEL
05 Exec VP for Acad Affairs/Provost ... Dr. Gretchen CAUGHMAN
10 Chief Business Ofcr/EVP Admin & Fin ... Mr. Anthony E. WAGNER
26 EVP Strategic Comm/Chf Mrktng Ofcr ... Ms. Karla LEEPER
31 Exec VP External Rel/Chief of Staff ... Mr. Russell KEEN
43 General Counsel ... Mr. Chris MELCHER
17 Int VP Clinical Affs/Dean Medicine ... Dr. Peter F. BUCKLEY
86 VP Gov Rel/Chief Advocacy Officer ... Mr. W. Michael SHAFFER
46 Senior Vice President for Research ... Dr. Michael DIAMOND
30 Sr VP Advance/Cmty Relations/CDO ... Ms. Susan L. BARCUS
15 Enterprise VP Human Resources ... Ms. Susan A. NORTON
88 VP Academic & Faculty Affairs ... Dr. Carol RYCHLY
28 VP Acad Plng/Strategic Initiative ... Dr. Quincy BYRDSONG
32 VP for Student Affairs ... Dr. Mark Allen POISEL
09 VP Institutional Effectiveness ... Mrs. Beth P. BRIGDON
18 VP Facilities Service ... Mr. Philip HOWARD
26 VP Communications & Marketing ... Mr. Jack EVANS
21 Vice Pres Finance ... Mr. Lee FRUITTICHER
58 Dean College of Graduate Studies ... Dr. Mitchell WATSKY
76 Dean College of Allied Health ... Dr. E. Andrew BALAS
52 Dean College of Dental Med ... Dr. Carol LEFEBVRE
66 Dean College of Nursing ... Dr. Lucy N. MARION
50 Int Dean Hull College of Business ... Dr. Mark THOMPSON
49 Dean College of Arts/Hum/Soc Sci ... Dr. Charles CLARK
53 Dean College of Education ... Dr. Zach KELEHEAR
81 Dean College of Science & Math ... Dr. Rickey P. HICKS
88 Chief Audit Officer ... Mr. Clay SPROUSE
88 Chief Integrity Officer ... Mr. James RUSH, JR.
13 Enterprise CIO ... Mr. Charles ENICKS
88 Director Cancer Center ... Dr. Samir KHLEIF
06 Registrar ... Ms. Heather METRESS
88 Bursar ... Ms. Beth WELSH
41 Director of Athletics ... Mr. Clint BRYANT
19 Int Director of Public Safety ... Maj. Eugene MAXWELL
08 Director of Libraries ... Dr. Brenda SEAGO
88 Director of Supply Chain Mgmt ... Mr. Clay TROVER
109 Director of Auxiliary Services ... Mr. Karl MUNSCHY
37 Director of Financial Aid ... Ms. Cynthia PARKS
07 Interim Director of Admissions ... Mr. Scott ARGO

† Part of the University System of Georgia.

Bainbridge State College (D)

2500 E Shotwell Street, PO Box 990, Bainbridge GA 39818-0990
County: Decatur | FICE Identification: 011074
Unit ID: 139010
Telephone: (229) 243-3000 | Carnegie Class: Assoc/Pub-R-M
FAX Number: (229) 248-2623 | Calendar System: Semester
URL: www.bainbridge.edu
Established: 1970 | Annual Undergrad Tuition & Fees (In-State): $3,227
Enrollment: 2,334 | Coed
Affiliation or Control: State | IRS Status: 501(c)3
Highest Offering: Baccalaureate
Program: Occupational; 2-Year Principally Bachelor's Creditable
Accreditation: SC, ADNUR

01 President ... Dr. Richard CARVAJAL
05 Vice Pres Academic Affairs ... Dr. Rodney CARR
10 Vice Pres of Business & Operations ... Mr. Shawn MCGEE
32 Vice President of Student Affairs ... Dr. Rodney CARR
49 Dean School of Arts & Sciences ... Ms. Joann SIMPSON
75 Dean Sch Health Sci/Profess Studies ... Ms. Kathleen KETTERER
35 Associate Dean of Student Affairs ... Mr. Spencer STEWART
08 Director Library ... Ms. Michelle BARSOM
26 Chief Public Relations Officer ... Vacant
37 Director of Financial Aid ... Vacant
21 Controller ... Mr. Steven MORRISON
18 Director of Plant Operations ... Mr. Wayne QUINN
91 Director of Technology Services ... Mr. Scott DUNN
88 Assistant Dean of Student Affairs ... Mr. Sam MAYHEW
30 Int Director of Inst Advancement ... Ms. Lauren HARRELL
07 Director of Admissions ... Ms. Melanie CLEVELAND
19 Director of Public Safety ... Mr. James SPOONER
06 Assistant Registrar ... Mr. Robert THOMPSON

† Part of the University System of Georgia.

Berry College (E)

2277 Martha Berry Highway, NW, Mount Berry GA 30149-0001
County: Floyd | FICE Identification: 001554
Unit ID: 139144
Telephone: (706) 232-5374 | Carnegie Class: Bac/A&S
FAX Number: (706) 236-2238 | Calendar System: Semester
URL: www.berry.edu
Established: 1902 | Annual Undergrad Tuition & Fees: $31,996
Enrollment: 2,177 | Coed
Affiliation or Control: Independent Non-Profit | IRS Status: 501(c)3
Highest Offering: Beyond Master's But Less Than Doctorate
Program: Liberal Arts And General; Teacher Preparatory; Professional
Accreditation: SC, BUS, MUS, NURSE, TED

01 President ... Dr. Stephen R. BRIGGS
05 Vice President & Provost ... Dr. Kathy Brittain RICHARDSON
10 Vice President Finance ... Mr. Brian I. ERB
32 VP Student Affairs and Enrollment ... Ms. Debbie HEIDA
30 Vice Pres Institutional Advancement ... Ms. Bettyann O'NEILL
84 VP of Enrollment Management ... Dr. Gary WATERS
100 Chief of Staff ... Mr. Whit WHITAKER
42 Chaplain ... Rev. Jonathan HUGGINS
35 Assoc Vice Pres Student Affairs ... Ms. Lindsey TAYLOR
26 Asst VP Public Rels and Marketing ... Ms. Jeanne MATHEWS
20 Associate Provost ... Dr. Andrew BRESSETTE
50 Dean Campbell School of Business ... Dr. John GROUT
53 Dean Charter School of Education ... Dr. Jackie MCDOWELL
79 Dean School Humanities/Arts/Soc Sci ... Dr. Thomas D. KENNEDY
66 Dean of Nursing ... Dr. Vanice ROBERTS
81 Dean School of Math/Nat Sci ... Dr. Gary BRETON
78 Dean Stdnt Work/Experiential Lrng ... Mr. Rufus MASSEY
07 Asst Vice Pres Admissions ... Mr. Brett E. KENNEDY
08 Director of the Library ... Ms. Sherre Lee HARRINGTON
29 Director of Alumni Affairs ... Ms. Jennifer SCHAKNOWSKI
13 Chief Information Officer ... Ms. Penny EVANS-PLANTS
38 Director of Counseling Center ... Dr. J. Marshall JENKINS
37 Director of Financial Aid ... Ms. Donna CHILDRES
36 Director of Career Center ... Mrs. Sue TARPLEY
09 Dir Institutional Research ... Dr. Bryce DURBIN
46 Dir Research & Sponsored Programs ... Mrs. Donna DAVIN
18 Director Physical Plant ... Mr. Mark HOPKINS
89 Director First Year Experience ... Mrs. Katherine POWELL
92 Director Honors Program ... Dr. Lara WHELAN
94 Director Women's Studies ... Dr. Susan CONRADSEN
96 Director Purchasing ... Mr. Brad BARRIS
85 Director International Programs ... Ms. Sarah EGERER
15 Director Human Resources ... Mr. Wayne PHIPPS
43 Director of Legal Services ... Mr. Danny PRICE
28 Director of Multicultural Affairs ... Dr. Tasha TOY
78 Dir Stdnt Work/Experiential Lrng ... Mr. Michael BURNES
88 Director of Employee Development ... Mr. Mark KOZERA
06 Registrar ... Dr. Bryce DURBIN
41 Director of Athletics ... Mr. Todd BROOKS

Beulah Heights University (F)

892 Berne Street, SE, PO Box 18145, Atlanta GA 30316-1873
County: Fulton | FICE Identification: 030763
Unit ID: 139153
Telephone: (404) 627-2681 | Carnegie Class: Spec/Faith
FAX Number: (404) 627-0702 | Calendar System: Semester
URL: www.beulah.org
Established: 1918 | Annual Undergrad Tuition & Fees: $9,390
Enrollment: 673 | Coed
Affiliation or Control: Other Protestant | IRS Status: 501(c)3
Highest Offering: Doctorate
Program: Religious Emphasis
Accreditation: BI, TRACS

01 President ... Dr. Benson M. KARANJA
05 Vice Pres/Dean Academic Affairs ... Dr. James B. KEILLER
32 VP Student Life/Enrollment Mgmt ... Pastor Shawn ADAMS
88 Vice Pres Academic Program Dev ... Dr. Angelita HOWARD
11 Assoc Vice Pres Operations ... Mr. Peter KARANJA
42 Dean of Chapel ... Bishop Johnathan E. ALVARADO
20 Associate Academic Officer ... Dr. Mark HARDGROVE
37 Director of Financial Aid ... Ms. Robin HARRELL
08 Director of Library Services ... Mr. Pradeep K. DAS
06 University Registrar ... Ms. NaTanya F. DOWELL
07 Director of Admissions ... Ms. Charlotte DUDLEY
18 Facilities Director ... Mr. Harvey BRUMELOW
21 Director of Finance ... Ms. Bernadette ASHER
58 Chair Div of Graduate Studies ... Dr. Mark HARDGROVE
73 Chair Dept of Religious Studies ... Mr. Walter TURNER
88 Chair Dept of Leadership Studies ... Ms. Betty G. PALMER
26 Director of Marketing/Recruiting ... Ms. Sonya YOUNG

Brenau University (G)

500 Washington Street, SE, Gainesville GA 30501-3668
County: Hall | FICE Identification: 001556
Unit ID: 139199
Telephone: (770) 534-6299 | Carnegie Class: Master's L
FAX Number: (770) 534-6114 | Calendar System: Semester
URL: www.brenau.edu
Established: 1878 | Annual Undergrad Tuition & Fees: $25,478
Enrollment: 2,789 | Coed
Affiliation or Control: Independent Non-Profit | IRS Status: 501(c)3
Highest Offering: Doctorate
Program: Liberal Arts And General; Teacher Preparatory; Professional
Accreditation: SC, ACBSP, CIDA, DANCE, NURSE, OT, @PTA, TED

01 President ... Dr. Ed L. SCHRADER
03 Sr VP/Chief Financial Ofcr ... Dr. David L. BARNETT
05 Provost & VP For Academic Affairs ... Dr. Nancy F. KRIPPEL
100 Chief of Staff ... Ms. Jody Y. WALL
10 Vice President Financial Services ... Mr. Toby R. HINTON
84 Vice Pres Enrollment Management ... Mr. Ray TATUM
30 Vice Pres External Relations ... Mr. J. Matthew THOMAS
13 Vice Pres Information Technology ... Mr. Chip L. ANDREWS
09 Director of Research & Planning ... Dr. Robert E. CUTTINO
37 Assoc VP of EM & Dir Financial Aid ... Ms. Pam J. BARRETT
21 Asst VP Financial Svcs/Controller ... Ms. Holly REYNOLDS
15 Director of Human Resources ... Ms. Kelley L. MADDOX
18 Director Facilities & Logistics ... Mr. Mike HOLLIMON
26 VP Communications/Publications ... Mr. David MORRISON
32 Dean of Student Success & Retention ... Ms. Valerie SIMMONS-WALSTON
36 Director of Career Services ... Mr. George BAGEL
24 Director of Learning Center ... Dr. Vince J. YAMILKOSKI
41 Athletic Director ... Mr. Mike LOCHSTAMPFOR
23 Chaplain ... Dr. Don HARRISON
53 Dean College of Education ... Dr. Sandra LESLIE
76 Dean College of Health Sciences ... Dr. Gale H. STARICH
50 Dean College Business/Mass Comm ... Dr. Suzanne ERICKSON
79 Dean College of Fine Arts & Human ... Dr. Andrea C. BIRCH
08 Dean of Library Svcs & SACS Liaison ... Ms. Marlene GIGUERE
88 Executive Director for Admissions ... Mr. Nathan R. GOSS
06 Registrar & Dir of Student Records ... Ms. Barbara WILSON
29 Exec Director Alumni & Events ... Ms. Jennifer DELL
19 Director Campus Safety & Security ... Ms. Paula DAMPIER

Brewton-Parker College (H)

201 David-Eliza Fountain Circle, Mount Vernon GA 30445-0197
County: Montgomery | FICE Identification: 001557
Unit ID: 139205

Telephone: (912) 583-2241 Carnegie Class: Bac/Diverse
FAX Number: (912) 583-4498 Calendar System: Semester
URL: www.bpc.edu
Established: 1904 Annual Undergrad Tuition & Fees: $16,180
Enrollment: 503 Coed
Affiliation or Control: Baptist IRS Status: 501(c)3
Highest Offering: Baccalaureate
Program: 2-Year Principally Bachelor's Creditable; Liberal Arts And General; Teacher Preparatory; Business Emphasis
Accreditation: SC, TED

01 President ... Dr. Steven F. ECHOLS
43 General Counsel ... Mr. John MANNING
10 Exec VP Finance ... Dr. Nicole SHEPARD
05 VP Academics ... Dr. Robert M. BRIAN
30 VP College Advancement ... Vacant
32 VP of Student Services ... Mr. Dave EPPLING
84 VP of Enrollment Services ... Mr. Chris DOOLEY
09 Dir of Assessment & Inst Research ... Dr. Patti WILLIAMS
15 Director Human Resources ... Ms. Leslie HARRELL
37 Director of Financial Aid ... Vacant
18 Director of Plant Operations ... Mr. Jim WAMPLER
06 Registrar ... Mrs. Elizabeth ADAMS
38 Dir Counseling & Career Services ... Vacant
41 Athletic Director ... Mr. Daniel PREVETT
08 Librarian ... Vacant
26 Marketing Associate ... Ms. Amanda CORBIN
35 Director of Student Activities ... Ms. Jennifer L. WOOTEN
39 Director of Housing ... Vacant
40 Bookstore Manager ... Mrs. Lynn ADDISON
50 Chair Business Division ... Dr. Nicole G. SHEPARD
53 Chair Education Division ... Dr. Susan E. WHITE
49 Chair Humanities & Social Sciences ... Dr. Farrah SENN
73 Chair Christian Studies ... Dr. Jerry RAY
42 Director of Campus Ministry ... Ms. Lauren PARNELL
07 Director of Admissions ... Mrs. Kim BELL
04 Administrative Asst to President ... Mrs. Jennifer J. BLAYLOCK
29 Director Alumni Relations ... Ms. Kim LAJINESS
96 Director of Purchasing ... Mrs. Evelyn CARPENTER

Brown College of Court Reporting (A)

1100 Spring Street NW, Suite 101, Atlanta GA 30309
County: Fulton FICE Identification: 020609
Unit ID: 139214
Telephone: (404) 876-1227 Carnegie Class: Assoc/PrivFP
FAX Number: (404) 876-4415 Calendar System: Quarter
URL: www.bccr.edu
Established: 1972 Annual Undergrad Tuition & Fees: $16,600
Enrollment: 208 Coed
Affiliation or Control: Proprietary IRS Status: Proprietary
Highest Offering: Associate Degree
Program: Occupational; 2-Year Principally Bachelor's Creditable
Accreditation: COE

01 President ... Russell FREEMAN
03 Director ... Marita CAREY
07 Director of Admissions ... Carlette JENNINGS
05 Director of Education ... Karen RENNER
06 Registrar ... Lisa LOWE

Brown Mackie College-Atlanta (B)

4370 Peachtree Road NE, Atlanta GA 30319
Telephone: (404) 799-4500 FICE Identification: 026214
Accreditation: ACICS, OTA

† Branch campus of The Art Institute of Phoenix, Phoenix, AZ.

Cambridge Institute of Allied Health and Technology (C)

5673 Peachtree Dunwoody Rd, Ste 450, Atlanta GA 30342
Telephone: (404) 255-4500 Identification: 770938
Accreditation: ABHES

† Branch campus of Cambridge Institute of Allied Health and Technology, Delray Beach, FL.

Carver College (D)

3870 Cascade Road SW, Atlanta GA 30331-2184
County: Fulton FICE Identification: 036353
Unit ID: 139287
Telephone: (404) 527-4520 Carnegie Class: Not Classified
FAX Number: (404) 527-4524 Calendar System: Semester
URL: www.carver.edu
Established: 1943 Annual Undergrad Tuition & Fees: $9,260
Enrollment: 88 Coed
Affiliation or Control: Independent Non-Profit IRS Status: 501(c)3
Highest Offering: Baccalaureate
Program: Occupational; Religious Emphasis
Accreditation: BI

01 President and CEO ... Mr. Robert W. CRUMMIE
05 Academic Dean ... Mr. Damon D. BYRD
10 Vice President of Business Affairs ... Mr. Terry ALEXANDER
30 Director of Advancement ... Mrs. Carla M. CRUMMIE
32 Dean of Students ... Mr. Thomas B. CAIN
84 Dir Enrollment Management ... Ms. Tonya CANNON
06 Registrar ... Mrs. Olive JACKS
09 Dir Institutional Effectiveness ... Mrs. Marriane GREENFIELD
29 Director Alumni Affairs ... Ms. Cathy REYNOLDS
42 Director of Chapel Services ... Mr. Teddy WRIGHT
73 Director of Bible/Theology Studies ... Dr. Benjamin JACKS
97 Director of General Studies ... Mrs. Amber BOGLIN
107 Director of Professional Studies ... Dr. John A. JENKINS
08 Director of Library Services ... Ms. Debra A. MILLIGAN
83 Director of Psychology Studies ... Ms. Patricia WESLEY
50 Director of Business Division ... Dr. Wynton HEYLIGER
18 Director of Physical Plant ... Mr. Herman PATE
41 Athletic Director ... Mr. Martin CARTER
40 Director of Bookstore ... Mr. Willie KITCHENS
04 Assistant to the President ... Ms. Iverna SHELTON
19 Chief of Police ... Capt. Ray COLLINS
27 Public Relations/Sports Information ... Mr. Augustus HOWARD

Central Georgia Technical College (E)

3300 Macon Tech Drive, Macon GA 31206
County: Bibb FICE Identification: 005763
Unit ID: 140304
Telephone: (478) 757-3400 Carnegie Class: Assoc/Pub-R-L
FAX Number: (478) 757-3454 Calendar System: Quarter
URL: www.centralgatech.edu
Established: 1966 Annual Undergrad Tuition & Fees (In-State): $3,000
Enrollment: N/A Coed
Affiliation or Control: State IRS Status: 501(c)3
Highest Offering: Associate Degree
Program: Occupational; Technical Emphasis
Accreditation: SC, CVT, DH, EMT, MLTAD, POLYT, RAD, SURGT

01 President ... Dr. Ivan ALLEN
05 Vice President Academic Affairs ... Dr. Amy HOLLOWAY
10 Vice President Admin/Fin Svcs ... Ms. Michelle SINIARD
32 Vice President Student Affairs ... Mr. Craig JACKSON
31 Vice President Econ Dev ... Ms. Rebecca LEE
11 AVP Facilities/Ancillary Svcs ... Mr. Jimmy FAIRCLOTH
13 Vice Pres Technology ... Mr. Gardner LONG, II
12 VP for Satellite Operations South ... Dr. Joan THOMPSON
35 Dean of Student Affairs ... Vacant
06 Registrar ... Ms. Sonja JENKINS
07 Exec Director of Admissions ... Mr. Dann WEBB
30 Asst VP for Advancement ... Ms. Tonya MCCLURE
36 Director Career Services ... Mr. Pat IVEY
08 Director Library & Media Services ... Mr. Neil MCARTHUR
37 Director of Financial Aid ... Ms. Jackie WHITE
15 Executive Director Human Resources ... Ms. Carol JONES
18 Facilities Director ... Mr. Robert DOMINY
13 Director of Information Technology ... Mr. Michael CLOUGH
51 Director of Continuing Education ... Mr. Clay TEAGUE

Central Georgia Technical College (F)

80 Cohen Walker Drive, Warner Robins GA 31088-2729
County: Houston FICE Identification: 025086
Unit ID: 140085
Telephone: (478) 988-6800 Carnegie Class: Assoc/Pub-R-M
FAX Number: (478) 988-6813 Calendar System: Quarter
URL: www.centralgatech.edu
Established: 1973 Annual Undergrad Tuition & Fees (In-State): $2,568
Enrollment: 7,625 Coed
Affiliation or Control: State IRS Status: 501(c)3
Highest Offering: Associate Degree
Program: Occupational; 2-Year Principally Bachelor's Creditable; Technical Emphasis
Accreditation: SC, CVT, DH, RAD, SURGT

01 President ... Dr. Ivan H. ALLEN
03 Executive Vice President ... Mr. Jeffrey SCRUGGS
05 Vice President for Academic Affairs ... Dr. Amy L. HOLLOWAY
32 Vice President for Student Affairs ... Mr. Craig JACKSON
09 VP Economic Development ... Ms. Becky LEE
11 VP Administrative Financial Svcs ... Mrs. Michelle SINIARD
88 Vice President for Adult Education ... Ms. Brenda L. BROWN
07 Director of Admissions ... Mr. Dann WEBB
37 Director of Financial Aid ... Ms. Shirley GLOVER
06 Registrar ... Ms. Sonja JENKINS
08 Director of Library Services ... Dr. Dumont C. BUNN
15 Director of Human Resources ... Ms. Carol F. JONES
30 Director of Advancement ... Ms. Janet H. KELLY
26 Marketing & PR Director ... Ms. Janet H. KELLY
18 Maintenance Superintendent ... Mr. Joe PETERSDORFF

Chamberlain College of Nursing-Atlanta (G)

5775 Peachtree Dunwoody Rd NE,A100,
Atlanta GA 30342
Telephone: (404) 250-8500 Identification: 770504
Accreditation: &NH, NURSE

† Branch campus of Chamberlain College of Nursing-Addison, Addison, IL.

Chattahoochee Technical College (H)

980 South Cobb Drive, Marietta GA 30060
County: Cobb FICE Identification: 030290
Unit ID: 140331
Telephone: (770) 528-4545 Carnegie Class: Not Classified
FAX Number: (770) 975-4126 Calendar System: Quarter
URL: www.chattahoocheetech.edu
Established: 1981 Annual Undergrad Tuition & Fees (In-State): $3,204
Enrollment: 9,942 Coed
Affiliation or Control: State IRS Status: 501(c)3
Highest Offering: Associate Degree
Program: Occupational
Accreditation: SC, ACFEI, MAC, MLTAD, OTA, PTAA, RAD

01 President ... Dr. Ron NEWCOMB
04 Administrative Asst to President ... Ms. Tammy COLLUM
03 Executive Vice President ... Dr. Trina BOTELER
05 Actg Vice President for Academics ... Dr. Trina BOTELER
11 Vice Pres for Administrative Svcs ... Ms. Catrice HUFSTETLER
32 VP Student Affairs/Technology ... Dr. Scott RULE
31 Vice Pres External Affairs ... Ms. Jennifer NELSON
18 Vice President for Facilities ... Mr. David SIMMONS
15 Vice President Human Resources ... Mr. Ron PRICE
30 Vice Pres Economic Development ... Mr. Rex BISHOP
26 Exec Dir External Affs/Brd Liaison ... Ms. Jennifer NELSON
27 Specialist for Public Relations ... Ms. Rebecca LONG

Clark Atlanta University (I)

223 James P. Brawley Drive, SW, Atlanta GA 30314-4391
County: Fulton FICE Identification: 001559
Unit ID: 138947
Telephone: (404) 880-8000 Carnegie Class: DRU
FAX Number: N/A Calendar System: Semester
URL: www.cau.edu
Established: 1988 Annual Undergrad Tuition & Fees: $21,945
Enrollment: 3,485 Coed
Affiliation or Control: United Methodist IRS Status: 501(c)3
Highest Offering: Doctorate
Program: Liberal Arts And General; Teacher Preparatory; Professional
Accreditation: SC, BUS, CACREP, SPAA, SW, TED

01 President ... Dr. Ronald A. JOHNSON
05 Provost/VP for Academic Affairs ... Dr. James A. HEFNER
30 VP for Inst Advancement/Univ Rels ... Ms. Trisa Long PASCHAL
10 VP for Finance/Business Svcs ... Ms. Lucille MAUGE
84 VP for Enroll Svcs/Student Affairs ... Dr. Carl JONES
46 Assoc VP/Research & Spon Pgms ... Dr. John HALL
20 Assoc VP for Academic Affairs ... Dr. Bettye CLARK
13 Interim Assoc VP/Chief Info Ofcr ... Mr. Joseph T. DIXON
21 Interim Assoc VP/Controller ... Mr. Leighton O'SULLIVAN
32 Dean of Students ... Ms. Ernita HEMMITT
09 Asst VP Planning Assess/Inst Rsrch ... Dr. Narendra H. PATEL
43 General Counsel ... Mr. Lance DUNNINGS
06 University Registrar ... Ms. Susan GIBSON
26 Director Strategic Communications ... Ms. Donna BROCK
29 Director Alumni Relations ... Ms. Gay-linn JASHO
15 EVP Human Resources ... Ms. Debra HOYT
07 Dir Recruitment & Admissions ... Ms. Lori RICE-SADDLER
38 Director University Counseling Ctr ... Dr. Joy BRADFORD
36 Career Planning/Placement ... Mr. Andre MCKINNEY
37 Director Student Financial Aid ... Mr. James STOTTS
96 Director of Purchasing ... Ms. Donna BYRD
41 Interim Director of Athletics ... Ms. Dana HARVEY
49 Dean Arts & Sciences ... Dr. Danielle GRAY-SINGH
50 Acting Dean Business Admin ... Dr. Charles MOSES
53 Interim Dean Education ... Dr. Moses NORMAN
70 Dean Social Work ... Dr. Vimala PILLARI
58 Dean Graduate Studies ... Dr. Shirley WILLIAMS-KIRKSEY
19 Chief of Public Safety ... Chief Thomas TRAWICK
23 Director Health Services ... Ms. Janet SINGLETON
25 Dir Accts Payable Grants/Contracts ... Ms. Rotesha HARRIS
39 Interim Director of Residence Life ... Ms. Camille STEPHENS
88 Director Instructional Media ... Mr. Frank EDWARDS
101 Coordinator for Board Relations ... Ms. Natalie BAKER
104 Dir International Educ/Study Abroad ... Dr. Luis MILETTI
22 University Compliance Officer ... Mr. Robert CLARK
18 Director of Facilities ... Mr. Victor PANCHUK
108 Director Institutional Assessment ... Dr. Tia MINNIS
04 Administrative Asst to President ... Ms. Carlethia TOWNSEND
100 Chief of Staff ... Ms. Marilyn DAVIS

Clayton State University (J)

2000 Clayton State Boulevard, Morrow GA 30260-0285
County: Clayton FICE Identification: 008976
Unit ID: 139311
Telephone: (678) 466-4000 Carnegie Class: Bac/Diverse
FAX Number: (770) 961-3700 Calendar System: Semester
URL: www.clayton.edu
Established: 1969 Annual Undergrad Tuition & Fees (In-State): $5,340
Enrollment: 7,022 Coed
Affiliation or Control: State IRS Status: 501(c)3
Highest Offering: Master's
Program: Occupational; Liberal Arts And General; Teacher Preparatory
Accreditation: SC, BUS, DH, MUS, NURSE, TED

01 President ... Dr. Thomas HYNES
05 Provost/Vice Pres Academic Affairs ... Dr. Kevin DEMMITT
10 VP for Operations/Planning/Budget ... Ms. Corlis CUMMINGS
32 Vice President for Student Affairs ... Dr. Elaine MANGLITZ
26 Vice President External Affairs ... Ms. Kate TROELSTRA
13 Vice Pres Information Tech & Svcs ... Mr. Bill GRUSZKA
20 Assoc Vice President Academic Affs ... Dr. Robert A. VAUGHAN, JR.
35 Assistant Vice Pres Student Affairs ... Dr. Allen WARD
84 Asst VP Enroll Mgmt/Acad Success ... Dr. Stephen SCHULTHEIS
41 Executive Director of Athletics ... Mr. Tim DUNCAN
88 Executive Director of Spivey Hall ... Mr. Samuel DIXON
15 Exec Dir Human Resources & Services ... Mr. Tom GAUSVIK
49 Dean of Arts & Sciences ... Dr. Nasser MOMAYEZI
36 Director Retention& Stdnt Placement ... Mr. Eric TACK
50 Dean of Business ... Dr. Avinandan MUKHERJEE

76 Dean of Health Sciences .... Dr. Lisa EICHELBERGER
81 Dean Information/Mathematical Sci .... Dr. Lila ROBERTS
08 Dean of Library Services .... Dr. Gordon BAKER
108 Dean Assessment/Instructional Dev .... Dr. Jill LANE
51 Director of Continuing Education .... Ms. Karen LAMARSH
06 University Registrar .... Ms. Rebecca GMEINER
07 Director of Admissions .... Mr. Stephen JENKINS
109 Director of Auxiliary Services .... Ms. Carolina AMERO
27 Asst VP Marketing/Communications .... Ms. Maritza FERREIRA
18 Director of Plant Operations .... Mr. Harun BISWAS
19 Director of Public Safety .... Mr. Bobby HAMIL
30 Director of Development .... Mr. Thomas GIFFIN
09 Director of Institutional Research .... Dr. Narem REDDY
24 Director Media Services .... Mr. Paul BAILEY
38 Director of Counseling Services .... Dr. Christine SMITH
37 Director Student Financial Aid .... Ms. Pat BARTON
96 Director of Purchasing .... Ms. Marcia JONES
29 Director Alumni Relations .... Ms. Leila TATUM
21 Acting Comptroller .... Dr. Narem REDDY

† Part of the University System of Georgia.

Coastal Pines Technical College (A)

1701 Carswell Avenue, Waycross GA 31503-4016

County: Ware FICE Identification: 005511
Unit ID: 248776
Telephone: (912) 287-6584 Carnegie Class: Assoc/Pub-R-M
FAX Number: (912) 287-4865 Calendar System: Semester
URL: www.coastalpines.edu
Established: 1965 Annual Undergrad Tuition & Fees (In-State): $4,782
Enrollment: 2,431 Coed
Affiliation or Control: State IRS Status: 501(c)3
Highest Offering: Associate Degree
Program: Occupational; 2-Year Principally Bachelor's Creditable; Technical Emphasis
Accreditation: SC, COARC, MAC, MLTAD, RAD, SURGT

01 President .... Dr. Glenn DEIBERT
05 Vice Pres for Academic Affairs .... Dr. Al CUNNINGHAM
11 VP of Administrative Services .... Ms. Monica O'QUINN
46 Vice Pres for Economic Development .... Dr. Pete SNELL
32 Vice President for Student Affairs .... Ms. Karla EUBANKS
06 Registrar .... Ms. Tara EICHFIELD
26 Director Public Relations .... Ms. Cindy TANNER
18 Facilities Director .... Mr. Chad BOYETT
36 Career Placement & Develop Coord .... Mr. Buck THIGPEN
37 Director Student Financial Aid .... Ms. Tina MANNING
09 VP for Institutional Effectiveness .... Dr. Teresa ALLEN
07 Director of Admissions .... Mr. Chris JEANCAKE
15 Human Resources Coordinator .... Ms. Cynthia LINDER
30 Vice President for Advancement .... Ms. Cindy TANNER

College of Coastal Georgia (B)

One College Drive, Brunswick GA 31520-3632

County: Glynn FICE Identification: 001558
Unit ID: 139250
Telephone: (912) 279-5700 Carnegie Class: Assoc/Pub-R-M
FAX Number: (912) 262-3072 Calendar System: Semester
URL: www.ccga.edu
Established: 1961 Annual Undergrad Tuition & Fees (In-State): $4,434
Enrollment: 3,008 Coed
Affiliation or Control: State IRS Status: 501(c)3
Highest Offering: Baccalaureate
Program: Occupational; 2-Year Principally Bachelor's Creditable; Liberal Arts And General; Teacher Preparatory; Professional
Accreditation: SC, ACFEI, ADNUR, MLTAD, NUR, RAD

01 President .... Dr. Gregory F. ALOIA
05 Vice President Academic Affairs .... Dr. Tracy PELLETT
30 Vice President Advancement .... Mr. Michael CUMBIE
10 Vice President Business Affairs .... Mr. Jeffrey H. PRESTON
32 Vice President Student Affairs .... Dr. Jason W. UMFRESS
20 Associate VP Academic Affairs .... Ms. Kay HAMPTON
21 Asst VP Business Affairs .... Mr. C. Tom SAUNDERS
84 Asst VP Enrollment Management .... Mr. Clayton DANIELS
13 Chief Information Officer .... Mr. Alan OURS
19 Chief of Police .... Mr. Bryan SIPE
08 Dean of Library Services .... Ms. Debra HOLMES
35 Dean of Students .... Dr. Michael BUTCHER
49 Dean School of Arts and Sciences .... Dr. Keith E. BELCHER
50 Dean Sch of Business & Public Affs .... Dr. William MOUNTS
53 Dean School of Education & Teacher .... Dr. Michael HAZELKORN
66 Dean School of Nursing & Health Sci .... Dr. Patricia KRAFT
41 Director of Athletics .... Dr. William CARLTON
12 Director Camden Center .... Ms. Holly CHRISTENSEN
106 Director of E-Learning .... Dr. Lisa MCNEAL
09 Director Institutional Effectivenes .... Dr. James LYNCH
104 Dir of International Initiatives .... Mr. Adam JOHNSON
15 Director of Human Resources .... Ms. Phyllis BROADWELL
18 Director of Facilities and Plant Op .... Mr. Gary STRICKLAND
26 Director of Marketing & Public Rels .... Mr. John CORNELL
37 Director Student Financial Aid .... Ms. Terral HARRIS
06 Registrar .... Ms. Lisa LESSEIG
07 Associate Director of Admissions .... Ms. Aerial DICKERSON
04 Executive Assistant President's Off .... Ms. Judy JOHNSTON
88 Coordinator Faculty & Admin Svcs .... Ms. Connie HIOTT
96 Purchasing Officer .... Ms. Karen O. MARTIN

† Part of the University System of Georgia.

Columbia Theological Seminary (C)

P.O. Box 520, 701 S Columbia Drive,
Decatur GA 30031-0520

County: DeKalb FICE Identification: 001560
Unit ID: 139348
Telephone: (404) 378-8821 Carnegie Class: Spec/Faith
FAX Number: (404) 377-9696 Calendar System: 4/1/4
URL: www.ctsnet.edu
Established: 1828 Annual Graduate Tuition & Fees: N/A
Enrollment: 333 Coed
Affiliation or Control: Presbyterian Church (U.S.A.) IRS Status: 501(c)3
Highest Offering: Doctorate; No Undergraduates
Program: Professional; Religious Emphasis
Accreditation: SC, THEOL

01 President .... Dr. Leanne VAN DYK
05 Exec VP Acad Affs/Dean of Faculty .... Dr. Deborah F. MULLEN
10 Vice Pres Business and Finance .... Mr. Martin SADLER
32 Vice President Student Services .... Dr. Skip JOHNSON
30 Interim VP Inst Advancement .... Mr. Arnie HULTEEN
20 Assoc Dean Academic Administration .... Dr. Ann Clay ADAMS
08 Director of Library .... Dr. Kelly D. CAMPBELL
107 Assoc Dean Advanced Prof Studies .... Dr. Kevin PARK
06 Registrar .... Mr. Mike MEDFORD
07 Director Recruitment and Admission .... Ms. Betsy LYLES
26 Director of Communications .... Mr. Michael THOMPSON

Columbus State University (D)

4225 University Avenue, Columbus GA 31907-5645

County: Muscogee FICE Identification: 001561
Unit ID: 139366
Telephone: (706) 507-8800 Carnegie Class: Master's L
FAX Number: (706) 568-2123 Calendar System: Semester
URL: www.columbusstate.edu
Established: 1958 Annual Undergrad Tuition & Fees (In-State): $7,056
Enrollment: 8,194 Coed
Affiliation or Control: State IRS Status: 501(c)3
Highest Offering: Doctorate
Program: 2-Year Principally Bachelor's Creditable; Liberal Arts And General; Teacher Preparatory; Professional
Accreditation: SC, ART, BUS, CACREP, MUS, NURSE, TED, THEA

01 President .... Dr. Chris MARKWOOD
05 Provost/VP Academic Affairs .... Dr. Tom HACKETT
10 Vice President Business & Finance .... Mr. Tom HELTON
32 VP Student Affairs & Enrollment Mgt .... Dr. Gina SHEEKS
30 VP University Advancement .... Dr. Alan MEDDERS
13 Chief Information Officer .... Mr. Abraham GEORGE
84 Asst VP for Enrollment Mgmt .... Mr. John MCELVEEN
26 Asst VP for University Relations .... Mr. John LESTER
50 Dean College of Business & Comp Sci .... Dr. Linda HADLEY
08 Dean of Libraries .... Mr. Mark FLYNN
35 AVP Student Affs/Dean of Students .... Mr. Aaron J. REESE
15 Human Resources Director .... Ms. Laurie S. JONES
09 Director Institutional Research .... Dr. Sri SITHARAMAN
41 Athletic Director .... Mr. Todd REESER
37 Director Financial Aid .... Mr. Russ ROMANDINI
07 Director of Admissions .... Ms. Susan LOVELL

† Part of the University System of Georgia.

Columbus Technical College (E)

928 Manchester Expressway, Columbus GA 31904-6572

County: Muscogee FICE Identification: 005624
Unit ID: 139357
Telephone: (706) 649-1800 Carnegie Class: Assoc/Pub-R-M
FAX Number: (706) 649-1885 Calendar System: Semester
URL: www.columbustech.edu
Established: 1961 Annual Undergrad Tuition & Fees (In-State): $2,694
Enrollment: 3,594 Coed
Affiliation or Control: State IRS Status: 501(c)3
Highest Offering: Associate Degree
Program: Occupational; 2-Year Principally Bachelor's Creditable; Technical Emphasis
Accreditation: SC, ADNUR, COARC, DA, DH, DMS, MAC, RAD, SURGT

01 President .... Ms. Lorette M. HOOVER
10 VP Admin/Chief Financial Svcs .... Ms. Karen THOMAS
05 Vice President Academic Affairs .... Dr. Melanie THORNTON
32 Vice President Student Affairs .... Ms. Tara ASKEW
18 Vice President Operations .... Mr. Tommy WILSON
46 VP Institutional Effectiveness .... Ms. Monique BAUCHAM
88 Vice President Economic Development .... Mr. James LOYD
51 Assoc VP of Adult Education .... Ms. April HOPSON
15 Director of Human Resources .... Ms. Patricia HOOD
26 Director of Communications .... Ms. Cheryl MYERS
37 Associate VP of Financial Aid .... Ms. Debbie HENSHAW
38 Director Student Counseling .... Ms. Olive VIDAL-KENDALL
30 Director Institutional Advancement .... Ms. Gloria DODDS

Covenant College (F)

14049 Scenic Highway, Lookout Mountain TN 30750-4164

County: Dade FICE Identification: 003484
Unit ID: 139393
Telephone: (706) 820-1560 Carnegie Class: Bac/Diverse
FAX Number: (706) 820-2165 Calendar System: Semester
URL: www.covenant.edu
Established: 1955 Annual Undergrad Tuition & Fees: $31,320
Enrollment: 1,173 Coed
Affiliation or Control: Presbyterian Church In America IRS Status: 501(c)3
Highest Offering: Master's
Program: Liberal Arts And General; Teacher Preparatory
Accreditation: SC

01 President .... Dr. J. Derek HALVORSON
05 Vice Pres Academic Affairs .... Dr. Jeffrey B. HALL
30 Vice President Development .... Mr. Jeff SANDHOFF
32 Vice Pres Student Development .... Mr. Brad VOYLES
10 Vice Pres for Business & Finance .... Mr. Dan WYKOFF
08 Librarian .... Mr. Tad MINDEMAN
06 Dean of Records .... Mr. Rodney E. MILLER
42 Chaplain .... Mr. Grant LOWE
58 Director of Master of Education Pgm .... Dr. Jim DREXLER
21 Controller .... Mr. Robert E. HARBERT
18 Director of Physical Plant .... Mr. David NORTHCUTT
37 Director of Student Financial Plng .... Mrs. Beth BAILEY
15 Director of Human Resources .... Mrs. Tonya GREESON
41 Athletic Director .... Mr. Kyle TAYLOR
13 Chief Information Officer .... Ms. Marjorie CROCKER
29 Director of Alumni Relations .... Ms. Kim COLLINS
24 Director of AV Services .... Mr. Matt WRIGHT
23 Director of Health Services .... Ms. Tina HOLT
07 Assoc Dir Admissions .... Mr. Scott SCHINDLER
09 Director of Institutional Research .... Dr. Karen NELSON
26 Chief Communications Officer .... Ms. Jen ALLEN
20 Director of Academic Support .... Mrs. Janet HULSEY
36 Dir of Center for Calling & Career .... Mr. John PLATING
04 Administrative Asst to President .... Mrs. Joan STANTON
19 Director Security/Safety .... Mr. Kevin PATTY
109 Director of Auxiliary Services .... Mr. Tom SCHREINER

Dalton State College (G)

650 College Drive, Dalton GA 30720-3797

County: Whitfield FICE Identification: 003956
Unit ID: 139463
Telephone: (706) 272-4436 Carnegie Class: Bac/Assoc
FAX Number: (706) 272-4588 Calendar System: Semester
URL: www.daltonstate.edu
Established: 1963 Annual Undergrad Tuition & Fees (In-State): $3,950
Enrollment: 4,854 Coed
Affiliation or Control: State IRS Status: 501(c)3
Highest Offering: Baccalaureate
Program: Occupational; 2-Year Principally Bachelor's Creditable; Liberal Arts And General; Teacher Preparatory; Professional
Accreditation: SC, ADNUR, BUS, COARC, MAC, MLTAD, NUR, PHLEB, RAD, SW, TED

01 Interim President .... Dr. Margaret VENABLE
05 Interim VP for Academic Affairs .... Dr. Andy MEYER
10 Vice President Fiscal Affairs .... Mr. Scott BAILEY
84 Vice Pres Enrollment & Student Svcs .... Dr. Jodi S. JOHNSON
20 Interim Asst VP Academic Affs .... Barbara TUCKER
37 Director of Financial Aid/Vet Svcs .... Ms. Kim JONES
08 Librarian .... Ms. Lydia KNIGHT
09 Director Inst Research & Planning .... Dr. Henry M. CODJOE
21 Asst Director of Business Office .... Mr. Nick HENRY
18 Chief Facilities/Physical Plant .... Mr. Jack REYNOLDS
26 Director Marketing & Communication .... Ms. Pam PARTAIN
102 Director Foundation .... Mr. David ELROD
32 Director Student Life .... Ms. Jami HALL
38 Director Student Counseling .... Ms. Linda WHEELER
15 Director Human Resources .... Ms. Faith MILLER
96 Purchasing Coordinator .... Ms. Penny CORDELL
13 Director Computing & Info Services .... Mr. Terry BAILEY
19 Director Public Safety .... Mr. Michael MASTERS
29 Director Alumni Relations .... Mr. Josh WILSON
39 Director Student Housing .... Mrs. Natalie BATES
50 Dean School of Business .... Dr. Larry JOHNSON
53 Dean School of Education .... Dr. Sharon HIXON
49 Dean School of Liberal Arts .... Ms. Mary NIELSEN
81 Dean School of Science/Tech/Math .... Mr. Randall GRIFFUS
76 Dean Health Professions .... Dr. Gina KERTULIS-TARTAR
06 Registrar .... Mr. Rob WINGFIELD
41 Director Intercollegiate Athletics .... Mr. Derek WAUGH

† Part of the University System of Georgia.

Darton State College (H)

2400 Gillionville Road, Albany GA 31707-3098

County: Dougherty FICE Identification: 001543
Unit ID: 138691
Telephone: (229) 317-6000 Carnegie Class: Assoc/Pub-R-M
FAX Number: (229) 317-6604 Calendar System: Semester
URL: www.darton.edu
Established: 1963 Annual Undergrad Tuition & Fees (In-State): $3,395
Enrollment: 5,623 Coed
Affiliation or Control: State IRS Status: 501(c)3
Highest Offering: Baccalaureate
Program: Occupational; 2-Year Principally Bachelor's Creditable
Accreditation: SC, ADNUR, CAHIIM, COARC, CSHSE, CVT, DH, EMT, HT, MLTAD, NUR, OTA, POLYT, PTAA, RAD

01 Interim President .... Dr. Paul JONES
10 Interim VP for Fiscal Affairs .... Mr. John CLEMENS
05 Interim VP Academic Affairs .... Dr. Joan DARDEN
32 Interim VP Student Affairs .... Dr. Allia CARTER
21 Asst VP Business/Financial Svcs .... Mr. Stan BROWN
08 Director Learning Resources Ctr .... Mrs. Mary WASHINGTON
07 Director Admissions .... Vacant

13 Director Office of Information Tech .... Mr. Tracy COSPER
18 Director Physical Plant .... Mr. Lee HOWELL
26 Interim Director College Relations .... Ms. Cynthia GEORGE
41 Interim Athletic Director .... Ms. Lea HENRY
06 Registrar .... Mrs. Frances CARR
37 Asst Director Financial Aid .... Ms. Haley HOOKS
15 Dir & Chief Human Resources Officer .... Mr. Kendall ISAAC
85 International Coordinator .... Ms. Cortney DOWDLE
29 Director Alumni Relations .... Vacant
36 Director Student Placement .... Ms. Gloria RIDGEWAY
96 Director of Purchasing .... Mrs. Joy CAUSEY
89 Director Freshmen Studies .... Ms. Gloria RIDGEWAY
92 Coordinator Honors Program .... Ms. Shani CLARK
93 Director Minority Students .... Ms. Wendy WILSON
09 Director of Institutional Research .... Dr. Shavecca SNEAD
106 Dir Online Education/E-learning .... Ms. Renita LUCK
19 Chief of Police/Public Safety .... Mr. James BRACKIN
22 Dir Affirmative Action/EEO .... Mr. Kendall ISAAC
25 Interim Director of Grants .... Ms. Shalonda HEARD
28 Director of Diversity .... Ms. Wendy WILSON
30 Interim Chief Advancement Officer .... Ms. Cynthia GEORGE
39 Director Residence Life .... Mr. Rocco CAPELLO
84 Interim Asst VP Enrollment Mgmt .... Mr. Frank MALINOWSKI
43 Legal Affairs Officer .... Mr. Kendall ISAAC

† Part of the University System of Georgia.

DeVry University - Decatur Campus (A)

One West Court Square, Ste. 100,
Decatur GA 30030-2556
Telephone: (404) 270-2700 FICE Identification: 009224
Accreditation: &NH, CAHIIM, ENGT

† Regional accreditation is carried under the parent institution in Downers Grove, IL.

East Georgia State College (B)

131 College Circle, Swainsboro GA 30401-3643
County: Emanuel FICE Identification: 010997
Unit ID: 139621
Telephone: (478) 289-2000 Carnegie Class: Assoc/Pub-R-S
FAX Number: (478) 289-2038 Calendar System: Semester
URL: www.ega.edu
Established: 1973 Annual Undergrad Tuition & Fees (In-State): $3,612
Enrollment: 2,910 Coed
Affiliation or Control: State IRS Status: 501(c)3
Highest Offering: Baccalaureate
Program: Occupational; 2-Year Principally Bachelor's Creditable
Accreditation: SC

01 President .... Dr. Robert G. BOEHMER
05 Vice President for Academic Affairs .... Dr. Timothy D. GOODMAN
10 Vice President for Business Affairs .... Mr. Cliff GAY
32 Vice Pres for Student Affairs .... Dr. Donald AVERY
13 Vice Pres Information Technology .... Mr. Mike ROUNTREE
100 Chief of Staff/Legal Counsel .... Mrs. Mary C. SMITH
04 Executive Assistant to President .... Mrs. Susan GRAY
08 Librarian .... Mrs. Amanda MCKENZIE
06 Registrar .... Mrs. Janet STRACHER
12 Director of EGSC -Augusta .... Ms. Jordyn NAIL
27 Director of Public Information .... Vacant
09 Director of Institutional Research .... Mr. David GRIBBIN
84 Assoc Vice Pres Enrollment Mgmt .... Mrs. Karen S. JONES
15 Director of Human Resources .... Mrs. Tracy WOODS
30 Director of External Affairs .... Ms. Elizabeth GILMER
11 Director of Business Operations .... Mrs. Michelle GOFF
26 Director of Marketing .... Ms. Norma KENNEDY
12 Director of EGSC-Statesboro .... Ms. Caroline MCMILLAN
19 Dir Public Safety/Chief of Police .... Mr. Wiley GAMMON
35 Director of Student Life .... Ms. Vicki SHERROD
07 Director of Admissions .... Ms. Georgia EDMOND
21 Comptroller .... Vacant
38 Dir Counseling/Disability Services .... Ms. Anna Marie REICH
39 Director of Housing .... Ms. Missie CRAWFORD
41 Director of Athletics .... Vacant
88 Dir Sudie A Fulford Cmty Lrng Ctr .... Mrs. Jean D. SCHWABE
18 Director of Plant Operations .... Mr. David STEPTOE
88 Director of Accounting Services .... Ms. Becky FOSKEY
106 Director of Distance Education .... Dr. Dee MCKINNEY
88 Director of Academic Advisement .... Ms. Deborah KITTRELL-MIKELL
88 Director Learning Support .... Ms. Jill KIRKLAND
88 Auditor .... Ms. Rebecca VINCENT
109 Director of Auxiliary Services .... Ms. Ruth UNDERWOOD
88 Director of Student Conduct .... Ms. Sherrie HELMS
81 Dean of Mathematics & Sciences .... Dr. Robert BROWN
79 Dean of Humanities .... Dr. Carmine PALUMBO
83 Dean of Social Sciences .... Dr. Lee CHEEK
81 Chair of Biology Department .... Dr. Jimmy WEDINCAMP
88 Dir of Ctr for Teaching & Learning .... Vacant
88 Dir of Military Resource Center .... Ms. Stacey KING

† Part of the University System of Georgia.

Emmanuel College (C)

181 Springs Street, Franklin Springs GA 30639
County: Franklin FICE Identification: 001563
Unit ID: 139630
Telephone: (706) 245-7226 Carnegie Class: Bac/Diverse
FAX Number: (706) 245-4424 Calendar System: Semester
URL: www.ec.edu
Established: 1919 Annual Undergrad Tuition & Fees: $18,540
Enrollment: 801 Coed
Affiliation or Control: Pentecostal Holiness Church IRS Status: 501(c)3
Highest Offering: Baccalaureate
Program: Liberal Arts And General; Teacher Preparatory; Professional; Business Emphasis
Accreditation: SC

01 President .... Dr. Ronald WHITE
32 Vice President for Student Life .... Mr. Jason CROY
05 Vice President for Academic Affairs .... Dr. John R. HENZEL, JR.
10 Vice President for Finance .... Mr. Greg K. HEARN
30 Vice President for Development .... Mr. W. Brian JAMES
84 Vice Pres Enrollment Mgmt/Marketing .... Ms. Wendy VINSON
08 Director of Library Services .... Ms. Austina JORDAN
06 Registrar .... Mrs. Debra F. GRIZZLE
37 Director of Financial Aid .... Mrs. Niki STINSON
13 Director of Information Technology .... Mr. Glenn TONEY
11 Assoc VP of Campus Operations .... Vacant
41 Athletics Director .... Mr. Nate MOORMAN
42 Dir Spiritual Life/Campus Pastor .... Mr. Chris MAXWELL
15 Director of Human Resources .... Mrs. Joann HARPER
26 Chief Public Relations Officer .... Mrs. Paula DIXON
38 Director of Student Counseling .... Mr. Sean WILLIAMSON
96 Director of Accounting Services .... Mrs. Anita RAY
18 Physical Plant Director .... Mr. Wayne CRIDER
09 Director of Institutional Research .... Dr. Brian PEEK
29 Director Alumni Relations .... Mr. Harrell W. QUEEN
36 Director Career Services .... Mr. Sean WILLIAMSON

Emory University (D)

201 Dowman Drive, Atlanta GA 30322-0001
County: DeKalb FICE Identification: 001564
Unit ID: 139658
Telephone: (404) 727-6123 Carnegie Class: RU/VH
FAX Number: (404) 727-5997 Calendar System: Semester
URL: www.emory.edu
Established: 1836 Annual Undergrad Tuition & Fees: $46,314
Enrollment: 14,769 Coed
Affiliation or Control: United Methodist IRS Status: 501(c)3
Highest Offering: Doctorate
Program: Occupational; 2-Year Principally Bachelor's Creditable; Liberal Arts And General; Teacher Preparatory; Professional
Accreditation: SC, AA, ARCPA, BUS, CLPSY, DENT, IPSY, LAW, MED, MIDWF, NURSE, PAST, PCSAS, PH, PTA, RAD, THEOL

01 President .... Dr. James W. WAGNER
05 Provost/Exec VP Acad Affs .... Dr. Claire E. STERK
11 Interim Exec VP for Business/Admin .... Dr. Richard A. MENDOLA
17 Exec Vice Pres Health Affairs .... Dr. S. Wright CAUGHMAN
101 VP/Secretary of the University .... Ms. Allison K. DYKES
04 VP/Deputy to the President .... Dr. Gary S. HAUK
43 Sr Vice Pres & General Counsel .... Mr. Stephen D. SENCER
30 Sr Vice Pres Devel/Alumni Rels .... Ms. Susan CRUSE
32 Sr Vice President/Dean Campus Life .... Dr. Ajay NAIR
88 Vice Provost International Affairs .... Dr. Philip WAINWRIGHT
46 Vice President for Research Admin .... Dr. David L. WYNES
10 Vice President for Finance .... Ms. Carol KISSAL
58 Vice Provost/Dean Graduate Sch .... Dr. Lisa A. TEDESCO
15 Vice President Human Resources .... Mr. Peter BARNES
26 Senior VP Comm/Public Affairs .... Mr. Jerry LEWIS
88 Sr Advisor to Provost and Director .... Dr. Lanny S. LIEBESKIND
86 Interim Vice President Govt Affairs .... Ms. Cameron TAYLOR
18 Vice President Campus Services .... Mr. Matthew EARLY
29 Sr Assoc Vice Pres Alumni Assn .... Ms. Sarah COOK
25 Assoc Vice Pres for Research Admin .... Ms. Kathleen BIENKOWSKI
21 Assoc VP Finance & Controller .... Ms. Allison S. BERG
35 Special Asst to Sr VP Campus Life .... Ms. Judith M. PANNELL
28 Assoc Vice Provost Equity/Inclusion .... Ms. Lynell CADRAY
20 Sr Vice Prov Academic Affairs .... Dr. Lynn ZIMMERMAN
109 Assoc Vice Prov Oper Student Svcs .... Ms. Heather MUGG
08 Interim Sr VP for Lib Svcs/CIO .... Mr. Marc OVERCASH
07 AVP Undergrad Enroll/Dean of Admiss .... Dr. John LATTING
21 Chief Univ Budget Officer .... Mr. Michael ANDRECHAK
49 Dean of Emory College .... Dr. Robin FORMAN
12 Dean & CEO Oxford College .... Dr. Stephen H. BOWEN
63 Dean of Medicine .... Dr. Christian P. LARSEN
66 Dean of Nursing .... Dr. Linda MCCAULEY
73 Dean of Theology .... Dr. Jan LOVE
61 Dean of Law .... Mr. Robert SCHAPIRO
50 Dean of Business School .... Ms. Erika JAMES
69 Dean of Public Health .... Dr. James W. CURRAN
85 Dir Intl Student Scholar Program .... Ms. Shinsaeng KO
80 Pres & CEO of the Carter Center .... Ms. Mary Ann PETERS
42 Dean of the Chapel & Spiritual Life .... Rev. Bridgette YOUNG ROSS
06 University Registrar .... Ms. JoAnn MCKENZIE
27 AVP Communications & Marketing .... Mr. David JOHNSON
36 Director Placement Service .... Mr. Paul FOWLER
19 Chief of Police .... Mr. Craig T. WATSON
23 Pres & CEO Emory Healthcare .... Mr. Michael J. MANDL
41 Director Athletics/Recreation .... Dr. Michael VIENNA
12 Director Yerkes Research Ctrs .... Dr. Paul JOHNSON
49 Director Institute Liberal Arts .... Dr. Kevin CORRIGAN
88 Director M C Carlos Museum .... Ms. Bonnie SPEED
40 University Bookstore Liaison .... Mr. Bruce COVEY
39 Exec Dir Res Life & Housing .... Dr. Andrea TRINKLEIN
38 Director Univ Counseling Center .... Dr. Mark MCLEOD
09 Director Institutional Research .... Dr. Melissa BOLYARD
96 Director Contract Admin/Compliance .... Mr. Rex HARDAWAY
44 Executive Director of Annual Giving .... Ms. Kimberly JULIAN BOWDEN
45 Vice Provost University Strategies .... Mr. Michael SACKS

88 Director Operations .... Ms. Carol A. FLOWERS
37 Director Student Financial Aid .... Mr. John LEACH

Fort Valley State University (E)

1005 State University Drive, Fort Valley GA 31030-4313
County: Peach FICE Identification: 001566
Unit ID: 139719
Telephone: (478) 825-6211 Carnegie Class: Bac/Diverse
FAX Number: (478) 825-6394 Calendar System: Semester
URL: www.fvsu.edu
Established: 1895 Annual Undergrad Tuition & Fees (In-State): $6,566
Enrollment: 2,594 Coed
Affiliation or Control: State IRS Status: 501(c)3
Highest Offering: Beyond Master's But Less Than Doctorate
Program: Occupational; Liberal Arts And General; Teacher Preparatory
Accreditation: SC, AAFCS, CACREP, CORE, ENGT, TED

01 Interim President .... Dr. Jessica BAILEY
10 Interim VP Business & Finance .... Ms. Dorothy STRIPLING
31 Vice President External Affairs .... Dr. Melody CARTER
84 Vice Pres Enroll Mgmt/Stdnt Success .... Dr. Angela HARRIS
05 Int Vice Pres for Academic Affairs .... Dr. Rayton SIANJINA
09 VP Inst Research/Plng & Effec .... Dr. B. Donta TRUSS
88 Assoc VP for Land Grant Affair .... Dr. Mark LATTIMORE
49 Dean Arts & Sciences .... Dr. Uppinder MEHAN
21 Comptroller .... Ms. Dorothy STRIPLING
06 Registrar .... Mrs. Sharee LAWRENCE
43 Chief Legal Officer/Dir Govt Rels .... Mr. Charles JONES
13 Director for Information Technology .... Mr. Gary MILLER
08 Director Hunt Memorial Library .... Mr. Frank MAHITAB
07 Director Admissions .... Ms. Calandra WRIGHT
37 Director Financial Aid .... Ms. Cynthia PARKS
29 Director Alumni Affairs .... Mr. Ed BOSTON
15 Director of Human Resources .... Ms. Tricia ADDISON
19 Director Campus Safety .... Mr. Ken MORGAN
47 Dean Agriculture .... Dr. Gavindarajan KANNAN
23 Dir Student Health & Behav Coun .... Mrs. Jacqueline CASKEY-JAMES
18 Director Plant & Maintenance .... Dr. Dwayne CREW
36 Director Counsel/Career Development .... Ms. Simmons ROMELDA
26 Director Marketing/ Communications .... Mrs. Pamela BERRY-JOHNSON
41 Director of Athletics .... Mr. Joshua MURFREE
88 Exec Dir Academic Success Ctr .... Vacant
58 Dean Grad Studies/Extended Educ .... Dr. Rayton SIANJINA
53 Dean College of Education .... Dr. Edward HILL
22 Dir Affirmative Act/EEO/Diversity .... Mrs. Denise w. EADY
25 Director of Sponsored Programs .... Mrs. Lisa WILSON
30 Development Director .... Mr. Robert STEPHENS
39 Director Student Housing .... Mr. Shawn MODENA
102 Director Foundation .... Mrs. Krisitie KENNEY
50 Director Business .... Dr. Samuel GYAPONG
54 Director Engineering .... Mr. Archie WILLIAMS
96 Director of Purchasing .... Ms. Becky HORTON

† Part of the University System of Georgia.

Georgia Christian University (F)

6789 Peachtree Industrial Boulevard, Atlanta GA 30360
County: DeKalb FICE Identification: 041565
Unit ID: 461236
Telephone: (770) 279-0507 Carnegie Class: Not Classified
FAX Number: (770) 279-0308 Calendar System: Semester
URL: www.gcuniv.edu
Established: 1993 Annual Undergrad Tuition & Fees: $25,010
Enrollment: 300 Coed
Affiliation or Control: Independent Non-Profit IRS Status: 501(c)3
Highest Offering: Doctorate
Program: Liberal Arts And General; Professional; Religious Emphasis
Accreditation: @THEOL, TRACS

00 Chancellor .... Dr. Paul C. KIM
01 President .... Dr. Young Ihl CHANG
07 Director of Admissions .... Ms. Jihyun KIM
05 Vice President for Academic Affairs .... Dr. Howoo LEE
10 Vice President for Business Affairs .... Dr. Hee Sook SONG
20 Chief Academic Officer .... Dr. Eun Moo LEE
45 Director Of Planning .... Rev. Don YANG
21 Chief Financial Officer .... Ms. Eunice KIM
12 Director of Branch Campus .... Ms. Sun Hee CHOI
12 Director of Virginia TS .... Dr. Nam Hong CHO
18 Chief Facilities/Physical Plant .... Rev. Min Soo KIM
19 Director Security/Safety .... Mr. Samuel KIM
21 Director of Business Affairs .... Mr. Daniel D. KIM
29 Director Alumni Relations .... Rev. Min Soo KIM
26 Chief Public Relations Officer .... Dr. Sam Young KIM
06 Registrar .... Ms. Sara KIM
37 Director Student Financial Aid .... Ms. Ji Hyun KIM
50 Dean School of Business .... Dr. Kyung-il GHYMN
73 Dean School of Christianity .... Dr. HeeSook SONG
88 Dean School of Divinity .... Dr. Ho Woo LEE
64 Dean School of Music .... Dr. Mi Sun CHUN
88 Dn Mission Stds/World Christianity .... Dr. Eun Moo LEE
63 Dean School of Oriental Medicine .... Dr. Byeong HYUN
88 International Student Advisor .... Ms. Jy Hyun KIM
30 Dir of Institutional Advancement .... Dr. Hee Sook SONG
42 Chaplain .... Dr. Sam Young KIM
08 Director of the Library .... Ms. Keum Ju CHO
04 Administrative Asst to President .... Ms. Donghui FERGUSON
32 Chief Student Affairs/Student Life .... Dr. Hyun Sung CHO

Georgia College & State University (A)

231 West Hancock Street, Milledgeville GA 31061-0490
County: Baldwin FICE Identification: 001602
Unit ID: 139861
Telephone: (478) 445-5004 Carnegie Class: Master's L
FAX Number: (478) 445-1191 Calendar System: Semester
URL: www.gcsu.edu
Established: 1889 Annual Undergrad Tuition & Fees (In-State): $9,170
Enrollment: 6,772 Coed
Affiliation or Control: State IRS Status: 501(c)3
Highest Offering: Doctorate
Program: Liberal Arts And General; Teacher Preparatory; Professional
Accreditation: SC, BUS, CAATE, MUS, NUR, NURSE, SPAA, TED

01 President ....Dr. Steve M. DORMAN
04 Exec Assistant to the President ....Ms. Monica STARLEY
05 Provost/VP for Academic Affairs ....Dr. Kelli BROWN
10 Interim VP Finance/Administration ....Ms. Susan ALLEN
32 Vice President for Student Affairs ....Dr. Bruce HARSHBARGER
30 VP for University Advancement ....Ms. Monica DELISA
88 Dir of Econ Dev/External Relations ....Mr. Johnny GRANT
20 Sr Assoc Provost for Acad Affs ....Dr. Tom ORMOND
88 Assoc Provost for Student Success ....Dr. Carolyn DENARD
51 Assoc VP for Extended University ....Dr. Mark PELTON
35 Dean of Students ....Dr. Andy LEWTER
26 Int AVP Strategic Communications ....Mr. Kyle CULLARS
84 Assoc VP for Enrollment Management ....Ms. Suzanne PITTMAN
109 Int Asst VP for Auxiliary Services ....Mr. Greg BROWN
21 Assistant Budget Director ....Ms. Lilia MCMICHAEL
49 Dean College of Arts & Sciences ....Mr. Ken PROCTER
50 Dean College of Business ....Dr. Jim PAYNE
53 Dean College of Education ....Dr. Joseph PETERS
76 Dean College of Health Sciences ....Dr. Sandra GANGSTEAD
39 Exec Director of University Housing ....Mr. Larry CHRISTENSON
88 Univ Architect/Dir Facilities Plng ....Mr. Michael RICKENBAKER
18 Director of Facilities Operations ....Mr. Mark DUCLOS
19 Director of Public Safety ....Mr. Scott BECKNER
09 Asst VP of Institutional Research ....Dr. Chris FERLAND
12 Director Macon Graduate Center ....Dr. Kendra RUSSELL
13 Chief Information Officer ....Mr. Robert ORR
08 Director of Libraries ....Dr. Joe MOCNIK
36 Director Career Center ....Ms. Mary ROBERTS
40 Bookstore Manager ....Ms. Barresa ADAMS
15 Chief Human Resources Officer ....Ms. Leslie PIERCE
28 Director of Instl Equity/Diversity ....Dr. Veronica WOMACK
90 Associate Chief Information Officer ....Dr. Howard WOODARD
07 Director of Admissions ....Mr. Ramon BLAKLEY
06 Registrar ....Ms. Kay ANDERSON
41 Director of Athetics ....Mr. Wendell STATON
29 Dir Alumni Relations/Annual Giving ....Mrs. Mindy MILLER
43 Interim General Counsel ....Ms. Qiana WILSON
38 Director of Counseling Services ....Dr. Stephen WILSON
37 Director of Financial Aid ....Ms. Cathy CRAWLEY
88 Sr Dir Materials Mgmt/Central Svcs ....Mr. Mark MEEKS
88 Dir for Internal Audit/Advisory Ser ....Ms. Julia HANN
35 Director of Campus Life ....Mr. Tom MILES
104 Asst VP for International Educ ....Dr. Eric SPEARS

Georgia Gwinnett College (B)

1000 University Center Lane, Lawrenceville GA 30043
County: Gwinnett FICE Identification: 041429
Unit ID: 447689
Telephone: (678) 407-5000 Carnegie Class: Bac/Diverse
FAX Number: N/A Calendar System: Semester
URL: www.ggc.edu
Established: 2005 Annual Undergrad Tuition & Fees (In-District): $5,352
Enrollment: 10,828 Coed
Affiliation or Control: State/Local IRS Status: 501(c)3
Highest Offering: Baccalaureate
Program: Liberal Arts And General
Accreditation: SC, TED

01 President ....Dr. Stanley PRECZEWSKI
05 Acting SVP for Academic Affairs ....Dr. Lois RICHARDSON
18 Vice Pres Facilities/Operations ....Mr. Eddie BEAUCHAMP
13 Vice Pres Educational Technology ....Dr. Mark IKEN
10 VP of Business & Finance/CFO ....Ms. Laura MAXWELL
30 Vice President Advancement ....Ms. Renee BYRD-LEWIS
32 Sr Assoc Provost Student Affairs ....Dr. Jim B. FATZINGER
15 Assoc VP Human Resources ....Mrs. Katherine KYLE
19 AVP of Public Safety/Police Chief ....Mr. Terrance SCHNEIDER
41 Athletic Director ....Dr. Darin WILSON
07 Associate Director Admissions ....Mrs. Kristi L. MCBRIDE
04 Administrative Asst to President ....Mrs. Luann CAUSLAND
06 Registrar ....Ms. Nancy GRATTAN
08 Dean of Library Services ....Mr. Gene RUFFIN
09 Director of Institutional Research ....Dr. Lily HWANG
108 Exec Director Instl Effectiveness ....Dr. Juliana LANCASTER
46 Dir Research & Sponsored Programs ....Mr. Glenn A. PFEIFER
26 Director for Public Relations ....Mrs. Sloan JONES
28 Director Legal Diversity Affairs ....Ms. L. S. JORDAN
29 Director Alumni Relations ....Mr. Andrew SCHMIDT
37 Director Student Financial Aid ....Ms. Kimberly JORDAN
38 Director Student Counseling ....Dr. Tamara D'ANJOU TURNER
50 Dean School of Business ....Dr. Victoria E. JOHNSON
53 Dean School of Education ....Dr. Cathy D. MOORE

Georgia Highlands College (C)

3175 Cedartown Highway SE, Rome GA 30161-3897
County: Floyd FICE Identification: 009507
Unit ID: 139700
Telephone: (706) 802-5000 Carnegie Class: Assoc/Pub-R-M
FAX Number: (706) 295-6341 Calendar System: Semester
URL: www.highlands.edu
Established: 1970 Annual Undergrad Tuition & Fees (In-State): $3,115
Enrollment: 5,365 Coed
Affiliation or Control: State IRS Status: 501(c)3
Highest Offering: Baccalaureate
Program: Occupational; 2-Year Principally Bachelor's Creditable
Accreditation: SC, ADNUR, DH, PNUR

01 President ....Dr. Donald J. GREEN
05 Vice President Academic Affairs ....Dr. Renva WATTERSON
10 Vice Pres Finance/Administration ....Mr. Jeff DAVIS
32 Vice President Student Affairs ....Dr. Todd JONES
15 Vice President Human Resources ....Ms. Ginni SILER
37 Director Financial Aid ....Ms. Megan SIMPSON
06 Director Admissions & Registrar ....Ms. Sandie DAVIS
08 Dean Libraries/College Testing ....Mr. Elijah SCOTT
30 Development Officer ....Vacant
12 Campus Dean Marietta Campus ....Mr. Ken REAVES
12 Campus Dean Paulding/Douglasville ....Dr. Cathy LEDBETTER
12 Campus Dean Floyd Campus ....Dr. Todd JONES
13 VP/Information Technology/CIO ....Mr. Jeff PATTY
41 Director of Athletics ....Mr. Phillip GAFFNEY
04 Assistant Exec to the President ....Ms. Joannie YARBROUGH
18 Director Plant Operations ....Mr. Phillip KIMSEY
26 VP/Advacement & Marketing ....Ms. Mary TRANSUE

† Part of the University System of Georgia.

Georgia Institute of Technology (D)

225 North Avenue, NW, Atlanta GA 30332-0002
County: Fulton FICE Identification: 001569
Unit ID: 139755
Telephone: (404) 894-2000 Carnegie Class: RU/VH
FAX Number: (404) 894-1277 Calendar System: Semester
URL: www.gatech.edu
Established: 1885 Annual Undergrad Tuition & Fees (In-State): $12,204
Enrollment: 23,109 Coed
Affiliation or Control: State IRS Status: 501(c)3
Highest Offering: Doctorate
Program: Professional
Accreditation: SC, ART, BUS, CEA, CONST, CS, ENG, IPSY, OPE, PLNG

01 President ....Dr. G. P. (Bud) PETERSON
05 Provost/Exec VP Academic Affairs ....Dr. Rafael BRAS
10 Executive Vice Pres Admin/Finance ....Mr. Steven SWANT
46 Executive Vice President Research ....Dr. Stephen CROSS
100 Assistant Vice Pres/Chief of Staff ....Ms. Lynn DURHAM
30 Vice President Development ....Mr. Barrett H. CARSON
26 Vice Pres Communications/Marketing ....Mr. Michael L. WARDEN
32 Int Vice President Student Affairs ....Mr. John STEIN
88 VP/Director GA Tech Res Inst ....Dr. Andrew GERBER
46 Vice President Research ....Ms. Jilda GARTON
86 Vice Pres Government/Cmty Relations ....Mr. Dene SHEHEANE
88 VP Enterprise Innovation Inst ....Mr. Stephen FLEMING
29 President Georgia Tech Alumni Assoc ....Mr. Joseph IRWIN
58 Vice Prov Grad Ed & Faculty Affairs ....Dr. Susan COZZENS
84 Vice Prov Enrollment Services ....Dr. Paul KOHN
20 Vice Prov Undergraduate Education ....Dr. Colin POTTS
43 Vice Pres Legal Affairs/Risk Mgt ....Mr. Patrick MCKENNA
28 Vice President Institute Diversity ....Dr. Archie ERVIN
15 Int Assoc VP Human Resources ....Dr. Kim HARRINGTON
18 Vice President Facilities ....Mr. Charles G. RHODE
11 Senior Vice Pres Admin/Finance ....Dr. Jeffrey SCOTT
31 Vice President Campus Services ....Mr. Paul STROUTS
13 Vice President Information Tech/CIO ....Mr. James O'CONNOR
41 Director of Athletics ....Mr. Michael BOBINSKI
22 Sr Director Diversity Management ....Ms. Pearl ALEXANDER
12 Dean Ivan Allen College ....Dr. Jacqueline J. ROYSTER
35 Dean of Students/Asst Vice Pres ....Mr. John STEIN
48 Dean College of Architecture ....Dr. Steve FRENCH
77 Dean College of Computing ....Dr. Zvi GALIL
54 Dean College of Engineering ....Dr. Gary S. MAY
08 Vice Prov Lrng Excel/Dean Libraries ....Ms. Catherine MURRAY-RUST
82 Dean Scheller College of Business ....Dr. Maryam ALAVI
81 Dean College of Sciences ....Dr. Paul GOLDBART
06 Registrar ....Ms. Reta PIKOWSKY
40 Director Bookstore ....Mr. Gerald J. MALONEY
19 Director of Security & Police ....Mr. Robert CONNOLLY
107 Dean Professional Education ....Dr. Nelson BAKER
36 Executive Director Career Develop ....Dr. Michelle TULLIER
37 Director Student Financial Aid ....Ms. Marie MONS
23 Sr Director Student Health Svcs ....Dr. Gregory MOORE
39 Executive Director Housing ....Mr. Michael BLACK
09 Exec Dir Inst Research/Decision Spt ....Ms. Sandra J. BRAMBLETT
85 Vice Prov International Initiatives ....Dr. Yves BERTHELOT
104 Exec Dir International Education ....Ms. Amy HENRY
38 Director Counseling Center ....Dr. Ruperto PEREZ
109 Senior Director Auxiliary Services ....Mr. Richard STEELE
07 Director Undergraduate Admission ....Mr. Richard CLARK
96 Director of Procurement Services ....Mr. Frans BARENDS
88 Exec Dir Inst Budget Plng & Admin ....Mr. James KIRK
88 Director Capital Planning/Spce Mgt ....Mr. Howard WERTHEIMER
88 Exec Director Strategic Consulting ....Dr. Sonia ALVAREZ-ROBINSON
88 Bursar ....Mr. Terry FAIR
21 Assoc Vice Pres Financial Services ....Mr. James FORTNER

† Part of the University System of Georgia.

Georgia Military College (E)

201 E Greene Street, Milledgeville GA 31061-3398
County: Baldwin FICE Identification: 001571
Unit ID: 139904
Telephone: (478) 387-4900 Carnegie Class: Assoc/Pub-Spec
FAX Number: N/A Calendar System: Quarter
URL: www.gmc.edu
Established: 1879 Annual Undergrad Tuition & Fees: $5,734
Enrollment: 7,262 Coed
Affiliation or Control: Independent Non-Profit IRS Status: 501(c)3
Highest Offering: Baccalaureate
Program: 2-Year Principally Bachelor's Creditable; Business Emphasis
Accreditation: SC

01 President ....LTG. William B. CALDWELL, IV
03 Executive Vice President/COO ....BGEN. Curt RAUHUT
05 Vice Pres Academic Affs/Dn Faculty ....Dr. Phillip M. HOLMES
10 Chief Financial Officer ....Mr. James WATKINS
84 Vice Pres for Enrollment Management ....Ms. Jody YEARWOOD
32 Vice Pres Student Svcs/Commandant ....COL. Patrick BEER
30 Chief College Relations Officer ....Mr. Mark STROM
13 VP Info Technology/Online Campus ....Mr. Jody YEARWOOD
21 Assoc Vice Pres Business Affairs ....Ms. Susan MEEKS
09 Director Institutional Research ....Dr. Susan ISAAC
41 Athletic Director ....Mr. Bert WILLIAMS
18 Director Facilities/Engineer ....Mr. Jeff GRAY
06 Registrar ....Mrs. Robin KNIGHT
08 Librarian ....Ms. Erin NEWTON
19 Chief of Security/Safety ....Mr. James HODNETT

Georgia Northwestern Technical College (F)

One Maurice Culberson Drive, Rome GA 30161
County: Floyd FICE Identification: 005257
Unit ID: 139384
Telephone: (706) 295-6963 Carnegie Class: Not Classified
FAX Number: (706) 295-6944 Calendar System: Semester
URL: www.gntc.edu
Established: 1966 Annual Undergrad Tuition & Fees (In-State): $2,674
Enrollment: 5,816 Coed
Affiliation or Control: State IRS Status: 501(c)3
Highest Offering: Associate Degree
Program: Occupational; 2-Year Principally Bachelor's Creditable
Accreditation: SC, ADNUR, CAHIIM, COARC, DA, DMS, EMT, MAC, OTA, RAD, SURGT

01 President ....Dr. Pete MCDONALD
05 Provost ....Vacant
11 Vice Pres Administrative Services ....Ms. Kelly BARNES
30 Vice Pres Econ Development ....Mr. Pete MCDONALD
20 Vice President Academic Affairs ....Dr. Mindy MCCANNON
09 Vice Pres Inst Effectiveness ....Ms. Heidi POPHAM
51 Vice President Adult Education ....Ms. Connie SMITH
32 Assoc Vice Pres Student Services ....Dr. Steve BRADSHAW
06 Registrar ....Ms. Selena MAGNUSSON
08 Director of Library Services ....Mr. John LASSITER
19 Director Safety & Security ....Mr. Bill BYARS
37 Exec Director of Financial Aid ....Mr. Stephen ANDERSEN
18 Director Facilities Management ....Mr. Jeffrey AGAN
26 Dir Marketing/Public Relations ....Ms. Amber JORDAN
15 Director of Human Resources ....Ms. Peggy CORDELL

Georgia Perimeter College (G)

3251 Panthersville Road, Decatur GA 30034-3897
County: DeKalb FICE Identification: 001562
Unit ID: 244437
Telephone: (678) 891-2300 Carnegie Class: Assoc/Pub-S-MC
FAX Number: N/A Calendar System: Semester
URL: www.gpc.edu
Established: 1963 Annual Undergrad Tuition & Fees (In-State): $3,758
Enrollment: 21,371 Coed
Affiliation or Control: State IRS Status: 501(c)3
Highest Offering: Baccalaureate
Program: Occupational; 2-Year Principally Bachelor's Creditable
Accreditation: SC, ADNUR, DH

01 Interim President ....Mr. Robert E. WATTS
05 Int Vice President Academic Affairs ....Mr. Philip A. SMITH
10 Exec Vice Pres Financial/Admin Affs ....Mr. Ronald B. STARK
30 Vice Pres Institutional Advancement ....Mr. Jeffrey TARNOWSKI
32 Vice Pres Student Affs/Enroll Svcs ....Dr. Vincent JUNE
21 Assoc Vice Pres Financial Affairs ....Ms. Diane HICKEY
13 Assoc VP/Chief Information Officer ....Mr. Mark HOETING
35 Asst VP Student Devel/Special Pgms ....Dr. Coletta CARTER
21 Asst VP Budgets/Strategic Planning ....Ms. Jamie FERNANDES
88 Dir Ctr for Teaching/Learning Spprt ....Mr. Christopher REDNOUR
12 Academic Dean Alpharetta Campus ....Dr. Susan CODY
106 Academic Dean Online Campus ....Dr. Ingrid THOMPSON-SELLERS
12 Academic Dean Decatur Campus ....Dr. Stuart NOEL
12 Academic Dean Dunwoody Campus ....Dr. Margaret EHRLICH
12 Academic Dean Newton Campus ....Dr. Paulos YOHANNES
12 Academic Dean Clarkston Campus ....Ms. Marla CALICO
15 Exec Director Human Resources ....Mr. James RASMUS
16 Dir HR Employment/Acad Svcs ....Ms. Eyvon MITCHELL
26 Director Public Relations ....Ms. Barbara OBRENTZ
88 Dir Human Res Conflict Management ....Ms. Karen TRUESDALE
09 Int Dir Institutional Research/Plng ....Ms. Patti GREGG

41 Director Athletics ... Mr. Alfred BARNEY
29 Director Alumni Relations ... Mr. Collins FOSTER
37 Dir Student Financial Services ... Ms. Robin WINSTON
25 Director Grants/Sponsored Programs ... Mr. Glenn PFEIFER
28 Director of Disability Services ... Ms. Bonnie MARTIN
22 Dir Hum Res Cmp/Aff Act/Opn Rec Ofr ... Ms. Amanda REDDICK
88 Director of College Services ... Mr. Brian Keith CHAPMAN
07 Int Dir Recruitment/Admissions ... Mr. Danny BELLINGER
06 Director of Records/Registrar ... Ms. Tarrah MIRRUS
18 Dir Facil/Physical Plant Operations ... Mr. Scott E. HARDY
45 Director Facilities/Planning ... Mr. Lewis GODWIN
19 Chief of Police ... Mr. Nicholas MARINELLI

† Part of the University System of Georgia.

Georgia Piedmont Technical College (A)

495 N Indian Creek Drive, Clarkston GA 30021-2397

County: DeKalb FICE Identification: 005622
Unit ID: 244446
Telephone: (404) 297-9522 Carnegie Class: Assoc/Pub-S-MC
FAX Number: (404) 297-4234 Calendar System: Semester
URL: www.gptc.edu
Established: 1961 Annual Undergrad Tuition & Fees (In-State): $3,362
Enrollment: 4,050 Coed
Affiliation or Control: State IRS Status: 501(c)3
Highest Offering: Associate Degree
Program: Occupational; 2-Year Principally Bachelor's Creditable; Technical Emphasis
Accreditation: SC, EMT, ENGT, MAC, MLTAD

01 President ... Dr. Jabari SIMAMA
04 Exec Dir & Spec Asst to President ... Mr. Keith SAGERS
10 Vice Pres of Business & Financial ... Ms. Heather PENCE
05 Vice President Academic Affairs ... Dr. Mariam DITTMANN
46 Vice Pres of Economic Development ... Dr. Jeff STEVENSON
31 VP Econonic Devel/Cmty Engagement ... Ms. Cynthia EDWARDS
32 Int Vice President Student Affairs ... Dr. Candice JONES
20 Dean of Academic Programs ... Mr. Marcus HICKS
20 Dean of Academic Programs ... Dr. Debra GORDON
15 Director of Human Resources ... Ms. Lolita MORRISON
26 Director of Public Relations & Info ... Ms. Zaundra BROWN
06 Registrar ... Ms. Joana BLANKSON
07 Director of Admissions/Records ... Mr. Corey PARKER
51 Director Continuing Education ... Ms. Loretta HICKS
37 Assistant VP of Financial Aid ... Ms. Lakisha SANDERS
18 Int Dir of Facilities & Auxil Svcs ... Mr. Raymond CLUNIE
88 Dean of Adult Literacy ... Dr. Jacqueline ECHOLS
36 Dir Adv/Career & Retention Svcs ... Ms. Angela CUMMINGS
35 Dean of Student Development ... Ms. Candice JONES
108 Dean of Quality Initiatives ... Dr. Catrenia MCLENDON
13 Director of Information Technology ... Mr. Keith PERRY

Georgia Southern University (B)

PO Box 8033, Statesboro GA 30460-8033

County: Bulloch FICE Identification: 001572
Unit ID: 139931
Telephone: (912) 478-4636 Carnegie Class: DRU
FAX Number: N/A Calendar System: Semester
URL: www.georgiasouthern.edu
Established: 1906 Annual Undergrad Tuition & Fees (In-State): $7,318
Enrollment: 20,517 Coed
Affiliation or Control: State IRS Status: 501(c)3
Highest Offering: Doctorate
Program: Liberal Arts And General; Teacher Preparatory; Professional
Accreditation: SC, ART, BUS, BUSA, CAATE, CACREP, CIDA, CLPSY, CONST, CS, DIETD, @DIETI, ENG, ENGT, MUS, NRPA, NURSE, PH, TED, THEA

01 President ... Dr. Brooks A. KEEL
05 Provost/Vice Pres Academic Affairs ... Dr. Jean BARTELS
10 Vice Pres Business & Finance ... Mr. Rob WHITAKER
32 VP Student Affairs & Enroll Mgmt ... Dr. Teresa THOMPSON
30 VP Univ Advance/GSU Foundation Pres ... Ms. Salinda ARTHUR
27 VP Information Technology/CIO ... Dr. Steve BURRELL
86 VP for External Affairs ... Mr. Russell KEEN
46 Vice Pres for Research ... Dr. Charles PATTERSON
09 Assoc VP Strategic Rsrch & Analysis ... Dr. Jayne PERKINS BROWN
20 Associate Provost ... Dr. Diana CONE
35 Assoc VP & Dean of Students ... Ms. Patrice BUCKNER JACKSON
43 Assoc Vice Pres for Legal Affairs ... Ms. Maura COPELAND
44 Assoc VP University Advancement ... Mr. Michael SHIPPAM
04 Exec Associate to the President ... Ms. Leigh PRICE
07 Director of Admissions ... Ms. Amy SMITH
58 Dean College of Graduate Studies ... Dr. Charles PATTERSON
50 Dean College Business Admin ... Dr. Allen AMASON
53 Dean College Education ... Dr. Thomas KOBALLA
76 Dean College Health/Human Sci ... Dr. Barry JOYNER
49 Dean Col Liberal Arts/Social Sci ... Dr. Curtis RICKER
81 Dean College Science & Mathematics ... Dr. Martha ABELL
54 Dean AEP Col Engr/Info Tech ... Dr. Mohammad DAVOUD
51 Exec Director Continuing Educ ... Dr. Belkis CAPELES
69 Dean College of Public Health ... Dr. R. Gregory EVANS
62 Dean University Library ... Dr. Bede MITCHELL
88 Dir NCAA Compliance ... Mr. Keith ROUGHTON
88 Chief Audit & Advisory Services ... Ms. Jana BRILEY
43 Associate University Attorney ... Mr. Geoffrey CARSON
26 Assoc VP Mktg & Comm ... Ms. Jan BOND
88 Director Academic Success Center ... Ms. Janet L. O'BRIEN
37 Director Financial Aid ... Ms. Connie MURPHEY
06 Registrar ... Dr. Velma BURDEN
109 Assoc VP Auxiliary Services ... Mr. Edward D. MILLS
21 Senior Assoc VP/Controller ... Ms. Kim THOMPSON BROWN
15 Interim Assoc VP Human Resources ... Dr. Ale KENNEDY
41 Athletic Director ... Mr. Tom KLEINLEIN
18 Assoc VP Facilities ... Mr. Marvin MILLS
19 Interim Director Public Safety ... Ms. Laura MCCULLOUGH
36 Director Career Services ... Mr. Philip BRUCE
38 Director Counseling Services ... Dr. Jodi K. CALDWELL
88 Director Educ Opportunity Programs ... Dr. Joyya SMITH
23 Director Health Services ... Ms. Elissa NORRIS
39 Director University Housing ... Mr. Christopher MACDONALD
28 Dir Multicultural Student Center ... Ms. Dorsey BALDWIN
88 Director Leadership/Outreach Pgms ... Dr. Todd DEAL
88 Interim Director Advancement IT ... Ms. Jill GERIG
29 Sr Director Alumni Relations ... Mr. Wendell TOMPKINS, JR.
88 Director Garden of Coastal Plain ... Ms. Carolyn ALTMAN
14 Director Technical Services ... Mr. Joey REEVES
90 Director Info Tech for Acad Affairs ... Ms. Pamela DEAL
88 Director Museum ... Dr. Brent THARP
88 Director Wildlife Educ/Raptor Ctr ... Mr. Steven M. HEIN
96 Interim Director of Materials Mgt ... Mr. John OGLESBY
28 Interim Dir Equal Opp/Title IX ... Mr. Joel WRIGHT
89 Director First-Year Experience ... Dr. Chris CAPLINGER
92 Director Univ Honors Program ... Dr. Steven ENGEL
85 Director Center for Intl Studies ... Dr. Jacek LUBECKI
13 Chief Information Tech Security Ofc ... Mr. Michael FOX
88 Director Centers for Teaching & Tec ... Dr. Rachel SCHWARTZ
88 Dir Student Disability Resource Ctr ... Mr. Mike CHAMBERS
102 Director Foundation Acct ... Ms. Jodi COLLINS

† Part of the University System of Georgia.

Georgia Southwestern State University (C)

800 GA Southwestern State Univ Dr, Americus GA 31709-4693

County: Sumter FICE Identification: 001573
Unit ID: 139764
Telephone: (877) 871-4594 Carnegie Class: Master's S
FAX Number: N/A Calendar System: Semester
URL: www.gsw.edu
Established: 1906 Annual Undergrad Tuition & Fees (In-State): $6,198
Enrollment: 2,666 Coed
Affiliation or Control: State IRS Status: 501(c)3
Highest Offering: Beyond Master's But Less Than Doctorate
Program: Occupational; Liberal Arts And General; Teacher Preparatory; Professional
Accreditation: SC, BUS, NUR, NURSE, TED

01 Interim President ... Dr. Charles E. PATTERSON
05 Vice President Academic Affairs ... Dr. Brian U. ADLER
10 Vice Pres Business & Finance ... Mr. W. Cody KING
32 Vice President for Student Affairs ... Dr. Samuel T. MILLER
84 Vice Pres Enroll Mgmt/Dir Admiss ... Dr. Gaye HAYES
09 Director Institutional Research ... Dr. Lisa A. COOPER
08 Dean Library Services ... Ms. Ru STORY-HUFFMAN
13 Dir Information Technology/CIO ... Mr. Royce HACKETT
102 GSW Foundation Executive Director ... Ms. Reda K. ROWELL
06 Registrar ... Ms. Krista SMITH
36 Director Career Services Center ... Ms. Sandra FOWLER
37 Director Student Financial Aid ... Ms. Angela V. BRYANT
26 Director University Relations ... Mr. Stephen E. SNYDER
35 Assistant Dean of Students ... Dr. Darcy BRAGG
41 Athletic Director ... Mr. Mike LEEDER
29 Coord Alumni Relations/Annual Fund ... Ms. Kimberly COMER
15 Director of Human Resources ... Ms. Gena WILSON
19 Director of Public Safety ... Mr. Michael TRACY

† Part of the University System of Georgia.

Georgia State University (D)

PO Box 3999, Atlanta GA 30302-3999

County: Fulton FICE Identification: 001574
Unit ID: 139940
Telephone: (404) 413-2000 Carnegie Class: RU/VH
FAX Number: (404) 413-1380 Calendar System: Semester
URL: www.gsu.edu
Established: 1913 Annual Undergrad Tuition & Fees (In-State): $10,686
Enrollment: 32,542 Coed
Affiliation or Control: State IRS Status: 501(c)3
Highest Offering: Doctorate
Program: Liberal Arts And General; Teacher Preparatory; Professional
Accreditation: SC, ART, BUS, BUSA, CACREP, CEA, CLPSY, COARC, COPSY, CORE, DIETC, DIETD, EXSC, HSA, IPSY, LAW, MUS, NURSE, PH, PTA, SCPSY, SP, SPAA, SW, TED

01 President ... Dr. Mark P. BECKER
05 Sr VP Academic Affairs & Provost ... Dr. Risa I. PALM
10 Sr VP Finance & Administration ... Dr. Jerry J. RACKLIFFE
84 Vice Provost & VP Enroll Mgt ... Dr. Timothy M. RENICK
46 Vice President Research & Econ Dev ... Dr. James A. WEYHENMEYER
32 Vice President Student Affairs ... Dr. Douglass F. COVEY
30 Vice President Development ... Mr. Walter T. MASSEY
26 VP PR & Mktg Communications ... Mr. Don HALE
43 University Attorney ... Dr. Kerry L. HEYWARD
49 Dean Arts & Sciences ... Dr. William J. LONG
50 Dean Business ... Dr. Richard D. PHILLIPS
53 Dean Education ... Dr. Paul A. ALBERTO
76 Interim Dean Nursing/Health Prof ... Dr. Andrew J. BUTLER
69 Dean Public Health ... Dr. Michael P. ERIKSEN
61 Dean Law ... Dr. Steven J. KAMINSHINE
80 Dean Policy Studies ... Dr. Mary Beth WALKER
92 Dean Honors College ... Dr. Larry S. BERMAN
08 Interim Dean Libraries ... Ms. Tammy S. SUGARMAN
88 Assoc Provost Strategic Initiatives ... Dr. Robert D. MORRIS
58 Interim Assoc Provost Grad Programs ... Dr. Lisa P. ARMISTEAD
09 Assoc Provost Inst Effectiveness ... Dr. Peter LYONS
82 Assc Prov International Initiatives ... Dr. Jun LIU
20 Assoc Provost Faculty Affairs ... Dr. Lynda BROWN WRIGHT
88 Assistant Provost Admin Operations ... Dr. Edgar C. TORBERT
45 Assoc VP Research Integrity ... Dr. Brenda J. CHAPMAN
88 Chief Innovation Officer for IT ... Mr. Phil VENTIMIGLIA
13 Assoc VP IS&T/Chief Technology Ofc ... Mr. Dennis ROSE
18 Assoc VP Facilities ... Mr. Ramesh VAKAMUDI
21 Assoc Vice President Finance ... Ms. Elizabeth R. JONES
21 Assoc VP Finance & Comptroller ... Mr. Bruce R. SPRATT
30 Assoc VP Central Development ... Mr. John D. CLARK
30 Assoc VP Advancement Resources ... Ms. Charlotte P. PARKS
30 Assoc VP Constituent Programs Dev ... Mr. David J. FRABONI
102 Assoc VP GSU Foundation ... Mr. Dale J. PALMER
35 Assoc VP Student Affairs ... Dr. Rebecca Y. STOUT
27 Assoc VP Public Relations ... Ms. Andrea JONES
07 Asst VP Undergraduate Admissions ... Mr. Scott M. BURKE
84 Asst VP Student Retention ... Dr. Allison CALHOUN-BROWN
35 Dean of Students ... Dr. Darryl B. HOLLOMAN
29 Asst VP Alumni Relations ... Ms. Christina C. MILLION
109 Asst VP Auxiliary Enterprises ... Mr. Wayne E. REED
15 Asst VP Human Resources ... Ms. Linda J. NELSON
22 Asst VP Opp Dev/Diversity Educ ... Ms. Linda J. NELSON
19 Asst VP/Chief University Police ... Ms. Connie B. SAMPSON
06 Registrar ... Ms. Shari P. SCHWARTZ
85 Dir Intl Students/Scholars Svcs ... Ms. Heather L. HOUSLEY
39 Director University Housing ... Ms. Marilyn A. DE LAROCHE
38 Director Psychological & Health Svc ... Dr. Jill LEE-BARBER
28 Director Diversity Programs ... Mr. John R. DAY
88 Director Application Engineering ... Mr. John M. BANDY, JR.
14 Director Technology Engineering ... Mr. Keith E. CAMPBELL
88 Interim Dir Research Computing ... Mr. Davide GAETANO
36 Director University Career Svcs ... Mr. Kevin E. GAW
37 Director Financial Aid ... Mr. Louis B. SCOTT
96 Director of Business Services ... Mr. Michael E. DAVIDSON
88 Dir Univ Auditing & Advisory Svcs ... Mr. Sterling ROTH
88 Director Design/Construction Svcs ... Ms. Kimberly P. BAUER
88 Director Emergency Management ... Mr. Keith P. SUMAS
26 Director Govt & Community Affairs ... Ms. Julia M. KERLIN
41 Athletic Director ... Mr. Charles G. COBB
88 Special Advisor to President ... Mr. Thomas C. LEWIS
04 Assistant to the President ... Ms. Ethel M. BROWN

† Part of the University System of Georgia.

Gordon State College (E)

419 College Dr., Barnesville GA 30204-1746

County: Lamar FICE Identification: 001575
Unit ID: 139968
Telephone: (678) 359-5555 Carnegie Class: Assoc/Pub4
FAX Number: (678) 359-5080 Calendar System: Semester
URL: www.gordonstate.edu
Established: 1972 Annual Undergrad Tuition & Fees (In-State): $4,164
Enrollment: 4,047 Coed
Affiliation or Control: State IRS Status: 501(c)3
Highest Offering: Baccalaureate
Program: Occupational; 2-Year Principally Bachelor's Creditable; Teacher Preparatory
Accreditation: SC, ADNUR, NUR, TED

01 President ... Dr. Max BURNS
05 Provost & VP Academic Affairs ... Dr. Margaret VENABLE
05 Int Provost & VP Academic Affairs ... Dr. Jeffery KNIGHTON
10 VP Finance and Administration ... Ms. Kristen ALBRITTON
32 VP Student Affairs ... Dr. Dennis R. CHAMBERLAIN
30 VP Institutional Advancement ... Mrs. Rhonda TOON
04 Administrative Asst to President ... Mrs. Dolores BELL
20 Associate VP Academic Affairs ... Dr. Richard BASKIN
08 Library Director ... Dr. Sonya GAITHER
88 Asst VP Institutional Effectiveness ... Mrs. Teresa BETKOWSKI
09 Director of Institutional Research ... Mr. Britt LIFSEY
49 Int Dean School of Arts & Sciences ... Dr. Susan FINAZZO
53 Dean School of Education ... Dr. Michael MAHAN
66 Dean School of Nursing ... Dr. Anne PURVIS
20 Director of Student Success Center ... Mr. Peter J. HIGGINS
40 Bookstore Manager ... Mrs. Connie H. WADE
21 Int Controller ... Mr. Walter GREEN
21 Director of Business Services ... Ms. Irene CELESTIN
18 Director of Facilities ... Mr. Richard VEREEN
37 Int Director of Financial Aid ... Mrs. Jody DEFORE
15 Int Director of Human Resources ... Mrs. Laura BOWEN
13 Director of Information Technology ... Mr. Jeff HAYES
19 Director of Public Safety ... Chief Jeff MASON
07 Director of Admissions ... Mr. Bennett FERGUSON
41 Athletic Director ... Mr. Todd DAVIS
38 Director of Counseling Services ... Mrs. Laura BOWEN
39 Director of Residence Life ... Ms. Tonya R. COLEMAN
35 Director of Student Activities ... Mrs. Sharon LLOYD
06 Registrar ... Mrs. Janet BARRAS
30 Development Officer ... Mr. Skipper BURNS
29 Director of Alumni Relations ... Vacant
26 Chief Public Information Officer ... Mrs. Tamara BOATWRIGHT

† Part of the University System of Georgia.

Gupton Jones College of Funeral Service (A)

5141 Snapfinger Woods Drive, Decatur GA 30035-4022
County: DeKalb FICE Identification: 010771
Unit ID: 139995
Telephone: (770) 593-2257 Carnegie Class: Assoc/PrivNFP
FAX Number: (770) 593-1891 Calendar System: Quarter
URL: www.gupton-jones.edu
Established: 1920 Annual Undergrad Tuition & Fees: $14,400
Enrollment: 115 Coed
Affiliation or Control: Independent Non-Profit IRS Status: 501(c)3
Highest Offering: Associate Degree
Program: Occupational; 2-Year Principally Bachelor's Creditable; Technical Emphasis
Accreditation: FUSER

01 President .... Mr. Walter L. CROX, JR.
05 Dean .... Mr. James HINZ
06 Registrar .... Ms. Felicia SMITH

Gwinnett College (B)

4230 Highway 29, Suite 11, Lilburn GA 30047-3447
County: Gwinnett FICE Identification: 025830
Unit ID: 140003
Telephone: (770) 381-7200 Carnegie Class: Assoc/PrivFP
FAX Number: (770) 381-0454 Calendar System: Other
URL: www.gwinnettcollege.com
Established: 1976 Annual Undergrad Tuition & Fees: $9,925
Enrollment: 325 Coed
Affiliation or Control: Proprietary IRS Status: Proprietary
Highest Offering: Associate Degree
Program: Occupational; 2-Year Principally Bachelor's Creditable
Accreditation: ACICS

01 President .... Mr. Michael DAVIS

Gwinnett Technical College (C)

5150 Sugarloaf Parkway, Lawrenceville GA 30043-5702
County: Gwinnett FICE Identification: 022884
Unit ID: 140012
Telephone: (770) 962-7580 Carnegie Class: Assoc/Pub-S-SC
FAX Number: (770) 962-7985 Calendar System: Semester
URL: www.gwinnetttech.edu
Established: 1984 Annual Undergrad Tuition & Fees (In-State): $3,330
Enrollment: 7,234 Coed
Affiliation or Control: State IRS Status: 501(c)3
Highest Offering: Associate Degree
Program: Occupational; 2-Year Principally Bachelor's Creditable; Technical Emphasis
Accreditation: SC, ACFEI, ADNUR, COARC, CVT, DA, DMS, EMT, MAC, RAD, SURGT

01 President .... Dr. Glen D. CANNON
10 Executive VP Finance/Administration .... Mr. David WELDEN
05 VP of Academic Affairs .... Dr. Victoria SEALS
26 VP of Economic Development .... Mr. Dave MCCULLOCH
32 VP of Student Affairs .... Dr. Julie POST
30 VP of Institutional Advancement .... Ms. Mary Beth BYERLY
103 Director State Workforce Programs .... Ms. Ann SECHRIST
15 Director of Human Resources .... Ms. Debbie GERARDO
21 Director of Accounting .... Mrs. Valerie STRICKLAND
06 Registrar .... Ms. Arlene CLARKE
36 Director of Career Services .... Ms. Ave MILLER
37 Director of Financial Aid .... Ms. Lisa MARTIN
53 Dean of Adult Education .... Ms. Stephanie ROOKS
07 Dir Admissions/Assessment/Advise .... Ms. Brenda PYLE
18 Supervisor of Facilities Operation .... Ms. Janice BOLTON
19 Chief of Campus Police & Security .... Mr. Joseph MARKHAM
08 Manager of Library Services .... Ms. Elissa CHECOV
09 Coord Institutional Effectiveness .... Mr. Stephen MAYFIELD
04 Admin Operations Specialist .... Ms. Melissa FLANAGAN

Herzing University (D)

3393 Peachtree Road NE, Suite 1003, Atlanta GA 30326-1332
Telephone: (404) 816-4533 FICE Identification: 020897
Accreditation: &NH, NURSE

† Regional accreditation is carried under the parent institution in Madison, WI.

Interactive College of Technology (E)

5303 New Peachtree Road, Chamblee GA 30341-2818
County: DeKalb FICE Identification: 022843
Unit ID: 138655
Telephone: (770) 216-2960 Carnegie Class: Assoc/PrivFP
FAX Number: (770) 216-2988 Calendar System: Semester
URL: www.ict.edu
Established: 1986 Annual Undergrad Tuition & Fees: $8,880
Enrollment: 784 Coed
Affiliation or Control: Proprietary IRS Status: Proprietary
Highest Offering: Associate Degree
Program: Occupational
Accreditation: #COE

01 President .... Mr. Elmer R. SMITH
05 Dean of the College .... Mr. Thomas BLAIR
12 Campus Director Pasadena Texas .... Mr. Richard BARROSO
12 Campus Dir SW Houston Texas .... Ms. Cynthia BRYSON
12 Campus Dir North Houston Texas .... Mr. Harry MAUZ
12 Campus Director - Newport KY .... Mr. Rich ELLISON
12 Campus Director - Morrow GA .... Mr. Greg KOCH
12 Campus Director - Gainesville GA .... Ms. Sophia LUCAS

Interactive College of Technology (F)

2323-C Browns Bridge Road, Gainesville GA 30504
Telephone: (678) 456-0550 Identification: 770533
Accreditation: COE

† Branch campus of Interactive College of Technology, Chamblee, GA.

Interactive College of Technology (G)

1580 Southdale Parkway, Suite C, Morrow GA 30260
Telephone: (770) 960-1298 Identification: 770534
Accreditation: COE

† Branch campus of Interactive College of Technology, Chamblee, GA.

Interdenominational Theological Center (H)

700 Martin L. King, Jr. Drive, SW, Atlanta GA 30314-4143
County: Fulton FICE Identification: 001568
Unit ID: 140146
Telephone: (404) 527-7700 Carnegie Class: Spec/Faith
FAX Number: (404) 527-0901 Calendar System: Semester
URL: www.itc.edu
Established: 1958 Annual Graduate Tuition & Fees: $11,780
Enrollment: 306 Coed
Affiliation or Control: Interdenominational IRS Status: 501(c)3
Highest Offering: Doctorate; No Undergraduates
Program: Professional; Religious Emphasis
Accreditation: #SC, THEOL

01 President .... Dr. Edward LORENZA WHEELER
05 Provost/VP for Academic Services .... Dr. Maisha HANDY
10 Vice Pres of Admin Services .... Dr. Charles E. THOMAS, JR.
30 VP for Institutional Advancement .... Mr. Charles WARD
84 AVP Enrollment Management/Registrar .... Ms. Bobbie HALL
37 Financial Aid Director .... Mr. Johnny NIMES
15 Human Resource Director .... Ms. Kathryn J. WEBB
29 Director Alumni Relations .... Ms. Timi C. SIMPSON
07 Director of Admissions/Recruitment .... Ms. Michelle DAVIS
42 Chaplain .... Dr. Keith SLAUGHTER

ITT Technical Institute (I)

485 Oak Place, Suite 800, Atlanta GA 30349
Telephone: (404) 765-4600 Identification: 666595
Accreditation: ACICS

† Branch campus of ITT Technical Institute, Indianapolis, IN.

ITT Technical Institute (J)

5905 Stewart Parkway, Douglasville GA 30135
Telephone: (678) 715-2100 Identification: 770655
Accreditation: ACICS

† Branch campus of ITT Technical Institute, Indianapolis, IN.

ITT Technical Institute (K)

10700 Abbotts Bridge Road, Ste. 190, Duluth GA 30097-8460
Telephone: (678) 957-8510 Identification: 666325
Accreditation: ACICS

† Branch campus of ITT Technical Institute, Indianapolis, IN.

ITT Technical Institute (L)

2065 ITT Tech Way N.W., Kennesaw GA 30144
Telephone: (770) 426-2300 Identification: 666378
Accreditation: ACICS

† Branch campus of ITT Technical Institute, Indianapolis, IN.

Kennesaw State University (M)

585 Cobb Avenue NW, Kennesaw GA 30144-5563
County: Cobb FICE Identification: 001577
Unit ID: 140164
Telephone: (770) 578-6000 Carnegie Class: Master's L
FAX Number: N/A Calendar System: Semester
URL: www.kennesaw.edu
Established: 1963 Annual Undergrad Tuition & Fees (In-State): $7,326
Enrollment: 25,714 Coed
Affiliation or Control: State IRS Status: 501(c)3
Highest Offering: Doctorate
Program: Liberal Arts And General; Teacher Preparatory; Professional
Accreditation: SC, ART, BUS, BUSA, CGTECH, CONST, CS, ENG, ENGR, ENGT, MACTE, MUS, NURSE, SPAA, SW, TED, THEA

01 President .... Dr. Daniel S. PAPP
10 Chief Business Officer .... Dr. Randy C. HINDS
05 Provost/Vice Pres Academic Affs .... Dr. W. Ken HARMON
30 VP University Advancement & Devel .... Mr. Michael HARDERS
32 Vice Pres Student Affairs .... Dr. Kathleen WHITE
11 Vice President for Operations .... Dr. Randy C. HINDS
58 VP Research/Dean Graduate College .... Dr. Charles J. AMLANER
26 VP Strategic Comm & Marketing .... Ms. Arlethia PERRY-JOHNSON
31 VP Economic Dev & Community Eng .... Mr. Charles ROSS
20 Senior Vice Provost Academic Affs .... Dr. John OMACHONU
43 Gen Counsel/Sp Asst Pres Leg Affs .... Dr. Flora B. DEVINE
04 Faculty Exec Assistant to President .... Dr. Jon PRESTON
20 Assoc Vice Pres for Curriculum .... Dr. Valerie D. WHITTLESEY
21 Assoc Vice Pres for Operations .... Ms. Maria BRITT
20 Dean University College .... Dr. Keisha L. HOERRNER
15 Asst Vice Pres Human Resources Svcs .... Mr. Rodney BOSSERT
84 Assoc Vice Pres Enrollment Services .... Mr. Kim WEST
08 Asst Vice Pres for Library Services .... Mr. J. David EVANS
18 Asst Vice Pres Facilities Services .... Mr. John A. ANDERSON
26 Asst VP Strategic Comm//Marketing .... Mr. Ronald RAMOS
46 Asst VP Enterprise Info Mgmt .... Dr. Robert SMITH
04 Exec Admin/Chief of Protocol .... Ms. Lynda K. JOHNSON
79 Dean Humanities/Social Science .... Dr. Robert DORFF
81 Dean Science & Mathematics .... Dr. Mark R. ANDERSON
53 Dean Bagwell College of Education .... Dr. Arlinda EATON
50 Dean Coles College of Business .... Dr. Kathy S. SCHWAIG
76 Dean WellStar Col Health/Human Svcs .... Ms. Monica NANDAN
49 Dean College of the Arts .... Dr. Patricia S. POULTER
35 Assoc VP Student Affairs .... Dr. Michael L. SANSEVIRO
51 Dean Continuing/Professional Educ .... Ms. Barbara S. CALHOUN
07 Sr Exec Director Enrollment Svcs .... Ms. Susan N. BLAKE
38 Assoc VP/Dir Student Success Svcs .... Dr. Robert J. MATTOX
28 Chief Diversity Officer .... Dr. Erik MALEWSKI
06 Registrar .... Mr. Kim WEST
13 Assoc CIO/CTO .... Dr. John L. ISENHOUR
91 Exec Dir Enterprise Systems & Svcs .... Ms. Rifka MAYANI
37 Director Student Financial Aid .... Mr. Rondall H. DAY
07 Dir Student Recruitment/Admissions .... Dr. Angela J. EVANS
25 Director Procurement & Contracting .... Ms. Laura MCMILLAN
36 Int Dir of Career Services Center .... Ms. Ana BAIDA
41 Director of Athletics .... Mr. Vaughn A. WILLIAMS
29 Director Alumni Affairs .... Ms. Pierrette MAILLET
44 Director Annual Giving .... Dr. Joan DUNCAN
19 AVP Public Safety/Chief of Police .... Mr. Roger STEARNS
35 Director Student Life .... Ms. Katherine E. ALDAY
88 Dir Enterprise Academic Reporting .... Ms. Donna R. HUTCHESON
96 Director of Purchasing .... Vacant

† Part of the University System of Georgia.

LaGrange College (N)

601 Broad Street, La Grange GA 30240-2999
County: Troup FICE Identification: 001578
Unit ID: 140234
Telephone: (706) 880-8000 Carnegie Class: Bac/Diverse
FAX Number: (706) 880-8358 Calendar System: 4/1/4
URL: www.lagrange.edu
Established: 1831 Annual Undergrad Tuition & Fees: $27,210
Enrollment: 963 Coed
Affiliation or Control: United Methodist IRS Status: 501(c)3
Highest Offering: Master's
Program: Liberal Arts And General; Teacher Preparatory; Professional
Accreditation: SC, ACBSP, NUR

01 President .... Dr. Dan MCALEXANDER
04 Executive Assistant to President .... Mrs. Carla RHODES
31 Events Coordinator .... Ms. Tammy ROGERS
41 Athletic Director .... Mrs. Jennifer D. CLAYBROOK
05 Provost .... Dr. David GARRISON
32 Dean of Student Engagement .... Dr. Mark SHOOK
06 Registrar .... Ms. Cindy SAINES
08 Co-Director Library .... Mr. Joseph MARCINIAK
08 Co-Director Library .... Ms. Charlene BAXTER
55 Dir Graduate/Degree Completion .... Mr. Jeff LUKKEN
09 Director Inst Effectiveness .... Dr. Carol YIN
36 Director Career Development Center .... Vacant
38 Director Counseling Center .... Mrs. Pamela TREMBLAY
20 Associate Provost .... Dr. Maranah SAUTER
104 Associate Provost and Professor .... Mrs. Sarah Beth MALLORY
39 Director Res Educ & Housing .... Mr. Vernon JAMES
30 Vice President External Relations .... Mr. William JONES
26 Sr Director Communications/Mktg .... Mr. Dean A. HARTMAN
37 Director Student Financial Aid .... Mrs. Michelle REEVES
44 Senior Director Development .... Ms. Rebecca ROTH
29 Director Alumni & Cmty Relations .... Mrs. Martha PIRKLE
84 Dean of Enrollment Management .... Mr. Joseph C. MILLER
44 Major Gift Officer .... Mr. Mark DAVIS
07 Director of Admission .... Mr. David MCGREAL
105 Asst Director Communications & Mktg .... Mr. David BEARD
10 Vice Pres Finance & Operations .... Mr. Martin E. PIRRMAN
21 Director of Finance .... Mrs. Patti D. HOXSIE
15 Senior Director Human Resources .... Mrs. Dawn COKER
13 Chief Information Officer .... Vacant
18 Manager Facilities/Physical Plant .... Mr. Michael CONIGLIO
19 Director of Security .... Mr. Michael A. THOMAS
14 Director Information Technology .... Mr. James BLACKWOOD
42 Director Spiritual Life & Chaplain .... Mr. Adam ROBERTS
106 Director Online Instruction .... Dr. Jon ERNSTBERGER
91 Database Administrator .... Mr. Brandon MOBLEY

Lanier Technical College (A)

2990 Landrum Education Drive, Oakwood GA 30566-3405
County: Hall FICE Identification: 005254
Unit ID: 140243
Telephone: (770) 533-7000 Carnegie Class: Assoc/Pub-R-M
FAX Number: (678) 989-3107 Calendar System: Semester
URL: www.laniertech.edu
Established: 1964 Annual Undergrad Tuition & Fees (In-State): $3,164
Enrollment: 3,695 Coed
Affiliation or Control: State IRS Status: 501(c)3
Highest Offering: Associate Degree
Program: Occupational; 2-Year Principally Bachelor's Creditable; Technical Emphasis
Accreditation: **SC**, DA, DH, EMT, MAC, #MLTAD, @PTAA, RAD, SURGT

01 President ... Dr. Ray PERREN
103 Vice President Economic Development ... Mr. Tim MCDONALD
05 Vice President Academic Affairs ... Dr. Tavarez HOLSTON
45 Vice President IE & Operations ... Dr. Joanne P. TOLLESON
32 Vice President Student Affairs ... Ms. Nancy BEAVER
10 Vice Pres Administrative Services ... Ms. Laura ELDER
13 Vice President Technology ... Mr. Robbie VICKERS
88 Vice President Adult Education ... Dr. Linda M. BARROW
04 Executive Assistant to President ... Ms. Karen MINOR
20 Asst Vice Pres Academic Affairs ... Dr. Dana NICHOLS
75 Dean of Professional Programs ... Ms. Donna BRINSON
76 Dean of Allied Health ... Dr. Deanne COLLINS
50 Dean of Business & Computer Science ... Ms. Lisa MALOOF
72 Dean of Technical & Industrial Pgms ... Mr. Troy LINSEY
97 Dean of General Education ... Dr. Howard LEDFORD
09 Dir of Institutional Effectiveness ... Mr. Brad GADBERRY
30 Exec Dir Institutional Advancement ... Ms. Cris PERKINS
26 Director of Marketing ... Mr. Dave PARRISH
07 Director of Admissions ... Ms. Sue CRONIC
06 Registrar ... Ms. Sandi J. BAKER
37 Director Student Financial Aid ... Ms. Kimberly KELLEY
21 Director Administrative Services ... Ms. Janet BOHANON
15 Director of Human Resources ... Ms. Jill CANTRELL
18 Director of Facilities ... Mr. Guy ABBS
36 Student Placement Specialist ... Ms. Melissa LAWRENCE
28 Coord Special Svcs/Minority Affairs ... Ms. Mallory SAFLEY

Le Cordon Bleu College of Culinary Arts in Atlanta (B)

1927 Lakeside Parkway, Tucker GA 30084-5865
Telephone: (770) 938-4711 Identification: 666298
Accreditation: **ACICS**, ACFEI

† Branch campus of Le Cordon Bleu College of Culinary Arts, Portland, OR.

Life University (C)

1269 Barclay Circle, Marietta GA 30060-2996
County: Cobb FICE Identification: 020748
Unit ID: 140252
Telephone: (770) 426-2600 Carnegie Class: Bac/A&S
FAX Number: (770) 429-4819 Calendar System: Quarter
URL: www.life.edu
Established: 1974 Annual Undergrad Tuition & Fees: $10,860
Enrollment: 2,754 Coed
Affiliation or Control: Independent Non-Profit IRS Status: 501(c)3
Highest Offering: Doctorate
Program: 2-Year Principally Bachelor's Creditable; Liberal Arts And General; Professional
Accreditation: **SC**, CAATE, CHIRO, DIETD, DIETI

01 President ... Dr. Guy F. RIEKEMAN
10 Exec VP for Finance ... Mr. William JARR
05 Provost and VP of Academic Affairs ... Dr. Rob SCOTT
30 VP of University Advancement ... Mr. Greg HARRIS
32 VP for Student Services ... Dr. Marc SCHNEIDER
11 VP of Operations ... Mr. John MCGEE
84 VP of Enrollment & Mktg ... Dr. Cynthia BOYD
88 VP of Professional Relations ... Dr. Gilles LAMARCHE
41 Director of Athletics ... Mr. Dan PAYNE
15 Director of Human Resources ... Ms. Stella PETERSON
13 Chief Information Officer ... Mr. John ALTIKULAC
13 Director Information Technology ... Mr. Thorton MUIR
104 Director of Global Initiatives ... Dr. John DOWNES
76 Dean College of Chiropractic ... Dr. Leslie KING
49 Asst Dean Grad & Undergrad Studies ... Dr. Micheal D. SMITH
23 Assistant Dean for Clinics ... Dr. Bernadette LAVENDER
06 Registrar ... Ms. Heather HOFFMAN
07 Director of Admissions Operations ... Ms. Stephanie BUCHANAN
08 Director of Learning Resources ... Ms. Karen PRESTON
46 Director of Research ... Dr. Stephanie SULLIVAN
29 Alumni Relations Manager ... Ms. Mary Ellen LEFFARD
108 Director of Inst Effectiveness ... Dr. Vince ERARIO
09 Director of Institutional Research ... Dr. Howard WRIGHT
18 Director Facilities/Physical Plant ... Mr. Larry RIDDLE
38 Director Student Success ... Dr. Lisa RUBIN
37 Director Student Financial Aid ... Ms. Melissa WATERS
35 Exec Dir of Student Services ... Ms. Jennifer VALTOS
36 Director of Career Planning ... Ms. Susan DUDT
88 Dir of Student Administrative Svcs ... Ms. Kay FREELAND
26 Director of Communications ... Mr. Will BROOKS
21 Budget Director ... Ms. Amy MCILVANE
44 Director of Development ... Ms. Erin DANCER
27 Director of Marketing ... Ms. Shelly BATCHER
44 Director of Advancement Services ... Ms. Lauren NELSON
88 Director of Life Force ... Dr. Cierra HOFFMAN
101 Board Secretary ... Ms. Nita LOONEY

Luther Rice College and Seminary (D)

3038 Evans Mill Road, Lithonia GA 30038-2454
County: DeKalb FICE Identification: 031009
Unit ID: 135364
Telephone: (770) 484-1204 Carnegie Class: Spec/Faith
FAX Number: (770) 484-1155 Calendar System: Semester
URL: www.lutherrice.edu
Established: 1962 Annual Undergrad Tuition & Fees: $7,920
Enrollment: 1,158 Coed
Affiliation or Control: Independent Non-Profit IRS Status: 501(c)3
Highest Offering: Doctorate
Program: Liberal Arts And General; Professional
Accreditation: **BI**, TRACS

01 President ... Dr. James L. FLANAGAN
10 Vice President Financial Affairs ... Mr. Louis B. HARDCASTLE
32 Vice Pres for Student Development ... Dr. Dennis D. DIERINGER
05 Vice President for Academic Affairs ... Dr. Ralph J. MCCANN
26 Director of Marketing ... Mr. Russell L. SORROW
09 VP for Institutional Effectiveness ... Dr. Ralph J. MCCANN
08 Director of Library Services ... Mr. Daryl FLETCHER
37 Director Student Financial Aid ... Mr. Gary W. COOK
85 Asst to the Pres Global Strategy ... Dr. Ronald B. LONG
58 Director Doctor of Ministry Program ... Dr. Brad K. ARNETT
20 Acting Assoc VP Academic Affairs ... Mr. Evan POSEY
11 VP for Administration ... Mr. Steven STEINHILBER

Medtech College (E)

4501 Circle 75, Pkwy SE, Ste D-4100, Atlanta GA 30339
County: Cobb FICE Identification: 038044
Unit ID: 444714
Telephone: (770) 859-9779 Carnegie Class: Not Classified
FAX Number: (770) 859-9778 Calendar System: Quarter
URL: www.medtech.edu
Established: Annual Undergrad Tuition & Fees: $14,830
Enrollment: 320 Coed
Affiliation or Control: Proprietary IRS Status: Proprietary
Highest Offering: Associate Degree
Program: Occupational
Accreditation: **COE**

01 Executive Director ... Pammie LAND

Medtech College (F)

2800 Century Pkwy NE, Suite 100, Atlanta GA 30345
Telephone: (678) 218-0600 Identification: 770536
Accreditation: **COE**

† Branch campus of Medtech College, Atlanta, GA.

Mercer University (G)

1501 Mercer University Drive, Macon GA 31207-0003
County: Bibb FICE Identification: 001580
Unit ID: 140447
Telephone: (478) 301-2700 Carnegie Class: Master's L
FAX Number: (478) 301-2108 Calendar System: Semester
URL: www.mercer.edu
Established: 1833 Annual Undergrad Tuition & Fees: $34,150
Enrollment: 8,557 Coed
Affiliation or Control: Independent Non-Profit IRS Status: 501(c)3
Highest Offering: Doctorate
Program: Liberal Arts And General; Teacher Preparatory; Professional
Accreditation: **SC**, ARCPA, BUS, CACREP, CS, ENG, LAW, MED, MFCD, MUS, NURSE, PH, PHAR, PTA, TED, THEOL

01 President and CEO ... Mr. William D. UNDERWOOD
00 Chancellor ... Dr. R. Kirby GODSEY
100 Senior VP and Chief of Staff ... Mr. Larry D. BRUMLEY
05 Provost ... Dr. D. Scott DAVIS
10 Executive VP for Admin & Finance ... Dr. James S. NETHERTON
30 Sr VP for University Advancement ... Mr. John A. PATTERSON
84 Sr Vice Pres Enrollment Mgmt ... Dr. Penny L. ELKINS
43 Vice President and General Counsel ... Mr. William G. SOLOMON
13 Chief Technology Officer ... Mr. Michael R. BELOTE
17 Sr VP Health Sciences/Dean Phar/HS ... Dr. Hewitt MATTHEWS
32 Vice President & Dean of Students ... Dr. Doug R. PEARSON
46 Sr V Prov Research/Dean Grad Stds ... Dr. Wayne C. GLASGOW
09 Vice Provost for Inst Effectiveness ... Dr. Susan C. MALONE
21 Treasurer & Assoc VP Finance ... Ms. Julia T. DAVIS
18 Assoc Vice President for Facilities ... Mr. Russell VULLO
15 Associate Vice Pres Personnel Admin . Ms. Rhonda W. LIDSTONE
26 Sr Asst VP for Marketing Commun ... Mr. Richard L. CAMERON
37 Assoc VP Student Financial Planning ... Ms. Maria A. HAMMETT
49 Int Dean College of Liberal Arts ... Dr. Keith E. HOWARD
61 Dean School of Law ... Ms. Daisy H. FLOYD
63 Dean School of Medicine ... Dr. William F. BINA, III
54 Dean School of Engineering ... Dr. Wade H. SHAW
50 Dean Sch Business/Econ ... Dr. Susan P. GILBERT
73 Int Dean School of Theology ... Dr. Robert N. NASH
53 Dean College of Education ... Dr. James J. BARTA
66 Dean College of Nursing ... Dr. Linda A. STREIT
51 Dean College Cont/Prof Stds ... Dr. Priscilla R. DANHEISER
64 Dean School of Music ... Dr. C. David KEITH
76 Int Dean Col of Health Professions ... Dr. Lisa M. LUNDQUIST
08 Dean of University Libraries ... Ms. Elizabeth D. HAMMOND
06 Registrar ... Ms. Lucy P. WILSON
41 Athletic Director ... Mr. Jim COLE
19 Chief Police Department ... Mr. Gary COLLINS
09 Director of Institutional Research ... Ms. Sarah E. MAY
96 Director of Purchasing ... Mr. Charles MIZE
04 Administrative Asst to President ... Ms. Vonne SHEFFIELD
29 Director Alumni Relations ... Ms. Jill H. KINSELLA
86 Director Government Relations ... Mr. Hugh D. SOSEBEE, JR.

Middle Georgia State University (H)

100 College Station Drive, Macon GA 31206-5145
County: Bibb FICE Identification: 007728
Unit ID: 482158
Telephone: (478) 471-2700 Carnegie Class: Bac/Diverse
FAX Number: (478) 471-2846 Calendar System: Semester
URL: www.mga.edu
Established: 1884 Annual Undergrad Tuition & Fees (In-State): $4,542
Enrollment: 7,927 Coed
Affiliation or Control: State IRS Status: 501(c)3
Highest Offering: Baccalaureate
Program: Liberal Arts And General
Accreditation: **SC**, ADNUR, COARC, CS, NUR, OTA, TED

01 President ... Dr. Christopher BLAKE
05 Provost ... Dr. Martha L. VENN
10 Exec VP Finance & Operations ... Ms. Nancy STROUD
84 VP Enrollment Management ... Dr. Sheri ROWLAND
40 Director Campus Stores ... Ms. Ashley EVANS
30 VP Univ Advancement/Exec Dir Fdn ... Mr. Raymond CARNLEY
20 Vice Provost Academic Initiatives ... Dr. Pamela BEDWELL
88 Assoc Provost Regional Coordination ... Dr. Deepa ARORA
108 Asst Provost Acad Planning/Policy ... Dr. Mary WEARN
31 Asst Provost Innovative Outreach ... Dr. Art RECESSO
100 Chief of Staff ... Mr. Albert J. ABRAMS
13 Chief Information Officer ... Mr. Roger DIXON
43 Dir Legal Services/General Counsel ... Ms. Frances DAVIS
88 Spec Asst to Pres/Comm & Bus Outrch ... Mr. David LANIER
26 Exec Dir Adv/Mktg/Comm ... Ms. Cheryl CARTY
15 Exec Dir Human Resources ... Dr. Lisa BURROUGHS
44 Exec Dir Major and Planning Giving ... Ms. Julie DAVIS
32 Asst VP Student Affairs ... Mr. Michael STEWART
18 Asst VP Facilities ... Mr. David SIMS
19 Asst VP Risk Mgmt and Police Svcs ... Mr. Shawn DOUGLAS
21 Controller ... Mr. Brian STANLEY
06 Registrar ... Ms. Brenda HOGAN
07 Director of Admissions ... Ms. Margo WOODHAM
29 Director Alumni Relations ... Ms. Natalie RISCHBIETER
109 Director Auxillary Services ... Mr. Kevin REID
38 Director Counseling ... Ms. Predita HOWARD
37 Director Financial Aid ... Ms. LeeAnn KIRKLAND
96 Director Purchasing ... Ms. Barbara BURNS
104 Director International Education ... Dr. Laura THOMASON
08 Director Library Services ... Ms. Pat BORCK
39 Director of Residence Life ... Mr. Brian HARRELL
41 Director Recreation and Athletics ... Mr. Charles MULLIS
88 Director Student Support Services ... Ms. Yolanda PETTY
12 Director Cochran/Eastman Campuses ... Mr. Henry WHITFIELD
12 Director Dublin Campus ... Dr. Stephen SVONAVEC
12 Director Warner Robins Campus ... Ms. Pella MURPHY
49 Dean Arts & Sciences ... Dr. Ron WILLIAMS
50 Dean of Business ... Dr. Varkey K. TITUS
53 Dean of Education ... Dr. David FULLER
76 Dean Health Sciences ... Dr. Rebecca J. CORVEY
72 Dean Information Technology ... Dr. Alex KOOHANG
04 Administrative Asst to President ... Ms. Carrie WIMBERLEY
09 Director of Institutional Research ... Vacant

† Part of the University System of Georgia.

Miller-Motte Technical College (I)

621 NW Frontage Road, Augusta GA 30907
Telephone: (706) 396-8000 Identification: 770710
Accreditation: **ACICS**

† Branch campus of Miller-Motte Technical College, Clarksville, TN.

Miller-Motte Technical College (J)

1800 Box Road, Columbus GA 31907
Telephone: (706) 225-5000 Identification: 770711
Accreditation: **ACICS**

† Branch campus of Miller-Motte Technical College, Clarksville, TN.

Miller-Motte Technical College (K)

175 Tom Hill Sr Boulevard, Macon GA 31210
Telephone: (478) 803-4800 Identification: 770844
Accreditation: **ACICS**

† Branch campus of McCann School of Business & Technology, Pottsville, PA.

Morehouse College (L)

830 Westview Drive SW, Atlanta GA 30314-3773
County: Fulton FICE Identification: 001582
Unit ID: 140553
Telephone: (404) 681-2800 Carnegie Class: Bac/A&S
FAX Number: (404) 681-2650 Calendar System: Semester
URL: www.morehouse.edu

Established: 1867 Annual Undergrad Tuition & Fees: $29,791
Enrollment: 2,109 Male
Affiliation or Control: Independent Non-Profit IRS Status: 501(c)3
Highest Offering: Baccalaureate
Program: Liberal Arts And General; Teacher Preparatory
Accreditation: SC, BUS, MUS

01 President Dr. John S. WILSON, JR.
05 Provost/SVP Academic Affairs Dr. Garikai CAMPBELL
18 Assoc Vice Pres Campus Operations Mr. Andre E. BERTRAND
30 Int VP Institutional Advancement Dr. John P. BROWN
11 Chief Operating Officer Mr. William TAGGART
32 Vice Pres Student Development Dr. Timothy SAMS
10 Vice Pres Business Affairs/CFO Dr. Alan ROBERTSON
15 AVP Human Resource Mrs. Amanda BAILEY
44 Special Asst Pres-Capital Campaign Ms. Kathleen L. JOHNSON
42 Dean Martin Luther King Jr Chapel Dr. Lawrence E. CARTER
06 Interim Dean/Registrar Ms. Kasi ROBINSON
07 Director Admissions & Recruitment Mr. Darryl ISOM
37 Director of Financial Aid Ms. Sheryl SPIVEY
29 Dir Alumni Rels/Annual Giving Pgm Mr. Henry GOODGAME
26 Interim Director of Communications Ms. Elise DURHAM
36 Director of Placement Mr. Doug COOPER
41 Athletic Director Mr. Andre PATTILLO
39 Director Student Housing Mr. Maurice WASHINGTON
19 Chief of Campus Police Chief Valerie DALTON
85 Interim Dir Andrew Young Ctr Mr. Julius COLES
20 Special Assistant to Provost Dr. Tafaya RANSOM
35 Director Student Services Mr. Kevin BOOKER
38 Director of Student Counseling Dr. Gary WRIGHT
96 Assoc VP/Chief Procurement Mgr Mr. Ralph JOHNSON
27 Publications Manager Ms. Vickie HAMPTON
84 Assoc VP of Enrollment Mangement Mr. Terrance DIXON
21 Director of Budgets Mr. David LERCH
21 Controller Ms. Robbie BISHOP-MONROE
13 Chief Information Officer Mr. Clifford RUSSELL
43 General Counsel & Chief of Staff Ms. Lacrecia CADE
88 Chief Internal Auditor Ms. Undria STALLINGS

Morehouse School of Medicine (A)

720 Westview Drive, SW, Atlanta GA 30310-1495
County: Fulton FICE Identification: 024821
Unit ID: 140562
Telephone: (404) 752-1500 Carnegie Class: Spec/Med
FAX Number: (404) 752-1027 Calendar System: Semester
URL: www.msm.edu
Established: 1975 Annual Graduate Tuition & Fees: $49,652
Enrollment: 398 Coed
Affiliation or Control: Independent Non-Profit IRS Status: 501(c)3
Highest Offering: Doctorate; No Undergraduates
Program: Professional
Accreditation: SC, MED, PH

01 President Dr. Valerie MONTGOMERY RICE
05 Dean Dr. Valerie MONTGOMERY RICE
86 Exec Director of Government Affairs Mr. Daniel DAWES
43 General Counsel Ms. Almeta COOPER
30 Sr Vice President of Institutional Dr. Bennie L. HARRIS
46 VP & Sr Assoc Dean OSRA Dr. Sandra HARRIS-HOOKER
26 VP of Marketing & Communications Ms. Pamela SIMMONS
15 Associate VP of Human Resources Ms. Denise BRITT
102 Assoc VP Development/Advance Dr. Ernie HUGHES
20 Sr Assoc Dean for Educ/Faculty UME Dr. Martha ELKS
88 Sr Assoc Dean for Clinical Affairs Dr. Derrick BEECH, JR.
20 Assoc Dean Faculty Affairs Dr. Erika BROWN
37 Director Student Fiscal Affairs Ms. Cynthia H. HANDY
08 Library Manager Mr. Joe SWANSON, JR.
09 Director II Planning & IR/Title 3 Ms. Andrea D. FOX
25 Director of Grants & Contracts Mr. Patrick THOMAS
29 Director Alumni Affairs Ms. Samra COOTE
07 Director Admissions Mr. Brandon HUNTER
96 Director Purchasing Mr. Philmon THOMAS
44 Major Gifts Officer Vacant
22 Chief Compliance Officer Ms. Desiree RAMIREZ
06 Registrar Ms. Angela FREEMAN
13 Chief Information Officer Ms. Annmarie EADES
19 Chief of Police Mr. Joseph CHEVALIER, JR.

North Georgia Technical College (B)

PO Box 65, Clarkesville GA 30523-0065
County: Habersham FICE Identification: 005619
Unit ID: 140678
Telephone: (706) 754-7700 Carnegie Class: Assoc/Pub-R-M
FAX Number: (706) 754-7777 Calendar System: Semester
URL: www.northgatech.edu
Established: 1943 Annual Undergrad Tuition & Fees (In-State): $4,887
Enrollment: 2,694 Coed
Affiliation or Control: State IRS Status: 501(c)3
Highest Offering: Associate Degree
Program: Occupational; 2-Year Principally Bachelor's Creditable; Technical Emphasis
Accreditation: SC, ACFEI, MAC, MLTAD

01 President Dr. Gail THAXTON
05 Vice President for Academic Affairs Kathie IVESTER
32 Vice President for Student Affairs Dr. Michael KING
11 Vice President for Administration Carol CARSON
30 Vice Pres of Economic Development Dr. Mark IVESTER
06 Registrar Caroline FRICK
07 Director of Admissions Michele SHIRLEY
15 Human Resources Coordinator Marcia PEYTON
18 Chief Facilities/Physical Plant Michael BOYD
26 Chief Public Relations Officer Vacant
29 Director Alumni Relations Cynthia BROWN
35 Campus Life Director Sherry SEAL
36 Director Job Placement Vacant
37 Financial Aid Director Audra JIMENEZ
96 Procurement Officer Jeannie BARRETT
09 Institutional Research Analyst Mark HARMON
46 Institutional Effectiveness Dir Janet HENDERSON
20 Dean for Academic Affairs Dan PRESSLEY
20 Dean for Academic Affairs Leslie MCFARLIN
20 Dean for Academic Affairs Mindy GLANDER
106 Distance Education Specialist Dr. Renee DEIBERT
13 Information Technology Director Savonda TURNER
19 Chief of Police Stan LOVEL

Oconee Fall Line Technical College-North Campus (C)

1189 Deepstep Road, Sandersville GA 31082-9337
County: Washington FICE Identification: 031555
Unit ID: 420431
Telephone: (478) 553-2050 Carnegie Class: Assoc/Pub-R-S
FAX Number: (478) 553-2118 Calendar System: Semester
URL: www.oftc.edu
Established: 1996 Annual Undergrad Tuition & Fees (In-State): $2,614
Enrollment: 1,866 Coed
Affiliation or Control: State IRS Status: 501(c)3
Highest Offering: Associate Degree
Program: Occupational
Accreditation: @SC, COE

01 President Dr. Lloyd HORADAN
05 Vice Pres Academic/Student Affs Ms. Erica HARDEN
10 Vice Pres Administrative Services Ms. Rosemary SELBY
30 Vice Pres Economic Development Mr. Joe GORE
49 Dean Arts & Sciences/Business Svcs Ms. Michele STRICKLAND
32 Dean Student Affairs Ms. Johnnie EDGE
06 Registrar Ms. Geri CLEMENTS
07 Director of Admissions Ms. Raydor CONEWAY
15 Director Human Resources Ms. Sharon O'NEAL
21 Director of Administrative Services Ms. Penny KITCHENS
18 Director Facilities/Physical Plant Mr. Jim HARRISON
26 Exec Director Marketing Ms. Lakeshia POOLE
37 Financial Aid Director Ms. Betty YOUNG
28 Dir of Spec Populations/Stdnt Life Ms. Susan HAMMOCK

Oconee Fall Line Technical College-South Campus (D)

560 Pinehill Road, Dublin GA 31021-1599
County: Laurens FICE Identification: 022795
Unit ID: 140076
Telephone: (478) 275-6589 Carnegie Class: Assoc/Pub-R-M
FAX Number: (478) 275-6642 Calendar System: Semester
URL: www.oftc.edu
Established: 1984 Annual Undergrad Tuition & Fees (In-State): $1,574
Enrollment: 1,869 Coed
Affiliation or Control: State IRS Status: 501(c)3
Highest Offering: Associate Degree
Program: Occupational; Technical Emphasis
Accreditation: @SC, COE, COARC, MAC, RAD

01 President Dr. Lloyd HORADAN
09 Vice Pres Inst Effectiveness Dr. Katie DAVIS
32 Dean Student Affairs Mr. Jay MULLIS
06 Assistant Registrar Ms. Kimberly NOLES
18 Director Facilities Mr. Ragan GREEN
30 Exec Dir Institutional Advancement Mrs. Jenny SHUMAN
19 Chief Security & Facilities Mr. Mark ROGERS
36 Director of Career Development Vacant
76 Dean Allied Health/Prof Svcs Ms. Tammy BAYTO
37 Asst Director Financial Aid Ms. Teresa CRAFTON
08 Director Library Services Ms. Wendi MORRIS
07 Director of Admissions Mr. Raydor CONEWAY

Ogeechee Technical College (E)

One Joseph E. Kennedy Boulevard, Statesboro GA 30458-8049
County: Bulloch FICE Identification: 030300
Unit ID: 366465
Telephone: (912) 681-5500 Carnegie Class: Assoc/Pub-R-M
FAX Number: (912) 486-7704 Calendar System: Semester
URL: www.ogeecheetech.edu
Established: 1987 Annual Undergrad Tuition & Fees (In-State): $3,396
Enrollment: 2,340 Coed
Affiliation or Control: State IRS Status: 501(c)3
Highest Offering: Associate Degree
Program: Occupational; 2-Year Principally Bachelor's Creditable; Technical Emphasis
Accreditation: SC, CAHIIM, DA, DMS, FUSER, MAC, OPD, RAD, SURGT

01 President Dr. Dawn H. CARTEE
04 Exec Assistant to the President Ms. Karen MOBLEY
05 Executive VP for Academic Affairs Dr. Charlene LAMAR
31 Vice President Economic Development Ms. Lori DURDEN
108 VP Institutional Effectiveness Ms. Brandy TAYLOR
32 Vice President Student Affairs Dr. Ryan FOLEY
10 Vice President for Administration Ms. Eyvonne HART
13 VP Technology & Institutional Supp Mr. Jeff DAVIS
30 VP for College Advancement Mr. Barry TURNER
09 Director Inst Research & Planning Ms. YLonne HODGES
20 Dean for Academic Affairs Mr. John GROOVER
08 Dean for Library Services Vacant
51 Dir Continuing Ed & Ind Training Ms. Kathleen KOSMOSKI
07 Director for Admissions Ms. Laura SAUNDERS
06 Registrar Ms. Michelle STUBBS
37 Director for Financial Aid Ms. Letrell THOMAS
21 Director for Accounting Ms. Patsy POWELL
15 Director for Human Resources Mr. Steve MILLER
109 Director for Auxiliary Services Mr. J.J ALTMAN
18 Director for Plant Operations Mr. Buddy SAPP
19 Director Campus Safety & Security Mr. Stan YORK
88 Dean for Adult Education Dr. Paul MIZELL
97 Dean Distance & General Education Ms. Jennifer WITHERINGTON
20 Dean for Academic Affairs Ms. Kelly KINGRY
35 Dean of Students Ms. Jan MOORE

Oglethorpe University (F)

4484 Peachtree Road, NE, Atlanta GA 30319-2797
County: DeKalb FICE Identification: 001586
Unit ID: 140696
Telephone: (404) 261-1441 Carnegie Class: Bac/A&S
FAX Number: (404) 364-8500 Calendar System: Semester
URL: www.oglethorpe.edu
Established: 1835 Annual Undergrad Tuition & Fees: $33,800
Enrollment: 1,094 Coed
Affiliation or Control: Independent Non-Profit IRS Status: 501(c)3
Highest Offering: Master's
Program: Liberal Arts And General; Teacher Preparatory; Business Emphasis
Accreditation: SC

01 President Dr. Lawrence M. SCHALL
05 Provost Dr. Glenn SHARFMAN
10 Vice Pres for Business & Finance Mr. Norman MCKAY
30 Vice Pres Devel & Alumni Relations Ms. Robyn FURNESS-FALLIN
84 VP Enrollment Mgmt/FinancialAid Ms. Lucy LEUSCH
32 VP Campus Life/Dean of Students Ms. Michelle HALL
20 Assoc Provost Dr. Keith AUFDERHEIDE
04 Exec Assistant to the President Ms. Colleen D'ALESSANDRO
20 Asst Provost Mr. Eric TACK
08 Librarian Ms. Anne SALTER
06 Registrar Mr. Brian COLDREN
09 Director of Institutional Research Dr. Amy PALDER
26 Exec Dir University Communications Mr. Todd BENNETT
41 Athletic Director Ms. Becky HALL
37 Director of Financial Aid Mr. Chris SUMMERS
39 Director of Residence Life Mr. Danny GLASSMAN
21 Director of Finance/Controller Ms. Amy KING
91 Director Administrative Computing Vacant
27 Dir University Communications Ms. Renee VARY KEELE
29 Director of Alumni/Donor Relations Ms. Susie SHARFMAN
36 Director of Career Counseling Vacant
44 Director of Major Gifts Mr. John CARR
15 Director Human Resources Mr. Wayne PHIPPS
31 Dir Center for Civic Engagement Ms. Tamara NASH
18 Director Facilities/Physical Plant Mr. Walter HALL
07 Associate Director of Admissions Ms. Katie PADEN
40 Bookstore Manager Ms. Ashley GANDY

Pacific Institute of Technology (G)

1380 Southlake Plaza Dr, Morrow GA 30260
County: Clayton Identification: 667239
Telephone: (678) 610-5900 Carnegie Class: Not Classified
FAX Number: (678) 610-5008 Calendar System: Quarter
URL: www.pacifictech.edu
Established: 1999 Annual Undergrad Tuition & Fees: N/A
Enrollment: N/A Coed
Affiliation or Control: Proprietary IRS Status: Proprietary
Highest Offering: Associate Degree
Program: Occupational
Accreditation: ACICS

Paine College (H)

1235 Fifteenth Street, Augusta GA 30901-3182
County: Richmond FICE Identification: 001587
Unit ID: 140720
Telephone: (706) 821-8200 Carnegie Class: Bac/Diverse
FAX Number: (706) 821-8373 Calendar System: Semester
URL: www.paine.edu
Established: 1882 Annual Undergrad Tuition & Fees: $14,224
Enrollment: 844 Coed
Affiliation or Control: Multiple Protestant Denominations
IRS Status: 501(c)3
Highest Offering: Baccalaureate
Program: Liberal Arts And General; Teacher Preparatory; Professional
Accreditation: #SC, ACBSP, TED

01 Interim President Dr. Samuel SULLIVAN
04 Office Manager/President's Office Mrs. Juanita HARPS
05 Provost/VP Academic Affairs Dr. Cheryl EVANS JONES
32 VP Student Affairs Dr. Elias ETINGE
10 VP Administrative & Fiscal Affairs Ms. Debra LATIMORE

30 VP of Institutional Advancement ... Ms. Sunya YOUNG
45 Executive Asst to the President ... Vacant
42 Campus Pastor ... Dr. Luther FELDER
41 Athletics Director ... Mrs. Selina KOHN
20 Exec Asst Provost/VP Acad Affairs ... Ms. Frances WIMBERLY
50 Chair Business Dept ... Dr. Okoroafor NZEH
53 Chair Education Dept ... Dr. LaShawnda LINDSAY-DENNIS
79 Chair Humanities Dept ... Dr. Catherine ADAMS
81 Chair Math Sci Tech Dept ... Dr. Raul PETERS
60 Chair Media Studies Dept ... Ms. Teri BURNETTE
83 Chair Social Sciences Dept ... Dr. Lawanda CUMMINGS
88 Sp Asst Acad Ctr for Excel/Success ... Ms. Andrea ANDERSON
55 Coord Center Advanced Prof Studies ... Mrs. Symphoni WIGGINS
09 Director Inst Research/QEP ... Mrs. Alice M. SIMPKINS
08 Director Library/LRC ... Ms. Eugenia MCALLISTER
06 Registrar ... Mrs. Castine RHOADES WILLIAMS
36 Director Career Services ... Mrs. April EWING
38 Director Counseling & Wellness Ctr ... Ms. Brooke ROBERTSON
39 Dir Residence Life/Stdnt Activities ... Mr. Kelwin WILLIAMS
19 Interim Chief of Campus Safety ... Lt. Leroy MORGAN, JR.
21 Controller ... Ms. Sherrell FLOURNOY
18 Dir Facilities Mgmt/Environ Svcs ... Mr. Jason DENNIS
37 Interim Director Financial Aid ... Ms. Consuelo QUINN
15 Director Human Resources ... Vacant
13 Dir Information Technology Svcs ... Mr. Michael HICKS
40 Manager The Lion's Shop ... Mr. Julius GORDON
96 Purchasing Manager ... Mr. Marc THOMPSON
44 Asst VP of Inst Advancement ... Ms. Helene CARTER
44 Director Institutional Advancement ... Mr. Reginald POWELL
44 Director Institutional Development ... Ms. Leadra COLLINS
29 Director Alumni Relations ... Ms. Alatorya CRANFORD
26 Dir Communications & Marketing ... Ms. Tonya WILLIAMS
88 Dir Hlth Educ Ath Learning Complex ... Vacant
25 Director Sponsored Progms/Title III ... Mr. Geno CLARK
104 Interim Dir Academic Support ... Dr. Sezilee REID
108 Director Inst Assessment & Eval ... Vacant
24 LRC Manager ... Mrs. Rosa L. MARTIN
07 Asst Dir Admissions/Recruitment ... Mr. Charles SINGLEY, III
23 College Nurse ... Vacant
106 Blackboard Administrator ... Mr. Ignace HIHEGLO
88 Director Athletics Compliance ... Ms. Taura HATNEY
27 Asst Dir Communications & Marketing ... Ms. Vonetta FLOWERS-HINTON

Philadelphia College of Osteopathic Medicine Georgia Campus (A)

625 Old Peachtree Road NW, Suwanee GA 30024
Telephone: (678) 225-7500 Identification: 770165
Accreditation: &M, OSTEO, PHAR

† Branch campus of Philadelphia College of Osteopathic Medicine, Philadelphia, PA.

Piedmont College (B)

PO Box 10, Demorest GA 30535-0010
County: Habersham FICE Identification: 001588
Unit ID: 140818
Telephone: (706) 778-3000 Carnegie Class: Master's L
FAX Number: (706) 776-0701 Calendar System: Semester
URL: www.piedmont.edu
Established: 1897 Annual Undergrad Tuition & Fees: $21,990
Enrollment: 2,120 Coed
Affiliation or Control: United Church Of Christ IRS Status: 501(c)3
Highest Offering: Doctorate
Program: Liberal Arts And General; Teacher Preparatory
Accreditation: SC, ACBSP, NUR

01 President ... Dr. James F. MELLICHAMP
05 Vice Pres Academic Affairs ... Dr. Perry RETTIG
03 Exec VP for Institutional Resources ... Dr. John MISNER
11 Asst VP for Administrative Services ... Mr. Parks MILLER
10 Asst VP Finance/Human Resources ... Ms. Margie MEANS
12 Vice President Athens Campus ... Dr. Mel PALMER
30 Vice President for Advancement ... Ms. Amy AMASON
07 Dean of Admiss/Undergrad Enrol Mgmt ... Ms. Cynthia L. PETERSON
88 Special Assistant to the President ... Ms. Jane KIDD
44 Director of Development ... Mr. Justin SCALI
09 Director of Institutional Research ... Ms. Kim LOVELL
29 Dir Special Projects/Community Rels ... Mr. Bill LOYD
04 Assistant to the President ... Ms. Kristen GRAY
32 Dean of Student Engagement ... Ms. Emily PETTIT
42 Chaplain ... Rev Dr. Ashley CLEERE
84 Director Graduate Enrollment Mgmt ... Ms. Kathleen ANDERSON
06 Registrar ... Mr. Anthony COX
08 Dean of Libraries/College Librarian ... Mr. Robert GLASS, JR.
37 Director of Financial Aid ... Mr. David MCMILLION
07 Director Undergraduate Admissions ... Ms. Brenda BOONSTRA
13 Director Information Technology ... Dr. Shahryar HEYDARI
15 Human Resources Specialist ... Ms. Elaina COCHRAN
26 Director of Public Relations ... Mr. David E. PRICE
41 Dir of Intercollegiate Athletics ... Mr. John L. DZIK
21 Compliance & Treasurery Officer ... Ms. Leesa P. ANDERSON
19 Director Security/Campus Police ... Mr. Richard D. MARTIN
66 Dean School of Nursing/Health Sci ... Dr. Linda SCOTT
50 Dean School of Business Admin ... Dr. John MISNER
49 Dean School of Arts & Sciences ... Dr. Steven NIMMO
53 Dean School of Education ... Dr. Donald GNECCO

Point University (C)

507 West 10th St, West Point GA 31833
County: Troup FICE Identification: 001547
Unit ID: 138868
Telephone: (706) 385-1000 Carnegie Class: Bac/Diverse
FAX Number: (706) 645-9473 Calendar System: Semester
URL: www.point.edu
Established: 1937 Annual Undergrad Tuition & Fees: $25,100
Enrollment: 1,522 Coed
Affiliation or Control: Christian Churches And Churches of Christ
IRS Status: 501(c)3
Highest Offering: Baccalaureate
Program: 2-Year Principally Bachelor's Creditable; Liberal Arts And General; Teacher Preparatory; Religious Emphasis
Accreditation: SC, TED

01 President ... Mr. Dean C. COLLINS
05 Chief Academic Officer ... Dr. W. Darryl HARRISON
108 Vice Pres for Inst Effectiveness ... Dr. Dennis E. GLENN
10 Vice Pres of Finance ... Mr. Dan FRAZIER
08 Library Director ... Mr. Michael L. BAIN
84 Vice Pres for Enrollment Management ... Dr. Stacy BARTLETT
07 Asst Vice President of Enrollment ... Mrs. Tiffany WOOD
06 Registrar ... Ms. Suzanne SHAW
07 Director of Admission ... Mr. Rusty HASSELL
37 Director of Financial Aid ... Ms. Janifer MORGAN
88 Director of Student Accounts ... Ms. Yolanda STEELE
32 Director of Student Life ... Mr. Chris BEIRNE
11 Chief Operations Officer ... Mr. Lance FRANCIS
15 Director of Human Resources ... Ms. Margaret HODGE
21 Controller ... Ms. Merinda THROWER
42 Vice Pres for Spiritual Formation ... Mr. Wye HUXFORD
30 Director of Development ... Mr. Richard BUMPERS
29 Director of Alumni Relations ... Ms. Pam ROSS
26 Director of Communications ... Ms. Weslynn BIGGERS
13 Vice Pres for Info Technology ... Mr. Bill DORMINY
41 Interim Athletic Director ... Mr. Alan WILSON
18 Dir of Facilities and Maintenance ... Mr. Jim ALDRIDGE
19 Director of Security ... Mr. Fred BERKELEY
88 Director of Student Finance ... Mr. John LANIER
106 Director of Online & Continuing Ed ... Mr. Chris DAVIS
39 Residence Life Manager ... Ms. Kasey BODINE

† Formerly Atlanta Christian College

Reformed University (D)

1700 North Brown Rd., Ste 104, Lawrenceville GA 30043
County: Gwinnett Identification: 667247
Telephone: (770) 232-2717 Carnegie Class: Not Classified
FAX Number: N/A Calendar System: Semester
URL: www.trsusa.org
Established: 1992 Annual Undergrad Tuition & Fees: $4,560
Enrollment: 47 Coed
Affiliation or Control: Presbyterian Church In America IRS Status: Exempt
Highest Offering: Master's
Program: Professional; Religious Emphasis
Accreditation: @TRACS

01 President ... Dr. Joshua PARK

Reinhardt University (E)

7300 Reinhardt Circle, Waleska GA 30183-2981
County: Cherokee FICE Identification: 001589
Unit ID: 140872
Telephone: (770) 720-5600 Carnegie Class: Bac/Diverse
FAX Number: (770) 720-5602 Calendar System: Semester
URL: www.reinhardt.edu
Established: 1883 Annual Undergrad Tuition & Fees: $20,266
Enrollment: 1,341 Coed
Affiliation or Control: United Methodist IRS Status: 501(c)3
Highest Offering: Master's
Program: Liberal Arts And General
Accreditation: SC, MUS

01 President ... Dr. Kina S. MALLARD
04 Executive Assistant to President ... Mrs. Bonnie H. DEBORD
05 VP & Dean for Academic Affairs ... Dr. Mark A. ROBERTS
10 Vice Pres Finance & Administration ... Mr. David R. LEOPARD
30 VP for Advancement ... Mr. Timothy A. NORTON
32 VP Student Affairs/Dean of Students ... Dr. Roger R. LEE
84 VP for Enrollment Mgmt ... Mrs. Julie C. FLEMING
58 Assoc Vice Pres Graduate Studies ... Dr. Margaret M. MORLIER
101 Asst Secretary Board of Trustees ... Mrs. Bonnie H. DEBORD
18 Director of Physical Plant ... Mrs. Missy H. DAYOUB
26 Exec Dir Marketing/Communications ... Mrs. Marsha S. WHITE
13 Dir of Info Tech/Chief Tech Officer ... Mr. David G. DOSTER
88 Exec Director of Funk Heritage Ctr ... Dr. Joseph H. KITCHENS
07 Director of Admissions ... Ms. Lacey L. SATTERFIELD
06 Registrar ... Ms. Janet M. RODNING
09 Dir Instnl Research/Effectiveness ... Mr. Daniel TEODORESCU
08 Director of Library Services ... Mr. Joel C. LANGFORD
19 Director of Public Safety ... Ms. Sherry N. MADER-CORNETT
29 Dir Alumni Rel & Alumni Giving ... Mrs. Kathy A. BOUYETT
42 University Chaplain ... Rev. Jordan S. THRASHER
21 Controller ... Mr. Charles B. GRAVITT
37 Director Student Financial Aid ... Mrs. Angie D. HARLOW
41 Director of Athletics ... Mr. William C. POPP
15 Director Human Resources ... Mrs. Kelly M. MORRIS
39 Director Residence Life ... Mr. Eric W. BOOTH
23 University Nurse ... Mrs. Alicia C. MILES
35 Asst Dean of Students/Dir Stdnt Act ... Dr. Walter P. MAY
38 Director of Counseling Svcs ... Mr. Derek L. STRUCHTEMEYER
88 Dir Center for Student Success ... Dr. Catherine B. EMANUEL
36 Director of Career Services ... Mrs. Peggy C. FEEHERY
40 Bookstore Manager ... Mrs. Janet SWEENEY
105 Web Communication Manager ... Mr. John C. PETTIBONE
106 Coordinator Online Education ... Dr. Katherine E. HYATT
49 Dean School of Arts & Humanities ... Dr. Arthur W. GLOWKA
81 Dean School of Maths & Sciences ... Dr. Jake P. HARNEY
50 Int Dean McCamish School Business ... Dr. Donald D. WILSON, JR.
53 Dean Price School of Education ... Dr. Cindy M. KIERNAN
64 Dean School of Performing Arts ... Dr. Fredrick A. TARRANT
107 Int Dean Sch Professional Studies ... Mr. Lester W. DRAWDY

SAE Institute Atlanta (F)

215 Peachtree St NE #300, Atlanta GA 30303-1739
County: Fulton FICE Identification: 042066
Unit ID: 476948
Telephone: (404) 526-9366 Carnegie Class: Not Classified
FAX Number: (404) 526-9367 Calendar System: Semester
URL: atlanta.sae.edu
Established: 1976 Annual Undergrad Tuition & Fees: $18,040
Enrollment: 374 Coed
Affiliation or Control: Proprietary IRS Status: Proprietary
Highest Offering: Associate Degree
Program: Occupational
Accreditation: ACICS

01 Int Campus Director ... Mr. Jerry MYERS
05 Director of Education ... Mr. Scott KIEKLAK

Sanford-Brown College (G)

500 Embassy Row NE, Atlanta GA 30328
County: Fulton FICE Identification: 021160
Unit ID: 420495
Telephone: (770) 576-4498 Carnegie Class: Assoc/PrivFP
FAX Number: (773) 601-3881 Calendar System: Other
URL: www.sanfordbrown.edu/Atlanta
Established: Annual Undergrad Tuition & Fees: $15,050
Enrollment: 428 Coed
Affiliation or Control: Proprietary IRS Status: Proprietary
Highest Offering: Associate Degree
Program: Occupational; Technical Emphasis
Accreditation: ACICS, CVT, DMS

01 Campus President ... Mr. Carter SMITH

† School is in teach-out plan.

Savannah College of Art and Design (H)

342 Bull Street, PO Box 3146, Savannah GA 31402-6263
County: Chatham FICE Identification: 021415
Unit ID: 140951
Telephone: (912) 525-5000 Carnegie Class: Spec/Arts
FAX Number: (912) 525-6263 Calendar System: Quarter
URL: www.scad.edu
Established: 1978 Annual Undergrad Tuition & Fees: $34,470
Enrollment: 11,973 Coed
Affiliation or Control: Independent Non-Profit IRS Status: 501(c)3
Highest Offering: Master's
Program: Fine Arts Emphasis
Accreditation: SC, CIDA

01 President ... Mrs. Paula WALLACE
03 COO ... Vacant
10 VP for Business Operations ... Mr. Steve MINEO
88 VP for Financial Growth ... Mr. J.J WALLER
88 VP for Student Financial Services ... Mr. Scott LINZEY
46 Sr Vice Pres University Resources ... Mr. Glenn E. WALLACE, JR.
05 Chief Academic Officer ... Dr. Gokhan OZAYSIN
20 Assoc VP for Academic Support ... Ms. Hannah FLOWERS
12 Vice President for SCAD Atlanta ... Dr. Teresa GRIFFIS
12 Assoc VP for SCAD Hong Kong ... Mr. Michael SHREVE
88 Exec Dir of Strategic Content ... Ms. Cassandra HANDLEY
13 VP for Educational Technology ... Mr. Andrew FULP
32 Vice President for Student Success ... Dr. Philip ALLETTO
15 Vice President for Human Resources ... Ms. Lesley HANAK
13 VP for Information Technology ... Mr. Brad GRANT
106 VP for Strategy & Innovation ... Mr. John Paul ROWAN
07 Associate Vice President Admission ... Mr. David PUGH
109 VP for Auxiliary Operations ... Mr. Jeff HARRIS
09 Assoc VP of Inst Effectiveness ... Ms. Erin O'LEARY
88 Dean of Academic Svcs (Atlanta) ... Mr. Steve AISHMAN
27 Director of Univ Communications ... Ms. Ally HUGHES
18 Exec Dir of Physical Resources ... Ms. Helen MORGAN
08 Senior Director of Library Services ... Mr. Darrell NAYLOR-JOHNSON
37 Director of Financial Aid ... Ms. Kim BEVERIDGE
07 Exec Dir Adm Recruit/Events ... Ms. Jenny JAQUILLARD
19 Director of Security (Savannah) ... Mr. John BUCKOVICH
88 Director of Security (Atlanta) ... Mr. John CROWE
41 Athletics Director (Savannah) ... Mr. Doug WOLLENBURG
41 Athletics Director (Atlanta) ... Ms. Stephany RAINES
38 Dir Counseling/Student Support Svc ... Dr. Tamara KNAPP-GROSZ
58 Sr Dir of Grad Studies & Registrar ... Ms. Sarah MCCARN

88	Dean of School of Building Arts	Mr. Christian SOTTILE
88	Dean of School Communication Arts	Mr. Anthony FISHER
88	Dean of School of Design	Mr. Victor ERMOLI
88	Dean of School of Digital Media	Ms. Tina O'HAILEY
57	Dean of School of Fine Arts	Mr. Steve BLISS
49	Dean of School of Liberal Arts	Dr. Beth CONCEPCION
88	Dean School of Fashion	Mr. Michael FINK
88	Dean School of Foundation Studies	Ms. Maureen GARVIN
88	Dean of Entertainment Arts	Mr. Gregory BECK
36	Exec Dir of Career & Alumni Success	Ms. Kimberly LOPEZ
44	Director of Development	Vacant
20	Dean of Academic Services	Mr. Jesus ROJAS
108	Dean of Inst Effectiv & Assessment	Dr. Tara OVIEDO
35	Dean of Students Atlanta	Mr. Art MALLOY
100	Chief of Staff	Mr. Len CRIPE

Savannah State University (A)

3219 College Street, Savannah GA 31404-5308

County: Chatham — FICE Identification: 001590

Unit ID: 140960

Telephone: (912) 358-3004 — Carnegie Class: Bac/A&S

FAX Number: N/A — Calendar System: Semester

URL: www.savannahstate.edu

Established: 1890 — Annual Undergrad Tuition & Fees (In-State): $6,616

Enrollment: 4,915 — Coed

Affiliation or Control: State — IRS Status: 501(c)3

Highest Offering: Master's

Program: Liberal Arts And General; Teacher Preparatory; Professional

Accreditation: SC, BUS, ENGT, JOUR, SPAA, SW

01	University President	Dr. Cheryl DOZIER
05	Interim Provost/VP Academic Affairs	Dr. Kimberly HOLMES
10	Vice Pres Business & Finance	Mr. Edward B. JOLLEY, JR.
32	Vice President Student Affairs	Dr. Carl WALTON
30	VP Advancement/Exec Dir SSU Found	Mr. Phillip D. ADAMS
20	Associate Provost	Dr. Kimberly HOLMES
13	Chief Information Officer	Dr. Mable MOORE
50	Dean College Business Admin	Dr. Mostafa SARHAN
81	Dean Col Science & Technology	Dr. Jonathan LAMBRIGHT
49	Dean Col Lib Arts/Soc Sci	Dr. Robert SMITH
53	Dean School of Teacher Education	Vacant
84	Assistant VP for Enrollment	Mr. Descatur POTIER
26	Director Marketing/Communications	Ms. Loretta HEYWARD
15	Assistant VP Human Resources	Dr. Sandra M. BEST
08	Librarian	Mrs. MaryJo FAYOYIN
19	Chief of Police	Mr. Coaxum JULIAN
18	Director Facilities/Physical Plant	Mr. Ervin OGDEN
43	Dir Legal Services/General Counsel	Mr. Joseph STEFFEN
09	Dir Inst Research/Plng/Assessment	Dr. Michael G. CROW
29	Director Alumni Relations	Ms. Barbara S. MYERS
37	Director Financial Aid	Mr. Kenneth WILSON
41	Director Athletics	Mr. Sterling STEWARD, JR.
35	Director of Student Development	Ms. Jacqueline AWE
06	Coordinator for Student Records	Ms. Carolyn DREISSEN

† Part of the University System of Georgia.

Savannah Technical College (B)

5717 White Bluff Road, Savannah GA 31405-5521

County: Chatham — FICE Identification: 005618

Unit ID: 140942

Telephone: (912) 443-5700 — Carnegie Class: Assoc/Pub-R-M

FAX Number: (912) 443-5705 — Calendar System: Quarter

URL: www.savannahtech.edu

Established: 1967 — Annual Undergrad Tuition & Fees (In-State): $3,966

Enrollment: 4,644 — Coed

Affiliation or Control: State — IRS Status: 501(c)3

Highest Offering: Associate Degree

Program: Occupational; 2-Year Principally Bachelor's Creditable; Technical Emphasis

Accreditation: SC, ACFEI, DA, DH, ENGT, MAC, PNUR, SURGT

01	President	Dr. Kathy S. LOVE
05	Vice Pres Academic Affairs	Dr. Ken BOYD
11	Vice Pres Administrative Services	Ms. Sue Z. TURNER
32	Vice President Student Affairs	Ms. Terrie O. SELLERS
45	Vice Pres Economic Development	Mr. Kevin WERNTZ
84	Exec Director Enroll Mgmt/Marketing	Ms. Gail EUBANKS
13	Exec Director Information Tech	Mr. Jamie DAVIS
07	Director Admissions	Ms. Gwendolyn MOORE
37	Director Financial Aid	Ms. Faith ANDERSON
06	Registrar	Ms. Regina THOMAS-WILLIAMS
18	Director Facilities/Operations	Dr. Vic BURKE
37	Exec Dir Student Financial Services	Ms. Teresa POTTS
38	Director Student Support Services	Vacant
15	Director Human Resources	Ms. Melissa BANKS
88	Director Learning Enrichment Center	Dr. Ethel BERKSTEINER
08	Library Services Director	Mr. Jim BURCH
26	Director of Communications	Ms. Amy SHAFFER
12	Campus Dean Liberty Campus	Mr. Lonnie GRIFFIN
12	Campus Dean Effingham Campus	Mr. Robert SOLOMON
96	Purchasing Manager	Mr. Kevin CHIEVES
88	Dean Public Services	Dr. Gayle TREMBLE
76	Dean Health Science	Mr. Scott KROELL
50	Dean Business and Technology	Mr. Brendan FERRARA
97	Dean General Studies	Mr. Brent STUBBS
88	Dean Industrial Technology	Mr. Joseph POWELL
20	Dean Curriculum/Special Projects	Dr. Kathleen MERRIGAN
88	Dean Aviation	Mr. Tal LOOS
56	Adult Education Coordinator	Dr. Charlene FORD

Shorter University (C)

315 Shorter Avenue, Rome GA 30165-4298

County: Floyd — FICE Identification: 001591

Unit ID: 140988

Telephone: (706) 291-2121 — Carnegie Class: Bac/A&S

FAX Number: (706) 236-1515 — Calendar System: Semester

URL: www.shorter.edu

Established: 1873 — Annual Undergrad Tuition & Fees: $20,906

Enrollment: 2,413 — Coed

Affiliation or Control: Baptist — IRS Status: 501(c)3

Highest Offering: Master's

Program: Liberal Arts And General; Teacher Preparatory; Professional

Accreditation: SC, MUS, NURSE

01	President	Dr. Donald V. DOWLESS
05	Executive Vice President & Provost	Dr. Donald L. MARTIN
11	VP for Administrative Affairs	Vacant
10	VP for Finance & CFO	Ms. Susan ZEIRD
84	Vice Pres Enrollment Management	Ms. Emily MESSER
30	Vice President for Advancement	Vacant
32	VP Student Affairs/Dean of Students	Mr. Corey HUMPHRIES
26	Assoc VP University Communications	Dr. Dawn C. TOLBERT
104	Asst Vice Pres International Pgms	Mrs. Linda PALUMBO-OLSZANSKI
06	Registrar	Mr. Justin MITCHELL
29	Director of Alumni Relations	Mrs. Sheri RANSOME
35	Director of Student Life & Conduct	Mr. Anthony CHATMAN
08	Director of Libraries	Ms. Linda FLOYD
09	Director of Inst Planning/Research	Mr. Matthew LE HEW
37	Director of Financial Aid	Ms. Colleen LASSITER
15	Director Human Resources	Mr. Tommy CURTIS
90	Director of Academic Computing	Mr. Anthony J. NICHOLS
56	Director Special Programs	Vacant
13	Director of Information Technology	Mr. Jeff BRAMLETTE
18	Director of Facilities Management	Mr. Bob BAGLEY
38	Director of Student Support Svcs	Ms. Sara BAKER
23	Director of Health Services	Mrs. Mary SHOTWELL SMITH
41	Athletic Director	Mr. Donald Kim GRAHAM
44	Director of Annual Giving	Vacant
07	Director of Admissions	Mr. Patrick MCELHANEY
39	Director Residence Life	Ms. Melanie LAWRIMORE
40	Bookstore Manager	Ms. Cassie POTTS
57	Dean School of the Arts	Dr. Alan B. WINGARD
50	Dean College of Business	Dr. Melissa HICKMAN
49	Dean College of Arts & Sciences	Dr. Kathi VOSEVICH
53	Dean School of Education	Dr. Norma HARPER
56	Dean Coll Adult/Professional Pgms	Dr. Amy AUSTIN
66	Dean School of Nursing	Dr. Angela HAYNES
106	Director of Online Programs	Ms. Liz MAHAFFEY
81	Chair of Natural Sciences	Dr. Susan MONTELEONE
73	Chair Dept of Christian Studies	Dr. Earle KELLETT
77	Chair Dept of Mathematics	Dr. Diana SWANAGAN
60	Chair Dept of Communication Arts	Dr. Cassandra JOHNSON
83	Chair Dept of Social Sciences	Dr. Barsha PICKELL
42	Campus Minister	Rev. David E. ROLAND

South Georgia State College (D)

100 W College Park Drive, Douglas GA 31533-5098

County: Coffee — FICE Identification: 001592

Unit ID: 140997

Telephone: (912) 260-4394 — Carnegie Class: Assoc/Pub-R-S

FAX Number: (912) 260-4454 — Calendar System: Semester

URL: www.sgsc.edu

Established: 1906 — Annual Undergrad Tuition & Fees (In-State): $3,756

Enrollment: 2,611 — Coed

Affiliation or Control: State — IRS Status: 501(c)3

Highest Offering: Baccalaureate

Program: 2-Year Principally Bachelor's Creditable; Liberal Arts And General

Accreditation: SC, ADNUR, NUR

01	President	Dr. Virginia M. CARSON
05	Vice Pres Academic Affairs	Dr. Robert PAGE
32	Vice President for Student Success	Mr. Wes S. BROWN
10	Vice President for Fiscal Affairs	Mr. Mark LATHAM
30	Vice President for External Affairs	Ms. Walda KIGHT
18	Vice President for Operations	Mr. Keith NEWELL
20	Asst Vice Pres for Academic Affairs	Dr. Rick REIMAN
13	Chief Info Technology Officer	Mr. Jimmy HARPER
08	Director of Libraries	Ms. Jacqueline VICKERS
06	Registrar	Ms. Ame WILKERSON
37	Director of Financial Aid	Ms. Latoya CURTIS
15	Director of Human Resources	Mr. Jamie TANNER
07	Director of Admissions	Ms. Angela WASDIN
12	Dir of Entry Programs and Planning	Ms. Valerie WEBSTER
40	Director of Bookstore	Ms. Daphne FRENCH
41	Athletic Director	Mr. Bud DREW
09	Dir of Institutional Effectiveness	Ms. Danielle SUTLIFF
35	Director of Campus Life	Ms. Sharon KOMANECKY
19	Director of Security	Ms. Sonja MCCULLOCH
26	Coordinator for Marketing	Ms. Hailey ELLIS

† Part of the University System of Georgia.

South Georgia Technical College (E)

900 South Georgia Tech Parkway, Americus GA 31709-8167

County: Sumter — FICE Identification: 005617

Unit ID: 141006

Telephone: (229) 931-2394 — Carnegie Class: Assoc/Pub-R-M

FAX Number: (229) 931-2924 — Calendar System: Semester

URL: www.southgatech.edu

Established: 1948 — Annual Undergrad Tuition & Fees (In-State): $4,887

Enrollment: 1,658 — Coed

Affiliation or Control: State — IRS Status: 501(c)3

Highest Offering: Associate Degree

Program: Occupational; Technical Emphasis

Accreditation: SC

01	President	Sparky REEVES
11	Vice Pres Administrative Services	Janice DAVIS
10	Vice Pres Business & Industry Svcs	Wally SUMMERS
05	Vice President for Academic Affairs	John WATFORD
09	Vice Pres of Institutional Support	Karen J. WERLING
04	Special Assistant to the President	Don SMITH
20	Asst Vice Pres Academic Affairs	David KUIPERS
20	Dean of Academic Affairs	Raymond HOLT
26	Vice Pres Resource Dev & Marketing	Su Ann BIRD
13	Technology Director	Wray SKIPPER
37	Director of Financial Aid	Carrie WILDER
15	Director Personnel Services	Sandy LARSON
36	Director of Career Services	Cynthia CARTER
32	Director of Campus Life	Cynthia CARTER
21	Director of Accounting	Lea COE
88	Director of Administrative Services	Mark BROOKS
55	Evening Coordinator	John WILDER
06	Registrar	Julie PARTAIN
08	Librarian	Jerry STOVALL
07	Director of Admissions	Whitney CRISP
41	Acting Athletic Director	Janice DAVIS
29	Director Alumni Relations	SuAnn BIRD
38	Director Student Counseling	LaKenya JOHNSON
84	Director Enrollment Management	Whitney CRISP
18	Chief Facilities/Physical Plant	Don SMITH
96	Purchasing Agent	Gail CLARY

South University (F)

709 Mall Boulevard, Savannah GA 31406-4881

County: Chatham — FICE Identification: 013039

Unit ID: 139579

Telephone: (912) 201-8000 — Carnegie Class: Master's L

FAX Number: (912) 201-8070 — Calendar System: Quarter

URL: www.southuniversity.edu

Established: 1899 — Annual Undergrad Tuition & Fees: $16,665

Enrollment: 21,882 — Coed

Affiliation or Control: Proprietary — IRS Status: Proprietary

Highest Offering: Doctorate

Program: Occupational; Professional; Nursing Emphasis

Accreditation: SC, AA, ACBSP, ARCPA, MAC, NURSE, PHAR, PTAA

01	Chancellor	Mr. John T. SOUTH, III
12	President Ai Charlotte Campus	Mr. Asher HAINES
12	President Ai Raleigh-Durham Campus	Mr. Christopher MESECAR
12	President Ai Dallas Campus	Ms. Barbara JANOWSKI
12	President Ai Fort Worth Campus	Ms. Lourdes GIPSON
11	Interim Vice Chanc South Campuses	Mr. David MCGURE
12	President Montgomery Campus	Mr. Victor K. BIEBIGHAUSER
12	President West Palm Beach Campus	Mr. Thomas CREOLA
12	President Columbia Campus	Dr. David SHOOP
12	President Novi Campus	Vacant
12	President Richmond Campus	Mr. Troy RALSTON
12	President Tampa Campus	Dr. Bob BOHMAN
12	President Virginia Beach Campus	Mr. Richard KRIOFSKY
12	President Austin Campus	Ms. Shelby FRUTCHEY
12	President Cleveland Campus	Mr. Scott BEHMER
12	President High Point Campus	Mr. Michael TREMBLEY
12	President Savannah Campus	Dr. Todd CELLINI
13	Assoc Chanc Information Technology	Mr. James FREYBURGER
14	Regional Campus Technology Manager	Mr. Dustin BARRETT
106	Vice Chanc Online & Strat Operation	Mr. Steven READ
05	Vice Chancellor Academic Affairs	Dr. Joseph HARM
20	Assoc Vice Chanc Academic Operation	Dr. Destini COPP
20	Assoc Vice Chan Academic Affairs	Dr. Jay STUBBLEFIELD
20	Assoc Vice Chan Academic Affairs	Dr. Devin BYRD
08	Interim Asst Vice Chanc Univ Libr	Ms. Nancy SPEISSER
06	University Registrar	Ms. Anita MACIAS
20	Asst Vice Chanc Academic Services	Dr. Lucas B. KAVLIE
09	Sr Dir Inst Effectiveness	Dr. Frances W. OBLANDER
108	Director for Academic Assessment	Ms. Elizabeth DEVITA
20	Dir QEP & Academic Project Manager	Dr. Reinhold GERBSCH
49	Dean College of Arts and Sciences	Vacant
50	Dean College of Business	Dr. Cheryl NOLL
107	Dean College of Health Professions	Dr. Scott MCPHEE
66	Dean College of Nursing	Dr. Mable H. SMITH
67	Dean School of Pharmacy	Dr. Curtis JONES
57	Dean College Creative Art & Design	Dr. Leslie BAUGHMAN
73	Dean College of Theology	Dr. Robert R. REDMAN, JR.
07	Vice Chancellor for Admissions	Mr. Matthew MILLS
84	Regional Director of Admissions	Mr. Matt SWANSON
84	Regional Director of Admissions	Mr. Charlie PARKER
88	ADA Training Manager	Ms. Ashley JOHNSON
15	Assoc Chancellor of Human Resources	Ms. Lynne HAINES
88	Senior Human Resources Generalist	Ms. Christy SHAPARD
88	Human Resources Generalist	Ms. Jamie FRAZIER-HELD
32	Asst Chancellor for Student Affairs	Ms. Alisa KROUSE
36	University Director Career Services	Ms. Paula REISING
10	Vice Chancellor for Finance	Mr. John PAPP
37	Asst Chanc Student Financial Svcs	Ms. Kacey ATKINSON
26	Associate Chancellor for Marketing	Mr. Bruce CHONG
88	Senior Marketing Manager	Ms. Kalani ROBINSON
88	Senior Marketing Manager	Ms. Hope DAVID

Southeastern Technical College (A)

3001 E First Street, Vidalia GA 30474-8817
County: Toombs FICE Identification: 030665
Unit ID: 368911
Telephone: (912) 538-3100 Carnegie Class: Assoc/Pub-R-S
FAX Number: (912) 538-3156 Calendar System: Semester
URL: www.southeasterntech.edu
Established: 1989 Annual Undergrad Tuition & Fees (In-State): $4,161
Enrollment: 1,625 Coed
Affiliation or Control: State IRS Status: 501(c)3
Highest Offering: Associate Degree
Program: Occupational; Technical Emphasis
Accreditation: SC, DH, EMT, MAC, MLTAD, RAD

01 President .... Dr. Cathryn MITCHELL
03 Provost .... Mr. Larry CALHOUN
05 Vice Pres Academic Affairs .... Ms. Teresa COLEMAN
11 Vice Pres Administrative Services .... Ms. Denise POWELL
10 Vice President Fiscal Affairs .... Vacant
32 Vice President Student Affairs .... Dr. Barry DOTSON
84 Director Enrollment Services .... Mr. Brad HART
06 Registrar .... Ms. Karen VEREEN
37 Director Financial Aid .... Mr. Mitchell FAGLER
36 Director Job Placement .... Mr. Lance HELMS
103 Special Populations Coordinator .... Ms. Helen THOMAS
40 Bookstore Manager .... Ms. Ashley MCINTYRE
26 Dir Marketing & Public Relations .... Ms. Krysta RUSHING
08 Head Librarian .... Mrs. Leah DASHER
19 Director Security/Safety .... Mr. Travis AKRIDGE

Southern Crescent Technical College (B)

501 Varsity Road, Griffin GA 30223-2042
County: Spalding FICE Identification: 005621
Unit ID: 139986
Telephone: (770) 228-7348 Carnegie Class: Assoc/Pub-S-MC
FAX Number: (770) 229-3227 Calendar System: Semester
URL: www.sctech.edu
Established: 1963 Annual Undergrad Tuition & Fees (In-State): $3,855
Enrollment: 4,899 Coed
Affiliation or Control: State IRS Status: 501(c)3
Highest Offering: Associate Degree
Program: Occupational; 2-Year Principally Bachelor's Creditable; Technical Emphasis
Accreditation: SC, CAHIIM, COARC, COARCP, DA, EMT, MAC, SURGT

01 President .... Dr. Randall PETERS
03 Executive Vice President .... Mr. Mark ANDREWS
05 Vice Pres for Academic Affairs .... Dr. Dawn HODGES
32 Vice Pres for Student Affairs .... Ms. Xenia JOHNS
10 Vice Pres Administrative Services .... Ms. Miriam CASLIN
18 Vice Pres Facilities/Operations .... Mr. Jim BROWN
30 Vice President Advancement .... Ms. Barbara Jo COOK
46 Vice Pres for Tech/Inst Research .... Mr. Brent MAYES
88 Vice Pres for Adult Education .... Ms. Melissa GORDON
08 Director of Library Services .... Ms. Kate WILLIAMS
06 Registrar .... Ms. Kathlyn BURDEN
26 Dir Marketing & Public Relations .... Ms. Anna TAYLOR
37 Director of Financial Aid .... Ms. Kimberly MORRIS
49 Dean Business Tech Arts & Sciences/ ..... Ms. Rebecca JOHNSON
76 Dean Allied Health .... Mr. Michael MELVIN
75 Dean Personal Svcs/Public Safety .... Mr. Lemuel MERCADO
75 Dean Industrial Technical Studies .... Mr. Steve CROMER
106 Dean Computer Info Services .... Ms. Tempie KITCHENS
84 Director of Enrollment Management .... Dr. Jasper FOUST
15 Director of Human Resources .... Ms. Sharon IRBY
35 Director of Student Affairs .... Ms. Cherryl GILBERT
21 Director of Administrative Services .... Ms. Gina BYRD
36 Director of Career Services .... Ms. Susan MURRAY
88 Director of Satellite Operations .... Mr. Scott ROSS
19 Campus Police Chief .... Mr. Kenneth TROISI
13 Chief Information Officer .... Mr. Michael SHIVER

Southern Regional Technical College (C)

15689 US Highway 19 N, Thomasville GA 31792-2622
County: Thomas FICE Identification: 005615
Unit ID: 141158
Telephone: (229) 225-4096 Carnegie Class: Assoc/Pub-R-S
FAX Number: (229) 225-4330 Calendar System: Semester
URL: www.southernregional.edu
Established: 2015 Annual Undergrad Tuition & Fees (In-State): $4,722
Enrollment: 3,623 Coed
Affiliation or Control: State IRS Status: 501(c)3
Highest Offering: Associate Degree
Program: Occupational
Accreditation: SC, ADNUR, #COARC, EMT, MAC, MLTAD, SURGT

01 President .... Dr. Craig R. WENTWORTH
11 Vice Pres Administrative Services .... Mr. Paul ROBERTS
05 Vice Pres Academic Affairs .... Dr. Annie L. MCELROY
32 Vice President Student Affairs .... Ms. Leigh WALLACE
30 Vice President Economic Development .... Mr. Dennis LEE
09 VP Institutional Effectiveness .... Dr. Debbie GOODMAN
76 Dean School of Health Sciences .... Ms. Carla BARROW
50 Dean School of Bus/Industrial Tech .... Ms. Abby CARTER
107 Dean School of Professional Svcs .... Ms. Becky RICHARDSON

49 Dean School of Art and Sciences .... Ms. Kathryn KENT
37 Executive Director Financial Aid .... Ms. Judi LOVVORN
26 VP Marketing/Inst Devel/Pub Rels .... Ms. Amy MAISON
88 Executive Director Adult Education .... Mr. Dale ALDRIDGE
07 Director of Admissions .... Ms. Wanda HANCOCK
35 Director Student Affairs .... Ms. Lisa GRIFFIN
06 Registrar .... Ms. Wendi TOSTENSON
08 Executive Director Library Services .... Ms. Udella SPICER
36 Dir Career Services & Counseling .... Dr. Jeanine LONG
15 Director Human Resources .... Mr. Michael HEARD
18 VP Operations .... Mr. David EVANS

Spelman College (D)

350 Spelman Lane, SW, Atlanta GA 30314-4399
County: Fulton FICE Identification: 001594
Unit ID: 141060
Telephone: (404) 681-3643 Carnegie Class: Bac/A&S
FAX Number: N/A Calendar System: Semester
URL: www.spelman.edu
Established: 1881 Annual Undergrad Tuition & Fees: $26,388
Enrollment: 2,135 Female
Affiliation or Control: Independent Non-Profit IRS Status: 501(c)3
Highest Offering: Baccalaureate
Program: Liberal Arts And General; Teacher Preparatory
Accreditation: SC, MUS

01 President .... Dr. Mary SCHMIDT CAMPBELL
05 Interim Provost & VP Academic Affs .... Dr. Myra BURNETT
20 Interim Vice Provost .... Dr. Karen BRAKKE
10 VP Business/Financial Affairs/ Treas .... Mr. Robert D. FLANIGAN, JR.
32 Vice President for Student Affairs .... Dr. Darnita KILLIAN
30 Vice Pres for College Relations .... Ms. Eloise ALEXIS
84 Vice Pres Enrollment Management .... Ms. Ingrid HAYES
30 VP of Institutional Advancement .... Ms. Kassandra JOLLEY
88 Dir Investments & Financial Plng .... Ms. Rhonda HONEGAN
21 Controller .... Ms. April AUSTIN
101 Secretary of College .... Vacant
26 Exec Dir of Communications .... Ms. Renita MATHIS
04 Assistant to President .... Ms. Yvonne SKILLINGS
13 VP & CIO Media & Information Tech .... Ms. Delores BARTON
105 Dir Bonner Comm Svcs/Student Dev .... Ms. Jilo TISDALE
20 Dean of Undergraduate Studies .... Dr. Desiree PEDESCLEAUX
42 Director Sisters Center for WISDOM .... Rev. Lisa D. RHODES
06 Registrar .... Mr. John BROWN
07 Director of Admissions .... Vacant
27 Director Publications .... Ms. Jo Moore STEWART
29 Director of Alumnae Affairs .... Ms. Sharon OWENS
37 Assoc Dir of Student Financial Svcs .... Ms. Thresa GAY
36 Director Career Planning/Devel .... Mr. Harold BELL
78 Director of Cooperative Education .... Mr. Keith WEBB
15 Director Human Resources .... Ms. Bernadette COHEN
38 Director Counseling Services .... Dr. Ave MARSHALL
09 Dir Inst Rsrch/Assessment/Planning .... Ms. Jill TRIPLETT
88 Director Women's Resource Center ... Dr. Beverly GUY-SHEFTALL
18 Director Facilities/Mgmt & Svcs .... Mr. Arthur E. FRAZIER, III
19 Director of Public Safety .... Mr. Steve BOWSER
24 Dir Educational Technology Svcs .... Vacant
46 Associate Provost of Research .... Dr. Carmen SIDBURY
102 Dir of Corp & Foundation Relations .... Ms. Shelese LANE
88 Director of Special Events .... Ms. Heather HAWES
39 Director Housing & Residential Life .... Ms. Alison CUMMINGS
86 Director Title III/Government Rels .... Ms. Helga GREENFIELD
88 Coordinator Commuter Students .... Ms. Letitia DENARD
85 Coordinator International Students .... Vacant
08 Library Director/CEO .... Ms. Loretta PARHAM
23 Director Health Services .... Ms. Brenda DALTON
25 Director Sponsored Programs .... Dr. Claudia SCHOLZ
35 Dean Students .... Ms. Kimberly FERGUSON
40 Bookstore Manager .... Ms. Tiffani HODGE
41 Interim Dir Phys Ed & Athletics .... Ms. Joyce TERRELL
96 Dir Adminstrative Support Svcs .... Ms. Jacqueline JAMES
44 Director of Donor Relations .... Ms. Stacy LYONS
88 Director of Budgets & Contracts .... Ms. Dawn ALSTON
88 Special Asst to President .... Ms. Tomika DEPRIEST
88 Director of Wellness .... Ms. Chavonne SHORTER

Thomas University (E)

1501 Millpond Road, Thomasville GA 31792-7499
County: Thomas FICE Identification: 001555
Unit ID: 141167
Telephone: (229) 226-1621 Carnegie Class: Bac/Diverse
FAX Number: (229) 226-1653 Calendar System: Semester
URL: www.thomasu.edu
Established: 1950 Annual Undergrad Tuition & Fees: $16,400
Enrollment: 1,138 Coed
Affiliation or Control: Independent Non-Profit IRS Status: 501(c)3
Highest Offering: Master's
Program: Liberal Arts And General; Professional
Accreditation: SC, CORE, IACBE, MT, NUR, SW

01 President .... Dr. Gary BONVILLIAN
05 Provost & Exec Vice President .... Dr. Ann LANDIS
30 Vice Pres for Instnl Advancement .... Dr. Grady ENLOW
08 Univ Librarian/Dir Info Services .... Ms. Lynn KELLY
06 Registrar .... Mrs. Lacey HARRISON
09 Director of Institutional Research .... Danae JOHNSON
84 Assoc VP Enrollment Management .... Dr. Jill DENNIS
38 Director of Student Support Svcs .... Mrs. Faye R. JOHNSON
37 Director of Financial Aid .... Ms. Chrissy GAINOUS
41 Director of Athletics .... Mr. Michael D. LEE
10 Controller .... Ms. Sue STONE
32 Student Life/Athletics Coordinator .... Vacant
44 Director of Annual Fund .... Mrs. Melinda FUDGE
26 Director of Communications .... Mrs. Cindy MONTGOMERY
04 Assistant to the President .... Mrs. Linda M. HERNDON

Toccoa Falls College (F)

107 Kincaid Drive, Toccoa Falls GA 30598-0068
County: Stephens FICE Identification: 001596
Unit ID: 141185
Telephone: (706) 886-6831 Carnegie Class: Bac/Diverse
FAX Number: (706) 282-6005 Calendar System: Semester
URL: www.tfc.edu
Established: 1907 Annual Undergrad Tuition & Fees: $20,110
Enrollment: 909 Coed
Affiliation or Control: The Christian And Missionary Alliance
IRS Status: 501(c)3
Highest Offering: Baccalaureate
Program: 2-Year Principally Bachelor's Creditable; Liberal Arts And General; Teacher Preparatory; Professional
Accreditation: SC, MUS

01 President .... Dr. Robert M. MYERS
04 Sr Exec Administrative Assistant .... Mrs. Paula S. ELKINS
32 VP Student Affairs .... Dr. Ken W. GASSIOT
30 VP for Advancement .... Mr. Lee P. YOWELL
10 Vice President for Finance .... Mr. R. Gregg SCHULTE
05 VP for Academic Affairs .... Dr. W. Brian SHELTON
84 VP for Enrollment Services .... Mr. James ZUGELDER
42 Director Spiritual Formation .... Mr. Chris STRATTON
09 Director Institutional Research .... Dr. Kieran CLEMENTS
08 Dean of Info Svcs/IT Dept/Library .... Miss Heather SAMSA
106 Director of Distance Education .... Ms. Anna MCCLATCHY
39 Director Residence/Community Life .... Mrs. Emily SPROWLS
29 Director Alumni Assoc/Col Relations .... Mrs. Deborah WILKES
38 Dir Stdnt Health/Career Servs .... Mr. Johnathan C. KERR
37 Director Student Financial Aid .... Mr. Stuart SPIRES
07 Director of Admissions .... Vacant
06 Registrar .... Mr. Kelly G. VICKERS
41 Athletic Director .... Vacant
18 Chief Facilities/Physical Plant .... Mr. Merlin SCHENCK
19 Director of Security/Safety .... Mr. Stephen JOHANNES
15 Director Human Resources .... Ms. Mary K. RITCHEY
40 Director of Business Services .... Mrs. Helen GENTRY

Truett McConnell College (G)

100 Alumni Drive, Cleveland GA 30528-1264
County: White FICE Identification: 001597
Unit ID: 141237
Telephone: (706) 865-2134 Carnegie Class: Bac/Assoc
FAX Number: (706) 243-4968 Calendar System: Semester
URL: www.truett.edu
Established: 1946 Annual Undergrad Tuition & Fees: $18,000
Enrollment: 1,682 Coed
Affiliation or Control: Baptist IRS Status: 501(c)3
Highest Offering: Master's
Program: Liberal Arts And General; Religious Emphasis
Accreditation: SC, MUS

01 President .... Dr. Emir CANER
05 Vice Pres Academic Services .... Dr. Brad REYNOLDS
11 Vice Pres Administrative Svcs .... Dr. David ARMSTRONG
32 Vice President of Student Services .... Mr. Chris EPPLING
20 Associate VP Academic Services .... Dr. Joe WIEGAND
04 Executive Assistant to President .... Ms. Cindy ERBELE
41 Athletic Director .... Dr. Stacy HALL
06 Registrar/Dir Inst Research .... Mrs. Melissa FORTNER
37 Director of Financial Aid .... Mr. Truitt FRANKLIN
08 Director of Library Resources .... Mrs. Teresa HAYMORE
29 Director of Alumni Relations .... Dr. John YARBROUGH
07 Director of Admissions .... Mr. Andrew GAILEY
42 Director of Collegiate Ministries .... Mr. Keith WADE
40 Bookstore Manager .... Mr. Eddie O'BRIEN

University of Georgia (H)

Athens GA 30602-0001
County: Clarke FICE Identification: 001598
Unit ID: 139959
Telephone: (706) 542-3000 Carnegie Class: RU/VH
FAX Number: N/A Calendar System: Semester
URL: www.uga.edu
Established: 1785 Annual Undergrad Tuition & Fees (In-State): $11,622
Enrollment: 35,197 Coed
Affiliation or Control: State IRS Status: 501(c)3
Highest Offering: Doctorate
Program: Liberal Arts And General; Teacher Preparatory; Professional
Accreditation: SC, AAFCS, ART, BUS, BUSA, CAATE, CACREP, CIDA, CLPSY, COPSY, CS, DANCE, DIETD, DIETI, ENG, JOUR, LAW, LSAR, MFCD, MUS, PCSAS, PH, PHAR, SCPSY, SP, SPAA, SW, TED, THEA, VET

01 President .... Dr. Jere W. MOREHEAD
100 Chief of Staff .... Dr. Kathy R. PHARR
04 Assistant to the President .... Dr. Kyle TSCHEPIKOW
04 Assistant to the President .... Mr. Matthew M. WINSTON, JR.
05 Sr VP Acad Affs/Provost .... Dr. Pamela WHITTEN
20 Vice Provost Academic Affairs .... Dr. Russ MUMPER
10 Vice Pres for Finance & Admin .... Mr. Ryan A. NESBIT

26 Vice Pres for Develop & Alumni Rel .... Mr. Kelly K. KERNER
20 Vice President for Instruction ....Dr. Rahul SHRIVASTAV
46 Vice President for Research .... Dr. David C. LEE
88 Vice Pres Public Svc/Outreach ....Dr. Jennifer L. FRUM
32 Vice President Student Affairs ....Dr. Victor K. WILSON
86 Vice President for Govt Relations ....Mr. J. Griffin DOYLE
26 Vice President Public Affairs .... Dr. Thomas H. JACKSON, JR.
92 Assoc Prov/Dir of Honors Program ....Dr. David S. WILLIAMS
104 Assoc Prov for International Educ ....Dr. Kavita K. PANDIT
28 Assoc Prov/Chief Diversity Officer ....Dr. Michelle G. COOK
45 Assoc Provost Academic Planning .... Dr. Jerome S. LEGGE
20 Assoc Provost Academic Programs ....Dr. Margaret AMSTUTZ
13 VP for Information Technology ....Dr. Timothy M. CHESTER
08 Assoc Provost/University Librarian .... Dr. Toby GRAHAM
88 Assoc Provost Faculty Affairs .... Ms. Sarah COVERT
07 Assoc VP Admissions/Enroll Mgmt .... Mr. Patrick WINTER
21 Assoc VP Univ Business & Acct Svcs ....Ms. Holley W. SCHRAMSKI
18 Assoc VP Facilities Management .... Mr. Ralph F. JOHNSON
15 Associate VP Human Resources ....Mr. Juan JARRETT
43 Executive Director Legal Affairs .... Mr. Michael RAEBER
49 Dean of Arts & Sciences ....Dr. Alan T. DORSEY
47 Dean of Agricultural & Environ Sci ....Dr. J. Scott ANGLE
61 Dean of Law .... Mr. Peter RUTLEDGE
67 Dean of Pharmacy ....Dr. Svein OIE
65 Dean Forestry & Natural Resources ....Dr. Dale GREENE
53 Dean of Education ....Dr. Craig H. KENNEDY
58 Dean of the Graduate School ....Dr. Suzanne BARBOUR
50 Dean of Business ....Dr. Benjamin C. AYERS
60 Dean Journalism & Mass Comm .... Dr. Charles N. DAVIS
59 Dean of Family & Consumer Sci .... Dr. Linda K. FOX
74 Dean of Veterinary Medicine .... Dr. Sheila W. ALLEN
70 Dean of Social Work ....Dr. Maurice C. DANIELS
48 Dean of Environment & Design .... Mr. Daniel J. NADENICEK
80 Dean of Public/International Affs ....Dr. Stefanie A. LINDQUIST
69 Dean of Public Health ....Dr. Phillip L. WILLIAMS
88 Dean School of Ecology ....Dr. John L. GITTLEMAN
88 Interim Dean GHSU/UGA Medical ....Dr. Leslie LEE
54 Dean of Engineering .... Dr. Donald LEO
41 Athletic Director ....Mr. William G. MCGARITY
22 Director of Equal Opportunity ....Ms. E. Janyce DAWKINS
06 Registrar ....Dr. Jan M. HATHCOTE
19 Chief of Police ....Chief James E. WILLIAMSON
37 Director of Student Financial Aid .... Ms. Bonnie C. JOERSCHKE
36 Director of Career Services Center .... Mr. Scott T. WILLIAMS
39 Executive Director of Housing ....Dr. Gerard J. KOWALSKI
23 Exec Director of Health Services ....Dr. Jean E. CHIN
35 Dean of Students ....Dr. William M. MCDONALD
38 Dir Counseling/Psychological Svcs .... Dr. Gayle M. ROBBINS
51 Dir of Georgia Ctr Continuing Educ ....Dr. William R. CROWE
29 Exec Dir of Alumni Relations .... Ms. Meredith G. JOHNSON
30 Assoc VP Develop for the Campaign .... Mr. Mac CORRY
09 Director of Institutional Research .... Dr. Meihua ZHAI
88 Director of Academic Enhancement ....Dr. Earl GINTER
94 Director Inst of Women's Studies . Dr. Juanita JOHNSON-BAILEY
96 Director of Purchasing .... Ms. Annette EVANS
106 Dir Online Education/E-learning .... Dr. Keith BAILEY
108 Director Institutional Assessment ....Mr. Allan AYCOCK
44 Exec Dir Annual or Planned Giving ....Mr. David JONES
88 Director Office of Economic Dev ....Mr. Sean MCMILLAN

† Part of the University System of Georgia.

University of North Georgia (A)

82 College Circle, Dahlonega GA 30597-1001

County: Lumpkin FICE Identification: 001585
Unit ID: 482680
Telephone: (706) 864-1400 Carnegie Class: Master's L
FAX Number: (706) 864-1478 Calendar System: Semester
URL: www.ung.edu
Established: 1873 Annual Undergrad Tuition & Fees (In-State): $4,551
Enrollment: 16,064 Coed
Affiliation or Control: State IRS Status: 501(c)3
Highest Offering: Doctorate
Program: 2-Year Principally Bachelor's Creditable; Liberal Arts And General; Teacher Preparatory; Professional
Accreditation: SC, ADNUR, BUS, CAATE, CACREP, CSHSE, NUR, PTA, TED

01 President ....Dr. Bonita JACOBS
11 Vice Pres of Exec Affairs ....Mr. Billy WELLS
05 Interim Provost & Sr Vice President .... Dr. Richard OATES
10 Sr VP Business & Finance ....Mr. Frank J. MCCONNELL
03 Interim VP University Affairs .... Dr. Eric SKIPPER
30 Vice Pres of University Advancement .... Mr. Jeff TARNOWSKI
32 Vice Pres Student Affairs ....Dr. Janet MARLING
20 Assoc Provost Acad Administration .... Dr. Richard OATES
20 Interim Asst VP for Acad Affairs .... Dr. Kelly MANLEY
84 Assoc VP Enrollment Management .... Ms. Jennifer CHADWICK
88 Int Assoc VP & Dean Univ College ....Dr. Harriet ALLISON
29 Assoc VP Alumni Relations & Annual ....Mr. Phil COLLINS
21 Associate VP for Financial Services ....Dr. Brenda FINDLEY
18 Assoc VP Facilities & Auxiliary Ent ....Mr. Gerald SULLIVAN
88 Assoc VP Univ Affairs & Academic ....Dr. Chaudron GILLE
88 Assoc VP for Executive Affairs ....Ms. Mary TRANSUE
44 Asst VP Development ....Mr. Perry ROBERTS
88 Asst VP Advancement Svcs .... Ms. Amanda BRIDGES
35 Asst VP Stdnt Affs & Dean of Stdnts ....Dr. Michelle BROWN
35 Asst VP Stdnt Affs & Dean of Stdnts ....Ms. Alyson PAUL
88 Assoc Provost Inst Effectiveness .... Dr. Denise YOUNG
106 Dir Distance Ed & Tech Integration .... Dr. Irene KOKKALA
07 Exec Director Undergrad Admissions .... Mr. Keith ANTONIA
07 Director of Cadet Admissions ....Mr. Anthony FRITCHLE
92 Dean Honors Pgm/Grad Studies .... Dr. Eric SKIPPER

41 Director of Athletics ....Ms. Lindsay REEVES
13 Chief Information Officer .... Mr. Brandon HAAG
88 Director of Internal Audit .... Ms. Jill HOLMAN
06 Acting University Registrar .... Mr. Steve STUBBS
25 Director of Grants & Contracts .... Dr. Kelley ROBERTS
37 Director of Financial Aid ....Ms. Jill RAYNER
09 Director Institutional Research .... Ms. Linda ROWLAND
88 Assoc Dean Academic Administration .... Dr. Kelly MANLEY
35 Dean of Students - Gainesville ....Dr. Cara RAY
08 Dean of Libraries .... Dr. Deborah PROSSER
88 Dir of Public Services .... Ms. Jane O'GORMAN
49 Dean College of Arts & Letters .... Dr. Christopher JESPERSEN
50 Dean M C College of Business .... Dr. Donna MAYO
53 Acting Dean of College of Education .... Dr. Susan AYERS
81 Dean College of Sci & Mathematics .... Dr. Michael BODRI
76 Dean College of Health Sciences ....Dr. Teresa CONNER-KERR
104 Exec Director Global Engagement ....Dr. John WILSON
15 Director Human Resources .... Ms. Beth ARBUTHNOT
18 Director of Facilities - North ....Mr. Todd BERMANN
18 Director of Facilities - South ....Mr. Bill MOODY
19 Director of Public Safety ....Mr. Justin GAINES
14 Assoc CIO IT Services-Dah .... Mr. Steve MCLEOD
26 Director of University Relations ....Ms. Kate MAINE
20 Commandant Corp of Cadets ....Col. James PALMER
36 Director of Career Services ....Ms. Dora DITCHFIELD
38 Director Counseling Services .... Dr. Simon CORDERY
39 Director of Residence Life ....Ms. Treva SMITH
23 Director of Student Health Services ....Ms. Karen TOMLINSON
12 Exec Dir Cumming Campus .... Mr. Jason PRUITT
12 Actg CEO Oconee Campus .... Dr. Eric SKIPPER
108 Dir Accreditation & Assessment .... Ms. Betsy CANTRELL
102 Dir Corporate & Foundation Relation ....Mr. Jeff BOGGAN
51 Dir Continuing Education .... Ms. Wendy THELLMAN
31 Dir Civic Engagement .... Ms. Sloan JONES
96 Director Purchasing ....Ms. Beverly LONG
88 Dir Student Disability Services .... Dr. Nicole DOVEY
22 Dir Multicultural Student Affairs ....Mr. Robert ROBINSON
44 Director Planned Giving ....Mr. Bruce HOWERTON
88 Executive Director NISTS ....Dr. Janet MARLING
04 Admin Asst to the President ....Ms. Linda SMITH

† Part of the University System of Georgia.

University of Phoenix Atlanta Campus (B)

8200 Roberts Drive, Sandy Springs GA 30350-4147
Telephone: (678) 731-0555 Identification: 770200
Accreditation: &NH, ACBSP

† Branch campus of University of Phoenix, Tempe, AZ.

University of Phoenix Augusta Campus (C)

3150 Perimeter Parkway, Augusta GA 30909-4583
Telephone: (706) 868-2000 Identification: 770198
Accreditation: &NH, ACBSP

† Branch campus of University of Phoenix, Tempe, AZ.

University of Phoenix Columbus GA Campus (D)

7200 North Lake Drive, Columbus GA 31909
Telephone: (706) 320-1266 Identification: 770199
Accreditation: &NH, ACBSP

† Branch campus of University of Phoenix, Tempe, AZ.

University of Phoenix Savannah Campus (E)

8001 Chatham Center Drive, Savannah GA 31405-7400
Telephone: (912) 232-0531 Identification: 770201
Accreditation: &NH, ACBSP

† No longer accepting campus-based students.

University of West Georgia (F)

1601 Maple Street, Carrollton GA 30118-0001

County: Carroll FICE Identification: 001601
Unit ID: 141334
Telephone: (678) 839-5000 Carnegie Class: Master's L
FAX Number: N/A Calendar System: Semester
URL: www.westga.edu
Established: 1906 Annual Undergrad Tuition & Fees (In-State): $7,188
Enrollment: 12,206 Coed
Affiliation or Control: State IRS Status: 501(c)3
Highest Offering: Doctorate
Program: Liberal Arts And General; Teacher Preparatory; Professional
Accreditation: SC, ART, BUS, BUSA, CACREP, CS, MUS, NURSE, SP, SPAA, TED, THEA

01 President ....Dr. Kyle MARRERO
05 Provost & VP for Academic Affairs ....Dr. Michael CRAFTON
10 Exec VP for Business & Finance ....Mr. Jim SUTHERLAND
32 VP for Student Affairs & Enroll Mgt .... Dr. Scott LINGRELL
26 VP for University Advancement ....Mr. Dave FRABONI
30 Director of Development ....Ms. Diane HOMESLEY
84 AVP for Enrollment Management ....Dr. John HEAD
20 Associate VP for Academic Affairs ....Dr. Myrna GANTNER
21 University Controller .... Mr. Richard SEARS
83 Dean Social Sciences .... Dr. N. Jane MCCANDLESS
50 Dean Richards College of Business ....Dr. Faye S. MCINTYRE
53 Dean Education ....Dr. Dianne HOFF

79 Dean Arts & Humanities ....Dr. Randy HENDRICKS
81 Interim Dean Science & Mathematics .... Dr. Scott GORDON
92 Dean Honors College ....Dr. Janet DONOHOE
06 Registrar ....Ms. Donna HALEY
07 Director Admissions .... Mr. Justin BARLOW
08 Dean of Libraries ....Ms. Lorene FLANDERS
37 Director Financial Aid .... Dr. Philip HAWKINS
36 Director Career Services ....Ms. Keri BURNS
13 Chief Information Officer ....Mrs. Kathy KRAL
51 Director Continuing Education .... Mr. Marty DAVIS
15 Dir of Human Resources ....Ms. Juanita HICKS
18 Asst VP Campus Planning/Facilities ....Mr. Brendan BOWEN
19 Chief of University Police ....Mr. Thomas J. MACKEL
23 Director Health Services .... Dr. Leslie COTTRELL
39 Director Housing & Residence Life .... Mr. Stephen WHITLOCK
41 Director of Athletics .... Mr. Daryl DICKEY
38 Director Counseling Center .... Dr. Lisa ADAMS
109 Asst VP Auxiliary Services .... Mr. Mark REEVES
108 AVP Inst Effectiveness & Assessment ....Dr. Catherine JENKS
29 Director of Alumni Relations ....Mr. H. Franklin PRITCHETT
27 Asst Vice President of UA ....Ms. Jami BOWER
25 Int AVP Research & Sponsored Proj .... Dr. Denise OVERFIELD
106 Dean USG eCore ....Dr. Melanie N. CLAY
44 Assoc Director of Legacy Giving .... Mr. Baylor BASSETT
24 Asst Director for Classroom Support ....Mr. Brian MCCRARY
43 University General Counsel .... Ms. Jane SIMPSON
102 Assoc Exec Dir of WG Foundation .... Mr. Bart GILLESPIE
66 Dean Tanner School of Nursing .... Dr. Jennifer SCHUESSLER
14 Director of User Services ....Mr. Blake ADAMS
16 Asst Director of Human Resources ....Mr. Rodney BYRD
96 Director of Purchasing ....Mr. Paul WILLIAMS
22 Social Equity Officer ....Mr. Willie BLACK
86 Gov & External Relations Spec ....Ms. Ashley JONES
12 Chief Admin Officer Off Campus Pgm .... Dr. Robert HEABERLIN
105 Manager Web Innovations .... Mr. Denny CHASTEEN
16 Asst Director of Human Resources .... Ms. Laquana MARRABLE
40 Bookstore Manager ....Ms. Bettina A. ROBINSON

† Part of the University System of Georgia.

*University System of Georgia Office (G)

270 Washington Street, SW, Atlanta GA 30334-9007

County: Fulton FICE Identification: 008290
Telephone: (404) 962-3000 Carnegie Class: N/A
FAX Number: (404) 962-3013
URL: www.usg.edu

01 Chancellor ....Mr. Henry M. HUCKABY
04 Executive Assistant to Chancellor ....Ms. Sabrina THOMPSON
11 Exec Vice Chanc Administration .... Mr. Steve WRIGLEY
05 Exec Vice Chanc/Chief Academic Ofcr ....Dr. Houston DAVIS
45 Assoc VC Planning & Implementation ....Ms. Shelley C. NICKEL
10 Vice Chancellor Fiscal Affairs ....Mr. John BROWN
21 Chief Audit Officer ....Mr. John M. FUCHKO, III
18 Vice Chancellor Facilities ....Mr. Jim JAMES
43 Vice Chancellor Legal Affairs .... Mr. Nels PETERSON
26 Vice Chanc Comm & Govt Relations .... Mr. Charles SUTLIVE
13 Vice Chanc/Chief Information Ofcr .... Dr. Robert LAURINE

Valdosta State University (H)

1500 N Patterson Street, Valdosta GA 31698-0010

County: Lowndes FICE Identification: 001599
Unit ID: 141264
Telephone: (229) 333-5800 Carnegie Class: Master's L
FAX Number: (229) 333-7400 Calendar System: Semester
URL: www.valdosta.edu
Established: 1906 Annual Undergrad Tuition & Fees (In-State): $6,297
Enrollment: 11,563 Coed
Affiliation or Control: State IRS Status: 501(c)3
Highest Offering: Doctorate
Program: 2-Year Principally Bachelor's Creditable; Liberal Arts And General; Teacher Preparatory
Accreditation: SC, ART, BUS, CAATE, CACREP, EXSC, LIB, MFCD, MUS, NURSE, SP, SPAA, SW, TED, THEA

01 Interim President ....Dr. Cecil STATON
05 Provost & VPAA ....Dr. Brian L. GERBER
10 Vice President for Finance & Admin ....Ms. Traycee F. MARTIN
30 Vice President for Advancement ....Mr. John D. CRAWFORD
32 Interim VP for Student Affairs ....Dr. James G. ARCHIBALD
84 VP for Enroll/Marketing & Comm ....Mr. Andy T. CLARK
58 Interim Asst VP Rsrch & Grad Dean ....Dr. James T. LAPLANT
20 Assoc VP Academic Affairs ....Dr. Sharon L. GRAVETT
20 Asst VP Academic Affairs .... Dr. Lai K. ORENDUFF
88 Asst VP for Development ....Ms. Hilary H. GIBBS
86 Asst to Pres Gov & Corp Relations ....Mr. Philip D. ALLEN
49 Dean College of Arts & Sciences ....Dr. Connie L. RICHARDS
50 Dean College of Business Admin ....Dr. Wayne L. PLUMLY
57 Dean College of the Arts ....Mr. Arthur B. PEARCE
53 Interim Dean College of Education .... Dr. Brian GERBER
66 Interim Dean College of Nursing ....Dr. Sheri R. NOVIELLO
92 Interim Dean of Honors College ....Dr. Michael P. SAVOIE
08 University Librarian .... Dr. Alan BERNSTEIN
06 Registrar ....Mr. Stanley JONES
106 Dir of Online Education/E-learning ....Ms. Meg H. GIDDINGS
27 Chief Information Officer .... Mr. Brian A. HAUGABROOK
13 Dir Infrastructure Support Services ....Mr. Joseph A. NEWTON
07 Director of Admissions .... Mr. Tee MITCHELL
39 Director Housing & Residence Life .... Dr. Thomas W. HARDY
88 Director of Off-Campus Learning .... Dr. Joseph WEAVER

41 Director of Athletics .... Mr. Herb REINHARD
37 Director of Financial Aid .... Mr. Douglas R. TANNER
88 Dir of Creative Design Services .... Mr. Jeff GRANT
36 Director of Career Opportunities .... Dr. Gerald WILLIAMS
29 Director Alumni Relations .... Vacant
15 Director of Human Resources .... Dr. Denise BOGART
88 Director Division Aerospace Studies .... LtCol. Melvin GREEN, III
22 Director of Social Equity .... Dr. Maggie J. VIVERETTE
43 University Attorney .... Ms. Laverne L. GASKINS
18 Dir Phys Plant & Facilities Plng .... Mr. Ray SABLE
26 Dir Univ Marketing & Cmty Relations .... Ms. Mary B. GOODING
38 Director of Counseling Center .... Dr. Tricia A. HALE
88 Director of Centralized Advising .... Ms. Alicia ROBERSON
40 Director of Bookstore .... Vacant
23 Director of Student Health Services .... Dr. Edwin L. HIATT
19 Director Public Safety/Police Chief .... Mr. Ronald SEACRIST
108 Director of Inst Effectiveness .... Dr. Michael M. BLACK
44 Director Advncmnt Info Services .... Ms. Karen A. JOHNSON
04 Administrative Asst to President .... Ms. Melinda CUTCHENS
96 Asst Director of Procurement .... Mr. John DARITY
09 Interim Director Inst Research .... Mr. Barrie D. FITZGERALD

† Part of the University System of Georgia.

Virginia College (A)

2807 Wylds Road Extension, Suite B, Augusta GA 30909
Telephone: (706) 288-2500 Identification: 770833
Accreditation: **ACICS**, MAAB, SURGT

† Branch campus of Virginia College, Birmingham, AL.

Virginia College (B)

5601 Veterans Parkway, Columbus GA 31904
Telephone: (762) 207-1600 Identification: 770835
Accreditation: **ACICS**, MAAB, SURGT

† Branch campus of Virginia College, Birmingham, AL.

Virginia College (C)

1901 Paul Walsh Drive, Macon GA 31206
Telephone: (478) 803-4600 Identification: 770834
Accreditation: **ACICS**, MAAB

† Branch campus of Virginia College, Birmingham, AL.

Virginia College (D)

14045 Abercorn Street, Suite 1503, Savannah GA 31419
Telephone: (912) 721-5600 Identification: 770836
Accreditation: **ACICS**, ACFEI, MAAB, SURGT

† Branch campus of Virginia College, Birmingham, AL.

Wesleyan College (E)

4760 Forsyth Road, Macon GA 31210-4462
County: Bibb FICE Identification: 001600
Unit ID: 141325
Telephone: (478) 477-1110 Carnegie Class: Bac/A&S
FAX Number: (478) 757-4030 Calendar System: Semester
URL: www.wesleyancollege.edu
Established: 1836 Annual Undergrad Tuition & Fees: $20,140
Enrollment: 711 Female
Affiliation or Control: United Methodist IRS Status: 501(c)3
Highest Offering: Master's
Program: Liberal Arts And General
Accreditation: **SC**, MUS

01 President .... Ms. Ruth A. KNOX
05 Provost/VP for Academic Affairs .... Dr. Vivia L. FOWLER
30 VP Institutional Advancement .... Ms. Andrea G. WILLIFORD
10 Vice Pres Finance/Treasurer .... Mr. Richard P. MAIER
32 Vice Pres for Student Affairs .... Ms. Patricia M. GIBBS
84 Vice Pres for Enrollment Services .... Mr. C. Stephen FARR
06 Assistant Dean/Registrar .... Ms. Angie WRIGHT
04 Assistant to the President .... Mrs. Denise W. HOLLOWAY
04 Assistant to the President .... Mrs. Carol A. PAYTON
08 Library Director .... Ms. Kristi PEAVY
13 Director of Information Services .... Mr. Kevin L. ULSHAFER
29 Director of Alumnae Affairs .... Ms. Cathy C. SNOW
26 Director of Communications .... Ms. Mary Ann HOWARD
44 Director of Annual Fund .... Ms. Whitney DAVIS
37 Director of Financial Aid .... Ms. Danielle LODGE
39 Director of Residence Life .... Ms. Stefanie SWANGER
18 Director of Physical Plant .... Ms. Kelly BLEDSOE
41 Athletic Director .... Ms. Patty GIBBS
42 Director of Campus Ministry .... Rev. Debra C. WILLIAMS
19 Director Security/Safety .... Mr. Lionel DOSS
15 Director Human Resources .... Ms. Meagon DAVIS
07 Director of Admissions .... Ms. Leslie B. GOODMAN
09 Director of Institutional Research .... Ms. Thelma SEXTON
35 Chief Student Life Officer .... Ms. Stefanie SWANGER
36 Director Career Development .... Ms. Kathleen CROWNOVER
38 Director Student Counseling .... Ms. Jamie THAMES
96 Director of Purchasing .... Mr. Brandon GOULD
20 Associate Academic Officer .... Dr. Matthew R. MARTIN
21 Associate Business Officer .... Ms. Dawn P. NASH
40 Bookstore Manager .... Mr. Brandon GOULD

West Georgia Technical College (F)

176 Murphy Campus Boulevard, Waco GA 30182-2407
County: Haralson FICE Identification: 010487
Unit ID: 139278
Telephone: (770) 537-6000 Carnegie Class: Assoc/Pub-S-SC
FAX Number: (770) 537-7976 Calendar System: Semester
URL: www.westgatech.edu
Established: 1968 Annual Undergrad Tuition & Fees (In-State): $3,328
Enrollment: 6,536 Coed
Affiliation or Control: State IRS Status: 501(c)3
Highest Offering: Associate Degree
Program: Occupational; 2-Year Principally Bachelor's Creditable; Technical Emphasis
Accreditation: **SC**, ACBSP, ADNUR, CAHIIM, DH, MAC, MLTAD, RAD, SURGT

01 President .... Mr. Steve G. DANIEL
05 Provost/COO .... Dr. Perrin ALFORD
11 Vice President Administrative Svcs .... Mr. Rick LEVEILLE
20 Vice President Academic Affairs .... Mr. Patrick K. HANNON
32 Vice President Student Affairs .... Dr. Tonya F. WHITLOCK
30 Exec Dir Institutional Advancement .... Ms. Kim LEARNARD
09 VP Institutional Effectiveness .... Dr. Kristen DOUGLAS
20 Asst Vice Pres For Curriculum .... Dr. Sindi MCGOWAN
08 Exec Director Library Services .... Mr. Emanuel MITCHELL
06 Registrar .... Mrs. Laura THORNTON
13 Exec Dir Information Technology .... Mr. Sam JENKINS
07 Director of Admissions .... Mrs. Mary ADERHOLD
18 Director Facilities .... Mr. Michael JILES
04 Administrative Asst to President .... Mrs. Julia WATSON
36 Manager Career Services .... Ms. Dawne WHITE
37 Director Student Financial Aid .... Mrs. Anna ENGLISH
41 Interim Athletic Director .... Mr. Todd PRATT

Westwood College-Atlanta Midtown (G)

1100 Spring Street, Suite 102, Atlanta GA 30309-2824
Telephone: (404) 745-9862 Identification: 666421
Accreditation: **ACICS**, CAHIIM

† Branch campus of Westwood College-DuPage, Woodbridge, IL.

Westwood College-Atlanta Northlake (H)

2309 Parklake Drive NE, Atlanta GA 30345-2906
Telephone: (866) 821-6145 Identification: 666597
Accreditation: **ACICS**

† Branch campus of Westwood College-O'Hare Airport, Chicago, IL.

Wiregrass Georgia Technical College (I)

4089 Val Tech Road, Valdosta GA 31602
County: Lowndes FICE Identification: 005256
Unit ID: 141255
Telephone: (229) 333-2100 Carnegie Class: Assoc/Pub-R-M
FAX Number: (229) 333-2129 Calendar System: Semester
URL: www.wiregrass.edu
Established: 1963 Annual Undergrad Tuition & Fees (In-State): $3,268
Enrollment: 3,629 Coed
Affiliation or Control: State IRS Status: 501(c)3
Highest Offering: Associate Degree
Program: Occupational; 2-Year Principally Bachelor's Creditable; Technical Emphasis
Accreditation: **SC**, CAHIIM, DA, DH, MLTAD, SURGT

01 President .... Dr. Tina K. ANDERSON
05 Exec Vice Pres Academic Affairs .... Dr. Shawn UTLEY
10 Vice President Operations .... Ms. Lisa TOMBERLIN
46 VP Research/Strategic Initiatives .... Dr. Ron O'MEARA
11 VP for Administrative Services .... Ms. Keren WYNN
84 VP for Enrollment Management .... Ms. Angela HOBBY
09 Exec Dir for Inst Effectiveness .... Dr. Bonnie KELLY
51 VP for Adult Education Services .... Mr. Alvin PAYTON
46 VP for Economic Development .... Ms. Lidell GREENWAY
13 Chief Info Technology Officer (CIO) .... Mr. Jarrod BROGDON
18 Chief of Facilities .... Mr. Michael FLETCHER
30 Exec Dir Advancement/Res Devel .... Dr. Penelope SCHMIDT
32 Dean of Student Affairs .... Ms. Shannon POLLOCK
26 Dir for Cmty/College Relations .... Ms. Lydia HUBERT
07 Director Recruitment .... Ms. Brooke JARAMILLO
04 Administrative Asst to President .... Ms. Cheryl ACREE
06 Assistant Registrar .... Ms. Julie SCOTT
08 Head Librarian .... Vacant
105 Director Web Services .... Vacant
106 Exec Director Online Education .... Ms. Sally DORMINY
15 Exec Dir of Human Resources .... Ms. Shalonda SANDERS
19 Chief of Police .... Mr. Mike KELLY
36 Director Student Placement .... Ms. Kay MORRIS
37 Financial Aid Coordinator .... Ms. Paula HERRING
96 Director of Purchasing .... Mr. Jim RAGO
50 Dean of Business/Education .... Ms. Lynn BOWEN
54 Dean of Engineering .... Vacant

Young Harris College (J)

1 College Street, Young Harris GA 30582-0098
County: Towns FICE Identification: 001604
Unit ID: 141361
Telephone: (706) 379-3111 Carnegie Class: Assoc/PrivNFP
FAX Number: (706) 379-4319 Calendar System: Semester
URL: www.yhc.edu
Established: 1886 Annual Undergrad Tuition & Fees: $27,012
Enrollment: 1,218 Coed
Affiliation or Control: United Methodist IRS Status: 501(c)3
Highest Offering: Baccalaureate
Program: Liberal Arts And General
Accreditation: **SC**, MUS

01 President .... Ms. Cathy COX
05 Vice Pres for Academic Affairs .... Dr. Gary MYERS
11 Senior VP for Finance & Admin .... Dr. Brooks SEAY
10 Vice Pres for Business/Controller .... Mr. Wade M. BENSON
32 Vice President for Student Affairs .... Ms. Angi SMITH
84 Vice Pres for Enrollment Management .... Mr. Clinton G. HOBBS
30 Vice President of Advancement .... Vacant
45 VP for Planning and Assessment .... Ms. Rosemary R. ROYSTON
13 Vice President of Campus Technology .... Mr. Ken FANEUFF
29 Director of Alumni Relations .... Ms. Dana ENSLEY
20 Associate Academic Officer .... Dr. Keith DEFOOR
08 Librarian .... Ms. Debra MARCH
38 Counselor .... Ms. Lynne GRADY
06 Registrar .... Ms. Tammy GIBSON
37 Director Student Financial Aid .... Ms. Linda ADAMS
15 Director Personnel Services .... Mr. Vince ROBELOTTO
26 Chief Public Relations Officer .... Ms. LeAnn WALDROUP
18 Chief Facilities/Physical Plant .... Mr. Jim RAWSKI
19 Director of Safety & Compliance .... Vacant
41 Athletic Director .... Mr. Randy DUNN
42 Campus Minister .... Rev. Tim MOORE
04 Administrative Asst to President .... Ms. Teresa HOBBS
39 Director Student Housing .... Mr. Stuart MILLER

HAWAII

Argosy University, Hawaii (K)

400 ABS Tower, 1001 Bishop Street, Honolulu HI 96813
Telephone: (808) 536-5555 Identification: 666787
Accreditation: **&WC**, ACBSP, CLPSY

† Regional accreditation is carried under the parent institution in Orange, CA.

Babel University Professional School of Translation (L)

1833 Kalakaua Avenue, #208, Honolulu HI 96815
County: Honolulu Identification: 666350
Telephone: (808) 946-3773 Carnegie Class: Not Classified
FAX Number: (808) 946-3993 Calendar System: Other
URL: www.babel.edu
Established: 2000 Annual Graduate Tuition & Fees: $12,000
Enrollment: N/A Coed
Affiliation or Control: Proprietary IRS Status: Proprietary
Highest Offering: Master's; No Undergraduates
Program: Professional
Accreditation: **DEAC**

01 Chancellor .... Dr. Miyoko YUASA
03 Vice Chancellor .... Mr. Tomoki HOTTA
05 Head of Deans .... Mr. Yoshiharu ISHIDA

Brigham Young University Hawaii (M)

55-220 Kulanui Street, Laie Oahu HI 96762-1294
County: Honolulu FICE Identification: 001606
Unit ID: 230047
Telephone: (808) 675-3211 Carnegie Class: Bac/Diverse
FAX Number: (808) 675-3329 Calendar System: Semester
URL: www.byuh.edu
Established: 1955 Annual Undergrad Tuition & Fees: $5,100
Enrollment: 2,787 Coed
Affiliation or Control: Latter-day Saints IRS Status: 501(c)3
Highest Offering: Baccalaureate
Program: Liberal Arts And General; Teacher Preparatory; Professional
Accreditation: **WC**, SW

01 President .... Dr. John S. TANNER
05 Vice President for Academics .... Dr. John D. BELL
11 VP Administrative Services .... Mr. Norman S. BLACK
32 VP for Student Development & Svcs .... Dr. Debbie HIPPOLITE WRIGHT
04 Administrative Asst to the Pres .... Mrs. Lisa FAONELUA
108 Assoc Academic VP for Assessment .... Dr. Rosalind RAM
20 Assoc Academic VP for Instruction .... Dr. David BYBEE
20 Assoc Academic VP for Curriculum .... Dr. Jennifer LANE
81 Dean College of Math and Sciences .... Dr. Mark B. CANNON
88 Dean College of Bus/Computing/Govt .... Dr. James D. LEE
88 Dean College of Human Development .... Dr. Mark WOLFERSBERGER
88 Dean College of Lang/Culture & Arts .... Dr. Phillip MCARTHUR
13 University Technology Officer .... Mr. Kevin SCHLAG
07 Director Enrollment Services .... Mr. Arapata MEHA
41 Director of Athletics .... Mr. Ken WAGNER
08 University Librarian .... Mr. Michael ALDRICH
88 Director Budget Services .... Mr. Steven TUELLER
96 Director of Purchasing & Travel .... Mr. Robert OWAN
19 Director Safety/Security & Risk Mgt .... Mr. Earl MORRIS
15 Director of Human Resources .... Mrs. Tessie FAUSTINO
18 Director Facilities Management .... Mr. Randy SHARP
10 Director Financial Services .... Mr. Eric MARLER
23 Director Health Center .... Dr. P. Douglas NIELSON

88 Dir Compliance & Internal Audit .... Mr. Christopher BEARD
36 Director Career Services .... Mr. Mark MACDONALD
38 Director of Counseling Services .... Mrs. Leilani AUNA
35 Director Student Leadership & Honor .... Ms. Alison WHITING
88 Director Food Services .... Mr. David KEALA
26 Director Communications .... Mr. Michael JOHANSON
88 Director Testing and Assessment .... Mr. Christopher WRIGHT
06 Registrar .... Mr. Daryl WHITFORD
39 Director Housing & Residential Life .... Mr. Edwin ROGERS
51 Manager of Educational Outreach .... Mrs. Edna OWAN
40 Manager Bookstore .... Mr. David FONOIMOANA

† Affiliated with Brigham Young University, Provo, UT.

Chaminade University of Honolulu (A)

3140 Waialae Avenue, Honolulu HI 96816-1578
County: Honolulu　FICE Identification: 001605
Unit ID: 141486
Telephone: (808) 735-4711　Carnegie Class: Master's L
FAX Number: (808) 735-4870　Calendar System: Semester
URL: www.chaminade.edu
Established: 1955　Annual Undergrad Tuition & Fees: $21,740
Enrollment: 2,466　Coed
Affiliation or Control: Independent Non-Profit　IRS Status: 501(c)3
Highest Offering: Master's
Program: Liberal Arts And General; Teacher Preparatory; Professional
Accreditation: WC, CIDA, IACBE, MACTE, NURSE

01 President .... Bro. Bernard PLOEGER, SM
88 Exec Director of Compliance & Pers .... Ms. Christine DENTON
05 Provost .... Dr. Helen WHIPPY
30 VP for Institutional Advancement ..... Ms. Diane PETERS-NGUYEN
10 Vice President Finance/Facilities .... Ms. Aulani KAANOI
13 Dean of Info Technologies & Support .... Mr. Kyle JOHNSON
84 Dean of Enrollment Management .... Ms. Joy BOUEY
32 Dean of Students .... Ms. Grissel BENITZ-HODGE
35 Associate Dean of Students .... Ms. Allison JEROME
90 Director Network/Desktop Services .... Mr. Eddie PANG
51 Dir Professional & Continuing Educ .... Ms. Cindy JANUS
91 Director of Management Info Svcs .... Mr. Jorge HERNANDEZ
29 Director of Alumni Relations .... Ms. Be-Jay KODAMA
41 Director of Athletics .... Mr. William VILLA
42 Director of Campus Ministry .... Mr. Danny O'REGAN
36 Dir Career Develop/Job Placement .... Ms. Angela COLORETTI
18 Director of Facilities Operations .... Mr. Michael HAISEN
11 Director of Administrative Services .... Ms. Elaine OISHI
21 Director of Finance .... Mr. Choong LIM
07 Director of Admissions .... Ms. Joy BOUEY
08 Director of Library .... Ms. Sharon LEPAGE
19 Director of Security .... Mr. Melvin DECOSTA
38 Director of Student Counseling .... Dr. June YASUHARA
06 Registrar .... Mr. John MORRIS
37 Director of Financial Aid .... Ms. Amy TAKIGUCHI
09 Dir of Institutional Research .... Mr. Hieu NGUYEN
26 Director of Communications .... Ms. Kapono RYAN

Hawaii Medical College (B)

1221 Kapiolani Blvd PH 35, Honolulu HI 96814
County: Honolulu　FICE Identification: 041822
Unit ID: 460756
Telephone: (808) 237-5140　Carnegie Class: Not Classified
FAX Number: N/A　Calendar System: Other
URL: www.hmi.edu
Established: 2007　Annual Undergrad Tuition & Fees: $14,425
Enrollment: 503　Coed
Affiliation or Control: Proprietary　IRS Status: Proprietary
Highest Offering: Associate Degree
Program: Occupational
Accreditation: CNCE

01 Executive Director .... Guy BENJAMIN

Hawaii Pacific University (C)

1164 Bishop Street, Suite 800, Honolulu HI 96813-2882
County: Honolulu　FICE Identification: 007279
Unit ID: 141644
Telephone: (808) 544-0200　Carnegie Class: Master's L
FAX Number: (808) 544-1136　Calendar System: Semester
URL: www.hpu.edu
Established: 1965　Annual Undergrad Tuition & Fees: $22,440
Enrollment: 5,827　Coed
Affiliation or Control: Independent Non-Profit　IRS Status: 501(c)3
Highest Offering: Master's
Program: Liberal Arts And General; Teacher Preparatory; Professional
Accreditation: WC, NURSE, SW, TEAC

01 President .... Dr. Geoffrey BANNISTER
00 President Emeritus .... Mr. Chatt G. WRIGHT
11 Exece Vice Pres Admin/Gen Counsel .... Ms. Janet S. KLOENHAMER
05 Provost & VP Academic Affairs .... Ms. Carolyn WEEKS-LEVY
10 VP/Chief Financial Officer .... Mr. Bruce EDWARDS
84 Vice Pres Enrollment Management .... Vacant
30 Vice Pres University Relations .... Mr. Samuel MOKU
20 Assoc VP Academic Affairs .... Mr. Joe SCHMIEDL
15 Int AVP of Human Resources .... Ms. Diana NILES-HANSEN
21 Associate VP/Controller .... Mr. James BRESE
50 Dean Business Administration .... Dr. Deborah CROWNE
66 Dean Nursing/Health Sciences .... Dr. Lynette LANDRY
81 Dean Natural/Computational Sciences .... Dr. David HORGEN
60 Dean Humanities & Social Sciences .... Dr. David LANOUE
89 Dean of Students .... Ms. Marites MCKEE
106 Assistant Dean Distance Ed Policy .... Dr. Asoke DATTA
07 Assoc Dir International Admissions ..... Mr. Jimmi HEMMENBACH
97 Assistant Dean General Education ... Dr. Valentina ABORDONADO
07 Director of Admissions .... Ms. Marissa BRATTON
104 Director Intl Exchange/Study Abroad ... Ms. Melissa MATSUBARA
36 Director Career Svcs Ctr/Co-op Educ .... Vacant
06 University Registrar .... Ms. Jean LANG
37 Assoc Director Financial Aid .... Ms. Alyson MACHADO
41 Executive Athletic Director .... Mr. Vince BALDEMOR
51 Assoc Dir Adult Learning Program .... Ms. Jill MERL
105 Director Web Services .... Vacant
08 Director of Libraries .... Ms. Nori LEONG
42 University Chaplain .... Rev. Dale BURKE
13 Director Computing Services .... Ms. Lisa CARPENTER
19 Assoc Director Security and Safety .... Mr. Wayne FERNANDEZ
18 Director Facilities Management .... Mr. John RUSSELL
29 Alumni/Parent Relations Coordinator .... Vacant
38 Director Counseling/Behavioral Hlth .... Dr. Kevin BOWMAN
96 Procurement Director .... Mr. Kevin WETTER
26 Chief Information Ofcr/Vice Pres .... Dr. Sharon BLANTON
100 Chief of Staff .... Mr. Mark E. DELOS REYES DAVIS

Hawaii Tokai International College (D)

2241 Kapiolani Boulevard, Honolulu HI 96826-4310
County: Honolulu　FICE Identification: 037603
Telephone: (808) 983-4100　Carnegie Class: Not Classified
FAX Number: (808) 983-4107　Calendar System: Quarter
URL: www.hawaiitokai.edu
Established: 1992　Annual Undergrad Tuition & Fees: $7,700
Enrollment: 183　Coed
Affiliation or Control: Independent Non-Profit　IRS Status: 501(c)3
Highest Offering: Associate Degree
Program: 2-Year Principally Bachelor's Creditable; Liberal Arts And General
Accreditation: WJ

01 Chancellor .... Dr. Takuya YOSHIMURA
05 Vice Chancellor .... Dr. Douglas FUQUA
10 Exec Director of Administration .... Mr. Yuzo OIDA
20 Dean of Instruction .... Dr. Deanna MADDEN
08 Librarian .... Ms. Heather KAUFMAN
32 Director of Student Services .... Dr. Yukari KUNISUE
15 Human Resources Specialist .... Mr. Jerome BURCH
21 Finance Department .... Ms. Miho BRADLEY
88 Academic Liaison Officer .... Ms. Erin SUKUMOTO

Institute of Clinical Acupuncture and Oriental Medicine (E)

100 N Beretania Street, Suite 203 B,
Honolulu HI 96817-4709
County: Honolulu　FICE Identification: 037353
Unit ID: 444699
Telephone: (808) 521-2288　Carnegie Class: Spec/Health
FAX Number: (808) 521-2271　Calendar System: Semester
URL: www.orientalmedicine.edu
Established: 1996　Annual Graduate Tuition & Fees: $12,810
Enrollment: 54　Coed
Affiliation or Control: Proprietary　IRS Status: Proprietary
Highest Offering: Master's; No Undergraduates
Program: Professional; Business Emphasis
Accreditation: ACUP

01 President .... Dr. Wai Hoa LOW
05 Chancellor Academic Affairs .... Dr. Edmund BERNAUER
63 Clinic Director .... Dr. Catherine Yu-Ling LOW

Pacific Rim Christian University (F)

290 Sand Island Access Road, Honolulu HI 96819
County: Honolulu　Identification: 667010
Unit ID: 457484
Telephone: (808) 853-1040　Carnegie Class: Not Classified
FAX Number: (808) 853-1042　Calendar System: Semester
URL: hawaii.newhope.edu/
Established: 1998　Annual Undergrad Tuition & Fees: $9,700
Enrollment: 108　Coed
Affiliation or Control: Independent Non-Profit　IRS Status: 501(c)3
Highest Offering: Master's
Program: Religious Emphasis
Accreditation: BI

00 Founder .... Dr. Wayne CORDEIRO
01 President .... Dr. Kent KEITH
58 Dean Grad Sch/Pres Emeritus .... Dr. Randall FURUSHIMA
05 Vice Pres Academic Affairs .... Martha STINTON
32 Vice Pres Student Services .... Mia BURKE
09 Vice Pres Institutional Support .... Danny CASEY
84 Director of Enrollment Management .... Vacant
06 Dir Admissions/Registrar .... Joshua MOORE

Remington College-Honolulu Campus (G)

1111 Bishop Street, Suite 400, Honolulu HI 96813-2811
Telephone: (808) 942-1000　Identification: 666028
Accreditation: ACCSC

† Branch campus of Remington College, Mobile, AL.

*University of Hawaii System Office (H)

2444 Dole Street, Honolulu HI 96822
County: Honolulu　FICE Identification: 007885
Unit ID: 141963
Telephone: (808) 956-8207　Carnegie Class: N/A
FAX Number: (808) 956-5286
URL: www.hawaii.edu

01 President .... Dr. David K. LASSNER
05 VP for Academic Affairs .... Dr. Risa E. DICKSON
46 VP for Research and Innovation .... Dr. Vassilis L. SYRMOS
43 VP for Legal Affs/Univ Gen Counsel .... Ms. Carrie OKINAGA
10 VP for Budget and Finance/CFO .... Mr. Kalbert K. YOUNG
88 VP for Community Colleges .... Dr. John F. MORTON
11 VP for Administration .... Ms. Jan GOUVEIA
13 VP for Information Tech/CIO .... Mr. Garrett YOSHIMI
32 Interim Assoc VP Student Affairs .... Dr. Jan M. JAVINAR
18 Director of Capital Projects .... Mr. Todd A. KANJA
102 President & CEO UH Foundation .... Ms. Donna VUCHINICH
21 Director of Budget .... Mr. Michael NG
15 System Director Human Resources .... Ms. Debra A. ISHII
14 Director Management Info Systems .... Ms. Susan K. INOUYE
45 Director Ofc of Research Services .... Ms. Yaa-Yin FONG
21 Dir Fin Mgmt & Controller .... Ms. Susan X. LIN
09 Director Data Govt & Operations .... Ms. Sandra K. FURUTO
22 Director EEO/AA .... Ms. Mie WATANABE
88 Director Media Production .... Mr. Dan T. MEISENZAHL
88 Director Communications .... Ms. Jodi C. LEONG
100 Executive Asst to President .... Mr. David W. LONBORG
101 Exec Administrator/Sec to the BOR .... Ms. Cynthia D. QUINN
86 Director Government Relations .... Ms. Stephanie KIM
100 Executive Asst to President .... Ms. Lynn K. MONACO
04 Administrative Asst to President .... Ms. Janelle L. MURAKAWA

*University of Hawaii at Hilo (I)

200 W Kawili Street, Hilo HI 96720-4091
County: Hawaii　FICE Identification: 001611
Unit ID: 141565
Telephone: (808) 932-7348　Carnegie Class: Bac/A&S
FAX Number: (808) 932-7347　Calendar System: Semester
URL: www.hilo.hawaii.edu
Established: 1947　Annual Undergrad Tuition & Fees (In-State): $6,912
Enrollment: 3,497　Coed
Affiliation or Control: State　IRS Status: 501(c)3
Highest Offering: Doctorate
Program: Liberal Arts And General; Teacher Preparatory; Professional
Accreditation: WC, BUS, CEA, NUR, NURSE, PHAR, @TEAC

02 Chancellor .... Dr. Donald O. STRANEY
05 Vice Chancellor Academic Affair .... Dr. Matthew PLATZ
10 Vice Chanc Administrative Affs .... Dr. Marcia SAKAI
46 Vice Chancellor for Research .... Vacant
32 Interim VC Student Affairs .... Ms. Gail MAKUAKANE-LUNDIN
20 Asst VC for Academic Affairs .... Vacant
21 Budget Director .... Ms. Lois M. FUJIYOSHI
88 Director University Disability Svcs .... Ms. Susan SHIRACHI
15 Director Human Resources .... Ms. Claire SHIGEOKA
18 Director Facilities Planning .... Mr. Lo-Li CHIH
26 Director University Relations .... Mr. Jerry CHANG
08 Interim University Librarian .... Ms. Helen ROGERS
24 Director Media Relations .... Ms. Alyson Y. KAKUGAWA-LEONG
07 Interim Director Admissions .... Mr. Zach STREET
38 Int Asst Director Counseling .... Mr. Andrew POLLOI
39 Exec Director Housing & Dining Svs .... Mr. Miles K. NAGATA
35 Director Campus Center .... Ms. Ellen I. KUSANO
37 Director Financial Aid .... Ms. Sherrie PADILLA
06 Interim University Registrar .... Ms. Chelsea KAY-WONG
49 Dean College of Arts & Sciences .... Dr. Randy HIROKAWA
50 Dean College of Business/Economics .... Dr. Krishna DHIR
67 Dean College of Pharmacy .... Dr. John PEZZUTO
47 Int Dean Col Agri/For/Nat Res Mgmt .... Dr. Bruce MATHEWS
51 Int Dean Cont Educ/Community Svcs ...... Dr. Farrahmarie GOMES
41 Interim Director of Athletics .... Mr. Joseph ESTRELLA, JR.
40 Bookstore Manager .... Mr. Jason K. TANAKA
85 Exex Dir Internatl Student Services .... Mr. James P. MELLON
36 Exec Director Career Services .... Ms. Kainoa ARIOLAN-SUKISAKI
22 Director EEO/AA .... Dr. Jennifer STOTTER
09 Institutional Research Analyst .... Ms. Kelli OKUMURA
29 Director Marketing & Alumni .... Ms. Yu Yok PEARRING
30 Exec Director of Development .... Ms. Mariko MIHO
94 Coordinator Women's Center .... Ms. Hannah WU
23 Asst Director Medical Services .... Ms. Heather HIRATA
92 Honors Director .... Vacant
88 Dir College of Hawaiian Language .... Ms. Keiki KAWAI`AE`A
19 Director Security/Safety .... Mr. Darrell MAYFIELD

*University of Hawaii at Manoa (J)

2500 Campus Road, Honolulu HI 96822-2217
County: Honolulu　FICE Identification: 001610
Unit ID: 141574
Telephone: (808) 956-8111　Carnegie Class: RU/VH
FAX Number: N/A　Calendar System: Semester
URL: www.manoa.hawaii.edu
Established: 1907　Annual Undergrad Tuition & Fees (In-State): $11,164
Enrollment: 19,507　Coed
Affiliation or Control: State　IRS Status: 501(c)3
Highest Offering: Doctorate
Program: Liberal Arts And General; Teacher Preparatory; Professional
Accreditation: WC, BUS, CAATE, CEA, CLPSY, CORE, DH, DIETD, ENG, IPSY, LAW, LIB, MED, MT, MUS, NURSE, PH, PLNG, SP, SW, TED

02 Chancellor ..... Dr. Robert BLEY-VROMAN
10 Vice Chanc Admin/Finance/ Operations ..... Ms. Kathleen D. CUTSHAW
05 Vice Chanc Academic Affairs ..... Dr. Reed W. DASENBROCK
45 Int Vice Chancellor for Research ..... Dr. Brian TAYLOR
32 Int Vice Chancellor for Students ..... Ms. Lori IDETA
06 University Registrar ..... Mr. Stuart LAU
08 University Librarian ..... Dr. Irene HEROLD
37 Director Financial Aid Services ..... Ms. Jodie M. KUBA
38 Director Counsel/Student Devel Ctr ..... Dr. Allyson M. TANOUYE
23 Director University Health Center ..... Dr. Andrew W. NICHOLS
39 Director Student Housing ..... Mr. Michael W. KAPTIK
40 Director Campus Svcs (Bookstore) ..... Ms. Deborah T. HEUBLER
41 Athletic Director ..... Mr. Ben JAY
86 Director of Cmty/Govt Affairs ..... Mr. Elmer KAAI
28 Dir Stdnt Equity/Exclnce/Diversity ..... Dr. Amefil AGBAYANI
36 Interim Dir Manoa Career Center ..... Ms. Wendy SORA
15 Director Human Resources ..... Ms. Tammy KUNIYOSHI
88 Director Cancer Center ..... Dr. Michele CARBONE
88 Director Institute for Astronomy ..... Dr. Guenther HASINGER
88 Director Waikiki Aquarium ..... Dr. Andrew ROSSITER
88 Int Assc Dr Pac Biosci Research Ctr ..... Dr. Marilyn DUNLAP
56 Int Dean Outreach College ..... Dr. William G. CHISMAR
50 Dean Shidler College of Business ..... Dr. V. Vance ROLEY
58 Dean Graduate Education ..... Dr. Krystyna AUNE
88 Int Dean Sch of Travel Industry Mgt ..... Dr. Tom BINGHAM
53 Dean College of Education ..... Dr. Donald B. YOUNG
54 Dean College of Engineering ..... Dr. Peter E. CROUCH
47 Dean Col Trop Agric & Human Res ..... Dr. Maria GALLO
63 Dean John A Burns Sch of Med ..... Dr. Jerris R. HEDGES
66 Dean Sch Nursing & Dental Hygiene ..... Dr. Mary G. BOLAND
70 Dean M P Thompson Sch of Soc Work ... Dr. Noreen K. MOKUAU
61 Dean Wm S Richardson Sch of Law ..... Mr. Aviam SOIFER
48 Dean School of Architecture ..... Mr. Daniel S. FRIEDMAN
49 Dean College Arts & Humanities ..... Mr. Peter ARNADE
65 Int Dean College Natural Sciences ..... Dr. Kristin KUMASHIRO
83 Dean College Social Sciences ..... Dr. Denise E. KONAN
79 Int Dean College Lang Ling & Lit ..... Dr. Jeffrey G. CARROLL
88 Dean Sch Ocean & Earth Sci & Tech ..... Dr. Brian TAYLOR
88 Dean Pacific and Asian Studies ..... Dr. R. Anderson SUTTON
88 Dn Hawaiinuiakea Sch Hawn Knowledge .... Dr. Maenette BENHAM

*University of Hawaii - West Oahu (A)

91-1001 Farrington Highway, Kapolei HI 96707

County: Honolulu FICE Identification: 021078
Unit ID: 141981
Telephone: (808) 689-2770 Carnegie Class: Bac/Diverse
FAX Number: (808) 689-2771 Calendar System: Semester
URL: www.uhwo.hawaii.edu
Established: 1976 Annual Undergrad Tuition & Fees (In-State): $7,152
Enrollment: 2,661 Coed
Affiliation or Control: State IRS Status: 501(c)3
Highest Offering: Baccalaureate
Program: Liberal Arts And General; Teacher Preparatory
Accreditation: WC, TED

02 Chancellor ..... Dr. Rockne C. FREITAS
05 Vice Chanc Academic Affairs ..... Dr. Doris CHING
32 Int Vice Chanc for Student Affairs ..... Dr. Judy OLIVEIRA
11 Int Vice Chanc for Administration ..... Ms. Kathy WONG-NAKAMURA
20 Int Acad Pgm Ofcr/Dir Stratg Init ..... Ms. Sherry PROPER
84 Director for Enrollment Management ..... Mr. James CROMWELL
09 Director of Institutional Research ..... Ms. Jacqueline HONDA
26 Director of Communications ..... Ms. Leila SHIMOKAWA
08 Head Librarian ..... Ms. Sarah S. GILMAN-SUR
06 Registrar ..... Ms. Robyn OSHIRO
37 Financial Aid Officer ..... Mr. Lester ISHIMOTO
15 Director of Human Resources ..... Ms. Nancy K. NAKASONE
18 Facilities/Mgmt/Operation Mgr ..... Mr. Dan FURUYA
10 Director of Business Affairs ..... Ms. Linda SAIKI

*University of Hawaii Community Colleges (B)

2444 Dole Street, Honolulu HI 96822-2411

County: Honolulu FICE Identification: 006751
Unit ID: 420592
Telephone: (808) 956-7038 Carnegie Class: N/A
FAX Number: (808) 956-9219
URL: www.hawaii.edu

01 Vice Pres for Community Colleges ..... Dr. John F. MORTON
05 Assoc Vice Pres Academic Affairs ..... Dr. Peter QUIGLEY
11 Assoc Vice Pres Admin/Cmty Col Oper ..... Mr. Michael T. UNEBASAMI
04 Executive Assistant to the VP & Dir ..... Ms. Deborah NAKAGAWA
10 Director Budget & Planning ..... Mr. Lance YAMAMOTO
108 Director Academic Plng Assessment ..... Ms. Cheryl CHAPPELL-LONG
15 Director Personnel Services ..... Ms. Sandra UYENO
18 Director Facilities/Physical Plant ..... Ms. Denise YOSHIMORI-YAMAMOTO
22 Dir Affirmative Action/EEO ..... Ms. Mary PERREIRA
26 Public Relations/Marketing ..... Ms. Susan LEE

*Kapiolani Community College (C)

4303 Diamond Head Road, Honolulu HI 96816-4496

County: Honolulu FICE Identification: 001613
Unit ID: 141796
Telephone: (808) 734-9000 Carnegie Class: Assoc/Pub2in4
FAX Number: (808) 734-9162 Calendar System: Semester
URL: www.kcc.hawaii.edu
Established: 1957 Annual Undergrad Tuition & Fees (In-State): $2,940
Enrollment: 7,994 Coed
Affiliation or Control: State IRS Status: 501(c)3
Highest Offering: Associate Degree
Program: Occupational; 2-Year Principally Bachelor's Creditable
Accreditation: WJ, ACBSP, ACFEI, ADNUR, COARC, EMT, MAC, MLTAD, OTA, PHLEB, PTAA, RAD, SURGT

02 Chancellor ..... Dr. Leon RICHARDS
05 Vice Chancellor Academic Affairs ..... Dr. Louise PAGOTTO
10 Vice Chancellor for Admin Services ..... Mr. Brian FURUTO
32 Vice Chanellor for Student Services ..... Dr. Brenda IVELISSE
49 Dean Arts and Sciences ..... Vacant
50 Dean Hospitality/Business/Legal ..... Mr. John RICHARDS
66 Dean Health Programs ..... Dr. Patricia O'HAGAN
51 Dir Continuing Educ & Training ..... Ms. Ann ISHIDA-HO
04 Special Asst to the Chancellor ..... Ms. Joanne WHITTAKER
88 Dir Culinary Inst of the Pacific ..... Mr. Conrad NONAKA
09 Dir Institutional Effectiveness ..... Dr. Robert FRANCO
08 Librarian ..... Ms. Susan KAZAMA
06 Registrar ..... Ms. Jerilyn ENOKAWA
37 Financial Aid Officer ..... Ms. Jennifer BRADLEY
109 Auxiliary Services Officer ..... Mr. Gordon MAN
29 Director Community Relations ..... Ms. Louise YAMAMOTO
30 Development Officer ..... Ms. Linh HOANG POE
15 Director Personnel Office ..... Ms. Kelli BRANDVOLD
21 Fiscal Officer ..... Vacant

*University of Hawaii Hawaii Community College (D)

200 W Kawili Street, Hilo HI 96720-4091

County: Hawaii FICE Identification: 005258
Unit ID: 383190
Telephone: (808) 934-2500 Carnegie Class: Assoc/Pub2in4
FAX Number: (808) 934-2501 Calendar System: Semester
URL: www.hawaii.hawaii.edu
Established: 1941 Annual Undergrad Tuition & Fees (In-State): $2,910
Enrollment: 3,186 Coed
Affiliation or Control: State IRS Status: 501(c)3
Highest Offering: Associate Degree
Program: Occupational; 2-Year Principally Bachelor's Creditable
Accreditation: WJ, ACFEI, ADNUR, CEA

02 Chancellor ..... Ms. Noreen R. YAMANE
05 Vice Chanc Academic Affairs ..... Ms. Joni Y. ONISHI
10 Vice Chanc Administrative Affairs ..... Mr. James M. YOSHIDA
32 Vice Chanc Student Affairs ..... Mr. Jason S. CIFRA
51 Int Dir Continuing Educ/Training ..... Ms. Deborah S. SHIGEHARA
37 Student Financial Aid Officer ..... Ms. Vivian LAMOTHE
12 Director UH Center at West Hawaii .Dr. Kenneth Marty FLETCHER
06 Registrar ..... Ms. Dorinna MANUEL-CORTEZ
15 Human Resource Manager ..... Ms. Mari CHANG
07 Registrar/Admissions/Records Mgr ..... Ms. Dorinna MANUEL-CORTEZ
21 Budget Analyst ..... Ms. Jodi MINE

*University of Hawaii Honolulu Community College (E)

874 Dillingham Boulevard, Honolulu HI 96817-4598

County: Honolulu FICE Identification: 001612
Unit ID: 141680
Telephone: (808) 845-9211 Carnegie Class: Assoc/Pub2in4
FAX Number: (808) 845-9173 Calendar System: Semester
URL: www.honolulu.hawaii.edu
Established: 1920 Annual Undergrad Tuition & Fees (In-State): $2,943
Enrollment: 4,144 Coed
Affiliation or Control: State IRS Status: 501(c)3
Highest Offering: Associate Degree
Program: Occupational; 2-Year Principally Bachelor's Creditable; Technical Emphasis
Accreditation: WJ

02 Chancellor ..... Ms. Erika LACRO
11 Vice Chancellor of Admin Svcs ..... Mr. Derek INAFUKU
05 Vice Chancellor of Academic Affairs ..... Ms. Katy HO
88 Director PCATT ..... Mr. Steven AUERBACH
88 Dean Transport & Trades ..... Mr. Keala CHOCK
27 Dean Communications & Services ..... Mr. Russell UYENO
08 Librarian in Charge ..... Ms. Irene MESINA
37 Financial Aid Officer ..... Ms. Jannine OYAMA
15 Human Resources Mgr/EEO/AA Coord ... Ms. Monique TINGKANG
32 Director Student Affairs ..... Ms. Emily Ann KUKULIES
06 Registrar ..... Ms. Josephine STENBERG
09 Director Management Info & Research .... Mr. Steven SHIGEMOTO
36 Dir Student Placement/Counselor ..... Ms. Silvan CHUNG
20 Dean University College ..... Ms. Marcia ROBERTS-DEUTSCH
07 Director of Admissions ..... Ms. Josephine STENBERG
10 Acting Chief Business Officer ..... Ms. Myrna PATTERSON
26 Chief Public Relations Officer ..... Ms. Billie LUEDER
38 Director Student Counseling ..... Ms. Lara SUGIMOTO
88 Dean of Academic Support ..... Mr. Wayne SUNAHARA
96 Acting Director of Purchasing ..... Ms. Myrna PATTERSON
88 Director Secondary Education Pgms ..... Ms. Lara SUGIMOTO
13 Chief Info Technology Officer (CIO) ..... Mr. Michael MEYER
35 Dean of Student Services ..... Ms. Lara SUGIMOTO

*University of Hawaii Kauai Community College (F)

3-1901 Kaumualii Highway, Lihue HI 96766-9500

County: Kauai FICE Identification: 001614
Unit ID: 141802
Telephone: (808) 245-8311 Carnegie Class: Assoc/Pub2in4
FAX Number: (808) 245-8220 Calendar System: Semester
URL: kauai.hawaii.edu/
Established: 1964 Annual Undergrad Tuition & Fees (In-State): $4,176
Enrollment: 1,424 Coed
Affiliation or Control: State IRS Status: 501(c)3
Highest Offering: Associate Degree
Program: Occupational; 2-Year Principally Bachelor's Creditable
Accreditation: WJ, ACFEI, ADNUR

02 Chancellor ..... Dr. Helen COX
05 Vice Chanc Academic Affairs ..... Dr. James DIRE
32 Vice Chanc Student Affairs ..... Mr. Earl K. NISHIGUCHI
11 Vice Chanc Administrative Services ..... Mr. Brandon SHIMOKAWA
20 Director Acad Supp/Univ Ctr Dir ..... Ms. Ramona KINCAID
51 Director Continuing Educ/Training ..... Mr. Bruce GETZEN
08 Librarian ..... Mr. Robert KAJIWARA
10 Chief Financial Officer ..... Mr. Leighton ORIDE
37 Financial Aid Officer ..... Mr. Jeff ANDERSON
18 Auxillary/Facilities Svc Specialist ..... Mr. Calvin SHIRAI
15 Human Resource Specialist ..... Ms. Jorae BAPTISTE
35 Counselor ..... Mr. John CONSTANTINO
09 Institutional Researcher ..... Mr. Jonathan KALK

*University of Hawaii Leeward Community College (G)

96-045 Ala Ike, Pearl City HI 96782-3393

County: Honolulu FICE Identification: 004549
Unit ID: 141811
Telephone: (808) 455-0011 Carnegie Class: Assoc/Pub2in4
FAX Number: (808) 455-0471 Calendar System: Semester
URL: www.leeward.hawaii.edu
Established: 1968 Annual Undergrad Tuition & Fees (In-State): $2,791
Enrollment: 7,742 Coed
Affiliation or Control: State IRS Status: 501(c)3
Highest Offering: Associate Degree
Program: Occupational; 2-Year Principally Bachelor's Creditable
Accreditation: WJ, ACFEI

02 Chancellor ..... Mr. Manuel J. CABRAL
05 Vice Chancellor Academic Affs/CAO ..... Mr. Michael PECSOK
11 Vice Chancellor Admin Services ..... Mr. Mark LANE
10 Chief Business Officer ..... Ms. Cecilia LUCAS
49 Dean Arts & Sciences ..... Mr. James GOODMAN
72 Dean Career & Tech Education ..... Mr. Ron UMEHIRA
32 Int Dean Student Services ..... Ms. Laurie LAWRENCE
20 Dean of Academic Services ..... Mr. Paul KUEHN
08 Librarian ..... Mr. Wayde OSHIRO
06 Registrar ..... Mr. Grant HELGESON
37 Financial Aid Officer ..... Ms. Aileen LUM-AKANA
18 Chief Facilities/Physical Plant ..... Ms. Sandy MAEDA
09 Int Dir Policy/Planning/Assessment ..... Ms. Harriet MIYASAKI
26 Chief Public Relations Officer ..... Ms. Kathleen CABRAL
15 Human Resources/EEO/AA Officer ..... Mr. Michael WONG
13 Computer Center Manager ..... Ms. Penny UYEHARA
19 Security Supervisor ..... Mr. Talbort HOOK
12 Int Coord Waianae Education Center ..... Mr. Danny WYATT
24 Media Coordinator ..... Ms. Leanne CHUN
35 Student Activities Coordinator ..... Ms. Lexer CHOU
36 Placement Officer ..... Vacant

*University of Hawaii Maui College (H)

310 Kaahumanu Avenue, Kahului HI 96732-1644

County: Maui FICE Identification: 001615
Unit ID: 141839
Telephone: (808) 984-3500 Carnegie Class: Assoc/Pub4
FAX Number: (808) 984-3546 Calendar System: Semester
URL: maui.hawaii.edu
Established: 1931 Annual Undergrad Tuition & Fees (In-State): $1,503
Enrollment: 3,809 Coed
Affiliation or Control: State IRS Status: 501(c)3
Highest Offering: Baccalaureate
Program: Occupational; 2-Year Principally Bachelor's Creditable; Nursing Emphasis
Accreditation: WC, ACFEI, ADNUR, DA, DH

02 Chancellor ..... Dr. Lui HOKOANA
05 Vice Chanc Academic Affairs ..... Dr. Jonathon MCKEE
32 Interim Vice Chanc of Student Affs ..... Ms. Debra NAKAMA
10 Vice Chanc of Administrative Affs ..... Mr. David TAMANAHA
20 Int Assistant Dean of Instruction ..... Mr. David GROOMS
51 Director Continuing Educ/Training ..... Ms. Lori TERAGAWACHI
08 Librarian ..... Ms. Ellen PETERSON
12 Director University Center Maui ..... Ms. Tamone Karen HANADA
07 Director of Admissions/Registrar ..... Ms. Flora MORA
09 Director of Institutional Research ..... Dr. Jean PEZZOLI
15 Director Personnel Services ..... Ms. Susan TOKUNAGA
18 Chief Facilities/Physical Plant ..... Mr. Robert BURTON
21 Associate Fiscal Officer ..... Ms. Cindy YAMAMOTO
30 Chief Development ..... Ms. Cordy MACLAUGHLIN
36 Director Student Placement ..... Ms. Cathy BIO
37 Interim Financial Aid Officer ..... Mr. Kilohana MILLER
38 Director Student Counseling ..... Mr. Shane PAYBA

*University of Hawaii Windward Community College (A)

45-720 Keaahala Road, Kaneohe HI 96744-3598
County: Honolulu FICE Identification: 011220
Unit ID: 141990
Telephone: (808) 235-7400 Carnegie Class: Assoc/Pub2in4
FAX Number: (808) 247-5362 Calendar System: Semester
URL: www.wcc.hawaii.edu
Established: 1972 Annual Undergrad Tuition & Fees (In-State): $2,776
Enrollment: 2,661 Coed
Affiliation or Control: State IRS Status: 501(c)3
Highest Offering: Associate Degree
Program: Occupational; 2-Year Principally Bachelor's Creditable
Accreditation: WJ

02 Chancellor Mr. Doug DYKSTRA
05 Vice Chancellor Academic Affs Ms. Ardis ESHENBERG
32 Int Vice Chancellor Student Affairs Mr. Tom DOI
11 Vice Chanc Administrative Services Mr. Kevin ISHIDA
20 Dean of Academic Affairs Div I Ms. Ellen ISHIDA-BABINEAU
20 Dean of Academic Affairs Div II Mr. Mike TOM
75 Dir Vocational/Cmty Education Mr. Mike MOSER
08 Head Librarian Ms. Nancy HEU
06 Registrar Ms. Geri IMAI
09 Director of Institutional Research Mr. Jeffrey HUNT
37 Director Student Financial Aid Mr. Steven CHIGAWA
15 Personnel Officer Ms. Karen CHO
26 Marketing/Public Relations Dir Ms. Bonnie BEATSON

University of Phoenix Hawaii Campus (B)

745 Fort Street, Suite 2000, Honolulu HI 96813-3800
Telephone: (808) 536-2686 Identification: 770202
Accreditation: &NH, ACBSP

† Branch campus of University of Phoenix, Tempe, AZ.

World Medicine Institute (C)

931 University Avenue, Suite 104,
Honolulu HI 96826-3266
County: Honolulu FICE Identification: 030725
Unit ID: 141936
Telephone: (808) 947-4788 Carnegie Class: Spec/Health
FAX Number: (808) 373-4341 Calendar System: Semester
URL: www.wmi.edu
Established: 1970 Annual Graduate Tuition & Fees: $11,100
Enrollment: 78 Coed
Affiliation or Control: Independent Non-Profit IRS Status: 501(c)3
Highest Offering: Master's; No Undergraduates
Program: Professional
Accreditation: ACUP

01 President Dr. Lillian CHANG
05 Academic Dean Dr. Wasim SIDDIQUI
10 Chief Operating Officer Dr. Eric ONO
09 Director of Institutional Research Dr. Catharina ANG
37 Director Student Financial Aid Mr. Hansford CHOCK
07 Director of Admissions Dr. Gayle TODOKI

IDAHO

Boise Bible College (D)

8695 W Marigold Street, Boise ID 83714-1220
County: Ada FICE Identification: 022345
Unit ID: 142090
Telephone: (208) 376-7731 Carnegie Class: Spec/Faith
FAX Number: (208) 376-7743 Calendar System: Semester
URL: www.boisebible.edu
Established: 1945 Annual Undergrad Tuition & Fees: $10,540
Enrollment: 177 Coed
Affiliation or Control: Christian Churches And Churches of Christ
IRS Status: 501(c)3
Highest Offering: Baccalaureate
Program: Religious Emphasis
Accreditation: BI

01 President Mr. Terry E. STINE
05 Academic Dean Mr. Charles FABER
32 Dean of Students Mr. Cody CHRISTENSEN
10 Business Officer Ms. Val WELCH
30 Director of Development Mr. David DAVOLT
06 Registrar Mr. Ross KNUDSEN
07 Director of Admissions Mr. Mike MAGLISH
08 Librarian Ms. Amber GROVE
37 Financial Aid Director Mrs. Joyce ANDERSON
18 Supt of Building & Grounds Mr. Jon SHINGLER
04 Executive Assistant Mrs. Mary REICH

Boise State University (E)

1910 University Drive, Boise ID 83725-1000
County: Ada FICE Identification: 001616
Unit ID: 142115
Telephone: (208) 426-1000 Carnegie Class: Master's L
FAX Number: (208) 426-3765 Calendar System: Semester
URL: www.boisestate.edu
Established: 1932 Annual Undergrad Tuition & Fees (In-State): $6,876
Enrollment: 22,259 Coed
Affiliation or Control: State IRS Status: 501(c)3
Highest Offering: Doctorate
Program: Liberal Arts And General; Teacher Preparatory; Professional; Business Emphasis
Accreditation: NW, ART, BUS, BUSA, CAATE, CACREP, COARC, CONST, CS, DMS, ENG, MUS, NUR, RAD, SPAA, SW, TED, THEA

01 President Dr. Robert W. KUSTRA
05 Provost/Vice Pres Academic Affairs Dr. Martin E. SCHIMPF
10 Vice Pres Finan/Administration Ms. Stacy PEARSON
32 Vice Pres Student Affairs Dr. Lisa B. HARRIS
30 Vice Pres University Advancement Ms. Laura SIMIC
43 Vice Pres Gen Counsel & Campus Op Mr. Kevin SATTERLEE
20 Vice Provost for Acad Planning Dr. James MUNGER
20 Vice Provost for Undergrad Studies Dr. Sharon MCGUIRE
21 Associate Vice Pres for Finance Ms. Jo Ellen DI NUCCI
35 Assoc Vice Pres Student Life Dr. Leslie WEBB
18 Acting Assoc VP Campus Plng/Facil Michael SUMPTER
46 Vice Pres for Research & Econ Devel Dr. Mark RUDIN
13 Assoc Vice Pres of IT Mr. Max DAVIS-JOHNSON
08 Dean of University Library Ms. Tracy BICKNELL-HOLMES
35 Dean of Students Dr. Chris WUTHRICH
84 Assoc Vice Pres Enrollment Services Mr. James ANDERSON
15 Asst VP Human Resources Mr. Jay STEPHENS
29 Executive Director Alumni Affairs Mr. Estevan ANDRADE
17 Medical Services Director Dr. Vincent SERIO
06 Registrar Ms. Kristine COLLINS
18 Exec Director Campus Security Mr. John KAPLAN
40 Director Bookstore Mr. Jim GOODMAN
24 Director Academic Technologies Mr. Dale PIKE
09 Director Institutional Research Dr. Shari ELLERTSON
07 Director of Admissions Dr. Kelly TALBERT
26 Assoc Vice Pres Comm & Market Mr. Greg HAHN
41 Exec Director Athletics Mr. Mark COYLE
22 Affirmative Action/EEO Ms. Jean SOLECKI
38 Director Counseling Services Dr. Karla WEST
37 Dir Financial Aid & Scholarships Ms. Diana FAIRCHILD
96 Director of Purchasing Ms. Terri SPINAZZA
51 Dean Extended Studies Mr. Mark WHEELER
49 Dean of Arts & Sciences Dr. Tony ROARK
83 Interim Dean of Social Sci/Pub Affs Dr. Shelton WOODS
50 Dean of Business & Economics Dr. Kenneth J. PETERSEN
53 Dean of Education Dr. Richard OSGUTHORPE
58 Dean of the Graduate College Dr. Jack PELTON
76 Dean of Health Sciences Dr. Tim DUNNAGAN
54 Dean of College of Engineering Dr. Amy MOLL
88 Dean Col of Innovation & Design Mr. Gordon JONES
92 Dean Honors College Dr. Andrew FINSTUEN
88 Dean School of Public Service Dr. Corey COOK
04 Exec Asst to President Ms. Melissa JENSEN
100 Chief of Staff Ms. Randi MCDERMOTT
104 Director Intl Learn Opps Ms. Corrine HENKE
39 Director Housing and Res Life Dr. Dean KENNEDY
86 Director Government Relations Mr. Bruce C. NEWCOMB
88 Director of IDEA Dr. Leslie MADSEN-BROOKS
103 Dir Workforce/Career Development Ms. Debbie KAYLOR
106 Dir Online Education/E-learning Ms. Janet ATKINSON
28 Director of Student Diversity Mr. Francisco SALINAS
44 Director Annual or Planned Giving Ms. Cara WALKER

Brigham Young University-Idaho (F)

525 South Center Street, Rexburg ID 83460
County: Madison FICE Identification: 001625
Unit ID: 142522
Telephone: (208) 496-1411 Carnegie Class: Bac/Diverse
FAX Number: (208) 496-1103 Calendar System: Semester
URL: www.byui.edu
Established: 1888 Annual Undergrad Tuition & Fees: $3,830
Enrollment: 24,196 Coed
Affiliation or Control: Latter-day Saints IRS Status: 501(c)3
Highest Offering: Baccalaureate
Program: Occupational; 2-Year Principally Bachelor's Creditable; Liberal Arts And General; Teacher Preparatory
Accreditation: NW, ADNUR, EMT, ENG, MAC, MUS, NUR, @PTAA, SW

01 President Dr. Clark G. GILBERT
05 Academic Vice President Dr. Fenton L. BROADHEAD
46 University Resources Vice President Mr. Charles N. ANDERSEN
35 Student Svcs & Activities Vice Pres Mr. Kevin T. MIYASAKI
30 Advancement Vice President Dr. Henry J. EYRING
20 Assoc Academic VP Instruction Mr. Kelly T. BURGENER
106 Assoc Acad VP Curriculum & Online Dr. Edwin A. SEXTON
20 Assoc Acad VP Support Services Dr. Richard K. PAGE
20 Assoc Acad VP Student Connections Dr. Ralph M. KERN
32 Dean of Students Mr. Kip B. HARRIS
32 Student Well Being Mng Director Mr. Wynn N. HILL
51 Continuing Education Director Mr. Chad P. PRICE
13 Chief Information Officer Mr. Joe TAYLOR
09 Inst Research & Assessment Director Dr. Scott J. BERGSTROM
06 Student Records & Registration Mr. Kyle R. MARTIN
37 Student Fin Aid/Scholarship Dir Mr. Aaron D. SANNS
08 University Librarian Mrs. Laurie S. FRANCIS
10 Univ Operations Managing Director Mr. Wayne N. CLARK
15 Human Resources Director Mr. Kevin L. PRICE
23 Student Health Services Director Mr. Shaun ORR
38 Student Counseling Center Director Mr. Reed J. STODDARD
19 University Security & Safety Dir Mr. Garth M. GUNDERSON
07 Admissions Director Mr. Tyler R. WILLIAMS
29 Alumni Director Mr. Steven J. DAVIS
35 Student Activities Mng Director Mr. Derek R. FAY
26 University Relations Mng Director Mr. Merv R. BROWN
30 Philanthropies Director Mr. Christopher W. MOORE
44 Annual Giving Director Mr. D. Alton HANSEN
39 Housing & Student Living Director Dr. Troy J. DOUGHERTY
43 Legal Counsel Mr. Michael R. ORME
21 Financial Services Mng Director Mr. Shane WEBSTER
88 Academic Discovery Center Director Mrs. Amy R. LABAUGH
96 Purchasing & Travel Director Mr. Mike B. THUESON
84 Enrollment Svcs Managing Director Mr. Rob J. GARRETT
40 University Store Manager Mr. Doug R. MASON
104 International Services Manager Mr. Mike R. OSWALD
04 Asst to Pres Strategy & Planning Mrs. Betty A. OLDHAM

Broadview University (G)

2750 East Gala Court, Meridian ID 83642
Telephone: (208) 577-2900 Identification: 770712
Accreditation: ACICS, MAAB

† Branch campus of Broadview University, West Jordan, UT.

Brown Mackie College-Boise (H)

9050 West Overland Road, Ste. 101, Boise ID 83709
Telephone: (208) 321-8800 Identification: 666780
Accreditation: ACICS, OTA

† Branch campus of Brown Mackie College, South Bend, IN.

Carrington College - Boise (I)

1122 N Liberty Street, Boise ID 83704-8742
Telephone: (208) 377-8080 FICE Identification: 022180
Accreditation: &WJ, DA, DH, MAAB, PNUR, PTAA

† Regional accreditation is carried under the parent institution in Sacramento, CA.

The College of Idaho (J)

2112 Cleveland Boulevard, Caldwell ID 83605-9990
County: Canyon FICE Identification: 001617
Unit ID: 142294
Telephone: (208) 459-5011 Carnegie Class: Bac/A&S
FAX Number: (208) 454-2077 Calendar System: Other
URL: www.collegeofidaho.edu
Established: 1891 Annual Undergrad Tuition & Fees: $25,400
Enrollment: 1,109 Coed
Affiliation or Control: Independent Non-Profit IRS Status: 501(c)3
Highest Offering: Master's
Program: Liberal Arts And General; Teacher Preparatory
Accreditation: NW

01 President Dr. Charlotte G. BORST
05 Vice President Academic Affairs Dr. John OTTENHOFF
10 Vice Pres Finance/Administration Mr. Richard ERNE
32 Vice President Student Affairs Mr. Paul BENNION
30 Vice President for Advancement Mr. Michael VANDERVELDEN
84 Vice President for Enrollment Ms. Lorna HUNTER
20 Associate Dean of Faculty Dr. Paul MOULTON
06 Registrar Ms. Susan HINES
41 Director of Athletics Mr. Marty HOLLY
26 Dir of Marketing & Communications Mr. Jordan RODRIGUEZ
29 Director of Alumni Ms. Sally SKINNER
44 Director of Boone Fund Ms. Annie MORRISON
08 Director of Library Ms. Christine SCHUTZ
18 Director of Facilities Mr. Kyle ABRAHAMSON
21 Controller Mr. Jesse HARRIS
37 Director of Financial Services Ms. Jennifer WORDEN
15 Human Resources Director Ms. Nancy JOHNSON-CASSULO
36 Director Student Placement Ms. Jennifer RIDDLE
92 Director of Honors Program Dr. Sue SCHAPER
39 Director of Residential Life Ms. Jen NELSON
93 Director of Multicultural Affairs Mr. Arnold HERNANDEZ
42 Campus Minister/Asc Dean Students Dr. Phil ROGERS
19 Director of Campus Safety Mr. Allan LAIRD
13 Director of Information Technology Mr. Fred WARR
09 Director Institutional Research Mr. Mark HEIDRICH
30 Director Development Mr. Jack CAFFERTY
07 Associate Director of Admissions Mr. Mike BURDINE
40 Bookstore Manager Ms. Susan HUNSPERGER
38 Counselor Ms. Cynthia MAUZERALL

College of Southern Idaho (K)

PO Box 1238, 315 Falls Avenue,
Twin Falls ID 83303-1238
County: Twin Falls FICE Identification: 001619
Unit ID: 142559
Telephone: (208) 733-9554 Carnegie Class: Assoc/Pub-R-L
FAX Number: (208) 736-3015 Calendar System: Semester
URL: www.csi.edu
Established: 1965 Annual Undergrad Tuition & Fees (In-District): $2,880
Enrollment: 8,357 Coed
Affiliation or Control: Local IRS Status: 501(c)3
Highest Offering: Associate Degree
Program: Occupational; 2-Year Principally Bachelor's Creditable
Accreditation: NW, ADNUR, DH, EMT, MAC, RAD, SURGA, SURGT

01 President Dr. D. Jeff FOX
00 Chairman of the Board Mr. Karl KLEINKOPF
05 Exec VP/Chief Academic Officer Dr. Todd SCHWARZ
10 Vice President of Administration Mr. J. Mike MASON
32 Assoc VP Student Services Dr. Michelle SCHUTT

Code	Title	Name
04	Exec Admin Asst to President	Ms. Kathy S. DEAHL
21	Dean of Finance	Mr. Jeff M. HARMON
20	Instructional Dean	Dr. Cindy R. BOND
20	Instructional Dean	Mr. Terry L. PATTERSON
20	Instructional Dean HSHS	Mr. Jayson LLOYD
09	Assoc Dean of IE/ALO	Mr. Chris BRAGG
35	Assoc Dean of Student Affairs	Mr. Nolan GOUBEAUX
56	Assoc Dean of Extended Studies	Mr. Cesar PEREZ
88	Assoc Dean of Student Success	Mr. John HUGHES
15	Director Human Resources	Mr. Eric NIELSON
06	Registrar	Dr. Michele MCFARLAND
07	Director of Admissions	Ms. Gail SCHULL
37	Director of Student Financial Aid	Ms. Jennifer J. ZIMMERS
08	Director Library	Ms. Teri L. FATTIG
13	Director Data Services	Mr. Jay N. SNEDDON
102	Executive Director Foundation	Ms. Debra J. WILSON
103	Director Workforce Development	Ms. Brandi TURNIPSEED
41	Athletic Director	Mr. Joel C. BATE
18	Director Physical Plant	Mr. Randy G. DILL
19	Director Security & Safety	Mr. Jim ELLINGTON
26	Public Information Director	Mr. Doug L. MAUGHAN
27	Public Information Specialist	Ms. Kim LAPRAY
40	Bookstore Manager	Ms. Jayme KETTERLING
92	Coordinator Honors Program	Mr. Brian DOBBS
39	Director Student Housing	Ms. Angela URSENBACH

College of Western Idaho (A)

P.O. Box 3010, Nampa ID 83653
County: Canyon FICE Identification: 042118
Unit ID: 455114
Telephone: (208) 562-3000 Carnegie Class: Assoc/Pub-R-M
FAX Number: (888) 562-3216 Calendar System: Semester
URL: cwidaho.cc
Established: 2007 Annual Undergrad Tuition & Fees (In-District): $3,264
Enrollment: 10,217 Coed
Affiliation or Control: Local IRS Status: 501(c)3
Highest Offering: Associate Degree
Program: Occupational; 2-Year Principally Bachelor's Creditable
Accreditation: @NW, ACFEI, ADNUR, DA, SURGT

Code	Title	Name
01	President	Dr. Bert GLANDON
10	VP Finance & Administration	Ms. Cheryl WRIGHT
05	EVP of Instruction/Student Services	Mr. David SHELLBERG
84	Dean Enrollment & Student Services	Mr. Kevin JENSEN
06	Registrar	Ms. Connie BLACK
09	Director Inst Effectiveness	Mr. Doug DEPRIEST
13	Chief Info Technology Officer	Dr. David HUNTER
26	Exec Dir Marketing/Advancement	Ms. Jennifer COUCH
07	Director of Admissions	Mr. Luis CALOCA

Eastern Idaho Technical College (B)

1600 S 25th E, Idaho Falls ID 83404-5788
County: Bonneville FICE Identification: 011133
Unit ID: 142179
Telephone: (208) 524-3000 Carnegie Class: Assoc/Pub-R-S
FAX Number: (208) 524-3007 Calendar System: Semester
URL: www.eitc.edu
Established: 1969 Annual Undergrad Tuition & Fees (In-State): $6,150
Enrollment: 686 Coed
Affiliation or Control: State IRS Status: 501(c)3
Highest Offering: Associate Degree
Program: Occupational; 2-Year Principally Bachelor's Creditable; Technical Emphasis
Accreditation: NW, MAC, SURGT

Code	Title	Name
01	President	Dr. Rick K. AMAN
10	Vice President of Finance and Admin	Dr. Christian GODFREY
05	VP of Instruction & Student Affairs	Dr. Sharee ANDERSON
06	Registrar	Mrs. Rae Lynn PATTERSON
21	Controller	Mr. Don E. BOURNE
103	Mgr Workforce Trng/Cmty Education	Mr. Kenneth W. ERICKSON
08	Librarian	Mrs. Suzy RICKS
37	Financial Aid Director	Mrs. Shayna SHARP
04	President Administrative Assistant	Mrs. Jacque LARSEN
26	Director of College Relations	Mr. Todd WIGHTMAN
102	Foundation Director	Mrs. Natalie J. HEBARD
07	Director of Admissions/Placement	Mrs. Hailey MACK
40	Bookstore Operator	Mr. Devon H. GLOVER
50	Business/Office/Technology Div Mgr	Mr. Leslie JERNBERG
97	General Education Division Manager	Mrs. Peggy L. NELSON
76	Health Care Technology Div Manager	Mr. Jared L. GARDNER
88	Trades/Industry Division Manager	Mr. Kent E. BERGGREN
88	Adult Basic Education Div Manager	Mrs. Melody CLEGG
09	Director of Institutional Research	Mrs. Marina MEIER
15	Director Human Resources	Vacant

Idaho State University (C)

921 S 8th, Pocatello ID 83209-0009
County: Bannock FICE Identification: 001620
Unit ID: 142276
Telephone: (208) 282-0211 Carnegie Class: RU/H
FAX Number: (208) 282-4000 Calendar System: Semester
URL: www.isu.edu
Established: 1901 Annual Undergrad Tuition & Fees (In-State): $6,784
Enrollment: 13,429 Coed
Affiliation or Control: State IRS Status: 501(c)3
Highest Offering: Doctorate
Program: Occupational; Liberal Arts And General; Teacher Preparatory; Professional
Accreditation: NW, ADNUR, ARCPA, AUD, BUS, BUSA, CAATE, CACREP, CAHIIM, CLPSY, COARC, COMTA, DENT, DH, DIETD, DIETI, EMT, ENG, ENGR, ENGT, MAC, MT, MUS, NAIT, NURSE, OT, PH, PHAR, PTA, PTAA, RAD, SP, SW, TED, THEA

Code	Title	Name
01	President	Dr. Arthur C. VAILAS
05	Provost/VP for Acad Affairs	Dr. Laura WOODWORTH-NEY
10	Vice President for Finance & Admin	Mr. James A. FLETCHER
30	Vice Pres University Advancement	Dr. Kent M. TINGEY
32	Vice Pres of Student Affairs	Dr. Patricia TERRELL
46	Vice President for Research	Dr. Cornelis VAN DER SCHYF
43	University Legal Counsel	Mr. David ALEXANDER
41	Athletic Director	Mr. Jeff TINGEY
20	Vice Provost	Dr. Lyle CASTLE
20	AVP/Exec Dean Div Health Sciences	Dr. Linda HATZENBUEHLER
20	AVP for Academic Affairs	Dr. Margaret JOHNSON
20	AVP for Academic Affairs	Ms. Selena GRACE
30	AVP for Development	Mr. Scott TURNER
18	AVP for Facilities Services	Mr. Phillip MOESSNER
58	Dean of Graduate School	Dr. Cornelis VAN DER SCHYF
54	Interim Dean College Science & Eng	Dr. Richard BREY
67	Dean College of Pharmacy	Dr. Paul S. CADY
50	Dean College of Business	Dr. Thomas OTTAWAY
49	Dean College of Arts & Letters	Dr. Kandi TURLEY-AMES
53	Dean College of Education	Dr. Deborah L. HEDEEN
75	Dean College of Technology	Dr. Scott RASMUSSEN
12	Dean of Academic Pgm ISU-Meridian	Dr. Bessie KATSILOMETES
12	Dean of Academic Pgm ISU-Id Falls	Dr. Lyle W. CASTLE
08	Dean & University Librarian	Mr. Karl BRIDGES
06	Registrar & Dir of Undergrad Admiss	Ms. Laura MCKENZIE
13	Chief Information Officer	Mr. Randy GAINES
29	Director Alumni Relations	Ms. K.C FELT
09	Director Institutional Research	Mr. Vince MILLER
37	Director Student Financial Aid	Mr. James MARTIN
15	Director Human Resources	Mr. Brian SAGENDORF
23	Director Student Health Center	Dr. Ronald SOLBRIG
22	Dir EEO/Affirm Action & Diversity	Ms. Stacey GIBSON
19	Director Public Safety	Mr. Lewis EAKINS
26	Director Marketing & Communication	Dr. Adrienne KING
86	Director Government Relations	Mr. Kent KUNZ
88	Director Events Management	Mr. George CASPER
35	Director of Student Life	Dr. Jane COE-SMITH
38	Director of Counseling & Testing	Dr. Don PAULSON
85	Director of International Programs	Ms. Maria FLETCHER
84	Director of Enrollment Services/IF	Ms. Ann HOWELL
07	Interim Director of Admissions	Ms. Nicole ROSEBERG
39	Director University Housing	Mr. Craig THOMPSON
96	Director of Purchasing Services	Mr. David BUCK

ITT Technical Institute (D)

12302 W Explorer Drive, Boise ID 83713-1529
Telephone: (208) 322-8844 FICE Identification: 004553
Accreditation: ACICS

† Branch campus of ITT Technical Institute, Indianapolis, IN.

Lewis-Clark State College (E)

500 8th Avenue, Lewiston ID 83501-2698
County: Nez Perce FICE Identification: 001621
Unit ID: 142328
Telephone: (208) 792-5272 Carnegie Class: Bac/Diverse
FAX Number: (208) 792-2831 Calendar System: Semester
URL: www.lcsc.edu
Established: 1893 Annual Undergrad Tuition & Fees (In-State): $6,000
Enrollment: 4,304 Coed
Affiliation or Control: State IRS Status: 501(c)3
Highest Offering: Baccalaureate
Program: Occupational; 2-Year Principally Bachelor's Creditable; Liberal Arts And General; Teacher Preparatory; Professional; Nursing Emphasis
Accreditation: NW, IACBE, MAC, NURSE, RAD, SW, TED

Code	Title	Name
01	President	Dr. J. Anthony FERNANDEZ
05	Provost/VP Academic Affairs	Dr. Lori STINSON
10	VP Finance and Administration	Mr. Chet HERBST
75	Dean Professional/Technical Pgms	Dr. Robert LOHRMEYER
51	Dean Community Programs	Ms. Kathy MARTIN
20	Dean Academic Programs	Ms. Mary FLORES
32	Vice President Student Affairs	Dr. Andrew HANSON
08	Director of Library Services	Ms. Susan NIEWENHOUS
103	Director of Workforce Training	Dr. Linda STRICKLIN
07	Director of Admissions/Registrar	Ms. Nikol ROUBIDOUX
09	Dir Planning/Research/Assessment	Mr. Sean GEHRKE
13	Chief Technology Officer	Mr. Allen SCHMOOCK
41	Athletic Director	Mr. Gary PICONE
15	Director of Human Resources	Ms. Vikki SWIFT
26	Director of College Communications	Mr. Logan FOWLER
29	Director of Alumni Relations	Ms. Renee OLSEN
37	Director of Student Financial Aid	Ms. Laura HUGHES
30	Director of College Advancement	Ms. Erika ALLEN
18	Director of Physical Plant	Mr. Matt GRAVES
36	Director Career & Advising Services	Ms. Debra LYBYER
96	Director of Purchasing	Ms. Sheila KOM

New Saint Andrews College (F)

PO Box 9025, Moscow ID 83843-1525
County: Latah Identification: 666166
Unit ID: 440396
Telephone: (208) 882-1566 Carnegie Class: Bac/A&S
FAX Number: (208) 882-4293 Calendar System: Other
URL: www.nsa.edu
Established: 1994 Annual Undergrad Tuition & Fees: $11,800
Enrollment: 178 Coed
Affiliation or Control: Independent Non-Profit IRS Status: 501(c)3
Highest Offering: Master's
Program: Liberal Arts And General; Religious Emphasis
Accreditation: TRACS

Code	Title	Name
01	President	Dr. Ben MERKLE
05	Academic Dean	Dr. Timothy EDWARDS
73	Director MA Program	Mr. Douglas WILSON
53	Dir Classical Christian Studies Pgm	Mr. Christopher SCHLECT
10	Dir Financial & Facility Services	Mr. Eric BURNETT
08	Library Manager	Mrs. Helen HOWELL
06	Registrar	Mr. Jacob MOYA
07	Director Admissions	Mrs. Brenda SCHLECT
09	Dir Institutional Effectiveness	Vacant
84	Director Student Recruitment	Mrs. Brenda SCHLECT

North Idaho College (G)

1000 W Garden Avenue, Coeur d'Alene ID 83814-2199
County: Kootenai FICE Identification: 001623
Unit ID: 142443
Telephone: (208) 769-3300 Carnegie Class: Assoc/Pub-R-M
FAX Number: (208) 765-2761 Calendar System: Semester
URL: www.nic.edu
Established: 1933 Annual Undergrad Tuition & Fees (In-District): $3,214
Enrollment: 5,779 Coed
Affiliation or Control: Local IRS Status: 501(c)3
Highest Offering: Associate Degree
Program: Occupational; 2-Year Principally Bachelor's Creditable
Accreditation: NW, ADNUR, MAC, @PTAA, RAD

Code	Title	Name
01	President	Dr. Joe H. DUNLAP
05	Vice President for Instruction	Dr. Lita BURNS
10	VP for Finance & Business Affairs	Mr. Christopher MARTIN
32	Vice President for Student Services	Mr. Graydon STANLEY
26	VP Cmty & Governmental Relations	Mr. Mark BROWNING
103	Dean of Prof/Tech/Workforce Educ	Mr. Mike MIRES
97	Dean of General Studies	Dr. Larry BRIGGS
66	Dean of Nursing & Health Prof	Ms. Christy DOYLE
88	Dean of Outreach & Ed Innovation	Ms. Kassie SILVAS
06	Director of Admissions/Registrar	Ms. Tami HAFT
09	Director of Inst Effectiveness	Ms. Ann LEWIS
08	Library Director	Mr. George MCALISTER
13	Chief Information Officer	Mr. Ken WARDINSKY
37	Director of Financial Aid	Ms. Stephanie HOUSE
15	Executive Dir of Human Resources	Ms. Laura HILL
18	Asst Director of Facilities	Mr. Garry STARK
26	Director of Comm & Marketing	Ms. Stacy HUDSON
30	Development Director	Ms. Rayelle ANDERSON
35	Director Student Development	Mr. Alex HARRIS
21	Controller	Ms. Sarah GARCIA
72	Technology Coordinator	Mr. Andy FINNEY
29	Alumni Relations Coordinator	Vacant
04	Sr Executive Assistant	Ms. Shannon GOODRICH
106	Director of E-learning	Mr. Thomas SCOTT
25	Grants Development Manager	Ms. Sara FLADELAND
41	Athletic Director	Mr. Alvin WILLIAMS

Northwest Nazarene University (H)

623 S. University Boulevard, Nampa ID 83686-5897
County: Canyon FICE Identification: 001624
Unit ID: 142461
Telephone: (208) 467-8011 Carnegie Class: Master's L
FAX Number: (208) 467-8099 Calendar System: Semester
URL: www.nnu.edu
Established: 1913 Annual Undergrad Tuition & Fees: $16,580
Enrollment: 2,249 Coed
Affiliation or Control: Church Of The Nazarene IRS Status: 501(c)3
Highest Offering: Doctorate
Program: Liberal Arts And General; Teacher Preparatory; Professional
Accreditation: NW, ACBSP, CACREP, MUS, NURSE, SW, TED

Code	Title	Name
01	President	Mr. Joel K. PEARSALL
05	Vice Pres Academic Affairs/Dean	Dr. Burton J. WEBB
10	Vice Pres Financial Affairs	Mr. David S. TARRANT
84	Vice Pres Enrollment & Marketing	Mrs. Stacey L. BERGGREN
32	Vice President Student Development	Dr. Carey W. COOK
88	Vice Pres Spiritual & Ldrshp Dev	Dr. Fred C. FULLERTON
30	AVP of Development	Mr. Mark WHEELER
06	Registrar	Mrs. Nancy A. AYERS
08	Director of the Library	Dr. Sharon I. BULL
29	Director of Alumni Relations	Mr. Darl L. BRUNER
51	Dir Center for Professional Devel	Mr. Dave R. COVINGTON
42	Dean of the Chapel	Rev. Dustin METCALF
42	Director of Campus Ministry	Ms. Julene M. TEGERSTRAND
40	Bookstore Manager	Ms. Gail D. WALKER
39	Director of Residential Life	Mrs. Karen L. PEARSON
38	Director of Wellness Center	Mrs. Terri BLACKBURN
07	Director of Admissions	Mr. Shawn A. BLENKER
21	Controller	Mrs. Shirley J. HAIDLE
26	Director of Marketing & Media	Vacant
35	Director of Community Life	Mr. Grant T. MILLER
36	Director of Career Center	Ms. Amanda F. MARBLE
13	Exec Director of Info Technology	Mr. Sal SIMILI
24	Director of Tech & Media Resources	Mr. Frank E. ESTELL
37	Director of Financial Aid	Mrs. Ann CRABB
93	Director of Multicultural Affairs	Vacant
15	Director of Human Resources	Ms. Sherry L. HARTMAN
41	Athletic Director	Ms. Kelli LINDLEY

91 Dir of Administrative Computing ....Mr. Brian C. STILLMAN
18 Chief Facilities/Physical Plant ....Mr. Jade ANDERSON
04 Administrative Asst to President ....Ms. Jill D. JONES

Stevens-Henager College (A)

901 Pier View Drive, Suite 105, Idaho Falls ID 83404
Telephone: (205) 522-0887 Identification: 770573
Accreditation: ACCSC

† Branch campus of Stevens-Henager College, Ogden, UT.

Stevens-Henager College-Boise (B)

1444 S. Entertainment Avenue, Boise ID 83709
Telephone: (208) 383-4540 Identification: 666329
Accreditation: ACCSC, #COARC

† Branch campus of Stevens-Henager College, Ogden, UT.

University of Idaho (C)

875 Perimeter Drive MS 3151, Moscow ID 83844-3151
County: Latah FICE Identification: 001626
Unit ID: 142285
Telephone: (208) 885-6111 Carnegie Class: RU/H
FAX Number: (208) 885-5540 Calendar System: Semester
URL: www.uidaho.edu
Established: 1889 Annual Undergrad Tuition & Fees (In-State): $7,020
Enrollment: 12,338 Coed
Affiliation or Control: State IRS Status: 501(c)3
Highest Offering: Doctorate
Program: Liberal Arts And General; Teacher Preparatory; Professional
Accreditation: NW, ART, BUS, BUSA, CAATE, CEA, CIDA, CORE, CS, DIETC, ENG, IPSY, JOUR, LAW, LSAR, MUS, NAIT, NRPA, TED

01 President ....Dr. Chuck A. STABEN
03 VP Infrastructure ....Mr. Dan EWART
05 Provost & Executive VP ....Dr. John M. WIENCEK
10 VP Finance ....Vacant
30 VP University Advancement .... Ms. Mary Kay MCFADDEN
46 VP Research & Econ Dev ....Dr. John MCIVER
32 VP Stdnt Affairs & Dir Enroll Mgmt ....Dr. Jean KIM
12 Assoc Vice Pres for Northern Idaho ....Dr. Charles BUCK
12 Executive Officer Boise Center ....Mr. Michael SATZ
12 Assoc Vice Pres Idaho Falls Center ....Vacant
18 Assistant Vice President Facilities ....Mr. Brian D. JOHNSON
109 Asst VP Auxiliary Services ....Mr. Tyrone W. BROOKS
84 Asst Vice Pres Enrollmnt Managemnt ....Vacant
20 Vice Provost Academic Affairs .... Dr. Jeanne M. STEVENSON
08 Dean Library Services ....Ms. Lynn N. BAIRD
15 Executive Director Human Resources ....Mr. Greg WALTERS
26 Executive Dir of Mktg & Comm ....Ms. Stefany BALES
35 Dean of Students ....Dr. Blaine ECKELS
22 Chief Diversity Ofcr/AVP Stdnt Affs ....Dr. Carmen A. SUAREZ
06 Registrar ....Ms. Heather A. CHERMAK
07 Director of Admissions ....Mr. Cezar MESQUITA
09 Director Inst Research & Assessment ....Dr. Archie A. GEORGE
27 AVP ITS/CIO ....Mr. Daniel EWART
29 Director Alumni Relations ....Mr. Steven C. JOHNSON
36 Director Career Center ....Ms. Suzanne BILLINGTON
37 Director Student Financial Aid ....Dr. Daniel D. DAVENPORT
38 Director Counseling & Testing Ctr .... Dr. Joan PULAKOS
39 Director University Residences .... Ms. Dee Dee KANIKKEBERG
41 Athletic Director ....Dr. Robert SPEAR
42 Director Campus Christian Center ....Ms. Sharon A. KEHOE
43 General Counsel ....Mr. Kent E. NELSON
44 Director Annual Giving ....Mr. James BROWNSON
87 Coord Summer & Dual Credit Pgm ....Ms. Linda GOLLBERG
92 Director Honors Program ....Dr. Alton CAMPBELL
93 Dir Multicultural Affairs ....Mr. Jesse MARTINEZ
94 Director Women's Center ....Ms. Lysa SALSBURY
40 Director Bookstore ....Mr. John BALES
96 Director Purchasing Services ....Ms. Julia MCILROY
47 Term Dean College of Ag/Life Sci ....Dr. John FOLTZ
48 Dean College of Art & Architecture ....Mr. Mark E. HOVERSTEN
49 Dean Col of Letters/Arts Soc Sci ....Dr. Andrew KERSTEN
50 Dean College of Business & Econ ....Dr. Mario S. REYES
53 Dean College of Education ....Dr. Corinne MANTLE-BROMLEY
54 Dean College of Engineering ....Dr. Larry STAUFFER
58 Dean Graduate Studies ....Dr. Jie CHEN
61 Dean College of Law ....Mr. Mark ADAMS
65 Dean College of Natural Resources .... Dr. Kurt PREGITZER
81 Dean College of Science ....Dr. Paul JOYCE
04 Executive Asst to the President ....Ms. Brenda HELBLING
25 Director Research Admin ....Ms. Polly KNUTSON
45 Exec Director Planning & Budget ....Vacant
86 Special Asst State Gov Relations ....Mr. Joe STEGNER

University of Phoenix Idaho Campus (D)

1420 South Tech Lane, Meridian ID 83642-5114
Telephone: (208) 898-2000 Identification: 770204
Accreditation: &NH, ACBSP

† No longer accepting campus-based students.

ILLINOIS

Adler University (E)

17 North Dearborn Street, Chicago IL 60602
County: Cook FICE Identification: 020681
Unit ID: 142832
Telephone: (312) 662-4000 Carnegie Class: Spec/Health
FAX Number: (312) 662-4099 Calendar System: Semester
URL: www.adler.edu
Established: 1952 Annual Graduate Tuition & Fees: $39,270
Enrollment: 1,004 Coed
Affiliation or Control: Independent Non-Profit IRS Status: 501(c)3
Highest Offering: Doctorate; No Undergraduates
Program: Professional
Accreditation: NH, CLPSY, CORE, IPSY

01 President ....Dr. Raymond E. CROSSMAN
101 Board Secy/Dir Ofc of the Pres ....Ms. Mitzi NORTON
11 Vice President Administration ....Mrs. Jo Beth CUP
05 Vice President Academic Affairs .... Dr. Wendy PASZKIEWICZ
10 Vice President Finance & IT ....Mr. Jeffrey GREEN
30 VP for Institutional Advancement .... Mr. Anthony CHIMERA
07 Vice President Admissions ....Mr. Craig HINES
26 Assoc Vice President Marketing .... Mr. Mark BRANSON
06 Registrar ....Ms. Sheba JONES
32 Assoc Vice President Student Affair ....Mr. Greg MACVARISH
88 Ex Dir Inst Pub Safety/Soc Justice ....Dr. Elena QUINTARA
35 Asst Director Student Affairs ....Ms. Jennifer POPE
37 Director Student Financial Aid ....Ms. Terri ESCH
13 Associate VP Technology ....Mr. Paul COLLINS
08 Director Library ....Ms. Kerry COCHRANE
09 Director of Institutional Research ....Mr. Don HUFFMAN
12 Dean Vancouver Campus ....Dr. Larry AXELROD

Ambria College of Nursing (F)

5210 Trillium Boulevard, Hoffman Estates IL 60192
County: Cook FICE Identification: 041247
Unit ID: 457527
Telephone: (847) 397-0300 Carnegie Class: Not Classified
FAX Number: (847) 397-0313 Calendar System: Other
URL: www.ambria.edu
Established: 2006 Annual Undergrad Tuition & Fees: $25,400
Enrollment: 432 Coed
Affiliation or Control: Proprietary IRS Status: Proprietary
Highest Offering: Baccalaureate
Program: Occupational; Nursing Emphasis
Accreditation: ACICS

01 President ....Jon OLIVEROS

American Academy of Art (G)

332 S Michigan Avenue, Chicago IL 60604-4302
County: Cook FICE Identification: 001628
Unit ID: 142887
Telephone: (312) 461-0600 Carnegie Class: Spec/Arts
FAX Number: (312) 294-9570 Calendar System: Semester
URL: www.aaart.edu
Established: 1923 Annual Undergrad Tuition & Fees: $30,220
Enrollment: 365 Coed
Affiliation or Control: Independent Non-Profit IRS Status: 501(c)3
Highest Offering: Baccalaureate
Program: Professional; Fine Arts Emphasis
Accreditation: NH, ACCSC

01 Director ....Mr. Richard H. OTTO
05 Academic Dean ....Mr. Duncan WEBB
06 Registrar ....Ms. Marcia R. THOMAS
36 Career Services Coordinator .... Ms. Lindsay SANDBOTHE
37 Financial Aid Director ....Ms. Ione FITZGERALD
08 Faculty Librarian ....Ms. Emily DECKER
88 Cultural Coordinator ....Ms. Lou Ann BURKHARDT
07 Director of Admissions ....Mr. Stuart ROSENBLOOM

American InterContinental University (H)

231 North Martingale Rd, 6th Fl, Schaumburg IL 60173
County: Cook FICE Identification: 021136
Unit ID: 445027
Telephone: (877) 701-3800 Carnegie Class: Master's L
FAX Number: N/A Calendar System: Quarter
URL: www.aiuonline.edu
Established: 1970 Annual Undergrad Tuition & Fees: $16,691
Enrollment: 11,900 Coed
Affiliation or Control: Proprietary IRS Status: Proprietary
Highest Offering: Master's
Program: 2-Year Principally Bachelor's Creditable; Professional
Accreditation: NH, ACBSP, TEAC

01 President & Chancellor ....Dr. George P. MILLER
05 Provost/Chief Academic Officer ....Dr. Robert A. MANZER
32 Vice President Student Affairs ....Ms. Betsy BALACHANDRAN
10 VP Finance/Strategy/Univ Operations ....Mr. John SPRINGER
07 Vice President Admissions .... Mr. Keith ARMSTRONG
09 Dir of Institutional Effectiveness ....Mr. Chris PERRY

Argosy University, Chicago (I)

225 North Michigan Ave., Suite 1300, Chicago IL 60601
Telephone: (312) 777-7600 Identification: 666736
Accreditation: &WC, ACBSP, CACREP, CLPSY

† Regional accreditation is carried under the parent institution in Orange, CA.

Argosy University, Schaumburg (J)

999 N. Plaza Drive, Suite 111, Schaumburg IL 60173-5403
Telephone: (847) 969-4900 Identification: 666789
Accreditation: &WC, ACBSP, CACREP, CLPSY

† Regional accreditation is carried under the parent institution in Orange, CA.

Augustana College (K)

639 38th Street, Rock Island IL 61201-2296
County: Rock Island FICE Identification: 001633
Unit ID: 143084
Telephone: (309) 794-7000 Carnegie Class: Bac/A&S
FAX Number: (309) 794-7422 Calendar System: Trimester
URL: www.augustana.edu
Established: 1860 Annual Undergrad Tuition & Fees: $38,466
Enrollment: 2,500 Coed
Affiliation or Control: Evangelical Lutheran Church In America
IRS Status: 501(c)3
Highest Offering: Baccalaureate
Program: Liberal Arts And General; Teacher Preparatory
Accreditation: NH, MUS, TED

01 President ....Mr. Steven C. BAHLS
05 Dean of College ....Dr. Pareena G. LAWRENCE
10 Vice Pres Business & Finance ....Mr. Thomas LEACH
30 Vice President Advancement ....Ms. Julie E. CROCKETT
32 Vice Pres/Dean of Student Services ...... Dr. Evelyn S. CAMPBELL
84 VP Enrollment/Communication/Plng ....Mr. W. Kent BARNDS
20 Associate Dean of the College . Dr. Wendy S. HILTON-MORROW
20 Associate Dean of the College ....Dr. Kristin DOUGLAS
20 Associate Dean of the College ....Dr. Jeffrey RATLIFF-CRAIN
42 Chaplain ....Rev. Richard W. PRIGGIE
06 College Registrar ....Ms. Liesl A. FOWLER
09 Asst Dean/Director Inst Research .... Mr. Mark SALISBURY
08 Director of the Library ....Ms. Carla B. TRACY
36 Associate VP Careers & Prof Devel ..... Dr. Michael EDMONDSON
13 Director of ITS ....Mr. Chris VAUGHAN
37 Director of Student Financial Aid ....Ms. Susan STANDLEY
96 Director of Purchasing ....Vacant
19 Chief of Public Safety ....Mr. Thomas M. PHILLIS
41 Director of Athletics ....Mr. Mike ZAPOLSKI
15 Director Human Resources ....Mrs. Laura C. FORD
18 Director Facilities Services ....Mr. Joe SCIFO
38 Director Student Counseling ....Mr. Michael W. TENDALL
35 Assistant Dean of Student Life .... Mr. Mark A. ANDERSON
26 Exec Director Public Relations C&M .... Ms. Keri RURSCH
28 Director of Multicultural & Intl .... Ms. Patricia SANTOYO-MARIN
29 Director Alumni/Parent Relations ....Ms. Kelly NOACK
07 Director of Admissions/Recruitment .... Ms. Meghan M. COOLEY
04 Administrative Asst to President ....Ms. Jennifer MOON
104 Director Study Abroad ....Dr. Allen P. BERTSCHE
43 Dir Legal Services/General Counsel ....Ms. Sheri L. CURRAN
100 Chief of Staff ....Mr. Kai SWANSON
102 Dir Foundation/Corporate Relations ....Ms. Lori RODERICK
44 Associate VP of Development ....Ms. Nancy A. JOHNSON

Aurora University (L)

347 S Gladstone Avenue, Aurora IL 60506-4892
County: Kane FICE Identification: 001634
Unit ID: 143118
Telephone: (630) 892-6431 Carnegie Class: Master's L
FAX Number: (630) 844-5463 Calendar System: Semester
URL: www.aurora.edu
Established: 1893 Annual Undergrad Tuition & Fees: $22,080
Enrollment: 5,027 Coed
Affiliation or Control: Independent Non-Profit IRS Status: 501(c)3
Highest Offering: Doctorate
Program: Liberal Arts And General; Teacher Preparatory; Professional
Accreditation: NH, CAATE, NURSE, SW, TED

01 President ....Dr. Rebecca L. SHERRICK
03 Executive Vice President ....Dr. Andrew P. MANION
30 Executive Vice President ....Mr. Theodore C. PARGE
05 Provost ....Dr. P. Joan POOR
10 Vice President for Finance ....Dr. David EISINGER
84 Vice President for Enrollment ....Dr. Donna DE SPAIN
32 Vice President for Student Life ....Dr. Lora DE LACEY
26 VP Univ Communications/Admin .... Mr. Steven MCFARLAND
31 Vice President Community Relations ....Ms. Sarah R. RUSSE
30 VP for Development/Alumni Relations ....Ms. Teri TOMASZKIEWICZ
35 Asst Vice Pres for Student Life ....Dr. Amy GRAY
21 Assistant VP/Controller ....Ms. Sharon MAXWELL
37 Dean of Student Financial Services ....Ms. Heather L. GRANART
13 Asst VP/Chief Information Officer ....Vacant
20 Assistant Provost ....Ms. Ellen J. GOLDBERG
06 Registrar ....Ms. Lisa WISNIOWICZ
08 Director of the Library ....Mr. John W. LAW
15 Director of Human Resources ....Ms. Mary WEIS
19 Director of Campus Safety ....Mr. Gary BOLT
44 Director Special Gifts ....Mr. Roger K. PAROLINI
41 Athletic Director ....Mr. James HAMAD
38 Director of Counseling Center ....Mr. David REETZ
66 Exec Director of School of Nursing ....Dr. Brenda SHOSTROM
70 Exec Dir of School of Social Work ....Dr. Fred R. MCKENZIE
49 Dean Graduate and Adult Studies .... Dr. Saib OTHMAN
88 Dean of Faculty Development ....Dr. Alicia C. COSKY
106 Dean Undergrad/Dean Aurora Online .... Dr. Carmella MORAN
53 Director of School of Education ....Dr. Jocelyn BOOTH

Benedictine University (A)

5700 College Road, Lisle IL 60532-0900
County: DuPage FICE Identification: 001767
Unit ID: 145619
Telephone: (630) 829-6000 Carnegie Class: DRU
FAX Number: (630) 960-1126 Calendar System: Semester
URL: www.ben.edu
Established: 1887 Annual Undergrad Tuition & Fees: $29,700
Enrollment: 4,448 Coed
Affiliation or Control: Roman Catholic IRS Status: 501(c)3
Highest Offering: Doctorate
Program: Liberal Arts And General; Teacher Preparatory; Professional
Accreditation: NH, DIETD, DIETI, NURSE, PH

01 President ... Dr. Michael S. BROPHY
03 Executive Vice President ... Mr. Charles GREGORY
05 Provost/Vice Pres Academic Affs ... Dr. Maria DE LA CAMARA
10 VP Business & Finance ... Mr. Allan GOZUM
88 Exec Dir of Stewardship Development ... Ms. Pat ARIANO
32 Vice Pres Student Life ... Mr. Marco MASINI
09 Assoc Prov/Dir Inst Effectiveness ... Dr. David SONNENBERGER
42 Director University Ministry ... Mr. Mark KUROWSKI
84 VP for Enrollment Services ... Ms. Kari GIBBONS
06 Registrar ... Ms. Betty MORRISON
08 Director Library Services ... Mr. Jack FRITTS
37 Sr Associate Dean Financial Aid ... Ms. Diane BATTISTELLA
09 Director Institutional Research ... Mr. Robert STANLEY
36 Director Career Development ... Ms. Julie COSIMO
23 Director Health Services ... Vacant
26 Exec Dir Marketing/Communications ... Ms. Mercy ROBB
50 Dean College of Business ... Dr. Sandra GILL
81 Dean College of Science ... Dr. Bart NG
49 Dean College of Liberal Arts ... Dr. Susan MIKULA
51 Dean Col of Adult Profess Studies ... Vacant
53 Dean Col Education/Health Services ... Dr. Ethel RAGLAND
19 Chief of Police ... Mr. Michael SALATINO
18 Director Campus Services ... Mr. Chet ILDEFONSO
31 Director Community Development ... Ms. Denise WEST
15 Director of Personnel Resources ... Ms. Betsy RHINESMITH
35 Student Activ & Commuter Svcs Coord ... Ms. Katie BUELL
13 Chief Information Officer ... Mr. Rodney FOWLKES
07 Director of Admissions ... Mr. Anthony SCOLA

Benedictine University at Springfield (B)

1500 N 5th Street, Springfield IL 62702
Telephone: (217) 525-1420 Identification: 770067
Accreditation: &NH

† Branch campus of Benedictine University, Lisle, IL.

Bexley Seabury (C)

8765 W. Higgins Road, Chicago IL 60631
County: Cook FICE Identification: 001754
Unit ID: 148724
Telephone: (773) 380-6780 Carnegie Class: Spec/Faith
FAX Number: (847) 328-9624 Calendar System: Semester
URL: www.bexleyseabury.edu
Established: 1858 Annual Graduate Tuition & Fees: N/A
Enrollment: 45 Coed
Affiliation or Control: Protestant Episcopal IRS Status: 501(c)3
Highest Offering: Doctorate; No Undergraduates
Program: Professional; Religious Emphasis
Accreditation: THEOL

01 President ... Rev. Roger A. FERLO
05 Vice Pres for Academic Affairs ... Rev. Thomas FERGUSON
30 Vice Pres Advancement/Church Rels ... Mr. Conrad SELNICK
10 Director of Finance ... Mr. Robert DOAK
04 Exec Assistant to the President ... Br. Ronald A. FOX, BSG
08 Director United Library ... Ms. Lucy CHUNG
06 Registrar & Admissions ... Ms. Peggy PEARSON
42 Dir of Congregational Development ... Ms. Susan HARLOW
15 Mgr Accting/Human Res/Spec Events ... Ms. Lynn BOWERS
44 Annual Campaign Coordinator ... Ms. Susan QUIGLEY

Black Hawk College (D)

6600 34th Avenue, Moline IL 61265-5899
County: Rock Island FICE Identification: 001638
Unit ID: 143279
Telephone: (309) 796-5000 Carnegie Class: Assoc/Pub-R-L
FAX Number: (309) 792-5976 Calendar System: Semester
URL: www.bhc.edu
Established: 1946 Annual Undergrad Tuition & Fees (In-District): $3,240
Enrollment: 5,562 Coed
Affiliation or Control: Local IRS Status: 501(c)3
Highest Offering: Associate Degree
Program: Occupational; 2-Year Principally Bachelor's Creditable
Accreditation: NH, ADNUR, EMT, PTAA

01 President ... Dr. Bettie TRUITT
05 Int VP of Instruction/Student Svcs ... Dr. Lee WEIMER
10 Chief Fin Ofcr/Board Treasurer ... Mr. Steve FROMMELT
32 Dean of Student Services ... Mr. Luis MORENO
12 Vice President for East Campus ... Ms. Chanda DOWELL
15 Director of Human Resources ... Ms. Stacey CARY
09 Director Plng & Inst Effectiveness ... Ms. Kathy MALCOLM
20 Dean Instruction/Academic Support ... Vacant
13 IT Systems Manager ... Mr. Ryan WHITE
50 Dean of Business & Health Sciences ... Ms. Betsey MORTHLAND
72 Dean of Math/Sciences/Technology ... Mr. Ken NICKELS
51 Dean Adult/Continuing Educ ... Ms. Glenda NICKE
88 Asst Dean of Student Support Svc/EC ... Mr. B. J MCCULLUM
102 Exec Dir BHC Foundation QC Campus ... Ms. Jessica MALCHEFF
88 Director Small Business Devel Ctr ... Mr. Joel YOUNGS
26 Director Marketing/Public Relations ... Mr. John MEINEKE
37 Director of Financial Aid ... Ms. Joanna DYE
36 Director Career Services Center ... Dr. Bruce STOREY
41 Division Director Athletics/Coach ... Mr. Gary HUBER
08 Librarian ... Ms. Ashtin TRIMBLE
19 Chief of Police ... Ms. Shawn CISNA
51 Director Adult Education ... Ms. Diane FALL
06 Registrar ... Ms. Heather BJORGAN
40 Bookstore Manager Quad Cities ... Ms. Aimee MUHLEMAN
96 Purchasing Manager ... Mr. Mike MELEG
50 Dept Chair Business & Technology ... Ms. Carrie DELCOURT
57 Dept Chair Comm & Fine Arts ... Ms. Melissa HERBERT-JOHNSON
79 Dept Chair Human/Languages/Journal ... Mr. Bill DESMOND
81 Dept Chair Mathematics ... Ms. Connie MCLEAN
54 Dept Chair Natural Science/Engrng ... Mr. Brian GLASER
83 Dept Chair Social Sciences ... Dr. Jay PEARCE
47 Department Chair Agriculture ... Dr. Jeffrey HAWES
66 Dept Chair Nursing ... Ms. Trudy STARR
76 Dept Chair Allied Health/HPE ... Ms. Diane ABELS
88 Dept Chair Counseling ... Ms. Wendy BOCK
62 Dept Chair Lrg Resource Center ... Vacant
49 Dean of Liberal Arts & Sciences ... Vacant
53 Dept Chair Psych/Sociology/Educ ... Dr. Traci DAVIS
72 Dept Chair Career Technologies ... Ms. Jamie HILL
18 Chief Facilities/Physical Plant ... Mr. Bob MCCHURCH

Black Hawk College East Campus (E)

26230 Black Hawk Road, Galva IL 61434
Telephone: (309) 854-1700 Identification: 770069
Accreditation: &NH

† Branch campus of Black Hawk College, Moline, IL.

Blackburn College (F)

700 College Avenue, Carlinville IL 62626-1498
County: Macoupin FICE Identification: 001639
Unit ID: 143288
Telephone: (217) 854-3231 Carnegie Class: Bac/Diverse
FAX Number: (217) 854-5700 Calendar System: Semester
URL: www.blackburn.edu
Established: 1837 Annual Undergrad Tuition & Fees: $20,364
Enrollment: 591 Coed
Affiliation or Control: Presbyterian Church (U.S.A.) IRS Status: 501(c)3
Highest Offering: Baccalaureate
Program: Liberal Arts And General; Teacher Preparatory
Accreditation: NH

01 President ... Dr. John COMERFORD
05 Provost ... Dr. John MCCLUSKY
10 Vice Pres Administration & Finance ... Vacant
30 VP for Institutional Advancement ... Vacant
32 Vice Pres of Student Affairs ... Ms. Heidi HEINZ
101 Exec Asst to Pres/Sec Bd Trustees ... Ms. Shawna POE
07 Director of Admissions ... Ms. Alisha KAPP
88 Director of Transfer Admissions ... Mr. John MALIN
29 Sr Develop Ofcr/Alumni/Staff Rels ... Mr. Nate RUSH
37 Director of Financial Aid ... Ms. Jane KELSEY
08 Head Librarian ... Mr. Spencer BRAYTON
38 College Counselor ... Mr. Tim MORENZ
06 College Registrar ... Ms. Dianna RUYLE
15 Director Personnel Services ... Ms. Melissa JONES
36 Director Student Placement ... Ms. Suzanne KRUPICA
18 Director Physical Plant ... Mr. Bill BERTETTO
41 Dir of Athletics/Recreational Pgms ... Mr. Vernon MUMMERT
42 Chaplain ... Rev. Erica BROWN
26 Director of Public Relations ... Mr. Peter OSWALD
09 Director of Institutional Research ... Dr. Kristi NELMS
21 Controller ... Ms. Dawn SHRYOCK
44 Director of Annual Giving ... Ms. Jodi ROWE
84 Enrollment Services Administrator ... Ms. Kathy RUITER
19 Director Security/Safety ... Mr. Morrison FRASER
28 Director of Diversity ... Mr. Jarrod GRAY

Blessing-Rieman College of Nursing (G)

Broadway at 11th, PO Box 7005, Quincy IL 62305-7005
County: Adams FICE Identification: 006214
Unit ID: 143297
Telephone: (217) 228-5520 Carnegie Class: Spec/Health
FAX Number: (217) 223-4661 Calendar System: Semester
URL: www.brcn.edu
Established: 1891 Annual Undergrad Tuition & Fees: $21,810
Enrollment: 258 Coed
Affiliation or Control: Independent Non-Profit IRS Status: 501(c)3
Highest Offering: Master's
Program: Professional; Nursing Emphasis
Accreditation: NH, #COARC, NURSE

01 President College of Nursing ... Dr. Pamela S. BROWN
06 Registrar ... Ms. Rachel CRAMSEY

Bradley University (H)

1501 W Bradley Avenue, Peoria IL 61625-0001
County: Peoria FICE Identification: 001641
Unit ID: 143358
Telephone: (309) 676-7611 Carnegie Class: Master's L
FAX Number: N/A Calendar System: Semester
URL: www.bradley.edu
Established: 1897 Annual Undergrad Tuition & Fees: $31,480
Enrollment: 5,300 Coed
Affiliation or Control: Independent Non-Profit IRS Status: 501(c)3
Highest Offering: Doctorate
Program: Liberal Arts And General; Teacher Preparatory; Professional
Accreditation: NH, ART, BUS, BUSA, CACREP, CONST, DIETD, DIETI, ENG, ENGT, MUS, NUR, PTA, SW, TED, THEA

01 Interim President ... Dr. Stanly R. LIBERTY
05 Int Provost/Vice Pres Academic Affs ... Dr. Joan L. SATTLER
20 Assistant Provost Academic Affairs ... Mrs. Linda J. PIZZUTI
10 Vice President Business Affairs ... Mr. Gary M. ANNA
30 Vice President Advancement ... Mr. Jacob HEUSER
32 Vice President Student Affairs ... Mr. Nathan THOMAS
84 VP Enrollment Management ... Vacant
26 Exec Dir Public Relations ... Ms. Renee CHARLES
88 Assoc VP Enrollment Management ... Mr. Justin BALL
58 Assoc Provost/Dean Res/Grad School ... Dr. Jeffrey BAKKEN
21 Assoc Business Officer/Controller ... Mrs. Pratima N. GANDHI
50 Dean Foster Col Business ... Dr. Darrell J. RADSON
57 Dean Slane Col Communic/Fine Arts ... Dr. Jeffrey H. HUBERMAN
53 Int Dean Educ & Health Sciences ... Dr. Maureen (Molly) CLUSKEY
54 Dean Engineering & Technology ... Dr. Lex A. AKERS
49 Dean Liberal Arts & Sciences ... Dr. Christopher JONES
13 Int Assoc Provost Info Res & Tech ... Mrs. Sandra BURY
08 Exec Director of the Library ... Ms. Barbara GALIK
39 Dir Ctr Residential Lvgn/Ldrshp ... Mr. Ryan BAIR
88 Exec Dir Student Involvement ... Mr. Mike KEUP
36 Exec Dir Smith Career Center ... Mr. Jon NEIDY
14 Exec Dir Computing Services ... Ms. Sandra BURY
24 Ex Dir Instruct Tech/Media Svcs ... Mr. Nial L. JOHNSON
29 Director of Alumni Relations ... Ms. Tory JENNETTEN
51 Executive Director Continuing Educ ... Ms. Janet LANGE
06 Registrar ... Mr. Andreas KINDLER
37 Exec Dir Enroll Mgmt/Dir Fin Asst ... Mr. David L. PARDIECK
19 Chief of Campus Police ... Mr. Brian JOSCHKO
15 Director of Human Resources ... Ms. Nena PEPLOW
18 Director Facilities Management ... Vacant
23 Medical Director Health Services ... Dr. Jessica HIGGS
27 Senior Director Public Relations ... Ms. Kathleen CONVER
41 Director Athletics ... Dr. Chris REYNOLDS
78 Director Springer Center ... Mrs. Dawn KOELTZOW
87 Dir Summer/Interim Sessions ... Ms. Janet LANGE
25 Exec Dir Sponsored Programs ... Ms. Sandra SHUMAKER
22 Director Affirmative Action/EEO ... Ms. Nena PEPLOW
28 Dir Multicultural Student Services ... Vacant
92 Director of Honors Program ... Dr. Kyle DZAPO
94 Director of Women's Studies ... Dr. Amy SCOTT
09 Dir of Institutional Improvement ... Ms. Jennifer G. BURGE
40 Manager Bookstore ... Mr. Paul KROENKE
88 Dir of PreProfessional Health Adv ... Dr. Valerie BENNETT
88 Dir Pre-Law Center ... Vacant
07 Asst Dir Admissions ... Mr. Joshua JONES
104 Director Study Abroad ... Dr. Christine BLOUCH

Carl Sandburg College (I)

2400 Tom L. Wilson Boulevard, Galesburg IL 61401-9576
County: Knox FICE Identification: 007265
Unit ID: 143613
Telephone: (309) 344-2518 Carnegie Class: Assoc/Pub-R-M
FAX Number: (309) 344-1395 Calendar System: Semester
URL: www.sandburg.edu
Established: 1966 Annual Undergrad Tuition & Fees: $4,390
Enrollment: 2,024 Coed
Affiliation or Control: Independent Non-Profit IRS Status: 501(c)3
Highest Offering: Associate Degree
Program: Occupational; 2-Year Principally Bachelor's Creditable
Accreditation: NH, ADNUR, DH, FUSER, PNUR

01 President ... Dr. Lori L. SUNDBERG
05 VP of Academic Services ... Ms. Julie GIBB
32 VP of Student Services ... Mr. Steve NORTON
04 Sr Exec Assistant to President ... Ms. Julie L. VAN FLEET
13 Director of Information Technology ... Ms. Christy PESCI
45 Dean HR/Institutional Effectiveness ... Dr. Constance THURMAN
10 Chief Financial Officer/Treasurer ... Ms. Lisa BLAKE
26 Director Marketing/Public Relations ... Ms. Robin DEMOTT
35 Dean of Student Success ... Ms. Misty LYON
19 Director of Public Safety ... Mr. Kipton CANFIELD
15 Director of Human Resources ... Ms. Gina KRUPPS
08 Coordinator of Library Services ... Ms. Amy CAULKINS
27 Public Relations Specialist ... Mr. Aaron FREY
20 Dean of Career & Corporate Dev ... Dr. Kyle CECIL
12 Dean of Extension Services ... Ms. Debra MILLER
56 Director of Extension Services ... Ms. Linda THOMAS
109 Director of Business Services ... Mr. Patrick MEREDITH
37 Director Financial Aid ... Ms. Lisa HANSON
30 Exec Director of Advancement ... Ms. Maureen DICKINSON
88 Director TRIO Upward Bound ... Mr. Tony BENTLEY
07 Director of Recruitment ... Ms. Dylana CARLSON
66 Associate Dean of Nursing ... Ms. Mischelle WEAVER
07 Director of Admissions & Records ... Mr. Rick EDDY
41 Athletic Director ... Mr. Mike BAILEY

79 Assoc Dean Humanities/Fine Arts .... Ms. Carol PETERSEN
81 Assoc Dean Math/Natural Sciences .... Mr. Dave BURNS
83 Assoc Dean Social & Behavioral Sci ....Ms. Jill JOHNSON
75 Interim Assoc Dean CTHE .... Ms. Diana HIGGINS
09 Coordinator of Institutional Rsrch ....Ms. Sara CREE

Carl Sandburg College The Branch Campus (A)

305 Sandburg Drive, Carthage IL 62321
Telephone: (217) 357-3129 Identification: 770071
Accreditation: &NH

† Branch campus of Carl Sandburg College, Galesburg, IL.

Carl Sandburg College The Extension Center (B)

380 E Main Street, Bushnell IL 61422
Telephone: (309) 772-2177 Identification: 770070
Accreditation: &NH

† Branch campus of Carl Sandburg College, Galesburg, IL.

Catholic Theological Union (C)

5401 S Cornell Avenue, Chicago IL 60615-5698
County: Cook FICE Identification: 009232
Unit ID: 143659
Telephone: (773) 371-5400 Carnegie Class: Spec/Faith
FAX Number: (773) 324-8490 Calendar System: Semester
URL: www.ctu.edu
Established: 1968 Annual Graduate Tuition & Fees: $19,680
Enrollment: 410 Coed
Affiliation or Control: Roman Catholic IRS Status: 501(c)3
Highest Offering: Doctorate; No Undergraduates
Program: Professional; Religious Emphasis
Accreditation: THEOL

01 President ....Rev. Mark R. FRANCIS, CSV
05 Vice President/Academic Dean ....Sr. Barbara E. REID, OP
10 Vice Pres Administration & Finance .... Mr. Michael W. CONNORS
30 Director of Development .... Ms. Anne M. TIRPAK
26 Dir of Marketing & Communications .... Ms. Nancy NICKEL
08 Director of the Library .... Ms. Melody L. MCMAHON
06 Registrar ....Mrs. Maria De Jesus LEMUS
07 Director of Admissions ....Ms. Angela PAVIGLIANITI
13 Director of Information Technology .... Mr. Darnell PAYNE
04 Assistant to the President .... Sr. Pam PAULOSKI, SP
32 Events & Student Services Manager ...Ms. Christine HENDERSON

*Chamberlain College of Nursing-Administrative Office (D)

3005 Highland Parkway, Downers Grove IL 60515
County: DuPage Identification: 667149
Telephone: (877) 751-5783 Carnegie Class: N/A
FAX Number: (630) 512-8888
URL: www.chamberlain.edu

01 President .... Dr. Susan GROENWALD
03 VP Campus Operations ....Marie HALLINAN
05 VP Academic Affairs ....Dr. Richard COWLING
10 VP Finance ....Sonya EVANOSKY
26 VP Marketing ....Thomas WILLIAMS
07 VP Enrollment Management .... Larry VEENEMAN
32 VP Student Services ....June MARLOWE

† Part of DeVry University, IL.

*Chamberlain College of Nursing-Addison (E)

1221 N. Swift Road, Addison IL 60101
County: DuPage FICE Identification: 006385
Unit ID: 466921
Telephone: (630) 953-3680 Carnegie Class: Spec/Health
FAX Number: (630) 628-1154 Calendar System: Semester
URL: www.chamberlain.edu
Established: 1889 Annual Undergrad Tuition & Fees: $18,160
Enrollment: 961 Coed
Affiliation or Control: Proprietary IRS Status: Proprietary
Highest Offering: Doctorate
Program: Nursing Emphasis
Accreditation: NH, NURSE

01 Campus President ....Dr. Jan SNOW
05 Associate Dean Academic Operations ....Debra SAVAGE
32 Manager Student Services .... Lisa PETSCHENKO
07 Director Admissions ....Roz CASTRO

† Master's and Doctorate programs are only offered online.

**Chamberlain College of Nursing-Chicago* (F)

3300 North Campbell Avenue, Chicago IL 60618
Telephone: (773) 961-3000 Identification: 770495
Accreditation: &NH, NURSE

† Branch campus of Chamberlain College of Nursing-Addison, Addison, IL.

**Chamberlain College of Nursing-Tinley Park* (G)

18624 West Creek Drive, Tinley Park IL 60477
Telephone: (708) 560-2000 Identification: 770496
Accreditation: &NH, NURSE

† Branch campus of Chamberlain College of Nursing-Addison, Addison, IL.

Chicago ORT Technical Institute (H)

5440 W. Fargo Avenue, Skokie IL 60077
County: Cook FICE Identification: 041184
Unit ID: 393180
Telephone: (847) 324-5588 Carnegie Class: Assoc/PrivNFP
FAX Number: (847) 324-5580 Calendar System: Other
URL: www.ortchicagotech.edu
Established: 1991 Annual Undergrad Tuition & Fees: $5,895
Enrollment: 433 Coed
Affiliation or Control: Independent Non-Profit IRS Status: 501(c)3
Highest Offering: Associate Degree
Program: Occupational; 2-Year Principally Bachelor's Creditable; Technical Emphasis
Accreditation: CNCE

01 Executive Director ....Michelle MOVITZ
26 Marketing Specialist ....Melissa LIEBOVICH

Chicago School of Professional Psychology-Chicago (I)

325 N Wells Street, Chicago IL 60654-8158
Telephone: (312) 329-6600 Identification: 770349
Accreditation: &WC, CLPSY

† Branch campus of Chicago School of Professional Psychology Los Angeles Campus, Los Angeles, CA.

Chicago State University (J)

9501 S King Drive, Chicago IL 60628-1598
County: Cook FICE Identification: 001694
Unit ID: 144005
Telephone: (773) 995-2000 Carnegie Class: Master's L
FAX Number: (773) 995-2563 Calendar System: Semester
URL: www.csu.edu
Established: 1867 Annual Undergrad Tuition & Fees (In-State): $11,610
Enrollment: 5,211 Coed
Affiliation or Control: State IRS Status: 501(c)3
Highest Offering: Doctorate
Program: Liberal Arts And General; Teacher Preparatory; Professional
Accreditation: NH, ACBSP, CACREP, CAHIIM, MUS, NRPA, NUR, OT, PHAR, SW, TED

01 President ....Dr. Wayne D. WATSON
05 Provost/Sr VP for Academic Affairs .... Dr. Angela HENDERSON
43 VP Gen Counsel for Labor/Legal Affs .... Mr. Patrick CAGE
10 VP of Administration and Finance ....Mr. Lawrence PINKELTON
21 Executive Director Budget/Resource ... Mrs. Arrileen PATAWARAN
13 Chief Information Officer .... Mr. Prashant SHINDE
84 Vice Pres of Enrollment Management ....Dr. Carol CORTILET-ALBRECHT
09 Dir Inst Effectiveness & Research .... Dr. Latrice E. EGGLESTON
32 Dean of Student Affairs .... Ms. Farah C. MUSCADIN
49 Dean Arts & Sciences ....Dr. Leroy JONES, II
53 Dean Education ....Dr. Satasha GREEN
67 Dean College of Pharmacy .... Dr. Miriam MOBLEY-SMITH
76 Dean Col of Health Sciences ....Dr. Leslie A. ROUNDTREE
50 Dean College of Business ....Mr. Derrick K. COLLINS
08 Dean of Library/Instruct Services .... Dr. Richard DARGA
51 Dean Cont Educ Nontrad Pgms .... Ms. Nelly MAYNARD
06 Registrar .... Mrs. Shawnice AVILEZ
21 Bursar .... Ms. Miesha V. DALEY
84 Assoc Vice President Enroll Mgmt .... Ms. Cheri SIDNEY
37 Director of Financial Aid .... Dr. Maureen CRUMP-PHILLIPS
07 Director of Admissions ....Vacant
29 Director Alumni Affairs ....Vacant
26 Director of Marketing & Communicati .... Mrs. Sabrina LAND
15 Director Human Resources .... Dr. Renee D. MITCHELL
36 Director of Career Development .... Dr. Renee D. MITCHELL
88 Dir Latino Resource Center ....Vacant
96 Director of Purchasing ....Ms. Janielle GRAHAM
18 Int Dir Facilities/Physical Plant .... Mr. Alan O'NEAL
20 Interim Assoc VP Academic Affairs ....Ms. Robin M. HAWKINS
35 Dir of Student Act & Leadership Dev .... Ms. MaToya MARSH
38 Director Counseling Center .... Dr. Yvonne PATTERSON
27 Dir of Public Relations & Communica .... Mr. Thomas WOGAN
108 Asst VP Curriculum & Assessment .... Dr. Bernard ROWAN
25 Interim Assoc VP of Sponsored Prgm .... Dr. David KANIS
28 Ethics & Diversity Officer ....Hon. Bernetta D. BUSH
86 Int Director Intergovernmental Affs .... Mr. Thomas WOGAN
19 Chief of Police .... Ms. Patricia WALSH
39 Director Student Housing ....Mr. Timothy LEE
41 Athletic Director/Associate VP .... Dr. Denisha HENDRICKS

Chicago Theological Seminary (K)

1407 East 60th Street, Chicago IL 60637-1284
County: Cook FICE Identification: 001661
Unit ID: 144014
Telephone: (773) 896-2400 Carnegie Class: Spec/Faith
FAX Number: (773) 643-1284 Calendar System: Semester
URL: www.ctschicago.edu
Established: 1855 Annual Graduate Tuition & Fees: $16,742
Enrollment: 290 Coed
Affiliation or Control: United Church Of Christ IRS Status: 501(c)3
Highest Offering: Doctorate; No Undergraduates
Program: Professional; Religious Emphasis
Accreditation: NH, THEOL

01 President ....Dr. Alice HUNT
05 Academic Dean .... Dr. Ken STONE
10 Vice President for Finance & Admin ....Ms. Julie FISHER
30 Vice President for Advancement .... Ms. Rhonda BROWN
06 Registrar ....Ms. Elena JIMENEZ
08 Head Librarian ....Mr. Evan BOYD
07 Director Recruitment/Admission .... Rev. Lisa SEIWERT
04 Assistant to the President .... Ms. Kim M. JOHNSON
26 Director of Marketing ....Ms. Susan CUSICK

Christian Life College (L)

400 E Gregory Street, Mount Prospect IL 60056-2522
County: Cook FICE Identification: 031993
Unit ID: 260947
Telephone: (847) 259-1840 Carnegie Class: Spec/Faith
FAX Number: (847) 259-3888 Calendar System: Semester
URL: www.christianlifecollege.edu
Established: 1950 Annual Undergrad Tuition & Fees: $11,000
Enrollment: 38 Coed
Affiliation or Control: Pentecostal/Charismatic Non-Denominational
IRS Status: 501(c)3
Highest Offering: Baccalaureate
Program: Religious Emphasis
Accreditation: TRACS

01 President .... Mr. Harry R. SCHMIDT
05 Academic Dean .... Mr. Wayne R. WACHSMUTH
08 Director of Library Services ....Mr. Christopher C. ULLMAN
10 Director of Finance .... Mr. Roger K. STEVENS
32 Dean of Students .... Mr. Michael BELL
06 Registrar ....Mrs. Christina BELL

*City Colleges of Chicago (M)

226 W Jackson Boulevard, Chicago IL 60606-6998
County: Cook FICE Identification: 001647
Unit ID: 144500
Telephone: (312) 553-2500 Carnegie Class: N/A
FAX Number: (312) 553-2699
URL: www.ccc.edu

01 Chancellor ....Ms. Cheryl L. HYMAN
05 Chief Academic Officer ....Ms. Vernese EDGHILL-WALDEN
10 Vice Chancellor Finance ....Ms. Joyce CARSON
13 Vice Chanc/Chief Information Ofcr ....Mr. Jerrold MARTIN
09 Vice Chanc Strategy & Instnl Intel ....Mr. Rasmus LYNNERUP
11 Vice Chanc Administrative Services ....Ms. Diane MINOR
04 Executive Board Administrator .... Ms. Candace MONTGOMERY
43 General Counsel ....Mr. Eugene MUNIN
30 Executive Vice Chancellor ....Mr. Laurent PERNOT

*City Colleges of Chicago Harold Washington College (N)

30 E Lake Street, Chicago IL 60601-2449
County: Cook FICE Identification: 001652
Unit ID: 144209
Telephone: (312) 553-5600 Carnegie Class: Assoc/Pub-U-MC
FAX Number: (312) 553-5964 Calendar System: Semester
URL: www.ccc.edu
Established: 1962 Annual Undergrad Tuition & Fees (In-District): $3,506
Enrollment: 9,392 Coed
Affiliation or Control: State/Local IRS Status: 501(c)3
Highest Offering: Associate Degree
Program: Occupational; 2-Year Principally Bachelor's Creditable; Business Emphasis
Accreditation: NH, ACBSP

02 President .... Dr. Margaret J. MARTYN
05 Interim Vice Pres Academic Affairs .... Mr. Armen SARRAFIAN
10 Exec Dir of Business/Operations .... Mr. Kent LUSK
37 Director of Financial Aid ....Ms. Elina FONSECA
18 Chief Facilities/Physical Plant ....Mr. Richard WREN
88 Dean of College to Careers ....Mr. Paul THOMPSON, III
08 Librarian .... Mr. John KIERALDO
15 Human Resources Admin ....Ms. Millie ADAN
20 Dean of Instruction ....Mr. Kevin SMITH
32 Dean of Student Services .... Mr. Wendell BLAIR
04 Assistant to the President .... Ms. Angela GUERNICA
20 Associate Dean of Instruction .... Dr. Cynthia CERRENTANO
13 Director Information Technology ....Ms. Ewa BEJNAROWICZ
35 Assoc Dean of Student Services ....Ms. Patricia CUEVAS
46 Asst Director Research/Planning ....Dr. George W. CALISTO
06 Registrar ....Ms. Courtney O'BRIEN
19 Director of Security ....Mr. Milton OWENS
09 Director Strategy/Initiatives .... Ms. Juliana TASHIRO

*City Colleges of Chicago Harry S Truman College (O)

1145 W Wilson Avenue, Chicago IL 60640-5691
County: Cook FICE Identification: 001648
Unit ID: 144184
Telephone: (773) 907-4700 Carnegie Class: Assoc/Pub-U-MC
FAX Number: (773) 907-4464 Calendar System: Semester

URL: www.trumancollege.edu
Established: 1956 Annual Undergrad Tuition & Fees (In-District): $3,070
Enrollment: 10,601 Coed
Affiliation or Control: State/Local IRS Status: 501(c)3
Highest Offering: Associate Degree
Program: Occupational; 2-Year Principally Bachelor's Creditable
Accreditation: NH, ADNUR

02 President ... Dr. Reagan F. ROMALI
03 Vice President ... Dr. Pervez RAHMAN
05 Dean of Instruction ... Ms. Susan MARCUS
06 Registrar ... Ms. My Linh TRAN
32 Dean of Student Services ... Ms. Marilyn DEMENT
35 Associate Dean of Student Services ... Ms. Indra PAOLA PELAEZ
56 Dean of Adult Education ... Mr. Armanda MATA
51 Director of Continuing Education ... Ms. Kyla WILSON
20 Dean of Instruction ... Ms. Loretta BAILES
20 Associate Dean of Instruction ... Ms. DeShaunta STEWART
20 Associate Dean of Instruction ... Ms. Maggie RICE AYALA
10 Exec Director Business Services ... Mr. Thomas DUNHAM
19 Director of Security ... Mr. Andres DURBAK
37 Director of Financial Aid ... Mr. Robert EVANS
15 Director Human Resource ... Mr. Michael ROBERTS
26 Director Public Relations/Marketing ... Mr. R. Scott BRIGHAM
109 Director Auxiliary Services ... Ms. Penelope VARNAVA
72 Director Information Technology ... Mr. Anthony GAMBOA
24 Director Lakeview Learning Center ... Vacant
09 Asst Dir of Research & Planning ... Ms. Ericka KILBURN
21 Business Manager ... Ms. Nina CAO
20 Director of Developmental Education ... Ms. Elizabeth ROSENTHAL

*City Colleges of Chicago Kennedy-King College (A)

6301 South Halsted Street, Chicago IL 60621-3798
County: Cook FICE Identification: 001654
Unit ID: 144157
Telephone: (773) 602-5000 Carnegie Class: Assoc/Pub-U-MC
FAX Number: N/A Calendar System: Semester
URL: www.ccc.edu/colleges/kennedy
Established: 1934 Annual Undergrad Tuition & Fees (In-District): $3,070
Enrollment: 5,313 Coed
Affiliation or Control: State/Local IRS Status: 501(c)3
Highest Offering: Associate Degree
Program: Occupational; 2-Year Principally Bachelor's Creditable
Accreditation: NH, DH

02 President ... Ms. Arshele STEVENS
05 Vice President for Academic Affairs ... Dr. Cristy LISLE
32 Dean Student Services ... Dr. Johnny CRAIG
12 Dean-Dawson Tech Institute ... Mr. Robert BARNETT
36 Dean College to Careers ... Mr. Kristopher MURRAY
51 Dean Adult/Continuing Education ... Ms. Latasha JOHSON
20 Dean of Instruction ... Ms. DeReere REID-HART
35 Assistant Dean Student Services ... Ms. Zalika LANDRUM
37 Director Financial Aid ... Ms. Tabitha O'NEIL
20 Director Academic Support Services ... Mr. Eugene ROBINSON
10 Exec Dir Business/Operations ... Mr. Baha AWADALLAH
06 Assistant Registrar ... Ms. Kasey MATHER
09 Director of Institutional Research ... Vacant
18 Chief Facilities/Physical Plant ... Mr. Jerome DABNEY
26 Marketing Director ... Vacant
15 Director Human Resources ... Mrs. Araceli CABRALES-MEDINA
27 Senior Director of Communications ... Ms. Katheryn HAYES
04 Assistant to the President ... Mrs. Roxanne BROWN

*City Colleges of Chicago Olive-Harvey College (B)

10001 S Woodlawn Avenue, Chicago IL 60628-1645
County: Cook FICE Identification: 009767
Unit ID: 144175
Telephone: (773) 291-6100 Carnegie Class: Assoc/Pub-U-MC
FAX Number: (773) 291-6304 Calendar System: Semester
URL: www.ccc.edu/colleges/olive-harvey/pages/default.aspx
Established: 1970 Annual Undergrad Tuition & Fees (In-District): $3,070
Enrollment: 4,572 Coed
Affiliation or Control: State/Local IRS Status: 501(c)3
Highest Offering: Associate Degree
Program: Occupational; 2-Year Principally Bachelor's Creditable
Accreditation: NH

02 President ... Ms. Angelia N. MILLENDER
04 Assistant to President ... Ms. Lexie TRIPP
05 VP Academic & Student Affairs ... Dr. David MARSHALL
88 Dean STEM/Ctr Teaching & Lrng ... Dr. Vera AVERYHART-FULLARD
32 Dean Student Services ... Dr. Mia HARDY
51 Dean Adult & Continuing Education ... Mr. Robert REIMER
36 Dean of College to Career ... Dr. Ruben HOWARD, II
35 Interim Dean of Student Services ... Ms. Tania WITTGENFELD
20 Assoc Dean of Instruction ... Ms. Tia ROBINSON
35 Assoc Dean of Student Services ... Dr. Ria PINKSTON-MCKEE
36 Assoc Dean of College to Career ... Ms. Joanne IVORY
10 Exec Dir Business/Admin/Aux Svc ... Ms. Angela ARRINGTON-JONES
09 Director of Strategic Initiative ... Ms. Nicole HOBBS
13 Director Information Technology ... Mr. Savio PINTO
36 Dir Career Planning/ Placement ... Ms. Kassandra MCGHEE JOHNSON
12 Director of South Chicago Lrng Ctr ... Mr. John ROSALES

37 Director Financial Aid ... Ms. Jolander JEFFRIES
06 Registrar ... Ms. Dorian THOMAS
19 Director Security ... Mr. Louis TORRES
88 Director Child Development Center ... Ms. Tiffany CARTER
41 Director of Athletics ... Mr. James COOPER
15 Human Resource Director ... Ms. Latasha LARRY
26 Director Public Relations ... Vacant
38 Manager Wellness Center ... Ms. TeraKesha HAMMOND
18 Chief Engineer ... Mr. Tom SIEFERT

*City Colleges of Chicago Richard J. Daley College (C)

7500 S Pulaski Road, Chicago IL 60652-1299
County: Cook FICE Identification: 001649
Unit ID: 144193
Telephone: (773) 838-7500 Carnegie Class: Assoc/Pub-U-MC
FAX Number: (773) 838-7524 Calendar System: Semester
URL: daley.ccc.edu
Established: 1960 Annual Undergrad Tuition & Fees (In-District): $3,070
Enrollment: 8,914 Coed
Affiliation or Control: State/Local IRS Status: 501(c)3
Highest Offering: Associate Degree
Program: Occupational; 2-Year Principally Bachelor's Creditable
Accreditation: NH, ADNUR

02 President ... Dr. Jose M. AYBAR
05 Vice Pres Academic/Student Affs ... Dr. Keith MCCOY
20 Dean of Instruction ... Mr. Michael CRAWFORD
36 Dean of College to Careers ... Mr. Ray PRENDERGAST
55 Dean Adult Education ... Mr. Victor CASTILLO
32 Dean of Student Services ... Dr. Edwardo GARZA
51 Dean Continuing Education ... Mrs. Jean JOHNSON
10 Exec Director Business Operations ... Ms. Crystal WASHINGTON
18 Chief Engineer/Physical Plant ... Mr. Tim SMITH
19 Director Security ... Mr. Frank LIMON
35 Assoc Dean Student Services ... Ms. Maria ACOSTA
35 Assoc Dean Student Services ... Ms. Eileen LYNCH
06 Registrar ... Mr. Milton WRIGHT
15 Director Human Resources ... Ms. Elinore MOORE
13 Director of Information Technology ... Mr. Ronald VERSETTO
26 Senior Director of Marketing ... Ms. Katheryn HAYES

*City Colleges of Chicago Wilbur Wright College (D)

4300 N Narragansett Avenue, Chicago IL 60634-1591
County: Cook FICE Identification: 001655
Unit ID: 144218
Telephone: (773) 777-7900 Carnegie Class: Assoc/Pub-U-MC
FAX Number: (773) 481-8185 Calendar System: Semester
URL: www.ccc.edu/wright
Established: 1934 Annual Undergrad Tuition & Fees (In-District): $3,070
Enrollment: 12,146 Coed
Affiliation or Control: State/Local IRS Status: 501(c)3
Highest Offering: Associate Degree
Program: Occupational; 2-Year Principally Bachelor's Creditable
Accreditation: NH, ACBSP, OTA, RAD

02 President ... Dr. David POTASH
05 VP of Academic & Student Affairs ... Ms. Nicole REAVES
32 Dean Student Services ... Ms. Romell MURDEN-WALDU
20 Dean of Instruction ... Mr. Kevin LI
35 Assoc Dean Student Svcs ... Ms. Maria LLOPIZ
35 Assoc Dean Student Svcs ... Ms. Linda HUERTAS
20 Associate Dean of Instruction ... Ms. Nancy KOLL
20 Associate Dean of Instruction ... Mr. Jeffrey JANULIS
88 Director Developmental Education ... Ms. Sara SCHUPACK
10 Executive Business Director ... Ms. Phoebe WOOD
37 Director Financial Aid ... Ms. Danielle HAAS
09 Dir Institutional Research/Plng ... Mr. Brian TRZEBIATOWSKI
13 Director Information Technology ... Mr. Anthony GAMBOA
18 Director of Facilities ... Ms. Dina LEILER
26 Director Public Relations ... Ms. Angela O'CONNOR
08 Library Department Chair ... Ms. Reina WILLIAMS
15 Human Resources Manager ... Ms. Griselda SILVA
38 Director of Wellness Center ... Ms. Anne WYSOGLAD
19 Director of Security ... Mr. Jack MURPHY
06 Registrar ... Ms. Mai ALY
41 Athletic Director ... Mr. John MCDONNELL
66 Dean of Nursing Programs ... Ms. Ines MONTERO
53 Dean Adult Education ... Ms. Magxina WAGEMAN
51 Dean of Continuing Education ... Ms. Alba PEZZAROSSI
12 Dean Humboldt Park Center ... Mr. Kenneth SANTIAGO
12 Assoc Dean Humboldt Park Center ... Ms. Maureen FITZPATRICK

*Malcolm X College, One of the City Colleges of Chicago (E)

1900 West Van Buren Street, Chicago IL 60612-3197
County: Cook FICE Identification: 001650
Unit ID: 144166
Telephone: (312) 850-7000 Carnegie Class: Assoc/Pub-U-MC
FAX Number: (312) 850-7039 Calendar System: Semester
URL: www.ccc.edu/malcolmx
Established: 1911 Annual Undergrad Tuition & Fees (In-District): $3,506
Enrollment: 6,245 Coed
Affiliation or Control: State/Local IRS Status: 501(c)3
Highest Offering: Associate Degree
Program: Occupational; 2-Year Principally Bachelor's Creditable
Accreditation: NH, COARC, EMT, FUSER, RAD, SURGT

02 President ... Mr. David A. SANDERS
05 Vice Pres Academic/Student Affairs ... Dr. Christopher Anne EASLEY
32 Dean Student Services ... Dr. Tasha WILLIAMS
10 Exec Director Business Operations ... Vacant
04 Executive Office Manager ... Mrs. Alanna S. WITHERSPOON
15 Director of Human Resources ... Mr. Stanley BEAMON
20 Dean Instruction ... Ms. Kimberly HOLLINGSWORTH
09 Assoc Dir Inst Research & Planning ... Mr. Byron A. JAVIER
13 Director Information Technology ... Ms. Debra CRONIN
06 Registrar ... Mr. Jeffery WONDERS
35 Assoc Dean Student Services ... Mr. Mario DIAZ
37 Director Financial Aid ... Ms. Tamika DAVENPORT
88 Director Child Care Center ... Ms. Aisha RUTHER
19 Director Security/Public Safety ... Mr. Michael HUNTER
18 Chief Facilites/Physical Plant ... Mr. John MORLEY
08 Librarian ... Vacant
21 Business Manager ... Mr. Richard SLATER
76 Dean Health Sciences Programs ... Dr. Vickie GUKENBERGER
56 Dean Adult Education Pgms ... Ms. Pamela LYNCH
51 Dean Continuing Education ... Vacant
66 Dean City Col Chicago/Nursing Pgm ... Dr. Marsha ATKINS
88 Assoc Dean Student Development ... Ms. Lisa WILLIS
76 Assoc Dean Health Careers ... Mr. Roy WALKER
36 Dir Career Planning/Placement ... Ms. Toya JOHNSON
103 Director Workforce Partnerships ... Ms. Rhonda HARDEMON
26 Director of Public Relations ... Mr. Aymen ABDELHALIM
46 Director of Strategic Initiatives ... Ms. Dhyia THOMPSON
109 Director of Auxilary Services ... Ms. Jessica HOLLOWAY

College of DuPage (F)

425 Fawell Boulevard, Glen Ellyn IL 60137-6599
County: DuPage FICE Identification: 006656
Unit ID: 144865
Telephone: (630) 942-2800 Carnegie Class: Assoc/Pub-S-SC
FAX Number: (630) 858-9399 Calendar System: Semester
URL: www.cod.edu
Established: 1965 Annual Undergrad Tuition & Fees (In-District): $4,200
Enrollment: 29,476 Coed
Affiliation or Control: State/Local IRS Status: 501(c)3
Highest Offering: Associate Degree
Program: Occupational; 2-Year Principally Bachelor's Creditable
Accreditation: NH, ACFEI, ADNUR, ART, CAHIIM, COARC, CONST, CSHSE, DH, DMS, MAC, NMT, #PTAA, RAD, SURGT

01 Interim President ... Dr. Joseph L. COLLINS
03 Executive Vice President ... Dr. Joseph COLLINS
05 Vice President Academic Affairs ... Dr. Jean V. KARTJE
10 Interim CFO ... Mr. John DISCHNER
13 Vice Pres Information Technology ... Mr. Chuck CURRIER
45 VP Planning & Inst Effectiveness ... Mr. James BENTE
15 Vice President Human Resources ... Ms. Linda SANDS-VANKERK
30 VP Develop/Exec Dir COD Foundation ... Ms. Catherine BROD
24 Asst VP Info Sys/Multimedia Svcs ... Ms. Donna BERLINER
20 Assoc VP Academic Affairs ... Mr. Emmanuel AWUAH
26 Vice Pres Marketing & Communication ... Mr. Joseph MOORE
32 Vice President Student Affairs ... Mr. Earl DOWLING
49 Dean Liberal Arts ... Dr. Daniel LLOYD
75 Dean Health & Sciences ... Mr. Thomas CAMERON
51 Dean Cont Ed/Extended Learning ... Dr. Joseph CASSIDY
08 Dean Learning Resources ... Ms. Ellen SUTTON
35 Dean Student Affairs ... Ms. Susan M. MARTIN
21 Interim Controller ... Mr. Kurt BECKEMAN
18 Dir Facilities Planning and Dev ... Mr. Bruce SCHMIEDL
06 Dean Admiss/Registration/Records ... Ms. Jane L. SMITH
09 Director Research & Analytics ... Mr. Eugene YE
30 Asst VP Resource Development ... Vacant
88 Internal Auditor ... Mr. James E. MARTNER
57 Director Performing Arts ... Mrs. Diana MARTINEZ
41 Director Athletics ... Mr. Paul ZAKOWSKI
25 Director of Grants ... Ms. Barbara ABROMITIS
86 Director Legislative Relations ... Ms. Mary Ann MILLUSH
19 Director & Chief COD Police Dept ... Mr. Joseph MULLIN
18 Director Facilities Operations ... Mr. Jim MA
79 Associate Dean Humanities ... Dr. Sandra MARTINS
60 Associate Dean English & Acad ESL ... Mr. Sheldon WALCHER
27 Dir Marketing & Creative Svcs ... Ms. Laurie JORGENSEN
66 Director Nursing Programs ... Vacant
16 Director Labor & Emp Relations ... Ms. Mia IGYARTO
72 Assoc Dean Technology ... Mr. John KRONENBURGER
83 Assoc Dean Social & Behav Sciences ... Ms. Marianne HUNNICUTT
81 Assoc Dean Math & Physical Sciences ... Mr. Thomas SCHRADER
88 Assoc Dean Health & Bio Sciences ... Ms. Karen SOLT
88 Assoc Dean Learn Resource ... Mr. Blakely WALTER
07 Manager Admissions & Outreach ... Ms. Julie MARLATT

College of Lake County (G)

19351 W Washington Street, Grayslake IL 60030-1198
County: Lake FICE Identification: 007694
Unit ID: 146472
Telephone: (847) 543-2000 Carnegie Class: Assoc/Pub-S-MC
FAX Number: (847) 223-1017 Calendar System: Semester
URL: www.clcillinois.edu
Established: 1967 Annual Undergrad Tuition & Fees (In-District): $4,290
Enrollment: 15,410 Coed
Affiliation or Control: Local IRS Status: 501(c)3
Highest Offering: Associate Degree
Program: Occupational; 2-Year Principally Bachelor's Creditable
Accreditation: NH, ADNUR, CAHIIM, DH, MAC, PHLEB, RAD, SURGT

01 President .... Dr. Girard W. WEBER
05 Vice President Educ Affairs .... Dr. Richard J. HANEY
11 Vice Pres Administrative Affs .... Mr. David AGAZZI
32 Assoc Vice Pres of Student Devel .... Ms. Karen HLAVIN
20 Asst Vice Pres Educational Affairs .... Ms. Alyssa O'BRIEN
88 Asst Dir Student Develop Operation .... Ms. Jennifer MALLER
12 Dean Southlake Campus .... Ms. Vicky CVITKOVIC
12 Dean Lakeshore Campus .... Dr. Alphonso BALDWIN
08 Dean Libraries/Instruction Svcs .... Mr. Brian BEECHER
21 Controller .... Mr. Andy WILLIAMS
50 Dean of Business/Workforce Bus Div .... Ms. Lourdene HUHRA
76 Dean Biological/Health Sciences .... Mr. Steven HOLMAN
83 Dean Social Sciences .... Dr. Jeffrey A. STOMPER
79 Dean Comm Arts/Humanities/Fine Arts .... Mr. Roland G. MILLER
54 Int Dean Engr/Math/Physical Science .... Mr. Rob TWARDOCK
51 Dean Adult Basic Education/GED/ESL .... Dr. Raiana MEARNS
38 Dean Counsel/Advising/Transfer Ctr .... Vacant
31 Assoc Dean Community Education .... Vacant
103 Exec Dir Workforce/Prof Dev Inst .... Ms. Roneida MARTIN
26 Exec Dir Public Relations & Mktg .... Ms. Evelyn R. SCHIELE
35 Int Executive Director Student Life .... Ms. Teresa AGUINALDO
102 Executive Director CLC Foundation .... Ms. Karen SCHMIDT
15 Exec Director Human Resources .... Ms. Julia GUINEY
88 Exec Dir James Lumber Ctr Perf Arts ... Ms. Gwethalyn BRONNER
09 Exec Dir/Inst Effect/Plan/Research .... Dr. Sean HOGAN
41 Director of Athletics/Title IX .... Mr. Nic SCANDRETT
86 Dir Resource Dev/Legislative Affrs .... Mr. Nick C. KALLIERIS
13 Chief Info Ofcr/Info Tech Svcs .... Ms. Lynn BUTLER
14 Director User Services/User Spport .... Mr. David AYKROID
88 Dir Workplace Lrng/Perform/Prof Dev .... Vacant
10 Dir Business & Auxilliary Svcs .... Ms. Michele REYNOLDS
88 Dir Application Svcs/Applic Develop .... Mr. Jay MEYER
88 Director Student Services Lakeshore .... Mr. David WEATHERSPOON
18 Director Facilities .... Mr. Greg EVANS
88 Dir Children's Learning Center .... Ms. Sandra GROENINGER
88 Dir Ofc Students with Disabilities .... Mr. Thomas CROWE
19 Chief of Police/CLC Police Dept .... Mr. Thomas GUENTHER
36 Exec Dir Career/Placement Services .... Ms. Sylvia M. JOHNSON JONES
88 Asst Dir Educational Affairs Oper .. Ms. Arlene SANTOS-GEORGE
66 Director Nursing Education .... Dr. Deborah JEZUIT
88 Director Judicial Services .... Ms. Margaret C. MILLER
29 Dir Alumni Relations/Special Events .... Ms. Julie SHROKA
23 Director Health Services .... Ms. Michelle M. GRACE
37 Director Financial Aid .... Ms. Erin FOWLES
88 Dir Active Lrng Technologies .... Mr. Scott RIAL
88 Director Continuing Prof Devel .... Ms. Carol EWING
88 Asst Director of Business Services .... Vacant
84 Asst Director Enrollment Services .... Ms. Debra MICHELINI
88 Director Green Jobs Initiative .... Mr. Stephen BELL
88 Director Student Support Services .... Ms. Zandra GENOUS
88 Director Technical Services .... Mr. James SENFT
38 Director of Advising .... Ms. Trisha ANDREWS
88 Project Dir IGEN Career Pathways .... Dr. Theresa BERRYMAN
100 Chief of Staff .... Mr. Derrick HARDEN
16 Manager Recruiting .... Ms. Kathleen SCATLIFFE-WALLACE

College of Lake County Lakeshore Campus (A)

33 North Genesee Street, Waukegan IL 60085
Telephone: (847) 543-2191 Identification: 770073
Accreditation: &NH

† Branch campus of College of Lake County, Grayslake, IL.

College of Lake County Southlake Campus (B)

1120 South Milwaukee Avenue, Vernon Hills IL 60061
Telephone: (847) 543-6501 Identification: 770072
Accreditation: &NH

† Branch campus of College of Lake County, Grayslake, IL.

Columbia College Chicago (C)

600 S Michigan Avenue, Chicago IL 60605-1996
County: Cook FICE Identification: 001665
Unit ID: 144281
Telephone: (312) 369-1000 Carnegie Class: Master's M
FAX Number: (312) 369-8069 Calendar System: Semester
URL: www.colum.edu
Established: 1890 Annual Undergrad Tuition & Fees: $23,544
Enrollment: 9,440 Coed
Affiliation or Control: Independent Non-Profit IRS Status: 501(c)3
Highest Offering: Master's
Program: Liberal Arts And General
Accreditation: NH, CIDA

01 President .... Dr. Kwang-Wu KIM
05 Sr VP Academic Affairs/Provost .... Dr. Stanley WEARDEN
10 VP Bus Affairs/Chief Financial Ofcr .... Ms. Michelle GATES
43 Senior Counsel .... Ms. Patricia BERGESON
30 Vice Pres Development .... Mr. Jonathan STERN
88 Vice President Campus Environment .... Ms. Alicia M. BERG
32 Vice President Student Affairs .... Mr. Mark KELLY
49 Int Dean Sch Liberal Arts/Sciences .... Dr. Steven COREY
57 Dean School of Fine/Performing Arts .... Mr. John GREEN
45 Assoc VP/Planning and Compliance .... Ms. Anne FOLEY
18 Assoc VP Facilities/Operations .... Mr. John KAVOURIS
35 Assoc Vice Pres/Dean of Students .... Ms. Sharon WILSON-TAYLOR
19 Assoc Vice Pres Safety & Security .... Mr. Robert KOVERMAN
15 Assoc Vice Pres of Human Res .... Ms. Patricia RIOS
09 AVP Institutional Effectiveness .... Mr. Royal DAWSON
84 AVP Enrollment Management .... Mr. Jeffrey MEECE
37 AVP Student Financial Svcs .... Ms. Jennifer WATERS
35 Asst Dean of Student Development .... Mr. William FRIEDMAN
26 Senior Director of Public Relations .... Mr. Steve KAUFFMAN
96 Director of Purchasing .... Mr. Thomas RUSSELL
28 Exec Director Multicultural Affs .... Ms. Sheila CARTER
85 Dir International Student Affairs .... Ms. Gigi POSEJPAL
06 Director of Records/Registrar .... Mr. Marvin COHEN
39 Director of Residence Life .... Ms. Mary OAKES

Concordia University Chicago (D)

7400 Augusta Street, River Forest IL 60305-1499
County: Cook FICE Identification: 001666
Unit ID: 144351
Telephone: (708) 771-8300 Carnegie Class: Master's L
FAX Number: (708) 209-3176 Calendar System: Semester
URL: www.cuchicago.edu
Established: 1864 Annual Undergrad Tuition & Fees: $29,520
Enrollment: 5,038 Coed
Affiliation or Control: Lutheran Church - Missouri Synod
IRS Status: 501(c)3
Highest Offering: Doctorate
Program: Liberal Arts And General; Teacher Preparatory; Professional
Accreditation: NH, CACREP, MUS, TED

01 President .... Dr. Daniel GARD
05 Sr Vice President for Academics .... Dr. John ZILLMAN
102 President for Foundation .... Mr. James M. MILLER
45 Sr VP for Planning & Research .... Dr. Alan E. MEYER
10 Vice President for Finance .... Mr. Tom HALLETT
11 Vice President for Administration .... Dr. Dennis E. WITTE
84 Sr VP Enrollment/Student Svcs .... Ms. Evelyn P. BURDICK
32 Vice President Student Services .... Mr. Jeff HYNES
84 Asst Vice President for Enrollment .... Ms. Gwen E. KANELOS
26 Asst Vice Pres Marketing .... Mr. Eric MATANYI
49 Dean College Arts & Sciences .... Dr. Pamela KALBFLEISCH
53 Dean College Education .... Dr. Kevin BRANDON
50 Dean College of Business .... Dr. Claudia SANTIN
58 Dean Col Graduate Innovative Pgms .... Dr. Thomas JANDRIS
09 Director Institutional Research .... Ms. Elizabeth OWOLABI
37 Director Financial Planning .... Ms. Aida ASENCIO-PINTO
06 Registrar .... Ms. Connie PETTINGER
08 Director of Library Services .... Ms. Yana V. SERDYUK
88 Director of Degree Completion .... Dr. Carol J. REISECK
36 Director Career Services .... Mr. Gerald PINOTTI
15 Director of Human Resources .... Ms. Peg O'BRIEN
18 Director of Physical Plant .... Ms. Linda HOLOWICKI
11 Assistant VP of Administration .... Mr. Glen D. STEINER
29 Director of Alumni Relations .... Ms. Paige CRAIG
38 Director Schmieding Counseling Ctr .... Dr. Carol A. JABS
109 Director of Auxiliary Services .... Mr. Pete D. BECKER
41 Director of Athletics .... Mr. Peter D. GNAN
21 Director of Business Services .... Ms. Aileen POL
88 Director of Budget Services .... Ms. Tina NEPOMUCENO
39 Director Campus Housing .... Mr. Alexander DECAMP
42 Campus Pastor .... Rev. Jeffrey LEININGER
24 Dir of Media Production Services .... Mr. James A. KOSINSKY
19 Asst Director of Public Safety .... Mr. John STEINER
88 Director of Academic Advising .... Ms. Rosemarie GARCIA-HILLS
96 Director of Purchasing .... Ms. Denise JAMES
91 Manager of Admin Information System .... Ms. Linda C. BERRY
85 International Student Coordinator .... Mr. Peter RENN
07 Exec Director Graduate Admissison .... Ms. Deborah NESS

Coyne College (E)

330 North Green Street, Chicago IL 60607-1300
County: Cook FICE Identification: 007549
Unit ID: 144485
Telephone: (773) 577-8100 Carnegie Class: Assoc/PrivFP
FAX Number: (312) 226-3818 Calendar System: Other
URL: www.coynecollege.edu
Established: 1899 Annual Undergrad Tuition & Fees: $15,712
Enrollment: 543 Coed
Affiliation or Control: Proprietary IRS Status: Proprietary
Highest Offering: Associate Degree
Program: Occupational; 2-Year Principally Bachelor's Creditable; Technical Emphasis
Accreditation: ACCSC, MAAB

01 President .... Mr. Russell T. FREEMAN
03 Director .... Mr. John L. MUELLER

Danville Area Community College (F)

2000 E Main Street, Danville IL 61832-5199
County: Vermilion FICE Identification: 001669
Unit ID: 144564
Telephone: (217) 443-3222 Carnegie Class: Assoc/Pub-R-L
FAX Number: (217) 443-8560 Calendar System: Semester
URL: www.dacc.edu
Established: 1949 Annual Undergrad Tuition & Fees (In-District): $3,900
Enrollment: 5,446 Coed
Affiliation or Control: State/Local IRS Status: 501(c)3
Highest Offering: Associate Degree
Program: Occupational; 2-Year Principally Bachelor's Creditable
Accreditation: NH, ADNUR, CAHIIM, RAD

01 President .... Dr. Alice M. JACOBS
04 Admin Asst to the Pres/Board Sec .... Ms. Kerri L. THURMAN
05 VP Instruction & Student Svcs .... Mr. David L. KIETZMANN
15 Director Human Resources/AA Ofcr .... Ms. Jill A. CRANMORE
10 Chief Financial Officer .... Ms. Tammy L. CLARK-BETANCOURT
11 Director Administrative Services ... Mr. R. Michael CUNNINGHAM
84 Dean Student Services .... Ms. Stacy L. EHMEN
25 Director Grants and Planning .... Mr. Patrick BAYARD
102 Foundation Executive Director .... Ms. Tracy D. WAHLFELDT
26 Director Marketing/Col Relations .... Ms. Lara L. CONKLIN
09 Dir Institutional Effectiveness .... Mr. Bob MATTSON
103 Executive Director of JTP .... Mr. Brian C. HENSGEN
21 Controller .... Ms. Debra L. KNIGHT
37 Director of Financial Aid .... Ms. Janet M. INGARGIOLA
31 Dir Corporate/Community Education .... Mr. Andy PERRY
91 Director of Admin Data Systems .... Mr. Kim H. COLWELL
90 Director Computer & Network Svcs .... Mr. Mark BARNES
88 Director of Adult Education .... Ms. Laura M. WILLIAMS
50 Dean Business & Technology .... Mr. Bruce M. RAPE
49 Dean Liberal Arts and Library Servi .... Dr. Penny J. MCCONNELL
81 Dean Math & Sciences .... Ms. Kathy R. STURGEON
41 Athletic Director .... Mr. Tim M. BUNTON
88 Director Small Business Development .... Ms. Carol NICHOLS
07 Director Admissions & Registrar .... Ms. Cindy J. PECK
38 Director Student Support Services .... Ms. Shanay M. HUERTA
36 Coordinator Career Services .... Ms. Carla M. BOYD
24 Director Instructional Media .... Mr. Jonathon L. SPORS
88 Coordinator Recruitment .... Ms. Dawn S. NASSER
19 Director Security/Safety .... Mr. Greg FEGETT

DePaul University (G)

1 E Jackson Boulevard, Chicago IL 60604-2287
County: Cook FICE Identification: 001671
Unit ID: 144740
Telephone: (312) 362-8610 Carnegie Class: DRU
FAX Number: (312) 362-5322 Calendar System: Quarter
URL: www.depaul.edu
Established: 1898 Annual Undergrad Tuition & Fees: $36,280
Enrollment: 23,799 Coed
Affiliation or Control: Roman Catholic IRS Status: 501(c)3
Highest Offering: Doctorate
Program: Liberal Arts And General; Teacher Preparatory; Professional
Accreditation: NH, ANEST, BUS, BUSA, CLPSY, LAW, MUS, NURSE, PH, SPAA, SW

01 President .... Rev. Dennis H. HOLTSCHNEIDER
00 Chancellor .... Rev. John T. RICHARDSON, CM
05 Provost .... Dr. Marten DEN BOER
03 Executive Vice President .... Mr. Robert L. KOZOMAN
101 Sec of Univ/VP Teaching & Learning .... Rev. Edward R. UDOVIC
32 VP Student Affairs .... Mr. Gene ZDZIARSKI
84 Sr Vice Pres Enroll Mgmt/Marketing .... Dr. David H. KALSBEEK
30 Sr Vice Pres for Advancement .... Ms. Erin MINNE
10 Vice President for Finance .... Ms. Bonnie FRANKEL
15 Vice President Human Resources .... Ms. Stephanie SMITH
18 Vice President Facilities Operation .... Mr. Robert J. JANIS
43 Vice President & General Counsel .... Dr. Jose D. PADILLA
29 Asst VP Alumni Engagement/Outreac .... Ms. Tracy KRAHL
28 VP Inst Diversity & Equity .... Ms. Elizabeth F. ORTIZ
26 VP Public Relations & Communication .... Ms. Cynthia LAWSON
20 Assoc Provost Academic Affairs .... Ms. Caryn CHADEN
106 Assoc VP Academic Affairs Online .... Mr. GianMario BESANA
45 VP Planning & Presidential Admin .... Dr. Jay BRAATZ
13 VP Information Services .... Mr. Robert MCCORMICK
35 Assoc Vice Pres Student Development .... Dr. Peggy BURKE
22 Assoc VP Diversity Education .... Mr. Rico TYLER
09 AVP Inst Research/Market Analytics .... Dr. Liz SANDERS
84 AVP Enrollment Management/ Marketing .... Mr. Jon BOECKENSTEDT
36 AVP Div Planning & Mgmt/Career Ctr .... Ms. Jane MCGRATH
42 Assoc VP University Ministry .... Mr. Mark LABOE
108 AVP Assessment/Planning & Comm .... Ms. Ellen MEENTS-DECAIGNY
27 Assoc VP Univ Marketing Comm .... Ms. Gwyn FRIEND
27 AVP Strategic Marketing & Branding .... Ms. Verna DONOVAN
27 Director News & Information Bureau .... Ms. Carol HUGHES
88 Senior Executive University Mission .... Rev. Edward R. UDOVIC, CM
88 Treasurer .... Mr. Jeffrey BETHKE
21 Controller .... Ms. Sherri SIDLER
90 Dir Faculty Instructional Tech Svcs .... Dr. Sharon GUAN
37 Assoc Vice Pres Financial Aid .... Ms. Paula LUFF
25 Director Sponsored Programs Rsrch .... Dr. Douglas PETCHER
07 Associate Director of Admission .... Ms. Cass JOHNSON
19 Director Public Safety .... Mr. Robert WACHOWSKI
38 Director Student Counseling .... Dr. Jeffery LANFEAR
39 Director of Housing Operations .... Mr. Rick MORECI
41 Athletics Director .... Ms. Jean PONSETTO
06 Director of Registration/Records .... Ms. Patricia HUERTA
104 Director Study Abroad .... Ms. Nobi HAYASHI
88 Asst VP Grad & Adult Recruit & Adm .... Ms. Suzanne DEPEDER
07 Dean of Undergraduate Admission .... Ms. Carlene KLAAS
77 Dean Computing & Digital Media .... Dr. David MILLER
49 Int Dean Liberal Arts & Sciences .... Dr. Lucy RINEHART
50 Dean Driehaus Business College .... Dr. Ray WHITTINGTON
60 Dean Col of Communication .... Dr. Salma GHANEM
64 Int Dean School of Music .... Dr. Judy I. BUNDRA
61 Interim Dean College of Law .... Ms. Jennifer R. PEREA
57 Dean Theatre School .... Mr. John CULBERT
53 Dean School of Education .... Dr. Paul ZIONTS
51 Dean School for New Learning .... Dr. Marisa ALICEA
76 Dean Col of Science & Health .... Dr. Gerald P. KOOCHER

08 Head Librarian ... Dr. Scott WALTER
04 Administrative Asst to President ... Ms. Phyllis GREGG

*DeVry University - Home Office (A)

3005 Highland Parkway, Downers Grove IL 60515-5799
County: DuPage FICE Identification: 001672
Unit ID: 144777
Telephone: (800) 733-3879 Carnegie Class: N/A
FAX Number: (630) 571-0317
URL: www.devry.edu

00 President & Chief Executive Officer ... Mr. Daniel HAMBURGER
01 President of DeVry University ... Mr. Robert PAUL
86 SVP External Relations ... Ms. Lisa SODEIKA
26 Chief Marketing Officer ... Ms. Melissa ESBENSHADE
32 VP of Student & Career Services ... Ms. Madeleine SLUTSKY
10 SVP/CFO/Treasurer ... Mr. Timothy WIGGINS
106 President DeVry Online Services ... Mr. Eric DIRST
43 SVP/General Counsel/Corp Secretary ... Mr. Gregory DAVIS
84 VP Enrollment Management ... Ms. Erika ORRIS
88 VP Enrollment Management - Online ... Mr. Mark BUCK
05 Provost/VP Academic Affairs ... Ms. Donna LORAINE
15 SVP Human Resources ... Ms. Donna JENNINGS
88 VP Regulatory Compliance Officer ... Mr. Thomas BABEL
88 President Prof & Intl Education ... Mr. Steven RIEHS
07 Vice President Admissions ... Mr. Russell GILL
07 Vice President Admissions ... Ms. Jamie JAYNES
07 Vice President Admissions ... Mr. Matt DEARSMAN
07 Vice President Admissions ... Mr. David WOOD
12 Group Vice President ... Mr. Mark CAMERON
12 Group Vice President ... Ms. Shelly DUBOIS
12 Group Vice President ... Mr. Darryl FIELD
12 Group Vice President ... Mr. Julio TORRES

*DeVry University - Chicago Campus (B)

3300 N Campbell Avenue, Chicago IL 60618-5994
County: Cook FICE Identification: 010727
Unit ID: 144759
Telephone: (773) 929-8500 Carnegie Class: Master's L
FAX Number: (773) 348-1780 Calendar System: Semester
URL: www.devry.edu
Established: 1931 Annual Undergrad Tuition & Fees: $17,132
Enrollment: 1,294 Coed
Affiliation or Control: Proprietary IRS Status: Proprietary
Highest Offering: Master's
Program: Occupational; Professional; Business Emphasis
Accreditation: NH, CAHIIM, ENGT

02 Campus President ... Ms. Candace GOODWIN
06 Registrar ... Ms. Kory RIDDLE
07 Director of Admissions ... Ms. Stacey KRAHE
05 Group DAA ... Ms. Deborah ZELECHOWSKI
36 Director of Career Services ... Ms. Carrie RUBIN
37 Dean Student Central ... Ms. Inesha KELLY
08 Director Library Services ... Mr. Jason ROSSI

† Regional accreditation is carried under the parent institution in Downers Grove, IL.

Dominican University (C)

7900 W Division Street, River Forest IL 60305-1099
County: Cook FICE Identification: 001750
Unit ID: 148496
Telephone: (708) 366-2490 Carnegie Class: Master's L
FAX Number: (708) 524-5990 Calendar System: Semester
URL: www.dom.edu
Established: 1901 Annual Undergrad Tuition & Fees: $30,670
Enrollment: 3,498 Coed
Affiliation or Control: Roman Catholic IRS Status: 501(c)3
Highest Offering: Doctorate
Program: Liberal Arts And General; Teacher Preparatory; Professional
Accreditation: NH, ACBSP, BUS, DIETC, DIETD, LIB, SW, TED

01 President ... Dr. Donna M. CARROLL
05 Provost ... Dr. Jeffrey BREESE
20 Associate Provost ... Dr. David H. KRAUSE
10 Sr VP for Finance & Administration ... Dr. Amy MCCORMACK
42 Vice Pres for Mission & Ministry ... Dr. Claire NOONAN
30 Vice Pres University Advancement ... Ms. Grace J. CICHOMSKA
84 Interim VP Enrollment Management ... Ms. Pam JOHNSON
13 VP Info Tech/Chief Information Ofcr ... Ms. Jill ALBIN-HILL
07 AVP Enroll Mgt/Dir Undergrad Admiss ... Mr. Glenn HAMILTON
26 Dir Marketing & Web Services ... Ms. Betsy BUTTERWORTH
32 Dean of Students ... Ms. Trudi GOGGIN
50 Dean Brennan School of Business ... Dr. Roberto CURCI
62 Dean Grad School Library Science ... Ms. Kate MAREK
53 Dean School of Education ... Dr. Victoria CHOU
70 Dean Graduate School Social Work ... Dr. Charles STOOPS
49 Dean College of Arts & Science ... Dr. Jeffrey CARLSON
88 Assistant Provost ... Mr. Matthew J. HLINAK
08 University Librarian ... Ms. Felice E. MACIEJEWSKI
06 Registrar ... Mr. Michael Patrick MILLER
36 Director Career Development ... Ms. Keli WOJCIECHOWSKI
29 Dir Alumnae/i Relations ... Ms. Alysha COMSTOCK
88 Promoter of Mission Integration ... Sr. Mary Ann MEUNINGHOFF, OP
09 Dir Institutional Rsch & Assessment ... Ms. Elizabeth SILK
15 Director Human Resources ... Ms. Roberta MCMAHON
18 Director/Physical Plant ... Mr. Daniel BULOW
07 Director Transfer/Adult Admission ... Mr. Michael MORSOVILLO
37 Director Financial Aid ... Ms. Victoria LAMICK
23 Director Wellness Center ... Ms. Elizabeth RITZMAN
41 Director Athletics ... Mr. Erick BAUMANN
104 Director International Studies ... Dr. Sue PONREMY

East-West University (D)

816 S Michigan Avenue, Chicago IL 60605-2185
County: Cook FICE Identification: 021686
Unit ID: 144883
Telephone: (312) 939-0111 Carnegie Class: Bac/A&S
FAX Number: (312) 939-0083 Calendar System: Quarter
URL: www.eastwest.edu
Established: 1980 Annual Undergrad Tuition & Fees: $19,545
Enrollment: 555 Coed
Affiliation or Control: Independent Non-Profit IRS Status: 501(c)3
Highest Offering: Baccalaureate
Program: Liberal Arts And General
Accreditation: #NH

01 Chancellor ... Dr. M. Wasiullah KHAN
05 Provost ... Dr. Madhu JAIN
20 Associate Provost ... Dr. Ekkehard T. WILKE
88 Assistant Provost for Acad Quality ... Dr. Lawrence J. GORMAN
30 Assoc Dean Development/Univ Rels ... Mr. Zafar A. MALIK
32 Director Counseling/Student Affairs ... Ms. Sonja M. SIMS
07 Director of Admissions ... Mr. Raul ANDRADE
37 Director of Financial Aid ... Mr. Cesar CAMPOS
06 Registrar ... Ms. Misha K. STARKS
04 Assistant to the Chancellor ... Ms. Carolyn J. FOWLKES
19 Director of Security ... Mr. Tasleem RAJA
10 Director of Business ... Dr. Madhu JAIN
44 Dir Devel/Univ Rels/Publications ... Ms. Barbara ABRAJANO
26 Manager Public Relations ... Mr. Joel D. INWOOD
18 Facilities Manager ... Mr. Tasleem RAJA
38 Academic Counselor ... Ms. Jennifer TAYLOR
85 International Student Advisor ... Mr. Rashed JAHANGIR

Eastern Illinois University (E)

600 Lincoln Avenue, Charleston IL 61920-3099
County: Coles FICE Identification: 001674
Unit ID: 144892
Telephone: (217) 581-5000 Carnegie Class: Master's L
FAX Number: (217) 581-2722 Calendar System: Semester
URL: www.eiu.edu
Established: 1895 Annual Undergrad Tuition & Fees (In-State): $11,312
Enrollment: 8,913 Coed
Affiliation or Control: State IRS Status: 501(c)3
Highest Offering: Beyond Master's But Less Than Doctorate
Program: Liberal Arts And General; Teacher Preparatory; Professional
Accreditation: NH, AAFCS, ART, BUS, BUSA, CAATE, CACREP, DIETD, DIETI, JOUR, MUS, NAIT, NRPA, NURSE, SP, TED, THEA

01 President ... Dr. David M. GLASSMAN
05 Provost/Vice Pres Academic Affairs ... Dr. Blair M. LORD
10 Int Vice Pres Bus Affairs/Treasurer ... Mr. Paul A. MCCANN
32 Vice President Student Affairs ... Dr. Daniel P. NADLER
30 Vice Pres University Advancement ... Mr. Robert K. MARTIN
20 Associate VP Academic Affairs ... Mr. Jeffrey F. CROSS
35 Special Asst to VP Student Affairs ... Ms. Jennifer L. SIPES
13 Asst VP for Information Tech Svcs ... Ms. Kathy S. REED
26 Asst VP Integ Marketing/Communic ... Vacant
08 Dean of Library Services ... Dr. Allen K. LANHAM
84 Asst VPAA/Enrollment Management ... Vacant
92 Dean Honors College ... Dr. Richard ENGLAND
15 Director Human Resources ... Dr. Richard K. ENYARD
43 General Counsel ... Mr. Robert L. MILLER
22 Director Civil Rights ... Vacant
45 Dir Planning/Budgeting/Research ... Mr. Michael S. MAURER
07 Director of Admissions ... Mr. Chris DEARTH
37 Interim Director of Financial Aid ... Ms. Carol WALDMANN
06 Registrar ... Ms. Amy J. LYNCH
29 Director Alumni Svc/Community Rels ... Mr. Steven W. RICH
18 Int Dir Facilities/Planning Mgmt ... Mr. Timothy P. ZIMMER
96 Dir Procur/Disburs/Contract Svc ... Ms. Kay E. MCELWEE
38 Director of Counseling Center ... Vacant
25 Director of Research & Grants ... Dr. Robert W. CHESNUT
41 Director of Athletics ... Mr. Thomas R. MICHAEL
93 Director of Minority Affairs ... Ms. Mona DAVENPORT
39 Director of Housing/Dining Service ... Mr. Mark A. HUDSON
21 Interim Director Business Services ... Ms. Linda C. HOLLOWAY
36 Director of Career Services ... Ms. Linda L. MOORE
51 Dean Continuing Education ... Dr. Regis M. GILMAN
58 Int Dean Graduate School ... Dr. Ryan C. HENDRICKSON
81 Dean College Sciences ... Dr. W. Harold ORNES
50 Dean Lumpkin Col Bus/Appl Sci ... Dr. Mahyar IZADI
79 Int Dean College Arts/Humanities ... Mr. Glenn J. HILD
53 Dean College Education ... Dr. Diane H. JACKMAN

Elgin Community College (F)

1700 Spartan Drive, Elgin IL 60123-7193
County: Kane FICE Identification: 001675
Unit ID: 144944
Telephone: (847) 697-1000 Carnegie Class: Assoc/Pub-S-MC
FAX Number: (847) 214-7995 Calendar System: Semester
URL: www.elgin.edu
Established: 1949 Annual Undergrad Tuition & Fees (In-District): $3,570
Enrollment: 10,937 Coed
Affiliation or Control: Local IRS Status: 501(c)3
Highest Offering: Associate Degree
Program: Occupational; 2-Year Principally Bachelor's Creditable
Accreditation: NH, ADNUR, COMTA, CSHSE, DA, HT, MLTAD, PTAA, RAD, RADMAG, SURGT

01 President ... Dr. David SAM
10 Vice Pres Business/Finance ... Ms. Sharon KONNY
05 VP Teaching/Learning/Stdnt Dev ... Ms. Rose DIGERLANDO
20 Asst VP Teach/Lrng/Stdnt Dev ... Ms. Marcy THOMPSON
20 Dean Academic Dev/Learning Resource ... Dr. Mi HU
88 Dean Sustain/Safety & Career Tech ... Dr. Ilio LOTT
83 Dean Comm/Behavioral Sciences ... Dr. Ruixuan MAO
57 Dean Liberal/Visual/Performing Arts ... Ms. Mary HATCH
81 Dean Math/Science & Engineer ... Dr. James MCGEE
32 Dean of Student Services ... Dr. Gregory ROBINSON
88 Dean Adult Basic Education ... Ms. Peggy HEINRICH
76 Dean Health Professions ... Ms. Wendy MILLER
84 Assoc Dean Enrollment Management ... Dr. Mary PERKINS
106 Assoc Dean Inst Improve/Dist Lrng ... Mr. Timothy MOORE
88 Asc Dean TRIO/Reten/Stdnt Outreach ... Dr. L. Bruce AUSTIN
18 Managing Director Facilities ... Mr. Cal BYRD
15 Chief Human Resources Officer ... Vacant
13 Chief Information Officer ... Mr. Ned COONEN
26 Exec Dir Communications ... Mr. Jeff JULIAN
30 Exec Dir Inst Advance/ECC Found ... Ms. Katherine SAWYER
88 Managing Dir Inst Comp/Curr ... Ms. Annamarie SCHOPEN
45 Executive Dir Planning/Inst Effect ... Dr. Philip GARBER
09 Director Institutional Research ... Mr. David RUDDEN
37 Director Financial Aid/Scholarships ... Ms. Amy PERRIN
19 Chief of Police ... Mr. Emad EASSA
21 Controller ... Ms. Heather SCHOLL
84 Managing Dir Enrollment Svcs ... Dr. Jennifer MCCLURE
90 Director Academic Computing ... Ms. Karin STACY
22 Paralegal/EEO/AA Title IX/FOIA Ofcr ... Ms. Marilyn PRENTICE
07 Director of Admissions/Recruitment ... Dr. Trevell EDDINS
41 Director Athletics & Wellness ... Mr. Kent PAYNE
109 Exec Dir Aux Enterprises & Cont Ed ... Mr. Frank HERNANDEZ
96 Director Business Services ... Ms. Melissa TAIT
36 Acad Advising/Transfer/Career Svcs ... Ms. Peggy GUNDRUM
26 Director of Marketing ... Ms. Heidi HEALY
35 Director Orientation/Student Life ... Ms. Amybeth MAURER
88 Dir Small Business Devel Center ... Ms. Sybil EGE
14 Sr Director Technology Services ... Mr. Phil HOWARD
86 Dir Cmty Engagemnt/Legislative Affs ... Ms. Paula AMENTA
101 Secretary to Board of Trustees ... Mr. John DUFFY
04 Sr Exec Asst to the President ... Ms. Diane KERRUISH

Elmhurst College (G)

190 Prospect, Elmhurst IL 60126-3296
County: DuPage FICE Identification: 001676
Unit ID: 144962
Telephone: (630) 279-4100 Carnegie Class: Master's M
FAX Number: (630) 617-3282 Calendar System: 4/1/4
URL: www.elmhurst.edu
Established: 1871 Annual Undergrad Tuition & Fees: $34,200
Enrollment: 3,257 Coed
Affiliation or Control: United Church Of Christ IRS Status: 501(c)3
Highest Offering: Master's
Program: Liberal Arts And General; Teacher Preparatory; Professional
Accreditation: NH, NURSE, @SP

01 Interim President ... Dr. Larry BRASKAMP
10 VP of Finance & Administration ... Ms. Denise JONES
05 Sr VP Acad Affs/Dean of Faculty ... Dr. Alzada TIPTON
13 VP and Chief Information Officer ... Dr. James KULICH
26 VP for Enrollment & Communications ... Mr. James W. WINTERS
29 VP for Development/Alumni Relations ... Mr. Joseph R. EMMICK
32 Dean of Students ... Dr. Eileen G. SULLIVAN
107 Dean School for Professional Stds ... Dr. Timothy RICORDATI
20 Associate Dean of Faculty ... Dr. Heather HALL
20 Associate Dean of Faculty ... Dr. Theodore LERUD
88 Exec Dir Center for Pro Excellence ... Dr. Lawrence B. CARROLL
18 Exec Director Facilities Management ... Mr. Bruce J. MATHER
42 Chaplain ... Rev. H. Scott MATHENEY
06 Registrar ... Mr. S. Dean ELLENS
08 Director of the Library ... Ms. Susan S. STEFFEN
36 Director of Career Education ... Ms. Peggy KILLIAN
21 Controller ... Mr. James STUART
38 Director of Counseling Services ... Dr. Amy SWARR
28 Director of Intercultural Education ... Vacant
14 Director of Computer Services ... Vacant
88 Director Development Services ... Ms. Emily TELFORD
29 Director of Alumni Engagement ... Ms. Samantha KILEY
88 Managing Dir of Public Affairs ... Ms. Desiree CHEN
15 Director of Human Resources ... Ms. Lynita GEBHARDT
19 Exec Director of Campus Security ... Mr. Jeff KEDROWSKI
37 Director of Financial Aid ... Ms. Ruth PUSICH
07 Executive Director of Admission ... Ms. Stephanie LEVENSON
07 Managing Dir Adult/Grad Admission ... Mr. Tim PANFIL
39 Director of Residence Life ... Ms. Christine J. SMITH
41 Director Intercollegiate Athletics ... Mr. Paul KROHN

Erikson Institute (H)

451 N. Lasalle Street, Chicago IL 60654
County: Cook FICE Identification: 035103
Unit ID: 409254
Telephone: (312) 755-2250 Carnegie Class: Spec/Other
FAX Number: (312) 755-0928 Calendar System: Semester
URL: www.erikson.edu
Established: 1966 Annual Graduate Tuition & Fees: $35,065
Enrollment: 260 Coed
Affiliation or Control: Independent Non-Profit IRS Status: 501(c)3

Highest Offering: Master's; No Undergraduates
Program: Professional
Accreditation: NH, @SW

01 President ..... Geoffrey A. NAGLE
05 Sr VP Academic Affs/Dean of Faculty ..... Aisha RAY
10 Vice President Finance/Operations ..... Susan WALLACE
30 Vice Pres Institutional Advancement ..... Randy L. HOLGATE
84 Dean of Enrollment Management ..... Michel FRENDIAN
32 Dean of Students ..... Colette DAVISON
13 Chief Information Officer ..... Jonathan FRANK
26 Int Director of Communications ..... Susan FARAONE
44 Asst Dir Data Systems/Donor Svcs ..... Madeleine HOLDSWORTH

Eureka College (A)

300 E College Avenue, Eureka IL 61530-1500
County: Woodford
FICE Identification: 001678
Unit ID: 144971
Telephone: (309) 467-3721
Carnegie Class: Bac/Diverse
FAX Number: (309) 467-6386
Calendar System: Semester
URL: www.eureka.edu
Established: 1855
Annual Undergrad Tuition & Fees: $24,745
Enrollment: 654
Coed
Affiliation or Control: Christian Church (Disciples Of Christ)
IRS Status: 501(c)3
Highest Offering: Baccalaureate
Program: Liberal Arts And General; Teacher Preparatory
Accreditation: NH

01 President ..... Dr. J. David ARNOLD
04 Administrative Asst to President ..... Mrs. Jyl ZUBIATE
05 Provost & Dean of the College ..... Dr. Daniel BLANKENSHIP
10 VP Fin/Fac/Chief Financial Officer ..... Mr. Marc PASTERIS
32 Assoc Provost/Dean of Students ..... Dr. Jeffrey COATS
30 Vice Pres of Institutional Advance ..... Mr. Michael MURTAGH
06 Registrar ..... Mr. Scott WIGNALL
08 Library Director ..... Mr. Tony GLASS
18 Director of Physical Plant ..... Mr. Daryle EGE
42 Chaplain ..... Rev. Bruce M. FOWLKES
13 Director of Computer Services ..... Dr. Kanaka VIJITHA-KUMARA
37 Director of Financial Aid ..... Mrs. Erin BLINE
41 Athletic Director ..... Mr. Steve THOMPSON
29 Director Alumni Relations ..... Mrs. Shellie SCHWANKE
15 Director Personnel Services ..... Mrs. Lori GUTH
39 Director Student Housing ..... Ms. Lisa FISCHER
28 Chief Diversity Officer ..... Dr. Jamel S. BELL

Fox College (B)

6640 South Cicero Avenue, Bedford Park IL 60638
County: Cook
FICE Identification: 025228
Unit ID: 145239
Telephone: (708) 444-4500
Carnegie Class: Assoc/PrivFP
FAX Number: (708) 802-6585
Calendar System: Semester
URL: www.foxcollege.edu
Established: 1932
Annual Undergrad Tuition & Fees: $17,570
Enrollment: 335
Coed
Affiliation or Control: Proprietary
IRS Status: Proprietary
Highest Offering: Associate Degree
Program: Occupational; 2-Year Principally Bachelor's Creditable; Business Emphasis
Accreditation: NH, MAAB, PTAA

01 President ..... Mr. Carey CRANSTON
11 Operations Administrator ..... Ms. Nicole BROWN

Garrett-Evangelical Theological Seminary (C)

2121 Sheridan Road, Evanston IL 60201-3298
County: Cook
FICE Identification: 001682
Unit ID: 145275
Telephone: (847) 866-3900
Carnegie Class: Spec/Faith
FAX Number: (847) 866-3884
Calendar System: Semester
URL: www.garrett.edu
Established: 1853
Annual Graduate Tuition & Fees: $19,040
Enrollment: 365
Coed
Affiliation or Control: United Methodist
IRS Status: 501(c)3
Highest Offering: Doctorate; No Undergraduates
Program: Professional; Religious Emphasis
Accreditation: NH, THEOL

01 President ..... Dr. Lallene J. RECTOR
11 VP for Administration ..... Dr. James A. NOSEWORTHY
05 Acad Dean/Vice Pres Acad Affairs ..... Dr. Luis J. RIVERA
30 Vice President for Development ..... Dr. David L. HEETLAND
10 Vice President Business Affairs/CFO ..... Mr. Dale MCCLAIN
32 Dean of Students ..... Rev. Cynthia A. WILSON
84 Associate VP for Enrollment Mgmt ..... Rev. Becky J. EBERHART
04 Dir of the President's Office ..... Ms. Erin B. MOORE
21 Controller ..... Mr. Bob SUTTON
06 Registrar/Dir of Academic Studies ..... Rev. Vince MCGLOTHIN-ELLER
08 Director of United Library ..... Dr. Jaeyeon L. CHUNG
18 Director of Buildings & Grounds ..... Ms. Cheryl LARSEN
39 Director of Housing & Food Service ..... Ms. Barbara B. ADAMS
29 Dir Annual Gvg/Alum Rel/ Hospitality ..... Mrs. April MCGLOTHIN-ELLER
88 Director of Stewardship ..... Ms. Elizabeth P. CAMPBELL
37 Director of Financial Aid ..... Mr. Jason GILL
26 Manager of Communications & Events ..... Mr. Shane NICHOLS

Governors State University (D)

1 University Parkway, University Park IL 60484-0975
County: Will
FICE Identification: 009145
Unit ID: 145336
Telephone: (708) 534-5000
Carnegie Class: Master's L
FAX Number: (708) 534-4107
Calendar System: Semester
URL: www.govst.edu
Established: 1969
Annual Undergrad Tuition & Fees (In-State): $10,246
Enrollment: 5,776
Coed
Affiliation or Control: State
IRS Status: 501(c)3
Highest Offering: Doctorate
Program: Liberal Arts And General; Teacher Preparatory; Professional
Accreditation: NH, ACBSP, CACREP, HSA, NUR, OT, PTA, SP, SPAA, SW, TED

01 President ..... Dr. Elaine P. MAIMON
03 Executive VP & Chief of Staff/Treas ..... Mr. David MEADOWS
05 Provost/VP Academic Affairs ..... Dr. Deborah BORDELON
10 Vice Pres Admininstration & Finance ..... Ms. Karen KISSEL
30 VP Advancement/CEO Foundation ..... Mr. William DAVIS
84 VP Enrollment Mgmt & Marketing ..... Mr. Charles NOLLEY
43 Legal Counsel ..... Ms. Alexis KENNEDY
22 Affirmative Action/EO ..... Ms. Alexis KENNEDY
45 Director Budget Planning/Inst Rsrch ..... Dr. Jeffrey SLOVAK
09 Assoc Dir of Institutional Research ..... Mr. Marco KRCATOVICH, II
29 Director of Alumni Assoc ..... Ms. Cheri GAREY
26 Asst VP of Marketing/Communication ..... Ms. Keisha DYSON
50 Dean Col Business/Public Admin ..... Dr. Ellen FOSTER CURTIS
49 Dean College Arts Sciences ..... Dr. Reinhold HILL
76 Dean Col Health Professions ..... Dr. Elizabeth CADA
53 Dean College Education ..... Dr. Andrea EVANS
32 Dean Student Affairs & Services ..... Dr. Aurelio VALENTE
08 Dean Library Svc/Academic Computing ..... Vacant
06 Registrar ..... Mr. Christopher HUANG
37 Director Financial Aid ..... Mr. John PERRY
20 Associate Provost/AVP Academic Affs ..... Dr. Colleen SEXTON
21 Director Business Operations ..... Ms. Karen KISSEL
13 Exec Director Information Tech Svcs ..... Mr. Peter J. MIZERA
15 Director Human Resources ..... Ms. Joyce COLEMAN
18 Director Physical Plant ..... Mr. Sajid MAIN
19 Int Director Dept Public Safety ..... Mr. James MCGEE
38 Dir Stdnt Develop/Counseling Center ..... Ms. Kelly MCCARTHY
36 Director of Career Services ..... Ms. Darcie R. CAMPOS
96 Dir of Procurement/Auxillary Svcs ..... Ms. Tracy SULLIVAN
04 Executive Asst to President ..... Ms. Penny PERDUE
39 Director Student Housing ..... Dr. Elizabeth JOSEPH
41 Athletic Director ..... Mr. Anthony BATES
86 Director Government Relations ..... Ms. Maureen KELLY

Greenville College (E)

315 E College, Greenville IL 62246
County: Bond
FICE Identification: 001684
Unit ID: 145372
Telephone: (618) 664-2800
Carnegie Class: Bac/Diverse
FAX Number: (618) 664-6841
Calendar System: 4/1/4
URL: www.greenville.edu
Established: 1892
Annual Undergrad Tuition & Fees: $33,376
Enrollment: 1,307
Coed
Affiliation or Control: Free Methodist
IRS Status: 501(c)3
Highest Offering: Master's
Program: Liberal Arts And General; Teacher Preparatory; Professional
Accreditation: NH, TEAC

01 President ..... Dr. Ivan FILBY
101 Executive Assistant to the Board ..... Mrs. Kristin KOEHNEMANN
05 Provost & Chief Operating Officer ..... Dr. Edwin ESTEVEZ
30 Vice Pres for Advancement ..... Mr. Scott GIFFEN
10 Vice President for Finance ..... Mrs. Dana FUNDERBURK
29 Sr Advis to Pres for Alumni Rels ..... Dr. Norman D. HALL
84 Vice Pres for Enrollment ..... Mr. Michael RITTER
88 Dean of Adult Studies ..... Dr. Dave HOLDEN
08 Director of Library ..... Ms. Jane L. HOPKINS
06 Registrar ..... Mrs. Michelle SUSSENBACH
37 Director of Financial Aid ..... Mrs. Marilae LATHAM
30 Director of Advancement ..... Mrs. Linda MYETTE
42 Dean Chapel & Dir Spiritual Form ..... Mrs. Lori GAFFNER
18 Director of Facilities ..... Mr. Mark OWENS
26 Director of Marketing ..... Vacant
49 Dean School Arts & Sciences ..... Dr. Brian HARTLEY
53 Dean School of Education ..... Dr. Mark LAMB
41 Athletic Director ..... Mr. Kent KROBER
28 Dean of Diversity ..... Dr. Eugene DUNKLEY
50 Dean of School of Business ..... Dr. Suzanne DAVIS

Harper College (F)

1200 W Algonquin Road, Palatine IL 60067-7398
County: Cook
FICE Identification: 003961
Unit ID: 149842
Telephone: (847) 925-6000
Carnegie Class: Assoc/Pub-S-SC
FAX Number: (847) 925-6034
Calendar System: Semester
URL: www.harpercollege.edu
Established: 1965
Annual Undergrad Tuition & Fees (In-District): $3,228
Enrollment: 15,830
Coed
Affiliation or Control: State/Local
IRS Status: 501(c)3
Highest Offering: Associate Degree
Program: Occupational; 2-Year Principally Bachelor's Creditable
Accreditation: NH, ACBSP, ADNUR, CAHIIM, CEA, DH, DIETT, DMS, MAC, MUS, RAD

01 President ..... Dr. Kenneth L. ENDER
100 Chief of Staff/VP Plng/Inst Effect ..... Dr. Sheila QUIRK-BAILEY
101 Sr Exec Pres/Brd Lia/VP Wkfrc Strat ..... Dr. Maria COONS
10 Exec VP Finance & Admin Services ..... Dr. Ron ALLY
05 Provost ..... Dr. Judith MARWICK
30 Chief Advancement Officer ..... Ms. Laura BROWN
26 Chief Communications Officer ..... Mr. Phil BURDICK
28 Assoc Provost/Spc Asst/Div & Inclus ..... Ms. Michele ROBINSON
20 Assoc Provost/Interdis Student Succ ..... Mr. Brian KNETL
15 Chief Human Resources Officer ..... Mr. Roger SPAYER
13 Chief Information Officer ..... Mr. Patrick BAUER
21 Controller ..... Mr. Bret BONNSTETTER
18 Exec Dir of Facilities Management ..... Mr. Thomas CRYLEN
84 Asst Provost/Dean Enrollment Svcs ..... Ms. Maria MOTEN
35 Asst Provost Student Development ..... Ms. Sheryl OTTO
75 Dean Career & Technical Programs ..... Dr. Mary Beth OTTINGER
76 Dean Health Careers ..... Ms. Kimberly CHAVIS
88 Dean Acad Enrichment/Engagement ..... Dr. Kenya AYERS
08 Dean Resources for Learning ..... Ms. Njambi KAMOCHE
32 Int Dean Sutdent Affs/Stdnt Develop ..... Dr. Travaris HARRIS
51 Dean Cont Education & Bus Outreach ..... Dr. Mark MROZINSKI
50 Dean Business & Social Science ..... Ms. Kathryn ROGALSKI
81 Dean Mathematics & Sciences ..... Ms. Kathy BRUCE
88 Assoc Dean Ctr Adjunct Fac Engag ..... Dr. Michael BATES
103 Int Dean Workforce & Economic Devel ..... Dr. Rebecca LAKE
49 Dean Liberal Arts ..... Dr. Jennifer BERNE
102 Asc Exec Dir Found/Dir Major Gifts ..... Ms. Heather ZOLDAK
88 Assoc Dean Interdisc Stdnt Success ..... Ms. Darice TROUT
72 Asst Dean Ctr for Adjunct Fac Engag ..... Dr. Jack HENDERSON
35 Assoc Dean Student Affairs ..... Dr. Keith O'NEILL
23 Director Health Services ..... Dr. Bridget CAHILL
88 Dir New Student Programs/Retention ..... Ms. Vicki ATKINSON
14 Director IT Enterprise Systems ..... Dr. Mike BABB
14 Director IT Technical Services ..... Mr. James BATSON
26 Director Marketing Services ..... Mr. Mike BARZACCHINI
36 Director Job Placement Resource Ctr ..... Ms. Kathleen CANFIELD
91 Director IT Client Services ..... Ms. Sue CONTARINO
09 Director Institutional Research ..... Dr. Katherine COY
106 Director Ctr for Innov Instruction ..... Mr. Matthew ENSENBERGER
88 Director Adult Educational Dev ..... Ms. Andrea FIEBIG
88 Acting Dir One Million Degrees Pgm ..... Ms. Kristin HOFFHINES
88 Dir One Stop Center/Student Svcs ..... Ms. Paula HANLEY
88 Director Physical Plant ..... Mr. Darryl KNIGHT
37 Dir Student Financial Assistance ..... Ms. Laura MCGEE
66 Director Nursing ..... Ms. Julie D'AGOSTINO
07 Dir Student Recruitment & Outreach ..... Mr. Robert PARZY
38 Dir Academic Advising & Counseling ..... Dr. Eric ROSENTHAL
108 Dir Inst Effect/Outcomes Assess ..... Ms. Darlene SCHLENBECKER
41 Director of Athletics & Fitness ..... Mr. Doug SPIWAK
19 Chief of Police ..... Mr. Paul LEBRECK
88 Campus Architect ..... Mr. Steve PETERSEN

Harrington College of Design (G)

200 W Madison, 2nd Floor, Chicago IL 60606-3433
County: Cook
FICE Identification: 020552
Unit ID: 145460
Telephone: (312) 939-4975
Carnegie Class: Spec/Arts
FAX Number: (312) 939-8005
Calendar System: Semester
URL: www.harrington.edu
Established: 1931
Annual Undergrad Tuition & Fees: N/A
Enrollment: 516
Coed
Affiliation or Control: Proprietary
IRS Status: Proprietary
Highest Offering: Master's
Program: Professional; Fine Arts Emphasis
Accreditation: NH, CIDA

01 President ..... Mr. Max S. SHANGLE
05 Director of Academic Affairs ..... Ms. Gretchen FRICKX
07 Director of Admissions ..... Ms. Jessie MCEWEN
10 Regional Controller ..... Ms. Gladys CHINCHILLA
13 Manager of IT & Facilities ..... Mr. Hector DORINO
36 Director Career Services ..... Ms. Camille HARRIS
08 Head Librarian ..... Ms. Leigh GATES
21 Campus Business Operations Manager ..... Mr. Ryan FROEHLE
06 Registrar ..... Mr. Sam DELAROSA
32 Director Student Services ..... Mr. Sam DELAROSA

† School is in teach-out plan and plans to close in May, 2018. All of Harrington's classes have been transferred to Columbia College Chicago.

Heartland Community College (H)

1500 W Raab Road, Normal IL 61761-9446
County: McLean
FICE Identification: 030838
Unit ID: 384342
Telephone: (309) 268-8000
Carnegie Class: Assoc/Pub-R-L
FAX Number: (309) 268-7999
Calendar System: Semester
URL: www.heartland.edu
Established: 1990
Annual Undergrad Tuition & Fees (In-District): $4,260
Enrollment: 5,064
Coed
Affiliation or Control: State/Local
IRS Status: 501(c)3
Highest Offering: Associate Degree
Program: Occupational; 2-Year Principally Bachelor's Creditable
Accreditation: NH, ADNUR, @PTAA, RAD

01 President ..... Mr. Robert D. WIDMER
05 Vice Pres Learning/Student Success ..... Dr. Rick PEARCE
10 Vice President Business Services ..... Mr. Douglas MINTER
30 Vice Pres Cont Educ/Advancement ..... Ms. Kelli HILL
20 Assoc VP for Academic Affairs ..... Dr. Sarah DIEL-HUNT
88 Dean Student Success ..... Vacant
84 Dean Enrollment Services ..... Mr. Padriac SHINVILLE

18 Executive Director of Facilities .... Mr. James HUBBARD
11 Director of Administrative Services ....Ms. Valerie CRAWFORD
13 Chief Information Officer ....Mr. Scott BROSS
21 Controller ....Ms. Sue GILPIN
37 Director of Financial Aid ....Mr. Todd BURNS
15 Exec Director Human Resources ....Mrs. Barb LEATHERS
86 Exec Dir Governmental Relations ....Ms. Janet HILL GETZ
09 Exec Director Inst Effectiveness ....Vacant
41 Director of Athletics ....Mr. Nate METZGER
29 Director Alumni Relations ....Ms. Colleen REYNOLDS
36 Director Student Success ....Ms. Kimberly KELLEY
06 Director of Records ....Ms. Cindy ALFANO
26 Director of Marketing ....Ms. Amy HUMPHREYS
32 Director of Student Engagement ....Mr. Marvin RASCH
38 Dir Advisement/Career Services ....Ms. Lindsay EICKHORST

Hebrew Theological College (A)

7135 N Carpenter Road, Skokie IL 60077-3263
County: Cook FICE Identification: 001685
Unit ID: 145497
Telephone: (847) 982-2500 Carnegie Class: Spec/Faith
FAX Number: (847) 674-6381 Calendar System: Semester
URL: www.htc.edu
Established: 1922 Annual Undergrad Tuition & Fees: $19,190
Enrollment: 465 Coordinate
Affiliation or Control: Independent Non-Profit IRS Status: 501(c)3
Highest Offering: Master's
Program: Liberal Arts And General; Teacher Preparatory; Professional; Religious Emphasis
Accreditation: NH

01 Interim Chancellor ....Rabbi Shmuel SCHUMAN
100 Chief of Staff ....Ms. Cheryl KARP
05 Rosh Hayeshiva-Chief Academic ....Rabbi Avraham FRIEDMAN
11 Vice President for Administration ....Rabbi Sender KUTNER
20 Dean AHS & LAS Men's Division ....Rabbi Hertzel YITZCHAK
33 Mashgiach Ruchani-Dean ....Rabbi Zvi ZIMMERMAN
34 Menahel Ruchani-Dean ....Rabbi Binyamin OLSTEIN
34 Assistant Dean Blitstein Institute ....Ms. Rita LIPSHITZ
06 Registrar ....Rabbi Shmuel SCHUMAN
07 Director of Admissions ....Rabbi Joshua ZISOOK
30 Director of Development ....Rabbi Gershon SEIF
44 Development Coordinator ....Rabbi Yaakov FRIEDMAN
08 Librarian ....Ms. Eti BERLAND

† Separate campuses for male and female students. Part of the Touro College and University System.

Highland Community College (B)

2998 W Pearl City Road, Freeport IL 61032-9341
County: Stephenson FICE Identification: 001681
Unit ID: 145521
Telephone: (815) 235-6121 Carnegie Class: Assoc/Pub-R-M
FAX Number: (815) 235-6130 Calendar System: Semester
URL: www.highland.edu
Established: 1962 Annual Undergrad Tuition & Fees (In-District): $4,260
Enrollment: 1,456 Coed
Affiliation or Control: State/Local IRS Status: 501(c)3
Highest Offering: Associate Degree
Program: Occupational; 2-Year Principally Bachelor's Creditable
Accreditation: NH, MAC

01 President ....Mr. Tim HOOD
03 Executive Vice President ....Ms. Chris KUBERSKI
10 Vice Pres Administrative Services ....Ms. Jill M. JANSSEN
32 Vice Pres Student Dev & Support Svc ...Ms. Elizabeth L. GERBER
15 Associate VP Human Resources ....Ms. Rose A. FERGUSON
50 Dean Business & Technology ....Mr. Scott R. ANDERSON
81 Dean Health/Nat Science & Math ....Ms. Donna KAUKE
51 Director Adult Education ....Mr. Mark JANSEN
41 Director Athletics ....Mr. Peter E. NORMAN
84 Director Enrollment/Records ....Mr. Jeremy BRADT
37 Director Financial Aid ....Ms. Kathy BANGASSER
09 Director Institutional Research ....Dr. Michelle THRUMAN
88 Director Learning & Transitional Ed ....Ms. Carolyn PETSCHE
08 Director Library Services ....Vacant
31 Director Marketing & Cmty Relations ....Mr. Pete WILLGING
18 Director Facilities & Safety ....Mr. Kurt SIMPSON
88 Director Retired & Senior Vol Pgm ....Ms. Cindi MIELKE
88 Director Title IV Student Support ....Mr. Anthony SAGO
21 Manager Accounting ....Ms. Mary J. LLOYD
40 Manager Bookstore ....Ms. Madonna KEENEY
101 Exec Asst to President/Board Sec ....Ms. Terri A. GRIMES
96 Purchasing & Insurance Specialist ....Ms. Teresa WILLIAMS
102 Executive Director Foundation ....Mr. James M. BERBERET
07 Director of Enrollment & Records ....Mr. Jeremy BRADT
13 Director ITS ....Mr. Nathan HENSAL

Illinois Central College (C)

1 College Drive, East Peoria IL 61635-0001
County: Tazewell FICE Identification: 006753
Unit ID: 145682
Telephone: (309) 694-5422 Carnegie Class: Assoc/Pub-R-L
FAX Number: (309) 694-5450 Calendar System: Semester
URL: www.icc.edu
Established: 1966 Annual Undergrad Tuition & Fees (In-District): $4,050
Enrollment: 10,770 Coed
Affiliation or Control: State/Local IRS Status: 501(c)3
Highest Offering: Associate Degree
Program: Occupational; 2-Year Principally Bachelor's Creditable
Accreditation: NH, ADNUR, COARC, DH, EMT, MAC, MLTAD, MUS, OTA, PTAA, RAD, SURGT

01 Interim President ....Dr. William TAMMONE
10 Exec VP Administration/Finance ....Mr. Bruce BUDDE
26 Vice President of Marketing & Comm ....Dr. Cheryl FLIEGE
05 Interim Provost ....Dr. Margaret A. SWANSON
102 VP of Education Foundation ....Dr. John MOSSER
15 Vice President of Human Resources .... Ms. Marti BLOODSAW
28 VP of Diversity/Intl & Adult Educ ....Dr. Rita ALI
32 Vice President Student Services ....Dr. Tracy MORRIS
09 Exec Dir Inst Research & Planning ....Mr. David COOK
13 Director Technology Services ....Dr. Susan WHEELER
35 Dean of Students ....Ms. Emily POINTS
37 Dean of Enrollment Management ....Ms. Beth MCCLAIN
35 Dean of Student Services ....Ms. Angela DREESSEN
51 Dean Corporate/Community Education .... Ms. Ellen GEORGE
88 Assoc Dean Organizational Learning ....Ms. Janice KINSINGER
83 Dean of Social Sciences ....Dr. Marwin SPILLER
79 Dean Eng/Humanities/Lang .... Ms. Jennifer SWARTOUT
81 Dean Math/Science/Engineering ....Mr. Joe BERGMAN
50 Dean Business/Hospitality/Info Sys ....Ms. Julie HOWAR
57 Dean Arts & Communications ....Dr. Christopher GRAY
47 Dean Agriculture/Industrial Tech ....Mr. Michael SLOAN
31 Dean Comm Outreach/Career Readiness ....Ms. Kay SUTTON
76 Dean Health Careers ....Ms. Wendee GUTH
106 Associate Dean Online Learning ....Dr. Patrice HESS
21 Director Business Services ....Ms. Kim MALCOLM
06 Registrar ....Ms. Nikisha WRIGHTANDERSON
29 Coordinator Alumni Relations ....Vacant
04 Administrative Asst to President ....Ms. Paula FRALEY
08 Director Library Services ....Ms. Cathryne KAUFMAN
19 Campus Police Chief ....Mr. Thomas LARSON
22 Dir Affirmative Action/EEO ....Dr. Rita ALI
25 Grants Development Officer ....Dr. Herbert DACOSTA
41 Athletic Director ....Ms. Sue SINCLAIR
104 Dir International Educ Program ....Dr. Barbara BURTON
88 Controller ....Mr. Ed BABCOCK
101 Secretary of the Institution/Board ....Ms. Paula FRALEY
86 Legislative Liaison ....Ms. Valerie WELSH

Illinois College (D)

1101 W College Avenue, Jacksonville IL 62650-2299
County: Morgan FICE Identification: 001688
Unit ID: 145691
Telephone: (217) 245-3000 Carnegie Class: Bac/A&S
FAX Number: (217) 245-3034 Calendar System: Semester
URL: www.ic.edu
Established: 1829 Annual Undergrad Tuition & Fees: $31,110
Enrollment: 957 Coed
Affiliation or Control: Independent Non-Profit IRS Status: 501(c)3
Highest Offering: Master's
Program: Liberal Arts And General; Teacher Preparatory
Accreditation: NH

01 President ....Dr. Barbara A. FARLEY
05 Provost and Dean of the College ....Dr. Elizabeth H. TOBIN
10 Vice President of Business Affairs ....Mr. Frank G. WILLIAMS
30 Vice President Development & Alumni ....Mr. William JOHNSON
84 Vice President of Enrollment ....Ms. Stephanie CHIPMAN
32 VP Student Affairs/Dean of Students ......Dr. Malinda L. CARLSON
20 Dean of the Faculty ....Dr. Adam PORTER
20 Dean of Student Success ....Dr. Andrew JONES
09 Exec Dir for Inst Research ....Dr. Robert A. SWEATMAN
06 Registrar ....Ms. Helen KUHN
13 Chief Info Technology Officer (CIO) ....Mr. Patrick BROWN
07 Senior Assoc Director Admissions ....Mr. Richard L. BYSTRY
37 Director of Financial Aid ....Ms. Katherine A. TAYLOR
88 Associate Director of Admissions ....Ms. Kristen REED
29 Dir Annual Giving/Alumni Relations ....Ms. Kristin E. JAMISON
26 Acting Dir Marketing/Communications ....Mr. Bryan LEONARD
08 Library Director ....Mr. Jan FIGA
18 Director of Campus Facilities ....Mr. Al DILLOW
36 Director of Career Services ....Ms. Susan K. DRAKE
21 Controller ....Ms. Melissa J. DYSON
35 Dir Center for Student Involvement ....Ms. Karen K. HOMOLKA
42 Chaplain ....Rev. Katrina E. JENKINS
15 Director of Human Resources ....Ms. Angela VALUCK
38 Dir Templeton Counseling Center ....Mr. William TENNILL
28 Director of Diversity ....Vacant
41 Athletic Director ....Mr. Mike SNYDER

Illinois College of Optometry (E)

3241 S Michigan Avenue, Chicago IL 60616-3878
County: Cook FICE Identification: 001689
Unit ID: 145628
Telephone: (312) 225-1700 Carnegie Class: Spec/Health
FAX Number: (312) 225-1724 Calendar System: Quarter
URL: www.ico.edu
Established: 1872 Annual Graduate Tuition & Fees: $36,464
Enrollment: 638 Coed
Affiliation or Control: Independent Non-Profit IRS Status: 501(c)3
Highest Offering: First Professional Degree; No Undergraduates
Program: Professional
Accreditation: NH, OPT, OPTR

01 President ....Dr. Arol R. AUGSBURGER
05 Vice Pres for Academic Affairs/Dean ....Dr. Stephanie MESSNER
10 VP for Finance & Business/CFO .... Mr. John BUDZYNSKI
11 Vice President Administration ....Mrs. Laura L. ROUNCE
17 Vice Pres for Patient Care Services ....Dr. Leonard V. MESSNER

30 VP Student/Alumni/College Devel ....Dr. Mark COLIP
22 VP Compliance/Cmty Based Services ....Dr. Valarie CONRAD
06 Asst Dean Academic Admin/Registrar ....Mrs. Lavern YOUNG
07 Director of Admissions ....Ms. Teisha JOHNSON
32 Sr Director Student Development ....Ms. Beth KARMIS
37 Director Student Financial Aid ....Ms. Melissa BARTOLD
29 Director Alumni Relations ....Ms. Connie M. SCAVUZZO
18 Chief Facilities/Physical Plant ....Mr. Opie NIMON
26 Director of Communications ....Ms. Jennifer SOPKO

*Illinois Eastern Community Colleges System Office (F)

233 E Chestnut Street, Olney IL 62450-2298
County: Richland FICE Identification: 009135
Unit ID: 443368
Telephone: (618) 393-2982 Carnegie Class: N/A
FAX Number: (618) 392-4816
URL: www.iecc.edu

01 Chief Executive Officer ....Mr. Terry BRUCE
05 Dean Acad/Student Support Svc/CAO ....Mrs. Chris CANTWELL
10 Chief Finance Officer/Treasurer ....Mr. Roger BROWNING
103 Dean Workforce Education ....Mr. Michael THOMAS
30 Assoc Dean Grants/Inst Development ..Mrs. LeAnn HARTLEROAD
20 Pgm Director College Support Svcs ....Ms. Rita S. ADAMS
88 Program Director SBDC ....Mr. Byron BRUMFIEL
85 Pgm Dir Intl Std/Dir Dist Std Rctmt ....Ms. Pamela SWANSON-MADDEN
15 Director of Human Resources ....Mrs. Tara BUERSTER
88 TRiO Upward Bound Director DO/OCC ....Ms. Tiffany COWGER
88 Pgm Dir Student Learning Assessment ....Mr. Brandon WEGER
88 Director Student Advantage Network ....Mr. Wain DAVIS
88 Dir Educational Talent Search/TRiO ....Ms. Elizabeth OLIVER
103 Associate Dean of Outreach ....Mrs. Jervaisc MCDANIEL

*Illinois Eastern Community Colleges Frontier Community College (G)

Frontier Drive, Fairfield IL 62837-9801
County: Wayne FICE Identification: 020744
Unit ID: 403469
Telephone: (618) 842-3711 Carnegie Class: Assoc/Pub-R-L
FAX Number: (618) 842-4425 Calendar System: Semester
URL: www.iecc.edu/fcc
Established: 1976 Annual Undergrad Tuition & Fees (In-District): $3,156
Enrollment: 2,218 Coed
Affiliation or Control: State/Local IRS Status: 501(c)3
Highest Offering: Associate Degree
Program: Occupational; 2-Year Principally Bachelor's Creditable
Accreditation: &NH, ADNUR

02 President ....Dr. Gerald EDGREN, JR.
05 Dean of Instruction ....Mr. Paul BRUINSMA
32 Asst Dean of Student Services ....Ms. Jan WILES
51 Director of Adult Education ....Ms. Cheryl HOLDER
10 Director of Business ....Mrs. Mary JOHNSTON
08 Director of Learning Resource Ctr ....Ms. Merna YOUNGBLOOD
41 Athletic Director ....Mr. Thomas KENT
88 Pgm Dir Emergency Preparedness Mgmt .... Mr. Scott MESEROLE
18 Supervisor of Building & Grounds ....Mr. Galen DUNN
37 Coordinator of Financial Aid ....Ms. Lori NOE
26 Coord of Public Info & Marketing ....Mrs. Karen BRYANT
88 Coord Literary Development Program ....Ms. Linda SARGENT
06 Coordinator of Registration/Records ....Ms. Amy LOSS

† Regional accreditation is carried under the parent institution Illinois Eastern Community Colleges System Office in Olney, IL.

*Illinois Eastern Community Colleges Lincoln Trail College (H)

11220 State Highway 1, Robinson IL 62454-5707
County: Crawford FICE Identification: 009786
Unit ID: 403478
Telephone: (618) 544-8657 Carnegie Class: Assoc/Pub-R-M
FAX Number: (618) 544-7423 Calendar System: Semester
URL: www.iecc.edu/ltc
Established: 1969 Annual Undergrad Tuition & Fees (In-District): $3,156
Enrollment: 1,032 Coed
Affiliation or Control: State/Local IRS Status: 501(c)3
Highest Offering: Associate Degree
Program: Occupational; 2-Year Principally Bachelor's Creditable
Accreditation: &NH, ADNUR

02 President ....Ms. Kathy HARRIS
05 Dean of the College ....Mr. David CARPENTER
37 Director of Financial Aid ....Mr. Aaron WHITE
32 Asst Dean of Student Services ....Ms. Megan BLACK
08 Director of Learning Resource Ctr ....Ms. Vicky BONELLI
10 Director of Business ....Ms. Jamie HENRY
41 Athletic Director ....Mr. Kevin BOWERS
18 Groundskeeper ....Mr. Dan LEGGITT
26 Coord Public Information/Marketing ....Mr. Christopher FORDE

† Regional accreditation is carried under the parent institution Illinois Eastern Community Colleges System Office in Olney, IL.

*Illinois Eastern Community Colleges Olney Central College (A)

305 North West Street, Olney IL 62450-1099
County: Richland FICE Identification: 001742
Unit ID: 145707
Telephone: (618) 395-7777 Carnegie Class: Assoc/Pub-R-M
FAX Number: (618) 392-3293 Calendar System: Semester
URL: www.iecc.edu/occ
Established: 1962 Annual Undergrad Tuition & Fees (In-District): $3,156
Enrollment: 1,398 Coed
Affiliation or Control: State/Local IRS Status: 501(c)3
Highest Offering: Associate Degree
Program: Occupational; 2-Year Principally Bachelor's Creditable
Accreditation: &NH, ADNUR, RAD

Code	Title	Name
02	President	Mr. Rodney RANES
05	Dean of Instruction	Mr. Jeff CUTCHIN
32	Assistant Dean Student Services	Mr. Adam GREATHOUSE
76	Assoc Dean Nursing Allied Health	Ms. Tamara FRALICKER
08	Director Learning Resource Center	Ms. Brittany BASS
88	Director Cosmetology	Ms. Linda MILLER
10	Director Business	Mr. Doug SHIPMAN
41	Athletic Director/Coach	Mr. Dennis CONLEY
37	Financial Aid Coordinator	Ms. Veralee HARRIS

† Regional accreditation is carried under the parent institution Illinois Eastern Community Colleges System Office in Olney, IL.

*Illinois Eastern Community Colleges Wabash Valley College (B)

2200 College Drive, Mount Carmel IL 62863-2657
County: Wabash FICE Identification: 001779
Unit ID: 403487
Telephone: (618) 262-8641 Carnegie Class: Assoc/Pub-R-L
FAX Number: (618) 262-5347 Calendar System: Semester
URL: www.iecc.edu/wvc
Established: 1960 Annual Undergrad Tuition & Fees (In-District): $3,156
Enrollment: 4,239 Coed
Affiliation or Control: State/Local IRS Status: 501(c)3
Highest Offering: Associate Degree
Program: Occupational; 2-Year Principally Bachelor's Creditable
Accreditation: &NH, ADNUR

Code	Title	Name
02	President	Mr. Matt FOWLER
05	Dean of Instruction	Mr. Robert CONN
32	Assistant Dean Student Services	Mrs. Diana SPEAR
20	Director of Academic Advising	Mr. Tim ZIMMER
08	Director of LRC	Ms. Sandy CRAIG
60	Director of Broadcasting	Mr. Kyle PEACH
41	Athletic Director	Mr. Mike CARPENTER
10	Director of Business	Mrs. Reilly BAUMGART
37	Financial Aid Coordinator	Ms. Mary JOHNSON
18	Groundskeeper	Mr. Adam ROESCH

† Regional accreditation is carried under the parent institution Illinois Eastern Community Colleges System Office in Olney, IL.

The Illinois Institute of Art (C)

350 N Orleans, Suite 136, Chicago IL 60654-1514
County: Cook FICE Identification: 012584
Unit ID: 148177
Telephone: (312) 280-3500 Carnegie Class: Spec/Arts
FAX Number: (312) 777-8780 Calendar System: Quarter
URL: www.artinstitutes.edu/chicago
Established: 1916 Annual Undergrad Tuition & Fees: $17,488
Enrollment: 1,807 Coed
Affiliation or Control: Proprietary IRS Status: Proprietary
Highest Offering: Baccalaureate
Program: Professional; Technical Emphasis
Accreditation: NH, ACFEI, CIDA

Code	Title	Name
01	President/Chicago	David W. RAY
05	Vice President Academic Affairs	Dr. Donna L. GRAY
20	Associate Dean of Academic Affairs	Karen JANKO
07	Senior Director of Admissions	Summer TOOMEY
06	Registrar	Donohue MICHAEL
08	Librarian	Sean MCCARTHY
79	Program Coordinator Humanities	Karine BRAVAIS-SLYMAN
81	Program Coordinator Math/Science	Deann GROSSI
10	Regional Director of Finance	Daniel LEAVITT
37	Director Student Financial Aid	Terry LEPPELLERE
32	Dean of Student Affairs	Catherine BROKENSHIRE
35	Asst Dean of Student Affairs	Valarie RAND
38	Student Support Coordinator	Sara SPIEGEL
40	Supply Store Manager	Ricardo OLAVE
36	Director of Career Services	Vanessa JACKSON
15	Human Resources Generalist	Rae DEROSE
13	Director of Technology	Terence HAHN
29	Director Alumni Relations	Anne CAMPION

The Illinois Institute of Art-Schaumburg (D)

1000 Plaza Drive, Suite 100, Schaumburg IL 60173-4913
Telephone: (847) 619-3450 Identification: 770074
Accreditation: &NH, CIDA

† Branch campus of The Illinois Institute of Art, Chicago, IL.

Illinois Institute of Technology (E)

3300 S Federal Street, Chicago IL 60616-3793
County: Cook FICE Identification: 001691
Unit ID: 145725
Telephone: (312) 567-3000 Carnegie Class: RU/H
FAX Number: (312) 567-3004 Calendar System: Semester
URL: www.iit.edu
Established: 1890 Annual Undergrad Tuition & Fees: $42,000
Enrollment: 7,898 Coed
Affiliation or Control: Independent Non-Profit IRS Status: 501(c)3
Highest Offering: Doctorate
Program: Liberal Arts And General; Teacher Preparatory; Professional; Technical Emphasis
Accreditation: NH, BUS, CLPSY, CORE, CS, ENG, LSAR

Code	Title	Name
01	President	Dr. Alan CRAMB
05	Provost	Ms. Frances BRONET
10	VP Finance & Administration	Dr. Patricia LAUGHLIN
21	AVP & Controller	Mr. Brian LAFFEY
18	VP Facilities & Public Safety	Mr. Bruce WATTS
30	Vice Pres Institutional Advancement	Ms. Elizabeth HUGHES
88	Vice Pres International Affairs	Dr. Darsh T. WASAN
86	Vice President External Affairs	Mr. David E. BAKER
43	Vice President General Counsel	Mr. Anthony D'AMATO
31	VP Community Affairs & Outreach	Mr. Leroy E. KENNEDY
26	Vice Pres Marketing/Communications	Ms. Jeanne HARTIG
88	Sr VP & Dir IIT Research Inst	Dr. David MCCORMICK
88	VP & Dir Inst Food Safety & Health	Dr. Robert BRACKETT
13	Chief Information Officer	Mr. Ophir TRIGALO
04	Director President's Office	Ms. Sandra LAPORTE
28	Vice Provost Student Diversity	Mr. Gerald DOYLE
15	Associate VP Human Resources	Ms. Antoinette MURRIL
07	Vice Provost Admission & Fin Aid	Dr. Michael GOSZ
20	Vice Provost Academic Affairs	Dr. Christopher WHITE
88	Vice Provost for Research	Mr. Dennis ROBERSON
32	Vice Provost Student Affairs	Ms. Katherine MURPHY-STETZ
61	Dean Chicago-Kent College of Law	Mr. Harold J. KRENT
49	Dean College of Science & Letters	Dr. Russell BETTS
54	Dean Armour Col of Engineering	Dr. Natacha DEPAOLA
50	Dean Stuart School of Business	Dr. Harvey KAHALAS
48	Dean College of Architecture	Mr. Wiel ARETS
83	Dean Lewis Col of Human Sciences	Dr. Christine HIMES
12	Dean Institute of Design	Mr. Patrick F. WHITNEY
58	Dean Graduate Col & VP Research	Dr. Ali CINAR
72	Dean School of Applied Technology	Dr. C. Robert CARLSON
08	Dean of Libraries	Ms. Sharon BOSTICK
88	Assoc Vice Provost UG Acad Affairs	Ms. Carole ORZE
88	Assoc Vice Provost Grad Acad Affs	Ms. Holli PRYOR-HARRIS
37	Assoc Vice Provost Financial Aid	Ms. Abigail MCGRATH
84	Assoc Vice Provost Enrollment Mgmt	Ms. Caryn SCHNIERLE
06	Assoc Vice Provost/Registrar & OII	Mr. Peter ZACHOCKI
84	Assoc Vice Provost Strat Intvs	Ms. April WELCH
36	Exec Dir Career Mgmt Ctr	Mr. Andres GARZA
25	Director Sponsored Research	Ms. Domenica G. PAPPAS
14	Director Enterprise Systems	Mr. Vince BATTISTA
07	Director UG Admissions	Ms. Toni RILEY
07	Director Graduate Admissions	Mr. Rishab MALHOTRA
108	Director of Assessment	Dr. Carol-Ann EMMONS
44	Director Annual Giving	Mr. Jason SMITH
29	Director Alumni & Donor Relations	Mr. James ACTON
41	Athletic Director	Mr. Joseph HAKES
19	Director Public Safety	Mr. Carl DOBRICH
22	Dir Equal Opp/Affirmative Action	Ms. Candida MIRANDA
96	Director of Purchasing	Mr. Frank FIORITO
28	Director Student Ctr for Diversity	Ms. Lisa MONTGOMERY
88	Director Student Conduct	Ms. Erin MCDONALD
88	Dir Environmental Health & Safety	Ms. Cynthia CHAFFEE
38	Director Student Health & Wellness	Ms. Anita OPDYCKE
105	Director Web Dvlpmt/Services	Mr. Brian BAILEY
106	Dir IITOnline Tech Svcs	Ms. Lauren WOODS

Illinois Institute of Technology Chicago-Kent College of Law (F)

565 W Adams Street, Chicago IL 60661
Telephone: (312) 906-5000 Identification: 770075
Accreditation: &NH, LAW

† Branch campus of Illinois Institute of Technology, Chicago, IL.

Illinois Institute of Technology Institute of Design (G)

350 N LaSalle Street, Chicago IL 60610
Telephone: (312) 595-4900 Identification: 770076
Accreditation: &NH

† Branch campus of Illinois Institute of Technology, Chicago, IL.

Illinois Institute of Technology Rice Campus (H)

201 East Loop Road, Wheaton IL 60189
Telephone: (630) 682-6000 Identification: 770077
Accreditation: &NH

† Branch campus of Illinois Institute of Technology, Chicago, IL.

Illinois State University (I)

School and North Streets, Normal IL 61790-0001
County: McLean FICE Identification: 001692
Unit ID: 145813
Telephone: (309) 438-2111 Carnegie Class: DRU
FAX Number: (309) 438-2768 Calendar System: Semester
URL: www.ilstu.edu
Established: 1857 Annual Undergrad Tuition & Fees (In-State): $13,666
Enrollment: 20,615 Coed
Affiliation or Control: State IRS Status: 501(c)3
Highest Offering: Doctorate
Program: Liberal Arts And General; Teacher Preparatory; Professional
Accreditation: NH, AAFCS, ART, AUD, BUS, BUSA, CAATE, CAHIIM, CIDA, CONST, CS, DIETD, DIETI, IPSY, MT, MUS, NAIT, NRPA, NURSE, SCPSY, SP, SW, TED, THEA

Code	Title	Name
01	President	Dr. Larry DIETZ
05	VP Academic Affairs & Provost	Dr. Janet KREJCI
10	Interim VP Finance & Planning	Mr. Greg ALT
32	Interim VP Student Affairs	Dr. Brent PATERSON
26	VP University Advancement	Mr. Pat VICKERMAN
20	Associate Provost	Dr. Jim JAWAHAR
35	Interim Asst VP Student Affairs	Dr. Danielle MILLER-SCHUSTER
21	Sr Assoc VP Finance & Planning	Ms. Debra K. SMITLEY
91	Chief Academic Technology Officer	Dr. Mark WALBERT
58	Assoc VP Grad Std/Res/Intern Educ	Dr. John BAUR
84	Assoc VP Enrollment Management	Dr. Troy JOHNSON
15	Asst VP Human Resources	Ms. Tammy CARLSON
08	Dean University Libraries	Dr. Dane WARD
06	University Registrar	Mr. Jess D. RAY
07	Director Admissions	Mr. Jeff MAVROS
20	Director University College	Ms. Amelia NOEL-ELKINS
30	Exec Director of Development	Ms. Joy D. HUTCHCRAFT
21	Interim Comptroller	Ms. JoEllen BAHNSEN
37	Director Financial Aid	Ms. Jana ALBRECHT
29	Exec Director Alumni Engagement	Ms. Doris GROVES
18	Exec Director Facilities Management	Mr. Charles SCOTT
19	Chief University Police	Mr. Aaron WOODRUFF
28	Dir Off of Eq Oppty/Ethics & Access	Mr. Shane MCCREERY
23	Director Student Health Services	Ms. Laura KNOBLAUCH
39	Director University Housing	Ms. Stacey MWILAMBWE
41	Director Intercollegiate Athletics	Mr. Larry LYONS
85	Director International Studies	Dr. Luis CANALES
92	Director Honors Program	Dr. Tim FREDSTROM
94	Director Women's Studies	Dr. Alison BAILEY
96	Director of Purchasing	Ms. Judy JOHNSON
49	Dean College Arts & Sciences	Dr. Gregory SIMPSON
50	Interim Dean College Business	Dr. Gerry MCKEAN
53	Dean College Education	Dr. Perry SCHOON
72	Dean College Applied Science/Tech	Dr. Jeffrey A. WOOD
57	Dean College Fine Arts	Ms. Jean M K. MILLER
66	Acting Dean Mennonite College	Dr. Catherine MILLER
100	Chief of Staff	Mr. Jay GROVES
35	Asst VP & Dean of Students	Dr. Art MUNIN
88	Asst VP Acad Admin	Dr. Sam CATANZARO
88	Interim Assoc VP Acad Fiscal Mgmt	Dr. Alan LACY
88	Asst VP Administrative Technologies	Mr. Matthew HELM
21	Dir of Budget Planning/Operations	Ms. Sandra CAVI
35	Asst VP Student Affairs	Mr. Dwayne SACKMAN
44	Exec Dir Annual Giving	Ms. Lora WEY
88	Chief Operations Ofcr Advancement	Ms. Jill JONES
27	Exec Dir University Marketing/Comm	Mr. Brian BEAM
45	Dir Planning/Rsch/Policy Analysis	Ms. Angela ENGEL
108	Director University Assessment	Dr. Ryan SMITH
38	Director Student Counseling	Dr. Sandy COLBS
43	General Counsel	Ms. Lisa HUSON

Illinois Valley Community College (J)

815 N Orlando Smith Road, Oglesby IL 61348-9692
County: La Salle FICE Identification: 001705
Unit ID: 145831
Telephone: (815) 224-2720 Carnegie Class: Assoc/Pub-R-L
FAX Number: (815) 224-3033 Calendar System: Semester
URL: www.ivcc.edu
Established: 1966 Annual Undergrad Tuition & Fees (In-District): $3,580
Enrollment: 3,525 Coed
Affiliation or Control: Local IRS Status: 501(c)3
Highest Offering: Associate Degree
Program: Occupational; 2-Year Principally Bachelor's Creditable
Accreditation: NH, ADNUR, DA

Code	Title	Name
01	President	Dr. Jerry M. CORCORAN
05	Vice Pres for Academic Affairs	Dr. Deborah L. ANDERSON
10	Vice Pres Business Svcs/Finance	Ms. Cheryl E. ROELFSEMA
20	AVP Academic Affs/Dean Wrkfce Devel	Ms. Sue L. ISERMANN
32	Assoc Vice Pres Student Svcs	Mr. Mark J. GRZYBOWSKI
24	Director of Learning Technologies	Ms. Emily B. VESCOGNI
31	Director Cmty Relations & Marketing	Mr. Francis R. BROLLEY
13	Dir of Information Technology Svcs	Mr. Harold B. BARNES
51	Dir Cont Educ/Business Services	Ms. Jamie L. GAHM
15	Director Human Resources	Ms. Glenna S. JONES
37	Director of Financial Aid	Ms. Patricia A. WILLIAMSON
07	Director of Admissions/Records	Mr. Quintin M. OVEROCKER
08	Head Librarian	Ms. Frances A. WHALEY
30	Director of Development	Mr. Francis R. BROLLEY
96	Director of Purchasing	Ms. Michelle L. CARBONI
18	Director of Facilities	Mr. Scott CURLEY
09	Director of Institutional Research	Mr. Matthew P. SUERTH
81	Dean Natural Science/Business	Mr. Ron W. GROLEAU
66	Dean Health Professions/ Nursing	Ms. Bonnie L. BENNETT-CAMPBELL
79	Dn Humanities/Fine Arts/Soc Sci	Mr. Brian R. HOLLOWAY
53	Dean English/Mathematics/Educ	Dr. Robyn L. SCHIFFMAN

Illinois Wesleyan University (A)

PO Box 2900, 1312 Park Street,
Bloomington IL 61702-2900
County: McLean FICE Identification: 001696
Unit ID: 145646
Telephone: (309) 556-1000 Carnegie Class: Bac/A&S
FAX Number: (309) 556-3411 Calendar System: Other
URL: www.iwu.edu
Established: 1850 Annual Undergrad Tuition & Fees: $42,290
Enrollment: 1,893 Coed
Affiliation or Control: Independent Non-Profit IRS Status: 501(c)3
Highest Offering: Baccalaureate
Program: Liberal Arts And General; Teacher Preparatory; Professional
Accreditation: NH, MUS, NURSE

01 President .... Dr. Richard F. WILSON
05 Provost & Dean of Faculty .... Dr. Jonathan D. GREEN
10 Vice President Business & Finance .... Mr. Daniel P. KLOTZBACH
30 Vice President for Advancement .... Mr. Martin W. SMITH
26 Vice President for Communications .... Mr. Matt KURZ
32 VP Student Affairs/Dean Students .... Dr. Karla CARNEY-HALL
07 Dean of Admissions .... Mr. Tony BANKSTON
84 Dean of Enrollment Management .... Mr. Robert MURRAY
09 AVP Instl Research/Plng/Evaluation .... Dr. Michael THOMPSON
86 Dir Government/Community Relations .... Mr. Carl F. TEICHMAN
04 Exec Assistant to the President .... Dr. Molly MUNSON-DRYER
20 Assoc Provost Acad Plng/Standards .... Dr. Frank A. BOYD
20 Assoc Dean Curricular/Faculty Devel .... Prof. Lynda DUKE
15 Assoc VP for Human Resources .... Ms. Catherine SPITZ
13 Asst Provost/Chief Technology Ofcr .... Mr. Trey SHORT
44 Associate Vice Pres Gift Planning .... Mr. Steve D. SEIBRING
35 Assoc Dean of Students .... Ms. Darcy L. GREDER
38 Asst Dean/Dir Student Counseling .... Dr. Annorrah MOORMAN
35 Asst Dean of Students .... Mr. Matthew DAMSCHRODER
08 University Librarian .... Dr. Karen SCHMIDT
06 Registrar .... Dr. Leslie BETZ
42 University Chaplain .... Rev. Elyse NELSON WINGER
21 Controller .... Mr. John BRYANT
37 Director of Financial Aid .... Mr. Scott SEIBRING
64 Director of School of Music .... Dr. Mario J. PELUSI
57 Director of School of Art .... Prof. Kevin STRANDBERG
57 Director of School of Theatre Arts .... Dr. Curtis C. TROUT
66 Director of School of Nursing .... Dr. Victoria FOLSE
41 Director of Athletics .... Prof. Mike WAGNER
29 Director of Alumni Relations .... Ms. Adriane POWELL
102 Dir Grants/Foundation Relations .... Mr. Dick FOLSE
44 Dir of Wesleyan Annual Fund .... Mr. Van MILLER
36 Director of Career Center .... Mr. Warren KISTNER
18 Director of Physical Plant .... Mr. James J. BLUMBERG
88 Director of Sports Information .... Mr. Stewart I. SALOWITZ
93 Director of Diversity & Inclusion .... Mr. Brandon H. COMMON
35 Dir Student Act/Leadership Programs .... Mr. Colin STEWART
94 Dir of Women's & Gender Studies .... Dr. Carole MYSCOFSKI
104 Director of International Office .... Ms. Stacey SHIMIZU
40 Bookstore Manager .... Mr. Thaddeus SUTTER

Institute for Clinical Social Work (B)

401 South State Street, Suite 822, Chicago IL 60605
County: Cook FICE Identification: 025737
Unit ID: 145886
Telephone: (312) 935-4232 Carnegie Class: Spec/Health
FAX Number: (312) 935-4255 Calendar System: Semester
URL: www.icsw.edu
Established: 1981 Annual Graduate Tuition & Fees: $19,200
Enrollment: 124 Coed
Affiliation or Control: Independent Non-Profit IRS Status: 501(c)3
Highest Offering: Doctorate; No Undergraduates
Program: Professional
Accreditation: NH

01 Dean/President .... Dr. Scott H. ROSE
05 Associate Dean .... Dr. Jennifer TOLLESON
03 Vice President of Operations .... Lynne GORDON
20 Director of Academic Administration .... Elizabeth OLLER
37 Director of Student Financial Svcs .... Sebastien BEAUDET
08 Librarian .... Vacant
07 Director of Admissions .... Jennifer TOLLESON

ITT Technical Institute (C)

3800 N. Wilke Road, Suite 100, Arlington Heights IL 60004
Telephone: (847) 454-1800 Identification: 666538
Accreditation: ACICS

† Branch campus of ITT Technical Institute, Indianapolis, IN.

ITT Technical Institute (D)

800 Jorie Blvd., Suite 100, Oak Brook IL 60523
Telephone: (630) 472-7000 Identification: 666118
Accreditation: ACICS

† Branch campus of ITT Technical Institute, Indianapolis, IN.

ITT Technical Institute (E)

11551 184th Place, Orland Park IL 60467-4900
Telephone: (708) 326-3200 Identification: 666539
Accreditation: ACICS

† Branch campus of ITT Technical Institute, Indianapolis, IN.

ITT Technical Institute (F)

2501 Wabash Avenue, Springfield IL 62704
Telephone: (217) 547-5700 Identification: 770649
Accreditation: ACICS

† Branch campus of ITT Technical Institute, Indianapolis, IN.

John A. Logan College (G)

700 Logan College Road, Carterville IL 62918-2500
County: Williamson FICE Identification: 008076
Unit ID: 146205
Telephone: (618) 985-3741 Carnegie Class: Assoc/Pub-R-L
FAX Number: (618) 985-2248 Calendar System: Semester
URL: www.jalc.edu
Established: 1967 Annual Undergrad Tuition & Fees (In-District): $3,267
Enrollment: 6,108 Coed
Affiliation or Control: State/Local IRS Status: 501(c)3
Highest Offering: Associate Degree
Program: Occupational; 2-Year Principally Bachelor's Creditable
Accreditation: NH, CAHIIM, CONST, DA, DH, DMS, MLTAD, OTA, SURGT

01 President .... Dr. Michael DREITH
05 Vice President Instruction Services .... Dr. Laurel KLINKENBERG
10 VP Business Svcs/College Facilities .... Mr. Brad MCCORMICK
32 VP Student Affairs & Community Educ .... Vacant
35 Dean Student Services .... Mr. Terry CRAIN
21 Dean Financial Operations .... Ms. Stacy BUCKINGHAM
20 Dean Academic Affairs .... Vacant
103 Dean Workforce Dev/Comm Educ .... Ms. Kay FLLEMING
88 Assoc Dean Baccalaureate Transfer .... Mr. Mark HENSON
72 Dean for Career and Technical Educ .... Mr. Michael COFFMAN
51 Dean for Continuing Education .... Dr. Barry HANCOCK
88 Assoc Dn Adult Basic/Secondary Educ .... Vacant
13 Assoc Dean Information Technology .... Vacant
07 Director of Admissions .... Ms. Lauralyn CIMA
37 Director of Student Financial Asst .... Ms. Sherry SUMMARY
08 Assoc Dean for Library Services .... Ms. Judy VINEYARD
30 Dean for Institutional Effectivenes .... Dr. Valerie BARKO
26 Dir Community Relations/Marketing .... Dr. Steve O'KEEFE
35 Director of Student Activities .... Ms. Adrienne BARKLEY-GIFFIN
36 Director of Placement .... Ms. Lisa HUDGENS
102 Executive Director of Foundation .... Ms. Staci SHAFER
66 Director of Nursing .... Ms. Marilyn FALASTER
36 Director of Career Dev/Acad Support .... Ms. Christy MCBRIDE
15 Director of Human Resources/AAO .... Dr. Clay BREWER
18 Dir Buildings and Grounds .... Mr. Tim GIBSON
09 Director Institutional Research .... Mr. Eric PULLEY
29 Dir of Scholarships/Alumni Svcs .... Ms. Stacy HOLLOWAY
04 Administrative Asst to President .... Ms. Sondra WALKER
101 Admin Asst Pres/Board of Trustees .... Ms. Donna GLODJO
19 Director Security/Safety .... Mr. Don PRIDDY
28 Director of Diversity & Inclusion .... Ms. Toyin FOX
41 Athletic Director .... Mr. Jerry HALSTEAD
88 Director of Emerg Plng & Risk Mgmt .... Mr. Don PRIDDY

Ellis University (H)

2 Mid America Plaza, Suite 824AB,
Oakbrook Terrace IL 60181
County: DuPage FICE Identification: 041433
Unit ID: 452133
Telephone: (877) 366-0321 Carnegie Class: Bac/A&S
FAX Number: (630) 873-3487 Calendar System: Semester
URL: www.ellis.edu
Established: 2008 Annual Undergrad Tuition & Fees: $7,500
Enrollment: 78 Coed
Affiliation or Control: Proprietary IRS Status: Proprietary
Highest Offering: Master's
Program: Professional; Business Emphasis
Accreditation: DEAC

01 President .... Dr. Virginia A. CARLIN
10 Chief Financial Officer .... Randy WILLY
05 Chair of Academic Programs .... Dr. Russell RADFORD
06 Director of Registrar Functions .... Yahana TEGEGNE

John Marshall Law School (I)

315 S Plymouth Court, Chicago IL 60604-3968
County: Cook FICE Identification: 001698
Unit ID: 146241
Telephone: (312) 427-2737 Carnegie Class: Spec/Law
FAX Number: (312) 427-8307 Calendar System: Semester
URL: www.jmls.edu
Established: 1899 Annual Graduate Tuition & Fees: $45,780
Enrollment: 1,319 Coed
Affiliation or Control: Independent Non-Profit IRS Status: 501(c)3
Highest Offering: First Professional Degree; No Undergraduates
Program: Professional
Accreditation: NH, LAW

01 Dean .... Mr. John E. CORKERY
05 Assoc Dean Academic Affairs .... Mr. Anthony NIEDWIECKI
07 Assoc Dean Admissions/Stdnt Affairs .... Mr. William B. POWERS
10 Chief Financial Officer .... Ms. Cynthia SAH
13 Dir Library & IT Operations .... Mr. Ramsey DONNELL
20 Asst Dean for Academic Services .... Ms. Jodie NEEDHAM
15 Asst Dean Human Resources .... Mr. Martin D'AMBROSE
36 Asst Dean Career Services .... Ms. Chante SPANN
06 Registrar .... Ms. Jodie NEEDHAM
29 Director Alumni Relations/Aux Svcs .... Ms. Sherri DZIK
37 Director Student Financial Aid .... Ms. Yara SANTANA
26 Exec Dir of Institutional Affairs .... Ms. Anna KRUG
88 Assoc Dean for Advanced Studies .... Ms. Kathryn KENNEDY
88 Assoc Dn Professional/Career Strat .... Hon. Margaret O'Mara FROSSARD, RET.
28 Dir Diversity Affairs and Outreach .... Mr. Troy RIDDLE
19 Director Security/Safety .... Mr. Ali HALEEM
88 Assoc Dean Faculty Affairs .... Ms. Julie SPANBAUER
11 Asst Dean for Administration .... Ms. Teresa DO

John Wood Community College (J)

1301 S 48th Street, Quincy IL 62305-8736
County: Adams FICE Identification: 012813
Unit ID: 146278
Telephone: (217) 224-6500 Carnegie Class: Assoc/Pub-R-M
FAX Number: (217) 224-4208 Calendar System: Semester
URL: www.jwcc.edu
Established: 1974 Annual Undergrad Tuition & Fees (In-District): $4,410
Enrollment: 1,900 Coed
Affiliation or Control: State/Local IRS Status: 501(c)3
Highest Offering: Associate Degree
Program: Occupational; 2-Year Principally Bachelor's Creditable
Accreditation: NH, SURGT

01 President .... Mr. Michael ELBE
05 Vice President for Instruction .... Vacant
10 Dean Business Svcs/Inst Effective .... Mr. Josh WELKER
32 Dean Student Services .... Vacant
49 Dean Arts and Sciences .... Mr. Ken TRZASKA
75 Dean Careers and Technology .... Mr. William STUFFLICK
84 Dean Enrollment Svcs/Dir Finan Aid .... Ms. Melanie LECHTENBERG
07 Director Admissions .... Mr. William SCHAFFER
06 Registrar/Dean of Students .... Mr. Cody BAGGETT
21 Director Fiscal Services .... Ms. Susan FIFER
35 Director Support Services .... Mr. Robert HODGSON
13 Director Information Technology .... Mr. Joshua BRUECK
08 Director Learning Resource Center .... Ms. Barbara LIEBER
26 Director Public Relations/Marketing .... Ms. Tracy ORNE
30 Director Advancement .... Ms. Barbara HOLTHAUS
15 Director Human Resources .... Vacant
18 Director Physical Plant .... Mr. Lou BARTA
37 Director Financial Aid .... Ms. Melanie LECHTENBERG
19 Chief of Campus Police .... Mr. Bill LATOUR
41 Manager Athletics & Intramurals .... Mr. Brad HOYT
40 Manager Campus Services .... Ms. Lynn BLICKHAN
96 Purchasing Coordinator .... Ms. Darla SNYDER
47 Dept Chair Ag Sciences .... Mr. Gary SHUPE
77 Dept Chair Ofc Technology/Comp Sci .... Mr. Nick KRIZMANIC
50 Dept Chair Business .... Ms. Cathy STEPHENS
57 Dept Chair Fine Arts .... Vacant
81 Department Chair Mathematics .... Mr. David RIGSBEE
65 Dept Chair Natural Sciences .... Dr. Ivan PAUL
79 Dept Chair Language/Literature/Hum .... Mr. Mike TERRY
88 Dept Chair Developmental Education .... Vacant
83 Dept Chair Social/Behavior Science .... Dr. Randall EGDORF
04 Administrative Asst to President .... Ms. Leah BENZ
102 Dir Foundation/Corporate Relations .... Ms. Barbara HOLTHAUS

Joliet Junior College (K)

1215 Houbolt Road, Joliet IL 60431-8938
County: Will FICE Identification: 001699
Unit ID: 146296
Telephone: (815) 729-9020 Carnegie Class: Assoc/Pub-S-SC
FAX Number: N/A Calendar System: Semester
URL: www.jjc.edu
Established: 1901 Annual Undergrad Tuition & Fees (In-District): $3,450
Enrollment: 16,870 Coed
Affiliation or Control: State/Local IRS Status: 501(c)3
Highest Offering: Associate Degree
Program: Occupational; 2-Year Principally Bachelor's Creditable
Accreditation: NH, ACBSP, ACFEI, ADNUR, CAHIIM, MUS

01 President .... Dr. Debra S. DANIELS
10 VP Administrative Services .... Dr. Judy MITCHELL
13 Exec Dir Information Technology .... Mr. Jim SERR
32 VP Student Development .... Dr. Yolanda ISAACS
31 Dean Community/Economic Development .... Vacant
07 Director Admissions & Recruitment .... Ms. Jennifer KLOBERDANZ
88 Dir Adult & Family Services .... Ms. Emilie MCCALLISTER
37 Director Financial Aid .... Vacant
15 Executive Director Human Resources .... Ms. Julie MCNEIL
06 Registrar .... Mr. Keith TILLMAN
18 Director Facility Services .... Mr. Patrick VAN DUYNE
21 Director Business/Auxiliary Svcs .... Ms. Janice REEDUS
26 Dir Commun/External Relations .... Ms. Kelly ROHDER
36 Director Career Services .... Ms. Bridgett LARKIN-BEENE
41 Director Athletics .... Mr. Wayne KING
21 Director Financial Svcs/Controller .... Mr. Jeffrey HEAP
19 Dir Campus Safety & Police Chief .... Mr. Peter COMANDA
30 Ex Dir Inst Adv Exec Dir JJC Found .... Ms. Kristin MULVEY
08 Director Library .... Vacant
09 Director of Institutional Research .... Mr. Joseph OFFERMANN
29 Director Alumni Relations .... Vacant
40 Manager Bookstore .... Vacant
88 Coord GSD .... Dr. Angie KAYSEN-LUZBETAK
74 Dept Chair Veterinary Medicine Tech .... Dr. Scott KELLER
38 Counselor/Dept Chair .... Ms. Jennifer KIMBAROVSKY

04 Administrative Asst to President Ms. Jennifer TENN
100 Chief of Staff Ms. Linda SMITH
101 Secretary of the Institution/Board Ms. Joan TIERNEY
103 Dir Workforce Development Ms. Paige VANDERHYDEN
104 Coordinator Study Abroad Ms. Tamara BRATTOLI
106 Dir Online Education/E-learning Mr. Chris OSTWINKLE
84 Dean of Enrollment Management Ms. Susan PADDOCK

Judson University (A)

1151 N State Street, Elgin IL 60123-1498

County: Kane | FICE Identification: 001700 | Unit ID: 146339
Telephone: (847) 628-2500 | Carnegie Class: Bac/Diverse
FAX Number: (847) 628-1027 | Calendar System: Semester
URL: www.judsonu.edu
Established: 1913 | Annual Undergrad Tuition & Fees: $28,170
Enrollment: 1,190 | Coed
Affiliation or Control: American Baptist | IRS Status: 501(c)3
Highest Offering: Doctorate
Program: Liberal Arts And General; Teacher Preparatory; Professional
Accreditation: NH

01 President Dr. Gene CRUME
04 Exec Assistant to the President Mrs. Tena ROBOTHAM
05 Provost/Chief Academic Officer Dr. Wilbert FRIESEN
10 Int Sr VP of Business Affs/CFO Mr. Randall PATTERSON
30 Assoc Vice President Advancement Mr. Roger BRIMMERMAN
06 Assoc VP and Univ Registrar Ms. Virginia GUTH
84 VP for Enrollment & Strategic Plan Ms. Nancy BINGER
49 Dean Liberal Arts & Sciences/ Educ Dr. Lanette POTEETE-YOUNG
48 Interim Dean Art/Design & Arch Dr. Jhennifer AMUNDSON
50 Dean Business & Professional Stds Dr. David COOK
32 Assistant VP for Student Life Mrs. Lisa JAROT
08 Library Director Mr. Larry WILD
13 Assistant VP Information Technology Mr. Brent RICHARDSON
44 Senior VP for External Relations Mr. Devlin DONALDSON
88 Director of Advancement Mr. Dan DICK
29 Director of Alumni Relations Mrs. Bonnie BIENERT
37 Director of Financial Aid Dr. Roberto SANTIZO
07 Director of Admissions Mr. Nate MCNEELY
26 Director of Comm & Marketing Ms. Mary DULABAUM
36 Director of Career Development Mrs. Doris HAUGEN
38 Dir of Student Health & Wellness Mr. Elliott ANDERSON
19 Director of Campus Safety Mr. Nick SALZMANN
41 Athletic Director Mr. Rich BENJAMIN
88 Director of Retention & Orientation Miss Jaimee BARTHA
39 Housing Coord/International Advisor Mr. Rafael HECK
85 Director of Intercultural Relations Vacant
35 Associate Dean of Students Ms. Casey SUNDSEDT
23 Director of Health Center Ms. Susan WEBER
88 Tutor/ADA Compliance Coordinator Ms. Gineen VARGAS
92 Honors Director Dr. Craig KAPLOWITZ
15 Director of Human Resources Mr. Jeremiah THOMPSON
101 Asst Sec to Board of Trustees Mrs. Tena ROBOTHAM
105 Webmaster Mr. Eric SECKER
28 Asst for Diversity/Spiritual Dev Dr. Curtis SARTOR
91 Interim Director of IT Mr. Ben GREENO

Kankakee Community College (B)

100 College Drive, Kankakee IL 60901-6505

County: Kankakee | FICE Identification: 007690 | Unit ID: 146348
Telephone: (815) 802-8100 | Carnegie Class: Assoc/Pub-R-L
FAX Number: (815) 802-8101 | Calendar System: Semester
URL: www.kcc.edu
Established: 1966 | Annual Undergrad Tuition & Fees (In-District): $4,050
Enrollment: 3,247 | Coed
Affiliation or Control: State/Local | IRS Status: 501(c)3
Highest Offering: Associate Degree
Program: Occupational; 2-Year Principally Bachelor's Creditable
Accreditation: NH, COARC, MLTAD, PHLEB, PTAA

01 President Dr. John AVENDANO
04 Executive Secretary to President Ms. Karen SLAGER
05 VP of Instructional & Stdnt Success Dr. Michael BOYD
06 Registrar Mr. David HERMANN
32 Dean of Student Development Ms. Julia WASKOSKY
09 Director Institutional Research Dr. Purva DEVOL
31 Director Adult & Community Educ Mr. Allen WEAVER
103 Director of Workforce Development Ms. Dana WASHINGTON
37 Director Financial Aid Ms. Deanna THOMPSON
35 Coordinator Student Life Ms. Laura GARDNER
88 Director Fitness Center Mr. Dennis CLARK
41 Director Athletics Mr. Ted PETERSEN
15 Director Human Resources Mr. David CAGLE
10 Director Financial Affairs Ms. Beth NUNLEY
50 Assoc Dean Business & Technology Mr. Paul CARLSON
51 Asst Dean Cont Educ & Career Svcs Ms. Mary POSING
18 Dir Campus Facilities & Security Mr. Rich SODERQUIST
88 Coordinator Small Business Devel Mr. Ken CRITE
81 Assoc Dean Math/Science Division Mr. Fred COOPER
76 Assoc Dean Health Careers Div Ms. Sheri CAGLE
88 Director Student Advisement Ms. Meredith PURCELL
76 Director Respiratory Therapist Pgm Ms. Nancy OZEE
76 Director Medical Lab Technology Ms. Glenda FORNERIS
83 Assoc Dean Humanities/Social Sci Dr. Jill CHANNING
76 Director Radiology Technology Pgm Ms. Darla JEPSON
13 Director Information Tech Svcs Mr. Michael O'CONNOR
102 Exec Director of KCC Foundation Ms. Kelly MYERS

07 Coord Admissions & Recruitment Ms. Lindsey ZERBIAN
88 Director Institutional Tech/Fac Dev Mr. Craig KEIGHER
62 Director Learning Resource Center Ms. Karen BECKER
26 Director Marketing Ms. Kari NUGENT
88 Dean of Sustainability Dr. Bert JACOBSON
101 Board Recording Secretary Ms. Karen SLAGER

Kaskaskia College (C)

27210 College Road, Centralia IL 62801-7878

County: Clinton | FICE Identification: 001701 | Unit ID: 146366
Telephone: (618) 545-3000 | Carnegie Class: Assoc/Pub-R-L
FAX Number: (618) 532-1990 | Calendar System: Semester
URL: www.kaskaskia.edu
Established: 1940 | Annual Undergrad Tuition & Fees (In-District): $3,930
Enrollment: 2,654 | Coed
Affiliation or Control: State/Local | IRS Status: 501(c)3
Highest Offering: Associate Degree
Program: Occupational; 2-Year Principally Bachelor's Creditable
Accreditation: NH, ADNUR, CAHIIM, COARC, DA, MLTAD, OTA, PTAA, RAD, SURGT

01 President Dr. Penny QUINN
11 Vice Pres Administrative Services Mrs. Nancy KINSEY
05 Vice Pres Instructional Services Dr. Gregory LABYAK
32 Vice President of Student Services Mrs. Susan BATCHELOR
75 Dean Career & Technical Education Mr. George EVANS
49 Dean of Arts & Sciences Ms. Kellie HENEGAR
66 Dean of Nursing Mrs. Janet GARRETSON
09 Dean Institutional Effectiveness Mr. Jeffrey EBEL
43 Dir Legal CounselRisk Mgt/Plan Giv Ms. Rhonda BOEHNE
15 Director of Human Resources Ms. Anna MOYER
18 Director Facilities/Physical Plant Mr. Jennings CARTER
96 Director Purchasing/Auxiliary Svcs Mr. Craig ROPER
06 Manager of Records & Registration Ms. Jan RIPPERDA
37 Director of Financial Aid Ms. Jill KLOSTERMANN
76 Director of Radiologic Technology Mrs. Mimi POLCZYNSKI
76 Dir Physical Therapist Asst Pgm Ms. Jane HERRMANN
13 Dean of Information Technology Ms. Gina SCHUETZ
27 Director of Public Information Ms. Cathy KARRICK
26 Director of Marketing Mr. Travis HENSON
40 Bookstore Manager Ms. Cheryl JOHNSON
51 Dean of Adult Education Vacant
88 Project Manager Business Svc Ctr Mr. Steve GRONER
50 Business Services Field Rep Mr. Art BORUM
41 Athletic Director Mr. Adam ESSES
10 Controller Ms. Mary DANT
88 Director of Student Recruitment Ms. Amy TROUTT
88 Dean of Student Success Dr. Scott CROTHERS
07 Dir Admissions/Records & Dual Cred Mrs. Cheryl BOEHNE
88 Dir Centralia Correctional Ctr Pgm Ms. Tina WOLFE
30 Dir Inst Advancement Programs Mrs. Suzanne CHRIST

Kendall College (D)

900 N North Branch Street, Chicago IL 60642

County: Cook | FICE Identification: 001703 | Unit ID: 146393
Telephone: (312) 752-2000 | Carnegie Class: Bac/Diverse
FAX Number: (312) 752-2021 | Calendar System: Quarter
URL: www.kendall.edu
Established: 1934 | Annual Undergrad Tuition & Fees: $25,945
Enrollment: 1,516 | Coed
Affiliation or Control: Proprietary | IRS Status: Proprietary
Highest Offering: Baccalaureate
Program: Occupational; 2-Year Principally Bachelor's Creditable; Liberal Arts And General; Teacher Preparatory; Professional; Business Emphasis
Accreditation: NH, ACFEI

01 President Ms. Emily WILLIAMS KNIGHT
05 Provost Dr. Agueda BENITO
26 Director of Marketing Ms. Genevieve BURKE
04 Executive Assistant to President Mr. Scott BRANDEL
10 Director of Finance Vacant
06 Registrar Ms. Amanda MOLLER
15 Manager of Human Resources Ms. Crystal KAMINSKI
29 Alumni Affairs Ms. Marguerite ALLGRETTI
38 Director of Advising Mr. Frank ARCE
08 Library Technician Ms. Alexis CARSCADDEN
84 Director of Enrollment Management Mr. Ross ROSENBERG
13 Director of Information Technology Ms. Laura WELMERS
37 Director of Financial Aid Mr. Lauren WALKER
39 Director of Housing Ms. Kenya HAWKINS
106 Academic Director Ms. Cheryl BONCUORE
97 Director of General Education Mr. Ryan BARTELMAY
18 Chief Facilities/Physical Plant Mr. Cliff HILL
32 Director Student Operations Ms. Jeanette KONIECZKA
09 Director of Institutional Research Mr. Patrick EGAN
96 Procurement Manager Ms. Lara ENGERT

Kishwaukee College (E)

21193 Malta Road, Malta IL 60150-9600

County: De Kalb | FICE Identification: 007684 | Unit ID: 146418
Telephone: (815) 825-2086 | Carnegie Class: Assoc/Pub-S-SC
FAX Number: (815) 825-2072 | Calendar System: Semester
URL: www.kishwaukeecollege.edu
Established: 1967 | Annual Undergrad Tuition & Fees (In-District): $3,930
Enrollment: 4,475 | Coed
Affiliation or Control: State/Local | IRS Status: 501(c)3
Highest Offering: Associate Degree
Program: Occupational; 2-Year Principally Bachelor's Creditable
Accreditation: NH, COMTA, RAD

01 President Dr. Thomas L. CHOICE
05 Vice President Instruction Mr. Mark LANTING
10 Vice Pres of Finance/Administration Mr. Robert GALICK
32 Vice President Student Services Mr. Sedgwick HARRIS
09 Assoc VP Institutional Effectivenes Mr. Kevin J. FUSS
83 Dean Arts/Communic/Social Science Ms. Jaime LONG
72 Dean Career Technologies Mrs. Sara POHL
76 Dean Health & Education Ms. Bette CHILTON
35 Dean of Student Services Ms. Nancy PARTCH
81 Dean Math/Science/Business Vacant
51 Dean Adult Educ/Transition Pgms Ms. Joanne KANTNER
21 Dean of Business Affairs Ms. Beth YOUNG
103 Dean of Workforce Dev & Cont Ed Ms. Michele BOLDEN
102 Exec Dir Kish Col Foundation Devel Mr. Marshall HAYES
07 Dir Admissions/Registration/Records Ms. Michelle ROTHMEYER
26 Dir of Marketing & Public Relations Ms. Kayte HAMEL
37 Director Student Financial Aid Ms. Cynthia STONESIFER
13 Director Information Technology Mr. Scott ARMSTRONG
40 Bookstore Manager Ms. Jessica ANDERSON
08 Director Library Services Ms. Anne-Marie GREEN
15 Director Human Resources Mr. John ACARDO
41 Athletic Director Mr. Craig JACKSON
18 Chief Facilities/Physical Plant Mr. Michael KUROPAS
04 Executive Asst to President Ms. Cindy MCCLUSKEY
108 Director Institutional Assessment Mr. Matthew CRULL
28 Coord Access/Equity and Diversity Mr. Keith BARNES
96 Purchasing Coordinator Ms. Kathleen JONES

Knowledge Systems Institute (F)

3420 Main Street, Skokie IL 60076-2453

County: Cook | FICE Identification: 026227 | Unit ID: 260956
Telephone: (847) 679-3135 | Carnegie Class: Spec/Tech
FAX Number: (847) 679-3166 | Calendar System: Semester
URL: www.ksi.edu
Established: 1978 | Annual Graduate Tuition & Fees: $7,900
Enrollment: 193 | Coed
Affiliation or Control: Independent Non-Profit | IRS Status: 501(c)3
Highest Offering: Master's; No Undergraduates
Program: Professional; Technical Emphasis
Accreditation: NH

01 Chancellor Dr. Shi-Kuo CHANG
03 Executive Director Ms. Judy PAN
05 Academic Dean Dr. Cheng-Yuan HSIEH
07 Chr Computer Sci/Admiss Committee Dr. Cheng-Yuan HSIEH
11 Administrative Manager Mr. Noorjhan ALI

Knox College (G)

2 E South Street, Galesburg IL 61401-4999

County: Knox | FICE Identification: 001704 | Unit ID: 146427
Telephone: (309) 341-7000 | Carnegie Class: Bac/A&S
FAX Number: (309) 341-7090 | Calendar System: Trimester
URL: www.knox.edu
Established: 1837 | Annual Undergrad Tuition & Fees: $41,847
Enrollment: 1,378 | Coed
Affiliation or Control: Independent Non-Profit | IRS Status: 501(c)3
Highest Offering: Baccalaureate
Program: Liberal Arts And General; Teacher Preparatory
Accreditation: NH, @TEAC

01 President Dr. Teresa L. AMOTT
05 VP Acad Affairs/Dean of College Dr. Laura L. BEHLING
10 Vice Pres for Finance & Admin Svcs Mr. Keith A. ARCHER
30 Vice President for Advancement Ms. Beverly HOLMES
07 Vice Pres Enrollment/Dean of Admiss Mr. Paul R. STEENIS
26 Assoc VP Communications Ms. Megan SCOTT
06 Registrar Dr. Chuck SCHULZ
32 Dean of Students Ms. Debbie SOUTHERN
20 Associate Dean of College Dr. Lori SCHROEDER
37 Director Financial Aid Ms. Ann BRILL
08 Librarian Mr. Jeffrey A. DOUGLAS
36 Director Ctr Career Pre-Prof Dev Ms. Terrie SALINE
13 VP/CIO Information Technology Svcs Mr. Steven HALL
15 Director Human Resources Vacant
18 Director Facilities Services Mr. Scott MAUST
21 Controller Ms. Bobby Jo MAURER
86 Dir Government & Community Relation Ms. Karrie HEARTLEIN
29 Dir Alumni & Constituent Programs Ms. Carol J. BROWN
38 Director of Counseling Services Dr. Daniel L. LARSON
41 Director of Athletics Mr. Chad EISELE
19 Director Campus Safety Mr. Mark A. WELKER
09 Dir Institutional Research/Assess Mr. Charles L. CLARK
102 Dir Corporate/Foundation Relations Ms. Anne-Marie BERK
43 Dir Legal Services/General Counsel Vacant
44 Director Annual or Planned Giving Mr. Scott PARK

Lake Forest College (H)

555 N Sheridan Road, Lake Forest IL 60045-2338

County: Lake | FICE Identification: 001706 | Unit ID: 146481
Telephone: (847) 234-3100 | Carnegie Class: Bac/A&S
FAX Number: (847) 735-6291 | Calendar System: Semester
URL: www.lakeforest.edu
Established: 1857 | Annual Undergrad Tuition & Fees: $42,644
Enrollment: 1,592 | Coed
Affiliation or Control: Independent Non-Profit | IRS Status: 501(c)3

Highest Offering: Master's
Program: Liberal Arts And General
Accreditation: NH

01	President	Mr. Stephen D. SCHUTT
05	Provost/Dean of Faculty	Dr. Michael ORR
10	VP for Finance/Planning & Treasurer	Ms. Lori SUNDBERG
30	VP of Development & Alumni Pgms	Mr. Philip HOOD
07	VP of Enrollment	Mr. Chris ELLERTSON
32	Vice President for Student Affairs	Mr. Rob FLOT
21	Controller and Payroll	Ms. Doris DUMAS
04	Executive Assistant to President	Ms. Elizabeth A. PALM
35	Assoc Dean Dir of Residence Life	Mr. Andrew POLLOM
28	Director Intercult Relelations	Ms. Erin HOFFMAN
20	Asc Dean Facul/Dir Ctr Chicago Pgms	Dr. Davis SCHNEIDERMAN
20	Assoc Dean Facul/Dir Lrng/Tchng Ctr	Dr. Ann ROBERTS
31	Director of Community Education	Mr. Dan LEMAHIEU
37	Associate VP of Financial Aid	Mr. Gerard J. CEBRZYNSKI
41	Athletic Director	Ms. Jacqueline SLAATS
08	Librarian & Director Info Svcs/Tech	Mr. James R. CUBIT
06	Registrar	Ms. Ruthane I. BOPP
38	Director of Counseling Services	Dr. Jennifer JEZIORSKI
29	Assoc Vice Pres for Alumni Relation	Ms. Kim FEIGH
09	Director of Institutional Research	Ms. Lori H. SUNDBERG
15	Director of Human Resources	Ms. Agnes STEPEK
36	Director of Career Services	Ms. Lisa HINKLEY
18	Director of Facilities Management	Mr. David J. SIEBERT
26	Assoc VP for Comm//Mktg	Ms. Elizabeth LIBBY
19	Director of Public Safety	Mr. Richard L. COHEN
101	Secretary of the Institution/Board	Ms. Carol LUEDERS
104	Director Study Abroad	Ms. Ashley SINCLAIR
44	Director Annual Giving	Ms. Katie ROTH

Lake Forest Graduate School of Management (A)

1905 W Field Court, Lake Forest IL 60045-4824
County: Lake — FICE Identification: 023192
Unit ID: 146490
Telephone: (847) 234-5005 — Carnegie Class: Spec/Bus
FAX Number: (847) 295-3656 — Calendar System: Semester
URL: www.lakeforestmba.edu
Established: 1946 — Annual Graduate Tuition & Fees: $20,220
Enrollment: 470 — Coed
Affiliation or Control: Independent Non-Profit — IRS Status: 501(c)3
Highest Offering: Master's; No Undergraduates
Program: Professional; Business Emphasis
Accreditation: NH

01	President	Mr. Jeffrey J. ANDERSON
05	VP and Chief Academic Officer	Dr. Bryan J. WATKINS
10	VP Finance & CFO	Mr. Malcolm C. DOUGLAS
26	Senior Director of Marketing	Ms. Barb SIEGEL
20	VP Corporate Learning Solutions	Ms. Carrie BUCHWALD
15	VP HR & External Relations	Ms. Stasia ZWISLER
13	VP IT/RDI & CIO	Mr. Gregory KOZAK
20	Dean Faculty & Degree Programs	Vacant
20	Dean Corporate Learning Solutions	Dr. Neil HOLMAN
06	Registrar	Ms. Christine L. PERLSTROM
37	Associate Director of Financial Aid	Ms. Rebecca KIM
07	Senior Director of Admissions	Ms. Carolyn BRUNE
32	Director of Student Services	Ms. Laura PALEY
35	Manager of Student Services	Mr. Richard DELEWSKY
04	Administrative Asst to President	Ms. Carol ELLIS
09	Sr Director R&D & Innovation	Mr. Manish SHAH
88	Mgr Faculty & Academic Planning	Ms. Rachel OLBUR
21	Mgr Student Financial Services	Mr. Kartik GURURAJAN

Lake Land College (B)

5001 Lake Land Boulevard, Mattoon IL 61938-9366
County: Coles — FICE Identification: 007644
Unit ID: 146506
Telephone: (217) 234-5253 — Carnegie Class: Assoc/Pub-R-L
FAX Number: (217) 234-5400 — Calendar System: Semester
URL: www.lakeland.cc.il.us
Established: 1966 — Annual Undergrad Tuition & Fees (In-District): $3,460
Enrollment: 6,895 — Coed
Affiliation or Control: State/Local — IRS Status: 501(c)3
Highest Offering: Associate Degree
Program: Occupational; 2-Year Principally Bachelor's Creditable
Accreditation: NH, ADNUR, DH, PNUR, PTAA

01	President	Dr. Josh BULLOCK
100	Senior Executive to the President	Ms. Jean Anne GRUNLOH
04	Admin Asst to the President's Ofc	Ms. Seirra LAUGHHUNN
10	VP for Business Services	Mr. Ray RIECK
05	VP for Academic Services	Dr. Jim HULL
32	Vice President for Student Services	Dr. Tina STOVALL
20	Assoc Vice Pres of Instruction	Ms. Leslie DEVORE
88	Dean of Correctional Pgms-South	Mr. Brandon YOUNG
20	Assoc Vice Pres Educational Svcs	Dr. Deb HUTTI
07	Dean of Admissions Services	Mr. Jon VAN DYKE
88	Assoc Dean Corrections-Taylorville	Mr. Robert EIFERT
88	Assoc Dean Corrections-Graham	Vacant
88	Assoc Dean Corrections-Western	Ms. Malea HARNEY
88	Assoc Dean Correction-IL River	Mr. Michael CHASE
88	Assoc Dean Corrections-Southwestern	Mr. Harvey GROENNERT
88	Assoc Dean Corrections-Jacksonville	Mr. Steve BAHNEY
88	Assoc Dean Corrections-Lawrence	Ms. Valerie PRATSCHER
88	Assoc Dean Corrections-Robinson	Vacant
88	Assc Dean Corrections-Vandalia	Mr. Steve DRAKE
44	Exec Dir for College Advancement	Ms. Jacqueline JOINES
88	Site Director Corrections-Hill	Vacant
88	Site Director Corr-Vienna & Shawnee	Mr. Blake MCCONNELL
21	Comptroller	Ms. Madge SHOOT
50	Dir Center for Business & Industry	Ms. Bonnie MOORE
08	Director of Library Services	Mr. Scott DRONE-SILVERS
26	Dir of Marketing/Public Relations	Mrs. Kelly ALLEE
13	Director of Information Systems	Mr. Lee SPANIOL
37	Dir of Financial Aid/Veteran Svcs	Ms. Paula CARPENTER
18	Director of Facilities Planning	Mr. Michael KASDORF
15	Director of Human Resources	Ms. Dawn SCHLECHTE
88	Director of Learning Technologies	Mr. Steve GARREN
25	Director of Grants Development	Ms. Emily RAMAGE
109	Director of Auxiliary Services	Ms. Chris KRAMER
29	Dir of Alumni Rels/Annual Giving	Mr. Dave COX
36	Director of Career Services	Ms. Tina MOORE
38	Chair of Counseling/Judicial Affs	Ms. Emily HARTKE
18	Dir of Physical Plant Operations	Mr. Scott RAWLINGS
41	Director of Athletics	Mr. William JACKSON
09	Director of Institutional Research	Dr. Mary BREER
84	Coordinator of Enrollment Services	Ms. Paula SMITH

Lakeview College of Nursing (C)

903 N Logan Avenue, Danville IL 61832-3788
County: Vermilion — FICE Identification: 010501
Unit ID: 146533
Telephone: (217) 709-0920 — Carnegie Class: Spec/Health
FAX Number: (217) 709-0954 — Calendar System: Semester
URL: www.lakeviewcol.edu
Established: 1987 — Annual Undergrad Tuition & Fees: $14,025
Enrollment: 322 — Coed
Affiliation or Control: Independent Non-Profit — IRS Status: 501(c)3
Highest Offering: Baccalaureate
Program: Professional; Nursing Emphasis
Accreditation: NH, NURSE

01	President	Ms. Sheila MINGEE
05	Dean of Nursing	Ms. Chastity OSBORN
06	Registrar/Dir Enrollment	Ms. Connie YOUNG
08	Library Dir/IT Coordinator	Ms. Miranda SHAKE

Le Cordon Bleu College of Culinary Arts in Chicago (D)

361 W Chestnut Street, Chicago IL 60610
County: Cook — FICE Identification: 023522
Unit ID: 144467
Telephone: (312) 944-0882 — Carnegie Class: Assoc/PrivFP
FAX Number: (312) 944-8557 — Calendar System: Quarter
URL: www.chefs.edu/chicago
Established: 1983 — Annual Undergrad Tuition & Fees: $40,050
Enrollment: 600 — Coed
Affiliation or Control: Proprietary — IRS Status: Proprietary
Highest Offering: Associate Degree
Program: Occupational; 2-Year Principally Bachelor's Creditable; Fine Arts Emphasis
Accreditation: NH, ACFEI

01	Campus President	Mrs. Maegan K. MURPHY
07	Director of Admissions	Mr. Kevin FERGUSON
08	Regional Librarian	Ms. Laura RICE
108	Director Institutional Effectivenes	Ms. Julianna DHANIE
36	Director of Career Services	Mrs. Mona YAEAGER
37	Business Operations Manager	Ms. Christina NELSON
53	Director of Education	Mr. Michael RILEY

Lewis and Clark Community College (E)

5800 Godfrey Road, Godfrey IL 62035-2466
County: Madison — FICE Identification: 010020
Unit ID: 146603
Telephone: (618) 468-7000 — Carnegie Class: Assoc/Pub-S-SC
FAX Number: (618) 466-2798 — Calendar System: Semester
URL: www.lc.edu
Established: 1970 — Annual Undergrad Tuition & Fees (In-District): $3,388
Enrollment: 7,903 — Coed
Affiliation or Control: State/Local — IRS Status: 501(c)3
Highest Offering: Associate Degree
Program: Occupational; 2-Year Principally Bachelor's Creditable
Accreditation: NH, ADNUR, DA, DH, OTA

01	President	Dr. Dale T. CHAPMAN
05	Vice President Academic Affairs	Dr. Linda CHAPMAN
84	Vice President Enrollment Services	Mr. Kent SCHEFFEL
32	Vice Pres Student Engagement	Dr. Sean HILL
11	Vice President Administration	Ms. Lori ARTIS
10	Vice President Finance	Mrs. Mary SCHULTE
21	Chief Budget Officer	Mrs. Nancy KAISER
88	Director Corp & Comm Learning	Mrs. Kathy WILLIS
13	Chief Information Officer	Mr. Mark TUCK
09	Dir Institutional Res/Library Svcs	Mr. Dennis KRIEB
06	Registrar	Ms. Heidi SCOTT
41	Director Athletics	Mr. Doug STOTLER

Lewis University (F)

One University Parkway, Romeoville IL 60446-2200
County: Will — FICE Identification: 001707
Unit ID: 146612
Telephone: (815) 838-0500 — Carnegie Class: Master's L
FAX Number: (815) 838-9456 — Calendar System: Semester
URL: www.lewisu.edu
Established: 1932 — Annual Undergrad Tuition & Fees: $28,940
Enrollment: 6,689 — Coed
Affiliation or Control: Roman Catholic — IRS Status: 501(c)3
Highest Offering: Doctorate
Program: Liberal Arts And General
Accreditation: NH, ACBSP, CAATE, NURSE, SW, TED

01	President	Br. James GAFFNEY, FSC
05	Provost	Dr. Stephany SCHLACHTER
32	Sr Vice President Student Services	Mr. Joseph FALESE
10	Senior Vice Pres/CFO	Mr. Robert DE ROSE
84	Sr VP Enrollment Mgmt/Marketing	Mr. Raymond KENNELLY
30	Vice Pres University Advancement	Mr. Leonard BERTOLINI
07	Director of Admission	Mr. Ryan COCKERILL
35	Dean of Student Services	Ms. Katheryn SLATTERY
28	VP Mission & Academic Services	Dr. Kurt SCHACKMUTH
49	Dean College Arts & Sciences	Dr. Bonnie BONDAVALLI
50	Dean College Business	Dr. Rami KHASAWNEH
66	Dean Col Nursing/Health Professions	Dr. Peggy RICE
53	Dean College of Education	Dr. Pamela JESSEE
15	Assoc Vice Pres Human Resources	Ms. Graciela DUFOUR
09	Assoc VP Inst Research/Planning	Dr. Jion YEN
08	Director of Library	Mr. Thomas URBANSKI
06	Registrar	Mr. Robert KEMPIAK
37	Director of Financial Aid	Ms. Janeen DECHARINTE
26	Director Marketing/Communications	Dr. Ramona LAMONTAGNE
41	Director of Athletics	Dr. John PLANEK
38	Director of Counseling Services	Ms. Michele MANASSAH
19	Chief of Police	Mr. James MONTANARI
42	Director of University Ministry	Mr. Steve ZLATIC
31	Dir of Meetings/Events/Conferences	Mr. Robert ARNOLD
85	Director International Student Svcs	Mr. Michael FEKETE
11	Director of Administrative Services	Mr. Charles PUSTZ
13	Associate Vice Pres/Technology	Dr. LeRoy BUTLER
29	Exec Dir Alumni/Development Svcs	Ms. Julie PENNER
96	Director of Opers and Purchasing	Ms. Jiennifer SKVARLA
36	Exec Director of Career Services	Ms. Mary MYERS
04	Administrative Asst to President	Ms. Margaret KIENTOP
102	Dir Foundation & Corp Relations	Ms. Jennifer DOHERTY
104	Director Study Abroad	Mr. Christopher SWANSON
105	Director Web Services	Mr. Syl GOYETTE
18	Assoc VP Facilities/Physical Plant	Mr. Donald CASTELLO
25	Director of Sponsored Programs	Mr. Jeffrey RITCHIE
23	Director Health Services	Ms. Michele RONCHETTI
39	Director of Residence Life	Mr. Fredrick GANDY
44	Director Planned Giving	Mr. Robert KANONIK

Lincoln Christian University (G)

100 Campus View Drive, Lincoln IL 62656-2167
County: Logan — FICE Identification: 001708
Unit ID: 146667
Telephone: (217) 732-3168 — Carnegie Class: Spec/Faith
FAX Number: (217) 732-5914 — Calendar System: Semester
URL: www.lincolnchristian.edu
Established: 1944 — Annual Undergrad Tuition & Fees: $20,900
Enrollment: 936 — Coed
Affiliation or Control: Christian Churches And Churches of Christ — IRS Status: 501(c)3
Highest Offering: Doctorate
Program: Liberal Arts And General; Religious Emphasis
Accreditation: NH, BI, CACREP, THEOL

01	President	Dr. Donald GREEN
10	Vice President of Finance	Mr. G. Steve POPENFOOSE
05	Vice Pres of Academics	Dr. Silas MCCORMICK
84	VP of Enrollment & Student Services	Mr. Randall INGMIRE
32	Dean of Students	Mr. Steve COLLINS
30	VP of University Advancement	Mr. Gordon D. VENTURELLA
29	VP of Alumni Services	Mr. Lynn LAUGHLIN
06	Registrar	Mr. Shawn SMITH
08	Librarian	Ms. Nancy OLSON
37	Director of Financial Aid	Ms. Nancy SIDDENS
101	Admin Asst to Pres/Secy Bd of Gov	Mrs. Linda SEGGELKE
13	Director of Campus Technology	Mr. Larry WOOLARD
07	Director of Enrollment Management	Mrs. Jessica HANSON
15	Director of Human Resources	Mrs. Marla BENNETT
41	Athletic Director	Mr. Mac INGMIRE

Lincoln College (H)

300 Keokuk Street, Lincoln IL 62656-1699
County: Logan — FICE Identification: 001709
Unit ID: 146676
Telephone: (217) 732-3155 — Carnegie Class: Bac/Assoc
FAX Number: (217) 732-8859 — Calendar System: Semester
URL: www.lincolncollege.edu
Established: 1865 — Annual Undergrad Tuition & Fees: $17,700
Enrollment: 1,264 — Coed
Affiliation or Control: Independent Non-Profit — IRS Status: 501(c)3
Highest Offering: Baccalaureate
Program: 2-Year Principally Bachelor's Creditable; Liberal Arts And General
Accreditation: NH, IACBE

01	President	Dr. David M. GERLACH
05	Vice President for Academic Affairs	Dr. A. Gigi FANSLER
30	Vice President for Advancement	Ms. Debbie ACKERMAN
84	VP for Enroll Mgmt & Student Svcs	Mr. Rick SAMUELS
10	Vice Pres Finance & Administration	Mr. Greg A. EIMER

07 Dean of Enrollment Management .... Mr. Joe HENDRIX
32 Dean of Students .... Mrs. Bridgett THOMAS
107 Exec Dir Center for Adult Learning .... Mr. Vance LAINE
88 Director of Academic Advising .... Ms. Susan BOEHLER
06 Registrar .... Mrs. Debra J. HARMON
08 Head Librarian .... Mr. Mike STARASTA
13 Director of Information Technology .... Mr. David LOLLING
21 Controller .... Mrs. Katherine PAPESCH
15 Director of Human Resources .... Ms. Sara SCHWANTZ
18 Director of Building & Grounds .... Ms. Ronda PIATT
37 Director of Financial Aid .... Mr. Chris STECKMANN
41 Athletic Director .... Mr. Dave KLEMM
40 Bookstore Manager .... Mrs. Donna HUTCHISON

Lincoln College - Normal (A)

715 W Raab Road, Normal IL 61761
Telephone: (309) 452-0500　Identification: 770078
Accreditation: &NH

† Branch campus of Lincoln College, Lincoln, IL.

Lincoln College of Technology (B)

8317 West North Avenue, Melrose Park IL 60160-1605
County: Cook　FICE Identification: 010316
Unit ID: 146700
Telephone: (708) 344-4700　Carnegie Class: Assoc/PrivFP
FAX Number: (708) 345-4065　Calendar System: Semester
URL: www.lincolnedu.com
Established: 1950　Annual Undergrad Tuition & Fees: $31,502
Enrollment: 497　Coed
Affiliation or Control: Proprietary　IRS Status: Proprietary
Highest Offering: Associate Degree
Program: Occupational; Technical Emphasis
Accreditation: ACCSC

01 Campus President .... Karen M. CLARK

Lincoln Land Community College (C)

5250 Shepherd Road, PO Box 19256,
Springfield IL 62794-9256
County: Sangamon　FICE Identification: 007170
Unit ID: 146685
Telephone: (217) 786-2200　Carnegie Class: Assoc/Pub-R-L
FAX Number: (217) 786-2468　Calendar System: Semester
URL: www.llcc.edu
Established: 1967　Annual Undergrad Tuition & Fees (In-District): $3,630
Enrollment: 7,006　Coed
Affiliation or Control: Local　IRS Status: 501(c)3
Highest Offering: Associate Degree
Program: Occupational; 2-Year Principally Bachelor's Creditable; Nursing Emphasis
Accreditation: NH, ADNUR, COARC, NDT, OTA, RAD, SURGT

01 President .... Dr. Charlotte J. WARREN
11 Vice President Administrative Svcs .... Mr. Todd MCDONALD
05 Vice President Academic Svcs .... Dr. Eileen G. TEPATTI
32 Vice President Student Services .... Ms. Lesley J. FREDERICK
103 Vice Pres Workforce Dev/Cmty Educ .... Dr. Judy JOZAITIS
13 Chief Information Officer .... Mr. Esteban CRUZ
15 Assoc Vice Pres Human Resources .... Ms. Junell A. RANSDELL
84 Assoc VP Enrollment Svcs/Registrar .... Ms. Lisa COLLIER
10 Associate Vice President Finance .... Ms. Karie L. LONGHTA
86 Asst VP Corp/Gov Trng & Econ Devel .... Ms. Paula J. LUEBBERT
18 Asst VP Construction .... Mr. Hugh GARVEY
12 Assoc Vice Pres LLCC Outreach .... Mr. Scott R. STALLMAN
102 Exec Director LLCC Foundation .... Ms. Karen A. SANDERS
26 Exec Dir Public Relations/Marketing .... Ms. Lynn WHALEN
24 Exec Director Learning Lab .... Mrs. Julie CLEVENGER
88 Director Small Business Devel Ctr .... Mr. Kevin LUST
07 Director Admissions/Records .... Mrs. Shanda R. BYER
22 Dir Employ Bnft Svc/Eq Opty Cmpl Of .... Ms. Nicole M. RALPH
09 Director Institutional Research .... Ms. Susan SIMPSON
102 Asst Director Foundation .... Ms. Barbara EADES
45 Dir Institutional Effectiveness .... Ms. Tricia A. KUJAWA
19 Police Chief .... Mr. Bradley D. GENTRY
50 Dean Business & Technologies .... Mr. David A. GREEN
83 Dean Social Sciences .... Dr. Victor K. BRODERICK
72 Assoc Vice Pres Academic Services .... Ms. Wendy L. HOWERTER
57 Dean Arts & Humanities .... Mr. J. Timothy HUMPHREY
81 Dean Mathematics and Sciences .... Mr. William D. BADE
76 Dean Health Professions .... Dr. Cynthia L. MASKEY
08 Assoc Dean Library .... Mrs. Tamara KUHN-SCHNELL
56 Asc Dean Instruct Tech/Distance Ed .... Mrs. Becky PARTON
14 Director IT and Infrastructure .... Mr. Ben ROTH
14 Director IT Service and Support .... Mrs. Joni BERNAHL
41 Director Athletics .... Mr. Ron RIGGLE
109 Director Campus Services .... Mr. Andrew BLAYLOCK
35 Asst Vice Pres Student Success .... Ms. Leslie R. JOHNSON
38 Dir Advising/Counseling/Career Svcs .... Ms. Mary Beth RAY
18 Director Facilities .... Mr. David BRETSCHER

Lindenwood University Belleville Campus (D)

2600 West Main Street, Belleville IL 62226
Telephone: (618) 239-6000　Identification: 770322
Accreditation: &NH, ACBSP

† Branch campus of Lindenwood University, Saint Charles, MO.

Loyola University Chicago (E)

1032 W. Sheridan Road, Chicago IL 60660
County: Cook　FICE Identification: 001710
Unit ID: 146719
Telephone: (773) 274-3000　Carnegie Class: RU/H
FAX Number: (312) 915-7003　Calendar System: Semester
URL: www.luc.edu
Established: 1870　Annual Undergrad Tuition & Fees: $40,426
Enrollment: 15,902　Coed
Affiliation or Control: Roman Catholic　IRS Status: 501(c)3
Highest Offering: Doctorate
Program: 2-Year Principally Bachelor's Creditable; Liberal Arts And General; Teacher Preparatory; Professional; Business Emphasis
Accreditation: NH, BUS, BUSA, CLPSY, COPSY, DENT, DIETI, EMT, FEPAC, LAW, MED, NURSE, SCPSY, SW, TED, THEA

00 Chancellor .... Rev. Michael J. GARANZINI, SJ
01 Interim President .... Dr. John P. PELISSERO
17 Provost Health Sciences .... Dr. Margaret F. CALLAHAN
05 Interim Provost .... Dr. Samuel ATTOH
10 Sr Vice President Finance & CFO .... Mr. Robert A. MUNSON
44 Vice President Advancement .... Rev. Justin DAFFRON, SJ
45 Sr VP Cap Planning & Campus Mgmt .... Mr. Wayne MAGDZIARZ
11 Sr VP Admin Svcs .... Mr. Thomas M. KELLY
43 Vice President & General Counsel .... Ms. Pam COSTAS
32 Vice President Student Development .... Ms. Jane NEUFELD
22 VP HR & Chief Diversity Officer .... Ms. Winifred WILLIAMS
88 Director Strategic Financing/Risk .... Ms. Susan BODIN
65 Director Environmental Services .... Mr. William CURTIN
88 Dir of Capital Business Operations .... Mr. David BEALL
88 Dir Institute Pastoral Studies .... Dr. Brian SCHMISEK
84 Dir Graduate/Professional Admiss .... Ms. Ann TALBOT
51 Director Adult & Transfer Center .... Ms. Jill SCHUR
88 Director Enrollment Marketing .... Ms. Nicole BARRON
19 Director Campus Safety .... Mr. Thomas MURRAY
29 Director Alumni Relations .... Ms. Leticia NIETO
88 Dir of Advancement Communication .... Mr. Brendan KEATING
105 Director of Web Communication .... Mr. John DREVS
88 Director of Student Complex .... Ms. Dawn M. COLLINS
96 Director of Payment Services .... Mr. Brian SLAVINSKAS
96 Director of Cash Management .... Mr. Corey O'BRIEN
18 Director of Facilities-HSD .... Mr. Tom EARLY
12 Vice President & Director Rome Ctr .... Mr. Emilio IODICE
86 Vice President Government Affairs .... Mr. Philip P. HALE
13 Vice President Information Services .... Ms. Susan M. MALISCH
04 Special Assistant to the President .... Rev. John COSTELLO, SJ
26 VP Marketing & Communications .... Ms. Kelly SHANNON
88 Sr VP for Health Sciences .... Mr. Steve BERGFELD
30 Assoc VP Development .... Mr. Kevin WILEY
88 Assoc VP Finance - HSD .... Mr. Roger RUSSELL
88 Assoc VP Informatics/System Devel .... Mr. Ronald N. PRICE
21 Assoc VP Finance & Controller .... Ms. Andrea SABITSANA
21 Assoc VP Finance Sponsored Pgm Acc .... Ms. Donna QUIRK
109 Associate VP Campus Services .... Mr. Timothy MCGURIMAN
31 Assoc VP Campus/Community Planning .... Ms. Jennifer R. CLARK
21 Assoc VP for Budget & Finance .... Ms. Lauren HAGAN
18 Associate VP of Capital Projects .... Ms. Kana WIBBENMEYER
35 Dean of Students .... Mr. Kenechukwu MMEJE
35 Assistant VP Student Development .... Dr. Jack MCLEAN
100 Asst VP/Asst to Pres/Chairman .... Dr. Donna B. CURIN
30 Asst VP Development Health Sciences .... Mr. Shawn VOGEN
27 Asst VP Marketing & Communication .... Ms. Kate HESSION
23 Vice Provost Health Sciences .... Dr. Richard KENNEDY
85 Vice Provost Acad Ctrs/Global Inits .... Dr. Patrick M. BOYLE
20 Vice Provost Academic Affairs .... Dr. David P. PRASSE
84 Assoc Provost Enrollment Management .... Mr. Paul G. ROBERTS
46 Assoc Provost Research Services .... Dr. Samuel A. ATTOH
88 Assoc Provost Academic Admin .... Dr. Marian A. CLAFFEY
88 Assoc Provost for Mission & Identit .... Dr. John HARDT
62 Assoc Provost & Dir HSD Library .... Ms. Gail HENDLER
88 Assoc Provost Curriculum Dev .... Dr. Jo Beth D'AGOSTINO
88 Asst Provost & Dir Faculty Admin .... Dr. Beverly KASPER
100 Special Assistant to the President .... Ms. Lorraine G. SNYDER
08 Dean University Libraries .... Mr. Robert A. SEAL
50 Dean School of Business Admin .... Dr. Kevin STEVENS
51 Dean Continuing & Professional Educ .... Dr. Janet DEATHERAGE
58 Dean of Graduate School .... Dr. Samuel A. ATTOH
60 Dean School of Communication .... Dr. Donald B. HEIDER
61 Dean School of Law .... Dr. David N. YELLEN
63 Dean School of Medicine .... Dr. Linda BRUBAKER
66 Dean School of Nursing .... Dr. Vicki A. KEOUGH
70 Interim Dean School of Social Work .... Dr. Susan GROSSMAN
16 Dean Faculty Rome Center .... Dr. Alexander EVERS
107 Dean School of Cont & Prof Stds .... Mr. Walter S. PEARSON
53 Interim Dean School of Education .... Dr. Teri PIGOTT
88 Dean & Exec Dir Arrupe College .... Rev. Stephen N. KATSOUROS, SJ
18 Superintendent Lakeside Facilities .... Mr. William SHERRY
88 Exec Director Conference Services .... Mr. Dana ADAMS
96 Manager of Purchasing .... Mr. Sam J. PERRY
90 Director Academic Tech Services .... Mr. Bruce A. MONTES
88 Asst Prov Dir Academic Business Ops .... Ms. Joanna PAPPAS
88 AVP Budgeting & Financial Planning .... Mr. Ben SMIGIELSKI
88 Dir Enrollment Systems & Analysis .... Mr. Timothy HEUER
28 Dir Student Diversity & Multicultur .... Ms. Sadika SULAIMAN-HARA
29 Director Alumni Relations HSD .... Ms. Mary WEINGARTNER
37 Director of Financial Aid .... Ms. Nancy MERZ
15 Director of Human Resources .... Ms. Joan C. STASIAK
90 Dir of System Implementation & Cons .... Mr. Kevin J. SMITH
102 Dir of Corporate & Foundation Rels .... Ms. Angela LIEGEL
88 Dir Advancement Info Services .... Vacant
21 Treasurer & Chief Inv Officer .... Mr. Eric JONES
23 Director Wellness Center .... Ms. Diane C. ASARO
09 Director Institutional Research .... Dr. Richard S. HURST
06 Director of Registration & Records .... Ms. Clare M. KORINEK
07 Director Undergraduate Admissions .... Ms. Erin T. MORIATY
36 Director Career Development Center .... Ms. Kathryn JACKSON
39 Director Residence Life .... Vacant
18 Director Infrastructure Services .... Mr. Dan VONDER HEIDE
88 Dir Enterprise Architecture & Promo .... Mr. Jim SIBENALLER
28 Dir Cultural Affairs & LUMA .... Ms. Pam AMBROSE
42 Director Campus Ministry .... Dr. Lisa REITER
41 Athletic Director .... Mr. Steve WATSON
85 Director Chicago Center .... Mr. Jason OBIN
88 Director Compensation & Benefits .... Ms. Debra MEISTER
88 Director Faculty Admin-HSD .... Ms. Martha KING

Loyola University Health Sciences Campus (F)

2160 S First Avenue, Maywood IL 60153
Telephone: (708) 216-9000　Identification: 770080
Accreditation: &NH, PAST

† Branch campus of Loyola University Chicago, Chicago, IL.

Loyola University Water Town Campus (G)

820 N Michigan Avenue, Chicago IL 60611
Telephone: (312) 915-6000　Identification: 770079
Accreditation: &NH

† Branch campus of Loyola University Chicago, Chicago, IL.

Lutheran School of Theology at Chicago (H)

1100 E 55th Street, Chicago IL 60615-5199
County: Cook　FICE Identification: 001712
Unit ID: 146728
Telephone: (773) 256-0700　Carnegie Class: Spec/Faith
FAX Number: (773) 256-0782　Calendar System: Semester
URL: www.lstc.edu
Established: 1860　Annual Graduate Tuition & Fees: $15,800
Enrollment: 229　Coed
Affiliation or Control: Evangelical Lutheran Church In America
IRS Status: 501(c)3
Highest Offering: Doctorate; No Undergraduates
Program: Professional; Religious Emphasis
Accreditation: NH, THEOL

01 President .... Dr. James NIEMAN
04 Assistant to the President .... Ms. Patti DEBIAS
108 Exec for Administration/Assess/Plng .... Ms. Laura WILHELM
05 Dean/Vice Pres for Academic Affairs .... Dr. Esther MENN
88 Director of the MDiv Programs .... Dr. Kathleen BILLMAN
88 Director of the MA Programs .... Rev. Jan RIPPENTROP
58 Director of Advanced Studies .... Dr. Ben STEWART
88 Pastor to the Community .... Dr. Harvard STEPHENS, JR.
11 Vice President for Operations .... Mr. Bob BERRIDGE
30 Vice President for Advancement .... Mr. Mark H. VAN SCHARREL
10 Vice President for Finance .... Mr. Robert EDER
07 Director of Admissions .... Dr. Scott CHALMERS
06 Registrar .... Ms. Patricia A. BARTLEY
26 Director of Communications/Mktg .... Ms. Janet BODEN
08 Director of Library .... Dr. Christine WENDEROTH
13 Dir of Information Technology Svcs .... Mr. Kenesa DEBELA

MacCormac College (I)

29 E Madison Street 2nd Floor, Chicago IL 60602-4405
County: Cook　FICE Identification: 001716
Unit ID: 146816
Telephone: (312) 922-1884　Carnegie Class: Assoc/PrivNFP
FAX Number: (312) 922-4286　Calendar System: Semester
URL: www.maccormac.edu
Established: 1904　Annual Undergrad Tuition & Fees: $12,820
Enrollment: 216　Coed
Affiliation or Control: Independent Non-Profit　IRS Status: 501(c)3
Highest Offering: Associate Degree
Program: 2-Year Principally Bachelor's Creditable
Accreditation: NH

01 President .... Dr. Marnelle ALEXIS
05 Dean of Academic & Student Affairs .... Dr. Mary Ann ROWAN
10 Dean of Finance & Operations .... Mr. Matt GAWENDA
06 Registrar .... Ms. Mariza SILVA
37 Director of Financial Aid .... Ms. Rathenia HUNTER
32 Assoc Dir Admission/Student Svcs .... Mr. Marcus TROUTMAN
84 Dean Enrollment Management .... Mr. Roberto TORRES
26 Dir Communications/Public Relations .... Ms. Natasha MEEAJANE

MacMurray College (J)

447 E College Avenue, Jacksonville IL 62650-2590
County: Morgan　FICE Identification: 001717
Unit ID: 146825
Telephone: (217) 479-7000　Carnegie Class: Bac/Diverse
FAX Number: (217) 245-0405　Calendar System: 4/1/4
URL: www.mac.edu
Established: 1846　Annual Undergrad Tuition & Fees: $22,900
Enrollment: 554　Coed
Affiliation or Control: United Methodist　IRS Status: 501(c)3
Highest Offering: Baccalaureate
Program: Liberal Arts And General; Teacher Preparatory; Professional

Accreditation: NH, NURSE, SW

01 President ..... Dr. Mark J. TIERNO
10 CFO ..... Ms. Kimberly STREIB
05 Provost ..... Dr. James MAXWELL
32 Director of Student Affairs ..... Ms. Beth OBERG
30 Exec Dir Institutional Advancement ..... Vacant
07 Enrollment Manager ..... Mr. Karl HATTON
21 Controller ..... Mr. Andrew SIDOCK
13 Director of IT/System Administrator ..... Ms. Nancy SULLIVAN
06 Registrar ..... Dr. Glen CLATTERBUCK
08 Librarian ..... Ms. Susan EILERING
37 Director of Financial Aid ..... Ms. Laci ENGELBRECHT
36 Director of Career Services ..... Ms. Anne GODMAN
29 Director Alumni Relations ..... Ms. Rikki LANGAN
09 Director of Institutional Research ..... Vacant
18 Director of Facilities ..... Mr. Kerry SATTERWHITE
26 Director of Public Relations ..... Mr. Ted ROTH
04 Executive Asst to President ..... Ms. Sharon SEYMOUR
41 Athletic Director ..... Mr. Justin FUHLER

McCormick Theological Seminary (A)

5460 S University Avenue, Chicago IL 60615-5108
County: Cook FICE Identification: 001721
Unit ID: 146977
Telephone: (773) 947-6300 Carnegie Class: Spec/Faith
FAX Number: (773) 288-2612 Calendar System: 4/1/4
URL: www.mccormick.edu
Established: 1829 Annual Graduate Tuition & Fees: $21,615
Enrollment: 181 Coed
Affiliation or Control: Presbyterian Church (U.S.A.) IRS Status: 501(c)3
Highest Offering: Doctorate; No Undergraduates
Program: Professional
Accreditation: NH, THEOL

01 President ..... Rev. Frank M. YAMADA
10 Exec Vice Pres/Chief Business Ofcr ..... Mr. David CRAWFORD
05 Vice Pres Acad Affs/Dean Faculty ..... Dr. Theodore HIEBERT
32 Vice President for Student Affairs ..... Vacant
30 Vice Pres Seminary Rels/Development ..... Ms. Lisa M. DAGHER
06 Registrar ..... Ms. Chandra WADE
29 Dir of Alumni/ae & Church Rels ..... Rev. Nannette BANKS
08 Director of JKM Library ..... Dr. Christine WENDEROTH
15 Director Human Resources ..... Ms. Ashley WOODFAULK
37 Dir Student Financial Aid/Planning ..... Ms. Tabitha CLARK
07 Sr Director Admissions/Enrollment ..... Ms. Veronica JOHNSON

McHenry County College (B)

8900 US Highway 14, Crystal Lake IL 60012-2796
County: McHenry FICE Identification: 007691
Unit ID: 147004
Telephone: (815) 455-3700 Carnegie Class: Assoc/Pub-S-SC
FAX Number: (815) 455-3999 Calendar System: Semester
URL: www.mchenry.edu
Established: 1967 Annual Undergrad Tuition & Fees (In-District): $3,314
Enrollment: 6,567 Coed
Affiliation or Control: State/Local IRS Status: 501(c)3
Highest Offering: Associate Degree
Program: Occupational; 2-Year Principally Bachelor's Creditable
Accreditation: NH, OTA

01 President ..... Dr. Vicky SMITH
30 VP Institutional Advancement ..... Vacant
10 CFO/Treasurer ..... Mr. Bob TENUTA
05 VP Academic & Student Affairs ..... Dr. Tony MIKSA
13 Chief Information Officer ..... Dr. Allen P. BUTLER
04 Asst to the President/Board Liaison ..... Mrs. Pat KRIEGERMEIER
19 Exec Dir Public Safety/Facilities ..... Mr. Michael CLESCERI
26 Chief Communications Officer ..... Mrs. Christina HAGGERTY
32 AVP Academic & Student Affairs ..... Ms. Juletta PATRICK
21 AVP of Finance ..... Ms. Lynn COWLIN
15 AVP of Human Resources ..... Ms. Angelina CASTILLO
79 Exec Dean Humanities & Soc Sciences ..... Mr. Brock FISCHER
81 Exec Dean Math/Sciences Health Pgm ..... Dr. Amy MAXEINER
103 Exec Dean Workforce Comm ..... Ms. Terri BERRMAN
75 Exec Dean Educ/Career/Technical Ed ..... Mr. James FALCO
102 Executive Director MCC Foundation ..... Ms. Katrina MCGUIRE
103 Exec Dir Workforce Community Pgm ..... Mr. David MATTS
88 Executive Director of Adult Ed ..... Mr. Tom PIERCE
20 Dean of Academic Development ..... Ms. Adriane HUTCHINSON
84 Dean Enrollment Services ..... Ms. Marianne DEVENNY
08 Dean of Library ..... Ms. Kathy HARGER
88 Dean of Student Development ..... Dr. Flecia THOMAS
66 Director Nursing ..... Vacant
88 Director Recruitment & Staffing ..... Ms. Sandra HESS MOLL
88 Director Institutional Effectivenes ..... Ms. Patricia STEJSKAL
14 Director Software Solutions ..... Mr. Todd SMITH
14 Director Technology Support Service ..... Mr. Geary SMITH
40 Director Bookstore ..... Ms. Karen SMITH
41 Director Athletics-Intramural & Rec ..... Ms. Karen WILEY
51 Dir of Continuing Education ..... Ms. Dori SULLINS
25 Director of Resource Development ..... Mr. Mark DOUGHER
23 Director of Health and Wellness ..... Ms. Lena KALEMBA
88 Director of Sustainability ..... Ms. Kim HANKINS
19 Director Public Safety Operations ..... Mr. Scott SOSNOWSKI
88 Director of Learning Support ..... Ms. Emma HENDRIETH
88 Director Food Services ..... Ms. Sandra JOHNSTON
96 Director of Business Services ..... Ms. Jennifer JONES
37 Director of Financial Aid ..... Ms. Leana DAVIS
06 Director of Registration & Records ..... Ms. Amy HALLER
14 Director Infrastructure Operations ..... Mr. Rob RASMUSSEN
106 Director of Online Learning ..... Dr. Raymond LAWSON
09 Director of Institutional Research ..... Dr. Amy HUMKE
88 Director of Maintenance ..... Mr. Steve KORMANAK
19 Director Facilities and Contracts ..... Mr. Todd WHEELAND
88 Dir Fieldwork Occ Therapy Asst Pgm ..... Ms. Marlene VOGT
88 Dir Health Info Technology Programs ..... Ms. Allison MINICZ
72 Assoc Dean Educ Career/Tech Educ ..... Ms. Diana SHARP
79 Assoc Dean Humanities/Social Sci ..... Ms. Loreen KELLER
81 Assoc Dean Math/Science/Health ..... Vacant
88 Assoc Dean College/Career Readiness ..... Mr. Tony CAPALBO
88 Mgr IL Small Business Development ..... Ms. Kristi PATTERSON
88 Manager of Customer Service ..... Mr. Frank GELASI
88 Manager of Nursing Laboratory ..... Ms. Ann STAUCHE
07 Manager New Student Transitions ..... Ms. Kellie CARPER
35 Mgr of Student Conduct/Campus Life . Ms. Talia KORONKIEWICZ
16 Director of Human Resources ..... Ms. Anita ROEWER
88 Manager Accounts & Production ..... Mr. Ryan KLOS
88 Manager Access & Disability Service ..... Ms. Lil O'CONNELL

McKendree University (C)

701 College Road, Lebanon IL 62254-9990
County: Saint Clair FICE Identification: 001722
Unit ID: 147013
Telephone: (618) 537-4481 Carnegie Class: Master's L
FAX Number: (618) 537-6259 Calendar System: Semester
URL: www.mckendree.edu
Established: 1828 Annual Undergrad Tuition & Fees: $27,900
Enrollment: 3,131 Coed
Affiliation or Control: United Methodist IRS Status: 501(c)3
Highest Offering: Doctorate
Program: Liberal Arts And General; Teacher Preparatory; Professional
Accreditation: NH, CAATE, IACBE, NURSE, TED

01 President ..... Dr. James M. DENNIS
03 Senior Vice President ..... Ms. Victoria A. DOWLING
04 Assistant to the President ..... Ms. Patti J. DANIELS
05 Provost/Dean of the University ..... Dr. Christine M. BAHR
10 Vice Pres Finance/Administration ..... Mrs. Sally A. MAYHEW
07 Vice Pres Admission & Financial Aid ..... Mr. Chris HALL
32 Vice President Student Affairs ..... Dr. Joni BASTIAN
09 Vice Pres Research Plng & Tech ..... Vacant
20 Associate Dean of the University ..... Dr. Tami EGGLESTON
12 Assoc Dean McKendree-at-Scott ..... Mrs. Tia CROWDER
56 External Programs ..... Dr. Joseph J. CIPFL
13 Director Technology Information ..... Mr. George KRISS
06 Registrar/Asst Dean ..... Ms. Debra LARSON
08 Librarian ..... Ms. Rebecca SCHREINER
21 Accounting Manager ..... Mrs. Shari B. KEFFER
26 Exec Dir Marketing/Communications ..... Mrs. Krysti H. CONNELLY
29 Director Alumni Relations ..... Mrs. Whitney FRAIER
44 Director of Annual Giving ..... Mr. Vincent PIAZZA
37 Director Financial Aid ..... Mrs. Elizabeth JUEHNE
36 Director Career Services ..... Ms. Jennifer K. PICKERELL
18 Director of Operations ..... Mr. Tom P. JENSEN
15 Director Human Resources ..... Ms. Shirley A. BAUGH
27 Director Media Relations ..... Ms. Lisa K. BRANDON
39 Director of Residence Life ..... Mr. Mitch NASSER
35 Director of Campus Activities ..... Mr. Craig L. ROBERTSON
41 Athletic Director ..... Mr. Chuck BRUEGGEMANN
42 Chaplain/Director Church Relations ..... Rev Dr. B. Timothy HARRISON
40 Bookstore Director ..... Vacant
30 Director of Advancement Services ..... Mr. Scott L. BILLHARTZ
19 Director Safety & Security ..... Mr. Ranodore M. FOGGS
44 Director of Major Gifts ..... Ms. Tricia POETTKER
88 Director of Student Accounts ..... Mrs. Marsha GILES
28 Director of Diversity ..... Mr. Brent W. REEVES

Meadville Lombard Theological School (D)

610 South Michigan Avenue, Chicago IL 60605
County: Cook FICE Identification: 001723
Unit ID: 147031
Telephone: (773) 256-3000 Carnegie Class: Spec/Faith
FAX Number: (312) 327-7002 Calendar System: Semester
URL: www.meadville.edu
Established: 1844 Annual Graduate Tuition & Fees: $2,232
Enrollment: 110 Coed
Affiliation or Control: Unitarian Universalist IRS Status: 501(c)3
Highest Offering: Doctorate; No Undergraduates
Program: Professional; Religious Emphasis
Accreditation: THEOL

01 President ..... Dr. Lee BARKER
05 Provost ..... Dr. Sharon WELCH
10 Vice Pres Finance & Administration ..... Ms. Deborah BIEBER
08 Director of Library and Information ..... Ms. Rana SALZMANN
32 Dean of Students ..... Rev. Darrick JACKSON
06 Registrar ..... Ms. Valencia PENN-HARGROVE
07 Director of Admissions ..... Ms. Heather NICHOLSON

Methodist College (E)

415 St. Mark Court, Peoria IL 61603
County: Peoria FICE Identification: 006228
Unit ID: 147129
Telephone: (309) 672-5530 Carnegie Class: Spec/Health
FAX Number: (309) 671-8303 Calendar System: Semester
URL: www.methodistcol.edu
Established: 2000 Annual Undergrad Tuition & Fees: $20,290
Enrollment: 595 Coed
Affiliation or Control: Independent Non-Profit IRS Status: 501(c)3
Highest Offering: Baccalaureate
Program: Nursing Emphasis
Accreditation: NH, NURSE

01 President ..... Dr. Kimberly JOHNSTON
05 Vice Pres Academic Affairs ..... Dr. Deborah GARRISON
84 Dean Enrollment Management ..... Dr. Keith BRANHAM
10 Director of Finance ..... Mr. Tim DIETZ
20 Director of Educational Tech ..... Mr. Matthew HERTZOG
29 Director Community/Alumni Affairs ..... Ms. Alyssa SELBURG
15 Director Human Resources ..... Ms. Linda MOORE
13 Dir Information/Instruct Technology ..... Dr. Matthew HERTZOG
06 Registrar ..... Ms. Melissa EARNEST
07 Director of Admissions and Advising ..... Ms. Abby REEL
37 Director Financial Aid ..... Ms. Angela ROBINSON
09 Institutional Research Coordinator ..... Ms. Kristin WOIWODE

Midstate College (F)

411 W Northmoor Road, Peoria IL 61614-3558
County: Peoria FICE Identification: 004568
Unit ID: 147165
Telephone: (309) 692-4092 Carnegie Class: Bac/Assoc
FAX Number: (309) 692-3893 Calendar System: Quarter
URL: www.midstate.edu
Established: 1888 Annual Undergrad Tuition & Fees: $16,495
Enrollment: 521 Coed
Affiliation or Control: Proprietary IRS Status: Proprietary
Highest Offering: Baccalaureate
Program: Occupational; 2-Year Principally Bachelor's Creditable; Business Emphasis
Accreditation: NH, CAHIIM, MAC

01 President and CEO ..... Meredith N. BUNCH
05 Dean of Academics ..... Ruth E. SHAFFER
32 Dean of Students ..... Vicki DRAKSLER
10 Controller ..... Angie HATTEN
06 Registrar ..... Angela K. KEPLER
37 Director of Financial Assistance ..... Irene BIMROSE
26 Director of Marketing & Enrollment ..... Ashley SPAIN
35 Exec Director of Student Affairs ..... Rhonda P. URBAN
36 Director of Career Services ..... Jennie GREENAN
08 Director of Library Services ..... Jane BRADBURY
07 Director of Admissions ..... Marisa LITHERLAND

Midwest College of Oriental Medicine (G)

4334 N Hazel, Suite 206, Chicago IL 60613-1429
Telephone: (773) 975-1295 Identification: 666090
Accreditation: ACUP

† Branch campus of Midwest College of Oriental Medicine, Racine, WI.

Midwestern University (H)

555 31st Street, Downers Grove IL 60515-1200
County: DuPage FICE Identification: 001657
Unit ID: 143853
Telephone: (630) 969-4400 Carnegie Class: Spec/Med
FAX Number: N/A Calendar System: Quarter
URL: www.midwestern.edu
Established: 1900 Annual Undergrad Tuition & Fees: N/A
Enrollment: 2,917 Coed
Affiliation or Control: Independent Non-Profit IRS Status: 501(c)3
Highest Offering: Doctorate
Program: Professional
Accreditation: NH, ARCPA, CLPSY, DENT, OSTEO, OT, PHAR, PTA, @SP

01 President/CEO ..... Dr. Kathleen H. GOEPPINGER
03 Exec VP/Chief Operating Officer ..... Dr. Arthur G. DOBBELAERE
10 Sr VP/Chief Financial Officer ..... Mr. Gregory J. GAUS
21 Vice President Finance ..... Mr. Dean P. MALONE
46 VP Research & Strategic Initiatives ..... Dr. Theresa W. FOSSUM
26 Vice President University Relations ..... Dr. Karen D. JOHNSON
05 VP/CAO Dental/Medical & Veterin Ed ..... Dr. Dennis J. PAULSON
05 VP/CAO Pharmacy & Optometry ..... Dr. Mary W L. LEE
05 VP/CAO Health Sci Ed & VP Clinic Op ..... Dr. Kathleen N. PLAYER
11 VP Human Resources & Administration ..... Ms. Angela L. MARTY
43 VP & General Counsel ..... Ms. Barbara L. MCCLOUD
63 Dean Chicago Col of Osteo Medicine ..... Dr. Karen J. NICHOLS
67 Dean Chicago College of Pharmacy ..... Dr. Nancy F. FJORTOFT
76 Dean Col Health Sci Dowers Grove ..... Dr. Fred D. ROMANO
88 Dean Optometry ..... Dr. Sunny M. SANDERS
52 Dean College of Dental Medicine IL ..... Dr. M. A. J. Lex MACNEIL
88 Dean Basic Sciences ..... Dr. Kyle H. RAMSEY
58 Dean Postdoctoral Education ..... Dr. Thomas A. BOYLE
32 Dean Student Services ..... Dr. Teresa A. DOMBROWSKI
07 Director of Admissions ..... Mr. Michael J. LAKEN
18 Director Campus Facilities ..... Mr. Kevin M. MCCORMICK
30 Director Development/Alumni ..... Ms. Barbara WYSOCKI
15 Director Human Resources ..... Ms. Amy B. GIBSON
13 Director Information Technology Svc ..... Mr. Erik P. CARROLL
09 Director of Institutional Research ..... Dr. Kevin P. HYNES
62 Director Library ..... Ms. Natalie K. REED
24 Director Media Resources ..... Ms. Kathleen A M. DOOLEY
06 Registrar ..... Vacant
46 Director Research & Sponsored Pgms ..... Dr. James M. WOODS
19 Director Security/Safety ..... Vacant
37 Director Student Financial Services ..... Mr. Nathan ERNST
27 Director of Communications ..... Ms. Dana FAY

† Tuition varies by degree program.

Millikin University (A)

1184 W Main Street, Decatur IL 62522-2084
County: Macon　FICE Identification: 001724
Unit ID: 147244
Telephone: (217) 424-6211　Carnegie Class: Bac/Diverse
FAX Number: (217) 424-3993　Calendar System: Semester
URL: www.millikin.edu
Established: 1901　Annual Undergrad Tuition & Fees: $29,838
Enrollment: 2,160　Coed
Affiliation or Control: Presbyterian Church (U.S.A.)　IRS Status: 501(c)3
Highest Offering: Doctorate
Program: Liberal Arts And General; Teacher Preparatory; Professional; Nursing Emphasis
Accreditation: NH, ACBSP, ANEST, CAATE, MUS, NURSE, TED

01 President .... Dr. Patrick E. WHITE
05 Provost .... Dr. Jeffery P. APER
10 Vice Pres Finance/Business Affs .... Mrs. Ruby F. BRASE
30 Vice Pres University Development .... Mr. Dave E. BRANDON
84 Vice President Enrollment/Marketing .... Ms. Sarah SHUPENUS
32 Dean of Student Development .... Mrs. Raphaella PRANGE
100 Chief of Staff/Board Secretary .... Ms. Marilyn S. DAVIS
49 Dean of Arts & Sciences .... Dr. Randy M. BROOKS
57 Dean of Fine Arts .... Ms. Laura LEDFORD
107 Dean Col of Professional Studies .... Dr. Deborah L. SLAYTON
50 Dean Tabor School Business .... Dr. Susan KRUML
06 Registrar .... Mr. Jason WICKLINE
29 Sr Director Alumni/Donor Engagement .... Ms. Gina L. BIANCHI
44 Director of Major Gifts/Grant Devel .... Ms. Dawn SANDONE
36 Director of Career Center .... Ms. Pamela M. FOLGER
13 Director of Technology .... Mrs. Amy BRILLEY
08 Director of the Library .... Ms. Cindy FULLER
44 Sr Director of Development .... Mrs. Amanda PODESCHI
41 Director of Athletics .... Dr. Craig WHITE
53 Director of School of Education .... Dr. Christina MAGOULIAS
88 Director Kirkland Fine Arts Center .... Mrs. Janiece L. SADDORIS-TRAUGHBER
28 Dir Inclusion/Student Engagement .... Mrs. Molly BERRY
104 Director Center for Intl Education .... Mrs. Carmen ARAVENA
15 Director Human Resources .... Ms. Diane L. LANE
21 Controller .... Mrs. Vicki A. WRIGLEY
38 Director of Counseling Services .... Mr. Kevin C. GRAHAM
92 Director of Honors Program .... Dr. Cheryl L. CHAMBLIN
35 Director Student Development .... Mr. Z. Paul REYNOLDS
37 Director of Financial Aid .... Ms. Cheryl L. HOWERTON
51 Director of PACE Program .... Mrs. Gail CROOKSHANK
58 Director of MBA Program .... Dr. Anthony F. LIBERATORE
64 Director School of Music .... Dr. Stephen B. WIDENHOFER
87 Director of Summer School .... Dr. Randy M. BROOKS
19 Dir Dept Public Safety/Chief Police .... Mr. Chris BALLARD
66 Director School of Nursing .... Dr. Pamela L. LINDSEY
07 Director of Admission .... Mr. Kevin MCINTYRE
39 Director of Residence Life .... Mr. Paul LIDY
18 Director of Facilities Services .... Mr. Ken JORDAN
26 Director of Marketing .... Ms. Samantha KOON
09 Coord of Institutional Research .... Mrs. Laura A. BIRCH
105 Web Developer .... Ms. Jessica LANDGREBE

Monmouth College (B)

700 E Broadway, Monmouth IL 61462-1963
County: Warren　FICE Identification: 001725
Unit ID: 147341
Telephone: (309) 457-2311　Carnegie Class: Bac/A&S
FAX Number: (309) 457-2141　Calendar System: Semester
URL: www.monmouthcollege.edu
Established: 1853　Annual Undergrad Tuition & Fees: $42,260
Enrollment: 1,295　Coed
Affiliation or Control: Presbyterian Church (U.S.A.)　IRS Status: 501(c)3
Highest Offering: Baccalaureate
Program: Liberal Arts And General; Teacher Preparatory
Accreditation: NH

01 President .... Dr. Clarence R. WYATT
05 Dean of Faculty .... Dr. David M. TIMMERMAN
10 Vice President Finance & Business .... Mr. Richard A. MARSHALL
30 Vice Pres Devel/College Relations .... Col. Stephen M. BLOOMER
32 Vice Pres Student Life/Dn Students .... Ms. Jacquelyn S. CONDON
84 Vice President for Enrollment Mgmt .... Mr. Trent GILBERT
06 Registrar .... Ms. Kristi HIPPEN
08 Director Hewes Library .... Mr. Richard SAYRE
37 Director of Financial Aid .... Ms. Jayne A. SCHRECK
29 Director of Alumni Engagement .... Ms. Hannah MAHER
26 Director College Communications .... Mr. Jeffrey D. RANKIN
07 Director of Admissions .... Mr. Nick SPAETH
44 Asst Director of Annual Giving .... Ms. Jennifer SANBERG
15 Director of Personnel Services .... Mr. Mike MCNALL
18 Director Facilities Management .... Vacant
20 Associate Dean of the Faculty .... Dr. Frank GERSICH
21 Controller .... Ms. Debbie CLARK

Moody Bible Institute (C)

820 N Lasalle Boulevard, Chicago IL 60610-3263
County: Cook　FICE Identification: 001727
Unit ID: 147369
Telephone: (312) 329-4000　Carnegie Class: Spec/Faith
FAX Number: (312) 329-4109　Calendar System: Semester
URL: www.moody.edu
Established: 1886　Annual Undergrad Tuition & Fees: $12,284
Enrollment: 3,954　Coed
Affiliation or Control: Independent Non-Profit　IRS Status: 501(c)3
Highest Offering: First Professional Degree
Program: Liberal Arts And General; Professional; Religious Emphasis
Accreditation: NH, BI, MUS, THEOL

01 President .... Dr. J. Paul NYQUIST
05 Provost & Dean of Education .... Dr. Junias V. VENUGOPAL
11 Exec VP & Chief Operating Officer .... Mr. Steven A. MOGCK
10 Chief Financial Officer .... Mr. Ken HEULITT
43 VP & General Counsel .... Mrs. Janet A. STIVEN
30 VP of Stewardship .... Mr. James ELLIOTT
13 VP of Information Systems .... Mr. Frank W. LEBER
15 VP of Human Resources .... Ms. Debbie ZELINSKI
26 VP of Corporate Communications .... Mrs. Christine GORZ
20 VP & Dean of Undergraduate School .... Dr. Larry J. DAVIDHIZAR
58 VP & Dean of Theo Sem & Grad School .... Dr. John A. JELINEK
106 VP & Dean of Dist Learning School .... Dr. James SPENCER
32 VP & Dean of Student Life .... Dr. Timothy E. ARENS
108 Dir of Accreditation & Assessment .... Ms. Camille WARD
08 Department Manager Library .... Mr. James PRESTON
84 Dean of Student/Enrollment Services .... Mr. Anthony TURNER
06 Registrar/Director of Acad Records .... Mr. George MOSHER
37 Director of Financial Aid .... Mrs. Heather SHALLEY
29 Exec Director Alumni Association .... Mrs. Nancy HASTINGS
38 Associate Dean Counseling Services .... Mr. Steve BRASEL
12 Campus Dean MBI Spokane WA .... Dr. Jack LEWIS
12 Campus Dean MTS Plymouth MI .... Mr. Christopher BROOKS
14 Technology Services Director .... Mr. Ben DALLMANN
39 Associate Dean Residence Life .... Mr. Bruce R. NORQUIST
36 Assoc Dean of Career Development .... Mr. Patrick FRIEDLINE
35 Associate Dean for Student Programs .... Mr. Joseph M. GONZALES, JR.
07 Dean of Admissions .... Vacant
88 Asst Dean Student Experience MDL .... Mr. John ENGELKEMIER
41 Athletic Director .... Mr. Daniel DUNN
23 Admin of Health Service .... Ms. Ann MEYER
104 Dean of International Study Program .... Dr. Gregg QUIGGLE
04 Executive Assistant to President .... Ms. Judy SANDIFORD
19 Deputy Chief of Public Safety .... Mr. Brian M. STOFFER
21 Controller .... Ms. Linda WAHR
96 Manager of Procurement Services .... Mr. Paul BRACKLEY
18 Division Manager of Facilities .... Mr. Bill BIELAWSKI

† Tuition is paid through donor contributions. Fees are $1,950.00 per year.

Moraine Valley Community College (D)

9000 W College Parkway, Palos Hills IL 60465-0937
County: Cook　FICE Identification: 007692
Unit ID: 147378
Telephone: (708) 974-4300　Carnegie Class: Assoc/Pub-S-SC
FAX Number: (708) 974-1184　Calendar System: Semester
URL: www.morainevalley.edu
Established: 1967　Annual Undergrad Tuition & Fees (In-District): $3,996
Enrollment: 15,286　Coed
Affiliation or Control: State/Local　IRS Status: 501(c)3
Highest Offering: Associate Degree
Program: Occupational; 2-Year Principally Bachelor's Creditable
Accreditation: NH, ACFEI, ADNUR, CAHIIM, COARC, COMTA, MAC, PHLEB, POLYT, RAD

01 President .... Dr. Sylvia JENKINS
05 Vice President Academic Affairs .... Dr. Pamela HANEY
32 Vice President Student Devel .... Dr. Normah SALLEH-BARONE
11 Exec Vice Pres Administrative Svcs .... Mr. Andrew M. DUREN
10 Chief Financial Officer .... Mr. Robert STERKOWITZ
13 Chief Information Officer .... Mr. Kamlesh SANGHVI
50 Dean Science/Business/Comp Tech .... Dr. Ryen NAGLE
49 Dean Liberal Arts .... Dr. Walter FRONCZEK
38 Dean Counseling & Advising .... Mr. Scott FRIEDMAN
84 Dean Enrollment Services .... Mr. Severo BALASON
51 Dean Corporate/Cmty & Cont Educ .... Mr. Albert LEWIS
36 Dean Career Programs .... Ms. Kiana BATTTLE
35 Dean Student Services .... Mr. Chester SHAW
88 Dean Learn Enrich & Col Readiness .... Mr. Michael MORSCHES
56 Asst Dean/Dir Academic Outreach .... Mr. Grant MATTHEWS
32 Asst Dean Code of Conduct & St Life .... Mr. Kent MARSHALL
37 Director Financial Aid .... Ms. Laurie ANEMA
09 Dir Institutional Research/Planning .... Ms. Elizabeth REIS
19 Chief of Police .... Mr. Patrick O'CONNOR
15 Director Human Resources .... Ms. Lynn HARRINGTON
07 Director of Admissions/Recruitment .... Mr. Andrew SARATA
26 Director College & Cmty Relations .... Mr. Mark HORSTMEYER
18 Director Campus Operations .... Mr. Rick BRENNAN
109 Director Auxiliary Services .... Mr. Kashif SHAH
88 Director Health Education Well Ctr .... Mr. William FINN
85 Asst Dean Intl Student Admissions .... Ms. Diane VIVERITO
27 Director Mktg & Creative Services .... Ms. Clare BRINER
44 Dir Res Devel/Extended Programs .... Dr. Sharon KATTERMAN
21 Controller .... Ms. Theresa O'CARROLL
88 Director Center Disability Services .... Ms. Debbie SIEVERS
96 Director of Purchasing .... Ms. Jane BENTLEY
102 Executive Director Foundation .... Ms. Susan LINN

Morrison Institute of Technology (E)

701 Portland Avenue, Morrison IL 61270-2959
County: Whiteside　FICE Identification: 008880
Unit ID: 147396
Telephone: (815) 772-7218　Carnegie Class: Assoc/PrivNFP
FAX Number: (815) 772-7584　Calendar System: Semester
URL: www.morrisontech.edu
Established: 1973　Annual Undergrad Tuition & Fees: $15,590
Enrollment: 86　Coed
Affiliation or Control: Independent Non-Profit　IRS Status: 501(c)3
Highest Offering: Associate Degree
Program: 2-Year Principally Bachelor's Creditable; Technical Emphasis
Accreditation: COE, ENGT

01 Chief Executive Officer .... Mr. Christopher D. SCOTT
05 Vice President of Academic Affairs .... Mr. Greg J. TULLY
10 Vice President for Finance .... Mr. Richard PARKINSON
06 Registrar .... Ms. Judy TURNEY

Morthland College (F)

202 East Oak St, PO Box 429, West Frankfort IL 62896
County: Franklin　FICE Identification: 042279
Telephone: (618) 937-2127　Carnegie Class: Not Classified
FAX Number: (618) 937-2137　Calendar System: Semester
URL: www.morthland.edu
Established: 2009　Annual Undergrad Tuition & Fees: $13,060
Enrollment: 63　Coed
Affiliation or Control: Independent Non-Profit　IRS Status: 501(c)3
Highest Offering: Baccalaureate
Program: Religious Emphasis
Accreditation: TRACS

01 President .... Dr. Tim MORTHLAND
03 Executive Vice President .... Ms. Emily HAYES
05 Provost .... Dr. Randy CARNEY
32 Dean of Student Affairs .... Ms. Cathie MIELDEZIS

Morton College (G)

3801 S Central Avenue, Cicero IL 60804-4398
County: Cook　FICE Identification: 001728
Unit ID: 147411
Telephone: (708) 656-8000　Carnegie Class: Assoc/Pub-S-SC
FAX Number: (708) 656-3297　Calendar System: Semester
URL: www.morton.edu
Established: 1924　Annual Undergrad Tuition & Fees (In-District): $3,640
Enrollment: 4,653　Coed
Affiliation or Control: State/Local　IRS Status: 501(c)3
Highest Offering: Associate Degree
Program: Occupational; 2-Year Principally Bachelor's Creditable
Accreditation: NH, ADNUR, PTAA

01 Interim President .... Dr. Muddassir SIDDIQI
45 VP of Inst Plng & Effectiveness .... Dr. Keith MCLAUGHLIN
32 Dean of Student Develpment & Ombuds .... Dr. Yesenia AVALOS
51 Dean Adult Educ/Cmty Prgms/Outreach .... Vacant
08 Director of Library .... Ms. Jennifer BUTLER
15 Director of Human Resources .... Mr. Anthony RAY
31 Director of Continuing Education .... Ms. Susan FELICE
09 Director Institutional Research .... Ms. Magda BANDA
18 Director of Facilities & Operations .... Mr. John POTEMPA
37 Director of Financial Aid .... Ms. Yolanda FREEMON
35 Director of Student Development .... Ms. Marlena AVALOS-THOMPSON
10 Director of Business Services .... Ms. Mireya PEREZ
19 Exec Director of Campus Safety .... Mr. Frank MARZULLO

National-Louis University (H)

122 S Michigan Avenue, Chicago IL 60603
County: Cook　FICE Identification: 001733
Unit ID: 147536
Telephone: (888) 658-8632　Carnegie Class: DRU
FAX Number: N/A　Calendar System: Quarter
URL: www.nl.edu
Established: 1886　Annual Undergrad Tuition & Fees: $15,990
Enrollment: 4,582　Coed
Affiliation or Control: Independent Non-Profit　IRS Status: 501(c)3
Highest Offering: Doctorate
Program: Teacher Preparatory; Professional
Accreditation: NH, CACREP, IACBE, TED

01 President .... Dr. Nivine MEGAHED
05 Provost .... Dr. Alison HILSABECK
30 Vice Pres Institutional Advancement .... Vacant
15 Vice President Human Resources .... Mr. Tom BERGMANN
10 Vice Pres Finance & Administration .... Mr. Marty MICKEY
84 Vice Pres Enrollment Mgmt .... Ms. Bobbi BIRINGER
26 Vice Pres Marketing/Communications .... Mr. Tom EHRHARDT
09 Vice Provost Institutional Effect .... Dr. Marsha WATSON
20 Vice Prov Acad Pgm & Fac Dev .... Dr. Ignacio LOPEZ
88 Exec Dir of Advising/Retention .... Mr. Stephen NEER
50 Dean CPSA .... Dr. Judah VIOLA
53 Dean NCE .... Dr. Robert MULLER
08 Dean University Library .... Dr. Robert MORRISON
32 VP Student Services .... Mr. Steve DIBENEDETTO
12 Exec Director Florida Regional .... Dr. Karen O'DONNELL
28 Director of Employment/Diversity .... Ms. Erin HAULOTTE
37 Director of Student Finance .... Ms. Rathenia HUNTER
07 Director of Admissions .... Mr. Ken KASPRZAK
36 Director of Career Development .... Vacant
51 Director Outreach Academic Pgm .... Ms. Karen HAWORTH
35 Director of Student Experience .... Ms. Danielle LABAN
04 Administrative Asst to President .... Ms. Diane M. TRAUSCH
06 Registrar .... Ms. Shannon MEGGERT
108 Director Institutional Assessment .... Dr. Kathleen GORSKI
13 Chief Info Technology Officer (CIO) .... Mr. Michael GRAHAM
18 Chief Facilities/Physical Plant .... Mr. Richard SORENSON
25 Assoc Dir of Grant Operations .... Ms. Lucille MORGAN

29	Director Alumni & Outreach Programs	Ms. Kimberly MICHAELSON
90	Director Academic Computing	Ms. Sonja STRAHL
91	Technical Director	Mr. John MAZARIEGOS
96	Purchasing Coordinator	Ms. Caryn SMITH
102	Dir Foundation/Corporate Relations	Mr. Brian RUSSELL

National-Louis University Elgin Campus (A)

620 Tollgate Road, Elgin IL 60123

Telephone: (800) 443-5522 Identification: 770083

Accreditation: &NH

† Branch campus of National-Louis University, Chicago, IL.

National-Louis University Lisle Campus (B)

850 Warrenville Road, Lisle IL 60532

Telephone: (800) 443-5522 Identification: 770084

Accreditation: &NH

† Branch campus of National-Louis University, Chicago, IL.

National-Louis University North Shore Campus (C)

5202 Old Orchard Road, Skokie IL 60077

Telephone: (800) 443-5522 Identification: 770085

Accreditation: &NH

† Branch campus of National-Louis University, Chicago, IL.

National-Louis University Wheeling Campus (D)

1000 Capitol Drive, Wheeling IL 60090

Telephone: (800) 443-5522 Identification: 770086

Accreditation: &NH

† Branch campus of National-Louis University, Chicago, IL.

National University of Health Sciences (E)

200 E Roosevelt Road, Lombard IL 60148-4583

County: DuPage FICE Identification: 001732

Unit ID: 147590

Telephone: (630) 629-2000 Carnegie Class: Spec/Health

FAX Number: (630) 889-6600 Calendar System: Trimester

URL: www.nuhs.edu

Established: 1906 Annual Undergrad Tuition & Fees: $11,368

Enrollment: 718 Coed

Affiliation or Control: Independent Non-Profit IRS Status: 501(c)3

Highest Offering: First Professional Degree

Program: Liberal Arts And General; Professional; Technical Emphasis

Accreditation: NH, ACUP, CHIRO, COMTA, NATUR

01	President	Dr. Joseph P D. STIEFEL
05	Vice President Academic Services	Dr. Randy L. SWENSON
10	Vice President Business Services	Mr. Ron MENSCHING
11	Vice Pres Administrative Services	Ms. Tracy MCHUGH
76	Dean College Allied Health Sciences	Dr. Randy L. SWENSON
51	Dean Col Postprofessional Educ	Dr. Jenna GLENN
23	Dean of Clinics	Dr. Theodore JOHNSON
107	Dean Col Professional Studies FL	Dr. Daniel STRAUSS
107	Dean Col Professional Studies IL	Dr. Robert SHIEL
46	Dean of Research	Dr. Gregory D. CRAMER
32	Dean of Students	Dr. Daniel R. DRISCOLL
108	Dean Academic Assessment	Vacant
88	Dean Accreditation	Vacant
08	Chair Learning Resource Center	Ms. Joyce E. WHITEHEAD
06	University Registrar	Ms. Izabela DUBAK
07	Dir Communication/Enrollment Svcs	Ms. Victoria SWEENEY
21	Director of Financial Services	Ms. Sue UNGER
37	Director of Financial Aid	Mr. Robert DAME
18	Director Maintenance & Facilities	Mr. Mark GALVANONI
15	Director of Human Resources	Mr. Andrew WOZNIAK
26	Chief Public Relations Officer	Ms. Marie OLBRYSH
30	Director Alumni & Development	Ms. Shawna MCDONOUGH
13	Dir Management Information Services	Mr. Ron MENSCHING
29	Director Alumni Relations	Ms. Shawna MCDONOUGH
40	Bookstore Manager	Ms. Sue ROBERTSON
39	Coordinator of Housing	Ms. Marilyn FREAD

North Central College (F)

30 N Brainard Street, Naperville IL 60540-4607

County: DuPage FICE Identification: 001734

Unit ID: 147660

Telephone: (630) 637-5100 Carnegie Class: Master's M

FAX Number: (630) 637-5121 Calendar System: Trimester

URL: www.northcentralcollege.edu

Established: 1861 Annual Undergrad Tuition & Fees: $35,421

Enrollment: 3,043 Coed

Affiliation or Control: United Methodist IRS Status: 501(c)3

Highest Offering: Master's

Program: Liberal Arts And General

Accreditation: NH, CAATE

01	President	Dr. Troy D. HAMMOND
04	Exec Secy/Assistant to President	Ms. Margaret A. WHITE
05	Vice President Academic Affairs	Dr. Abiodun GOKE-PARIOLA
10	Vice President Business Affairs	Mr. Paul H. LOSCHEIDER
30	Vice Pres Institutional Advancement	Mr. Rick E. SPENCER
84	VP Enrollment Management/Athletics	Mr. Marty R. SAUER
32	VP Student Affairs/Dean of Students	Ms. Kimberly SLUIS
15	Asst Vice Pres Human Resources	Ms. Michelle M. SKINDER
26	Asst Vice President Mktg/Communic	Mr. James GODO
21	Asst VP for Business Operations	Mr. Michael J. HUDSON
20	Associate Academic Dean	Dr. Marti S. BOGART
07	Dean of Admissions	Ms. Martha A. STOLZE
58	Dean of Graduate Pgms/Continuing Ed	Dr. Pamela MONACO
06	Registrar	Vacant
08	Director of the Library	Mr. John J. SMALL
36	Director of Career Development	Mr. Jeffrey D. DENARD
37	Director of Financial Aid	Mr. Martin REBA
23	Director of the Wellness Center	Ms. Tatiana SIFRI
31	Director of Cmty Educ/Conf/Camps	Vacant
41	Athletic Director	Mr. James MILLER
21	AVP Finance/Controller	Mr. David S. MISSURELLI
39	Director of Residence Life	Ms. Sarah E. AVERY
42	Campus Chaplain	Rev. Eric DOOLITTLE
13	AVP/Chief Information Officer	Mr. Matthew BURDEN
44	Director of Planned Giving	Mr. Bruce NORTELL
09	Director of Institutional Research	Mr. Peter S. BARGER
29	Director Alumni Relations	Mr. Adrian M. ALDRICH
28	Director of Multicultural Affairs	Ms. Dorothy J. PLEAS

North Park University (G)

3225 W Foster Avenue, Chicago IL 60625-4895

County: Cook FICE Identification: 001735

Unit ID: 147679

Telephone: (773) 244-6200 Carnegie Class: Master's L

FAX Number: N/A Calendar System: Semester

URL: www.northpark.edu

Established: 1891 Annual Undergrad Tuition & Fees: $25,740

Enrollment: 3,193 Coed

Affiliation or Control: Evangelical Covenant Church Of America

IRS Status: 501(c)3

Highest Offering: Doctorate

Program: Liberal Arts And General; Teacher Preparatory; Professional

Accreditation: NH, CAATE, IACBE, MUS, NURSE, THEOL

01	President	Dr. David L. PARKYN
10	Executive Vice President/CFO	Mr. Carl E. BALSAM
05	Provost	Dr. Michael O. EMERSON
84	Vice Pres for Enrollment/Marketing	Mr. Genaro BALCAZAR
30	Vice President for Development	Ms. Mary K. SURRIDGE
73	Seminary Dean	Dr. David W. KERSTEN
49	Dean of Arts & Sciences	Dr. Charles I. PETERSON
51	Interim Dean School of Adult Lrng	Mr. Neale MURRAY
50	Dean School of Business & NFP Mgmt	Dr. Wesley LINDAHL
53	Dean School of Education	Dr. Rebecca NELSON
64	Dean School of Music	Dr. Craig JOHNSON
66	Dean School of Nursing	Dr. Linda DUNCAN
28	Dean of Diversity & Intercult Pgm	Dr. Terry LINDSAY
32	VP for Student Engagement	Dr. Jodi KOSLOW MARTIN
08	Dean Library & Academic Technology	Ms. Kathryn MAIER-O'SHEA
07	Senior Director of UG Enrollment	Mr. Jared CHRISTENSEN
23	Director Health Services	Ms. Hannah AZEVEDO
37	Director Financial Aid Services	Ms. Carolyn LACH
13	Director of Computer Center	Mr. Steven P. CLARK
15	Director of Human Resources	Ms. Ingrid K. TENGLIN
18	Director of Physical Plant	Mr. Carl H. WISTROM
19	Director of Security	Mr. Daniel GOORIS
21	Director of Finance	Mr. Lester H. CARLSTROM
26	University Marketing & Communic	Ms. Marcia MAWE
41	Athletic Director	Mr. Jack F. SURRIDGE
42	Director University Ministries	Mr. Anthony ZAMBLE
36	Senior Director of Career Planning	Ms. Pamela BOZEMAN-EVANS
06	Registrar	Mr. Aaron D. SCHOOF
29	Alumni Relations Manager	Ms. Melissa VELEZ LUCE
04	Assistant to the President	Mrs. Karen P. MEARS
104	Director of International Office	Dr. Sumie SONG
39	Director Student Housing	Ms. Sherry SIMMONS
44	Annual Fund Manager	Mr. Justin PREVOST-SCHULTZ

Northeastern Illinois University (H)

5500 N Saint Louis Avenue, Chicago IL 60625-4699

County: Cook FICE Identification: 001693

Unit ID: 147776

Telephone: (773) 583-4050 Carnegie Class: Master's L

FAX Number: (773) 442-4900 Calendar System: Semester

URL: www.neiu.edu

Established: 1867 Annual Undergrad Tuition & Fees (In-State): $9,351

Enrollment: 10,275 Coed

Affiliation or Control: State IRS Status: 501(c)3

Highest Offering: Master's

Program: Liberal Arts And General; Teacher Preparatory; Professional; Fine Arts Emphasis

Accreditation: NH, ART, CACREP, CORE, MUS, SW, TED

01	President	Dr. Sharon K. HAHS
05	Provost & VP Academic Affairs	Dr. Richard J. HELLDOBLER
10	Vice Pres Finance & Administration	Mr. Michael J. PIERICK
32	Vice President for Student Affairs	Vacant
30	Vice President Inst Advancement	Ms. Melba RODRIGUEZ
35	Associate VP for Student Affairs	Dr. Daniel LOPEZ, JR.
35	Asst VP Stdnt Aff/Dean of Students	Mr. Matthew F. SPECHT
07	Associate VP Enrollment Services	Dr. Janice M. HARRING-HENDON
21	Director of Univ Budgets	Ms. Ann M. MCNABB
08	Dean Libraries & Learning Res	Mr. Carlos MELIAN
09	Exec Dir Inst Rsrch & Assessment	Mr. Blase E. MASINI
15	Dir of HR Empl & Labor Relations	Ms. Marta E. MASO
25	Coordinator Sponsored Programs	Ms. Stephanie M. LOGARAS
26	Chief Communication Officer/Dir	Mr. Michael M. DIZON
37	Director Financial Aid	Ms. Maureen T. AMOS
50	Dean College Bus/Management	Dr. Michael D. BEDELL
58	Dean College Graduate Studies & Res	Dr. Michael J. STERN
53	Dean College of Education	Dr. Maureen D. GILLETTE
49	Dean College of Arts & Sciences	Dr. Wamucii E. NJOGU
13	Chief Information Officer	Vacant
18	Asst Vice Pres Facilities Mgmt	Ms. Nancy MEDINA
19	Director University Police Dept	Mr. James C. LYON, JR.
21	Director Controller's Office	Ms. Fe LENON
22	Dir Equal Opportunity/AA & Ethics	Ms. Natalie BROUWER POTTS
86	Executive Dir Government Relations	Dr. Suleyma PEREZ
06	University Registrar	Mr. Daniel R. WEBER
29	Director of Alumni Relations	Ms. Damaris TAPIA
38	Dir Student Health & Counseling	Dr. Sue STOCK
96	Asst VP Procurement & Support Svcs	Mr. Robert B. FILIPP
44	Director Institutional Advancement	Mr. John BUTLER-LUDWIG
96	Director Purchasing	Ms. Rosalinda CASTILLO

Northern Illinois University (I)

1425 W. Lincoln Way, De Kalb IL 60115-2828

County: De Kalb FICE Identification: 001737

Unit ID: 147703

Telephone: (815) 753-1000 Carnegie Class: RU/H

FAX Number: (815) 753-0198 Calendar System: Semester

URL: www.niu.edu

Established: 1895 Annual Undergrad Tuition & Fees (In-State): $12,344

Enrollment: 20,611 Coed

Affiliation or Control: State IRS Status: 501(c)3

Highest Offering: Doctorate

Program: Liberal Arts And General; Teacher Preparatory; Professional

Accreditation: NH, ART, AUD, BUS, BUSA, CAATE, CACREP, CLPSY, CORE, DIETD, DIETI, ENG, ENGT, IPSY, LAW, MFCD, MT, MUS, NAIT, NURSE, PH, PTA, SCPSY, SP, SPAA, TED, THEA

01	President	Douglas D. BAKER
05	Executive Vice Pres & Provost	Lisa FREEMAN
20	Vice Provost Academic Planning/Dev	Carolinda DOUGLASS
10	VP Administration & Finance	Alan PHILLIPS
45	Vice Prov Resource Planning	Susan MINI
51	VP University Outreach	Anne C. KAPLAN
32	Vice Pres Student Affs/Enroll Mgmt	Eric WELDY
46	VP for Research/Innv Prtnrsh	Lesley RIGG
26	Interim VP Marketing & Comm	Harlan TELLER
43	VP/General Counsel/Legal Svcs	Jerry D. BLAKEMORE
102	Vice Pres University Advancement	Catherine SQUIRES
13	VP Chief Information Officer	Brett CORYELL
18	VP Facilities Planning & Opers	Alan PHILLIPS
15	AVP Administration/HR	Celeste LATHAM
35	Assoc VP Stdnt Affs & Dean of Stdnt	Kelley WESENER-MICHAEL
23	Director Health Services	Christine GRADY
28	Asst Vice Pres Diversity/Equity	Katrina CALDWELL
20	Vice Provost	Anne BIRBERICK
50	Dean of Business	Denise SCHOENBACHLER
53	Dean of Education	La Vonne NEAL
54	Dean of Engineering/Engr Tech	Promod VOHRA
61	Dean of Law	Jennifer ROSATO
49	Dean Liberal Arts & Sciences	Christopher MCCORD
76	Dean Health & Human Sciences	Derryl BLOCK
57	Dean Visual & Performing Arts	Richard HOLLY
58	Dean Grad Sch/AVP Grad Studies	Bradley BOND
85	Actg Assoc VP International Pgms	Bradley BONE
84	Asst Vice Prov Enrollment Services	Vacant
88	Asst VP Outreach Rockford	Rena COTSONES
12	Director Lorado Taft Field Campus	Diana DENNIS
12	Director NIU Naperville	Gina KENYON
06	Director Registration & Records	Jerry MONTAG
09	Director of Institutional Research	J. Daniel HOUSE
24	Director of Media Services	Vacant
25	Director of Sponsored Projects	David STONE
36	Exec Director of Career Services	Cindy HENDERSON
37	Director of Student Financial Aid	Rebecca BABEL
38	Director of Counseling/Student Dev	Brooke RUXTON
40	Director of University Bookstore	Vacant
19	Police Chief/Public Safety	Thomas R. PHILLIPS, SR.
41	Athletic Director	Sean FRAZIER
91	Director Enterprise Info Systems	Vacant
39	Executive Director Housing & Dining	Michael STANG
88	Dir Disability Resources Center	Jennifer PIPPIN
29	Director Alumni Relations	Joseph MATTY
96	Director of Purchasing	Vacant

Northern Seminary (J)

660 E Butterfield Road, Lombard IL 60148-5698

County: DuPage FICE Identification: 001736

Unit ID: 147697

Telephone: (630) 620-2180 Carnegie Class: Spec/Faith

FAX Number: (630) 620-2190 Calendar System: Quarter

URL: www.seminary.edu

Established: 1913 Annual Graduate Tuition & Fees: $13,860

Enrollment: 218 Coed

Affiliation or Control: American Baptist IRS Status: 501(c)3

Highest Offering: Doctorate; No Undergraduates

Program: Professional; Religious Emphasis

Accreditation: THEOL

01 Interim President .... Dr. Karen WALKER FREEBURG
00 President (on sabbatical) .... Dr. Alistair BROWN
04 Executive Asst to President .... Ms. Jennifer OULD
05 Vice President of Academic Affairs .... Dr. Karen WALKER FREEBURG
30 Vice President of Advancement .... Vacant
44 Director of Development .... Mr. Ben WATERMAN
84 Admissions & Enrollment Counselor .... Mr. Isaac AMPIL
10 Director of Finance & Operations .... Ms. Christie LINSNER
06 Registrar .... Ms. Marilyn R. MAST HEWITT
88 Director Doctoral Studies .... Dr. Karen WALKER-FREEBURG
32 Director Student Services .... Ms. Marilyn MAST HEWITT
15 Director Human Resources .... Vacant
13 Director of Information Technology .... Mr. Ace MCCLINTON

Northwest Suburban College (A)

5999 S. New Wilke Rd, Rolling Meadows IL 60008
County: Cook | Identification: 667240
Telephone: (847) 290-6425 | Carnegie Class: Not Classified
FAX Number: (847) 290-1441 | Calendar System: Semester
URL: www.nwsc.edu
Established: 2008 | Annual Undergrad Tuition & Fees: $11,760
Enrollment: N/A | Coed
Affiliation or Control: Independent Non-Profit | IRS Status: 501(c)3
Highest Offering: Associate Degree
Program: Occupational
Accreditation: ACICS

01 President .... Dr. M. T. ALINIAZEE
05 Provost/Dean of Acad & Student Affs .... Dr. Maksood AKBAR
76 Dean Allied Health Sciences .... Dr. Liliyea HERNANDEZ
07 Admissions Representative .... Ms. Kalene EVANS

Northwestern College (B)

9501 Technology Blvd; Suite 425, Rosemont IL 60018
County: Cook | FICE Identification: 012362
Unit ID: 147749
Telephone: (847) 233-7700 | Carnegie Class: Assoc/PrivFP
FAX Number: (847) 233-7705 | Calendar System: Quarter
URL: www.nc.edu
Established: 1902 | Annual Undergrad Tuition & Fees: $23,100
Enrollment: 1,081 | Coed
Affiliation or Control: Proprietary | IRS Status: Proprietary
Highest Offering: Associate Degree
Program: Occupational; 2-Year Principally Bachelor's Creditable
Accreditation: NH, ACBSP, CAHIIM, MAC, RAD

01 President .... Mr. Lawrence SCHUMACHER
03 Executive VP of Operations .... Mrs. Gail SCHUMACHER
11 Chief Operations Officer .... Mr. Dimitrios KRIARAS
10 Controller .... Ms. Leslie RODRIGUEZ
108 VP of Accreditation and Compliance .... Mrs. Diane MAREK
05 VP of Academic Success .... Mr. William BELL
09 Dean of Institutional Research .... Vacant
13 Chief Information & Digital Officer .... Mr. David HOMAN
32 VP of Student Affairs .... Mrs. Barbara ANDERSON-SAPATA
86 Government and Public Relations Dir .... Ms. Laura POLLASTRINI
08 Director of Library Services .... Ms. Sarah DULAY
12 Director of Bridgeview Campus .... Mrs. Christa HOLTON
12 Director of NC Online .... Ms. Mary REYNOLDS
12 Director of Chicago Campus .... Mr. Todd LASOTA
15 Director of Human Resources .... Mrs. Margie BENNECKE
37 Director of Financial Assistance .... Ms. Patricia KILIAN
105 Institutional Initiatives Director .... Ms. Lauren SCHUMACHER
38 Director of Counseling .... Ms. Alexandra DELLUTRI
106 Distance Education Director .... Ms. Jenifer VIENCEK
07 Director of Admissions NC Online .... Ms. Emily HAYDON
07 Enrollment Services Manager .... Mrs. Theresa VALDES
11 Dir of Administration Bridgeview .... Vacant
66 Dean of Nursing .... Ms. Richae MURO
06 Registrar .... Ms. Tina MARFOE
36 Career Development Coordinator .... Ms. Amy BUOSCIO
36 Career Development Coordinator .... Mr. Greg NORTON
97 Program Director - GE .... Mr. David COOPER
61 Program Director - LS .... Mr. John LOMBARDI
50 Program Director - SC&T .... Ms. Ali BAKER
76 Program Director - SHS .... Ms. Chandra HURT
04 Executive Asst to President .... Ms. Vilma FRANCO

Northwestern College-SW Campus (C)

7725 S Harlem Avenue, Bridgeview IL 60455
Telephone: (888) 205-2283 | Identification: 770089
Accreditation: &NH

† Branch campus of Northwestern College, Rosemont, IL.

Northwestern University (D)

633 Clark Street, Evanston IL 60208-3854
County: Cook | FICE Identification: 001739
Unit ID: 147767
Telephone: (847) 491-8400 | Carnegie Class: RU/VH
FAX Number: (847) 491-7364 | Calendar System: Quarter
URL: www.northwestern.edu
Established: 1851 | Annual Undergrad Tuition & Fees: $52,243
Enrollment: 21,403 | Coed
Affiliation or Control: Independent Non-Profit | IRS Status: 501(c)3
Highest Offering: Doctorate
Program: Liberal Arts And General; Teacher Preparatory; Professional
Accreditation: NH, ARCPA, AUD, BUS, CACREP, CLPSY, ENG, IPSY, JOUR, LAW, MED, MFCD, MUS, OPE, PCSAS, PH, PTA, SP

01 President .... Dr. Morton O. SCHAPIRO
05 Provost .... Dr. Daniel I. LINZER
10 Exectutive Vice President .... Mr. Nim S. CHINNIAH
32 Vice President Student Affairs .... Dr. Patricia TELLES-IRVIN
26 Vice President University Relations .... Mr. Alan K. CUBBAGE
45 Vice Pres Administration & Planning .... Ms. Marilyn MCCOY
13 Vice Pres Information Technology .... Mr. Sean B. REYNOLDS
30 Vice Pres for Alumni Rel & Devel .... Mr. Robert MCQUINN
46 Vice President Research .... Mr. Joseph T. WALSH
88 Vice Pres/Chief Investment Officer .... Mr. William H. MCLEAN
43 Vice President/General Counsel .... Mr. Thomas G. CLINE
84 Associate Provost Univ Enrollment .... Mr. Michael E. MILLS
53 Associate Provost Undergrad Educ .... Dr. Ronald R. BRAEUTIGAM
20 Associate Provost Faculty Affairs .... Vacant
20 Assoc VP & Assoc Provost Academic .... Mr. Jake JULIA
21 Assoc Prov Budget/Facil/Analysis .... Ms. Jean E. SHEDD
86 Spec Asst to Pres for Govt Rels .... Mr. Bruce LAYTON
04 Assistant to the President .... Mr. Eugene Y. LOWE, JR.
100 Director Office of the President .... Ms. Judith V. REMINGTON
41 Vice Pres Athletics and Recreation .... Mr. James J. PHILLIPS
72 Dean Sch Engr/Applied Science .... Dr. Julio M. OTTINO
50 Dean Graduate School of Management .... Dr. Sally E. BLOUNT
60 Dean School of Journalism .... Dr. Bradley J. HAMM
64 Dean School of Music .... Dr. Toni-Marie MONTGOMERY
63 Lewis Landsberg Deanship/Deans Ofc .... Dr. Eric G. NEILSON
51 Dean/Assoc Prov Conting Educ .... Dr. Thomas F. GIBBONS
58 Dean Graduate School .... Mr. Dwight A. MCBRIDE
60 Dean School of Communication .... Dr. Barbara J. O'KEEFE
53 Dean School of Ed & Social Policy .... Dr. Penelope L. PETERSON
49 Interim Dean College Arts & Science .... Mr. Mark C. RATNER
61 Dean School of Law .... Dr. Daniel B. RODRIGUEZ
08 University Librarian .... Ms. Sarah M. PRITCHARD
36 Exec Dir of Univ Career Svcs .... Mr. Mark PRESNELL
35 Assistant VP of Student Engagement .... Mr. Burgwell HOWARD
29 Assoc VP Alumni Relations & Develop .... Mr. Simon GREENWOLD
88 Assoc Vice President for Research .... Mr. Lewis SMITH
88 Assoc Vice President for Research .... Mr. Jian CAO
88 Assoc VP for Rsrch Innov & New Vent .... Ms. Alicia LOFFLER
88 Assoc Vice President for Research .... Ms. Ann ADAMS
88 Assoc Vice Pres for Research .... Mr. Rex CHISHOLM
21 Assoc Vice Pres Budget Planning .... Mr. James M. HURLEY
18 Assoc Vice Pres Facilities Mgmt .... Mr. Ronald NAYLER
15 Assoc Vice Pres for Human Resources .... Ms. Pamela BEEMER
21 Assoc Vice Pres Finance/Controller .... Ms. Ingrid S. STAFFORD
07 Dean of Undergraduate Admissions .... Mr. Christopher WATSON
88 Exec Dir Intl Research Partnerships .... Ms. Indrani MUKHARJI
23 Medical Director of Health Services .... Dr. John ALEXANDER
39 Asst Dean of Students .... Ms. Mary GOLDENBERG
38 Director of Counseling/Psych Svcs .... Dr. John H. DUNKLE
42 University Chaplain .... Dr. Timothy S. STEVENS
09 Director Analytical Studies .... Mr. Bill HAYWARD
88 Dir Program Review/Spec Project .... Mr. Jeremy HUNSUCKER
71 Planning/Special Projects Director .... Ms. Evelyn CALIENDO
109 Ex Dir Univ Center/Student Aux Svcs .... Ms. Kelly A. SCHAEFER
88 Director University Services .... Mr. Brian S. PETERS
06 University Registrar .... Ms. Jacqualyn CASAZZA
37 Director Financial Aid .... Ms. Carolyn V. LINDLEY
16 Dir HR Consulting Svcs/Staffing .... Ms. Eva ERSKINE
19 Chief of University Police .... Mr. Bruce LEWIS
21 Assoc VP of Audit & Advisory Svcs .... Ms. Betty L. MCPHILIMY
22 Dir Equal Emply Oppprty/Affirm Act .... Ms. Tasha SHELTON
96 Director University Svcs Purchasing .... Mr. Jim KONRAD
28 Asst Provost Diversity & Inclusion .... Ms. Dona CORDERO

Oakton Community College (E)

1600 E Golf Road, Des Plaines IL 60016-1256
County: Cook | FICE Identification: 009896
Unit ID: 147800
Telephone: (847) 635-1600 | Carnegie Class: Assoc/Pub-S-MC
FAX Number: (847) 635-1992 | Calendar System: Semester
URL: www.oakton.edu
Established: 1969 | Annual Undergrad Tuition & Fees (In-District): $3,285
Enrollment: 5,479 | Coed
Affiliation or Control: Local | IRS Status: 501(c)3
Highest Offering: Associate Degree
Program: Occupational; 2-Year Principally Bachelor's Creditable; Business Emphasis
Accreditation: NH, ADNUR, CAHIIM, MLTAD, PTAA

01 President .... Dr. Joianne L. SMITH
05 Vice President Academic Affairs .... Dr. Thomas HAMEL
20 Assistant VP Academic Affairs .... Dr. Nancy PRENDERGAST
20 Assistant VP Academic Affairs .... Dr. Michael CARR
32 Vice President Student Affairs .... Dr. Karl BROOKS
28 AVP for Access/Equity & Diversity .... Dr. Michael ANTHONY
10 Vice President Business & Finance .... Mr. Robert NOWAK
51 Interim AVP Cont Ed/Trng/Wrkfrc Dev .... Dr. Colette HANDS
13 Vice Pres Information Technology .... Ms. Bonnie LUCAS
76 Dean Science & Health Careers .... Vacant
81 Dean Math & Technology .... Dr. Robert SOMPOLSKI
60 Dean Language/Humanities & the Arts .... Ms. Linda KORBEL
83 Dean Social Science/Business .... Mr. Bradley WOOTEN
26 Director of College Relations .... Mr. Paul PALIAN
09 Director Research .... Dr. Maya EVANS
08 Director Library & Media Svcs .... Mr. Gary NEWHOUSE
84 Dir of Student Recruitment/Outreach .... Ms. Michele BROWN
06 Director of Registrar Services .... Mr. Bruce OATES
35 Director of Student Life .... Ms. Ann Marie BARRY
88 Director of Student Success .... Mr. Sebastian CONTRERAS, JR.
88 Dir of Student Learning/Engagement .... Ms. Leana CUELLAR
41 Director of Athletics .... Mr. Bruce OATES
103 Dir Workforce Dev & Corp Training .... Dr. Colette HANDS
21 Dir of Budget & Accounting Services .... Ms. Karen EPPS
21 Director of Business Services .... Ms. Doreen SCHWARTZ
15 Chief Human Resources Officer .... Ms. Mums MARTENS
18 Director of Facilities .... Ms. Leah SWANQUIST
14 Director Systems & Network Svcs .... Mr. John WADE
14 Dir of Educ Computing/End User Svcs .... Ms. Renee KOZIMOR
07 Director of Enrollment Services .... Ms. Cheryl WARMANN
25 Dir of Grants & Alternative Funding .... Ms. Roxann MARSHBURN
11 Dir of Operations and Admin .... Ms. Robyn BAILEY
28 Ethics Officer .... Ms. Mum MARTENS
38 Director of Counseling .... Dr. Mark KIEL

Oakton Community College Ray Hartstein Campus (F)

7701 N Lincoln Avenue, Skokie IL 60077
Telephone: (847) 635-1600 | Identification: 770091
Accreditation: &NH

† Branch campus of Oakton Community College, Des Plaines, IL.

Olivet Nazarene University (G)

One University Avenue, Bourbonnais IL 60914-2345
County: Kankakee | FICE Identification: 001741
Unit ID: 147828
Telephone: (815) 939-5011 | Carnegie Class: Master's L
FAX Number: (815) 935-4998 | Calendar System: Semester
URL: www.olivet.edu
Established: 1907 | Annual Undergrad Tuition & Fees: $32,790
Enrollment: 4,877 | Coed
Affiliation or Control: Church Of The Nazarene | IRS Status: 501(c)3
Highest Offering: Doctorate
Program: Liberal Arts And General; Teacher Preparatory; Professional
Accreditation: NH, CAATE, DIETD, ENG, MUS, NURSE, SW, TED

01 President .... Dr. John C. BOWLING
05 Vice President Academic Affairs .... Vacant
10 Vice President for Finance .... Dr. Douglas E. PERRY
32 Vice President Student Development .... Dr. Walter W. WEBB
26 Vice Pres Institutional Advancement .... Dr. Brian ALLEN
88 Vice Pres of Strategic Expansion .... Mr. Ryan SPITTAL
49 Dean College of Arts & Sciences .... Dr. Jim UPCHURCH
73 Dn Sch Theology/Christian Ministry .... Dr. Mark QUANSTROM
53 Dean School of Education .... Dr. Robert HULL
20 Assoc VP for Academic Affairs .... Dr. Houston THOMPSON
29 Dir Alumni & University Relations .... Mr. Gary GRIFFIN
07 Director of Admissions .... Mrs. Susan WOLFF
06 Dean of Inst Effect & Registrar .... Mr. Jonathan PICKERING
08 Dean of Library Services .... Mrs. Kathy R. BOYENS
37 Director of Financial Aid .... Mr. Greg BRUNER
13 Chief Information Officer .... Mr. Dennis SEYMOUR
41 Athletic Director .... Mr. Gary NEWSOME
42 Chaplain .... Rev. Mark HOLCOMB
30 Director of Development .... Mr. John MONGERSON
35 Director Student Activities .... Mrs. Kathy STEINACKER
38 Director Student Counseling .... Mrs. Lisa VANDER VEER
15 Director of Human Resources .... Mr. David PICKERING
18 Chief Facilities/Physical Plant .... Mr. Matt WHITIS
40 Bookstore Manager .... Mrs. Rachel PIAZZA
36 Assoc Director of Career Services .... Miss Poppy MILLER
85 International Student Advisor .... Dr. Mark MOUNTAIN
27 Director of Marketing .... Mr. Remington ANKSORUS
19 Director Security/Safety .... Mr. Dale NEWSOME
76 Dean School of Life/Health Sciences .... Mrs. Amber RESIDORI
64 Dean School of Music .... Dr. Don REDDICK
50 Dean School of Business .... Dr. Glen REWERTS
54 Dean School of Engineering & Tech .... Dr. Shane RITTER
58 Dean School Grad/Continuing Studies .... Dr. Jonathan BARTLING

Pacific College of Oriental Medicine (H)

65 East Wacker Place 21st Floor, Chicago IL 60601
Telephone: (888) 729-4811 | Identification: 666615
Accreditation: ACCSC, ACUP

† Branch campus of Pacific College of Oriental Medicine, San Diego CA.

Parkland College (I)

2400 W Bradley Avenue, Champaign IL 61821-1899
County: Champaign | FICE Identification: 007118
Unit ID: 147916
Telephone: (217) 351-2200 | Carnegie Class: Assoc/Pub-R-L
FAX Number: (217) 351-2581 | Calendar System: Semester
URL: www.parkland.edu
Established: 1966 | Annual Undergrad Tuition & Fees (In-District): $4,215
Enrollment: 8,443 | Coed
Affiliation or Control: State/Local | IRS Status: 501(c)3
Highest Offering: Associate Degree
Program: Occupational; 2-Year Principally Bachelor's Creditable
Accreditation: NH, ADNUR, COARC, DH, EMT, OTA, RAD, SURGT

01 President .... Dr. Thomas R. RAMAGE
04 Asst to President/Board of Trustees .... Ms. Nancy R. WILLAMON
05 Int Vice President Academic Svcs .... Dr. Pam LAU
32 Int Vice President Student Services .... Dr. Mike TRAME
10 Vice Pres Administrative Svcs/CFO .... Mr. Christopher M. RANDLES

30 Vice Pres Institutional Advancement Dr. Seamus REILLY
35 Dean of Students Ms. Marietta TURNER
106 Dean Adult Basic Educ/Workforce Dev Ms. Tawanna NICKENS
75 Dean of Career & Transfer Prgms Mr. Randy FLETCHER
50 Dept Chair Bus & Agri Industries Mr. Bruce HENRIKSON
77 Department Chair Comp Science & IT Ms. Maria MOBASSERI
54 Dept Chair Engineering Science/Tech Ms. Catherine STALTER
79 Dept Chair Humanities Mr. Tom BARNARD
57 Dept Chair Fine & Applied Arts Ms. Nancy SUTTON
76 Dept Chair Health Professions Ms. Roberta SCHOLZE
81 Department Chair Mathematics Mr. Geoffrey GRIFFITHS
65 Dept Chair Natural Sciences Ms. Sheryl DRAKE
83 Dept Chair Social Sci & Human Svcs Mr. Paul SARANTAKOS
88 Dir Center for Academic Success Vacant
09 Director Accountability & Research Mr. Kevin KNOTT
26 Dir Marketing & Public Relations Ms. Patty LEHN
103 Exec Director Workforce Development Mr. Tawanna NICKENS
102 Exec Dir Foundation/Alumni Affairs Ms. Ellen SCHMIDT
08 Director Library Ms. Anna Maria S. WATKIN
31 Director Community Education Ms. Amy FLESHNER
25 Director Grants and Contracts Mr. Joshua BIRKY
07 Director Admissions/Enrollment Mgmt Mr. Reo WILHOUR
35 Director Student Life Dr. Thomas M. CAULFIELD
41 Director Athletics Mr. Rod M. LOVETT
36 Director Career Center Ms. Sandra L. SPENCER
38 Dir Counseling & Advising Center Mr. John SHEAHAN
37 Director Financial Aid Mr. Tim WENDT
19 Director Public Safety Mr. William COLBROOK
18 Director Physical Plant Mr. James BUSTARD
15 Director Human Resources Ms. Kathleen CHARLESTON
21 Controller Mr. Dave DONSBACH
40 Manager of Bookstore Ms. Diane M. KIEST
88 Director Assessment Center Dr. Michael TRAME

Prairie State College (A)

202 S Halsted Street, Chicago Heights IL 60411-8226
County: Cook FICE Identification: 001640
Unit ID: 148007
Telephone: (708) 709-3500 Carnegie Class: Assoc/Pub-S-SC
FAX Number: (708) 755-2587 Calendar System: Semester
URL: www.prairiestate.edu
Established: 1957 Annual Undergrad Tuition & Fees (In-District): $4,290
Enrollment: 4,571 Coed
Affiliation or Control: State/Local IRS Status: 501(c)3
Highest Offering: Associate Degree
Program: Occupational; 2-Year Principally Bachelor's Creditable
Accreditation: NH, ADNUR, DH, SURGT

01 President Dr. Terri L. WINFREE
10 Vice Pres Finance & Administration Dr. Thomas SABAN
05 Vice Pres Acad Affs/Dean Faculty Dr. Marie C. HANSEL
31 Vice Pres Community/Economic Devel Mr. Craig D. SCHMIDT
32 VP Student Affairs/Dean of Students Dr. Gregory A. THOMAS
49 Interim Dean Liberal Arts Mr. Elighie WILSON
50 Dean Business/Mathematics & Science Dr. Debra L. PRENDERGAST
72 Dean Health/Industrial Tech Ms. Patty ZUCCARELLO
15 Exec Dir Human Resources Mr. David CRONAN
16 Asst Dir of Human Resources Mr. Leo ALEXANDER
13 Exec Dir Info Technology Resources Mr. Gregory KAIN
56 Dean Adult Education Ms. Kim M. KUNCE
21 Controller/Dir of Business Svcs Ms. Marina KIBARDINA
88 Assistant Controller Vacant
08 Assoc Dean/Library Ms. Kristina HOWARD
51 Dean Corporate/Continuing Ed Ms. Kelly LAPETINO
35 Dean Student Dev/Campus Life Mr. Felix SIMPKINS
18 Exec Dir Facilities and Operations Mr. Timothy J. KOZIEK
26 Exec Dir Public Relations/Marketing Ms. Jennifer E. STONER
102 Executive Director Foundation Ms. Deborah S. HAVIGHORST
07 Exec Dir Enrollment/Fin Aid Svcs Ms. Jaime M. MILLER
19 Dir Police/Campus Safe/Chief Police Vacant
88 Director Advising/Disability Svcs Ms. Diane J. JANOWIAK
37 Director Financial Aid Ms. Grace MCGINNIS
09 Director Inst Research/Planning Dr. Adane G. KASSA
88 Director Institutional Support Svcs Ms. Paulette A. MAURER
41 Director of Athletics Mr. Christopher ZORICH
04 Admin Dir Pres Office/Board Ms. Patricia G. TROST
88 Director Develop/Special Projects Vacant
89 Director First Year Experience Dr. Loretta KUCHARCZYK
88 Director Children's Learning Center Ms. Alison DRAKE
20 Associate Dean Faculty Affairs Dr. Dave NAZE

Prince Institute - Southeast (B)

1300 East Woodfield Road, Suite 110,
Schaumburg IL 60173
FICE Identification: 022960
Unit ID: 101958
Telephone: (847) 592-6600 Carnegie Class: Assoc/PrivFP
FAX Number: N/A Calendar System: Quarter
URL: www.princeinstitute.edu
Established: 1976 Annual Undergrad Tuition & Fees: $12,600
Enrollment: 84 Coed
Affiliation or Control: Proprietary IRS Status: Proprietary
Highest Offering: Associate Degree
Program: Occupational; Business Emphasis
Accreditation: ACICS

01 Campus Director Mr. Gerald C. ACEVEDO
05 Dean of Academic Affairs Ms. Debbie FIELD
10 Office Manager Ms. Vivian HAN
07 Admissions Representative Vacant

Principia College (C)

1 Maybeck Place, Elsah IL 62028-9799
County: Jersey FICE Identification: 001744
Unit ID: 148016
Telephone: (618) 374-2131 Carnegie Class: Bac/A&S
FAX Number: (618) 374-5500 Calendar System: Semester
URL: www.principiacollege.edu
Established: 1898 Annual Undergrad Tuition & Fees: $26,940
Enrollment: 500 Coed
Affiliation or Control: Independent Non-Profit IRS Status: 501(c)3
Highest Offering: Baccalaureate
Program: Liberal Arts And General; Teacher Preparatory
Accreditation: NH

01 President Dr. Jonathan PALMER
05 Dean of Academics Dr. Joseph RITTER
88 Chief Investment Officer Mr. Howard E. BERNER, JR.
10 Vice President Finance & Operations Mr. Doug GIBBS
11 Vice President Administration Mrs. Karen D. GRIMMER
20 Assistant Dean of Academics Dr. Libby SCHEIERN
06 Registrar Ms. Alice DERVIN
32 Dean of Students Ms. Debra JONES
08 Director of Libraries Mrs. Lisa ROBERTS
13 Director Information Technology Mr. Chris HUFFORD
104 Director of Principia Abroad Ms. Linda A. BOHAKER
41 Director of Athletics Mr. Lee ELLIS
15 Human Resources Director Ms. SharonAnn SMITH
18 Director of Facilities Mr. Ed GOEWERT
21 Controller Mr. Don MILLER
29 Dir of Alumni & Field Relations Mrs. Donna GIBBS
37 Director of College Financial Aid Mrs. Tami GAVALETZ
96 Purchasing Agent Mrs. Susan CURRY
38 Director Academic Career Advising Mrs. Midge BROWNING
09 Institutional Effectiveness Mrs. Cindy SHEDD
30 Admissions Vice Pres Rels Mr. Peter STEVENS
26 Marketing and Communications Mrs. Laurel WALTERS

Quincy University (D)

1800 College Avenue, Quincy IL 62301-2699
County: Adams FICE Identification: 001745
Unit ID: 148131
Telephone: (217) 222-8020 Carnegie Class: Master's S
FAX Number: (217) 228-5257 Calendar System: Semester
URL: www.quincy.edu
Established: 1860 Annual Undergrad Tuition & Fees: $26,998
Enrollment: 1,279 Coed
Affiliation or Control: Roman Catholic IRS Status: 501(c)3
Highest Offering: Master's
Program: Liberal Arts And General; Teacher Preparatory
Accreditation: NH

01 President Dr. Robert GERVASI
05 VP for Academic Affairs Dr. Ann BEHRENS
42 VP for Mission & Ministry Fr. John DOCTOR, OFM
10 VP for Business/Finance Mr. Tim WEIS
84 VP Enrollment Mgmt & Academic Supp Dr. Soumitra GHOSH
32 VP for Student Engagement/Success Dr. Tiffany NOLAN
30 VP for Univ Advancement Mrs. Julie BELL
04 Exec Assistant to the President Mrs. Julie BUDINE
101 Corporate Secretary Fr. John DOCTOR, OFM
21 Assoc VP for Finance/Controller Mrs. Jean GREEN
50 Dean School of Business Dr. Cynthia HALIEMUN
53 Dean School of Education Dr. Bruce SPITZER
79 Acting Chair Division of Humanities Dr. Daniel STRUDWICK
81 Chair Division Science & Technology Dr. Lee ENGER
83 Chair Div Behavioral/Social Sci Dr. Wendy BELLER
57 Chair Div Communication/Fine Arts Mr. Karl WARMA
08 Dean Library/Info Resources Ms. Patricia TOMCZAK
92 Director Honors Program Dr. Daniel STRUDWICK
06 Registrar Ms. Barbara WELLMAN
09 Institution Research Specialist Mr. David SHINN
42 Director Campus Ministry Vacant
29 Director Development/Alumni Svc Mr. Matthew BERGMAN
37 Director Financial Aid Ms. Lisa FLACK
13 Director Information Technology Svc Mr. Tony HAYES
26 Director Communications Mrs. Heidi MEYER
36 Director Career Services Mrs. Kristen LIESEN
41 Director of Athletics Mr. Marty BELL
18 Director Facilities Management Mr. Rob GOEBEL
39 Director Residence Life/Community Mr. Jason AMEZCUA
28 Dir Multicultural/Leadership Pgms Vacant
19 Director Safety & Security Mr. Sam LATHROP
15 Director Human Resources Ms. Tanya HARVEY
38 Director Counseling Center Mrs. Molly DUNN-STEINKE
07 Director of Admissions Ms. Abby WAYMAN
88 Director Student Success Center Ms. Melinda GARRICK
35 Director Campus & Community Events Mrs. Crystal SUTTER
104 Director Career Services/Study Abr Ms. Kristen LIESEN
96 Purchasing Ms. Jennifer TRUITT
25 Grant Writer Ms. Julie BOLL
40 Manager Bookstore Mr. Ben MEANS

Rasmussen College - Aurora (E)

2363 Sequoia Drive, Suite 131, Aurora IL 60506
Telephone: (630) 888-3500 Identification: 667060
Accreditation: &NH, CAHIIM, MAAB

† Regional accreditation is carried under the parent institution in Saint Cloud, MN. The tuition figure is an average, actual tuition may vary.

Rasmussen College - Mokena/Tinley Park (F)

8650 W. Spring Lake Drive, Mokena IL 60448
Telephone: (815) 534-3300 Identification: 667064
Accreditation: &NH, MAAB

† Regional accreditation carried under the parent institution in Saint Cloud, MN. The tuition figure is an average, actual tuition may vary.

Rasmussen College - Rockford (G)

6000 E. State Street, 4th Floor, Rockford IL 61108
Telephone: (815) 316-4800 Identification: 667065
Accreditation: &NH, CAHIIM, MAAB

† Regional accreditation carried under the parent institution in Saint Cloud, MN. The tuition figure is an average, actual tuition may vary.

Rasmussen College - Romeoville/Joliet (H)

1400 West Normantown Road, Romeoville IL 60446
Telephone: (815) 306-2600 Identification: 667066
Accreditation: &NH, MAAB

† Regional accreditation carried under the parent institution in Saint Cloud, MN. The tuition figure is an average, actual tuition may vary.

Rend Lake College (I)

468 N Ken Gray Parkway, Ina IL 62846-9801
County: Jefferson FICE Identification: 007119
Unit ID: 148256
Telephone: (618) 437-5321 Carnegie Class: Assoc/Pub-R-L
FAX Number: (618) 437-5677 Calendar System: Semester
URL: www.rlc.edu
Established: 1967 Annual Undergrad Tuition & Fees (In-District): $3,300
Enrollment: 2,781 Coed
Affiliation or Control: State/Local IRS Status: 501(c)3
Highest Offering: Associate Degree
Program: Occupational; 2-Year Principally Bachelor's Creditable
Accreditation: NH, MLTAD, OTA, RAD, SURGT

01 President Mr. Terry WILKERSON
05 VP Career Technical Education Mrs. Lori RAGLAND
10 VP of Finance & Administration Mrs. Angie KISTNER
09 VP of Institutional Effectiveness Mrs. Andrea WITTHOFT
32 Vice Pres of Student Services Ms. Lisa PRICE
26 Director Marketing & Information Mr. Chad COPPLE
37 Director Student Financial Aid Ms. Cheri RUSHING
41 Athletic Director Mr. Tim WILLS
18 Director Physical Plant Mr. C. Randall SHIVELY
102 CEO of RLC Foundation Mrs. Shawna BULLARD
06 Director of Student Records Mrs. Kelly DOWNES
09 Director of Institutional Research Ms. Vickie SCHULTE
07 Dean Admissions/Enrollment Mgmt Mr. Jason SWANN

Resurrection University (J)

1431 N. Claremont Street, 6th Floor, Chicago IL 60622
County: Cook FICE Identification: 006250
Unit ID: 149763
Telephone: (773) 252-6464 Carnegie Class: Spec/Health
FAX Number: (773) 227-3838 Calendar System: Semester
URL: www.resu.edu
Established: 1982 Annual Undergrad Tuition & Fees: $25,142
Enrollment: 509 Coed
Affiliation or Control: Independent Non-Profit IRS Status: 501(c)3
Highest Offering: Master's
Program: Professional; Nursing Emphasis
Accreditation: NH, CAHIIM, NURSE, RAD

01 President Dr. Beth A. BROOKS
05 Chief Academic Officer Dr. Adam HAYASHI
26 Dir of Marketing & Communications Ms. Jeri BINGHAM
10 Chief Operating Officer Dr. Therese A. SCANLAN
32 Director of Student Services Ms. Heather PIERCE
29 Asst Dir Alumni Rels/Career Svcs Ms. Esther WALLEN
04 Assistant to President Ms. Angela M. MCCOY
90 Program Analyst Mr. Zbigniew KUSNIERZ
37 Student Financial Aid Ms. Shirley HOWELL
06 Registrar Mr. Michael SHERMAN
07 Dir of Admissions/Enrollment Mgmt Mr. Ron DE LOS SANTOS
08 Manager of Library Services Ms. Liesl COTTRELL
15 Director of Human Resources Mr. Brian BOLLENBACHER
66 Dean of Nursing Dr. Rebecca S. ZUKOWSKI

Richland Community College (K)

One College Park, Decatur IL 62521-8513
County: Macon FICE Identification: 010879
Unit ID: 148292
Telephone: (217) 875-7200 Carnegie Class: Assoc/Pub-R-M
FAX Number: (217) 875-6961 Calendar System: Semester
URL: www.richland.edu
Established: 1971 Annual Undergrad Tuition & Fees (In-District): $3,444
Enrollment: 3,369 Coed
Affiliation or Control: State/Local IRS Status: 501(c)3
Highest Offering: Associate Degree
Program: Occupational; 2-Year Principally Bachelor's Creditable
Accreditation: NH, ACFEI, ADNUR, CAHIIM, RAD, SURGT

01 President Dr. Gayle M. SAUNDERS

10 Vice President of Finance & Admin ... Mr. Greg E. FLORIAN
05 Vice Pres Academic Services ... Dr. Denise CREWS
32 Vice Pres of Student Success ... Mr. Marcus BROWN
103 VP Econ Dev/Innov Wkfce Solutions ... Dr. Douglas BRAUER
106 Director Online Learning ... Mrs. Kona JONES
30 Exec Director Foundation & Develop ... Mr. Richard MCGOWAN
29 Dir Scholarships/Alumni Development ... Mrs. Tricia CORDULACK
51 Dean Continuing & Prof Educ Div ... Mrs. Darbe BRINKOETTER
26 Exec Dir Public Info/Chief of Staff ... Ms. Lisa GREGORY
07 Dean Enrollment Services ... Mr. Marcus BROWN
06 Director Advising & Registrar ... Mr. Richard KERR
35 Director Student Success ... Ms. Kathryn MAST
38 Director Student Development ... Mrs. Deborah MCGEE
81 Dean of Math & Sciences ... Dr. Andy HYNDS
72 Dean of Business & Technology ... Dr. Jack ADWELL
37 Asst Dir Financial Aid/Veteran Affs ... Ms. Jody BURTNETT
36 Director Career Services ... Mr. Michael DIGGS
15 Director Human Resources ... Mr. Richard GSCHWEND
57 Dean Commun/Fine Arts/Education/Hum ... Dr. Lily SIU
76 Dean of Health Professions ... Ms. Ellen COLBECK

Robert Morris University - Illinois (A)

401 South State Street, Chicago IL 60605-1225
County: Cook FICE Identification: 001746
Unit ID: 148335
Telephone: (312) 935-6800 Carnegie Class: Master's M
FAX Number: (312) 935-6660 Calendar System: Other
URL: www.robertmorris.edu
Established: 1913 Annual Undergrad Tuition & Fees: $25,200
Enrollment: 23,700 Coed
Affiliation or Control: Independent Non-Profit IRS Status: 501(c)3
Highest Offering: Master's
Program: Occupational; 2-Year Principally Bachelor's Creditable; Liberal Arts And General; Professional; Business Emphasis
Accreditation: NH, ADNUR, IACBE, MAC, SURGT

01 President ... Michael P. VIOLLT
05 Provost ... Mablene KRUEGER
45 Sr VP for Resource Administration ... Deborah BRODZINSKI
84 Sr VP for Enrollment Management ... Nicole FARINELLA
84 VP for Graduate Enrollment ... Catherine LOCKWOOD
20 VP of Academic Administration ... Kathleen SUHAJDA
88 VP of Brand and Image ... Christine FISHER
10 VP of Business Affairs ... Ronald M. ARNOLD
41 VP of Extracurricular Activities ... Megan SMITH-EGGERT
37 VP of Financial Services ... Leigh BRINSON
15 VP of Human Resources ... Ann BRESINGHAM
13 VP of Information Systems ... Lisa CONTRERAS
88 VP of Student Accounts ... Arlene REGNERUS
32 VP of Student Affairs ... Angela JORDAN
97 Dean of College of Liberal Arts ... Jill MCCINTY
66 Dean College of Nurs & Health Stds ... Lora TIMMONS
49 Dean of Professional Arts ... Nancy ROTUNNO
72 Dean of Inst of Technology & Media ... Basim KHARTABIL
58 Dean of Morris Grad School of Mgmt ... Kayed AKKAWI
50 Dean of Business Administration ... Larry NIEMAN
88 Exec Dir/Dean Inst of Culinary Arts ... Nancy ROTUNNO
106 Dean of Experiential Technolgy ... Deanna HO
07 Dean of Admissions ... Ana MENDEZ
26 VP of Marketing & Recruitment ... Danielle NAFFZIGER
88 Sr Dir of Academic Administration ... Kathleen VIOLLT
88 Dir of Admissions Info Systems ... Damaris RIVERA
88 Director of Data Administration ... Deana MIRANDA
109 VP of Auxiliary Operations ... Nick JARMUZ
88 Director of Academic Programming ... Carmen CUEVAS
14 Director of Networking Services ... Adrian CEPEDA
26 Director of Public Relations ... Nancy DONOHOE
88 Director of Student Center ... Daniel MARTIN
06 Dean of Student Information ... Stella MACH
39 Dir of Student Life and Housing ... Janely RIVERA
35 Dir of Student Support Services ... Angelia CASTANDEA
88 Director of Title VII Grant ... Lauren MILLER
88 Dir of Upward Bound and ETS ... Angelica CASTANEDA
88 Associate Registrar ... Nancy SMITH-IRONS
21 Controller ... Melanie CARLIN
08 Institutional Library Director ... Sue DUTLER
18 Institutional Operations Director ... Nino RANDAZZO
19 Director Security/Safety ... Paul HUERTA

Rock Valley College (B)

3301 N Mulford Road, Rockford IL 61114-5699
County: Winnebago FICE Identification: 001747
Unit ID: 148380
Telephone: (815) 921-7821 Carnegie Class: Assoc/Pub-R-L
FAX Number: N/A Calendar System: Semester
URL: www.rockvalleycollege.edu
Established: 1964 Annual Undergrad Tuition & Fees (In-District): $7,944
Enrollment: 7,737 Coed
Affiliation or Control: Local IRS Status: 501(c)3
Highest Offering: Associate Degree
Program: Occupational; 2-Year Principally Bachelor's Creditable
Accreditation: NH, COARC, DH, SURGT

01 President ... Mr. Michael MASTROIANNI
05 Provost/Chief Academic Officer ... Dr. Carmen COBALLES-VEGA
11 Vice Pres Administrative Services ... Mr. Sam OVERTON, JR.
32 Dean of Students/Title IX Coord ... Dr. Amy DIAZ
51 VP Career & Technical Education ... Mr. Ronald GEARY
15 Vice President of Human Resources ... Ms. Jessica JONES
09 VP Institutional Effectiveness ... Dr. Lisa MEHLIG
30 VP/Chief Development Officer ... Ms. Susan GLENN
84 AVP Enrollment Management/Retention ... Mr. Howard SPEARMAN
20 Assoc VP Academic Affairs ... Vacant
13 Chief Information Officer ... Ms. Diann JABUSCH
35 Dean of Students ... Ms. Lynn PERKINS
18 Director Facilities Planning & POM ... Mr. Michael PHILLIPS
26 Exec Dir Col Comm/Marketing ... Ms. Nancy CHAMBERLAIN
88 Director Theatre & Arts Park ... Mr. Michael WEBB
19 Director Public Safety ... Mr. Joe DROUGHT
06 Registrar/Director Records/Rgstn ... Mr. Brooke JOHNSON
36 Manager Career Svcs/Placement ... Ms. Kelly COOPER
04 Assistant to the President ... Ms. Ann KERWITZ

Rockford Career College (C)

1130 S. Alpine Road, Suite 100, Rockford IL 61108
County: Winnebago FICE Identification: 008545
Unit ID: 148399
Telephone: (815) 965-8616 Carnegie Class: Assoc/PrivFP
FAX Number: (815) 965-0360 Calendar System: Quarter
URL: www.rockfordcareercollege.edu
Established: 1862 Annual Undergrad Tuition & Fees: $10,964
Enrollment: 434 Coed
Affiliation or Control: Proprietary IRS Status: Proprietary
Highest Offering: Associate Degree
Program: Occupational; 2-Year Principally Bachelor's Creditable
Accreditation: ACCSC, ACICS, MAC

01 President/CEO ... Mr. Kevin PULS
10 Vice President/Dir of Finance ... Mr. Guary BERNADELLE
05 Academic Dean ... Mr. Tom LEU
12 Campus President ... Mr. Mick O'HERRON
32 Student Services Director ... Ms. Danielle HARRIOTT
06 Registrar/Director of Compliance ... Ms. Christine LOTT
07 Director of Admissions ... Mr. Kevin PARTELOW
15 Director of Human Resources ... Mr. Jim LAIBLE
36 Director Career Services ... Ms. Ann STITES
37 Director of Financial Aid ... Mr. Shane MALONEY
26 Director of College Relations ... Mr. Jeff SWANBERG
27 Marketing Coordinator ... Mr. Dusten CARLSON

Rockford University (D)

5050 E State Street, Rockford IL 61108-2393
County: Winnebago FICE Identification: 001748
Unit ID: 148405
Telephone: (815) 226-4000 Carnegie Class: Master's L
FAX Number: (815) 226-4119 Calendar System: Semester
URL: www.rockford.edu
Established: 1847 Annual Undergrad Tuition & Fees: $28,200
Enrollment: 1,110 Coed
Affiliation or Control: Independent Non-Profit IRS Status: 501(c)3
Highest Offering: Master's
Program: Liberal Arts And General; Teacher Preparatory; Professional
Accreditation: NH, IACBE, NUR

01 President ... Dr. Robert L. HEAD
05 Int VP of Academic Affairs/Provost ... Dr. Belinda WHOLEBEN
30 VP for Institutional Advancement ... Mr. Bernard SUNDSTEDT
88 Senior Development Officer ... Mr. John MCNAMARA
10 VP for Business/Operations/CFO ... Ms. Christina ANDERSON
21 Business Office Accounting Manager ... Mr. Justin KRUEGER
84 VP Enrollment Management ... Dr. Eric FULCOMER
07 Assoc VP Undergraduate Admission ... Ms. Jennifer NORDSTROM
37 Assistant VP for SAS ... Mr. Todd FISCHER-FREE
11 Associate Vice President Operations ... Mr. Matthew PHILLIPS
13 Director of Information Technology ... Mr. Ryan CUSHING
32 Dean of Students ... Ms. Lisa HETZEL
58 Director of MBA ... Mr. Jeffrey FAHRENWALD
58 Director of MAT ... Vacant
06 Registrar ... Ms. Anna J. JATTKOWSKI-HUDSON
04 Exec Assistant to the President ... Ms. Brenda PERRONE
04 Special Assistant to the President ... Ms. Teddy PHILLIPS
41 Athletic Director ... Mrs. Kristyn KING
15 Director of Human Resources ... Ms. Monique LINDSTEDT
36 Director Career Services ... Mr. Maurice WEST, II
26 Director of Communications ... Ms. Rita ELLIOTT
09 Coordinator of IR ... Mr. Todd FISCHER-FREE
88 Director of ESL ... Mr. Sam BANDY
38 Director Counseling ... Mrs. Sallyann ROBERTS
23 Director Health Services ... Mrs. Cecelia M. BRISTOL
18 Director Facilities/Custodial Svcs ... Mr. Joshua SMITH
19 Director Campus Safety & Security ... Mr. Jeffrey SCHELLING
08 Head Librarian ... Ms. Kelly JAMES

Roosevelt University (E)

430 S Michigan Avenue, Chicago IL 60605-1394
County: Cook FICE Identification: 001749
Unit ID: 148487
Telephone: (312) 341-3500 Carnegie Class: Master's L
FAX Number: (312) 341-3655 Calendar System: Semester
URL: www.roosevelt.edu
Established: 1945 Annual Undergrad Tuition & Fees: $27,300
Enrollment: 6,113 Coed
Affiliation or Control: Independent Non-Profit IRS Status: 501(c)3
Highest Offering: Doctorate
Program: Liberal Arts And General; Teacher Preparatory; Professional
Accreditation: NH, ACBSP, CACREP, CLPSY, MUS, PHAR, TED

01 President ... Dr. Ali MALEKZADEH
05 Exec Vice President/Univ Provost ... Vacant
88 Vice Provost Acad Supt/Retention ... Mr. Michael FORD
20 Interim Provost/VP Academic ... Dr. Samuel ROSENBERG
10 Sr VP of Finance/Admin and CFO ... Ms. Miroslava MEJIA KRUG
86 VP Govt Relations/Univ Outreach ... Ms. Lesley SLAVITT
84 Interim VP Enrollment Mgmt ... Mr. David RHODES
15 Vice President Human Resources ... Vacant
100 Chief of Staff & Asst Secy to BOT ... Mr. Michael FORD
30 Interim VP Inst Advancement ... Ms. Jan PARKIN
29 Asst VP Alumni Relations/Campaigns ... Ms. Janice PARKIN
44 Asst Vice President Planned Giving ... Ms. Denise A. BRANSFORD
32 Assoc Provost Student Success ... Ms. Sheila COFFIN
26 Asst VP Public Relations ... Mr. Thomas R. KAROW
35 Asst VP Student Development ... Ms. Sharron EVANS
09 Assoc Provost Inst Research ... Mr. Joseph P. REGAN
21 Associate VP Finance ... Ms. Tangella MADDOX
18 Assoc VP Campus Planning & Op ... Mr. Steven A. HOSELTON
88 Asst Provost Adult & Exp Learning ... Ms. Laurie CASHMAN
85 Asst Dir of International Programs ... Ms. Dawn HOUGLAND
13 Chief Information Officer ... Mr. Neeraj KUMAR
58 Assoc Provost Research & Grad Stds ... Dr. Kimberly N. RUFFIN
49 Dean College Arts & Sciences ... Dr. Bonnie GUNZENHAUSER
50 Dean College Business Admin ... Dr. Joe CHAN
64 Dean College of Performing Arts ... Mr. Henry FOGEL
107 Dean College of Professional Stds ... Dr. D. Bradford HUNT
53 Dean College of Education ... Dr. Thomas PHILION
67 Dean College of Pharmacy ... Dr. George MACKINNON
88 Exec Dir of Auditorium Theatre/RU ... Mr. Brett BATTERSON
08 Head Pub Svcs/Dir Rob Lib ... Ms. Linda WILKINSON
06 University Registrar ... Ms. Lakisha YOUNG
38 Director Counseling Center ... Dr. Susan STOCK
36 Director Career & Prof Development ... Ms. Jennifer WONDERLY
04 Asst to President ... Ms. Cheryl GOULDSBY
19 Director Security/Safety ... Ms. Maureen FRONCEK
41 Asst VP Health & Dir Athletic ... Mr. Michael CASSIDY
88 Director Intl Programs ... Mr. Justin OSADJAN
07 Assoc Director of Admissions ... Mr. Victor SANCHEZ
105 Senior Web Developer ... Ms. Vickie BERTINI

Roosevelt University Albert A. Robin Campus (F)

1400 N Roosevelt Boulevard, Schaumburg IL 60173
Telephone: (847) 619-7300 Identification: 770092
Accreditation: &NH

† Branch campus of Roosevelt University, Chicago, IL.

Rosalind Franklin University of Medicine & Science (G)

3333 Green Bay Road, North Chicago IL 60064-3095
County: Lake FICE Identification: 001659
Unit ID: 145558
Telephone: (847) 578-3000 Carnegie Class: Spec/Med
FAX Number: (847) 578-3401 Calendar System: Quarter
URL: www.rosalindfranklin.edu
Established: 1912 Annual Undergrad Tuition & Fees: N/A
Enrollment: 2,191 Coed
Affiliation or Control: Independent Non-Profit IRS Status: 501(c)3
Highest Offering: Doctorate; No Lower Division
Program: Professional; Technical Emphasis
Accreditation: NH, ANEST, ARCPA, CLPSY, MED, PA, PHAR, POD, PTA

01 President/CEO ... Dr. Michael WELCH
05 Provost ... Dr. Wendy RHEAULT
10 VP Finance & Admin ... John NYLEN
67 Dean Col of Pharmacy ... Dr. Marc ABEL
58 Dean Sch Grad PostDoc Stds ... Dr. Joseph X. DIMARIO
63 Dean Medical School ... Dr. John TOMKOWIAK
63 Dean Scholl Col Podiatric Med ... Dr. Nancy L. PARSLEY
107 Dean College Health Professions ... Dr. James CARLSON
20 VP Academic/Faculty Affairs ... Dr. Judity STOECKER
46 VP Research ... Dr. Ronald S. KAPLAN
32 VP Student Affairs & Inclusion ... Ms. Rebecca DURKIN
26 VP Marketing/Brand Management ... Ms. Lee CONCHA
13 Chief Information Officer ... Mr. Richard LOESCH
88 Chief Compliance Officer ... Mr. Bret MOBERG
35 AVP Student Affairs ... Mr. Steve WEIAND
08 AVP Accreditation/Assessment ... Dr. Glenda GALLISATH
37 AVP Student Financial Services ... Ms. Maryann DECAIRE
106 AVP Online/Distance Education ... Ms. Marilyn HANSON
88 AVP Faculty Development ... Dr. Rea KATZ
31 Exec Dir Community Relations ... Ms. Christine LOPEZ
29 Exec Dir Alumni Relations ... Ms. Martha KELLY BATES
15 Exec Dir of Human Resources ... Ms. Sherry BAGNO
100 Dir Office of the President ... Ms. Donna AGNEW
102 Dir Foundation & Grant Relations ... Ms. Shella BLUE
44 Dir Annual Giving ... Mr. Mark RUSSELL
96 Dir Materials Management ... Mr. Vince BUTERA
28 Dir Diversity & Inclusion Programs ... Ms. Monica CUMMINGS
39 Dir Student Housing ... Ms. Jennifer LOGAN
09 Dir Institutional Research ... Ms. Renee FRANCISCO
18 Dir Facilities Management ... Mr. Robert D. JACKSON
88 Dir Academic/Retention Svcs ... Mr. Steven WEIAND
07 Dir Admissions/Recruitment ... Ms. Amanda NOASCONO
35 Dir Student Life ... Ms. Shelly BRZYCKI
19 Dir Campus Security ... Mr. Gordon BLANCHARD
25 Dir Sponsored Research ... Ms. Dora ESPINOZA
06 Registrar ... Mr. Timothy CARROLL
04 Executive Administrative Assistant ... Ms. Anita DIAZ MORALES

Rush University (A)

600 S Paulina, Chicago IL 60612-3832
County: Cook FICE Identification: 009800
Unit ID: 148511
Telephone: (312) 942-7100 Carnegie Class: Spec/Med
FAX Number: (312) 942-2219 Calendar System: Quarter
URL: www.rushu.rush.edu
Established: 1971 Annual Undergrad Tuition & Fees: $33,421
Enrollment: 2,457 Coed
Affiliation or Control: Independent Non-Profit IRS Status: 501(c)3
Highest Offering: Doctorate
Program: Professional
Accreditation: NH, ANEST, ARCPA, AUD, BBT, COARC, DIETI, DMS, HSA, IPSY, MED, MT, NURSE, OT, PAST, PERF, SP

01 CEO RUMC & Pres Rush University .... Dr. Larry J. GOODMAN
17 President RUMC .... Mr. Peter W. BUTLER
03 Executive Vice President .... Mr. Michael DANDORPH
05 Provost .... Dr. Thomas A. DEUTSCH
26 Vice Pres Corp/External Affairs .... Mr. Terry PETERSON
10 Senior Vice President Finance .... Mr. John MORDACH
30 Senior Vice President Philanthropy ...... Ms. Diane M. MCKEEVER
13 Sr Vice Pres/Chief Information Ofcr .... Mr. Lac VAN TRAN
43 Sr Vice President Legal Affairs .... Ms. Anne MURPHY
15 Sr Vice President Human Resource .... Ms. Mary E. SCHOPP
46 Vice President .... Dr. James L. MULSHINE
25 Vice Pres Chief Compliance Office .... Dr. Cynthia E. BOYD
22 Mgr Diversity & Inclusion/EOO .... Ms. Paula J. BROWN
20 Vice Provost .... Dr. Lois A. HALSTEAD
32 Assoc Prov Student Svcs/Registrar .... Dr. Gayle WARD
108 Assoc Prov Inst Res/Assess/Accred .... Dr. Rosemarie SUHAYDA
76 Dean Col of Health Sciences .... Dr. Charlotte ROYEEN
58 Acting Dean Graduate College .... Dr. James L. MULSHINE
66 Dean College of Nursing .... Dr. Marquis D. FOREMAN
63 Dean Rush Medical College .... Dr. Thomas A. DEUTSCH
20 Assoc Dean Med/Student Pgm .... Dr. Keith BOYD
27 Asst Vice President Marketing .... Ms. Lori ALLEN
08 Director Library .... Ms. Christine D. FRANK
35 Director Student Life & Engagement .... Ms. Angela BRANSON
37 Director Student Financial Aid .... Mr. Michael FRECHETTE
09 Director of Institutional Research .... Dr. James L. MULSHINE
38 Director Student Counsel Center .... Dr. Hilarie TEREBESSY
29 Director Alumni Relations .... Mr. Roscoe CRAMPTON
85 International Student Coordinator .... Mr. Melvin HARRIS
96 Director of Purchasing .... Mr. Michael MULROE
106 Director METC .... Mr. Frank TOMSIC
21 Manager of Financial Affairs .... Ms. Diane HEALY
06 Registrar .... Ms. Marvell NESMITH
102 Dir Foundation/Corporate Relations .... Ms. Sophia WOROBEC
105 Assoc VP IS Clinical Systems .... Mr. Steven P. WIGHTKIN
19 Director Security Services .... Mr. Lauris FREIDENFELDS
50 Director Business .... Mr. Richard K. DAVIS
54 Director Med Ctr Engineering .... Mr. Mike WISNIEWSKI

Saint Anthony College of Nursing (B)

5658 E State Street, Rockford IL 61108-2425
County: Winnebago FICE Identification: 009987
Unit ID: 149028
Telephone: (815) 395-5091 Carnegie Class: Spec/Health
FAX Number: (815) 395-2275 Calendar System: Semester
URL: www.sacn.edu
Established: 1915 Annual Undergrad Tuition & Fees: $22,808
Enrollment: 309 Coed
Affiliation or Control: Roman Catholic IRS Status: 501(c)3
Highest Offering: Doctorate
Program: Professional; Nursing Emphasis
Accreditation: NH, NURSE

01 President .... Dr. Sandie SOLDWISCH
05 Dean Undergraduate Affairs .... Dr. Elizabeth M. CARSON
58 Dean Graduate Affairs & Research .... Dr. Shannon K. LIZER
32 Associate Dean Support Services .... Ms. Nancy A. SANDERS
08 College LRC/Med Library Director ...... Ms. Heather A. KLEPITSCH
37 Financial Aid/Alumni Res Officer .... Ms. Serrita WOODS

St. Augustine College (C)

1333-45 W Argyle Street, Chicago IL 60640-3501
County: Cook FICE Identification: 021854
Unit ID: 148876
Telephone: (773) 878-8756 Carnegie Class: Assoc/PrivNFP4
FAX Number: (773) 878-0937 Calendar System: Semester
URL: www.staugustine.edu
Established: 1980 Annual Undergrad Tuition & Fees: $9,840
Enrollment: 1,529 Coed
Affiliation or Control: Independent Non-Profit IRS Status: 501(c)3
Highest Offering: Baccalaureate
Program: 2-Year Principally Bachelor's Creditable; Liberal Arts And General
Accreditation: NH, COARC, SW

01 President .... Dr. Andrew C. SUND
05 Dean of Academic & Student Affairs .... Dr. Bruno BONDAVALLI
20 Dean of Instruction .... Mr. Lee MALTBY
10 VP for Finance .... Ms. Saundra K. FLEMING
30 VP for Marketing/Advancement .... Mr. David CORDOVA
103 VP Institute Workforce Development .... Mr. Norman RUANO
09 VP Technology/Research & Systems .... Mr. Paul HECK
37 Director of Financial Aid .... Ms. Maria ZAMBONINO
15 Director Human Resources .... Mr. Teofilo CALERO
18 Director of Physical Facilities .... Mr. Francisco MICHEL
07 Director of Admission .... Ms. Gloria QUIROZ
12 Director West Satellite .... Ms. Carmen RIVERA
12 Director South Satellite .... Ms. Gloria QUIROZ
12 Director of Southeast Satellite .... Ms. Patricia VEGA
12 Director of Aurora Satallite .... Ms. Elizabeth CARDENAS
24 Dir of Learning Resources Center .... Ms. Elizabeth GRUBY

Saint Francis Medical Center College of Nursing (D)

511 NE Greenleaf Street, Peoria IL 61603-3783
County: Peoria FICE Identification: 006240
Unit ID: 148575
Telephone: (309) 655-2201 Carnegie Class: Spec/Health
FAX Number: (309) 624-8973 Calendar System: Semester
URL: www.sfmccon.edu
Established: 1985 Annual Undergrad Tuition & Fees: $19,419
Enrollment: 676 Coed
Affiliation or Control: Roman Catholic IRS Status: 501(c)3
Highest Offering: Doctorate
Program: Professional; Nursing Emphasis
Accreditation: NH, NUR

01 President of the College .... Dr. Patricia A. STOCKERT
05 Dean Undergraduate Program .... Dr. Sue C. BROWN
58 Dean Graduate Program .... Dr. Kimberly A. MITCHELL
32 Asst Dean of Support Services .... Mr. Kevin N. STEPHENS
07 Director of Admissions/Registrar .. Ms. Janice E. FARQUHARSON
08 Librarian .... Mr. William KOMANECKI
38 College Counselor .... Mrs. Jennifer CARLOCK
37 Coord Student Fin/Financial Assist .... Mrs. Nancy S. PERRYMAN
10 Coord Student Finance/Accts Rec .... Ms. Laura L. SIMMONS
04 Administrative Assistant .... Ms. Luann MORELOCK
108 Inst Effectiveness/Assess Specialist .... Mr. Ryan A. WILLIAMS

St. John's College (E)

729 E. Carpenter Street, Springfield IL 62702-5317
County: Sangamon FICE Identification: 030980
Unit ID: 148593
Telephone: (217) 525-5628 Carnegie Class: Spec/Health
FAX Number: (217) 757-6870 Calendar System: Semester
URL: www.stjohnscollegespringfield.edu
Established: 1991 Annual Undergrad Tuition & Fees: $19,237
Enrollment: 119 Coed
Affiliation or Control: Independent Non-Profit IRS Status: 501(c)3
Highest Offering: Baccalaureate
Program: Professional; Nursing Emphasis
Accreditation: NH, NUR

01 Chancellor .... Dr. Brenda R. JEFFERS
05 Academic Dean .... Dr. Jane DIERS
07 Admissions Officer/Registrar .... Ms. Britni CARUSO
30 Development Officer .... Ms. Allyson STRAUCH
51 Director of Continuing Education .... Dr. Mary Jo BROWN
37 Financial Aid Officer .... Mr. Timothy MARTEN

Saint Xavier University (F)

3700 W 103rd Street, Chicago IL 60655-3105
County: Cook FICE Identification: 001768
Unit ID: 148627
Telephone: (773) 298-3000 Carnegie Class: Master's L
FAX Number: (773) 779-9061 Calendar System: Semester
URL: www.sxu.edu
Established: 1846 Annual Undergrad Tuition & Fees: $30,920
Enrollment: 4,073 Coed
Affiliation or Control: Roman Catholic IRS Status: 501(c)3
Highest Offering: Master's
Program: Liberal Arts And General; Professional
Accreditation: NH, ACBSP, BUS, MUS, NURSE, SP, TED

01 President .... Ms. Christine M. WISEMAN
05 Provost .... Dr. Paul L. DEVITO
10 Vice President Business & Finance .... Mr. Robert H. FISHER
30 Vice President Advancement .... Mr. Shereitte C. STOKES, III
26 Vice President University Relations . Mr. Robert C. TENCZAR, JR.
32 Vice President Student Affairs .... Mr. John P. PELRINE, JR.
09 Exec Dir Institutional Research .... Dr. Kathleen CARLSON
35 Asst Vice Pres Student Affairs .... Ms. Carrie SCHADE
18 Director of Facilities Management .... Mr. Peter SKACH
20 Associate Provost .... Dr. Richard VENNERI
20 Asst Provost/Director Retention .... Ms. Maureen WOGAN
35 Dean of Students .... Dr. Eileen DOHERTY
109 Director Auxiliary Services .... Ms. Linda MORENO
37 Director Financial Aid .... Ms. Susan SWISHER
21 Controller .... Ms. Diane STALLMANN
43 General Counsel .... Ms. Kathleen A. RINEHART
07 Director of Admission .... Mr. Brian HOTZFIELD
27 Executive Director Media Relation .... Ms. Karla THOMAS
24 Director CIDAT .... Mr. Christopher ZAKREWSKI
08 Director Library .... Mr. David STERN
06 Director Records/Registration Svcs .... Ms. Barbara SUTTON
19 Dir Public Safety/Chief of Police .... Mr. Jack TOUHY
29 Director Alumni/Parent Relations .... Ms. Jamie MANAHAN
41 Director Athletics .... Mr. Robert HALLBERG
42 VP University Mission & Ministry ..... Mr. Graziano MARCHESCHI
85 Dir Center International Education .... Ms. Kelly REIDY-FOX
36 Director of Career Services .... Ms. Jean RIORDAN
51 Dean School Cont Prof Studies .... Dr. Leslie PETTY
49 Dean College Arts/Sciences .... Dr. Kathleen ALAIMO
53 Interim Dean School of Education .... Dr. Suzanne LEE
50 Dean Graham School of Management .... Dr. Asghar SABBAGHI
66 Dean School of Nursing .... Dr. Gloria JACOBSON
04 Executive Assistant to President .... Ms. Gail B. YOUNG

Saint Xavier University Orland Park Campus (G)

18230 Orland Parkway, Orland Park IL 60467
Telephone: (708) 802-6200 Identification: 770093
Accreditation: &NH

† Branch campus of Saint Xavier University, Chicago, IL.

Sanford-Brown College (H)

1 N State Street, Suite 500, Chicago IL 60602-9736
County: Cook FICE Identification: 021603
Unit ID: 146010
Telephone: (312) 980-9200 Carnegie Class: Spec/Arts
FAX Number: (312) 541-3929 Calendar System: Quarter
URL: www.sanfordbrown.edu
Established: 1977 Annual Undergrad Tuition & Fees: $14,401
Enrollment: 229 Coed
Affiliation or Control: Proprietary IRS Status: Proprietary
Highest Offering: Baccalaureate
Program: Occupational
Accreditation: ACICS

01 President .... Mr. Anthony WILLIAMS
05 Campus Director of Education .... Mr. Michael GORMAN
06 Associate Registrar .... Ms. Wildanette MOLLFULLEDA
08 Regional Director Library Services .... Ms. Amanda HENDERSON
36 Director of Career Services .... Mr. Elliott REASONER
10 Business Operations Manager .... Mr. Willis JORDAN

† School is in teach-out plan through November 2017.

Sauk Valley Community College (I)

173 Illinois Route 2, Dixon IL 61021-9188
County: Lee FICE Identification: 001752
Unit ID: 148672
Telephone: (815) 288-5511 Carnegie Class: Assoc/Pub-R-M
FAX Number: (815) 288-1880 Calendar System: Semester
URL: www.svcc.edu
Established: 1965 Annual Undergrad Tuition & Fees (In-District): $3,146
Enrollment: 2,211 Coed
Affiliation or Control: State/Local IRS Status: 501(c)3
Highest Offering: Associate Degree
Program: Occupational; 2-Year Principally Bachelor's Creditable
Accreditation: NH, RAD

01 President .... Dr. George J. MIHEL
05 Provost .... Mr. Alan A. PFEIFER
20 Dean of Academics & Student Svcs .... Mr. Jon D. MANDRELL
09 Dean Inst Research/Marketing .... Mr. Steve C. NUNEZ
76 Dean Health & Sciences .... Ms. Janet L. LYNCH
10 Dean of Business Services .... Ms. Melissa DYE
18 Director Buildings & Grounds .... Mr. Frank J. MURPHY
15 Director of Human Resources .... Ms. Kathryn C. SNOW
84 Director Enrollment Services .... Ms. Pamela S. MEDEMA
102 Foundation Manager .... Ms. Sharri K. MILLER
13 Dean of Information Services .... Ms. Chris A. SHELLEY
41 Director of Athletics .... Mr. Russ K. DAMHOFF
37 Financial Assistance Specialist .. Ms. Kimberlee L. MCCLANAHAN
91 Instructional Technology Sppt Spec .... Ms. Kathleen M. DIRKS

School of the Art Institute of Chicago (J)

37 S Wabash, Chicago IL 60603-3103
County: Cook FICE Identification: 001753
Unit ID: 143048
Telephone: (312) 899-5100 Carnegie Class: Spec/Arts
FAX Number: (312) 263-0141 Calendar System: Semester
URL: www.saic.edu
Established: 1866 Annual Undergrad Tuition & Fees: $42,230
Enrollment: 3,599 Coed
Affiliation or Control: Independent Non-Profit IRS Status: 501(c)3
Highest Offering: Master's
Program: Teacher Preparatory; Fine Arts Emphasis
Accreditation: NH, ART

01 President .... Dr. Walter E. MASSEY
05 Provost .... Dr. Elissa TENNY
84 Vice Pres Enrollment Management .... Ms. Rose MILKOWSKI
30 VP for Institutional Advancement .... Ms. Cheryl JESSOGNE
10 Vice Pres Finance & Administration .... Mr. Brian ESKER
15 Vice President for Human Resources .... Mr. Michael NICOLAI
32 Vice Pres/Dean of Student Affairs .... Dr. Felice DUBLON
20 Vice Provost .... Mr. Paul COFFEY
18 Assoc VP Facilities/Operations .... Mr. Thomas BUECHELE
20 Dean of Faculty/VP Acad Affs .... Ms. Lisa WAINWRIGHT
35 Dean of Student Life .... Ms. Deborah MARTIN
21 Exec Dir Academic Accounting .... Ms. Sherry MISGEN
26 Exec Dir Enroll Mktg & Operations .... Ms. Maryann SCHAEFER
29 Assoc Director Alumni Relations .... Ms. Jennifer JANSEN
38 Exec Director Wellness Center .... Dr. Joseph BEHEN
84 Exec Director Enrollment Services .... Ms. Jane BRUMITT
06 Director Registration & Records .... Mr. Brad ERZ

08 Director of School Library .... Ms. Claire EIKE
36 Asst Dean/Dir Career Development .... Ms. Katharine SCHUTTA
07 Director of Undergrad Admissions .... Ms. Asia MITCHELL
07 Director of Graduate Admissions .... Mr. Scott RAMON
37 Director of Student Financial Svcs .... Mr. Patrick JAMES
28 Director of Multicultural Affairs .... Ms. Rashayla BROWN
88 Director of Learning Center .... Ms. Valerie ST. GERMAIN
49 Dean of Undergraduate Studies .... Ms. Tiffany HOLMES
58 Int Dean of Graduate Studies .... Mr. David GETSY

Shawnee Community College (A)

8364 Shawnee College Road, Ullin IL 62992-2206
County: Pulaski　FICE Identification: 007693
Unit ID: 148821
Telephone: (618) 634-3200　Carnegie Class: Assoc/Pub-R-L
FAX Number: (618) 634-3300　Calendar System: Semester
URL: www.shawneecc.edu
Established: 1967　Annual Undergrad Tuition & Fees (In-District): $3,168
Enrollment: 1,799　Coed
Affiliation or Control: Local　IRS Status: 501(c)3
Highest Offering: Associate Degree
Program: Occupational; 2-Year Principally Bachelor's Creditable
Accreditation: NH, CAHIIM, MLTAD, OTA, SURGT

01 President .... Dr. Tim BELLAMEY
05 Vice Pres Instructional Services .... Dr. Vickie ARTMAN
32 Vice President Student Svcs .... Ms. Jipaum ASKEW-ROBINSON
04 Asst to President .... Ms. Becky CASPER
20 Dean Instructional Services .... Ms. Jean Ellen BOYD
51 Dean Adult Educ/Alternative Instruc .... Mr. James DARDEN
10 Chief Financial Officer .... Ms. Tiffiney RYAN
38 Student Support Services Director .... Ms. Amber SUGGS
35 Dean of Student Services .... Ms. Dee BLAKELY
37 Dir Fin Aid/Coord Vet & Mil Personl .... Dr. Tammy CAPPS
41 Athletic Director .... Vacant
13 Director MIS .... Mr. Chris CLARK
12 Director Metro Center .... Ms. Faye JOYNER-KEENE
66 Director of Nursing .... Ms. Denise GRIFFITH
08 Head Librarian .... Ms. Tracey JOHNSON
06 Registrar .... Ms. Danielle BOYD
102 Dir Resource Development/Foundation .... Vacant
21 Director of Business Services .... Ms. Brandy WOODS
18 Facilities Director .... Mr. Don KOCH
09 Director of Institutional Research .... Vacant
40 Bookstore Manager .... Ms. Erica POAT
88 Special Needs Counselor .... Ms. Lee Ann GEORGE
88 Coord Ctr for Cmty/Economic Devel .... Ms. Candy EASTWOOD
26 Public Relations Coordinator .... Ms. Emily ELLIOT
36 Career Services Coordinator .... Ms. Leslie WELDON
50 Div Chair Business/Occup/Tech Dp .... Mr. Jerry AINSWORTH
81 Division Chair Math/Science .... Ms. Rhonda DILLOW
79 Div Chr Social Stds/Humanities/Comm .... Ms. Sharon WALKER
76 Div Chair Allied Health .... Ms. Tracy LOHSTROH
15 Human Resources Director .... Ms. Emily FORTHMAN

Shimer College (B)

3424 S State Street, Second Floor,
Chicago IL 60616-3893
County: Cook　FICE Identification: 001756
Unit ID: 148849
Telephone: (312) 235-3500　Carnegie Class: Bac/A&S
FAX Number: (312) 235-3502　Calendar System: Semester
URL: www.shimer.edu
Established: 1853　Annual Undergrad Tuition & Fees: $33,746
Enrollment: 80　Coed
Affiliation or Control: Independent Non-Profit　IRS Status: 501(c)3
Highest Offering: Baccalaureate
Program: Liberal Arts And General
Accreditation: NH

01 President .... Dr. Susan HENKING
11 Chief Operating Officer .... Mr. James ULRICH
05 Dean of the College .... Dr. Harold STONE
32 Director of Student Life .... Ms. Samantha BENNETT
30 Director of Development .... Vacant
37 Director of Financial Aid .... Ms. Janet HENTHORN
07 Dean of Admission .... Vacant
10 Chief Financial Officer .... Ms. Phyllis DOBBS
06 Registrar .... Mr. James ULRICH
26 Dir of Strategic Communications .... Ms. Isabella WINKLER

SOLEX College (C)

350 East Dundee Road, Wheeling IL 60090
County: Cook　FICE Identification: 045816
Unit ID: 459356
Telephone: (847) 229-9595　Carnegie Class: Not Classified
FAX Number: (847) 229-1919　Calendar System: Other
URL: www.solex.edu
Established: 1995　Annual Undergrad Tuition & Fees: $17,500
Enrollment: 234　Coed
Affiliation or Control: Proprietary　IRS Status: Proprietary
Highest Offering: Associate Degree
Program: Occupational; 2-Year Principally Bachelor's Creditable; Technical Emphasis
Accreditation: ACICS, COMTA, PTAA

01 Executive Director .... Mr. Leon E. LINTON

South Suburban College of Cook County (D)

15800 S State Street, South Holland IL 60473-1270
County: Cook　FICE Identification: 001769
Unit ID: 149365
Telephone: (708) 596-2000　Carnegie Class: Assoc/Pub-S-SC
FAX Number: (708) 210-5710　Calendar System: Semester
URL: www.ssc.edu
Established: 1927　Annual Undergrad Tuition & Fees (In-District): $4,133
Enrollment: 4,329　Coed
Affiliation or Control: State/Local　IRS Status: 501(c)3
Highest Offering: Associate Degree
Program: Occupational; 2-Year Principally Bachelor's Creditable
Accreditation: NH, OTA, PHLEB

01 President .... Mr. Don MANNING
05 Vice President Academic Services .... Dr. Linda STOKES-WILSON
11 Vice Pres Administration .... Mr. Martin LAREAU
32 Vice President Student Development .... Ms. Songie ADEBIYI
84 VP Enrollment/Community Education .... Mrs. Jane Ellen STOCKER
35 Dean Student Services .... Ms. Patrice BURTON
20 AVP Academic Svcs/Instl Effect .... Mr. Ronald KAWANNA, JR.
50 Dean Business & Technology .... Mr. James COATES
76 Dean Health Professions & Sciences .... Mr. Jeff WADDY
57 Dean Fine Arts/Soc & Behav Sci/Bus .... Mr. Tom GOVAN, JR.
66 Dean Nursing/Fine Arts/English/Hum .... Ms. Miriam ANTHONY
51 Director Continuing Education .... Ms. Shirley DREWENSKI
10 Treasurer/Controller .... Mr. Tim POLLERT
26 Director Public Rels/Pub & Found .... Mr. Patrick RUSH
13 Exec Dir Information Technology .... Mr. John MCCORMACK
88 Dir New Student Ctr & Retenion Svcs .... Mrs. Jazaer FARRAR
84 Director Enrollment Services .... Mrs. Robin RIHACEK
37 Director of Financial Aid .... Mr. John SEMPLE
18 Director Physical Plant Services .... Mr. Justin PAPP
24 Dir Communication Svcs/Media Design .... Mrs. Lisa MILLER
41 Athletic Director .... Mr. Steve RUZICH
09 Director of Institutional Research .... Mr. Kevin RIORDAN
15 Director Human Resources .... Ms. Kimberly PIGATTI
06 Manager for Registration/Records .... Ms. Tenial WHITTED
07 Mgr of Admissions/Recruitment .... Ms. Tiffane JONES

South Suburban College of Cook County University and College Center (E)

16333 Kilbourne Avenue, Oak Forest IL 60452
Telephone: (708) 225-6029　Identification: 770094
Accreditation: &NH

† Branch campus of South Suburban College of Cook County, South Holland, IL.

Southeastern Illinois College (F)

3575 College Road, Harrisburg IL 62946-4925
County: Saline　FICE Identification: 001757
Unit ID: 148937
Telephone: (618) 252-5400　Carnegie Class: Assoc/Pub-R-L
FAX Number: (618) 252-3156　Calendar System: Semester
URL: www.sic.edu
Established: 1960　Annual Undergrad Tuition & Fees (In-District): $3,120
Enrollment: 1,834　Coed
Affiliation or Control: State/Local　IRS Status: 501(c)3
Highest Offering: Associate Degree
Program: Occupational; 2-Year Principally Bachelor's Creditable
Accreditation: NH, MLTAD, OTA, SURGT

01 President .... Dr. Jonah RICE
05 Vice President Instruction .... Dr. Dana KEATING
10 Dean Administration/Business Affs .... Mr. David WRIGHT
32 Dean Student Servicess/Enrollment .... Mr. Chad FLANNERY
20 Dean of Career & Technical Educ .... Mrs. Karen WEISS
103 Assoc Dean of Workforce & Cmty Ed .... Mrs. Lori COX
08 Librarian/LRC Director .... Mr. Gary JONES
84 Director Enrollment Services .... Ms. Kyla BURFORD
26 Marketing Coordinator .... Ms. Angela WILSON
37 Financial Aid Director .... Ms. Emily HENSON
13 Chief Information Officer .... Mr. Greg MCCULLOCH
76 Director Allied Health & Nursing .... Ms. Gina SIRACH
15 Exec Asst to Pres/Human Res Mgr .... Mrs. Barbara POTTER
06 Registrar .... Ms. Kyla BURFORD
18 Director of Environmental Services .... Mr. Ed FITZGERALD

*Southern Illinois University (G)

Stone Center - 1400 Douglas Drive, Carbondale IL 62901
County: Jackson　FICE Identification: 008237
Unit ID: 149240
Telephone: (618) 536-3331　Carnegie Class: N/A
FAX Number: (618) 536-3404
URL: www.southernillinois.edu

01 President .... Dr. Randy J. DUNN
05 Vice President Academic Affairs .... Dr. Paul SARVELA
10 Sr VP Financial/Admin Affs/Bd Treas .... Dr. Duane STUCKY
88 Director Risk Management .... Ms. Chris GLIDEWELL
86 Exec Dir Governmental/Public Affs .... Mr. John CHARLES
21 Exec Dir of Internal Audits .... Ms. Kim LABONTE
43 Interim General Counsel .... Mr. Lucas CRATER
04 Assistant to the President .... Ms. Paula S. KEITH

*Southern Illinois University Carbondale (H)

1265 Lincoln Drive, Carbondale IL 62901-6899
County: Jackson　FICE Identification: 001758
Unit ID: 149222
Telephone: (618) 453-2121　Carnegie Class: RU/H
FAX Number: (618) 453-3250　Calendar System: Semester
URL: siu.edu
Established: 1869　Annual Undergrad Tuition & Fees (In-State): $13,137
Enrollment: 17,989　Coed
Affiliation or Control: State　IRS Status: 501(c)3
Highest Offering: Doctorate
Program: Occupational; 2-Year Principally Bachelor's Creditable; Liberal Arts And General; Teacher Preparatory; Professional
Accreditation: NH, ARCPA, ART, BUS, BUSA, CACREP, CEA, CIDA, CLPSY, COPSY, CORE, CS, DH, DIETD, DIETI, DMS, ENG, ENGT, FUSER, IFSAC, IPSY, JOUR, LAW, MED, MUS, NAIT, PH, PTAA, RAD, RADDOS, RADMAG, RTT, SP, SPAA, SW, TED, THEA

02 Interim Chancellor .... Dr. William B. COLWELL
05 Acting Provost & Vice Chancellor .... Dr. Susan FORD
32 Dean of Students .... Vacant
30 VC for Development & Alumni Rels .... Mr. Jim SALMO
10 VC for Administration and Finance .... Mr. Kevin BAME
46 Interim VC for Research .... Dr. James GARVEY
28 Assoc Chancellor Diversity .... Dr. Linda MCCABE-SMITH
102 CFO SIU Foundation .... Mr. Stephen NAGLE
13 Asst Provost & Chief Info Officer .... Mr. Scott D. BRIDGES
84 Asst Provost Enrollment Mgmt .... Vacant
20 Assoc Provost for Academic Admin .... Dr. David DILALLA
20 Assoc Provost for Academic Programs .... Dr. James S. ALLEN
04 Assistant to the Chancellor .... Mr. Matthew BAUGHMAN
49 Interim Dean Liberal Arts .... Dr. Meera KOMARRAJU
50 Interim Dean College of Business .... Dr. Jason T. GREENE
53 Dean Educ & Human Services .... Dr. Lyle WHITE
54 Dean Engineering .... Dr. John J. WARWICK
58 Dean Graduate School .... Dr. Yueh-TIng LEE
61 Dean School of Law .... Dr. Cynthia FOUNTAINE
81 Dean College of Science .... Dr. Laurie ACHENBACH
63 Dean School of Medicine .... Dr. John K. DORSEY
47 Dean Agricultural Sciences .... Dr. Mickey A. LATOUR
72 Dean Col Applied Sciences & Arts .... Dr. JuAn WANG
57 Dean Mass Comm/Media Arts .... Dr. Dafna P. LEMISH
08 Dean Library Affairs .... Vacant
07 Director Undergrad Admissions .... Ms. Josephine KOONCE-EVANS
37 Director Student Financial Aid .... Ms. Terry HARFST
29 Associate VC Alumni Services .... Ms. Michelle SUAREZ
88 Interim Budget Director .... Ms. Judith MARSHALL
09 Dir Institutional Research .... Dr. John EVANS
21 Executive Director for Finance .... Ms. Judith MARSHALL
26 Chief Marketing & Comm Officer .... Ms. Rae GOLDSMITH
15 Director Human Resources .... Ms. Jennifer WATSON
39 Interim Director University Housing .... Mr. Jon L. SHAFFER
36 Director Univ Career Services .... Mr. Douglas C. REICHENBERGER
85 Director International Education .... Ms. Carla E. COPPI
18 Director Plant/Service Operations .... Mr. Philip S. GATTON
19 Director of Public Safety .... Mr. Benjamin NEWMAN
23 Director Student Health Services .... Dr. Ted W. GRACE
41 Dir Intercollegiate Athl .... Mr. Tommy BELL
106 Director Distance Education .... Dr. Mandara SAVAGE
06 Director Registrar's Office .... Ms. Tamara WORKMAN
38 Asst Dir Student Counseling Cntr .... Dr. Frank KOSMICKI
96 Int Director Procurement Services .... Ms. Debbie ABELL
35 Acting Assoc Dean of Students .... Mr. Andy L. MORGAN
25 Chief Contracts/Grants Admin .... Mr. Wayne GLASS

*Southern Illinois University Edwardsville (I)

Edwardsville IL 62026
County: Madison　FICE Identification: 001759
Unit ID: 149231
Telephone: (618) 650-2000　Carnegie Class: Master's L
FAX Number: (618) 650-2270　Calendar System: Semester
URL: www.siue.edu
Established: 1957　Annual Undergrad Tuition & Fees (In-State): $10,247
Enrollment: 14,265　Coed
Affiliation or Control: State　IRS Status: 501(c)3
Highest Offering: Doctorate
Program: Liberal Arts And General; Teacher Preparatory; Professional
Accreditation: NH, ANEST, BUS, BUSA, CONST, CS, DENT, ENG, EXSC, JOUR, MUS, NURSE, PHAR, SP, SPAA, SW, TED, THEA

02 Interim Chancellor .... Dr. Stephen L. HANSEN
05 Prov & VC for Academic Affs .... Dr. Parviz H. ANSARI
10 Vice Chancellor for Administration .... Mr. Kenneth R. NEHER
30 VC Univ Adv & CEO SIUE Foundation .... Ms. Rachel C. STACK
32 Vice Chanc for Student Affairs .... Dr. Jeffrey N. WAPLE
100 Chief of Staff .... Ms. Kimberly H. DURR
22 Dir Equal Opp/Access & Title IX .... Mr. Chad MARTINEZ
20 Assoc Prov for Acad Plng & Pgm Dev .... Dr. P. Denise COBB
20 Assoc Prov Rsch/Dean Grad Sch .... Dr. Jerry B. WEINBERG
35 Assoc VC Stdnt Affs/Dean of Stdnts .... Dr. James W. KLENKE
35 Assoc VC for Student Affairs .... Ms. Lora MILES
13 Interim Assoc VC for IT & CIO .... Mr. Steven HUFFSTUTLER
28 Asc Chanc Inst Diversity/Inclusion .... Dr. Venessa BROWN
88 Asst Prov for Acad Innov & Eff .... Dr. Erin BEHNEN
41 Asst VC Athletic Dev/Dir Athletics .... Dr. Bradley L. HEWITT
84 Assoc VC for Enrollment Mgmt .... Mr. Scott BELOBRAJDIC
45 Asst VC for Planning & Budgeting .... Mr. Richard WALKER

49 Dean College of Arts & Sciences .... Dr. Gregory BUDZBAN
50 Dean School of Business .... Dr. John NAVIN
52 Dean Sch of Dental Medicine .... Dr. Bruce E. ROTTER
53 Dean Sch of Educ/Hlth & Human Behav .... Dr. Curt LOX
54 Dean School of Engineering .... Dr. Hasan SEVIM
66 Interim Dean School of Nursing .... Dr. Laura BERNAIX
67 Dean School of Pharmacy .... Dr. Gireesh V. GUPCHUP
62 Dean Library & Information Services .... Dr. Regina MCBRIDE
21 Budget Director .... Mr. William F. WINTER, JR.
26 Exec Dir Univ Mktg & Comm .... Mr. Doug MCILHAGGA
88 Dir Grant Funded Pgm East StL Ctr .... Mr. Jesse DIXON
88 Director Academic Advising .... Ms. Cheryle L. TUCKER
07 Director Admissions .... Mr. Todd C. BURRELL
29 Director Alumni Affairs .... Mr. Stephen E. JANKOWSKI
36 Director Career Dev Center .... Ms. Susan SEIBERT
38 Director Counseling Services .... Dr. James LINSIN
18 Director Facilities Management .... Mr. Paul FULIGNI
23 Director Health Services .... Ms. Riane B. GREENWALT
15 Director Human Resources .... Ms. Sherrie SENKFOR
09 Dir Institutional Rsrch & Studies .... Mr. Phillip M. BROWN
85 Exec Dir International Affairs .... Dr. Mary WEISHAAR
96 Director of Purchasing .... Ms. Nancy J. UFERT FAIRLESS
37 Dir Student Financial Aid .... Ms. Sally MULLEN
102 Dir Univ Advancement/Foundation Ops .... Mr. Kevin MARTIN
39 Director University Housing .... Mr. Michael J. SCHULTZ
19 Director University Police .... Mr. Kevin SCHMOLL
06 Registrar .... Ms. Laura A. STROM

* *Southern Illinois University Carbondale School of Medicine* (A)

PO Box 19620, Springfield IL 62794-9620
Telephone: (217) 545-8000 Identification: 770181
Accreditation: &NH

† Branch campus of Southern Illinois University Carbondale, Carbondale, IL.

Southwestern Illinois College (B)

2500 Carlyle Avenue, Belleville IL 62221-5899
County: Saint Clair FICE Identification: 001636
Unit ID: 143215
Telephone: (618) 235-2700 Carnegie Class: Assoc/Pub-S-MC
FAX Number: (618) 277-0631 Calendar System: Semester
URL: www.swic.edu
Established: 1946 Annual Undergrad Tuition & Fees (In-District): $3,420
Enrollment: 10,545 Coed
Affiliation or Control: State/Local IRS Status: 501(c)3
Highest Offering: Associate Degree
Program: Occupational; 2-Year Principally Bachelor's Creditable
Accreditation: NH, ACFEI, ADNUR, CAHIIM, COARC, EMT, MAC, MLTAD, PTAA, RAD

01 President - District .... Dr. Georgia COSTELLO
10 Controller .... Ms. Missy ROCHE
11 VP Administrative Svcs/Treasurer .... Mr. Bernie J. YSURSA, JR.
05 Vice Pres Instruction .... Mr. Clay L. BAITMAN
31 Vice Pres Community Svcs .... Dr. Mark P. EICHENLAUB
26 Vice Pres Mktg/Institutional Adv .... Mr. Mike R. FLEMING
15 Director Human Resources .... Ms. Sherry FAVRE
32 Vice Pres Student Development .... Ms. Staci G. CLAYBORNE
20 Assoc Dean Instructional Services .... Ms. Patricia POU
12 Executive Director SWGCC .... Ms. Nancy LEVAULT
12 Executive Director Red Bud Campus .... Mr. Mike REED
08 Dean Learning Resources .... Mrs. Laurie A. BINGEL
37 Director of Financial Aid/Placement .... Mr. Robert TEBBE
13 Chief Information Officer .... Dr. James RIHA
18 Director of Physical Plant .... Mr. Ron R. HENDERSON
19 Director of Public Safety .... Mr. Mark A. GREEN
96 Director of Purchasing .... Mr. Mike R. THOMAS
76 Dean Hlth Sci and Homeland Security .... Ms. Julie A. MUERTZ
50 Dean of Business Division .... Dr. Janet S. FONTENOT
72 Dean of Technical Education .... Mr. Brad SPARKS
81 Dean of Math & Science .... Mr. Steve L. HOLMAN
49 Dean of Liberal Arts .... Mr. Richard SPENCER
51 Director Adult Education/Cont Educ .... Dr. Lea MAUE
07 Dean of Enrollment Services .... Ms. Michelle L. BIRK
88 Dean of Success Programs .... Ms. Deborah ALFORD
88 Treasurer IL Green Economy Network .... Mr. Robert J. HILGENBRINK
06 Specialist for Registration/Records .... Ms. Debra RAHN

Southwestern Illinois College Red Bud Campus (C)

500 W South 4th Street, Red Bud IL 62278
Telephone: (618) 282-6682 Identification: 770096
Accreditation: &NH

† Branch campus of Southwestern Illinois College, Belleville, IL.

Southwestern Illinois College Sam Wolf Granite City Campus (D)

4950 Maryville Road, Granite City IL 62040
Telephone: (618) 931-0600 Identification: 770095
Accreditation: &NH

† Branch campus of Southwestern Illinois College, Belleville, IL.

Spertus Institute for Jewish Learning and Leadership (E)

610 S Michigan Avenue, Chicago IL 60605-1994
County: Cook FICE Identification: 001663
Unit ID: 148982
Telephone: (312) 322-1700 Carnegie Class: Spec/Other
FAX Number: (312) 922-6406 Calendar System: Quarter
URL: www.spertus.edu
Established: 1924 Annual Graduate Tuition & Fees: $20,000
Enrollment: 250 Coed
Affiliation or Control: Independent Non-Profit IRS Status: 501(c)3
Highest Offering: Doctorate; No Undergraduates
Program: Liberal Arts And General; Teacher Preparatory; Professional
Accreditation: NH

01 President .... Dr. Hal M. LEWIS
05 Provost/Vice President .... Dr. Dean BELL
20 Assistant Dean .... Ms. Beth SCHENKER
10 Controller .... Mr. Doug PETERSON
88 Director Nonprofit Admin Program .... Dr. Karen BAIRD
37 Financial Aid Mgr .... Ms. Pamela FELTON
84 Director of Enrollment Management .... Ms. Stacey FLINT

Spoon River College (F)

23235 N County Road 22, Canton IL 61520-9801
County: Fulton FICE Identification: 001643
Unit ID: 148991
Telephone: (309) 647-4645 Carnegie Class: Assoc/Pub-R-M
FAX Number: (309) 649-6235 Calendar System: Semester
URL: www.src.edu
Established: 1959 Annual Undergrad Tuition & Fees (In-District): $4,200
Enrollment: 1,733 Coed
Affiliation or Control: Local IRS Status: 501(c)3
Highest Offering: Associate Degree
Program: Occupational; 2-Year Principally Bachelor's Creditable
Accreditation: NH

01 President .... Mr. Curt OLDFIELD
05 Vice Pres Inst/Student Services .... Vacant
10 Vice Pres Administrative Services .... Mr. Brett STOLLER
04 Executive Asst to the President .... Ms. Julie HAMPTON
36 Dean Career & Technical Education .... Vacant
32 Dean Student Services .... Ms. Missy WILKINSON
66 Director Nursing .... Ms. Tamatha SCHLEICH
88 Dean Transfer Education .... Ms. Holly NORTON
06 Dir of Records & Admissions .... Ms. Melissa WILKINSON
18 Director Facilities .... Mr. Bob A. HAILE
55 Dir Adult and Outreach Education .... Mr. Chad MURPHY
08 Director Library Services .... Vacant
13 Chief Information Officer .... Mr. Raj SIDDARAJU
41 Director Athletics/Student Life .... Mr. Ron CLARK
21 Director Business Services .... Ms. Sarah GRAY
37 Director Financial Aid .... Ms. Salinda Jo BRANSON
96 Dir Purchasing & Auxiliary Services .... Mr. Brad T. O'BRIEN
15 Director Human Resources .... Ms. Michelle L. BUGOS
14 Director Technology Services .... Mr. Dean CLARY
84 Director Enrollment Services .... Ms. Janet MUNSON
09 Coord Institutional Reporting .... Mr. Aaron ROE
26 Director Marketing .... Ms. Sherri RADER
27 Coordinator Public Information .... Ms. Sally SHIELDS
102 Director Foundation .... Mr. Colin DAVIS
30 Director Institutional Advancement .... Vacant

Spoon River College-Macomb Campus (G)

208 S Johnston Street, Macomb IL 61455
Telephone: (309) 837-5727 Identification: 770097
Accreditation: &NH

† Branch campus of Spoon River College, Canton, IL.

Taylor Business Institute (H)

318 W Adams Street, Suite 500, Chicago IL 60606
County: Cook FICE Identification: 011810
Unit ID: 149310
Telephone: (312) 658-5100 Carnegie Class: Assoc/PrivFP
FAX Number: (312) 658-0867 Calendar System: Quarter
URL: www.tbiil.edu
Established: 1962 Annual Undergrad Tuition & Fees: $13,500
Enrollment: 280 Coed
Affiliation or Control: Proprietary IRS Status: Proprietary
Highest Offering: Associate Degree
Program: Occupational; Technical Emphasis
Accreditation: @NH, ACICS

01 President .... Mrs. Janice C. PARKER

Telshe Yeshiva-Chicago (I)

3535 W Foster Avenue, Chicago IL 60625-5598
County: Cook FICE Identification: 020732
Unit ID: 149329
Telephone: (773) 463-7738 Carnegie Class: Spec/Faith
FAX Number: (773) 463-2849 Calendar System: Semester
Established: 1960 Annual Undergrad Tuition & Fees: $13,500
Enrollment: 81 Male
Affiliation or Control: Independent Non-Profit IRS Status: 501(c)3
Highest Offering: Second Talmudic Degree
Program: Professional; Business Emphasis
Accreditation: RABN

01 President .... Rabbi Avrohom C. LEVIN
03 Executive Vice President .... Rabbi Yitzchok LEVIN
05 Vice President .... Rabbi Chaim D. KELLER
05 Vice President .... Rabbi Moshe SCHMELCZER
11 Administrative Director/Secretary .... Rabbi Shmuel ADLER

Toyota Technological Institute at Chicago (J)

6045 South Kenwood Avenue, Chicago IL 60637
County: Cook Identification: 666367
Unit ID: 445054
Telephone: (773) 834-2500 Carnegie Class: Assoc/PrivNFP4
FAX Number: (773) 834-9881 Calendar System: Quarter
URL: www.ttic.edu
Established: 2003 Annual Graduate Tuition & Fees: $30,000
Enrollment: 20 Coed
Affiliation or Control: Independent Non-Profit IRS Status: 501(c)3
Highest Offering: Doctorate; No Undergraduates
Program: Professional; Technical Emphasis
Accreditation: NH

01 President .... Dr. Sadaoki FURUI
05 Chief Academic Officer .... Dr. David MCALLESTER
10 Treasurer/Secretary of the Board .... Mr. Masashi HISAMOTO
58 Admin Director of Graduate Studies .... Ms. Christina NOVAK
21 Controller .... Ms. Anna RUFFOLO

Tribeca Flashpoint Media Arts Academy (K)

28 North Clark Street, Suite 500, Chicago IL 60602
County: Cook Identification: 667083
Unit ID: 460747
Telephone: (312) 332-0707 Carnegie Class: Not Classified
FAX Number: (312) 506-0708 Calendar System: Semester
URL: www.tfa.edu
Established: 2007 Annual Undergrad Tuition & Fees: $25,600
Enrollment: 353 Coed
Affiliation or Control: Proprietary IRS Status: Proprietary
Highest Offering: Baccalaureate
Program: Occupational; 2-Year Principally Bachelor's Creditable
Accreditation: ACICS

01 President .... Todd STEELE
05 Exec VP/Dean Academic Affairs .... Peter HAWLEY
10 Exec VP/Chief Financial Officer .... Erik PARKS
11 Sr Vice President Operations .... Ernesto PARAS
20 Sr VP/Dean of Faculty .... John MURRAY
30 VP Strategy/Development .... Kyle O'MEARA
07 Vice President Admissions .... Bill BECKLY
06 Registrar .... Jason CALIZ

Trinity Christian College (L)

6601 W College Drive, Palos Heights IL 60463-0929
County: Cook FICE Identification: 001771
Unit ID: 149505
Telephone: (708) 597-3000 Carnegie Class: Bac/Diverse
FAX Number: (708) 385-5665 Calendar System: 4/1/4
URL: www.trnty.edu
Established: 1959 Annual Undergrad Tuition & Fees: $26,190
Enrollment: 1,406 Coed
Affiliation or Control: Independent Non-Profit IRS Status: 501(c)3
Highest Offering: Master's
Program: Liberal Arts And General; Teacher Preparatory; Professional
Accreditation: NH, ACBSP, NURSE, SW

01 President .... Mr. Kurt D. DYKSTRA
05 Interim Provost .... Dr. Sharon ROBBERT
10 Vice Pres for Finance & Admin .... Mr. James E. BELSTRA
32 Vice Pres for Student Life .... Mrs. Rebekah L. STARKENBURG
30 Vice Pres for Development .... Vacant
08 Director of Library Services .... Vacant
06 Registrar .... Ms. Jaynn TOBIAS-JOHNSON
07 Director of Admissions .... Mr. Jeremy KLYN
36 Director Career Planning/Placement .... Mr. John BALDAUFF
55 Dean Adult Studies & Grad Programs .... Dr. Lori SCREMENTI
29 Director of Alumni Relations .... Mr. Bill DERUITER
26 Dir of Marketing and Communications .... Ms. Kim FABIAN
88 Asst Dir Marketing/Graphic Designer .... Mr. Peter CLEVERING
13 Director of Computer Services .... Mr. Joe VELDERMAN
41 Director of Athletics .... Mr. Bill SCHEPEL
31 Director of Community Partnerships .... Ms. Tabitha MATTHEWS
42 Chaplain .... Dr. Willis VAN GRONINGEN
85 Director of Off-Campus Programs .... Dr. Burton J. ROZEMA
37 Director Financial Aid .... Mr. Ryan ZANTINGH
18 Director of Building/Grounds .... Mr. Tim TIMMONS
44 Director of Planned Giving .... Mr. Ken BOSS
21 Controller .... Mr. Mike TROCHUCK
28 Dir of Diversity/Dir AS Psychology .... Dr. Tiffany KING
92 Director of Honors Program .... Dr. Craig MATTSON
38 Director Cooper Ctr Counseling .... Dr. Dan SARTOR
84 Exec Director of College Enrollment .... Mr. Adam ASHER
09 Asst Registar for Inst Research .... Ms. Kimberly WILLIAMS
15 Human Resources Manager .... Ms. Julia FOUST
20 Assoc Dean Academics .... Dr. John FRY
04 Exec Admin Asst to President .... Ms. Deborah S. VINCENT
19 Director Security/Safety .... Mr. Dale GUSTAFSON

Trinity College of Nursing & Health Sciences (A)

2122 25th Avenue, Rock Island IL 61201-5317

County: Rock Island FICE Identification: 006225
Unit ID: 146755
Telephone: (309) 779-7700 Carnegie Class: Spec/Health
FAX Number: (309) 779-7748 Calendar System: Semester
URL: www.trinitycollegeqc.edu
Established: 1994 Annual Undergrad Tuition & Fees: $27,067
Enrollment: 246 Coed
Affiliation or Control: Independent Non-Profit IRS Status: 501(c)3
Highest Offering: Master's
Program: Professional; Nursing Emphasis
Accreditation: **NH**, ADNUR, COARC, NURSE, RAD

01 Chancellor ... Dr. Tracy L. POELVOORDE
05 Int Dean of Nursing & Health Sci ... Ms. Tracy L. POELVOORDE
06 Registrar ... Ms. Cara BANKS

Trinity International University (B)

2065 Half Day Road, Deerfield IL 60015-1284

County: Lake FICE Identification: 001772
Unit ID: 149514
Telephone: (847) 945-8800 Carnegie Class: DRU
FAX Number: (847) 317-8090 Calendar System: Semester
URL: www.tiu.edu
Established: 1897 Annual Undergrad Tuition & Fees: $28,700
Enrollment: 2,686 Coed
Affiliation or Control: Evangelical Free Church Of America
IRS Status: 501(c)3
Highest Offering: Doctorate
Program: Liberal Arts And General; Teacher Preparatory; Professional
Accreditation: **NH**, CAATE, THEOL

01 President ... Dr. David S. DOCKERY
03 Exec Vice President & Provost ... Vacant
05 VP Education/Dean TEDS ... Dr. Graham COLE
05 VP Academic Affairs/Dean TC & TGS ... Dr. Thomas CORNMAN
84 Sr VP for Enrollment Management ... Mr. Rich GRIMM
32 VP Student Life/Dean of Students ... Mr. Feliy THEONUGRAHA
13 Sr VP Information Technology/Plng ... Mr. Steven GEGGIE
30 Sr Vice Pres University Advancement ... Dr. David HOAG
10 Sr VP of Business & Finance/CFO ... Mr. Mike PICHA
44 Spec Asst to Pres Church/Cmty Rels ... Mr. Carl JOHNSON
26 VP for University Communication ... Mr. Mark KAHLER
21 VP for Fin/Inst Research/Controller ... Mr. Paul EISENMENGER
73 Assoc Academic Dean Divinity School ... Dr. H. Wayne JOHNSON
88 Interim Dean of Nontraditional Educ ... Mr. Jay SIMALA
35 Assoc Dean of Undergraduate Stdnts ... Ms. Karen WROBBEL
90 Director of Acad/Desktop Computing ... Mr. Chris MILLER
91 Director Administrative Computing ... Ms. Katie KEMP
58 Assoc Dean of Graduate School ... Dr. Don HEDGES
61 Dean of Law School ... Mr. Myron R. STEEVES
42 VP Spiritual Life/Univ Ministries ... Dr. Taylor WORLEY
07 Director Undergraduate Admissions ... Mr. Jordan BRYANT
19 Director of Security Services ... Mr. Bob TOPOREK
96 Director of Facilities ... Ms. Julie WONG
15 Interim Director of Human Resources ... Mrs. Linda BRUNDIDGE
06 University Registrar ... Mr. David SKINNER
37 Executive Director Student Services ... Ms. Rachel RUSSIAKY
36 Director of Career Services ... Ms. Jan VICTOR
36 Director of Placement ... Dr. Phil SELL
08 University Librarian ... Dr. Robert H. KRAPOHL
29 Director of Alumni Relations ... Mr. Michael GORSLINE
27 Asst VP University Communication ... Mr. Chris DONOTO
92 Director of Honors Program ... Dr. Matt HELLER
35 Director of Student Activities ... Ms. Heather CORDERO

Triton College (C)

2000 Fifth Avenue, River Grove IL 60171-1995

County: Cook FICE Identification: 001773
Unit ID: 149532
Telephone: (708) 456-0300 Carnegie Class: Assoc/Pub-S-SC
FAX Number: (708) 583-3112 Calendar System: Semester
URL: www.triton.edu
Established: 1964 Annual Undergrad Tuition & Fees (In-District): $3,638
Enrollment: 11,577 Coed
Affiliation or Control: Local IRS Status: 501(c)3
Highest Offering: Associate Degree
Program: Occupational; 2-Year Principally Bachelor's Creditable; Business Emphasis
Accreditation: **NH**, ADNUR, DMS, NMT, RAD, SURGT

01 Interim President ... Ms. Mary-Rita MOORE
05 VP Academic and Student Affairs ... Dr. Douglas OLSON
10 Vice President Business Services ... Mr. Sean SULLIVAN
101 Secretary for Brd of Trustees ... Ms. Susan PAGE
100 Chief of Staff ... Ms. Lindsey WESTLEY
13 Assoc VP Information Systems ... Mr. Michael GARRITY
21 Assoc VP Business Operations ... Mr. Kevin KENNEDY
18 Director of Facilities ... Mr. John LAMBRECHT
32 AVP of Student Affairs ... Dr. Quincy MARTIN
45 AVP of Strategic Planning ... Ms. Mary Rita MOORE
35 Dean of Student Services ... Mr. Corey WILLIAMS
84 Dean of Enrollment Services ... Dr. Amanda TURNER
37 Assoc Dean of Financial Aid ... Ms. Patricia ZINGA
21 Director Finance ... Mr. James REYNOLDS
88 Director Teaching & Learning ... Dr. Mary Ann TOBIN
26 Executive Director Marketing ... Mr. Sam TOLIA
07 Director Admissions Services ... Ms. Izabela ZURAWSKA
29 Director Alumni Relations ... Ms. Lisa SCALESSI
19 Chief of Police ... Mr. Jeffrey SARGENT
09 Dir Institutional Effectiveness ... Ms. Hannah BALLAS
14 Sr Data and System Admin ... Mr. Robert HAUSKNECHT
88 Public Relations Associate ... Ms. Brenda JONES WATKINS
72 Instructional Technologist ... Ms. Marie-Ange ZICHER
49 Dean Arts & Sciences ... Mr. Ricardo SEGOVIA
51 Dean of Continuing Education ... Mr. Paul JENSEN
55 Dean of Adult Education ... Dr. Virginia CABASA-HESS
09 Dean of Academic Success ... Dr. Deborah BANESS KING
49 Asst Dean of Arts & Sciences ... Mr. Gabriel GUZMAN
51 Asst Dean Continuing Education ... Ms. Colleen MAZZUCA-PESCE

University of Chicago (D)

5801 S Ellis Avenue, Chicago IL 60637-1496

County: Cook FICE Identification: 001774
Unit ID: 144050
Telephone: (773) 702-1234 Carnegie Class: RU/VH
FAX Number: N/A Calendar System: Quarter
URL: www.uchicago.edu
Established: 1890 Annual Undergrad Tuition & Fees: $50,193
Enrollment: 15,312 Coed
Affiliation or Control: Independent Non-Profit IRS Status: 501(c)3
Highest Offering: Doctorate
Program: Liberal Arts And General; Teacher Preparatory; Professional
Accreditation: **NH**, BUS, IPSY, LAW, MED, SW, THEOL

01 President ... Mr. Robert J. ZIMMER
05 Provost ... Dr. Eric D. ISAACS
03 Executive Vice President ... Mr. David B. FITHIAN
17 EVP for Medical Affairs/Dean of BSD ... Dr. Kenneth POLONSKY
100 Associate VP and Chief of Staff ... Ms. Katie CALLOW-WRIGHT
101 VP/Sec of the University ... Mr. Darren REISBERG
46 VP for Research/Natl Lab ... Mr. Donald LEVY
10 VP of Operations/CFO ... Mr. Rowan MIRANDA
30 VP for Alumni Rels & Development ... Mr. Ken MANOTTI
43 Vice President & General Counsel ... Ms. Kim TAYLOR
88 Vice Pres/Chief Investment Officer ... Mr. Mark A. SCHMID
88 VP for Global Engagement ... Mr. Ian H. SOLOMON
84 VP/Dean Col Enroll/Financial Aid ... Mr. James NONDORF
07 Director of Admissions ... Mr. James NONDORF
32 VP/Campus Life Student Services ... Ms. Karen W. COLEMAN
31 Vice President for Civic Engagement ... Mr. Derek DOUGLAS
26 Vice Pres for Communications ... Mr. John LONGBRAKE
49 Dean of the College ... Mr. John W. BOYER
81 Dean Physical Sciences Division ... Mr. Edward W. KOLB
83 Dean of Social Sciences Division ... Mr. David NIRENBERG
42 Dean Rockefeller Memorial Chapel ... Ms. Elizabeth DAVENPORT
79 Dean of Humanities Division ... Ms. Martha T. ROTH
54 Dean of Molecular Engineering ... Mr. Matthew TIRRELL
50 Dean of Booth School of Business ... Mr. Sunil KUMAR
35 Dean of Students ... Ms. Michele RASMUSSEN
61 Interim Dean of the Law School ... Mr. Geoffrey STONE
73 Interim Dean of the Divinity School ... Mr. Richard A. ROSENGARTEN
51 Dean of Graham School ... Mr. Mark R. NEMEC
56 Dean Extension ... Mr. Mark NEMEC
63 Dean Medicine ... Mr. Kenneth POLONSKY
80 Dean Harris Sch of Public Policy ... Mr. Daniel DIERMEIER
70 Dean Social Svcs Admin ... Mr. Neil GUTERMAN
21 Senior Advisor for Finance & Admin ... Mr. John R. KROLL
20 Assoc Provost and Budget Director ... Mr. David L. MURPHY
13 VP and CIO ... Mr. Cole W. CAMPLESE
18 Assoc VP University Architect ... Mr. Steve WIESENTHAL
25 Chief Contracts/Grants Admin ... Mr. Donald LEVY
15 Interim Associate VP HR ... Mr. Mike KNITTER
20 Senior Associate Provost ... Mr. Larry HILL
28 Deputy Provost for Minority Issues ... Mr. William MCDADE
88 Vice Provost for Acad Initiatives ... Ms. Sian BEILOCK
06 Registrar ... Mr. Scott CAMPBELL
37 Executive Director University Aid ... Ms. Amanda FIJAL
57 Deputy Provost for the Arts ... Mr. Lawrence ZBIKOWSKI
22 Assoc Provost/Affirm Action Ofcr ... Vacant
09 Dir Institutional Research ... Mr. William GREENLAND
29 Senior AVP Alumni Rels & Develop ... Mr. Damon CATES
36 Exec Dir Career Advancement ... Ms. Meredith DAW
41 Athletic Director ... Ms. Erin MCDERMOTT
08 Director University Library ... Ms. Brenda JOHNSON
38 Dir Student Counseling Services ... Mr. David ALBERT
96 Exec Dir Payroll/Procurement ... Mr. Mark FEHLBERG
39 Exec Director Student Housing ... Ms. Jennifer LUTTIG-KOMROSKY

*University of Illinois University Administration (E)

506 S Wright Street, Urbana IL 61801-3689

County: Champaign FICE Identification: 008001
Unit ID: 149587
Telephone: (217) 333-6400 Carnegie Class: N/A
FAX Number: (217) 333-5733
URL: www.uillinois.edu

01 President ... Dr. Timothy L. KILLEEN
12 Chancellor/Vice President (Chicago) ... Dr. Michael AMIRIDIS
12 Chancellor/Vice President (Sprfld) ... Dr. Susan KOCH
12 Chancellor/Vice President (Urbana) ... Dr. Phyllis WISE
10 VP & Chief Financial Officer ... Mr. Walter KNORR
05 Vice Pres for Academic Affairs ... Dr. Christophe PIERRE
09 Vice Pres for Research ... Dr. Lawrence SCHOOK
43 University Counsel ... Mr. Thomas R. BEARROWS
26 Exec Dir for University Relations ... Mr. Thomas P. HARDY
13 CIO & Sr Assoc VP ... Dr. Michael HITES
15 Assoc VP Human Resources ... Ms. Maureen PARKS
101 Secretary Board of Trustees/Univ ... Dr. Susan M. KIES
102 President/CEO Univ Foundation ... Mr. James H. MOORE, JR.
29 Pres/CEO Univ Alumni Association ... Mr. Loren R. TAYLOR

*University of Illinois at Chicago (F)

601 S Morgan, M/C 102, Chicago IL 60607-7128

County: Cook FICE Identification: 001776
Unit ID: 145600
Telephone: (312) 996-7000 Carnegie Class: RU/VH
FAX Number: (312) 413-3393 Calendar System: Semester
URL: www.uic.edu
Established: 1896 Annual Undergrad Tuition & Fees (In-State): $13,762
Enrollment: 27,969 Coed
Affiliation or Control: State IRS Status: 501(c)3
Highest Offering: Doctorate
Program: Liberal Arts And General; Teacher Preparatory; Professional
Accreditation: **NH**, BUS, BUSA, CAHIIM, CEA, CLPSY, CS, DENT, DIETC, DIETD, ENG, ENGR, FEPAC, HSA, IPSY, MED, MIDWF, MIL, NURSE, OT, PAST, PH, PHAR, PLNG, PTA, SPAA, SW

02 Chancellor ... Dr. Michael AMIRIDIS
05 Interim VC Acad Affs and Provost ... Dr. Eric A. GISLASON
32 Vice Chancellor for Student Affairs ... Dr. Barbara HENLEY
11 Vice Chanc for Administrative Svcs ... Mr. Mark DONOVAN
46 Vice Chancellor for Research ... Dr. Mitra DUTTA
26 Exec Assoc Chanc External Affairs ... Mr. Michael REDDING
17 CEO Hospital Administration ... Dr. Avijit GHOSH
29 Vice President Alumni Relations ... Ms. Arlene NORSYM
30 Vice Chancellor Development ... Mr. Jeff NEARHOOF
84 Vice Prov Acad/Enrollment Svcs ... Mr. Kevin BROWNE
15 Vice Provost for Faculty Affairs ... Dr. Renee TAYLOR
20 Int Vice Prov Undergrad Affairs ... Dr. Emanuel POLLACK
45 Vice Provost Planning & Programs ... Dr. Saul WEINER
21 Vice Provost Resource Plng/Mgmt ... Ms. Janet PARKER
35 Assoc Vice Chanc/Dean Student Affs ... Dr. Linda DEANNA
27 Senior Exec Director Public Affrs ... Ms. Sherri MCGINNIS GONZALEZ
23 Interim Vice Pres Health Affairs ... Dr. Jerry BAUMAN
10 Interim Asst VP Business/Finance ... Ms. Vanessa PEOPLES
48 Dean Col of Architect/Design/Arts ... Dr. Steve EVERETT
50 Dean College of Business Admin ... Dr. Michael B. MIKHAIL
52 Dean College of Dentistry ... Dr. Clark STANFORD
53 Dean College of Education ... Dr. Alfred TATUM
54 Dean College of Engineering ... Dr. Peter C. NELSON
76 Dean Col Applied Health Sciences ... Dr. Bo FERNHALL
58 Dean Graduate College ... Dr. Karen COLLEY
92 Dean Honors College ... Dr. Bette L. BOTTOMS
49 Dean College Liberal Arts/Sciences ... Dr. Astrida O. TANTILLO
63 Dean College of Medicine ... Dr. Dimitri AZAR
66 Dean College of Nursing ... Dr. Terri E. WEAVER
67 Dean College of Pharmacy ... Dr. Jerry BAUMAN
70 Dean College of Social Work ... Dr. Creasie HAIRSTON
69 Dean School of Public Health ... Dr. Paul BRANDT-RAUF
27 Dean Urban Planning/Public Affrs ... Dr. Michael A. PAGANO
43 University Counsel ... Mr. Thomas R. BEARROWS
08 University Librarian ... Ms. Mary CASE
88 Asst Univ Librarian Health Sciences ... Ms. Kathryn H. CARPENTER
07 Managing Director Admissions ... Ms. Malinda LORKOVICH
41 Director Athletics ... Mr. James W. SCHMIDT
38 Director Counseling Services ... Dr. Joseph HERMES
37 Interim Director Financial Aid ... Ms. Shirley RODRIGUEZ-VEGA
09 Director of Institutional Research ... Mr. Lance Cortney KENNEDY-PHILLIPS
16 Assoc Vice Provost Faculty Affairs ... Ms. Angela L. YUDT
22 Director Access/Equity ... Ms. Caryn A. BILLS-WINDT
36 Director Career Services ... Mr. Thy NGUYEN
13 CIO/Exec Dir Acad Computing ... Ms. Cynthia E. HERRERA LINDSTROM
51 Exec Dir School Continuing Studies ... Ms. Gayla M. STONER
06 Registrar ... Mr. Robert DIXON
96 Director of Purchasing ... Ms. Debra MATLOCK
18 Exec Dir Operations/Maintenance ... Mr. Clarence F. BRIDGES
28 Vice Provost for Diversity ... Dr. Tyrone A. FORMAN

*University of Illinois at Springfield (G)

One University Plaza, Springfield IL 62703-5407

County: Sangamon FICE Identification: 009333
Unit ID: 148654
Telephone: (217) 206-6600 Carnegie Class: Master's L
FAX Number: (217) 206-6511 Calendar System: Semester
URL: www.uis.edu
Established: 1969 Annual Undergrad Tuition & Fees (In-State): $11,413
Enrollment: 5,431 Coed
Affiliation or Control: State IRS Status: 501(c)3
Highest Offering: Doctorate
Program: Liberal Arts And General; Teacher Preparatory; Professional
Accreditation: **NH**, BUS, CACREP, MT, SPAA, SW

02 Chancellor ... Dr. Susan KOCH
05 Vice Chancellor Acad Affs ... Ms. Lynn PARDIE
32 Interim Vice Chanc Student Affairs ... Dr. Clarice FORD
20 Assc Vice Chanc Undergrad Education ... Ms. Karen MORANSKI
29 Assoc Vice Chanc for Alumni Rels ... Mr. Charles SCHRAGE
30 Vice Chanc Dev/Sr VP UL Found ... Dr. Jeffrey D. LORBER
35 Asst Vice Chanc for Student Service ... Dr. Van VIEREGGE
18 Exec Dir Facility Services ... Mr. David BARROWS

22	Asc Chanc Access/Equal Opportunity	Ms. Deanie BROWN
27	Assoc Chancellor for Public Affairs	Mr. Ryan CROKE
49	Dean College Liberal Arts/Science	Dr. James ERMATINGER
50	Dean College Business/Management	Dr. Ronald D. MCNEIL
80	Acting Dean Col Public Affs/Admin	Mr. David RACINE
53	Dean College Educ/Human Svcs	Dr. Hanfu MI
15	Senior Director of Human Resources	Ms. Laura ALEXANDER
84	Director of Enrollment Management	Vacant
43	Legal Counsel	Ms. Rhonda PERRY
08	University Librarian	Ms. Jane B. TREADWELL
26	Director Public Information	Mr. Derek SCHNAPP
10	Assc Provost Budget and Admin Plng	Dr. Jerry JOSEPH
19	Chief Campus Police Department	Mr. Donald MITCHELL
06	Registrar	Mr. Brian CLEVENGER
35	Director of Student Life	Ms. Cynthia THOMPSON
41	Director of Athletics	Ms. Kim PATE
90	Director Campus Technology Service	Vacant
09	Director Institutional Research	Ms. Laura DORMAN
96	Director of Purchasing	Mr. Michael BLOECHLE
37	Acting Dir Financial Assistance	Ms. Carolyn SCHLOEMANN
38	Exec Director Counseling Center	Dr. Judith SHIPP
85	Director International Programs	Dr. Jonathan GOLDBERGBELLE
13	Assoc Prov Information Technology	Mr. Farokh ESLAHI
39	Director Campus Housing	Mr. John RINGLE
07	Director of Admissions	Mr. Fernando PLANAS
21	Sr Business/Financial Coordinator	Mr. Jason BANE

*University of Illinois at Urbana-Champaign (A)

601 E John Street, Champaign IL 61820-5711
County: Champaign FICE Identification: 001775
Unit ID: 145637
Telephone: (217) 333-1000 Carnegie Class: RU/VH
FAX Number: (217) 333-9758 Calendar System: Semester
URL: www.illinois.edu
Established: 1867 Annual Undergrad Tuition & Fees (In-State): $15,626
Enrollment: 43,603 Coed
Affiliation or Control: State IRS Status: 501(c)3
Highest Offering: Doctorate
Program: Occupational; Liberal Arts And General; Teacher Preparatory; Professional
Accreditation: NH, ART, AUD, BUS, BUSA, CEA, CLPSY, COPSY, CS, DANCE, DIETD, DIETI, ENG, IPSY, JOUR, LAW, LIB, LSAR, MUS, NRPA, PCSAS, PH, PLNG, SP, SW, THEA, VET

02	Interim Chancellor	Dr. Barbara J. WILSON
05	Vice Chancellor Acad Affs & Provost	Dr. Ilesanmi ADESIDA
46	Vice Chancellor Research	Dr. Peter E. SCHIFFER
32	Vice Chancellor Student Affairs	Dr. C. Renee ROMANO
30	Vice Chanc for Inst Advancement	Mr. Daniel C. PETERSON
31	Associate Chanc Public Engagement	Dr. Pradeep KHANNA
20	Vice Provost Academic Affairs	Dr. Elabbas BENMAMOUN
88	Associate Chancellor	Mr. Michael DELORENZO
88	Associate Chancellor	Dr. Menah PRATT-CLARKE
26	Associate Chanc Public Affairs	Ms. Robin KALER
04	Associate Chancellor	Dr. Reginald ALSTON
29	Associate Chanc Alumni Relations	Vacant
15	Associate Provost Human Resources	Ms. Elyne COLE
84	Int Assoc Prov Enrollment Mgmt	Mr. Keith MARSHALL
104	Vice Provost Intl Pgms/Studies	Ms. Reitumetse MABOKELA
21	Assoc Provost Budgetary Planning	Ms. Vicky GRESS
09	Asst Provost Management Info	Dr. Amy EDWARDS
49	Dean Liberal Arts & Sciences	Dr. Barbara WILSON
61	Dean Law	Dr. Vikram AMAR
74	Dean Veterinary Medicine	Dr. Peter CONSTABLE
54	Dean Engineering	Dr. Andreas C. CANGELLARIS
47	Dean Agric/Consumer/Environ Sci	Dr. Robert HAUSER
50	Dean Business	Dr. Jeffrey BROWN
57	Dean Fine & Applied Arts	Dr. Edward FESER
70	Dean School of Social Work	Dr. Wynne S. KORR
68	Dean Col Applied Health Sciences	Dr. Tanya M. GALLAGHER
60	Dean College of Media	Dr. Janet SLATER
58	Dean Graduate College	Dr. Wojciech CHODZKO-ZAJKO
62	Int Dean Grad Sch Library/Info Sci	Dr. Allen H. RENEAR
53	Dean Education	Dr. Mary KALANTZIS
63	Reg Dean Col Med/Urbana-Champ	Dr. Michele MARISCALCO
88	Int Dean Labor & Employment Rels	Dr. Fritz DRASGOW
08	University Librarian & Dean	Mr. John P. WILKIN
13	Chief Information Officer	Mr. Mark HENDERSON
35	Dean of Students	Dr. Kenneth BALLOM
56	Assoc Dean Extension & Outreach	Dr. George CZAPAR
41	Director Athletics	Mr. Michael J. THOMAS
10	Asst Vice Pres Bus/Fin Affairs	Ms. Ginger VELAZQUEZ
43	Campus Legal Counsel	Mr. Scott RICE
88	Deputy CIO Information Technology	Mr. Joseph G. GULICK
22	Dir Equal Opportunity & Access	Dr. Menah PRATT-CLARKE
19	Director Public Safety	Mr. Jeffrey T. CHRISTENSEN
18	Exec Director Facilities	Mr. Allan M. STRATMAN
23	Director McKinley Health Center	Dr. Robert D. PALINKAS
36	Director Career Services Center	Dr. Gail ROONEY
37	Director Student Financial Aid	Mr. Daniel R. MANN
38	Director Counseling Center	Dr. Carla MCCOWAN
39	Director Housing Division	Ms. Alma SEALINE
51	Int Dir Cont Educ/Public Service	Dr. Faye LESHT
06	Int Registrar	Mr. Rodney E. HOEWING

*University of Illinois at Chicago College of Medicine at Peoria (B)

Box 1649, Peoria IL 61656-1649
Telephone: (309) 671-3000 Identification: 770182
Accreditation: &NH

† Branch campus of University of Illinois at Chicago, Chicago, IL.

*University of Illinois Chicago College of Medicine at Rockford (C)

1601 Parkview Avenue, Rockford IL 61107
Telephone: (815) 395-0600 Identification: 770183
Accreditation: &NH

† Branch campus of University of Illinois at Chicago, Chicago, IL.

*University of Illinois at Chicago College of Medicine at Urbana (D)

506 South Matthews Avenue, Urbana IL 61801
Telephone: (217) 333-5465 Identification: 770184
Accreditation: &NH

† Branch campus of University of Illinois at Chicago, Chicago, IL.

University of Phoenix Chicago Campus (E)

1500 McConnor Parkway, Suite 700, Schaumburg IL 60173-4395
Telephone: (847) 413-1922 Identification: 770205
Accreditation: &NH, ACBSP

† No longer accepting campus-based students.

University of St. Francis (F)

500 N Wilcox Street, Joliet IL 60435-6188
County: Will FICE Identification: 001664
Unit ID: 148584
Telephone: (815) 740-3400 Carnegie Class: Master's L
FAX Number: (815) 740-4285 Calendar System: Semester
URL: www.stfrancis.edu
Established: 1920 Annual Undergrad Tuition & Fees: $29,950
Enrollment: 3,762 Coed
Affiliation or Control: Roman Catholic IRS Status: 501(c)3
Highest Offering: Doctorate
Program: Liberal Arts And General; Teacher Preparatory; Professional
Accreditation: NH, ACBSP, NRPA, NURSE, RTT, SW, TED

01	President	Dr. Arvid C. JOHNSON
05	Provost/VP Academic Affairs	Dr. Frank H. PASCOE
10	VP Finance & Administration	Ms. Elizabeth A. LAKEN
84	VP Admissions/Mktg/Enrollment Svcs	Mr. Charles M. BEUTEL
88	VP Mission Int & Univ Ministry	Sr. Mary Elizabeth IMLER
32	VP Student & Alumni Affairs	Mr. Damon N. SLOAN
13	CIO/Info Tech & Library Services	Mr. Terrance L. COTTRELL
31	Exec Dir Cmty Relations/Grants	Ms. Nancy A. POHLMAN
30	Chief Development Officer	Ms. Regina M. BLOCK
21	Controller	Ms. Michelle L. MAHONEY
49	Dean Col Arts & Sciences	Dr. Robert KASE
50	Interim Dean Col Business/Health	Dr. Anthony ZORDAN
53	Dean Col Education	Dr. John S. GAMBRO
66	Dean Leach Col Nursing	Dr. Carol J. WILSON
29	Dir Alumni Relations	Ms. Aubrey L. KNIGHT
41	Dir Athletics	Mr. Dave LAKETA
36	Dir Career Success Center	Ms. Maribeth HEARN
38	Dir Counseling & Wellness	Mr. Carlos AQUINO
15	Dir Human Resources	Vacant
28	Dir Institutional Diversity	Ms. Bernadette TIAPO
09	Dir Institutional Effectiveness	Ms. Janine M. HICKS
07	Dir Undergrad Admissions	Ms. Cynthia A. LAMBERT
07	Dir Grad/Degree Completion Admiss	Ms. Sandra L. SLOKA
104	Dir Intl Programs Office	Ms. Angie MAFFEO
26	Dir Marketing Services	Ms. Julie FUTTERER
14	Dir Network Support Services	Mr. Mark T. SNODGRASS
18	Dir Operations & Facilities	Mr. Mike DECMAN
39	Dir Residence Education	Ms. Mollie ROCKAFELLOW
19	Dir Safety/Security & Transport	Mr. Joseph W. KRIPP
35	Dir Student Engagement/Leadership	Ms. Dominique A. ANNIS
42	Dir University Ministry	Mr. Joseph T. WYSOCKI
06	Registrar	Ms. Laura A. KOGA
108	Assessment Coordinator	Dr. Pamela STEINKE
23	Coordinator of Health Services	Ms. Phyllis M. PETERSON
24	Head of Tech Svcs	Ms. Gail GAWLIK
105	Web Communications Manager	Mr. Michael PLANETA
37	Exec Dir Financial Aid	Mr. Bruce FOOTE
90	Dir Dept Academic Technology	Mr. Steve WETTERGREN

University of Saint Mary of the Lake-Mundelein Seminary (G)

1000 E Maple Avenue, Mundelein IL 60060-1174
County: Lake FICE Identification: 001765
Unit ID: 148885
Telephone: (847) 566-6401 Carnegie Class: Spec/Faith
FAX Number: (847) 566-7330 Calendar System: Semester
URL: www.usml.edu
Established: 1844 Annual Graduate Tuition & Fees: $24,875
Enrollment: 209 Male
Affiliation or Control: Roman Catholic IRS Status: 501(c)3
Highest Offering: Doctorate; No Undergraduates
Program: Professional; Religious Emphasis
Accreditation: THEOL

00	Chancellor	ArBish. Blase CUPICH
01	Rector/President	Rev. Robert BARRON
11	Vice Rector for Admin/Dir Admission	Rev. James PRESTA
05	Vice Rector for Academic Affairs	Rev. Thomas A. BAIMA
73	Pres/Pontifical Faculty of Theology	Rev. John KARTJE
32	Dean of Formation	Rev. Brian WELTER
10	Vice President for Finance	Mr. John F. LEHOCKY
30	Vice President Inst Advancement	Mr. Ryan BUTTS
20	Assoc Acad Dean Sem/Grad Sch	Dr. Christopher MCATEE
73	Director Pre-Theology Program	Rev. James PRESTA
08	Library Director	Mrs. Lorraine OLLEY EUSTICE
06	Registrar	Mrs. Mary Ann ULZ
88	Director of Pastoral Internships	Rev. Martin BARNUM
88	Director of Liturgy	Rev. John GUTHRIE
88	Director of Spiritual Life	Rev. Brendan LUPTON
85	Director of International Students	Rev. Martin BARNUM
18	Chief Facilities/Physical Plant	Mr. Clayton KALWEIT

VanderCook College of Music (H)

3140 S Federal Street, Chicago IL 60616-3731
County: Cook FICE Identification: 001778
Unit ID: 149639
Telephone: (312) 225-6288 Carnegie Class: Spec/Arts
FAX Number: (312) 225-5211 Calendar System: Semester
URL: www.vandercook.edu
Established: 1909 Annual Undergrad Tuition & Fees: $26,300
Enrollment: 246 Coed
Affiliation or Control: Independent Non-Profit IRS Status: 501(c)3
Highest Offering: Master's
Program: Teacher Preparatory; Professional; Music Emphasis
Accreditation: NH, MUS

01	President	Dr. Charles T. MENGHINI
08	Head Librarian	Mr. Robert DELAND
05	Dean of Undergraduate Studies	Ms. Stacey L. DOLAN
58	Dean of Graduate Studies	Mr. Robert L. SINCLAIR
07	Director of Admissions & Retention	Ms. Amy L. LENTING
10	Chief Financial Officer	Ms. Michelle ANDERSON
37	Director of Financial Aid	Ms. Sirena COVINGTON
13	Director Information Technologies	Mr. Rick MALIK
04	President's Assistant	Ms. Cindy TOVAR
51	Director of Continuing Education	Mr. Patrick BENSON
09	Director of Institutional Reports	Mr. Gregor MEYER
25	Grants Administrator	Ms. Sue G'SELL
06	Registrar/EPO Director	Mrs. Carolyn BERGHOFF
30	Director of Philanthropy	Mr. Jeffrey SADOWSKI

Vatterott College-Fairview Heights (I)

110 Commerce Lane, Fairview Heights IL 62208
Telephone: (618) 489-2400 Identification: 770943
Accreditation: ACCSC

† Branch campus of Vatterott College-NorthPark, Berkeley, MO.

Vatterott College-Quincy (J)

3609 North Marx Drive, Quincy IL 62305
County: Adams FICE Identification: 020693
Unit ID: 148140
Telephone: (217) 224-0600 Carnegie Class: Assoc/PrivFP
FAX Number: (217) 223-6771 Calendar System: Other
URL: www.vatterott-college.edu
Established: 1995 Annual Undergrad Tuition & Fees: $12,027
Enrollment: 140 Coed
Affiliation or Control: Proprietary IRS Status: Proprietary
Highest Offering: Associate Degree
Program: Occupational; 2-Year Principally Bachelor's Creditable
Accreditation: ACCSC

01	CEO & President	Ms. Pam BELL
10	Chief Financial Officer	Mr. Dennis BEAVERS
05	Vice President Academic Affairs	Mr. Brandon SHEDRON
30	VP Regulatory Affs/Strategic Devel	Mr. Aaron LACEY
43	General Counsel/Chief Administrator	Mr. Scott CASANOVER
12	Campus Director	Mr. Tom LOCKETT

Waubonsee Community College (K)

Route 47 at Waubonsee Drive, Sugar Grove IL 60554-9799
County: Kane FICE Identification: 006931
Unit ID: 149727
Telephone: (630) 466-7900 Carnegie Class: Assoc/Pub-S-SC
FAX Number: (630) 466-7550 Calendar System: Semester
URL: www.waubonsee.edu
Established: 1966 Annual Undergrad Tuition & Fees (In-District): $2,688
Enrollment: 9,814 Coed
Affiliation or Control: Local IRS Status: 501(c)3
Highest Offering: Associate Degree
Program: Occupational; 2-Year Principally Bachelor's Creditable
Accreditation: NH, ADNUR, CAHIIM, EMT, MAC, SURGT

01	President	Dr. Christine J. SOBEK
05	Exec VP Educ Affs/Chief Lrng Ofcr	Dr. Deborah F. LOVINGOOD
10	Exec VP Finance & Operations	Mr. David QUILLEN
45	VP Strategic Development	Dr. Jamal SCOTT
32	Vice Pres of Student Development	Dr. Melinda L. JAMES
21	Asst Vice President of Finance	Ms. Darla S. CARDINE
106	Asst VP Onlne Lrng/Instruction Sup	Ms. Renee TONIONI
36	Asst VP Workforce Sol/Comm Learning	Mr. Gary KECSKÉS
75	Asst VP Career/Technical Education	Ms. Suzette MURRAY
88	Asst VP Transfer/Development Educ	Dr. William MARZANO
13	Chief Information Officer	Mr. Terence FELTON
35	Dean for Students	Dr. Scott PESKA

15 Exec Director Human Resources — Ms. Michele NEEDHAM
26 Exec Dir Marketing/Communications — Mr. James SIBLEY
76 Dean Health Professions/Public Svc — Dr. Jess TOUSSAINT
83 Dean Social Sciences/Edu/World Lang — Dr. Laura ORTIZ
79 Dean Communic/Humanities/Fine Arts — Ms. Cynthia SPARR
88 Dean Development Ed/Coll Read — Dr. Medea RAMBISH
81 Dean Mathematics/Sciences — Ms. Mary Edith BUTLER
38 Dean Counseling/Careers/Student Sup — Ms. Kelli SINCLAIR
56 Dean Adult Education — Ms. Jeri L. DIXON
30 Chief Advancement Officer — Vacant
50 Dean Business/Career Technologies — Mr. Michael CERMAK
103 Dean Workforce Development — Ms. Lesa NORRIS
84 Dean Enrollment Management — Ms. Faith LASHURE
31 Dean Community Education — Mr. Douglas L. GRIER
04 Dir Pres Communications/Operations — Ms. Kimberly CAPONI
37 Dir Student Financial Aid Services — Dr. Charles BOUDREAU
09 Dir Institutional Effectiveness — Dr. Stacey RANDALL
28 Dir Governmental/Multicultural Affa — Dr. Lourdes BLACKSMITH
19 Dir Emergency Management/Safety — Mr. John WU
88 Dir Accounting/Business Services — Mr. Bruce HARTMANN
18 Director Campus Operations — Mr. Daniel LARSEN
06 Dir Registration/Records/Registrar — Mr. Marc DALE
07 Admissions Manager — Ms. Joy SANDERS

Western Illinois University (A)

1 University Circle, Macomb IL 61455-1390
County: McDonough | FICE Identification: 001780 | Unit ID: 149772
Telephone: (309) 298-1414 | Carnegie Class: Master's L
FAX Number: (309) 298-2400 | Calendar System: Semester
URL: www.wiu.edu
Established: 1899 | Annual Undergrad Tuition & Fees (In-State): $11,509
Enrollment: 11,458 | Coed
Affiliation or Control: State | IRS Status: 501(c)3
Highest Offering: Doctorate
Program: Liberal Arts And General; Teacher Preparatory
Accreditation: NH, ART, BUS, BUSA, CAATE, CACREP, CEA, DIETD, ENG, MUS, NAIT, NRPA, NURSE, SP, SW, TED, THEA

01 President — Dr. Jack THOMAS
05 Interim Provost/Academic VP — Dr. Kathleen NEUMANN
20 Int Assoc Prov/Assoc VP Acad Affs — Dr. Russell MORGAN
20 Asst VP for Academic Affairs — Dr. Ronald WILLIAMS
20 Assoc Provost/Undergrad & Grad — Dr. Nancy P. PARSONS
10 VP Administrative Services — Ms. Julie DEWEES
32 Vice President Student Services — Dr. Gary M. BILLER
30 Vice Pres Advancement/Public Svcs — Mr. Bradley BAINTER
29 Director Alumni Programs — Ms. Amy SPELMAN
23 General Counsel Attorney — Ms. Rica CALHOUN
39 Assoc Vice Pres Student Services — Mr. John BIERNBAUM
45 VP for QC & Planning — Dr. Joseph RIVES
86 Asst to Pres Government Relations — Ms. Jeanette MALAFA
49 Dean College Arts/Sciences — Dr. Susan MARTINELLI-FERNANDEZ
50 Interim Dean College Business/Tech — Dr. Kathleen NEUMANN
53 Interim Dean Col Educ & Human Svcs — Dr. Erskine SMITH
57 Dean Fine Arts & Comm — Mr. William T. CLOW
08 Dean University Libraries — Dr. Michael LORENZEN
92 Dir Illinois Centennial Honors Col — Dr. Richard J. HARDY
64 Director School of Music — Dr. Bart SHANKLIN
06 Registrar — Dr. Angela LYNN
21 Interim Director Business Services — Mr. Matthew J. BIERMAN
13 Dir Admin Information Mgmt Systems — Ms. Brenda PARKS
90 Director of University Technology — Mr. Daniel A. ROMANO
27 Director University Relations — Ms. Darcie R. SHINBERGER
09 Director Inst Research & Planning — Ms. Angela BONIFAS
22 Director Equal Opportunity & Access — Ms. Andrea HENDERSON
37 Director Financial Aid — Mr. Robert ANDERSEN
36 Director Placement — Mr. Martin J. KRAL
15 Director Human Resources — Ms. Pamela L. BOWMAN
18 Director Physical Plant — Mr. Scott A. COKER
19 Director Public Safety — Mr. Scott HARRIS
23 Director Health Center — Ms. John W. SMITH
31 Dir Distance Learning and Outreach — Dr. Richard CARTER
40 Interim Dir University Bookstore — Ms. Ann COMERFORD
41 Interim Director Athletics — Mr. Matt TANNEY
102 Director WIU Foundation — Mr. Bradley BAINTER
07 Director Admissions — Dr. Andrew BORST
38 Director Student Counseling — Mr. James E. DITULIO
85 Dir Center International Studies — Dr. Richard CARTER
88 Director Budget — Mr. Matthew J. BIERMAN

Western Illinois University Quad Cities (B)

3300 River Drive, Moline IL 61265
Telephone: (309) 762-9481 | Identification: 770100
Accreditation: &NH

† Branch campus of Western Illinois University, Macomb, IL.

Westwood College-Chicago Loop (C)

1 North State Street, Suite 1000, Chicago IL 60602
Telephone: (312) 739-0890 | Identification: 666424
Accreditation: ACICS

† Branch campus of Westwood College-Los Angeles, Los Angeles, CA.

Westwood College-DuPage (D)

7155 Janes Avenue, Woodridge IL 60517-2321
County: DuPage | FICE Identification: 030792 | Unit ID: 406194
Telephone: (630) 434-7655 | Carnegie Class: Bac/Diverse
FAX Number: (630) 963-1425 | Calendar System: Other
URL: www.westwood.edu
Established: | Annual Undergrad Tuition & Fees: $26,448
Enrollment: 157 | Coed
Affiliation or Control: Proprietary | IRS Status: Proprietary
Highest Offering: Baccalaureate
Program: Occupational; 2-Year Principally Bachelor's Creditable; Liberal Arts And General
Accreditation: ACICS

01 Campus President — Jeff HILL
05 Campus Academic Dean — Jennifer SHARP
11 Director of Campus Operations — Diana GARCIA
07 Director of Admissions — Vacant
36 Assistant Director of Career Svcs — Marina TEDRIS
37 Director of Student Finance — Pertrina BRIGGS

Westwood College-O'Hare Airport (E)

8501 W Higgins Road, Suite 100, Chicago IL 60631-2814
County: Cook | FICE Identification: 023139 | Unit ID: 178226
Telephone: (773) 380-6800 | Carnegie Class: Bac/Diverse
FAX Number: (773) 380-6820 | Calendar System: Other
URL: www.westwood.edu
Established: 2000 | Annual Undergrad Tuition & Fees: $17,802
Enrollment: 304 | Coed
Affiliation or Control: Proprietary | IRS Status: Proprietary
Highest Offering: Baccalaureate
Program: Occupational; 2-Year Principally Bachelor's Creditable; Professional; Technical Emphasis
Accreditation: ACICS

01 President — Ms. Deann FITZGERALD
05 Academic Dean — Ms. Katherine GROTH
32 Director of Student Support — Ms. Tracy WALKER
07 Director of Admissions — Mr. James GALAS
36 Director of Career Services — Ms. Hope GREEN
37 Director of Student Finance — Ms. Tracy WALKER

Westwood College-River Oaks (F)

96 River Oaks Center Drive, Dept 45, Calumet City IL 60409-5555
Telephone: (708) 832-1988 | Identification: 666440
Accreditation: ACICS

† Branch campus of Westwood College-Los Angeles, Los Angeles, CA.

Wheaton College (G)

501 College Avenue, Wheaton IL 60187-5593
County: DuPage | FICE Identification: 001781 | Unit ID: 149781
Telephone: (630) 752-5000 | Carnegie Class: Bac/A&S
FAX Number: (630) 752-5555 | Calendar System: Semester
URL: www.wheaton.edu
Established: 1860 | Annual Undergrad Tuition & Fees: $32,950
Enrollment: 2,914 | Coed
Affiliation or Control: Independent Non-Profit | IRS Status: 501(c)3
Highest Offering: Doctorate
Program: Liberal Arts And General; Teacher Preparatory; Professional
Accreditation: NH, CLPSY, MUS, TED

01 President — Dr. Philip G. RYKEN
05 Provost — Dr. Stanton L. JONES
10 Vice President for Finance — Mr. Dale A. KEMP
32 Vice President Student Development — Mr. Paul O. CHELSEN
30 VP Advancement/Alumni Rels — Mr. Kirk FARNEY
13 Chief Information Officer — Ms. Wendy WOODWARD
29 Sr Dir Vocation & Alum Engagement — Ms. Cindra STACKHOUSE TAETZSCH
04 Exec Asst to the President — Miss Marilee A. MELVIN
58 Dean of the Graduate School — Dr. Nicholas PERRIN
79 Dean Humanities/Theol Studies — Dr. Jill P. BAUMGAERTNER
49 Dean Conservatory/Arts & Comm — Dr. Michael WILDER
83 Dean Natural & Social Sciences — Dr. Dorothy F. CHAPPELL
104 Dean Global & Exper Learning — Dr. Laura M. MONTGOMERY
35 Dean of Student Engagement — Dr. Steve IVESTER
08 College Librarian — Mrs. Lisa T. RICHMOND
21 Controller — Mr. Mark AHRENHOLZ
20 Interim Dir Billy Graham Center — Mr. Paul ERICKSEN
09 Dir Inst Research & Acad Support — Dr. Gary N. LARSON
06 Registrar — Mrs. Peggy KING
109 Auxilary Services Director — Mr. Tony DAWSON
24 Director Academic Media & Tech — Mr. J. R. SMITH
36 Interim Dir Ctr Vocation & Career — Ms. Dee PIERCE
15 Director of Human Resources — Mrs. Karen TUCKER
07 Director Undergraduate Admissions — Ms. Shawn B. LEFTWICH
07 Director Graduate Admissions — Mr. Dusty DI SANTO
37 Director of Student Financial Aid — Ms. Karen BELLING
41 Director of Athletics — Ms. Julie DAVIS
39 Associate Dean of Residence Life — Mr. Justin HETH
38 Director of Counseling — Dr. Toussaint WHETSTONE
42 Chaplain — Rev. Timothy BLACKMON
23 Director of Student Health Services — Ms. Britt BLACK
27 Director of Media Relations — Ms. LaTonya TAYLOR
40 Manager of Bookstore — Ms. Jennifer HAMPTON
18 Director of Facilities Management — Mr. James M. JOHNSON
19 Chief of Public Safety — Mr. Robert F. NORRIS
26 Director Marketing Communications — Ms. Kimberly MEDAGLIA
93 Director Multicultural Development — Mr. Rodney K. SISCO

96 Director of Purchasing — Mr. John CLASS
88 Director Risk Management — Mr. Daniel CLARK
105 Director Web Communications — Mrs. Rebecca LARSON
25 Academic Grants Officer — Mrs. Virginia SHAFFER

Worsham College of Mortuary Science (H)

495 Northgate Parkway, Wheeling IL 60090-2646
County: Cook | FICE Identification: 001783 | Unit ID: 369455
Telephone: (847) 808-8444 | Carnegie Class: Assoc/PrivFP
FAX Number: (847) 808-8493 | Calendar System: Quarter
URL: www.worshamcollege.com
Established: 1911 | Annual Undergrad Tuition & Fees: $20,700
Enrollment: 109 | Coed
Affiliation or Control: Proprietary | IRS Status: Proprietary
Highest Offering: Associate Degree
Program: Occupational
Accreditation: FUSER

01 Director — Ms. Stephanie J. KANN

INDIANA

American College of Education (I)

101 West Ohio Street, Suite 1200, Indianapolis IN 46204
County: Marion | Identification: 666242 | Unit ID: 449889
Telephone: (800) 280-0307 | Carnegie Class: Spec/Other
FAX Number: (317) 829-9401 | Calendar System: Semester
URL: www.ace.edu
Established: 2005 | Annual Undergrad Tuition & Fees: $7,955
Enrollment: 2,902 | Coed
Affiliation or Control: Proprietary | IRS Status: Proprietary
Highest Offering: Doctorate
Program: Teacher Preparatory
Accreditation: NH, TEAC

01 Interim President — Dr. Shawntel D. LANDRY
05 Provost — Dr. Shawntel D. LANDRY
43 Assoc Counsel & VP Reg Affairs — Ms. Amber YING
26 Sr VP Marketing and Enrollment — Mr. Dan HOLESTINE
84 VP Enrollment Operations — Ms. Monica CARSON
07 Director of Admissions — Ms. Courtney SHELTON
06 Registrar — Ms. Stephanie HINSHAW
09 Dir Inst Research/Effectiveness — Dr. Kathryn TALLEY
04 Administrative Asst to President — Ms. Jill ALGATE
08 Librarian — Dr. Sandra QUIATKOWSKI
10 Chief Financial Officer — Mr. Howard ROUSE
13 Chief Information Officer — Mr. Randy DAVIS
15 Manager Human Resources — Ms. KK BYLAND
53 Acad Dean & Dir Grad Programs — Dr. Lee TINCHER

American National University (J)

6131 N Clinton Street, Fort Wayne IN 46825
Telephone: (260) 483-1605 | Identification: 770696
Accreditation: ACICS, MAC

† Branch campus of American National University, Indianapolis, IN.

American National University (K)

6060 Castleway West Drive, Indianapolis IN 46250
County: Marion | FICE Identification: 010489
Telephone: (317) 578-7353 | Carnegie Class: Not Classified
FAX Number: (317) 578-7721 | Calendar System: Quarter
URL: www.an.edu
Established: 1886 | Annual Undergrad Tuition & Fees: N/A
Enrollment: N/A | Coed
Affiliation or Control: Proprietary | IRS Status: Proprietary
Highest Offering: Master's
Program: Occupational
Accreditation: ACICS, CAHIIM, MAC, SURGT

01 Campus Director — Mr. Jim ABRAHAM
04 Admin Asst to Campus Director — Ms. Paula PYNM

American National University (L)

1030 E Jefferson Boulevard, South Bend IN 46617
Telephone: (574) 307-7100 | Identification: 770695
Accreditation: ACICS, MAC

† Branch campus of American National University, Indianapolis, IN.

Anabaptist Mennonite Biblical Seminary (M)

3003 Benham Avenue, Elkhart IN 46517-1999
County: Elkhart | FICE Identification: 001823 | Unit ID: 151865
Telephone: (574) 295-3726 | Carnegie Class: Spec/Faith
FAX Number: (574) 295-0092 | Calendar System: 4/1/4
URL: www.ambs.edu
Established: 1946 | Annual Graduate Tuition & Fees: $14,190
Enrollment: 106 | Coed
Affiliation or Control: Mennonite Church | IRS Status: 501(c)3
Highest Offering: Master's; No Undergraduates

Program: Professional
Accreditation: NH, THEOL

01 President ..... Dr. Sara W. SHENK
05 Academic Dean ..... Dr. Rebecca SLOUGH
11 Administrative Vice President ..... Mr. Ron RINGENBERG
30 Director of Development ..... Ms. Missy K. SCHROCK
10 Chief Financial Officer ..... Mr. Jeff MILLER
06 Registrar ..... Mr. Scott JANZEN
08 Director of Library Services ..... Ms. Eileen SANER
84 Dir Enrollment Mgmt/Financial Aid ..... Mr. Daniel GRIMES
73 Director of Inst Mennonite Studies ..... Dr. Mary H. SCHERTZ

Ancilla College (A)

PO Box 1, Donaldson IN 46513-0001
County: Marshall FICE Identification: 001784
Unit ID: 150048
Telephone: (574) 936-8898 Carnegie Class: Assoc/PrivNFP
FAX Number: (574) 935-1773 Calendar System: Semester
URL: www.ancilla.edu
Established: 1937 Annual Undergrad Tuition & Fees: $14,100
Enrollment: 390 Coed
Affiliation or Control: Roman Catholic IRS Status: 501(c)3
Highest Offering: Associate Degree
Program: 2-Year Principally Bachelor's Creditable
Accreditation: NH

01 President ..... Dr. Ken ZIRKLE
04 Assistant to the President ..... Ms. Diana CALDWELL
05 VP of Academic Affairs ..... Dr. Joanna BLOUNT
10 VP of Finance & Admin ..... Mr. Mike BROWN
30 Vice President of Development ..... Mr. Todd ZELTWANGER
84 Vice President of Enrollment Mgmt ..... Mr. Eric WIGNALL
42 Vice President Mission Integration ..... Sr. Jolise MAY, PHJC
21 Director of Business Affairs ..... Mr. Raymond GIRRES
37 Director of Financial Aid ..... Mrs. Marcella HOPPLE
41 Athletic Director ..... Mr. Robert REESE
30 Assoc Dir Inst Advancement/Alumni ..... Mr. Thomas SIBAL
13 Director of Information Technology ..... Mr. John LINBACK
09 Dir Institutional Effectiveness ..... Mr. Brian WELCH
18 Chief Facilities/Physical Plant ..... Mr. Tom NOWAK
32 Director Student Development ..... Mr. Jim CAWTHON
06 Registrar ..... Ms. Tiffany FISHER
40 Bookstore Manager ..... Ms. Kim WEHR
08 Librarian ..... Ms. Cassaundra BASH
17 Director Nursing & Health Science ..... Ms. Ann FITZGERALD
26 Dir of Marketing & Social Media ..... Ms. Amanda PETRUCELLI

Anderson University (B)

1100 E Fifth Street, Anderson IN 46012-3495
County: Madison FICE Identification: 001785
Unit ID: 150066
Telephone: (765) 649-9071 Carnegie Class: Master's L
FAX Number: (765) 641-3851 Calendar System: Semester
URL: www.anderson.edu
Established: 1917 Annual Undergrad Tuition & Fees: $36,990
Enrollment: 2,399 Coed
Affiliation or Control: Church Of God IRS Status: 501(c)3
Highest Offering: Doctorate
Program: Liberal Arts And General; Teacher Preparatory; Professional
Accreditation: NH, ACBSP, CAATE, MUS, NURSE, SW, TED, THEOL

01 President ..... Mr. John S. PISTOLE
05 Provost ..... Dr. Marie S. MORRIS
10 Vice President Finance/Treasurer ..... Mrs. Dana S. STUART
30 Vice President for Advancement ..... Mr. Robert L. COFFMAN
32 VP Student Affairs ..... Dr. Brent A. BAKER
73 Dean School of Theology ..... Dr. James W. LEWIS
50 Dean Falls School of Business ..... Dr. Terry C. TRUITT
53 Dean School of Education ..... Dr. Janice L. FULKERSON
81 Dean School of Humanities ..... Dr. Joel D. SHROCK
64 Dean School Music/Theatre & Dance ..... Dr. Jeffrey E. WRIGHT
66 Dean Sch Nursing/Kines/Behav Sci ..... Dr. Karen S. WILLIAMS
54 School of Science & Engineering ..... Dr. Chad E. WALLACE
58 Ex Dir Graduate Admn/Adult Studies ..... Dr. Jeff M. BUCK
28 Dean Intercultural Engagement ..... Dr. Aleza D. BEVERLY
42 Campus Pastor ..... Rev. J. Todd FAULKNER
33 Dean of Students ..... Dr. Christopher L. CONFER
06 University Registrar ..... Mr. Arthur J. LEAK
26 Exec Director for Advancement ..... Vacant
08 Director of Libraries ..... Dr. Janet L. BREWER
07 Director of Admissions ..... Dr. Joe M. DAVIS
21 Assistant Treasurer/Controller ..... Mrs. Vanessa J. TIJERINA
36 Director of Career Development ..... Mrs. Laurie L. JUDGE
13 Director of Info Technology Svcs ..... Mr. Michael A. TUCKER
37 Student Financial Services ..... Mr. Kenneth F. NIEMAN
27 Dir Univ Communications/Cmty Rels ..... Mr. Chris J. WILLIAMS
18 Exec Dir Facilities & Property Mgmt ..... Mr. Joseph M. ROYER
15 Director of Human Resources ..... Mrs. Denise A T. KRIEBEL
19 Director Police & Security Services ..... Mr. Rick A. GARRETT
40 Bookstore Manager ..... Mr. Dustin L. MARTIN
41 Athletic Director ..... Ms. Marcie J. TAYLOR
38 Director Counseling Services ..... Ms. Christal R. HELVERING
29 Director of Alumni Relations ..... Mr. Colin W. SHORT
109 Manager Business & Auxiliary Svcs ..... Mrs. Suahil HOUSHOLDER
04 Administrative Asst to President ..... Mrs. Ronda S. REEMER
104 Director Study Abroad ..... Mr. Willi E. KANT
105 Director Web Services ..... Mrs. Stefanie K. LEITER
108 Director Institutional Assessment ..... Dr. Jaye L. ROGERS
39 Director Student Housing ..... Ms. Tamara SHELTON

The Art Institute of Indianapolis (C)

3500 Depauw Boulevard Suite 1010,
Indianapolis IN 46268
Telephone: (317) 613-4800 Identification: 666247
Accreditation: ACICS

† Branch campus of The Art Institute of Phoenix, AZ.

Ball State University (D)

2000 W. University Avenue, Muncie IN 47306-1099
County: Delaware FICE Identification: 001786
Unit ID: 150136
Telephone: (765) 289-1241 Carnegie Class: RU/H
FAX Number: (765) 285-1461 Calendar System: Semester
URL: www.bsu.edu
Established: 1918 Annual Undergrad Tuition & Fees (In-State): $9,498
Enrollment: 20,655 Coed
Affiliation or Control: State IRS Status: 501(c)3
Highest Offering: Doctorate
Program: Occupational; Liberal Arts And General; Teacher Preparatory; Professional
Accreditation: NH, AAFCS, ART, #AUD, BUS, BUSA, CAATE, CACREP, CEA, CIDA, CONST, COPSY, CORE, DANCE, DIETD, DIETI, IPSY, JOUR, LSAR, MUS, NURSE, PLNG, RAD, SCPSY, SP, SW, TED, THEA

01 President ..... Dr. Paul W. FERGUSON
05 Provost/Vice Pres Academic Affs ..... Dr. Terry KING
84 VP Marketing/Comm/Enroll Mgmt ..... Vacant
10 VP Business Affairs & Treasurer ..... Mr. Bernard M. HANNON
30 Vice Pres University Advancement ..... Mr. Hudson AKIN
13 VP for Information Technology ..... Mr. Philip C. REPP
32 VP Student Affairs/Dean of Students ..... Dr. Kay BALES
41 Dir Intercollegiate Athletics ..... Mr. Mark SANDY
43 VP & General Counsel ..... Ms. Sali K. FALLING
109 Assoc VP Business/Auxiliary Svcs ..... Ms. Leisa JULIAN
86 Assoc VP Governmental Relations ..... Ms. Julie HALBIG
21 Assoc VP Finance/Asst Treasurer ..... Vacant
85 Exec Director International Pgms ..... Mr. Imara V. DAWSON
20 Assoc Provost/Dean Univ College ..... Dr. Marilyn M. BUCK
18 Assoc VP Facilities Planning/Mgmt ..... Mr. Kevin S. KENYON
07 Director Admissions & Orientation . Mr. Christopher T. MUNCHEL
35 Assoc VP Student Affs/Dir Housing ..... Dr. Alan L. HARGRAVE
29 Assoc VP of Alumni Programs ..... Ms. Julie STROH
26 Assoc VP Marketing & Communications ..... Vacant
38 Director Counseling/Health Services ..... Dr. June P. PAYNE
14 Asst VP IT for Strategic/Fiscal Mgt ..... Mr. Donald KING, JR.
88 Dir Unified Techonology Support ..... Mr. Dan LUTZ
36 Director Career Center ..... Mr. Jim MCATEE
37 Director Scholarships/Financial Aid ..... Dr. John MCPHERSON
06 Reg/Dir Registration/Acad Pgms ..... Mrs. Nancy L. CRONK
09 Int Dir Inst Effectiveness ..... Mrs. Andrea INGLE
30 Exec Director Univ Development ..... Vacant
96 Director of Purchasing Services ..... Mr. Roger HASSENZAHL
24 Director of Teleplex ..... Vacant
88 Asst to VP/Coord Title IX ..... Mrs. Katie SLABAUGH
25 Director Contracts & Grants ..... Ms. Kathy A. LUCAS
19 Director Public Safety ..... Mr. James DUCKHAM
15 Director of Human Resources Svcs ..... Ms. Judith A. BURKE
28 Asst Provost Diversity ..... Dr. Charlene ALEXANDER
08 Dean University Libraries ..... Vacant
57 Dean College of Fine Arts ..... Dr. Robert A. KVAM
50 Dean Miller College of Business ..... Dr. Rajib N. SANYAL
48 Dean College Architecture/
Planning ..... Dr. Guillermo P. VASQUEZ DE VELASCO
53 Dean of Teachers College ..... Dr. John E. JACOBSON
58 Asc Provost/Research/Dean Grad Sch ..... Dr. Robert J. MORRIS
49 Dean Col of Science/Humanities ..... Dr. Michael A. MAGGIOTTO
60 Dean Col of Comm/Info/Media ..... Mr. Roger LAVERY
72 Dean Col Applied Science/Technology ..... Dr. Mitchell H. WHALEY
92 Dean of Honors College ..... Dr. James S. RUEBEL
103 Assoc VP Econ Dev/Community Engage . Dr. John A. FALLON, III
88 Assoc Provost Learning Initiatives ..... Dr. Jennifer BOTT

Bethany Theological Seminary (E)

615 National Road W, Richmond IN 47374-4019
County: Wayne FICE Identification: 001637
Unit ID: 143233
Telephone: (800) 287-8822 Carnegie Class: Spec/Faith
FAX Number: (765) 983-1840 Calendar System: Semester
URL: www.bethanyseminary.edu
Established: 1905 Annual Graduate Tuition & Fees: $12,690
Enrollment: 65 Coed
Affiliation or Control: Church Of The Brethren IRS Status: 501(c)3
Highest Offering: Master's; No Undergraduates
Program: Professional
Accreditation: NH, THEOL

01 President ..... RevDr. Jeffrey W. CARTER
05 Academic Dean ..... Dr. Steven J. SCHWEITZER
10 Exec Dir of Student/Business Svcs ..... Ms. Brenda J. REISH
30 Exec Dir Institutional Advancement ..... Mr. Mark A. LANCASTER
20 Director of Academic Services ..... Ms. April VANLONDEN
26 Director of Communications ..... Ms. Jennifer L. WILLIAMS
32 Director of Student Development ..... Ms. Amy S. GALL RITCHIE
12 Exec Director Brethren Academy ..... Ms. Julie M. HOSTETTER
88 Director Inst Ministry with Youth ..... Mr. Russell HAITCH
07 Interim Director of
Admissions ..... Mr. Jim GROSSNICKLE-BATTERTON
88 Dir Peace/Cross Cultural Studies ..... Mr. Scott HOLLAND
88 Director of the MA Program ..... Vacant
88 Dir of Educational Technology ..... Mr. Dan POOLE

Bethel College (F)

1001 Bethel Circle, Mishawaka IN 46545-5509
County: Saint Joseph FICE Identification: 001787
Unit ID: 150145
Telephone: (574) 807-7000 Carnegie Class: Bac/Diverse
FAX Number: (574) 807-7957 Calendar System: Semester
URL: www.bethelcollege.edu
Established: 1947 Annual Undergrad Tuition & Fees: $26,590
Enrollment: 1,792 Coed
Affiliation or Control: Missionary Church IRS Status: 501(c)3
Highest Offering: Master's
Program: 2-Year Principally Bachelor's Creditable; Liberal Arts And General; Religious Emphasis
Accreditation: NH, ADNUR, IACBE, MUS, NUR, TED

01 President ..... Dr. Gregg A. CHENOWETH
05 VP for Academic Services ..... Dr. Barbara K. BELLEFEUILLLE
30 VP for Institutional Advancement ..... Mr. Richard A. MUNROE
10 Interim VP for Business Affairs ..... Dr. Raymond E. WHITEMAN
32 VP for Student Development ..... Dr. Shawn M. HOLTGREN
36 Director of Student Success ..... Dr. Joel D. BOEHNER
84 Asst VP for Enrollment/Marketng ..... Vacant
13 Senior Director of IT ..... Ms. Patti J. FISHER
66 Dean of Nursing ..... Dr. Deborah GILLUM
49 Dean of Arts & Sciences ..... Dr. Janna MCLEAN
53 Dean of Education ..... Vacant
83 Dean of Humanities/Social Sciences ..... Dr. Bradley D. SMITH
35 Director of Student Life ..... Mrs. Julie BEAM
06 Registrar ..... Mrs. Jeanne E. FOX
36 Director Student Enrichment ..... Vacant
37 Director Financial Aid ..... Mrs. Jody P. WALKER
26 Director Public Relations ..... Mrs. Erin C. KINZEL
41 Director Athletics ..... Dr. Thomas VISKER
08 Director Library Services ..... Mr. Mark J. ROOT
88 Director Teacher Certification ..... Mrs. Kimberly J. MEYER
109 Senior Dir Auxil Svcs/Phys Plant ..... Mr. Edward E. BERNHARD
09 Director Institutional Research ..... Dr. Raymond E. WHITEMAN
19 Director Campus Safety ..... Mr. Paul E. NEEL
85 Director International Students ..... Mrs. Emily S. SHERWOOD
91 Director Administrative Computing ..... Mr. Harold E. RODGERS
23 Director Wellness Center ..... Vacant
29 Director Alumni Services ..... Mrs. Emily S. SHERWOOD
28 Director Intercultural Development ..... Vacant
84 AVP of Traditional Enroll/Fin Aid ..... Ms. Andrea M. HELMUTH
15 Director Human Resources ..... Mr. Mike L. NICHOLAS
04 Administrative Asst to President ..... Mrs. Barbara J. RODGERS
104 Director Study Abroad ..... Ms. Laura A. WINNINGHAM

Brown Mackie College-Fort Wayne (G)

3000 E Coliseum Boulevard, Ste 100,
Fort Wayne IN 46805-1565
Telephone: (260) 484-4400 Identification: 666435
Accreditation: ACICS, OTA, #PTAA, SURGT, SURTEC

† Branch campus of Brown Mackie-South Bend, South Bend, IN.

Brown Mackie College-Indianapolis (H)

1200 N. Meridian Street, Suite 100, Indianapolis IN 46204
Telephone: (317) 554-8300 Identification: 666394
Accreditation: ACICS, OTA

† Branch campus of Brown Mackie College-Findlay, Findlay, OH.

Brown Mackie College-Merrillville (I)

1000 E 80th Place, Suite 205M, Merrillville IN 46410-5602
Telephone: (219) 769-3321 FICE Identification: 021032
Accreditation: ACICS, OTA, SURGT

† Branch campus of Brown Mackie College-Cincinnati, Cincinnati, OH.

Brown Mackie College-Michigan City (J)

1001 E. US Highway 20, Michigan City IN 46360-7362
Telephone: (219) 877-3100 Identification: 666426
Accreditation: ACICS

† School is in teach-out plan. Branch campus of Brown Mackie College-Cincinnati, Cincinnati, OH.

Brown Mackie College-South Bend (K)

3454 Douglas Road, South Bend IN 46635
Telephone: (574) 237-0774 FICE Identification: 004583
Accreditation: ACICS, OTA, PTAA

† Branch campus of The Art Institute of Phoenix, Phoenix, AZ.

Butler University (L)

4600 Sunset Avenue, Indianapolis IN 46208-3443
County: Marion FICE Identification: 001788
Unit ID: 150163
Telephone: (317) 940-8000 Carnegie Class: Master's M
FAX Number: (317) 940-9930 Calendar System: Semester
URL: www.butler.edu
Established: 1855 Annual Undergrad Tuition & Fees: $37,010
Enrollment: 4,848 Coed

Affiliation or Control: Independent Non-Profit IRS Status: 501(c)3
Highest Offering: Doctorate
Program: Liberal Arts And General; Teacher Preparatory; Professional
Accreditation: NH, ARCPA, BUS, CACREP, DANCE, IPSY, MUS, PHAR, TED, THEA

01 President ... Mr. James M. DANKO
05 Provost/VP Academic Affairs ... Dr. Kathryn MORRIS
10 Vice President for Finance ... Mr. Bruce E. ARICK
30 VP University Advancement ... Ms. Shari ALEXANDER RICHEY
26 VP Marketing & Communication ... Mr. Matthew S. MINDRUM
32 Vice President of Student Affairs ... Dr. Levester JOHNSON
41 VP & Director of Athletics ... Mr. Barry S. COLLIER
84 VP of Enrollment Management ... Ms. Lori GREENE
100 Chief of Staff/Exec Dir Pub Safety ... Mr. Ben D. HUNTER
43 General Counsel ... Ms. Claire KONOPA AIGOTTI
20 Assoc Provost Student Acad Affs ... Dr. Mary M. RAMSBOTTOM
57 Dean Jordan College Fine Arts ... Dr. Ronald CALTABIANO
50 Dean College of Business ... Dr. Stephen STANDIFIRD
49 Dean Liberal Arts & Science ... Dr. Jay R. HOWARD
53 Dean Education ... Dr. Ena M. SHELLEY
67 Dean Pharmacy & Health Sciences ... Dr. Mary H. GRAHAM
60 Dean College of Communication ... Dr. Gary EDGERTON
08 Dean of Libraries ... Dr. Julie L. MILLER
35 Dean Student Services ... Dr. Sally E. CLICK
35 Dean Student Life ... Dr. Anne G. FLAHERTY
38 Asst Dean & Director Counseling Ctr ... Dr. Keith B. MAGNUS
44 Assoc VP Advancement Administration ... Ms. Rachael STEPHENS BURT
18 Executive Director of Facilities ... Mr. Richard MICHAL
29 Exec Dir Alumni/Development Pgms ... Ms. Nikki MAZELIN
15 Exec Dir HR/Chief Diversity Officer ... Ms. La Veda D. HOWELL
88 Exec Director Clowes Memorial Hall ... Ms. Elise J. KUSHIGIAN
21 Executive Budget Director ... Mr. Robert J. MARCUS
37 Director Financial Aid ... Ms. Melissa J. SMURDON
101 Dir Confs & Events/Board Liason ... Ms. Beth A. ALEXANDER
39 Director Residence Life ... Ms. Karla K. CUNNINGHAM
09 Director Institutional Research ... Dr. Nandini RAMASWAMY
85 Director Global Education ... Ms. Jill MCKINNEY
36 Director Career Services ... Mr. Gary R. BEAULIEU
27 Director of Creative Services ... Ms. Nancy LYZUN
28 Director of Diversity Programs ... Ms. Valerie J. DAVIDSON
31 Director of External Relations ... Mr. Michael KALTENMARK
07 Director of Admission ... Ms. Aimee SCHEUERMANN
06 Registrar ... Ms. Michele NEARY
13 Chief Information Officer ... Mr. Peter WILLIAMS
21 Controller ... Ms. Susan M. WESTERMEYER
40 Manager Bookstore ... Ms. Janine L. FRAINIER
96 Manager of Purchasing ... Ms. Shelly S. RABIDEAU
04 Exec Assistant to the President ... Ms. Emily KENNEY

Calumet College of Saint Joseph (A)

2400 New York Avenue, Whiting IN 46394-2195
County: Lake FICE Identification: 001834
Unit ID: 150172
Telephone: (219) 473-7770 Carnegie Class: Master's S
FAX Number: (219) 473-4259 Calendar System: Semester
URL: www.ccsj.edu
Established: 1951 Annual Undergrad Tuition & Fees: $17,000
Enrollment: 1,072 Coed
Affiliation or Control: Roman Catholic IRS Status: 501(c)3
Highest Offering: Master's
Program: Liberal Arts And General; Teacher Preparatory; Professional; Business Emphasis
Accreditation: NH, TED

01 President ... Dr. Daniel LOWERY
05 Vice President Academic Affairs ... Dr. Ginger RODRIGUEZ
30 Dir of Institutional Advancement ... Ms. Ester DIAZ
10 VP Business & Finance ... Ms. Lynn MISKUS
32 VP of Student Affairs & Retention .. Ms. Dionne JONES-MALONE
06 Registrar ... Ms. Diana FRANCIS
08 Librarian ... Ms. Qi CHIN
09 Institutional Researcher ... Mr. Darren HENDERSON
26 Dir of Marketing & Public Relations ... Ms. Linda GAJEWSKI
41 Athletic Director ... Mr. Peter HARING
42 Director of Campus Ministry ... Br. Jerry SCHWIETERMAN
18 VP of Facilities & Technology ... Mr. Gene KESSLER
84 Director of Enrollment Management ... Mr. Carl CUTTONE
37 Dir of Business Office & Fin Aid Op ... Ms. Gina PIRTLE
13 Director of Computer Services ... Mr. Kevin KRIEPS
29 Alumni Relations ... Ms. Angela HUGHES
38 Dir of Academic Advising ... Ms. Sally LOBO-TORRES
105 Director Web Services ... Mr. Jesus AVALOS

Chamberlain College of Nursing-Indianapolis Campus (B)

9100 Keystone Crossing, Suite 600, Indianapolis IN 46240
Telephone: (317) 816-7335 Identification: 770503
Accreditation: &NH, NURSE

† Branch campus of Chamberlain College of Nursing-Addison, Addison, IL.

Christian Theological Seminary (C)

1000 W. 42nd Street, Indianapolis IN 46208-3301
County: Marion FICE Identification: 001789
Unit ID: 150215
Telephone: (317) 924-1331 Carnegie Class: Spec/Faith
FAX Number: (317) 923-1961 Calendar System: Semester
URL: www.cts.edu
Established: 1925 Annual Graduate Tuition & Fees: $15,306
Enrollment: 173 Coed
Affiliation or Control: Christian Church (Disciples Of Christ) IRS Status: 501(c)3
Highest Offering: Doctorate; No Undergraduates
Program: Professional; Religious Emphasis
Accreditation: NH, MFCD, THEOL

01 President ... Dr. Matthew M. BOULTON
03 Executive Vice President ... Rev. Verity JONES
05 Int Vice Pres of Academics ... Dr. Bill KINCAID
30 Vice President Development ... Rev. Sarah LUND
32 Dean of Students ... Rev. Mary HARRIS
10 Vice President Finance and Business ... Mr. Curtis SHORT
11 Director Finance & Administration ... Mr. Patrick ZULKOWSKI
04 Executive Administrator ... Ms. Sarah EVANS
07 Director of Admissions ... Rev. Brenda FREIJE
44 Director Annual Fund ... Ms. Aimee LARAMORE
21 Director of Business Affairs ... Mr. Chuck CORBIN
08 Director of Library ... Mr. Anthony ELIA
06 Registrar ... Mr. Matt SCHLIMGEN
75 Director of Field Education ... Dr. William KINCAID
18 Director of Facilities ... Mr. Richard DAVIS
37 Int Dir of Student Financial Aid ... Mr. Rodney DUNN
26 Director of Communications ... Ms. Liz JOSS
40 Bookstore Manager ... Mr. Nick BUCK

College of Court Reporting, Inc. (D)

111 W 10th, Suite 111, Hobart IN 46342-5969
County: Lake FICE Identification: 026158
Unit ID: 150251
Telephone: (866) 294-3974 Carnegie Class: Assoc/PrivFP
FAX Number: (219) 942-1631 Calendar System: Semester
URL: www.ccr.edu
Established: 1984 Annual Undergrad Tuition & Fees: $13,550
Enrollment: 229 Coed
Affiliation or Control: Proprietary IRS Status: Proprietary
Highest Offering: Associate Degree
Program: Occupational
Accreditation: ACICS

01 President ... Mr. Jeff T. MOODY
03 Executive Director ... Mr. Jay VETTICKAL
05 Director of Education ... Ms. Kay MOODY
07 Director of Admissions ... Ms. Nicky M. RODRIQUEZ
37 Director of Financial Aid ... Ms. Lisa MORTON
32 Director of Student Services ... Ms. Kathleen LAZART

Concordia Theological Seminary (E)

6600 N Clinton Street, Fort Wayne IN 46825-4996
County: Allen FICE Identification: 020876
Unit ID: 150288
Telephone: (260) 452-2100 Carnegie Class: Spec/Faith
FAX Number: (260) 452-2121 Calendar System: Quarter
URL: www.ctsfw.edu
Established: 1846 Annual Graduate Tuition & Fees: $27,201
Enrollment: 322 Male
Affiliation or Control: Lutheran Church - Missouri Synod IRS Status: 501(c)3
Highest Offering: Doctorate; No Undergraduates
Program: Professional
Accreditation: NH, THEOL

01 President ... Dr. Lawrence R. RAST
05 Academic Dean ... Dr. Charles A. GIESCHEN
36 Dean Pastoral Education/ Placement ... Dr. Carl C. FICKENSCHER, II
32 Dean of Students ... Rev. Thomas P. ZIMMERMAN
10 Vice President Business Affairs ... Rev. Albert B. WINGFIELD
06 Registrar ... Mrs. Barbara A. WEGMAN
07 Director of Admissions ... Rev. John M. DREYER
08 Head Librarian ... Prof. Robert V. ROETHEMEYER

Crossroads Bible College (F)

601 N Shortridge Road, Indianapolis IN 46219-4912
County: Marion FICE Identification: 034567
Unit ID: 439613
Telephone: (317) 789-8255 Carnegie Class: Spec/Faith
FAX Number: (317) 789-8253 Calendar System: Semester
URL: www.crossroads.edu
Established: 1980 Annual Undergrad Tuition & Fees: $12,400
Enrollment: 241 Coed
Affiliation or Control: Independent Non-Profit IRS Status: 501(c)3
Highest Offering: Baccalaureate
Program: Religious Emphasis
Accreditation: BI

01 President ... Dr. A. Charles WARE
03 Executive Vice President ... Dr. John A. CRABTREE, JR.
05 Dean of Educational Svcs ... Dr. Joel BADAL
11 Dean of Administration ... Mr. Marcus SCHRADER
84 Dean of Enrollment Management ... Mr. John CROWDER
06 Registrar ... Ms. Cheryl PIOTROWSKI
18 Facilities Director ... Mr. Nelson POYNTER

DePauw University (G)

313 S Locust Street, Greencastle IN 46135-1772
County: Putnam FICE Identification: 001792
Unit ID: 150400
Telephone: (765) 658-4800 Carnegie Class: Bac/A&S
FAX Number: (765) 658-4177 Calendar System: 4/1/4
URL: www.depauw.edu
Established: 1837 Annual Undergrad Tuition & Fees: $44,678
Enrollment: 2,215 Coed
Affiliation or Control: United Methodist IRS Status: 501(c)3
Highest Offering: Baccalaureate
Program: Liberal Arts And General
Accreditation: NH, MUS

01 President ... Dr. Brian W. CASEY
04 Executive Assistant to President ... Ms. Elizabeth DEMMINGS
100 Chief of Staff/Assoc VP for Comm ... Mr. Jonathan COFFIN
05 VP for Academic Affairs ... Dr. Larry STIMPERT
32 VP Student Life ... Dr. Christopher J. WELLS
10 VP for Finance/Administration ... Mr. Bradley A. KELSHEIMER
84 VP for Admissions/Financial Aid ... Dr. Cindy BABINGTON
30 VP for Development ... Ms. Melanie NORTON
20 Dean of the Faculty ... Dr. Carrie F. KLAUS
88 Dean of Experiential Learning ... Dr. Raj BELLANI
64 Dean of the School of Music ... Dr. Mark MCCOY
13 Chief Information Officer ... Ms. Carol L. SMITH
35 Dean of Campus Life ... Mr. Dorian SHAGER
06 Registrar ... Dr. Kenneth J. KIRKPATRICK
89 Director of First Year Programs ... Ms. Cara SETCHELL
20 Dean of Academic Life ... Dr. David A. BERQUE
15 Director of Human Resources ... Ms. Amy HAUG
37 Director of Financial Aid ... Mr. Craig A. SLAUGHTER
41 Director of Athletics ... Ms. Stevie BAKER-WATSON
29 Associate VP for Alumni Engagement ... Mr. Steven J. SETCHELL
21 Assoc VP for Finance ... Mr. Kevin S. KESSINGER
08 Director of Libraries ... Mr. Rick E. PROVINE
44 Director of Annual Giving ... Ms. Kristin CHAMPA
19 Director of Public Safety ... Ms. Angela D. NALLY
07 Director of Admission ... Ms. Dani WEATHERFORD
96 Director of Purchasing ... Mr. Richard SHUCK
18 Assoc VP for Facilities ... Mr. Richard N. VANCE
21 Exec Director of Finance/Controller ... Mr. Keith ARCHER
35 Assoc Dean of Students ... Vacant
26 Exec Director of Media Relations ... Mr. Ken OWEN
09 Director of Institutional Research ... Dr. William M. TOBIN
23 Director of Health Services ... Vacant
38 Director of Student Counseling ... Dr. Julie D'ARGENT
39 Director of Housing ... Mr. Greg DILLON
28 Director of Diversity ... Ms. Renee MADISON

Earlham College and Earlham School of Religion (H)

801 National Road W, Richmond IN 47374-4095
County: Wayne FICE Identification: 001793
Unit ID: 150455
Telephone: (765) 983-1200 Carnegie Class: Bac/A&S
FAX Number: (765) 983-1304 Calendar System: Semester
URL: www.earlham.edu
Established: 1847 Annual Undergrad Tuition & Fees: $53,510
Enrollment: 984 Coed
Affiliation or Control: Friends IRS Status: 501(c)3
Highest Offering: Master's
Program: Liberal Arts And General; Teacher Preparatory; Professional; Religious Emphasis
Accreditation: NH, THEOL

01 President ... John David DAWSON
05 Vice President Academic Affairs ... Greg MAHLER
10 Vice President Business Affairs ... Sena LANDEY
30 Vice President Advancement ... Avis STEWART
88 Vice President School of Religion ... Jay MARSHALL
07 VP of Enrollment & Communications ... Jonathan STROUD
32 VP/Dean of Student Life ... Laura HUTCHINSON
20 Associate Academic Dean ... Andrew MOORE
44 Assoc VP for Institutional Advance ... Kim TANNER
29 Director of Alumni Relations ... Gail CLARK
21 Controller ... Cathy HABSCHMIDT
06 Registrar ... Bonita WASHINGTON-LACEY
88 Director Academic Support Services ... Donna KEESLING
84 Director of Admissions ... Shenita PIPER
73 Admissions School of Religion ... Matt HISRICH
41 Athletic Director ... Mike BERGUM
42 Director of Religious Life ... Kelly BURK
13 Director of Computing Services ... Thomas STEFFES
37 Director of Financial Aid ... Katherine GOTTSCHALK
23 Director of Health Services ... Mary Ann STIENBARGER
15 Director of Human Resources/Ops ... Dana NORTH
85 Director of International Programs ... Patty O'MALEY-LAMSON
18 Director of Physical Plant ... Ian SMITH
26 AVP for Marketing & Communications ... Vacant
27 Director of Media Relations ... Brian ZIMMERMAN
19 Director of Public Safety ... Tom KEARNS
08 Director of Library ... Neal BAKER
35 Director Student Leadership ... Tracy DUBS
28 Director of Diversity & Inclusion ... Susan LEE
36 Director Center Integrated Learning ... Jay ROBERTS
04 Administrative Asst to President ... Lyn THOMAS
25 Chief Contracts/Grants Admin ... Sally SOUTHWICK
39 Director Residence Life ... Shane PETERS

Faith Bible Seminary (I)

5526 State Road 26 East, Lafayette IN 47905
County: Tippecanoe Identification: 667250
Telephone: (765) 448-1986 Carnegie Class: Not Classified
FAX Number: N/A Calendar System: Other
URL: www.faithlafayette.org/seminary

Established: 2005 Annual Graduate Tuition & Fees: $3,000
Enrollment: 97 Coed
Affiliation or Control: Independent Non-Profit IRS Status: 501(c)3
Highest Offering: Master's; No Undergraduates
Program: Religious Emphasis
Accreditation: @BI

01 President .... Dr. Brent AUCOIN

Fortis College (A)

9001 N Wesleyan Road, Indianapolis IN 46268
Telephone: (317) 808-4800 Identification: 770574
Accreditation: ACCSC, ADNUR, MAAB

† Branch campus of Fortis Colleg, Winter Park, FL.

Franklin College of Indiana (B)

101 Branigin Boulevard, Franklin IN 46131-2623
County: Johnson FICE Identification: 001798
Unit ID: 150604
Telephone: (317) 738-8000 Carnegie Class: Bac/Diverse
FAX Number: (317) 736-6030 Calendar System: 4/1/4
URL: www.franklincollege.edu
Established: 1834 Annual Undergrad Tuition & Fees: $28,840
Enrollment: 1,075 Coed
Affiliation or Control: American Baptist IRS Status: 501(c)3
Highest Offering: Master's
Program: Liberal Arts And General; Teacher Preparatory; Fine Arts Emphasis
Accreditation: NH, CAATE, TED

01 President .... Dr. Thomas J. MINAR
04 Assistant to the President .... Ms. Janet D. SCHANTZ
10 Vice President Business/Finance .... Mr. Daniel SCHLUGE
05 Vice Pres Academic Affs/Dean of Col .... Dr. David G. BRAILOW
84 Interim VP Enrollment & Marketing .... Dr. Timothy L. GARNER
30 VP of Development/Alumni Engagement .... Mrs. Gail LOWRY
20 Int Assoc VP Acad Affs/Inst Effect .... Dr. Denise BAIRD
32 VP Stdnt Affs/Dean of Students .... Mr. Ellis F. HALL
29 Dean Alumni/Student Engagement .... Mrs. Brooke A. WORLAND
06 Registrar .... Ms. Lisa MAHAN
18 Dir Facilities/Energy Management .... Mr. Thomas PATZ
39 Director of Residence Life .... Mr. Jacob E. KNIGHT
38 Director of Counseling Center .... Dr. John R. SHAFER
35 Asst Dean Student Involvement .... Ms. Keri ELLINGTON
46 Dir of Development Research .... Ms. Betsy SCHMIDT
44 Sr Dir Development/Planned Giving .... Mr. Thomas W. ARMOR
37 Director of Financial Aid .... Mrs. Elizabeth SAPPENFIELD
42 Campus Minister .... Rev. Leah PARSELL RUMSEY
41 Athletic Director .... Mr. Kerry N. PRATHER
13 Dir of Information Tech Services .... Mr. Larry J. STOFFEL
36 Dir Career Svcs/Asst Dean Students .... Mr. Kirk J. BIXLER
88 Director of Leadership Development .... Mr. Dale REBHORN
104 Dir Intercultural/Off-Campus Stds .... Ms. Jennifer CATALDI
88 Director of Dining Services-Sodexo .... Mr. Les PETROFF
44 Annual Fund Director .... Mrs. Jane HOWARD
07 Director of Admissions .... Ms. Jennifer BOSTROM
27 Director of Communications .... Ms. Deidra BAUMGARDNER
26 Director of Marketing .... Ms. Theresa LEHMAN
08 Director of the Library .... Mr. Ronald L. SCHUETZ
19 Director of Campus Security .... Mr. Steve LEONARD
105 Website Administrator .... Ms. Ann KISH
15 Manager of Employee Resources .... Mrs. Maureen PINNICK
22 Director Physical Facilities .... Mr. Thomas PATZ
40 Bookstore Manager (Follett) .... Ms. Rebecca RAUSCH
21 Business Office Manager .... Mr. Bradley JONES
23 Coordinator Student Health Center .... Ms. Catherine DECLEENE
28 Coord Multicultural/Diversity Svcs .... Ms. Terri L. ROBERTS-LEONARD
50 Head Business/Computing/Math Div .... Mr. James C. WILLIAMS
53 Head Education Division .... Dr. Linda AIREY
79 Head Humanities Division .... Dr. Susan CRISAFULLI
60 Head Journalism Division .... Mr. Joel CRAMER
65 Head Natural Sciences Division .... Dr. Steven K. BROWDER
83 Head Social Sciences Division .... Dr. Denise M. BAIRD
57 Head Fine Arts Division .... Mr. Robin ROBERTS

Goshen College (C)

1700 S Main Street, Goshen IN 46526-4794
County: Elkhart FICE Identification: 001799
Unit ID: 150668
Telephone: (574) 535-7000 Carnegie Class: Bac/A&S
FAX Number: (574) 535-7060 Calendar System: Semester
URL: www.goshen.edu
Established: 1894 Annual Undergrad Tuition & Fees: $30,900
Enrollment: 843 Coed
Affiliation or Control: Mennonite Church IRS Status: 501(c)3
Highest Offering: Master's
Program: Liberal Arts And General; Teacher Preparatory; Professional
Accreditation: NH, NURSE, SW, TED

01 President .... Dr. James E. BRENNEMAN
03 Executive Vice President .... Dr. Ken F. NEWBOLD
05 VP Academic Affairs/Academic Dean .... Dr. Ross PETERSON-VEATCH
10 Vice President for Finance .... Mr. James L. HISTAND
30 Vice Pres Institutional Advancement .... Mr. James K. CASKEY
84 VP for Enroll Management/Marketing .... Dr. Scott BARGE
28 Director of Intercultural Dev .... Mr. Gilberto PEREZ, JR.
66 Director of Undergraduate Nursing .... Ms. Vicki S. KIRKTON
58 Director of Graduate Nursing .... Dr. Brenda S. SROF
70 Director of Social Work .... Dr. Jeanne M. LIECHTY
53 Director of Elementary Teacher Educ .... Dr. Kathryn MEYER REIMER
08 Librarian .... Vacant
82 Director of International Education .... Dr. Tom J. MEYERS
88 Director of Secondary Education .... Ms. Suzanne EHST
13 Director of Information Tech Svcs .... Mr. Michael SHERER
09 Director of Institutional Research .... Dr. Scott BARGE
06 Interim Registrar .... Ms. Becky HORST
37 Director Student Financial Aid .... Mr. Joel D. SHORT
26 Dir of Public Relations .... Ms. Jodi BEYELER
29 Director of Alumni/Parent Relations .... Mr. Dan LIECHTY
42 Campus Minister .... Mr. Robert E. YODER
36 Director of Career Services .... Ms. Melissa KINSEY
18 Director of Facilities .... Mr. Clay E. SHETLER
15 Director of Human Resources .... Mr. Norm BAKHIT
106 Director of Adult/Online Pgms .... Mr. Phil MASON
39 Director of Residence Life .... Mr. Chad COLEMAN
04 Exec Assistant to the President .... Ms. Kathleen YODER
108 Director Institutional Assessment .... Mr. Scott BARGE
41 Athletic Director .... Mr. Josh GLEASON
38 Director Student Counseling .... Ms. Launa ROHR

Grace College and Seminary (D)

200 Seminary Drive, Winona Lake IN 46590-1294
County: Kosciusko FICE Identification: 001800
Unit ID: 150677
Telephone: (574) 372-5100 Carnegie Class: Bac/Diverse
FAX Number: (574) 372-5139 Calendar System: Semester
URL: www.grace.edu
Established: 1937 Annual Undergrad Tuition & Fees: $22,450
Enrollment: 2,185 Coed
Affiliation or Control: Fellowship Of Grace Brethren Churches
IRS Status: 501(c)3
Highest Offering: Doctorate
Program: 2-Year Principally Bachelor's Creditable; Liberal Arts And General; Teacher Preparatory; Religious Emphasis
Accreditation: NH, CACREP, IACBE, TED, THEOL

01 President .... Dr. William J. KATIP
04 Exec Assistant to the President .... Mrs. Nancy L. WEIMER
05 Exec VP Academic Affairs .... Dr. John R. LILLIS
88 Exec Assistant Academic Affairs .... Mrs. Elma C. SHERMAN
20 Exec Officer Academic Affairs .... Mr. Timothy J. ZIEBARTH
73 VP & Dean Seminary & School of Min .... Dr. Jeffery A. GILL
30 VP Advancement .... Mr. Andrew R. FLAMM
11 VP Administration & Compliance .... Dr. Carrie A. YOCUM
84 VP Enrollment Management .... Mrs. Cindy N. SISSON
10 VP Financial Affairs/CFO .... Mr. Paul G. BLAIR
45 VP Strategic Initiatives & Planning .... Vacant
32 VP Student Affairs & Academic Svcs .... Dr. James E. SWANSON
51 Dean of Adult & Community Educ .... Dr. Stephen A. GRILL
49 Dean of School of Arts & Sciences .... Dr. Mark M. NORRIS
83 Dean of Sch of Behavioral Science .... Dr. Thomas J. EDGINGTON
50 Dean of School of Business .... Dr. Jeffrey K. FAWCETT
53 Dean of School of Education .... Dr. Laurinda A. OWEN
106 Dean of School of Prof/Online Educ .... Mr. Timothy J. ZIEBARTH
42 Dean of Chapel & Global Ministries .... Mr. J. Carlos TELLEZ
06 Registrar .... Mr. Steven T. CARLSON
08 Librarian .... Mrs. Tonya L. FAWCETT
13 Dir Information Technology .... Mr. Donald W. FLUKE
23 Dir Student Health & Counseling .... Dr. Debra S. MUSSER
37 Dir Student Financial Aid .... Mrs. Charlette R. SAUDERS
15 Dir of Human Resource .... Mrs. Lisa F. HARMAN
26 Dir of Marketing & Communication .... Mr. David GROUT
18 Director Physical Plant .... Mr. Randy KLEINHANS
29 Director Alumni Relations .... Mr. Dennis L. DUNCAN
41 Athletic Director .... Mr. Chad BRISCOE
36 Director Career Connections .... Mrs. Denise TERRY
09 Dir Institutional Effectiveness .... Dr. Mark H. RAIKES

Hanover College (E)

PO Box 108, Hanover IN 47243-0108
County: Jefferson FICE Identification: 001801
Unit ID: 150756
Telephone: (812) 866-7000 Carnegie Class: Bac/A&S
FAX Number: (812) 866-2164 Calendar System: Other
URL: www.hanover.edu
Established: 1827 Annual Undergrad Tuition & Fees: $34,514
Enrollment: 1,148 Coed
Affiliation or Control: Presbyterian Church (U.S.A.) IRS Status: 501(c)3
Highest Offering: Baccalaureate
Program: Liberal Arts And General; Teacher Preparatory
Accreditation: NH, TED

01 President .... Dr. Lake LAMBERT, III
04 Executive Asst to the President .... Treva SHELTON
10 Vice President Business Affairs .... J. Michael BRUCE
41 Director of Athletics .... Lynn HALL
30 Vice President College Advancement .... Vacant
05 Vice President Academic Affairs .... Dr. Steve JOBE
84 Vice Pres Enrollment Management .... Jon RIESTER
32 Vice President Student Life .... Dr. David YEAGER
88 Exec Dir Business Scholars Program .... Jerry JOHNSON
07 Dean of Admission .... Chris GAGE
06 Registrar .... Dr. Ken PRINCE
13 Chief Technology Officer .... John COLLINS
35 Associate Dean of Students .... Katy LOWE-SCHNEIDER
42 Chaplain .... Vacant
29 Director of Alumni Engagement .... Ann INMAN
19 Director of Campus Safety .... Jim HICKERSON
36 Director of Career Center .... Margaret KRANTZ
26 Dir of Communications & Marketing .... Rhonda BURCH
08 Director of Duggan Library .... Kelly JOYCE
37 Director of Financial Aid .... Richard NASH
23 Director of Health Services .... Sandi ALEXANDER-LEWIS
15 Director of Human Resources .... Shelley PREOCANIN
28 Assoc Dir Multi-Cultural Affairs .... Vacant
18 Director of Physical Plant .... Scott KLEIN
104 Director of Study Abroad .... Uschi APPELT
38 Director of Student Counseling .... Catherine LE SAUX
39 Director of Student Housing .... Casey HECKLER
35 Asst Dir Fraternities/Sororities .... Matthew DEEG

Harrison College - Anderson Campus (F)

140 E 53rd Street, Anderson IN 46013-1717
Telephone: (765) 644-7514 Identification: 666030
Accreditation: ACICS, MAC

† Regional accreditation is carried under the parent institution in Indianapolis (Downtown Campus), IN.

Harrison College - Columbus Indiana Campus (G)

2222 Poshard Drive, Columbus IN 47203-1843
Telephone: (812) 379-9000 Identification: 666428
Accreditation: ACICS, MAC

† Regional accreditation is carried under the parent institution in Indianapolis (Downtown Campus), IN.

Harrison College - Elkhart Campus (H)

56075 Parkway Avenue, Elkhart IN 46516-9325
Telephone: (574) 522-0397 Identification: 666143
Accreditation: ACICS, MAC

† Regional accreditation is carried under the parent institution in Indianapolis (Downtown Campus), IN.

Harrison College - Evansville Campus (I)

4601 Theater Drive, Evansville IN 47715-3901
Telephone: (812) 476-6000 Identification: 666429
Accreditation: ACICS, MAC

† Regional accreditation is carried under the parent institution in Indianapolis (Downtown Campus), IN.

Harrison College - Fort Wayne Campus (J)

6413 N Clinton Street, Fort Wayne IN 46825-4911
Telephone: (260) 471-7667 Identification: 666029
Accreditation: ACICS, MAC, SURGT

† Regional accreditation is carried under the parent institution in Indianapolis (Downtown Campus), IN.

Harrison College - Indianapolis Downtown Campus (K)

550 E Washington Street, Indianapolis IN 46204-2611
County: Marion FICE Identification: 021584
Unit ID: 151166
Telephone: (317) 447-6200 Carnegie Class: Bac/Assoc
FAX Number: (317) 686-9190 Calendar System: Quarter
URL: www.harrison.edu
Established: 1902 Annual Undergrad Tuition & Fees: $17,025
Enrollment: 3,498 Coed
Affiliation or Control: Proprietary IRS Status: Proprietary
Highest Offering: Baccalaureate
Program: Occupational; 2-Year Principally Bachelor's Creditable; Business Emphasis
Accreditation: ACICS, ACFEI, MAC, NURSE

01 President .... Dr. James D. HUTTON
12 Campus President .... Mr. Steve D. HARDIN

† Includes online and The Chef's Academy.

Harrison College - Indianapolis East Campus (L)

8150 Brookville Road, Indianapolis IN 46239-8903
Telephone: (317) 375-8000 Identification: 666430
Accreditation: ACICS, ADNUR, MAC, MLTAD, SURGT

† Regional accreditation is carried under the parent institution in Indianapolis (Downtown Campus), IN.

Harrison College - Indianapolis Northwest Campus (M)

6300 Technology Center Drive,
Indianapolis IN 46278-6022
Telephone: (317) 873-6500 Identification: 666388
Accreditation: ACICS

† Regional accreditation is carried under the parent institution in Indianapolis (Downtown Campus), IN.

Harrison College - Lafayette Campus (A)

4705 Meijer Court, Lafayette IN 47905-4859
Telephone: (765) 447-9550 Identification: 666431
Accreditation: ACICS, MAC

† Regional accreditation is carried under the parent institution in Indianapolis (Downtown Campus), IN.

Harrison College - Terre Haute Campus (B)

1378 S State Road 46, Terre Haute IN 47803-9787
Telephone: (812) 877-2100 Identification: 666433
Accreditation: ACICS, MAC

† Regional accreditation is carried under the parent institution in Indianapolis (Downtown Campus), IN.

Holy Cross College (C)

PO Box 308, Notre Dame IN 46556-0308
County: Saint Joseph FICE Identification: 007263
Unit ID: 150774
Telephone: (574) 239-8400 Carnegie Class: Bac/A&S
FAX Number: (574) 239-8323 Calendar System: Semester
URL: www.hcc-nd.edu
Established: 1966 Annual Undergrad Tuition & Fees: $27,950
Enrollment: 532 Coed
Affiliation or Control: Roman Catholic IRS Status: 501(c)3
Highest Offering: Baccalaureate
Program: Liberal Arts And General
Accreditation: NH

01 President ... Bro. John R. PAIGE, CSC
11 VP for Administration ... Mr. Daniel HAVERTY
26 VP for Commun/Marketing/Enrollment ... Vacant
04 Executive Assistant ... Ms. Jodie L. SWEET
05 VP for Academic Affairs ... Dr. Justin WATSON
32 VP for Student Affairs ... Dr. Kelly JORDAN
30 VP for College Relations ... Ms. Charmaine TORMA
20 Assoc VP of Academic Affairs ... Bro. Jesus ALONSO, CSC
06 Registrar ... Mrs. Hiroko TEZUKA
84 Director of Enrollment Management ... Mr. Brian STUDEBAKER
37 Director of Financial Aid ... Mr. Michael SCHMALTZ
38 Director of Student Counseling Svcs ... Vacant
13 Director of Campus Technology ... Mr. Doug BLAIR
39 Director of Residence Life ... Mr. William MCKENNEY
08 Director of Library Services ... Mrs. Mary Ellen HEGEDUS
36 Director of Career Development ... Mr. Charles BALL
42 Director of Campus Ministry ... Mr. Andrew POLANIECKI
41 Athletic Director ... Ms. Aimee NIESPODZIANY
09 Director of Institutional Research ... Bro. Charles DREVON

Huntington University (D)

2303 College Avenue, Huntington IN 46750-9986
County: Huntington FICE Identification: 001803
Unit ID: 150941
Telephone: (260) 356-6000 Carnegie Class: Bac/Diverse
FAX Number: (260) 359-4086 Calendar System: 4/1/4
URL: www.huntington.edu
Established: 1897 Annual Undergrad Tuition & Fees: $24,822
Enrollment: 1,209 Coed
Affiliation or Control: United Brethren Church IRS Status: 501(c)3
Highest Offering: Doctorate
Program: Liberal Arts And General; Teacher Preparatory; Professional
Accreditation: NH, NURSE, SW, TED

01 President ... Dr. Sherilyn R. EMBERTON
05 Vice President Academic Affairs ... Dr. Michael K. WANOUS
10 VP for Business/Finance/Treasurer ... Mr. Gregory A. SMITLEY
84 VP Enrollment Mgmt & Marketing ... Mr. Daniel SOLMS
45 VP Strategy & Grad/Professionl Pgms ... Dr. Ann C. MCPHERREN
30 Vice President for Advancement ... Mr. Vincent D. HAUPERT
32 Vice President for Student Life ... Dr. Ron L. COFFEY
04 Administrative Secy to President ... Mrs. Cindy H. GEDERS
42 Campus Pastor ... Rev. Arthur L. WILSON
58 Dir of Grad & Professional Programs ... Mrs. Julie K. GOETZ
36 Assoc Dean Student Life/Career Dev ... Ms. Martha J. SMITH
35 Assoc Dean of Student Development ... Mr. Jesse M. BROWN
21 Controller/Dir of Fin Services ... Mrs. Connie C. BONNER
37 Director of Financial Aid ... Mr. Jerry W. DAVIS
06 Registrar ... Mrs. Sarah J. HARVEY
08 Director of Library Services ... Ms. Anita GRAY
13 Dir Information/Technology Services ... Mr. Adam L. SKILES
38 Director of Learning Assistance ... Mrs. Kris L. CHAFIN
41 Athletic Director ... Ms. Lori L. CULLER
18 Director of Physical Plant ... Mr. Jerry A. GRESSLEY
29 Director of Alumni Relations ... Mrs. Marcy T. HAWKINS
19 Director of Campus Police ... Mr. Barry A. COCHRAN
88 Dir of Horizon Leadership Program ... Mr. Jesse M. BROWN

Indiana State University (E)

200 N 7th Street, Terre Haute IN 47809-1902
County: Vigo FICE Identification: 001807
Unit ID: 151324
Telephone: (812) 237-6311 Carnegie Class: DRU
FAX Number: (812) 237-2291 Calendar System: Semester
URL: web.indstate.edu
Established: 1865 Annual Undergrad Tuition & Fees (In-State): $8,580
Enrollment: 13,183 Coed
Affiliation or Control: State IRS Status: 501(c)3
Highest Offering: Doctorate
Program: Liberal Arts And General; Teacher Preparatory; Professional
Accreditation: NH, AAFCS, ARCPA, ART, BUS, CAATE, CACREP, CIDA, CLPSY, CONST, COPSY, DIETC, ENGT, MUS, NAIT, NUR, OT, @PTA, SCPSY, SP, SW, TED

01 President ... Dr. Daniel J. BRADLEY
100 Chief of Staff ... Ms. Teresa D. EXLINE
86 Exec Dir of Government Relations ... Mr. Greg J. GOODE
88 Exec Dir Strat Initiat/Dir Ent Svc ... Mr. Michael (Mike) SNYDER
05 Provost/Vice Pres Academic Affs ... Dr. Michael J. LICARI
10 Sr VP Finance & Admin/Univ Treas ... Ms. Diann E. MCKEE
84 Sr VP Enrollment Mgmt/Mktg/Comm ... Mr. John BEACON
32 VP Student Affairs ... Dr. Willie BANKS
88 Vice Pres Univ Engagement ... Dr. Nancy B. ROGERS
43 General Counsel Legal Affairs ... Ms. Bridget K. BUTWIN
20 Assoc VP Academic Affairs ... Dr. Joshua POWERS
13 Assoc VP Chief Info Officer ... Dr. Lisa SPENCE
18 Assoc VP Univ Facilities Management ... Mr. Kevin L. RUNION
26 Asst VP Comm/Marketing ... Mr. Santhana NAIDU
07 Assoc VP Enroll/Mgmt/Adm/HS Rel ... Mr. Richard J. TOOMEY
29 Director of Alumni Affairs ... Mr. Rex KENDALL
15 Assoc VP Human Resources ... Mr. Wil DOWNS
14 Exec Dir Information Technology ... Mr. Yancy PHILLIPS
21 Business Officer ... Ms. Diann E. MCKEE
06 Registrar ... Ms. April HAY
22 Int Dir Equal Opportunity/Title IX ... Ms. Channon BROWN
28 University Diversity Officer ... Ms. Elonda ERVIN
41 Director of Athletics ... Mr. Ronald PRETTYMAN
36 Executive Dir Career Svcs ... Dr. Darby C. SCISM
25 Director Sponsored Programs ... Ms. Dawn UNDERWOOD
09 Director of Institutional Research ... Ms. Patty MCCLINTOCK
19 Director of Public Safety ... Mr. Joseph M. NEWPORT
96 Dir Purchasing/Central Receiving ... Mr. Kevin BARR
39 Executive Dir of Residential Life ... Ms. Amanda KNERR
38 Director of Student Counseling ... Dr. Kenneth CHEW
37 Director Student Financial Aid ... Ms. Crystal BAKER
49 Dean of Arts & Sciences ... Dr. John MURRAY
50 Dean of Business ... Dr. Brien N. SMITH
53 Dean of Education ... Dr. Kandi HILL-CLARKE
68 Dean Nursing/Health & Human Svcs ... Dr. Jack E. TURMAN, JR.
72 Dean of Technology ... Dr. Robert ENGLISH
58 Dean of Grad/Professional Studies ... Dr. Lynn MAURER
08 Dean of Library Services ... Dr. Robin CRUMRIN
56 Dean of Extended Learning ... Dr. Ken BRAUCHLE

Indiana Tech (F)

1600 E Washington Boulevard, Fort Wayne IN 46803-1297
County: Allen FICE Identification: 001805
Unit ID: 151290
Telephone: (260) 422-5561 Carnegie Class: Spec/Bus
FAX Number: (260) 420-1453 Calendar System: Semester
URL: www.IndianaTech.edu
Established: 1930 Annual Undergrad Tuition & Fees: $25,180
Enrollment: 6,133 Coed
Affiliation or Control: Independent Non-Profit IRS Status: 501(c)3
Highest Offering: Doctorate
Program: Professional; Business Emphasis
Accreditation: NH, ENG

01 President ... Dr. Arthur E. SNYDER
15 Human Resources Director ... Mr. Christopher B. BLACK
100 Director Executive Operations ... Ms. Jennifer A. ROSS
04 Executive Operations Coordinator ... Ms. Penny J. EGLY
10 Exec VP Finance & Administration ... Ms. Judy K. ROY
21 Controller ... Ms. Shelly R. MUSOLF
13 Director of Information Technology ... Mr. Jeff S. LEICHTY
18 Dir Security & Facilities Mgmt ... Mr. R. Michael TOWNSLEY
37 Financial Aid Director ... Mr. Scott W. THUM
05 Vice President for Academic Affairs ... Dr. John F. SHANNON
54 Dean of Engineering/Computer Sci ... Mr. David A. ASCHLIMAN
50 Dean of Business ... Dr. Jeffrey A. ZIMMERMAN
97 Interim Dean of General Studies ... Dr. Joshua C. FRANCIS
58 Director Global Leadership Program ... Dr. Kenneth E. RAUCH
09 Director of Academic Research ... Mr. Christopher D. DOUSE
08 Director McMillen Library ... Ms. Constance E. SCOTT
06 Registrar ... Mr. Esaeas J. RODRIGUEZ
108 Director of Institutional Planning ... Mr. Henry D. KING
77 Assoc Dean of Computer Sciences ... Mr. Gary A. MESSICK
61 Dean Law School ... Mr. Charles P. CERCONE
08 Associate Dean for Library Affairs ... Ms. Phebe E. POYDRAS
84 VP for Enrollment Management ... Mr. Steve A. HERENDEEN
88 Director of International Admiss ... Ms. Maya H. TSAI
88 CPS Development Manager ... Ms. A. Nicole SCOTT
84 Enrollment Manager-Fort Wayne ... Mr. Yiani DEMITSAS
106 Director of Online Learning ... Dr. Y. Ben LEE
11 Associate VP for Operations ... Ms. Sharon LOKUTA
07 CPS Director of Admissions ... Mr. Duncan L. MCCORQUODALE
32 VP for Student Affairs ... Dr. Daniel J. STOKER
41 Athletic Director ... Ms. Debra P. WARREN
39 Assoc VP Student Services ... Mr. Chris M. DICKSON
35 Director Student Life ... Ms. Andrea G. CHECK
88 Director Learning Support Services ... Ms. Cynthia P. VERDUCE
42 Faith Services Coordinator ... Mr. Gregory P. BYMAN
26 VP University Relations ... Mr. Brian W. ENGELHART
30 Associate VP Advancement ... Ms. Mary V. SLAFKOSKY
29 Dir Annual Fund & Alumni Relations ... Ms. Arienne B. JULIANO
88 Exec Dir C3 ... Mr. Mark H. RICHTER
102 Dir Foundation/Corporate Relations ... Ms. Tracina A. SMITH
25 Chief Contracts/Grants Admin ... Ms. Barbara B. DANIELS
44 Director Annual or Planned Giving ... Ms. Lisa M. BIERS

Indiana Tech-Elkhart (G)

3333 Middleburg Street, Elkhart IN 46516
Telephone: (574) 296-7075 Identification: 770102
Accreditation: &NH

† Branch campus of Indiana Tech, Fort Wayne, IN.

Indiana Tech-Indianapolis (H)

3500 DePaul W Boulevard, Indianapolis IN 46268
Telephone: (317) 466-2121 Identification: 770103
Accreditation: &NH

† Branch campus of Indiana Tech, Fort Wayne, IN.

*Indiana University (I)

107 S. Indiana Ave., Bryan Hall 200,
Bloomington IN 47405-7000
County: Monroe FICE Identification: 008002
Unit ID: 151351
Telephone: (812) 855-4613 Carnegie Class: N/A
FAX Number: (812) 855-9586
URL: www.indiana.edu

01 President ... Dr. Michael A. MCROBBIE
05 Exec Vice President/Provost IUB ... Ms. Lauren ROBEL
03 Exec Vice Chancellor IUPUI ... Dr. Nasser PAYDAR
21 Exec VP Univ Academic Affairs ... Mr. John APPLEGATE
46 Vice Pres for Research ... Dr. Fred CATE
28 VP Diversity/Equity/Multicultural ... Dr. James WIMBUSH
18 Vice Pres Capital Planning & Facil ... Dr. Thomas MORRISON
10 Vice President/CFO ... Ms. MaryFrances MCCOURT
26 VP Public Affairs & Govt Relations ... Mr. Michael SAMPLE
100 Chief of Staff ... Dr. Karen H. ADAMS
13 Vice President Info Tech/CIO ... Dr. Brad C. WHEELER
43 Vice Pres and University Counsel ... Ms. Jacqueline A. SIMMONS
104 Vice Pres for International Affairs ... Dr. David ZARET
88 Vice Pres for Engagement ... Mr. William B. STEPHAN
41 VP & Dir of Intercoll Athletics ... Mr. Fred GLASS
63 VP Univ Clinical Affs/Dean Sch Med ... Dr. Jay HESS
21 University Treasurer ... Ms. Mary Frances MCCOURT
22 Director of Affirmative Action ... Ms. Julie KNOST
29 Exec Dir IU Alumni Association ... Mr. J. Thomas FORBES
15 Director of Human Resources ... Mr. John WHELAN
27 Director of Media Relations ... Mr. Mark LAND
102 President IU Foundation ... Dr. Dan SMITH

*Indiana University Bloomington (J)

107 S. Indiana Avenue, Bloomington IN 47405-7000
County: Monroe FICE Identification: 001809
Unit ID: 151351
Telephone: (812) 855-4848 Carnegie Class: RU/VH
FAX Number: (812) 855-5678 Calendar System: Semester
URL: www.iub.edu
Established: 1820 Annual Undergrad Tuition & Fees (In-State): $10,388
Enrollment: 46,416 Coed
Affiliation or Control: State IRS Status: 501(c)3
Highest Offering: Doctorate
Program: Liberal Arts And General; Teacher Preparatory; Professional
Accreditation: NH, ART, AUD, BUS, BUSA, CAATE, CACREP, CEA, CIDA, CLPSY, COPSY, DIETD, IPSY, JOUR, LAW, LIB, MUS, NRPA, OPD, OPT, OPTR, OPTT, PCSAS, PH, SCPSY, SP, SPAA, TED, THEA

02 President ... Dr. Michael MCROBBIE
05 Exec Vice Pres & Provost ... Ms. Lauren ROBEL
03 Exec Vice Pres & Chanc IUPUI ... Dr. Charles BANTZ
05 Exec VP Univ Academic Affairs ... Mr. John S. APPLEGATE
10 Vice President/CFO & Treasurer ... Ms. MaryFrances MCCOURT
63 VP Univ Clin Affrs/Dean Sch of Med ... Dr. Jay HESS
18 Vice Pres Capital Plng/Facilities ... Dr. Tom MORRISON
28 VP Diversity/Equity & Multicul Affs ... Dr. James WIMBUSH
46 Vice President for Research ... Dr. Jorge JOSE
26 VP for Public Affs & Govt Relations ... Mr. Mike SAMPLE
88 Vice President for Engagement ... Mr. William B. STEPHAN
20 Vice Provost for Undergraduate Educ ... Dr. Dennis GROTH
20 Vice Prov Faculty & Academic Affs ... Dr. Thomas GIERYN
09 Interim Vice Provost Research ... Dr. Rick VAN KOOTEN
84 Vice Provost Enrollment Mgmt ... Dr. David JOHNSON
88 Vice Prov Grad Educ & Health Sci ... Dr. David DALEKE
88 Vice Provost Strategic Initiatives ... Dr. Munirpallam VENKATARAMANAN
30 Exec Vice Pres Development/IU Fdn ... Mr. Richard K. DUPREE
15 Associate Vice Pres Univ Human Res ... Mr. John WHELAN
88 Assoc VP Client Services & Support ... Mr. Dennis CROMWELL
13 Vice Pres Info Technology & CIO ... Dr. Brad WHEELER
58 Dean University Graduate School ... Dr. James WIMBUSH
102 Pres & CEO IU Foundation ... Dr. Daniel C. SMITH
85 Assoc VP for International Svcs ... Mr. Christopher VIERS
49 Dean College Arts & Sciences ... Dr. Larry SINGELL
08 Ruth Lilly Dean Univ Libraries ... Ms. Carolyn WALTERS
32 Dean of Students ... Dr. Pete GOLDSMITH
50 Dean Kelley School of Business ... Dr. Idalene KENSER
53 Dean School of Education ... Dr. Gerardo GONZALEZ
68 Dean School of Public Health ... Dr. Mohammed TORABI
88 Dean School of Optometry ... Dr. Joseph BONANNO
61 Dean School of Law ... Mr. Austen L. PARRISH
64 Dean Jacobs School of Music ... Mr. Gwyn RICHARDS
60 Interim Dean Media School ... Dr. Lesa H. MAJOR
88 Dean School of Informatics and Comp ... Dr. Robert B. SCHNABEL
88 Dean School of Global and Intl Stds ... Mr. Lee FEINSTEIN

80 Dean SPEA Dr. John D. GRAHAM
82 Vice Pres International Affairs Dr. David ZARET
92 Dean Hutton Honors College Dr. Andrea CICCARELLI
35 Assoc Dean for Student Affairs Ms. Carol MCCORD
29 Exec Dir IU Alumni Association Mr. J.T FORBES
39 Exec Dir Residential Pgm & Svcs Mr. Pat CONNOR
36 Director Career Dev Center Mr. Patrick DONAHUE
16 Bloomington Dir Employee Rels Svcs Ms. Suzanne RYAN
06 Assoc Vice Provost/Registrar Mr. Mark MCCONAHAY
23 Exec Dir IU Health Center Dr. Pete GROGG
43 VP & General Counsel Ms. Jacqueline SIMMONS
88 Director IU Press Dr. Gary DUNHAM
22 Director Affirmative Action Ms. Julie KNOST
19 Chief of Police Ms. Laury FLINT
88 Exec Dir Indiana Memorial Union Vacant
88 Exec Director Radio/TV Services Mr. Perry METZ
88 Operations Mgr Campus Bus Service Mr. Perry MAULL
88 Director IU Auditorium Mr. Doug BOOHER
18 Asst VP Facilities Mr. Hank HEWETSON
38 Director Counseling & Psych Svs Dr. Nancy STOCKTON
41 VP & Dir Intercollegiate Athletics Mr. Fred GLASS
96 Asst VP for Procurement Ms. Jill SCHUNK
25 Exec Dir Grant & Contract Services Mr. Jim BECKER
90 Assoc Dean Rsrch Tech/ED PTI/Prof Dr. Craig STEWART
88 Director IU Art Museum Ms. Adelheid GEALT
07 Director of Admissions Ms. Sacha THIEME
100 Chief of Staff Dr. Karen ADAMS
101 Secretary of the Institution/Board Ms. Deborah A. LEMON
104 Assoc VP Overseas Study Dr. Kathleen SIDELI
106 Senior Dir Online Education Dr. Barbara A. BICHELMEYER

*Indiana University East (A)

2325 Chester Boulevard, Richmond IN 47374-1289
County: Wayne FICE Identification: 001811
Unit ID: 151388
Telephone: (765) 973-8200 Carnegie Class: Bac/Diverse
FAX Number: (765) 973-8364 Calendar System: Semester
URL: www.iue.edu
Established: 1946 Annual Undergrad Tuition & Fees (In-State): $6,787
Enrollment: 4,573 Coed
Affiliation or Control: State IRS Status: 501(c)3
Highest Offering: Master's
Program: Liberal Arts And General; Teacher Preparatory
Accreditation: NH, ACBSP, NUR, TED

02 Chancellor Dr. Kathyrn CRUZ-URIBE
05 Int Vice Chanc Academic Affairs Dr. Mary BLAKEFIELD
26 Vice Chanc External Affs/Marketing Mr. Jason TROUTWINE
10 Vice Chancellor Admin & Finance Mr. Dan DOOLEY
32 Int Dean Students/Academic Affairs Ms. Carrie REISNER
13 Director Information Technology Mr. Todd DUKE
30 Director of Gift Development Ms. Stephanie HAYS-MUSSOINI
06 Registrar Mr. Dennis HICKS
08 Director Library/Media Services Dr. Frances YATES
15 Director Human Resources Mr. Andrew LENHARDT
36 Experiential Learning Coordinator Ms. Liz FERRIS
07 Director of Admissions Ms. Molly VANDERPOOL
37 Dir Fin Aid & Scholarships Ms. Sarah SOPER
20 Director University College Ms. Carrie REISNER
40 Manager of Barnes & Noble Bookstore Ms. Kristy FRASHER
35 Director of Campus Life Ms. Rebeckah HESTER
21 Bursar Ms. Shelley DODSON
22 Director Affirmative Action Ms. Patricia CRAWFORD
70 Director Social Work/Human Services Mr. Ed FITZGERALD
27 Director Communications & Marketing Mr. John DALTON
97 Assoc VC & Director General Studies Dr. Ross ALEXANDER
29 Director Alumni Relations Ms. Terry WIESEHAN
28 Director of Multicultural Affairs Mr. Tim WILLIAMS
50 Dean Business/Technology Dr. David FRANTZ
79 Dean Humanities & Social Sciences Dr. Ross ALEXANDER
81 Dean Natural Science & Math Dr. Neil SABINE
66 Dean of Nursing Ms. Karen CLARK
53 Interim Dean Education Dr. Jerry WILDE

*Indiana University Kokomo (B)

2300 S Washington, Box 9003, Kokomo IN 46904-9003
County: Howard FICE Identification: 001814
Unit ID: 151333
Telephone: (765) 453-2000 Carnegie Class: Bac/Diverse
FAX Number: (765) 455-9444 Calendar System: Semester
URL: www.iuk.edu
Established: 1945 Annual Undergrad Tuition & Fees (In-State): $6,941
Enrollment: 4,180 Coed
Affiliation or Control: State IRS Status: 501(c)3
Highest Offering: Master's
Program: Occupational; Liberal Arts And General; Teacher Preparatory; Professional
Accreditation: NH, BUS, NUR, NURSE, RAD, TED

02 Chancellor Dr. Susan SCIAME-GIESECKE
05 Vice Chanc Academic Affairs Dr. Mark CANADA
32 Vice Chanc Student Affs/Enroll Mgmt Dr. Todd GAMBILL
30 Vice Chancellor for Advancement Ms. Jan HALPERIN
72 Director Division Purdue Tech Mr. Jeff GRIFFIN
08 Dean of the Library Ms. Polly BORUFF-JONES
37 Director Financial Aid Ms. Karen SHAW
10 Director of Budget Administration Dr. Philemon YEBEI
26 Dir External Rels/Public Affairs Ms. Cathy VALCKE
06 Registrar Ms. Stacey THOMAS
100 Chief of Staff Ms. Gerry G. STROMAN
36 Manager Career/Accessibility Center Ms. Tracy SPRINGER
27 Director Communications & Marketing Ms. Marie RADEL
07 Director of Admissions Ms. Angie SIDERS
28 Director of Diversity Ms. Maria AHMAD
35 Dean of Students Ms. Sarah SARBER
18 Director Facilities/Physical Plant Mr. John SARBER
50 Dean School of Business Dr. Alan KRABBENHOFT
49 Dean Sch Humanities/Social Sciences Dr. Scott JONES
66 Dean School of Nursing Dr. Linda WALLACE
53 Dean Division of Education Dr. Paul PAESE
81 Dean Sch Sciences/Math/Information Dr. Christian CHAURET
79 Chair Humanities Dr. Joe KEENER

*Indiana University Northwest (C)

3400 Broadway, Gary IN 46408-1197
County: Lake FICE Identification: 001815
Unit ID: 151360
Telephone: (219) 980-6500 Carnegie Class: Master's M
FAX Number: (219) 980-6670 Calendar System: Semester
URL: www.iun.edu
Established: 1921 Annual Undergrad Tuition & Fees (In-State): $6,962
Enrollment: 6,052 Coed
Affiliation or Control: State IRS Status: 501(c)3
Highest Offering: Master's
Program: Occupational; Liberal Arts And General; Teacher Preparatory; Professional
Accreditation: NH, BUS, CAHIIM, DA, DH, NUR, RAD, RTT, SPAA, TED

02 Chancellor Dr. William J. LOWE
04 Exec Asst to the Chancellor Mrs. Kathy MALONE
05 Exec Vice Chanc Academic Affairs Dr. Mark MCPHAIL
11 Exec Dir of Facilities/Operations Vacant
32 Vice Chanc Student Svcs/Enroll Mgmt Dr. Alexis S. MONTEVIRGEN
10 Campus Chief Financial Officer Mrs. Marianne MILICH
26 Vice Chanc Advancement & Ext Affs Ms. Jeri Pat GABBERT
13 Chief Information Officer Ms. Beth VAN GORDON
20 Assoc Vice Chanc Academic Affs Dr. Cynthia O'DELL
09 Asst VC Inst Effectiveness & Rsrch Mr. John NOVAK
49 Dean College of Arts & Sciences Dr. Mark HOYERT
88 Dean Col of Health & Human Svcs Dr. Patrick BANKSTON
50 Dean School of Business & Economics Dr. Anna ROMINGER
53 Interim Dean School of Education Dr. Patrick BANKSTON
80 Interim Dir Public & Environ Affs Dr. Linda DELUNAS
70 Director Social Work Dr. Darlene LYNCH
06 Registrar Mr. Craig DEMYER
88 Director Pre-Professional Pgm Dr. Michael LAPOINTE
07 Director of Admissions Ms. Dorothy FRINK
37 Director Financial Aid Mr. Harold BURTLEY
36 Director Career & Placement Ms. Sharese DUDLEY
35 Director Student Activities Mr. Scott FULK
19 Director Security Ms. Patricia NOWAK
29 Director Alumni Relations Ms. Paulette LAFATA-JOHNSON
66 Director Division of Nursing Dr. Linda DELUNAS
24 Director Instr Media Mr. Aaron PIGORS
08 Director Library Mr. Timothy SUTHERLAND
18 Director Physical Plant Mr. Otto JEFIMENKO
21 Manager Student Accounts Ms. Sandra MENDOZA
25 Director Research/Sponsored Pgms Ms. T.J STOOPS
15 Interim Director Human Resources Ms. Mianta' DIMING
28 Director Diversity Programming Mr. James WALLACE, JR.
38 Director of Counseling Services Ms. Barbara A. DAHL
22 Director Affirmative Action Ms. Ida GILLIS
88 Dir Schlrshp in Teaching & Learning Dr. Christopher YOUNG
88 Dir Urban & Regional Excellence Dr. Ellen SZARLETA
105 Director Web Services Ms. Myriam YOUNG
106 Dir Online Education/E-learning Mr. Christopher YOUNG
41 Athletic Director Mr. Kristofer SCHNATZ

*Indiana University-Purdue University Fort Wayne (D)

2101 E Coliseum Boulevard, Fort Wayne IN 46805-1499
County: Allen FICE Identification: 001828
Unit ID: 151102
Telephone: (260) 481-6100 Carnegie Class: Master's L
FAX Number: (260) 481-6880 Calendar System: Semester
URL: www.ipfw.edu
Established: 1964 Annual Undergrad Tuition & Fees (In-State): $8,079
Enrollment: 13,214 Coed
Affiliation or Control: State IRS Status: 501(c)3
Highest Offering: Doctorate
Program: Liberal Arts And General; Teacher Preparatory; Professional
Accreditation: NH, ART, BUS, CS, DA, DH, DT, ENG, ENGT, MUS, NUR, RAD, TED, THEA

02 Chancellor Dr. Vicky L. CARWEIN
05 Vice Chanc Academic Affairs Dr. Carl DRUMMOND
10 Vice Chanc Financial/Admin Affairs Dr. David WESSE
32 Vice Chancellor Student Affairs Dr. George S. MCCLELLAN
09 Assoc Vice Chanc Inst Effectiveness Dr. Robert WILKINSON
30 Vice Chancellor for Advancement Vacant
13 Chief Information Officer Mr. Mitch DAVIDSON
18 Director Physical Plant Mr. Jay H. HARRIS
29 Director Alumni Relations Ms. Debra BOGGS
08 Library Dean Ms. Cheryl B. TRUESDELL
15 Director Human Resources Ms. Tamarah D. BROWNLEE
41 Director of Athletics Ms. Kelley HARTLEY
06 Registrar Mr. Patrick A. MCLAUGHLIN
96 Director Purchasing Ms. Cynthia M. ELICK
19 Chief University Police Ms. Julie YUNKER
22 Director Institutional Equity Ms. Christine M. MARCUCCILLI
85 Director International Program Mr. Brian MYLREA
37 Director Financial Aid Mr. David PETERSON
07 Director of Admissions Ms. Tonishea JACKSON
49 Dean Arts & Sciences Dr. Eric C. LINK
76 Dean Health Sciences Dr. Ann OBERGFELL
51 Exec Director Continuing Stds Ms. Karen VANGORDER
26 Director of Marketing Mr. Jack PATTON
72 Dean Engr Tech/Computer Science Mr. S.C. Max YEN
53 Dean Educ & Public Policy Dr. James BURG
50 Dean Business Dr. Michael EIKENBERRY
57 Dean Visual/Performing Arts Dr. John O'CONNELL
46 Assoc Vice Chanc Rsrch Ext Support Vacant
35 Dean of Students Dr. Eric M. NORMAN
28 Assoc Vice Chancellor Diversity Mr. Kenneth C. CHRISTMON
100 Chief of Staff Ms. Kimberly WAGNER

*Indiana University-Purdue University Indianapolis (E)

301 University Blvd., Suite 5010, Indianapolis IN 46202-5146
County: Marion FICE Identification: 001813
Unit ID: 151111
Telephone: (317) 274-5555 Carnegie Class: RU/H
FAX Number: N/A Calendar System: Semester
URL: www.iupui.edu
Established: 1969 Annual Undergrad Tuition & Fees (In-State): $9,065
Enrollment: 30,690 Coed
Affiliation or Control: State IRS Status: 501(c)3
Highest Offering: Doctorate
Program: Occupational; Liberal Arts And General; Teacher Preparatory; Professional
Accreditation: NH, #ARCPA, CACREP, CAHIIM, CIDA, CLPSY, CS, CYTO, DA, DENT, DH, DIETI, EMT, ENG, ENGT, FEPAC, HSA, HT, IPSY, LAW, MED, MT, MUS, NMT, NUR, NURSE, OT, PA, PAST, PH, PTA, RAD, RADDOS, RTT, SPAA, SW

02 Chancellor Dr. Charles R. BANTZ
100 Chief of Staff Dr. Jeffrey A. DEAN
28 Vice Chanc Diversity/Equity/Incl Dr. Karen L. DACE
04 Assistant to Chancellor for Comm Mr. Vernon A. WILLIAMS
05 Exec Vice Chanc/Chief Academic Ofcr Dr. Nasser H. PAYDAR
10 Vice Chanc Administration & Finance Ms. Dawn M. RHODES
26 Vice Chancellor External Affairs Ms. Amy C. WARNER
32 Vice Chancellor Student Life Dr. Zebulun R. DAVENPORT
46 Vice Chancellor Research Dr. Kody VARAHRAMYAN
13 Dean Information Technologies Dr. Anastasia MORRONE
08 Dean University Library Mr. David W. LEWIS
84 Director Enrollment Services Dr. Rebecca E. PORTER
06 Registrar Ms. Mary Beth MYERS
21 Bursar Mr. Dan YOUNGBLOOD
22 Director Equal Opportunity Ms. Kim D. KIRKLAND
38 Director Student Counseling Dr. Julie LASH
39 Director Campus Housing Mr. Aaron HART
40 Bookstore Manager Ms. Michele GRETCH-CARTER
36 Career Services Council Mr. Joshua D. KILLEY
41 Athletic Director Mr. Michael R. MOORE
29 Director Alumni Relations Mr. Stefan S. DAVIS
27 Director News & Media Ms. Margie SMITH-SIMMONS
09 Director Institutional Research Dr. Gary PIKE
07 Dir of Undergraduate Admissions Mr. Chris J. FOLEY
37 Director Student Financial Aid Mr. Marvin L. SMITH
15 Asst Vice Chanc Human Resources Ms. Carlene M. THOMPSON
23 Medical Director Student Health Svc Dr. Stephen F. WINTERMEYER
18 Director Campus Facility Services Ms. Emily C. WREN
19 Chief Campus Police Mr. Robert L. TRUE
92 Dean Honors College Dr. E. Jane LUZAR
96 Director Purchasing Mr. Robert HALTER
45 Senior Advisor/Academic Planning Dr. Trudy W. BANTA
12 Dean Columbus Campus Dr. Marwan A. WAFA
76 Dean School Health/Rehab Sci Dr. Austin O. AGHO
57 Dean Herron School of Art Ms. Valerie EICKMEIER
52 Dean School of Dentistry Dr. John N. WILLIAMS
54 Dean School of Engr/Technology Dr. David J. RUSSOMANNO
88 Exec Assoc Dean of Informatics Dr. Mathew J. PALAKAL
61 Dean McKinney Sch of Law Mr. Andrew R. KLEIN
49 Dean School of Liberal Arts Dr. William A. BLOMQUIST
63 Dean School of Medicine Dr. Jay L. HESS
66 Dean School of Nursing Dr. Robin P. NEWHOUSE
68 Dean School of Physical Education Dr. James M. GLADDEN
81 Dean School of Science Dr. Simon RHODES
70 Dean School of Social Work Dr. Michael PATCHNER
69 Dean Fairbanks Sch of Public Health Dr. Paul K. HALVERSON
88 Dean Lilly Fam Sch of Philanthropy Dr. Amir PASIC
53 Exec Assoc Dean School of Education Dr. Patricia M. ROGAN
60 Int Ex Assoc Dean Sch of Journalism Dr. Dan DREW
62 Int Ex Assoc Dean Library/Info Sci Dr. Rachel APPLEGATE
80 Exec Assoc Dean Public/Environ Affs Dr. Lilliard RICHARDSON
85 Assoc Vice Chanc International Affs Dr. Gil LATZ
50 Assoc Dean School of Business Dr. Philip L. COCHRAN
58 Associate Dean Graduate School Dr. Sherry F. QUEENER
89 Dean University College Dr. Kathy JOHNSON

*Indiana University South Bend (F)

1700 Mishawaka Avenue, South Bend IN 46634-7111
County: Saint Joseph FICE Identification: 001816
Unit ID: 151342
Telephone: (574) 520-4872 Carnegie Class: Master's M
FAX Number: (574) 520-4834 Calendar System: Semester
URL: www.iusb.edu
Established: 1940 Annual Undergrad Tuition & Fees (In-State): $6,986

Enrollment: 7,859 Coed
Affiliation or Control: State IRS Status: 501(c)3
Highest Offering: Master's
Program: Occupational; Liberal Arts And General; Teacher Preparatory; Professional
Accreditation: NH, BUS, CACREP, DH, MUS, NURSE, RAD, SPAA, TED

02 Chancellor .... Dr. Terry L. ALLISON
05 Exec Vice Chanc Acad Affairs .... Dr. Jann JOSEPH
10 Vice Chancellor Finance & Admin .... Mr. Bill J. O'DONNELL
26 Vice Chanc Public Affs/Univ Advance .... Dr. Ilene SHEFFER
32 Vice Chanc Student Affs/Enroll Mgmt .... Vacant
13 Regional Chief Information Officer .... Ms. Elizabeth VAN GORDON
20 Int Assoc Vice Chanc Academic Affs .... Dr. Linda CHEN
88 Assoc VC Student Acad Support Svcs .... Ms. Karen L. WHITE
84 Asst Vice Chanc for Enrollment Svcs .... Ms. Cathy M. BUCKMAN
06 Registrar .... Mr. Keith DAWSON
36 Director Career Services Office .... Vacant
35 Dir Student Activit Ctr/Athletics .... Mr. Steve BRUCE
18 Director Facilities Management .... Mr. Michael PRATER
19 Director of Safety & Security .... Mr. Martin L. GERSEY
15 Director of Human Resources .... Vacant
24 Dir of Instructional Media Svcs .... Mr. Jim YOCOM
29 Dir Alumni Affs/Campus Ceremonies .... Ms. Jeanie METZGER
27 Director Communications/Marketing .... Mr. Kenneth W. BAIERL
52 Director of Dental Auxiliary Educ .... Ms. Kristyn QUIMBY
51 Director of Extended Learning .... Mr. Mike MANCINI
97 Director of General Studies .... Dr. David A. VOLLRATH
85 Director of International Programs .... Dr. Scott SERNAU
38 Director Student Counseling Ctr .... Vacant
07 Director of Admissions .... Vacant
09 Director of Institutional Research .... Mr. Biniam TESFAMARIAM
28 Director of Diversity .... Vacant
30 Director of Development .... Ms. Dina HARRIS
39 Director of Student Housing .... Vacant
21 Director of Accounting .... Ms. Kathleen PIZANA
37 Associate Director of Financial Aid .... Ms. Cyndi LANG
49 Dean of Liberal Arts & Science .... Dr. Elizabeth E. DUNN
50 Dean of Business & Economics .... Dr. Robert DUCOFFE
53 Dean of Education .... Dr. Marvin LYNN
57 Dean of the Arts .... Dr. Marvin CURTIS
66 Dean of Nursing/Health Profess .... Dr. Mario ORTIZ
08 Dean of Library Services .... Ms. Vicki BLOOM

*Indiana University Southeast (A)

4201 Grant Line Road, New Albany IN 47150-2158
County: Floyd FICE Identification: 001817
Unit ID: 151379
Telephone: (812) 941-2333 Carnegie Class: Master's L
FAX Number: (812) 941-2475 Calendar System: Semester
URL: www.ius.edu
Established: 1941 Annual Undergrad Tuition & Fees (In-State): $6,950
Enrollment: 6,442 Coed
Affiliation or Control: State IRS Status: 501(c)3
Highest Offering: Master's
Program: Liberal Arts And General; Teacher Preparatory; Professional
Accreditation: NH, BUS, NURSE, TED

02 Chancellor .... Dr. Ray WALLACE
05 Executive VC Academic Affairs .... Dr. Uric DUFRENE
10 VC Administration/Finance .... Mr. Dana C. WAVLE
84 VC Enrollment Mgmt/Student Affairs .... Mr. Jason L. MERIWETHER
30 VC Advancment .... Ms. Betty S. RUSSO
20 Assoc VC Academic Affairs .... Dr. Annette M. WYANDOTTE
88 Asst VC Academic Affairs .... Dr. Angela M. SALAS
32 Asst VC Retention/Student Services .... Ms. Amanda G. STONECIPHER
13 Chief Information Officer .... Ms. Elizabeth VAN GORDON
07 Director Admissions .... Mr. Chris CREWS
04 Admin Assistant to the Chancellor .... Ms. Sara R. JAMES
35 Dean for Student Life .... Mr. Seuth CHALEUNPHONH
06 Interim Registrar .... Ms. Mary Beth NANZ
37 Director Student Financial Aid .... Ms. Traci ARMES
08 Director Library Services .... Mr. C. Martin ROSEN
36 Interim Director Career Development .... Ms. Danielle LEFFLER
18 Director Physical Plant .... Mr. Robert C. POFF
14 Dir IT Communications & Support .... Mr. Nicholas T. RAY
41 Director Athletics .... Mr. Joseph M. GLOVER
72 Dir Purdue College of Technology .... Andrew B. TAKAMI
15 Director Human Resources .... Mr. Ray KLEIN
09 Int Dir Institutional Effectiveness .... Mr. Ronald E. SEVERTIS, JR.
19 Chief Safety & Security .... Mr. Charles EDELEN
38 Dir Personal Counseling .... Dr. Michael DAY
26 Dir of Mktg & Communications .... Mr. Steven KROLAK
97 Manager General Studies .... Ms. Saundra E. GORDON
79 Dean School Arts & Letters .... Dr. Samantha EARLEY
81 Dean School Natural Sciences .... Dr. Elaine HAUB
83 Dean School Social Sciences .... Dr. Joseph L. WERT
50 Dean School Business .... Dr. A. Jay WHITE
53 Dean School Education .... Dr. Doyin COKER-KOLO
66 Interim Dean School Nursing .... Dr. Donna J. BOWLES
46 Dean for Research .... Dr. Diane E. WILLE
28 Director Staff Equity & Diversity .... Ms. Darlene P. YOUNG
29 Interim Director Alumni Relations .... Mrs. Lynn L. PRINZ
88 Dir Advising Ctr Explrtry Students .... Ms. Rebecca TURNER
88 Director Academic Accting Services .... Ms. Melissa D. HILL
88 Director Student Accting Services .... Ms. Ashley M. MCKAY

*Indiana University-Purdue University Columbus (B)

4601 Central Avenue, Columbus IN 47203
Telephone: (812) 348-7271 Identification: 770185
Accreditation: &NH

† Branch campus of Indiana University-Purdue University Indianapolis, Indianapolis, IN.

Indiana Wesleyan University (C)

4201 S Washington Street, Marion IN 46953-4999
County: Grant FICE Identification: 001822
Unit ID: 151801
Telephone: (765) 674-6901 Carnegie Class: Master's L
FAX Number: (765) 677-2499 Calendar System: 4/1/4
URL: www.indwes.edu
Established: 1920 Annual Undergrad Tuition & Fees: $24,728
Enrollment: 14,941 Coed
Affiliation or Control: Wesleyan Church IRS Status: 501(c)3
Highest Offering: Doctorate
Program: Liberal Arts And General; Teacher Preparatory; Professional; Business Emphasis
Accreditation: NH, CAATE, CACREP, EXSC, MFCD, MUS, NURSE, SW, TED, THEOL

01 President .... Dr. David WRIGHT
88 CEO for Residential Education .... Dr. Keith NEWMAN
88 CEO for Non-Residential Education .... Mrs. Audrey HAHN
05 Exec VP for Academic Affairs .... Dr. Don SPROWL
28 VP for Multicultural Enrichment .... Ms. Diane MCDANIEL
10 Vice President Business Affs/CFO .... Mrs. Nancy SCHOONMAKER
88 VP Wesley Seminary .... Dr. Wayne SCHMIDT
20 VP for Academic Affairs/CAPS .... Dr. Brock REIMAN
30 VP for Advancement .... Dr. Brian GARDNER
26 VP Enroll Mgmt & Mktg/Residential .... Mrs. Janelle VERNON
84 VP Enroll Mgmt & Mktg/Non-Resident .... Mr. David ROSE
11 VP of Operations/Residential Campus .... Mr. John JONES
04 Sr Counsel to the President/Ombudsm .... Mrs. Karen ROORBACH
66 Dean of the School of Nursing .... Dr. Barbara IHRKE
58 Dean Graduate School .... Dr. Joanne BARNES
88 Dean of the Seminary .... Dr. David SMITH
76 Dean School of Health Sciences .... Dr. Scott MCPHEE
32 Int Vice Pres Student Development .... Mr. Andrew PARKER
37 Associate VP Financial Aid .... Mr. Thomas RATLIFF
08 Director Library Resources .... Mrs. Shelia CARLBLOM
08 Director Off-campus Library Svcs .... Mrs. Jule KIND
29 Director of Alumni .... Mr. Rick CARDER
07 Director Admissions/Residential Ed .... Mr. Adam FARMER
15 Exec Director Human Resources .... Mr. Mark PEDERSON
06 University Registrar .... Mrs. Kim NICHOLSON
21 Controller .... Mrs. Tiffany LEWIS
36 Exec Director Ctr for Life Calling .... Dr. Bill MILLARD
41 Athletic Director .... Mr. Mark DEMICHAEL
42 Dean of the Chapel .... Dr. Jim LO
44 Director Planned Giving .... Mr. Brian LEWIS
92 Exec Director of Honors College .... Mr. David RIGGS
09 Acting Dir Institutional Research .... Mr. Tony PARANDI
18 AVP Facilities Services .... Mr. Don ROWLEY
19 Director Campus Police .... Mr. Mario RANGEL
25 Director of Research Support .... Dr. Ken BIELEN

International Business College (D)

5699 Coventry Lane, Fort Wayne IN 46804-9990
County: Allen FICE Identification: 004579
Unit ID: 151458
Telephone: (260) 459-4500 Carnegie Class: Bac/Assoc
FAX Number: (260) 436-1896 Calendar System: Semester
URL: www.ibcfortwayne.edu
Established: 1889 Annual Undergrad Tuition & Fees: $13,880
Enrollment: 372 Coed
Affiliation or Control: Proprietary IRS Status: Proprietary
Highest Offering: Baccalaureate
Program: Occupational; 2-Year Principally Bachelor's Creditable
Accreditation: ACICS, MAC

01 President .... Mr. Steve KINZER
05 Director of Education .... Ms. Amee AUGENSTEIN
07 Director of Admissions .... Ms. Gena HOPKINS
32 Student Services Director .... Ms. Roxanna SHULL
36 Director of Placement .... Vacant
06 Registrar .... Ms. Jan WILCOXEN

International Business College (E)

7205 Shadeland Station, Indianapolis IN 46256-3997
Telephone: (317) 813-2300 Identification: 666929
Accreditation: ACICS, DA, MAC

† Branch campus of International Business College, Fort Wayne, IN.

ITT Technical Institute (F)

2810 Dupont Commerce Court, Fort Wayne IN 46825-2393
Telephone: (260) 497-6200 FICE Identification: 008329
Accreditation: ACICS

† Branch campus of ITT Technical Institute, Indianapolis, IN.

ITT Technical Institute (G)

9511 Angola Court, Indianapolis IN 46268-1119
County: Marion FICE Identification: 007329
Unit ID: 151519
Telephone: (317) 875-8640 Carnegie Class: Master's S
FAX Number: (317) 875-8641 Calendar System: Quarter
URL: www.itt-tech.edu
Established: 1956 Annual Undergrad Tuition & Fees: N/A
Enrollment: 3,486 Coed
Affiliation or Control: Proprietary IRS Status: Proprietary
Highest Offering: Master's
Program: Technical Emphasis
Accreditation: ACICS, CAHIIM

ITT Technical Institute (H)

2525 N Shadeland Avenue, Suite 103, Indianapolis IN 46219
Telephone: (317) 351-3800 Identification: 770651
Accreditation: ACICS

† Branch campus of ITT Technical Institute, Indianapolis, IN.

ITT Technical Institute (I)

8488 Georgia Street, Merrillville IN 46410
Telephone: (219) 738-6100 Identification: 770650
Accreditation: ACICS

† Branch campus of ITT Technical Institute, Indianapolis, IN.

ITT Technical Institute (J)

10999 Stahl Road, Newburgh IN 47630-7429
Telephone: (812) 858-1600 FICE Identification: 007327
Accreditation: ACICS

† Branch campus of ITT Technical Institute, Indianapolis, IN.

ITT Technical Institute (K)

17390 Dugdale Drive, Suite 100, South Bend IN 46635
Telephone: (574) 247-8300 Identification: 666700
Accreditation: ACICS

† Branch campus of ITT Technical Institute, Indianapolis, IN.

*Ivy Tech Community College of Indiana-Central Office (L)

50 W Fall Creek Parkway N Drive, Indianapolis IN 46208-5752
County: Marion FICE Identification: 008546
Unit ID: 363563
Telephone: (317) 921-4882 Carnegie Class: N/A
FAX Number: (317) 921-4753
URL: www.ivytech.edu

01 President .... Mr. Thomas J. SNYDER
05 Sr VP Academic Affairs/Provost .... Dr. Mary E. OSTRYE
102 Sr Vice Pres Ivy Tech Foundation .... Mr. John MURPHY
11 Exec Vice Pres/COO .... Mr. Jeff TERP
10 VP Finance/Treasurer/Gen Counsel .... Mr. Chris RUHL
32 Vice Pres Stdnt Affairs/Enrol Mgmt .... Dr. Benjamin YOUNG
26 Sr Vice Pres Mktg/Comm/Stdnt Exp .... Mr. Jeff FANTER
88 Vice Pres of Univ & Transfer Div .... Dr. Russell D. BAKER
86 Vice Pres Business/Public Svcs Div .... Dr. Steven TINCHER
18 AVP Facilities Inst Planning .... Ms. Amanda WILSON
36 AVP Stdnt Affairs/Career Placement .... Dr. John HOGAN
84 Vice Pres for Student Experience .... Ms. Anne P. VALENTINE
06 College Registrar .... Mrs. Ann YATER
37 Chief Fin Student Resources Ofcr .... Mr. Ben BURTON
15 Executive Director Human Resources .... Mrs. Julie LORTON-ROWLAND
09 Exec Dir Institutional Research .... Mrs. Jill KRAMER
21 Assistant Treasurer .... Mr. Mark A. HUSK
13 Chief Technology Officer .... Mrs. Anne BRINSON
07 Asst Vice President Admissions .... Ms. Seana MURPHY

*Ivy Tech Community College of Indiana-Central Indiana (M)

50 W Fall Creek Parkway North Drive, Indianapolis IN 46208-5752
County: Marion FICE Identification: 009917
Unit ID: 150987
Telephone: (317) 921-4882 Carnegie Class: Assoc/Pub-U-SC
FAX Number: (317) 921-4753 Calendar System: Semester
URL: www.ivytech.edu/indianapolis/
Established: 1966 Annual Undergrad Tuition & Fees (In-State): $4,115
Enrollment: 21,714 Coed
Affiliation or Control: State IRS Status: 501(c)3
Highest Offering: Associate Degree
Program: Occupational; 2-Year Principally Bachelor's Creditable
Accreditation: NH, ACBSP, ACFEI, ADNUR, ART, CAHIIM, COARC, CSHSE, FUSER, MAC, NAIT, PNUR, RAD, SURGT

02 Chancellor .... Dr. Kathleen F. LEE
05 VC of Academic Affairs .... Dr. Frank MOMAN
32 Vice Chancellor of Student Affairs .... Dr. Darrell CAIN
10 Executive Director of Finance .... Mr. Michael DAVIDSON
15 Exec Director of Human Resources .... Ms. Sara MCKEE
11 Exec Dir of Administrative Services .... Mr. James N. BARNEY
103 Exec Dir Workforce & Economic Devel .... Vacant
30 Exec Dir Institutional Advancement .... Mr. Thomas KILIAN
35 Asst Vice Chanc Student Affairs .... Mr. Jerry H. HARRELL
35 Asst Vice Chanc Student Affairs .... Dr. Tracy FUNK

84 Assoc Vice Pres Enrollment ... Ms. Anne P. VALENTIINE
37 Director of Financial Aid ... Vacant
06 Registrar ... Ms. Amanda OWEN
09 Director of Institutional Research ... Dr. Jeff CORNETT
36 Director of Career Services ... Ms. Rebecca PATTEN-LEMONS
96 Director of Purchasing ... Mr. Jerry L. KOENIG
20 Asst Vice Chanc Academic Affairs ... Mr. Gary PELLICO
26 Director Marketing/Communications ... Ms. Kelli FORD
46 Director of Resource Development ... Vacant

***Ivy Tech Community College of Indiana-Anderson** (A)
104 West 53rd Street, Anderson IN 46013-1502
Telephone: (800) 644-4882 Identification: 770239
Accreditation: &NH

† Branch campus of Ivy Tech Community College of Indiana-Central Office, Indianapolis, IN.

***Ivy Tech Community College of Indiana-Bloomington** (B)
200 N Daniels Way, Bloomington IN 47404-9772
Telephone: (812) 332-1559 FICE Identification: 035213
Accreditation: &NH, ACBSP, ACFEI, ADNUR, CAHIIM, COARC, CSHSE, EMT, NAIT, PNUR, RTT

† Branch campus of Ivy Tech Community College of Indiana-Central Office, Indianapolis, IN.

***Ivy Tech Community College of Indiana-Columbus** (C)
4475 Central Avenue, Columbus IN 47203-1868
Telephone: (812) 372-9925 FICE Identification: 010038
Accreditation: &NH, ART, ACBSP, ADNUR, CSHSE, DA, EMT, MAC, NAIT, PNUR, SURGT

† Branch campus of Ivy Tech Community College of Indiana-Central Office, Indianapolis, IN.

***Ivy Tech Community College of Indiana-East Central** (D)
4301 Cowan Road, Muncie IN 47302-9448
Telephone: (765) 289-2291 FICE Identification: 009924
Accreditation: &NH, ACBSP, ACFEI, ADNUR, COARC, CSHSE, DA, DH, MAC, NAIT, PNUR, PTAA, RAD, SURGT

† Branch campus of Ivy Tech Community College of Indiana-Central Office, Indianapolis, IN.

***Ivy Tech Community College of Indiana-East Chicago** (E)
410 East Columbus Drive, East Chicago IN 46312
Telephone: (219) 392-3600 Identification: 770240
Accreditation: &NH

† Branch campus of Ivy Tech Community College of Indiana-Central Office, Indianapolis, IN.

***Ivy Tech Community College of Indiana-Elkhart** (F)
22531 County Road 18, Goshen IN 46528
Telephone: (574) 830-0375 Identification: 770241
Accreditation: &NH

† Branch campus of Ivy Tech Community College of Indiana-Central Office, Indianapolis, IN.

***Ivy Tech Community College of Indiana-Kokomo** (G)
1815 E Morgan Street, Box 1373, Kokomo IN 46903-1373
Telephone: (765) 459-0561 FICE Identification: 010041
Accreditation: &NH, ACBSP, ADNUR, CSHSE, DA, EMT, MAC, NAIT, PNUR, SURGT

† Branch campus of Ivy Tech Community College of Indiana-Central Office, Indianapolis, IN.

***Ivy Tech Community College of Indiana-Lafayette** (H)
3101 S Creasy Lane, Box 6299, Lafayette IN 47903-6299
Telephone: (765) 269-5000 FICE Identification: 010039
Accreditation: &NH, ACBSP, ADNUR, CAHIIM, COARC, CSHSE, DA, MAC, NAIT, PNUR, SURGT

† Branch campus of Ivy Tech Community College of Indiana-Central Office, Indianapolis, IN.

***Ivy Tech Community College of Indiana-Lawrenceburg-Riverfront** (I)
50 Walnut Street, Lawrenceburg IN 47025
Telephone: (812) 537-4010 Identification: 770242
Accreditation: &NH, MAC

† Branch campus of Ivy Tech Community College of Indiana-Central Office, Indianapolis, IN.

***Ivy Tech Community College of Indiana-Logansport** (J)
1 Ivy Tech Way, Logansport IN 46947
Telephone: (866) 753-5102 Identification: 770243
Accreditation: &NH

† Branch campus of Ivy Tech Community College of Indiana-Central Office, Indianapolis, IN.

***Ivy Tech Community College of Indiana-Marion** (K)
261 S Commerce Drive, Marion IN 46953
Telephone: (800) 644-4882 Identification: 770244
Accreditation: &NH, MAC

† Branch campus of Ivy Tech Community College of Indiana-Central Office, Indianapolis, IN.

***Ivy Tech Community College of Indiana-Michigan City** (L)
3714 Franklin Drive, Michigan City IN 46360
Telephone: (219) 879-9137 Identification: 770245
Accreditation: &NH, ACFEI, MAC

† Branch campus of Ivy Tech Community College of Indiana-Central Office, Indianapolis, IN.

***Ivy Tech Community College of Indiana-North Central** (M)
220 Dean Johnson Boulevard, South Bend IN 46601-3415
Telephone: (574) 289-7001 FICE Identification: 008423
Accreditation: &NH, ART, ACBSP, ACFEI, ADNUR, COARC, CSHSE, DA, DH, EMT, MAC, MLTAD, NAIT, PNUR

† Branch campus of Ivy Tech Community College of Indiana-Central Office, Indianapolis, IN.

***Ivy Tech Community College of Indiana Northeast** (N)
3800 N Anthony Boulevard, Fort Wayne IN 46805-1489
Telephone: (260) 482-9171 FICE Identification: 009926
Accreditation: &NH, ACBSP, ACFEI, ADNUR, COARC, CSHSE, EMT, MAC, NAIT, PNUR

† Branch campus of Ivy Tech Community College of Indiana-Central Office, Indianapolis, IN.

***Ivy Tech Community College of Indiana-Northwest** (O)
1440 E 35th Avenue, Gary IN 46409-1499
Telephone: (219) 981-1111 FICE Identification: 010040
Accreditation: &NH, ACBSP, ADNUR, COARC, CSHSE, FUSER, MAC, NAIT, PNUR, PTAA, SURGT

† Branch campus of Ivy Tech Community College of Indiana-Central Office, Indianapolis, IN.

***Ivy Tech Community College of Indiana-Richmond** (P)
2357 Chester Boulevard, Richmond IN 47374-1298
Telephone: (765) 966-2656 FICE Identification: 010037
Accreditation: &NH, ACBSP, ADNUR, CSHSE, MAC, NAIT, PNUR

† Branch campus of Ivy Tech Community College of Indiana-Central Office, Indianapolis, IN.

***Ivy Tech Community College of Indiana-Southeast** (Q)
590 Ivy Tech Drive, Madison IN 47250-1883
Telephone: (812) 265-2580 FICE Identification: 009923
Accreditation: &NH, ACBSP, ADNUR, CSHSE, EMT, MAC, PNUR

† Branch campus of Ivy Tech Community College of Indiana-Central Office, Indianapolis, IN.

***Ivy Tech Community College of Indiana-Southern Indiana** (R)
8204 Highway 311, Sellersburg IN 47172-1897
Telephone: (812) 246-3301 FICE Identification: 010109
Accreditation: &NH, ACBSP, ADNUR, ART, COARC, CSHSE, MAC, MLTAD, NAIT, PNUR, PTAA

† Branch campus of Ivy Tech Community College of Indiana-Central Office, Indianapolis, IN.

***Ivy Tech Community College of Indiana-Southwest** (S)
3501 First Avenue, Evansville IN 47710-1881
Telephone: (812) 426-2865 FICE Identification: 009925
Accreditation: &NH, ACBSP, ADNUR, ART, CSHSE, EMT, MAC, NAIT, PNUR, SURGT

† Branch campus of Ivy Tech Community College of Indiana-Central Office, Indianapolis, IN.

***Ivy Tech Community College of Indiana-Valparaiso** (T)
3100 Ivy Tech Drive, Valparaiso IN 46383
Telephone: (219) 464-8514 Identification: 770246
Accreditation: &NH

† Branch campus of Ivy Tech Community College of Indiana-Central Office, Indianapolis, IN.

***Ivy Tech Community College of Indiana-Wabash** (U)
277 N Thorne Street, Wabash IN 46992
Telephone: (260) 563-8828 Identification: 770247
Accreditation: &NH

† Branch campus of Ivy Tech Community College of Indiana-Central Office, Indianapolis, IN.

***Ivy Tech Community College of Indiana-Wabash Valley** (V)
8000 S. Education Drive, Terre Haute IN 47802-4833
Telephone: (812) 299-1121 FICE Identification: 008547
Accreditation: &NH, ACBSP, ADNUR, ART, COARC, CSHSE, DMS, EMT, MAC, MLTAD, NAIT, PNUR, RAD, SURGT

† Branch campus of Ivy Tech Community College of Indiana-Central Office, Indianapolis, IN.

***Ivy Tech Community College of Indiana-Warsaw** (W)
2545 Silreus Crossing, Warsaw IN 46582
Telephone: (574) 267-5428 Identification: 770248
Accreditation: &NH

† Branch campus of Ivy Tech Community College of Indiana-Central Office, Indianapolis, IN.

Kaplan College (X)

7833 Indianapolis Boulevard, Hammond IN 46324-3347
County: Lake FICE Identification: 022018
Unit ID: 152415
Telephone: (219) 844-0100 Carnegie Class: Assoc/PrivFP
FAX Number: (219) 844-0105 Calendar System: Quarter
URL: www.getinfo.kaplancollege.com
Established: 1969 Annual Undergrad Tuition & Fees: $15,555
Enrollment: 299 Coed
Affiliation or Control: Proprietary IRS Status: Proprietary
Highest Offering: Associate Degree
Program: Occupational
Accreditation: ACICS

01 Campus President ... Mr. Chris ARTIM

Kaplan College (Y)
4200 South East Street, Indianapolis IN 46227
Telephone: (317) 782-0315 Identification: 770575
Accreditation: ACICS, MAAB

† Branch campus of Kaplan College, Hammond, IN.

Lincoln College of Technology (Z)

7225 Winton Drive, Building 128,
Indianapolis IN 46268-4198
County: Marion FICE Identification: 007938
Unit ID: 151661
Telephone: (317) 632-5553 Carnegie Class: Assoc/PrivFP
FAX Number: (317) 687-0475 Calendar System: Semester
URL: www.lincolntech.com
Established: 1962 Annual Undergrad Tuition & Fees: $30,000
Enrollment: 1,199 Coed
Affiliation or Control: Proprietary IRS Status: Proprietary
Highest Offering: Associate Degree
Program: Occupational; 2-Year Principally Bachelor's Creditable; Technical Emphasis
Accreditation: ACCSC

01 Campus President ... Todd CLARK
05 Vice President of Education ... Stephanie MILLER
11 Director Administrative Services ... Linda WILKINS
37 Director Student Financial Aid ... Sheila ANDREWS
07 Director of Admissions ... Melissa DURKIN

Manchester University (a)

604 E College Avenue, North Manchester IN 46962-1225
County: Wabash FICE Identification: 001820
Unit ID: 151777
Telephone: (260) 982-5000 Carnegie Class: Bac/Diverse
FAX Number: (260) 982-5043 Calendar System: 4/1/4
URL: www.manchester.edu
Established: 1889 Annual Undergrad Tuition & Fees: $28,840
Enrollment: 1,479 Coed
Affiliation or Control: Church Of The Brethren IRS Status: 501(c)3
Highest Offering: Doctorate
Program: Liberal Arts And General; Teacher Preparatory; Professional

Accreditation: NH, CAATE, @PHAR, SW, TED

01 President .... Dr. David F. MCFADDEN
05 Vice President Academic Affairs .... Dr. Tim MCELWEE
10 Vice Pres Financial Affairs/Treas .... Mr. Jack A. GOCHENAUR
30 Vice President College Advancement .... Mrs. Melanie HARMON
84 VP Enrollment & Marketing .... Mr. Scott OCHANDER
84 Asst VP for Enrollment/Marketing .... Mr. Adam HOHMAN
20 Associate Academic Dean .... Vacant
29 Exec Director of Alumni Relations .... Ms. Jennifer SHEPHERD
08 Director of the Library .... Ms. Jill LICHTSINN
06 Registrar .... Ms. Lila D. HAMMER
24 Director of Audio-Visual Services .... Mr. Stanley G. PITTMAN
38 Director of Counseling .... Ms. Danette NORMAN TILL
36 Director of Career Services .... Vacant
39 Director of Residence Life .... Mr. Allen J. MACHIELSON
42 Campus Pastor .... Mr. Walt WILTSCHEK
41 Director of Athletics .... Mr. Rick ESPESET
13 Director of Mgmt Info Services .... Mr. Michael CASE
19 Director of Security .... Mr. Harold NAPIER
44 Director of the Manchester Fund .... Ms. Janeen W. KOOI
37 Director of Student Financial Aid .... Ms. Sherri L. SHOCKEY
85 Director of Multicultural Affairs .... Mr. Michael G. DIXON
26 Director of Public Relations .... Ms. Anne GREGORY
18 Director of Physical Plant .... Mr. Christopher W. GARBER
23 Director of Health Services .... Ms. Anna C. RICHISON
21 Senior Accountant .... Mr. Michael J. LECKRONE
32 Director Student Affairs .... Ms. Shanon L. FAWBUSH
96 Director of Purchasing .... Mr. Quentin J. MOUDY
40 Bookstore Manager .... Ms. Heather K. GOCHENAUR

Marian University (A)

3200 Cold Spring Road, Indianapolis IN 46222-1997
County: Marion FICE Identification: 001821
Unit ID: 151786
Telephone: (317) 955-6000 Carnegie Class: Bac/Diverse
FAX Number: (317) 955-6448 Calendar System: Semester
URL: www.marian.edu
Established: 1851 Annual Undergrad Tuition & Fees: $30,500
Enrollment: 2,771 Coed
Affiliation or Control: Roman Catholic IRS Status: 501(c)3
Highest Offering: Doctorate
Program: Liberal Arts And General; Teacher Preparatory; Professional
Accreditation: NH, IACBE, NURSE, @OSTEO, TED

01 President .... Mr. Daniel J. ELSENER
05 Executive VP and Provost .... Dr. Thomas ENNEKING
45 SVP Planning/Mission/Identity .... Mr. Dan CONWAY
10 SVP for Personnel/Fin/Facil/Tech .... Mr. Greg GINDER
26 VP for Marketing Communications .... Mr. Mark APPLE
30 SVP for Institutional Advancement .... Dr. Kenith BRITT
32 VP Student Life and Success .... Ms. Ruth RODGERS
63 VP and Dean College of Osteopathic .... Dr. Paul EVANS
84 VP Enrollment Management .... Dr. Paul (PJ) WOOLSTON
37 Dean Financial Aid/Enroll Mgmt .... Mr. Chad BIR
20 Dean for Academic Affairs .... Mr. William HARTING
18 Director of Projects & Procurement .... Ms. Audra BLASDEL
41 Director of Athletics .... Mr. Steve DOWNING
29 Director of Alumni Relations .... Ms. Nicholle ELLIS
06 Registrar .... Ms. Jennifer SCHWARTZ
08 Director of Library Services .... Vacant
35 Director of Student Act/Orientation .... Mr. Ben BRAKSICK
19 Director of Safety & Police Svcs .... Mr. Scott RALPH
13 Chief Information Office .... Vacant
27 Manager of Event Marketing and Spon .... Ms. Maggie KUCIK
36 Executive Director The Exchange .... Ms. Ellen WHITT
42 Director of Campus Ministry .... Mr. Adam SETMEYER
38 Director Academic Support Services .... Mrs. Marjorie BATIC
07 AVP for Enrollment Management .... Vacant
55 Exec Director Adult Programs .... Ms. Amy BENNETT
38 Director of Counseling Services .... Dr. Marla SMITH
88 Director of Advancement Information .... Vacant
23 Director of Health & Wellness Svcs .... Ms. Jan CARNAGHI
09 Director of Institutional Research .... Mr. William HARTING
15 Director of Human Resources .... Ms. Anita HERBERTZ
21 Director of Business Services .... Ms. Alice SHELTON
40 Bookstore Manager .... Ms. Allison BONEZ
04 Executive Asst to President .... Ms. Cyndi KAMP
11 VP of Administration/General Counse ... Ms. Deborah LAWRENCE

Martin University (B)

2171 Avondale Place, Indianapolis IN 46218
County: Marion FICE Identification: 021408
Unit ID: 151810
Telephone: (317) 543-3235 Carnegie Class: Bac/A&S
FAX Number: (317) 543-3257 Calendar System: Semester
URL: www.martin.edu
Established: 1977 Annual Undergrad Tuition & Fees: $12,536
Enrollment: 402 Coed
Affiliation or Control: Independent Non-Profit IRS Status: 501(c)3
Highest Offering: Master's
Program: Liberal Arts And General
Accreditation: #NH

01 President .... Dr. Eugene WHITE
05 VP Academic Affs/Student Svc .... Dr. Charlesetta SMITH STALEY
09 VP of Institutional Effectiveness .... Dr. Brian STEUERWALD
10 VP Fiscal Affairs .... Mr. Michael MOOS
37 Director Financial Aid .... Ms. Virginia GOODWIN
32 Director Student Services .... Ms. Dana L. MUDROW
26 Dir of Univ Rels/Communications .... Ms. Jennifer MCCLOUD

21 Bursar .... Ms. Angela HARRINGTON-MARTIN
06 Registrar .... Ms. Dana DODSON

MedTech College (C)

7230 Engle Road, Suite 200, Fort Wayne IN 46804
Telephone: (260) 436-3272 Identification: 666677
Accreditation: ACICS, MAC, MLTAD

† Branch campus of MedTech College, Indianapolis, IN.

MedTech College (D)

1500 American Way, Greenwood IN 46143
Telephone: (317) 534-0322 Identification: 666678
Accreditation: ACICS, MAC, MLTAD

† Branch campus of MedTech College, Indianapolis, IN.

MedTech College (E)

6612 East 75th Street Suite 300, Indianapolis IN 46250
County: Marion FICE Identification: 007362
Unit ID: 448415
Telephone: (317) 845-0100 Carnegie Class: Assoc/PrivFP
FAX Number: (317) 845-1800 Calendar System: Quarter
URL: www.medtech.edu
Established: 2004 Annual Undergrad Tuition & Fees: $44,100
Enrollment: 529 Coed
Affiliation or Control: Proprietary IRS Status: Proprietary
Highest Offering: Associate Degree
Program: Occupational
Accreditation: ACICS, #MAC, MLTAD, PNUR

01 Interim Campus President .... Mr. Bill WINKOWSKI

Mid-America College of Funeral Service (F)

3111 Hamburg Pike, Jeffersonville IN 47130-9630
County: Clark FICE Identification: 010618
Unit ID: 151962
Telephone: (812) 288-8878 Carnegie Class: Spec/Other
FAX Number: (812) 288-5942 Calendar System: Quarter
URL: www.mid-america.edu
Established: 1905 Annual Undergrad Tuition & Fees: $11,100
Enrollment: 71 Coed
Affiliation or Control: Independent Non-Profit IRS Status: 501(c)3
Highest Offering: Associate Degree
Program: Occupational
Accreditation: FUSER

01 President .... Ms. Lauren M. BUDROW
32 Dean of Students .... Ms. Alisa PERKINS
06 Registrar/Director of Admissions .... Ms. Angela PERSINGER
29 Director Alumni Relations .... Vacant
37 Director Student Financial Aid .... Mr. Richard D. NELSON

Mid-America Reformed Seminary (G)

229 Seminary Drive, Dyer IN 46311-1069
County: Lake FICE Identification: 039893
Unit ID: 373030
Telephone: (219) 864-2400 Carnegie Class: Not Classified
FAX Number: (219) 864-2410 Calendar System: Semester
URL: www.midamerica.edu
Established: 1981 Annual Graduate Tuition & Fees: $8,940
Enrollment: 35 Coed
Affiliation or Control: Independent Non-Profit IRS Status: 501(c)3
Highest Offering: Master's; No Undergraduates
Program: Religious Emphasis
Accreditation: THEOL, TRACS

01 President .... Dr. Cornelius VENEMA
32 Dean of Students .... Rev. Alan STRANGE
30 Director of Development .... Mr. Keith LEMAHIEU
96 Office Manager/Director Purchasing .... Ms. Florence KOOIMAN
36 Director of Apprenticeship Program .... Rev. Mark VANDERHART
07 Director of Admissions .... Rev. Jeffrey DEBOER
09 Director Institutional Assessment .... Rev. Marcus MININGER

National American University-Indianapolis (H)

3600 Woodview Terrace, Suite 200, Indianapolis IN 46268
Telephone: (800) 609-1430 Identification: 770393
Accreditation: &NH

† Branch campus of National American University, Rapid City, SD.

Oakland City University (I)

138 N Lucretia Street, Oakland City IN 47660-1099
County: Gibson FICE Identification: 001824
Unit ID: 152099
Telephone: (812) 749-4781 Carnegie Class: Master's M
FAX Number: (812) 749-1233 Calendar System: Semester
URL: www.oak.edu
Established: 1885 Annual Undergrad Tuition & Fees: $22,800
Enrollment: 2,101 Coed
Affiliation or Control: Baptist IRS Status: 501(c)3
Highest Offering: Doctorate
Program: Occupational; 2-Year Principally Bachelor's Creditable; Liberal Arts And General; Teacher Preparatory; Professional; Business Emphasis
Accreditation: NH, IACBE, TED, THEOL

01 President .... Dr. Ray G. BARBER
11 Vice Pres Administration & Finance .... Dr. Robert E. YEAGER
05 Provost .... Dr. Jeffrey MCNABB
10 Chief Financial Officer .... Mrs. Elizabeth BARBER
30 Director of Advancement .... Mr. Brian BAKER
73 Vice Provost/Dean Religious Studies .... Dr. Daniel DUNIVAN
50 Dean School of Business .... Dr. John SUTTON
53 Dean School of Education .... Dr. Steven DEGEORGE
49 Dean School of Arts & Sciences .... Dr. Claudine CUTCHIN
108 Director of Assessment .... Mrs. Katheryn WEBB
32 Director of Campus Life .... Dr. James PRATT
106 Coordinator of Online Learning .... Dr. Mark SIMPSON
07 Director of Admissions .... Mr. Caleb FENDRICH
37 Director of Financial Aid .... Mrs. Cassie SCRAPER
56 Coordinator Adult Extend Learning .... Dr. Cathy ROBB
22 Compliance Officer .... Ms. Patricia ENDICOTT
88 Director of Correctional Education .... Mr. Theodore PEARSON
06 Registrar .... Ms. Betty BURNS
08 Director of Library .... Mrs. Denise PINNICK
26 Director of Mktg/Athletic Director .... Dr. Mike SANDIFAR
42 Campus Minister .... Rev. Marc GRIMES
18 Director of Maintenance .... Mr. Nelson ROWLAND
88 Payroll Coordinator .... Mrs. Cheryl YATES
15 Human Resources Coordinator .... Mrs. Melissa MARTIN
13 Director of Information Technology .... Mr. Clint WOOLSEY
19 Chief of Security .... Mr. Alec HENSLEY
29 Director of Alumni Affairs .... Ms. Susan SULLIVAN
36 Director of Directions Program .... Mrs. Charity JULIAN
35 Director Student Support Services .... Mrs. Tamara MILEY
21 Assistant Chief Financial Officer .... Mrs. Elizabeth CARLISLE
88 Supervisor of Collections .... Mrs. Anita MISKELL
88 Director of Housekeeping .... Mrs. Dorothy GRAPER

Ottawa University Jeffersonville (J)

287 Quarter Master Court, Jeffersonville IN 47130-3669
Telephone: (785) 242-5200 Identification: 666088
Accreditation: &NH

† Regional accreditation is carried under the parent institution in Ottawa, KS.

Purdue University Main Campus (K)

610 Purdue Mall, West Lafayette IN 47907-2040
County: Tippecanoe FICE Identification: 001825
Unit ID: 243780
Telephone: (765) 494-4600 Carnegie Class: RU/VH
FAX Number: N/A Calendar System: Semester
URL: www.purdue.edu
Established: 1869 Annual Undergrad Tuition & Fees (In-State): $10,002
Enrollment: 38,770 Coed
Affiliation or Control: State IRS Status: 501(c)3
Highest Offering: Doctorate
Program: Liberal Arts And General; Teacher Preparatory; Professional
Accreditation: NH, AAB, ART, AUD, BUS, CAATE, CACREP, CIDA, CLPSY, CONST, COPSY, CS, DIETC, DIETD, ENG, ENGR, ENGT, IPSY, LSAR, NAIT, NURSE, PHAR, SP, TED, THEA, VET

01 President .... Mr. Mitchell E. DANIELS, JR.
10 Exec Vice President & Treasurer .... Mr. William E. SULLIVAN
05 Provost/Exec VP for Acad Affairs .... Dr. Debasish DUTTA
21 Sr VP Business Svcs/Asst Treas .... Mr. James S. ALMOND
13 Vice Pres Information Technology .... Dr. William G. MCCARTNEY
15 Vice President Human Resources .... Mr. Trent KLINGERMAN
26 Vice President for Public Affairs .... Ms. Julie K. GRIFFITH
20 Int Vice Prov Student Acad Affairs .... Dr. Frank J. DOOLEY
20 Interim VP Faculty Affairs .... Dr. Alyssa PANITCH
08 Dean of Libraries .... Dr. James L. MULLINS
29 Interim Pr & CEO Alumni Association .... Mr. Jim KARL
07 Dean Admiss/VP Enroll Mgmt .... Dr. Pamela T. HORNE
37 Director Financial Aid .... Mr. Ted E. MALONE

Purdue University Calumet (L)

2200 169th Street, Hammond IN 46323-2094
County: Lake FICE Identification: 001827
Unit ID: 152248
Telephone: (219) 989-2204 Carnegie Class: Master's L
FAX Number: (219) 989-2581 Calendar System: Semester
URL: www.purduecal.edu
Established: 1946 Annual Undergrad Tuition & Fees (In-State): $7,359
Enrollment: 9,501 Coed
Affiliation or Control: State IRS Status: 501(c)3
Highest Offering: Doctorate
Program: Liberal Arts And General; Teacher Preparatory; Professional
Accreditation: NH, BUS, CACREP, CEA, CS, ENG, ENGR, ENGT, IACBE, MFCD, NAIT, NUR, TED

01 Chancellor .... Dr. Thomas L. KEON
05 Int Vice Chanc Acad Affs & Provost .... Dr. Karen SCHMID
10 Vice Chanc Finance & Admin .... Mr. Steve TURNER
30 Vice Chanc for Inst Advancement .... Dr. Regina D. BIDDINGS-MURO
13 Vice Chanc Info Services .... Dr. Sarah HOWARD
32 Vice Chanc Enroll Mgmt & Stdnt Affs .... Dr. Carmen PANLILIO
46 Interim Assoc VC Rsrch & Grad Stds .... Dr. Chenn ZHOU
26 Assoc Vice Chanc Marketing .... Ms. Kris FALZONE
09 Asst VC Academic Quality & Outreach .... Ms. M. Beth PELLICCIOTTI

11 Asst Vice Chancellor for Admin Svcs ... Mr. Michael KULL
27 Asst Vice Chanc Advance/Univ Rels ... Mr. Wes K. LUKOSHUS
35 Assoc Vice Chanc Stdnt Affs/EOP ... Mr. Roy HAMILTON
21 Asst VC Business Svcs/Comptroller ... Mr. Phillip JANKOWSKI
15 Asst Vice Chanc Human Resources ... Ms. Susan MILLLER
49 Dean College of Lib Arts/Social Sci ... Dr. Ronald CORTHELL
54 Dean College of Engr/Math/Sci ... Dr. William R. LAW
72 Dean College of Technology ... Dr. Niaz LATIF
50 Dean College of Business ... Dr. Jane MUTCHLER
66 Interim Dean College of Nursing ... Dr. Lisa HOPP
53 Interim Dean College of Education ... Dr. John ROWAN
06 Registrar ... Ms. Cheryl ARROYO
21 Asst Comptroller/Budget/Fiscal Plng .. Ms. Donna ADELSPERGER
37 Director Student Financial Services ... Ms. Mary Ann BISHEL
41 Director of Athletics ... Mr. Richard J. COSTELLO
38 Director Counseling Center ... Dr. Kenneth JACKSON
08 Dir Research/Learning & Res Svcs ... Ms. Tammy GUERRERO
29 Dir Alumni Affairs & Advancement ... Ms. Jennifer CAMPBELL
19 University Police ... Chief Anthony MARTIN, SR.
85 Asst Vice International Affairs ... Dr. Dallas KENNY
96 Dir of Procurement/General Services ... Ms. Phillip BROWN
39 Director of Housing Residental Educ ... Ms. Scott IVERSON
92 Dean Honors Program ... Dr. Rowan JOHN
84 Assoc Dean Enroll Mgmt & Grad Pgms ... Dr. Lori FELDMAN
04 Executive Asst to Chancellor ... Ms. Daphne D. ROBINSON
100 Chief of Staff ... Mr. Robert E. ENNIS
102 Dir Advance Resource/Donor Steward ... Ms. Mary Jane DOPP
104 Education Abroad Coordinator ... Ms. Judy MOORE
105 Dir Tech Infrastructure Services ... Mr. Mahendra VERMA
25 Chief Contracts/Grants Admin ... Dr. Chenn ZHOU
28 Director Ofc Equity & Diversity ... Ms. Linda B. KNOX
36 Director Career Dev & Services ... Ms. Natalie CONNORS
90 Dir Acdemic Research & Computng ... Ms. Heather ZAMOJSKI
07 Executive Director of Admissions ... Mr. Eric FELVER

Purdue University North Central Campus (A)

1401 S US 421, Westville IN 46391-9542
County: La Porte FICE Identification: 001826
Unit ID: 152266
Telephone: (219) 785-5200 Carnegie Class: Bac/Diverse
FAX Number: (219) 785-5355 Calendar System: Semester
URL: www.pnc.edu
Established: 1943 Annual Undergrad Tuition & Fees (In-State): $7,381
Enrollment: 6,177 Coed
Affiliation or Control: State IRS Status: 501(c)3
Highest Offering: Master's
Program: Liberal Arts And General; Teacher Preparatory; Professional
Accreditation: NH, ACBSP, ENG, ENGR, ENGT, NUR, TED

01 Chancellor ... Dr. James B. DWORKIN
04 Executive Asst to the Chancellor ... Mrs. Debra A. NIELSEN
30 Director of Advancement ... Mrs. Marie C. FOSTER
05 Vice Chanc Academic Affairs ... Dr. Karen L. SCHMID
20 Int Assoc Vice Chanc Acad Affairs ... Dr. Michael LYNN
10 Vice Chanc for Finance & Admin ... Mr. Stephen R. TURNER
84 VC for Enroll Mgmt & Student Svcs .. Mr. Paul M. MCGUINNESS
32 Asst VC & Dean of Students ... Mr. John WEBER
26 Asst VC of Mktg & Campus Relations ... Ms. Judy N. JACOBI
10 Assoc VC Business Svcs/Budget ... Mr. Phillip E. JANKOWSKI
15 Assoc Vice Chanc Human Resources ... Mrs. Susan T. MILLER
50 Dean College of Business ... Dr. Cynthia ROBERTS
72 Dean College of Engr & Tech ... Dr. Thomas F. BRADY
49 Dean College of Liberal Arts ... Dr. S. Rex MORROW
88 Dean College of Science ... Dr. K. Chris HOLFORD
66 Chair Nursing Department ... Dr. Diane SPOLJORIC
83 Chair Social Sciences Department ... Dr. Michael LYNN
81 Int Chair Biology/Chem Department ... Dr. Robin SCRIBAILO
81 Chair Math/Physics/Statistics Dept ... Dr. Purna DAS
53 Acting Chair Education Department ... Dr. David FEIKES
88 Chair English/Foreign Language Dept ... Dr. Jerry HOLT
60 Chair Communication Dept ... Dr. V. Scott SMITHSON
54 Chair Engr Tech Dept ... Dr. Mark L. SMITH
88 Interim Chr Business & Leadershp ... Dr. Carolyn ROPER
22 Asst Dir EEO & Training ... Ms. Laura ODOM
21 Bursar ... Mrs. Beverly J. PULLER
21 Accounting Manager ... Mr. Brock MARTIN
96 Dir Auxiliary Svcs & Resource Plng ... Mrs. Elizabeth DEPEW
08 Librarian ... Ms. Tammy GUERRERO
07 Director Enroll & Outreach ... Mrs. Janice WHISLER
06 Associate Registrar ... Mrs. Jennifer WOLSZCZAK
36 Director of Career Services ... Ms. Natalie CONNORS
37 Dir of Financial Aid & Compliance ... Mr. Brad REMMENGA
38 Director Student Counseling ... Ms. Diana MAROVICH
19 Director of Public Safety ... Mr. Brian MILLER
27 Director Media & Comm Services ... Mrs. Carol CONNELLY
41 Director Student Athletics ... Mr. Thomas ALBANO
35 Director Student Activities ... Mrs. Amanda SCHACHT
18 Director Facilities Management ... Mr. L. James SALLEE
09 Institutional Research Specialist ... Mr. Joseph P. WARD
88 Coord Special Events & Marketing ... Ms. Liz BERNEL
29 Coord Alumni & Annual Giving ... Ms. Erika JONES
58 Coord Graduate & Extended Learning .. Mrs. Cassandra BOEHLKE
88 Director of Food Service ... Mr. Keith PEFFERS
40 Bookstore Manager ... Mr. Isaiah HENDERSON
88 Coord Service Learning ... Ms. Laura WEAVER
88 Dir School Partnerships ... Mrs. Susan WILSON
88 Dir Student Success Center ... Dr. Jane BROOKS
88 Asst Dean of Enroll Access ... Ms. Mary A. BISHEL
13 Chief Information Officer ... Mrs. Robin BROWN
88 Wellness Coordinator ... Ms. Kendra GARDIN
88 Dir of Academic Advising ... Ms. Kathleen JOHNSON

Radiological Technologies University-VT (B)

100 E. Wayne St., Ste 140, South Bend IN 46601
County: St. Joseph Identification: 667156
Telephone: (574) 232-2408 Carnegie Class: Not Classified
FAX Number: (574) 232-2200 Calendar System: Semester
URL: www.rtuvt.com
Established: 2009 Annual Graduate Tuition & Fees: $25,150
Enrollment: N/A Coed
Affiliation or Control: Proprietary IRS Status: Proprietary
Highest Offering: Master's; No Undergraduates
Program: Professional
Accreditation: ACICS

01 President ... Brent D. MURPHY
11 Dir of Administrative Services ... Betsy DATEMA

Rose-Hulman Institute of Technology (C)

5500 Wabash Avenue, Terre Haute IN 47803-3920
County: Vigo FICE Identification: 001830
Unit ID: 152318
Telephone: (812) 877-1511 Carnegie Class: Spec/Engg
FAX Number: (812) 877-9925 Calendar System: Quarter
URL: www.rose-hulman.edu
Established: 1874 Annual Undergrad Tuition & Fees: $41,865
Enrollment: 2,388 Coed
Affiliation or Control: Independent Non-Profit IRS Status: 501(c)3
Highest Offering: Master's
Program: Professional; Technical Emphasis
Accreditation: NH, CS, ENG

01 President ... Dr. James C. CONWELL
10 Senior VP/Chief Admin Officer ... Mr. Robert A. COONS
05 Int Vice Pres Academic Affairs ... Dr. Richard E. STAMPER
30 Int VP Inst Advancement ... Mr. J Douglas SMITH
32 Vice President Student Affairs ... Mr. Erik Z. HAYES
26 VP Communications/Marketing ... Mr. James A. GOECKER
21 Assoc VP for Finance/Controller ... Mr. Matthew D. DAVIS
84 Vice President Enrollment Mgmt ... Mr. James A. GOECKER
03 Vice Pres for Rose-Hulman Ventures ... Dr. Elizabeth M. HAGERMAN
88 Dean of Innovation/Engagement ... Dr. William KLINE
20 Interim Dean of Faculty ... Dr. Jameel AHMED
20 Associate Dean of Faculty ... Dr. Azad SIAHMAKOUN
88 Assoc Dean Learning/Technology ... Dr. Kay C. DEE
104 Dir of Study Abroad/Intl Exchanges ... Mr. Christopher DIXON
13 Vice Pres Info Tech and CIO ... Dr. Wayne DENNISON
18 Sr Director Facilities Operations ... Mr. Michael A. TAYLOR
36 Dir Career Services/Employer Rels ... Mr. Kevin L. HEWERDINE
07 Dean of Admissions ... Ms. Lisa M. NORTON
29 Executive Director Alumni Affairs ... Mr. Jim BERTOLI
45 Exec Dir Inst Rsrch/Plng/Assessment ... Dr. Julia M. WILLIAMS
15 Director of Human Resources ... Ms. Kimberly D. MILLER
37 Director of Financial Aid ... Ms. Melinda L. MIDDLETON
41 Director of Athletics ... Mr. Jeffrey L. JENKINS
28 Director Center for Diversity ... Dr. Luanne TILSTRA
44 Director of Planned Giving ... Mr. Chris AIMONE
44 Annual Fund Coordinator ... Ms. Jennifer KENZOR
06 Registrar ... Ms. Jan LIND
08 Library Director ... Ms. Bernadette EWEN
19 Director of Public Safety ... Mr. John S. WOLFE
40 Bookstore Manager ... Ms. Sheryl E. FULK
85 Dir Intl Stdnt Svcs/Disability Svcs ... Ms. Karen A. DEGRANGE
04 Exec Assistant to the President ... Ms. Kerry SCHAFFER
25 Dir Fin Svcs/Sponsored Programs ... Ms. Linda L. PRICE
109 Director Administrative Services ... Mr. Bryan T. BROMSTRUP
09 Director of Institutional Research ... Dr. Timothy CHOW
102 Director of Corporate Relations ... Mr. Brandon M. ZOLLNER
39 Associate Dean of Student Affairs ... Mr. Erik Z. HAYES
35 Dean of Student Affairs ... Mr. Thomas D. MILLER
35 Dean of Student Services ... Ms. Kristen J. LOYD
101 Dir Donor Relations/Exec Asst Board ... Ms. Tammy SHAFFER
105 Sr Director Interactive Marketing ... Ms. Julie T. DAVIS
24 Instructional Technology Manager ... Ms. Janie SZABO
24 Emerging Digital Technologies Mgr ... Mr. Alan WARD
38 Director of Counseling Services ... Dr. Michael LATTA

St. Anthony School of Echocardiography (D)

1201 S. Main Street, Crown Point IN 46307
County: Lake Identification: 667119
Telephone: (219) 757-6132 Carnegie Class: Not Classified
FAX Number: (219) 681-6725 Calendar System: Semester
URL: www.franciscanalliance.org/hospitals/crownpoint
Established: 2004 Annual Undergrad Tuition & Fees: $7,000
Enrollment: 10 Coed
Affiliation or Control: Independent Non-Profit IRS Status: 501(c)3
Highest Offering: Associate Degree
Program: Occupational; 2-Year Principally Bachelor's Creditable; Technical Emphasis
Accreditation: DMS

01 Co-Program Director ... Lori HULT
01 Co-Program Director ... Karin KOLISZ

Saint Joseph's College (E)

PO Box 870, US Highway 231, Rensselaer IN 47978-0870
County: Jasper FICE Identification: 001833
Unit ID: 152363
Telephone: (219) 866-6000 Carnegie Class: Bac/Diverse
FAX Number: (219) 866-6100 Calendar System: Semester
URL: www.saintjoe.edu
Established: 1889 Annual Undergrad Tuition & Fees: $28,920
Enrollment: 1,013 Coed
Affiliation or Control: Roman Catholic IRS Status: 501(c)3
Highest Offering: Master's
Program: Liberal Arts And General; Teacher Preparatory; Professional
Accreditation: NH, IACBE, NURSE, TED

01 President ... Dr. Robert A. PASTOOR
04 Admin Asst to the President ... Mrs. Sheila K. HANEWICH
05 Int Vice Pres for Academic Affairs ... Dr. Chad A. PULVER
10 Int Vice President Business Affairs ... Mr. Spencer CONROY
30 Vice Pres Inst Advancement/Mrktng ... Mr. Gregory ROBERTS
44 Asst VP Institutional Advancement ... Mrs. Elizabeth GRAF
32 VP Student Development ... Dr. Leslie FRERE
06 Registrar ... Mrs. Maureen HEALEY
07 Director of Admissions ... Mr. Michael RAMIAN
08 Librarian ... Mrs. Jody TAYLOR-WATKINS
13 Director of Computer Center ... Mr. Jon MESSMAN
38 Director of Counseling Services ... Ms. Laura WAGNER
18 Chief Facilities/Physical Plant ... Mr. Randal FLINN
15 Director Human Resources ... Ms. Nancy STUDER
26 Director of Integrated Marketing ... Vacant
29 Director Alumni Relations ... Mrs. Kendra ILLINGWORTH
37 Director Student Financial Services ... Mrs. Debra SIZEMORE
28 Director of Diversity ... Mr. Ernest WATSON
36 Director Career Development ... Vacant
41 Athletic Director ... Mr. William MASSOELS
40 Director Bookstore ... Mrs. Rhonda ELIJAH
42 Chaplain/Director Campus Ministry ... Vacant

Saint Mary-of-the-Woods College (F)

1 St Mary of Woods College,
St Mary of the Woods IN 47876-1099
County: Vigo FICE Identification: 001835
Unit ID: 152381
Telephone: (812) 535-5151 Carnegie Class: Bac/Diverse
FAX Number: (812) 535-5231 Calendar System: Semester
URL: www.smwc.edu
Established: 1840 Annual Undergrad Tuition & Fees: $28,932
Enrollment: 932 Coed
Affiliation or Control: Roman Catholic IRS Status: 501(c)3
Highest Offering: Master's
Program: Liberal Arts And General
Accreditation: NH, MUS, TED

01 President ... Dr. Dottie KING
30 VP for Advancement ... Ms. Karen DYER
10 CFO/Controller ... Mr. Cory CAMPBELL
05 Vice President for Academic Affairs ... Dr. Janet CLARK
11 Vice President for Operations ... Ms. Vicki KOSOWSKY
84 Vice Pres for Enrollment Management ... Mr. Brennan RANDOLPH
06 Registrar ... Ms. Deanna TROTZKE
08 Director of the Library ... Ms. Judy TRIBBLE
29 Senior Dir Advancement/Alumni Rels ... Ms. Susan TURNER
26 Executive Dir of College Relations ... Ms. Dee REED
07 Executive Director of Admissions ... Vacant
106 Director Woods Online Program ... Ms. Gwen HAGEMEYER
13 Exec Dir Information Technology ... Vacant
36 Director of Career Development ... Ms. Susan GRESHAM
15 Director Human Resources ... Ms. Diana WARREN
32 Director Campus Life ... Mr. Jeffrey MALLOY
37 Director Financial Aid ... Ms. Darla HOPPER
44 Dir Major and Planned Gifts ... Ms. April SIMMA
64 Dir Grad Pgm Music Therapy ... Ms. Tracy RICHARDSON
88 Dir Grad Pgm Art Therapy ... Ms. Kathy GOTSHALL
88 Dir Grad Pgm Leadership Development ... Ms. Susan DECKER
09 Director of Institutional Research ... Mr. Mike KING

Saint Mary's College (G)

Notre Dame IN 46556
County: Saint Joseph FICE Identification: 001836
Unit ID: 152390
Telephone: (574) 284-4000 Carnegie Class: Bac/A&S
FAX Number: (574) 284-4716 Calendar System: Semester
URL: www.saintmarys.edu
Established: 1844 Annual Undergrad Tuition & Fees: $37,400
Enrollment: 1,519 Female
Affiliation or Control: Roman Catholic IRS Status: 501(c)3
Highest Offering: Doctorate
Program: Liberal Arts And General; Teacher Preparatory; Professional
Accreditation: NH, ART, MUS, NURSE, @SP, SW, TED

01 President ... Dr. Carol Ann MOONEY
04 Special Asst to the President ... Ms. Susan C. DAMPEER
05 Provost/Sr VP Academic Affairs ... Dr. Patricia A. FLEMING
26 Vice President College Relations ... Ms. Shari M. RODRIGUEZ
32 Vice President for Student Affairs ... Ms. Karen A. JOHNSON
10 Vice Pres Finance & Administration ... Ms. Susan BOLT
84 Vice Pres for Enrollment Management ... Ms. Mona BOWE
88 Vice President for Mission ... Ms. Judith FEAN
89 Associate Dean for Advising ... Ms. Susan VANEK

06 Registrar Mr. Todd NORRIS
07 Director of Admission Ms. Sarah DVORAK
08 Director of Library Ms. Janet S. FORE
09 Director of Institutional Research Mr. Daniel FLOWERS
29 Director of Alumnae Relations Ms. Kara O'LEARY
37 Director of Financial Aid Ms. Kathleen M. BROWN
27 Director of Media Relations Ms. Gwen O'BRIEN
38 Director of Women's Health Ms. Elizabeth FOURMAN
13 Chief Information Officer Mr. Michael BOEHM
15 Director of Human Resources Mr. Richard NUGENT
19 Director of Safety & Security Mr. David GARIEPY
40 Manager Bookstore Vacant
41 Director of Athletics Ms. Julie SCHROEDER-BIEK
42 Director of Campus Ministry Vacant
18 Director of Facilities Mr. Benjamin BOWMAN
96 Director of Purchasing Ms. Kathleen CARLSON
88 Director of Student Involvement Ms. Brittany HOUSE
85 Director of Multicultural Program Ms. Gloria JENKINS

Saint Meinrad School of Theology (A)

200 Hill Drive, St. Meinrad IN 47577-1030
County: Spencer FICE Identification: 007276
Unit ID: 152451
Telephone: (812) 357-6611 Carnegie Class: Spec/Faith
FAX Number: (812) 357-6964 Calendar System: Semester
URL: www.saintmeinrad.edu
Established: 1861 Annual Graduate Tuition & Fees: $24,900
Enrollment: 224 Coed
Affiliation or Control: Roman Catholic IRS Status: 501(c)3
Highest Offering: Master's; No Undergraduates
Program: Professional; Religious Emphasis
Accreditation: NH, THEOL

01 President & Rector Rev. Denis ROBINSON, OSB
03 Vice Rector Rev. Tobias COLGAN, OSB
05 Academic Dean Dr. Robert ALVIS
84 Director of Enrollment Rev. Luke WAUGH, OSB
42 Director of Spiritual Formation Rev. Peter MARSHALL
20 Director of Lay Degree Programs Sr. Jeana VISEL, OSB
30 Vice President of Development Mr. Michael ZIEMIANSKI
10 Business Manager & Treasurer Mrs. Lisa CASTLEBURY
08 Library Director Dr. Daniel KOLB
06 Registrar Mrs. Donna BALBACH
88 Dir Inst for Priests & Presbyterate Vacant
21 Director of Budget Mrs. Pam DOWLAND
37 Director of Student Financial Aid Mrs. Ruth KRESS
26 Director of Communications Mrs. Mary Jeanne SCHUMACHER
29 Director of Alumni Relations Mr. Christian MOCEK
38 Director of Student Counseling Ctr Sr. Diane PHARO, SCN
09 Director of Institutional Research Rev. Bede CISCO, OSB
23 Director of Health Services Ms. Ann ROHLEDER
108 Director of Assessment Mr. John SCHLACHTER
04 Administrative Asst to President Mrs. Karen SCHERZER
13 Chief Info Technology Officer (CIO) Mr. Aaron STETTER
18 Chief Facilities/Physical Plant Mr. Andy HAGEDORN
44 Director Annual or Planned Giving Mr. Darren SROUFE

Taylor University (B)

West 236 Reade Avenue, Upland IN 46989-1001
County: Grant FICE Identification: 001838
Unit ID: 152530
Telephone: (765) 998-2751 Carnegie Class: Bac/Diverse
FAX Number: (765) 998-4910 Calendar System: 4/1/4
URL: www.taylor.edu
Established: 1846 Annual Undergrad Tuition & Fees: $30,270
Enrollment: 2,104 Coed
Affiliation or Control: Independent Non-Profit IRS Status: 501(c)3
Highest Offering: Master's
Program: Liberal Arts And General; Teacher Preparatory; Fine Arts Emphasis
Accreditation: NH, CEA, ENG, MUS, SW, TED

01 President Dr. Eugene B. HABECKER
05 Provost Dr. Jeffrey MOSHIER
11 VP Business Administration Mr. Ronald SUTHERLAND
30 VP University Advancement Dr. Ben SELLS
32 VP Student Development Dr. Skip TRUDEAU
84 VP Enroll Mgmt & Marketing Mr. Stephen MORTLAND
10 VP Finance & CFO Mr. Stephen OLSON
20 Vice Provost Dr. Jeff GROELING
49 Dean Sch Hum/Arts & Biblical Stds Dr. Michael HAMMOND
83 Dean Sch of Soc Sci/Educ & Bus Dr. Connie LIGHTFOOT
81 Dean Sch Natural & Applied Sciences Dr. William TOLL
104 Dean International Programs Dr. Charles BRAINER
13 Chief Information Officer Mr. Rob LINEHAN
41 Director of Athletics Vacant
20 Dean Faculty Development/Dir BCTLE Dr. Faye CHECHOWICH
26 Assoc VP for University Relations Ms. Joyce WOOD
44 Senior Director for Campaigns Mr. David RITCHIE
44 Assoc VP for Major & Planned Gifts Mr. Mike FALDER
29 Exec Dir for Alumni Relations Ms. Dara JOHNSON
37 Assoc Dean Enroll Mgmt/Dir Fin Aid Mr. Timothy NACE
08 University Librarian Mr. Daniel BOWELL
35 Dean of Students Mr. Steve MORLEY
39 Dir Residence Life Mr. Scott BARRETT
06 Registrar Ms. Janet ROGERS
106 Director of Online Learning Ms. Carrie MEYER
42 Campus Pastor Mr. Jon CAVANAGH
15 Asst Director of Human Resources Ms. April EVANS
07 Director Admissions Ms. Amy BARNETT
18 Director of Physical Plant Mr. Greg ELEY
38 Director of Counseling Center Mr. Robert NEIDECK
19 Chief of Police/Taylor Police Mr. Jeff WALLACE
09 Director IR/Assoc Registrar Dr. Edwin WELCH
21 Controller Mr. David LLOYD
108 Director Assessment/Quality Improv Dr. Kim CASE
88 Payroll Manager Ms. Toni NEWLIN
88 University Bursar Ms. Cathy MOORMAN
24 Director of Tech & Learning Ctr Dr. Ken BOYD
103 Dn Exper Lrng/Dir Calling & Career Dr. Drew MOSER
105 Assoc Dir of Enterprise Systems Mr. Corey COOPER

TCM International Institute (C)

6337 Hollister Drive, Indianapolis IN 46224
County: Marion Identification: 666333
Telephone: (317) 299-0333 Carnegie Class: Not Classified
FAX Number: (317) 290-8607 Calendar System: Semester
URL: www.tcmi.org
Established: 1991 Annual Graduate Tuition & Fees: N/A
Enrollment: N/A Coed
Affiliation or Control: Independent Non-Profit IRS Status: 501(c)3
Highest Offering: Master's; No Undergraduates
Program: Religious Emphasis
Accreditation: NH

01 President Dr. Tony TWIST
05 Academic Affairs Manager Ms. Victoria BOJONCA
06 Registrar Vacant
10 Director of Finance Ms. Julie RICE

Trine University (D)

1 University Avenue, Angola IN 46703-1764
County: Steuben FICE Identification: 001839
Unit ID: 152567
Telephone: (260) 665-4100 Carnegie Class: Bac/Diverse
FAX Number: (260) 665-4292 Calendar System: Semester
URL: www.trine.edu
Established: 1884 Annual Undergrad Tuition & Fees: $29,900
Enrollment: 3,700 Coed
Affiliation or Control: Independent Non-Profit IRS Status: 501(c)3
Highest Offering: Doctorate
Program: Teacher Preparatory; Professional; Business Emphasis
Accreditation: NH, ACBSP, ENG, @PTA, TED

01 President Dr. Earl D. BROOKS, II
03 Senior Vice President Mr. Mike BOCK
05 Vice President for Academic Affairs Dr. Allen HERSEL
10 Vice President Finance Ms. Jody GREER
30 Vice Pres for Alumni & Development Mr. Kent D. STUCKY
84 Vice Pres Enrollment Management Dr. Stuart JONES
32 Vice President for Student Services Mr. Randy WHITE
51 Asst Vice Pres for Adult Learning Dr. Jean DELLER
49 Dean Jannen School of Arts & Sci Mr. Craig LAKER
107 Dean of Professional Studies Ms. Mersiha ALIC
15 Human Resources Ms. Jamie NORTON
41 Athletic Director Mr. Matt LAND
06 Registrar Ms. Debra F. HELMSING
27 Dir Integrated & Brand Marketing Ms. Jill BOGGS
04 Assistant to the President Ms. Gretchen MILLER
37 Director Student Financial Planning Ms. Kim BENNETT
08 Director of the Library Ms. Kristina BREWER
36 Int Director of Placement/Coop Educ Ms. Linda BATEMAN
09 Director Inst Planning/Analysis Ms. Christina ZUMBRUN

Trine University-Fort Wayne Regional Campus (E)

9910 Dupont Circle Dr East, Ste 130,
Fort Wayne IN 46825
Telephone: (260) 483-4949 Identification: 770105
Accreditation: &NH

† Branch campus of Trine University, Angola, IN.

Trine University-South Bend Regional Campus (F)

4101 Edison Lakes Parkway, Ste 250,
Mishawaka IN 46545
Telephone: (574) 243-0500 Identification: 770106
Accreditation: &NH

† Branch campus of Trine University, Angola, IN.

Union Bible College (G)

PO Box 900, Westfield IN 46074
County: Hamilton Identification: 667253
Telephone: (317) 896-9324 Carnegie Class: Not Classified
FAX Number: (317) 867-0784 Calendar System: Semester
URL: www.ubca.org
Established: 1911 Annual Undergrad Tuition & Fees: $4,550
Enrollment: 61 Coed
Affiliation or Control: Interdenominational IRS Status: 501(c)3
Highest Offering: Baccalaureate
Program: Religious Emphasis
Accreditation: @BI

01 President C. Adam BUCKLER
05 Academic Dean John WHITAKER
10 Finance Director Merton RUNDELL, III
32 Dean of Student Affairs Joe CAREY
09 Director of Institutional Research Isabel RUNDELL
06 Registrar Lisa BURKET

University of Evansville (H)

1800 Lincoln Avenue, Evansville IN 47722-1586
County: Vanderburgh FICE Identification: 001795
Unit ID: 150534
Telephone: (812) 488-2000 Carnegie Class: Master's S
FAX Number: (812) 488-2320 Calendar System: Semester
URL: www.evansville.edu
Established: 1854 Annual Undergrad Tuition & Fees: $32,473
Enrollment: 2,591 Coed
Affiliation or Control: United Methodist IRS Status: 501(c)3
Highest Offering: Doctorate
Program: Liberal Arts And General; Teacher Preparatory; Professional
Accreditation: NH, BUS, CAATE, CS, ENG, MUS, NUR, PTA, PTAA, TED

01 President Dr. Thomas A. KAZEE
05 Sr Vice President Academic Affairs Dr. Michael CULLEN
30 VP Development Ms. Abigail WERLING
10 Vice President Fiscal Affairs/Admin Mr. Jeffery M. WOLF
32 VP Student Affairs/Dean of Students Dr. Dana CLAYTON
84 Vice President Enrollment Services Dr. Shane DAVIDSON
26 VP Marketing and Communication Mr. Donald JONES
25 Assoc VP Academic Affs Dr. Jennifer L. GRABAN
35 Asst VP Student Affs/Dir Res Life Mr. Michael A. TESSIER
21 Asst VP for Fiscal Affairs Ms. Donna O. TEAGUE
13 Dir of Technology Services Mr. Michael SMITH
49 Dean of Arts & Sciences Dr. Ray LUTGRING
50 Dean of Business Administration Dr. Greg RAWSKI
53 Assoc Dean of Educ/Health Science Ms. Mary KESSLER
54 Dean Engineering/Computer Science Dr. Phillip M. GERHART
51 Director of Adult Education Ms. Kristie BYRNS
85 Exec Dir International Programs Dr. Wesley MILNER
41 Director of Athletics Mr. Mark SPENCER
88 Dir of Content Development Ms. Amanda CAMPBELL
09 Dir Institutional Effectiveness Mr. Chul LEE
06 University Registrar Ms. Jennifer BRIGGS
08 University Librarian Mr. Steven A. MUSSETT
42 University Chaplain Rev. Tammy GIESELMAN
11 Director of Administrative Services Mr. Mark J. LOGEL
29 Director of Alumni/Parent Relations Ms. Sylvia Y. DEVAULT
36 Director of Career Svcs/Placement Mr. C. Gene WELLS
38 Director of Counseling/Health Educ Ms. Sylvia T. BUCK
37 Director of Financial Aid Ms. Cathleen WRIGHT
15 Director of Human Resources Mr. Keith GEHLHAUSEN
18 Dir of Facilities Mgmt & Planning Mr. Chad MILLER
19 Director of Safety & Security Mr. Harold P. MATTHEWS
104 Assoc Director of Study Abroad Ms. Barbara PIERONI
40 Director of Bookstore Mr. Douglas GUSTWILLER
28 Director of Diversity Ms. LaNeeca WILLIAMS
44 Director of Annual Giving Mr. Scott A. GILREATH
88 Director of Academic Advising Ms. Deborah A. KASSENBROCK
37 Director of Student Engagement Mr. Geoffrey M. EDWARDS
07 Dean of Admissions Mr. Scott HENNE
04 Assistant to the President Ms. Patricia A. LIPPERT
101 Assistant Secretary of the Board Ms. Rebecca SIMPSON

University of Indianapolis (I)

1400 E Hanna Avenue, Indianapolis IN 46227-3697
County: Marion FICE Identification: 001804
Unit ID: 151263
Telephone: (317) 788-3368 Carnegie Class: Master's L
FAX Number: (317) 788-3300 Calendar System: Semester
URL: www.uindy.edu
Established: 1902 Annual Undergrad Tuition & Fees: $25,910
Enrollment: 5,540 Coed
Affiliation or Control: United Methodist IRS Status: 501(c)3
Highest Offering: Doctorate
Program: Occupational; Liberal Arts And General; Teacher Preparatory; Professional; Business Emphasis
Accreditation: NH, ACBSP, ADNUR, ART, CAATE, CLPSY, EXSC, MIDWF, MUS, NURSE, OT, PTA, PTAA, SW, TED

01 President Dr. Robert L. MANUEL
05 Exec VP Academic Affairs/Provost Dr. Deborah Ware BALOGH
84 Exec VP for Campus Affs/Enroll Svcs Mr. Mark T. WEIGAND
10 VP of Business & Finance/Treasurer Mr. Michael L. HOLSTEIN
26 VP Communications & Marketing Dr. Jeanette DEDIEMAR
30 Vice President for Univ Advancement Mr. Christopher H. MOLLOY
31 Assoc VP of Community Relations Dr. David W. WANTZ
41 VP for Intercollegiate Athletics Dr. Sue C. WILLEY
42 Dean Ecumenical and Interfaith Pgm Dr. Michael G. CARTWRIGHT
43 Vice President & General Counsel Ms. Samantha KARN
32 VP for Stdnt/Campus Affs/Dn of Std Ms. Kory M. VITANGELI
100 Special Asst to the President Ms. Lara G. MANN
04 Executive Administrative Asst Ms. Angela PRESNELL
36 Assoc VP of Professional Edge Mr. Corey L. WILSON
09 Asst VP of Inst Planning & Rsrch Dr. Patrick ALLES
35 Assistant Dean of Students Joseph THOMAS
06 Registrar Ms. Kristine L. DOZIER
13 Associate VP Information Systems Mr. Steven R. HERRIFORD
49 Dean College of Arts & Sciences Dr. Jennifer A. DRAKE
50 Dean School of Business Dr. Lawrence BELCHER
53 Dean School of Education Dr. Kathryn A. MORAN

66 Dean School of Nursing ..... Dr. Anne C. THOMAS
76 Dean College of Health Sciences ..... Dr. Stephanie KELLY
51 Dean School of Adult Learning ..... Dr. Judy APPLE VANALSTINE
55 Dean Psychological Sciences ..... Dr. Anita J. THOMAS
20 Assoc Provost for Academic Systems ..... Dr. Mary Beth BAGG
20 Int Assoc Prov Rsrch/Grad/Acad Ptnr ..... Ms. Ellen MILLER
108 Assoc VP for Accreditation ..... Dr. Mary C. MOORE
07 Associate VP for Admissions ..... Mr. Ronald W. WILKS
08 Library Director ..... Mr. Matthew SHAW
15 Director Human Resources ..... Mrs. Chris RAISOVICH
26 Director of Marketing ..... Mr. Joe P. SOLARI
37 Assoc VP or Financial Aid ..... Mrs. Linda B. HANDY
58 Director Graduate Business Pgms ..... Mr. Stephen A. TOKAR
18 Executive Director Physical Plant ..... Mrs. Pamela L. FOX
19 Director Safety & Police Services ..... Mr. David K. SELBY
31 Director of Service Learning ..... Dr. Marianna K. FOULKROD
42 Co-Chaplain ..... Rev. L. Lang BROWNLEE
42 Co-Chaplain/Dir Lantz Center ..... Rev. Jeremiah GIBBS
29 Assoc VP Alumni Engagement ..... Mr. Andy M. KOCHER
85 Director International Division ..... Ms. Marilyn O. CHASE
24 Asst VP of Information Systems ..... Mr. Robert A. JONES
38 Director Counseling Center ..... Dr. Kelly M. MILLER
40 Bookstore Manager ..... Vacant
96 Procurement & Ancillary Services ..... Ms. Stacie L. NEUHAUS
45 Director of Facilities & Planning ..... Ms. Andrea NEWSOM

University of Notre Dame (A)

400 Main Building, Notre Dame IN 46556
County: Saint Joseph FICE Identification: 001840
Unit ID: 152080
Telephone: (574) 631-5000 Carnegie Class: RU/VH
FAX Number: (574) 631-6700 Calendar System: Semester
URL: www.nd.edu
Established: 1842 Annual Undergrad Tuition & Fees: $47,929
Enrollment: 12,179 Coed
Affiliation or Control: Roman Catholic IRS Status: 501(c)3
Highest Offering: Doctorate
Program: Liberal Arts And General; Professional; Business Emphasis
Accreditation: NH, ART, BUS, BUSA, CS, ENG, IPSY, LAW, THEOL

01 President ..... Rev. John I. JENKINS, CSC
05 Provost ..... Dr. Thomas G. BURISH
03 Executive Vice President ..... Dr. John F. AFFLECK-GRAVES
20 Vice Pres/Sr Associate Provost ..... Dr. Christine M. MAZIAR
20 Vice Pres/Associate Provost ..... Dr. Daniel J. MYERS
89 VP/Assoc Prov/Dean First Year Stdts ..... Dr. Hugh R. PAGE, JR.
82 VP/Provost Internationalization ..... Dr. Nicholas ENTRIKIN
32 Vice President for Student Affairs ..... Ms. Erin HOFFMANN HARDING
10 Vice President for Finance ..... Mr. John A. SEJDINAJ
46 Vice President for Research ..... Dr. Robert J. BERNHARD
43 Vice President & General Counsel ..... Ms. Marianne CORR
88 Vice Pres/Chief Investment Ofcr ..... Mr. Scott C. MALPASS
41 Vice Pres & Director of Athletics ..... Mr. John 'Jack' B. SWARBRICK, JR.
15 Vice Pres Human Resources ..... Mr. Robert K. MCQUADE
26 Vice President University Relations ..... Mr. Louis M. NANNI
13 VP & Chief Information Officer ..... Mr. Ronald D. KRAEMER
88 VP Mission Engagmnt/Church Affairs ..... Rev. William M. LIES, CSC
58 VP/Assoc Prov/Dean Graduate Sch ..... Dr. Laura CARLSON
100 Chief of Staff ..... Ms. Ann M. FIRTH
28 Chief Diversity Officer ..... Mr. Eric LOVE
84 Assoc VP Undergraduate Enrollment ..... Mr. Donald C. BISHOP
18 Assoc VP Facilities & Design ..... Mr. Douglas K. MARSH
06 Registrar ..... Mr. Charles T. HURLEY
96 Director Procurement ..... Mr. Vaibhav AGARWAL
50 Dean of College of Business ..... Dr. Roger D. HUANG
61 Dean of Law School ..... Prof. Nell J. NEWTON
54 Dean College of Engineering ..... Dr. Peter K. KILPATRICK
49 Dean of Arts & Letters ..... Dr. John T. MCGREEVY
81 Dean of Science ..... Dr. Gregory P. CRAWFORD
48 Dean of Architecture ..... Dr. Michael N. LYKOUDIS
88 Dean First Year of Studies ..... Dr. Hugh R. PAGE
29 Exec Director Alumni Assoc ..... Ms. Dolly DUFFY
08 Dir of University Libraries ..... Ms. Diane PARR WALKER
27 Chief Communications Executive ..... Mr. Paul BROWNE
42 Director of Campus Ministry ..... Rev. Peter M. MCCORMICK, CSC
37 Dir of Student Financial Aid ..... Ms. Mary B. NUCCIARONE
36 Director of Career Center ..... Mr. Lee J. SVETE
38 Director of Counseling Center ..... Dr. Susan C. STEIBE-PASALICH
45 Assoc VP Strategic Planning ..... Mr. David C. BAILEY
19 Director of Security/Police ..... Mr. Phillip A. JOHNSON
07 Director of Admissions ..... Mr. Robert MUNDY
101 Secretary of the Institution/Board ..... Ms. Demetra C. SCHOENIG
09 Director of Institutional Research ..... Ms. Eva NANCE
102 Dir Foundation/Corporate Relations ..... Mr. Rudy REYES
104 Director Study Abroad ..... Ms. Kathleen OPEL
39 Director Student Housing ..... Ms. Karen M. KENNEDY

University of Phoenix Indianapolis Campus (B)

7999 Knue Road, Indianapolis IN 46250-1932
Telephone: (317) 585-8610 Identification: 770206
Accreditation: &NH, ACBSP

† No longer accepting campus-based students.

University of Saint Francis (C)

2701 Spring Street, Fort Wayne IN 46808-3994
County: Allen FICE Identification: 001832
Unit ID: 152336
Telephone: (260) 399-7700 Carnegie Class: Master's S
FAX Number: N/A Calendar System: Semester
URL: www.sf.edu
Established: 1890 Annual Undergrad Tuition & Fees: $27,220
Enrollment: 2,308 Coed
Affiliation or Control: Roman Catholic IRS Status: 501(c)3
Highest Offering: Master's
Program: Occupational; 2-Year Principally Bachelor's Creditable; Liberal Arts And General; Teacher Preparatory; Professional
Accreditation: NH, ACBSP, ADNUR, ARCPA, ART, @DIETC, NURSE, PTAA, RAD, SURGT, SW, TED

01 President ..... Sr. M. Elise KRISS, OSF
05 Vice President Academic Affairs ..... Dr. J. Andrew PRALL
11 Vice President Administration ..... Mrs. Teresa A. SORDELET
30 Vice Pres Institutional Advancement ..... Dr. Matthew J. SMITH
10 Vice President Finance & Operations ..... Mr. Richard A. BIENZ
106 Assoc VP Academic Affairs ..... Dr. Joseph M. FRIONA
84 Assoc VP Enrollment Management ..... Mr. Jean Paul SPAGNOLO
45 Assoc VP Inst Research/Planning ..... Dr. Stephanie J. OETTING
26 Assoc Vice President Marketing ..... Mrs. Trois K. HART
88 Assistant VP Mission Integration ..... Sr. M. Anita HOLZMER, OSF
50 Dean Keith Busse School of Business ..... Mr. Robert W. LEE
57 Dean School of Creative Arts ..... Mr. Rick E. CARTWRIGHT
17 Dean School of Health Sciences ..... Dr. Mindy J. YODER
49 Dean School Liberal Arts & Sciences ..... Dr. Lance D. RICHEY
12 Dean Crown Point Site ..... Dr. Marsha M. KING
32 Dean of Students ..... Mr. Donald B. APPIARIUS
35 Associate Dean of Students ..... Mrs. Elizabeth A. GROMAN
21 Controller ..... Mr. Craig M. TEETSEL
06 Registrar ..... Mr. Francis P. CONNOR
29 Exec Dir Alumni & Career Outreach ..... Mr. Jason S. LIPSCOMB
07 Executive Dir Enrollment Services ..... Mrs. Jamie M. MCGRATH
08 Exec Dir Information/Instruc Svcs ..... Mrs. Karla K. ALEXANDER
53 Chair Department of Education ..... Dr. Daniel J. TORLONE
88 Dir Adult/Online Enrollment Svcs ..... Mrs. Michelle L. KUHLHORST
44 Dir Annual Fund ..... Mrs. Alexandra ELLIS KREAGER
41 Dir Athletics ..... Mr. Michael H. MCCAFFREY
42 Director Campus Ministry ..... Mr. Scott R. OPPERMAN
42 Chaplain ..... Fr. David L. MEINZEN
102 Dir Corp/Found Relations and Grants ..... Mrs. Lynnette M. MCKENNA FRAZIER
44 Director Development ..... Mr. Matthew C. ROWAN
15 Dir Employer Relations ..... Mrs. Natalie M. WAGONER
88 Dir Environ Health/Safety/Risk Mgt ..... Mr. Randy D. TROY
37 Director Financial Aid ..... Mrs. Michelle L. NISUN
88 Dir Health Science Sim Lab ..... Dr. Dawn M. MABRY
88 Dir Hlth Sci Strategic Initiatives ..... Dr. Lorene R. ARNOLD
92 Dir Honors Program ..... Dr. Kenneth A. BUGAJSKI
16 Dir Human Resources & Org Develop ..... Ms. Jennifer M. FAWBUSH
16 Assistant Director Human Resources ..... Mr. Andy MCKEE
108 Dir Inst Effectiveness/Accredit ..... Vacant
105 Dir Marketing & Creative Services ..... Mrs. Carla S. PYLE
28 Dir Retention/Diversity Programming ..... Mr. Garien L. HUDSON
88 Dir Service & Social Action ..... Mrs. Katrina P. BOEDEKER
88 Dir Sports Information ..... Mr. William J. SCOTT
88 Dir Student Academic Services ..... Mrs. Tricia J. VANDERLEE BUGAJSKI
91 Dir Tech Network & Information Mgmt ..... Mr. Mark ROBBINS
14 Dir Tech User Support Services ..... Mr. A. Drew REPP
13 Senior Tech Help Desk Analyst ..... Mr. George R. IJAMES
19 Supervisor Campus Safety/Security ..... Mr. Richard E. ROBBINS
18 Supervisor Maintenance/Grounds ..... Mr. Rex A. BERCOT
09 Research/Assessment Analyst ..... Mrs. Kim E. DIETRICH
04 Admin Liaison Office of Pres ..... Miss Vicki L. JACOBS, OFS
88 Mgr & Exec Chef AVI Food Service ..... Mr. Brian D. SMITH
40 Mgr Barnes & Noble Campus Shoppe ..... Mrs. Robin HUFFMAN

University of Southern Indiana (D)

8600 University Boulevard, Evansville IN 47712-3596
County: Vanderburgh FICE Identification: 001808
Unit ID: 151306
Telephone: (812) 464-8600 Carnegie Class: Master's L
FAX Number: (812) 464-1960 Calendar System: Semester
URL: www.usi.edu
Established: 1965 Annual Undergrad Tuition & Fees (In-State): $6,837
Enrollment: 9,364 Coed
Affiliation or Control: State IRS Status: 501(c)3
Highest Offering: Doctorate
Program: Liberal Arts And General; Teacher Preparatory; Professional
Accreditation: NH, ART, BUS, BUSA, COARC, DA, DH, DIETD, DMS, ENG, JOUR, NURSE, OT, OTA, RAD, SW, TED

01 President ..... Dr. Linda L M. BENNETT
100 Exec Assistant to the President ..... Ms. Miekka M. COX
05 Provost ..... Dr. Ronald S. ROCHON
10 Vice President Business Affairs ..... Mr. Steven J. BRIDGES
86 Vice Pres Govt and Univ Relations ..... Ms. Cynthia S. BRINKER
26 Asst VP Marketing/Communications ..... Ms. Kindra STRUPP
56 Assoc Provost Outreach Engagement ..... Dr. Mark C. BERNHARD
20 Asst Provost for Academic Affairs ..... Dr. Shelly B. BLUNT
32 Assoc Provost for Student Affairs ..... Dr. Marcia K. KIESSLING
21 Assoc Vice Pres Business Affairs ..... Ms. Mary A. HUPFER
09 Exec Director Plng/Research/Assess ..... Dr. Katherine A. DRAUGHON
58 Director of Graduate Studies ..... Dr. Mayola ROWSER
06 Registrar ..... Ms. Sandy K. FRANK
07 Interim Director of Admission ..... Mr. Mark A. RUSK
08 Director of Library Svcs ..... Ms. Marna M. HOSTETLER
30 Director of Development/USI Fndtn ..... Mr. David A. BOWER
92 Director Honors Program ..... Dr. Antonia D. BAMBINA
38 Director of Counseling ..... Dr. B. Thomas LONGWELL
29 Director of Alumni Affairs ..... Mrs. Janet L. JOHNSON
37 Director of Student Financial Asst ..... Ms. Mary J. HARPER
15 Director of Human Resources ..... Ms. Donna J. EVINGER
36 Director Career Svcs & Internships ..... Mr. Philip L. PARKER
35 Dean of Students ..... Dr. Bryan RUSH
85 Director of Intl Programs & Svcs ..... Mrs. Heidi GREGORI-GAHAN
28 Director Multicultural Center ..... Ms. Pamela F. HOPSON
13 Exec Dir of Information Technology ..... Mr. Richard TOENISKOETTER
90 Academic Services Coordinator ..... Mr. Juzar AHMED
18 Director of Facilities Operations ..... Mr. James E. WOLFE
96 Director Procurement Services ..... Mr. Daniel R. MARTENS
27 Director of Univ Communication ..... Mr. John A. FARLESS
19 Director of Public Safety ..... Mr. Stephen WOODALL
39 Director of Residence Life ..... Vacant
40 Campus Store Manager ..... Mr. Michael J. GOELZHAUSER
41 Athletic Director ..... Mr. Jon Mark HALL
50 Dean Romain College of Business ..... Dr. Mohammed KHAYUM
49 Dean College of Liberal Arts ..... Mr. Michael K. AAKHUS
66 Dean College Nursing/Health Profess ..... Dr. Ann H. WHITE
81 Dean College of Science/Engineering ..... Dr. Scott A. GORDON
51 Exec Dir Continuing Education ..... Ms. Linda L. CLEEK
106 Asst Provost for Distance Learning ..... Ms. Megan W. LINOS

Valparaiso University (E)

1700 Chapel Drive, Valparaiso IN 46383-9978
County: Porter FICE Identification: 001842
Unit ID: 152600
Telephone: (219) 464-5000 Carnegie Class: Master's L
FAX Number: (219) 464-5381 Calendar System: Semester
URL: valpo.edu
Established: 1859 Annual Undergrad Tuition & Fees: $36,160
Enrollment: 4,520 Coed
Affiliation or Control: Lutheran IRS Status: 501(c)3
Highest Offering: Doctorate
Program: Liberal Arts And General; Teacher Preparatory; Professional
Accreditation: NH, BUS, CACREP, ENG, LAW, MUS, NURSE, SW, TED

01 President ..... Dr. Mark A. HECKLER
05 Provost/Exec VP for Acad Affs ..... Dr. Mark BIERMANN
20 Assoc Provost for Intl Affairs ..... Dr. Jaishankar RAMAN
32 VP for Student Affairs ..... Dr. Bonnie L. HUNTER
10 VP for Finance & Administration ..... Mr. John PALMUCCI
84 VP for Enrollment Mgt & Mktg ..... Mr. Michael JOSEPH
58 Asc Provost/Dean Grad Sch/Cont Ed ..... Dr. Jennifer ZIEGLER
30 VP for Advancement ..... Ms. Lisa HOLLANDER
43 VP University Counsel ..... Mr. Darron C. FARHA
11 VP for Administration & Finance ..... Ms. Susan SCROGGINS
92 Dean of Christ College ..... Dr. Peter KANELOS
49 Dean College Arts & Sciences ..... Dr. Jon T. KILPINEN
61 Dean School of Law ..... Dr. Andrea LYON
54 Dean College of Engineering ..... Dr. Eric JOHNSON
50 Dean College of Business Admin ..... Dr. James BRODZINSKI
66 Dean College of Nursing ..... Dr. Janet M. BROWN
08 Dean Library Services ..... Dr. Bradford L. EDEN
35 Dean of Students ..... Dr. Timothy S. JENKINS
84 AVP Enrollment Management ..... Mr. David FEVIG
42 Exec Dir of Campus Ministries ..... Rev. Brian T. JOHNSON
06 Registrar ..... Ms. Stephanie MARTIN
19 Chief University Police ..... Ms. Rebecca A. WALKOWIAK
39 Asst Dean Students/Residential Life ..... Mr. Ryan BLEVINS
104 Director of Study Abroad Programs ..... Ms. Julie A. MADDOX
85 Assoc Dir of International Program ..... Ms. Janice LIN
29 Director Alumni Relations ..... Ms. Linda ROETTGER
15 Dir Human Resource Services ..... Mr. Scott HARRISON
88 Exec Dir for Capital Planning ..... Mr. Fred W. PLANT
36 Director Career Center ..... Mr. Tom CATH
38 Director of Counseling Services ..... Dr. Stewart E. COOPER
41 Director Athletics ..... Mr. Mark LABARBERA
20 Asst Provost for Faculty Affairs ..... Dr. Rick GILLMAN
21 Controller ..... Ms. Diana BLANEY
28 Director of Multicultural Programs ..... Mr. Byron MARTIN
96 Director of Procurement ..... Ms. Nancy K. MURRAY
09 Exec Dir Instnl Effectiveness ..... Mr. Greg STINSON
42 University Pastor ..... Rev. Charlene COX
42 University Pastor ..... Rev. James WETZSTEIN
37 Director of Financial Aid ..... Ms. Karen KLIMCZYK
100 Chief of Staff ..... Mr. Rick AMRHEIN
04 Administrative Asst to President ..... Ms. Gwen GRAHAM
07 Director of Admissions ..... Ms. Barb LIESKE
101 Secretary of the Institution/Board ..... Mr. Darron FARHA
102 Dir Foundation/Corporate Relations ..... Ms. Kathy GROTH
13 Chief Info Technology Officer (CIO) ..... Mr. Rick AMRHEIN
18 Chief Facilities/Physical Plant ..... Mr. Gary GREINER
44 Director Annual or Planned Giving ..... Mr. David NOVAK
86 Director Government Relations ..... Ms. Diane NOE

Vincennes University (F)

1002 N First Street, Vincennes IN 47591-1504
County: Knox FICE Identification: 001843
Unit ID: 152637
Telephone: (812) 888-8888 Carnegie Class: Assoc/Pub4
FAX Number: (812) 888-5868 Calendar System: Semester
URL: www.vinu.edu
Established: 1801 Annual Undergrad Tuition & Fees (In-State): $5,173
Enrollment: 10,351 Coed
Affiliation or Control: State IRS Status: 501(c)3
Highest Offering: Baccalaureate
Program: Occupational; 2-Year Principally Bachelor's Creditable; Liberal Arts And General
Accreditation: NH, ACBSP, ADNUR, ART, CAHIIM, EMT, FUSER, NUR, PNUR, PTAA, SURGT, TED, THEA

01	President	Dr. Richard E. HELTON
05	Provost/Vice Pres Institutional Svc	Dr. Charles R. JOHNSON, JR.
10	Vice Pres Financial Svcs/Govt Rels	Mr. Phillip S. RATH
103	VP Workforce Dev/Comm Services	Mr. David C. TUCKER
12	Assistant VP/Dean Jasper Campus	Vacant
21	Associate Vice President/Controller	Ms. Linda L. WALDROUP
32	Asst Provost Student Affairs	Ms. Lynn WHITE
20	Int Asst Provost Curriculum & Inst	Dr. Laurel A. SMITH
35	Dean of Students	Mr. John T. LIVERS
26	Sr Director External Relations	Ms. Kristi R. DEETZ
07	Director of Admissions	Mrs. Heidi M. WHITEHEAD
08	Director of Learning Resources/Tech	Mr. David M. PETER
09	Director of Institutional Research	Ms. Kimela A. MEEKS
13	Director of Mgmt Information Center	Mr. Carmin A. SCHNARR
27	Director Public Information	Mr. Duane H. CHATTIN
88	Director of University Events	Ms. Cynthia A. BEAMAN
36	Dir Ctr for Career & Empl Relations	Mr. Richard A. COLEMAN
37	Director of Student Financial Aid	Mr. Stanley J. WERNE
88	Director Disability Services	Ms. Leslie M. SMITH
38	Director of Student Counseling	Dr. Lisa J. BISHOP
40	Manager of Bookstore	Mr. Alan RAGGO
102	President of VU Foundation	Mr. Bumper R. HOSTETLER
41	Athletic Director	Mr. Harry L. MEEKS
88	Director of Project Excel/Proj Link	Ms. Heather MOFFAT
29	Director of Alumni Programs	Ms. Jennifer D. GILMORE
85	Dir Multicultural Affairs	Mr. Charles M. SURRETT
18	Director of Physical Plant	Mr. Andrew YOUNG
19	Director of Campus Police	Mr. James M. JONES
88	Bursar	Ms. Lori J. HOSTETLER
24	Director of Media Services	Mr. Jay D. WOLF
06	Registrar	Ms. Rebecca K. LITTLE
39	Director Residential Life	Ms. Dawn M. BREWER
88	Director Marketing Services	Ms. Andrea G. TSCHERTER
96	Director of Procurement	Mr. Michael L. MORRISON
38	Director Student Success Ctr	Ms. Michelle CUMMINS
88	Director Architectural Services	Mr. Andrew YOUNG
15	Director Human Res/AAO	Ms. Regina L. MCCORD-FITHIAN
76	Dean College Health Sci/Human Perf	Dr. Jana L. VIECK
50	Int Dean Col of Business/Public Svc	Ms. Anna MILLER
72	Int Dean College of Technology	Mr. Dean ACKERMAN
81	Dean College of Science/Engr/Math	Dr. Paul J. WILDER
83	Dean Social Sci/Performing Arts	Mr. Eric W. MARGERUM
51	Dean Extended Studies	Mr. Donald E. KAUFMAN
79	Int Dean College of Humanities	Ms. Joan PUCKETT
88	Dir Avia Tech Ctr Indianapolis	Mr. Michael D. GEHRICH
88	Dir Marketing Communications	Ms. Krystal F. SPENCER
88	Dir Institutional Effectiveness	Mr. Michael E. GRESS
20	Interim Dir Early College	Dr. Carolyn K. JONES
88	Director Military Education Pgm	Mr. Matthew J. SCHWARTZ
88	Director Veterans Affairs	Ms. Kristen PHILLIPS
88	Dir Gibson Ctr Adv Mfg/Logistics	Mr. Rob HUDSON
88	Dir Plainfield Logistics Ctr	Mr. James E. DOLAN
04	Administrative Asst to President	Ms. Patricia A. KONKLE
88	Dir International Recruitment	Ms. Valerie M. ALLEN
23	Dir Univ Primary Care Clinic	Ms. Denah PERRY

Vincennes University-Jasper Center (A)

850 College Avenue, Jasper IN 47546

Telephone: (812) 482-3030 Identification: 770107

Accreditation: &NH

† Branch campus of Vincennes University, Vincennes, IN.

Wabash College (B)

301 W Wabash, PO Box 352,
Crawfordsville IN 47933-0352

County: Montgomery FICE Identification: 001844
Unit ID: 152673

Telephone: (765) 361-6100 Carnegie Class: Bac/A&S
FAX Number: (765) 361-6461 Calendar System: Semester
URL: www.wabash.edu
Established: 1832 Annual Undergrad Tuition & Fees: $39,330
Enrollment: 917 Male
Affiliation or Control: Independent Non-Profit IRS Status: 501(c)3
Highest Offering: Baccalaureate
Program: Liberal Arts And General
Accreditation: NH

01	President	Dr. Gregory D. HESS
05	Dean of the College	Dr. Scott FELLER
10	Chief Financial Officer & Treasurer	Mr. Larry GRIFFITH
32	Dean of Students	Mr. Michael P. RATERS
30	Dean for Advancement	Ms. Michelle L. JANSSEN
84	Dean for Enrollment Management	Dr. Michael F. THORP
36	Dean for Professional Development	Mr. Alan P. HILL
100	Chief of Staff	Mr. James L. AMIDON
20	Sr Associate Dean of the College	Dr. Todd F. MCDORMAN
08	Head Librarian & Dir Lilly Library	Mr. John E. LAMBORN
06	Registrar and Assoc Dean	Dr. Jonathon D. JUMP
13	Director of IT Services	Mr. Bradley K. WEAVER
37	Director of Financial Aid	Ms. Heidi A. CARL
35	Associate Dean of Students	Mr. Marc WELCH
36	Director of Career Development	Mr. R. Scott CRAWFORD
29	Dir of Alumni & Parent Relations	Mr. Thomas G. RUNGE
109	Director of Business Auxilaries	Mr. Thomas E. KEEDY
41	Dir of Athletics & Campus Wellness	Mr. Joseph R. HAKLIN
44	Associate Dean for Advancement	Mr. Joseph R. KLEN
15	Director of Human Resources	Ms. Catherine A. METZ
18	Director of Campus Services	Mr. David MORGAN
21	Controller	Ms. Cathy VANARSDALL
38	Director of Counseling Services	Mr. Kevin C. SWAIM
28	Int Director of Malcolm X Institute	Mr. Willyerd R. COLLIER
88	Director of Inquiries CILA	Dr. Charles F. BLAICH
88	Dir Wabash Ctr Teaching/Learning	Dr. Nadine S. PENCE
19	Director of Safety and Security	Mr. Richard G. WOODS
09	Director of Institutional Research	Dr. Preston R. BOST
101	Secretary of the Institution/Board	Mr. James L. AMIDON, JR.
102	Dir Foundation/Corporate Relations	Ms. Deborah WOODS
104	Director International Programs	Ms. Amy WEIR
26	Chief Public Relations/Marketing	Ms. Kimberly JOHNSON
96	Director of Purchasing	Mr. Thomas E. KEEDY

IOWA

AIB College of Business (C)

2500 Fleur Drive, Des Moines IA 50321-1799

County: Polk FICE Identification: 003963
Unit ID: 152822

Telephone: (515) 244-4221 Carnegie Class: Spec/Bus
FAX Number: (515) 244-6773 Calendar System: Quarter
URL: www.aib.edu
Established: 1921 Annual Undergrad Tuition & Fees: $15,300
Enrollment: 1,014 Coed
Affiliation or Control: Independent Non-Profit IRS Status: 501(c)3
Highest Offering: Baccalaureate
Program: Business Emphasis
Accreditation: NH

01	President	Ms. Nancy WILLIAMS
05	Vice Pres/Chief Academic Officer	Ms. Christy ROLAND
11	Vice President for Administration	Mr. Kirk TROW
30	Vice President for Advancement	Ms. Dawn ROBERTS
32	Vice President for Student Life	Mr. Terry WILSON
18	Vice President for Facilities	Mr. Al DORENKAMP
10	Controller	Mr. Tim HORSCH
26	Chief Communications Officer	Ms. Jane MEISNER
04	Executive Assistant to President	Ms. Ronette SMITH
106	Asst Dean of Online Education	Ms. Danielle EDWARDS
18	Chief Facilities Officer	Mr. Chris SCHMIDT
06	Registrar	Mr. Randy TERRONEZ
08	Library Director	Ms. Leslie BINTNER
21	Director of Financial Services	Ms. Laurie SANDERS
36	Director of Career Services	Ms. Toni HUMPFER
37	Director of Financial Aid Services	Mr. Tristan LYNN
38	Director of Student Counseling	Ms. Sheila KEENE
40	Bookstore Manager	Ms. Cassandra HUFF
18	Director of Facilities Management	Mr. Mike LARSON
19	Director Safety & Risk Management	Mr. Karl FENTON

Allen College (D)

1825 Logan Avenue, Waterloo IA 50703-1999

County: Black Hawk FICE Identification: 030691
Unit ID: 152798

Telephone: (319) 226-2000 Carnegie Class: Spec/Health
FAX Number: (319) 226-2010 Calendar System: Semester
URL: www.allencollege.edu
Established: 1989 Annual Undergrad Tuition & Fees: $19,645
Enrollment: 575 Coed
Affiliation or Control: Independent Non-Profit IRS Status: 501(c)3
Highest Offering: Doctorate
Program: Professional; Nursing Emphasis
Accreditation: NH, DMS, MT, NMT, NURSE, RAD

01	Chancellor	Dr. Jerry DURHAM
05	Vice Chancellor of Academic Affairs	Dr. Nancy KRAMER
10	Dir Business/Administrative Svcs	Ms. Denise HANSON
66	Dean School of Nursing	Dr. Kendra WILLIAMS-PEREZ
76	Dean School of Health Sciences	Dr. Peggy FORTSCH
32	Director of Student Services	Ms. Joanna RAMSDEN-MEIER
37	Financial Aid Coordinator	Ms. Kathie ASWEGAN
37	Financial Aid Coordinator	Ms. Molly CORDES
24	Media Specialist	Ms. Robin NICHOLSON
06	Registrar	Ms. Michelle KOEHN
08	Director of Library Services	Dr. Ruth YAN
07	Director of Admissions	Ms. Molly QUINN
09	Coord Inst Research/Effectiveness	Vacant

Antioch School of Church Planting and Leadership Development (E)

2400 Oakwood Road, Ames IA 50014

County: Story Identification: 667026
Telephone: (515) 292-9694 Carnegie Class: Not Classified
FAX Number: (515) 292-1933 Calendar System: Other
URL: www.antiochschool.edu
Established: 2006 Annual Undergrad Tuition & Fees: $1,800
Enrollment: N/A Coed
Affiliation or Control: Independent Non-Profit IRS Status: 501(c)3
Highest Offering: Doctorate
Program: Religious Emphasis
Accreditation: DEAC

01	President	Jeff REED
05	Academic Dean	Stephen KEMP

*Board of Regents, State of Iowa (F)

11260 Aurora Avenue, Urbandale IA 50322-7905

County: Polk FICE Identification: 033443
Telephone: (515) 281-3934 Carnegie Class: N/A
FAX Number: (515) 281-6420
URL: www.regents.iowa.gov

01	Executive Director	Mr. Bob DONLEY
05	Chief Academic Officer	Dr. Diana GONZALEZ
10	Chief Business Officer	Mrs. Patrice M. SAYRE
43	General Counsel	Mr. Thomas A. EVANS

*Iowa State University (G)

Ames IA 50011-0002

County: Story FICE Identification: 001869
Unit ID: 153603

Telephone: (515) 294-4111 Carnegie Class: RU/VH
FAX Number: (515) 294-2592 Calendar System: Semester
URL: www.iastate.edu
Established: 1858 Annual Undergrad Tuition & Fees (In-State): $7,736
Enrollment: 34,435 Coed
Affiliation or Control: State IRS Status: 501(c)3
Highest Offering: Doctorate
Program: Liberal Arts And General; Teacher Preparatory; Professional
Accreditation: NH, ART, BUS, BUSA, CAATE, CIDA, COPSY, CS, DIETD, DIETI, ENG, IPSY, JOUR, LSAR, MUS, NAIT, PLNG, VET

02	President	Dr. Steven LEATH
100	Assoc VP/Chief of Staff	Mr. Miles LACKEY
04	Assistant to the President	Ms. Shirley J. KNIPFEL
43	University Counsel	Mr. Paul N. TANAKA
05	Sr Vice President and Provost	Dr. Jonathan A. WICKERT
10	Sr Vice Pres for Business & Finance	Mr. Warren R. MADDEN
32	Sr Vice Pres for Student Affairs	Dr. Thomas L. HILL
88	Vice Pres for Ec Dev/Bus Engagement	Dr. Michael R. CRUM
46	Vice Pres Research	Dr. Sarah M. NUSSER
56	Vice Pres Extension/Outreach	Dr. Cathann A. KRESS
13	Int Vice President Info Tech Svcs	Dr. Jim KURTENBACH
20	Associate Provost Academic Programs	Dr. David K. HOLGER
20	Assoc Prov Faculty	Dr. Dawn BRATSCH-PRINCE
21	Associate Vice President/Univ Sec	Ms. Pam ELLIOTT CAIN
18	Assoc Vice Pres Facilities	Dr. David L. MILLER
15	Vice President Human Resources	Dr. Julie L. NUTER
84	Assoc Vice Pres Student Affairs	Dr. Martino HARMON
38	Asst VP for Student Counseling Svcs	Vacant
30	President of ISU Foundation	Ms. Larissa HOLTMYER-JONES
29	President of Alumni Association	Dr. Jeffrey W. JOHNSON
41	Director of Athletics	Mr. Jamie B. POLLARD
26	Exec Director of University Rels	Mr. John F. MCCARROLL
06	Registrar	Ms. Laura J. DOERING
37	Director of Financial Aid	Ms. Roberta L. JOHNSON
07	Director of Admissions	Ms. Katharine JOHNSON SUSKI
22	Director of Equal Opportunity	Ms. Robinette KELLEY
09	Director of Institutional Research	Dr. Gebre H. TESFAGIORGIS
19	Director of Public Safety	Mr. Jerry D. STEWART
35	Dean of Students	Dr. Pamela ANTHONY
23	Int Director of Student Health	Ms. Mary HENSLEY
104	Director Study Abroad	Dr. Trevor NELSON
39	Director of Residence	Dr. Peter D. ENGLIN
91	Associate CIO	Mr. David M. POPELKA
25	Int Director/Sponsored Pgm Admin	Ms. Tamara R. POLASKI
88	Director Ames Laboratory	Dr. Adam SCHWARTZ
96	Director of Purchasing	Ms. Nancy S. BROOKS
40	Director University Bookstore	Ms. Rita M. PHILLIPS
58	Dean Graduate College	Dr. David K. HOLGER
08	Dean of Library Services	Ms. Mary E. MCNEIL
47	Dean College of Agriculture	Dr. Wendy WINTERSTEEN
50	Dean College of Business	Mr. David P. SPALDING
48	Dean College of Design	Mr. Luis C. RICO-GUTIERREZ
53	Dean College of Human Sciences	Dr. Pamela J. WHITE
54	Dean College of Engineering	Dr. Sarah RAJALA
49	Dean Col of Lib Arts & Sciences	Dr. Beate SCHMITTMANN
74	Dean College of Veterinary Medicine	Dr. Lisa K. NOLAN
106	Assoc Director for Online Education	Dr. Ralph E. NAPOLITANO
102	Sr Dir Dev-Corp & Found Relations	Mr. Mark BOECK
102	Sr Dir Dev-Corp & Found Relations	Ms. Donna VAN PELT
44	Exec Dir of Annual & Special Giving	Ms. Melissa ROWAN
27	Director of University Marketing	Ms. Carole A. CUSTER

*University of Iowa (H)

Iowa City IA 52242-0001

County: Johnson FICE Identification: 001892
Unit ID: 153658

Telephone: (319) 335-3500 Carnegie Class: RU/VH
FAX Number: (319) 335-0807 Calendar System: Semester
URL: www.uiowa.edu
Established: 1847 Annual Undergrad Tuition & Fees (In-State): $8,104
Enrollment: 31,387 Coed
Affiliation or Control: State IRS Status: 501(c)3
Highest Offering: Doctorate
Program: Liberal Arts And General; Teacher Preparatory; Professional
Accreditation: NH, ANEST, ARCPA, AUD, BUS, BUSA, CAATE, CACREP, CEA, CLPSY, COPSY, CORE, DANCE, DENT, DIETI, DMS, EMT, ENG, ENGR, HSA, IPSY, JOUR, LAW, LIB, MED, MUS, NMT, NURSE, PAST, PCSAS, PERF, PH, PHAR, PLNG, PTA, RAD, RTT, SCPSY, SP, SW, THEA

02	President	Mr. Bruce HARRELD
05	Exec Vice President & Provost	Dr. Patrick B. BUTLER
46	VP Research & Economic Development	Dr. Daniel REED
10	Interim VP Chief Fin Officer	Mr. Terry JOHNSON
32	VP Student Life	Dr. Thomas R. ROCKLIN
17	Vice President for Medical Affairs	Dr. Jean E. ROBILLARD
30	Vice Pres & Development Officer	Mr. David R. DIERKS
26	VP Univ Communications & Marketing	Dr. Joseph A. BRENNAN

20 Associate Provost Faculty .... Dr. Kevin KREGEL
51 Assoc Provost Continuing Education .... Dr. Chet S. RZONCA
28 Chief Diversity Officer/AP .... Dr. Georgina DODGE
88 Assoc Provost/Dean Univ College .... Mr. Lon MOELLER
45 Assoc Vice President Research .... Dr. Richard D. HICHWA
11 Assoc VP/Dir of Admin and Planning .. Mr. Donald J. SZESZYCKI
15 Int Assoc VP Finance/Dir HR .... Mr. Kevin WARD
18 Assoc VP/Dir Facilities Management .... Mr. Donald J. GUCKERT
13 Assoc Vice President & CIO .... Mr. Steven R. FLEAGLE
23 Assoc VP/CEO Univ Hosp & Clinics .... Mr. Kenneth KATES
25 Exec Director Sponsored Programs .... Ms. Jennifer LASSNER
19 Interim Director Public Safety .... Mr. David VISIN
85 Dean International Programs .... Dr. Downing THOMAS
43 VP Legal Affairs & General Counsel .... Ms. Carroll REASONER
08 University Librarian .... Mr. John P. CULSHAW
29 Exec Director Alumni Association .... Mr. Jeffrey D. KUETER
102 President University Foundation .... Ms. Lynette L. MARSHALL
07 Director Admissions/Enrollment .... Mr. Kirk R. KLUVER
37 Director Student Financial Aid .... Mr. Mark S. WARNER
06 Registrar .... Mr. Lawrence J. LOCKWOOD
36 Director Career Center .... Mr. David A. BAUMGARTNER
38 Director Univ Counseling Services .... Dr. Sam V. COCHRAN, III
39 Director Residence Services .... Mr. Von STANGE
41 Director Athletics Administration .... Mr. Gary BARTA
49 Dean Col of Liberal Arts & Sciences .... Dr. Chaden DJALALI
50 Dean College of Business Admin .... Dr. Sarah GARDIAL
52 Dean College of Dentistry .... Dr. David C. JOHNSEN
53 Dean College of Education .... Dr. Nicholas COLANGELO
54 Dean College of Engineering .... Dr. Alec SCRANTON
58 Dean Graduate College .... Dr. John C. KELLER
61 Dean College of Law .... Dr. Gail B. AGRAWAL
66 Dean College of Nursing .... Dr. Rita A. FRANTZ
67 Dean College of Pharmacy .... Dr. Donald E. LETENDRE
69 Dean College of Public Health .... Dr. Susan CURRY
04 Special Assistant to President .... Dr. Thomas K. DEAN
22 Dir Equal Opportunity/Diversity .... Ms. Jennifer A. MODESTOU
86 Director State Relations .... Mr. Keith SAUNDERS
40 Director University Bookstore .... Mr. George E. HERBERT
96 Director Purchasing .... Ms. Deborah J. ZUMBACH
92 Director Honors Program .... Dr. Art L. SPISAK
87 Director Summer Session .... Dr. Marlys BOOTE
35 Dean of Students .... Vacant
84 Assoc VP/Enrollment Management .... Dr. Brent GAGE
100 Chief of Staff .... Mr. Peter MATTHES
104 Director Study Abroad .... Mr. Douglas LEE

*University of Northern Iowa (A)

1227 W 27th Street, Cedar Falls IA 50614-0001

County: Black Hawk — FICE Identification: 001890
Unit ID: 154095
Telephone: (319) 273-2311 — Carnegie Class: Master's L
FAX Number: (319) 273-2885 — Calendar System: Semester
URL: www.uni.edu
Established: 1876 — Annual Undergrad Tuition & Fees (In-State): $7,817
Enrollment: 11,928 — Coed
Affiliation or Control: State — IRS Status: 501(c)3
Highest Offering: Doctorate
Program: Liberal Arts And General; Teacher Preparatory
Accreditation: NH, BUS, CAATE, CACREP, CEA, ENGT, MUS, NAIT, NRPA, SP, SW, THEA

02 President .... Dr. William N. RUUD
05 Exec Vice President & Provost .... Dr. A. James WOHLPART
10 Sr VP Admin/Financial Svcs .... Dr. Michael A. HAGER
32 Vice Pres for Student Affairs .... Dr. Terrence HOGAN
30 Vice President for Univ Advancement .... Ms. Lisa B. BARONIO
84 Assoc VP for Enrollment Management .... Mr. Matthew KROEGER
18 Asst VP Fac Planning/Campus Archite .... Mr. Philip A. SIMPSON
04 Spec Asst to Pres for Board/Gov Rel .... Dr. Patricia L. GEADELMANN
26 Director Univ Relations .... Mr. Scott KETELSEN
39 Asst VP & Exec Dir of Residence .... Mr. Glenn GRAY
20 Int Assoc Provost for Acad Affairs .... Dr. Kavita R. DHANWADA
20 Assoc Provost for Faculty Affairs .... Dr. Nancy COBB
13 Chief Information Officer .... Ms. Marty MARK
09 Int Dir Inst Res & Effectiveness .... Dr. Kristin M. MOSER
62 Dean of Library Services .... Mr. Christopher COX
06 University Registrar .... Mr. Philip L. PATTON
29 Director Alumni Relations .... Ms. Leslie J. PRIDEAUX
37 Director of Financial Aid .... Ms. Joyce MORROW
15 Dir Human Resource Services .... Ms. Michelle C. BYERS
36 Director of Career Services .... Mr. Robert J. FREDERICK
83 Dean Col Social/Behav Science .... Dr. Brenda BASS
53 Int Dean Col Education .... Dr. Victoria L. ROBINSON
49 Int Dean Col Hum/Arts & Science .... Dr. John FRITCH
51 Dean Cont Educ/Special Programs .... Dr. Kent M. JOHNSON
50 Int Dean Col Business Admin .... Dr. Leslie K. WILSON
35 Dean of Students .... Dr. Leslie K. WILLIAMS
10 Controller/Secretary/Treasurer .... Mr. Gary B. SHONTZ
38 Counseling Center Director .... Dr. David C. TOWLE
22 Asst to Pres Compliance/Equity Mgmt .. Ms. Leah K. GUTKNECHT
41 Athletic Director .... Mr. Troy A. DANNEN
21 Director of Business Operations .... Ms. Kelly A. FLEGE
86 State Relations Officer .... Ms. Mary BRAUN
104 Int Assoc Provost for Intl Programs .... Mr. Philip D. PLOURDE
88 Director Undergraduate Studies .... Dr. Deirdre A. HEISTAD
108 Univ Accreditation Administrator .... Dr. Donna E. VINTON
19 Chief of Police/Dir Public Safety .... Ms. Helen M. HAIRE
25 Grants and Contracts Administrator .... Mr. Tolif R. HUNT
43 University Counsel .... Mr. Timothy J. MCKENNA

Briar Cliff University (B)

3303 Rebecca Street, Sioux City IA 51104-2324

County: Woodbury — FICE Identification: 001846
Unit ID: 152992
Telephone: (712) 279-5321 — Carnegie Class: Bac/Diverse
FAX Number: (712) 279-5410 — Calendar System: 4/1/4
URL: www.briarcliff.edu
Established: 1929 — Annual Undergrad Tuition & Fees: $27,910
Enrollment: 1,135 — Coed
Affiliation or Control: Roman Catholic — IRS Status: 501(c)3
Highest Offering: Doctorate
Program: Liberal Arts And General; Teacher Preparatory; Professional
Accreditation: NH, NURSE, @PTA, SW

01 President .... Mrs. Beverly A. WHARTON
05 Vice President Academic Affairs .... Dr. William MANGAN
10 Vice President Finance & Treasurer .... Mrs. Beth GRIGSBY
30 Vice Pres University Relations .... Mrs. Tina STROUD
84 Vice Pres Enrollment Management .... Mr. Brian EBEN
32 Vice President Student Development .... Mrs. Louise PASKEY
06 Registrar .... Mrs. Deidre ENGEL
08 Librarian/Dir Information Services .... Mr. Julius FLESCHNER
13 Director Computer Center .... Ms. Leah WARD
29 Activities/Events & E-Coordinator .... Ms. Lorna KOHN
36 Director Career Development .... Mr. Joshua COBBS
37 Director Financial Aid .... Mrs. Shelby REED
40 Director Bookstore .... Ms. Nancy WATSON
41 Athletic Director .... Mr. Steve GAST
42 Director Campus Ministry .... Sr. Janet MAY
18 Director Physical Plant .... Mr. Eric HOLMQUIST
26 Director Marketing & Communications .... Mrs. Amanda MAYO
07 Director of Admissions .... Vacant
15 Director Human Resources .... Mr. Beau SUDTELGTE
39 Director Residence Life .... Mr. Dave ARENS
38 Director Student Counseling .... Ms. Jessica DOMINOWSKI
09 Director of Institutional Research .... Ms. Deidre ENGEL
44 Director of Development .... Mrs. Tina STROUD
19 Director Security/Safety .... Mr. Dean REYNOLDS

Brown Mackie College-Quad Cities (C)

2119 East Kimberly Road, Bettendorf IA 52722

Telephone: (563) 344-1500 — Identification: 666792
Accreditation: ACICS, OTA

† Branch campus of The Art Institute of Phoenix, Phoenix, AZ.

Buena Vista University (D)

610 W Fourth Street, Storm Lake IA 50588-1798

County: Buena Vista — FICE Identification: 001847
Unit ID: 153001
Telephone: (712) 749-2351 — Carnegie Class: Bac/Diverse
FAX Number: (712) 749-2037 — Calendar System: 4/1/4
URL: www.bvu.edu
Established: 1891 — Annual Undergrad Tuition & Fees: $31,318
Enrollment: 1,759 — Coed
Affiliation or Control: Presbyterian Church (U.S.A.) — IRS Status: 501(c)3
Highest Offering: Master's
Program: Liberal Arts And General; Teacher Preparatory
Accreditation: NH, CAATE, SW

01 President .... Dr. Frederick V. MOORE
04 Assistant to the President .... Ms. Emily A. WILLIAMS
05 VP Academic Affairs/Dean of Faculty .... Dr. Barbara BYRNE
10 Vice President Business Services .... Ms. Elizabeth MERTEN
84 Vice Pres for Enrollment Management .... Mr. Michael FRANTZ
32 VP Student Affairs/DOS .... Mr. Dale SCULLY
30 Vice Pres for Inst Advancement .... Mr. Kenneth L. CONVERSE
81 Dean School of Science .... Mr. Ben DONATH
50 Dean HWS School of Business .... Dr. Ashok SUBRAMANIAN
53 Dean School of Education .... Dr. Paul THEOBALD
60 Dean School Communication & Arts . Dr. Michael D. WHITLATCH
83 Dean School Social Sci/Phil/Relig .... Dr. Dixee BARTHOLOMEW-FEIS
20 Associate Dean of Faculty .... Dr. Peter K. STEINFELD
20 AVP Acad Affs/Dn Graduate/Prof Stds .... Dr. Jill RHEA
06 Registrar .... Ms. Nila HOUSKA
07 Director of Admissions .... Ms. Bridget KURKOWSKI
15 Human Resources Manager .... Ms. Meghann HENRICH
08 Actg Dir of Library/Ref Librarian .... Ms. Jodie MORIN
26 Dir University Marketing & Comm .... Ms. Jennifer FELTON
29 Director of Alumni Rels/Annual Fund .... Ms. Amy J. JONES
13 Managing Director Univ Info Svcs .... Mr. Pat LEPORE
18 Director of Physical Plant .... Mr. Keith E. SCHMIDT
36 Director of Career Services .... Vacant
37 Director of Financial Assistance .... Ms. Leanne VALENTINE
28 Director of Intercultural Programs .... Ms. Carol WILLIAMS
41 Athletic Director .... Ms. Christyn ABARAY
42 Chaplain .... Rev. Ken MEISSNER
19 Director of Campus Security .... Mr. Mark KIRKHOLM
38 Director of Counseling Services .... Ms. Mandy BOOTHBY
09 Institutional Researcher .... Mr. James E. HEWETT
96 Purchasing Administrator .... Ms. Tanya LANDGRAF

Central College (E)

812 University, Pella IA 50219-1999

County: Marion — FICE Identification: 001850
Unit ID: 153108
Telephone: (641) 628-9000 — Carnegie Class: Bac/A&S
FAX Number: (641) 628-5316 — Calendar System: Semester
URL: www.central.edu
Established: 1853 — Annual Undergrad Tuition & Fees: $33,345
Enrollment: 1,411 — Coed
Affiliation or Control: Reformed Church In America — IRS Status: 501(c)3
Highest Offering: Baccalaureate
Program: Liberal Arts And General
Accreditation: NH, CAATE, MUS

01 President .... Dr. Mark L. PUTNAM
05 VP Academic Affairs/Dean of Faculty .... Dr. Mary M. STREY
30 Vice President Advancement .... Mr. Bill NORTHUP
84 Vice Pres Enrollment Management .... Mrs. Carol WILLIAMSON
32 Vice Pres Student Development .... Dr. Peggy FITCH
10 Vice Pres for Finance & Admin .... Mr. Thomas JOHNSON
20 Director of Academic Resources .... Mr. Eric JONES
35 Dean of Students .... Mr. Charles STREY
07 Director of Admission .... Mr. Chevy FREIBURGER
38 Director of Counseling .... Ms. Michelle KELLAR
39 Director of Residence Life .... Ms. Melissa SHARKEY
08 Director of Library .... Ms. Beth MCMAHON
88 Associate Dean for Global Education .... Ms. Lyn R. ISAACSON
36 Director of Career Center .... Mrs. Patricia JOACHIM KITZMAN
29 Director of Alumni Relations .... Ms. Kathy THOMPSON
37 Director Financial Aid .... Mr. Wayne DILLE
104 Director of Study Abroad .... Mr. Blaire MODIC
13 Chief Information Officer .... Ms. Debra BRUXVOORT
42 Chaplain .... Rev. Joe BRUMMEL
44 Dir Development/Planned Giving .... Mr. Don MORRISON
15 Director of Human Resources .... Ms. Paula RYAN
41 Athletics Director .... Mr. Eric VAN KLEY
18 Dir Facilities Planning/Management .... Mr. Mike LUBBERDEN
06 Registrar .... Ms. Stephanie HENNING
04 Administrative Asst to President .... Ms. Carma STURTZ
09 Institutional Research Director .... Mr. Thomas WALKER

Clarke University (F)

1550 Clarke Drive, Dubuque IA 52001-3198

County: Dubuque — FICE Identification: 001852
Unit ID: 153126
Telephone: (563) 588-6300 — Carnegie Class: Bac/Diverse
FAX Number: (563) 588-6789 — Calendar System: Semester
URL: www.clarke.edu
Established: 1843 — Annual Undergrad Tuition & Fees: $29,940
Enrollment: 1,200 — Coed
Affiliation or Control: Roman Catholic — IRS Status: 501(c)3
Highest Offering: Doctorate
Program: Liberal Arts And General; Teacher Preparatory; Professional
Accreditation: NH, CAATE, MUS, NURSE, PTA, SW

01 President .... Dr. Joanne M. BURROWS, SC
04 Exec Admin Assistant to President .... Ms. Kathy TEIG
05 Vice Pres Academic Affs .... Dr. Susan R. BURNS
30 Vice Pres Institutional Advancement .... Mr. Bill BIEBUYCK
32 Vice President Student Life .... Ms. Kate ZANGER
10 Vice President Business & Finance .... Ms. Daisy HALVORSON
84 Vice President Enrollment Mgmt .... Dr. Beth TRIPLETT
88 Assistant to the President .... Ms. Megan STULL
06 Registrar .... Ms. Kristi BAGSTAD
08 Director of Library .... Ms. Susanne LEIBOLD
20 Dean of Undergraduate Studies .... Dr. Graciela CANEIRO-LIVINGSTON
58 Acad Dean of Adult & Grad Studies .... Dr. Jo LOBERTINI
37 Director of Financial Aid .... Ms. Amy NORTON
26 Exec Director of Marketing & Comm .... Mr. Ken BROWN
13 Chief Technology Officer .... Mr. Andy BELLILNGS
18 Exec Dir of Facilities Management .... Mr. Chris DRESSLER
38 Asst Dir of Counseling/Career Svcs .... Ms. Becky HERRIG
15 Director of Human Resources .... Ms. Megan LUCAS
41 Director of Athletics .... Mr. Curt LONG
42 Director of Campus Ministry .... Vacant
40 Director of the Bookstore .... Ms. Sarah MERZ
23 Director of Health Services .... Ms. Julie BURGMEIER
90 Asst Dean Acad Affairs/Inst Supp .... Mr. Pat MADDUX
07 Asst Director of Admissions .... Ms. Emily KRUSE
44 Director of Development .... Ms. Kari NICKOL
29 Assoc Dir of Alumni Relations .... Ms. Alissa RIEGLER
85 International Students Advisor .... Ms. Evelyn NADEAU
39 Dean of Students .... Mr. Kevin UTT

Coe College (G)

1220 1st Avenue, NE, Cedar Rapids IA 52402-5092

County: Linn — FICE Identification: 001854
Unit ID: 153144
Telephone: (319) 399-8000 — Carnegie Class: Bac/A&S
FAX Number: (319) 399-8830 — Calendar System: Semester
URL: www.coe.edu
Established: 1851 — Annual Undergrad Tuition & Fees: $47,590
Enrollment: 1,436 — Coed
Affiliation or Control: Independent Non-Profit — IRS Status: 501(c)3
Highest Offering: Master's
Program: Liberal Arts And General; Teacher Preparatory; Professional
Accreditation: NH, CAATE, MUS, NURSE

01 President .... Dr. David W. MCINALLY
03 Executive Vice President .... Mr. Michael L. WHITE
05 Vice Pres Acad Affs/Dean of Faculty .... Dr. Marie BAEHR
32 Vice President for Student Affairs .... Mr. Erik ALBINSON
30 Vice President for Advancement .... Mr. David HAYES
07 Associate VP/Dean of Admission .... Ms. Julie STAKER
06 Registrar .... Mr. Jason CLAPP
08 Director Library Services .... Ms. Jill JACK

29 Director Alumni Programs .... Ms. Jean A. JOHNSON
09 Director of Institutional Research .... Dr. Wendy L. DUNN
26 Dir of Marketing/Public Relations .... Mr. Rod PRITCHARD
37 Director of Financial Aid .... Ms. Barbara HOFFMAN
20 Associate Dean .... Dr. Terry MCNABB
35 Dean of Students .... Mr. Tom HICKS
85 International Student Advisor .... Ms. Rebecca STONAWSKI
42 Chaplain .... Rev. Kristin E. HUTSON
23 Director of Health Services .... Ms. Lindsay SHEDEK
41 Director of Athletics .... Mr. John M. CHANDLER
18 Director of Physical Plant .... Ms. Lisa CIHA
36 Career Services Coordinator .... Ms. Michelle MCILLECE
36 Dir of Internships/Career Services .... Ms. Diana R. PATTEN
15 Director of Human Resources .... Ms. Kristina BRIDGES
04 Administrative Asst to President .... Ms. Kim PRIBYL
13 Chief Info Technology Officer (CIO) .... Mr. Tony BATA
19 Director Security/Safety .... Mr. Carlos VELEZ
44 Director Annual or Planned Giving .... Ms. Barb TUPPER

Cornell College (A)

600 First Street SW, Mount Vernon IA 52314-1098

County: Linn — FICE Identification: 001856
Unit ID: 153162
Telephone: (319) 895-4000 — Carnegie Class: Bac/A&S
FAX Number: (319) 895-4492 — Calendar System: Other
URL: www.cornellcollege.edu
Established: 1853 — Annual Undergrad Tuition & Fees: $47,400
Enrollment: 1,070 — Coed
Affiliation or Control: United Methodist — IRS Status: 501(c)3
Highest Offering: Baccalaureate
Program: Liberal Arts And General; Teacher Preparatory
Accreditation: NH

01 President .... Mr. Jonathan BRAND
05 VP Acad Affairs/Dean of College .... Dr. R. Joseph DIEKER
10 Vice President Business Affairs .... Ms. Kay LANGSETH
84 Vice President for Enrollment .... Ms. Colleen MURPHY
32 Vice President Student Affairs .... Mr. John W. HARP
44 VP for Alumni & College Advancement .... Ms. Pam GERARD
35 Interim Dean of Students .... Ms. Gwendolyn SCHIMEK
20 Associate Dean of the College .... Dr. Benjamin GREENSTEIN
09 Director of Institutional Research .... Dr. Becki S. ELKINS
37 Director of Student Financial Asst .... Ms. Shannon AMUNDSON
06 Registrar .... Dr. Becki ELKINS
08 College Librarian .... Mr. Paul WAELCHLI
29 Director of Alumni & Annual Giving . Mr. RJ HOLMES-LEOPOLD
30 Senior Director of Development .... Ms. Kristi COLUMBUS
26 Senior Dir Marketing/Communications .... Ms. Jen VISSER
42 Chaplain .... Ms. Catherine M. QUEHL-ENGEL
22 Affirmative Action Officer .... Ms. Lindsey HOTZ
41 Athletics Director .... Mr. John T. COCHRANE
18 Director of Facilities .... Mr. Joel C. MILLER
36 Director Career Engagement Center .... Mr. Jason NAPOLI
38 Director Student Counseling .... Dr. Brenda C. LOVSTUEN
15 Human Resource Coordinator .... Ms. Lindsey HOTZ
07 Director of Admission .... Ms. Marie SCHOFER
13 Director of Information Technology .... Vacant
40 Manager Bookstore .... Ms. Lee Ann GRIMLEY
04 Administrative Asst to President .... Ms. RuthAnn SCHEER

Des Moines Area Community College (B)

2006 S Ankeny Boulevard, Ankeny IA 50023-3993

County: Polk — FICE Identification: 007120
Unit ID: 153214
Telephone: (515) 964-6200 — Carnegie Class: Assoc/Pub-R-L
FAX Number: N/A — Calendar System: Semester
URL: www.dmacc.edu
Established: 1966 — Annual Undergrad Tuition & Fees (In-District): $4,290
Enrollment: 23,526 — Coed
Affiliation or Control: State/Local — IRS Status: 501(c)3
Highest Offering: Associate Degree
Program: Occupational; 2-Year Principally Bachelor's Creditable
Accreditation: NH, ACBSP, ACFEI, ADNUR, COARC, DA, DH, FUSER, MAC, MLTAD, SURGT

01 President/CEO .... Dr. Rob DENSON
05 Exec Vice Pres Academic Affairs .... Dr. Kim LINDUSKA
10 Vice President Business Svcs .... Mr. Greg MARTIN
13 Exec Dir Information Solutions .... Mr. Mark CLARK
12 Provost Urban Campus .... Dr. Laura DOUGLAS
12 Provost Boone Campus .... Mr. Tom LEE
12 Provost Carroll Campus .... Mr. Joel LUNDSTROM
12 Provost Newton Campus .... Ms. Mary ENTZ
12 Provost West Campus .... Dr. Tony PAUSTIAN
32 Exec Dean Student Services .... Dr. Laurie WOLF
15 Executive Director Human Resources .... Dr. Sandy TRYON
102 Executive Director Foundation .... Ms. Tara CONNOLLY
09 Exec Director Inst Effectiveness .... Dr. Joe DEHART
51 Exec Dir Continuing Education .... Mr. Michael HOFFMAN
50 Exec Dir Business Resources .... Ms. Kim DIDIER
37 Director Financial Aid .... Ms. DeLores HAWKINS
26 Director of Marketing .... Mr. Todd JONES
25 Director Grants/Contracts .... Ms. Deb KOUA
06 Registrar .... Ms. Rachel ERKKILA
18 Chief Facilities/Physical Plant .... Mr. Ned MILLER
38 Director Student Development .... Vacant
96 Director of Purchasing .... Mr. Tim HAGER
27 Media Liaison .... Mr. Dan IVIS
70 Dean Sciences & Humanities .... Mr. Jim STICK
72 Dean Industrial & Technology .... Mr. Scott OCKEN
76 Dean Health Service & Science .... Ms. Sally SCHROEDER
50 Dean Business/Mgmt/Information Tech .... Mr. MJ ISLEY
55 Dean Evening & Weekend College .... Ms. Andrea ISEMINGER
08 Head Librarian .... Ms. Rebecca FUNKE
41 Athletic Director .... Mr. Orv SALMON
101 Secretary of the Institution/Board .... Ms. Carolyn FARLOW

Des Moines Area Community College Boone Campus (C)

1125 Hancock Drive, Boone IA 50036

Telephone: (515) 432-7203 — Identification: 770048
Accreditation: &NH

† Branch campus of Des Moines Area Community College, Ankeny, IA.

Des Moines Area Community College Carroll Campus (D)

906 North Grant Road, Carroll IA 51401-2525

Telephone: (712) 792-1755 — Identification: 770049
Accreditation: &NH

† Branch campus of Des Moines Area Community College, Ankeny, IA.

Des Moines Area Community College Newton Campus (E)

600 N 2nd Avenue West, Newton IA 50208

Telephone: (641) 791-3622 — Identification: 770051
Accreditation: &NH

† Branch campus of Des Moines Area Community College, Ankeny, IA.

Des Moines Area Community College Urban Campus (F)

1100 7th Street, Des Moines IA 50314

Telephone: (515) 244-4226 — Identification: 770050
Accreditation: &NH

† Branch campus of Des Moines Area Community College, Ankeny, IA.

Des Moines Area Community College West Des Moines Campus (G)

5959 West Grand Avenue, West Des Moines IA 50266

Telephone: (515) 633-2407 — Identification: 770052
Accreditation: &NH

† Branch campus of Des Moines Area Community College, Ankeny, IA.

Des Moines University (H)

3200 Grand Avenue, Des Moines IA 50312-4198

County: Polk — FICE Identification: 001855
Unit ID: 154156
Telephone: (515) 271-1400 — Carnegie Class: Spec/Med
FAX Number: (515) 271-1532 — Calendar System: Other
URL: www.dmu.edu
Established: 1898 — Annual Graduate Tuition & Fees: $45,630
Enrollment: 1,542 — Coed
Affiliation or Control: Independent Non-Profit — IRS Status: 501(c)3
Highest Offering: First Professional Degree; No Undergraduates
Program: Professional
Accreditation: NH, ARCPA, OSTEO, PH, POD, PTA

01 President/CEO .... Dr. Angela L. WALKER FRANKLIN
05 Provost .... Dr. Karen P. MCLEAN
32 Vice President Student Services .... Ms. Mary Ann ZUG
86 VP External and Government Affairs .... Ms. Susan HUPPERT
46 Vice President for Research .... Dr. Jeffrey GRAY
06 Registrar .... Ms. Kathy L. SCAGLIONE
08 Director of Library .... Ms. Natalie HUTCHINSON
15 Chief Human Resources Officer .... Ms. Becky LADE
13 Chief Information Officer .... Ms. Carolyn WEAVER
37 Director of Financial Aid .... Ms. Mary PAYNE
18 Director of Facilities Management .... Mr. David MCNERNEY
19 Director University Services .... Mr. John BRUECKEN
88 Chief Compliance Officer .... Ms. Erika LINDEN
10 Chief Financial Officer .... Mr. Mark J. PEIFFER
69 Director Public Health Program .... Dr. Rachel REIMER
76 Director Healthcare Administration .... Dr. Carla STEBBINS
26 Director Marketing & Communication .... Ms. Kendall DILLON
38 Dir Center for Teaching & Learning .... Dr. Kerry GREGORYK
76 Dean College Health Sciences .... Dr. Jodi CAHALAN
63 Dean Col Podiatric Medicine/Surg .... Dr. Robert YOHO
63 Dean Col Osteopathic Medicine/Surg .... Dr. JD POLK
04 Executive Asst to President .... Ms. Christina HENDERSON
07 Director of Admissions .... Ms. Gina SMITH
28 Director of Multicultural Affairs .... Dr. Richard SALAS
29 Director Alumni Relations .... Ms. Ronnette VONDRAK
30 Chief Development Officer .... Ms. Stephanie GREINER
101 Secretary of the Institution/Board .... Ms. Linda KADING

† Tuition varies by degree program.

Divine Word College (I)

102 Jacoby Drive, SW, PO Box 380, Epworth IA 52045-0380

County: Dubuque — FICE Identification: 001858
Unit ID: 153241
Telephone: (563) 876-3353 — Carnegie Class: Spec/Faith
FAX Number: (563) 876-3407 — Calendar System: Semester
URL: www.dwci.edu
Established: 1918 — Annual Undergrad Tuition & Fees: $12,500
Enrollment: 115 — Male
Affiliation or Control: Roman Catholic — IRS Status: 501(c)3
Highest Offering: Baccalaureate
Program: Religious Emphasis
Accreditation: NH

01 President .... Fr. Timothy A. LENCHAK
05 Academic Dean/Vice President ..... Dr. Mathew KANJIRATHINKAL
10 Vice Pres for Finances/Fin Aid Dir .... Mr. Mark PASKER
32 Dean of Students .... Rev. Bang TRAN
07 Director Admissions/VP Recruitment .... Mr. Len UHAL
30 Development Director .... Mr. Terrance SYKORA
26 Public Relations Director .... Ms. Sandy WILGENBUSCH
08 Librarian .... Mr. Daniel BOICE
06 Registrar .... Mr. Paul STAMM
38 Counselor .... Mrs. Nan PECK
104 Director Study Abroad .... Rev. Kenneth ANICH
13 Chief Info Technology Officer (CIO) .... Mr. Brad FLORENCE
45 Chief Institutional Planning .... Rev. John SZUKALSKI, SVD

Dordt College (J)

498 4th Avenue, NE, Sioux Center IA 51250-1697

County: Sioux — FICE Identification: 001859
Unit ID: 153250
Telephone: (712) 722-6000 — Carnegie Class: Bac/Diverse
FAX Number: (712) 722-6035 — Calendar System: Semester
URL: www.dordt.edu
Established: 1955 — Annual Undergrad Tuition & Fees: $28,280
Enrollment: 1,459 — Coed
Affiliation or Control: Christian Reformed Church — IRS Status: 501(c)3
Highest Offering: Master's
Program: 2-Year Principally Bachelor's Creditable; Liberal Arts And General; Teacher Preparatory
Accreditation: NH, ENG, NURSE, SW

01 President .... Dr. Erik HOEKSTRA
05 Provost .... Dr. Eric A. FORSETH
30 Vice President College Advancement .... Mr. John BAAS
10 Exec Dir of Finance & Facilities .... Mr. Arlan NEDERHOFF
11 Vice President for Administration .... Mr. Howard WILSON
88 Dean of Off Campus Programs .... Vacant
37 Director Financial Aid .... Mr. Michael EPEMA
06 Registrar .... Mr. James BOS
88 Director for Research & Scholarship .... Dr. Nathan TINTLE
20 Dean for Curriculum & Instruction .... Dr. Leah ZUIDEMA
58 Director Graduate Education .... Dr. Timothy VAN SOELEN
36 Career Services Coordinator .... Mrs. Sarah MOSS
26 Marketing and Public Relations .. Ms. Sonya JONGSMA KNAUSS
18 Director Physical Plant .... Mr. Stan OORDT
32 Dean of Campus Life .... Mr. Robert TAYLOR
42 Campus Pastor .... Rev. Aaron BAART
41 Director of Athletics .... Mr. Glenn BOUMA
40 Director Bookstore/Purchasing .... Ms. Lora DEVRIES
44 Director of Planned Giving .... Mr. Dave VANDER WERF
29 Director Alumni/External Relations .... Mr. Brandon HUISMAN
15 Director Human Resources .... Mrs. Sue DROOG
96 Director of Purchasing .... Mr. Fred HAAN
91 Director of Computer Services .... Mr. Brian VAN DONSELAAR
08 Director of Library Services .... Vacant
23 Director of Health Sciences .... Ms. Deb BOMGAARS
88 Director Academic Skills Center .... Ms. Pamala S. DE JONG
04 Administrative Asst to President .... Mrs. LeeAnn MOERMAN

Drake University (K)

2507 University Avenue, Des Moines IA 50311-4505

County: Polk — FICE Identification: 001860
Unit ID: 153269
Telephone: (515) 271-2011 — Carnegie Class: Master's L
FAX Number: (515) 271-3016 — Calendar System: Semester
URL: www.drake.edu
Established: 1881 — Annual Undergrad Tuition & Fees: $33,550
Enrollment: 5,062 — Coed
Affiliation or Control: Independent Non-Profit — IRS Status: 501(c)3
Highest Offering: Doctorate
Program: Liberal Arts And General; Teacher Preparatory; Professional
Accreditation: NH, ART, CACREP, CORE, JOUR, LAW, MUS, PHAR

01 President .... Mr. Earl F. MARTIN
05 Interim Provost .... Dr. Joseph LENZ
10 Chief Financial Officer .... Ms. Teresa KREJCI
11 Chief Administrative Officer .... Ms. Venessa MACRO
30 Vice Pres Alumni and Development .... Mr. John SMITH
07 Vice Pres Admissions/Financial Aid .... Mr. Tom DELAHUNT
20 Associate Provost of Curriculum .... Mr. Art SANDERS
32 Interim Vice Prov Student Affairs ..... Ms. Melissa STURM-SMITH
35 Dean of Students .... Dr. Sentwali BAKARI
15 Human Resources Director .... Mr. Gary JOHNSON
13 Chief Tech Information Officer .... Mr. Chris GILL
04 Executive Asst to Pres/Secy of Univ .... Ms. Linda S. RYAN
18 Director Facility Services .... Ms. Jolene SCHMIDT
09 Dir of Inst Research & Assessment .... Mr. Kevin SAUNDERS
06 Director of Student Records .... Mr. Kevin P. MOENKHAUS
08 Dean Cowles Library .... Mr. Rodney N. HENSHAW
85 Vice Provost of Intl Programs .... Dr. Christa OLSON
91 Director Campus Information Svcs .... Vacant
19 Chief Campus Security Services .... Mr. Scott LAW

26 VP University Communications ... Ms. Debra LUKEHART
29 Alumni/Parent Programs ... Mr. Blake CAMPBELL
49 Interim Dean Arts & Sciences ... Dr. Keith SUMMERVILLE
53 Dean School Education ... Dr. Janet M. MCMAHILL
61 Dean Law School ... Mr. Ben ULLEM
50 Dean Business/Public Administration ... Ms. Terri VAUGHAN
67 Int Dean Pharmacy/Health Science ... Dr. Renae CHESNUT
60 Dean Journ/Mass Communications ... Ms. Kathleen RICHARDSON
41 Director Intercollegiate Athletics ... Ms. Sandy Hatfield CLUBB
37 Director Financial Aid ... Ms. Susan K. LADD
38 Director University Counseling Ctr ... Dr. Mark KLOBERDANZ
92 Assistant Director Honors Program ... Ms. Charlene SKIDMORE
94 Director Women's Studies ... Dr. Nancy REINCKE
31 Dir Community Outreach/ Development ... Ms. Amanda MCREYNOLDS
39 Director Office of Residence Life ... Ms. Lorissa LIEURANCE

*Eastern Iowa Community College District (A)

306 W River Drive, Davenport IA 52801-1221
County: Scott FICE Identification: 004075
Unit ID: 153311
Telephone: (563) 336-3300 Carnegie Class: N/A
FAX Number: (563) 336-3350
URL: www.eicc.edu

01 Chancellor ... Dr. Donald S. DOUCETTE
30 Exec Dir Resource Development ... Dr. Ellen KABAT LENSCH
05 Vice Chanc for Education & Training ... Dr. Joan KINDLE
26 Associate Director for Marketing ... Ms. Karen FARLEY
09 Dir Institutional Effectiveness ... Ms. Laurie R. HANSON
27 Associate Director Communications ... Mr. Alan CAMPBELL
10 Chief Business Officer ... Mr. Suteesh TANDON
101 Secretary of the Institution/Board ... Ms. Honey BEDELL
15 Director Personnel Services ... Ms. Deb SULLIVAN
18 Chief Facilities/Physical Plant ... Mr. Matt SCHMIT
84 Director Enrollment Management ... Ms. Erin SNYDER

*Clinton Community College (B)

1000 Lincoln Boulevard, Clinton IA 52732-6299
County: Clinton FICE Identification: 001853
Unit ID: 153135
Telephone: (563) 244-7001 Carnegie Class: Not Classified
FAX Number: (563) 244-7107 Calendar System: Semester
URL: www.eicc.edu
Established: 1966 Annual Undergrad Tuition & Fees (In-District): $140
Enrollment: 1,898 Coed
Affiliation or Control: State/Local IRS Status: 501(c)3
Highest Offering: Associate Degree
Program: Occupational; 2-Year Principally Bachelor's Creditable
Accreditation: &NH, EMT

02 President ... Dr. Karen VICKERS
05 Dean of the College ... Mr. Ron SERPLISS
32 Dean of Student Development ... Ms. Lisa MILLER
102 Asst to Pres/Exec Dir Sharar Found ... Ms. Ann EISENMAN
04 Assistant to President/Admin ... Ms. Deborah RICHTER

† Regional accreditation is carried under the parent institution Eastern Iowa Community College District in Davenport, IA.

*Muscatine Community College (C)

152 Colorado Street, Muscatine IA 52761-5396
County: Muscatine FICE Identification: 001882
Unit ID: 154040
Telephone: (563) 288-6001 Carnegie Class: Not Classified
FAX Number: (563) 288-6074 Calendar System: Semester
URL: www.eicc.edu
Established: 1929 Annual Undergrad Tuition & Fees (In-District): $140
Enrollment: 1,611 Coed
Affiliation or Control: State/Local IRS Status: 501(c)3
Highest Offering: Associate Degree
Program: Occupational; 2-Year Principally Bachelor's Creditable
Accreditation: &NH, EMT

02 President ... Mr. Bob ALLBEE
04 Assistant to the President ... Ms. Lisa WIEGEL
05 Dean of the College ... Dr. Gail SPIES
32 Dean of Student Development ... Ms. Shelly CRAM-RAHLF
31 Director Business/Industry Center ... Mr. Marvin SMITH
06 Registrar ... Ms. Robin MITCHELL
08 Library Specialist ... Ms. Nancy LUIKART

† Regional accreditation is carried under the parent institution Eastern Iowa Community College District in Davenport, IA.

*Scott Community College (D)

500 Belmont Road, Bettendorf IA 52722-6804
County: Scott FICE Identification: 001885
Unit ID: 154314
Telephone: (563) 441-4001 Carnegie Class: Not Classified
FAX Number: (563) 441-4154 Calendar System: Semester
URL: www.eicc.edu
Established: 1966 Annual Undergrad Tuition & Fees (In-District): $140
Enrollment: 4,634 Coed
Affiliation or Control: State/Local IRS Status: 501(c)3
Highest Offering: Associate Degree
Program: Occupational; 2-Year Principally Bachelor's Creditable
Accreditation: &NH, CAHIIM, DA, EMT, NDT, RAD, SURGT

02 President ... Dr. Teresa A. PAPER
32 Dean of Student Development/Affs ... Ms. LaDrina WILSON
36 Dean Career Assistance Center ... Ms. Peg GARRISON
05 Dean of the College ... Ms. Janet COOGAN
08 Librarian ... Ms. Michelle BAILEY
11 Asst to President Administration ... Mr. Matt SCHMIT
06 Registrar ... Mr. Arnold THODE
37 Director Student Financial Aid ... Ms. Jeannine INGELSON
36 Job Placement Specialist ... Mr. Wayne COLE

† Regional accreditation is carried under the parent institution Eastern Iowa Community College District in Davenport, IA.

Emmaus Bible College (E)

2570 Asbury Road, Dubuque IA 52001-3096
County: Dubuque FICE Identification: 023289
Unit ID: 153302
Telephone: (563) 588-8000 Carnegie Class: Spec/Faith
FAX Number: (563) 588-1216 Calendar System: Semester
URL: www.emmaus.edu
Established: 1941 Annual Undergrad Tuition & Fees: $15,920
Enrollment: 216 Coed
Affiliation or Control: Independent Non-Profit IRS Status: 501(c)3
Highest Offering: Baccalaureate
Program: Liberal Arts And General; Teacher Preparatory; Professional
Accreditation: NH, BI

01 President ... Mr. Philip BOOM
10 VP for Administration and Finance ... Mr. Mark A. PRESSON
05 Vice President for Academic Affairs ... Mrs. Lisa L. BEATTY
30 Vice President for Advancement ... Mr. Jon W. GLOCK
32 Dean for Student Development ... Mr. Israel CHAVEZ
88 Dean for Biblical Studies ... Dr. David J. MACLEOD
08 Librarian ... Mr. John H. RUSH
37 Financial Aid Officer ... Mr. Steve C. SEEMAN
21 Controller ... Mr. Steve M. JENSEN
06 Registrar ... Mrs. Janice G. BENNETT
84 Dir of Marketing & Enrollment ... Mr. Jesse LANGE

Faith Baptist Bible College and Seminary (F)

1900 NW 4th Street, Ankeny IA 50023-2152
County: Polk FICE Identification: 007121
Unit ID: 153320
Telephone: (515) 964-0601 Carnegie Class: Spec/Faith
FAX Number: (515) 964-1638 Calendar System: Semester
URL: www.faith.edu
Established: 1921 Annual Undergrad Tuition & Fees: $16,600
Enrollment: 262 Coed
Affiliation or Control: Independent Non-Profit IRS Status: 501(c)3
Highest Offering: First Professional Degree
Program: Liberal Arts And General; Teacher Preparatory; Religious Emphasis
Accreditation: NH, BI

01 President ... Rev. James R. TILLOTSON
05 VP for Academic Services ... Vacant
73 Dean of Seminary ... Dr. Douglas E. BROWN
10 VP for Business/CFO ... Mr. Daniel H. BJOKNE
30 VP for Advancement/Church Rels ... Vacant
34 Dean of Women ... Mrs. Carrie A. AUGSBURGER
32 Dean of Students ... Mr. Lance A. AUGSBURGER
26 Director of Communications ... Mr. Don K. ANDERSON
06 Registrar ... Mr. Andrew L. STEARNS
37 Director Student Financial Aid ... Mr. Breck H. APPELL
08 Head Librarian ... Dr. Paul A. HARTOG
04 Administrative Asst to President ... Miss Briana K. HARRIER
07 VP for Enrollment and Student Life ... Mr. Mark L. DAVIS
106 Dir Online Education/E-learning ... Dr. Christopher E. ELLIS
41 Athletic Director ... Mr. Brian S. FINCHAM

Graceland University (G)

1 University Place, Lamoni IA 50140-1699
County: Decatur FICE Identification: 001866
Unit ID: 153366
Telephone: (641) 784-5000 Carnegie Class: Master's L
FAX Number: (641) 784-5480 Calendar System: Semester
URL: www.graceland.edu
Established: 1895 Annual Undergrad Tuition & Fees: $25,890
Enrollment: 2,407 Coed
Affiliation or Control: Other IRS Status: 501(c)3
Highest Offering: Doctorate
Program: Liberal Arts And General; Teacher Preparatory
Accreditation: NH, CAATE, NURSE, TED

01 President ... Dr. John SELLARS
05 Vice Pres Acad Affs/Dean of Faculty ... Dr. Tammy EVERETT
09 VP Institutional Effectiveness ... Dr. Kathleen M. CLAUSON BASH
10 CIO/Vice Pres Business & Admin Svc ... Mr. Paul DAVIS
32 VP Student Life/Dean of Students ... Mr. Dave SCHAAL
84 Int Vice Pres Enrollment ... Mr. Joe WORLAND
30 Vice Pres Institutional Advancement ... Mr. Kelly EVERETT
51 Director for Graduate/Continuing Ed ... Mr. Paul BINNICKER
39 Director of Residence Life ... Ms. Deb SKINNER
06 Registrar ... Mrs. M. Joyce LIGHTHILL
29 Director of Alumni Relations ... Mr. Paul DAVIS
36 Director Career/Acad/CAP Couns Ctr ... Ms. Catharine CRAIG
15 Director Human Resources ... Mrs. Ondrea DORY
04 Executive Asst to President ... Mrs. Jodi L. SEYMOUR
44 Director of Annual Fund/Stewardship ... Mrs. Peggy STURDEVANT
85 Director International Programs ... Ms. Diana JONES
86 Director Government Relations ... Dr. Tom MORAIN
50 Dean School of Business ... Dr. Steven ANDERS
53 Int Dean School of Education ... Dr. Scott HUDDLESTON
66 Dean School of Nursing ... Dr. Claudia HORTON
07 Director of Admissions ... Mr. Kevin BROWN
09 Director of Institutional Research ... Mr. James UHLENKAMP

Grand View University (H)

1200 Grandview Avenue, Des Moines IA 50316-1599
County: Polk FICE Identification: 001867
Unit ID: 153375
Telephone: (515) 263-2800 Carnegie Class: Bac/Diverse
FAX Number: (515) 263-6095 Calendar System: Semester
URL: www.grandview.edu
Established: 1896 Annual Undergrad Tuition & Fees: $24,544
Enrollment: 2,064 Coed
Affiliation or Control: Evangelical Lutheran Church In America
IRS Status: 501(c)3
Highest Offering: Master's
Program: Liberal Arts And General; Professional
Accreditation: NH, NURSE

01 President ... Mr. Kent L. HENNING
04 Executive Asst to the President ... Mr. Lucas J. CASEY
05 Provost/Vice Pres Academic Affairs ... Dr. Mary Elizabeth STIVERS
79 Dean College of Humanities & Educ ... Dr. Ross WASTVEDT
83 Dean College of Social/Nat Science ... Vacant
10 Vice Pres Administration & Finance ... Mr. Adam J. VOIGTS
30 Vice President Advancement ... Mr. William H. BURMA
84 Vice Pres Enrollment Management ... Ms. Debbie M. BARGER
26 Vice Pres Marketing/Communications ... Ms. Carol M. BAMFORD
32 Vice President Student Affairs ... Dr. Jay B. PRESCOTT
37 Director Financial Aid ... Ms. Michele A. DUNNE
20 Special Assistant to the Provost ... Ms. Pamela M. CHRISTOFFERS
51 Dean Graduate/Adult Programs ... Dr. Patricia A. WILLIAMS
35 Associate VP for Student Affairs ... Mr. Jason K. BAUER
06 Registrar ... Ms. Debbie K. GANNON
42 Senior Campus Pastor ... Rev. Russell L. LACKEY
09 Director Inst Planning/Research ... Ms. Debbie M. BARGER
36 Director Career Center ... Ms. Susan M. STEARNS
91 Vice President Information Svcs/CIO ... Mr. Tim T. WHEELDON
08 Director of the Library ... Ms. Pamela D. REES
40 Director Bookstore & Campus Svcs ... Mr. Michael D. SHUPP
07 Director of Admissions ... Mr. Ryan THOMPSON
18 Director Buildings & Grounds ... Ms. Kim I. BUTLER
38 Director Leadership & Counseling ... Mr. Kent A. SCHORNACK
28 Dir Multicultural & Cmty Outreach ... Mr. Alex H. PIEDRAS
41 Athletic Director ... Mr. Troy A. PLUMMER
15 Human Resources Manager ... Ms. Erica L. KLUVER

Grinnell College (I)

1121 Park Street, Grinnell IA 50112-1690
County: Poweshiek FICE Identification: 001868
Unit ID: 153384
Telephone: (641) 269-4000 Carnegie Class: Bac/A&S
FAX Number: (641) 269-3408 Calendar System: Semester
URL: www.grinnell.edu
Established: 1846 Annual Undergrad Tuition & Fees: $46,990
Enrollment: 1,692 Coed
Affiliation or Control: Independent Non-Profit IRS Status: 501(c)3
Highest Offering: Baccalaureate
Program: Liberal Arts And General; Teacher Preparatory
Accreditation: NH

01 President ... Raynard S. KINGTON
100 Chief of Staff/VP Planning ... Angela VOOS
05 Vice Pres Acad Affs/Dean Col ... Michael LATHAM
30 Vice President Dev/Alumni Rel ... Shane JACOBSON
88 Chief Investment Officer ... Scott L. WILSON
88 Vice President of College Services ... John KALKBRENNER
10 Vice President for Finance/Treas ... Kate E. WALKER
20 Associate Dean of College ... Maria TAPIAS
20 Associate Dean of College ... Heather LOBBAN-VIRAVONG
07 VP Enroll/Dean Adm & Fin Aid ... Joseph P. BAGNOLI
30 Director of Development Operations ... Adam LAUG
37 Director of Student Financial Aid ... Brad LINDBERG
15 Director of Human Resources ... Vacant
26 Director of Communication ... Jim REISCHE
06 Registrar ... Jason MAHER
08 Librarian ... Richard FYFFE
29 Director of Alumni Relations ... Jayn CHANEY
13 Chief Information Tech Officer ... Dave ROBINSON
09 Assoc VP Analytics/Inst Rsch ... Randall STILES
85 Director Intl Student Services ... Karen K. EDWARDS
40 Manager/Bookstore ... Cassandra J. WHERRY
41 Athletic Director ... Greg WALLACE
23 Dir Stdnt Health & Counsel Service ... Deb SHILL
38 Dean Student Success/Acad Advising ... Joyce STERN
18 Director Facilities Mgmt ... Richard WHITNEY
19 Director of Safety & Security ... Stephen A. BRISCOE
42 Chaplain/Dean of Rel Life ... Deanna SHORB
102 Director Corp/Found/Govt Rels ... Susan FERRARI
32 Assoc VP Student Affairs ... Andrea CONNER
35 Dean of Students ... Sarah MOSCHENROSS
31 Dir Community Enhancement/Engagemnt ... Monica CHAVEZ-SILVA
36 Dean & Director/Career Life & Svcs ... Mark PELTZ

04 Executive Asst to President ....Tammy PRUSHA
101 Secretary of the College ....Susan SCHOEN
104 Director Study Abroad ....Richard BRIGHT
28 Director of Diversity ....Lakeshia JOHNSON
39 Director Student Housing ....Jon SEXTON
44 Director Annual or Planned Giving ....Mae TURLEY

Hamilton Technical College (A)

1011 E 53rd Street, Davenport IA 52807-2616
County: Scott FICE Identification: 012064
Unit ID: 153427
Telephone: (563) 386-3570 Carnegie Class: Spec/Tech
FAX Number: (563) 386-6756 Calendar System: Semester
URL: www.hamiltontechcollege.com
Established: 1969 Annual Undergrad Tuition & Fees: $12,165
Enrollment: 143 Coed
Affiliation or Control: Proprietary IRS Status: Proprietary
Highest Offering: Baccalaureate
Program: Occupational; Technical Emphasis
Accreditation: ACCSC

01 President ....Mrs. Maryanne HAMILTON

Hawkeye Community College (B)

Box 8015, Waterloo IA 50704-8015
County: Black Hawk FICE Identification: 004595
Unit ID: 153445
Telephone: (319) 296-2320 Carnegie Class: Assoc/Pub-R-L
FAX Number: (319) 296-2874 Calendar System: Semester
URL: www.hawkeyecollege.edu
Established: 1966 Annual Undergrad Tuition & Fees (In-District): $4,785
Enrollment: 5,291 Coed
Affiliation or Control: State/Local IRS Status: 501(c)3
Highest Offering: Associate Degree
Program: Occupational; 2-Year Principally Bachelor's Creditable
Accreditation: NH, COARC, DA, DH, MLTAD, OTA, PTAA

01 President ....Dr. Linda A. ALLEN
05 Vice Pres Academic Affairs ....Dr. Jane BRADLEY
10 Vice Pres Administration & Finance ....Mr. Dan GILLEN
30 Vice Pres Institutional Advancement ....Ms. Kathy A. FLYNN
102 Executive Director Foundation ....Ms. Holly JOHNSON
15 Exec Dir Human Resource Services ....Mr. John D. CLOPTON
81 Dean Math/Natural & Social Sciences ....Dr. Cynthia BOTTRELL
79 Dean Comm/Humanities/Educ/Fine Arts . Ms. Catharine FREEMAN
75 Dean Applied Science/Eng Technology ....Mr. A. Ray BEETS
76 Dean Health Sciences ....Dr. Candace CROFT
50 Dean Business & Public Services ....Mr. Bryan RENFRO
32 Dean of Students ....Ms. Nancy HENDERSON
07 Director Admissions & Recruitment ....Mr. Dave BALL
21 Director Business Services ....Ms. Julie THOMAS
13 Director Communication/Info Systems ....Mr. Brian MCCORMICK
62 Director Library Services ....Ms. Candace HAVELY
51 Exec Director Business & Cmty Ed ....Mr. Aaron SAUERBREI
18 Director Plant & Facilities ....Ms. Lindsey NISSEN
06 Dir Student Records & Registration ....Ms. Patricia A. EAST
24 Director Teaching/Learning Services ....Mr. Robin GALLOWAY
09 Director Institutional Research ....Ms. Connie BUHR
26 Director Public Relations/Mktg ....Ms. Mary Pat MOORE
28 Assoc Dir of Multicultural Affairs ....Mr. Quentin HART
35 Assoc Dir of Student Life ....Ms. Stephanie CHERRY
44 Development Officer ....Ms. Karen GEBEL
101 Board Secretary ....Ms. Denise A. DUNN
19 Dir Public Safety/Emergency Mgr ....Mr. John BECKMAN
88 Director Urban Ctrs/Adult Literacy ....Ms. Sandra JENSEN
88 Dean of Transitional Programs ....Mr. Tom MUELLER
103 Dir Workforce/Career Development ....Ms. Christina MASON
37 Director Student Financial Aid ....Ms. Gisella BAKER

Indian Hills Community College (C)

525 Grandview Avenue, Ottumwa IA 52501-1398
County: Wapello FICE Identification: 008403
Unit ID: 153472
Telephone: (641) 683-5111 Carnegie Class: Assoc/Pub-R-M
FAX Number: (641) 683-5184 Calendar System: Quarter
URL: www.indianhills.edu
Established: 1966 Annual Undergrad Tuition & Fees (In-District): $3,720
Enrollment: 4,412 Coed
Affiliation or Control: State/Local IRS Status: 501(c)3
Highest Offering: Associate Degree
Program: Occupational; 2-Year Principally Bachelor's Creditable
Accreditation: NH, ACFEI, CAHIIM, DA, EMT, MLTAD, OTA, PTAA, RAD

01 President ....Dr. Marlene SPROUSE
10 Chief Financial Officer ....Mr. Bill MECK
05 Vice Pres Acad Affs/Instl Effect ....Dr. Matt THOMPSON
49 Executive Dean Arts & Sciences ....Ms. Darlas SHOCKLEY
103 Exec Dean Reg Economic Advancement ....Mr. Tom RUBEL
32 Dean Student Services ....Mr. Chris BOWSER
76 Dean Health Sciences ....Dr. Jill BUDDE
12 Dean Centerville Campus ....Mr. Joe STARCEVICH
86 Assoc Dean Govt Affs & Cmty Rels ....Ms. Martha WICK
102 Assoc Dean Foundation/Cmty Rels ....Ms. Rhonda CONRAD
15 Director Human Resources ....Ms. Bonnie CAMPBELL
18 Director Maintenance ....Mr. Rick FOSDYCK
06 Registrar ....Ms. Joni KELLEY
41 Athletic Director ....Mr. Mike HAGEN
26 Director for Media/Public Rels ....Mr. Kevin PINK
88 Chair Aviation Programs ....Mr. Darren GRAHAM
07 Director of Admissions ....Mr. Mark THOMPSON
09 Director of Institutional Research ....Dr. Stephanie HOLLIMAN
29 Director of Alumni Relations ....Dr. Bianca MYERS
35 Chief Development ....Ms. Rhonda CONRAD

Indian Hills Community College Centerville (D)

721 N First Street, Centerville IA 52544
Telephone: (641) 856-2143 Identification: 770054
Accreditation: &NH

† Branch campus of Indian Hills Community College, Ottumwa, IA.

Inste Bible College (E)

2302 SW 3rd Street, Ankeny IA 50023-2453
County: Polk Identification: 666461
Telephone: (515) 289-9200 Carnegie Class: Not Classified
FAX Number: (515) 289-9201 Calendar System: Semester
URL: www.inste.edu
Established: 1982 Annual Undergrad Tuition & Fees: $2,520
Enrollment: 17 Coed
Affiliation or Control: Interdenominational IRS Status: 501(c)3
Highest Offering: Baccalaureate
Program: Liberal Arts And General; Religious Emphasis
Accreditation: DEAC

01 President ....Dr. Nicholas VENDITTI
05 Vice President ....Dr. Leona VENDITTI
20 Assistant Dean ....Rev. Victor COLÓN
20 Academic Dean ....Mr. Caleb PAHL

Iowa Central Community College (F)

One Triton Circle, Fort Dodge IA 50501-5798
County: Webster FICE Identification: 001865
Unit ID: 153524
Telephone: (515) 576-7201 Carnegie Class: Assoc/Pub-R-M
FAX Number: (515) 576-7207 Calendar System: Semester
URL: www.iowacentral.edu
Established: 1966 Annual Undergrad Tuition & Fees (In-District): $4,890
Enrollment: 5,686 Coed
Affiliation or Control: Local IRS Status: 501(c)3
Highest Offering: Associate Degree
Program: Occupational; 2-Year Principally Bachelor's Creditable
Accreditation: NH, DH, EMT, MAC, MLTAD, RAD

01 President ....Dr. Daniel P. KINNEY
04 Assistant to the President ....Mrs. Karen L. LOMBARD
05 Vice President of Instruction ....Mr. David E. GROSLAND
32 Vice Pres Enroll Mgmt/Student Devel ....Mr. Thomas J. BENEKE
10 Vice President of Business Affairs ....Mrs. Angela A. MARTIN
86 VP External Affairs/Govt Rels ....Mr. James B. KERSTEN
30 VP Development/Alumni Rels ....Mrs. Laurie M. HENDRICKS
72 Dean Business & Ind Technology ....Mr. Neale J. ADAMS
66 Dean Health Sciences ....Mrs. Trina J. STATON
49 Dean Liberal Arts & Sciences ....Mrs. Jennifer M. CONDON
106 Dean Distance Learning ....Mr. Timothy J. MARTIN
09 Institutional Effectiv Exec Dir ....Mrs. Stacy L. MENTZER
06 Registrar ....Ms. Courtney A. KOPP
84 Director Enrollment Management ....Ms. Sara A. CONDON
37 Director Financial Aid ....Mrs. Darci M. BANGERT
21 Director Business Office ....Mr. Luke J. GROVE
15 Director Human Resources ....Mrs. Kimberly N. WHITMORE
16 Coordinator Human Resources ....Ms. Sandi J. PIEPER
41 Director Intercollegiate Athletics ....Mr. Rick A. SANDQUIST
39 Director Housing ....Mr. Jeremy D. CONLEY
35 Dir Student Life & Activities ....Mr. David L. PEARSON
88 Director Academic Resource Services ....Ms. Lori L. WALTON
18 Director Physical Facilities ....Mr. Shan L. BEECHER
12 Director Storm Lake Center ....Mr. Dan J. ANDERSON
12 Director Webster City Center ....Mrs. Kelly J. WIRTZ
26 Director Public Information ....Mr. Paul A. DECOURSEY
13 Director Institutional Technology ....Mr. Jeff A. NELSEN
13 Director Institutional Technology ....Mr. Troy D. CRAMPTON
14 Computer System Analyst ....Mr. Warren K. BAUER
40 Bookstore Manager ....Mrs. Samantha E. MCCLAIN

Iowa Lakes Community College (G)

19 S Seventh Street, Estherville IA 51334-2234
County: Emmet FICE Identification: 001864
Unit ID: 153533
Telephone: (712) 362-2604 Carnegie Class: Assoc/Pub-R-M
FAX Number: (712) 362-8363 Calendar System: Semester
URL: www.iowalakes.edu
Established: 1967 Annual Undergrad Tuition & Fees (In-District): $5,676
Enrollment: 2,391 Coed
Affiliation or Control: State/Local IRS Status: 501(c)3
Highest Offering: Associate Degree
Program: Occupational; 2-Year Principally Bachelor's Creditable
Accreditation: NH, MAC, SURGT

01 President ....Ms. Valerie K. NEWHOUSE
11 Vice President of Administration ....Mr. Robert W. L'HEUREUX
12 Exec Dean Emmetsburg Campus ....Mr. Thomas S. BROTHERTON
12 Exec Dean Estherville Campus ....Mr. Robert A. LEIFELD
26 Exec Director of Marketing ....Ms. Jane S. CAMPBELL
05 Exec Dean Instruction/Development ....Mr. Scott M. STOKES
18 Exec Dir of Facilities Management ....Ms. Delaine S. HINEY
51 Exec Dir Cmty & Business Relations ....Ms. Jolene R. ROGERS
32 Executive Dean of Students ....Ms. Julie R. WILLIAMS

Iowa Lakes Community College Emmetsburg Campus (H)

3200 College Drive, Emmetsburg IA 50536
Telephone: (712) 852-3554 Identification: 770055
Accreditation: &NH

† Branch campus of Iowa Lakes Community College, Estherville, IA.

Iowa Lakes Community College Spencer Campus (I)

Gateway N 1900 Grand Ave, Ste B-1, Spencer IA 51301
Telephone: (712) 262-7141 Identification: 770056
Accreditation: &NH

† Branch campus of Iowa Lakes Community College, Estherville, IA.

*Iowa Valley Community College District (J)

3702 S Center Street, Marshalltown IA 50158-4760
County: Marshall FICE Identification: 033436
Telephone: (641) 752-4643 Carnegie Class: N/A
FAX Number: (641) 754-1336
URL: www.iavalley.edu

01 Chancellor ....Mr. Christopher DUREE
11 Vice Chanc Administrative Services ....Ms. Colleen SPRINGER
51 Vice Chanc Continuing Educ/Training ....Ms. Jacque GOODMAN
10 Chief Financial Officer ....Ms. Kathleen PINK
12 Provost of ECC ....Vacant
12 Provost of MCC ....Dr. Robin SHAFFER LILIENTHAL
12 Dean of Iowa Valley Grinnell ....Ms. Mary Anne NICKLE
26 Director of Marketing ....Ms. Robin ANCTIL
09 Institutional Researcher ....Dr. Lisa BREJA
04 Admin Assistant to the Chancellor ....Ms. Barbara JENNINGS
13 Chief Information Officer ....Mr. Jim WILSON
86 Director Government Relations ....Ms. Cynthia SCHULTE

*Ellsworth Community College (K)

1100 College Avenue, Iowa Falls IA 50126-1199
County: Hardin FICE Identification: 001862
Unit ID: 153296
Telephone: (641) 648-4611 Carnegie Class: Assoc/Pub-R-S
FAX Number: (641) 648-3128 Calendar System: Semester
URL: www.iavalley.edu/ecc
Established: 1890 Annual Undergrad Tuition & Fees (In-District): $4,296
Enrollment: 949 Coed
Affiliation or Control: State/Local IRS Status: 501(c)3
Highest Offering: Associate Degree
Program: Occupational; 2-Year Principally Bachelor's Creditable
Accreditation: &NH, MAC

02 Provost ....Dr. Nancy MUECKE
05 Dean of Students & Academic Affairs ....Dr. Lisa STOCK
08 Director of Libraries ....Ms. Sandra GREUFE
32 Director of Athletics/Student Life ....Mr. Nate FORSYTH
39 Director Student Housing ....Mr. O. J. PAYNE
37 Director Financial Aid ....Ms. Tara MILLER
44 Dir Annual Plan Giving/Dir Alum Rel ....Ms. Kaitlyn BARTLING
07 Director of Admissions ....Ms. Adriane SEITSEMA
84 Dean Enrollment Mgmt/Registrar ....Dr. Barb KLEIN

† Regional accreditation is carried under the parent institution Iowa Valley Community College District in Marshalltown, IA.

*Marshalltown Community College (L)

3700 S Center Street, Marshalltown IA 50158-4760
County: Marshall FICE Identification: 001875
Unit ID: 153922
Telephone: (641) 752-7106 Carnegie Class: Assoc/Pub-R-S
FAX Number: (641) 752-8149 Calendar System: Semester
URL: www.mcc.iavalley.edu
Established: 1927 Annual Undergrad Tuition & Fees (In-District): $5,520
Enrollment: 2,041 Coed
Affiliation or Control: State/Local IRS Status: 501(c)3
Highest Offering: Associate Degree
Program: Occupational; 2-Year Principally Bachelor's Creditable
Accreditation: &NH, DA

02 Chancellor ....Dr. Christopher A. DUREE
05 Provost ....Dr. Robin SHAFFER LILIENTHAL
11 Vice Chanc Administrative Services ....Ms. Colleen SPRINGER
10 Chief Financial Officer ....Ms. Kathy PINK
51 Vice Chancellor of Cont Educ/Trng ....Jacque GOODMAN
20 Dean of Students & Academic Affairs ....Dr. Chris A. RUSSELL
20 Dir of Retention/Learning Svcs/TRIO ....Mr. Nate CHUA
06 Registrar/Dir of Operations ....Ms. Mandy BROWN
76 Assoc Dean of Health Occupations ....Ms. Linda HANSON
102 Executive Director MCC Foundation ....Ms. Carol GEIL
84 Dean Enrollment/Student Life ....Ms. Angie REDMOND
37 Director Student Financial Aid ....Mr. Matt DANIELS
26 Director of Marketing ....Vacant
09 Dir of Institutional Research ....Vacant
41 Athletic Director ....Mr. Daniel HUNTLEY
32 Director of Student Engagement ....Mr. Chris BREES
38 Senior Student Success Specialist ....Mr. Dan KEY
08 Library Services Manager ....Ms. Mara EGHERMAN

40 MCC Bookstore Supervisor .... Ms. Meghan TOMLINSON

† Regional accreditation is carried under the parent institution Iowa Valley Community College District in Marshalltown, IA.

Iowa Wesleyan University (A)

601 N Main, Mount Pleasant IA 52641-1398

County: Henry FICE Identification: 001871
Unit ID: 153621
Telephone: (319) 385-8021 Carnegie Class: Bac/Diverse
FAX Number: (319) 385-6296 Calendar System: Semester
URL: www.iwc.edu
Established: 1842 Annual Undergrad Tuition & Fees: $26,806
Enrollment: 482 Coed
Affiliation or Control: United Methodist IRS Status: 501(c)3
Highest Offering: Baccalaureate
Program: Liberal Arts And General; Teacher Preparatory; Professional
Accreditation: NH, NUR

01 President .... Dr. Steven E. TITUS
10 VP/Chief Financial Officer .... Ms. Chris PLUNKET
84 Sr VP for Enrollment/Communications .... Mr. Scott BRIELL
05 VP Academic Affairs and Dean .... Dr. DeWayne FRAZIER
30 Sr VP University Advancement .... Ms. Meg RICHTMAN
32 Dean for Student Development .... Dr. Wes BROOKS
13 Assoc VP/Chief Information Officer .... Dr. Kit NIP
06 Registrar .... Ms. Catherine ASHTON
37 Director of Financial Aid .... Ms. Julie DUPLESSIS
07 Director of Admissions .... Vacant
21 Controller .... Ms. Deb LILLIE
08 Library Director .... Ms. Paula KINNEY
15 Director of Human Resources .... Ms. Kathy MOOTHART
44 Director of Annual Fund .... Ms. Holly JONES
26 Director of Marketing/Communication .... Ms. Ashlee WHIPPLE
27 Publications Manager .... Ms. Sheri MICHAELS
29 Director of Alumni/Parent Relations .... Ms. Anita HAMPTON
41 Athletic Director .... Mr. Steve WILLIAMSON
18 Director of Physical Plant .... Mr. Bob VITALE
35 Director of Student Activities .... Ms. Kat NIEMANN
36 Director of Career Development .... Ms. Erin MAFRA
40 Bookstore Director .... Ms. Amy MABEUS
04 Senior Exec Asst to the President .... Ms. Mary NOTESTEIN
105 Director Web Services .... Vacant
09 Director of Institutional Research .... Mr. Michelle PARKEVICH
102 Dir Corporate/Foundation Relations .... Mr. Jim PEDRICK

Iowa Western Community College (B)

2700 College Road, Council Bluffs IA 51503-0567

County: Pottawattamie FICE Identification: 004598
Unit ID: 153630
Telephone: (712) 325-3200 Carnegie Class: Assoc/Pub-S-MC
FAX Number: (712) 325-3424 Calendar System: Semester
URL: www.iwcc.edu
Established: 1966 Annual Undergrad Tuition & Fees (In-District): $4,560
Enrollment: 6,547 Coed
Affiliation or Control: State/Local IRS Status: 501(c)3
Highest Offering: Associate Degree
Program: Occupational; 2-Year Principally Bachelor's Creditable
Accreditation: NH, ACFEI, DA, DH, EMT, #MAC, @PTAA, SURGT

01 President .... Dr. Dan KINNEY
04 Assistant to the President .... Ms. Erin STOPAK
05 Vice President for Academic Affairs .... Dr. Marjorie WELCH
10 Vice President of Finance .... Mr. Edwin HOLTZ
32 Vice President for Student Services .... Ms. Tori CHRISTIE
26 Vice Pres of Marketing/Public Rels .... Mr. Donald KOHLER
30 Vice Pres Institutional Advancement .... Ms. Molly NOON
103 VP Economic/Workforce Devel .... Mr. Mark STANLEY
09 Dean Institutional Research/Accred .... Ms. Barb GODDEN
84 Dean Enrollment Services .... Ms. Chris LAFERLA
35 Dean Student Life/Student Success .... Ms. Kimberly HENRY
12 Director of Clarinda Campus .... Mr. Chad WELLHAUSEN
06 Registrar .... Ms. Jill CLARK
15 Director of Human Resources .... Ms. Kelly FISCHER
29 Director of Alumni Relations .... Ms. Stacy SHOCKEY
37 Director of Student Financial Aid .... Vacant
21 Asst Director Accounting .... Ms. Randi PAPE
13 Dir Information Technology .... Mr. James A. MAHLBERG
88 Exec Dir Economic Development .... Mr. Mark STANLEY
41 Athletic Director .... Ms. Brenda HAMPTON
39 Director of Residence Life .... Ms. Elizabeth LUIKEN
18 Director Physical Plant .... Mr. Greg CLAUSEN
07 Director of Admissions/Advising .... Ms. Cara TREDE
96 Director of Purchasing .... Mrs. Diane OSBAHR
40 Director Food Svcs/Bookstore Mgr .... Ms. Eddie HOLTZ
76 Area Nursing Coordinator .... Ms. Rita BERTHELSEN

Iowa Western Community College Clarinda Center (C)

923 East Washington Street, Clarinda IA 51632

Telephone: (712) 542-5117 Identification: 770057
Accreditation: &NH

† Branch campus of Iowa Western Community College, Council Bluffs, IA.

ITT Technical Institute (D)

1860 NW 118th Street, Suite 110, Clive IA 50325-8278

Telephone: (515) 327-5500 Identification: 666596
Accreditation: ACICS

† Branch campus of ITT Technical Institute, Indianapolis, IN.

Kaplan University (E)

3165 Edgewood Parkway SW, Cedar Rapids IA 52404-2998

Telephone: (319) 363-0481 FICE Identification: 004220
Accreditation: &NH, ACBSP, MAC

† Regional accreditation is carried under the parent institution in Davenport, IA.

Kaplan University (F)

1801 East Kimberly Road, Suite 1, Davenport IA 52807-2095

County: Scott FICE Identification: 004586
Unit ID: 260901
Telephone: (563) 355-3500 Carnegie Class: Master's L
FAX Number: (563) 355-1320 Calendar System: Quarter
URL: www.kaplanuniversity.edu/davenport-iowa.aspx
Established: 1937 Annual Undergrad Tuition & Fees: $13,956
Enrollment: 52,018 Coed
Affiliation or Control: Proprietary IRS Status: Proprietary
Highest Offering: Doctorate
Program: Occupational
Accreditation: NH, ACBSP, MAC, NURSE

01 Campus President .... Ms. Liza ZERBONIA
31 Campus Relations Manager .... Ms. Angela BOWERS
32 Director of Student Services .... Vacant
37 Director of Financial Aid .... Ms. Sharon BARBER
07 Director of Admissions .... Mr. Jason WILEBSKI
36 Employment Search Coordinator .... Ms. Sandra WAKEFIELD
08 Librarian .... Ms. Marlene METZGAR
06 Registrar .... Ms. Janet GEHRLS

Kaplan University (G)

Plaza West 2570 4th Street, SW, Mason City IA 50401-3102

Telephone: (641) 423-2530 Identification: 666438
Accreditation: &NH, ACBSP, MAC

† Regional accreditation is carried under the parent institution in Davenport, IA.

Kaplan University (H)

4655 121st Street, Urbandale IA 50323-2311

Telephone: (515) 727-2100 Identification: 666437
Accreditation: &NH, ACBSP, MAC

† Regional accreditation is carried under the parent institution in Davenport, IA.

Kaplan University-Cedar Falls (I)

7009 Nordic Drive, Cedar Falls IA 50613

Telephone: (319) 277-0220 Identification: 770058
Accreditation: &NH, ACBSP, MAC

† Branch campus of Kaplan University, Davenport, IA.

Kirkwood Community College (J)

PO Box 2068, Cedar Rapids IA 52406-2068

County: Linn FICE Identification: 004076
Unit ID: 153737
Telephone: (319) 398-5411 Carnegie Class: Assoc/Pub-R-L
FAX Number: (319) 398-1037 Calendar System: Semester
URL: www.kirkwood.edu
Established: 1966 Annual Undergrad Tuition & Fees (In-District): $4,440
Enrollment: 14,708 Coed
Affiliation or Control: Local IRS Status: 501(c)3
Highest Offering: Associate Degree
Program: Occupational; 2-Year Principally Bachelor's Creditable; Technical Emphasis
Accreditation: NH, ACBSP, ACFEI, CAHIIM, COARC, DA, DH, DT, EMT, MAC, NDT, OTA, PTAA, SURGT

01 President .... Dr. Mick STARCEVICH
51 VP Cont Education/Training Svcs .... Dr. Kim BECICKA
10 Vice President/Chief Fin/Oper Ofcr .... Mr. Jim CHOATE
30 Vice President Development .... Ms. Kathy HALL
05 Vice President Academic Affairs .... Dr. Bill LAMB
32 Vice President Student Services .... Dr. Jon BUSE
20 Assoc Vice President Acad Affairs .... Mr. John HENIK
12 Dean Iowa City Campus .... Dr. Ann VALENTINE
35 Dean of Students .... Dr. Melissa PAYNE
15 Director Human Resources .... Mr. Mike ROBERTS
13 Associate VP IT .... Mr. Jon NEFF
09 Associate VP Institutional Research .... Mr. Al ROWE
106 Dean Distance Lrng & Secondary Pgm .... Mr. Todd PRUSHA
84 Director Enrollment Management .... Ms. Peg JULIUS
08 Director Library .... Mr. Arron WINGS
07 Director Admissions .... Mr. Douglas F. BANNON
18 Associate VP Facilities .... Mr. Tom KALDENBERG
25 Director Grants & Fed Programs .... Ms. Heather CONLEY
41 Athletic Director .... Mr. Doug WAGEMESTER
06 Registrar .... Ms. Dena RAUCH
29 Scholarship & Alumni Director .... Ms. Jody DONALDSON
37 Director Student Financial Aid .... Ms. Peg JULIUS
47 Dean Agriculture .... Mr. Scott ERMER
72 Dean Industrial Technology .... Mr. Jeff MITCHELL
79 Dean Humanities & English .... Dr. Jennifer BRADLEY
76 Dean Allied Health .... Dr. Nicky CLINE
83 Dean Social Sciences/Career Option .... Ms. Brooke STRAHN-KOLLER
81 Dean Math/Science .... Mr. Marvin BAUSMAN
66 Dean Nursing .... Vacant
76 Dean Health Occupations .... Dr. Mike MCLAUGHLIN
50 Dean Business & Information Tech .... Ms. Lisa DUTCHIK
88 Dean Learning Services .... Mr. Arron WINGS
04 Administrative Asst to President .... Ms. Sheryl COOK
104 Director Study Abroad .... Ms. Dawn WOOD
19 Director Security/Safety .... Mrs. Melissa JENSEN
26 Chief Public Relations/Marketing .... Mrs. Kathy KAISER
44 Director Annual or Planned Giving .... Mrs. Susan OVEL

Kirkwood Community College Iowa City (K)

1816 Lower Muscatine Road, Iowa City IA 52240

Telephone: (819) 887-3658 Identification: 770062
Accreditation: &NH

† Branch campus of Kirkwood Community College, Cedar Rapids, IA.

Loras College (L)

1450 Alta Vista, Dubuque IA 52004-0178

County: Dubuque FICE Identification: 001873
Unit ID: 153825
Telephone: (563) 588-7100 Carnegie Class: Bac/Diverse
FAX Number: (563) 588-7964 Calendar System: Semester
URL: www.loras.edu
Established: 1839 Annual Undergrad Tuition & Fees: $30,628
Enrollment: 1,536 Coed
Affiliation or Control: Roman Catholic IRS Status: 501(c)3
Highest Offering: Master's
Program: Liberal Arts And General; Teacher Preparatory
Accreditation: NH, CAATE, ENG, SW

01 President .... Mr. James E. COLLINS
05 Interim Academic Dean .... Rev. Douglas WATHIER
10 Vice President Finance/Admin Svcs .... Mr. Brock EVEN
03 Senior Vice President .... Dr. Mary Ellen CARROLL
30 Vice Pres Institutional Advancement .... Mr. Michael J. DOYLE
32 Vice President Student Development .... Dr. Arthur W. SUNLEAF
04 Executive Assistant to President .... Ms. Barbara J. SIMON
42 Dean of Campus Spiritual Life .... Rev. William JOENSEN
91 Sr Dir Technology Support Services .... Vacant
29 Exec Dir Alumni & Communications .... Ms. Bobbi L. EARLES
15 Dir Human/Organization Development .... Mr. Troy WRIGHT
09 Director of Institutional Research .... Ms. Katie THARP
38 Director Center for Counseling .... Ms. Tricia BORELLI
07 Dean of Admissions/Financial Aid .... Mr. Jason WOODS
08 Director of Academic Resource Ctr .... Ms. Joyce A. MELDREM
35 Assistant Dean of Students .... Ms. Molly BURROWS-SCHUMACHER
44 Director of Major & Planned Giving .... Mr. Eric J. SOLBERG
41 Director of Athletics .... Ms. Denise UDELHOFEN
18 Director of Physical Plant .... Mr. John R. MCDERMOTT
40 Director of Bookstore .... Ms. Renee A. MENNE
23 Director of Health Center .... Mrs. Tammy S. MARTI
42 Director of Campus Ministry .... Ms. Colleen M. KUHL
06 Registrar .... Mr. JT BROWN
39 Dir of Residence Life/Campus Safety .... Ms. Molly A. BURROWS-SCHUMACHER
35 Director of Student Life .... Ms. Kimberly A. WALSH
37 Director of Financial Planning .... Ms. Julie A. DUNN
25 Grant Writing Director .... Ms. Valorie A. WOERDEHOFF
26 Dir Communications/Marketing .... Ms. Susan P. HAFKEMEYER
96 Controller for Business Office .... Ms. Rennie ROOT
36 Academic Internship Coordinator .... Ms. Faye A. FINNEGAN

Luther College (M)

700 College Drive, Decorah IA 52101-1045

County: Winneshiek FICE Identification: 001874
Unit ID: 153834
Telephone: (563) 387-2000 Carnegie Class: Bac/A&S
FAX Number: (563) 387-2158 Calendar System: 4/1/4
URL: www.luther.edu
Established: 1861 Annual Undergrad Tuition & Fees: $39,190
Enrollment: 2,385 Coed
Affiliation or Control: Evangelical Lutheran Church In America
IRS Status: 501(c)3
Highest Offering: Baccalaureate
Program: Liberal Arts And General; Teacher Preparatory; Professional
Accreditation: NH, CAATE, MUS, NURSE, SW, TED

01 President .... Dr. Paula J. CARLSON
05 Vice Pres Acad Affs/Dean of College .... Dr. Kevin KRAUS
20 Assistant Dean .... Ms. Arleen ORVIS
30 Vice President for Development .... Vacant
10 Vice President for Finance & Admin .... Mr. Eric RUNESTAD
32 Vice Pres/Dean for Student Life .... Mr. Corey LANDSTROM
84 Vice Pres Enrollment Management .... Mr. Scot SCHAEFFER
26 Vice Pres Communications/Marketing .... Dr. Rob K. LARSON
13 Exec Dir Library & Information Svcs .... Mr. Paul R. MATTSON
21 Controller .... Ms. Peggy LENSING
18 Director of Facilities Services .... Mr. Jay L. UTHOFF
91 Director Information Systems .... Ms. Marcia A. GULLICKSON
44 Senior Development Officer .... Mr. Doug NELSON
06 Registrar .... Vacant

20 Associate Dean/Dir Faculty Devel ... Dr. Jeffrey WILKERSON
15 Director Human Resources ... Ms. Marsha WENTHOLD
41 Director Intercollegiate Athletics ... Ms. Renae HARTL
29 Exec Director of Alumni Relations ... Ms. Sherry B. ALCOCK
27 Director of Publications ... Ms. Ellen E. MODERSOHN
27 Coordinator of Campus News ... Ms. Julie SHOCKEY
04 Assistant to the President ... Ms. Karen B. MARTIN-SCHRAMM
35 Assistant Dean Student Life ... Ms. Jane HILDEBRAND
36 Director Career Center ... Ms. Brenda RANUM
38 Director Counseling Service ... Ms. Meg HAMMES
37 Director Student Financial Planning ... Ms. Janice K. CORDELL
42 Dir Campus Ministry & Cong Rels ... Rev. Michael R. BLAIR
40 Director Book Shop/Union Services ... Ms. Deanna CASTERTON
39 Assistant Dean & Dir Res Life ... Ms. Kristine FRANZEN
85 Exec Dir Ctr Global Learn & Int Adm ... Mr. Jon LUND
23 Director Health Services ... Ms. Diane TAPPE
19 Director Security/Safety ... Mr. Robert HARRI
88 Director Campus Programing ... Ms. Tanya M. GERTZ
28 Director of Diversity ... Vacant
09 Director Assessment/Inst Research ... Dr. Jon A. CHRISTY
07 Senior Assoc Director of Admissions ... Mr. Kirk NEUBAUER
35 Coordinator Student Activities ... Ms. Trish NEUBAUER
88 Asst Dean & Health Res Adv ... Ms. Janet HUNTER

Maharishi University of Management (A)

1000 N 4th Street, Fairfield IA 52557-0001

County: Jefferson FICE Identification: 011113
Unit ID: 153861
Telephone: (641) 472-7000 Carnegie Class: Master's L
FAX Number: (641) 472-1179 Calendar System: Semester
URL: www.mum.edu
Established: 1971 Annual Undergrad Tuition & Fees: $26,530
Enrollment: 1,323 Coed
Affiliation or Control: Independent Non-Profit IRS Status: 501(c)3
Highest Offering: Doctorate
Program: Liberal Arts And General; Teacher Preparatory; Professional
Accreditation: NH, IACBE

01 President ... Dr. Bevan H. MORRIS
03 Executive Vice President ... Dr. Craig PEARSON
45 Vice President of Expansion ... Mr. Thomas BROOKS
05 Dean of Faculty ... Dr. Cathy GORINI
10 Treasurer ... Mr. Michael SPIVAK
88 International Vice President ... Dr. Michael DILLBECK
88 International Vice President ... Dr. Susan DILLBECK
11 Chief Administrative Officer ... Mr. David TODT
43 Legal Counsel/Dean Global Develop ... Mr. Bill GOLDSTEIN
07 Fellow-Dean of Admissions ... Ms. Gwendolyn STOWE
07 Fellow-Dean of Admissions ... Ms. Aster HESSE
32 Dean of Students ... Mr. Rod EASON
33 Associate Dean of Men ... Mr. Alwin HESSE
34 Associate Dean of Women ... Ms. Amellia HESSE
06 Registrar ... Ms. Mary KING
26 Media Relations ... Mr. Norman ZIEROLD
51 Dir Distance Educ/Intl Programs ... Mr. Dennis HEATON
27 Director of Press ... Mr. Harry BRIGHT
39 Director of Housing ... Ms. Leslie HARRIS
37 Director of Student Financial Aid ... Mr. Dan WASIELEWSKI
13 Director of Information Services ... Mr. Tom HIRSCH
09 Director Evaluation ... Dr. Chris JONES
15 Director/Human Resources ... Mr. Stan LAMOTHE
29 Director Alumni ... Mr. Joshua WILSON
30 Co-Exec Director Inst Advancement ... Mr. Nick ROSANIA
30 Co-Exec Director Inst Advancement ... Ms. Sandra ROSANIA
36 Director Career Services ... Dr. Steve LANGERUD
18 Chief Facilities/Physical Plant ... Mr. Craig WAGNER
49 Dean College of Arts & Sciences ... Dr. Chris JONES
77 Dean College of Computer Sci & Math ... Mr. Gregory GUTHRIE
58 Dean of Graduate School ... Dr. Frederick TRAVIS
04 Administrative Asst to President ... Ms. Jane AIKENS
08 Head Librarian ... Ms. Rouzanna VARDANYAN
41 Athletic Director ... Mr. Ken DALEY
44 Director of Major Gifts ... Mr. Brad MYLETT
101 Secretary of the Board of Trustees ... Ms. Susan TRACY
19 Director of Security and Safety ... Ms. Beata NACSA
106 Dir Online Education/E-learning ... Ms. Cheryl MICHIE
38 Director Student Support Services ... Mr. Jonathan SHAPIRO

Mercy College of Health Sciences (B)

928 Sixth Avenue, Des Moines IA 50309-1239

County: Polk FICE Identification: 006273
Unit ID: 153977
Telephone: (515) 643-3180 Carnegie Class: Spec/Health
FAX Number: (515) 643-6698 Calendar System: Semester
URL: www.mchs.edu
Established: 1995 Annual Undergrad Tuition & Fees: $16,268
Enrollment: 774 Coed
Affiliation or Control: Roman Catholic IRS Status: 501(c)3
Highest Offering: Baccalaureate
Program: Liberal Arts And General; Professional; Nursing Emphasis
Accreditation: NH, ADNUR, DMS, EMT, MAC, MT, NURSE, POLYT, PTAA, RAD, SURGT

01 President ... Dr. Barbara Q. DECKER
05 VP of Academic Affairs and Provost ... Dr. Steven D. LANGDON
26 VP of External Affairs ... Mr. Brian P. TINGLEFF
10 VP of Business & Regulatory Affairs ... Dr. Thomas LEAHY
84 VP Enroll Mgmt & Student Affairs ... Dr. Karen ANDERSON
66 Dean of Nursing ... Dr. Shirley BEAVER
49 Dean of Liberal Arts & Sciences ... Dr. Jeannine MATZ
76 Dean of Allied Health ... Dr. Robert LOCH
09 Dean Inst Rsrch & Effectiveness ... Dr. Jeanette MCGREEVY
08 Dir of Library and Media Services ... Mr. Roy MEADOR
06 Registrar ... Ms. Carolyn BUCKLIN
15 Human Resources Business Partner ... Ms. Anne DENNIS
37 Director of Financial Aid ... Mr. Joe BROOKOVER
38 Manager of Student Success ... Dr. Kristine OWENS
13 Director of Information Technology ... Mr. David VON ARB
18 Facilities Manager ... Mr. David STEENHOEK
07 Director of Admissions ... Ms. Melinda TINGLE-WILLIAMS
26 Marketing Coordinator ... Mr. Jim TAGYE
04 Administrative Asst to President ... Ms. Carole ADAMS
106 Dir Distance Ed/Teaching & Learning ... Dr. Vanessa PREAST

Morningside College (C)

1501 Morningside Avenue, Sioux City IA 51106-1751

County: Woodbury FICE Identification: 001879
Unit ID: 154004
Telephone: (712) 274-5000 Carnegie Class: Bac/Diverse
FAX Number: (712) 274-5101 Calendar System: Semester
URL: www.morningside.edu
Established: 1894 Annual Undergrad Tuition & Fees: $28,155
Enrollment: 2,824 Coed
Affiliation or Control: United Methodist IRS Status: 501(c)3
Highest Offering: Master's
Program: Liberal Arts And General; Teacher Preparatory; Professional
Accreditation: NH, MUS, NURSE

01 President ... Mr. John C. REYNDERS
05 Provost ... Dr. William C. DEEDS
10 Vice President Business & Finance ... Mr. Ronald A. JORGENSEN
32 Vice Pres Student Life & Enrollment ... Mrs. Terri A. CURRY
30 Vice Pres Institutional Advancement ... Mrs. Kari L. WINKLEPLECK
35 Dean of Students ... Ms. Karmen TEN NAPEL
20 Associate Dean for Acad Affairs ... Dr. Beth HINGA
09 Assoc VP Grad Pgm & Inst Assessment ... Dr. John PINTO
88 Vice President Advising ... Dr. Lillian LOPEZ
06 Registrar ... Mrs. Jen DOLPHIN
37 Director Student Financial Planning ... Ms. Karen GAGNON
13 Exec Dir of Information Services ... Mr. Mike HUSMANN
26 Vice Pres Communications & Mktg ... Mr. Rick G. WOLLMAN
29 Director of Alumni Relations ... Mr. Gene AMBROSON
07 Director of Admissions ... Ms. Steph PETERS
18 Director of Physical Plant ... Mr. Kirk JOHNSON
19 Director of Security ... Mr. Jim CORNELIA
23 Director of Student Health ... Ms. Carol GARVEY
36 Director of Career Services ... Ms. Stacie HAYS
40 Director of Bookstore ... Mr. Duane BENSON
41 Athletic Director ... Mr. Tim JAGER
42 Campus Ministry ... Mr. Ryan M. RUSSELL
44 Director of Gift Planning ... Mr. Fred S. ERBES
15 Director Human Resources ... Ms. Cindy WELP
21 Controller ... Mr. Paul TREFT
04 Administrative Asst to President ... Mrs. Lisa KROHN
102 Senior Writer & Foundation Mgr ... Ms. Laura L. FLORIO
105 Digital Communications Mgr ... Mr. Kevin POTTEBAUM
39 Asst Director Residence Life ... Ms. Sheri HINEMAN
08 Library Director ... Mr. Adam FULLERTON
38 Personal Counselor ... Ms. Bobbi MEISTER

Mount Mercy University (D)

1330 Elmhurst Drive, NE, Cedar Rapids IA 52402-4797

County: Linn FICE Identification: 001880
Unit ID: 154013
Telephone: (319) 363-8213 Carnegie Class: Bac/Diverse
FAX Number: (319) 363-5270 Calendar System: 4/1/4
URL: www.mtmercy.edu
Established: 1928 Annual Undergrad Tuition & Fees: $28,226
Enrollment: 1,762 Coed
Affiliation or Control: Roman Catholic IRS Status: 501(c)3
Highest Offering: Master's
Program: Liberal Arts And General; Teacher Preparatory; Professional; Nursing Emphasis
Accreditation: NH, NURSE, SW

01 President ... Ms. Laurie HAMEN
05 Provost ... Dr. Jan HANDLER
10 VP of Finance & Business Operations ... Mr. Doug BROCK
21 Executive Dir Business Services ... Vacant
84 VP of Enrollment Management ... Mr. Robert CALLAHAN
30 VP of Development & Alumni Relation ... Ms. Brenda DUELLO
42 VP of Mission and Ministry ... Sr. Shari SUTHERLAND
20 Associate Provost ... Dr. Tom CASTLE
07 Dean of Admissions ... Ms. Terri CRUMLEY
06 Registrar ... Mr. Chance MCWORTHY
08 Director of Library Services ... Mrs. Marilyn J. MURPHY
36 Director of Career Services ... Ms. Cheryl TABARELLA-REED
44 Assistant VP of Development ... Ms. Lonna DREWELOW
37 Director of Financial Aid ... Ms. Bethany RINDERKNECHT
26 Asst VP Communications/Marketing ... Ms. Lisa LAFLER
41 Director of Athletics ... Mr. Scot H. REISINGER
32 Dean of Students ... Ms. Malinda JENSEN
88 Director of Faculty Development ... Dr. Edy PARSONS
38 Counselor ... Ms. Karol WHITE
13 Director of Technology Operations ... Ms. Connie SNITKER
19 Director of Public Safety ... Mr. Nicholas HEINTZ
24 Academic Technology Librarian ... Ms. Nadia STENNES-SPIDAHL
35 Assoc Dean & Dir Student Engagement ... Vacant
15 Director Human Resources ... Mr. Thomas DOERMANN
18 Director Facilities/Physical Plant ... Mr. Dave D. DENNIS
92 Director Honors Program ... Dr. Joy E. OCHS
40 Bookstore Manager ... Ms. Janie A. MILLS
04 Assistant to President ... Ms. Kim BLANKENHEIM
09 Exec Dir of Institutional Research ... Ms. Lori HEYING
25 Chief Contracts/Grants Admin ... Mr. Walter CHIEN

North Iowa Area Community College (E)

500 College Drive, Mason City IA 50401-7299

County: Cerro Gordo FICE Identification: 001877
Unit ID: 154059
Telephone: (641) 423-1264 Carnegie Class: Assoc/Pub-R-M
FAX Number: (641) 423-1711 Calendar System: Semester
URL: www.niacc.edu
Established: 1917 Annual Undergrad Tuition & Fees (In-District): $4,792
Enrollment: 2,950 Coed
Affiliation or Control: State/Local IRS Status: 501(c)3
Highest Offering: Associate Degree
Program: Occupational; 2-Year Principally Bachelor's Creditable
Accreditation: NH, ADNUR, MAC, PTAA

01 President ... Dr. Steve D. SCHULZ
05 Interim VP Academic Affairs ... Mrs. Donna J. ORTON
10 Vice Pres Administrative Services ... Mrs. Kathy M. GROVE
32 Vice President of Student Services ... Dr. Terri L. EWERS
30 Director of Inst Advancement ... Mrs. Molly H. KNOLL
88 Director of JPEC ... Mr. Timothy J. PUTNAM
15 VP Organiz Develop & Human Resource ... Dr. Shelly M. SCHMIT
06 Registrar ... Mrs. Michelle L. PETZNICK
83 Chair Humanities & Social Science ... Mr. Joe D. DAVIS
81 Chair Math/Science & Wellness ... Dr. Kathy M. ROGOTZKE
72 Chair Industrial Division ... Mr. Josh J. BYRNES
50 Chair Business/Ag Division ... Ms. Laura L. WOOD
51 Dean of Continuing Education ... Mr. Terry W. SCHUMAKER
37 Director of Financial Aid ... Mrs. Mary E. BLOOMINGDALE
20 Director Learning Services ... Mrs. Jessica J. PUTNAM
13 Dir of Technology Svcs/Assoc CIO ... Mr. Mark D. GREENWOOD
103 Regional WIA Director ... Mrs. Angela A. KONIG
38 Dir Student Develop/Counselor ... Ms. Trudy G. LABARR
40 Bookstore Manager ... Mrs. Rhonda K. NESHEIM-KAUFFMAN
41 Director of Athletics ... Mr. Dan J. MASON
18 Director of Facilities Management ... Mr. Tony A. PAPPAS
21 Director Business Services ... Ms. Mindy R. EASTMAN
39 Director Student Housing ... Mr. Travis J. HERGERT
08 Librarian ... Ms. Angie L. SCHAPER
26 Dir Marketing/Public Rel/Govt Affs ... Mrs. Valerie F. ZAHORSKI-SCHMIDT
88 Director Accelerator/Incubator ... Mr. Daniel J. WINEGARDEN
88 Director SBDC ... Mr. Brook S. BOEHMLER
88 Director of School Partnerships ... Mr. Brian M. WOGEN
88 Dir of Operations/Continuing Educ ... Mrs. Constance J. GLANDON
88 Director of Sales & Programming ... Mrs. Jody L. EAST
88 Business & Industry Program Manager ... Mr. Eric M. NEITZKE
09 Director of Institutional Research ... Dr. Shelly M. SCHMIT
102 Grant Writer/Inst Fund Develop Spec ... Ms. Jana T. BARRACKS
106 Instructional Tech Coordinator ... Mr. Bruce G. MCKEE
29 Director Alumni Relations ... Mrs. Molly H. KNOLL
07 Director of Admissions ... Mrs. Rachel L. MCGUIRE
28 Director of Diversity ... Dr. Kathy M. ROGOTZKE

Northeast Iowa Community College (F)

Box 400, Calmar IA 52132-0400

County: Winneshiek FICE Identification: 004587
Unit ID: 154110
Telephone: (563) 562-3263 Carnegie Class: Assoc/Pub-R-M
FAX Number: (563) 562-3719 Calendar System: Semester
URL: www.nicc.edu
Established: 1966 Annual Undergrad Tuition & Fees (In-District): $5,344
Enrollment: 4,959 Coed
Affiliation or Control: Local IRS Status: 501(c)3
Highest Offering: Associate Degree
Program: Occupational; 2-Year Principally Bachelor's Creditable; Technical Emphasis
Accreditation: NH, CAHIIM, COARC, DA

01 President ... Dr. Liang C. WEE
10 Vice Pres Finance & Administration ... Mr. John D. NOEL
05 Chief Acad Ofcr/VP Academic Affairs ... Dr. Kathy J. NACOS-BURDS
46 Vice Pres Bus & Community Solutions ... Dr. Wendy A. MIHM-HEROLD
12 Peosta Provost ... Dr. Jeffrey M. ARMSTRONG
12 Calmar Provost ... Ms. Rhonda K. SEIBERT
32 Vice Pres Student Services ... Dr. Linda M. PETERSON
51 Exec Dir Town Clock/Dubuque Centers ... Ms. Wendy S. KNIGHT
102 Exec Director of NICC Foundation ... Ms. Julie A. WURTZEL
21 Executive Director of Finance ... Mr. Thomas M. RIDOUT
45 Exec Dir of Inst Effectiveness ... Ms. Kristin A. DIETZEL
15 Exec Director of Human Resources ... Dr. Julie G. HUISKAMP
106 Director Distance Learning ... Vacant
13 Director Computer Information Sys ... Mr. Craig R. MEIRICK
09 Director of Institutional Research ... Ms. Dolores M. MILLER
88 Director Economic Devel/Peosta ... Mr. Gregory A. WILLGING
37 Director of Financial Aid ... Ms. Kim M. BAUMLER
06 District Registrar ... Ms. Karla R. WINTER
06 Dir of Advising/Registr/Persistence ... Ms. Sheila R. BECKER
36 Career Services Manager ... Mr. Chris E. ENTRINGER

07 Director of Admissions ... Ms. Kristi L. STRIEF
26 Dir Marketing/News/Publications ... Ms. Shea A. HERBST

Northwest Iowa Community College (A)

603 W Park Street, Sheldon IA 51201-1046
County: Sioux FICE Identification: 004600
Unit ID: 154129
Telephone: (712) 324-5061 Carnegie Class: Assoc/Pub-R-S
FAX Number: (712) 324-4136 Calendar System: Semester
URL: www.nwicc.edu
Established: 1966 Annual Undergrad Tuition & Fees (In-District): $5,600
Enrollment: 1,568 Coed
Affiliation or Control: State/Local IRS Status: 501(c)3
Highest Offering: Associate Degree
Program: Occupational; 2-Year Principally Bachelor's Creditable; Technical Emphasis
Accreditation: NH, CAHIIM

01 President ... Dr. Alethea F. STUBBE
05 VP Student & Academic Services ... Dr. John HARTOG
30 VP Inst Adv & External Affairs ... Dr. Jan E. SNYDER
10 VP Operations & Finance ... Mr. Mark BROWN
49 Dean Arts & Sci/Business/Health ... Dr. Rhonda R. PENNINGS
72 Dean Applied Technology ... Mr. Steve WALDSTEIN
53 Dean Center for Teaching & Learning ... Ms. Gretchen G. BARTELSON
21 Director of Business Services ... Ms. Jessica WILLIAMS
37 Director Financial Aid ... Ms. Karna HOFMEYER
84 Director Enrollment Management ... Ms. Lisa L. STORY
08 Director of Library Services ... Ms. Molly D. GALM
13 Director of Technology & Info Svcs ... Mr. Mike OLDENKAMP
88 Director of TRIO ... Ms. Laurie L. EDWARDS
51 Dean Workforce and Continuing Educ ... Vacant
06 Registrar/Assoc Dean of Students ... Ms. Beth SIBENALLER-WOODALL
15 Director of Human Resources ... Ms. Sandy BRUNS
88 Director of Alt HS/Learning Center ... Ms. Susan SCHMIDT
26 Director Community Relations ... Ms. Kristin E. KOLLBAUM
18 Director Physical Facilities ... Mr. Doug RODGER

Northeast Iowa Community College Peosta Campus (B)

8342 NICC Drive, Peosta IA 52068
Telephone: (800) 728-7367 Identification: 770063
Accreditation: &NH, EMT, RAD

† Branch campus of Northeast Iowa Community College, Calmar, IA.

Northwestern College (C)

101 Seventh Street, SW, Orange City IA 51041-1996
County: Sioux FICE Identification: 001883
Unit ID: 154101
Telephone: (712) 707-7000 Carnegie Class: Bac/Diverse
FAX Number: (712) 707-7247 Calendar System: Semester
URL: www.nwciowa.edu
Established: 1882 Annual Undergrad Tuition & Fees: $28,750
Enrollment: 1,205 Coed
Affiliation or Control: Reformed Church In America IRS Status: 501(c)3
Highest Offering: Master's
Program: Liberal Arts And General; Teacher Preparatory; Professional
Accreditation: NH, CAATE, IACBE, NURSE, SW, TED

01 President ... Mr. Gregory E. CHRISTY
05 Provost ... Vacant
20 Dean of Faculty ... Dr. Adrienne M. FORGETTE
32 Dean of Student Life ... Dr. Julie VERMEER ELLIOTT
10 Vice President Financial Affairs ... Mr. Doug D. BEUKELMAN
30 Vice President Advancement ... Mr. Jay WIELENGA
84 Dean of Enrollment Management ... Vacant
88 Assoc Dean of Spiritual Formation ... Ms. Barb DEWALD
42 Chaplain ... Rev. Harlan VAN OORT
41 Director of Athletics ... Mr. Earl WOUDSTRA
08 Director of the Library ... Ms. Greta GROND
06 Registrar ... Ms. Sandy VAN KLEY
37 Director of Financial Aid ... Mr. Eric ANDERSON
13 Director of Computing Services ... Mr. Harlan R. JORGENSEN
26 Director of Public Relations ... Mr. Duane L. BEESON
36 Director of Career Development ... Mr. William C. MINNICK
38 Dir Student Counseling Services ... Dr. Sally EDMAN
18 Director of Maintenance/Operations ... Mr. Scott K. SIMMELINK
29 Director Alumni Relations ... Mr. Mark R. BLOEMENDAAL
15 Director of Human Resources ... Mrs. Deb SANDBULTE
09 Director of Institutional Research ... Mr. Michael WALLINGA
04 Administrative Asst to President ... Ms. Jill HAARSMA
19 Director Security/Safety ... Vacant

Palmer College of Chiropractic (D)

1000 Brady Street, Davenport IA 52803-5287
County: Scott FICE Identification: 012300
Unit ID: 154174
Telephone: (563) 884-5000 Carnegie Class: Spec/Health
FAX Number: (563) 884-5409 Calendar System: Trimester
URL: www.palmer.edu
Established: 1897 Annual Undergrad Tuition & Fees: $33,459
Enrollment: 2,181 Coed
Affiliation or Control: Independent Non-Profit IRS Status: 501(c)3
Highest Offering: First Professional Degree
Program: Professional
Accreditation: NH, CHIRO

01 Chancellor ... Dr. Dennis M. MARCHIORI
05 College Provost ... Dr. Daniel J. WEINERT
108 Vice Chancellor for Inst Effect ... Dr. Robert E. PERCUOCO
32 Vice Chancellor Student Success ... Dr. Kevin A. CUNNINGHAM
84 Vice Chancellor for Enrollment ... Mr. Thomas STEMPEK
10 Vice Chancellor for Administration ... Mr. Thomas L. TIEMEIER
46 Vice Chancellor for Research ... Dr. Christine GOERTZ
26 Vice Chancellor for Mktg & Comm ... Mr. James O'CONNOR
29 Exec Director Alumni & Development ... Dr. Mickey G. BURT
20 Dean of Academic Affairs ... Dr. Kevin PAUSTIAN
88 Director of Undergrad Studies ... Ms. Cathy EBERHART
06 Senior Director/Registrar ... Ms. Mindy S. LEAHY
09 Sr Dir Institutional Research & Eff ... Dr. Dustin C. DERBY
21 Senior Dir for Financial Affairs ... Ms. Alexis A. VANDER HORN
13 Senior Director of IT ... Mr. Mike A. BENEDICT
15 Senior Director of Human Resources ... Ms. Michelle K. WALKER
18 Senior Director of Facilities ... Mr. Stanley E. CARLSON
07 Sr Dir of Admissions & Recruitment ... Ms. Julie BEHN
37 Senior Dir of Financial Planning ... Ms. Abbey NAGLE-KUCH
108 Senior Director for Assessment ... Dr. Andrea HAAN
24 Sr Dir/Center for Teaching/Lrng ... Dr. Dana J. LAWRENCE
51 Senior Dir of Continuing Education ... Vacant
38 Sr Dir of Academic Support Services ... Dr. Ann MARGRAVE
08 Senior Director of Library ... Ms. Chabha TEPE
40 Manager of Bookstores ... Ms. Leann MCDONALD
88 Sr Dir Quality Assurance/Sys Organ ... Ms. Earlye A. JULIEN
96 Purchasing Manager ... Ms. Cheryl L. KOFRON
101 Secretary of the Institution/Board ... Ms. Lynne LINDSTROM
104 Sr Director Clinic Administration ... Dr. Julie SCHRAD
105 Manager of Web Design ... Mr. Mike REKEMEYER
19 Manager of Security ... Mr. Jesse MOODY
41 Athletic & Rec Coordinator ... Mr. Ron O'BRIEN

St. Ambrose University (E)

518 W Locust Street, Davenport IA 52803-2898
County: Scott FICE Identification: 001889
Unit ID: 154235
Telephone: (563) 333-6000 Carnegie Class: Master's L
FAX Number: (563) 333-6243 Calendar System: Semester
URL: www.sau.edu
Established: 1882 Annual Undergrad Tuition & Fees: $28,240
Enrollment: 3,507 Coed
Affiliation or Control: Roman Catholic IRS Status: 501(c)3
Highest Offering: Doctorate
Program: Liberal Arts And General; Fine Arts Emphasis
Accreditation: NH, ACBSP, #ARCPA, ENG, NURSE, OT, PTA, SP, SW, TEAC

01 President ... Sr. Joan LESCINSKI, CSJ
05 Provost & VP for ASA ... Dr. Paul KOCH
10 Vice President Finance ... Mr. Michael C. POSTER
42 Chaplain ... Rev. Charles A. ADAM
30 Vice President Advancement ... Mr. James R. STANGLE
84 Vice Pres Enrollment Management ... Mr. John D. COOPER
88 Assoc Vice Pres for Advancement ... Mr. Edward J. FINN
46 Assoc Vice Pres Assess/Research ... Dr. Tracy SCHUSTER-MATLOCK
11 Director Administrative Services ... Ms. Carol A. GLINES
26 Asst Vice Pres Communications/Mktg ... Ms. Linda R. HIRSCH
32 Asst VP Student Svcs/Dean of Stdnts ... Mr. Timothy PHILLIPS
15 Director Human Resources ... Ms. Audrey D. BLAIR
13 Exec Dir of Information Resources ... Ms. Mary B. HEINZMAN
29 Director Alumni Rels & Spec Project ... Ms. Anne A. GANNAWAY
37 Director Financial Aid ... Ms. Julie A. HAACK
38 Director Counseling ... Mr. Stephen TENDALL
18 Director Physical Plant ... Mr. Jim M. HANNON
06 Registrar ... Mr. Dan L. ZEIMET
23 Director of Health Services ... Ms. Nancy A. HINES
19 Director of Security ... Mr. Robert CHRISTOPHER
39 Director of Resident Life ... Mr. Matt B. HANSEN
08 Director Library ... Ms. Mary B. HEINZMAN
36 Director Career Development ... Ms. Angela P. ELLIOTT
41 Athletic Director ... Mr. Raymond J. SHOVLAIN
94 Director of Women's Studies ... Ms. Katy A. STRZEPEK
40 Manager of Bookstore ... Mr. Cory W. SAMBDMAN
85 Asst VP International Education ... Dr. Ryan D. DYE
88 Chair Masters Pastoral Studies ... Dr. Micah KIEL
88 Chair Masters Criminal Justice ... Dr. Chris C. BARNUM
49 Int Dean College Arts & Sciences ... Dr. Sarah R. VORDRIEDE-PATTON
50 Dean College Business ... Dr. William J. LESCH
71 Dean Health & Human Services ... Dr. Sandra L. CASSADY
88 Dean Academic Adult & Graduate Pgm ... Dr. Regina M. MATHESON
54 Dir Industrial & Mechinical Engr ... Dr. Michael E. OPAR
57 Director Fine Arts ... Mr. Lance A. SADLEK
88 Director Occupational Therapy ... Dr. Lynn J. KILBURG
88 Director Masters of Accounting ... Mr. Lew D. MARX
58 Director Academic Svcs MBA Pgm ... Ms. Teresa L. HUTCHINSON
58 Director Graduate Student Recruit ... Ms. Michelle L. KRONFELD
28 Director of Diversity ... Mr. Ryan C. SADDLER
04 Senior Asst to President ... Ms. Kathleen M. ANDERSON
09 Director Institutional Research ... Ms. Clare M. HOLLADAY
44 Assoc VP Gift Planning/Campaign Dir ... Ms. Sally E. CRINO
53 Director Education ... Dr. Thomas CARPENTER
86 Director Government Relations ... Mr. Paul J. FOLEY

St. Luke's College (F)

2720 Stone Park Boulevard, Sioux City IA 51104-0010
County: Woodbury FICE Identification: 007291
Unit ID: 154262
Telephone: (712) 279-3149 Carnegie Class: Assoc/PrivNFP
FAX Number: (712) 233-8017 Calendar System: Semester
URL: www.stlukescollege.edu
Established: 1995 Annual Undergrad Tuition & Fees: $19,900
Enrollment: 261 Coed
Affiliation or Control: Independent Non-Profit IRS Status: 501(c)3
Highest Offering: Baccalaureate
Program: Occupational; 2-Year Principally Bachelor's Creditable; Nursing Emphasis
Accreditation: NH, ADNUR, COARC, MT, PAST, RAD

01 Chancellor ... Mr. Michael D. STILES
05 Chief Academic Officer ... Dr. Susan BOWERS
32 Dean Student Services ... Ms. Danelle D. JOHANNSEN
66 Dean Nursing Education ... Dr. Susan BOWERS
76 Dean Health Sciences ... Dr. Dan JENSEN
06 Registrar ... Ms. Michelle FITCH
10 Bursar ... Ms. Shannelle BREWSTER
26 Director of Communications ... Vacant
07 Director of Admissions ... Ms. Sherry MCCARTHY
08 Head Librarian ... Ms. Nancy ZUBROD
29 Director Alumni Relations ... Ms. Patricia ROGERS
37 Director Student Financial Aid ... Ms. Danelle JOHANNSEN

Shiloh University (G)

100 Shiloh Drive, Kalona IA 52247
County: Washington Identification: 667095
Unit ID: 480499
Telephone: (319) 656-2447 Carnegie Class: Not Classified
FAX Number: (319) 656-2448 Calendar System: Trimester
URL: www.shilohuniversity.edu
Established: 2006 Annual Undergrad Tuition & Fees: $4,510
Enrollment: 38 Coed
Affiliation or Control: Independent Non-Profit IRS Status: 501(c)3
Highest Offering: Master's
Program: 2-Year Principally Bachelor's Creditable; Liberal Arts And General; Professional; Religious Emphasis
Accreditation: DEAC

00 Chancellor ... Mr. Gary HARGRAVE
01 President ... Mr. Christopher REEVES
05 Vice President of Academics ... Dr. Wesley PINKHAM
24 Vice President of Inst Services ... Dr. Daniel SALVADOR
13 Vice President of Technology ... Mr. James WIRTHLIN
58 Dean ... Dr. John BUCKINGHAM
06 Registrar ... Mrs. Judy BREWER
07 Admissions Coordinator ... Mr. Andy THOMPSON
108 Manager of Academic Effectiveness ... Mrs. Gayle WIRTHLIN
08 Library Director ... Ms. Julie MCPHAIL

Simpson College (H)

1450 SW Vintage Pkwy, Ankeny IA 50023
Telephone: (515) 965-9355 Identification: 770849
Accreditation: &NH

† Branch campus of Simpson College, Indianola, IA.

Simpson College (I)

701 North C Street, Indianola IA 50125-1297
County: Warren FICE Identification: 001887
Unit ID: 154350
Telephone: (515) 961-6251 Carnegie Class: Bac/A&S
FAX Number: (515) 961-1498 Calendar System: Other
URL: www.simpson.edu
Established: 1860 Annual Undergrad Tuition & Fees: $33,532
Enrollment: 1,660 Coed
Affiliation or Control: United Methodist IRS Status: 501(c)3
Highest Offering: Master's
Program: Liberal Arts And General; Teacher Preparatory; Business Emphasis
Accreditation: NH, CAATE, MUS

01 President ... Dr. Jay K. SIMMONS
05 Vice Pres/Dean Academic Affairs ... Dr. Steven J. GRIFFITH
10 Vice President Business/Finance ... Mr. Kenneth I. BIRKENHOLTZ
30 Vice President College Advancement ... Mr. Robert J. LANE
45 Int VP Student Devel/Strategic Plng ... Mr. James HAYES
84 Vice President Enrollment ... Ms. Deborah J. TIERNEY
13 VP Info Svcs/Chief Info Officer ... Ms. Kelley L. BRADDER
37 Asst VP Enrollment/Financial Aid ... Ms. Tracie PAVON
06 Registrar & Associate Dean ... Ms. Jody RAGAN
32 Dean of Students ... Mr. Luke BEHAUNEK
26 Executive Director Marketing and PR ... Ms. Jill JOHNSON
08 Director of Library ... Ms. Cynthia M. DYER
14 Director of Information Services ... Vacant
44 Director of Annual Giving ... Ms. Brenna STOFFA
15 Director of Human Resources ... Ms. Mary E. BARTLEY
36 Director of Career Services ... Vacant
07 Director of Admissions ... Ms. Alison SWANSON
41 Athletic Director ... Mr. Brian NIEMUTH
96 Director of Procurement ... Ms. Marilyn J. LEEK
35 Assistant Dean of Students ... Mr. Richard O. RAMOS
42 Chaplain ... Rev. Mara BAILEY
18 Director Campus Services ... Mr. John HARRIS
21 Controller ... Mr. Logan EDEL
19 Coordinator of Campus Security ... Mr. Chris FRERICHS
51 Associate Dean Adult Learning ... Dr. Rosemary J. LINK
28 International Educ Coordinator ... Mr. Jay WILKINSON
04 Administrative Asst to President ... Ms. Brenda K. WICKETT
29 Director Alumni Relations ... Mr. Andy ENGLISH

Simpson College West Des Moines (A)

1415 28th Street, #250, West Des Moines IA 50266
Telephone: (515) 309-3099 Identification: 770064
Accreditation: &NH

† Branch campus of Simpson College, Indianola, IA.

Southeastern Community College (B)

1500 W Agency Road, PO Box 180,
West Burlington IA 52655-0180
County: Des Moines FICE Identification: 001848
Unit ID: 154378
Telephone: (319) 752-2731 Carnegie Class: Assoc/Pub-R-M
FAX Number: (319) 752-4957 Calendar System: Semester
URL: www.scciowa.edu
Established: 1966 Annual Undergrad Tuition & Fees (In-District): $4,950
Enrollment: 2,987 Coed
Affiliation or Control: State/Local IRS Status: 501(c)3
Highest Offering: Associate Degree
Program: Occupational; 2-Year Principally Bachelor's Creditable
Accreditation: NH, COARC, EMT, MAC

01 President ..... Dr. Michael ASH
05 Vice Pres of Academic Affairs ..... Dr. Carole RICHARDSON
32 Vice President of Student Services ..... Ms. Joan WILLIAMS
11 Vice Pres Administrative Services ..... Mr. Kevin CARR
30 Exec Director for Inst Advancement ..... Ms. Rebecca RUMP
37 Financial Aid Officer ..... Mr. Ean FREELS
84 Enrollment Coordinator ..... Ms. Dana CHRISMAN
06 Registrar ..... Mr. Tim GRAY
15 Director Human Resources ..... Ms. Michelle FOSTER
49 Dean Arts and Sciences ..... Vacant
12 Dean Keokuk Campus/Trans Studies ..... Dr. Teresa GARCIA
75 Dean Career/Tech/Health Educ ..... Vacant
26 Dir Marketing/Communications ..... Mr. Jeff EBBING

Southeastern Community College Keokuk Campus (C)

335 Messenger Road, PO Box 6007, Keokuk IA 52632
Telephone: (319) 524-3221 Identification: 770065
Accreditation: &NH

† Branch campus of Southeastern Community College, West Burlington, IA.

Southwestern Community College (D)

1501 W Townline Street, Creston IA 50801-1098
County: Union FICE Identification: 001857
Unit ID: 154396
Telephone: (641) 782-7081 Carnegie Class: Assoc/Pub-R-S
FAX Number: (641) 782-3312 Calendar System: Semester
URL: www.swcciowa.edu
Established: 1966 Annual Undergrad Tuition & Fees (In-State): $4,920
Enrollment: 1,606 Coed
Affiliation or Control: State IRS Status: 501(c)3
Highest Offering: Associate Degree
Program: Occupational; 2-Year Principally Bachelor's Creditable
Accreditation: NH

01 President/CEO ..... Dr. Barbara J. CRITTENDEN
03 Vice President Economic Development ..... Mr. Thomas L. LESAN
10 Chief Financial Officer ..... Mr. Randy COOK
05 Vice President Instruction ..... Mr. Bill TAYLOR
32 Dean Stdnt Svcs/Dir Inst Advance ..... Ms. Beth KULOW
20 Asst Vice Pres of Instruction ..... Mrs. Lindsay STOAKS
106 Director of Distance Education ..... Mr. Doug GREENE
15 Director of Human Resources ..... Mrs. Jolene GRIFFITH
26 Director of Marketing ..... Mrs. Terri HIGGINS
08 Head Librarian ..... Mrs. Ann COULTER
13 Director of Information Technology ..... Mr. Scott HELM
37 Director of Financial Aid ..... Ms. Rebecca SLICK
06 Registrar ..... Ms. Sandy WEBB
04 Administrative Asst to President ..... Ms. Mary Jo SKARDA
07 Director of Admissions ..... Ms. Caitlyn LESAN

University of Dubuque (E)

2000 University Avenue, Dubuque IA 52001-5099
County: Dubuque FICE Identification: 001891
Unit ID: 153278
Telephone: (563) 589-3000 Carnegie Class: Master's S
FAX Number: (563) 589-3682 Calendar System: 4/1/4
URL: www.dbq.edu
Established: 1852 Annual Undergrad Tuition & Fees: $27,896
Enrollment: 2,118 Coed
Affiliation or Control: Presbyterian Church (U.S.A.) IRS Status: 501(c)3
Highest Offering: Doctorate
Program: Liberal Arts And General; Teacher Preparatory; Professional
Accreditation: NH, AAB, NURSE, THEOL

01 President ..... Dr. Jeffrey F. BULLOCK
04 Exec Assistant to the President ..... Mrs. Deborah L. BUOL
05 Vice President/Dean of the College ..... Dr. Mark WARD
10 Vice President Finance & Treasurer ..... Mr. James D. STEINER
84 Vice Pres Enrollment/Univ Rels ..... Mr. Peter L. SMITH
20 Vice Pres/Dean of Seminary ..... Dr. Bradley J. LONGFIELD
32 Vice President/Dean of Student Life ... Dr. Michael H. MIYAMOTO
13 Network Administrator ..... Ms. Sherry CUSICK
30 Sr AVP Enroll Mgmt/Univ Relations ..... Mr. Jesse L. JAMES
06 Registrar ..... Ms. Diane HANTEN
08 Director of Libraries ..... Ms. Mary Anne KNEFEL
15 Director of Human Resources ..... Ms. Julie MACTAGGART
37 Dean of Student Financial Planning ..... Mr. Timothy KREMER
09 Dir Institutional Research ..... Ms. Keri SAMSON
36 Director of Career Services ..... Dr. Amy BAUS
29 Director Alumni Relations ..... Ms. Katie KRAUS
40 Director Bookstore ..... Ms. Margo KETELS
41 Athletic Director ..... Mr. Dan RUNKLE
18 Director of Facilities ..... Mr. Craig KLOFT
04 Special Assistant to the President ..... Dr. John R. STEWART
88 Exec Dir Heritage Center ..... Mr. Thomas J. ROBBINS
07 Director of First-year Admissions ..... Mr. Robert D. BROSHOUS

University of Phoenix Des Moines Campus (F)

317 6th Avenue, Suite 102, Des Moines IA 50309-4109
Telephone: (866) 229-5743 Identification: 770203
Accreditation: &NH, ACBSP

† No longer accepting campus-based students.

Upper Iowa University (G)

605 Washington, Box 1857, Fayette IA 52142-1857
County: Fayette FICE Identification: 001893
Unit ID: 154493
Telephone: (563) 425-5200 Carnegie Class: Master's M
FAX Number: (563) 425-5271 Calendar System: Semester
URL: www.uiu.edu
Established: 1857 Annual Undergrad Tuition & Fees: $27,323
Enrollment: 5,859 Coed
Affiliation or Control: Independent Non-Profit IRS Status: 501(c)3
Highest Offering: Master's
Program: Liberal Arts And General; Teacher Preparatory; Business Emphasis
Accreditation: NH, CAATE, NURSE

01 President ..... Dr. William R. DUFFY, II
05 Provost ..... Dr. Kurt WOOD
10 CFO ..... Ms. Leslie ANDERSON
82 VP International Education ... Mr. Ismael J. BETANCOURT VELEZ
84 SVP Strategic Pos/Chief Enroll Ofcr ..... Vacant
07 Exec Dir of Admissions ..... Mr. Storm SCHMITT
30 VP of External Affairs ..... Mr. Andrew WENTHE
09 Assoc Provost ..... Ms. Janet SHEPHERD
88 AVP for Military Affs/Business Dev ..... Mr. Wayne CONVERSE
32 Dean of Student Development ..... Ms. Louise SCOTT
36 Assoc Dean Stdnts/Dir Res Life ..... Ms. Jean MERKLE
12 Dir Mid-West/South Central Region ..... Mr. Walter BEMBRY
12 Dir North Central/Mid-Central Reg ..... Ms. Jen WEBB
06 Registrar ..... Mrs. Holly STREETER
08 Director Library Services ..... Mrs. Becky WADIAN
41 Athletic Director ..... Mr. David MILLER
04 Exec Assistant to the President ..... Ms. Holly D. WOLFF
56 Asst VP Center for Distance Educ ..... Ms. Barb SCHULTZ
105 Director Internet Development ..... Mr. Joel KUNZE
21 Associate Business Ofcr/Controller ..... Ms. Kathy FRANKEN
36 Int Director of Career Development ..... Ms. Hope TRAINOR
35 Dir Student Leadership & Activities ..... Mr. Daryl GROVE
26 Assoc VP for Comm and Marketing ..... Ms. Monica HEATON
86 Director External Affairs ..... Mr. Andrew WENTHE
29 Director of Alumni Relations ..... Mr. Josem DIAZ
13 Director Information Technology ..... Mr. Terry SMID
15 Director Human Resources ..... Ms. Amanda DUVAL
88 Director Sports Info Services ..... Mr. Howard THOMPSON
18 Chief Facilities/Physical Plant ..... Mr. Justin MARCHANT
40 Bookstore Manager ..... Ms. Becky WISSMILLER

Vatterott College-Des Moines (H)

7000 Fleur Drive, Des Moines IA 50321-2414
County: Polk FICE Identification: 026092
Unit ID: 373058
Telephone: (515) 309-9000 Carnegie Class: Assoc/PrivFP
FAX Number: (515) 309-0366 Calendar System: Other
URL: www.vatterott-college.edu
Established: 1997 Annual Undergrad Tuition & Fees: $12,839
Enrollment: 200 Coed
Affiliation or Control: Proprietary IRS Status: Proprietary
Highest Offering: Associate Degree
Program: Occupational
Accreditation: ACCSC, DA, MAAB

01 CEO & President ..... Ms. Pam BELL
12 Campus Director ..... Ms. Kimber DAVIS

Waldorf College (I)

106 S 6th Street, Forest City IA 50436-1713
County: Winnebago FICE Identification: 001895
Unit ID: 154518
Telephone: (641) 585-2450 Carnegie Class: Bac/Diverse
FAX Number: (641) 585-8194 Calendar System: Semester
URL: www.waldorf.edu
Established: 1903 Annual Undergrad Tuition & Fees: $20,884
Enrollment: 1,116 Coed
Affiliation or Control: Proprietary IRS Status: Proprietary
Highest Offering: Master's
Program: Liberal Arts And General
Accreditation: NH

01 President ..... Dr. Robert ALSOP
05 Int Dean of Col/Vice Pres Acad Affs ..... Mr. David R. BEHLING
10 Vice President Business Affairs ..... Mr. Mason HARMS
04 Assistant to the President ..... Ms. Cindy CARTER
32 Dean of Students ..... Mr. Jason RAMAKER
92 Dean of Honors Program ..... Dr. Suzanne FALCK-YI
07 Director Admissions ..... Mr. Scott PITCHER
08 Library Director ..... Mr. Derrick BURTON
29 Director of Alumni Affairs ..... Ms. Rita GILBERTSON
06 Registrar ..... Mr. Darrell BARBOUR
37 Director of Financial Aid ..... Mr. Duane POLSDOFER
18 Director of Facilities Services ..... Mr. Allan EGGEBRAATEN
26 Communications Director ..... Ms. Cassie CHRISTIANSON
44 Director of Annual Fund ..... Ms. Nancy OLSON
38 Counselor ..... Mr. James AMELSBERG
41 Athletic Director ..... Mr. Bart GRAY
36 Director Student Placement ..... Ms. Mary REISETTER
40 Bookstore Manager ..... Ms. Karla SCHAEFER
15 Director Human Resources ..... Ms. Dawn RAMAKER

Wartburg College (J)

PO Box 1003, 100 Wartburg Boulevard,
Waverly IA 50677-0903
County: Bremer FICE Identification: 001896
Unit ID: 154527
Telephone: (319) 352-8200 Carnegie Class: Bac/A&S
FAX Number: (319) 352-8514 Calendar System: Other
URL: www.wartburg.edu
Established: 1852 Annual Undergrad Tuition & Fees: $37,190
Enrollment: 1,661 Coed
Affiliation or Control: Evangelical Lutheran Church In America
IRS Status: 501(c)3
Highest Offering: Baccalaureate
Program: Liberal Arts And General; Teacher Preparatory
Accreditation: NH, MUS, SW, TED

01 President ..... Dr. Darrel D. COLSON
05 VP Acad Affs/Dean Faculty ..... Dr. Brian ERNSTING
32 VP Student Life/Dean Students ..... Dr. Daniel KITTLE
10 VP for Finance and Administration ..... Mr. Richard SEGGERMAN
30 Vice Pres Institutional Advancement ..... Mr. Scott C. LEISINGER
84 Vice Pres Enrollment Management ..... Dr. Edith J. WALDSTEIN
07 Asst VP Admiss/Alumni/Parent Pgms ..... Mr. Jay T. COLEMAN
06 Registrar ..... Ms. Sheree S. COVERT
26 VP for Mktg and Comm ..... Mr. Graham GARNER
91 Dir of Info Technology Svcs/CIO ..... Mr. Gary L. WIPPERMAN
08 College Librarian ..... Mr. Curtis BRUNDY
29 Dir of Alumni/Parent Rel & Ann Giv ..... Ms. Renee VOVES
37 Director of Financial Aid ..... Ms. Jen L. SASSMAN
41 Exec Dir of Athletics and Wellness ..... Mr. Eric R. WILLIS
42 Dean of the Chapel ..... Rev. Ramona S. BOUZARD
18 Director of Physical Plant ..... Mr. John A. WUERTZ
39 Asst Dean/Dir of Residential Life ..... Vacant
36 Dir of Pathways/Career Svcs ..... Mr. Derek N. SOLHEIM
38 Director of Counseling Svcs ..... Mrs. Stephanie R. NEWSOM
40 Bookstore Manager ..... Ms. Janet HUEBNER
85 Director of International Programs ..... Ms. Helen LEONG
35 Director of Campus Programming ..... Ms. Ashley LANG
88 Campus Pastor ..... Rev. Brian A. BECKSTROM
21 Chief Business Officer & Treasurer ..... Mr. Richard W. SEGGERMAN
15 Director of Human Resources ..... Ms. Jamie HOLLAWAY
30 Director of Development ..... Mr. Donald J. MEYER
09 Dir of Inst Research/Prof of Psych ..... Dr. Fred D. RIBICH
92 Director Honors Program ..... Dr. Leilani ZART
04 Assistant to the President ..... Ms. Janeen K. STEWART
20 Asst Dean for Academic Affairs ... Mr. Douglas D. KOSCHMEDER

Wartburg Theological Seminary (K)

333 Wartburg Place, PO Box 5004,
Dubuque IA 52004-5004
County: Dubuque FICE Identification: 001897
Unit ID: 154536
Telephone: (563) 589-0200 Carnegie Class: Spec/Faith
FAX Number: (563) 589-0333 Calendar System: 4/1/4
URL: www.wartburgseminary.edu
Established: 1854 Annual Graduate Tuition & Fees: $15,900
Enrollment: 153 Coed
Affiliation or Control: Evangelical Lutheran Church In America
IRS Status: 501(c)3
Highest Offering: Master's; No Undergraduates
Program: Professional
Accreditation: NH, THEOL

01 President ..... Rev. Louise N. JOHNSON
05 Academic Dean of the Seminary ..... Dr. Craig L. NESSAN
10 Vice Pres for Finance & Operations ... Mr. Andy B. WILLENBORG
30 Vice President for Mission Support ..... Ms. Janelle KOEPKE
15 Assistant to President & Dir of HR ..... Ms. Eileen LEMAY
88 Dean for Vocation ..... Rev. Amy L. CURRENT
08 Library Director ..... Ms. Susan J S. EBERTZ
06 Registrar/Admin Assistant to Dean ..... Dr. Kevin L. ANDERSON
13 Director of Information Technology ..... Mr. Richard ROBLEDO
04 Asst to President ..... Ms. Eileen LEMAY

Western Iowa Tech Community College (A)

PO Box 5199, 4647 Stone Avenue,
Sioux City IA 51102-5199

County: Woodbury | FICE Identification: 007316
Unit ID: 154572
Telephone: (712) 274-6400 | Carnegie Class: Assoc/Pub-R-L
FAX Number: (712) 274-6412 | Calendar System: Semester
URL: www.witcc.edu
Established: 1966 | Annual Undergrad Tuition & Fees (In-District): $4,104
Enrollment: 6,399 | Coed
Affiliation or Control: State/Local | IRS Status: 501(c)3
Highest Offering: Associate Degree
Program: Occupational; 2-Year Principally Bachelor's Creditable
Accreditation: NH, DA, EMT, MAC, PNUR, PTAA, SURGT

01 President .... Dr. Terry MURRELL
05 VP Learning .... Ms. Juline ALBERT
10 VP Finance/Administrative Svcs .... Mr. Troy JASMAN
32 Dean of Student Support .... Mr. Martin REIMER
15 Dean of Quality and Human Resources .... Ms. Brenda BRADLEY
13 Dean of Information Technologies .... Mr. Mike LOGAN
30 Exec Director College Development .... Ms. Carolyn ELLWANGER
84 Dean of Completion/Students .... Dr. Tricia SUTHERLAND
88 Dean of Outreach .... Ms. Janet GILL
20 Executive Dean of Instruction .... Mr. Darin MOELLER
08 Library Manager .... Ms. Sharon DYKSHOORN
88 KWIT/KOJI-FM General Manager .... Ms. Gretchen GONDEK
88 Director Small Business Devel Ctr .... Mr. Todd RAUSCH
18 Director Physical Plant .... Mr. Kyle HUESER
06 Registrar .... Ms. Lora VANDER ZWAAG
26 Director Marketing/Publications .... Ms. Emma HEWITT
37 Director of Financial Aid .... Ms. LeAnn HOFFMAN

William Penn University (B)

201 Trueblood Avenue, Oskaloosa IA 52577-1799

County: Mahaska | FICE Identification: 001900
Unit ID: 154590
Telephone: (641) 673-1001 | Carnegie Class: Bac/Diverse
FAX Number: (641) 673-1396 | Calendar System: Semester
URL: www.wmpenn.edu
Established: 1873 | Annual Undergrad Tuition & Fees: $23,680
Enrollment: 1,463 | Coed
Affiliation or Control: Friends | IRS Status: 501(c)3
Highest Offering: Master's
Program: 2-Year Principally Bachelor's Creditable; Liberal Arts And General; Teacher Preparatory
Accreditation: NH, NURSE

01 President .... Mr. John OTTOSSON
05 Vice Pres for Academic Affairs .... Dr. Noel STAHLE
30 Interim VP for Advancement .... Ms. Marsha RIORDAN
10 VP Financial Operations .... Ms. Bonnie JOHNSON
11 VP of Operations .... Mr. Greg HAFNER
84 VP for Enrollment Management .... Ms. Kerra STRONG
56 Interim Vice President of CWA .... Ms. Linda PARKER
29 Assoc Vice Pres Alumni Relations .... Vacant
108 Director of Assessment .... Dr. Jared PEARCE
06 Registrar .... Ms. DeAnne DOLL
37 Director of Financial Aid .... Ms. Cyndi PEIFFER
36 Career Services Coordinator .... Ms. Debbie STEVENS
08 Head Librarian .... Ms. Julie HANSEN
15 Human Resource Director .... Vacant
35 Director of Student Activities .... Mr. Levi TARBELL
09 Director of Institutional Research .... Mr. Michael EDWARDS
42 Campus Minister .... Vacant
40 Bookstore Manager .... Ms. Heidi PARKER
18 Director of Buildings & Grounds .... Mr. Milt CAMPBELL
83 Chair Div of Social/Behavioral Sci .... Dr. Michael COLLINS
72 Co-Chair Div of Applied Technology .... Dr. Jim DROST
72 Co-Chair Div of Applied Technology .... Mr. Jim HOEKSEMA
53 Co-Chair Division of Education .... Ms. Susan BOXLER
53 Co-Chair Division of Education .... Ms. Cathy WILLIAMSON
50 Chair Div of Business Admin .... Dr. Lance EDWARDS
79 Chair Division of Humanities .... Dr. Anita MEINERT
76 Chair Div of Health & Life Sciences .... Dr. Gary CHRISTOPHER
66 Chair Div of Nursing .... Dr. Brenda KROGH-DUREE
04 Executive Asst to President .... Ms. Angella DURIAN-GAMBELL
13 Director of Information Services .... Mr. Mike FOSTER
19 Director of Security .... Mr. Tim REYNOLDS
32 Director of Student Activities .... Mr. Levi TARBELL
38 Campus Counselor .... Ms. Tyne SMITH
39 Co-Director of Residence Life .... Ms. Dianne BURNS
39 Co-Director of Residence Life .... Mr. Matt CROONQUIST
41 Athletic Director .... Mr. Greg HAFNER

KANSAS

Allen County Community College (C)

1801 N Cottonwood, Iola KS 66749-1698

County: Allen | FICE Identification: 001901
Unit ID: 154642
Telephone: (620) 365-5116 | Carnegie Class: Assoc/Pub-R-M
FAX Number: (620) 365-7406 | Calendar System: Semester
URL: www.allencc.edu
Established: 1923 | Annual Undergrad Tuition & Fees (In-District): $2,720
Enrollment: 2,776 | Coed
Affiliation or Control: State/Local | IRS Status: 501(c)3
Highest Offering: Associate Degree
Program: 2-Year Principally Bachelor's Creditable
Accreditation: NH

01 President .... Mr. John A. MASTERSON
05 Vice Pres for Academic Affairs .... Mr. Jon MARSHALL
10 Vice Pres for Finance & Operations .... Mr. Brian COUNSIL
32 Vice Pres Student Affairs .... Ms. Cynthia JACOBSON
12 Dean for the Iola Campus .... Mrs. Tosca HARRIS
12 Dean for the Burlingame Campus .... Mr. Bob REAVIS
106 Dean for Online Learning .... Mrs. Regena BAILEY-AYE
08 Director of Library .... Mrs. Sandy MOORE
13 Director of MIS .... Mr. Doug DUNLAP
37 Director of Financial Aid .... Mrs. Vicki CURRY
30 Director of Development .... Mrs. Cynthia ADAMS
18 Director of Physical Plant Opers .... Mr. Kent TOMSON
07 Director of Admissions .... Ms. Rebecca BILDERBACK
41 Director of Athletics .... Dr. Doug DESMARTEAU
40 Director of Bookstore .... Mrs. Donna CASON
17 Allied Health Director .... Ms. Tera SOLOMAN
85 Foreign Student Advisor .... Mrs. Nichole PETERS
90 Director Academic Computing .... Mrs. Christy CUTSHAW
09 Director Inst Research/Assessment .... Vacant
35 Director Student Life .... Mr. Ryan BILDERBACK
06 Registrar .... Mrs. Bobbie HAVILAND
26 Public Relations Coordinator .... Mrs. Nancy FORD

Allen County Community College Burlingame Campus (D)

100 Bloomquist, Burlingame KS 66413

Telephone: (785) 654-2416 | Identification: 770249
Accreditation: &NH

† Branch campus of Allen County Community College, Iola, KS.

The Art Institutes International - Kansas City (E)

8208 Melrose Drive, Lenexa KS 66214

Telephone: (913) 217-4600 | Identification: 666765
Accreditation: ACICS

† Branch campus of The Art Institute of Phoeniz, AZ.

Baker University (F)

618 Eighth Street, Baldwin City KS 66006-0065

County: Douglas | FICE Identification: 001903
Unit ID: 154688
Telephone: (785) 594-6451 | Carnegie Class: Master's L
FAX Number: (785) 594-2522 | Calendar System: 4/1/4
URL: www.bakeru.edu
Established: 1858 | Annual Undergrad Tuition & Fees: $27,160
Enrollment: 3,116 | Coed
Affiliation or Control: United Methodist | IRS Status: 501(c)3
Highest Offering: Doctorate
Program: Liberal Arts And General; Teacher Preparatory; Professional
Accreditation: NH, ACBSP, MUS, NURSE, TED

01 President .... Dr. Lynne MURRAY
05 Provost .... Dr. Brian POSLER
30 VP of University Advancement .... Ms. Danielle YEAROUT
13 CIO/VP Strateg Plng & Academic Res .... Mr. Andy JETT
10 Chief Financial Officer .... Mr. Ray HAUKE
53 Dean School of Education .... Dr. Tes MEHRING
66 Dean of School of Nursing .... Dr. Bernadette M. FETTEROLF
49 Dean of CAS .... Ms. Martha HARRIS
107 Associate Dean SPGS .... Dr. Jake BUCHER
41 Director Of Athletics .... Ms. Theresa YETMAR
44 VP for Endowment/Planned Giving .... Mr. Jerry WEAKLEY
84 Senior Director of Admissions .... Mr. Kevin KROPF
27 Director of Marketing & Comm .... Mr. Chris SMITH
31 Director of Corporate Relations .... Mr. Ivan HUNTOON
06 University Registrar .... Ms. Ruth MILLER
21 Chief Accounting Officer/Controller .... Ms. Melissa VAN LEIDEN
18 Dir of Physical Plant & Facility Op .... Mr. Jeremy PORTLOCK
42 Minister to the University .... Rev. Kevin HOPKINS
37 Senior Director of Financial Aid .... Ms. Jeanne MOTT
15 Chief Human Resources Officer .... Ms. Connie DEEL
88 Senior Dir of University Relations .... Ms. Cheryl MCCRARY
32 Dean of Students .... Dr. Cassy BAILEY
88 Senior Dir of Development .... Ms. Amy PIERSOL
09 Dir of Inst Research/Math Prof .... Dr. Jean JOHNSON
35 Assoc Dean Students & Dir Diversity .... Dr. Teresa CLOUNCH
88 Asst Dean Stdnt Engage & Success .... Dr. Judith SMRHA
26 Director Public Relations .... Mr. Steve ROTTINGHAUS
29 Dir of Alumni Relations .... Mr. Doug BARTH
36 Director of Career Services .... Ms. Susan WADE
38 Dir of Health & Counseling Center .... Dr. Tim HODGES
08 Interim Dir of Library Services .... Mr. Ray WALLING

Baker University School of Professional and Graduate Studies (G)

8001 College Boulevard, Suite 100,
Overland Park KS 66210

Telephone: (913) 491-4432 | Identification: 770250
Accreditation: &NH

† Branch campus of Baker University, Baldwin City, KS.

Barclay College (H)

607 N Kingman, Haviland KS 67059-0288

County: Kiowa | FICE Identification: 001917
Unit ID: 155070
Telephone: (620) 862-5252 | Carnegie Class: Spec/Faith
FAX Number: (620) 862-5242 | Calendar System: Semester
URL: www.barclaycollege.edu
Established: 1917 | Annual Undergrad Tuition & Fees: $11,495
Enrollment: 251 | Coed
Affiliation or Control: Independent Non-Profit | IRS Status: 501(c)3
Highest Offering: Master's
Program: Liberal Arts And General; Religious Emphasis
Accreditation: @NH, BI

01 President .... Dr. Royce FRAZIER
05 VP Academics .... Dr. Jim LE SHANA
10 VP Business Services .... Mr. Lee ANDERS
32 VP Student Services .... Mr. Kevin LEE
30 VP Institutional Advancement .... Mr. Larry LEWIS
06 VP Registration and Records .... Dr. Glenn W. LEPPERT
37 Director Student Financial Aid .... Mr. Ryan HAASE
07 Admissions Counselor .... Mr. Justin KENDALL
08 Librarian .... Mr. Pat HALL
29 Alumni Relations .... Dr. Herb FRAZIER
106 Dir Online Education/E-learning .... Mrs. Angela WETMORE
13 Chief Info Technology Officer (CIO) .... Mr. Trent MAGGARD
15 Director Personnel Services .... Mrs. Gayle MORTIMER
18 Chief Facilities/Physical Plant .... Mr. CD FITCH
19 Director Security/Safety .... Mr. Kevin LEE
41 Athletic Director .... Mr. Royce BRYAN
09 Director of Institutional Research .... Dr. Glenn LEPPERT
25 Chief Contracts/Grants Admin .... Mr. Larry LEWIS

Barton County Community College (I)

245 NE 30th Road, Great Bend KS 67530-9107

County: Barton | FICE Identification: 004608
Unit ID: 154697
Telephone: (620) 792-2701 | Carnegie Class: Assoc/Pub-R-L
FAX Number: (620) 792-5624 | Calendar System: Semester
URL: www.bartonccc.edu
Established: 1965 | Annual Undergrad Tuition & Fees (In-District): $3,347
Enrollment: 8,615 | Coed
Affiliation or Control: State/Local | IRS Status: 501(c)3
Highest Offering: Associate Degree
Program: Occupational; 2-Year Principally Bachelor's Creditable
Accreditation: NH, ADNUR, EMT, MLTAD

01 President .... Dr. Carl R. HEILMAN
05 VP of Instruction & Student Svcs .... Dr. Robin GARRETT
11 Dean of Administration .... Mr. Mark E. DEAN
13 Dean of Information Services .... Mr. Charles PERKINS
32 Dean of Student Services .... Mrs. Angela M. MADDY
20 Dean of Academics .... Dr. Richard L. ABEL
88 Dean Ft Riley Lrng Svcs/Mil Ops .... Ms. Ashley ARNOLD
103 Dean Workforce Training & Cmty Educ .... Mrs. Elaine R. SIMMONS
37 Asst Dean Stndt Svcs/Dir Fin Aid .... Mrs. Myrna L. PERKINS
30 Exec Dir Institutional Advancement .... Ms. Nancy WIEBE
66 Exec Dir of Nursing & Healthcare Ed .... Dr. Kathy KOTTAS
50 Exec Dir of Business/Tech/Cmty Educ .... Ms. Jane HOWARD
103 Exec Dir of Workforce Trn & Cmty Ed .... Ms. Mary FOLEY
26 Dir of Public Relations & Marketing .... Mr. Brandon STEINERT
04 Assistant to President .... Mrs. Amye SCHNEIDER
41 Director of Athletics .... Mr. Trevor ROLFS
08 Director of Learning Resources .... Mrs. ReGina REYNOLDS-CASPER
15 Director of Human Resources .... Mrs. Julie A. KNOBLICH
07 Director of Admissions .... Ms. Tana COOPER
19 Coordinator of Facility Management .... Mr. Jim D. IRELAND
25 Director of Grants .... Ms. Cathie R. OSHIRO
06 Registrar .... Mrs. Lori D. CROWTHER
40 Bookstore Manager .... Mrs. Connie M. KERNS
09 Coord of Instruct & Instnl Research .... Mrs. Caicey L. CRUTCHER
39 Coordinator of Student Housing .... Mr. Jonathan DIETZ

Barton County Community College Fort Riley Campus (J)

PO Box 2463, Bldg 217, Rm 105, Fort Riley KS 66442

Telephone: (877) 620-6606 | Identification: 770251
Accreditation: &NH

† Branch campus of Barton County Community College, Great Bend, KS.

Benedictine College (K)

1020 N 2nd Street, Atchison KS 66002-1499

County: Atchison | FICE Identification: 010256
Unit ID: 154712
Telephone: (913) 367-5340 | Carnegie Class: Bac/Diverse
FAX Number: (913) 367-6566 | Calendar System: Semester
URL: www.benedictine.edu
Established: 1858 | Annual Undergrad Tuition & Fees: $26,690
Enrollment: 1,825 | Coed
Affiliation or Control: Roman Catholic | IRS Status: 501(c)3
Highest Offering: Master's
Program: Liberal Arts And General; Teacher Preparatory; Business Emphasis
Accreditation: NH, CAATE, MUS, NURSE, TED

01 President .... Mr. Stephen D. MINNIS
05 Dean of the College .... Dr. Kimberly C. SHANKMAN
10 Chief Financial Officer .... Mr. Ronald J. OLINGER
30 Vice President Advancement .... Ms. Kelly J. VOWELS
84 Dean of Enrollment Management .... Mr. Pete HELGESEN

32 Vice President of Student Life ..... Dr. Linda HENRY
35 Dean of Students ..... Dr. Joseph WURTZ
42 Director for Mission and Ministry ..... Mr. David TROTTER
41 Athletic Director ..... Mr. Charles GARTENMAYER
26 Vice President for College Rels ..... Mr. Tom HOOPES
20 Assoc Dean & Registrar ..... Sr. Linda HERNDON, OSB
09 Director of Institutional Research ..... Dr. Jennifer HELLER
58 Exec Dir of Grad Business Programs ..... Mr. Dave GEENENS
58 Director of MASL/Asst Prof Educ ..... Dr. Cheryl REDING
37 Director of Student Financial Aid ..... Mr. Tony TANKING
27 Dir of Marketing & Communications ..... Mr. Steve JOHNSON
38 Director of Counseling Center ..... Mr. Kerry A. MARVIN
23 Director of Student Health Services ..... Ms. Janet ADRIAN
18 Director of Operations ..... Mr. Matt FASSERO
13 Dir of Tech & Information Sys ..... Mr. Randy ROWLAND
88 Director of International Program ..... Mr. Daniele MUSSO
08 Librarian ..... Mr. Steven GROMATZKY
39 Director of Residence Life ..... Mr. Sean MULCAHY
21 Bursar ..... Ms. Becky MILLER
36 Director of Career Development ..... Ms. Katie MCDOWELL
29 Director of Planned Giving & Alumni ..... Mr. Tim ANDREWS
04 Executive Asst to President ..... Ms. Brianna SLUDER
15 Director of Human Resources ..... Ms. Michelle COURY
19 Security Account Manager ..... Mr. Danny FAIRLEY
53 Co-Chair Education Department ..... Dr. Charles OSBORN
54 Chair Engineering Department ..... Dr. Darrin MUGGLI

Bethany College (A)

335 E Swensson Street, Lindsborg KS 67456-1895
County: McPherson FICE Identification: 001904
Unit ID: 154721
Telephone: (785) 227-3311 Carnegie Class: Bac/Diverse
FAX Number: (785) 227-2004 Calendar System: 4/1/4
URL: www.bethanylb.edu
Established: 1881 Annual Undergrad Tuition & Fees: $25,250
Enrollment: 717 Coed
Affiliation or Control: Evangelical Lutheran Church In America
IRS Status: 501(c)3
Highest Offering: Baccalaureate
Program: Liberal Arts And General; Teacher Preparatory; Professional
Accreditation: #NH, CAATE, MUS, TED

01 Interim President ..... Dr. Robert VOGEL
05 Int Provost & Dean of the College ..... Robert CARLSON
30 VP for Advancement ..... Mr. Galen BUNNING
44 Assoc Vice Pres for Development ..... Mr. Warren OLSON
10 VP for Finance and Operations ..... Mr. Dennis STUGELMEYER
21 Controller ..... Mr. Dale BURGE
32 Int Dean for Student Development ..... Dane PAVLOVICH
35 Assoc Dean for Student Development ..... Vacant
84 Dean of Admissions/Financial Aid ..... Mr. Matt PHANNENSTIEL
37 Director of Financial Aid ..... Ms. Amy HOSS
06 Registrar ..... Ms. Jill MEGREDY
08 Dir of Wallerstedt Learning Center ..... Ms. Denise K. CARSON
41 Dean of Athletics ..... Mr. Dane PAVLOVICH
18 Director of Campus Facilities ..... Mr. Randy JIRAK
13 Director of Technology Services ..... Mr. Matthew CARVER
88 Exec Dir of Information Services ..... Ms. Christi PAULSEN
26 Exec Dir of Communications & Mktg ..... Ms. Tina M. GOODWIN
29 Director Alumni Relations ..... Ms. Molly B. JOHNSON
36 Director Career Services ..... Ms. Diane MILLER
39 Residential Education Director ..... Mr. Matt RIORDAN
42 Int Campus Pastor ..... Rev. Anita STROMMEN
35 Director Campus Activities ..... Ms. Roxie L. SJOGREN
88 Program Dir Athletic Training ..... Vacant
53 Program Director Teacher Education ..... Prof. Gail KONZEM
64 Music Department Chair ..... Dr. Dan MASTERSON
15 Director of Human Resources ..... Ms. Lisa EASTER
09 Research Analyst ..... Ms. Sarah ZEHNDER
40 Bookstore Manager ..... Ms. Brenda C. SMITH
92 Honors Program Coordinator ..... Dr. Kristin VAN TASSEL
38 Student Counselor ..... Mr. David OLSEN
85 Coord Student Dev & Intl Program ..... Ms. Charlotte ANDERSON
04 Admin Assistant to President ..... Ms. Linda BALL
108 Director Institutional Assessment ..... Dr. Anders GARDESTIG
07 Associate Director of Admissions ..... Mr. Richard STRANGE

Bethel College (B)

300 E 27th Street, North Newton KS 67117-0531
County: Harvey FICE Identification: 001905
Unit ID: 154749
Telephone: (316) 283-2500 Carnegie Class: Bac/Diverse
FAX Number: (316) 284-5286 Calendar System: 4/1/4
URL: www.bethelks.edu
Established: 1887 Annual Undergrad Tuition & Fees: $25,410
Enrollment: 483 Coed
Affiliation or Control: Mennonite Church IRS Status: 501(c)3
Highest Offering: Baccalaureate
Program: Liberal Arts And General; Teacher Preparatory; Professional
Accreditation: NH, CAATE, NURSE, SW, TED

01 President ..... Dr. Perry D. WHITE
04 Assistant to the President ..... Ms. Rosa M. BARRERA
05 Vice President Academic Affairs ..... Dr. Robert W. MILLIMAN
32 Vice President Student Life ..... Mr. Aaron L. AUSTIN
41 Athletic Director ..... Mr. Kent ALLSHOUSE
30 Vice President Advancement ..... Ms. Pamela TIESZEN
10 Vice President for Business Affairs ..... Mr. Allen WEDEL
26 VP for Marketing and Communications ..... Ms. Lori LIVENGOOD
06 Registrar ..... Ms. Marcia K. MILLER
44 Director of Development ..... Vacant
07 Vice President for Admissions ..... Mr. Andrew W. JOHNSON
37 Director of Financial Aid ..... Mr. Tony GRABER
29 Director of Alumni Relations ..... Mr. David LINSCHEID
08 Head Librarian ..... Ms. Gail STUCKY
42 Director of Church Relations ..... Mr. Peter GOERZEN
18 Chief Facilities/Physical Plant ..... Mr. Les GOERZEN
13 Chief Info Technology Officer (CIO) ..... Mr. Rus ROGERS
36 Dir Student Placement/Counseling ..... Ms. Joanna BJERUM
84 Enrollment Activities ..... Ms. Jane SCHMIDT

Brown Mackie College-Kansas City (C)

9705 Lenexa Drive, Lenexa KS 66215-1345
Telephone: (913) 768-1900 Identification: 666091
Accreditation: &NH, OTA

† Regional accreditation is carried under the parent institution in Salina, KS.

Brown Mackie College-Salina (D)

2106 S 9th Street, Salina KS 67401-7307
County: Saline FICE Identification: 006755
Unit ID: 154776
Telephone: (785) 825-5422 Carnegie Class: Assoc/PrivFP
FAX Number: (785) 827-7623 Calendar System: Other
URL: www.brownmackie.edu
Established: 1892 Annual Undergrad Tuition & Fees: $12,672
Enrollment: 299 Coed
Affiliation or Control: Proprietary IRS Status: Proprietary
Highest Offering: Baccalaureate
Program: Occupational; 2-Year Principally Bachelor's Creditable; Business Emphasis
Accreditation: NH, OTA

01 President ..... Ms. Judy HOLMES
05 Dean of Academic Affairs ..... Ms. Ralynn ERNEST
07 Senior Director of Admissions ..... Ms. Diann HEATH
06 Registrar ..... Ms. Kristi HAYS
36 Director of Career Services ..... Ms. Robin NASH

Bryan University (E)

1527 SW Fairlawn Road, Topeka KS 66604
County: Shawnee FICE Identification: 030662
Unit ID: 154794
Telephone: (785) 272-0889 Carnegie Class: Assoc/PrivFP
FAX Number: (785) 272-4538 Calendar System: Other
URL: www.bryanu.edu
Established: 1982 Annual Undergrad Tuition & Fees: $15,336
Enrollment: 63 Coed
Affiliation or Control: Proprietary IRS Status: Proprietary
Highest Offering: Associate Degree
Program: Occupational; 2-Year Principally Bachelor's Creditable
Accreditation: ACICS

01 Executive Director ..... Mr. Wayne MAJOR

Butler Community College (F)

901 S. Haverhill Road, El Dorado KS 67042-3225
County: Butler FICE Identification: 001906
Unit ID: 154800
Telephone: (316) 321-2222 Carnegie Class: Assoc/Pub-S-MC
FAX Number: (316) 322-3109 Calendar System: Semester
URL: www.butlercc.edu
Established: 1927 Annual Undergrad Tuition & Fees (In-District): $2,396
Enrollment: 9,239 Coed
Affiliation or Control: Local IRS Status: 501(c)3
Highest Offering: Associate Degree
Program: Occupational; 2-Year Principally Bachelor's Creditable; Liberal Arts And General
Accreditation: NH, ACBSP, ADNUR, ENGT

01 President ..... Dr. Kimberly KRULL
05 Vice President of Academics ..... Dr. Karla FISHER
10 Vice President of Finance ..... Mr. Kent WILLIAMS
32 Vice President of Student Services ..... Mr. Bill RINKENBAUGH
30 Vice President for Inst Advancement ..... Ms. Stacy COFER
08 Reference Librarian ..... Ms. Judy BASTIN
06 Registrar ..... Ms. Willow DEAN
09 Director of Institutional Research ..... Dr. Gene GEORGE
15 Director Personnel Services ..... Ms. Vicki LONG
21 Associate Business Officer ..... Ms. Edith WAUGH
29 Director Alumni Relations ..... Vacant
36 Director Student Placement ..... Vacant
37 Director Student Financial Aid ..... Ms. Heather WARD
35 Associate VP of Student Services ..... Ms. Jessica OHMAN
26 Director of Institutional Marketing ..... Ms. Kelly SNEDDEN
18 Director Facilities ..... Mr. Lynn UMHOLTZ
96 Director of Purchasing ..... Ms. Regina KIEFFER
07 Director of Admissions ..... Ms. Kirsten ALLEN
38 Director Student Counseling ..... Ms. Jessica OHMAN
13 Chief Info Technology Officer (CIO) ..... Mr. Tom ERWIN
19 Director Security/Safety ..... Mr. James BRYAN
39 Director Residence Life ..... Ms. Heather RINKENBAUGH
41 Athletic Director ..... Mr. Todd CARTER

Butler of Andover (G)

1810 N Andover Road, Andover KS 67002
Telephone: (316) 733-0071 Identification: 770253
Accreditation: &NH

† Branch campus of Butler Community College, El Dorado, KS.

Butler of Council Grove (H)

131 West Main, Council Grove KS 66846
Telephone: (620) 767-5158 Identification: 770254
Accreditation: &NH

† Branch campus of Butler Community College, El Dorado, KS.

Butler of Marion (I)

412 N Second Street, Marion KS 66861
Telephone: (620) 382-2183 Identification: 770255
Accreditation: &NH

† Branch campus of Butler Community College, El Dorado, KS.

Butler of McConnell (J)

Ed Ctr, Bldg 412, 53474 Lawrence Ct, McConnell AFB KS 67221
Telephone: (316) 681-3522 Identification: 770257
Accreditation: &NH

† Branch campus of Butler Community College, El Dorado, KS.

Butler of Rose Hill (K)

712 Rose Hill Road, Rose Hill KS 67133
Telephone: (316) 776-9429 Identification: 770256
Accreditation: &NH

† Branch campus of Butler Community College, El Dorado, KS.

Central Baptist Theological Seminary (L)

6601 Monticello Road, Shawnee KS 66226-3513
County: Johnson FICE Identification: 001907
Unit ID: 154837
Telephone: (913) 667-5700 Carnegie Class: Spec/Faith
FAX Number: (913) 371-8110 Calendar System: Semester
URL: www.cbts.edu
Established: 1901 Annual Graduate Tuition & Fees: $9,140
Enrollment: 391 Coed
Affiliation or Control: Baptist IRS Status: 501(c)3
Highest Offering: Doctorate; No Undergraduates
Program: Professional; Religious Emphasis
Accreditation: NH, THEOL

01 President ..... Dr. Molly T. MARSHALL
05 Dean of the Seminary ..... Dr. Robert E. JOHNSON
03 Executive Vice President ..... Mr. George TOWNSEND
30 VP for Institutional Advancement ..... Dr. John W. GRAVLEY
06 Assistant to the Dean/Registrar ..... Mr. Stephen GUINN
26 Director of Seminary Relations ..... Ms. Robin SANDBOTHE
07 Dir Recruitment/Foundation Coord ..... Vacant

Central Christian College of Kansas (M)

1200 S Main, PO Box 1403, McPherson KS 67460-5799
County: McPherson FICE Identification: 001908
Unit ID: 154855
Telephone: (620) 241-0723 Carnegie Class: Bac/Diverse
FAX Number: (620) 241-6032 Calendar System: 4/1/4
URL: www.centralchristian.edu
Established: 1884 Annual Undergrad Tuition & Fees: $22,500
Enrollment: 1,172 Coed
Affiliation or Control: Free Methodist IRS Status: 501(c)3
Highest Offering: Baccalaureate
Program: Liberal Arts And General
Accreditation: NH

01 President ..... Col. Hal HOXIE
05 Provost ..... Dr. Leonard FAVARA, JR.
30 VP/Chief Development Officer ..... Vacant
32 Chief Student Affairs Officer ..... Rev. Chris SMITH
10 Business Office Manager ..... Mr. Phil NELSON
11 Chief Operations Officer ..... Mr. Tom GRECO
41 Athletic Director ..... Vacant
06 Registrar ..... Mrs. Michele AUGUST
09 Director of Institutional Research ..... Mr. AJ ELLIS
37 Int Director of Financial Aid ..... Mrs. Nicole CARVER
08 Head Librarian ..... Ms. Bev KELLEY
20 Associate Academic Officer ..... Mr. Cheyenne KROEKER
18 Chief Facilities/Physical Plant ..... Mr. Bob BAILEY

Cleveland University - Kansas City (N)

10850 Lowell Avenue, Overland Park KS 66210
County: Johnson FICE Identification: 020907
Unit ID: 177038
Telephone: (913) 234-0600 Carnegie Class: Spec/Health
FAX Number: (913) 234-0904 Calendar System: Trimester
URL: www.cleveland.edu

Established: 1922 Annual Undergrad Tuition & Fees: $9,120
Enrollment: 483 Coed
Affiliation or Control: Independent Non-Profit IRS Status: 501(c)3
Highest Offering: First Professional Degree
Program: Professional
Accreditation: NH, CHIRO

01 President ... Dr. Carl S. CLEVELAND, III
10 Chief Operating Officer ... Mr. Jeff KARP
05 Int Provost/DeanClinical Education ... Dr. Julia BARTLETT
26 VP of Campus and Alumni Relations ... Dr. Clark BECKLEY
15 Vice Pres HR/Organizational Devel ... Mr. Dale MARRANT
20 Dean of Pre-Clinical Education ... Dr. Paul BARLETT
20 Dean of Clinical Education ... Dr. Julia BARTLETT
21 Controller ... Ms. Marla COPE
06 Director of Academic Records ... Mr. David FOOSE
37 Director of Financial Aid ... Ms. Caprice CALAMAIO
09 Director of Institutional Reporting ... Dr. Christena NICHOLSON
09 Director of Research ... Dr. Mark T. PFEFER
32 Director of Student Services ... Ms. Jalonna BOWIE
07 Director of Admissions ... Ms. Melissa DENTON
08 Library Director ... Ms. Simone BRIAND
13 Systems Administrator ... Mr. Calvin DANIELS
04 Assistant to the President ... Ms. Marjorie BRADSHAW
18 Director of Facilities Mgmt ... Mr. Frank HANEY

Cloud County Community College (A)

2221 Campus Drive, Concordia KS 66901-1002
County: Cloud FICE Identification: 001909
Unit ID: 154907
Telephone: (785) 243-1435 Carnegie Class: Assoc/Pub-R-M
FAX Number: (785) 243-1459 Calendar System: Semester
URL: www.cloud.edu
Established: 1965 Annual Undergrad Tuition & Fees (In-District): $2,970
Enrollment: 2,438 Coed
Affiliation or Control: State/Local IRS Status: 501(c)3
Highest Offering: Associate Degree
Program: Occupational; 2-Year Principally Bachelor's Creditable
Accreditation: NH, ADNUR

01 President ... Dr. Danette TOONE
05 Vice President for Academic Affairs ... Dr. William BACKLIN
84 VP Enrollment Mgmt/Student Services ... Mr. Joel FIGGS
11 Vice Pres for Administrative Svcs ... Ms. Amy LANGE
30 Director Institutional Advancement ... Vacant
07 Director of Admissions ... Vacant
08 Director of Library Services ... Ms. Jennifer SCHROEDER
41 Athletic Director ... Mr. Matthew BECHARD
06 Registrar ... Mrs. Linda PETERSEN
18 Chief Facilities/Physical Plant ... Mr. Rex E. SICARD
26 Chief Public Relations Officer ... Ms. Jenny ACREE
102 Ex Dir Cloud County Cmty Col Found .. Ms. Kimberly REYNOLDS
37 Director Student Financial Aid ... Ms. Suzi KNOETTGEN
38 Director Advising & Retention ... Ms. Rebecca MURROW
15 Coordinator of Human Resources ... Ms. Christine WILSON
09 Director Institutional Research ... Dr. Mitch STIMERS

Cloud County Community College Geary County Campus (B)

631 Caroline Avenue, Junction City KS 66441
Telephone: (785) 238-8010 Identification: 770258
Accreditation: &NH

† Branch campus of Cloud County Community College, Concordia, KS.

Coffeyville Community College (C)

400 W 11th Street, Coffeyville KS 67337-5064
County: Montgomery FICE Identification: 001910
Unit ID: 154925
Telephone: (620) 251-7700 Carnegie Class: Assoc/Pub-R-S
FAX Number: (620) 252-7098 Calendar System: Semester
URL: www.coffeyville.edu
Established: 1923 Annual Undergrad Tuition & Fees (In-District): $2,160
Enrollment: 1,608 Coed
Affiliation or Control: State/Local IRS Status: 501(c)3
Highest Offering: Associate Degree
Program: Occupational; 2-Year Principally Bachelor's Creditable
Accreditation: NH, EMT, MAC

01 President ... Ms. Linda MOLEY
05 Vice President for Academic Service ... Ms. Aron POTTER
10 Vice Pres for Operations & Finance ... Mr. Jeff MORRIS
88 VP for Innovation/Bus Initiatives ... Mr. Marlon THORNBURG
12 Director Columbus Technical Campus ... Mrs. Cindy HARROLD
102 Exec Director-CCC Foundation ... Mr. Dickie ROLLS
32 Dean of Student Life ... Mr. Ryan MCCUNE
09 Dean Institutional Research/Records ... Mrs. Deborah OESTMANN
26 Director of Marketing ... Ms. Kris ADAMS
20 Director Academic Advising/SSC ... Mrs. Kim LAY
45 Director Institutional Effectivenes ... Mr. Marty EVENSVOLD
37 Director of Financial Aid ... Mrs. Pam FEERER
15 Director of Human Resources ... Mrs. Kelli BAUER
41 Athletics Director ... Mr. Jeff LEIKER
18 Director of Maintenance ... Ms. Vivian FROST
106 Director of Distance Learning ... Mr. Brad WEBER
40 Bookstore Manager ... Mrs. Karen STRIMPLE
07 Admissions Representative ... Ms. Kristin HORNER

Colby Community College (D)

1255 S Range, Colby KS 67701-4099
County: Thomas FICE Identification: 001911
Unit ID: 154934
Telephone: (785) 462-3984 Carnegie Class: Assoc/Pub-R-M
FAX Number: (785) 460-4699 Calendar System: Semester
URL: www.colbycc.edu
Established: 1964 Annual Undergrad Tuition & Fees (In-District): $3,300
Enrollment: 1,514 Coed
Affiliation or Control: State/Local IRS Status: 501(c)3
Highest Offering: Associate Degree
Program: Occupational; 2-Year Principally Bachelor's Creditable
Accreditation: #NH, ADNUR, PTAA

01 President ... Mr. Seth M. CARTER
05 Vice President of Academic Affairs ... Mr. Gregory NICHOLS
32 Vice President of Student Affairs ... Dr. George MCNULTY
10 Vice President of Business Affairs ... Ms. Carolyn KASDORF
06 Registrar ... Mr. Christopher LEE
08 Librarian ... Mrs. Tara SCHROER
26 Director of Public Information ... Mr. Doug JOHNSON
09 Director of Data Management ... Mrs. Angel MORRISON
07 Director of Admissions ... Mrs. Amy MELIKOVA
37 Director of Financial Aid ... Mrs. Cindi KRISS
29 Director Alumni Relations ... Ms. Jennifer SCHOENFELD
41 Athletic Director ... Mr. Ryan STURDY
13 Director of IT ... Mr. Douglass MCDOWALL
04 Administrative Asst to President ... Mrs. Lisa FAILLA

Cowley County Community College (E)

125 S Second, PO Box 1147,
Arkansas City KS 67005-1147
County: Cowley FICE Identification: 001902
Unit ID: 154952
Telephone: (620) 442-0430 Carnegie Class: Assoc/Pub-R-M
FAX Number: (620) 441-5350 Calendar System: Semester
URL: www.cowley.edu
Established: 1922 Annual Undergrad Tuition & Fees (In-District): $2,820
Enrollment: 3,185 Coed
Affiliation or Control: Local IRS Status: 501(c)3
Highest Offering: Associate Degree
Program: Occupational; 2-Year Principally Bachelor's Creditable
Accreditation: NH, EMT

01 President ... Dr. Dennis C. RITTLE
05 Vice President of Academic Affairs ... Dr. Harold ARNETT
10 Vice Pres of Finance/Administration ... Dr. Gloria WALKER
13 Vice Pres Information Technology ... Mr. Paul ERDMANN
30 Vice Pres Institutional Development ... Mr. Ben SCHEARS
41 Athletic Director ... Mr. Shane LARSON
35 Director of Student Affairs ... Ms. Kristi SHAW
20 Director of Academics ... Ms. Janice STOVER
84 Exec Director Enrollment Management ... Mr. Josh COBBLE
32 Executive Director of Student Life ... Mr. Jason O'TOOLE
106 Assoc VP Mulvane/Online Operations ... Ms. Stephanie JOHNS-HINES
26 Dir Inst Comm/Public Relations ... Mr. Rama PEROO
06 Registrar ... Mr. Devin GRAVES
15 Director of Human Resources ... Ms. Linda KREUTZER

Dodge City Community College (F)

2501 N 14th Avenue, Dodge City KS 67801-2399
County: Ford FICE Identification: 001913
Unit ID: 154998
Telephone: (620) 225-1321 Carnegie Class: Assoc/Pub-R-M
FAX Number: (620) 227-9366 Calendar System: Semester
URL: www.dc3.edu
Established: 1935 Annual Undergrad Tuition & Fees (In-District): $2,100
Enrollment: 1,768 Coed
Affiliation or Control: State/Local IRS Status: 501(c)3
Highest Offering: Associate Degree
Program: Occupational; 2-Year Principally Bachelor's Creditable
Accreditation: NH, ADNUR

01 President ... Vacant
05 Exec VP Academic Affairs ... Mr. Danny GILLUM
10 Vice Pres of Operations & Finance ... Ms. Vada HERMON
31 VP Community & Industry Relations ... Mr. Anthony LYONS
32 Dean of Students & Registrar ... Ms. Stephanie LANNING
102 Exec Director of DCCC Foundation ... Mr. Roger PROFFITT
51 Dir Bus/Technology/Continuing Educ ... Vacant
24 Director Adult Learning Center ... Mrs. Brandi FERGUSON
26 Dir of Marketing/Human Resources ... Mr. David WETMORE
07 Dir of Admissions ... Mrs. Alisha ONTIBEROS
08 Director Learning Resource Center ... Mrs. Shelly HUELSMAN
66 Director Nursing Allied Health ... Mrs. Mary BENJAMIN
41 Athletic Director ... Mr. Casey MALEK
37 Director of Financial Aid ... Mr. Russ MCBEE
21 Director of Business Services ... Ms. Debbie BISCH
40 Director Bookstore ... Mrs. Debby MALEK
13 Director Information Technology ... Mrs. Judith MAXFIELD
39 Director of Residence Life ... Ms. Ashley WETMORE
18 Director of Facilities & Operations ... Mr. Greg PATEE
15 Asst Director of Human Resources ... Ms. Sheila BERGKAMP
04 Exec Assistant to the President ... Mrs. Carla PATEE
20 Dean of Instruction & Outreach ... Mr. Ryan AUSMUS
72 Dean of Instruction & Technology ... Mr. Paul YAROSLASKI

103 Dean of Innovation/Workforce Dev ... Mr. Nick WELLS
09 Dir of Inst Research/Accreditation ... Ms. Deanna MANN
21 Comptroller ... Ms. Sandy MOORE

Donnelly College (G)

608 N 18th Street, Kansas City KS 66102-4298
County: Wyandotte FICE Identification: 001914
Unit ID: 155007
Telephone: (913) 621-8700 Carnegie Class: Bac/Assoc
FAX Number: (913) 621-8719 Calendar System: Semester
URL: www.donnelly.edu
Established: 1949 Annual Undergrad Tuition & Fees: $7,590
Enrollment: 670 Coed
Affiliation or Control: Roman Catholic IRS Status: 501(c)3
Highest Offering: Baccalaureate
Program: Occupational; 2-Year Principally Bachelor's Creditable; Liberal Arts And General
Accreditation: NH

01 President ... Msgr. Stuart SWETLAND
03 Vice President ... Mrs. Frances SANDERS
84 Vice President of Enrollment Mgmt ... Ms. Sydney BEELER
30 Vice President of Advancement ... Mrs. Emily BUCKLEY
10 Vice President of Business Affairs ... Ms. Laurie LOETHEN
32 Director Student Success ... Dr. Mary PFLANZ
06 Registrar ... Ms. Jennifer BALES
36 Career Center Coord/Library Dir ... Mrs. Jane BALLAGH DE TOVAR
37 Director of Financial Aid ... Ms. Erin ANDERSON
09 Dir Institutional Rsrch/Plng/Assess ... Mrs. Frances SANDERS
13 Director of Computer Services ... Mr. Birdell MCCALL
29 Alumni Relations ... Mr. Roger BERG

Emporia State University (H)

1 Kellogg Circle, Emporia KS 66801-5415
County: Lyon FICE Identification: 001927
Unit ID: 155025
Telephone: (620) 341-1200 Carnegie Class: Master's L
FAX Number: (620) 341-5553 Calendar System: Semester
URL: www.emporia.edu
Established: 1863 Annual Undergrad Tuition & Fees (In-State): $6,139
Enrollment: 6,114 Coed
Affiliation or Control: State IRS Status: 501(c)3
Highest Offering: Doctorate
Program: Liberal Arts And General; Teacher Preparatory
Accreditation: NH, ART, BUS, CAATE, CACREP, CEA, CORE, LIB, MUS, NUR, TED

01 Interim President ... Dr. Jacqueline VIETTI
05 Provost/VP for Academic Affairs ... Dr. David CORDLE
11 Vice President Admin & Fiscal Affs ... Mr. Werner GOLLING
32 Vice President Student Affairs ... Dr. James E. WILLIAMS
13 Assoc Vice Pres Info Technology ... Mr. Cory FALLDINE
09 Asst Provost Inst Research/Assess ... Dr. JoLanna KORD
85 Dean of International Education ... Mr. Gonzalo BRUCE
35 Dean of Students ... Ms. Lynn M. HOBSON
10 Assoc Vice Pres Fiscal Affairs ... Ms. Diana E. KUHLMANN
102 President ESU Foundation ... Vacant
29 Director of Alumni/Govt Rels ... Mr. K. Tyler CURTIS
88 Director Natl Teachers Hall of Fame ... Ms. Carol STRICKLAND
22 Affirmative Action Officer ... Ms. Judy ANDERSON
53 Dean/The Teachers College ... Dr. Kenneth WEAVER
49 Dean College of Liberal Arts/Sci ... Dr. R. Brent THOMAS
50 Interim Dean School of Business ... Dr. John RICH
62 Dean School of Library/Info Mgmt ... Dr. Gwendolyn ALEXANDER
58 Dean Graduate Studies ... Dr. Kathy ERMLER
88 Exec Dir Jones Inst Educ Excel ... Dr. Roger CASWELL
06 Registrar ... Ms. M. Elaine HENRIE
08 Dean University Libraries/Archives ... Mr. John SHERIDAN
106 Director Distance Education ... Dr. Kathy ERMLER
37 Director Student Financial Aid ... Ms. M. Elaine HENRIE
07 Director Admissions ... Ms. Laura M. EDDY
36 Director Career Services ... Ms. June COLEMAN
38 Director Stdnt Wellness/ Counseling ... Ms. Sally CRAWFORD-FOWLER
26 Exec Dir Marketing & Media Relation ... Mr. Umair ABBASI
41 Director Athletics ... Mr. Kent L. WEISER
18 Director Facilities/Physical Plant ... Mr. Mark S. RUNGE
15 Director Human Resources ... Ms. Judy ANDERSON
23 Director Health Services ... Ms. Mary MCDANIEL
39 Dir Residential Life/Orientation ... Mr. Wade REDEKER
40 Manager Bookstore ... Mr. Michael MCRELL
19 Director Police & Safety ... Capt. Chris HOOVER
43 General Counsel ... Mr. Kevin JOHNSON
21 Controller ... Ms. Mary MINGENBACK
92 Associate Provost Honors College ... Dr. Gary WYATT
28 Director Diversity & Inclusion ... Mr. Jason BROOKS
04 Administrative Asst to President ... Ms. Sarah MCKERNAN
86 Director Government Relations ... Mr. Brian DENTON
91 Assoc CIO Academic & User Support ... Dr. Rob GIBSON

Flint Hills Technical College (I)

3301 W 18th Avenue, Emporia KS 66801-5957
County: Lyon FICE Identification: 005264
Unit ID: 155052
Telephone: (620) 343-4600 Carnegie Class: Assoc/Pub-R-S
FAX Number: (620) 343-4610 Calendar System: Semester
URL: www.fhtc.edu
Established: 1965 Annual Undergrad Tuition & Fees (In-District): $5,120
Enrollment: 836 Coed

Affiliation or Control: State/Local IRS Status: 501(c)3
Highest Offering: Associate Degree
Program: Occupational; Technical Emphasis
Accreditation: NH, DA, DH

01 President .... Dr. Dean HOLLENBECK
05 Vice Pres Instructional Services .... Mr. Steve LOEWEN
32 Vice Pres Student Services .... Ms. Lisa KIRMER
10 Vice Pres Business Services .... Mrs. Nancy THOMPSON
06 Registrar .... Ms. Brenda CARMICHAEL
15 Director Personnel Services .... Mrs. Sheri KNIGHT
37 Director Student Financial Aid .... Ms. Sandra SCHROEDER
84 Director Enrollment Management .... Ms. Brenda CARMICHAEL

Fort Hays State University (A)

600 Park Street, Hays KS 67601-4099
County: Ellis FICE Identification: 001915
Unit ID: 155061
Telephone: (785) 628-4000 Carnegie Class: Master's L
FAX Number: (785) 628-4096 Calendar System: Semester
URL: www.fhsu.edu
Established: 1902 Annual Undergrad Tuition & Fees (In-State): $4,654
Enrollment: 13,825 Coed
Affiliation or Control: State IRS Status: 501(c)3
Highest Offering: Beyond Master's But Less Than Doctorate
Program: Liberal Arts And General; Teacher Preparatory; Professional
Accreditation: NH, CAATE, MUS, NURSE, RAD, SP, SW, TED

01 President .... Dr. Mirta M. MARTIN
05 Provost .... Dr. Graham GLYNN
10 Vice Pres Administration & Finance .... Mr. Mike BARNETT
32 Vice Pres Student Affairs .... Dr. Joseph G. LINN
35 Asst Vice Pres Student Affairs .... Ms. Keegan NICHOLS
09 Asst Provost Quality Improvement .... Vacant
58 Dean Graduate Studies and Research .... Dr. Tim CROWLEY
04 Assistant to the President .... Ms. Lisa M. KARLIN
06 Interim Registrar .... Mr. Craig KARLIN
07 Admissions Director .... Ms. Tricia CLINE
29 Exec Director Alumni & Govt Rels .... Ms. Debra K. PRIDEAUX
45 Director Budget & Planning .... Mr. Larry R. GETTY
36 Director Career Services .... Mr. Daniel B. RICE
37 Interim Dir Student Financial Aid . Ms. Wendy ROHLEDER-SOOK
26 Director University Relations .... Mr. Kent L. STEWARD
13 Vice President for Technology .... Dr. Joy HATCH
08 Director Library .... Ms. Deborah LUDWIG
15 Director Personnel Services .... Ms. Shannon LINDSEY
51 Dean Virtual College .... Mr. Dennis KING
53 Dean College Education .... Dr. Paul ADAMS
49 Dean College Liberal Arts/Sciences .... Dr. Paul W. FABER
50 Dean College Business .... Dr. Mark BANNISTER
76 Dean Coll Health/Life Science .... Dr. Jeff BRIGGS
18 Co-Dir Chief Facil/Physical Plant .... Mr. Jim SCHREIBER
18 Co-Dir Chief Facil/Physical Plant .... Mr. Ken JACOBS
38 Dir Acad Advis/Career Exploration .... Dr. Patricia L. GRIFFIN
28 Diversity Coordinator .... Ms. Amber K. WHITE
19 Director Security/Safety .... Mr. Ed HOWELL
22 Dir Affirmative Action/EEO .... Ms. Carrie LANE
102 Dir Foundation/Corporate Relations .... Mr. Tim CHAPMAN
25 Chief Contracts/Grants Admin .... Ms. Leslie PAIGE
41 Athletic Director .... Mr. Curtis HAMMEKE

Fort Scott Community College (B)

2108 S Horton, Fort Scott KS 66701-3140
County: Bourbon FICE Identification: 001916
Unit ID: 155098
Telephone: (620) 223-2700 Carnegie Class: Assoc/Pub-R-M
FAX Number: (620) 223-4927 Calendar System: Semester
URL: www.fortscott.edu
Established: 1919 Annual Undergrad Tuition & Fees (In-District): $2,820
Enrollment: 1,816 Coed
Affiliation or Control: State/Local IRS Status: 501(c)3
Highest Offering: Associate Degree
Program: Occupational; 2-Year Principally Bachelor's Creditable
Accreditation: NH, ADNUR

01 President .... Alysia JOHNSTON
05 Dean of Instruction .... Regena LANCE
32 Dean of Student Services .... Robert GOLTRA
10 Dean of Finance and Operations .... Julie EICHENBERGER
13 Dean of Research & Technology .... Charles MCKOWN
07 Director Admissions .... Tom HAVRON
08 Library Director .... Stacy DZBENSKI
06 Registrar .... Courtney METCALF
26 Director Public Relations .... Jason HOGUE
66 Director Nursing .... Bill RHOADS
41 Athletic Director .... JD ETTORE
14 Information Technology Director .... Jacob REICHARD
12 Associate Dean Crawford Campuses .... Santos MANRIQUE
12 Associate Dean Paola .... Buddy Jo TANCK
38 Director of Advising .... Janet FANCHER
15 Human Resource Director .... Juley MCDANIEL
18 Director Facilities & Operations .... Darly ADAMS
30 Director of Development/Alumni .... Bailey LYONS
37 Director Student Financial Aid .... Lillie GRUBB
28 Director of Diversity .... Jill WARFORD
35 Director of Student Life .... Marci MYERS
21 Director Business Operations .... Mindy RUSSELL

Friends University (C)

2100 W University Avenue, Wichita KS 67213-3397
County: Sedgwick FICE Identification: 001918
Unit ID: 155089
Telephone: (316) 295-5000 Carnegie Class: Master's L
FAX Number: (316) 295-5060 Calendar System: Semester
URL: www.friends.edu
Established: 1898 Annual Undergrad Tuition & Fees: $25,965
Enrollment: 1,955 Coed
Affiliation or Control: Independent Non-Profit IRS Status: 501(c)3
Highest Offering: Master's
Program: Liberal Arts And General; Teacher Preparatory; Professional
Accreditation: NH, MFCD, MUS, TED

01 President .... Dr. Amy CAREY
04 Executive Asst to the President .... Ms. Natasha PEREZ
05 VP of Academic Affairs .... Vacant
10 Interim VP of Finance .... Ms. Julia CAPPS
32 VP of Student Affairs .... Dr. Carole OBERMEYER
30 VP of University Advancement .... Dr. Joan M. GALLAGHER
84 Interim VP Enrollment Mgmt & Mktg .... Ms. Deb STOCKMAN
11 VP of Administration .... Ms. Kelley WILLIAMS
06 University Registrar .... Mr. Mark BRITTON
49 Int Dean Col of Bus/Art/Sci & Educ .... Dr. Bill ALLAN
107 Int Dean Adult and Prof Studies .... Dr. David HOFMEISTER
58 Dean Graduate School .... Dr. David HOFMEISTER
50 Chair Business & IT .... Dr. Arlen HONTS
57 Chair Fine Arts .... Dr. Stephen EAVES
81 Chair Natural Science/Math .... Dr. Nora STRASSER
73 Chair Religion/Humanities .... Dr. Jeremy GALLEGOS
53 Chair Teacher Education .... Dr. Jan WILSON
83 Chair Social/Behavioral Science .... Dr. Bill ALLAN
08 Director Library .... Mr. Max BURSON
18 Chief Facilities/Physical Plant .... Mr. Paul WINCHESTER
96 Director of Business Operations .... Mr. Ryan ARCHER
07 Sr Dir Admissions & Fin Aid .... Mr. Brandon PIERCE
41 Director Athletics .... Dr. Carole OBERMEYER
37 Int Director Financial Aid .... Mr. Tony LUBBERS
42 Chaplain & Dir Campus Ministries .... Dr. Patrick SEHL, JR.
35 Asst Dean Student Affairs .... Mr. Gary RAPP
39 Dir Community & Res Development .... Ms. Kelley MARTIN
27 Director of Marketing .... Ms. Gisele MCMINIMY
29 Director of Alumni Relations .... Ms. Brie BOULANGER
88 Site Director - Topeka .... Ms. Hilary AUBEY
88 Site Manager - Kansas City .... Ms. Monica HASHEMI-BOZARTH
44 Director of Planned Giving .... Mr. Eric LITWILLER

Garden City Community College (D)

801 Campus Drive, Garden City KS 67846-6398
County: Finney FICE Identification: 001919
Unit ID: 155104
Telephone: (620) 276-7611 Carnegie Class: Assoc/Pub-R-M
FAX Number: (620) 276-9573 Calendar System: Semester
URL: www.gcccks.edu
Established: 1919 Annual Undergrad Tuition & Fees (In-District): $2,816
Enrollment: 2,086 Coed
Affiliation or Control: Local IRS Status: 501(c)3
Highest Offering: Associate Degree
Program: Occupational; 2-Year Principally Bachelor's Creditable
Accreditation: NH, ADNUR, EMT

01 President .... Dr. Herbert SWENDER
11 Exec Vice Pres Admin Svcs .... Ms. Dee WIGNER
05 Vice Pres of Instructional Services .... Vacant
32 Vice Pres of Student Services/AD .... Mr. Ryan RUDA
08 Library Director .... Mr. Trent SMITH
06 Registrar .... Ms. Nancy UNRUH
07 Director of Admissions & Assessment .... Ms. Jayre ZIMMERMAN
15 Director of Human Resources .... Ms. Cricket TURLEY
18 Director of Facilities .... Mr. Derek RAMOS
26 Exec Director Marketing & PR .... Vacant
37 Director Student Financial Aid .... Ms. Kathy BLAU
39 Director Residential Life .... Ms. Christine DILLINGHAM
35 Asst VP Student Services/Athletics .... Mr. Colin LAMB
103 Director of Workforce Development .... Mr. Jerrad WEBB
04 Executive Assistant to President .... Ms. Debra J. ATKINSON
09 Director of Institutional Research .... Vacant
10 Comptroller .... Ms. Debra NICHOLSON
13 Director of Information Technology .... Mr. Jeff SOUTHERN
19 Campus Police Chief .... Mr. Rodney DOZIER
41 Athletic Director .... Mr. Ryan RUDA
44 Executive Director Endowment .... Mr. Jeremy GIGOT
38 Coordinator Advising .... Ms. Tammy TABOR

Grantham University (E)

16025 W 113th Street, Lenexa KS 66219
County: Johnson FICE Identification: 004283
Unit ID: 442569
Telephone: (888) 947-2684 Carnegie Class: Master's S
FAX Number: (913) 309-4949 Calendar System: Other
URL: www.grantham.edu
Established: 1951 Annual Undergrad Tuition & Fees: $8,090
Enrollment: 12,577 Coed
Affiliation or Control: Proprietary IRS Status: Proprietary
Highest Offering: Master's
Program: Occupational; Professional; Technical Emphasis
Accreditation: DEAC

01 President .... Joseph C. MCGRATH
88 VP University Partnerships .... Dr. Marilyn BARTELS
26 Vice President of Marketing .... Alex BACH
10 Chief Financial Officer .... Ed SAMMARCO
05 Chief Academic Officer/Provost .... Dr. Cheryl HAYEK
30 Vice Pres of Strategic Initiatives .... Dr. Jeffrey CROPSEY
22 Vice President of Compliance .... Harry DOTSON
84 Vice Pres Student Enrollment .... Jared PARLETTE
15 Vice President of Human Resources .... Kip ESRY
37 Vice President of Financial Aid .... Roman YAGNITINSKY
13 Chief Information Officer .... Anthony SCHLINSOG
11 Chief Operating Officer .... Steve WALDRON
06 Registrar .... Mary HANOVER
103 Director Education Outreach .... Angela HUNT

Haskell Indian Nations University (F)

155 Indian Avenue, #5030, Lawrence KS 66046-4800
County: Douglas FICE Identification: 010438
Unit ID: 155140
Telephone: (785) 749-8404 Carnegie Class: Tribal
FAX Number: (785) 749-8406 Calendar System: Semester
URL: www.haskell.edu
Established: 1884 Annual Undergrad Tuition & Fees: $715
Enrollment: 809 Coed
Affiliation or Control: Federal IRS Status: Exempt
Highest Offering: Baccalaureate
Program: 2-Year Principally Bachelor's Creditable; Liberal Arts And General; Teacher Preparatory
Accreditation: NH, TED

01 President .... Dr. Venida CHENAULT
05 Acting Vice Pres Academic Affairs .... Ms. Cheryl CHUCKLUCK
11 Vice President University Services .... Ms. Tonia SALVINI
10 Chief Finance Officer .... Ms. Brenda RACEHORSE
13 Chief Information Officer .... Mr. Joshua ARCE
08 Acting Dir Academic Support Ctr .... Ms. Beverly FORTNER
39 Dir Resident Housing/Mgr Stdnt Life .... Mr. Jim TUCKER
37 Financial Aid Officer .... Ms. Carlene MORRIS
06 Registrar .... Ms. Lou HARA
07 Director of Admissions .... Ms. Dorothy D. STITES
09 Dir Instl Research/Sponsored Pgms .... Ms. Cynthia GROUNDS
36 Actg Career Development Specialist .... Mr. Burgess TAPEDO
38 Director Student Counseling .... Vacant
15 Human Resources Liason .... Ms. Mona FRANKLIN
96 Acquisitions .... Ms. Janice BEGAY
26 Executive Asst/Public Relations .... Mr. Stephen PRUE
18 Director Facilities Management .... Mr. Lee PAHCODDY, JR.

Heritage College-Wichita (G)

2800 South Rock Road, Wichita KS 67210
Telephone: (316) 681-1615 Identification: 770529
Accreditation: ABHES

† Branch campus of Heritage College, Denver, CO.

Hesston College (H)

Box 3000, Hesston KS 67062-2093
County: Harvey FICE Identification: 001920
Unit ID: 155177
Telephone: (620) 327-4221 Carnegie Class: Assoc/PrivNFP
FAX Number: (620) 327-8300 Calendar System: Semester
URL: www.hesston.edu
Established: 1909 Annual Undergrad Tuition & Fees: $25,234
Enrollment: 428 Coed
Affiliation or Control: Mennonite Church IRS Status: 501(c)3
Highest Offering: Baccalaureate
Program: Occupational; 2-Year Principally Bachelor's Creditable
Accreditation: NH, ADNUR

01 President .... Dr. Howard KEIM
05 Vice Pres of Academics .... Mr. Brent YODER
30 Vice Pres of Advancement .... Mrs. Tonya DETWEILER
07 Vice President of Admissions .... Mrs. Rachel S. MILLER
10 Vice Pres of Finance & Auxil Svcs .... Mr. Mark LANDES
32 Vice Pres of Student Development .... Mr. Rob RAMSEYER
29 Director of Alumni & Church Rels .... Mr. Dallas STUTZMAN
06 Registrar .... Mr. Justin HEINZEKEHR
21 Business Manager .... Mr. Karl BRUBAKER

Highland Community College (I)

606 W Main, Highland KS 66035-0068
County: Doniphan FICE Identification: 001921
Unit ID: 155186
Telephone: (785) 442-6000 Carnegie Class: Assoc/Pub-R-M
FAX Number: (785) 442-6100 Calendar System: Semester
URL: www.highlandcc.edu
Established: 1858 Annual Undergrad Tuition & Fees (In-District): $3,300
Enrollment: 3,217 Coed
Affiliation or Control: Local IRS Status: 501(c)3
Highest Offering: Associate Degree
Program: Occupational; 2-Year Principally Bachelor's Creditable
Accreditation: NH

01 President .... Mr. David REIST
05 Vice President for Academic Affairs .... Ms. Peggy FORSBERG
32 Vice President for Student Services .... Dr. Cheryl RASMUSSEN
10 Vice Pres for Finance/Operations .... Mr. Daniel ERBERT
88 Director of Technical Education .... Mr. Lucas HUNZIGER

30 Vice Pres Institutional Advancement .... Dr. Craig E. MOSHER
06 Registrar .... Ms. Alice HAMILTON
37 Financial Aid Director .... Ms. Amy LACKEY
13 Director of Information Systems .... Mr. Josh BERRY
09 Director of Institutional Research .... Vacant
38 Director Student Counseling .... Ms. Kristin WOODRUFF
41 Athletic Director .... Mr. Greg DELZEIT
08 Library Director .... Ms. Penny DONALDSON
18 Supervisor of Buildings & Grounds .... Vacant
26 Chief Public Relations Officer .... Dr. Craig MOSHER
29 Director Alumni Relations .... Dr. Craig MOSHER
35 Director of Student Life .... Mr. Tyler NORDMAN
15 Human Resource Manager .... Ms. Eileen C. GRONNIGER
40 Bookstore Coordinator .... Ms. Stephanie HARSHBERGER
07 Director of Admissions .... Ms. Vanetta GEIGER
39 Director Student Housing .... Mr. Tyler NORDMAN
106 Dir Online Education/E-learning .... Ms. Denise PETERS

Hutchinson Community College (A)

1300 N Plum Street, Hutchinson KS 67501-5894

County: Reno FICE Identification: 001923
Unit ID: 155195
Telephone: (620) 665-3500 Carnegie Class: Assoc/Pub-R-L
FAX Number: (620) 665-3310 Calendar System: Semester
URL: www.hutchcc.edu
Established: 1928 Annual Undergrad Tuition & Fees (In-District): $2,136
Enrollment: 5,718 Coed
Affiliation or Control: State/Local IRS Status: 501(c)3
Highest Offering: Associate Degree
Program: Occupational; 2-Year Principally Bachelor's Creditable
Accreditation: NH, ACBSP, ADNUR, CAHIIM, #COARC, EMT, PNUR, PTAA, RAD, SURGT

01 President .... Dr. Carter FILE
05 Vice President of Academic Affairs .... Dr. Cindy HOSS
10 Vice President Finance/Operations .... Ms. Julie BLANTON
103 VP Workforce Development/Outreach .... Mr. Steve PORTER
32 Vice President of Students .... Mr. Brett BRIGHT
26 Director of Marketing & Info .... Mr. Denny STOECKLEIN
13 Director of Data Processing .... Mr. Loren L. MORRIS
06 Registrar .... Mrs. Christina LONG
41 Athletic Director .... Mr. Josh GOOCH
15 Director of Personnel .... Mr. Brooks E. MANTOOTH
37 Financial Aid Officer .... Mr. Nathan BUCHE
07 Director of Admissions .... Mr. Corbin STROBEL
18 Director of Plant Facilities .... Mr. Don ROSE
39 Director of Residence Life .... Ms. Dana HINSHAW
29 Director Alumni Relations .... Mrs. Cindy KEAST
08 Coordinator of Library Services .... Mr. Robert KELLY
09 Coord of Institutional Research .... Mr. Rex CHEEVER

Independence Community College (B)

1057 West College Avenue,
Independence KS 67301-0708

County: Montgomery FICE Identification: 001924
Unit ID: 155201
Telephone: (620) 331-4100 Carnegie Class: Assoc/Pub-R-S
FAX Number: (620) 331-5344 Calendar System: Semester
URL: www.indycc.edu
Established: 1925 Annual Undergrad Tuition & Fees (In-District): $2,685
Enrollment: 945 Coed
Affiliation or Control: State/Local IRS Status: 501(c)3
Highest Offering: Associate Degree
Program: Occupational; 2-Year Principally Bachelor's Creditable
Accreditation: NH

01 President .... Dr. Daniel W. BARWICK
10 Contoller .... Ms. Wendy ISLE
05 VP Academic Affairs .... Vacant
32 VP Student Affairs/Athletics .... Ms. Tammie GELDENHUYS
13 IT Director .... Mr. Eric MONTGOMERY
26 Marketing Director/Instructor .... Mr. Brad HENDERSON
102 Foundation Director .... Ms. Lori SHAW
20 Dean of Instruction .... Mr. David SMITH
06 Registrar .... Ms. Sonja CONLEY
08 Director Library/Lrng Resource Ctr .... Mr. Drew BEISSWENGER
18 Maintenance/Custodial Supervisor .... Ms. Chris MCDIARMID
07 Recruiting/Admissions Specialist .... Ms. Brittany THORNTON
37 Financial Aid Coordinator .... Ms. Wendy ISLE
09 Dir of Institutional Research .... Ms. Debbie PHELPS
04 Executive Asst to President .... Ms. Beverly HARRIS
40 Bookstore Manager .... Ms. Teresa VESTAL
88 Upward Bound Program Director .... Ms. Stacia KAYLOR
15 Human Resources Coordinator .... Ms. Keli TUSCHMAN
51 Associate Dean On-line/Cont Educ .... Ms. Kara WHEELER
88 Associate Dean Acad Support Svcs .... Ms. Taylor CRAWSHAW

ITT Technical Institute (C)

7600 West 119th Street, Suite 100,
Overland Park KS 66213

Telephone: (913) 253-1300 Identification: 770652
Accreditation: ACICS

† Branch campus of ITT Technical Institute, Indianapolis, IN.

ITT Technical Institute (D)

8111 E. 32nd St. N, Suite 103, Wichita KS 67226

Telephone: (316) 609-4100 Identification: 666168
Accreditation: ACICS

† Branch campus of ITT Technical Institute, Indianapolis, IN.

Johnson County Community College (E)

12345 College Boulevard, Overland Park KS 66210-1299

County: Johnson FICE Identification: 008244
Unit ID: 155210
Telephone: (913) 469-8500 Carnegie Class: Assoc/Pub-S-SC
FAX Number: (913) 469-2559 Calendar System: Semester
URL: www.jccc.edu
Established: 1969 Annual Undergrad Tuition & Fees (In-District): $2,730
Enrollment: 19,429 Coed
Affiliation or Control: State/Local IRS Status: 501(c)3
Highest Offering: Associate Degree
Program: Occupational; 2-Year Principally Bachelor's Creditable
Accreditation: NH, ACBSP, ACFEI, ADNUR, COARC, DH, EMT, IFSAC

01 President .... Dr. Joe SOPCICH
10 Exec Vice Pres Finance & Admin Svcs .... Dr. Barbara LARSON
05 Exec VP Instruction/Operations .... Dr. Judy KORB
11 Exec VP Administrative Services .... Ms. Barbara LARSON
32 Vice Pres Student Success/Engagemnt .... Dr. Randy WEBER
13 Vice President Information Services .... Ms. Denise MOORE
20 Vice Pres Instruction/CAO .... Mr. Andy ANDERSON
04 Exec Asst to the President & Board .... Ms. Terri SCHLICHT
21 AVP Financial Services .... Mr. Don PERKINS
18 AVP Campus Services .... Mr. Rex HAYS
96 AVP Business Services .... Mr. Mitch BORCHERS
31 AVP College & Community Relations .... Ms. Julie HAAS
72 Dean Technology .... Mr. Bill BROWN
50 Dean of Business .... Mr. Mike WEST
14 Director Admin Computing Services .... Ms. Sandra WARNER
26 Int Exec Dir Mktg/Communications .... Ms. Christy WARD
35 Dean Student Success .... Mr. Paul KYLE
41 Asst Dean Athletics .... Mr. Carl HEINRICH
84 Asst Dean Enrollment Management .... Ms. MargE SHELLEY
35 Asst Dean Student Life/Ldrshp Dev .... Ms. Pam VASSAR
37 Director Student Financial Aid .... Vacant
36 Director Testing and Assessment .... Ms. Mary Ann DICKERSON
06 Registrar .... Ms. Leslie QUINN
08 Director Library Services .... Mr. Mark DAGANAAR
07 Director of Admissions .... Mr. Peter BELK
92 Program Facilitator Honors .... Dr. Pat DECKER
09 Director of Institutional Research .... Ms. Natalie ALLEMAN-BEYERS
38 Director Student Counseling .... Ms. Kate ALLEN

Kansas Christian College (F)

7401 Metcalf, Overland Park KS 66204-1995

County: Johnson Identification: 667134
Telephone: (913) 722-0272 Carnegie Class: Not Classified
FAX Number: (913) 403-0595 Calendar System: Semester
URL: www.kccbs.edu
Established: 1938 Annual Undergrad Tuition & Fees: $4,900
Enrollment: 30 Coed
Affiliation or Control: Independent Non-Profit IRS Status: 501(c)3
Highest Offering: Baccalaureate
Program: Religious Emphasis
Accreditation: @BI

01 President .... Mr. Delbert L. SCOTT

Kansas City Kansas Community College (G)

7250 State Avenue, Kansas City KS 66112-3003

County: Wyandotte FICE Identification: 001925
Unit ID: 155292
Telephone: (913) 334-1100 Carnegie Class: Assoc/Pub-U-SC
FAX Number: (913) 288-7609 Calendar System: Semester
URL: www.kckcc.edu
Established: 1923 Annual Undergrad Tuition & Fees (In-District): $3,024
Enrollment: 6,198 Coed
Affiliation or Control: State/Local IRS Status: 501(c)3
Highest Offering: Associate Degree
Program: Occupational; 2-Year Principally Bachelor's Creditable
Accreditation: NH, ACBSP, ADNUR, COARC, EMT, FUSER, PTAA

01 President .... Dr. Doris F. GIVENS
10 Chief Financia Ofcr/Chief Oper Ofcr .... Dr. Susan LINDAHL
05 VP Academic Affairs & Student Svcs .... Dr. Michael VITALE
81 Dean Math/Sci/CompTech/Bus/CEB .... Dr. Edward KREMER
84 Interim Dean Enrollment Management .... Dr. Michael BURNS
36 Dean Academic Workforce Programs .... Ms. Leota MARKS
103 Director of Workforce Development .... Ms. Marisa GRAY
88 Director of Entrepreneurship .... Ms. Alicia HOOKS
79 Dean Arts/Humanities/Social Science .... Dr. Cherilee WALKER
13 Dean Information Services .... Mr. Baz ABOUELENEIN
45 Dean Institutional Services .... Dr. Sangki MIN
66 Interim Dean Nursing/Allied Health .... Dr. Anita KRONKAK
32 Dean of Student Services .... Dr. Jonathan LONG
75 Dean Technical Operations .... Mr. Cliff SMITH
88 Exec Director Leavenworth Center .... Vacant
88 Director of Academic Resource Ctr .... Dr. Michael BURNS
41 Director of Athletics .... Mr. Anthony (Tony) TOMPKINS
40 Director of Bookstore Operations .... Vacant
18 Director of Buildings/Grounds .... Mr. Jeff SIXTA
19 Director of Campus Police .... Mr. Greg SCHNEIDER
30 Director of Endowment .... Mr. Patrick S. MCCARTNEY
14 Director of Computing .... Mr. James BENNETT
31 Director of Cont Educ & Cmty Svcs .... Ms. Rosemary L. LISCHKA
38 Director of Student Advising .... Mr. Shawn DERRITT
88 Director Counseling-Advocacy Ctr .... Ms. Linda WARNER
09 Director Institutional Research .... Vacant
37 Director of Financial Aid .... Ms. Mary I. DORR
21 Director of Financial Records .... Ms. Marie BRANSTETTER
92 Director of Honors/Phi Theta Kappa .... Dr. Stacy TUCKER
28 Director of Intercultural Center .... Ms. Barbara CLARK-EVANS
08 Director of Library .... Vacant
24 Director Media Services Technology .... Vacant
106 Director of Online Services .... Ms. Susan STUART
96 Director of Purchasing & Risk Mgr .... Mr. David ROOT
35 Director of Student Activities .... Ms. Andrica WILCOXEN
07 Director of Admissions .... Ms. Tami A. BARTUNEK
06 Assistant Registrar .... Ms. Theresa HOLLIDAY
15 Director Human Resources .... Ms. Abigail DILLARD
88 Director Forensic Laboratory .... Ms. D.C BROIL
88 Director Wellness Center .... Mr. Rob M. CRANE
103 Director of Cultural Outreach .... Mr. Brian PATRICK
66 Director Nursing .... Ms. Anita M. KRONDAK
66 Director Practical Nursing .... Ms. Susan K. WHITE
88 Assistant Director Student Develop .... Ms. Tamara D. MILLER
88 Director Technical Programs .... Mr. Richard PIPER
88 Director Technical Programs Perkins .... Ms. Donna S. SHAWN
88 Assistant Director Academic Resourc .... Ms. Amanda WILLIAMS
88 Director Performing Arts Center .... Dr. Cherilee WALKER
04 Administrative Asst to President .... Ms. Peggy L. FRIEDMANN
105 Director Web Services .... Ms. Lisa CLINE
26 Chief Public Relations/Marketing .... Dr. Susan LINDAHL
22 Dir Affirmative Action/EEO .... Mrs. Abigail DILLARD
39 Director Student Housing .... Dr. Jonathan LONG
43 Dir Legal Services/General Counsel .... Mr. Deryl WYNN

Kansas State University (H)

919 Mid-Campus Drive North, Manhattan KS 66506

County: Riley FICE Identification: 001928
Unit ID: 155399
Telephone: (785) 532-6250 Carnegie Class: RU/H
FAX Number: (785) 532-2120 Calendar System: Semester
URL: www.k-state.edu
Established: 1863 Annual Undergrad Tuition & Fees (In-State): $9,350
Enrollment: 24,766 Coed
Affiliation or Control: State IRS Status: 501(c)3
Highest Offering: Doctorate
Program: Liberal Arts And General; Teacher Preparatory; Professional
Accreditation: NH, ART, BUS, BUSA, CAATE, CACREP, CEA, CIDA, CONST, CS, DIETC, DIETD, ENG, IPSY, JOUR, LSAR, MFCD, MUS, NRPA, PH, PLNG, SP, SPAA, SW, TED, THEA, VET

01 President .... Dr. Kirk H. SCHULZ
04 Admin Asst to the President .... Ms. Dana M. HASTINGS
05 Provost and Senior Vice President .... Dr. April C. MASON
10 VP Admin & Finance .... Ms. Cindy A. BONTRAGER
46 Vice President Research .... Dr. Karen J. BURG
32 VP Student Life/Dean of Students .... Dr. Pat J. BOSCO
26 VP for Communications & Marketing .... Mr. Jeffery B. MORRIS
15 VP Human Capital .... Ms. Cheryl L. JOHNSON
102 President/CEO of Foundation .... Mr. Greg WILLEMS
29 Alumni Association President .... Ms. Amy Button RENZ
41 Athletic Director .... Mr. John CURRIE
100 Chief of Staff/Dir Community Rels .... Dr. Jackie L. HARTMAN
86 Dir for Governmental Relations .... Dr. Susan K. PETERSON
88 Exec Dir Military/Veterans Affairs .... Mr. Arthur S. DE GROAT
43 General Counsel .... Ms. Cheryl G. STRECKER
20 Senior Vice Provost .... Dr. Ruth DYER
13 Vice Provost Info Tech Svcs .... Mr. Kenneth STAFFORD
108 Assoc Prov Institutional Effectiv .... Dr. Brian A. NIEHOFF
28 Assoc Prov for Diversity .... Dr. Myra E. GORDON
09 Director Planning & Analysis .... Ms. Kelli S. COX
08 Dean of Libraries .... Dr. Lori A. GOETSCH
47 Dean of Agriculture .... Dr. John FLOROS
48 Dean Architecture/Planning/Design .... Mr. Timothy DE NOBLE
49 Dean of Arts & Sciences .... Dr. Peter K. DORHOUT
50 Interim Dean of Business Admin .... Dr. Kevin P. GWINNER
51 Dean of Continuing Education .... Dr. Sue C. MAES
53 Dean of Education .... Dr. Debbie K. MERCER
54 Dean of Engineering .... Dr. Darren M. DAWSON
58 Dean of Graduate School .... Dr. Carol SHANKLIN
59 Dean of Human Ecology .... Dr. John B. BUCKWALTER
72 CEO/Dean of Technology & Aviation .... Dr. Verna M. FITZSIMMONS
74 Dean of Veterinary Medicine .... Dr. Tammy R. BECKHAM
12 Interim CEO K-State Olathe .... Dr. Ralph C. RICHARDSON
56 Dir Research and Extension .... Dr. John FLOROS
18 Assoc VP Facilities Planning/Mgmt .... Mr. Ryan F. SWANSON
21 Asst VP for Budget Planning .... Mr. Ethan E. ERICKSON
19 Asst VP Univ Police & Public Safety .... Mr. Ronnie D. GRICE
96 Director of Purchasing .... Ms. Carla BISHOP
07 Assoc VP/Director of Admissions .... Mr. Lawrence E. MOEDER
06 Registrar .... Dr. Monty E. NIELSEN
37 Assoc VP/Dir Student Fin Assist .... Mr. Lawrence E. MOEDER
39 Asst VP/Dir Housing & Dining Svs .... Mr. Derek A. JACKSON
36 Exec Dir Career & Employment Svcs .... Ms. Kerri D. KELLER

Kansas State University-Salina, College of Technology and Aviation (I)

2310 Centennial Road, Salina KS 67401-8196

Telephone: (785) 826-2601 FICE Identification: 004611
Accreditation: &NH, AAB, ENGT

† Regional accreditation is carried under the parent institution in Manhattan, KS.

Kansas Wesleyan University (A)

100 E Claflin Avenue, Salina KS 67401-6196
County: Saline　FICE Identification: 001929
Unit ID: 155414
Telephone: (785) 827-5541　Carnegie Class: Bac/Diverse
FAX Number: (785) 827-0927　Calendar System: Semester
URL: www.kwu.edu
Established: 1886　Annual Undergrad Tuition & Fees: $26,600
Enrollment: 710　Coed
Affiliation or Control: United Methodist　IRS Status: 501(c)3
Highest Offering: Master's
Program: Liberal Arts And General; Teacher Preparatory; Professional
Accreditation: NH, TED

01 President and CEO ... Dr. Matthew R. THOMPSON
04 Executive Assistant to President ... Ms. Jan M. SHIRK
03 Executive Vice President ... Dr. Nancy CUMMINGS
10 Vice Pres Finance/Administration ... Mr. Wayne R. SCHNEIDER
45 VP Strategic Inst Init & Planning ... Dr. Rob SCOTT
21 Controller/Business Officer ... Mr. John W. COYKENDALL
84 Vice Pres Enrollment Management ... Dr. Mark A. BANDRE
37 Director Student Financial Planning ... Mrs. Lois MADSEN
06 Registrar ... Mrs. Krista L. LOUGH
07 Director of Admissions ... Mr. Esteban PAREDES
05 Provost ... Dr. Nancy CUMMINGS
30 Vice Pres Institutional Development ... Mr. Bill GREVES
29 Director of Alumni Relations ... Ms. Jennifer L. REIN
26 Sr Director Advanc & Communications ... Mrs. Paula HERMANN
27 Director of Marketting & Commun ... Mr. John ELMORE
44 Institutional Development ... Ms. Sara NETTLEINGHAM
32 Exec Director Student Development ... Ms. Bridget R. WEISER
36 Career Planning & Exper Educ Spec ... Vacant
39 Director of Residence Life ... Mr. Neal JEFFERY
38 Dir Student Succ & Testing Ctr ... Mrs. Jennifer BARRETT
88 Dir of Spiritual Development ... Mr. Cameron JACKSON
108 Director of Assessment ... Prof. Raymond A. TUCKER
08 Director of Library Svcs ... Ms. Ruth MIRTZ
24 Production Manager ... Mr. Paul GREEN
13 Director of Information Systems ... Mr. Jay C. KROB
19 Director of Emergency Management ... Dr. Lonnie BOOKER
18 Director of Plant Operations ... Mr. Darrell D. VICTORY
40 Manager Yotee's Bookstore ... Mr. Steve G. CARRIER
42 Chaplain Univ United Meth Church ... Vacant
41 Athletic Director ... Mr. Michael HERMANN
58 Director of MBA Program ... Prof. Joyce KELLEY
66 Division Nursing Education Chair ... Dr. Debra LOGAN
53 Director of Teacher Education ... Vacant
79 Division Chair Humanities ... Dr. Michael RUSSELL
49 Div Chair Applied Art & Sciences ... Prof. Bryan K. MINNICH
83 Division Chair Social Sciences ... Dr. Paul HEDLUND
57 Division Chair Fine Arts ... Prof. Barbara J. NICKELL
81 Division of Natural Sciences Chair ... Dr. Stephanie WELTER
106 Dir Online Education/E-learning ... Dr. Rob SCOTT

Labette Community College (B)

200 S 14th, Parsons KS 67357-4299
County: Labette　FICE Identification: 001930
Unit ID: 155450
Telephone: (620) 421-6700　Carnegie Class: Assoc/Pub-R-M
FAX Number: (620) 421-0921　Calendar System: Semester
URL: www.labette.edu
Established: 1923　Annual Undergrad Tuition & Fees (In-District): $2,700
Enrollment: 1,891　Coed
Affiliation or Control: Local　IRS Status: 501(c)3
Highest Offering: Associate Degree
Program: Occupational; 2-Year Principally Bachelor's Creditable
Accreditation: NH, ADNUR, COARC, DA, DMS, PTAA, RAD

01 President ... Dr. George C. KNOX
04 Executive Assistant to President ... Ms. Megan A. FUGATE
05 Vice President Academic Affairs ... Mr. Joe BURKE
10 Vice President Finance & Operations ... Ms. Leanna J. DOHERTY
32 Vice President Student Affairs ... Ms. Tammy FUENTEZ
84 Assoc Dean Enrollment Mgmt ... Ms. Kathy JOHNSTON
20 Dean of Instruction ... Mr. Mark WATKINS
13 Director of Information Technology ... Mrs. Jody BURZINSKI
30 Dir Resource Devel/Alumni Rels ... Mrs. Lindi D. FORBES
08 Director of Library Services ... Mr. Scott M. ZOLLARS
18 Director of Physical Plant ... Mr. Kevin DOHERTY
66 Director of Nursing ... Mrs. Delyna BOHNENBLUST
41 Athletic Director ... Mr. Aaron J. KEAL
31 Director of Community Services ... Vacant
26 Director of Public Relations ... Mrs. Bethany KENDRICK
06 Registrar/Dir Student Financial Aid ... Ms. Kathy JOHNSTON
15 Director of Human Relations ... Ms. Janice S. GEORGE
37 Director Student Financial Aid ... Ms. Kathy JOHNSTON
35 Student Life Coordinator ... Mrs. Melissa NANCE
40 Bookstore Specialist ... Mrs. Lois D. HEMBREE

Manhattan Area Technical College (C)

3136 Dickens Avenue, Manhattan KS 66503-2499
County: Riley　FICE Identification: 005500
Unit ID: 155487
Telephone: (785) 587-2800　Carnegie Class: Assoc/Pub-R-S
FAX Number: (785) 587-2804　Calendar System: Semester
URL: www.matc.net
Established: 1965　Annual Undergrad Tuition & Fees (In-District): $4,895
Enrollment: 766　Coed
Affiliation or Control: State/Local　IRS Status: 501(c)3
Highest Offering: Associate Degree
Program: Occupational; 2-Year Principally Bachelor's Creditable; Technical Emphasis
Accreditation: NH, ADNUR, DH, MLTAD

01 President/CEO ... Dr. Jim J. GENANDT
05 Vice Pres of Instructional Affairs ... Ms. Marilyn MAHAN
10 Vice President of Business Services ... Mr. Keith ZACHARIASEN
32 Vice President of Student Services ... Mr. Joel LUNDSTROM
30 Assoc VP Institutional Advancement ... Dr. Richard FOGG
06 Registrar ... Ms. Leslie SNEAD
15 Director Human Resources ... Ms. Trysta WILLIAMS
07 Director of Admissions ... Ms. Nicole BOLLIG
37 Director Financial Aid ... Ms. Laura WEISS-COOK

Manhattan Christian College (D)

1415 Anderson, Manhattan KS 66502-4081
County: Riley　FICE Identification: 001931
Unit ID: 155496
Telephone: (785) 539-3571　Carnegie Class: Spec/Faith
FAX Number: (785) 539-0832　Calendar System: Semester
URL: www.mccks.edu
Established: 1927　Annual Undergrad Tuition & Fees: $14,240
Enrollment: 311　Coed
Affiliation or Control: Christian Churches And Churches of Christ
IRS Status: 501(c)3
Highest Offering: Baccalaureate
Program: Liberal Arts And General; Professional; Religious Emphasis
Accreditation: NH, BI

01 President ... Mr. J. Kevin INGRAM
05 Int Vice President Academic Affairs ... Dr. Greg DELORT
10 Vice President Business Affairs ... Ms. Lori J. STANFIELD
32 Vice President Student Life ... Dr. Rick L. WRIGHT
06 Registrar ... Mr. Jeff DAVIS
30 Director Institutional Advancement ... Mrs. Jolene K. RUPE
37 Director of Financial Aid ... Ms. Jenna KECK
08 Library Director ... Mrs. Mary Ann BUHLER
41 Athletic Director ... Mr. Shawn M. CONDRA
29 Alumni Relations Director ... Mrs. Genae DENVER
04 Admin Asst to President ... Ms. Shalin KLEIN
07 Director of Admissions ... Mr. Nick BROWN

McPherson College (E)

1600 E Euclid, PO Box 1402, McPherson KS 67460-1402
County: McPherson　FICE Identification: 001933
Unit ID: 155511
Telephone: (620) 242-0400　Carnegie Class: Bac/Diverse
FAX Number: (620) 241-8443　Calendar System: 4/1/4
URL: www.mcpherson.edu
Established: 1887　Annual Undergrad Tuition & Fees: $25,300
Enrollment: 659　Coed
Affiliation or Control: Church Of The Brethren　IRS Status: 501(c)3
Highest Offering: Master's
Program: Liberal Arts And General; Teacher Preparatory
Accreditation: NH, TED

01 President ... Mr. Michael P. SCHNEIDER
05 Provost/VP Academic Affairs ... Dr. Bruce CLARY
30 Vice President for Advancement ... Mr. Steve GUSTAFSON
10 Vice President for Finance ... Mr. Rick TUXHORN
84 Vice Pres Enrollment Management ... Ms. Christi HOPKINS
100 Chief of Staff ... Ms. Abby ARCHER-RIERSON
32 Dean of Students ... Dr. Sharonda MACLIN
41 Athletic Director ... Mr. Doug QUINT
06 Registrar ... Ms. Tricia HARTSHORN
37 Director Financial Aid/Admissions ... Ms. Sara BRUBAKER
08 Director of Library Services ... Ms. Mary HESTER
29 Director Alumni Relations ... Mrs. Karlene TYLER

MidAmerica Nazarene University (F)

2030 E College Way, Olathe KS 66062-1899
County: Johnson　FICE Identification: 007032
Unit ID: 155520
Telephone: (913) 782-3750　Carnegie Class: Master's M
FAX Number: (913) 971-3290　Calendar System: Semester
URL: www.mnu.edu
Established: 1966　Annual Undergrad Tuition & Fees: $26,150
Enrollment: 1,870　Coed
Affiliation or Control: Church Of The Nazarene　IRS Status: 501(c)3
Highest Offering: Master's
Program: Liberal Arts And General; Teacher Preparatory; Professional
Accreditation: NH, ACBSP, CAATE, CACREP, MUS, NURSE, TED

01 President ... Dr. David J. SPITTAL
05 Provost and Chief Academic Officer ... Dr. Mary JONES
10 Vice President Finance ... Mr. Kevin P. GILMORE
30 Vice Pres University Advancement ... Mr. Jon D. NORTH
32 VP Student Development ... Mrs. Kristi KEETON
42 University Chaplain ... Dr. Randy BECKUM
58 Associate VP Grad & Professional ... Dr. Mark C. FORD
13 Associate VP for Technology ... Dr. Martin CROSSLAND
84 Assoc VP Enrollment Management ... Mr. Derry EBERT
09 Dir Institutional Effectiveness ... Mrs. Patricia J. WALSH
53 Dean School of Education ... Dr. Nancy DAMRON
66 Dean Sch Nursing/Health Sci ... Dr. Susan LARSON
50 Dean School of Business ... Mrs. Jamie MYRTLE
83 Dean Sch Behav Sci/Counseling ... Dr. Todd FRYE
49 Dean College Arts & Sciences ... Dr. Cindy PETERSON
06 Registrar ... Mr. James R. GARRISON
08 Director of the Library ... Mr. Bruce FLANDERS
26 Assoc VP University Advancement ... Mr. Tim KEETON
29 Director of Alumni ... Mr. Kevin S. GARBER
37 Director of Student Financial Svcs ... Mr. Paul GORDON
41 Athletic Director ... Mr. Kevin L. STEELE
15 Director of Human Resources ... Ms. Nancy S. MERIMEE
27 Marketing Strategist ... Mrs. Kimberly CAMPBELL
18 Director of Facility Services ... Mr. Denis JOHNSON
40 Bookstore Manager ... Mr. Nikos KELLEPOURIS
19 Director of Campus Safety ... Mr. Emil F. SCHELLACK

National American University-Overland Park (G)

10310 Mastin Street, Overland Park KS 66212
Telephone: (913) 981-8700　Identification: 770394
Accreditation: &NH, MAC

† Branch campus of National American University, Rapid City, SD.

National American University-Wichita (H)

7309 E 21st Street, Suite G40, Wichita KS 67206
Telephone: (316) 448-5400　Identification: 770395
Accreditation: &NH, MAC

† Branch campus of National American University, Rapid City, SD.

National American University-Wichita West (I)

8428 W 13th Street N, Suite 120, Wichita KS 67212
Telephone: (316) 448-3150　Identification: 770396
Accreditation: &NH

† Branch campus of National American University, Rapid City, SD.

Neosho County Community College (J)

800 W 14th Street, Chanute KS 66720-2699
County: Neosho　FICE Identification: 001936
Unit ID: 155566
Telephone: (620) 431-2820　Carnegie Class: Assoc/Pub-R-M
FAX Number: (620) 431-0082　Calendar System: Semester
URL: www.neosho.edu
Established: 1935　Annual Undergrad Tuition & Fees (In-District): $2,850
Enrollment: 2,214　Coed
Affiliation or Control: Local　IRS Status: 501(c)3
Highest Offering: Associate Degree
Program: Occupational; 2-Year Principally Bachelor's Creditable
Accreditation: NH, ACBSP, ADNUR, CAHIIM, OTA, SURGT

01 President ... Dr. Brian L. INBODY
05 Vice President Student Learning ... Ms. Sarah ROBB
11 Vice President for Operations ... Mr. Benjamin J. SMITH
10 Chief Financial Officer ... Ms. Sondra K. SOLANDER
103 Dean Outreach/Workforce Development ... Ms. Brenda L. KRUMM
12 Dean Ottawa Campus ... Mr. Dale E. ERNST
32 Dean of Student Services ... Ms. Kerrie COOMES
15 Director of Human Resources ... Ms. Kathy MCMILLEN
106 Dean for Online Campus ... Ms. Marie GARDNER
13 Dean for Operations/CIO ... Mr. Kerry D. RANABARGAR
30 Director of Development/Alumni Rels ... Ms. Claudia CHRISTIANSEN
08 Coordinator of Library Services ... Mr. Caleb PUCKETT
37 Director Student Financial Aid ... Ms. Kara B. HALE
66 Director of Nursing ... Ms. Pamela COVAULT
13 Dir of Tech Services/Webmaster ... Mr. Jon SEIBERT
46 Director of Assessment/Research ... Mr. Ethan SMILIE
41 Athletic Director ... Mr. Mike SADDLER
85 Dir International Student Services ... Ms. Sarah CADWALLADER
06 Registrar ... Ms. Amy MORRIS
09 Coordinator/Institutional Research ... Ms. LuAnn HAUSER
40 Chanute Bookstore Coordinator ... Ms. Mary Jo SECHLER
40 Ottawa Bookstore Coordinator ... Ms. Julie VINEYARD
26 Advertising/Media Coordinator ... Ms. Nancy ISAAC
39 Residence/Student Life Coordinator ... Ms. Allison OUELLETTE
04 AA to the President/Board Clerk ... Ms. Denise GILMORE
18 Director of Facilities ... Mr. Kyle SEUFERT

Newman University (K)

3100 McCormick, Wichita KS 67213-2097
County: Sedgwick　FICE Identification: 001939
Unit ID: 155335
Telephone: (316) 942-4291　Carnegie Class: Master's L
FAX Number: (316) 942-4483　Calendar System: Semester
URL: www.newmanu.edu
Established: 1933　Annual Undergrad Tuition & Fees: $25,928
Enrollment: 3,687　Coed
Affiliation or Control: Roman Catholic　IRS Status: 501(c)3
Highest Offering: Master's
Program: Occupational; 2-Year Principally Bachelor's Creditable; Liberal Arts And General; Teacher Preparatory; Professional
Accreditation: NH, ANEST, COARC, NURSE, OTA, RAD, SW, TED

01 President ... Dr. Noreen CARROCCI
04 Exec Assistant to the President ... Ms. Tracy MCGAREY
05 Provost & Vice Pres Acad Affairs ... Dr. Michael AUSTIN
30 Vice Pres University Advancement ... Mr. J.V JOHNSTON
10 Vice Pres Finance/Administration ... Ms. Jennifer GANTZ
32 VP Student Affairs/Dir Athletics ... Mr. Victor TRILLI
84 Vice Pres Enrollment Management ... Vacant

20 Assoc VP Acad Svcs/Student Dev .... Ms. Rosemary NIEDENS
42 Director of Campus Ministry .... Fr. John FOGLIASSO
29 Director of Alumni Relations ....Ms. Sarah CUNDIFF
09 Director of Institutional Research ....Dr. Lori STEINER
08 Library Director .... Mr. Steve HAMERSKY
06 Registrar .... Ms. Shirley RUEB
37 Director of Financial Aid ....Ms. Charly SMITH
40 Director of Bookstore ....Mr. Larry WILLIAMS
13 Chief Information Officer ....Mr. Icer VAUGHAN
19 Director of Security ....Mr. Maurice FLOYD
21 Controller ....Mr. Don WIESNER
35 Dean of Students ....Mr. Levi ESSES
58 Dean College of Grad/Cont Studies ....Fr. Joseph GILE
49 Dean College of Undergrad Studies ....Dr. David SHUBERT
104 Director Study Abroad ....Dr. Cheryl GOLDEN
18 Chief Facilities/Physical Plant .... Mr. Bruce SANDERSON
26 Chief Public Relations/Marketing .... Mr. Clark SCHAFER

North Central Kansas Technical College (A)

PO Box 507, Beloit KS 67420-0507
County: Mitchell FICE Identification: 005265
Unit ID: 155593
Telephone: (785) 738-2276 Carnegie Class: Assoc/Pub-R-S
FAX Number: (785) 738-2903 Calendar System: Semester
URL: www.ncktc.edu
Established: 1964 Annual Undergrad Tuition & Fees (In-District): $5,021
Enrollment: 455 Coed
Affiliation or Control: State/Local IRS Status: 501(c)3
Highest Offering: Associate Degree
Program: Occupational; 2-Year Principally Bachelor's Creditable; Technical Emphasis
Accreditation: NH, ADNUR

01 President ....Mr. Eric BURKS
05 Dean of Instruction ....Mr. Corey ISBELL
11 Dean of Administrative Services .... Mrs. Brandi ZIMMER
12 Dean of Hays Campus .... Mrs. Sandy GOTTSCHALK
06 Registrar .... Ms. Judy HEIDRICK
09 Coordinator Institutional Research .... Mrs. Jennifer BROWN
32 Dean of Student Services ....Ms. Angel PRESCOTT
37 Director Student Financial Aid ....Mr. Gary ODLE
04 Administrative Asst to President ....Ms. Bobette ROESTI
102 Dir Foundation/Marketing ....Vacant
101 Secretary of the Institution/Board ....Ms. Bobette ROESTI

North Central Kansas Technical College (B)

2205 Wheatland Avenue, Hays KS 67601
Telephone: (785) 625-2437 Identification: 770259
Accreditation: &NH

† Branch campus of North Central Kansas Technical College, Beloit, KS.

Northwest Kansas Technical College (C)

1209 Harrison Street, PO Box 668,
Goodland KS 67735-3441
County: Sherman FICE Identification: 005267
Unit ID: 155618
Telephone: (785) 890-3641 Carnegie Class: Assoc/Pub-R-S
FAX Number: (785) 899-5711 Calendar System: Semester
URL: www.nwktc.edu
Established: 1964 Annual Undergrad Tuition & Fees (In-District): $16,400
Enrollment: 647 Coed
Affiliation or Control: State/Local IRS Status: 501(c)3
Highest Offering: Associate Degree
Program: Occupational; Technical Emphasis
Accreditation: NH, COARC, MAC

01 President ....Dr. Ed MILLS
05 Vice Pres Academic/Student Affairs ......Ms. Brenda L. CHATFIELD
20 Asst Vice Pres Academic Affairs ....Mr. Scott SEARCY
10 Chief Financial Officer ....Ms. Sherri KNITIG
06 Registrar ....Ms. Sylvia SHORES

Ottawa University (D)

1001 S Cedar Street, Ottawa KS 66067-3399
County: Franklin FICE Identification: 001937
Unit ID: 155627
Telephone: (785) 242-5200 Carnegie Class: Bac/Diverse
FAX Number: (785) 229-1020 Calendar System: Semester
URL: www.ottawa.edu
Established: 1865 Annual Undergrad Tuition & Fees: $26,204
Enrollment: 896 Coed
Affiliation or Control: American Baptist IRS Status: 501(c)3
Highest Offering: Master's
Program: Liberal Arts And General; Teacher Preparatory
Accreditation: NH, NURSE, TED

01 President ....Mr. Kevin EICHNER
05 Exec VP & University Provost ....Dr. Terry HAINES
76 Dean of Health Sciences ....Dr. Dennis TYNER
10 Exec VP & Chief Financial Officer ....Mr. J. Clark RIBORDY
26 VP & Chief Marketing Officer ....Ms. Nancy WINGER
30 Vice Pres University Advancement ....Mr. Paul BEAN
32 Dean Student Affairs ....Mr. Tom TALDO
07 Director of Admissions ....Ms. Jessica HOMOLKA
06 University Registrar ....Ms. Karen ADAMS
21 Director Finance/Controller ....Ms. Noelle TESTA
21 Director Business Operations ....Mr. Thomas CORLEY
15 Director Human Resources ....Ms. Joanna WALTERS
37 Director Financial Aid ....Mr. Howard FISCHER
29 Director Alumni Programs ....Ms. Nori HALE
08 Director Library Services ....Ms. Gloria CREED-DIKEOGU
41 Director Athletics ....Ms. Arabie CONNER
18 Chief Facilities/Physical Plant ....Mr. Herb ORR
04 Executive Assistant to President ....Ms. Gaynia MENNINGER
11 Chief Operations Officer ....Mr. Keith JOHNSON
20 Dean of Instruction ....Dr. Teresa KRILEY
53 Dean School of Education ....Dr. Amy HOGAN
84 Director of Enrollment Management ....Mr. Bill HAMMOND
50 Dean Angell Snyder Sch of Business ....Dr. Marylou DEWALD
49 Dean School of Arts & Sciences ....Dr. Beverly RODGERS
86 Director Govt/Reg & Legal Affairs ....Ms. Lisa JOHNSON

† The Online division is included in the institution's enrollment count.

Ottawa University Kansas City (E)

4370 W. 109th Street, Suite 200,
Overland Park KS 66211-1302
Telephone: (913) 266-8600 Identification: 666083
Accreditation: &NH

† Regional accreditation is carried under the parent institution in Ottawa, KS.

Pinnacle Career Institute (F)

1601 W. 23rd Street, Ste 200, Lawrence KS 66046
County: Douglas FICE Identification: 026130
Unit ID: 367097
Telephone: (785) 841-9640 Carnegie Class: Assoc/PrivFP
FAX Number: (785) 841-4854 Calendar System: Quarter
URL: www.pcitraining.edu
Established: 1953 Annual Undergrad Tuition & Fees: $16,105
Enrollment: 113 Coed
Affiliation or Control: Proprietary IRS Status: Proprietary
Highest Offering: Associate Degree
Program: Occupational
Accreditation: ACICS

01 Executive Director ....Ms. Colleen SCHNEIDER

Pittsburg State University (G)

1701 S Broadway, Pittsburg KS 66762-7500
County: Crawford FICE Identification: 001926
Unit ID: 155681
Telephone: (620) 231-7000 Carnegie Class: Master's L
FAX Number: (620) 235-4080 Calendar System: Semester
URL: www.pittstate.edu
Established: 1903 Annual Undergrad Tuition & Fees (In-State): $6,530
Enrollment: 7,479 Coed
Affiliation or Control: State IRS Status: 501(c)3
Highest Offering: Doctorate
Program: Liberal Arts And General; Teacher Preparatory; Professional
Accreditation: NH, BUS, CACREP, CEA, ENGT, MUS, NRPA, NURSE, SW, TED

01 President ....Dr. Steven A. SCOTT
05 Provost & VP for Academic Affairs ....Dr. Lynette OLSON
11 VP Administration & Finance ....Mr. John D. PATTERSON
30 Interim VP University Advancement .... Ms. Kathleen FLANNERY
06 Registrar ....Ms. Debbie GREVE
32 VP Student Life ....Dr. Steve ERWIN
88 Assoc VP for Communication & Mktg ....Mr. Chris KELLY
84 Assoc VP Enroll Mgmt/Stdnt Success ....Mr. Lee YOUNG
51 Dean Graduate & Continuing Studies ....Dr. Pawan KAHOL
49 Dean of Arts & Sciences ....Dr. Karl KUNKEL
50 Dean of Business ....Dr. Paul GRIMES
53 Dean of Education ....Dr. Howard W. SMITH
72 Dean of Technology ....Dr. Bruce D. DALLMAN
08 Dean of Library Services ....Mr. Randy ROBERTS
108 Director of Assessment ....Ms. Nora HATTON
26 Director of Media Relations ....Mr. Ron WOMBLE
29 Dir Alumni Rels/Constituent Svcs ....Mr. Jon A. BARTLOW
13 Chief Information Officer ....Ms. Angela NERIA
15 Director Human Resource Svcs/Budget .... Dr. Michele D. SEXTON
85 Director of International Affairs ....Dr. Cathy L. ARCUINO
04 Dir of Community & Govt Relations .... Mr. Shawn NACCARATO
18 Director of Trades & Landscape Svcs ....Mr. Tom AMERSHEK
18 Director Gen & Custodial Services ....Mr. Tim SENECAUT
19 Director of University Police ....Mr. Mike MCCRACKEN
22 Dir Equal Opportunity/Affirm Action ....Ms. Cindy JOHNSON
37 Director of Financial Aid ....Ms. Tammy HIGGINS
41 Dir of Intercollegiate Athletics ....Mr. James JOHNSON
07 Director of Admissions ....Ms. Melinda A. ROELFS
36 Director Career Services ....Ms. Mindy E. CLONINGER
09 Director of Institutional Research ....Dr. Dai LI
38 Dir University Counseling Services ....Dr. Steven MAYHEW
96 Director of Purchasing ....Mr. Jim HUGHES
28 Director of Diversity ....Ms. Deatrea ROSE
10 Controller ....Ms. Barbara J. WINTER
39 Director of University Housing ....Ms. Connie D. MALLE
88 Exec Dir Innovation & Bus Dev ....Dr. Shawn NACCARATO

Pratt Community College (H)

348 NE SR 61, Pratt KS 67124-8432
County: Pratt FICE Identification: 001938
Unit ID: 155715
Telephone: (620) 672-5641 Carnegie Class: Assoc/Pub-R-S
FAX Number: (620) 672-5288 Calendar System: Semester
URL: www.prattcc.edu
Established: 1938 Annual Undergrad Tuition & Fees (In-District): $5,940
Enrollment: 1,383 Coed
Affiliation or Control: State/Local IRS Status: 501(c)3
Highest Offering: Associate Degree
Program: Occupational; 2-Year Principally Bachelor's Creditable
Accreditation: NH, ACBSP

01 President ....Dr. Mike CALVERT
05 Vice President Instruction ....Vacant
10 Vice President Finance/Operations ....Mr. Kent ADAMS
84 Vice Pres Student Enroll Management ....Ms. Lisa MILLER
41 Director of Athletics ....Mr. Kurt MCAFEE
07 Director of Admissions ....Mr. Brian ELKINS
06 Registrar ....Ms. Erin LACIO
13 Director of Information Technology ....Mr. Jerry SANKO
37 Director of Financial Aid ....Ms. Nikki POWELL
30 Director Development ....Vacant
08 Dir Linda Hunt Memorial Library ....Ms. Sandra WAGNER
15 Director of Personnel .... Ms. Rita PINKALL
38 Director Student Success Center ....Ms. Amy JACKSON
21 Controller ....Ms. Christy ALLEY
18 Director of Buildings & Grounds ....Mr. Dan PETZ
39 Director of Residence Life ....Vacant
04 Administrative Asst to President ....Ms. Debbie HEARN
29 Director Alumni Relations ....Ms. Ann RUDER
108 Director Institutional Assessment ....Mr. Eric WEBB

Rasmussen College-Kansas City/Overland Park (I)

11600 College Boulevard, Overland Park KS 66210
Telephone: (913) 491-7870 Identification: 770489
Accreditation: &NH, MAAB

† Regional accreditation carried under the parent institution in Saint Cloud, MN. The tuition figure is an average, actual tuition may vary.

Rasmussen College Topeka (J)

620 SW Governor View, Topeka KS 66606
Telephone: (785) 228-7320 Identification: 770490
Accreditation: &NH, MAAB

† Regional accreditation carried under the parent institution in Saint Cloud, MN. The tuition figure is an average, actual tuition may vary.

Saint Paul School of Theology (K)

4370 West 109th Street, Suite 300,
Overland Park KS 66211
County: Johnson FICE Identification: 002509
Unit ID: 179317
Telephone: (913) 253-5000 Carnegie Class: Spec/Faith
FAX Number: (913) 253-5075 Calendar System: Semester
URL: www.spst.edu
Established: 1958 Annual Graduate Tuition & Fees: $22,320
Enrollment: 157 Coed
Affiliation or Control: United Methodist IRS Status: 501(c)3
Highest Offering: Doctorate; No Undergraduates
Program: Professional; Religious Emphasis
Accreditation: NH, THEOL

01 President ....Rev. H. Sharon HOWELL
05 Interim VP Academic Affairs/Dean ....Dr. Elaine A. ROBINSON
30 Vice President for Advancement ....Mr. David SISNEY
12 Academic Dean for OCU Site ....Dr. Elaine A. ROBINSON
32 Associate Dean of Students .... Rev. Margaretta S. NARCISSE
15 Director of Human Resources ....Vacant
06 Registrar ....Ms. Tahmeka THOMPSON
37 Dir of Student Financial Services ....Ms. Kim WARREN
07 Dir of Student Recruitment Services .....Mr. Brian GREEN-YOUNG
26 Director of Communications .... Ms. Heather CHAMBERLIN
108 Assessment & Compliance Coordinator .... Ms. Jayme LAWLOR
08 Librarian ....Ms. Maggie MUELLER
04 Executive Assistant to President ....Ms. Melissa WHALEN
10 Director of Accounting & Finance ....Mr. Barney BARRY
101 Secretary of the Institution/Board ....Ms. Ashley CHEUNG

Salina Area Technical College (L)

2562 Centennial Road, Salina KS 67401
County: Saline FICE Identification: 005499
Unit ID: 155830
Telephone: (785) 309-3100 Carnegie Class: Not Classified
FAX Number: (785) 309-3101 Calendar System: Semester
URL: www.salinatech.edu
Established: 1965 Annual Undergrad Tuition & Fees (In-District): $4,893
Enrollment: 537 Coed
Affiliation or Control: State/Local IRS Status: 501(c)3
Highest Offering: Associate Degree
Program: Occupational; Technical Emphasis
Accreditation: @NH, DA

01	President	Mr. Gregg R. GOODE
05	Vice Pres of Instruction	Mr. Monte COUCHMAN
11	Vice Pres of Administrative Svcs	Mr. Andrew MANLEY
32	Vice Pres of Student Services	Mrs. Susan EBERWEIN
09	Director of Inst Research/Registrar	Mrs. Denise R. HOEFFNER
07	Director of Recruitment	Mr. Blane SCHLOO
15	Director Human Resources	Mrs. Tamera WILCOX
18	Director of Facilities	Vacant
25	Director of Grants and Planning	Vacant
102	Exec Dir of SATC Foundation	Ms. Morgan POWELL
37	Director Student Financial Aid	Mrs. Susan EBERWEIN

Seward County Community College/Area Technical School (A)

1801 N Kansas Avenue, Liberal KS 67901-2054

County: Seward　FICE Identification: 008228
Unit ID: 155858
Telephone: (620) 624-1951　Carnegie Class: Assoc/Pub-R-S
FAX Number: (620) 417-1169　Calendar System: Semester
URL: www.sccc.edu
Established: 1967　Annual Undergrad Tuition & Fees (In-District): $2,370
Enrollment: 1,852　Coed
Affiliation or Control: State/Local　IRS Status: 501(c)3
Highest Offering: Associate Degree
Program: Occupational; 2-Year Principally Bachelor's Creditable
Accreditation: NH, ACBSP, ADNUR, COARC, MLTAD, SURGT

01	President	Dr. Ken J. TRZASKA
05	Dean of Academic Affairs	Dr. Todd CARTER
10	Dean of Finance & Operations	Mr. Dennis M. SANDER
32	Dean of Student Services	Ms. Celeste DONOVAN
88	Dean of Career & Technical Educ	Vacant
06	Registrar	Ms. Alaina M. RICE
13	Director of Information Technology	Mr. J. J. WIDENER
37	Financial Aid Director	Mrs. Donna M. FISHER
26	Dir of Public and Alumni Relations	Ms. Rachel C. COLEMAN
50	Director of Business & Industry	Mrs. Norma Jean DODGE
24	Director of Multi-media Technology	Mr. Doug BROWNE
08	Director of Library	Mr. Matthew PANNKUK
41	Athletic Director	Mr. Galen W. MCSPADDEN
18	Dir of Buildings Grounds & Security	Mr. Roger SCHEIB
40	Director of Bookstore	Ms. Jerri L. LYDDON
30	Director of Development/Alumni Rels	Ms. Tammy DOLL
39	Student Housing Manager	Ms. Kate A. MULLIGAN
09	Institutional Research/Data Analyst	Ms. Teresa WEHMEIER
19	Safety and Security Supervisor	Mr. Dennis K. MULANAX
15	Director of Human Resources	Ms. Deborah WEILERT
07	Admissions Coordinator/Recruiting	Ms. Alyson CALL
36	Career Services & Admissions Coord	Vacant
38	Counselor/Retention Specialist	Ms. Rhonda L. KINSER
35	Director Student Activities	Mr. Wade LYON
04	Adm Asst to Pres & Brd of Trustees	Mrs. Lois B. MAGNER
66	Dir of Nursing and Allied Health	Ms. Jennifer LANDIS
75	Div Chair of Industrial Technology	Mr. Larry A. MCLEMORE
105	Website and Portal Manager	Mr. Craig DUSEK
108	Director of Research and Assessment	Mr. Adam BORTH
84	Director of Admissions	Mr. Bert LUALLEN

Southwestern College (B)

100 College Street, Winfield KS 67156-2499

County: Cowley　FICE Identification: 001940
Unit ID: 155900
Telephone: (620) 229-6000　Carnegie Class: Master's M
FAX Number: (620) 229-6224　Calendar System: Semester
URL: www.sckans.edu
Established: 1885　Annual Undergrad Tuition & Fees: $25,946
Enrollment: 1,627　Coed
Affiliation or Control: United Methodist　IRS Status: 501(c)3
Highest Offering: Doctorate
Program: Liberal Arts And General; Teacher Preparatory; Professional
Accreditation: NH, CAATE, MUS, NURSE, TED

01	President	Dr. Bradley J. ANDREWS
05	Provost	Dr. James A. SHEPPARD
10	Vice President Finance	Ms. Sheila R. KRUG
32	Vice President Student Life	Dr. Dawn E. PLEAS-BAILEY
107	Vice Pres Enroll Mgmt for Prof Stds	Ms. Susan BACKOFEN
45	VP Planning/New Programs	Dr. Stephen K. WILKE
30	Vice Pres Institutional Advancement	Ms. DeAnn DOCKERY
26	Vice President Communications	Ms. Sara S. WEINERT
13	Vice Pres Information Technology	Mr. Ben LIM
35	Dean of Student Life	Mr. Dan FALK
29	Director Alumni Programs	Ms. Susan G. LOWE
08	Library Director	Ms. Dalene MCDONALD
84	Vice President for Enrollment Mgmt	Ms. Marla SEXSON
37	Director Financial Aid	Ms. Brenda D. HICKS
06	Registrar	Ms. Linda WEIPPERT
09	Director of Institutional Research	Ms. Joni RANKIN
41	Director Athletics	Mr. David DENLY
15	Director Human Resources	Ms. Lonnie BOYD
96	Director of Purchasing	Mr. David H. DOLSEN
04	Exec Asst to President & Provost	Ms. Becky MANGUS

Southwestern College Wichita East (C)

2040 S Rock Road, Wichita KS 67207

Telephone: (316) 684-5335　Identification: 770260
Accreditation: &NH

† Branch campus of Southwestern College, Winfield, KS.

Sterling College (D)

125 W Cooper Street, Sterling KS 67579-1533

County: Rice　FICE Identification: 001945
Unit ID: 155937
Telephone: (620) 278-2173　Carnegie Class: Bac/Diverse
FAX Number: (620) 278-4411　Calendar System: 4/1/4
URL: www.sterling.edu
Established: 1887　Annual Undergrad Tuition & Fees: $23,350
Enrollment: 718　Coed
Affiliation or Control: Presbyterian　IRS Status: 501(c)3
Highest Offering: Baccalaureate
Program: Liberal Arts And General; Teacher Preparatory
Accreditation: NH, CAATE, TED

01	President	Mr. Scott RICH
05	Vice President Academic Affairs	Dr. Ken BROWN
30	Vice President for Inst Advancement	Mr. Scott CARTER
32	Vice President Student Life	Ms. Tina WOHLER
41	Athletic Director	Mr. Gary KEMPF
26	Dir Marketing/Pres Communications	Mr. Brad EVENSON
10	Director of Finance & Admin	Ms. Rita OWNBEY
37	Director of Financial Aid	Ms. Mitzi SUHLER
06	Registrar	Ms. Janet CAYWOOD
44	Director of Planned Giving	Ms. Sheila BIRD
29	Alumni & Marketing Manager	Ms. Teryn IRVIN
18	Chief Facilities/Physical Plant	Mr. Steven CAYWOOD
38	Director Student Counseling	Ms. Loida LEONE
08	Library Director	Mr. Jeremy LABOSIER
36	Director of Career Services	Mr. Terry EHRESMAN
07	Vice President Enrollment	Mr. Dennis DUTTON
04	Administrative Asst to President	Ms. Erica TREMAINE
42	Chaplain	Mr. Christian DASHIELL
108	Director Institutional Assessment	Dr. Felicia SQUIRES
13	Chief Info Technology Officer (CIO)	Mr. Mykeal PITTS
15	Director Personnel Services	Ms. Terri RIDGE

Tabor College (E)

400 S Jefferson Street, Hillsboro KS 67063-1753

County: Marion　FICE Identification: 001946
Unit ID: 155973
Telephone: (620) 947-3121　Carnegie Class: Bac/Diverse
FAX Number: (620) 947-2607　Calendar System: 4/1/4
URL: www.tabor.edu
Established: 1908　Annual Undergrad Tuition & Fees: $23,900
Enrollment: 766　Coed
Affiliation or Control: Mennonite Brethren Church　IRS Status: 501(c)3
Highest Offering: Master's
Program: Liberal Arts And General; Teacher Preparatory
Accreditation: NH, CAATE, MUS, NURSE, @SW, TED

01	President	Dr. Jules GLANZER
05	Vice President Academic Affairs	Dr. Frank JOHNSON
10	Sr Vice President Business/Finance	Mr. Kirby FADENRECHT
30	Vice President Advancement	Mr. Ronald BRAUN
41	Vice President of Athletics	Mr. Rusty ALLEN
32	Vice President of Student Life	Dr. Jim PAULUS
06	Registrar	Mr. Scott FRANZ
08	Director of Library Services	Vacant
84	Director Enrollment Management	Mr. Rusty ALLEN
37	Dir of Student Financial Services	Ms. Sommer SMITH
29	Director Alumni Relations	Mr. Rod HAMM
27	Director of Communications	Ms. Katrina HANCOCK
18	Director Facilities/Physical Plant	Mr. Doug GRABER
35	Director Student Success	Vacant
09	Institutional Research	Mrs. Deborah PENN
13	Director of Information Technology	Mr. Chris GLANZER
14	Chief Information Officer	Mrs. Joy MARK
15	Human Resources Coordinator	Mrs. Ruth FUNK

University of Kansas Edwards Campus (F)

12600 Quivira Road, Overland Park KS 66213

Telephone: (913) 897-8400　Identification: 770261
Accreditation: &NH

† Branch campus of University of Kansas Main Campus, Lawrence, KS.

University of Kansas Main Campus (G)

1450 Jayhawk Boulevard, Room 230, Lawrence KS 66045-7518

County: Douglas　FICE Identification: 001948
Unit ID: 155317
Telephone: (785) 864-3131　Carnegie Class: RU/VH
FAX Number: (785) 864-4120　Calendar System: Semester
URL: www.ku.edu
Established: 1866　Annual Undergrad Tuition & Fees (In-State): $10,824
Enrollment: 27,983　Coed
Affiliation or Control: State　IRS Status: 501(c)3
Highest Offering: Doctorate
Program: Liberal Arts And General; Teacher Preparatory; Professional
Accreditation: NH, ART, AUD, BUS, BUSA, CAATE, CEA, CLPSY, COPSY, CS, ENG, HSA, IPSY, JOUR, LAW, MUS, PH, PHAR, PLNG, SCPSY, SP, SPAA, SW, TED

01	Chancellor	Dr. Bernadette GRAY-LITTLE
05	Exec Vice Chancellor/Provost	Dr. Jeffrey S. VITTER
12	Vice Chancellor/Dean Edwards Campus	Dr. David COOK
26	Vice Chancellor for Public Affairs	Dr. Timothy CABONI
04	Executive Assistant to Chancellor	Ms. Mary G. BURG
43	General Counsel	Mr. James P. POTTORFF, JR.
20	Sr Vice Provost Academic Affairs	Dr. Sara ROSEN
20	Vice Provost	Dr. Mary Lee HUMMERT
20	Vice Provost	Ms. Diane H. GODDARD
32	Vice Provost for Student Affairs	Dr. Tammara DURHAM
46	Vice Prov Research/Grad Studies	Dr. James W. TRACY
28	Vice Provost Diversity & Equity	Dr. E. Nathan THOMAS, III
84	VP Enrollment Management	Dr. Matt MELVIN
13	Chief Information Officer	Mr. Bob LIM
45	Asst Vice Provost Research	Ms. Kristi M. BILLINGER
58	Assoc VP/Dean Research & Grad Stds	Dr. Michael C. ROBERTS
104	Assoc VP International Programs	Ms. Susan GRONBECK-TEDESCO
11	Assoc Vice Provost of Operations	Mr. Barry K. SWANSON
30	President Endowment Association	Mr. Dale SEUFERLING
29	President Alumni Association	Mr. Kevin J. CORBETT
07	Director Admissions	Ms. Lisa P. KRESS
10	Chief Business/Financial Plng Ofcr	Ms. Theresa K. GORDZICA
21	Comptroller	Ms. Katrina M. YOAKUM
21	Director Budget Office	Mr. Richard L. MCKINNEY
06	University Registrar	Ms. Cindy SANDERS
09	Univ Director Inst Research Plng	Ms. Deborah J. TEETER
15	AVP for Human Resource Management	Mr. Michael ROUNDS
85	Director International Student Svcs	Dr. Chuck OLCESE
38	Director Counseling/Psych Services	Dr. Michael LYNCH MAESTAS
18	Director Design & Construction Mgmt	Mr. James E. MODIG
37	Director Student Financial Aid	Ms. Brenda MAIGAARD
36	Director Career/Employment Svcs	Mr. David GASTON
41	Director Intercollegiate Athletics	Dr. Sheahon ZENGER
18	Interim Director Facilities Service	Mr. Vince AVILA
22	Director Inst Oppty & Access	Ms. Jane MCQUEENY
28	Interim Dir Multicultural Affairs	Ms. Precious PORRAS
23	Director Student Health Services	Dr. Douglas C. DECHARIO
14	Asst Director Information Tech	Ms. Anne MADDEN JOHNSON
39	Director Housing	Dr. Diana ROBERTSON
86	Director State Relations	Ms. Lindsey DOUGLAS
92	Director Honors Program	Dr. C. Bryan YOUNG
86	Director Federal Relations	Mr. Jack CLINE
40	Director Bookstores	Ms. Estella MCCOLLUM
51	Exec Dir Continuing Education	Ms. Sharon D. GRAHAM
25	Manager Contract Negotiations	Ms. Lucille MARINO
91	Project Coord Information Systems	Mr. David M. GARDNER
49	Interim Dean Liberal Arts/Science	Dr. Don W. STEEPLES
61	Dean of Law	Mr. Stephen W. MAZZA
54	Dean of Engineering	Dr. Michael BRANICKY
48	Dean Architecture/Design/Planning	Dr. Mahesh DAAS
50	Dean of Business	Dr. Neeli BENDAPUDI
67	Dean of Pharmacy	Dr. Kenneth L. AUDUS
60	Dean of Journalism	Dr. Ann M. BRILL
53	Dean of Education	Dr. Rick GINSBERG
64	Dean of Music	Dr. Robert L. WALZEL, JR.
70	Dean of Social Welfare	Dr. Paul SMOKOWSKI
08	Interim Dean Libraries	Ms. Mary ROACH
08	Interim Dean Libraries	Mr. Kent MILLER
57	Assoc Dean School of the Arts	Dr. Henry BIAL
19	Director Security/Safety	Mr. Ralph OLIVER

† Medical Center and Main campus enrollments should be combined for the total institution enrollment.

University of Kansas Medical Center (H)

3901 Rainbow Boulevard, Kansas City KS 66160-0001

Telephone: (913) 588-5000　FICE Identification: 024579
Accreditation: &NH, ANEST, CAHIIM, COARC, CYTO, DIETI, DMOLS, DMS, MED, MIDWF, MT, NMT, NURSE, OT, PTA

† Medical Center and Main campus enrollments should be combined for the total institution enrollment. Regional accreditation is carried under the parent institution in Lawrence, KS.

University of Saint Mary (I)

4100 S 4th Street Trafficway, Leavenworth KS 66048-5082

County: Leavenworth　FICE Identification: 001943
Unit ID: 155812
Telephone: (913) 682-5151　Carnegie Class: Master's M
FAX Number: (913) 758-6140　Calendar System: Semester
URL: www.stmary.edu
Established: 1923　Annual Undergrad Tuition & Fees: $25,620
Enrollment: 1,438　Coed
Affiliation or Control: Roman Catholic　IRS Status: 501(c)3
Highest Offering: Doctorate
Program: Liberal Arts And General; Teacher Preparatory; Professional; Nursing Emphasis
Accreditation: NH, CAHIIM, IACBE, NURSE, PTA, TED

01	President	Sr. Diane STEELE
05	Academic Vice President	Dr. Bryan LEBEAU
10	Vice President for Finance	Ms. Nancy BRAMLETT
30	Vice President of Development	Ms. Karolyn DREILING
07	VP Admissions & Marketing	Mr. John SHULTZ
32	Vice President for Student Life	Mr. Daniel DENTINO
88	Director Operations of Enrollment	Mrs. Kitti O'DONNELL
06	Registrar	Mr. Russell PERKINS
08	Director of the Library	Ms. Danielle THEISS
09	Data Analyst	Ms. Veronica DONOVAN
29	Alumni and Events Coordinator	Ms. Sharon CLAY
37	Director of Financial Aid	Ms. Annissa EPPERSON
42	Director of Campus Ministry	Mr. Robert KILLION

44 Development Officer Planned Giving .... Ms. Jane LIEBERT
41 Athletic Director .... Mr. Rob MILLER
15 Director Human Resources .... Ms. Teresa LEE
39 Director of Residence Life .... Mr. Josh CASE
21 Controller .... Ms. Sherry WELLS
38 Counselor .... Ms. Deborah SHADDY
18 Plant Manager .... Mr. Mark GIESEMAN
40 Bookstore Manager .... Ms. Cynthia FORRESTER
12 Site Coordinator Johnson County .... Ms. Patricia HOWARD
13 Coordinator of Computer Operations .... Mr. Kevin GANTT
04 Executive Administrative Assistant .... Ms. Kathy TATOM
35 Director of Student Activities .... Ms. Lisa POTOKA
19 Lead Public Safety Officer .... Mr. Vernon SHEAFFER

Vatterott College - Wichita (A)

8853 East 37th Street North, Wichita KS 67226-2018
Telephone: (316) 634-0066 Identification: 666583
Accreditation: ACCSC

† Branch campus of Vatterott College-North Park, Berkeley, MO.

Washburn University (B)

1700 SW College Avenue, Topeka KS 66621-0001
County: Shawnee FICE Identification: 001949
Unit ID: 156082
Telephone: (785) 670-1010 Carnegie Class: Master's M
FAX Number: (785) 670-1089 Calendar System: Semester
URL: www.washburn.edu
Established: 1865 Annual Undergrad Tuition & Fees (In-District): $6,350
Enrollment: 6,722 Coed
Affiliation or Control: Local IRS Status: 501(c)3
Highest Offering: Doctorate
Program: Liberal Arts And General; Teacher Preparatory; Professional
Accreditation: NH, ART, BUS, CAATE, CAHIIM, COARC, DMS, LAW, MUS, NURSE, OTA, PTAA, RAD, SW, TED

01 President .... Dr. Jerry B. FARLEY
05 Vice President Acad Affairs .... Dr. Randall G. PEMBROOK
10 Vice Pres Admin & Treasurer .... Mr. Rick L. ANDERSON
32 Vice President for Student Life .... Dr. Denise OTTINGER
04 Special Assistant to the President .. Dr. Cynthia A. HORNBERGER
84 Director Enrollment Management .... Dr. Richard W. LIEDTKE
43 University Legal Counsel .... Mr. Marc FRIED
35 Assoc Vice Pres of Student Life .... Mr. Joel BLUML
20 Assoc Vice Pres Acad Affairs .... Dr. Nancy A. TATE
21 Assoc Vice Pres & Dir of Finance .... Mr. Chris LEACH
102 President WU Foundation .... Dr. Juliann MAZACHEK
06 Registrar .... Ms. Kelly RUSSELL
08 Dean of Libraries .... Dr. Alan BEARMAN
37 Director Student Financial Aid .... Ms. Gail PALMER
07 Director of Admissions .... Ms. Kris KLIMA
15 Director of Human Resources .... Ms. Rhonda CANTRELL
90 Director Info Systems & Services .... Mr. Floyd DAVENPORT
09 Director Strategic Analysis & Rep .... Dr. Robert L. HANDLEY
49 Dean College Arts/Sciences .... Dr. Laura STEPHENSON
88 Dean School Applied Studies .... Dr. Pat MUNZER
61 Dean School of Law .... Mr. Thomas J. ROMIG
50 Dean School of Business .... Dr. David SOLLARS
66 Dean School of Nursing .... Dr. Monica S. SCHEIBMEIR
41 Director of Athletics .... Mr. Loren FERRE
35 Director Student Services .... Ms. Jeanne D. KESSLER
22 Director Equal Opportunity .... Ms. Pam FOSTER
18 Director Facilities Services .... Mr. Rich CONNELL
23 Director Health Services .... Dr. Shirley DINKEL
29 Alumni Association Director .... Ms. Susie HOFFMANN
92 Dean Honors Program .... Dr. Michael J. MCGUIRE
39 Director Student Housing .... Ms. Mindy P. RENDON
40 Director Bookstore .... Ms. Kay FARLEY
35 Director Student Activities .... Ms. Jessica BARRACLOUGH
38 Interim Director Student Counseling .... Ms. Jamie OLSEN
26 Director of University Relations .... Mr. Patrick EARLY
36 Director Student Placement .... Mr. Kent MCANALLY

Wichita Area Technical College (C)

4004 N Webb Road, Wichita KS 67226-8101
County: Sedgwick FICE Identification: 005498
Unit ID: 156107
Telephone: (316) 677-9400 Carnegie Class: Assoc/Pub-U-MC
FAX Number: (316) 677-9510 Calendar System: Semester
URL: www.watc.edu
Established: 1965 Annual Undergrad Tuition & Fees (In-District): $7,169
Enrollment: 3,373 Coed
Affiliation or Control: State/Local IRS Status: 501(c)3
Highest Offering: Associate Degree
Program: 2-Year Principally Bachelor's Creditable; Technical Emphasis
Accreditation: NH, DA, MAC, PNUR, SURGT

01 Interim President .... Ms. Sheree UTASH
05 Vice Pres Academic Affairs .... Ms. Sheree UTASH
10 Vice Pres Finance/Administration .... Mr. Greg UNRUH
26 VP Marketing/Recruit/Advancement .... Mr. Joe ONTJES
32 Vice President Student Services .... Mr. Justin PFEIFER
13 Exec Dir Tech/Instl Effectiveness .... Mr. Randy ROEBUCK
15 Exec Director Human Resources .... Ms. Judy MOUNT
06 Registrar .... Ms. Bonnie ENGELKEN

Wichita State University (D)

1845 N Fairmount, Wichita KS 67260-0001
County: Sedgwick FICE Identification: 001950
Unit ID: 156125
Telephone: (316) 978-3456 Carnegie Class: RU/H
FAX Number: (316) 978-3770 Calendar System: Semester
URL: www.wichita.edu
Established: 1895 Annual Undergrad Tuition & Fees (In-State): $7,750
Enrollment: 15,003 Coed
Affiliation or Control: State IRS Status: 501(c)3
Highest Offering: Doctorate
Program: Liberal Arts And General; Teacher Preparatory; Professional
Accreditation: NH, ARCPA, ART, AUD, BUS, BUSA, CAATE, CLPSY, CS, DANCE, DENT, DH, ENG, IPSY, MT, MUS, NURSE, PTA, SP, SPAA, SW, TED

01 President .... Dr. John W. BARDO
05 Provost/Senior VP Academic Affairs .... Dr. Anthony VIZZINI
10 VP Administration & Finance .... Ms. Mary L. HERRIN
32 VP Student Affairs/Athletics .... Dr. Eric L. SEXTON
43 General Counsel .... Mr. David MOSES
26 VP Strategic Communications .... Mr. Lou HELDMAN
20 Assoc VP Academic Affairs .... Dr. David WRIGHT
20 Assoc VP Academic Affairs .... Dr. Richard D. MUMA
13 Chief Information Officer .... Mr. Toney FLACK
20 Associate VP Academic Affairs .... Dr. Linnea GLENMAYE
46 VP Research & Technology Transfer .... Dr. John S. TOMBLIN
49 Dean Liberal Arts & Sciences .... Dr. Ronald R. MATSON
50 Dean Barton School of Business .... Dr. Anand DESAI
53 Dean Education .... Dr. Shirley LEFEVER-DAVIS
54 Dean Engineering .... Dr. Royce BOWDEN
57 Dean Fine Arts .... Dr. Rodney E. MILLER
76 Dean Health Professions .... Dr. Sandra BIBB
58 Interim Dean Graduate School .... Dr. Kerry WILKS
08 Dean Libraries .... Dr. Don GILSTRAP
35 Dean of Students .... Ms. Christine SCHNEIKART-LUEBBE
86 Exec Director Government Relations .... Mr. Andrew SCHLAPP
24 Dir Media Resources Center .... Mr. John JONES
102 CEO & President WSU Foundation .... Ms. Elizabeth H. KING
41 Athletic Director .... Dr. Eric L. SEXTON
88 Director Creative Services .... Mr. Craig LINDEMAN
15 Director Human Resources .... Mrs. Frankie M. KIRKENDOLL
21 Director Budgets .... Mr. Paul F. WERNER
06 Registrar .... Ms. Gina D. CRABTREE
07 Director Admissions .... Mr. Bobby GANDU
37 Director Financial Aid .... Ms. Sheelu M. SURENDER
36 Director Placement/Career Services .... Ms. Jill M. PLETCHER
38 Director Counseling & Testing ... Dr. Maureen DASEY-MORALES
18 Director Physical Plant .... Mr. Woodrow DEPONTIER
45 Director of Facilities Planning .... Mr. Eric KING
19 Campus Police Chief .... Ms. Sara B. MORRIS
23 Director Student Health Services .... Ms. Camille CHILDERS
39 Director Stdnt Housing & Resid Life .... Mr. Scott JENSEN
28 Director Diversity & Inclusion .... Ms. Alicia SANCHEZ
40 Manager Bookstore .... Mr. Kevin J. KONDA
21 Assoc VP Financial Operations .... Ms. Lois TATRO
42 Campus Minister .... Rev. Christopher ESHELMAN
96 Director of Purchasing .... Mr. Steven WHITE
29 Executive Director Alumni Assoc .... Ms. Courtney MARSHALL
22 Interim Director of EEO .... Ms. Jane J. LINK
04 Assistant to President .... Ms. Anna LANIER WEYERS
106 Dir Online Education/E-learning .... Mr. Mark D. PORCARO

Wichita Technical Institute (E)

2051 South Meridian Avenue, Wichita KS 67213-1927
County: Sedgwick FICE Identification: 010503
Unit ID: 156134
Telephone: (316) 943-2241 Carnegie Class: Not Classified
FAX Number: (316) 943-5438 Calendar System: Quarter
URL: www.wti.edu
Established: Annual Undergrad Tuition & Fees: $20,600
Enrollment: 1,000 Coed
Affiliation or Control: Proprietary IRS Status: Proprietary
Highest Offering: Associate Degree
Program: Occupational
Accreditation: ACCSC

01 Director .... Mr. Rod MOORE

Wright Career College (F)

10700 Metcalf Avenue, Overland Park KS 66210
County: Johnson FICE Identification: 025909
Unit ID: 406200
Telephone: (913) 385-7700 Carnegie Class: Assoc/PrivNFP
FAX Number: (913) 385-1711 Calendar System: Other
URL: www.wrightcc.edu
Established: 1997 Annual Undergrad Tuition & Fees: $20,858
Enrollment: 1,200 Coed
Affiliation or Control: Independent Non-Profit IRS Status: 501(c)3
Highest Offering: Baccalaureate
Program: Occupational
Accreditation: ACICS, SURTEC

01 Campus Director .... Ms. Thecla WOOLCOTT

Wright Career College (G)

7700 East Kellogg, Wichita KS 67207
Telephone: (913) 381-2577 Identification: 770721
Accreditation: ACICS, SURTEC

† Branch campus of Wright Career College, Overland Park, KS.

KENTUCKY

Alice Lloyd College (H)

Purpose Road, Pippa Passes KY 41844-9703
County: Knott FICE Identification: 001951
Unit ID: 156189
Telephone: (606) 368-2101 Carnegie Class: Bac/Diverse
FAX Number: (606) 368-6212 Calendar System: Semester
URL: www.alc.edu
Established: 1923 Annual Undergrad Tuition & Fees: $9,600
Enrollment: 619 Coed
Affiliation or Control: Independent Non-Profit IRS Status: 501(c)3
Highest Offering: Baccalaureate
Program: Liberal Arts And General; Teacher Preparatory
Accreditation: SC

01 President .... Dr. Joe A. STEPP
03 Executive Vice President .... Dr. Jim STEPP
05 Vice President Academic Affairs .... Dr. Claude CRUM
10 Vice President of Business Affairs .... Mr. David JOHNSON
32 Dean of Students & Community Life .... Mr. Scott CORNETT
07 Director of Admissions .... Ms. Angela PHIPPS
06 Registrar .... Ms. Dana DOTSON
08 Director of Library .... Mr. Andrew BUSROE
37 Director of Financial Aid .... Mrs. Jacqueline STEWART
88 Director of Student Work Program .... Mr. Kerry RATLIFF
53 Director of Teacher Education .... Mr. Norman BISHOP
18 Director of Physical Plant .... Mr. Ryan GIBSON
39 Director of Student Housing .... Mr. John MILLS
29 Director of Alumni Relations .... Mrs. Teresa GRENDER
35 Director of Student Activities .... Ms. Christine STUMBO
26 Dir of Marketing & Communications .... Ms. Katelin HYLTON
09 Director of Institutional Research .... Mr. Norman BISHOP
30 Director of Development .... Mrs. Margo SPARKMAN

† Cost of tuition is guaranteed for students from 108 county territories.

American National University (I)

115 E Lexington Avenue, Danville KY 40422-1517
Telephone: (859) 236-6991 Identification: 666441
Accreditation: ACICS, MAC

† Branch campus of American National University, Indianapolis, IN.

American National University (J)

8095 Connector Drive, Florence KY 41042-1466
Telephone: (859) 525-6510 Identification: 666442
Accreditation: ACICS, MAC, SURGT

† Branch campus of American National University, Indianapolis, IN.

American National University (K)

2376 Sir Barton Way, Lexington KY 40509-2256
Telephone: (859) 253-0621 Identification: 667202
Accreditation: ACICS, MAC, SURGT

† Branch campus of American National University, Indianapolis, IN.

American National University (L)

4205 Dixie Highway, Louisville KY 40216-4147
Telephone: (502) 447-7634 Identification: 666443
Accreditation: ACICS, CAHIIM, MAC, SURGT

† Branch campus of American National University, Indianapolis, IN.

American National University (M)

50 National College Boulevard, Pikeville KY 41501-3176
Telephone: (606) 478-7200 Identification: 666444
Accreditation: ACICS, MAC

† Branch campus of American National University, Indianapolis, IN.

American National University (N)

125 S Killarney Lane, Richmond KY 40475-2309
Telephone: (859) 623-8956 Identification: 666445
Accreditation: ACICS, MAC

† Branch campus of American National University, Indianapolis, IN.

Asbury Theological Seminary (O)

204 N Lexington Avenue, Wilmore KY 40390-1199
County: Jessamine FICE Identification: 001953
Unit ID: 156222
Telephone: (859) 858-3581 Carnegie Class: Spec/Faith
FAX Number: N/A Calendar System: 4/1/4
URL: www.asburyseminary.edu
Established: 1923 Annual Graduate Tuition & Fees: $4,455
Enrollment: 1,470 Coed
Affiliation or Control: Independent Non-Profit IRS Status: 501(c)3
Highest Offering: Doctorate; No Undergraduates
Program: Professional; Religious Emphasis
Accreditation: SC, THEOL

01 President .... Dr. Timothy C. TENNENT

11 Vice President/COO ... Mr. Robert S. LANDREBE
05 Provost/VP Academic for Affairs ... Dr. Douglas K. MATTHEWS
10 Vice Pres Finance/Admin/CFO ... Mr. Bryan P. BLANKENSHIP
30 Vice President for Advancement ... Mr. Jay MANSUR
31 Vice President Community Formation ... Dr. Marilyn ELLIOTT
84 Vice Pres Enrollment Management ... Mr. Kevin BISH
13 Chief Technology Officer ... Mr. Patrick GARDELLA
06 Registrar ... Ms. Christine L. JOHNSON
07 Director of Admissions ... Mr. Randy OZAN
37 Director of Student Financial Aid ... Mrs. Jenny BURKHART
18 Director of Physical Plant ... Mr. Lanny SPEARS
09 Dir Inst Effectiveness/Assessment ... Dr. Alexandra HENCHY
15 Director of Human Resources ... Mrs. Barbara ANTROBUS
29 Director Alumni/Church Relations ... Ms. Tammy CESSNA
73 Dean School of Theology & Formation ... Dr. James THOBABEN
88 Dean Beeson Center ... Dr. Tom TUMBLIN
88 Dean ESJ School World of Missions ... Dr. Gregg OKESSON
88 Dean School Biblical Interpretation ... Dr. David BAUER
73 Actg Dean School Practical Theology ... Dr. Chris KIESLING
88 Dean Advanced Research Programs ... Dr. Lalsangkima PACHUAU

Asbury University (A)

1 Macklem Drive, Wilmore KY 40390-1198
County: Jessamine FICE Identification: 001952
Unit ID: 156213
Telephone: (859) 858-3511 Carnegie Class: Bac/Diverse
FAX Number: (859) 858-3921 Calendar System: Semester
URL: www.asbury.edu
Established: 1890 Annual Undergrad Tuition & Fees: $27,736
Enrollment: 1,622 Coed
Affiliation or Control: Independent Non-Profit IRS Status: 501(c)3
Highest Offering: Beyond Master's But Less Than Doctorate
Program: Liberal Arts And General; Teacher Preparatory
Accreditation: SC, MUS, SW, TED

01 President ... Dr. Sandra C. GRAY
05 Provost ... Dr. Jon S. KULAGA
10 Vice Pres Business Affairs & Treas ... Mr. Glenn R. HAMILTON
84 Vice Pres of Enrollment Management ... Dr. Mark J. TROYER
32 Vice Pres Student Dev/Dean Students ... Dr. Sarah T. BALDWIN
30 Vice President for Inst Advancement ... Mr. Charles SHEPARD
20 Academic Dean ... Dr. Timothy G. CAMPBELL
49 Dir of College of Arts & Sciences ... Dr. Stephen K. CLEMENTS
53 Director of School of Education ... Dr. Sherry W. POWERS
60 Dir of School of Communication Arts ... Dr. James R. OWENS
58 Dir of School of Grad & Prof Stud ... Dr. William HALL, JR.
51 Dir of Adult Professional Studies ... Mr. T. Joshua FEE
106 Director of Online Education ... Vacant
44 Senior Advancement Director ... Rev. Stuart A. SMITH
37 Director of Financial Aid ... Mr. Ronald M. ANDERSON
42 Assoc Dean for Campus Ministries ... Rev. Gregory K. HASELOFF
39 Assoc Dean for Residence Life ... Mr. Joe W. BRUNER
06 Registrar ... Mrs. Sheryl VOIGTS
29 Dir of Alumni Relations/Parents Pgm ... Mrs. Lisa D. HARPER
08 Director of Library Services ... Mr. Morgan A. TRACY
13 Director of Information Services ... Mr. Paul J. DUPREE
07 Director of Admissions ... Mr. Brandon COMBS
26 Dir of Marketing & Communications ... Mr. Brad JOHNSON
18 Director of Physical Plant ... Mr. Eric C. MCMILLION
23 Supervisor of Clinic ... Miss Carol J. AMEY
36 Dir Center for Career & Calling ... Ms. Michelle KRATZER
38 Director of Counseling Center ... Mrs. Melissa COZART
19 Dir of Security & Environ Safety ... Mr. David HAY
40 Manager of Bookstore ... Mr. C. David TRAMMELL
21 Associate Business Officer ... Mr. Gary E. HOWARD
04 Admin Asst to the President ... Mrs. Dana MOUTZ
85 Coordinator of Intercultural Pgms ... Rev. Esther JADHAV
41 Athletics Director ... Mr. Mark PERDUE
09 Director of Institutional Research ... Dr. Gay HOLCOMB
104 Coordinator Global Engagement Ofc ... Ms. Rosanna WILLHITE
15 Dir of Human Resources/Risk Mgt ... Mrs. Jan CRAIGMILES
45 Director Institutional Planning ... Mr. Paul STEPHENS
50 Dean Howard Dayton Sch Business ... Dr. Michael KANE

ATA College (B)

10180 Linn Station Road, Ste A-200, Louisville KY 40223
County: Jefferson FICE Identification: 040383
Unit ID: 447935
Telephone: (502) 371-8330 Carnegie Class: Assoc/PrivFP
FAX Number: (502) 371-8598 Calendar System: Quarter
URL: www.ata.edu
Established: 1994 Annual Undergrad Tuition & Fees: $11,550
Enrollment: 439 Coed
Affiliation or Control: Proprietary IRS Status: Proprietary
Highest Offering: Associate Degree
Program: Occupational
Accreditation: ABHES

01 President ... Mr. Donald A. JONES

Baptist Seminary of Kentucky (C)

400 E. College St, Box 358, Georgetown KY 40324
County: Scott Identification: 667211
Telephone: (502) 863-8300 Carnegie Class: Not Classified
FAX Number: N/A Calendar System: Semester
URL: www.bsky.org
Established: Annual Graduate Tuition & Fees: $7,500
Enrollment: 31 Coed
Affiliation or Control: Independent Non-Profit IRS Status: 501(c)3
Highest Offering: Master's; No Undergraduates
Program: Religious Emphasis
Accreditation: THEOL

01 President ... Dr. Greg C. EARWOOD
05 Academic Dean ... Dr. Dalen C. JACKSON
07 Director of Admissions ... Mr. Jarrod LOPEZ

Beckfield College (D)

16 Spiral Drive, Florence KY 41042-4866
County: Boone FICE Identification: 024911
Unit ID: 247065
Telephone: (859) 371-9393 Carnegie Class: Assoc/PrivFP4
FAX Number: (859) 371-5096 Calendar System: Quarter
URL: www.beckfield.edu
Established: 1984 Annual Undergrad Tuition & Fees: $12,906
Enrollment: 712 Coed
Affiliation or Control: Proprietary IRS Status: Proprietary
Highest Offering: Baccalaureate
Program: Professional; Business Emphasis
Accreditation: ACICS

00 Chief Executive Officer ... Ms. Diane G. WOLFER
01 President Florence Campus ... Mr. Richard F. COSTA, JR.
05 Dean of Academic Affairs ... Mr. Steven LAKES
12 Campus Director of Florence ... Mr. Keith GRANT
32 Director of Student Services ... Ms. Alisha WOODESHICK
37 Director of Financial Aid ... Ms. Patricia A. NETTLETON
13 Director of Information Technology ... Mr. James BRUN
07 Director Admissions ... Mr. John AVILES
36 Director Career Services ... Ms. Christin JACKSON
22 Director of Compliance ... Mr. Peter NETTLETON
06 Registrar ... Ms. Jocelyn ROY
08 Librarian ... Ms. Emily STEELE
12 Campus Dean-Florence ... Ms. Rachel MCARTHUR
50 Dean of Business/Technology ... Mr. Scott BURRELL
66 Assoc Dean of Nursing ... Mr. Tim CURL
76 Dean of Allied Health ... Ms. Dolores DOMINGUEZ
97 Dean of General Education ... Ms. Brittaney HARP
88 Dean of Criminal Justice ... Ms. Brandy TAYLOR
04 Assistant to the President ... Ms. Cheryl A. KUNKEL

Bellarmine University (E)

2001 Newburg Road, Louisville KY 40205-0671
County: Jefferson FICE Identification: 001954
Unit ID: 156286
Telephone: (502) 272-8000 Carnegie Class: Master's L
FAX Number: (502) 272-8033 Calendar System: Semester
URL: www.bellarmine.edu
Established: 1950 Annual Undergrad Tuition & Fees: $37,650
Enrollment: 3,609 Coed
Affiliation or Control: Independent Non-Profit IRS Status: 501(c)3
Highest Offering: Doctorate
Program: Liberal Arts And General; Teacher Preparatory; Professional
Accreditation: SC, BUS, COARC, MT, NURSE, PTA, TED

01 President ... Dr. Joseph J. MCGOWAN
03 Executive Vice President ... Dr. Doris A. TEGART
05 Provost ... Dr. Carole PFEFFER
20 Vice Provost ... Dr. Graham ELLIS
20 Vice Provost ... Dr. Jay D. GATRELL
10 Vice President for Admin & Finance ... Mr. Robert L. ZIMLICH
32 Vice President for Student Affairs ... Dr. Helen G. RYAN
30 VP for Dev & Alumni Relations ... Mr. Glenn F. KOSSE
26 VP for Comm & Public Affairs ... Mr. Hunt C. HELM
84 Vice President for Enrollment Mgmt ... Dr. Sean J. RYAN
100 Exec Assistant to the President ... Ms. Marisa ZOELLER
04 Administrative Asst to President ... Ms. Lucy BURNS
66 Dn Lansing Sch of Nursing/Hlth Sci ... Dr. Mark WIEGAND
50 Dean Rubel School of Business ... Dr. Robert BROWN
107 Dean of Continuing and Prof Studies ... Dr. Sean J. RYAN
53 Dean Annsley Frazier Thornton Ed ... Dr. Robert B. COOTER
65 Dean Sch of Environmental Studies ... Dr. Robert KINGSOLVER
49 Dean Bellarmine College ... Dr. William E. FENTON
15 Chief Human Resources Officer ... Ms. Lynn M. BYNUM
21 Asst VP Business Affairs ... Ms. Denise BROWN-CORNELIUS
28 Asst VP Stdnt & Multicultural Affs ... Dr. Hannah CLAYBORNE
85 Chief International Officer ... Ms. Gabriele BOSLEY
35 Dean of Students ... Vacant
92 Director Honors Program ... Dr. Hank J. ROTHGERBER
41 Athletic Director ... Mr. Scott P. WIEGANDT
18 Asst VP Facilities Management ... Mr. Jeffrey DEAN
07 Dean of Admission ... Mr. Timothy A. STURGEON
08 Director of the Library ... Mr. John K. STEMMER
19 Director of Safety & Security ... Mr. Joseph FRYE
07 Dean of Graduate Admission ... Dr. Sara Y. PETTINGILL
06 Registrar ... Ms. Ann E. OLSEN
96 Purchasing Manager ... Mr. Patrick COONS
42 Director Campus Ministry ... Dr. Melanie P. SULLIVAN
39 Associate Dean Residence Life ... Ms. Leslie M. MAXIE-ASHFORD
13 Vice Provost Information Technology ... Mr. Eric SATTERLY
37 Director Student Financial Aid ... Ms. Heather BOUTELL
36 Director of Career Services ... Vacant
29 Executive Director Alumni Relations ... Mr. Peter W. KREMER
26 Director of News/Media/Social Netwk ... Mr. Jason A. CISSELL
38 Director of Counseling Center ... Dr. Gary PETIPRIN
92 Director of Brown Scholars Program ... Dr. Conor A. PICKEN

Berea College (F)

101 Chestnut Street, Berea KY 40404-0003
County: Madison FICE Identification: 001955
Unit ID: 156295
Telephone: (859) 985-3000 Carnegie Class: Bac/A&S
FAX Number: (859) 985-3917 Calendar System: Semester
URL: www.berea.edu
Established: 1855 Annual Undergrad Tuition & Fees: $570
Enrollment: 1,577 Coed
Affiliation or Control: Independent Non-Profit IRS Status: 501(c)3
Highest Offering: Baccalaureate
Program: Liberal Arts And General; Teacher Preparatory; Professional
Accreditation: SC, NURSE, TED

01 President ... Dr. Lyle D. ROELOFS
10 Vice President Finance ... Mr. Jeff S. AMBURGEY
30 VP Alumni & College Relations ... Ms. Bernadine DOUGLAS
32 VP Labor and Student Life ... Mr. Virgil BURNSIDE
11 VP Operations and Sustainability ... Mr. Derrick SINGLETON
04 Assistant to President ... Ms. Rebecca PARRISH
35 Asst Vice Pres for Student Life ... Mr. Gus GERASSIMIDES
05 Academic VP/Dean of the Faculty ... Dr. Chad BERRY
37 Dir of Student Financial Aid Svcs ... Ms. Theresa LOWDER
38 Dir Counseling/Psychological Svcs ... Ms. Sue REIMONDO
44 Director of Gift Planning ... Ms. Amy SHEHEE
108 Director of Academic Assessment ... Dr. Robert SMITH
20 Dean of Curriculum/Student Learning ... Dr. Scott STEELE
13 Interim Chief Information Officer ... Mr. V. Lavoyed HUDGINS
07 Director of Admissions Operations ... Mr. Luke HODSON
29 Director of Alumni Relations ... Vacant
15 Director of Human Resources ... Mr. Steve LAWSON
18 Director of Facilities Management ... Mr. Wayne ORR
88 Director of Appalachian Center ... Mr. Chris GREEN
09 Director of Inst Rsrch/Assessment ... Ms. Judith WECKMAN
26 Publications and Project Manager ... Mr. J. MORGAN
08 Director of Library Services ... Ms. Anne CHASE
41 Dir Athletics/Seabury Ctr Complex ... Mr. Mark CARTMILL
42 Director Campus Christian Center ... Rev. Gail BOWMAN
43 General Counsel ... Mr. Judge WILSON
19 Director of Public Safety ... Mr. V. Lavoyed HUDGINS
28 Director Black Cultural Center ... Ms. Monica JONES
88 Dean of Labor ... Mr. David K. TIPTON
85 Director International Center ... Dr. Richard CAHILL
40 College Bookstore Director ... Mr. Nate DANIELS
96 Purchasing Manager ... Ms. Aurelia BRANDENBURG
24 Media Services Coordinator ... Mr. Rob LEWIS
06 Director of Academic Services ... Mr. Curtis SANDBERG
88 Center for Transformative Learning ... Ms. Leslie ORTQUIST-AHRENS
88 Woodson Center for Interracial Educ ... Dr. Alicestyne TURLEY
88 Director of CELTS ... Ms. Ashley COCHRANE
23 Director of Health and Wellness ... Ms. Jill GURTATOWSKI
88 Director of Internships ... Ms. Esther LIVINGSTON
103 Director of Career Development ... Vacant
104 Education Abroad Adviser ... Ms. Ann BUTWELL
22 VP for Diversity and Inclusion ... Dr. Linda LEEK

Brescia University (G)

717 Frederica Street, Owensboro KY 42301-3023
County: Daviess FICE Identification: 001958
Unit ID: 156356
Telephone: (270) 685-3131 Carnegie Class: Bac/Diverse
FAX Number: (270) 686-6422 Calendar System: Semester
URL: www.brescia.edu
Established: 1950 Annual Undergrad Tuition & Fees: $19,950
Enrollment: 1,059 Coed
Affiliation or Control: Roman Catholic IRS Status: 501(c)3
Highest Offering: Master's
Program: Liberal Arts And General; Teacher Preparatory
Accreditation: SC, SW

01 President ... Rev. Larry HOSTETTER
05 Vice President & Academic Dean ... Dr. Cheryl CLEMONS
10 Vice President Business & Finance ... Mr. Dale CECIL
84 Vice President of Enrollment ... Mr. Christopher HOUK
30 Vice Pres Institutional Advancement ... Ms. Tracy NAYLOR
32 Vice Pres/Dean Student Development ... Mr. Joshua R. CLARY
39 Director Residence Life ... Mr. Issac DUNCAN
35 Director Stdnts Act/Leadership Dev ... Ms. Patricia LOVETT
06 Registrar ... Sr. Helena FISCHER, OSU
106 Director of BU Online ... Ms. Shanda LARUE
38 Director of Counseling Center ... Ms. Eva G. ATKINSON
08 Director of Library Services ... Sr. Judith N. RINEY, OSU
88 Director Student Support Services ... Ms. Kaye CASTLEN
15 Director of Human Resources ... Ms. Tammy S. KELLER
13 Director of Information Technology ... Mr. Chris FORD
18 Director of Physical Plant ... Mr. Mike WARD
37 Director of Financial Aid ... Ms. Kristi EIDSON
41 Director of Athletics ... Mr. Brian SKORTZ
26 Director of Public Relations ... Ms. Kayla CRUSE
29 Sr Director of Alumni & Donor Rels ... Mr. Mike GOETZ
44 Director of Annual Giving ... Ms. Sydney WARREN
09 Director of Institutional Research ... Ms. Stephanie CLARY
58 Director of Graduate Program-MBA ... Dr. Sandra O. OBILADE
58 Director of Graduate Program-MSCI ... Dr. Patricia A. AKOJIE
42 Director of Campus Ministry ... Sr. Pam MUELLER, OSU
07 Director of Admissions ... Ms. Christy ROHNER
21 Asst Director Business & Finance ... Ms. Nancy W. REYNOLDS
36 Coordinator of Career Services ... Ms. Sarah JACKSON
20 Associate Academic Dean for Online ... Mr. Jeffrey BARNETTE
40 Bookstore Manager ... Ms. Beverly MCCANDLESS
25 Grants Writer/Special Asst to Pres ... Ms. Jayme WALTERS

Brown Mackie College-Hopkinsville (A)

4001 Fort Campbell Boulevard,
Hopkinsville KY 42240-4948
Telephone: (270) 886-1302 Identification: 666516
Accreditation: ACICS, OTA

† Branch campus of Brown Mackie College-Findlay, Findlay, OH.

Brown Mackie College-Louisville (B)

3605 Fern Valley Road, Louisville KY 40219-1916
Telephone: (502) 810-6000 FICE Identification: 021082
Accreditation: ACICS, OTA, SURTEC

† Branch campus of Brown Mackie College-Findlay, Findlay, OH.

Brown Mackie College-Northern Kentucky (C)

309 Buttermilk Pike, Fort Mitchell KY 41017-2191
Telephone: (859) 341-5627 Identification: 666446
Accreditation: ACICS, OTA

† School is in teach-out plan. Branch campus of Brown Mackie College, Cincinnati, OH.

Campbellsville University (D)

1 Universty Drive, Campbellsville KY 42718-2799
County: Taylor FICE Identification: 001959
Unit ID: 156365
Telephone: (270) 789-5000 Carnegie Class: Master's M
FAX Number: (270) 789-5050 Calendar System: Semester
URL: www.campbellsville.edu
Established: 1906 Annual Undergrad Tuition & Fees: $23,828
Enrollment: 3,484 Coed
Affiliation or Control: Baptist IRS Status: 501(c)3
Highest Offering: Master's
Program: Liberal Arts And General; Teacher Preparatory; Professional
Accreditation: SC, IACBE, MUS, SW, TED

01 President .... Dr. Michael CARTER
10 Vice Pres Finance & Administration .... Mr. Otto TENNANT
05 Vice President Academic Affairs .... Dr. Donna HEDGEPATH
30 Vice President for Development .... Mr. Benji KELLY
26 VP for Church & External Rels .... Mr. John E. CHOWNING
07 VP for Admissions/Student Svcs .... Mr. Dave WALTERS
32 Dean of Student Services .... Vacant
20 Associate Academic Officer .... Vacant
21 Comptroller .... Mr. Tim JUDD
09 Director of Institutional Research .... Mrs. Anna PAVY
38 Director of Student Counseling .... Vacant
28 Director of Diversity .... Mr. John E. CHOWNING
92 Director of Honors Program .... Dr. Craig L. ROGERS
41 Director of Athletics .... Mr. Rusty HOLLINGSWORTH
40 Director of Bookstore .... Mrs. Donna WRIGHT
42 Director of Campus Ministries .... Mr. Edwin C. PAVY
13 Director of Computing/Communication .... Mr. Hermano QUEIROZ
37 Director of Financial Aid .... Ms. Chris TOLSON
29 Director of Alumni Relations .... Mrs. Paula SMITH
08 Director of Library Services .... Mr. John BURCH
15 Director of Personnel Services .... Mr. Terry VANMETER
18 Director of Maintenance .... Mr. Steve MORRIS
27 Director of News Information .... Mrs. Joan C. MCKINNEY
06 Director of Student Records .... Mrs. Rita A. CREASON
04 Secretary to the President .... Mrs. Kellie VAUGHN
96 Dir of Purchasing/Special Projects .... Vacant
88 Director of Custodial Services .... Mr. Bob STOTTS

Centre College (E)

600 W Walnut Street, Danville KY 40422-1394
County: Boyle FICE Identification: 001961
Unit ID: 156408
Telephone: (859) 238-5200 Carnegie Class: Bac/A&S
FAX Number: (859) 238-6977 Calendar System: Other
URL: www.centre.edu
Established: 1819 Annual Undergrad Tuition & Fees: $47,820
Enrollment: 1,388 Coed
Affiliation or Control: Independent Non-Profit IRS Status: 501(c)3
Highest Offering: Baccalaureate
Program: Liberal Arts And General; Teacher Preparatory
Accreditation: SC

01 President .... Dr. John A. ROUSH
05 Vice President & Dean of College .... Dr. Stephanie L. FABRITIUS
10 Vice Pres for Finance & Treasurer .... Mr. Robert L. KEASLER
26 Vice President College Relations .... Dr. Richard W. TROLLINGER
32 Vice Pres/Dean of Student Life .... Mr. Wm. Randy HAYS
30 Assoc VP Development/Alumni Affairs .... Mr. Shawn LYONS
43 Assoc VP for Legal Affs/Gift Plng .... Mr. James P. LEAHEY
53 Professor of Education .... Dr. Donna M. PLUMMER
28 Asst Vice Pres Diversity .... Vacant
07 Dean of Admissions & Financial Aid .... Mr. Robert M. NESMITH
20 Associate Dean of the College .... Dr. Beth GLAZIER-MCDONALD
38 Director of Counseling Services .... Ms. Ann E. GOODWIN
45 Asst to the President for Planning .... Dr. J. Patrick NOLTEMEYER
104 Director of International Programs .... Dr. Milton M. REIGELMAN
08 Director of Library Services .... Mr. Stanley R. CAMPBELL
04 Exec Assistant to the President .... Ms. Yvonne Y. MORLEY
37 Director of Financial Aid .... Mr. Kevin D. LAMB
06 Registrar .... Mr. Timothy P. CULHAN
15 Director Human Resources/Admin Svcs .... Mrs. Kay L. DRAKE
27 Director of Communications .... Dr. Michael P. STRYSICK
36 Director of Career Services .... Ms. Joy ASHER
39 Director Student Life & Housing .... Ms. Ann S. YOUNG
41 Director of Athletics & Recreation .... Mr. W. Bradley FIELDS
19 Co-Director of Public Safety .... Mr. Kevin S. MILBY
19 Co-Director of Public Safety .... Mr. Gary D. BUGG
09 Director of Institutional Research .... Mr. J. Patrick NOLTEMEYER
13 Director of Info Technology Service .... Mr. J. Keith FOWLKES
24 Director Ctr for Teaching/Learning .... Dr. Sarah E. LASHLEY
18 Director of Facilities Management .... Mr. D. Wayne KING
21 Controller .... Mr. R. Scott OWENS
42 College Chaplain .... Dr. Richard D. AXTELL
96 Dir Purchasing/Campus Interiors .... Ms. Ann T. SMITH
29 Director of Alumni Affairs .... Ms. Megan H. MILBY
57 Director Norton Center for Arts .... Mr. Steven A. HOFFMAN

Clear Creek Baptist Bible College (F)

300 Clear Creek Road, Pineville KY 40977-9754
County: Bell FICE Identification: 025356
Unit ID: 156417
Telephone: (606) 337-3196 Carnegie Class: Spec/Faith
FAX Number: (606) 337-2372 Calendar System: Semester
URL: www.ccbbc.edu
Established: 1926 Annual Undergrad Tuition & Fees: $6,724
Enrollment: 156 Coed
Affiliation or Control: Southern Baptist IRS Status: 501(c)3
Highest Offering: Baccalaureate
Program: Religious Emphasis
Accreditation: SC, BI

01 President .... Dr. Donnie S. FOX
05 Academic Dean .... Dr. Jay SULFRIDGE
32 Dean of Students .... Rev. Charlie GOODMAN
11 Dean of Administrative Affairs .... Mr. Jeremy ANDERSON
30 Dean of Institutional Advancement .... Rev. David WADE
08 Director of Library .... Mrs. Marge CUMMINGS
42 Christian Service Director .... Rev. Gerald SIMMONS
18 Director of Physical Plant .... Mr. Ronnie WASHAM
37 Director Financial Aid .... Mr. Sam RISNER
06 Registrar .... Mr. Jacob YATES
07 Director of Admissions .... Rev. Shannon BENEFIEL
26 Director of College Relations .... Rev. Richard L. WITHERITE
13 Director of Computer Services .... Mr. Shane KAHKOLA
56 Director of Distance Education .... Dr. Jay BARNETT

Daymar College Online (G)

4112 Fern Valley Road, Louisville KY 40219
Telephone: (502) 495-1040 Identification: 770615
Accreditation: ACICS

† Branch campus of Daymar College-Owensboro, Owensboro, KY.

Daymar College-Bellevue (H)

119 Fairfield Avenue, Bellevue KY 41073
Telephone: (859) 291-0800 Identification: 666390
Accreditation: ACICS

† Branch campus of Daymar College, Owensboro, KY.

Daymar College-Bowling Green (I)

2421 Fitzgerald Industrial Drive,
Bowling Green KY 42101-4071
Telephone: (270) 843-6750 Identification: 666439
Accreditation: ACICS

† Branch campus of Daymar Institute, Nashville, TN.

Daymar College-Madisonville (J)

1105 National Mine Drive, Madisonville KY 42431
Telephone: (270) 643-0312 Identification: 667079
Accreditation: ACICS

† Branch campus of Daymar College, Owensboro, KY.

Daymar College-Owensboro (K)

3361 Buckland Square, PO Box 22150,
Owensboro KY 42304-2150
County: Daviess FICE Identification: 009313
Unit ID: 157465
Telephone: (270) 926-4040 Carnegie Class: Assoc/PrivFP
FAX Number: (270) 685-4090 Calendar System: Quarter
URL: www.daymarcollege.edu
Established: 1963 Annual Undergrad Tuition & Fees: $17,000
Enrollment: 94 Coed
Affiliation or Control: Proprietary IRS Status: Proprietary
Highest Offering: Baccalaureate
Program: Technical Emphasis
Accreditation: ACICS

01 Area President .... Richard HORTWITZ
66 Director of Nursing .... Dr. Michael RAGER

Eastern Kentucky University (L)

521 Lancaster Avenue, Richmond KY 40475-3102
County: Madison FICE Identification: 001963
Unit ID: 156620
Telephone: (859) 622-1000 Carnegie Class: Master's L
FAX Number: (859) 622-1020 Calendar System: Semester
URL: www.eku.edu
Established: 1906 Annual Undergrad Tuition & Fees (In-State): $4,075
Enrollment: 16,305 Coed
Affiliation or Control: State IRS Status: 501(c)3
Highest Offering: Doctorate
Program: Occupational; Liberal Arts And General; Teacher Preparatory; Professional
Accreditation: SC, AAFCS, ADNUR, BUS, CAATE, CACREP, CAHIIM, CONST, CS, DIETD, DIETI, EMT, FEPAC, IFSAC, MLTAD, MT, MUS, NAIT, NRPA, NURSE, OT, PH, SP, SPAA, SW, TED

01 President .... Dr. Michael BENSON
05 Provost/Vice Pres Academic Affairs .... Dr. Janna VICE
32 Assoc VP/Dean of Students .... Ms. Kenna MIDDLETON
10 VP Financial Affs/Treasurer/Admin .... Mr. Barry POYNTER
30 Vice Pres University Advancement .... Mr. Nick PERLICK
84 Act VP Enrol Mgt/Mrktng/Univ Rels .... Mr. Brett MORRIS
45 Assoc VP University Programs .... Dr. Sara ZEIGLER
26 Asst VP Branding & Marketing .... Mr. Doug CORNETT
35 Exec Director Student Affairs .... Dr. Salome NNOROMELE
76 Dean Health Sciences .... Dr. Deborah WHITEHOUSE
49 Dean Arts & Sciences .... Dr. John WADE
50 Dean Business & Technology .... Dr. Thomas EREKSON
53 Dean Education .... Vacant
88 Dean Justice & Safety .... Dr. Victor KAPPELER
86 Exec Dir Government Relations .... Mr. David MCFADDIN
43 University Counsel .... Dr. Laurie CARTER
19 Chief of Police .... Mr. Brian MULLINS
08 Director Libraries .... Ms. Betina GARDNER
06 Registrar .... Ms. Tina DAVIS
27 Director Advising .... Mr. Benton SHIREY
07 Director Admissions .... Mr. Brett MORRIS
36 Director Career Services .... Mrs. Gladys MILLER
25 Director Sponsored Programs .... Mr. Gus BENSON
92 Director Honors Program .... Dr. David COLEMAN
09 Asst VP Inst Research/Effectiveness .... Ms. Tanlee WESSON
85 Director International Education .... Vacant
38 Director Counseling Center .... Dr. Jen C. WALKER
39 Exec Director Housing .... Mr. Billy MARTIN
88 Director Judicial Affairs/Disabled .... Mrs. Betsy BOHANNON
37 Dir Student Financial Assistance .... Mr. Bryan ERSLAN
23 Director Student Health Services .... Dr. Pradeep BOSE
40 Director Bookstore .... Mr. Timothy GOGNAT
15 Interim Director Equity/Inclusion .... Mr. Brandon WILLIAMS
90 Director Info Tech/Delivery Svcs .... Ms. Jean MARLOW
29 Asst VP Alumni/Donor Engagement .... Mrs. Kari MARTIN
109 Exec Dir Stdnt Life/Auxiliary Svcs .... Mr. Billy MARTIN
18 Director Facilities Services .... Mr. David WILLIAMS
28 Interim Chief Diversity Officer .... Mr. Sherwood THOMPSON
41 Athletic Director .... Mr. Stephen LOCHMUELLER
96 Director of Purchasing .... Ms. Lora SNIDER
42 Chaplain .... Dr. Patrick C. NNOROMELE
04 Admin Asst to the President .... Ms. Lisa KELLEY
04 Exec Asst to Pres/Asst Sec to BoR .... Mrs. Dreidre DE LEON

Frontier Nursing University (M)

195 School Street, Hyden KY 41749
County: Leslie FICE Identification: 030070
Unit ID: 156727
Telephone: (606) 672-2312 Carnegie Class: Spec/Health
FAX Number: (606) 672-3776 Calendar System: Quarter
URL: www.frontier.edu
Established: 1939 Annual Graduate Tuition & Fees: $16,640
Enrollment: 1,478 Coed
Affiliation or Control: Independent Non-Profit IRS Status: 501(c)3
Highest Offering: Doctorate; No Undergraduates
Program: Professional; Nursing Emphasis
Accreditation: SC, MIDWF, NUR

01 President & Dean .... Dr. Susan STONE
05 Associate Dean of Academic Affairs .... Dr. Anne COCKERHAM
66 Dean of Nursing .... Dr. Julie MARFELL
46 Associate Dean of Research .... Vacant
88 PM-DNP Program Director .... Dr. Susan YOUNT
88 Bridge Option Director .... Dr. Trish VOSS
37 Director of Financial Aid .... Ms. Rainie BOGGS

Galen College of Nursing (N)

1031 Zorn Avenue, Louisville KY 40207-1064
County: Jefferson FICE Identification: 030837
Unit ID: 156471
Telephone: (502) 410-6200 Carnegie Class: Assoc/PrivFP
FAX Number: (502) 568-1271 Calendar System: Quarter
URL: www.galencollege.edu
Established: 1989 Annual Undergrad Tuition & Fees: $17,866
Enrollment: 655 Coed
Affiliation or Control: Proprietary IRS Status: Proprietary
Highest Offering: Baccalaureate
Program: 2-Year Principally Bachelor's Creditable; Nursing Emphasis
Accreditation: SC

01 Chief Executive Officer .... Mr. Mark A. VOGT
05 Academic President .... Dr. Anne MCNAMARA
06 Director of Academic Records .... Ms. Jonda BRINNER
106 Dean of Online Programs .... Ms. Kathy BURLINGAME
66 ADN Program Director of Main Campus .... Dr. Constance COOPER
03 Senior VP .... Dr. Audria DENKER
11 VP of Operations and Reg Affairs .... Ms. Kathleen DWYER

84	VP of Enrollment Management	Vacant
66	Dean of Main Campus	Dr. Joan L. FREY
10	VP of Finance	Mr. Thomas DWYER
14	Director of Information Technology	Mr. Duane HELLUMS
20	Executive VP	Dr. Steve HYNDMAN
26	Director of Marketing	Ms. Anna KITSON
15	Director of Human Resources	Ms. Robin BERRY
66	PN Program Director of Main Campus	Ms. Lisa PEAK
37	Director of Financial Aid	Ms. Joni M. PENLAND
03	Executive VP and CAO	Mr. Joseph R. PETERS
13	VP of Technology and Planning	Mr. David RAY
108	Director of Inst Effectiveness	Dr. Carissa SHAFTO
07	Director of Admissions	Ms. Terri THOMAS

Georgetown College (A)

400 E College Street, Georgetown KY 40324-1696

County: Scott FICE Identification: 001964
Unit ID: 156745
Telephone: (502) 863-8000 Carnegie Class: Bac/A&S
FAX Number: (502) 868-8891 Calendar System: Semester
URL: www.georgetowncollege.edu
Established: 1829 Annual Undergrad Tuition & Fees: $34,280
Enrollment: 1,262 Coed
Affiliation or Control: Baptist IRS Status: 501(c)3
Highest Offering: Master's
Program: Liberal Arts And General
Accreditation: SC, CAATE, TED

01	President	Dr. Dwaine GREENE
05	Provost/Dean of the College	Dr. Rosemary ALLEN
10	Vice President/CFO/Treasurer	Mr. James A. MOAK, JR.
101	Asst to President/Board Secretary	Mr. Robin OLDHAM
30	VP Institutional Advancement	Dr. Todd RASBERRY
32	Dean of Students/Title IX Coord	Ms. Laura JOHNSON
84	Vice President for Enrollment	Ms. Michelle LYNCH
13	Assoc VP for Info Tech Services	Mr. Donald L. BLAKEMAN
26	Assoc VP for Comm & Marketing	Mr. Jim ALLISON
21	Controller	Mr. David WILHITE
88	Bursar	Ms. Marianne RIDDLE
06	Registrar	Ms. Winnie BRATCHER
88	Dir Ctr for Culturally Rel Pedagogy	Dr. Rebecca POWELL
15	Director of Human Resources	Ms. Tracie SHAPIRO
53	Dean of Education	Dr. Joy BOWERS-CAMPBELL
07	Director of Admissions	Vacant
37	Dir of Student Financial Planning	Ms. Tiffany H. JOHNSON
30	Director of Development	Ms. Lori MATTHEWS
09	Director of Institutional Research	Dr. David FORMAN
08	Director of Library Services	Mr. Benjamin RAWLINS
29	Director of Alumni Relations	Ms. Laura OWSLEY
41	Director of Athletics	Mr. Brian EVANS
88	Dir Comm/Mktg & Church Relations	Mr. H.K KINGKADE
36	Dir Graves Ctr for Calling & Career	Ms. Holly JAMES
19	Director Campus Safety	Mr. Dan BROWN
38	Director of Counseling/Health Svcs	Dr. Lloyd CLARK
18	Dir Facilities and Grounds	Mr. Bart HORNE
28	Director of Diversity Initiatives	Ms. Beth PURDY

Indiana Tech-Louisville (B)

11855 Commonwealth Drive, Louisville KY 40299
Telephone: (502) 708-2363 Identification: 770104
Accreditation: &NH

† Branch campus of Indiana Tech, Fort Wayne, IN.

Interactive College of Technology (C)

76 Caruthers Road, Newport KY 41071
Telephone: (859) 282-8989 Identification: 770535
Accreditation: COE

† Branch campus of Interactive College of Technology, Chamblee, GA.

ITT Technical Institute (D)

2473 Fortune Drive, Suite 180, Lexington KY 40509-4253
Telephone: (859) 246-3300 Identification: 666158
Accreditation: ACICS

† Branch campus of ITT Technical Institute, Indianapolis, IN.

ITT Technical Institute (E)

9500 Ormsby Station Road, Suite 100, Louisville KY 40223
Telephone: (502) 327-7424 Identification: 666540
Accreditation: ACICS

† Branch campus of ITT Technical Institute, Indianapolis, IN.

Kentucky Christian University (F)

100 Academic Parkway, Grayson KY 41143-2205

County: Carter FICE Identification: 001965
Unit ID: 157100
Telephone: (606) 474-3000 Carnegie Class: Bac/Diverse
FAX Number: (606) 474-3189 Calendar System: Semester
URL: www.kcu.edu
Established: 1919 Annual Undergrad Tuition & Fees: $18,970
Enrollment: 519 Coed
Affiliation or Control: Christian Churches And Churches of Christ
IRS Status: 501(c)3
Highest Offering: Master's
Program: Liberal Arts And General; Fine Arts Emphasis
Accreditation: SC, NURSE, SW

01	President/CEO	Dr. Jeff K. METCALF
05	VP of Academic Affairs	Dr. Marvin L. ELLIOTT
30	Director of Development	Mr. Tim DAVIS
88	Director of Church Relations	Mr. Jeff W. GREENE
06	Registrar	Mrs. Andrea L. STAMPER
13	Director of Campus Technology	Mr. Greg C. RICHARDSON
08	Library Director	Mrs. Naulayne R. ENDERS
108	Director Institutional Assessment	Mr. Kenneth L. BECK
32	Dean of Student Services	Mr. Ron W. ARNETT
42	Campus Minister	Mr. Larry W. MARSHALL
37	Director Financial Aid	Mrs. Jennie M. BENDER
15	Human Resource Officer	Mr. Terry L. YANKEY
38	Student Counseling Coordinator	Vacant
41	Athletic Director	Mr. Bruce W. DIXON
39	Director of Residence Services	Mr. Kris A. LANGSTAFF
18	Director of Facilities	Mr. John R. SEAGRAVES
29	Alumni Relations Officer	Mr. Jeff W. GREENE
58	Dean of the Graduate School	Dr. David A. FIENSY
07	Director of Enrollment Services	Miss Heather J. STACY
40	Manager of Retail Operations	Mrs. Patty J. SERHAL
105	Website Manager	Mr. David A. BENNETT
106	Specialist/Online-learning	Mrs. Terry A. GOLIGHTLY
10	Director of Business	Mr. Daniel R. WHITE

*Kentucky Community and Technical College System (G)

300 N Main Street, Versailles KY 40383-1245

County: Woodford FICE Identification: 006724
Unit ID: 157854
Telephone: (859) 256-3100 Carnegie Class: N/A
FAX Number: (859) 256-3119
URL: www.kctcs.edu

01	President	Dr. Jay BOX
00	Chancellor	Dr. Rhonda TRACY
05	VC Academic Affairs	Dr. Michael QUILLEN
10	Vice President	Mr. Wendell FOLLOWELL
13	Vice President	Mr. Paul CZARAPATA
30	Vice President	Mr. Timothy R. BURCHAM, CFRE
32	Vice President	Dr. Gloria MCCALL
103	VC Econ Dev/Workforce Solutions	Dr. Larry FERGUSON
09	VC Research and Analysis	Dr. Christina WHITFIELD
04	Sr Exec Assistant to the President	Ms. Beth HILLIARD

*Ashland Community and Technical College (H)

1400 College Drive, Ashland KY 41101-3617

County: Boyd FICE Identification: 001990
Unit ID: 156231
Telephone: (606) 326-2000 Carnegie Class: Assoc/Pub-R-M
FAX Number: (606) 326-2187 Calendar System: Semester
URL: www.ashland.kctcs.edu
Established: 1938 Annual Undergrad Tuition & Fees (In-State): $4,650
Enrollment: 3,345 Coed
Affiliation or Control: State IRS Status: 501(c)3
Highest Offering: Associate Degree
Program: Occupational; 2-Year Principally Bachelor's Creditable
Accreditation: SC, ADNUR, EMT, IFSAC, SURGT

02	President & CEO	Dr. Kay ADKINS
05	Dean of Academic Affairs	Dr. Janie KITCHEN
32	Dean of Student Affairs	Mr. Steven WOODBURN
10	Dean of Business Affairs	Ms. Karen J. BLEVINS
30	Dean Resource Dev/External Affairs	Ms. Willie MCCULLOUGH
09	Dean of Institutional Effectivemess	Mr. Steve FLOUHOUSE
86	Dean of Public Services	Mr. John MCGLONE
26	Director of Marketing	Ms. Allison GOBLE
08	Director of Library Services	Mr. Matthew ONION
06	Registrar	Mr. Kevin COOTS
13	Assoc Dean Information Technology	Mr. Farnoosh RAFIEE
28	Director of Cultural Diversity	Mr. Alvin BAKER
15	Director of Human Resources	Ms. Kellie ALLEN
25	Director of Grants & Contracts	Ms. Sarah DIAMOND BURROWAY
37	Director of Financial Aid	Ms. Robin LEWIS
36	Coordinator of Career Services	Ms. Nancy MENSHOUSE
79	Division Chair Humanities	Dr. Carol GREENE
76	Division Chair Health Sciences	Ms. Michelle NAPIER
81	Div Chair Math & Natural Sciences	Ms. Nicole GRIFFITH-GREEN

*Big Sandy Community and Technical College (I)

1 Bert T. Combs Drive, Prestonburg KY 41653-9502

County: Floyd FICE Identification: 001996
Unit ID: 157553
Telephone: (606) 886-3863 Carnegie Class: Assoc/Pub-R-M
FAX Number: (606) 886-2677 Calendar System: Semester
URL: www.bigsandy.kctcs.edu
Established: 1964 Annual Undergrad Tuition & Fees (In-State): $3,528
Enrollment: 4,659 Coed
Affiliation or Control: State IRS Status: 501(c)3
Highest Offering: Associate Degree
Program: Occupational; 2-Year Principally Bachelor's Creditable
Accreditation: SC, COARC, DH

02	President/CEO	Dr. Devin STEPHENSON
03	Vice Pres Institutional Services	Mr. Bobby MCCOOL
05	Provost	Dr. Nancy JOHNSON
35	Dean of Student Affairs	Mr. Jimmy WRIGHT
10	Chief Business Affairs Officer	Ms. Michelle MEEK
08	Director of Library Services	Ms. Kathy LOWE
15	Director of Human Resources	Ms. Bryen GOBLE
06	Registrar	Ms. Della PACK
37	Director of Financial Aid	Ms. Denise TRUSTY
09	Dean of Institutional Effectiveness	Dr. Chris DANIEL
13	Dean of Information Technology	Mr. John DOVE
18	Dir Facilities/Safety/Auxil Svcs	Mr. John HERALD
40	Bookstore Manager	Ms. Stephanie WEST
26	Public Relations	Mr. Joshua BALL
30	Director of Advancement	Mr. Randall ROBERTS
20	Dean of Academic Affairs	Ms. Myra ELLIOTT
28	Director of Cultural Diversity	Ms. Tina TERRY
103	Director Workforce Solutions	Ms. Kelli HALL
32	Mgr Transformation Communications	Ms. Melinda JUSTICE

*Bluegrass Community and Technical College (J)

470 Cooper Drive, Lexington KY 40506-0001

County: Fayette FICE Identification: 009707
Unit ID: 156392
Telephone: (859) 246-6200 Carnegie Class: Assoc/Pub-R-L
FAX Number: (859) 246-4664 Calendar System: Semester
URL: www.bluegrass.kctcs.edu
Established: 1965 Annual Undergrad Tuition & Fees (In-State): $3,516
Enrollment: 10,961 Coed
Affiliation or Control: State IRS Status: 501(c)3
Highest Offering: Associate Degree
Program: Occupational; 2-Year Principally Bachelor's Creditable
Accreditation: SC, ADNUR, COARC, DH, IFSAC, MAC, NMT, RAD, SURGT

02	President & CEO	Dr. Augusta A. JULIAN
13	VP of Information Technology	Mr. Ren BATES
05	Interim VP of Academics	Mr. Frances (Tri) ROBERTS
32	VP Student Dev/Enrollment Svcs	Dr. Palisa WILLIAMS RUSHIN
10	VP Finance & Administration	Ms. Lisa G. BELL
28	VP Multiculturalism & Inclusion	Ms. Charlene WALKER
56	VP Regional Campuses/Outreach	Vacant
20	Dean of Academic Affairs	Dr. Gregory FEENEY
20	Dean of Academic Affairs	Ms. Rebecca SIMMS
06	Registrar	Ms. Becky HARP-STEPHENS
37	Financial Aid Director	Ms. Runan PENDERGRAST
07	Admissions Director	Ms. Shelbie HUGLE
15	Associate VP Institutional Develop	Ms. Deborrah L. CATLETT
26	PR and Marketing Coordinator	Ms. Jennifer TYSON
38	Director of Advising & Assessment	Ms. Pamela BATES
30	Associate Vice President for Advanc	Ms. Laurel MARTIN
79	Assistant Dean Humanities	Ms. Angella KING
88	Asst Dean Natural Science	Ms. Tammy LILES
66	Assistant Dean Nursing	Ms. Susan HAYES
76	Assistant Dean Allied Health	Ms. Tammy LILES
81	Asst Dean Mathematics/Statistics	Ms. Jackie WISEMAN
77	Asst Dean Business/CIS	Ms. Debbie HOLT
72	Asst Dean Advanced Mfg and Trade	Mr. Kevin DUNN
83	Asst Dean Comm/Hist/Lang/Social Sci	Ms. Vicki WILSON
08	Director Learning Resources Center	Mr. Steve STONE
88	Asst Dean Adult Educ/Opportunity	Vacant
106	Assistant Dean Distance Learning	Mr. Ben WORTH
18	Director of Maintenance/Operations	Mr. Michael BALL
96	Director of Purchasing	Vacant

*Elizabethtown Community and Technical College (K)

600 College Street Road, Elizabethtown KY 42701

County: Hardin FICE Identification: 001991
Unit ID: 156648
Telephone: (270) 769-2371 Carnegie Class: Assoc/Pub-R-M
FAX Number: (270) 769-0736 Calendar System: Semester
URL: www.elizabethtown.kctcs.edu
Established: 1963 Annual Undergrad Tuition & Fees (In-State): $3,624
Enrollment: 7,353 Coed
Affiliation or Control: State IRS Status: 501(c)3
Highest Offering: Associate Degree
Program: Occupational; 2-Year Principally Bachelor's Creditable
Accreditation: SC, ADNUR, COARC, IFSAC, RAD

02	President	Dr. Thelma WHITE
05	Provost/CAO	Dr. Tiffany EVANS
32	Chief Student Affairs Officer	Dr. Dale BUCKLES
11	Chief Operations	Mr. Keith JOHNSON
12	Campus Education Center Director	Mr. Darrin POWELL
103	Dean of Workforce Development	Dr. Thomas DAVENPORT
10	Dean of Business Affairs	Mr. John WHITE
20	Dean of Instruction/Prof Develop	Ms. Sue FRENCH
08	Library Director	Ms. Ann THOMPSON
15	Director of Human Resources	Ms. Kris WOOD
06	Registrar	Mr. Bryan SMITH
13	Director of Information Technology	Mr. Chris LEE
37	Director of Financial Aid	Mr. Michael BARLOW
30	Chief Development	Mr. Ronald HARRELL
26	Director of Public Relations	Ms. Mary Jo KING
24	Learning Center Coordinator	Ms. Pam HARPER
36	Counselor	Ms. Sharon SPRATT
38	Counselor	Ms. Suzanne DARLAND
40	Bookstore Manager	Ms. Pamela BENTLEY

46 Assoc Dean of Inst Effectiveness ....Dr. Jack DILBECK
18 Maintenance/Operations Supervisor ....Mr. Charles COBB
57 Chair Div of Arts/Humanities ....Ms. Jacqueline HAWKINS
81 Chair Div of Biological Science ......Ms. Tiffany MCFALLS-SMITH
81 Chair Div of Physical Science ....Mr. Paul STURGEON
75 Chair Div Occupational Technology .... Mr. Mike HAZZARD
83 Chair Div Social & Behavioral Sci ....Ms. Ramona BARROW
28 Director of Diversity ....Ms. Felicia TOLIVER
109 Campus Administrative Coordinator ....Dr. David DONATHAN

*Gateway Community and Technical College (A)

500 Technology Way, Florence KY 41042

County: Boone FICE Identification: 005273
Unit ID: 157438
Telephone: (859) 441-4500 Carnegie Class: Assoc/Pub-S-MC
FAX Number: (859) 341-6859 Calendar System: Semester
URL: www.gateway.kctcs.edu
Established: 1961 Annual Undergrad Tuition & Fees (In-State): $4,410
Enrollment: 4,594 Coed
Affiliation or Control: State IRS Status: 501(c)3
Highest Offering: Associate Degree
Program: Occupational; 2-Year Principally Bachelor's Creditable
Accreditation: SC, IFSAC

02 Interim President/CEO ....Dr. Keith BIRD
88 Special Assistant to the Pres/CEO ....Mr. Jack KELLER
88 Special Assistant to the Pres/CEO ....Mr. Mike BAKER
04 Executive Assistant to President ....Ms. Sharon POORE
03 Exec VP of Strategic Initiatives ....Dr. Patricia GOODMAN
09 Associate VP for Knowledge Mgt .... Mr. Jeremy BERBERICH
05 VP Academic Affairs .... Dr. Teri VONHANDORF
20 Associate VP for Academic Affairs ....Vacant
49 Dean of Arts and Sciences ....Dr. Susan SANTOS
50 Dean of Business/IT/Prof Services .... Dr. Amy CARRINO
76 Dean of Health Professions ....Ms. Amber CARTER
72 Dean of Manufacturing & Technology ....Mr. Dee WRIGHT
75 Dean of Transportation Technologies ....Mr. Sam COLLIER
30 VP Devel & Strategic Partnerships ....Dr. Amber DECKER
32 VP Student Development ....Ms. Ingrid WASHINGTON
35 Associate VP for Student Dev ....Ms. Mallis GRAVES
38 Director of Counseling ....Ms. Tiffany MINARD
10 VP Admin & Business Affairs ....Mr. James YOUNGER
103 VP Corporate College ....Ms. Carissa SCHUTZMAN
84 Dean of Enrollment Services ....Mr. Andre WASHINGTON
06 Registrar ....Ms. Robin WRIGHT
15 Director of Human Resources ....Ms. Phyllis YEAGER
18 Director Maintenance & Operations ....Mr. George HALL
26 Director of Communications ....Ms. Michelle SJOGREN
37 Director of Financial Aid ....Ms. Zana SMITH
13 Director of Information Services ....Ms. Melissa SEARS
88 Director Early College Initiatives ....Ms. Shelby KRENTZ
08 Director Library/Information Svcs ....Ms. Denise FRITSCH
25 Director of Grants ....Vacant
27 Public Relations Coordinator ....Mr. Patrick LAMPING
105 Web Services Manager ....Mr. Jonathan WILBURN

*Hazard Community and Technical College (B)

One Community College Drive, Hazard KY 41701-2402

County: Perry FICE Identification: 006962
Unit ID: 156790
Telephone: (606) 436-5721 Carnegie Class: Assoc/Pub-R-M
FAX Number: (606) 439-2988 Calendar System: Semester
URL: www.hazard.kctcs.edu
Established: 1968 Annual Undergrad Tuition & Fees (In-State): $3,720
Enrollment: 3,479 Coed
Affiliation or Control: State IRS Status: 501(c)3
Highest Offering: Associate Degree
Program: Occupational; 2-Year Principally Bachelor's Creditable
Accreditation: SC, CAHIIM, DMS, IFSAC, PTAA, RAD, SURGT

02 President/CEO ....Dr. Stephen GREINER
05 Provost/Vice Pres of Academic Svcs ....Dr. Kathy SMOOT
32 Vice President of Student Affairs ....Ms. Germaine SHAFFER
10 Chief Financial Officer ....Ms. Connie WATTS
04 Asst to President Special Projects ....Ms. Delcie COMBS
13 Chief Information Officer ....Ms. Donna ROARK
15 Senior Director of Human Resources ....Ms. Vickie COMBS
21 Dean of Business Services ....Ms. Jackie HALL
08 Director Library Services ....Mrs. Cathy BRANSON
97 Dean General Education ....Ms. Leila SMITH
103 Dean Occup Tech & Workforce Sol ....Ms. Jennifer LINDON
76 Dean Allied Health Science Tech ....Ms. Anna NAPIER
56 Dean Distance Learning ....Ms. Ella STRONG
26 Director of Public Relations ....Mrs. Evelyn WOOD
37 Director of Financial Aid ....Mr. Charles ANDERSON, JR.
06 Registrar ....Ms. Libby PETERS
07 Director of Admissions ....Mr. Scott GROSS
108 Dir of Effect/Planning & Research ....Ms. Alexis MALEPEAI
18 Dir of Maintenance and Operations ....Mr. Stu FUGATE

*Henderson Community College (C)

2660 S Green Street, Henderson KY 42420-4699

County: Henderson FICE Identification: 001993
Unit ID: 156851
Telephone: (270) 827-1867 Carnegie Class: Assoc/Pub-R-M
FAX Number: (270) 831-9600 Calendar System: Semester
URL: www.henderson.kctcs.edu
Established: 1960 Annual Undergrad Tuition & Fees (In-State): $3,720
Enrollment: 2,000 Coed
Affiliation or Control: State IRS Status: 501(c)3
Highest Offering: Associate Degree
Program: Occupational; 2-Year Principally Bachelor's Creditable
Accreditation: SC, ADNUR, DH, MAC, MLTAD

02 President ....Dr. Kris WILLIAMS
05 Interim Chief Academic Officer ....Mr. Paul KASENOW
32 Chief Student Officer ....Mr. Keith SAYLES
10 Chief Business Affairs Officer ....Mr. Jerry H. GENTRY
08 Library Director ....Mr. Mike W. KNECHT
13 Chief Information Technology Ofcr ....Ms. Kimberley S. CONLEY
15 Director of Human Resources ....Ms. Doris J. LAKE
57 Director of Fine Arts Center ....Ms. Rachael BAAR
06 Assistant Registrar ....Ms. Sarah DONOHUE
20 Assoc Dean of Academics/Dir of Nurs .....Ms. Debbie WHITAKER
88 Dean Success Grants ....Ms. Pamala P. WILSON
28 Director of Cultural Diversity ....Mr. William DIXON
30 Chief Advancement Officer ....Ms. Jennifer PRESTON
09 Dir Institutional Research & Effect ....Mr. Brian MCMURTRAY
18 Maintenance/Oper Supervisor ....Mr. Lance CONYERS
35 Student Activities Coordinator ....Mr. Larry TUTT
36 Career Services Coordinator ....Ms. Angela WATSON
37 Director Financial Aid ....Mr. Andrew ZELLERS
84 Assoc Dean for Enrollment Mgmt ....Mr. Cary CONLEY
88 Professional Development Coord ....Ms. Katie GRIFFIS
49 Div Chair Liberal Arts/Prof Studies ....Ms. Sharon BURTON
76 Div Chair Allied Health ....Ms. Kim DEAN
81 Div Chair STEM .... Mr. Eugene PATSALIDES
04 Administrative Asst to President ....Ms. Malinda S. HUDSON
103 Dir Community/Workforce/Econ Dev .... Mr. Eric AHLBRAND

*Hopkinsville Community College (D)

720 North Drive, PO Box 2100,
Hopkinsville KY 42241-2100

County: Christian FICE Identification: 001994
Unit ID: 156860
Telephone: (270) 707-3700 Carnegie Class: Assoc/Pub-R-M
FAX Number: (270) 886-0237 Calendar System: Semester
URL: www.hopkinsville.kctcs.edu
Established: 1965 Annual Undergrad Tuition & Fees (In-State): $3,528
Enrollment: 3,568 Coed
Affiliation or Control: State IRS Status: 501(c)3
Highest Offering: Associate Degree
Program: Occupational; 2-Year Principally Bachelor's Creditable
Accreditation: SC, ADNUR

02 President ....Dr. Jay S. ALLEN
04 Exec Admin Asst to President ....Ms. Cheryle DYMEK
05 Chief Academic Affairs Officer ....Dr. Alissa YOUNG
06 Registrar ....Ms. Melissa STEVENSON
08 Library Services Director ....Ms. Ann NICHOLS
09 Dir Institutional Effectiveness ....Dr. Sara S. PHILLIPS
10 Chief Business Affairs Officer ....Mr. Jeff HORTON
12 Campus/Educ Center Director FTC ....Ms. Allisha LEE
13 Technology Solutions Director ....Mr. Terry DUNCAN
15 Human Resources Director ....Ms. Yvonne GLASMAN
18 Maintence/Operations Director ....Mr. Dan HAMBY
19 Safety and Security Director ....Vacant
21 Business Affairs Associate Dean ....Ms. Ann T. HOLLAND
26 Marketing & Communication Director ....Ms. Rena YOUNG
28 Cultural Diversity Director ....Ms. Tracey Y. FOLDEN
30 Chief Institutional Advancement Ofc ....Ms. Yvette EASTHAM
32 Chief Student Affairs Officer ....Dr. Jason D. WARREN
36 Career & Transfer Director ....Ms. Kanya ALLEN
37 Financial Aid Director ....Ms. Janet GUNTHER
38 Advising Center Director ....Ms. Deloria SCOTT
40 Bookstore Director .... Ms. Diane CUNNINGHAM
57 Arts and Sciences Division Chair ....Dr. Ken CASEY
72 Professional & Technical Studies .... Mr. Gregory BRIDGEMAN
76 Allied Health Div Chair ....Ms. Peggy I. BOZARTH
81 Mathmatics & Sciences Div Chair ....Mr. Ted H. WILSON
103 Chief CWED Officer ....Ms. Carol KIRVES

*Jefferson Community and Technical College (E)

109 E Broadway, Louisville KY 40202-2000

County: Jefferson FICE Identification: 006961
Unit ID: 156921
Telephone: (502) 213-5333 Carnegie Class: Assoc/Pub-U-MC
FAX Number: (502) 213-2115 Calendar System: Semester
URL: www.jefferson.kctcs.edu
Established: 1967 Annual Undergrad Tuition & Fees (In-State): $4,410
Enrollment: 13,680 Coed
Affiliation or Control: State IRS Status: 501(c)3
Highest Offering: Associate Degree
Program: Occupational; 2-Year Principally Bachelor's Creditable
Accreditation: SC, ACFEI, ADNUR, CAHIIM, COARC, #DMS, IFSAC, MAC, MLTAD, OTA, PTAA, RAD, SURGT

02 Interim President ....Dr. Gwendolyn G. JOSEPH
05 Provost/Chief Academic Affairs
Ofcr ....Dr. Diane CALHOUN-FRENCH
10 Chief Business Officer ....Ms. Norma NORTHERN
20 Int Dean Academic Affs Tech Pgms ....Dr. Telly SELLARS
20 Dean Academic Affs Downtown ....Dr. Randy DAVIS
20 Dean Academic Affairs Southwest ....Vacant
32 Dean of Student Affairs Southwest ....Dr. Denise GRAY
32 Dean Student Affairs Downtown ....Dr. Laura SMITH
21 Associate Dean of Business Affairs ....Mr. Bill NOWAK
08 Library Services Director ....Ms. Sheree WILLIAMS
13 Director Information Technology ....Mr. Thomas ROGERS
09 VP of Institutional Research ....Dr. Mary C. JONES
06 Registrar ....Ms. Amanda TINDALL
28 Director Cultural Diversity ....Ms. Lea DORSEY-MUCKER
26 VP of Marketing/Public Relations ....Ms. Lisa BROSKY
15 Director of Human Resources ....Ms. Toni WHALEN
18 Facilities Director ....Mr. Craig TURPIN
37 Director of Financial Aid ....Ms. Angela JOHNSON
30 Dir Inst Advance/Development Coord ....Ms. Lisa BROSKY
103 VP Workforce Sol CE/CS/Bus/
Industry ....Ms. Mary Ann HYLAND-MURR
07 Director of Admissions ....Vacant
38 Director of Student Counseling ....Dr. Telly SELLARS
96 Director of Purchasing ....Ms. Pamela DUMM
12 Director of Carrollton Campus ....Ms. Susan CARLISLE
12 Director of Shelby Campus ....Dr. John WIELAND
12 Director of Bullitt County Campus ....Ms. Donna MILLER
44 Manager of Advancement ....Ms. Karla HALL
24 Learning Center Coord Downtown ....Ms. Reneau WAGGONER
79 Chairperson Humanities Southwest ....Ms. Meg MATHENY
50 Chairperson Business Downtown ....Dr. Pamela BESSER
65 Div Chair Natural Sci Downtown ....Ms. Kathy LOWERY
66 Dean Nursing/Allied Health ....Dr. Carolyn O'DANIEL
76 Chair Allied Health Jefferson Tech ....Ms. Eva OLTMAN
83 Div Chair Behav/Soc Sci Downtown ....Mr. Charlie MCCOMBS
83 Chair Behav/Soc Sci Southwest ....Ms. Cathy WRIGHT
79 Chairperson Humanities Downtown ....Ms. Marlisa AUSTIN
81 Chrpsn Natural Science Southwest ....Mr. Charlie PURVIS
72 Chair Technology/Related Sci-SW ....Mr. Bruce JOST
72 Chair Technology & Industry ....Mr. Andrew KORNOWSKI

*Madisonville Community College (F)

2000 College Drive, Madisonville KY 42431-9199

County: Hopkins FICE Identification: 009010
Unit ID: 157304
Telephone: (270) 824-8562 Carnegie Class: Assoc/Pub-R-M
FAX Number: (270) 824-1866 Calendar System: Semester
URL: www.madisonville.kctcs.edu
Established: 1968 Annual Undergrad Tuition & Fees (In-State): $3,552
Enrollment: 4,434 Coed
Affiliation or Control: State IRS Status: 501(c)3
Highest Offering: Associate Degree
Program: Occupational; 2-Year Principally Bachelor's Creditable
Accreditation: SC, ADNUR, COARC, IFSAC, MLTAD, OTA, PTAA, RAD, SURGA, SURGT

02 President ....Dr. Judith L. RHOADS
05 Chief Academic Officer ....Dr. Deborah M. COX
10 Chief Business Affairs Officer ....Mr. Ray GILLASPIE
32 Chief Student Affairs Officer ....Dr. Jay V. PARRENT
72 Division Chair Applied Technology ....Mr. David ALSIP
66 Div Chr Nursing/Related Tech ....Ms. Shannon ALLEN
79 Div Chr Humanities/Related Tech ....Dr. Mary B. WERNER
83 Div Chr Social Science/Related Tech ....Ms. Natalie F. COOPER
81 Div Chr Mathematics and Sciences ....Dr. John D. LOWBRIDGE
76 Div Chr Allied Health/Related Tech ......Ms. Stephanie A. TAYLOR
08 Director of Library Services ....Ms. Cherry L. BERGES
06 Registrar ....Ms. Tiffanie WITT
15 Director of Human Resources ....Ms. May F. WRIGHT
36 Director of Counseling Services ....Ms. Cathy A. VAUGHAN
30 Director of Advancement ....Mr. Chris WOODALL
37 Director of Financial Aid ....Ms. Martha PHELPS
26 Public Relations Director ....Ms. Joyce RIGGS
56 Extended Campus Director ....Dr. George G. HUMPHREYS
25 Dir Grants/Planning & Effectiveness ... Mr. David A. SCHUERMER
28 Director of Cultural Diversity ....Mr. James H. BOWLES
103 Director Workforce Solutions ....Mr. Mike DAVENPORT
20 Dean of Academic Affairs ....Ms. Lisa A. HOWERTON
21 Dean of Business Affairs ....Mr. Michael L. JOHNSON
40 Bookstore Manager ....Ms. Sonya L. BURNS
84 Director of Enrollment Management ....Ms. Aimee J. WILKERSON

*Maysville Community and Technical College (G)

1755 US Highway 68, Maysville KY 41056-8910

County: Mason FICE Identification: 006960
Unit ID: 157331
Telephone: (606) 759-7141 Carnegie Class: Assoc/Pub-R-M
FAX Number: (606) 759-7176 Calendar System: Semester
URL: www.maysville.kctcs.edu
Established: 1966 Annual Undergrad Tuition & Fees (In-State): $3,624
Enrollment: 3,478 Coed
Affiliation or Control: State IRS Status: 501(c)3
Highest Offering: Associate Degree
Program: Occupational; 2-Year Principally Bachelor's Creditable
Accreditation: SC, IFSAC, MAC

02 President ....Dr. Steve VACIK
05 Provost ....Dr. Juston PATE
10 Chief Finance & Facilities Officer ....Mr. George A. JONES
84 Chief Ofcr Enrollment/Student Svc ....Ms. Jessica KERN
20 Assoc Dean Academic Support Svc ....Dr. Dana CALLAND
09 Assoc Dean Institutional Rsch/Plng ....Ms. Pam STAFFORD
08 Director Library Services ....Ms. Sonja EADS
13 Director Information Technology ....Mr. Henry JEFFERSON
30 Dir Resource Development/Foundation ....Ms. Cara CLARKE
103 Chief Officer Workforce Solutions ....Ms. Barbara CAMPBELL
37 Director Student Financial Aid ....Ms. Sandy POWER
06 Registrar ....Ms. Lori GAUNCE

26 Dir Marketing & Public Relations ... Ms. Jessica KERN
28 Director of Diversity ... Ms. Millicent HARDING
15 Director of Human Resources ... Ms. Sandi L. ESTILL
25 Director Grants & Contracts ... Ms. Andrea CALLAND
106 Coordinator Distance Learning ... Ms. Kim SPARKS
20 Coordinator of Academic Programs ... Mr. Stanley CLICK
50 Div Chr Business/Info Technologies ... Ms. Darla HUNT
49 Div Chair Liberal Arts/Education ... Ms. Kathleen MELLENKAMP
81 Div Chair Math/Science/Agriculture ... Dr. Angela FULTZ
66 Division Chair of Health Sciences ... Ms. Deborah NOLDER
72 Division Chair Industrial Tech ... Mr. Stanley W. CLICK

*Owensboro Community and Technical College (A)

4800 New Hartford Road, Owensboro KY 42303-1899
County: Daviess FICE Identification: 030345
Unit ID: 247940
Telephone: (270) 686-4400 Carnegie Class: Assoc/Pub-R-M
FAX Number: (270) 686-4496 Calendar System: Semester
URL: www.octc.kctcs.edu
Established: 1986 Annual Undergrad Tuition & Fees (In-State): $3,720
Enrollment: 4,162 Coed
Affiliation or Control: State IRS Status: 501(c)3
Highest Offering: Associate Degree
Program: Occupational; 2-Year Principally Bachelor's Creditable
Accreditation: **SC**, ACBSP, EMT, IFSAC, RAD, SURGT

02 President ... Dr. Scott WILLIAMS
04 Assistant to the President ... Ms. Kittridge MIDKIFF
05 Interim VP of Academic Affairs ... Mr. Mike RODGERS
32 VP of Student Affairs ... Mr. Kevin BEARDMORE
30 VP Institutional Advancement ... Mr. Larry S. MILLER
10 VP of Business Affairs ... Ms. Sarah PRICE
13 VP Information Technology ... Mr. James HARTZ
103 VP Workforce Solutions ... Ms. Cynthia FIORELLA
35 Assoc Dean of Student Affairs ... Ms. Sandy CARDEN
08 Library Services Director ... Ms. Donna ABELL
06 Registrar ... Ms. Sandy CARDEN
15 Director of Human Resources ... Ms. Victoria HOHIEMER
09 Director of Institutional Research ... Mr. Kevin BEARDMORE
29 Dir Advancement/Alumni Relations ... Vacant
37 Financial Aid Director ... Ms. Bernice AYER
26 Director of Public Relations ... Ms. Bernadette TOYE-HALE
28 Director of Diversity ... Mr. Lewatis MCNEAL
38 Director Student Counseling ... Ms. Barbara TIPMORE
84 Director Enrollment Management ... Mr. Kevin BEARDMORE
96 Director of Purchasing ... Ms. Sarah PRICE
24 Dir of Teaching & Learning Center ... Vacant
40 Bookstore Manager ... Ms. Sonya SOUTHARD
88 TV Production Manager ... Mr. John BRYENTON
07 Senior Admissions Advisor ... Ms. Linda CALHOUN
36 Career Resource/Placemnt Ctr Coord ... Ms. Katie BALLARD
79 Associate Dean Humanities ... Dr. Julia LEDFORD
83 Assoc Dean Soc Sci/Bus/Public Svc ... Dr. Marc MALTBY
81 Assoc Dean Math/Sci/Allied Health ... Dr. Veena SALLAN
75 Assoc Dean Advanced Technologies ... Mr. Dean AUTRY
66 Associate Dean Nursing ... Ms. Terri LANHAM
88 Assc Dean Personal Svc/Skill Trades ... Mr. Mike RODGERS
20 Assoc Dean Academic Affairs ... Dr. Stacy EDDS-ELLIS
09 Coord Institutional Effectiveness ... Ms. Joy BOWLDS
19 Director Security/Safety ... Mr. Jeff WILLIAMS

*Somerset Community College (B)

808 Monticello Street, Somerset KY 42501-2973
County: Pulaski FICE Identification: 001997
Unit ID: 157711
Telephone: (877) 629-9722 Carnegie Class: Assoc/Pub-R-L
FAX Number: N/A Calendar System: Semester
URL: somerset.kctcs.edu
Established: 1965 Annual Undergrad Tuition & Fees (In-State): $3,456
Enrollment: 7,504 Coed
Affiliation or Control: State IRS Status: 501(c)3
Highest Offering: Associate Degree
Program: Occupational; 2-Year Principally Bachelor's Creditable
Accreditation: **SC**, ADNUR, COARC, IFSAC, MLTAD, PTAA, #RAD, SURGT

02 President/CEO ... Dr. Jo MARSHALL
05 Provost ... Dr. Tony L. HONEYCUTT
10 Chief Business Affairs Officer ... Dr. Timothy ZIMMERMAN
11 Chief Operations Officer ... Mr. Larry ABBOTT
49 Dean of Arts and Sciences ... Vacant
76 Dean for Health Sciences ... Ms. Nancy L. POWELL
88 Dean of Applied Technology ... Mr. Roger L. ANGEVINE
09 Dir of Institutional Effectiveness ... Dr. Clint HAYES
32 Dean of Student Affairs ... Ms. Tracy L. CASADA
106 Assoc Dean for Distance Education ... Ms. Linda D. BOURNE
103 Chief Cmty Wkfc & Economic Dev Ofc ... Ms. Alesa JOHNSON
79 Assoc Dean Humanities/Fine Arts/SS ... Mr. Jon BURLEW
83 Assoc Dean Math/Natural Science ... Dr. Clint R. HAYES
88 Assoc Dean Const/Manuf/Trans ... Mr. Daniel C. BURNETT
50 Assoc Dean Bus/IT/Crim Just/Ed/ Cons ... Ms. Lois A. MCWHORTER
88 Dean Academic Support Services ... Mr. Bruce GOVER
30 Dir of Institutional Advancement ... Ms. Cindy D. CLOUSE
20 Assoc Dean for Learning ... Vacant
37 Director of Financial Aid ... Mr. Daniel PATTERSON
06 Registrar ... Ms. Paula J. LATHAM
15 Director of Human Resources ... Ms. Jill N. MEECE
26 Director of Public Relations ... Ms. Cindy D. CLOUSE
28 Director of Cultural Diversity ... Ms. Elaine WILSON

12 Director of McCreary Center ... Mr. Steve HAMMONS
12 Director of Clinton Center ... Ms. Judy TALLENT
12 Director of Casey Center ... Ms. Judy SAPP
12 Director of Russell Center ... Ms. Winfrey BATES

*Southcentral Kentucky Community and Technical College (C)

1845 Loop Drive, Bowling Green KY 42101-9202
County: Warren FICE Identification: 005271
Unit ID: 156338
Telephone: (270) 901-1000 Carnegie Class: Assoc/Pub-R-M
FAX Number: (270) 901-1145 Calendar System: Semester
URL: www.bowlinggreen.kctcs.edu
Established: 1939 Annual Undergrad Tuition & Fees (In-State): $3,720
Enrollment: 4,115 Coed
Affiliation or Control: State IRS Status: 501(c)3
Highest Offering: Associate Degree
Program: Occupational; 2-Year Principally Bachelor's Creditable; Technical Emphasis
Accreditation: **SC**, ACFEI, COARC, DMS, IFSAC, RAD, SURGT

02 President & CEO ... Dr. Phillip W. NEAL
05 Provost ... Dr. Maggie SHELTON
32 Vice President Student Success ... Vacant
10 Vice President Finance/Admin ... Mr. Chris CUMENS
31 Int Vice Pres Outreach/Cmty Dev ... Dr. James B. MCCASLIN
06 Registrar ... Ms. Brooke JUSTICE
15 Director of Human Resources ... Ms. Sherri L. FORESTER
26 Director of Public Relations ... Mr. Mark D. BROOKS
30 Director of Inst Advancement ... Ms. Donna P. MARTIN
37 Director of Financial Aid ... Ms. Jennifer WELLS
09 Director Instituion Effectiveness ... Mr. Mark GARRETT

*Southeast Kentucky Community and Technical College (D)

700 College Road, Cumberland KY 40823-1099
County: Harlan FICE Identification: 001998
Unit ID: 157739
Telephone: (606) 589-2145 Carnegie Class: Assoc/Pub-R-M
FAX Number: (606) 589-3175 Calendar System: Semester
URL: www.southeast.kctcs.edu
Established: 1960 Annual Undergrad Tuition & Fees (In-State): $3,624
Enrollment: 3,660 Coed
Affiliation or Control: State IRS Status: 501(c)3
Highest Offering: Associate Degree
Program: Occupational; 2-Year Principally Bachelor's Creditable
Accreditation: **SC**, ADNUR, COARC, FUSER, MLTAD, PNUR, PTAA, #RAD, SURGT

02 President ... Dr. Lynn MOORE
05 Chief Academic Officer ... Dr. Wheeler CONOVER
30 VP Advancement ... Mr. Scott SHERMAN
15 Human Resources Director ... Ms. Billie FRANKS
08 Head Librarian ... Mr. Warren GRAY
13 Director of Information Technology ... Mr. Merrill GALLOWAY
28 Director of Diversity ... Ms. Carolyn SUNDY
32 Chief Student Affairs Officer ... Ms. Rebecca PARROTT
10 VP & Chief Financial Officer ... Ms. Angela SIMPSON
07 Director of Admissions ... Ms. Veria BALDWIN
37 Coordinator Financial Aid ... Ms. Charlotte LOCKABY

*West Kentucky Community and Technical College (E)

4810 Alben Barkley Drive, Paducah KY 42002-7380
County: McCracken FICE Identification: 001979
Unit ID: 157483
Telephone: (270) 554-9200 Carnegie Class: Assoc/Pub-R-L
FAX Number: (270) 554-6217 Calendar System: Semester
URL: www.westkentucky.kctcs.edu
Established: 1909 Annual Undergrad Tuition & Fees (In-State): $4,650
Enrollment: 6,505 Coed
Affiliation or Control: State IRS Status: 501(c)3
Highest Offering: Associate Degree
Program: Occupational; 2-Year Principally Bachelor's Creditable
Accreditation: **SC**, ACBSP, ACFEI, ADNUR, DA, DMS, IFSAC, MLTAD, PNUR, PTAA, RAD, SURGT

02 President ... Dr. Barbara VEAZEY
103 VP of Workforce Solutions ... Mr. Jim PAPE
05 VP of Academic Affairs ... Dr. Tena PAYNE
32 VP of Student Development ... Dr. Belinda DALTON-RUSSELL
11 VP of Administrative Services ... Mr. John CARRICO
88 VP Learning Initiatives ... Ms. Sherry ANDERSON
45 VP Institutional Development ... Dr. Steve FREEMAN
10 VP Business Affairs ... Ms. Susan GRAVES
08 Library Services Director ... Mr. Ken BRADSHAW
37 Interim Financial Aid Director ... Ms. Angel RHODES
26 Public Relations Director ... Ms. Janett BLYTHE
13 Director Information Technology ... Ms. Ruby RODGERS
15 Director Human Resources ... Ms. Bridget CANTER
30 Dir Institutional Advancement ... Ms. Ashley WRIGHT
40 Bookstore Manager ... Mr. Todd MITCHELL
06 Registrar/Dir of Admissions ... Ms. Jess PUFFENBARGER
84 Dean of Enrollment ... Mr. Nate SLATON
35 Student Activities Coordinator ... Ms. Amy ELMORE
79 Dean Humanities/Fine Arts/Soc Sci ... Ms. Sharla KRUPANSKY
66 Dean Nursing Division ... Ms. Shari GHOLSON

50 Dean Business/Comp Related Tech Div ... Ms. Tammy POTTER
76 Dean Allied Health Division ... Ms. Peggy BLOCK
75 Dean Applied Tech Division ... Ms. Stephanie MILLIKEN
81 Dean Science & Math Division ... Dr. Karen HLINKA
97 Dean Transition Education Div ... Ms. Maria FLYNN
09 Associate VP of IE ... Dr. Renea AKIN
04 Administrative Asst to President ... Ms. Barbara MAXEY
19 Director Security/Safety ... Mr. David WALLACE

Kentucky Mountain Bible College (F)

855 Highway 541, Jackson KY 41339
County: Breathitt FICE Identification: 030021
Unit ID: 157030
Telephone: (606) 693-5000 Carnegie Class: Spec/Faith
FAX Number: (606) 693-4884 Calendar System: Semester
URL: www.kmbc.edu
Established: 1931 Annual Undergrad Tuition & Fees: $7,460
Enrollment: 84 Coed
Affiliation or Control: Independent Non-Profit IRS Status: 501(c)3
Highest Offering: Baccalaureate
Program: 2-Year Principally Bachelor's Creditable; Liberal Arts And General; Religious Emphasis
Accreditation: **BI**

01 President ... Dr. Philip E. SPEAS
05 Academic Dean/Exec Vice Pres ... Rev. Thomas H. LORIMER
10 Chief Business Manager ... Ms. Joy PAUL
32 Dean of Student Affairs ... Mr. Jim NELSON
13 Director IT ... Mr. Stephen A. LORIMER
08 Head Librarian ... Ms. Patricia A. BOWEN
06 Registrar ... Dr. Richard E. ENGLEHARDT
07 Chief Admissions Counselor ... Mr. David W. LORIMER
37 Director Student Financial Aid ... Ms. Rosita MARSHALL
26 Dir PR/Foreign Stdnts/Dean of Men ... Mr. James H. NELSON
34 Dean of Women ... Ms. Wanda SPEAS
18 Chief Facilities/Physical Plant ... Mr. Jonathan MATHES
20 Associate Academic Officer ... Mr. David PAUL
29 Director of Alumni Relations ... Ms. Donna WOODRING
106 Dir Online Education/E-learning ... Mr. Jason GOBEN

Kentucky State University (G)

400 E Main Street, Frankfort KY 40601-2355
County: Franklin FICE Identification: 001968
Unit ID: 157058
Telephone: (502) 597-6000 Carnegie Class: Bac/A&S
FAX Number: (502) 597-6490 Calendar System: Semester
URL: www.kysu.edu
Established: 1886 Annual Undergrad Tuition & Fees (In-State): $7,364
Enrollment: 1,895 Coed
Affiliation or Control: State IRS Status: 501(c)3
Highest Offering: Doctorate
Program: Liberal Arts And General; Teacher Preparatory; Business Emphasis
Accreditation: **SC**, ACBSP, ADNUR, MUS, NUR, SPAA, SW, TED

01 President ... Dr. Raymond M. BURSE
05 VP Academic Affairs ... Dr. Beverly L. DOWNING
10 VP for Business Affairs ... Mr. Curtis E. CREAGH
32 VP Student Affairs ... Dr. Vernell A. BENNETT
30 Interim VP External Relations & Dev ... Mr. Max A. MAXWELL
43 General Counsel ... Ms. Lori A. DAVIS
13 Interim Chief Information Officer ... Ms. Wendy D. DIXIE
45 Special Asst to Pres Strategic Plan ... Ms. Melinda A. IMPELLIZZERI
20 Dean of the University ... Dr. Lorna L. SHAW
19 Asst to Pres for Risk and Police ... Mr. George R. BAKER
06 Interim Registrar ... Ms. Yolanda C. BENSON
07 Director of Admissions ... Vacant
25 Associate VP Grants Sponsored Pgm ... Dr. Mary W. SPOR
21 Assistant VP Business Affairs ... Mr. Paul S. EDWARDS
47 Assoc VP Land Grant & Dean CAFSS ... Dr. Teferi D. TSEGAYE
27 Assistant to the VP Public Relation ... Ms. Felicia Y. LEWIS
18 Acting Facilities Director ... Mr. Russell L. SMITH
15 Director Human Resource Services ... Mr. Gary A. MEISELES
37 Director Student Financial Aid ... Ms. Victoria G. OWENS
41 Interim Director Athletics ... Mr. Harry O. STINSON, III
08 Director Library ... Ms. Sheila A. STUCKEY
96 Purchasing Manager ... Ms. Tonya Y. MONTGOMERY
58 Graduate Studies Director ... Dr. James B. OBIELODAN
39 Director Residence Life ... Vacant
23 Director Health Services ... Ms. Floarine A. WILSON
36 Director Counsel & Placement ... Mr. Ronald BANKS
29 Director Alumni Affairs ... Mr. Wendell C. THOMAS
56 Associate Ext Admin ... Dr. Javiette V. SAMUEL
09 Int Dir Institutional Research Eff ... Ms. Yuliana SUSANTO
46 Associate Director Research ... Dr. Kirk W. POMPER
109 Interim Director Auxiliary Entrprs ... Ms. Kathy O. PEALE
106 Academic Technology Trainer ... Ms. Jennifer P. MILES
16 Asst Director HR Disability Srvcs ... Ms. Corlia H. LOGSDON
50 Chair Business ... Dr. Abdul M. TURAY
53 Chair Education ... Dr. Sylvia A. MASON
57 Interim Chair Fine Arts ... Dr. Roosevelt O. SHELTON
66 Chair Nursing ... Dr. Indira D. TYLER
77 Chair Computer Sciences ... Dr. Chi SHEN
80 Interim Chair Public Adminstration ... Dr. Stephen GRAHAM-HILL
81 Chair Mathematics ... Dr. Fariba BIGDELI-JAHED
83 Acting Chair Social Sciences ... Dr. Tierra M. FREEMAN
92 Chair Whitney Young Honors ... Dr. Thomas J. MCPARTLAND

Kentucky Wesleyan College (A)

3000 Frederica Street, Owensboro KY 42301
County: Daviess FICE Identification: 001969
Unit ID: 157076
Telephone: (270) 926-3111 Carnegie Class: Bac/Diverse
FAX Number: (270) 926-3112 Calendar System: Semester
URL: www.kwc.edu
Established: 1858 Annual Undergrad Tuition & Fees: $22,230
Enrollment: 709 Coed
Affiliation or Control: United Methodist IRS Status: 501(c)3
Highest Offering: Baccalaureate
Program: Liberal Arts And General; Teacher Preparatory
Accreditation: SC, IACBE

01 President ... Dr. Bart DARRELL
05 VP Acad Affairs/Dean of the College ... Dr. Paula DEHN
10 Vice President for Finance ... Ms. Cindra K. STIFF
32 VP of Student Svcs/Dean of Students ... Mr. Scott E. KRAMER
31 Vice Pres External Affairs ... Ms. Jodie MAJORS
13 Dir Information Tech Services ... Mr. Kevin PAYNE
30 Vice President for Development ... Mr. Thomas W. KEITH
07 Director of Admissions ... Mr. Rashad SMITH
06 Registrar ... Ms. Lou Ann BOWERSOX
09 Dir of Institutional Effective/Rsch ... Mr. Randy PETERSON
15 Director of Human Resources ... Mrs. Linda B. KELLER
37 Director of Financial Aid ... Ms. Samantha HAYS
89 Director of the PLUS Center ... Ms. Donna HANLEY
08 Director of Library Learning Center . Mrs. Patricia G. MCFARLING
41 Director of Athletics ... Mr. Rob MALLORY
21 Controller ... Ms. Stephanie WILLIAMS
26 Director of Public Relations ... Ms. Kathy RUTHERMAN
42 KWC Chaplain/Dir Church Relations ... Mr. Kent LEWIS
30 Dir Development/Donor Rels ... Mr. M. Blake HARRISON

Lexington Theological Seminary (B)

230 Lexington Green Circle, Ste 300, Lexington KY 40503
County: Fayette FICE Identification: 001971
Unit ID: 157207
Telephone: (859) 252-0361 Carnegie Class: Spec/Faith
FAX Number: (859) 281-6042 Calendar System: Semester
URL: www.lextheo.edu
Established: 1865 Annual Graduate Tuition & Fees: $12,340
Enrollment: 87 Coed
Affiliation or Control: Christian Church (Disciples Of Christ)
IRS Status: 501(c)3
Highest Offering: Doctorate; No Undergraduates
Program: Professional; Religious Emphasis
Accreditation: THEOL

01 President ... Dr. Charisse L. GILLETT
05 VP Academic Affairs/Dean ... Dr. Richard WEIS
30 Vice President for Advancement ... Mr. Mark V. BLANKENSHIP
10 Chief Financial Officer ... Mrs. Karen C. WAGERS
06 Registrar ... Ms. Windy KIDD
08 Librarian ... Ms. Dolores YILIBUW
13 Director Information Services ... Mr. Ben WYATT
07 Director Admission ... Rev. Erin CASH
15 Director Personnel Services ... Ms. Karen C. WAGERS
18 Chief Facilities/Physical Plant ... Ms. Karen C. WAGERS
29 Director Alumni Relations ... Mr. Mark V. BLANKENSHIP
37 Director Student Financial Aid ... Ms. Windy KIDD
96 Director of Purchasing ... Ms. Robin VARNER

Lindsey Wilson College (C)

210 Lindsey Wilson Street, Columbia KY 42728-1298
County: Adair FICE Identification: 001972
Unit ID: 157216
Telephone: (270) 384-2126 Carnegie Class: Master's M
FAX Number: (270) 384-8200 Calendar System: Semester
URL: www.lindsey.edu
Established: 1903 Annual Undergrad Tuition & Fees: $22,920
Enrollment: 2,650 Coed
Affiliation or Control: United Methodist IRS Status: 501(c)3
Highest Offering: Doctorate
Program: 2-Year Principally Bachelor's Creditable; Liberal Arts And General; Teacher Preparatory
Accreditation: SC, CACREP, IACBE, NURSE, TED

01 President ... Dr. William T. LUCKEY, JR.
00 Chancellor ... Dr. John B. BEGLEY
05 Vice President Academic Affairs ... Dr. Bettie C. STARR
10 Vice President Administration ... Dr. Mark COLEMAN
30 Vice President Advancement ... Mr. Kevin A. THOMPSON
04 Executive Assistant ... Mrs. Nancy SINCLAIR
32 Vice Pres Student Svcs/Enroll Mgmt ... Dr. Dean ADAMS
37 VP Educ Outreach/Stdnt Finan Svcs ... Mrs. Denise G. FUDGE
35 Dean of Students ... Mr. Christopher SCHMIDT
20 Associate Academic Dean ... Vacant
88 Dean of Chapel ... Dr. Terry W. SWAN
07 Dean of Admissions ... Mrs. Traci M. POOLER
07 Director of Admissions ... Mrs. Charity F. FERGUSON
55 Director of Evening College ... Mrs. Regina HAUGEN
41 Athletic Director ... Mr. Willis POOLER, III
06 Registrar ... Mrs. Sue B. COOMER
15 Director of Human Resources ... Mrs. Karen F. WRIGHT
31 Dir of Civic Engagement & Std Ldrsp ... Mrs. Amy C. THOMPSON-WELLS
36 Director Career Services ... Mrs. Ashley MILLER
08 Librarian ... Mr. C. Phil HANNA
18 Director of Physical Plant ... Mr. Michael L. NEWTON
109 Director of Auxiliary Services ... Mr. Jeff WILLIS
40 Bookstore Manager ... Mrs. Amy M. COOPER
35 Director of Student Activities ... Ms. Lafawn NETTLES
85 Dir International Student Programs ... Ms. Sabine EASTHAM
14 Director Information Services ... Mrs. Harriet B. GOLD
13 Director of Information Systems ... Mr. Anthony MOORE
26 Public Relations Officer ... Mr. Duane BONIFER
29 Assistant to Pres Alumni Affairs ... Mr. Randy BURNS
19 Director Safety/Security ... Mr. Michael STATEN
42 Chaplain ... Rev. Troy A. ELMORE
37 Director Student Financial Services ... Ms. Marilyn RADFORD
38 Director Student Counseling ... Dr. Jeff CRANE
66 Director of Nursing ... Mrs. Marian SMITH

Louisville Bible College (D)

8011 Restoration Drive, Louisville KY 40228
County: Jefferson FICE Identification: 041418
Unit ID: 157234
Telephone: (502) 231-5221 Carnegie Class: Spec/Faith
FAX Number: (502) 231-5222 Calendar System: Semester
URL: louisvillebiblecollege.org
Established: 1948 Annual Undergrad Tuition & Fees: $12,830
Enrollment: 85 Coed
Affiliation or Control: Independent Non-Profit IRS Status: 501(c)3
Highest Offering: Master's
Program: Religious Emphasis
Accreditation: BI

01 President ... Dr. Tracy W. MARX
30 VP for Advancement ... Dr. Barry S. THORNTON
32 VP for Student Affairs ... Ms. Melissa PATRICK
05 Academic Dean ... Mr. Matthew SULLIVAN
10 Director of Finance ... Ricka CLAYCOMB
06 Registrar ... Angela K. MARX
07 Director of Admissions ... John BOHNENKAMP
08 Director of Library ... Tony JONES
26 Dir of Marketing & Technology ... Mr. Rob RASOR

Louisville Presbyterian Theological Seminary (E)

1044 Alta Vista Road, Louisville KY 40205-1798
County: Jefferson FICE Identification: 001974
Unit ID: 157298
Telephone: (502) 895-3411 Carnegie Class: Spec/Faith
FAX Number: (502) 895-1096 Calendar System: 4/1/4
URL: www.lpts.edu
Established: 1853 Annual Graduate Tuition & Fees: $10,546
Enrollment: 165 Coed
Affiliation or Control: Presbyterian Church (U.S.A.) IRS Status: 501(c)3
Highest Offering: Doctorate; No Undergraduates
Program: Professional; Religious Emphasis
Accreditation: SC, MFCD, THEOL

01 President ... Dr. Michael JINKINS
30 Vice Pres for Inst Advancement ... Ms. Linda S. MEDLEY
10 Vice President & CFO ... Mr. Patrick A. CECIL
05 Dean of the Seminary ... Dr. Susan R. GARRETT
32 Dean of Students ... Rev. Kilen GRAY
06 Registrar/OIRE ... Dr. Steve COOK
102 Sr Director of Development ... Ms. Sally PENDLETON
29 Director of Church Relations ... Mr. Greg CLARK
44 Director of Seminary Fund ... Vacant
14 Director of Data Management ... Ms. Heather GRIFFIN
26 Director of Communications ... Mr. Chris WOOTON
08 Director of Library Services ... Dr. Matthew COLLINS
21 Controller ... Ms. Angela TRAYLOR
51 Director of DMin & Continuing Ed ... Vacant
07 Director of Recruitment & Admiss ... Mr. Grant CRUSOR
13 Director of IT Services ... Mr. Jack SHARER
18 Director of Facilities ... Mr. Tim WILLIAMS
04 Administrative Asst to President ... Ms. Susan A. DILUCA

MedTech College-Lexington (F)

1648 McGrathiana Pkwy, Suite 200, Lexington KY 40511
Telephone: (859) 410-2110 Identification: 770722
Accreditation: ACICS, MAC, MLTAD

† Branch campus of MedTech College, Indianapolis, IN.

Midway University (G)

512 E Stephens Street, Midway KY 40347-1120
County: Woodford FICE Identification: 001975
Unit ID: 157377
Telephone: (859) 846-4421 Carnegie Class: Bac/Diverse
FAX Number: (859) 846-5349 Calendar System: Semester
URL: www.midway.edu
Established: 1847 Annual Undergrad Tuition & Fees: $22,250
Enrollment: 1,140 Female
Affiliation or Control: Christian Church (Disciples Of Christ)
IRS Status: 501(c)3
Highest Offering: Master's
Program: 2-Year Principally Bachelor's Creditable; Liberal Arts And General; Teacher Preparatory; Professional
Accreditation: SC, ADNUR, MAAB, NUR

01 President ... Dr. John P. MARSDEN
05 Provost and VP of Academic Affairs ... Dr. Laura ARMESTO
04 Exec Assistant to the President ... Ms. Sheila K. HOLSCLAW
10 Vice Pres of Finance and Admin ... Dr. Heather BIGARD
30 Vice President of Advancement ... Mr. Scott B. FITZPATRICK
84 Dean Enrollment Services ... Ms. Stephanie E. WHALEY
26 Vice Pres of Marketing & Comm ... Mrs. Ellen D. GREGORY
20 Associate Provost ... Dr. William (Bill) BROWN
32 Asst VP of Stdnt Affs/Dean Wom Col ... Mrs. Karen PETKO
07 Admissions System Manager/Enroll ... Mr. Andrew KUNG
58 Director of Graduate/Adult/Online ... Mrs. Jessica NEALEY
13 Chief Information Officer ... Dr. Salah SHAKIR
06 Registrar ... Mrs. Linda P. ELDRIDGE
08 Director of Library Services ... Ms. Catherine L. REILENDER
41 Athletic Director ... Vacant
14 Technical Support Specialist ... Vacant
15 Director of Human Resources ... Mrs. Ann M. ELKIN
29 Asst Director of Development ... Vacant
37 Director Student Financial Planning ... Mrs. Kate WARE
18 Director of Campus Services ... Mr. John HAYES
09 Director Compliance & Research ... Dr. Johnie DEAN
28 Dir Ofc of Multicultural & Int Affs . Mrs. Rosa PONCE-SANABRIA
50 Dean Business/Equine & Sport Stds ... Dr. Charles W. WILLIAMS
49 Dean School of Arts & Sciences ... Dr. Charles H. ROBERTS
76 Dean School of Health Sciences ... Dr. Barbara KITCHEN

Morehead State University (H)

150 University Boulevard, Morehead KY 40351-1689
County: Rowan FICE Identification: 001976
Unit ID: 157386
Telephone: (800) 585-6781 Carnegie Class: Master's L
FAX Number: N/A Calendar System: Semester
URL: www.moreheadstate.edu
Established: 1887 Annual Undergrad Tuition & Fees (In-State): $8,098
Enrollment: 11,053 Coed
Affiliation or Control: State IRS Status: 501(c)3
Highest Offering: Doctorate
Program: Occupational; 2-Year Principally Bachelor's Creditable; Liberal Arts And General; Teacher Preparatory; Professional
Accreditation: SC, ADNUR, ART, BUS, DMS, MUS, NAIT, NURSE, RAD, RADMAG, SPAA, SW, TED, THEA

01 President ... Dr. Wayne D. ANDREWS
05 Provost & VP Academic Affairs ... Dr. Steven M. RALSTON
10 Chief Financial Officer/VP AFS ... Ms. Beth G. PATRICK
32 Vice President Student Life ... Ms. Madonna B. WEATHERS
30 Vice Pres for Univ Advancement ... Mr. James A. SHAW
45 Executive Assistant to President ... Dr. John P. ERNST
20 Assoc VP Academic Affairs/Programs .. Dr. Clarenda M. PHILLIPS
04 Assistant to the President ... Ms. Sharon S. REYNOLDS
06 Registrar ... Ms. Roslyn PERRY
58 AVP & Dean of Graduate School ... Dr. Michael C. HENSON
51 Asst VP Adult Educ & College Access ... Dr. Dan J. CONNELL
84 Asst Vice Pres Enrollment Services ... Mr. Jeffrey R. LILES
20 Asst VP Academic Affs/Inst Effectiv ... Ms. Jill C. RATLIFF
26 Asst VP Communication & Marketing ... Ms. Jami M. HORNBUCKLE
18 Asst VP Facilities Management ... Mr. Richard T. LINIO
109 Asst Vice Pres Auxiliary Services ... Mr. William REDWINE
29 Asst VP Alumni Relations & Develop ... Ms. Melinda C. HIGHLEY
13 Asst VP Technology ... Mr. Steve RICHMOND
35 AVP Student Life/Dean of Students ... Vacant
08 Dean of Library Services ... Dr. David L. GREGORY
07 Dir of Undergraduate Admissions ... Ms. Holly L. POLLOCK
09 Dir Inst Research & Analysis ... Dr. Jennifer S. TISON
15 Director of Human Resources ... Mr. Harold D. NALLY
19 Chief of Police ... Mr. Merrell J. HARRISON
21 Director Accounting/Financial Svcs ... Ms. Kelli D. OWEN
21 Exec Dir Budgets & Financial Plng ... Ms. Teresa C. LINDGREN
88 Dir Stdnt Act Inclusion/Ldrshp Dev ... Mr. Ricardo NAZARIO-COLON
37 Director Financial Aid ... Ms. Denise M. TRUSTY
36 Director Career Services ... Ms. Julia L. HAWKINS
39 Director of Housing/Residence Educ ... Dr. Christopher A. SUMMERLIN
41 Director of Athletics ... Mr. Brian A. HUTCHINSON
43 General Counsel ... Dr. Jane FITZPATRICK
27 Media Relations Director ... Mr. Jason BLANTON
79 Director of DIIS ... Dr. Philip KRUMMRICH
96 Director Procurement Services ... Ms. Ladonna M. PURCELL
38 Director of Counseling & Health Svc ... Dr. Shannon L. SMITH-STEPHENS
50 Dean Col of Business & Public Affs ... Dr. Robert ALBERT
53 Dean College of Education ... Dr. Margo E. DELLI CARPINI
72 Dean College Science & Technology ... Dr. Roger R. MCNEIL
79 Dean Col of Arts/Human/Soc Studies ... Dr. Scott MCBRIDE
105 Web Director ... Ms. April H. NUTTER
106 Director Distance Education & Instr ... Ms. Misty HANKS

Murray State University (I)

218 Wells Hall, Murray KY 42071-3318
County: Calloway FICE Identification: 001977
Unit ID: 157401
Telephone: (270) 809-3011 Carnegie Class: Master's L
FAX Number: (270) 809-3413 Calendar System: Semester
URL: www.murraystate.edu
Established: 1922 Annual Undergrad Tuition & Fees (In-State): $7,608
Enrollment: 11,207 Coed
Affiliation or Control: State IRS Status: 501(c)3
Highest Offering: Doctorate
Program: 2-Year Principally Bachelor's Creditable; Liberal Arts And General; Teacher Preparatory; Professional

Accreditation: **SC**, ANEST, ART, BUS, CAATE, CACREP, DIETD, DIETI, ENG, ENGR, ENGT, EXSC, JOUR, MUS, NURSE, SP, SW, TED, THEA

01 President ... Dr. Robert O. DAVIES
101 Sr Exec Coord for Pres/Coord Bd Rel ... Ms. Jill HUNT
05 Interim Provost/VP Academic Affairs ... Dr. Timothy TODD
10 VP Finance & Admin Svcs ... Ms. Jacklyn K. DUDLEY
32 VP Student Affairs ... Dr. Don E. ROBERTSON
30 VP Marketing & Outreach ... Vacant
20 Assoc Provost Grad Educ & Research ... Dr. Robert PERVINE
20 Assoc Provost Undergrad Education ... Dr. Renae D. DUNCAN
35 Interim Assoc VP Student Affairs ... Mr. Michael E. YOUNG
26 Communications Director ... Vacant
43 General Counsel ... Mr. John P. RALL
50 Interim Dean Col of Business ... Dr. Gerry MUUKA
53 Dean Col of Education & Human Svcs ... Dr. David WHALEY
79 Interim Dean Col Humanities & Arts ... Dr. Staci STONE
81 Dean Col Science/Engineering & Tech ... Dr. Stephen H. COBB
47 Dean Hutson School of Agriculture ... Dr. Tony L. BRANNON
66 Dean School Nursing & Health Profes ... Dr. Marcia B. HOBBS
08 Dean University Libraries ... Ms. Asheley IRELAND
51 Dean Regional Academic Outreach ... Dr. Brian W. VAN HORN
106 Asst Dean RAO/Dir Dist Learning ... Mr. Daniel A. LAVIT
97 Coordinator University Studies ... Dr. Peter F. MURPHY
92 Director Honors Program ... Dr. Warren EDMINSTER
85 Exec Dir Institute for Intl Studies ... Dr. Guangming ZOU
104 Assoc Director Education Abroad ... Ms. Melanie C. MCCALLON
84 Assoc VP Enrollment Mgmt ... Mr. Fred K. DIETZ
07 Dir Undgrad Admissions Svcs ... Ms. Lesa C. HARRIS
06 Registrar ... Ms. Tracy ROBERTS
37 Dir Student Financial Aid ... Vacant
39 Director Housing ... Dr. J. David WILSON
38 Dir University Counseling Services ... Dr. Angie TRZEPACZ
28 Dir Multicultural Affairs ... Mr. Sidney G. CARTHELL
36 Director Career Services ... Dr. Ross B. MELOAN
23 Director Health Services ... Ms. Kimberly S. PASCHALL
21 Dir Fiscal Plng/Analysis/Budget ... Mr. Carl F. PRESTFELDT
96 Director Procurement Services ... Ms. Jan R. FUQUA
22 Ex Dir Inst Diversity/Equity/Access ... Ms. Cami DUFFY
88 Exec Director Regional Outreach ... Ms. Gina S. WINCHESTER
13 Interim Chief Information Officer ... Mr. Brian PURCELL
91 Dir Enterprise Application Services ... Mr. Brantly D. TRAVIS
90 Dir Ctr Teaching/Learning/Tech ... Mr. Howard T. RICE
09 Dir Institutional Effectiveness ... Dr. Kelley C. WEZNER
41 Athletic Director ... Mr. C. Allen WARD
18 Interim Chief Facilities Officer ... Mr. David BURDETTE
19 Dir Public Safety/Emergency Mgmt ... Mr. Roy J. DUNAWAY
40 Director University Store ... Ms. R. Karol HARDISON
25 Director Sponsored Programs ... Mr. John A. ROARK
29 Assoc Director Alumni Affairs ... Ms. Katie W. PAYNE
105 Manager Web Services ... Ms. Charley B. ALLEN
100 Pres Advisor Stratregic Initiative ... Dr. K. Renee FISTER
102 President MSU Foundation ... Dr. Robert JACKSON
86 Director Government Relations ... Mr. Jordan SMITH

Northern Kentucky University (A)

Nunn Drive, Highland Heights KY 41099-0000
County: Campbell FICE Identification: 009275
Unit ID: 157447
Telephone: (859) 572-5100 Carnegie Class: Master's L
FAX Number: (859) 572-5566 Calendar System: Semester
URL: www.nku.edu
Established: 1968 Annual Undergrad Tuition & Fees (In-State): $8,736
Enrollment: 15,114 Coed
Affiliation or Control: State IRS Status: 501(c)3
Highest Offering: Doctorate
Program: 2-Year Principally Bachelor's Creditable; Liberal Arts And General; Teacher Preparatory; Professional
Accreditation: **SC**, BUS, CAATE, CACREP, COARC, CONST, ENGT, LAW, MUS, NUR, RAD, SPAA, SW, TED

01 President ... Mr. Geoffrey S. MEARNS
04 Exec Asst to President ... Dr. Kathryn J. HERSCHEDE
05 Provost/Exec VP Academic Affairs ... Ms. Sue OTT ROWLANDS
10 Sr Vice Pres Admin & Finance ... Dr. Sue Hodges MOORE
32 Vice Pres Student Affairs ... Vacant
30 Vice Pres University Advancement ... Mr. Eric C. GENTRY
43 VP Legal Affairs & General Counsel ... Ms. Sara L. SIDEBOTTOM
20 Vice Provost University Programs ... Mr. J. Patrick MOYNAHAN
84 VP Enrollment/Degree Management ... Ms. Kimberly SCRANAGE
88 Vice Provost Grad Educ/ Research ... Ms. Samantha LANGLEY-TURNBAUGH
20 Assoc Provost Academic Affs/Admin ... Ms. Beth SWEENEY
13 Chief Information Officer ... Mr. Timothy FERGUSON
08 Assoc Provost Library Services ... Mr. Arne J. ALMQUIST
35 AVP Student Engage/Dean of Students ... Vacant
29 AVP Development & Alumni Relations ... Ms. Julie DIALS
49 Dean College of Arts & Sciences ... Dr. Katherine FRANK
50 Dean College of Business ... Dr. Rebecca PORTERFIELD
88 Dean College of Informatics ... Dr. Kevin KIRBY
53 Dean College of Ed/Human Svcs ... Dr. Cynthia REED
61 Dean Chase College of Law ... Mr. Jeffrey STANDEN
66 Dean College of Health Professions ... Dr. Dale SCALISE-SMITH
11 Director of Administration ... Vacant
18 Asst VP Facilities Management ... Mr. Larry BLAKE
18 Director Operations & Maintenance ... Mr. Ray MIRIZZI
26 Asst VP Marketing & Communications ... Ms. Kelly MARTIN
21 Dir Fin & Operational Auditing ... Mr. Larry MEYER
109 Dir BusinessOps/Auxiliary Services ... Mr. Andy MEEKS
88 Dir Univ Architect/Design/Const Mgt ... Mr. Steve NIENABER
88 Director Campus Space and Planning ... Ms. Mary Paula SCHUH
15 Senior Director Human Resources ... Ms. Lori SOUTHWOOD
21 Comptroller ... Mr. Russell A. KERDOLFF
19 Director University Police ... Vacant
96 Director Procurement Services ... Mr. Jeffrey STRUNK
92 Interim Director Honors Program ... Ms. Belle ZEMBRODT
07 Director Undergraduate Admissions ... Ms. Melissa GORBANDT
104 Exec Dir Intl Education Center ... Dr. Francois LEROY
06 Registrar ... Ms. Marla HERRON
88 Int AVP Degree/Enrollment Mgmt ... Ms. Leah STEWART
78 Exec Dir Ctr for Civic Engagement ... Mr. Mark NEIKIRK
51 Director Community Connections ... Ms. Melinda SPONG
25 Director Research/Grants/Contracts ... Mr. William THOMPSON
89 Assoc Director First Year Programs ... Ms. Jeanne PETTIT
88 Sr Director Office of the Budget ... Vacant
09 AVP Planning/Institutional Research ... Ms. Vickie NATALE
88 Assoc Dir Institutional Research ... Ms. Erin MULLIGAN
88 Director Campus Recreation ... Mr. Matthew HACKETT
38 Dir Health/Counseling/Prevention ... Ms. Lisa BARRESI
35 Student leadership Development ... Ms. Tiffany MAYSE
38 Disability Programs & Services ... Mr. Ben ANDERSON
39 Director University Housing ... Mr. Arnie SLAUGHTER
36 Director Career Services ... Mr. Bill FROUDE
41 Athletic Director ... Mr. Ken BOTHOF
22 Sr Advisor to Pres Inclusive Excell ... Dr. Kathleen ROBERTS

St. Catharine College (B)

2735 Bardstown Road, Saint Catharine KY 40061-9499
County: Washington FICE Identification: 001983
Unit ID: 157632
Telephone: (859) 336-5082 Carnegie Class: Bac/Assoc
FAX Number: (859) 336-5031 Calendar System: Semester
URL: www.sccky.edu
Established: 1931 Annual Undergrad Tuition & Fees: $19,732
Enrollment: 961 Coed
Affiliation or Control: Roman Catholic IRS Status: 501(c)3
Highest Offering: Master's
Program: 2-Year Principally Bachelor's Creditable; Liberal Arts And General; Teacher Preparatory
Accreditation: **SC**, ADNUR, DMS, RAD, RTT, SURGT

01 President ... Dr. Cindy GNADINGER
05 Provost ... Vacant
10 Vice President Finance ... Mr. Lyen CREWS
30 Vice President for Advancement ... Ms. Kristen BENNETT
32 Dean of Students ... Mr. Ticha CHIKUNI
06 Registrar ... Ms. Anita FOSTER
07 Director of Admissions ... Ms. Lauren BUCKMAN
08 Head Librarian ... Ms. Ilona BURDETTE
37 Director of Financial Aid ... Mr. Jeremy PITTMAN
15 Director of Personnel Services ... Mrs. Carlotta BRUSSELL
18 Chief Facilities/Physical Plant ... Mr. Brad PENN
21 Associate Business Officer ... Ms. Kathy WEYHING
26 Chief Public Rels Ofcr/Dir Comm ... Mr. Jesse OSBOURNE
09 Director of Institutional Research .. Mrs. Margaret HOCKENSMITH
29 Director of Alumni Relations ... Ms. Angela HOFFMAN
04 Administrative Asst to President ... Ms. Katrina L. HAYDON
105 Director Web Services ... Mr. Ming LI
19 Director Security/Safety ... Mr. Craig MATTINGLY
41 Athletic Director ... Mr. Tom BYSTREK
43 Dir Legal Services/General Counsel .... Sr. Angie SHAUGHNESSY

Simmons College of Kentucky (C)

1018 South 7th Street, Louisville KY 40203-3322
County: Jefferson FICE Identification: 041780
Unit ID: 461759
Telephone: (502) 776-1443 Carnegie Class: Not Classified
FAX Number: (502) 776-2227 Calendar System: Semester
URL: www.simmonscollegeky.edu
Established: 1879 Annual Undergrad Tuition & Fees: $5,310
Enrollment: 221 Coed
Affiliation or Control: Baptist IRS Status: 501(c)3
Highest Offering: Baccalaureate
Program: Liberal Arts And General; Religious Emphasis
Accreditation: **BI**

01 President ... Dr. Kevin W. COSBY
03 Executive Vice President ... Dr. Frank M. SMITH, JR.
05 Vice Pres Academic Affairs ... Dr. Brian J. WELLS
32 Vice Pres Student Affs/Dir Admiss ... Dr. Christine COSBY-GAITHER
06 Registrar ... Ms. Deborah THOMAS
09 Director of Institutional Research ... Dr. Ken B. JOBST

The Southern Baptist Theological Seminary (D)

2825 Lexington Road, Louisville KY 40280-2899
County: Jefferson FICE Identification: 001982
Unit ID: 157748
Telephone: (502) 897-4011 Carnegie Class: Spec/Faith
FAX Number: (502) 899-1770 Calendar System: Other
URL: www.sbts.edu
Established: 1859 Annual Undergrad Tuition & Fees: $17,080
Enrollment: 3,820 Coed
Affiliation or Control: Southern Baptist IRS Status: 501(c)3
Highest Offering: Doctorate
Program: Professional; Religious Emphasis
Accreditation: **SC**, MUS, THEOL

01 President ... Dr. R. Albert MOHLER, JR.
100 Chief of Staff to the President ... Dr. Thomas HELLAMS
04 Sr Admin Asst Office of President ... Mrs. Rachel BROCK
05 Sr VP Academic Administration ... Dr. Randy STINSON
11 Sr VP Institutional Administration ... Mr. Dan DUMAS
10 Vice Pres of Business & Strategy ... Mr. Geoff DENNIS
11 Vice President of Operations ... Mr. Andrew VINCENT
26 Vice President Communications ... Mr. Steve WATTERS
13 VP CampusTechnology ... Mr. Jason HEATH
30 VP Institutional Advancement ... Mr. Craig PARKER
32 Vice President Academic Services ... Dr. Matthew HALL
106 Assoc VP Online Education ... Dr. Timothy Paul JONES
20 Vice President of Academic Services ... Dr. Matthew HALL
108 Assoc VP Institutional Assessment ... Dr. Joseph C. HARROD
15 Director Human Resources ... Mr. Richard MCRAE
18 Chief Facilities/Physical Plant ... Mr. Bob SNIP
41 Director of Health & Recreation ... Mr. Blake ROGERS
07 Director of Admissions ... Mr. Kody GIBSON
08 Librarian ... Dr. Berry DRIVER
37 Manager of Financial Aid ... Mrs. Erin JOINER
73 Dean of School of Theology ... Dr. Greg WILLS
88 Dean Missions Evang Ch Growth ... Mr. Adam GREENWAY
88 Dean Boyce College ... Dr. Dan DEWITT
06 Registrar ... Mr. Norm CHUNG
39 Director Student Housing ... Vacant

Spalding University (E)

845 S Third Street, Louisville KY 40203-2213
County: Jefferson FICE Identification: 001960
Unit ID: 157757
Telephone: (502) 585-9911 Carnegie Class: DRU
FAX Number: (502) 585-7158 Calendar System: Other
URL: www.spalding.edu
Established: 1814 Annual Undergrad Tuition & Fees: $23,887
Enrollment: 2,311 Coed
Affiliation or Control: Independent Non-Profit IRS Status: 501(c)3
Highest Offering: Doctorate
Program: Liberal Arts And General; Teacher Preparatory; Professional
Accreditation: **SC**, CLPSY, IACBE, NURSE, OT, SW, TED

01 President ... Ms. Tori MURDEN MCCLURE
05 Provost ... Dr. Randy STRICKLAND
30 Chief Advancement Officer ... Mr. Bert GRIFFIN
32 Dean of Students ... Dr. Richard HUDSON
10 Interim Chief Financial Officer ... Mr. Ezra KRUMHANSL
43 General Counsel ... Ms. Emily NORRIS
84 Dean of Enrollment Management ... Mr. Chris HART
53 Dean of College of Education ... Dr. Beverly C. KEEPERS
83 Assoc Dean College Social Sci/Hum ... Dr. Melissa CHASTAIN
88 Director Adult Accelerated Program ... Ms. Katherine WALKER-PAYNE
76 Dean Kosair Col Health & Nat Sci ... Dr. Joanne BERRYMAN
26 Chief Marketing Officer ... Mr. Rick BARNEY
88 Director Academic Resource Center ... Mr. Sam MEYER
88 Director Academic Advising Center ... Mr. Robert GIESTING
06 Registrar ... Ms. Jennifer GOHMANN
13 Chief Information Officer ... Mr. Ezra KRUMHANSL
08 Director Library ... Ms. Jackie YOUNG
37 Interim Director Financial Aid ... Ms. Michelle STANDRIDGE
15 Human Resources Manager ... Ms. Jennifer BROCKHOFF
09 Dir of Institutional Effectiveness ... Ms. Kay VETTER
26 Director of Executive Communication ... Ms. Beth NEWBERRY
41 Director of Athletics ... Mr. Roger BURKMAN
88 Admin Dir/Mstr Fin Arts in Writing ... Ms. Karen MANN
21 Controller ... Ms. Anne-Marie HOGAN
18 JLL Facilities Manager ... Mr. Kevin WEBER
40 Bookstore Manager ... Ms. Ann BRODERICK
88 Director Applied Behavior Analysis ... Dr. Erick DUBUQUE
88 Director Masters of Business Commu ... Dr. Robin HINKLE

Spencerian College (F)

2355 Harrodsburg Rd, Lexington KY 40504
Telephone: (859) 223-9608 Identification: 666448
Accreditation: **ACICS**, MAC, MLTAB, RAD

† Branch campus of Spencerian College, Louisville, KY.

Spencerian College (G)

4627 Dixie Highway, Louisville KY 40216-2605
County: Jefferson FICE Identification: 004618
Unit ID: 157766
Telephone: (502) 447-1000 Carnegie Class: Assoc/PrivFP
FAX Number: (502) 447-4574 Calendar System: Quarter
URL: www.spencerian.edu
Established: 1892 Annual Undergrad Tuition & Fees: $17,940
Enrollment: 500 Coed
Affiliation or Control: Proprietary IRS Status: Proprietary
Highest Offering: Baccalaureate
Program: Occupational
Accreditation: **ACICS**, #COARC, COMTA, CVT, MAC, MLTAB, RAD, SURGT

01 Executive Director ... Ms. Jan M. GORDON
05 Academic Dean ... Ms. Linda BLAIR
06 Registrar ... Ms. Paula O'LEARY
37 Director of Financial Planning ... Ms. Jill SCHULER
07 Director of Admissions ... Ms. Charmaine POWELL
36 Director of Career Services ... Ms. Lauren KING
32 Director of Student Services ... Ms. Amanda HICKERSON

Sullivan College of Technology and Design (A)

3901 Atkinson Square Drive, Louisville KY 40218-4549
County: Jefferson FICE Identification: 012088
Unit ID: 157270
Telephone: (502) 456-6509 Carnegie Class: Spec/Arts
FAX Number: (502) 456-2341 Calendar System: Quarter
URL: www.sctd.edu
Established: 1961 Annual Undergrad Tuition & Fees: $19,080
Enrollment: 366 Coed
Affiliation or Control: Proprietary IRS Status: Proprietary
Highest Offering: Baccalaureate
Program: Occupational
Accreditation: ACICS, CIDA

00 Chancellor .... Dr. A. R. SULLIVAN
01 President .... Mr. Glenn D. SULLIVAN
11 Chief Operations Officer .... Mr. Thomas F. DAVISSON
05 Dean of Academic Affairs .... Mr. Robert MITCHELL
10 Vice President Finance .... Mr. Shelton BRIDGES
84 Vice Pres Enrollment Management .... Mr. James CRICK
12 Executive Director .... Mr. Chris ERNST
06 Registrar .... Ms. Brittany LEACH
07 Director of Admissions .... Ms. Heather WILSON
37 Dir of Student Financial Planning .... Ms. Michelle SMITH
08 Head Librarian .... Ms. Jill SHERMAN
36 Placement Director .... Mr. Gerald BEAVERS
55 Evening Division Dean .... Mr. Robert MITCHELL
96 Director of Purchasing .... Ms. Ann VEST
13 Chief Technology Officer .... Mr. Mike GROSSE
29 Director Alumni Relations .... Ms. Hazel MATTHEWS

Sullivan University (B)

3101 Bardstown Road, Louisville KY 40205-3000
County: Jefferson FICE Identification: 004619
Unit ID: 157793
Telephone: (502) 456-6504 Carnegie Class: Master's M
FAX Number: (502) 456-0040 Calendar System: Quarter
URL: www.sullivan.edu
Established: 1962 Annual Undergrad Tuition & Fees: $19,200
Enrollment: 4,442 Coed
Affiliation or Control: Proprietary IRS Status: Proprietary
Highest Offering: Doctorate
Program: Occupational; Professional
Accreditation: SC, ACFEI, #ARCPA, IACBE, MAC, NURSE, PHAR

00 Chancellor .... Dr. A. R. SULLIVAN
01 President .... Mr. Glenn D. SULLIVAN
03 Chief Executive Officer .... Dr. Jay MARR
05 Provost .... Dr. Ken MILLER
88 Senior Vice President .... Mr. Thomas F. DAVISSON
10 Vice President Finance .... Mr. Shelton BRIDGES
84 Vice Pres Enrollment Management .... Mr. James CRICK
07 Vice President of Admissions .... Ms. Nina MARTINEZ
58 Assoc Provost/Dean Graduate School .... Dr. Tim SWENSON
32 Dean of Students .... Mr. Gabe GHAMMACHI
88 Dir Natl Ctr Hospitality Studies .... Mr. David DODD
06 Registrar .... Ms. Kim MITCHELL
08 Librarian .... Mr. Charles BROWN
13 Chief Technology Officer .... Mr. Mike GROSSE
36 Director of Career Services .... Mr. Sam MANNINO
37 Director Student Financial Planning .... Ms. Amanda MCANINCH
55 Director Evening Division .... Mr. James TAYLOR
40 Bookstore Manager .... Mr. Bryan NEEDY
12 Director Lexington Branch .... Mr. David KEENE
96 Director of Purchasing .... Ms. Ann VEST
56 Director of Extension Campus .... Ms. Barbara DEAN
88 University Ombudsman .... Mr. Jim KLEIN
29 Director Alumni Relations .... Ms. Hazel MATTHEWS
09 Director Institutional Research .... Dr. Mark WILJANEN
18 Manager Campus Facilities .... Mr. Mike FOWLER
35 Student Life Coordinator .... Ms. Kim ATWOOD
67 Dean College of Pharmacy .... Dr. Cindy STOWE
50 Dean College of Business Admin .... Dr. Ken MORAN
72 Dean Col Information/Computer Tech .... Dr. Emmanuel UDOH

Thomas More College (C)

333 Thomas More Parkway,
Crestview Hills KY 41017-3495
County: Kenton FICE Identification: 002001
Unit ID: 157809
Telephone: (859) 341-5800 Carnegie Class: Master's S
FAX Number: (859) 344-3345 Calendar System: Semester
URL: www.thomasmore.edu
Established: 1921 Annual Undergrad Tuition & Fees: $27,325
Enrollment: 1,308 Coed
Affiliation or Control: Roman Catholic IRS Status: 501(c)3
Highest Offering: Master's
Program: Liberal Arts And General; Teacher Preparatory; Professional
Accreditation: SC, ACBSP, NUR, TED

01 President .... Mr. David A. ARMSTRONG
04 Assistant to the President .... Ms. Charlene BARLOW
10 CFO .... Mr. Jeff BRIGGS
05 Vice President for Academic Affairs .... Dr. Kathleen JAGGER
30 Vice Pres for Inst Advancement .... Ms. Cathy SILVERS
11 Vice Pres of Operations/Cmty Affs .... Vacant
32 Dean of Students .... Ms. Amy WYLIE
09 Dir of Inst Planning/Effectiveness .... Ms. Kelly FRENCH
06 Registrar .... Ms. Michelle VEZINA
08 Director of Library .... Ms. Leoma DUNN
37 Director of Financial Aid .... Ms. Mary GIVHAN
13 Director of IT .... Mr. Sean KAPSAL
26 Dir Communications/Media Relations .... Ms. Amy WAGNER
38 Director of Counseling .... Ms. Veronica A. LUBBE
42 Chaplain .... Rev. Gerald E. TWADDELL
84 Exec Director of Enrollment Mgmt .... Vacant
41 Athletic Director .... Mr. Terry D. CONNOR
19 Director of Campus Safety .... Mr. Robert MARSHALL
15 Director of Human Resources .... Ms. Laura CUSTER
18 Director of Facilities .... Mr. Doug PARKER
29 Director of Alumni .... Ms. Monica GINNEY
36 Dir of Career Planning/Coop Educ .... Ms. Julie MUELLER
73 Director of Campus Ministry .... Mr. Robert SHEARN
21 Controller .... Ms. Beth MALEY
51 Director of Lifelong Learning .... Mr. Nathan HARTMAN
92 Director of Honors Program .... Dr. Catherine SHERRON
44 Dir Annual Giving/Special Events .... Vacant
07 Associate Director of Admissions .... Mr. Justin VOGEL
35 Director of Student Engagement .... Mr. Kevin REYNOLDS
39 Coordinator of Residence Life .... Vacant

Transylvania University (D)

300 N Broadway, Lexington KY 40508-1797
County: Fayette FICE Identification: 001987
Unit ID: 157818
Telephone: (859) 233-8300 Carnegie Class: Bac/A&S
FAX Number: (859) 233-8797 Calendar System: Other
URL: www.transy.edu
Established: 1780 Annual Undergrad Tuition & Fees: $34,370
Enrollment: 1,015 Coed
Affiliation or Control: Christian Church (Disciples Of Christ)
IRS Status: 501(c)3
Highest Offering: Baccalaureate
Program: Liberal Arts And General; Teacher Preparatory
Accreditation: SC, TED

01 President .... Dr. Seamus CAREY
05 Vice Pres & Dean of the University .... Dr. Laura BRYAN
10 Vice President Finance & Business .... Mr. Marc MATHEWS
32 Interim VP for SA/Dean of Students .... Dr. Michael COVERT
84 Interim VP for Enrollment .... Dr. Rhyan M. CONYERS
30 VP for Advancement .... Mr. Kirk PURDOM
13 VP for Information Technology .... Mr. Jason WHITAKER
26 Vice President for Marketing & Comm .... Ms. Michele SPARKS
41 Vice President for Athletics .... Dr. Holly SHEILLEY
28 Dir Diversity/Incl & Intl Students .... Ms. Serenity WRIGHT
03 Executive Asst to President .... Ms. Rachel MILLARD
06 Registrar .... Ms. Michelle RAWLINGS
08 Librarian .... Ms. Susan M. BROWN
09 Director of Institutional Research .... Mr. Rhyan M. CONYERS
104 Director of Study Abroad .... Ms. Kathryn C. SIMON
36 Director of Career Development .... Ms. Susan S. RAYER
15 Assoc VP & Director Human Resources .... Mr. Jeff MUDRAK
18 Chief Facilities/Physical Plant .... Mr. Charlie L. REDMON
19 Director Security/Safety .... Mr. Gregg MURAVCHICK
96 Director of Purchasing .... Ms. Shawn T. SINGLETON
39 Director Student Housing .... Mr. Bob BROWN
37 Director of Financial Aid .... Mr. David J. CECIL
29 Director Alumni Relations .... Ms. Natasa PAJIC

Union College (E)

310 College Street, Barbourville KY 40906-1499
County: Knox FICE Identification: 001988
Unit ID: 157863
Telephone: (606) 546-4151 Carnegie Class: Master's L
FAX Number: (606) 546-1217 Calendar System: Other
URL: www.unionky.edu
Established: 1879 Annual Undergrad Tuition & Fees: $24,000
Enrollment: 1,139 Coed
Affiliation or Control: United Methodist IRS Status: 501(c)3
Highest Offering: Master's
Program: Liberal Arts And General; Teacher Preparatory
Accreditation: SC, CAATE, NURSE, SW

01 President .... Dr. Marcia HAWKINS
05 VP for Academic Affairs .... Dr. David JOHNS
30 Vice President for Advancement .... Ms. Jessica BERGMAN
84 Director Undergraduate Enrollment .... Mr. Craig GROOMS
32 Dean of Students .... Mr. Justin KITTS
53 Head of Educational Studies Dept .... Dr. Jason REEVES
55 Associate Dean Student Life .... Ms. Barbara TEAGUE
10 Chief Business Officer .... Mr. Steve HOSKINS
21 Controller .... Ms. Elisabeth RICHARDSON
06 Registrar .... Ms. Kathy INKSTER
18 Director of Physical Plant (NMRC) .... Mr. James JAMERSON
41 Athletic Director .... Mr. Tim CURRY
29 Director of Alumni Relations .... Mr. Brian STRUNK
09 Director of Institutional Research .... Ms. Anisa JAMES
26 Director of Public Relations .... Mr. Jay STANCIL
88 Director of Sports Information .... Mr. John GATTO
88 Associate Dean for Student Success .... Ms. Stephanie SMITH
08 Head Librarian .... Ms. Tara L. COOPER
42 College Minister .... Rev. David MILLER
31 Director of Center for Civic Engage .... Ms. Jodi CARROLL
37 Director of Financial Aid .... Ms. Andra BUTLER
15 Benefits Coordinator .... Ms. Lynn SMITH
19 Safety Team Leader .... Mr. Jurgin MCRIGHT
50 Chair Department of Business .... Dr. Carolyn PAYNE
88 Chair Dept Wellness/Human Perf/Rec .... Dr. Larry INKSTER
79 Chair Dept Engr/Comm/Language .... Dr. Jimmy D. SMITH
57 Chr Dpt Hist/Relig Std/Fn/Perf Arts .... Dr. Russell SISSON
81 Chair Dept of Natural Sciences .... Dr. Dan COVINGTON
83 Chair Dept Social/Behav Science .... Dr. Robert ARMOUR
04 Assistant to the President .... Ms. Sherry PARTIN
88 Events Coordinator .... Ms. Bobbie DOOLIN
102 Dir Foundation/Corporate Relations .... Ms. Monica CLOUSE
105 Director Web Services .... Mr. Kevin SIMPSON
108 Director Institutional Effectivenes .... Dr. Barry PELPHREY

University of the Cumberlands (F)

6191 College Station Drive, Williamsburg KY 40769-1372
County: Whitley FICE Identification: 001962
Unit ID: 156541
Telephone: (606) 549-2200 Carnegie Class: Master's M
FAX Number: (606) 539-4280 Calendar System: Semester
URL: www.ucumberlands.edu
Established: 1888 Annual Undergrad Tuition & Fees: $21,640
Enrollment: 5,736 Coed
Affiliation or Control: Baptist IRS Status: 501(c)3
Highest Offering: Doctorate
Program: Liberal Arts And General; Teacher Preparatory; Professional
Accreditation: SC, #ARCPA

01 President .... Dr. Larry L. COCKRUM
30 Vice Pres Institutional Advancement .... Ms. Jamirae HAMMONS
05 Vice President Academic Affairs .... Dr. Barbara KENNEDY
32 Vice President Student Services .... Dr. Emily COLEMAN
23 Vice President Medical Services .... Dr. Eddie PERKINS
10 Vice President Business Services .... Mr. Steve MORRIS
21 Vice President Finance .... Ms. Jana K. BAILEY
11 Vice President Operations .... Mr. Kyle GILBERT
37 Vice Pres Student Financial Plng .... Mr. Steve ALLEN
41 Vice Pres Athletics/Athletic Dir .... Mr. Randy VERNON
13 VP for Information Technology .... Mr. Donnie GRIMES
07 VP for Enrollment & Communication .... Dr. Jerry JACKSON
06 Registrar .... Mr. Charles DUPIER
20 Associate Dean .... Dr. Thomas E. FISH
88 Vice President of Compliance .... Dr. Verna LOWE
26 Dir Multimedia/Athletic Services .... Ms. Jennifer FLOYD
35 Dean Student Life .... Ms. Linda CARTER
15 Director of Human Resources .... Ms. Pearl BAKER
42 Dir International Pgm/Church Rels .... Dr. Rick FLEENOR
36 Director of Career Services .... Ms. Debbie HARP
08 Director of Library .... Ms. Jan WREN
58 Graduate Enrollment Manager .... Dr. Summer JACKSON
29 Director Alumni Relations .... Mr. Paul STEPP
18 Director of Physical Plant .... Mr. David ROOT
21 Bursar .... Ms. Jo DUPIER

University of Kentucky (G)

101 Main Building, Lexington KY 40506-0003
County: Fayette FICE Identification: 001989
Unit ID: 157085
Telephone: (859) 257-9000 Carnegie Class: RU/VH
FAX Number: (859) 257-4000 Calendar System: Semester
URL: www.uky.edu
Established: 1865 Annual Undergrad Tuition & Fees (In-State): $10,780
Enrollment: 29,203 Coed
Affiliation or Control: State IRS Status: 501(c)3
Highest Offering: Doctorate
Program: Liberal Arts And General; Teacher Preparatory; Professional
Accreditation: SC, AAFCS, ARCPA, ART, BUS, BUSA, CAATE, CIDA, CLPSY, COPSY, CORE, CS, DENT, DIETC, DIETD, DIETI, ENG, HSA, IPSY, JOUR, LAW, LIB, LSAR, MED, #MFCD, MT, MUS, NURSE, PAST, PCSAS, PH, PHAR, PTA, SCPSY, SP, SPAA, SW, TED, THEA

01 President .... Dr. Eli I. CAPILOUTO
46 Vice President Research .... Dr. Lisa A. CASSIS
05 Provost .... Dr. Tim S. TRACY
100 Chief of Staff .... Dr. Bill K. SWINFORD
11 Exec VP Finance/Administration .... Mr. Eric N. MONDAY
17 Executive VP for Health Affairs .... Dr. Michael KARPF
13 Sr Vice Provost Univ Tech/Analytics .... Dr. Vincent J. KELLEN
32 Vice Pres Student Affairs .... Dr. Robert C. MOCK, JR.
28 Interim VP Institutional Diversity .... Mr. Terry D. ALLEN
30 Vice President for Development .... Dr. D. Michael RICHEY
10 VP Health Affs/Chief Financial Ofcr .... Mr. Murray B. CLARK
45 VP Financial Planning & CBO .... Ms. Angela S. MARTIN
18 VP Facilities Mgmt & Chief Facil .... Ms. Mary S. VOSEVICH
22 Assoc VP Institutional Equity .... Mr. Terry D. ALLEN
26 VP University Relations .... Mr. Thomas W. HARRIS
35 Assoc VP Stdnt Affs/Dean of Stdnts .... Dr. Victor A. HAZARD
15 VP Human Resources Admin & CHRO .... Ms. Kimberly P. WILSON
88 Asst Vice Pres Public Safety .... Mr. Anthony BEATTY
109 Interim Assoc VP Auxiliary Services .... Ms. Sarah F. NIKIRK
25 Assoc VP Res Admin & Fiscal Affs .... Mr. Jack SUPPLEE, JR.
25 Exec Director Sponsored Projects .... Ms. Kim C. CARTER
88 Assoc Provost Internationalization .... Dr. Susan E. CARVALHO
88 Assoc VP Clinical Network Devel .... Mr. Joe CLAYPOOL
58 Interim Dean Graduate School .... Dr. Susan E. CARVALHO
20 Assoc Provost Undergrad Education .... Dr. Ben C. WITHERS
20 Assoc Provost Faculty Advancement .... Dr. Gene T. LINEBERRY
84 Assoc Provost Enroll Mgmt/Registrar .... Mr. Don E. WITT
08 Dean of Libraries .... Dr. Terry L. BIRDWHISTELL
27 Exec Director Public Relations .... Mr. Jay D. BLANTON
27 Director University Press .... Dr. Stephen M. WRINN
43 General Counsel .... Mr. William E. THRO

41 Director Athletics .... Mr. Mitch S. BARNHART
37 Director Student Financial Aid .... Dr. Nimmi K. WIGGINS
09 Director of Institutional Research .... Dr. Roger P. SUGARMAN
36 Asst Dean for Career & Academic Exp .... Mr. Ray R. CLERE
38 Director Counseling & Testing .... Dr. Mary C. BOLIN
29 Director Alumni Affairs .... Mr. Stan R. KEY
21 Controller .... Ms. Ronda S. BECK
47 Dean of Agriculture/Food & Envir .... Dr. Nancy M. COX
19 Chief of Police .... Mr. Joseph W. MONROE
88 Dean of Design .... Ms. Mitzi VERNON
88 Exec Director Student Center .... Mr. John H. HERBST
49 Dean of Arts & Sciences .... Dr. Mark L. KORNBLUH
50 Dean of Business & Economics .... Dr. David W. BLACKWELL
53 Dean of Education .... Dr. Mary John O'HAIR
54 Dean of Engineering .... Dr. John Y. WALZ
57 Dean of Fine Arts .... Dr. Michael TICK
60 Dean of Communication/Information .... Dr. H. Dan O'HAIR
61 Dean of Law .... Dr. David A. BRENNEN
70 Dean of Social Work .... Dr. James ADAMS, JR.
76 Dean of Health Sciences .... Dr. Scott M. LEPHART
52 Dean of Dentistry .... Dr. Stephanos KYRKANIDES
63 Dean of Medicine/VP Clinical Affs .... Dr. Fredrick C. DE BEER
66 Dean of Nursing .... Dr. Janie H. HEATH
67 Interim Dean of Pharmacy .... Dr. Kelly M. SMITH
69 Interim Dean Public Health .... Dr. Wayne SANDERSON
96 Exec Director Purchasing & CPO .... Mr. William L. HARRIS
23 Director Univ Student Health Svcs .... Vacant
108 Director of Assessment .... Ms. Tara A. ROSE
44 Director Annual Giving .... Ms. Anne V. LICHTENBERG

University of Louisville (A)

2301 S Third Street, Louisville KY 40292-0001
County: Jefferson FICE Identification: 001999
Unit ID: 157289
Telephone: (502) 852-5555 Carnegie Class: RU/VH
FAX Number: (502) 852-7013 Calendar System: Semester
URL: www.louisville.edu
Established: 1798 Annual Undergrad Tuition & Fees (In-State): $10,702
Enrollment: 21,561 Coed
Affiliation or Control: State IRS Status: 501(c)3
Highest Offering: Doctorate
Program: Liberal Arts And General; Teacher Preparatory; Professional
Accreditation: SC, AUD, BUS, BUSA, CACREP, #CIDA, CLPSY, COPSY, CS, DENT, DH, ENG, EXSC, IPSY, LAW, #MED, MFCD, MUS, NURSE, PH, PLNG, SP, SPAA, SW, TED, THEA

01 President .... Dr. James R. RAMSEY
05 Exec Vice Pres/University Prov .... Dr. Shirley C. WILLIHNGANZ
17 Exec Vice Pres for Health Affairs .... Dr. David DUNN
46 Executive VP for Research .... Dr. Bill PIERCE
10 Sr VP Finance & Admin & COO .... Mr. Harlan SANDS
32 Acting VP Student Affairs .... Dr. Michael MARDIS, JR.
30 Vice Pres Univ Advancement .... Mr. Keith INMAN
13 Vice Pres Information Tech .... Dr. Priscilla HANCOCK
86 VP for Community Engagement .... Mr. Daniel HALL
15 Vice Pres Human Resources .... Vacant
41 Vice President for Athletics .... Mr. Tom JURICH
44 Sr Assoc VP Advancement .... Ms. Rebecca SIMPSON
18 Assoc VP Facilities/Physical Plant .... Mr. Larry DETHERAGE
29 Assoc VP for Alumni Relations .... Ms. Deborah DIETZLER
100 Chief of Staff for the President .... Ms. Kathleen M. SMITH
43 Interim University Counsel .... Ms. Dana B. MAYTON
20 Vice Prov Undergraduate Affairs .... Dr. Dale B. BILLINGSLEY
58 Dean Graduate School .... Dr. Beth A. BOEHM
28 Vice Prov for Diversity/Intl Affs .... Dr. Mordean TAYLOR-ARCHER
09 Vice Provost IR Effect & Analytics .... Mr. Robert S. GOLDSTEIN
106 Assoc Univ Provost Distance Ed/Delp .... Dr. Gale RHODES
88 Asst Prov for Accreditation .... Ms. Connie C. SHUMAKE
21 Controller .... Mr. Larry W. ZINK
07 Executive Director Admissions .... Ms. Jenny L. SAWYER
06 University Registrar .... Mr. Scott A. BURKS
37 Director Financial Aid .... Ms. Sandra NEEL
26 Director of Comm/Marketing .... Ms. Cindy HESS
25 Director Contract Admin/Risk Mgmt .... Mr. David MARTIN
16 Dir of Staff Dev/Employee Rel .... Ms. Mary E. MILES
19 Director Public Safety .... Mr. Wayne HALL
09 Exec Director Inst Res & Plng .... Ms. Becky PATTERSON
45 Exec Director Inst Effectiveness .... Dr. Cheryl B. GILCHRIST
39 Director Student Housing .... Ms. Shannon D. STATEN
105 Director of Digital Media .... Mr. Jeffery A. RUSHTON
27 Director Media Relations .... Mr. Mark HEBERT
88 Assoc Vice Pres for Audit Services .... Mr. David F. BARKER
14 Exec Dir IT Infrastructure .... Ms. Brenda B. GOMBOSKY
92 Exec Director of Honors Program .... Dr. Joy HART
96 Director Purchasing .... Mr. David MARTIN
88 Dir Planning/Design & Construction .... Mr. Kenneth DIETZ
36 Director Career Development .... Mr. Trey LEWIS
38 Director Counseling Center .... Ms. Aesha TYLER
08 Dean of University Libraries .... Mr. Robert FOX
49 Dean College Arts & Sciences .... Dr. Kimberly KEMPF-LEONARD
50 Int Dean College of Business .... Dr. Rohan M. CHRISTIE-DAVID
52 Dean School of Dentistry .... Dr. John J. SAUK
53 Dean Col of Educ/Human Develop .... Dr. Ann LARSON
70 Dean Kent School Social Work .... Dr. Terry L. SINGER
64 Dean School of Music .... Dr. Christopher DOANE
61 Dean Brandeis School of Law .... Ms. Susan DUNCAN
66 Dean School of Nursing .... Dr. Marcia J. HERN
54 Dean Speed School of Engineering .... Dr. Neville PINTO
63 Dean School of Medicine .... Dr. Toni GANZEL
69 Dean Public Health/Information Sci .... Dr. Craig H. BLAKELY
35 Dean of Students/Assoc VP Stdnt Aff .... Dr. Michael MARDIS
04 Assistant to the President .... Ms. Debra K. DOUGHERTY

University of Phoenix Louisville Campus (B)

10400 Linn Station Road, Louisville KY 40223-3839
Telephone: (502) 423-0149 Identification: 770207
Accreditation: &NH, ACBSP

† No longer accepting campus-based students.

University of Pikeville (C)

147 Sycamore Street, Pikeville KY 41501-1194
County: Pike FICE Identification: 001980
Unit ID: 157535
Telephone: (606) 218-5250 Carnegie Class: Bac/A&S
FAX Number: (606) 218-5269 Calendar System: Semester
URL: www.upike.edu
Established: 1889 Annual Undergrad Tuition & Fees: $18,840
Enrollment: 2,458 Coed
Affiliation or Control: Presbyterian Church (U.S.A.) IRS Status: 501(c)3
Highest Offering: Doctorate
Program: Liberal Arts And General; Teacher Preparatory; Professional
Accreditation: SC, NUR, OSTEO, SW

00 Chancellor/Interim President .... Mr. Paul E. PATTON
01 President .... Vacant
05 VPAA/Dean College Arts/Sciences .... Dr. Thomas R. HESS
88 Dean College of Optometry .... Dr. Andrew BUZZELLI
50 Dean College of Business .... Dr. Howard V. ROBERTS
10 Vice Pres Finance/Business Affairs .... Mr. Douglas J. LANGE
30 Vice President for Advancement .... Vacant
26 Asst Vice President Public Affairs .... Mrs. Lucy HOLMAN
63 VP Health Affairs/Dean KYCOM .... Dr. Boyd R. BUSER
32 Dean of Students .... Ms. Renee WATSON
84 VP for Enrollment Management .... Mrs. Teresa LOCKHART
07 Director Admissions .... Mrs. Amber COLLINS
08 Director of Library Services .... Ms. Karen S. CHAFIN-EVANS
06 Asst VP Academic Affairs/Registrar .... Mrs. Gia POTTER
09 Director of Institutional Research .... Dr. Meg SIDLE
13 Senior Info Services Administrator .... Mr. Randy SCARBERRY
18 Asst VP for Facilities .... Mr. John HOLMAN
37 Director of Student Financial Svcs .... Mrs. Judy BRADLEY
15 Director of Human Resources .... Mr. Michael PACHECO
04 Executive Asst to President .... Mrs. Sherrie MARRS
19 Director Security/Safety .... Mr. Allen ABSHIRE
41 Athletic Director .... Mr. Robert STAGGS
105 Director Web Services .... Mr. Bruce PARSONS
25 Chief Contracts/Grants Admin .... Mrs. Tiffany BAKER
29 Director Alumni Relations .... Mr. Jordan GIBSON
38 Director Student Success .... Mrs. Ambria RAY
39 Housing Operations Supervisor .... Mr. Robert ENDEAN
44 Director Annual or Planned Giving .... Mr. Ronald DAMRON
53 Dean College of Education .... Dr. David BARNETT
90 Director Academic Computing .... Mrs. Corrine BOLT

Western Kentucky University (D)

1906 College Heights Blvd, Bowling Green KY 42101-3576
County: Warren FICE Identification: 002002
Unit ID: 157951
Telephone: (270) 745-0111 Carnegie Class: Master's L
FAX Number: (270) 745-5387 Calendar System: Semester
URL: www.wku.edu
Established: 1906 Annual Undergrad Tuition & Fees (In-State): $9,482
Enrollment: 20,171 Coed
Affiliation or Control: State IRS Status: 501(c)3
Highest Offering: Doctorate
Program: 2-Year Principally Bachelor's Creditable; Liberal Arts And General; Teacher Preparatory; Professional
Accreditation: SC, ADNUR, ART, BUS, BUSA, CACREP, CAHIIM, CONST, DANCE, DH, DIETD, @DIETI, ENG, JOUR, MUS, NAIT, NRPA, NURSE, PH, @PTA, SP, SPAA, SW, TED, THEA

01 President .... Dr. Gary A. RANSDELL
05 Provost/VP Academic Affairs .... Dr. A. Gordon EMSLIE
46 VP for Research .... Dr. Gordon BAYLIS
26 VP for Public Affairs .... Ms. Robbin M. TAYLOR
30 VP Development & Alumni Rels .... Ms. Kathryn COSTELLO
32 Vice President Student Affairs .... Mr. Howard E. BAILEY
10 Vice President Finance & Admin .... Ms. K. Ann MEAD
100 Chief of Staff/General Counsel .... Ms. Deborah T. WILKINS
20 Vice Provost Academic Affairs .... Dr. Richard C. MILLER
84 Chief Enrollment/Grad Officer .... Dr. Brian MEREDITH
106 Assoc VP Ext Learning & Outreach .... Dr. Beth LAVES
79 Dean Arts & Letters .... Dr. David D. LEE
50 Dean Business .... Dr. Jeffrey KATZ
53 Dean Education/Behavioral Sci .... Dr. Sam EVANS
76 Dean Health & Human Services .... Dr. Neale R. CHUMBLER
81 Dean Science/Engineering .... Dr. Cheryl L. STEVENS
58 Assc Provost/Dean Grad Studies .... Dr. Carl A. FOX
97 Assc Provost Regional Hgh Ed/Dean .... Dr. Dennis K. GEORGE
62 Dean Libraries .... Ms. Connie FOSTER
88 Assoc VP Enrichment & Effectiveness .... Dr. Doug MCELROY
88 Assoc VP Planning & Program Develop .... Dr. Sylvia GAIKO
21 Chief Financial Officer .... Mr. Jim CUMMINGS
21 Budget Director .... Ms. Kimberly REED
07 Director Admissions .... Dr. Jace T. LUX
88 Assoc VP Academic Budgets & Admin .... Mrs. Ladonna L. HUNTON
30 Assoc VP Research and Development .... Mr. Douglas ROHRER
06 University Registrar .... Ms. Tiffany ROBINSON
13 Chief Information Tech Officer .... Mr. Gordon L. JOHNSON
15 Director Human Resources .... Mr. Tony L. GLISSON
18 Director Facilities Management .... Mr. Trent BLAIR
12 Regional Chancellor .... Dr. Sally RAY
12 Regional Chancellor .... Dr. Gene E. TICE
90 Director Academic Technology .... Mr. John BOWERS
88 Dir Acad Advising & Retention Ctr .... Dr. Russell L. CURLEY
28 Director Diversity & Inclusion .... Ms. Andrea GARR-BARNES
39 Director Housing & Residence Life .... Mr. Brian KUSTER
19 Chief of Police .... Mr. Robert DEANE
102 President College Heights Found .... Mr. Donald SMITH
29 Asst VP/Exec Dir Alumni Relations .... Mr. Richard A. DUBOSE
44 Associate VP Major Gifts .... Mr. John P. BLAIR
36 Director Ctr for Career & Prof Dev .... Dr. Lynne HOLLAND
37 Dir Student Financial Assistance .... Ms. Cindy BURNETTE
88 Director Student Support Svcs .... Mr. Terrance C. GEORGE
40 Director WKU Store .... Ms. Ann-Marie FLORESCA
09 Director Institutional Research .... Dr. Tuesdi HELBIG
22 Equal Oppty/ADA/Compliance Director .... Vacant
24 Director Public Radio Services .... Mr. David BRINKLEY
41 Athletics Director .... Mr. Todd M. STEWART
85 Director International Enrollment .... Ms. Stephanie SIEGGREEN
92 Executive Director Honors College .... Dr. Craig COBANE
96 Director Purchasing/Accts Payable .... Mr. Ken BAUSHKE
101 Assistant to the President .... Ms. Julia J. MCDONALD
101 Executive Administrative Assistant .... Ms. Torie COCKRIEL
104 Dir Study Abroad/Global Learning .... Ms. Laura M. MONARCH
27 Director of Media Relations .... Mr. Bob SKIPPER
86 Dir Govt/Community Relations .... Ms. Jennifer B. SMITH
04 Executive Admininstrative Assistant .... Ms. Shelia E. HOUCHINS

LOUISIANA

Baton Rouge School of Computers (E)

9352 Interline Avenue, Baton Rouge LA 70809-1909
County: East Baton Rouge FICE Identification: 021975
Unit ID: 158343
Telephone: (225) 923-2524 Carnegie Class: Assoc/PrivFP
FAX Number: (225) 923-2979 Calendar System: Other
URL: www.brsc.edu
Established: 1979 Annual Undergrad Tuition & Fees: $16,354
Enrollment: 60 Coed
Affiliation or Control: Proprietary IRS Status: Proprietary
Highest Offering: Associate Degree
Program: Occupational
Accreditation: ACCSC

01 President/Director .... Mrs. Betty D. TRUXILLO
05 Chief Academic Officer .... Ms. Pauline ROBERTS
06 Registrar .... Ms. Diane MCNABB

Blue Cliff College (F)

120 James Comeaux Road, Lafayette LA 70508
County: Lafayette FICE Identification: 034226
Unit ID: 439491
Telephone: (337) 269-0620 Carnegie Class: Assoc/PrivFP
FAX Number: (337) 269-0688 Calendar System: Quarter
URL: www.bluecliffcollege.com
Established: 1987 Annual Undergrad Tuition & Fees: $18,050
Enrollment: 307 Coed
Affiliation or Control: Proprietary IRS Status: Proprietary
Highest Offering: Associate Degree
Program: Occupational; Technical Emphasis
Accreditation: ACCSC

01 Director .... Mr. Donald MONTGOMERY
07 Director of Admissions .... Ms. Kimberly BELL
37 Director of Financial Aid .... Mrs. Verna TAYLOR

Blue Cliff College (G)

3200 Cleary Avenue, Metairie LA 70002-5714
County: Jefferson FICE Identification: 032943
Unit ID: 434821
Telephone: (504) 456-3141 Carnegie Class: Assoc/PrivFP
FAX Number: (504) 456-7849 Calendar System: Quarter
URL: www.bluecliffcollege.edu
Established: 1987 Annual Undergrad Tuition & Fees: $15,047
Enrollment: 892 Coed
Affiliation or Control: Proprietary IRS Status: Proprietary
Highest Offering: Associate Degree
Program: Occupational
Accreditation: ACCSC

01 President/CEO .... Mr. Reggie MOORE
05 Campus Director .... Mr. Doug ROBERTSON

Blue Cliff College (H)

8731 Park Plaza Drive, Shreveport LA 71105-5682
County: Caddo FICE Identification: 034225
Unit ID: 439482
Telephone: (318) 798-6868 Carnegie Class: Assoc/PrivFP
FAX Number: (318) 798-6880 Calendar System: Quarter
URL: www.bluecliffcollege.com
Established: 1995 Annual Undergrad Tuition & Fees: $8,100
Enrollment: 211 Coed
Affiliation or Control: Proprietary IRS Status: Proprietary
Highest Offering: Associate Degree
Program: Occupational

Accreditation: ACCSC

01 Campus Director .... Mr. Simon J. LUMLEY
05 Director of Education .... Dr. Cassandra DANIEL

Cameron College (A)

2740 Canal Street, New Orleans LA 70119-5500
County: Orleans FICE Identification: 022340
Unit ID: 158440
Telephone: (504) 821-5881 Carnegie Class: Assoc/PrivFP
FAX Number: (504) 822-3467 Calendar System: Other
URL: www.cameroncollege.com
Established: 1981 Annual Undergrad Tuition & Fees: $18,150
Enrollment: 20 Coed
Affiliation or Control: Proprietary IRS Status: Proprietary
Highest Offering: Associate Degree
Program: Occupational
Accreditation: COE

01 President .... Ms. Eleanor W. CAMERON

Career Technical College (B)

2319 Louisville Avenue, Monroe LA 71201-6126
County: Ouachita FICE Identification: 026068
Unit ID: 367112
Telephone: (318) 323-2889 Carnegie Class: Assoc/PrivFP
FAX Number: (318) 324-9883 Calendar System: Quarter
URL: www.careertc.edu
Established: 1988 Annual Undergrad Tuition & Fees: $14,160
Enrollment: 500 Coed
Affiliation or Control: Proprietary IRS Status: Proprietary
Highest Offering: Associate Degree
Program: Occupational; 2-Year Principally Bachelor's Creditable; Technical Emphasis
Accreditation: ACICS, MAC, SURGT

01 College Director .... Ms. Cheryl P. LOKEY

Career Technical College (C)

1227 Shreveport-Barksdale Highway,
Shreveport LA 71105
Telephone: (318) 629-2889 Identification: 770723
Accreditation: ACICS, MAC, SURGT

† Branch campus of Career Technical College, Monroe, LA.

Centenary College of Louisiana (D)

PO Box 41188, Shreveport LA 71134-1188
County: Caddo FICE Identification: 002003
Unit ID: 158477
Telephone: (318) 869-5011 Carnegie Class: Bac/A&S
FAX Number: (318) 869-5010 Calendar System: Semester
URL: www.centenary.edu
Established: 1825 Annual Undergrad Tuition & Fees: $33,900
Enrollment: 619 Coed
Affiliation or Control: United Methodist IRS Status: 501(c)3
Highest Offering: Master's
Program: Liberal Arts And General; Teacher Preparatory; Professional
Accreditation: SC, MUS, TEAC, TED

01 President .... Dr. B. David ROWE
04 Exec Assistant to the President .... Mrs. Connie WHITTINGTON
05 Provost & Dean of the College .... Dr. Jenifer WARD
50 Dean of the School of Business .... Vacant
64 Dean of the School of Music .... Dr. Gale ODOM
10 Vice President for Finance/Admin .... Mr. Bob BLUE
30 VP for Advancement .... Mr. Fred LANDRY
84 Vice President for Enrollment .... Mr. Calhoun ALLEN
20 Vice Provost .... Dr. Karen SOUL
13 Director of Information Technology .... Mr. Scott MERRITT
21 Controller .... Mrs. Diane ROTHERY
41 Director of Athletics & Wellness .... Mrs. Ronda SEAGRAVES
32 Dean of Students .... Mr. Mark MILLER
38 Director of Counseling .... Ms. Tina FELDT
37 Director of Financial Aid .... Mrs. Lynette VISKOZKI
06 Registrar/Director of Re-Enrollment .... Vacant
08 Librarian .... Ms. Christy WRENN
26 Dir of Strategic Communications .... Mrs. Kate PEDROTTY
29 Director of Alumni Relations .... Ms. Saige WILHITE
38 Director of Professional Success .... Mrs. Rachael PETERS
18 Director of Facilities .... Mr. Chris SAMPITE
46 Director Sponsored Research .... Ms. Patty J. ROBERTS
44 Sr Director of Philanthropy .... Ms. Margo SHIDELER
07 Director of Admissions .... Vacant
15 Human Resources Director .... Ms. Edie CUMMINGS
19 Director of Public Safety .... Mr. Eddie WALKER

Delta School of Business & Technology, DBA Delta Tech (E)

517 Broad Street, Lake Charles LA 70601-4334
County: Calcasieu FICE Identification: 020555
Unit ID: 158723
Telephone: (337) 439-5765 Carnegie Class: Assoc/PrivFP
FAX Number: (337) 436-5151 Calendar System: Quarter
URL: www.deltatech.edu
Established: 1970 Annual Undergrad Tuition & Fees: $9,590
Enrollment: 300 Coed
Affiliation or Control: Proprietary IRS Status: Proprietary
Highest Offering: Associate Degree
Program: Occupational; 2-Year Principally Bachelor's Creditable; Technical Emphasis
Accreditation: ACICS

01 Chief Executive Officer .... Mr. Jeff EDWARDS
10 Chief Fiscal Officer/Corp Secretary .... Mrs. Nina LEBLANC

Dillard University (F)

2601 Gentilly Boulevard, New Orleans LA 70122-3097
County: Orleans FICE Identification: 002004
Unit ID: 158802
Telephone: (504) 283-8822 Carnegie Class: Bac/A&S
FAX Number: N/A Calendar System: Semester
URL: www.dillard.edu
Established: 1869 Annual Undergrad Tuition & Fees: $15,860
Enrollment: 1,200 Coed
Affiliation or Control: United Methodist IRS Status: 501(c)3
Highest Offering: Baccalaureate
Program: Liberal Arts And General; Professional; Fine Arts Emphasis
Accreditation: SC, NUR

01 President .... Dr. Walter M. KIMBROUGH
03 Executive Vice President .... Mr. Marc BARNES
05 Provost/Sr VP for Academic Affairs .... Dr. Yolanda PAGE
32 Vice President for Student Success .... Dr. Toya BARNES-TEAMER
43 VP for Legal Affairs .... Dr. Denise WALLACE
10 VP for Finance & CFO .... Mr. Gregory LEWIS
20 Associate Provost .... Dr. Christopher JEFFRIES
07 Asst VP of Admissions & Programming .... Ms. Monica WHITE
18 Assoc Vice Pres Facilities Mgmt .... Mr. Randy YEAGER
36 Director of Career/Prof Services .... Ms. Caretta COOKE
06 Dir of Records & Registration .... Mr. Robert MITCHELL, JR.
37 Int Dir Financial Aid/Scholarships .... Ms. Shannon NEAL
102 Assoc VP Research & Spons Programs .... Mr. Theodore CALLIER
30 Director of Development .... Dr. Lupita ROY-RASHEED
04 ExecutiveAssistant to the President .... Ms. Kathy TAYLOR
09 Director of Institutional Research .... Dr. Willie KIRKLAND
31 Director Community Development .... Mr. Nick L. HARRIS
19 Chief of Police .... Vacant
15 Director of Human Resources .... Mrs. Brittany RICHARDSON
26 Sr Dir of Marketing Communications .... Ms. Mona DUFFEL-JONES
97 Dean of College of General Studies .... Dr. Dorothy SMITH
08 Interim Dean of Library/Learning .... Ms. Cynthia CHARLES
49 Dean of College of Arts & Sciences .... Dr. John WILSON
96 Purchasing Officer .... Ms. Anlatear KIRKLIN
103 Dir Workforce/Career Development .... Ms. Caretta COOKE
105 Director Web Services .... Mr. Norward SEARS
13 Chief Info Technology Officer (CIO) .... Mr. Cederic KONYAOLE
22 Dir Affirmative Action/EEO .... Ms. Denise WALLACE
25 Chief Contracts/Grants Admin .... Mr. Theodore CALLIER
39 Director Student Housing .... Dr. Demetrius JOHNSON
41 Athletic Director .... Mrs. Kiki BARNES
50 Dean of Business .... Dr. Richard IGWIKI
91 Director Administrative Computing .... Vacant

Fortis College (G)

9255 Interline Avenue, Baton Rouge LA 70809
County: East Baton Rouge FICE Identification: 034803
Unit ID: 439738
Telephone: (225) 248-1015 Carnegie Class: Assoc/PrivFP
FAX Number: (225) 248-9517 Calendar System: Other
URL: www.fortis.edu
Established: 1991 Annual Undergrad Tuition & Fees: $13,316
Enrollment: 382 Coed
Affiliation or Control: Proprietary IRS Status: Proprietary
Highest Offering: Associate Degree
Program: Occupational
Accreditation: ABHES, MLTAD, RAD, SURGT, SURTEC

01 Campus Director .... Mr. Vaughn HARTUNIAS

Herzing University (H)

2500 Williams Boulevard, Kenner LA 70062
Telephone: (504) 733-0074 Identification: 666450
Accreditation: &NH, MAAB, SURTEC

† Regional accreditation is carried under the parent institution in Madison, WI.

ITI Technical College (I)

13944 Airline Highway, Baton Rouge LA 70817-5998
County: East Baton Rouge FICE Identification: 021662
Unit ID: 159197
Telephone: (225) 752-4230 Carnegie Class: Assoc/PrivFP
FAX Number: (225) 756-0903 Calendar System: Quarter
URL: www.iticollege.edu
Established: 1973 Annual Undergrad Tuition & Fees: $27,950
Enrollment: 695 Coed
Affiliation or Control: Proprietary IRS Status: Proprietary
Highest Offering: Associate Degree
Program: Occupational; 2-Year Principally Bachelor's Creditable; Technical Emphasis
Accreditation: ACCSC

01 President .... Mr. Earl Joe MARTIN, III
03 Vice President .... Mr. Mark WORTHY
05 Dean of Education .... Mr. Louis BABIN
88 Director of Compliance .... Mr. Michael CHAMPAGNE
06 Registrar .... Ms. Teresa MAYEUX
07 Director of Admissions .... Mr. Shawn NORRIS
37 Director Student Financial Aid .... Ms. Connie ROUBIQUE

ITT Technical Institute (J)

14111 Airline Hwy, Suite 101,
Baton Rouge LA 70817-6241
Telephone: (225) 754-5800 Identification: 666164
Accreditation: ACICS

† Branch campus of ITT Technical Institute, Indianapolis, IN.

ITT Technical Institute (K)

140 James Drive East, Saint Rose LA 70087-4005
Telephone: (504) 463-0338 Identification: 666031
Accreditation: ACICS

† Branch campus of ITT Technical Institute, Indianapolis, IN.

Louisiana College (L)

1140 College Drive, Pineville LA 71359-0001
County: Rapides FICE Identification: 002007
Unit ID: 159568
Telephone: (318) 487-7011 Carnegie Class: Bac/Diverse
FAX Number: (318) 487-7191 Calendar System: Semester
URL: www.lacollege.edu
Established: 1906 Annual Undergrad Tuition & Fees: $15,070
Enrollment: 1,256 Coed
Affiliation or Control: Southern Baptist IRS Status: 501(c)3
Highest Offering: Master's
Program: Liberal Arts And General; Teacher Preparatory
Accreditation: #SC, ACBSP, CAATE, MUS, NURSE, PTAA, SW, TEAC

01 President .... Dr. Rick BREWER
03 VP Integration Faith/Learning .... Dr. Philip CAPLES
05 Interim Vice Pres Academic Affairs .... Dr. Cheryl CLARK
10 Vice President for Business Affairs .... Mr. Randall HARGIS
30 VP Inst Advancement/New Projects .... Mr. Byron MCGEE
32 Dean of Students .... Dr. Michael SHAMBLIN
06 Registrar .... Ms. Eileen DEBOER
84 Director Enrollment Mgmt/Admissions .... Mr. Byron MCGEE
37 Director of Financial Aid .... Mr. David BARNARD
08 Director of the Library .... Mr. Terry MARTIN
26 Exec Asst to Pres Comm/Marketing .... Mr. Norm MILLER
13 Director Computer Services .... Mr. Shane DAVIS
18 Director of Physical Plant .... Mr. Randall HARGIS
21 Director of Business Office .... Ms. Beverly INGRAM
39 Director of Housing .... Mr. Dayne REEVES
41 Athletic Director .... Mr. Dennis DUNN
42 Baptist Student Union Director .... Mr. Shannon LANE
44 Director Constituent Relations .... Vacant
35 Director Student Activities .... Ms. K. B THOMAS
36 Director Career Development .... Mrs. Leneil MERCER
09 Director of Institutional Research .... Vacant
38 Director Student Counseling .... Ms. Leneil MERCER
07 Director of Admissions .... Mr. Byron MCGEE
15 Director Personnel Services .... Ms. Shannon TASSIN
40 Bookstore Manager .... Mrs. Linda BILLINGSLEY
29 Coord Alumni Affairs/Fdn Rels .... Ms. Kathy OVERTURF
19 Coordinator of Safety & Security .... Mr. Charles ROBERTSON
23 Coordinator of Health Services .... Ms. Janet SANDERS
04 Assistant to the President .... Ms. Susan NIXON

*Louisiana Community & Technical College System (M)

265 S Foster Drive, Baton Rouge LA 70806-4104
County: East Baton Rouge Identification: 666188
Telephone: (225) 922-2800 Carnegie Class: N/A
FAX Number: (225) 922-2392
URL: www.lctcs.edu

01 President .... Dr. Monty SULLIVAN
03 Executive Vice President .... Dr. Neil MATKIN
10 Sr Vice Pres Finance & Admin .... Mr. Joseph F. MARIN
05 Int VP Academic Affs/Inst Rsch .... Dr. Paul CARLSEN
103 VP Workforce/Career/Tech Education .... Mr. David HELVESTON
30 Sr Vice Pres System Advancement .... Mr. Glen DUNCAN
26 Exec Director Media Relations .... Mr. Quinton TAYLOR
04 Special Assistant to President .... Ms. Jan JACKSON
106 Director of Client Services .... Ms. Tiffany SNELL

*Baton Rouge Community College (N)

201 Community College Drive,
Baton Rouge LA 70806-4156
County: East Baton Rouge FICE Identification: 037303
Unit ID: 437103
Telephone: (225) 216-8000 Carnegie Class: Assoc/Pub-U-SC
FAX Number: (225) 216-8100 Calendar System: Semester
URL: www.mybrcc.edu
Established: 1998 Annual Undergrad Tuition & Fees (In-District): $4,053
Enrollment: 10,458 Coed
Affiliation or Control: State/Local IRS Status: 501(c)3
Highest Offering: Associate Degree
Program: Occupational; 2-Year Principally Bachelor's Creditable

Accreditation: SC, ACBSP, ACFEI, ADNUR, DMS, NAIT, SURGT

02 Chancellor .... Dr. Andrea L. MILLER
04 Int Exec Asst to the Chancellor .... Mr. Tommy A. MORRIS
26 Spec Asst to the Chanc for Med Rels .... Mr. Steve MITCHELL
84 Vice Chanc Enroll Mgmt/Stdnt Supp .... Dr. Albert TEZENO
86 Spec Asst to the Chanc for Gov Rels .... Ms. Phyllis MOUTON
45 Vice Chanc Plng/Assess & Account .... Dr. Cristi CARSON
46 Dir of Business Process Improv .... Ms. Dionne ANDRUS
05 Vice Chanc Acad Affairs .... Vacant
75 Vice Chanc for Tech Educ .... Dr. Kay MCDANIEL
10 Vice Chanc for Finance .... Ms. Helen HARRIS
13 Chief Information Officer .... Mr. Ron SOLOMON
31 Director of Community Rels .... Ms. Gerri HOBDY
15 Director of HR .... Ms. Terri RICKS
19 Chief of Police .... Ms. Genoria TILLEY
25 Dir Grants Resource Center .... Ms. Ann ZANDERS
18 Dir of Facilities/Phys Plant .... Mr. Aurel BOTA
88 Events Manager .... Ms. Georgia SCOBEE
32 Dean of Students .... Mr. Harry THOMPSON
35 Int Exec Dir of Student Svcs .... Dr. Steven ANDRUS
88 Int Exec Dir of Enroll Mgmt .... Dr. Teresa A. JONES
88 Dir Student Support Services .... Ms. Stacia HARDY
36 Director Career and Job Placement .... Ms. Lisa HIBNER
37 Director Student Financial Aid .... Ms. Amy CABLE
41 Athletic Director .... Mr. Neil HAYHURST
38 Dir of Counseling & Disability Svcs .... Ms. Wendy DEVALL
88 Dir of Academic Learning Center .... Ms. Jeanne STACY
88 Upward Bound Program Director .... Ms. Darica SIMON
96 Director of Purchasing .... Mr. Michael CONSTANTIN
06 Registrar .... Ms. Erin BLAKE

*Bossier Parish Community College (A)

6220 E Texas Street, Bossier City LA 71111-6922
County: Bossier FICE Identification: 020554
Unit ID: 158431
Telephone: (318) 678-6000 Carnegie Class: Assoc/Pub-R-M
FAX Number: (318) 678-6389 Calendar System: Semester
URL: www.bpcc.edu
Established: 1966 Annual Undergrad Tuition & Fees (In-District): $6,800
Enrollment: 8,695 Coed
Affiliation or Control: State/Local IRS Status: 501(c)3
Highest Offering: Associate Degree
Program: Occupational; 2-Year Principally Bachelor's Creditable
Accreditation: SC, ACFEI, ADNUR, COARC, EMT, MAC, NAIT, OTA, PHLEB, PTAA, SURGT

02 Interim Chancellor .... Dr. Douglas R. BATEMAN
05 VC for Academic Affairs .... Ms. Lesa TAYLOR DUPREE
11 VC Business Affs/Economic Devel .... Mr. Tom WILLIAMS
32 VC of Student Services .... Ms. Karen RECCHIA
10 Assoc VC Finance .... Mr. Raymond ABRAHAM
20 Assoc VC Planning/Instruction .... Ms. Lesa TAYLOR-DUPREE
60 Dean of Comm & Performing Arts .... Dr. Ray Scott CRAWFORD
103 Dean of Workforce Develop/Cont Educ .... Ms. Lisa WARGO
08 Dean of Learning Resources .... Ms. Brenda BRANTLEY
88 Assoc VC for Innov Learning/WF .... Ms. Donna WOMACK
21 Comptroller .... Ms. Carol BATES
38 Student Counselor .... Ms. Jennifer MCMULLEN
37 Director Student Financial Aid .... Ms. Vicki TEMPLE
06 Registrar .... Mr. Richard COCKERHAM
26 Director of Public Relations .... Ms. Tracy MCGILL
15 Director of Human Resources .... Ms. Teri BASHARA
35 Director of Student Life .... Ms. Marjoree HARPER
13 Chief Information Officer .... Mr. Gary HOLLATZ
22 Diversity/Multicultural Affairs .... Ms. Cindy DARBY
72 Director of Educational Technology .... Vacant
18 Dir Physical Plant & Maintenance .... Mr. Joe ST. ANDRE
29 Director Alumni Relations .... Ms. Stephanie ROGERS
09 Dir Inst Research/Assessment/Grants .... Ms. Lisa WHEELER
96 Director of Purchasing .... Ms. Gayle DOUCET
04 Exec Assistant to Chancellor .... Ms. Christy MOORE
07 Dean of Enrollment Management .... Ms. Kathy VERCHER
108 Dir Institutional Effectiveness .... Ms. Allison MARTIN
19 Director Security/Safety .... Mr. Mike MAY
50 Dean of Business .... Ms. Peggy FULLER
54 Dean of TEM .... Ms. Sandra PARTAIN

*Central Louisiana Technical College Avoyelles Campus (B)

508 Choupique Street, Cottonport LA 71327-3743
County: Avoyelles FICE Identification: 008317
Unit ID: 158237
Telephone: (318) 876-2401 Carnegie Class: Not Classified
FAX Number: (318) 876-2634 Calendar System: Semester
URL: www.ltc.edu
Established: 1938 Annual Undergrad Tuition & Fees (In-District): $1,282
Enrollment: 378 Coed
Affiliation or Control: State/Local IRS Status: 501(c)3
Highest Offering: Associate Degree
Program: Occupational; Technical Emphasis
Accreditation: COE

02 Campus Dean .... Ms. Jacqueline AUSBON

*Central Louisiana Technical College Oakdale Campus (C)

117 Highway 1152, Oakdale LA 71463-3536
County: Allen FICE Identification: 030026
Unit ID: 160047
Telephone: (318) 335-3944 Carnegie Class: Assoc/Pub-R-S
FAX Number: (318) 335-3347 Calendar System: Quarter
URL: www.cltcc.edu
Established: 1999 Annual Undergrad Tuition & Fees (In-District): $3,566
Enrollment: 456 Coed
Affiliation or Control: State/Local IRS Status: 501(c)3
Highest Offering: Associate Degree
Program: Occupational; Technical Emphasis
Accreditation: COE

02 Acting Campus Administrator .... Ms. Kim ANDREWS

*Central Louisiana Technical Community College (D)

4311 S. Macarthur Drive, Alexandria LA 71301
County: Rapides FICE Identification: 005489
Unit ID: 158088
Telephone: (318) 487-5443 Carnegie Class: Assoc/Pub-R-S
FAX Number: (318) 487-5970 Calendar System: Trimester
URL: www.cltcc.edu
Established: 1965 Annual Undergrad Tuition & Fees (In-State): $1,783
Enrollment: 2,049 Coed
Affiliation or Control: State IRS Status: 501(c)3
Highest Offering: Associate Degree
Program: Occupational; Technical Emphasis
Accreditation: COE

02 Chancellor .... Dr. James (Jimmy) R. SAWTELLE, III
05 Chief Academic/Student Svcs Officer .... Mr. William TULAK
10 Controller .... Ms. Elizabeth BYNOG

*Central Louisiana Technical & Community College-Huey P. Long Campus (E)

5960 Highway 167 N, Winnfield LA 71483-5075
County: Winn FICE Identification: 005480
Unit ID: 159090
Telephone: (318) 628-4342 Carnegie Class: Not Classified
FAX Number: (318) 628-7768 Calendar System: Semester
URL: www.cltcc.edu
Established: 1938 Annual Undergrad Tuition & Fees (In-District): $1,961
Enrollment: 258 Coed
Affiliation or Control: State/Local IRS Status: 501(c)3
Highest Offering: Associate Degree
Program: Occupational; Technical Emphasis
Accreditation: COE

02 Campus Dean .... Mr. Jeff JOHNSON

*Delgado Community College (F)

615 City Park Avenue, New Orleans LA 70119-4399
County: Orleans FICE Identification: 004625
Unit ID: 158662
Telephone: (504) 671-5000 Carnegie Class: Assoc/Pub-U-MC
FAX Number: (504) 361-6699 Calendar System: Semester
URL: www.dcc.edu
Established: 1921 Annual Undergrad Tuition & Fees (In-District): $4,970
Enrollment: 17,138 Coed
Affiliation or Control: State/Local IRS Status: 501(c)3
Highest Offering: Associate Degree
Program: Occupational; 2-Year Principally Bachelor's Creditable
Accreditation: SC, ACBSP, ACFEI, ADNUR, CAHIIM, COARC, DIETT, DMS, EMT, ENGT, FUSER, MLTAD, NAIT, NMT, OTA, PHLEB, POLYT, PTAA, RAD, RTT, SURGT

02 Chancellor .... Ms. Joan Y. DAVIS
10 Int VC Business/Admin Affairs .... Mr. Steven H. CAZAUBON
05 Vice Chanc Acad Affs/Col Provost .... Dr. Kathleen CURPHY
103 Vice Chanc Workforce Dev/Tech Educ .... Dr. Larissa LITTLETON-STEIB
30 VC for Inst Advancement/Public Rels .... Dr. Stanton F. MCNEELY, III
66 Exec Dean School of Nursing Campus .... Dr. Cheryl MYERS
76 Dean of Allied Health .... Mr. Harold GASPARD
50 Dean Business & Technology .... Mr. Warren PUNEKY
60 Dean of Communication Division .... Dr. Lester ADELSBERG
81 Dean Science & Math .... Mr. Thomas GRUBER
79 Dean of Arts and Humanities .... Ms. Patrice MOORE
106 Dean of Dist Learn and Instr Tech .... Ms. Jeanne SAMUEL
12 Exec Dean Northshore .... Ms. Ashley CHITWOOD
12 Exec Dean West Bank Campus .... Dr. Kristine STRICKLAND
32 Exec Dn City Pk Camp/VC Stdnt Affs .... Dr. Arnel COSEY
15 Asst Vice Chanc for Human Resources .... Ms. Carla MAJOR
13 Exec Dn SC Camp/Asst VC Info Tech .... Mr. Thomas LOVINCE
21 Asst VC Financial Services .... Mr. Steven H. CAZAUBON
18 Asst VC of Dir Facilities/Planning .... Mr. Matthew ALTIER
21 Asst VC/Controller .... Mr. Rodney JOHNSON
04 Executive Asst to the Chancellor .... Ms. Traci SMOTHERS
72 Int Asst Dean Business & Technology .... Ms. Karen MUHSIN

09 Int Exec Dir Planning & Research .... Mr. Rene CINTRON
88 Exec Dir of Curriculum & Pgm Devel .... Mr. Timothy STAMM
08 Librarian .... Mr. Timothy STAMM
37 Director Financial Aid .... Ms. Rhonda KING
41 Athletic Director .... Mr. Joe SCHEUERMANN
06 College Registrar .... Ms. Maria CISNEROS
07 Director Admissions/Enrollment Svcs .... Ms. Gwen BOUTTE
44 Director of Restricted Funds .... Mr. Ron RUSSO
35 Director of Student Life .... Mrs. Michelle GRECO
88 Director Ofc of Advising & Testing .... Ms. Tania CARRADINE
96 Director of Purchasing .... Ms. Susan VARBLE
19 Interim Director of Campus Police .... Mr. Alvin FLINT

*L.E. Fletcher Technical Community College (G)

1407 Highway 311, Schriever LA 70395
County: Terrebonne FICE Identification: 005761
Unit ID: 160481
Telephone: (985) 448-7900 Carnegie Class: Assoc/Pub-U-MC
FAX Number: (985) 446-3308 Calendar System: Semester
URL: www.fletcher.edu
Established: 1948 Annual Undergrad Tuition & Fees (In-State): $3,911
Enrollment: 2,417 Coed
Affiliation or Control: State IRS Status: Exempt
Highest Offering: Associate Degree
Program: Occupational; 2-Year Principally Bachelor's Creditable
Accreditation: SC, COARC, NAIT, PHLEB, PNUR

02 Chancellor .... Mr. Earl W. MEADOR
03 Executive Vice Chancellor .... Dr. Derrick MANNS
10 Vice Chancellor of Finance .... Vacant
05 Vice Chancellor of Academic Affairs .... Dr. Derrick MANNS
06 Registrar .... Ms. Lisa HIDALGO
09 Director of Inst Research & Effect .... Ms. Carrie CORTEZ
21 Director of Accounting .... Mr. Andrew BOYNE
32 Associate VC Student Services .... Vacant
75 Dean of Technical Education .... Ms. Fathia WILLIAMS
66 Dean of Nursing and Allied Health .... Ms. Sonia CLARKE
07 Director of Admissions .... Ms. Ana NANNEY
15 HR Manager .... Ms. Gina MARCEL
37 Director of Financial Aid .... Mr. Derrick PROCELL
04 Assistant to the Chancellor .... Ms. Brenda FAUCHEUX
08 Head Librarian .... Mrs. Suzanne MARTIN
30 Exec Dir of Inst Advancement .... Ms. Jessica THORNTON
49 Dean Art and Sciences .... Mrs. Donna ESTRADA
103 Director of Workforce Education .... Mrs. Catherine BARBER
75 Dean of LAMPI .... Mr. Carl MOORE
96 Director of Purchasing .... Ms. Nancy CLEMENT

*Louisiana Delta Community College (H)

7500 Millhaven Road, Monroe LA 71203
County: Ouachita Parish FICE Identification: 041301
Unit ID: 440624
Telephone: (318) 345-9000 Carnegie Class: Assoc/Pub-R-S
FAX Number: N/A Calendar System: Semester
URL: www.ladelta.edu
Established: 2001 Annual Undergrad Tuition & Fees (In-District): $3,634
Enrollment: 2,973 Coed
Affiliation or Control: State/Local IRS Status: 501(c)3
Highest Offering: Associate Degree
Program: Occupational; 2-Year Principally Bachelor's Creditable; Business Emphasis
Accreditation: SC, ADNUR, NAIT

02 Chancellor .... Dr. Barbara M. HANSON
05 Vice Chanc of Academic Affairs .... Vacant
10 VC of Finance & Administration .... Mr. Troy CASERTA
84 Dir of Enrollment Mgmt/Registrar .... Mr. Adam ABERCROMBIE
32 Vice Chanc of Student Affairs .... Mr. John TURNER
30 Exec Dir of Dev/Alumni Relations .... Mr. James JOPLING
13 Chief Information Officer .... Mr. Bradley MASTERS

*Northshore Technical Community College (I)

1710 Sullivan Drive, Bogalusa LA 70427-5866
County: Washington FICE Identification: 006756
Unit ID: 160667
Telephone: (985) 732-6640 Carnegie Class: Assoc/Pub-U-MC
FAX Number: (985) 732-6603 Calendar System: Semester
URL: www.northshorecollege.edu
Established: 1930 Annual Undergrad Tuition & Fees (In-District): $3,945
Enrollment: 4,030 Coed
Affiliation or Control: State/Local IRS Status: 501(c)3
Highest Offering: Associate Degree
Program: Occupational; 2-Year Principally Bachelor's Creditable; Technical Emphasis
Accreditation: COE

02 Chancellor .... Dr. William S. WAINWRIGHT
10 Vice Chancellor Finance & Admin .... Mr. Marc CHAUVIN
72 Dean of Technical Studies .... Mr. Dewayne LAMBERT
32 Vice Provost of Student Affairs .... Ms. Christy MONTGOMERY
08 Director of Library Services .... Ms. Margaret KELLER
76 Dean of Health Sciences & Nursing .... Ms. Katherine M. LYONS
81 Dean of Academic and STEM Programs .... Dr. Tina TINNEY
12 Dean of Campus Administration .... Ms. Sharon HORNSBY

12 Dean of Campus Administration .... Ms. Bridget LABORDE
103 Executive Director of Workforce Dev .... Mr. David LLOYD
09 Dir of Inst Rsrch & Eff/Vice Prov .... Ms. Shelia SINGLETARY
15 Human Resources Director .... Ms. Joanna DILLMAN
06 Registrar .... Ms. Kim FINCH
18 Chief Facilities/Physical Plant .... Mr. Gerald BLAPPERT
96 Director of Purchasing .... Mr. Danny STEWART

*Northwest Louisiana Technical College Northwest Campus (A)

9500 Industrial Drive, Minden LA 71055
County: Webster FICE Identification: 009975
Unit ID: 160010
Telephone: (318) 371-3035 Carnegie Class: Assoc/Pub-R-S
FAX Number: (318) 371-3026 Calendar System: Trimester
URL: www.nwltc.edu
Established: 1952 Annual Undergrad Tuition & Fees (In-District): $2,566
Enrollment: 2,694 Coed
Affiliation or Control: State/Local IRS Status: 501(c)3
Highest Offering: Associate Degree
Program: Occupational; 2-Year Principally Bachelor's Creditable; Technical Emphasis
Accreditation: COE

02 Interim Campus Dean .... Mrs. Dianne CLARK
05 Assistant Dean .... Mr. Charles SCOTT PRICE
09 Director Institutional Research .... Mr. David RHODES
15 Chief Human Resources Officer .... Ms. Amber SAUNDERS
37 Dir Student Fin Aid/Admissions .... Ms. Annette CHANLER

*Nunez Community College (B)

3710 Paris Road, Chalmette LA 70043-1297
County: Saint Bernard FICE Identification: 021661
Unit ID: 158884
Telephone: (504) 278-6200 Carnegie Class: Assoc/Pub-S-SC
FAX Number: (504) 278-6480 Calendar System: Semester
URL: www.nunez.edu
Established: 1992 Annual Undergrad Tuition & Fees (In-District): $3,938
Enrollment: 2,500 Coed
Affiliation or Control: State/Local IRS Status: 501(c)3
Highest Offering: Associate Degree
Program: Occupational; 2-Year Principally Bachelor's Creditable
Accreditation: SC, NAIT

02 Chancellor .... Dr. Thomas R. WARNER
05 Vice Chanc Academic & Student Affs .... Mrs. Annette ACCOMANDO
30 VC for Institutional Advancement .... Ms. Teresa L. SMITH
10 Chief Financial Officer .... Mr. Louis LEHR
15 Dir Human Res/Exec Asst to Chanc .... Mr. Richard GREENE
20 Dean of Academic Affairs .... Ms. Tonia LORIA
32 Dean for Student Affairs .... Ms. Becky MAILLET
45 Dean Planning/Inst Effectiveness .... Mr. Leonard UNBEHAGEN
103 Director Workforce Development .... Mr. Ernest T. FRAZIER, JR.
06 Registrar .... Ms. Meg GREENFIELD
07 Director of Admissions .... Ms. Angie JONES
37 Director Financial Aid .... Mr. John WHISNANT
27 Public Information Officer .... Ms. Lindsay JAKIEL DIULUS
18 Coordinator of Facilities .... Ms. Dawn HART-THORE
25 Director of Sponsored Programs ...... Ms. Kimberly RUTHERFORD
13 IT Manager .... Mr. Jason HOSCH

*River Parishes Community College (C)

PO Box 2367, Gonzales LA 70707
County: Ascension FICE Identification: 037894
Unit ID: 436304
Telephone: (225) 743-8500 Carnegie Class: Assoc/Pub-S-SC
FAX Number: (225) 644-8210 Calendar System: Semester
URL: www.rpcc.edu
Established: 1999 Annual Undergrad Tuition & Fees (In-District): $3,911
Enrollment: 1,992 Coed
Affiliation or Control: State/Local IRS Status: 501(c)3
Highest Offering: Associate Degree
Program: Occupational; 2-Year Principally Bachelor's Creditable
Accreditation: SC, NAIT

02 Chancellor .... Dr. Dale DOTY
10 VC Business/Finance/Administration .... Khalli HAGAN
84 VC of Students/Enrollment Mgmt .... Allison D. VICKNAIR
05 VC of Academic Studies .... Dr. Crystal LEE
21 Director of Accounting & Payroll .... Lisa JACKSON
06 Registrar .... Cara LANDRY
37 Director Financial Aid .... Terry MARTIN
38 Director Student Counseling .... Jennifer KLEINPETER
08 Director of Library Services .... Wendy JOHNSON
15 Human Resource Manager .... Donna WHITTINGTON
07 Admissions Counselor .... Dianna GILBERT
09 Director of Institutional Research .... Melba KENNEDY

*South Central Louisiana Technical College Young Memorial Campus (D)

900 Youngs Road, Morgan City LA 70380-2931
County: Saint Mary FICE Identification: 005526
Unit ID: 160913
Telephone: (985) 380-2957 Carnegie Class: Assoc/Pub-S-MC
FAX Number: (985) 380-2440 Calendar System: Semester
URL: www.scl.edu
Established: 1965 Annual Undergrad Tuition & Fees (In-District): $2,414
Enrollment: 2,039 Coed
Affiliation or Control: State/Local IRS Status: 501(c)3
Highest Offering: Associate Degree
Program: Occupational; Technical Emphasis
Accreditation: COE

02 Campus Dean .... Mr. Anthony L. BAHAM
05 Chief Academic Officer .... Ms. Melanie HENRY
07 Dir of Admissions/Student Affairs .... Ms. Tammie L. MOORE
09 Director of Institutional Research .... Ms. Katherine FALGOUT
15 Director Human Resources .... Ms. Pam MILLER

*South Louisiana Community College (E)

1101 Bertrand Drive, Lafayette LA 70506-4124
County: Lafayette FICE Identification: 039563
Unit ID: 434061
Telephone: (337) 521-9000 Carnegie Class: Assoc/Pub-R-M
FAX Number: (337) 521-9061 Calendar System: Semester
URL: www.solacc.edu
Established: 1998 Annual Undergrad Tuition & Fees (In-District): $3,916
Enrollment: 6,332 Coed
Affiliation or Control: State/Local IRS Status: 501(c)3
Highest Offering: Associate Degree
Program: Occupational; 2-Year Principally Bachelor's Creditable
Accreditation: SC, ACFEI, EMT, MLTAD, NAIT, SURGT

02 Chancellor .... Dr. Natalie HARDER
04 Assistant to the Chancellor .... Ms. Holly GREER
05 Vice Chanc of Academic Affairs .... Dr. Micheal GLISSON
10 Vice Chanc Finance & Administration .... Mr. Bryan GLATTER
103 Vice Chanc Economic & Workforce Dev .... Dr. Willie SMITH
32 Vice Chanc for Student Services .... Dr. David VOLPE
07 Director of Admissions .... Mr. Chris STUTES
37 Director of Financial Aid .... Ms. Kelly KNIGHT
08 Director of Library Services .... Ms. Katherine ROLFES
21 Business Manager .... Ms. Janet LAGRANGE
96 Director of Accounting .... Ms. Carla ORTEGO
18 Facilities Coordinator .... Mr. Ed LOPEZ
15 Human Resources Director .... Ms. Alicia HULIN

*Sowela Technical Community College (F)

PO Box 16950, Lake Charles LA 70616-6950
County: Calcasieu FICE Identification: 005467
Unit ID: 160579
Telephone: (337) 421-6565 Carnegie Class: Assoc/Pub-R-S
FAX Number: (337) 491-2135 Calendar System: Semester
URL: www.sowela.edu
Established: 1938 Annual Undergrad Tuition & Fees (In-District): $4,669
Enrollment: 3,521 Coed
Affiliation or Control: State/Local IRS Status: 501(c)3
Highest Offering: Associate Degree
Program: 2-Year Principally Bachelor's Creditable; Technical Emphasis
Accreditation: SC, ACFEI, COE, NAIT

02 Chancellor .... Dr. Neil ASPINWALL
04 Assistant to the Chancellor .... Ms. Mary REEDER
05 Int VC Acad Affs/Stdnt Success .... Ms. Paula HELLUMS
10 Vice Chancellor Finance .... Ms. Jeanine NEWMAN
46 Vice Chancellor Economic Devel .... Vacant
13 Int Chief Info Res & Tech Officer ..... Dr. Martha J. SCHEXNEIDER
84 Exec Dir Enroll Mgmt & Student Affs .... Vacant
21 Controller .... Mr. Francis PORCHE, JR.
37 Director of Financial Aid .... Ms. Anna DAIGLE
08 Director of Library Services .... Ms. Mary Frances SHERWOOD
15 Director of Human Resources .... Dr. FitzPatrick ANYANWU
103 Director of Workforce Development .... Dr. Joseph FLEISHMAN
32 Director of Student Support Svcs .... Ms. Christine COLLINS
18 Director Facilities Planning & Mgmt .... Mr. Davidson DARBONE
09 Exec Director Planning & Analysis ... Dr. Fitzpatrick U. ANYANWU
30 Exec Dir Institutional Advancement .... Ms. Marianne WHITE

*Northwest Louisiana Technical College Natchitoches Campus (G)

6587 Highway 1 Bypass (3110), Natchitoches LA 71458-0657
Telephone: (318) 357-3162 FICE Identification: 021602
Accreditation: COE

† Branch campus of Northwest Louisiana Technical College Northwest Campus, Minden, LA.

*Northwest Louisiana Technical College Shreveport Campus (H)

Box 78527, 2010 N Market Street, Shreveport LA 71137-8527
Telephone: (318) 676-7811 FICE Identification: 005469
Accreditation: COE

† Branch campus of Northwest Louisiana Technical College Northwest Campus, Minden, LA.

*South Central Louisiana Technical College Lafourche Campus (I)

1425 Tiger Drive, Thibodaux LA 70301-4336
Telephone: (985) 447-0924 FICE Identification: 030091
Accreditation: COE, SURGT

† Branch campus of South Central Louisiana Technical College Young Memorial Campus.

*South Central Louisiana Technical College Reserve Campus (J)

PO Drawer AQ, 181 Regala Park Road, Reserve LA 70084-0542
Telephone: (985) 536-4418 FICE Identification: 023334
Accreditation: COE, NAIT

† Branch campus of South Central Louisiana Technical College Young Memorial Campus.

Louisiana Culinary Institute (K)

10550 Airline Highway, Baton Rouge LA 70816-4109
County: East Baton Rouge FICE Identification: 041123
Unit ID: 449612
Telephone: (225) 769-8820 Carnegie Class: Assoc/PrivFP
FAX Number: (225) 769-8792 Calendar System: Semester
URL: www.lci.edu
Established: 2002 Annual Undergrad Tuition & Fees: $14,575
Enrollment: 208 Coed
Affiliation or Control: Proprietary IRS Status: Proprietary
Highest Offering: Associate Degree
Program: Occupational
Accreditation: COE, ACFEI

01 Chief Executive Officer .... Keith RUSH

*Louisiana State University Administration (L)

3810 W Lakeshore Drive, Baton Rouge LA 70808-4600
County: East Baton Rouge FICE Identification: 002009
Unit ID: 159638
Telephone: (225) 578-2111 Carnegie Class: N/A
FAX Number: (225) 578-5524
URL: www.lsu.edu

01 President .... Dr. F. King ALEXANDER
05 VP Academic Affairs/Tech Trans .... Dr. Carolyn H. HARGRAVE
17 Exec VP HC/Med Educ Redesign .... Dr. Frank OPELKA
88 Asst Vice Pres for System Relations . Dr. Robert H. RASMUSSEN
10 Assoc Vice Pres Finance/Admin .... Mrs. Wendy SIMONEAUX
18 System Director Facility Planning .... Mr. Danny MAHAFFEY
43 LSU Lead Counsel .... Mr. W. Shelby MCKENZIE
15 System Dir Human Resource/Risk Mgt ... Ms. Sharyon LIPSCOMB
21 System Director Internal Audit .... Mr. Chad BRACKIN

*Louisiana State University and Agricultural and Mechanical College (M)

Baton Rouge LA 70803-0100
County: East Baton Rouge FICE Identification: 002010
Unit ID: 159391
Telephone: (225) 578-3202 Carnegie Class: RU/VH
FAX Number: (225) 578-6400 Calendar System: Semester
URL: www.lsu.edu
Established: 1860 Annual Undergrad Tuition & Fees (In-State): $9,714
Enrollment: 30,451 Coed
Affiliation or Control: State IRS Status: 501(c)3
Highest Offering: Doctorate
Program: Liberal Arts And General; Teacher Preparatory; Professional
Accreditation: SC, ART, BUS, CAATE, CACREP, CIDA, #CLPSY, CONST, CS, DIETD, ENG, IPSY, JOUR, LIB, LSAR, MUS, SCPSY, SP, SPAA, SW, TED, THEA, VET

02 President .... Dr. King ALEXANDER
05 Int Exec Vice Pres/Provost .... Dr. Richard KOUBEK
43 General Counsel .... Mr. Thomas SKINNER
26 VP of Strategic Communication .... Mrs. Linda BONNIN
10 Vice Pres Finance & Admin .... Mr. Daniel LAYZELL
46 Vice Pres Research & Econ Dev .... Dr. Kalliat T. VALSARAJ
45 Vice Pres Strategic Initiatives .... Dr. Isiah M. WARNER
32 Vice Pres Student Life/Enroll Svcs .... Dr. Kurt J. KEPPLER
102 President/CEO LSU Foundation .... Mr. Stephen MORET
28 Vice Prov Campus Equity/Diversity .... Mr. Dereck ROVARIS
20 Vice Prov Academic Affairs .... Dr. Jane CASSIDY
20 Vice Provost Academics & Planning .... Dr. Gilmore REEVE
15 Assoc VP Human Resources Mgmt .... Mr. A.G MONACO
84 Int Assoc VP Enrollment Management ...... Mrs. Charlotte TULLOS
30 Exec Director Inst Advancement .... Ms. Bunnie CANNON
86 External & Legislative Affairs Dir .... Dr. Jason DRODDY
85 Assoc VP International Programs .... Dr. Hector ZAPATA
37 Assoc Dir Student Aid/Scholarships .... Ms. Amy MARIX
08 Dean LSU Libraries .... Mr. Stanley WILDER
79 Dean Col of Humanities & Soc Sci .... Dr. Stacia HAYNIE
58 Dean of Graduate School .... Dr. Michelle MASSE
54 Dean College of Engineering .... Dr. Richard KOUBEK
47 Dean College of Agriculture .... Dr. William RICHARDSON

50 Dean Ourso College of Business .... Dr. Richard D. WHITE
64 Dean College Music & Dramatic Arts .... Mr. Todd QUEEN
81 Dean College of Science .... Dr. Cynthia PETERSON
62 Dean Sch of Library & Info Science .... Dr. Beth M. PASKOFF
53 Int Dean Col of Human Sci & Educ .... Dr. Damon P. ANDREW
49 Int Dean College of Art & Design .... Mr. Alcibiades TSOLAKIS
74 Dean Veterinary Medicine .... Dr. Joel D. BAINES
60 Dean Manship Sch of Mass Comm .... Dr. Jerry CEPPOS
92 Dean Honors College .... Dr. Jonathan EARLE
65 Dean Sch of Coast & Environ .... Dr. Christopher D'ELIA
88 Assoc Dean University College .... Mr. Paul IVEY
38 Assc Dean Advising & Counseling Ctr .... Mr. R. Paul IVEY
35 Assistant Dean Student Services .... Ms. Angela GUILLORY
88 Sr Ex Dir SN Ctr Security Rsch Trng .... Mr. Jim FERNANDEZ
88 Exec Director Center Energy Stds .... Mr. David DISMUKES
51 Exec Director Continuing Education .... Mr. Doug WEIMER
29 President Alumni Association .... Mr. Cliff VANNOY
59 Director School Human Ecology .... Dr. Roy J. MARTIN
88 Exec Director Museum of Art .... Dr. Jordana POMEROY
18 Exec Director Facility Services .... Mr. Tony LOMBARDO
13 Int Chief Info Ofcr/Info Tech Svcs .... Mr. Brian NICHOLS
75 Dir Sch Human Res Ed/Workforce Dev .. Dr. Michael F. BURNETT
80 Director Public Admin Institute .... Dr. James A. RICHARDSON
88 Director LSU Press .... Ms. MaryKatherine CALLAWAY
41 Athletic Director .... Mr. Joe ALLEVA
06 Registrar .... Mr. Robert K. DOOLOS
36 Dir Olinde Career Center .... Mr. Jesse G. DOWNS
09 Director of Institutional Research .... Mr. Thomas M. SMITH
93 Director Multicultural Affairs .... Ms. Chaunda ALLEN
94 Director Women's/Gender Studies .... Ms. Summer STEIB
65 Director Museum of Natural Science .... Mr. Robb BRUMFIELD
88 Director Rural Life Museum .... Mr. David FLOYD
96 Exec Dir of Purch & Property Mgmt .... Ms. Sally MCKECHNIE
07 Assoc Director of Admissions .... Ms. Lupe LAMADRID
19 Chief LSU Police .... Mr. Lawrence RABALAIS
39 Exec Director Residential Life .... Mr. Steven WALLER

*Louisiana State University at Alexandria (A)

8100 Highway 71 S, Alexandria LA 71302-9121

County: Rapides   FICE Identification: 002011
Unit ID: 159382
Telephone: (318) 445-3672   Carnegie Class: Bac/A&S
FAX Number: (318) 473-6418   Calendar System: Semester
URL: www.lsua.edu
Established: 1959   Annual Undergrad Tuition & Fees (In-State): $6,611
Enrollment: 2,707   Coed
Affiliation or Control: State   IRS Status: 501(c)3
Highest Offering: Baccalaureate
Program: Liberal Arts And General; Teacher Preparatory
Accreditation: SC, ADNUR, MLTAD, NUR, RAD, TED

02 Chancellor .... Dr. Daniel HOWARD
05 Vice Chanc Academic & Student Affs .... Dr. Barbara S. HATFIELD
10 Int Vice Chanc Finance/Admin Svcs .... Mr. Deron THAXTON
30 Director Institutional Advancement .... Ms. Melinda F. ANDERSON
20 Asst VC Academic/Student Affairs .... Dr. Eamon HALPIN
21 Asst VC Finance/Admin Services .... Vacant
50 Int Dept Chair Business Admin .... Dr. Haywood JOINER
49 Dept Chair Arts/English/Humanities .... Dr. Holly WILSON
83 Dept Chair Behavioral & Social Sci .... Dr. Jerry SANSON
81 Dept Chair Math & Physical Sciences .... Dr. Nathan PONDER
53 Int Deparment Chair Education .... Dr. Patsy JENKINS
76 Department Chair Allied Health .... Dr. Haywood JOINER
66 Department Chair Nursing .... Dr. Cathy CORMIER
49 Dept Chair Biological Sciences .... Dr. Carol CORBAT
18 Exec Director of Facility Services .... Vacant
08 Director Library Services .... Dr. Bonnie HINES
37 Director of Financial Aid .... Mr. Jeff MASSEY
13 Exec Dir Info Educational Tech Svcs .... Mr. Deron THAXTON
15 Director Human Resource Management .... Ms. Lynette BURLEW
51 Director Continuing Education .... Vacant
32 Director Student Services .... Dr. Eamon HALPIN
09 Dir Inst Research/Effectiveness .... Vacant
96 Dir Procurement Svcs/Property Mgmt .... Vacant
41 Director Athletics .... Mr. Brent PORCHE
07 Director of Admissions & Recruiting .... Ms. Shelly KIEFFER
06 Registrar .... Ms. Stephanie CAGE
26 Director of University Relations .... Ms. Sarah BLACK

*Louisiana State University at Eunice (B)

2048 Johnson Highway, Eunice LA 70535-6726

County: Acadia   FICE Identification: 002012
Unit ID: 159407
Telephone: (337) 457-7311   Carnegie Class: Assoc/Pub2in4
FAX Number: (337) 546-6620   Calendar System: Semester
URL: www.lsue.edu
Established: 1964   Annual Undergrad Tuition & Fees (In-State): $3,528
Enrollment: 2,738   Coed
Affiliation or Control: State   IRS Status: 501(c)3
Highest Offering: Associate Degree
Program: Occupational; 2-Year Principally Bachelor's Creditable
Accreditation: SC, ADNUR, #COARC, DMS, RAD

02 Chancellor .... Dr. William J. NUNEZ, III
05 Vice Chancellor Academic Affairs .... Dr. Renee ROBICHAUX
32 Vice Chancellor Student Affairs .... Ms. Judy DANIELS
10 Vice Chancellor Business Affairs .... Ms. Arlene C. TUCKER
26 Director of Public Relations .... Mr. Van REED
08 Director of the Library .... Mr. Gerald PATOUT
06 Registrar/Dir of Admissions .... Dr. Kenneth ELLIOTT
37 Director of Financial Aid .... Ms. Jacqueline LA CHAPELLE
30 Dir Foundation & Institutional Dev .... Ms. Madelaine LANDRY
09 Dir Inst Effect/Devel Educ .... Dr. Paul FOWLER
51 Director of Continuing Education .... Mr. David PULLING
18 Director Physical Plant .... Mr. Michael BROUSSARD
25 Director Grants .... Ms. Jane SPRADLING
15 Director Personnel Services .... Ms. Angel MCGEE
81 Head Division of Sciences .... Dr. John HAMLIN
50 Head Div Bus/Nursing/Allied Health .... Ms. Dotty MCDONALD
49 Head Division of Liberal Arts .... Dr. Randall ESTERS
13 Chief Info Technology Officer (CIO) .... Mr. Fred FRUGE
41 Athletic Director .... Mr. Jeff WILLIS

*Louisiana State University Health Sciences Center-New Orleans (C)

433 Bolivar Street, New Orleans LA 70112-2223

County: Orleans   FICE Identification: 002014
Unit ID: 159373
Telephone: (504) 568-4808   Carnegie Class: Spec/Med
FAX Number: N/A   Calendar System: Semester
URL: www.lsuhsc.edu
Established: 1931   Annual Undergrad Tuition & Fees (In-State): $7,608
Enrollment: 2,769   Coed
Affiliation or Control: State   IRS Status: 501(c)3
Highest Offering: Doctorate
Program: Occupational; 2-Year Principally Bachelor's Creditable; Professional
Accreditation: SC, ANEST, #ARCPA, AUD, COARC, CORE, CVT, DENT, DH, DT, IPSY, MED, MT, NURSE, OT, PH, PTA, SP

02 Chancellor .... Dr. Larry H. HOLLIER
05 Vice Chanc Acad Aff/Dean Grad Stds .... Dr. Joseph M. MOERSCHBAECHER
10 Vice Chancellor Finance .... Mr. Terry ULLRICH
11 Vice Chancellor for Administration .... Mr. John R. PEGUES
17 Vice Chanc Clinic/Cmty/Security Aff .... Mr. Ronald E. GARDNER
63 Dean Medicine NO .... Dr. Steve NELSON
52 Dean School of Dentistry .... Dr. Henry GREMILLION
66 Dean of Nursing .... Dr. Demetrius PORCHE
69 Int Dean of Public Health .... Dr. Richard CULBERTSON
76 Dean Allied Health Professions .... Dr. Jim R. CAIRO
04 Assistant to the Chancellor .... Mrs. Christine MANALLA
86 Director of International Services .... Ms. Remy E. ALLEN
14 Director Computer Services .... Ms. Bettina OWENS
13 Director Information Services .... Ms. Leslie L. CAPO
08 Director Library Administration .... Ms. Debra H. SIBLEY
15 Director Human Resource Mgmt .... Mr. Danielle LOMBARD-SIMS
06 Registrar .... Mr. William Bryant FAUST
37 Assoc Dir Student Financial Aid .... Ms. Kimberly BRUNO
09 Director of Institutional Research .... Dr. Ken KRATZ
31 Director of Community Relations .... Ms. Diane E. BAJOIE
18 Chief Facilities/Physical Plant .... Mr. John BALL
96 Exec Director of Purchasing .... Mr. Brent HEROLD
26 Director of External Relations .... Mr. Christopher VIDRINE

*Louisiana State University Health Sciences Center at Shreveport (D)

1501 Kings Highway, Shreveport LA 71103

County: Caddo   FICE Identification: 008067
Unit ID: 435000
Telephone: (318) 675-5241   Carnegie Class: Spec/Med
FAX Number: (318) 675-5244   Calendar System: Semester
URL: www.lsuhscshreveport.edu
Established: 1973   Annual Undergrad Tuition & Fees: $7,723
Enrollment: 870   Coed
Affiliation or Control: Other   IRS Status: Exempt
Highest Offering: Doctorate
Program: Professional
Accreditation: SC, COARC, DENT, MED, MT, OT, PTA, SP

02 Chancellor .... Dr. Robert A. BARISH
11 Vice Chancellor Administration .... Mr. John T. DAILEY
05 Chief Academic Officer .... Dr. Jane EGGERSTEDT
10 Chief Financial Officer .... Ms. Sheila FAOUR
43 Senior Legal Counsel .... Ms. Susan ARMSTRONG
63 Interim Dean School of Medicine .... Dr. John V. MARYMONT
76 Dean Sch Allied Health Professions .... Dr. Joseph MCCULLOCH
58 Dean School of Graduate Studies .... Dr. Sandra C. ROERIG
07 Director of Admissions .... Dr. F. Scott KENNEDY
08 Head Librarian .... Mrs. Dixie JONES
09 Director of Institutional Research .... Dr. Sandra ROERIG
06 Registrar .... Dr. Kim CARMEN
13 Chief Info Technology Officer (CIO) .... Mr. Timothy MAGNER
15 Director Personnel Services .... Mrs. Lisa EBARB
18 Chief Facilities/Physical Plant .... Mr. Marc GIBSON
19 Director Security/Safety .... Mr. Willie BUFFINGTON
25 Exec Dir Government Affairs .... Ms. Mimi HEDGCOCK
26 Exec Dir Comm/Public Relations .... Mrs. Sally CROOM
28 Director of Diversity .... Mr. Roosevelt SEABERRY
29 Director Alumni Relations .... Mrs. Marianne COMEGYS
37 Director Student Financial Aid .... Mrs. Sherry GLADNEY

† Tuition varies by degree program.

*Louisiana State University Paul M. Hebert Law Center (E)

1 East Campus Drive, Baton Rouge LA 70803

County: East Baton Rouge   Identification: 667028
Telephone: (225) 578-5292   Carnegie Class: Not Classified
FAX Number: (225) 578-8202   Calendar System: Semester
URL: www.law.lsu.edu
Established: 1906   Annual Graduate Tuition & Fees: $21,947
Enrollment: 681   Coed
Affiliation or Control: State   IRS Status: 501(c)3
Highest Offering: Doctorate; No Undergraduates
Program: Professional
Accreditation: SC, LAW

02 Interim Co-Dean .... William R. CORBETT
02 Interim Co-Dean .... Cheney C. JOSEPH, JR.
10 Assoc Dean Business/Financial Affs .... N. Gregory SMITH
05 Assoc Dean Inst Assess/Faculty Dev .... Raymond T. DIAMOND
20 Director Student Academic Services .... Michele FORBES
29 Dir Alumni/Communications/Ext Rels .... Karen SONIAT
07 Director of Admissions .... Jake T. HENRY, III
09 Director of Institutional Research .... Shana L. CORVERS

*Louisiana State University in Shreveport (F)

One University Place, Shreveport LA 71115-2399

County: Caddo   FICE Identification: 002013
Unit ID: 159416
Telephone: (318) 797-5000   Carnegie Class: Master's M
FAX Number: (318) 797-5180   Calendar System: Semester
URL: www.lsus.edu
Established: 1967   Annual Undergrad Tuition & Fees (In-State): $6,903
Enrollment: 4,186   Coed
Affiliation or Control: State   IRS Status: 501(c)3
Highest Offering: Doctorate
Program: Liberal Arts And General; Teacher Preparatory; Professional
Accreditation: SC, ARCPA, BUS, CS, TED

02 Chancellor .... Mr. Lawrence S. CLARK
05 Provost/VC Academic Affairs .... Dr. John S. VASSAR
10 Vice Chancellor Business Affairs .... Mr. Michael T. FERRELL
32 Vice Chancellor for Student Affairs . Dr. Randy R. BUTTERBAUGH
102 Executive Director LSUS Foundation .... Ms. Laura PERDUE
29 Director Alumni Affairs .... Ms. Dianne B. HOWELL
09 Director Planning/Inst Research .... Vacant
06 Registrar .... Ms. Darlenna M. ATKINS
15 Director of Human Resource Mgmt .... Mr. Bill WOLFE
08 Dean Noel Memorial Library .... Dr. Alan D. GABEHART
37 Director of Student Financial Aid .... Ms. Chelsea CHANCE
07 Director of Admissions .... Ms. Tara B. SULLIVAN
36 Dir Student Devel & Counseling .... Mrs. Paula B. ATKINS
13 Director of Computing Services .... Mr. Shelby C. KEITH
18 Director of Facility Services .... Mr. Bruce NELMS
40 Director of Bookstore .... Ms. Brenda P. BARTLEBAUGH
96 Interim Director of Purchasing .... Mr. Bill WOLFE
26 Director of Media/Public Relations .... Mrs. Brooke H. RINAUDO
04 Assistant to the Chancellor .... Mrs. Viki P. FENTRESS
19 Interim Dir of University Police .... Mr. Lance COLE
41 Athletic Director .... Mr. Chad MCDOWELL
49 Dean of Arts and Sciences .... Dr. Larry ANDERSON
58 Dean of Graduate Studies .... Dr. Paul D. SISSON
51 Director of Continuing Education .... Mrs. Tisha L. SAMHAN
53 Interim Dean Business/Ed/Human Dev .... Dr. Doug S. BIBLE

*University of New Orleans (G)

2000 Lakeshore Drive, New Orleans LA 70148-2000

County: Orleans   FICE Identification: 002015
Unit ID: 159939
Telephone: (504) 280-6000   Carnegie Class: RU/H
FAX Number: (504) 280-5522   Calendar System: Semester
URL: www.uno.edu/
Established: 1958   Annual Undergrad Tuition & Fees (In-State): $4,077
Enrollment: 9,199   Coed
Affiliation or Control: State   IRS Status: 501(c)3
Highest Offering: Doctorate
Program: Liberal Arts And General; Teacher Preparatory
Accreditation: SC, ART, BUS, BUSA, CACREP, CS, ENG, MUS, PLNG, SPAA, TED, THEA

02 President .... Dr. Peter J. FOS
05 Provost/VP Academic Affairs .... Dr. John W. NICKLOW
46 Int Dir for Research/Economic Devel .... Dr. Emir MACARI
10 VP Business Affairs .... Mr. Gregg LASSEN
32 Vice President of Student Affairs .... Dr. Brett KEMKER
13 Chief Information Officer .... Mr. David DUPREE
85 Asst VP/Director International Educ .... Ms. Alea COT
19 Asst Vice Chanc for Public Safety .... Mr. Thomas HARRINGTON
50 Dean of Business Administration .... Dr. John A. WILLIAMS
54 Interim Dean of Engineering .... Dr. Emir MACARI
49 Int Dean Liberal Arts & Sch of Educ .... Dr. Kevin GRAVES
08 Interim Dean of Library .... Dr. Lora AMSBERRYAUGIER
81 Dean of Sciences .... Dr. Steve JOHNSON
06 University Registrar .... Mr. Matt MOORE
29 Director Alumni Affairs .... Ms. Pamela MEYER
27 Director of Public Relations .... Mr. Adam NORRIS
96 Associate Director of Purchasing .... Ms. Heather CASSELL
41 Director Athletics .... Mr. Derek MOREL
39 Director Student Housing .... Mr. Mike BRAUNINGER

Loyola University New Orleans (A)

6363 Saint Charles Avenue, New Orleans LA 70118-6195
County: Orleans FICE Identification: 002016
Unit ID: 159656
Telephone: (504) 865-2011 Carnegie Class: Master's L
FAX Number: (504) 865-3851 Calendar System: Semester
URL: www.loyno.edu
Established: 1912 Annual Undergrad Tuition & Fees: $37,700
Enrollment: 4,396 Coed
Affiliation or Control: Roman Catholic IRS Status: 501(c)3
Highest Offering: Doctorate
Program: Liberal Arts And General; Teacher Preparatory; Professional; Fine Arts Emphasis
Accreditation: SC, BUS, CACREP, JOUR, LAW, MUS, NUR, NURSE

01 President .... Rev. Kevin W. WILDES, SJ
101 Exec Asst to Pres for Board Rels .... Ms. Kristine D. LELONG
04 Executive Asst to Pres .... Ms. Gail HOWARD
05 Provost/Vice Pres Academic Affs .... Dr. Marc MANGANARO
10 Vice Pres Finance/Administration .... Mr. John J. CALAMIA
30 Vice Pres Institutional Advance .... Mr. William BISHOP
32 VP Student Affairs/Assoc Provost .... Dr. Marcia L. PETTY
88 Vice Pres for Mission & Ministry .... Dr. John SEBASTIAN
84 Vice Pres for Enrollment Management .... Ms. Roberta KASKEL
13 Vice Prov Information Tech/CIO .... Mr. Bret JACOBS
21 Assoc Vice Pres Financial Affairs .... Mr. Leon MATHES
44 Assoc Vice Pres Development .... Mr. Chris WISEMAN
26 VP Marketing/Communications .... Ms. Laura KURZU
11 Asst Vice Pres Administration .... Mr. Paul C. FLEMING
35 Asst Vice Pres of Student Affairs .... Mr. Robert A. REED
09 Sr Dir for Inst Rsrch & Stdnt Sccs .... Dr. Brad PETITFILS
42 Director of University Ministry .... Mr. Kurt BINDEWALD
108 Coord Internal Reporting/Assessment .... Ms. Donna BOURGEOIS
27 Assoc Dir Public Affs/External Rels .... Ms. Patricia MURRET
43 General Counsel .... Ms. Gita BOLT
29 Director Alumni Relations .... Ms. Laurie LEIVA
06 Dir Stdnt Records/Registration Svcs .... Ms. Kathy R. GROS
15 Director of Human Resources .... Mr. Ross D. MATTHEWS
40 Bookstore Manager .... Ms. Maleta WILSON
41 Director Athletics & Wellness .... Mr. Brett SIMPSON
36 Director Career Development Center .... Ms. Tamara BAKER
23 Director of Student Health Services .... Dr. Alicia BOURQUE
19 Director University Police .... Mr. Patrick X. BAILEY
37 Director Scholarships/Financial Aid .... Ms. Carrie GLASS
08 Director of the Law Library .... Mr. P. Michael WHIPPLE
85 Director Ctr for International Ed .... Ms. Debra DANNA
86 Dir Government Relations .... Mr. Tommy SCREEN
38 Director Student Counseling .... Dr. Alicia BOURQUE
96 Director of Purchasing .... Mr. Robert NELSON
06 Dir Admin Services-Student Records .... Mr. Michael RACHAL
39 Director of Residential Life .... Ms. Amy BOYLE
08 Interim Dean of Libraries .... Ms. Deborah POOLE
79 Dean Humanities/Natural Science .... Dr. Maria CALZADA
61 Interim Dean of Law .... Rev. Lawrence MOORE, SJ
64 Dean of Music and Fine Arts .... Mr. Anthony DECUIR
50 Dean of Business .... Dr. William LOCANDER
83 Dean of Social Sciences .... Dr. Roger WHITE
88 Interim Director of Svc Learning .... Ms. Jennifer N. JEANFREAU
88 Interim Dir of Women's Resource Ctr .... Ms. Patricia BOYETT
92 Dir of University Honors Program .... Ms. Naomi YAVNEH
88 Dir of Common Curriculum .... Dr. Lydia VOIGT
35 Dir of Student Services .... Ms. Maria MCBRIDE
88 Dir of Campus Dining .... Ms. Heather BACQUE

NationsUniversity (B)

650 Poydras St., Ste 1400, PMB 133,
New Orleans LA 70130
County: Orleans Identification: 667257
Telephone: (866) 617-6446 Carnegie Class: Not Classified
FAX Number: N/A Calendar System: Other
Established: 1996 Annual Undergrad Tuition & Fees: $480
Enrollment: N/A Coed
Affiliation or Control: Independent Non-Profit IRS Status: 501(c)3
Highest Offering: Master's
Program: Religious Emphasis
Accreditation: DEAC

01 President .... Dr. Mac LYNN

New Orleans Baptist Theological Seminary (C)

3939 Gentilly Boulevard, New Orleans LA 70126
County: Orleans FICE Identification: 002019
Unit ID: 159948
Telephone: (504) 282-4455 Carnegie Class: Spec/Faith
FAX Number: (504) 283-3631 Calendar System: Semester
URL: www.nobts.edu
Established: 1917 Annual Undergrad Tuition & Fees: $6,810
Enrollment: 2,806 Coed
Affiliation or Control: Southern Baptist IRS Status: 501(c)3
Highest Offering: Doctorate
Program: Professional; Religious Emphasis
Accreditation: SC, MUS, THEOL

01 President .... Dr. Charles S. KELLEY, JR.
05 Provost .... Dr. Steve W. LEMKE
09 Dir Institutional Effectiveness .... Dr. Jimmy DUKES
10 Vice President for Business Affairs .... Mr. Clay L. CORVIN
30 Vice President for Development .... Mr. Randy DRIGGERS
58 Dean Graduate Studies .... Dr. Mike EDENS
12 Dean Leavell College .... Dr. L. Thomas STRONG, III
32 Dean of Students .... Dr. J. Craig GARRETT
07 Dean of Admissions & Registrar .... Dr. Paul E. GREGOIRE, JR.
08 Dean of Libraries .... Dr. Jeff D. GRIFFIN
18 Associate VP of Facilities .... Dr. Jim O. PARKER
13 Assoc VP Information Technology .... Dr. Laurie S. WATTS
73 Assoc Dean Prof Doctoral Pgms .... Dr. Reggie R. OGEA
106 Associate Dean of Online Learning .... Dr. W. Craig PRICE
58 Assoc Dean Research Doctoral Pgms .... Dr. Charles A. RAY, JR.
35 Assoc Dean of Students .... Dr. Judi JACKSON
15 Director of Human Resources .... Ms. Pattie SHOENER
26 Chief Public Relations Officer .... Mr. Gary D. MYERS
29 Director of Alumni Relations .... Dr. Dennis L. PHELPS
36 Director of Student Enlistment .... Dr. Jonathan C. KEY
37 Director of Student Financial Aid .... Mr. Michael WANG
38 Director of Testing & Counseling .... Dr. Jeffery W. NAVE
88 Director of Innovative Learning .... Dr. Donna B. PEAVEY
39 Director Student Housing .... Mrs. Julie BARENTINE
41 Athletic Director .... Mr. Brad WINTER

Notre Dame Seminary, Graduate School of Theology (D)

2901 S Carrollton Avenue, New Orleans LA 70118-4391
County: Orleans FICE Identification: 002022
Unit ID: 160029
Telephone: (504) 866-7426 Carnegie Class: Spec/Faith
FAX Number: (504) 866-3119 Calendar System: Semester
URL: www.nds.edu
Established: 1923 Annual Undergrad Tuition & Fees: $20,916
Enrollment: 208 Coed
Affiliation or Control: Roman Catholic IRS Status: 501(c)3
Highest Offering: Master's
Program: Professional; Religious Emphasis
Accreditation: SC, THEOL

01 President - Rector .... V.Rev. James A. WEHNER, STD
05 Academic Dean .... Dr. Thomas J. NEAL
08 Director of Library .... Mr. Thomas B. BENDER, IV
09 Director IE/Planning/Faculty Devel .... Dr. Rebecca S. MALONEY
10 Business Manager .... Ms. Michelle W. KLEIN

Our Lady of Holy Cross College (E)

4123 Woodland Drive, New Orleans LA 70131-7399
County: Orleans FICE Identification: 002023
Unit ID: 160065
Telephone: (504) 394-7744 Carnegie Class: Master's S
FAX Number: (504) 391-2421 Calendar System: Semester
URL: www.olhcc.edu
Established: 1916 Annual Undergrad Tuition & Fees: $10,912
Enrollment: 1,133 Coed
Affiliation or Control: Roman Catholic IRS Status: 501(c)3
Highest Offering: Doctorate
Program: Liberal Arts And General; Teacher Preparatory; Professional; Nursing Emphasis
Accreditation: SC, CACREP, IACBE, NUR, RAD, TED

01 President .... Dr. David M. LANDRY
05 Provost/VP Academic Affairs .... Dr. Victoria DAHMES
03 Executive Vice President .... Mr. Kenneth TEDESCO
10 Vice Pres for Finance & Operations .... Mrs. Arlean WEHLE
30 Vice Pres for Philanthropy .... Mr. David CATHERMAN
84 VP for Enrollment Management .... Ms. Meredith REED
88 VP for Mission Integration .... Sr. Rochelle PERRIER
08 Director of Library Services .... Ms. Diana SCHAUBHUT
83 Dean Couns/Educ/Business .... Dr. Carolyn WHITE
66 Dean Nursing/Allied Health .... Dr. Patricia PRECHTER
49 Dean Liberal Arts and Science .... Dr. Michael LABRANCHE
06 Registrar .... Ms. Kobi SLOANE
09 Director Inst Research & Planning .... Dr. Fawn UKPOLO
42 Director of Campus Ministry .... Sr. Keri BURKE
15 Human Resources Manager .... Ms. Cathy WAGUESPACK
44 Director of Annual Fund .... Mr. David CATHERMAN
13 Director of Technology Services .... Ms. Rosalind CHESTER
37 Director of Financial Aid .... Ms. Catherine SIMONEAUX
04 Administrative Asst to President .... Ms. Peggy BOURGEOIS
07 Director of Admissions .... Ms. Nikki COLLETTI
106 Dir Online Education/E-learning .... Dr. Tess O'NEILL
19 Director Security/Safety .... Mr. Bernard NELSON
26 Chief Public Relations/Marketing .... Ms. Erin SULLIVAN
29 Director Alumni Relations .... Mr. Steve MORGAN
32 Chief Student Affairs/Student Life .... Mr. Andre CARPENTER

Our Lady of the Lake College (F)

5414 Brittany Drive, Baton Rouge LA 70808
County: East Baton Rouge FICE Identification: 031062
Unit ID: 160074
Telephone: (225) 768-1700 Carnegie Class: Spec/Health
FAX Number: (225) 768-0811 Calendar System: Semester
URL: www.ololcollege.edu
Established: 1923 Annual Undergrad Tuition & Fees: $12,984
Enrollment: 1,722 Coed
Affiliation or Control: Roman Catholic IRS Status: 501(c)3
Highest Offering: Master's
Program: Occupational; 2-Year Principally Bachelor's Creditable; Liberal Arts And General; Professional
Accreditation: SC, ADNUR, ANEST, ARCPA, COARC, MT, NUR, PTAA, RAD

01 President .... Dr. Tina HOLLAND
05 Vice Pres for Academic Affairs .... Dr. Ed VIOLETT
30 VP for Institutional Advancement .... Ms. Judith ROBERSON
10 Vice Pres Operations & Finance .... Ms. Beverly S. PLAISANCE
84 VP Stdnt Affairs/Enrollment Mgmt .... Ms. Rebecca CANNON
66 Interim Dean School of Nursing .... Dr. Phyllis PEDERSEN
49 Dean School of A&S and Health Prof .... Dr. Katherine KRIEG
32 Dean Of Students .... Dr. Allison WELLS
44 Director Institutional Advancement .... Ms. Denise BOURGEOIS
37 Director Financial Aid .... Vacant
06 Registrar .... Mr. Brad DUFFY
88 Director Physician Asst Studies .... Mr. John ALLGOOD
88 Int Dir Nurse Anesthetist Program .... Ms. Aimee BADEAUX
76 Director Radiologic Technology .... Ms. Liza MAYEUX
76 Director Clinical Lab Sciences .... Dr. Debbie FOX
76 Director Physical Therapist Asst .... Ms. Leah GEHEBER
88 Dir Health Service Administration .... Ms. Elizabeth BERZAS
76 Director Respiratory Therapy .... Ms. Sue DAVIS
88 Director Writing Center .... Mr. Angus WOODWARD
72 Director CollegeTechnology .... Mr. Eric SENECA
07 Assistant Director of Admissions .... Vacant
91 Manager Student Info System .... Mr. Janssen BURRIS
26 Marketing Coordinator .... Mr. Thien-Kieu LAM

Remington College-Baton Rouge Campus (G)

10551 Coursey Boulevard, Baton Rouge LA 70816-4040
Telephone: (225) 236-3200 Identification: 666449
Accreditation: ACCSC

† Branch campus of Remington College, Cleveland, OH.

Remington College-Lafayette Campus (H)

303 Rue Louis XIV, Lafayette LA 70508-5700
Telephone: (337) 981-4010 FICE Identification: 005203
Accreditation: ACCSC

† Branch campus of Remington College, Cleveland, OH.

Remington College-Shreveport (I)

2106 Bert Kouns Industrial Loop, Shreveport LA 71118
Telephone: (318) 671-4001 Identification: 666302
Accreditation: ACCSC

† Branch campus of Remington College, Cleveland, OH.

Saint Joseph Seminary College (J)

75376 River Road, Saint Benedict LA 70457-9999
County: Saint Tammany FICE Identification: 002027
Unit ID: 160409
Telephone: (985) 867-2238 Carnegie Class: Spec/Faith
FAX Number: (985) 867-2270 Calendar System: Semester
URL: www.sjasc.edu
Established: 1891 Annual Undergrad Tuition & Fees: $30,690
Enrollment: 135 Male
Affiliation or Control: Roman Catholic IRS Status: 501(c)3
Highest Offering: Baccalaureate
Program: Liberal Arts And General; Religious Emphasis
Accreditation: SC

01 President - Rector .... V.Rev. Gregory M. BOQUET, OSB
05 Academic Dean .... Dr. Daniel P. BURNS
03 Vice-Rector .... Rev. Matthew CLARK, OSB
08 Librarian .... Ms. Bonnie WOOD
10 Business Officer .... Mrs. Jennifer WHITEHOUSE
37 Director Financial Aid .... Mrs. Katie PLUDE
29 Director of Alumni Affairs .... Rev. Matthew CLARK, OSB
30 Director of Development .... Mrs. Victoria BERGER
26 Director of Communications .... Vacant
32 Dean of Students .... Rev. Jude ISRAEL, OSB
06 Registrar .... Mr. Casey EDLER
108 Director Institutional Assessment .... Mrs. Katie MURPHY
13 Chief Info Technology Officer (CIO) .... Mr. Todd RUSSELL
18 Chief Facilities/Physical Plant .... Mr. Jim ROBEAUU

*Southern University and Agricultural & Mechanical College System Office (K)

JS Clark Admin Building, 4th Floor,
Baton Rouge LA 70813-0001
County: East Baton Rouge FICE Identification: 009637
Unit ID: 160533
Telephone: (225) 771-4680 Carnegie Class: N/A
FAX Number: (225) 771-5522
URL: www.sus.edu

01 President .... Dr. Ray L. BELTON
10 System VP/Finance/Business Affairs .... Vacant
13 System VP/Information Technology .... Vacant
15 System VP/Human Resources .... Mr. Lester A. POURCIAU
84 System Dir Enroll/Online Processes .... Ms. Michelle HILL
30 System Dir Dev/Exec Dir Foundation .... Mr. Alfred E. HARRELL, III
43 General Counsel to the System/Board .... Ms. Tracie J. WOODS
29 System Director of Alumni Affairs .... Ms. Robyn M. MERRICK
26 System Director of Communications .... Mr. Henry J. TILLMAN
18 System Dir of Facilities Planning .... Mr. Endas W. VINCENT
21 System Director of Internal Audit .... Ms. Linda H. CATALON
09 System Dir/Institutional Research .... Vacant

*Southern University and A&M College (A)

Harding Boulevard, Baton Rouge LA 70813-0001
County: East Baton Rouge FICE Identification: 002025
Unit ID: 160621
Telephone: (225) 771-4500 Carnegie Class: Master's L
FAX Number: (225) 771-2018 Calendar System: Semester
URL: www.subr.edu
Established: 1880 Annual Undergrad Tuition & Fees (In-State): $7,444
Enrollment: 6,330 Coed
Affiliation or Control: State IRS Status: 501(c)3
Highest Offering: Doctorate
Program: Liberal Arts And General; Teacher Preparatory; Nursing Emphasis
Accreditation: SC, AAFCS, BUS, CACREP, CORE, CS, #DIETD, DIETI, ENG, ENGT, JOUR, MUS, NURSE, SP, SPAA, SW, TED

02 Acting Chancellor .... Mr. Flandus MCCLINTON, JR.
05 Int Vice Chanc for Academic Affairs .... Dr. VerJanis PEOPLES
32 Vice Chanc Stdnt Affs/Enroll Mgmt .... Dr. Brandon DUMAS
10 Vice Chanc of Finance & Admin ... Mr. Flandus MCCLINTON, JR.
46 VC Research & Strategic Initiative .... Dr. Michael A. STUBBLEFIELD
20 Assoc Vice Chanc/Dn Honors College .... Vacant
21 AVP Finance/Admin/Controller .... Ms. Gwendolyn A. BENNETT
26 Asst to Chanc for Media Relations .... Mr. Edward PRATT
45 Dir Planning Assess/Instnl Research .... Mr. Urban WIGGINS
29 Dir Alumni Aff/Exec Dir SU Alum Fed .... Ms. Robyn MERRICK
15 Director Human Resources .... Mr. Lester POURCIAU
06 Registrar .... Mrs. Caronda BEAN
07 Exec Dir Admissions/Recruitment .... Mr. Anthony JACKSON
35 Dean of Students .... Mr. Marcus A. COLEMAN
39 Director Residential Housing .... Ms. Tracie A. ABRAHAM
37 Director of Financial Aid .... Ms. Ursula SHORTY
13 Chief Information Officer .... Dr. Carlos THOMAS
51 Dir Intl Educ/Dir Svc Learning/CE .... Dr. Barbara CARPENTER
41 Athletic Director .... Mr. William BROUSSARD
18 Dir Facilities Svcs/Physical Plant .... Mr. Eli G. GUILLORY, III
88 Director School of Accountancy .... Ms. Mary A. DARBY
96 Director of Purchasing .... Mrs. Linda B. ANTOINE
38 Director Student Counseling .... Dr. ValaRay IRVIN
62 Dean of Libraries .... Mrs. Emma BRADFORD-PERRY
88 Dean University College .... Dr. Dana CARPENTER
92 Dean of Honors College .... Dr. Ella KELLEY
58 Interim Dean of the Graduate School .... Dr. Doze BUTLER
54 Dean College of Engineering .... Dr. Habib P. MOHAMADIAN
50 Dean College of Business .... Dr. Donald R. ANDREWS
53 Interim Dean College of Education .... Dr. Luria YOUNG
59 Chair Dept Family/Consumer Sciences .... Dr. Grace NAMWAMBA
49 Int Dean Col Educ/Arts/Humanities .... Dr. Luria YOUNG
83 Int Dean Col Social/Behavioral Sci .... Dr. William ARP
48 Coordinator School of Architecture .... Mr. Lonnie WILKINSON
66 Dean College of Nursing/Allied Hlth .... Dr. Janet RAMI
47 Int Dn Col of Sciences/Agriculture .... Dr. Robert H. MILLER

*Southern University at New Orleans (B)

6400 Press Drive, New Orleans LA 70126-1009
County: Orleans FICE Identification: 002026
Unit ID: 160630
Telephone: (504) 286-5000 Carnegie Class: Master's M
FAX Number: (504) 286-5131 Calendar System: Semester
URL: www.suno.edu
Established: 1956 Annual Undergrad Tuition & Fees (In-State): $6,827
Enrollment: 2,674 Coed
Affiliation or Control: State IRS Status: 501(c)3
Highest Offering: Master's
Program: Liberal Arts And General; Teacher Preparatory; Business Emphasis
Accreditation: SC, AAFCS, BUS, CAHIIM, SW, TED

02 Chancellor .... Dr. Victor UKPOLO
04 Exec Assoc to the Chancellor .... Mr. Harold E. CLARK
05 VC for Academic Affairs & SACS .... Dr. David S. ADEGBOYE
10 VC for Admin & Finance .... Mr. Jullin RENTHROPE
09 Dir IR/IE & Strategic Planning .... Dr. Donalyn L. LOTT
09 Director Quality Enhancement Plan .... Dr. Dionne NICHOLS
108 Learning Outcomes/Assessment Coord .... Mr. Ashu BENJAMIN
84 VC Student Affs & Enroll Services .... Dr. Donna GRANT
29 Vice Chan Cmty Outreach/Univ Advanc .... Mrs. Gloria B. MOULTRIE
21 Director of Facilities Management .... Mr. Shaun M. LEWIS
25 Dir Grants & Sponsored Programs .... Dr. William R. BELISLE
06 Registrar .... Ms. Gilda DAVIS
21 Comptroller .... Ms. Shawn M. CHARLES
08 Director of Library .... Mrs. Shatiqua A. MOSBY-WILSON
36 Dir Career Counseling & Vet Liaison .... Mr. Joseph MARION
13 Director of Information Technology .. Mr. Edmond M. CUMMINGS
15 Director of Human Resources .... Ms. Evelyn MASTERS-DUBUCLET
19 Police Captain Campus Police .... Mr. Kevin BANKS
20 Assoc VC Academic Affairs Faculty .... Mr. Wesley T. BISHOP
41 Director of Athletics .... Mr. Elston H. KING
07 Asst VC for Enrollment Management ... Ms. Leatrice D. LATIMORE
26 Director of Public Relations .... Ms. Tammy BARNEY
96 Director of Purchasing .... Ms. Marilyn G. MANUEL
106 Director of E-Learning .... Ms. Shelia WOOD
70 Dean School of Social Work .... Dr. Ronald MANCOSKE
50 Dean College of Business/Pub Admin .... Dr. Igwe E. UDEH
88 Director of Museum Studies .... Mr. Haithum EID
58 Dean of Graduate Studies .... Vacant
49 Dean College of Arts & Sciences .... Dr. Lisa MIMS-DEVEZIN
53 Dean College Educ & Human Dev .... Dr. Mwalimu SHUJAA
88 Dir Services for Students w/Disab .... Ms. Yolanda L. MIMS
32 Int Dir of Student Activities/Orgs .... Mr. Gerald BROOKS
38 Dir of Student Development Center .... Mrs. Josephine OKORONKWO
88 Director of Title III Programs .... Dr. Brenda W. JACKSON
88 Dir Student Support Services Pgm .... Ms. Linda D. FREDERICK
88 Dir Ctr for African & American Stds .... Dr. Romanus EJIAGA

*Southern University at Shreveport-Louisiana (C)

3050 Martin Luther King Drive, Shreveport LA 71107-4795
County: Caddo FICE Identification: 007686
Unit ID: 160649
Telephone: (318) 670-6000 Carnegie Class: Assoc/Pub2in4
FAX Number: (318) 670-6374 Calendar System: Semester
URL: www.susla.edu
Established: 1964 Annual Undergrad Tuition & Fees (In-State): $3,634
Enrollment: 2,952 Coed
Affiliation or Control: State IRS Status: 501(c)3
Highest Offering: Associate Degree
Program: Occupational; 2-Year Principally Bachelor's Creditable
Accreditation: SC, ADNUR, CAHIIM, COARC, DH, MLTAD, PHLEB, RAD, SURGT

02 Chancellor .... Dr. Ray L. BELTON
26 Spec Asst to Chanc IR/Div Univ Rels .... Theron JACKSON
04 Admin Assistant to the Chancellor .... Mrs. Linzola WINZER
05 Vice Chanc Academic/Student Affs .... Dr. Rosetta JONES
10 Vice Chanc Finance/Administration .... Mr. Benjamin W. PUGH
103 VC Cmty Outreach/Workforce Develop .... Mrs. Janice B. SNEED
32 Asst Vice Chanc Student Affairs .... Dr. Fatina ELLIOTT
84 Asst Vice Chanc Enrollment Mgmt .... Mr. Terence VINSON
20 Asst Vice Chanc for Academic Affs .... Dr. Regina ROBINSON
21 Comptroller .... Mrs. Brandy JACOBSEN
21 Bursar .... Ms. Tomeka K. BROWN
06 Registrar .... Dr. Lalita ROGERS
08 Library Director .... Mrs. Jane O'RILEY
35 Director of Student Activities .... Mrs. Rebecca GILLIAM
51 Director of Continuing Education .... Mrs. Beverly J. PARKER
07 Director of Admission & Recruitment .... Ms. Annie MOSS
37 Director of Financial Aid .... Ms. Katraya WILLIAMS
27 Dir Office of University Relations .... Ms. Krystle GRINDLEY
19 Chief University Police .... Mr. Marshall NELSON
13 Dir Information Technology Center .... Dr. Gabriel FAGBEYIRO
88 Director Student Support Services .... Ms. Karen COCO
75 Director Aerospace Technology .... Mr. David FOGLEMAN
38 Director Counseling Center .... Vacant
15 Director Human Resources .... Mr. Wayne H. BRYANT
96 Director of Purchasing .... Ms. Sophia JACKSON-LEE
18 Dir Physical Plant Facilities .... Mr. Joseph LACOUR
88 Director of Testing Center .... Ms. Kaye WASHINGTON
21 University Budget Officer .... Ms. Regina WINN
72 Director Radiologic Technology .... Ms. Sheila SWIFT
88 Exec Dir TRIO Community Outreach .... Ms. Betty C. FAGBEYIRO
88 Director Dental Hygiene .... Mrs. Kheysia H. WASHINGTON
88 Director Biomedical Research Devel .... Dr. Joseph ORBAN
09 Director Inst Plng/Assessment/Rsrch .... Mr. Martin FORTNER
50 Division Chair Business Studies .... Vacant
79 Division Chair for Humanities .... Ms. Wanda M. WALLER
72 Div Chair Science & Technology .... Dr. Barry C. HESTER
76 Div Chair Allied Health Sci .... Mrs. JoAnn BROWN
83 Div Ch Behav Sci/Educ/Bus Standards .... Dr. Rosalyn J. HOLT
66 Dean of School of Nursing .... Dr. Tiffany VARNER

*Southern University Law Center (D)

PO Box 9294, Baton Rouge LA 70813
County: East Baton Rouge Identification: 667233
Unit ID: 440916
Telephone: (225) 771-2552 Carnegie Class: Not Classified
FAX Number: N/A Calendar System: Semester
URL: www.sulc.edu
Established: 1947 Annual Graduate Tuition & Fees: $16,000
Enrollment: 644 Coed
Affiliation or Control: State IRS Status: 501(c)3
Highest Offering: First Professional Degree; No Undergraduates
Program: Professional
Accreditation: SC, LAW

02 Interim Chancellor .... Mr. John K. PIERRE

Southwest University (E)

2200 Veterans Memorial Boulevard, Kenner LA 70062-4005
County: Jefferson Identification: 666310
Telephone: (504) 468-2900 Carnegie Class: Not Classified
FAX Number: (504) 468-3213 Calendar System: Semester
URL: www.southwest.edu
Established: 1982 Annual Undergrad Tuition & Fees: $9,000
Enrollment: 415 Coed
Affiliation or Control: Proprietary IRS Status: Proprietary
Highest Offering: Master's
Program: 2-Year Principally Bachelor's Creditable; Liberal Arts And General; Professional; Business Emphasis
Accreditation: DEAC

01 President .... Dr. Grayce LEE
11 Chief Administrative Officer .... Mr. Neil FESER
07 Admissions .... Mrs. Lydia OCMAND

Tulane University (F)

6823 St. Charles Avenue, New Orleans LA 70118-5698
County: Orleans FICE Identification: 002029
Unit ID: 160755
Telephone: (504) 865-5000 Carnegie Class: RU/VH
FAX Number: (504) 865-5202 Calendar System: Semester
URL: www.tulane.edu
Established: 1834 Annual Undergrad Tuition & Fees: $49,638
Enrollment: 13,531 Coed
Affiliation or Control: Independent Non-Profit IRS Status: 501(c)3
Highest Offering: Doctorate
Program: Liberal Arts And General; Teacher Preparatory; Professional
Accreditation: SC, BUS, DIETI, ENG, ENGR, HSA, IPSY, LAW, MED, PH, SCPSY, SW, TEAC

01 President .... Mr. Michael A. FITTS
05 Sr Vice Pres Acad Affairs/Provost .... Prof. Michael BERNSTEIN
26 COO/Sr VP External Affairs .... Ms. Yvette M. JONES
10 Sr Vice Pres for Operations & CFO .... Mr. Anthony P. LORINO
63 Sr Vice Pres/Dn School of Medicine .... Dr. L. L. HAMM
17 VP/Vice Dean Health Sciences .... Ms. Mary BROWN
43 General Counsel .... Ms. Victoria D. JOHNSON
13 VP Information Technology/CTO .... Mr. Charles P. MCMAHON
20 Senior Associate Provost .... Dr. Ana LOPEZ
32 VP Student Affairs .... Dr. J. Davidson PORTER
20 Assoc Provost Health Sciences .... Dr. M. A. 'Tonette' KROUSEL-WOOD
58 Assoc Prov Graduate Studies .... Dr. Michael CUNNINGHAM
100 Chief of Staff & Vice President .... Ms. Anne BANOS
22 VP Inst Equity/Asst to Pres Dvrsity .... Ms. Deborah E. LOVE
84 Vice Pres Enrollment Mgmt/Registrar .... Mr. Earl RETIF
18 VP Operations & Facilities Services .... Vacant
26 Vice Pres University Communications .... Ms. Deborah L. GRANT
46 Vice President for Research .... Dr. Laura LEVY
30 Vice Pres Constituency Programs .... Ms. Luann D. DOZIER
86 Assoc VP Government Relations .... Ms. Sharon P. COURTNEY
35 Assoc VP Auxiliary Svcs/Student Ctr .... Mr. Robert C. HAILEY
18 Assoc Vice President Facilities .... Mr. Sylvester C. JOHNSON
37 Assoc Vice President Financial Aid .... Mr. Michael GOODMAN
21 Director Budget .... Mr. Gene MEYERS
29 VP for Alumni Affairs .... Mr. James STOFAN
21 Controller .... Mr. Frank (Doug) HARRELL
19 Director of Public Safety .... Mr. Jon BARNWELL
08 Dean Library & Academic Information .... Mr. David BANUSH
38 Exec Dir Educ Resources/Couns .... Dr. Donna BENDER
36 Exec Director Career Svcs Ctr .... Dr. Amjad AYOUBI
12 Dir Tulane Natl Primate Res Ctr .... Dr. Andrew LACKNER
24 Executive Director Publications .... Ms. Carol J. SCHLUETER
39 Assoc VP Housing Services/Residence .... Dr. Brian JOHNSON
96 Director Central Procurement Svcs .... Mr. William VAN CLEAVE
91 Asst VP Academic & Admin Computing .... Ms. Mary T. WALSH
41 Director Athletics .... Mr. Richard P. DICKSON
51 Dean Sch Cont Stds/Summer Sch .... Dr. Rick MARKSBURY
49 Dean School of Liberal Arts .... Dr. Carole HABER
49 Dean Newcomb-Tulane College .... Dr. James MACLAREN
61 Dean School of Law .... Mr. David D. MEYER
69 Dean Sch Public Health/Trop Med .... Dr. Pierre BUEKENS
54 Dean School Science & Engineering .... Dr. Nicholas J. ALTIERO
48 Dean School of Architecture .... Mr. Kenneth SCHWARTZ
50 Dean AB Freeman School of Business .... Dr. Ira SOLOMON
70 Dean School of Social Work .... Dr. Ronald MARKS
09 Director of Institutional Research .... Mr. Shawn POTTER
88 Exec Dir of CELT .... Dr. Susann LUSNIA
85 Assoc Dean Ctr for Global Education .... Dr. Scott PENTZER
35 Assoc VP Student Affairs .... Dr. John NONNAMAKER
108 Asst Provost Assessment and IR .... Dr. Katie BUSBY
20 Assoc Provost International Affairs .... Ms. Tania TETLOW
88 CPS Executive Director .... Dr. Agnieszka NANCE

*University of Louisiana System Office (G)

1201 N Third Street, Suite 7-300, Baton Rouge LA 70802-5243
County: East Baton Rouge FICE Identification: 033444
Unit ID: 247083
Telephone: (225) 342-6950 Carnegie Class: N/A
FAX Number: (225) 342-6473
URL: www.ulsystem.net

01 President .... Dr. Sandra K. WOODLEY
03 Executive Vice President & Provost .... Dr. Karla HUGHES
10 VP for Business and Finance .... Dr. Edwin LITOLFF
26 VP of External Affairs .... Ms. Rachel KINCAID

*Grambling State University (H)

403 Main Street, Grambling LA 71245
County: Lincoln FICE Identification: 002006
Unit ID: 159009
Telephone: (318) 247-3811 Carnegie Class: Master's M
FAX Number: (318) 274-6172 Calendar System: Semester
URL: www.gram.edu
Established: 1901 Annual Undergrad Tuition & Fees (In-State): $7,063
Enrollment: 4,504 Coed
Affiliation or Control: State IRS Status: 501(c)3
Highest Offering: Doctorate
Program: 2-Year Principally Bachelor's Creditable; Liberal Arts And General; Teacher Preparatory; Professional

Accreditation: SC, BUS, CS, ENGT, JOUR, MUS, NRPA, NUR, SPAA, SW, TED, THEA

02 President .... Dr. Willie D. LARKIN
05 Provost/Vice Pres Academic Affairs .... Dr. Janet GUYDEN
10 Vice President for Finance and Admn .... Mr. Leon SANDERS
84 VP Inst Effect & Dir Enroll Mgmt .... Dr. Damon R. WADE
32 Interim Assoc VP Student Affairs .... Dr. David C. PONTON, JR.
30 Int VP Research Advanc/Econ Dev .... Mr. Otto MEYERS, III
86 Exec Assoc VP of CIAP .... Vacant
18 Director of Facilties Management .... Mr. Tremmel TURNER
13 Assoc VP of Information Technology .... Mr. Winfred JONES
09 Director of Institutional Research .... Ms. Ulrica S. EDWARDS
19 University Police Chief .... Mr. Howard CAVINESS
15 AVP of Human Resources .... Mrs. Monica BRADLEY
53 Dean College of Education .... Dr. Larnell FLANNAGAN
50 Dean College of Business .... Dr. Tsegai EMMANUEL
58 Dean Division Grad Studies/Research .... Dr. Larnell FLANNAGAN
107 Dean Col of Prof Studies .... Dr. Larnell FLANNAGAN
49 Interim Dean College of Arts & Sci .... Dr. King D. GODWIN
92 Assistant Dean Honors College .... Dr. Ellen SMILEY
41 Interim Director of Athletics .... Dr. Obadiah SIMMONS
22 EEO Officer & Wage & Salary Officer .... Mrs. Monica BRADLEY
07 Director of Admissions .... Vacant
06 University Registrar .... Mrs. Patricia J. HUTCHERSON
37 Dir Student Financial Aid .... Mr. Gavin HAMM
91 Dir of Administrative Computing .... Mrs. Peggy HANLEY
04 Executive Asst to the President .... Vacant
29 Director Alumni Relations .... Vacant
23 Director of Health Services .... Mrs. Patrice OUTLEY
38 Director Counseling Center .... Dr. Coleen SPEED
39 Interim Dir of Residential Life .... Ms. Dana K. HOWARD
42 Director of Campus Ministry .... Vacant
96 Director of Purchasing .... Mr. Alvin BRADLEY
40 Manager University Bookstore .... Ms. Rosalyn LEWIS
106 Director of Distance Learning .... Mr. Eldrie HAMILTON
20 Special Assistant to Provost and VP .... Vacant
36 Director of Career Services .... Mr. Johnny PATTERSON
44 Dir Annual Fund Coord .... Vacant

*Louisiana Tech University (A)

PO Box 3168, Ruston LA 71272-0001

County: Lincoln FICE Identification: 002008
Unit ID: 159647
Telephone: (318) 257-0211 Carnegie Class: RU/H
FAX Number: (318) 257-2928 Calendar System: Quarter
URL: www.latech.edu
Established: 1894 Annual Undergrad Tuition & Fees (In-State): $8,823
Enrollment: 11,271 Coed
Affiliation or Control: State IRS Status: 501(c)3
Highest Offering: Doctorate
Program: Liberal Arts And General; Teacher Preparatory; Professional
Accreditation: SC, AAB, AAFCS, ADNUR, ART, AUD, BUS, BUSA, CACREP, CAHIIM, CIDA, COPSY, CS, DIETD, DIETI, ENG, ENGT, MUS, SP, TED

02 President .... Dr. Leslie K. GUICE
05 Vice Pres Academic Affairs .... Dr. Terry M. MCCONATHY
32 Vice Pres for Student Advancement .... Dr. Jim M. KING
11 AVP of Administration & Facilities .... Mr. Sam G. WALLACE
30 Vice President for Univ Advancement .... Vacant
10 AVP of Finance & Comptroller .... Mrs. Lisa L. COLE
50 Dean of Business .... Dr. Chris MARTIN
49 Dean of Liberal Arts .... Dr. Don KACZVINSKY
53 Dean of Education .... Dr. Don N. SCHILLINGER
54 Dean of Engineering & Science .... Dr. Hisham HEGAB
65 Dean of Applied & Natural Sciences .... Dr. Gary A. KENNEDY
84 Dean of Enrollment Management .... Mrs. Pamela R. FORD
26 Exec Dir University Communications .... Dr. David GUERIN
07 Interim Director of Admissions .... Mrs. Joan B. EDINGER
13 Director of Computer Center .... Mr. Roy S. WATERS
37 Director Student Financial Aid .... Ms. Aimee F. BAXTER
09 Director Institutional Research .... Mrs. Lori C. THEIS
06 Registrar .... Mr. Robert D. VENTO
08 Interim Director of Libraries .... Ms. Rita FRANKS
15 Director of Human Resoures .... Mrs. Sheila TRAMMEL
29 Director of Alumni Relations .... Mr. Wesley CAVIN
36 Dir Career Ctr/Student Counseling .... Mr. Ron CATHEY
89 Director of Freshmen Studies .... Vacant
92 Director of Honors Program .... Dr. Rick SIMMONS
93 Director of Multicultural Affairs .... Vacant
96 Director of Purchasing .... Ms. Melissa HUGHES
18 Chief Facilities/Physical Plant .... Vacant
41 Athletics Director .... Mr. Thomas H. MCCLELLAND, II

*McNeese State University (B)

4205 Ryan Street, Lake Charles LA 70609-4510

County: Calcasieu FICE Identification: 002017
Unit ID: 159717
Telephone: (337) 475-5000 Carnegie Class: Master's L
FAX Number: (337) 475-5012 Calendar System: Semester
URL: www.mcneese.edu
Established: 1939 Annual Undergrad Tuition & Fees (In-State): $6,968
Enrollment: 8,242 Coed
Affiliation or Control: State IRS Status: 501(c)3
Highest Offering: Beyond Master's But Less Than Doctorate
Program: Liberal Arts And General; Teacher Preparatory; Professional
Accreditation: SC, ADNUR, ART, BUS, CAATE, CS, DIETD, DIETI, ENG, ENGT, MT, MUS, NURSE, RAD, TED

02 President .... Dr. Philip C. WILLIAMS
05 Provost/VP Academic & Student Affs .... Dr. Jeanne M. DABOVAL
10 VP Business Affairs/University Svcs .... Mr. Eddie P. MECHE
30 Vice Pres University Advancement .... Mr. Richard H. REID
84 Assoc VP Enrollment Management .... Ms. Stephanie B. TARVER
32 AVP University Services .... Dr. Christopher THOMAS
81 Dean College of Science .... Dr. George F. MEAD, JR.
50 Dean College Business .... Dr. Musa M. ESSAYYAD
53 Dean of College of Education .... Dr. Wayne R. FETTER
49 Dean College Liberal Arts .... Dr. Ray MILES
54 Dean Col of Engr & Engr Technology .... Dr. Nikos KIRITSIS
66 Dean of College of Nursing .... Dr. Peggy L. WOLFE
18 Director Facilities & Plant Opers .... Mr. Richard R. RHODEN
13 Chief Information Technology .... Mr. Chad THIBODEAUX
31 Dir Community Service and Outreach .... Mrs. Betty H. ANDERSON
15 Dir Human Res/Student Employment .... Ms. Charlene R. ABBOTT
09 Director Institutional Research .... Vacant
37 Director Student Financial Aid .... Ms. Taina J. SAVOIT
08 Director of Library .... Ms. Debbie L. JOHNSON-HOUSTON
19 University Police Chief .... Mr. Robert SPINKS
29 Director Alumni Affairs .... Ms. Joyce D. PATTERSON
88 Director of Scholarships .... Mrs. Ralynn F. CASTETE
07 Dir of Admissions and Recruiting .... Ms. Kara SMITH
41 Athletic Director .... Mr. F. Bruce HEMPHILL
45 Dir Inst Research and Effectiveness .... Ms. Jessica HUTCHINGS
96 Director Purchasing/Property Cntrl .... Ms. Roxane FONTENOT
92 Director of Honors College .... Dr. Scott E. GOINS
14 Director of Univ Computing Services .... Mr. Stanley HIPPLER
46 Dir Ofc of Research/Sponsored Pgm .... Ms. Janet R. WOOLMAN
85 International Student Advisor .... Vacant
26 Director Public Relations .... Ms. Candace V. TOWNSEND
23 RN Supervisor-Student Health .... Vacant
40 Bookstore Manager .... Ms. Donna LUNDQUIST
106 Director of Electronic Learning .... Ms. Helen B. WARE
28 Chief Diversity Officer .... Dr. Michael T. SNOWDEN
04 Administrative Asst to President .... Ms. Lisa SULLIVAN

*Nicholls State University (C)

University Station, Thibodaux LA 70310-0001

County: Lafourche FICE Identification: 002005
Unit ID: 159966
Telephone: (985) 446-8111 Carnegie Class: Master's M
FAX Number: (985) 448-4920 Calendar System: Semester
URL: www.nicholls.edu
Established: 1948 Annual Undergrad Tuition & Fees (In-State): $7,349
Enrollment: 6,298 Coed
Affiliation or Control: State IRS Status: 501(c)3
Highest Offering: Beyond Master's But Less Than Doctorate
Program: 2-Year Principally Bachelor's Creditable; Liberal Arts And General; Teacher Preparatory
Accreditation: SC, AAFCS, ART, BUS, BUSA, CAATE, CACREP, DIETD, ENGR, JOUR, MUS, NAIT, NURSE, TED

02 President .... Dr. Bruce T. MURPHY
05 Provost/VP for Academic Affairs .... Dr. Lynn GILLETTE
32 Vice Pres Student Affs/Enroll Svcs .... Dr. Eugene A. DIAL
30 VP for University Advancement .... Dr. Neal WEAVER
18 Director Facility Services .... Mr. Michael G. DAVIS
10 Assoc Vice Pres for Finance/CFO .... Mr. Ronald RODRIGUEZ
45 Exec Dir of Planning/Effectiveness .... Mrs. Renee G. HICKS
49 Dean of Arts & Sciences .... Dr. John DOUCET
66 Dean of Nursing and Allied Health .... Dr. Velma S. WESTBROOK
50 Dean Business Administration .... Dr. Shawn MAULDIN
53 Dean of Education .... Dr. Leslie JONES
88 Int Dean of University College .... Mr. David ZERANGUE
09 Dir Assess/Institutional Research .... Mrs. Leslie B. DISHMAN
08 Co-Director of Library .... Dr. Van VIATOR
08 Co-Director of Library .... Ms. Anke TONN
08 Co-Director of Library .... Mr. Clifton THERIOT
19 Director of University Police .... Mr. Craig M. JACCUZZO
36 Director of Career Services .... Ms. Kristie R. TAUZIN
37 Director of Student Financial Aid .... Ms. Casie TRICHE
13 Director of Computing Center .... Mr. Charles R. ORDOYNE
15 Director of Human Resources .... Ms. Annette ARBONEAUX
26 Director of University Relations .... Ms. Stephanie VERDIN
51 Dir of Continuing Education .... Mr. Jason EIERMANN
41 Athletic Director .... Mr. Robert BERNARDI
29 Director of Alumni Affairs .... Miss Monique CROCHET
06 Director Records & Registration .... Mr. Kelly J. RODRIGUE
07 Director of Admissions .... Mrs. Becky L. DUROCHER
23 Director University Health Services .... Vacant
35 Dean of Student Services .... Dr. Michele E. CARUSO
39 Director Residence Life .... Mr. Hayward GUENARD
84 Director of Enrollment Services .... Mrs. Courtney CASSARD
96 Director of Purchasing .... Mr. Terry G. DUPRE
46 Director Research & Sponsored Pgms .... Mrs. Debra BENOIT
58 Director of Graduate Programs .... Mrs. DesLey PLAISANCE
88 Director of Printing & Design .... Mr. Bruno RUGGIERO
109 Director of Auxiliary Services .... Mrs. Brenda HASKINS
88 Coordinator of Veterans Services .... Mr. Gilberto BURBANTE
106 Co-Dir Online Education/E-learning .... Dr. Lori SOULE
106 Co Dir Online Education/E-learning .... Dr. Andrew SIMONCELLI

*Northwestern State University (D)

310 Sam Sibley Drive, Suite 223, Natchitoches LA 71497-0002

County: Natchitoches FICE Identification: 002021
Unit ID: 160038
Telephone: (318) 357-6011 Carnegie Class: Master's L
FAX Number: (318) 357-4223 Calendar System: Semester
URL: www.nsula.edu
Established: 1884 Annual Undergrad Tuition & Fees (In-State): $6,877
Enrollment: 9,002 Coed
Affiliation or Control: State IRS Status: 501(c)3
Highest Offering: Doctorate
Program: Liberal Arts And General; Teacher Preparatory; Professional
Accreditation: SC, AAFCS, ADNUR, ART, BUS, CACREP, ENGT, MUS, NURSE, RAD, SW, TED, THEA

02 President .... Dr. James B. HENDERSON
05 Provost/VP Academic & Student Affs .... Dr. Lisa ABNEY
11 Vice Pres for University Affairs .... Dr. Marcus JONES
26 Vice President for External Affairs .... Mr. Jerry D. PIERCE
46 Vice Pres for Tech/Research/Eco Dev .... Dr. Darlene WILLIAMS
10 Vice President Business Affairs .... Mr. Carl JONES
20 Vice Provost .... Dr. Steve HORTON
32 Dean of Students .... Mrs. Frances CONINE
53 Dean Col of Education & Human Dev .... Dr. Vickie GENTRY
49 Dean Col of Arts/Letters/Grad Stds .... Dr. Steve HORTON
66 Dean Col of Nursing & Allied Health .... Dr. Dana CLAWSON
72 Dean Col of Business & Technology .... Vacant
88 Interim Director Scholars College .... Dr. William HOUSEL
12 Exec Dir CENLA & Ft Polk Campuses .... Mr. Jason PARKS
09 Director Institutional Research .... Mrs. Lily PHARIS
06 Registrar .... Mrs. Lillie F. BELL
08 Director of Libraries .... Ms. Abbie LANDRY
29 Director Alumni Affairs & Devel .... Dr. Chris MAGGIO
37 Director Student Financial Aid .... Ms. Lauren JACKSON
27 Director News Bureau .... Mr. David WEST
36 Director Counseling & Career Svcs .... Mrs. Rebecca BOONE
41 Athletic Director .... Mr. Greg BURKE
23 Director of Health Services .... Mrs. Stephanie CAMPBELL
07 Director of University Recruiting .... Mrs. Jana LUCKY
15 Director Human Resources .... Mr. Cecil KNOTTS
18 Physical Plant Director .... Mr. Dale WOHLETZ
96 Director of Purchasing .... Mr. Dale MARTIN
21 Associate Business Officer .... Ms. Rita GRAVES

*Southeastern Louisiana University (E)

548 Ned McGehee Drive, Hammond LA 70402-0001

County: Tangipahoa FICE Identification: 002024
Unit ID: 160612
Telephone: (985) 549-2000 Carnegie Class: Master's L
FAX Number: (985) 549-2061 Calendar System: Semester
URL: www.southeastern.edu/
Established: 1925 Annual Undergrad Tuition & Fees (In-State): $6,938
Enrollment: 14,498 Coed
Affiliation or Control: State IRS Status: 501(c)3
Highest Offering: Doctorate
Program: Liberal Arts And General; Teacher Preparatory; Professional
Accreditation: SC, AAFCS, ART, BUS, BUSA, CAATE, CACREP, CS, ENGR, MUS, NAIT, NURSE, SP, SW, TED

02 President .... Dr. John L. CRAIN
05 Provost/VP Academic Affairs .... Dr. Tammy BOURG
10 VP Administration/Finance .... Mr. Sam DOMIANO
30 Vice Pres University Advancement .... Ms. Wendy LAUDERDALE
32 Vice President Student Affairs .... Dr. Marvin L. YATES
20 Asst VP Academic Affairs .... Vacant
13 Chief Information Officer .... Dr. Mike M. ASOODEH
86 Exec Asst Public & Govt Affairs .... Mr. Erin K. COWSER
21 Controller .... Ms. Nettie L. BURCHFIELD
06 Director Records & Registration .... Ms. Paulette M. POCHE
08 Director of Library .... Mr. Eric W. JOHNSON
36 Director Career Development Svcs .... Mr. Ken W. RIDGEDELL
109 Interim Director Auxiliary Services .... Ms. Connie DAVIS
29 Director of Alumni Services .... Ms. Kathy L. PITTMAN
39 Dir Student Housing & Resident Svcs .... Dr. Kay MAURIN
15 Director Human Resources .... Vacant
19 Director University Police .... Mr. Harold TODD
46 Dir Sponsored Research/Programs .... Ms. Cheryl HALL
41 Athletic Director .... Mr. Jay ARTIGUES
18 Director Facility Planning .... Mr. Ken D. HOWE
92 Director Honors Program .... Dr. Kent NEUERBURG
23 Director Health Services .... Ms. Michelle REED
38 Director Counseling Center .... Vacant
07 Director Admissions .... Vacant
37 Director Financial Aid .... Vacant
09 Director Inst Research/Assessment .... Dr. Michelle HALL
26 Director Public Information .... Mr. Rene G. ABADIE
96 Dir Purchasing/Property Control .... Mr. Richard HIMBER
85 Dir Multicultural/Intl Stdnt Affs .... Mr. Eric J. SUMMERS
22 Coordinator EEO/ADA .... Mr. Gene E. PREGEANT
49 Int Dn Col Arts/Human/Soc Sciences .... Dr. Karen FONTENOT
50 Int Dean of College of Business .... Dr. Antoinette PHILLIPS
53 Interim Dean College Education .... Dr. Shirley JACOB
66 Dean Col of Nursing & Health Sci .... Dr. Ann CARRUTH
72 Dean Col of Science & Technology .... Dr. Daniel MCCARTHY

*University of Louisiana at Lafayette (F)

104 University Circle, Lafayette LA 70503-0001

County: Lafayette FICE Identification: 002031
Unit ID: 160658
Telephone: (337) 482-1000 Carnegie Class: RU/H
FAX Number: (337) 482-6195 Calendar System: Semester
URL: www.louisiana.edu
Established: 1898 Annual Undergrad Tuition & Fees (In-State): $8,256
Enrollment: 17,195 Coed
Affiliation or Control: State IRS Status: 501(c)3
Highest Offering: Doctorate
Program: Liberal Arts And General; Teacher Preparatory; Professional

Accreditation: SC, ART, BUS, BUSA, CAATE, CACREP, CAHIIM, CIDA, CS, DIETD, DIETI, ENG, JOUR, MUS, NAIT, NURSE, SP, TED

02 President ..... Dr. E. Joseph SAVOIE
05 Provost/VP for Academic Affairs ..... Dr. James HENDERSON
10 VP Administration & Finance ..... Mr. Jerry L. LEBLANC
32 VP for Student Affairs ..... Ms. Patricia COTTONHAM
30 VP University Advancement ..... Mr. John BLOHM
46 Vice Pres for Research ..... Dr. Ramesh KOLLURU
84 VP for Enrollment Mgmt ..... Dr. DeWayne BOWIE
13 Chief Information Officer ..... Mr. Gene FIELDS
11 Director of Administrative Services ..... Ms. Lisa C. LANDRY
21 Asst Vice Pres Financial Services ..... Ms. Debra CALAIS
21 Comptroller ..... Vacant
108 Asst VP Institutional Plng & Effect ..... Vacant
20 Asst VP Academic Affairs ..... Ms. Ellen D. COOK
35 Dean of Students ..... Ms. Margarita PEREZ
35 Assoc Dean Students/Dir Stdnt Life ..... Ms. Heidie LINDSEY
25 Assoc Dir Research/Sponsored Pgms ..... Ms. Abby GUILLORY
91 Director of Information Systems ..... Mr. Sam F. BULLARD
14 Director Computing Support Services ..... Mr. Patrick LANDRY
08 Dean of University Libraries ..... Dr. Charles W. TRICHE, III
07 Dir of UN Admissions & Recruitment ..... Mr. Andy BENOIT
88 Director Information Networks ..... Mr. Stephen J. MAHLER
09 Director of Institutional Research ..... Ms. Lisa LORD
55 Director University Connection ..... Ms. Amanda DOYLE
37 Director of Financial Aid ..... Ms. Cindy SHOWS-PEREZ
96 Director Purchasing ..... Ms. Marie FRANK
27 Assoc Director Publications ..... Ms. Kathleen A. THAMES
36 Director Career Services ..... Ms. Kim A. BILLEAUDEAU
19 Chief of Police ..... Chief Joey STURM
23 Director Student Health Svcs .. Ms. Madeline HUSBAND-ARDOIN
49 Dean Liberal Arts ..... Dr. Jordan KELLMAN
54 Dean of Engineering ..... Dr. Mark E. ZAPPI
53 Dean of Education ..... Dr. Gerald P. CARLSON
66 Dean of Nursing ..... Dr. Gail P. POIRRIER
58 Dean of Graduate School ..... Dr. Mary FARMER-KAISER
50 Dean of Business Administration ..... Ms. Gwen FONTENOT
81 Dean of Sciences ..... Dr. Azmy ACKLEH
97 Dean of University College ..... Dr. Bobbie DECUIR
57 Dean College of the Arts ..... Mr. H. Gordon BROOKS, II
77 Director Ctr Adv Computer Studies ..... Dr. Magdy A. BAYOUMI
18 Director Physical Plant ..... Mr. William J. CRIST
22 Director Operational Review/EEO Off ..... Ms. Christine BRASHER
39 Director Housing ..... Mr. Jules BREAUX
40 Manager Bookstore ..... Mr. Robert RICHARD
24 Director Univ Media/Printing Svcs ..... Mr. Steve MAHLER
41 Athletic Director ..... Mr. Scott FARMER
85 Director Office of Intl Affairs ..... Dr. Rose HONEGGER
51 Director of Continuing Education ..... Ms. Dawn PROVOST
31 Dean of Community Service ..... Mr. David YARBROUGH
86 Coordinator Governmental Relations ..... Vacant
26 Dir of Communication and Marketing ..... Mr. Aaron MARTIN
29 Director Alumni Affairs ..... Ms. Jennifer LEMEUNIER
44 Planned Giving Officer ..... Mr. David P. COMEAUX
38 Director Counseling and Testing ..... Mr. Brian FREDERICK
15 Director of Human Resources ..... Mr. Paul THOMAS
06 Registrar ..... Mr. Mickey DIEZ
106 Director of Distance Learning ..... Dr. Luke DOWDEN
92 Director of Honors Program ..... Dr. Julia FREDERICK
89 Director of First-Year Experience ..... Dr. Jennifer FAUST
28 Director of Diversity ..... Ms. Taniecea MALLERY
108 Director Institutional Assessment ..... Ms. Alise HAGAN

*University of Louisiana at Monroe (A)

700 University Avenue, Monroe LA 71209-0001
County: Ouachita | FICE Identification: 002020
Unit ID: 159993
Telephone: (318) 342-1000 | Carnegie Class: Master's L
FAX Number: (318) 342-5161 | Calendar System: Semester
URL: www.ulm.edu
Established: 1931 | Annual Undergrad Tuition & Fees (In-State): $6,963
Enrollment: 8,517 | Coed
Affiliation or Control: State | IRS Status: 501(c)3
Highest Offering: Doctorate
Program: 2-Year Principally Bachelor's Creditable; Liberal Arts And General; Teacher Preparatory; Professional; Business Emphasis
Accreditation: SC, BUS, BUSA, CACREP, CONST, CS, DH, EXSC, MFCD, MT, MUS, NURSE, OT, OTA, PHAR, RAD, SP, SW, TED

02 President ..... Dr. Nick J. BRUNO
03 Executive VP ..... Dr. Stephen P. RICHTERS
10 Chief Business Officer ..... Mr. William T. GRAVES
32 Vice President for Student Affairs ..... Mr. Camile CURRIER
05 Vice President for Academic Affairs ..... Dr. Eric A. PANI
84 Asst VP for Mktg/Recruit/Cmty Engag ..... Mrs. Lisa R. MILLER
07 Director Enrollment & Scholarship ..... Ms. Mary SCHMEER
41 Director of Athletics ..... Mr. Brian WICKSTROM
26 Director Media Relations ..... Ms. Donna BERNARD
88 Director Internal Audit ..... Mr. Kirby D. CAMPBELL
49 Dean Arts/Education & Sciences ..... Dr. Sandra M. LEMOINE
50 Dean Business and Social Sciences ..... Dr. Ronald BERRY
67 Dean Health and Pharmaceutical Sci ..... Dr. Benny BLAYLOCK
58 Director Graduate School ..... Dr. Leonard CLARK
108 Director Assessment and Evaluation .. Mrs. Allison L. THOMPSON
09 Exec Dir Univ Planning/Analysis ..... Mr. Jeffrey HENDRIX
08 Dean of the Library ..... Mr. Donald R. SMITH
51 Director eULM ..... Ms. Paula THORNHILL
06 Registrar ..... Mr. Anthony MALTA
37 Director Financial Aid Services ..... Ms. Frankie EVERETT
85 Dir Intl Student Program and Svcs ..... Ms. Sami OWENS
88 Director of University Retention ..... Mrs. Barbara MICHAELIDES
102 Executive Director Foundation ..... Ms. Susan CHAPPELL
39 Director Residential Life ..... Ms. Tresea L. BUCKHAULTS
45 Budget Officer ..... Ms. Gail C. PARKER
21 Controller ..... Ms. Sarah WALKER
15 Director Human Resources ..... Mr. Fred BARAGONA
13 Director Computer Center ..... Mr. Chance W. EPPINETTE
109 Exec Dir Auxiliary Enterprises ..... Mr. Tommy WALPOLE
40 Manager University Bookstore ..... Ms. Rebecca BOOTHBY
18 Director Physical Plant Admin ..... Mr. Lawrence B. THORN
88 Director Facilities Mgmt & Ehs ..... Mr. Jason S. ROUBIQUE
35 Dean Student Life/Title IX ..... Ms. Pamela JACKSON
38 Director Counseling Center ..... Ms. Karen FOSTER
19 Officer in Charge Univ Police ..... Mr. Steven MAHON
36 Director Career Connections ..... Ms. Roslynn POGUE
88 Dir Recreational Svcs/Facilities ..... Ms. Treina LANDRUM
88 Director of Special Projects ..... Mr. Lindsey S. WILKERSON
29 Director of Alumni Affairs ..... Ms. Robin S. UNDERWOOD

University of Phoenix Baton Rouge Campus (B)

2431 S Acadian Thruway, Baton Rouge LA 70808-2300
Telephone: (225) 927-4443 | Identification: 770208
Accreditation: &NH, ACBSP

† No longer accepting campus-based students.

Virginia College (C)

9501 Cortana Place, Baton Rouge LA 70815-8604
Telephone: (225) 236-3900 | Identification: 770826
Accreditation: ACICS, ACFEI, MAAB, SURGT

† Tuition varies by degree program.

Virginia College (D)

2950 East Texas Street, Suite C, Bossier City LA 71111
Telephone: (888) 342-0014 | Identification: 770827
Accreditation: ACICS, MAAB

† Branch campus of Virginia College, Birmingham, AL.

Xavier University of Louisiana (E)

One Drexel Drive, New Orleans LA 70125-1098
County: Orleans | FICE Identification: 002032
Unit ID: 160904
Telephone: (504) 486-7411 | Carnegie Class: Bac/A&S
FAX Number: (504) 520-7904 | Calendar System: Semester
URL: www.xula.edu
Established: 1925 | Annual Undergrad Tuition & Fees: $19,800
Enrollment: 2,976 | Coed
Affiliation or Control: Roman Catholic | IRS Status: 501(c)3
Highest Offering: Doctorate
Program: Liberal Arts And General; Teacher Preparatory; Professional
Accreditation: SC, ACBSP, CACREP, MUS, PHAR, TED

01 President ..... Dr. Norman C. FRANCIS
11 Sr Vice Pres for Administration ..... Mr. Ralph JOHNSON
05 Interim VP for Academic Affairs ..... Dr. Deidre LABAT
46 Assoc VP Research/Sponsored Pgms ..... Dr. Deborah MARSHALL
32 Vice President for Student Services ..... Mr. Joseph K. BYRD
30 Vice President for Inst Advancement ... Dr. Kenneth ST. CHARLES
10 Vice President for Finance ..... Mr. Edward PHILLIPS
13 VP for Office of Technology ..... Mr. Tony MOORE
45 VP Planning Inst Res & Assessment .... Dr. Ronald R. DURNFORD
18 Vice President Facilities Planning ..... Mr. Marion BRACY
20 Assoc VP for Academic Affairs ..... Dr. Marguerite GIGUETTE
109 Assoc Vice Pres Auxiliary Services ..... Mr. William JEFFRION
07 Dean of Admissions ..... Mr. Winston D. BROWN
06 Registrar ..... Ms. Avis STUARD
42 University Chaplain ..... Fr. Etido S. JEROME
21 Director of Accounting ..... Ms. Joyce SANDIFER
21 Director of Operations ..... Ms. Lori GIE
21 Dir Fin Reporting & External Audit ..... Mrs. Ingenue S. SCHEXNIDER-FIELDS
15 Director of Human Resources ..... Mr. Larry CALVIN
49 Dean of Arts & Sciences ..... Dr. Anil KUKREJA
67 Dean of College of Pharmacy ..... Dr. Kathleen KENNEDY
89 Director of Freshmen Studies ..... Dr. Wendy GAUDIN
108 Dir of Inst Effectiv & Assessment ..... Dr. Danielle DUFFOURC
09 Dir Inst Compliance & Plng Init ..... Dr. Treva A. LEE
08 Director of the Library ..... Dr. Lynette RALPH
36 Director of Career Services ..... Mrs. Carolyn D. THOMAS
37 Director of Financial Aid ..... Ms. Emily LONDON-JONES
19 Director of Campus Police ..... Mr. Duane CARKUM
23 Med Dir Student Health Services ..... Dr. Robert MERCADEL
38 Director of Counseling Services ..... Ms. Eloise DOXIE-DIXON
29 Director of Alumni Relations ..... Ms. Kimberly REESE
40 Manager Bookstore ..... Ms. Rose NAQUIN
41 Athletic Director ..... Mr. Jason HORN
04 Administrative Asst to President ..... Mrs. Karen WATKINA
101 Secretary of the Institution/Board ..... Mrs. Isabella THOMPSON
104 Director Study Abroad ..... Mr. Torian LEE
106 Dir Online Education/E-learning ..... Dr. Karen NICHOLS
39 Director Student Housing ..... Mrs. Judy BRACY
44 Director Annual or Planned Giving ..... Ms. Lacrecia JAMES

MAINE

Bates College (F)

2 Andrews Road, Lewiston ME 04240-6047
County: Androscoggin | FICE Identification: 002036
Unit ID: 160977
Telephone: (207) 786-6255 | Carnegie Class: Bac/A&S
FAX Number: (207) 786-6123 | Calendar System: Other
URL: www.bates.edu
Established: 1855 | Annual Undergrad Tuition & Fees: $62,540
Enrollment: 1,773 | Coed
Affiliation or Control: Independent Non-Profit | IRS Status: 501(c)3
Highest Offering: Baccalaureate
Program: Liberal Arts And General
Accreditation: EH

01 President ..... Dr. A. Clayton SPENCER
05 VP Academic Affairs/Dean of Faculty ..... Dr. Matthew R. AUER
10 VP Finance & Admin/Treasurer ..... Mr. Geoffrey SWIFT
08 VP Info & Libr Services/Librarian ..... Vacant
30 VP Advancement ..... Ms. Sarah R. PEARSON
32 Dean of Students ..... Mr. Joshua MCINTOSH
21 Asst Vice Pres Financial Planning ..... Mr. Douglas W. GINEVAN
20 Associate Dean of Faculty ..... Dr. Kathryn G. LOW
20 Assoc Dean of Faculty ..... Mr. Kirk D. READ
31 Director of Community Partnerships ..... Ms. Darby K. RAY
06 Registrar ..... Ms. Mary MESERVE
09 Dir Inst Rsch/Analysis and Planning ..... Ms. Anne Marie T. RUSSELL
15 Asst VP Human Resources ..... Ms. Mary MAIN
18 Dir of Facilities Svcs Operations ..... Mr. Jay PHILLIPS
88 Dir Capital Planning/Construction ..... Ms. Pamela J. WICHROSKI
07 Dean of Admissions & Financial Aid ..... Ms. Leigh WEISENBURGER
19 Dir Security & Campus Safety ..... Mr. Thomas P. CAREY
23 Dir Health Services ..... Ms. Christy TISDALE
26 Asst VP Communications/Media Rels ..... Vacant
37 Dir Student Financial Services ..... Ms. Wendy G. GLASS
40 Dir Bookstore/Contract Officer ..... Ms. Sarah POTTER
36 Dir of Career Services ..... Mr. David MCDONOUGH
91 Dir Sys Development & Integration ... Ms. Eileen P. ZIMMERMAN
24 Dir of Academic Technology Services ..... Mr. Andrew W. WHITE
41 Athletic Director ..... Mr. Kevin MCHUGH
42 College Chaplain ..... Ms. Brittany LONGSDORF
39 Asst Dean of Students/Housing ..... Ms. Erin FOSTER ZSIGA
102 Dir of the Office for External Grnt ..... Vacant
104 Assoc Dean of Students/Study Abroad ..... Mr. Stephen SAWYER
100 Chief of Staff ..... Mr. Michael HUSSEY
28 AVP and Chief Diversity Officer ..... Ms. Crystal WILLIAMS
84 Asst Dean of Admiss/Intl Enrollment ..... Ms. Misha GARG
04 Exec Assistant to the President ..... Ms. Claire B. SCHMOLL
101 Secretary of the Institution/Board ..... Mr. Michael HUSSEY

† Tuition figure is a comprehensive fees figure.

Beal College (G)

99 Farm Road, Bangor ME 04401-6831
County: Penobscot | FICE Identification: 005204
Unit ID: 160995
Telephone: (207) 947-4591 | Carnegie Class: Assoc/PrivFP
FAX Number: (207) 947-0208 | Calendar System: Other
URL: www.bealcollege.edu
Established: 1891 | Annual Undergrad Tuition & Fees: $8,210
Enrollment: 429 | Coed
Affiliation or Control: Proprietary | IRS Status: Proprietary
Highest Offering: Associate Degree
Program: 2-Year Principally Bachelor's Creditable; Business Emphasis
Accreditation: ACICS, CAHIIM, MAC

01 President ..... Mr. Allen T. STEHLE
03 Campus Director ..... Mr. Corey LEIGHTON
10 Chief Financial Officer ..... Ms. Renee DUNTON
05 Director of Education ..... Ms. Deborah CROCKETT
07 Director of Admissions ..... Ms. Sue BORDEN
37 Director Student Financial Aid ..... Ms. Maggie MAGEE
32 Director of Student Affairs ..... Ms. Stephanie MISHOU
08 Chief Librarian ..... Ms. Tegan C. MILLS
18 Superintendent Physical Plant ..... Mr. Kevin HARDY
88 Dir Early Child Ed/Hospitality Svcs ..... Ms. Susan XIRINACHS
76 Director Allied Health ..... Ms. Barbara MARCHELLETTA
88 Director Criminal Justice ..... Mr. Allen STEHLE
40 Director Bookstore ..... Ms. Wandamae CLEAVES
36 Director Student Placement ..... Ms. Donna GILLETTE
06 Registrar ..... Ms. Ellen EDWARDS
50 Director Business Studies ..... Ms. Katrin TEEL
83 Director Social & Human Svcs Asst ..... Ms. Susan POLYOT
75 Director Welding Technology ..... Mr. Jesse CROSBY

Bowdoin College (H)

3500 College Station, Brunswick ME 04011-8448
County: Cumberland | FICE Identification: 002038
Unit ID: 161004
Telephone: (207) 725-3000 | Carnegie Class: Bac/A&S
FAX Number: (207) 725-3123 | Calendar System: Semester
URL: www.bowdoin.edu
Established: 1794 | Annual Undergrad Tuition & Fees: $48,212
Enrollment: 1,797 | Coed
Affiliation or Control: Independent Non-Profit | IRS Status: 501(c)3
Highest Offering: Master's
Program: Liberal Arts And General

Accreditation: EH

01 President .... Dr. Clayton ROSE
11 Sr VP Finance/Admin & Treasurer ..... Ms. S. Catherine LONGLEY
46 Sr VP Devel & Alumni Relations .... Mr. Rick GANONG
10 Vice President for Finance a .... Mr. Matthew ORLANDO
15 Vice President of Human Resources .... Ms. Tamara D. SPOERRI
32 Dean of Student Affairs .... Mr. Timothy W. FOSTER
05 Dean for Academic Affairs .... Dr. Jennifer SCANLON
07 Dean of Admissions .... Mr. Scott A. MEIKLEJOHN
26 VP/Dir Comm/Public Affairs .... Mr. Scott W. HOOD
09 VP Inst Rsrch/Analytics Consulting ....Dr. Christina M. FINNERAN
13 Chief Information Officer .... Mr. Mitchel W. DAVIS
29 Director Alumni Relations .... Ms. Rodie F. LLOYD
08 College Librarian .... Ms. Marjorie HASSEN
37 Director of Student Aid .... Mr. Michael D. BARTINI
06 Registrar .... Ms. Martina DUNCAN
19 Director of Security .... Mr. Randall NICHOLS
36 Director of Career Planning .... Mr. Timothy DIEHL
38 Director of Counseling Service .... Dr. Bernie HERSHBERGER
41 Director of Athletics .... Mr. Timothy M. RYAN
23 Director of Health Services .... Dr. Birgit POLS
18 Director Facilities Ops/Maintenance .... Mr. Theodore R. STAM
24 Instructional Media Librarian .... Ms. Carmen M. GREENLEE
21 Director of Finance & Campus Svcs .... Mr. Delwin C. WILSON
39 Director of Residential Life .... Ms. Meadow DAVIS
40 Dir Dining & Bookstore Services .... Ms. Mary M. KENNEDY
35 Director of Student Activities .... Dr. Allen W. DELONG
35 Sr Associate Dean Student Affairs .... Ms. Kimberly A. PACELLI
88 Co-Dir of the Museum of Art .... Ms. Anne GOODYEAR
88 Co-Dir of the Musuem of Art .... Mr. Frank GOODYEAR
18 Director of Capital Projects .... Mr. Donald V. BORKOWSKI
20 Assoc Dean for Academic Affairs .... Dr. Barry LOGAN
88 Associate Dean for Faculty .... Dr. Jennifer SCANLON

Colby College (A)

4000 Mayflower Hill, Waterville ME 04901-8840
County: Kennebec FICE Identification: 002039
Unit ID: 161086
Telephone: (207) 859-4000 Carnegie Class: Bac/A&S
FAX Number: (207) 859-4603 Calendar System: 4/1/4
URL: www.colby.edu
Established: 1813 Annual Undergrad Tuition & Fees: $47,350
Enrollment: 1,847 Coed
Affiliation or Control: Independent Non-Profit IRS Status: 501(c)3
Highest Offering: Baccalaureate
Program: Liberal Arts And General
Accreditation: EH

01 President .... Dr. David A. GREENE
05 Provost and Dean of Faculty .... Dr. Lori G. KLETZER
10 Vice President Admin & CFO .... Mr. Douglas C. TERP
30 VP College & Student Advancement .... Dr. Daniel LUGO
32 VP Student Affairs/Dean of Students .... Mr. James S. TERHUNE
26 Vice President for Communications .... Ms. Ruth JACKSON
07 Vice Pres/Dean Admiss & Fin Aid .... Dr. Matthew PROTO
20 Sr Assoc Provost & Dean of Faculty .... Dr. Paul G. GREENWOOD
32 Asst Vice Pres/Sr Associate Dean .... Ms. Barbara E. MOORE
35 Sr Assoc/DOS/Dir Campus Life .... Mr. Jed WARTMAN
06 Registrar .... Ms. Elizabeth N. SCHILLER
08 Director of Libraries .... Mr. Clement P. GUTHRO
36 Director of Career Center .... Ms. Alisa M. JOHNSON
88 Director of Special Programs .... Mr. Jacques MOORE
37 Director of Financial Aid .... Mr. Elreo CAMPBELL
29 Director of Alumni Relations .... Vacant
15 Director Human Resources .... Mr. Mark CROSBY
19 Director of Security .... Mr. Peter S. CHENEVERT
13 Director of Info-Tech Services .... Dr. Raymond B. PHILLIPS
18 Asst VP Facilities and Campus Plng .... Ms. Minakshi M. AMUNDSEN
23 Medical Director .... Dr. Paul D. BERKNER
38 Director of Counseling Services .... Mr. Eric S. JOHNSON
41 Director of Athletics .... Mr. Timothy W. WHEATON
09 Dir Inst Research & Assessment .... Ms. Rebecca H. BRODIGAN
21 Controller .... Mr. Ruben L. RIVERA
40 Director of the Bookstore .... Ms. Barbara C. SHUTT
104 Director of Off-Campus Study .... Dr. Nancy DOWNEY
102 Director of Grants .... Mr. William C. LAYTON, III
04 Asst to the Pres/Dir of Planning .... Mr. Brian J. CLARK

College of the Atlantic (B)

105 Eden Street, Bar Harbor ME 04609-1198
County: Hancock FICE Identification: 011385
Unit ID: 160959
Telephone: (207) 288-5015 Carnegie Class: Bac/A&S
FAX Number: (207) 288-3780 Calendar System: Trimester
URL: www.coa.edu
Established: 1969 Annual Undergrad Tuition & Fees: $40,491
Enrollment: 386 Coed
Affiliation or Control: Independent Non-Profit IRS Status: 501(c)3
Highest Offering: Master's
Program: Liberal Arts And General; Teacher Preparatory
Accreditation: EH

01 President .... Dr. Darron COLLINS
05 Academic Dean .... Dr. Ken HILL
10 Administrative Dean .... Mr. Andy GRIFFITHS
32 Dean for Student Life .... Ms. Sarah LUKE
30 Dean Institutional Advancement .... Ms. Lynn BOULGER
07 Dean of Admission .... Ms. Heather ALBERT-KNOPP
06 Registrar .... Ms. Judy ALLEN
08 Director of Thorndike Library .... Ms. Jane HULTBERG
21 Comptroller .... Mrs. Melissa COOK
37 Director of Financial Aid .... Mr. Bruce HAZAM
36 Director of Internship/Career Svcs .... Ms. Jill BARLOW-KELLEY
26 Public Relations Manager .... Vacant

Husson University (C)

1 College Circle, Bangor ME 04401-2929
County: Penobscot FICE Identification: 002043
Unit ID: 161165
Telephone: (207) 941-7000 Carnegie Class: Master's M
FAX Number: (207) 941-7139 Calendar System: Semester
URL: www.husson.edu
Established: 1898 Annual Undergrad Tuition & Fees: $16,060
Enrollment: 3,414 Coed
Affiliation or Control: Independent Non-Profit IRS Status: 501(c)3
Highest Offering: Doctorate
Program: Professional
Accreditation: EH, CACREP, IACBE, NURSE, OT, PHAR, PTA

01 President .... Dr. Robert A. CLARK
05 VP for Academic Affairs/Provost .... Dr. Lynne COY-OGAN
10 VP Finance & Admin/Treasurer .... Craig HADLEY
30 Vice President for Advancement .... Thomas MARTZ
84 VP Enrollment Management .... Jonathan HENRY
50 Dean College of Business .... Dr. Marie HANSEN
67 Dean School of Pharmacy .... Dr. Rodney LARSON
53 Dean College of Health & Education .... Dr. Rhonda WASKIEWICZ
49 Dean Science/Humanities .... Dr. Patricia BIXEL
26 Exec Dir of Marketing and Comm .... Eric GORDON
32 Dean of Student Life .... Carl STILES
53 Director School of Education .... Barbara MOODY
07 Director of Admissions .... Carlena BEAN
37 Director of Financial Aid .... Anne TABOR
13 Exec Dir of Information Resources .... Garth CORMIER
06 Registrar .... Nancy FENDERS
09 Director of Institutional Research .... Dr. Gail TUDOR
108 Director Institutional Assessment .... Travis E. ALLEN
106 Dir Online and Extended Learning .... Richard PUSHARD
36 Director Career Services .... James WESTHOFF
41 Director of Athletics .... Francis PERGOLIZZI
26 Dir of Comm and Student Engagement .... Julia GREEN
15 Human Resources Director .... Mary DEMERS
29 Director of Alumni Relations .... Amanda CUMMINGS
18 Director of Maintenance .... Lewis MCEACHARN
08 Librarian .... Amy AVERRE
31 Dir of Special Programs .... Mike FOSTER
44 Director of Advancement Services .... Lynda ROHMAN
04 Administrative Asst to President .... Nancy BUBAR
100 Chief of Staff .... Mary Ann HAAS
19 Director Safety and Security .... Ray BESSETTE
38 Director of Counseling Services .... Dr. Joshua LAWRENCE
105 Website Manager & Social Media Dir . Matthew GREEN-HAMANN

Institute for Doctoral Studies in the Visual Arts (D)

130 Neal Street, Portland ME 04102
County: Cumberland FICE Identification: 041888
Unit ID: 462044
Telephone: (207) 879-8757 Carnegie Class: Not Classified
FAX Number: N/A Calendar System: Semester
URL: www.idsva.org
Established: 2007 Annual Graduate Tuition & Fees: $30,500
Enrollment: 57 Coed
Affiliation or Control: Independent Non-Profit IRS Status: 501(c)3
Highest Offering: Doctorate; No Undergraduates
Program: Professional
Accreditation: @EH

01 President .... George SMITH
03 Executive Vice President .... Amy CURTIS

Kaplan University-Augusta (E)

14 Marketplace Drive, Augusta ME 04330
Telephone: (207) 213-2500 Identification: 770060
Accreditation: &NH

† Branch campus of Kaplan University, Davenport, IA.

Kaplan University-Lewiston (F)

475 Lisbon Street, Lewiston ME 04240
Telephone: (207) 333-3300 Identification: 770061
Accreditation: &NH

† Branch campus of Kaplan University, Davenport, IA.

Kaplan University-Maine (G)

265 Western Avenue, South Portland ME 04106
Telephone: (207) 774-6126 FICE Identification: 009292
Accreditation: &NH, ACBSP

† Regional accreditation is carried under the parent institution in Davenport, IA.

The Landing School (H)

286 River Road, Arundel ME 04046
County: York FICE Identification: 023613
Unit ID: 161208
Telephone: (207) 985-7976 Carnegie Class: Not Classified
FAX Number: (207) 985-7942 Calendar System: Semester
URL: www.landingschool.edu
Established: 1978 Annual Undergrad Tuition & Fees: $21,694
Enrollment: 82 Coed
Affiliation or Control: Independent Non-Profit IRS Status: 501(c)3
Highest Offering: Associate Degree
Program: Occupational; 2-Year Principally Bachelor's Creditable; Technical Emphasis
Accreditation: ACCSC

01 President .... Dr. Richard J. SCHUHMANN
05 Director of Education .... Mr. Richard WOODMAN
10 Dir of Administration & Finance .... Ms. Kristy LANK
07 Director of Admissions .... Ms. Janet ACKER
37 Director Student Financial Aid .... Ms. Jennifer BECHARD

Maine College of Art (I)

522 Congress St, Portland ME 04101
County: Cumberland FICE Identification: 011673
Unit ID: 161509
Telephone: (207) 699-5521 Carnegie Class: Spec/Arts
FAX Number: (207) 775-5087 Calendar System: Semester
URL: www.meca.edu
Established: 1882 Annual Undergrad Tuition & Fees: $32,290
Enrollment: 427 Coed
Affiliation or Control: Independent Non-Profit IRS Status: 501(c)3
Highest Offering: Master's
Program: Liberal Arts And General; Professional; Fine Arts Emphasis
Accreditation: EH, ART

01 President .... Mr. Donald TUSKI
03 Executive Vice President .... Ms. Beth ELICKER
05 Dean/Vice Pres Academic Affairs .... Mr. Ian ANDERSON
30 VP for Institutional Advancement .... Ms. Rebecca CONRAD
06 Registrar .... Ms. Anne DENNISON
32 Director of Student Life .... Ms. Adrea JAEHNIG
07 Director of Admissions .... Mr. Liam SULLIVAN
13 Director Technology .... Mr. Seth CLAYTER
26 Dir of Marketing & Communications ..... Mr. Raffi DER SIMONIAN
10 Director of Business Services .... Mr. Phil STEVENS
37 Director of Financial Aid .... Ms. Carri FRECHETTE
51 Director Continuing Studies .... Ms. Courtney COOK
18 Chief Facilities/Physical Plant .... Mr. Douglas DOERING
08 Librarian .... Ms. Moira STEVENS
04 Executive Assistant .... Ms. Melissa SULLIVAN
29 Director Alumni Relations .... Ms. Jill DALTON
36 Director of Artists at Work .... Ms. Jessica TOMLINSON

Maine College of Health Professions (J)

70 Middle Street, Lewiston ME 04240-7027
County: Androscoggin FICE Identification: 006305
Unit ID: 161022
Telephone: (207) 795-2840 Carnegie Class: Assoc/PrivNFP
FAX Number: (207) 795-2849 Calendar System: Semester
URL: www.mchp.edu
Established: 1891 Annual Undergrad Tuition & Fees: $9,890
Enrollment: 210 Coed
Affiliation or Control: Independent Non-Profit IRS Status: 501(c)3
Highest Offering: Associate Degree
Program: 2-Year Principally Bachelor's Creditable; Nursing Emphasis
Accreditation: EH, ADNUR, NMT, RAD

01 President .... Dr. Richard E. FARMER
10 Director of Financial Affairs .... Mr. Otis VANCE
05 Director of General Education .... Mrs. Judith RIPLEY
07 Director of Admissions .... Ms. Erica WATSON
06 Registrar .... Mrs. Kathleen C. JACQUES
37 Student Financial Aid Specialist .... Mrs. Nicole DEBLOIS
66 Director of Nursing .... Ms. Carol FACKLER

*Maine Community College System (K)

323 State Street, Augusta ME 04330-7131
County: Kennebec Identification: 666092
Unit ID: 409713
Telephone: (207) 629-4000 Carnegie Class: N/A
FAX Number: (207) 629-4048

01 Interim President .... Mr. Derek LANGHAUSER
05 Chief Academic Officer .... Ms. Janet SORTOR
10 Chief Financial Officer .... Mr. David DAIGLER

*Central Maine Community College (L)

1250 Turner Street, Auburn ME 04210-6498
County: Androscoggin FICE Identification: 005276
Unit ID: 161077
Telephone: (207) 755-5100 Carnegie Class: Assoc/Pub-R-M
FAX Number: (207) 755-5491 Calendar System: Semester
URL: www.cmcc.edu
Established: 1964 Annual Undergrad Tuition & Fees (In-State): $3,600
Enrollment: 3,000 Coed
Affiliation or Control: State IRS Status: 501(c)3
Highest Offering: Associate Degree
Program: Occupational; 2-Year Principally Bachelor's Creditable; Technical Emphasis
Accreditation: EH, ADNUR, ENGT

02 President ....Dr. Scott E. KNAPP
05 Dean Academic Affairs ....Ms. Betsy LIBBY
06 Registrar ....Ms. Sonya SAMPSON
10 Dean of Finance and General Service ....Ms. Pamela REMIERES-MORIN
37 Director of Financial Aid ....Mr. John BOWIE
31 Dean Corporate/Community Services ....Ms. Diane DOSTIE
32 Dean of Student Services ....Mr. Nicholas HAMEL
26 Dean Planning/Development/PR ....Mr. Roger PHILIPPON
07 Director of Admissions ....Mr. Andrew MORONG
08 Head Librarian ....Ms. Judith FROST
18 Chief Physical Plant ....Mr. Raymond MASSE
22 Affirmative Action Officer ....Ms. Barbara OWEN
39 Director of Housing/Athletic Dir ....Mr. David GONYEA
40 Director of Bookstore ....Ms. Christine MORIN
15 Dean of Human Resources ....Ms. Barbara OWEN
30 Director of Development ....Vacant
27 Director of Communications ....Ms. Heather B. SEYMOUR

*Eastern Maine Community College (A)

354 Hogan Road, Bangor ME 04401-4280
County: Penobscot　FICE Identification: 005277
Unit ID: 161138
Telephone: (207) 974-4600　Carnegie Class: Assoc/Pub-R-M
FAX Number: (207) 974-4608　Calendar System: Semester
URL: www.emcc.edu
Established: 1966　Annual Undergrad Tuition & Fees (In-State): $3,920
Enrollment: 2,613　Coed
Affiliation or Control: State　IRS Status: 501(c)3
Highest Offering: Associate Degree
Program: Occupational; 2-Year Principally Bachelor's Creditable; Technical Emphasis
Accreditation: EH, ADNUR, EMT, MAC, RAD, SURGT

02 President ....Dr. Lawrence M. BARRETT
05 Academic Dean ....Ms. Elizabeth RUSSELL
10 Dir Finance & Auxiliary Services ....Mr. Jerry HAYMAN
09 Dean Inst Research/Enrollment Mgmt ....Mr. Daniel CROCKER
88 Professional Services Coordinator ....Mr. Matt MCLAUGHLIN
07 Director of Admissions ....Ms. Stacy GREEN
15 Director of Human Resources ....Ms. Jody VAIL
08 Librarian ....Ms. Janet ELVIDGE
37 Director of Financial Aid ....Ms. Candace WARD
13 Dean of Communication/Info Tech ....Mr. Timothy CONROY
18 Dir Facilities Mgmt/Student Life ....Mr. Daniel BELYEA
20 Assistant Academic Dean ....Vacant
30 Dir of Institutional Advancement ....Ms. CarolAnne DUBE

*Kennebec Valley Community College (B)

92 Western Avenue, Fairfield ME 04937-1367
County: Somerset　FICE Identification: 009826
Unit ID: 161192
Telephone: (207) 453-5000　Carnegie Class: Assoc/Pub-R-M
FAX Number: (207) 453-5010　Calendar System: Semester
URL: www.kvcc.me.edu
Established: 1970　Annual Undergrad Tuition & Fees (In-State): $3,318
Enrollment: 2,401　Coed
Affiliation or Control: State　IRS Status: 501(c)3
Highest Offering: Associate Degree
Program: Occupational; 2-Year Principally Bachelor's Creditable
Accreditation: EH, ACBSP, ADNUR, CAHIIM, COARC, DMS, EMT, MAC, OTA, PTAA, RAD

02 President ....Dr. Richard HOPPER
05 Academic Dean/Vice President ....Dr. Jon CONNOLLY
13 Dean of Information Technology ....Mr. Kevin CASEY
32 Dean of Student Affairs ....Ms. Karen NORMANDIN
10 Dean of Finance & Administration ....Mr. Douglas MITCHELL
06 Registrar ....Mrs. Lisa YORK-LEMELIN
30 Director of Development ....Ms. Michelle WEBB
07 Director of Admissions ....Vacant
37 Director Student Financial Aid ....Ms. Anne CONNORS
09 Director of Institutional Research ....Ms. Karen GLEW
84 Enrollment Services Coordinator ....Mr. Crichton MCKENNA

*Northern Maine Community College (C)

33 Edgemont Drive, Presque Isle ME 04769-2099
County: Aroostook　FICE Identification: 005760
Unit ID: 161484
Telephone: (207) 768-2700　Carnegie Class: Assoc/Pub-R-S
FAX Number: (207) 768-2831　Calendar System: Semester
URL: www.nmcc.edu
Established: 1961　Annual Undergrad Tuition & Fees (In-State): $3,588
Enrollment: 758　Coed
Affiliation or Control: State　IRS Status: 501(c)3
Highest Offering: Associate Degree
Program: Occupational; 2-Year Principally Bachelor's Creditable
Accreditation: EH, ACBSP, ADNUR, EMT, MAC

02 President ....Mr. Timothy D. CROWLEY
05 Academic Dean ....Dr. Dorothy MARTIN
32 Dean of Students ....Dr. William G. EGELER
10 Dean of Finance ....Mr. Michael WILLIAMS
51 Dean of Continuing Education ....Ms. Leah BUCK
30 Dean of Development & College Rels ....Ms. Sue BERNARD

07 Director of Admissions ....Mr. Eugene MCCLUSKEY
06 Registrar ....Ms. Betsy A. HARRIS
37 Asst Director for Financial Aid ....Ms. Norma M. SMITH
39 Director of Housing & Resident Life ....Mr. Jon A. BLANCHARD
38 Director of Counseling ....Ms. Tammy NELSON
18 Dean of Tech and Facilities ....Mr. Barry INGRAHAM
21 Business Manager ....Mr. Philip R. BROWN
15 Human Resource Manager ....Vacant
40 Bookstore Manager ....Ms. Rebecca A. MAYNARD
08 Head Librarian ....Ms. Gail ROY

*Southern Maine Community College (D)

2 Fort Road, South Portland ME 04106-1698
County: Cumberland　FICE Identification: 005525
Unit ID: 161545
Telephone: (207) 741-5500　Carnegie Class: Assoc/Pub-R-M
FAX Number: (207) 741-5751　Calendar System: Semester
URL: www.smccme.edu
Established: 1946　Annual Undergrad Tuition & Fees (In-State): $3,755
Enrollment: 6,734　Coed
Affiliation or Control: State　IRS Status: 501(c)3
Highest Offering: Associate Degree
Program: Occupational; 2-Year Principally Bachelor's Creditable
Accreditation: EH, ACFEI, ADNUR, COARC, DIETT, EMT, RAD, RTT

02 President/CEO ....Ronald G. CANTOR
05 Vice President/Academic Dean ....Janet M. SORTOR
32 Dean of Student Life/Affiirm Action ....Tiffanie L. BENTLEY
26 Dean of Effectiveness & Engagement ....Kaylene MITCHELL
04 Asst to the Pres/Strategic Initiat ....Darla JEWETT
04 Exec Assistant to the President ....Lori HALL
12 Dean of the Midcoast Campus ....James WHITTEN
10 Dean of Finance ....Robert COOMBS
11 Dean of Administration ....Scott BEATTY
13 Dean of Information Technology/CIO ....Timothy DUNNE
88 Int Dean Bus & Cmty Partnerships ....Julie CHASE
20 Associate Dean of Academic Affairs ....Paul CHARPENTIER
06 Asst Dean of Records/Retention ....Jeremy DILL
21 Director of Budget & Financial Rpt ....Shaun GRAY
37 Director of Financial Aid Systems ....Michel LUSSIER
07 Director of Admissions ....Amy LEE
88 Assistant Dean of Student Success ....Kathleen DOAN
39 Dir of Residence Life & Stdnt Dev ....Shane LONG
19 Director Campus Security ....Joseph MANHARDT
41 Director of Athletics ....Matthew RICHARDS
18 Plant Maintenance Engineer III ....James RENY
40 Manager Campus Store ....Cherie BRYANT
21 Business Mgr Student Billing/Bursar ....Leslie GUERRETTE
15 HR & Benefits Manager ....Denise RENY
38 Dir Counseling & Disability Svcs ....Sandra LYNHAM
27 Director of Communitcations ....Clarke CANFIELD
102 Dir Foundation Corporate Relations ....Joan COHEN
105 Director Web Services ....Ken POOLEY

*Washington County Community College (E)

One College Drive, Calais ME 04619-9704
County: Washington　FICE Identification: 009231
Unit ID: 161581
Telephone: (207) 454-1000　Carnegie Class: Assoc/Pub-R-S
FAX Number: (207) 454-1092　Calendar System: Semester
URL: www.wccc.me.edu
Established: 1969　Annual Undergrad Tuition & Fees (In-State): $3,500
Enrollment: 470　Coed
Affiliation or Control: State　IRS Status: 501(c)3
Highest Offering: Associate Degree
Program: Occupational; 2-Year Principally Bachelor's Creditable
Accreditation: EH, MAC

02 President ....Mr. Joseph CASSIDY
05 Academic Dean ....Mr. Alexander CLIFFORD
10 Dean of Finance & Admin Services ....Ms. Desiree THOMPSON
15 Director of HR and Public Relations ....Mrs. Tina ERSKINE
84 Assoc Dean Enroll/Retention Svcs ....Mrs. Susan MINGO
37 Financial Aid Director ....Ms. Linda WINCHESTER
07 Director of Admissions ....Mrs. Susan MINGO
39 Director Student Housing ....Ms. Karen GOOKIN

*York County Community College (F)

112 College Drive, Wells ME 04090-0529
County: York　FICE Identification: 031229
Unit ID: 420440
Telephone: (207) 646-9282　Carnegie Class: Assoc/Pub-R-S
FAX Number: (207) 646-9675　Calendar System: Semester
URL: www.yccc.edu
Established: 1994　Annual Undergrad Tuition & Fees (In-State): $3,480
Enrollment: 1,699　Coed
Affiliation or Control: State　IRS Status: 501(c)3
Highest Offering: Associate Degree
Program: Occupational; 2-Year Principally Bachelor's Creditable
Accreditation: EH

02 President ....Dr. Barbara FINKELSTEIN
05 Vice President/Academic Dean ....Ms. Paula GAGNON
32 Dean of Students ....Mr. Jason AREY
10 Dean of Finance & Administration ....Ms. Nancy DROUIN
26 Dir of Marketing/Communications ....Ms. Stacy CHILICKI

31 Dir of Business/Community Programs ....Ms. Paulette MILLETTE
04 Exec Assistant to the President ....Ms. Erin HAYE
20 Associate Academic Dean ....Ms. Doreen ROGAN
08 Director Library/Learning Resources ....Ms. Amber TATNALL
88 Faculty Development Coordinator ....Ms. Stefanie FORSTER
07 Director of Admissions ....Mr. Fred QUISTGARD
84 Director of Enrollment Services ....Ms. Jessica MASI
37 Director Financial Aid ....Mr. David DAIGLE
13 Director of Technology ....Mr. Eric BOURQUE
21 Business Manager ....Mr. Samuel ELLIS
15 Human Resources & Benefits Manager ....Ms. Ellen HARFORD
18 Manager of Facilities ....Mr. Dana PETERSEN
09 Assoc Dean of Inst Research ....Mr. Nicholas GILL

Maine Maritime Academy (G)

Pleasant Street, Castine ME 04420-0001
County: Hancock　FICE Identification: 002044
Unit ID: 161299
Telephone: (207) 326-4311　Carnegie Class: Bac/Diverse
FAX Number: (207) 326-2218　Calendar System: Semester
URL: www.mma.edu
Established: 1941　Annual Undergrad Tuition & Fees (In-State): $20,154
Enrollment: 292　Coed
Affiliation or Control: State　IRS Status: 501(c)3
Highest Offering: Master's
Program: Professional
Accreditation: EH, ENG, ENGT

01 President ....Dr. William J. BRENNAN
05 Academic Dean ....Dr. David GARDNER
11 Vice Pres of Operations ....Mr. Darrell DONAHUE
84 VP Stdnt Svcs/Enrollment Mgmt ....Dr. Elizabeth TRUE
30 Vice President for Advancement ....Vacant
15 Human Resource Officer ....Mrs. Carrie MARGRAVE
32 Chief Student Life Officer ....Ms. Amanda NGUYEN
35 Dean of Student Services ....Ms. Deidra DAVIS
36 Placement Director ....Mr. Timothy LEACH
07 Director of Admissions ....Mr. Jeffrey WRIGHT
06 Registrar ....Ms. Christina STEPHENS
29 Director Alumni Relations ....Mr. Paul MERCER
37 Director Student Financial Aid ....Ms. Kathy HEATH
38 Director Student Counseling ....Mr. Paul FERREIRA
08 Head Librarian ....Ms. Wendy GIRVEN
10 Chief Business Officer ....Ms. Diana SNAPP
18 Chief Facilities/Physical Plant ....Mr. Adam POTTER
20 Associate Academic Dean ....Dr. Joceline BOUCHER
26 Chief Public Relations Officer ....Mrs. Jennifer DEJOY
09 Director of Institutional Research ....Vacant
96 Director of Purchasing ....Mrs. Alice HERRICK
28 Dir Policy/Institutional Equity ....Vacant

Saint Joseph's College of Maine (H)

278 Whites Bridge Road, Standish ME 04084-5236
County: Cumberland　FICE Identification: 002051
Unit ID: 161518
Telephone: (207) 892-6766　Carnegie Class: Master's M
FAX Number: (207) 893-7861　Calendar System: Semester
URL: www.sjcme.edu
Established: 1912　Annual Undergrad Tuition & Fees: $32,620
Enrollment: 1,633　Coed
Affiliation or Control: Roman Catholic　IRS Status: 501(c)3
Highest Offering: Master's
Program: Liberal Arts And General; Teacher Preparatory; Professional
Accreditation: EH, NURSE

01 President ....Dr. James S. DLUGOS
05 VP & Chief Officer of Learning ....Dr. Michael PARDALES
30 VP & Chief Advancement Officer ....Ms. Joanne BEAN
84 Vice Pres Enrollment ....Ms. Lynne ROBINSON
88 Vice Pres for Sponsorship & Mission ....Sr. Kathleen SULLIVAN
10 VP & Chief Financial Officer ....Ms. Yvonne BERRY
32 Dean of Campus Life ....Mr. Matthew GAWEL
06 Dir of Academic Records/Registrar ....Mr. Kevin PAQUETTE
08 Director of the Library ....Ms. Shelly DAVIS
13 Director Information Systems ....Ms. Gayle LANGIS
23 Director Health Services ....Dr. Sue-Anne HAMMOND
15 Director Human Resources ....Ms. Kristine AVERY

Thomas College (I)

180 W River Road, Waterville ME 04901-5097
County: Kennebec　FICE Identification: 002052
Unit ID: 161563
Telephone: (207) 859-1111　Carnegie Class: Bac/Diverse
FAX Number: (207) 859-1114　Calendar System: Semester
URL: www.thomas.edu
Established: 1894　Annual Undergrad Tuition & Fees: $24,300
Enrollment: 1,404　Coed
Affiliation or Control: Independent Non-Profit　IRS Status: 501(c)3
Highest Offering: Master's
Program: Liberal Arts And General; Teacher Preparatory; Professional; Business Emphasis
Accreditation: EH

01 President ....Ms. Laurie G. LACHANCE
05 Provost ....Dr. Thomas EDWARDS
10 Senior Vice President/CFO/Treasurer ....Ms. Beth B. GIBBS
30 Vice Pres Advancement ....Mr. Robert M. MOORE
84 Vice Pres Enrollment Management ....Mr. Jonathan KENT

32 Vice President Student Affairs .. Ms. Lisa DESAUTELS-POLIQUIN
13 Vice Pres Information Services/CIO ... Mr. Christopher RHODA
88 Dean of Advancement ... Ms. Erin BALTES
20 Dean of Academic Affairs ... Dr. James LIBBY
35 Dean of Students ... Ms. Hannah GLADSTONE
20 Assistant Academic Dean ... Ms. Merlene SANBORN
15 Chief Human Resources Officer ... Ms. Michelle JOLER-LABBE
08 Director Library Services ... Ms. Lisa AURIEMMA
37 Director Student Financial Services ... Ms. Jeannine BOSSE
29 Director Alumni/Career Services ... Mr. Corey PELLETIER
18 Director Physical Plant ... Mr. James PARSONS
26 Director Public Relations ... Ms. Jennifer BUKER
06 Registrar ... Ms. Lindsey NELSON
04 Executive Asst to President ... Ms. Mikaela ZIOBRO
41 Director of Athletics ... Mr. David ROUSSEL

Unity College (A)

90 Quaker Hill Road, Unity ME 04988-9502
County: Waldo FICE Identification: 006858
Unit ID: 161572
Telephone: (207) 509-7100 Carnegie Class: Bac/Diverse
FAX Number: (207) 512-1192 Calendar System: Semester
URL: www.unity.edu
Established: 1965 Annual Undergrad Tuition & Fees: $35,400
Enrollment: 601 Coed
Affiliation or Control: Independent Non-Profit IRS Status: 501(c)3
Highest Offering: Master's
Program: Occupational; 2-Year Principally Bachelor's Creditable; Liberal Arts And General; Teacher Preparatory
Accreditation: EH

01 President ... Dr. Stephen MULKEY
03 Executive VP/Liaison to BOT ... Dr. Melik Peter KHOURY
05 Provost & VP for Academic Affairs ... Vacant
101 Secretary to Board ... Ms. Chris MELANSON
04 Executive Assistant ... Ms. Kimberly SHEFF
10 Vice Pres Finance & Administration ... Ms. Deborah CRONIN
06 Registrar ... Ms. Heather A. MCANIRLIN
32 Dean of Student Affairs ... Mr. Gary ZANE
07 Director of Admissions ... Mr. Joseph SALTALAMACHIA
41 Director of Athletics ... Mr. Chris KEIN
30 Dir College Development/Alumni ... Ms. Julie CUNNINGHAM
88 Director Dining Services ... Ms. Lorey DUPREY
36 Director Career Services ... Ms. Nicole COLLINS
18 Director Facilities & Public Safety ... Mr. Daniel LAFORGE
37 Director Financial Aid ... Mr. Rand E. NEWELL
23 Director Health & Wellness Center ... Ms. Anna MCGALLIARD
15 Director Human Resources ... Ms. Sarah CONROY
13 Director Information Technology ... Mr. Bert AUDETTE
24 Director Learning Resource Center ... Dr. James HECK
08 Director Quimby Library ... Ms. Sandra ABBOTT-STOUT
26 Director of Marketing/Communication ... Vacant
106 Dir Online Education/E-learning ... Mr. Howard DAVIS
88 Director Outdoor Adventure Center ... Ms. Jessica STEELE
39 Director Residence Life ... Mr. Stephen S. NASON
35 Director Student Accounts ... Ms. Jeri ROBERTS
88 Director Writing Center ... Ms. Judy WILLIAMS
88 Director of Sustainability ... Ms. Jennifer DEHART
53 Director of Teacher Education ... Dr. Jennifer CARTIER
88 Assoc Dir College Communications ... Mr. Bob MENTZINGER
19 Chief Public Safety Officer ... Mr. Dean BESSEY
88 Community-Based/Internship Coord ... Ms. Reeta BENEDICT
40 Manager Bookstore ... Ms. Leigh JUSKEVICE
09 Director of Institutional Research ... Ms. Holly HEIN

*University of Maine System Office (B)

16 Central Street, Bangor ME 04401-5106
County: Penobscot FICE Identification: 008012
Unit ID: 161280
Telephone: (207) 973-3200 Carnegie Class: N/A
FAX Number: (207) 973-3296
URL: www.maine.edu

01 Chancellor ... Dr. James H. PAGE
10 CFO & Treasurer ... Mr. Ryan LOW
43 University Counsel ... Mr. James B. THELEN
86 Asst to Chanc Governmental Rels ... Mr. John LISNIK
101 Clerk of the Board ... Ms. Tracy BIGNEY
32 Chief Student Affairs Officer ... Ms. Rosa REDONNETT
13 Chief Information Officer ... Mr. Dick THOMPSON
18 Director of Facilities ... Mr. M. F. Chip GAVIN
15 Chief Human Resources Officer ... Ms. Lynda DEC
26 Exec Director of Public Affairs ... Mr. Daniel DEMERITT

*University of Maine (C)

Orono ME 04469-0001
County: Penobscot FICE Identification: 002053
Unit ID: 161253
Telephone: (207) 581-1110 Carnegie Class: RU/H
FAX Number: (207) 581-1604 Calendar System: Semester
URL: www.umaine.edu
Established: 1865 Annual Undergrad Tuition & Fees (In-State): $10,610
Enrollment: 11,286 Coed
Affiliation or Control: State IRS Status: 501(c)3
Highest Offering: Doctorate
Program: Liberal Arts And General; Teacher Preparatory; Professional
Accreditation: EH, ART, BUS, CAATE, CEA, CLPSY, CS, DIETD, DIETI, ENG, ENGT, IPSY, MUS, NURSE, SP, SW, TED

02 President ... Dr. Susan J. HUNTER
05 Exec VP Academic Affairs/Provost ... Dr. Jeffrey E. HECKER
10 Assoc VC & Chief Financial Officer ... Mr. Ryan LOW
102 Pres Univ of Maine Foundation ... Dr. Jeffery N. MILLS
32 VP Student Affs/Dean of Students ... Dr. Robert Q. DANA
46 Vice President for Research ... Dr. Carol H. KIM
84 Vice Pres Enrollment Management ... Vacant
88 VP Innovation/Economic Development ... Mr. James WARD, IV
15 AVP Human Resources ... Vacant
21 Asst VP of Financial/Budget Svcs ... Mrs. Claire I. STRICKLAND
20 Assoc Provost/Dean Undergrad Educ ... Dr. Jeffrey E. ST. JOHN
100 Chief of Staff ... Ms. Megan A. SANDERS
08 Dean of Libraries ... Ms. Joyce V. RUMERY
13 Exec Dir of Information Technology ... Ms. Cindy MITCHELL
18 Exec Dir Facilities/Capital Mgt Svc ... Mr. Stewart A. HARVEY
26 Sr Dir Univ Relations/Operations ... Ms. Margaret A. NAGLE
109 Exec Director of Auxiliary Services ... Mr. Daniel H. STURRUP
25 Dir Research & Sponsored Programs .. Mr. Michael M. HASTINGS
06 Director Student Records ... Ms. Kimberly D. PAGE
07 Senior Director of Admissions ... Ms. Sharon M. OLIVER
37 Director of Financial Aid ... Ms. Sarah DOHENY
36 Director of Career Center ... Ms. Patricia B. COUNIHAN
09 Director Institutional Studies ... Mr. Ted T. COLADARCI
85 Int Director International Programs ... Ms. Orlina BOTEVA
41 Athletic Director ... Mr. Karlton W. CREECH
28 Director Equal Employment Diversity ... Ms. Karen D. KEMBLE
19 Chief Police Dept ... Chief Roland J. LACROIX
29 Int President Alumni Association ... Mr. John N. DIAMOND
40 Interim Director of Bookstore ... Mr. Richard YOUNG
96 Acting Dir of Procurment Services ... Mr. Kevin CARR
38 Director Student Counseling ... Mr. Douglas P. JOHNSON
49 Dean Liberal Arts & Sciences ... Dr. Emily A. HADDAD
50 Dean Maine Business School ... Dr. Ivan M. MANEV
53 Int Dean Educ/Human Development ... Dr. Susan K. GARDNER
54 Dean Engineering ... Dr. Dana N. HUMPHREY
65 Dean Natural Science/Forestry/Agric .. Dr. Edward N. ASHWORTH
51 Dean Lifelong Learning ... Dr. Monique M. LAROCQUE
58 Dean Graduate School ... Dr. Carol KIM

*University of Maine at Augusta (D)

46 University Drive, Augusta ME 04330-9410
County: Kennebec FICE Identification: 006760
Unit ID: 161217
Telephone: (207) 621-3000 Carnegie Class: Bac/Assoc
FAX Number: (207) 621-3116 Calendar System: Semester
URL: www.uma.edu
Established: 1965 Annual Undergrad Tuition & Fees (In-State): $7,448
Enrollment: 4,664 Coed
Affiliation or Control: State IRS Status: 501(c)3
Highest Offering: Baccalaureate
Program: 2-Year Principally Bachelor's Creditable; Liberal Arts And General; Professional
Accreditation: EH, ADNUR, DA, DH, MLTAD, NUR

02 President ... Dr. Rebecca WYKE
05 Vice President/Provost ... Dr. Joe S. SZAKAS
10 Chief Business Officer ... Mr. Tim BROKAW
84 Dean of Enrollment Services ... Ms. Sheri FRASER
11 Exec Director of Admin Services ... Ms. Sheri R. STEVENS
100 Chief of Staff ... Ms. Joyce BLANCHARD
08 Librarian ... Ms. Ana NORIEGA
32 Dean of Students ... Ms. Kathleen A. DEXTER
107 Dean College of Prof Studies ... Ms. Brenda MCALEER
37 Director of Financial Aid ... Ms. Sherry MCCOLLETT
06 Registrar ... Ms. Ann CORBETT
15 Director Personnel Services ... Mr. David LANE
18 Chief Facilities/Physical Plant ... Mr. Peter ST. MICHEL
38 Dir of Cornerstone & Counseling ... Ms. Dorrea FELLMAN
88 Director of Advising ... Ms. Tricia DYER
35 Director of Student Life ... Vacant
40 Director Bookstore ... Mr. Jerry GARTHOFF
26 Exec Director of External Relations ... Mr. Bob STEIN
09 Exec Director of IR & Planning ... Mr. Gregory LAPOINTE
49 Dean College of Arts & Sciences ... Mr. Greg FAHY

*University of Maine at Farmington (E)

224 Main Street, Farmington ME 04938-1911
County: Franklin FICE Identification: 002040
Unit ID: 161226
Telephone: (207) 778-7000 Carnegie Class: Bac/Diverse
FAX Number: (207) 778-7247 Calendar System: Semester
URL: www.umf.maine.edu
Established: 1864 Annual Undergrad Tuition & Fees (In-State): $9,217
Enrollment: 1,960 Coed
Affiliation or Control: State IRS Status: 501(c)3
Highest Offering: Master's
Program: Liberal Arts And General; Teacher Preparatory
Accreditation: EH, TED

02 President ... Dr. Kathryn A. FOSTER
05 Vice Pres Academic Affairs/Provost ... Dr. Joseph P. MCGINN
10 Exec Dir Finance & Administration ... Ms. Laurie A. GARDNER
32 Vice Pres Student & Community Svcs ... Ms. Celeste BRANHAM
44 VP for University Advancement ... Mr. Kelly L. DODGE
07 Assoc Director of Admissions ... Ms. Eileen READING
88 Sustainability Coordinator ... Dr. Lucas C. KELLETT
53 Assoc Provost & Dean of Education ... Dr. Katherine W. YARDLEY
20 Assoc Provost & Dean of Acad Svcs ... Dr. Robert L. LIVELY
92 Director of Honors Program ... Dr. Eric BROWN
88 Dir of Learning Assistance Center ... Ms. Jessica BERRY
37 Financial Aid Director ... Mr. Ronald P. MILLIKEN
15 Dir Human Resources & Finance ... Ms. Kathleen P. FALCO
06 Director Adm Sys/Student Records ... Ms. Sharon L. NADEAU
88 Dir Center for Student Development ... Mr. Robert A. PEDERSON
26 Assoc Director of Media Relations ... Ms. April C. MULHERIN
13 Ex Dir Innov/Campus Tech/Strategy ... Mr. Frederick L. BRITTAIN
41 Dir Athletics/Fitness & Recreation ... Ms. Julie A. DAVIS
88 Dir Fitness & Recreation Center ... Mr. James D. TONER
32 Director Student Life ... Mr. Brian K. UFFORD
35 Dir Student Leadership/Services ... Ms. Kirsten SWAN
23 Director Student Health Center ... Dr. Susan E. COCHRAN
18 Director of Facilities Management ... Mr. Jeffrey MCKAY
19 Director of Public Safety ... Mr. Brock E. CATON
26 Dir of Marketing and Communications ... Ms. Jennifer A. ERIKSEN
88 Director of Dining Services ... Mr. Andrew HUTCHINS
09 Interim Dir of Inst Research ... Ms. Rachel GROENHOUT

*University of Maine at Fort Kent (F)

23 University Drive, Fort Kent ME 04743-1292
County: Aroostook FICE Identification: 002041
Unit ID: 161235
Telephone: (207) 834-7500 Carnegie Class: Bac/Diverse
FAX Number: (207) 834-7503 Calendar System: Semester
URL: www.umfk.maine.edu
Established: 1878 Annual Undergrad Tuition & Fees (In-State): $7,575
Enrollment: 1,327 Coed
Affiliation or Control: State IRS Status: 501(c)3
Highest Offering: Baccalaureate
Program: Occupational; 2-Year Principally Bachelor's Creditable; Liberal Arts And General; Teacher Preparatory; Professional; Nursing Emphasis
Accreditation: EH, IACBE, NURSE

02 Interim President ... Mr. John D. MURPHY
05 Vice President Academic Affairs ... Dr. Robert M. DIXON
10 Vice President for Administration ... Mr. John D. MURPHY
31 Dean of Community Education ... Mr. Scott A. VOISINE
84 Dean Enrollment Svcs/Student Life ... Ms. Ellia SABLAN-ZEBEDY
36 Assistant Dean of Student Success ... Vacant
06 Registrar ... Mr. Mark SCHENK
15 Acting Director of Human Resources ... Mr. John D. MURPHY
66 Nursing Division Director ... Ms. Erin SOUCY
08 Dir of Information Svcs/Library ... Ms. Leslie E. KELLY
07 Director of Admissions ... Ms. Jill CAIRNS
37 Director of Financial Aid ... Ms. Lisa M. LIPE
18 Director of Facilities Management ... Mr. Andrew C. JACOBS
21 Director of Business Systems ... Ms. Leslie R. GUERRETTE
29 Director Alumni Relations ... Vacant
32 Assoc Dean Student Life/Development . Mr. Raymond R. PHINNEY
09 Assoc Dir of Institutional Research ... Mr. Joseph R. BJERKLIE
30 Development Officer ... Ms. Linda DEPREY

*University of Maine at Machias (G)

116 O'Brien Avenue, Machias ME 04654-1397
County: Washington FICE Identification: 002055
Unit ID: 161244
Telephone: (207) 255-1200 Carnegie Class: Bac/A&S
FAX Number: (207) 255-4864 Calendar System: Semester
URL: www.umm.maine.edu
Established: 1909 Annual Undergrad Tuition & Fees (In-State): $7,480
Enrollment: 810 Coed
Affiliation or Control: State IRS Status: 501(c)3
Highest Offering: Baccalaureate
Program: 2-Year Principally Bachelor's Creditable; Liberal Arts And General; Teacher Preparatory; Professional
Accreditation: EH, NRPA

02 Interim President ... Dr. Joyce HEDLUND
05 Vice Pres Academic Affairs/Provost ... Dr. Stuart G. SWAIN
10 Chief Financial Officer ... Mr. Mark HATT
32 Dean of Students and Admissions ... Dr. Melvin ADAMS
06 Registrar ... Ms. Mary STOVER
08 Director Library ... Ms. Marianne THIBODEAU
15 Director Human Resources ... Ms. Kim PAGE
37 Director Student Financial Aid ... Mrs. Katie KURZ
18 Director Physical Facilities ... Mr. Robert FARRIS
26 Director Public Relations ... Ms. Sharon K. MACK
41 Director Athletics ... Ms. Betsy HAYDEN

*University of Maine at Presque Isle (H)

181 Main Street, Presque Isle ME 04769-2888
County: Aroostook FICE Identification: 002033
Unit ID: 161341
Telephone: (207) 768-9400 Carnegie Class: Bac/Diverse
FAX Number: (207) 768-9608 Calendar System: Semester
URL: www.umpi.edu
Established: 1903 Annual Undergrad Tuition & Fees (In-State): $7,436
Enrollment: 1,138 Coed
Affiliation or Control: State IRS Status: 501(c)3
Highest Offering: Baccalaureate
Program: Liberal Arts And General; Teacher Preparatory; Professional
Accreditation: EH, CAATE, MLTAD, PTAA, SW

02 President ... Dr. Linda K. SCHOTT
05 Vice President Academic Affairs ... Dr. Raymond J. RICE
10 Vice Pres Administration & Finance ... Mr. Marty PARSONS
32 Dean of Students ... Mr. James D. STEPP
07 Director of Admissions ... Ms. Erin V. BENSON
15 Director of Human Resources ... Vacant

13 Director of Information Services ... Vacant
06 Director of Student Records ... Ms. Kathy K. DAVIS
37 Director of Financial Services ... Mr. Christopher BELL
36 Director of Career Preparation ... Ms. Nicole FOURNIER
39 Director Residence Life ... Mr. Dennis KOCH
41 Director of Athletics ... Mr. Michael S. HOLMES
26 Director of Media Relations ... Ms. Rachel RICE
30 Exec Dir of University Advancement ... Ms. Debbie ROARK
40 Bookstore Manager ... Mr. Greg DOAK
18 Director of Facilities Management ... Mr. Gregg BOUCHARD
19 Director Security/Safety ... Mr. Frederick A. THOMAS

*University of Southern Maine (A)

96 Falmouth Street, PO Box 9300,
Portland ME 04101-9300

County: Cumberland — FICE Identification: 002054
Unit ID: 161554
Telephone: (207) 780-4141 — Carnegie Class: Master's L
FAX Number: (207) 780-4933 — Calendar System: Semester
URL: www.usm.maine.edu
Established: 1878 — Annual Undergrad Tuition & Fees (In-State): $8,920
Enrollment: 8,428 — Coed
Affiliation or Control: State — IRS Status: 501(c)3
Highest Offering: Doctorate
Program: Liberal Arts And General; Teacher Preparatory; Professional
Accreditation: EH, ART, BUS, CAATE, CACREP, CORE, CS, ENG, EXSC, HSA, LAW, MUS, NAIT, NURSE, OT, SW, TEAC

02 President ... Mr. Glenn T. CUMMINGS
05 Provost/VPAA ... Vacant
10 Chief Financial Officer/VP Admin ... Mr. Buster NEEL
84 VP Enrollment Management ... Dr. Nancy GRIFFIN
30 Vice President for Advancement ... Vacant
09 Assoc Dir Institutional Research ... Ms. Patricia DAVIS
18 Exec Director Facilities Management ... Mr. Bob BERTRAM
96 Director of Purchasing and Paybles ... Mr. Gregg N. ALLEN
08 University Librarian ... Mr. David NUTTY
108 Director Academic Assessment Ctr ... Ms. Susan L. KING
38 Director of Health & Counseling ... Dr. Kristine BERTINI
15 Chief Human Resources Office ... Vacant
26 Executive Director Public Affairs ... Mr. Christopher QUINT
37 Director of Financial Aid ... Mr. Keith DUBOIS
32 Executive Director Student Success ... Ms. Elizabeth HIGGINS
07 Interim Director Admissions ... Ms. Rachel MORALES
06 Registrar ... Mr. Steven RAND
22 Director of Equal Opportunity ... Mr. Daryl MCLLWAIN
72 Interim Director CTEL ... Ms. Barbara STEBBINS
25 Dir of Office of Sponsored Programs ... Mr. Lawrence WAXLER
31 Director of Community Standards ... Ms. Joy PUFHAL
41 Director of Athletics & Rec Sports ... Mr. Al BEAN
39 Director of Residential Life ... Ms. Joy PUFHAL
40 Director of USM Bookstore ... Ms. Nicole PIAGET
61 Dean School of Law ... Mr. Peter PITEGOFF
50 Dean College of Mgmt & Human Svcs ... Dr. Joseph MCDONNELL
72 Dean College of Sci/Tech & Health ... Dr. James GRAVES
49 Dean of Arts/Humanities & Soc Sci ... Dr. Manuel AVALOS
12 Dean Lewiston-Auburn College ... Dr. Joyce GIBSON
88 Director of Community-Based Lrng ... Mr. Joseph M. AUSTIN
24 Manager Audiovisual/Media Services ... Ms. Angela COOK
94 Director of Women's Studies ... Dr. Lucinda COLE
20 Assoc Provost Undergraduate Educ ... Dr. Dahlia LYNN
85 Coordinator Multicultural Affairs ... Mr. Reza JALALI
29 Director of Alumni Relations ... Ms. Betsy UHUAD
27 Director of Marketing ... Ms. Traci ST. PIERRE
102 President & CEO USM Foundation ... Ms. Cecile AITCHISON
58 Assoc Provost of Grad Stds/RSCA ... Dr. Samantha LANGLEY-TURNBAUGH

University of New England (B)

11 Hills Beach Road, Biddeford ME 04005-9988

County: York — FICE Identification: 002050
Unit ID: 161457
Telephone: (207) 283-0171 — Carnegie Class: Master's L
FAX Number: (207) 282-6379 — Calendar System: Semester
URL: www.une.edu
Established: 1831 — Annual Undergrad Tuition & Fees: $34,760
Enrollment: 6,429 — Coed
Affiliation or Control: Independent Non-Profit — IRS Status: 501(c)3
Highest Offering: Doctorate
Program: Occupational; 2-Year Principally Bachelor's Creditable; Liberal Arts And General; Teacher Preparatory; Professional
Accreditation: EH, ACBSP, ADNUR, ANEST, ARCPA, CAATE, DENT, DH, NUR, OSTEO, OT, PH, PHAR, PTA, SW

01 President ... Dr. Danielle RIPICH
04 Executive Asst to the President ... Ms. Holly HAMMOND NASS
05 Provost & Senior Vice President ... Dr. James KOELBL
06 Registrar ... Ms. Joan MONAHAN
07 Dean of University Admissions ... Mr. Scott STEINBERG
23 Sr Vice Pres for Health Affairs ... Mr. Douglas WOOD
58 VP Strategic Initiatives ... Ms. Ellen BEAULIEU
18 Vice Pres of Operations ... Mr. William BOLA
88 Vice President Clinical Affairs ... Dr. Dora MILLS
10 Vice Pres Fiscal Affairs ... Ms. Nicole TRUFANT
30 Vice Pres Institutional Advancement ... Mr. Bill CHANCE
32 Vice Pres Student Affairs ... Dr. Cynthia FORREST
26 Vice Pres of Communications ... Vacant
102 Asst VP Institutional Advancement ... Ms. Amy HAILLE
15 Exec Dir Human Resources ... Ms. Sharen BEAULIEU
82 VP Global Affairs & Communications ... Dr. Anouar MAJID
46 VP for Research & Scholarship ... Dr. Edward BILSKY
106 Dean College of Grad/Prof Studies ... Dr. Martha WILSON
49 Dean College Arts & Sciences ... Dr. Jeanne HEY
17 Dean College Health Professions ... Dr. Elizabeth FRANCIS-CONNOLLY
63 Dean College Osteopathic Medicine ... Dr. Douglas WOOD
67 Dean College of Pharmacy ... Dr. Gayle BRAZEAU
52 Int Dean of College Dental Medicine ... Dr. Jon RYDER
63 Director School of Nurse Anesthesia ... Dr. Maribeth MASSIE
62 Dean Library Services ... Mr. Andrew GOLUB
35 Dean of Students ... Mr. Mark NAHORNEY
88 Asst Dean Student Support Svcs ... Mr. John LANGEVIN
17 Assoc Dean College Health Prof ... Mrs. Karen PARDUE
66 Director of Nursing ... Dr. Jennifer MORTON
49 Assoc Dean College Arts & Sciences ... Ms. Paulette ST. OURS
76 Assoc Dean Health Professions ... Dr. Clay GRAYBEAL
29 Director Alumni Relations ... Ms. Amy HAIL
39 Asst Dean of Students Res Life ... Ms. Jennifer DEBURRO
41 Assoc VP & Director of Athletics ... Mr. Jack MCDONALD
09 Director for Institutional Research ... Ms. Margaret MOREMEN
88 Director Campus Planning ... Mr. Alan THIBEAULT
19 Director Campus Safety & Security ... Mr. Donald CLARK
52 Int Director of Dental Hygiene ... Ms. Marji HARMER-BEEM
88 Director Exercise & Sport Perf ... Mr. Wayne LAMARRE
75 Director Occupational Therapy ... Dr. Jane O'BRIEN
75 Director of Physical Therapy ... Dr. Michael SHELDON
96 Director Purch/Risk Mgmt/Contract ... Mr. William BOLA
62 Director Reference Services ... Ms. Barbara SWARTZLANDER
28 Director Multi-Cultural Affairs ... Ms. Donna GASPAR JARVIS
70 Director Social Work ... Dr. Danielle WOZNIAK
25 Director Sponsored Programs ... Mr. Nicholas GERE
38 Director Student Counseling ... Dr. John LANGEVIN
37 Exec Director Student Fiscal Svcs ... Mr. Paul HENDERSON

MARYLAND

Allegany College of Maryland (C)

12401 Willowbrook Road, SE,
Cumberland MD 21502-2596

County: Allegany — FICE Identification: 002057
Unit ID: 161688
Telephone: (301) 784-5000 — Carnegie Class: Assoc/Pub-R-M
FAX Number: (301) 784-5050 — Calendar System: Semester
URL: www.allegany.edu
Established: 1961 — Annual Undergrad Tuition & Fees (In-District): $3,420
Enrollment: 3,227 — Coed
Affiliation or Control: Local — IRS Status: 501(c)3
Highest Offering: Associate Degree
Program: Occupational; 2-Year Principally Bachelor's Creditable
Accreditation: M, ADNUR, COARC, COMTA, CSHSE, DH, MAC, MLTAD, OTA, PTAA, RAD

01 President ... Dr. Cynthia S. BAMBARA
05 Vice Pres Instructional Affairs ... Dr. David HINDS
10 Vice President Finance ... Mr. David DEWITT
30 VP Col Advancement/Enroll Mgmt ... Mrs. Linda A. PRICE
11 VP Administrative Services ... Dr. Mona CLITES
32 VP Student Services ... Dr. B. Renee CONNER
51 VP of Continuing Education ... Mr. Jeff KIRK
13 Assoc Dean Computer Services ... Vacant
30 Vice Pres of Grants & Development ... Mr. David R. JONES
37 Director Student Financial Aid ... Mrs. Vicki SMITH
07 Director Admissions/Registration ... Ms. Carol KAUFFMAN
18 Director of Physical Plant ... Mr. Adam PHIPPS
08 Director Learning Resources ... Mr. Matthew HAY
26 Dir Public Relations/Recruitment ... Ms. Shauna N. MCQUADE
41 Athletic Director ... Mr. Steve BAZARNIC
51 Director Professional Cont Educ ... Mrs. Becky L. RUPPERT
09 Director of Institutional Research ... Mr. Scott HARRAH
69 Director Health Prof Cont Education ... Ms. Linda ATKINSON
38 Director Student Counseling ... Vacant
15 Director Personnel ... Mrs. Melinda DUCKWORTH

Ana G. Mendez University System Capital Area Campus (D)

11006 Veirs Mill Road, Wheaton MD 20902

Telephone: (301) 949-2224 — Identification: 770924
Accreditation: &M

† Branch campus of Sistema Universitario Ana G. Mendez, Rio Piedras, PR.

Anne Arundel Community College (E)

101 College Parkway, Arnold MD 21012-1895

County: Anne Arundel — FICE Identification: 002058
Unit ID: 161767
Telephone: (410) 777-2222 — Carnegie Class: Assoc/Pub-S-SC
FAX Number: (410) 777-2489 — Calendar System: Semester
URL: www.aacc.edu
Established: 1961 — Annual Undergrad Tuition & Fees (In-District): $3,895
Enrollment: 15,274 — Coed
Affiliation or Control: State/Local — IRS Status: 501(c)3
Highest Offering: Associate Degree
Program: Occupational; 2-Year Principally Bachelor's Creditable
Accreditation: M, ACFEI, ADNUR, ARCPA, CAHIIM, CSHSE, EMT, MAC, MLTAD, PTAA, RAD, SURGT

01 President ... Dr. Dawn S. LINDSAY
05 VP for Learning ... Dr. Karen L. HAYS
10 VP Learning Resources Management ... Ms. Melissa A. BEARDMORE
03 VP for Learner Support Services ... Ms. Felicia L. PATTERSON
106 Dean of Virtual Campus ... Ms. Jean M. RUNYON
20 Associate VP for Learning ... Dr. Michael H. GAVIN
30 Director of Development ... Mr. Vollie D. MELSON
32 Dean of Student Services ... Dr. Jacqueline S. JACKSON
76 Dean School Health/Wellness/Phys Ed ... Dr. Claire L. SMITH
66 Director of Nursing ... Ms. Beth Anne BATTURS
49 Dean School of Liberal Arts ... Dr. Alicia MORSE
50 Dean School of Business & Law ... Ms. Karen COOK
81 Dean School of Science & Technology ... Dr. Bruce A. BOWMAN
51 Dean Sch Cont Educ & Workforce Dev ... Dr. Faith A. HARLAND-WHITE
22 Controller ... Ms. Martha D. ROTHSCHILD
21 Executive Director of Finance ... Mr. Andrew P. LITTLE
13 Chief Technology Officer/Info Svcs ... Ms. Shirin M. GOODARZI
08 Director of Library ... Ms. Cynthia K. STEINHOFF
06 Registrar ... Ms. Nancy A. BEIER
09 Dean Plng/Rsrch/Inst Assess ... Dr. Ricka K. FINE
15 Exec Director of Human Resources ... Ms. Suzanne L. BOYER
26 Exec Director PR & Marketing ... Mr. Daniel B. BAUM
37 Director of Financial Aid ... Mr. Richard C. HEATH
07 Dir Admissions/Enroll Development ... Mr. Thomas J. MCGINN, III
11 Exec Dir of Administrative Services ... Mr. Maury L. CHAPUT, JR.
35 Asst Dean Student Devel & Success ... Vacant
84 Dean Enrollment Services ... Dr. John F. GRABOWSKI
36 Dir Counseling/Advising/Reten Svcs ... Ms. Bonnie J. GARRETT
35 Director of Student Life ... Ms. Christine M. STORCK
22 Federal Compliance Officer ... Ms. Suzanne L. BOYER
40 College Bookstore Manager ... Mr. Steven M. PEGG
19 Director Public Safety ... Mr. J. Gary LYLE
96 Director Purchasing/Contracting ... Ms. Melanie L. SCHERER
29 Manager Major Giving ... Ms. Jo Ann MATTSON
23 Coordinator Health Services ... Ms. Beth A. MAYS
41 Athletic Director ... Mr. Duane HERR
28 Coordinator of Minority Recruitment ... Mr. James T. JACKSON, JR.
94 Coordinator of Women's Studies ... Dr. Suzanne J. SPOOR
88 Director of Environmental Center ... Dr. M. Stephen AILSTOCK
88 Director Center Study Local Issues ... Dr. Daniel D. NATAF
88 Dir Homeland Sec/Crim Justice Inst ... Dr. Tyrone POWERS
53 Director TEACH Institute ... Ms. Colleen K. EISENBEISER
88 Director Hosp/Cul Arts/Tourism Inst ... Ms. Mary Ellen MASON
38 Coordinator Inst for the Future ... Mr. Steven T. HENICK
88 Dir Sarbanes Center/Pub & Cmty Svc ... Ms. Cathleen H. DOYLE
28 Chief Diversity Officer ... Mr. James A. FELTON, III
04 Administrative Asst to President ... Ms. Judy HEATH
18 Dir Facilities Planning & Construc ... Mr. James TAYLOR
25 Director Sponsored Programs ... Ms. Deborah A. MERCADO

Bais HaMedrash & Mesivta of Baltimore (F)

6823 Old Pimlico Road, Baltimore MD 21209

County: Baltimore — FICE Identification: 041884
Unit ID: 476601
Telephone: (410) 486-0006 — Carnegie Class: Not Classified
FAX Number: (410) 602-9738 — Calendar System: Semester
Established: 1997 — Annual Undergrad Tuition & Fees: $17,000
Enrollment: 59 — Male
Affiliation or Control: Independent Non-Profit — IRS Status: 501(c)3
Highest Offering: First Talmudic Degree
Program: Professional; Religious Emphasis
Accreditation: RABN

01 Rosh Yeshiva ... Rabbi Zvi Dov SLANGER

Baltimore City Community College (G)

2901 Liberty Heights Avenue, Baltimore MD 21215-7893

County: Baltimore City — FICE Identification: 002061
Unit ID: 161864
Telephone: (410) 462-8300 — Carnegie Class: Assoc/Pub-U-MC
FAX Number: (410) 462-7795 — Calendar System: Semester
URL: www.bccc.edu
Established: 1947 — Annual Undergrad Tuition & Fees (In-State): $2,112
Enrollment: 5,550 — Coed
Affiliation or Control: State — IRS Status: 501(c)3
Highest Offering: Associate Degree
Program: Occupational; 2-Year Principally Bachelor's Creditable
Accreditation: M, ACBSP, ADNUR, CAHIIM, #COARC, DH, PTAA, SURGT

01 President and CEO ... Dr. Gordon F. MAY
10 Int VP Business & Finance ... Mr. Calvin HARRIS, JR.
32 Vice President for Student Affairs ... Mr. Ronald SMITH
05 VP Academic Affairs ... Dr. Tonja RINGGOLD
51 Vice Pres Business & Cont Educ ... Mr. Gregory MASON
84 Dean of Enrollment Management ... Ms. Robin WASHINGTON-SCOTT
30 VP of Institutional Advancement ... Ms. Maureen K. CORNEAL
18 Dir Facilities/Plng/Operations ... Mr. Jamiel FARRAR
21 Controller/Chief of Accounting ... Ms. Sabina SILKWORTH
37 Director Student Financial Aid ... Ms. Vera BROOKS
13 Chief Information Tech Officer ... Mr. Antonio HERRERA
08 Director Library/Media Services ... Vacant
06 Exec Director Records/Registrar ... Ms. Sylvia ROCHESTER
15 Executive Director of HR ... Ms. Sheryl NELSON
09 Director of Institutional Research ... Mr. Gerard REICHENBERG
96 Chief Procurement Officer ... Mr. Daniel COLEMAN
04 Executive Asst to the President ... Ms. Valerie MCQUEEN-BEY

07 Director of Admissions ... Ms. Deneen DANGERFIELD
101 Asst to President Board Relations ... Ms. Nikita LEMON
106 Director of E-Learning ... Dr. Diana ZILBERMAN
19 Director of Public Safety ... Mr. William BOOTH
36 Coordinator Job Placement ... Mr. Vincent WHITMORE
41 Director Intercollegiate Athletics ... Ms. Tara OWENS
86 Director Government Relations ... Mr. Christopher FALKENHAGEN

Capitol Technology University (A)

11301 Springfield Road, Laurel MD 20708-9759
County: Prince Georges FICE Identification: 001436
Unit ID: 162061
Telephone: (301) 369-2800 Carnegie Class: Spec/Engg
FAX Number: (301) 953-1442 Calendar System: Semester
URL: www.captechu.edu
Established: 1927 Annual Undergrad Tuition & Fees: $23,460
Enrollment: 804 Coed
Affiliation or Control: Independent Non-Profit IRS Status: 501(c)3
Highest Offering: Doctorate
Program: Technical Emphasis
Accreditation: M, ENG, ENGT, IACBE

01 President ... Dr. Michael T. WOOD
05 Vice President for Academic Affairs ... Dr. W. Vic MACONACHY
10 Vice Pres Finance/Administration ... Jeffrey L. WILLIAMS
46 Vice Pres for Planning/Assessment ... Dianne M. O'NEILL
30 Vice President Advancement ... Dr. Donna THOMAS
88 Dean Mgmt and Info Sciences ... Dr. Helen G. BARKER
32 Dean Student Life & Retention ... Melinda A. BUNNELL-RHYNE
54 Dean Engineering/Computer Sci/Tech ... Dr. Robert WEILER
06 Director of Registration & Records ... Greg HUGHES
08 Dir Library/Information Literacy ... Rick A. SAMPLE
11 Dir Administration/Human Resources ... Vacant
07 Senior Director Admissions ... George H. WALLS
26 Director Communications ... Robert HERSCHBACH
29 Assistant Dir Development ... Leah CAPUTO
07 Dir Admissions Operations ... Meghan YOUNG
37 Director of Financial Aid ... Kim WITTLER
21 Director of Finance ... Kathleen WERNER
51 Director of Continuing Education ... Vacant
90 Director Academic Computing ... Allen EXNER
18 Director of Maintenance ... Bruce RIBB
04 Administrative Asst to President ... Aletha R. WADE

Carroll Community College (B)

1601 Washington Road, Westminster MD 21157-6913
County: Carroll FICE Identification: 031007
Unit ID: 405872
Telephone: (410) 386-8000 Carnegie Class: Assoc/Pub-S-SC
FAX Number: (410) 386-8181 Calendar System: Semester
URL: www.carrollcc.edu
Established: 1993 Annual Undergrad Tuition & Fees (In-District): $3,446
Enrollment: 4,999 Coed
Affiliation or Control: Local IRS Status: 501(c)3
Highest Offering: Associate Degree
Program: Occupational; 2-Year Principally Bachelor's Creditable
Accreditation: M, PTAA

01 President ... Dr. James D. BALL
10 Exec Vice Pres Administration ... Mr. Alan M. SCHUMAN
05 VP of Academic & Student Affairs ... Dr. Jan OHLEMACHER
45 VP Planning Marketing & Assessment ... Dr. Craig A. CLAGETT
51 VP Continuing Education/Training ... Ms. Karen L. MERKLE
30 Exec Dir Inst Devel/College Found ... Mr. Steven WANTZ
26 Dir of Communication & Media Rels ... Ms. Sylvia BLAIR
88 Integrity & Judicial Affairs Advoca ... Mr. Joel M. HOSKOWITZ
50 Div Chair Business & Technology ... Mr. Robert BROWN
60 Div Chair English & Humanities ... Ms. Siobhan WRIGHT
76 Div Chair Allied Health ... Dr. Nancy PERRY
83 Div Chair Social Sciences ... Dr. Michael STOVALL
81 Div Chair Mathematics/Engineer ... Ms. Maria BURNESS
81 Div Chair Sciences ... Dr. Raza KHAN
53 Div Chair Education ... Ms. Susan SIES
97 Div Chair Trans & Acad Svvcs ... Ms. Magdeleine VANDAL
88 Sr Director Student Engage/Compl ... Dr. Kristie CRUMLEY
38 Dir of Advise/Transfer/Stdnt Plcmnt ... Ms. Janenne CORCORAN
88 Director Transfer ... Mr. Paul HUNTER
84 Sr Director Enrollment Develop ... Ms. Candace EDWARDS
06 Registrar ... Ms. Lauren SHIELDS
37 Director of Financial Aid ... Mr. John GAY
08 Sr Dir Library/Media/Dist Lrn ... Mr. Alan BOGAGE
106 Director Distance Lrng Programs ... Dr. Susan BIRO
26 Director Publications/Comm Design ... Ms. Eleni SWENGLER
09 Director Institutional Research ... Ms. Janet NICKELS
103 Sr Dir CET/Wkforce Trng & Bus Svcs ... Ms. Libby TROSTLE
31 Sr Dir Lifelong Lrng/Pgm Supp Sys ... Ms. Jean MARRIOTT
105 Director of Network & Tech Services ... Ms. Patti DAVIS
21 Director Fiscal Affairs ... Mr. Timothy LEAGUE
15 Director Human Resources ... Ms. Donna MARRIOTT
18 Director Facilities Management ... Ms. Terry BOWEN
86 Chief Compliance & Integrity Ofcr ... Dr. Michael KIPHART
19 Chief of Public Safety & Security ... Mr. Wayne LIVESAY
88 Director Disability Support Svcs ... Mr. Joseph TATELA

Cecil College (C)

One Seahawk Drive, North East MD 21901-1999
County: Cecil FICE Identification: 008308
Unit ID: 162104
Telephone: (410) 287-6060 Carnegie Class: Assoc/Pub-S-SC
FAX Number: (410) 287-1026 Calendar System: Semester
URL: www.cecil.edu
Established: 1968 Annual Undergrad Tuition & Fees (In-District): $3,540
Enrollment: 2,552 Coed
Affiliation or Control: State/Local IRS Status: 501(c)3
Highest Offering: Associate Degree
Program: Occupational; 2-Year Principally Bachelor's Creditable
Accreditation: M, ADNUR, EMT, MAC, @PTAA

01 Interim President ... Dr. Mary WAY BOLT
05 Vice President Academic Programs ... Dr. David LINTHICUM
11 Vice Pres Administrative Services ... Dr. Christine A. VALUCKAS
32 VP Students/Inst Effectiveness ... Dr. Diane C. LANE
13 VP/Chief Information Officer ... Vacant
30 Vice Pres Institutional Advancement ... Ms. Chris Ann SZEP
15 Director Human Resources ... Ms. Colleen CASHILL
20 Dean of Academic Programs ... Vacant
31 Dean of Career/Community Education ... Mr. Miles DEAN
66 Dean Nursing Ed/Alld Hlth/Hlth Sci ... Dr. Christy DRYER
18 Director of Facilities ... Mr. Christopher SHERLOCK
37 Director of Financial Aid Services ... Ms. Amanda SOLECKI
26 Director of Marketing ... Ms. Charlene CONOLLY
84 Director of Enrollment Management ... Ms. Cindy MISHOE
93 Director Minority Student Services ... Ms. Laney HOXTER
09 Director of Institutional Research ... Mr. Dan STOICESCU
06 Registrar/Dir Admiss & Registration ... Ms. S. Tomeka SWAN
08 Director of Library Services ... Ms. Lorraine MARTORANA
41 Director Athletics ... Mr. Ed DURHAM
29 Coordinator Alumni Relations ... Ms. Mary MOORE
04 Assistant to the President ... Ms. Robin MCMANN
10 Dean of Business Services ... Vacant
19 Director Security/Safety ... Mr. William WOOLSTON

Chesapeake College (D)

PO Box 8, 1000 College Circle, Wye Mills MD 21679-0008
County: Queen Annes FICE Identification: 004650
Unit ID: 162168
Telephone: (410) 822-5400 Carnegie Class: Assoc/Pub-R-M
FAX Number: (410) 827-5875 Calendar System: Semester
URL: www.chesapeake.edu
Established: 1965 Annual Undergrad Tuition & Fees (In-District): $4,520
Enrollment: 2,426 Coed
Affiliation or Control: State/Local IRS Status: 501(c)3
Highest Offering: Associate Degree
Program: Occupational; 2-Year Principally Bachelor's Creditable
Accreditation: M, ADNUR, EMT, PTAA, RAD, SURGT

01 President ... Dr. Barbara A. VINIAR
05 VP Academic Affairs & Econ Develop ... Dr. Kathryn A. BARBOUR
11 Vice Pres for Administrative Svcs ... Mr. Tim JONES
32 VP Student Success/Enrollment Svcs ... Dr. Richard D. MIDCAP
72 VP Technology & Academic Support ... Mr. Douglass P. GRAY
18 Director of Facilities ... Mr. Anthony PATTERSON
51 Continuing Education Dean ... Mr. Michael DUGAN
49 Dean for Liberal Arts & Sciences ... Dr. Eleanor WELSH
107 Dean for Career & Professional Stds ... Ms. Maureen A. GILMARTIN
08 Dean Lrng Res/Acad Sppt Svcs ... Ms. Chandra M. GIGLIOTTI-GURIDI
15 Director of Human Resources ... Ms. Susan A. CIANCHETTA
37 Director of Financial Aid ... Ms. Mindy M. SCHAFFER
30 Director Resource Development ... Ms. Lauren C. HALTERMAN
09 Dir Inst Planning/Research & Assmnt ... Mr. Vincent MARUGGI
07 Director Admissions ... Ms. Kathleen J. PETRICHENKO
26 Director of Public Information ... Ms. Marcie A. MOLLOY
06 Registrar ... Mr. James A. DAVIDSON
20 Dean for Retention Services ... Ms. Joan M. SEITZER
04 Executive Associate to President ... Ms. Jane THOMAS

College of Southern Maryland (E)

PO Box 910, La Plata MD 20646-0910
County: Charles FICE Identification: 002064
Unit ID: 162122
Telephone: (301) 934-2251 Carnegie Class: Assoc/Pub-S-MC
FAX Number: (301) 934-7698 Calendar System: Semester
URL: www.csmd.edu
Established: 1958 Annual Undergrad Tuition & Fees (In-District): $3,543
Enrollment: 8,426 Coed
Affiliation or Control: Local IRS Status: 501(c)3
Highest Offering: Associate Degree
Program: Occupational; 2-Year Principally Bachelor's Creditable
Accreditation: M, ACBSP, ADNUR, EMT, MLTAD, PNUR, PTAA

01 President ... Dr. Bradley GOTTFRIED
05 Vice Pres Academic Affairs ... Dr. Eileen ABEL
12 Vice President Leonardtown Campus ... Dr. Tracy HARRIS
12 VP Prince Frederick Campus ... Dr. Richard FLEMING
103 VP Cmty Educ & Workforce Dev ... Dr. Daniel MOSSER
10 VP Financial & Admin Services ... Mr. Tony JERNIGAN
32 VP Student/Instruc Support Svcs ... Dr. William COMEY
30 Vice President for Advancement ... Ms. Michelle GOODWIN
43 Vice President/General Counsel ... Mr. Craig PATENAUDE
20 Assoc VP Academic Affairs ... Mr. Rob FARINELLI
09 Assoc VP Plng/Inst Effective/Rsrch ... Dr. Kelly MCMURRAY
84 Assoc VP Enrollment Mgmt Team ... Vacant
13 Assoc VP Info Management ... Mr. James FINGER
18 Director of Facilities ... Mr. Ron TOWARD
15 Assoc VP of Human Resources ... Dr. Mychal COLEMAN
26 Asst Vice Pres Community Relations ... Ms. Karen SMITH-HUPP
37 Director Financial Assistance ... Mr. Christian ZIMMERMANN
06 Registrar ... Ms. Carol HARRISON
08 Director of Library ... Mr. Thomas REPENNING
66 Chair Nursing Dept ... Dr. Laura POLK
35 Director of Athletics/Student Life ... Ms. Michelle RUBLE
40 General Mgr College Store ... Ms. Marcy GANNON
07 Director Admissions Department ... Mr. Brian HAMMOND
38 Director Advisement/Career Services ... Ms. Helene CAMERON
96 Director of Procurement ... Mr. Joe PICCOLO
28 Assoc VP Diversity/Equal Oppty ... Ms. Makeba CLAY
04 Exec Asst to President & Board ... Ms. Kim YELLMAN
19 Exec Director Security/Safety ... Mr. Don FRICK
25 Grants Coordinator ... Ms. Becky COCKERHAM
44 Director Development ... Ms. Chelsea BROWN
27 Marketing Director ... Ms. Theresa JOHNSON

The Community College of Baltimore County (F)

7201 Rossville Blvd., Baltimore MD 21237-3899
County: Baltimore FICE Identification: 002063
Unit ID: 434672
Telephone: (443) 840-2222 Carnegie Class: Assoc/Pub-S-MC
FAX Number: (443) 840-1100 Calendar System: Semester
URL: www.ccbcmd.edu
Established: 1957 Annual Undergrad Tuition & Fees (In-District): $3,791
Enrollment: 22,887 Coed
Affiliation or Control: Local IRS Status: 501(c)3
Highest Offering: Associate Degree
Program: Occupational; 2-Year Principally Bachelor's Creditable
Accreditation: M, ACBSP, ADNUR, ART, CAHIIM, COARC, COMTA, CSHSE, DH, EMT, FUSER, MLTAD, MUS, OTA, POLYT, RAD, RTT, SURGT, THEA

01 President ... Dr. Sandra L. KURTINITIS
30 Vice Pres Institutional Advancement ... Mr. Kenneth WESTARY
10 Vice Pres Finance/Administration ... Ms. Melissa HOPP
05 Vice Pres Instruction ... Dr. Mark MCCOLLOCH
84 VP Enrollment & Student Services ... Dr. Richard LILLEY
26 Sr Director for Public Relations ... Ms. Mary DELUCA
15 Senior Director Human Resources ... Ms. Penny MILSOM

Faith Theological Seminary (G)

529 Walker Avenue, Baltimore MD 21212
County: Baltimore City Identification: 667016
Unit ID: 212452
Telephone: (410) 323-6211 Carnegie Class: Not Classified
FAX Number: (410) 323-6331 Calendar System: Semester
URL: www.faiththeological.org
Established: 1937 Annual Undergrad Tuition & Fees: $6,900
Enrollment: 142 Coed
Affiliation or Control: Non-denominational IRS Status: 501(c)3
Highest Offering: Doctorate; No Lower Division
Program: Religious Emphasis
Accreditation: #@TRACS

01 President ... Dr. Norman J. MANOHAR
05 Academic Dean ... Dr. Stephen T. HAGUE
06 Registrar ... Ms. Aruna S. MANOHAR
07 Dir Admissions/Distance Education ... Mr. Michael DEWALT
08 Head Librarian ... Ms. Anita TAYLOR
108 Director Institutional Assessment ... Mrs. Margaret P. PROCH
10 Business Manager ... Ms. Susan J. WOOD
13 IT Manager/Financial Aid Advisor ... Mr. John MANOHAR

Fortis College (H)

4351 Garden City Drive, Landover MD 20785
Telephone: (301) 459-3650 Identification: 770731
Accreditation: ACICS, DH, MLTAD

† Branch campus of Fortis Institute, Erie, PA.

Frederick Community College (I)

7932 Opossumtown Pike, Frederick MD 21702-2097
County: Frederick FICE Identification: 002071
Unit ID: 162557
Telephone: (301) 846-2400 Carnegie Class: Assoc/Pub-S-SC
FAX Number: (301) 846-2498 Calendar System: Semester
URL: www.frederick.edu
Established: 1957 Annual Undergrad Tuition & Fees (In-District): $4,165
Enrollment: 6,031 Coed
Affiliation or Control: State/Local IRS Status: 501(c)3
Highest Offering: Associate Degree
Program: Occupational; 2-Year Principally Bachelor's Creditable
Accreditation: M, ADNUR, COARC, NMT, SURGT

01 President ... Ms. Elizabeth BURMASTER
05 Provost/VP for Academic Affairs ... Dr. Tony HAWKINS
51 Vice Pres for CE/Workforce Develop ... Mr. David CROGHAN
10 Vice Pres Finance & Human Resources ... Ms. Dana MCDONALD
32 Vice Pres & Chief Student Affairs ... Dr. Wayne BARBOUR
30 Exec Dir Office of Inst Advance ... Ms. Marcelena HOLMES
13 Chief Technology Officer ... Mr. Wayne KELLER
28 Director of Diverstity ... Ms. Shezwae FLEMING
20 Assoc VP of Academic Affairs ... Dr. Alanka BROWN
84 Assoc VP Enrollment Management ... Ms. Laura MEARS
15 Assoc VP for Human Resources ... Ms. MaryRose WILSON
21 Assistant Director Fiscal Services ... Ms. Angela LUDEMAN
06 Exec Dir of Welcome Center/Registar . Ms. Deidre WEILMINSTER
49 Interim AVP/Dean of Arts & Science ... Dr. Kenneth KERR
20 Assoc VP Teaching/Learning ... Dr. Kelly TRIGGER
35 Interim Assoc VP/Dean of Students . Ms. Jeanni WINSTON-MUIR

88 Spec Asst to Pres Inst Effectiv ... Mr. Gerald L. BOYD
18 Exec Dir Facilities Planning ... Ms. Diane BRANSON
08 Exec Dir Library ... Mr. Mick O'LEARY
09 Exec Dir Assessment and Research ... Dr. Gohar FARAHANI
19 Chief of Operations ... Mr. Greg SOLBERG
26 Director of Marketing ... Mr. Michael BAISEY
27 Exec Dir Communicat & Community ... Mr. Michael PRITCHARD
37 Exec Dir Financial Aid ... Ms. Brenda DAYHOFF
04 Exec Assoc to the President & Board ... Ms. Kari MELVIN
36 Director Workforce Training ... Ms. Patricia MEYER
14 Exec Dir of Enterprise Application ... Mr. Adam RENO
41 Director of Athletics ... Mr. Rodney BENNETT
88 Director Children's Center ... Ms. Teri BICKEL
90 Director Learning Technologies ... Mr. Alberto RAMIREZ
106 Exec Director Distributed Learning ... Mr. Jurgen HILKE
88 Asst Dir Student Development ... Ms. Melissa MAIN
28 Dir Multicultural Student Services ... Mr. Chad ADERO
88 Director Office of Adult Services ... Ms. Janice BROWN
88 Dir Svcs for Students w/ Disbilities ... Ms. Kate KRAMER-JEFFERSON
07 Director of Admissions ... Ms. Lisa FREEL
14 Exec Dir Network Services ... Mr. Joe MARSHALL
105 Director Web Services ... Ms. Cindy OSBON
88 Coordinator Veterans Services ... Ms. Rachel NACHLAS
109 Exec Director Auxiliary Services ... Mr. Frederick HOCKENBERRY
103 Int AVP/Dean CE/Workforce Develpmnt ... Ms. Karen REILLY
88 Director Administrative Projects ... Ms. Linda SEEK
102 Asst Dir Corporate Relations ... Ms. Michelle NUSUM-SMITH
88 Manager Food Services ... Ms. Donna S. SOWERS
29 Asst Dir of Alumni Relations ... Ms. Christina PETERMAN

Garrett College (A)

687 Mosser Road, McHenry MD 21541-1265
County: Garrett FICE Identification: 010014
Unit ID: 162609
Telephone: (301) 387-3000 Carnegie Class: Assoc/Pub-R-S
FAX Number: (301) 387-3038 Calendar System: Semester
URL: www.garrettcollege.edu
Established: 1966 Annual Undergrad Tuition & Fees (In-District): $3,584
Enrollment: 712 Coed
Affiliation or Control: State/Local IRS Status: 501(c)3
Highest Offering: Associate Degree
Program: Occupational; 2-Year Principally Bachelor's Creditable
Accreditation: M, EMT

01 President ... Dr. Richard MACLENNAN
04 Executive Assistant to President ... Ms. Marcia KNEPP
10 Dean of Administration & Finance ... Ms. Josephine GILMAN
05 VP of Academic Affairs ... Dr. Sarah GARRETT
20 Associate VP of Instruction ... Mr. Alexander TUEL
51 Dean of Cont Educ/Workforce Devel ... Ms. Julie YODER
13 Director of IT ... Ms. Jami REYNOLDS
32 Dean of Student Services ... Dr. Kelly HALL
30 Dir Develop/Exec Dir Foundation ... Ms. Cherie KRUG
06 Director of Records & Registration ... Ms. Kim DEGIOVANNI
37 Director of Financial Aid ... Ms. Cissy VANSICKLE
08 Interim Library Director ... Ms. Ellen SHEAFFER
21 Director of Business Office ... Ms. Katherine BROWNING
18 Plant Manager ... Mr. Hugh SCHRIER
15 Director of Human Resources ... Ms. Linda K. FIKE
65 Dir of Natural Res/Wildlife Tech ... Mr. Kevin DODGE
41 Director of Athletics ... Mr. Dennis GIBSON
50 Director of Business/Info Tech ... Dr. Qing YUAN
36 Coordinator of Academic Support ... Ms. Rhonda SCHWINABART
96 Purchasing/Accounts Payable ... Ms. Bonnie BROADWATER
09 IR Analyst ... Mr. Zachery BEITZEL
40 Interim Bookstore Manager ... Ms. Lois ANDERSON
84 Director of Enrollment Management ... Ms. Rachelle DAVIS
38 Coordinator of Counseling Services ... Ms. Madonna POOL
39 Coordinator of Residential Services ... Ms. Tracy BARCUS
45 Director of Institutional Planning ... Mr. James ALLEN, JR.
105 Webmaster ... Ms. Linda STEVANUS
79 Dir of Humanities & Social Sciences ... Vacant
88 Director of Adventure Sports ... Mr. Michael LOGSDON
106 Coordinator of Distance Learning ... Ms. Denise FRIEND
19 Coordinator of Security/Safety ... Ms. Shelley MENEAR
35 Director of Student Life ... Ms. Tracie ELLIS
26 Coordinator of Marketing and PR ... Ms. Stacy HOLLER

Goucher College (B)

1021 Dulaney Valley Road, Towson MD 21204-2780
County: Baltimore FICE Identification: 002073
Unit ID: 162654
Telephone: (410) 337-6000 Carnegie Class: Bac/A&S
FAX Number: (410) 337-6123 Calendar System: Semester
URL: www.goucher.edu
Established: 1885 Annual Undergrad Tuition & Fees: $42,180
Enrollment: 2,114 Coed
Affiliation or Control: Independent Non-Profit IRS Status: 501(c)3
Highest Offering: Master's
Program: Liberal Arts And General; Teacher Preparatory
Accreditation: M

01 President ... Dr. Jose A. BOWEN
05 Provost & Chief Academic Officer ... Dr. Leslie W. LEWIS
45 Sr VP for Strategic Initiatives ... Mr. Marty SWEIDEL
32 Vice Pres/Dean of Students ... Dr. Bryan F. COKER
30 Vice Pres Advancement ... Ms. Trishana E. BOWDEN
10 VP for Finance & Administration ... Ms. Tammi JACKSON
26 Vice President for Communications ... Ms. Allie LABAN-BAKER
13 VP for Technology and Planning ... Mr. Bill LEIMBACH
88 VP New Ventures/Bus Strategies ... Ms. Lynne LOCHTE
43 General Counsel ... Ms. Barbara STOB
20 Associate Provost for UG Affairs ... Ms. La Jerne CORNISH
82 Assoc Dean International Studies ... Mr. Eric SINGER
35 Asst VP for Student Affairs ... Ms. Emily PERL
15 Vice President for Human Resources ... Ms. Deborah LUPTON
21 Controller ... Mr. Alex ANTKOWIAK
07 Director of Admissions ... Mr. Carlton E. SURBECK, III
08 Librarian ... Ms. Nancy MAGNUSON
29 Exec Dir for Alumnae/i Engagement ... Ms. Holly SELBY
36 Director of Career Development ... Ms. Traci MARTIN
58 Director Grad Program in Education ... Ms. Phyllis SUNSHINE
06 Registrar ... Mr. Andrew WESTFALL
09 Dir for Institutional Effectiveness ... Ms. Shuang LIU
10 Dir Business/Auxiliary Services ... Mr. Calvin GLADDEN
18 Dir Facilities Management Services ... Mr. Terence MCCANN, JR.
37 Director Financial Aid ... Ms. Stephanie BENDER
105 Webmaster ... Mr. John PERRELLI
106 Dir Online Education/E-learning ... Ms. Linda BRUCE
28 Asst Dean Stdnts Intercultural Affs ... Ms. Luz BURGOS-LOPEZ
39 Director Student Housing ... Mr. Pavan PURSWANI
41 Athletic Director ... Mr. Geoff MILLER

Hagerstown Community College (C)

11400 Robinwood Drive, Hagerstown MD 21742-6590
County: Washington FICE Identification: 002074
Unit ID: 162690
Telephone: (240) 500-2000 Carnegie Class: Assoc/Pub-R-M
FAX Number: (301) 393-3682 Calendar System: Semester
URL: www.hagerstowncc.edu
Established: 1946 Annual Undergrad Tuition & Fees (In-District): $3,930
Enrollment: 4,716 Coed
Affiliation or Control: State/Local IRS Status: 501(c)3
Highest Offering: Associate Degree
Program: Occupational; 2-Year Principally Bachelor's Creditable
Accreditation: M, ADNUR, DA, DH, EMT, PNUR, RAD

01 President ... Dr. Guy ALTIERI
05 Vice President of Academic Affairs ... Dr. David WARNER
10 Vice Pres Administration/Finance ... Ms. Christina S. KILDUFF
32 Dean of Students ... Dr. Jessica A. CHAMBERS
09 Dean of Plng/Inst Effectiveness ... Ms. Barbara E. MACHT
51 Dean Continuing Educ/Bus Svcs ... Ms. Theresa M. SHANK
18 Dir Facilities Management & Plng ... Mr. Jonathan G. METCALF
07 Dir Admissions/Records/ Registration ... Ms. Robin A. BECKER-CORNBLATT
30 Exec Director College Advancement ... Ms. Stacey L. LOWMAN
26 Director Marketing/Public Info ... Ms. Elizabeth L. KIRKPATRICK
37 Director of Financial Aid ... Ms. Carolyn S. COX
106 Dean Academic Services & Online Ed ... Dr. Julian K. HORTON
14 Dir Technology/Computer Studies ... Mr. Daniel T. VOGEL
21 Director of Finance ... Mr. David C. BITTORF
21 Director of Business Services ... Ms. Lita J. ORNER
66 Director of Nursing ... Ms. Karen S. HAMMOND
15 Director of Human Resources ... Ms. Jennifer A. KNIGHT
41 Dir Athletics/Phys Ed/Leisure Stds ... Mr. Bernard A. JOHNSON
20 Director of Instruction ... Vacant
13 Director of Information Technology ... Mr. Craig M. FENTRESS
76 Director of Health Sciences ... Ms. Angela D. STOOPS

Harford Community College (D)

401 Thomas Run Road, Bel Air MD 21015-1698
County: Harford FICE Identification: 002075
Unit ID: 162706
Telephone: (443) 412-2000 Carnegie Class: Assoc/Pub-S-SC
FAX Number: (443) 412-2120 Calendar System: Semester
URL: www.harford.edu
Established: 1957 Annual Undergrad Tuition & Fees (In-District): $4,176
Enrollment: 6,748 Coed
Affiliation or Control: Local IRS Status: 501(c)3
Highest Offering: Associate Degree
Program: Occupational; 2-Year Principally Bachelor's Creditable
Accreditation: M, ADNUR, HT, MAC

01 President ... Dr. Dennis GOLLADAY
05 Vice President Academic Affairs ... Dr. M. Annette HAGGRAY
10 Vice President Finance & Operations ... Mr. Fredrick P. JOHNSON
32 VP Student Affairs/Inst Effective ... Dr. Deborah J. CRUISE
31 VP Mkting/Dev/Community Relations ... Ms. Brenda M. MORRISON
13 Chief Information Officer ... Dr. Thomas FRANZA
96 Asst Vice Pres Procurement ... Mr. Victor H. DODSON
84 Assoc VP Enrollment Services ... Dr. Alexandra VICTOR
35 Assoc VP Student Development ... Dr. Diane L. RESIDES
21 Assoc VP Finance & Budget ... Mr. Stephen S. PHILLIPS
51 Assoc VP Continuing Educ & Training ... Dr. Zoann J. PARKER
18 Assoc VP Campus Operations ... Mr. Stephen P. GAREY
37 Director Financial Aid ... Ms. D. Lynn LEE
06 Assistant Registrar ... Ms. Monisha T. GIDDINGS
26 Dir Marketing & Public Relations ... Ms. Nancy J. DYSARD
15 Dir Human Resources/Employee Dev ... Ms. Kathleen M. CALLAN
29 Director College/Alumni Development ... Ms. Denise M. DREGIER
08 Director Library & Info Resources ... Ms. Carol M. ALLEN
106 Dir eLearning & Instr Resources ... Vacant
09 Dir Inst Research/Plng/Effective ... Ms. Valerie T. SWAIN
38 Dir Advising/Career/Transfer Svcs ... Ms. J. Bonnie SULZBACH
40 Coordinator College Store ... Ms. Linda L. FIFE
07 Director for Admissions ... Ms. Megan CORNETT
29 Alumni Coordinator ... Ms. Jean Marie KRYGOWSKI
81 Dean Science/Tech/Engr/Math ... Ms. Deborah R. WROBEL
83 Dean Behavioral & Social Sciences ... Mr. Avery W. WARD
79 Dean Humanities ... Dr. Karry L. HATHAWAY
57 Dean Visual/Performing/Applied Arts ... Mr. Paul E. LABE
50 Dean Bus/Computing/Applied Tech ... Mr. John F. MAYHORNE
88 Dean Educ & Transitional Studies ... Mr. Carl E. HENDERSON
66 Dean Nursing & Allied Health Profs ... Ms. Laura C. PRESTON

Hood College (E)

401 Rosemont Avenue, Frederick MD 21701-8575
County: Frederick FICE Identification: 002076
Unit ID: 162760
Telephone: (301) 663-3131 Carnegie Class: Master's M
FAX Number: (301) 694-7653 Calendar System: Semester
URL: www.hood.edu
Established: 1893 Annual Undergrad Tuition & Fees: $35,150
Enrollment: 2,240 Coed
Affiliation or Control: Independent Non-Profit IRS Status: 501(c)3
Highest Offering: Master's
Program: Liberal Arts And General; Teacher Preparatory; Professional; Fine Arts Emphasis
Accreditation: M, ACBSP, NURSE, SW, TED

01 President ... Dr. Andrea E. CHAPDELAINE
05 Interim Provost/Dean of Faculty ... Dr. Edgar SCHICK
10 Vice Pres Finance ... Mr. Charles G. MANN
30 VP for Institutional Advancement ... Ms. Nancy E. GILLECE
32 VP Student Life/Dean of Students ... Dr. Olivia G. WHITE
84 VP Undergrad/Grad Enrollment ... Mr. William BROWN
07 Director of Admissions ... Ms. Jennifer DECKER
58 Dean of Graduate School ... Dr. Maria GREEN COWLES
20 Director CAAR ... Mr. Matthew HOLSAPPLE
26 Exec Dir Marketing/Communications ... Mr. Dave DIEHL
29 Director of Alumnae/i Programs ... Ms. Linda ROTH
06 Registrar ... Mrs. Nanette MARKEY
08 Librarian ... Mrs. Jan SAMET
37 Director of Financial Aid ... Ms. Brenda DISORBO
15 Director of Human Resources ... Ms. Carol M. WUENSCHEL
18 Director of Facilities ... Mr. John WICHSER
13 Chief Technology Officer ... Mr. Cornelius R. FAY, III
09 Director of Institutional Research ... Ms. Cynthia EMORY
04 Administrative Asst to President ... Ms. Diane K. WISE
104 Director Study Abroad ... Ms. Kathleen EMORY
19 Director Security/Safety ... Mr. Thurmond MAYNARD
38 Director Student Counseling ... Ms. Delores GRIGSBY
39 Director Student Housing ... Mr. Matthew TROUTMAN
41 Athletic Director ... Mr. Tom DICKMAN

Howard Community College (F)

10901 Little Patuxent Parkway, Columbia MD 21044-3197
County: Howard FICE Identification: 008175
Unit ID: 162779
Telephone: (443) 518-1000 Carnegie Class: Assoc/Pub-S-SC
FAX Number: N/A Calendar System: Semester
URL: www.howardcc.edu
Established: 1966 Annual Undergrad Tuition & Fees (In-District): $4,648
Enrollment: 10,184 Coed
Affiliation or Control: State/Local IRS Status: 501(c)3
Highest Offering: Associate Degree
Program: Occupational; 2-Year Principally Bachelor's Creditable
Accreditation: M, ACFEI, ADNUR, CVT, DH, DMS, EMT, MLTAD, MUS, PNUR, PTAA, RAD

01 President ... Dr. Kathleen B. HETHERINGTON
32 Vice President of Student Services ... Dr. Cynthia J. PETERKA
05 Vice President of Academic Affairs ... Dr. Sharon J. PIERCE
10 Vice Pres of Administration/Finance ... Ms. Lynn C. COLEMAN
13 Vice Pres Information Technology ... Mr. Thomas J. GLASER
51 AVP Cont Education/Workforce Dev ... Mr. Eddie SWAIN
84 Assoc Vice Pres Enrollment Services ... Ms. Alison BUCKLEY
35 Assoc Vice Pres for Student Devel ... Ms. Janice L. MARKS
15 Associate Vice Pres Human Resources ... Mr. Dave JORDAN
21 Associate Vice Pres of Finance ... Ms. Janet L. CULLISON
09 Exec Dir Plng/Research & Org Dev ... Ms. Zoe A. IRVIN
18 Exec Dir Capital Proj/Facilities ... Mr. Charles NIGHTINGALE
101 Executive Associate to President ... Ms. Linda EMMERICH
26 Exec Dir Public Relations/Mktg ... Ms. Elizabeth HOMAN
88 Director of Finance ... Ms. Amanda HUFFMAN
30 Exec Director of Development ... Ms. Melissa MATTEY
109 Director Auxiliary Services ... Ms. Arla J. WEBB
19 Director of Public Safety ... Mr. Ken MCGLYNN
35 Director Student Life ... Ms. Llatetra D. BROWN
04 Exec Assistant to the President ... Ms. Farida P. GUZDAR
96 Director of Purchasing ... Ms. Elizabeth H. MOSS
06 Registrar ... Ms. Catherine MUND
07 Director of Admissions & Advising ... Ms. Dorothy B. PLANTZ

ITT Technical Institute (G)

7030 Dorsey Road, Suite 100, Hanover MD 21076
Telephone: (410) 694-4700 Identification: 770644
Accreditation: ACICS

† Branch campus of ITT Technical Institute, Indianapolis, IN.

ITT Technical Institute (H)

11301 Red Run Boulevard, Owings Mills MD 21117-3246
Telephone: (443) 394-7115 Identification: 666377
Accreditation: ACICS

† Branch campus of ITT Technical Institute, Indianapolis, IN.

Johns Hopkins University (A)

3400 N. Charles Street, Baltimore MD 21218-2680
County: Independent City FICE Identification: 002077
Unit ID: 162928
Telephone: (410) 516-8000 Carnegie Class: RU/VH
FAX Number: N/A Calendar System: Semester
URL: www.jhu.edu
Established: 1876 Annual Undergrad Tuition & Fees: $48,710
Enrollment: 27,038 Coed
Affiliation or Control: Independent Non-Profit IRS Status: 501(c)3
Highest Offering: Doctorate
Program: Liberal Arts And General; Teacher Preparatory; Professional
Accreditation: M, BBT, CACREP, CS, DIETC, DMS, ENG, ENGR, HSA, IPSY, MED, MIL, MUS, NMT, NURSE, PDPSY, PH, TED

01 President ... Mr. Ronald J. DANIELS
100 Sr Vice President/Chief of Staff ... Ms. Kerry A. ATES
05 Provost & Sr VP Acad Affs ... Dr. Robert LIEBERMAN
17 CEO Johns Hopkins Medicine ... Dr. Paul D. ROTHMAN
10 Sr VP Finance & Administration ... Mr. Daniel G. ENNIS
29 VP for Development & Alum Relations ... Mr. Fritz SCHROEDER
45 Vice Pres Strategic Initiatives ... Mr. Phillip SPECTOR
26 Vice Pres Comm/Public Affairs ... Mr. Glenn M. BIELER
43 Vice Pres/General Counsel ... Mr. Mark B. ROTENBERG
43 Deputy General Counsel ... Mr. Frederick SAVAGE
86 Vice Pres Govt/Community Affairs ... Mr. Thomas LEWIS
18 Vice Pres Real Estate/Campus Svcs ... Mr. Alan FISH
15 Vice Pres Human Resources ... Ms. Charlene M. HAYES
21 Vice Pres Finance & CFO ... Ms. Helene GRADY
21 Vice Pres Chief Investment Officer ... Dr. Kathryn J. CRECELIUS
21 Chief Risk Officer ... Dr. Jonathan LINKS
32 Vice Provost for Student Affairs ... Dr. Kevin SHOLLENBERGER
20 Vice Provost Faculty Affairs ... Dr. Cheryl HOLCOMB-MCCOY
20 Vice Provost Academic Services ... Mr. Philip TANG
07 Vice Provost for Admiss & Fin Aid ... Mr. David PHILLIPS
88 Vice Provost Education ... Dr. Kelly GEBO
13 Vice Provost Info Technology/CIO ... Ms. Stephanie REEL
22 Vice Provost Institutional Equity ... Ms. Caroline LAGUERRE-BROWN
46 Vice Provost Research ... Dr. Denis WIRTZ
09 Asst Provost Institutional Research ... Dr. Cathy J. LEBO
88 Asst Prov International Services ... Mr. James BRAILER
88 Vice Provost for Digital Initiative ... Vacant
06 Registrar ... Ms. Mary Ellen FLAHERTY
82 Dean Nitze School Adv Intl Studies ... Dr. Vali NASR
49 Dean Krieger School Arts & Sciences ... Dr. Beverly WENDLAND
50 Dean Carey Business School ... Dr. Bernard FERRARI
53 Dean School of Education ... Dr. David W. ANDREWS
54 Dean Whiting Sch Engineering ... Dr. Ed SCHLESINGER
63 Dean School of Medicine ... Dr. Paul ROTHMAN
66 Dean School of Nursing ... Dr. Patricia DAVIDSON
69 Dean Bloomberg School Public Health ... Dr. Michael J. KLAG
08 Dean Sheridan Libraries and Museums ... Mr. Winston G. TABB
64 Director Peabody Institute ... Mr. Fred BRONSTEIN
81 Director Applied Physics Lab ... Mr. Ralph SEMMEL
96 Director Purchasing ... Mr. Paul N. BEYER
21 Controller ... Mr. Scott JONES
19 Exec Director Safety & Security ... Mr. Leroy "Lee" JONES
21 Exec Director Internal Audits ... Mr. James JARRELL
27 Exec Director Comm & Public Affairs ... Mr. Dennis O'SHEA
88 Exec Director JH Real Estate ... Mr. Brian B. DEMBECK
04 Administrative Asst to President ... Ms. Gillian RATHBONE-WEBBER
104 Director Study Abroad ... Dr. Lori A. CITTI
28 Chair Diversity Leadership Council ... Mr. Ashley J. LLORENS
36 Executive Director Career Center ... Ms. Trudy VAN ZEE
41 Athletic Director ... Mr. Tom CALDER

Kaplan University (B)

18618 Crestwood Drive, Hagerstown MD 21742-2797
Telephone: (301) 766-3600 FICE Identification: 007946
Accreditation: &NH, ACBSP, CAHIIM, MAC, PHLEB

† Regional accreditation is carried under the parent institution in Davenport, IA.

Lincoln College of Technology (C)

9325 Snowden River Parkway, Columbia MD 21046
County: Howard FICE Identification: 007936
Unit ID: 163028
Telephone: (410) 290-7100 Carnegie Class: Assoc/PrivFP
FAX Number: (410) 290-7880 Calendar System: Quarter
URL: www.lincolntech.com
Established: 1978 Annual Undergrad Tuition & Fees: $30,564
Enrollment: 647 Coed
Affiliation or Control: Proprietary IRS Status: Proprietary
Highest Offering: Associate Degree
Program: Occupational
Accreditation: ACCSC

01 Campus President ... Mr. Glen JOHANNESEN

Loyola University Maryland (D)

4501 N Charles Street, Baltimore MD 21210-2694
County: Independent City FICE Identification: 002078
Unit ID: 163046
Telephone: (410) 617-2000 Carnegie Class: Master's L
FAX Number: (410) 322-2768 Calendar System: Semester
URL: www.loyola.edu
Established: 1852 Annual Undergrad Tuition & Fees: $44,090
Enrollment: 5,967 Coed
Affiliation or Control: Roman Catholic IRS Status: 501(c)3
Highest Offering: Doctorate
Program: Liberal Arts And General; Teacher Preparatory
Accreditation: M, BUS, BUSA, CACREP, CLPSY, CS, ENG, SP, TED

01 President ... Rev. Brian F. LINNANE, SJ
03 Executive Vice President ... Dr. Susan DONOVAN
04 Acting Assistant to the President ... Mr. Darryl COWARD
05 Vice President for Academic Affairs ... Ms. Amy WOLFSON
10 Vice Pres for Finance & Treasurer ... Mr. Randall GENTZLER
11 Vice President for Administration ... Dr. Terrence M. SAWYER
30 Vice President Advancement ... Ms. Megan GILLICK
32 VP Student Devel/Dean of Students ... Dr. Sheilah SHAW HORTON
84 Vice Pres Enrollment Management ... Mr. Marc CAMILLE
20 Assoc Vice Pres Academic Affairs ... Ms. Jenny LOWRY
28 Asst VP Academic Affrs/Diversity ... Dr. Martha L. WHARTON
37 Asst Vice Pres of Financial Aid ... Mr. Mark L. LINDENMEYER
09 Asst VP of Institutional Research ... Ms. Terra SCHEHR
18 Assoc VP Facilities/Campus Services ... Ms. Helen SCHNEIDER
13 Asst VP of Technology Services/CIO ... Ms. Louise FINN
26 Dir Marketing and Communications ... Ms. Rita BUETTNER
15 Asst Vice Pres for Human Resources ... Ms. Kathleen PARNELL
21 Asst Vice Pres for Administration ... Ms. Joan FLYNN
27 Asst VP Marketing/Communications ... Ms. Sharon HIGGINS
41 Asst VP/Director of Athletics ... Mr. James PAQUETTE
38 Assoc VP Student Development ... Dr. Donelda COOK
102 Dir Corporation & Foundation Rels ... Mr. Thomas BRUSH
07 Director Undergraduate Admissions ... Ms. Elena HICKS
07 Director of Graduate Admissions ... Ms. Maureen FAUX
06 Director of Records ... Ms. Rita L. STEINER
85 Dean of International Programs ... Dr. Andre COLOMBAT
08 Director of Library ... Ms. Barbara PREECE
42 Interim Director of Campus Ministry ... Rev. Timothy BROWN, SJ
88 Dir Center Community Svc/Justice ... Sr. Catherine GUGERTY, SSND
36 Director of The Career Center ... Dr. CreSaundra SILLS
88 Dir Alcohol/Drug Ed/Support Svcs ... Mr. Jan WILLIAMS
88 Director Recreational Sports ... Ms. Pamela WETHERBEE-METCALF
35 Director Student Activities ... Mr. Mark C. BRODERICK
88 Director ALANA Services ... Mr. Rodney PARKER
21 Asst VP Controller ... Ms. Jare ALLOCCO ALLEN
45 Director of Resource Management ... Mr. David DAUGHADAY
109 Director Event Svcs/Auxiliary Mgmt ... Mr. Joseph BRADLEY
88 Director of Project Management ... Mr. Laszlo PELY
88 Director Environment Health/Safety ... Mr. Thomas HETTLEMAN
19 Dir of Public Safety/Campus Police ... Mr. Timothy FOX
29 Director Alumni Relations ... Mr. Daniel BARNETT
30 Asst VP Advancement ... Ms. Jane Curley HOGGE
88 Director of Creative Services ... Mr. Brian HATCHER
88 Director Advancement Services ... Mr. Ian WEBSTER
89 Dean of Freshman & Academic Svcs ... Dr. Ilona MCGUINESS
49 Dean College of Arts & Sciences ... Rev. James F. MIRACKY, SJ
50 Dean Sellinger Sch Business & Mgmt ... Ms. Karyl LEGGIO
49 Assoc Dean Arts & Sciences ... Dr. Suzanne KEILSON
50 Asst Dean for Business Programs ... Ms. Ann ATTANASIO
88 Associate Dean of Students ... Ms. Michelle CHEATEM
58 AVP for Graduate Studies ... Ms. Amanda THOMAS
18 Dir Facilities Management ... Ms. Kiki WILLIAMS
44 Director of Annual Giving ... Ms. Dianne THOMPSON
88 Director Budget and Planning ... Mr. Sean FRANCIS
88 Director Budget & Data Management ... Ms. Lorie HOLTGRAVE
88 Director of Bangkok Programs ... Mr. James KELLY
105 Dir Web Communications ... Ms. Amy FILARDO

Maple Springs Baptist Bible College & Seminary (E)

4130 Belt Road, Capitol Heights MD 20743-5712
County: Prince Georges FICE Identification: 038224
Unit ID: 446394
Telephone: (301) 736-3631 Carnegie Class: Spec/Faith
FAX Number: (301) 735-6507 Calendar System: Semester
URL: www.msbbcs.edu
Established: 1986 Annual Undergrad Tuition & Fees: $4,590
Enrollment: 101 Coed
Affiliation or Control: Baptist IRS Status: 501(c)3
Highest Offering: Doctorate
Program: Religious Emphasis
Accreditation: TRACS

01 President ... Dr. Larry W. JORDAN
05 Vice President Academic Affairs ... Dr. Vivian BESS
11 Vice Pres Administration & Finance ... Dr. Jerrye B. FELICIANA
73 Academic Dean College Division ... Dr. Carl KEELS
88 Academic Dean Seminary Div ... Vacant
06 Director Records and Admissions ... Dr. Esther BIRCH
09 Dir Institutional Plng/Assessment ... Dr. David CLARK
10 Director Business Affairs ... Mrs. Fannie G. THOMPSON
32 Director Student Affairs ... Dr. Jerrye FELICIANA
08 Dir Library/Instrnl Resource Center ... Mr. Darren JONES
37 Financial Aid Coordinator ... Mrs. Patricia JONES

Maryland Institute College of Art (F)

1300 Mount Royal Avenue, Baltimore MD 21217-4191
County: Independent City FICE Identification: 002080
Unit ID: 163295
Telephone: (410) 669-9200 Carnegie Class: Spec/Arts
FAX Number: (410) 669-9206 Calendar System: Semester
URL: www.mica.edu
Established: 1826 Annual Undergrad Tuition & Fees: $42,280
Enrollment: 2,262 Coed
Affiliation or Control: Independent Non-Profit IRS Status: 501(c)3
Highest Offering: Master's
Program: Fine Arts Emphasis
Accreditation: M, ART

01 President ... Mr. Samuel HOI
05 Vice Pres Academic Affairs/Provost ... Dr. David BOGEN
10 Vice Pres Finance/CFO ... Mr. Douglas MANN
30 Vice Pres Advancement ... Ms. Rita WALTERS
32 Vice Pres Student Affairs ... Mr. Michael PATTERSON
07 VP Admissions/Financial Aid ... Ms. Theresa BEDOYA
13 Vice Pres Technology Systems & Svcs ... Mr. Tom HYATT
11 Vice Pres Operations ... Mr. Mike MOLLA
20 Vice Prov Undergrad Studies/Faculty ... Ms. Jan STINCHCOMB
107 Vice Prov Professional Stds/Cont Ed ... Mr. David GRACYALNY
46 Vice Provost Research/Grad Studies ... Ms. Gwynne KEATHLEY
04 Executive Assistant to President ... Ms. Marian SMITH
37 Assoc VP Financial Aid ... Ms. Diane PRENGAMAN
44 Assoc VP Dev/Constituent Rels ... Ms. Lillian BURKE
14 Assoc VP Technology ... Ms. Susan MILTENBERGER
18 Assoc VP Facilities Management ... Mr. Timothy MILLNER
15 Human Resources Director ... Ms. Laura ROSSI
20 Dean Academic Services ... Ms. Cynthia BARTH
53 Dean Art Education ... Ms. Karen CARROLL
35 Assoc Dean Stdnt Life/Judicial Affs ... Ms. Kelly HOOVER
88 Assoc Dean Student Health Wellness ... Mr. James DAVIS
07 Assoc Dean Undergraduate Admissions ... Ms. Christine SEESE
88 Assoc Dean Graduate Admissions ... Mr. Scott KELLY
51 Assoc Dean Continuing Studies ... Mr. Peter DUBEAU
06 Assoc Dean Enrollment Svs/Registrar ... Ms. Christine PETERSON
28 Asst Dean Diversity Intercultur Dev ... Mr. Clyde JOHNSON, JR.
21 Director Accounting ... Ms. Jessica RURKA
88 Director Budget ... Ms. Brigitte SULLIVAN
26 Dir Marketing/Communications ... Ms. Allyson MOREHEAD
39 Director Residence Life ... Mr. Scott STONE
36 Director Career Development ... Ms. Megan MILLER
31 Director Community Engagement ... Ms. Karen STULTS
38 Director Counseling Center ... Ms. Pat FARRELL
35 Director Student Activities ... Ms. Karol MARTINEZ
88 Director Admissions Operations ... Ms. Cheryl ISSOD
08 Director & Head Librarian ... Vacant
88 Director Annual Fund ... Ms. Carolyn STRATFORD-YOUNCE
88 Director Advancement Services ... Ms. Dana COSTELLO
88 Director Stewardships ... Ms. Erin CHREST
27 Asst Director Public Relations ... Ms. Dionne MCCONKEY
88 Director Exhibitions ... Mr. Gerald ROSS
85 Director International Affairs ... Ms. Mary ALLEN
88 Director Writing St/Learn Res Cnt ... Mr. Daniel GUTSTEIN
88 Dir Data Mgmt/Registration Cont Std ... Ms. Sarah MARAVETZ
84 Dir Enroll Svcs/Stdnt Records/Rsrch ... Mr. Hadley GARBART
19 Director of Campus Safety ... Mr. Stephen DAVIS
88 Director Events ... Ms. Anne SOUTH
88 Director Operation Services ... Mr. Chris BOHASKA
29 Dir Alumni & Parent Rels ... Ms. Lindsay DORRANCE
102 Director Corp/Found/Govt Relations ... Ms. Sara WARREN
105 Director of Web Communications ... Mr. Justin CODD
24 Director Technical Support Services ... Mr. John RHODES
91 Director Administrative Systems ... Vacant
105 Director Network Services ... Mr. David APAW
90 Dir Instructional Advance & Tech ... Ms. Pamela STEFANUCA
40 Manager College Store ... Ms. Kerri LITZ

Maryland University of Integrative Health (G)

7750 Montpelier Road, Laurel MD 20723-6010
County: Howard FICE Identification: 025784
Unit ID: 164085
Telephone: (410) 888-9048 Carnegie Class: Master's S
FAX Number: (410) 888-9004 Calendar System: Trimester
URL: www.muih.edu
Established: 1981 Annual Graduate Tuition & Fees: $24,500
Enrollment: 1,066 Coed
Affiliation or Control: Independent Non-Profit IRS Status: 501(c)3
Highest Offering: Doctorate; No Undergraduates
Program: Professional
Accreditation: M, ACUP

01 President & CEO ... Mr. Frank VITALE
05 Provost/Exec VP Academic Affairs ... Dr. Judith BROIDA
11 VP Administration/General Counsel ... Ms. Louise GUSSIN
30 VP Inst Adv & Chief Values Officer ... Ms. Cheryl WALKER SHAPERO
26 VP Marketing/Enrollment Mgmt ... Ms. Gail DOERR
10 VP/CFO & Treasurer ... Mr. Marc LEVIN
88 Assoc Provost Digital Learning ... Ms. Mary Ellen HRUTKA
108 Asst Provost Acad Assessment & Accr ... Ms. Deneb FALABELLA
09 Asst Provost Research ... Mr. James SNOW
88 Acad Dir Acupuncture/Oriental Med ... Mr. Jeffrey MILLISON
88 Acad Dir Herbal Programs ... Dr. Michael TIMS
88 Acad Dir Nutrition ... Dr. Kathy WARNER
37 Director Student Financial Aid ... Ms. Kristina DEAN
08 Director of Library Services ... Ms. Jenifer KIRIN
29 Director Cont Ed & Alumni Affairs ... Ms. Patricia DELORENZO
15 Director Human Enrichment ... Mr. Fredrick SMOCK
84 Director Enrollment Management ... Mr. Chad EGRESI
106 Director of Online Learning ... Ms. Yan (Sunny) SUN
06 Registrar ... Mr. Reginald GARCON
04 Administrative Asst to President ... Ms. Olga MADIOU-BEALE
43 Dir Legal Services/General Counsel ... Ms. Louise GUSSIN

McDaniel College (A)

2 College Hill, Westminster MD 21157-4390
County: Carroll FICE Identification: 002109
Unit ID: 164270
Telephone: (410) 848-7000 Carnegie Class: Bac/A&S
FAX Number: (410) 857-2279 Calendar System: Semester
URL: www.mcdaniel.edu
Established: 1867 Annual Undergrad Tuition & Fees: $39,500
Enrollment: 3,187 Coed
Affiliation or Control: Independent Non-Profit IRS Status: 501(c)3
Highest Offering: Master's
Program: Liberal Arts And General; Teacher Preparatory
Accreditation: M, SW, TED

01 President ... Dr. Roger N. CASEY
04 Chief Exec Asst to the President ... Mr. Geoff PEARSON
05 Acting Provost/Dean of Faculty ... Dr. Julia JASKEN
10 Vice Pres Administration & Finance ... Mr. Thomas PHIZACKLEA
30 Vice Pres Institutional Advancement ... Ms. Lori LEWIS
32 Vice Pres/Dean of Student Affairs ... Ms. Beth R. GERL
84 VP Enroll Mgt/Dean of Admissions ... Ms. Florence W. HINES
13 Chief Information Officer ... Dr. Greg DUMONT
26 Assoc Vice Pres Comm/Marketing ... Ms. Gina PIELLUSCH
58 Dean Graduate/Professional Stds ... Dr. Michael TYLER
20 Assoc Dean/International Programs ... Dr. Amy MCNICHOLS
88 Assoc Dean/Student Academic Life ... Ms. Lisa BRESLIN
89 Assoc Dean/First Year Program ... Ms. Karen VIOLANTI
35 Assoc Dean/Student Affairs ... Ms. Elizabeth TOWLE
44 Executive Director of Major/Planned ... Mr. Robert CONRAD
29 Executive Director of Alumni Relati ... Ms. Heather WILENSKY
102 Dir Corp & Foundation Relations ... Ms. Bonnie SCHILLING
08 Director of Library ... Ms. Jessame E. FERGUSON
37 Director Financial Aid ... Ms. Zhanna GOLTSER
06 Registrar ... Vacant
41 Director Athletics ... Mr. Paul MOYER
36 Director Center for Exper and Opp ... Ms. Constance SGARLATA
38 Director Counseling ... Ms. Susan J. GLORE
35 Director Student Engagement ... Ms. Christine WORKMAN
39 Director of Residence Life ... Mr. Michael ROBBINS
21 Director Financial Services/Treas ... Mr. Arthur S. WISNER
15 Director Human Resources ... Ms. Jennifer GLENNON
45 Dir Facility Plng/Capital Projects ... Mr. Edgar S. SELL, JR.
18 Director Physical Plant ... Mr. Stafford TORGESEN
19 Director of Campus Safety ... Mr. James HAMRICK
40 Manager Bookstore ... Mr. Kyle MELOCHE
109 Dir Conferences/Auxiliary Services ... Ms. Mary J. COLBERT
28 Director of Multicultural Services ... Ms. Jennifer MARANA
92 Director of Honors Program ... Dr. Bryn UPTON
96 Director of Purchasing/Receiving ... Ms. Ellen RUGEMER
88 Coord of Deaf Education Program ... Dr. Mark M. RUST
09 Director Institutional Research ... Vacant
86 Director of Government Relations ... Dr. Herbert C. SMITH
07 Director of Admissions ... Ms. Heidi REIGEL
104 Coord of International Programs ... Ms. Jennifer QUIJANO SAX
105 Director Digital Comm/Social Media ... Mr. Vince BUSCEMI
25 Director Academic/Government Grants ... Ms. Robin DEWEY

Montgomery College (B)

900 Hungerford Drive, Rockville MD 20850-1733
County: Montgomery FICE Identification: 006911
Unit ID: 163426
Telephone: (240) 567-5000 Carnegie Class: Assoc/Pub-S-MC
FAX Number: (240) 567-6397 Calendar System: Semester
URL: www.montgomerycollege.edu
Established: 1946 Annual Undergrad Tuition & Fees (In-District): $4,728
Enrollment: 25,520 Coed
Affiliation or Control: Local IRS Status: 501(c)3
Highest Offering: Associate Degree
Program: Occupational; 2-Year Principally Bachelor's Creditable
Accreditation: M, ADNUR, CAHIIM, DMS, MUS, POLYT, PTAA, RAD, SURGT

01 President ... Dr. DeRionne P. POLLARD
100 Chief of Staff/Chief Strategy Ofcr ... Dr. Stephen D. CAIN
05 Sr VP for Academic Affairs ... Dr. Sanjay RAI
32 Sr VP for Student Services ... Dr. Monica R. BROWN
11 Sr VP for Admin & Fiscal Svcs ... Dr. Janet WORMACK
30 Sr VP for Advance & Comm Engagement ... Mr. David SEARS
86 Chief Government Relations Officer ... Ms. Susan MADDEN
43 General Counsel ... Mr. Clyde H. SORRELL
04 Assistant to the President ... Ms. Ida BRITTON
12 VP/Prov Rockville Campus ... Dr. Judy ACKERMAN
12 VP/Prov Germantown Campus ... Ms. Margaret LATIMER
12 VP/Prov Takoma Park Campus ... Dr. Brad J. STEWART
103 VP/Prov Workforce Dev & Cont Ed ... Mr. George M. PAYNE
45 VP of Planning and Inst Effective ... Ms. Kathleen WESSMAN
13 VP of Instructional & IT/CIO ... Mr. Carl E. WHITMAN
15 VP of Human Res/Dev & Engagement ... Ms. Nadine PORTER
18 VP of Facilities & Security ... Dr. Dewey YEATTS
37 Chief Enrollment Svcs/Fin Aid Ofc ... Ms. Melissa GREGORY
109 Dir of Auxiliary Services ... Vacant
26 VP of Communications ... Mr. Ray GILMER
10 VP of Finance/CFO ... Ms. Ruby SHERMAN
88 VP of Audit & Business Process Mgmt ... Mr. Robert PRESTON
88 Deputy Chief of Staff and Strategy ... Dr. Brian K. BAKER
88 Deputy Chief of Staff and Strategy ... Dr. Michelle T. SCOTT
41 Athletic Director ... Mr. Derek A. CARTER
44 Dir of MC Foundation/Dir of Dev ... Ms. Carol ROGNRUD
88 Exec Dir Hercules Pinkney Life SP ... Ms. Martha SCHOONMAKER
09 Dir Institutional Rsrch & Analysis ... Dr. Robert LYNCH
96 Director of Procurement ... Mr. Patrick JOHNSON

06 Asst Dir of Enrollment & Registrar ... Mr. Ernest CARTLEDGE
19 Dir Public Safety/Emergency Mgmt ... Vacant
102 Dir Corporate/Foundation Relats ... Ms. Rose GARVIN AQUILINO
29 Alumni Coordinator ... Mr. John LIBBY

Morgan State University (C)

1700 East Cold Spring Lane, Baltimore MD 21251-0001
County: Independent City FICE Identification: 002083
Unit ID: 163453
Telephone: (443) 885-3333 Carnegie Class: DRU
FAX Number: (443) 885-3698 Calendar System: Semester
URL: www.morgan.edu
Established: 1867 Annual Undergrad Tuition & Fees (In-State): $7,508
Enrollment: 7,698 Coed
Affiliation or Control: State IRS Status: 501(c)3
Highest Offering: Doctorate
Program: Liberal Arts And General; Teacher Preparatory; Professional
Accreditation: M, BUS, BUSA, DIETD, ENG, ENGR, LSAR, MT, MUS, NURSE, PH, PLNG, SW, TED

01 President ... Dr. David WILSON
05 Provost/Vice Pres Academic Affs ... Dr. Gloria GIBSON
88 VP Academic Outreach and Engagement ... Dr. Maurice TAYLOR
10 Vice Pres Finance & Management ... Mr. Sidney EVANS
45 Vice President Planning ... Dr. Joseph POPOVICH
32 Vice Pres Student Affairs ... Dr. Kevin BANKS
30 Vice Pres Institutional Advancement ... Ms. Cheryl Y. HITCHCOCK
20 Assoc VP for Academic Affairs ... Dr. Kara TURNER
21 Asst Vice President for Finance ... Mr. Bickram JANAK
35 Associate VP Student Affairs ... Ms. Tanya RUSH
100 Chief of Staff ... Vacant
49 Acting Dean College of Liberal Arts ... Dr. Pamela SCOTT-JOHNSON
50 Dean School Business & Management ... Dr. Fikru BOGHOSSIAN
53 Dean School of Education ... Dr. Patricia WELCH
54 Dean School of Engineering ... Dr. Eugene DELOATCH
58 Dean of the Graduate School ... Dr. Mark GARRISON
48 Dean School of Architecture ... Dr. Mary Anne AKERS
70 Dean School of Social Work ... Dr. Anna MCPHATTER
69 Dean School of Community Health ... Dr. Kim SYDNOR
37 Director of Financial Aid ... Ms. Tanya WILKERSON
38 Director of Counseling Services ... Ms. Nina DOBSON-HOPKINS
08 Director of Library ... Dr. Richard BRADBERRY
06 Director of Records/Registration ... Mr. Hans COOPER
07 Director of Admissions ... Ms. Shonda GRAY
36 Director of Placement ... Ms. Seana COULTER
15 Director Human Resources ... Mrs. Armada GRANT
29 Director Alumni Association ... Mrs. Joyce BROWN
13 Director Computer Center ... Mr. Gilbert MORGAN
86 Director State Relations ... Mr. Claude E. HITCHCOCK
09 Director of Institutional Research ... Ms. Cheryl ROLLINS
18 Acting Director Physical Plant ... Mr. Premdat KOKILEPERSAUD
26 Director Public Relations ... Mr. Clinton R. COLEMAN
84 Director Enrollment Management ... Vacant
96 Interim Director of Purchasing ... Ms. Lois WHITAKER
28 Director of Diversity ... Ms. Tanyka BARBER

Mount St. Mary's University (D)

16300 Old Emmitsburg Road,
Emmitsburg MD 21727-7799
County: Frederick FICE Identification: 002086
Unit ID: 163462
Telephone: (301) 447-6122 Carnegie Class: Master's M
FAX Number: (301) 447-5634 Calendar System: Semester
URL: www.msmary.edu
Established: 1808 Annual Undergrad Tuition & Fees: $37,500
Enrollment: 2,305 Coed
Affiliation or Control: Roman Catholic IRS Status: 501(c)3
Highest Offering: Master's
Program: Liberal Arts And General; Teacher Preparatory; Professional; Religious Emphasis
Accreditation: M, IACBE, TED, THEOL

01 President ... Mr. Simon NEWMAN
03 Vice President/Rector ... Vacant
03 Executive Vice President ... Mr. Dan SOLLER
88 Vice President University Affairs ... Ms. Pauline ENGLESTATTER
05 Provost ... Dr. David B. REHM
10 Vice Pres for Business & Finance ... Mr. William E. DAVIES
30 Vice President for Advancement ... Mr. Robert J. BRENNAN
84 Vice Pres Enrollment Management ... Mr. Michael POST
20 Assoc Provost ... Dr. Leona SEVICK
50 Dean Richard J Bolte Sr Sch of Bus ... Dr. Karl W. EINOLF
53 Dean Sch Education & Human Services ... Dr. Barbara MARTIN PALMER
81 Dean School Natural Science & Math ... Dr. Jeffrey SIMMONS
79 Dean College of Liberal Arts ... Dr. Joshua HOCHSCHILD
41 Director of Athletics ... Ms. Lynne P. ROBINSON
42 Chaplain ... Fr. Brian NOLAN
32 Dean of Students ... Mr. Michael TABERSKI
51 Director Professional/Cont Studies ... Mr. Joe LEBHERZ
08 Dean of the Library ... Mr. Charles KUHN
09 Director Institutional Research ... Ms. Linda K. SITES
06 Registrar ... Mr. Chris WEBER
50 Director of Grad/Adult Business Pgm ... Ms. Deborah POWELL
88 Director Conferences/Special Pgms ... Ms. Marianne DEMPSEY
23 Director of Health Services ... Dr. Bonnie PORTIER
24 Director of the Media Center ... Mr. John B. BREWER, JR.
37 Director of Financial Aid ... Mr. David C. REEDER
36 Director Career Center ... Ms. Claire TAURIELLO

13 Chief Information Officer ... Mr. Bobby L. FLACK
26 Director of Communications ... Mr. Duffy ROSS
44 Director of Annual Giving ... Ms. Marie CACACE
15 Director of Human Resources ... Ms. Barbara R. MILLER
19 Director of Public Safety ... Mr. R. Barry TITLER
29 Director of Alumni Relations ... Ms. Maureen C. PLANT
18 Director of Physical Plant ... Mr. Bruce NORMAN
88 Director Office of Social Justice ... Mr. Ian VANANDEN
28 Director Ctr for Student Diversity ... Ms. Chianti BLACKMON
35 Dir Campus Activ/Student Ldrshp ... Mr. Kenneth MCVEARRY
92 Director of the Honors Program ... Dr. Thane NABERHAUS
40 Manager of College Store ... Ms. Amanda CASALE
96 Purchasing Agent ... Ms. Maria L. TOPPER

Ner Israel Rabbinical College (E)

400 Mount Wilson Lane, Baltimore MD 21208-1198
County: Baltimore FICE Identification: 002087
Unit ID: 163532
Telephone: (410) 484-7200 Carnegie Class: Spec/Faith
FAX Number: (410) 484-3060 Calendar System: Semester
Established: 1933 Annual Undergrad Tuition & Fees: $10,900
Enrollment: 512 Male
Affiliation or Control: Independent Non-Profit IRS Status: 501(c)3
Highest Offering: Doctorate
Program: Teacher Preparatory; Professional; Religious Emphasis
Accreditation: RABN

01 President ... Rabbi Sheftel M. NEUBERGER
05 Chief Academic Officer ... Rabbi Aharon FELDMAN
03 Executive Director ... Mr. Jerome H. KADDEN
04 Assistant to the President ... Rabbi Boruch NEUBERGER
07 Director of Admissions ... Rabbi Beryl WEISBORD
13 Director of Administrative Services ... Mr. Larry RIBAKOW
06 Registrar ... Rabbi Chaim D. LAPIDUS
37 Director Student Financial Aid ... Rabbi Shmuel SCHACHTER
85 Foreign Student Advisor ... Rabbi Eliyahu HAKKAKIAN
30 Director of Development ... Rabbi Louis HOFFMAN
45 Director of Planning ... Rabbi Leonard OBERSTEIN
26 Director Community Relations ... Rabbi Jonathan SEIDEMANN
18 Chief Physical Plant ... Mr. David FRIEDMAN
08 Head Librarian ... Rabbi Avrohom SHNIDMAN
39 Director of Student Housing ... Rabbi Emanuel GOLDFEIZ
29 Associate Director Alumni Relations ... Rabbi Eli GREENGART

Notre Dame of Maryland University (F)

4701 N Charles Street, Baltimore MD 21210-2404
County: Independent City FICE Identification: 002065
Unit ID: 163578
Telephone: (410) 435-0100 Carnegie Class: Master's L
FAX Number: (410) 532-5791 Calendar System: Semester
URL: www.ndm.edu
Established: 1873 Annual Undergrad Tuition & Fees: $32,548
Enrollment: 2,764 Female
Affiliation or Control: Roman Catholic IRS Status: 501(c)3
Highest Offering: Doctorate
Program: Liberal Arts And General; Teacher Preparatory; Professional
Accreditation: M, NUR, PHAR, TED

01 President ... Dr. Marylou YAM
05 Int Vice President Academic Affairs ... Dr. Russell WARREN
32 Vice President Student Life ... Dr. Rebecca SAWYER
30 Vice Pres Institutional Advancement ... Dr. Tanya EASTON
84 Vice Pres Enrollment Management ... Ms. Heidi L. FLETCHER
10 Vice Pres for Finance & Admin ... Ms. Debbie ASBURY
20 Associate VP Academic Affairs ... Dr. Kathryn DOHERTY
88 Assoc VP Enrollment Mgmt ... Ms. Sharon BOGDAN
35 Dean of Students ... Vacant
100 Chief of Staff ... Dr. Candace CARACO
06 Registrar ... Ms. Irma WILLIAMS
37 Director of Financial Aid ... Ms. Audrey BROOKS
36 Director Career Center ... Mr. Ammad SHEIKH
13 Director Information Technology ... Mr. Warren SZELISTOWSKI
29 Director of Alumnae Relations ... Ms. Emilia POITER
08 Librarian ... Ms. Barbara PREECE
85 Director International Program ... Mr. Eleftherios MICHAEL
07 Director of Admissions ... Ms. Angela BAUMLER
09 Dir Inst Research/Effectiveness ... Ms. Luz CACEDA
15 Director of Human Resources ... Ms. Geri LARSEN
18 Director of Facility Management ... Mr. Martin KAJIC
21 Controller ... Ms. Barbara MORRIS
38 Director Counseling Center ... Ms. Amy PROVAN
19 Director of Public Safety ... Mr. Jeff MUNCHEL
40 Bookstore Manager ... Ms. Allegra WOODALL
41 Athletic Director ... Ms. Erin FOLEY
42 Director Campus Ministry ... Ms. Melissa LEES
67 Dean School of Pharmacy ... Dr. Anne LIN
07 Director Pharmacy Admissions ... Mr. Larry SHATTUCK
25 Chief Contracts/Grants Admin ... Ms. Joan WISNER-CARLSON
26 Chief Public Relations/Marketing ... Ms. Susan REPKO

Prince George's Community College (G)

301 Largo Road, Largo MD 20774-2199
County: Prince Georges FICE Identification: 002089
Unit ID: 163657
Telephone: (301) 336-6000 Carnegie Class: Assoc/Pub-S-SC
FAX Number: (301) 808-0960 Calendar System: Semester
URL: www.pgcc.edu
Established: 1958 Annual Undergrad Tuition & Fees (In-District): $3,650
Enrollment: 13,678 Coed

Affiliation or Control: Local IRS Status: 501(c)3
Highest Offering: Associate Degree
Program: Occupational; 2-Year Principally Bachelor's Creditable
Accreditation: M, ADNUR, CAHIIM, #COARC, EMT, #NMT, RAD

01 President ... Dr. Charlene M. DUKES
05 Vice Pres Academic Affairs ... Dr. Sandra F. DUNNINGTON
32 Vice Pres Student Services ... Dr. Tyjaun A. LEE
10 Vice Pres Administrative Services ... Mr. Thomas E. KNAPP
103 Interim VP Workforce Devel/Cont Ed . Mr. Joseph L. MARTINELLI
72 Vice Pres Technology Services ... Dr. Joseph G. ROSSMEIER
20 Sr Acad Admin to VP for Acad Affs ... Ms. Catherine LAPALOMBARA
38 Dean Student Development Svcs ... Dr. Scheherazade W. FORMAN
84 Dean of Enrollment Services ... Ms. Cindy D. CHILDS
09 Int Dean Planning/Instl Research ... Mr. William RICHMAN
51 Dean Wrkfrce Dev/Cont Educ Pgms ... Mr. Joseph I. MARTINELLI
15 Dean Human Resources ... Ms. Lark T. DOBSON
88 Dean of Learning Foundations ... Dr. Beverly S. REED
21 Dean Financial Affairs ... Ms. Nancy E. BURGESS
100 Chief of Staff ... Ms. Alonia C. SHARPS
08 Dir Library/Learning Resources ... Ms. Priscilla C. THOMPSON
06 Registrar ... Ms. Nilaya BACCUS-HAIRSTON
07 Director Recruitment ... Vacant
18 Dean Facilities Management ... Dr. David C. MOSBY
88 Director Physical Facilities ... Mr. John DETISTH
86 Dir Community & Government Affairs ... Dr. Jacqueline L. BROWN
30 Exec Dir Institutional Advancement ... Ms. Brenda S. MITCHELL
26 Director Marketing & Creative Svcs ... Ms. Joyce X. BENTZMAN
13 Chief Technology Officer ... Mr. William L. ANDERSON
96 Interim Director of Procurement ... Mrs. LaTonya HOLLAND
37 Director Financial Aid ... Vacant
36 Manager Career & Job Services ... Ms. Stephanie S. PAIR-CUNNINGHAM
79 Dean of Liberal Arts ... Dr. Carolyn F. HOFFMAN
35 Dean College Life Services ... Mr. Malverse A. NICHOLSON, JR.
76 Dean of Health Science ... Ms. Angela D. ANDERSON
81 Dean Science/Tech/Engr/Math ... Dr. Christine E. BARROW
83 Int Dean Soc Sci/Bus Studies Div ... Dr. Lorraine P. BASSETTE

St. John's College (A)

60 College Avenue, Annapolis MD 21401
County: Anne Arundel FICE Identification: 002092
Unit ID: 163976
Telephone: (410) 263-2371 Carnegie Class: Bac/A&S
FAX Number: (410) 626-2886 Calendar System: Semester
URL: www.sjc.edu
Established: 1784 Annual Undergrad Tuition & Fees: $49,019
Enrollment: 472 Coed
Affiliation or Control: Independent Non-Profit IRS Status: 501(c)3
Highest Offering: Master's
Program: Liberal Arts And General
Accreditation: M

01 President ... Mr. Christopher B. NELSON
30 Vice Pres Advancement Annapolis ... Ms. Barbara GOYETTE
05 Dean ... Ms. Pamela KRAUS
10 Treasurer ... Mr. Joseph SMOLSKIS
06 Registrar ... Ms. Jacqueline THOMS
07 Director of Admissions ... Mr. Thomas WEEDE
102 Director Corporate/Foundation Rels ... Ms. Susan BORDEN
37 Director of Financial Aid ... Ms. Dana KENNEDY
08 Library Director ... Ms. Catherine DIXON
15 Director of Human Resources ... Ms. Deborah ANAWALT
18 Supt of Buildings & Grounds ... Mr. Sid PHIPPS
19 Chief of Security ... Mr. Timon LINN
23 Director of Student Health ... Ms. Nancy CALABRESE
26 Director of Communications ... Ms. Patricia DEMPSEY
32 Director of Student Services ... Ms. Taylor WATERS
20 Assistant Dean ... Ms. Heather LATHAM
36 Director of Career Services ... Ms. Jaime DUNN
40 Bookstore Manager ... Mr. Robin DUNN
41 Director of Athletics ... Mr. Michael MCQUARRIE
58 Director of Graduate Institute ... Mr. Jeff BLACK
21 Controller ... Ms. Diane SAWYER
29 Director of Alumni Relations ... Mr. Leo PICKENS
04 Executive Asst to President ... Ms. Ashleigh CADMUS

† See Affiliate: St. John's College at Santa Fe, NM.

St. Mary's College of Maryland (B)

18952 E Fisher Road, Saint Mary's City MD 20686-3001
County: Saint Mary's FICE Identification: 002095
Unit ID: 163912
Telephone: (240) 895-2000 Carnegie Class: Bac/A&S
FAX Number: (240) 895-4462 Calendar System: Semester
URL: www.smcm.edu
Established: 1840 Annual Undergrad Tuition & Fees (In-State): $13,895
Enrollment: 1,804 Coed
Affiliation or Control: State IRS Status: 501(c)3
Highest Offering: Master's
Program: Liberal Arts And General
Accreditation: M

01 President ... Dr. Tuajuanda JORDAN
05 Acting Provost/Dean of Faculty ... Dr. Laraine M. GLIDDEN
10 VP Business & Finance ... Mr. Charles C. JACKSON
30 VP for Institutional Advancement ... Ms. Carolyn CURRY
84 Vice Pres Enrollment Management ... Mr. Gary SHERMAN
21 Asst Vice President for Finance ... Mr. Christopher J. TRUE
11 Asst VP for Campus Operations ... Mr. Derek K. THORNTON
88 Exec Assoc to Pres/Trustee Liaison ... Ms. Ledesa J. EDDINS
26 Assoc VP of Marketing/ Communication ... Ms. Cheryl A. BATES-LEE
29 Director Alumni Relations ... Mr. David M. SUSHINSKY
09 Assoc Dir Institutional Research ... Mr. Ross P. CONOVER
06 Registrar ... Mr. Nickolas B. TULLEY
20 Assoc Dean of Faculty ... Dr. Ruth P. FEINGOLD
37 Director of Financial Aid ... Ms. Nadine L. HUTTON
07 Director of Admissions ... Mr. Michael J. CUMMINGS
88 Acting Dir Institutional Research ... Dr. Anne Marie BRADY
32 VP for Student Affairs ... Mr. Leonard E. BROWN, JR.
38 Exec Dir of the Wellness Center ... Dr. Kyle K. BISHOP
41 Director of Athletics/Recreation ... Mr. Scott W. DEVINE
83 Chair Anthropology ... Dr. William C. ROBERTS
57 Chair of Arts & Art History ... Vacant
88 Chair of Biology ... Dr. Jeffrey J. BYRD
88 Chair of Chemistry ... Dr. Randolph K. LARSEN, III
88 Chair of Economics ... Dr. Russell M. RHINE
83 Chair Educational Studies ... Dr. Katy ARNETT
79 Chair of English ... Dr. Christine A. WOOLEY
83 Chair of History ... Dr. Adriana M. BRODSKY
79 Chair of Intl Languages/Cultures ... Dr. Katie L. GANTZ
81 Chair of Math/Computer Science ... Dr. Sandy GANZELL
64 Chair of Music ... Dr. Deborah A. LAWRENCE
79 Chair Philosophy/Religious Studies ... Dr. Michael S. TABER
77 Chair of Physics ... Dr. Joshua M. GROSSMAN
82 Chair of Political Science ... Dr. Todd E. EBERLY
83 Chair of Psychology ... Dr. Elizabeth N. WILLIAMS
83 Chair of Sociology ... Dr. Louis E. HICKS
57 Chair of Theatre/Film/Media Stds ... Dr. Joanne R. KLEIN
20 Assoc Dean of Academic Services ... Dr. Donald R. STABILE
18 Assoc VP Planning & Facilities ... Mr. Daniel S. BRANIGAN
19 Interim Director of Public Safety ... Mr. Sean D. KENNEDY
40 Director of the Campus Store ... Mr. Richard T. WAGNER
15 Director of Human Resources ... Ms. Catherine A. PRATSON
23 Director of Health Services ... Ms. Linda L. SKUTKA
35 Associate Dean of Students ... Ms. Joanne A. GOLDWATER
13 Asst VP of Information Technology ... Vacant
44 Senior Development Officer ... Mr. Richard J. EDGAR
08 Director of the Library/Media Svcs ... Vacant
102 Director of Development & Campaigns ... Vacant
21 Comptroller/Director of Accounting ... Mr. Gabriel A. MBOMEH
43 Assistant Attorney General ... Ms. Erin O. MILLAR
22 Affirm Act/Equal Opportunity Office .. Mr. Melvin A. MCCLINTOCK
25 Director of Sponsored Research ... Ms. Sabine DILLINGHAM
96 Procurement Officer/Director of Aux ... Mr. Patrick G. HUNT
92 Director DeSousa Brent Scholars Pgm ... Dr. Frederico J. TALLEY
88 Director Events and Conferences ... Ms. Linda T. JONES
44 Dir Advancement/Prospect Management ... Vacant
102 Dir Foundation Finance/Admin ... Ms. Jacqueline A. WRIGHT
104 Director International Education ... Ms. Amanda R. REINIG
36 Director of Career Development ... Ms. Dana L. BURKE

Saint Mary's Seminary and University (C)

5400 Roland Avenue, Baltimore MD 21210-1994
County: Independent City FICE Identification: 002096
Unit ID: 163842
Telephone: (410) 864-4000 Carnegie Class: Spec/Faith
FAX Number: (410) 864-4278 Calendar System: Semester
URL: www.stmarys.edu
Established: 1791 Annual Undergrad Tuition & Fees: $29,450
Enrollment: 208 Coed
Affiliation or Control: Roman Catholic IRS Status: 501(c)3
Highest Offering: First Professional Degree
Program: Liberal Arts And General; Professional; Religious Emphasis
Accreditation: M, THEOL

01 President/Rector ... Rev. Thomas R. HURST
10 Vice President for Finance ... Mr. Richard G. CHILDS
30 Vice Pres Advancement/Human Res ... Mrs. Elizabeth L. VISCONAGE
05 Dean School Theology ... Rev. Timothy A. KULBICKI, OFM CONV
73 Dean Ecumenical Institute Theology ... Dr. D. Brent LAYTHAM
73 Dean Ecclesiastical Faculty ... Rev. Timothy A. KULBICKI, OFM CONV
06 University Registrar ... Ms. Paula M. THIGPEN
37 Director Financial Aid ... Mrs. Victoria F. GAUNT
08 Director of Knott Library ... Mr. Thomas RASZEWSKI
13 Director Information Services ... Mr. Arryn MILNE

The SANS Technology Institute (D)

8120 Woodmont Avenue, Suite 205, Bethesda MD 20814
County: Montgomery Identification: 667006
Telephone: (301) 654-7267 Carnegie Class: Not Classified
FAX Number: (301) 951-0140 Calendar System: Other
URL: www.sans.edu
Established: 2006 Annual Graduate Tuition & Fees: $15,750
Enrollment: 95 Coed
Affiliation or Control: Proprietary IRS Status: Proprietary
Highest Offering: Master's; No Undergraduates
Program: Professional; Technical Emphasis
Accreditation: M

01 President ... Mr. Alan PALLER
03 Executive Director ... Mr. Bill LOCKHART
05 Provost ... Dr. Toby GOUKER

Stevenson University (E)

1525 Greenspring Valley Road, Stevenson MD 21153-0641
County: Baltimore FICE Identification: 002107
Unit ID: 164173
Telephone: (410) 486-7000 Carnegie Class: Master's S
FAX Number: (410) 486-3552 Calendar System: Semester
URL: www.stevenson.edu
Established: 1947 Annual Undergrad Tuition & Fees: $30,998
Enrollment: 4,322 Coed
Affiliation or Control: Independent Non-Profit IRS Status: 501(c)3
Highest Offering: Master's
Program: Liberal Arts And General; Teacher Preparatory
Accreditation: M, CSHSE, MT, NURSE, TED

01 President ... Dr. Kevin J. MANNING
04 Assistant to President ... Ms. Ruth HUBBARD
05 Executive VP for Academic Affairs ... Dr. Paul D. LACK
10 Exec Vice Pres/Chief Financial Ofcr .. Mr. Timothy M. CAMPBELL
30 Vice Pres University Advancement ... Mr. Steve CLOSE
84 Vice Pres Enrollment Management ... Mr. Mark J. HERGAN
32 Vice President Student Affairs ... Ms. Claire E. MOORE
26 VP Marketing & Digital Comm ... Ms. Glenda G. LEGENDRE
15 Vice Pres for Human Resources ... Ms. Brenda BALZER
100 Vice President & Chief of Staff ... Ms. Sue KENNEY
20 Associate VP for Academic Affairs ... Dr. Jo-Ellen ASBURY
36 VP for Career Services ... Ms. Anne SCHOLL-FIEDLER
58 Dean Graduate/Professional Studies ... Ms. Joyce K. BECKER
50 Dean School of Business ... Vacant
81 Dean School of Science ... Dr. Susan GORMAN
83 Dean Sch of Humanities/Social Sci ... Dr. James SALVUCCI
88 Dean School of Design ... Ms. Amanda HOSTALKA
53 Dean School of Education ... Dr. Deborah KRAFT
18 Asst VP Fac & Campus Svcs ... Mr. Leland BEITEL
21 Asst VP Finan Affs/Controller ... Ms. Melanie M. EDMONDSON
37 Director of Financial Aid ... Ms. Barbara MILLER
35 Assoc VP/Dean of Students ... Dr. Jeffrey M. KELLY
13 Chief Information Officer/Asst VP ... Mr. Tom ALLEN
88 Associate Dean Academic Support ... Vacant
09 Director Institutional Research ... Dr. Bonnie THOMAS
108 Director for Assessment ... Dr. Natasha MILLER
23 Assoc Dean/Dir of Wellness Center ... Ms. Linda REYMANN
66 Associate Dean GPS Nursing ... Dr. Judith FEUSTLE
66 Interim Chair Nursing ... Ms. Ellen CLAYTON
106 Associate Dean Distance Education ... Dr. Barbara ZIRKIN
08 Director of Library Services ... Ms. Susan BONSTEEL
06 Registrar ... Ms. Tracy L. BOLT
19 Director of Safety & Security ... Mr. Timothy OSTENDARP
41 Athletic Director ... Mr. Brett C. ADAMS
109 Director Auxiliary Services ... Mr. Robert REED
28 Director of Multicultural Affairs ... Mr. Alvin ROBERTS
29 Director Alumni Relations ... Mr. James MYERS
88 Director Academic Link and PASS ... Ms. Christine FLAX
88 Director of Developmental Studies ... Dr. Terri WRIGHT

Stratford University Baltimore Campus (F)

219 S. Central Avenue, Baltimore MD 21202
Telephone: (410) 752-4710 Identification: 770616
Accreditation: ACICS, ACFEI

† Branch campus of Stratford University, Falls Church, VA.

TESST College of Technology (G)

1520 S Caton Avenue, Baltimore MD 21227-1063
County: Baltimore City FICE Identification: 007491
Unit ID: 163736
Telephone: (410) 644-6400 Carnegie Class: Assoc/PrivFP
FAX Number: (410) 644-6481 Calendar System: Quarter
URL: www.tesst.com
Established: 1956 Annual Undergrad Tuition & Fees: $15,258
Enrollment: 582 Coed
Affiliation or Control: Proprietary IRS Status: Proprietary
Highest Offering: Associate Degree
Program: Occupational
Accreditation: ACICS

01 President ... Mr. Matthew DIACONT
05 Director of Education ... Ms. Greta BONAPARTE

TESST College of Technology (H)

4600 Powder Mill Road, Suite 500, Beltsville MD 20705-2649
County: Prince Georges FICE Identification: 020836
Unit ID: 164058
Telephone: (301) 937-8448 Carnegie Class: Assoc/PrivFP
FAX Number: (301) 937-5327 Calendar System: Quarter
URL: www.tesst.com
Established: 1956 Annual Undergrad Tuition & Fees: $18,659
Enrollment: 388 Coed
Affiliation or Control: Proprietary IRS Status: Proprietary
Highest Offering: Associate Degree
Program: Occupational
Accreditation: ACICS

01 Campus Director ... Mr. Kevin BEAVER

TESST College of Technology (A)

803 Glen Eagles Court, Towson MD 21286-2201
County: Baltimore FICE Identification: 010410
Unit ID: 161776
Telephone: (410) 296-5350 Carnegie Class: Assoc/PrivFP
FAX Number: (410) 296-5356 Calendar System: Quarter
URL: www.tesst.com
Established: 1956 Annual Undergrad Tuition & Fees: $15,272
Enrollment: 318 Coed
Affiliation or Control: Proprietary IRS Status: Proprietary
Highest Offering: Associate Degree
Program: Occupational
Accreditation: ACICS

01 Executive Director .... Ms. Sue SHERWOOD
07 Director of Admissions .... Mr. Dru YOKUM

University of Phoenix Maryland Campus (B)

8830 Stanford Boulevard, Suite 100,
Columbia MD 21045-5423
Telephone: (410) 872-9001 Identification: 770210
Accreditation: &NH, ACBSP

† No longer accepting campus-based students.

*The University System of Maryland Office (C)

3300 Metzerott Road, Adelphi MD 20783-1690
County: Prince George's FICE Identification: 007959
Unit ID: 164146
Telephone: (301) 445-1901 Carnegie Class: N/A
FAX Number: (301) 445-1931
URL: www.usmd.edu

01 Chancellor .... Dr. Robert L. CARET
05 Sr VC Academic Affairs .... Dr. Joann BOUGHMAN
11 COO/Vice Chanc Admin & Finance .... Mr. Joseph F. VIVONA
30 VC Advancement & CEO USM Foundation .... Mr. Leonard R. RALEY
86 VC Governmental Relations .... Mr. Patrick J. HOGAN
26 VC for Communications .... Ms. Anne MOULTRIE
100 USM Chief of Staff .... Ms. Janice B. DOYLE
20 Assoc Vice Chanc Academic Affairs .... Ms. Teri HOLLANDER
13 Assoc VC & CIO .... Mr. Donald Z. SPICER
21 Assoc VC Administration & Finance .... Ms. JoAnn GOEDERT
21 Director Internal Audit .... Mr. David MOSCA
21 Director Budget Analysis .... Ms. Monica WEST

*University of Maryland College Park (D)

1101 Main Administration Building,
College Park MD 20742-0001
County: Prince Georges FICE Identification: 002103
Unit ID: 163286
Telephone: (301) 405-1000 Carnegie Class: RU/VH
FAX Number: (301) 314-9560 Calendar System: Semester
URL: www.umd.edu
Established: 1856 Annual Undergrad Tuition & Fees (In-State): $9,966
Enrollment: 26,222 Coed
Affiliation or Control: State IRS Status: 501(c)3
Highest Offering: Doctorate
Program: Liberal Arts And General; Teacher Preparatory; Professional; Business Emphasis
Accreditation: M, AUD, BUS, CEA, CLPSY, COPSY, DIETD, DIETI, ENG, IACBE, IPSY, JOUR, LIB, LSAR, MFCD, MUS, PH, PLNG, SCPSY, SP, SPAA, TED

02 President .... Dr. Wallace D. LOH
05 Sr Vice President & Provost .... Dr. Mary Ann RANKIN
11 Vice President Administrative Affs .... Mr. Carlo COLELLA
43 Vice President and General Counsel ... Mr. Michael R. POTERALA
26 Vice President University Relations .... Mr. Peter B. WEILER
32 Vice President Student Affairs .... Dr. Linda M. CLEMENT
13 Vice Pres Info Tech & CIO .... Dr. Eric DENNA
46 Vice President Research .... Dr. Patrick G. O'SHEA
47 Dean Col Agric/Natural Resources .... Dr. Cheng-I WEI
48 Dean Sch Architecture/Plng/Preserv .... Mr. David CRONRATH
79 Dean College Arts & Humanities .... Dr. Bonnie T. DILL
83 Dean Col Behavioral/Social Sciences .... Dr. Gregory F. BALL
50 Dean Smith School of Business .... Dr. Alexander J. TRIANTIS
81 Dean Computer/Math/Natural Science .... Dr. Jayanth R. BANAVAR
53 Dean of College of Education .... Dr. Donna WISEMAN
54 Dean Clark School of Engineering .... Dr. Darryll J. PINES
69 Dean School of Public Health .... Dr. Jane E. CLARK
60 Dean Merrill College of Journalism .... Ms. Lucy DALGLISH
62 Dean College Info Studies .... Dr. Jennifer J. PREECE
80 Dean School Public Policy .... Dr. Robert ORR
20 Dean Undergraduate Studies .... Dr. Donna B. HAMILTON
58 Dean Graduate School .... Dr. Charles A. CARAMELLO
08 Dean of Libraries .... Dr. Patricia A. STEELE
104 Assoc Provost International Affairs .... Dr. Ross LEWIN
09 Assoc VP/Inst Research & Planning .... Ms. Sharon A. LA VOY
18 Int Assoc VP Facilities/Management .... Mr. John FARLEY
28 Assoc VP & Chief Diversity Officer .... Dr. Kumea SHORTER-GOODEN
39 Asst VP/Director Resident Life .... Dr. Deborah F. GRANDNER
25 Assoc VP/Dir Research Adv & Admin .... Ms. Denise CLARK
35 Asst Vice Pres Student Affairs .... Mr. John ZACKER
07 Asst Vice Pres Admissions .... Ms. Barbara A. GILL
06 Asst VP Records/Registration .... Mr. Chuck A. WILSON
37 Asst VP Student Financial Aid .... Ms. Barbara A. GILL
27 Asst VP Marketing & Communications .... Mr. Brian ULLMANN
20 Professor/Assoc Prov Faculty Affs .... Dr. Juan URIAGEREKA
29 Exec Director Alumni Association .... Ms. Amy EICHHORST
36 Executive Director Career Center .... Kelley BISHOP
64 Director School of Music .... Dr. Robert L. GIBSON
85 Int Dir International Services .... Ms. Barbara VARSA
41 Director Athletics .... Mr. Kevin ANDERSON
40 Director University Book Center .... Mr. Mike GORE
23 Director Health Center .... Dr. David MCBRIDE
38 Director Counseling Center ... Dr. Sharon E. KIRKLAND-GORDON
19 Chief Campus Police .... Mr. David B. MITCHELL
15 Director University Human Resources ... Ms. Jewel WASHINGTON
92 Director University Honors Program .... Dr. William DORLAND
31 Asst Director Community Service .... Mr. Craig SLACK

*University of Maryland Baltimore (E)

620 W. Lexington Street, Baltimore MD 21201-1508
County: Independent City FICE Identification: 002104
Unit ID: 163259
Telephone: (410) 706-7004 Carnegie Class: Spec/Med
FAX Number: (410) 706-0500 Calendar System: 4/1/4
URL: www.umaryland.edu
Established: 1807 Annual Undergrad Tuition & Fees (In-State): $10,143
Enrollment: 6,276 Coed
Affiliation or Control: State IRS Status: 501(c)3
Highest Offering: Doctorate
Program: Professional
Accreditation: M, ANEST, DENT, DH, DIETI, IPSY, LAW, MED, MT, NURSE, PA, PH, PHAR, PTA, RADDOS, SW

02 President .... Dr. Jay A. PERMAN
05 Sr VP/Chief Acad & Research Officer .... Dr. Bruce E. JARRELL
11 Sr VP/Chief Operating Officer .... Vacant
17 Vice President Medical Affairs/Dean .... Dr. E. Albert REECE
10 Chief Admin & Finance Officer/VP .... Ms. Kathleen M. BYINGTON
13 Vice President and CIO .... Dr. Peter J. MURRAY
46 Chief Enterprise & Econ Dev Ofcr/VP .... Mr. James L. HUGHES
26 Chief Communications Officer/VP .... Ms. Jennifer B. LITCHMAN
30 Chief Development Officer/VP .... Mr. Michael B. DOWDY
43 Chief University Counsel .... Ms. Susan GILLETTE
20 Assoc VP AA/Ch Accountability Ofc .... Dr. Roger J. WARD
18 Assoc VP Facilities & Operations .... Mr. Robert M. ROWAN
15 Assoc VP Human Resource Services .... Vacant
86 Int AVP Govt & Community Affairs .... Mr. Kevin P. KELLY
21 Assoc Vice Pres Budget & Finance .... Mr. Scott BITNER
14 Asst VP Information Technology ...... Mr. Christopher G. PHILLIPS
24 Asst VP Technology Svcs & Support .... Vacant
22 Asst Vice President for Compliance .... Vacant
09 Asst VP Institutional Research .... Mr. Gregory C. SPENGLER
37 Asst VP Student Financial Assist .... Ms. Patricia A. SCOTT
27 Asst VP Communications & Ext Aff .... Ms. Laura A. KOZAK
32 AVP Student Affairs & Wellness .... Mr. Flavius R. LILLY
88 AVP Sponsored Projects Accounting ...... Ms. Lynn M. MCGINLEY
19 Chief of Police/AVP Public Safety .... Mr. Antonio WILLIAMS
08 Exec Dir Health Sci/Human Svc Libr .... Ms. Mary J. TOOEY
06 Director Records & Registration .... Mr. Ryan HOLTZ
41 Dir Univ Recreation & Fitness .... Mr. William P. CROCKETT
88 Director Benefits & Compensation .... Ms. Patricia HOFFMAN
31 Coordinator Community Affairs .... Mr. Brian C. STURDIVANT
16 Exec Dir Human Resource Services .... Mr. Joseph T. SMITH
38 Director Counseling .... Ms. Emilia K. PETRILLO
35 Director Student Services .... Ms. Cynthia E. RICE
88 Director of Financial Services .... Ms. Susan E. MCKECHNIE
96 Director of Procurement Services .... Mr. Joseph EVANS
52 Dean School of Dentistry .... Dr. Mark A. REYNOLDS
58 Dean Graduate School .... Dr. Bruce E. JARRELL
61 Dean School of Law .... Mr. Donald TOBIN
63 Dean School of Medicine .... Dr. E. Albert REECE
66 Dean School of Nursing .... Dr. Jane M. KIRSCHLING
67 Dean School of Pharmacy .... Dr. Natalie D. EDDINGTON
70 Dean School of Social Work .... Dr. Richard P. BARTH
84 Asst Dean Grad Admin/Enrollment Mgt .... Mr. Keith BROOKS
45 Dir of Capital Budget and Planning .... Ms. Angela FOWLER-YOUNG
31 Exec Dir Cmty Initiatives/Engage .... Ms. Ashley R. VALIS
07 Associate Dean of Admissions .... Mr. Milford M. FOXWELL, JR.

*University of Maryland Baltimore County (F)

1000 Hilltop Circle, Baltimore MD 21250-0001
County: Baltimore FICE Identification: 002105
Unit ID: 163268
Telephone: (410) 455-1000 Carnegie Class: RU/H
FAX Number: (410) 455-1210 Calendar System: 4/1/4
URL: www.umbc.edu
Established: 1966 Annual Undergrad Tuition & Fees (In-State): $11,006
Enrollment: 13,979 Coed
Affiliation or Control: State IRS Status: 501(c)3
Highest Offering: Doctorate
Program: Liberal Arts And General; Teacher Preparatory; Fine Arts Emphasis
Accreditation: M, CLPSY, CS, DANCE, DMS, EMT, ENG, IPSY, MUS, SPAA, SW, TED

02 President .... Dr. Freeman A. HRABOWSKI
05 Provost/Sr Vice Pres Acad Affs .... Dr. Philip ROUS
10 Vice Pres Finance/Administration .... Ms. Lynne SCHAEFER
32 Vice President Student Affairs .... Dr. Nancy YOUNG
30 Vice Pres Institutional Advancement .... Mr. Gregory SIMMONS
13 Vice Pres Information Technology .... Mr. Jack J. SUESS
46 Vice President of Research .... Dr. Karl V. STEINER
49 Dean Col of Arts/Humanities/Soc Sci .... Dr. Scott CASPER
81 Int Dean Col Natural/Math Sciences .... Dr. William LACOURSE
54 Dean College of Engr/Info Tech .... Dr. Julia ROSS
84 Asst Dean Graduate Enrollment Mgmt .... Ms. K. Jill BARR
20 Vice Provost/Dean Undergrad Educ .... Dr. Diane M. LEE
51 VP Cont/Prf Std/Ex Dir Shriver Ctr .... Vacant
20 Vice Provost Academic Affairs .... Dr. Antonio R. MOREIRA
58 Dean/Vice Provost for Graduate Educ .... Dr. Janet RUTLEDGE
15 Vice Provost Faculty Affairs .... Dr. Patrice MCDERMOTT
84 Vice Provost Enrollment Mgmt .... Dr. Yvette MOZIE-ROSS
21 Assoc VP Financial Services .... Mr. Benjamin LOWENTHAL
26 Assistant to Pres/Assoc VP Mktg/PR .... Ms. Lisa G. AKCHIN
11 Assoc VP Administrative Services .... Ms. Terry COOK
16 Associate VP for Human Resources .... Ms. Valerie A. THOMAS
29 Director Alumni Relations .... Ms. Stanyell BRUCE
88 Asst VP New Media/Instruction Tech .... Mr. John FRITZ
18 Asst VP Facilities Management .... Mr. Rusty POSTLEWATE
04 Senior Advisor to the President .... Dr. Peter HENDERSON
96 Director of Procurement .... Ms. Sharon QUINN
92 Director Honors College .... Dr. Simon STACEY
41 Director Physical Educ & Recreation .... Dr. Tim HALL
19 Director University Police .... Mr. Mark SPARKS
36 Asst VP Career & Corp Partnership .... Ms. Caroline BAKER
23 Director Health Services .... Ms. Jennifer LEPUS
37 Director Financial Aid .... Ms. Jane HICKEY
27 Senior Manager Communications .... Ms. Chelsea HADDAWAY-WILLIAMS
25 Director Sponsored Programs .... Ms. Christina STANGER
40 Director of UMBC Bookstore .... Mr. Robert J. SOMERS
85 Director International Educ Svcs .... Dr. Arlene WERGIN ODENWALD
08 Director Library .... Vacant
06 Registrar .... Vacant
35 Director Student Life .... Ms. Lee CALIZO
43 General Counsel .... Mr. David GLEASON
07 Assistant Vice Provost .... Mr. Dale BITTINGER
39 Director Residential Life .... Vacant
09 Director of Institutional Research .... Dr. Connie PIERSON
38 Director Student Counseling .... Dr. Bruce HERMAN
100 Chief of Staff President's Office .... Ms. Elyse ASHBURN

*University of Maryland Center for Environmental Science (G)

PO Box 775, Cambridge MD 21613
County: Dorchester Identification: 667159
Telephone: (410) 228-9250 Carnegie Class: Not Classified
FAX Number: (410) 228-3843 Calendar System: Semester
URL: www.umces.edu
Established: 1925 Annual Graduate Tuition & Fees: N/A
Enrollment: 80 Coed
Affiliation or Control: State IRS Status: 501(c)3
Highest Offering: Doctorate; No Undergraduates
Program: Professional
Accreditation: @M

02 President .... Dr. Donald BOESCH
05 Vice Pres for Education .... Dr. Edward HOUDE

*University of Maryland Eastern Shore (H)

11868 Academic Oval, Princess Anne MD 21853-1299
County: Somerset FICE Identification: 002106
Unit ID: 163338
Telephone: (410) 651-2200 Carnegie Class: Master's S
FAX Number: (410) 651-6105 Calendar System: Semester
URL: www.umes.edu
Established: 1886 Annual Undergrad Tuition & Fees (In-State): $7,625
Enrollment: 4,281 Coed
Affiliation or Control: State IRS Status: 501(c)3
Highest Offering: Doctorate
Program: Liberal Arts And General; Teacher Preparatory; Professional
Accreditation: M, #ARCPA, BUS, CONST, CORE, DIETD, DIETI, ENG, PHAR, PTA, TED

02 President .... Dr. Juliette B. BELL
03 Executive Vice President .... Ms. Kimberly C. DUMPSON
05 Provost/VP Academic Affairs .... Dr. Patrick R. LIVERPOOL
10 Vice Pres Administrative Affairs .... Mr. Kevin APPLETON
30 Vice President Inst Advancement .... Mr. Stephen L. MCDANIEL
32 Vice President Student Affairs .... Dr. D Jason DESOUSA
88 VP Research/Economic Development .... Dr. Garlen D. WESSON
13 Chief Information Officer .... Mr. Ken F. KUNDELL
20 Int Assoc Vice Pres Acad Affairs ..... Dr. Kimberly D. WHITEHEAD
11 Asst Vice President Admin Affairs .... Vacant
88 Asst to VP Administrative Affairs .... Dr. Maurice C. NGWABA
21 Asst VP Admin Affs/Budget Director .... Ms. Nelva G. COLLIER-WHITE
15 Asst VP Human Resources .... Ms. Marie H. BILLIE
84 Assoc VP Student Life/Enroll Mgt .... Dr. James M. WHITE
04 Special Assistant to the President .... Vacant
91 Director Administrative Computing .... Mr. Kenneth GASTON
56 Int Assoc Extension Administrator .... Dr. Enrique N. ESCOBAR
29 Director Alumni Affairs .... Mr. James G. LUNNERMON, II
08 Dean Library Services .... Mr. Tracy J. HUNTER-HAYES
37 Director Financial Aid .... Mr. James W. KELLAM

23 Director Student Health Services ....Ms. Sharone V. GRANT
96 Director Procurement ....Ms. Jacqueline M. COLLINS
07 Int Director of Strategic Enroll ....Ms. Jinawa A. MCNEIL
06 Registrar ....Ms. Cheryl HOLDEN-DUFFY
12 Gen Mgr Richard A Henson Center ....Ms. Kimberly A. MILLS
36 Director Career Services ....Dr. Theresa QUEENAN
09 Director Inst Research/Plng/Assess ......Dr. Stanley M. NYIRENDA
19 Director Public Safety ....Mr. Ernest LEATHERBURY, JR.
18 Director Physical Plant ....Mr. Kenny B. BELTON
39 Director Residence Life ....Mr. Marvin L. JONES
41 Athletic Director ....Mr. Keith S. DAVIDSON
21 Comptroller ....Ms. Bonita E. BYRD
46 Director Sponsored Research ....Ms. Catherine BOLEK
88 Director Student Retention & Svcs ....Dr. Angela L. WILLIAMS
88 Director Rural Development ....Vacant
88 Director Upward Bound ....Dr. Nicole L. GALE
35 Director Student Activities ....Ms. Qiana J. DRUMMOND
88 Director Title III Program ....Dr. Frances H. MCKINNEY
26 Director Public Relations ....Mr. William ROBINSON
44 Director Development ....Dr. Veronique L. DIRIKER
88 Director Advancement Services ....Ms. Chenita R. REDDICK
51 Coordinator Continuing Education ....Ms. Gretchen M. BOGGS
38 Coordinator Counseling Services ....Dr. Patricia E. TILGHMAN
58 Dean Graduate Studies ....Dr. Jennifer M. KEANE-DAWES
47 Dean School Agric/Natural Sciences ....Dr. Moses T. KAIRO
49 Dean School of Arts & Professions ....Dr. Ray J. DAVIS
50 Dean School Business & Technology ....Dr. Ayodele J. ALADE
67 Int Dean Sch Pharmacy/Health Prof ....Dr. Rondall E. ALLEN

*University of Maryland University College (A)

3501 University Boulevard East, Adelphi MD 20783-7998
County: Prince Georges FICE Identification: 011644
Unit ID: 163204
Telephone: (301) 985-7000 Carnegie Class: Master's L
FAX Number: (301) 985-7678 Calendar System: Semester
URL: www.umuc.edu
Established: 1947 Annual Undergrad Tuition & Fees (In-State): $6,696
Enrollment: 47,906 Coed
Affiliation or Control: State IRS Status: 501(c)3
Highest Offering: Doctorate
Program: Liberal Arts And General; Professional
Accreditation: M, CAHIIM

02 President ....Mr. Javier MIYARES
11 Chief Operating Officer ....Mr. George SHOENBERGER
10 Vice Pres Chief Financial Officer .... Mr. Eugene D. LOCKETT, JR.
05 Provost/Sr Vice Pres Academic Affs ....Dr. Marie CINI
26 Sr Vice President Communications ....Mr. Michael FREEDMAN
45 Sr VP Institutional Effectiveness ....Vacant
88 Sr VP Military & Veteran Operations ....Mr. Lloyd MILES
13 Sr Vice Pres Analytics/Plng/Tech ....Mr. Peter C. YOUNG
43 Vice President & General Counsel ....Ms. Maureen DAVID
15 VP/Chief Human Resources Officer ....Mr. John PETROV
86 Vice Pres Federal Govt Relations ....Ms. Sarah DUFENDACH
28 Ombudsman/VP Diversity Programs ....Dr. Blair HAYES
18 Associate Vice President Facilities ....Mr. George TRUJILLO
88 Director of State Govt Relations ....Vacant
37 AVP Student Financial Aid ....Ms. Cheryl STORIE
58 Vice Prov/Dean The Graduate School ....Mr. Aric KRAUSE
08 Assoc Provost of Library Services ....Mr. Stephen MILLER
06 Assoc Vice Provost/Registrar ....Ms. Joellen SHENDY
49 Dean The Undergrad School ....Dr. Matthew PRINEAS
09 Sr Director Institutional Research ....Wei ZHOU
07 Director of Admissions ....Ms. Insiya JIWANJI
84 Sr VP Strategic Enrollment Mgmt ....Mr. Joseph ADAMS

*Bowie State University (B)

14000 Jericho Park Road, Bowie MD 20715-3318
County: Prince Georges FICE Identification: 002062
Unit ID: 162007
Telephone: (301) 860-4000 Carnegie Class: DRU
FAX Number: (301) 860-3510 Calendar System: Semester
URL: www.bowiestate.edu
Established: 1865 Annual Undergrad Tuition & Fees (In-State): $7,658
Enrollment: 5,695 Coed
Affiliation or Control: State IRS Status: 501(c)3
Highest Offering: Doctorate
Program: Liberal Arts And General; Teacher Preparatory
Accreditation: M, ACBSP, CS, NUR, SPAA, SW, TED

02 President ....Dr. Mickey L. BURNIM
05 Provost/Vice Pres Academic Affs ....Dr. Weldon JACKSON
10 Vice Pres Finance & Administration ....Dr. Karl B. BROCKENBROUGH
30 Vice Pres Institutional Advancement ....Dr. Richard LUCAS, JR.
32 VP Student Affairs/Campus Life ....Dr. Artie L. TRAVIS
43 Vice Pres & General Counsel ....Ms. Karen JOHNSON-SHAHEED
35 Student Code of Conduct ....Mrs. Thomaice BOARDLEY
13 VP Office of Information Technology ....Mr. E. Wayne ROSE
84 Asst VP Enrollment Management ....Dr. Clayton STEEN
88 Asst to Prov Institutional Effec ....Ms. Gayle M. FINK
06 University Registrar ....Ms. Patricia MITCHELL
08 Assoc Library Dir/Interim Dean ...... Ms. Marian RUCKER-SHAMU
36 Director Career Services ....Ms. April JOHNOSON
15 Sr Director of Human Resources ....Ms. Sheila HOBSON
19 Chief of Campus Police ....Mr. Ernest WAITERS
58 Int Dean Sch of Grad Stds/Research ....Dr. Cosmos NWOKEAFOR
49 Dean School of Arts & Sciences ....Dr. George ACQUAAH
50 Dean School of Business ....Dr. Anthony NELSON

53 Dean Sch of Education ....Dr. Traki TAYLOR
107 Dean School of Professional Studies ....Dr. Jerome H. SCHIELE
92 Director UCE Honors Program ....Dr. Monika GROSS
23 Director University Wellness Center ....Dr. Rita WUTOH
41 Director Athletics ....Mr. Clyde DOUGHTY, JR.
26 Dir University Relations/ Marketing ....Ms. Cassandra M. ROBINSON
88 Director University Wiseman Centre ....Mr. Frank WALLER
37 Director Financial Aid ....Vacant
18 Director Facilities ....Mr. Darryl WILLIFORD
07 Director Undergraduate Admissions ....Mr. Derrick DAVIS
29 Director of Alumni Relations ....Ms. Anette WEDDERBURN
96 Director of Purchasing ....Mr. Steve A. JOST
09 Director of Institutional Research ....Dr. Doug NUTTER
100 Chief of Staff ....Ms. Tammi L. THOMAS

*Coppin State University (C)

2500 W North Avenue, Baltimore MD 21216-3698
County: Baltimore City FICE Identification: 002068
Unit ID: 162283
Telephone: (410) 951-3000 Carnegie Class: Master's S
FAX Number: (410) 333-5369 Calendar System: Semester
URL: www.coppin.edu
Established: 1900 Annual Undergrad Tuition & Fees (In-State): $7,346
Enrollment: 3,133 Coed
Affiliation or Control: State IRS Status: 501(c)3
Highest Offering: Doctorate
Program: Liberal Arts And General; Teacher Preparatory; Professional
Accreditation: M, CAHIIM, CORE, NUR, NURSE, SW, TED

02 President ....Dr. Maria THOMPSON
05 Provost/VP Academic Affairs ....Dr. Sadie R. GREGORY
30 VP Institutional Advancement ....Mr. Douglas DALZELL
10 Int VP Administration & Finance ....Ms. Julie PHELPS
32 Int Vice Pres Student Affairs ....Dr. Joann M. CHRISTOPHER-HICKS
13 VP Information Systems/CIO ....Dr. Ahmed EL-HAGGAN
84 Assoc VP Enrollment Management ....Mr. Troy MILLER
45 Assoc VP Planning/Assessment ....Vacant
20 Actg Assoc Vice Pres Academic Affs ....Dr. Habtu BRAHA
21 Assoc Vice Pres Admin/Finance ....Vacant
18 Assoc VP Capital Plng/Constr & Cont ....Mr. Maqbool PATEL
86 Assoc VP of Pub Policy & Govt Rel ....Dr. Monica E. RANDALL
15 Assoc VP of Human Resorces ....Mrs. Lisa EARLY
07 Director of Admissions ....Ms. Michelle R. GROSS
06 Interim Registrar ....Ms. Karen BARLAND
21 Controller ....Mrs. Crystal MOSLEY
08 Director of the Library ....Dr. Mary WANZA
37 Director of Financial Aid ....Ms. Thelma ROSS
36 Director of Career Services Center ....Mrs. Linda BOWIE
19 Chief of Public Safety ....Chief Leonard HAMM
39 Director of Housing/Residence Life ....Mrs. Vallyn MERRICK
41 Director of Athletics ....Mr. Derrick RAMSEY
35 Director Student Support Services ....Ms. Leila WASHINGTON
44 Director Major Gifts/Planned Giving ....Ms. Tara TURNER
96 Director of Purchasing ....Mr. Thomas E. DAWSON, JR.
26 Director of University Relations ....Vacant
88 Director Client Computing Services ....Mr. Emmanuel OWUSU-SEKYERE
88 Director Coppin Academy ....Vacant
35 Director of Student Activities ....Mrs. Jocelyn BRYANT
14 Director Telecommunications ....Mr. Claude K. RADER
105 Director Web & Multimedia ....Mr. Andrew C. BAIN
31 Exec Dir of Community Partnerships ....Vacant
92 Dean Honors College & McNair Pgms ....Mr. Ronnie L. COLLINS, SR.
58 Dean Graduate School ....Dr. Mary E. OWENS-SOUTHHALL
66 Dean of Nursing ....Dr. Tracey L. MURRAY
04 Executive Assistant to President ....Mrs. Sherie JOHNSON
88 Chair Interdisciplinary Studies ....Ms. Tondelaya BLACKSTONE
97 Chair General & Adult Education ......Dr. Jacqueline H. WILLIAMS
88 Int Chr Applied Psych/Rehab Counsel ....Mr. James STEWART
61 Chair Crim Justice/Law Enforcement ....Dr. Dilip DAS
53 Chair Curriculum & Instruction ....Dr. Glynis BARBER
57 Chair Fine Arts ....Dr. Garey HYATT
82 Chair History Geography/Global Stds ....Dr. Katherine BANKOLE-MEDINA
79 Interim Chair Humanities ....Dr. Seth FORREST
50 Chr Mgmt Sci & Economics (Business) ....Dr. Habtu BRAHA
77 Int Chair Math & Computer Science ....Dr. Sean BROOKS
65 Chair Natural Sciences ....Dr. Gilbert OGONJI
83 Chair Social Sciences ....Dr. John L. HUDGINS
70 Chair Social Work ....Dr. Errol BOLDEN
68 Chair Health/Physical Education ....Vacant
88 Chair Special Education ....Dr. Daniel P. JOSEPH

*Frostburg State University (D)

101 Braddock Road, Frostburg MD 21532-2303
County: Allegany FICE Identification: 002072
Unit ID: 162584
Telephone: (301) 687-4000 Carnegie Class: Master's L
FAX Number: (301) 687-4737 Calendar System: Semester
URL: www.frostburg.edu
Established: 1898 Annual Undergrad Tuition & Fees (In-State): $8,488
Enrollment: 5,645 Coed
Affiliation or Control: State IRS Status: 501(c)3
Highest Offering: Doctorate
Program: Liberal Arts And General; Teacher Preparatory
Accreditation: M, BUS, CAATE, ENG, NRPA, NURSE, SW, TED

02 Interim President ....Dr. Thomas BOWLING
05 Provost & VP Academic Affairs ....Vacant
32 Int VP Student/Education Svcs ....Dr. Jay HEGEMAN
10 Vice President for Admin & Finance ....Mr. David C. ROSE
30 Vice Pres Univ Advancement ....Mr. John SHORT
84 Assoc VP for Enrollment Management ....Mr. Wray BLAIR
100 Senior VP/Chief of Staff ....Mr. Steven SPAHR
15 Vice President Human Resources ....Ms. Katherine SNYDER
43 University Counsel ....Ms. Karen A. TREBER
20 Associate Provost ....Vacant
21 Assoc VP Finance & Controller ....Mr. Richard A. REPAC
35 Asst VP Student Svcs/Dean of Stdnts ....Dr. Jesse KETTERMAN
88 Associate VP Univ Advancement ....Ms. Colleen STUMP
45 Assoc Director Budget & Planning ....Ms. Denise MURPHY
20 Vice Provost ....Dr. John BOWMAN
49 Dean Col Liberal Arts & Science ....Dr. Joseph M. HOFFMAN
50 Dean College of Business ....Dr. Ahmad TOOTOONCHI
53 Dean College of Education ....Dr. Clarence GOLDEN
08 Director of the Library .... Ms. Lea MESSMAN-MANDICOTT
37 Director of Financial Aid ....Mrs. Angela L. HOVATTER
108 Asst Vice Pres Planning and Assess ....Vacant
09 Dir of Research/Sponsored Programs ....Mr. Aaron HOEL
58 Director of Graduate Services ....Ms. Vickie MAZER
18 Director Facilities/Physical Plant ....Mr. Robert BOYCE
26 Director News & Media Services ....Ms. Elizabeth MEDCALF
36 Director Career Services ....Dr. Robbie L. CORDLE
38 Director Counseling & Psyc Svcs ....Dr. Spencer F. DEAKIN
40 Asst Mgr Bookstore & ID Services ....Mr. Kenneth EMERICK
41 Athletic Director ....Mr. Troy DELL
19 Chief University Police ....Col. Cynthia SMITH
13 Chief Information Officer ....Mr. Troy DONOWAY
91 Director of Technology Services ....Ms. Beth KENNEY
29 Director of Alumni ....Ms. Shannon L. GRIBBLE
22 Director of AA/EEO ....Mrs. Beth HOFFMAN
07 Director of Admissions ....Ms. Trisha GREGORY
28 Director of Diversity ....Ms. Robin WYNDER
44 Director of Development ....Ms. Laura C. MCCULLOUGH
14 Dir Networking/Telecommunications ....Mr. Brian JENKINS
96 Coord Procurement/Material Handling ....Mr. Alan R. SNYDER
23 Director Health Services ....Ms. Darlene SMITH
39 Director Residence Life ....Mr. Dana A. SEVERANCE
06 Registrar ....Dr. Jay HEGEMAN

*Salisbury University (E)

1101 Camden Avenue, Salisbury MD 21801-6860
County: Wicomico FICE Identification: 002091
Unit ID: 163851
Telephone: (410) 543-6000 Carnegie Class: Master's L
FAX Number: (410) 548-2587 Calendar System: Semester
URL: www.salisbury.edu
Established: 1925 Annual Undergrad Tuition & Fees (In-State): $9,086
Enrollment: 8,770 Coed
Affiliation or Control: State IRS Status: 501(c)3
Highest Offering: Doctorate
Program: Liberal Arts And General; Teacher Preparatory; Professional
Accreditation: M, BUS, BUSA, CAATE, COARC, EXSC, MT, MUS, NURSE, SW, TED

02 President ....Dr. Janet E. DUDLEY-ESHBACH
05 Provost & Sr VP of Acad Affairs ....Dr. Diane D. ALLEN
100 Chief of Staff ....Ms. Amy S. HASSON
10 Vice Pres Administration/Finance ....Mrs. Betty P. CROCKETT
32 Vice Pres of Student Affairs ....Dr. Dane R. FOUST
30 Vice Pres Advancement/External Affs ....Mr. T. Greg PRINCE
84 Asst VP of Enrollment Management ....Mr. Aaron M. BASKO
28 Chief Diversity Officer ....Mr. Humberto X. ARISTIZABAL
35 Associate VP of Student Affairs . Ms. Mentha A. HYNES-WILSON
20 Interim Associate Provost ....Dr. Jason MCCARTNEY
20 Asst Vice Pres Academic Affairs ....Ms. Melissa M. BOOG
18 Assoc VP Facilities & Cap Mgmt ....Mr. Eric J. BERKHEIMER
35 Asst VP Student Affs/Dean Students ....Ms. Valerie J. RANDALL-LEE
13 Chief Information Officer ....Mr. Simeon ANANOU
26 Director of Public Relations ....Mr. Richard W. CULVER
41 Director of Athletics ....Vacant
92 Director Honors Program ....Dr. James J. BUSS
06 Registrar ....Ms. Jacqueline M. MAISEL
07 Director of Admissions ....Ms. Elizabeth A. SKOGLUND
09 Special Asst to Pres/UARA ....Dr. Kara O. SIEGERT
08 Dean of Libraries & Instr Resources ....Dr. Beatriz B. HARDY
38 Director of Counseling Center ....Dr. Kathleen J. SCOTT
36 Director of Career Services ....Vacant
37 Director of Financial Aid ....Ms. Barri ZIMMERMAN
15 Assoc VP for HR ....Ms. Nancy L. SIEGERT
29 Dir Alumni Relations & Gift Develop ....Mr. Jayme E. BLOCK
23 Director of Student Health Services ....Ms. Victoria A. LENTZ
35 Director of Student Activities ....Ms. Tricia G. SMITH
86 Dir of Govt & Community Relations ....Mr. Robert J. SHEEHAN
43 General Counsel ....Ms. Susan A. GRIISSER
39 Director Housing/Residence Life ....Mr. David P. GUTOSKEY
19 Director of Public Safety ....Mr. Edwin L. LASHLEY
40 Director of Bookstore ....Ms. Lisa G. GRAY
18 Director of Physical Plant ....Mr. Kevin J. MANN
96 Director of Purchasing ....Ms. Tonia NIXON
75 Dean Henson Sch Science/Tech ....Dr. Karen L. OLMSTEAD
50 Dean Perdue School of Business ....Dr. Christy H. WEER
49 Dean Fulton School of Liberal Arts .... Dr. Maarten L. PEREBOOM
53 Int Dean Seidel Sch Ed/Prof Studies ....Dr. Kelly FIALA
58 Dean Graduate Studies/Research ....Dr. Clifton P. GRIFFIN
88 Dir Ctr for Student Achievement ....Dr. Heather W. HOLMES

*Towson University (A)

8000 York Road, Baltimore MD 21252-0001

County: Baltimore　FICE Identification: 002099
Unit ID: 164076
Telephone: (410) 704-2000　Carnegie Class: Master's L
FAX Number: N/A　Calendar System: 4/1/4
URL: www.towson.edu
Established: 1866　Annual Undergrad Tuition & Fees (In-State): $8,650
Enrollment: 22,285　Coed
Affiliation or Control: State　IRS Status: 501(c)3
Highest Offering: Doctorate
Program: Liberal Arts And General; Teacher Preparatory; Professional
Accreditation: M, #ARCPA, AUD, BUS, BUSA, CAATE, CS, DANCE, FEPAC, IPSY, MUS, NURSE, OT, SP, TED, THEA

02 Interim President ..... Dr. Timothy CHANDLER
05 Act Provost/Vice Pres Acad Affairs ..... Dr. S. Maggie REITZ
10 Vice Pres Admin & Finance ..... Mr. Joseph J. OSTER
30 Vice Pres University Advancement ..... Dr. Gary N. RUBIN
32 Vice President Student Affairs ..... Dr. Deb MORIARTY
46 VP Div of Innovation/Applied Rsrch ... Ms. Dyan L. BRASINGTON
100 Chief of Staff ..... Ms. Jennifer GAJEWSKI
88 Deputy Chief of Staff ..... Ms. Marina COOPER
04 Asst to the Pres Div & Equ Opp ..... Dr. Debbie SEEBERGER
20 Interim Provost ..... Dr. S. Maggie REITZ
84 Assoc VP Enrollment Mgmt/Registrar ..... Mr. Robert GIORDANI
44 Assoc Vice President Development ..... Mr. Michael CATHER
26 VP Univ Marketing/ Communications ..... Ms. Josianne E. PENNINGTON
29 Assoc Vice Pres Alumni Relations ..... Ms. Lori B. ARMSTRONG
13 Assoc Vice President OTS/CIO ..... Mr. Jeffrey SCHMIDT
109 Assoc Vice Pres Auxiliary Svcs ..... Mr. Daniel SLATTERY
18 Assoc VP Facilities Management ..... Mr. Kevin PETERSEN
21 Assoc VP Fiscal Planning & Svcs ..... Mr. Robert CAMPBELL
15 Assoc Vice Pres Human Resources ..... Mr. Phillip ROSS, III
35 Assoc Vice Pres Student Affairs ..... Dr. Jana VARWIG
45 Assoc Prov Academic Res & Plng ..... Dr. Gary LEVY
88 Assoc Vice President Campus Life ..... Dr. Teresa HALL
28 Asst VP Student Affairs/Diversity ..... Mr. L. Victor COLLINS
39 Asst VP Housing/Residence Life ..... Mr. Jerry T. DIERINGER
37 Director for Financial Aid ..... Mr. David HORNE
25 Asst VP Sponsored Programs/Research ..... Ms. Amy L. TAYLOR
07 Director of Admissions ..... Mr. David FEDORCHAK
19 Asst VP Public Sfty/Chief of Police ..... Chief Bernard GERST
53 Dean College of Education ..... Dr. Laurie MULLEN
50 Dean College of Business/Economics .. Dr. Shohreh A. KAYNAMA
49 Dean College of Liberal Arts ..... Dr. Terry COONEY
81 Dean J&M Fisher Col of Science/Math ..... Dr. David VANKO
57 Dean Col Fine Arts/Communications ..... Ms. Susan PICINICH
76 Dean College of Health Professions ..... Dr. Lisa PLOWFIELD
92 Interim Dean Honors College ..... Dr. Terry COONEY
43 University Counsel ..... Mr. Michael A. ANSELMI
08 Dean of University Libraries ..... Ms. Deborah NOLAN
104 Director Study Abroad ..... Ms. Liz SHEARER
94 Chair Women's & Gender Studies .Dr. Cindy H. GISSENDANNER
09 Director Institutional Research ..... Mr. Tim BIBO, JR.
27 Dir Communications/Media Relations ..... Mr. Raymond C. FELDMANN
41 Director of Athletics ..... Mr. Timothy LEONARD
23 Director of Health Services ..... Dr. Matthias GOLDSTEIN
40 Director of University Store ..... Ms. Stacey ELOFIR
96 Director of Procurement ..... Ms. Lucy SLAICH
38 Director Counseling Center ..... Dr. Gregory REISING
36 Director of Career Center ..... Ms. Lorie LOGAN-BENNETT
06 Assoc Director Records/Registration ..... Ms. Susan HYMAN

*University of Baltimore (B)

1420 N Charles Street, Baltimore MD 21201-5779

County: Independent City　FICE Identification: 002102
Unit ID: 161873
Telephone: (410) 837-4200　Carnegie Class: Master's L
FAX Number: N/A　Calendar System: Semester
URL: www.ubalt.edu
Established: 1925　Annual Undergrad Tuition & Fees (In-State): $9,219
Enrollment: 6,422　Coed
Affiliation or Control: State　IRS Status: 501(c)3
Highest Offering: Doctorate
Program: Liberal Arts And General; Professional
Accreditation: M, BUS, LAW, SPAA

02 President ..... Mr. Kurt L. SCHMOKE
05 Provost & Sr VP Academic Affairs ..... Dr. Joseph S. WOOD
10 Sr VP Admin & Finance ..... Mr. Harry SCHUCKEL
100 Executive Director ..... Ms. Susan SCHUBERT
84 Sr Vice Pres Enrollment Management ..... Ms. Miriam E. KING
30 Vice Pres Institutional Advancement ..... Ms. Theresa SILANSKIS
27 Vice Pres University Advance/Comm ..... Mr. Peter TORAN
86 VP Government & Community Relations ... Ms. Anita HAREWOOD
18 VP Facil Mgmt/Capital Planning ..... Mr. Neb SERTSU
13 Vice Pres Technology/CIO ..... Mr. David BOBART
15 Asst Vice Pres Human Resources ..... Ms. Mary MAHER
20 Associate Provost ..... Ms. Catherine ANDERSEN
09 AVP for Institutional Research ..... Mr. Paul MONIODIS
35 Assoc Vice Pres Student Affairs ..... Ms. Shelia BURKHALTER
32 Dean of Students ..... Ms. Kathleen ANDERSON
35 Coord Center Student Involvement ..... Mr. Joe SLIDER
28 Dir Diversity and Culture Center ..... Ms. Karla M. SHEPHERD
07 Actg Executive Director Admissions ..... Ms. Janet WHELAN
08 Director of Library ..... Ms. Lucy HOLMAN
19 Chief of Police ..... Mr. Samuel D. TRESS
84 AVP Enrollment Services ..... Mr. Mark JACQUE
96 Director of Procurement & Supply ..... Mr. Blair BLANKINSHIP
44 Dir Annual Giving/Alumni Relations ..... Ms. Kate CRIMMINS
38 Director Counseling Services ..... Dr. Myra WATERS
36 Director Career & Professional Dev ..... Ms. Lakeisha MATHEWS
06 Registrar ..... Mr. Michael DRISCOLL
09 Director Institutional Research ..... Vacant
26 Manager Public Information ..... Mr. Chris HART
80 Dean College of Public Affairs ..... Dr. Roger HARTLEY
49 Interim Dean College of Arts & Sci ..... Dr. Christine SPENCER
61 Dean of the School of Law ..... Dr. Ronald WEICH
50 Dean School of Business ..... Mr. Murray DALZIEL
88 Dir Center for Education Access ..... Ms. Karyn SCHULZ
21 AVP Admin & University Budget Dir ..... Ms. Barbara AUGHENBAUGH
07 AVP Admissions ..... Mr. David WAGGONER

Washington Adventist University (C)

7600 Flower Avenue, Takoma Park MD 20912-7794

County: Montgomery　FICE Identification: 002067
Unit ID: 162210
Telephone: (301) 891-4000　Carnegie Class: Bac/Diverse
FAX Number: (301) 270-1618　Calendar System: Semester
URL: www.wau.edu
Established: 1904　Annual Undergrad Tuition & Fees: $22,790
Enrollment: 1,057　Coed
Affiliation or Control: Seventh-day Adventist　IRS Status: 501(c)3
Highest Offering: Master's
Program: Liberal Arts And General; Teacher Preparatory; Professional
Accreditation: M, MUS, RAD

01 President ..... Dr. Weymouth SPENCE
10 Exec Vice Pres Finance ..... Mr. Patrick FARLEY
05 Provost ..... Dr. Cheryl HARRIS KISUNZU
32 Vice Pres Student Life ..... Mr. Bruce PEIFER
42 Vice President Ministry ..... Baraka MUGANDA
13 VP Information Technology ..... Mr. James BUTLER
15 Assoc VP of Human Resources ..... Ms. Rythee JONES
09 Assoc VP Inst Research/Effect ..... Ms. Janette NEUFVILLE
58 Dean Sch Grad/Professional Studies ..... Vacant
33 Dean of Men ..... Mr. Tim NELSON
34 Dean of Women ..... Ms. Adrienne MATTHEWS
08 Library Director ..... Mr. Don ESSEX
30 Director of Development ..... Vacant
06 Director of Records/Admissions ..... Ms. Wanda COLON-CANALES
19 Director Safety & Security ..... Vacant
41 Athletic Director ..... Mr. Patrick CRAREY, II
84 Director of Student Recruiting ..... Vacant
29 Director of Alumni ..... Vacant
26 Director Marketing & Communications ..... Mr. William JACKSON
78 Dir Coop Educ/Acad Support & Test ..... Mr. Fitzroy THOMAS
18 Chief Facilities/Physical Plant ..... Mr. Steve LAPHAM
37 Director Student Financial Aid ..... Ms. Sharon CONWAY
38 Campus Counseling ..... Ms. Madge QUESENBERRY
40 Manager the College Bookstore ..... Mr. Lloyd YUTUC

Washington College (D)

300 Washington Avenue, Chestertown MD 21620-1197

County: Kent　FICE Identification: 002108
Unit ID: 164216
Telephone: (410) 778-2800　Carnegie Class: Bac/A&S
FAX Number: (410) 778-7850　Calendar System: Semester
URL: www.washcoll.edu
Established: 1782　Annual Undergrad Tuition & Fees: $43,850
Enrollment: 1,467　Coed
Affiliation or Control: Independent Non-Profit　IRS Status: 501(c)3
Highest Offering: Master's
Program: Liberal Arts And General; Teacher Preparatory; Fine Arts Emphasis
Accreditation: M

01 President ..... Ms. Sheila C. BAIR
05 Provost/Dean of College ..... Dr. Emily CHAMLEE-WRIGHT
100 Chief of Staff ..... Mr. Joseph L. HOLT
10 Vice Pres Finance/Administration ..... Dr. Mark C. HAMPTON
30 Vice Pres College Advancement ..... Vacant
44 Sr AVP College Advancement ..... Mrs. Barbara H. HECK
84 Vice Pres Enrollment Mgmt ..... Mr. Satyajit DATTAGUPTA
26 AVP College Relations/Marketing ..... Mr. Michael O'CONNOR
32 Vice President & Dean of Students ..... Dr. Xavier A. COLE
35 Assoc Vice Pres Student Affairs ..... Dr. Sarah R. FEYERHERM
29 Dir Alumni Rels/Ldrship Annual Gvng ..... Ms. Rebekah L. HARDY
09 Asst Provost Inst Research & Assmt ..... Mr. Victor SENSENIG
20 Asst Dean Academic Initiatives ..... Dr. Andrea G. LANGE
31 Director of Campus Special Events ..... Mrs. Laura J. WILSON
41 Director of Athletics ..... Dr. Bryan L. MATTHEWS
06 Registrar ..... Ms. Ashley TURLINGTON
08 Director of Miller Library ..... Dr. Ruth C. SHOGE
27 Chief Information Officer ..... Mr. Scott COWDREY
91 Director of Admin Computing ..... Mr. Kenneth W. SUTTON
58 Director of Graduate Program ..... Dr. Andrea G. LANGE
21 Controller ..... Ms. Penelope L. FARLEY
18 Director of Physical Plant ..... Mr. Reid C. RAUDENBUSH
15 Director of Human Resources ..... Vacant
19 Director of Public Safety ..... Mr. Gerald K. RODERICK
07 Director of Admissions ..... Mr. Bradly BOOKE
37 Director of Financial Aid ..... Ms. Jeani M. NARCUM
39 Dir Resid Life/Assoc Dean of Stdnts ..... Mr. Carl CROWE
85 Director International Programs ..... Vacant
23 Clinical Director Health Services ..... Mrs. Lisa M. MARX
38 Director of Counseling Center ..... Ms. Miranda ALTMAN
36 Director of Career Development ..... Mr. James M. ALLISON, JR.
28 Asst Dean for Multi-Cultural Affs ..... Vacant
27 Director of Media Relations ..... Mrs. Kay H. MACINTOSH
40 Bookstore Manager ..... Ms. Shannon WYBLE

Wor-Wic Community College (E)

32000 Campus Drive, Salisbury MD 21804-1486

County: Wicomico　FICE Identification: 020739
Unit ID: 164313
Telephone: (410) 334-2800　Carnegie Class: Assoc/Pub-R-M
FAX Number: (410) 334-2951　Calendar System: Semester
URL: www.worwic.edu
Established: 1975　Annual Undergrad Tuition & Fees (In-District): $3,600
Enrollment: 3,107　Coed
Affiliation or Control: Local　IRS Status: 501(c)3
Highest Offering: Associate Degree
Program: Occupational; 2-Year Principally Bachelor's Creditable
Accreditation: M, ACFEI, EMT, @PTAA, RAD

01 President ..... Dr. Murray K. HOY
05 Sr Vice Pres Academic Affairs ..... Dr. Stephen L. CAPELLI
84 Vice Pres Enroll Mgmt & Student Aff ..... Mr. Bryan NEWTON
10 Vice Pres Administrative Services ..... Ms. Jennifer A. SANDT
26 Vice Pres Institutional Affairs ..... Dr. Reenie MCCORMICK
51 Dean Continuing Education ..... Mrs. Ruth E. BAKER
97 Dean General Education ..... Dr. Colleen C. DALLAM
75 Dean Occupational Education ..... Dr. Trevor H. JONES
07 Director Admissions ..... Mr. Richard C. WEBSTER
13 Director Information Technology ..... Ms. Ruth GILL
36 Director Career Services ..... Ms. Lori SMOOT
37 Director Financial Aid ..... Ms. Deborah D. JENKINS
21 Director Accounting ..... Mr. Thomas N. TYSON
15 Director Human Resources ..... Ms. Karen BERKHEIMER
38 Director Counseling ..... Ms. Annette BROWN
27 Director Marketing ..... Ms. Janet S. KENNINGTON
09 Director Institutional Research ..... Ms. Carol A. MENZEL
30 Director Development ..... Ms. Janice MURPHY
06 Registrar ..... Ms. Kelly HEWETT
88 Dir Retention & Student Success ..... Ms. Deirdra G. JOHNSON
32 Director Student Activities ..... Ms. Katherine JONES
08 Director of Library Services ..... Ms. Cheryl MICHAEL
18 Director Facilities Management ..... Mr. Angelo FONTANAZZA
96 Director Purchasing & Auxiliary Svc ..... Ms. Allison M. CANADA
105 Webmaster ..... Mr. Joshua W. TOWNSEND
19 Director Public Safety ..... Mr. Linnie VANN

Yeshiva College of the Nation's Capital (F)

1216 Arcola Avenue, Silver Spring MD 20902-3408

County: Montgomery　FICE Identification: 039373
Unit ID: 434937
Telephone: (301) 649-7077　Carnegie Class: Spec/Faith
FAX Number: (301) 649-7053　Calendar System: Semester
Established: 1995　Annual Undergrad Tuition & Fees: $9,700
Enrollment: 35　Male
Affiliation or Control: Independent Non-Profit　IRS Status: 501(c)3
Highest Offering: Second Talmudic Degree
Program: Teacher Preparatory; Professional; Religious Emphasis
Accreditation: RABN

01 President ..... Rabbi Yitzchok MERKIN
05 Rosh Yeshiva ..... Rabbi Aaron LOPIANSKY
37 Financial Aid Director ..... Ms. Maryanna WALLS
11 Administrator ..... Rabbi Yehoshua SINGER

MASSACHUSETTS

American International College (G)

1000 State Street, Springfield MA 01109-3155

County: Hampden　FICE Identification: 002114
Unit ID: 164447
Telephone: (413) 737-7000　Carnegie Class: Master's L
FAX Number: (413) 205-3084　Calendar System: Semester
URL: www.aic.edu
Established: 1885　Annual Undergrad Tuition & Fees: $31,870
Enrollment: 3,629　Coed
Affiliation or Control: Independent Non-Profit　IRS Status: 501(c)3
Highest Offering: Doctorate
Program: Liberal Arts And General; Teacher Preparatory; Professional; Nursing Emphasis
Accreditation: EH, IACBE, NURSE, OT, PTA

01 President ..... Dr. Vincent M. MANIACI
05 Acting Chief Academic Officer ..... Dr. Susanne SWANKER
11 Exec VP Administration ..... Mr. Mark R. BERMAN
13 Chief Information Officer ..... Ms. Mimi ROYSTON
15 Vice President for Human Resources ..... Ms. Nicolle M. CESTERO
09 VP for Institutional Effectiveness ..... Dr. Gregory T. SCHMUTTE
10 Vice President for Finance ..... Mr. Thomas DYBICK
51 VP for Graduate and Adult Education ..... Ms. Ellen R. NOONAN
30 VP for Institutional Advancement ..... Ms. Maureen FITZGERALD
18 VP for Facilities ..... Mr. Floyd YOUNG
07 Director of Admissions ..... Vacant
41 Athletic Director ..... Mr. Matthew JOHNSON
88 Dean of Academic Success ..... Dr. Marianne REIFF
76 Dean Health Sciences ..... Dr. Cesarina THOMPSON

49 Dean Business/Arts/Sciences .... Dr. Susanne SWANKER
32 Dean of Students .... Mr. Brian J. O'SHAUGHNESSY
06 Registrar .... Mr. Paul KLESCHICK
08 Director of Library .... Ms. Estelle H. SPENCER
26 Dir for Marketing & Communications .... Mr. Timothy GRADER
38 Director Counseling Center .... Dr. Rose L. ANDREJCZYK
36 Dir of Career Services .... Mr. J. A. MARSHALL
76 Director Occupational Therapy Pgm .... Dr. Cathy A. DOW-ROYER
76 Director Physical Therapy Program .... Dr. Cindy BUCHANAN
66 Director of Division of Nursing .... Ms. Karen S. ROUSSEAU
37 Director for Financial Aid .... Ms. Sage CRARY-STACHOWIAK
21 Comptroller .... Mr. Christopher GARRITY
04 Admin Asst to President .... Ms. Lani KRETSCHMAR
19 Director Security/Safety .... Mr. David KUZMESKI
91 Director Administrative Computing .... Mr. Jeremy ANDERSON

Amherst College (A)

PO Box 5000, Amherst MA 01002-5000
County: Hampshire FICE Identification: 002115
Unit ID: 164465
Telephone: (413) 542-2000 Carnegie Class: Bac/A&S
FAX Number: (413) 542-2621 Calendar System: Semester
URL: www.amherst.edu
Established: 1821 Annual Undergrad Tuition & Fees: $49,730
Enrollment: 1,792 Coed
Affiliation or Control: Independent Non-Profit IRS Status: 501(c)3
Highest Offering: Baccalaureate
Program: Liberal Arts And General
Accreditation: EH

01 President .... Dr. Carolyn (Biddy) A. MARTIN
100 Chief of Staff/Sec of the Board .... Ms. Susan PIKOR
05 Dean of the Faculty .... Dr. Catherine A. EPSTEIN
32 Chief Student Affairs Officer .... Dr. Suzanne R. COFFEY
07 Dean Admission/Financial Aid .... Ms. Katharine L. FRETWELL
37 Dean of Financial Aid .... Ms. Gail W. HOLT
20 Associate Dean of the Faculty .... Dr. John CHENEY
20 Associate Dean of the Faculty .... Dr. Austin D. SARAT
10 Chief Financial Officer .... Mr. Kevin C. WEINMAN
30 Chief Advancement Officer .... Ms. Megan MOREY
43 Chief Policy Ofcr/General Counsel .... Ms. Lisa H. RUTHERFORD
29 Exec Dir Alumni Pgms/Annual Giving .... Ms. Elizabeth A. ANEMA
06 Registrar .... Ms. Kathleen KILVENTON
15 Director of Human Resources .... Ms. Maria-Judith RODRIGUEZ
21 Controller .... Mr. Stephen M. NIGRO
09 Chief Inst Research/Planning Ofcr .... Dr. Hanna S. SPINOSA
26 Chief Communications Officer .... Dr. Peter F. MACKEY
08 College Librarian .... Mr. Bryn GEFFERT
13 Chief Information Officer .... Mr. David L. HAMILTON
23 Director of Student Health Services .... Dr. Warren H. MORGAN
38 Director of Counseling Center .... Dr. Jacqueline ALVAREZ
36 Director of the Career Center .... Ms. Ursula J. OLENDER
41 Director of Athletics .... Mr. Donald R. FAULSTICK
18 Chief of Campus Operations .... Mr. James D. BRASSORD
19 Chief of Campus Police .... Mr. John B. CARTER
88 Director of Dining Services .... Mr. Charles G. THOMPSON

Andover Newton Theological School (B)

210 Herrick Road, Newton Centre MA 02459-2243
County: Middlesex FICE Identification: 002116
Unit ID: 164474
Telephone: (617) 964-1100 Carnegie Class: Spec/Faith
FAX Number: (617) 965-9756 Calendar System: Semester
URL: www.ants.edu
Established: 1807 Annual Graduate Tuition & Fees: $16,700
Enrollment: 261 Coed
Affiliation or Control: Independent Non-Profit IRS Status: 501(c)3
Highest Offering: Doctorate; No Undergraduates
Program: Professional; Religious Emphasis
Accreditation: EH, THEOL

01 President .... Rev. Martin COPENHAVER
05 Dean of the Faculty .... Dr. Sarah B. DRUMMOND
10 Vice President for Finance .... Mr. Peter CHINETTI
30 Vice Pres Institutional Advance .... Ms. Jennifer CRAIG
29 Director of the Annual Fund .... Rev. Ruth EDENS
06 Registrar .... Ms. Nayda G. AGUILA
84 Director of Recruitment .... Ms. Alison MCCARTY
08 Co-Director of the Library .... Rev. Nancy LOIS
08 Co-Director of the Library .... Mr. Jeffrey BRIGHAM
32 Dean of Students .... Dr. Nancy E. NIENHUIS
04 Assistant to the President .... Ms. Marjorie BELL
18 Director Physical Plant .... Mr. Frank CAVACO
13 Chief Information Officer .... Mr. Mugur ROZ
37 Coordinator Financial Aid .... Ms. Rosemary TURANO
39 Director Housing & Events Planning .... Mr. Frank NOVO

Anna Maria College (C)

50 Sunset Lane, Paxton MA 01612-1198
County: Worcester FICE Identification: 002117
Unit ID: 164492
Telephone: (508) 849-3300 Carnegie Class: Master's M
FAX Number: (508) 849-3334 Calendar System: 4/1/4
URL: www.annamaria.edu
Established: 1946 Annual Undergrad Tuition & Fees: $35,074
Enrollment: 1,455 Coed
Affiliation or Control: Roman Catholic IRS Status: 501(c)3
Highest Offering: Beyond Master's But Less Than Doctorate
Program: Liberal Arts And General; Teacher Preparatory; Professional
Accreditation: EH, MUS, NUR, SW

01 President .... Ms. Mary Louise RETELLE
03 Executive Vice President .... Vacant
10 VP for Finance and Admin/CFO .... Mr. David M. ROSATI
21 Controller .... Ms. Yvonnie MALCOLM
05 Interim VP for Academic Affairs .... Dr. Christine HOLMES
32 VP for Student Affairs .... Mr. Andrew O. KLEIN
26 Director of College Relations .... Ms. Tricia M. OLIVER
09 Director of Institutional Research .... Ms. Irene IRUDAYAM
06 Registrar .... Ms. Barbara ZAWALICH
30 Director Institutional Advancement .... Ms. Susan A. WOJTAS
88 Director of the Learning Center .... Mr. Dennis VANASSE
23 Director of Health Services .... Ms. Linda ARONSON
08 Director of Library .... Ms. Janice WILBUR
29 Director Alumni Relations .... Mr. Wesley DUNHAM
36 Director Career Counsel/Placement .... Vacant
37 Director Financial Aid .... Ms. Sandra PEREIRA
13 Chief Information Officer .... Mr. Michael MIERS
04 Executive Asst to the President .... Ms. Kay FLICK
18 Director Physical Plant .... Mr. Matthew SIMPSON
41 Athletic Director .... Ms. Laura HABACKER
42 Director Campus Ministry .... Fr. Manuel CLAVIJO
15 Director of Human Resources .... Ms. Lisa DRISCOLL
88 Dean of Mission Effectiveness .... Sr. Rollande QUINTAL
07 Dean of Admissions & Financial Aid .... Mr. Peter MILLER
28 Director of Multicultural Affairs .... Mr. Joshua DODDS

Assumption College (D)

500 Salisbury Street, Worcester MA 01609-1296
County: Worcester FICE Identification: 002118
Unit ID: 164562
Telephone: (508) 767-7000 Carnegie Class: Master's M
FAX Number: (508) 767-7169 Calendar System: Semester
URL: www.assumption.edu
Established: 1904 Annual Undergrad Tuition & Fees: $36,160
Enrollment: 2,706 Coed
Affiliation or Control: Roman Catholic IRS Status: 501(c)3
Highest Offering: Beyond Master's But Less Than Doctorate
Program: Liberal Arts And General; Teacher Preparatory; Professional
Accreditation: EH, CORE

01 President .... Dr. Francesco C. CESAREO
10 VP for Finance and Administratoin .... Mr. Peter D. WELLS
05 Provost/Academic Vice Pres .... Dr. Louise Carroll KEELEY
32 Vice President for Student Affairs .... Dr. Catherine M. WOODBROOKS
30 Vice Pres Institutional Advancement .... Mr. Timothy R. STANTON
42 Vice President Mission .... Rev. Dennis M. GALLAGHER, AA
84 Vice Pres for Enrollment Management .... Mr. Evan E. LIPP
43 General Counsel .... Dr. Michael H. RUBINO
20 Associate Provost .... Dr. Kimberly A. SCHANDEL
51 Dir of Career and Continuing Ed .... Mr. Dennis BRAUN
07 Dean of Admissions .... Ms. Kathleen M. MURPHY
20 Dean of Undergraduate Studies .... Dr. Eloise KNOWLTON
58 Assistant Provost/Dean of Grad Stds .... Mr. Joseph B. MORRISON
89 Assistant Dean for the First Year .... Dr. Jennifer K. MORRISON
42 Director of Campus Ministry .... Mr. Paul F. COVINO
35 Dean of Student Development .... Dr. Neil R. CASTRONOVO
08 Director of Library Services .... Ms. Doris Ann SWEET
10 Director of Finance .... Ms. Cathleen R. CULLEN
21 Dir of Facilities Planning & Projs .... Vacant
09 Director Inst Research and Ac Asst .... Mr. Stuart J. MUNRO
107 Director Opers Grad & Prof Studies .... Dr. Landy C. JOHNSON
06 Registrar .... Mr. David W. AALTO
13 Exec Dir Info Tech & Media Svcs .... Dr. Dawn M. THISTLE
15 Director of Human Resources/AAO .... Ms. Grace BLUNT
26 Executive Director of Communication .... Mr. Michael K. GUILFOYLE
29 Director of Alumni Relations .... Ms. Diane LASKA-NIXON
44 Director of Assumption Fund .... Mr. Timothy R. MARTIN
88 Director of Academic Support Center .... Dr. Allen A. BRUEHL
35 Dean of Campus Life .... Mr. Conway CAMPBELL
39 Assoc Dean Campus Life/Dir Res Life .... Mr. Joseph ZITO
41 Director of Athletics .... Mr. Nichloas A. SMITH
19 Director of Public Safety .... Mr. Steven B. CARL
23 Director of Health Services .... Ms. Elizabeth DREXLER-HINES
24 Director of Media Services .... Mr. Ted HALEY
37 Director of Financial Aid .... Mr. William C. SMITH
109 Director of Auxiliary Services .... Vacant
25 Director of Grant Development .... Dr. Landy C. JOHNSON
35 Dean of Students .... Mr. Robert G. RAVENELLE
28 Director Cross Cultural Center .... Ms. Beatriz PATINO
96 Director of Purchasing .... Ms. Gail M. RACINE
86 Exec Asst for Govt/Cmty Relations .... Mr. Daniel F. DITULLIO
36 Director of Career Services .... Ms. Nicole DIORIO
04 Exec Admin Asst to President .... Ms. Sharon A. MAHONEY

Babson College (E)

231 Forest Street, Babson Park MA 02457-0310
County: Norfolk FICE Identification: 002121
Unit ID: 164580
Telephone: (781) 235-1200 Carnegie Class: Spec/Bus
FAX Number: (781) 239-5231 Calendar System: Semester
URL: www.babson.edu
Established: 1919 Annual Undergrad Tuition & Fees: $46,784
Enrollment: 3,049 Coed
Affiliation or Control: Independent Non-Profit IRS Status: 501(c)3
Highest Offering: Master's
Program: Professional; Business Emphasis
Accreditation: EH, BUS

01 President .... Dr. Kerry MURPHY HEALEY
12 CEO Babson Global .... Dr. Shahid ANSARI
05 Acting Provost .... Dr. Gordon PRICHETT
10 Chief Administrative Officer .... Ms. Katherine CRAVEN
45 Chf of Stf/VP Strategic Initiatives .... Mr. Steve MOORE
18 AVP Facilities Mgmt & Contruction .... Ms. Janet FISHSTEIN
101 VP for Governance .... Ms. Jane EDMONDS
30 Vice President of Development .... Ms. Diana P. ZAIS
29 VP Alumni and Friends Network .... Ms. Carol J. HACKER
15 Vice Pres Human Resources .... Ms. Donna BONAPARTE
43 VP and General Counsel .... Mr. Jonathan MOLL
36 Dir Graduate Center for Career Dev .... Ms. Cheri PAULSON
06 Registrar .... Ms. Linda KEAN
36 Dir Ungrad Center for Career Dev .... Ms. Donna SOSHOWSKI
26 Sr Dir Institutional Communication .... Ms. Kelly LYNCH
26 Sr Dir Integrated Marketing .... Mr. Gene BEGIN
27 Director of Public Relations .... Mr. Michael CHMURA
13 Chief Information Officer .... Mr. Phillip KNUTEL
26 Chief Marketing Officer .... Ms. Sarah SYKORA
32 VP/Dean of Students .... Dr. Lawrence P. WARD
20 Dean of Faculty .... Ms. Carolyn HOTCHKISS
07 Dean Undergraduate Admissions .... Ms. Courtney MINDEN
97 Interim Dean Undergraduate School .... Dr. Henry DENEAULT
107 Dean of Babson Exec Education .... Ms. Elaine EISENMAN
37 Assoc Dean UG Sch/Dir Std Fin Svcs .... Ms. Melissa J. SHAAK
94 Exec Dir Ctr for Wms Entrep Lship .... Dr. Susan DUFFY
07 Director Graduate Admissions .... Ms. Petia WHITMORE
09 Director of Institutional Research .... Ms. Anne Marie DELANEY
96 Director of Business Services .... Ms. Teresa PITARO
28 Chief Diversity & Inclusion Officer .... Dr. Sadie BURTON-GOSS
58 Dean Graduate School .... Dr. Will LAMB
19 Director Public Safety .... Mr. James POLLARD
41 Director of Athletics .... Mr. Josh MACARTHUR

Bard College at Simon's Rock (F)

84 Alford Road, Great Barrington MA 01230-9702
County: Berkshire FICE Identification: 009645
Unit ID: 167792
Telephone: (413) 644-4400 Carnegie Class: Bac/Assoc
FAX Number: (413) 528-7365 Calendar System: Semester
URL: www.simons-rock.edu
Established: 1964 Annual Undergrad Tuition & Fees: $49,752
Enrollment: 329 Coed
Affiliation or Control: Independent Non-Profit IRS Status: 501(c)3
Highest Offering: Baccalaureate
Program: Liberal Arts And General
Accreditation: EH

01 President .... Dr. Leon BOTSTEIN
03 Executive Vice President .... Mr. Dimitri PAPADIMITRIOU
05 Vice President/Provost .... Dr. Peter LAIPSON
04 Asst to Vice President & Provost .... Ms. Lisa CLAYTON
32 Dean of the College .... Ms. Leslie DAVIDSON
20 Dean of Academic Affairs .... Dr. Anne O'DWYER
35 Dean of Student Affairs .... Mr. Robert GRAVES
10 Director of Finance/Admin/HR .... Mr. Bryant MORGAN
20 Assoc Dean of Academic Affairs .... Dr. Sue LYON
26 Director of Communications .... Ms. Kimberly ROCK
30 Chief Development/Advancement .... Vacant
07 Director of Admissions .... Ms. Chandra JOOS DEKOVEN
06 Registrar .... Ms. Heidi ROTHBERG
08 Library Director .... Mr. Brian MIKESELL
37 Director of Financial Aid .... Ms. Ellen MAMMEN
18 Director Physical Plant .... Mr. Steven CARIGNAN
38 Director Counseling Services .... Ms. Sharon HARTUNIAN
23 Director of Health Services .... Ms. Jodi TULLER
13 Director of Information Technology .... Ms. Janice GILDAWIE
19 Director of Security .... Mr. Kenneth GEREMIA
39 Director or Residence Life .... Ms. Cindy EFINGER
44 Director of Annual Fund/Alumni .... Mr. Richard MONTONE
41 Athletic Center Manager .... Mr. David COLLOPY
57 Division Head Arts .... Ms. Aimee MICHEL
81 Division Head Science/Math/Computer .... Dr. Eric KRAMER
83 Division Head Social Studies .... Dr. Asma ABBAS
79 Division Head Language/ Literature .... Dr. Colette VAN KERCKVOORDE

Bay Path University (G)

588 Longmeadow Street, Longmeadow MA 01106-2292
County: Hampden FICE Identification: 002122
Unit ID: 164632
Telephone: (413) 565-1000 Carnegie Class: Bac/A&S
FAX Number: (413) 565-1105 Calendar System: Semester
URL: www.baypath.edu
Established: 1897 Annual Undergrad Tuition & Fees: $31,785
Enrollment: 2,593 Female
Affiliation or Control: Independent Non-Profit IRS Status: 501(c)3
Highest Offering: Master's
Program: Liberal Arts And General; Teacher Preparatory; Professional
Accreditation: EH, #ARCPA, OT

01 President .... Dr. Carol A. LEARY
05 Vice Pres Academic Affairs/ Provost .... Dr. Melissa MORRISS-OLSON
10 VP Finance/Administrative Services .... Mr. Michael GIAMPIETRO
30 VP for Institutional Advancement .... Ms. Kathleen BOURQUE
45 Chief Strategy Officer Springfield .... Ms. Caron T. HOBIN
04 Assistant to the President .... Ms. Barbara KOCHON
21 Associate Vice President Finance .... Ms. Donna GUERTIN
46 Founding Dean of Research .... Ms. Ann DOBMEYER

12 Director of the Burlington Campus ....Ms. Amy CARMACK
12 Director of CMC Campus ....Ms. Laura HUNTER
26 Director of Communications ....Ms. Kathleen WROBLEWSKI
37 Director of Student Financial Svcs ....Ms. Stephanie KING
36 Exec Dir Career & Life Planning ....Ms. Laureen CIRILLO
08 Director of the Library ....Mr. Michael MORAN
06 Registrar ....Ms. Stephanie SANCHEZ
29 Dir of Alumni Relations ....Ms. Amanda SBRISCIA
23 Director of Health Services ....Vacant
19 Captain Campus Public Safety ....Mr. Danilo FELICIANO
15 Asst VP & Dir of Human Resources ....Ms. Kathleen HALPIN-ROBBINS
13 Mgr of Info Systems and Telecommun ...Mrs. Linda A. SIMONDS
18 Director Facilities/Campus Svcs ....Mr. Paul E. STANTON
13 Exec Director Info Technology ....Mr. Brian BASGEN
41 Director of Athletics ....Mr. Steven J. SMITH
88 Dir Masters of Sci Commun/Info Mgmt ....Mr. Richard BRIOTTA
32 Director of Student Life ....Ms. Natalie STOTHART
88 Sr Dir Bus Pgm Online/Ongrnd Spfld ....Vacant
88 Dir MBA Entrepr Thnkg/Innov Practic ....Mr. Mo SATTAR
88 Dir Grad Pgms Nonprofit Mgmt/Philan ....Mr. Jeffrey GREIM
20 Assistant Provost ....Ms. Kathleen MARTIN
88 Director of Health & Wellness ....Ms. Katie JONES
88 Dir Center for Teaching & Learning ....Dr. Charlotte BRIGGS
17 Director of Clinical Education ....Vacant
96 Exec Dir of Purchasing/Office Svcs ......Mr. Ted LETH-STEENSEN
102 Dir Foundation/Corporate Relations ....Ms. Janine MCVAY
53 Assoc Prov Sch Educ/Human/Hlth Sci ....Dr. Elizabeth FLEMING
88 Dean School Art/Science/Mgmt ....Dr. Thomas LOPER
107 Chief Learning Officer Springfield ....Dr. Vana NESPOR
88 Dean of Planning & Student Develop ....Mr. Dave YELLE
83 Found Dean Sch Health Sci/Hum Behav ....Vacant
88 Dir Occupational Therapy Program ....Dr. Lori VAUGHN
07 Dean Graduate Admissions ....Ms. Diane RANALDI
108 Exec Dir Academic Ops/Assessment ....Vacant
88 Deputy Chief Operational Effect ....Ms. Amanda GOULD
57 Director MFA Program ....Ms. Leanna JAMES BLACKWELL
53 Director ABA Program ....Dr. Susan AINSLEIGH
88 Director PA Program ....Ms. Theresa RIETHLE
44 Dir of Annual Giving & Alumni Rel ....Ms. Amanda SBRISCIA
88 Director of Cybersecurity Program ....Mr. Lawrence SNYDER

Bay State College (A)

122 Commonwealth Avenue, Boston MA 02116-2975
County: Suffolk FICE Identification: 003965
Unit ID: 164641
Telephone: (617) 217-9000 Carnegie Class: Assoc/PrivFP4
FAX Number: (617) 249-0400 Calendar System: Semester
URL: www.baystate.edu
Established: 1946 Annual Undergrad Tuition & Fees: $20,324
Enrollment: 1,108 Coed
Affiliation or Control: Proprietary IRS Status: Proprietary
Highest Offering: Baccalaureate
Program: Occupational; 2-Year Principally Bachelor's Creditable
Accreditation: EH, ADNUR, MAAB, PTAA

01 President ....Stacy SWEENEY
05 Vice President of Academic Affairs ....Dr. William CARROLL
10 Vice Pres Administration & Finance ....Meg TRANT
32 Vice Pres Student Affs/Dean Stdnts ....Kate O'HARA
84 Vice Pres Enrollment Management ....Senthil KUMAR
26 VP of Marketing/Communications ....Chip BERGSTROM
37 Director Student Financial Services ....Jeanne DEVANI
06 Registrar ....Mary Ann D'ENTREMONT
08 Librarian ....Jessica NEAVE
32 Director Student Success ....Sarah WOOD
07 Director of Admissions ....Vacant
21 Student Account Administrator ....Melissa PETERSEN
36 Director Career Services ....Tom CORRIGAN
38 Director Student Counseling ....Cheryl RAICHE
15 Director Human Resources ....Donna GAFFEY
35 Asst Dir Student Activities ....Kristin STAINE
18 Facilities Manager ....Marquis WALKER

Bay State College (B)

101 Industrial Park Road, Taunton MA 02780
Telephone: (617) 217-9829 Identification: 770927
Accreditation: &EH, MAAB

† Main campus is Bay State College in Boston, MA.

Becker College (C)

61 Sever Street, Worcester MA 01609-2165
County: Worcester FICE Identification: 002123
Unit ID: 164720
Telephone: (508) 791-9241 Carnegie Class: Bac/Diverse
FAX Number: (508) 831-7505 Calendar System: Semester
URL: www.becker.edu
Established: 1784 Annual Undergrad Tuition & Fees: $34,080
Enrollment: 2,021 Coed
Affiliation or Control: Independent Non-Profit IRS Status: 501(c)3
Highest Offering: Baccalaureate
Program: Occupational; Liberal Arts And General; Technical Emphasis
Accreditation: EH, ADNUR, NUR

01 President ....Dr. Robert E. JOHNSON
10 Senior Vice President & CFO ....Dr. David A. ELLIS
05 Provost & VP of Academic Affairs ....Dr. Leonidis IRAKLIOTIS
30 Vice President Advancement ....Ms. Veronica L. ROSA
32 Vice President of Student Affairs ....Dr. Nancy P. CRIMMIN
84 Vice Pres of Enrollment Management ....Mr. Kevin MAYNE
13 Chief Information Officer ....Ms. Patty L. PATRIA
15 Assoc Vice Pres of Human Resources .Mrs. Kathleen M. GARVEY
20 Assoc VP of Academic Affairs ....Dr. Elizabeth V. FULLER
41 Asst Vice Pres/Athletics Director ....Mr. Frank E. MILLERICK
11 Assistant VP for Administration ....Mr. Kenneth CAMERON
07 Dean of Admissions ....Mr. Michael PERRON
66 Dean of Nursing ....Dr. Judith M. PARE
88 Dean of Animal Studies ....Dr. Richard FRENCH
107 Dean of Accelerated & Prof Studies ....Ms. Colleen BIELITZ
06 Registrar ....Ms. Nikki ANDREWS
09 Director of Institutional Research ....Dr. Yun XIANG
88 Director for BA in Design ....Dr. Paul D. COTNOIR
27 Communications Director ....Ms. Sandy LASHIN-CUREWITZ
96 Director of Business Services ....Mr. Mike MONGEON
26 Director Marketing/Strategic Comm ....Ms. Amy DEAN
38 Director of Counseling ....Vacant
88 Director of Data Science ....Mr. Feyzi R. BAGIROV
36 Director of Career Services ....Mr. Richard DAVINO
37 Director Student Financial Aid ....Ms. Heather RULAND
39 Director Student Housing ....Mr. Joe LOMASTRO
88 Director of Enrollment Management ....Mr. Robert OUTERBRIDGE, JR.
88 Director of Clinical Services ....Dr. Julie BAILEY
08 Director of the Libraries ....Mr. Garrett EASTMAN
66 Director and Professor of Nursing ....Dr. Linda L. ESPER
29 Dir Alumni Relations & Annual Fund ....Ms. Elizabeth CULLEN
88 Director of Campus Activities ....Dr. Tracey PAKSTIS
88 Director of Creative Services ....Ms. Judith TONELLI-BROWN
53 Director of Education ....Ms. Nina MAZLOFF
88 Director of Equine Facilities ....Ms. Nicole EASTMAN
26 Dir Media Relation & Public Affairs ....Ms. Kimberly DUNBAR
23 Director of Health Services ....Ms. Catherine MELOCHE
89 Director of First Year Experience ....Ms. Sarah MOSIER
106 Dir of Online and In-House Training ....Mr. Paul CHASE
88 Director of Program Development ....Mr. Timothy LOEW
88 Director of Student Accounts ....Mr. Alexander HARTMAN
35 Dir of Student and Admin Services ....Ms. Sheila SOLOPERTO
04 Special Asst to President ....Ms. Anne A. SROKA
21 Controller ....Mr. Richard NAYLOR
19 Campus Police Chief ....Mr. David J. BOUSQUET

Benjamin Franklin Institute of Technology (D)

41 Berkeley Street, Boston MA 02116-6296
County: Suffolk FICE Identification: 002151
Unit ID: 165884
Telephone: (617) 588-1368 Carnegie Class: Spec/Tech
FAX Number: (617) 778-6499 Calendar System: Semester
URL: www.bfit.edu
Established: 1908 Annual Undergrad Tuition & Fees: $16,950
Enrollment: 518 Coed
Affiliation or Control: Independent Non-Profit IRS Status: 501(c)3
Highest Offering: Baccalaureate
Program: Occupational; 2-Year Principally Bachelor's Creditable; Technical Emphasis
Accreditation: EH, OPD

01 President ....Anthony BENOIT
05 Dean of Academic Affairs ....Brian BICKNELL
32 Dean of Student Services ....Mike BOSCO
10 Chief Financial & Admin Officer ....Keith DROPKIN
06 Registrar ....James KLASEN
08 Librarian ....Sharon B. BONK
07 Associate Dean of Admissions ....Marvin LOISEAU
30 Chief Development Officer ....Anne CADEMENOS
20 Director of Student Success ....Ashley LINKER
09 Director of Institutional Research ....James KLASEN
15 Director Human Resources ....Shelley DROPKIN
19 Director of Facilities ....Myftar MYRTAJ
36 Director of Career Services ....Phyllis MOLTA
37 Director Student Financial Services ....Ozie RATCLIFF
04 Administrative Asst to President ....Carole ANDREOTTI

Bentley University (E)

175 Forest Street, Waltham MA 02452-4705
County: Middlesex FICE Identification: 002124
Unit ID: 164739
Telephone: (781) 891-2000 Carnegie Class: Master's L
FAX Number: (781) 891-2569 Calendar System: Semester
URL: www.bentley.edu
Established: 1917 Annual Undergrad Tuition & Fees: $44,085
Enrollment: 5,568 Coed
Affiliation or Control: Independent Non-Profit IRS Status: 501(c)3
Highest Offering: Doctorate
Program: Liberal Arts And General; Professional; Business Emphasis
Accreditation: EH, BUS, BUSA

01 President ....Ms. Gloria C. LARSON
43 General Counsel ....Ms. Judith MALONE
102 Director Foundation Relations ....Mr. Paul CARBERRY
05 VP Academic Affairs/Provost ....Dr. Michael PAGE
10 VP Business/Finance/Treas ....Mr. Kenneth CODY
30 VP University Advancement ....Mr. William TORREY
32 VP Student Affairs ....Dr. J. Andrew SHEPARDSON
13 Chief Information Officer ....Vacant
84 VP Enrollment Management ....Ms. Joann MCKENNA
49 Dean of Arts and Sciences ....Dr. Daniel EVERETT
50 Dean of Business/Grad Sch ....Dr. Roy WIGGINS
20 Assoc Dean for Academic Affairs ....Dr. Vicki LAFARGE
88 Assoc Dean Academic Services ....Ms. Catherina CARLSON
58 Asst Dean/Director GSAS ....Mr. George THOMPSON
29 Exec Director of Adv Relations ....Ms. Leigh GASPAR
26 Chief Marketing Officer ....Vacant
15 Assoc VP of Human Resources ....Ms. Ann DEXTER
11 Assoc Dean of Business Programs ....Dr. Dorothy FELDMANN
21 Controller Financial Operations ....Ms. Nancy ANTUNES
06 Registrar ....Ms. Patricia ROGERS
22 Spec Advisor to the Pres/Ombudsman ....Dr. Earl AVERY
38 Assoc Dean/Dir Couns & Student Dev ....Vacant
41 Director of Athletics ....Mr. Robert DEFELICE
09 Director of Institutional Research ....Ms. Kelly GIARDULLO
37 Exec Dir Enroll Mgmt & Fin Assist ....Ms. Donna KENDALL
39 Asst Dean Residential Center ....Mr. John PIGA
90 Dir Academic Tech/Library/Rsch Svcs ....Ms. Laurie SUTCH
31 Director Service-Learning Center ....Dr. Jonathon WHITE
19 Executive Director of Public Safety ....Mr. Ernest LEFFLER
27 Director Public & Media Relations ....Ms. Michele WALSH
36 Exec Dir Corp Rel & Career Services ....Ms. Susan BRENNAN
23 Asst Dean/Dir Health & Wellness ....Ms. Geraldine TAYLOR
25 Director of Sponsored Programs ....Vacant
07 Director Undergrad Admission ....Vacant
07 Asst Dean/Dir of Grad Admission ....Ms. Sharon HILL
88 Director of MBA Programs ....Dr. David SCHWARZKOPF
18 Director Facilities Management ....Mr. Thomas KANE
96 Director Purchasing/Contract Svcs ....Ms. Julianne BRITT
44 Sr Assoc Dir Annual Giving ....Mr. Brian READ
35 Director Student Activities ....Ms. Nicole CHABOT-WIEFERICH
04 Administrative Asst to President ....Ms. Katherine CONNOLLY
104 Director Study Abroad ....Ms. Natalie SCHLEGEL

Berklee College of Music (F)

1140 Boylston Street, Boston MA 02215-3693
County: Suffolk FICE Identification: 002126
Unit ID: 164748
Telephone: (617) 266-1400 Carnegie Class: Spec/Arts
FAX Number: (617) 247-6878 Calendar System: Semester
URL: www.berklee.edu
Established: 1945 Annual Undergrad Tuition & Fees: $40,082
Enrollment: 4,908 Coed
Affiliation or Control: Independent Non-Profit IRS Status: 501(c)3
Highest Offering: Master's
Program: Music Emphasis
Accreditation: EH

01 President ....Roger H. BROWN
100 Chief of Staff ....Melissa HOWE
05 Sr Vice Pres Academic Affs/Provost ....Lawrence J. SIMPSON
32 Vice Pres Student Affs/Dean Stdnts ....Betsy NEWMAN
102 Sr VP Institutional Advancement ....Cindy ALBERT LINK
10 Chief Financial Officer ....Richard M. HISEY
13 Sr VP Innovation/Strategy/Tech ....David MASH
84 Vice President Enrollment ....Mark CAMPBELL
14 Assoc VP Information Technology ....Scott V. STREET
15 Vice Pres Human Res/Diversity/Incl ....Christine M. CONNORS
88 Assoc Ed Outreach/Ex Dir BC Music ....J. Curtis WARNER, JR.
88 Vice President Global Initiatives ....Guillermo CISNEROS
20 VP Academic Affs/Vice Provost ....S. Jay KENNEDY
26 Asst VP for External Affairs ....Rob HAYES
88 Dean of Profes Performance Division ....Matt MARVUGLIO
88 Dean Prof Writing Div/Music Tech ....Kari JUUSELA
53 Dean of Prof Education Division ....Darla S. HANLEY
06 Registrar ....Michael HAGERTY
39 Director of Housing ....Marguerite SHARKEY
37 Asst VP Student Financial Services ....Tod OLIVIERE
38 Director of Counseling ....Toni BLACKWELL
07 Dean of Admissions ....Damien S. BRACKEN
36 Director Career Development Center ....Peter SPELLMAN
18 Senior Director of Physical Plant ....Kevin ANDERSON

Boston Architectural College (G)

320 Newbury Street, Boston MA 02115-2795
County: Suffolk FICE Identification: 003966
Unit ID: 164872
Telephone: (617) 262-5000 Carnegie Class: Spec/Arts
FAX Number: (617) 585-0111 Calendar System: Semester
URL: www.the-bac.edu
Established: 1889 Annual Undergrad Tuition & Fees: $20,666
Enrollment: 754 Coed
Affiliation or Control: Independent Non-Profit IRS Status: 501(c)3
Highest Offering: Master's
Program: Professional; Technical Emphasis
Accreditation: EH, CIDA, LSAR

01 Acting President ....Ms. Julia HALEVY
05 Provost ....Ms. Julia HALEVY
10 Vice President for Finance/Admin ....Ms. Kathleen C. ROOD
30 VP Institutional Advancement ....Mr. Evan GALLIVAN
18 Associate VP of Facilities ....Mr. Arthur BYERS
88 Dean of School of Interior Design ....Mr. Crandon GUSTAFSON
88 Dean School of Landscape Architect ....Ms. Maria BELLALTA
88 Dean School of Design Studies ....Mr. Donald HUNSICKER
48 Dean School of Architecture ....Ms. Karen L. NELSON
88 Dean & Faculty of Practice ....Mr. Len CHARNEY
32 Assoc Vice Pres/Dean of Students .....Mr. Richard M. GRISWOLD
13 Chief Information Officer ....Mr. Timothy OGAWA
88 Dir of Master's Thesis Arch ....Mr. Ian TABERNER
88 Director of Design Media ....Mr. Aidan ACKERMAN
88 Director of Media Arts ....Mr. Luis MONTALVO

88 Director of Distance M Arch ... Mr. Tom PARKS
08 Library Director ... Ms. Susan A. LEWIS
06 Assoc Registrar ... Mr. Joseph DIDONATO
07 VP Enrollment & Student Fin Svcs ... Mr. James RYAN
11 Dir of Administrative Operations ... Ms. Patti VAUGHN
88 Dean of Advising Services ... Ms. Rebecca CHABOT-WIEFERICH
88 Director of Foundation Studies ... Mr. Lee PETERS
106 Director of Distance MArch ... Mr. Michael WOLFSON
88 Director of Practice Instruction ... Mr. Ben PETERSON
88 Director of the Landscape Institute ... Ms. Heather HEIMARCK
58 Dean Grad Studies & Dir of Liberal ... Ms. Diana RAMIREZ-JASSO
35 Dean of Student Svcs & Registrar ... Mrs. Bethany FANTASIA
88 Exec Asst Governance & Development ... Ms. Lauren GRANT
15 Director of Human Resources ... Ms. Jondelle DEVEAUX
26 Enrollment Marketing Director ... Ms. Alice LIN
29 Alumni & Development Officer ... Ms. Catalina IANETTA

Boston Baptist College (A)

950 Metropolitan Avenue, Boston MA 02136-4000

County: Suffolk FICE Identification: 032483
Unit ID: 164614
Telephone: (617) 364-3510 Carnegie Class: Spec/Faith
FAX Number: (775) 245-1498 Calendar System: Semester
URL: www.boston.edu
Established: 1976 Annual Undergrad Tuition & Fees: $13,500
Enrollment: 98 Coed
Affiliation or Control: Baptist IRS Status: 501(c)3
Highest Offering: Baccalaureate
Program: Occupational; Religious Emphasis
Accreditation: TRACS

01 President ... Rev. David V. MELTON
05 Vice President for Academics ... Rev. Kenneth D. GILLMING
32 Vice President for Student Affairs ... Vacant
11 Vice President for Operations ... Mr. Randall WARD
84 Director of Enrollment Services ... Mrs. Wendi WEBBER
07 Director of Admissions ... Ms. Brianna VILLANUEVA
08 Head Librarian ... Mr. Fred TATRO

Boston College (B)

140 Commonwealth Avenue, Chestnut Hill MA 02467-3934

County: Middlesex FICE Identification: 002128
Unit ID: 164924
Telephone: (617) 552-8000 Carnegie Class: RU/H
FAX Number: (617) 552-8828 Calendar System: Semester
URL: www.bc.edu
Established: 1863 Annual Undergrad Tuition & Fees: $48,540
Enrollment: 14,125 Coed
Affiliation or Control: Roman Catholic IRS Status: 501(c)3
Highest Offering: Doctorate
Program: Occupational; Liberal Arts And General; Teacher Preparatory; Professional
Accreditation: EH, ANEST, BUS, COPSY, LAW, NURSE, SW, TEAC, THEOL

01 President ... Rev. William P. LEAHY, SJ
00 Chancellor ... Rev. J. Donald MONAN, SJ
05 Provost & Dean of Faculties ... Dr. David QUIGLEY
03 Executive Vice President ... Mr. Michael J. LOCHHEAD
26 Senior Vice President ... Dr. James P. MCINTYRE
30 Senior VP University Advancement ... Mr. James J. HUSSON
04 Executive Assistant to President ... Mr. Kevin J. SHEA
10 Financial Vice President/Treasurer ... Mr. Peter C. MCKENZIE
101 Vice President/University Secretary . Rev. Terrence P. DEVINO, SJ
32 Vice Pres Student Affairs ... Dr. Barbara JONES
15 Vice President for Human Resources ... Mr. David TRAINOR
13 Vice Pres Information Technology ... Mr. Michael J. BOURQUE
88 Vice Pres Univ Mission & Ministry ... Rev. John T. BUTLER, SJ
86 Vice Pres Govt/Community Affairs ... Mr. Thomas J. KEADY
18 Vice Pres Facilities Management ... Mr. Daniel F. BOURQUE
45 Vice Pres Planning & Assessment ... Dr. Kelli J. ARMSTRONG
20 Vice Provost for Undergrad Affairs ... Vacant
46 Vice Provost for Research ... Dr. Thomas CHILES
20 Vice Provost for Faculties ... Dr. Patricia DE LEEUW
44 Assoc VP Development ... Ms. Beth MCDERMOTT
20 Assoc Vice Provost Undergrad Acad ... Dr. J. Joseph BURNS
18 Assoc VP Capital Projects ... Ms. Mary S. NARDONE
29 Associate VP Alumni Relations ... Ms. Joy MOORE
16 Assoc VP Human Resources ... Mr. Robert J. LEWIS
21 Assoc VP Finance ... Mr. John D. BURKE
109 Assoc VP Auxiliary Services ... Ms. Patricia A. BANDO
49 Int Dean College Arts & Sciences ... Rev. Gregory KALSCHEUR, SJ
87 Int Dn Col Adv Stds/Summer Session ... Rev. James R. BURNS
53 Dean School of Education ... Ms. Maureen E. KENNY
61 Dean Law School ... Mr. Vincent D. ROUGEAU
50 Dean School of Management ... Dr. Andrew C. BOYNTON
66 Dean of School of Nursing ... Dr. Susan GENNARO
70 Dean Grad School of Social Work ... Dr. Alberto A. GODENZI
88 Dean School of Theology & Ministry ... Rev. Mark S. MASSA, SJ
84 Dean of Enrollment Management ... Mr. Robert S. LAY
35 Assoc VP Student Affairs Engagement ... Dr. Katherine G. O'DAIR
08 University Librarian ... Dr. Thomas WALL
28 Exec Dir Institutional Diversity ... Mr. Richard P. JEFFERSON
06 Exec Director Student Services ... Dr. Louise M. LONABOCKER
07 Director of Admission ... Mr. John L. MAHONEY, JR.
26 Exec Dir/Special Asst to Pres/Mktg ... Mr. Ben BIRNBAUM
27 Dir Office of News & Public Affairs ... Mr. John B. DUNN
102 Exec Director School Development ... Mrs. Ginger K. SAARIAHO
41 Director Athletic Department ... Dr. Brad BATES
36 Assoc VP Career Center ... Mr. Joseph DUPONT
42 Director Campus Ministry ... Rev. Anthony PENNA
31 Director of Community Affairs ... Mr. William R. MILLS
38 Assoc VP Univ Counseling Svcs ... Dr. Thomas P. MCGUINNESS
37 Director Financial Aid ... Ms. Mary S. MCGRANAHAN
23 Director Health Services ... Dr. Thomas I. NARY
39 Assoc VP Residential Life ... Mr. George A. AREY
25 Dir Pre-Award Admin Sponsored Pgms ... Mrs. Sharon COMVALIUS-GODDARD
25 Dir Post-Award Admin Sponsored Pgms ... Ms. Susan ZIPKIN
19 Dir Public Safety/Chief of Police ... Mr. John M. KING
40 Director Bookstore ... Mr. Robert STEWART
43 General Counsel ... Mr. Joseph M. HERLIHY
24 Director Media Technology Services ... Mr. David CORKUM
85 Director International Programs ... Dr. Nick GOZIK
88 Director Presidential Scholars Pgms .. Rev. James F. KEENAN, SJ
93 Director AHANA Student Programs ... Dr. Ines MATURANA SENDOYA
86 Director Governmental Relations ... Ms. Jeanne LEVESQUE
96 Director Procurement Services ... Mr. Paul MCGOWAN
09 Director Inst Research & Assessment ... Dr. Jessica A. GREENE
88 Exec Dir Irish Pgms & Institute ... Vacant

The Boston Conservatory (C)

8 The Fenway, Boston MA 02215-4006

County: Suffolk FICE Identification: 002129
Unit ID: 164933
Telephone: (617) 536-6340 Carnegie Class: Spec/Arts
FAX Number: (617) 912-9101 Calendar System: Semester
URL: www.bostonconservatory.edu
Established: 1867 Annual Undergrad Tuition & Fees: $40,900
Enrollment: 730 Coed
Affiliation or Control: Independent Non-Profit IRS Status: 501(c)3
Highest Offering: Master's
Program: Teacher Preparatory; Professional; Music Emphasis
Accreditation: EH, MUS

01 President ... Mr. Richard ORTNER
05 VP Academic Affairs/Dean/CAO ... Dr. Joe BENNETT
11 VP for Finance and Planning ... Mr. Eric NORMAN
84 Vice Pres Enrollment/Student Svcs ... Mr. Terry WHITTUM
30 VP for Institutional Advancement ... Ms. Leslie JACOBSON KAYE
10 Director of Finance ... Ms. Leigh Ann LUETZEN
32 Dean of Students ... Dr. Christopher READE
20 Assoc Dean Academic Operations ... Dr. James O'DELL
35 Assoc Dean for Student Affairs ... Mr. Felix FERNANDEZ PIZZI
07 Director of Admissions ... Mr. Brian CALHOON
64 Director Music Division ... Dr. Abra BUSH
88 Director Dance Division ... Ms. Cathy YOUNG
57 Director Theater Division ... Mr. Neil DONOHOE
06 Registrar ... Ms. Florence BERGERON
37 Director Student Financial Aid ... Ms. Nicole BRENNAN
08 Library Director ... Ms. Jennifer HUNT
13 Director of Information Technology ... Mr. Bob XAVIER
18 Director Facilities ... Mr. Christopher HAYDEN
26 Director Marketing & Communications ... Ms. Andrea DICOCCO
85 Director International Student Svcs ... Mr. Gordon HOMANN
29 Dir of Alumni and Parent Relations ... Vacant
26 Director of External Relations ... Ms. Kim HAACK
15 Human Resource Manager ... Ms. Carrie BOURQUE
16 Manager HR Benefits ... Mr. Lee AVALLONE

Boston Graduate School of Psychoanalysis (D)

1581 Beacon Street, Brookline MA 02446-4602

County: Norfolk FICE Identification: 031943
Unit ID: 164915
Telephone: (617) 277-3915 Carnegie Class: Spec/Health
FAX Number: (617) 277-0312 Calendar System: Semester
URL: www.bgsp.edu
Established: 1973 Annual Graduate Tuition & Fees: $24,585
Enrollment: 136 Coed
Affiliation or Control: Independent Non-Profit IRS Status: 501(c)3
Highest Offering: Doctorate; No Undergraduates
Program: Professional
Accreditation: EH

01 President ... Dr. Jane SYNDER
10 Vice President Finance ... Dr. Carol PANETTA
58 Dean of Graduate Studies ... Dr. Lynn PERLMAN
07 Director of Admissions ... Dr. Jill SOLOMON
26 Director of Marketing ... Ms. Priscilla BENNETT
06 Registrar ... Ms. Allison WILLIAMS
37 Director of Financial Aid ... Ms. Stephanie WOOLBERT
21 Controller ... Ms. Gayle DOLAN
08 Head Librarian ... Ms. Amy COHEN-ROSE
09 Director of the Center for Research ... Dr. Stephen SOLDZ

Boston University (E)

One Silber Way, Boston MA 02215-1700

County: Suffolk FICE Identification: 002130
Unit ID: 164988
Telephone: (617) 353-2000 Carnegie Class: RU/VH
FAX Number: (617) 353-2053 Calendar System: Semester
URL: www.bu.edu
Established: 1839 Annual Undergrad Tuition & Fees: $48,436
Enrollment: 33,119 Coed
Affiliation or Control: Independent Non-Profit IRS Status: 501(c)3
Highest Offering: Doctorate
Program: Liberal Arts And General; Teacher Preparatory; Professional
Accreditation: EH, #ARCPA, BUS, CAATE, CACREP, CEA, CLPSY, DENT, DIETD, DIETI, ENG, FEPAC, HSA, IPSY, LAW, MED, MUS, OT, PH, PTA, SP, SW, THEOL

01 President ... Robert A. BROWN
05 University Provost ... Jean MORRISON
17 Provost Medical Campus ... Karen H. ANTMAN
100 VP & Chief of Staff to President ... Douglas SEARS
49 Dean Col/Grad Sch Arts & Sciences ... Anne E. CUDD
60 Dean College of Communication ... Thomas FIEDLER
53 Dean School of Education ... Hardin L. COLEMAN
54 Dean College of Engineering ... Kenneth R. LUTCHEN
57 Interim Dean College of Fine Arts ... Lynne ALLEN
97 Dean College General Studies ... Natalie MCKNIGHT
61 Dean of School of Law ... Maureen A. O'ROURKE
50 Dean Questrom School of Business ... Kenneth W. FREEMAN
55 Interim Dean Met Col/Ext Educ ... Tanya ZLATEVA
76 Dean SAR Health & Rehab Science ... Christopher A. MOORE
88 Dean School of Hospitality Admin ... Arun UPNEJA
70 Dean School of Social Work ... Gail STEKETEE
73 Dean School of Theology ... Mary E. MOORE
63 Dean School of Medicine ... Karen H. ANTMAN
52 Dean Sch of Dental Medicine ... Jeffery W. HUTTER
69 Dean School of Public Health ... Sandro GALEA
32 Dean of Students ... Kenneth ELMORE
42 Dean of Marsh Chapel ... Robert A. HILL
88 VP/Assoc Provost Global Programs ... Willis G. WANG
84 VP Enrollment & Student Affairs ... Laurie POHL
46 VP & Assoc Provost Research ... Gloria WATERS
20 Assoc Provost Graduate Affairs ... Timothy BARBARI
20 Assoc Provost Strategic Initiatives ... Nicole HAWKES
20 Assoc Provost Undergraduate Affairs ... Elizabeth LOIZEAUX
20 Assoc Provost for Faculty Affairs ... Julie SANDELL
18 Senior Vice President Operations ... Gary W. NICKSA
10 Senior Vice Pres/CFO & Treasurer ... Martin J. HOWARD
26 Senior VP Marketing & Comm ... Stephen P. BURGAY
43 Sr VP/General Counsel & Board Secy ... Todd L C. KLIPP
30 Senior VP Devel/Alumni Relations ... Scott G. NICHOLS
90 VP Information Systems & Technology ... Tracy SCHROEDER
45 Vice President Budget and Planning ... Derek HOWE
88 Associate VP Budget & Planning ... Ines GARRANT
109 Vice President Auxiliary Services ... Peter SMOKOWSKI
86 Vice Pres Government & Cmty Rels ... Robert DONAHUE
88 Vice President Federal Relations ... Jennifer GRODSKY
11 Vice Pres Administrative Services ... Peter FIEDLER
41 Director of Athletics ... Drew MARROCHELLO
06 Assistant VP & Registrar ... Jeffrey VON MUNKWITZ-SMITH
07 Assoc VP/Exec Dir Undergraduate Adm ... Kelly WALTER
08 University Librarian ... Robert HUDSON
09 Asst VP Institutional Research ... Melanie MADAIO-O'BRIEN
09 Director Institutional Research ... Linette DECARIE
15 Chief Human Resouce Officer ... Diane P. TUCKER
19 Chief of Police ... Thomas G. ROBBINS
20 Assoc Provost Budget & Planning ... Christopher GOSS
23 Interim Dir Student Health Services ... Judy PLATT
27 VP Strategic Communication ... Amy HOOK
28 Director Thurman Center ... Katherine KENNEDY
29 VP Alumni Relations ... Steven A. HALL
35 Assoc VP Enroll & Student Affairs ... Denise MOONEY
35 Asst Dean & Exec Dir Student Affair ... John BATTAGLINO
35 Assoc Director Student Activities ... Raul FERNANDEZ
36 Director Career Planning Services ... Kimberley DELGIZZO
37 Assoc VP/Exec Dir Financial Assist ... Christine MCGUIRE
39 Exec Director of Housing/Dining ... Marc ROBILLARD
44 Assistant VP Annual Giving ... Daniel ALLENBY
44 Assoc VP Sch-based Dev & Alum Rels ... Adam K. WISE
46 VP Research Finance & Operations ... Vacant
68 Exec Director Physical Education ... Timothy MOORE
85 Director Intl Student/Scholars Ofc ... Jeanne KELLEY
87 Assistant Dean Summer Term ... Donna SHEA
96 Exec Dir Sourcing/Procurement ... Walter WICKERSHAM
88 Chief Investment Officer ... Lila HUNNEWELL
43 General Counsel ... Erika GEETTER

Brandeis University (F)

415 South Street, Waltham MA 02453

County: Middlesex FICE Identification: 002133
Unit ID: 165015
Telephone: (781) 736-2000 Carnegie Class: RU/VH
FAX Number: (781) 736-8699 Calendar System: Semester
URL: www.brandeis.edu
Established: 1948 Annual Undergrad Tuition & Fees: $49,298
Enrollment: 5,945 Coed
Affiliation or Control: Independent Non-Profit IRS Status: 501(c)3
Highest Offering: Doctorate
Program: Liberal Arts And General; Professional
Accreditation: EH, BUS

01 Interim President ... Dr. Lisa LYNCH
05 Interim Provost ... Dr. Irving R. EPSTEIN
11 Senior Vice President and COO ... Mr. Steve MANOS
03 Sr Vice Pres/Spec Advisor to Pres ... Dr. Steve GOLDSTEIN
30 Sr Vice Pres Inst Advancement ... Ms. Nancy K. WINSHIP
84 Sr Vice Pres for Students/Enroll ... Mr. Andrew FLAGEL
43 Sr VP and General Counsel ... Mr. Steven S. LOCKE
88 Chief Legal Officer ... Mr. David A. BUNIS
10 Sr VP for Finance and CFO ... Ms. Marianne CWALINA
13 CIO/Vice Provost Univ Librarian ... Mr. John UNSWORTH
18 Vice Pres for Operations ... Mr. James GRAY
15 Int Vice Pres Human Resources ... Ms. Michelle SCICHILONE
18 VP for Capital Projects ... Mr. Dan FELDMAN
49 Dean of Arts & Sciences ... Dr. Susan J. BIRREN

70 Int Dn Heller Sch Social Pol & Mgt .... Dr. Marty KRAUSS
50 Dean International Business School .... Dr. Bruce R. MAGID
06 University Registrar ....Dr. Mark S. HEWITT

Cambridge College (A)

1000 Massachusetts Avenue, Cambridge MA 02138-5304
County: Middlesex FICE Identification: 021829
Unit ID: 165167
Telephone: (800) 877-4723 Carnegie Class: Master's L
FAX Number: (617) 349-3545 Calendar System: Trimester
URL: www.cambridgecollege.edu
Established: 1971 Annual Undergrad Tuition & Fees: $14,004
Enrollment: 2,841 Coed
Affiliation or Control: Independent Non-Profit IRS Status: 501(c)3
Highest Offering: Doctorate
Program: Liberal Arts And General; Professional
Accreditation: EH, TEAC

01 President .... Deborah JACKSON
05 Provost ....Vacant
10 CFO/Vice President of Finance .... John SPINARD
43 Acting General Counsel .... Judith SIZER
30 Vice Pres Institutional Advancement .... Carson BERGLUND
15 Director of Human Resources .... Lauretta SIGGERS
37 Director of Financial Aid .... Frank LAUDER
21 Controller .... Lynn WOOD
06 Registrar .... Amy CAVALIER
84 Vice Pres of Enrollment Management .... Robin PEEVEY
90 Director of Information Technology .... Achal KHATRI
18 Director of Business Operations ....Vacant
12 Director of Lawrence MA .... Joseph MIGLIO
12 Director Springfield MA .... Teresa (Terrie) FORTE
12 Director of Southern California .... Rita CLEMONS
12 Director of Puerto Rico .... Dr. Jose R. IRIZARRY
12 Director of Memphis TN .... Jeremy WHITTAKER
12 Director of Augusta GA .... Sharlotte EVANS
20 Dean Undergraduate .... James LEE
26 Dir of Mktg/Communications & PR .... Jacqueline CONRAD
86 Dir of Govt/Bus & Comm Partnership .... Phillip PAGE
04 Administrative Asst to President .... Robyn CARROLL
07 Director of Admissions .... Carol LOMBARDI
09 Associate Provost .... Mark ROTONDO
102 Dir Foundation/Corporate Relations .... Sonnya ESPINAL
29 Dir Alumni Relations/Annual Fund .... Kevin DRISCOLL
32 Dean Student Affairs/Student Life .... Regina ROBINSON
50 Dean School of Management .... Mary Ann JOSEPH
53 Dean School of Education .... Dr. Sheila WRIGHT
54 Dean School of Psychology .... Dr. Niti SETH

Clark University (B)

950 Main Street, Worcester MA 01610-1477
County: Worcester FICE Identification: 002139
Unit ID: 165334
Telephone: (508) 793-7711 Carnegie Class: RU/H
FAX Number: (508) 793-7780 Calendar System: Semester
URL: www.clarku.edu
Established: 1887 Annual Undergrad Tuition & Fees: $41,940
Enrollment: 3,423 Coed
Affiliation or Control: Independent Non-Profit IRS Status: 501(c)3
Highest Offering: Doctorate
Program: Liberal Arts And General; Teacher Preparatory; Professional
Accreditation: EH, BUS, CLPSY

01 President .... Dr. David P. ANGEL
03 Executive Vice President .... Ms. Julie L. DOLAN
10 Chief Investment Officer .... Mr. James E. COLLINS
05 Provost & Vice Pres Academic Affs .... Dr. Davis BAIRD
30 Vice Pres University Advancement .... Mr. Jeffrey GILLOOLY
26 Vice Pres Marketing & Communication .... Ms. Paula DAVID
13 Vice Pres for Information Tech/CIO .... Ms. Pennie TURGEON
86 VP Government/Cmty Affs/Campus Svcs .... Mr. John FOLEY
32 Interim Dean of Students .... Dr. Kevin MCKENNA
46 Assoc Provost/Dean of Research .... Dr. Nancy BUDWIG
58 Assoc Provost/Dean Graduate Studies .... Dr. William FISHER
49 Assoc Provost/Dean of College .... Dr. Matthew MALSKY
88 Interim Dir Academic Advisement .... Ms. Jennifer PLANTE
50 Dean Graduate School Mgmt .... Dr. Catherine USOFF
07 Dean of Admissions & Financial Aid .... Mr. Donald HONEMAN
37 Director of Financial Aid .... Ms. Mary Ellen SEVERANCE
08 University Librarian .... Dr. Gwendolynne ARTHUR
21 Controller .... Ms. Katherine CANNON
36 Director Career Services .... Ms. Victoria COX-LANYON
06 Registrar .... Ms. Rebecca HUNTER
15 Dir of Human Resources/Affirm Act .... Ms. Jacqueline CAPOMACCHIO
18 Director of Physical Plant ....Vacant
41 Director of Athletics .... Ms. Trish CRONIN
19 Chief of Campus Police .... Mr. Stephen P. GOULET
23 Director of Health Services .... Ms. Robin MCNALLY
28 Chief Officer Diversity/Inclusion .... Dr. Betsy HUANG
04 Assistant to the President .... Ms. Joanne MILLER
21 Business Manager .... Mr. Paul WYKES
09 Manager of Institutional Research .... Mr. Jeffrey HIMMELBERGER
104 Director Study Abroad .... Ms. Adriane VAN GILS-PIERCE
39 Director Student Housing .... Mr. Adam KEYES
44 Director Annual or Planned Giving .... Ms. Lindsay ALLEN

College of the Holy Cross (C)

1 College Street, Worcester MA 01610-2322
County: Worcester FICE Identification: 002141
Unit ID: 166124
Telephone: (508) 793-2011 Carnegie Class: Bac/A&S
FAX Number: (508) 793-3030 Calendar System: Semester
URL: www.holycross.edu
Established: 1843 Annual Undergrad Tuition & Fees: $47,176
Enrollment: 2,904 Coed
Affiliation or Control: Roman Catholic IRS Status: 501(c)3
Highest Offering: Baccalaureate
Program: Liberal Arts And General
Accreditation: EH, THEA

01 President .... Rev. Philip L. BOROUGHS, SJ
03 Senior Vice President .... Dr. Frank VELLACCIO
05 VP Academic Affairs/Dean of Col .... Dr. Margaret FREIJE
10 VP Admin & Finance/Treasurer .... Ms. Dottie HAUVER
88 Chief Investment Officer .... Mr. Timothy JARRY
32 VP Student Affairs/Dean of Students .... Ms. Jacqueline D. PETERSON
30 VP for Development/Alumni Relations .... Ms. Tracy BARLOK
42 Vice President for Mission .... Rev. Paul F. HARMAN, SJ
20 Associate Dean of the College .... Mr. Ronald JARRET
21 Director of Finance/Asst Treasurer ....Vacant
06 Registrar .... Ms. Patricia RING
07 Director of Admissions .... Ms. Ann B. MCDERMOTT
08 Interim Dir of Library Services .... Ms. Karen REILLY
37 Director of Financial Aid .... Ms. Lynne M. MYERS
25 Director of Sponsored Research .... Ms. Stacy RISEMAN
42 Director Ofc of College Chaplains .... Ms. Marybeth KEARNS-BARRETT
71 Director Ctr Interdisc/Spec Studies .... Dr. Richard E. MATLAK
36 Director of Career Planning .... Ms. Amy MURPHY
13 Director Information Tech Services .... Ms. Ellen J. KEOHANE
26 Chief Marketing & Comm Officer .... Ms. Ellen RYDER
29 Director of Alumni Relations .... Ms. Kristyn M. DYER
19 Director of Public Safety .... Mr. Robert HART
35 Director of Campus Center .... Mr. Jeremiah O'CONNOR
15 Director of Employee Relations .... Ms. Donna C. WRENN
18 Director of Physical Plant .... Mr. Scott M. MERRILL
41 Director of Athletics .... Mr. Nathan PINE
21 Controller .... Mr. Charles F. ESTAPHAN
45 Director of Planning .... Ms. Judy A. HANNUM
38 Director Counseling Center .... Dr. Paul GALVINHILL
23 Director Student Health Services .... Ms. Martha SULLIVAN
11 Director Administrative Services .... Mr. William J. CONLEY
96 Manager of Purchasing .... Ms. Joan E. ANDERSON
09 Ofc of Assessment/Research .... Ms. Denise BELL
86 Dir of Govt/Cmty Relations .... Mr. Jamie D. HOAG
43 General Counsel ....Vacant
88 Dir Ofc of Strategic Initiatives .... Dr. Charles WEISS

College of Our Lady of the Elms (D)

291 Springfield Street, Chicopee MA 01013-2839
County: Hampden FICE Identification: 002140
Unit ID: 167394
Telephone: (413) 594-2761 Carnegie Class: Bac/Diverse
FAX Number: (413) 592-4871 Calendar System: Semester
URL: www.elms.edu
Established: 1928 Annual Undergrad Tuition & Fees: $32,052
Enrollment: 1,717 Coed
Affiliation or Control: Roman Catholic IRS Status: 501(c)3
Highest Offering: Doctorate
Program: Liberal Arts And General; Teacher Preparatory; Professional
Accreditation: EH, IACBE, NURSE, SW

01 President .... Dr. Mary REAP
05 Vice President of Academic Affairs .... Dr. Walter C. BREAU
10 Vice Pres Finance/Administration .... Mr. Brian E. DOHERTY
32 Dean of Students .... Ms. Teresa WINTERS DUNN
30 Vice Pres of Instl Advancement .... Dr. Carla OLESKA
07 Director of Admissions .... Mr. Joseph WAGNER
06 Registrar .... Ms. Frances BLISS
08 Director of Library .... Mr. Anthony FONSECA
26 Director of Institutional Marketing .... Ms. Nancy FARRELL
37 Director of Financial Aid .... Ms. Kristin HMIELESKI
13 Director Information Technology .... Ms. Mary KASELOUSKAS
15 Director Human Resources/Personnel .... Ms. Marie PHILLIPS

Conway School of Landscape Design (E)

332 S Deerfield Road, PO Box 179,
Conway MA 01341-0179
County: Franklin FICE Identification: 022743
Unit ID: 165495
Telephone: (413) 369-4044 Carnegie Class: Spec/Arts
FAX Number: (413) 369-4032 Calendar System: Trimester
URL: www.csld.edu
Established: 1972 Annual Graduate Tuition & Fees: $31,450
Enrollment: 17 Coed
Affiliation or Control: Independent Non-Profit IRS Status: 501(c)3
Highest Offering: Master's; No Undergraduates
Program: Professional
Accreditation: EH

01 President/Director .... Mr. Paul C. HELLMUND
11 Administrative Director .... Mr. David NORDSTROM
07 Director Admissions/Marketing .... Mr. Adrian DAHLIN
30 Director of Advancement .... Ms. Nina ANTONETTI

Curry College (F)

1071 Blue Hill Avenue, Milton MA 02186-2395
County: Norfolk FICE Identification: 002143
Unit ID: 165529
Telephone: (617) 333-0500 Carnegie Class: Master's M
FAX Number: (617) 979-3540 Calendar System: Semester
URL: www.curry.edu
Established: 1879 Annual Undergrad Tuition & Fees: $36,445
Enrollment: 3,141 Coed
Affiliation or Control: Independent Non-Profit IRS Status: 501(c)3
Highest Offering: Master's
Program: Liberal Arts And General; Professional
Accreditation: EH, NURSE

01 President .... Mr. Kenneth K. QUIGLEY, JR.
05 Vice President Academic Affairs .... Dr. David SZCZERBACKI
30 Vice Pres Institutional Advancement ...... Mr. Christopher LAWSON
10 Chief Financial Officer .... Mr. Richard F. SULLIVAN, JR.
07 Dean of Admission .... Ms. Jane P. FIDLER
32 Dean of Student Affairs .... Ms. Maryellen M. KILEY
45 Dean for Institutional Planning .... Dr. Susan W. PENNINI
04 Assistant to the President .... Ms. Amy M. BIANCHI
08 Director Library .... Mr. Edward TALLENT
13 Chief Information Officer .... Mr. Dennis THIBEAULT
15 Director of Human Resources .... Ms. Kim HOWARD
06 Registrar ....Vacant
18 Chief Facilities/Physical Plant .... Mr. Robert G. O'CONNELL
26 Chief Public Relations Officer .... Ms. Frances L. JACKSON
29 Director of Alumni Relations ....Vacant
36 Director of Student Placement .... Ms. Kerrie ABORN
37 Dir of Student Financial Services .... Ms. Stephanny J. ELIAS
38 Director of Student Counseling .... Dr. Alison W. MARKSON
51 Dean of Continuing Ed/Graduate Stds ....Vacant
09 Director of Institutional Research .... Ms. Jennifer DUNNE
105 Director Web Services .... Mr. John EAGAN
19 Director Security/Safety .... Mr. Brian G. GREELEY
41 Athletic Director .... Mr. Vincent ERUZIONE

Dean College (G)

99 Main Street, Franklin MA 02038-1994
County: Norfolk FICE Identification: 002144
Unit ID: 165574
Telephone: (508) 541-1508 Carnegie Class: Assoc/PrivNFP4
FAX Number: (508) 541-8726 Calendar System: Semester
URL: www.dean.edu
Established: 1865 Annual Undergrad Tuition & Fees: $35,420
Enrollment: 1,325 Coed
Affiliation or Control: Independent Non-Profit IRS Status: 501(c)3
Highest Offering: Baccalaureate
Program: 2-Year Principally Bachelor's Creditable; Liberal Arts And General
Accreditation: EH

01 President .... Dr. Paula M. ROONEY
04 Exec Assistant to President .... Ms. Sandra CAIN
84 VP Enrollment Services/Marketing .... Mr. John MARCUS
10 Vice Pres Financial Svcs/Treasurer .... Mr. Dan MODELANE
32 VP Student Development & Retention .... Ms. Cindy T. KOZIL
30 Vice Pres Institutional Advancement .... Ms. Coleen RESNICK
13 VP/Chief Information Officer .... Mr. Darrell KULESZA
15 VP/Chief Human Resources Officer .... Dr. Gary CONVERTINO
44 Assoc Vice Pres Leadership Gifts .... Mr. Ryan MCDONALD
21 Assoc VP/Controller/Asst Treasurer .... Ms. Kathleen MCGUIRE
07 Asst VP Enrollment/Dean Admission .... Ms. Iris GODES
20 Asst VP Student Success/Career Plng .... Ms. Wendy ADLER
05 Asst Vice Pres Academic Affairs .... Ms. Melissa P. READ
45 Asst VP Capital Planning/Facilities .... Mr. Brian KELLY
26 AVP Marketing/Communications .... Mr. Gregg CHALK
35 Dean of Students .... Mr. David DRUCKER
51 Dean School of Continuing Studies .... Ms. Diletta MASIELLO
50 Dean School of Business .... Dr. Robert CUOMO
49 Dean Sch of Liberal Arts/Sciences .... Dr. Dawn POIRIER
57 Dean School of Dance .... Ms. Julianne O'BRIEN PEDERSEN
57 Dean School of the Arts .... Dr. David KRASNER
06 Registrar .... Mr. Daniel O'DRISCOLL
19 Dir Public Safety/Risk Management ...... Mr. Kenneth F. CORKRAN
08 Director of the Library .... Mr. Ted BURKE
41 Athletic Director .... Mr. John A. JACKSON
39 Director of Residence Life .... Ms. Shannon VALVERDE
35 Dir Student Activities/Orientation .... Ms. Jennifer BOTHWELL
40 Director of Bookstore .... Ms. Kathleen EKBOLM
37 Dean Student & Financial Plng/Svcs .... Mr. Frank MULLEN
84 Director Enrollment Operations .... Ms. Kathleen RYAN
36 Dir Career Planning/Internships .... Ms. Thea CERIO
38 Director of Counseling Services .... Ms. Mary Ann SILVESTRI

Eastern Nazarene College (H)

23 E Elm Avenue, Quincy MA 02170-2999
County: Norfolk FICE Identification: 002145
Unit ID: 165644
Telephone: (617) 745-3000 Carnegie Class: Bac/A&S
FAX Number: (617) 745-3907 Calendar System: 4/1/4
URL: www.enc.edu
Established: 1918 Annual Undergrad Tuition & Fees: $29,000
Enrollment: 1,211 Coed
Affiliation or Control: Church Of The Nazarene IRS Status: 501(c)3
Highest Offering: Master's
Program: Liberal Arts And General; Teacher Preparatory
Accreditation: EH, SW

01 President ... Dr. Corlis A. MCGEE
05 Provost & Dean of the College ... Dr. Timothy T. WOOSTER
10 Vice President for Finance ... Mr. Jan G. WEISEN
32 Vice Pres Student Development ... Mr. Jeff KIRKSEY
84 Director of Enrollment ... Mr. Brian PARKER
30 Vice President Inst Advancement ... Dr. Scott TURCOTT
39 Assoc Dean Students/Residence Life ... Mr. Marion MASON
06 Registrar ... Mrs. Margaret BALLARD
37 Director Financial Aid ... Ms. Lisa SEALS
08 Director of Library Services ... Ms. Susan J. WATKINS
19 Director Safety/Security/Risk Mgmt ... Mr. John GELORMINI
38 Dir Counseling & Career Services ... Mr. Bradford E. THORNE
58 Dean of Div of Graduate/Prof Stds ... Vacant
41 Athletic Director ... Mr. Bradford ZARGES
18 Maintenance Manager ... Mr. Mike JOHNSTON
45 Supervisor Instructional Resources ... Ms. Patricia VASQUEZ
21 Controller ... Mrs. Myrna GIBERTSON
42 Director Church Relations ... Mr. Stephen DILLMAN
22 Director Human Resources ... Vacant
40 Director Bookstore ... Vacant
13 Chief Information Officer ... Mr. Charles BURT
58 Director Adult/Graduate Studies ... Dr. Jossie OWENS
04 Admin Assistant to the President ... Mrs. Sheryl WEISEN
39 Dir Resident Life/Multicultural Aff ... Mr. Robert BENJAMIN

Emerson College (A)

120 Boylston Street, Boston MA 02116-4624
County: Suffolk FICE Identification: 002146
Unit ID: 165662
Telephone: (617) 824-8500 Carnegie Class: Master's L
FAX Number: (617) 824-8511 Calendar System: Semester
URL: www.emerson.edu
Established: 1880 Annual Undergrad Tuition & Fees: $36,650
Enrollment: 4,518 Coed
Affiliation or Control: Independent Non-Profit IRS Status: 501(c)3
Highest Offering: Doctorate
Program: Liberal Arts And General; Professional
Accreditation: EH, SP

01 President ... Mr. M. Lee PELTON
43 Vice President & General Counsel ... Ms. Christine HUGHES
11 Vice President for Admin & Finance ... Ms. Maureen MURPHY
05 Vice President for Academic Affairs ... Ms. Michaele WHELAN
13 VP for Information Technology ... Dr. William GILLIGAN
26 Vice Pres Communications/Marketing ... Mr. Andrew TIEDEMANN
28 VP Diversity & Inclusion ... Ms. Sylvia SPEARS
10 Assoc Vice Pres for Finance ... Mr. Marc MILLER
15 Assoc Vice Pres for Human Resources ... Ms. Alexa JACKSON
29 AVP Inst Advance/Dir Alumni Affrs ... Ms. Barbara RUTBERG
86 Assoc Vice Pres Govt/Community Rels ... Ms. Margaret Ann INGS
58 Dean Grad Studies/AVP Acad Affairs ... Ms. Carol PARKER
32 Dean of Students ... Ms. Sharon DUFFY
107 Exec Director Professional Studies ... Vacant
08 Exec Director of Library Services ... Mr. Robert FLEMING
07 Director of Graduate Admission ... Mr. Sean GANAS
36 Director of Career Services ... Ms. Carol SPECTOR
38 Director Counseling Center ... Dr. Elise HARRISON
41 Director Athletics ... Ms. Patricia NICOL
85 Director International Student Affs ... Ms. Virga MOHSINI
96 Director Purchasing/Risk Management ... Ms. Margaret ROGAN
39 Assoc Dean Housing/Residence Life ... Mr. David W. HADEN
21 Controller ... Vacant
06 Registrar ... Mr. William DEWOLF
42 Chair Center for Spiritual Life ... Vacant
101 Exec Asst to the Board of Trustees ... Ms. Anne SHAUGHNESSY
18 Int Assoc Director of Facilities ... Mr. Joseph KNOLL
37 Director Financial Aid ... Vacant
07 Director of Admissions ... Mr. Christopher WRIGHT
09 Director of Institutional Research ... Mr. Michael DUGGAR

Emmanuel College (B)

400 The Fenway, Boston MA 02115-5798
County: Suffolk FICE Identification: 002147
Unit ID: 165671
Telephone: (617) 277-9340 Carnegie Class: Master's S
FAX Number: (617) 735-9877 Calendar System: Semester
URL: www.emmanuel.edu
Established: 1919 Annual Undergrad Tuition & Fees: $36,504
Enrollment: 2,311 Coed
Affiliation or Control: Roman Catholic IRS Status: 501(c)3
Highest Offering: Master's
Program: Liberal Arts And General; Teacher Preparatory; Professional
Accreditation: EH, NURSE

01 President ... Sr. Janet EISNER, SND
03 Exec Asst to the President ... Ms. Michelle ERICKSON
04 Senior Assistant to the President ... Ms. Lori SIMMONS
10 VP of Finance/Treasurer (CFO) ... Sr. Anne DONOVAN, SND
05 VP of Academic Affairs ... Vacant
32 VP of Student Affairs ... Dr. Patricia RISSMEYER
86 VP for Government & Cmty Relations ... Ms. Sarah WELSH
30 VP of Development & Alumni Rels ... Vacant
37 Assoc VP for Student Financial Svcs ... Ms. Jennifer PORTER
42 Assoc VP of Mission & Ministry ... Fr. John SPENCER, SJ
26 Assoc VP of Marketing Communication ... Ms. Molly HONAN
07 Dean of Enrollment ... Ms. Sandra ROBBINS
35 Dean of Students ... Dr. Joseph ONOFRIETTI
49 Dean of Arts & Sciences ... Dr. William LEONARD
06 Assoc VP for Inst Rsrch/Registrar ... Ms. Elizabeth ROSS
20 Assoc Dean of Academic Pgm Support ... Ms. Cindy O'CALLAGHAN
88 Asst Dean Cmty Stdrds & Family Pgms ... Ms. Mary Beth THOMAS
88 Assoc Dean of Academic Advising ... Sr. Susan THORNELL, SND
88 Assoc Dean Natural Sciences ... Dr. Josef KURTZ
08 Director of Library Services ... Ms. Susan VON DAUM THOLL
15 Director of Human Resources ... Ms. Erin FARMER NOONAN
41 Director of Athletics & Recreation ... Ms. Pamela ROECKER
38 Director of Counseling ... Dr. Brenda HAWKS
90 Director of Academic Resource Ctr ... Ms. Wendy LABRON
09 Director of Institutional Research ... Ms. Alison VALLEREUX
13 Chief Info Technology Officer (CIO) ... Mr. Sean PHILPOTT
19 Director Security/Safety ... Mr. John KELLY
29 Director Alumni Relations ... Ms. Molly M. ZUCCARINI

Endicott College (C)

376 Hale Street, Beverly MA 01915-2098
County: Essex FICE Identification: 002148
Unit ID: 165699
Telephone: (978) 927-0585 Carnegie Class: Master's M
FAX Number: (978) 927-0084 Calendar System: 4/1/4
URL: www.endicott.edu
Established: 1939 Annual Undergrad Tuition & Fees: $30,492
Enrollment: 4,655 Coed
Affiliation or Control: Independent Non-Profit IRS Status: 501(c)3
Highest Offering: Doctorate
Program: Liberal Arts And General; Professional
Accreditation: EH, ART, CAATE, CIDA, NUR

01 President ... Dr. Richard E. WYLIE
05 Vice President & Academic Dean ... Dr. Laura ROSSI-LE
10 Executive VP/Vice President Finance ... Ms. Lynne B. O'TOOLE
84 Vice Pres Admissions/Financial Aid ... Mr. Thomas J. REDMAN
58 VP/Dean Graduate & Prof Stds ... Dr. Mary HUEGEL
30 Vice Pres Institutional Advancement ... Mr. David VIGNERON
20 VP/Dean of Academic Resources ... Dr. Kathleen BARNES
04 Assistant to the President ... Ms. Joanne L. WALDNER
90 Assoc Dean of Academic Technology ... Mr. Kent BARCLAY
07 Associate Dean of Admission ... Mr. George M. SHERMAN
45 Executive Director of Research ... Mr. Peter L. HART
15 Director Human Resources ... Ms. Sally ARNOLD
21 Treasurer ... Mr. Anthony FERULLO
06 Registrar ... Ms. Rosa CADENA
08 Library Director ... Mr. Brian COURTEMANCHE
37 Director Financial Aid ... Ms. Marcia D. TOOMEY
41 Athletic Director ... Dr. Brian WYLIE
91 Chief Information Systems Officer ... Mr. Gary F. KELLEY
38 Senior Counselor ... Ms. Karen THOMPKINS
18 Director of Physical Plant ... Mr. Dennis MONACO
26 Director Communications ... Ms. Carol RAICHE
36 Director of Career Services ... Ms. Dale MCLENNAN
09 Assoc Dir of Institutional Research ... Mr. Donald FEMINO
96 Purchasing Agent ... Ms. Susan AYERS
85 Dean of Undergrad International Ed ... Dr. Warren JAFERIAN
49 Dean of Arts & Sciences ... Dr. Gene WONG
53 Dean of Education ... Dr. Sara QUAY
57 Dean of Visual & Performing Arts ... Mr. Mark TOWNER
59 Dean of Hospitality Management ... Dr. William H. SAMENFINK
68 Dean of Sports Science/Fitness Stds ... Dr. Deborah SWANTON
66 Dean of Nursing ... Dr. Kelly FISHER
50 Dean of Business ... Dr. Michael PAIGE
60 Dean of Communication ... Dr. Laurel HELLERSTEIN
88 Director Internship ... Ms. Cindy RICHARD
101 Secretary of the Institution/Board ... Ms. Amy ASTOLFI
105 Director Web Services ... Ms. Jeanne COMMETTE
19 Director Security/Safety ... Mr. Charles FEMINO
43 Dir Legal Services/General Counsel ... Ms. Karen ABBOTT
44 Director Annual or Planned Giving ... Ms. Jennifer JONES

Episcopal Divinity School (D)

99 Brattle Street, Cambridge MA 02138-3494
County: Middlesex FICE Identification: 002149
Unit ID: 165705
Telephone: (617) 868-3450 Carnegie Class: Spec/Faith
FAX Number: (617) 864-5385 Calendar System: Semester
URL: www.eds.edu
Established: 1857 Annual Graduate Tuition & Fees: $15,610
Enrollment: 62 Coed
Affiliation or Control: Protestant Episcopal IRS Status: 501(c)3
Highest Offering: Doctorate; No Undergraduates
Program: Professional; Religious Emphasis
Accreditation: THEOL

01 Interim President and Dean ... Rev. Frank FORNARO
05 Academic Dean ... Dr. Angela BAUER-LEVESQUE
32 Dean of Student & Comm Life ... Rev. Thomas EOYANG
30 VP Institutional Advancement ... Mr. Christopher HARTLEY
08 Director of the Library ... Vacant
27 Dir of Communications & Marketing ... Mr. Brendan HUGHES
10 Chief Financial and Planning Office ... Mr. William JUDGE
21 Comptroller ... Ms. Joanne MANNING
07 Mgr of Admissions & Recruitment ... Ms. Hillary KODY
06 Registrar/Manager Academic Affairs ... Ms. Cecelia CULL
88 Interim Director Field Education ... Rev. Amy MCCREATH
18 Buildings & Grounds ... Ms. Denise MARDER
04 Exec Assistant to President & Dean ... Ms. Jane WAGNER
37 Director Student Financial Aid ... Ms. Valerie PATERSON
15 Director of Human Resources ... Ms. Samaria WILSON-STALLINGS

FINE Mortuary College (E)

150 Kerry Place, Norwood MA 02062
County: Norfolk FICE Identification: 033164
Unit ID: 436599
Telephone: (781) 762-1211 Carnegie Class: Assoc/PrivFP
FAX Number: (781) 762-7177 Calendar System: Quarter
URL: www.fine-ne.com
Established: 1996 Annual Undergrad Tuition & Fees: $22,890
Enrollment: 80 Coed
Affiliation or Control: Proprietary IRS Status: Proprietary
Highest Offering: Associate Degree
Program: Occupational; Business Emphasis
Accreditation: FUSER

01 President ... Mrs. Sherry JONES
03 Executive Vice President ... Mr. Kevin KOCH
05 Chief Academic Officer ... Ms. Susan BURKE
37 Director Financial Aid ... Ms. Kerry GREENE

Fisher College (F)

118 Beacon Street, Boston MA 02116-1500
County: Suffolk FICE Identification: 002150
Unit ID: 165802
Telephone: (617) 236-8800 Carnegie Class: Bac/Assoc
FAX Number: (617) 236-8858 Calendar System: Semester
URL: www.fisher.edu
Established: 1903 Annual Undergrad Tuition & Fees: $28,942
Enrollment: 1,875 Coed
Affiliation or Control: Independent Non-Profit IRS Status: 501(c)3
Highest Offering: Master's
Program: Occupational; 2-Year Principally Bachelor's Creditable; Liberal Arts And General; Business Emphasis
Accreditation: EH, CAHIIM

01 President ... Dr. Thomas MCGOVERN
05 Vice President Academic Affairs ... Dr. Janet KUSER
10 VP for Finance ... Mr. Steven RICH
84 VP of Enrollment Management ... Mr. Robert MELARAGNI
11 General Counsel/VP Operations ... Ms. Carolina AVELLANEDA
32 Dean of Students ... Ms. Shiela LALLY
88 Dean Intl Acad Oper/Curriculum Dev ... Ms. Nancy PITHIS
49 Asst Dean School of Liberal Arts ... Dr. Dean WALTON
06 College Registrar ... Ms. Alissa BERTRAM
41 Director of Athletics ... Mr. Scott DULIN
21 Director of Accounting ... Mr. Jeffrey CONRAD
13 Director of Information Services ... Mr. Jonathan BARTSCH
18 Director of Facilities ... Mr. Paul MCBRINE
37 Director of Financial Aid ... Ms. Pamela WALKER
45 VP of Strategy and Planning ... Dr. Melinda COOK
20 Assistant Dean for Academic Affairs ... Mr. Carla DELUCIA
35 Director Student Involvement ... Ms. Lisa JACKSON
19 Chief Dept of Public Safety ... Ms. Deborah CRAFTS
36 Director of Career Services ... Ms. Barbara ZERILLO
88 Director of Accessibility Service ... Dr. Wanda CAMACHO-MARON
21 College Bursar ... Ms. Kristen MARTINEZ
08 College Librarian ... Mr. Joshua MCKAIN
30 Assoc Dir Advancement & Alumni Rels ... Ms. Amanda MATAREZE
09 Director of Institutional Research ... Mr. Alex WAGNER
58 Dean Grad Studies ... Dr. Neil TROTTA
39 Director Student Housing ... Mr. Kyle GRENIER
04 Manager Office of President/HR Mgr ... Ms. Ellen LYONS

Franklin W. Olin College of Engineering (G)

Olin Way, Needham MA 02492-1200
County: Norfolk FICE Identification: 039463
Unit ID: 441982
Telephone: (781) 292-2300 Carnegie Class: Spec/Engg
FAX Number: (781) 292-2210 Calendar System: Semester
URL: www.olin.edu
Established: 2002 Annual Undergrad Tuition & Fees: $45,525
Enrollment: 350 Coed
Affiliation or Control: Independent Non-Profit IRS Status: 501(c)3
Highest Offering: Baccalaureate
Program: Professional
Accreditation: EH, ENG

01 President ... Dr. Richard K. MILLER
04 Asst to President ... Ms. Nancy SULLIVAN
05 Provost/Dean of Faculty ... Dr. Vincent P. MANNO
32 Dean of Student Life ... Ms. Rae-Anne BUTERA
06 Assoc Dean Student Life & Registrar ... Ms. Linda T. CANAVAN
07 Dean of Admission and Financial Aid ... Ms. Emily ROPER-DOTEN
37 Director of Financial Aid ... Ms. Jean RICKER
08 Library Director ... Mr. Jeff GOLDENSON
03 Executive Vice President ... Mr. Stephen P. HANNABURY
10 VP for Financial Affairs ... Ms. Patricia GALLAGHER
11 VP Operations/Chief Info Officer ... Ms. Joanne KOSSUTH
26 Chief Marketing Officer ... Ms. Michelle DAVIS
09 Dir Inst Research & Eval ... Mr. Jeremy GOODMAN
30 VP Development/Family & Alumni Rel ... Vacant
29 Director Family & Alumni Relations ... Ms. Kristina RAPOSA

† All admitted students who enroll at Olin College receive an Olin Scholarship covering half tuition during the eight semesters of the baccalaureate program.

Gordon College (A)

255 Grapevine Road, Wenham MA 01984-1899
County: Essex FICE Identification: 002153
Unit ID: 165936
Telephone: (978) 927-2300 Carnegie Class: Bac/A&S
FAX Number: (978) 867-4659 Calendar System: Semester
URL: www.gordon.edu
Established: 1889 Annual Undergrad Tuition & Fees: $35,386
Enrollment: 1,736 Coed
Affiliation or Control: Independent Non-Profit IRS Status: 501(c)3
Highest Offering: Master's
Program: Liberal Arts And General
Accreditation: EH, MUS, SW

01 President ... Dr. D. Michael LINDSAY
03 Exec VP and Chief of Staff ... Mr. Daniel TYMANN
05 Provost ... Dr. Janel CURRY
10 VP for Finance and Administration ... Mr. Michael J. AHEARN
07 AVP Enrollment ... Ms. June BODONI
32 Vice President for Student Life ... Mrs. Jennifer JUKANOVICH
26 VP of Marketing and Communications ... Mr. Rick SWEENEY
45 Legal Counsel ... Vacant
08 Director of Library Services ... Mr. Myron SCHIRER-SUTER
06 Registrar ... Mrs. Alice A. FALCONE
13 AVP of Techonology & Operations ... Mr. Christopher JONES
37 Sr Dir of Student Financial Svcs ... Mr. Daniel O'CONNELL
15 Director of Human Resources ... Ms. Nancy ANDERSON
18 Dir of Plant Operations and Sustain ... Mr. Paul HELGESEN
21 Controller ... Ms. Kim MATHER
29 AVP College Relations & Annual Fund ... Mrs. Britt CARLSON
36 Director of Career Services ... Ms. Pam LAZARAKIS
96 Dir of Purchasing and Distribution ... Mr. Michael NAWOICHIK
09 Exec Dir Institutional Research ... Mr. Robert VAN CLEEF
19 Director Security/Safety ... Mr. Glenn DECKERT
30 Dir of Development Information Tech ... Mr. Rick HOUSTON
41 Director of Athletics ... Mr. Jon TYMANN
44 Chief Development Officer ... Mr. Paul EDWARD

Gordon-Conwell Theological Seminary (B)

130 Essex Street, South Hamilton MA 01982-2317
County: Essex FICE Identification: 009747
Unit ID: 165945
Telephone: (978) 468-7111 Carnegie Class: Spec/Faith
FAX Number: (978) 468-6691 Calendar System: Semester
URL: www.gordonconwell.edu
Established: 1884 Annual Graduate Tuition & Fees: $17,100
Enrollment: 2,067 Coed
Affiliation or Control: Independent Non-Profit IRS Status: 501(c)3
Highest Offering: Doctorate; No Undergraduates
Program: Professional; Religious Emphasis
Accreditation: EH, THEOL

01 President ... Dr. Dennis HOLLINGER
10 Vice Pres Finance/Operations ... Mr. Jay S. TREWERN
05 Vice Pres for Academic Affairs ... Dr. Richard LINTS
30 Vice President of Advancement ... Mr. Kurt W. DRESCHER
12 Dean of Boston Campus ... Dr. Mark HARDEN
12 Academic Dean - Charlotte ... Dr. Timothy S. LANIAK
32 Dean of Students/Dir Stdnt Life Svc ... Ms. Michelle D. WILLIAMS
15 Director of Human Resources ... Ms. Susan ARSLANIAN
13 Chief Information Officer ... Mrs. Amy E. DONOVAN
84 Dean Enrollment Mgmt/Registrar ... Mr. Scott B. POBLENZ
18 Director of Physical Plant ... Mr. Timothy INGRAHAM
08 Director of Goddard Library ... Mr. Meredith KLINE
42 Dir Doctor of Ministry Programs ... Mr. Dave CURRIE
88 Director of the Ockenga Institute ... Dr. David G. HORN
37 Director of Financial Aid ... Mr. Stacey T. GLIDDEN
40 Director of Support Services ... Mr. David SHOREY
19 Director of Campus Safety ... Mr. Cabot W. DODGE
26 Dir of Communications & Marketing ... Mr. Michael L. COLARERI
07 Asst Director of Admissions ... Ms. Jill M. BENSON
21 Controller & Dir Financial Svcs ... Mr. Gregg HANSEN
30 Chief Advancement Ofcr Charlotte ... Dr. Neely GASTON

Hampshire College (C)

893 West Street, Amherst MA 01002-3372
County: Hampshire FICE Identification: 004661
Unit ID: 166018
Telephone: (413) 549-4600 Carnegie Class: Bac/A&S
FAX Number: (413) 559-5584 Calendar System: 4/1/4
URL: www.hampshire.edu
Established: 1965 Annual Undergrad Tuition & Fees: $48,738
Enrollment: 1,400 Coed
Affiliation or Control: Independent Non-Profit IRS Status: 501(c)3
Highest Offering: Baccalaureate
Program: Liberal Arts And General
Accreditation: EH

01 President ... Dr. Jonathan LASH
101 Secretary of the College ... Ms. Beth I. WARD
05 Vice President & Dean of Faculty ... Dr. Eva RUESCHMANN
32 Dean of Students ... Mr. Byron MCCRAE
10 Vice Pres for Finance & Admin ... Mr. Mary MCENEANY
15 Assoc Vice Pres Human Resources ... Ms. Ann Michele RUOCCO
30 Chief Advancement Officer ... Mr. Clay BALLANTINE
07 Dean of Admissions & Financial Aid ... Ms. Meredith TWOMBLY
08 Director of Library/Info Services ... Ms. Jennifer KING
06 Director of Central Records ... Ms. Roberta P. STUART
37 Director of Financial Aid ... Ms. Jennifer G. LAWTON
09 Director of Institutional Research ... Ms. Meredith TWOMBLY
18 Director of Facilities and Grounds ... Mr. Larry ARCHEY
20 Sr Assc Dean Faculty Acad Fin/Admin ... Ms. Yaniris FERNANDEZ
26 Chief Creative Officer ... Mr. David GIBSON
29 Director Alumni & Family Relations ... Ms. Melissa MILLS-DICK
36 Director Student Placement ... Ms. Carin RANK
38 Director Student Counseling ... Dr. Eliza MCARDLE
100 Chief of Staff ... Ms. Joanna OLIN
28 Director of Diversity ... Ms. Diana FERNANDEZ

Harvard University (D)

1350 Massachusetts Ave, Cambridge MA 02138-3800
County: Middlesex FICE Identification: 002155
Unit ID: 166027
Telephone: (617) 495-1000 Carnegie Class: RU/VH
FAX Number: (617) 495-0500 Calendar System: Semester
URL: www.harvard.edu
Established: 1636 Annual Undergrad Tuition & Fees: $45,278
Enrollment: 21,430 Coed
Affiliation or Control: Independent Non-Profit IRS Status: 501(c)3
Highest Offering: Doctorate
Program: Liberal Arts And General; Teacher Preparatory; Professional
Accreditation: EH, BUS, CLPSY, DENT, ENG, IPSY, LAW, LSAR, MED, PCSAS, PH, PLNG, THEOL

01 President ... Drew GILPIN FAUST
05 Provost ... Alan GARBER
49 Dean Arts and Sciences ... Michael D. SMITH
58 Dean Graduate School of A&S ... Xiao-Li MENG
50 Dean Harvard Business School ... Nitin NOHRIA
49 Dean Harvard College ... Rakesh KHURANA
56 Dean Continuing Educ and Extension ... Huntington D. LAMBERT
52 Dean School of Dental Medicine ... R. Bruce DONOFF
48 Dean Graduate School of Design ... Moshen MOSTAFAVI
73 Dean Harvard Divinity School ... David N. HEMPTON
53 Dean Graduate School of Education ... James E. RYAN
54 Dean Engineering/Applied Sciences ... Vacant
80 Dean Kennedy School of Government ... Vacant
61 Dean Harvard Law School ... Martha MINOW
63 Dean Harvard Medical School ... Jeffrey S. FLIER
69 Dean School of Public Health ... Julio FRENK
88 Dean Inst for Advanced Studies ... Lizabeth COHEN
88 Treasurer ... Paul J. FINNEGAN
03 Executive Vice President ... Katherine N. LAPP
29 VP Alumni Affairs/Development ... Tamara ROGERS
10 VP for Finance and CFO ... Thomas HOLLISTER
101 VP and Secretary of the University ... Marc GOODHEART
88 VP for Strategy and Programs ... Leah ROSOVSKY
43 VP and General Counsel ... Robert IULIANO
26 VP Public Affairs and Communication ... Paul ANDREW
15 VP for Human Resources ... Marilyn HAUSAMMANN
45 VP Planning and Project Management ... Mark R. JOHNSON
08 VP for the Harvard Library ... Sarah E. THOMAS
13 VP and CIO ... Anne MARGULIES
18 VP for Campus Services ... Meredith WEENICK

Hebrew College (E)

160 Herrick Road, Newton Centre MA 02459-2237
County: Middlesex FICE Identification: 002157
Unit ID: 166045
Telephone: (617) 559-8600 Carnegie Class: Spec/Faith
FAX Number: (617) 559-8601 Calendar System: Semester
URL: www.hebrewcollege.edu
Established: 1921 Annual Undergrad Tuition & Fees: $26,360
Enrollment: 172 Coed
Affiliation or Control: Independent Non-Profit IRS Status: 501(c)3
Highest Offering: Beyond Master's But Less Than Doctorate
Program: Professional; Religious Emphasis
Accreditation: EH

01 President ... Rabbi Daniel LEHMANN
10 Vice Pres Finance & Administration ... Mr. Leon ZAIMES
05 Provost ... Vacant
84 Director of Enrollment Management ... Ms. Barbara SELWYN
06 Registrar/Dir Student Financial Aid ... Ms. Marilyn JAYE
30 Director of Development ... Vacant
15 Director Personnel Services ... Ms. Steffi BOBBIN
04 Assistant to the President ... Ms. Jessica EISENBERG

Hellenic College-Holy Cross Greek Orthodox School of Theology (F)

50 Goddard Avenue, Brookline MA 02445-7496
County: Norfolk FICE Identification: 002154
Unit ID: 166054
Telephone: (617) 731-3500 Carnegie Class: Spec/Faith
FAX Number: (617) 850-1460 Calendar System: Semester
URL: www.hchc.edu
Established: 1937 Annual Undergrad Tuition & Fees: $21,940
Enrollment: 179 Coed
Affiliation or Control: Greek Orthodox IRS Status: 501(c)3
Highest Offering: Master's
Program: Teacher Preparatory; Professional
Accreditation: EH, THEOL

01 President ... RevDr. Christopher T. METROPULOS
73 Dean School of Theology ... Dr. James SKEDROS
05 Dean Hellenic College ... Dr. Demetrios KATOS
32 Dean of Students ... Dean Nicholas BELCHER
11 Chief Operating Officer ... Mr. James D. KARLOUTSOS
10 Chief Financial Officer ... Mr. Kevin DERRIVAN
07 Director of Admissions & Records ... Mr. Gregory FLOOR
08 Director Library ... Rev. Joachim COTSONIS
37 Financial Aid Director ... Mr. Michael KIRCHMAIER
06 Registrar ... Ms. Alba PAGAN
13 Director Computing/Information Mgmt ... Mr. Mugur ROZ
42 Chaplain ... Rev. Peter CHAMBERAS
38 Director Student Counseling ... Ms. Athina-Eleni MAVROUDHIS
30 Director Institutional Advancement ... Rev. James KATINAS
29 Director of Alumni Office ... Mr. Gregory FLOOR
21 Controller ... Mr. Paul HUBBARD
40 Bookstore Manager ... Ms. Tanya CONTOS
26 Marketing/Communications Manager ... Vacant
39 Director of Housing/Security ... Mr. George GEORGENES
04 Administrator of President's Office ... Vacant
15 Director of Human Resources ... Mr. David VOLZ

Hult International Business School (G)

One Education Street, Cambridge MA 02141-1805
County: Middlesex FICE Identification: 041432
Unit ID: 164368
Telephone: (617) 746-1990 Carnegie Class: Not Classified
FAX Number: (617) 746-1991 Calendar System: Other
URL: www.hult.edu
Established: 1964 Annual Undergrad Tuition & Fees: $69,800
Enrollment: 814 Coed
Affiliation or Control: Proprietary IRS Status: Proprietary
Highest Offering: Master's
Program: Professional; Business Emphasis
Accreditation: EH

01 President ... Dr. Stephen J. HODGES
05 Vice Provost ... Ms. Margaret ANDREWS
10 Chief Financial Officer ... Mr. Anders LJUNGDAHL
11 Chief Operations Officer ... Mr. Chris HOLMES
20 Dean of Faculty ... Mr. Nick AMDUR
12 Dean Boston Campus ... Dr. Henrik TOTTERMAN
12 Dean San Francisco Campus ... Mr. Larry LOUIE
84 Regional Director Enrollment ... Mr. Steve WYNN
36 Dir of Career Services Boston ... Ms. Joanne MARKOW
32 Dir Student Services Boston ... Ms. Emily BURKE
06 Senior Registrar Boston Campus ... Mr. Alec FISHER
06 Registrar San Francisco Campus ... Ms. Caroline CONNOR
37 Director Student Financial Aid ... Ms. Karen VAN DYNE

ITT Technical Institute (H)

333 Providence Highway, Norwood MA 02062
Telephone: (781) 278-7200 Identification: 666541
Accreditation: ACICS

† Branch campus of ITT Technical Institute, Indianapolis, IN.

ITT Technical Institute (I)

200 Ballardvale Street, Suite 200, Wilmington MA 01887
Telephone: (978) 658-2636 Identification: 666119
Accreditation: ACICS

† Branch campus of ITT Technical Institute, Indianapolis, IN.

Laboure College (J)

303 Adams Street, Milton MA 02186-4253
County: Suffolk FICE Identification: 006324
Unit ID: 165264
Telephone: (617) 322-3500 Carnegie Class: Assoc/PrivNFP
FAX Number: (617) 296-7947 Calendar System: Semester
URL: www.laboure.edu
Established: 1892 Annual Undergrad Tuition & Fees: $33,015
Enrollment: 767 Coed
Affiliation or Control: Roman Catholic IRS Status: 501(c)3
Highest Offering: Baccalaureate
Program: Occupational; 2-Year Principally Bachelor's Creditable; Nursing Emphasis
Accreditation: EH, ADNUR, CAHIIM, #DIETT, NDT, NURSE, RTT

01 President ... Maureen A. SMITH
05 Vice President of Academic Affairs ... Albert DECICCIO
30 Vice Pres Institutional Advancement ... Catherine PHILBIN
84 Vice Pres Enrollment Management ... Nora SHERIDAN
04 Administrative Asst to President ... Megan D. COX
06 Registrar ... John SACCO
07 Director of Admissions ... Amy ROWAN
08 Director of Library ... Andrew CALO
10 Chief Financial Officer ... Mark VIRELLO
13 Chief Info Technology Officer (CIO) ... Eric ELLIS
15 Chief Human Resource Officer ... Martha DOVE
19 Director Security/Safety ... Yvonne HALL
26 Chief Marketing Officer ... Katelyn DWYER
29 Director Alumni Relations ... Abigail JARVIS
37 Director Student Financial Aid ... Erin HANLON

Lasell College (K)

1844 Commonwealth Avenue, Newton MA 02466-2716
County: Middlesex FICE Identification: 002158
Unit ID: 166391
Telephone: (617) 243-2000 Carnegie Class: Bac/Diverse

FAX Number: (617) 243-2389 Calendar System: Semester
URL: www.lasell.edu
Established: 1851 Annual Undergrad Tuition & Fees: $32,000
Enrollment: 2,070 Coed
Affiliation or Control: Independent Non-Profit IRS Status: 501(c)3
Highest Offering: Master's
Program: Liberal Arts And General
Accreditation: EH, ACBSP, CAATE, EXSC

01 President .... Michael B. ALEXANDER
04 Exec Assistant to the President .... Pamela FARIA
05 VP Academic Affairs .... James OSTROW
10 VP Business & Finance .... Michael HOYLE
84 VP Enrollment Management .... Kathleen O'CONNOR
88 VP Lasell Village .... Paula PANCHUCK
32 VP Student Affairs .... Diane AUSTIN
26 VP Comm/Community & Govt Rels .... Vacant
30 VP Development & Alumni Relations .... Dean HICKEY
21 Assistant Vice President Finance .... Diane PARKER
20 Assoc VP/Dean Undergraduate Educ .... Steven BLOOM
07 Dean Undergraduate Admission .... James TWEED
58 Dean Grad & Prof Studies .... Joan DOLAMORE
89 Dean Advis & First Year Programs .... Helena SANTOS
35 Dean Student Affairs .... David HENNESSEY
37 Dir Student Financial Planning .... Michele KOSBOTH
09 Dir Institutional Research .... Melanie LARSON
06 Registrar .... Dianne POLIZZI
18 Director Plant Operations .... Wayne LAMOUREUX
27 Dir Communications .... Michelle GASSEAU
30 Dir Development .... Mark LAFRANCE
30 Senior Advancement Officer .... Katharine URNER-JONES
29 Dir Alumni Relations/Annual Giving .... Lauren MCCAUSLIN
35 Dir Student Act & Orientation .... Jennifer GRANGER
23 Dir Health Center .... Lisa PEARLMAN
08 Dir Library .... Marilyn NEGIP
41 Dir Athletics .... Kristy WALTER
15 Dir Human Resources .... Donna DANIELS
38 Dir Counseling Center .... Janice FLETCHER
07 Dir Graduate Admission .... Adrienne FRANCIOSI
42 Dir Center for Spirtual Life .... Thomas SULLIVAN
13 Chief Information Officer .... Deborah GELCH
44 Annual Giving Officer .... Rebecca BRENNER
39 Dir Residential Life .... Vacant

Le Cordon Bleu College of Culinary Arts in Cambridge (A)

215 First Street, Cambridge MA 02142
Telephone: (617) 218-8000 Identification: 770576
Accreditation: ACCSC, ACICS

† Branch campus of Le Cordon Bleu College of Culinary Arts in Scottsdale, Scottsdale, AZ.

Lesley University (B)

29 Everett Street, Cambridge MA 02138-2790
County: Middlesex FICE Identification: 002160
Unit ID: 166452
Telephone: (617) 868-9600 Carnegie Class: Master's L
FAX Number: (617) 349-8717 Calendar System: Semester
URL: www.lesley.edu
Established: 1909 Annual Undergrad Tuition & Fees: $24,720
Enrollment: 4,859 Coed
Affiliation or Control: Independent Non-Profit IRS Status: 501(c)3
Highest Offering: Doctorate
Program: Liberal Arts And General; Teacher Preparatory; Professional
Accreditation: EH, ART, TEAC

01 President .... Dr. Joseph B. MOORE
05 Provost .... Dr. Selase W. WILLIAMS
11 Vice President for Administration .... Ms. Marylou BATT
10 Vice President/CFO .... Ms. Bernice BRADIN
30 Vice President of Advancement .... Ms. Janis MARTINSON
84 VP of Enrollment Management .... Mr. Timothy ROBISON
21 VP for Budgeting & Fin Planning .... Ms. M. L. DYMSKI
43 General Counsel .... Ms. Shirin PHILIPP
100 Chief of Staff .... Dr. MaryPat LOHSE
20 Associate Provost .... Dr. Lisa IJIRI
58 Dean Grad Sch Arts & Social Sci .... Dr. Catherine KOVEROLA
53 Dean School of Education .... Dr. Jack GILLETTE
32 Dean of Student Life & Academic Dev .... Dr. Nathaniel MAYS
49 Dean College of Liberal Arts & Sci .... Dr. Mary COLEMAN
57 Dean of College of Art and Design .... Dr. Richard ZAUFT
07 Director of Graduate Admissions .... Ms. Barbara SELMO
15 Director of Human Resources .... Ms. Jane JOYCE
37 Director of Financial Aid .... Mr. Scott JEWELL
21 Controller .... Mr. Stephen MICARELLI
08 Interim Director of Libraries .... Ms. Constance VRATTOS
07 Dir Undergrad Admissions .... Ms. Deb KOCAR
09 Dir of Assessment/Inst Research .... Dr. Linda PURSLEY
04 Assistant to the President .... Ms. Kathleen SAMMARTINO
06 Registrar .... Ms. Adrianne ZONDERMAN
28 Dir Equal Opportunity & Inclusion .... Dr. Barbara ADDISON REID

Longy School of Music of Bard College (C)

27 Garden Street, Cambridge MA 02138
Telephone: (617) 876-0956 Identification: 770137
Accreditation: &M

† Branch campus of Bard College, Annandale-On-Hudson, NY.

*Massachusetts Board of Higher Education (D)

One Ashburton Place, Room 1401,
Boston MA 02108-1696
County: Suffolk FICE Identification: 029283
Unit ID: 166531
Telephone: (617) 994-6950 Carnegie Class: N/A
FAX Number: (617) 727-6397
URL: www.mass.edu

01 Commissioner .... Dr. Carlos SANTIAGO
103 Assoc Comm of Workforce Development .... Mr. David C. CEDRONE
05 Sr Deputy Comm Academic Policy .... Vacant
43 General Counsel .... Ms. Constantia PAPANIKOLAOU
10 Dep Comm Administration and Finance .... Mr. Sean NELSON
09 Sr Dep Comm Institutional Research .... Dr. Jonathan KELLER
37 Sr Dep Comm Student Financial Aid .... Dr. Clantha MCCURDY

*University of Massachusetts System Office (E)

225 Franklin Street, 33rd Floor, Boston MA 02110
County: Suffolk FICE Identification: 008017
Unit ID: 166665
Telephone: (617) 287-7050 Carnegie Class: N/A
FAX Number: (617) 287-7167
URL: www.massachusetts.edu

01 President .... Mr. Martin MEEHAN
03 Exec VP/Chief Operating Officer .... Mr. James JULIAN
05 Sr VP Acad Affs/Stdnt & Intl Affs .... Dr. Marcellette WILLIAMS
10 Sr VP Administration and Finance .... Ms. Christine WILDA
30 Vice President for Advancement .... Mr. Charles PAGNAM
46 Vice President Economic Development .... Mr. Thomas CHMURA
26 VP Strategic Comm/Univ Spokesperson .... Mr. Robert CONNOLLY
104 Deputy Chief Operating Officer .... Ms. Susan KELLY
86 Special Asst to Pres Govt Relation .... Mr. David MCDERMOTT
43 General Counsel .... Ms. Deirdre HEATWOLE
13 Assoc VP and Chief Info Officer .... Mr. Robert SOLIS
101 Secretary to Board of Trustees .... Ms. Zunilka BARRETT
21 Director for University Auditing .... Mr. Kyle DAVID
15 Human Resources Officer .... Mr. Andrew RUSSELL
106 Interim CEO UMass Online .... Dr. John CUNNINGHAM

*University of Massachusetts (F)

Amherst MA 01003-0001
County: Hampshire FICE Identification: 002221
Unit ID: 166629
Telephone: (413) 545-0111 Carnegie Class: RU/VH
FAX Number: N/A Calendar System: Semester
URL: www.umass.edu
Established: 1863 Annual Undergrad Tuition & Fees (In-State): $14,171
Enrollment: 28,635 Coed
Affiliation or Control: State IRS Status: 501(c)3
Highest Offering: Doctorate
Program: Liberal Arts And General; Teacher Preparatory; Professional
Accreditation: EH, AUD, BUS, BUSA, CLPSY, DIETD, DIETI, ENG, IPSY, LSAR, MUS, NURSE, PH, PLNG, SCPSY, SP, TED

02 Chancellor .... Dr. Kumble R. SUBBASWAMY
03 Deputy Chancellor .... Dr. Robert S. FELDMAN
05 Sr VC/Provost Academic Affairs .... Dr. Katherine S. NEWMAN
10 Vice Chancellor Admin/Finance .... Mr. James P. SHEEHAN
30 VC Development & Alumni Relations .... Mr. Michael A. LETO
46 Vice Chancellor Research .... Dr. Michael F. MALONE
32 VC Student Affairs & Campus Life .... Ms. Enku GELAYE
26 Vice Chanc University Relations .... Mr. John KENNEDY
41 Director of Athletics .... Mr. Ryan BAMFORD
43 Senior Counsel .... Mr. Brian W. BURKE
13 VC Information Services & CIO .... Ms. Julie L. BUEHLER
22 Exec Dir EO&D/Chief Diversity Ofcr .... Ms. Debora D. FERREIRA
28 Faculty Adv Diversity & Excellence .... Dr. Amilcar SHABAZZ
04 Senior Asst to the Chancellor .... Ms. Natalie BLAIS
20 Vice Provost for Acad Affairs .... Dr. Elizabeth R. DUMONT
20 Vice Provost Undegrad & Cont Educ .... Dr. Carol A. BARR
58 Vice Provost/Dean of Grad School .... Dr. John J. MCCARTHY
88 Assoc Provost Academic Personnel .... Mr. John BRYAN
85 Assoc Provost Intl Programs .... Dr. Jack AHERN
84 Assoc Provost Enrollment Management .... Dr. James ROCHE
45 Assoc Chancellor/Chf Planning Ofcr .... Dr. Bryan C. HARVEY
20 Asst Provost Advising/Acad Advising .... Dr. Pamela R. MARSH-WILLIAMS
09 Asst Chanc Institutional Research .... Dr. Marilyn H. BLAUSTEIN
108 Asst Provost Assessment/Educ Effect .... Dr. Martha L. STASSEN
51 Exec Director Continuing Education .... Mr. William S. MCCLURE
07 Director Undergraduate Admissions .... Mr. Kevin KELLY
37 Director Financial Aid Services .... Ms. Suzanne PETERS
06 University Registrar .... Mr. John LENZI
92 Dean Commonwealth Honors Col .... Dr. Gretchen GERZINA
79 Dean Col Humanities & Fine Arts .... Dr. Julie C. HAYES
81 Dean Col Natural Science .... Dr. Steve GOODWIN
53 Dean School of Education .... Dr. Christine B. MCCORMICK
54 Dean College of Engineering .... Dr. Timothy J. ANDERSON
50 Dean School of Management .... Dr. Mark A. FULLER
66 Dean School of Nursing .... Dr. Stephen CAVANAGH
69 Dean Sch Public Health/Health Sci .... Dr. C. Marjorie AELION
08 Director of Libraries .... Mr. Jay SCHAFER
56 Director of Extension .... Ms. Nancy GARRABRANTS
47 Dir Stockbridge School Agriculture .... Dr. Wesley AUTIO
88 Director Fine Arts Center .... Dr. Willie L. HILL, JR.
15 Asst Vice Chanc Human Resources .... Ms. Marie H. BOWEN
21 Assoc VC Finance & Budget Director .... Mr. Andrew P. MANGELS
18 Assoc VC Facilities & Campus Svcs .... Ms. Juanita M. HOLLER
19 Director Public Safety/Chief Police .... Mr. Patrick T. ARCHBALD
96 Director Procurement & Campus Svcs .... Mr. John O. MARTIN
40 Manager Univ Store/Retail Services .... Mr. Ken KAHLER
35 VC Student Affairs/Campus Life .... Ms. Enku GELAYE
39 Exec Director Residential Life .... Mr. Edward C. HULL
23 Director University Health Services .... Dr. George A. COREY
38 Director Mental Health/Health Svcs .... Dr. Harry S. ROCKLAND-MILLER
36 Interim Director Career Services .... Ms. Candice J. SERAFINO
29 Exec Director Alumni Relations .... Dr. JC SCHNABL
86 Exec Dir Public/Constituent Rels .... Mr. Christopher DUNN
31 Assoc VC for University Relations .... Dr. Nancy BUFFONE
25 Acting Dir Grant & Contract Admin .... Ms. Carol SPRAGUE
91 Deputy CIO/Dir Admin Applics .... Ms. Heidi DOLLARD
90 Assoc Dir OIT Academic Computing .... Mr. Fred ZINN
24 Director Educational Media .... Mr. Stephen PIELOCK
105 Web Manager .... Ms. Nina SOSSEN

*University of Massachusetts Boston (G)

100 Morrissey Boulevard, Boston MA 02125-3393
County: Suffolk FICE Identification: 002222
Unit ID: 166638
Telephone: (617) 287-5000 Carnegie Class: RU/H
FAX Number: (617) 265-7173 Calendar System: Semester
URL: www.umb.edu
Established: 1964 Annual Undergrad Tuition & Fees (In-State): $12,682
Enrollment: 16,756 Coed
Affiliation or Control: State IRS Status: 501(c)3
Highest Offering: Doctorate
Program: Liberal Arts And General; Teacher Preparatory; Professional; Business Emphasis
Accreditation: EH, BUS, CLPSY, CORE, CS, MFCD, NURSE, @TEAC

02 Chancellor .... Dr. J. Keith MOTLEY
88 Assistant Chancellor .... Dr. Theresa MORTIMER
100 Chief of Staff .... Mr. Christopher HOGAN
05 Provost .... Dr. Winston LANGLEY
10 Vice Chanc for Admin & Finance .... Ms. Ellen O'CONNOR
30 VC Chanc for Univ Advancement .... Ms. Gina CAPPELLO
84 Vice Chanc Enrollment Mgmt .... Ms. Lisa JOHNSON
32 Int Vice Chancellor for Student Aff .... Ms. Lisa BUENAVENTURA
32 Int Vice Chancellor for Student Aff .... Mr. James OVERTON
41 VC for Athletics & Special Projects .... Mr. Charlie TITUS
86 VC for Govt Rel/Public Aff .... Mr. Edward LAMBERT
13 Vice Provost Info Tech/CIO .... Mr. Robert WEIR
84 Assoc Vice Chanc Enrollment Mgmt .... Vacant
15 Asst Vice Chanc for Human Resources .... Ms. Becky HSU
29 Assoc VC Alumni Relations .... Ms. Elizabeth FREEDMAN DOHERTY
31 Asst Vice Chanc Community Relations .... Ms. Gail HOBIN
23 Exec Dir Univ Health Services .... Mr. Robert POMALES
20 Associate Provost .... Ms. Kristine ALSTER
20 Assoc Provost Assess and Planning .... Dr. Peter LANGER
53 Dean Col of Educ & Human Dev .... Mr. Michael MIDDLETON
51 Dean of University College .... Dr. Philip DISALVIO
81 Dean of Math & Science .... Dr. Andrew GROSOVSKY
79 Dean of Liberal Arts .... Dr. David TERKLA
50 Dean College of Management .... Dr. Jorge HADDOCK
66 Dean College of Nursing & Health Sc .... Dr. Anahid KULWICKI
80 Int Dean of CPCS .... Dr. Anna MADISON
35 Dean of Students .... Vacant
43 Interim General Counsel .... Ms. Deirdre HEATWOLE
26 Director of Communications .... Mr. DeWayne LEHMAN
38 Director Univ Advising Center .... Ms. Gail STUBBS
09 Director Institutional Research .... Dr. Jennifer A. BROWN
06 Director of Registration & Records .... Mr. David R. CESARIO
07 Director of Undergrad Admissions .... Mr. John DREW
37 Director Financial Aid Services .... Ms. Judy KEYES
08 Dean of University Libraries .... Dr. Daniel ORTIZ
22 Int Chief Diversity Officer-ODI .... Ms. Georgianna MELENDEZ
18 Director of Facilities Devel & Mgmt .... Ms. Dorothy RENAGHAN
19 Int Director of Public Safety .... Mr. Donald BAYNARD
40 Director of Campus Services .... Ms. Diane D'ARRIGO
41 Senior Assoc Director of Athletics .... Ms. Terry CONDON
36 Director of Career Services .... Mr. Mark KENYON
96 Director of Procurement .... Mr. Darryl MAYERS
92 Dean of Honors College .... Ms. Rajini SRIKANTH
20 Asst Vice Provost Undergrad Studies .... Ms. Maura MAST

*University of Massachusetts Dartmouth (H)

285 Old Westport Road, North Dartmouth MA 02747-2300
County: Bristol FICE Identification: 002210
Unit ID: 167987
Telephone: (508) 999-8000 Carnegie Class: Master's L
FAX Number: (508) 999-8901 Calendar System: Semester
URL: www.umassd.edu
Established: 1895 Annual Undergrad Tuition & Fees (In-State): $11,681
Enrollment: 9,111 Coed
Affiliation or Control: State IRS Status: 501(c)3
Highest Offering: Doctorate
Program: Liberal Arts And General; Teacher Preparatory; Professional
Accreditation: EH, ART, BUS, CS, ENG, #LAW, MT, NURSE

02 Chancellor .... Dr. Divina GROSSMAN

05 Provost/VC Acad & Student Affairs ... Dr. Mohammad KARIM
10 VC Admin & Finance/CFO ... Mr. Mark PREBLE
30 Int Vice Chancellor Advancement ... Mr. Jack MOYNIHAN
04 Executive Office Director ... Ms. Lori NICKERSON
51 Executive Director Univ Extension ... Dr. Karen RHODA
20 Vice Provost for Academic Affairs ... Dr. Magali CARRERA
58 Assoc Provost Grad Studies ... Dr. Tesfay MERESSI
84 Assc VC Enrollment Management ... Mr. Ian DAY
21 Assoc Vice Chancellor Finance ... Vacant
18 Associate VC Facilities Management ... Mr. Peter DUFFY
58 Dir Graduate Studies/Admissions ... Mr. Scott WEBSTER
22 Asst Chanc Diversity/Equity/Inc ... Ms. Deborah MAJEWSKI
88 Assistant VC Student Success ... Ms. Carol SPENCER
32 Assoc Vice Chanc Student Affairs ... Dr. David M. MILSTONE
13 Interim Assoc VC IT/CIO ... Mr. Holger DIPPEL
91 Asst VC IT System & Planning ... Vacant
88 Asst VC for Pgm Planning/Fiscal Mgt ... Ms. Joanne ZANELLA-LITKE
49 Dean College Arts & Science ... Dr. Jeannette RILEY
50 Dean Charlton Col of Business ... Dr. Angappa GUNASEKARAN
54 Dean College of Engineering ... Dr. Robert PECK
66 Dean College of Nursing ... Dr. Kimberly CHRISTOPHER
57 Dean College Visual Perform Arts ... Mr. Adrian TIO
88 Dean School Marine Science/Tech ... Dr. Steven LOHRENZ
61 Dean School of Law ... Ms. Mary Lu BILEK
96 Asst VC for Administrative Services ... Mr. Michael LAGRASSA
21 Asst Financial Controller ... Ms. Suzanne AUDET
92 Director Honors Program ... Dr. Avery PLAW
94 Dir Center Women/Gender/Sexuality ... Dr. Juli PARKER
88 Assoc Dir Academic Advising Center ... Ms. Suzanne MELLONI
06 Interim University Registrar ... Ms. Christine KAYLOR
07 Director of Admissions ... Mr. Michael LYNCH
09 Director of Institutional Research ... Ms. Tammy A. SILVA
08 Dean Library Services ... Mr. Terrance BURTON
19 Dir Public Safety/Chief of Police ... Col. Emil FIORAVANTI
36 Director Career Development Center ... Ms. Linda KENT DAVIS
37 Director Financial Aid ... Ms. Audra CALLAHAN
38 Dir Counseling/Stdnt Develop Ctr ... Dr. Christine FRIZZELL
90 Exec Dir IT Quality Assurance ... Ms. Margaret S. DIAS
29 Asst VC Alumni Relations ... Mr. Robert SALTZMAN
29 Director of Alumni Relations ... Ms. Nancy VANASSE
15 Asst VC Human Resources ... Ms. Carol SANTOS
18 Director Facilities/Physical Plant ... Mr. Jeffrey LOURO
41 Director of Athletics ... Ms. Amanda VAN VOORHIS
23 Director of Health Services ... Ms. Sheila DORGAN
39 Director of Housing/Residence Life ... Ms. Lucinda POUDRIER-AARONSON
44 Director Annual Funds ... Ms. Leanne BARKLEY
26 Vice Chancellor for Univ Marketing ... Ms. Renee BUISSON
88 Bursar ... Ms. Kathleen L. EUBANKS
35 Asst VC Student Affairs ... Ms. Cynthia CUMMINGS
35 Associate Dean of Students ... Ms. Shelly METIVIER SCOTT
104 Dir International Programs Office ... Ms. Kristen KALBRENER
85 Dir International Student Center ... Ms. Christina M. BRUEN
93 Director Fred Douglas Unity House ... Ms. Nicole WILLIAMS
88 Director Academic Resource Center ... Mr. Sokratis KOUMAS
105 Webmaster ... Mr. Donald KING
108 Dir of Learning Assessment ... Vacant
100 Assistant Chancellor ... Mr. John HOEY
101 Senior VC Strategic Management ... Mr. Gerard KAVANAUGH
102 Public Affairs Specialist ... Mr. Joseph SULLIVAN
103 Dir Experiential Learning & Intern ... Ms. Amelia SCOTT
106 Dir Center for Access & Success ... Ms. Wendi CHAKA
25 Dir Sponsored Projects Admin ... Ms. Elena GLATMAN
28 Diversity and Outreach Manager ... Ms. Chantal BOUCHEREAU
45 Assoc VC Campus Master Planning/Cap ... Mr. Michael HAYES

*University of Massachusetts Lowell (A)

1 University Avenue, Lowell MA 01854-2881
County: Middlesex FICE Identification: 002161
Unit ID: 166513
Telephone: (978) 934-4000 Carnegie Class: RU/H
FAX Number: (978) 934-3000 Calendar System: Semester
URL: www.uml.edu
Established: 1894 Annual Undergrad Tuition & Fees (In-State): $13,427
Enrollment: 17,184 Coed
Affiliation or Control: State IRS Status: 501(c)3
Highest Offering: Doctorate
Program: 2-Year Principally Bachelor's Creditable; Liberal Arts And General; Teacher Preparatory; Professional
Accreditation: EH, ART, BUS, ENG, ENGR, ENGT, MT, MUS, NURSE, PTA, TED

02 Chancellor ... Dr. Jacqueline MOLONEY
05 Provost ... Dr. Donald E. PIERSON
10 Vice Chancellor Finance & Operation ... Ms. Joanne YESTRAMSKI
26 VC University Relations ... Ms. Patricia MCCAFFERTY
30 Vice Chancellor for Advancement ... Mr. Edward CHIU
84 Dean Enrollment & Student Success ... Mr. Thomas TAYLOR
41 Director of Athletics ... Mr. Dana SKINNER
46 Vice Provost for Research ... Dr. Julie CHEN
15 Assoc VC Human Resources and EOO ... Ms. Lauren TURNER
44 Assoc VC Principal Gifts ... Mr. John DAVIS
106 Exec Dir Acad Svcs Online/Cont Ed ... Ms. Pauline CARROLL
21 Assoc Vice Chancellor for Finance ... Mr. Steven O'RIORDAN
106 Sr Exec Dir Online/Cont Educ ... Ms. Catherine KENDRICK
88 Vice Provost for Enrollment ... Dr. John TING
58 Vice Provost Graduate Education ... Dr. Donald PIERSON
20 Vice Provost Undergrad Education ... Dr. Charlotte MANDELL
18 Assoc VC Facilities Mgmt ... Mr. Thomas DREYER
88 Assoc VC Entrepreneurship Econ Dev ... Mr. Steven TELLO
31 Exec Dir Comm & Cultrl Affairs ... Mr. Paul MARION
49 Dean Col Fine Arts/Hum/Soc Sci ... Dr. Luis FALCON
81 Dean College of Sciences ... Dr. Mark HINES
53 Dean of Education ... Dr. Anita GREENWOOD
54 Dean College of Engineering ... Dr. Joseph HARTMAN
76 Dean College of Health Sciences ... Dr. Shortie MCKINNEY
50 Dean Manning School of Business ... Dr. Kathryn CARTER
09 Director of Institutional Research ... Dr. Julie ALIG
08 Director of Libraries ... Mr. George HART
06 Registrar ... Ms. Kerry DONOHOE
37 Director of Financial Aid ... Ms. Joyce MCLAUGHLIN
32 Assoc VC Student Affs/Univ Events ... Mr. Larry SIEGEL
38 Director of Counseling Svcs ... Dr. John PAKSTIS
29 Dir of Alumni Relations ... Ms. Heather MAKREZ
19 Chief Univ Police Dir Public Safe ... Mr. Randolph BRASHEARS
88 Dir Graduate Admissions ... Ms. Linda SOUTHWORTH
96 Dir Purchasing & Campus Services ... Mr. Thomas HOOLE
88 Dir Outreach & Recruitment ... Mr. Michael BELCHER
07 Assoc Dean Enroll & Dir UG Admiss ... Ms. Kerri JOHNSTON
88 Assoc Director UCAPS ... Mr. Jon VICTORINE
28 Dir Equal Opportunity & Outreach ... Ms. Clara ORLANDO
36 Asst Dean of Stdnt Affs/Career Dev ... Mr. Gregory DENON
88 Director Student Disability Svcs ... Ms. Jody GOLDSTEIN
35 Dean Student Affs & Enrich ... Mr. James KOHL
23 Assoc Dir Student Health Svcs ... Ms. Diana WALKER MOYER
108 Director of Assessment ... Ms. Paula HAINES
35 Dean Student Affairs & Event Svcs ... Ms. Brenda EVANS
13 Chief Information Officer ... Mr. Michael CIPRIANO
85 Exec Dir Intl Administration ... Ms. Maria CONLEY
104 Director Intl Exper/Study Abroad ... Ms. Fern MACKINNON

*University of Massachusetts Medical School (B)

55 Lake Avenue N, Worcester MA 01655-0001
County: Worcester FICE Identification: 009756
Unit ID: 166708
Telephone: (508) 856-8989 Carnegie Class: Spec/Med
FAX Number: (508) 856-8181 Calendar System: Semester
URL: www.umassmed.edu
Established: 1962 Annual Graduate Tuition & Fees: $25,510
Enrollment: 1,103 Coed
Affiliation or Control: State IRS Status: 501(c)3
Highest Offering: Doctorate; No Undergraduates
Program: Professional
Accreditation: EH, IPSY, MED, NURSE

02 Chancellor & SVP Health Sciences ... Dr. Michael F. COLLINS
05 Dean Provost & Exec Dep Chancellor ... Dr. Terence R. FLOTTE
10 Exec VC Administration & Finance ... Mr. Robert E. JENAL
88 Exec VC Innovation and Business Dev ... Dr. Brendan O'LEARY
30 Interim VC for Development ... Mr. John J. HAYES
88 Exec Vice Chancellor MassBiologics ... Dr. Mark D. KLEMPNER
11 Exec VC Commonwealth Medicine ... Ms. Joyce A. MURPHY
15 VC Diversity & Inclusion ... Dr. Deborah L. PLUMMER
86 VC Government/Community Relations ... Mr. James LEARY
26 Vice Chancellor of Communications ... Ms. Jennifer BERRYMAN
88 Vice Provost Faculty Affairs ... Dr. Luanne THORNDYKE
88 Vice Provost School Services ... Dr. Deborah Harmon HINES
53 Sr Assoc Dean Educational Affairs ... Dr. Michele P. PUGNAIRE
63 Sr Assc Dean Clin Aff/Assc Dean GME ... Dr. Deborah DEMARCO
66 Dean Graduate School of Nursing ... Dr. Paulette SEYMOUR-ROUTE
32 Assoc Dean Student Affairs ... Dr. Sonia CHIMIENTI
58 Dean Grad School Biomedical Science ... Dr. Anthony CARRUTHERS
06 Registrar ... Mr. Michael F. BAKER
13 Chief Information Officer ... Mr. Greg WOLF
07 Assoc Dean for Admissions ... Dr. Mariann M. MANNO
37 Director Financial Aid ... Mr. Shawn MORRISSEY
08 Director of Library ... Ms. Elaine R. MARTIN
100 Chancellor's Chief of Staff ... Mr. Brendan H. CHISHOLM
04 Exec Assistant to the Chancellor ... Ms. Jennifer HALSTROM
88 Vice Provost for Clin/Trans Science ... Dr. Katherine LUZURIAGA
88 Asst Dean Admin/Chief of Staff ... Ms. Lisa B. BEITTEL
20 Exec Asst Dean Provost & Exec Dep ... Ms. Kimberly LAPERLE
88 Assc Provost Basic Sci Research ... Dr. Jean KING

*Bridgewater State University (C)

131 Summer Street, Bridgewater MA 02325-0001
County: Plymouth FICE Identification: 002183
Unit ID: 165024
Telephone: (508) 531-1000 Carnegie Class: Master's L
FAX Number: N/A Calendar System: Semester
URL: www.bridgew.edu
Established: 1840 Annual Undergrad Tuition & Fees (In-State): $8,773
Enrollment: 11,187 Coed
Affiliation or Control: State IRS Status: 501(c)3
Highest Offering: Master's
Program: Liberal Arts And General; Teacher Preparatory; Professional
Accreditation: EH, AAB, ART, CAATE, CACREP, CS, MUS, SPAA, SW, TED

02 President ... Mr. Frederick CLARK
03 Exec VP/VP for External Affs ... Vacant
05 Provost & VP Academic Affairs ... Dr. Barbara FELDMAN
05 Vice Provost and Sr Intl Officer ... Dr. Karim ISMAILI
11 Vice Pres Administration/Finance ... Mr. Miguel GOMES, JR.
32 Vice President Student Affairs ... Dr. Jason PINA
30 VP University Advancement ... Dr. Brenda MOLIFE
10 Assoc Vice President Finance ... Mr. Douglas SHROPSHIRE
15 VP Human Resources & Talent Mgmt ... Ms. Keri POWERS
22 Director Title IX Coordinator ... Ms. Erin DEBOBES
32 Asst Vice Pres Student Affairs ... Mr. Brian SALVAGGIO
35 Assoc Vice Pres Student Affairs ... Vacant
84 Assoc Vice Pres for Enrollment Svcs ... Dr. Heather C. SMITH
20 Assoc Provost Faculty Affs ... Dr. Pamela M. WITCHER
45 Assoc Provost Academic Plng/Admin ... Dr. Michael YOUNG
79 Dean Col of Humanities/Social Sci ... Dr. Paula M. KREBS
53 Dean Col Education/Allied Stds ... Dr. Lisa BATTAGLINO
51 Dean Col of Continuing Studies ... Dr. David CRANE
50 Dean Ricciardi College of Business ... Dr. Elmore ALEXANDER
100 Chief of Staff ... Dr. Deniz LEUENBERGER
07 Dean of University Admissions ... Mr. Gregg A. MEYER
13 Acting Chief Information Officer ... Mr. Raymond LEFEBVRE
06 Acting Registrar ... Ms. Elizabeth COLLINS
88 Director Academic Achievement Ctr ... Ms. Alicia D'OYLEY
29 Director Alumni Relations ... Ms. Shana MURRELL
30 Assistant VP for Development ... Mr. Todd AUDYATIS
41 Director Athletics/Recreation ... Dr. Marybeth LAMB
21 Director University Services ... Ms. Margarida VIEIRA
19 Chief of Police ... Mr. David TILLINGHAST
36 Director Career Services ... Mr. John PAGANELLI
88 Acting Director Children's Center ... Ms. Joanne HOGAN
37 Director of Financial Aid ... Ms. Janet GUMBRIS
23 Sr Dir Counseling/Health Services ... Dr. Mary Lou FRIAS
08 Director Library Administration ... Mr. Michael SOMERS
51 Dir Continuing/Distance Education ... Dr. Mary FULLER
22 Director Multicultural Affairs ... Ms. Sydne M. MARROW
27 Director of Publications ... Ms. Marie MURPHY
25 Director Grants/Sponsored Projects ... Ms. Mia ZOINO
96 Director of Purchasing ... Ms. Jennifer PACHECO
28 Director of Institutional Diversity .. Dr. Sabrina GENTLEWARRIOR
18 Assoc VP Facilities Management/Plng ... Ms. Karen JASON
81 Dean Bartlett Col Science & Math ... Dr. Arthur GOLDSTEIN
88 Exec Dir University Initiatives ... Dr. Anna BRADFIELD
58 Int Dean College of Graduate Stds ... Dr. Wendy HAYNES
09 Director of Institutional Research ... Dr. Kate MCLAREN
88 Director Teaching and Learning ... Dr. Roben TOROSYAN
46 Director Undergraduate Research ... Dr. Jenny SHANAHAN
85 Dir International Students/Scholar ... Dr. Roopa RAWJEE
88 Dir Regional Partnerships ... Dr. Diana E. JENNINGS
104 Director Study Abroad ... Mr. Michael SANDY
88 Asst VP Applications & Development ... Vacant
91 Dir Administrative Systems ... Ms. Kelley BARAN
88 Asst VP Infrastructure Netwk Sy ... Mr. Steven ZUROMSKI
105 Director of Web Development ... Ms. Eileen O'SULLIVAN
26 Dir Intergrated Marketing and Comm ... Ms. Eva GAFFNEY
26 VP Marketing & Communications ... Mr. Paul JEAN
27 Director of University News ... Mr. John WINTERS
38 Clinical Dir Counseling Center ... Mr. Philip ROBERTS
39 Dir Residence Life and Housing ... Ms. Beth MORIARTY
88 Deputy Chief of Staff ... Ms. Mary DELGADO
108 Director of Assessment ... Dr. Ruth SLOTNICK
04 Staff Associate to the President ... Ms. Kelly HESS
43 General Counsel ... Ms. Elizabeth SMALL

*Fitchburg State University (D)

160 Pearl Street, Fitchburg MA 01420-2697
County: Worcester FICE Identification: 002184
Unit ID: 165820
Telephone: (978) 345-2151 Carnegie Class: Master's L
FAX Number: (978) 665-3693 Calendar System: Semester
URL: www.fitchburgstate.edu
Established: 1894 Annual Undergrad Tuition & Fees (In-State): $9,935
Enrollment: 6,818 Coed
Affiliation or Control: State IRS Status: 501(c)3
Highest Offering: Master's
Program: Liberal Arts And General; Teacher Preparatory; Professional
Accreditation: EH, CS, CSHSE, IACBE, NURSE, TED

02 President ... Dr. Richard S. LAPIDUS
05 Vice President Academic Affairs ... Dr. Paul I. WEIZER
10 Vice Pres Finance & Administration ... Mr. Jay BRY
20 Associate VP Academic Affairs ... Dr. Catherine CANNEY
26 Exec Asst to Pres for External Affs ... Mr. Michael V. SHANLEY
32 Dean of Student & Academic Life ... Dr. Stanley BUCHOLC
84 Assistant VP Enrollment Mgmt ... Ms. Pamela MCCAFFERTY
53 Dean of Education ... Dr. Annette S. SULLIVAN
30 Vice President of Inst Advancement ... Mr. Christopher HENDRY
35 Assistant Dean for Student Devel ... Dr. Henry C. PARKINSON, III
06 Registrar ... Ms. Linda DUPELL
09 Director of Institutional Research ... Mr. Anthony WILCOX
08 Director Library ... Dr. Sean GOODLETT
41 Director Athletics ... Ms. Sue M. LAUDER
07 Director of Admissions ... Mr. Sean GANAS
36 Director of Career Services ... Ms. Erin C. KELLEHER
38 Director Counseling ... Dr. Robert HYNES
23 Director Student Health Services ... Ms. Martha FAVRE
29 Asst Director of Alumni Relations ... Ms. Emily AUSTIN-BRUNS
19 Director of Campus Police ... Chief Karen LEARY
44 Director of Annual Giving ... Mr. Michael KUSHMEREK
96 Director of Procurement ... Ms. Doreen ARES
15 Asst VP of Human Resources/Payroll ... Ms. Jessica MURDOCH
18 Dir of Operations & Maint ... Mr. Richard MCCLUSKEY
18 Dir Capital Planning & Construction ... Mr. Doug THOMAS
102 Director Grants & Sponsored Pgm ... Ms. Karen FRANK MAYS
37 Director Financial Aid ... Ms. Denise BRINDLE
104 Director Study Abroad ... Mr. Papa SARR
106 Dir Online Education/E-learning ... Dr. Michael B. LEAMY
108 Director Institutional Assessment ... Dr. Christopher CRATSLEY
13 Chief Info Technology Officer (CIO) ... Mr. Stephen E. SWARTZ
39 Director Student Housing ... Ms. Kristin MURPHY

*Framingham State University (A)

100 State Street, PO Box 9101,
Framingham MA 01701-9101
County: Middlesex FICE Identification: 002185
Unit ID: 165866
Telephone: (508) 620-1220 Carnegie Class: Master's L
FAX Number: (508) 626-4592 Calendar System: Semester
URL: www.framingham.edu
Established: 1839 Annual Undergrad Tuition & Fees (In-State): $8,700
Enrollment: 6,499 Coed
Affiliation or Control: State IRS Status: 501(c)3
Highest Offering: Master's
Program: Liberal Arts And General; Teacher Preparatory
Accreditation: EH, ART, DIETC, DIETD, NURSE

02 President .... Dr. F. Javier CEVALLOS
03 Executive Vice President .... Dr. Dale M. HAMEL
05 Vice President Academic Affairs .... Dr. Linda VADEN-GOAD
88 Vice President Enrollment & Student .... Dr. Lorretta HOLLOWAY
43 Vice President General Counsel .... Ms. Rita COLUCCI
20 Associate Vice President .... Dr. Scott B. GREENBERG
13 Associate Vice President .... Mr. Patrick LAUGHRAN
18 Assistant Vice President .... Mr. Warren FAIRBANKS
84 Dean of Enrollment Management .... Mr. Jeremy SPENCER
32 Dean of Student Affairs .... Dr. Melinda K. STOOPS
39 Associate Dean Student Affairs .... Mr. Glenn COCHRAN
07 Associate Dean Undergrad Admissions .... Ms. Shayna EDDY
35 Assistant Dean Student Affairs .... Mr. David N. BALDWIN
88 Assistant Dean Student Affairs .... Dr. Christopher GREGORY
06 Executive Director/Registrar .... Mr. Mark R. POWERS
15 Director Human Resources .... Ms. Erin NECHIPURENKO
19 Chief Public Safety .... Mr. Brad MEDEIROS
88 Director Academic Support .... Ms. LaDonna BRIDGES
108 Director Assessment .... Dr. Mark NICHOLAS
41 Director Athletics .... Mr. Thomas KELLEY
36 Director Career Services .... Mrs. Dawn ROSS
37 Director Financial Aid .... Ms. Deborah ALTSHER
10 Director Financial Services .... Ms. Rachel TRANT
89 Director First Year Programs .... Mr. Benjamin J. TRAPANICK
23 Director Health Services .... Ms. Ilene HOFRENNING
104 Director International Education .... Ms. Jane DECATUR
08 Director Library Services .... Mrs. Bonnie MITCHELL
38 Director Counseling Center .... Dr. Paul WELCH
35 Director Student Involvement .... Ms. Rachel LUCKING
88 Director Student Accounts .... Ms. Deborah DALTON
30 Director Development .... Mr. Eric GUSTAFSON
25 Director Grants Sponsored Programs .... Mr. Jonathan LEE
09 Director Institutional Research .... Ms. Ann CASO
04 Administrative Assistant .... Ms. Katie RESTUCCIA
22 Director of Equal Opportunity .... Ms. Kimberly DEXTER
58 Dean of Graduate Studies .... Dr. Yasar NAJJAR
26 Chief Public Relations Officer .... Mr. Daniel MAGAZU
28 Chief Diversity & Inclusion Officer .... Mr. Sean HUDDLESTON
29 Director of Alumni Relations .... Mr. Steve WHITTEMORE

*Massachusetts College of Art and Design (B)

621 Huntington Avenue, Boston MA 02115-5882
County: Suffolk FICE Identification: 002180
Unit ID: 166674
Telephone: (617) 879-7000 Carnegie Class: Spec/Arts
FAX Number: (617) 566-4034 Calendar System: Semester
URL: www.massart.edu
Established: 1873 Annual Undergrad Tuition & Fees (In-State): $11,725
Enrollment: 2,098 Coed
Affiliation or Control: State IRS Status: 501(c)3
Highest Offering: Master's
Program: Teacher Preparatory; Professional; Fine Arts Emphasis
Accreditation: EH, ART

02 Acting President .... Mr. Kurt STEINBERG
03 Associate VP of Administration .... Mr. Robert PERRY
05 Provost/Vice Pres Academic Affairs .... Mr. Ken STRICKLAND
32 Vice President Student Development .... Dr. Maureen KEEFE
30 Vice Pres Institutional Advancement .... Ms. Marjorie O'MALLEY
09 Assoc VP for Planning/Research .... Ms. Kathleen KEENAN
10 Asst Vice Pres of Fiscal Affairs .... Mr. Donald ARPINO
100 Chief of Staff President's Office .... Ms. Susana SEGAT
07 Interim Dean of Admissions .... Ms. Kathleen KEENAN
88 Assoc VP/Dean Multi-Cultural Affs .... Dr. Jamie COSTELLO
06 Registrar .... Mr. Jonathan RAND
37 Director of Financial Aid .... Mr. Aurelio RAMIREZ
88 Dir Curatorial Pgms/Prof Galleries .... Ms. Lisa TUNG
08 Director Library .... Mr. Paul DOBBS
15 Director Human Resources .... Ms. Elaine O'SULLIVAN
22 Dir Civil Rights Compliance/Dvrsty .... Ms. Mercedes EVANS
18 Director Facilities/Physical Plant .... Mr. Howie LAROSEE
11 Director of Administrative Services .... Mr. James MCDAID
26 Exec Dir Marketing/Communications .... Ms. Ellen CARR
13 Chief Info Technology Officer .... Mr. Patrick O'CONNOR
19 Director Security/Safety .... Mr. Dwayne FARLEY

*Massachusetts College of Liberal Arts (C)

375 Church Street, North Adams MA 01247-4100
County: Berkshire FICE Identification: 002187
Unit ID: 167288
Telephone: (413) 662-5000 Carnegie Class: Bac/A&S
FAX Number: (413) 662-5010 Calendar System: Semester
URL: www.mcla.edu
Established: 1894 Annual Undergrad Tuition & Fees (In-State): $9,475
Enrollment: 1,765 Coed
Affiliation or Control: State IRS Status: 501(c)3
Highest Offering: Master's
Program: Liberal Arts And General; Teacher Preparatory; Professional
Accreditation: EH, CAATE

02 Interim President .... Dr. Cynthia F. BROWN
03 Executive Vice President .... Ms. Denise RICHARDELLO
05 Interim VP Academic Affairs .... Dr. Monica JOSLIN
10 VP Administration & Finance .... Dr. James M. STAKENAS
30 Chief Advancement Officer .... Ms. Marianne DRAKE
32 VP Student Affairs .... Dr. Catherine B. HOLBROOK
13 Chief Information Officer .... Mr. Curt KING
58 Dean Gradaute & Continuing Educ .... Dr. Howard EBERWEIN
20 Assoc Dean Academic Affairs .... Dr. Kristina BENDIKAS
35 Assoc Dean Student Affairs .... Ms. Theresa M. O'BRYANT
15 Director Human Resources .... Ms. Mary Ellen OLENYK
26 Dir Marketing & Communications .... Ms. Bernadette LUPO
04 Assistant to President .... Ms. Ginger MENARD
08 Assoc Dean Library Services .... Ms. Maureen HORAK
14 Assoc Dean Information Technology .... Mr. Peter ALLMAKER
88 Assoc Dean of CSSE .... Ms. Suzanne HUNGER
06 Asst Dean Registrar .... Mr. Steven KING
21 Director Fiscal Affairs .... Ms. Laura BROWN
37 Director Financial Aid .... Ms. Elizabeth PETRI
21 Director Student Accounts/Bursar .... Ms. Jennifer MACKSEY
07 Director Admissions .... Ms. Gina PUC
41 Director Athletics .... Ms. Laura MOONEY
09 Institutional Research Analyst .... Mr. Jason G. CANALES
23 Director Health Services .... Ms. Jacki KRZANIK
39 Director Residential Programs .... Ms. Dianne M. MANNING
18 Director Facilities Management .... Mr. Charles L. KIMBERLING
38 Director Counseling Services .... Ms. Heidi A. RIELLO
29 Dir Alumni Relations & Development .... Ms. Christine NAUGHTON
102 Dir Corporate & Foundation Rels .... Ms. Theresa MILLER
108 Director Assessment .... Ms. Erin M. MILNE
36 Asst Dir Career Services .... Ms. Manat WOOTEN

*Massachusetts Maritime Academy (D)

101 Academy Drive, Buzzards Bay MA 02532-3400
County: Barnstable FICE Identification: 002181
Unit ID: 166692
Telephone: (508) 830-5000 Carnegie Class: Bac/Diverse
FAX Number: (508) 830-5004 Calendar System: Semester
URL: www.maritime.edu
Established: 1891 Annual Undergrad Tuition & Fees (In-State): $7,656
Enrollment: 1,497 Coed
Affiliation or Control: State IRS Status: 501(c)3
Highest Offering: Master's
Program: Professional
Accreditation: EH, IACBE

02 President .... RADM. Francis X. MCDONALD
05 Vice President/Dean .... CAPT. Brad LIMA
10 Vice Pres Finance .... Ms. Rose CASS
30 Vice Pres Advancement .... Ms. Holly KNIGHT
27 Vice President/CIO .... Ms. Anne Marie FALLON
32 Dean of Students .... CAPT. Edward ROZAK
36 Assoc Dir Career/Professional Svcs .... CDR. Maryanne RICHARDS
84 Vice Pres Enrollment Management .... CAPT. Elizabeth STEVENSON
06 Director Student Records/Registrar .... Mr. Michael CUFF
08 Director Library .... Ms. Susan BERTEAUX
108 Dir of Institutional Effectiveness .... Dr. Kate MCLAREN
15 Director Personnel Services .... Mrs. Elizabeth BENWAY
18 Chief Facilities/Physical Plant .... Mr. Paul O'KEEFE
26 Chief Public Relations Officer .... Mr. Christopher RYAN
29 Director Alumni Relations .... Mr. Ian MACLEOD
37 Director Student Financial Aid .... Mrs. Cathy KEDSKI
96 Director of Purchasing .... Mr. Paul AIROZO

*Salem State University (E)

352 Lafayette Street, Salem MA 01970-5353
County: Essex FICE Identification: 002188
Unit ID: 167729
Telephone: (978) 542-6000 Carnegie Class: Master's L
FAX Number: (978) 542-6970 Calendar System: Semester
URL: www.salemstate.edu
Established: 1854 Annual Undergrad Tuition & Fees (In-State): $9,246
Enrollment: 9,267 Coed
Affiliation or Control: State IRS Status: 501(c)3
Highest Offering: Master's
Program: Liberal Arts And General; Teacher Preparatory; Professional
Accreditation: EH, ART, CAATE, CS, MUS, NMT, NURSE, OT, SW, TED, THEA

02 President .... Dr. Patricia M. MESERVEY
05 Interim Provost & Academic VP .... Dr. David J. SILVA
84 VP Enrollment Mgmt & Student Life .... Dr. Scott JAMES
30 VP Institutional Advancement .... Ms. Cynthia MCGURREN
100 Chief of Staff .... Ms. Beth A. BOWER
26 VP Marketing & Communications .... Mr. Tom TORELLO
13 CIO-CISO/Interim Exec Dir Finance .... Ms. Patricia AINSWORTH
10 Assoc VP Financial Svcs .... Mr. Joseph DONOVAN
15 Int Assistant VP for HR & EEO .... Mr. Mark R. QUIGLEY
20 Assoc Provost and Dean Human Svcs .... Dr. Neal DECHILLO
20 Asst Provost .... Vacant
86 Director of External Affairs .... Ms. Adria LEACH
08 Dean Library & Instr/Learning Supp .... Dr. Susan E. CIRILLO
50 Dean School of Business .... Dr. K. Brewer DORAN
58 Interim Dean of Graduate Studies .... Dr. Mary CHURCHILL
53 Dean of Education .... Mr. Joseph CAMBONE
51 Dean Sch Cont & Prof Studies .... Dr. Mary CHURCHILL
49 Int Dean School of Arts & Sciences .... Dr. Michele SWEENEY
32 Assoc VP & Dean of Student Life .... Dr. James G. STOLL
44 Asst VP Alumni Affairs/Annual Giv .... Ms. Eileen M. O'BRIEN
101 Exec Asst to President/Secy to BOT .... Ms. Katrina SADOWSKI
19 Dir Public Safety/Int Ex Dir Facil .... Mr. Gene R. LABONTE
41 Director Athletics .... Ms. Peggy CARL
06 Registrar .... Ms. Megan M. MILLER
84 Assistant VP for Enroll Mgmt .... Ms. Bonnie GALINSKI
18 Director of Facilities .... Mr. Daniel BURKE
28 Dir Diversity & Multicult Affairs .... Ms. Rebecca COMAGE
29 Director Alumni Affairs .... Ms. Mandy RAY
37 Director of Financial Aid .... Ms. Judy CRAMER
38 Dir Counseling and Health Service .... Ms. Elisa CASTILLO
96 Director Purchasing & Vendor Rel .... Ms. Evelyn WILSON
25 Dir Sponsored Programs & Res Adm .... Ms. Mary MADER

*Westfield State University (F)

577 Western Avenue, Westfield MA 01086-1630
County: Hampden FICE Identification: 002189
Unit ID: 168263
Telephone: (413) 572-5300 Carnegie Class: Master's M
FAX Number: (413) 572-8147 Calendar System: Semester
URL: www.westfield.ma.edu
Established: 1838 Annual Undergrad Tuition & Fees (In-State): $8,682
Enrollment: 6,370 Coed
Affiliation or Control: State IRS Status: 501(c)3
Highest Offering: Beyond Master's But Less Than Doctorate
Program: Liberal Arts And General; Teacher Preparatory
Accreditation: EH, CAATE, CS, EXSC, MUS, NURSE, SW, TED

02 Interim President .... Dr. Elizabeth PRESTON
05 Interim Vice Pres Academic Affairs .... Dr. Marsha MAROTTA
32 Vice Pres Student Affairs .... Dr. Carlton PICKRON
84 Vice Pres Enrollment Management .... Vacant
10 Interim Vice Pres Admin & Finance .... Dr. Kimberly TOBIN
30 VP Advancement & University Rels .... Mr. Kenneth LEMANSKI
21 Assoc VP Administration/Finance .... Ms. Lisa FREEMAN
11 Assoc Vice Pres Facil & Operations .... Dr. Curt ROBIE
15 Assistant VP Human Resources .... Mr. Rafael BONES
20 Dean of Faculty .... Dr. Stephen ADAMS
49 Interim Dean of Undergrad Studies .... Dr. Diane PRUSANK
51 Interim Dean Graduate/Cont Educ .... Dr. Shelley TINKHAM
53 Dean of Education .... Dr. Cheryl STANLEY
35 Dean of Students .... Ms. Susan LAMONTAGNE
06 Registrar .... Mr. John OHOTNICKY
09 Assoc Dean Institutional Reseach .... Dr. Lisa PLANTEFABER
88 Assoc Dean Academic Achievement .... Ms. Maureen MCCARTNEY
08 Dean Acad Info Svcs/Dir Library .... Mr. Thomas RAFFENSPERGER
39 Exec Director Residential Life .... Dr. Jon CONLOGUE
19 Director Public Safety .... Mr. Tony CASCIANO
36 Director Career Services .... Mr. Junior DELGADO
90 Exec Director Acad Tech Services .... Mr. Christopher HIRTLE
72 Director Information Technology .... Mr. Alan BLAIR
91 Director Admin Systems .... Mr. Rudolph HEBERT
18 Director Facilities/Operations .... Mr. Terry FENSTAD
41 Director Athletics .... Mr. Richard LENFEST
38 Director Counseling Center .... Ms. Tammy BRINGAZE
23 Director Health Services .... Ms. Patricia BERUBE
37 Director of Financial Aid .... Ms. Catherine RYAN
07 Director of Admissions .... Dr. Kelly HART
96 Director of Purchasing .... Mr. Chris RAYMOND
25 Director Grants Sponsored Programs .... Ms. Louann D'ANGELO
102 Director of WSU Foundation .... Mr. Michael KNAPIK
04 Executive Assistant to President .... Ms. Azanda SEYMOUR
101 Secretary of the Institution/Board .... Mrs. Adele GAMELLI
104 Director of International Program .... Ms. Cynthia SIEGLER
28 Director of Diversity & Inclusion .... Ms. Lizette RIVERA
88 Veteran & Military Svcs Coord .... Ms. Lisa DUCHARME

*Worcester State University (G)

486 Chandler Street, Worcester MA 01602-2597
County: Worcester FICE Identification: 002190
Unit ID: 168430
Telephone: (508) 929-8000 Carnegie Class: Master's M
FAX Number: (508) 929-8191 Calendar System: Semester
URL: www.worcester.edu
Established: 1874 Annual Undergrad Tuition & Fees (In-State): $8,857
Enrollment: 6,350 Coed
Affiliation or Control: State IRS Status: 501(c)3
Highest Offering: Master's
Program: Occupational; Liberal Arts And General; Teacher Preparatory; Professional
Accreditation: EH, NMT, NURSE, OT, SP, TEAC

02 President .... Mr. Barry M. MALONEY
05 Provost/VP of Academic Affairs .... Dr. Lois A. WIMS
10 Vice Pres Administration & Finance .... Ms. Kathleen EICHELROTH
32 Dean of Student Affairs .... Ms. Julie KAZARIAN
30 Vice Pres University Advancement .... Mr. Thomas MCNAMARA
84 Vice Pres for Enrollment Mgmt .... Dr. Ryan FORSYTHE
20 Assoc VP for Academic Affairs .... Dr. Patricia A. MARSHALL
21 Assoc VP Administration & Finance .... Ms. Robin QUILL
13 Assoc VP/CIO Univ Technology Svcs .... Dr. Anthony ADADE
58 Acting Assoc VP CE & Dean Grad Stds .... Dr. Roberta KYLE
108 Asst VP for Assessment & Planning .... Dr. Carol LERCH
22 Int Dir Diversity/Inclusion & Eq Op .... Dr. Sybil BROWNLEE
53 Dean Sch of Educ/Health/Nat Sci .... Dr. Linda LARRIVEE
79 Dean Sch of Hum & Social Sciences .... Vacant

88 Assoc Dean Sch Educ/Heath/Nat Sci ....Dr. Raynold LEWIS
66 Associate Dean of Nursing ....Dr. Stephanie CHALUPKA
51 Acting Assoc Dean of Grad/Cont Ed ....Ms. Sara GRADY
35 Assoc Dean & Dir Stdnt Ctr/Activ ....Mr. Timothy J. SULLIVAN
93 Asst Dean/Dir Multicultural Affairs ....Ms. Marcela URIBE-JENNINGS
19 Chief of Campus Police ....Mr. Michael NOCKUNAS
86 Asst to Pres for Intl/Cmty & Govt ....Mr. Carl HERRIN
26 Asst to Pres for Camp Communication ....Ms. Renae LIAS CLAFFEY
08 Executive Director of the Library ....Mr. Matthew BEJUNE
29 Exec Dir Univ Advancement & Alumni ....Ms. Karen SHARPE
15 Asst VP of HR/Payroll/Aff Act/Eq ...Ms. Stacey DEBOISE LUSTER
18 Director of Facilities ....Ms. Sandra OLSON
37 Director of Financial Aid ....Ms. Jayne MCGINN
07 Director of Admissions ....Mr. Joseph DICARLO
06 Registrar ....Ms. Julie CHAFEE
39 Director Residence Life & Housing ....Mr. Adrian GAGE
88 Manager of Student Accounts ....Ms. Julie CARMEL
96 Director of Procurement/Bus Mgr ....Ms. Brenda BUSSEY
09 Director of Institutional Research ....Mr. Kenneth SMITH
38 Director Student Counseling ....Ms. Laura MURPHY
85 Director of International Students ....Ms. Katey PALUMBO
36 Director of Career Services ....Ms. Jillian ANDERSON
41 Director of Athletics ....Mr. Michael A. MUDD
24 Director of Media Services ....Mr. Thomas R. WHITE
109 Director of Admin Support Services ....Ms. Nancy M. RAMSDELL

*Berkshire Community College (A)

1350 West Street, Pittsfield MA 01201-5786

County: Berkshire FICE Identification: 002167

Unit ID: 164775

Telephone: (413) 499-4660 Carnegie Class: Assoc/Pub-R-M

FAX Number: (413) 447-7840 Calendar System: Semester

URL: www.berkshirecc.edu

Established: 1960 Annual Undergrad Tuition & Fees (In-State): $4,866

Enrollment: 2,230 Coed

Affiliation or Control: State IRS Status: 501(c)3

Highest Offering: Associate Degree

Program: Occupational; 2-Year Principally Bachelor's Creditable

Accreditation: EH, ADNUR, COARC, PTAA

02 President ....Dr. Ellen KENNEDY
05 Vice President for Academic Affairs ....Dr. Frances FEINERMAN
10 Vice President for Admin/Finance ....Mr. John LAW
32 Vice Pres Student Affs/Enroll Svcs ....Mr. Michael BULLOCK
30 Vice Pres Institutional Advancement ....Mr. Craig SMITH
103 VP Community Ed/Workforce Dev .....Mr. William MULHOLLAND
15 VP Human Res/Affirm Action Officer ....Ms. Deborah COTE
66 Dean Nursing/Allied Hlth ....Ms. Anna FOSS
06 Registrar ....Mr. Adam EMERSON
102 Exec Dir BCC Foundation ....Mr. Craig SMITH
13 Director Information Technology ....Mr. Richard WIXSOM
07 Dir of Marketing/Stdnt Recruitment ....Ms. Christina BARRETT
37 Director Student Financial Aid ....Ms. Anne MOORE
38 Senior Academic Counselor ....Ms. Lisa MATTILA

*Bristol Community College (B)

777 Elsbree Street, Fall River MA 02720-7395

County: Bristol FICE Identification: 002176

Unit ID: 165033

Telephone: (508) 678-2811 Carnegie Class: Assoc/Pub-U-MC

FAX Number: (508) 730-3270 Calendar System: Semester

URL: www.bristolcc.edu

Established: 1965 Annual Undergrad Tuition & Fees (In-State): $4,478

Enrollment: 9,189 Coed

Affiliation or Control: State IRS Status: 501(c)3

Highest Offering: Associate Degree

Program: Occupational; 2-Year Principally Bachelor's Creditable

Accreditation: EH, ADNUR, CAHIIM, COMTA, DH, MAC, MLTAD, OTA

02 President ....Dr. John J. SBREGA
03 Executive Vice President ....Mr. David F. FEENEY
05 Vice President of Academic Affairs ....Mr. Greg SETHARES
50 Dean of Business & Info Tech ....Mr. William BERARDI
79 Dean of Humanities & Education ....Dr. Ulli RYDER
83 Dean of Behavioral & Soc Sciences ....Dr. Kathleen PEARLE
76 Dean of Health Sciences ....Ms. Patricia DENT
81 Dean of Math/Science & Engineering ....Dr. Sarmad SAMAN
10 VP of Administration & Finance ....Mr. Steven KENYON
30 VP of Resource Development ....Ms. Elizabeth K. MCCARTHY
84 VP of Students and Enrollment Mgt ....Mr. Steve OZUG
91 VP of Information Technology ....Ms. Jo-Ann M. PELLETIER
103 Acting VP of Workforce Development ....Mr. Paul VIGEANT
32 Director Student Engagement ....Ms. Kathleen BURNS
07 Dean of Admissions ....Ms. Shilo HENRIQUES
12 Interim Dean of New Bedford Campus ....Mr. Robert REZENDES
12 Dean of Attleboro Center ....Mr. Rodney CLARK
06 Registrar ....Mr. Benjamin BAUMANN
08 Associate Dean Library Sciences ....Mr. Robert REZENDES
25 Dean of Grant Development ....Ms. Jennifer MENARD
37 Dean of Financial Aid & Technology ....Mr. David ALLEN
38 Director Counseling Services ....Mr. Michael BENSINK
15 VP of Human Resources/Affirm Action ....Mr. Tafa AWOLAJU
18 Director of Facilities Management ....Mr. Leo RACINE
19 Director of Public Safety ....Mr. Wayne WOOD
21 Comptroller ....Mr. Keith TONI
11 Associate VP of Administration ....Ms. Linda DANZELL
20 Assoc VP of Academic Affairs ....Mr. Anthony UCCI
20 Assoc VP of Academic Affairs ....Dr. Ana GAILLAT

84 Acting VP Enrollment Services ....Ms. Kathleen TORPEY GARGANTA
26 VP College Communications ....Ms. Sally C. CAMERON
29 Assoc VP Development Alumni Affairs .....Ms. Katherine BREZINA
88 Dean Disability Svcs & Student Engm ....Ms. Susan BOISSONEAULT
78 Director Coop Education ....Ms. Nicole HEANEY
31 Dean Ctr for Workforce/Community Ed ......Ms. Carmen AGUILAR
23 Health Services Coordinator ....Ms. Carol CONSTANTINE
56 Asst Dean Instructional Lrng Tech ....Ms. April BELLAFIORE
09 VP Inst Research/Plng & Assesssment ..Ms. Rhonda GABOVITCH
92 Director Honors Program ....Ms. Susan MCCOURT
96 Director of Purchasing ....Ms. Philicia PACHECO
36 Coord Career Planning Placement ....Ms. Patricia CONDON
41 Athletic Director ....Mr. Derek VIVEIROS
04 Executive Assistant to President ....Ms. Kathleen A. WORDELL
88 Dean Access and Transition ....Ms. Sarah MORRELL

*Bunker Hill Community College (C)

250 New Rutherford Avenue, Boston MA 02129-2925

County: Suffolk FICE Identification: 011210

Unit ID: 165112

Telephone: (617) 228-2000 Carnegie Class: Assoc/Pub-U-MC

FAX Number: (617) 228-2082 Calendar System: Semester

URL: www.bhcc.mass.edu

Established: 1973 Annual Undergrad Tuition & Fees (In-State): $4,470

Enrollment: 14,253 Coed

Affiliation or Control: State IRS Status: 501(c)3

Highest Offering: Associate Degree

Program: Occupational; 2-Year Principally Bachelor's Creditable

Accreditation: EH, ADNUR, DMS, MLTAD, RAD, SURGT

02 President ....Dr. Pam Y. EDDINGER
10 VP of Administration and Finance ....Mr. John PITCHER
05 VP Academic Affairs/Student Service ....Dr. James F. CANNIFF
28 Director Diversity & Inclusion ....Mr. Thomas L. SALTONSTALL
09 Exec Dean Inst Effectiveness ....Vacant
20 Associate Academic Dean ....Ms. Judith GRAHAM-ROBEY
32 Dean of Students ....Ms. Julie B. ELKINS
26 Exec Director of Communications ....Ms. Karen NORTON
18 Director Facilities Management ....Mr. Paul A. RIGHI
81 Dean of Mathematics/Behav Sciences ....Dr. Valerie T. SMITH
79 Dean of Humanities ....Ms. Lori A. CATALLOZZI
54 Dean Science/Engineering ....Dr. Laurie K. MCCORRY
107 Dean of Professional Studies ......Dr. Bogusia WOJCIECHOWSKA
66 Interim Dean Nurse Education ....Dr. Patti-Ann COLLINS
12 Interim Dean Chelsea Campus ....Dr. Vanessa SHANNON
21 Comptroller ....Mr. Weusi A. TAFAWA
25 Director of Grants Development ....Mr. Steven A. ROLLER
84 Director Enrollment Systems ....Ms. Debra A. BOYER
06 Registrar ....Ms. Nadira DOOKHARAN
08 Director Library/Info Center ....Dr. Vivica D. PIERRE
13 Chief Information Officer ....Ms. Laura GRANDGENETT
15 Dir Human Resources/Labor Relations ....Ms. Molly B. AMBROSE
27 Director of Public Relations ....Ms. Patricia J. BRADY
19 Director of Public Safety ....Mr. Robert BARROWS
37 Director of Financial Aid ....Ms. Melissa HOLSTER
96 Director of Purchasing ....Mr. Richard J. PISHKIN
38 Dir Advising/Counseling/Assessment ....Ms. Anne BROWN
30 Executive Director of Development ....Ms. Marilyn KUHAR
07 Director of Admissions ....Ms. Vanessa ROWLEY
100 Exec Asst to the President ....Mr. George HALLSMITH
108 Exec Dir Institutional Research ....Mr. David LEAVITT

*Cape Cod Community College (D)

2240 Iyannough Road, West Barnstable MA 02668-1599

County: Barnstable FICE Identification: 002168

Unit ID: 165194

Telephone: (508) 362-2131 Carnegie Class: Assoc/Pub-R-M

FAX Number: (508) 362-3988 Calendar System: Semester

URL: www.capecod.edu

Established: 1960 Annual Undergrad Tuition & Fees (In-State): $7,284

Enrollment: 3,818 Coed

Affiliation or Control: State IRS Status: 501(c)3

Highest Offering: Associate Degree

Program: Occupational; 2-Year Principally Bachelor's Creditable

Accreditation: EH, ADNUR, DH, MAC

02 President ....Dr. John L. COX
05 Vice Pres Academic/Student Affairs ....Dr. Susan MILLER
10 Vice President Finance & Operations ....Mr. Walter T. BROOKS
21 Asst VP Administration & Finance ....Ms. Cynthia CROSSMAN
18 Director Facilities ....Mr. Jeffrey MARCOTTE
13 Asst VP Information Technology ....Mr. Gregory BANWARTH
49 Dean Arts & Humanities ....Dr. Lore DEBOWER
81 Dean Science/Tech/Math/Business ....Dr. Robert CODY
08 Dean Learning Res & Student Success ....Mr. David ZIEMBA
84 Dean Enroll Mgmt/Advising Services ....Ms. Susan KLINE-SYMINGTON
83 Dean Health/Social Sci/Human Svcs ....Ms. Susan MADDIGAN
15 Asst VP Human Resources ....Mr. Victor SANTOS
08 Assoc Dean Library ....Ms. Jeanmarie FRASER
07 Director Admissions ....Mr. Matthew CORMIER
37 Director of Financial Aid ....Ms. Sherry ANDERSEN
26 Director College Communications ....Mr. Michael GROSS
06 Acting Registrar ....Ms. Lucina HOLMES
19 Chief Public Safety ....Ms. Karen AHERN
04 Exec Assisstant to President ....Ms. Mia HAZLETT
36 Coord Career Plng & Placement ....Ms. Kristina IERARDI
09 Dir Institutional Research & Effec ....Ms. Maureen O'SHEA

*Greenfield Community College (E)

1 College Drive, Greenfield MA 01301-9739

County: Franklin FICE Identification: 002169

Unit ID: 165981

Telephone: (413) 775-1000 Carnegie Class: Assoc/Pub-S-SC

FAX Number: (413) 774-4676 Calendar System: Semester

URL: www.gcc.mass.edu

Established: 1962 Annual Undergrad Tuition & Fees (In-State): $6,482

Enrollment: 2,127 Coed

Affiliation or Control: State IRS Status: 501(c)3

Highest Offering: Associate Degree

Program: 2-Year Principally Bachelor's Creditable

Accreditation: EH, ADNUR

02 President ....Dr. Robert L. PURA
05 Chief Academic/Student Affairs Ofcr ....Dr. Sheryl HRUSKA
10 Chief Financial Officer ....Mr. Barry BRAIM
103 Int Dean of Workforce & Cmty Educ ....Ms. Alyce STILES
84 Dean of Enrollment Services ....Ms. Elaine LAPOMARDO
79 Dean Humanities ....Mr. Leo HWANG
81 Dean Engr/Math/Nurs & Sciences .. Ms. Mary Ellen FYDENKEVEZ
50 Dean Bus/IT/Soc Sci/Prof Stds ....Ms. Kathleen VRANOS
15 Exec Dir of Human Resources ....Mr. Peter SENNETT
30 Exec Director Resource Development ....Ms. Regina CURTIS
13 Chief Information Officer ....Mr. Michael ASSAF
28 Chief Diversity Officer ....Mr. Peter SENNETT
18 Director Physical Plant ....Mr. Jeffrey MARQUES
07 Interim Admissions Director ....Mr. Mark HUDGIK
37 Director Financial Aid ....Ms. Linda DESJARDINS
19 Director Public Safety ....Vacant
96 Director of Purchasing ....Mr. Ryan AIKEN
08 Director Library ....Ms. Deborah CHOWN
21 Comptroller ....Ms. Karen PHILLIPS
06 Registrar ....Ms. Holly FITZPATRICK
38 Co-Coord Learning Asst Programs ....Ms. Cynthia SNOW
38 Co-Coord Learning Asst Programs ....Mr. Norman BEEBE
36 Coordinator of Student Assessment ....Ms. Catherine DEVLIN
32 Coordinator of Student Activities ....Ms. Mary MCENTEE
04 Administrative Asst to President ....Ms. Wendy GAY
31 Interim Dir Cmty & Workforce Educ ....Mr. Jermiah RIORDON
108 Director Institutional Assessment ....Ms. Marie BREHENY
26 Marketing Coordinator ....Ms. Liz CARROLL

*Holyoke Community College (F)

303 Homestead Avenue, Holyoke MA 01040-1099

County: Hampden FICE Identification: 002170

Unit ID: 166133

Telephone: (413) 538-7000 Carnegie Class: Assoc/Pub-S-SC

FAX Number: (413) 552-2045 Calendar System: Semester

URL: www.hcc.edu

Established: 1946 Annual Undergrad Tuition & Fees (In-State): $4,166

Enrollment: 6,604 Coed

Affiliation or Control: State IRS Status: 501(c)3

Highest Offering: Associate Degree

Program: Occupational; 2-Year Principally Bachelor's Creditable

Accreditation: EH, ACFEI, ADNUR, MUS, RAD

02 President ....Dr. William F. MESSNER
11 Vice Pres Administration & Finance .... Mr. William FOGARTY
05 Vice President Academic Affairs ....Ms. Monica PEREZ
32 Vice President Student Affairs ....Ms. Yanina VARGAS
30 Vice Pres Institutional Development ....Ms. Erica BROMAN
28 Assistant Vice Pres of Diversity ....Ms. Idelia SMITH
08 Dean Library ....Ms. Mary DIXEY
84 Dean of Enrollment Management ....Ms. Renee TASTAD
15 Dean Human Resources ....Ms. Clara ELLIOTT
36 Dean Coop Education & Career Svcs ....Vacant
06 Registrar ....Ms. Christine HOLBROOK
37 Director of Financial Aid ....Ms. Karen DEROUIN
91 Director Administrative Computing ....Vacant
18 Dir Facilities & Engineering Svcs .... Mr. Dan CAMPBELL
10 Comptroller ....Mr. John O'ROURKE
13 Chief Information Officer ....Ms. Linda SZALANKIEWICZ
21 Dir Business Services/Purchasing ....Ms. Karen DESJEANS
09 Director Institutional Research ....Ms. Veena DHANKHER
26 Dir of Marketing/Public Relations ....Ms. JoAnne ROME
29 Dir Alumni Relations/Special Events .....Ms. Bonniez ZIMA DOWD
35 Int Dean of Student Services ....Mr. Tony SBALBI
20 Director of Academic Administration ....Ms. Idelia SMITH
38 Dir Retention & Adult Support Svcs ....Vacant

*Massachusetts Bay Community College (G)

50 Oakland Street, Wellesley Hills MA 02481-5357

County: Norfolk FICE Identification: 002171

Unit ID: 166647

Telephone: (781) 239-3000 Carnegie Class: Assoc/Pub-S-MC

FAX Number: (781) 237-1061 Calendar System: Semester

URL: www.massbay.edu

Established: 1961 Annual Undergrad Tuition & Fees (In-State): $4,176

Enrollment: 5,369 Coed

Affiliation or Control: State IRS Status: 501(c)3

Highest Offering: Associate Degree

Program: Occupational; 2-Year Principally Bachelor's Creditable

Accreditation: EH, ADNUR, RAD, SURGT

02 President ....Dr. John O'DONNELL
05 Provost/Chief Academic Officer ....Dr. Francesca PURCELL

10 VP Finance & Administrative Svcs ....Ms. Kathleen KIRLEIS
15 VP for HR/Empl Rels & Compliance ....Ms. Robin NELSON-BAILEY
84 VP for Enroll Mgmt & Student Svcs ....Mr. Stephen SULLIVAN
22 Affirmative Action Officer ....Ms. Robin NELSON-BAILEY
09 VP for Strat Plng/Inst Eff & Grants ....Dr. Yves SALOMON-FERNÁNDEZ
30 Asst VP of Inst Adv & Alumni Rel ....Ms. Mary SHIA
84 Asst VP Enrol Mgmt/Student Affairs ....Ms. Marva PERRY
106 Asst Provost/Dean of eLearning ....Dr. Lynn HUNTER
04 Exec Assistant to the President ....Ms. Vivian ORTIZ
76 Dean Health Sciences Division ....Dr. Lynne DAVIS
107 Dean Soc Sciences & Prof Studies ....Dr. Jane O'BRIEN FRIEDERICHS
81 Dean STEM Division ....Dr. Chitra JAVDEKAR
51 Dean Ctr for Corp Training/Comm Ed ....Ms. Carol STAFFIER
79 Dean Humanities Division ....Dr. Christopher LA BARBERA
88 Director Acad Achievement Ctr ....Ms. Jennifer JEFFERSON
88 Project Director Title III ....Dr. Linda GRISHAM
41 Dir Athletics Recreation & Wellness ....Mr. Bill RAYNOR
35 Coordinator of Student Activities ....Ms. Julie SCHLEICHER
20 Director of Academic Advising ....Ms. Sarah READING
32 Dean of Students ....Dr. Elizabeth BLUMBERG
06 Registrar ....Mr. Ali GUVENDIREN
07 Director of Admissions ....Ms. Donna RAPOSA
38 Director of Counseling ....Mr. Jon EDWARDS
37 Director of Financial Aid ....Ms. Elizabeth ENOS
36 Director of Career Services ....Ms. Julie FURBISH
16 Assistant Director Human Resources ....Ms. Kim PRATT
21 Controller ....Ms. Eileen GERENZ
96 Budget Analyst ....Mr. Kevin FLYNN
96 Purchasing Supervisor ....Ms. Lauren CURLEY
25 Director of Grants Development ....Ms. Laura BROWN
13 Chief Information Officer ....Mr. Michael LYONS
91 Director Administrative Computing ....Mr. Terry KRAMER
08 Director of Learning Services ....Mr. Timothy RIVARD
18 Director of Facilities ....Mr. Marco BRANCATO
19 Manager of Public Safety ....Mr. John MCCUNE

*Massasoit Community College (A)

1 Massasoit Boulevard, Brockton MA 02302-3996

County: Plymouth FICE Identification: 002177
Unit ID: 166823

Telephone: (508) 588-9100 Carnegie Class: Assoc/Pub-R-L
FAX Number: (508) 427-1202 Calendar System: Semester
URL: www.massasoit.mass.edu
Established: 1966 Annual Undergrad Tuition & Fees (In-State): $4,296
Enrollment: 7,905 Coed
Affiliation or Control: State IRS Status: 501(c)3
Highest Offering: Associate Degree
Program: Occupational; 2-Year Principally Bachelor's Creditable
Accreditation: EH, ADNUR, COARC, DA, MAC, RAD

02 President ....Dr. Charles WALL
05 VP Faculty & Instruction ....Dr. Barbara MCCARTHY
10 Chief Financial Officer ....Mr. William MITCHELL
32 Vice Pres Student Svcs/Enroll Mgmt ....Mr. David TRACY
12 Vice Pres/Dean of Canton Campus ......Mr. Nicholas PALANTZAS
15 VP & Director of Human Resources ....Vacant
09 Assoc Dean Institutional Research ...Ms. Mary GOODHUE LYNCH
25 Associate Dean of Grants ....Ms. Hollyce STATES
04 Exec Dir Extrnl Affs/Asst to Pres ....Mr. Phillip SHEPPARD
26 Public Relations Director ....Ms. Laurie MAKER
84 Dean of Enrollment Management ....Ms. Nancy SULLIVAN
35 Dean Student Affairs ....Vacant
07 Director of Admissions ....Ms. Michelle HUGHES
37 Director Student Financial Aid ....Mr. Todd HUGHES
06 Registrar ....Ms. Jannie GILSON
38 Director Student Counseling ....Ms. Christine DYMENT
28 Director of Diversity ....Ms. Yolanda DENNIS
13 CIO ....Mr. Alfred WILLIAMS
21 Comptroller ....Ms. Patricia MARCELLA
36 Director of Career Placement ....Ms. Kathyrn PRYLES
18 Director Facilities/Physical Plant ....Mr. Richard HADLEY
96 Director of Purchasing ....Ms. Diane PIQUETTE
41 Director of Athletics ....Ms. Julie MULVEY
29 Director Alumni Relations ....Vacant
50 Acting Dean Business & Technology ....Ms. Lynda THOMPSON
79 Dean Humanities/Social Science ....Ms. Deanna YAMEEN
76 Dean Allied Health ....Dr. Anne SCALZO-MCNEIL
83 Dean Public Svc/Social Science ....Ms. Karyn BOUTIN
81 Dean Science & Math ....Mr. Douglas BROWN
72 Dean of Emergent Technologies ....Ms. Carine SAUVIGNON
88 Dean of Academic Advising ....Mr. Peter JOHNSTON

*Middlesex Community College (B)

591 Springs Road, Bedford MA 01730-1197

County: Middlesex FICE Identification: 009936
Unit ID: 166887

Telephone: (781) 280-3200 Carnegie Class: Assoc/Pub-S-MC
FAX Number: (781) 275-0741 Calendar System: Semester
URL: www.middlesex.mass.edu
Established: 1969 Annual Undergrad Tuition & Fees (In-State): $4,464
Enrollment: 9,502 Coed
Affiliation or Control: State IRS Status: 501(c)3
Highest Offering: Associate Degree
Program: Occupational; 2-Year Principally Bachelor's Creditable
Accreditation: EH, ADNUR, DA, DH, DMS, DT, MAC, RAD

02 President ....Dr. James L. MABRY
05 Provost/VP of Academic Affairs ....Mr. Philip J. SISSON
03 Executive Vice President ....Mr. James F. LINNEHAN, JR.
84 VP Enrollment Svcs/Rsrch & Plng ....Dr. Paula R. PITCHER
04 Assistant to the President ....Ms. Lura SMITH
20 Associate Provost ....Vacant
32 Dean of Students ....Ms. Pamela B. FLAHERTY
79 Dean Humanities and Social Sciences ....Mr. Matthew OLSON
72 Dean of Business/Education & Publi ....Ms. Judith HOGAN
17 Dean of Health and STEM ....Ms. Kathleen J. SWEENEY
88 Dean Professional/Instructional Dev ....Ms. Susan ANDERSON
22 Asst Dir HR/Affirm Action Officer ....Ms. Darcy ORELLANA
12 Dean of Lowell Campus ....Ms. Colleen COX
12 Dir Fac Mgmt/Bedford Campus Mgr ....Mr. John LYONS
84 Dean of Enrollment Services ....Ms. Audrey NAHABEDIAN
26 Dean External Affs/Col Advancement ....Mr. Dennis MALVERS
07 Dean of Admissions ....Ms. Marilynn GALLAGAN
35 Associate Dean of Students ....Ms. Susan WOODS
09 Assoc Dean Institutional Planning ....Vacant
27 Exec Director Public Affairs ....Mr. Patrick COOK
27 Director Marketing Communication .....Ms. Jennifer M. ARADHYA
10 Director of Budget & Financial Svcs ....Ms. Gina SPAZIANI
15 Director Human Resources ....Ms. Kimberley MCMAHON
37 Director of Financial Aid ....Mr. Robert BAUMAL
21 Comptroller ....Ms. Kathy RICH
21 Bursar ....Mr. Christopher FIORI
08 Director Library Services ....Ms. Maryann NILES
23 Director of Health Services ....Vacant
06 Registrar ....Mr. Daniel MOYNIHAN
96 Coordinator of Purchasing ....Ms. Maureen HUDSON

*Mount Wachusett Community College (C)

444 Green Street, Gardner MA 01440-1000

County: Worcester FICE Identification: 002172
Unit ID: 166957

Telephone: (978) 632-6600 Carnegie Class: Assoc/Pub-R-M
FAX Number: (978) 632-6155 Calendar System: Semester
URL: www.mwcc.edu
Established: 1963 Annual Undergrad Tuition & Fees (In-State): $5,068
Enrollment: 4,336 Coed
Affiliation or Control: State IRS Status: 501(c)3
Highest Offering: Associate Degree
Program: Occupational; 2-Year Principally Bachelor's Creditable; Business Emphasis
Accreditation: EH, ADNUR, DA, DH, MAC, MLTAD, PNUR, PTAA

02 President ....Dr. Daniel M. ASQUINO
84 Exec VP & VP of Enrollment Services ...Ms. Ann M. MCDONALD
05 Vice Pres of Academic Affairs ....Dr. Melissa FAMA
51 VP Lifelong Learning/Workforce Dev .....Ms. Jacqueline BELROSE
10 VP Finance & Administration ....Mr. Robert LABONTE
15 VP HR/Affirmative Action Officer ....Ms. Diane RUKSNAITIS
26 Vice Pres Marketing/Communications ....Vacant
30 Assoc VP Institutional Advancement ....Mr. Joseph STISO
12 Dean Leominster Campus ....Mr. John WALSH
72 Dean Academic & Inst Technology ....Mr. Vincent IALENTI
76 Dean School of Health Sciences ....Ms. Eileen COSTELLO
08 Dean Library and Academic Support ....Vacant
09 Asst Dean of Records/Instl Research ....Ms. Rebecca FOREST
36 Dir North Central Career Services ....Ms. Cynthia KRUSEN
18 Director Maintenance/Mechanical Sys ....Mr. William SWIFT
68 Director Fitness & Wellness Center ....Mr. Stephen WASHKEVICH
19 Chief Public Safety & Security ....Ms. Karen KOLIMAGA
32 Assistant Dean of Student Services ....Mr. Gregory CLEMENT
38 Director of Counseling ....Vacant
29 Dir Alumni Affairs/Annual Giving ....Ms. Carol JACOBSON
06 Registrar ....Ms. Rebecca FOREST

*North Shore Community College (D)

1 Ferncroft Road, PO Box 3340, Danvers MA 01923-0840

County: Essex FICE Identification: 002173
Unit ID: 167312

Telephone: (978) 762-4000 Carnegie Class: Assoc/Pub-S-MC
FAX Number: (978) 762-4020 Calendar System: Semester
URL: www.northshore.edu
Established: 1965 Annual Undergrad Tuition & Fees (In-State): $5,670
Enrollment: 7,412 Coed
Affiliation or Control: State IRS Status: 501(c)3
Highest Offering: Associate Degree
Program: 2-Year Principally Bachelor's Creditable
Accreditation: EH, ADNUR, COARC, #MAC, OTA, PNUR, PTAA, RAD, SURGT

02 President ....Dr. Patricia A. GENTILE
05 Vice Pres Academic Affairs ....Dr. Karen HYNICK
10 Vice Pres Administration/Finance .....Ms. Janice M. FORSSTROM
84 Vice Pres Student Affairs ....Mr. Jermaine WILLIAMS
30 Vice Pres Institutional Advancement ....Mr. Mark REIMER
45 Asst Vice Pres Budget/Planning ....Ms. Mariflor UVA
15 Vice President Human Res/Affirm Act ....Ms. Madeline WALLIS
31 Dean of Community Svcs/Corp Ed ....Ms. Dianne PALTER-GILL
90 Dean Academic Technology ....Mr. Michael BADOLATO
84 Dean of Enrollment Services ....Mr. John DUFF
32 Dean of Students ....Mr. Stephen CREAMER
20 Assistant Dean Academic Affairs ....Vacant
08 Director Library/Tutoring ....Ms. Karen PANGALLO
13 Dir of Networking/Info Services ....Mr. Gary HAM
37 Dean of Financial Aid ....Mr. Stephen CREAMER
09 Asst Vice Pres Planning & Research ......Ms. Laurie LACHAPELLE
18 Asst Vice Pres Facilities Mgmt ....Mr. Richard RENEY
19 Campus Police Chief ....Mr. Douglas P. PUSKA
21 Comptroller ....Ms. Patricia CALLAHAN
26 Director Public Relations/New Media ....Ms. Linda BRANTLEY
29 Director Alumni Relations ....Ms. Sandra ROCHON
35 Chief Student Life Officer ....Ms. Lisa MILSO
36 Director Student Placement ....Ms. Lynn MARCUS
07 Director of Recruitment ....Vacant
38 Director Student Support & Advising ....Mr. Daniel O'NEILL
27 Director Marketing Communications ....Ms. Samantha MCGILLOWAY
40 Bookstore Manager ....Mr. Shawn CRONIN
06 Registrar ....Ms. Mel POTOCZAK

*Northern Essex Community College (E)

100 Elliott Street, Haverhill MA 01830-2399

County: Essex FICE Identification: 002174
Unit ID: 167376

Telephone: (978) 556-3000 Carnegie Class: Assoc/Pub-S-MC
FAX Number: (978) 556-3723 Calendar System: Semester
URL: www.necc.mass.edu
Established: 1960 Annual Undergrad Tuition & Fees (In-State): $5,560
Enrollment: 6,963 Coed
Affiliation or Control: State IRS Status: 501(c)3
Highest Offering: Associate Degree
Program: Occupational; 2-Year Principally Bachelor's Creditable
Accreditation: EH, ADNUR, COARC, CSHSE, DA, MAC, MLTAD, PNUR, POLYT, RAD

02 President ....Dr. Lane A. GLENN
05 Vice President of Academic Affairs ....Dr. William HEINEMAN
30 Vice Pres Institutional Advancement ....Ms. Jean C. POTH
10 Vice Pres Finance & Administration ....Mr. David GINGERELLA
15 Vice President of Human Resources . Mr. Stephen W. FABBRUCCI
07 Dean of Enroll Services ....Ms. Tina FAVARA
12 Exec Dir of Lawrence Campus ....Dr. Noemi CUSTODIA-LORA
09 Dean of Institutional Research ....Mr. Thomas FALLON
44 Dean of Development ....Ms. Wendy SHAFFER
88 Dean of Acad Support/Transfer ....Ms. Grace YOUNG
103 Exec Dir Workforce Devel/Cont Ed ....Mr. George MORIARTY
13 Chief Information Officer ....Mr. Jeffrey BICKFORD
06 Registrar ....Ms. Sue SHAIN
37 Director of Financial Aid ....Ms. Alexis FISHBONE
26 Director of Public Relations ....Ms. Ernestine GREENSLADE
29 Director Alumni Relations ....Ms. Lindsey MAYO
32 Chief Student Life Officer ....Ms. Nita LAMBORGHINI
35 Director Student Affairs ....Ms. Dina BROWN
18 Chief Facilities/Physical Plant ....Vacant
96 Director of Purchasing ....Vacant
04 Sr Exec Asst to President ....Ms. Cheryl GOODWIN

*Quinsigamond Community College (F)

670 W Boylston Street, Worcester MA 01606-2092

County: Worcester FICE Identification: 002175
Unit ID: 167534

Telephone: (508) 853-2300 Carnegie Class: Assoc/Pub-U-SC
FAX Number: (508) 852-6943 Calendar System: Semester
URL: www.qcc.edu
Established: 1963 Annual Undergrad Tuition & Fees (In-State): $5,640
Enrollment: 8,453 Coed
Affiliation or Control: State IRS Status: 501(c)3
Highest Offering: Associate Degree
Program: Occupational; 2-Year Principally Bachelor's Creditable
Accreditation: EH, ADNUR, COARC, DA, DH, MAC, OTA, PNUR, RAD, SURGT

02 President ....Dr. Gail E. CARBERRY
05 VP of Academic Affairs ....Ms. Patricia A. TONEY
10 VP of Administration ....Mr. Stephen T. MARINI
84 VP of Student Enrollment/Develop ....Dr. Lillian M. ORTIZ
26 VP for Community Engagement ....Dr. Dale ALLEN
101 Asst VP for Policy & Governance ....Ms. Susan LAPRADE
20 Assistant VP Academic Affairs ....Dr. Nancy SCHOENFELD
20 Assistant VP Academic Affairs ....Ms. Jane SHEA
04 Assistant to President ....Ms. Selina M. BORIA
21 Asst VP for Finance/Comptroller ....Ms. Debra A. LAFLASH
83 Dean Public Service & Social Sci ....Dr. James BROWN
79 Dean Humanities & Education ....Dr. Clarence ATES
76 Dean Health Care ....Dr. Jane JUNE
50 Dean Business/Engineer/Technology ....Ms. Kathleen RENTSCH
81 Dean Science & Mathematics ....Dr. Leslie HORTON
15 Assoc VP of Human Resources ....Mr. William DARING
06 Assoc Dean Enrollment/Registrar ....Ms. Tara F. JENKINS
62 Dean of Library Services ....Ms. Andrea MACRITCHIE
09 Dean of Inst Research/Planning ....Dr. Ingrid SKADBERG
84 Dean of Enrollment Management ....Ms. Michelle TUFAU-AFRIYIE
13 Chief Technology Officer ....Mr. Ken DWYER
31 Dir Community Affs & Site Facilit ....Mr. Victor SOMMA
32 Director Student Life ....Mr. Jonathan MILLER
18 Director of Facilities ....Mr. Don HALL
37 Director Student Financial Aid ....Ms. Karen GRANT
96 Purchasing Manager ....Ms. Stacey TATA
19 Chief of Campus Police ....Mr. Kevin RITACCO
88 Dir Institutional Communications ....Mr. Joshua MARTIN
22 Dean for Employment & Equity ....Ms. Anita BOWDEN
38 Coordinator of Counseling Services ....Ms. Karen COX
88 Director Disability Services ....Ms. Kristen PROCTOR
35 Dean of Students ....Ms. Elizabeth WOODS
07 Director of Admissions ....Ms. Mishawn DAVIS-EYENE

*Roxbury Community College (A)

1234 Columbus Avenue,
Roxbury Crossing MA 02120-3423

County: Suffolk FICE Identification: 011930
Unit ID: 167631
Telephone: (617) 427-0060 Carnegie Class: Assoc/Pub-S-MC
FAX Number: (617) 541-5351 Calendar System: Semester
URL: rcc.mass.edu
Established: 1973 Annual Undergrad Tuition & Fees (In-State): $4,351
Enrollment: 2,393 Coed
Affiliation or Control: State IRS Status: 501(c)3
Highest Offering: Associate Degree
Program: Occupational; 2-Year Principally Bachelor's Creditable
Accreditation: EH, ADNUR, RAD

02 President ... Dr. Valerie R. ROBERSON
04 Executive Asst to the President ... Ms. Martha LAMBERT
05 VP Academic And Student Affairs ... Ms. Cecile REGNER
30 VP Advancement/Cmty Engagemenet ... Ms. Lorita WILLIAMS
10 Vice President of Admin & Finance ... Mr. Kevin HEPNER
13 Chief Information Tech Officer ... Mr. Patrick JEAN-LOUIS
41 Director of RLTAC ... Mr. A. Keith MCDERMOTT
37 Assoc Director Financial Aid ... Mr. Alex JEAN-JACQUES
08 Director of Library ... Mr. William HOAG
23 Director of Health Services ... Ms. Ruth HINES
06 Registrar ... Ms. Cheryl MARTIN
32 Director of Student Life ... Ms. Elizabeth CLARK
15 Chief Human Res/Affirm Action Ofcr ... Mr. Charles WALKER
26 Director Marketing/Communications ... Mr. Jordan SMOCK
25 Grants Research Specialist ... Ms. Yvonne E. ANTHONY
57 Dir of Visual/Performing/Media Arts ... Mr. Marshall HUGHES
88 Director of the Writing Center Lab ... Ms. Judith KAHALAS

*Springfield Technical Community College (B)

Armory Square, Springfield MA 01105-1296

County: Hampden FICE Identification: 008078
Unit ID: 167905
Telephone: (413) 781-7822 Carnegie Class: Assoc/Pub-U-SC
FAX Number: (413) 755-6309 Calendar System: Semester
URL: www.stcc.edu
Established: 1967 Annual Undergrad Tuition & Fees (In-State): $5,436
Enrollment: 6,622 Coed
Affiliation or Control: State IRS Status: 501(c)3
Highest Offering: Associate Degree
Program: Occupational; 2-Year Principally Bachelor's Creditable; Technical Emphasis
Accreditation: EH, ADNUR, CA, COARC, DA, DH, DMS, ENGT, MAC, MLTAD, OTA, PTAA, RAD, SURGT

02 President ... Dr. Ira H. RUBENZAHL
05 Int Vice Pres Academic Affairs ... Dr. Arlene RODRIGUEZ
10 VP of Finance/CFO ... Mr. Joseph DASILVA
20 Dean of Curriculum ... Mr. Matthew GRAVEL
32 VP Student/Multicultural Affairs ... Mrs. Myra D. SMITH
04 Assistant to the President ... Mr. Michael J. SUZOR
50 Dean School of Business/Info Tech ... Dr. Leona R. ITTLEMAN
66 Director of Nursing ... Ms. Lisa FUGIEL
72 Dean Engineering/Mathematics ... Ms. Adrienne SMITH
76 Dean School of Health ... Mr. Michael C. FOSS
79 Dean Arts/Humanities/Social Sci ... Dr. Arlene RODRIGUEZ
81 Dean Sciences/Engineering Transfer ... Dr. Robert DICKERMAN
51 Dean of Business Services ... Dr. Debbie BELLUCCI
35 Dean of Student Affairs ... Vacant
07 Dean of Admissions ... Ms. Louisa M. DAVIS FREEMAN
09 Dean of Institutional Effectiveness ... Dr. Barb CHALFONTE
06 Registrar ... Mrs. Theresa REMILLARD
41 Director of Athletics ... Mr. J. Vincent GRASSETTI
102 VP Foundation/Workforce Options ... Mr. Bob LEPAGE
19 Chief of Police/Dir Public Safety ... Ms. E. Shawn DEJONG
18 Sr Director of Facilities ... Mrs. Maureen SOCHA
20 Dean Acad Advising/Student Success ... Mr. Kamari COLLINS
23 Coordinator of Health Services ... Mr. Jonathan L. MILLER
26 Director of Marketing ... Mrs. Joan THOMAS
36 Director of Coop/Career Placement ... Ms. Pamela WHITE
15 Senior Director of Human Resouces ... Ms. Joan D. NADEAU
16 Director of Human Resources ... Vacant
37 Director Student Financial Aid ... Mr. Jeremy GREENHOUSE
88 Fiscal/Financial Project Manager ... Mr. Jason COHEN
35 Coord Student Activities/Devel ... Ms. Andrea TARPEY
27 Coordinator of Media Relations ... Ms. Carla POTTS
88 Senior Director Finance/Budgets ... Mrs. Cathy OLSON
14 Sr Director of IT Applications ... Mr. Clifton PORTER
13 Sr Director of IT Infrastructure ... Mr. Robert TRUSCH
62 Dean Library Services ... Ms. Barbara WURTZEL
88 Controller ... Mr. Jonathan TUDRYN
09 Director of Institutional Research ... Ms. Suzanne SMITH
108 Director of Assessment ... Dr. Tracey TROTTIER
88 Director of Grants ... Vacant
96 Director of Purchasing ... Mr. Roger BESSETTE
88 Director of Access/Student Success ... Mr. Roosevelt CHARLES
88 Int Director of Gateway to College ... Ms. Jennifer SANCHEZ
44 Dir Alumni Relations/Annual Giving ... Ms. Christina TUOHEY
76 Assistant Dean Health ... Mr. Christopher SCOTT
102 Director of Foundation ... Ms. Jessica PROKOP
88 Director of Great Ideas ... Ms. Kerri KANE
37 Director of Student Accounts ... Ms. Dorothy UNGERER

Massachusetts Institute of Technology (C)

77 Massachusetts Avenue, Cambridge MA 02139-4307

County: Middlesex FICE Identification: 002178
Unit ID: 166683
Telephone: (617) 253-1000 Carnegie Class: RU/VH
FAX Number: N/A Calendar System: 4/1/4
URL: web.mit.edu
Established: 1861 Annual Undergrad Tuition & Fees: $46,704
Enrollment: 11,319 Coed
Affiliation or Control: Independent Non-Profit IRS Status: 501(c)3
Highest Offering: Doctorate
Program: Technical Emphasis
Accreditation: EH, BUS, CS, ENG, PLNG

01 President ... Dr. L. Rafael REIF
88 Chairman of the Corporation ... Mr. Robert B. MILLARD
05 Provost ... Prof. Martin SCHMIDT
00 Chancellor ... Prof. Cynthia BARNHART
03 Exec Vice President & Treasurer ... Mr. Israel RUIZ
46 Vice President for Research ... Prof. Maria T. ZUBER
43 Vice President & General Counsel ... Mr. Mark DIVINCENZO
20 Chancellor for Academic Advancement ... Mr. W. Eric L. GRIMSON
101 Vice President ... Dr. Kirk D. KOLENBRANDER
26 VP for Communications ... Mr. Nate NICKERSON
30 VP for Resource Development ... Ms. Julie LUCAS
88 Senior VP & Secretary of the Corp ... Mr. R. Gregory MORGAN
88 Deputy Executive Vice President ... Mr. Anthony P. SHARON
15 VP for Human Resources ... Ms. Lorraine GOFFE-RUSH
13 Vice President IS&T ... Mr. John CHARLES
10 Vice President for Finance ... Mr. Glen SHOR
29 Exec VP & CEO Alumni Association ... Ms. Judith M. COLE
88 President MIT Investment Mgmt Co ... Mr. Seth ALEXANDER
48 Dean Sch of Architecture & Planning ... Prof. Hashim SARKIS
54 Dean School of Engineering ... Prof. Ian A. WAITZ
79 Dean Sch Hum/Arts/Soc Sciences ... Prof. Melissa NOBLES
81 Dean School of Science ... Prof. Michael SIPSER
50 Dean Sloan School of Management ... Prof. David C. SCHMITTLEIN
20 Associate Provost ... Dr. Karen GLEASON
20 Associate Provost ... Prof. Philip S. KHOURY
20 Associate Provost ... Prof. Richard K. LESTER
08 Director of Libraries ... Mr. Chris BOURG
28 Institute Community & Equity Ofcr ... Prof. Edmund BERTSCHINGER
58 Dean Graduate for Education ... Dr. Christine ORTIZ
88 Dean for Undergraduate Education ... Prof. Dennis FREEMAN
32 Dean for Student Life ... Mr. Chris COLOMBO
106 Director of Digital Learning ... Prof. Sanjay SARMA
88 Director Lincoln Laboratory ... Dr. Eric D. EVANS
86 Director MIT Washington Office ... Mr. William B. BONVILLIAN
07 Dean of Admissions ... Mr. Stuart SCHMILL
37 Exec Dir Student Financial Services ... Ms. Elizabeth M. HICKS
23 Medical Dir & Head MIT Medical ... Dr. William M. KETTYLE
18 Dir Facilities Operations/Security ... Chief John DI FAVA
45 Director of Campus Planning ... Mr. Dennis SWINFORD
102 Exec Dir Foundation Relations ... Ms. Lindley HUEY
25 Dir Office of Sponsored Programs ... Ms. Michelle D. CHRISTY
96 Asst Dir of Strategic Sourcing ... Ms. Sara MALCONIAN
41 Director of Athletics ... Ms. Julie SORIERO
09 Director of Institutional Research ... Mrs. Lydia S. SNOVER
85 Dir International Students Office ... Mr. David ELWELL
36 Exec Dir Global Educ/Career Dev Ctr ... Ms. Melanie L. PARKER
93 Associate Dean and Director OME ... Ms. DiOnetta CRAYTON
06 Registrar ... Ms. Mary CALLAHAN
40 Director MIT Press ... Ms. Amy BRAND
39 Director of Housing Operations ... Mr. Daniel RODERICK
42 Chaplain to the Institute ... Dr. Robert M. RANDOLPH
38 Assoc Dean Student Support Services ... Mr. David RANDALL
94 Women's and Gender Studies Director ... Prof. Emma TENG
104 Associate Dean Global Education ... Ms. Malgorzata HEDDERICK
24 Manager Audio Visual ... Mr. Louis W. GRAHAM, JR.
04 Exec Assistant to the President ... Ms. Karla CASEY

Massachusetts School of Law at Andover (D)

500 Federal Street, Andover MA 01810-1094

County: Essex FICE Identification: 032353
Unit ID: 369002
Telephone: (978) 681-0800 Carnegie Class: Spec/Law
FAX Number: (978) 681-6330 Calendar System: Semester
URL: www.mslaw.edu
Established: 1988 Annual Graduate Tuition & Fees: $19,500
Enrollment: 408 Coed
Affiliation or Control: Independent Non-Profit IRS Status: 501(c)3
Highest Offering: Doctorate; No Undergraduates
Program: Professional
Accreditation: EH

00 Dean Emeritus ... Mr. Lawrence R. VELVEL
01 Dean ... Prof. Michael COYNE
10 Chief Business Officer ... Prof. Paula KALDIS
37 Director Student Financial Aid ... Ms. Lynn BOWAB
06 Registrar ... Ms. Louise ROSE
07 Director of Admissions ... Ms. Paula COLBY CLEMENTS
26 Chief Public Relations Officer ... Vacant
36 Director of Career Services ... Ms. Ursula FURI-PERRY
29 Director of Alumni Relations ... Ms. Ursula FURI-PERRY

MCPHS University (E)

179 Longwood Avenue, Boston MA 02115-5896

County: Suffolk FICE Identification: 002165
Unit ID: 166656
Telephone: (617) 732-2800 Carnegie Class: Spec/Health
FAX Number: (617) 732-2801 Calendar System: Semester
URL: www.mcphs.edu
Established: 1823 Annual Undergrad Tuition & Fees: $30,530
Enrollment: 6,935 Coed
Affiliation or Control: Independent Non-Profit IRS Status: 501(c)3
Highest Offering: Doctorate
Program: Professional
Accreditation: EH, ARCPA, DH, NMT, NURSE, @OPT, PHAR, PTA, RAD, RTT

01 President ... Mr. Charles F. MONAHAN, JR.
05 VP Academic Affairs/Provost ... Dr. Douglas J. PISANO
10 Exec Vice Pres Finance & Admin/COO .. Mr. Richard J. LESSARD
30 VP for Development & Chief of Staff ... Ms. Marguerite JOHNSON
12 Vice President Wor/Manch Campuses ... Vacant
107 Assoc Provost Professional Affairs ... Dr. Lily HSU
20 Assoc VP Academic Affs/Assoc Prov ... Dr. Michael MONTAGNE
106 Assoc Provost Online Education/CEO ... Dr. Barbara MACAULAY
43 Legal Counsel ... Ms. Deborah A. O'MALLEY
32 Dean of Students-Boston ... Dr. Craig MACK
32 Dean of Students-W/M ... Dr. Shuli XU
67 Dean Pharmacy Boston ... Dr. Paul DIFRANCESCO
67 Dean Pharmacy Worcester ... Dr. Michael J. MALLOY
08 Dean Library & Learning Resources ... Mr. Richard KAPLAN
49 Dean School of Arts and Sciences ... Dr. Delia C. ANDERSON
66 Dean School of Nursing ... Dr. Carol ELIADI
52 Dean Forsyth School for Dental Hyg ... Dr. Linda D. BOYD
88 Dean School of Physical Therapy ... Dr. Linda J. TSOUMAS
76 Assoc Provost Health Professions ... Dr. Maryann J. CLARK
15 Chief Human Resources Officer ... Ms. Mary LILLY
11 Admin Dean/Chief Retention Officer ... Ms. Stacey TAYLOR
06 Registrar ... Ms. Aeri MEYERS
13 Director of Information Services ... Mr. Tom SCANLON
21 Chief Business Officer ... Mr. Keith BELLUCCI
12 Exec Director Wor/Manch Campuses ... Mr. Seth P. WALL
29 Exec Director Alumni Relations ... Ms. Dawn BALLOU
07 Chief Enrollment Officer ... Ms. Kathleen RYAN
96 Director of Purchasing ... Ms. Margaret EATON-CRAWFORD
38 Director Counseling Services ... Ms. Molly PAYNE
26 Director of Communications ... Mr. Michael RATTY
39 Asst Dean Residential Living ... Mr. Joshua CHENEY
35 Asst Dean Campus Life & Leadership ... Ms. Jennifer MICHAEL
18 Director of Facilities ... Mr. Jeff WARD
19 Chief of Public Safety ... Mr. Jack KELLY
105 Manager of Web Services ... Ms. Charlene ROBERTSON
09 Dir Inst Research & Assessment ... Mr. Rajiv MALHOTRA
04 Administrative Asst to President ... Ms. Sheryl CHEAL

MCPHS-Worcester Campus (F)

19 Foster Street, Worcester MA 01608-1715

Telephone: (508) 890-8855 Identification: 770112
Accreditation: &EH

† Branch campus of MCPHS University, Boston, MA.

Merrimack College (G)

315 Turnpike Street, North Andover MA 01845-5800

County: Essex FICE Identification: 002120
Unit ID: 166850
Telephone: (978) 837-5000 Carnegie Class: Bac/Diverse
FAX Number: (978) 837-5222 Calendar System: Semester
URL: www.merrimack.edu
Established: 1947 Annual Undergrad Tuition & Fees: $37,270
Enrollment: 3,337 Coed
Affiliation or Control: Roman Catholic IRS Status: 501(c)3
Highest Offering: Master's
Program: Liberal Arts And General; Teacher Preparatory; Professional
Accreditation: EH, CAATE, ENG

01 President ... Dr. Christopher E. HOPEY
100 Chief of Staff ... Mr. Jeffrey DOGGETT
04 Director Office of the President ... Ms. Lisa JEBALI
05 Provost & Sr VP Academic Affairs ... Dr. Carol GLOD
10 Vice Pres Finance & Budget/CFO ... Mr. William KLINE
88 Special Assistant to the President ... Dr. Russell MAYER
11 VP of Administration & Campus Svcs ... Mr. Mark COLLINS
84 VP for Enrollment & Retention ... Mr. David HAUTANEN
32 Vice Pres Mission/Student Affairs .. Rev. Raymond DLUGOS, OSA
30 VP Development and Alumni Affairs ... Ms. Sara BRAZDA
06 AVP Planning/Research & Registrar ... Dr. Nancy LUDWIG
88 Assoc VP/Chief of Staff to Provost ... Mr. Mark GOULD
27 Assoc VP Communications ... Mr. James CHIAVELLI
86 AVP for External Affairs ... Mr. Felipe SCHWARZ
20 Senior Vice Provost ... Dr. Cynthia MCGOWAN
43 Internal General Counsel ... Mr. Nicholas MCDONALD
88 Asst VP for Marketing ... Ms. Zoe COHEN
21 Asst VP & Controller Fiscal Affair ... Ms. Paula CONNOLLY
29 Assoc VP Develop & Alumni Relations ... Ms. Joanne MERMELSTEIN
35 AVP Stdnt Engage/Dean 1st Yr Stdnts ... Ms. Allison GILL
104 AVP Intl/Grad/Multicul Students ... Ms. Lauren BENT
36 Assoc VP Corporate & Career Engage ... Dr. Heather MAIETTA
50 Dean Girard School of Business ... Dr. Mark CORDANO
54 Dean Science & Engineering ... Dr. Alan WEATHERWAX
49 Dean of Liberal Arts ... Dr. Kathleen TIEMANN

53	Dean School of Education	Dr. Dan BUTIN
88	AVP for Wellness/Dean of Students	Ms. Stephanie KENDALL
37	Director of Student Financial Aid	Ms. Adrienne MONTGOMERY
13	Chief Information Officer	Mr. Chip STILES
07	Director of Undergraduate Admission	Mr. Darren CONINE
41	Director of Athletics	Mr. Jeremy GIBSON
09	Dir Institutional Research & Plng	Ms. Kristen SULLIVAN
15	Director Human Resources	Ms. Denice BAKER
08	Director of the Library	Ms. Kathryn GEOFFRION-SCANNELL
42	Director of Campus Ministry	Rev. Keith HOLLIS
23	Director Counseling & Health Svcs	Vacant
39	Director of Residence Life	Mr. Cameron SMITH
19	Director of Police Services	Mr. Michael DELGRECO
31	Dir of Stevens Service Learning Ctr	Ms. Mary MCHUGH
24	Dir of Media Instructional Services	Mr. Kevin SALEMME
96	Director of Purchasing	Mr. Michael MAGNER
105	Director of Web Services	Ms. Stacie BOWMAN
28	Director Diversity Education	Mr. J. Scott GAGE
88	Special Asst Acad Affairs/Provost	Mr. Michael ACCARDI

MGH Institute of Health Professions (A)

36 1st Avenue, Boston MA 02129-4557

County: Suffolk FICE Identification: 022316
Unit ID: 166869

Telephone: (617) 726-2947 Carnegie Class: Spec/Health
FAX Number: (617) 726-3716 Calendar System: Semester
URL: www.mghihp.edu
Established: 1977 Annual Undergrad Tuition & Fees: N/A
Enrollment: 1,166 Coed
Affiliation or Control: Independent Non-Profit IRS Status: 501(c)3
Highest Offering: Doctorate
Program: Professional
Accreditation: EH, #ARCPA, NURSE, PTA, SP

† Tuition varies by degree program.

Montserrat College of Art (B)

23 Essex Street, Beverly MA 01915-4508

County: Essex FICE Identification: 020630
Unit ID: 166911

Telephone: (978) 921-4242 Carnegie Class: Spec/Arts
FAX Number: (978) 922-4268 Calendar System: Semester
URL: www.montserrat.edu
Established: 1970 Annual Undergrad Tuition & Fees: $29,550
Enrollment: 380 Coed
Affiliation or Control: Independent Non-Profit IRS Status: 501(c)3
Highest Offering: Baccalaureate
Program: Fine Arts Emphasis
Accreditation: EH, ART

01	President	Dr. Stephen D. IMMERMAN
05	Dean Faculty/Academic Affairs	Ms. Laura TONELLI
32	Dean of Students	Ms. Maureen WARK
30	Dean of Development	Mr. Howard AMIDON
26	Dean College Rels/Spec Asst to Pres	Ms. Jo BRODERICK
10	Chief Financial Officer	Ms. Cara CALLANAN
13	Director of Information Technology	Mr. Jake SYNDER
08	Librarian	Ms. Cheri COE
06	Registrar	Mrs. Theresa SKELLY
37	Director of Financial Aid	Ms. Emma PUGLISI
15	Human Resources Generalist	Ms. Christin BOURANIS
07	Director of Admissions	Mr. Jeffrey NEWELL
04	Executive Asst to the President	Ms. Margaret WAUGH

Mount Holyoke College (C)

50 College Street, South Hadley MA 01075-1424

County: Hampshire FICE Identification: 002192
Unit ID: 166939

Telephone: (413) 538-2000 Carnegie Class: Bac/A&S
FAX Number: (413) 538-2391 Calendar System: Semester
URL: www.mtholyoke.edu
Established: 1837 Annual Undergrad Tuition & Fees: $43,716
Enrollment: 2,255 Female
Affiliation or Control: Independent Non-Profit IRS Status: 501(c)3
Highest Offering: Master's
Program: Liberal Arts And General; Teacher Preparatory
Accreditation: EH

01	President	Lynn PASQUERELLA
05	Dean of Faculty/VP for Acad Affairs	Sonya STEPHENS
10	VP for Finance and Administration	Shannon GUREK
84	VP for Enrollment	Diane ANCI
30	VP for Advancement	MaryAnne YOUNG
32	Dean of the College/VP Student Affs	Cerri BANKS
26	VP for Communication and Marketing	Christine HUTCHINS
101	Sr Advisor/Secretary of the Board	Lenore REILLY
06	Registrar	Elizabeth PYLE

Mount Ida College (D)

777 Dedham Street, Newton MA 02459

County: Middlesex FICE Identification: 002193
Unit ID: 166948

Telephone: (617) 928-4500 Carnegie Class: Bac/Diverse
FAX Number: (617) 928-4746 Calendar System: Semester
URL: www.mountida.edu
Established: 1899 Annual Undergrad Tuition & Fees: $32,300
Enrollment: 1,320 Coed
Affiliation or Control: Independent Non-Profit IRS Status: 501(c)3
Highest Offering: Master's
Program: Liberal Arts And General; Professional
Accreditation: EH, ART, CIDA, DH, FUSER

01	President	Mr. Barry BROWN
05	Provost and Chief Academic Officer	Mr. Ronald E. AKIE
30	Vice President for Advancement	Ms. Jill WIERBICKI ABRAHAMS
10	Vice Pres & Chief Financial Officer	Mr. Jason POTTS
32	Vice President of Student Affairs	Ms. Laura DEVEAU
21	Controller	Mr. Richard ROGAN
88	Asst Dean Student Engage/ Leadership	Mr. Patrick ROMERAO-ALDAZ
06	Registrar	Ms. Kathy POSEY
88	Director of Disability Services	Mr. Nick FARANDA
29	Dir Alumni Relations/Annual Giving	Vacant
37	Director Financial Aid	Ms. Dyan TEEHAN
36	Director of Career Services	Mr. Robert BROOKS
15	Interim Director of Human Resources	Ms. Denise DORGAN
26	Associate VP Mkting & Communication	Ms. Fran BERGER
85	Dir Ctr Gbl Connections/Cont Educ	Ms. Robin MALAVALIN
41	Athletic Director	Mr. Matthew BURKE
19	Acting Director of Public Safety	Mr. John KENNEDY
18	Director of Facilities	Mr. Andrew PAIGE
09	Director of Institutional Research	Mr. Jerome DEAN
35	Dean of Student Services	Ms. Mary Anne MILLER
24	Director of Educational Media	Mr. Manouche MADANIPOUR
96	Director of Business Services	Ms. Leah WEBBER
07	Dean of Admissions	Mr. Jeff CUTTING
28	Asst Director Diversity & Inclusion	Vacant
42	College Chaplain	Vacant
13	Director Network Services	Mr. David VALENTINE
23	Dir Student Health Services	Ms. Beth GRAMPETRO
35	Director Student Activities	Ms. Adebimpe DARE
58	Assistant Dean Graduate Studies	Mr. Scott BURKE
04	Administrative Asst to President	Ms. Nylana C. THOME
43	Dir Legal Services/General Counsel	Ms. Suzanne GALLAGHER

The National Graduate School of Quality Management (E)

186 Jones Road, Falmouth MA 02540-2908

County: Barnstable FICE Identification: 035043
Unit ID: 441478

Telephone: (508) 457-1313 Carnegie Class: Spec/Bus
FAX Number: (508) 457-5347 Calendar System: Other
URL: www.ngs.edu
Established: 1993 Annual Undergrad Tuition & Fees: $20,500
Enrollment: 239 Coed
Affiliation or Control: Independent Non-Profit IRS Status: 501(c)3
Highest Offering: Doctorate
Program: Business Emphasis
Accreditation: EH

01	President/CEO	Dr. R. Clinton MINER
05	Dean of Academic Affairs	Dr. Eileen SULLIVAN
84	Dean Enrollment Management	Vacant
88	Director of Compliance	Mr. Jay BEIRN
06	Registrar	Mr. Jay BEIRNE

New England College of Business and Finance (F)

10 High Street, Suite 204, Boston MA 02110

County: Suffolk FICE Identification: 039653
Unit ID: 164438

Telephone: (617) 951-2350 Carnegie Class: Assoc/PrivFP4
FAX Number: (617) 951-2533 Calendar System: Other
URL: www.necb.edu
Established: 1909 Annual Undergrad Tuition & Fees: $10,525
Enrollment: 841 Coed
Affiliation or Control: Proprietary IRS Status: Proprietary
Highest Offering: Master's
Program: Business Emphasis
Accreditation: EH

01	President	Mr. Howard E. HORTON
05	Provost	Ms. Debra LEAHY
10	Sr VP Operations/Finance	Mr. Dennis J. MADIGAN
32	Sr Vice Pres of Student Services	Ms. Paula BRAMANTE
21	Controller	Ms. Cassie LAMPSHIRE
97	Dean of Undergraduate Studies	Mr. Roger PAO
88	Program Chair MBE	Ms. Michele JURGENS
88	Program Chair MBA	Dr. Carla PATALANO
04	Asst to the President/Office Mgr	Ms. Kathy CANTALUPA
06	Registrar	Mr. Robert WAGSTAFF
88	Dean of Students	Ms. Caitrin BRISSON
84	Director of Enrollment	Ms. Kirsten THOMPSON
37	Student Finance Supervisor	Ms. Renee JORDON

New England College of Optometry (G)

424 Beacon Street, Boston MA 02115-1129

County: Suffolk FICE Identification: 002164
Unit ID: 167093

Telephone: (617) 266-2030 Carnegie Class: Spec/Health
FAX Number: (617) 424-9202 Calendar System: Semester
URL: www.neco.edu
Established: 1894 Annual Undergrad Tuition & Fees: $44,840
Enrollment: 520 Coed
Affiliation or Control: Independent Non-Profit IRS Status: 501(c)3
Highest Offering: Doctorate
Program: Professional
Accreditation: EH, OPT, OPTR

01	President	Dr. Clifford SCOTT
05	VP & Dean of Academic Affairs	Dr. Barry FISCH
10	Sr VP CFO/COO	Ms. Traci LOGAN
17	Chief Pracrice Management & Clinic	Dr. David MILLS
30	VP of Institutional Advancement	Ms. Nancy BROUDE
32	Assoc Dean Students/Dir Stdnt Svcs	Ms. Barbara MCGINLEY
07	Director of Admissions	Ms. Kristen HARRINGTON
37	Director Student Financial Aid	Ms. Carol RUBEL
15	Director of Human Resources	Ms. Patricia DAHILL
06	Registrar	Ms. Glenda UNDERWOOD
08	Director of Library Services	Ms. Kristin MOTTE
04	Executive Asst to the President	Ms. Marie HILL

New England Conservatory of Music (H)

290 Huntington Avenue, Boston MA 02115-5018

County: Suffolk FICE Identification: 002194
Unit ID: 167057

Telephone: (617) 585-1100 Carnegie Class: Spec/Arts
FAX Number: (617) 262-0500 Calendar System: Semester
URL: www.necmusic.edu
Established: 1867 Annual Undergrad Tuition & Fees: $42,600
Enrollment: 786 Coed
Affiliation or Control: Independent Non-Profit IRS Status: 501(c)3
Highest Offering: Doctorate
Program: Liberal Arts And General; Teacher Preparatory; Professional; Music Emphasis
Accreditation: EH

01	Interim President	Mr. Thomas NOVAK
05	Provost/Dean of the College	Mr. Thomas NOVAK
10	Sr Vice Pres Finance/Operations	Mr. Edward R. LESSER
30	Exec Vice Pres Institutional Advanc	Mr. Don JONES
26	Vice Pres Marketing/Communications	Ms. Carol PHELAN
100	Chief of Staff	Ms. Kairyn RAINER
56	Dean/Exec Dir Sch Continuing Educ	Ms. Leslie Wu FOLEY
32	Dean of Students	Ms. Suzanne HEGLAND
07	Asst Dean for Admissions	Mr. Alex POWELL
21	Controller	Ms. Amanda GATES
18	Exec Dir Facilities/Engrng/Constr	Mr. Michael RYAN
06	Registrar	Mr. Robert WINKLEY
08	Director of Libraries	Mr. Alan KARASS
37	Director Financial Aid	Ms. Lauren URBANEK
35	Director Residence Life	Ms. Allesandra C. PALMER
29	Senior Director of Alumni Relations	Ms. Katrina DEBONVILLE
15	Director of Human Resources	Ms. Marianne WISHEART
13	Director ITS	Mr. Charles MEMBRINO
09	Director of Institutional Research	Ms. Sarah DOW
20	Asst Dean of Stdnts/Dir Intl Stdnts	Ms. Rebecca TEETERS
38	Director Student Counseling	Ms. Jan LERBINGER
88	Dir of Entrepreneurial Musicianship	Ms. Rachel ROBERTS

The New England Institute of Art (I)

10 Brookline Place West, Brookline MA 02445-7295

County: Norfolk FICE Identification: 007486
Unit ID: 167321

Telephone: (617) 739-1700 Carnegie Class: Spec/Arts
FAX Number: (617) 582-4500 Calendar System: Semester
URL: www.artinstitutes.edu/boston
Established: 1952 Annual Undergrad Tuition & Fees: $18,760
Enrollment: 555 Coed
Affiliation or Control: Proprietary IRS Status: Proprietary
Highest Offering: Baccalaureate
Program: Occupational; Fine Arts Emphasis
Accreditation: EH

01	President	Dr. John LAY
05	Dean of Academic Affairs	Mr. Chris PREVITA
32	Dean of Student Affairs	Ms. Michele TRACIA
06	Registrar	Ms. Maria SARDINAS
13	Campus Technology Manager	Mr. Sayed KHODIER
15	Human Resources Generalist	Ms. Camile BATEMAN
36	Director of Career Services	Mr. John LAY
10	Director Financial Services	Mr. Eric MESSINA

New England Law | Boston (J)

154 Stuart Street, Boston MA 02116-5687

County: Suffolk FICE Identification: 008916
Unit ID: 167215

Telephone: (617) 451-0010 Carnegie Class: Spec/Law
FAX Number: (617) 422-7333 Calendar System: Semester
URL: www.nesl.edu
Established: 1908 Annual Undergrad Tuition & Fees: $45,606
Enrollment: 871 Coed
Affiliation or Control: Independent Non-Profit IRS Status: 501(c)3
Highest Offering: First Professional Degree
Program: Professional
Accreditation: LAW

01	Dean	Mr. John F. O'BRIEN
05	Associate Dean	Mr. Victor M. HANSEN
11	Associate Dean of Administration	Ms. Susan S. CALAMARE
20	Assistant Dean	Ms. Sandra GOLDSMITH

07 Director of Admission ....Ms. Michelle L'ETOILE
10 Chief Financial Officer ....Mr. David M. ROSATI
08 Director of the Law Library ....Ms. Anne ACTON
30 Dir Career Svcs/Dev/Alumni Rels ....Ms. Mandie A. LEBEAU
37 Director of Financial Aid ....Mr. Eric A. KRUPSKI
06 Registrar ....Mr. David M. BERTI
18 Director of Facilities/Security ....Mr. Miguel ALVARADO
32 Director of Student Services ....Ms. Jacqueline PILGRIM

New England School of Acupuncture (A)

150 California Street, Newton MA 02458-1005
County: Middlesex FICE Identification: 025798
Unit ID: 167181
Telephone: (617) 558-1788 Carnegie Class: Spec/Health
FAX Number: (617) 558-1789 Calendar System: Trimester
URL: www.nesa.edu
Established: 1975 Annual Undergrad Tuition & Fees: $20,600
Enrollment: 180 Coed
Affiliation or Control: Independent Non-Profit IRS Status: 501(c)3
Highest Offering: Master's; No Lower Division
Program: Professional
Accreditation: ACUP

01 Executive Director ....Susan L. GORMAN
05 Academic Dean ....Meredith ST. JOHN
10 Controller ....Katherine DECELLES
07 Admissions Director ....Jason POWERS
06 Registrar ....Julia MABUCHI

Newbury College (B)

129 Fisher Avenue, Brookline MA 02445-5796
County: Norfolk FICE Identification: 007484
Unit ID: 167251
Telephone: (617) 730-7000 Carnegie Class: Bac/Diverse
FAX Number: (617) 731-9618 Calendar System: Semester
URL: www.newbury.edu
Established: 1962 Annual Undergrad Tuition & Fees: $29,930
Enrollment: 874 Coed
Affiliation or Control: Independent Non-Profit IRS Status: 501(c)3
Highest Offering: Baccalaureate
Program: Liberal Arts And General
Accreditation: EH

01 President ....Mr. Joseph L. CHILLO
05 Vice President Academic Affairs ....Dr. Douglas FLOR
10 Vice President Finance/CFO ....Ms. Joyce HANLON
11 Vice President of Administration ....Mr. Paul MARTIN
30 Vice President for Advancement ....Ms. Clare MCCULLY
84 Vice Pres Enrollment Management ....Mr. Salvadore LIBERTO
106 Assoc VP for Online & Cont Educ ....Mr. Bill BOOZANG
32 Dean of Student Affairs ....Ms. Anne-Marie KENNEY
20 Assoc Dean for Academic Services ....Ms. Sara D'ANJOU
08 Director of Library Services ....Mr. Anthony VIOLA
37 Dean of Student Financial Services ....Mr. Elreo CAMPBELL
06 Registrar ....Ms. Rachelle E. MAZZA
15 Director Human Resources ....Ms. Amy DOWNING
26 Dir of Marketing and Communications .Ms. Valerie STURTEVANT
36 Director of Career Services ....Ms. Sara SHECKELLS
38 Director Counseling/Health Educ ....Ms. Susan CHAMANDY
18 Director of Facilities ....Mr. Ron MINERVINI
41 Director of Athletics ....Mr. Jonathan HARPER
07 Director of Admissions ....Ms. Jillian HALL
39 Dir of Res Life & Community Stds ....Ms. Jennifer FORRY
04 Executive Asst to President ....Ms. Cory LANDIS
19 Director Campus Safety ....Mr. Paul NOONAN

Nichols College (C)

Center Road, PO Box 5000, Dudley MA 01571-5000
County: Worcester FICE Identification: 002197
Unit ID: 167260
Telephone: (508) 213-1560 Carnegie Class: Bac/Diverse
FAX Number: N/A Calendar System: Semester
URL: www.nichols.edu
Established: 1815 Annual Undergrad Tuition & Fees: $33,300
Enrollment: 1,476 Coed
Affiliation or Control: Independent Non-Profit IRS Status: 501(c)3
Highest Offering: Master's
Program: Liberal Arts And General; Teacher Preparatory; Professional; Business Emphasis
Accreditation: EH, IACBE

01 President ....Susan WEST ENGELKEMEYER
05 Provost and Senior Vice President ....Alan J. REINHARDT
10 Vice President Administration ....Michael J. STANTON
30 Vice President for Advancement ....William C. PIECZYNSKI
84 Vice President for Enrollment ....William BOFFI
32 Dean of Students ....Pamela J. BOGGIO
26 Assoc VP Marketing/Communications ....Cynthia G. BROWN
13 Chief Information Officer ....Kevin F. BRASSARD
58 Exec Dir Graduate & Prof Studies ....Kerry CALNAN
04 Assistant to the President ....Lynn S. LOOBY
06 Assoc Dean Academic Admin/Records ....Peter M. ENGH
41 Director of Athletics ....Christopher COLVIN
07 Asst Dean for Enrollment ....Paul O. BROWER
06 Registrar ....Betin ROBICHAUD
08 Director of Library ....Jim DOUGLAS
15 Asst Director of Human Resources ....Katie CUSHING

29 Director of Alumni Relations ....Brianne S. CALLAHAN
21 Controller ....Jamie SKOWYRA
35 Dir Student Activities/Orientation ....Brian QUINLAN
36 Director of Career Services ....Elizabeth HORGAN
37 Interim Director of Financial Aid ....Jennifer BIANCO
38 Director Mental Health Services . Monica GOODRICH PELLETIER
26 Director of Communications ....Ronald SCHACHTER
18 Assoc VP for Facilities Management ....Robert W. LAVIGNE
07 Associate Director of Admissions ....Emily REARDON
96 Director Procurement & Contract Svc ....Kay F. YOUNG
19 Director Public Safety ....Jack CAULFIELD
23 Director Health Services ....Katherine NICOLETTI
39 Director Residence Life ....Marney BUSS
104 Director Study Abroad ....Susan WAYMAN
105 Director Web & Social Media ....Claudia SNELL

Northeastern University (D)

360 Huntington Avenue, Boston MA 02115-0195
County: Suffolk FICE Identification: 002199
Unit ID: 167358
Telephone: (617) 373-2000 Carnegie Class: RU/H
FAX Number: N/A Calendar System: Semester
URL: www.northeastern.edu
Established: 1898 Annual Undergrad Tuition & Fees: $45,530
Enrollment: 19,798 Coed
Affiliation or Control: Independent Non-Profit IRS Status: 501(c)3
Highest Offering: Doctorate
Program: Liberal Arts And General; Teacher Preparatory; Professional
Accreditation: EH, ANEST, ARCPA, AUD, BUS, ENG, ENGT, LAW, NURSE, PH, PHAR, PSPSY, PTA, SCPSY, SP, SPAA

01 President ....Dr. Joseph E. AOUN
04 Executive Asst to the President ....Ms. Susie C. GUSZCZA
05 Sr VP Academic Affairs and Provost ....Dr. James C. BEAN
100 Chief of Staff ....Mr. J.D LAROCK
88 Sr VP Enroll Mgmt & CEO NUGN ..Dr. Philomena V. MANTELLA
30 Sr VP University Advancement ....Ms. Diane N. MACGILLIVRAY
43 Sr VP and General Counsel ....Mr. Ralph C. MARTIN, II
26 Sr VP External Affairs ....Mr. Michael A. ARMINI
11 Sr VP & Chief Operating Officer ....Vacant
12 Seattle Campus Dean & CEO ....Mr. Tayloe WASHBURN
12 Charlotte Campus Dean & CEO ....Dr. Cheryl RICHARDS
08 Dean University Libraries ....Mr. William M. WAKELING
46 Sr Vice Provost Research & Grad Ed ....Dr. Melvin BERNSTEIN
88 Sr Vice Prov UG Ed & Exp Learning ....Dr. Susan AMBROSE
32 Chief Integrated Stdnt Engmt Ofcr ....Dr. Laura A. WANKEL
88 VP & Senior Counsel ....Mr. Vincent J. LEMBO
13 VP & CIO ....Mr. Rehan KHAN
84 VP Enrollment Management ....Mr. Sundar KUMARASAMY
35 VP Student Affs & Dean of Students ....Ms. Madeleine A. ESTABROOK
88 VP Development ....Ms. Luanne KIRWIN
15 VP Human Resources Management ....Ms. Katherine N. PENDERGAST
18 VP Facilities ....Ms. Nancy S. MAY
86 VP Government Relations ....Mr. Tim E. LESHAN
88 VP Public Affairs ....Mr. Robert P. GITTENS
88 VP Business Affs Graduate Campuses .Mr. M. Seamus HARREYS
88 VP Advancement & Campaign Director ....Mr. Joseph DONNELLY, JR.
31 VP City & Community Affairs ....Mr. John M. TOBIN
88 VP Enterprise Risk Management ....Ms. Deloris PETTIS
88 VP & Chief Campus Planning and Dev . Ms. Kathy SPIEGELMAN
20 Vice Provost Academic Affairs ....Dr. Mary LOEFFELHOLZ
20 Vice Provost Budget/Planning/Admin ....Dr. Anthony RINI
28 Vice Prov Inst Diversity & Inclsn ....Dr. John ARMENDARIZ
76 Interim Dean Health Sciences ....Mr. Jack REYNOLDS
07 AVP Enrollment ....Ms. Ronne PATRICK-TURNER
37 Dean Student Financial Services ....Mr. Tony ERWIN
36 Assoc VP Career Services & Co-Op Ed ....Ms. Maria K. STEIN
88 Assoc VP & Deputy General Counsel ....Ms. Lisa SINCLAIR
58 AVP Graduate Affairs ....Dr. Phil HE
21 Assoc VP of Finance ....Mr. Greg CONDELL
88 AVP Research Administration ....Vacant
09 Interim AVP Inst Rsrch & Data Admin ....Mr. David NAVICK
06 Asst VP & University Registrar ....Ms. Linda D. ALLEN
27 Asst VP Communications ....Ms. Renata NYUL
88 AVP Interdisc Initiatives/Spec Proj ....Mr. Robert DIETRICH
44 Asst VP of Treasury Mgmt ....Ms. Alysa GERLACH
92 Director of University Honors Pgm ....Dr. Paola CESARINI
42 Exec Dir Sprituality & Dialogue ....Mr. Alexander KERN
19 Director of Public Safety ....Mr. Michael DAVIS
41 Director of Athletics ....Mr. Peter P. ROBY
10 Sr VP Finance & Treasurer ....Mr. Thomas NEDELL
88 Sr Advisor to the President ....Mr. Jack H. MCCARTHY
77 Dean Col Computer & Info Science ....Dr. Carla E. BRODLEY
54 Dean College of Engineering ....Dr. Nadine AUBRY
81 Dean College of Science ....Dr. J. Murray GIBSON
50 Dean D'Amore-McKim School of Bus ....Dr. Hugh COURTNEY
57 Dean Col Arts/Media/Design ....Dr. Elizabeth HUDSON
61 Dean School of Law ....Dr. Jeremy PAUL
83 Dean Col of Soc Sci & Humanities ....Dr. Uta POIGER
107 Dean Col Prof Studies/VP Prof Educ ....Dr. John G. LABRIE

Northpoint Bible College (E)

320 South Main Street, Haverhill MA 01835
County: Essex FICE Identification: 035705
Unit ID: 217606
Telephone: (978) 478-3400 Carnegie Class: Spec/Faith
FAX Number: (978) 478-3406 Calendar System: Semester
URL: www.northpoint.edu
Established: 1924 Annual Undergrad Tuition & Fees: $11,150
Enrollment: 316 Coed
Affiliation or Control: Assemblies Of God Church IRS Status: 501(c)3
Highest Offering: Master's
Program: Religious Emphasis
Accreditation: BI

01 President ....Rev Dr. David J. ARNETT
03 Senior Vice President ....Rev Dr. Patrick G. GALLAGHER
32 Dean of Student Affairs ....Rev. David HANSHUMAKER
10 Director of Finance ....Mr. Ed LAUGHLIN
07 Director of Enrollment ....Rev. Chris CLEVELAND
08 Head Librarian ....Miss Ginger MCDONALD
37 Director of Financial Aid ....Miss Patricia STAUFFER

Pine Manor College (F)

400 Heath Street, Chestnut Hill MA 02467-2332
County: Norfolk FICE Identification: 002201
Unit ID: 167455
Telephone: (617) 731-7000 Carnegie Class: Bac/A&S
FAX Number: (617) 731-7199 Calendar System: Semester
URL: www.pmc.edu
Established: 1911 Annual Undergrad Tuition & Fees: $26,360
Enrollment: 420 Coed
Affiliation or Control: Independent Non-Profit IRS Status: 501(c)3
Highest Offering: Master's
Program: Liberal Arts And General
Accreditation: EH

01 Interim President ....Dr. Rosemary ASHBY
05 Dean of College ....Dr. Diane MELLO-GOLDNER
10 Vice President for Finance ....Mr. Tim JOHNSON
11 Vice President for Administration ....Mr. William OPAVA
30 Chief Development Officer ....Ms. Susan FUGLIESE
32 Interim Dean of Student Affairs ....Mr. Craig HUTCHINSON
84 Vice President for Enrollment ....Mr. Glen THOMAS
21 Director of Finance ....Mr. Timothy JOHNSON
06 Interim Registrar ....Ms. Liz DORAN
26 Dir Publications/Media Relations ....Ms. Efrat ZINNAR-SHAVIT
08 Interim Library Director ....Ms. Sarah WOOLF

Pope St. John XXIII National Seminary (G)

558 South Avenue, Weston MA 02493-2699
County: Middlesex FICE Identification: 002202
Unit ID: 167464
Telephone: (781) 899-5500 Carnegie Class: Spec/Faith
FAX Number: (781) 899-9057 Calendar System: Semester
URL: www.psjs.edu
Established: 1964 Annual Graduate Tuition & Fees: $31,500
Enrollment: 67 Male
Affiliation or Control: Roman Catholic IRS Status: 501(c)3
Highest Offering: Master's; No Undergraduates
Program: Professional
Accreditation: THEOL

01 Rector and President ....Rev. William B. PALARDY
05 Academic Dean ....Dr. Anthony KEATY
08 Librarian ....Mr. Joel PETTIT
10 Business Manager ....Mrs. Kyle RYAN
06 Registrar ....Dr. Anthony KEATY
30 Chief Development Officer ....Mr. Richard MURPHY
32 Chief Student Life Officer ....Rev. Paul MICELI

Quincy College (H)

1250 Hancock Street, Quincy MA 02169-4324
County: Norfolk FICE Identification: 002205
Unit ID: 167525
Telephone: (617) 984-1700 Carnegie Class: Assoc/Pub-S-MC
FAX Number: (617) 984-1779 Calendar System: Semester
URL: www.quincycollege.edu
Established: 1958 Annual Undergrad Tuition & Fees (In-District): $6,856
Enrollment: 4,705 Coed
Affiliation or Control: Local IRS Status: 501(c)3
Highest Offering: Associate Degree
Program: Occupational; 2-Year Principally Bachelor's Creditable
Accreditation: EH, ADNUR, MLTAD, PNUR, @PTAA, SURGT

01 President ....Dr. Peter H. TSAFFARAS
05 SVP/Academic Affairs ....Ms. Aundrea E. KELLEY
11 SVP/Administration/Finance ....Mr. Joseph MERCURIO
100 Assistant to the President ....Mr. Stephen KEARNEY
10 Chief Financial Officer ....Mr. Joseph MERCURIO
04 Admin Asst to President ....Ms. Donna M. BRUGMAN
06 Dir of Student Records & Registrar ....Ms. Catherine MALONEY
66 Dean of Nursing ....Ms. Linda PENDERGAST
49 Dean of Liberal Arts ....Dr. Robert BAKER
50 Dean of Professional Programs ....Mr. William BRENNAN
81 Dean of Natural & Health Sciences ....Capt. Vincent VANJOOLEN
21 Director of Finance ....Mr. Martin AHERN
13 VP/Technology & Mission Support ....Mr. Tom C. PHAM
12 Dean of Plymouth Campus ....Ms. Mary BURKE
37 Assoc VP for Financial Aid ....Ms. Rose M. DEVITO
18 Dir of Admin Services & Facilities ....Mr. William C. HALL
32 Assoc VP for Student Development ....Ms. Susan G. BOSSA
15 Vice Pres for Human Resources ....Ms. Mary SCOTT
26 Assoc VP of Comm & Marketing ....Mr. Taggart BOYLE
07 Director of Admissions ....Ms. Eileen KNIGHT
88 Director of Academic Advising ....Mr. Arthur ESPOSITO

85 Director of Int'l Student Services .... Ms. Lisa STACK
30 Director of Development .... Ms. Tina CAHILL
09 Assoc VP for Inst Research & Assess .... Dr. Kimberly PUHALA
35 Director of Student Development .... Ms. Amanda DECK
08 Director of Library Services .... Ms. Susan WHITEHEAD
106 Dean/Online Learning & Inst Affairs ..... Mr. Michael MARRAPODI

Regis College (A)

235 Wellesley Street, Weston MA 02493-1571
County: Middlesex FICE Identification: 002206
Unit ID: 167598
Telephone: (781) 768-7000 Carnegie Class: Spec/Health
FAX Number: (781) 768-8339 Calendar System: Semester
URL: www.regiscollege.edu
Established: 1927 Annual Undergrad Tuition & Fees: $37,540
Enrollment: 1,912 Coed
Affiliation or Control: Independent Non-Profit IRS Status: 501(c)3
Highest Offering: Doctorate
Program: 2-Year Principally Bachelor's Creditable; Liberal Arts And General; Teacher Preparatory; Professional; Nursing Emphasis
Accreditation: EH, ADNUR, NMT, NUR, RAD, SW

01 President .... Dr. Antoinette M. HAYS
10 Vice President Finance/Business .... Mr. Thomas G. PISTORINO
84 Vice Pres Enrollment & Marketing .... Mr. Paul VACCARO
05 Vice President Academic Affairs .... Dr. Malcolm O. ASADOORIAN, III
07 Director of Admission .... Vacant
37 Director of Financial Aid .... Ms. Bonnie QUINN
06 Registrar .... Ms. Esther A. GHAZARIAN
09 Vice Pres of Institutional Research .... Dr. Susan TAMMARO
15 Director of Human Resources .... Ms. Joan D. SULLIVAN
18 Director of Physical Plant .... Mr. Joseph SHAUGHNESSY
21 Director Finance & Business .... Ms. Nancy PLASKER
29 Director of Alumni Relations .... Mrs. Christina DUGGAN
32 Vice President Student Affairs .... Ms. Kara KOLOMITZ
23 Director of Health Services .... Ms. Dianna JONES
04 Special Assistant to President .... Ms. Mary Jane DOHERTY
08 Director of Library .... Vacant
13 Chief Information Officer .... Ms. Marla BOTELHO
41 Director Athletics & Physical Ed .... Mr. Robert RILEY
42 Director Campus Ministry .... Vacant
96 Director of Purchasing .... Ms. Diep SHEEHAN
31 Director of Community Living .... Ms. Kelly TRESELER
35 Director of Student Programs .... Mr. Paul MURPHY
30 Chief Development Officer .... Ms. Miriam FINN-SHERMAN

Saint John's Seminary (B)

127 Lake Street, Brighton MA 02135-3898
County: Suffolk FICE Identification: 002214
Unit ID: 167677
Telephone: (617) 254-2610 Carnegie Class: Spec/Faith
FAX Number: (617) 787-2336 Calendar System: Semester
URL: www.sjs.edu
Established: 1884 Annual Undergrad Tuition & Fees: $30,900
Enrollment: 207 Coed
Affiliation or Control: Roman Catholic IRS Status: 501(c)3
Highest Offering: Master's
Program: Professional; Religious Emphasis
Accreditation: EH, THEOL

01 Rector .... Msgr. James MORONEY
03 Vice Rector .... Rev. Christopher K. O'CONNOR
05 Dean of Faculty .... Prof. Paul METILLY
32 Dean of Students .... Rev. Edward RILEY
07 Director of Admissions & Records ... Mrs. Maureen DEBERNARDI
08 Librarian .... Rev. Raymond VAN DE MOORTELL
10 Director Finance and Operations .... Mr. Richard A. FLAHERTY
73 Director Pre-Theology Program .... Rev. David PIGNATO
21 Asst Finance Director .... Mr. Armand DILANDO

Salter College (C)

645 Shawinigan Drive, Chicopee MA 01020-3744
Telephone: (508) 853-1074 Identification: 770724
Accreditation: ACICS

† Branch campus of Salter College, West Boylston, MA.

Salter College (D)

184 West Boylston Street, West Boylston MA 01583
County: Worcester FICE Identification: 004666
Unit ID: 167738
Telephone: (508) 853-1074 Carnegie Class: Assoc/PrivFP
FAX Number: (508) 853-1674 Calendar System: Semester
URL: www.saltercollege-us.com
Established: 1937 Annual Undergrad Tuition & Fees: $16,100
Enrollment: 555 Coed
Affiliation or Control: Proprietary IRS Status: Proprietary
Highest Offering: Associate Degree
Program: Occupational; 2-Year Principally Bachelor's Creditable
Accreditation: ACICS, ACFEI, MAC

01 Campus Director .... Mr. Kenneth RICHARDS

School of the Museum of Fine Arts, Boston (E)

230 The Fenway, Boston MA 02115-5518
County: Suffolk FICE Identification: 004667
Unit ID: 166984
Telephone: (617) 267-6100 Carnegie Class: Spec/Arts
FAX Number: (617) 424-6271 Calendar System: Semester
URL: www.smfa.edu
Established: 1876 Annual Undergrad Tuition & Fees: $41,228
Enrollment: 548 Coed
Affiliation or Control: Independent Non-Profit IRS Status: 501(c)3
Highest Offering: Master's
Program: Liberal Arts And General; Teacher Preparatory; Fine Arts Emphasis
Accreditation: @EH, ART

01 President .... Chris BRATTON
04 Executive Asst to the President .... Christine WILLIS
05 Senior VP for Academic Affairs/Dean .... Sarah MCKINNON
06 Registrar .... Taylor HORNER
30 VP for Inst Advance/Ext Relations .... Anne COWIE
84 VP and Dean of Enrollment .... Karen TOWNSEND
10 Chief Financial Officer .... Mark KERWIN
21 Director of Financial Operations .... Barbara DONNELLAN
09 Assoc VP Operations and Research .... Mary ROETZEL
32 Vice President and Dean of Students .... Robert CHAMBERS
45 Budget and Planning Officer .... Christopher FOX
88 Assoc VP Non-Degree Programs .... Debra SAMDPERIL
20 Assoc VP Academic Administration .... Greg D'ANGELO
58 Assoc Dean Graduate Studies .... Lisa BYNOE
37 Director of Financial Aid .... Shaun THOMAS
20 Assoc Dean Undergraduate Studies .... Susan LUSH
88 Bursar .... Rosalyn NAZZARO
07 Director of Admissions .... Angela JONES
26 Dir of Marketing & Communications .... Amanda KARR
44 Senior Development Officer .... Alexandra HUFF
27 Communications Officer .... Brooke DANIELS
29 Dir Alum Relations/Special Projects .... Vacant
08 Director of Library Services .... Darin MURPHY
90 Mgr of Instructional Technology .... Matthew GIRARD
40 School Store Manager .... Terri NORDONE
36 Career Services Manager .... Catherine TUTTER
35 Asst Director of Student Life .... Vacant
39 Asst Dir of Residential Life .... Holly GOULD
18 Director SMFA Campus Facilities .... Arthur TRENOWETH
15 Director Human Resources .... Jane O'REILLY
96 Director of Purchasing .... Brendan MULLIGAN
19 Director of Protective Services .... Nicki LUONGO
88 Interim Curator .... Carol STAKENAS
13 Sr Dir Info Systems & Technology .... Tom CATALINI
91 Database Administrator .... Tom THORNTON
38 Director Student Counseling .... Pamela CRISWELL

Simmons College (F)

300 The Fenway, Boston MA 02115-5898
County: Suffolk FICE Identification: 002208
Unit ID: 167783
Telephone: (617) 521-2000 Carnegie Class: Master's L
FAX Number: (617) 521-3065 Calendar System: Semester
URL: www.simmons.edu
Established: 1899 Annual Undergrad Tuition & Fees: $36,320
Enrollment: 4,802 Coordinate
Affiliation or Control: Independent Non-Profit IRS Status: 501(c)3
Highest Offering: Doctorate
Program: Liberal Arts And General; Teacher Preparatory; Professional
Accreditation: EH, BUS, DIETD, DIETI, HSA, LIB, NURSE, PTA, SW

01 President .... Helen G. DRINAN
04 Assistant to the President .... Marianne FIGUEIREDO
05 Provost .... Sheila (Katie) CONBOY
20 Deputy Provost .... Stefan KRUG
62 Dean Grad Sch Library/Info Science .... Eileen G. ABELS
76 Dean Sch Nursing & Health Sciences .... Judy BEAL
50 Dean School of Management .... Cathy MINEHAN
49 Dean College of Arts & Sciences .... Renee WHITE
104 Director of Study Abroad .... Joseph STANLEY
06 Asst VP Acad Operations & Registrar .... Donna M. DOLAN
08 Director Library .... Daphne HARRINGTON
25 Director Sponsored Programs .... Jon KIMBALL
09 Director Institutional Research .... Lan GAO
36 Director Career Education Center .... Andrea WOLF
10 Sr VP Finance/Admin/Treasurer .... Stefano FALCONI
21 Asst VP Finance .... Vacant
37 Asst VP Admission/Student Fin Svcs .... Daniel FORSTER
13 Executive Director Technology CIO .... Debra ORR
14 Sr Dir Enterprise Applications & Sv .... Michael PENNACHIO
86 AVP Government Relations .... Vacant
19 Director Public Safety .... Sean COLLINS
96 Director Purchasing & Procurement ... Kathy PERONI-CALLAHAN
26 VP Marketing & Admission .... Cheryl HOWARD
07 Director of Undergraduate Admission .... Ellen JOHNSON
07 Assistant VP Graduate Admissions .... Kristen HAACK
26 Sr Director Marketing .... Allyson IRISH
30 VP Advancement .... Marianne E. LORD
30 Assoc VP Advancement .... Laura BRINK
44 Director of Capital Giving .... Vacant
88 Event Strategist .... Janice TAYLOR
32 VP Student Affairs Dean of Students .... Sarah NEILL
42 Spiritual Life Program Manager .... Bonnie-Jeanne CASEY
38 Clinical Director Counseling Svcs .... Sherri ETTINGER

39 Director Residence Life .... Jessica FAULK
41 Director Athletics .... Ali KANTOR
35 Assoc Dean Office for Student Life .... Vacant
43 VP & General Counsel .... Kathleen R. ROGERS
15 VP Talent & Human Capital Strategy .... Regina SHERWOOD
100 Chief of Staff .... Lynda CONNOLLY
28 Assistant Provost for Diversity .... Lisa SMITH-MCQUEENIE

Smith College (G)

Northampton MA 01063-0001
County: Hampshire FICE Identification: 002209
Unit ID: 167835
Telephone: (413) 584-2700 Carnegie Class: Bac/A&S
FAX Number: (413) 585-2123 Calendar System: Semester
URL: www.smith.edu
Established: 1871 Annual Undergrad Tuition & Fees: $46,010
Enrollment: 2,989 Female
Affiliation or Control: Independent Non-Profit IRS Status: 501(c)3
Highest Offering: Doctorate
Program: Liberal Arts And General; Teacher Preparatory; Professional
Accreditation: EH, ENG, SW

01 President .... Kathleen MCCARTNEY
04 Secretary to the President .... Beth BERG
10 Vice Pres Finance & Administration .... Ruth H. CONSTANTINE
05 Provost & Dean of the Faculty .... Katherine ROWE
84 VP for Enrollment .... Audrey Y. SMITH
20 Dean for Academic Development .... Bill PETERSON
32 Dean of the College .... Donna LISKER
35 Dean of Students .... Julianne OHOTNICKY
70 Dean School for Social Work .... Marianne YOSHIOKA
39 Director of Residence Life .... Becky SHAW
85 Assoc Dean International Students .... Caitlin B. SZYMKOWICZ
30 Associate VP for Development .... Sandra DOUCETT
38 Assoc Dir Health Svcs/Stdnt Counsel .... Pamela MCCARTHY
26 VP for Public Affairs .... Laurie FENLASON
29 Exec Director Alumnae Association .... Jennifer S. CHRISLER
13 Exec Director Info Technology Svcs .... David D. GREGORY
09 Exec Dir Inst Research .... Cate ROWEN
08 Director of Libraries .... Christopher LORING
15 Assoc VP for Human Resources .... Lawrence HUNT
07 Dean of Admission .... Debra D. SHAVER
58 Director of Graduate Study .... Danielle D. RAMDATH
37 Dir Student Financial Services .... David J. BELANGER
06 Registrar .... Gretchen B. HERRINGER
36 Director Career Development Office .... Stacie HAGENBAUGH
28 Dir for Inst Diversity and Equity .... Dwight K. HAMILTON
88 Associate Dean of the Faculty .... Danielle D. RAMDATH
18 Assoc VP for Facilities Management .... Roger MOSIER
23 Director of Health Services .... Leslie R. JAFFE
41 Director of Athletics .... Krisin HUGHES
42 Dean of Religious Life .... Jennifer L. WALTERS
96 Procurement Director .... Linda HIESIGER
104 Dean for International Study .... Rebecca HOVEY
108 Assoc Director of Assessment .... Minh LY

Springfield College (H)

263 Alden Street, Springfield MA 01109-3797
County: Hampden FICE Identification: 002211
Unit ID: 167899
Telephone: (413) 748-3000 Carnegie Class: Master's L
FAX Number: N/A Calendar System: Semester
URL: www.springfieldcollege.edu
Established: 1885 Annual Undergrad Tuition & Fees: $34,455
Enrollment: 3,408 Coed
Affiliation or Control: Independent Non-Profit IRS Status: 501(c)3
Highest Offering: Doctorate
Program: Liberal Arts And General; Professional
Accreditation: EH, ARCPA, CAATE, CORE, EMT, EXSC, IACBE, NRPA, OT, PTA, SW

01 President .... Dr. Mary-Beth A. COOPER
05 Provost & VP Academic Affairs .... Dr. Jean A. WYLD
29 Vice President Devel & Alumni Rels .... Mr. John A. WHITE
10 Sr VP for Finance & Admin .... Mr. John MAILHOT
32 VP of Student Affairs .... Dr. Shannon FINNING
43 VP & General Counsel .... Mr. Christopher NERONHA
88 VP for Inclusion & Com Engagement .... Dr. Calvin R. HILL
20 Assoc VP Academic Affairs .... Dr. Mary Ann COUGHLIN
21 Asst VP Finance/Admin .... Ms. Rosanne CAPTAIN
30 Associate VP Development .... Mr. Scott M. BERG
84 Dir Enrollment Management .... Ms. Mary DEANGELO
06 Registrar .... Mr. Keith INGALLS
07 Dir Undergrad Admission .... Mr. Richard VERES
08 Director Library .... Ms. Andrea S. TAUPIER
29 Director Alumni Relations .... Ms. Tamie KIDESS LUCEY
37 Director of Financial Aid .... Mr. Edward CIOSEK
36 Director Career Center .... Ms. Jeanette M. DOYLE
13 Chief Information Officer .... Mr. Danny DAVIS
90 Sr Dir Networking/AC & Clnt Comp .... Mr. Thomas F. LARKIN
26 Exec Dir Marketing/Communication .... Mr. Stephen ROULIER
38 Director of Counseling Center .... Mr. Brian KRYLOWICZ
19 Exec Dir Public Safety/Chief Police ...... Mr. Michael D. SULLIVAN
88 Director YMCA Programs .... Mr. Harry ROCK
85 Director of International Center .... Dr. Deborah ALM
42 Director Campus Ministry .... Mr. David MCMAHON
18 Director of Facilities & Campus Svc .... Vacant
41 Director of Athletics .... Dr. Craig POISSON
96 Director of Purchasing .... Ms. Lita ADAMS

Stonehill College (A)

320 Washington Street, Easton MA 02357-6110

County: Bristol FICE Identification: 002217
Unit ID: 167996
Telephone: (508) 565-1000 Carnegie Class: Bac/A&S
FAX Number: (508) 565-1500 Calendar System: Semester
URL: www.stonehill.edu
Established: 1948 Annual Undergrad Tuition & Fees: $53,270
Enrollment: 2,382 Coed
Affiliation or Control: Roman Catholic IRS Status: 501(c)3
Highest Offering: Master's
Program: Liberal Arts And General; Teacher Preparatory; Professional
Accreditation: EH, BUS

01 President ... Rev. John F. DENNING, CSC
05 Provost/VP for Acad Affairs ... Dr. Joseph FAVAZZA
10 Vice Pres for Finance & Treasurer ... Ms. Jeanne FINLAYSON
30 Vice President for Advancement ... Mr. Francis X. DILLON
32 Vice President of Student Affairs ... Ms. Pauline DOBROWSKI
88 Vice President for Mission ... Rev. James LIES, CSC
84 VP for Enrollment Mgmt & Marketing ... Vacant
21 AVP for Finance & Operations ... Mr. Craig BINNEY
35 Assoc VP for Students Affairs ... Mr. Kevin PISKADLO
37 Asst VP/Dir of Student Aid/Finance ... Mrs. Eileen K. O'LEARY
04 Sr Executive Asst to the President ... Mrs. Jessica L. GRACIA
20 Dean of the Faculty ... Dr. Maria CURTIN
43 General Counsel ... Mr. Thomas V. FLYNN
21 Controller ... Ms. Jennifer MATHEWS
07 Dean of Admissions ... Mr. David TOBIAS
06 Registrar ... Mr. John PESTANA
09 Director Planning/Inst Research ... Ms. Laura J. UERLING
08 Director of College Library ... Ms. Cheryl MCGRATH
26 Dir of Media Rels & Communications ... Mr. Martin P. MCGOVERN
29 Director of Alumni Affairs ... Ms. Anne M. SANT
15 Director of Human Resources ... Ms. Maryann B. PERRY
38 Dir of Counseling & Testing Center ... Ms. Maria A. KAVANAUGH
13 Chief Information Officer ... Ms. Tamara ANDERSON
19 Chief of Police ... Mr. Peter CARNES
42 Director Campus Ministry ... Rev. Anthony SZAKALY, CSC
90 Manager of Instructional Technology ... Ms. Janice HARRISON
45 Director of Academic Development ... Ms. Bonnie L. TROUPE
88 Dir of Enterprise Infrastructure ... Mr. Thomas MCGRATH
23 Director of Health Services ... Mrs. Maria SULLIVAN
36 Director of Career Services ... Ms. Heather HEERMAN
41 Dir of Intercollegiate Athletics ... Mr. Brendan SULLIVAN
92 Interim Director of Honors Program ... Prof. Allyson SHECKLER
44 Director of Development ... Mr. Douglas J. SMITH
20 Interim Asst Dean for Acad Svcs ... Mr. John PESTANA
96 Director of Purchasing ... Mr. Gregory WOLFE
45 Asst VP for Planning & Budgeting ... Mr. Stephen BEAUREGARD
39 Director of Residence Life ... Ms. Kristen PIERCE
24 Dir of Media/Videography Services ... Mr. Michael PIETROWSKI
40 Manager of College Bookstore ... Mrs. Mary DUNCKLEE
88 Dean of Academic Achievement ... Dr. Craig ALMEIDA
97 Asst Dean Gen Educ & Acad Achievmnt ... Dr. Todd S. GERNES
18 Dir of Facilities Management ... Mr. Bruce BOYER
104 Director International Programs ... Ms. Alice CRONIN
31 Campus Minister for Community Svc ... Vacant
28 Director of Intercultural Affairs ... Vacant

Suffolk University (B)

8 Ashburton Place, Boston MA 02108-2770

County: Suffolk FICE Identification: 002218
Unit ID: 168005
Telephone: (617) 573-8000 Carnegie Class: Master's L
FAX Number: (617) 573-8353 Calendar System: Semester
URL: www.suffolk.edu
Established: 1906 Annual Undergrad Tuition & Fees: $33,800
Enrollment: 8,215 Coed
Affiliation or Control: Independent Non-Profit IRS Status: 501(c)3
Highest Offering: Doctorate
Program: Liberal Arts And General; Teacher Preparatory; Professional
Accreditation: EH, ART, BUS, BUSA, CIDA, CLPSY, ENG, IPSY, LAW, RADDOS, RTT, SPAA

01 President ... Ms. Margaret A. MCKENNA
05 Sr VP Academic Affs/Provost ... Dr. Marisa KELLY
10 Sr VP Finance/Admin/Treasurer ... Ms. Danielle MANNING
30 Sr Vice Pres for Advancement ... Vacant
84 Vice Pres Enrollment Mgmt ... Vacant
26 VP Marketing/Communications ... Mr. Greg GATLIN
86 VP Government/Community Affairs ... Mr. John A. NUCCI
20 Vice Prov Faculty Devel/Curriculum ... Mr. Jeffrey POKORAK
37 AVP/Dir of Financial Aid ... Ms. Christine M. PERRY
100 Chief of Staff ... Dr. Carol S. STREIT
32 Dean of Student Affairs ... Dr. Nancy C. STOLL
50 Dean Sawyer Business School ... Mr. William J. O'NEILL, JR.
61 Dean of the Law School ... Mr. Andrew PERLMAN
49 Dean College Arts & Science ... Dr. Maria TOYADA
22 Chief Diversity/Inclusion Officer ... Ms. Nicole G. PRICE
07 Director Undergraduate Admission ... Mr. John HAMEL
07 Director Graduate Admission ... Mr. Cory J. MEYERS
08 Director of Sawyer Library ... Ms. Sharon BRITTON
06 University Registrar ... Ms. Mary LALLY
36 Director Career Development Center ... Ms. Teresa DIMAGNO
15 Chief Human ResourcesOfficer ... Ms. Katherine WHIDDEN
29 Director of Alumni Affairs/Law Sch ... Ms. Kate GOGGINS
13 Chief Information Officer ... Mr. Thomas LYNCH, III
19 Cheif University Police ... Mr. Gerard COLETTA

35 Director of Student Activities ... Mr. John SILVERIA
41 Int Director of Athletics ... Mr. Cary MCCONNELL
18 Sr Dir Facilites Plng & Mgmt ... Mr. Gordon B. KING
88 Asst Dean for Acad Svcs Law School ... Ms. Lorraine D. COVE
08 Law Librarian ... Ms. Elizabeth MCKENZIE
09 Assoc Provost/Inst Research ... Ms. Melanie JENKINS

Tufts University (C)

Medford MA 02155-5555

County: Middlesex FICE Identification: 002219
Unit ID: 168148
Telephone: (617) 628-5000 Carnegie Class: RU/VH
FAX Number: N/A Calendar System: Semester
URL: www.tufts.edu
Established: 1852 Annual Undergrad Tuition & Fees: $50,604
Enrollment: 10,907 Coed
Affiliation or Control: Independent Non-Profit IRS Status: 501(c)3
Highest Offering: Doctorate
Program: Liberal Arts And General; Teacher Preparatory; Professional
Accreditation: EH, #ARCPA, CS, DENT, DIETI, ENG, IPSY, MED, OT, PH, PLNG, VET

01 President ... Dr. Anthony P. MONACO
100 Chief of Staff ... Mr. Michael BAENEN
03 Executive Vice President ... Ms. Patricia CAMPBELL
05 Provost & Senior Vice President ... Mr. David R. HARRIS
26 SVP Univ Relations & Gen Counsel ... Ms. Mary R. JEKA
30 Vice Pres University Advancement ... Mr. Eric C. JOHNSON
11 Vice President for Operations ... Ms. Linda SNYDER
10 Vice President Finance/Treasurer ... Mr. Thomas S. MCGURTY
15 VP for Human Resources ... Mr. Julien C. CARTER
13 VP & Chief Information Officer ... Mr. David J. KAHLE
20 Vice Provost ... Mr. Kevin DUNN
46 Vice Provost for Research ... Ms. Diane SOUVAINE
09 Assoc Provost Inst Res & Eval ... Dr. Dawn G. TERKLA
88 Associate Provost ... Mr. Boris HASSELBLATT
21 Assistant Provost for Admin/Finance ... Ms. Celia K. CAMPBELL
29 Exec Director Alumni Relations ... Mr. Tim BROOKS
45 Exec Dir Planning & Administration ... Ms. Martha POKRAS
22 Assoc Prov/Chief Diversity Officer ... Dr. Mark BRIMHALL-VARGAS
23 Sr Director Health/Wellness Svcs ... Ms. Michelle D. BOWDLER
37 Director of Financial Aid ... Ms. Patricia REILLY
26 Director Public Relations ... Ms. Kimberly M. THURLER
36 Director Career Center ... Ms. Jean M. PAPALIA
08 Director Tisch Library ... Ms. Laura WOOD
18 Senior Facilities Director ... Mr. Stephen NASSON
28 Director Equal Opportunity ... Ms. Jill A. ZELLMER
38 Director Mental Health Services ... Dr. Julie S. ROSS
19 Director Public & Env Safety ... Mr. Kevin C. MAGUIRE
49 Dean Arts & Sciences ... Mr. James GLASER
54 Dean of Engineering ... Dr. Jianmin QU
58 Dean Grad School of A&S ... Mr. Robert G. COOK
82 Dean Fletcher Sch Law & Diplomacy ... Adm. James STAVRIDIS
52 Dean of Dental Medicine ... Dr. Huw F. THOMAS
74 Dean Cummings Sch of Veterinary Med ... Dr. Deborah KOCHEVAR
63 Dean Medical School ... Dr. Harris BERMAN
88 Dean Sackler School ... Dr. Naomi ROSENBERG
88 Dean Friedman School ... Dr. Dariush MOZAFFARIAN
88 Dean Tisch College ... Mr. Alan SOLOMONT
53 Dean Undergrad & Grad Educ ... Mr. John BARKER
88 Dean Academic Adv & Undergrad Study ... Dr. Carmen LOWE
32 Dean of Student Affairs ... Ms. Mary Pat MCMAHON
35 Dean of Student Services/Art & Sci ... Mr. Paul STANTON
07 Dean Undergrad Admiss/Enroll Mgt ... Mr. Lee A. COFFIN
06 Registrar ASE & Stdnt Svcs Desk Mgr ... Ms. Jo Ann JACK
96 Purchasing Director ... Mr. John HOMICH
41 Director Athletics ... Mr. John MORRIS
42 University Chaplain ... Rev. Gregory MCGONIGLE
102 Dir Foundation/Corporate Relations ... Mr. Donald A. MCGOWAN
104 Director Study Abroad ... Ms. Sheila BAYNE
39 Director Residential Life ... Ms. Yolanda M. KING
44 Senior Director Gift Planning ... Ms. Brooke ANDERSON
31 Director Community Relations ... Ms. Barbara G. RUBEL

University of Phoenix Boston Campus (D)

2 Adams Place, Suite 300, Quincy MA 02169

Telephone: (866) 867-3678 Identification: 770209
Accreditation: &NH, ACBSP

† No longer accepting campus-based students.

Urban College of Boston (E)

178 Tremont Street, Boston MA 02111-1006

County: Suffolk FICE Identification: 031305
Unit ID: 429128
Telephone: (617) 449-7070 Carnegie Class: Assoc/PrivNFP
FAX Number: (617) 423-4758 Calendar System: Semester
URL: www.urbancollege.edu
Established: 1993 Annual Undergrad Tuition & Fees: $8,170
Enrollment: 810 Coed
Affiliation or Control: Independent Non-Profit IRS Status: 501(c)3
Highest Offering: Associate Degree
Program: 2-Year Principally Bachelor's Creditable
Accreditation: EH

01 President ... Mr. Michael TAYLOR
05 Academic Dean ... Ms. Nancy C. DANIEL
84 Dean Enrollment Svcs & Registrar ... Mr. Avanti SEYMOUR
32 Dean of Students/Dir Student Affs ... Ms. Carmen PINEDA
37 Director of Financial Aid ... Ms. Mia TAYLOR
20 Curriculum Coordinator ... Ms. Tong FENG
10 Business Manager ... Ms. Kathleen BARDELL

Wellesley College (F)

106 Central Street, Wellesley MA 02481-8203

County: Norfolk FICE Identification: 002224
Unit ID: 168218
Telephone: (781) 283-1000 Carnegie Class: Bac/A&S
FAX Number: (781) 283-3639 Calendar System: Semester
URL: www.wellesley.edu
Established: 1875 Annual Undergrad Tuition & Fees: $46,836
Enrollment: 2,323 Female
Affiliation or Control: Independent Non-Profit IRS Status: 501(c)3
Highest Offering: Baccalaureate
Program: Liberal Arts And General
Accreditation: EH

01 President ... Kim BOTTOMLY
05 Provost & Dean of the College ... Andrew SHENNAN
30 VP for Resources & Public Affairs ... Cameran MASON
10 VP Finance Administration/Treasurer ... Ben HAMMOND
18 Asst VP Facilities Management/Plng ... Peter ZURAW
15 Asst VP/Director Human Resources/EO ... Carolyn SLABODEN
13 Chief Information Officer ... Ganesan RAVISHANKER
07 Dean of Admission/Financial Aid ... Joy ST. JOHN
32 Interim Dean of Students ... Adele WOLFSON
42 Dn Intercult Educ/Relig/Spirit Life ... Vacant
20 Dean of Academic Affairs ... Ann VELENCHIK
20 Dean of Faculty Affairs ... Kathryn LYNCH
09 Asc Prov Institutional Plng/Assess ... Elena BERNAL
28 Assc Prov/Acad Dir Dvrsty/Inclusion ... Robbin CHAPMAN
06 Registrar ... Carol SHANMUGARATNAM
29 Executive Director Alumnae Assn ... Susan CHALLENGER
37 Director of Student Financial Svcs ... Scott JUEDES
36 Director Center for Work & Service ... Joanne S. MURRAY
26 Chief Public Relations Officer ... Elizabeth T. GILDERSLEEVE
35 Assoc Director Student Involvement ... Megan K. JORDAN
38 Administrative Counseling Svcs ... Robin COOK-NOBLES
101 Clerk Board of Trustees ... Marianne B. COOLEY
96 Purchasing Manager ... Tina M. DOLAN

Wentworth Institute of Technology (G)

550 Huntington Avenue, Boston MA 02115-5998

County: Suffolk FICE Identification: 002225
Unit ID: 168227
Telephone: (617) 989-4590 Carnegie Class: Bac/Diverse
FAX Number: (617) 989-4591 Calendar System: Semester
URL: www.wit.edu
Established: 1904 Annual Undergrad Tuition & Fees: $3,760
Enrollment: 4,558 Coed
Affiliation or Control: Independent Non-Profit IRS Status: 501(c)3
Highest Offering: Master's
Program: Professional; Technical Emphasis
Accreditation: EH, ART, CIDA, CONST, CS, ENG, ENGT, IACBE

01 President ... Dr. Zorica PANTIC
100 Chief of Staff ... Ms. Amy INTILLE
05 Interim Provost ... Dr. Richard HANSEN
10 Vice Pres Finance ... Mr. Robert TOTINO
21 Vice President Business ... Mr. David A. WAHLSTROM
30 Vice Pres Institutional Advancement ... Ms. Paula SAKEY
32 VP Enrollment Mgmt/Student Affairs ... Ms. Keiko BROOMHEAD
15 Vice Pres Human Resources ... Ms. Anne M. GILL
13 VP of Information Technology ... Mr. Mark STAPLES
88 Exec Asst to the Chief of Staff ... Ms. Rebecca COAKLEY
20 Assoc Provost ... Vacant
35 Assoc Vice Pres of Student Affairs ... Ms. Annamaria WENNER
21 Assoc Vice President Finance ... Mr. Peter MADDOCKS
84 Assoc VP of Enrollment Management ... Ms. Dianne PLUMMER
31 Assoc VP Community Affairs ... Ms. Sandra E. PASCAL
14 Assoc VP Information Technology ... Mr. Leslie VAUGHAN
88 AVP Innovation & Entrepreneurship ... Ms. Monique FUCHS
20 Assoc Provost for Acad Operations ... Ms. Susan PARIS
51 Dean of College of Prof & Cont Educ ... Ms. Deborah WRIGHT
07 Executive Director of Admissions ... Ms. Maureen DISCHINO
06 Interim Registrar ... Mr. Darnell GRAHAM
08 Director of Library ... Mr. Kevin KIDD
35 Dir Student Financial Services ... Ms. Patricia OSGOOD
18 Associate VP Physical Facilities ... Mr. Michael PANKIEVICH
29 Director of Alumni Programs ... Ms. Monica KEY
27 Director of Publications ... Mr. Caleb COCHRAN
35 Associate Dean of Students ... Mr. Peter FOWLER
102 Dir Corp Foundation/Govt Rels ... Ms. Lori FRIEDMAN
37 Director Financial Aid ... Ms. Anne-Marie CARUSO
38 Director of Counseling ... Ms. Maura MULLIGAN
19 Director of Public Safety ... Mr. William POWERS
41 Associate Athletic Director ... Mr. William P. GORMAN
36 Dir Of Cooperative Educ/Career Svcs ... Ms. Robbin BEAUCHAMP
39 Director Housing & Residential Life ... Mr. Philip BERNARD
41 Director of Athletics ... Mr. Stan VIEIRA
09 Director of Institutional Research ... Mr. Bradford WILD
96 Director of Purchasing ... Mr. Gerald INMAN
09 Institutional Researcher ... Mr. Alan T. WHITEMORE
49 Dean for Arts & Sciences ... Dr. Patrick HAFFORD
48 Dean for Arch/Design & Const Mgmt ... Dr. Charles HOTCHKISS
54 Dean for Engineering & Technology ... Mr. Frederick DRISCOLL
18 Director of Physical Plant ... Mr. Robert FERRO
88 Director Office of Campus Life ... Ms. Carissa DURFEE

Western New England University (A)

1215 Wilbraham Road, Springfield MA 01119-2684
County: Hampden FICE Identification: 002226
Unit ID: 168254
Telephone: (413) 782-3111 Carnegie Class: Master's M
FAX Number: (413) 782-1746 Calendar System: Semester
URL: www.wne.edu
Established: 1919 Annual Undergrad Tuition & Fees: $34,030
Enrollment: 3,950 Coed
Affiliation or Control: Independent Non-Profit IRS Status: 501(c)3
Highest Offering: Doctorate
Program: Liberal Arts And General; Professional
Accreditation: EH, BUS, ENG, LAW, PHAR, SW

01 President .... Dr. Anthony S. CAPRIO
04 Administrative Asst to President .... Ms. Marie IRZYK
05 Provost/Vice Pres Academic Affairs .... Dr. Linda E. JONES
26 Vice Pres Marketing & External Affs .... Mrs. Barbara A. MOFFAT
10 Vice Pres Finance & Administration .... Mr. William J. KELLEHER
84 Vice President for Enrollment Mgmt .... Mr. Bryan J. GROSS
32 VP Student Affairs/Dean of Students .... Dr. Jeanne S. HART-STEFFES
30 Vice President Advancement .... Ms. Beverly J. DWIGHT
88 Vice Pres for Strategic Initiatives .... Dr. Richard S. KEATING
13 Asst Vice Pres Information Tech .... Mr. Scott J. COOPEE
15 Asst VP & Dir of Human Resources .... Ms. Joanne OLLSON
61 Dean of the School of Law .... Prof. Eric J. GOUVIN
67 Dean of the College of Pharmacy .... Dr. Evan ROBINSON
49 Dean of the College of Arts & Sci .... Dr. Saeed GHAHRAMANI
50 Dean of the College of Business .... Dr. Julie SICILIANO
54 Dean of the College of Engineering .... Dr. S. Hossein CHERAGHI
89 Dean First Year/Transfer Students .... Ms. Kerri P. JARZABSKI
08 Assoc Dean Law Library/Info Res .... Ms. Patricia NEWCOMBE
39 Asst Dean of Students and Res Life .... Mr. Jerry ROEDER
28 Asst Dean of Diversity Programs .... Mrs. Yvonne BOGLE
06 Director of Student Admin Services .... Mr. Rodney W. PEASE
37 Director of Financial Aid .... Ms. Kathleen CHAMBERS
41 Director of Athletics .... Dr. Michael THEULEN
36 Director Career Development Center .... Ms. Andrea ST. JAMES
38 Director of Counseling Services .... Dr. Wayne D. CARPENTER
08 Director of D'Amour Library .... Mrs. Priscilla L. PERKINS
23 Director of Health Services .... Mrs. Kathleen A. REID
18 Director of Facilities Management .... Mr. C. Michael DUNCAN
90 Dir Educational Technology Center .... Mr. Steven NARMONTAS
91 Dir of Administrative Info Systems .... Mr. Anthony MUTTI
29 Director of Alumni Relations .... Ms. Katherine PAPPAS
102 Dir of Foundation Relations .... Mr. Matthew VANHEYNIGEN
42 Spiritual Life Coordinator .... Ms. Sheila HANIFIN
19 Director of Public Safety .... Mr. Adam WOODROW
11 Director Administrative Services .... Ms. Arlene M. ROCK
07 Dir of Undergraduate Admissions .... Mr. Christopher WYSTEPEK
20 Academic Scheduling Controller .... Dr. Linda M. CHOJNICKI
09 Director Inst Research & Planning .... Dr. Richard A. WAGNER
43 General Counsel .... Mrs. Cheryl SMITH

Wheaton College (B)

26 E Main Street, Norton MA 02766-2322
County: Bristol FICE Identification: 002227
Unit ID: 168281
Telephone: (508) 286-8200 Carnegie Class: Bac/A&S
FAX Number: (508) 286-8270 Calendar System: Semester
URL: www.wheatoncollege.edu
Established: 1834 Annual Undergrad Tuition & Fees: $47,700
Enrollment: 1,587 Coed
Affiliation or Control: Independent Non-Profit IRS Status: 501(c)3
Highest Offering: Baccalaureate
Program: Liberal Arts And General
Accreditation: EH

01 President .... Dr. Dennis HANNO
05 Provost .... Dr. Linda EISENMANN
10 Vice Pres Finance/Administration .... Mr. Brian DOUGLAS
30 Vice President College Advancement .... Vacant
84 Vice President Enrollment/Marketing .... Mr. Grant GOSSELIN
32 VP Student Affairs/Dean of Students .Ms. Kathryn E. MCCAFFREY
37 Asst VP Enroll/Stdnt Finan Svcs .... Ms. Robin RANDALL
26 Asst Vice Pres for Communications .... Mr. Michael GRACA
06 Registrar/Dean Academic Systems .... Ms. Michelle SANTOS
29 Dir Alumni Rels/Annual Giving .... Ms. Susan W. DOYLE
105 Director of Creative Technology .... Mr. Christopher PADDOCK
15 Asst VP/Director Human Resources .... Ms. Barbara LEMA
38 Assoc Dean/Director Counseling Ctr .... Mr. Jeffrey KLUG
07 Director of Admission .... Ms. Amy E. MARKHAM
18 Asst VP Business Svcs/Phys Plant .... Mr. John M. SULLIVAN
09 Director of Institutional Research .... Dr. Paul PREWITT-FREILINO
39 Director Stdnt Life/Housing .... Mr. Edward T. BURNETT
19 Director Public Safety .... Chief Christopher SANTIAGO
101 Asst to President/Sec Brd Trustees .... Ms. Ellen E. HALLETT
41 Athletic Director .... Mr. John SUTYAK
104 Director Study Abroad .... Ms. Gretchen YOUNG
13 Chief Info Technology Officer (CIO) .... Ms. Susan V. WAWRZASZEK
91 Director Administrative Computing .... Ms. Susan A. MORGADO

Wheelock College (C)

200 The Riverway, Boston MA 02215-4176
County: Suffolk FICE Identification: 002228
Unit ID: 168290
Telephone: (617) 879-2000 Carnegie Class: Master's M
FAX Number: (617) 566-7369 Calendar System: Semester
URL: www.wheelock.edu
Established: 1888 Annual Undergrad Tuition & Fees: $33,835
Enrollment: 1,331 Coed
Affiliation or Control: Independent Non-Profit IRS Status: 501(c)3
Highest Offering: Beyond Master's But Less Than Doctorate
Program: Liberal Arts And General; Teacher Preparatory
Accreditation: EH, SW, TED

01 President .... Ms. Jackie JENKINS-SCOTT
04 Executive Assistant to President .... Ms. Valerie THORNHILL-HUDSON
11 VP Admin/Inst Effect/Innovation .... Mr. Roy SCHIFILLITI
05 VP for Academic Affairs .... Vacant
30 VP for Development/Alumni Affairs .... Ms. Jennifer RICE
10 VP/Chief Financial Officer .... Ms. Anne Marie MARTORANA
84 VP Student Success and Engagement .... Dr. Adrian K. HAUGABROOK
86 Dir of Government and Ext Affairs .... Ms. Marta ROSA
32 Dean of Students .... Ms. Barbara MORGAN
49 Interim Dean of Arts & Sciences .... Dr. Detris Honora ADELABU
104 Dean International Pgms/Prtrnshp .... Dr. Linda DAVIS
53 Assoc Dean of Education .... Dr. Donna MCKIBBENS
70 Assoc Dean of Social Work .... Dr. Hope HASLAM STRAUGHAN
07 Sr Assoc Dir Undergrad Admissions .... Mr. Calvin CONYERS
07 Director of Graduate Admissions .... Mr. Brian MINCHELLO
06 Registrar .... Ms. Michelle ORMEROD
08 Interim Director of Library .... Ms. Ann GLANNON
15 Director of Human Resources .... Ms. Michele CREWS
13 Director of Information Technology .... Mr. Jonathan LAPIERRE
36 Dir Center for Career Development .... Vacant
18 Chief Facilities/Physical Plant .... Mr. Ed JACQUES
38 Director Counseling Center .... Ms. Eileen THOMPSON
29 Dir of Development/Alumni Relations .... Ms. Lauren MARQUIS
09 Institutional Research Analyst .... Mr. Lance ANGELL
26 Marketing Manager .... Mr. Stephen DILL
41 Athletic Director .... Mr. Dwight DATCHER
42 Spiritual Life Coordinator .... Dr. Adrienne KISNER
39 Director of Residence Life .... Ms. Darcy DUBOIS
26 Communications Manager .... Ms. Beth KAPLAN
107 Interim Dean of Grad/Prof Programs .Dr. Linda BANKS-SANTILLI

William James College (D)

1 Wells Avenue, Newton MA 02459-3211
County: Norfolk FICE Identification: 021636
Unit ID: 166717
Telephone: (617) 327-6777 Carnegie Class: Spec/Health
FAX Number: (617) 327-4447 Calendar System: Semester
URL: www.williamjames.edu
Established: 1974 Annual Graduate Tuition & Fees: $38,240
Enrollment: 700 Coed
Affiliation or Control: Independent Non-Profit IRS Status: 501(c)3
Highest Offering: Doctorate; No Undergraduates
Program: Professional
Accreditation: EH, CLPSY, IPSY

01 President .... Dr. Nicholas COVINO
04 Executive Asst to the President .... Ms. Lilly MANOLIS
10 VP Finance .... Mr. Daniel BRENT
05 Vice Pres Academic Affairs .... Dr. Stanley BERMAN
30 Vice Pres Institutional Advance .... Ms. Susan LINN
11 Chief Operations Officer .... Mr. Robert CATALANOTTI
46 Assoc VP for Research .... Dr. Edward DEVOS
37 Director Financial Aid .... Mrs. Elaine TOOMEY
06 Registrar .... Ms. Eileen O'DONNELL
32 Dean of Students .... Mr. Josh COOPER
88 Director of Multicultural Affairs .... Dr. Mari Carmen BENNASAR
07 Director of Admissions .... Mr. Mario MURGA
51 Director Continuing Prof Education .... Mr. Dean ABBY
27 Director of Marketing .... Mrs. Katie O'HARE
13 Dir Information Technology .... Mr. Jeff CHOO
08 Head Librarian .... Mr. Matt KRAMER
15 Human Resource Director .... Mrs. Mary-Alice HOWARD
18 Facilities Manager .... Mr. Kevin COSTELLO
26 Chief Public Relations Officer .... Ms. Patti JACOBS
96 Director of Purchasing .... Ms. Marice NICHOLS
29 Director Alumni Relations .... Dr. Alan BECK
09 Director of Institutional Research .... Dr. Ed DEVOS

† Formerly Massachusetts School of Professional Psychology

Williams College (E)

880 Main Street, Williamstown MA 01267
County: Berkshire FICE Identification: 002229
Unit ID: 168342
Telephone: (413) 597-3131 Carnegie Class: Bac/A&S
FAX Number: N/A Calendar System: 4/1/4
URL: www.williams.edu
Established: 1793 Annual Undergrad Tuition & Fees: $50,070
Enrollment: 2,099 Coed
Affiliation or Control: Independent Non-Profit IRS Status: 501(c)3
Highest Offering: Master's
Program: Liberal Arts And General
Accreditation: EH

01 President .... Adam F. FALK
05 Dean of Faculty .... Denise K. BUELL
45 Provost .... William C. DUDLEY
10 VP for Fin & Admin and Treasurer .... Frederick W. PUDDESTER
32 Vice President for Campus Life .... Stephen P. KLASS
30 Vice Pres for College Relations .... John M. MALCOLM
28 VP for Inst Diversity & Equity .... Leticia HAYNES
26 Chief Communications Officer .... Angela P. SCHAEFFER
04 Asst to Pres/Secretary of the Col .... Keli A. GAIL
20 Dean of the College .... Sarah R. BOLTON
18 Exec Director Facilities Management .... Robert F. WRIGHT
06 Registrar .... Barbara A. CASEY
07 Director of Admission .... Richard L. NESBITT
37 Director of Financial Aid .... Paul J. BOYER
08 Librarian .... David M. PILACHOWSKI
21 Controller .... Susan S. HOGAN
29 Director Alumni Relations .... Brooks L. FOEHL
15 Director of Human Resources .... Martha R. TETRAULT
36 Director of Career Center .... Vacant
88 Director of Dining Services .... Robert P. VOLPI
13 Chief Technology Officer .... Barron KORALESKY
09 Director of Institutional Research .... Courtney WADE
23 Director of Health Admin Services .... Angie MARANO
35 Director Office of Student Life .... Douglas J. SCHIAZZA
41 Director of Athletics/PE .... Lisa M. MELENDY
42 Chaplain .... Richard E. SPALDING

Woods Hole Oceanographic Institution (F)

266 Woods Hole Road, Woods Hole MA 02543-1535
County: Barnstable FICE Identification: 002230
Unit ID: 166610
Telephone: (508) 289-2252 Carnegie Class: Not Classified
FAX Number: N/A Calendar System: 4/1/4
URL: www.whoi.edu
Established: 1930 Annual Graduate Tuition & Fees: $59,620
Enrollment: 124 Coed
Affiliation or Control: Independent Non-Profit IRS Status: 501(c)3
Highest Offering: Doctorate; No Undergraduates
Program: Professional
Accreditation: EH

01 President and Director .... Dr. Mark A. ABBOTT
09 Exec Vice Pres/Director of Research .... Dr. Laurence P. MADIN
05 VP of Academic Programs and Dean .... Dr. James A. YODER
10 Vice Pres of Operations/CFO .... Mr. Jeffrey FERNANDEZ
20 Associate Dean .... Dr. Margaret K. TIVEY
06 Registrar .... Ms. Julia WESTWATER
08 Research Librarian .... Ms. Holly N. MILLER

Worcester Polytechnic Institute (G)

100 Institute Road, Worcester MA 01609-2280
County: Worcester FICE Identification: 002233
Unit ID: 168421
Telephone: (508) 831-5000 Carnegie Class: DRU
FAX Number: (508) 831-5753 Calendar System: Semester
URL: www.wpi.edu
Established: 1865 Annual Undergrad Tuition & Fees: $45,590
Enrollment: 6,057 Coed
Affiliation or Control: Independent Non-Profit IRS Status: 501(c)3
Highest Offering: Doctorate
Program: Liberal Arts And General; Professional; Technical Emphasis
Accreditation: EH, BUS, CS, ENG

01 President .... Dr. Laurie LESHIN
05 Sr Vice President and Provost .... Dr. Bruce BURSTEN
10 Executive Vice President & CFO .... Mr. Jeffrey S. SOLOMON
30 VP for University Advancement .... Mr. William J. MCAVOY
26 Chief Marketing Officer .... Ms. Amy M. MORTON
13 Chief Information Officer (CIO) .... Ms. Deborah C. SCOTT
03 Senior Vice President .... Ms. Kristin R. TICHENOR
18 Asst Vice President for Facilities .... Mr. Alfred DIMAURO, JR.
15 Vice President of Human Resources .... Ms. A. Tracy HASSETT
20 VP Academics & Corporate Devel .... Mr. Stephen P. FLAVIN
32 Vice President of Student Affairs .... Mr. Philip N. CLAY
22 University Compliance Officer .... Vacant
36 Exec Director Career Devel Center .... Mr. Stefan KOPPI
100 Asst VP/Chief of Staff .... Ms. Stephanie PASHA
07 Interim Dean of Admissions .... Ms. Jennifer A. CLUETT
06 University Registrar .... Ms. Heather L. JACKSON
27 Director of Research/Communications .... Mr. Michael W. DORSEY
96 Manager of Procurement Services .... Ms. Laurie COLELLA
21 University Controller .... Ms. Amy L. RODERICK
09 Assistant VP of Budget Planning .... Ms. Judith L. TRAINOR
38 Asst Dean of Stdnt Dev/Dir SDCC .... Mr. Charles C. MORSE
88 Director Life Sciences Center .... Mr. David D. EASSON
37 Director Student Financial Aid .... Ms. Monica M. BLONDIN
19 Mgr Env Occupational Safety .... Mr. David H. MESSIER
28 Director of Multicultural Affair .... Ms. Bonnie HALL
29 Exec Dir Alumni Rels/Annual Giving .... Mr. Peter A. THOMAS

MICHIGAN

Adrian College (H)

110 S Madison Street, Adrian MI 49221-2575
County: Lenawee FICE Identification: 002234
Unit ID: 168528
Telephone: (517) 265-5161 Carnegie Class: Bac/Diverse
FAX Number: (517) 264-3331 Calendar System: Semester
URL: www.adrian.edu
Established: 1859 Annual Undergrad Tuition & Fees: $33,210
Enrollment: 1,641 Coed
Affiliation or Control: United Methodist IRS Status: 501(c)3
Highest Offering: Master's
Program: 2-Year Principally Bachelor's Creditable; Liberal Arts And General; Teacher Preparatory

Accreditation: NH, CAATE, SW, TEAC

01 President ....Dr. Jeffrey R. DOCKING
05 Vice Pres/Dean for Academic Affairs ....Dr. Agnes CALDWELL
30 Vice Pres Institutional Advancement ....Mr. James MAHONY
84 Vice President of Enrollment ....Mr. Frank J. HRIBAR
10 Vice Pres Business Affairs/CFO ....Mr. Jerry WRIGHT
32 Dean of Student Affairs ....Mr. Troy SCHMIDLI
20 Asst Dean of Academic Affairs ....Ms. Bridgette WINSLOW
21 Asst Vice Pres of Business Affairs ....Mr. David DREWS
44 Asst Vice President for Development ....Mr. Ryan EFF
07 Associate Director of Admissions ....Ms. Erin VANDERWORP
42 Chaplain/Director Church Relations ..Dr. Christopher P. MOMANY
26 Director of Public Relations ....Ms. Jennifer COMPTON
06 Registrar ....Ms. Kristen MILLER
35 Associate Dean for Student Life ....Ms. Mallory FRAILING
21 Controller ....Ms. Nicole MEGALE
86 Dir of Govt & Foundation Relations ....Ms. Amy CAMPBELL
15 Director of Human Resources ....Mrs. Ann FORRISTER
40 Bookstore Manager ....Ms. Rachelle M. DUFFY
93 Dir Multicultural Cultural Programs ....Ms. Idali FELICIANO
29 Director Alumni Relations ....Mrs. Marsha FIELDER
41 Director of Athletics ....Mr. Michael DUFFY
19 Director of Campus Safety ....Mr. Wade BIETELCHIES
36 Director of Career Planning ....Mrs. Janna D'AMICO
88 Director of Conferences ....Ms. Denise HEIN
38 Director of Counseling ....Ms. Monique J. SAVAGE
08 Head Librarian ....Mr. David CRUSE
23 Director of Health Center ....Ms. Dawn MARSH
96 Director of Purchasing ....Ms. Robin RUMLER
37 Director of Financial Aid ....Mr. Matt RHEINECKER
18 Director of Facilities ....Mr. John E. JOHNSTON
09 Director of Institutional Research ....Ms. Beth L. HEISS
88 Director of Academic Services ....Ms. Linda JACOBS
88 Asst Director of Academic Services ....Ms. Danielle WARD
13 Asst Dir of Information Services ....Mr. Bradley MAGGARD
04 Administrative Asst to President ....Mrs. Andrea BURT

Albion College (A)

611 E Porter Street, Albion MI 49224-1831

County: Calhoun FICE Identification: 002235
Unit ID: 168546
Telephone: (517) 629-1000 Carnegie Class: Bac/A&S
FAX Number: (517) 629-0509 Calendar System: Semester
URL: www.albion.edu
Established: 1835 Annual Undergrad Tuition & Fees: $50,188
Enrollment: 1,250 Coed
Affiliation or Control: United Methodist IRS Status: 501(c)3
Highest Offering: Baccalaureate
Program: Liberal Arts And General; Teacher Preparatory
Accreditation: NH, CAATE, MUS, TEAC

01 President ....Dr. Mauri A. DITZLER
10 Vice Pres Business & Finance ....Mr. Jerry WHITE
05 Provost ....Dr. Marc ROY
30 Vice Pres Institutional Advancement ....Mr. Robert ANDERSON
84 Vice Pres Enrollment Mgmt ....Mr. Steven KLEIN
32 Vice Pres & Dean Student Affairs ....Dr. Sally J. WALKER
13 Assoc Vice Pres Info Svcs/CIO ....Mr. Michael DEVER
07 Director of Admissions ....Ms. Mandy DUBIEL
39 Director Residential Life ....Mr. Michael WADSWORTH
08 Director of Libraries ....Dr. Michael VAN HOUTEN
26 Director of Communications ....Mr. John THOMPSON
29 Director of Alumni Engagement ....Ms. Elinor MARSH
38 Director of Counseling ....Dr. Frank KELEMEN
37 Director of Financial Aid ....Ms. Ann WHITMER
06 Registrar ....Dr. Andrew M. DUNHAM
88 Director Dining & Hospitality Svcs ....Mrs. Pat MILLER
18 Director of Facilities Operations ....Mr. Donald MASTERNAK
19 Director of Campus Safety ....Mr. Kenneth SNYDER
41 Athletic Director ....Mr. Matthew AREND
42 College Chaplain ....Rev. Daniel MCQUOWN
15 Director of Human Resources ....Mrs. Lisa LOCKE
09 Director of Institutional Research ....Dr. Andrew DUNHAM
96 Director of Purchasing ....Mrs. Susan CLARK
20 Associate Academic Officer ....Dr. John WOELL
28 Assoc Director Multicultural Affs ....Vacant
40 Manager of Bookstore ....Vacant

Alma College (B)

614 W Superior, Alma MI 48801-1599

County: Gratiot FICE Identification: 002236
Unit ID: 168591
Telephone: (989) 463-7111 Carnegie Class: Bac/A&S
FAX Number: (989) 463-7277 Calendar System: Other
URL: www.alma.edu
Established: 1886 Annual Undergrad Tuition & Fees: $35,428
Enrollment: 1,396 Coed
Affiliation or Control: Independent Non-Profit IRS Status: 501(c)3
Highest Offering: Baccalaureate
Program: Liberal Arts And General; Teacher Preparatory
Accreditation: NH, CAATE, MUS, TEAC

01 President ....Dr. Jeff ABERNATHY
05 Provost & Vice Pres for Acad Affs ....Dr. Michael L. SELMON
10 VP for Finance & Administration ....Mr. Todd FRIESNER
30 Vice President for Advancement ....Mr. Matt VANDENBERG
84 Vice President for Enrollment ....Mr. Bob GARCIA
32 Vice President for Student Life ....Dr. Nicholas A. PICCOLO
26 Vice Pres Communication/Marketing ....Ms. Ann HALL
04 Executive Asst to the President ....Ms. Sandee A. GADDE
06 Associate Provost & Registrar ....Ms. Julie WILLIAMS
20 Assistant Provost ....Ms. Susan M. DEEL
42 Chaplain ....Rev. Noel SNYDER
37 Dir Stdnt Financial Assistance ....Ms. Michelle MCNIER
08 Director of Library ....Ms. Carol ZEILE
27 Director of College Communications ....Mr. Mike SILVERTHORN
13 Chief Technology Officer ....Dr. Keith R. NELSON
18 Director Facilities & Service Mgmt ....Mr. Douglas DICE
15 Director Human Resources ....Mr. Kenneth L. BORGMAN
21 Controller ....Mr. Dan HENRIS
29 Director Alumni Relations ....Ms. Amanda SLENSKI
35 Director Campus Life ....Mr. David K. BLANDFORD
38 Director Counseling & Wellness ....Ms. Anne K. LAMBRECHT
07 Director Admissions ....Vacant
09 Research Analyst ....Mr. John MACARTHUR

Alpena Community College (C)

665 Johnson Street, Alpena MI 49707-1495

County: Alpena FICE Identification: 002237
Unit ID: 168607
Telephone: (989) 356-9021 Carnegie Class: Assoc/Pub-R-M
FAX Number: (989) 358-7553 Calendar System: Semester
URL: www.alpenacc.edu
Established: 1952 Annual Undergrad Tuition & Fees (In-District): $4,140
Enrollment: 1,638 Coed
Affiliation or Control: Local IRS Status: 501(c)3
Highest Offering: Associate Degree
Program: Occupational; 2-Year Principally Bachelor's Creditable
Accreditation: NH, MAC

01 President ....Dr. Donald MACMASTER
05 Vice Pres Academic/Student Affairs ....Ms. Kathleen MARSH
10 Vice President Admin & Finance ....Mr. Richard SUTHERLAND
32 Dean of Students ....Ms. Nancy SEGUIN
21 Controller ....Ms. Lyn KOWALEWSKY
20 Dean Learning Resource Center ....Ms. Wendy BROOKS
25 Director of TAACCT Grants ....Ms. Dawn STONE
13 Co-Director Mgmt Info Systems ....Ms. Vicky KROPP
13 Co-Director Mgmt Info Systems ....Mr. Mark GRUNDER
26 Dir Marketing & Public Information ....Mr. Jay WALTERREIT
40 Director Bookstore ....Mr. William MATZKE
102 Foundation Executive Director ....Ms. Penny BOLDREY
18 Director of Facilities Management ....Mr. Nicholas BREGE
88 Director Volunteer Center ....Ms. Kathleen BRUSKI
06 Registrar ....Ms. Lori DZIESINSKI
15 Director Human Resources ....Ms. Carolyn DAOUST
07 Director of Admissions ....Mr. Mike KOLLIEN
37 Director Student Financial Aid ....Mr. Robert ROOSE

Andrews University (D)

8975 U.S. 31, Berrien Springs MI 49104-0001

County: Berrien FICE Identification: 002238
Unit ID: 168740
Telephone: (269) 471-7771 Carnegie Class: DRU
FAX Number: (269) 471-6900 Calendar System: Semester
URL: www.andrews.edu
Established: 1874 Annual Undergrad Tuition & Fees: $27,000
Enrollment: 3,418 Coed
Affiliation or Control: Seventh-day Adventist IRS Status: 501(c)3
Highest Offering: Doctorate
Program: Liberal Arts And General; Teacher Preparatory; Professional
Accreditation: NH, CACREP, CS, DIETD, DIETI, ENG, IACBE, MT, MUS, NUR, PTA, @SP, SW, TED, THEOL

01 President ....Dr. Niels-Erik A. ANDREASEN
05 Provost ....Dr. Andrea T. LUXTON
20 Associate Provost for Faculty Dev ....Dr. Christon ARTHUR
20 Assistant Provost Inst Assessment ....Dr. Lynn MERKLIN
10 Vice President for Financial Admin ....Mr. Lawrence E. SCHALK
32 Vice President for Student Life ....Dr. Frances M. FAEHNER
26 Vice Pres Marketing & Communication ....Mr. Stephen D. PAYNE
84 Vice Pres for Enrollment Management ....Mr. Randy K. GRAVES
30 Vice President for Advancement ....Dr. David A. FAEHNER
43 General Counsel ....Ms. Gwendolyn POWELL BRASWELL
06 Registrar ....Ms. Aimee VITANGCOL REGOSO
49 Dean College Arts & Sciences ....Dr. Keith E. MATTINGLY
76 Dean School of Health Professions ....Dr. Emmanuel RUDATSIKIRA
50 Dean School of Business Admin ....Dr. Allen F. STEMBRIDGE
53 Dean School of Education ....Dr. Robson MARINHO
48 Dean Sch Architecture/Art & Design ....Mr. Carey CARSCALLEN
73 Dean of Theological Seminary ....Dr. Jiri MOSKALA
58 Dean School of Grad Studies ....Dr. Christon ARTHUR
106 Dean School of Distance Education ....Dr. Alayne THORPE
08 Dean of Libraries ....Mr. Lawrence W. ONSAGER
21 Associate Business Officer ....Mr. Glenn A. MEEKMA
39 Dir of University Apartment Life ....Mr. Alfredo RUIZ
34 Dir of the Women's Residence Halls ....Ms. Jennifer R. BURRILL
33 Dir of the Men's Residence Halls ....Mr. Spencer D. CARTER
85 Dir of International Student Svcs ....Mr. Robert BENJAMIN
92 Director of Honors Program ....Dr. L. Monique PITTMAN
15 Director of Human Resources ....Mr. Daniel E. AGNETTA
37 Director Student Financial Aid ....Ms. Elynda A. BEDNEY
07 Director of Undergrad Admissions ....Ms. Shanna LEAK
07 Director of Graduate Admissions ....Ms. Monica WRINGER
88 Media Relations Specialist ....Ms. Becky ST. CLAIR
29 Director of Alumni Services ....Ms. Tami CONDON
38 Dir of Counseling/Testing Center ....Dr. Judith FISHER
40 Manager of Bookstore ....Ms. Cynthia SWANSON
19 Director of Campus Safety ....Mr. Dale B. HODGES
23 Director of Medical Services ....Dr. Daniel REICHERT
42 University Chaplain ....Ms. June M. PRICE
09 Director Institutional Research ....Mr. James R. MASSENA
18 Director of Facilities Management ....Mr. Paul ELDER
04 Executive Asst to President ....Ms. Dalry B. PAYNE
41 Athletic Director ....Mr. David JARDINE
44 Director of Planned Giving ....Ms. Tari POPP
104 Director Study Abroad ....Dr. Pedro NAVIA
105 Director Web Services ....Mr. Robert FUSTE
13 Chief Information Officer ....Ms. Lorena L. BIDWELL
28 Director of Diversity ....Ms. Deborah WEITHERS

Aquinas College (E)

1607 Robinson Road, SE, Grand Rapids MI 49506-1799

County: Kent FICE Identification: 002239
Unit ID: 168786
Telephone: (616) 632-8900 Carnegie Class: Master's M
FAX Number: (616) 732-4469 Calendar System: Semester
URL: www.aquinas.edu
Established: 1886 Annual Undergrad Tuition & Fees: $28,820
Enrollment: 1,933 Coed
Affiliation or Control: Roman Catholic IRS Status: 501(c)3
Highest Offering: Master's
Program: 2-Year Principally Bachelor's Creditable; Liberal Arts And General; Teacher Preparatory; Professional
Accreditation: NH, CAATE, TEAC

01 President ....Dr. Juan OLIVAREZ
05 Provost/Dean of Faculty ....Dr. Gilda GELY
30 Vice Pres Institutional Advancement ....Mr. Greg MEYER
10 Vice President Finance ....Dr. Leonard KOGUT
84 Vice Pres Enrollment Management ....Ms. Paula T. MEEHAN
04 Assistant to President ....Ms. Monica EDISON
26 Assoc VP Marketing & Communication ....Ms. Meg DERRER
07 Assoc VP for Admissions ....Mr. Thomas MIKOWSKI
32 Assoc VP for Student Services ....Mr. Brian MATZKE
21 Controller ....Ms. Cathy LUCK
09 Dean of Institutional Effectiveness ....Dr. Susan ENGLISH
53 Dean of School of Education ....Vacant
06 Registrar ....Mrs. Cecelia MESLER
38 Director of Career/Counseling Svcs ....Ms. Sharon E. SMITH
51 Director of Continuing Education ....Dr. Deborah WICKERING
104 Dir International Education Pgms ....Ms. Joelle BALDWIN
94 Director of Women's Studies ....Ms. Amy DUNHAM STRAND
92 Director of Honors Program ....Dr. Michelle DEROSE
58 Director of Graduate Management ....Mr. Brian DIVITA
08 Co-Director Woodhouse Library ....Ms. Shellie JEFFRIES
08 Co-Director Woodhouse Library ....Ms. Francine PAOLINI
18 Director of Maintenance ....Mr. Dale HAISMA
39 Director Residence Life ....Ms. Julie BLASZAK
07 Director of Admissions ....Ms. Angela SCHLOSSER-BACON
37 Director of Financial Aid ....Mr. David J. STEFFEE
41 Director Athletics ....Mr. Terry M. BOCIAN
42 Director Campus Ministry ....Ms. Mary CLARK-KAISER
13 Dir Information Technology & Svcs ....Mr. Doug MACNEIL
29 Director of Alumni Relations ....Ms. Brigid AVERY
35 Director of Campus Life ....Ms. Heather HALL
44 Director of Major Gifts ....Ms. Cecelia CUNNINGHAM
44 Director of Corporate Giving ....Dr. Ali ERHAN
20 Director of Academic Advising ....Ms. Cecelia MESLER
28 Director of Diversity & Inclusion ....Ms. Latoya BOOKER
40 Director Bookstore ....Ms. Marian TODISH
23 Manager of Health and Wellness ....Ms. Veronica BEITNER
24 Media Coordinator ....Ms. Francine PAOLINI
42 Campus Chaplain ....Rev. Stanley DRONGOWSKI, OP

The Art Institute of Michigan (F)

28125 Cabot Drive, Suite 120, Novi MI 48377

Telephone: (248) 675-3800 Identification: 666692
Accreditation: &NH, ACFEI

† Regional accreditation is carried under the parent institution The Illinois Institute of Art, Chicago, IL.

*Baker College System (G)

1050 W Bristol Road, Flint MI 48507-5508

County: Genesee Identification: 666923
Unit ID: 419572
Telephone: (810) 766-4280 Carnegie Class: N/A
FAX Number: (810) 766-4279
URL: www.baker.edu

00 Chairman of the Board ....Mr. Edward J. KURTZ
01 CEO/President of System ....Mr. F. James CUMMINS
05 Vice President for Academics ....Dr. Denise A. BANNAN
13 Vice President for Computer Systems ....Ms. Jacqueline SPICER
15 Vice President of Human Resources ....Ms. Dana CLARK
26 Vice Pres Marketing/Admissions/PR ....Mr. Bruce LUNDEEN
10 Vice President for Finance ....Ms. Tiffany DAVIS
32 Director of Student Life ....Vacant
20 Director Curriculum ....Ms. Kim L. LUTZ
36 Director of Career Services ....Vacant
14 Director Computer Operations ....Mrs. Sheryl L. DEAN
08 Director of Library Services ....Mr. Eric PALMER
58 President Graduate Studies ....Dr. Jill LANGEN

*Baker College of Flint (H)

1050 W Bristol Road, Flint MI 48507-5508

County: Genesee FICE Identification: 004673
Unit ID: 168847
Telephone: (810) 766-4000 Carnegie Class: Bac/Assoc

FAX Number: (810) 766-4293 Calendar System: Quarter
URL: www.baker.edu
Established: 1911 Annual Undergrad Tuition & Fees: $8,640
Enrollment: 4,002 Coed
Affiliation or Control: Independent Non-Profit IRS Status: 501(c)3
Highest Offering: Doctorate
Program: Occupational; 2-Year Principally Bachelor's Creditable; Liberal Arts And General; Business Emphasis
Accreditation: NH, CAHIIM, CSHSE, ENG, ENGT, IACBE, MAC, NURSE, OT, POLYT, PTAA, SURGT, TEAC

02 President .... Mrs. Wen HEMINGWAY
05 Vice President of Academics .... Dr. Candace JOHNSON
07 Vice President of Admissions .... Ms. Jodi CUNEAZ
15 Vice President of Human Resources .... Ms. Dana CLARK
32 Vice President of Student Services .... Mr. Gerald MCCARTY, II
50 Dean of Business Administration .... Dr. John C. COTE
97 Dean of General Education .... Dr. Mary Ann THAYER
76 Dean of Health/Human Services .... Vacant
72 Dean of Technical Division .... Mrs. Anca SALA
08 Director of Library Services .... Vacant
06 Registrar .... Mr. Robert MARTIN
13 Director of Computer Operations .... Mr. Michael MEYERS
18 Director of Facilities .... Mr. Marvin DEAN
38 Director of Counseling/Assessment .... Mr. Paul ZANG
19 Director of Safety/Security .... Mr. John JOSEPH
40 Director of Bookstore .... Mr. James ROTTA
54 Dir Engineering/Computer Science .... Mrs. Anca SALA
26 Director Community Relations .... Vacant
10 Business Officer .... Mrs. Rebecca AYRE-BOGGS
36 Director of Career Services .... Mrs. Janie STEWART
37 Director Student Financial Aid .... Ms. Veta NORRIS
31 Director Corporate/Community Svcs .... Ms. Karen EASTERLING
23 Director of Health and Fitness .... Ms. Maureen PARMANN
39 Housing Coordinator .... Mr. Leon CARTER

* Baker College of Allen Park (A)

4500 Enterprise Drive, Allen Park MI 48101-3033
Telephone: (313) 425-3700 Identification: 666996
Accreditation: &NH, CAHIIM, COMTA, CSHSE, IACBE, MAC, MLTAD, OTA, PTAA, SURGT

† Branch campus of Baker College of Flint, Flint, MI.

* Baker College of Auburn Hills (B)

1500 University Drive, Auburn Hills MI 48326-2642
Telephone: (248) 340-0600 Identification: 666940
Accreditation: &NH, COARC, CSHSE, DA, DH, DMS, IACBE, MAC, PHLEB, PTAA

† Branch campus of Baker College of Flint, Flint, MI.

* Baker College of Cadillac (C)

9600 E 13th Street, Cadillac MI 49601-9600
Telephone: (231) 876-3100 Identification: 666941
Accreditation: &NH, COMTA, CSHSE, IACBE, MAC, SURGT

† Branch campus of Baker College of Flint, Flint, MI.

* Baker College of Clinton Township (D)

34950 Little Mack Avenue,
Clinton Township MI 48035-4701
Telephone: (586) 791-6610 Identification: 666942
Accreditation: &NH, CAHIIM, COMTA, CSHSE, IACBE, MAC, RAD, SURGT

† Branch campus of Baker College of Flint, Flint, MI.

* Baker College of Jackson (E)

2800 Springport Road, Jackson MI 49202-1290
Telephone: (517) 788-7800 FICE Identification: 004680
Accreditation: &NH, CAHIIM, COMTA, CSHSE, IACBE, MAC, OPD, RTT, SURGT

† Branch campus of Baker College of Flint, Flint, MI.

* Baker College of Muskegon (F)

1903 Marquette Avenue, Muskegon MI 49442-1490
Telephone: (231) 777-5200 FICE Identification: 002296
Accreditation: &NH, ACFEI, ADNUR, COMTA, CSHSE, IACBE, MAC, OTA, PTAA, RAD, SURGT

† Branch campus of Baker College of Flint, Flint, MI.

* Baker College of Owosso (G)

1020 S Washington Street, Owosso MI 48867-4400
Telephone: (989) 729-3370 Identification: 666937
Accreditation: &NH, ADNUR, COMTA, CSHSE, DMS, IACBE, MAC, MLTAD, PHLEB, RAD

† Branch campus of Baker College of Flint, Flint, MI.

* Baker College of Port Huron (H)

3403 Lapeer Road, Port Huron MI 48060-2597
Telephone: (810) 985-7000 Identification: 666943
Accreditation: &NH, CSHSE, DH, IACBE, MAC

† Branch campus of Baker College of Flint, Flint, MI.

Bay College West Campus (I)

PO Box 130, Iron Mountain MI 49801
Telephone: (906) 774-8547 Identification: 770262
Accreditation: &NH

† Branch campus of Bay de Noc Community College, Escanaba, MI.

Bay Mills Community College (J)

12214 W Lakeshore Drive, Brimley MI 49715-9750
County: Chippewa FICE Identification: 030666
Unit ID: 380359
Telephone: (906) 248-3354 Carnegie Class: Tribal
FAX Number: (906) 248-3351 Calendar System: Semester
URL: www.bmcc.edu
Established: 1984 Annual Undergrad Tuition & Fees: $3,180
Enrollment: 555 Coed
Affiliation or Control: Tribal Control IRS Status: 501(c)3
Highest Offering: Associate Degree
Program: Occupational; 2-Year Principally Bachelor's Creditable; Business Emphasis
Accreditation: NH

01 President .... Michael C. PARISH
05 Vice President of Academic Affairs .... Samantha CAMERON
10 Vice Pres Business & Finance .... Laura POSTMA
32 Dean of Student Services .... Debra J. WILSON
13 Director Technology .... Chet KASPER
06 Registrar/Inst Info Systems Mgr .... Sherri SCHOFIELD
37 Director Student Financial Aid .... Tina MILLER
07 Director of Admissions .... Elaine LEHRE
88 Land Grant Director .... Stephen YANNI
30 Director of Development .... Kathy ADAIR

Bay de Noc Community College (K)

2001 N Lincoln Road, Escanaba MI 49829-2510
County: Delta FICE Identification: 002240
Unit ID: 168883
Telephone: (906) 786-5802 Carnegie Class: Assoc/Pub-R-M
FAX Number: (906) 789-6952 Calendar System: Semester
URL: www.baycollege.edu
Established: 1962 Annual Undergrad Tuition & Fees (In-District): $4,040
Enrollment: 2,024 Coed
Affiliation or Control: Local IRS Status: 501(c)3
Highest Offering: Associate Degree
Program: Occupational; 2-Year Principally Bachelor's Creditable
Accreditation: NH, ADNUR

01 President .... Dr. Laura COLEMAN
11 VP of Operations .... Ms. Christine WILLIAMS
12 VP of West Campus .... Dr. Patrick KENNEDY
10 Chief Financial Officer .... Mr. Kevin CARLSON
49 Dean of Arts & Sciences .... Dr. Matthew BARRON
50 Int Exec Dean of Business/Tech/WD .... Mr. Mark KINNEY
30 VP of College Advancement .... Ms. Kim CARNE
37 Director of Financial Aid .... Ms. Laurie SPANGENBERG
07 Interim Dean Admission Services .... Ms. Cynthia CARTER
15 Director of Human Resources .... Mrs. Bridget DEGROOT
18 Director of Buildings & Grounds .... Mr. Ralph CURRY
76 Dean of Allied Health .... Ms. Jeanette STEBELTON
32 Director of Student Life .... Mr. Dave LAUR
103 Exec Dir Professional Workforce Dev .... Mr. Robert PONTIUS
04 Exec Admin Asst to President .... Mrs. Laura JOHNSON
84 Int Dean Enrollment Management .... Mr. Travis BLUME
08 Head Librarian .... Mr. Oscar DELONG

Calvin College (L)

3201 Burton Street, SE, Grand Rapids MI 49546-4388
County: Kent FICE Identification: 002241
Unit ID: 169080
Telephone: (616) 526-6000 Carnegie Class: Bac/A&S
FAX Number: (616) 526-8551 Calendar System: 4/1/4
URL: www.calvin.edu
Established: 1876 Annual Undergrad Tuition & Fees: $30,425
Enrollment: 3,993 Coed
Affiliation or Control: Christian Reformed Church IRS Status: 501(c)3
Highest Offering: Master's
Program: Liberal Arts And General; Teacher Preparatory; Professional
Accreditation: NH, CS, ENG, MUS, NURSE, @SP, SW, TEAC

01 President .... Dr. Michael K. LE ROY
04 Senior Executive Associate .... Mr. Robert A. BERKHOF
05 Provost .... Dr. Cheryl BRANDSEN
10 Vice Pres Admin/Finance .... Ms. Sally VANDER PLOEG
30 Vice President for Advancement .... Mr. Kenneth ERFFMEYER
84 Vice Pres Enrollment Management .... Mr. Russell J. BLOEM
32 Vice President Student Life .... Dr. Sarah VISSER
21 Director of Finance .... Mr. Joel DEBRUIN
08 Director of the Library .... Mr. Glenn A. REMELTS
29 Director Alumni/Parent Relations .... Mr. Michael J. VAN DENEND
06 Director Academic Svcs/Registrar .... Mr. Thomas L. STEENWYK
39 Dean of Residence Life .... Mr. John WITTE
35 Dean of Student Development .... Mr. C. Robert CROW
88 Dean of Students for Judicial Affs .... Ms. Jane E. HENDRIKSMA
46 Dean of Research & Scholarship .... Dr. Matthew WALHOUT
108 Dean Institutional Effectiveness .... Dr. Michael STOB
83 Acad Dean Lang/Soc Sci/Context Disc .. Dr. Elizabeth VANDERLEI
81 Acad Dean Educ/Kinesio/Nat Sci/Math .... Dr. Stanley L. HAAN
28 Exec Assoc for Diversity/Inclusion .... Dr. Michelle LOYD-PAIGE
15 Vice President People/Strategy & IT .... Mr. Todd K. HUBERS
36 Director of Career Development .... Vacant
09 Dir Institutional/Enroll Research .... Mr. Thomas A. VAN ECK
26 Dir Communications & Brand Strategy .... Mr. Timothy L. ELLENS
26 Director of Marketing .... Ms. Jeanne NIENHUIS
88 Director Social Research Center .... Dr. Neil CARLSON
19 Director of Campus Safety .... Mr. William T. CORNER
18 Director Physical Plant .... Mr. Philip D. BEEZHOLD
24 Director Instruc Resources Center .... Mr. Randal G. NIEUWSMA
38 Director Broene Counseling Center .... Dr. Cynthia KOK
23 Director Health Services .... Dr. Laura CHAMPION
92 Director Honors Program .... Dr. Bruce BERGLUND
42 College Chaplain .... Dr. Mary HULST
41 Athletic Director Men .... Dr. James TIMMER, JR.
41 Athletic Director Women .... Dr. Nancy L. MEYER
102 Dir Foundation/Corporate Relations .... Ms. Megan BERGLUND
104 Director Study Abroad .... Dr. Donald DEGRAAF
105 Director Web Services .... Mr. Luke ROBINSON
13 Assoc Vice President for IT .... Mr. Brian PAIGE
37 Director Student Financial Aid .... Mr. Paul R. WITTE, III
44 Director Annual Giving & Engagement .... Mr. Rick TREUR
53 Dean of Education .... Dr. James ROOKS
07 Director of Admissions/Counseling .... Mr. Ben ARENDT

Calvin Theological Seminary (M)

3233 Burton Street, SE, Grand Rapids MI 49546-4387
County: Kent FICE Identification: 002242
Unit ID: 169099
Telephone: (616) 957-6036 Carnegie Class: Spec/Faith
FAX Number: (616) 957-8621 Calendar System: Semester
URL: www.calvinseminary.edu
Established: 1876 Annual Graduate Tuition & Fees: $14,619
Enrollment: 291 Coed
Affiliation or Control: Christian Reformed Church IRS Status: 501(c)3
Highest Offering: Doctorate; No Undergraduates
Program: Professional; Religious Emphasis
Accreditation: THEOL

01 President .... Rev. Julius T. MEDENBLIK
05 Dean of Academic Programs .... Dr. Ronald J. FEENSTRA
20 Assoc Academic Dean .... Ms. Mary L. VANDENBERG
06 Registrar .... Ms. Joan BEELEN
32 Dean of Students .... Rev. Jeff SAJDAK
08 Theological Librarian .... Rev. Lugene L. SCHEMPER
10 Chief Financial & Operations Ofcr .... Ms. Jinny DE JONG
30 Director of Development .... Mr. Robert KNOOR
36 Director of Mentored Ministries .... Rev. Alvern GELDER
07 Dir of Admissions/Enrollment Mgmt .... Mr. Aaron EINFELD
37 Director of Financial Aid .... Mrs. Jennifer SETTERGREN

Career Quest Learning Center (N)

3215 S. Pennsylvania Ave, Lansing MI 48910
County: Ingham FICE Identification: 039153
Unit ID: 446136
Telephone: (517) 318-3330 Carnegie Class: Not Classified
FAX Number: (517) 318-3331 Calendar System: Other
URL: www.careerquest.edu
Established: 1995 Annual Undergrad Tuition & Fees: $16,100
Enrollment: 408 Coed
Affiliation or Control: Proprietary IRS Status: Proprietary
Highest Offering: Associate Degree
Program: Occupational
Accreditation: COE

01 President & CEO .... Robert MCCART

Central Michigan University (O)

1200 S. Franklin Street, Mount Pleasant MI 48859
County: Isabella FICE Identification: 002243
Unit ID: 169248
Telephone: (989) 774-4000 Carnegie Class: DRU
FAX Number: (989) 774-3537 Calendar System: Semester
URL: www.cmich.edu
Established: 1892 Annual Undergrad Tuition & Fees (In-State): $11,850
Enrollment: 26,879 Coed
Affiliation or Control: State IRS Status: 501(c)3
Highest Offering: Doctorate
Program: Liberal Arts And General; Teacher Preparatory; Professional
Accreditation: NH, ART, ACAE, #ARCPA, AUD, BUS, BUSA, CAATE, CIDA, CLPSY, DIETD, DIETI, ENG, JOUR, #MED, MUS, NAIT, NRPA, PTA, SCPSY, SP, SPAA, SW, TEAC

01 President .... Dr. George E. ROSS
05 Executive VP/Provost .... Dr. Michael A. GEALT
10 Vice Pres Finance/Admin Svcs .... Mr. Barrie J. WILKES
30 Vice Pres Development/Ext Relations .... Ms. Kathleen M. WILBUR
84 Vice Pres Enrollment & Student Svcs .... Mr. Steven L. JOHNSON
88 Vice Pres Global Campus .... Mr. Peter G. ROSS
13 Vice President Info Technology/CIO .... Dr. Roger E. REHM
21 AVP Fin Svcs & Reporting/Controller .... Ms. Mary M. HILL
26 AVP University Communications .... Ms. Sherry S. KNIGHT
18 Assoc Vice Pres Facilities Mgmt .... Mr. Stephen P. LAWRENCE
39 Assoc VP Residence/Auxiliary Svcs .... Mr. John S. FISHER
28 Assoc Vice Pres Diversity .... Ms. Carolyn M. DUNN
15 Assoc VP Human Resources .... Ms. Lori L. HELLA
20 Vice Provost Academic Effectiveness .... Dr. Claudia B. DOUGLASS
88 Sr Vice Provost Academic Admin .... Dr. Ray L. CHRISTIE

58 Interim VP Rsrch & Dean Grad Stds .... Dr. Ian R. DAVISON
44 Asst VP Major & Planned Giving Pgm .. Mr. Edward A. TOLCHER
08 Dean of Libraries .... Mr. Thomas J. MOORE
32 Assoc VP Student Affairs .... Mr. Anthony A. VOISIN
88 Exec Dir Acad Advis/Assistance .... Ms. Michelle L. HOWARD
29 Exec Dir of Alumni Relations .... Ms. Marcie M. OTTEMAN
09 Exec Dir Institutional Research .... Dr. Robert M. ROE
22 Exec Dir Civil Rights/Inst Equity .... Ms. Katherine M. LASHER
07 Director Undergraduate Admissions .. Mr. Thomas W. SPEAKMAN
43 Vice President & General Counsel .... Dr. Manuel R. RUPE
06 Registrar .... Mr. Keith J. MALKOWSKI
37 Director Scholarships/Financial Aid .... Mr. Kirk M. YATS
36 Director Career Services .... Ms. Julia B. SHERLOCK
41 Assoc VP/Director of Athletics .... Mr. David W. HEEKE, JR.
38 Director Counseling Center .... Mr. Ross J. RAPAPORT
45 Director Financial Plan & Budgets .... Ms. Carol A. HAAS
27 Director PR & Internal Comm .... Mr. Steven F. SMITH
19 Chief of Police .... Mr. William YEAGLEY, JR.
40 Director CMU Bookstore .... Mr. Barry D. WATERS
81 Dean College of Sci & Tech .... Dr. Ian R. DAVISON
76 Interim Dean Health Professions .... Dr. Tom J. MASTERSON
63 Dean College of Medicine .... Dr. George E. KIKANO
83 Dean Col Hum/Soc/Behav Sci .... Dr. Pamela S. GATES
57 Dean College Comm/Fine Arts .... Dr. Janet HETHORN
50 Dean College of Business Admin .... Dr. Charles T. CRESPY
53 Dean College Education/Human Svcs .... Dr. Dale-Elizabeth PEHRSSON
04 Executive Assistant to President .... Ms. Mary Jane FLANAGAN
85 Exec Dir International Affairs .... Mr. William A. HOLMES
96 Dir Contract & Purchasing Svcs .... Mr. Thomas P. TRIONFI
92 Director Honors Program .... Dr. Phame M. CAMARENA
93 Dir Multicultural Acad/Stdnt Sv .... Dr. Traci L. GUINN
86 Director Government Relations .... Mr. Toby ROTH, JR.
102 Dir Corp & Foundation Relations .... Ms. Kimberly R. HOUSTON-PHILPOT
104 Director Study Abroad .... Ms. Dianne S. DESALVO

Chamberlain College of Nursing-Troy (A)

200 Kirfs Blvd, Ste C, Troy MI 48084
Telephone: (248) 817-4140 Identification: 770851
Accreditation: &NH, NURSE

† Branch campus of Chamberlain College of Nursing-Addison, Addison, IL.

Cleary University (B)

3750 Cleary Drive, Howell MI 48843
County: Livingston FICE Identification: 002246
Unit ID: 169327
Telephone: (800) 686-1883 Carnegie Class: Spec/Bus
FAX Number: N/A Calendar System: Semester
URL: www.cleary.edu
Established: 1883 Annual Undergrad Tuition & Fees: $625
Enrollment: 538 Coed
Affiliation or Control: Independent Non-Profit IRS Status: 501(c)3
Highest Offering: Master's
Program: Occupational; Professional; Business Emphasis
Accreditation: NH

01 President & CEO .... Mr. Jayson BOYERS
05 VP Academic Affairs & Provost .... Dr. Lance LEWIS
10 VP Finance & Administration .... Ms. Judy WALKER
26 VP Communications & Enrollment Mgmt .... Dr. Matt BENNETT
06 Asst VP Academic Svcs/Registrar .... Ms. Dawn M. FISER
04 Exec Asst to Pres/Board of Trustees .... Ms. Linda T. RENTZ
20 Dn Col Bus Innovation/Applied Tech .... Ms. Dawn MARKELL
85 Dean International Students .... Ms. Sadhana ALANGAR
13 Exec Director/Chief Info Officer .... Mr. David G. BOWERS
09 Dir Institutional Research/Analysis .... Mr. Tim VEENSTRA
109 Chief Auxiliary Services Officer .... Mr. Gary BACHMAN
30 Exec Dir Development/Alumni Rel .... Ms. Janet FILIP
37 Director Financial Aid .... Ms. Vesta SMITH-CAMPBELL
36 Dir Career Services & Placement .... Ms. Peggy SIMPSON
40 Director Bookstore Services .... Ms. Sheila THOMPSON
07 Director of Admissions .... Ms. Carrie BONOFIGLIO
15 Chief Human Resource Officer .... Ms. Julie SVERID
41 Athletic Director .... Mr. Karl KLING
44 Director Annual or Planned Giving .... Ms. Josephine JABARA

Cleary University-Livingston Campus (C)

3750 Cleary Drive, Howell MI 48843
Telephone: (800) 686-1883 Identification: 770263
Accreditation: &NH

† Branch campus of Cleary University, Howell, MI.

College for Creative Studies (D)

201 E Kirby, Detroit MI 48202-4034
County: Wayne FICE Identification: 006771
Unit ID: 169442
Telephone: (313) 664-7400 Carnegie Class: Spec/Arts
FAX Number: (313) 872-8377 Calendar System: Semester
URL: www.collegeforcreativestudies.edu
Established: 1906 Annual Undergrad Tuition & Fees: $37,560
Enrollment: 1,382 Coed
Affiliation or Control: Independent Non-Profit IRS Status: 501(c)3
Highest Offering: Master's
Program: Teacher Preparatory; Professional; Fine Arts Emphasis
Accreditation: NH, ART, CIDA

01 President .... Mr. Richard L. ROGERS
100 Exec Asst to Pres & Sec to Board .... Ms. Sandra WILSON
04 Admin Assistant to the President .... Ms. Brigette NEAL
05 Provost & VP for Academic Affairs .... Mr. Sooshin CHOI
10 Vice Pres Administration & Finance .... Ms. Anne D. BECK
84 Vice Pres Enrollmnt & Student Svcs .... Ms. Julie HINGELBERG
30 Vice Pres Institutional Advancement .... Ms. Nina HOLDEN
20 Assoc Provost .... Ms. Sharon PROCTER
58 Dean Graduate Studies .... Ms. Joanne HEALY
57 Dean Undergraduate Studies .... Mr. Vince CARDUCCI
32 Dean of Students .... Mr. Daniel LONG
06 Registrar & Acad Advising Director .... Ms. Nadine ASHTON
07 Director of Admissions .... Ms. Carla GONZALEZ
37 Director Financial Aid .... Ms. Kristin MOSKOVITZ
35 Director Student Life .... Mr. Michael COLEMAN
85 Director Intl Student Services .... Mr. Francisco LOPEZ
28 Director of Multicultural Affairs .... Mr. Cliff HARRIS
51 Dir Continuing & Precollege Studies .... Ms. Alicia SIMON
31 Dir of Community Arts Partnerships .... Mr. Mikel BRESEE
08 Director Library .... Ms. Beth WALKER
19 Director of Safety & Security .... Mr. Garrett OCHALEK
18 Director Facilities & Admin Svcs .... Mr. Geoffrey SLEEMAN
13 Director Information Technology .... Mr. Greg FRASER
90 Director of Academic Technologies .... Ms. Laurie EVANS
21 Director Business Services .... Ms. Kerri MCKAY
15 Director Human Resources .... Mr. Gregory KNOFF
26 Director Marketing & Communications ..... Mr. Marcus POPIOLEK
44 Dir Annual Giving/Donor Services .... Ms. Elizabeth KLOS
36 Director Career Services .... Ms. Terese NEHRA
29 Asst Dir Annual Giv/Alumni Rels .... Mr. Anthony SPANGLER
38 Personal Counselor .... Ms. Valerie WEISS
40 Manager Bookstore .... Ms. Lauren HART
39 Director of Residence Life .... Mr. Ryan HARRISON
102 Dir Foundation/Corporate Relations .... Ms. Shannon MCPARTLON

Compass College of Cinematic Arts (E)

41 Sheldon Boulevard, SE, Grand Rapids MI 49503
County: Kent FICE Identification: 041633
Unit ID: 459417
Telephone: (616) 988-1000 Carnegie Class: Not Classified
FAX Number: (616) 458-4676 Calendar System: Other
URL: www.compass.edu
Established: 2003 Annual Undergrad Tuition & Fees: $13,835
Enrollment: 98 Coed
Affiliation or Control: Independent Non-Profit IRS Status: 501(c)3
Highest Offering: Baccalaureate
Program: Occupational; 2-Year Principally Bachelor's Creditable; Fine Arts Emphasis
Accreditation: ACCSC

01 President .... Keri LOWE
05 Director of Education .... Dr. Mark VANDERMEER
15 Compliance & HR Manager .... Kim D. BUSH
30 Director of Development .... Greg VANDERGOOT
10 Finance Manager .... Laura COULIER
26 Director Marketing & Recruiting .... Tom LOWE
32 Student Affairs Specialist .... Austin MORSE
07 Admissions Representative .... Amy HILLS

Concordia University Ann Arbor (F)

4090 Geddes Road, Ann Arbor MI 48105-2797
County: Washtenaw FICE Identification: 002247
Unit ID: 169363
Telephone: (734) 995-7300 Carnegie Class: Bac/Diverse
FAX Number: (734) 995-4610 Calendar System: Semester
URL: www.cuaa.edu
Established: 1962 Annual Undergrad Tuition & Fees: $24,930
Enrollment: 829 Coed
Affiliation or Control: Lutheran Church - Missouri Synod
IRS Status: 501(c)3
Highest Offering: Master's
Program: Liberal Arts And General; Teacher Preparatory; Professional; Religious Emphasis
Accreditation: NH, TED

01 President .... Rev. Patrick FERRY
03 Executive VP & Chief Oper Ofcr .... Mr. Allen PROCHNOW
11 VP of Admin/Campus Chief Exec .... Mr. Curt GIELOW
05 VP Academic Affairs .... Dr. William CARIO
07 Director of Enrollment Services .... Mr. Jonathon BAHR
32 Executive Director Student Life .... Rev. John RATHJE
38 Director Student Counseling .... Mrs. Gina VERSEMAN
39 Director Residence Life .... Mr. Dauthan KEENER
41 Director of Athletics .... Mr. Lonnie PRIES
42 Director of Spiritual Life .... Mr. Robert MCKINNEY
18 Director Buildings & Grounds .... Mr. Jerry NOVAK
19 Director Security/Safety .... Mr. James STEPHENSON
13 Director IT Services .... Mr. Christopher RAASCH
30 Director of Development .... Mr. Martin MORO
09 Director of Institutional Research .... Dr. Mae KELLER
08 Coordinator of Library Services .... Mr. Michael O'LEARY
15 Human Resources Generalist .... Mrs. Barb WALTHER
53 Campus Dean School of Education .... Dr. Harvey SCHMIT
50 Campus Dean School of Business .... Dr. Suzanne SIEGLE
66 Campus Dean School of Nursing .... Dr. Cynthia FENSKE
49 Campus Dean School Arts & Sciences ... Dr. Robert MCCORMICK
09 Campus Coord of Acad Operations .... Dr. Kelsi ANDERSON

Cornerstone University (G)

1001 E Beltline Avenue, NE, Grand Rapids MI 49525-5897
County: Kent FICE Identification: 002266
Unit ID: 170037
Telephone: (616) 949-5300 Carnegie Class: Master's L
FAX Number: (616) 222-1540 Calendar System: Semester
URL: www.cornerstone.edu
Established: 1941 Annual Undergrad Tuition & Fees: $26,100
Enrollment: 2,770 Coed
Affiliation or Control: Independent Non-Profit IRS Status: 501(c)3
Highest Offering: Master's
Program: Liberal Arts And General; Teacher Preparatory; Professional
Accreditation: NH, MUS, SW, TEAC, THEOL

01 President .... Dr. Joseph M. STOWELL
03 Executive Vice President .... Mr. Marc FOWLER
05 Chief Academic Officer .... Dr. John VERBERKMOES
30 Vice President Donor Relations .... Mr. William KNOTT
88 Vice President of Broadcasting .... Mr. Chris LEMKE
88 Vice Pres Student Development .... Mr. Gerald LONGJOHN
97 Dean of Undergraduate Education .... Dr. Martin HUGHES
73 Dean Grand Rpds Theol Seminary ...... Mr. John VER BERKMOES
32 Dean of Student Engagement .... Mr. Chip HUBER
09 Dean Institutional Effectiveness .... Dr. Tim DETWILER
35 Director of Student Services .... Mr. Keith DEBOER
08 Director of Miller Library .... Mr. Fred SWEET
37 Director Financial Services .... Mrs. Carol CARPENTER
21 Controller .... Mr. Scott STEWART
88 Director of Retention .... Mrs. Kay LANDRUM
41 Athletic Director .... Mr. Dave GRUBE
15 Director of Human Resources .... Mrs. Emilie AZKOUL
18 Director of Campus Services .... Mr. Bob PRIOLO
19 Director of Campus Safety .... Mr. Brandan BISHOP
29 Director of Alumni .... Mr. Nate CLASON
06 Registrar .... Mrs. Gail DUHON
24 Director of Technical Support .... Mr. Dan MILLS
38 Director of the Counseling Center .... Mr. Scott COUREY
92 Director of Honors Program .... Mr. Michael STEVENS
07 Director of Admissions .... Mr. Dave EMERSON
10 Chief Financial Officer .... Mrs. Dee MOONEY
26 Chief Public Relations Officer .... Mr. Bob SACK
04 Administrative Asst to President .... Mrs. Beth LONGJOHN

Cranbrook Academy of Art (H)

39221 Woodward Avenue, PO Box 801, Bloomfield Hills MI 48303-0801
County: Oakland FICE Identification: 002248
Unit ID: 169424
Telephone: (248) 645-3300 Carnegie Class: Spec/Arts
FAX Number: (248) 645-3591 Calendar System: Semester
URL: www.cranbrook.edu
Established: 1932 Annual Graduate Tuition & Fees: $35,886
Enrollment: 150 Coed
Affiliation or Control: Independent Non-Profit IRS Status: 501(c)3
Highest Offering: Master's; No Undergraduates
Program: Professional; Fine Arts Emphasis
Accreditation: NH, ART

01 Director .... Mr. Christopher SCOATES
06 Registrar/Fin Aid & Admiss Mgr .... Ms. Leslie TOBAKOS

Davenport University (I)

6191 Kraft Avenue, S.E., Grand Rapids MI 49512
County: Kent FICE Identification: 002249
Unit ID: 169479
Telephone: (616) 698-7111 Carnegie Class: Master's M
FAX Number: N/A Calendar System: Semester
URL: www.davenport.edu
Established: 1866 Annual Undergrad Tuition & Fees: $18,990
Enrollment: 8,985 Coed
Affiliation or Control: Independent Non-Profit IRS Status: 501(c)3
Highest Offering: Master's
Program: Professional; Business Emphasis
Accreditation: NH, CAHIIM, IACBE, MAC, NUR, NURSE, PNUR

01 President .... Dr. Richard J. PAPPAS
30 Exec VP Advancement .... Ms. Peg LUY
46 Exec VP of Quality & Effectiveness .... Dr. Scott EPSTEIN
15 Exec VP Human/Organizational Devel .... Mr. Dave VENEKLASE
07 Exec VP Admission & Student Svcs .... Mr. Walter O'NEILL
10 Exec Vice President for Finance/CFO .... Mr. Michael S. VOLK
05 Exec VP Academics/Provost .... Dr. Linda RINKER
13 Vice Pres Information Technology .... Mr. Brian MILLER
09 VP for Institutional Research .... Dr. Kathy ABOUFADEL
18 Vice President for Plant & Security ...... Mr. Shallan SPIELMAKER
50 Dean College of Business .... Vacant
72 Interim Dean College of Technology .... Mr. Brian MILLER
76 Dean College of Health Professions .... Dr. Karen DALEY
49 Dean College of Arts and Sciences .... Dr. Thomas LONERGAN
106 Dean Online .... Mr. Brian MILLER
107 Dean College of Urban Education .... Ms. Susan GUNN
37 Exec Director Financial Aid .... Mr. David DE BOER
26 Executive Dir of Communications .... Mr. Robyn LUYMES
29 Director of Alumni Relations .... Mr. Jason MADDON
21 Controller .... Mr. Michael SLEVA
06 University Registrar .... Ms. Donna MILHAM
41 Director of Athletics .... Mr. Paul LOWDEN
04 Administrative Asst to President .... Ms. Rose KARSTEN
28 Director of Diversity .... Dr. RhaeAnn BOOKER

Davenport University Battle Creek (A)

200 West Van Buren Street, Battle Creek MI 49017
Telephone: (269) 968-6105 Identification: 770264
Accreditation: &NH, MAC

† School is in teach-out and plans to close in August, 2016.

Davenport University Holland (B)

643 S Waverly Road, Holland MI 49423
Telephone: (616) 395-4600 Identification: 770266
Accreditation: &NH

† Branch campus of Davenport University, Grand Rapids, MI.

Davenport University Kalamazoo (C)

4123 West Main Street, Kalamazoo MI 49006
Telephone: (269) 382-2835 Identification: 770267
Accreditation: &NH

† Branch campus of Davenport University, Grand Rapids, MI.

Davenport University Lansing (D)

220 E Kalamazoo, Lansing MI 48933
Telephone: (517) 484-2600 Identification: 770268
Accreditation: &NH, MAC

† Branch campus of Davenport University, Grand Rapids, MI.

Davenport University Livonia (E)

19499 Victor Parkway, Livonia MI 48152
Telephone: (734) 943-2800 Identification: 770269
Accreditation: &NH, CAHIIM

† Branch campus of Davenport University, Grand Rapids, MI.

Davenport University Midland (F)

3555 E Patrick Road, Midland MI 48642
Telephone: (989) 835-5588 Identification: 770270
Accreditation: &NH

† Branch campus of Davenport University, Grand Rapids, MI.

Davenport University Saginaw (G)

5300 Bay Road, Saginaw MI 48604
Telephone: (989) 799-7800 Identification: 770271
Accreditation: &NH, CAHIIM

† Branch campus of Davenport University, Grand Rapids, MI.

Davenport University Warren (H)

27650 Dequindre Road, Warren MI 48092
Telephone: (586) 558-8700 Identification: 770272
Accreditation: &NH

† Branch campus of Davenport University, Grand Rapids, MI.

Delta College (I)

1961 Delta Rd., University Center MI 48710-0001
County: Bay FICE Identification: 002251
Unit ID: 169521
Telephone: (989) 686-9000 Carnegie Class: Assoc/Pub-R-L
FAX Number: (989) 667-0620 Calendar System: Semester
URL: www.delta.edu
Established: 1961 Annual Undergrad Tuition & Fees (In-District): $3,395
Enrollment: 9,843 Coed
Affiliation or Control: Local IRS Status: 501(c)3
Highest Offering: Associate Degree
Program: Occupational; 2-Year Principally Bachelor's Creditable
Accreditation: NH, ADNUR, COARC, DA, DH, DMS, PTAA, RAD, SURGT

01 President ... Dr. Jean GOODNOW
10 Vice President Finance/Treasurer ... Ms. Debra K. LUTZ
32 Vice President Student & Educ Svcs ... Ms. Margarita MOSQUEDA
05 VP Instruction/Learning Svcs ... Dr. Reva CURRY
30 Ex Dir Delta Col Found/Inst Advance ... Ms. Pam CLARK
20 Dean of Teaching & Learning ... Mr. David PERUSKI
35 Dean of Students ... Dr. Amie ANDERSON
36 Dean Career Educ/Learning Part ... Ms. Ginny PRZYGOCKI
84 Dean of Enrollment ... Vacant
26 Marketing & Public Info Director ... Ms. Leanne GOVITZ
11 Dir Institutional Effectiveness ... Ms. Andrea L. URSUY
101 Assistant to Pres/Board Secretary ... Ms. Andrea URSUY
25 Director of Corporate Services ... Ms. Jennifer CARROLL
37 Director of Student Financial Aid ... Mr. David URBANIAK
15 Director of Human Resources ... Ms. Mary L. GMEINER
18 Director of Facilities Management ... Mr. Larry E. RAMSEYER
07 Director of Admissions ... Vacant
19 Director of Public Safety ... Vacant
88 Director of Learning Centers ... Ms. Kristy NELSON
38 Dir Counseling Advising/Career Svcs ... Ms. Diana GUTIERREZ
21 Business Services Director ... Ms. Barbara WEBB
09 Director of Institutional Research ... Mr. Wm. Michael WOOD
06 Registrar ... Vacant
13 Chief Information Officer ... Mr. Jason STAHL
40 Bookstore Manager ... Ms. Barbara POWERS
08 Mgr of Library Programs & Services ... Ms. Michele PRATT

Eastern Michigan University (J)

Ypsilanti MI 48197-2207
County: Washtenaw FICE Identification: 002259
Unit ID: 169798
Telephone: (734) 487-1849 Carnegie Class: Master's L
FAX Number: (734) 481-1095 Calendar System: Semester
URL: www.emich.edu
Established: 1849 Annual Undergrad Tuition & Fees (In-State): $10,417
Enrollment: 22,430 Coed
Affiliation or Control: State IRS Status: 501(c)3
Highest Offering: Doctorate
Program: Liberal Arts And General; Teacher Preparatory; Professional
Accreditation: NH, #ARCPA, BUS, CAATE, CACREP, CEA, CIDA, CLPSY, CONST, DIETC, ENGT, MT, MUS, NURSE, OPE, OT, PLNG, SP, SPAA, SW, TED

01 Interim President ... Dr. Kim SCHATZEL
05 Provost/Exec VP Acad/Stdnt Affs ... Dr. Kim SCHATZEL
10 Chief Financial Officer ... Mr. Michael VALDES
26 Vice President Communications ... Mr. Walter KRAFT
30 Interim VP Advancement ... Ms. Linda MCGILL
101 VP & Sec to the Board of Regents ... Ms. Vicki REAUME
41 VP/Dir Intercollegiate Athletics ... Ms. Heather LYKE
32 Assoc Vice Pres Student Affairs ... Mr. Calvin PHILLIPS
20 Assoc Prov/Assoc VP Acad Pgm Svcs ... Dr. Rhonda KINNEY LONGWORTH
20 Assoc Prov/Assoc VP Admin ... Dr. James J. CARROLL, III
58 Int Assc Prov/AVP Grad Studies/Rsrc ... Dr. Wade TORNQUIST
27 Assoc VP Marketing & Communication ... Mr. Theodore G. COUTILISH
84 Assoc Vice Pres Enrollment Mgmt ... Mr. Kevin KUCERA
86 Exec Dir Govt/Community Relations ... Mr. Ken DOBSON
18 VP for Operations and Facilities ... Mr. John P. DONEGAN
15 VP for University Human Resources ... Mr. David TURNER
69 Dean Col Health & Human Svcs ... Dr. Murali NAIR
106 Int Dir EMU Online/Exten/Reg Sites ... Ms. Julie KNUTSON-GARCIA
49 Dean Col of Art & Sciences ... Dr. Thomas VENNER
50 Dean Col of Business ... Dr. Michael TIDWELL
53 Dean Col of Education ... Dr. Michael SAYLER
72 Dean Col of Technology ... Dr. Mohamad QATU
43 General Counsel/University Attorney ... Ms. Gloria HAGE
13 Asst VP/CIO Information Technolog ... Dr. Carl POWELL
23 Asst VP of Student Well-Being ... Ms. Ellen GOLD
09 Asst VP & Exec Dir Inst Rsrch/Info ... Dr. Bin NING
20 Asst VP for Academic Affairs ... Dr. David WOIKE
21 Asst VP Bus Oper/Student Svcs ... Mr. Brian KULPA
102 Exec Dir Foundation Operations/CFO ... Ms. Laura WILBANKS
88 Ombuds ... Dr. Chiara HENSLEY
29 Exec Dir Alumni Relations ... Ms. Ann THOMPSON
19 Exec Dir Public Safety ... Mr. Robert HEIGHES
08 Interim University Librarian ... Dr. Susann DEVRIES
88 Dir Charter Schools Program ... Dr. Malverne WINBORNE
92 Director Honors College ... Dr. Rebecca SIPE
39 Dir Residence Life ... Vacant
27 Executive Director Media Relations ... Mr. Geoffrey LARCOM
21 Exec Dir Financial Plng & Budget ... Mr. Todd OHMER
88 Dir University Convocation Center ... Mr. Mark MONAHAN
44 Sr Development Officer/Central Svcs ... Ms. Susan RINK
88 Chief Development Officer ... Ms. Jill HUNSBERGER
88 Exec Dir Integrated Content ... Ms. Darcy GIFFORD
88 Dir Presidential Events & Protocol ... Ms. Kelly BRENNAN
88 Gen Mgr WEMU-FM Public Rad ... Ms. Mary MOTHERWELL
06 Registrar ... Ms. Christina SHELL
37 Director Financial Aid ... Ms. Donna HOLUBIK
38 Dir Diversity & Affirmative Action ... Ms. Sharon ABRAHAM
96 Director Purchasing ... Mr. Dean BACKOS
88 Title IX Coordinator ... Dr. Melody A. WERNER

Ecumenical Theological Seminary (K)

2930 Woodward Avenue, Detroit MI 48201-3035
County: Wayne FICE Identification: 040024
Unit ID: 247162
Telephone: (313) 831-5200 Carnegie Class: Spec/Faith
FAX Number: (313) 831-1353 Calendar System: Quarter
URL: www.etseminary.edu
Established: 1980 Annual Undergrad Tuition & Fees: $14,304
Enrollment: 103 Coed
Affiliation or Control: Independent Non-Profit IRS Status: 501(c)3
Highest Offering: Doctorate
Program: Professional; Technical Emphasis
Accreditation: THEOL

01 President ... Dr. Stephen B. MURRAY
05 Vice Pres Academic Affs/Acad Dean ... Dr. Kenneth HARRIS
11 Vice President of Administration ... Rev. Margaret PRIEST
30 Office Manager Inst Advancement ... Ms. Jacquelyn HINES
06 Registrar ... Ms. Elle FOLSON
08 Library Director ... Mr. Joshua PIKKA
07 Director of Admissions/Recruitment ... Dr. Patricia CHUNN
10 Finance Officer ... Ms. Porsha MALLETT

Ferris State University (L)

1201 S. State Street, Big Rapids MI 49307-2295
County: Mecosta FICE Identification: 002260
Unit ID: 169910
Telephone: (231) 591-2000 Carnegie Class: Master's L
FAX Number: (231) 591-3592 Calendar System: Semester
URL: www.ferris.edu
Established: 1884 Annual Undergrad Tuition & Fees (In-State): $11,610
Enrollment: 14,600 Coed
Affiliation or Control: State IRS Status: 501(c)3
Highest Offering: First Professional Degree
Program: Occupational; 2-Year Principally Bachelor's Creditable; Liberal Arts And General; Teacher Preparatory; Professional
Accreditation: NH, ACBSP, ART, CAHIIM, CIDA, COARC, CONST, DH, DMS, ENG, ENGT, MLTAD, MT, NMT, NUR, OPT, OPTR, PHAR, RAD, SW, TEAC

01 President ... Dr. David L. EISLER
05 Provost & VPAA ... Dr. Paul A. BLAKE
43 Vice President & General Counsel ... Mr. Miles J. POSTEMA
10 VP of Administration & Finance ... Mr. Jerry L. SCOBY
30 VP of Advancement & Mktg ... Ms. Shelly ARMSTRONG
32 Vice President Student Affairs ... Dr. Jeanine WARD-ROOF
12 President of KCAD & VP of Ferris ... Dr. Leslie BELLAVANCE
12 Interim Dean Extended and Intl ... Ms. Cheryl CLUCHEY
28 VP for Diversity and Inclusion ... Dr. David PILGRIM
20 Assoc Provost of Accreditation ... Dr. Roberta TEAHEN
20 Assoc Provost Retention ... Dr. William POTTER
21 Assistant VP of Finance ... Mr. Mike GRANDY
30 Assoc Vice Pres Advancement ... Mr. David LEPPER
15 Assoc Vice Pres Human Resources ... Ms. Tamie GRUNOW
30 Assoc Vice Pres for Advancement ... Ms. Carla MILLER
18 Assoc Vice Pres Plant Management ... Mr. Mike HUGHES
84 Associate Dean Enrollment Services ... Ms. Kathy LAKE
07 Dean of Enrollment Services ... Dr. Kristen SALOMONSON
109 Associate VP Auxiliary Enterprises ... Mr. James HESSLER
45 Director Budget Planning/Analysis ... Ms. Sally DEPEW
13 Chief Technology Officer ... Mr. John URBANICK
22 Director of Equal Opportunity ... Mr. Matthew OLOVSON
19 Director of Public Safety ... Mr. Bruce BORKOVICH
88 Mgr Stdnt Empl & Financial Aid Adv ... Mr. John RANDLE
88 Director of University Center ... Mr. Mark SCHUELKE
38 Director Counseling & Health Center ... Ms. Renee VANDER MYDE
35 Dean of Student Life ... Mr. Leroy WRIGHT
88 Dir Multicultural Student Svcs ... Dr. Matthew CHANEY
88 Dir for CLACS ... Ms. Angela ROMAN
88 Director University Recreation ... Ms. Cindy HORN
29 Assoc VP for External Affairs ... Mr. Jeremy MISHLER
09 Dir of Inst Research & Testing ... Ms. Mitzi DAY
39 Director Residential Life ... Mr. Brian MARQUARDT
40 Director Bookstore ... Ms. Karen BOHREN
41 Director of Athletics ... Mr. Perk WEISENBURGER
44 Dir Annual Giving & Advance Svcs ... Ms. Jennifer YONTZ
96 Director Purchasing ... Mr. Michael PETHICK
49 Interim Dean of Arts & Sciences ... Dr. Andy KARAFA
50 Dean of Business ... Dr. David NICOL
53 Interim Dean Educ & Human Svcs ... Mr. Steve REIFERT
67 Dean of Pharmacy ... Dr. Steve DURST
76 Dean of Health Professions ... Dr. Matthew ADEYANJU
63 Dean Michigan College Optometry ... Dr. David DAMARI
72 Dean of Engineering Technology ... Mr. Larry SCHULT
08 Dean of FLITE ... Dr. Scott GARRISON
04 Executive Asst to the President ... Ms. Elaine KAMPTNER
101 Secretary to the Board ... Ms. Karen HUISMAN
37 Director Financial Aid ... Ms. Sara DEW

Finlandia University (M)

601 Quincy Street, Hancock MI 49930-1882
County: Houghton FICE Identification: 002322
Unit ID: 172440
Telephone: (906) 482-5300 Carnegie Class: Bac/Diverse
FAX Number: (906) 487-7366 Calendar System: Semester
URL: www.finlandia.edu
Established: 1896 Annual Undergrad Tuition & Fees: $22,110
Enrollment: 493 Coed
Affiliation or Control: Evangelical Lutheran Church In America
IRS Status: 501(c)3
Highest Offering: Baccalaureate
Program: Liberal Arts And General; Professional
Accreditation: NH, MAC, NURSE, PTAA

01 President ... Dr. Philip JOHNSON
10 Vice Pres Business/Finance ... Mr. Nick STEVENS
05 Vice Pres Academic & Student Affs ... Dr. Fredi DE YAMPERT
26 VP University Relations ... Ms. Karin VAN DYKE
30 Vice Pres Advancement & Enrollment ... Dr. Lenny KLAVER
04 Executive Administrative Assistant ... Ms. Doreen KORPELA
27 Director Marketing/Communications ... Mr. Michael BABCOCK
102 Dir Grants and Foundation Affairs ... Ms. Terri MARTIN
08 Librarian ... Ms. Rebecca DALY
32 Dir Academic Success & Student Life ... Ms. Erin BARNETT
42 University Chaplain ... Mr. Soren SCHMIDT
06 Registrar ... Mr. Jason SULLIVAN
13 Director Information Technology ... Mr. Scott BLAKE
41 Athletic Director ... Mr. Chris SALANI
18 Director of Plant and Facilities ... Mr. Curt HAHKA
21 Controller ... Ms. Lori BAAKKO
37 Director Student Financial Aid ... Ms. Sandra TURNQUIST
36 Career Services Manager ... Mr. Mark CAVIS
09 Institutional Research Analyst ... Mr. Hannu LEPPANEN
40 Bookstore Manager ... Ms. Alana EVANS
96 Purchaser ... Ms. Janine NOTTKE
15 Human Resources Specialist ... Mr. Craig KANGAS
07 Director of Admissions ... Mr. Travis HANSON
19 Director of Campus Safety/Security ... Mr. Jim HARDEN
39 Residence Life Coordinator ... Ms. Leann FOGLE
49 Dean College of Arts & Sciences ... Dr. Christine O'NEIL
57 Dean Intl School of Art & Design ... Ms. Denise VANDEVILLE
76 Dean College of Health Science ... Dr. Cam WILLIAMS
104 Dean Intl School of Business ... Mr. Kevin MANNINEN
28 Director of Diversity ... Dr. Shana PORTEEN

Glen Oaks Community College (A)

62249 Shimmel Road, Centreville MI 49032-9719

County: Saint Joseph FICE Identification: 002263
Unit ID: 169974
Telephone: (269) 467-9945 Carnegie Class: Assoc/Pub-R-S
FAX Number: (269) 467-4114 Calendar System: Semester
URL: www.glenoaks.edu
Established: 1965 Annual Undergrad Tuition & Fees (In-District): $4,148
Enrollment: 1,104 Coed
Affiliation or Control: Local IRS Status: 501(c)3
Highest Offering: Associate Degree
Program: Occupational; 2-Year Principally Bachelor's Creditable
Accreditation: NH, MAC

01 President ... Dr. David DEVIER
05 Dean of Academics/Extended Learning ... Dr. Patricia MORGENSTERN
10 Dean of Finance/Administrative Svcs ... Mr. Bruce ZAKRZEWSKI
32 Assistant Dean of Student Services ... Ms. Tonya HOWDEN
66 Interim Dean of Nursing ... Mr. Bill LEDERMAN
84 Asst Dean Enrollment Svcs/Registrar ... Ms. Beverly ANDREWS
08 Director Learning Resources Center ... Ms. Betsy S. MORGAN
21 Accountant ... Ms. Jennifer DODSON
18 Director of Buildings/Grounds ... Vacant
07 Director of Admissions ... Vacant
37 Dir of Financial Aid/Scholarships ... Ms. Jean ZIMMERMAN
41 Director of Athletics ... Mr. Bruce ZAKRZEWSKI
09 Institutional Effect/Rsrch Analyst ... Ms. Tammy RUSSELL
15 Personnel Coordinator ... Ms. Candy BOHACZ
26 Public Relations/Marketing ... Ms. Valorie JUERGENS

Gogebic Community College (B)

E4946 Jackson Road, Ironwood MI 49938-1366

County: Gogebic FICE Identification: 002264
Unit ID: 169992
Telephone: (906) 932-4231 Carnegie Class: Assoc/Pub-R-S
FAX Number: (906) 932-5541 Calendar System: Semester
URL: www.gogebic.edu
Established: 1931 Annual Undergrad Tuition & Fees (In-District): $4,344
Enrollment: 1,122 Coed
Affiliation or Control: Local IRS Status: 501(c)3
Highest Offering: Associate Degree
Program: Occupational; 2-Year Principally Bachelor's Creditable
Accreditation: NH

01 President ... Mr. James A. LORENSON
05 Dean of Instruction/Dir Exten Pgm ... Vacant
10 Dean of Business Services ... Mr. Erik M. GUENARD
32 Dean of Student Services ... Ms. Jeanne GRAHAM
37 Dir Financial Aid/Veterans Svcs ... Ms. Suzetta R. FORBES
76 Director of Allied Health Program ... Ms. Nicole ROWE
88 Director of Ski Area Management ... Mr. James VANDERSPOEL
08 Dir Learning Resource/Instruct Tech .. Ms. Kathryn MACIEJEWSKI
13 Director of Computer Services ... Ms. Kathie A. MUNN
07 Dir of Admission/Public Information ... Ms. Kim ZECKOVICH
30 Dir of Institutional Development ... Ms. Kelly MARZCAK
15 Director of Human Resources ... Ms. Ashley PAQUETTE
88 Transfer Coordinator ... Ms. Jennifer FORSHEY
06 Asst Registrar/Institutional Rschr ... Ms. Miranda LAWVER
04 Administrative Asst to President ... Ms. Linda M. GUSTAFSON
36 Director Student Placement ... Ms. Kelly MARCZAK

Grace Bible College (C)

1011 Aldon Street, SW, Grand Rapids MI 49509-1998

County: Kent FICE Identification: 002265
Unit ID: 170000
Telephone: (616) 538-2330 Carnegie Class: Bac/Diverse
FAX Number: (616) 538-0599 Calendar System: Semester
URL: www.gbcol.edu
Established: 1939 Annual Undergrad Tuition & Fees: $18,000
Enrollment: 318 Coed
Affiliation or Control: Independent Non-Profit IRS Status: 501(c)3
Highest Offering: Baccalaureate
Program: Liberal Arts And General; Teacher Preparatory; Religious Emphasis
Accreditation: NH, BI

01 President ... Dr. Kenneth B. KEMPER
05 Vice President for Academics ... Mrs. Kim PILIECI
10 Vice Pres Finance/Bus Operations ... Mr. Douglas VRIESMAN
11 Vice Pres Cmty Life/Operations ... Mr. Brian P. SHERSTAD
106 Vice Pres Adult & Online Education ... Mr. Mike STOWELL
32 Dean of Students ... Mr. Kyle BOHL
04 Executive Assistant to President ... Mrs. Joyce A. STORMS
06 Registrar ... Ms. Linda K. SILER
44 Fund Development Director ... Mr. Steve HILBRANDS
08 Director Library Services ... Vacant
37 Director of Financial Aid ... Mr. Kurt POSTMA
84 Assoc Vice Pres for Enrollment ... Mr. Kevin E. GILLIAM
13 Information Technology Coordinator ... Mr. James PETERS
18 Director of Maintenance ... Mr. Nathan JOHNSON
41 Athletic Director ... Mr. Gary BAILEY
42 Campus Ministry Coordinator ... Mr. Jim GAMBLE
88 Dir Recruitment Online & Adult Stds ... Mr. Zak SORENSEN
108 Director Institutional Assessment ... Mr. Timothy RUMLEY
15 Human Resources Coordinator ... Mrs. Sherea LACY
29 Alumni Services Coordinator ... Ms. Julianne POORT

Grand Rapids Community College (D)

143 Bostwick Avenue, NE, Grand Rapids MI 49503-3295

County: Kent FICE Identification: 002267
Unit ID: 170055
Telephone: (616) 234-4000 Carnegie Class: Assoc/Pub-U-SC
FAX Number: (616) 234-4005 Calendar System: Semester
URL: www.grcc.edu
Established: 1914 Annual Undergrad Tuition & Fees (In-District): $3,699
Enrollment: 15,719 Coed
Affiliation or Control: Local IRS Status: 501(c)3
Highest Offering: Associate Degree
Program: Occupational; 2-Year Principally Bachelor's Creditable
Accreditation: NH, ACFEI, ADNUR, ART, DA, DH, MAC, MUS, OTA, PNUR, RAD

01 President ... Dr. Steven C. ENDER
05 Prov/Exec VP Academic Affairs ... Dr. Laurie CHESLEY
10 Exec VP Business/Financial Services ... Ms. Lisa FREIBURGER
13 VP & CIO Lrng Res/Tech Solutions ... Mr. David ANDERSON
30 Assoc VP Advancement/Exec Dir Found ... Dr. Kathryn MULLINS
88 Dean of Adult & Developmental Educ ... Mr. John COWLES
103 Director of Workforce Training ... Ms. Julie PARKS
32 Dean Student Affairs ... Ms. Tina OEN-HOXIE
09 Dean Inst Research & Planning ... Ms. Donna KRAGT
49 Dean School of Arts & Sciences ... Dr. Michael VARGO
72 Dean Instruct Design/Info Tech ... Ms. Patti TREPKOWSKI
07 Assoc Dean Admiss/Enrollment Mgmt ... Ms. Diane D. PATRICK
26 Director of Communications ... Ms. Leah NIXON
37 Director of Financial Aid ... Ms. Ann ISACKSON
15 Executive Director Human Resources ... Ms. Cathy WILSON
06 Registrar ... Ms. Diane PATRICK
35 Director Student Activities ... Mr. Eric MULLEN
36 Assoc Director Student Employment ... Ms. Luann WEDGE
08 Director of Library Services ... Ms. Pat INGERSOLL
18 Executive Director of Facilities ... Mr. Thomas J. SMITH
19 Chief of Campus Police ... Ms. Rebecca R. WHITMAN
43 General Counsel ... Ms. Kathy KEATING
96 Director Purchasing ... Mr. Mansfield MATTHEWSON
12 Dean of Lakeshore Campus & Outreach ... Mr. Daniel CLARK
22 Exec Dir Equity/Community/Legis ... Mr. Eric WILLIAMS
28 Dir Diversity Learning Center ... Ms. Christina ARNOLD

Grand Valley State University (E)

1 Campus Drive, Allendale MI 49401-9403

County: Ottawa FICE Identification: 002268
Unit ID: 170082
Telephone: (616) 331-5000 Carnegie Class: Master's L
FAX Number: (616) 331-3503 Calendar System: Semester
URL: www.gvsu.edu
Established: 1960 Annual Undergrad Tuition & Fees (In-State): $11,078
Enrollment: 25,094 Coed
Affiliation or Control: State IRS Status: 501(c)3
Highest Offering: Doctorate
Program: Liberal Arts And General; Teacher Preparatory; Professional
Accreditation: NH, ARCPA, ART, BUS, BUSA, CAATE, CS, CVT, DMS, ENG, IPSY, MT, MUS, NURSE, OT, PTA, RTT, @SP, SPAA, SW, TED

01 President ... Dr. Thomas J. HAAS
05 Provost/Exec VP Acad & Student Affs ... Dr. Gayle R. DAVIS
10 Vice President Finance/Admin ... Mr. James BACHMEIER
26 Vice President University Relations ... Mr. Matthew E. MCLOGAN
84 Vice President Enrollment Develop ... Ms. Lynn BLUE
30 Vice President of Development ... Ms. Karen M. LOTH
28 Vice President Inclusion and Equity ... Dr. Jesse BERNAL
43 Vice President and General Counsel ... Mr. Thomas A. BUTCHER
04 Exec Assoc to the President ... Ms. Teri LOSEY
32 Vice Provost/Dean Student Services ... Dr. H. Bart MERKLE
20 Vice Provost for Student Success ... Dr. Nancy GIARDINA
88 Vice Provost for Research Admin ... Dr. Robert SMART
20 V Prov Instruct Develop & Innov ... Dr. Christine RENER
23 Vice Provost for Health ... Dr. Jean NAGELKERK
20 Assoc Vice Pres Academic Affairs ... Mr. Jon A. JELLEMA
20 Assoc Vice Pres Academic Affairs ... Dr. Julia GUEVARA
20 Asst Vice Pres Academic Affairs ... Ms. Kathleen GULEMBO
20 Asst Vice Pres Academic Affairs ... Dr. Maria CIMITILE
21 Associate VP Business/Finance ... Mr. Brian COPELAND
21 Asst VP for University Budgets ... Mr. Jeff MUSSER
15 Assoc VP Human Resources ... Mr. D. Scott RICHARDSON
88 Assoc VP Institutional Marketing ... Ms. Rhonda LUBBERTS
27 Assoc VP for Univ Communications ... Ms. Mary Eilleen LYON
18 Assoc Vice Pres Facilities Services ... Mr. Timothy THIMMESCH
88 Assoc VP for Facilities Planning ... Mr. James MOYER
12 Asst VP for Pew Campus Operations ... Ms. Lisa HAYNES
88 Asst VP for Inclusion & Equity ... Ms. Kathleen VANDERVEEN
88 Interim Asst VP Inclusion & Equity ... Ms. Beverly GRANT
49 Dean Col of Liberal Arts & Sciences ... Dr. Frederick ANTCZAK
50 Dean Seidman Col of Business ... Dr. Diana LAWSON
70 Dean College of Cmty/Public Service ... Dr. George GRANT
53 Interim Dean College of Education ... Dr. John SHINSKY
54 Dean Padnos Col Engr & Computing ... Dr. Paul PLOTKOWSKI
76 Dean College of Health Professions ... Dr. Roy OLSSON
88 Dean College Interdisciplin Studies ... Dr. Anne HISKES
66 Dean Kirkhof College of Nursing ... Dr. Cynthia MCCURREN
58 Dean Graduate Studies ... Dr. Jeffrey POTTEIGER
08 Dean University Libraries ... Dr. Lee VAN ORSDEL
07 Director of Admissions ... Ms. Jodi CHYCINSKI
29 Director of Alumni Relations ... Mr. Chris W. BARBEE
36 Director Career Center ... Mr. Troy FARLEY
37 Director of Financial Aid ... Ms. Michelle RHODES
88 Director of Hauenstein Center ... Mr. Gleaves WHITNEY
39 Dir of Housing and Residence Life ... Dr. Andrew J. BEACHNAU
13 Director of Information Technology ... Ms. Sue KORZINEK
09 Director of Institutional Analysis ... Dr. Philip BATTY
28 Director of Multicultural Affairs ... Ms. Connie DANG
96 Director of Procurement Services ... Mr. Kim PATRICK
19 Dir of Public Safety/Police Chief ... Ms. Renee FREEMAN
88 Dir Small Business Development Ctr ... Mr. Dante VILLARREAL
38 Director Univ Counseling Center ... Dr. Amber ROBERTS
41 Athletic Director ... Mr. Tim SELGO
40 Bookstore Manager ... Mr. Jerrod NICKELS
85 Chief International Officer ... Dr. Mark SCHAUB
88 Controller ... Ms. Pam BRENZING
88 Exec Dir Van Andel Global Trade Ctr ... Ms. Sonja JOHNSON
88 General Manager WGVU ... Mr. Michael WALENTA
06 Interim Registrar ... Dr. Sherril SOMAN
88 Spec Asst for Charter Schools ... Mr. Tim WOOD
22 Interim Title IX Coordinator ... Ms. Theresa ROWLAND

Grand Valley State University Meijer Campus (F)

515 South Waverly Road, Holland MI 49423

Telephone: (616) 331-3910 Identification: 770275
Accreditation: &NH

† Branch campus of Grand Valley State University, Allendale, MI.

Grand Valley State University Pew Campus (G)

401 Fulton Street, Grand Rapids MI 49504

Telephone: (616) 331-7220 Identification: 770274
Accreditation: &NH

† Branch campus of Grand Valley State University, Allendale, MI.

Great Lakes Christian College (H)

6211 Willow Highway, Lansing MI 48917-1299

County: Eaton FICE Identification: 002269
Unit ID: 170091
Telephone: (517) 321-0242 Carnegie Class: Spec/Faith
FAX Number: (517) 321-5902 Calendar System: Semester
URL: www.glcc.edu
Established: 1949 Annual Undergrad Tuition & Fees: $14,630
Enrollment: 160 Coed
Affiliation or Control: Christian Churches And Churches of Christ
IRS Status: 501(c)3
Highest Offering: Baccalaureate
Program: Professional; Religious Emphasis
Accreditation: NH, BI

01 President ... Mr. Lawrence L. CARTER
10 Vice President Finance/Operations ... Mr. James A. LOCKWOOD
05 Vice President of Academic Affairs ... Mr. David J. RICHARDS
30 Vice Pres Institutional Advancement ... Mr. Philip E. BEAVERS
84 Vice Pres of Enrollment Management ... Mr. Lloyd S. SCHARER
06 Registrar ... Mr. James ORME
08 Director of Library Services ... Mr. James ORME
37 Financial Aid Director ... Prof. Ryan APPLE
32 Dean of Students/Dir Student Life ... Mr. Ryan BUSHNELL
41 Athletic Director ... Ms. Sasha LOCKWOOD
88 Director of Outreach Ministries ... Mrs. Judy BEAVERS
18 Maintenance Supervisor ... Mr. Chris ADLEMAN

Henry Ford College (I)

5101 Evergreen Road, Dearborn MI 48128-1495

County: Wayne FICE Identification: 002270
Unit ID: 170240
Telephone: (313) 845-9615 Carnegie Class: Assoc/Pub-S-MC
FAX Number: (313) 845-9658 Calendar System: Semester
URL: www.hfcc.edu
Established: 1938 Annual Undergrad Tuition & Fees (In-District): $3,270
Enrollment: 13,790 Coed
Affiliation or Control: Local IRS Status: 501(c)3
Highest Offering: Associate Degree
Program: Occupational; 2-Year Principally Bachelor's Creditable
Accreditation: NH, ACFEI, ADNUR, COARC, MAC, PTAA, RAD, SURGT

01 President ... Dr. Stanley C. JENSEN
10 Vice President Financial Services ... Dr. John SATKOWSKI
32 Vice Pres/Dean Student Services ... Dr. Lisa COPPRUE
05 Vice Pres Academic/Career Education ... Dr. Tracy PIERNER
30 Vice President of Development ... Mr. A. Reginald BEST, JR.
11 Vice President Admin Services ... Dr. Cynthia ESCHENBURG
26 Vice President Info/Mktg/Effectiv ... Ms. Becky J. CHADWICK
06 Director of Registration and Record ... Ms. Holly DIAMOND
38 Assoc Dean Counseling ... Mr. Imad NOURI
103 Director of Workforce Development ... Vacant
66 Director of Nursing ... Ms. Susan SHUNKWILER
08 Director Library ... Mr. Terrence POTVIN
13 Director Data & Voice ... Mr. Sandro SILVESTRI
27 Director Marketing/Communications ... Mr. Gary ERWIN
37 Director Student Financial Aid ... Mr. Kevin J. CULLER
92 Director Honors Program ... Dr. Michael DAHER
96 Director Purchasing ... Mr. Fred STEINER
40 Manager of College Store ... Ms. Pamela HALL

Hillsdale College (J)

33 East College Street, Hillsdale MI 49242-1298

County: Hillsdale FICE Identification: 002272
Unit ID: 170286
Telephone: (517) 437-7341 Carnegie Class: Bac/A&S
FAX Number: (517) 437-3923 Calendar System: Semester
URL: www.hillsdale.edu

Established: 1844 Annual Undergrad Tuition & Fees: $23,840
Enrollment: 1,504 Coed
Affiliation or Control: Independent Non-Profit IRS Status: 501(c)3
Highest Offering: Doctorate
Program: Liberal Arts And General
Accreditation: NH

01 President .... Dr. Larry ARNN
11 Chief Administrative Officer .... Mr. Rich PEWE
05 Provost .... Dr. David WHALEN
26 VP External Affairs .... Mr. Douglas JEFFREY
10 VP Finance .... Mr. Patrick FLANNERY
30 VP Institutional Advancement .... Mr. John CERVINI
88 VP Marketing .... Mr. Matt SCHLIENTZ
32 VP Student Affairs/Dean of Women .... Ms. Diane PHILIPP
43 General Counsel .... Mr. Robert NORTON
100 Chief Staff Officer .... Mr. Mike HARNER
07 Associate VP Admissions .... Mr. Doug BANBURY
27 Associate VP External Affairs .... Mr. Timothy CASPAR
36 Executive Director Career Services .... Mr. Michael MURRAY
15 Executive Director Human Resources .... Ms. Janet MARSH
90 Executive Director ITS .... Mr. David ZENZ
29 Director Alumni Affairs .... Mr. Grigor HASTED
41 Director Athletics .... Mr. Don BRUBACHER
19 Director Campus Security .... Mr. William WHORLEY
40 Director College Bookstore .... Ms. Cindy WILLING
105 Director Digital and Social Media .... Mr. Brad LOWREY
37 Director Financial Aid .... Mr. Rich MOEGGENBERG
23 Director Health Services .... Mr. Brock LUTZ
09 Director Institutional Research .... Mr. George ALLEN
08 Director Library .... Mr. Dan KNOCH
27 Director Marketing .... Mr. Bill GRAY
18 Director Physical Plant .... Mr. Todd CLOW
35 Director Student Activities .... Mr. Anthony MANNO
42 Chaplain .... RtRev. Peter BECKWITH
21 Controller .... Ms. LeAnn CREGER
33 Dean of Men .... Mr. Aaron PETERSEN
06 Registrar .... Mr. Douglas MCARTHUR
04 Admin Assistant to the President .... Ms. Victoria BERGEN
20 Assistant to the Provost .... Mr. Mark MAIER

Hope College (A)

141 E 12th Street, Holland MI 49423-3607
County: Ottawa FICE Identification: 002273
Unit ID: 170301
Telephone: (616) 395-7000 Carnegie Class: Bac/A&S
FAX Number: (616) 395-7922 Calendar System: Semester
URL: www.hope.edu
Established: 1866 Annual Undergrad Tuition & Fees: $30,550
Enrollment: 3,388 Coed
Affiliation or Control: Reformed Church In America IRS Status: 501(c)3
Highest Offering: Baccalaureate
Program: Liberal Arts And General; Teacher Preparatory; Professional
Accreditation: NH, ART, CAATE, DANCE, ENG, MUS, NURSE, SW, TEAC, THEA

01 President .... Dr. John C. KNAPP
05 Provost .... Dr. R. Richard RAY, JR.
10 Vice Pres and Chief Fiscal Officer .... Mr. Thomas W. BYLSMA
07 Vice President for Admissions .... Mr. William VANDERBILT
30 VP for Develop & Alumni Engagement .... Mr. Jeffrey PUCKETT
32 VP Student Devel/Dean of Students .... Dr. Richard A. FROST
20 Associate Provost .... Mr. Alfredo M. GONZALES
26 VP Public Affairs & Marketing .... Mrs. Jennifer FELLINGER
08 Librarian .... Ms. Kelly G. JACOBSMA
39 Dir of Residential Life & Housing .... Dr. John E. JOBSON
22 Director of Multicultural Life .... Ms. Vanessa GREENE
94 Director of Women's Studies .... Ms. Priscilla D. ATKINS
81 Dean for Natural Sciences .... Dr. David G. VANWYLEN
79 Dean for Arts & Humanities .... Dr. Patrice RANKINE
83 Dean for Social Sciences .... Dr. Scott D. VANDER STOEP
88 Dean of the Chapel .... Rev. Trygve D. JOHNSON
06 Registrar .... Ms. Carol DEJONG
37 Director of Financial Aid .... Ms. Jill NUTT
36 Director Career Services .... Mr. Dale F. AUSTIN
21 Director of Finance & Business Svcs .... Mr. Douglas VAN DYKEN
13 Director of Operations & Technology .... Mr. Greg MAYBURY
14 Director of Computing & Info Tech .... Mr. Carl E. HEIDEMAN
15 Director Human Resources .... Mrs. Lori MULDER
18 Director Physical Plant .... Mr. Greg MAYBURY
40 Manager of Bookstore .... Mr. Craig THELEN
29 Dir of Parent & Alumni Relations .... Mr. Scott TRAVIS
41 Co-Director of Athletics .... Mr. Tim SCHOONVELD
41 Co-Director of Athletics .... Ms. Melinda LARSON
42 Senior Chaplain .... Rev. Paul H. BOERSMA
38 Asst Dean/Director Counseling Ctr .... Dr. Kristen GRAY
04 Administrative Asst to President .... Mrs. Jan SOMMERVILLE
19 Director Security/Safety .... Mr. Chad WOLTERS
25 Chief Contracts/Grants Admin .... Ms. Tracey NALLY

ITT Technical Institute (B)

1905 S Haggerty Road, Canton MI 48188-2025
Telephone: (734) 397-7800 Identification: 666323
Accreditation: ACICS

† Branch campus of ITT Technical Institute, Indianapolis, IN.

ITT Technical Institute (C)

19855 West Outer Drive, L10W, Dearborn MI 48124
Telephone: (313) 278-5208 Identification: 770645
Accreditation: ACICS

† Branch campus of ITT Technical Institute, Indianapolis, IN.

ITT Technical Institute (D)

26700 Lahser Road, Suite 100, Southfield MI 48033
Telephone: (248) 603-6100 Identification: 770647
Accreditation: ACICS

† Branch campus of ITT Technical Institute, Indianapolis, IN.

ITT Technical Institute (E)

6359 Miller Road, Swartz Creek MI 48473-1520
Telephone: (810) 628-2500 Identification: 666146
Accreditation: ACICS

† Branch campus of ITT Technical Institute, Indianapolis, IN.

ITT Technical Institute (F)

1522 E Big Beaver Road, Troy MI 48083-1905
Telephone: (248) 524-1800 Identification: 666542
Accreditation: ACICS

† Branch campus of ITT Technical Institute, Indianapolis, IN.

ITT Technical Institute (G)

1980 Metro Court S.W., Wyoming MI 49519
Telephone: (616) 406-1200 FICE Identification: 010627
Accreditation: ACICS

† Branch campus of ITT Technical Institute, Indianapolis, IN.

Jackson College (H)

2111 Emmons Road, Jackson MI 49201-8399
County: Jackson FICE Identification: 002274
Unit ID: 170444
Telephone: (517) 787-0800 Carnegie Class: Assoc/Pub-R-L
FAX Number: (517) 796-8630 Calendar System: Semester
URL: www.jccmi.edu
Established: 1928 Annual Undergrad Tuition & Fees (In-District): $3,648
Enrollment: 5,487 Coed
Affiliation or Control: Local IRS Status: 501(c)3
Highest Offering: Baccalaureate
Program: Occupational; 2-Year Principally Bachelor's Creditable
Accreditation: NH, ACBSP, COARC, DMS, MAC, RAD

01 President/CEO .... Dr. Daniel J. PHELAN
10 Vice President of Finance/CFO .... Mr. Dale DOPP
32 Executive Dean of Students .... Mrs. Kristi HOTTENSTEIN
05 Provost .... Dr. Rebekah WOODS
11 Vice Pres of Administration .... Ms. Cindy ALLEN
102 President of JCC Foundation .... Mr. Jason VALENTE
04 Administrative Asst to President .... Ms. Julie NAU
06 Registrar .... Mr. Zakary MCNITT
07 Director of Admissions .... Ms. Karen CUZYDLO
08 Head Librarian .... Ms. Stephanie DAVIS
09 Director of Institutional Research .... Mr. Elias SAMUELS
100 Chief of Staff .... Ms. Sara JOHNSON
103 Dir Workforce/Career Development .... Ms. Tina MATZ
18 Chief Facilities/Physical Plant .... Mr. Rob HARRIS
19 Director Security/Safety .... Mr. Jeffrey WHIPPLE
28 Director of Diversity .... Mr. Lee HAMPTON
29 Director Alumni Relations .... Ms. Brigette ROBINSON
37 Director Student Financial Aid .... Ms. Kimberley CVITKOVIC
39 Director Student Housing .... Ms. Tasha WARFIELD
41 Athletic Director .... Ms. Heather BATEMAN

Kalamazoo College (I)

1200 Academy Street, Kalamazoo MI 49006-3295
County: Kalamazoo FICE Identification: 002275
Unit ID: 170532
Telephone: (269) 337-7000 Carnegie Class: Bac/A&S
FAX Number: (269) 337-7251 Calendar System: Quarter
URL: www.kzoo.edu
Established: 1833 Annual Undergrad Tuition & Fees: $51,732
Enrollment: 1,448 Coed
Affiliation or Control: Independent Non-Profit IRS Status: 501(c)3
Highest Offering: Baccalaureate
Program: Liberal Arts And General
Accreditation: NH

01 President .... Dr. Eileen B. WILSON-OYELARAN
05 Provost .... Dr. Michael A. MCDONALD
10 Vice President Business & Finance .... Mr. James E. PRINCE
30 Vice President College Advancement .... Mr. Albert J. DESIMONE
32 VP Student Devel & Dean of Students .... Dr. Sarah B. WESTFALL
85 Associate Provost for Intl Pgms .... Dr. Joseph L. BROCKINGTON
13 Associate Provost for Info Services .... Mr. Gregory S. DIMENT
09 Asst Provost Inst Support/Research .... Ms. Anne T. DUEWEKE
89 Dean of First Year & Advising .... Dr. Zaide E. PIXLEY
06 Registrar .... Mr. Ted WITRYK
15 Human Resources Manager .... Ms. Renee E. BOELCKE
07 Dean of Admission and Financial Aid .... Mr. Eric P. STAAB
37 Director of Financial Aid .... Ms. Marian STOWERS
26 Director of College Communication .... Mr. James A. VANSWEDEN
18 Director of Facilities Management .... Mr. Paul W. MANSTROM
40 Director Bookstore .... Ms. Deborah L. THOMPSON
29 Director of Alumni Relations .... Ms. Kimberly J. ALDRICH
38 Director of Student Counseling .... Dr. Patricia A. PONTO
36 Dir Ctr Career/Professional Devel .... Ms. Joan C. HAWXHURST
20 Associate Provost .... Dr. Michael J. SOSULSKI

04 Administrative Asst to President .... Ms. Melanie K. WILLIAMS
08 Head Librarian .... Dr. Stacy A. NOWICKI
102 Dir Foundation/Corporate Relations .... Ms. Ann M. JENKS
19 Director Security/Safety .... Mr. Eric L. WIMBLEY
41 Athletic Director .... Ms. Kristen J. SMITH
84 Enrollment Data Specialist .... Ms. Linda WIRGAU

Kalamazoo Valley Community College (J)

6767 West O Avenue, PO Box 4070,
Kalamazoo MI 49003-4070
County: Kalamazoo FICE Identification: 006949
Unit ID: 170541
Telephone: (269) 488-4400 Carnegie Class: Assoc/Pub-R-L
FAX Number: (269) 488-4220 Calendar System: Semester
URL: www.kvcc.edu
Established: 1966 Annual Undergrad Tuition & Fees (In-District): $3,060
Enrollment: 11,472 Coed
Affiliation or Control: Local IRS Status: 501(c)3
Highest Offering: Associate Degree
Program: Occupational; 2-Year Principally Bachelor's Creditable
Accreditation: NH, COARC, DH, EMT, MAC

01 President .... Dr. Marilyn J. SCHLACK
05 Vice President Academic Services .... Dr. Dennis BERTCH
10 Vice President Finance & Business .... Ms. Louise ANDERSON
32 Exec VP Instructional/Student Svcs .... Mr. Michael COLLINS
15 Vice President of Human Resources .... Ms. Sandra BOHNET
13 Vice Pres for Admin Svc/Info Tech .... Mr. Terrel F. HUTCHINS
45 VP for Strategic & Econ Development .... Mr. Craig JBARA
35 Assoc VP for Student Success .... Ms. Laura COSBY
86 Exec Dir Govt Rels/Special Projects .... Ms. Kathy JOHNSON
19 Director of Public Safety .... Mr. Richard IVES
08 Director of Libraries .... Vacant
07 Dir Admissions/Records/Registrar .... Vacant
09 Dir Planning/Research/Assessment .... Mr. Stephen CANNELL
30 Director Development .... Mr. Steve DOHERTY
37 Director Financial Aid .... Mr. Roger MILLER
18 Facilities/Construction Management .... Mr. Daniel MALEY
96 Director of Purchasing .... Vacant
21 Business Manager .... Ms. Muriel HICE
66 Director of Nursing .... Ms. Susan MOTT

Kalamazoo Valley Community College Arcadia Commons Campus (K)

202 North Rose St, Kalamazoo MI 49007
Telephone: (269) 373-7800 Identification: 770276
Accreditation: &NH

† Branch campus of Kalamazoo Valley Community College, Kalamazoo, MI.

Kellogg Community College (L)

450 North Avenue, Battle Creek MI 49017-3397
County: Calhoun FICE Identification: 002276
Unit ID: 170550
Telephone: (269) 965-3931 Carnegie Class: Assoc/Pub-R-L
FAX Number: (269) 962-4290 Calendar System: Semester
URL: www.kellogg.edu
Established: 1956 Annual Undergrad Tuition & Fees (In-District): $3,488
Enrollment: 4,764 Coed
Affiliation or Control: Local IRS Status: 501(c)3
Highest Offering: Associate Degree
Program: Occupational; 2-Year Principally Bachelor's Creditable
Accreditation: NH, DH, MLTAD, PTAA, RAD

01 Interim President .... Mr. Mark O'CONNELL
05 Vice President Instruction .... Ms. Catherine HENDLER
11 Vice Pres Administration/Finance .... Mr. Mark O'CONNELL
32 Vice Pres Student & Community Svcs .... Dr. Kay KECK
10 Chief Financial Officer .... Mr. Richard SCOTT
13 Chief Information Officer .... Mr. Robert REYNOLDS
57 Chair Arts & Communication Dept .... Ms. Barbara SUDEIKIS
81 Chair Math & Science Dept .... Ms. Carole DAVIS
49 Dean Arts/Sciences/Regional Educ .... Dr. Kevin RABINEAU
102 Executive Director KCC Foundation .... Ms. Teresa DURHAM
96 Director Purchasing .... Ms. Angela CLEVELAND
06 Registrar .... Ms. Colleen WRIGHT
08 Director Library Services .... Ms. Martha STILWELL
41 Director Athletics & PE .... Mr. Tom SHAW
12 Director of Grahl Center .... Ms. Roberta GAGNON
12 Director of Fehsenfeld Center .... Mr. Colin MCCALEB
15 Director Human Resources .... Ms. Ali ROBERTSON
18 Dir Inst Facilities/Public Safety .... Mr. John DIPIERRO
51 Director Lifelong Learning .... Ms. Mary GREEN
09 Director Inst Compliance Reporting .... Ms. Naomi LIVENGOOD
21 Director of Finance .... Ms. Tracy BEATTY
12 Int Dir Regional Mfg Tech Center .... Mr. Tom LONGMAN
35 Dean Student Services .... Ms. Terah ZAREMBA
26 Dir Public Information & Marketing .... Mr. Eric GREENE
07 Director of Admissions .... Ms. Meredith STRAVERS
40 Bookstore Manager .... Ms. Catherine JAMES
28 Director of Diversity .... Dr. Jorge ZEBALLOS

Kendall College of Art & Design (M)

17 Fountain Street, NW, Grand Rapids MI 49503
Telephone: (800) 676-2787 Identification: 770273
Accreditation: &NH

† Branch campus of Ferris State University, Big Rapids, MI.

Kettering University (A)

1700 University Avenue, Flint MI 48504-6214
County: Genesee FICE Identification: 002262
Unit ID: 169983
Telephone: (810) 762-9500 Carnegie Class: Master's M
FAX Number: (810) 762-9837 Calendar System: Semester
URL: www.kettering.edu
Established: 1919 Annual Undergrad Tuition & Fees: $38,430
Enrollment: 2,079 Coed
Affiliation or Control: Independent Non-Profit IRS Status: 501(c)3
Highest Offering: Master's
Program: Professional; Technical Emphasis
Accreditation: NH, ACBSP, CS, ENG, ENGR

01 President ... Dr. Robert K. MCMAHAN
04 Executive Assistant to President ... Ms. Evelyn YAEGER
04 Assistant to President ... Ms. Tabitha BOURASSA
05 Provost & VP Academic Affairs ... Dr. James ZHANG
10 VP Administration & Finance ... Mr. Tom AYERS
84 VP Enrollment Services ... Mr. Kip DARCY
32 VP Student Life & Dean of Students ... Ms. Betsy E. HOMSHER
30 VP Univ Advancement/Ext Relations ... Ms. Susan DAVIES
13 VP Instruct/Admin & Info Technology ... Ms. Viola SPRAGUE
20 Vice Provost/Assoc VP Acad Services ... Vacant
15 Director Human Resources ... Ms. Beth EWALD
102 Dir of Philanthropy Corp/Found ... Ms. Eve VITALE
29 Dir of Alumni Engagement ... Mr. Robert NICHOLS
88 Dir of Philanthropy Indiv Giving ... Mr. Jack P. STOCK
19 Chief Campus Safety ... Mr. James R. BENFORD
37 Director Student Financial Aid ... Ms. Diane K. BICE
21 Controller ... Ms. Beth A. COVERS
09 Director Institution Effectiveness ... Dr. Edwin IMASUEN
58 Director Graduate Programs ... Vacant
18 Director Physical Plant ... Mr. Joseph ASPERGER
08 Director Library Services ... Dr. Charles D. HANSON
07 Director Intl & Undergrad Admiss ... Ms. Tracie JONES
41 Director Athletics/Rec Service ... Mr. Michael L. SCHAAL
93 Director Minority Student Affairs ... Mr. Dwight L. TAVADA
104 Director International Office ... Dr. Basem ALZAHABI
109 Director Auxilliary Services ... Ms. Nadine L. THOR
26 Director of Marketing ... Ms. Julie A. ULSETH
06 Registrar ... Mr. Michael MOSHER
23 Director Wellness Center ... Ms. Cristina REED
39 Director Residence Life ... Ms. Katherine BOSIO
78 Director Coop Educ & Career Svcs ... Ms. Venetia PETTEWAY
88 MI SBTDC Regional Director ... Ms. Marsha J. LYTTLE
96 Purchasing Manager ... Ms. Kathleen A. REMENDER
44 Director of Annual Giving ... Ms. Michelle D. LOPER
14 Director of IT Operations ... Mr. Daniel GARCIA
25 Contract/Grant Specialist ... Ms. Jodi L. DORR
105 Webmaster ... Ms. Donna WICKS
88 Dir Center Excellence Teach & Learn ... Dr. Terri LYNCH-CARIS
88 Dir Enrollment Events/Visitor Rels ... Ms. Sheila ADAMS COWES
88 Director Special Events ... Ms. Diane ALDERSON
88 Director Academic Service Center ... Ms. Natalie CANDELA

Keweenaw Bay Ojibwa Community College (B)

111 Beartown Rd, PO Box 519, Baraga MI 49908
County: Baraga FICE Identification: 041647
Unit ID: 461315
Telephone: (906) 353-4640 Carnegie Class: Not Classified
FAX Number: (906) 353-8107 Calendar System: Semester
URL: www.kbocc.edu
Established: 1975 Annual Undergrad Tuition & Fees (In-District): $2,700
Enrollment: 89 Coed
Affiliation or Control: Local IRS Status: 501(c)3
Highest Offering: Associate Degree
Program: Occupational; 2-Year Principally Bachelor's Creditable
Accreditation: NH

01 President ... Ms. Debra J. PARRISH
05 Dean of Instruction ... Ms. Lynn AHO
07 Admissions Officer ... Mr. Patrick RACETTE
10 Business Officer ... Ms. Megan SHANAHAN
32 Dean of Student Services ... Ms. Elizabeth VEKER KING
37 Director Financial Aid ... Ms. Liz JULIO
88 Cultural Advisor ... Ms. Liz JULIO

Kirtland Community College (C)

10775 N Saint Helen Road, Roscommon MI 48653-9721
County: Roscommon FICE Identification: 007171
Unit ID: 170587
Telephone: (989) 275-5000 Carnegie Class: Assoc/Pub-R-M
FAX Number: (989) 275-6706 Calendar System: Semester
URL: www.kirtland.edu
Established: 1966 Annual Undergrad Tuition & Fees (In-District): $3,445
Enrollment: 1,773 Coed
Affiliation or Control: Local IRS Status: 501(c)3
Highest Offering: Associate Degree
Program: Occupational; 2-Year Principally Bachelor's Creditable
Accreditation: NH, CVT

01 President ... Dr. Thomas QUINN
05 Vice Pres of Instructional Services ... Dr. Julie LAVENDER
32 Vice Pres of Student Svcs/Registrar ... Ms. Michelle VYSKOCIL
97 Dean of General Education/Transfer ... Mr. Jason TETZLOFF
75 Dean of Occupational Programs ... Ms. Laura PERCIVAL
08 Director of Library & Tutoring Svcs ... Ms. Deb SHUMAKER
37 Director of Financial Aid ... Ms. Christin BATES
10 Vice Pres of Business Services ... Mr. Jason BROGE
13 Chief Info Ofcr/Title III Proj Dir ... Mr. Tim SCHERER
18 Director of Facilities ... Ms. Evelyn SCHENK
15 Dir of Human Resources/Talent Dev ... Mr. Dale SHANTZ
09 Director of Institutional Research ... Mr. Nick BAKER
102 Foundation Director ... Ms. Lynne RUDEN
07 Admissions Coordinator ... Ms. Michelle DEVINE
26 Director of Public Information ... Ms. Sarah HOLECHECK

Kuyper College (D)

3333 East Beltline Avenue, NE,
Grand Rapids MI 49525-9749
County: Kent FICE Identification: 002311
Unit ID: 171881
Telephone: (616) 222-3000 Carnegie Class: Bac/Diverse
FAX Number: (616) 988-3608 Calendar System: Semester
URL: www.kuyper.edu
Established: 1939 Annual Undergrad Tuition & Fees: $19,514
Enrollment: 245 Coed
Affiliation or Control: Independent Non-Profit IRS Status: 501(c)3
Highest Offering: Baccalaureate
Program: Professional; Religious Emphasis
Accreditation: NH, BI, SW

01 President ... Dr. Nicholas V. KROEZE
05 Provost ... Dr. Patricia R. HARRIS
06 Registrar ... Mr. Kyle WIGBOLDY
10 Vice Pres Business Administration ... Mr. Duane BRAS
84 Vice Pres Enrollment Management ... Mr. Dale KUIPER
07 Director of Admissions ... Mr. Luke MORGAN
37 Financial Aid Director ... Ms. Agnes M. RUSSELL
30 Vice Pres College Advancement ... Mr. Ken CAPISCIOLTO
44 Director Annual/Planned Giving ... Ms. Teresa JANZEN
04 Assistant to the President ... Ms. Dawn A. LYNEMA
08 Librarian ... Ms. Dianne V. ZANDBERGEN
32 Director of Student Life ... Mr. Curt ESSENBURG
18 Director of Physical Plant ... Mr. Tim CHUPP
29 Director of Alumni/Public Relations ... Ms. Hannah SCHIERBEEK
15 Director Personnel Services ... Ms. Mary CARLSON
13 Director Computing/Info Management ... Mr. Keith TORNO
49 Arts and Sciences ... Ms. Teresa RENKEMA
64 Music ... Dr. Carol HOCHHALTER
70 Social Work ... Mr. Greg SCOTT
73 Theology ... Dr. Branson PARLER
85 International Student Services ... Ms. Mary VANDERMEER
50 Director of Business Leadership ... Mr. Marc ANDREAS

Lake Michigan College (E)

2755 E Napier, Benton Harbor MI 49022-1899
County: Berrien FICE Identification: 002277
Unit ID: 170620
Telephone: (269) 927-1000 Carnegie Class: Assoc/Pub-R-M
FAX Number: N/A Calendar System: Semester
URL: www.lakemichigancollege.edu
Established: 1946 Annual Undergrad Tuition & Fees (In-District): $4,005
Enrollment: 4,219 Coed
Affiliation or Control: Local IRS Status: 501(c)3
Highest Offering: Baccalaureate
Program: Occupational; 2-Year Principally Bachelor's Creditable
Accreditation: NH, ADNUR, DA, DMS, RAD

01 President ... Dr. Robert HARRISON
11 VP Administrative Services ... Ms. Anne C. ERDMAN
30 VP Institutional Advance/Planning ... Vacant
10 Vice President Finance ... Ms. Kelli HAHN
04 Exec Assistant to the President ... Ms. Rebecca STEFFEN
75 VP Instruction Career Technical ... Ms. Leslie KELLOGG
49 VP Instruction Arts & Sciences ... Mr. Christopher SPRADLIN
103 Dean Career Education Workforce ... Mr. Ken FLOWERS
12 Exec Dean South Haven Campus ... Mr. Doug SCHAFFER
12 Exec Dean Bertrand Crossing ... Ms. Barbara CRAIG
32 Vice President Student Services ... Dr. Clinton GABBARD
88 Manager Mainstage Services ... Mr. Mike NADOLSKI
18 Director Facilities Management ... Mr. Lee H. VAN GINHOVEN
13 Exec Dir Informational Technology ... Mr. Randall MELTON
26 Director Marketing & Communications ... Ms. Candice ELDERS
37 Director of Financial Aid ... Ms. Anne TEWS
06 Registrar ... Ms. Helen HAYS-THOMAS
44 Director Major Gifts/Estate Plng ... Vacant
102 President College Foundation ... Mr. Mike WELCH
96 Purchasing Manager ... Mr. Nathan MAIN
91 Network Administrator ... Ms. Alecia LIN
90 Director Teaching/Learning Center ... Mr. Mark KELLY
84 Interim Director Enrollment Mgmt ... Ms. Larissa HUNT
08 Head Librarian ... Ms. Diane BAKER
09 Director of Institutional Research ... Mr. John HULSEBUS
19 Director Security/Safety ... Mr. Steve SILCOX
39 Director Student Housing ... Mr. Matt KREVDA
41 Athletic Director ... Mr. Jason COOPER

Lake Michigan College Bertrand Crossing (F)

1905 Foundation Drive, Niles MI 49120
Telephone: (269) 695-1391 Identification: 770277
Accreditation: &NH

† Branch campus of Lake Michigan College, Benton Harbor, MI.

Lake Michigan College South Haven (G)

125 Veterans Boulevard, South Haven MI 49090
Telephone: (269) 639-8442 Identification: 770278
Accreditation: &NH

† Branch campus of Lake Michigan College, Benton Harbor, MI.

Lake Superior State University (H)

650 W Easterday Avenue,
Sault Sainte Marie MI 49783-1699
County: Chippewa FICE Identification: 002293
Unit ID: 170639
Telephone: (906) 632-6841 Carnegie Class: Bac/Diverse
FAX Number: (906) 635-2111 Calendar System: Semester
URL: www.lssu.edu
Established: 1946 Annual Undergrad Tuition & Fees (In-State): $10,502
Enrollment: 2,406 Coed
Affiliation or Control: State IRS Status: 501(c)3
Highest Offering: Master's
Program: Liberal Arts And General; Teacher Preparatory; Professional
Accreditation: NH, ACBSP, CAATE, ENG, ENGT, IFSAC, NUR, TEAC

01 President ... Dr. Thomas C. PLEGER
05 Vice President/Provost ... Mr. Maurice WALWORTH
32 Vice President Student Affairs ... Dr. Kenneth PERESS
10 Vice President Finance ... Ms. Sherry L. BROOKS
108 Assoc Provost Assess/Grad/Educ ... Dr. David MYTON
49 Dean ALSS & Emerg Svcs ... Dr. Paige GORDIER
81 Dean Natural & Math Sciences ... Dr. Barbara KELLER
66 Interim Dean Nursing ... Mr. Ronald HUTCHINS
50 Dean Business & Engineering ... Dr. David FINLEY
53 Asst Dean Education ... Dr. Donna FIEBELKORN
13 Director IT/Network Admin ... Mr. Scott OLSON
18 Director Physical Plant ... Mr. Steve GREGORY
06 Registrar ... Ms. Nancy NEVE
07 Director of Admissions ... Mr. Allan CASE
15 Associate VP for Human Resources ... Mr. Philip ESPINOSA
36 Director of Career Services ... Ms. Theresa WEAVER
37 Director of Financial Aid ... Ms. Deborah FAUST
38 Director of Counseling ... Ms. Kristin LARSON
39 Director Housing/Residential Life ... Mr. Scott M. KORB
26 Director of Public Affairs ... Mr. Thomas A. PINK
29 Director Alumni Relations ... Ms. Susan FITZPATRICK
102 Director of Foundation ... Mr. Tom COATES
96 Director of Purchasing ... Ms. Colleen RYE
23 Director Health Services ... Ms. Karen STOREY
28 Dir Native American Ctr/Diversity ... Ms. Stephanie SABATINE
41 Athletic Director ... Ms. Kristin DUNBAR
35 Director Student Life ... Mr. Scott KORB
40 Bookstore Manager ... Ms. Amber MCLEAN
09 Institutional Research Analyst ... Vacant

Lansing Community College (I)

610 N Capitol Avenue, Lansing MI 48933
County: Ingham FICE Identification: 002278
Unit ID: 170657
Telephone: (517) 483-1200 Carnegie Class: Assoc/Pub-R-L
FAX Number: (517) 483-1845 Calendar System: Semester
URL: www.lcc.edu
Established: 1957 Annual Undergrad Tuition & Fees (In-District): $3,020
Enrollment: 18,000 Coed
Affiliation or Control: Local IRS Status: 501(c)3
Highest Offering: Associate Degree
Program: Occupational; 2-Year Principally Bachelor's Creditable
Accreditation: NH, ADNUR, COMTA, DH, DMS, EMT, HT, IFSAC, RAD, SURGT

01 President ... Dr. Brent KNIGHT
05 Provost ... Dr. Richard PRYSTOWSKY
10 Sr VP Finance/Admin & Advancement ... Dr. Lisa WEBB SHARPE
21 Chief Financial Officer ... Mr. Don WILSKE
13 Chief Information Officer ... Mr. Kevin BUBB
11 Exec Dir Administrative Svcs ... Ms. Patricia ENGLE
20 Associate VP Academic Affairs ... Dr. Vicki DEKETELAERE
30 Assoc VP External Affs/Development ... Ms. Elva REVILLA
88 Dean Health & Human Services ... Ms. Margie CLARK
103 Dean Community Educ/Workforce Dev ... Mr. Bo GARCIA
49 Dean Arts & Sciences ... Ms. Elaine POGONCHEFF
84 Exec Dir Enrollment Mgmt ... Ms. Khallai TAYLOR
49 Assoc VP Engaged Student Learning ... Dr. Michael NEALON
32 Dean Student Affairs ... Dr. Tanya MCFADDEN
72 Dean Technical Careers ... Mr. Mark COSGROVE
15 Exec Director Human Resources ... Ms. Ann KRONEMAN
26 Director Public Affairs ... Ms. Devon BRADLEY
77 Director Center for Data Science ... Mr. Matt FALL

Lawrence Technological University (J)

21000 W Ten Mile Road, Southfield MI 48075-1058
County: Oakland FICE Identification: 002279
Unit ID: 170675
Telephone: (248) 204-4000 Carnegie Class: Master's L
FAX Number: (248) 204-3727 Calendar System: Semester
URL: www.ltu.edu
Established: 1932 Annual Undergrad Tuition & Fees: $31,500
Enrollment: 4,015 Coed
Affiliation or Control: Independent Non-Profit IRS Status: 501(c)3
Highest Offering: Doctorate
Program: Liberal Arts And General; Professional
Accreditation: NH, ACBSP, ART, CIDA, ENG, IACBE

01 President ....Dr. Virinder K. MOUDGIL
04 Exec Assistant to the President ....Ms. Karen EMERSON
05 Provost ....Dr. Maria J. VAZ
10 Vice Pres Finance/Admin ....Ms. Linda L. HEIGHT
30 Interim VP of Univ Advancement ....Mr. Dennis J. HOWIE
88 Assoc VP Advance/Chief Dev Officer ....Mr. Dennis J. HOWIE
20 Assistant Provost ....Mr. Jim JOLLY
84 Asst Provost Enrollment Management ....Ms. Lisa R. KUJAWA
48 Dean of Architecture & Design ....Mr. Glen S. LEROY
49 Dean of Arts & Sciences ....Dr. Hsiao-Ping H. MOORE
54 Dean of Engineering ....Dr. Nabil F. GRACE
50 Dean of Management ....Dr. Bahman MIRSHAB
32 Dean of Students ....Mr. Kevin FINN
26 Assoc Vice Pres Mktg & Public Affs ....Mr. Bruce J. ANNETT, JR.
13 Ex Dir IT Svc Delivery Organization ....Mr. Tim CHAVIS
07 Director Admissions ....Ms. Jane T. ROHRBACK
06 University Registrar ....Ms. Noreen FERGUSON
08 Director Library ....Mr. Gary R. COCOZZOLI
18 Director Campus Facilities ....Mr. Carey G. VALENTINE
14 Director Help Desk/Services ....Ms. Charlene RAMOS
37 Dir Financial Aid & Vet Affs ....Ms. Dee KING
41 Athletic Director ....Mr. Scott TRUDEAU
36 Director of Career Services ....Ms. Peg PIERCE
35 Assistant Dean of Students ....Ms. Cyndi MCMICHAEL
24 Director Audio Visual Media Svcs ....Mr. Walter G. BIZON
39 Director Residence Life ....Ms. Kimberly OSANTOWSKI
86 Exec Dir Econ Dev & Govt Relations ....Mr. Mark J. BRUCKI
102 Dir of Corp & Foundation Relations ....Mr. Howard DAVIS
44 Philanthropy Director ....Ms. Julie VULAJ
44 Philanthropy Director ....Ms. Angeline ZELENAK
28 Director of Diversity ....Mr. Kevin FINN
15 Exec Director of Human Resources ....Ms. Deshawn JOHNSON
40 Manager Campus Bookstore ....Ms. Adria RAHN
88 Manager Dining Services ....Ms. Nancy THOMAS
27 Dir Univ Comm & Academic Editor ....Ms. Anne M G. ADAMUS
27 Managing Editor News Bureau ....Mr. Eric POPE
19 Director of Campus Safety ....Mr. Steven J. BOGDALEK
29 Manager Alumni Rels/Alumni Giving ....Ms. Lauren N. MORRIS
31 Dir of University Special Events ....Ms. Robin LECLERC
44 Coordinator of Advancement Services ....Ms. Deborah A. FARINA
88 University Architect ....Mr. Joseph C. VERYSER
88 Student Engagement Coordinator ....Mr. Phil LUCAS
88 Dir of Academic Achievement Center ....Dr. Gladys M. AVILES
09 Dir of Inst Research/Academic Plng ....Ms. Noreen FERGUSON
96 Purchasing Agent ....Ms. Michelle BUTKOVICH
105 Manager of Web Services ....Mr. Christian FORREST
106 Dir Online Education/E-learning ....Mr. Richard G. BUSH

Macomb Community College (A)

14500 Twelve Mile Road, Warren MI 48088-9838
County: Macomb FICE Identification: 008906
Unit ID: 170790
Telephone: (586) 445-7241 Carnegie Class: Assoc/Pub-S-MC
FAX Number: (586) 445-7886 Calendar System: Semester
URL: www.macomb.edu
Established: 1954 Annual Undergrad Tuition & Fees (In-District): $3,170
Enrollment: 23,370 Coed
Affiliation or Control: Local IRS Status: 501(c)3
Highest Offering: Associate Degree
Program: Occupational; 2-Year Principally Bachelor's Creditable
Accreditation: NH, ACFEI, ADNUR, CAHIIM, COARC, EMT, MAC, OTA, PTAA, SURGT

01 President ....Dr. James JACOBS
05 Senior VP/Provost Learning Unit ....Dr. James SAWYER
10 Vice President for Business ....Ms. Elizabeth ARGIRI
15 Vice President for Human Resources ....Ms. Denise WILLIAMS
30 VP College Adv/Community Relations ....Dr. Casandra ULBRICH
88 Dean University Relations ....Ms. Donna PETRAS
32 Vice President for Student Services .Ms. Jill M. THOMAS-LITTLE
49 Dean Arts & Sciences ....Dr. Marie PRITCHETT
76 Dean Health/Public Services ....Ms. Charlene MCPEAK
54 Dean Engineering & Adv Tech ....Mr. Joseph PETROSKY
50 Dean Business & Info Technology ....Mr. David CORBA
35 Dean of Student Success ....Dr. Susan BOYD
31 Dean Student & Community Services ....Mr. Geary MAIURI
45 Exec Director Planning & Research ....Ms. Gerri Lynn PAVONE
21 Director Finance & Investments ....Ms. Roberta REMIAS
19 Captain College Police ....Mr. Thomas WILK
88 Director Public Service Institute ....Mr. Carl SEITZ
26 Director Marketing & Recruitment ....Ms. Audrey TAKACS
09 Director Institutional Research ....Ms. Deirdre SYMS
88 Director Special Research Projects ....Mr. Randall HICKMAN
06 Registrar/Dir Enrollment Services ....Ms. Carrie JEFFERS
102 Director Macomb College Foundation ....Ms. Dawn MAGRETTA
38 Dir Counseling & Academic Advising ....Ms. Michelle KOSS
96 Purchasing Administrator ....Mr. Dennis COSTELLO
41 Manager Athletics/Sports Clubs ....Mr. Randall NELSON
18 Director Facilities Management ....Mr. Stevan ALTON
37 Director of Financial Aid ....Mr. Douglas LEVY
36 Director Career Employment Services ....Mr. Robert PENKALA
51 Dir Workforce Continuing Education ....Ms. Elise JOHNSON
13 CIO/Exec Dir Communications & IT ....Mr. Michael ZIMMERMAN
08 Dean Libraries/Learning Resources ....Mr. Michael BALSAMO
43 General Counsel/Exec Dir Col Police ....Mr. Hunter WENDT

Madonna University (B)

36600 Schoolcraft Road, Livonia MI 48150-1176
County: Wayne FICE Identification: 002282
Unit ID: 170806
Telephone: (734) 432-5300 Carnegie Class: Master's M
FAX Number: (734) 432-5333 Calendar System: Semester
URL: www.madonna.edu
Established: 1947 Annual Undergrad Tuition & Fees: $18,740
Enrollment: 4,428 Coed
Affiliation or Control: Roman Catholic IRS Status: 501(c)3
Highest Offering: Doctorate
Program: Liberal Arts And General; Teacher Preparatory; Professional; Religious Emphasis
Accreditation: NH, DIETD, DMS, FEPAC, NURSE, SW, TED

01 President ....Dr. Michael GRANDILLO
30 Vice President for Advancement ....Ms. Andrea NODGE
05 Provost and VP for Academic Admin ....Dr. Ernest NOLAN
10 Vice Pres for Finance/Operations ....Dr. David HOULE
32 Vice President for Student Affairs ... Dr. Connie TINGSON-GATUZ
84 Vice Pres Planning/Enrollment Mgmt ....Dr. Michael KENNEY
12 Dean Outreach and Distance Learning ....Vacant
42 Director of Campus Ministry ....Mr. Patrick WATERS
06 Registrar ....Ms. Dina DUBUIS
07 Director of Admissions ....Mr. Mike QUATTRO
28 Director Diversity/Multicultural ....Mr. Bryant GEORGE
08 Director of Library Services ....Ms. Joanne LUMETTA
37 Director of Financial Aid ....Mr. Chris ZIEGLER
13 Director Information Systems ....Sr. Serafina Marie DIXON
15 Director of Human Resources ....Ms. Tracey DURDEN
36 Director of Career Services ....Ms. Christine BRANT
30 Director Corp Devel/Special Events ....Ms. Katie ALEXANDER
19 Director Public Safety ....Mr. David HAMMERSCHMIDT
41 Director Athletics ....Mr. Bryan RIZZO
40 Bookstore Manager ....Ms. Debbie MITCHELL
39 Director Residence Hall ....Ms. Tanisha MCINTOSH
24 Director Media Services ....Ms. Patricia DERRY
23 Director Instruction Center ....Ms. Susan GREEN
09 Director of Institutional Research ....Dr. Phillip OLLA
18 Chief Facilities/Physical Plant ....Vacant
29 Director Alumni Relations ....Ms. Carole BOOMS
26 Director of Marketing ....Ms. Karen SANBORN
79 Dean Arts & Humanities ....Dr. Kathleen EDELMAYER
50 Dean Business ....Dr. Cleamon MOORER
58 Dean Graduate Studies ....Dr. Deborah DUNN
66 Dean Nursing & Health ....Dr. Deborah VARGO
72 Dean Science & Mathematics ....Dr. Theodore BIERMANN
83 Dean Social Sciences ....Dr. Karen ROSS
53 Dean Education ....Dr. Karen OBSNIUK
101 Secretary of the Institution/Board ....Vacant
102 Dir Foundation/Corporate Relations ....Ms. Lisa COMBEN
104 Director Study Abroad ....Dr. James NOVAK
105 Director Web Services ....Ms. Sheryl HERRON
106 Dir Online Education/E-learning ....Vacant
25 Chief Contracts/Grants Admin ....Ms. Lisa COMBEN
44 Director Annual or Planned Giving ....Mr. Dean ADKINS
91 Chief Info Technology Officer ....Ms. Carol HALL
96 Director of Operations ....Ms. Diane SEVIGNY-LEFEBVRE

Manthano Christian College (C)

6420 Newburgh Road, Westland MI 48185
County: Wayne Identification: 667140
Unit ID: 480754
Telephone: (734) 895-3280 Carnegie Class: Not Classified
FAX Number: (734) 895-7241 Calendar System: Other
URL: manthanochristian.org
Established: 2011 Annual Undergrad Tuition & Fees: $7,960
Enrollment: 32 Coed
Affiliation or Control: Non-denominational IRS Status: 501(c)3
Highest Offering: Baccalaureate
Program: Religious Emphasis
Accreditation: TRACS

01 President ....Dr. John A. MCLEAN
05 Academic Dean ....Mr. Bruce H. SNELL

Marygrove College (D)

8425 W McNichols Road, Detroit MI 48221-2599
County: Wayne FICE Identification: 002284
Unit ID: 170842
Telephone: (313) 927-1200 Carnegie Class: Master's L
FAX Number: (313) 927-1345 Calendar System: Semester
URL: www.marygrove.edu
Established: 1905 Annual Undergrad Tuition & Fees: $20,930
Enrollment: 1,774 Coed
Affiliation or Control: Roman Catholic IRS Status: 501(c)3
Highest Offering: Master's
Program: 2-Year Principally Bachelor's Creditable; Liberal Arts And General; Teacher Preparatory; Professional
Accreditation: NH, SW, TEAC

01 Interim President ....Dr. James F. BIRGE
04 Exec Assistant to the President ....Ms. Maryann S. KUMMER
05 Interim Provost ....Dr. Elizabeth A. BURNS
30 Int VP Institutional Advancement ....Dr. Gregory CASCIONE
10 VP Finance/Admin & CFO ....Mr. David L. NELSON
20 Dean of Academic Programs ....Dr. Judith A. HEINEN
20 Dean of the Faculty ....Dr. Frank D. RASHID
20 Interim Dean New Program Dev ....Dr. Sally WELCH
06 Registrar ....Ms. Gladys SMITH
07 Chief Recruitment & Enrollment Ofcr ....Vacant
09 Director of Institutional Research ....Mr. John SENKO
29 Dir of Alumni Relations/Annual Giv ....Ms. Janice M. MACHUSAK
37 Director Enrollment Center ....Ms. Isis TAYLOR-THOMPKINS
41 Athletic Director ....Mr. Stephen BLOOMFIELD
42 Director of Mission Integration ....Mr. Jesse COX
21 Controller ....Vacant
15 Director of Human Resources ....Vacant
32 Director Success Center ....Ms. Robyn TSUKAYAMA
38 Assistant Dean for Student Develop ....Dr. Carolyn ROBERTS
11 Director of Administrative Services ....Mr. Horace DANDRIDGE
88 Senior Editor/Mgr of Spec Projects ....Ms. Erin PISCOPINK
36 Director of Career Services ....Vacant
106 Director Online Education ....Dr. Mitali CHAUDHERY
51 Continuing Education Coordinator ....Ms. Theresa JORDAN

MIAT College of Technology (E)

2955 South Haggerty Road, Canton MI 48188
County: Wayne FICE Identification: 020603
Unit ID: 169655
Telephone: (734) 423-2139 Carnegie Class: Not Classified
FAX Number: (734) 858-5000 Calendar System: Other
URL: www.miat.edu
Established: Annual Undergrad Tuition & Fees: $13,763
Enrollment: 382 Coed
Affiliation or Control: Proprietary IRS Status: Proprietary
Highest Offering: Associate Degree
Program: Occupational
Accreditation: ACCSC

01 Campus President ....Mr. Kevin BURCHETT

Michigan Jewish Institute (F)

6890 West Maple Road, West Bloomfield MI 48322
County: Oakland FICE Identification: 032843
Unit ID: 434414
Telephone: (248) 414-6900 Carnegie Class: Bac/A&S
FAX Number: (248) 414-6907 Calendar System: Semester
URL: www.mji.edu
Established: 1994 Annual Undergrad Tuition & Fees: $11,200
Enrollment: 837 Coed
Affiliation or Control: Independent Non-Profit IRS Status: 501(c)3
Highest Offering: Baccalaureate
Program: Religious Emphasis
Accreditation: ACICS

01 President/CFO/VP Financial Affs ....Rabbi Kasriel SHEMTOV
10 COO ....Mr. Fred LEEB
06 Registrar ....Ms. Alicia JAMES
05 Director of Academics ....Mr. Dov STEIN
37 Financial Aid Administrator ....Ms. Sandra KITTLE
13 IT Manager ....Mr. James JEMISON

Michigan School of Professional Psychology (G)

26811 Orchard Lake Road,
Farmington Hills MI 48334-4512
County: Oakland FICE Identification: 021989
Unit ID: 169220
Telephone: (248) 476-1122 Carnegie Class: Spec/Health
FAX Number: (248) 476-1125 Calendar System: Semester
URL: www.mispp.edu
Established: 1981 Annual Graduate Tuition & Fees: $29,185
Enrollment: 150 Coed
Affiliation or Control: Independent Non-Profit IRS Status: 501(c)3
Highest Offering: Doctorate; No Undergraduates
Program: Professional
Accreditation: NH

01 President/Chief Executive Officer ....Dr. Diane BLAU
03 Vice President/Chief Operating Ofcr ....Ms. Diane ZALAPI
05 Program Director/Chief Academic Ofc ....Dr. Fran BROWN
13 Director of Info Tech & Bldg Svcs ....Mr. Jeffrey CROSS
08 Head Academic Librarian ....Ms. Michelle WHEELER
06 Registrar ....Ms. Amanda MING
07 Admissions/Recruitment Coordinator ....Ms. Tori HOLMES
11 Dir of Administrative Operations ....Ms. Laura LANE
88 Interim Dir of Clinical Training ....Dr. Jill CASTRO

Michigan State University (H)

426 Auditorium Road, East Lansing MI 48824-1046
County: Ingham FICE Identification: 002290
Unit ID: 171100
Telephone: (517) 355-1855 Carnegie Class: RU/VH
FAX Number: N/A Calendar System: Semester
URL: www.msu.edu
Established: 1855 Annual Undergrad Tuition & Fees (In-State): $23,136
Enrollment: 50,081 Coed
Affiliation or Control: State IRS Status: 501(c)3
Highest Offering: Doctorate
Program: Liberal Arts And General; Teacher Preparatory; Professional
Accreditation: NH, ANEST, BUS, BUSA, CAATE, CEA, CIDA, CLPSY, CONST, CORE, CS, DIETD, DIETI, DMOLS, ENG, FEPAC, IPSY, JOUR, LAW, LSAR, MED, MFCD, MT, MUS, NURSE, OSTEO, PLNG, SCPSY, SP, SW, TEAC, VET

01 President ....Dr. Lou Anna K. SIMON
05 Provost/Exec VP Academic Affairs ....Dr. June P. YOUATT
11 Exec Vice Pres for Admin Services ....Dr. Satish S. UDPA
101 Vice President/Secretary to Board ....Mr. William R. BEEKMAN
46 Vice President Research & Grad Stds ....Dr. Stephen HSU
32 VP Student Affairs & Svcs ....Dr. Denise B. MAYBANK
86 Vice President Governmental Affairs ....Mr. Mark A. BURNHAM
10 Vice Pres Finance Opers/Treasurer ....Mr. Mark HAAS

30 Vice Pres Univ Advancement ... Mr. Robert GROVES
43 VP Legal Affairs & General Counsel ... Mr. Robert A. NOTO
18 VP Infrastructure Planning & Facil ... Mr. Dan BOLLMAN
109 Vice President Auxiliary Services ... Mr. Vennie GORE
26 VP Communication & Brand Strategy ... Ms. Heather C. SWAIN
22 Dir Incl/Intrcult Init/Sr Adv P Dvr ... Ms. Paulette GRANBERRY-RUSSELL
88 Assoc VP Research/Graduate Studies ... Dr. Paul M. HUNT
58 Assoc Prov and Dean Grad School ... Dr. Karen L. KLOMPARENS
20 Assoc Prov & Dean Ungrad Educ ... Dr. Douglas ESTRY
88 Assoc Prov Univ Outreach/ Engagement ... Dr. Hiram E. FITZGERALD
88 Assoc Provost Academic Svcs ... Dr. John D. GABOURY
16 Assoc Prov/VP Academic Human Res ... Mr. Theodore H. CURRY, II
45 Asst VP & Director of Plng/Budgets ... Mr. David S. BYELICH
15 Asst Vice Pres for Human Resources ... Ms. Sharon BUTLER
13 CIO & VP of Information and Tech ... Ms. Joanna YOUNG
88 Asst VP Ofc of Sponsored Programs ... Dr. Twila REIGHLEY
21 Controller ... Mr. Greg DEPPONG
07 Director of Admissions ... Mr. James W. COTTER
29 Assoc VP for Alumni Relations ... Mr. W. Scott WESTERMAN, III
25 Director Contract & Grant Admin ... Mr. Daniel T. EVON
36 Assoc Dir Career Services/Placement ... Dr. Linda GROSS
38 Acting Director Counseling Center ... Dr. Scott BECKER
88 Dir MI AgBioResearch ... Dr. Doug BUHLER
56 Interim Assoc Dir MSU Extension ... Mr. Ray HAMMERSCHMIDT
37 Director of Financial Aid ... Mr. Richard SHIPMAN
06 Registrar ... Dr. Nicole ROVIG
85 Director Intl Students/Scholars ... Mr. Peter F. BRIGGS
23 Director MSU Student Health Ctr ... Dr. Glynda M. MOORER
92 Dean Honors College ... Dr. Cynthia JACKSON-ELMOORE
41 Director Intercollegiate Athletics ... Mr. Mark J. HOLLIS
08 Director of Libraries ... Mr. Clifford H. HAKA
88 Dir Natl Supercond Cyclotron Lab ... Dr. Konrad GELBKE
19 Police Chf/Dir Police & Pub Safety ... Mr. James H. DUNLAP
88 Director Undergraduate Univ Div ... Dr. Bonita P. CURRY
47 Dean Col Ag & Nat Resources ... Dr. Fred POSTON
79 Dean College Arts & Letters ... Dr. Christopher P. LONG
79 Dean Res Col Arts/Humanities ... Dr. Stephen L. ESQUITH
50 Dean Eli Broad Col of Business ... Dr. Sanjay GUPTA
60 Dean Col Comm/Arts & Sci ... Dr. Prabu DAVID
53 Dean College of Education ... Dr. Donald E. HELLER
54 Dean College of Engineering ... Dr. Leo KEMPEL
63 Dean College Human Medicine ... Dr. Marsha D. RAPPLEY
82 Dean James Madison College ... Dr. Sherman W. GARNETT
61 Dean College of Law ... Ms. Joan W. HOWARTH
81 Dean Lyman Briggs College ... Dr. Elizabeth H. SIMMONS
64 Dean College of Music ... Mr. James FORGER
81 Dean College Natural Science ... Dr. R. James KIRKPATRICK
66 Dean College of Nursing ... Dr. Randolph RASCH
63 Dean College Osteopathic Medicine ... Dr. William D. STRAMPEL
83 Interim Dean College of Social Sci ... Dr. Neal SCHMITT
74 Dean College Veterinary Medicine ... Dr. John C. BAKER
82 Dean Intl Studies & Programs ... Dr. Steven D. HANSON

Michigan Technological University (A)

1400 Townsend Drive, Houghton MI 49931-1295
County: Houghton FICE Identification: 002292
Unit ID: 171128
Telephone: (906) 487-1885 Carnegie Class: RU/H
FAX Number: (906) 487-2935 Calendar System: Semester
URL: www.mtu.edu
Established: 1885 Annual Undergrad Tuition & Fees (In-State): $14,286
Enrollment: 7,100 Coed
Affiliation or Control: State IRS Status: 501(c)3
Highest Offering: Doctorate
Program: Liberal Arts And General; Teacher Preparatory; Professional
Accreditation: NH, BUS, CEA, CONST, CS, ENG, ENGT, TEAC

01 President ... Dr. Glenn D. MROZ
05 Provost/Vice Pres Academic Affairs ... Vacant
86 Vice Pres Governmental Relations ... Dr. Dale R. TAHTINEN
11 Vice President for Administration ... Ms. Ellen S. HORSCH
46 Vice President for Research ... Dr. David D. REED
32 VP for Student Affairs/Advancement ... Dr. Les P. COOK
84 Asst VP for Enrollment Services ... Mr. John B. LEHMAN
35 Dean of Students ... Ms. Bonnie GORMAN
10 Treasurer ... Ms. Julie SEPPALA
26 Director Marketing/Communications ... Mr. Ian REPP
08 Director of the Library ... Ms. Ellen MARKS
09 Institutional Analysis ... Mr. Richard ELENICH
29 Director Alumni Association ... Ms. Brenda RUDIGER
06 Registrar ... Ms. Theresa K. JACQUES
07 Director Undergraduate Recruitment ... Ms. Allison A. CARTER
15 Director Human Resources ... Ms. Renee HILLER
37 Director of Financial Aid ... Mr. William R. ROBERTS
36 Director University Career Center ... Mr. Steve PATCHIN
18 Dir Facilities/Physical Plant ... Ms. Kerri SLEEMAN
21 Director Planning & Budgeting ... Ms. Deborah L. SHELDEN
38 Director Counseling Services ... Mr. Donald S. WILLIAMS
19 Director Public Safety ... Mr. Daniel P. BENNETT
22 Director Affirmative Programs ... Dr. Jill HODGES
96 Director of Purchasing ... Mr. Raymond E. LASANEN
58 Dean Graduate School ... Dr. Jacqueline E. HUNTOON
50 Dean Business & Economics ... Dr. Gene KLIPEL
54 Dean of Engineering ... Dr. Wayne PENNINGTON
65 Dean of Forestry ... Dr. Terry SHARIK
49 Dean Sciences/Arts ... Dr. Bruce E. SEELY
72 Dean of Technology ... Dr. James FRENDEWEY, JR.
100 Chief of Staff ... Ms. Roberta M. DESSELLIER
13 Chief Info Technology Officer (CIO) ... Dr. Walter MILLIGAN

41 Athletic Director ... Ms. Suzanne SANREGRET
25 Chief Contracts/Grants Admin ... Ms. Julie SEPPALA
30 Chief Development/Advancement ... Dr. Les COOK

Mid Michigan Community College (B)

1375 S Clare Avenue, Harrison MI 48625-9447
County: Clare FICE Identification: 006768
Unit ID: 171155
Telephone: (989) 386-6622 Carnegie Class: Assoc/Pub-R-M
FAX Number: (989) 386-2411 Calendar System: Semester
URL: www.midmich.edu
Established: 1965 Annual Undergrad Tuition & Fees (In-District): $3,609
Enrollment: 4,422 Coed
Affiliation or Control: State/Local IRS Status: 501(c)3
Highest Offering: Associate Degree
Program: Occupational; 2-Year Principally Bachelor's Creditable
Accreditation: NH, MAC, PHLEB, PTAA, RAD

01 President ... Dr. Christine M. HAMMOND
05 Vice President of Academic Services ... Dr. Michael W. JANKOVIAK
32 VP Community/Student Relations ... Dr. Matt MILLER
10 Vice President for Admin & Finance ... Ms. Lillian K. FRICK
04 Executive Assistant to President ... Ms. Tonya M. CLAYTON
15 Exec Director of Human Resources ... Ms. Gail NUNAMAKER
26 College Info/Org Dev Officer ... Mr. Anthony FREDS
20 Dean of Instruction ... Mr. Chris GOFFNETT
35 Exec Dean of Student Services ... Ms. Kimberly BARNES
81 Assoc Dean of Math & Science ... Mr. Peter VELGUTH
69 Associate Dean of Health Sciences ... Dr. Maggie MAGOON
14 IT Systems Manager ... Mr. Chris KLIEWONEIT
13 Director IT ... Mr. Kirk A. LEHR
88 Dir Grants Mgmt & Resource Dev ... Ms. Carol DARLINGTON
06 Assoc Dean of Student Services ... Mr. Scott MERTES
21 Director of Accounting ... Mr. Gene SCHMIDT
88 SBDC Director ... Mr. Anthony FOX
07 Director of Marketing & Admissions ... Ms. Jessica GORDON
08 Dir Library/Learning Services ... Mr. Corey GOETHE
37 Director of Financial Aid ... Mr. Gale M. CRANDELL
109 Director Auxiliary Services ... Ms. Kelly KOCH
18 Director of Facilities ... Mr. William D. WHITMAN
76 Director Radiology ... Ms. LouAnn GOODWIN
25 Title III Coordinator ... Ms. Rhonda LINN
88 Radiology Tech Clinical Coordinator ... Mr. Galen P. MILLER
49 Associate Dean Liberal Arts ... Mr. Shawn TROY
103 Exec Dir Econ/Workforce Dev ... Mr. Scott GOVITZ
25 NSF Plastics Grant Coordinator ... Mr. Steven FOSGARD
88 Dir Of Educational Talent Search ... Ms. Marilee KUJAT
09 Director of Institutional Research ... Mr. Kim OREN
35 Student Advancement Coordinator ... Ms. Tammy ALVARO

Monroe County Community College (C)

1555 S Raisinville Road, Monroe MI 48161-9746
County: Monroe FICE Identification: 002294
Unit ID: 171225
Telephone: (734) 242-7300 Carnegie Class: Assoc/Pub-S-SC
FAX Number: (734) 242-9711 Calendar System: Semester
URL: www.monroeccc.edu
Established: 1964 Annual Undergrad Tuition & Fees (In-District): $3,730
Enrollment: 3,482 Coed
Affiliation or Control: Local IRS Status: 170(c)1
Highest Offering: Associate Degree
Program: Occupational; 2-Year Principally Bachelor's Creditable
Accreditation: NH, ADNUR, COARC

01 President ... Dr. Kojo QUARTEY
05 Vice President of Instruction ... Dr. Grace B. YACKEE
10 Vice Pres of Admin ... Ms. Suzanne M. WETZEL
32 Vice Pres Student & Information Svc ... Mr. Randell W. DANIELS
50 Dean of Business ... Mr. Paul L. KNOLLMAN
76 Dean of Health Sciences ... Ms. Kimberly LINDQUIST
79 Dean of Humanities/Social Science ... Dr. Paul HEDEEN
72 Dean of Applied Sci & Eng Tech ... Mr. Parmeshwar COOMAR
81 Dean of Science/Mathematics ... Mr. Vincent MALTESE
31 Dean of Corporate/Cmty Svcs ... Vacant
08 Director Learning Resources ... Ms. Barbara MCNAMEE
06 Registrar ... Ms. Tracy VOGT
07 Director of Admissions/Guidance ... Mr. Mark HALL
88 Director of Upward Bound ... Mr. Anthony QUINN
88 Director of Respiratory Therapy ... Ms. Bonnie B. BOGGS
21 Director of Financial Services ... Vacant
18 Director Physical Plant ... Mr. Jack BURNS
96 Dir Auxiliary Services/Purchasing ... Ms. Jean FORD
14 Director Data Processing Services ... Mr. James A. ROSS
37 Director of Financial Aid ... Ms. Valerie CULLER
36 Dir Business Devel/Employment Svcs ... Mr. Barry C. KINSEY
56 Director of Extension Centers ... Vacant
88 Director of Lifelong Learning ... Ms. Tina PILLARELLI
13 Manager Information Services ... Mr. Brian K. LAY
26 Director of Marketing/Communication ... Mr. Joseph VERKENNES
15 Director of Human Resources ... Ms. Molly M. MCCUTCHAN
04 Executive Asst to President ... Ms. Penny R. DORCEY
09 Coord Inst Research/Eval & Assess ... Miss Jamie DELEEUW
102 Exec Director Foundation ... Mr. Joshua MYERS

Montcalm Community College (D)

2800 College Drive, Sidney MI 48885-9723
County: Montcalm FICE Identification: 002295
Unit ID: 171234
Telephone: (989) 328-2111 Carnegie Class: Assoc/Pub-R-M
FAX Number: (989) 328-2950 Calendar System: Semester
URL: www.montcalm.edu
Established: 1965 Annual Undergrad Tuition & Fees (In-District): $3,540
Enrollment: 1,832 Coed
Affiliation or Control: Local IRS Status: 501(c)3
Highest Offering: Associate Degree
Program: Occupational; 2-Year Principally Bachelor's Creditable; Liberal Arts And General
Accreditation: NH, MAC

01 President ... Mr. Robert C. FERRENTINO
05 Vice Pres for Student/Acad Affairs ... Mr. Robert SPOHR
102 Executive Director of Foundation ... Ms. Therese A. SMITH
32 Dean Student & Enrollment Svcs ... Ms. Debra ALEXANDER
37 Director of Financial Aid ... Ms. Traci NICHOLS
13 Director Information Tech Svcs ... Mr. Rodney C. MIDDLETON
09 Director Institutional Effectivenes ... Ms. Lisa LUND
26 Communications Director ... Ms. Shelly STRAUTZ-SPRINGBORN
15 Director of Human Resources ... Ms. Connie STEWART

Moody Theological Seminary-Michigan (E)

41550 E Ann Arbor Trail, Plymouth MI 48170-4308
Telephone: (734) 207-9581 FICE Identification: 031353
Accreditation: &NH, THEOL

† Regional accreditation is carried under the parent institution Moody Bible Institute, Chicago, IL.

Mott Community College (F)

1401 E Court Street, Flint MI 48503-2089
County: Genesee FICE Identification: 002261
Unit ID: 169275
Telephone: (810) 762-0200 Carnegie Class: Assoc/Pub-R-L
FAX Number: (810) 762-0257 Calendar System: Semester
URL: www.mcc.edu
Established: 1923 Annual Undergrad Tuition & Fees (In-District): $4,300
Enrollment: 9,385 Coed
Affiliation or Control: Local IRS Status: 501(c)3
Highest Offering: Associate Degree
Program: Occupational; 2-Year Principally Bachelor's Creditable; Business Emphasis
Accreditation: NH, ACBSP, ADNUR, COARC, DA, DH, OTA, PTAA

01 President ... Dr. Beverly WALKER-GRIFFEA
30 Exec Dir Inst Developmnt/Foundation ... Ms. Lennetta CONEY
05 Vice Pres Academic Affairs ... Dr. Amy FUGATE
11 VP Student & Administrative Svcs ... Mr. Scott JENKINS
10 Chief Financial Officer ... Mr. Larry GAWTHROP
15 Chief Human Resources Officer ... Vacant
88 Exec Dean Regional Tech Ctr Project ... Mr. Tom CRAMPTON
51 Exec Dir Corporate Svcs & Cont Educ ... Mr. Chuck THIEL
32 Interim Exec Dean Student Services ... Mr. Troy BOQUETTE
37 Exec Dir Student Fin Svcs ... Ms. Jennifer DOW-MCDONALD
81 Dean of Math & Science ... Dr. Todd TROUTMAN
76 Dean of Health Sciences ... Dr. Rebecca MYSZENSKI
83 Dean Social Sciences & Fine Arts ... Ms. Mary CUSACK
50 Dean of Business ... Dr. Jeff LIVERMORE
72 Dean of Technology ... Mr. Clark HARRIS
26 Exec Director Marketing & PR ... Vacant
13 Chief Technology Officer ... Ms. Cheryl BASSETT
06 Registrar ... Mr. Chris ENGLE
36 Exec Dir Career Ctr/Job Placement ... Vacant
62 Executive Director Library ... Mrs. Jill SODT
18 Exec Dir Physical Plant/Architect ... Mr. Larry KOEHLER
41 Director Athletics/Campus Rec ... Mr. Tom HEALEY
09 Exec Dir Institutional Research ... Mrs. Lori HANCOCK
35 Director Student Life ... Ms. Dawn VANNIMAN
96 Director of Purchasing ... Ms. Jody MICHAEL
04 Administrative Asst to President ... Ms. Lisa M. POMA

Muskegon Community College (G)

221 S Quarterline Road, Muskegon MI 49442-1493
County: Muskegon FICE Identification: 002297
Unit ID: 171304
Telephone: (231) 773-9131 Carnegie Class: Assoc/Pub-U-SC
FAX Number: (231) 777-0440 Calendar System: Semester
URL: www.muskegoncc.edu
Established: 1926 Annual Undergrad Tuition & Fees (In-District): $5,123
Enrollment: 4,640 Coed
Affiliation or Control: Local IRS Status: Exempt
Highest Offering: Associate Degree
Program: Occupational; 2-Year Principally Bachelor's Creditable
Accreditation: NH, ADNUR, COARC

01 President ... Dr. Dale K. NESBARY
05 VP of Academic Affairs and Finance ... Ms. Teresa STURRUS
32 VP Student Svcs and Administration ... Dr. John SELMON
06 Dean of Academic Svcs/Registrar ... Ms. Jean ROBERTS
20 Dean of Instruction & Assessment ... Dr. Edward BREITENBACH
31 Dean of Community Outreach ... Ms. Trynette Lottie HARPS
84 Dean of Enrollment Services ... Ms. Cindy REUSS
10 Director of Finance ... Mr. Kenneth LONG
13 Chief Information Officer ... Mr. Mike ALSTROM
37 Director Financial Aid ... Mr. Bruce WIERDA
09 Dir Institutional Research & Grants ... Mr. Eduardo BEDOYA
102 Dir Foundation/Strategic Initiative ... Ms. Tina DEE
15 Adm Dir of Human Resources ... Ms. Kristine ANDERSON
41 Athletic Director ... Mr. Marty MCDERMOTT
18 Physical Plant Director ... Mr. Gerald NYLAND

29 Alumni Relations Manager ....Ms. Julie WELLER
04 Executive Assistant to President ....Ms. Cindy S. DEBOEF

North Central Michigan College (A)

1515 Howard Street, Petoskey MI 49770-8717
County: Emmet FICE Identification: 002299
Unit ID: 171395
Telephone: (231) 348-6600 Carnegie Class: Assoc/Pub-R-M
FAX Number: (231) 348-6628 Calendar System: Semester
URL: www.ncmich.edu
Established: 1958 Annual Undergrad Tuition & Fees (In-District): $2,856
Enrollment: 2,581 Coed
Affiliation or Control: Local IRS Status: 501(c)3
Highest Offering: Associate Degree
Program: Occupational; 2-Year Principally Bachelor's Creditable
Accreditation: NH

01 President ....Dr. Cameron BRUNET-KOCH
05 VP Academic Affairs/Student Success ....Dr. Peter OLSON
10 VP of Finance & Facilities ....David HARTNETT
32 VP of Student Services ....Vacant
102 Executive Director Foundation ....Sean POLLION
08 Librarian ....Leland PARSONS
37 Director of Financial Aid ....Virginia PANOFF
18 Director of Physical Plant ....Jeff GARDNER
84 Dir Enrollment Services/Registrar ....Renee DEYOUNG
21 Controller ....Troy SLATER
29 Director Alumni Relations ....Sean POLLION
35 Dir Student Activities/Camp Housing ....Josh DEAL
15 Human Resources ....Diana SOUZA
40 Bookstore Manager ....Julie WEAVER
09 Assoc Dean Research & Assessment ....Dr. Robert MARSH
49 Assoc Dean Liberal Arts ....Dr. Sara GLASGOW
66 Assoc Dean Nurs/Allied Hlth/Sci ....Rene BIEGANOWSKI
50 Assoc Dean Business/Manuf/Tech ....Dr. Pamela MILLER
27 Director of College Communications ....Carol LAENEN
07 Director of Student Outreach ....Wendy FOUGHT
13 Director of Information Services ....David BORING
88 Director of Resource Center ....Dallas CULVAHOUSE

Northern Michigan University (B)

1401 Presque Isle Avenue, Marquette MI 49855-5301
County: Marquette FICE Identification: 002301
Unit ID: 171456
Telephone: (906) 227-1000 Carnegie Class: Master's M
FAX Number: (906) 227-2204 Calendar System: Semester
URL: www.nmu.edu
Established: 1899 Annual Undergrad Tuition & Fees (In-State): $9,620
Enrollment: 8,781 Coed
Affiliation or Control: State IRS Status: 501(c)3
Highest Offering: Doctorate
Program: Occupational; 2-Year Principally Bachelor's Creditable; Liberal Arts And General; Teacher Preparatory; Professional
Accreditation: NH, BUS, CA, CAATE, CGTECH, DMOLS, ENGT, MLTAD, MT, MUS, NURSE, RAD, SURGT, SW, TEAC

01 President ....Dr. Fritz J. ERICKSON
10 VP for Finance & Administration ....Mr. R. Gavin LEACH
30 Vice Pres Advancement ....Ms. Martha B. HAYNES
84 Vice Pres Enroll Mgmt/Student Svcs ....Dr. Steven NEIHEISEL
09 Assoc VP for Inst Research ....Dr. Linda WANG
05 Provost/VP Academic Affairs ....Dr. Kerri SCHUILING
31 VP Extended Lrng/Cmty Engagement .. Dr. Steve VANDENAVOND
20 Asc Provost Acad Affs/Undergrad Pgm ....Dr. Dale P. KAPLA
58 Asst Provost Graduate Educ/Research ....Dr. Brian CHERRY
90 Dean Academic Information Services ....Ms. Leslie A. WARREN
32 Assistant VP/Dean of Students ....Dr. Christine G. GREER
49 Dean of Arts & Sciences ....Dr. Michael J. BROADWAY
50 Dean Walker L Cisler Col Bus ....Dr. David RAYOME
107 Interim Dean College Prof Studies ....Dr. Charles MESLOH
06 Registrar ....Ms. Kim M. ROTUNDO
44 Director Major/Planned Giving ....Ms. Amy M. HUBINGER
45 Asst to Pres Strategic Initiatives ....Ms. Cindy L. PAAVOLA
36 Dir of Acad & Career Advisement ....Mr. James G. GADZINSKI
37 Director of Financial Aid ....Mr. Michael R. ROTUNDO
38 Acting Director Counseling Center ....Ms. Marie AHO
88 Director Glenn T Seaborg Center ....Ms. Chris STANDERFORD
41 Athletic Director ....Mr. Forrest KARR
19 Dir Public Safety/Police Services ....Mr. Michael J. BATH
39 Director Housing/Residence Life ....Mr. Gary BICE
07 Director of Admissions ....Ms. Gerri L. DANIELS
23 Chief of Staff/Physician ....Dr. David M. LUOMA
15 Director of Human Resources ....Ms. Rhea DEVER
26 Asst VP Marketing & Communications ....Mr. Derek HALL
28 Dir Multicult Educ/Resource Center ....Ms. Shirley A. BROZZO
85 Director International Programs ....Mr. Kevin J. TIMLIN
92 Director of Honors Program ....Dr. David H. WOOD
88 Director of Support/Consulting Svcs ....Ms. Felecia J. FLACK
24 Director Broadcast & AV Services ....Mr. Eric L. SMITH
29 Exec Dir Alumni Ops/Annual Giving ....Ms. Robyn L. STILLE
40 Bookstore Manager ....Mr. Michael J. KUZAK
18 Associate VP Eng & Plan/Facilities ....Ms. Kathy A. RICHARDS
13 Chief Technology Officer ....Mr. David W. MAKI
96 Manager of Purchasing ....Mr. Steven D. BROWN
86 Director of Government Relations ....Ms. Deanna HEMMILA
04 Executive Assistant to President ....Ms. Laura GLOVER
101 Secretary Board of Trustees ....Ms. Cathy NIEMI

Northwestern Michigan College (C)

1701 E Front Street, Traverse City MI 49686-3061
County: Grand Traverse FICE Identification: 002302
Unit ID: 171483
Telephone: (231) 995-1000 Carnegie Class: Assoc/Pub-R-M
FAX Number: (231) 995-1339 Calendar System: Semester
URL: www.nmc.edu
Established: 1951 Annual Undergrad Tuition & Fees (In-District): $3,876
Enrollment: 4,542 Coed
Affiliation or Control: Local IRS Status: 501(c)3
Highest Offering: Baccalaureate
Program: 2-Year Principally Bachelor's Creditable
Accreditation: NH, ACFEI, ADNUR, DA, PNUR

01 President ....Mr. Timothy J. NELSON
05 VP for Educational Services ....Dr. Stephen N. SICILIANO
107 VP Lifelong/Professional Learning ....Ms. Marguerite C. COTTO
10 VP of Finance & Administration ....Ms. Vicki COOK
32 VP for Enrollment & Student Svcs ....Dr. Chris WEBER
04 Exec Assistant to President & Board ....Ms. Holly J. GORTON
08 Exec Director Lrng Res/Technologies ....Mr. Todd NEIBAUER
15 Director of Human Resources ....Vacant
88 Exec Dir of Dennos Museum Center ... Mr. Eugene A. JENNEMAN
24 Director Educational Media Tech ....Vacant
12 Supt Great Lakes Maritime Academy ....RAdm. Gerard ACHENBACH, USMS
20 Dir Academic Affairs/Business Div ....Ms. Susan DECAMILLIS
56 Director Extended Educ Services ....Mr. Don CUNNINGHAM
06 Registrar ....Mr. Michael STALKER
23 Director of Health Services ....Ms. Renee R. JACOBSON
09 Dir Research Planning Effectiveness ....Ms. Joy EVANS
18 Director of Campus Services ....Mr. Paul PERRY
26 Exec Dir of PR/Marketing/ Communic ....Ms. Diana FAIRBANKS LAWSON
102 Exec Dir of Resource Dev & Found ....Ms. Rebecca M. TEAHEN
62 Director of Library Services ....Ms. Tina J. ULRICH
88 Director Great Lakes Culinary Inst ....Mr. Frederick L. LAUGHLIN
88 Director Upward Bound ....Ms. Patty ROTH
88 Director Training & Research ....Mr. Richard R. WOLIN
21 Controller ....Ms. Cheryl SULLIVAN
96 Purchasing Manager ....Mr. Donald LOEFFLER
19 Asst Dir Campus Safety & Security ....Mr. Jim WHITE
07 Director of Admissions ....Ms. Cathryn CLAERHOUT
37 Director of Financial Aid ....Ms. Pam PALERMO
36 Director of Learning Services ....Ms. Kari L. KAHLER
68 Coordinator Physical Education ....Mr. Peter W. LACOURSE
60 Communications Chair ....Ms. Deirdre M. MAHONEY
75 Director of Technical Division ....Mr. Ed BAILEY
88 Director of Aviation ....Mr. Alex BLOYE
79 Humanities Chair ....Mr. Jim PRESS
81 Science & Math Chair ....Mr. Keith OVERBAUGH
76 Health Occupations Chair ....Ms. Jean M. ROKOS

Northwood University (D)

4000 Whiting Drive, Midland MI 48640-2398
County: Midland FICE Identification: 004072
Unit ID: 171492
Telephone: (989) 837-4200 Carnegie Class: Spec/Bus
FAX Number: (989) 837-4111 Calendar System: Semester
URL: www.northwood.edu
Established: 1959 Annual Undergrad Tuition & Fees: $24,170
Enrollment: 5,326 Coed
Affiliation or Control: Independent Non-Profit IRS Status: 501(c)3
Highest Offering: Master's
Program: Liberal Arts And General; Business Emphasis
Accreditation: NH, ACBSP

01 President & Chief Executive Officer ....Dr. Keith A. PRETTY
03 EVP/CAO/COO ....Dr. Kristin STEHOUWER
10 Vice President Finance & Treasurer ....Mr. W. Karl STEPHAN
88 VP Strategic/Corporate Alliances ....Dr. Timothy G. NASH
84 VP Enrollment Management ....Dr. Brian SANDUSKY
12 President Northwood Texas ....Dr. Kevin G. FEGAN
26 Associate VP Mktg/Comm/PR ....Mr. William GAGLIARDI
51 Associate Dean Adult Degree Program ....Ms. Rhonda C. ANDERSON
07 Director of Admissions ....Mr. Gregory S. STIFFLER
32 Dean of Students ....Mr. Stephen A. CRIPE
85 Dean International Programs ....Ms. Mamiko REEVES
96 Director of Asset Management ....Mr. David L. BENDER
88 Director of Communications ....Ms. Barbara J. MUESSIG
06 Registrar ....Dr. Marisa L. TOSCHKOFF
09 Dir of Institutional Effectiveness ....Ms. Rachel R. VALDISERRI
37 System Financial Aid Director ....Mr. Mark A. MARTIN
15 Director of Human Resources ....Ms. Pamela L. CHRISTIE
21 Business Office Mgr/System Director ....Ms. Susan M. RIDGWAY
29 Executive Director Alumni Relations ....Ms. Julie L. FELSKE
04 Administrative Asst to President ....Ms. Sue A. NOWICKI
41 Athletic Director ....Mr. David F. MARSH

Oakland Community College (E)

2480 Opdyke Road, Bloomfield Hills MI 48304-2266
County: Oakland FICE Identification: 002303
Unit ID: 171535
Telephone: (248) 341-2000 Carnegie Class: Assoc/Pub-S-MC
FAX Number: (248) 341-2099 Calendar System: Semester
URL: www.oaklandcc.edu
Established: 1964 Annual Undergrad Tuition & Fees (In-District): $4,364
Enrollment: 20,585 Coed
Affiliation or Control: State/Local IRS Status: 501(c)3
Highest Offering: Associate Degree
Program: Occupational; 2-Year Principally Bachelor's Creditable
Accreditation: NH, ACFEI, ADNUR, COARC, DH, DMS, MAC, RAD, SURGT

01 Chancellor ....Dr. Timothy R. MEYER
05 Vice Chanc Academic & Student Affs ....Dr. Mary C. MAZE
10 Int Vice Chanc of Business/Finance ....Mr. Charles THOMAS
11 Vice Chanc Administrative Svcs ....Mr. Peter PROVENZANO
26 Vice Chancellor External Affairs ....Ms. Sharon E. MILLER
15 Vice Chancellor Human Resources ....Mr. William J. MACQUEEN
32 Assoc Vice Chanc Acad/Student Affs ....Dr. Timothy SHERWOOD
04 Exec Assistant to Chancellor ....Ms. Cherie A. FOSTER
12 President Highland Lakes Campus ....Dr. Cynthia ROMAN
12 President Royal Oak/Southfield Camp ....Dr. Steven J. REIF
12 President Auburn Hills Campus ....Dr. Timothy L. TAYLOR
12 Interim Pres Orchard Ridge Campus ....Dr. Steven J. REIF
09 Exec Dir Inst Research/Quality/Plng ....Ms. Nancy C. SHOWERS
88 Exec Director IE ....Mr. Martin A. ORLOWSKI
13 Vice Chanc Info Technologies/CIO ....Mr. Robert MONTGOMERY
84 Exec Director Enrollment Mgmt ....Mrs. Carla R. SIMS
66 Interim Acad Dean Nursing ....Ms. Nancy A. WONG
26 Exec Dir Marketing/Communications ....Ms. Janet E. ROBERTS
72 Exec Dir Information Technologies ....Mr. Chuck S. FLAGG
06 Registrar ....Mr. Stephen M. LINDEN
18 Director Physical Facilities ....Mr. Daniel P. CHEREWICK
19 Director Public Safety ....Mr. Terry L. MCCAULEY
21 Director Financial Services ....Ms. Sharon K. CONVERSE
21 Director Budget & Financial Plng ....Mrs. Renee OSZUST
22 Director Employee Relations ....Mr. Gary S. CASEY
102 Interim Director OCC Foundation ....Ms. Candy GEETER
36 Director Placement/Coop Education ....Mr. Willie L. LLOYD
41 Athletic Director ....Ms. Laurie G. HUBER
96 Int Director Purch/Auxiliary Svcs ....Ms. Sarah L. ROWLEY
37 Director Financial Res/Scholarships ....Ms. Wilma B. PORTER
16 Director Personnel Services ....Mrs. Margaret R. CARROLL
29 Director Alumni & Annual Giving ....Vacant
81 Academic Dean Math/Nat Life Sci ....Mr. Michael M. GOLDIN
54 Int Academic Dean Eng/Mfg/Ind Tech ....Ms. Deborah A. BAYER
80 Academic Dean Public Services/CREST ....Ms. Deborah A. BAYER
62 Academic Dean Learning Resources ....Ms. Mary Ann SHEBLE
83 Int Academic Dean Social Sciences ....Ms. Mary Ann SHEBLE
66 Academic Dean Nursing/Health Prof ....Vacant
79 Acad Dean Humanities/Art & Design ....Mr. Henry Y. TANAKA
88 Academic Dean College Readiness ....Ms. Beverly J. STANBROUGH
60 Int Acad Dean English/Lit/ Commun ....Ms. Beverly J. STANBROUGH
50 Acad Dean Bus & Info Technologies ....Mr. Tom M. HENDRICKS

Oakland Community College Auburn Hills (F)

2900Featherstone Road, Auburn Hills MI 48326-2845
Telephone: (248) 232-4100 Identification: 770281
Accreditation: &NH

† Branch campus of Oakland Community College, Bloomfield Hills, MI.

Oakland Community College Highland Lakes (G)

7350 Cooley Lake Road, Waterford MI 48327-4187
Telephone: (248) 942-3100 Identification: 770285
Accreditation: &NH

† Branch campus of Oakland Community College, Bloomfield Hills, MI.

Oakland Community College Orchard Ridge (H)

27055 Orchard Lake Road,
Farmington Hills MI 48334-4579
Telephone: (248) 522-3400 Identification: 770282
Accreditation: &NH

† Branch campus of Oakland Community College, Bloomfield Hills, MI.

Oakland Community College Royal Oak (I)

739 South Washington, Royal Oak MI 48067-3898
Telephone: (248) 246-2400 Identification: 770283
Accreditation: &NH

† Branch campus of Oakland Community College, Bloomfield Hills, MI.

Oakland Community College Southfield (J)

22322 Rutland Drive, Southfield MI 48075-4793
Telephone: (248) 233-2700 Identification: 770284
Accreditation: &NH

† Branch campus of Oakland Community College, Bloomfield Hills, MI.

Oakland University (K)

2200 N. Squirrel Road, Rochester MI 48309-4401
County: Oakland FICE Identification: 002307
Unit ID: 171571
Telephone: (248) 370-2100 Carnegie Class: DRU
FAX Number: N/A Calendar System: Semester
URL: www.oakland.edu
Established: 1957 Annual Undergrad Tuition & Fees (In-State): $11,512
Enrollment: 20,519 Coed
Affiliation or Control: State IRS Status: 501(c)3
Highest Offering: Doctorate
Program: Liberal Arts And General; Teacher Preparatory; Professional

Accreditation: NH, ANEST, BUS, BUSA, CACREP, CS, DANCE, ENG, ENGR, MED, MUS, NURSE, PTA, SPAA, SW, TEAC, THEA

01 President .... Dr. George W. HYND
04 Executive Asst to the President .... Vacant
05 Sr VP Academic Affairs/Provost .... Dr. James P. LENITNI
32 VP Student Affairs .... Mr. Glenn MCINTOSH
30 VP Dev/Alumni Community Engagement .... Mr. Geoffrey C. UPWARD
10 VP Finance & Administration .... Mr. John W. BEAGHAN
86 VP Government & Comm Relations .... Ms. Rochelle A. BLACK
12 Exec Dir OU Macomb .... Julie TRUBE
66 Interim Dean of Nursing .... Dr. Gary MOORE
54 Dean Engineer & Computer Science .... Dr. Louay M. CHAMRA
76 Interim Dean School Health Sciences .... Dr. Richard J. ROZEK
53 Dean Educ & Human Services .... Dr. Jon MARGERUM-LEYS
49 Dean College Arts & Sciences .... Dr. Kevin J. CORCORAN
50 Dean School of Business Admin .... Dr. Michael A. MAZZEO
63 Dean School of Medicine .... Dr. Robert FOLBERG
08 Interim Dean of the Library .... Ms. Nancy T. BULGARELLI
20 Senior Associate Provost .... Dr. Susan M. AWBREY
46 Interim Vice Provost Research .... Dr. Arik DVIR
24 Asst VP Classrm Spprt/Instruct Tech .... Mr. George T. PREISINGER
20 Asst VP Academic Affairs .... Ms. Peggy S. COOKE
88 Dir Ctr Excellence Tchg Lrng .... Dr. Judith ABLESER
88 Dir Eye Research Institute .... Dr. Frank GIBLIN
88 Director FAJRI .... Dr. Sayed NASSAR
21 Asst VP Finance & Administration .... Mr. Thomas P. LEMARBE
18 Assoc VP Facilities Mgmt .... Mr. Terry STOLLSTEIMER
15 Asst VP University Human Resources .... Mr. Ronald P. WATSON
102 Interim Campaign Director .... Ms. Angie SCHMUCKER
35 Asst VP SA/Dean Students .... Ms. Nancy A. SCHMITZ
19 Chief of Police .... Mr. Mark B. GORDON
06 Registrar .... Mr. Steven J. SHABLIN
44 Interim Exec Dir Planned/Annual Giv .... Ms. Kelly N. BRAULT
37 Director of Financial Aid .... Ms. Cindy L. HERMSEN
29 Dir Alumni Cmty Engagement .... Ms. Sue HELDEROP
27 Vice President Univ Comm & Mktg .... Mr. John O. YOUNG
41 Director of Athletics .... Mr. Jeffrey F. KONYA
28 Dir Inclus Intercu Initiatives/Atty .... Ms. Joi M. CUNNINGHAM
39 Director of University Housing .... Mr. James R. ZENTMEYER
36 Director Career Services .... Mr. Wayne J. THIBODEAU
38 Director Counseling Center .... Dr. David J. SCHWARTZ
85 Director International Students .... Mr. David J. ARCHBOLD
88 Director Disability Support Svcs .... Ms. Linda G. SISSON
96 Purchasing Manager .... Ms. Maria E. EBNER-SMITH
88 Sr Adv to Pres/Div Equity Incl .... Dr. Patricia A. DOLLY
106 Int Dir E-Learning/Instr Support .... Mr. John COUGHLIN
108 Dir Inst Research & Assessment .... Ms. Laura A. SCHARTMAN
101 VP Legal Affairs & General Counsel .... Mr. Victor A. ZAMBARDI
13 Chief Information Officer .... Ms. Theresa M. ROWE
84 Int Asst VP Student Affs/Admissions .... Ms. Dawn M. AUBRY
58 Dean Graduate Education .... Dr. Claudia A. PETRESCU

Olivet College (A)

320 S Main Street, Olivet MI 49076-9406
County: Eaton — FICE Identification: 002308
Unit ID: 171599
Telephone: (269) 749-7000 — Carnegie Class: Bac/Diverse
FAX Number: (269) 749-7600 — Calendar System: Semester
URL: www.olivetcollege.edu
Established: 1844 — Annual Undergrad Tuition & Fees: $24,816
Enrollment: 1,058 — Coed
Affiliation or Control: Independent Non-Profit — IRS Status: 501(c)3
Highest Offering: Master's
Program: Liberal Arts And General; Teacher Preparatory
Accreditation: NH, TEAC

01 President .... Dr. Steven M. COREY
05 Provost and Dean of the College .... Dr. Maria DAVIS
10 Vice Pres Finance/Administration .... Ms. Jackie LOOSER
84 Vice Pres Enrollment Management .... Vacant
32 Vice President/Dean Student Life .... Dr. Linda LOGAN
30 Vice Pres Advancement .... Mr. William HULL
13 Asst Vice President Technology .... Mr. Suresh ACHARYA
06 Registrar .... Ms. Leslie SULLIVAN
41 Interim Athletic Director .... Mr. Ryan SHOCKEY
42 Director of Campus Ministries .... Mr. Michael F. FALES
36 Int Dir Career Services Network .... Ms. Joanne WILLIAMS
37 Director of Student Financial Aid .... Ms. Libby JEAN
18 Director of Facilities .... Mr. Frank SCHUMACHER
94 Director of Women's Resource Center .... Ms. Cynthia NOYES
39 Student Housing .... Ms. Tamyra WALTERS
15 Director of Human Resources .... Mrs. Terri GLASGOW
29 Director of Alumni Engagement .. Ms. Martha MASON JENNINGS
04 Administrative Asst to President .... Ms. Barbara SPENCER

Puritan Reformed Theological Seminary (B)

2965 Leonard St NE, Grand Rapids MI 49525
County: Kent — Identification: 667099
Telephone: (616) 977-0599 — Carnegie Class: Not Classified
FAX Number: (616) 285-3246 — Calendar System: Semester
URL: www.prts.edu
Established: 1995 — Annual Graduate Tuition & Fees: $7,500
Enrollment: 82 — Coed
Affiliation or Control: Independent Non-Profit — IRS Status: 501(c)3
Highest Offering: Master's; No Undergraduates
Program: Religious Emphasis
Accreditation: THEOL

01 President .... Dr. Joel R. BEEKE
05 Academic Dean/VP Academic Affairs .... Dr. Michael BARRETT
06 Registrar .... Mr. Jonathon BEEKE
10 Vice President for Operations .... Mr. Henk KLEYN
58 Dean of Stu-dents/Spir-i-tual Form .... Rev. Mark KELDERMAN
04 Administrative Asst to President .... Ms. Ann C. DYKEMA
26 Chief Public Relations/Marketing .... Mr. Chris HANNA
07 Director of Admissions .... Mr. Jonathon D. BEEKE
08 Head Librarian .... Mrs. Laura LADWIG
106 Dir Online Education/E-learning .... Mr. Chris ENGELSMA

Robert B. Miller College (C)

450 North Avenue, Battle Creek MI 49017-3397
County: Calhoun — FICE Identification: 040943
Unit ID: 448804
Telephone: (269) 660-8021 — Carnegie Class: Bac/Diverse
FAX Number: (269) 565-2180 — Calendar System: Semester
URL: www.millercollege.edu
Established: 2002 — Annual Undergrad Tuition & Fees: $11,970
Enrollment: 276 — Coed
Affiliation or Control: Independent Non-Profit — IRS Status: 501(c)3
Highest Offering: Baccalaureate
Program: Liberal Arts And General; Teacher Preparatory; Business Emphasis
Accreditation: NH, NURSE, @TEAC

01 President .... Dr. Evon WALTERS
05 Vice President/Provost .... Ms. Gloria ROBERTSON
10 Chief Financial Officer .... Mr. John COAKES
06 Registrar/Teacher Cert Officer .... Ms. Jackie WASHBURN
07 VP Admissions & Enrollment Svcs .... Mr. Jeremy GIBBONS

Rochester College (D)

800 W Avon Road, Rochester Hills MI 48307-2764
County: Oakland — FICE Identification: 002288
Unit ID: 170967
Telephone: (248) 218-2000 — Carnegie Class: Bac/Diverse
FAX Number: (248) 218-2025 — Calendar System: Semester
URL: www.rc.edu
Established: 1959 — Annual Undergrad Tuition & Fees: $21,263
Enrollment: 1,113 — Coed
Affiliation or Control: Independent Non-Profit — IRS Status: 501(c)3
Highest Offering: Master's
Program: Liberal Arts And General
Accreditation: NH, NURSE, @TEAC

00 Chancellor .... Dr. Rubel SHELLY
01 President .... Dr. John N. TYSON
05 Provost .... Dr. Brian STOGNER
07 Vice Pres Admissions/Athletic Dir .... Mr. Klint PLEASANT
30 Vice President Development .... Mr. Tom RELLINGER
10 Chief Financial Officer .... Mr. Mark VANRHEENEN
07 Dean of Enrollment .... Ms. Mackenzie RELLINGER
21 Controller .... Ms. Susan IDE
18 Director Operational Support .... Mr. Mark JOHNSON
50 Int Dir School of Bus/Prof Studies .... Mr. Danny CAGNET
79 Dean School of Humanities .... Dr. David KELLER
15 Director of Human Resources .... Ms. Lindsey M. DUNFEE
26 Dir of Communication Services .... Mr. Elliot JONES
32 Dean of Students .... Ms. Candace CAIN
37 Director of Student Financial Svcs .... Ms. Jessica BRISTOW
08 Director of Library Services .... Ms. Alison KELLER
06 Registrar .... Ms. Rebekah PINCHBACK
108 Director of Assessment .... Mr. J. Mark MANRY
29 Director of Alumni/Bookstore Mgr .... Mr. Larry STEWART
35 Assoc Dean of Students/Campus Life .... Mr. Cole YOAKUM
41 Director of Athletics .... Mr. Klint PLEASANT
42 Campus Minister .... Mr. Chris SHIELDS
19 Director of Safety & Security .... Mr. Shawn WESTAWAY
04 Assistant to the President .... Ms. Karen HART

Sacred Heart Major Seminary (E)

2701 Chicago Boulevard, Detroit MI 48206-1799
County: Wayne — FICE Identification: 002313
Unit ID: 172033
Telephone: (313) 883-8500 — Carnegie Class: Spec/Faith
FAX Number: (313) 868-6440 — Calendar System: Semester
URL: www.shms.edu
Established: 1919 — Annual Undergrad Tuition & Fees: $17,507
Enrollment: 424 — Coed
Affiliation or Control: Roman Catholic — IRS Status: 501(c)3
Highest Offering: Master's
Program: Liberal Arts And General; Professional
Accreditation: NH, THEOL

01 Rector & President .... Msgr. Todd LAJINESS
32 Vice Rector/Dean of Seminarians .... Rev. Gerard BATTERSBY
05 Dean of Studies .... Rev. Timothy LABOE
73 Dean of the Institute for Ministry .... Mrs. Janet DIAZ
10 Director Finance/Treasurer .... Ms. Ann Marie CONNOLLY
06 Registrar .... Mr. John MELDRUM
35 Director Undergraduate Seminarians .... Rev. Stephen BURR
38 Graduate Spiritual Director .... Rev. Daniel TRAPP
08 Library Director .... Mr. Christopher SPILKER
38 Undergraduate Spiritual Director .... Rev. Robert SPEZIA
58 Dir Graduate Pastoral Formation .... Rev. John VANDENAKKER
13 Dir of Educational Technology .... Mr. Chad HUGHES
30 Dir Development/Stewardship .... Mr. David KELLEY

18 Facilities Director .... Mr. John DUNCAN
07 Director of Admissions .... Mrs. Tamra HULL FROMM

Saginaw Chippewa Tribal College (F)

2274 Enterprise Drive, Mount Pleasant MI 48858-2335
County: Isabella — FICE Identification: 037723
Unit ID: 441070
Telephone: (989) 775-4123 — Carnegie Class: Tribal
FAX Number: (989) 775-4528 — Calendar System: Semester
URL: www.sagchip.edu
Established: 1998 — Annual Undergrad Tuition & Fees: $2,040
Enrollment: 141 — Coed
Affiliation or Control: Tribal Control — IRS Status: 501(c)3
Highest Offering: Associate Degree
Program: 2-Year Principally Bachelor's Creditable
Accreditation: NH

01 President .... Ms. Carla SINEWAY
05 Dean of Instruction .... Mr. Andrew WAGNER
32 Dean of Student Services .... Mr. Nathaniel LAMBERTSON
07 Admissions Officer/Registrar .... Ms. Amanda FLAUGHER
37 Financial Aid Officer .... Ms. Patricia ALONZO
09 Dean of Research .... Ms. Tracy REED
25 Grants and Special Projects Coord .... Ms. Amanda GEORGE-DYE

Saginaw Valley State University (G)

7400 Bay Road, University Center MI 48710-0001
County: Saginaw — FICE Identification: 002314
Unit ID: 172051
Telephone: (989) 964-4000 — Carnegie Class: Master's L
FAX Number: (989) 964-0180 — Calendar System: Semester
URL: www.svsu.edu
Established: 1963 — Annual Undergrad Tuition & Fees (In-State): $8,969
Enrollment: 9,829 — Coed
Affiliation or Control: State — IRS Status: 501(c)3
Highest Offering: Doctorate
Program: Liberal Arts And General; Teacher Preparatory; Professional; Business Emphasis
Accreditation: NH, BUS, CAATE, CEA, ENG, MT, MUS, NURSE, OT, SW, TED

01 President .... Dr. Donald J. BACHAND
05 Provost/VP Academic Affairs .... Dr. Deborah R. HUNTLEY
10 Exec VP Admin & Business Affairs .... Mr. James G. MULADORE
30 Executive Director Alumni Relations .... Mr. James P. DWYER
32 Assoc Prov Student Affs/Dn Students .... Ms. Merry Jo BRANDIMORE
86 Director of External Affairs .... Dr. Eugene J. HAMILTON
28 Spec Asst to Pres/Diversity Pgms .... Dr. Mamie T. THORNS
04 Assoc Dean Arts/Behavioral Sciences .... Dr. Carlos RAMET
45 Assoc Provost Intl/Advanced Studies .... Dr. Marc H. PERETZ
21 Assoc VP Admin & Business Affairs .... Mr. Ronald E. PORTWINE
18 AVP Campus Facilities Plng/Const .... Mr. Stephen L. HOCQUARD
21 Business & Financial Analyst .... Ms. Susan L. CRANE
13 Exec Dir Information Tech Svcs .... Mr. James M. MAHER
07 Director of Admissions .... Ms. Jennifer K. PAHL
06 Registrar .... Dr. Clifford DORNE
36 Director Career Services .... Mr. Michael W. MAJOR
21 Director Business Services .... Ms. Connie J. SCHWEITZER
88 University Ombudsman .... Mr. Richard P. THOMPSON
29 Director of Alumni Relations .... Mr. Kevin J. SCHULTZ
14 Dir Enterprise Applications & Devel .... Mr. Patrick C. SAMOLEWSKI
31 Dir Media & Community Relations .... Mr. J. J BOEHM
08 Int Dir of Melvin J Zahnow Library .... Ms. Anita DEY
25 Dir Sponsored Pgms/IRB Rsrch Compl .... Ms. Janet D. RENTSCH
15 Director of Human Resources .... Dr. Jack VANHOORELBEKE
19 Chief of University Police .... Mr. Ronald E. TREPKOWSKI
37 Director Scholarships/Financial Aid .... Mr. Robert L. LEMUEL
22 Director of Disability Services .... Ms. Monica B. REYES
38 Dir Student Counseling Center .... Mr. Eddie V. JONES
41 Athletic Director .... Mr. Michael E. WATSON
44 Director of Annual Giving .... Mr. Joseph A. VOGL
53 Dean College of Education .... Mr. Craig DOUGLAS
88 Dir Enviornmental Health & Safety .... Mr. Robert J. TUTSOCK
88 Exec Dir Ctr for Business/Econ Dev .... Mr. Harold L. LEAVER
93 Director Multicultural Services .... Mr. Shawn WILSON
20 Associate Provost .... Dr. David M. CALLEJO PEREZ
102 Executive Director SVSU Foundation .... Mr. Andrew J. BETHUNE
40 Bookstore Manager .... Mr. Chris J. PAWLOSKI
96 Purchasing Manager .... Mr. Joshua M. WEBB
35 Asst Dean Stdnt Life/Leadership Pgm .... Mr. Bryan E. CRAINER
49 Exec Asst to Dean Arts/Behav Sci .... Dr. Joni M. BOYE-BEAMAN
50 Dean Business & Management .... Dr. Rama YELKUR
88 Professor of English .... Dr. Mary R. HARMON
76 Dean of Health & Human Services .... Dr. Judith P. RULAND
54 Assoc Dean College of Sci/Engr/Tech .... Dr. Andrew M. CHUBB

St. Clair County Community College (H)

323 Erie Street, PO Box 5015, Port Huron MI 48061-5015
County: St. Clair — FICE Identification: 002310
Unit ID: 172291
Telephone: (810) 984-3881 — Carnegie Class: Assoc/Pub-S-SC
FAX Number: (810) 984-4730 — Calendar System: Semester
URL: www.sc4.edu
Established: 1923 — Annual Undergrad Tuition & Fees (In-District): $3,546
Enrollment: 4,127 — Coed
Affiliation or Control: Local — IRS Status: 501(c)3
Highest Offering: Associate Degree
Program: Occupational; 2-Year Principally Bachelor's Creditable

Accreditation: NH, ADNUR, RAD

01 President .... Dr. Kevin A. POLLOCK
04 Executive Assistant to President .... Ms. Mary L. HAWTIN
10 Vice Pres Administrative Services .... Mr. Kirk A. KRAMER
05 Vice President Academic Services .... Mrs. Denise M. MCNEIL
32 Vice President Student Services .... Mr. Pete LACEY
23 Director of Health/Human Services .... Ms. Cindy NICHOLSON
37 Dir of Financial Assistance/Svcs .... Ms. Josephine R. CASSAR
06 Registrar .... Ms. Carrie BEARSS
21 Controller .... Ms. Mary K. BRUNNER
41 Dir Campus Activities/Athletics .... Mr. Dale R. VOS
88 Dean of Instructional Support .... Ms. Linda DAVIS
08 Director of Library Services .... Mr. Christopher RENNIE
20 Associate Dean .... Mr. James NEESE

Schoolcraft College (A)

18600 Haggerty Road, Livonia MI 48152-2696
County: Wayne FICE Identification: 002315
Unit ID: 172200
Telephone: (734) 462-4400 Carnegie Class: Assoc/Pub-S-SC
FAX Number: (734) 462-4507 Calendar System: Semester
URL: www.schoolcraft.edu
Established: 1961 Annual Undergrad Tuition & Fees (In-District): $3,680
Enrollment: 11,542 Coed
Affiliation or Control: Local IRS Status: 501(c)3
Highest Offering: Baccalaureate
Program: Occupational; 2-Year Principally Bachelor's Creditable
Accreditation: NH, ACFEI, ADNUR, CAHIIM, MAC

01 President .... Dr. Conway A. JEFFRESS
10 Vice Pres/Chief Financial Officer .... Mr. Glenn CERNY
05 Vice Pres/CAO .... Mr. Richard WEINKAUF
32 Vice Pres/Chief Student Affs Ofcr .... Ms. Cheryl M. HAGEN
49 Dean Liberal Arts & Sciences .... Dr. Cheryl HAWKINS
75 Dean Occupational Prog/Econ Dev .... Dr. Robert LEADLEY
20 Dean of Educ & Lrng Support .... Dr. Deborah DAIEK
88 Assoc Dean College Centers .... Dr. Bonnie HECKARD
51 Assoc Dean Cont Educ/Prof Develop .... Dr. Leslie PETTY
38 Assoc Dean Counseling/Student Sppt .... Dr. Michael OLIVER
11 Assoc Dean Opers/Curriculum/Assess .... Ms. Cindy CICCHELLI
84 Assoc Dean Enroll Mgmt/Student Rels .... Mr. Martin HEATOR
53 Assoc Dean Education Programs .... Dr. Dennis GENIG
81 Assoc Dean Sciences .... Mr. Charles HAYES
88 Assoc Dean Public Safety Programs .... Mr. Gerald CHAMPAGNE
88 Assoc Dean Advising & Partnerships .... Ms. Laurie KATTUAH-SNYDER
72 Asst Dean Occupational Programs .... Ms. Amy JONES
15 Exec Director of Human Resources .... Ms. Laura SENSING
06 Registrar .... Ms. Nicole WILSON-FENNELL
37 Exec Dir Student Financial Services .... Ms. Regina MOSLEY
19 Campus Police Authority Chief .... Mr. Steven KAUFMAN
96 Dir of Purchasing/Business Ops .... Mr. Matthew WILSON
21 Controller/Director of Finance .... Mr. Jon LAMB
27 Chief Information Officer .... Mr. Patrick TURNER
13 Exec Dir of Information Technology .... Mr. Christopher DENNY
07 Assoc Dean Admissions/Stdnt Engage .... Ms. Stacey STOVER
88 Exec Dir Info Security & Networking .... Mr. Jeffrey BORTON
88 Exec Dir of Enterprise Applications .... Ms. Laura CULLEN
04 Executive Asst to President .... Ms. Karla W. FRENTZOS
18 Exec Dir/Facilities Operations .... Mr. John WRIGHT
26 Exec Dir Marketing & Advancement .... Mr. Frank RUGGIRELLO
41 Director of Athletics .... Mr. Sidney FOX
44 Director of Development .... Ms. Elizabeth KOHLER
91 Director Administrative Systems .... Mr. Scott HEUSNER

Siena Heights University (B)

1247 Siena Heights Drive, Adrian MI 49221-1796
County: Lenawee FICE Identification: 002316
Unit ID: 172264
Telephone: (517) 263-0731 Carnegie Class: Master's M
FAX Number: (517) 264-7704 Calendar System: Semester
URL: www.sienaheights.edu
Established: 1919 Annual Undergrad Tuition & Fees: $23,750
Enrollment: 2,058 Coed
Affiliation or Control: Roman Catholic IRS Status: 501(c)3
Highest Offering: Beyond Master's But Less Than Doctorate
Program: Liberal Arts And General; Teacher Preparatory; Professional; Fine Arts Emphasis
Accreditation: NH, ART, NURSE, SW, TEAC

01 President .... Dr. Peg ALBERT, OP
10 Sr Vice Pres for Business/Finance .... Dr. J. Lee JOHNSON
30 Vice President for Advancement .... Mr. Mitchell P. BLONDE
05 Vice President for Academic Affairs .... Dr. Sharon R. WEBER, OP
84 Vice Pres of Enrollment Mgmt Svcs .... Mr. George WOLF
44 Assoc Vice Pres Advancement .... Mrs. Jennifer H. CHURCH
58 Dean of Graduate Studies .... Dr. Linda PETTIT
107 Dean College Professional Studies .... Mrs. Deborah CARTER
49 Dean College of Arts and Science .... Dr. Mark SCHERSTEN
32 Dean for Students .... Mr. Michael ORLANDO
06 Registrar .... Ms. Joy GARROW
07 Director of Admissions .... Ms. Trudy MOHRE
08 Director of Library .... Ms. Jennifer DEAN
13 Chief Information Officer .... Mr. Robert C. METZ
41 Director of Athletics .... Mr. Frederick M. SMITH
15 Human Resource Director .... Mr. Michael L. KARABETSOS
42 Director of Campus Ministry .... Fr. John GRACE
38 Director of Counseling Services .... Mrs. Sandy MORLEY
20 Director of Academic Advising .... Ms. Wiona PORATH
18 Supt of Buildings & Grounds .... Mr. Brian BERTRAM
09 Director of Institutional Research .... Mr. Jason HARTZ
39 Director of Residence Life .... Ms. Rachel RICKINGER
19 Director of Campus Security .... Mrs. Cindy A. BIRDWELL
23 Director of Health Services .... Ms. Marlene WALDVOGEL
29 Director of Alumni Relations .... Mrs. Jennifer H. CHURCH
36 Director of Career Services .... Mrs. Melissa A. GROWDEN
44 Director of Donor Relations .... Mrs. Jenn BROOKET
28 Director of Immersion & Diversity .... Mr. Tom PUSZCZEWICZ
88 Dir of Integrated Univ Marketing .... Mr. Doug GOODNOUGH
37 Director Student Financial Aid .... Mrs. Lori KOSARUE
21 Controller .... Ms. Mary KRUSE
44 Coordinator of Annual Fund .... Mrs. Kate HAMILTON
04 Executive Assistant to President .... Ms. Deborah KELLER

South University (C)

41555 Twelve Mile Road, Novi MI 48377
Telephone: (248) 675-0200 Identification: 770914
Accreditation: &SC, ACBSP, NURSE, PTAA

† Branch campus of South University, Savannah, GA.

Southwestern Michigan College (D)

58900 Cherry Grove Road, Dowagiac MI 49047-9793
County: Cass FICE Identification: 002317
Unit ID: 172307
Telephone: (269) 782-1000 Carnegie Class: Assoc/Pub-R-M
FAX Number: (269) 782-8414 Calendar System: Semester
URL: www.swmich.edu
Established: 1964 Annual Undergrad Tuition & Fees (In-District): $5,775
Enrollment: 2,567 Coed
Affiliation or Control: State/Local IRS Status: 501(c)3
Highest Offering: Associate Degree
Program: Occupational; 2-Year Principally Bachelor's Creditable
Accreditation: NH, CAHIIM

01 President .... Dr. David MATHEWS
100 Chief of Staff .... Mr. Thomas ATKINSON
10 Vice President/Chief Business Ofcr .... Ms. Susan COULSTON
13 Vice President/Chf Information Ofcr .... Mr. Ronald YOUNG
05 Vice President of Instruction .... Dr. David FLEMING
32 Vice President of Student Services .... Ms. Eileen CROUSE
35 Executive Dir Student Services .... Ms. Angela PALSAK
49 Dean of Arts and Sciences .... Dr. Scott TOPPING
50 Dean NAC/School of Business .... Dr. Stacy HORNER
66 Dean School Nursing/Human Services .... Ms. Rebecca JELLISON
88 Dir of Acad Assess & Testing Svcs .... Ms. Charlotte MCGOWAN
18 Director of Buildings & Grounds .... Mr. John EBERHART
44 Director of Development .... Ms. Eileen TONEY
88 Dir of Educational Talent Srch Pgm .... Ms. Amy ANDERSON
07 Director of Admissions .... Mr. Jason SMITH
35 Director of EXCEL .... Ms. Laura SKILLINGS
37 Director of Financial Aid .... Ms. Christine PASSER
15 Director of Human Resources .... Ms. Kate DORNER
09 Director of Institutional Research .... Dr. Angela EVANS
08 Director of Library Services .... Ms. Colleen WELSCH
06 Interim Director Records/Registrar .... Ms. Christine PASSER
39 Director of Student Housing .... Mr. Jason WILT
21 Controller .... Ms. Michelle KITE
88 Manager of Accounting .... Ms. Christy MANGUS
26 Manager of Marketing .... Ms. Michelle BOGUE
88 Manager of Student Activity Center .... Ms. Bethany WHITTAKER

Southwestern Michigan College Niles Area Campus (E)

33890 U.S. Highway 12, Niles MI 49120
Telephone: (800) 456-8675 Identification: 770286
Accreditation: &NH

† Branch campus of Southwestern Michigan College, Dowagiac, MI.

Spring Arbor University (F)

106 E Main Street, Spring Arbor MI 49283-9799
County: Jackson FICE Identification: 002318
Unit ID: 172334
Telephone: (517) 750-1200 Carnegie Class: Master's L
FAX Number: (517) 750-6620 Calendar System: 4/1/4
URL: www.arbor.edu
Established: 1873 Annual Undergrad Tuition & Fees: $24,910
Enrollment: 3,732 Coed
Affiliation or Control: Free Methodist IRS Status: 501(c)3
Highest Offering: Master's
Program: Liberal Arts And General
Accreditation: NH, MUS, NURSE, SW, TEAC

01 University President .... Dr. Brent ELLIS
05 Provost/Chief Academic Officer .... Dr. Kimberly RUPERT
03 Excutive Vice President .... Dr. Douglas A. WILCOXSON
10 Vice Pres Finance & Administration .... Mr. Keven W. ROSE
32 VP Student Success & Calling .... Dr. Kimberly K. HAYWORTH
100 Chief of Staff .... Mr. Damon M. SEACOTT
07 VP Enroll & Marketing .... Mr. Malachi D. CRANE
12 Assistant Provost SAU Global .... Dr. Linda G. SHERRILL
15 Director of Human Resources .... Mrs. Melissa MONTGOMERY
91 Chief Technology Officer .... Vacant
20 Associate Provost .... Mr. Rod S. STEWART
30 Assistant VP Advancement Operations .... Mrs. Rhonda R. SAURBEK
49 Dean School Arts & Sciences .... Vacant
50 Dean Gainey School of Business .... Dr. Caleb K. CHAN
53 Dean School of Education .... Dr. Reuben A. RUBIO
88 Dean School of Human Services .... Mrs. Tamara L. DINDOFFER
35 Asst VP Student Development .... Mr. Dan VANDERHILL
06 Registrar .... Vacant
84 Director of Enrollment Operations .... Mrs. Jill M. RAYMOND
21 Assistant VP Financial Services .... Mrs. Dawn I. SCHNITKEY
44 Executive Director of Development .... Mrs. Linda SCHAUB
41 Athletic Director .... Mr. Ryan T. COTTINGHAM
42 Chaplain .... Mr. Ronald L. KOPICKO
37 Director of Financial Aid .... Mr. Herbert K. ROTICH
09 Director Institutional Research .... Mr. Thomas P. KORMAN
108 Director of Assessment .... Vacant
08 Director Library .... Mr. Robert D. BOLTON
18 Director of Physical Plant .... Mr. Larry OUSLEY
89 Director Retention & Fresh Programs .... Vacant
104 Director Cross Cultural Studies .... Mrs. Diane L. KURTZ
23 Exec Dir Student Health/Wellness .... Mrs. Mary A. RICK
31 Asst Dean Students/Dir of Outreach .... Vacant
39 Asst Dean Students/Dir of Housing .... Mr. Robert C. PRATT
36 Director Career Svcs/Acad Advising .... Vacant
19 Director Campus Safety .... Mr. Scott L. KREBILL
106 Assoc Dean External/SAUonline .... Mr. Gary R. TUCKER
28 Director Intercultural Relations .... Mr. Eric A. BEDA
29 Director Alumni Relations .... Mrs. Irene L. PRICE
105 Web Architect .... Mr. Peter J. SHACKELFORD
04 Dir Operations Pres/Provost Office .... Mrs. Sarah R. CRANE

SS. Cyril and Methodius Seminary (G)

3535 Indian Trail, Orchard Lake MI 48324-1623
County: Oakland FICE Identification: 037384
Unit ID: 260211
Telephone: (248) 683-0310 Carnegie Class: Not Classified
FAX Number: (248) 738-6735 Calendar System: Semester
URL: www.sscms.edu
Established: 1885 Annual Graduate Tuition & Fees: $17,372
Enrollment: 44 Coed
Affiliation or Control: Roman Catholic IRS Status: 501(c)3
Highest Offering: Master's; No Undergraduates
Program: Professional
Accreditation: THEOL

01 Rector/President .... RevMsg. Thomas MACHALSKI
05 Interim Academic Dean .... Rev. Leonard OBLOY
06 Registrar .... Ms. Joanna OLEJNICZAK-CAUSHAJ

University of Detroit Mercy (H)

4001 W McNichols Road, Detroit MI 48221-3038
County: Wayne FICE Identification: 002323
Unit ID: 169716
Telephone: (313) 993-1000 Carnegie Class: Master's L
FAX Number: (313) 993-1229 Calendar System: Semester
URL: www.udmercy.edu
Established: 1877 Annual Undergrad Tuition & Fees: $38,626
Enrollment: 4,944 Coed
Affiliation or Control: Roman Catholic IRS Status: 501(c)3
Highest Offering: Doctorate
Program: Liberal Arts And General; Teacher Preparatory; Professional
Accreditation: NH, ANEST, ARCPA, BUS, CACREP, CLPSY, DENT, DH, ENG, NURSE, SW, TEAC

01 President .... Dr. Antoine M. GARIBALDI
05 Provost and VP for Academic Affairs .... Ms. Pamela ZARKOWSKI
10 VP for Business & Finance and CFO . Mr. Vincent ABATEMARCO
30 VP for University Advancement .... Ms. Barbara MILBAUER
84 VP Enrollment & Student Affairs .... Ms. Deborah STIEFFEL
101 University Secretary & Senior Atty .... Ms. Monica BARBOUR
18 Assoc Vice Pres Facil Management .... Ms. Tamara BATCHELLER
15 Associate Vice Pres Human Resources .... Mr. Steven J. NELSON
26 Assoc VP Marketing & Public Affairs .... Ms. Liz PATTERSON
13 Associate Vice President ITS .... Mr. Edward TRACY, II
06 Associate VP/Registrar .... Ms. Diane M. PRAET
44 Exec Director of Annual Giving .... Ms. Ann FISHER
88 Exec Director of Major Gifts .... Ms. Nikki BORGES
32 Dean of Students .... Ms. Monica WILLIAMS
08 Dean of Libraries .... Ms. Margaret AUER
09 Interim Dir Institutional Research .... Ms. Shelley WAGNON
37 Director Scholarships & Aid .... Ms. Jenny MCALONAN
35 Associate Director of Student Life .... Ms. Dorothy STEWART
41 Director of Athletics .... Mr. Robert VOWELS
49 Dean College of Liberal Arts/Ed .... Dr. Mark DENHAM
61 Dean School of Law .... Ms. Phyllis CROCKER
54 Dean College Engineering & Science .... Dr. Gary KULECK
48 Dean School of Architecture .... Mr. William WITTIG
50 Dean Col Business Admin .... Dr. Joseph EISENHAUER
52 Dean School of Dentistry .... Dr. Mert AKSU
76 Dean CHP/Nursing .... Dr. Christine PACINI
88 Dean Coop Education/Career Ctr .... Ms. Sheryl JOHNSON-ROULHAC
39 Director Residence Life .... Ms. Lanae GILL
04 Exec Asst to the President .... Ms. Lisa MACDONNELL
85 Dir of International Services .... Ms. Weihong SUN
38 Director of Wellness Center .... Ms. Annmarie SILVERI
92 Director of Honors Program .... Mr. J. Todd HIBBARD
96 Director of Procurement Services .... Ms. Tina A. MAITLAND
88 Coordinator of Advancement Systems .... Ms. Stephanie LANDERS
07 Director of Admissions .... Ms. Tyra ROUNDS
108 Director Institutional Assessment .... Dr. Elizabeth ROBERTS-KIRCHOFF
19 Director Public Safety .... Ms. Letitia WILLIAMS
25 Dir of Sponsored Research .... Ms. Catherine CALDWELL

53 Chair Education Department ... Dr. Lorri MACDONALD
106 Dir Online Education/E-learning ... Ms. Margaret AUER
29 Director Alumni Relations ... Ms. Eileen PAWLOWSKI

University of Detroit Mercy Corktown Campus (A)

2700 Martin Luther King Jr. Blvd, Detroit MI 48208-2576
Telephone: (313) 494-6700　Identification: 770291
Accreditation: &NH

† Branch campus of University of Detroit Mercy, Detroit, MI.

University of Detroit Mercy School of Law (B)

651 E Jefferson Avenue, Detroit MI 48226-4349
Telephone: (313) 596-0200　Identification: 770292
Accreditation: &NH, LAW

† Branch campus of University of Detroit Mercy, Detroit, MI.

University of Michigan-Ann Arbor (C)

500 S. State Street, Ann Arbor MI 48109
County: Washtenaw　FICE Identification: 002325
Unit ID: 170976
Telephone: (734) 764-1817　Carnegie Class: RU/VH
FAX Number: N/A　Calendar System: Trimester
URL: umich.edu
Established: 1817　Annual Undergrad Tuition & Fees (In-State): $13,486
Enrollment: 43,625　Coed
Affiliation or Control: State　IRS Status: 501(c)3
Highest Offering: Doctorate
Program: Liberal Arts And General; Teacher Preparatory; Professional
Accreditation: NH, ART, BUS, CAATE, CLPSY, CS, DANCE, DENT, DH, DIETD, DIETI, ENG, ENGR, HSA, IPSY, LAW, LIB, LSAR, MED, MIDWF, MUS, NURSE, PDPSY, PH, PHAR, PLNG, SW, TEAC

01 President ... Dr. Mark S. SCHLISSEL
05 Provost/Exec VP Academic Affs ... Dr. Martha E. POLLACK
10 Interim Exec VP/CFO ... Mr. Kevin HEGARTY
17 Interim Exec VP for Medical Affairs ... Dr. Marschall S. RUNGE
30 Vice President Development ... Mr. Jerry A. MAY
32 Vice President Student Life ... Dr. E. Royster HARPER
46 Interim Vice President for Research ... Dr. S. Jack HU
86 Vice Pres Governmental Relations ... Ms. Cynthia H. WILBANKS
26 Vice Pres Global Communications ... Ms. Lisa M. RUDGERS
43 Vice Pres/General Counsel ... Mr. Timothy G. LYNCH
101 Vice Pres/Sec of the University ... Ms. Sally J. CHURCHILL
04 Exec Asst to the President ... Ms. Erika J. HRABEC
100 Special Counsel to the Provost ... Ms. Kelly L. CUNNINGHAM
20 Vice Provost Acad/Budget Affairs ... Dr. Alfred FRANZBLAU
20 Vice Provost Acad & Faculty Affairs ... Dr. Lori J. PIERCE
20 Vice Provost Acad & Faculty Affairs ... Dr. Sara B. BLAIR
58 Vice Provost Acad Affs Grad Stds ... Dr. Janet A. WEISS
104 Vice Provost Global & Engaged Educ .. Dr. James P. HOLLOWAY
20 Vice Prov Equity/Inclus & Acad Affs ... Dr. Robert M. SELLERS
20 Vice Prov Dig Educ & Univ Librarian ... Dr. James L. HILTON
09 Assoc Vice Provost & Exec Dir OBP ... Ms. Glenna L. SCHWEITZER
07 Interim Dir UG Admissions ... Ms. Erica L. SANDERS
15 Assoc Vice Provost & Sr Dr Acad HR ... Mr. Jeffery R. FRUMKIN
22 Assoc Vice Prov/Sr Dir Inst Equity ... Mr. Anthony J. WALESBY
18 Assoc VP Facilities/Operations ... Mr. Henry D. BAIER
21 Interim Assoc VP Finance ... Ms. Nancy A. HOBBS
88 Chief Investment Officer ... Mr. Erik LUNDBERG
30 Assoc VP for Development ... Mr. Dondi L. CUPP
17 Assoc VP for Medical Affairs ... Dr. John E. BILLI
46 Assoc VP for Research ... Dr. Volker SICK
46 Assoc VP for Research ... Dr. J. Brian FOWLKES
46 Assoc VP for Research ... Dr. Toni C. ANTONUCCI
46 Assoc VP for Research ... Mr. Daryl C. WEINERT
46 Assoc VP for Research ... Dr. Eric MICHIELSSEN
46 Assoc VP Research ... Mr. Kenneth J. NISBET
46 Assoc VP Research ... Dr. James A. ASHTON-MILLER
35 Assoc VP Student Life/Dean Stdnts ... Ms. Laura B. JONES
35 Assoc VP Student Life ... Ms. Anjali N. ANTURKAR
35 Assoc VP Student Life ... Dr. Simone HIMBEAULT-TAYLOR
35 Assoc VP Student Life ... Mr. Loren J. RULLMAN
16 Assoc VP for Human Resources ... Ms. Laurita E. THOMAS
13 Assoc VP Info Tech/Chief Info Ofcr ... Ms. Laura M. PATTERSON
06 University Registrar ... Mr. Paul A. ROBINSON
96 Interim Dir Procurement Services ... Mr. Colin T. ANDERSON
38 Director Counseling & Psych Service ... Dr. Todd D. SEVIG
39 Director University Housing ... Ms. Linda L. NEWMAN
23 Director University Health Service ... Dr. Robert A. WINFIELD
19 Exec Dir Pub Safety/Security ... Mr. Eddie L. WASHINGTON
37 Exec Director Financial Aid ... Ms. Pamela W. FOWLER
18 Executive Director Plant Operations ... Mr. Richard W. ROBBEN
41 Interim Director of Athletics ... Mr. Jim HACKETT
48 Dean Col Architecture & Urban Plng ... Ms. Monica PONCE DE LEON
49 Dean Col Literature/Science/Arts ... Dr. Andrew D. MARTIN
54 Dean College of Engineering ... Dr. David C. MUNSON
61 Dean Law School ... Mr. Mark D. WEST
63 Dean Medical School ... Dr. James O. WOOLLISCROFT
67 Dean College of Pharmacy ... Dr. James T. DALTON
65 Dean Sch Natural Resrc/Environ ... Dr. Marie L. MIRANDA
64 Dean School Music Theatre & Dance ... Mr. Christopher W. KENDALL
57 Dean School of Art & Design ... Dr. Gunalan L. NADARAJAN
50 Dean School of Business ... Dr. Alison DAVIS-BLAKE
52 Dean School of Dentistry ... Dr. Laurie K. MCCAULEY
53 Dean School of Education ... Dr. Deborah L. BALL
62 Dean School of Information ... Dr. Jeffrey K. MACKIE-MASON
68 Dean School of Kinesiology ... Dr. Ronald F. ZERNICKE
66 Dean School of Nursing ... Dr. Kathleen M. POTEMPA
80 Dean School of Public Policy ... Dr. Susan M. COLLINS
70 Dean School of Social Work ... Dr. Laura LEIN
69 Dean School of Public Health ... Dr. Martin A. PHILBERT
29 President Alumni Association ... Mr. Steve C. GRAFTON

University of Michigan-Dearborn (D)

4901 Evergreen Road, Dearborn MI 48128-1491
County: Wayne　FICE Identification: 002326
Unit ID: 171137
Telephone: (313) 593-5000　Carnegie Class: Master's L
FAX Number: (313) 593-5452　Calendar System: Trimester
URL: www.umd.umich.edu
Established: 1959　Annual Undergrad Tuition & Fees (In-State): $11,562
Enrollment: 9,193　Coed
Affiliation or Control: State　IRS Status: 501(c)3
Highest Offering: Doctorate
Program: Liberal Arts And General; Teacher Preparatory; Professional
Accreditation: NH, BUS, CEA, CS, ENG, TEAC

01 Chancellor ... Dr. Daniel LITTLE
05 Prov/Vice Chanc Academic Affs ... Dr. Catherine A. DAVY
10 Vice Chancellor Business Affairs ... Mr. Jeffrey L. EVANS
84 Interim Vice Chanc Enroll Mgmt ... Mr. Ray E. METZ
30 Vice Chanc Inst Advancement ... Ms. Mallory M. SIMPSON
31 Vice Chanc for External Relations ... Mr. Kenneth KETTENBEIL
21 Director of Financial Services ... Mr. Noel HORNBACHER
06 Registrar ... Ms. Janice LEWIS-BOYD
100 Chief of Staff ... Mr. Ray METZ
26 Director Communications/Marketing ... Ms. Beth MARMARELLI
86 Government Relations Manager ... Mr. Mike LATVIS
15 Director of Human Resources ... Ms. Ana GRBIC
29 Alumni Engagement ... Ms. Peggy PATTISON
20 Associate Provost Undergraduate ... Dr. Mitchel SOLLENBERGER
20 Associate Provost Graduate ... Dr. Ilir MITEZA
13 Director IT Strategy/Operations ... Mr. Robert GOFFENEY
08 Director of Library ... Ms. Elaine LOGAN
09 Director of Institutional Research ... Ms. Roma E. HEANEY
84 Asst VC for Enrollment Management ... Dr. Monica PORTER
07 Director of Admissions ... Ms. Deb PEFFER
37 Director of Financial Aid ... Ms. Katherine ALLEN
38 Interim Director of Counseling ... Dr. Debra HUTTON
36 Director of Career Services ... Ms. Regina M. STORRS
85 Director of International Affairs ... Dr. Monica PORTER
32 Director of Student Engagement ... Ms. Reetha PERANANAMGAM
18 Exec Dir of Facilities Operations ... Ms. Carol GLICK
19 Chief of Police ... Mr. Kevin WILLIAMS
22 Institutional Equity Officer ... Ms. Anita GREEN
28 Asst to Chancellor for Inclusion ... Dr. Ann LAMPKIN-WILLIAMS
49 Dean Col Arts/Science/Letters ... Dr. Martin HERSHOCK
54 Dean Col of Engr/Comp Sci ... Dr. A. W. ENGLAND
50 Dean College of Business ... Dr. Raju BALAKRISHNAN
53 Dean College of Ed/Health/HS ... Dr. Janine JANOSKY
88 Director of Enrollment Research ... Mr. Dan MERIAN
41 Athletic Director ... Mr. Matt BEAUDRY

University of Michigan-Flint (E)

303 E Kearsley Street, Flint MI 48502-1950
County: Genesee　FICE Identification: 002327
Unit ID: 171146
Telephone: (810) 762-3000　Carnegie Class: Master's L
FAX Number: (810) 762-5725　Calendar System: Semester
URL: www.umflint.edu
Established: 1956　Annual Undergrad Tuition & Fees (In-State): $9,936
Enrollment: 8,574　Coed
Affiliation or Control: State　IRS Status: 501(c)3
Highest Offering: Doctorate
Program: Liberal Arts And General; Teacher Preparatory; Professional
Accreditation: NH, ANEST, BUS, CEA, ENG, MUS, NURSE, PTA, RTT, SW, TED

01 Chancellor ... Dr. Susan E. BORREGO
05 Provost/VC Academic Affairs ... Dr. Douglas KNERR
32 Vice Chancellor for Student Affairs ... Dr. Mary Jo S. SEKELSKY
10 Vice Chanc for Business and Finance ... Mr. Greg TEWKSBURY
35 Asst VC for Student Affairs ... Ms. Michelle ROSYNSKY
21 Asst Vice Chanc Business & Finance .. Mr. William C. WEBB, JR.
58 Sr Vice Provost/Dean Grad Pgms ... Dr. Vahid LOTFI
20 Asst Prov/Dean Undergrad Studies ... Dr. Christine WATERS
26 Exec Director University Relations ... Ms. Jennifer HOGAN
86 Director Government Relations ... Mr. David E. LOSSING
28 Int Exec Director Educational Oppty ... Dr. Douglas KNERR
08 Director of Library ... Mr. Robert L. HOUBECK, JR.
06 Registrar ... Ms. Karen A. ARNOULD
07 Admissions Director ... Mr. Jon DAVIDSON
37 Director Financial Aid ... Ms. Lori VEDDER
15 Director Human Res/Affirm Action ... Ms. Beth MANNING
49 Int Dean College Arts & Sciences ... Dr. Susasn GANO-PHILLIPS
50 Dean School of Management ... Dr. Scott JOHNSON
66 Director Nursing Program ... Dr. Margaret ANDREWS
76 Int Dean Sch Health Prof & Studies ... Dr. Keith MORELAND
53 Dean Sch Education & Human Svcs ... Dr. Robert BARNETT
51 Director of Extended Learning ... Ms. Deborah WHITE
19 Director of Public Safety ... Mr. Raymond D. HALL
18 Director Facilities Mgmt/Auxil Svcs ... Mr. George HAKIM
13 Director Info Technology Services ... Mr. Scott ARNST
36 Director Acad Advis & Career Center ... Ms. Aimi MOSS
46 Director of Research ... Dr. Terry VAN ALLEN

21 Director of Financial Svcs & Budget ... Mr. Gerald GLASCO
88 Int Director University Outreach ... Dr. Doug KNERR
30 Exec Dir of Dev and Alumni Relation ... Ms. Linda MOXAM
96 Procurement Agent Senior ... Ms. Brenda ROTH
09 Director of Institutional Analysis ... Ms. Fawn SKARSTEN
38 Director CAPS ... Ms. Tamara MCKAY
39 Director Student Housing ... Vacant
100 Chief of Staff ... Dr. Maria T. BARKER

University of Phoenix Detroit Main Campus (F)

26261 Evergreen Road, Southfield MI 48076-4400
Telephone: (248) 675-3700　Identification: 770211
Accreditation: &NH

† Branch campus of University of Phoenix, Tempe, AZ.

Van Andel Institute Graduate School (G)

333 Bostwick Avenue NE, Grand Rapids MI 49503
County: Kent　Identification: 667085
Telephone: (616) 234-5708　Carnegie Class: Not Classified
FAX Number: (616) 234-5709　Calendar System: Semester
URL: www.vai.org/en/vaei/graduate-school.aspx
Established: 1996　Annual Graduate Tuition & Fees: $25,000
Enrollment: 22　Coed
Affiliation or Control: Independent Non-Profit　IRS Status: 501(c)3
Highest Offering: Doctorate; No Undergraduates
Program: Professional
Accreditation: NH

01 President/Dean of the Graduate Sch . Dr. Steven J. TRIEZENBERG
05 Associate Dean of Graduate School ... Dr. Julie D. TURNER
06 Enrollment and Records Admin ... Ms. Carol RAPPLEY
04 Administrative Asst to President ... Ms. Kristie VANDERHOOF

Walsh College Novi Campus (H)

41500 Gardenbrook Road, Novi MI 48375-1313
Telephone: (248) 349-5454　Identification: 770293
Accreditation: &NH

† Branch campus of Walsh College of Accountancy and Business Administration, Troy, MI.

Walsh College of Accountancy and Business Administration (I)

3838 Livernois Road, Box 7006, Troy MI 48007-7006
County: Oakland　FICE Identification: 004071
Unit ID: 172608
Telephone: (248) 689-8282　Carnegie Class: Spec/Bus
FAX Number: (248) 689-9066　Calendar System: Semester
URL: www.walshcollege.edu
Established: 1922　Annual Undergrad Tuition & Fees: $12,820
Enrollment: 2,753　Coed
Affiliation or Control: Independent Non-Profit　IRS Status: 501(c)3
Highest Offering: Doctorate
Program: Professional; Business Emphasis
Accreditation: NH, ACBSP

01 President & CEO ... Ms. Stephanie W. BERGERON
05 Exec VP/Chief Academic Officer ... Dr. David SHIELDS
10 Vice President/CFO/Treasurer . Ms. Helen C. KIEBA-TOLKSDORF
26 Asst VP/Director of Marketing ... Ms. Brenda MELLER
15 VP/Chief Human Resources/Admin Ofcr ... Ms. Elizabeth A. BARNES
30 Vice President/Chief Devel Officer ... Ms. Audrey OLMSTEAD
04 Exec Assistant to the President ... Vacant
32 Asst VP Student Services/Marketing ... Ms. Victoria R. SCAVONE
106 Director Office of Online Learning ... Mr. Thomas PETZ
20 Director Academic Administration ... Ms. Monique CARDENAS
37 Director Financial Aid ... Ms. Catherine BERRAHOU
18 Director Facilities/Auxiliary Svcs ... Ms. Chris STOUT
21 Controller ... Mr. Ryan KUNZELMAN
07 Director Admissions/Acad Advising ... Ms. Heather RIGBY
06 Director of Records/Registrar ... Ms. Stacy JOHNSON
13 Exec Dir Ofc of Info Technology ... Mr. Jacob KLEIN
12 Director Novi Campus ... Vacant
36 Director Career Services ... Ms. Brenda PAINE
88 Chair Management ... Dr. Sheila R. RONIS
88 Chair Business Comm/Dir DM ... Dr. Linda HAGAN
88 Chair Marketing/Info Systems/QM ... Dr. Michael LEVENS
88 Director Corporate Rel/BLI ... Ms. Janet HUBBARD
88 Dir Center for Entrepreneurship ... Vacant
29 Manager of Alumni Relations ... Vacant
88 Chair Accounting/Taxation ... Ms. Jennifer SANDERSON
88 Chair Finance & Economics ... Mr. Greg TODD

Washtenaw Community College (J)

4800 E Huron River Dr, Ann Arbor MI 48105-4800
County: Washtenaw　FICE Identification: 002328
Unit ID: 172617
Telephone: (734) 973-3300　Carnegie Class: Assoc/Pub-U-SC
FAX Number: (734) 677-5413　Calendar System: Semester
URL: www.wccnet.edu
Established: 1965　Annual Undergrad Tuition & Fees (In-District): $2,424
Enrollment: 12,295　Coed
Affiliation or Control: Local　IRS Status: 501(c)3
Highest Offering: Associate Degree
Program: Occupational; 2-Year Principally Bachelor's Creditable

Accreditation: NH, ACFEI, ADNUR, DA, PTAA, RAD

01 President ... Dr. Rose BELLANCA
10 VP & Chief Financial Officer ... Mr. William JOHNSON
05 VP for Instruction ... Dr. William ABERNETHY
15 VP Human Resources Mgmt ... Mr. Douglas KRUZEL
32 VP Student & Academic Services ... Ms. Linda BLAKEY
18 VP Facilities Devel & Opers ... Mr. Damon FLOWERS
30 Vice Pres of College Advancement ... Ms. Julaine LEDUC
31 VP Economic/Community & College Dev ... Ms. Michelle MUELLER
07 AVP Recruitment & Enrollment ... Dr. Evan MONTAGUE
45 Exec Dir Inst Effect Plng & Accred ... Ms. Julie MORRISON
79 Dean Humanities & Social Sci ... Ms. Dena BLAIR
20 Dean Supp Svcs & Student Advocacy ... Dr. Patricia TAYLOR
62 Dean Learning Resources ... Mr. Victor LIU
50 Dean Business & Computer Tech ... Dr. Kimberly HURNS
81 Dean Math & Natural Science ... Ms. Kristin BRANDEMUEHL
36 Dean Career Svc/UA Programs ... Ms. Marilyn DONHAM
28 Dean Diversity & Inclusion ... Mr. Arnett CHISHOLM
88 Dean Adv Tech/Public Service ... Mr. Brandon TUCKER
13 Chief Information Officer ... Mr. Amin LADHA
10 Controller ... Ms. Lynn MARTIN
96 Dir Budget Purchasing Aux Svcs ... Ms. Barbara FILLINGER
16 Director Human Resource Svcs ... Ms. Christine MIHALY
37 Director Financial Aid ... Ms. Lori TRAPP
09 Director Institutional Research ... Dr. Roger MOURAD
19 Director Safety & Security ... Mr. Jacques DESROSIERS
35 Dir Student Development/Activities ... Mr. Peter LESHKEVICH
84 Dean of Enrollment Management ... Mr. Larry AEILTS
26 Executive Dir of Marketing ... Mr. Bryan FREEMAN
86 Dir of Governement Relations ... Mr. Jason MORGAN
43 General Counsel ... Mr. Larry BARKOFF
03 Exec Associate to President ... Ms. Vanessa BROOKS
04 Executive Admin Asst to President ... Ms. Robin GEMBACZ
100 Chief of Staff ... Dr. Katherine THIROLF

Wayne County Community College District (A)

801 W Fort Street, Detroit MI 48226-3010

County: Wayne FICE Identification: 009230
Unit ID: 172635
Telephone: (313) 496-2600 Carnegie Class: Assoc/Pub-U-MC
FAX Number: (313) 961-9439 Calendar System: Semester
URL: www.wcccd.edu
Established: 1967 Annual Undergrad Tuition & Fees (In-District): $2,780
Enrollment: 26,702 Coed
Affiliation or Control: State/Local IRS Status: 501(c)3
Highest Offering: Associate Degree
Program: Occupational; 2-Year Principally Bachelor's Creditable
Accreditation: NH, DA, DH, EMT, SURGA, SURGT

01 Chancellor ... Dr. Curtis L. IVERY
05 Interim Dist VC Educ Affairs/DL ... Dr. George W. SWAN, III
32 Dist VC Student Svcs/Dual Enrollmnt ... Mr. Brian SINGLETON
51 Dist VC Sch Cont Ed/Wrkforce Dev ... Ms. Shawna FORBES
10 Dist VC Finance & Admin ... Ms. Kim DICARO
15 Dist VC HR/Accountability ... Mr. Mirza F. AHMED
09 Dist VC IE & Info Mgmt ... Ms. Johnesa HODGE
12 Campus President/CAO Downriver ... Mr. Anthony ARMINIAK
12 Campus President/CAO Downtown ... Ms. Denise SHANNON
12 Campus President/CAO Western ... Mr. Michael P. DOTSON
12 Campus President Northwest ... Dr. Letitia UDUMA
12 Campus President/CAO Eastern ... Ms. Mawine DIGGS
88 Dist Asst to Chanc Instr/Stdnt Succ ... Dr. Patrick J. MCNALLY
12 Provost University Center ... Dr. Sandra T. ROBINSON
72 Provost of Learning Technology ... Ms. Kiran SEKHRI
30 Dist VC Institutional Advancement ... Ms. Muna KHOURY

Wayne County Community College District Downriver Campus (B)

21000 Northline Road, Taylor MI 48180

Telephone: (734) 946-3500 Identification: 770297
Accreditation: &NH

† Branch campus of Wayne County Community College District, Detroit, MI.

Wayne County Community College District Downtown Campus (C)

1001 West Fort Street, Detroit MI 48226

Telephone: (313) 496-2758 Identification: 770926
Accreditation: @NH

† Branch campus of Wayne County Community College District, Detroit, MI.

Wayne County Community College District Eastern Campus (D)

5901 Conner, Detroit MI 48213

Telephone: (313) 922-3311 Identification: 770295
Accreditation: &NH

† Branch campus of Wayne County Community College District, Detroit, MI.

Wayne County Community College District Northwest Campus (E)

8200 West Outer Drive, Detroit MI 48219

Telephone: (313) 943-4000 Identification: 770296
Accreditation: &NH

† Branch campus of Wayne County Community College District, Detroit, MI.

Wayne County Community College District Western Campus (F)

9555 Haggerty Road, Belleville MI 48111

Telephone: (734) 699-7008 Identification: 770294
Accreditation: &NH, SURGT

† Branch campus of Wayne County Community College District, Detroit, MI.

Wayne State University (G)

656 W. Kirby Street, Room # 4070, Detroit MI 48202-4095

County: Wayne FICE Identification: 002329
Unit ID: 172644
Telephone: (313) 577-2424 Carnegie Class: RU/VH
FAX Number: (313) 577-8154 Calendar System: Semester
URL: www.wayne.edu
Established: 1868 Annual Undergrad Tuition & Fees (In-State): $12,745
Enrollment: 27,578 Coed
Affiliation or Control: State IRS Status: 501(c)3
Highest Offering: Doctorate
Program: Occupational; Liberal Arts And General; Teacher Preparatory; Professional
Accreditation: NH, ANEST, ARCPA, AUD, BUS, CACREP, CLPSY, CORE, DANCE, DIETC, ENG, ENGR, ENGT, FUSER, LAW, LIB, MED, MIDWF, MT, MUS, NURSE, OT, PA, PH, PHAR, PLNG, PTA, RAD, RTT, SP, SPAA, SW, TEAC, THEA

01 President ... Dr. M. Roy WILSON
100 Chief of Staff/VP Marketing & Comm ... Mr. Michael G. WRIGHT
05 Provost/Sr VP Academic Affairs ... Dr. Margaret E. WINTERS
10 VP Finance & Business/Treasurer/CFO ... Mr. William DECATUR
43 Vice President and General Counsel ... Mr. Louis A. LESSEM
46 Vice President for Research ... Dr. Stephen M. LANIER
30 VP Development and Alumni Affairs ... Ms. Chacona JOHNSON
86 VP Government and Community Affairs ... Mr. Patrick O. LINDSEY
20 Associate VP Undergraduate Affairs ... Mr. Joseph RANKIN
88 VP for Economic Development ... Mr. Ned STAEBLER
84 Int Assoc VP for Enrollment Mgmt ... Mr. Robert KOHRMAN
101 Secretary to the BOG ... Ms. Julie H. MILLER
04 Assistant to the President ... Ms. Allison GUILLIOM
29 Executive Director Alumni Relations ... Mr. Ty S. STEVENSON
15 Associate VP of Human Resources ... Ms. Alicia PENDELTON
18 Assoc VP Facilities/Planning/Mgmt ... Mr. James R. SEARS
21 Assoc VP Budget/Planning/Analysis ... Mr. Robert KOHRMAN
44 Asst VP of Individual Giving ... Ms. Tracy UTECH
32 Dean of Students ... Dr. David J. STRAUSS
07 Int Sr Director of UG Admissions ... Ms. LaJoyce BROWN
26 Director of Communications ... Mr. Matthew T. LOCKWOOD
25 Asst VP Sponsored Program Admin ... Ms. Gail L. RYAN
37 Sr Director Student Financial Aid ... Ms. Gabriela GARFIELD
62 Dean University Library System ... Dr. Sandra G. YEE
06 University Registrar ... Ms. Linda K. FALKIEWICZ
09 Associate VP for Research ... Dr. Gloria HEPPNER
49 Dean College of Liberal Arts/Sci ... Dr. Wayne RASKIND
61 Dean Law School ... Ms. Jocelyn BENSON
63 Dean School of Medicine ... Dr. Jack SOBEL
66 Dean College of Nursing ... Dr. Laurie LAUZON CLABO
54 Dean College of Engineering ... Dr. Farshad FOTOUHI
50 Dean School of Business Admin ... Dr. Robert E. FORSYTHE
70 Dean School of Social Work ... Dr. Cheryl E. WAITES
67 Int Dean College of Pharm & Health ... Dr. Howard J. NORMILE
53 Int Dean College of Education ... Dr. R. Douglas WHITMAN
57 Dean College Fine/Perf & Comm Arts ... Dr. Matthew SEEGER
92 Dean Honors College ... Dr. Jerry HERRON
58 Dean Graduate School ... Dr. Ambika MATHUR
96 Assistant VP of Procurement ... Mr. Kenneth DOHERTY
104 Associate VP Outreach & Intl Pgms ... Dr. Ahmad EZZEDDINE
21 Associate VP Business & Aux Ops ... Mr. Timothy MICHAEL
88 Assoc VP Tech Commerc & Research ... Dr. Joan DUNBAR
13 Associate VP CIO ... Mr. Joseph SAWASKY
41 Director of Athletics ... Mr. Robert FOURNIER
105 Director of Web Communications ... Mr. Nick DENARDIS
19 Chief of Police ... Mr. Anthony HOLT
22 Director Ofc of Equal Opportunity ... Mr. Christopher JONES
28 Provost Diversity and Inclusion ... Ms. Marquita CHAMBLEE
36 Dean of Career Services ... Mr. Ronald KENT
39 Director Housing and Residence Life ... Ms. Jeanine BESSETTE
108 Director Institutional Assessment ... Dr. Catherine BARRETTE
38 Director Student Counseling ... Dr. Jeffrey KUENTZEL
45 Asst VP Institutional Research ... Mr. Mark A. BYRD

West Shore Community College (H)

3000 N. Stiles Road, Scottville MI 49454-0277

County: Mason FICE Identification: 007950
Unit ID: 172671
Telephone: (231) 845-6211 Carnegie Class: Assoc/Pub-R-S
FAX Number: (231) 843-5803 Calendar System: Semester
URL: www.westshore.edu
Established: 1967 Annual Undergrad Tuition & Fees (In-District): $2,478
Enrollment: 1,333 Coed
Affiliation or Control: Local IRS Status: 501(c)3
Highest Offering: Associate Degree
Program: Occupational; 2-Year Principally Bachelor's Creditable
Accreditation: NH

01 President ... Dr. Kenneth URBAN
11 VP of Administrative Services ... Mr. Scott WARD
05 VP of Academic and Student Services ... Ms. Lisa STICH
20 Dean of Instruction ... Dr. Brooke PORTMANN
32 Dean of Student Services ... Mr. Chad E. INABINET
40 Director of Bookstore & Food Svcs ... Ms. Cheryl HOGAN
04 Exec Assistant to the President ... Ms. Lisa STANKOWSKI
37 Director Financial Aid ... Ms. Juliann MURPHY
91 Manager of Adm Computing Systems ... Ms. Bonnie CHALTRON
88 Director of Criminal Justice ... Mr. Dan DELLAR
88 Director of Recreational Services ... Mr. Michael A. MOORE
15 Director of Human Resources ... Ms. Debra CAMPBELL
88 Director Student Resources ... Ms. Carla E. SHAY
08 Director of Library Services ... Ms. Renee SNODGRASS
26 Director of College Relations ... Mr. Thomas A. HAWLEY
23 Director of Wellness Center ... Ms. Julie PAGE-SMITH
10 Director of Accounting ... Ms. Kristen BIGGS
106 Director Distance Learning & Info ... Mr. John GERTS

Western Michigan University (I)

1903 W Michigan Avenue, Kalamazoo MI 49008-5202

County: Kalamazoo FICE Identification: 002330
Unit ID: 172699
Telephone: (269) 387-1000 Carnegie Class: RU/H
FAX Number: (269) 387-0958 Calendar System: Semester
URL: wmich.edu
Established: 1903 Annual Undergrad Tuition & Fees (In-State): $10,106
Enrollment: 23,914 Coed
Affiliation or Control: State IRS Status: 501(c)3
Highest Offering: Doctorate
Program: Liberal Arts And General; Teacher Preparatory; Professional
Accreditation: NH, AAB, ARCPA, ART, AUD, BUS, BUSA, CAATE, CACREP, CEA, CIDA, CLPSY, COPSY, CORE, CS, DANCE, DIETD, DIETI, ENG, ENGT, IPSY, MUS, NURSE, OT, SP, SPAA, SW, TED, THEA

01 President ... Dr. John M. DUNN
05 Provost/Vice Pres Academic Affairs ... Dr. Timothy J. GREENE
10 Vice Pres Business & Finance/CFO ... Ms. Jan VAN DER KLEY
32 VP Student Affairs/Dean of Students ... Dr. Diane K. ANDERSON
46 Vice President for Research ... Dr. Daniel M. LITYNSKI
30 VP Development & Alumni Relations ... Mr. James THOMAS
43 VP Legal Affairs & General Counsel ... Dr. Carol L J. HUSTOLES
86 VP Govt Affairs & Univ Relations ... Mr. Gregory J. ROSINE
28 VP for Diversity and Inclusion ... Dr. Martha B. WARFIELD
27 Vice Prov Budget & Personnel/CIO ... Dr. James A. GILCHRIST
84 Assoc Prov for Enrollment Mgmt . Dr. Christopher W. TREMBLAY
09 Assoc Provost Inst Effectiveness ... Dr. Jody BRYLINSKY
108 Assoc Prov Assessmt/UG Studies ... Dr. David S. REINHOLD
21 Assoc Vice Pres for Bus & Finance ... Ms. Patti VANWALBECK
15 Assoc Vice Pres Human Resources ... Dr. Warren L. HILLS
18 Assoc Vice Pres Facilities Mgmt ... Mr. Peter J. STRAZDAS
35 Assoc VP for Student Affairs ... Dr. Suzie NAGEL
35 Assoc VP for Student Affairs ... Mr. Vernon PAYNE
45 Exec Dir University Budgets ... Ms. Colleen SCARFF
31 Assoc VP for Community Outreach ... Mr. Robert MILLER
101 Secretary Board of Trustees ... Ms. Betty A. KOCHER
58 Dean Graduate College ... Dr. Susan R. STAPLETON
49 Interim Dean of Arts & Sciences ... Dr. Keith M. HEARIT
88 Dean of Aviation ... Capt. David M. POWELL
50 Dean of Business ... Dr. Kay PALAN
53 Dean of Education & Human Dev ... Dr. Ming LI
54 Int Dean of Engr & Applied Sciences ... Dr. Edmund TSANG
57 Dean of Fine Arts ... Mr. Daniel GUYETTE
76 Dean Health & Human Services ... Dr. Earlie WASHINGTON
92 Dean of Lee Honors College ... Dr. Carla M. KORETSKY
08 Dean of Libraries ... Dr. Joseph G. REISH
26 Exec Dir of University Relations ... Ms. Cheryl ROLAND
29 VP Development & Alumni Relations ... Mr. James THOMAS
36 Exec Dir Professional & Career Dev ... Ms. Lynn C. KELLY-ALBERTSON
06 Registrar ... Ms. Carrie CUMMING
07 Director Admissions/Orientation ... Ms. Dachea HILL
37 Int Dir Student Financial Aid ... Dr. Terrell L. HODGE
38 Dir Counseling Services ... Dr. Geniene M. GERSH
41 Dir Athletics ... Ms. Kathy B. BEAUREGARD
88 Assoc Prov for Global Education ... Dr. Wolfgang SCHLOER
85 Dir Intl Admissions & Services ... Mr. Juan TAVARES
106 Assoc Prov Extended Univ Programs ... Dr. Dawn M. GAYMER
13 Chief Technology Officer ... Mr. Thomas WOLF, JR.
22 Exec Dir Institutional Equity ... Dr. Evelyn B. WINFIELD-THOMAS

Western Michigan University Cooley Law School (J)

300 S Capitol Avenue, Lansing MI 48933

County: Ingham FICE Identification: 012627
Unit ID: 172477
Telephone: (517) 371-5140 Carnegie Class: Spec/Law
FAX Number: (517) 334-5718 Calendar System: Semester
URL: www.cooley.edu
Established: 1972 Annual Graduate Tuition & Fees: $47,890
Enrollment: 1,742 Coed
Affiliation or Control: Independent Non-Profit IRS Status: 501(c)3
Highest Offering: First Professional Degree; No Undergraduates
Program: Professional
Accreditation: NH, LAW

01 President ... Don LEDUC

04 Executive Asst to the President ... Cherie BECK
05 Dean ... Don LEDUC
10 Chief Financial Officer ... Kathleen CONKLIN
11 Chief Operating Officer ... Kathleen CONKLIN
07 Associate Director of Admissions ... Julia DUHAN
08 Associate Dean Library/Info Svcs ... Duane STROJNY
20 Associate Dean Lansing Campus ... Christine CHURCH
108 Assoc Dean Planning/Accreditation ... Laura LEDUC
36 Assoc Dean Career Prof Development ... Charles TOY
32 Assoc Dean Students/Professionalism ... Amy TIMMER
26 Assoc Dean External Aff/Gen Counsel ... James ROBB
13 Associate Dean for Information Tech ... Charles MICKENS
84 Assoc Dean for Enrollment Services ... Paul ZELENSKI
12 Associate Dean Grand Rapids ... Nelson MILLER
12 Associate Dean Tampa Bay ... Jeffrey MARTLEW
12 Associate Dean Auburn Hills Campus ... Joan VESTRAND
88 Assistant Dean Auburn Hills Campus ... Lisa HALUSHKA
88 Assistant Dean Lansing Campus ... Kathy SWEDLOW
88 Assistant Dean Grand Rapids Campus ... Tracey BRAME
88 Assistant Dean Tampa Bay Campus ... Ronald SUTTON
06 Registrar/Dir of Student Records ... Mohammad SOHAIL
37 Director Financial Aid ... Richard BORUSZEWSKI
40 Bookstore Manager ... Joelle TOPP
21 Controller ... Ronda BECK
29 Director Alumni Donor Relations ... Pamela HEOS
27 Director Communications ... Terry CARELLA
35 Director Student Services ... Christopher LEWIS

Western Michigan University Cooley Law School Auburn Hills Campus (A)

2630 Featherstone, Auburn Hills MI 48326
Telephone: (248) 751-7800 Identification: 770288
Accreditation: &NH

† Branch campus of Western Michigan University Cooley Law School, Lansing, MI.

Western Michigan University Cooley Law School Grand Rapids Campus (B)

111 Commerce Avenue, SW, Grand Rapids MI 49503
Telephone: (606) 301-6800 Identification: 770289
Accreditation: &NH

† Branch campus of Western Michigan University Cooley Law School, Lansing, MI.

Western Theological Seminary (C)

101 E 13th Street, Holland MI 49423-3622
County: Ottawa FICE Identification: 002331
Unit ID: 172705
Telephone: (616) 392-8555 Carnegie Class: Spec/Faith
FAX Number: (616) 392-7717 Calendar System: Semester
URL: www.westernsem.edu
Established: 1866 Annual Graduate Tuition & Fees: $13,376
Enrollment: 272 Coed
Affiliation or Control: Reformed Church In America IRS Status: 501(c)3
Highest Offering: Doctorate; No Undergraduates
Program: Professional; Religious Emphasis
Accreditation: THEOL

01 President ... Dr. Timothy BROWN
05 Interim Dean/VP Academic Affairs ... Dr. Jim BROWNSON
30 Vice Pres of Operations/Advancement ... Rev. Jeffrey MUNROE
10 Vice President of Finance ... Mr. Norman DONKERSLOOT
08 Interim Director of the Library ... Mrs. Ann E. NIEUWKOOP
06 Registrar ... Mrs. Pat DYKHUIS
07 Director of Admissions ... Dr. Mark POPPEN

Yeshiva Beth Yehuda - Yeshiva Gedolah of Greater Detroit (D)

24600 Greenfield, Oak Park MI 48237-1544
County: Oakland FICE Identification: 023638
Unit ID: 247773
Telephone: (248) 968-3360 Carnegie Class: Spec/Faith
FAX Number: (248) 968-8613 Calendar System: Semester
Established: 1985 Annual Undergrad Tuition & Fees: $6,200
Enrollment: 62 Male
Affiliation or Control: Independent Non-Profit IRS Status: 501(c)3
Highest Offering: Doctorate
Program: Professional
Accreditation: RABN

01 Dean ... Rabbi Y. BAKST
05 Assistant Dean ... Rabbi M. S. BAKST
11 Executive Administrator ... Rabbi P. RUSHNAWITZ
37 Director of Financial Aid ... Rabbi Y. BLITZ

MINNESOTA

Academy College (E)

1600 W. 82nd Street, Suite 100, Bloomington MN 55431
County: Hennepin FICE Identification: 020503
Unit ID: 172866
Telephone: (952) 851-0066 Carnegie Class: Bac/Assoc
FAX Number: (952) 851-0094 Calendar System: Quarter
URL: www.academycollege.edu
Established: 1936 Annual Undergrad Tuition & Fees: $17,075
Enrollment: 127 Coed
Affiliation or Control: Proprietary IRS Status: Proprietary
Highest Offering: Baccalaureate
Program: 2-Year Principally Bachelor's Creditable
Accreditation: ACICS, MAC

07 President ... Nancy GRAZZINI-OLSON
37 Director of Financial Aid ... Kellye MACLEOD

Adler Graduate School (F)

1550 E 78th Street, Richfield MN 55423
County: Hennepin FICE Identification: 030519
Unit ID: 374024
Telephone: (612) 861-7554 Carnegie Class: Spec/Health
FAX Number: (612) 861-7559 Calendar System: Semester
URL: www.alfredadler.edu
Established: 1969 Annual Graduate Tuition & Fees: $12,500
Enrollment: 380 Coed
Affiliation or Control: Independent Non-Profit IRS Status: 501(c)3
Highest Offering: Master's; No Undergraduates
Program: Professional
Accreditation: NH

01 President ... Dr. Daniel HAUGEN
05 Academic Vice President ... Mr. Chris HELGESTAD
10 Director of Business ... Ms. Kathy BENGTSON
07 Director of Admissions ... Ms. Evelyn HAAS
37 Director of Student Financial Aid ... Ms. Jeanette MAYNARD NELSON
06 Registrar ... Ms. Debbie VELASCO
08 Head Librarian ... Ms. Nicole MARCHAND

American Academy of Acupuncture and Oriental Medicine (G)

1925 W County Road B2, Roseville MN 55113-2703
County: Ramsey FICE Identification: 038333
Unit ID: 446002
Telephone: (651) 631-0204 Carnegie Class: Spec/Health
FAX Number: (651) 631-0361 Calendar System: Trimester
URL: www.aaaom.edu
Established: 1997 Annual Graduate Tuition & Fees: $11,212
Enrollment: 57 Coed
Affiliation or Control: Proprietary IRS Status: Proprietary
Highest Offering: Master's; No Undergraduates
Program: Professional
Accreditation: ACUP

01 President ... Dr. Changzhen GONG
11 Administrative Director ... Leila NIELSEN
37 Financial Aid Officer ... Cate LARSON

Argosy University, Twin Cities (H)

1515 Central Parkway, Eagan MN 55121-1756
Telephone: (888) 844-2004 FICE Identification: 007619
Accreditation: &WC, ACBSP, CLPSY, DH, DMS, HT, MAC, MFCD, MLTAD, MT, RTT

† Regional accreditation is carried under the parent institution in Orange, CA.

The Art Institutes International Minnesota (I)

15 S 9th Street, Minneapolis MN 55402-2808
County: Hennepin FICE Identification: 010248
Unit ID: 173887
Telephone: (612) 332-3361 Carnegie Class: Spec/Arts
FAX Number: (612) 332-3934 Calendar System: Quarter
URL: www.artinstitutes.edu/minneapolis
Established: 1964 Annual Undergrad Tuition & Fees: $23,088
Enrollment: 914 Coed
Affiliation or Control: Proprietary IRS Status: Proprietary
Highest Offering: Baccalaureate
Program: Occupational
Accreditation: ACICS, ACFEI

01 President ... Jennifer SORENSON
05 Dean of Academic Affairs ... Debra NEWGARD
32 Dean of Student Affairs ... Pam BOERSIG
36 Director of Career Services ... Becky BATES
07 Director of Admissions ... Amanda KARLSTAD

Association Free Lutheran Bible School and Seminary (J)

3134 East Medicine Lake Blvd, Plymouth MN 55441
County: Hennepin Identification: 667235
Telephone: (763) 544-9501 Carnegie Class: Not Classified
FAX Number: (763) 412-2047 Calendar System: Semester
URL: www.aflbs.org
Established: 1964 Annual Graduate Tuition & Fees: $9,970
Enrollment: N/A Coed
Affiliation or Control: Independent Non-Profit IRS Status: 501(c)3
Highest Offering: Master's; No Undergraduates
Program: Religious Emphasis
Accreditation: @TRACS

01 President ... Wade MOBLEY
05 Chief Academic Officer ... Mark OLSON

Augsburg College (K)

2211 Riverside Avenue, Minneapolis MN 55454-1398
County: Hennepin FICE Identification: 002334
Unit ID: 173045
Telephone: (612) 330-1000 Carnegie Class: Master's L
FAX Number: (612) 330-1649 Calendar System: Semester
URL: www.augsburg.edu
Established: 1869 Annual Undergrad Tuition & Fees: $35,465
Enrollment: 3,463 Coed
Affiliation or Control: Evangelical Lutheran Church In America IRS Status: 501(c)3
Highest Offering: Doctorate
Program: Liberal Arts And General; Teacher Preparatory; Professional
Accreditation: NH, ARCPA, MUS, NURSE, SW, TED

01 President ... Dr. Paul C. PRIBBENOW
05 Provost and Chief Academic Officer ... Dr. Karen KAIVOLA
10 CFO/VP Finance & Admin ... Dr. Beth REISSENWEBER
30 VP Institutional Advancement ... Ms. Heather RIDDLE
84 VP Enrollment Management ... Dr. William MULLEN
32 VP Student Affairs ... Ms. Ann L. GARVEY
26 VP Marketing/Communication ... Ms. Rebecca JOHN
13 VP & Chief Information Officer ... Mr. Leif B. ANDERSON
29 AVP Institutional Advancement ... Ms. Kim STONE
88 AVP Major Gifts ... Mr. Keith STOUT
58 AVP/Dean Grad & Prof Studies ... Vacant
49 AVP/Dean of Arts & Sciences ... Dr. Amy GORT
88 Dean of Global Education ... Mr. Eric CANNY
35 Dean of Students ... Dr. Sarah GRIESSE
12 Director Rochester Program ... Vacant
41 Athletic Director ... Mr. Jeffrey F. SWENSON
42 Campus Pastor ... Rev. Sonja HAGANDER
28 Chief Diversity Officer/Dir CAO ... Ms. Joanne REECK
37 Director of Financial Aid ... Ms. Carly EICHHORST
06 Registrar ... Ms. Crystal COMER
07 Director Undergraduate Admissions ... Mr. Rick ELLIS
07 Director Graduate Admissions ... Mr. Nathan GORR
18 Director of Facilities ... Mr. Dennis STUCKEY
14 Director of Information Technology ... Mr. Scott KRAJEWSKI
38 Director Ctr Wellness & Counseling . Ms. Nancy G. GUILBEAULT
15 Director & Chief HR Officer ... Ms. Lisa STOCK
08 Director Library Services ... Ms. Mary HOLLERICH
19 Director Public Safety & Risk Mgmt ... Mr. Scott BROWNELL
31 Director Community Relations ... Mr. Steve PEACOCK
88 Director Parent/Family Relations ... Ms. Sally DANIELS HERRON
88 Director StepUp Program ... Ms. Patrice SALMERI
88 Director Advancement Services ... Mr. Kevin HEALY
44 Director of Leadership Gifts ... Ms. Amy ALKIRE
85 Director International Student Svc ... Mr. James TRELSTAD-PORTER
21 Controller ... Mr. Matthew KSEPKA
21 Director of Budget ... Mr. Tom CARROLL
88 Director Event & Conf Planning ... Ms. Jodi COLLEN
20 Senior Analyst Academic Affairs ... Dr. Nathan HALLANGER
27 Director News and Media Services ... Ms. Stephanie WEISS
27 Director Marketing Communication .... Mr. Stephen JENDRASZAK
36 Director Strommen Career Center ... Mr. Keith MUNSON
39 Director Residence Life ... Ms. Amanda ERDMAN
104 Director Global Initiatives ... Ms. Leah SPINOSA DE VEGA
25 Director Sponsored Programs ... Ms. Erica SWIFT
102 Asst Dir Foundation/Corporate Rels ... Ms. Amanda SCHERER
04 Special Assistant to President ... Ms. Beth HELGEN
88 Operations Manager Admissions .... Ms. Keri VANOVERSCHELDE
40 Bookstore Manager ... Mr. Josh SCHWEITZER

Bethany Global University (L)

6820 Auto Club Road, Suite C, Bloomington MN 55438
County: Hennepin Identification: 667136
Telephone: (952) 944-2121 Carnegie Class: Not Classified
FAX Number: (952) 829-2753 Calendar System: Semester
URL: www.bcom.org
Established: 1948 Annual Undergrad Tuition & Fees: $9,970
Enrollment: 95 Coed
Affiliation or Control: Interdenominational IRS Status: 501(c)3
Highest Offering: Master's
Program: Religious Emphasis
Accreditation: @BI

01 President ... Dan BROKKE

Bethany Lutheran College (M)

700 Luther Drive, Mankato MN 56001-6163
County: Blue Earth FICE Identification: 002337
Unit ID: 173142
Telephone: (507) 344-7000 Carnegie Class: Bac/A&S
FAX Number: (507) 344-7376 Calendar System: Semester
URL: www.blc.edu
Established: 1911 Annual Undergrad Tuition & Fees: $25,460
Enrollment: 507 Coed
Affiliation or Control: Evangelical Lutheran Synod IRS Status: 501(c)3
Highest Offering: Baccalaureate
Program: Liberal Arts And General
Accreditation: NH

01 President ....Dr. Gene R. PFEIFER
42 Dir Campus Spiritual Life/Chaplain ....Rev. Donald L. MOLDSTAD
05 Vice President of Academic Affairs ....Dr. Eric K. WOLLER
32 Vice President of Student Affairs ....Dr. Theodore E. MANTHE
10 VP of Finance & Administration ....Mr. Daniel L. MUNDAHL
30 Vice President of Advancement ....Mr. Arthur P. WESTPHAL
37 Director of Financial Aid ....Mr. Jeffrey W. YOUNGE
06 Registrar ....Ms. Mary Jo H. STARKSON
07 Vice President of Enrollment ....Mr. Daniel P. TOMHAVE
15 Manager of Human Resources ....Ms. Paulette L. TONN BOOKER
08 Interim Dir of Library Services ....Ms. Alyssa K. INNIGER
13 Director of Information Technology ....Mr. John M. SEHLOFF
26 Dir of Institutional Communication ....Mr. Lance W. SCHWARTZ
41 Director of Athletics ....Mr. Donald M. WESTPHAL
29 Manager of Alumni Relations ....Mr. Jacob C. KRIER
09 Mgr Acad & Institutional Research ....Ms. Lisa A. SHUBERT
90 Manager of Academic Computing ....Vacant
40 Bookstore Manager ....Mr. Paul G. WOLD
21 Controller ....Mr. Gregory W. COSTELLO
28 Coord Ctr for Intercultural Develop ....Vacant
38 Coord of Student Counseling ....Vacant
18 Director of Facilities ....Mr. Juel O. MERSETH
108 Director of Assessment ....Dr. Theodore E. MANTHE

Bethel University (A)

3900 Bethel Drive, Saint Paul MN 55112-6999
County: Ramsey FICE Identification: 009058
Unit ID: 173160
Telephone: (651) 638-6400 Carnegie Class: Master's L
FAX Number: (651) 638-6001 Calendar System: Semester
URL: www.bethel.edu
Established: 1871 Annual Undergrad Tuition & Fees: $34,140
Enrollment: 4,917 Coed
Affiliation or Control: Baptist IRS Status: 501(c)3
Highest Offering: Doctorate
Program: Liberal Arts And General; Teacher Preparatory; Professional
Accreditation: NH, #ARCPA, CAATE, MFCD, @MIDWF, NURSE, SW, TEAC, THEOL

01 President ....Dr. James H. BARNES, III
100 Executive Assistant to President ....Dr. Randy BERGEN
05 Executive Vice Pres and Provost ....Dr. Debra HARLESS
10 Chief Financial Officer ....Mr. Patrick BROOKE
46 Sr VP Strategic Plng & Opers Effect ....Mr. Joseph LALUZERNE
26 Sr VP Communications/Marketing ....Vacant
30 Sr VP University Relations ....Mr. Mark MILES
07 VP for Admiss/Fin Aid & Retention ....Mr. Daniel NELSON
90 Vice President Information Tech ....Mr. Mark POSNER
29 Exec Minister for Church Relations ....Mr. Ralph GUSTAFSON
32 Vice President Student Life ....Dr. William WASHINGTON
49 Vice President & Dean of CAS ....Dr. Deborah SULLIVAN-TRAINOR
58 Vice Pres Dean Cont Stds/Grad Pgm ....Mr. Richard CROMBIE
73 VP and Dean BSSP ....Dr. David CLARK
79 Dean Arts & Humanities ....Dr. Barrett FISHER
108 Assoc Dean Inst Assess/Accred ....Dr. Joel FREDERICKSON
81 Acting Dean Natural/Behavioral Sci ....Dr. Dick PETERSON
107 Dean of Professional Programs ....Dr. Pamela ERWIN
104 Assoc Dean Off-Campus Programs ....Mr. Vincent PETERS
12 Actg Dn/Exec Ofcr BU Sem San Diego ....Dr. Arnell MOTZ
35 Dean of Students ....Dr. Marie WISNER
08 Director of Libraries ....Mr. David R. STEWART
15 Director of Human Resources ....Ms. Cara WALD
41 Athletic Director ....Mr. Robert B. BJORKLUND
37 Financial Aid Officer ....Mr. Jeffery D. OLSON
42 Dean Campus Ministrs/Campus Pastor ....Ms. Laurel BUNKER
07 Director of CAS Admissions ....Mr. Bret HYDER
07 Dir Seminary Admissions ....Ms. Jennifer NISKA
07 Director of CAPS/GS Admissions ....Ms. Vickie BAKKEN
06 University Registrar ....Ms. Katrina CHAPMAN
36 Director Career Counsel/Placement ....Mr. Dave BROZA
19 Chief of Security and Safety ....Mr. Andrew LUCHSINGER
40 Director Campus Stores ....Ms. Jill SONSTEBY
23 Director of Health Services ....Mrs. Elizabeth K. MILLER
96 Director of Purchasing ....Vacant
38 Director Student Counseling ....Dr. Miriam HILL
18 Interim Director of Facilities Mgmt ....Ms. Molly HOLMES
28 Chief Diversity Officer ....Dr. Ruben RIVERA
84 Director Enrollment Management ....Vacant

† The marriage and family therapy master's program at Bethel Seminary San Diego is accredited by the Commission on Accreditation for Marriage and Family Therapy Education (COAMFTE) of the American Association for Marriage and Family Therapy (AAMFT)

Bethlehem College and Seminary (B)

720 13th Avenue South, Minneapolis MN 55415
County: Hennepin Identification: 667249
Telephone: (612) 455-3420 Carnegie Class: Not Classified
FAX Number: N/A Calendar System: Semester
URL: bethlehemcollegeandseminary.org
Established: 2009 Annual Undergrad Tuition & Fees: $5,760
Enrollment: 183 Coed
Affiliation or Control: Independent Non-Profit IRS Status: 501(c)3
Highest Offering: Master's
Program: Religious Emphasis
Accreditation: BI

01 President ....Dr. Timothy TOMLINSON
05 Academic Dean ....Tom STELLER
11 VP of Administration ....Jason ABELL
30 VP of Advancement ....Rick SEGAL
07 Director of Admissions ....Will BARKLEY

Capella University (C)

225 S 6th Street, 9th Floor, Minneapolis MN 55402-4319
County: Hennepin FICE Identification: 032673
Unit ID: 413413
Telephone: (888) 227-3552 Carnegie Class: DRU
FAX Number: (612) 977-5066 Calendar System: Other
URL: www.capella.edu
Established: 1993 Annual Undergrad Tuition & Fees: $12,816
Enrollment: 35,061 Coed
Affiliation or Control: Proprietary IRS Status: Proprietary
Highest Offering: Doctorate
Program: Professional
Accreditation: NH, ACBSP, CACREP, CS, MFCD, NURSE, TED

01 President ....Mr. Scott KINNEY
05 VP Academic Affairs/Innovation ....Dr. Deborah BUSHWAY
26 Sr Vice Pres/Chief Marketing Ofcr ....Ms. Mary MILLER

Carleton College (D)

1 N College Street, Northfield MN 55057-4001
County: Rice FICE Identification: 002340
Unit ID: 173258
Telephone: (507) 222-4000 Carnegie Class: Bac/A&S
FAX Number: (507) 222-4204 Calendar System: Trimester
URL: www.carleton.edu
Established: 1866 Annual Undergrad Tuition & Fees: $49,263
Enrollment: 2,042 Coed
Affiliation or Control: Independent Non-Profit IRS Status: 501(c)3
Highest Offering: Baccalaureate
Program: Liberal Arts And General; Teacher Preparatory
Accreditation: NH

01 President ....Mr. Steven G. POSKANZER, JR.
05 Dean of the College ....Ms. Beverly NAGEL
10 VP Business & Finance/Treasurer ....Mr. Fred A. ROGERS
30 Vice President External Relations ....Mr. Tommy BONNER
32 VP for Student Dev/Dean of Students ..Ms. Carolyn LIVINGSTON
07 VP and Dean of Admissions/Fin Aid ....Mr. Paul THIBOUTOT
100 Assoc Vice President/Chief of Staff ....Ms. Elise ESLINGER
26 Assoc VP Ext Relations/Dir Develop ....Ms. Gayle MCJUNKIN
26 Assoc VP Ext Relations/Dir Col Comm ....Mr. Joe HARGIS
20 Associate Dean of the College ....Mr. Fernan JARAMILLO
20 Associate Dean of the College ....Mr. George SHUFFELTON
20 Assoc Dean and Director of Advising ....Mr. Louis NEWMAN
88 Director of Student Fellowships ....Ms. Marynel RYAN VAN ZEE
35 Associate Dean of Students ....Ms. Julie THORNTON
35 Associate Dean of Students ....Mr. Joseph BAGGOT
35 Associate Dean of Students ....Ms. Cathy CARLSON
37 Assoc Dean Admiss/Dir Stdnt Fin Svc ....Mr. Rod M. OTO
42 Chaplain ....Rev. Carolyn FURE-SLOCUM
06 Registrar ....Ms. Emy FARLEY
08 College Librarian ....Mr. Bradley SCHAFFNER
09 Dir of Inst Research and Assessment ....Mr. James FERGERSON
44 Asst VP Alum/Par Rel/Annual Giving ....Ms. Becky ZRIMSEK
29 Director of Alumni Relations ....Ms. Sarah FORSTER
44 Director of Alumni Annual Fund ....Ms. Maggie PATRICK
44 Director of Gift Planning ....Ms. Lynne WILMOT
13 Chief Technology Officer ....Ms. Janet SCANNELL
105 Dir Marketing Comm/Content Dvlpmt ....Ms. Jaye LAWRENCE
27 Director of Media/Public Relations ....Mr. Eric SIEGER
15 Director of Human Resources ....Ms. Kerstin CARDENAS
39 Director of Residential Life ....Ms. Andrea ROBINSON
88 Dir Intercult/International Life ....Ms. Joy KLUTTZ
104 Director of Off-Campus Studies ....Ms. Helena KAUFMAN
36 Director of the Career Center ....Ms. Kimberly BETZ
23 Dir Student Health and Counseling ....Ms. Marit LYSNE
18 Dir of Facilities/Capital Planning ....Mr. Steven SPEHN
21 Comptroller ....Ms. Linda THORNTON
102 Dir Corporate/Foundation Relations ....Mr. Mark GLEASON
88 Dir of Educational Research ....Ms. Andrea NIXON
88 Dir Center for Learning/Teaching ....Mr. Fred HAGSTROM
109 Director of Auxiliary Services ....Mr. Daniel BERGESON
41 Athletic Director ....Mr. Gerald YOUNG
19 Director of Security Services ....Mr. Wayne EISENHUTH
105 Director of Web Services ....Ms. Julie ANDERSON
88 Dir of Enterprise Information Svcs ....Ms. Julie CREAMER
88 Director of Technology Support ....Mr. Austin ROBINSON-COOLIDGE

Central Baptist Theological Seminary of Minneapolis (E)

900 Forestview Lane N, Plymouth MN 55441-5934
County: Hennepin Identification: 666050
Telephone: (763) 417-8250 Carnegie Class: Not Classified
FAX Number: (763) 417-8258 Calendar System: Semester
URL: www.centralseminary.edu
Established: 1956 Annual Undergrad Tuition & Fees: $7,100
Enrollment: 49 Coed
Affiliation or Control: Baptist IRS Status: 501(c)3
Highest Offering: Doctorate
Program: Religious Emphasis
Accreditation: TRACS

01 President ....Dr. Matthew D. MORRELL
03 Provost ....Dr. Brent A. BELFORD
05 VP of Academic Affairs ....Dr. Jonathan R. PRATT
06 Registrar ....Mr. Jeff P. STRAUB

*College of Medicine, Mayo Clinic (F)

200 First Street, Rochester MN 55905-3712
County: Olmsted Identification: 666719
Telephone: (507) 284-2511 Carnegie Class: N/A
FAX Number: (507) 284-0999
URL: www.mayo.edu

01 Chief Executive Officer ....Dr. John H. NOSEWORTHY
05 Exec Dean for Education Mayo Clinic ....Dr. Mark WARNER
46 Exec Dean for Research Mayo Clinic ....Dr. Greg GORES
22 Affirmative Action Administrator ....Mr. Kenneth J. SCHNEIDER
26 Chief Marketing Officer ....Mr. John H. WESTON
37 Financial Aid Officer ....Mr. David L. DAHLEN
08 Director of Libraries ....Mr. J. Michael HOMAN
29 Director Mayo Clinic Alumni Center ....Ms. Judith ANDERSON
30 Director of Development ....Dr. Michael CAMILLERI
86 Director Government Relations ....Dr. Patricia SIMMONS

*Mayo Medical School (G)

200 1st Street, SW, Rochester MN 55905-0001
County: Olmsted FICE Identification: 011732
Unit ID: 173957
Telephone: (507) 538-4897 Carnegie Class: Spec/Med
FAX Number: (507) 284-2634 Calendar System: Other
URL: www.mayo.edu/mms
Established: 1971 Annual Undergrad Tuition & Fees: $29,355
Enrollment: 228 Coed
Affiliation or Control: Independent Non-Profit IRS Status: 501(c)3
Highest Offering: First Professional Degree
Program: Professional
Accreditation: NH, MED

02 Interim Dean ....Dr. Michelle HALYARD
05 Assoc Dean Academic Affairs ....Dr. Darcy REED
32 Assoc Dean Student Affairs ....Dr. Alexandra A. WOLANSKYJ
20 Assoc Dean Faculty Affairs ....Dr. Geoffry THOMPSON
11 Administrator for Mayo Med School ....Ms. Marcia ANDERSON-REID
22 Chief Human Resources ....Ms. Jill RAGSDALE
26 Chief Mrktng Ofcr/Chair Public Affs ....Mr. John W. LAFORGIA
88 Internatl Personnel Practice Group ....Ms. Ann H. LANCE
37 Financial Aid Officer ....Mr. David L. DAHLEN
08 Head Librarian ....Mr. J. Michael HOMAN

*_Mayo Clinic College of Medicine-Mayo Graduate School_ (H)

200 First Street, SW, Rochester MN 55905-0001
Telephone: (507) 538-1160 FICE Identification: 011516
Accreditation: &NH, DENT, PDPSY

† Regional accreditation is carried under College of Medicine, Mayo Clinic.

*_Mayo School of Health Sciences_ (I)

200 First St. SW, Siebens Bldg 3,
Rochester MN 55905-0001
Telephone: (507) 284-3293 FICE Identification: 008182
Accreditation: &NH, ANEST, COARC, CVT, CYTO, DIETI, DMS, HT, MT, NDT, NMT, PAST, PHLEB, PTA, RAD, RTT, SURGA

† Regional accreditation is carried under College of Medicine, Mayo Clinic.

College of Saint Benedict (J)

37 S College Avenue, Saint Joseph MN 56374-2099
County: Stearns FICE Identification: 002341
Unit ID: 174747
Telephone: (320) 363-5011 Carnegie Class: Bac/A&S
FAX Number: (320) 363-6099 Calendar System: Semester
URL: www.csbsju.edu
Established: 1913 Annual Undergrad Tuition & Fees: $40,846
Enrollment: 2,020 Coordinate
Affiliation or Control: Roman Catholic IRS Status: 501(c)3
Highest Offering: Baccalaureate
Program: Liberal Arts And General; Teacher Preparatory
Accreditation: NH, DIETD, MUS, NURSE, TED

01 President ....Dr. Mary HINTON
05 Interim Provost Academic Affairs ....Dr. Richard ICE
32 Vice President Student Development ....Ms. Mary A. GELLER
30 VP Institutional Advancement ....Ms. Kathy HANSEN
84 VP Planning and Public Affairs ....Mr. Jon D. MCGEE
10 Vice Pres Finance/Administration ....Ms. Susan M. PALMER
07 VP Admission & Financial Aid ....Dr. Calvin MOSLEY
18 Exec Director Facilities ....Mr. Brad SINN
20 Academic Dean ....Dr. Karen ERICKSON
26 Chief Mktg & Comm Officer ....Ms. Tammy MOORE
34 Dean of Students ....Ms. Jody L. TERHAAR
06 Registrar ....Ms. Julie E. GRUSKA
08 Director Library ....Ms. Kathleen PARKER
37 Exec Director Financial Aid ....Mr. Stuart PERRY
15 Director Human Resources ....Ms. Carol ABELL
38 Director of Counseling ....Dr. Mike J. EWING
42 Director of Campus Ministry ....Sr. Sharon NOHNER, OSB

41 Athletic Director .... Ms. Glennis WERNER
13 Director of Info Technology Svc .... Ms. Casey GORDON
19 Director of Security .... Mr. Darren SWANSON
21 Controller .... Ms. Anne OBERMAN
44 Director of Planned Giving .... Mr. Bill HICKEY
36 Director of Career Services .... Dr. Heidi HARLANDER
09 Assoc Dir of Institutional Research .... Ms. Karen KNUTSON
40 Director of Bookstores .... Ms. Tina STREIT
100 Chief of Staff/Exec Asst to Pres .... Dr. Kathryn ENKE
88 Director/Student Human Rights .... Mr. Brandyn WOODARD
29 Asst Director Alumnae Relations .... Ms. Kristin LYMAN

The College of Saint Scholastica (A)

1200 Kenwood Avenue, Duluth MN 55811-4199
County: Saint Louis — FICE Identification: 002343
Unit ID: 174899
Telephone: (218) 723-6000 — Carnegie Class: Master's M
FAX Number: (218) 723-6290 — Calendar System: Semester
URL: www.css.edu
Established: 1912 — Annual Undergrad Tuition & Fees: $33,784
Enrollment: 4,237 — Coed
Affiliation or Control: Roman Catholic — IRS Status: 501(c)3
Highest Offering: Doctorate
Program: Liberal Arts And General; Teacher Preparatory; Professional
Accreditation: NH, CAATE, CAEP, CAHIIM, NURSE, OT, PTA, SW, TEAC

01 President .... Dr. Larry GOODWIN
10 Vice President Finance .... Ms. Susan KERRY
05 Vice Pres Academic Affairs .... Dr. Elizabeth DOMHOLDT
30 Vice Pres College Advancement .... Mr. John LABOSKY
32 Vice President for Student Affairs .... Mr. Steve LYONS
84 Vice Pres for Enrollment Management .... Mr. Eric BERG
15 VP for HR & Chief Diversity Officer .... Ms. Patricia PRATT-COOK
88 Assoc Vice Pres College Advancement .... Ms. Janet S. ROSEN
06 Registrar .... Mr. George A. BEATTIE
26 Exec Dir Public & Media Relations .... Mr. Robert J. ASHENMACHER
13 Chief Information Officer .... Mr. Xavier KNIGHT
08 Director of Library .... Mr. Kevin MCGREW
09 Director of Institutional Research .... Dr. Iwalani ELSE
18 Director of Facilities Services .... Mr. Tom BREKKE
88 Director OneStop Student Service .... Ms. Linda ROGENTINE
29 Director Alumni Relations .... Ms. Lisa ROSETH
07 Dir of Undergraduate Admissions .... Mr. Bryan KARL
07 Assoc Dir of Transfer Admissions .... Ms. Brenda PANGER
41 Athletic Director .... Mr. Don OLSON
42 Director of Campus Ministry .... Mr. Nathan LANGER
37 Director Student Financial Aid .... Mr. Jon ERICKSON
38 Dir Stdnt Ctr Health/Well-Being .... Mr. Tad SEARS
96 Purchasing Manager .... Ms. Lisa ANDERSON
79 Dean School of Arts & Letters .... Dr. Tammy OSTRANDER
50 Dean Sch of Buiness & Tech .... Dr. Lynne HAMRE
53 Dean School of Education .... Dr. Jo OLSEN
76 Dean School of Health Sciences .... Dr. Rondell BERKELAND
66 Dean School of Nursing .... Dr. Julie ANDERSON
81 Dean School of Sciences .... Dr. Aileen BEARD
85 International Student Advisor .... Ms. Alison CHAMPEAUX
104 Director of International Eduction .... Vacant
45 Vice Pres for Strategic Initiatives .... Mr. Donald WORTHAM
04 Exec Admin Asst to President .... Ms. Joan HOLTER
19 Safety and Security Manager .... Mr. Michael TURNER
39 Director of Residential Life .... Ms. Mickey FITCH
92 Director Honors Program .... Dr. Debra SCHROEDER
44 Exec Dir of Planned Giving .... Ms. Karen FINSETH
40 Bookstore Manager .... Ms. Ksenia OLSON
97 Director of General Education .... Dr. Bret AMUNDSON
88 Assoc VP of Mission Integration .... Sr. Mary ROCHEFORT
88 Virtual Campus Director .... Mr. Craig BRIDGES
35 Dean of Students .... Ms. Megan PERRY-SPEARS
88 Asst Dean Advising & Retention .... Mr. David BAUMAN
28 Director of Institutional Diversity .... Vacant
101 Secretary of the Institution/Board .... Ms. Joan HOLTER
105 Director Web Services .... Ms. Chris JUGASEK
106 Dir Academic Tech & Online Learning .... Mr. Peter PRUEFER
36 Director Career Services .... Ms. Mary ANDERSON
102 Assoc Vice Pres College Advancement .... Ms. Janet ROSEN

Concordia College (B)

901 8th Street S, Moorhead MN 56562-0001
County: Clay — FICE Identification: 002346
Unit ID: 173300
Telephone: (218) 299-4000 — Carnegie Class: Bac/A&S
FAX Number: (218) 299-3947 — Calendar System: Semester
URL: www.cord.edu
Established: 1891 — Annual Undergrad Tuition & Fees: $35,464
Enrollment: 2,358 — Coed
Affiliation or Control: Evangelical Lutheran Church In America — IRS Status: 501(c)3
Highest Offering: Master's
Program: Liberal Arts And General; Teacher Preparatory
Accreditation: NH, DIETD, DIETI, MUS, NURSE, SW

01 President .... Dr. William J. CRAFT
05 Dean of College/VP Academic Affairs .... Dr. Eric J. ELIASON
10 Vice Pres Finance/Treasurer .... Ms. Linda J. BROWN
84 Vice Pres Enrollment and Marketing .... Mr. Karl A. STUMO
30 Vice Pres Advancement .... Ms. Teresa L. HARLAND
32 VP Student Affairs/Dean of Students .... Dr. J. Sue OATEY
04 Senior Associate to the President .... Ms. Tracey A. MOORHEAD
13 Chief Info Ofcr/Assoc Vice Pres .... Mr. Bruce W. VIEWEG
07 Director of Admissions .... Mr. Scott D. ELLINGSON
06 Registrar .... Ms. Ericka K. PETERSON
37 Director Financial Aid .... Mr. Eric J. ADDINGTON
08 Librarian .... Mrs. Laura K. PROBST
36 Exec Dir of the Career Initiative .... Ms. Carly NELSON
15 Director Human Resources .... Ms. Peggy L. TORRANCE
29 Director Alumni Relations .... Mr. Eric P. JOHNSON
26 Sr Dir of Communications/Marketing .... Mr. Roger E. DEGERMAN
09 Dir of Institutional Effectiveness .... Ms. Jasi O'CONNOR
18 Director of Facilities Management .... Mr. Wayne R. FLACK
38 Director of Student Counseling .... Ms. Monica R. KERSTING
41 Athletic Director .... Mr. Rich GLAS
42 Campus Pastor .... Rev. Timothy M. MEGORDEN
85 Director Intercultural Affairs .... Dr. Per ANDERSON
19 Director of Public Safety .... Mr. William MACDONALD

Concordia University, St. Paul (C)

1282 Concordia Ave, Saint Paul MN 55104-5494
County: Ramsey — FICE Identification: 002347
Unit ID: 173328
Telephone: (651) 641-8278 — Carnegie Class: Master's L
FAX Number: (651) 659-0207 — Calendar System: Semester
URL: www.csp.edu
Established: 1893 — Annual Undergrad Tuition & Fees: $20,750
Enrollment: 4,057 — Coed
Affiliation or Control: Lutheran Church - Missouri Synod — IRS Status: 501(c)3
Highest Offering: Doctorate
Program: Liberal Arts And General; Teacher Preparatory
Accreditation: NH, ACBSP, OPE, @PTA, TED

01 President .... Rev.Dr. Thomas Karl RIES
03 Executive Vice President .... Dr. Cheryl T. CHATMAN
05 Vice President Academic Affairs .... Dr. Marilyn REINECK
10 Vice President for Finance .... Rev. Michael H. DORNER
30 Vice President for Advancement .... Mr. Mark HILL
11 Sr Vice Pres for Administration .... Dr. Eric E. LAMOTT
84 Assoc VP Cohort Enrollment Mgmt .... Ms. Kim CRAIG
07 Assc VP Traditional Enrollment Mgmt .... Mrs. Kristin M. VOGEL
32 Assoc VP Sudent Life .... Mr. Jason M. RAHN
108 Assoc VP for Assessment/Accred .... Dr. Miriam LUEBKE
53 Dean College of Education & Science .... Dr. Donald W. HELMSTETTER
49 Dean College of Arts & Letters .... Dr. David A. LUMPP
58 Dean of Graduate School .... Dr. Michael WALCHESKI
50 Dean College of Bus/Org Leadership .... Dr. Kevin HALL
28 Dean of Diversity .... Dr. Cheryl T. CHATMAN
39 Associate Dean of Residence Life .... Ms. Sharon R. SCHEWE
06 Registrar .... Mrs. Toni SQUIRES
08 Director of Library Services .... Dr. Charlotte M. KNOCHE
26 Dir Univ Communications/Mrktng .... Mr. Jason DEBOER-MORAN
15 Director of Human Resources .... Mrs. Mary M. ARNOLD
37 Director of Financial Aid .... Ms. Jeanie PECK
04 Executive Assistant to President .... Ms. Jill K. SIMON
42 University Pastor .... Rev. Thomas GUNDERMANN
88 Director of Traditional Advising .... Ms. Gretchen WALTHER
09 Director of Institutional Research .... Ms. Beth C. PETER
29 Director of Alumni Relations .... Mrs. Rhonda K. PALMERSHEIM
41 Director of Athletics .... Mr. Thomas J. RUBBELKE
18 Director of Operations .... Mr. James P. ORCHARD
36 Director of Placement/Prof .... Ms. Jacquelyn MAGNUSON
40 Bookstore Manager .... Mr. Anthony J. ROSS
90 Director of Computer Services .... Mr. Jonathan S. BREITBARTH
91 Director Administrative Computing .... Ms. Beth C. PETER
19 Risk Manager .... Mrs. Sara K. MULSO
24 Help Desk Coordinator .... Ms. Brianna TRAQUAIR

Crossroads College (D)

920 Mayowood Road, SW, Rochester MN 55902-2382
County: Olmsted — FICE Identification: 002366
Unit ID: 174206
Telephone: (507) 288-4563 — Carnegie Class: Spec/Faith
FAX Number: (507) 288-9046 — Calendar System: Semester
URL: www.crossroadscollege.edu
Established: 1913 — Annual Undergrad Tuition & Fees: $15,580
Enrollment: 109 — Coed
Affiliation or Control: Christian Churches And Churches of Christ — IRS Status: 501(c)3
Highest Offering: Baccalaureate
Program: 2-Year Principally Bachelor's Creditable; Religious Emphasis
Accreditation: @TRACS

01 President .... Michael KILGALLIN
05 Vice President of Academics .... Mark KRAUSE
10 Vice Pres Administration & Finance .... Roger LANGSETH
32 VP of Student Development .... Brad JORDE
06 Registrar .... Emily HOLTER
08 Director of the Library .... Vacant
07 Director of Admissions .... Todd LOONEY
37 Director of Financial Aid .... Polly KELLOGG-BRADLEY
21 Business Manager .... Roger W. LANGSETH

Crown College (E)

8700 College View Drive, Saint Bonifacius MN 55375-9001
County: Carver — FICE Identification: 002383
Unit ID: 174862
Telephone: (952) 446-4100 — Carnegie Class: Bac/Diverse
FAX Number: (952) 446-4149 — Calendar System: Semester
URL: www.crown.edu
Established: 1916 — Annual Undergrad Tuition & Fees: $31,600
Enrollment: 1,278 — Coed
Affiliation or Control: The Christian And Missionary Alliance — IRS Status: 501(c)3
Highest Offering: Master's
Program: Liberal Arts And General; Teacher Preparatory
Accreditation: NH, NURSE

01 President .... Dr. David J. WIGGINS
04 Exec Assistant to the President .... Mrs. Shirley M. GRANLUND
10 VP Finance .... Mrs. Susan WILSON
05 VP Academic Affairs/Provost .... Dr. Scott MOATS
32 VP Student Development .... Dr. Paul BLEZIEN
84 Int VP Enrollment & Marketing Svcs .... Dr. Paul BLEZIEN
30 Director of External Relations .... Ms. Shannon SCHAAF
20 Dean for Undergraduate Pgms .... Dr. Scott MOATS
66 Director of Nursing .... Mrs. Teresa NEWBY
21 Controller .... Mr. Ronald STRAKA
41 Athletic Director .... Vacant
08 Director of Media Services .... Dr. Dennis INGOLFSLAND
06 Registrar .... Mrs. Cheryl FISK
37 Interim Director of Financial Aid .... Mrs. Judy BEDFORD
35 Dir Leadership Dev/Student Activit .... Vacant
07 Director of Graduate Admissions .... Ms. Maggie UNGER
18 Director of Facilities Services .... Mr. Rick LARSON
40 Director of Bookstore Services .... Vacant
58 Dean Sch Online Studies/Grad School .... Dr. Fawn MCCRACKEN
42 Chaplain .... Mr. Bill KUHN
07 Dean of SAS Enrollment .... Ms. Korey COMPAAN
15 Director of Human Resources .... Mrs. Amy LUESSE
36 Dir Career Services .... Mr. Darren NOBLE
13 Director of Technology Services .... Mr. Paul FLAGSTAD
26 Marketing/Communications Manager .... Ms. Jessica ARTIBEE
29 Director Alumni Relations .... Vacant

Duluth Business University, Inc. (F)

4724 Mike Colalillo Drive, Duluth MN 55807-2723
County: Saint Louis — FICE Identification: 009892
Unit ID: 173489
Telephone: (218) 722-4000 — Carnegie Class: Assoc/PrivFP
FAX Number: (218) 628-2127 — Calendar System: Quarter
URL: www.dbumn.edu
Established: 1891 — Annual Undergrad Tuition & Fees: $16,285
Enrollment: 197 — Coed
Affiliation or Control: Proprietary — IRS Status: Proprietary
Highest Offering: Baccalaureate
Program: Occupational; 2-Year Principally Bachelor's Creditable; Technical Emphasis
Accreditation: ACICS, MAC

01 President .... Mr. James R. GESSNER
12 Campus Director .... Mrs. Bonnie L. KUPCZYNSKI
05 Associate Director .... Mr. David LUTZKA
08 Librarian .... Ms. Joyce C. PETERSON
36 Career Services Manager .... Mr. David E. COOK
37 Financial Aid Advisor .... Mrs. Gloria G. COOLE

Dunwoody College of Technology (G)

818 Dunwoody Boulevard, Minneapolis MN 55403-1192
County: Hennepin — FICE Identification: 004641
Unit ID: 175227
Telephone: (612) 374-5800 — Carnegie Class: Assoc/PrivNFP4
FAX Number: (612) 381-9620 — Calendar System: Semester
URL: www.dunwoody.edu
Established: 1914 — Annual Undergrad Tuition & Fees: $20,905
Enrollment: 1,070 — Coed
Affiliation or Control: Independent Non-Profit — IRS Status: 501(c)3
Highest Offering: Baccalaureate
Program: 2-Year Principally Bachelor's Creditable; Technical Emphasis
Accreditation: NH, CIDA, RAD

01 President .... Mr. Rich WAGNER
05 Provost .... Mr. Jeff YLINEN
20 Associate Provost .... Ms. Ann IVERSON
10 Chief Financial Officer .... Mr. James MCDONALD
84 Vice President Enrollment Mgmt .... Ms. Collette GARRITY
30 VP of Institutional Advancement .... Mr. Stuart LANG
15 Vice President of Human Resources .... Ms. Patricia EDMAN

Globe University (H)

80 South Eighth Street, Suite 51, Minneapolis MN 55402
Telephone: (651) 332-8042 — Identification: 770734
Accreditation: ACICS

† Branch campus of Globe University, Woodbury, MN.

Globe University (I)

2777 34th Street South, Moorhead MN 56560
Telephone: (218) 422-1000 — Identification: 770717
Accreditation: ACICS

† Branch campus of Minnesota School of Business, Richfield, MN.

Globe University (J)

8089 Globe Drive, Woodbury MN 55125-3388
County: Washington — FICE Identification: 004642
Unit ID: 173629
Telephone: (651) 730-5100 — Carnegie Class: Bac/Assoc
FAX Number: (651) 730-5151 — Calendar System: Quarter
URL: www.globeuniversity.edu

Established: 1885 Annual Undergrad Tuition & Fees: $14,400
Enrollment: 776 Coed
Affiliation or Control: Proprietary IRS Status: Proprietary
Highest Offering: Master's
Program: Occupational
Accreditation: ACICS, MAAB

01 Campus Director .... Ms. Lisa PALERMO
05 Dean of Education .... Ms. Kelley ALIFFI
37 Financial Aid Manager .... Ms. Holly WEBERG
07 Director of Admissions .... Ms. Tiffany SIMMONS

Gustavus Adolphus College (A)

800 W College Avenue, Saint Peter MN 56082-1498
County: Nicollet FICE Identification: 002353
Unit ID: 173647
Telephone: (507) 933-8000 Carnegie Class: Bac/A&S
FAX Number: (507) 933-7041 Calendar System: Semester
URL: www.gustavus.edu
Established: 1862 Annual Undergrad Tuition & Fees: $41,140
Enrollment: 2,456 Coed
Affiliation or Control: Evangelical Lutheran Church In America
IRS Status: 501(c)3
Highest Offering: Baccalaureate
Program: Liberal Arts And General
Accreditation: NH, CAATE, MUS, NURSE, TED

01 President .... Ms. Rebecca M. BERGMAN
05 Provost and Dean of the College .... Dr. Mark J. BRAUN
10 VP for Finance and Treasurer .... Mr. Kenneth C. WESTPHAL
07 VP for Enrollment Management .... Dr. Thomas M. CRADY
30 VP for Institutional Advancement .... Mr. Thomas W. YOUNG
32 VP for Student Life .... Dr. JoNes R. VANHECKE
26 VP Marketing & Communication .... Mr. Timothy R. KENNEDY
28 Dir Multicultural Programs .... Vacant
09 Director Institutional Research .... Mr. David A. MENK
08 Head Librarian .... Mr. Daniel J. MOLLNER
88 Director Church Relations .... Rev. Grady I. ST. DENNIS
29 Dir Alumni and Parent Engagement .... Mr. Glen D. LLOYD
36 Director Career Development .... Ms. Cynthia L. FAVRE
06 Registrar .... Ms. Kristianne R. WESTPHAL
13 Dir Gustavus Technology Services .... Mr. Bruce N. AARSVOLD
18 Director Physical Plant .... Mr. Warren P. WUNDERLICH
37 AVP and Dean of Financial Aid .... Mr. Doug O. MINTER
39 Director Residential Life .... Mr. Lawrence C. POTTS
42 Chaplain .... Rev. Siri C. ERICKSON
42 Chaplain .... Rev. Brian E. KONKOL
35 Associate Dean of Students .... Dr. Stephen R. BENNETT
41 Athletics Director .... Mr. Thomas W. BROWN
15 Director Human Resources .... Vacant
19 Director Campus Security .... Ms. Carol A. BREWER
40 Manager Book Mark .... Ms. Molly L. YONKERS
27 Director Media Relations .... Mr. Matthew D. THOMAS
04 Asst to the Pres & Sec of the Board .... Ms. Jolene D. CHRISTENSEN

Hamline University (B)

1536 Hewitt Avenue, Saint Paul MN 55104-1284
County: Ramsey FICE Identification: 002354
Unit ID: 173665
Telephone: (651) 523-2800 Carnegie Class: Master's L
FAX Number: (651) 523-2899 Calendar System: 4/1/4
URL: www.hamline.edu
Established: 1854 Annual Undergrad Tuition & Fees: $36,888
Enrollment: 4,469 Coed
Affiliation or Control: United Methodist IRS Status: 501(c)3
Highest Offering: Doctorate
Program: Liberal Arts And General; Teacher Preparatory; Professional
Accreditation: NH, LAW, MUS, TED

01 President .... Dr. Fayneese S. MILLER
05 Provost .... Dr. Eric JENSEN
10 Sr VP Business/Finance/Technology .... Ms. Margaret TUNGSETH
26 Vice Pres Marketing/Enrollment Mgmt .... Ms. Ann NESS
30 VP Development & Alumni Relations .... Mr. Tony GRUNDHAUSER
32 Dean of Students .... Dr. Alan A. SICKBERT
43 VP HR/General Counsel .... Ms. Catherine WASSBERG
13 Assoc VP/Dir IT .... Mr. Mark KONDRAK
26 Assoc VP Marketing Communications .... Ms. JacQui GETTY
28 Dir Multicult and Div Initiatives .... Dr. Veena DEO
18 Assoc VP Facilities/Physical Plant .... Mr. Lowell BROMANDER
61 Interim Dean School of Law .... Ms. Marie FAILINGER
50 Dean School of Business .... Ms. Anne MCCARTHY
53 Dean School of Education .... Dr. Nancy SORENSON
49 Dean College Liberal Arts .... Dr. John MATACHEK
28 Ast Dn/Dir Multicult/Intl Stdt Affs .... Mr. Carlos SNEED
06 Registrar Undergrad/Grad Schools .... Ms. Gwen SHERBURNE
29 Exec Director Assoc of Hamline Alum .... Ms. Elizabeth L. RADTKE
37 Director Financial Aid .... Ms. Lynette WAHL
06 Registrar Law School .... Ms. Colleen CLISH
07 Director Law School Admissions .... Ms. Robin C. INGLI
07 Director Undergraduate Admission .... Ms. Mai Nhia XIONG-CHAN
15 Director Human Resources .... Ms. Julie KLINE
36 Interim Dir Career Development .... Mr. Terry MIDDENDORF
41 Athletic Director .... Mr. Jason VERDUGO
19 Director of Safety & Security .... Mr. James SCHUMANN
23 Director Counseling & Health Center .... Ms. Hussein RAJPUT
35 Dir Student Leadership & Activities .... Ms. Wendy BURNS
42 Chaplain & Director .... Ms. Nancy M. VICTORIN-VANGERUD
96 Director of Purchasing .... Ms. Susan BORNUS
04 Exec Assistant to the President .... Ms. Jane A. TELLEEN
09 Director of Institutional Research .... Ms. Tracy WILLIAMS
08 Head Librarian .... Mr. Terry METZ
39 Director Student Housing .... Mr. Javier GUTIERREZ

Hazelden Betty Ford Graduate School of Addiction Studies (C)

PO Box 11 (CO9), Center City MN 55012-0011
County: Chisago FICE Identification: 040443
Unit ID: 173683
Telephone: (651) 213-4175 Carnegie Class: Spec/Health
FAX Number: (651) 213-4710 Calendar System: Semester
URL: www.hazelden.edu
Established: 1999 Annual Graduate Tuition & Fees: $32,734
Enrollment: 126 Coed
Affiliation or Control: Independent Non-Profit IRS Status: 501(c)3
Highest Offering: Master's; No Undergraduates
Program: Professional
Accreditation: NH

01 President and CEO .... Mr. Mark MISHEK
05 Chief Academic Officer & Provost .... Dr. Valerie SLAYMAKER
04 Asst to the Chief Academic Officer .... Ms. Denell BELLE ISLE
20 Dean .... Dr. Roy KAMMER
07 Mgr Enrollment & Student Services .... Ms. LeAnn BROWN
06 Registrar .... Ms. Debra MATTISON
09 Dir of Institutional Effectiveness .... Dr. Timothy SHEEHAN
06 Registrar of Administrative Service .... Ms. Twyla RAMSDELL

Herzing University (D)

5700 West Broadway, Minneapolis MN 55428
Telephone: (763) 535-3000 FICE Identification: 011017
Accreditation: &NH, DA, DH, NURSE, OTA

† Regional accreditation is carried under the parent institution in Madison, WI.

Institute of Production and Recording (E)

300 N. 1st Avenue, Suite 500, Minneapolis MN 55401
County: Hennepin FICE Identification: 041302
Unit ID: 454616
Telephone: (612) 244-2800 Carnegie Class: Assoc/PrivFP
FAX Number: (612) 244-2801 Calendar System: Other
URL: www.ipr.edu
Established: 2002 Annual Undergrad Tuition & Fees: $16,560
Enrollment: 243 Coed
Affiliation or Control: Proprietary IRS Status: Proprietary
Highest Offering: Associate Degree
Program: Occupational
Accreditation: ACCSC

01 President .... Vacant
12 Campus Director .... Norbert KRUEZER
05 Dean of Education .... Rebecca BULLER
07 Director of Admissions .... Suzanne FERKINGSTAD
36 Director of Career Services .... Sandra ROBINSON
08 Librarian .... Tina HALFMANN

ITT Technical Institute (F)

6120 Earle Brown Drive, Suite 100,
Brooklyn Center MN 55430
Telephone: (763) 549-5900 Identification: 770653
Accreditation: ACICS

† Branch campus of ITT Technical Institute, Indianapolis, IN.

ITT Technical Institute (G)

7905 Golden Triangle Dr, Ste 100,
Eden Prairie MN 55344-7220
Telephone: (952) 914-5300 Identification: 666319
Accreditation: ACICS

† Branch campus of ITT Technical Institute, Indianapolis, IN.

Le Cordon Bleu College of Culinary Arts in Minneapolis/St Paul (H)

1315 Mendota Heights Road,
Mendota Heights MN 55120-1129
Telephone: (651) 675-4700 Identification: 666370
Accreditation: ACICS, ACFEI

† Branch campus of Le Cordon Bleu College of Culinary Arts, Portland, OR.

Leech Lake Tribal College (I)

P.O. Box 180, Cass Lake MN 56633-0180
County: Cass FICE Identification: 030964
Unit ID: 413626
Telephone: (218) 335-4200 Carnegie Class: Tribal
FAX Number: (218) 335-4282 Calendar System: Semester
URL: www.lltc.edu
Established: 1990 Annual Undergrad Tuition & Fees: $5,000
Enrollment: 297 Coed
Affiliation or Control: Tribal Control IRS Status: 501(c)3
Highest Offering: Associate Degree
Program: Occupational; 2-Year Principally Bachelor's Creditable
Accreditation: NH

01 President .... Vacant
05 Vice President of Academics .... Dr. Sharon MARCOTTE
10 Chief Financial Officer .... Shelly PEMBERTON
32 Dean of Students .... Devin BATES
30 Director Institutional Advancement .... Bill BLACKWELL, JR.

Luther Seminary (J)

2481 Como Avenue, Saint Paul MN 55108-1496
County: Ramsey FICE Identification: 002357
Unit ID: 173896
Telephone: (651) 641-3456 Carnegie Class: Spec/Faith
FAX Number: (651) 641-3425 Calendar System: Semester
URL: www.luthersem.edu
Established: 1869 Annual Graduate Tuition & Fees: $15,304
Enrollment: 622 Coed
Affiliation or Control: Evangelical Lutheran Church In America
IRS Status: 501(c)3
Highest Offering: Doctorate; No Undergraduates
Program: Professional; Religious Emphasis
Accreditation: NH, THEOL

01 President .... Rev. Robin STEINKE
05 Dean of Academic Affairs .... Dr. Craig KOESTER
10 VP Admininstration & Finance .... Mr. Michael MORROW
26 VP Seminary Relations .... Ms. Heidi DROEGEMUELLER
32 VP Student Affairs & Enrollment .... Ms. Carrie CARROLL
15 Director of Human Resources .... Ms. Arnita WALLS
42 Seminary Pastor .... Dr. Laura THELANDER
07 Director of Admissions .... Ms. Jennifer OLSEN KRENGEL
06 Registrar .... Ms. Diane DONCITS
27 Dir of Marketing/Communications .... Ms. Diane HUMMON

Lutheran Brethren Seminary (K)

815 West Vernon Avenue, Fergus Falls MN 56537-2676
County: Otter Tail Identification: 666644
Telephone: (218) 739-3375 Carnegie Class: Not Classified
FAX Number: (218) 739-1259 Calendar System: Semester
URL: www.lbs.edu
Established: 1903 Annual Graduate Tuition & Fees: $10,206
Enrollment: 25 Coed
Affiliation or Control: Other IRS Status: 501(c)3
Highest Offering: Master's; No Undergraduates
Program: Liberal Arts And General; Religious Emphasis
Accreditation: TRACS

01 President .... Dr. David VEUM
05 Dean of the Seminary .... Dr. Eugene BOE
06 Registrar .... Dr. Gaylan MATHIESEN

Macalester College (L)

1600 Grand Avenue, Saint Paul MN 55105-1801
County: Ramsey FICE Identification: 002358
Unit ID: 173902
Telephone: (651) 696-6000 Carnegie Class: Bac/A&S
FAX Number: (651) 696-6689 Calendar System: Semester
URL: www.macalester.edu
Established: 1874 Annual Undergrad Tuition & Fees: $48,887
Enrollment: 2,073 Coed
Affiliation or Control: Presbyterian Church (U.S.A.) IRS Status: 501(c)3
Highest Offering: Baccalaureate
Program: Liberal Arts And General
Accreditation: NH

01 President .... Dr. Brian C. ROSENBERG
05 Dean of the Faculty & Provost .... Dr. Karine F. MOE
88 Chief Investment Officer .... Mr. Gary D. MARTIN
30 VP Advancement .... Mr. Andrew BROWN
32 Vice President Student Affairs .... Ms. Donna LEE
10 Vice President for Admin/Finance .... Mr. David M. WHEATON
13 Associate VP ITS/CIO .... Mr. Jerry R. SANDERS
07 Dean of Admissions/Financial Aid .... Mr. Lorne T. ROBINSON
85 Inst for Global Citizenship .... Ms. Christy L. HANSON
20 Director of Academic Programs .... Ms. Ann M. MINNICK
28 Dean of Multicultural Life .... Mr. Chris A. MACDONALD-DENNIS
09 Director Inst Research .... Ms. Polly A. FASSINGER
35 Dean of Students .... Mr. Jim HOPPE
37 Director Student Financial Aid .... Mr. Brian LINDEMAN
06 Registrar .... Ms. Jayne L. NIEMI
36 Assoc Dean for Student Services .... Ms. Denise WARD
15 Director Human Resources .... Mr. Bob GRAF
18 Director Facilities Management .... Mr. Nathan P. LIEF
41 Athletic Director .... Ms. Kim CHANDLER
04 Assistant to the President .... Ms. Cynthia L. HENDRICKS
21 Assistant Vice President Finance .... Ms. Patricia M. LANGER
26 Asst VP Communications and PR .... Mr. David P. WARCH
29 Director Alumni Relations .... Ms. Gabrielle S. LAWRENCE
38 Director Health and Wellness Center .... Ms. Denise WARD
96 Dir Purchasing/Accounts Payable .... Mr. Matthew D. RUMPZA
105 Director Web Services .... Ms. Sara C. SUELFLOW
84 Manager of Enrollment Systems .... Mr. Abraham NOEL
08 Head Librarian .... Ms. Teresa FISHEL
102 Dir Foundation/Corporate Relations .... Ms. Michelle EPP

Martin Luther College (A)

1995 Luther Court, New Ulm MN 56073-3300

County: Brown | FICE Identification: 002361 | Unit ID: 173452

Telephone: (507) 354-8221 | Carnegie Class: Bac/Diverse

FAX Number: (507) 354-8225 | Calendar System: Semester

URL: www.mlc-wels.edu

Established: 1995 | Annual Undergrad Tuition & Fees: $13,570

Enrollment: 857 | Coed

Affiliation or Control: Wisconsin Evangelical Lutheran Synod | IRS Status: 501(c)3

Highest Offering: Master's

Program: Liberal Arts And General; Teacher Preparatory

Accreditation: NH

Code	Title	Name
01	President	Rev. Mark G. ZARLING
05	Vice President for Academics	Dr. Jeffery P. WIECHMAN
11	Vice President for Administration	Prof. Steven R. THIESFELDT
84	Vice President for Enrollment Mgmt	Vacant
32	Vice President Student Life	Prof. Jeffrey L. SCHONE
53	Academic Dean Educational Ministry	Prof. Earl R. HEIDTKE
73	Academic Dean Pastoral Ministry	Prof. Daniel N. BALGE
10	Director of Finance	Mrs. Carla J. HULKE
08	Director of Library Services	Mrs. Linda KRAMER
37	Director of Financial Aid	Mr. Mark D. BAUER
07	Director of Admissions	Prof. Mark A. STEIN
58	Director Graduates Studies/Cont Edu	Prof. John E. MEYER
88	Director of Clinical Experiences	Prof. Paul A. TESS
41	Director of Athletics	Prof. James M. UNKE
42	Campus Pastor	Rev. John C. BOEDER
13	Director of Technology	Mr. James A. RATHJE
26	Director of Public Relations	Prof. William A. PEKRUL
40	Bookstore Manager	Mrs. Linette M. SCHARLEMANN
90	Director of Academic Computing	Dr. James R. GRUNWALD
29	Director Alumni Relations	Mr. Stephen J. BALZA
108	Director Institutional Assessment	Prof. Larry W. LOTITO

McNally Smith College of Music (B)

19 Exchange Street, Saint Paul MN 55101-2220

County: Ramsey | FICE Identification: 030012 | Unit ID: 367194

Telephone: (651) 291-0177 | Carnegie Class: Spec/Arts

FAX Number: (651) 291-0366 | Calendar System: Semester

URL: www.mcnallysmith.edu

Established: 1985 | Annual Undergrad Tuition & Fees: $25,210

Enrollment: 518 | Coed

Affiliation or Control: Proprietary | IRS Status: Proprietary

Highest Offering: Baccalaureate

Program: Occupational; Liberal Arts And General; Professional; Music Emphasis

Accreditation: @NH, MUS

Code	Title	Name
01	President	Harry CHALMIERS
10	Chief Financial Officer	Jakki EDWARDS
37	Financial Aid Director	Jeffrey R. AALBERS
07	Admissions Director	Matthew EDLUND

Minneapolis Business College (C)

1711 W County Road B, Roseville MN 55113-4056

County: Ramsey | FICE Identification: 004645 | Unit ID: 174118

Telephone: (651) 636-7406 | Carnegie Class: Assoc/PrivFP

FAX Number: (651) 636-8185 | Calendar System: Semester

URL: www.minneapolisbusinesscollege.edu

Established: 1874 | Annual Undergrad Tuition & Fees: $14,720

Enrollment: 150 | Coed

Affiliation or Control: Proprietary | IRS Status: Proprietary

Highest Offering: Associate Degree

Program: Occupational; 2-Year Principally Bachelor's Creditable; Business Emphasis

Accreditation: ACICS, MAC

Code	Title	Name
01	President	Mr. David WHITMAN
05	Director of Education	Mr. Jon BLUMENTHAL
32	Director of Student Services	Mrs. Marie MARTIN
36	Placement Coordinator	Mrs. Suzanne ERICKSON

Minneapolis College of Art and Design (D)

2501 Stevens Avenue, Minneapolis MN 55404-4343

County: Hennepin | FICE Identification: 002365 | Unit ID: 174127

Telephone: (612) 874-3700 | Carnegie Class: Spec/Arts

FAX Number: (612) 874-3704 | Calendar System: Semester

URL: www.mcad.edu

Established: 1886 | Annual Undergrad Tuition & Fees: $35,326

Enrollment: 783 | Coed

Affiliation or Control: Independent Non-Profit | IRS Status: 501(c)3

Highest Offering: Master's

Program: Liberal Arts And General; Professional; Fine Arts Emphasis

Accreditation: NH, ART

Code	Title	Name
01	President	Mr. Jay COOGAN
04	Executive Assistant to President	Ms. Sarah HARDING
05	Vice President Academic Affairs	Ms. Karen WIRTH
11	Vice President Administration	Ms. Pam NEWSOME
30	AVP Institutional Advancement	Ms. Cindy THEIS
84	Assoc VP Enrollment Management	Ms. Melissa HUYBRECHT
18	Assoc VP Facilities/Public Safety	Mr. Brock RASMUSSEN
13	Assoc Vice President Technology	Mr. R. Hal WELLS
32	Dean of Student Affairs	Ms. Jen ZUCCOLA
06	Registrar	Mr. River GORDON
51	Director of Continuing Education	Ms. Lara ROY
08	Director of Library	Ms. Amy NAUGHTON
24	Director of Media Center	Mr. Scott BOWMAN
36	Director of Career Services	Ms. Meghana SHROFF
29	Director Alumni and Annual Giving	Mr. Seth GOODSPEED
39	Director Student Housing	Mr. Nate K. LUTZ
26	Director Communications	Ms. Ann BENRUD
37	Director Student Financial Aid	Ms. Laura LINK
40	Manager of Bookstore	Ms. Allyson R. HARPER
108	Director Accreditation & Assessment	Mr. Colin O'NEILL
19	Director of Public Safety	Mr. Steve MCLAUGHLIN

Minneapolis Media Institute (E)

4100 West 76th Street, Edina MN 55435

Telephone: (952) 897-1111 | Identification: 770578

Accreditation: ACCSC, ACICS

† Branch campus of Madison Media Institute-College of Media Arts, Madison, WI.

Minnesota School of Business (F)

3680 Pheasant Ridge Drive NE, Blaine MN 55449

Telephone: (763) 225-8000 | Identification: 770718

Accreditation: ACICS, MAAB

† Branch campus of Minnesota School of Business, Richfield, MN.

Minnesota School of Business (G)

5910 Shingle Creek Parkway, #200, Brooklyn Center MN 55430-2319

Telephone: (763) 566-7777 | Identification: 666453

Accreditation: ACICS, MAAB

† Branch campus of Minnesota School of Business, Richfield, MN.

Minnesota School of Business (H)

11500 193rd Avenue NW, Elk River MN 55330

Telephone: (763) 367-7000 | Identification: 770719

Accreditation: ACICS, MAAB

† Branch campus of Minnesota School of Business, Richfield, MN.

Minnesota School of Business (I)

17685 Juniper Path, Lakeville MN 55044

Telephone: (952) 892-9000 | Identification: 770720

Accreditation: ACICS, MAAB

† Branch campus of Minnesota School of Business, Richfield, MN.

Minnesota School of Business (J)

1455 County Road 101 North, Plymouth MN 55447

Telephone: (763) 476-2000 | Identification: 770713

Accreditation: ACICS

† Branch campus of Minnesota School of Business, Richfield, MN.

Minnesota School of Business (K)

1401 W 76th Street, Suite 500, Richfield MN 55423-3846

County: Hennepin | FICE Identification: 004646 | Unit ID: 174279

Telephone: (800) 752-4223 | Carnegie Class: Master's S

FAX Number: (612) 861-5548 | Calendar System: Quarter

URL: www.msbcollege.edu

Established: 1877 | Annual Undergrad Tuition & Fees: $14,040

Enrollment: 763 | Coed

Affiliation or Control: Proprietary | IRS Status: Proprietary

Highest Offering: Master's

Program: Occupational

Accreditation: ACICS, MAAB, NURSE

Code	Title	Name
01	Campus Director	Mrs. Stacy SEVERSON
05	Dean of Education	Ms. Miraim WILLIAMS
32	Assoc Dean of Students	Mr. Patrick SHAY
07	Director of Admissions	Mr. Michael POSTER
36	Director of Career Services	Ms. Elizabeth ASHANTIZA
37	Director of Financial Aid	Ms. Carol BARTA

Minnesota School of Business (L)

2521 Pennington Drive NW, Rochester MN 55901

Telephone: (507) 536-9500 | Identification: 770716

Accreditation: ACICS, MAAB

† Branch campus of Minnesota School of Business, Richfield, MN.

Minnesota School of Business (M)

1201 2nd Street South, Waite Park MN 56387

Telephone: (320) 257-2000 | Identification: 770715

Accreditation: ACICS, MAAB

† Branch campus of Minnesota School of Business, Richfield, MN.

*Minnesota State Colleges and Universities System Office (N)

30 7th Street East, Suite 350, Saint Paul MN 55101-4901

County: Ramsey | FICE Identification: 009346 | Unit ID: 428453

Telephone: (651) 201-1800 | Carnegie Class: N/A

FAX Number: (651) 297-5550

URL: www.mnscu.edu

Code	Title	Name
01	Chancellor	Steven J. ROSENSTONE
03	Vice Chancellor	Mark CARLSON
05	Vice Chanc Academic/Student Affairs	Ron ANDERSON
10	Vice Chanc Finance/CFO	Laura M. KING
13	Vice Chanc Information Tech/CIO	Ramon PADILLA
30	Vice Chanc Advancement	Vacant
18	Assoc Vice Chancellor Facilities	Brian D. YOLITZ
46	Assoc Vice Chanc Research/Planning	Leslie K. MERCER
32	Assoc Vice Chanc Student Affairs	Toyia YOUNGER
100	Chief of Staff	Nancy JOYER
15	Chief Human Resource Officer	Vicki DEFORD
28	Chief Diversity Officer	Leon RODRIGUES
102	Exec Dir System/Foundation Rels	Maria R. MCLEMORE
43	Interim General Counsel	Kristine LEGLER KAPLAN
45	Program Director for Planning	Todd HARMENING
21	Exec Director of Internal Auditing	Beth H. BUSE

*Alexandria Technical & Community College (O)

1601 Jefferson Street, Alexandria MN 56308-2796

County: Douglas | FICE Identification: 005544 | Unit ID: 172918

Telephone: (320) 762-0221 | Carnegie Class: Assoc/Pub-R-M

FAX Number: (320) 762-4501 | Calendar System: Semester

URL: www.alextech.edu

Established: 1961 | Annual Undergrad Tuition & Fees (In-State): $5,400

Enrollment: 2,525 | Coed

Affiliation or Control: State | IRS Status: 501(c)3

Highest Offering: Associate Degree

Program: Occupational; 2-Year Principally Bachelor's Creditable; Technical Emphasis

Accreditation: NH, MLTAD

Code	Title	Name
02	President	Dr. Laura URBAN
05	Exec VP Academic/Student Affairs	Dr. Jan DOEBBERT
41	Vice Pres/Athletic Director	Vacant
51	Dean of Customized Training	Mr. Robert DEFRIES
10	Chief Financial Officer	Mr. David BJELLAND
05	Sr Dean Academic Affairs & Students	Mr. Gregg RAISANEN
32	Dean of Student Affairs	Vacant
72	Dean of Technology	Mr. Steve RICHARDS
20	Associate Dean of Academic Affairs	Vacant
19	Dean of Law Enforcement	Mr. Scott BERGER
37	Financial Aid Director	Mr. Steve RICHARDS
22	Human Rights Officer	Ms. Tamzin BUKOWSKI
36	Director Student Placement	Mr. Patrick RUNNING
102	Foundation Executive Director	Ms. Amy ALLEN
06	Registrar	Ms. Debra LEDOUX
18	Director of Facilities	Mr. Alan HALBUR
15	Chief Human Resources Officer	Ms. Shari MALONEY
09	Director of Institutional Research	Ms. Rebekah SUMMER
07	Director of Admissions	Mr. Scott BERGER
35	Director of Student Activities	Ms. Michelle AHLQUIST
38	Director of K-12 Initiatives	Ms. Mary LENZ
04	Asst to Pres/Dir of Office Services	Ms. Annette PAVEK
21	Director of Financial Operations	Ms. Julie FENLASON
40	Bookstore Manager	Ms. Karen SLACK
44	Development Officer	Ms. Linda DOLAN
88	Director of Support Services	Ms. Kaye MADIGAN
28	Chief Diversity Officer	Ms. Debra LEDOUX

*Anoka-Ramsey Community College (P)

11200 Mississippi Boulevard NW, Coon Rapids MN 55433-3499

County: Anoka | FICE Identification: 002332 | Unit ID: 172963

Telephone: (763) 433-1100 | Carnegie Class: Assoc/Pub-S-MC

FAX Number: (763) 433-1121 | Calendar System: Semester

URL: www.anokaramsey.edu

Established: 1965 | Annual Undergrad Tuition & Fees (In-State): $5,019

Enrollment: 7,877 | Coed

Affiliation or Control: State | IRS Status: 501(c)3

Highest Offering: Associate Degree

Program: 2-Year Principally Bachelor's Creditable; Liberal Arts And General

Accreditation: NH, ADNUR, MUS, PTAA

Code	Title	Name
02	President	Dr. Kent HANSON
10	VP Finance & Administration	Mr. Don LEWIS
05	VP Academic/Student Affairs	Ms. Deidra PEASLEE
32	Dean of Student Affairs	Ms. Lisa HARRIS
35	Dean of Student Affairs	Mr. Steve CRITTENDEN
18	Physical Plant Manager	Mr. Roger FREEMAN
15	Chief HR Director	Mr. Jay NELSON
57	Dean of Arts & Letters	Mr. Greg RATHERT
88	Dean CE/CT/Bus/Tech/Wellness	Ms. Luanne KANE
35	Dean Student Life	Vacant
76	Dean of Allied Health	Ms. Natasha BAER

21 Director Fiscal & Auxiliary Svcs ... Ms. Marilyn SMITH
81 Dean of STEM ... Ms. Kim LYNCH
09 Dean of Research & Assessment ... Ms. Nora MORRIS
28 Director of Multicultural Affairs ... Ms. Venoreen BROWNE-BOATSWAIN
102 Director of Foundations ... Vacant
26 Director of Mktg/Public Relations ... Ms. Mary JACOBSON
19 Int Director of Safety & Security ... Mr. Ed WILBERG
35 Director of Student Life ... Ms. Joyce TRACZYK
13 Interim Director of Technology ... Mr. Tim ZONDLO
21 Business Manager ... Ms. Kim BIENFANG
37 Director Financial Aid ... Mr. Sean JOHNS

*Anoka Technical College (A)

1355 W Highway 10, Anoka MN 55303-1590
County: Anoka FICE Identification: 007350
Unit ID: 172954
Telephone: (763) 576-4700 Carnegie Class: Assoc/Pub-S-MC
FAX Number: (763) 576-4715 Calendar System: Semester
URL: www.anokatech.edu
Established: 1967 Annual Undergrad Tuition & Fees (In-District): $5,584
Enrollment: 2,205 Coed
Affiliation or Control: State/Local IRS Status: 501(c)3
Highest Offering: Associate Degree
Program: Occupational; 2-Year Principally Bachelor's Creditable; Technical Emphasis
Accreditation: NH, CAHIIM, MAC, OTA, SURGT

02 President ... Dr. Kent HANSON
05 Int Vice Pres of Acad/Student Affs ... Heidi HAAGENSON
13 Chief Information Officer ... William BEAR
10 Vice Pres Finanance & Admin ... Donald LEWIS
20 Academic Dean ... Sherry WICKSTROM
04 Assistant to the President ... Vacant
15 Chief Human Res Ofcr/Dir Diversity ... Jay NELSON
26 Director of Marketing ... Mary JACOBSON
06 Director of Records ... Jamaica DELMAR
32 Intermin Dean of Student Affairs ... Elena FAVELA
37 Financial Aid Director ... Sean JOHNS
08 Head Librarian ... Vacant
18 Chief Facilities/Physical Plant ... Roger FREEMAN
19 Director Security/Safety ... Ed WILBERG
84 Director of Enrollment Services ... Leann BROWN
09 Director of Institutional Research ... Elizabeth PALMER

*Bemidji State University (B)

1500 Birchmont Drive NE, Bemidji MN 56601-2699
County: Beltrami FICE Identification: 002336
Unit ID: 173124
Telephone: (218) 755-2001 Carnegie Class: Master's S
FAX Number: N/A Calendar System: Semester
URL: www.bemidjistate.edu
Established: 1919 Annual Undergrad Tuition & Fees (In-State): $8,366
Enrollment: 4,906 Coed
Affiliation or Control: State IRS Status: 501(c)3
Highest Offering: Master's
Program: Liberal Arts And General; Teacher Preparatory
Accreditation: NH, IACBE, MUS, NAIT, NURSE, SW

02 President ... Dr. Richard A. HANSON
05 Provost & VP Acad & Student Affairs ... Dr. Martin TADLOCK
10 VP Finance & Administration ... Ms. Karen SNOREK
20 VP Innovation & Ext Learning ... Mr. Robert J. GRIGGS
20 Interim Asst VP Academic Affairs ... Dr. Randall WESTHOFF
84 Int Dean of Student Support Svcs ... Ms. Michelle FRENZEL
32 Interim Dean of Student Success ... Dr. Mary WARD
49 Dean Arts & Sciences ... Dr. Colleen GREER
50 Dean Business/Tech & Communication ... Dr. Shawn STRONG
76 Int Dean Health Sci/Human Ecology ... Dr. Troy GILBERTSON
94 Director Gender Studies ... Dr. Carla NORRIS-RAYNBIRD
92 Director Honors Program ... Dr. Marsha DRISCOLL
06 Registrar ... Vacant
09 Director Inst Rsrch/Effectiveness ... Mr. Douglas P. OLNEY
106 Director Distance Learning ... Ms. Lynn JOHNSON
07 Director Admissions/Enrollment ... Mr. Michael HEITKAMP
36 Director Career Services ... Ms. Margie T. GIAUQUE
85 Director International Program Ctr ... Ms. Cherish HAGEN-SWANSON
39 Director Housing & Residential Life ... Dr. Jodi MONERSON
88 Director American Indian Ctr ... Dr. Bill BLACKWELL
37 Director Financial Aid ... Ms. Lesa LAWRENCE
15 Interim Director Human Resources ... Ms. Marybeth CHRISTENSON-JONES
21 Business Manager ... Ms. Diane ILLIES
96 Director Procurement & Logistics ... Ms. Belinda S. LINDELL
19 Director Public Safety ... Mr. Casey J. MCCARTHY
18 Director Physical Plant ... Mr. Jeff A. SANDE
22 Affirmative Action & Accreditation ... Dr. Debra PETERSON
30 Exec Dir for University Advancement ... Mr. Robert D. BOLLINGER
29 Interim Director Alumni Relations ... Mr. Brett BAHR
13 Chief Information Officer ... Vacant
26 Director Communications & Marketing ... Mr. Scott FAUST
41 Athletic Director ... Mr. Tracy DILL

*Central Lakes College (C)

501 W College Drive, Brainerd MN 56401-3900
County: Crow Wing FICE Identification: 002339
Unit ID: 173203
Telephone: (218) 855-8000 Carnegie Class: Assoc/Pub-R-M
FAX Number: (218) 855-8057 Calendar System: Semester
URL: www.clcmn.edu
Established: 1938 Annual Undergrad Tuition & Fees (In-State): $5,393
Enrollment: 1,391 Coed
Affiliation or Control: State IRS Status: 501(c)3
Highest Offering: Associate Degree
Program: Occupational; 2-Year Principally Bachelor's Creditable; Technical Emphasis
Accreditation: NH, DA, MAC

02 President ... Dr. Larry A. LUNDBLAD
05 Interim Vice Pres Academic Affairs ... Dr. David HIETALA
10 VP Administrative Svcs/Facilities ... Ms. Kari CHRISTIANSEN
12 Dean Technical Pgms/Staples Campus ... Mr. Christopher HADFIELD
32 Dean of Students ... Vacant
13 Dean Computer Tech & Online ... Mr. Michael AMICK
49 Dean of Liberal Arts ... Ms. Martha KUEHN
30 Dir Resource Development/CLC Found ... Ms. Pamela THOMSEN
15 Director of Human Resources ... Ms. Nancy PAULSON
07 Director of Enrollment Services ... Mr. Nick HEISSERER
06 Registrar ... Ms. Michelle KANGAS
08 Librarian ... Mr. David BISSONETTE
37 Director Financial Aid ... Mr. Mike BARNABY
26 Director Marketing & PR ... Mr. Kenn DOLS
21 Director of Business Services ... Ms. Christina ANDERSON
18 Physical Plant Director ... Mr. James MCARDELL
28 Director of Diversity ... Ms. Mary SAM
04 Administrative Asst to President ... Ms. Debra K. WESP
09 Director of Institutional Research ... Ms. Wendy ADAMSON
19 Director Security/Safety ... Mr. Dave DAVIS

*Century College (D)

3300 Century Avenue N, White Bear Lake MN 55110-1894
County: Ramsey FICE Identification: 010546
Unit ID: 175315
Telephone: (651) 779-3200 Carnegie Class: Assoc/Pub-S-SC
FAX Number: (651) 779-3417 Calendar System: Semester
URL: www.century.edu
Established: 1967 Annual Undergrad Tuition & Fees (In-State): $5,391
Enrollment: 9,386 Coed
Affiliation or Control: State IRS Status: 501(c)3
Highest Offering: Associate Degree
Program: Occupational; 2-Year Principally Bachelor's Creditable; Technical Emphasis
Accreditation: NH, ADNUR, DA, DH, EMT, MAC, RAD

02 Interim President ... Dr. Patrick OPATZ
05 VP Academic Affairs/CAO ... Mr. Michael BERNDT
32 Int VP Enroll Mgmt/Student Svcs ... Mr. Greg MCCALLEY
51 VP Advancement & Innovation ... Ms. Jeralyn JARGO
10 Acting VP Finance & Administration ... Ms. Bonnie MEYERS
13 Assoc VP Information Tech/Admn Svcs ... Mr. John ROHLEDER
96 Purchasing & Auxiliary Svcs Suprvr ... Mr. Todd OSEBY
21 Acting Director of Finance ... Ms. Deborah MAYNE
102 Executive Director Foundation ... Ms. Jill GREENHALGH
06 Registrar ... Ms. Susan DICKENS
15 Director of Human Resources ... Ms. Mary NIENABER
07 Director of Admissions ... Ms. Christine PAULOS
45 Director of Resource Development ... Mr. Donald LONG
37 Director of Financial Aid ... Ms. Pam ENGEBRETSON
18 Mgr of Physical Plant/Super of Bld ... Mr. Michael HOUFER
19 Director of Public Safety ... Mr. Mark HOLPER
66 Dean Nursing/Allied Health ... Ms. Kathleen BELL
75 Dean Trades/Public Safety/Svcs ... Ms. Jane NICHOLSON
72 Dean Science/Technology ... Ms. Brenda LYSENG
81 Dean English/ESOL/Reading/Math ... Mr. Andrew NESSET
83 Dean Soc & Beh Sci/Lang/Com ... Dr. Jesse MASON
35 Dean of Student Services ... Mr. Jason CARDINAL
35 Dean of Student Services ... Ms. Andrea RYSTROM
35 Dean of Student Services ... Ms. Kristin HAGEMAN
09 Dean of Institutional Effectiveness ... Ms. Lisa SCHLOTTERHAUSEN
04 Administrative Asst to President . Ms. Laurel KARTARIK MARTIN
26 Director of Marketing ... Mr. James STUMNE
28 Director/Chief Diversity Officer ... Ms. Nickyia COGSHELL

*Dakota County Technical College (E)

145th Street E, Rosemount MN 55068-2999
County: Dakota FICE Identification: 010402
Unit ID: 173416
Telephone: (651) 423-8000 Carnegie Class: Assoc/Pub-S-SC
FAX Number: (651) 423-8775 Calendar System: Semester
URL: www.dctc.edu
Established: 1970 Annual Undergrad Tuition & Fees (In-District): $5,712
Enrollment: 2,910 Coed
Affiliation or Control: State/Local IRS Status: 501(c)3
Highest Offering: Associate Degree
Program: Occupational; 2-Year Principally Bachelor's Creditable; Technical Emphasis
Accreditation: NH, DA, MAC

02 President ... Mr. Tim WYNES
05 VP Academic & Student Affairs ... Dr. Mike OPP
88 Dean Transportation Indust Careers ... Mr. Chad SHEETS
50 Dean of Business/Technology and GE ... Ms. Gayle LARSON
32 Director Student Success ... Mr. Patrick LAIR
06 Registrar ... Ms. Jodie SWEARINGEN
18 Director of Operations ... Mr. Paul DEMUTH
35 Director Student Life/Activities ... Ms. Nicole MEULEMANS
103 Dean Customized Training/Cont Educ ... Mr. Pat MCQUILLAN
07 Admissions Coordinator ... Ms. Karianne LOULA
30 Director Institutional Advancement ... Ms. Erin EDLUND
37 Director Financial Aid ... Mr. Scott ROELKE
09 Dir Institutional Research/Planning ... Ms. Carrie SCHNEIDER
15 Chief Human Resource Officer ... Ms. Suzanne BRUSOE

*Fond du Lac Tribal and Community College (F)

2101 14th Street, Cloquet MN 55720-2984
County: Carlton FICE Identification: 031291
Unit ID: 380368
Telephone: (218) 879-0800 Carnegie Class: Tribal
FAX Number: (218) 879-0814 Calendar System: Semester
URL: www.fdltcc.edu
Established: 1987 Annual Undergrad Tuition & Fees (In-State): $5,256
Enrollment: 2,253 Coed
Affiliation or Control: State IRS Status: 501(c)3
Highest Offering: Associate Degree
Program: Occupational; 2-Year Principally Bachelor's Creditable; Liberal Arts And General
Accreditation: NH

02 President ... Mr. Larry ANDERSON
05 Vice President of Academics ... Dr. Don CARLSON
10 Chief Financial Officer ... Ms. Stephanie HAMMITT
32 Dean of Student Affairs ... Mr. Keith TURNER
26 Director of Public Information ... Mr. Tom URBANSKI
06 Registrar ... Ms. Leah TOLLEFSON
88 Disability Services/Student Service ... Ms. Shelia SUMNER
13 Information Technology Specialist ... Mr. Loran WAPPES
37 Director of Financial Aid ... Mr. David SUTHERLAND
07 Director of Admissions ... Ms. Susan BUMANN
09 Director of Institutional Research ... Ms. Sherry SANCHEZ-TIBBETTS
35 Dir of Student Support Services ... Ms. Peggy POITRA
62 Library Services ... Ms. Nancy BROUGHTON
30 Director of Development ... Mr. Larry ANDERSON
39 Director of Housing ... Mr. Jesse STIREWALT
15 Director of Human Resources ... Ms. Louise LIND
18 Chief Facilities/Physical Plant ... Mr. Mark BERNHARDSON
40 Bookstore Coordinator ... Ms. Bonnie BERNHARDSON
04 Executive Assistant to President ... Ms. Mary SOYRING

*Hennepin Technical College (G)

9000 Brooklyn Boulevard, Brooklyn Park MN 55445-2399
County: Hennepin FICE Identification: 010491
Unit ID: 173708
Telephone: (952) 995-1300 Carnegie Class: Assoc/Pub-S-MC
FAX Number: (763) 488-2956 Calendar System: Semester
URL: www.hennepintech.edu
Established: 1972 Annual Undergrad Tuition & Fees (In-District): $5,122
Enrollment: 5,985 Coed
Affiliation or Control: State/Local IRS Status: 501(c)3
Highest Offering: Associate Degree
Program: Occupational; 2-Year Principally Bachelor's Creditable; Technical Emphasis
Accreditation: NH, ACBSP, ACFEI, DA, IFSAC, MAC

02 President ... Dr. Merrill IRVING, JR.
05 Vice Pres Academic & Student Affs ... Dr. Lisa LARSON
11 Vice Pres Administrative Services ... Mr. Craig ERICKSON
06 Registrar ... Ms. Julie HIGDEM
15 Chief Human Resources Officer ... Ms. Sharon MOHR
30 Dir Development/Alumni Relations ... Vacant
28 Director of Diversity ... Ms. Jean MAIERHOFER
07 Director of Admissions ... Ms. Monir JOHNSON
09 Dir of Institutional Effectiveness ... Ms. Donna S. STATZELL
26 Exec Dir Inst Adv & Marketing ... Ms. Annette ROTH
37 Director of Financial Aid ... Mr. Tim JACOBSON
84 Dean of Enrollment ... Ms. Kristine RAMOS-WALKER
88 Dean of Student Success ... Ms. Dara HAGAN
04 Administrative Asst to President ... Ms. Lisa OPEM
13 Chief Info Technology Officer (CIO) ... Mr. Randy BAYERL
08 Head Librarian ... Ms. Jennie SIMNING
22 Dir Affirmative Action/EEO ... Ms. Jean MAIERHOFER

*Hibbing Community College, A Technical and Community College (H)

1515 E 25th Street, Hibbing MN 55746-3300
County: Saint Louis FICE Identification: 002355
Unit ID: 173735
Telephone: (218) 262-7200 Carnegie Class: Assoc/Pub-R-S
FAX Number: (218) 262-6717 Calendar System: Semester
URL: www.hibbing.edu
Established: 1916 Annual Undergrad Tuition & Fees (In-State): $5,308
Enrollment: 1,310 Coed
Affiliation or Control: State IRS Status: 501(c)3
Highest Offering: Associate Degree
Program: Occupational; 2-Year Principally Bachelor's Creditable
Accreditation: NH, ADNUR, DA, MLTAD

02 President ... Mr. Bill MAKI
05 Provost ... Dr. Michael RAICH
32 Int Dean of Lib Arts & Student Svcs ... Ms. Lisa BESTUL
10 Chief Fiscal Officer ... Mr. Bill MANNEY
09 Institutional Research ... Ms. Tracey ROY
37 Director Student Financial Aid ... Mrs. Ann JOHNSTON
18 Plant Maintenance Engineer ... Mr. Jimmer HODGE

26 Marketing Specialist/Public Info ..... Ms. Jessica MATVEY
06 Registrar ..... Ms. Kari DOUCETTE
13 Chief Info Technology Officer (CIO) ..... Ms. Linda RASKOVICH
39 Director Student Housing ..... Mr. Eric THORSON
41 Athletic Director ..... Mr. Mike FLATEN

*Inver Hills Community College (A)

2500 80th Street E, Inver Grove Heights MN 55076-3224
County: Dakota FICE Identification: 009740
Unit ID: 173799
Telephone: (651) 450-3000 Carnegie Class: Assoc/Pub-S-SC
FAX Number: (651) 450-3679 Calendar System: Semester
URL: www.inverhills.edu
Established: 1970 Annual Undergrad Tuition & Fees (In-State): $5,272
Enrollment: 59,588 Coed
Affiliation or Control: State IRS Status: 501(c)3
Highest Offering: Associate Degree
Program: Occupational; 2-Year Principally Bachelor's Creditable
Accreditation: NH, ACBSP, ADNUR, EMT

02 President ..... Mr. Timothy WYNES
05 Prov/VP Academic Affs & Student Dev ..... Dr. Christina ROYAL
11 Vice Pres Administrative Services ..... Ms. Dee BERNARD
32 Interim VP for Student Affairs ..... Dr. Jessica STUMPF
10 Chief Financial Officer ..... Mr. Scott ERICKSON
45 Int Assc VP of Strategic Initiative ..... Ms. Anne JOHNSON
06 Registrar ..... Mr. Matt TRAXLER
50 Dean of Business & Social Sci ..... Vacant
76 Dean of Allied Health Sci ..... Dr. Lynne HVIDSTEN
79 Dean of Fine Arts/Humanities ..... Ms. Ann DEIMAN-THORNTON
81 Dean of STEM ..... Dr. Stephen L. STROM
102 Exec Dir of Foundation & Advancemnt ..... Mrs. Gail MORRISON
15 Director of Human Resources ..... Ms. Elizabeth NEWBERRY
103 Dean Ctr Prof/Workforce Development ..... Mr. Pat MCQUILLAN
08 Librarian ..... Ms. Julie BENOLKEN
84 Director of Enrollment Services ..... Mr. Matt TRAXLER
88 Dir Paralegal Pgm/Ofc Sys-Legal ..... Ms. Sally DAHLQUIST
90 Director Acad Tech/Computing Svcs ..... Mr. Mark PETERSON
18 Director Facilities Plng/Management ..... Mr. Pat BUHL
88 Interim Dir of Emer Health Svcs ..... Mr. Brad WRIGHT
28 Director of Equity & Inclusion ..... Vacant
37 Director of Financial Aid ..... Mr. Steve YANG
09 Director of Institutional Research ..... Ms. Wendy MARSON
26 Dir of Inst Advance/Mktg & PR ..... Ms. Erin EDLUND
88 Director of Service Learning ..... Ms. Katie HALCROW
20 Interim Assoc Dean of Acad Affair ..... Ms. Susan DION

*Itasca Community College (B)

1851 E Highway 169, Grand Rapids MN 55744-3397
County: Itasca FICE Identification: 002356
Unit ID: 173805
Telephone: (800) 996-6422 Carnegie Class: Assoc/Pub-R-S
FAX Number: (218) 322-2332 Calendar System: Semester
URL: www.itascacc.edu
Established: 1922 Annual Undergrad Tuition & Fees (In-State): $5,324
Enrollment: 1,222 Coed
Affiliation or Control: State IRS Status: 501(c)3
Highest Offering: Associate Degree
Program: 2-Year Principally Bachelor's Creditable
Accreditation: NH

02 Chief Executive Officer ..... Mr. William D. MAKI
03 Executive Vice President ..... Ms. Karen KEDROWSKI
05 Interim Provost ..... Dr. Michael RAICH
20 Academic Dean ..... Mr. Bart JOHNSON
10 Accounting Officer Finance ..... Ms. Kristen LIND
84 Dir of Enrollment Mgmt/Admissions ..... Mr. William MARSHALL
06 Registrar ..... Ms. Allison GEISLER
29 Director of Alumni Relations ..... Ms. Beth ANDERSON
30 Director of College Development ..... Ms. Janet NEURAUTER
37 Director of Student Financial Aid ..... Mr. Nathan WRIGHT
08 Head Librarian ..... Mr. Steve BEAN
18 Director of Facilities & Info Tech ..... Mr. Chad HAATVEDT
40 Bookstore Manager ..... Ms. Faith MCBRIDE
28 Director of Diversity ..... Mr. Harold ANNETTE
09 Director of Institutional Research ..... Ms. Tracey ROY
39 Director Student Housing ..... Mr. Weldon BRAXTON
32 Dean of Student & Admin Services ..... Mr. Richard KANGAS

*Lake Superior College (C)

2101 Trinity Road, Duluth MN 55811-3399
County: Saint Louis FICE Identification: 005757
Unit ID: 173461
Telephone: (218) 733-7600 Carnegie Class: Assoc/Pub-R-L
FAX Number: (218) 733-4921 Calendar System: Semester
URL: www.lsc.edu
Established: 1995 Annual Undergrad Tuition & Fees (In-State): $5,083
Enrollment: 5,101 Coed
Affiliation or Control: State IRS Status: 501(c)3
Highest Offering: Associate Degree
Program: Occupational; 2-Year Principally Bachelor's Creditable
Accreditation: NH, ADNUR, COARC, DH, MAC, MLTAD, PNUR, PTAA, RAD, SURGT

02 President ..... Dr. Patrick JOHNS
05 Vice Pres Academic/Student Affairs ..... Mr. Michael SEYMOUR
10 Vice Pres Finance & Administration ..... Mr. Al FINLAYSON
49 Dean of Liberal Arts & Sciences ..... Ms. Hanna ERPESTAD
75 Dean of Business/Industry Division ..... Ms. Jenni SWENSON
76 Dean of Allied Health & Nursing ..... Ms. Laurie JENSEN
103 Exec Dir Workforce/Cmty Develop ..... Mr. Steve WAGNER
09 Dir IR/Accred Assessment/Research ..... Mr. Kent RICHARDS
15 Director of Human Resources ..... Ms. Audra FLANAGAN
26 Dir of Public Affairs/Advancement ..... Vacant
84 Director of Enrollment Mgmt ..... Ms. Melissa LENO
18 Director Physical Plant ..... Mr. Gary ADAMS
32 Dir Safety/Security & Student Life ..... Mr. Wade GORDON
36 Director Career Services ..... Mr. Eric BRANDT
37 Director Student Financial Aid ..... Ms. LaNita ROBINSON
21 Director Business Services ..... Ms. Kathy DUGDALE
102 Foundation Director ..... Ms. Kim PARMETER
13 Director Information Technology ..... Mr. Steve FUDALLY
96 Purchasing Agent ..... Ms. Michelle PHERNETTON
04 Administrative Asst to President ..... Ms. Debbie JOHNSON

*Mesabi Range College (D)

1001 Chestnut Street West, Virginia MN 55792-3401
County: Saint Louis FICE Identification: 004009
Unit ID: 173993
Telephone: (218) 741-3095 Carnegie Class: Assoc/Pub-R-S
FAX Number: (218) 748-2419 Calendar System: Semester
URL: www.mesabirange.edu
Established: 1963 Annual Undergrad Tuition & Fees (In-State): $5,293
Enrollment: 1,265 Coed
Affiliation or Control: State IRS Status: Exempt
Highest Offering: Associate Degree
Program: Occupational; 2-Year Principally Bachelor's Creditable
Accreditation: NH, EMT

02 President ..... Mr. William MAKI
05 Provost ..... Ms. Carol HELLAND
32 Dean of Student Affairs ..... Mr. David DAILEY
10 Director of Finance ..... Mr. Roy TROUSDELL
15 Director Human Resources ..... Ms. Carmen BRADACH
37 Director Student Financial Aid ..... Ms. Jodi PONTINEN
06 Registrar ..... Mrs. Rebecca STEVINSON
07 Director of Admissions ..... Ms. Brenda KOCHEVAR
09 Director of Institutional Research ..... Ms. Tracey ROY
26 Chief Public Relations Officer ..... Ms. Brenda KOCHEVAR
38 Director Student Counseling ..... Ms. Kelly BAKK
36 Director Student Placement ..... Ms. Shari CHRISTENSON
84 Director Enrollment Management ..... Ms. Brenda KOCHEVAR
13 Chief Info Technology Officer (CIO) ..... Mrs. Shelly MCCAULEY-JUGOVICH

*Metropolitan State University (E)

700 E 7th Street, Saint Paul MN 55106-5000
County: Ramsey FICE Identification: 010374
Unit ID: 174020
Telephone: (651) 793-1300 Carnegie Class: Master's M
FAX Number: (651) 793-1235 Calendar System: Semester
URL: www.metrostate.edu
Established: 1971 Annual Undergrad Tuition & Fees (In-State): $7,560
Enrollment: 8,354 Coed
Affiliation or Control: State IRS Status: 501(c)3
Highest Offering: Doctorate
Program: Liberal Arts And General; Teacher Preparatory; Professional
Accreditation: NH, NURSE, SW

02 Interim President ..... Dr. Devinder MALHOTRA
05 Provost/Vice Pres Academic Affs ..... Ms. Virginia ARTHUR
11 Vice Pres Administrative Affairs ..... Mr. Murtuza SIDDIQUI
32 Vice Pres Student Affs/Enroll Mgmt ..... Vacant
30 Interim VP Advancement/Planning ..... Ms. Anne SONNEE
35 Dean of Students ..... Mr. Herbert KING
18 Assoc Vice Pres Admin Affairs ..... Mr. Daniel HAMBROCK
13 Assoc VP Info/Telecom/Tech/CIO ..... Vacant
10 Assoc VP Financial Management ..... Vacant
15 Director Human Resources ..... Ms. Deb GEHRKE
06 Registrar ..... Mr. Daryl JOHNSON
37 Director Financial Aid ..... Ms. Lois LARSON
26 Director Communications/Marketing ..... Ms. Poh Lin KHOO
27 Publication/News Services Director ..... Ms. Susan M. AMOS PALMER
29 Director Alumni Relations ..... Ms. Kristine HANSEN
22 Director Affirmative Action ..... Mr. Craig MORRIS
09 Director Institutional Research ..... Ms. Cynthia DEVORE
07 Director of Admissions ..... Mr. Julio VARGAS-ESSEX
49 Dean College of Arts & Sciences ..... Dr. Thomas NELSON
58 Dean of College of Management ..... Dr. Kat LUI
107 Act Dean Col Health/Cmty/Prof Stds ..... Dr. Shonda CRAFT
88 Dean Col Individualized Stds ..... Dr. Carl POLDING
88 Dean School of Urban Education .. Dr. Rene ANTROP-GONZALEZ
88 Int Dean Sch Law Enforce/Crim Just ..... Dr. Carl POLDING

*Minneapolis Community and Technical College (F)

1501 Hennepin Avenue, Minneapolis MN 55403-9810
County: Hennepin FICE Identification: 002362
Unit ID: 174136
Telephone: (612) 659-6000 Carnegie Class: Assoc/Pub-U-SC
FAX Number: (612) 659-6210 Calendar System: Semester
URL: www.minneapolis.edu
Established: 1996 Annual Undergrad Tuition & Fees (In-State): $5,364
Enrollment: 9,159 Coed
Affiliation or Control: State IRS Status: 501(c)3
Highest Offering: Associate Degree
Program: Occupational; 2-Year Principally Bachelor's Creditable
Accreditation: NH, ADNUR, DA, NDT, PNUR, POLYT

02 Interim President ..... Dr. Avelino MILLS-NOVOA
05 Vice Pres Academic Affairs ..... Dr. Gail O'KANE
10 Vice President Finance/Operations ..... Mr. Scott ERICKSON
32 Int Vice President Student Affairs ..... Mr. Patrick TROUP
103 Assoc VP Workforce Development ..... Mr. Mike CHRISTENSON
84 Dean of Enrollment Management ..... Vacant
49 Dean of Liberal Arts ..... Mr. Derrick LINDSTROM
81 Dean of Science & Math ..... Mr. Chuck PAULSON
51 Dean of Continuing Education ..... Mr. Reede WEBSTER
66 Int Dean of Nursing & Allied Health ..... Ms. Yvette TROTMAN
35 Dean of Students ..... Ms. Becky NORDIN
20 Interim Dean Academic Foundations ..... Ms. Kristine SNYDER
43 CHRO and Director Legal Affairs ..... Ms. Dianna CUSICK
13 Chief Information Officer ..... Ms. Tiffni DEEB
06 Interim Registrar ..... Ms. Michele COPELAND
08 Librarian ..... Mr. Tom ELAND
37 Financial Aid Director ..... Ms. Angela CHRISTENSEN
09 Director of Institutional Research ..... Ms. Jessica SHRAYCK
18 Director Facilities ..... Mr. Roger BROZ
19 Director of Public Safety ..... Mr. Curt SCHMIDT
26 Chief Public Relations Officer ..... Ms. Dawn SKELLY
32 Chief Student Life Officer ..... Ms. Tara MARTINEZ

*Minnesota State College-Southeast Technical (G)

1250 Homer Road, Winona MN 55987-4897
County: Winona FICE Identification: 002393
Unit ID: 175263
Telephone: (507) 453-2700 Carnegie Class: Assoc/Pub-R-M
FAX Number: (507) 453-2715 Calendar System: Semester
URL: www.southeastmn.edu
Established: 1949 Annual Undergrad Tuition & Fees (In-District): $6,064
Enrollment: 1,097 Coed
Affiliation or Control: State/Local IRS Status: 501(c)3
Highest Offering: Associate Degree
Program: Occupational; 2-Year Principally Bachelor's Creditable; Technical Emphasis
Accreditation: NH, MLTAD, RAD

02 President ..... Dr. Dorothy DURAN
04 Assistant to President ..... Ms. Mary DONLIN
05 Vice President Academic Affairs ..... Dr. Leslie BLESKACHEK
32 Vice Pres Student Affairs/Life ..... Mr. Nate EMERSON
10 Vice Pres Finance/Administration ..... Mr. Mike KROENING
13 Chief Information Officer ..... Mr. Rick NAHRGANG
30 Chief Development/Advancement ..... Mr. Chris SCHABOW
20 Dean of Academic Affairs ..... Dr. Jolene PONCELET
49 Dean of Liberal Arts & Sciences ..... Dr. Jolene PONCELET
26 Director of Communications ..... Ms. Joanne THOMPSON
06 Registrar ..... Ms. Mary JOHNSON
37 Director Financial Aid ..... Ms. Tammy VONDRASEK
09 Director of Institutional Research ..... Vacant
84 Director of Recruitment ..... Ms. Shannon SCHELL
07 Director of Admissions ..... Ms. Gale LANNING
18 Chief Facilities/Physical Plant ..... Mr. Thomas HOFFMAN
84 Dir of Enrollment Svcs/Stdnt Plcmt ..... Ms. Gale LANNING
29 Director of Alumni Relations ..... Ms. Casie JOHNSON

*Minnesota State Community and Technical College (H)

1414 College Way, Fergus Falls MN 56537-1000
County: Otter Tail FICE Identification: 005541
Unit ID: 173559
Telephone: (218) 736-1500 Carnegie Class: Assoc/Pub-R-L
FAX Number: (218) 736-1510 Calendar System: Semester
URL: www.minnesota.edu
Established: 1960 Annual Undergrad Tuition & Fees (In-State): $5,824
Enrollment: 6,416 Coed
Affiliation or Control: State IRS Status: 501(c)3
Highest Offering: Associate Degree
Program: Occupational; 2-Year Principally Bachelor's Creditable; Liberal Arts And General
Accreditation: NH, CAHIIM, DA, MLTAD, RAD

02 President ..... Dr. Peggy KENNEDY
05 Chief Academic Officer ..... Dr. Carrie BRIMHALL
15 Director of Human Resources ..... Mrs. Dacia JOHNSON
06 Registrar ..... Ms. Sharlene ALLEN
13 Chief Information Officer ..... Mr. Dan KNUDSON
10 Chief Financial Officer ..... Mr. Pat NORDICK
32 VP of Student Devel & Marketing ..... Dr. Peter WIELINSKI
84 Dean of Student Access ..... Mr. Anthony SCHAFFHAUSER
20 Assoc VP of Acad & Stdnt Affs ..... Dr. Jill ABBOTT
18 Supt of Buildings & Grounds ..... Mr. Matt SHEPPARD
35 Senior Dean for Student Success ..... Mr. Shawn ANDERSON
12 Academic Dean-Detroit Lakes ..... Mr. Tom WHELIHAN
12 Acad Dean Lib Arts/Sci-Fergus Falls ..... Dr. Gary HENRICKSON
12 Academic Dean-Wadena ..... Mr. Monty JOHNSON
88 Dean of CTS/BES ..... Mr. G.L TUCKER
66 Dean of Health ..... Mrs. Jennifer JACOBSON
09 Dean of Institutional Effectiveness ..... Mr. Steve ERICKSON
07 Director of Admissions ..... Mr. Kyle JOHNSTON

*Minnesota State University, Mankato (A)

309 Wigley Administration Center,
Mankato MN 56001-6062

County: Blue Earth FICE Identification: 002360
Unit ID: 173920
Telephone: (507) 389-1111 Carnegie Class: Master's L
FAX Number: (507) 389-6200 Calendar System: Semester
URL: www.mnsu.edu
Established: 1868 Annual Undergrad Tuition & Fees (In-State): $15,616
Enrollment: 15,000 Coed
Affiliation or Control: State IRS Status: Exempt
Highest Offering: Doctorate
Program: Liberal Arts And General; Teacher Preparatory; Professional
Accreditation: NH, AAB, ART, BUS, CAATE, CACREP, CONST, CORE, DH, DIETD, ENG, ENGT, MUS, NRPA, NURSE, SP, SW, TED

02 President ... Dr. Richard DAVENPORT
05 VP Academic & Student Affairs ... Dr. Marilyn WELLS
10 Vice Pres Finance & Administration ... Mr. Richard STRAKA
30 VP University Advancement ... Mr. Kent CLARK
13 VP Technology/CIO ... Mr. Ed CLARK
88 VP Strategic/Busnss/Ed/Reg Prtrshps ... Mr. Michael GUSTAFSON
32 VP for Student Affairs ... Dr. David JONES
20 Interim VP for Academic Affairs ... Dr. Kim GREER
04 Interim Assistant to the President ... Dr. Sandra KING
20 Interim Asst VP Undergrad Studies ... Dr. Ginger ZIERDT
27 Asst VP Integrated Marketing/Comm ... Mr. Jeff ISEMINGER
28 Dean Institutional Diversity ... Mr. Henry MORRIS
18 Facilities Service Director ... Mr. David COWAN
06 University Registrar ... Mr. Marcius BROCK
07 Director of Admissions ... Mr. Brian JONES
08 Dean Library Services ... Dr. Joan ROCA
15 Director of Human Resources ... Ms. DeeAnn SNAZA
36 Director Career Development ... Ms. Pamela WELLER-DENGEL
26 Director Media Relations ... Mr. Daniel BENSON
41 Dir of Intercollegiate Athletics ... Mr. Kevin BUISMAN
29 Director of Alumni Relations ... Mr. Ramon PINERO
22 Interim Director Affirmative Action ... Ms. Mary DOWD
37 Director Student Financial Services ... Ms. Jan MARBLE
58 AVP Graduate Studies/Research ... Dr. Barry RIES
79 Interim Dean of Arts & Humanities ... Dr. Kimberly CONTAG
53 Dean of Education ... Dr. Jean HAAR
50 Dean of Business ... Dr. Brenda FLANNERY
76 Dean Allied Health/Nursing ... Dr. Kristine RETHERFORD
81 Dean Science/Engineering/Technology ... Dr. Brian MARTENSEN
83 Dean Social/Behavioral Science ... Dr. Maria BEVACQUA
38 Director Student Counseling ... Ms. Kari MUCH
09 Asst VP of Institutional Research ... Ms. Lynn AKEY
19 Director Security/Safety ... Ms. Suzanne DUGAN
39 Director Student Housing ... Ms. Cindy JANNEY

*Minnesota State University Moorhead (B)

1104 7th Avenue S, Moorhead MN 56563-2996

County: Clay FICE Identification: 002367
Unit ID: 174358
Telephone: (218) 477-4000 Carnegie Class: Master's M
FAX Number: (218) 477-2168 Calendar System: Semester
URL: www.mnstate.edu
Established: 1887 Annual Undergrad Tuition & Fees (In-State): $8,092
Enrollment: 6,306 Coed
Affiliation or Control: State IRS Status: 501(c)3
Highest Offering: Doctorate
Program: Liberal Arts And General; Teacher Preparatory; Professional
Accreditation: NH, ART, BUS, CAATE, CACREP, CONST, DH, MUS, NAIT, NURSE, SP, SW, TED

02 President ... Dr. Anne BLACKHURST
05 Provost/Sr VP Academic Affairs ... Dr. Joseph BESSIE
10 VP Finance & Administration ... Ms. Jean HOLLAAR
84 VP Enrollment Mgmt/Student Affairs ... Dr. Yvette UNDERDUE MURPH
29 VP Alumni Foundation ... Ms. Laura L. HUTH
04 Assistant to the President ... Ms. Kathleen J. MCNABB
20 AVP Academic Affairs ... Dr. John (Jack) HEALY
28 Chief Diversity Officer ... Dr. Donna L. BROWN
09 Dir Institutional Effectiveness ... Mr. Kevin BROWN
41 Director of Athletics ... Mr. Doug D. PETERS
13 Chief Information Officer ... Mr. Daniel A. HECKAMAN
21 Comptroller ... Ms. Karen K. LESTER
50 Dean Business & Innovation ... Dr. Marsha L. WEBER
49 Int Dean Arts/Media/Communication ... Ms. Denise M. GORSLINE
53 Actg Dean Educ/Human Svcs/Grad Stds ... Dr. Boyd BRADBURY
83 Dean Sciences/Health/Environment ... Dr. Michelle L. MALOTT
79 Dean of Col Humanities/Soc Sci ... Dr. Randy L. CAGLE
15 Director Human Resources ... Ms. Ann HIEDEMAN
06 Registrar ... Ms. Heather M. SOLEIM
26 Director Marketing/Communications ... Mr. David C. WAHLBERG
19 Director of Security ... Vacant
37 Dir Financial Aid & Scholarships ... Ms. Carolyn F. ZEHREN
23 Dir Health/Wellness/Counseling Ctrs ... Ms. Carol M. GRIMM
88 Director Disabilities ... Mr. Greg A. TOUTGES
36 Director of Career Development ... Vacant
07 Director of Admissions ... Mr. Shaun MANNING
32 Exec Dir Student Union ... Mr. Layne ANDERSON
39 Dir Housing & Residential Life ... Ms. Heather PHILLIPS
85 Director International Student Affs ... Ms. Janet M. HOHENSTEIN
18 Manager Physical Plant ... Mr. Jeffrey D. GOEBEL
40 Bookstore Supervisor ... Ms. Kim M. SAMSON

*Minnesota West Community and Technical College (C)

1450 Collegeway, Worthington MN 56187

County: Nobles FICE Identification: 005263
Unit ID: 173638
Telephone: (800) 658-2330 Carnegie Class: Assoc/Pub-R-M
FAX Number: (507) 372-5803 Calendar System: Semester
URL: www.mnwest.edu
Established: 1985 Annual Undergrad Tuition & Fees (In-State): $5,660
Enrollment: 3,182 Coed
Affiliation or Control: State IRS Status: 501(c)3
Highest Offering: Associate Degree
Program: Occupational; 2-Year Principally Bachelor's Creditable
Accreditation: NH, ADNUR, DA, MAC, MLTAD, RAD, SURGT

02 President ... Dr. Terry GAALSWYK
05 College Provost ... Dr. Jeff WILLIAMSON
11 Vice President of Administration ... Ms. Lori VOSS
106 Dean Technology/Distance Learning ... Ms. Kayla WESTRA
84 Director of Enrollment Management ... Vacant
37 Director of Student Financial Aid ... Ms. Jodi LANDGAARD
18 Chief Facilities/Physical Plant ... Vacant
06 Registrar ... Ms. Crystal STROUTH
15 Director Human Resources ... Ms. Karen MILLER
102 Foundation Director ... Ms. Lori VOSS
08 Head Librarian ... Mr. Kip THORSON
10 Chief Business Officer ... Ms. Diana FLISS
26 Chief Public Relations/Marketing ... Ms. Amber LUINENBURG

*Normandale Community College (D)

9700 France Avenue S, Bloomington MN 55431-4399

County: Hennepin FICE Identification: 007954
Unit ID: 174428
Telephone: (952) 358-8200 Carnegie Class: Assoc/Pub-S-SC
FAX Number: (952) 358-8101 Calendar System: Semester
URL: www.normandale.edu
Established: 1968 Annual Undergrad Tuition & Fees (In-State): $6,436
Enrollment: 9,539 Coed
Affiliation or Control: State IRS Status: 501(c)3
Highest Offering: Associate Degree
Program: Occupational; 2-Year Principally Bachelor's Creditable; Liberal Arts And General
Accreditation: NH, ACBSP, ADNUR, ART, DH, DIETT, MUS, THEA

02 President ... Dr. Joyce C. ESTER
04 Executive Assistant to President ... Mrs. Amanda RYAN-SCHMOLL
10 Vice President Finance & Operations ... Dr. Lisa WHEELER
05 Vice President of Academic Affairs ... Mrs. Julie GUELICH
32 Vice President of Student Affairs ... Dr. Orinthia MONTAGUE
15 Chief Human Resources Officer ... Mrs. Dionne DOERING
09 Dir of Research & Planning ... Dr. Mark LEWIS
50 Dean of Business & Social Sci ... Dr. Michael KIRCH
79 Dean of Humanities ... Dr. Jeffrey JUDGE
81 Dean of STEME ... Dr. Cary KOMOTO
76 Dean of Health Sciences ... Dr. Colleen BRICKLE
08 Dean of Academic Svcs & Library ... Dr. Erin DALY
35 Interim Dean of Students ... Ms. Wanda L. KANWISCHER
21 Interim Associate VP of Fin & Acct ... Mrs. Catherine BREUER
13 Chief Information Officer ... Mr. Stephen WINCKELMAN
16 Assistant Human Resources Director ... Ms. Victoria SCHWAB
18 Assoc VP of Operations ... Mr. Patrick BUHL
102 Executive Director of Foundation ... Ms. Colleen SIMPSON
35 Dean of Student Affairs ... Mr. Matthew CRAWFORD
26 Chief Public Relations Officer ... Mr. Steve GELLER
06 Registrar ... Ms. Tonya HANSON
07 Director of Admissions ... Ms. Nancy PATES
37 Director of Financial Aid & Scholar ... Mrs. Susan ANT
38 Director of Advising & Counseling ... Mr. Torrion AMIE
19 Director of Public Safety ... Mr. Erik BENTLEY
106 Director of Online Learning ... Mrs. Sheri HUTCHINSON
26 Director of Marketing Communication ... Mr. Geoffrey JONES
88 Accounting Supervisor ... Mrs. Cindy LADD
40 Bookstore Manager ... Ms. Peggy BACALL
25 Grant Development Director ... Mrs. Angela ARNOLD
29 Alumni & Donor Relations Manager ... Mrs. Nichole AXTMAN

*North Hennepin Community College (E)

7411 85th Avenue N, Brooklyn Park MN 55445-2299

County: Hennepin FICE Identification: 002370
Unit ID: 174376
Telephone: (763) 424-0702 Carnegie Class: Assoc/Pub-S-SC
FAX Number: (763) 424-0929 Calendar System: Semester
URL: www.nhcc.edu
Established: 1966 Annual Undergrad Tuition & Fees (In-State): $5,477
Enrollment: 7,384 Coed
Affiliation or Control: State IRS Status: 501(c)3
Highest Offering: Associate Degree
Program: Occupational; 2-Year Principally Bachelor's Creditable
Accreditation: NH, ACBSP, ADNUR, HT, MLTAD

02 President ... Dr. Barbara MCDONALD
05 VP Academic & Student Affairs ... Dr. Landon PIRIUS
10 VP Finance & Facilities ... Mr. Daniel HALL
13 Chief Information Officer ... Ms. Kristine BOIKE
32 Dean Student Development ... Vacant
84 Dean of Enrollment ... Ms. Jackie OLSSON
08 Librarian ... Mr. Craig LARSON
06 Director of Admissions & Records ... Ms. Melissa LEIMBEK
15 Chief Human Resources Officer ... Mr. Michael FREER
18 Director of Plant Services ... Mr. Joseph MORAN
30 Director of Advancement ... Ms. Jennifer LAMBRECHT
28 Director Diversity/Multiculturalism ... Mr. Michael BIRCHARD
26 Dir Marketing/Communications ... Ms. Liz HOGENSON
09 Director of Institutional Research ... Ms. Sheryl OLSON
19 Director of Public Safety ... Mr. Erik PAKIESER
21 Business Manager ... Ms. Dawn BELKO
49 Dean of Liberal Arts ... Mr. Michael DUEÑES
50 Int Dean Business & Career Programs ... Mr. Brady PRENZLOW
81 Dean of Math/Science ... Dr. Elaina BLEIFIELD
76 Dean of Health Sciences ... Ms. Doris HILL
60 Dean of Comm/Language & Fine Arts ... Ms. Jan MCFALL
51 Dean of Cont Educ/Custom Trng ... Ms. Cherie ROLLINGS
38 Director Student Advising ... Ms. Sarah DOMAN-FLYGARE
04 Administrative Asst to President ... Ms. Nicole CARLSON
36 Director Student Placement ... Ms. Deb ATKINS

*Northland Community and Technical College (F)

1101 Highway 1 E, Thief River Falls MN 56701-2598

County: Pennington FICE Identification: 002385
Unit ID: 174473
Telephone: (218) 683-8800 Carnegie Class: Assoc/Pub-R-M
FAX Number: (218) 683-8980 Calendar System: Semester
URL: www.northlandcollege.edu
Established: 1965 Annual Undergrad Tuition & Fees (In-State): $3,554
Enrollment: 3,584 Coed
Affiliation or Control: State IRS Status: 501(c)3
Highest Offering: Associate Degree
Program: Occupational; 2-Year Principally Bachelor's Creditable; Technical Emphasis
Accreditation: NH, ADNUR, COARC, CVT, EMT, OTA, PTAA, RAD, SURGT

02 President ... Dr. Dennis BONA
05 VP Academic Affairs/Student Svcs ... Mr. Carey CASTLE
10 VP of Admin Services/CFO ... Ms. Shannon JESME
04 Asst to President/Int Exec Dir Fdn ... Ms. Sheila BRUHN
11 Campus Dean Administration ... Dr. Brian HUSCHLE
20 Dean Thief River Falls Campus ... Mr. Mike CURFMAN
32 Dean of Students East Grand Forks ... Dr. Mary FONTES
103 Dean Workforce & Econ Development ... Mr. James RETKA
66 Dean Health/Nursing & Public Svcs ... Ms. Jodi STASSEN
08 Academic Success Ctr Director ... Ms. Heather MENG
38 Counselor ... Ms. Kelsy BLOWERS
38 Counselor ... Ms. Kate SCHMALENBERG
84 Dir of Enrollment Mgmt & Admission ... Ms. Nicki CARLSON
37 Director Student Financial Aid ... Mr. Gerald SCHULTE
09 Director of Institutional Research ... Dr. Mary FONTES
15 Chief Humand Resource Officer ... Ms. Kristi LANE
18 Chief Facilities/Physical Plant ... Mr. Clinton CASTLE
26 Interim Director Marketing ... Mr. Chad SPERLING
44 Dir Annual Giving/Alumni Relations ... Mr. Lars DYRUD
06 Registrar ... Ms. Lisa BOTTEM
28 Diversity Coordinator ... Ms. Heather MENG
30 Interim Chief Development Officer ... Ms. Sheila BRUHN
13 Director of Technology ... Ms. Stacey HRON
41 Dir of Student Life & Athletics ... Mr. Richard SPEAS

*Northwest Technical College (G)

905 Grant Avenue, SE, Bemidji MN 56601-4907

County: Beltrami FICE Identification: 005759
Unit ID: 173115
Telephone: (218) 333-6600 Carnegie Class: Assoc/Pub-R-S
FAX Number: (218) 333-6694 Calendar System: Semester
URL: www.ntcmn.edu
Established: 1966 Annual Undergrad Tuition & Fees (In-State): $5,482
Enrollment: 1,080 Coed
Affiliation or Control: State IRS Status: 501(c)3
Highest Offering: Associate Degree
Program: Occupational; 2-Year Principally Bachelor's Creditable
Accreditation: NH, DA

02 President ... Dr. Richard HANSON
05 Provost/Vice President ... Mr. Robert GRIGGS

*Pine Technical and Community College (H)

900 Fourth Street, SE, Pine City MN 55063-2198

County: Pine FICE Identification: 005535
Unit ID: 174570
Telephone: (320) 629-5100 Carnegie Class: Assoc/Pub-R-S
FAX Number: (320) 629-5101 Calendar System: Semester
URL: www.pine.edu
Established: 1965 Annual Undergrad Tuition & Fees (In-State): $5,081
Enrollment: 1,530 Coed
Affiliation or Control: State IRS Status: 501(c)3
Highest Offering: Associate Degree
Program: Occupational; 2-Year Principally Bachelor's Creditable; Technical Emphasis
Accreditation: NH, MAC

02 President ... Mr. Joe MULFORD
05 Chief Academic Officer ... Dr. Joan BLOEMENDAAL-GRUETT
13 Chief Information Officer ... Mr. Kenneth RIES

10 Chief Financial Officer ..... Ms. Janis WEGNER
32 Dean Student Affairs ..... Ms. Paula HOFFMAN
51 Dean of Continuing Edu/Custom Trng ..... Mr. Jason SPAETH
103 Dean of Economic/Work Devel ..... Ms. Stephanie SCHROEDER
36 Exec Dir Employment/Training Ctr ..... Mr. Dwayne GREEN
06 Registrar ..... Ms. Darla CAVERLEY
15 Chief Human Resources Officer ..... Ms. Amy KRUSE
07 Director of Admissions ..... Ms. Shawnda SCHELINDER
37 Director Student Financial Aid ..... Mr. Shawn REYNOLDS
18 Physical Plant Supervisor ..... Mr. Steven LANGE
04 Administrative Asst to President ..... Ms. Sandra CARLISLE

*Rainy River Community College (A)

1501 Highway 71, International Falls MN 56649-2187

County: Koochiching FICE Identification: 006775
Unit ID: 174604
Telephone: (218) 285-7722 Carnegie Class: Assoc/Pub-R-S
FAX Number: (218) 285-2239 Calendar System: Semester
URL: www.rrcc.mnscu.edu
Established: 1967 Annual Undergrad Tuition & Fees (In-State): $5,324
Enrollment: 325 Coed
Affiliation or Control: State IRS Status: 501(c)3
Highest Offering: Associate Degree
Program: Occupational; 2-Year Principally Bachelor's Creditable
Accreditation: NH

02 Provost ..... Ms. Carol HELLAND
06 Registrar ..... Ms. Berta HAGEN
37 Dir of Financial Aid/Housing ..... Mr. Scott T. RILEY
13 Dir Information Technology ..... Mr. James BUJOLD
10 Business Manager ..... Mrs. Emily AHRENS

*Ridgewater College (B)

PO Box 1097, 2101 15th Ave NW,
Willmar MN 56201-1097

County: Kandiyohi FICE Identification: 005252
Unit ID: 175236
Telephone: (320) 222-5200 Carnegie Class: Assoc/Pub-R-M
FAX Number: (320) 222-5212 Calendar System: Semester
URL: www.ridgewater.edu
Established: 1961 Annual Undergrad Tuition & Fees (In-State): $5,400
Enrollment: 3,753 Coed
Affiliation or Control: State IRS Status: 501(c)3
Highest Offering: Associate Degree
Program: Occupational; 2-Year Principally Bachelor's Creditable
Accreditation: NH, ADNUR, CAHIIM, EMT, MAC, PNUR

02 President ..... Dr. Douglas W. ALLEN
05 Vice Pres Acad Affs/Student Svcs ..... Dr. Betty J. STREHLOW
10 Vice President Finance & Operations ..... Mr. Daniel F. HOLTZ
51 Dean of Cust Trng & Cont Education ..... Mr. Sam BOWEN
20 Dean of Instruction/Technical Pgms ..... Mr. Michael J. BOEHME
20 Dean of Instruction ..... Mr. Mike KUTZKE
20 Dean Instruction/Liberal Arts/Sci ..... Mr. Alan STAGE
32 Dean of Student Services ..... Ms. Heidi L. OLSON
21 Director of Business Services ..... Ms. Cheryl A. NORLIEN
15 Int Chief Human Resource Officer ..... Ms. Denise CARPENTER
66 Director of Nursing ..... Ms. C. Lynn JOHNSON
37 Director of Financial Aid ..... Mr. James W. RICE
07 Admissions Director ..... Ms. Sally KERFELD
41 Athletic Director ..... Mr. Todd M. THORSTAD
06 Registrar ..... Ms. Kelli S. KIENITZ
13 Chief Information Officer ..... Mr. Timothy L. FURR
26 Director of Communication/Marketing ..... Ms. Liz VANDERBILL
102 Foundation Executive Director ..... Ms. Kelly J. MAGNUSON
09 Director of Institutional Research ..... Dr. Mary L. MYERS
28 Multicultural Outreach/Academic Adv ..... Ms. Jehana KHAN
18 Physical Plant Director ..... Mr. Kip R. OVESON

*Riverland Community College (C)

1900 8th Avenue, NW, Austin MN 55912-1473

County: Mower FICE Identification: 002335
Unit ID: 173063
Telephone: (507) 433-0600 Carnegie Class: Assoc/Pub-R-M
FAX Number: (507) 433-0665 Calendar System: Semester
URL: www.riverland.edu
Established: 1940 Annual Undergrad Tuition & Fees (In-State): $5,530
Enrollment: 3,242 Coed
Affiliation or Control: State IRS Status: 501(c)3
Highest Offering: Associate Degree
Program: Occupational; 2-Year Principally Bachelor's Creditable; Liberal Arts And General
Accreditation: NH, ACBSP, ADNUR, RAD

02 President ..... Dr. Adenuga ATEWOLOGUN
05 VP of Academic & Student Affairs ..... Dr. Mary DAVENPORT
10 Chief Financial Officer ..... Mr. Brad DOSS
15 VP of Employees & Tech Resources ..... Ms. Celeste RUBLE
66 Director of Nursing ..... Ms. Nancy GENELIN
49 Dean of Arts/Humanities/Social Sci ..... Mr. Kelly MCCALLA
75 Dean of Bus Tech/Trade/Industry ..... Mr. Matt BISSONETTE
32 Dean of Student Affairs ..... Mr. Gary SCHINDLER
30 Dean for Institutional Advancement ..... Mr. Steve BOWRON
06 Dir of Enrollment Svcs/Registrar ..... Ms. Sue JECH
07 Dir of Admissions & New Student Rel ..... Ms. Nel ZELLAR
26 Dir of Communications/Media & Mktg ..... Mr. James DOUGLASS
37 Director of Financial Aid ..... Mr. Gary SCHINDLER
36 Dir of College Partnerships & Trans ..... Ms. Lori JENSEN

13 Director of Technology ..... Mr. Dan HARBER
18 Facilities Supervisor ..... Ms. Judy ENRIGHT
96 Purchasing Agent ..... Ms. Page PETERSEN
28 Regional Diversty Trainer/Investgtr ..... Ms. Ricki WALTERS
08 Head Librarian ..... Ms. Jeannie KEARNEY
19 Director Security/Safety ..... Mr. Mike HOWE
29 Director Alumni Relations ..... Vacant
41 Athletic Director ..... Mr. David LILLEMON

*Rochester Community and Technical College (D)

851 30th Avenue, SE, Rochester MN 55904-4999

County: Olmsted FICE Identification: 002373
Unit ID: 174738
Telephone: (507) 285-7210 Carnegie Class: Assoc/Pub-R-M
FAX Number: (507) 285-7496 Calendar System: Semester
URL: www.rctc.edu
Established: 1915 Annual Undergrad Tuition & Fees (In-State): $5,760
Enrollment: 5,889 Coed
Affiliation or Control: State IRS Status: 501(c)3
Highest Offering: Associate Degree
Program: Occupational; 2-Year Principally Bachelor's Creditable; Liberal Arts And General
Accreditation: NH, ACBSP, ADNUR, CAHIIM, DA, DH, PNUR, SURGT

02 President ..... Ms. Leslie R. MCCLELLON
05 Vice President Academic Affairs ..... Dr. Greg MOSIER
10 Vice Pres Finance and Facilities ..... Mr. Steve SCHMALL
76 Dean Allied Health ..... Dr. Nirmala KOTAGAL
49 Dean of Art & Design ..... Vacant
20 Dean of Academic Affairs ..... Ms. Michelle PYFFEROEN
15 Chief Human Resources Officer ..... Mrs. Renee ENGELMEYER
13 Chief Information Technology Ofcr ..... Mr. Scott SAHS
32 Chief Student Affairs Officer ..... Mr. Alex HERZOG
88 Dir of Business/Econ Development ..... Ms. Michelle PYFFEROEN
35 Student Life Coordinator ..... Mr. Scott KROOK
06 Registrar ..... Ms. Nancy SHUMAKER
07 Director Admissions ..... Vacant
37 Director Financial Aid ..... Ms. Beth DIEKMANN
09 Director of Institutional Research ..... Vacant
04 Assistant to President ..... Mrs. Judy KINGSBURY
21 Business Office Supervisor ..... Ms. Ruth SIEFERT
26 Chief Public Relations Officer ..... Mr. Nate STOLTMAN
19 Security Officer ..... Mr. Andrew HAMANN
40 Bookstore Coordinator ..... Ms. Michelle DANIELSON
96 Director of Purchasing ..... Ms. June MEITZNER
29 Dir Alumni Rels/Found Exec Dir ..... Vacant
18 Chief Facilities/Physical Plant ..... Mr. Mark FASS
38 Director Student Counseling ..... Ms. Lisa MOHR

*St. Cloud State University (E)

720 4th Avenue S, Saint Cloud MN 56301-4498

County: Stearns FICE Identification: 002377
Unit ID: 174783
Telephone: (320) 308-0121 Carnegie Class: Master's L
FAX Number: N/A Calendar System: Semester
URL: www.stcloudstate.edu
Established: 1869 Annual Undergrad Tuition & Fees (In-State): $7,814
Enrollment: 15,416 Coed
Affiliation or Control: State IRS Status: 501(c)3
Highest Offering: Doctorate
Program: Occupational; 2-Year Principally Bachelor's Creditable; Liberal Arts And General; Teacher Preparatory; Professional
Accreditation: NH, ART, BUS, CAATE, CACREP, CORE, CS, ENG, ENGR, JOUR, MFCD, MT, MUS, NAIT, NURSE, SP, SW, TED, THEA

02 President ..... Dr. Earl H. POTTER, III
04 Executive Asst to President ..... Ms. Linda CONWAY
05 Provost/VP Academic Affairs ..... Dr. Ashish VAIDYA
20 Dir of Academic Operations ..... Ms. Michele MUMM
10 Vice Pres Finance/Admin ..... Ms. Tammy L. MCGEE
21 Interim Assoc VP Finance/Admin ..... Mr. Jeff WAGNER
88 AVP Safety/Risk Mgmt ..... Mr. Jesse CASHMAN
32 Vice Pres Student Life Development ..... Dr. Wanda OVERLAND
30 Vice Pres University Advancement ..... Mr. Matthew ANDREW
43 Special Advisor to the President ..... Dr. Judith P. SIMINOE
22 Equity and Affirmative Action Ofc ..... Ms. Ellyn BARTGES
41 Athletic Director ..... Ms. Heather WEEMS
86 Dir Univ Relations/Legislative Rel ..... Mr. Bernie OMANN
45 AVP/AP Strategy/Planning & Effect ..... Dr. Lisa FOSS
26 Asst VP Marketing & Communications ..... Mr. Loren BOONE
13 Chief Info Technology Officer (CIO) ..... Mr. Henry MAY
50 Dean Herberger Business School ..... Dr. David HARRIS
53 Interim Dean School of Education ..... Dr. Steve HOOVER
76 Dean Health/Human Service ..... Dr. Monica DEVERS
49 Dean College of Liberal Arts ..... Dr. Mark SPRINGER
88 Dean School of Public Affairs ..... Dr. King BANAIAN
81 Dean Science & Engineering ..... Dr. Dan GREGORY
51 Interim Dir of Continuing Studies ..... Ms. Gail RUHLAND
08 Dean Learning Resources ..... Mr. Mark VARGAS
88 Interim AP for Research/Dean ..... Dr. Marilyn HART
88 Interim AP University College ..... Mr. Adam KLEPETAR
35 Interim AP Faculty/Student Affairs ..... Ms. Nancy MILLS
84 AP Undergrad Recruit & Transition ..... Dr. Amber SCHULTZ
88 Assoc VP International Studies ..... Ms. Thy YANG
06 Registrar ..... Ms. Sue BAYERL
91 Dir Info Technology Services ..... Mr. Phil THORSON
29 Director of Constituent Engagement ..... Ms. Terri MISCHE
36 Interim Director Career Services ..... Mr. Bobbie MURPHY
37 Director of Financial Aid ..... Mr. Mike T. URAN

38 Director of Counseling ..... Dr. John M. EGGERS
39 Director of Student Housing ..... Mr. Daniel T. PEDERSEN
09 Dir Analytics and Bus Intelligence ..... Mr. Brent DONNAY
15 Director Human Resources ..... Ms. Holly SCHOENHERR
18 Director Facilities Management ..... Mr. John FRISCHMANN
104 Director Education Abroad ..... Ms. Nichole PAZDERNIK
88 Director American Indian Center . Mr. Jim KNUTSON-KOLODZNE
88 Director of Atwood Services ..... Ms. Anne BUTTKE
88 Director LGBT Resources ..... Mr. Brandon JOHNSON
88 Director Lindgren Child Care Center ..... Ms. Debra CARLSON
88 Director Multicultural Student Svcs ..... Mr. Shahzad AHMED
88 Director Student Disability Service ..... Mr. Owen ZIMPEL
23 Director Student Health Services ..... Ms. Corie BECKERMANN
88 Director Womens Center ..... Ms. Jane OLSEN
19 Director Public Safety ..... Mr. Kevin WHITLOCK
40 Bookstore Manager ..... Mr. Ted MEARS

*Saint Cloud Technical and Community College (F)

1540 Northway Drive, Saint Cloud MN 56303-1240

County: Stearns FICE Identification: 005534
Unit ID: 174756
Telephone: (320) 308-5000 Carnegie Class: Assoc/Pub-R-M
FAX Number: (320) 308-5981 Calendar System: Semester
URL: www.sctcc.edu
Established: 1948 Annual Undergrad Tuition & Fees (In-State): $5,301
Enrollment: 4,924 Coed
Affiliation or Control: State IRS Status: 501(c)3
Highest Offering: Associate Degree
Program: 2-Year Principally Bachelor's Creditable; Technical Emphasis
Accreditation: NH, CAHIIM, CVT, DA, DH, DMS, EMT, PNUR, SURGT

02 President ..... Ms. Joyce M. HELENS
05 VP of Academic Affairs ..... Ms. Margaret (Peg) SHROYER
04 Assistant to the President ..... Ms. Karen A. HIEMENZ
32 Vice President of Student Affairs ..... Mr. Jonathan EICHTEN
10 Vice Pres Admin/Chief Finan Officer ..... Ms. Lori KLOOS
75 Dean Trade/Industry ..... Mr. Darrin STROSAHL
81 Dean of Math/Sciences/Technology ..... Ms. Tarryl CLARK
50 Dean of Business/Comm/Humanities ..... Ms. Kristina KELLER
66 Dean of Nursing/Health ..... Ms. Carolyn OLSON
06 Registrar ..... Ms. Lana L. FEDDEMA
15 Dir Personnel Services/Aff Action ..... Ms. Deb A. HOLSTAD
84 Dir of Enroll Management/Admissions ..... Ms. Jodi M. ELNESS
08 Head Librarian ..... Ms. Patricia AKERMAN
19 Security/Safety Officer ..... Mr. Joseph RICK
37 Director Student Financial Aid ..... Ms. Anita G. BAUGH
20 Curriculum/Faculty Development ... Ms. Margaret (Peg) SHROYER
36 Director Student Placement ..... Ms. Jackie BAUER
40 Director Bookstore ..... Mr. James SCHOLLA
38 Director Student Counseling ..... Ms. Judy JACOBSON-BERG
35 Activ Dir/Chief Student Life Ofcr ..... Ms. Melissa MAJERUS
18 Chief Facilities/Physical Plant ..... Mr. Jason THEISEN
13 Chief Information Officer ..... Ms. Viola BERGQUIST
88 Director of Academic Accountability ..... Ms. Norma KONSCHAK
21 Associate Business Officer ..... Mr. Duane DAHLSTROM
96 Director of Purchasing ..... Ms. Susan MEYER
14 Director Library & Info Technology ..... Ms. Viola BERGQUIST
22 Director Affirm Action/Equal Oppty ..... Ms. Deb HOLSTAD
30 Chief Devel/Dir Annual/Planned Giv ..... Ms. Lori GRESS
28 Director of Diversity ..... Mr. Jonathan EICHTEN

*Saint Paul College-A Community & Technical College (G)

235 Marshall Avenue, Saint Paul MN 55102-1800

County: Ramsey FICE Identification: 005533
Unit ID: 175041
Telephone: (651) 846-1600 Carnegie Class: Assoc/Pub-U-SC
FAX Number: (651) 846-1451 Calendar System: Semester
URL: www.saintpaul.edu
Established: 1910 Annual Undergrad Tuition & Fees (In-State): $5,478
Enrollment: 5,825 Coed
Affiliation or Control: State IRS Status: 501(c)3
Highest Offering: Associate Degree
Program: Occupational; 2-Year Principally Bachelor's Creditable
Accreditation: NH, ACBSP, ACFEI, CAHIIM, COARC, MLTAD, PNUR

02 President ..... Dr. Rassoul DASTMOZD
05 VP Academic Affs/Chief Acad Ofcr ..... Dr. Kelly MURTAUGH
10 Vice President Finance & Operations ..... Mr. Scott WILSON
30 Chief Development Officer ..... Ms. Laura SAVIN
32 Vice Pres Student Development/Svcs ..... Mr. Thomas MATOS
103 Dean Workforce Trng/Continuing Educ ..... Ms. Tracy WILSON
84 Dean Enrollment Management ..... Ms. Sarah CARRICO
90 Assoc Dean of Academic Services ..... Ms. Shelley BIBEAU
15 Chief Human Resources Officer ..... Ms. Rachelle M. SCHMIDT
06 Registrar ..... Ms. Katie YEP
07 Director of Admissions ..... Mr. Ger VUE
09 Dean of Institutional Research ..... Ms. Laura KING
29 Director of Alumni Relations ..... Ms. Laura SAVIN
36 Director Student Placement ..... Ms. Sheryl SAUL
38 Director Student Counseling ..... Dr. Lisa HANES-GOODLANDER
96 Director of Purchasing ..... Ms. Teresa SORENSEN
18 Director Facilities/Physical Plant ..... Mr. Daniel KIRK
21 Business Manager ..... Mr. John PALMER
28 Director of Diversity ..... Mr. John PARKER-DER BOGHOSSIAN
28 Director of Diversity ..... Ms. Rachelle SCHMIDT
37 Director of Student Financial Aid ..... Mr. Adam JOHNSON
102 Exec Dir of Foundation/Alumni Rels ..... Ms. Laura SAVIN

13 Chief Information Officer .... Mr. Najam SAEED
26 Director of Marketing .... Ms. Audrey BERGENGREN
17 Dean of Health & Services .... Mr. Brendan ASHBY
81 Dean Science/Technology/Eng & Math .... Dr. Linda KINGSTON
50 Dean Business/Career Tech Educ .... Mr. Frank BRASWELL
88 Dean Liberal & Fine Arts .... Dr. Milford MUSKETT
19 Director Security/Safety .... Mr. Thomas BERGS

*South Central College (A)

1920 Lee Boulevard, PO Box 1920,
North Mankato MN 56002-1920

County: Nicollet | FICE Identification: 005537
Unit ID: 173911
Telephone: (507) 389-7200 | Carnegie Class: Assoc/Pub-R-M
FAX Number: (507) 388-9951 | Calendar System: Semester
URL: www.southcentral.edu
Established: 1946 | Annual Undergrad Tuition & Fees (In-District): $5,378
Enrollment: 3,660 | Coed
Affiliation or Control: State/Local | IRS Status: 501(c)3
Highest Offering: Associate Degree
Program: Occupational; 2-Year Principally Bachelor's Creditable; Liberal Arts And General
Accreditation: NH, DA, EMT, MAC, MLTAD

02 President .... Dr. Annette PARKER
04 Exec Assistant to the President .... Ms. Carol FREED
05 Vice Pres Student/Academic Affs .... Dr. Susan TARNOWSKI
10 Interim VP Finance/Facilities .... Ms. Dee BERNARD
09 Assoc VP Rsrch/Inst Effectivenes .... Dr. Peter WRUCK
13 Vice Pres of Technology .... Dr. Mark BAAS
32 Dean of Student Affairs .... Vacant
103 Dean of Workforce Ed/Training .... Ms. Barb EMBACHER
49 Interim Dean of LAS .... Ms. Ramona BEISWANGER
26 Public Relations/Marketing Director .... Ms. Shelly MEGAW
28 Interim Chief Diversity Officer .... Ms. Vicky SCHWAB
15 Interim CHRO .... Ms. Vicky SCHWAB
37 Director of Financial Aid .... Ms. Jayne DINSE
07 Director of Admissions/Advising .... Mr. Anthony RIESBERG
08 Director of Library/Media Services .... Ms. Johnna HORTON
19 Director of Safety & Security .... Mr. Al KLUEVER

*Southwest Minnesota State University (B)

1501 State Street, Marshall MN 56258-1598

County: Lyon | FICE Identification: 002375
Unit ID: 175078
Telephone: (507) 537-7678 | Carnegie Class: Master's M
FAX Number: (507) 537-7154 | Calendar System: Semester
URL: www.smsu.edu
Established: 1963 | Annual Undergrad Tuition & Fees (In-State): $8,334
Enrollment: 7,069 | Coed
Affiliation or Control: State | IRS Status: 501(c)3
Highest Offering: Master's
Program: Liberal Arts And General; Teacher Preparatory; Professional
Accreditation: NH, MUS, NURSE, SW

02 President .... Dr. Connie J. GORES
05 Provost .... Dr. Dwight WATSON
10 VP Finance and Admin .... Ms. Debra KERKAERT
32 AVP Stdnt Affairs/Dean of Students .... Mr. Scott CROWELL
30 VP Advance/Foundation Ex Dir .... Mr. William MULSO
49 Dean Arts/Letters/Sciences .... Dr. Jan LOFT
50 Dean Bus/Ed/Grad/Prof Stud .... Dr. Raphael ONYEAGHALA
41 Athletic Director .... Mr. Christopher HMIELEWSKI
13 Chief Information Officer .... Mr. Dan BAUN
07 VP EMSS .... Mr. Allan VOGEL
14 Director of Computer Services .... Mr. Shawn HEDMAN
06 Registrar .... Ms. Patricia CARMODY
19 Director University Public Safety .... Mr. Michael MUNFORD
28 Director Cultural Diversity .... Mr. Jay LEE
15 Dir Human Resources/Affirm Action .... Ms. Deb ALMER
29 Director of Alumni .... Mr. Michael VANDREHLE
18 Facilities & Physical Plant Manager .... Ms. Cyndi HOLM
36 Interim Director of Career Services .... Mr. Gary GILLIN
37 Director of Student Financial Aid .... Mr. David VIKANDER
38 Associate Professor of Counseling .... Ms. Sara FIER
96 Buyer Supervisor .... Ms. Barb BERKENPAS
21 Business Manager .... Mr. Eric RUNESTAD
26 Dir Communications/Marketing .... Mr. James TATE
04 Administrative Asst to President .... Ms. Chris ANDERSON
09 Director of Institutional Research .... Mr. Alan MATZNER
102 Dir Development .... Ms. Stacy FROST
44 Director Annual or Planned Giving .... Mr. Erik VOGEL

*Vermilion Community College (C)

1900 E Camp Street, Ely MN 55731-1998

County: Saint Louis | FICE Identification: 002350
Unit ID: 175157
Telephone: (218) 365-7200 | Carnegie Class: Assoc/Pub-R-S
FAX Number: (218) 235-2173 | Calendar System: Semester
URL: www.vcc.edu
Established: 1922 | Annual Undergrad Tuition & Fees (In-State): $5,323
Enrollment: 712 | Coed
Affiliation or Control: State | IRS Status: 501(c)3
Highest Offering: Associate Degree
Program: Occupational; 2-Year Principally Bachelor's Creditable
Accreditation: NH

02 Provost/Chief Academic Officer .... Mr. Shawn BINA
07 Director of Admissions/Student Affs .... Mr. Jeff NELSON
09 Director of Institutional Research .... Ms. Tracey ROY
10 Business Manager .... Ms. Kristi L'ALLIER
15 Director of Human Resources .... Ms. Carmen BRADACH
32 Dir Student Life/Facil/Phy Plant .... Mr. Dave MARSHALL
36 Director of Student Placement .... Mr. Doug FURNSTAHL
37 Director of Student Financial Aid .... Ms. Kristi L'ALLIER
38 Director of Student Counseling .... Ms. Cindy ANDERSON-BINA
29 Director Alumni Relations .... Ms. Patti ZUPANCICH
28 Director of Diversity .... Ms. Patti ZUPANCICH
26 Chief Public Relations Officer .... Mr. Jeff NELSON

*Winona State University (D)

PO Box 5838, Winona MN 55987-0838

County: Winona | FICE Identification: 002394
Unit ID: 175272
Telephone: (507) 457-5000 | Carnegie Class: Master's M
FAX Number: (507) 457-5586 | Calendar System: Quarter
URL: www.winona.edu
Established: 1858 | Annual Undergrad Tuition & Fees (In-State): $9,047
Enrollment: 8,701 | Coed
Affiliation or Control: State | IRS Status: 501(c)3
Highest Offering: Doctorate
Program: Liberal Arts And General; Teacher Preparatory; Professional
Accreditation: NH, BUS, CAATE, CACREP, ENG, MT, MUS, NURSE, SW, TED, THEA

02 President .... Dr. Scott R. OLSON
05 Provost/VP Academic Affairs/CAO .... Dr. Patricia ROGERS
10 VP Finance & Administration .... Mr. Scott ELLINGHUYSEN
30 Interim VP University Advancement .... Mr. Gary EVANS
32 VP Enrollment & Student Life & Dev .... Ms. Denise MCDOWELL
13 AVP Academic Affairs/CIO .... Mr. Kenneth JANZ
26 Asst VP Marketing & Communications .... Vacant
38 Interim Director of Counseling Svcs .... Ms. Patricia FERDEN
54 Dean Col of Science/Engr .... Dr. Charla MIERTSCHIN
49 Dean College of Liberal Arts .... Dr. Ralph TOWNSEND
50 Dean College of Business .... Dr. Hamid AKBARI
53 Dean College of Education .... Dr. Tarrell PORTMAN
66 Dean Col of Nursing/Health Science .... Dr. William MCBREEN
35 Dean of Students .... Ms. Karen JOHNSON
06 Sr Associate Registrar .... Ms. Tania SCHMIDT
84 Director Warrior Success Center .... Ms. Barbara OERTEL
37 Assistant Director of Financial Aid .... Ms. Charlene KREUZER
36 Associate Director Career Services .... Ms. Deanna GODDARD
07 Director of Admissions .... Mr. Carl STANGE
39 Residential College Program Coord .... Ms. Sarah OLCOTT
51 Exec Dir Outreach/Continuing Educ .... Ms. Diane DINGFELDER
29 Associate Director Alumni Relations .... Ms. Heather KOSIK
40 Bookstore Manager .... Ms. Karen KRAUSE
44 Director Development .... Ms. Debbie BLOCK
88 Director of International Svcs .... Ms. Kemale PINAR
19 Director of Security .... Mr. Don WALSKI
41 Athletic Director .... Mr. Eric SCHOH
18 Asst VP for Facilities Management .... Mr. Michael PIEPER
27 Director University Public Info .... Ms. Andrea NORTHAM
94 Director of Women's Studies .... Dr. Tamara BERG
96 Director of Purchasing .... Ms. Laura MANN
28 Director of Cultural Diversity .... Mr. Alexander HINES
15 Director of Human Resources .... Ms. Lori REED

*Anoka-Ramsey Community College Cambridge Campus (E)

300 Spirit River Drive South, Cambrdige MN 55008-5704
Telephone: (763) 433-1100 | Identification: 770298
Accreditation: &NH

† Branch campus of Anoka-Ramsey Community College, Coon Rapids, MN.

*Hennepin Technical College (F)

131000 College View, Eden Prairie MN 55347
Telephone: (952) 995-1300 | Identification: 770299
Accreditation: &NH, ACFEI

† Branch campus of Hennepin Technical College, Brooklyn Park, MN.

*Mesabi Range College Eveleth (G)

1100 Industrial Park Drive, Eveleth MN 55734
Telephone: (218) 741-3095 | Identification: 770300
Accreditation: &NH

† Branch campus of Mesabi Range College, Virginia, MN.

*Metropolitan State University (H)

1300 Harmon Place, Minneapolis MN 55403
Telephone: (651) 793-1300 | Identification: 770301
Accreditation: &NH

† Branch campus of Metropolitan State University, Saint Paul, MN.

*Minnesota State College-Southeast Technical Red Wing Campus (I)

308 Pioneer Road, Red Wing MN 55066
Telephone: (651) 385-6300 | Identification: 770302
Accreditation: &NH

† Branch campus of Minnesota State College-Southeast Technical, Winona, MN.

*Minnesota State Community and Technical College Detroit Lakes (J)

9-- Highway 34 E, Detroit Lakes MN 56501
Telephone: (218) 846-3700 | Identification: 770303
Accreditation: &NH

† Branch campus of Minnesota State Community and Technical College, Fergus Falls, MN.

*Minnesota State Community and Technical College Moorhead (K)

1900 28th Avenue S, Moorhead MN 56560
Telephone: (218) 299-6500 | Identification: 770304
Accreditation: &NH

† Branch campus of Minnesota State Community and Technical College, Fergus Falls, MN.

*Minnesota State Community and Technical College Wadena (L)

405 Colfax Avenue SW, Wadena MN 56482
Telephone: (213) 631-7800 | Identification: 770305
Accreditation: &NH

† Branch campus of Minnesota State Community and Technical College, Fergus Falls, MN.

*Minnesota West Community and Technical College Canby Campus (M)

1011 First Street, Canby MN 56220
Telephone: (507) 223-7252 | Identification: 770306
Accreditation: &NH

† Branch campus of Minnesota West Community and Technical College, Worthington, MN.

*Minnesota West Community and Technical College Granite Falls Campus (N)

1593 11th Avenue, Granite Falls MN 56241
Telephone: (320) 564-5000 | Identification: 770307
Accreditation: &NH

† Branch campus of Minnesota West Community and Technical College, Worthington, MN.

*Minnesota West Community and Technical College Jackson Campus (O)

401 West Street, Jackson MN 56143
Telephone: (547) 847-7920 | Identification: 770308
Accreditation: &NH

† Branch campus of Minnesota West Community and Technical College, Worthington, MN.

*Minnesota West Community and Technical College Pipestone Campus (P)

1314 North Hiawatha Avenue, Pipestone MN 56164
Telephone: (507) 825-6800 | Identification: 770309
Accreditation: &NH

† Branch campus of Minnesota West Community and Technical College, Worthington, MN.

*Minnesota West Community and Technical College Worthington Campus (Q)

1450 College Way, Worthington MN 56187
Telephone: (507) 372-3400 | Identification: 770310
Accreditation: &NH

† Branch campus of Minnesota West Community and Technical College, Worthington, MN.

*Northland Community and Technical College-East Grand Forks (R)

2022 Central Avenue NE, East Grand Forks MN 56721
Telephone: (218) 793-2800 | Identification: 770311
Accreditation: &NH

† Branch campus of Northland Community and Technical College, Thief River Falls, MN.

*Ridgewater College Hutchinson Campus (S)

2 Century Avenue SE, Hutchinson MN 55350
Telephone: (320) 234-8500 | Identification: 770312
Accreditation: &NH

† Branch campus of Ridgewater College, Willmar, MN.

*Riverland Community College Albert Lea Campus (T)

2200 Riverland Drive, Albert Lea MN 56007
Telephone: (507) 379-3300 | Identification: 770313

Accreditation: &NH

† Branch campus of Riverland Community College, Austin, MN.

* South Central College Faribault Campus (A)

1225 Third Street SW, Faribault MN 55021
Telephone: (507) 332-5800 Identification: 770314
Accreditation: &NH

† Branch campus of South Central College, North Mankato, MN.

* Winona State University-Rochester (B)

859 30th Avenue SE, Rochester MN 55904
Telephone: (800) 366-5418 Identification: 770317
Accreditation: &NH

† Branch campus of Winona State University, Winona, MN.

National American University-Bloomington (C)

7801 Metro Pkwy, Suite 200, Bloomington MN 55425
Telephone: (952) 356-3600 Identification: 770397
Accreditation: &NH, MAC

† Branch campus of National American University, Rapid City, SD.

National American University-Brooklyn Center (D)

6200 Shingle Creek Pkwy, Suite 130,
Brooklyn Center MN 55430
Telephone: (763) 852-7500 Identification: 770398
Accreditation: &NH, MAC

† Branch campus of National American University, Rapid City, SD.

National American University-Burnsville (E)

501 West Travelers Trail, #617, Burnsville MN 55337
Telephone: (952) 563-1250 Identification: 770399
Accreditation: &NH

† Branch campus of National American University, Rapid City, SD.

National American University-Rochester (F)

3906 East Frontage Highway 52 Road,
Rochester MN 55901
Telephone: (866) 628-6387 Identification: 770400
Accreditation: &NH

† Branch campus of National American University, Rapid City, SD.

National American University-Roseville (G)

1550 W Highway 36, Roseville MN 55113
Telephone: (651) 855-6300 Identification: 770401
Accreditation: &NH, MAC

† Branch campus of National American University, Rapid City, SD.

North Central University (H)

910 Elliot Avenue, Minneapolis MN 55404-1391
County: Hennepin FICE Identification: 002369
Unit ID: 174437
Telephone: (612) 343-4400 Carnegie Class: Bac/Diverse
FAX Number: (612) 343-4778 Calendar System: Semester
URL: www.northcentral.edu
Established: 1930 Annual Undergrad Tuition & Fees: $20,776
Enrollment: 1,191 Coed
Affiliation or Control: Assemblies Of God Church IRS Status: 501(c)3
Highest Offering: Master's
Program: Liberal Arts And General
Accreditation: NH, @SW

01 President ....Dr. Gordon L. ANDERSON
04 Executive Assistant of President ....Mrs. Bridgett KNISELY
05 Vice Pres Academic Affs/Acad Dean ....Dr. Tom A. BURKMAN
10 Vice President Business/Finance ....Mrs. Cheryl A. BOOK
30 Vice President Advancement ....Dr. Paul A. FREITAG
32 Vice President Student Development ....Mr. Mike A. NOSSER
26 VP University Relations ....Mr. Andrew DENTON
57 Executive Director Fine Arts ....Dr. Larry C. BACH
21 Director of Accounting ....Mr. Bruce JENSEN
39 Dean of Residence Life ....Mr. Juice MONTEZON
31 Dean of Community Life ....Mr. Greg J. LEEPER
41 Interim Director of Athletics ....Mr. Jake SMITH
37 Director of Financial Aid ....Mr. Eric AUSTIN
08 Library Director ....Mr. Edwin SCHENK
13 Exec Dir Information Technology ....Mr. Michael CAPPELLI
06 Registrar ....Ms. Mary MURPHY
44 Director Plannned Giving ....Mr. Wes BOOK
09 Dir Inst Research/Effectiveness ....Mr. Casey ROZOWSKI
07 Assoc Director of Recruitment ....Ms. Beth HARSHBARGER
38 Director of Student Success Center ....Mr. Todd MONGER
18 Facilities/Campus Housing Manager ....Mr. Jordon ROBERTSON

Northwestern Health Sciences University (I)

2501 W 84th Street, Bloomington MN 55431-1599
County: Hennepin FICE Identification: 012328
Unit ID: 174507
Telephone: (952) 888-4777 Carnegie Class: Spec/Health
FAX Number: (952) 888-6713 Calendar System: Trimester
URL: www.nwhealth.edu
Established: 1941 Annual Undergrad Tuition & Fees: $9,408
Enrollment: 882 Coed
Affiliation or Control: Independent Non-Profit IRS Status: 501(c)3
Highest Offering: First Professional Degree
Program: Professional
Accreditation: NH, ACUP, CHIRO, COMTA

01 President and CEO ....Dr. Christopher CASSIRER
05 Interim Provost and VPAA ....Dr. Pat CASELLO-MADDOX
10 VP Administrative Affairs/CFO ....Mr. Ross DUGAS
32 Vice Pres Student Affs/Enroll Mgmt ....Dr. Emily TWEED
07 Director of Admissions ....Vacant
08 Director of Library Services ....Ms. Anne MACKERETH
29 Dir Alumni Relations/Career Svcs ....Ms. Kim BAILEY
15 VP of Human Resources ....Ms. Mary GALE
51 Director Continuing Education ....Vacant
26 VP of Marketing & Institutional Adv ....Mr. Jeffrey RICH
13 Chief Technology Officer ....Vacant
38 University Counselor ....Ms. Becky LAWYER
18 Director Facilities Management ....Mr. Kevin WOLPERN
96 Director Bookstore & Purchasing ....Ms. Jan HALLEEN
04 Administrative Asst to President ....Ms. Nancy JOHNSON
11 Chief Operating Officer ....Ms. Lesllie BRONK
25 Executive Director of Partnerships ....Ms. Kim TAMBLE
28 Director of Diversity and Inclusion ....Dr. Alejandra DASHE

Oak Hills Christian College (J)

1600 Oak Hills Road, SW, Bemidji MN 56601-8826
County: Beltrami FICE Identification: 009992
Unit ID: 174525
Telephone: (218) 751-8670 Carnegie Class: Spec/Faith
FAX Number: (218) 751-8825 Calendar System: Semester
URL: www.oakhills.edu
Established: 1946 Annual Undergrad Tuition & Fees: $16,165
Enrollment: 141 Coed
Affiliation or Control: Interdenominational IRS Status: 501(c)3
Highest Offering: Baccalaureate
Program: Liberal Arts And General; Religious Emphasis
Accreditation: BI

01 President ....Dr. Steve J. HOSTETTER
05 Dean of the College ....Dr. Steven J. WARE
30 Vice President for Advancement ....Mrs. Joan L. BERNTSON
84 VP Enrollment Management ....Mr. Mike RASCH
32 Dean of Student Life ....Mr. Randy MCKAIN
10 Business Manager ....Mrs. Carol NELSON
06 Registrar ....Mrs. Mary HANNAH
08 Library Director ....Mr. Keith BUSH
37 Director of Financial Aid ....Mr. Matt MYRICK
26 Dir of Marketing & Communications ....Ms. Rachel JOHNSON

Presentation College Fairmont (K)

115 S Park Street, Suite 117, Fairmont MN 56031
Telephone: (507) 235-4658 Identification: 770418
Accreditation: &NH

† Branch campus of Presentation College, Aberdeen, SD.

* Rasmussen College Corporate Office (L)

8300 Norman Center Drive, Suite 300,
Bloomington MN 55437
County: Washington Identification: 667034
Unit ID: 17501405
Telephone: (952) 806-3910 Carnegie Class: N/A
FAX Number: (952) 831-0624
URL: www.rasmussen.edu

01 President ....Kristi WAITE

* Rasmussen College - St. Cloud (M)

226 Park Avenue South, Saint Cloud MN 56301-3713
County: Stearns FICE Identification: 008694
Unit ID: 175014
Telephone: (320) 251-5600 Carnegie Class: Assoc/PrivFP4
FAX Number: (320) 251-3702 Calendar System: Quarter
URL: www.Rasmussen.edu
Established: 1902 Annual Undergrad Tuition & Fees: $15,700
Enrollment: 5,395 Coed
Affiliation or Control: Proprietary IRS Status: Proprietary
Highest Offering: Baccalaureate
Program: Occupational; 2-Year Principally Bachelor's Creditable
Accreditation: NH, CAHIIM, MAAB, MLTAD, NURSE, SURGT

02 Campus Director ....Ms. Mary SWINGLE

† Regional accreditation carried under the parent institution in Lake Elmo, MN.

* Rasmussen College - Blaine (N)

3629 95th Avenue Northeast, Blaine MN 55014
Telephone: (763) 795-4720 Identification: 667061
Accreditation: &NH, MAAB

† Regional accreditation is carried under the parent institution in Saint Cloud, MN. The tuition figure is an average, actual tuition may vary.

* Rasmussen College - Bloomington (O)

4400 W 78th St, 6th Floor, Bloomington MN 55435
Telephone: (952) 545-2000 FICE Identification: 011686
Accreditation: &NH, CAHIIM, MAAB

† Regional accreditation carried under the parent institution in Saint Cloud, MN. The tuition figure is an average, actual tuition may vary.

* Rasmussen College - Brooklyn Park (P)

8301 93rd Avenue North, Brooklyn Park MN 55445-1512
Telephone: (763) 493-4500 Identification: 666769
Accreditation: &NH, CAHIIM, MAAB, SURGT

† Regional accreditation carried under the parent institution in Saint Cloud, MN. The tuition figure is an average, actual tuition may vary.

* Rasmussen College - Eagan (Q)

3500 Federal Drive, Eagan MN 55122-1346
Telephone: (651) 687-9000 FICE Identification: 004648
Accreditation: &NH, CAHIIM, MAAB

† Regional accreditation carried under the parent institution in Saint Cloud, MN. The tuition figure is an average, actual tuition may vary.

* Rasmussen College - Lake Elmo/Woodbury (R)

8565 Eagle Point Circle, Lake Elmo MN 55042
Telephone: (651) 259-6600 Identification: 770486
Accreditation: &NH, CAHIIM, MAC, MLTAD

† Regional accreditation carried under the parent institution in Saint Cloud, MN. The tuition figure is an average, actual tuition may vary.

* Rasmussen College - Mankato (S)

130 Saint Andrews Drive, Mankato MN 56001
Telephone: (507) 625-6556 FICE Identification: 025033
Accreditation: &NH, CAHIIM, MAAB, MLTAD

† Regional accreditation carried under the parent institution in Saint Cloud, MN.

* Rasmussen College - Moorhead Park (T)

1250 29th Avenue South, Moorhead MN 56560
Telephone: (218) 304-6200 Identification: 770487
Accreditation: &NH, MAC, MLTAD, SURGT

† Regional accreditation carried under the parent institution in Saint Cloud, MN. The tuition figure is an average, actual tuition may vary.

St. Catherine University (U)

601 25th Avenue S, Minneapolis MN 55454
Telephone: (651) 690-6000 Identification: 770315
Accreditation: &NH

† Branch campus of St. Catherine University, Saint Paul, MN.

St. Catherine University (V)

2004 Randolph Avenue, Saint Paul MN 55105-1789
County: Ramsey FICE Identification: 002342
Unit ID: 175005
Telephone: (651) 690-6000 Carnegie Class: Master's L
FAX Number: (651) 690-6024 Calendar System: 4/1/4
URL: www.stkate.edu
Established: 1905 Annual Undergrad Tuition & Fees: $37,842
Enrollment: 5,055 Female
Affiliation or Control: Roman Catholic IRS Status: 501(c)3
Highest Offering: Doctorate
Program: Liberal Arts And General; Teacher Preparatory; Professional
Accreditation: NH, ADNUR, #ARCPA, CAHIIM, COARC, DIETD, DMS, EXSC, LIB, NUR, NURSE, OT, OTA, PHLEB, PTA, PTAA, RAD, SW

01 President ....Dr. Andrea J. LEE, IHM
05 Exec Vice Pres and Provost ....Dr. Colleen HEGRANES
11 Exec Vice Pres and COO ....Dr. Brian BRUESS
10 Vice Pres Finance/Administration ....Mr. Thomas ROONEY
26 Vice Pres for External Relations ....Ms. Blanche ABDALLAH
04 Exec Assistant to the President ....Ms. Stacy JACOBSON
49 AVP/Dean Sch Humanities/Arts/Sci ....Dr. Alan SILVA
76 Dean Hen Schmoll Sch Hlth/Grad Col ....Dr. Penelope MOYERS
20 Associate Dean Academic Affairs ....Ms. Bonnie LADUCA
50 Dean Sch Business/Professional Stds ....Dr. Joann BANGS
51 Dean Adult and Applied Education ....Dr. Anne WEYANDT
32 Dean of Student Affairs ....Mr. Curt GALLOWAY
83 Dean School of Social Work ....Dr. Barbara SHANK
08 Library Director ....Ms. Emily ASCH
84 Dean of Enrollment Management ....Mr. Daniel THOMPSON
30 Director of Development ....Ms. Elizabeth RIEDEL CARNEY
21 Business Manager ....Ms. Tracey GRAN

13 Director of Computing Services ... Mr. John JERIES
06 Registrar ... Ms. Cynthia EGENESS
29 Director of Alumnae Relations ... Ms. Karen G. JOTHEN
27 Dir of Marketing & Communications ... Ms. Kristin CUMMINGS
07 Associate Dean of Admissions ... Ms. Marlene MOHS
37 Director of Financial Aid ... Ms. Elizabeth STEVENS
07 Assoc Dean Admiss/Market Devel ... Mr. Greg STEENSON
36 Director of Career Development ... Ms. Tina WAGNER
35 Associate Dean of Students ... Ms. Ellen RICHTER-NORGEL
15 Director of Human Resources ... Ms. Susan SEXTON
38 Director of Student Counseling ... Ms. Heide MALAT
92 Director of Honors Program ... Dr. Rafael CERVANTES
94 Director of Women's Studies ... Dr. Sharon DOHERTY
96 Director of Purchasing ... Ms. Gail BLIVEN
09 Dir Inst Rsrch/Plng/Assessment . Dr. Jennifer ROBINSON KLOOS
18 Chief Facilities/Physical Plant ... Mr. James MANSHIP

Saint John's University (A)

2850 Abbey Plaza, Box 2000, Collegeville MN 56321-2000
County: Stearns FICE Identification: 002379
Unit ID: 174792
Telephone: (320) 363-2011 Carnegie Class: Bac/A&S
FAX Number: (320) 363-2504 Calendar System: Semester
URL: www.csbsju.edu
Established: 1857 Annual Undergrad Tuition & Fees: $40,226
Enrollment: 1,895 Coordinate
Affiliation or Control: Roman Catholic IRS Status: 501(c)3
Highest Offering: Master's
Program: Liberal Arts And General; Teacher Preparatory; Professional
Accreditation: NH, DIETD, MUS, NURSE, THEOL

01 President ... Dr. Michael HEMESATH
05 Interim Provost Academic Affairs ... Dr. Richard ICE
20 Academic Dean ... Dr. Karen ERICKSON
30 Vice President for Inst Advancement ... Mr. Rob CULLIGAN
32 Vice President Student Development ... Fr. Douglas MULLIN, OSB
10 Vice Pres Finance/Admin Services ... Mr. Richard ADAMSON
46 VP Inst Plng/Research/Communication ... Mr. Jon MCGEE
07 Vice Pres Admissions/Financial Aid ... Dr. Cal MOSLEY
73 Dean School Theology ... Dr. William CAHOY
35 Dean of Students ... Mr. Michael CONNOLLY
26 Exec Director of Comm & Marketing ... Mr. Michael HEMMESCH
08 Director of Library ... Ms. Kathleen PARKER
06 Registrar ... Ms. Julie GRUSKA
36 Director of Career Services ... Ms. Heidi HARLANDER
37 Exec Director of Financial Aid ... Mr. Stuart PERRY
13 Director of Info Technology Svcs ... Ms. Casey GORDON
29 Director of Alumni Relations ... Mr. Adam HERBST
15 Director Human Resources ... Ms. Carol ABELL
09 Assoc Director Inst Research ... Ms. Karen G. KNUTSON

Saint Mary's University of Minnesota (B)

700 Terrace Heights, Winona MN 55987-1399
County: Winona FICE Identification: 002380
Unit ID: 174817
Telephone: (507) 452-4430 Carnegie Class: DRU
FAX Number: (507) 457-1633 Calendar System: Semester
URL: www.smumn.edu
Established: 1912 Annual Undergrad Tuition & Fees: $31,335
Enrollment: 5,825 Coed
Affiliation or Control: Roman Catholic IRS Status: 501(c)3
Highest Offering: Doctorate
Program: Liberal Arts And General; Teacher Preparatory
Accreditation: NH, ANEST, IACBE, MFCD, MUS, NMT, NURSE

01 President ... Bro. William MANN, FSC
18 Vice President of Facilities ... Mr. James BEDTKE
84 VP Enroll/Mktg/Strat Initiatives ... Dr. John PYLE
30 Vice Pres for Devel & Alumni Rels ... Ms. Audrey KINTZI
32 Vice President Student Life ... Mr. Chris KENDALL
10 Vice President Financial Affairs ... Mr. Ben MURRAY
43 Exec Vice Pres/General Counsel ... Ms. Ann E. MERCHLEWITZ
05 Vice President for Academic Affairs ... Dr. Donna ARONSON
58 VP Schs of Graduate/Prof Pgms ... Bro. Robert SMITH
26 Assoc VP Marketing & Communications ... Mr. Nick LEMMER
20 Academic Dean/Assoc Vice President ... Ms. Linka HOLEY
35 Dean of Students/Dir Resident Life ... Mr. Tim GOSSEN
04 Exec Assistant to the President ... Ms. Mary BECKER
06 Registrar ... Mr. Christopher VERCH
13 Chief Information Officer ... Mr. Scott COWDREY
07 Director of Admissions ... Ms. Suzanne DERANEK
37 Director of Financial Aid ... Ms. Jayne WOBIG
88 Director of Conferencing & Camps ... Ms. Terrie LUECK
36 Dir Career Services & Internships ... Vacant
38 Director of Counseling Center ... Dr. Ruth MATHEWS
08 Director of Library ... Ms. Laura OANES
22 Affirmative Action Officer ... Ms. Genelle GROH BECK
19 Director of Security ... Vacant
18 Director of Physical Plant ... Mr. John SCHOLLMEIER
23 Director of Health Services ... Ms. Angela WEISBROD
29 Director Alumni Relations ... Mr. Robert FISHER
41 Director of Athletics ... Ms. Nicole FENNERN
15 Director of Human Resources ... Ms. Genelle GROH BECK
09 Institutional Researcher ... Ms. Kara WENER
53 Dean School Education ... Dr. Scott SORVAAG
79 Dean School of the Arts ... Mr. Michael CHARRON

St. Olaf College (C)

1520 St. Olaf Avenue, Northfield MN 55057-1098
County: Rice FICE Identification: 002382
Unit ID: 174844
Telephone: (507) 786-2222 Carnegie Class: Bac/A&S
FAX Number: N/A Calendar System: 4/1/4
URL: wp.stolaf.edu
Established: 1874 Annual Undergrad Tuition & Fees: $42,940
Enrollment: 3,034 Coed
Affiliation or Control: Evangelical Lutheran Church In America
IRS Status: 501(c)3
Highest Offering: Baccalaureate
Program: Liberal Arts And General; Teacher Preparatory; Professional
Accreditation: NH, ART, DANCE, MUS, NURSE, SW, TED, THEA

01 President ... Dr. David R. ANDERSON
05 Provost & Dean of the College ... Dr. Marci J. SORTOR
10 Vice Pres & Chief Financial Officer ... Ms. Janet K. HANSON
30 Vice Pres for Advancement ... Mr. Enoch BLAZIS
32 Vice Pres of Student Life ... Mr. Greg KNESER
84 Vice Pres Enrollment/Col Relations ... Mr. Michael KYLE
88 Vice Pres for Mission ... Dr. Jo M. BELD
15 Vice Pres for Human Resources ... Mr. Michael GOODSON
18 Asst Vice President for Facilities ... Mr. Peter SANDBERG
28 Asst to the Pres for Inst Diversity ... Mr. Bruce KING
20 Associate Provost ... Dr. Dan DRESSEN
06 Asst VP/Registrar ... Dr. Steve MCKELVEY
89 Assoc Dean Interdisciplin/Gen Stds ... Dr. Dana GROSS
81 Assoc Dean Natural Sciences & Math ... Dr. Mary WALCZAK
79 Assoc Dean Humanities ... Dr. Corliss SWAIN
57 Assoc Dean Fine Arts ... Ms. Mary GRIEP
83 Assoc Dean Social Sciences ... Dr. Rebecca JUDGE
21 Asst VP/Chief Investment Officer ... Mr. Mark GELLE
109 Asst VP/Budget & Auxiliary Ops ... Ms. Angela MATHEWS
07 Dean of Admissions & Financial Aid ... Mr. Chris GEORGE
35 Dean of Students ... Dr. Rosalyn EATON-NEEB
35 Assoc Dean of Students ... Mr. Justin FLEMING
35 Assoc Dean of Students ... Mr. Timothy SCHROER
42 Campus Pastor ... Dr. Matthew MAROHL
42 Associate College Pastor ... Ms. Katherine FICK
13 Director of IT and Libraries ... Ms. Roberta LEMBKE
08 Director of IT and Libraries ... Ms. Roberta LEMBKE
44 Director Annual Giving ... Vacant
29 Dir of Engage/Alum/Parent Relations ... Mr. Brad HOFF
19 Director of Public Safety ... Mr. Fred C. BEHR
41 Director of Athletics ... Mr. Matt C. MCDONALD
38 Director of Counseling ... Dr. Stephen O'NEILL
26 Dir of Marketing & Communications ... Mr. Steve BLODGETT
75 Int Dir Ctr for Vocation and Career ... Ms. Kirsten CAHOON
36 Sr Assoc Dir Career Ed & Coaching ... Ms. Kirsten CAHOON
108 Director of Evaluation & Assessment ... Dr. Gary MUIR
09 Director of Institutional Research ... Ms. Susan CANON
39 Director of Residence Life ... Ms. Pamela MCDOWELL
40 Bookstore Director ... Ms. Victoria BEUSSMAN
37 Director of Student Financial Aid ... Ms. Sandra SUNDSTROM
102 Dir of Govt/Fndtn & Corp Relations ... Ms. Helen WARREN
104 Dir of Intl & Off Campus Studies ... Dr. Jodi MALMGREN
85 International Student Coordinator ... Ms. Kham VANG
04 Exec Assistant to the President ... Ms. Jennifer WHITSON

Sanford-Brown College (D)

5951 Earle Brown Drive, Brooklyn Center MN 55430
Telephone: (763) 279-2400 Identification: 770733
Accreditation: ACICS

† School is in teach-out plan.

Sanford-Brown College-Mendota Heights (E)

1340 Mendota Heights Road, Mendota Heights MN 55120
County: Dakota FICE Identification: 007351
Unit ID: 174394
Telephone: (651) 905-3400 Carnegie Class: Bac/Assoc
FAX Number: (651) 905-3550 Calendar System: Other
URL: www.browncollege.edu
Established: 1946 Annual Undergrad Tuition & Fees: $13,140
Enrollment: 150 Coed
Affiliation or Control: Proprietary IRS Status: Proprietary
Highest Offering: Baccalaureate
Program: Occupational; 2-Year Principally Bachelor's Creditable; Professional; Business Emphasis
Accreditation: ACICS

01 President/Dir Brooklyn Ctr Campus ... Dr. Michelle ERNST
05 Dean of Education ... Ms. Lisa THOMAS
36 Director of Career Services ... Mr. Paul KRAIMER
13 Director of Information Technology ... Mr. John HANS
06 Registrar ... Ms. Debra NEWGARD
08 Librarian ... Mr. Philip DUDAS
10 Business Office Manager ... Ms. Jennifer BOLISH

† School is in teach-out plan through 2017.

United Theological Seminary of the Twin Cities (F)

3000 5th Street, NW, New Brighton MN 55112-2598
County: Ramsey FICE Identification: 002386
Unit ID: 175139
Telephone: (651) 633-4311 Carnegie Class: Spec/Faith
FAX Number: (651) 633-4315 Calendar System: Semester
URL: www.unitedseminary.edu
Established: 1962 Annual Graduate Tuition & Fees: $15,500
Enrollment: 141 Coed
Affiliation or Control: United Church Of Christ IRS Status: 501(c)3
Highest Offering: Doctorate; No Undergraduates
Program: Professional; Religious Emphasis
Accreditation: NH, THEOL

01 President ... Rev. Barbara A. HOLMES
05 VP for Academic Affairs/Dean ... Dr. Sharon M. TAN
10 VP for Finance and Administration ... Mr. Peter LEE
30 VP for Advancement ... Mr. Bradley O. REINERS
20 Associate Dean ... Dr. Paul CAPETZ
37 Asst Dean Stdnts/Dir Fin Aid & Hous ... Ms. Michelle TURNAU
107 Director of Advanced Studies ... Dr. Thorsten MORITZ
44 Director of Development ... Ms. Kit BRIEM
07 Director of Admissions ... Ms. Maria FRENCH
06 Registrar ... Ms. Susan HASTINGS
08 Director of the Library ... Ms. Susan EBBERS
51 Community Programing Director ... Mr. Brian BRASKICH
42 Chaplain ... Rev. John LEE
18 Director Physical Plant ... Mr. Brandon KROSCH
28 Dir Diversity/Blck Chrch Leadershp ... Ms. Margaree LEVY
29 Director of Alumni Relations ... Ms. Kiely TODD ROSKA
15 Dir of Human Resources & Operations ... Ms. Vonda PEARSON
25 Dir of Church Relations & Grants ... Rev. Kathleen REMUND
27 Director of Communications ... Ms. Liz WARD
04 Admin Assistant to the President ... Ms. Meredythe JONES ROSSI

University of Minnesota Duluth (G)

1049 University Drive, Duluth MN 55812-3011
County: Saint Louis FICE Identification: 002388
Unit ID: 174233
Telephone: (218) 726-8000 Carnegie Class: Master's M
FAX Number: (218) 726-6254 Calendar System: Semester
URL: www.d.umn.edu
Established: 1947 Annual Undergrad Tuition & Fees (In-State): $13,082
Enrollment: 11,093 Coed
Affiliation or Control: State IRS Status: 501(c)3
Highest Offering: Doctorate
Program: Liberal Arts And General; Teacher Preparatory; Professional
Accreditation: NH, ART, BUS, CAATE, CEA, CS, ENG, MUS, SP, SW, TED

01 Chancellor ... Dr. Lendley C. BLACK
05 Exec Vice Chanc Academic Affairs ... Dr. Andrea SCHOKKER
32 Vice Chanc Stdnt Life/Dean Stdnts ... Dr. Lisa ERWIN
10 Vice Chanc Finance/Operations ... Mr. Stephen W. KETO
06 Registrar ... Ms. Carla L. BOYD
08 Director of Library ... Mr. Matt ROSENDAHL
37 Director Financial Aid ... Ms. Brenda H. HERZIG
36 Director Career Services ... Ms. Julie A. WESTLUND
13 Director Info Tech Sys/Services ... Dr. Jason DAVIS
09 Director Institutional Research ... Ms. Mary KEENAN
25 Senior Grant Administrator ... Ms. Elizabeth RUMSEY
51 Director Continuing Education ... Ms. Lynn BURBANK
41 Athletic Director ... Mr. Josh BERLO
15 Int Dir Human Resources/Equal Opp ... Ms. Mary CAMERON
07 Assistant Director Admissions ... Mr. Scott SCHULZ
18 Dir Facilities/Physical Plant ... Mr. John RASHID
29 Director Alumni Relations ... Ms. Lisa PRATT
30 Director Development ... Ms. Tricia BUNTEN
21 Interim Director of Finance ... Ms. Elaine HANSEN
86 Director of External Affairs ... Ms. Lynne WILLIAMS
63 Associate Dean School of Med ... Dr. Paula TERMUHLEN
81 Dean College Science/Engineering ... Dr. Joshua HAMILTON
49 Dean College Liberal Arts ... Dr. Susan MAHER
53 Dean Col Education/Human Svc Prof ... Dr. Jill PINKNEY-PASTRANA
50 Dean School of Business & Economics ... Dr. Amy HIETAPELTO
57 Dean School Fine Arts ... Mr. William PAYNE
58 Interim Director of Grad Programs ... Dr. Erik BROWN

University of Minnesota-Crookston (H)

2900 University Avenue, Crookston MN 56716-5001
County: Polk FICE Identification: 004069
Unit ID: 174075
Telephone: (218) 281-6510 Carnegie Class: Bac/Diverse
FAX Number: (218) 281-8040 Calendar System: Semester
URL: www.crk.umn.edu
Established: 1965 Annual Undergrad Tuition & Fees (In-State): $11,465
Enrollment: 1,876 Coed
Affiliation or Control: State IRS Status: 501(c)3
Highest Offering: Baccalaureate
Program: Occupational; Business Emphasis
Accreditation: NH

01 Chancellor ... Dr. Fred WOOD
05 VC for Academic Affairs ... Dr. Barbara KEINATH
32 Assoc VC Student Affs/Enrollment ... Dr. Peter PHAIAH
18 Director Facilities/Operations ... Mr. Dave DANFORTH
10 Dir of Finance/University Services ... Ms. Tricia SANDERS
15 Director Human Resources ... Mr. Les JOHNSON
37 Director Financial Aid ... Ms. Melissa DINGMANN
26 Director of Communications ... Mr. Andrew SVEC
30 Dir Development/Alumni Relations ... Mr. Corby KEMMER
08 Director Library ... Mr. Owen WILLIAMS
36 Director Career/Counseling ... Mr. Donald R. CAVALIER
49 Head of Arts/Humanities/Soc Sci ... Dr. Soo-Yin LIM-THOMPSON
47 Head Agriculture & Nat Resources ... Dr. Ron DEL VECCHIO

72 Head Math/Science/Technology .... Dr. Joseph SHOSTELL
50 Head Business .... Vacant
51 Director Center for Adult Learning .... Ms. Michelle CHRISTOPHERSON
06 Registrar .... Dr. Ken MYERS
07 Director of Admissions .... Ms. Carola THORSON
28 Director of Diversity .... Ms. Lorna HOLLOWELL
85 Dir of International Programs .... Dr. Kimberly GILLETTE

University of Minnesota-Morris (A)

600 E 4th Street, Morris MN 56267-2132
County: Stevens FICE Identification: 002389
Unit ID: 174251
Telephone: (320) 589-2211 Carnegie Class: Bac/A&S
FAX Number: (320) 589-6399 Calendar System: Semester
URL: www.morris.umn.edu
Established: 1959 Annual Undergrad Tuition & Fees (In-State): $12,485
Enrollment: 1,899 Coed
Affiliation or Control: State IRS Status: 501(c)3
Highest Offering: Baccalaureate
Program: Liberal Arts And General; Teacher Preparatory
Accreditation: NH, TED

01 Chancellor .... Dr. Jacqueline JOHNSON
05 Vice Chanc Academic Affs/Dean .... Dr. Bart FINZEL
32 Vice Chanc for Student Affairs .... Ms. Sandra OLSON-LOY
18 Vice Chanc for Finance & Facilities .... Mr. Bryan HERRMANN
10 Director for Finance .... Ms. Colleen MILLER
08 Head Librarian .... Ms. LeAnn DEAN
06 Registrar's Office .... Ms. Judy KORN
26 Director of Communications .... Ms. Melissa WEBER
29 Director of Alumni Relations .... Ms. Carla RILEY
09 Director of Institutional Research .... Ms. Nancy HELSPER
36 Director Career Center .... Mr. Gary L. DONOVAN
13 Director of Information Technology .... Mr. James HALL
38 Director of Counseling .... Dr. Henry FULDA
37 Director of Financial Aid .... Ms. Jill BEAUREGARD
93 Dir Multi Ethnic Student Program .... Ms. Hilda LADNER
24 Director Educational Media .... Mr. Michael CIHAK
07 Director of Admissions .... Vacant
53 Chair of Education Division .... Dr. Gwen RUDNEY
81 Chair of Science/Math Division .... Dr. Peh Peh NG
79 Chair of Humanities Division .... Dr. Pieranno GARAVASO
83 Chair of Social Science Division .... Dr. Arne KILDEGAARD

University of Minnesota-Rochester Campus (B)

111 South Broadway, Suite 300, Rochester MN 55904
Telephone: (800) 947-0117 Identification: 770316
Accreditation: &NH, OT

† Branch campus of University of Minnesota-Twin Cities, Minneapolis, MN.

University of Minnesota-Twin Cities (C)

100 Church Street, SE, Minneapolis MN 55455-0213
County: Hennepin FICE Identification: 003969
Unit ID: 174066
Telephone: (612) 625-5000 Carnegie Class: RU/VH
FAX Number: (612) 624-6369 Calendar System: Semester
URL: www.umn.edu
Established: 1851 Annual Undergrad Tuition & Fees (In-State): $13,840
Enrollment: 51,147 Coed
Affiliation or Control: State IRS Status: 501(c)3
Highest Offering: Doctorate
Program: Occupational; Liberal Arts And General; Teacher Preparatory; Professional
Accreditation: NH, ANEST, AUD, BUS, CIDA, CLPSY, COARC, CONST, COPSY, DANCE, DENT, DH, DIETC, DIETD, DIETI, ENG, ENGR, FUSER, HSA, IPSY, JOUR, LAW, LSAR, MED, MFCD, MIDWF, MT, MUS, NURSE, OT, PCSAS, PH, PHAR, PLNG, PTA, RTT, SCPSY, SP, SPAA, SW, TED, THEA, VET

01 President .... Dr. Eric W. KALER
100 Chief of Staff .... Ms. Amy PHENIX
05 Sr VP for Academic Affairs/Provost .... Dr. Karen HANSON
17 Vice President for Health Sciences .... Dr. R. Brooks JACKSON
10 Vice President/Chief Financial Ofcr .... Mr. Richard H. PFUTZENREUTER
46 Vice President for Research .... Dr. Brian HERMAN
58 Vice Prov/Dean Graduate Education .... Dr. Henning SCHROEDER
20 Vice Prov/Dean Undergrad Education .... Dr. Robert MCMASTER
15 Vice President Human Resources .... Ms. Kathryn F. BROWN
88 Vice Pres for University Services .... Ms. Pam WHEELOCK
28 Vice Pres for Equity and Diversity .... Dr. Katrice ALBERT
13 Interim VP/Chief Info Officer .... Mr. Bernard GULACHEK
43 General Counsel .... Mr. William DONOHUE
102 President Univ Minnesota Foundation .... Ms. Katherine SCHMIDLKOFER
25 Assoc VP Sponsored Projects Admin .... Ms. Frances LAWRENZ
86 Assoc Vice Pres for Govt Relations .... Ms. Erin DADY
18 Associate VP/Chief of Facilities .... Mr. Mike BERTHELSEN
32 Vice Provost for Student Affairs .... Ms. Danita BROWN YOUNG
19 Asst VP Pub Safety/Chief of Police .... Mr. Matthew CLARK
08 University Librarian .... Dr. Wendy P. LOUGEE
06 Registrar .... Ms. Sue N. VAN VOORHIS
07 Director of Admissions .... Ms. Rachelle HERNANDEZ
09 Director of Institutional Research .... Dr. John KELLOGG
22 Director Equal Oppty/Affirm Action .. Ms. Kimberly HEWITT BOYD
37 Interim Director of Student Finance .... Ms. Tina FALKNER
40 Director of the U of M Bookstores .... Mr. Ross ROSATI
39 Dir of Housing & Residential Life .... Ms. Laurie L. MCLAUGHLIN
48 Dean of the College of Design .... Dr. Thomas R. FISHER
86 Director of Federal Relations .... Ms. Channing RIGGS
29 CEO Alumni Association .... Ms. Lisa LEWIS
38 Dir of Counseling & Consulting Srvc .... Dr. Glenn HIRSCH
87 Director of the Summer Session .... Michelle KOKER
21 Associate VP for Budget/Finance .... Ms. Julie A. TONNESON
36 Director of Student Placement .... Vacant
96 Interim Director of Purchasing .... Mr. Tim BRAY
49 Dean of the College of Liberal Arts .... Mr. John COLEMAN
51 Dean College of Continuing Educ .... Dr. Mary L. NICHOLS
61 Dean of the Law School .... Mr. David WIPPMAN
74 Dean College of Veterinary Medicine .... Dr. Trevor R. AMES
63 Dean of the Medical School .... Dr. Brooks JACKSON
66 Dean of the School of Nursing .... Dr. Connie J. DELANEY
53 Dean College Education/Human Devel .... Dr. Jean K. QUAM
52 Dean of the School of Dentistry .... Dr. Leon ASSAEL
69 Dean of the School Public Health .... Dr. John FINNEGAN
72 Dean College of Science/Engineering .... Dr. Steven CROUCH
67 Dean of the College Pharmacy .... Dr. Marilyn K. SPEEDIE
50 Dean Carlson School of Management .... Dr. Srilata A. ZAHEER
80 Dean Humphrey Sch of Pub Aff .... Dr. Eric SCHWARTZ
81 Dean College of Biological Science .... Dr. Valery E. FORBES
47 Dean Col Food/Agric/Nat Resourc Sci .... Mr. Brian BUHR
41 Int Dir Intercollegiate Athletics .... Ms. Beth GOETZ
26 Chief Public Relations Officer .... Mr. Chuck TOMBARGE

University of Northwestern - St. Paul (D)

3003 Snelling Avenue N, Saint Paul MN 55113-1598
County: Ramsey FICE Identification: 002371
Unit ID: 174491
Telephone: (651) 631-5100 Carnegie Class: Bac/Diverse
FAX Number: (651) 628-3339 Calendar System: Semester
URL: www.unwsp.edu
Established: 1902 Annual Undergrad Tuition & Fees: $32,676
Enrollment: 3,322 Coed
Affiliation or Control: Independent Non-Profit IRS Status: 501(c)3
Highest Offering: Master's
Program: Liberal Arts And General; Teacher Preparatory
Accreditation: NH, MUS, NURSE

01 President .... Dr. Alan S. CURETON
05 Senior Vice Pres Academic Affairs .... Dr. Janet B. SOMMERS
27 Senior Vice President Media .... Dr. Paul H. VIRTS
32 Vice Pres Student Life & Athletics .... Dr. Mathew B. HILL
30 Vice President Advancement .... Vacant
10 Vice President Finance/CFO .... Mr. Douglas R. SCHROEDER
15 Assoc Vice President of HR .... Mr. Timothy A. RICH
18 Assoc VP Facility Ops & Planning .... Mr. Brian L. HUMPHRIES
79 Dean College of Arts & Humanities .. Dr. Jeremy W. KOLWINSKA
83 Dean College Behave & Nat Sciences .... Dr. Daniel R. CRANE
107 Dean College Professional Studies .... Dr. Richard C. THOMAN
58 Sr Dean Col Adult & Grad Studies .... Vacant
20 Sr Dean Academic Administration .... Dr. Fengling M. JOHNSON
35 Dean of Student Life .... Mr. Paul A. BRADLEY
35 Assoc Dean Student Life .... Dr. Katie J. SMITH
39 Associate Dean for Residence Life .... Mr. Jerod L. CORNELIUS
88 Assoc Dean Commuter Life/Transition .... Mr. Jeff B. SNYDER
13 CIO .... Mr. David G. RICHERT
88 Controller .... Mr. Bryon D. KRUEGER
09 Institutional Researcher Rprt Spec .... Mr. Russell E. ERICKSON
20 Director Academic Operations .... Mr. Kevin B. MCGAUGHEY
90 Director Academic Technology .... Mr. Joel T. JOHNSON
29 Sr Dir Dev & Constituent Relations .... Mr. James K. JOHNSON
38 Director of Counseling/Student Svcs . Ms. Dannette C. WILFAHRT
88 Dir Dept of Support Servces .... Mr. David P. GOLIAS
37 Director of Financial Aid .... Mr. Richard L. BLATCHLEY
23 Director of Health Services .... Mrs. Cynthia P. REEDSTROM
08 Director of Library Services .... Mrs. Ruth A. MCGUIRE
44 Director Major Gifts .... Mr. John T. DELICH
44 Director of Planned Giving .... Mr. David D. DANIELSON
19 Director of Public Safety .... Mr. Peter L. SOLA
106 Dir Undergraduate Pathways .... Dr. Tanya L. GROSZ
96 Manager of Purchasing .... Ms. Cheryl A. GLASS
40 Manager Campus Store .... Mrs. Julienne N. ENTINGER
88 Asst to Pres for ADA Initiatives .... Dr. Yvonne R. BANKS
101 Exec Secy to Pres & Bd of Trustees .... Ms. Mona S. GRELLSON
00 President Emeritus .... Dr. Donald O. ERICKSEN
04 Administrative Asst to President .... Mrs. Rachel A. MORGAN
102 Sr Dir Advancement/VP of Foundation .... Mr. Kirby R. STOLL
103 Dir Ctr for Calling & Career .... Mrs. Diann L. LLOYD-DENNIS
26 Director Marketing & Communication .. Ms. Marita K. MEINERTS
108 Special Asst/Director of Assessment .... Dr. Barbara A. LINDMAN
28 Director/GRACE .... Dr. David E. FENRICK
41 Asst Athletic Director .... Vacant
06 Registrar .... Mr. Andy L. SIMPSON
104 Asst Dir Center for Global Programs .... Ms. Veelie P. ABBA
50 Asst Dean School of Business .... Mr. Richard F. ELLIOTT
53 Asst Dean School of Education .... Dr. Susan N. JOHNSON
84 Vice President Enrollment Mgt .... Mr. Michael R. MORONEY

† Formerly Northwestern College

University of Phoenix Minneapolis/St. Paul Campus (E)

435 Ford Road, St. Louis Park MN 55426-4915
Telephone: (952) 487-7226 Identification: 770212
Accreditation: &NH, ACBSP

† No longer accepting campus-based students.

University of Saint Thomas (F)

2115 Summit Avenue, Saint Paul MN 55105-1096
County: Ramsey FICE Identification: 002345
Unit ID: 174914
Telephone: (651) 962-5000 Carnegie Class: DRU
FAX Number: (651) 962-6360 Calendar System: 4/1/4
URL: www.stthomas.edu
Established: 1885 Annual Undergrad Tuition & Fees: $37,264
Enrollment: 10,229 Coed
Affiliation or Control: Roman Catholic IRS Status: 501(c)3
Highest Offering: Doctorate
Program: Liberal Arts And General; Teacher Preparatory; Professional
Accreditation: NH, BUS, COPSY, ENG, HSA, IPSY, LAW, MUS, SW, TED, THEOL

01 President .... Dr. Julie H. SULLIVAN
04 Executive Advisor to President .... Dr. Susan L. ALEXANDER
05 Provost .... Dr. Richard G. PLUMB
88 Rector/Vice Pres School of Divinity .... Msgr. Aloysius R. CALLAGHAN
32 Vice President for Student Affairs .... Dr. Karen M. LANGE
10 Vice Pres for Business Affairs/CFO .... Mr. Mark D. VANGSGARD
26 Vice President University Relations .... Mr. Doug E. HENNES
13 Int VP Information Resources & Tech .... Mr. Chris S. GREGG
20 Int Assoc Vice Pres Academic Affs .... Dr. Robert J. RILEY
84 VP Enrollment Services .... Mr. Dan MEYER
15 Assoc VP Human Res/General Counsel .... Ms. Sara E. GROSS METHNER
21 Assoc VP/Finance & Controller .... Mr. Gary L. THYEN
18 Associate Vice Pres Facilities .... Mr. James M. BRUMMER
109 Associate VP for Auxiliary Services .... Mr. Gerald M. ANDERLEY
49 Dean College Arts & Sciences .... Dr. Terrence G. LANGAN
50 Dean Opus College of Business .... Dr. Stefanie A. LENWAY
53 Int Dean of School of Education .... Dr. Joseph L. KREITZER
83 Dean of School of Social Work .... Dr. Barbara W. SHANK
73 Dean St Paul Seminary School of Div .... Dr. Christopher J. THOMPSON
61 Dean School of Law .... Mr. Robert VISCHER
35 Dean of Student Life .... Vacant
88 Assoc Dean Grad Prof Psychology .... Dr. Christopher VYE
58 Dir Graduate Programs/Business Comm .... Dr. Michael PORTER
88 Sr Assoc Dean College of Business .... Dr. Michael GARRISON
54 Dean School of Engineering .... Dr. Donald H. WEINKFAUF
30 Sr VP Institutional Advancement .... Ms. Kimberly J. MOTES
06 Registrar .... Mr. Paul M. SIMMONS
07 Director Admissions & Financial Aid .... Ms. Kris A. GETTING
09 Director of Institutional Research .... Dr. Michael F. COGAN
35 Executive Director Campus Life .... Ms. Mary A. RYAN
36 Director of Career Services .... Ms. Diane G. CRIST
27 Director of the News Service .... Mr. James C. WINTERER
29 Exec Dir Alumni/Constituent Rels .... Ms. Rachel A. WOBSCHALL
41 Athletic Director .... Mr. Stephen J. FRITZ
40 Director Bookstore .... Mr. Tony W. ERICKSON
42 Director Campus Ministry .... Fr. Erich RUTTEN
19 Director Safety/Security .... Mr. Daniel J. MEUWISSEN
39 Director Campus Life .... Ms. Margaret D. CAHILL
38 Director Student Counseling .... Dr. Jeri M. ROCKETT
96 Director Purchasing Services .... Ms. Karen M. HARTHORN
28 Director of Diversity .... Dr. MariAnn GRAHAM

Walden University (G)

100 Washington Ave S, Suite 900, Minneapolis MN 55401
County: Hennepin FICE Identification: 025042
Unit ID: 125231
Telephone: (612) 338-7224 Carnegie Class: DRU
FAX Number: (612) 338-5092 Calendar System: Other
URL: www.waldenu.edu
Established: 1970 Annual Undergrad Tuition & Fees: $14,970
Enrollment: 52,188 Coed
Affiliation or Control: Proprietary IRS Status: Proprietary
Highest Offering: Doctorate
Program: Teacher Preparatory
Accreditation: NH, ACBSP, CACREP, CS, NURSE, @SW, TED

00 Chief Executive Officer .... Mr. Jonathan A. KAPLAN
01 Interim President .... Mr. Jonathan A. KAPLAN
05 Chief Academic Officer .... Dr. Eric RIEDEL
69 VP College Health Sciences .... Dr. Melanie STORMS
83 VP College Soc & Behav Sciences .... Dr. Melanie STORMS
50 VP College of Mgmt & Tech .... Dr. Gregory WASHINGTON
26 VP Marketing .... Mr. Christian SCHINDLER
43 VP and Assistant General Counsel .... Ms. Deborah L. ZIMIC
20 VP of Undergrad Programs .... Dr. L. Ward ULMER
27 Div VP for Ext Rel & Pub Policy .... Dr. John A. SABATINI, JR.
13 CIO .... Mr. Jorge ELGUERA
10 CFO .... Mr. Roger MCKINNEY
53 Dean RWR College of Education .... Dr. Kate STEFFENS
46 Exec Dir Office of IR & Assesment .... Mr. Jim LENIO
32 Exec Dir Ctr for Student Success .... Ms. Susanna DAVIDSEN
88 Interim Exec Dir Ctr for Fac Exc .... Dr. Laurie BEDFORD
88 Exec Dir Ctr for Research Support .... Dr. Laura LYNN
104 Exec Dir International Programs .... Ms. Lauren STONE
15 Exec Director of Human Resources .... Ms. Paola MADRISOTTI
14 Director of IT .... Ms. Terri THOMPSON
07 Interim Director of Admissions .... Ms. Reena LICHTENFELD
21 Bursar .... Ms. Linda ANTHONY
37 Director of Financial Aid .... Ms. Melvina JOHNSON
06 Registrar .... Ms. Devon LOETZ
08 Director of Library Services .... Ms. Jennie VER STEEG
09 Director of Inst Research .... Ms. Nicole HOLLAND

108 Director Institutional Assessment ... Dr. Shari JORISSEN
29 Director Alumni Relations ... Ms. Valescia LEE-COLLICK

White Earth Tribal and Community College (A)

PO Box 478, Mahnomen MN 56557-0478
County: Mahnomen FICE Identification: 039214
Unit ID: 434751
Telephone: (218) 935-0417 Carnegie Class: Tribal
FAX Number: (218) 936-5814 Calendar System: Semester
URL: www.wetcc.edu
Established: 1997 Annual Undergrad Tuition & Fees: $3,285
Enrollment: 69 Coed
Affiliation or Control: Tribal Control IRS Status: 501(c)3
Highest Offering: Associate Degree
Program: 2-Year Principally Bachelor's Creditable; Liberal Arts And General
Accreditation: NH

01 President ... Terry JANIS
05 Academic Dean ... Sheila MICHAELS
32 Dean of Student Services ... Karen BRANDEN
10 Finance Director ... Landa MOORE
15 Human Resources Technician ... Denise ASKELSON
37 Financial Aid Specialist ... Patrick VOIGHT
56 Director of Extension ... Steve DAHLBERG
13 IT Director ... Cody COAUETTE
06 Registrar ... Martha ALLEN
07 Admissions Coordinator ... Loreen STANLEY
30 Special Projects/Interim Devel Dir ... Deb MCARTHUR

William Mitchell College of Law (B)

875 Summit Avenue, Saint Paul MN 55105-3076
County: Ramsey FICE Identification: 002391
Unit ID: 175281
Telephone: (651) 227-9171 Carnegie Class: Spec/Law
FAX Number: (651) 290-6414 Calendar System: Semester
URL: www.wmitchell.edu
Established: 1900 Annual Graduate Tuition & Fees: $39,560
Enrollment: 668 Coed
Affiliation or Control: Independent Non-Profit IRS Status: 501(c)3
Highest Offering: First Professional Degree; No Undergraduates
Program: Professional
Accreditation: LAW

01 President & Dean ... Mr. Mark GORDON
04 Exec Asst to President & Board ... Ms. Deb CALVERT
11 Assoc Dean for Administration ... Ms. Mary Pat BYRN
30 VP of Institutional Advancement ... Ms. Linda K. BERG
15 Int Vice President Human Resources ... Ms. Kate LAW
13 Director of Information Technology ... Mr. Chad JOHNSON
10 Vice President Finance ... Ms. Kathy PANCIERA
32 Vice President of Student Affairs ... Ms. Christine SZAJ
08 Assoc Dean of Info Resources ... Mr. Simon CANICK
28 Asst Dean/Multicultural Inclusion ... Ms. Luiza DREASHER
36 Asst Dean for Career Development . Ms. Karen VANDER SANDEN
07 Asst Dean/Director of Admissions ... Ms. Julie EKKERS
06 Registrar ... Mr. Jim STEVENS
26 Director of Marketing/Alumni Rels ... Ms. Louise COPELAND
37 Director of Financial Aid ... Ms. Patty HARRIS
96 Purchasing Manager ... Ms. Paula B. MERTH
19 Asst Director Security ... Mr. David HELLERMANN

MISSISSIPPI

Alcorn State University (C)

1000 ASU Drive, #359, Lorman MS 39096-7500
County: Claiborne FICE Identification: 002396
Unit ID: 175342
Telephone: (601) 877-6100 Carnegie Class: Master's M
FAX Number: (601) 877-2975 Calendar System: Semester
URL: www.alcorn.edu
Established: 1871 Annual Undergrad Tuition & Fees (In-State): $6,384
Enrollment: 3,639 Coed
Affiliation or Control: State IRS Status: 501(c)3
Highest Offering: Beyond Master's But Less Than Doctorate
Program: 2-Year Principally Bachelor's Creditable; Liberal Arts And General; Teacher Preparatory; Professional
Accreditation: SC, AAFCS, ACBSP, ADNUR, #DIETD, MUS, NAIT, NUR, NURSE, SW, TED

01 President ... Dr. Alfred RANKINS, JR.
05 Provost/VP Academic Affairs ... Dr. Donzell LEE
11 Sr VP for Univ Operations/COO ... Vacant
04 Exec Asst to the President ... Mrs. Karen R. SHEDRICK
88 Special Asst for Univ Initiatives ... Vacant
88 Director of Internal Audit ... Mr. Permy K. THUHA
46 Chief Research Officer ... Dr. Babu P. PATLOLLA
10 VP for Finance & Administrative Svc ... Mrs. Carolyn DUPRE'
32 VP for Student Affairs ... Mr. Emanuel BARNES
30 VP Institutional Advancement ... Mr. Marcus D. WARD
26 VP Marketing/Communications ... Mrs. Clara R. STAMPS
20 Vice Provost Academic Affs/GS ... Dr. John IGWEBUIKE
18 Assoc VP for Facilities Management ... Mr. Marlin KING
39 Director of Residence Life ... Ms. Jessica L. FOXWORTH
28 Dir of Educational Equity/Inclusion ... Mrs. Lljuna WEIR
21 Director of Accounting ... Mrs. Cassandra B. LEWIS
96 Purchasing Agent ... Ms. Mertha V. GEORGE
07 Director of Admissions/Recruiting ... Mrs. Katangela TENNER
37 Director of Financial Aid ... Mrs. Juanita RUSSELL-EDWARDS
06 Registrar ... Mr. Jimmy L. SMITH
08 Dean University Libraries ... Dr. Blanche SANDERS
47 Interim Dean School of Agriculture ... Dr. Ivory LYLES
49 Dean School of Arts & Science ... Dr. Babu P. PATLOLLA
50 Dean School of Business ... Dr. Vivek BHARGAVA
53 Dean School of Education ... Dr. Robert CARR
66 Dean School of Nursing ... Dr. Yolanda POWELL-YOUNG
88 Dean University College ... Dr. Valerie THOMPSON
13 CIO for Ctr for Info Tech Svcs ... Mrs. Donna G. HAYDEN
15 Director of Human Resources ... Mrs. Carla WILLIAMS
36 Director Career Services ... Dr. Joey MITCHELL
23 Director of Health Services ... Ms. Dorothy G. JACKSON-DAVIS
41 Director of Athletics ... Mr. Derek HORNE
40 Manager Barnes and Noble ... Mr. Domonic RABY
38 Director of Counseling & Testing ... Mrs. Dyann W. MOSES
09 Director Institutional Res/Assess ... Dr. Ramesh MADDALI
108 Dir Institutional Effectiveness ... Dr. LaToya HART
19 Chief of Campus Police ... Mr. Douglas STEWART
88 General Manager Sodexo ... Mr. Corey D. YOUNG
102 Exec Dir ASU Foundation ... Mr. Marcus D. WARD
31 Dir Ctr Rural Life/Econ Dev ... Mr. Alfred GALTNEY
92 Director of Pre-Prof/Honors Program ... Dr. Thomas C. STURGIS
25 Grants/Contract Administrator ... Ms. Sallie GRIFFIN
88 Senior Dir Community Outreach ... Dr. Ruth R. NICHOLS
106 Director Online Educ Vicksburg ... Dr. Ivan BANKS
104 Director Study Abroad ... Dr. Dovi ALIPOE

Antonelli College (D)

1500 N 31st Avenue, Hattiesburg MS 39401-3056
Telephone: (601) 583-4100 Identification: 666517
Accreditation: ACCSC

† Branch campus of Antonelli College, OH.

Antonelli College (E)

2323 Lakeland Drive, Jackson MS 39208-9549
Telephone: (601) 362-9991 Identification: 666518
Accreditation: ACCSC

† Branch campus of Antonelli College, OH.

Belhaven University (F)

1500 Peachtree Street, Jackson MS 39202-1798
County: Hinds FICE Identification: 002397
Unit ID: 175421
Telephone: (601) 968-5940 Carnegie Class: Master's M
FAX Number: (601) 968-9998 Calendar System: Semester
URL: www.belhaven.edu
Established: 1883 Annual Undergrad Tuition & Fees: $21,626
Enrollment: 4,120 Coed
Affiliation or Control: Presbyterian Church (U.S.A.) IRS Status: 501(c)3
Highest Offering: Master's
Program: Liberal Arts And General; Teacher Preparatory; Professional; Fine Arts Emphasis
Accreditation: SC, ART, DANCE, IACBE, MUS, @SW, THEA

01 President ... Dr. Roger PARROTT
05 Exec Vice President & Provost ... Dr. Dan FREDERICKS
30 Vice Pres Institutional Advancement ... Mr. Kevin RUSSELL
88 VP of Adult & Graduate Marketing ... Dr. Audrey KELLEHER
10 Chief Financial Officer ... Mrs. Virginia HENDERSON
32 VP for Student Affairs and Athletic ... Mr. Scott LITTLE
11 Asst Vice Pres Campus Operations ... Mr. David POTVIN
51 Assistant VP for Adult Studies ... Dr. Rick UPCHURCH
20 Assoc Provost ... Dr. Lee SKINKLE
20 Assoc Provost ... Dr. Dennis WATTS
12 Academic Dean/Houston Campus ... Dr. Larry RUDDELL
12 Academic Dean/Orlando ... Dr. Tracie LAMBETH
12 Academic Dean/Mississippi ... Dr. Ken ELLIOTT
12 Academic Dean/Memphis Tennessee ... Dr. Paul CRISS
12 Academic Dean/Chattanooga-Atlanta ... Dr. Kym CHAVEZ
50 Dean of the School of Business ... Dr. Chip MASON
08 Librarian ... Mr. Chris CULLNANE
07 Asst VP Trad & Online Admissions ... Mrs. Suzanne SULLIVAN
06 Registrar ... Mrs. Donna WEEKS
26 Director of Integrated Marketing ... Mr. Bryant BUTLER
35 Director of Student Leadership ... Ms. JoBeth PETTY
13 Director Institutional Technology ... Mr. Bo MILLER
19 Director Security/Safety ... Mr. Steve FARMER
40 Bookstore Manager ... Ms. Sheila LYONS
36 Dean of Student Development ... Mr. Ron PIRTLE
35 Dean of Student Life ... Mr. Greg HAWKINS

Blue Mountain College (G)

201 W Main Street, PO Box 160,
Blue Mountain MS 38610-0160
County: Tippah FICE Identification: 002398
Unit ID: 175430
Telephone: (662) 685-4771 Carnegie Class: Bac/Diverse
FAX Number: (662) 685-4776 Calendar System: Semester
URL: www.bmc.edu
Established: 1873 Annual Undergrad Tuition & Fees: $10,968
Enrollment: 544 Coed
Affiliation or Control: Southern Baptist IRS Status: 501(c)3
Highest Offering: Master's
Program: Liberal Arts And General; Teacher Preparatory; Religious Emphasis
Accreditation: SC

01 President ... Dr. Barbara C. MCMILLIN
05 Vice President for Academic Affairs ... Dr. Sharon B. ENZOR
32 VP for Student Services ... Mr. Jack T. MOSER
07 Vice Pres for Enrollment Services ... Mr. Lynn GIBSON
10 Chief Financial Officer ... Mr. Steve ROBBINS
11 Chief Operating Officer ... Mrs. Joyce PETERS
04 Admin Assistant to the President ... Mrs. Pam BOWMAN
58 Dean Graduate Studies ... Dr. Jenetta WADDELL
06 Registrar ... Mrs. Sheila D. FREEMAN
08 Director of Library Services ... Dr. Derek J. CASH
37 Director of Financial Aid ... Mrs. Janice PRATHER
40 Director Campus Store ... Mrs. Dot M. LOCKE
41 Athletic Director ... Mr. Lavon DRISKELL
42 Director Baptist Student Union ... Mrs. Tracy S. MOSER
09 Director of Institutional Research ... Mr. Robert E. RUCKER
13 Director of Information Services ... Mr. Kevin BAREFIELD
26 Dir of PR/Publications ... Ms. Emma L. AINSWORTH
29 Director of Alumni Affairs ... Mrs. Nancy H. MCDONALD

Coahoma Community College (H)

3240 Friars Point Road, Clarksdale MS 38614-9700
County: Coahoma FICE Identification: 002401
Unit ID: 175519
Telephone: (662) 627-2571 Carnegie Class: Assoc/Pub-R-S
FAX Number: (662) 627-9451 Calendar System: Semester
URL: www.coahomacc.edu
Established: 1949 Annual Undergrad Tuition & Fees (In-District): $2,440
Enrollment: 2,040 Coed
Affiliation or Control: State/Local IRS Status: 501(c)3
Highest Offering: Associate Degree
Program: Occupational; 2-Year Principally Bachelor's Creditable
Accreditation: SC, ADNUR, #COARC, POLYT

01 President ... Dr. Valmadge T. TOWNER
05 Dean of Academics ... Dr. Rolanda BROWN
10 Chief Financial Officer ... Ms. Deborah MCNEAL
32 Dir of Enrollment & Student Svcs ... Mrs. Karen DONE
09 Dir Inst Effectiveness/SACS Liaison ... Mrs. Margaret DIXON
30 Coordinator for Federal Programs ... Mrs. Marilyn STARKS
75 Dean of Career & Technical Educ ... Mrs. Anne SHELTON-CLARK
07 Director of Admissions/Registrar ... Mr. Michael HOUSTON
08 Dir Library/Instructional Resources ... Mrs. Rose LOCKETT
13 Director Computer Services ... Mr. Matt LOGAN
19 Director of Safety/Transportation ... Vacant
26 Chief Communication Officer ... Mr. Matthew KILLEBREW
37 Director of Financial Aid ... Mr. Luke HOWARD
15 Director of Employee Services ... Mrs. Wanda HOLMES
18 Chief Facilities/Physical Plant ... Mr. Jerone SHAW
51 Director of Educational Outreach ... Ms. Letha RICHARDS
29 Director Alumni Relations ... Mr. Emanuel LACKEY
36 Director Student Placement ... Mr. Orlando PADEN
38 Director Student Counseling ... Vacant
96 Director of Purchasing ... Mrs. Deborah MCNEAL
04 Administrative Asst to President ... Ms. Yolanda D. MILLER
100 Chief of Staff ... Mr. Jerone SHAW
103 Dir Workforce/Career Development ... Mr. Steven JOSSELL
105 Director Web Services ... Mr. Ezra HOWARD
106 Dir Online Education/E-learning ... Ms. Shanelle FRAZIER
41 Athletic Director ... Mr. Freeman HORTON

Concorde Career College (I)

7900 Airways Boulevard, Suite 103, Southaven MS 38671
Telephone: (662) 429-9909 Identification: 770540
Accreditation: COE

† Branch campus of Concorde Career College, Memphis, TN.

Copiah-Lincoln Community College (J)

PO Box 649, Wesson MS 39191-0649
County: Copiah FICE Identification: 002402
Unit ID: 175573
Telephone: (601) 643-5101 Carnegie Class: Assoc/Pub-R-M
FAX Number: (601) 643-8212 Calendar System: Semester
URL: www.colin.edu
Established: 1928 Annual Undergrad Tuition & Fees (In-State): $2,390
Enrollment: 3,040 Coed
Affiliation or Control: State IRS Status: 501(c)3
Highest Offering: Associate Degree
Program: Occupational; 2-Year Principally Bachelor's Creditable
Accreditation: SC, ADNUR, COARC, MLTAD, RAD

01 President ... Dr. Ronald E. NETTLES
04 Assistant to the President ... Mrs. Brenda J. PARRETT
10 Vice President Business Affairs ... Mr. Stan PATRICK
05 Vice Pres of Instructional Services ... Dr. Jane HULON
12 VP of the Simpson County Center ... Dr. Dewayne MIDDLETON
12 Vice Pres of the Natchez Campus ... Ms. Teresa BUSBY
20 Academic Dean ... Dr. Jill B. LOGAN
32 Dean of Student Services ... Mrs. Brenda SMITH
75 Dean Career & Technical Educ ... Ms. Jackie L. MARTIN
31 Dean of Community Programs ... Dr. Brenda B. ORR
41 Athletic Director ... Mr. Gwyn YOUNG
38 Director of Counseling/Recruitment ... Mrs. Lea Ann KNIGHT
35 Assistant Dean of Students ... Mr. Bryan NOBILE
37 Director Student Financial Aid ... Mrs. Leslie SMITH
40 Director Bookstore ... Mr. Charles HART

08 Director of Library Resources ....Mr. Kendall P. CHAPMAN
26 Director of Public Relations ....Mrs. Natalie DAVIS
13 Information Systems Specialist .... Ms. Deemie LETCHWORTH
19 Director of Security ....Mr. Wayne ROBERTS
09 Dir Inst Effectiv/Facilities Plng ....Dr. Jeff POSEY
07 Director of Admissions ....Mr. Chris WARREN
102 Executive Dir Foundation/Alumni ....Mr. David CAMPBELL
18 Director of Physical Plant .... Mr. Daniel CASE
66 Director of Assoc Degree Nursing . Mrs. Mary Ann CANTERBURY
06 Student Records Manager ....Mrs. Gay LANGHAM
57 Chair Fine Arts Division ....Mrs. Janet SMITH
50 Chair Business Division ....Mr. Richard BAKER
68 Chair Physical Education Division ....Dr. Stephanie DUGUID
81 Chair Math/Computer Science Div .... Mr. Eddie BRITT
79 Chair Humanities Division .... Mrs. Pam REID
82 Chair Social Science Division ....Mr. David HIGGS
88 Chair Science Division ....Dr. Kevin MCKONE
96 Director of Purchasing ....Mrs. Erin LIKENS
106 Director of E-learning ....Ms. Vanessa ALEXANDER
108 QEP Director .... Ms. Glenda SILVERII
15 Human Resources Director ....Ms. Julia PARKER
39 Director Student Housing .... Mr. Allen KENT
91 Director of Technology/Info Systems ....Mr. James P. MCINNIS

Delta State University (A)

1003 W. Sunflower Rd., Cleveland MS 38733
County: Bolivar FICE Identification: 002403
Unit ID: 175616
Telephone: (662) 846-3000 Carnegie Class: Master's L
FAX Number: (662) 846-4014 Calendar System: Semester
URL: www.deltastate.edu
Established: 1924 Annual Undergrad Tuition & Fees (In-State): $6,112
Enrollment: 3,614 Coed
Affiliation or Control: State IRS Status: 501(c)3
Highest Offering: Doctorate
Program: Liberal Arts And General; Teacher Preparatory; Professional
Accreditation: SC, AAB, AAFCS, ACBSP, ART, CAATE, CACREP, #DIETC, MUS, NURSE, SW, TED

01 President ....Dr. William (Bill) LAFORGE
05 Provost/VP Academic Affairs ....Dr. Charles MCADAMS
10 Vice President for Finance ....Mr. Steve MCCLELLAN
32 Interim VP for Student Affairs ....Dr. E.E CASTON
100 Chief of Staff/VP Univ Relations ....Dr. Michelle A. ROBERTS
15 Assoc VP for Finance/Director HR ....Dr. Myrtis TABB
41 Director of Athletics ....Mr. Ronnie MAYERS
84 Dean Enrollment Mgt/Director Ad Mkt ....Dr. Debbie S. HESLEP
29 Exec Dir of Alumni/Foundation ....Mr. D. Keith FULCHER
49 Dean College of Arts & Sciences .... Dr. David BREAUX
50 Dean College of Business ....Dr. Billy MOORE
53 Dean College of Education ....Dr. Leslie GRIFFIN
66 Dean School of Nursing ....Dr. Libby L. CARLSON
08 Dean Library Services ....Mr. Jeff SLAGELL
58 Dean Grad/Cont Studies & Research .... Dr. Beverly MOON
06 Registrar .... Ms. Becky FINLEY
09 Dir of Inst Research & Planning ....Ms. Emily C. DABNEY
13 Chief Information Officer ....Mr. Edwin CRAFT
30 Chief Development Officer ....Mr. Gary BOUSE
21 Comptroller/Accounting ....Mr. James RUTLEDGE
88 Internal Auditor .... Ms. Vicki WILLIAMS
88 Executive Director BPAC ....Ms. Laura HOWELL
88 Executive Director Student Success .... Ms. Christy RIDDLE
88 Director Coahoma County Higher Educ .... Ms. Jennifer WALLER
20 Director Academic Support Services ....Vacant
37 Director Student Financial Assist ....Ms. Christie ROCCONI
38 Director Counsel/Stdnt Health Svcs .... Dr. Richard HOUSTON
36 Director Career Services/Placement ....Mr. Davlon MILLER
19 Director of Police Department ....Mr. N. Lynn BUFORD
39 Director of Housing .... Ms. Julie JACKSON
26 Coordinator of Communication & Mktg ..Ms. Caitlyn THOMPSON
29 Director of Alumni Affairs ....Mr. Jeffery FARRIS
25 Director Institutional Grants ....Ms. Robin BOYLES
88 Int Director Student Business Svcs .... Ms. Camesha BENSON
88 Director Field Experiences ....Dr. Cheryl CUMMINS
106 Director of E-Learning ....Dr. Angela BRIDGES
31 Director Delta Center Culture Learn .... Dr. Rolando HERTS
88 Director of Recruiting .... Mr. Christopher GAINES
88 Director of Administrative Systems ....Mr. Chris GIGER
88 Director of Donor Relations ....Ms. Ann GIGER
88 Director of H L Nowell Union ....Ms. Linda ROSS
88 Director of Facilities Operations ....Mr. Ted HOCHRADEL
88 Director of Post Office ....Mr. Michael MARTIN
88 Assoc Director Human Resources ....Ms. Lisa GIGER
18 Director of Facilities Management ....Mr. Greg KORB
96 Assistant Comptroller ....Ms. Beverly LINDSEY
35 Ast to VP Stdnt Affs/Dir Stdnt Life ....Vacant
40 Manager of Bookstore ....Ms. Tina GLADDEN
44 Director of Annual Giving .... Ms. Melissa PEARCE

East Central Community College (B)

PO Box 129, Decatur MS 39327-0129
County: Newton FICE Identification: 002404
Unit ID: 175643
Telephone: (601) 635-2111 Carnegie Class: Assoc/Pub-R-M
FAX Number: (601) 635-4011 Calendar System: Semester
URL: www.eccc.edu
Established: 1928 Annual Undergrad Tuition & Fees (In-District): $2,190
Enrollment: 2,544 Coed
Affiliation or Control: Local IRS Status: 501(c)3
Highest Offering: Associate Degree
Program: Occupational; 2-Year Principally Bachelor's Creditable
Accreditation: SC, ADNUR, EMT, SURGT

01 President ....Dr. Billy W. STEWART
05 Vice President for Instruction ....Dr. Teresa L. HOUSTON
10 Vice Pres for Business Operations .... Mr. Mickey VANCE
32 Vice President for Student Services .... Dr. Randall LEE
09 VP Institutional Research/Effective .... Mr. David CASE
26 Associate VP for Public Information ....Mr. Bill WAGNON
51 Director of ABE/GED ....Mr. Ryan CLARKE
103 Director of Workforce Education ....Mr. Wayne EASON
07 Director Admissions and Records ....Vacant
15 Dean of Personnel Svcs/Athletics ....Mr. Chris HARRIS
18 Superintendent of Physical Plant .... Mr. Artie FOREMAN
13 Dean of Information Technology .... Mr. Derek PACE
38 Academic Counselor ....Mr. Michael D. ALEXANDER
37 Director of Financial Aid ....Mrs. Brenda B. CARSON
08 Dean of Learning Resources .... Mr. Leslie HUGHES
14 Assoc Dir Information Technology .... Mrs. Regena BOYKIN
19 Chief of Police ....Mr. John HARRIS
39 Director of Hous/Student Activities ....Vacant
29 Exec Dir Foundation/Alumni Rels .. Dr. Stacey HOLLINGSWORTH
57 Chairperson Fine Arts Division ....Mrs. Vicki BLAYLOCK
83 Chairperson Social Sciences .... Mrs. Wanda HURLEY
81 Chrpn Mathematics/Computer Science ....Dr. Lisa MCMILLIN
66 Dean of Healthcare Education ....Mrs. Denita THOMAS
81 Chairperson Science ....Mr. Curt SKIPPER
60 Chairperson Communications/ Language ....Mrs. Carol SHACKELFORD

East Mississippi Community College (C)

PO Box 158, Scooba MS 39358-0158
County: Kemper FICE Identification: 002405
Unit ID: 175652
Telephone: (662) 476-8442 Carnegie Class: Assoc/Pub-R-M
FAX Number: (662) 476-5058 Calendar System: Semester
URL: www.eastms.edu
Established: 1927 Annual Undergrad Tuition & Fees (In-District): $2,710
Enrollment: 4,127 Coed
Affiliation or Control: State/Local IRS Status: 501(c)3
Highest Offering: Associate Degree
Program: Occupational; 2-Year Principally Bachelor's Creditable
Accreditation: SC, ADNUR, EMT, FUSER

01 President ....Dr. Thomas M. HUEBNER, JR.
05 Vice Pres for Instruction ....Dr. Thomas WARE
12 Vice President for GT Campus ....Dr. Paul MILLER
12 Vice President for Scooba Campus ....Mr. Mickey STOKES
10 Chief Financial Officer .... Ms. Melissa MOSLEY
32 VP for SC Student Affs & Athletics ....Mr. Mickey E. STOKES
30 VP Institutional Advanc/Alumni Affs .... Mr. Nick CLARK
103 VP of Workforce & Cmty Services .... Dr. Raj SHAUNAK
37 Vice Pres for Financial Aid .... Mr. James GIBSON
04 Administrative Asst to President ....Mrs. Lauren CLAY
09 Dist Dir Instl Research/Effective .... Mrs. Diana PRUETT
08 District Librarian ....Ms. Donna BALLARD
13 Dist Director of Info Technology .... Mr. Michael TVARKUNAS
18 Physical Plant Director-Scooba ....Vacant
37 Director of Financial Aid GT .... Mr. Garry JONES
06 Registrar-Scooba ....Mrs. Melinda SCIPLE
07 Director of Admissions-SC ....Mrs. Karen BRIGGS
56 Director of MNAS Extension ....Vacant
40 District Bookstore Manager ....Ms. Gennie CODY
26 Director of Public Information ....Ms. Suzanne MONK
35 Dean of Student Affairs .... Mr. Tony MONTGOMERY

Hinds Community College (D)

PO Box 1100, Raymond MS 39154-1100
County: Hinds FICE Identification: 002407
Unit ID: 175786
Telephone: (601) 857-5261 Carnegie Class: Assoc/Pub-R-L
FAX Number: (601) 857-3392 Calendar System: Semester
URL: www.hindscc.edu
Established: 1917 Annual Undergrad Tuition & Fees (In-District): $2,500
Enrollment: 11,839 Coed
Affiliation or Control: State/Local IRS Status: 501(c)3
Highest Offering: Associate Degree
Program: Occupational; 2-Year Principally Bachelor's Creditable
Accreditation: SC, ADNUR, CAHIIM, COARC, DA, DMS, EMT, MAC, MLTAD, PTAA, RAD, SURGT

01 President ....Dr. Clyde MUSE
11 VP Admin Svcs/VP Utica/Vicksburg .. Dr. Debra MAYS-JACKSON
10 Vice President Business Services ....Mr. Russell SHAW
12 VP Raymond/NSG/AH/Parallel Pgm .... Dr. Theresa HAMILTON
12 VP Rankin/Jackson/Dir Occup Pgm ....Dr. Norman SESSION
31 Vice Pres Community Relations ....Ms. Colleen C. HARTFIELD
88 VP for Economic Dev & Training ....Mr. John J. WOODS
18 VP Physical Plant & Aux Services ....Mr. Thomas WASSON
30 VP for Advancement & Stdnt Success .... Ms. Jacqueline M. GRANBERRY
103 Vice Pres Workforce Development .... Dr. Chad STOCKS
35 Assoc Vice President for Students .... Dr. Tyrone JACKSON
84 Director of Enrollment Services ....Ms. Kathryn B. COLE
32 District Dean of Student Affairs .... Dr. Tyrone JACKSON
08 Dean of Learning Resources .... Ms. Mary Beth APPLIN
05 Academic Dean .... Dr. Thomas KELLY
15 Director of Human Resources .... Ms. Gay Lynn CASTON
37 Dir of Financial Aid & VA Affairs ....Ms. Joy WILLIS
38 Director of Counseling Services ....Ms. Mary Lee MCDANIEL

41 Athletic Director .... Mr. Gene MURPHY
09 Director of Institutional Research ....Ms. Carley DEAR
26 Public Relations Director ....Ms. Cathy C. HAYDEN
96 Director of Purchasing ....Mr. Samuel LEMONIS
04 Executive Secretary to President ....Mrs. Alesia PORCH
06 Assistant Registrar ....Mrs. Norma Jean SCRIVENER
105 Director Web Services .... Ms. Jil WRIGHT
106 Dean Online Education/E-learning .... Mrs. Keri COLE
13 Chief Info Technology Officer (CIO) .... Mr. Hamp SHIVE
25 Chief Contracts/Grants Admin .... Mr. Donald SLABACH
29 Alumni Coordinator ....Ms. Libby POSEY
39 Director Student Housing ....Mr. DeAndre HOUSE

Holmes Community College (E)

Hill Street, PO Box 369, Goodman MS 39079-0369
County: Holmes FICE Identification: 002408
Unit ID: 175810
Telephone: (662) 472-2312 Carnegie Class: Assoc/Pub-R-L
FAX Number: (662) 472-9152 Calendar System: Semester
URL: www.holmescc.edu
Established: 1925 Annual Undergrad Tuition & Fees (In-District): $5,230
Enrollment: 6,186 Coed
Affiliation or Control: Local IRS Status: 501(c)3
Highest Offering: Associate Degree
Program: Occupational; 2-Year Principally Bachelor's Creditable
Accreditation: SC, ADNUR, EMT, FUSER, OTA, SURGT

01 President ....Dr. Jim HAFFEY
04 Asst to President/Dir Inst Rsch ....Dr. Lindy MCCAIN
05 Vice Pres for Academic Programs ....Dr. Fran COX
12 Vice President Ridgeland Campus ....Dr. Don BURNHAM
12 Vice President Grenada Center .... Mrs. Michelle BURNEY
72 Vice Pres Career/Technical Educ ....Mrs. Sherrie CHEEK
10 Vice Pres of Financial Services ....Mr. Sonny SPARKS
32 Dir Goodman Campus & Athletic Dir ....Mr. Andy WOOD
07 Director of Admissions & Records .... Mr. Joshua GUEST
08 Librarian ....Mrs. Joan TIERCE
26 District Director of Communications ....Mr. Steve DIFFEY
31 Director Community/Workforce Devel .....Mr. Mike BLANKENSHIP
37 Director Student Financial Aid ....Mrs. Gail MUSE
15 Director Personnel Services ....Ms. Julia BROWN
09 Director of Institutional Research ....Mrs. Stephanie DIFFEY
18 Chief Facilities/Physical Plant ....Vacant
96 Director of Purchasing .... Ms. Roxanne CHISOLM
06 Registrar .... Mr. Joshua GUEST
29 Director Alumni Relations ....Mrs. Hilliary O'BRIANT
21 Business Manager ....Mr. Matt SURRELL

Itawamba Community College (F)

602 W Hill Street, Fulton MS 38843-1022
County: Itawamba FICE Identification: 002409
Unit ID: 175829
Telephone: (662) 862-8000 Carnegie Class: Assoc/Pub-R-M
FAX Number: (662) 862-8036 Calendar System: Semester
URL: www.iccms.edu
Established: 1948 Annual Undergrad Tuition & Fees (In-District): $2,400
Enrollment: 5,654 Coed
Affiliation or Control: Local IRS Status: 501(c)3
Highest Offering: Associate Degree
Program: Occupational; 2-Year Principally Bachelor's Creditable
Accreditation: SC, ADNUR, CAHIIM, COARC, EMT, OTA, PTAA, RAD, SURGT

01 President .... Mr. Michael B. EATON
05 Vice President of Instruction .... Dr. Sara JOHNSON
10 Vice President of Business Services .... Mr. Jerry SENTER
32 Vice President of Student Services ....Mr. Buddy COLLINS
30 Vice Pres Dev/Plng/Telecom/Info Svc ....Mr. Wayne SULLIVAN
07 Dir Admission/Registration ....Ms. Cay LOLLAR
26 Dir Commnuicty Relations .... Dr. Jan REID-BUNCH
37 Director of Financial Aid .... Mr. Terry BLAND
24 Director of Learning Resources .... Dr. Glenda SEGARS
08 Librarian/Tupelo ....Ms. Janet Y. ARMOUR
51 Director of Adult & Continuing Educ ....Mr. Scott BLACKLEY
41 Athletic Director .... Ms. Carrie BALL-WILLIAMSON
102 Director of Foundation ....Mr. Jim INGRAM
44 Director of Development .... Mr. Tyler CAMP
18 Chief Facilities/Physical Plant .... Mr. Thomas BONDS
35 Director Student Affairs .... Mr. Brad BOGGS
09 Director of Institutional Research ....Mrs. Elizabeth EDWARDS
15 Director Personnel Services ....Mr. Timothy C. SENTER
106 Dir Online Education/E-learning ....Dr. Michelle SUMEREL
108 Director Strategic Assessment ....Mrs. Amy CAPPLEMAN
39 Director Student Housing ....Mr. Chad CASE

ITT Technical Institute (G)

382 Galleria Parkway, Suite 100, Madison MS 39110
Telephone: (601) 607-4500 Identification: 666701
Accreditation: ACICS

† Branch campus of ITT Technical Institute, Indianapolis, IN.

Jackson State University (H)

1400 J. R. Lynch Street, Jackson MS 39217
County: Hinds FICE Identification: 002410
Unit ID: 175856
Telephone: (601) 979-2121 Carnegie Class: RU/H
FAX Number: (601) 979-2358 Calendar System: Semester
URL: www.jsums.edu
Established: 1877 Annual Undergrad Tuition & Fees (In-State): $6,866
Enrollment: 9,508 Coed

Affiliation or Control: State IRS Status: 501(c)3
Highest Offering: Doctorate
Program: Liberal Arts And General; Teacher Preparatory; Professional
Accreditation: SC, ART, BUS, CACREP, CLPSY, CORE, CS, ENG, MUS, NAIT, PH, PLNG, SP, SPAA, SW, TED

01 President ... Dr. Carolyn MEYERS
05 Sr VP/Prov Acad & Student Affairs ... Dr. James RENICK
10 VP for Business & Finance ... Mr. Michael THOMAS
46 VP for Rsrch/Federal Relations ... Dr. Loretta A. MOORE
30 VP Institutional Advancement ... Mr. Anthony L. HOLLOMAN
13 VP for Information Management ... Dr. Deborah F. DENT
32 VP for Student Life ... Dr. Charles SMITH
84 VP Enroll Mgmt/Inst Research ... Dr. Nicole EDWARDS- EVANS
43 General Counsel ... Mr. Matthew A. TAYLOR
88 Internal Auditor ... Ms. Ella HOLMES
18 Assoc VP for Facil/Construct/Mgmt ... Mr. Wayne GOODWIN
21 Assoc VP for Business & Finance ... Ms. Dana BROWN
20 Assoc Provost for Academic Affairs ... Dr. Evelyn LEGGETTE
106 Executive Director JSU Online ... Mrs. Andrea DAVIS-JONES
35 Assoc VP for Student Life/Dean Std ... Dr. Phillip COCKRELL
46 Assoc VP for Research Development ... Dr. Safiya OMARI
88 Assoc VP for Research & Admin ... Mrs. Tracy STAPLETON
14 Assoc VP Information Mgmt ... Dr. Ivory GRISKELL
19 Assoc VP for Campus Safety ... Mr. Lindsey HORTON
53 Dean College Educ/Human Devel ... Dr. Daniel WATKINS
58 Dean Division of Graduate Studies ... Dr. Dorris R. ROBINSON-GARDNER
89 Dean Division Undergrad Studies ... Dr. Robert BLAINE
49 Dean College of Liberal Arts ... Dr. Mario AZEVEDO
85 Int Director JSU Global ... Ms. Shirley J. HARRISON
50 Dean College of Business ... Dr. Raymin MAYSAMI
80 Dean College of Public Service ... Dr. Ricardo BROWN
72 Dean College of Sci/Engr/Tech ... Dr. Richard ALO
51 Director of Lifelong Learning ... Dr. Millard BINGHAM
08 Dean Div of Library & Info Res ... Dr. Melissa DRUCKREY
20 Assoc Dean University College .. Dr. Marie O'BANNER-JACKSON
92 Assoc Dean Div of Honors College ... Dr. Loria BROWN GORDAN
88 Asst Director Testing & Assessment ... Dr. Arthur JEFFERSON
31 Assoc Dir Ctr Svc & Comm/Eng Lrng ... Dr. Gisele GENTRY
29 Dir Alumni/Constituency Rels ... Dr. Steven SMITH
15 Executive Director Human Resources ... Mrs. Robin SPANN-PACK
44 Asst VP of Development ... Mrs. Patricia MITCHELL
39 Int Director of Residence Life ... Dr. Erin VAUGHN
37 Director of Financial Aid ... Mrs. Betty MONCURE
21 Dir Budget & Financial Analysis ... Mrs. Tammiko HARRISON
06 Registrar ... Mr. Alfred B. JACKSON
23 University Physician ... Dr. Robert SMITH
23 University Physician ... Dr. Samuel JONES
89 Director of First Year Experience ... Mrs. Patricia SHERIFF-TAYLOR
07 Dir Undergraduate Admissions ... Mrs. Janieth ADAMS
07 Director Student Recruitment ... Dr. Juanita MORRIS
41 Int Director of Athletics ... Mr. Robert M. WALKER
88 Director of Title III ... Dr. Fredrick WHITE
88 Director MS Urban Research Ctr ... Dr. Melvin DAVIS
19 Director Public Safety ... Mr. Thomas ALBRIGHT
26 Int Director Communications ... Mr. Robert JEUITT
22 Asst Dir for ADA Services ... Ms. Monica WALL JONES
109 Exec Dir Auxiliary Enterprises ... Ms. Alicina PUGH
88 Director of Planning & Construction ... Mr. Robert WATTS
35 Assoc Director of Campus Life ... Vacant
40 Manager Bookstore ... Mr. Mark PERSON
88 Spec Asst to the Prov for Cmty Col ... Dr. Priscilla SLADE
108 Director Academic Assessment ... Dr. Shemeka MCCLUNG
04 Administrative Asst to President ... Mrs. Joyce JORDAN-GOODEN
36 Executive Director Career Services ... Ms. Lashanda JORDAN
38 Director Student Counseling ... Ms. Frances WHITE
21 Executive Director Business Office ... Ms. Jewell HARRIS
22 Chief Diversity Officer/EEO-AA Off ... Mr. Thomas HUDSON
105 Webmaster ... Mr. Gerard L. HOWARD
86 Exec Director Institutions of Govt ... Dr. Otha BURON
90 Director Academic IT ... Ms. Emily A. BISHOP

Jones County Junior College (A)

900 S Court Street, Ellisville MS 39437-3999
County: Jones FICE Identification: 002411
Unit ID: 175883
Telephone: (601) 477-4000 Carnegie Class: Assoc/Pub-R-M
FAX Number: (601) 477-4017 Calendar System: Semester
URL: www.jcjc.edu
Established: 1927 Annual Undergrad Tuition & Fees (In-District): $2,722
Enrollment: 4,507 Coed
Affiliation or Control: State/Local IRS Status: Exempt
Highest Offering: Associate Degree
Program: Occupational; 2-Year Principally Bachelor's Creditable
Accreditation: SC, ACBSP, ADNUR, EMT, RAD

01 President ... Dr. Jesse R. SMITH
05 VP Instructional Affrs/Assessment ... Ms. Candace WEAVER
10 Vice President of Business Affairs ... Mr. Rick YOUNGBLOOD
32 Vice President of Student Affairs ... Dr. Sam JONES
30 VP of Institutional Advancement ... Mr. Charlie GARRETSON
13 Director of Information Technology ... Mr. Paul SPELL
26 Director of Marketing ... Ms. Finee RUFFIN
04 Assistant to the President ... Ms. Gwen MAGEE
04 Director of Campus Operations ... Mr. Michael BRADSHAW
35 Dean of Student Affairs ... Mr. Mark EASLEY
75 Dean of Career & Technical Educ ... Mr. Jason DEDWYLDER
92 Dean of Arts and Honors ... Dr. Mark TAYLOR
103 Director of the Adv Tech Center ... Mr. Greg BUTLER
07 Director of Admissions & Records ... Mr. Rick HAMILTON
38 Dir of Student Success Center ... Mr. Andrew SHARP
37 Director of Student Financial Aid ... Ms. Jennifer SUBER
39 Director of Housing-Women ... Ms. Ashley HILL
39 Director of Housing-Men ... Mr. Joseph TUGGLE
40 Bookstore Manager ... Mr. Kevin KUHN
41 Athletic Director ... Ms. Katie HERRINGTON
15 Human Resources Manager ... Mr. Luke HAMMONDS
96 Director of Purchasing ... Ms. LeAnne NIXON
106 Dean of eLearning ... Ms. Jennifer POWELL
08 Head Librarian ... Ms. Julie ATWOOD
19 Chief Campus Police ... Mr. Stan LIVINGSTON

Meridian Community College (B)

910 Highway 19 N, Meridian MS 39307-5890
County: Lauderdale FICE Identification: 002413
Unit ID: 175935
Telephone: (601) 483-8241 Carnegie Class: Assoc/Pub-R-M
FAX Number: (601) 481-1305 Calendar System: Semester
URL: www.meridiancc.edu
Established: 1937 Annual Undergrad Tuition & Fees (In-District): $2,250
Enrollment: 3,366 Coed
Affiliation or Control: Local IRS Status: 501(c)3
Highest Offering: Associate Degree
Program: Occupational; 2-Year Principally Bachelor's Creditable
Accreditation: SC, ADNUR, CAHIIM, COARC, DA, DH, EMT, MLTAD, PNUR, PTAA, RAD, SURGT

01 President ... Dr. Scott D. ELLIOTT
10 Assoc Vice President for Finance ... Mrs. Amy BRAND
03 Vice President of Operations ... Mrs. Barbara JONES
07 Director of Admissions ... Dr. Angela PAYNE
09 Dir Institutional Effectiveness ... Mrs. Cathy PARKER
32 Dean of Students ... Mrs. Soraya WELDEN
05 Dean of Academic Affs/General Educ ... Mr. Michael THOMPSON
62 Assoc Vice Pres Learning Resources ... Mr. Billy BEAL
30 Assoc Vice Pres for Development ... Mrs. Kathy BROOKSHIRE
18 Director Physical Plant ... Mr. Terry WILLIAMS
37 Director Financial Aid ... Ms. Nedra BRADLEY
15 Director Human Resources ... Ms. Shellye ESPEY
41 Athletic Director ... Mr. Sander ATKINSON
19 Chief of Security ... Mr. Shane WILLIAMS
40 Bookstore Manager ... Mrs. Martha WILLIAMS
26 Dir Marketing/Public Relations ... Ms. Kay THOMAS
36 Career Center Development Director ... Ms. Darlene MAYATT
103 Assoc Vice Pres for Workforce Educ ... Dr. Richie MCALISTER
06 Registrar ... Ms. Deborah OLDHAM
105 Director Web Services ... Ms. Inga BASS
13 Chief Info Technology Officer (CIO) ... Mr. Chris EDWARDS
39 Director Student Housing ... Mr. Calvin BENNETT
106 Director of E-Learning ... Mrs. Haley DUCK

Miller-Motte Technical College (C)

12121 Highway 49, Gulfport MS 39503
Telephone: (228) 273-3400 Identification: 770845
Accreditation: ACICS

† Branch campus of McCann School of Business & Technology, Pottsville, PA.

Millsaps College (D)

1701 N State Street, Jackson MS 39210-0001
County: Hinds FICE Identification: 002414
Unit ID: 175980
Telephone: (601) 974-1000 Carnegie Class: Bac/A&S
FAX Number: (601) 974-1059 Calendar System: Semester
URL: www.millsaps.edu
Established: 1890 Annual Undergrad Tuition & Fees: $35,510
Enrollment: 771 Coed
Affiliation or Control: United Methodist IRS Status: 501(c)3
Highest Offering: Master's
Program: Liberal Arts And General; Teacher Preparatory; Professional
Accreditation: SC, BUS, TED

01 President ... Dr. Rob PEARIGEN
05 VP/Dean of the College ... Dr. Keith DUNN
10 Vice Pres for Planning & Assesment ... Ms. Terri HUDSON
30 VP for Institutional Advancement ... Mr. Michael HUTCHISON
32 VP Student Life/Dean Students ... Dr. Brit KATZ
50 Dean of the School of Management ... Dr. Kimberly G. BURKE
84 Vice Pres Enrollment/Communications ... Dr. Robert ALEXANDER
79 Assoc Dean Arts & Letters ... Dr. David DAVIS
81 Associate Dean Sciences Division ... Dr. Timothy J. WARD
82 Assoc Dean International Education ... Dr. George J. BEY
37 Director of Financial Aid ... Mrs. Isabelle HIGBEE
20 Director Academic Support Services ... Dr. Melissa LEA
51 Director of Continuing Education ... Dr. Nola R. GIBSON
08 College Librarian ... Mr. Thomas W. HENDERSON
36 Director of Career Center ... Ms. Tonya CRAFT
41 Director of Athletics ... Mr. Josh BROOKS
15 Dir of Human Resource Services ... Ms. Julie DANIELS
42 Chaplain ... Rev. Christopher DONALD
28 International Student Advisor ... Ms. Christina PHILLIPS
21 Controller ... Vacant
06 Registrar ... Ms. Elizabeth GIDDENS
09 Director of Institutional Reseraach ... Dr. Ken THOMPSON
18 Director of Physical Plant ... Mr. W. David WILKINSON
29 Director Alumni Relations ... Ms. Maribeth KITCHINGS
19 Director Security/Safety ... Mr. John CONWAY
26 Director of Communications & Market ... Mr. John SEWELL
07 Director of Admission ... Mr. Jonathan FERRELL

Mississippi College (E)

200 W College Street, Clinton MS 39058-0001
County: Hinds FICE Identification: 002415
Unit ID: 176053
Telephone: (601) 925-3000 Carnegie Class: Master's L
FAX Number: (601) 925-3276 Calendar System: Semester
URL: www.mc.edu
Established: 1826 Annual Undergrad Tuition & Fees: $16,114
Enrollment: 4,984 Coed
Affiliation or Control: Southern Baptist IRS Status: 501(c)3
Highest Offering: Doctorate
Program: Liberal Arts And General; Teacher Preparatory; Professional
Accreditation: SC, ACBSP, ARCPA, CACREP, CIDA, LAW, MUS, NURSE, SW, TED

01 President ... Dr. Lee G. ROYCE
04 Sr Exec Assistant to President ... Ms. Shelia CARPENTER
10 Chief Financial Officer ... Ms. Donna LEWIS
05 Vice President Academic Affairs ... Dr. Ronald HOWARD
32 VP Enrollment Svcs/Dean of Students ... Dr. Jim TURCOTTE
45 Vice President Planning/Assessment ... Dr. Debbie NORRIS
42 Vice Pres Christian Development ... Dr. Eric PRATT
30 VP Inst Advan/Alum/Leg Coun to Pres ... Dr. Bill TOWNSEND
11 Vice Pres Admin/Government Rels ... Dr. Steve STANFORD
84 Director Enrollment Services ... Mr. Mark HUGHES
06 Registrar ... Ms. Ginger ROBBINS
09 Director of Institutional Research ... Ms. Cassandra SESSUMS
08 Librarian ... Ms. Kathleen HUTCHISON
21 Comptroller ... Vacant
13 Chief Information Officer ... Mr. Bill CRANFORD
38 Director Counseling/Testing Center ... Dr. Morgan BRYANT
15 Director Human Resources ... Ms. Donna SMITH
29 Interim Director Alumni Affairs ... Ms. Lori BOBO
26 Director Public Relations ... Ms. Tracey HARRISON
18 Director of Physical Plant ... Mr. Billy THORNTON
39 Coordinator of Residence Life ... Ms. Sharia BROCK
37 Director Student Financial Aid ... Ms. Karon MCMILLAN
07 Director of Admissions ... Mr. Kyle BRANTLEY
35 Assistant Director Student Life ... Ms. Dannie WOODS
19 Director of Public Safety ... Mr. Steven MCCRANEY
41 Director of Athletics ... Mr. Mike JONES
96 Director of Purchasing ... Ms. Dana ELMORE
40 Manager Bookstore ... Ms. Karen BARNES
36 Director of Career Services ... Ms. Jennifer MCGILL
81 Dean School of Science/Mathematics ... Dr. Stan BALDWIN
50 Dean School of Business Admin ... Dr. Marcelo EDUARDO
79 Dean School of Humanities ... Dr. Jonathan RANDLE
53 Dean School of Education ... Dr. Don LOCKE
73 Dean Sch Christian Studies/Fine Art ... Dr. Wayne VAN HORN
61 Dean School of Law ... Prof. Wendy SCOTT
58 Dean Grad School/Special Programs ... Dr. Debbie NORRIS
66 Dean School of Nursing ... Dr. Mary Jean PADGETT
86 Director Government Relations ... Dr. Steve STANFORD

Mississippi Delta Community College (F)

PO Box 668, Moorhead MS 38761-0668
County: Sunflower FICE Identification: 002416
Unit ID: 176008
Telephone: (662) 246-6322 Carnegie Class: Assoc/Pub-R-M
FAX Number: (662) 246-6321 Calendar System: Semester
URL: www.msdelta.edu
Established: 1926 Annual Undergrad Tuition & Fees (In-District): $2,490
Enrollment: 2,783 Coed
Affiliation or Control: Local IRS Status: 501(c)3
Highest Offering: Associate Degree
Program: Occupational; 2-Year Principally Bachelor's Creditable
Accreditation: SC, ADNUR, DH, MLTAD, PNUR, RAD

01 President ... Dr. Larry NABORS
03 Executive Vice President ... Dr. Charles BARNETT
05 Vice President of Instruction ... Mrs. Carol WALDEN
10 Vice President of Business Services ... Mrs. Marsha LEE
32 Vice President of Student Services ... Dr. Edward RICE
88 Assoc VP GHEC Operations ... Dr. MaryAnne BROCATO
84 Associate Vice Pres of Enrollment ... Dr. Brent GREGORY
30 Assoc VP College Advancement ... Mr. Reed ABRAHAM
15 Director of Human Resources ... Ms. Brenda VANLANDINGHAM
37 Director of Financial Aid ... Mrs. Mary P. RODGERS
07 Director of Admissions ... Dr. Brent GREGORY
13 Director Computer & Info Tech Svcs ... Mr. Jim H. AYCOCK
08 Director of Library Services ... Mrs. Kristi BARIOLA
07 Director Counseling/Recruiting ... Mrs. Kate FAILING
18 Director of Maintenance ... Mr. Rick DAVIS
88 Director of Special Events ... Mrs. Corey SMITH
09 Director of Institutional Research ... Mrs. Rosemary LAMB
04 Admin Asst to the President ... Mrs. Debra BAKER
41 Athletic Director ... Mr. Domino BELLIPANNI
19 Director Security/Safety ... Mr. Henry MANUEL

Mississippi Gulf Coast Community College (G)

PO Box 609, Perkinston MS 39573-0012
County: Stone FICE Identification: 002417
Unit ID: 176071
Telephone: (601) 928-5211 Carnegie Class: Assoc/Pub-R-L
FAX Number: (601) 928-6386 Calendar System: Semester
URL: www.mgccc.edu
Established: 1911 Annual Undergrad Tuition & Fees (In-District): $3,292
Enrollment: 9,799 Coed

Affiliation or Control: Local IRS Status: 501(c)3
Highest Offering: Associate Degree
Program: Occupational; 2-Year Principally Bachelor's Creditable
Accreditation: SC, ADNUR, EMT, FUSER, MLTAD, PNUR, RAD

01 President ... Dr. Mary S. GRAHAM
05 VP Teaching & Lrng/Stdnt Svcs/CC ... Dr. Jason PUGH
10 VP Administration/Finance ... Dr. Michael J. HEINDL
12 VP Perkinston Campus (PC) ... Dr. Ladd TAYLOR
12 VP Jefferson Davis Campus (JDC) ... Dr. Jonathan WOODWARD
12 VP Jackson County Campus (JCC) ... Dr. Carmen WALTERS
30 VP Institutional Advancement ... Ms. Caroline RAMAGOS
75 AVP Cmty Campus/CareerTech Ed ... Mr. John SHOWS
09 Director Inst Research & Planning ... Mr. Adam SWANSON
41 College Dean for Athletics ... Mr. Bert PICKARD
106 Director of Distance Learning ... Ms. Jennifer LEIMER
50 Director of Business Services ... Mr. Wayne KUNTZ
21 Comptroller ... Ms. Shelly FORD
06 Records Clerk - PC ... Ms. Latrice MCDONALD
06 Records Clerk - JCC ... Ms. Linda OTIS
06 Records Clerk - JDC ... Ms. Mary JOYCE
20 Dean of Instruction - JCC ... Dr. Cedric BRADLEY
20 Dean of Instruction - JDC ... Mr. Larry MILLER
20 Dean of Instruction - PC ... Dr. Jan MOODY
50 Dean of Business Services - PC ... Dr. Vanessa DEDEAUX
50 Dean of Business Services - JCC ... Ms. Tammy FRANKS
50 Dean of Busines Services - JDC ... Ms. Stacy CARMICHAEL
66 Dean of Nursing/Allied Health ... Dr. Joan HENDRIX
75 Dn Career Tech/Wrkfc/Cmty Ed - PC ... Mr. Bobby GHOSAL
75 Dn Career/Tech/Wrkf/Cmty Ed - JDC ... Dr. Beverly CLARK
75 Dn Career/Tech/Wrkf/Cmty Ed - JCC ... Mr. Brock CLARK
08 Asst Dean LRC - PC ... Dr. Brenda RIVERO
08 Asst Dean LRC - JCC ... Dr. Pam LADNER
08 Asst Dean LRC - JDC ... Ms. Nancy WILCOX
32 Dn Stdnt Svcs/Enroll Mgmt - PC ... Dr. Jason BEVERLY
32 Dn Stdnt Svcs/Enroll Mgmt - JCC ... Ms. Michelle SEKUL
32 Dn Stdnt Svcs/Enroll Mgmt - JDC ... Dr. Phil BONFANTI
88 Dean George County Center ... Ms. Cheryl BALIUS
07 Director of Admissions/Rec - PC ... Mr. Trey ROBERTSON
07 Director of Admissions/Rec - JCC ... Mr. William EVERITT
07 Director of Admissions/Rec - JDC ... Mr. Christopher BAGWELL
29 Coord College Events/Special Proj ... Ms. Jenifer FRERIDGE
37 Financial Aid Director - JDC ... Ms. Angela BRADLEY
37 Financial Aid Director - PC ... Ms. LeighAnn HUSSEY
37 Financial Aid Director - JCC ... Ms. LaShanda CHAMBERLAIN
15 District Director Human Resources ... Ms. Tenesha BATISTE
96 Dir Purchasing/Property Control ... Ms. Lynn DEEGEN
18 Construction Manager ... Mr. Jason BRELAND
44 Director Institutional Development ... Ms. Brenda DAVIS
04 Exec Assistant to the President ... Ms. Tracey WALTERS

Mississippi State University (A)

Lee Boulevard, Mississippi State MS 39762-5708
County: Oktibbeha FICE Identification: 002423
Unit ID: 176080
Telephone: (662) 325-2323 Carnegie Class: RU/VH
FAX Number: (662) 325-7455 Calendar System: Semester
URL: www.msstate.edu
Established: 1878 Annual Undergrad Tuition & Fees (In-State): $7,142
Enrollment: 20,138 Coed
Affiliation or Control: State IRS Status: 501(c)3
Highest Offering: Doctorate
Program: Liberal Arts And General; Teacher Preparatory; Professional
Accreditation: SC, AAFCS, ART, BUS, BUSA, CACREP, CIDA, CORE, CS, DIETD, DIETI, ENG, LSAR, MUS, SCPSY, SPAA, SW, TED, VET

01 President ... Dr. Mark E. KEENUM
05 Provost/Executive Vice President ... Dr. Jerome A. GILBERT
46 Vice Pres Research & Economic Devel ... Dr. David SHAW
88 Vice Pres Agricult/Forestry/Vet Med ... Dr. Gregory BOHACH
10 VP for Budget and Planning ... Mr. Don ZANT
32 VP for Student Affairs ... Dr. Regina HYATT
30 VP for Development and Alumni ... Mr. John P. RUSH
18 VP for Campus Services ... Ms. Amy TUCK
41 Athletic Director ... Mr. Scott STRICKLIN
43 General Counsel ... Ms. Joan LUCAS
28 Chief Diversity Officer ... Dr. Tommy STEVENSON, JR.
04 Assistant to the President ... Mr. Joe R. FARRIS
15 Director Human Resources Mgmt ... Ms. Judith SPENCER
26 Exec Dir External Affairs ... Mr. Kyle STEWARD
84 Interim Exec Director Enrollment ... Dr. John DICKERSON
27 Director Public Affairs ... Mr. Sid SALTER
86 Director Government Relations ... Mr. John A. TOMLINSON
20 Assoc Provost Academic Affairs ... Dr. Peter RYAN
13 Chief Information Officer ... Mr. J. Mike RACKLEY
88 Exec Dir International Institute ... Dr. Jon REZEK
48 Dean of Architecture/Art/Design ... Mr. James L. WEST
49 Dean College Arts & Sciences ... Dr. Greg DUNAWAY
50 Dean College Business ... Dr. Sharon OSWALD
53 Dean of Education ... Dr. Richard L. BLACKBOURN
58 Dean of Graduate Studies ... Dr. Lori BRUCE
54 Dean College of Engineering ... Dr. Jason KEITH
65 Dean of Forest Resources ... Dr. George M. HOPPER
47 Dean College Agriculture & Life Sci ... Dr. George M. HOPPER
74 Dean of Veterinary Medicine ... Dr. Kent H. HOBLET
12 Interim Dean Meridian Campus ... Dr. Meghan MILLEA
08 Dean of Libraries ... Ms. Frances N. COLEMAN
92 Dean Honors College ... Dr. Christopher SNYDER
56 Dir University Extension Service ... Dr. Gary JACKSON
88 Dir Agricultural Experiment Station ... Dr. George M. HOPPER
06 Registrar ... Dr. John R. DICKERSON
106 Dir Center for Distance Learning ... Dr. Steve TAYLOR
36 Director Career Services/Coop Educ ... Mr. Scott MAYNARD
35 Asst Vice Pres of Student Affairs ... Mr. Bill BROYLES
35 Dean of Students ... Dr. Thomas BOURGEOIS
38 Director of Counseling Center ... Dr. Leigh JENSEN
37 Director Student Financial Aid ... Mr. Paul MCKINNEY
39 Director Housing/Residence Life ... Dr. Ann BAILEY
09 Director Institutional Research ... Dr. Tim CHAMBLEE
23 Director Student Health Center ... Dr. Robert K. CADENHEAD
29 Director of Alumni Association ... Mr. Jeffrey DAVIS
44 Director of Planned Giving ... Mr. Vance BRISTOW
25 Director Sponsored Programs ... Mrs. Jennifer EASLEY
88 Director Internal Audit ... Ms. Leisa ERVIN
96 Director Procurement/Contracts ... Mr. Don BUFFUM
19 Police Chief ... Mr. Vance RICE
07 Interim Exec Dir Enrollment Service ... Dr. John DICKERSON

Mississippi University for Women (B)

1100 College Street, Columbus MS 39701-5800
County: Lowndes FICE Identification: 002422
Unit ID: 176035
Telephone: (877) 462-8439 Carnegie Class: Master's S
FAX Number: (662) 329-7297 Calendar System: Semester
URL: www.muw.edu
Established: 1884 Annual Undergrad Tuition & Fees (In-State): $5,781
Enrollment: 2,696 Coed
Affiliation or Control: State IRS Status: 501(c)3
Highest Offering: Doctorate
Program: Liberal Arts And General; Teacher Preparatory; Professional
Accreditation: SC, ACBSP, ADNUR, ART, MUS, NURSE, SP, TED

01 President ... Dr. Jim BORSIG
05 Interim Provost/VP Academic Affairs ... Dr. Thomas RICHARDSON
10 Sr Vice Pres Administration & CFO ... Ms. Nora R. MILLER
30 Exec Dir of University Relations ... Ms. Maridith GEUDER
32 Vice Pres for Student Affairs ... Dr. Jennifer MILES
20 Assoc Vice Pres Academic Affairs ... Dr. Martin HATTON
43 University Counsel ... Ms. Karen CLAY
49 Dean College Arts/Sciences ... Dr. Brian ANDERSON
50 Dean Business/Professional Studies ... Dr. Scott TOLLISON
53 Int Dean College Educ/Human Sci ... Dr. Martin HATTON
66 Dean College Nursing/SLP ... Dr. Sheila V. ADAMS
08 Dean of Library Services ... Ms. Gail P. GUNTER
58 Director Graduate Studies ... Dr. Martin HATTON
88 Int Director Outreach & Innovation ... Ms. Melinda LOWE
06 Interim Registrar ... Dr. Martin HATTON
09 Director Inst Research & Assessment ... Ms. Jennifer MOORE
92 Interim Director Honors College ... Dr. Kim WHITEHEAD
25 Director Sponsored Programs ... Mr. James DENNEY
29 Director Alumni Relations ... Ms. Lyndsay CUMBERLAND
30 Exec Dir Development/Alumni Rels ... Ms. Andrea N. STEVENS
44 Director Annual Giving ... Ms. Brandy WILLIAMS
26 Director Public Affairs ... Ms. Anika M. PERKINS
105 Dir Web Development/Univ Webmaster ... Mr. Rich SOBOLEWSKI
21 Director University Accounting ... Ms. Susan SOBLEY
88 Internal Auditor ... Mr. Kenneth WIDNER
13 Director of Information Systems ... Ms. Lisa MCDANIEL
07 Director Admissions ... Ms. Shelley MCNEES MOSS
37 Director Financial Aid ... Ms. Nicole PATRICK
15 Director Human Resources ... Ms. Melanie H. FREEMAN
27 Chief Information Officer ... Ms. Carla LOWERY
19 Chief of Police ... Mr. Danny PATTON
18 Director of Facilities Management ... Mr. Dewey BLANSETT
96 Director Resources Management ... Ms. Angie S. ATKINS
35 Director Student Life ... Ms. Jessica HARPOLE
35 Dean of Students ... Ms. Sirena CANTRELL
41 Director Campus Recreation ... Ms. LeAnn ALEXANDER
40 Director Bookstore ... Ms. Helana ROBINSON
88 Director Student Success Center ... Dr. David BROOKING
88 General Manager of MUW Dining Svcs ... Mr. Alan JOHNSON
84 Enrollment Certification Officer ... Ms. Laura L. BLACK
14 Director of Systems & Networks ... Mr. Rodney GODFREY
104 Director Study Abroad ... Dr. Kim WHITEHEAD
39 Director Housing & Residence Life ... Mr. Andrew MONEYMAKER

Mississippi Valley State University (C)

14000 Highway 82 W, Itta Bena MS 38941-1400
County: Leflore FICE Identification: 002424
Unit ID: 176044
Telephone: (662) 254-9041 Carnegie Class: Master's M
FAX Number: (662) 254-6709 Calendar System: Semester
URL: www.mvsu.edu
Established: 1950 Annual Undergrad Tuition & Fees (In-State): $5,936
Enrollment: 2,222 Coed
Affiliation or Control: State IRS Status: 501(c)3
Highest Offering: Master's
Program: Liberal Arts And General; Teacher Preparatory; Professional
Accreditation: SC, ACBSP, ART, CS, MUS, SW, TED

01 President ... Dr. William BYNUM, JR.
05 VP Academic Affairs ... Dr. Constance BLAND
11 Exec Vice Pres/COO ... Dr. Jerryl BRIGGS, SR.
32 Vice Pres for Student Affairs ... Dr. Jacqueline GIBSON
35 Assoc VP for Student Affairs ... Mr. Renardo HALL
20 Assoc VP Academic Affairs ... Dr. Kathie STROMILE-GOLDEN
20 Asst VP for IRE/Strat Planning ... Dr. Sharon FREEMAN
10 VP Business & Finance/CFO ... Ms. Joyce A. DIXON
100 Chief of Staff/Legislative Liaison ... Mrs. LaShon F. BROOKS
30 Vice President for Univ Advancement ... Ms. Veronica COHEN
106 Asst VP for Distance & Online ... Dr. Kenneth DONE
58 Dean of Graduate College ... Vacant
41 Director of Athletics ... Mrs. Dianthia FORD-KEE
06 Director of Student Records ... Mr. Jeff LOGGINS
07 Director Admission/Recruitment ... Ms. Jacqueline A. WILLIAMS
08 Head Librarian ... Ms. Mantra HENDERSON
15 Director of Human Resources ... Mrs. Elizabeth HURSSEY
13 Director of Computer Center ... Mr. Steven L. PITCHFORD
37 Director of Financial Aid ... Mr. Lloyd E. DIXON
29 Manager of Alumni Relations ... Ms. Latacha DAVIS-JACKSON
26 Director of Comm/Mktg ... Mrs. Maxine GREENLEAF
19 Director University Police ... Mr. Leron WEEKS
18 Director Facilities/Physical Plant ... Mr. Tommy VERDELL
39 Asst Director Residential Life ... Ms. Glenda RANSOM
36 Director Career Development ... Ms. Tiffany WALLACE
38 Director Student Counseling ... Dr. Yolanda JONES
50 Acting Chair of Business Department ... Dr. Curressia BROWN
53 Chair of Education Dept ... Dr. Lula COLLIER
65 Chair Nat Sci/Env Health Dept ... Dr. Louis J. HALL
49 Dean College of Arts & Sciences ... Vacant
88 Chair English/Foreign Language ... Dr. John ZHENG
57 Chair Fine Arts Department ... Dr. Alphonso SANDERS
68 Chair Health/Phys Ed/Rec Dept ... Dr. Gloria ROSS
81 Chair of Math/Computer Science Dept ... Dr. Latonya GARNER
54 Acting Chair of EngineeringTech ... Mr. Antonio BROWNLOW
60 Chair Mass Communication Dept ... Dr. Samuel OSUNDE
88 Chair Criminal Justice ... Dr. Emmanual AMADI
70 Chair Social Work Department ... Dr. Catherine SINGLETON-WALKER
96 Director of Purchasing ... Mr. Billy SCOTT
04 Executive Asst to President ... Mrs. Augustер WALLACE
25 Director Sponsored Pgm/Title III ... Mr. Samuel MELTON, JR.
44 Executive Director of Development ... Mr. Dameon SHAW

Northeast Mississippi Community College (D)

101 Cunningham Boulevard, Booneville MS 38829-1731
County: Prentiss FICE Identification: 002426
Unit ID: 176169
Telephone: (662) 728-7751 Carnegie Class: Assoc/Pub-R-M
FAX Number: (662) 728-1165 Calendar System: Semester
URL: www.nemcc.edu
Established: 1948 Annual Undergrad Tuition & Fees (In-District): $2,484
Enrollment: 3,459 Coed
Affiliation or Control: State/Local IRS Status: 501(c)3
Highest Offering: Associate Degree
Program: Occupational; 2-Year Principally Bachelor's Creditable
Accreditation: SC, ADNUR, COARC, DH, MAC, MLTAD, RAD

01 President ... Ricky G. FORD
03 Executive Vice President ... Craig-Ellis SASSER
103 Vice Pres Wrkfrce Training/Econ Dev ... Nadara L. COLE
26 Assoc Vice Pres of Public Info ... Tony FINCH
05 Dean of Instruction ... Rilla c. JONES
35 Assoc Dean of Student Activities ... Angie LANGLEY
08 Director Learning Resources ... Glenice STONE
96 Director of Purchasing ... Sheila OWENS
37 Director of Financial Aid ... Greg WINDHAM
38 Director Student Counseling ... Joey WILLIFORD
13 Director Computer Center ... Gregory SMITH
18 Director Facilities/Maintenance ... Mark HATFIELD
39 Director Residential Housing ... Rod COGGIN
32 Dean of Students ... David ROBBINS
75 Director of Vocational Tech Educ ... Jody PRESLEY
84 Dir of Enrollment Svcs/Registrar ... Chassie KELLY
15 Human Resources Officer ... Tammie HARDIN
04 Administrative Asst to President ... Mary A. COATS
102 Dir Foundation/Corporate Relations ... Patrick D. EATON
106 Dir Online Education/E-learning ... Kim HARRIS
19 Director Security/Safety ... Randy A. BAXTER
10 Director of Finance ... Chris MURPHY

Northwest Mississippi Community College (E)

4975 Highway 51 N, Senatobia MS 38668-1703
County: Tate FICE Identification: 002427
Unit ID: 176178
Telephone: (662) 562-3200 Carnegie Class: Assoc/Pub-R-L
FAX Number: (662) 562-3911 Calendar System: Semester
URL: www.northwestms.edu
Established: 1927 Annual Undergrad Tuition & Fees (In-State): $1,275
Enrollment: 8,000 Coed
Affiliation or Control: State IRS Status: 501(c)3
Highest Offering: Associate Degree
Program: Occupational; 2-Year Principally Bachelor's Creditable
Accreditation: SC, ADNUR, COARC, EMT, FUSER

01 President ... Dr. Gary Lee SPEARS
10 Vice President for Fiscal Affairs ... Mr. Gary MOSLEY
32 VP Student Affairs/Chief of Staff ... Mr. Dan SMITH
05 Vice Pres for Educational Affairs ... Mr. Richie LAWSON
20 Academic Dean ... Dr. Matthew S. DOMAS
103 Dean Career Tech Ed/Wrkfce Dev Trng ... Mr. David CAMPBELL
51 Dir Division of Continuing Educ ... Ms. Pam WOOTEN
84 Dean Enrollment Mgmt & Registrar ... Mr. Larry SIMPSON
35 Director of Student Personnel ... Mr. Mike DOTTOREY
26 Director of Communications ... Mrs. Sarah SAPP
37 Director of Financial Aid ... Mr. Reginald SMITH
36 Dir Student Development Center ... Ms. Meg ROSS
08 Director of Learning Resources ... Mrs. Maggie MORAN
13 Director Management Information Sys ... Mrs. Amy LATHAM

07 Director of Recruiting ....Mrs. Jere HERRINGTON
09 Director Planning/Inst Research ....Dr. Carolyn WARREN
18 Director of Physical Plant Building ....Mr. Mike ROBISON
19 Chief of Campus Security ....Mr. Zabe DAVIS
30 Director of Development/Alumni Rels ....Mrs. Sybil CANON
39 Director of Campus Life and Housing ....Mrs. Aime ANDERSON
40 Director Bookstore ....Mr. Joel BOYLES
41 Director of Athletics/Intramurals ....Mr. Don SKELTON
96 Director of Purchasing ....Mrs. Barbara YOUNG
15 Personnel Officer ....Mrs. Erica STANFORD
29 Director Alumni Relations ....Mrs. Dolores WOOTEN
21 Business Manager ....Ms. Ruthie CASTLE

Pearl River Community College (A)

101 Highway 11 N, Poplarville MS 39470-2298
County: Pearl River FICE Identification: 002430
Unit ID: 176239
Telephone: (601) 403-1000 Carnegie Class: Assoc/Pub-R-M
FAX Number: (601) 403-1339 Calendar System: Semester
URL: www.prcc.edu
Established: 1909 Annual Undergrad Tuition & Fees (In-District): $2,650
Enrollment: 4,798 Coed
Affiliation or Control: State/Local IRS Status: 501(c)3
Highest Offering: Associate Degree
Program: 2-Year Principally Bachelor's Creditable
Accreditation: SC, ADNUR, COARC, DA, DH, MLTAD, OTA, PTAA, RAD, SURGT

01 President ....Dr. William A. LEWIS
05 VP for General Educ & Technology ....Dr. Martha L. SMITH
32 VP Poplarville Campus/Hancock Ctr ....Dr. Adam BREERWOOD
10 VP for Business/Admn Services ....Mr. Roger A. KNIGHT
08 Director of College Libraries ....Ms. Tracy SMITH
26 Director of Public Relations ....Mr. Chuck ABADIE
84 Director of Admissions and Records ....Ms. Tonia MOODY
12 VP for Forrest County Operations ....Dr. Jana CAUSEY
18 Director of Physical Plant ....Mr. Craig TYNES
30 Director Development/Alumni Rels ....Mr. Ernest L. LOVELL, JR.
37 Director Student Financial Aid ....Ms. Valerie HORNE
41 Interim Director of Athletics ....Mr. Jason FRANCIS
07 Director of Recruitment/Marketing ....Ms. Delana HARRIS
09 VP for Planning & Inst Research ....Dr. Jennifer SEAL
36 Dir Student Placement/Counselor ....Dr. Ann MOORE
31 VP Econ/Comm Development ....Dr. David S. ALSOBROOKS
04 Administrative Asst to President ....Ms. Marilyn DILLARD
105 Webmaster ....Mr. Eric REID

Reformed Theological Seminary (B)

5422 Clinton Boulevard, Jackson MS 39209-3099
County: Hinds FICE Identification: 009193
Unit ID: 176284
Telephone: (601) 923-1600 Carnegie Class: Not Classified
FAX Number: (601) 923-1654 Calendar System: 4/1/4
URL: www.rts.edu
Established: 1965 Annual Graduate Tuition & Fees: $14,150
Enrollment: 329 Coed
Affiliation or Control: Independent Non-Profit IRS Status: 501(c)3
Highest Offering: Doctorate; No Undergraduates
Program: Professional; Religious Emphasis
Accreditation: SC, MFCD, THEOL

00 Chancellor Emeritus ....Dr. Robert C. CANNADA, JR.
01 Chancellor/CEO ....Dr. J. Ligon DUNCAN
10 Chief Opertations Financial Officer ....Mr. Bradley TISDALE
05 Provost and Chief Academic Officer ....Dr. Robert CARA
30 Chief Advancement Officer ....Rev. Lynwood C. PEREZ
12 President Charlotte Campus ....Dr. Michael J. KRUGER
12 President Orlando Campus ....Dr. Don W. SWEETING
12 President Jackson Campus ....Dr. Guy L. RICHARDSON
12 President RTS Global Campus ....Dr. Andrew J. PETERSON
12 President Atlanta Campus ....Mr. John T. SOWELL
12 President Washington DC ....Dr. Scott REDD
06 Registrar Jackson Campus ....Ms. Kim LEE
08 Library Director ....Mr. John MUETHER
32 Dean of Student Affairs/Admissions ....Mr. Brian C. GAULT
29 Dir Alum Rels/Dev/Supt Svcs Jackson ....Mrs. Stephanie J. HARTLEY
04 Assistant to Pres Jackson Campus ....Mrs. Wanda RUSHING
88 Dir Marriage & Fam Ther Jackson ....Dr. James B. HURLEY
18 Maintenance Director Jackson Campus ....Mr. Kyle SANDIDGE
108 Chief Institutional Assessment Ofcr ....Ms. Polly STONE
15 Director Personnel Svcs Jackson ....Ms. Linda COCHRAN
07 Institutional Dir of Enrollment ....Rev. Kevin COLLINS

Rust College (C)

150 Rust Avenue, Holly Springs MS 38635-2328
County: Marshall FICE Identification: 002433
Unit ID: 176318
Telephone: (662) 252-8000 Carnegie Class: Bac/A&S
FAX Number: (662) 252-6107 Calendar System: Semester
URL: www.rustcollege.edu
Established: 1866 Annual Undergrad Tuition & Fees: $9,500
Enrollment: 1,028 Coed
Affiliation or Control: United Methodist IRS Status: 501(c)3
Highest Offering: Baccalaureate
Program: Liberal Arts And General
Accreditation: SC, SW, @TEAC

01 President ....Dr. David L. BECKLEY
30 Vice President for College Relation ....Dr. Ishmell H. EDWARDS
10 Vice President for Finance ....Mr. Donald MANNING-MILLER
108 Asst to Vice Pres Assessment/Plng ....Dr. Vida MAYS
05 VP for Academic Affairs ....Dr. Sandra C. VAUGHN
06 Registrar ....Mr. Clarence E. SMITH
08 Library Director ....Mrs. Anita W. MOORE
13 Director Computer Center ....Ms. Barbara NAYLOR MOORE
32 Vice Pres for Student Affairs ....Mr. Carllos LASSITER
35 Director Student Activities ....Mr. Frederick TAYLOR
37 Director of Financial Aid ....Mrs. Helen STREET
25 Director Contracts & Grants ....Mrs. Christine L. RATCLIFF
29 Director Alumni Development ....Ms. Jo Ann SCOTT
89 Chair First Year Experience ....Dr. Kenneth E. JONES
26 Director of Public Relations ....Vacant
21 Comptroller ....Ms. Glenda KING
84 Dean of Enrollment Services ....Mr. Braque TALLEY
23 Director Student Health Services ....Dr. Dianna HUGHES-MARION
39 Director Student Housing ....Ms. Tanya K. KIRK
36 Director of Career Development ....Mr. Robert WILLIAMS
18 Director Physical Plant ....Mr. Robert CURRY
83 Division Chair Social Science ....Dr. Alfred J. STOVALL
15 Director Personnel Services ....Ms. Patricia PEGUES
19 Chief of Security ....Mr. Claude GLEETON
30 Director of Development ....Ms. Jo Ann SCOTT
40 Bookstore Manager ....Mrs. Patricia HARRIS
42 College Chaplain ....Rev. Annie TRAVIS
96 Director of Purchasing ....Ms. Ollie BOWENS
28 Director of Diversity ....Miss Patricia PEGUES
50 Division Chair Business ....Mr. Richard FREDERICK
53 Division Chair Education ....Dr. Leon HOWARD
79 Division Chair Humanities ....Dr. Alisea MCLEOD
81 Chair Division Science & Math ....Dr. Doris WARD
70 Chair Department of Social Work ....Dr. Gemma BECKLEY
105 Director Web Services ....Mrs. Nilse F. GILLIAM
41 Athletic Director ....Dr. Ishmell H. EDWARDS
101 Secretary of the Institution/Board ....Mrs. Willa TERRY
106 Dir Online Education/E-learning ....Dr. Helen OLIVER
38 Director Student Counseling ....Mr. Carllos LASSITER

Southeastern Baptist College (D)

4229 Highway 15 N, Laurel MS 39440-1096
County: Jones FICE Identification: 002435
Unit ID: 176336
Telephone: (601) 426-6346 Carnegie Class: Spec/Faith
FAX Number: (601) 426-6347 Calendar System: Semester
URL: www.southeasternbaptist.edu
Established: 1948 Annual Undergrad Tuition & Fees: $4,790
Enrollment: 51 Coed
Affiliation or Control: Baptist IRS Status: 501(c)3
Highest Offering: Baccalaureate
Program: 2-Year Principally Bachelor's Creditable; Liberal Arts And General; Religious Emphasis
Accreditation: BI

01 President ....Vacant
05 Academic Dean ....Dr. Aaron L. PARKER
32 Dean of Student Services ....Dr. Daryle COATS
13 Director Information Technology ....Mr. Hubert DYESS
07 Director of Admissions ....Mr. Ronnie KITCHENS
06 Registrar ....Mrs. Emma BOND
37 Financial Aid Administrator ....Mr. Ronnie KITCHENS
08 Director of Library ....Mrs. Amy E. HINTON

Southwest Mississippi Community College (E)

1156 College Drive, Summit MS 39666-9029
County: Pike FICE Identification: 002436
Unit ID: 176354
Telephone: (601) 276-2000 Carnegie Class: Assoc/Pub-R-S
FAX Number: (601) 276-3888 Calendar System: Semester
URL: www.smcc.edu
Established: 1918 Annual Undergrad Tuition & Fees (In-District): $2,620
Enrollment: 1,973 Coed
Affiliation or Control: Local IRS Status: 501(c)3
Highest Offering: Associate Degree
Program: Occupational; 2-Year Principally Bachelor's Creditable
Accreditation: SC, ADNUR, CAHIIM

01 President ....Dr. Steve BISHOP
05 Vice President of Academic Affairs ....Ms. Alicia SHOWS
10 Vice President of Financial Affairs ....Mr. Grady SMITH
32 Vice President of Student Affairs ....Dr. Bill ASHLEY
75 Vice Pres Career & Tech Education ....Mr. Jeremy SMITH
06 Registrar/Vice President Admissions ....Mr. Matthew CALHOUN
37 Financial Aid Director ....Ms. Joni WILKINSON
09 Director of Institutional Research ....Dr. Bill TUCKER
08 Library Director ....Mrs. Natalie MCMAHON
39 Dir Student Activities/Housing ....Ms. Ashley GRAY

Tougaloo College (F)

500 West County Line Road, Tougaloo MS 39174-9999
County: Madison FICE Identification: 002439
Unit ID: 176406
Telephone: (601) 977-7730 Carnegie Class: Bac/A&S
FAX Number: (601) 977-7739 Calendar System: Semester
URL: www.tougaloo.edu
Established: 1869 Annual Undergrad Tuition & Fees: $10,600
Enrollment: 882 Coed
Affiliation or Control: United Church Of Christ IRS Status: 501(c)3
Highest Offering: Master's
Program: Liberal Arts And General
Accreditation: SC

01 President ....Dr. Beverly W. HOGAN
05 Provost/Vice Pres Academic Affairs ....Dr. Bettye Parker SMITH
32 Interim VP for Student Affairs ....Ms. Gladys JONES
30 Vice Pres Institutional Advance ....Dr. Delores Bolden STAMPS
10 Vice Pres Finance Administration ....Dr. Cynthia MELVIN
18 Vice Pres for Facilities Management ....Mr. Kelle MENOGAN
20 Asst Provost/VP Academic Affairs ....Dr. Candice Love JACKSON
84 Asst VP for Enrollment Management ....Ms. Linda DANIELS
35 Asst Vice Pres for Student Affairs ....Vacant
88 Ex Dir Ntnl Transp Sec Ctr of Excel ....Vacant
08 Director of Library Services ....Mrs. Orthella P. MOMAN
13 Chief Information Officer ....Ms. Denese CARROLL
37 Director of Student Financial Aid ....Ms. Maria THOMAS
09 Director Inst Research/Assess/Plng ....Dr. Larry JOHNSON
06 Registrar ....Ms. Carolyn L. EVANS
15 Director Human Resources ....Ms. Doretha PRESLEY
26 Dir Communications/Public Affairs ....Vacant
29 Director of Alumni Affairs ....Mrs. Doris BRIDGEMAN
07 Director of Admissions ....Ms. Junoesque JACOBS
36 Director of Career Services ....Ms. Whitney MCDOWELL
44 Director of Advancement Services ....Ms. Johnetta LINDSEY
46 Dir of Sponsored Programs/Research ....Dr. Motice BRUCE
88 Director of TRiO ....Dr. Valvia WILSON
38 Director of Counseling Services ....Dr. Rosie HARPER
96 Purchasing Agent ....Ms. Easter COMMON
102 Dir Corporation & Foundation Rels ....Vacant
19 Director Security/Safety ....Ms. Edna DRAKE
39 Director Student Housing ....Mr. Albert GOINS

University of Mississippi (G)

P.O. Box 1848, University MS 38677
County: Lafayette FICE Identification: 002440
Unit ID: 176017
Telephone: (662) 915-7211 Carnegie Class: RU/H
FAX Number: (662) 915-7010 Calendar System: Semester
URL: www.olemiss.edu
Established: 1844 Annual Undergrad Tuition & Fees (In-State): $7,444
Enrollment: 20,112 Coed
Affiliation or Control: State IRS Status: 501(c)3
Highest Offering: Doctorate
Program: Liberal Arts And General; Teacher Preparatory; Professional
Accreditation: SC, ART, BUS, BUSA, CACREP, CLPSY, CS, @DIETC, DIETD, ENG, FEPAC, JOUR, LAW, MUS, NRPA, PHAR, SP, SW, TED, THEA

01 Acting Chancellor ....Dr. Morris STOCKS
26 Chief Communications Officer ....Mr. Thomas E. EPPES
05 Acting Provost/VC Academic Affairs ....Dr. Noel E. WILKIN
10 Vice Chanc Administration & Finance ....Mr. Larry D. SPARKS
32 Vice Chancellor Student Life ....Dr. Brandi Hephner LABANC
46 Vice Chanc Research/Sponsored Pgms ....Dr. Alice M. CLARK
35 Asst VC Student Affs/Dean Students ....Dr. Melinda SUTTON
51 Int Dir Outreach/Continuing Studies ....Dr. Tony AMMETER
06 Asst Provost & Registrar ....Dr. Charlotte Fant PEGUES
20 Assoc Provost/Dir of Accreditation ....Dr. Maurice R. EFTINK
20 Associate Provost ....Dr. Noel E. WILKIN
85 Ast Prov/Ast to Chanc Multicul Affs ....Dr. Donald R. COLE
08 Dean of Libraries ....Ms. Julia RHOLES
13 Chief Information Officer ....Dr. Kathryn F. GATES
30 Chief Development Officer ....Mrs. Deborah S. VAUGHN
29 Int Exec Director Alumni Affairs ....Ms. Sheila D. DOSSETT
37 Director of Financial Aid ....Ms. Laura DIVEN-BROWN
36 Director Career Center ....Ms. Toni D. AVANT
41 Director Intercollegiate Athletics ....Mr. Ross BJORK
15 Director of Human Resources ....Mr. Clayton H. JONES
18 Director of Facilities Management ....Mr. Ashton PEARSON
19 Director Univ Police/Campus Safety ....Mr. Tim POTTS
38 Dir of University Counseling Center ....Dr. Quinton T. EDWARDS, JR.
23 Director University Health Service ....Dr. Travis W. YATES
39 AVC Student Affs/Student Housing ....Mr. Lionel MATEN
09 Int Director Institutional Research ....Ms. Tiffany GREGORY
22 Dir Equal Oppty/Reg Compliance ....Ms. Rebecca B. BRESSLER
04 Assistant to the Chancellor ....Ms. Sue T. KEISER
43 General Counsel/Chief of Staff ....Dr. Lee TYNER
96 Director of Procurement Services ....Ms. Rachel R. BOST
06 Associate Registrar ....Mrs. Denise KNIGHTON
21 Interim Controller ....Ms. Nina JONES
07 Director of Admissions ....Mr. Whitman SMITH
50 Dean School of Business Admin ....Dr. Kendall B. CYREE
49 Int Dean College of Liberal Arts ....Dr. Richard G. FORGETTE
81 Dean School of Applied Sciences ....Dr. Velmer S. BURTON, JR.
53 Dean School of Education ....Dr. David ROCK
54 Dean School of Engineering ....Dr. Alex CHENG
61 Interim Dean School of Law ....Dr. Deborah H. BELL
67 Dean of the School of Pharmacy ....Dr. David D. ALLEN
88 Dean School of Accountancy ....Dr. W. Mark WILDER
60 Dean Meek Sch Journalism/New Media ....Dr. H. Will NORTON

University of Mississippi Medical Center (H)

2500 N State Street, Jackson MS 39216-4505
County: Hinds FICE Identification: 004688
Unit ID: 176026
Telephone: (601) 984-1000 Carnegie Class: Spec/Med
FAX Number: (601) 984-1013 Calendar System: Semester
URL: www.umc.edu
Established: 1955 Annual Undergrad Tuition & Fees (In-State): $7,344
Enrollment: 2,391 Coed
Affiliation or Control: State IRS Status: 501(c)3

Highest Offering: Doctorate
Program: Professional; Nursing Emphasis
Accreditation: SC, CAHIIM, CYTO, DENT, DH, IPSY, MED, MT, NMT, NURSE, OT, PHAR, PTA, RAD

01 Vice Chancellor Health Affairs .... Dr. LouAnn WOODWARD
100 Chief of Staff to Vice Chancellor .... Dr. Brian RUTLEDGE
10 Chief Financial Officer .... Mr. James WENTZ
21 Comptroller .... Mr. Sam E. SMITH
25 Director Contract Management .... Ms. Stacy BALDWIN
11 Chief Administrative Officer .... Dr. Jonathan WILSON
86 Director Governmental Affairs .... Ms. Kristy SIMMS
46 Associate Vice Chanc Research .... Dr. Richard SUMMERS
05 Assoc VC for Academic Affairs .... Dr. Ralph H. DIDLAKE
20 Deputy Chief Academic Officer .... Dr. Robin ROCKHOLD
28 Assoc Vice Chanc Multicultural Affs .... Vacant
88 Assoc VC for Population Health .... Dr. Bettina BEECH
23 Assoc Vice Chanc Clinical Affairs .... Dr. Charles O'MARA
17 CEO Univ Hosp & Health Systems .... Mr. Kevin COOK
88 Sr Advisor to VC for External Aff .... Dr. Claude BRUNSON
17 Chief Medical Officer .... Dr. John M. HENDERSON
43 Chief Legal Officer .... Mr. Jeffrey WALKER
26 Chief Public Affs & Comm Officer .... Mr. Tom FORTNER
27 Chief Marketing Officer .... Ms. Rondah MARKS
13 Chief Information Officer .... Mr. David CHOU
15 Chief Human Resources Officer .... Mr. Michael ESTES
22 Director Employee Relations .... Ms. Barbara A. SMITH
66 Dean School of Nursing .... Dr. Kim HOOVER
58 Dean Sch Grad Stds Health Sciences .... Dr. Joey GRANGER
76 Dean Sch Health Related Profess .... Dr. Jessica H. BAILEY
52 Dean of School of Dentistry .... Dr. Gary W. REEVES
67 Assoc Dean for Clinical Affrs/SOPH .... Dr. Leigh A. ROSS
63 Assoc Dean-Graduate Medical Educ .. Dr. Shirley SCHLESSINGER
09 Chief Institutional Research Office .... Dr. David G. FOWLER
19 Chief of Police .... Mr. Michael T. STAMPS
18 Exec Director Facilities Mgmt .... Mr. Ivory BOGAN
30 Exec Dir & Chief Development Ofcr .... Ms. Sara MERRICK
88 Exec Dir for Academic Effectiveness .... Dr. Mitzi NORRIS
108 Director of Assessment .... Dr. Kimberly SIMPSON
96 Chief Supply Chain Mgmt .... Mr. Mitch HARRIS
29 Director Alumni Affairs .... Ms. April S. MANN
38 Director Office of Academic Support .... Dr. Natalie W. GAUGHF
37 Director Student Financial Aid .... Ms. Carrie COOPER
32 Chief Student Affairs Officer .... Dr. Jerry CLARK
06 Dir Student Records & Registrar . Ms. Barbara M. WESTERFIELD
08 Director Rowland Medical Library .... Ms. Susan B. CLARK
88 Chief Integrety/Compliance Officer .... Ms. Carol DENTON

University of Phoenix Jackson Campus (A)

120 Stone Creek Blvd, Suite 200,
Flowood MS 39232-8205
Telephone: (601) 664-9500 Identification: 770215
Accreditation: &NH, ACBSP

† No longer accepting campus-based students.

University of Southern Mississippi (B)

118 College Drive, #5001, Hattiesburg MS 39406-0001
County: Forrest FICE Identification: 002441
Unit ID: 176372
Telephone: (601) 266-1000 Carnegie Class: RU/H
FAX Number: (601) 266-5756 Calendar System: Semester
URL: www.usm.edu
Established: 1910 Annual Undergrad Tuition & Fees (In-State): $7,334
Enrollment: 14,792 Coed
Affiliation or Control: State IRS Status: 501(c)3
Highest Offering: Doctorate
Program: Liberal Arts And General; Teacher Preparatory; Professional
Accreditation: SC, AAFCS, ANEST, ART, AUD, BUS, BUSA, CAATE, CIDA, CLPSY, CONST, COPSY, CS, DANCE, DIETD, DIETI, ENGT, JOUR, KIN, LIB, MFCD, MT, MUS, NURSE, PH, PHLEB, SCPSY, SP, SW, TED, THEA

01 President .... Dr. Rodney D. BENNETT
04 Assistant to the President .... Vacant
05 Provost & VP for Academic Affairs .... Vacant
10 VP of Finance & Administration .... Dr. Douglas VINZANT
12 VP for Gulf Coast Campus .... Dr. Steven G. MILLER
32 Vice President for Student Affairs .... Dr. Thomas BURKE
30 Vice President Advancement .... Mr. Bob PIERCE
108 Assoc Prov Assessment/Accreditation ..... Dr. William W. POWELL
46 Vice President Research .... Dr. Gordon CANNON
84 Assoc VP Enrollment Management .... Ms. Becky VINZANT
35 Assoc Vice President Student Affs .... Mr. Sid GONSOULIN
53 Dean College Education/Psychology .... Dr. Ann BLACKWELL
49 Dean College Arts & Letters .... Dr. Steven MOSER
50 Dean College Business .... Dr. Faye GILBERT
66 Dean College Nursing .... Dr. Katherine NUGENT
72 Dean College Science/Technology .... Dr. David HAYHURST
92 Dean of Honors College .... Dr. Ellen WEINAUER
76 Dean College Health .... Dr. Michael FORSTER
58 Dean Graduate School .... Dr. Karen COATS
08 Dean/University Librarian .... Dr. John EYE
18 Asst VP Planning & Facilities Mgmt .... Dr. Chris CRENSHAW
13 Chief Information Officer .... Mr. David SLIMAN
41 Director Intercollegiate Athletics .... Mr. Bill MCGILLIS
06 Registrar .... Mr. Greg PIERCE
25 Asst VP for Research Administration .... Ms. Marcia LANDEN
09 Director of Institutional Research .... Mrs. Michelle ARRINGTON
45 Dir of Institutional Effectiveness .... Mrs. Kathryn LOWERY
29 Alumni Activities/Exec Director .... Mr. Jerry DEFATTA
36 Director Career Services .... Mr. Russell ANDERSON
21 Asc VP for Finance & Controller .... Ms. Allyson EASTERWOOD
22 Title IX Coordinator .... Dr. Rebecca WOODRICK
38 Director of Counseling Center .... Dr. Deena CRAWFORD
23 Director of Health Services .... Dr. Virginia CRAWFORD
39 Director of Residence Life .... Dr. Scott BLACKWELL
15 Director of Human Resources .... Mrs. Linda RASMUSSEN
96 Director Procurement & Contracts .... Mr. Steve BALLEW
07 Dir of Admissions for Operations .... Vacant
26 Chief Communication Officer .... Mr. James P. COLL
88 Asst to Pres Military/Vet Stdnt Aff .... Gen. Jeff HAMMOND
102 Exec Dir USM Foundation .... Vacant
104 Assoc VP for Intl Programs .... Dr. Daniel NORTON
106 Dir Learning Enhancement Ctr .... Ms. Sheri LYONS
19 Chief of Police .... Mr. Bob HOPKINS
43 Dir Legal Services/General Counsel .... Mr. Jon M. WEATHERS
86 Exec Asst to Pres External Affairs .... Mr. Chad DRISKELL
37 Director Student Financial Aid .... Mr. David WILLIAMSON

Virginia College (C)

920 Cedar Lake Road, Biloxi MS 39532-2107
Telephone: (228) 546-9100 Identification: 666073
Accreditation: ACICS, MAAB, SURGT

† Branch campus of Virginia College, Birmingham, AL.

Virginia College (D)

5841 Ridgewood Road, Jackson MS 39211
Telephone: (601) 977-0960 Identification: 666032
Accreditation: ACICS, MAAB, SURGT

† Branch campus of Virginia College, Birmingham, AL.

Wesley Biblical Seminary (E)

787 E Northside Drive, Jackson MS 39206-4945
County: Hinds FICE Identification: 025162
Unit ID: 176451
Telephone: (601) 366-8880 Carnegie Class: Spec/Faith
FAX Number: (601) 366-8832 Calendar System: Semester
URL: www.wbs.edu
Established: 1974 Annual Graduate Tuition & Fees: $12,750
Enrollment: 51 Coed
Affiliation or Control: Interdenominational IRS Status: 501(c)3
Highest Offering: Master's; No Undergraduates
Program: Professional; Religious Emphasis
Accreditation: THEOL

01 President .... Dr. John E. NEIHOF, JR.
05 Vice President Academic Affairs .... Dr. Gareth COCKERILL
10 Vice Pres Business Affairs .... Mr. Ralph BROWN
07 VP Recruitment/Student Services .... Rev. Rob POCAI
30 Vice President Development .... Mr. John GAINEY
08 Director of Library Services .... Ms. Beth NEIHOF
08 Director of Library Services .... Mr. David STEVELINE
18 Director of Operations .... Mr. Ken MONEY
06 Registrar/Director Financial Aid .... Mr. Karl LUMEN

William Carey University (F)

498 Tuscan Avenue, Hattiesburg MS 39401-5461
County: Forrest FICE Identification: 002447
Unit ID: 176479
Telephone: (601) 318-6051 Carnegie Class: Master's L
FAX Number: (601) 318-6494 Calendar System: Trimester
URL: www.wmcarey.edu
Established: 1892 Annual Undergrad Tuition & Fees: $15,900
Enrollment: 3,936 Coed
Affiliation or Control: Southern Baptist IRS Status: 501(c)3
Highest Offering: Doctorate
Program: Liberal Arts And General; Teacher Preparatory; Professional
Accreditation: SC, MUS, NURSE, @OSTEO, TED

01 President/Chief Executive Officer .... Dr. Tommy KING
03 Executive Vice President .... Dr. Scott HUMMEL
05 Vice President of Academic Affairs .... Dr. Garry M. BRELAND
10 Vice Pres Business Affs/CFO .... Mr. Grant GUTHRIE
32 Vice Pres for Student Support .... Mrs. Valerie BRIDGEFORTH
46 Vice President Inst Effectiveness .... Dr. Bennie R. CROCKETT
30 Interm Director of Advancement .... Mrs. Monica MARLOWE
63 Dean College Osteopathic Medicine .... Dr. James TURNER
12 Admin Dean Tradition Campus .... Mr. Gerald BRACEY
04 Executive Assistant to President .... Ms. Barbara HAMILTON
50 Dean School of Business .... Dr. Cheryl DALE
53 Dean School of Education .... Dr. Benjamin BURNETT
83 Dean Sch Natural/Behavioral Science .... Dr. Frank BAUGH
66 Dean School of Nursing .... Dr. Janet WILLIAMS
49 Dean School of Arts & Letters .... Dr. Myron NOONKESTER
64 Dean School of Music & Ministry .... Dr. Don ODOM
73 Chair School of Ministry Studies .... Dr. Daniel CALDWELL
84 Dean of Enrollment Management .... Mr. William N. CURRY
58 Dean of Graduate Studies .... Dr. Frank BAUGH
20 Assoc Dean of Academic Services .... Dr. Cassandra CONNOR
09 Interim Dir Institutional Research .... Mrs. Susan CURRY
06 Registrar .... Mrs. Gayle KNIGHT
08 Director of Libraries .... Mr. Reese POWELL
29 Alumni Director .... Mrs. Pam SHEARER
26 Chief Public Relations Officer .... Vacant
13 Director of Information Technology .... Mr. Jeff ANDREWS
92 Director of Honors Program .... Dr. Tyler HODGES
21 Director of Budget Management .... Mr. Grant GUTHRIE
41 Athletic Director .... Mr. Steven H. KNIGHT
18 Dir Facilities/Grounds/Maintenance .... Mr. Robert BLEVINS
35 Dir Student Svcs Tradition Campus .... Mr. James M. HARRISON
66 Associate Dean Nursing NO Campus .... Vacant
21 Dir Business Svcs Tradition Campus .... Mr. Gerald BRACEY
12 Director of Keesler Center .... Ms. Amanda KNESAL
15 Director Personnel Services .... Ms. Deidre SHOWS
19 Director Campus Security .... Mr. Bob BLEVINS
88 Coord of Instructional Technology .... Mr. David J. BROCKWAY
12 Coordinator New Orleans Campus .... Vacant
07 Director of Admissions .... Mrs. Alissa KING

MISSOURI

A. T. Still University of Health Sciences (G)

800 W Jefferson Street, Kirksville MO 63501-1497
County: Adair FICE Identification: 002477
Unit ID: 177834
Telephone: (660) 626-2391 Carnegie Class: Spec/Med
FAX Number: (660) 626-2672 Calendar System: Semester
URL: www.atsu.edu
Established: 1892 Annual Graduate Tuition & Fees: N/A
Enrollment: 3,213 Coed
Affiliation or Control: Independent Non-Profit IRS Status: 501(c)3
Highest Offering: First Professional Degree; No Undergraduates
Program: Professional
Accreditation: NH, DENT, OSTEO, PH

01 President .... Dr. Craig PHELPS
05 Sr VP Academic Affairs .... Dr. Norman GEVITZ
63 Dean KCOM .... Dr. Margaret WILSON
32 VP Student Affairs .... Mrs. Lori HAXTON
30 VP University Advancement .... Dr. Shaun SOMMERER
43 VP & General Counsel .... Mr. Matthew HEEREN
46 VP Inst Res Grants & Info Systems .... Dr. John HEARD
52 Dean MO Sch of Dentistry/Oral Hlth .... Dr. Chris HALLIDAY
88 Dean Col of Graduate Hlth Studies .... Dr. Don ALTMAN
52 Dean AZ Sch of Dentistry/Oral Hlth .... Dr. Jack DILLENBERG
76 Dean AZ Sch of Health Sciences .... Dr. Randy DANIELSEN
63 Acting Dean Sch of Osteo Med in AZ .... Dr. Jeffrey MORGAN
10 Vice President Finance/CFO .... Mr. Rick RIEDER
35 Assoc VP AZ Student Affairs .... Mrs. Beth POPPRE
13 Asst VP Info Technologies/Services .... Mr. Bryan KRUSNIAK
07 Asst VP Admissions .... Dr. David KOENECKE
88 VP Strategic Univ Partnerships .... Dr. Gary CLOUD
88 Sr VP Strategic Univ Initiatives .... Dr. O.T WENDEL
88 Associate VP Sponsored Programs .... Mrs. Gaylah SUBLETTE
04 Asst to Pres & Secretary to BoT .... Mrs. Norine EITEL
06 Registrar .... Dr. Deanna HUNSAKER
08 Director Library .... Mr. Michael KRONENFIELD
15 Asst VP Human Resources .... Mrs. Donna BROWN
18 Director Facilities/Plant Operation .... Mr. Robert EHRLICH
22 Affirmative Action Officer .... Mrs. Donna BROWN
37 Dir Student Financial Assistance .... Mr. Steven JORDEN
38 Director Student Counseling .... Mr. Thomas VAN VLECK
96 Director Purchasing .... Mr. Corey LOUDER
19 Director Security .... Mr. Bob FRAIZER
28 Director of Diversity .... Mr. Clinton NORMORE
20 Associate VP Academic Affairs .... Dr. Ann BOYLE
44 Associate VP University Advancement .... Mr. Randy ROGERS
88 Assistant VP Academic Affairs .... Dr. Leonard GOLDSTEIN
21 Assistant VP for Finance .... Mrs. Tonya GRIMM
09 Director ATStill Research Institute .... Dr. Brian DEGENHARDT

† Arizona campus accreditation includes ARPCA, AUD, DENT, OSTEO, OT, PTA.

American Business & Technology University (H)

1018 West Saint Maartens Drive, Saint Joseph MO 64506
County: Buchanan FICE Identification: 041187
Unit ID: 457688
Telephone: (816) 279-7000 Carnegie Class: Not Classified
FAX Number: (888) 890-8190 Calendar System: Other
URL: www.abtu.edu
Established: 2001 Annual Undergrad Tuition & Fees: $6,976
Enrollment: 580 Coed
Affiliation or Control: Proprietary IRS Status: Proprietary
Highest Offering: Master's
Program: Occupational; 2-Year Principally Bachelor's Creditable; Technical Emphasis
Accreditation: DEAC

01 President .... Mr. Sam ATIEH
11 Vice President .... Mr. Lute ATIEH
45 VP of Strategic Iniatives .... Mr. Eddie COLON
37 VP of Financial Aid .... Dr. Michael CAMPBELL
13 Chief Information Officer .... Mr. Ramsey ATIEH
10 Chief Financial Officer .... Mr. Dan MARLOW
05 Director Of Education .... Dr. Luanne HAGGARD
20 Assoc Dean of Undergrad Programs .... Dr. Donald LADER
108 Director of Compliance .... Mr. Chad BREAZILE
06 Registrar .... Mrs. Kourtney DRAKE
07 Director of Admissions .... Mr. Richard LINGLE

American Trade School (A)

3925 Industrial Dr, Saint Ann MO 63074
County: Saint Louis FICE Identification: 041748
Unit ID: 461573
Telephone: (314) 423-1900 Carnegie Class: Not Classified
FAX Number: (314) 423-1911 Calendar System: Quarter
URL: www.americantradeschool.edu
Established: 2003 Annual Undergrad Tuition & Fees: $16,600
Enrollment: 113 Coed
Affiliation or Control: Proprietary IRS Status: Proprietary
Highest Offering: Associate Degree
Program: Occupational; 2-Year Principally Bachelor's Creditable
Accreditation: ACCSC

Aquinas Institute of Theology (B)

23 S Spring Avenue, Saint Louis MO 63108-3323
County: City of Saint Louis FICE Identification: 001632
Unit ID: 176600
Telephone: (314) 256-8800 Carnegie Class: Spec/Faith
FAX Number: (314) 256-8888 Calendar System: Semester
URL: www.ai.edu
Established: 1951 Annual Graduate Tuition & Fees: $19,950
Enrollment: 156 Coed
Affiliation or Control: Roman Catholic IRS Status: 501(c)3
Highest Offering: Doctorate; No Undergraduates
Program: Professional; Religious Emphasis
Accreditation: NH, THEOL

01 President .... Rev. Sean MARTIN
05 Academic Dean .... Rev. Gregory HEILLE
10 Director of Finance .... Mr. Thomas BARBARAK
06 Registrar .... Mrs. Erin HAMMOND
30 Director of Inst Advancement .... Mrs. Stacey KRIEG
32 Dean of Students .... Rev. George BOUDREAU
07 Director Admissions .... Mr. David WERTHMANN
26 Dir Communications/Financial Aid .... Mrs. Jan LINGUA

The Art Institute of St. Louis (C)

1520 South Fifth Street, Suite 107,
Saint Charles MO 63303
Telephone: (636) 688-9281 Identification: 770738
Accreditation: ACICS

† Branch campus of The Art Institute of Phoenix, Phoenix, AZ.

Assemblies of God Theological Seminary (D)

1435 N Glenstone Avenue, Springfield MO 65802-2131
County: Greene FICE Identification: 012120
Unit ID: 176619
Telephone: (417) 268-1000 Carnegie Class: Spec/Faith
FAX Number: (417) 268-1001 Calendar System: Semester
URL: www.agts.edu
Established: 1972 Annual Graduate Tuition & Fees: $14,232
Enrollment: 327 Coed
Affiliation or Control: Assemblies Of God Church IRS Status: 501(c)3
Highest Offering: Doctorate; No Undergraduates
Program: Professional; Religious Emphasis
Accreditation: THEOL

01 President .... Dr. Mark A. HAUSFELD
05 Dean of Faculty .... Dr. James H. RAILEY
58 Dir Intercultural Doctoral Studies .... Dr. DeLonn L. RANCE
58 Director DMin Program .... Dr. Cheryl A. TAYLOR
10 Director of Finance & Opers .... Mr. Dan M. SHAFFER
29 Dir of Institutional & Alumni Rels .... Mrs. Dorothea J. LOTTER
08 Director of Library Services .... Mr. Joseph F. MARICS
27 Promotions Coordinator .... Mrs. Jennifer S. HALL
42 Director of Spiritual Formation .... Dr. Jay P. TAYLOR
51 Director of Continuing Education .... Dr. Randy C. WALLS
06 Registrar .... Mrs. Connie CROSS
37 Financial Aid Coordinator .... Mrs. Samantha JONES

† The Seminary continues to offer its educational programs as a distinct unit within the consolidated Evangel University, Springfield, MO.

Avila University (E)

11901 Wornall Road, Kansas City MO 64145-9990
County: Jackson FICE Identification: 002449
Unit ID: 176628
Telephone: (816) 942-8400 Carnegie Class: Master's M
FAX Number: (816) 942-3362 Calendar System: Semester
URL: www.avila.edu
Established: 1916 Annual Undergrad Tuition & Fees: $26,450
Enrollment: 1,676 Coed
Affiliation or Control: Roman Catholic IRS Status: 501(c)3
Highest Offering: Master's
Program: Liberal Arts And General; Teacher Preparatory; Professional
Accreditation: NH, IACBE, NURSE, RAD, SW

01 President .... Dr. Ron SLEPITZA
05 Vice Pres Academic Affairs .... Dr. Cathryn PRIDAL
20 Vice Provost for Academic Affairs .... Dr. Sue KING
10 Vice Pres for Finance/Admin Svcs .... Mr. Paul TOLER
26 Asst VP Marketing/Communication .... Mrs. Ann O'MEARA
30 Chief Development Officer .... Ms. Angela HEER
32 Dean of Students .... Darby GOUGH
84 VP Enrollment/Director of Admission .... Mr. Brandon JOHNSON
06 Registrar .... Ms. Michelle DRISCOLL
08 Librarian .... Ms. Kathleen FINEGAN
37 Director of Financial Aid .... Ms. Crystal BRUNTZ
42 Dir Mission Effect & Campus Ministr .... Mr. David M. ARMSTRONG
21 Controller .... Mr. Joseph H. SJUTS
29 Director Alumni .... Mrs. Bailey CARR
41 Athletic Director .... Vacant
15 Director of Human Resources .... Ms. Janet MCMANUS
18 Chief Facilities/Physical Plant .... Mr. Mike STUCKEY
40 Bookstore Manager .... Mr. John A. TARANTO
38 Coord Counseling & Career Services .... Ms. Elizabeth MCKINLEY

Baptist Bible College (F)

628 E Kearney St, Springfield MO 65803-3498
County: Greene FICE Identification: 013208
Unit ID: 176664
Telephone: (417) 268-6000 Carnegie Class: Spec/Faith
FAX Number: (800) 819-8330 Calendar System: Semester
URL: www.gobbc.edu
Established: 1950 Annual Undergrad Tuition & Fees: $11,340
Enrollment: 320 Coed
Affiliation or Control: Baptist IRS Status: 501(c)3
Highest Offering: First Professional Degree
Program: Teacher Preparatory; Professional; Religious Emphasis
Accreditation: NH, BI

01 President .... Mr. Mark L. MILIONI
05 Vice President of Academic Affairs .... Dr. Greg T. CHRISTOPHER
10 Chief Financial Officer .... Mr. Jason L. TODD
32 Executive Director of Student Svcs .... Mr. Nathaniel S. HARMON
18 Chief Facilities/Physical Plant .... Mr. Chris C. WILLIAMS
88 Director of Campus Advising .... Mr. Joseph K. GLEASON
06 Registrar .... Mr. Terry A. ALLCORN
07 Dir Enrollment Services .... Mr. John DECKER
37 Director of Financial Aid .... Mr. Bob L. KOTULSKI
38 Campus Counselor .... Mr. Bill A. PIATT
39 Director of Resident Life .... Mr. Bill J. LEVERGOOD
15 Director of Human Resources .... Mrs. Hope GOFFNEY
19 Director Security/Safety .... Vacant
41 Athletic Director .... Mr. Mark HEDGER
40 Virtual Bookstore .... Mrs. Julie BECK
08 Director of Library Services .... Mr. Jon JONES
51 Dean of Continuing Education .... Ms. Cheryl PAGE

Bolivar Technical College (G)

2001 W Broadway Street, 2nd Floor, Bolivar MO 65613
Telephone: (417) 777-5062 Identification: 667033
Accreditation: ACICS

† Branch campus of Texas County Technical College, Houston, MO.

Brookes Bible College (H)

10257 St. Charles Rock Road, St. Ann MO 63074
County: St. Louis Identification: 667137
Telephone: (314) 773-0083 Carnegie Class: Not Classified
FAX Number: (314) 736-6293 Calendar System: Semester
URL: www.brookesbible.com
Established: 1909 Annual Undergrad Tuition & Fees: $2,840
Enrollment: N/A Coed
Affiliation or Control: Independent Non-Profit IRS Status: 501(c)3
Highest Offering: Associate Degree
Program: Religious Emphasis
Accreditation: @BI

01 Interim President .... Mr. Larry HARDER
05 Academic/Student Dean .... Dr. Allan HENDERSON

Brown Mackie College-St. Louis (I)

2 Soccer Park Road, Fenton MO 63026-2564
Telephone: (636) 651-3290 Identification: 666793
Accreditation: ACICS, OTA, SURGT, SURTEC

† Branch campus of Brown Mackie College, Tucson, AZ.

Bryan University (J)

3215 LeMone Industrial Boulevard, Columbia MO 65201
Telephone: (573) 777-5550 Identification: 770725
Accreditation: ACICS

† Branch campus of Bryan University, Springfield, MO.

Bryan University (K)

4255 Nature Center Way, Springfield MO 65804
County: Greene FICE Identification: 030663
Unit ID: 369516
Telephone: (417) 862-5700 Carnegie Class: Assoc/PrivFP
FAX Number: (417) 865-7144 Calendar System: Other
URL: www.bryanu.edu
Established: 1982 Annual Undergrad Tuition & Fees: $15,321
Enrollment: 322 Coed
Affiliation or Control: Proprietary IRS Status: Proprietary
Highest Offering: Master's
Program: Occupational; 2-Year Principally Bachelor's Creditable; Business Emphasis
Accreditation: ACICS

01 Executive Director .... Mr. Scott HAAR

Calvary Bible College and Theological Seminary (L)

15800 Calvary Road, Kansas City MO 64147-1341
County: Cass FICE Identification: 002450
Unit ID: 176789
Telephone: (816) 322-0110 Carnegie Class: Spec/Faith
FAX Number: (816) 331-4474 Calendar System: Semester
URL: www.calvary.edu
Established: 1932 Annual Undergrad Tuition & Fees: $9,480
Enrollment: 314 Coed
Affiliation or Control: Independent Non-Profit IRS Status: 501(c)3
Highest Offering: First Professional Degree
Program: Teacher Preparatory; Religious Emphasis
Accreditation: NH, BI

01 President .... Dr. James L. CLARK
10 Vice President of Operations .... Mr. Randy GRIMM
05 Academic Dean of the College .... Dr. Teddy BITNER
20 Seminary Academic Dean .... Dr. Victor "Skip" HESSEL
32 Dean of Students .... Mr. Cory D. TROWBRIDGE
34 Dean of Women .... Miss Arely PEREZ
07 Director of Admissions .... Mr. Brian MASON
06 Registrar .... Mr. Larry SPRY
08 Head Librarian .... Miss Hannah BITNER
88 Dir of Adult & Graduate Studies .... Mr. Mike PIBURN
18 Director of Maintenance .... Vacant
41 Athletic Director .... Miss Jeanette REGIER
91 Director Administrative Computing .... Mr. Aaron HEATH
38 Director Biblical Counsel/Educ Ctr .... Dr. Mark HAGER
30 Director of Development .... Mr. Mervin WAGNER
19 Director of Security .... Mr. Glenn WILLIAMS
37 Director of Financial Aid .... Mr. Robert CRANK
26 Director of Public Relations/Market .... Mr. Jeff CAMPA
09 Institutional Research Coordinator .... Mr. Charles KURTZ
15 Human Resources Coordinator .... Mrs. Jolayne ROGERS
29 Alumni Relations Coordinator .... Mrs. Sara KLAASSEN
88 Director of The Learning Center .... Dr. Terri STRICKER
42 Director of Christian Ministries .... Mr. Joe EVERETT
88 Director of Food Service .... Mr. Joe DAPRA
04 Administrative Asst to President .... Mrs. Maryjean SPRY
105 Director Web Services .... Vacant
106 Dir Online Education/E-learning .... Mr. Mike PIBURN
44 Director Annual or Planned Giving .... Mr. Mervin WAGNER
50 Program Director Business .... Dr. Skip HESSEL
53 Dept Chair Education .... Ms. Rose HENNESS

Central Christian College of the Bible (M)

911 E Urbandale Drive, Moberly MO 65270-1997
County: Randolph FICE Identification: 022664
Unit ID: 176910
Telephone: (660) 263-3900 Carnegie Class: Spec/Faith
FAX Number: (660) 263-3936 Calendar System: Semester
URL: www.cccb.edu
Established: 1957 Annual Undergrad Tuition & Fees: $11,900
Enrollment: 290 Coed
Affiliation or Control: Christian Churches And Churches of Christ
IRS Status: 501(c)3
Highest Offering: Baccalaureate
Program: 2-Year Principally Bachelor's Creditable; Liberal Arts And General; Professional; Religious Emphasis
Accreditation: @NH, BI

01 President .... Dr. David B. FINCHER
05 Academic Dean .... Dr. Eric A. STEVENS
10 VP of Business & Finance .... Mrs. Lara LAWRENCE
07 Associate Director of Admissions .... Mr. Michael BUTRUM
07 Executive Director of Admissions .... Mr. Rocky CHRISTENSEN
88 Director of Stewardship .... Mr. Alan G. WILSON
04 Exec Assistant to the President .... Mrs. Sherry L. WALLIS
32 Exec Dir of Student Development .... Mr. Darryl C. AMMON
34 Dean of Women .... Mrs. Anne P. MENEAR
41 Athletic Director .... Mr. Jack DEFREITAS
08 Head Librarian .... Mrs. Patty A. AGEE
06 Registrar .... Mrs. Faith M. AXTON
37 Director of Financial Aid .... Mrs. Rhonda J. DUNHAM
13 Director of Information Technology .... Mr. Aaron MERRITT
18 Physical Plant Manager .... Mr. Mark E. DUNHAM
40 Bookstore Manager .... Mrs. Kelly HARDING
35 Director of Student Services .... Mrs. Lori PETER
39 Residence Director - Women .... Mrs. Anne MENEAR
39 Residence Director - Men .... Mr. Rocky CHRISTENSEN
21 Director of Accounting .... Mr. Matt DOUGLASS
04 Administrative Executive Assistant .... Mrs. Cindy MEYER
33 Dean of Men .... Mr. Darryl C. AMMON
101 Secretary of the Institution/Board .... Mr. Ronald SELF
106 Online Education Coordinator .... Mr. James FRANKE

† Onsite students accepted into a degree or certificate program will receive Full-Tuition Scholarship which equals cost of tuition up to 18 hrs/semester. Scholarship may be reduced from deficiencies in grades, Christian service, or chapel attendance.

Central Methodist University (N)

411 Central Methodist Square, Fayette MO 65248-1198
County: Howard FICE Identification: 002453
Unit ID: 445267

Telephone: (660) 248-3391 Carnegie Class: Bac/Diverse
FAX Number: (660) 248-2287 Calendar System: 4/1/4
URL: www.centralmethodist.edu
Established: 1854 Annual Undergrad Tuition & Fees: $29,700
Enrollment: 5,702 Coed
Affiliation or Control: United Methodist IRS Status: 501(c)3
Highest Offering: Master's
Program: Liberal Arts And General; Teacher Preparatory
Accreditation: NH, CAATE, MUS, NURSE

01 President .... Dr. Roger D. DRAKE
05 Provost/VP Acad Affairs/Dn Faculty .... Dr. Rita GULSTAD
10 Vice Pres Finance & Administration .... Ms. Julee SHERMAN
30 Vice Pres Advancement/Alumni Rels .... Dr. Joshua JACOBS
32 VP Instl Growth/Student Engagement .... Mr. Kenneth R. OLIVER
20 Assoc Dean for Academics/Assesment .... Dr. Barbara ANDERSON
13 Vice President Information Services .... Mr. Chad GAINES
09 Institutional Research/Reporting .... Ms. Amber MONNIG
07 Director of Admission .... Mr. Adam JENKINS
41 Athletic Director .... Mr. Brian SPIELBAUER
04 Administrative Asst to President .... Ms. Catherine SHANAHAN
29 Director Development/Alumni Pgms .... Ms. Deanna COOPER
06 Registrar .... Ms. Kathryn WINEGARD
37 Director of Financial Assistance .... Ms. Kristen GIBBS
18 Chief Facilities/Physical Plant .... Mr. Derry WISWALL
26 Exec Dir Marketing Communications .... Mr. Kent PROPST
36 Director Student Placement .... Ms. Nicolette YEVICH
15 Director of Human Resources .... Ms. Kimberly THOMSON

Chamberlain College of Nursing - St. Louis (A)

11830 Westline Industrial, Ste 106, St. Louis MO 63146
Telephone: (314) 991-6200 Identification: 770494
Accreditation: &NH, NURSE

† Branch campus of Chamberlain College of Nursing-Addison, Addison, IL.

City Vision University (B)

3101 Troost Ave. Suite 200, Kansas City MO 64109-1845
County: United States FICE Identification: 041191
Unit ID: 457697
Telephone: (816) 960-2008 Carnegie Class: Not Classified
FAX Number: (816) 256-8471 Calendar System: Other
URL: www.cityvision.edu
Established: 1998 Annual Undergrad Tuition & Fees: $6,000
Enrollment: 78 Coed
Affiliation or Control: Other IRS Status: 501(c)3
Highest Offering: Master's
Program: Professional; Religious Emphasis
Accreditation: DEAC

01 Executive Director/President .... Dr. Andrew SEARS
05 Academic Dean .... Dr. Kenneth HEITLAND
10 Financial Accounting Manager .... Mrs. AnnMarie CAMERON-THOMPSON
07 Director of Admissions .... Ms. Nancy YOUNG

† Mail address is 31 Torrey St, Dorchester, MA 02124-3543.

College of the Ozarks (C)

PO Box 17, Point Lookout MO 65726-0017
County: Taney FICE Identification: 002500
Unit ID: 178697
Telephone: (417) 334-6411 Carnegie Class: Bac/Diverse
FAX Number: (417) 335-2618 Calendar System: Semester
URL: www.cofo.edu
Established: 1906 Annual Undergrad Tuition & Fees: $430
Enrollment: 1,433 Coed
Affiliation or Control: Independent Non-Profit IRS Status: 501(c)3
Highest Offering: Baccalaureate
Program: Liberal Arts And General
Accreditation: NH, ACFEI, DIETD, NURSE

01 President .... Dr. Jerry C. DAVIS
03 Vice President .... Dr. Howell W. KEETER
05 Dean of the College .... Dr. Eric BOLGER
30 Director of Development .... Mrs. Natalie RASNICK
10 Treasurer .... Mr. Charles F. HUGHES
11 Dean of Administration .... Dr. Marvin SCHOENECKE
103 Dean of Work Education .... Dr. Chris LARSEN
32 Dean of Student Services .... Mr. Nick SHARP
07 Dean of Admissions and Financial Ai .... Dr. Marci LINSON
06 Registrar .... Mrs. Fran FORMAN
29 Director of Alumni Affairs .... Mrs. Angela WILLIAMSON
36 Director of Career Placement .... Mr. Jim FREEMAN
37 Director of Financial Aid .... Mr. Brad FULLER
26 Director of Public Relations .... Mrs. Valorie COLEMAN
96 Director of Purchasing .... Mr. Kurt MCDONALD
38 Student Counseling .... Mrs. Pat MCLEAN
04 Administrative Asst to President .... Ms. Elizabeth HUDSON

Columbia College (D)

1001 Rogers Street, Columbia MO 65216-0001
County: Boone FICE Identification: 002456
Unit ID: 177065
Telephone: (573) 875-8700 Carnegie Class: Master's M
FAX Number: (573) 875-7209 Calendar System: Semester
URL: www.ccis.edu
Established: 1851 Annual Undergrad Tuition & Fees: $20,936
Enrollment: 16,567 Coed
Affiliation or Control: Christian Church (Disciples Of Christ) IRS Status: 501(c)3
Highest Offering: Master's
Program: Liberal Arts And General; Teacher Preparatory; Professional
Accreditation: NH

01 President .... Dr. Scott DALRYMPLE
04 Sr Exec Assistant to the President .... Ms. Mary BROWN
05 Provost/VP Academic Affairs .... Dr. David STARRETT
51 VP Adult Higher Education .... Dr. Jeff MUSGROVE
84 VP of Enrollment & Marketing .... Mr. Kevin PALMER
32 Dean for Student Affairs .... Ms. Faye C. BURCHARD
10 Chief Financial Officer .... Mr. Bruce E. BOYER
30 Exec Director of Devel/Alumni Svcs .... Mr. Mike KATEMAN
18 Exec Director of Plant/Facilities .... Mr. Bob C. HUTTON
27 Executive Director of Marketing .... Ms. Lana POOLE
07 Director of Admissions .... Ms. Stephanie JOHNSON
06 Registrar .... Ms. Jennifer THORPE
29 Senior Director of Alumni Relations .... Ms. Susan Y. DAVIS
26 Senior Director of Public Relations .... Ms. Suzanne ROTHWELL
37 Director of Financial Aid .... Ms. Sharon A. ABERNATHY
08 Director of Stafford Library .... Ms. Janet CARUTHERS
35 Director of Student Activities .... Vacant
36 Director Career Services Center .... Mr. Dan GOMEZ-PALACIO
15 Executive Director Human Resources .... Ms. Patty FISCHER
23 Director of Health Services .... Ms. Judy WOOD
13 Chief Information Officer .... Mr. Gary STANOWSKI
55 Assoc Dean Adult Higher Education .... Mr. Eric CUNNINGHAM
58 Associate Dean Graduate Studies .... Dr. Steve C. WIEGENSTEIN
41 Athletic Director .... Mr. Bob P. BURCHARD
09 Director Institutional Research .... Ms. Misty HASKAMP
19 Director of Campus Safety .... Mr. Robert KLAUSMEYER
21 Associate Controller .... Mr. Randal SCHENEWERK

Conception Seminary College (E)

37174 State Highway VV, PO Box 502,
Conception MO 64433-0502
County: Nodaway FICE Identification: 002467
Unit ID: 177083
Telephone: (660) 944-3105 Carnegie Class: Spec/Faith
FAX Number: (660) 944-2829 Calendar System: Semester
URL: www.conception.edu
Established: 1883 Annual Undergrad Tuition & Fees: $20,104
Enrollment: 92 Male
Affiliation or Control: Roman Catholic IRS Status: 501(c)3
Highest Offering: Baccalaureate
Program: Liberal Arts And General; Religious Emphasis
Accreditation: NH

01 Rector & President .... Rev. Brendan MOSS
11 Director of Administration .... Mrs. Amy K. SCHIEBER
32 Dean of Students .... Rev. Patrick YORK
05 Dean of Academic Affairs .... Dr. William BROWNSBERGER
10 Business Manager/Dir Auxiliary Svcs .... Rev. Benedict T. NEENAN
30 Development Director .... Rev. Benedict T. NEENAN
07 Director of Admissions .... Vacant
37 Director of Student Financial Aid .... Bro. Justin J. HERNANDEZ
06 Registrar .... Mrs. Jeanette SCHIEBER
29 Director of Alumni .... Rev. Daniel PETSCHE
08 Librarian .... Bro. Thomas SULLIVAN
26 Director of Communications .... Mrs. Jenny HUARD
13 Director of Information Technology .... Mr. Tony MEISTER
38 Director of Counseling Services .... Rev. Duane REINERT
41 Director of Wellness Program .... Mr. Skip SHEAR

Concorde Career College (F)

3239 Broadway Boulevard, Kansas City MO 64111-2407
County: Jackson FICE Identification: 023616
Unit ID: 155283
Telephone: (816) 531-5223 Carnegie Class: Assoc/PrivFP
FAX Number: (816) 756-3231 Calendar System: Other
URL: www.concorde.edu
Established: 1986 Annual Undergrad Tuition & Fees: $30,270
Enrollment: 350 Coed
Affiliation or Control: Proprietary IRS Status: Proprietary
Highest Offering: Baccalaureate
Program: Occupational
Accreditation: ACCSC, CAHIIM, COARC, DH, PTAA

01 President .... Colleen MCDERMOTT
05 Academic Dean .... April RAHE
07 Director Student Recruitment .... Jeff HARRIS

Concordia Seminary (G)

801 Seminary Place, Saint Louis MO 63105-3168
County: Saint Louis FICE Identification: 002457
Unit ID: 177092
Telephone: (314) 505-7000 Carnegie Class: Spec/Faith
FAX Number: (314) 505-7001 Calendar System: Quarter
URL: www.csl.edu
Established: 1839 Annual Graduate Tuition & Fees: $27,105
Enrollment: 602 Coed
Affiliation or Control: Lutheran Church - Missouri Synod IRS Status: 501(c)3
Highest Offering: Doctorate; No Undergraduates
Program: Professional; Religious Emphasis
Accreditation: NH, THEOL

01 President .... Dr. Dale A. MEYER
03 Executive Vice President .... Mr. Michael LOUIS
05 Provost .... Dr. Jeffrey KLOHA
10 Sr VP for Finance/Administration .... Mr. Chad A. CATTOOR
30 Senior VP for Advancement .... Mr. Paul GRAY
58 Dean of Advanced Studies .... Dr. Gerhard BODE
06 Registrar .... Mrs. Beth R. MENNEKE
08 Director of Library Services .... Rev. Benjamin HAUPT
51 Director Continuing Education .... Dr. Anthony COOK
88 Director Center for Hispanic Study .... Dr. Leopoldo A. SANCHEZ
15 Director of Human Resources .... Mr. Thomas MYERS
18 Director Facilities/Physical Plant .... Mr. Stephen B. MUDD
36 Director of Placement .... Rev. Wayne KNOLHOFF
37 Director of Student Financial Aid .... Mrs. Laura HEMMER
13 Chief Information Officer .... Mr. John KLINGER
29 Director of Alumni Relations .... Rev. Michael REDEKER
04 Executive Asst to President .... Mrs. Michelle CHRIST
07 Director of Admissions .... Rev. William WREDE
09 Director of Institutional Research .... Rev. Alan BORCHERDING

Cottey College (H)

1000 W Austin Boulevard, Nevada MO 64772-2763
County: Vernon FICE Identification: 002458
Unit ID: 177117
Telephone: (417) 667-8181 Carnegie Class: Assoc/PrivNFP
FAX Number: (417) 667-8103 Calendar System: Semester
URL: www.cottey.edu
Established: 1884 Annual Undergrad Tuition & Fees: $19,300
Enrollment: 270 Female
Affiliation or Control: Independent Non-Profit IRS Status: 501(c)3
Highest Offering: Baccalaureate
Program: 2-Year Principally Bachelor's Creditable; Liberal Arts And General; Fine Arts Emphasis
Accreditation: NH, MUS

01 President .... Dr. Jann WEITZE
05 Vice President for Academic Affairs .... Dr. Chioma R. UGOCHUKWU
88 Dir Center Women's Leadership .... Ms. Denise C. HEDGES
36 Coord Career & Transfer Planning .... Ms. Renee HAMPTON
04 Assistant to the President .... Mrs. Tricia BOBBETT
10 VP for Administration & Finance .... Mrs. Amy RUETTEN
30 VP for Institutional Advancement .... Vacant
32 VP for Student Life .... Dr. Mari Anne PHILLIPS
42 Dir Spiritual Life & Diversity .... Ms. Erica SIGAUKE
84 VP for Enrollment Management .... Vacant
07 Director of Admissions .... Ms. Judi STEEGE
06 Registrar .... Ms. Marcia MORTON
08 Library Director .... Ms. Courtney TRAUTWEILER
18 Director Physical Plant/Security .... Mr. Neal R. SWARNES
26 Director of Public Information .... Mr. Steve E. REED
15 Director of Human Resources .... Ms. Betsy A. MCREYNOLDS
91 Director Administratrive Computing .... Mr. Keith J. SPENCER
37 Director of Financial Aid .... Mrs. Sherry R. PENNINGTON
90 Director Academic Computing .... Mr. Adam S. DEAN
39 Director of Student Housing .... Ms. Helen LODGE
41 Director of Athletics .... Ms. Stephanie BEASON
40 Bookstore Manager .... Mrs. Lois J. WITTE
09 Coordinator Institutional Research .... Mrs. Nancy KERBS
29 Alumnae Relations Manager .... Ms. Tracy HASS CORDOVA
38 Coordinator of Counseling .... Ms. Jeanna BRAUER
44 Assoc VP for Marketing .... Ms. Carla FARMER
88 Director of Food Service .... Mr. Michael RICHARDSON
88 PEO Relations Manager .... Ms. Margaret HAVERSTIC
88 Coordinator Academic Advising .... Ms. Stephanie MCGHEE
85 Coord International Student Svcs .... Ms. Jennifer CORNWELL

Court Reporting Institute of St. Louis (I)

7730 Carondelet, Clayton MO 63105
County: Saint Louis Identification: 770617
Unit ID: 481766
Telephone: (314) 290-0200 Carnegie Class: Not Classified
FAX Number: (314) 721-4085 Calendar System: Quarter
URL: www.cri.edu
Established: Annual Undergrad Tuition & Fees: $13,000
Enrollment: 247 Coed
Affiliation or Control: Proprietary IRS Status: Proprietary
Highest Offering: Associate Degree
Program: 2-Year Principally Bachelor's Creditable; Technical Emphasis
Accreditation: ACICS

01 Campus Director .... Darrell JOY

Covenant Theological Seminary (J)

12330 Conway Road, Saint Louis MO 63141-8697
County: Saint Louis FICE Identification: 004707
Unit ID: 177126
Telephone: (314) 434-4044 Carnegie Class: Spec/Faith
FAX Number: (314) 434-4819 Calendar System: 4/1/4
URL: www.covenantseminary.edu
Established: 1956 Annual Graduate Tuition & Fees: $14,880
Enrollment: 541 Coed
Affiliation or Control: Presbyterian Church In America IRS Status: 501(c)3
Highest Offering: Doctorate; No Undergraduates
Program: Professional; Religious Emphasis
Accreditation: NH, THEOL

01 President .... Dr. Mark DALBEY
05 VP of Academic Administration .... Rev. Christopher FLORENCE
10 VP of Business and Finance .... Ms. Alice EVANS
30 VP of Advancement .... Mr. John RANHEIM
88 VP of Strategic Academic Projects .... Dr. Daniel DORIANI
88 Dean of Faculty .... Dr. Jay SKLAR
32 Dean of Students .... Rev. Michael HIGGINS
20 Dean of Academic Services .... Dr. Tasha CHAPMAN
18 Director of Facilities & Operations .... Mr. David BROWN
84 Sr Director of Enrollment Services .... Mr. Brian TIEMEIER
07 Director of Admissions .... Mr. John PATTON
08 Library Director .... Rev. James C. PAKALA
13 Director of Information Technology .... Mr. Richard HIERS
21 Controller .... Mr. Jason ROBEY
29 Alumni/Placement Services Director .... Mr. Joel HATHAWAY
37 Director of Financial Aid .... Ms. Melinda CONN
06 Registrar .... Ms. Betsy GASOSKE

Cox College (A)

1423 N Jefferson Avenue, Springfield MO 65802-1917
County: Greene FICE Identification: 020682
Unit ID: 176770
Telephone: (417) 269-3401 Carnegie Class: Spec/Health
FAX Number: (417) 269-3581 Calendar System: Semester
URL: www.coxcollege.edu
Established: 1995 Annual Undergrad Tuition & Fees: $12,480
Enrollment: 807 Coed
Affiliation or Control: Independent Non-Profit IRS Status: 501(c)3
Highest Offering: Master's
Program: Occupational; 2-Year Principally Bachelor's Creditable; Professional
Accreditation: NH, ADNUR, DIETI, DMS, NURSE, RAD

01 President .... Dr. Lance RATCLIFF
05 Vice President of Academic Affairs .... Dr. Amy DEMELO
09 Vice Pres College Svcs/Inst Rsrch .... Dr. Jim MOORE
10 Vice Pres Business/Finance .... Ms. Jayne BULLARD
97 Dean Gen Educ/Student Advancement .... Sonya HAYTER
58 Dean Interprof Graduate Studies .... Dr. Kathleen JACKSON
30 Exec Dir College Comm & Development .... Todd RUTLEDGE
21 Comptroller .... Deborah ADKINS
37 Director of Financial Aid .... Steve NICHOLS
07 Director of Admissions .... Lindy BIGLIENI
08 Director Library Services .... Wilma C. BUNCH

Crowder College (B)

601 Laclede Avenue, Neosho MO 64850-9165
County: Newton FICE Identification: 002459
Unit ID: 177135
Telephone: (417) 451-3223 Carnegie Class: Assoc/Pub-R-M
FAX Number: (417) 455-5702 Calendar System: Semester
URL: www.crowder.edu
Established: 1963 Annual Undergrad Tuition & Fees (In-District): $2,880
Enrollment: 5,710 Coed
Affiliation or Control: Local IRS Status: 501(c)3
Highest Offering: Associate Degree
Program: Occupational; 2-Year Principally Bachelor's Creditable
Accreditation: NH, ADNUR, CAHIIM, EMT, OTA

01 President .... Dr. Jennifer METHVIN
10 Vice President of Finance .... Mrs. Amy RAND
05 Vice President of Academic Affairs .... Dr. Glenn COLTHARP
32 Vice President of Student Affairs .... Mrs. Tiffany SLINKARD
27 Assoc VP of Information Services .... Mrs. Mickie MAHAN
75 Assoc VP of Careers & Tech Ed .... Mr. Edward STEPHENS
07 Director of Admissions .... Mr. Jim RIGGS
09 Director of Institutional Research .... Mrs. Bobbie AUGSPURGER
08 Director of Lee Library .... Mr. Eric DEATHERAGE
26 Director of Public Information .... Mrs. Cindy BROWN
41 Athletic Director .... Mr. John SISEMORE
37 Director of Financial Aid .... Mrs. Stephanie FERGUSON
15 Director of Human Resources .... Mrs. Michelle PAUL
25 Dir of Institutional Advancement .... Mrs. Cindy BRANSCUM
40 Bookstore Manager .... Ms. Colleen HOLLAND
36 Career Services Coordinator .... Vacant
13 Director of Information Technology .... Mr. Chris WOITOWITZ

Culver-Stockton College (C)

1 College Hill, Canton MO 63435-1257
County: Lewis FICE Identification: 002460
Unit ID: 177144
Telephone: (573) 288-6000 Carnegie Class: Bac/Diverse
FAX Number: (573) 288-6611 Calendar System: Semester
URL: www.culver.edu
Established: 1853 Annual Undergrad Tuition & Fees: $24,500
Enrollment: 971 Coed
Affiliation or Control: Christian Church (Disciples Of Christ)
IRS Status: 501(c)3
Highest Offering: Master's
Program: Liberal Arts And General; Teacher Preparatory; Professional
Accreditation: NH, CAATE, IACBE, MUS

01 President .... Dr. Kelly M. THOMPSON
05 Vice Pres Academic Affs/Dean of Col .... Dr. Daniel K. SILBER
32 Dean of Student Life .... Dr. D. Christopher GILL
07 Director of Admission .... Mrs. Misty MCBEE
30 Sr Director of Advancement & Alumni .... Mrs. Marjorie ELLISON
06 Registrar/Director Inst Research .... Mrs. Chris HUEBOTTER

08 Librarian .... Ms. Katherine MARNEY
26 Director of College Communications .... Ms. Jessica M. CATE
37 Director Financial Aid .... Mrs. Tina WISEMAN
29 Director of Alumni Programs .... Mrs. Jennifer SOUSA
91 Exec Dir Admin Systems & Service .... Mr. Joseph LIESEN
10 Chief Financial Officer .... Mrs. Diane BOZARTH
15 Director of Human Resources .... Mrs. Amy BAKER
35 Coordinator of Student Activities .... Mr. Bill BOXDORFER
42 Chaplain .... Rev. Amanda SORENSON
41 Athletic Director .... Mr. Patrick ATWELL
40 Wildcat Warehouse Manager .... Mrs. Sharon FARR
04 Assistant to the President .... Ms. Cindy FREELS
19 Director Campus Security & Facil .... Mr. Michael BRINGER
49 Chair Applied Liberal Arts/ Sciences .... Dr. Lauren SCHELLENBERGER
50 Chair Business Education & Law .... Dr. Kimberly GAITHER
57 Chair Fine Applied & Literary Arts .... Mr. Kent MILLER
88 Assoc Dean/Experiential Education .... Dr. Dell Ann JANNEY
92 Director of Honors Program .... Dr. Haidee HEATON
93 Director of Minority Students .... Dr. Mohamed EL-BERMAWY
24 Media Coordinator .... Mrs. Julie WRIGHT
44 Director of the Annual Fund .... Mr. Steve MILLER
36 Coord of Career Services/Internship .... Vacant
39 Director of Residential Life .... Ms. Megan CATALANO
20 Associate Dean Academic Success .... Dr. Holly ANDRESS-MARTIN
38 Dir Counseling/Student Wellness .... Ms. Susan MOON
09 Director of Institutional Research .... Mrs. Karla MCREYNOLDS
88 Director of Advancement Operations .... Mrs. Marjorie ELLISON
104 Director Study Abroad .... Dr. C. Patrick HOTLE

DeVry University - Kansas City Campus (D)

11224 Holmes Road, Kansas City MO 64131-3626
Telephone: (816) 943-7300 FICE Identification: 002455
Accreditation: &NH, ENGT

† Regional accreditation is carried under the parent institution in Downers Grove, IL.

Drury University (E)

900 N Benton Avenue, Springfield MO 65802-3791
County: Greene FICE Identification: 002461
Unit ID: 177214
Telephone: (417) 873-7879 Carnegie Class: Master's M
FAX Number: (417) 873-7529 Calendar System: Semester
URL: www.drury.edu
Established: 1873 Annual Undergrad Tuition & Fees: $23,750
Enrollment: 3,028 Coed
Affiliation or Control: Independent Non-Profit IRS Status: 501(c)3
Highest Offering: Master's
Program: Liberal Arts And General; Teacher Preparatory; Professional
Accreditation: NH, ACBSP, BUS, MUS, TED

01 President .... Dr. David MANUEL
05 Vice President for Academic Affairs .... Dr. Steven COMBS
11 Vice President for Administration .... Mr. Bill SCORSE
32 Vice President for Student Services .... Dr. Tijuana S. JULIAN
30 Vice Pres Alumni & Develop .... Ms. Dianne JOHNSON
10 Chief Financial Officer .... Mr. Rob FRIDGE
20 Assoc VP Academic Affairs .... Dr. Peter K. MEIDLINGER
84 Vice President Enrollment Mgt .... Mr. Jay FEDJE
51 Dean of Continuing Studies .... Mr. Aaron JONES
20 Assoc VP Academic Affairs .... Dr. Bruce CALLEN
06 Registrar .... Mrs. Cindy M. JONES
26 Exec Dir Marketing/Communications .... Ms. Jann HOLLAND
37 Director of Financial Aid .... Ms. Rebecca AHRENS
88 Director of Facilities Services .... Mr. Ron CUSHMAN
08 Director of Library/Info Services .... Mr. William GARVIN
36 Dir Career Development .... Ms. Emily BUCKMASTER
15 Director of Human Resources .... Ms. Scotti SIEBERT
09 Director of Institutional Research .... Vacant
38 Dir of Counseling/Student Devel .... Mr. Ed DERR
19 Director Safety/Security .... Ms. Sarene DEEDS
105 Director Web Communications .... Ms. Amanda SEAMAN
35 Director Student Affairs .... Ms. Emily GIVENS
39 Dir of Student Housing .... Ms. Holly BINDER
40 Director Univ Bookstore .... Ms. Valerie RAINS
41 Athletic Director .... Mr. Mark FISHER
42 Chaplain .... Dr. Peter BROWNING
04 Administrative Asst to President .... Ms. Donna HANLEY
101 Secretary of the Institution/Board .... Ms. Bonnie WILCOX
104 Director Study Abroad .... Dr. Thomas RUSSO
106 Dir Online Education/E-learning .... Mr. Steve HYNDS
50 Dean of Business Administration .... Dr. Robin SRONCE
53 Dean Sch of Educ & Child Develop .... Dr. Lauren EDMONDSON
91 Director Administrative Computing .... Mr. Val SERAFIMOV

Drury University Cabool Campus (F)

620 Peabody Avenue, Cabool MO 65689
Telephone: (417) 962-5314 Identification: 770318
Accreditation: &NH

† Branch campus of Drury University, Springfield, MO.

Drury University Ft. Leonard Wood Campus (G)

6002 Cikiradi Ave., Ft. Leonard Wood MO 65473
Telephone: (573) 329-4400 Identification: 770319
Accreditation: &NH

† Branch campus of Drury University, Springfield, MO.

Drury University Lebanon Campus (H)

PO Box 509, Lebanon MO 65536
Telephone: (417) 532-9828 Identification: 770320
Accreditation: &NH

† Branch campus of Drury University, Springfield, MO.

Drury University Rolla Campus (I)

1034 S. Bishop Avenue, Rolla MO 65401
Telephone: (573) 368-4959 Identification: 770321
Accreditation: &NH

† Branch campus of Drury University, Springfield, MO.

East Central College (J)

1964 Prairie Dell Road, Union MO 63084-0529
County: Franklin FICE Identification: 008862
Unit ID: 177250
Telephone: (636) 584-6500 Carnegie Class: Assoc/Pub-S-MC
FAX Number: (636) 583-1897 Calendar System: Semester
URL: www.eastcentral.edu
Established: 1968 Annual Undergrad Tuition & Fees (In-District): $2,850
Enrollment: 3,606 Coed
Affiliation or Control: Local IRS Status: 501(c)3
Highest Offering: Associate Degree
Program: Occupational; 2-Year Principally Bachelor's Creditable
Accreditation: NH, ACFEI, ART, CAHIIM, EMT, MAC, MUS, NAIT, OTA

01 President .... Dr. C. Jon BAUER
10 Vice Pres Finance/Administration .... Mr. Phil PENA
05 Vice President Instruction .... Ms. Jean A. MCCANN
32 Vice President Student Development .... Ms. Shelli R. ALLEN
88 VP External Relations .... Mr. Joel DOEPKER
12 Director ECC/Rolla & Sullivan .... Ms. Christina M. AYRES
30 Dir of Institutional Development .... Ms. Shannon M. GRUS
18 Director Facilities & Grounds .... Mr. Mark A. EATON
08 Director of Library Services .... Ms. Lisa M. FARRELL
96 Purchasing Manager .... Ms. Melissa D. POPP
83 Div Chair Educ/Humanities/Soc Sci .... Ms. Mary B. HUXEL
79 Div Chair Math & English .... Ms. Ann BOEHMER
81 Div Chair Science & Engineering .... Ms. Fatemeh NICHOLS
75 Division Chair Business & Industry .... Vacant
15 Director Human Resources .... Ms. Wendy HARTMANN
66 Director of Nursing/Allied Health .... Ms. Robyn C. WALTER
37 Director Financial Aid .... Ms. Karen GRIFFIN
06 Registrar .... Ms. Marcia BAILEY
21 Director Financial Svcs/Comptroller .... Ms. Shirley A. HOFSTETTER
09 Director of Institutional Research .... Ms. Bethany L. LOHDEN
26 Director of Public Relations .... Ms. Dorothy A. SCHOWE
13 Director Information Technology .... Mr. Doug HOUSTON
40 Bookstore/Mail/Imaging Coordinator .... Mr. Doug A. AGEE
36 Coordinator Advisement Services .... Mr. Paul LAMPE
103 Executive Director Workforce Devel .... Mr. Mardy LEATHERS
51 Coordinator Adult Educ & Literacy .... Ms. Alice WHALEN
24 Coordinator Instructional Design .... Mr. R. Chad BALDWIN
35 Coordinator Student Activities .... Vacant
04 Executive Asst to President .... Ms. Bonnie S. GARDNER
41 Athletic Director .... Mr. Jay MEHRHOFF

Eden Theological Seminary (K)

475 E Lockwood Avenue,
Webster Groves MO 63119-3192
County: Saint Louis FICE Identification: 002462
Unit ID: 177278
Telephone: (314) 961-3627 Carnegie Class: Spec/Faith
FAX Number: (314) 918-2626 Calendar System: 4/1/4
URL: www.eden.edu
Established: 1850 Annual Graduate Tuition & Fees: $16,530
Enrollment: 152 Coed
Affiliation or Control: United Church Of Christ IRS Status: 501(c)3
Highest Offering: Doctorate; No Undergraduates
Program: Professional; Religious Emphasis
Accreditation: NH, THEOL

01 President .... Dr. David M. GREENHAW
30 Vice Pres Institutional Advancement .... Mr. Bryce KRUG
05 Academic Dean .... Dr. Deborah KRAUSE
06 Registrar .... Ms. Michelle WOBBE
08 Director Eden Library .... Mr. Michael BODDY
07 Director of Admissions .... Rev. Tiffany PITTMAN
40 Director Eden Bookstore .... Ms. Hannah RICE
04 Admin Asst to the President .... Ms. Danita CARTER
15 Director of Human Resouces .... Ms. Denise STAUFFER
18 Director of Facilities .... Ms. Beverly SCANLON
85 Dir International Student Pgms .... Rev. Stephanie DELONG
101 Secretaty to Board of Trustees .... Ms. Denise STAUFFER
108 Director of Assessment .... Ms. Michelle WOBBE
32 Dean of Students .... Rev. Carol SHANKS

Evangel University (L)

1111 N Glenstone, Springfield MO 65802-2191
County: Greene FICE Identification: 002463
Unit ID: 177339
Telephone: (417) 865-2815 Carnegie Class: Bac/Diverse
FAX Number: (417) 865-9599 Calendar System: Semester
URL: www.evangel.edu
Established: 1955 Annual Undergrad Tuition & Fees: $21,436
Enrollment: 2,006 Coed
Affiliation or Control: Assemblies Of God Church IRS Status: 501(c)3

Highest Offering: Doctorate
Program: Liberal Arts And General; Teacher Preparatory
Accreditation: NH, CAATE, MUS, SW, TED

01 President .... Dr. Carol A. TAYLOR
10 Vice Pres for Business/Finance .... Ms. Linda ALLEN
32 VP for Student Development .... Dr. Sheri PHILLIPS
30 VP for University Advancement .... Dr. Michael KOLSTAD
05 VP for Academic Affairs/Provost .... Dr. Michael MCCORCLE
84 Vice Pres Enrollment Management .... Mr. Chris BELCHER
18 Director of Physical Plant .... Mr. Tom KELTNER
41 Interim Director of Athletics .... Mr. Brenton ILLUM
06 Registrar .... Mrs. Cathy WILLIAMS
27 Chief Information Officer .... Mr. Gary BLACKARD
08 Librarian .... Mr. Dale JENSEN
19 Director of Public Safety .... Mr. Roger MOORE
38 Director of Counseling Services .... Mr. Brian UPTON
29 Director Alumni Relations .... Mr. Chuck COX
37 Dir of Student Financial Services .... Mrs. Valerie SHARP
36 Career Development/Placement .... Mrs. Tina MOORE
42 Campus Pastor .... Rev. Greg JOHNS
26 Director of Public Relations .... Mr. Paul LOGSDON
07 Director of Admissions .... Mr. Josh CINCOTTA
23 Director of Health Services .... Ms. Susan BRYAN
21 Controller .... Mr. Jeff HUINDA
35 Director Student Life .... Miss Gina RENTSCHLER
15 Supervisor Human Resources .... Mrs. Ocki HAAS
39 Housing Coordinator .... Mrs. Pamela SMALLWOOD
09 Director of Institutional Research .... Dr. Linda WELLBORN
04 Executive Asst to President .... Mrs. Angela DENSE
101 Secretary of the Institution/Board .... Mrs. Joanne STROM

Everest College (A)

1010 W Sunshine, Springfield MO 65807-2488
County: Greene FICE Identification: 022506
Unit ID: 179070
Telephone: (417) 864-7220 Carnegie Class: Bac/Assoc
FAX Number: (417) 864-5697 Calendar System: Quarter
URL: www.everestcollege.com
Established: 1976 Annual Undergrad Tuition & Fees: $13,500
Enrollment: 232 Coed
Affiliation or Control: Proprietary IRS Status: Proprietary
Highest Offering: Baccalaureate
Program: Occupational; 2-Year Principally Bachelor's Creditable; Business Emphasis
Accreditation: ACICS, MAC

01 President .... Ms. Wendy WOOSLEY
05 Academic Dean .... Mr. Greg WEAVER
07 Director of Admissions .... Ms. Tricia WOODS
06 Registrar .... Ms. Roxanne KUTCH
37 Financial Aid Director .... Ms. Erica SEAMEN
10 Director of Student Accounts .... Ms. Brendy MERRILL
08 Librarian .... Mr. Trenton TUBBS

Fontbonne University (B)

6800 Wydown Boulevard, Saint Louis MO 63105-3098
County: Saint Louis FICE Identification: 002464
Unit ID: 177418
Telephone: (314) 862-3456 Carnegie Class: Master's L
FAX Number: (314) 889-1451 Calendar System: Semester
URL: www.fontbonne.edu
Established: 1923 Annual Undergrad Tuition & Fees: $23,790
Enrollment: 1,819 Coed
Affiliation or Control: Roman Catholic IRS Status: 501(c)3
Highest Offering: Master's
Program: Liberal Arts And General; Teacher Preparatory
Accreditation: NH, ACBSP, DIETD, SP, SW, TED

01 President .... Dr. J. Michael PRESSIMONE
05 Vice Pres for Academic Affairs .... Dr. Carey ADAMS
30 Vice President Inst Advancement .... Mrs. Kitty LOHRUM
32 Vice President Student Affairs .... Mr. Joseph DEIGHTON
10 Vice President Finance & Admin/CFO .... Dr. Gary L. ZACK
84 Vice President Enrollment Mgt .... Mr. Joseph HAVIS
13 Vice Pres Information Technology .... Mr. Mark FRANZ
35 Associate Vice Pres Student Affairs .... Ms. Carla HICKMAN
20 Associate VP Acad Affairs .... Dr. Heather NORTON
58 Director of Graduate Studies .... Dr. Heather NORTON
53 Dean of Education .... Dr. Gale RICE
50 Dean of Global Business & Prof Stds .... Mr. Jay JOHNSON
88 Asst to the Pres for Mission Integ .... Dr. Mary Beth GALLAGHER
06 Registrar .... Ms. Mazie MOORE
15 Director of Human Resources .... Ms. Linda PIPITONE
08 University Librarian .... Dr. Sharon MCCASLIN
45 Director of Academic Resources .... Vacant
09 Dir of Inst Research & Assessment .... Mrs. Meaghan ONG
26 Director Communications/Marketing .... Mr. Mark JOHNSON
106 Director of Online Program .... Ms. Jo MATTSON
37 Director of Financial Aid .... Mr. Matthew KEARNEY
88 Director of Academic Advising .... Ms. Lee DELAET
85 Director of International Affairs .... Ms. Rebecca GRANT BAHAN
29 Director of Alumni Relations .... Ms. Michelle SIEGEL
41 Director of Athletics .... Ms. Maria EFTINK
28 Director of Multicultural Affairs .... Ms. Leslie DOYLE
88 Dir Ldrshp Educ & Stdnt Activities .... Dr. Janelle DENSBERGER
42 Director of Campus Ministry .... Mrs. Lori HELFRICH
19 Director of Public Safety .... Mr. Larry VERTREES
21 Controller .... Mr. Dennis JOHNSON
07 Director of Admissions .... Ms. Michelle PALUMBO
18 Director Physical Plant .... Mr. Brent SPIES

Global University (C)

1211 South Glenstone Avenue,
Springfield MO 65804-1894
County: Greene Identification: 666687
Unit ID: 247296
Telephone: (800) 443-1083 Carnegie Class: Not Classified
FAX Number: (417) 865-7167 Calendar System: Other
URL: www.globaluniversity.edu
Established: 2000 Annual Undergrad Tuition & Fees: $4,449
Enrollment: 4,527 Coed
Affiliation or Control: Assemblies Of God Church IRS Status: 501(c)3
Highest Offering: Doctorate
Program: Occupational; 2-Year Principally Bachelor's Creditable; Liberal Arts And General; Professional; Religious Emphasis
Accreditation: NH, DEAC

01 President .... Dr. Gary SEEVERS, JR.
03 Executive Vice President .... Rev. Keith HEERMANN
05 Provost .... Dr. John (Jack) NILL
20 Vice Provost .... Dr. Randy HUDLUN
58 Graduate School Dean .... Dr. David DEGARMO
73 UG School of Bible & Theology .... Dr. Willard TEAGUE
13 VP Info Tech/Media Dept .... Mr. Wade PETTENGER
20 Dean of Education .... Rev. Brad AUSBURY
07 Director of Enrollment Services .... Rev. Todd WAGGONER
06 Registrar .... Mrs. Lynne KROH
10 Chief Financial Officer .... Mr. Mark PERRY
15 Director of Human Resources .... Ms. Jami NEMETI
04 Administrative Asst to President .... Ms. Kristin DEGARMO
08 Head Librarian .... Rev. Russ LANGFORD
09 Director of Institutional Research .... Rev. Brad AUSBURY
18 Chief Facilities/Physical Plant .... Mr. Bruce HAVENS
29 Director Alumni Relations .... Ms. Nicole VICARI

Goldfarb School of Nursing at Barnes-Jewish College (D)

4483 Duncan Avenue, Saint Louis MO 63110-1111
County: Saint Louis FICE Identification: 006389
Unit ID: 177719
Telephone: (314) 454-7055 Carnegie Class: Spec/Health
FAX Number: (314) 362-9250 Calendar System: Trimester
URL: www.barnesjewishcollege.edu
Established: 1902 Annual Undergrad Tuition & Fees: $29,975
Enrollment: 715 Coed
Affiliation or Control: Independent Non-Profit IRS Status: 501(c)3
Highest Offering: Doctorate
Program: Professional; Nursing Emphasis
Accreditation: NH, ANEST, NURSE

01 Dean .... Dr. Michael BLEICH
03 Assoc Dean for Practice Engagement .... Dr. Shirley A. THORN
10 Vice Dean for Finance/Admin .... Mr. Philip DANIELS
32 Vice Dean Stdnt Affairs/Diversity .... Dr. Michael WARD
46 Associate Dean for Research .... Dr. Jean DAVIS
05 Associate Dean Academic Affairs .... Dr. Gretchen DRINKARD
15 Vice Dean/HR .... Ms. Janet SANTOS
08 Library & Info Services Director .... Ms. Renee GORRELL
13 Information System Director .... Mr. Wade LEHDE
06 Registrar .... Vacant
84 Director Enrollment Mgmnt .... Mr. Jason CROWE
04 Administrative Asst to President .... Ms. Debbie METTLACH
29 Director Alumni Relations .... Dr. June COWELL-OATES

Graceland University (E)

1401 West Truman Road, Independence MO 64050-3434
Telephone: (816) 833-0524 Identification: 666262
Accreditation: &NH

† Regional accreditation is carried under the parent institution in Lamoni, IA.

Hannibal-LaGrange University (F)

2800 Palmyra Road, Hannibal MO 63401-1999
County: Marion FICE Identification: 009089
Unit ID: 177542
Telephone: (573) 221-3675 Carnegie Class: Bac/Diverse
FAX Number: (573) 221-6594 Calendar System: Semester
URL: www.hlg.edu
Established: 1858 Annual Undergrad Tuition & Fees: $21,110
Enrollment: 1,216 Coed
Affiliation or Control: Southern Baptist IRS Status: 501(c)3
Highest Offering: Master's
Program: Liberal Arts And General; Teacher Preparatory; Professional
Accreditation: NH, ADNUR, NURSE

01 President .... Dr. Anthony W. ALLEN
05 VP for Academic Administration .... Dr. Miles S. MULLIN, II
45 VP for Institutional Effectiveness .... Dr. Raymond W. CARTY
84 VP for Enrollment Management .... Dr. Raymond M. SUMMERLIN
10 VP for Business & Finance .... Mrs. Betty L. ANDERSON
30 VP for Institutional Advancement .... Mr. Jason GEIKEN
32 Dean of Student Development .... Mr. Bradley D. NEWBOLD
26 Director Public Relations .... Mrs. Carolyn A. CARPENTER
06 Registrar/Director of Records .... Ms. Beth A. CRUM
37 Director of Financial Aid .... Mr. Brice D. BAUMGARDNER
29 Director Alumni Services .... Ms. Lauren YOUSE
36 Director Student Placement .... Dr. Karry D. RICHARDSON

08 Library Director .... Mrs. Julie A. ANDRESEN
18 Chief Facilities/Physical Plant .... Mr. Kevin RUSHING
19 Director Public Safety .... Mr. Albert HIGDON
39 Director of Residential Life .... Mr. Joshua PIERCE
41 Athletic Director .... Mr. Jason D. NICHOLS
40 University Bookstore Manager .... Mrs. Susan A. BOOTH

Harris-Stowe State University (G)

3026 Laclede Avenue, Saint Louis MO 63103-2199
County: Independent City FICE Identification: 002466
Unit ID: 177551
Telephone: (314) 340-3366 Carnegie Class: Bac/Diverse
FAX Number: (314) 340-3399 Calendar System: Semester
URL: www.hssu.edu
Established: 1857 Annual Undergrad Tuition & Fees (In-State): $4,926
Enrollment: 1,280 Coed
Affiliation or Control: State IRS Status: 501(c)3
Highest Offering: Baccalaureate
Program: Liberal Arts And General; Teacher Preparatory; Professional; Business Emphasis
Accreditation: NH, ACBSP, IACBE, TED

01 President .... Dr. Dwaun WARMACK
05 Provost & VP Academic Affairs .... Dr. Dwayne SMITH
10 VP for Administration & Finance .... Vacant
26 Exec Dir Instittutional Advancement .... Ms. Leslie HOLLOWAY
06 Registrar .... Ms. Chauvette MCELMURRY
84 Exec Dir Enrollment Management .... Mr. Reynolda BROWN
08 Director Library Services .... Mrs. Barbara NOBLE
37 Director of Financial Aid .... Mr. James GREEN
15 Director Human Resources .... Mrs. Tammy KIMBROUGH
38 Director Counseling Services .... Mrs. Vicki BERNARD
56 Exec Dir Title III/Sponsored Pgms .... Mrs. Heather BOSTIC
20 Dir Center for Excel & Retention .... Vacant
41 Director of Athletics .... Mr. Jamaal MAYO
18 Director of Physical Plant .... Vacant
88 Director of Business Services .... Ms. Barbara A. MORROW
13 VP Strategic Plan & IT Services .... Mr. James FOGT
36 Director of Career Services .... Mrs. Wanda MCNEIL
21 Comptroller/Grants Officer .... Mr. Brian HUGGINS
38 Dean of Student Success .... Mr. Emmanuel LALANDE
53 Dean College of Education .... Vacant
50 Dean Busch School of Business .... Ms. Fatemeh ZAKERY
49 Dean College of Arts & Sciences .... Dr. Lateef ADELANI
101 Secretary of the Institution/Board .... Mrs. Lea SUTHERLIN
19 Director Security/Safety .... Vacant
30 Chief Development/Advancement .... Ms. Leslie HOLLOWAY
32 Chief Student Affairs/Student Life .... Mr. Emmanuel LALANDE

Heartland Christian College (H)

500 New Creation Rd, Newark MO 63458
County: Knox Identification: 667091
Telephone: (660) 284-4800 Carnegie Class: Not Classified
FAX Number: (680) 284-4098 Calendar System: Semester
URL: www.heartlandcollege.org
Established: 1992 Annual Undergrad Tuition & Fees: $1,185
Enrollment: 34 Coed
Affiliation or Control: Non-denominational IRS Status: 501(c)3
Highest Offering: Associate Degree
Program: 2-Year Principally Bachelor's Creditable; Religious Emphasis
Accreditation: @BI

01 President .... Kris R. PALMER
05 Chief Academic Officer .... Martha PALMER
10 CFO .... David BARTON
06 Registrar .... Judi BARTON
08 Head Librarian .... Molly NICKERSON

Heritage College (I)

1200 E 104th Street, Suite 300,
Kansas City MO 64131-4557
Telephone: (816) 942-5474 Identification: 666155
Accreditation: ABHES

† Branch campus of Heritage College, Denver, CO.

Hickey College (J)

2700 North Lindbergh Boulevard, Saint Louis MO 63114
County: Saint Louis FICE Identification: 010279
Unit ID: 177579
Telephone: (314) 434-2212 Carnegie Class: Bac/Assoc
FAX Number: (314) 434-1974 Calendar System: Other
URL: www.hickeycollege.edu
Established: 1933 Annual Undergrad Tuition & Fees: $13,850
Enrollment: 415 Coed
Affiliation or Control: Proprietary IRS Status: Proprietary
Highest Offering: Baccalaureate
Program: Business Emphasis
Accreditation: ACICS, ACFEI

01 President .... Mr. Christopher A. GEARIN
11 Director of Operations .... Mr. Ken SIMONS
05 Director of Education .... Ms. Connie L. SCOTT
32 Director of Student Services .... Ms. Deanna L. PECORONI
07 Director of Admissions .... Mr. Bill E. LEWIS

ITT Technical Institute (A)

1930 Meyer Drury Drive, Arnold MO 63010-6004
Telephone: (636) 464-6600 Identification: 666033
Accreditation: ACICS

† Branch campus of ITT Technical Institute, Indianapolis, IN.

ITT Technical Institute (B)

3640 Corporate Trail Drive, Earth City MO 63045-1122
Telephone: (314) 298-7800 FICE Identification: 007557
Accreditation: ACICS

† Branch campus of ITT Technical Institute, Indianapolis, IN.

ITT Technical Institute (C)

9150 East 41st Terrace, Kansas City MO 64133-1448
Telephone: (816) 276-1400 Identification: 666380
Accreditation: ACICS

† Branch campus of ITT Technical Institute, Indianapolis, IN.

ITT Technical Institute (D)

3216 South National Avenue, Springfield MO 65807
Telephone: (417) 877-4800 Identification: 666702
Accreditation: ACICS

† Branch campus of ITT Technical Institute, Indianapolis, IN.

Jefferson College (E)

1000 Viking Drive, Hillsboro MO 63050-2441
County: Jefferson FICE Identification: 002468
Unit ID: 177676
Telephone: (636) 797-3000 Carnegie Class: Assoc/Pub-S-MC
FAX Number: (636) 789-4012 Calendar System: Semester
URL: www.jeffco.edu
Established: 1963 Annual Undergrad Tuition & Fees (In-District): $3,000
Enrollment: 4,918 Coed
Affiliation or Control: State/Local IRS Status: 501(c)3
Highest Offering: Associate Degree
Program: Occupational; 2-Year Principally Bachelor's Creditable
Accreditation: NH, OTA, PTAA, RAD

01 President .... Dr. Raymond V. CUMMISKEY
05 VP Instruction .... Dr. Caron DAUGHERTY
10 VP Finance & Administration .... Mr. Daryl GEHBAUER
32 Associate VP Student Services .... Ms. Julie FRASER
49 Dean of Arts & Sciences .... Ms. Shirley DAVENPORT
75 Dean Career/Technical Ed .... Dr. Dena MCCAFFREY
15 Director of Human Resources .... Ms. Tasha D. WELSH
26 Director of PR & Marketing .... Mr. Roger A. BARRENTINE
81 Division Chair Math/Sci/Business .... Ms. Linda ABERNATHY
83 Division Chair Social Sciences .... Dr. Sandy FREY
60 Division Chair Comm/Fine Arts .... Dr. Michael BOOKER
75 Div Chair Business/Technical Educ .... Mr. Christopher DEGEARE
35 Director Student Support Services .... Ms. Diane ARNZEN
21 Controller .... Mr. Richard H. HARDIN
41 Director Athletics .... Mr. Greg MCVEY
31 Director Business & Community Devel .... Mr. Bryan D. HERRICK
12 Director Outreach/Educational Sites .... Ms. Patricia AUMANN
08 Director Library Services .... Ms. Lisa PRITCHARD
90 Dir Online Learning/Inst Tech .... Mr. Allan A. WAMSLEY
18 Director Buildings & Grounds .... Mr. Ed TOMASZKIEWICZ
96 Procurement Coordinator .... Ms. Sheree BELL
13 Director Information Technology .... Mr. Tracy JAMES
74 Director Veterinary Technology .... Ms. Dana A. NEVOIS
88 Director Child Care Center .... Ms. Sandra K. BASLER
76 Director Health Occupation Programs .... Mr. Kenny WILSON
06 Director Admissions/Student Records .... Dr. Kim M. HARVEY
37 Director Student Financial Services .... Ms. Sarah BRIGHT
66 Director of Nursing .... Ms. Linda BOEVINGLOH
38 Director Advising & Retention .... Ms. Kathy JOHNSTON
39 Director Residential & Student Life .... Ms. Kristen YELTON
09 Resarch Analyst .... Ms. Joan WARREN
19 Director Public Safety Programs .... Ms. Diane SCANGA
04 Admin Asst to the President & Board .... Ms. Lisa VINYARD

Kansas City Art Institute (F)

4415 Warwick Boulevard, Kansas City MO 64111-1874
County: Jackson FICE Identification: 002473
Unit ID: 177746
Telephone: (816) 472-4852 Carnegie Class: Spec/Arts
FAX Number: (816) 472-3439 Calendar System: Semester
URL: www.kcai.edu
Established: 1885 Annual Undergrad Tuition & Fees: $35,120
Enrollment: 618 Coed
Affiliation or Control: Independent Non-Profit IRS Status: 501(c)3
Highest Offering: Baccalaureate
Program: Fine Arts Emphasis
Accreditation: NH, ART

01 Interim President .... Mr. Tony JONES
10 Int VP for Administration/CFO .... Ms. Laura SNOW
05 Vice President for Academic Affairs .... Dr. Bambi BURGARD
30 Vice President for Advancement .... Ms. Nicolle RATLIFF
07 Director of Admissions .... Ms. Julia WELLES
26 Vice President for Communications .... Vacant
13 Vice Pres/Chief Information Officer .... Mr. Larry DICKERSON
20 Assoc Vice Pres Academic Affairs .... Mr. Milton KATZ
51 Dir Continuing/Professional Studies .... Ms. Sonja GARRETT
06 Registrar .... Ms. Nancy EASTMAN
15 Director of Human Resources .... Vacant
18 Facilities Director/Plant Services .... Mr. Larry STUCKEY
29 Director of Alumni Relations .... Mr. Marcus CAIN
37 Director of Financial Aid .... Ms. Darci WEBSTER
21 Controller .... Ms. Suzette NAYLOR
36 Dir of Acad Advising & Career Svcs .... Ms. Tori SINCLAIR
08 Director of Library .... Ms. M.J POEHLER
32 Dean of Student Affairs .... Ms. Gina GOLBA
24 Director of Media Center .... Mr. Aldo BACCHETTA
19 Director of Safety & Security .... Mr. Robert BAYLESS
109 Director of Auxiliary Services .... Mr. Ed RODRIGUEZ
88 Director of Block Artspace Gallery .... Ms. Raechell SMITH

Kansas City University of Medicine & Biosciences (G)

1750 East Independence Avenue, Kansas City MO 64119
County: Jackson FICE Identification: 002474
Unit ID: 179812
Telephone: (816) 654-7000 Carnegie Class: Spec/Med
FAX Number: (816) 654-7101 Calendar System: Semester
URL: www.kcumb.edu
Established: 1916 Annual Graduate Tuition & Fees: $43,288
Enrollment: 1,064 Coed
Affiliation or Control: Independent Non-Profit IRS Status: 501(c)3
Highest Offering: First Professional Degree; No Undergraduates
Program: Professional
Accreditation: NH, OSTEO

01 President & CEO .... Dr. Marc B. HAHN
05 Exec VP Acad & Med Affairs/Dean COM .... Dr. Bruce D. DUBIN
30 Vice Pres for Advancement .... Dr. Jane LAMPO
10 Director of Finance & Admin .... Mr. Pete STOBIE
20 Sr Assoc Dean Clin Educ & Med Affs .... Dr. John DOUGHERTY
21 Chief Financial Officer .... Mr. Joseph MASSMAN
20 Assoc Dean for Curriculum Affairs .... Ms. Linda ADKISON
32 Vice Prov Student/Enrollment Svcs .... Dr. Richard P. WINSLOW
35 Asst Dean for Student Affairs .... Ms. LeAnn K. CARLTON
08 Director of Libraries .... Miss Marilyn J. DEGEUS
15 Dir of Human Resources .... Ms. Sarah TATE
18 Facilities Manager .... Ms. Anna GRAETHER
96 Director of Purchasing .... Ms. Carrie L. SIMSHEUSER
13 Interim Chief Information Officer .... Mr. Lance HUGGINS
37 Asst Director Financial Aid .... Mr. Jerry BELCHER
88 Adm Dir Community Clin Educ .... Ms. Valorie L. MILLICAN
19 Director Security .... Mr. James HERRINGTON
28 Director Learning Enhancement .... Mr. Stan VIEBROCK
29 Asst Director of Alumni Programs .... Mr. Patrick ALLEN
35 Exec Dir Comm of Student Affairs .... Ms. Sara E. SELKIRK
09 Exec Dir Institutional/Acad Rsrch .... Dr. Maria COLE
76 Dean of College of Biosciences .... Dr. Douglas R. RUSHING
76 Assoc Dean College of Biosciences .... Dr. Robert E. STEPHENS
24 Instructional Tech Media Technician .... Mr. Wade W. GLOSSER
07 Director Admissions .... Ms. Patricia HARPER

Kenrick-Glennon Seminary-Kenrick School of Theology (H)

5200 Glennon Drive, Saint Louis MO 63119-4399
County: Saint Louis FICE Identification: 002476
Unit ID: 177816
Telephone: (314) 792-6100 Carnegie Class: Spec/Faith
FAX Number: (314) 792-6500 Calendar System: Semester
URL: www.kenrick.edu
Established: 1893 Annual Undergrad Tuition & Fees: $35,310
Enrollment: 136 Male
Affiliation or Control: Roman Catholic IRS Status: 501(c)3
Highest Offering: Master's
Program: Professional; Religious Emphasis
Accreditation: NH, THEOL

01 President/Rector .... Rev. James MASON
42 Dir Pre-Theology/Vice Rector .... Msgr. Gregory MIKESCH
05 Academic Dean .... Dr. John GRESHAM
32 Dean of Seminarians .... Rev. Paul HOESING
08 Director of Library .... Ms. Mary Ann AUBIN
88 Director of Spiritual Formation .... Rev. Mark KRAMER, SJ
42 Director of Worship .... Rev. Donald ANSTOETTER
30 Director of Development .... Ms. Kate GUYOL
06 Registrar/Financial Aid .... Deacon Joseph MEIERGERD
18 Chief Facilities/Physical Plant .... Mr. Gerry KLAAS
04 Administrative Asst to President .... Ms. Mary Ann FOX
10 Chief Business Officer .... Mr. Greg NOVAK

L'Ecole Culinaire (I)

9811 South Forty Drive, Saint Louis MO 63124
Telephone: (314) 587-2433 Identification: 666275
Accreditation: ACCSC, ACFEI

† Branch campus of Vatterott College, Des Moines, IA.

L'Ecole Culinaire Kansas City (J)

310 Ward Parkway, Kansas City MO 64112
Telephone: (816) 627-0100 Identification: 770579
Accreditation: ACCSC

† Branch campus of Vatterott College-Des Moines, Des Moines, IA.

Lincoln University (K)

820 Chestnut Street, Jefferson City MO 65101-3537
County: Cole FICE Identification: 002479
Unit ID: 177940
Telephone: (573) 681-5000 Carnegie Class: Master's S
FAX Number: (573) 681-5566 Calendar System: Semester
URL: www.lincolnu.edu
Established: 1866 Annual Undergrad Tuition & Fees (In-State): $7,042
Enrollment: 3,117 Coed
Affiliation or Control: State IRS Status: 501(c)3
Highest Offering: Beyond Master's But Less Than Doctorate
Program: 2-Year Principally Bachelor's Creditable; Liberal Arts And General; Teacher Preparatory; Professional; Music Emphasis
Accreditation: NH, ACBSP, ADNUR, MUS, NUR, SURGT, SW, TED

01 President .... Dr. Kevin D. ROME
11 Dean Administration/Student Affairs .... Dr. Jerome OFFORD, JR.
05 VP Academic Affairs/Provost .... Dr. Said SEWELL
30 Exec Director of Philanthropy .... Mr. Willie JUDE
83 Dean College of Arts & Sciences .... Dr. Ruthie STURDEVANT
107 Dean Col of Professional Studies .... Dr. Linda S. BICKEL
47 Interim Dean of Ag/Natural Sciences .... Dr. Albert ESSEL
08 University Librarian .... Dr. Rinalda FARRAR
10 Chief Financial Officer .... Mrs. Sandy KOETTING
51 Director Continuing Education .... Mr. Brandon HILDRETH
15 Director Human Resources .... Mr. James MARCANTONIO
18 Director of Facilities and Planning .... Mrs. Sheila GASSNER
19 Director Police Department .... Mr. Bill NELSON
41 Interim Director of Athletics .... Mr. John MOSELEY
29 Director Alumni Affairs .... Mrs. Sylvia WILSON
26 Director of University Relations .... Ms. Misty YOUNG
06 Director of Records/Registrar .... Ms. Liz MORROW
36 Director Career & Academic Support .... Mrs. Ruth CANADA
07 Director of Admissions .... Ms. Annette CROWDER
09 Director Ctr Assess/Inst Rsrch .... Mrs. Beth NOLTE
23 Director Student Health Services .... Vacant
32 Director of Student Activities .... Vacant
43 Director Legal Svcs/Genl Counsel .... Mr. Kent BROWN
37 Dir Financial Aid/Stdnt Employment .... Mr. Alfred L. ROBINSON
96 Director of Purchasing .... Ms. Debra KIDWELL
13 Chief Information Officer .... Dr. Kevin HARRIS
39 Director of Residential Life .... Mr. Khalilah DOSS
12 Director Fort Leonard Wood Site .... Mrs. Barbara LANE
24 Dir of Center Teaching/Learning .... Dr. Rachel SALE
40 Manager LU Bookstore .... Mr. James HOWARD
101 Exec Asst to President & Curators .... Ms. Rose Ann ORTMEYER
85 International Student Advisor .... Mr. Duwon CLARK
105 Web Content Manager .... Mr. Derek SCHWARTZE
22 Dir Affirmative Action/EEO .... Mr. James MARCANTONIO

Lindenwood University (L)

209 S Kingshighway, Saint Charles MO 63301-1695
County: Saint Charles FICE Identification: 002480
Unit ID: 177968
Telephone: (636) 949-2000 Carnegie Class: Master's L
FAX Number: (636) 949-4910 Calendar System: Semester
URL: www.lindenwood.edu
Established: 1827 Annual Undergrad Tuition & Fees: $15,640
Enrollment: 12,151 Coed
Affiliation or Control: Independent Non-Profit IRS Status: 501(c)3
Highest Offering: Doctorate
Program: Liberal Arts And General; Teacher Preparatory; Professional
Accreditation: NH, ACBSP, CAATE, SW, @TEAC

01 President .... Dr. Michael D. SHONROCK
04 Exec Asst Pres & Asst Secy to BOD .... Mrs. Stefani M. SCHUETTE
05 Acting Provost .... Dr. Marilyn ABBOTT
11 Vice Pres Operations/Finance & COO .... Ms. Julie MUELLER
30 Vice Pres Institutional Advancement .... Dr. Susan MANGELS
32 Vice President Student Development .... Dr. Ryan GUFFEY
15 Vice Pres Human Resources .... Dr. Deb AYRES
84 Vice Pres for Enrollment Management .... Dr. Joe PARISI
12 President Belleville Campus .... Mr. Jerry BLADDICK
09 Dean of Institutional Research .... Dr. Jeannie THIES
06 Registrar .... Ms. Christine HANNAR
10 Chief Financial Officer .... Dr. Greg PHELPS
29 Director Alumni Relations .... Ms. Elizabeth WIKOFF
26 Dir Community & Public Relations .... Mr. Scott QUEEN
31 Director Community Development .... Ms. Charlsie FLOYD
13 Chief Information Director .... Mr. Shawn HAGHIGHI
08 Dean of Library Services .... Ms. Elizabeth MACDONALD
37 Director of Financial Aid .... Ms. Lori BODE
35 Dir of Student Life & Leadership .... Ms. Angela ROYAL
35 Dean of Students .... Mr. Terry RUSSELL
39 Director of Student Housing .... Ms. Michelle GIESSMAN
92 Director of Honors Program .... Dr. Michael WHALEY
43 In-House Legal Counsel .... Mr. Eric STUHLER
102 Dir Corporate Relations .... Ms. Jessica GATEWOOD
86 Dir of Outreach & Govt Relations .... Vacant
109 Director of Auxiliary Services .... Mr. David DICKHERBER
22 Director of Compliance .... Ms. Anna GIRDWOOD
89 Dean First Year Programs .... Dr. Shane WILLIAMSON
51 Dean Distance Learning .... Mr. Willie BROUSSARD
88 Dean of American Studies .... Dr. David KNOTTS
20 Dean of Academic Services .... Mr. Barry FINNEGAN
55 Dean Evening/Ext Campus Admissions .... Vacant
36 Director of Career Placement .... Ms. Dana WEHRLI
41 Dean of Intercol Ath & Rec Sports .... Mr. John CREER
42 Chaplain .... Mr. Timothy BUTLER
79 School Dean Humanities .... Dr. Michael WHALEY

81 School Dean Sciences .... Dr. Ricardo DELGADO
53 School Dean Education .... Dr. Cynthia BICE
57 School Dean Fine & Performing Arts .... Mr. Joe ALSOBROOK
50 Sch Dean Business/Entrepreneurship .... Dr. Roger ELLIS
60 School Dean Communications .... Mr. Mike WALL
83 School Dean Human Services .... Dr. Carla MUELLER
51 School Dean LCIE(Adult Learning) .... Dr. Gina GANAHL
68 Sch Dean Sport/Rec/Exercise Science ... Dr. Cynthia SCHROEDER
108 Chief Assessment Officer .... Dr. David WILSON
19 Director Security/Safety .... Mr. John BOWMANN
25 Chief Contracts/Grants Admin .... Ms. Vicki SCHRADER
44 Director Annual or Planned Giving .... Ms. Donna BABER

Logan University (A)

1851 Schoettler Road, Chesterfield MO 63017

County: Saint Louis FICE Identification: 004703
Unit ID: 177986
Telephone: (800) 782-3344 Carnegie Class: Spec/Health
FAX Number: (636) 207-2424 Calendar System: Trimester
URL: www.logan.edu
Established: 1935 Annual Undergrad Tuition & Fees: $10,320
Enrollment: 899 Coed
Affiliation or Control: Independent Non-Profit IRS Status: 501(c)3
Highest Offering: First Professional Degree
Program: Professional
Accreditation: NH, CHIRO

01 President .... Dr. Clay MCDONALD
05 VP Academic Affairs .... Dr. Kimberly PADDOCK-O'REILLY
84 VP Enrollment Management .... Dr. Boyd BRADSHAW
30 VP Chiropractic/Alumni Relations .... Dr. Ralph BARRALE
43 Gen Counsel/VP Strategic Perf .... Ms. Laura MCLAUGHLIN
10 Chief Financial Officer .... Mr. Adil KHAN
13 Chief Information Officer .... Dr. Bradley HOUGH
107 Dean College of Chiropractic .... Dr. Vincent DEBONO
76 Dean College of Health Sciences .... Dr. Sherri COLE
17 Dean of Clinics .... Dr. Muriel PERILLAT
32 Dean of Students .... Dr. Shelley SAWALICH
88 Director Logan Health Centers .... Dr. Michael WITTMER
88 Dir Human Perf Ctr/Sports Rehab Pgm .... Dr. David PARISH
88 Director Integrated Health Centers .... Dr. Barry WIESE
23 Director of Student Health Centers .... Dr. Eugene SPILKER
76 Director of Science & Nutrition .... Dr. Robert DAVIDSON
14 Associate VP for Educational Tech .... Mr. Vincent J. MCGEE
21 Controller .... Ms. Lori FULFORD
26 Director Marketing/Public Relations .... Ms. Jennifer R. REED
108 Director of Academic Assessment .... Dr. Martha KAESER
07 Asst VP Admissions & Development .... Ms. Stacey TILL
29 Director Alumni and Friends House .... Ms. Barb CRONIN
06 Registrar .... Mr. John-Herbert JAFFRY
41 Director Sports and Activities .... Mr. Robert POWELL
37 Director Financial Aid .... Ms. Kerry HALLAHAN
08 Director Learning Resource Center .... Ms. Ellen DICKMAN
15 Director of Human Resources .... Ms. Shelly CHANITZ
96 Director of Purchasing .... Mr. Charles FELTMANN
18 Physical Plant Superintendent .... Mr. Bill WHARTON
09 Director of Strategic Performance .... Ms. Laurinda SMITH
38 Director Counseling and Psych Svcs .... Dr. Jameca FALCONER
04 Executive Secretary .... Ms. Haydee MANONI

Maryville University of Saint Louis (B)

650 Maryville University Drive,
Saint Louis MO 63141-7299

County: Saint Louis FICE Identification: 002482
Unit ID: 178059
Telephone: (314) 529-9300 Carnegie Class: DRU
FAX Number: (314) 542-9085 Calendar System: Semester
URL: www.maryville.edu
Established: 1872 Annual Undergrad Tuition & Fees: $26,958
Enrollment: 5,931 Coed
Affiliation or Control: Independent Non-Profit IRS Status: 501(c)3
Highest Offering: Doctorate
Program: Liberal Arts And General; Teacher Preparatory; Professional
Accreditation: NH, ACBSP, ART, CIDA, CORE, MUS, NURSE, OT, PTA, TED

01 President .... Dr. Mark LOMBARDI
05 Vice Pres Academic Affairs .... Dr. Mary Ellen FINCH
45 VP of Planning/Research/Tech .... Mr. Jerry BRISSON
10 Vice Pres Finance & Facilities .... Mr. Steve MANDEVILLE
84 Vice President Enrollment .... Mr. Jeffrey MILLER
30 VP Inst Advancemnt & Chief Dev Ofcr .... Mr. Thomas ESCHEN
32 VP for Student Life .... Dr. Nina CALDWELL
20 Associate VP Academic Affairs .... Dr. Tammy GOCIAL
100 Chief of Staff .... Ms. Kathy LUNAN
50 Dean School of Business .... Dr. Melissa GRISWOLD
53 Dean School of Education .... Dr. Catherine BEAR
76 Dean School Health Professions .... Dr. Charles GULAS
49 Dean College Arts & Sciences .... Ms. Cherie FISTER
08 Dean University Library .... Dr. Eugenia MCKEE
106 Dean Adult & Online Education .... Mr. Dan VIELE
06 Exec Dir Student Svcs Ctr .... Ms. Stephanie ELFRINK
88 Dir Acad Advising & Life Coaching .... Ms. Kelly MOCK
07 Assoc VP Enrollment .... Ms. Shani LENORE-JENKINS
29 Director of Alumni Affairs .... Ms. Erin VERRY
41 Director of Athletics .... Mr. Marcus MANNING
42 Dir Campus Ministry & Comm Service .... Mr. Stephen DISALVO
35 Dean of Students .... Ms. Kathy QUINN
36 Director Career & Prof Development .... Ms. Leigh DEUSINGER
35 Asst Dean/Dir Student Involvement .... Mr. Brian GARDNER
21 Controller/Dir Finance .... Ms. Nikki PAYNE
102 Director of Development .... Ms. Megan HOLMES
37 Dir Student Svcs Ctr/Financial Aid .... Ms. Martha HARBAUGH
23 Director of Health & Wellness .... Ms. Pamela CULLITON
22 Assoc Dean/Affirm Action Officer .... Dr. Christie CRUISE
13 Director Technology Services .... Mr. Richard KUBB
91 Dir Enterprise Information Systems .... Mr. David SCHULTE
09 Director Institutional Research .... Ms. Mary MERRIFIELD
90 Dir Learning Design & Technology .... Ms. Pamela BRYAN WILLIAMS
26 VP Integrated Mktg & Communications .... Ms. Marcia SULLIVAN
18 Director of Physical Plant .... Mr. Tom BENNING
44 Director of Planned Gifts .... Mr. Mark ROOCK
102 Dir Foundation/Corp Relations .... Ms. Peggy MICHELSON
19 Director of Public Safety .... Mr. Michael PARKINSON
39 Director of Residential Life .... Ms. Amy HOWARD
88 VP for Student Success .... Dr. Jennifer MCCLUSKEY
104 Assoc VP/Dir Ctr for Global Educ .... Dr. James HARF
88 Asst Athletic Dir-Communications .... Mr. Charles YAHNG
53 Assoc Dean & Dir Teacher Education .... Dr. Mascheal SCHAPPE
21 Dir Student Svcs Ctr/Student Accts .... Ms. DJuana KING
88 Director Fresh Ideas Food Services .... Ms. Linda THACKER
38 Director Personal Counseling .... Ms. Jennifer HENRY
44 Director of Development .... Ms. Fay FETICK
88 Assoc VP Ctr for Institution Values .... Dr. Alden CRADDOCK
04 Administrative Asst to President .... Ms. Jan JOHNSTON
109 Director of Auxiliary Operations .... Ms. Laura STEVENS

Metro Business College (C)

1732 N Kingshighway, Cape Girardeau MO 63701-2122

County: Cape FICE Identification: 021802
Unit ID: 178110
Telephone: (573) 334-9181 Carnegie Class: Assoc/PrivFP
FAX Number: (573) 334-0617 Calendar System: Quarter
URL: www.metrobusinesscollege.edu
Established: 1981 Annual Undergrad Tuition & Fees: $15,000
Enrollment: 110 Coed
Affiliation or Control: Proprietary IRS Status: Proprietary
Highest Offering: Associate Degree
Program: Occupational; 2-Year Principally Bachelor's Creditable; Business Emphasis
Accreditation: ACICS

01 President .... Ms. Mary BUCKLEY
12 Campus Director .... Mrs. Jan REIMANN
05 Education Director .... Mr. Shannon BUFORD
37 Financial Aid Director .... Mrs. Janie WARNE
36 Career Services Coordinator .... Ms. Diane JORDAN

Metro Business College (D)

210 El Mercado Plaza, Jefferson City MO 65109
Telephone: (573) 635-6600 Identification: 666454
Accreditation: ACICS

† Branch campus of Metro Business College, Cape Girardeau, MO.

Metro Business College (E)

1202 E Highway 72, Rolla MO 65401-3938
Telephone: (573) 364-8464 Identification: 666455
Accreditation: ACICS

† Branch campus of Metro Business College, Cape Girardeau, MO.

*Metropolitan Community College - Kansas City Administrative Center (F)

3200 Broadway, Kansas City MO 64111-2429

County: Jackson FICE Identification: 009137
Unit ID: 178129
Telephone: (816) 604-1000 Carnegie Class: N/A
FAX Number: (816) 759-1158
URL: www.mcckc.edu

01 Chancellor .... Mr. Mark S. JAMES
101 Chancellor's Asst/Board Secretary .... Ms. Cindy K. JOHNSON
05 Int Vice Chanc of Academic Affairs .... Dr. Michel HILLMAN
32 Vice Chanc Student Success/Engagmnt ... Dr. Kathrine SWANSON
10 Vice Chanc Financial & Admin Svcs .... Mrs. Shelley TEMPLE KNEUVEAN
100 Chief of Staff/Associate VC HR .... Ms. Kathy WALTER-MACK
88 Performance Director Resource Dev .... Ms. Kendra EDWARDS
45 Director Budget and Planning .... Ms. Deborah BALL
13 Director Computer Services .... Mr. Gary W. SCHIEBER
102 Exec Director MCC Foundation .... Mr. Kent HUYSER
96 Manager Purchasing .... Ms. Diane PACHECO
18 Director Facility Services .... Mr. Douglas LIGHTFOOT
103 Exec Dir Workforce Dev .... Ms. Nancy RUSSELL
88 Director Educational Services .... Ms. Fran A. PADOW
106 Director Distance Education .... Dr. Leo J. HIRNER
09 Director Inst Research/Assessment .... Dr. Kristy A. BISHOP
35 Director of Student Dev .... Vacant
37 Director Student Financial Services .... Ms. Dena NORRIS
21 Director of Accounting .... Vacant
14 Dir Admin Systems/Management Svcs .... Ms. Patricia A. AMICK
88 Dir of Support Services PS .... Mr. Domenick R. BROUILLETTE
19 Chief of Campus Police .... Mr. Londell JAMERSON, JR.
88 Dir of CTE Accountability & Comp .... Ms. Teresa A. LONEY
109 Director Auxiliary Services .... Mr. Scott GEORGE
36 Director Career Education .... Mr. Tristan LONDRE

*Metropolitan Community College - Blue River (G)

20301 E 78 Highway, Independence MO 64057-2053

County: Jackson FICE Identification: 032613
Unit ID: 440305
Telephone: (816) 604-6550 Carnegie Class: Assoc/Pub-U-MC
FAX Number: (816) 759-6582 Calendar System: Semester
URL: www.mcckc.edu
Established: 1997 Annual Undergrad Tuition & Fees (In-District): $2,300
Enrollment: 2,963 Coed
Affiliation or Control: State/Local IRS Status: 501(c)3
Highest Offering: Associate Degree
Program: Occupational; 2-Year Principally Bachelor's Creditable
Accreditation: &NH

02 President .... Dr. Michael BANKS
04 Assistant to the President .... Mrs. Kimberly A. MORICONI
05 Dean of Instruction .... Mr. Mickey MCCLOUD
32 Dean of Student Development .... Dr. Jonathan L. BURKE
51 Assoc Dean of Instruction .... Mr. Steven D. JOHNSON
35 Assoc Dean of Student Development .... Mr. Basil LISTER
08 Head Librarian .... Mr. Jared RINCK
19 Campus Police Captain .... Mr. Gary WILSON
18 Facilities Superintendent .... Mr. Tom COOLEY
38 Lead Counselor .... Dr. Victorie KELLEY
84 Enrollment Manager .... Mr. Rowdy PYLE
105 Campus Network Coordinator .... Mr. Tim POHOLSKY
26 Marketing Coordinator .... Mr. Bob K. FLORENCE
37 Assoc Dir of Financial Aid Ops .... Ms. Marion KRAFT
09 Senior Research Analyst .... Ms. Denise JACOBSEN

† Regional accreditation is carried under the parent institution Metropolitan Community College-Kansas City Administrative Center in Kansas City, MO.

*Metropolitan Community College - Business and Technology (H)

1775 Universal Avenue, Kansas City MO 64120-2429

County: Jackson Identification: 666295
Unit ID: 442000
Telephone: (816) 604-1000 Carnegie Class: Assoc/Pub-U-MC
FAX Number: (816) 482-5256 Calendar System: Semester
URL: www.mcckc.edu/btc
Established: 1995 Annual Undergrad Tuition & Fees (In-District): $2,850
Enrollment: 1,133 Coed
Affiliation or Control: Local IRS Status: 501(c)3
Highest Offering: Associate Degree
Program: Occupational; 2-Year Principally Bachelor's Creditable; Technical Emphasis
Accreditation: &NH

02 President .... Dr. Hasan NAIMA
05 Dean of Instruction .... Dr. Thomas WHEELER
32 Dean of Student Development .... Dr. Ryan MEADOR
103 Exec Dir Workforce Development .... Ms. Nancy RUSSELL
84 Enrollment Manager .... Ms. Rene BENNETT
04 Assistant to the Provost .... Ms. Laurena CALDERON
37 Assoc Dir of Financial Aid Ops .... Ms. Marian KRAFT

† Regional accreditation is carried under the parent institution Metropolitan Community College-Kansas City Administrative Center in Kansas City, MO.

*Metropolitan Community College - Longview (I)

500 SW Longview Road, Lee's Summit MO 64081-2105

County: Jackson FICE Identification: 009140
Unit ID: 177995
Telephone: (816) 604-1000 Carnegie Class: Assoc/Pub-U-MC
FAX Number: (816) 672-2025 Calendar System: Semester
URL: www.mcckc.edu
Established: 1969 Annual Undergrad Tuition & Fees (In-District): $2,830
Enrollment: 5,205 Coed
Affiliation or Control: Local IRS Status: 501(c)3
Highest Offering: Associate Degree
Program: Occupational; 2-Year Principally Bachelor's Creditable
Accreditation: &NH

02 President .... Dr. Kirk A. NOOKS
05 Dean of Instruction .... Dr. Arminda MCCALLUM
32 Dean Student Devel/Support Services .... Dr. Karen GOOS
20 Associate Dean Instruction .... Mr. Gurbhushan SINGH
35 Assoc Dean Student Dev/Support Svcs .... Mrs. Linda NELSON
37 Manager of Student Financial Aid .... Ms. Lisa L. FANNAN
10 Business Office Supervisor .... Ms. Dianna M. CARPENTER
18 Physical Facilities Superintendent .... Mr. Steve B. GREIFE
36 Coordinator Student Employment Svcs .Ms. Linda S. ANDERSON
38 Director Student Counseling .... Mrs. Gretchen S. BLYTHE

† Regional accreditation is carried under the parent institution Metropolitan Community College-Kansas City Administrative Center in Kansas City, MO.

*Metropolitan Community College - Maple Woods (J)

2601 NE Barry Road, Kansas City MO 64156-1299

County: Clay FICE Identification: 009139
Unit ID: 178022
Telephone: (816) 604-1000 Carnegie Class: Assoc/Pub-U-MC
FAX Number: (816) 437-3049 Calendar System: Semester
URL: www.mcckc.edu

Established: 1968 Annual Undergrad Tuition & Fees (In-District): $2,938
Enrollment: 9,050 Coed
Affiliation or Control: Local IRS Status: 501(c)3
Highest Offering: Associate Degree
Program: Occupational; 2-Year Principally Bachelor's Creditable
Accreditation: &NH

02 President Dr. Utpal K. GOSWAMI
05 Dean Instruction Mr. David OEHLER
32 Dean Student Development Ms. Karen MOORE
20 Associate Dean Mrs. Dawn K. HATTERMAN
20 Associate Dean Dr. Brian BECHTEL
08 Librarian Mrs. Linda CARTER
41 Athletic Director Dr. Brian BECHTEL
37 Manager Student Financial Aid Mrs. Robin STIMAC
18 Physical Facilities Superintendent Mr. Tom HULETT
10 Business Office Supervisor Ms. Emily THOMPSON
31 Community Relations Coordinator Mrs. Heather K. PEREZ
36 Student Employment Service Coord Ms. Mary Lynn MUNGER
84 Dean of Enrollment Services Ms. Ingrid BERLIN

† Regional accreditation is carried under the parent institution Metropolitan Community College-Kansas City Administrative Center in Kansas City, MO.

*Metropolitan Community College - Penn Valley (A)

3201 Southwest Trafficway, Kansas City MO 64111-2764
County: Jackson FICE Identification: 002484
Unit ID: 178785
Telephone: (816) 604-1000 Carnegie Class: Assoc/Pub-U-MC
FAX Number: (816) 759-4161 Calendar System: Semester
URL: www.mcckc.edu
Established: 1915 Annual Undergrad Tuition & Fees (In-District): $2,880
Enrollment: 6,000 Coed
Affiliation or Control: Local IRS Status: 501(c)3
Highest Offering: Associate Degree
Program: Occupational; 2-Year Principally Bachelor's Creditable; Nursing Emphasis
Accreditation: &NH, ADNUR, CAHIIM, DA, EMT, OTA, PTAA, RAD, SURGT

02 President Dr. Joe SEABROOKS
05 Dean of Instruction Dr. Cheryl CARPENTER-DAVIS
32 Dean of Student Services Ms. Yvette SWEENEY
84 Dean of Enrollment Services Ms. Ingrid BERLIN
20 Assoc Dean Instructional Svc Ms. Tarana CHAPPLE
35 Assoc Dean Student Development Mrs. Mindy JOHNSON
23 Director of Health Sciences Ms. Sandy MCILNAY
06 Registrar/Director of Admissions Mr. Carlton FOWLER
08 Librarian Vacant
13 NUS Department Director Vacant
18 Facilities Services Support Mr. Lloyd HALE
19 Campus Police Captain Cpt. Booker ARMSTRONG
41 Athletic Programs Manager Mr. Marcus HARVEY
37 Student Financial Aid Manager Ms. Rossann DOWNING
40 College Bookstore Manager Ms. Selin GAONA
10 Business Office Supervisor Ms. Michele ALLEN
26 Community & Public Relations Coord Ms. Kimberly RILEY
36 Career Coordinator Ms. Margaret STEGMAN

† Regional accreditation is carried under the parent institution Metropolitan Community College-Kansas City Administrative Center in Kansas City, MO.

Midwest Institute (B)

964 S. Highway Drive, Fenton MO 63026
County: St. Louis FICE Identification: 021211
Unit ID: 178183
Telephone: (314) 965-8363 Carnegie Class: Assoc/PrivFP
FAX Number: (636) 326-1059 Calendar System: Other
URL: www.midwestinstitute.com
Established: 1965 Annual Undergrad Tuition & Fees: $14,680
Enrollment: 225 Coed
Affiliation or Control: Proprietary IRS Status: Proprietary
Highest Offering: Associate Degree
Program: Occupational
Accreditation: ABHES

01 Director Dr. Adam EPSTEIN

Midwest Institute-Earth City (C)

4260 Shoreline Drive, Earth City MO 63045
County: Saint Louis Identification: 667074
Telephone: (314) 344-4440 Carnegie Class: Not Classified
FAX Number: (314) 344-0495 Calendar System: Other
URL: www.midwestinstitute.com
Established: 1970 Annual Undergrad Tuition & Fees: N/A
Enrollment: N/A Coed
Affiliation or Control: Proprietary IRS Status: Proprietary
Highest Offering: Associate Degree
Program: Occupational
Accreditation: ABHES

01 President Ms. Christine SHREFFLER

Midwest University (D)

851 Parr Road, Wentzville MO 63385-0365
County: Saint Charles FICE Identification: 035283
Unit ID: 440253
Telephone: (636) 327-4645 Carnegie Class: Spec/Faith
FAX Number: (636) 327-4715 Calendar System: Semester
URL: www.midwest.edu
Established: 1986 Annual Undergrad Tuition & Fees: $7,950
Enrollment: 275 Coed
Affiliation or Control: Non-denominational IRS Status: 501(c)3
Highest Offering: Doctorate
Program: Professional; Religious Emphasis
Accreditation: BI

01 President Dr. James SONG
11 Executive Assistant to President Ms. Taylor J. BUMILLER
05 Academic Dean Dr. Myeong H. OH
09 Dir of Institutional Effectiveness Mr. Rolfe E. KIEHNE
32 Director of Student Affairs Mr. Kyong S. YEOM
42 Chaplin Dr. Dae G. KIM
06 Registrar/Admission Mr. Jeoung H. HAM
08 Director of Library Services Mrs. Hyun Shim JUNG
106 Director of E-Learning Dr. Hee C. LEE
10 Director of Finance Mr. Kyong S. YEOM
21 Business Office Manager Ms. Bok H. SONG
45 Director of Planning & Marketing Mr. Jae P. SONG
13 Director of Information Technology Dr. Hee C. LEE
12 Korea Office Regional Director Dr. Jae M. SONG
12 Washington DC Regional Director Dr. Yoo K. KO
07 Admission Counselor Mr. Sang Bae SEO
85 International Student Officer Mr. Kyong S. YEOM
85 International Student Officer Mr. Kyoo W. SEO
104 Director of International Devel Dr. Hee C. LEE
50 Director of Business School Dr. Young S. PARK

Midwestern Baptist Theological Seminary (E)

5001 N Oak Trafficway, Kansas City MO 64118-4697
County: Clay FICE Identification: 002485
Unit ID: 178208
Telephone: (816) 414-3700 Carnegie Class: Spec/Faith
FAX Number: (816) 414-3724 Calendar System: Semester
URL: www.mbts.edu
Established: 1957 Annual Undergrad Tuition & Fees: $7,500
Enrollment: 1,821 Coed
Affiliation or Control: Southern Baptist IRS Status: 501(c)3
Highest Offering: Doctorate
Program: Professional; Religious Emphasis
Accreditation: NH, THEOL

01 President Dr. Jason K. ALLEN
05 Provost Dr. Jason DUESING
10 VP for Institutional Administration Mr. Gary CRUTCHER
20 Undergraduate Dean Dr. John Mark YEATS
58 Graduate Dean Dr. Thor MADSEN
09 Vice President Inst Effectiveness Dr. Rodney A. HARRISON
30 VP of Institutional Relations Mr. Charles SMITH
13 Director of Info Technology Mr. David MEYER
06 Registrar Dr. Mike HAWKINS
08 Librarian Ms. Kenette HARDER
73 Director of Doctoral Studies Dr. Rodney A. HARRISON
21 Director Financial Services Mrs. Cheryl HICKS
15 Human Resources Mr. Gary CRUTCHER
04 Exec Assistant to the President Mr. Patrick HUDSON
18 Director of Campus Operations Mr. Merv CHAPMAN
37 Financial Aid Director Mrs. Cheryl HICKS
84 Dir Student Recruitment & Admission Mr. Camden PULLIAM
20 Associate Dean Dr. Rustin UMSTATTD

Mineral Area College (F)

5270 Flat River Road, Park Hills MO 63601-2224
County: Saint Francois FICE Identification: 002486
Unit ID: 178217
Telephone: (573) 431-4593 Carnegie Class: Assoc/Pub-R-M
FAX Number: (573) 518-2164 Calendar System: Semester
URL: www.mineralarea.edu
Established: 1922 Annual Undergrad Tuition & Fees (In-District): $3,280
Enrollment: 4,637 Coed
Affiliation or Control: Local IRS Status: 501(c)3
Highest Offering: Associate Degree
Program: Occupational; 2-Year Principally Bachelor's Creditable
Accreditation: NH, EMT, PTAA, RAD

01 President Dr. Steve KURTZ
03 Vice Pres/Dean Career/Tech Educ Mr. John (Gil) KENNON
49 Dean of Arts & Sciences Ms. Carolyn (Kay) CRECELIUS
32 Dean Student Services Ms. Jean MERRILL-DOSS
10 Business Manager Vacant
13 Director of Computer Services Mr. Chad PIPKIN
06 Registrar Ms. Pam REEDER
07 Director of Admissions Ms. Julie SHEETS
09 Director of Institutional Research Ms. Lisa EDBURG
26 Chief Public Relations Officer Ms. Sarah HAAS
29 Director Alumni Relations Mr. Kevin THURMAN
15 Chief Human Resource Officer Ms. Kathryn NEFF
37 Director Student Financial Aid Ms. Denise SEBASTIAN
38 Director Student Counseling Mr. Michael EASTER
88 General Services Supervisor Mr. Rodney RESINGER
21 Director Payroll Ms. Lisa CLAUSER
04 Administrative Asst to President Ms. Amy MCKENNA-JONES
08 Head Librarian Ms. Melissa HOPKINS
19 Director Security/Safety Mr. Jeff MCCREARY
39 Director Student Housing Ms. Debi BAYLESS
41 Athletic Director Mr. Chad MILLS

Missouri Baptist University (G)

One College Park Drive, Saint Louis MO 63141-8698
County: Saint Louis FICE Identification: 007540
Unit ID: 178244
Telephone: (314) 434-1115 Carnegie Class: Master's L
FAX Number: (314) 434-7596 Calendar System: Semester
URL: www.mobap.edu
Established: 1964 Annual Undergrad Tuition & Fees: $23,750
Enrollment: 5,321 Coed
Affiliation or Control: Baptist IRS Status: 501(c)3
Highest Offering: Doctorate
Program: Liberal Arts And General; Teacher Preparatory; Professional
Accreditation: NH, EXSC, MUS, TED

01 President Dr. R. Alton LACEY
04 Assistant to the President Mrs. Susan RUTLEDGE
05 Senior VP of Academic Affs/Provost Dr. Arlen R. DYKSTRA
30 Senior VP of Inst Advancement Dr. Keith ROSS
32 Senior VP of Student Development Dr. Andy CHAMBERS
10 Senior VP for Business Affairs Mr. Ken REVENAUGH
58 VP of Grad Stds/Academic Pgm Review Dr. Clark TRIPLETT
29 Director for Alumni Relations Mr. Brian KNAPP
85 Director of International Services Mrs. Kari SAUNDERS
09 Director Institutional Research Mrs. Heather BRASE
08 Librarian Ms. Nitsa HINDELEH
37 Director Financial Services Mr. John BRANDT
26 Director University Communications Mr. Bryce CHAPMAN
36 Dir Career Svcs/Assoc Dean Students Ms. Kimberly GREY
41 Athletic Director Dr. Thomas SMITH
20 Associate Academic Dean Vacant
18 Director Campus Operations Mr. Stu LINDLEY
06 Director of Records Mrs. Thea ABRAHAM
15 Director Personnel Services Mrs. Barb BURNS
13 Director of Information Systems Mr. Jerry MCKITTRICK
19 Director Public Safety Mr. Stephen HEIDKE
35 Director Student Activities Mrs. Lara HINES
21 Controller Mrs. Pam SAVAGE
44 Development Officer Mrs. Ashlee JOHNSON
07 Director of Admissions Mrs. Cynthia SUTTON

Missouri College (H)

1405 South Hanley Road, Brentwood MO 63144-2902
County: St. Louis FICE Identification: 009795
Unit ID: 178305
Telephone: (314) 768-7800 Carnegie Class: Bac/Assoc
FAX Number: (314) 768-7900 Calendar System: Semester
URL: www.missouricollege.com
Established: 1963 Annual Undergrad Tuition & Fees: $14,702
Enrollment: 586 Coed
Affiliation or Control: Proprietary IRS Status: Proprietary
Highest Offering: Baccalaureate
Program: Occupational; 2-Year Principally Bachelor's Creditable
Accreditation: ACICS, DA, DH

01 President Mr. Karl PETERSEN
05 Dean of Academics Mrs. Nicole GRAMLICH
07 Admissions Director Ms. Heidi HOLMES
06 Registrar Ms. Brandi MENKE

Missouri Southern State University (I)

3950 E Newman Road, Joplin MO 64801-1595
County: Jasper FICE Identification: 002488
Unit ID: 178341
Telephone: (417) 625-9300 Carnegie Class: Bac/Diverse
FAX Number: (417) 625-3121 Calendar System: Semester
URL: www.mssu.edu
Established: 1965 Annual Undergrad Tuition & Fees (In-State): $5,523
Enrollment: 5,613 Coed
Affiliation or Control: State IRS Status: 501(c)3
Highest Offering: Master's
Program: Liberal Arts And General; Teacher Preparatory; Professional
Accreditation: NH, ACBSP, COARC, DH, EMT, ENGT, NUR, NURSE, RAD, TED

01 President Dr. Alan MARBLE
05 Provost/Vice Pres Academic Affairs Dr. Paula CARSON
32 Vice Pres Stdnt Affs/Enrollment Mr. Darren S. FULLERTON
10 Vice President Business Affairs Mr. Rob YUST
30 Exec Vice Pres for Development Dr. Brad HODSON
20 Int Prov/Vice Pres Academic Affairs Dr. Wendy MCGRANE
35 Dean of Students Dr. Ronald S. MITCHELL
06 Registrar Ms. Cheryl DOBSON
08 Interim Library Director Mr. James CAPECI
37 Director Student Financial Aid Ms. Becca L. DISKIN
38 Director of ACTS Mrs. Kelly WILSON
21 Treasurer Mrs. Linda EIS
15 Director Human Resources Mr. Evan JEWSBURY
18 Director Facilities/Physical Plant Mr. Robert HARRINGTON
76 Dean School Health Sciences Dr. Tia STRAIT
49 Dean School of Arts & Sciences Dr. Richard B. MILLER
53 Interim Dean School Education Dr. Deborah BROWN
50 Dean Plaster School of Business Dr. John GROESBECK
04 Administrative Asst to President Ms. Sharon ODEM
07 Director of Admissions Mr. Derek S. SKAGGS
103 Dir Workforce/Career Development Ms. Nicole R. BROWN
104 Director Study Abroad Dr. Chad STEBBINS
106 Director Distance Learning Mr. Scott SNELL
108 Dir Institutional Effectiveness Ms. Josie WELSH
19 Chief of Campus Police Mr. Kenneth KENNEDY
25 Grant Writer Ms. Sandra LOVETT

41 Director of Athletics .... Mr. Jared BRUGGEMAN
44 Director Annual or Planned Giving .... Ms. Elisa BRYANT
91 Dir of Information Technology Svcs .... Mr. Albert (Al) STADLER
88 Dir Budget & Operations .... Mr. Jeff GIBSON
03 Executive Vice President .... Dr. Brad HODSON
101 Secretary of the Institution/Board .... Mrs. Sharon ODEM
26 Dir University Relations/Marketing .... Ms. Cassie MATHES
29 Director Alumni Relations .... Ms. Lee ELLIFF POUND

Missouri State University (A)

901 S National Avenue, Springfield MO 65897-0027

County: Greene FICE Identification: 002503
Unit ID: 179566
Telephone: (417) 836-8500 Carnegie Class: Master's L
FAX Number: (417) 836-7669 Calendar System: Semester
URL: www.missouristate.edu
Established: 1905 Annual Undergrad Tuition & Fees (In-State): $7,060
Enrollment: 24,489 Coed
Affiliation or Control: State IRS Status: 501(c)3
Highest Offering: Doctorate
Program: Liberal Arts And General; Teacher Preparatory; Professional; Business Emphasis
Accreditation: NH, ADNUR, ANEST, ARCPA, AUD, BUS, BUSA, CAATE, CACREP, CEA, CONST, CS, DIETD, @DIETI, MUS, NRPA, NURSE, PH, PLNG, PTA, SP, SPAA, SW, TED, THEA

01 President .... Mr. Clifton M. SMART, III
05 Provost .... Dr. Frank E. EINHELLIG
12 Chancellor West Plains Campus .... Dr. Drew A. BENNETT
46 VP for Research/Economic Devel .... Dr. James P. BAKER
11 Vice Pres Administrative/Info Svcs .... Mr. Ken MCCLURE
30 Vice Pres University Advancement .... Mr. W. Brent DUNN
32 VP Student Affairs & Dean of Stdts .... Dr. Dee SISCOE
28 Vice Pres Diversity/Inclusion .... Dr. Kenneth COOPWOOD, SR.
20 Associate Provost .... Dr. Christopher J. CRAIG
20 Associate Provost .... Dr. Rachelle DARABI
20 Associate Provost .... Dr. Joye NORRIS
58 Dean of Grad College .... Dr. Julie J. MASTERSON
10 Chief Financial Officer .... Mr. Steve FOUCART
84 Associate VP Enrollment Mgmt & Svcs .. Mr. Donald E. SIMPSON
08 Dean Library Services .... Mr. Thomas A. PETERS
09 Director of Institutional Research .... Dr. Michelle D. OLSEN
29 Exec Dir of Alumni Relations .... Ms. Lori FAN
15 Director of Human Resources .... Mr. Edward CHOATE
37 Director of Student Financial Aid .... Ms. Vicki S. MATTOCKS
19 Director of Safety & Transportation .... Mr. Donald A. CLARK
36 Director of the Career Center .... Ms. Jill WIGGINS
13 Chief Information Officer .... Mr. Jeff P. MORRISSEY
22 Equal Opportunity Officer .... Mr. Harold W. PRATT
100 Chief of Staff .... Mr. Ryan DEBOEF
23 Director of Health & Wellness Svcs .... Dr. Dave MUEGGE
92 Director Honors College .... Dr. John F. CHUCHIAK
18 Director Facilities Management .... Mr. Brad B. KIELHOFNER
96 Director of Procurement .... Mr. Mike WILLS
07 Director of Admissions .... Ms. Nechell T. BONDS
06 Asst VP Enrollment Mgmt/Registrar .... Mr. Rob HORNBERGER
49 Dean College Arts & Letters .... Dr. Gloria GALANES
79 Dean Col Humanities/Public Affairs .... Dr. Victor MATTHEWS
76 Dean Col Health/Human Services .... Dr. Helen C. REID
81 Dean Col Natural/Applied Science .... Dr. Tamera S. JAHNKE
53 Dean College of Education .... Dr. David HOUGH
50 Dean College of Business .... Dr. Stephanie BRYANT
85 Associate VP International Program ... Mr. Stephen H. ROBINETTE
105 Director of Web and New Media .... Ms. Sara M. CLARK
26 VP Marketing and Communications .... Ms. Suzanne SHAW
41 Athletic Director .... Mr. Kyle MOATS
43 General Counsel .... Ms. Rachael M. DOCKERY

Missouri State University - West Plains (B)

128 Garfield, West Plains MO 65775-2715

County: Howell FICE Identification: 031060
Unit ID: 179344
Telephone: (417) 255-7255 Carnegie Class: Assoc/Pub2in4
FAX Number: (417) 255-7962 Calendar System: Semester
URL: www.wp.missouristate.edu
Established: 1963 Annual Undergrad Tuition & Fees (In-State): $3,880
Enrollment: 2,193 Coed
Affiliation or Control: State IRS Status: 501(c)3
Highest Offering: Associate Degree
Program: Occupational; 2-Year Principally Bachelor's Creditable
Accreditation: NH, COARC

01 Chancellor .... Dr. Drew A. BENNETT
05 Dean of Academics .... Dr. Dennis LANCASTER
32 Dean of Student Services .... Dr. Angela TOTTY
20 Assistant Dean of Academic Affairs .... Dr. Michael ORF
10 Director of Business Services .... Mr. Scott SCHNEIDER
30 Director of Development .... Mr. Joe KAMMERER
27 Director of Univ Communications .... Mrs. Cheryl CALDWELL
31 Director of Univ/Community Pgms .... Ms. Brenda POLYARD
13 Director of Computer Services .... Vacant
06 Registrar .... Mrs. Laurie WALL
07 Coord of Admissions .... Mrs. Melissa JETT
09 Coord of Institutional Research .... Vacant
26 Chief Public Relations Officer .... Mrs. Cheryl CALDWELL
36 Coord of Career Services .... Mr. Jared CATES
37 Coord of Student Financial Aid .... Mrs. Donna BASSHAM
18 Chief Facilities/Physical Plant .... Mr. Ron HENSLEY
04 Executive Asst to Chancellor .... Ms. Kristy LAWRENCE

08 Head Librarian .... Mrs. Sylvia KUHLMEIER
15 Procurement/Human Resources Spec .... Mrs. Alyssa D. COLLINS
39 Coord Student Life and Development .... Mr. Rogers L. TAYLOR

Missouri Tech (C)

1690 Country Club Plaza Drive, Saint Charles MO 63303

County: Saint Louis FICE Identification: 023040
Unit ID: 178350
Telephone: (636) 573-9300 Carnegie Class: Spec/Tech
FAX Number: (636) 573-9398 Calendar System: Semester
URL: www.motech.edu
Established: 1932 Annual Undergrad Tuition & Fees: $15,530
Enrollment: 105 Coed
Affiliation or Control: Proprietary IRS Status: Proprietary
Highest Offering: Baccalaureate
Program: Technical Emphasis
Accreditation: ACCSC

01 President .... Ms. Cynthia DODGE
05 Dean of Education .... Vacant
37 Director Financial Aid .... Ms. Cindy Ann SINNOTT

Missouri Valley College (D)

500 E College, Marshall MO 65340-3197

County: Saline FICE Identification: 002489
Unit ID: 178369
Telephone: (660) 831-4000 Carnegie Class: Bac/Diverse
FAX Number: (660) 831-4039 Calendar System: Semester
URL: www.moval.edu
Established: 1889 Annual Undergrad Tuition & Fees: $19,750
Enrollment: 1,695 Coed
Affiliation or Control: Presbyterian Church (U.S.A.) IRS Status: 501(c)3
Highest Offering: Master's
Program: Liberal Arts And General; Teacher Preparatory
Accreditation: NH, CAATE, NURSE

01 President .... Dr. Bonnie HUMPHREY
00 Chancellor Emeritus .... Dr. Earl J. REEVES
10 Chief Financial Officer .... Mr. Greg SILVEY
30 Vice Pres Institutional Advancement .... Mr. Eric SAPPINGTON
32 Vice Pres Student Affairs .... Mr. Heath MORGAN
05 VP Academic Affairs/Chief Acad Ofcr .... Dr. Parris WATTS
18 Asst VP of Operations .... Mr. Tim SCHULTE
07 Dean of Admissions .... Ms. Tennille LANGDON
06 Registrar .... Ms. Marsha LASHLEY
21 Business Officer .... Mrs. Tonia BARTEL
08 Head Librarian .... Mrs. Pamela K. REEDER
41 Athletic Director/Dir of Operations .... Mr. Tom FIFER
42 Director Campus Ministry .... Rev. Pam SEBASTIAN
09 Director of Institutional Research .... Ms. Diane BARTHOLOMEW
37 Director Student Financial Aid .... Mrs. Rachel ROBINSON
38 Director Student Counseling .... Ms. Teresa CESELSKI
13 Director of Systems Administration .... Mr. Jason RINNE
26 Dir of Marketing & Media Relations .... Ms. Danielle DURHAM
04 Administrative Asst to President .... Ms. Brandy SCHULTE

Missouri Western State University (E)

4525 Downs Drive, Saint Joseph MO 64507-2294

County: Buchanan FICE Identification: 002490
Unit ID: 178387
Telephone: (816) 271-4200 Carnegie Class: Bac/Diverse
FAX Number: N/A Calendar System: Semester
URL: www.missouriwestern.edu
Established: 1915 Annual Undergrad Tuition & Fees (In-State): $5,465
Enrollment: 5,742 Coed
Affiliation or Control: State IRS Status: 501(c)3
Highest Offering: Master's
Program: Liberal Arts And General; Teacher Preparatory
Accreditation: NH, BUS, CAHIIM, ENGT, MUS, NURSE, PTAA, SW, TED

01 President .... Dr. Robert A. VARTABEDIAN
05 Provost/VP Academic Affairs .... Dr. Jeanne DAFFRON
30 Vice Pres University Advancement .... Mr. Jerry PICKMAN
10 VP Financial Planning and Admin .... Mr. Cale FESSLER
32 Vice Pres for Student Affairs .... Ms. Shana MEYER
20 Assoc Vice Pres Academic Affairs .... Dr. Doug DAVENPORT
21 Assoc VP Financial Plng/Admin .... Ms. Carey MCMILLIAN
35 Dean of Students .... Dr. Judith GRIMES
57 Dean of Fine Arts .... Dr. Bob WILLENBRINK
49 Dean Liberal Arts & Science .... Dr. Murray NABORS
107 Dean Professional Studies .... Dr. Kathleen O'CONNOR
51 Dean of Western Institute .... Dr. Gordon MAPLEY
06 Registrar .... Ms. Susan BRACCIANO
07 Director of Admissions .... Mr. Tyson SCHANK
08 Director of Library .... Ms. Julia SCHNEIDER
37 Director Student Financial Aid .... Ms. Marilyn BAKER
13 Director of Information Technology .... Mr. Mark MABE
38 Director Student Counsel & Testing .... Mr. H. David BROWN
18 Director Physical Plant .... Mr. Jerry GENTRY
41 Director of Athletics .... Mr. Kurt MCGUFFIN
15 Director of Human Resources .... Ms. Sally SANDERS
26 Dir of Public Relations & Marketing .... Vacant
29 Director of Alumni Services .... Ms. Colleen KOWICH
96 Director of Purchasing .... Ms. Letha NOLD
04 Administrative Asst to President .... Ms. Connie BROCK
103 Dir Workforce/Career Development .... Ms. Kay-lynne TAYLOR
39 Director Student Housing .... Mr. Nathan ROBERTS
50 Dean of Business .... Dr. Mike LANE

84 Director Enrollment Management .... Mr. Howard MCCAULEY
88 Chief of University Police .... Ms. Yvonne MEYER

Moberly Area Community College (F)

101 College Avenue, Moberly MO 65270-1304

County: Randolph FICE Identification: 002491
Unit ID: 178448
Telephone: (660) 263-4110 Carnegie Class: Assoc/Pub-R-M
FAX Number: (660) 263-6252 Calendar System: Semester
URL: www.macc.edu
Established: 1927 Annual Undergrad Tuition & Fees (In-District): $3,060
Enrollment: 5,431 Coed
Affiliation or Control: State/Local IRS Status: 501(c)3
Highest Offering: Associate Degree
Program: Occupational; 2-Year Principally Bachelor's Creditable
Accreditation: NH, MLTAD, OTA

01 President .... Dr. Jeffery LASHLEY
10 Vice President for Finance .... Mr. Gary STEFFES
05 Vice President of Instruction .... Ms. Paula GLOVER
75 Dean of Career/Technical Educ .... Ms. Jo FEY
32 Dean of Student Services .... Dr. James GRANT
12 Dean Off-Camp Pgms/Instr Tech .... Ms. Michele MCCALL
20 Dean of Academic Affairs .... Ms. Jacqueline FISCHER
09 Director Inst Effectiveness/Plng .... Ms. Meghan HOLLERAN
21 Director Business Services .... Ms. Sandra MAREK
26 Dir of Mktg and Public Relations .... Mr. Scott MCGARVEY
18 Director of Plant Operations .... Mr. Eric ROSS
13 Chief Information Officer .... Mr. Lloyd MARCHANT
08 Director of Library Services .... Ms. Valerie DARST
15 Director of Human Resources .... Ms. Ann PARKS
40 Director of Inst Svcs/Bookstore Mgr .... Ms. Virginia GEBHARDT
37 Director of Financial Aid .... Mrs. Amy HAGER
06 Registrar .... Ms. Lynn WALKER
29 Director Alumni Services .... Mr. Chad JAECQUES
36 Dir of Career and Technical Pgms .... Ms. Suzi MCGARVEY
88 Dir of Academic Services .... Ms. Katelyn BRANDKAMP

National American University-Independence (G)

3620 Arrowhead Avenue, Independence MO 64057

Telephone: (816) 418-7700 Identification: 770402
Accreditation: &NH, MAC, OTA

† Branch campus of National American University, Rapid City, SD.

National American University-Lee's Summit (H)

401 NW Murray Road, Lee's Summit MO 64081

Telephone: (816) 600-3900 Identification: 770404
Accreditation: &NH

† Branch campus of National American University, Rapid City, SD.

National American University-Weldon Spring (I)

Triad Crossing, 1030 Wolfrum Rd,
Weldon Spring MO 63304

Telephone: (623) 229-3200 Identification: 770405
Accreditation: &NH

† Branch campus of National American University, Rapid City, SD.

National American University-Zona Rosa (J)

7490 NW 87th Street, Kansas City MO 64153

Telephone: (816) 412-5500 Identification: 770403
Accreditation: &NH, ADNUR, MAC, MLTAD

† Branch campus of National American University, Rapid City, SD.

Nazarene Theological Seminary (K)

1700 E Meyer Boulevard, Kansas City MO 64131-1263

County: Jackson FICE Identification: 002494
Unit ID: 178518
Telephone: (816) 268-5400 Carnegie Class: Spec/Faith
FAX Number: (816) 268-5500 Calendar System: Semester
URL: www.nts.edu
Established: 1945 Annual Graduate Tuition & Fees: $8,370
Enrollment: 239 Coed
Affiliation or Control: Church Of The Nazarene IRS Status: 501(c)3
Highest Offering: Doctorate; No Undergraduates
Program: Professional; Religious Emphasis
Accreditation: THEOL

01 President .... Dr. Carl SUNBERG
05 Dean of the Faculty .... Dr. Roger HAHN
11 Dean for Administration .... Rev. Chet DECKER
08 Director Library Service .... Mrs. Debra BRADSHAW
06 Registrar .... Mrs. Pamela ASHER
37 Financial Aid Coordinator .... Mr. Jeremy SHUNK
26 Director of Communications .... Ms. Marsha SAILORS

North Central Missouri College (L)

1301 Main Street, Trenton MO 64683-1824

County: Grundy FICE Identification: 002514
Unit ID: 179715
Telephone: (660) 359-3948 Carnegie Class: Assoc/Pub-R-S
FAX Number: (660) 359-2211 Calendar System: Semester
URL: www.ncmissouri.edu
Established: 1925 Annual Undergrad Tuition & Fees (In-District): $3,870

Enrollment: 1,742 Coed
Affiliation or Control: Local IRS Status: 501(c)3
Highest Offering: Associate Degree
Program: Occupational; 2-Year Principally Bachelor's Creditable
Accreditation: NH, DH, OTA

01 President ... Dr. Neil NUTTALL
09 VP Institutional Effectiveness ... Dr. Jamie HOOYMAN
10 Chief Financial Officer ... Mr. Tyson OTTO
32 Dean of Student Services ... Dr. Kristen ALLEY
05 Dean of Instruction ... Dr. Sharon WEISER
76 Dean Allied Health Sciences ... Vacant
06 Registrar ... Ms. Linda BROWN
13 Chief Information Officer ... Mr. Alan BARNETT
08 Librarian ... Ms. Beth CALDARELLO
37 Director of Financial Aid ... Ms. Megan DEWITT
30 Director Development ... Ms. Teresa CROSS
40 Director Bookstore ... Ms. Cecilia MARSH
39 Director Student Housing ... Mr. Donnie HILLERMAN
41 Athletic Director ... Mr. Steve RICHMAN
18 Director of Facilities ... Mr. Randy YOUNG
101 Sec of Inst/Board of Governors ... Ms. Kristi HARRIS
105 Director Web Services ... Mr. Anthony ALEXANDER
09 Director of Institutional Research ... Ms. Tara NOAH

Northwest Missouri State University (A)

800 University Drive, Maryville MO 64468-6015
County: Nodaway FICE Identification: 002496
Unit ID: 178624
Telephone: (660) 562-1212 Carnegie Class: Master's L
FAX Number: (660) 562-1900 Calendar System: Trimester
URL: www.nwmissouri.edu
Established: 1905 Annual Undergrad Tuition & Fees (In-State): $7,894
Enrollment: 6,720 Coed
Affiliation or Control: State IRS Status: 501(c)3
Highest Offering: Beyond Master's But Less Than Doctorate
Program: Liberal Arts And General; Teacher Preparatory; Business Emphasis
Accreditation: NH, ACBSP, DIETD, MUS, NRPA, TED

01 President ... Dr. John JASINSKI
05 Provost ... Dr. Timothy MOTTET
10 Vice Pres for Finance ... Ms. Stacy CARRICK
32 VP Student Affairs/Dean of Students ... Dr. Matt BAKER
13 Vice Pres for Information Systems ... Mr. Rob THOMAS, JR.
26 Vice President University Relations ... Vacant
15 Vice Pres of Human Resources ... Ms. Nola BOND
30 VP University Advancement ... Mr. Michael JOHNSON
84 Dean Enrollment Management ... Ms. Beverly S. SCHENKEL
09 Assoc Dir Institutional Research ... Ms. Mary Ann PENNISTON
08 Dir of Academic & Library Services ... Dr. Leslie GALBREATH
06 Registrar ... Ms. Terri VOGEL
37 Director Financial Aid ... Mr. Del MORLEY
36 Director of Career Services ... Ms. Joan SCHNEIDER
29 Director Alumni Relations ... Mr. Robert MACHOVSKY
19 Chief University Police Department ... Mr. Clarence GREEN
41 Director Athletics/HPERD ... Mr. Mel TJEERDSMA
23 Director Wellness Services ... Dr. Gerald WILMES
96 Director of Purchasing ... Ms. Ann MARTIN
18 Director Facility Services ... Mr. Allen MAYS
58 Dean of Graduate School ... Dr. Gregory HADDOCK
53 Dean Col of Education & Human Svcs ... Dr. Joyce PIVERAL
49 Dean Col of Arts & Sciences ... Dr. Michael STEINER
50 Int Dean Col of Business/Prof Stds ... Dr. Greg HADDOCK
38 Director Student Counseling Center ... Vacant
07 Associate Director of Admissions ... Ms. Tamara J. GROW
04 Administrative Asst to President ... Ms. Lynne GILBERT

Ozark Christian College (B)

1111 N Main Street, Joplin MO 64801-4804
County: Jasper FICE Identification: 022027
Unit ID: 178679
Telephone: (417) 626-1234 Carnegie Class: Spec/Faith
FAX Number: (417) 624-0090 Calendar System: Semester
URL: www.occ.edu
Established: 1942 Annual Undergrad Tuition & Fees: $11,110
Enrollment: 743 Coed
Affiliation or Control: Independent Non-Profit IRS Status: 501(c)3
Highest Offering: Baccalaureate
Program: Religious Emphasis
Accreditation: BI

01 President ... Matt PROCTOR
03 Executive Vice President ... Damien SPIKEREIT
04 Executive Asst to the President ... Kathy BOWERS
05 Exec VP Academic Affairs/Dean ... Doug ALDRIDGE
06 Registrar ... Jennifer MCMILLIN
32 Vice Pres of Student Life ... Monte SHOEMAKE
10 Vice Pres of Campus Operations ... David MCMILLIN
84 Vice Pres of Enrollment Management ... Troy NELSON
09 Vice Pres Effectiveness/Gen Counsel ... Doug MILLER
29 Vice Pres of Alumni Relations ... Dru ASHWELL
30 Interim Vice Pres of Development ... Travis HURLEY
20 Assistant Academic Dean ... Chad RAGSDALE
26 Vice Pres of College Relations ... Jim DALRYMPLE
37 Director of Student Financial Aid ... Kim BALENTINE
90 LMS Administrator ... David FISH
07 Director of Recruitment ... Marley BUTLER
08 Director of Library Services ... John HUNTER
106 Associate Dean Online Learning ... Shawn LINDSAY
64 Coordinator of Music Department ... Scott HANDLEY
38 Student Counselor ... Sharon ENGELBRECHT
88 Director of Food Services ... Teresa BAKER
23 Campus Nurse ... Sara WOOD
34 Dean of Women ... Lisa WHITE
42 Director Campus Ministry ... Kevin GREER
88 Director of Ministry Center ... Bob WITTE
40 Director of Bookstore ... Bob HEATH
41 Director of Athletics ... Chris LAHM
18 Director Physical Plant ... Tim RUNYON
13 Director of College Technology Dept ... Mitchell PIERCY
07 Director of Enrollment Services ... Ashley NEGRON
105 Web Developer/Network Admin ... Matt DICKEY
14 Coordinator of Data Processing ... Gary WHEAT

Ozarks Technical Community College (C)

1001 E Chestnut Expressway, Springfield MO 65802-3625
County: Greene FICE Identification: 030830
Unit ID: 177472
Telephone: (417) 447-7500 Carnegie Class: Assoc/Pub-R-L
FAX Number: N/A Calendar System: Semester
URL: www.otc.edu
Established: 1990 Annual Undergrad Tuition & Fees (In-District): $2,784
Enrollment: 14,396 Coed
Affiliation or Control: State/Local IRS Status: 501(c)3
Highest Offering: Associate Degree
Program: Occupational; 2-Year Principally Bachelor's Creditable
Accreditation: NH, ACFEI, ADNUR, CAHIIM, COARC, DA, DH, EMT, IFSAC, MLTAD, OTA, PTAA, SURGT

01 Chancellor ... Dr. Hal L. HIGDON
100 Chief of Staff ... Ms. Stephanie SUMNERS
101 Secretary to the Chancellor ... Ms. Janel GRASSI
05 Vice Chancellor Academic Affairs ... Dr. Steve BISHOP
11 Vice Chancellor Admin Services ... Mr. Rob RECTOR
32 Vice Chancellor Student Affairs ... Ms. Joan BARRETT
10 Vice Chancellor Finance ... Ms. Marla MOODY
12 President Table Rock Campus ... Mr. Cliff DAVIS
12 President Richwood Valley Campus ... Dr. Jeff JOCHEMS
13 Chief Technology Officer ... Mr. David ESPING
15 Assoc VC Human Resources/Workforce ... Mr. Tim BALTES
20 Dean of Academic Services ... Dr. Vivian ELDER
76 Dean of Allied Health Programs ... Dr. Sherry TAYLOR
97 Dean of General Education ... Mr. Lance RENNER
72 Dean of Technical Education ... Dr. Matthew HUDSON
103 Exec Dir Workforce Development ... Mr. James ABRAMOVITZ
88 Director Business Development ... Ms. Sherry COKER
06 Asst Registrar Records/Registration ... Ms. Katie MOORE
38 Director of Counseling Services ... Ms. Joyce BATEMAN
26 College Dir Comm & Marketing ... Mr. Mark MILLER
18 College Director Facilities/Grounds ... Mr. Rickie TAYLOR
91 College Dir Tech/Admin Computing ... Mr. Jack DOZIER
28 College Director Equity & Complianc ... Ms. Julie EDWARDS
37 College Director of Financial Aid ... Mr. Jeff FORD
08 Director College Library ... Mr. Corky MCCORMACK
88 Director College Library RVC/TRC ... Ms. Angela SWIFT
36 Director of Career Employment Svcs ... Ms. Kathy CHRISTY
102 Exec Director of OTC Foundation ... Ms. Stephanie SUMNERS
44 College Director of Development ... Ms. Amy BACON
88 College Dir Organizational Systems ... Mr. John CLAYTON
09 College Dir Research/Strategic Plng ... Mr. Matthew SIMPSON
19 College Director Safety & Security ... Mr. Scott LEVEN
35 Dean of Students ... Ms. Karla GREGG
88 Director Dual Credit/HS Admissions ... Ms. Kimberly GREENE

Ozarks Technical Community College Richwood Valley (D)

3369 W Jackson Street, Nixa MO 65714
Telephone: (417) 447-7700 Identification: 770324
Accreditation: &NH

† Branch campus of Ozarks Technical Community College, Springfield, MO.

Ozarks Technical Community College Table Rock Campus (E)

10698 Historic Highway 165, Hollister MO 65672
Telephone: (417) 447-7500 Identification: 770325
Accreditation: &NH

† Branch campus of Ozarks Technical Community College, Springfield, MO.

Park University (F)

8700 River Park Drive, Parkville MO 64152-3795
County: Platte FICE Identification: 002498
Unit ID: 178721
Telephone: (816) 741-2000 Carnegie Class: Master's M
FAX Number: (816) 746-6423 Calendar System: Semester
URL: www.park.edu
Established: 1875 Annual Undergrad Tuition & Fees: $11,070
Enrollment: 9,892 Coed
Affiliation or Control: Independent Non-Profit IRS Status: 501(c)3
Highest Offering: Master's
Program: Liberal Arts And General; Teacher Preparatory; Professional
Accreditation: NH, ACBSP, ADNUR, CAATE, NUR, SW

01 President ... Dr. Jeff EHRLICH
05 Provost & Senior Vice President ... Dr. Jerry JORGENSEN
10 Chief Financial Officer ... Mr. Matthew VAN HOESEN
30 VP University Relations/Development ... Ms. Laurie MCCORMACK
84 VP Enrollment Mgt/Student Services ... Vacant
43 Vice President & General Counsel ... Ms. Courtney GODDARD
20 Associate VP for Academic Affairs ... Dr. Rebekkah STUTEVILLE
29 Assoc VP Alumni & Constit Engagemnt ... Mr. Erik BERGRUD
32 Dean of Student Life ... Dr. Jayme UDEN
58 Dean School of Grad & Prof Studies ... Dr. Laurie DIPADOVA-STOCKS
06 Registrar ... Ms. Jody MANCHION
37 Exec Dir for Enrollment Operations ... Ms. Cathy COLAPIETRO
08 Interim Director of Library Systems ... Ms. Ann SCHULTIS
07 Exec Dir of Enrollment Services ... Mr. Eric BLAIR
44 Director of Advancement Services ... Ms. Jessica GREASON
15 Director of Human Resources ... Mr. Roger DUSING
41 Director of Athletics ... Mr. Claude ENGLISH
66 Director of Nursing Program ... Ms. Gerry WALKER
85 Dir of Intl Student Admissions ... Ms. Emily BRATTIN
13 CIO Technical Services ... Vacant
108 Director Academic Assessment ... Dr. Christopher MESEKE
19 Director of Campus Safety ... Mr. Christopher LOOS
50 Director MBA Program ... Dr. Nick KOUDOU
04 Exec Asst to the President ... Ms. Laure CHRISTENSEN
50 Dean School of Business/Mgmt ... Dr. Brad KLEINDL
106 Assoc VP Park Distance Learning ... Dr. Charles KATER
49 Dean Liberal Arts & Sciences ... Dr. Emily DONNELLI-SALLEE
53 Dean School for Education ... Dr. Michelle MYERS

Pinnacle Career Institute (G)

1001 E 101st Terrace, Suite 325, Kansas City MO 64131-3368
County: Jackson FICE Identification: 010405
Unit ID: 177302
Telephone: (816) 331-5700 Carnegie Class: Assoc/PrivFP
FAX Number: (816) 331-2026 Calendar System: Quarter
URL: www.pcitraining.edu
Established: 1953 Annual Undergrad Tuition & Fees: $14,048
Enrollment: 580 Coed
Affiliation or Control: Proprietary IRS Status: Proprietary
Highest Offering: Associate Degree
Program: Occupational; Technical Emphasis
Accreditation: ACICS

01 Executive Director ... Guy A. COGNET, II
05 Director of Education ... Debra BARNES
36 Director Student and Career Service ... Elisabeth O'BRIEN

Pinnacle Career Institute (H)

11500 Ambassador Road, Suite 221, Kansas City MO 64153
Telephone: (816) 270-5300 Identification: 770737
Accreditation: ACICS

† Branch campus of Pinnacle Career Institute, Kansas City, MO.

Ranken Technical College (I)

4431 Finney Avenue, Saint Louis MO 63113-2898
County: Saint Louis FICE Identification: 012500
Unit ID: 178891
Telephone: (314) 371-0236 Carnegie Class: Assoc/PrivNFP4
FAX Number: (314) 371-0241 Calendar System: Semester
URL: www.ranken.edu
Established: 1907 Annual Undergrad Tuition & Fees: $14,232
Enrollment: 1,852 Coed
Affiliation or Control: Independent Non-Profit IRS Status: 501(c)3
Highest Offering: Baccalaureate
Program: Occupational; 2-Year Principally Bachelor's Creditable; Technical Emphasis
Accreditation: NH

01 President ... Mr. Stan SHOUN
10 Vice President for Finance & Admin ... Mr. Peter T. MURTAUGH
03 Executive Vice President ... Mr. Don POHL
51 Dean of Continuing Education ... Mr. Keyvan GERAMI
05 Dean Academic Affairs ... Ms. Crystal HERRON
07 Admissions Director ... Mr. Michael E. HAWLEY
06 Registrar ... Ms. Carol J. WINKLER
18 Director Buildings & Grounds ... Mr. David CADLE
29 Director of Alumni Relations ... Ms. Kathy T. FERN
37 Director Financial Aid ... Ms. Michelle L. WILLIAMS
21 Business Office Manager ... Ms. Sara M. DAMINSKI
36 Career Services Coordinator ... Ms. Janie K. SUMMERS
15 Human Resources Coordinator ... Ms. Janice A. BOLLMANN
04 Administrative Asst to President ... Ms. Patricia CAPPS

Research College of Nursing (J)

2525 E Meyer Boulevard, Kansas City MO 64132-1133
County: Jackson FICE Identification: 006392
Unit ID: 178989
Telephone: (816) 995-2800 Carnegie Class: Spec/Health
FAX Number: (816) 995-2817 Calendar System: Semester
URL: www.researchcollege.edu
Established: 1980 Annual Undergrad Tuition & Fees: $34,000
Enrollment: 415 Coed
Affiliation or Control: Proprietary IRS Status: Proprietary
Highest Offering: Master's
Program: Liberal Arts And General; Professional; Nursing Emphasis

Accreditation: NH, NURSE

01 President .... Dr. Nancy O. DEBASIO
05 Dean .... Dr. Julie NAUSER
07 Director Admissions .... Ms. Leslie MENDENHALL
28 Director Diversity .... Vacant
37 Director Financial Aid .... Ms. Stacie WITHERS
24 Director LRC .... Ms. Tobey STOSBERG
32 Director Student Affairs .... Vacant
105 Director Web Based Education .... Ms. Sheryl MAX
09 Senior Technology Analyst .... Mr. Will GIVENS
04 Administrative Asst to President .... Mrs. Sherry L. OWEN
06 Registrar .... Ms. Camelia WILLIAMS

Rockbridge Seminary (A)

3111 East Battlefield Street, Springfield MO 65804

County: Greene Identification: 667151
Telephone: (866) 931-4300 Carnegie Class: Not Classified
FAX Number: (866) 931-4300 Calendar System: Other
URL: www.rockbridge.edu
Established: 2002 Annual Graduate Tuition & Fees: $5,132
Enrollment: 174 Coed
Affiliation or Control: Independent Non-Profit IRS Status: 501(c)3
Highest Offering: Doctorate; No Undergraduates
Program: Professional; Religious Emphasis
Accreditation: DEAC

01 President .... Dr. Daryl ELDRIDGE
05 Chief Learning Officer .... Dr. Sam SIMMONS
08 Head Librarian .... Seth ALLEN
04 Administrative Asst to President .... Heather WILLIAMSON
29 Director Alumni Relations .... Linda GRABER

Rockhurst University (B)

1100 Rockhurst Road, Kansas City MO 64110-2561

County: Jackson FICE Identification: 002499
Unit ID: 179043
Telephone: (816) 501-4000 Carnegie Class: Master's L
FAX Number: (816) 501-4588 Calendar System: Semester
URL: www.rockhurst.edu
Established: 1910 Annual Undergrad Tuition & Fees: $34,000
Enrollment: 3,002 Coed
Affiliation or Control: Roman Catholic IRS Status: 501(c)3
Highest Offering: Doctorate
Program: Liberal Arts And General; Teacher Preparatory; Professional; Business Emphasis
Accreditation: NH, BUS, OT, PTA, SP, TEAC

01 President .... Rev. Thomas B. CURRAN
30 Vice Pres University Advancement .... Mr. Robert GRANT
10 Chief Financial Officer .... Mr. Gerald MOENCH
05 Vice Pres for Academic Affairs .... Dr. Douglas N. DUNHAM
88 Asst to Pres for Mission & Ministry .... Dr. Ellen SPAKE
32 VP Student Development/Athletics .... Dr. Matthew D. QUICK
18 Assoc VP Facilities & Technology .... Mr. Matt W. HEINRICH
84 Associate Vice Pres Enrollment .... Mr. Lane RAMEY
20 Assoc VP Academic Affairs/Planning .... Dr. Paula SHORTER
35 Director of Student Life .... Ms. Angie CARR ROBINETT
88 Assistant Dean of Students .... Mrs. Sandy WADDELL
39 Associate Dean of Students .... Mr. Mark HETZLER
04 Assistant to the President .... Ms. Kathy J. SOLODUCHA
50 Dean Helzberg Sch of Management ... Dr. Cheryl M. MCCONNELL
49 Int Dean Arts & Sciences .... Dr. Renee MICHAEL
58 Int Dean Sch Graduate/Prof Studies .... Dr. Michael CLUMP
66 Pres Research College of Nursing .... Dr. Nancy DEBASIO
08 Director Library .... Ms. Laurie E. HATHMAN
06 Registrar .... Ms. Minda THROWER
37 Director Student Financial Aid .... Ms. Maureen MCKINNON
41 Director of Athletics .... Mr. Gary BURNS
15 Director of Human Resources .... Ms. Jennifer VARGO
13 Director of Infrastructure Services .... Mr. Michael CRAIG
36 Director of Career Center .... Mr. Michael J. THEOBALD
102 Director Foundation/Corp Relations .... Ms. Amy DROUIN
26 Director of Public Relations .... Ms. Katherine FROHOFF
29 Director of University Engagement .... Ms. Mary MOONEY BURNS
88 Director of Marketing .... Ms. Lauren DEBIAK HANNAWALD
42 Director of Campus Ministry .... Ms. Cindy SCHMERSAL
19 Director Security/Safety .... Mr. Randy HOPKINS
38 Director of Student Counseling .... Dr. Elbert DARDEN
31 Director Community Relations .... Ms. Alicia R. DOUGLAS
07 Director of Operations-Admission .... Ms. Annie LEHWALD
40 Director Bookstore .... Ms. Sarah STEENO
92 Director Honors Program .... Dr. Mindy WALKER
108 Assessment Coordinator .... Ms. Annalisa GRAMLICH
09 Institutional Research Coordinator .... Ms. Wendy PICKEL
28 Area & Diversity Coordinator .... Ms. Emily J. KEMPF
14 Support Manager - Computer Services .... Mr. Darnell JONES
88 Controller .... Ms. Kris PACE
88 Dean Research College of Nursing .... Ms. Julie NAUSER
105 Web Development Director .... Mr. Jeremiah BARBER

St. Charles Community College (C)

4601 Mid Rivers Mall Drive, Cottleville MO 63376-2865

County: Saint Charles FICE Identification: 025306
Unit ID: 262031
Telephone: (636) 922-8000 Carnegie Class: Assoc/Pub-S-SC
FAX Number: (636) 922-8352 Calendar System: Semester
URL: www.stchas.edu
Established: 1986 Annual Undergrad Tuition & Fees (In-District): $2,940
Enrollment: 7,214 Coed
Affiliation or Control: State/Local IRS Status: 501(c)3
Highest Offering: Associate Degree
Program: Occupational; 2-Year Principally Bachelor's Creditable
Accreditation: NH, ADNUR, CAHIIM, OTA

01 President .... Dr. Ronald CHESBROUGH
04 Exec Assistant to the President .... Ms. Julie PARCEL
05 VP Academic and Student Affairs .... Mr. Chris BREITMEYER
30 VP College Advancement/Planning .... Ms. Kasey MCKEE
10 VP Administrative Services .... Mr. Todd GALBIERZ
15 VP Human Resources .... Ms. Donna DAVIS
26 VP Marketing/Enrollment Services .... Ms. Heather MCDORMAN
18 Director of Facilities .... Mr. Al KOEHLER
20 AVP for Academic/Student Affairs ...... Dr. Michael B. DOMPIERRE
62 Dean Learning Resources & Acad Sup ...... Dr. Stephanie TOLSON
09 Director Grants and Research .... Dr. Chris JACKSON
13 AVP Technology/Online Learning .... Mr. William STRECKER
84 Dean Enrollment Services .... Ms. Kathy BROCKGREITENS
19 Director Public Safety .... Mr. Bob RONKOSKI
90 Director Technology Support .... Ms. Lisa MOUSER
32 Dean of Student Success .... Vacant
51 Assoc Dean Continuing Education .... Ms. Tina SIEKER
50 Dean Bus/Sci/Educ/Math & Comp Sci ..... Dr. John BOOKSTAVER
57 Dean Arts/Humanities & Soc Sci .... Ms. Karen JONES
40 Director Bookstore and Food Service .... Ms. Patricia A. HAYNES
41 Athletic Director .... Mr. Chris G. GOBER
96 Director Purchasing .... Ms. Christine E. ROMER
91 Director Administrative Computing .... Mr. Jerry BAUER
06 Registrar .... Ms. Kathy BROCKGREITENS
21 Director Financial Services .... Ms. Susan RUBEMEYER
36 Job Placement Coordinator .... Ms. Martha A. TOEBBEN
51 Dean Corporate & Community Dev .... Ms. Amanda SIZEMORE
88 Assoc Dean Student Success .... Ms. Kelley PFEIFFER

Saint Louis Christian College (D)

1360 Grandview Drive, Florissant MO 63033-6499

County: Saint Louis FICE Identification: 012580
Unit ID: 179256
Telephone: (314) 837-6777 Carnegie Class: Spec/Faith
FAX Number: (314) 837-8291 Calendar System: Semester
URL: www.slcconline.edu
Established: 1956 Annual Undergrad Tuition & Fees: $9,750
Enrollment: 173 Coed
Affiliation or Control: Other Protestant IRS Status: 501(c)3
Highest Offering: Baccalaureate
Program: 2-Year Principally Bachelor's Creditable; Religious Emphasis
Accreditation: BI

00 Chancellor .... Mr. Thomas W. MCGEE
01 President .... Dr. Guthrie VEECH
05 Academic Dean .... Dr. Eddy SANDERS
10 Vice Pres of Finance/Operations .... Dr. Judy LINCOLN
32 Dean of Students .... Ms. Christine CABLE
08 Library Manager .... Dr. Michael PABARCUS
41 Athletic Director .... Mr. Scott WOMBLE
06 Registrar .... Ms. Cindy BINGAMON
37 Financial Aid Director .... Ms. Pam RALLS
40 Bookstore Manager .... Ms. Jeri Ann JERALDS
07 Admissions Counselor .... Ms. Haley WOMBLE

Saint Louis College of Health Careers-Fenton Campus (E)

1297 N Highway Drive, Fenton MO 63026-1909

Telephone: (636) 529-0000 Identification: 666274
Accreditation: ABHES, COARC, OTA, PTAA

† Branch campus of Saint Louis College of Health Careers-South Taylor, Saint Louis, MO.

Saint Louis College of Health Careers-South Taylor (F)

909 S Taylor Avenue, Saint Louis MO 63110-1511

County: Saint Louis FICE Identification: 023405
Unit ID: 179511
Telephone: (314) 652-0300 Carnegie Class: Assoc/PrivFP
FAX Number: (314) 652-2125 Calendar System: Semester
URL: www.slchc.com
Established: 1981 Annual Undergrad Tuition & Fees: $15,250
Enrollment: 205 Coed
Affiliation or Control: Proprietary IRS Status: Proprietary
Highest Offering: Associate Degree
Program: Occupational; Technical Emphasis
Accreditation: ABHES

06 Registrar .... Ms. Jackie JENKINS
07 Director of Admissions .... Ms. Joanna FINCH
11 Chief of Administration .... Dr. Rush ROBINSON
36 Director Student Placement .... Mrs. Judy DRY
53 Dean or Director Education .... Ms. Melissa BROWN

St. Louis College of Pharmacy (G)

4588 Parkview Place, Saint Louis MO 63110-1088

County: Independent City FICE Identification: 002504
Unit ID: 179265
Telephone: (314) 367-8700 Carnegie Class: Spec/Health
FAX Number: (314) 446-8304 Calendar System: Semester
URL: www.stlcop.edu
Established: 1864 Annual Undergrad Tuition & Fees: $31,429
Enrollment: 1,366 Coed
Affiliation or Control: Independent Non-Profit IRS Status: 501(c)3
Highest Offering: First Professional Degree
Program: Professional
Accreditation: NH, PHAR

01 President .... Dr. John A. PIEPER
30 Vice Pres Devel/Alumni Relations .... Mr. Brett T. SCHOTT
10 VP Finance/Administration/CFO .... Ms. Heather FLABIANO
07 Vice Pres of Enrollment Services .... Ms. Gloria J. VERTREES
90 Vice Pres Info Technology & CIO .... Mr. Chad SHEPHERD
11 Vice President Administration .... Mr. Marcus LONG
49 Dean Arts & Science/Student Affairs ...... Dr. Kimberly J. KILGORE
67 Dean of Pharmacy .... Dr. Bruce CANADAY
15 Director of Human Resources .... Mr. Daniel C. BAUER
30 Senior Development Officer .... Ms. Colleen WATERMON
06 Registrar .... Ms. Penny J. BRYANT
08 Library Director .... Ms. Jill NISSEN
37 Director of Financial Aid .... Mr. Daniel J. STIFFLER
41 Director of Athletics .... Ms. Jill JOKERST-HARTER
04 Special Assistant to the President .. Sr. Mary Louise DEGENHART

*Saint Louis Community College Center (H)

300 S Broadway, Saint Louis MO 63102-2820

County: Saint Louis FICE Identification: 002471
Unit ID: 179283
Telephone: (314) 539-5000 Carnegie Class: N/A
FAX Number: (314) 539-5170
URL: www.stlcc.edu

01 Chancellor .... Dr. Jeff PITTMAN
05 Vice Chanc Academic Affairs .... Vacant
10 Vice Chanc Finance/Administration .... Mr. Kent KAY
103 Assoc VC Workforce & Cmty Develop .... Mr. Stephen LONG
102 Executive Director Foundation .... Ms. Jo-Ann DIGMAN
84 Director Enrollment Management .... Vacant
15 Assoc Vice Chanc HR .... Mr. Bill MILLER
26 Director Public Info/Marketing .... Mr. Dan KIMACK
09 Director of Institutional Research .... Ms. Kelli BURNS
20 Director Instructional Resources .... Ms. Sheila OUELLETTE
30 Director of Grants .... Ms. Gina BENESH
06 Sr Mgr/Enrollment Processing .... Ms. Karla GABLE
04 Administrative Asst to Chancellor .... Ms. Yvonne HELBERG
101 Secretary of the Board .... Ms. Rebecca GARRISON
106 Director Online Education .... Ms. Robin E. GREBING
37 Dir Dist Financial Aid/Scholarships . Ms. Regina G. BLACKSHEAR
96 Assistant Controller .... Ms. Cindy GREEN
19 Director Security/Safety .... Mr. Mark POTRATZ
41 Athletic Director .... Mr. Shawn SUMME
43 Dir Legal Services/General Counsel .... Ms. Mary NELSON

**Saint Louis Community College at Forest Park* (I)

5600 Oakland Avenue, Saint Louis MO 63110-1393

Telephone: (314) 644-9100 Identification: 770946
Accreditation: NH, ACFEI, ADNUR, CAHIIM, COARC, DA, DH, DMS, EMT, MLTAD, RAD, SURGT

† Branch campus of Saint Louis Community College Center, Saint Louis, MO.

**Saint Louis Community College at Florissant Valley* (J)

3400 Pershall Road, Saint Louis MO 63135-1499

Telephone: (314) 513-4200 FICE Identification: 002470
Accreditation: &NH, ADNUR, ART, DIETT, ENGT

† Branch campus of Saint Louis Community College Center, Saint Louis, MO.

**Saint Louis Community College at Meramec* (K)

11333 Big Bend Road, Kirkwood MO 63122-5799

Telephone: (314) 984-7500 FICE Identification: 002472
Accreditation: &NH, ADNUR, ART, OTA, PTAA

† Branch campus of Saint Louis Community College Center, Saint Louis, MO.

**Saint Louis Community College at Wildwood* (L)

2645 Generations Drive, Wildwood MO 63040-1168

Telephone: (636) 422-2000 Identification: 667084
Accreditation: &NH

† Branch campus of Saint Louis Community College Center, Saint Louis, MO.

Saint Louis University (M)

One Grand Boulevard, Saint Louis MO 63103-2097

County: Independent City FICE Identification: 002506
Unit ID: 179159
Telephone: (314) 977-2500 Carnegie Class: RU/H
FAX Number: (314) 977-3874 Calendar System: Semester
URL: www.slu.edu
Established: 1818 Annual Undergrad Tuition & Fees: $39,266
Enrollment: 13,287 Coed
Affiliation or Control: Roman Catholic IRS Status: 501(c)3
Highest Offering: Doctorate
Program: Liberal Arts And General; Teacher Preparatory; Professional

Accreditation: NH, AAB, ARCPA, ART, BUS, CAATE, CAHIIM, CLPSY, CYTO, DENT, DIETD, DIETI, ENG, HSA, LAW, MED, MFCD, MT, NMT, NURSE, OT, PH, PTA, RTT, SP, SPAA, SW, TED

01 President .... Dr. Fred P. PESTELLO
05 Provost .... Dr. Nancy BRICKHOUSE
10 Vice Pres/Chief Financial Officer .... Mr. David HEIMBURGER
18 Int Assoc VP Facilities Management .... Mr. Michael LUCIDO
84 Vice President Enrollment & Ret .... Mr. Jay GOFF
12 Director Madrid Campus .... Dr. Paul VITA
15 VP Human Resources .... Mr. Mickey LUNA
26 VP Marketing and Communications .... Mr. Jeffrey FOWLER
43 Vice President/General Counsel .... Mr. William R. KAUFFMAN
32 Vice President Student Development .... Dr. Kent PORTERFIELD
30 VP Development .... Ms. Sheila M. MANION
42 Spcl Asst to Pres Mission/Identity .... Vacant
13 Vice Pres Information Tech Svcs/CIO .... Mr. David HAKANSON
23 Vice President for Medical Affairs .... Dr. Philip O. ALDERSON
26 Asst VP for Marketing & Creat Svcs .... Ms. Laura GEISER
29 Assoc VP for Alumni Relations .... Ms. Meg CONNOLLY
21 Controller .... Mr. David GRABE
35 Associate VP and Dean of Students .... Dr. Ramona HICKS
54 Assoc Dean Parks Col Engr/Aviation .... Vacant
76 Dean Doisy College of Health Scis .... Dr. Mardell WILSON
49 Dean Arts & Sciences .... Dr. Christopher DUNCAN
50 Dean Cook School of Business .... Dr. Mark HIGGINS
61 Dean of Law .... Mr. Michael A. WOLFF
63 Dean of Medical School .... Dr. Philip O. ALDERSON
79 Dean Philosophy & Letters .... Bro. William REHG, SJ
69 Col for Pub Health & Soc Justice .... Dr. Don LINHORST
53 Dean Col of Educ & Public Svc .... Dr. Anne RULE
08 University Librarian .... Mr. David CASSENS
88 Exec Dir Ctr for Health Care Ethics .... Dr. Jeffrey BISHOP
52 Exec Dir Ctr Advanced Dental Educ .... Dr. John HATTON
46 Vice President for Research .... Dr. Raymond TAIT
19 Asst VP Pub Safety & Emergency Prep .... Mr. James MORAN
06 University Registrar .... Mr. Jay HAUGEN
07 Dean of Undergraduate Admission .... Ms. Jean GILMAN
37 Director Financial Aid .... Ms. Cari S. WICKLIFFE
39 Director Housing & Res Life .... Ms. Melinda CARLSON
41 Athletics Director .... Mr. Christopher V. MAY
36 Director Career Services .... Ms. Kim REITTER
85 Director International Center .... Mr. Tim HERCULES
92 Director Honors Program .... Ms. Jessica PEROLIO
23 Director Student Health Center .... Ms. Deborah M. SCHEFF
31 Pgm Mgr Leadership Community Svcs .... Dr. Bryan SOKOL
100 Director of the Pres Office .... Ms. Barb SAPIENZA
88 Director Univ Museums/Galleries .... Dr. Petruta LIPAN
44 Director Planned Giving .... Mr. Kent G. LEVAN
40 Manager Bookstore .... Ms. Debbie SCHNEIDER
20 Asst Academic Vice President .... Dr. Steven SANCHEZ
96 Director of Business Services .... Mr. Jeff HOVEY
22 Dir Ofc of Inst Equity & Diversity .... Ms. Michelle LEWIS
86 Director Government Relations .... Mr. Marc SCHEESSELE
28 Spcl Asst to Pres Diversity/Com Eng .... Dr. Jonathan C. SMITH

Saint Luke's College of Health Sciences (A)

624 Westport Road, Kansas City MO 64111

County: Jackson — FICE Identification: 009782 — Unit ID: 179450
Telephone: (816) 936-8700 — Carnegie Class: Spec/Health
FAX Number: N/A — Calendar System: Semester
URL: www.saintlukescollege.edu
Established: 1903 — Annual Undergrad Tuition & Fees: $14,305
Enrollment: 453 — Coed
Affiliation or Control: Independent Non-Profit — IRS Status: 501(c)3
Highest Offering: Master's
Program: Nursing Emphasis
Accreditation: NH, NURSE

01 Interim President .... Dr. Dean L. HUBBARD
05 Chief Financial Officer .... Ms. Rebecca PECK
10 Chief Financial Officer .... Ms. Rebecca PECK
09 Dean of Students .... Ms. Marcia LADAGE
88 Director Accreditation/Quality Mgmt .... Ms. Tere NAYLOR
30 Director of Development .... Dr. Melody MESSNER
06 Registrar/Dir Records Mgmt .... Ms. Jean SUMMERS
26 Communications/Alumni Rels Mgr .... Ms. Laurie DELONG
26 Director of Admissions .... Mr. Josh RICHARDS

Southeast Missouri Hospital College of Nursing and Health Sciences (B)

2001 William Street, 2nd Floor, Cape Girardeau MO 63703-5815

County: Cape Girardeau — FICE Identification: 030709 — Unit ID: 417734
Telephone: (573) 334-6825 — Carnegie Class: Assoc/PrivNFP
FAX Number: (573) 339-7805 — Calendar System: Other
URL: www.southeastmissourihospitalcollege.edu
Established: 1990 — Annual Undergrad Tuition & Fees: $15,690
Enrollment: 233 — Coed
Affiliation or Control: Independent Non-Profit — IRS Status: 501(c)3
Highest Offering: Baccalaureate
Program: 2-Year Principally Bachelor's Creditable; Nursing Emphasis
Accreditation: NH, ADNUR, MT, RAD, SURGT

01 President .... Dr. Tonya BUTTRY
05 Dean for General Education .... Dr. Leon BOOK
66 Dean of Nursing .... Dr. Donna SHIRRELL
06 Registrar .... Ms. Debbie HOWEY
37 Financial Aid Coordinator .... Ms. Margie SCHWENT
07 Admissions/Instl Research Officer .... Ms. Rhonda VANDERGRIFF

Southeast Missouri State University (C)

One University Plaza, Cape Girardeau MO 63701-4799

County: Cape Girardeau — FICE Identification: 002501 — Unit ID: 179557
Telephone: (573) 651-2000 — Carnegie Class: Master's L
FAX Number: (573) 651-2200 — Calendar System: Semester
URL: www.semo.edu
Established: 1873 — Annual Undergrad Tuition & Fees (In-State): $6,990
Enrollment: 12,087 — Coed
Affiliation or Control: State — IRS Status: 501(c)3
Highest Offering: Beyond Master's But Less Than Doctorate
Program: Liberal Arts And General; Teacher Preparatory; Professional
Accreditation: NH, BUS, CAATE, CACREP, CS, DIETD, DIETI, ENG, ENGT, JOUR, MUS, NAIT, NRPA, NURSE, SP, SW, TED, THEA

01 President .... Dr. Carlos VARGAS-ABURTO
05 Interim Provost/Chief Academic Ofcr .... Dr. Gerald MCDOUGALL
10 VP Finance & Administration .... Mrs. Kathy M. MANGELS
84 VP Enrollment Mgmt/Student Success .... Dr. Debbie BELOW
30 Vice Pres University Advancement .... Mr. Bill HOLLAND
20 Vice Provost .... Dr. Charles MCALLISTER
108 Asst Provost for Inst Rsch & Assess .... Dr. Kang BAI
04 Associate to the President .... Ms. Diane O. SIDES
100 Sr Assoc to the President/Board Sec .... Mr. Brady L. BARKE
22 Coord of Inst Equity & Diversity .... Ms. Sonia RUCKER
13 Asst Vice Pres Information Tech .... Vacant
106 Dean Online Lrng .... Dr. Allen GATHMAN
58 Dean Sch of Grad Studies .... Dr. Charles MCALLISTER
89 Dean of University Studies .... Dr. Francisco BARRIOS
50 Interim Dean DL Harrison Col Bus .... Dr. Gary JOHNSON
53 Dean College of Education .... Dr. Diana ROGERS-ADKINSON
76 Dean College Health & Human Svc .... Dr. Morris JENKINS
79 Dean College of Liberal Arts .... Dr. Francisco BARRIOS
72 Dean College of Science/Tech & Ag .... Dr. Chris MCGOWAN
32 Dean of Students .... Dr. Debbie BELOW
88 Dean Academic Information Svcs .... Vacant
08 Interim Director of Kent Library .... Ms. Cathy ROEDER
07 Director of Admissions .... Ms. Lenell HAHN
109 AVP Stdnt Success & Auxiliary Svcs .... Dr. Bruce SKINNER
35 Director of Campus Life .... Ms. Michele IRBY
26 Exec Dir Univ Comm & Mktg .... Mr. Jeff HARMON
41 Interim Director of Athletics .... Mr. Brady L. BARKE
29 Director Alumni Services .... Mr. Jay WOLZ
85 Exec Dir Intl Education & Svcs .... Mr. Zahir AHMED
51 Dir Extended & Continuing Education .... Ms. Joyce D. BECKER
12 Director Malden Campus .... Dr. Nicholas THIELE
12 Director Kennett Campus .... Ms. Marsha L. BLANCHARD
12 Director Sikeston Campus .... Mr. Stephen BORGSMILLER
18 Director of Facilities Management .... Ms. Angela MEYER
37 Director of Financial Aid .... Ms. Karen WALKER
27 Director of News Bureau .... Ms. Ann K. HAYES
15 Director of Human Resources .... Mr. Jim COOK
19 Director of Public Safety/Transit .... Mr. Doug RICHARDS
06 Registrar .... Ms. Sandy L. HINKLE
88 Director of Show Me Center .... Mr. Wil GORMAN
92 Director Jane Stephens Honors Pgm .... Dr. Kevin DICKSON
38 Dir Counseling & Disability Svcs .... Ms. Torie GROGRAN
96 Purchasing Manager .... Ms. Sarah STEINNERD
102 Director of Corporate Relations .... Mr. Chris MARTIN
39 Director of Residence Life .... Dr. Kendra SKINNER

Southwest Baptist University (D)

1600 University Avenue, Bolivar MO 65613-2597

County: Polk — FICE Identification: 002502 — Unit ID: 179326
Telephone: (417) 328-5281 — Carnegie Class: Master's L
FAX Number: (417) 328-1514 — Calendar System: Semester
URL: www.sbuniv.edu
Established: 1878 — Annual Undergrad Tuition & Fees: $21,840
Enrollment: 3,696 — Coed
Affiliation or Control: Southern Baptist — IRS Status: 501(c)3
Highest Offering: Doctorate
Program: Liberal Arts And General; Teacher Preparatory; Professional
Accreditation: NH, ACBSP, ADNUR, CAATE, CS, MUS, NUR, PTA, RAD, SW

01 President .... Dr. Pat TAYLOR
05 Interim Provost .... Dr. Allison LANGFORD
11 Vice President Administration .... Mrs. Tara PARSON
30 Vice President University Relations .... Dr. Brad JOHNSON
84 Dean of Enrollment Management .... Mr. Darren CROWDER
32 Vice Pres for Student Development .... Dr. Rob HARRIS
88 Vice Pres Oper Mercy Col Nurs & HS .... Dr. Robert MCGLASSON
20 Associate Provost .... Dr. Allison LANGFORD
10 Controller .... Vacant
29 Director of Alumni Engagement .... Ms. Holly STOCKARD
07 Director Admissions .... Vacant
41 Athletic Director .... Mr. Mike PITTS
06 Registrar .... Mr. John CREDILLE
35 Director Student Activities .... Mr. Nathan PENLAND
39 Director Residence Life .... Ms. Landee NEVILLS
42 Director University Ministries .... Mr. Kurt CADDY
15 Director of Human Resources .... Mrs. Carolyn O'KELLEY
18 Director Physical Plant .... Mr. Bob GLIDWELL
19 Director Campus Security .... Mr. Mark GRABOWSKI
08 Director of Library Services .... Dr. Ed WALTON
50 Dean College Business/Computer Sci .... Dr. Troy BETHARDS
73 Dean College Theology/Ministry .... Dr. Rodney REEVES
53 Dean Education/Social Sciences .... Dr. Kevin SCHRIVER
57 Dean Music/Arts/Letters .... Dr. Jeff WATERS
81 Dean Science/Math .... Dr. Perry TOMPKINS
36 Director of Career Services .... Mrs. Suzanne POWERS
13 Network Administrator .... Mr. Kevin KELLEY
90 Director Instructional Technology .... Mr. Neal CROSS
91 Chief Technology Officer .... Mr. David BOLTON
38 Director Counseling Services .... Vacant
37 Director Student Financial Planning .... Mr. Brad GAMBLE
56 Director Extended Learning .... Mr. Scott MCNEAL
26 Chief Public Relations Officer .... Mrs. Charlotte MARSCH
09 Director of Institutional Research .... Dr. Duke JONES
96 Director of Purchasing .... Vacant
40 Book Store Manager .... Ms. Carol SHOEMAKER
04 Administrative Asst to President .... Mrs. Ashley DINWIDDIE

Southwest Baptist University Mountain View Center (E)

209 W First Street, Mountain View MO 65548

Telephone: (417) 934-2999 — Identification: 770326
Accreditation: &NH

† Branch campus of Southwest Baptist University, Bolivar, MO.

Southwest Baptist University Salem Center (F)

501 S Grand, Salem MO 65560

Telephone: (573) 729-7071 — Identification: 770327
Accreditation: &NH

† Branch campus of Southwest Baptist University, Bolivar, MO.

Southwest Baptist University Springfield Center (G)

4431 S Fremont, Springfield MO 65804

Telephone: (417) 820-5049 — Identification: 770328
Accreditation: &NH

† Branch campus of Southwest Baptist University, Bolivar, MO.

State Fair Community College (H)

3201 W 16th Street, Sedalia MO 65301-2199

County: Pettis — FICE Identification: 008080 — Unit ID: 179539
Telephone: (660) 596-7222 — Carnegie Class: Assoc/Pub-R-M
FAX Number: (660) 596-7335 — Calendar System: Semester
URL: www.sfccmo.edu
Established: 1966 — Annual Undergrad Tuition & Fees (In-District): $2,352
Enrollment: 4,983 — Coed
Affiliation or Control: Local — IRS Status: 501(c)3
Highest Offering: Associate Degree
Program: Occupational; 2-Year Principally Bachelor's Creditable
Accreditation: NH, CAHIIM, CONST, DH, OTA, RAD

01 President .... Dr. Joanna ANDERSON
05 VP for Educ/Student Support Svcs .... Dr. Brent BATES
10 VP for Finance/Administration & HR .... Mr. Garry SORRELL
13 CIO Information Systems & Tech .... Mr. Mark HAVERLY
20 Dean of Academic Affairs .... Mr. Steve SCHEINER
75 Dean Vocational/Technical Studies .... Mr. Mark KELCHNER
38 Dean Student Support .... Dr. Joe GILGOUR
30 Exec Director for Development .... Ms. Mary TEURNER
06 Registrar .... Mrs. Jennifer WILBANKS
37 Director of Financial Aid .... Ms. Lana DEJAYNES
18 Chief Facilities/Physical Plant .... Mr. Justin O'NEAL
21 Controller Business Officer .... Mrs. Diane BROCKMAN
26 Director of Marketing/Communication .... Mrs. Dana KELCHNER
07 Director of Admissions .... Mrs. Amanda STOECKLEIN
04 Administrative Asst to President .... Ms. Toni WALTER
41 Athletic Director .... Mr. Darren PAMMIER

State Technical College of Missouri (I)

One Technology Drive, Linn MO 65051-0479

County: Osage — FICE Identification: 004711 — Unit ID: 177977
Telephone: (573) 897-5000 — Carnegie Class: Assoc/Pub-R-S
FAX Number: (573) 897-4656 — Calendar System: Semester
URL: www.statetechmo.edu
Established: 1961 — Annual Undergrad Tuition & Fees (In-State): $5,872
Enrollment: 1,484 — Coed
Affiliation or Control: State — IRS Status: 501(c)3
Highest Offering: Associate Degree
Program: Occupational; 2-Year Principally Bachelor's Creditable; Technical Emphasis
Accreditation: NH, DA, ENGT, NAIT, PTAA, RAD

01 President .... Dr. Donald M. CLAYCOMB
05 Dean Academic Affairs/Student Svcs .... Victoria SCHWINKE
13 Dean Information Technology .... Don LLOYD
09 Dean Institutional Research/Plng .... Dr. Rick MIHALEVICH
30 Executive Director Development .... Scott PETERS
08 Int College Librarian .... Fran STUMPF
37 Director Student Financial Aid .... Becky WHITHAUS
06 Registrar .... Elaine BRANDT

07 Director Admissions .... Kathy SCHEULEN
10 Director of Finance .... Jennifer JACOBS
20 Associate Academic Officer .... Janet CLANTON
21 Controller .... Jennifer JACOBS
29 Dir Alumni Relations/Chief PR Ofcr .... Scott PETERS
32 Director Student Affairs .... Richard PEMBERTON
36 Director Student Placement .... Glenda WHITNEY
28 Director of Diversity .... Richard PEMBERTON
15 Director Personnel Services .... Jennifer JACOBS
84 Director Enrollment Management .... Kathy SCHEULEN
18 Chief Facilities/Physical Plant .... Don LLOYD
38 Student Counselor .... Rebecca MEHMERT
101 Secretary of the Institution/Board .... Sue GOVE
86 Director Government Relations .... Becky DUNN

Stephens College (A)

1200 E Broadway, Columbia MO 65215-0001
County: Boone FICE Identification: 002512
Unit ID: 179548
Telephone: (573) 442-2211 Carnegie Class: Bac/Diverse
FAX Number: (573) 876-7248 Calendar System: Semester
URL: www.stephens.edu
Established: 1833 Annual Undergrad Tuition & Fees: $28,976
Enrollment: 873 Female
Affiliation or Control: Independent Non-Profit IRS Status: 501(c)3
Highest Offering: Master's
Program: Liberal Arts And General; Teacher Preparatory; Professional; Fine Arts Emphasis
Accreditation: NH, CAHIIM

01 President .... Dr. Dianne LYNCH
10 Vice Pres Finance/Business/CFO .... Dr. Lindi OVERTON
05 Vice Pres Academic Affairs .... Dr. Suzan HARKNESS
30 Vice Pres Institutional Advancement .... Ms. Meichele FOSTER
32 Vice President for Student Services .... Vacant
26 VP of Marketing/Public Relations .... Ms. Rebecca KLINE
06 Registrar .... Ms. Linda SHARP
13 IT Director .... Mr. Mark BRUNNER
41 Interim Athletic Director .... Mr. Ray FRON
21 Director of Accounting .... Mr. Josh HENGGLER
37 Interim Director of Financial Aid .... Ms. Kimberly STONECIPHER-FISHER
04 Administrative Asst to President .... Ms. Lita PISTONO
07 Director of Admissions .... Vacant
08 Head Librarian .... Mr. Dan KAMMER
18 Director of Facilities Mgmt .... Mr. Gregory MANKEY
19 Director Security/Safety .... Mr. Tony COLEMAN
39 Director of Residence Life .... Ms. Alissa PEI

Stevens Institute of Business & Arts (B)

1521 Washington Avenue, Saint Louis MO 63103
County: Saint Louis FICE Identification: 008552
Unit ID: 178767
Telephone: (314) 421-0949 Carnegie Class: Bac/Diverse
FAX Number: (314) 421-0304 Calendar System: Quarter
URL: www.siba.edu
Established: 1947 Annual Undergrad Tuition & Fees: $17,640
Enrollment: 143 Coed
Affiliation or Control: Proprietary IRS Status: Proprietary
Highest Offering: Baccalaureate
Program: Occupational
Accreditation: ACICS

01 President .... Ms. Cynthia A. MUSTERMAN
05 Academic Dean & Registrar .... Ms. Emilee SCHNEFKE
37 Director of Financial Aid .... Ms. Christa SIAMPOS
07 Dir Admissions/Cmty Development .... Ms. Christina EVANS

Texas County Technical College (C)

6915 S Highway 63 PO Box 314, Houston MO 65483
County: Texas FICE Identification: 035793
Unit ID: 441487
Telephone: (417) 967-5466 Carnegie Class: Assoc/PrivNFP
FAX Number: (417) 967-4604 Calendar System: Semester
URL: www.texascountytech.edu
Established: 1986 Annual Undergrad Tuition & Fees: $16,044
Enrollment: 125 Coed
Affiliation or Control: Independent Non-Profit IRS Status: 501(c)3
Highest Offering: Associate Degree
Program: Occupational; 2-Year Principally Bachelor's Creditable
Accreditation: ACICS

01 President .... Ms. Charlotte GRAY
07 Director of Admissions/Registrar .... Ms. Clarice CASEBEER
37 Acting Financial Aid Director .... Ms. Clarice CASEBEER

Three Rivers Community College (D)

2080 Three Rivers Boulevard,
Poplar Bluff MO 63901-2350
County: Butler FICE Identification: 004713
Unit ID: 179645
Telephone: (573) 840-9600 Carnegie Class: Assoc/Pub-R-M
FAX Number: (573) 840-9604 Calendar System: Semester
URL: www.trcc.edu
Established: 1966 Annual Undergrad Tuition & Fees (In-State): $3,348
Enrollment: 4,201 Coed
Affiliation or Control: State IRS Status: 501(c)3
Highest Offering: Associate Degree
Program: Occupational; 2-Year Principally Bachelor's Creditable
Accreditation: NH, ACBSP, ADNUR, MLTAD, OTA

01 President .... Dr. Wesley A. PAYNE
10 Chief Financial Officer .... Ms. Charlotte EUBANK
05 Vice President for Learning .... Dr. Wesley A. PAYNE
08 Director Library Services .... Ms. Kathy SANDERS
37 Director Financial Aid .... Ms. Laura MILLIGAN
06 Registrar .... Ms. Melanie HAMANN
32 Dean of Student Services .... Ms. Ann MATTHEWS
09 Dean of Institutional Effectiveness .... Dr. Maribeth PAYNE
09 Director of Institutional Research .... Ms. Bridgett BARNHILL
18 Chief Facilities/Physical Plant .... Mr. Rob TOMLINSON
15 Director Human Resources .... Ms. Kristina D. MCDANIEL
26 Chief Public Relations Officer .... Ms. Teresa JOHNSON
30 Chief Development/Dir Alumni Rels .... Mr. Brad THIELEMIER
84 Director Enrollment Management .... Mr. Chris ADAMS
96 Dir Procurement/Risk Management .... Ms. Cambrea HALCUMB
04 Administrative Asst to President .... Ms. Janine HEATH
103 Dir Workforce/Career Development .... Dr. Brenda RUSSELL
13 Chief Info Technology Officer (CIO) .... Mr. Steve ATWOOD
22 Dir Affirmative Action/EEO .... Ms. Kristina D. MCDANIEL
39 Director Student Housing .... Mr. Brad PIERCY

Truman State University (E)

100 E Normal, Kirksville MO 63501-4221
County: Adair FICE Identification: 002495
Unit ID: 178615
Telephone: (660) 785-4000 Carnegie Class: Master's M
FAX Number: (660) 785-4030 Calendar System: Semester
URL: www.truman.edu
Established: 1867 Annual Undergrad Tuition & Fees (In-State): $7,430
Enrollment: 6,248 Coed
Affiliation or Control: State IRS Status: 501(c)3
Highest Offering: Master's
Program: Liberal Arts And General; Teacher Preparatory; Professional
Accreditation: NH, BUS, BUSA, CAATE, MUS, NURSE, SP, TED

01 President .... Dr. Troy D. PAINO
05 Exec VP Academic Affairs & Provost .... Dr. Susan L. THOMAS
30 Vice Pres University Advancement .... Mr. Mark GAMBAIANA
10 VP for Admin Finance & Planning .... Mr. David RECTOR
84 VP for Enrollment Management .... Mrs. Regina MORIN
32 Dean of Student Affairs .... Dr. Lou Ann GILCHRIST
43 General Counsel .... Mr. Warren WELLS
21 Comptroller .... Mrs. Judy MULLINS
41 Athletic Director .... Mr. Jerry WOLLMERING
15 Executive Dir of Human Resources .... Ms. Sally HERLETH
07 Director of Admissions .... Mrs. Melody CHAMBERS
37 Financial Aid Director .... Mrs. Kathy ELSEA
06 Registrar .... Mrs. Margaret HERRON
13 Director Information Technology .... Mrs. Donna LISS
26 Director of Public Relations .... Mrs. Heidi TEMPLETON
88 Dir of Institute for Acad Outreach .... Dr. Kevin MINCH
38 Dir Student Health/Counseling Svcs .... Dr. Brenda HIGGINS
83 Dean Sch of Soc & Cultural Studies .... Dr. Elizabeth CLARK
49 Dean School of Arts & Letters .... Dr. James O'DONNELL
81 Dean Sch of Science & Mathematics .... Dr. Jon GERING
53 Dean Sch of Health Sciences & Educ .... Dr. Janet GOOCH
08 Dean of Libraries & Museums .... Mr. Richard COUGHLIN
50 Dean School of Business .... Dr. Debra KERBY

University of Central Missouri (F)

Administration Building, room 101,
Warrensburg MO 64093-5299
County: Johnson FICE Identification: 002454
Unit ID: 176965
Telephone: (660) 543-4255 Carnegie Class: Master's L
FAX Number: (660) 543-4200 Calendar System: Semester
URL: www.ucmo.edu
Established: 1871 Annual Undergrad Tuition & Fees (In-State): $7,340
Enrollment: 13,379 Coed
Affiliation or Control: State IRS Status: 501(c)3
Highest Offering: Beyond Master's But Less Than Doctorate
Program: Liberal Arts And General; Teacher Preparatory; Professional
Accreditation: NH, AAB, AAFCS, ART, BUS, BUSA, CAATE, CACREP, CEA, CIDA, CONST, CS, DIETD, ENGR, MUS, NAIT, NURSE, SP, SW, TED, THEA

01 President .... Dr. Charles M. AMBROSE
101 Exec Asst to Pres/Asst Sec to Board .... Ms. Monica R. HUFFMAN
05 Provost/Chief Learning Officer .... Dr. Deborah J. CURTIS
32 Vice Prov Student Experience/Engage .... Dr. Sharlene GARBER BAX
20 Vice Prov Academic Program/Services .... Dr. Kim ANDREWS
35 Assoc Vice Prov Student Services .... Dr. Corey L. BOWMAN
84 Vice Prov Recruitment/Outreach .... Dr. Mike GODARD
30 Vice Pres Univ Development .... Mr. Jason S. DRUMMOND
08 Dean of Library Services .... Dr. Gail STAINES
49 Dean College of Arts/Humanities/Sci .... Dr. Gersham NELSON
72 Dean College of Health/Science/Tech .... Dr. Alice L. GREIFE
50 Dean Harmon Col Business/Prof Stds .... Dr. Roger J. BEST
92 Dean Honors College & Intl Affairs .... Dr. Joseph D. LEWANDOWSKI
53 Dean of College of Education .... Dr. Michael D. WRIGHT
10 Vice Pres Finance/Chief Ops Ofcr .... Mr. John MERRIGAN
13 Vice Provost for Technology & CIO .... Dr. James F. GRAHAM
41 Athletic Director .... Mr. Jerry M. HUGHES
06 Director of Registrar .... Ms. Teri A. BOWMAN
26 Interim Chief Comm Officer .... Mr. Dennis CRYDER
09 Director Testing Services .... Ms. Carole NIMMER
36 Dir Career Development Services .... Mr. Kenneth SCHUELLER
37 Dir Student Financial Assistance .... Ms. Angela L. KARLIN
19 Director of Public Safety .... Mr. Scott RHOAD
109 AVP Student Auxiliary Services .... Mr. Patrick J. BRADLEY
21 Director Accounting Services .... Ms. Toni L. KREKE
18 Dir Facilities & Planning Op .... Mr. Chris BAMMAN
96 Director Purchasing .... Ms. Lisa BUTLER
15 Director Human Resources .... Mr. Rick L. DIXON
40 Director of Univ Store & Textbooks .... Mr. Charles D. RUTT
56 Vice Provost of Extended Studies .... Ms. Laurel HOGUE
07 Director Admissions .... Ms. Ann A. NORDYKE
16 Asst Director of Human Resources .... Ms. Cheryl D. TRELOW
29 Asst VP Resources Development .... Ms. Jennifer L. VANDERBOUT
38 Director Counseling Center .... Dr. Paul D. POLYCHRONIS
24 Director CentralNET .... Mr. Michael JEFFRIES

*University of Missouri System Administration (G)

321 University Hall, Columbia MO 65211-3020
County: Boone FICE Identification: 002515
Unit ID: 178439
Telephone: (573) 882-2011 Carnegie Class: N/A
FAX Number: (573) 882-2721
URL: www.umsystem.edu

01 President .... Mr. Tim M. WOLFE
100 Chief of Staff .... Ms. Zora Z. MULLIGAN
10 Vice President Finance .... Dr. Brian D. BURNETT
05 Exec Vice Pres Acad Affairs .... Dr. Henry C. FOLEY
13 Vice President Info Technology .... Dr. Gary K. ALLEN
86 Vice President University Relations .... Mr. Stephen C. KNORR
15 Vice Pres Human Resource Services .... Ms. Elizabeth RODRIGUEZ
20 Sr Assoc Vice Pres Academic Affairs .... Dr. Steven W. GRAHAM
43 General Counsel .... Mr. Stephen J. OWENS
26 Chief Communications Officer .... Mr. John FOUGERE
17 CEO/COO UM Health Care .... Mr. Mitch WASDEN
23 Vice Chancellor for Health Sciences .... Dr. Harold A. WILLIAMSON
21 Treasurer .... Mr. Tom F. RICHARDS
21 Controller .... Mr. Ryan RAPP
04 Executive Asst to President .... Ms. Regina A. MAY
101 Secretary of the Board of Curators .... Ms. Cindy S. HARMON

*University of Missouri - Columbia (H)

Columbia MO 65211-0001
County: Boone FICE Identification: 002516
Unit ID: 178396
Telephone: (573) 882-2121 Carnegie Class: RU/VH
FAX Number: (573) 882-9907 Calendar System: Semester
URL: www.missouri.edu
Established: 1839 Annual Undergrad Tuition & Fees (In-State): $9,808
Enrollment: 35,441 Coed
Affiliation or Control: State IRS Status: 501(c)3
Highest Offering: Doctorate
Program: Liberal Arts And General; Teacher Preparatory; Professional
Accreditation: NH, BUS, BUSA, CIDA, CLPSY, COARC, COPSY, CS, DIETC, DMS, ENG, HSA, IPSY, JOUR, LAW, MED, MUS, NMT, NRPA, NURSE, OT, PCSAS, PH, PTA, RAD, SCPSY, SP, SPAA, SW, TEAC, VET

02 Chancellor .... Mr. R. Bowen LOFTIN
03 Deputy Chancellor .... Mr. Michael A. MIDDLETON
05 Exec Vice Chanc Acad Affs/Provost .... Dr. Garnett STOKES
20 Deputy Provost .... Mr. Kenneth D. DEAN
32 Vice Chancellor Student Affairs .... Dr. Catherine C. SCROGGS
11 VC Administrative Services .... Ms. Jacquelyn K. JONES
10 Vice Chancellor for Finance & CFO .... Ms. Rhonda GIBLER
58 Assoc VC Grad Stds/Assoc VP Acad Af .... Dr. Leona RUBIN
04 Asst to Chanc for University Affs .... Ms. Christine H. KOUKOLA
30 Vice Chancellor University Advance .... Dr. Tom HILES
29 Assoc VC Alumni Relations/Devel .... Mr. Todd A. MCCUBBIN
17 Vice Chancellor for Health Sciences .... Dr. Harold A. WILLIAMSON, JR.
57 Director School of Music .... Dr. Robert SHAY
84 Vice Provost for Enrollment Mgmt .... Dr. Ann J. KORSCHGEN
56 Vice Provost for Extension .... Dr. Michael D. OUART
85 Vice Provost International Pgms .... Dr. Handy WILLIAMSON
46 Sr VC Research & Grad Studies .... Mr. Hank FOLEY
13 Chief Information Officer .... Dr. Gary K. ALLEN
15 Int AVP Human Resources .... Ms. Jatha SADOWSKI
18 Chief Operations Officer .... Mr. Gary L. WARD
46 Spec Asst to Vice Chanc of Research .... Vacant
35 Asst Vice Chanc Student Affairs .... Dr. Jeffrey ZEILENGA
06 University Registrar .... Ms. Brenda V. SELMAN
09 VProv Inst Research & Quality Impr .... Dr. Mardy T. EIMERS
08 Director of Libraries .... Mr. James A. COGSWELL
37 Director Student Financial Aid .... Mr. Nick PREWETT
47 Vice Chanc/Dean Agric/Food/Nat Res .... Dr. Thomas L. PAYNE
49 Dean Arts & Science .... Dr. Michael J. O'BRIEN
50 Dean of Business .... Ms. Joan GABEL
88 Director School of Accountancy .... Dr. Vairam ARUNACHALAM
53 Dean of Education .... Dr. Daniel CLAY
54 Interim Dean of Engineering .... Dr. Robert W. SCHWARTZ
65 Dir School of Natural Resources .... Dr. Mark R. RYAN
76 Dean School of Health Professions .... Dr. Richard E. OLIVER
59 Dean Human Environmental Science .... Dr. Stephen R. JORGENSEN
60 Dean of Journalism .... Dr. R. Dean MILLS
61 Dean of Law .... Dr. Gary MYERS
63 Dean of Medicine .... Dr. Robert CHURCHILL
66 Dean of Nursing .... Dr. Judith FITZGERALD MILLER
70 Director School of Social Work .... Dr. Marjorie SABLE
74 Dean of Veterinary Medicine .... Dr. Neil OLSON

19 Director of University Police ... Mr. Jack W. WATRING
27 VC for Marketing & Communications ... Ms. Ellen DE GRAFFENREID
41 Athletic Director ... Mr. Mack RHOADES
39 Director Residential Life ... Mr. Frankie D. MINOR
25 Director Sponsored Program Admin ... Mr. David CRAIG
40 Regional Director Retail Operations ... Ms. Sherry POLLARD
38 Director Counseling Services ... Dr. David WALLACE
88 Assoc Vice Provost Intl Initiatives ... Dr. James K. SCOTT
36 Director Career Services ... Dr. Matthew REISKE
23 Director Student Health Services ... Dr. Susan E. EVEN
92 Director Honors College ... Dr. Stuart B. PALONSKY
94 Director Women's/Gender Studies ... Dr. Jacquelyn S. LITT
88 Director Info Science Learning Tech ... Dr. John WEDMAN
80 Director Truman Schl Public Affairs ... Dr. Barton J. WECHSLER
07 Director of Admissions ... Mr. Charles A. MAY
35 Director Student Life ... Dr. Mark L. LUCAS
28 Chief Diversity Officer ... Ms. Noor AZIZAN-GARDNER
104 Director Study Abroad ... Ms. Barbara LINDEMAN
105 Director Web Services ... Ms. Lori CROY
106 Dir Online Education/E-learning ... Ms. Kim SIEGENTHALER
108 Director Institutional Assessment ... Dr. Gera C. BURTON

*University of Missouri - Kansas City (A)

5100 Rockhill Road, Kansas City MO 64110-2499
County: Jackson FICE Identification: 002518
Unit ID: 178402
Telephone: (816) 235-1000 Carnegie Class: RU/H
FAX Number: (816) 235-1717 Calendar System: Semester
URL: www.umkc.edu
Established: 1929 Annual Undergrad Tuition & Fees (In-State): $7,838
Enrollment: 16,160 Coed
Affiliation or Control: State IRS Status: 501(c)3
Highest Offering: Doctorate
Program: Liberal Arts And General; Teacher Preparatory; Professional
Accreditation: NH, AA, ARCPA, BUS, CLPSY, COPSY, CS, DANCE, DENT, DH, ENG, IPSY, LAW, MED, MUS, NURSE, OTA, PHAR, SPAA, SW, TED, THEA

02 Chancellor ... Mr. Leo E. MORTON
28 Vice Chanc Diversity & Inclusion ... Dr. Susan WILSON
05 Provost ... Dr. Barbara BICHELMEYER
32 Vice Chanc Stdnt Affs/Enroll Mgmt ... Mr. Melvin C. TYLER
10 Vice Chanc Finance/Administration ... Ms. Sharon LINDENBAUM
21 Director Budgeting and Planning ... Ms. Karen D. WILKERSON
102 Pres UMKC Foundation ... Mr. Steven NORRIS
30 Vice Chanc for Univ Advancement ... Mr. Curt J. CRESPINO
41 Athletic Director ... Ms. Carla WILSON
13 CIO & Senior Vice Prov ... Dr. Mary Lou A. FRITTS
20 Deputy Prov for Academic Affairs ... Dr. Cynthia L. PEMBERTON
20 Vice Prov for Faculty Affairs ... Dr. Denis M. MEDEIROS
49 Dean College of Arts & Sciences ... Dr. Wayne VAUGHT
50 Dean Bloch School of Management ... Dr. David DONNELLY
81 Dean Sch of Biological Sciences ... Dr. Theodore WHITE
64 Dean Conservatory of Music & Dance ... Mr. Peter T. WITTE
52 Dean School of Dentistry ... Dr. Marsha A. PYLE
53 Interim Dean School of Education ... Dr. Chrisanthia BROWN
54 Dean Sch of Computing/Engineering ... Dr. Kevin Z. TRUMAN
61 Dean School of Law ... Ms. Ellen Y. SUNI
63 Dean School of Medicine ... Dr. Steven KANTER
66 Dean Sch of Nursing & Health Stds ... Dr. Ann CARY
67 Dean School of Pharmacy ... Dr. Russell B. MELCHERT
62 Dean University Libraries ... Dr. Bonnie POSTLETHWAITE
58 Dean School of Graduate Studies ... Dr. Denis M. MEDEIROS
108 Director of Assessment ... Dr. Ruth CAIN
09 Director Institutional Research ... Dr. Larry BUNCE
15 Vice Chanc Human Resources ... Ms. Carol HINTZ
84 Assoc Vice Chanc Enrollment Mgmt ... Ms. Jennifer DEHAEMERS
32 Dean of Students ... Dr. Eric GROSPITCH
35 Assistant Dean of Students ... Dr. Jeff TRAIGER
35 Assistant Dean of Students ... Ms. Tiffany S. WILLIAMS
88 Director Student Involvement ... Dr. Angela COTTRELL
88 Vice Chan Strategic Market & Comm ... Ms. Anne SPENNER
26 Director Media Relations ... Mr. John MARTELLARO
29 Asst VC AlumniConstituent Relations ... Ms. Lisen TAMMEUS
86 Asst Vice Chanc External Relations ... Mr. Troy LILLEBO
22 Title IX Coordinator ... Dr. Mikah THOMPSON
88 Dir Acad Support and Mentoring ... Dr. Marion STONE
07 Director of Admissions ... Ms. Tamara C. BYLAND
85 Director Internatl Student Affairs ... Ms. Sandra GAULT
37 Director Student Financial Aid ... Mr. Scott YOUNG
06 Registrar ... Mr. Doug SWINK
19 Chief Campus Police ... Mr. Michael BONGARTZ
40 Director Bookstore ... Mr. Pete EISENTRAGER
38 Dir Counseling/Health/Disability ... Dr. Arnold ABELS
88 Director Women's Center ... Dr. Brenda BETHMAN
36 Director Career Services ... Mr. Greg HAYES
39 Director Residential Life ... Mr. Sean GRUBE
88 Dir Multicultural Student Affairs ... Ms. Keichanda DEES-BURNETT
96 Manager Campus Procurement ... Ms. Catherine A. SIMONDS
25 Business Manager for Admin Services ... Mr. Jeffery ROSS
18 Assoc Vice Chanc Campus Facilities ... Mr. Robert A. SIMMONS
104 Director International Acad Pgms ... Dr. Linna F. PLACE
106 Vice Provost Online Education ... Dr. Devon CANCILLA

*University of Missouri - Saint Louis (B)

One University Boulevard, Saint Louis MO 63121-4400
County: Saint Louis FICE Identification: 002519
Unit ID: 178420
Telephone: (314) 516-5000 Carnegie Class: RU/H
FAX Number: (314) 516-5378 Calendar System: Semester
URL: www.umsl.edu
Established: 1963 Annual Undergrad Tuition & Fees (In-State): $10,065
Enrollment: 12,134 Coed
Affiliation or Control: State IRS Status: 501(c)3
Highest Offering: Doctorate
Program: Liberal Arts And General; Teacher Preparatory; Professional
Accreditation: NH, BUS, BUSA, CACREP, CLPSY, ENG, IPSY, MUS, NURSE, OPT, OPTR, SPAA, SW, TED

02 Chancellor ... Dr. Thomas F. GEORGE
05 Provost/Vice Chanc Academic Affairs ... Dr. Glen H. COPE
10 Vice Chanc Managerial/Tech Svcs ... Dr. James M. KRUEGER
30 Vice Chancellor Univ Advancement ... Mr. Martin F. LEIFELD
26 Sr Assoc Vice Chanc Univ Marketing ... Mr. Ronald H. GOSSEN
27 Asst Vice Chanc Univ Communications ... Mr. Robert D. SAMPLES
22 Dir of Equal Opportunity/Diversity ... Ms. Deborah J. BURRIS
46 Vice Provost Research Admin ... Dr. Nasser ARSHADI
32 Vice Provost Student Affairs ... Dr. Curtis C. COONROD
58 Vice Prov Acad Affs/Dean Grad Sch ... Dr. Judith WALKER DE FELIX
13 Assoc VC Information Technology/CIO ... Mr. Lawrence W. FREDERICK
88 Dir Center for Teaching & Learning ... Mr. J. Andy GOODMAN
85 Director International Studies ... Dr. Joel N. GLASSMAN
49 Dean College Arts & Sciences ... Dr. Ronald YASBIN
50 Dean College Business Admin ... Mr. Charles E. HOFFMAN
53 Dean College of Education ... Dr. Carole G. BASILE
57 Int Dean College of Fine Arts/Comm ... Dr. James RICHARDS
66 Dean College of Nursing ... Dr. Susan DEAN-BAAR
92 Int Dean Honors College ... Dr. Daniel GERTH
88 Dean College of Optometry ... Dr. Larry J. DAVIS
08 Dean of Libraries ... Mr. Christopher DAMES
54 Dean Engineering Program ... Dr. Joseph O'SULLIVAN
88 Assistant to Provost Public Affairs ... Ms. Elizabeth VAN UUM
23 Asst Vice Provost Hlth/Wellness ... Dr. Nancy M. MAGNUSON
88 Asst Dean of Students/Stdnt Conduct ... Dr. D'Andre BRADDIX
93 Asst Dean of Stdnts/MultiCultural ... Ms. Natissia SMALL
35 Asst Dean of Students/Student Life ... Ms. Miriam I. ROCCIA
41 Director of Athletics ... Ms. Lori FLANAGAN
07 Dean of Enrollment ... Mr. Alan BYRD
40 Manager Bookstore ... Ms. Stephanie EATON
36 Director Career Services ... Ms. Teresa A. BALESTRERI
06 Acting Registrar ... Ms. Theresa KEUSS
39 Director Residential Life ... Mr. Jonathan A. LIDGUS
37 Director Student Financial Aid ... Dr. Anthony C. GEORGES
88 Director Ctr Nanoscience ... Dr. George W. GOKEL
88 Director Center Neurodynamics ... Dr. Sonya BAHAR
88 Dir Scientific & Computing/ITE ... Mr. William J. LEMON
88 Dir MO Inst of Mental Health ... Dr. Robert H. PAUL
25 Manager Bus/Fiscal/Research Admin ... Ms. Karen O. BOYD
88 Director Business Services ... Ms. Gloria J. LEONARD
18 Asst Vice Chancellor Facilities Mgt ... Mr. Larry A. EISENBERG
88 Director Budget Services ... Ms. Joann F. WIILKINSON
88 Director of Finance & Accounting ... Mr. Randall VOGAN
88 Director Cashiers/Student Accounts ... Mr. Mitchell R. HESS
15 Assoc VC Human Resources ... Mr. Peter A. HEITHAUS
19 Director Institutional Safety ... Mr. Forrest L. VAN NESS
09 Director Institutional Research ... Mr. Lawrence W. WESTERMEYER
102 Assoc VC Development ... Dr. Brenda M. MCPHAIL
88 Director St Louis Public Radio ... Mr. Tim J. EBY
29 Dir Alumni Community Engagement ... Ms. Linda CARTER
94 Director Women's & Gender Studies ... Dr. Kathy J. GENTILE
70 Director Social Work ... Dr. Lois PIERCE
44 Sr Director Planned Giving ... Mr. Lyle W. BRIZENDINE
88 Dir Public Policy Administration ... Dr. Deborah B. BALSER
88 Director Public Policy Research Ctr ... Dr. Mark TRANEL
88 Dir Sue Shear Institite for Women ... Ms. Vivian EVELOFF
31 Director Community College Relation ... Ms. Melissa HATTMAN
88 Managing Dir Performing Arts Center ... Mr. John R. CATTANACH
88 Dir Des Lee Collaborative Vision ... Ms. Patricia ZAHN
108 Assoc Provost Planning/Assesment ... Dr. Paulette E. ISAAC-SAVAGE
88 Center for Ethics in Public Life ... Dr. Walter M. STEWART

*Missouri University of Science & Technology (C)

300 W 13th Street, Rolla MO 65409-0001
County: Phelps FICE Identification: 002517
Unit ID: 178411
Telephone: (573) 341-4111 Carnegie Class: RU/H
FAX Number: (573) 341-4307 Calendar System: Semester
URL: www.mst.edu
Established: 1870 Annual Undergrad Tuition & Fees (In-State): $10,402
Enrollment: 8,642 Coed
Affiliation or Control: State IRS Status: 501(c)3
Highest Offering: Doctorate
Program: Professional; Technical Emphasis
Accreditation: NH, BUS, CEA, CS, ENG

02 Chancellor ... Dr. Cheryl B. SCHRADER
05 Provost/Exec Vice Chanc Acad Affs ... Dr. Robert MARLEY
10 Vice Chanc Finance/Admin Services ... Mr. Walter J. BRANSON
30 Vice Chanc University Advancement ... Ms. Joan M. NESBITT
32 Vice Chancellor Student Affairs ... Dr. Debra A G. ROBINSON
88 Vice Chanc Global/Strat Partnershp ... Dr. Warren K. WRAY
15 Vice Chanc Human Resources ... Ms. Shenethia MANUEL
46 Vice Provost for Research Services ... Dr. K. KRISHNAMURTHY
20 Vice Provost Undergrad Studies ... Dr. Jeffrey CAWLFIELD
58 Vice Provost Graduate Studies ... Dr. Venkata ALLADA
56 Interim Ast Vice Chanc/Global Learn ... Dr. Matt O'KEEFE
84 Vice Prov & Dean of Enrollment Mgmt ... Ms. Laura K. STOLL
54 VP/Dean Coll of Engr & Computing ... Dr. Ian FERGUSON
49 VP/Dean Coll of Arts/Sci & Bus ... Dr. Stephen ROBERTS
08 Director of Library ... Ms. Tracy PRIMICH
13 Interim Chief Information Officer ... Mr. Dan UETRECHT
06 Registrar ... Ms. Deanne JACKSON
38 AVC Student Affairs/Support Svcs ... Dr. Carl F. BURNS
41 Director of Athletics ... Mr. Mark E. MULLIN
36 Dir Career Opportunities Center ... Dr. Edna GROVER-BISKER
85 Director Intl/Cultural Affairs ... Ms. Jeanie H. HOFER
35 Director Student Life/Univ Center-R ... Mr. Mark POTRAFKA
39 Director Residential Life ... Dr. Dorie PAINE
09 Director Inst Research & Assessment ... Dr. Oyebanjo LAJUBUTU
07 Director of Admissions ... Ms. Lynn STICHNOTE
29 Ast Vice Chanc Advancement Services ... Ms. Darlene RAMSAY
37 Director Student Financial Aid ... Ms. Bridgette K. BETZ
26 Director of Communications ... Mr. Andrew P. CAREAGA
18 Director of Physical Facilities ... Mr. James PACKARD
88 Dir of Womens Leadership Institute ... Ms. Cecilia ELMORE
40 Manager of University Bookstore ... Mr. Mark GALLARDO
19 Director University Police ... Vacant
100 Chief of Staff ... Ms. Elizabeth SMITH

*Missouri University of Science & Technology Engineering Education Center (D)

12837 Flushing Meadows Drive, St. Louis MO 63131
Telephone: (314) 835-9822 Identification: 770323
Accreditation: &NH

† Branch campus of Missouri University of Science & Technology, Rolla, MO.

University of Phoenix Kansas City Campus (E)

1310 E 104th Street, Kansas City MO 64131-4504
Telephone: (816) 943-9600 Identification: 770213
Accreditation: &NH, ACBSP

† No longer accepting campus-based students.

University of Phoenix St. Louis Campus (F)

13801 Riverport Drive, St. Louis MO 63043
Telephone: (314) 298-9755 Identification: 770214
Accreditation: &NH, ACBSP

† Branch campus of University of Phoenix, Tempe, AZ.

Urshan Graduate School of Theology (G)

704 Howdershell Road, Florissant MO 63031-7526
County: St. Louis FICE Identification: 041461
Unit ID: 455099
Telephone: (314) 921-9290 Carnegie Class: Spec/Faith
FAX Number: (314) 921-9203 Calendar System: Semester
URL: www.ugst.edu
Established: 2001 Annual Undergrad Tuition & Fees: $9,775
Enrollment: 55 Coed
Affiliation or Control: Other Protestant IRS Status: 501(c)3
Highest Offering: Master's
Program: Professional; Religious Emphasis
Accreditation: THEOL

01 President ... Dr. David K. BERNARD
03 Executive Vice President ... Mrs. Jennie RUSSELL
05 Academic Dean ... Dr. Chris PARIS
32 Dean of Students ... Mr. David REID

Vatterott College-Joplin (H)

809 Illinois, Joplin MO 64801-9538
Telephone: (417) 781-5633 Identification: 666060
Accreditation: ACCSC

† Branch campus of Vatterott College-North Park, Berkeley, MO.

Vatterott College-Kansas City (I)

4131 N. Corrington Avenue, Kansas City MO 64117-1681
Telephone: (816) 861-1000 Identification: 666519
Accreditation: ACCSC

† Branch campus of Vatterott College-North Park, Berkeley, MO.

Vatterott College-NorthPark (J)

8580 Evans Avenue, Berkeley MO 63134-2900
County: Saint Louis FICE Identification: 025997
Unit ID: 245342
Telephone: (314) 264-1000 Carnegie Class: Assoc/PrivFP4
FAX Number: (314) 522-6174 Calendar System: Other
URL: www.vatterott-college.edu
Established: 1969 Annual Undergrad Tuition & Fees: $12,644
Enrollment: 1,287 Coed
Affiliation or Control: Proprietary IRS Status: Proprietary
Highest Offering: Baccalaureate
Program: Occupational; 2-Year Principally Bachelor's Creditable; Technical Emphasis
Accreditation: ACCSC

01 Campus President .... Robert DONNELL
10 Chief Financial Officer .... Dennis BEAVERS
05 Director of Education .... Charles MERRELL
06 Registrar .... Brenda LINCOLN-PENZEL
07 Director of Admissions .... Harvey CHAMBERLAIN

Vatterott College-St. Charles (A)

3550 West Clay Street, St. Charles MO 63301
Telephone: (636) 940-4100 Identification: 666584
Accreditation: ACCSC

† Branch campus of Vatterott College-North Park, Berkeley, MO.

Vatterott College-Saint Joseph (B)

3709 N. Belt Highway, Saint Joseph MO 64506-1364
Telephone: (816) 558-7500 Identification: 666520
Accreditation: ACCSC

† Branch campus of Vatterott College-Des Moines, Des Moines, IA.

Vatterott College-Springfield (C)

3850 S Campbell Avenue, Springfield MO 65807-5340
Telephone: (417) 831-8116 Identification: 666521
Accreditation: ACCSC

† Branch campus of Vatterott College-North Park, Berkeley, MO.

Vatterott College-Sunset Hills (D)

12900 Maurer Industrial Drive, Sunset Hills MO 63127
Telephone: (314) 843-4200 Identification: 666522
Accreditation: ACCSC

† Branch campus of Vatterott College-North Park, Berkeley, MO.

Washington University in St. Louis (E)

One Brookings Drive, Saint Louis MO 63130-4899
County: Saint Louis FICE Identification: 002520
Unit ID: 179867
Telephone: (314) 935-5000 Carnegie Class: RU/VH
FAX Number: N/A Calendar System: Semester
URL: www.wustl.edu
Established: 1853 Annual Undergrad Tuition & Fees: $48,093
Enrollment: 14,348 Coed
Affiliation or Control: Independent Non-Profit IRS Status: 501(c)3
Highest Offering: Doctorate
Program: Liberal Arts And General; Professional
Accreditation: NH, ACAE, ART, AUD, BUS, CLPSY, ENG, LAW, LSAR, MED, OT, PCSAS, PH, PTA, SW

01 Chancellor .... Dr. Mark S. WRIGHTON
05 Provost/Exec VC Academic Affairs .... Dr. Herbert Holden THORP
11 Exec VC Administration .... Mr. Henry S. WEBBER
63 Exec Vice Chanc/Dean of Medicine .... Dr. Larry J. SHAPIRO
43 Exec Vice Chanc/General Counsel .... Mr. Michael R. CANNON
30 Exec VC Alumni & Development .... Mr. David T. BLASINGAME
10 Vice Chancellor for Finance/CFO .... Ms. Barbara A. FEINER
46 Vice Chancellor for Research .... Dr. Jennifer K. LODGE
15 Vice Chanc for Human Resources .... Ms. Legail P. CHANDLER
13 Vice Chanc & Chief Info Officer .... Mr. John L. GOHSMAN, JR.
32 Vice Chancellor for Students .... Dr. Lori S. WHITE
26 Vice Chanc for Public Affairs .... Ms. Jill D. FRIEDMAN
86 VC Government & Community Relations . Ms. Pamela S. LOKKEN
88 Chief Investment Officer .... Ms. Kimberly G. WALKER
21 Assoc VC for Finance and Treasurer .... Ms. Amy B. KWESKIN
49 Dean Faculty of Arts & Sciences .... Dr. Barbara A. SCHAAL
61 Dean School of Law .... Dr. Nancy STAUDT
54 Dean Engineering & Applied Sciences .... Dr. Aaron F. BOBICK
57 Dean Sam Fox Sch Design/Visual Arts .... Prof. Carmon COLANGELO
58 Dir College & Grad Sch of Art .... Prof. Heather A. CORCORAN
50 Dean Olin School of Business .... Prof. Mahendra R. GUPTA
58 Dean Graduate School of A & S .... Prof. William F. TATE
70 Dean Brown School of Social Work .... Prof. Edward F. LAWLOR
55 Interim Dean University College .... Dr. Steven M. EHRLICH
48 Dean Architecture .... Prof. Bruce M. LINDSEY
100 Assoc Vice Chanc/Chief of Staff .... Mr. Steven J. GIVENS
101 Secretary to the Board of Trustees .... Ms. Ida H. EARLY
07 Vice Chancellor for Admissions .... Mr. John A. BERG
20 Vice Provost/Assoc VC Academic Affs .... Prof. Gerhild S. WILLIAMS
88 Assoc VC for Development .... Mr. William S. STOLL
29 Assoc VC Alumni & Development Pgm ..Ms. Pamella A. HENSON
26 Assoc VC Medical Public Affairs .... Ms. Joni L. WESTERHOUSE
28 Vice Provost .... Prof. Adrienne D. DAVIS
85 VC for International Affairs .... Prof. James V. WERTSCH
08 University Librarian .... Mr. Jeffrey G. TRZECIAK
39 Assoc VC Students/Dean Students .... Mr. Justin X. CARROLL
35 Assoc Vice Chanc for Students .... Dr. Robert M. WILD
92 Assoc VC & Dean Ervin Scholars Pgm .... Ms. Robyn S. HADLEY
13 Assoc VC Info Services & Tech .... Vacant
27 Asst VC for Campus Communications .... Ms. Julie A. FLORY
85 Asst VC/Dir International Students .... Ms. Kathy STEINER-LANG
96 Asst Vice Chanc Resource Management .... Mr. Alan S. KUEBLER
36 Assoc VC/Director Career Center .... Mr. Mark W. SMITH
18 Assoc VC Facilities Planning/Mgmt ... Mr. Arthur J. ACKERMANN
88 Asst VC Environ Health & Safety .... Mr. Bruce D. BACKUS
88 Assoc VC Real Estate .... Ms. Mary B. CAMPBELL
72 Interim Asst VC/Tech Management .... Ms. Nichole R. MERCIER
14 Asst VC Univ Admin/Acad Computing .... Ms. Denise R. HIRSCHBECK
23 Asst VC/Dir Stdnt Hlth Counslng Svc .... Dr. Alan I. GLASS
37 Director Student Financial Services .... Mr. Michael J. RUNIEWICZ
41 Director of Athletics .... Mr. Joshua H. WHITMAN
19 Director of Campus Police .... Mr. Donald STROM
07 Director of Admissions .... Ms. Julie SHIMABUKURO
06 University Registrar .... Ms. Susan E. HOSACK
38 Director of Mental Health Services .... Dr. Thomas M. BROUNK

Washington University in St. Louis-School of Medicine (F)

660 Euclid Avenue, Saint Louis MO 63110
Telephone: (314) 360-5000 Identification: 770329
Accreditation: &NH

† Branch campus of Washington University in St. Louis, Saint Louis, MO.

Webster University (G)

470 E Lockwood, Webster Groves MO 63119-3141
County: Saint Louis FICE Identification: 002521
Unit ID: 179894
Telephone: (800) 981-9801 Carnegie Class: Master's L
FAX Number: N/A Calendar System: Semester
URL: www.webster.edu
Established: 1915 Annual Undergrad Tuition & Fees: $25,500
Enrollment: 19,034 Coed
Affiliation or Control: Independent Non-Profit IRS Status: 501(c)3
Highest Offering: Doctorate
Program: Liberal Arts And General
Accreditation: NH, ACBSP, ANEST, MUS, NUR, TED

01 President .... Dr. Elizabeth J. STROBLE
05 Provost .... Dr. Julian Z. SCHUSTER
30 Vice Pres Advancement .... Mr. Charles HAHN
84 Interim Chief Enrollment Officer .... Mr. Robert PARRENT
10 VP & Chief Financial Officer .... Dr. Greg GUNDERSON
13 VP & Chief Information Officer .... Mr. Kenneth FREEMAN
20 AVP Academic Affairs .... Vacant
32 Asst Provost Student Affairs/Athls .... Dr. Paul CARNEY
58 Asst Provost for Graduate Studies .... Dr. Elizabeth RUSSELL
32 Associate VP/Dean of Students .... Dr. Ted HOEF
106 AVP/Dir OnLine Learning Center .... Mr. Michael COTTAM
82 AVP Academic Affairs/Dir Intl Pgms .... Dr. Peter MAHER
15 AVP & Chief Human Resources Officer .... Ms. Betsy SCHMUTZ
29 AVP Alumni Programs .... Ms. Jennifer JEZEK-TAUSSIG
86 AVP Military & Government Programs .... Mr. Mike CALLAN
27 AVP & Chief Communications Officer ...... Ms. Barbara O'MALLEY
46 AVP & Chief Strategic Initiatives .... Mr. Tom JOHNSON
20 Vice Provost .... Ms. Nancy HELLERUD
50 Dean School Business & Technology .... Dr. Benjamin O. AKANDE
53 Dean School of Education .... Dr. Brenda S. FYFE
57 Dean Leigh Gerdine Col of Fine Arts .... Mr. Peter E. SARGENT
49 Dean Col of Arts & Sciences .... Dr. David C. WILSON
60 Dean School of Communications .... Mr. Eric ROTHENBUHLER
08 Dean of University Library .... Ms. Laura REIN
39 Assoc Dean Stdts/Housing/Res Life .... Dr. John BUCK
20 Director of Academic Advising .... Vacant
21 Dir Resource Plng & Budget .... Ms. Kathleen PARDO
19 Director Public Safety .... Mr. Rick GERGER
06 Registrar .... Mr. Don MORRIS
26 Dir Public Relations/Global Mktg .... Mr. Patrick GIBLIN
24 Dir of Media & Acad Tech Services .... Mr. Dewey MARTIN
88 Director International Recruitment .... Mr. Calvin SMITH
41 Director Athletics .... Mr. Scott KILGALLON
36 Dir Career Planning & Dev Center . Ms. Tamara GEGG-LAPLUME
23 Director Student Health Svcs .... Ms. Ann BROPHY
35 Director Student Engagement .... Ms. Jennifer STEWART
37 AVP UG Admiss/Dir Financial Aid .... Mr. James MYERS
38 Director Counsel & Life Development .... Dr. Patrick STACK
96 Director of Procurement Services .... Ms. Maria HEIN
09 Director Institutional Effectivenes .... Dr. Julie WEISSMAN
88 Senior Project Manager .... Mr. Steven STRANG
18 Director Facilities Planning .... Mr. Craig MILLER
101 University Secretary .... Ms. Jeanelle WILEY
104 Dir Study Abroad & Intl Projects .... Mr. Guillermo RODRIGUEZ
28 AVP Diversity & Inclusion .... Ms. Nicole ROACH
04 Executive Assistant to President .... Ms. Shari SKRABACZ
102 Dir Foundation/Corporate Relations .... Mr. Mark KENT
44 Director Annual or Planned Giving .... Mr. Kenneth NICKLESS

WellSpring School of Allied Health-Kansas City (H)

9140 Ward Pkwy Ste 100, Kansas City MO 64114
County: Jackson FICE Identification: 039704
Unit ID: 447999
Telephone: (816) 523-9140 Carnegie Class: Not Classified
FAX Number: (816) 523-0741 Calendar System: Other
URL: www.wellspring.edu
Established: Annual Undergrad Tuition & Fees: $17,300
Enrollment: 133 Coed
Affiliation or Control: Proprietary IRS Status: Proprietary
Highest Offering: Associate Degree
Program: Occupational
Accreditation: ABHES

01 President .... Donald FARQUHARSON

Wentworth Military Academy and College (I)

1880 Washington Avenue, Lexington MO 64067-1799
County: Lafayette FICE Identification: 002522
Unit ID: 179919
Telephone: (800) 962-7682 Carnegie Class: Assoc/PrivNFP
FAX Number: (660) 259-2677 Calendar System: Semester
URL: www.wma.edu
Established: 1880 Annual Undergrad Tuition & Fees: $5,335
Enrollment: 851 Coed
Affiliation or Control: Independent Non-Profit IRS Status: 501(c)3
Highest Offering: Associate Degree
Program: Occupational; 2-Year Principally Bachelor's Creditable
Accreditation: NH

01 President/Superintendent .... Col. Michael LIERMAN
05 Chief Academic Officer .... Col. Timothy CASEY
30 Vice Pres for Advancement & Alumni ...... LtCol. Marnie MORGAN
32 Commandant of Cadets .... LtCol. Darren FITZGERALD
84 Vice Pres for Enrollment Managment .... Col. Rick COTTRELL
41 Athletic Director .... LtCol. Tom HUGHES
10 CFO .... LtCol. Glenn MILLER
81 Professor of Military Science .... LtCol. Grant MONTGOMERY
29 Alumni Director .... Maj. Cheney PARRISH
04 Executive Assistant .... Maj. Cheney PARRISH
06 Registrar .... Capt. Beth SCHLESSELMAN
08 Librarian .... Maj. Linda CHRISTIAN
37 Director Student Financial Aid .... Maj. Cindy HOWARD
85 Director Foreign Students .... Maj. Christhina STARKE
23 Director Health Services .... Capt. Barb PIERCE
35 Director Student Affairs .... LtCol. Darren FITZGERALD
09 Director of Institutional Research .... Col. Rick COTTRELL
15 Director Personal Services .... Capt. Cindy MIKOYCHIK
18 Chief Facilities/Physical Plant .... Mr. Wally RATLIFFE
40 Director Bookstore .... Capt. Jerry MAGGERT

Westminster College (J)

501 Westminster Avenue, Fulton MO 65251-1230
County: Callaway FICE Identification: 002523
Unit ID: 179946
Telephone: (573) 642-3361 Carnegie Class: Bac/A&S
FAX Number: (573) 592-5227 Calendar System: Semester
URL: www.westminster-mo.edu
Established: 1851 Annual Undergrad Tuition & Fees: $23,480
Enrollment: 935 Coed
Affiliation or Control: Independent Non-Profit IRS Status: 501(c)3
Highest Offering: Baccalaureate
Program: Liberal Arts And General; Teacher Preparatory
Accreditation: NH, ACBSP

01 President .... Dr. Benjamin AKANDE
05 Sr Vice President/Dean of Faculty .... Dr. Carolyn J. PERRY
30 VP for Advancement .... Dr. William F. SHEEHAN, JR.
10 Interim VP for Business and CFO .... Mr. Joey STONER
84 VP/Dean of Enrollment Management .... Dr. Stephanie MILLER
26 Director of College Relations .... Mr. Robert CROUSE
32 VP & Dean of Student Life .... Dr. Stephanie KRAUTH
20 Associate Dean .... Dr. David JONES
08 Director of Library Services .... Ms. Angela GROGAN
06 Registrar .... Mrs. Phyllis J. MASEK
13 Executive Director of IT .... Mr. Mike MCNELLIS
37 Director of Financial Aid .... Ms. Aimee BRISTOW
15 Director of Human Resources .... Ms. Lisa REFFETT
39 Director of Residential/Greek Life .... Ms. Jacqueline J. WEBER
41 Athletic Director .... Mr. Matt MITCHELL
23 Exec Director Wellness Center .... Dr. Kasi LACEY
88 Exec Dir Marketing/Communications ... Ms. Jennifer BONDURANT
29 Dir Alumni Engagement .... Ms. Sarah MUNNS
36 Director of Career Services .... Ms. Meg LANGLAND
18 Assoc VP of Inst Operations .... Mr. Daniel HASLAG
07 Director of Admissions .... Ms. Kelle SILVEY
09 Director of Institutional Research .... Dr. Ray BROWN
19 Dir Campus Safety & Security .... Mr. Jack BENKE
42 Chaplain .... Rev. Jamie HASKINS

William Jewell College (K)

500 College Hill, Liberty MO 64068-1896
County: Clay FICE Identification: 002524
Unit ID: 179955
Telephone: (816) 781-7700 Carnegie Class: Bac/A&S
FAX Number: (816) 415-5027 Calendar System: Semester
URL: www.jewell.edu
Established: 1849 Annual Undergrad Tuition & Fees: $32,330
Enrollment: 1,072 Coed
Affiliation or Control: Independent Non-Profit IRS Status: 501(c)3
Highest Offering: Master's
Program: Liberal Arts And General; Teacher Preparatory; Professional
Accreditation: NH, MUS, NURSE

01 President .... Dr. David L. SALLEE
05 Provost .... Dr. Anne C. DEMA
10 Vice Pres for Finance & Operations .... Mr. Brian CLEMONS
30 Vice Pres Institutional Advancement .... Mr. Clark MORRIS
88 Vice Pres for Social Responsibility .... Dr. Andrew L. PRATT
32 Dean of Student Life .... Ms. Shelly KING
07 Dean of Admission .... Mr. Cory SCHEER
06 Registrar .... Dr. Edwin H. LANE
08 Interim Director of the Library .... Ms. Rebecca HAMLETT

21 Controller .... Mr. Ron DEMPSEY
13 Director of Information Technology .... Ms. Lan GUO
97 Assoc Dean Core Curriculum .... Dr. Gary ARMSTRONG
37 Director of Financial Aid .... Mr. Daniel HOLT
15 Director of Human Resources .... Ms. Cherie SMITH
18 Director of Facilities Mgmt .... Vacant
57 Executive Director Harriman-Jewell .... Mr. Clark W. MORRIS
41 Director of Athletics .... Dr. Darlene BAILEY
36 Director of Career Development .... Ms. Marissa BLAND
38 Director of Counseling Services .... Vacant
29 Director of Alumni Relations .... Ms. Andrea MELOAN
104 Director of Global Studies .... Ms. Sara ROUND
04 Executive Asst to President .... Ms. Dayna BEINKE
19 Director of Campus Safety .... Mr. Chad MARTIE
26 Director of Communications .... Ms. Cara DAHLOR
39 Director of Residence Life .... Mr. Ernie STUFFLEBEAN
44 Director of Annual Giving .... Ms. Tanna CAMPBELL
90 Director of Teaching/Learning Tech .... Ms. Elise FISHER

William Woods University (A)

One University Avenue, Fulton MO 65251-1098

County: Callaway FICE Identification: 002525
Unit ID: 179964

Telephone: (800) 995-3159 Carnegie Class: Master's L
FAX Number: (573) 592-1146 Calendar System: Semester
URL: www.williamwoods.edu
Established: 1870 Annual Undergrad Tuition & Fees: $22,160
Enrollment: 2,042 Coed
Affiliation or Control: Christian Church (Disciples Of Christ)
IRS Status: 501(c)3
Highest Offering: Doctorate
Program: 2-Year Principally Bachelor's Creditable; Liberal Arts And General; Teacher Preparatory; Professional; Business Emphasis
Accreditation: NH, ACBSP, CAATE, SW, TEAC

01 President .... Dr. Jahnae H. BARNETT
03 University Vice President .... Scott GALLAGHER
11 Vice President Administration .... Kathy GROVES
30 Vice President of Advancement .... Dan DIEDRIECH
32 Vice President/Dean of Student Life .... Dr. Venita MITCHELL
58 VP and Dean of Grad Studies .... Dr. Michael W. WESTERFIELD
04 Executive Assistant to President .... Kenda E G. SHINDLER
05 Academic Dean .... Dr. Aimee SAPP
07 Dean of Admissions .... Vacant
53 Dean of Education .... Dr. E. Douglas EBERSOLD
50 Dean of Business .... Lee BAILEY
41 Director of Athletics .... Jason VITTONE
20 Assoc Dean Academic Services .... Dr. Tom FRANKMAN
09 Director of Institutional Research .... Dr. Paul STURGIS
108 Assoc Dean Assessment .... Dr. Carrie MCCRAY
08 Director Libraries .... Erlene DUDLEY
26 Director of University Relations .... Mary Ann BEAHON
27 Director of Marketing .... Vacant
18 Director of Buildings & Grounds .... Mike DILLON
13 Director of Technology .... Jim LONG
06 Director of Records/Registrar .... Tara EMERSON
10 Chief Financial Officer .... Julie HOUSEWORTH
37 Director Student Financial Services .... Deana READY
36 Dir Career Svcs/Student Success .... Amy DITTMER
39 Dir Residential Life/Campus Safety .... Mike WILLS
29 Director of Alumni Activities .... Becky STINSON
53 Chair Education Division .... Dr. Tim HANRAHAN
49 Chair Arts and Humanities .... Dr. Caroline BOYER FERHAT
88 Chair Equestrian Studies Division .... Jennifer PETTERSON
88 Chair Undergraduate Business .... Dr. Linda DAVIS
88 Chair Human Performance Division .... Raymond HUNE
83 Chair Behavioral/Soc Sciences Div .... Dr. Shawn HULL
35 Coord Greek Life/Student Involvemnt .... Lacy SWEETEN
42 Chaplain/Faith & Service Director .... Rev. Travis TAMERIUS
88 ADA Coordinator/Interpreter .... Margie COATNEY
28 Coordinator Multicultural Affairs .... Cyndi KOONSE
38 Counselor .... Rebecca SEITZ
106 Dir Online Education/E-learning .... Dr. Betsy TUTT

MONTANA

Aaniiih Nakoda College (B)

PO Box 159, Harlem MT 59526-0159

County: Blaine FICE Identification: 025175
Unit ID: 180203

Telephone: (406) 353-2607 Carnegie Class: Tribal
FAX Number: (406) 353-2898 Calendar System: Semester
URL: www.ancollege.edu
Established: 1984 Annual Undergrad Tuition & Fees: $2,410
Enrollment: 130 Coed
Affiliation or Control: Tribal Control IRS Status: 501(c)3
Highest Offering: Associate Degree
Program: Occupational; 2-Year Principally Bachelor's Creditable
Accreditation: NW

01 President .... Dr. Carole FALCON-CHANDLER
05 Dean of Academic Affairs .... Ms. Carmen CORNELIUS TAYLOR
32 Dean of Student Affairs .... Ms. Clarena BROCKIE
10 Comptroller .... Ms. Debra EVE
06 Registrar/Admissions Officer .... Mrs. Dixie BROCKIE
37 Financial Aid Director .... Ms. Toma CAMPBELL-HOOPS
08 Director of Library Services .... Ms. Eva ENGLISH
25 Director Sponsored Programs .... Mr. Scott FRISKICS
13 Information Systems Manager .... Mr. Harold H. HEPPNER
40 Bookstore Manager .... Ms. Kimberly BROCKIE
04 Assistant to the President .... Ms. Michele BROCKIE
09 Institutional Research Assistant .... Ms. Danielle JACKSON

Blackfeet Community College (C)

Box 819, Browning MT 59417-0819

County: Glacier FICE Identification: 025106
Unit ID: 180054

Telephone: (406) 338-5441 Carnegie Class: Tribal
FAX Number: (406) 338-3272 Calendar System: Semester
URL: www.bfcc.edu
Established: 1976 Annual Undergrad Tuition & Fees: $2,919
Enrollment: 484 Coed
Affiliation or Control: Independent Non-Profit IRS Status: 501(c)3
Highest Offering: Associate Degree
Program: Occupational; 2-Year Principally Bachelor's Creditable
Accreditation: NW

01 President .... Dr. Billie Jo KIPP
05 Dean Academic Affairs .... Mrs. Carol MURRAY
32 Dean Student Services .... Mrs. Anne RACINE
10 Chief Financial Officer .... Mr. James LORAN
37 Director of Financial Aid .... Mrs. Gaylene DUCHARME
06 Registrar/Admissions Officer .... Ms. Deana M. MCNABB
15 Director Human Resources .... Mr. Lyle W. MACDONALD
07 Director of Admissions .... Vacant
09 Director of Institutional Research .... Mr. Brad R. HALL
18 Chief Facilities/Physical Plant .... Mr. Curtis HENRIKSEN

Carroll College (D)

1601 N Benton Avenue, Helena MT 59625-0002

County: Lewis And Clark FICE Identification: 002526
Unit ID: 180106

Telephone: (406) 447-4300 Carnegie Class: Bac/Diverse
FAX Number: (406) 447-4533 Calendar System: Semester
URL: www.carroll.edu
Established: 1909 Annual Undergrad Tuition & Fees: $30,754
Enrollment: 1,430 Coed
Affiliation or Control: Roman Catholic IRS Status: 501(c)3
Highest Offering: Baccalaureate
Program: Occupational; Liberal Arts And General; Teacher Preparatory; Professional
Accreditation: NW, ENG, IACBE, NURSE

01 President .... Dr. Thomas EVANS
05 Vice President Academic Affairs .... Dr. Colin IRVINE
10 VP for Finance & Administration .... Ms. Lori PETERSON
31 VP Community Relations .... Mr. Thomas J. MCCARVEL
32 Vice President for Student Life .... Dr. James D. HARDWICK
30 VP of Philanthropy .... Ms. Karin OLSEN
84 Vice Pres of Enrollment Mgmt .... Ms. Nina LOCOCO
42 Chaplain/Director .... Rev. Marc LENNEMAN
26 Director of PR .... Ms. Sarah LAWLOR
26 Director of Marketing .... Ms. Patty WHITE
06 Registrar .... Ms. Cassie HALL
08 Director of Library .... Mr. Christian FRAZZA
37 Financial Aid Director .... Ms. Janet RIIS
36 Dir of Career Services/Testing .... Ms. Rosalie K. WALSH
07 Director Admissions/Enrollment Ops .... Ms. Cynthia J. THORNQUIST
15 Director of Human Res & Adm Svcs .... Ms. Renee M. MCMAHON
18 Director of Facilities .... Mr. Walter H. BISKUPIAK
39 Director of Community Living .... Ms. Maureen WARD
35 Dir Student Activities/Ldrshp .... Mr. Patrick HARRIS
38 Director of Counseling .... Dr. James ROGERS
21 Controller .... Ms. Kari BRUSTKERN
13 Director Information Technology .... Ms. Loretta ANDREWS
29 Director Alumni Relations .... Ms. Kathy RAMIREZ
09 Dir Research/Planing/Assess .... Dr. Dawn GALLINGER
41 Athletic Director .... Mr. Curt APSEY

Chief Dull Knife College (E)

One College Drive, PO Box 98, Lame Deer MT 59043

County: Rosebud FICE Identification: 025452
Unit ID: 180160

Telephone: (406) 477-6215 Carnegie Class: Tribal
FAX Number: (406) 477-6219 Calendar System: Semester
URL: www.cdkc.edu
Established: 1975 Annual Undergrad Tuition & Fees: $2,260
Enrollment: 192 Coed
Affiliation or Control: Independent Non-Profit IRS Status: 501(c)3
Highest Offering: Associate Degree
Program: Occupational; 2-Year Principally Bachelor's Creditable
Accreditation: NW

01 President/Int Dean Cultural Affairs .... Dr. Richard LITTLEBEAR
03 Vice President .... Mr. William WERTMAN
05 Dean Academic Affairs .... Vacant
32 Dean Student Affairs .... Mr. Zane SPANG
37 Director Student Financial Aid .... Mr. Devin WERTMAN
08 Head Librarian .... Mrs. Joan HANTZ

Dawson Community College (F)

Box 421, Glendive MT 59330-0421

County: Dawson FICE Identification: 002529
Unit ID: 180151

Telephone: (406) 377-3396 Carnegie Class: Assoc/Pub-R-S
FAX Number: (406) 377-8132 Calendar System: Semester
URL: www.dawson.edu
Established: 1940 Annual Undergrad Tuition & Fees (In-District): $4,965
Enrollment: 261 Coed
Affiliation or Control: State/Local IRS Status: 501(c)3
Highest Offering: Associate Degree
Program: Occupational; 2-Year Principally Bachelor's Creditable
Accreditation: NW

01 Interim President .... Dr. J. Vincent NIX
05 Vice President of Academic Affairs .... Ms. Marjorie PRICE-SEEGER
11 Vice President of Administration .... Ms. Kathleen ZANDER
32 Vice President of Student Affairs .... Mr. John BOLE
06 Registrar .... Ms. Virginia BOYSUN
08 Library Director .... Mr. Todd KNISPEL
37 Director of Financial Aid .... Mr. Rory SEEGER
13 Director of Information Technology .... Mr. Shane BISHOP
15 Human Resources Assistant .... Ms. Barb ROEHL

Flathead Valley Community College (G)

777 Grandview Drive, Kalispell MT 59901

County: Flathead FICE Identification: 006777
Unit ID: 180197

Telephone: (406) 756-3822 Carnegie Class: Assoc/Pub-R-M
FAX Number: (406) 756-3815 Calendar System: Semester
URL: www.fvcc.edu
Established: 1967 Annual Undergrad Tuition & Fees (In-District): $3,837
Enrollment: 2,161 Coed
Affiliation or Control: Local IRS Status: 501(c)3
Highest Offering: Associate Degree
Program: Occupational; 2-Year Principally Bachelor's Creditable
Accreditation: NW, EMT, MAC, PTAA, SURGT

01 President .... Dr. Jane A. KARAS
05 Vice President Academic Affairs .... Dr. Bradly ELDREDGE
10 Vice Pres Administration & Finance .... Mr. Charles JENSEN
12 Director Lincoln County Campus .... Mr. Patrick PEZZELLE
32 Dean of Students .... Ms. Brenda HANSON
51 Exec Dir Economic Dev/Continuing Ed .... Ms. Susan BURCH
30 Exec Dir Institutional Advancement .... Ms. Colleen UNTERREINER
13 Exec Dir Mgmt Information Services .... Mr. Bill E. BOND
15 Exec Director of Human Resources .... Ms. Karen GLASSER
06 Registrar/Coord/Admissions/Records .... Ms. Marlene STOLTZ
20 Director TRIO .... Ms. Lynn L. FARRIS
37 Director Student Financial Aid .... Ms. Cindy KIEFER
88 Director of Adult Basic Education .... Ms. Margaret L. GIRKINS
18 Director Maintenance Service .... Mr. Jack ROARK
21 Controller .... Mr. Kirk ZANDER
26 Director Communications .... Ms. Tara E. ROTH
96 Director of Purchasing .... Mr. Steve LARSON
09 Director of Institutional Research .... Vacant
20 Coord Advising & Retention .... Ms. Mary JORDT
24 Coord Instructional Media Services .... Ms. Malinda CRAWFORD
36 Coord Career Development .... Ms. Karen DARROW

Fort Peck Community College (H)

PO Box 398, Poplar MT 59255-0398

County: Roosevelt FICE Identification: 023430
Unit ID: 180212

Telephone: (406) 768-6300 Carnegie Class: Tribal
FAX Number: (406) 768-6301 Calendar System: Semester
URL: www.fpcc.edu
Established: 1978 Annual Undergrad Tuition & Fees: $2,250
Enrollment: 346 Coed
Affiliation or Control: Tribal Control IRS Status: 501(c)3
Highest Offering: Associate Degree
Program: Occupational; 2-Year Principally Bachelor's Creditable; Business Emphasis
Accreditation: NW

01 President .... Ms. Haven GOURNEAU
05 Vice President Academic Affairs .... Mr. Wayne TWO BULLS
32 Vice President Student Services .... Mr. Elijah HOPKINS
30 Director Institutional Development .... Mr. Craig SMITH
10 Business Manager .... Ms. Rose ATKINSON
06 Registrar .... Ms. Linda L. HANSEN
37 Financial Aid Officer .... Ms. Lanette CLARK
40 Bookstore Manager .... Ms. Jackie AZURE
08 Head Librarian .... Mrs. Anita A. SCHEETZ

Little Big Horn College (I)

PO Box 370, Crow Agency MT 59022-0370

County: Big Horn FICE Identification: 022866
Unit ID: 180328

Telephone: (406) 638-3104 Carnegie Class: Tribal
FAX Number: (406) 638-3169 Calendar System: Semester
URL: www.lbhc.edu
Established: 1980 Annual Undergrad Tuition & Fees: $2,850
Enrollment: 280 Coed
Affiliation or Control: Tribal Control IRS Status: 501(c)3
Highest Offering: Associate Degree
Program: Occupational; 2-Year Principally Bachelor's Creditable; Business Emphasis
Accreditation: NW

01 President .... Dr. David YARLOTT, JR.
05 Academic Dean .... Miss Frederica LEFT HAND
32 Dean of Student Services .... Miss Te-Atta OLD BEAR
11 Dean of Administration .... Mr. David SMALL

06 Registrar .... Ms. Dionne PRETTY ON TOP
08 Director of Library .... Mr. Tim BERNARDIS
13 Chief Information Officer .... Mr. Franklin COOPER
10 Chief Finance Officer .... Ms. Aldean GOOD LUCK
15 Director Human Resources .... Ms. Shaleen OLD COYOTE
07 Admissions Officer .... Ms. Arlene DAWES
97 Dept Head/General Stds/Crow Stds .... Dr. Tim MCCLEARY
81 Dept Head/Math/Science/Technology .... Dr. Dianna HOOKER

Miles Community College (A)

2715 Dickinson, Miles City MT 59301-4799

County: Custer FICE Identification: 002528
Unit ID: 180373
Telephone: (406) 874-6100 Carnegie Class: Assoc/Pub-R-S
FAX Number: (406) 874-6282 Calendar System: Semester
URL: www.milescc.edu
Established: 1939 Annual Undergrad Tuition & Fees (In-District): $3,945
Enrollment: 421 Coed
Affiliation or Control: State/Local IRS Status: 501(c)3
Highest Offering: Associate Degree
Program: Occupational; 2-Year Principally Bachelor's Creditable
Accreditation: NW, ADNUR, PHLEB

01 President .... Dr. Stacy KLIPPENSTEIN
10 VP Administration & Finance .... Ms. Lisa SMITH
05 Vice Pres of Academic Affairs .... Vacant
32 VP Student Success/Inst Research .... Ms. Jessie DUFNER
08 Director of Library .... Ms. Paula DEMARS
13 Director Information Technology .... Mr. Donald D. WARNER
37 Director Student Financial Aid .... Mr. Loren LANCASTER
18 Chief Facilities/Physical Plant .... Mr. Ross LAWRENCE
21 Controller .... Ms. Nancy AABERGE
06 Registrar .... Ms. Lisa BLUNT
15 Director Human Resources .... Ms. Kylene PHIPPS
66 Director Nursing .... Ms. Karla LUND
20 Associate Academic Officer .... Mr. Garth SLEIGHT
40 Manager Bookstore .... Ms. Karmalee YOUNG
04 Administrative Asst to President .... Ms. Candy LANEY

Montana Bible College (B)

3625 South 19th Avenue, Bozeman MT 59718-9108

County: Gallatin FICE Identification: 041403
Unit ID: 262165
Telephone: (406) 586-3585 Carnegie Class: Not Classified
FAX Number: (406) 586-3585 Calendar System: Semester
URL: www.montanabiblecollege.edu
Established: 1987 Annual Undergrad Tuition & Fees: N/A
Enrollment: 121 Coed
Affiliation or Control: Independent Non-Profit IRS Status: 501(c)3
Highest Offering: Baccalaureate
Program: Religious Emphasis
Accreditation: BI

01 President .... Mr. Jim CARLSON
05 Academic Dean .... Dr. Gale HEIDE
06 Registrar .... Mrs. Louise TURNER
07 Admissions Coordinator .... Mrs. Susan JACKSON
08 Head Librarian .... Mrs. Jessica CARLSON
32 Dean of Students .... Mr. Scott MORNINGSTAR
10 Business Manager .... Mrs. Leota FRED
21 Office Manager .... Mrs. Tasha OARD
18 Facilities Manager .... Mr. Danny JOHNSON
84 Enrollment Management .... Mr. Dan HOVESTOL
30 Advancement .... Ms. Jenni O'BRIAN
26 Church Relations .... Mr. Ryan WARD
105 Director Web Services .... Mr. Austin RUHL

*Montana University System Office (C)

2500 Broadway, Helena MT 59601-3201

County: Lewis And Clark FICE Identification: 029072
Unit ID: 180470
Telephone: (406) 444-6570 Carnegie Class: N/A
FAX Number: (406) 444-1469
URL: www.mus.edu

01 Commissioner Higher Education .... Mr. Clayton T. CHRISTIAN
05 Deputy Comm Academic/Student Affs .... Dr. John CECH
10 Dpty Comm Fiscal Affs/Chf of Staff .... Mr. Mick ROBINSON
45 Deputy Comm for Plng/Public Policy .... Mr. Tyler TREVOR
15 Deputy Comm Communications/HR .... Mr. Kevin MCRAE
43 Chief Legal Counsel/Deputy Comm .... Ms. Viv HAMMILL
103 Deputy Comm Two-Year Educ .... Mr. John CECH
88 Director of Benefits .... Ms. Connie WELSH
21 Chief Financial Officer .... Ms. Robin GRAHAM
21 Director Accounting & Budget .... Ms. Frieda HOUSER
88 Director of Work Comp Risk Mgmt .... Ms. Leah Jo TIETZ
93 Dir Minority/Amer Ind Achievement .... Ms. Brandi FOSTER
13 OCHE IT Manager .... Ms. Edwina MORRISON

*University of Montana - Missoula (D)

32 Campus Drive, Missoula MT 59812-0001

County: Missoula FICE Identification: 002536
Unit ID: 180489
Telephone: (406) 243-2311 Carnegie Class: RU/H
FAX Number: (406) 243-2797 Calendar System: Semester
URL: www.umt.edu
Established: 1893 Annual Undergrad Tuition & Fees (In-State): $6,158
Enrollment: 13,952 Coed
Affiliation or Control: State IRS Status: 501(c)3
Highest Offering: Doctorate
Program: 2-Year Principally Bachelor's Creditable; Liberal Arts And General; Teacher Preparatory; Professional
Accreditation: NW, ART, BUS, BUSA, CAATE, CACREP, CLPSY, COARC, CS, JOUR, LAW, MUS, PH, PHAR, PTA, SP, SW, TED, THEA

02 President .... Dr. Royce C. ENGSTROM
88 VP for Integrated Communications .... Ms. Peggy KUHR
05 Provost/VP Academic Affairs .... Dr. Perry BROWN
10 Vice President Finance/Admin .... Mr. Michael REID
32 Vice President for Student Affairs .... Dr. Teresa S. BRANCH
46 Vice Pres Research/Development .... Dr. Scott WHITTENBURG
84 AVP Enrollment & Student Success .... Ms. Sharon O'HARE
26 Asst Vice Pres Marketing .... Mr. Mario SCHULZKE
45 AVP for Plng/Budget Analysis .... Ms. Dawn RESSEL
15 AVP Human Resource Services .... Ms. Terri PHILLIPS
20 Associate Provost .... Dr. Nathan LINDSAY
58 Dean of the Graduate School .... Dr. Sandy ROSS
35 Dean of Students .... Ms. Rhondie VOORHEES
43 Legal Counsel .... Ms. Lucy FRANCE
12 Director Mansfield Center .... Mr. Abraham KIM
104 Assoc Provost Global Century Educ .... Mr. Paulo ZAGALO-MELO
88 Interim Dir Broadcast Media Center .... Ms. Linda TALBOTT
22 Dir Equal Opportunity/Affirm Action .... Ms. Jessica WELTMAN
06 Registrar .... Mr. Joseph HICKMAN
18 Interim Director Facilities Svcs .... Mr. Kevin KREBSBACH
13 CIO .... Mr. Matt RILEY
38 Director Counseling .... Mr. Mike FROST
36 Director Career Services .... Ms. Laurie FISHER
37 Director of Financial Aid .... Mr. Kent MCGOWAN
29 Director of Alumni Relations .... Mr. William S. JOHNSTON
102 President & CEO/UM Foundation .... Mr. Shane GIESE
19 Director of Public Safety .... Mr. Martin LUDEMANN
23 Director Curry Health Center .... Dr. Rick CURTIS
39 Director Residence Life .... Ms. Sandra SCHOONOVER
41 Athletic Director .... Mr. Kent HASLAM
85 Dir Foreign Student & Scholar Svcs .... Ms. Effie F. KOEHN
21 Interim Director Business Services .... Mr. John MCCORMICK
88 Exec Director Student Success .... Mr. Brian FRENCH
08 Dean Mansfield Library .... Dr. Sha Li ZHANG
51 Dean Continuing Education .... Dr. Roger MACLEAN
49 Dean College Humanities & Sciences .... Dr. Christopher COMER
61 Dean School of Law .... Mr. Paul KIRGIS
65 Dean College Forestry/Conservation .... Dr. James BURCHFIELD
50 Dean School of Business Admin .... Dr. Larry D. GIANCHETTA
76 Dean Col Health Prof & Biomed Sci .... Dr. Reed HUMPHREY
60 Dean School of Journalism .... Mr. Larry ABRAMSON
53 Dean College of Educ & Human Svcs .... Dr. Roberta EVANS
57 Dean College Visual/Performing Arts .... Mr. Stephen KALM
75 Dean Missoula College .... Dr. Shannon O'BRIEN
92 Dean Honors College .... Dr. Brock TESSMAN

*The University of Montana Western (E)

710 S Atlantic St, Dillon MT 59725-3598

County: Beaverhead FICE Identification: 002537
Unit ID: 180692
Telephone: (406) 683-7011 Carnegie Class: Bac/Diverse
FAX Number: (406) 683-7493 Calendar System: Other
URL: www.umwestern.edu
Established: 1893 Annual Undergrad Tuition & Fees (In-State): $5,610
Enrollment: 1,200 Coed
Affiliation or Control: State IRS Status: 501(c)3
Highest Offering: Baccalaureate
Program: 2-Year Principally Bachelor's Creditable; Liberal Arts And General; Teacher Preparatory
Accreditation: NW, IACBE, TED

02 Chancellor .... Dr. Beth WEATHERBY
05 Interim Provost/VC Academic Affairs .... Dr. Sylvia MOORE
10 Vice Chanc Administration/Finance .... Ms. Susan BRIGGS
26 Director Marketing/Univ Relations .... Mr. Kent J. ORD
20 Interim Assistant Provost .... Ms. Anneliese RIPLEY
06 Registrar .... Ms. Charity WALTERS
07 Interim Director of Admissions .... Mr. Matt ALLEN
08 Librarian .... Mr. Michael SCHULZ
36 Director of Field Learning .... Mr. Michael MILLER
26 Public Relations Manager .... Vacant
41 Director of Athletics .... Mr. Ryan NOURSE
13 Director of Information Technology .... Mr. Chad BAVER
18 Director of Facilities Services .... Vacant
32 Dean of Students .... Ms. Nicole HAZELBAKER
88 Dean School of Outreach .... Ms. Laura STRAUS
30 Director of Devel/Alumni Relations .... Ms. Roxanne ENGELLANT
37 Director Student Financial Aid .... Ms. Erica JONES
38 Director Student Counseling .... Ms. Lynn MEIER WELTZIEN
15 Personnel Services .... Ms. Patti LAKE
04 Administrative Asst to Chancellor .... Ms. Shelly KESSEL
22 Dir Affirmative Action/EEO .... Ms. Liane FORRESTER

*Helena College University of Montana (F)

1115 N Roberts, Helena MT 59601-3098

County: Lewis and Clark FICE Identification: 007570
Unit ID: 180276
Telephone: (406) 447-6900 Carnegie Class: Assoc/Pub2in4
FAX Number: (406) 447-6397 Calendar System: Semester
URL: www.umhelena.edu
Established: 1939 Annual Undergrad Tuition & Fees (In-State): $3,080
Enrollment: 1,564 Coed
Affiliation or Control: State IRS Status: 501(c)3
Highest Offering: Associate Degree
Program: Occupational; 2-Year Principally Bachelor's Creditable; Technical Emphasis
Accreditation: NW, ADNUR

02 Dean/CEO .... Dr. Daniel J. BINGHAM
04 Administrative Assoc to Dean/CEO .... Ms. Summer S. MARSTON
05 Assoc Dean of Academic Affairs/VP .... Vacant
07 Director of Admissions and Records .... Ms. Sarah DELLWO
08 Director of Library Services .... Ms. Della DUBBE
51 Director of Continuing Education .... Ms. Mary LANNERT
18 Assistant Dean of Fiscal & Plant .... Mr. Russ FILLNER
13 Director of IT Services .... Mr. Jeff BLOCK
40 Bookstore Manager .... Mr. Josh BENNETT
32 Assistant Dean of Student Services .... Ms. Elizabeth STEARNS-SIMS
26 Director of Marketing .... Ms. Barb MCALMOND
37 Director Financial Aid .... Ms. Valerie CURTIN
88 Director of Student Success .... Mr. Rick CARON
15 Director of Human Resources .... Ms. Kimberly WORTHY
36 Career Services Coordinator .... Mr. Alan THOMPSON
09 Director of Institutional Research .... Mr. Michael BROWN

*Montana State University (G)

PO Box 172190, Bozeman MT 59717-2190

County: Gallatin FICE Identification: 002532
Unit ID: 180461
Telephone: (406) 994-2452 Carnegie Class: RU/VH
FAX Number: (406) 994-1923 Calendar System: Semester
URL: www.montana.edu
Established: 1893 Annual Undergrad Tuition & Fees (In-State): $6,801
Enrollment: 15,421 Coed
Affiliation or Control: State IRS Status: 501(c)3
Highest Offering: Doctorate
Program: Occupational; 2-Year Principally Bachelor's Creditable; Liberal Arts And General; Teacher Preparatory; Professional
Accreditation: NW, ART, BUS, CACREP, CS, DIETD, DIETI, ENG, ENGT, IPSY, MT, MUS, NURSE, TEAC

02 President .... Dr. Waded CRUZADO
05 Provost/Vice Pres Academic Affairs .... Dr. Martha POTVIN
20 Assoc Provost .... Dr. David SINGEL
88 Assoc Provost Accreditation .... Dr. Ron LARSEN
10 Vice Pres Admin/Finance .... Mr. Terry LEIST
32 Vice Pres Student Success .... Dr. Chris KEARNS
56 Director Extension .... Dr. Jeff BADER
46 VP Research/Creat/Tech Transf .... Dr. Renee REIJO PERA
04 Special Assistant to the President .... Dr. Henrietta MANN
18 Assoc Vice Pres University Services .... Mr. Robert V. LASHAWAY
88 Assoc VP Res/Creativity/Tch Trnsfer .... Dr. Lee SPANGLER
15 Chief Human Resources Officer .... Mr. Dennis DEFA
21 Assoc Vice Pres Financial Services .... Ms. Laura HUMBERGER
102 President/CEO MSU Foundation .... Mr. Christopher D. MURRAY
104 Assoc Prov International Education .... Dr. David DI MARIA
26 Exec Director Univ Communications .... Mr. Tracy ELLIG
88 Exec Director Museum of the Rockies .... Mr. Sheldon MCKAMEY
50 Dean Business .... Dr. Kregg AYTES
53 Dean Education/Health/Human Dev .... Dr. Alison HARMON
54 Dean Engineering .... Dr. Brett GUNNINK
49 Dean Letters & Science .... Dr. Nicol RAE
66 Dean Nursing .... Dr. Helen MELLAND
08 Dean Libraries .... Mr. Kenning ARLITSCH
35 Dean Students .... Dr. Matthew CAIRES
58 Dean Graduate School .... Dr. Karlene HOO
47 VP and Dean Agriculture .... Dr. Charles BOYER
48 Dean Arts/Architecture .... Dr. Nancy CORNWELL
70 Dean Gallatin College Programs .... Mr. Robert HIETALA
07 Director Admissions .... Ms. Ronda RUSSELL
22 Director Institutional Equity .... Ms. Kate GRIMES
29 Pres/CEO Alumni Foundation .... Mr. Christopher D. MURRAY
41 Director Athletics .... Mr. Peter FIELDS
109 Director Auxiliary Services .... Mr. Tom STUMP
36 Director Career Services .... Dr. Carina BECK
38 Director Counseling/Psych Services .... Dr. Patrick DONAHOE
88 Dir Disability/Re-ent/Veteran Svcs .... Ms. Brenda YORK
56 Exec Director Extended University .... Dr. Kim OBBINK
37 Director Financial Aid .... Ms. Brandi PAYNE
43 Legal Counsel .... Ms. Kellie PETERSON
45 Director Planning & Analysis .... Dr. Chris FASTNOW
96 Director Procurement .... Mr. Brian O'CONNOR
06 Registrar .... Mr. Tony CAMPEAU
27 Director Marketing/Creative Service .... Ms. Julie KIPFER
19 Director University Police .... Mr. Robert PUTZKE
100 Asst to the President .... Ms. Maggie HAMMETT
105 Dir Web Communications .... Mr. Jacob DOLAN
13 Chief Information Officer .... Mr. Jerry SHEEHAN
25 Asst Vice Pres for Research .... Ms. Leslie SCHMIDT
39 Chief Housing Officer .... Ms. Tammie BROWN
14 Asst CEO IT .... Mr. Adam EDELMAN

*Montana State University - Billings (H)

1500 University Drive, Billings MT 59101-0245

County: Yellowstone FICE Identification: 002530
Unit ID: 180179
Telephone: (406) 657-2011 Carnegie Class: Master's M
FAX Number: (406) 657-2302 Calendar System: Semester
URL: www.msubillings.edu
Established: 1927 Annual Undergrad Tuition & Fees (In-State): $5,807
Enrollment: 4,781 Coed
Affiliation or Control: State IRS Status: 501(c)3
Highest Offering: Master's
Program: Occupational; Liberal Arts And General; Teacher Preparatory; Business Emphasis

Accreditation: NW, ART, BUS, CAATE, CORE, EMT, MUS, TED

02 Chancellor ..... Dr. Mark NOOK
10 Administrative Vice Chancellor ..... Ms. Terrie IVERSON
05 Academic Vice Chancellor & Provost ..... Dr. Robert HOAR
32 Vice Chancellor for Student Affairs ..... Dr. Joseph ORAVECZ
20 Vice Provost Academic Affairs ..... Dr. Matthew REDINGER
102 President/CEO Foundation ..... Mr. Chuck WENDT
08 Director Library Services ..... Mr. Brent ROBERTS
84 Director Enrollment Management ..... Vacant
07 Director Admiss/Records/Registrar ..... Dr. Cheri JOHANNES
15 Director Human Resources/EEO AA ..... Ms. Janet SIMON
36 Interim Director Career Services ..... Dr. Becky LYONS
13 Chief Information Officer ..... Dr. Michael J. BARBER
56 Director Extended Campus ..... Mr. Kevin NEMETH
25 Dir Grants & Sponsored Pgms ..... Dr. David MCGINNIS
26 Director University Relations ..... Mr. Aaron CLINGINGSMITH
09 Director Institutional Research ..... Ms. Joann STRYKER
18 Director Facility Services ..... Mr. Jason MCGIMPSEY
58 Int Director Graduate Programs ..... Dr. Diane DUIN
41 Athletic Director ..... Ms. Krista MONTAGUE
19 Chief of Campus Police ..... Mr. Scott FORSHEE
29 Director Alumni Relations ..... Ms. Sarah BROCKEL
37 Director Student Financial Aid ..... Ms. Emily WILLIAMSON
40 Director Bookstore ..... Mr. Chad SCHREIER
39 Int Dean Student Life & Auxiliaries ..... Ms. Kathy KOTECKI
31 Coordinator Community Involvement ..... Ms. Jennifer RANDALL
21 University Budget Director ..... Ms. Trudy COLLINS
96 Director of Business Services ..... Ms. Barb SHAFER
20 Dir Academic Support Center ..... Mr. Benjamin BARCKHOLTZ
28 Dir Montana Ctr for Inclusive Educ ..... Ms. Marsha SAMPSON
89 Dir New Student/Retention Services ..... Ms. Tammi WATSON
38 Director of Advising ..... Dr. Becky LYONS
88 Director American Indian Outreach ..... Reno CHARETTE
85 Exec Dir Intl Studies/Outreach ..... Dr. Paul FOSTER
106 Director e-Learning ..... Dr. Susan BALTER-REITZ
92 Dir of University Honors Program ..... Dr. David CRAIG
104 Dir ESL Pgm/Intl Studies & Outreach ..... Ms. Xia CHAO
49 Dean of Arts & Sciences ..... Dr. Christine SHEARER
53 Dean of Education ..... Dr. Mary Susan FISHBAUGH
50 Dean College of Business ..... Dr. Barbara WHEELING
12 Dean City College MSU Billings ..... Dr. Clifford COPPERSMITH
76 Dean College of Allied Health Prof ..... Dr. Diane DUIN
88 Asc Dean City College MSU Billings ..... Dr. Florence GARCIA

*Montana State University - Northern (A)

PO Box 7751, Havre MT 59501-7751
County: Hill | FICE Identification: 002533
Unit ID: 180522
Telephone: (406) 265-3700 | Carnegie Class: Bac/Diverse
FAX Number: N/A | Calendar System: Semester
URL: www.msun.edu
Established: 1929 | Annual Undergrad Tuition & Fees (In-State): $5,480
Enrollment: 1,245 | Coed
Affiliation or Control: State | IRS Status: 501(c)3
Highest Offering: Master's
Program: Liberal Arts And General; Teacher Preparatory; Professional; Music Emphasis
Accreditation: NW, ADNUR, ENGT, NUR

02 Chancellor ..... Mr. Gregory D. KEGEL
05 Provost/Vice Chanc Academic Affairs ..... Dr. William RUGG
10 VC Finance & Administration ..... Mr. Brian SIMONSON
102 Executive Director of Foundation ..... Mr. Jim BENNETT
72 Dean College Technical Sciences ..... Dr. Larry STRIZICH
32 Dean of Student Engagement ..... Ms. Kim WATSON
53 Dean Col Educ/Arts & Sci/Nursing ..... Dr. Carol REIFSCHNEIDER
06 Registrar ..... Ms. Alisha SCHROEDER
66 Director of Nursing ..... Dr. Janice STARR
21 Director of Business Services ..... Ms. Jamie MCBRYAN
41 Athletic Director ..... Mr. Christian OBERQUELL
36 Director Career Center ..... Ms. Mary HELLER
13 Dir Information Technology Svcs ..... Vacant
37 Director of Financial Aid ..... Ms. Cindy SMALL
26 Director of University Relations ..... Mr. James POTTER
08 Director of Library ..... Ms. Vicki GIST
38 Director Student Support Services ..... Mr. John A. DONALDSON
07 Director of Admissions ..... Ms. Kristi PETERSON
15 Director Human Resources ..... Ms. Kathy JAYNES
35 Sr Director Student Success ..... Ms. Tracey JETTE
18 Facilities Manager ..... Mr. Dan ULMEN
29 Alumni Coordinator ..... Vacant

*Great Falls College Montana State University (B)

2100 16th Avenue South, Great Falls MT 59405-4909
County: Cascade | FICE Identification: 009314
Unit ID: 180249
Telephone: (406) 771-4300 | Carnegie Class: Assoc/Pub2in4
FAX Number: (406) 771-4317 | Calendar System: Semester
URL: gfcmsu.edu
Established: 1969 | Annual Undergrad Tuition & Fees (In-State): $3,130
Enrollment: 1,770 | Coed
Affiliation or Control: State | IRS Status: 501(c)3
Highest Offering: Associate Degree
Program: 2-Year Principally Bachelor's Creditable
Accreditation: NW, CAHIIM, COARC, DA, DH, EMT, MAC, PTAA, SURGT

02 CEO/Dean ..... Dr. Susan J. WOLFF
04 Executive Assistant to the CEO/Dean ..... Ms. Lorene JAYNES
10 Chief Financial Officer ..... Dr. Darryl STEVENS
05 Chief Academic Officer ..... Dr. Heidi PASEK
32 Associate Dean Student Services ..... Dr. Camille CONSOLVO
15 Exec Director Human Resources ..... Ms. Mary Kay BONILLA
26 Exec Dir Development/Comm & Mktg ..... Mr. Lewis CARD
31 Int Exec Dir of Business & Cmty Dev ..... Mr. Mel LEHMAN
13 Director IT Services-Interim ..... Mr. David BONILLA
18 Director of Facilities Services ..... Mr. Dennis DEVINE
36 Director Advising & Career Center ..... Mr. Troy STODDARD
37 Director Student Financial Aid ..... Ms. Leah HABEL
40 Bookstore Manager ..... Mr. Steve HALSTED
96 Budget & Purchasing Analyst ..... Ms. Carmen ROBERTS
09 Research Analyst ..... Dr. Grace ANDERSON
08 Director of eLearning & Library ..... Ms. Laura WIGHT
88 Trades Division & Pathways Coord ..... Ms. Charla MERJA
49 Director of Gen Ed & Transfer ..... Ms. Leanne FROST
76 Director of Health Sciences ..... Dr. Frankie LYONS
06 Registrar ..... Ms. Dena WAGNER-FOSSEN
07 Interim Director of Admissions ..... Mr. Joe SIMONSEN

*Montana Tech of The University of Montana (C)

1300 W Park Street, Butte MT 59701-8997
County: Silver Bow | FICE Identification: 002531
Unit ID: 180416
Telephone: (800) 445-8324 | Carnegie Class: Bac/Diverse
FAX Number: (406) 496-4710 | Calendar System: Semester
URL: www.mtech.edu
Established: 1893 | Annual Undergrad Tuition & Fees (In-State): $6,797
Enrollment: 2,945 | Coed
Affiliation or Control: State | IRS Status: 501(c)3
Highest Offering: Master's
Program: 2-Year Principally Bachelor's Creditable; Liberal Arts And General; Professional; Technical Emphasis
Accreditation: NW, ADNUR, CS, ENG, ENGR, NURSE

02 Chancellor ..... Dr. Donald M. BLACKKETTER
05 Provost ..... Dr. Douglas M. ABBOTT
10 Business Officer/Controller ..... Mr. John C. BADOVINAC
11 VC for Administration & Finance ..... Ms. Maggie PETERSON
30 VC for Development & Univ Relations ..... Mr. Joseph MCCLAFFERTY
32 Assoc VC for Student Affairs ..... Mr. Paul V. BEATTY
46 VC Research & Dean Grad Sch ..... Dr. Beverly HARTLINE
65 Director Bureau of Mines & Geology ..... Dr. John J. METESH
84 Director of Enrollment Management ..... Ms. Leslie DICKERSON
31 Dir Inst of Educational Opportunity ..... Ms. Amy VERLANIC
36 Director Career Services ..... Ms. Sarah RAYMOND
08 Director Library ..... Mr. Scott JUSKIEWICZ
37 Director of Financial Aid ..... Mr. Michael W. RICHARDSON
18 Director of Physical Facilities ..... Mr. Michael ALLEN
29 Director Alumni Affairs ..... Ms. Peggy S. MCCOY
41 Athletic Director ..... Mr. Chuck MORRELL
72 Dean College of Technology ..... Mr. John GARIC
81 Dean Col Letters/Sci/Prof Studies ..... Dr. Douglas A. COE
54 Dean School of Mines & Engineering ..... Dr. H. Peter KNUDSEN
44 Director of Development ..... Mr. Michael BARTH
39 Director Residence Life ..... Mr. Scott FORTHOFER
26 Director Public Relations ..... Ms. Amanda BADOVINAC
40 Bookstore Director ..... Ms. Laurie VANDEL
09 Director Institutional Research ..... Ms. Melissa KUMP
06 Interim Registrar ..... Ms. Leslie DICKERSON
07 Director of Recruiting ..... Ms. Stephanie CROWE
105 Webmaster ..... Mr. David NOLT
106 Distance Learning Coordinator ..... Ms. Kathy STEVENS
13 Director of Network Services ..... Mr. Mike KUKAY
91 Director of Information Services ..... Ms. Jennifer SIMON
96 Dir Purchasing & Budgets ..... Ms. Marissa BENTLEY
15 Dir Human Resources ..... Ms. Vanessa VAN DYK

† Granted candidacy at the Doctorate level.

*City College at Montana State University Billings (D)

3803 Central Avenue, Billings MT 59102-4398
Telephone: (406) 247-3000 | FICE Identification: 010166
Accreditation: &NW

† Regional accreditation is carried under the parent institution Montana State University-Billings, Billings, MT.

*Highlands College of Montana Tech (E)

25 Basin Creek Road, Butte MT 59701-9704
Telephone: (406) 496-3701 | FICE Identification: 009282
Accreditation: &NW

† Regional accreditation is carried under the parent institution Montana Tech of The University of Montanna, Butte, MT.

*The University of Montana - Missoula College (F)

909 South Avenue West, Missoula MT 59801
Telephone: (406) 243-7811 | FICE Identification: 007561
Accreditation: &NW, ACFEI, ADNUR, SURGT

† Regional accreditation is carried under the parent institution The University of Montana-Missoula, Missoula, MT.

Rocky Mountain College (G)

1511 Poly Drive, Billings MT 59102-1796
County: Yellowstone | FICE Identification: 002534
Unit ID: 180595
Telephone: (406) 657-1000 | Carnegie Class: Bac/Diverse
FAX Number: (406) 259-9751 | Calendar System: Semester
URL: www.rocky.edu
Established: 1878 | Annual Undergrad Tuition & Fees: $25,742
Enrollment: 1,031 | Coed
Affiliation or Control: Interdenominational | IRS Status: 501(c)3
Highest Offering: Master's
Program: Liberal Arts And General; Teacher Preparatory
Accreditation: NW, AAB, ARCPA

01 President ..... Dr. Robert WILMOUTH
05 Academic Vice President ..... Dr. Stephen A. GERMIC
32 Vice President for Student Life ..... Mr. Bradley A. NASON
84 Vice Pres Enrollment Services ..... Mrs. Kelly EDWARDS
30 Vice President of Advancement ..... Mrs. Kelly EDWARDS
10 Chief Financial Officer ..... Vacant
88 Director of Educational Leadership ..... Dr. Stevie SCHMITZ
08 Director of the Library ..... Ms. Bobbi OTTE
44 Director of Major Gifts ..... Mr. Peter BOLENBAUGH
26 Dir Marketing/Communications/PR ..... Ms. Jenny MCPHAIL
13 Director of Information Technology ..... Mr. Daniel WOLTERS
18 Director of Campus Facilities ..... Mr. Richard STRYKER
41 Director of Athletics ..... Mr. Bruce PARKER
30 Director of Annual Fund ..... Mrs. Jill HIRSCHI
09 Institutional Research Analyst ..... Miss Erica WALL
06 Registrar ..... Mr. Erik WILLBORG
37 Director of Financial Assistance ..... Ms. Jessica FRANCISCHETTI
39 Director of Residence Life ..... Ms. Shaydean SAYE
04 Executive Assistant to the Pres ..... Ms. Tracy DAVIDSON
29 Director of Alumni Relations ..... Mrs. Jillian SHOEMAKER
07 Director of Admissions ..... Mr. Austin MAPSTON

Salish Kootenai College (H)

PO Box 70, Pablo MT 59855-0070
County: Lake | FICE Identification: 021434
Unit ID: 180647
Telephone: (406) 275-4800 | Carnegie Class: Tribal
FAX Number: (406) 275-4801 | Calendar System: Quarter
URL: www.skc.edu
Established: 1977 | Annual Undergrad Tuition & Fees: $6,549
Enrollment: 859 | Coed
Affiliation or Control: Independent Non-Profit | IRS Status: 501(c)3
Highest Offering: Baccalaureate
Program: Occupational; 2-Year Principally Bachelor's Creditable; Liberal Arts And General
Accreditation: NW, ADNUR, DA, NUR, SW

01 President ..... Mr. Robert DEPOE
05 Vice President of Academic Affairs ..... Mrs. Sandra BOHAM
10 Vice Pres Finance/Business/Admin ..... Ms. Audrey PLOUFFE
06 Registrar ..... Ms. Cleo KENMILLE
37 Financial Aid Director ..... Ms. Jackie SWAIN
09 Dir Institutional Effectiveness ..... Dr. Stacey SHERWIN
15 Director Personnel Services ..... Mrs. Dawn BENSON
30 Development Director ..... Ms. Angelique ALBERT
32 Dean of Students ..... Ms. Tracie MCDONALD
13 Director of Information Technology ..... Mr. Al ANDERSON
18 Facilities/Physical Plant Manager ..... Mr. Michael BIGCRANE
04 Exec Admin Assistant to President ..... Mr. Victor MONTOYA

Stone Child College (I)

8294 Upper Box Elder Road, Box Elder MT 59521-9796
County: Hill | FICE Identification: 026109
Unit ID: 366340
Telephone: (406) 395-4875 | Carnegie Class: Tribal
FAX Number: (406) 395-4836 | Calendar System: Semester
URL: www.stonechild.edu/
Established: 1984 | Annual Undergrad Tuition & Fees: $2,505
Enrollment: 458 | Coed
Affiliation or Control: Tribal Control | IRS Status: 501(c)3
Highest Offering: Associate Degree
Program: 2-Year Principally Bachelor's Creditable; Business Emphasis
Accreditation: NW

01 President ..... Mr. Nathaniel ST. PIERRE
05 Dean of Academics ..... Ms. Cory SANGREY-BILLY
32 Dean of Student Services ..... Ms. Clarice MORSETTE
10 Business Office/Finance Manager ..... Ms. Jewel L. WHITFORD
04 Admin Asst to the President ..... Ms. Wanda ST. MARKS
06 Registrar ..... Ms. Gaile TORRES
13 Management Information Specialist ..... Mr. Jeffery HENRY
40 Bookstore Manager ..... Ms. Shannon MONTEAU
37 Financial Aid Officer ..... Ms. Tiffany GALBAVY
18 Facilities Manager ..... Mr. Frank HENRY
08 Head Librarian ..... Ms. Joy BRIDWELL

University of Great Falls (J)

1301 Twentieth Street S, Great Falls MT 59405-4996
County: Cascade | FICE Identification: 002527
Unit ID: 180258
Telephone: (800) 856-9544 | Carnegie Class: Bac/Diverse
FAX Number: (406) 791-5209 | Calendar System: Semester
URL: www.ugf.edu
Established: 1932 | Annual Undergrad Tuition & Fees: $23,000
Enrollment: 1,138 | Coed

Affiliation or Control: Roman Catholic IRS Status: 501(c)3
Highest Offering: Master's
Program: Liberal Arts And General; Teacher Preparatory; Professional
Accreditation: NW, NURSE

01 President .... Dr. Eugene J. MCALLISTER
05 VP for Academic Affairs .... Dr. Timothy LAURENT
10 Vice President for Finance .... Ms. Stacey EVE
84 VP for Enrollment Management .... Ms. Julie EDSTROM
20 Academic Dean .... Dr. Gregory MADSON
37 Director Financial Aid .... Ms. Kelli ENGELHARDT
06 Registrar .... Vacant
14 Director Administrative Computing .... Ms. Kathryn CARBIS
26 Director of Marketing and PR .... Ms. Leslie DAWSON
18 Director Physical Plant .... Mr. Chet PIETRYKOWSKI
38 Director Student Counseling .... Ms. Linda FAGENSTROM
21 Director of the Business Office .... Ms. Amber OBRESLEY
51 Director of Continuing Education .... Vacant
106 Director of Distance Learning .... Mr. Jim GRETCH
15 Director of Human Resources .... Ms. Kristen RANTZ
09 Director of Institutional Research .... Mr. Greg MADSON
40 Campus Store Manger .... Mr. Lance LOHNSON
13 Operations Manager/IT Services .... Mr. John KOEHLER
88 Director Student Support Services .... Mr. Matthew HAUK
88 Director of Special Projects .... Ms. Barbara PALACIOS

Yellowstone Christian College (A)

1515 S. Shiloh Road, Billings MT 59106
County: Yellowstone Identification: 667254
Telephone: (406) 656-9950 Carnegie Class: Not Classified
FAX Number: N/A Calendar System: Semester
URL: www.yellowstonechristian.edu
Established: 1880 Annual Undergrad Tuition & Fees: $6,840
Enrollment: 39 Coed
Affiliation or Control: Independent Non-Profit IRS Status: 501(c)3
Highest Offering: Baccalaureate
Program: Religious Emphasis
Accreditation: @BI

01 President .... Bruce CANNON

NEBRASKA

Bellevue University (B)

1000 Galvin Road S, Bellevue NE 68005-3098
County: Sarpy FICE Identification: 009743
Unit ID: 180814
Telephone: (402) 293-2000 Carnegie Class: Master's L
FAX Number: (402) 293-2020 Calendar System: Other
URL: www.bellevue.edu
Established: 1966 Annual Undergrad Tuition & Fees: $8,700
Enrollment: 8,475 Coed
Affiliation or Control: Independent Non-Profit IRS Status: 501(c)3
Highest Offering: Doctorate
Program: Liberal Arts And General
Accreditation: NH, IACBE

01 President .... Dr. Mary B. HAWKINS
18 Vice President Facilities .... Mr. Jerry A. BLASIG
10 VP Finance .... Ms. Debbie Kay WARD
05 Vice President Academic Affairs .... Ms. Donna N. MCDANIEL
45 Exec VP Strategic Initiatives .... Dr. Mike ECHOLS
11 Chief Operating Officer .... Mr. Matthew DAVIS
106 Dean Ctr Learning Innovation .... Vacant
72 Dean of College of Science & Tech .... Ms. Mary DOBRANSKY
50 Dean College of Business .... Dr. Rebecca MURDOCK
49 Dean College of Arts & Sciences .... Dr. Clif MASON
51 Dean of Continuing and Profess Educ .... Dr. Michelle EPPLER
13 Asst VP of Information Technology .... Mr. James S. VEREBELY
04 Exec Assistant to the President .... Ms. Christine HOW
32 VP Community & Student Affairs .... Mr. Russ LANE
37 Director Student Financial Svcs .... Ms. Janet YALE
08 Sr Dir Library Services .... Ms. Robin BERNSTEIN
102 Foundation CEO .... Mr. Russ RUPIPER
41 Director of Athletics .... Mr. Ed LEHOTAK
40 Director Bookstore .... Mr. Mark RIGGERT
18 Director of Facilities .... Mr. Ralph (Sam) J. BORER
30 VP Development Programs .... Ms. Dorothy MORROW
21 Asst VP Financial Strategies .... Ms. Lori PIRSCH
15 Sr Director Human Resources .... Ms. Lora IOSSI
19 Director of Security/Safety .... Mr. Greg ALLEN
88 Quality Assurance Programs Director .... Mr. Pete HEINEMAN
85 Director International Admissions .... Mr. Lee WESTPHAL
26 Associate Dir Public Relations .... Mr. Jim MAXWELL
49 Dean College Arts & Sciences .... Vacant
105 Director Web Services .... Ms. Geri MASON
06 Registrar .... Mr. Scott BIERMAN

Bryan College of Health Sciences (C)

5035 Everett Street, Lincoln NE 68506-1315
County: Lancaster FICE Identification: 006399
Unit ID: 180878
Telephone: (402) 481-8697 Carnegie Class: Spec/Health
FAX Number: N/A Calendar System: Semester
URL: www.bryanhealthcollege.edu
Established: 2001 Annual Undergrad Tuition & Fees: $15,450
Enrollment: 691 Coed
Affiliation or Control: Independent Non-Profit IRS Status: 501(c)3
Highest Offering: Doctorate
Program: Professional; Nursing Emphasis
Accreditation: NH, ANEST, CVT, DMS, NUR

01 President .... Dr. Marilyn MOORE
05 Provost .... Dr. Kay MAIZE
97 Dean General Studies/Acad Avance .... Dr. Kristy PLANDER
11 Dean of Operations .... Dr. June SMITH
66 Dean of Undergraduate Nursing .... Dr. Theresa DELAHOYDE
76 Dean of Health Professions .... Ms. Diane KATHOL
58 Dean of Graduate Studies .... Dr. Sharon HADENFELDT
32 Dean of Students .... Ms. Debra BORDER
08 Director of Library Services .... Ms. Anne HEIMANN
07 Director of Admissions .... Ms. Kelli BACKMAN
06 Registrar .... Ms. Pam MCMASTER

Central Community College (D)

PO Box 4903, Grand Island NE 68802-4903
County: Hall FICE Identification: 020995
Unit ID: 180902
Telephone: (308) 398-4222 Carnegie Class: Assoc/Pub-R-L
FAX Number: (308) 398-7398 Calendar System: Semester
URL: www.cccneb.edu
Established: 1966 Annual Undergrad Tuition & Fees (In-District): $2,820
Enrollment: 6,377 Coed
Affiliation or Control: Local IRS Status: 501(c)3
Highest Offering: Associate Degree
Program: Occupational; 2-Year Principally Bachelor's Creditable
Accreditation: NH, ADNUR, CAHIIM, DA, DH, EMT, MAC, MLTAD, OTA

01 College President .... Dr. Greg P. SMITH
05 Exec Vice Pres/Chief Academic Ofcr .... Dr. Deb BRENNAN
12 Columbus Campus President .... Dr. Matt R. GOTSCHALL
12 Grand Island Campus President .... Dr. Thomas A. WALKER
12 Hastings Campus President .... Mr. Bill HITESMAN
26 Public Relations/Marketing Director .... Mr. James E. STRAYER
10 College Business Officer .... Mr. Joel KING
13 Dir Information Technology Services .... Mr. Tom D. PETERS
102 Foundation Director .... Mr. Dean MOORS
15 Human Resource Manager .... Dr. Chris WADDLE
06 Registrar .... Ms. Barb LARSON
29 Director Alumni Relations .... Ms. Cheri BEDA
37 Director Student Financial Aid .... Ms. Hylee ASCHE
84 Director Enrollment Management .... Mr. Jerry RACIOPPI
09 Director Institutional Research .... Mr. Brian MCDERMOTT
28 Director Diversity .... Dr. Chris WADDLE
32 Director Student Affairs .... Mr. Jerry RACIOPPI
96 Director of Purchasing .... Ms. Marilyn BOTTRELL
29 Alumni Coordinator .... Ms. Pat STANGE

Central Community College Columbus Campus (E)

PO Box 1027, 4500 63rd Street,
Columbus NE 68602-1027
Telephone: (402) 564-7132 Identification: 770331
Accreditation: &NH

† Branch campus of Central Community College, Grand Island, NE.

Central Community College Hastings Campus (F)

550 S Technical Blvd, PO Box 1024,
Hastings NE 68902-1024
Telephone: (402) 463-9811 Identification: 770332
Accreditation: &NH

† Branch campus of Central Community College, Grand Island, NE.

CHI Health School of Radiologic Technology (G)

7500 Mercy Road, Omaha NE 68124
County: Douglas FICE Identification: 008492
Unit ID: 181145
Telephone: (402) 398-5527 Carnegie Class: Assoc/PrivNFP
FAX Number: (402) 398-6650 Calendar System: Semester
URL: www.chihealth.com/school-of-radiologic-technology
Established: 1953 Annual Undergrad Tuition & Fees: $5,050
Enrollment: 22 Coed
Affiliation or Control: Independent Non-Profit IRS Status: 501(c)3
Highest Offering: Associate Degree
Program: Occupational; 2-Year Principally Bachelor's Creditable
Accreditation: RAD

01 Program Director .... Robert A. HUGHES
10 Chief Financial Officer .... Jeanette WOJTALEWICZ

Clarkson College (H)

101 S 42nd Street, Omaha NE 68131-2739
County: Douglas FICE Identification: 009862
Unit ID: 180832
Telephone: (402) 552-3100 Carnegie Class: Spec/Health
FAX Number: (402) 552-3369 Calendar System: Semester
URL: www.clarksoncollege.edu
Established: 1888 Annual Undergrad Tuition & Fees: $15,210
Enrollment: 1,210 Coed
Affiliation or Control: Independent Non-Profit IRS Status: 501(c)3
Highest Offering: Doctorate
Program: Liberal Arts And General; Professional; Nursing Emphasis
Accreditation: NH, ANEST, CAHIIM, IACBE, NUR, PTAA, RAD

01 President .... Dr. Louis W. BURGHER
05 Interim VP of Academic Affairs .... Dr. Andriea NEBEL
11 VP of Operations .... Tony M. DAMEWOOD
10 Controller .... Megan WICKLESS
06 Registrar .... Michele D. STIRTZ
15 Director Human Resources .... Deb TOMEK
13 Director Technology .... Larry J. VINSON
26 Director of Marketing .... Jina PAUL
28 Director Diversity Services .... Aubray D. ORDUNA
37 Director Student Financial Services .... Dale BROWN
08 Director Library Services .... Nancy M. RALSTON
38 Director Success Center .... Chuck C. MACDONELL
97 Director General Education .... Lori BACHLE
66 Dean Nursing/Dir BS & Grad Nursing .... Dr. Aubray ORDUNA
50 Dir of Business & HIM .... Carla DIRKSCHNEIDER
76 Dir Medical Imaging/Radiologic Tech .... Ellen COLLINS
76 Dir Physical Therapist Asst Pgm .... Andreia NEBEL
07 Director Admissions .... Denise WORK
51 Director of Professional Dev .... Judi B. DUNN
29 Director Alumni Relations .... Rita VANFLEET
106 Coordinator Online Education .... Linda A. NIETO
88 Dir Center of Teaching Excellence .... Vacant
09 Coord Inst Effect/Quality Assurance .... Chris SWANSON

College of Saint Mary (I)

7000 Mercy Road, Omaha NE 68106-2606
County: Douglas FICE Identification: 002540
Unit ID: 181604
Telephone: (402) 399-2400 Carnegie Class: Master's S
FAX Number: (402) 399-2647 Calendar System: Semester
URL: www.csm.edu
Established: 1923 Annual Undergrad Tuition & Fees: $28,964
Enrollment: 1,018 Female
Affiliation or Control: Roman Catholic IRS Status: 501(c)3
Highest Offering: Doctorate
Program: 2-Year Principally Bachelor's Creditable; Liberal Arts And General; Teacher Preparatory; Professional
Accreditation: NH, ADNUR, IACBE, NUR, OT

01 President .... Dr. Maryanne STEVENS, RSM
32 Vice President Student Development .... Dr. Tara KNUDSON-CARL
05 Vice Pres Academic Affairs/Dean .... Vacant
07 Vice President Marketing .... Mr. Greg FRITZ
10 Vice Pres Financial Services/CFO .... Ms. Sarah KOTTICH
04 Executive Asst to the President .... Ms. Brenda ELLIOTT
84 Associate Vice President Enrollment .... Ms. Sara HANSON
06 Registrar .... Mrs. Deb NUGEN
08 Director of Library .... Ms. Sara WILLIAMS
13 Director of Computer Center .... Mrs. Victoria HOSKOVEC
29 Director of Alumnae .... Ms. Diane PROULX
37 Director Student Financial Aid .... Ms. Beth SISK
26 Public Relations Director .... Mr. Brittney LONG
35 Director Student Affairs .... Mrs. Katty PETAK
39 Director Student Housing .... Ms. Kate BRANSTETTER
40 Director Bookstore .... Mr. Steve WESTENBROEK
41 Athletic Director .... Mr. Jim KRUEGER
42 Director Campus Ministry .... Ms. Vickie ZOBRIST
18 Director Physical Plant .... Mr. Dan SPARGEN
44 Director Annual Giving .... Vacant
21 Associate Business Officer .... Ms. Bridgette RENBARGER
15 Director Personnel Services .... Ms. Sarah M. LIVINGSTON
11 Chief of Administration .... Mrs. Kim SAVICKY
19 Director Security/Safety .... Mr. David FERBER

Concordia University (J)

800 N Columbia Avenue, Seward NE 68434-1599
County: Seward FICE Identification: 002541
Unit ID: 180984
Telephone: (402) 643-3651 Carnegie Class: Master's S
FAX Number: (402) 643-4073 Calendar System: Other
URL: www.cune.edu
Established: 1894 Annual Undergrad Tuition & Fees: $27,110
Enrollment: 2,332 Coed
Affiliation or Control: Lutheran Church - Missouri Synod
IRS Status: 501(c)3
Highest Offering: Master's
Program: Liberal Arts And General; Teacher Preparatory
Accreditation: NH, IACBE, MUS, TED

01 President .... Rev Dr. Brian L. FRIEDRICH
05 Provost .... Dr. Jenny MUELLER-ROEBKE
30 Vice President Inst Advancement .... Mr. Kurth BRASHEAR
84 VP Enroll Mgt/Stdnt Svcs/Athletics .... Mr. Scott SEEVERS
10 Chief Financial Officer .... Mr. David KUMM
53 Dean of Educ/Health & Human Svcs .... Dr. Nancy ELWELL
49 Dean of Arts & Sciences .... Dr. Brent ROYUK
13 Co-Dean Information Technology .... Dr. Donald SYLWESTER
13 Co-Dean Information Technology .... Dr. Kent EINSPAHR
58 Dean College Grad Studies/Adult Ed .... Mr. Jonathon MOBERLY
08 Director of Library Services .... Mr. Philip HENDRICKSON
36 Synodical & Education Placement Dir .... Mr. William SCHRANZ
29 Director Alumni/University Rels .... Mr. Adam HENGEVELD
32 VP for Student Affairs & Athletics .... Mr. Gene BROOKS
36 Career Counselor .... Mr. Corey GRAY
41 Athletic Director .... Mr. Devin SMITH
42 Campus Pastor .... Rev. Ryan MATTHIAS
37 Director of Financial Aid .... Mrs. Gloria HENNIG
18 Chief Facilities/Physical Plant .... Mr. Rick IHDE
15 Director of Human Resources .... Mrs. Connie BUTLER

07 Director Undergraduate Admissions .... Mr. Aaron ROBERTS
26 Director of Marketing .... Mr. Seth MERANDA
21 Dir Invest/Student Admin Svcs .... Mr. Curt SHERMAN
44 Coord of Resource Devel Ops .... Vacant
38 Director of Counseling .... Vacant
106 Dir Classroom Innov & Online Educ .... Ms. Angie WASSENMILLER

Creative Center (A)

10850 Emmet Street, Omaha NE 68164-2911
County: Douglas FICE Identification: 031643
Unit ID: 430485
Telephone: (402) 898-1000 Carnegie Class: Spec/Arts
FAX Number: (402) 898-1301 Calendar System: Semester
URL: www.creativecenter.edu
Established: 1993 Annual Undergrad Tuition & Fees: N/A
Enrollment: 78 Coed
Affiliation or Control: Proprietary IRS Status: Proprietary
Highest Offering: Baccalaureate
Program: Occupational; 2-Year Principally Bachelor's Creditable; Fine Arts Emphasis
Accreditation: ACCSC

01 President .... Mr. Ray DOTZLER
05 Director .... Ms. Kim GUYER
07 Director of Admissions .... Mr. Richard CALDWELL
10 Chief Business Officer .... Ms. Beth CONNOR
37 Director Student Financial Aid .... Ms. Sandy LAROCCA

Creighton University (B)

2500 California Plaza, Omaha NE 68178-0001
County: Douglas FICE Identification: 002542
Unit ID: 181002
Telephone: (402) 280-2700 Carnegie Class: Master's L
FAX Number: N/A Calendar System: Semester
URL: www.creighton.edu
Established: 1878 Annual Undergrad Tuition & Fees: $34,810
Enrollment: 8,236 Coed
Affiliation or Control: Roman Catholic IRS Status: 501(c)3
Highest Offering: Doctorate
Program: Liberal Arts And General; Teacher Preparatory; Professional
Accreditation: NH, BUS, BUSA, DENT, EMT, LAW, MED, NURSE, OT, PHAR, PTA, SW, TED

00 Chairman Creighton University Board .... Mr. Michael R. MCCARTHY
101 Corporate Secretary .... Mr. James S. JANSEN
01 President .... Rev. Daniel S. HENDRICKSON, SJ
100 Associate Vice President .... Ms. Colette O'MEARA-MCKINNEY
04 Sr Exec Assistant President Office .... Ms. Terri L. KILGARIN
04 Asst to the President for Mission .... Rev. Richard J. HAUSER, SJ
05 Provost .... Dr. Edward R. O'CONNOR
03 Sr Vice President Operations .... Mr. Daniel E. BURKEY
42 Vice Provost Mission & Ministry .... Dr. Eileen C. BURKE-SULLIVAN
30 Vice President University Relations .... Mr. Richard P. VIRGIN
45 Director Strategic Planning .... Ms. Colette O'MEARA-MCKINNEY
108 Assoc VP Acad Excel & Assessment .... Dr. Mary Ann DANIELSON
08 University Librarian .... Mr. James BOTHMER
106 Exec Dir Ctr for Acad Innovation .... Dr. Tracy A. CHAPMAN
09 Director Institutional Research .... Dr. Somchan VUTHIPADADON
06 Registrar .... Vacant
88 Dir Military/Veterans Liaison Svcs .... Mr. Mark P. TURNER
88 Director Disability Accommodations .... Ms. Denise Y. LE CLAIR
36 Interim Director Career Center .... Mr. Jeremy M. FISHER
103 Assoc Director Career Development .... Ms. Lisa L. BROCKHOFF FITZSIMMONS
43 General Counsel .... Mr. James S. JANSEN
17 Sr Vice Provost Clinical Affairs .... Dr. Donald R. FREY
88 Assoc VP Multicultr & Comm Affairs .... Dr. Sade KOSOKO-LASAKI
51 Assoc VP Continuing Education .... Dr. Sally C. O'NEIL
88 Dir Ctr for Hlth Policy & Ethics .... Dr. Amy M. HADDAD
32 Vice Provost Student Life .... Dr. Tanya C. WINEGARD
39 Assoc VP Resident Life .... Dr. Richard E. ROSSI
35 Assoc VP Student Life .... Dr. Wayne YOUNG
35 Assoc VP Student Life .... Dr. Michele K. BOGARD
41 Athletic Director .... Mr. Bruce D. RASMUSSEN
46 Assoc VP Research & Scholarship .... Dr. Thomas F. MURRAY
88 Assoc VP Hlth Sc Mission & Identity .... Rev. James F. CLIFTON, SJ
46 Dir Ctr UG Research & Scholarship .... Dr. Juliane K. STRAUSS-SOUKUP
84 Vice Provost Enrollment Management .... Dr. Mary E. CHASE
84 Director Enrollment Services .... Dr. Lori K. GIGLIOTTI
07 Director Admissions/Scholarships .... Ms. Sarah D. RICHARDSON
37 Director Student Financial Aid .... Ms. Paula S. KOHLES
88 Director Academic Success .... Dr. Joe ECKLUND
49 Dean Arts & Sciences .... Dr. Bridget M. KEEGAN
50 Dean Heider College of Business .... Dr. Anthony R. HENDRICKSON
107 Dean College of Prof Studies .... Dr. Gail M. JENSEN
52 Dean Dentistry .... Dr. Mark A. LATTA
58 Dean Graduate School .... Dr. Gail M. JENSEN
61 Dean Law .... Mr. Paul E. MCGREAL
63 Dean Medicine .... Dr. Robert W. DUNLAY
66 Dean Nursing .... Dr. Catherine M. TODERO
67 Dean Pharmacy & Health Professions .... Dr. J. Chris BRADBERRY
26 Chief Marketing & Comm Officer .... Mr. Jim BERSCHEIDT
27 Director Public Relations .... Ms. Cindy R. WORKMAN
11 Vice President Administration .... Mr. John L. WILHELM
18 Asst VP Facility Mgmt & Planning .... Mr. Timothy P. NORTON
19 Director Public Safety .... Mr. Richard J. MCAULIFFE
10 Vice President Finance .... Vacant
21 Assoc VP Finance .... Mr. John J. JESSE, III
96 Director Purchasing .... Mr. Joseph J. ZABOROWSKI
15 Assoc VP Human Resources .... Mr. Jeffrey C. BRANSTETTER
13 Vice Preside Information Technology .... Mr. Tim BROOKS
14 Asst VP Information Technology .... Mr. Mark J. MONGAR
90 Executive Director IT .... Mr. Ryan M. CAMERON
91 Director IT Service & Support .... Mr. J. D. RUMMEL
88 Site Dir Alegent/CU Hlth Systems .... Mr. Thomas HALEY
22 Exec Director Equity & Inclusion .... Ms. Allison S. TAYLOR
88 Sr Philanthropic Advisor .... Mr. Steven A. SCHOLER
44 Asst VP Office of Development .... Mr. Matthew C. GERARD
44 Asst VP Office of Development .... Ms. Kelly K. PTACEK
29 Asst VP Alumni Relations .... Ms. Anna NUBEL
102 Dir Corp & Foundation Relations .... Mr. Jeremy J. BOUMAN
23 Sr Director Student Health Services .... Ms. Debra C. SAURE
24 Director Learning Environment .... Mr. Charles A. LENOSKY
25 Director Sponsored Programs Admin .... Ms. Beth J. HERR
28 Director Multicultural Affairs .... Mr. Ricardo M. ARIZA
38 Sr Director Counseling Services .... Dr. Michael KELLEY
40 Bookstore Manager .... Mr. Calvin PETERSEN
85 Exec Dir Global Engagement Office .... Dr. Rene PADILLA
86 Director Cmty & Govt Relationships .... Mr. Chris T. RODGERS
87 Director Summer Session .... Ms. Christine BILLINGS
92 Director Honors Program .... Dr. Jeffrey P. HAUSE
94 Director Women's & Gender Studies .... Dr. Susan A. CALEF
104 Global Programs Coordinator .... Ms. Lizzy E. CURRAN
20 Vice Provost Learning & Assessment .... Dr. Gail M. JENSEN
88 Assoc Provost Academic Admin .... Ms. Tricia A. BRUNDO-SHARRAR
88 Assoc Provost Academic Finance .... Ms. Jessica M. GRANER
89 Director Advising and Operation .... Ms. Sandy V. CIRIACO

Doane College (C)

1014 Boswell Avenue, Crete NE 68333
County: Saline FICE Identification: 002544
Unit ID: 181020
Telephone: (402) 826-2161 Carnegie Class: Bac/A&S
FAX Number: (402) 826-8600 Calendar System: 4/1/4
URL: www.doane.edu
Established: 1872 Annual Undergrad Tuition & Fees: $28,790
Enrollment: 2,626 Coed
Affiliation or Control: United Church Of Christ IRS Status: 501(c)3
Highest Offering: Doctorate
Program: Liberal Arts And General; Teacher Preparatory
Accreditation: NH, NURSE, TED

01 President .... Dr. Jacque CARTER
05 Vice President Academic Affairs .... Dr. John BURNEY
10 Vice President Financial Affairs .... Ms. Julie SCHMIDT
30 Vice President for Advancement .... Mr. Kevin C. MEYER
32 Vice President Student Affairs .... Vacant
13 VP for Information Technology .... Mr. Mike CARPENTER
07 VP for Enrollment Svcs & Marketing .... Mr. Joel WEYAND
88 Dean of Educational Leadership .... Dr. Jed JOHNSTON
20 Dean of Curriculum & Instruction .... Dr. Lyn FORESTER
58 Dean of Grad Studies in Mgmt .... Ms. Janice M. HADFIELD
51 Dean Adult Undergraduate Studies .... Ms. Janice M. HADFIELD
35 Asst Dean for Student Affairs .... Dr. Carrie PETR
06 Registrar .... Ms. Denise ELLIS
37 Director of Financial Aid .... Ms. Peggy TVRDY
08 Director of the Library .... Ms. Julie PINNELL
21 Controller .... Mr. Ned TUCKER
36 Director College to Career Center .... Mr. Dennis HEFNER
26 Sr Director of Strategic Comm .... Mr. Mike LEFLER
29 Director of Alumni Relation .... Ms. Anne ZIOLA
44 Dir of Annual Fund & Advance Opers .... Ms. Amy JURGENS
15 Director of Human Resources .... Ms. Laura SEARS
18 Dir of Facilities & Constr Proj .... Mr. Wayne SPARY
58 Dir Master of Counseling/Assoc Dean .... Dr. Don BELAU
12 Director of Omaha Campus .... Ms. Colleen HAACK
12 Director of Grand Island Campus .... Ms. Jennifer WORTHINGTON
41 Athletic Director .... Ms. Jill MCCARTNEY
42 Chaplain .... Ms. Karla COOPER
40 Bookstore Manager .... Ms. Lynette NEWTON
28 Director of Multicultural Pgm & Edu .... Ms. Wilma JACKSON
23 Director of Health and Wellness .... Ms. Kelly JIROVEC
35 Director of Student Support Service .... Ms. Sherri HANIGAN
09 Director of Institutional Research .... Dr. Raja TAYEH
19 Dir of Campus Safety/Assoc Dean .... Mr. Russ HEWITT

Doane College (D)

3180 W U.S. Highway 34, Grand Island NE 68801
Telephone: (308) 398-0800 Identification: 770333
Accreditation: &NH

† Branch campus of Doane College, Crete, NE.

Doane College (E)

303 North 52nd Street, Lincoln NE 68504
Telephone: (402) 466-4774 Identification: 770334
Accreditation: &NH

† Branch campus of Doane College, Crete, NE.

Grace University (F)

1311 S 9th Street, Omaha NE 68108-3629
County: Douglas FICE Identification: 002547
Unit ID: 181093
Telephone: (402) 449-2800 Carnegie Class: Bac/Diverse
FAX Number: (402) 449-2999 Calendar System: Semester
URL: www.graceuniversity.edu
Established: 1943 Annual Undergrad Tuition & Fees: $19,708
Enrollment: 469 Coed
Affiliation or Control: Independent Non-Profit IRS Status: 501(c)3
Highest Offering: Master's
Program: Liberal Arts And General; Teacher Preparatory; Religious Emphasis
Accreditation: NH, BI

01 President .... Dr. David M. BARNES
10 Chief Financial Officer .... Vacant
05 Vice Pres of Academic Affairs .... Dr. Karl PAGENKEMPER
32 VP Christian Formation/Student Svcs .... Dr. Gary NEBEKER
84 Chief Enrollment Officer .... Mr. Bill HAMMOND
21 Director of Finance .... Ms. Anita RODRIGUEZ
06 Registrar .... Dr. Kris J. UDD
58 Dean Professional & Graduate Stds .... Mr. C. James SANTORO
09 Dir of Assessment & Inst Research .... Dr. Ronald J. SHOPE
37 Director of Financial Aid .... Vacant
15 Director Human Resources .... Ms. Deb OSMANSON
08 Librarian .... Mr. Harold (Ben) B. BRICK, III
04 Admin Assistant to the President .... Ms. Joanne R. FAST
33 Dean of Men .... Vacant
34 Dean of Women .... Dr. Tara RYE
41 Interim Athletic Director .... Mr. Willie WILLIAMS
30 Vice Pres Advancement .... Ms. Meredith SEAMAN
11 Asst VP Administration .... Ms. Deb OSMANSON
108 Director Institutional Assessment .... Dr. Ronald J. SHOPE

Hastings College (G)

710 N Turner Avenue, Box 269, Hastings NE 68902-0269
County: Adams FICE Identification: 002548
Unit ID: 181127
Telephone: (402) 463-2402 Carnegie Class: Bac/Diverse
FAX Number: (402) 461-7490 Calendar System: 4/1/4
URL: www.hastings.edu
Established: 1882 Annual Undergrad Tuition & Fees: $27,300
Enrollment: 1,149 Coed
Affiliation or Control: Presbyterian Church (U.S.A.) IRS Status: 501(c)3
Highest Offering: Master's
Program: Liberal Arts And General; Teacher Preparatory
Accreditation: NH, MUS, TED

01 President .... Mr. Donald JACKSON
00 Chairman of the Board .... Mr. Harold (Hal) E. DITTMER
30 CFO and VP for Advancement .... Mr. Gary FREEMAN
10 Assoc VP for Finance .... Mr. Tony BEATA
84 VP for Enrollment and Marketing .... Ms. Susan MEESKE
05 Vice Pres Acad Affs/Dean Faculty .... Dr. Gary C. JOHNSON
32 Vice President for Student Affairs .... Vacant
20 Assoc VP for Academic Affairs .... Dr. Liz FROMBGEN
100 Chief of Staff .... Mr. Matt FONG
41 Interim Athletic Director .... Ms. Patty SITORIUS
35 Assoc VP for Student Affairs .... Mr. Dan PETERS
44 Assoc VP for Planned & Major Gifts .... Mr. Michael KARLOFF
88 Assoc VP of Scholarship Development .... Ms. Patty SITORIUS
102 Assoc VP for Development .... Ms. Judee L. KONEN
06 Registrar .... Mr. Shawn BAKER
37 Director of Financial Aid .... Ms. Terri GRAHAM
39 Director of Housing .... Ms. Erica HABERMAN
15 Director of Human Resources .... Ms. Margo BUSBOOM
105 Director of Marketing .... Mr. Michael HOWIE
08 Director of Libraries .... Ms. Susan FRANKLIN
29 Director of Alumni Relations .... Ms. Hauli SABATKA
26 Chief Information Officer .... Mr. Steve HUTCHINSON
105 Network Administrator .... Mr. Jim MACKIN
90 Acad Computer Support Specialist .... Mr. Erik NIELSEN
18 Director Physical Plant Services .... Mr. James RUZICKA
93 Minority Students .... Dr. Moses DOGBEVIA
28 International Studies/Diversity Pgm .... Dr. Liz FROMBGEN
36 Director of Career Services .... Ms. Kimberly K. GRAVIETTE
23 Director Campus Health Services .... Ms. Beth LITTRELL
42 Chaplain .... Rev. Damen HEITMANN
21 Director of Accounting .... Mr. Dan LAUX
35 Director of Student Life .... Mr. Colt KRAUS
19 Director of Security/Safety .... Mr. John SILVESTER
38 Director of Counseling Services .... Mr. Jon LOETTERLE
40 Bookstore Manager .... Ms. Nicole KIMURA
88 News Service/Writer/Editor .... Ms. Alicia O'DONNELL
88 Graphic Designer/Publisher .... Mrs. Camille KASTL
85 Foreign Students/Student Life .... Dr. Antje ANDERSON
04 Executive Asst to President .... Ms. Marin SUHR
07 Director of Admissions .... Ms. Traci BOEVE

ITT Technical Institute (H)

1120 North 103rd Plaza, Ste. 200, Omaha NE 68114
Telephone: (402) 331-2900 Identification: 666543
Accreditation: ACICS

† Branch campus of ITT Technical Institute, Indianapolis, IN.

Kaplan University (I)

1821 K Street, PO Box 82826, Lincoln NE 68501-2826
Telephone: (402) 474-5315 FICE Identification: 004721
Accreditation: &NH, ACBSP, MAC

† Regional accreditation is carried under the parent institution in Davenport, IA.

Kaplan University **(A)**
5425 N. 103rd Street, Omaha NE 68134-1002
Telephone: (402) 431-6100 FICE Identification: 008491
Accreditation: &NH, ACBSP, DA, MAC

† Regional accreditation is carried under the parent institution in Davenport, IA.

Little Priest Tribal College (B)
601 East College Drive, PO Box 270, Winnebago NE 68071-0270
County: Thurston FICE Identification: 033233
Unit ID: 434016
Telephone: (402) 878-2380 Carnegie Class: Tribal
FAX Number: (402) 878-2355 Calendar System: Semester
URL: www.littlepriest.edu
Established: 1996 Annual Undergrad Tuition & Fees: $5,355
Enrollment: 127 Coed
Affiliation or Control: Independent Non-Profit IRS Status: 501(c)3
Highest Offering: Associate Degree
Program: Occupational; 2-Year Principally Bachelor's Creditable
Accreditation: NH

01 President ...... Mr. Ron HIS HORSE IS THUNDER
05 Academic Dean ...... Ms. Janyce WOODARD
10 Controller ...... Vacant
37 Director of Financial Aid ...... Ms. Yatty MOHAMMAD
13 IT Director ...... Mr. Morrie CONWAY
09 Dir Inst Research/Stdnt Records ...... Vacant
06 Registrar ...... Ms. Cherie HEISE

Mary Lanning Healthcare School of Radiology (C)
715 North St. Joseph Avenue, Hastings NE 68901
County: Adams FICE Identification: 004431
Unit ID: 181251
Telephone: (402) 461-5177 Carnegie Class: Not Classified
FAX Number: (402) 460-5059 Calendar System: Other
URL: www.marylanning.org
Established: 1952 Annual Undergrad Tuition & Fees: $4,353
Enrollment: 20 Coed
Affiliation or Control: Independent Non-Profit IRS Status: 501(c)3
Highest Offering: Associate Degree
Program: Occupational; 2-Year Principally Bachelor's Creditable; Technical Emphasis
Accreditation: RAD

01 Program Director ...... Cristi L. ENGEL
10 Chief Financial Officer ...... Shawn NORDBY
26 Dir of Public Rels/Marketing Svcs ...... Lisa BRANDT

McCook Community College **(D)**
1205 East Third Street, McCook NE 69001
Telephone: (308) 345-8100 Identification: 770337
Accreditation: &NH, EMT

† Branch campus of Mid-Plains Community College, North Platte, NE.

Metropolitan Community College (E)
PO Box 3777, Omaha NE 68103-0777
County: Douglas FICE Identification: 012586
Unit ID: 181303
Telephone: (402) 457-2400 Carnegie Class: Assoc/Pub-U-MC
FAX Number: (402) 457-2395 Calendar System: Quarter
URL: www.mccneb.edu
Established: 1974 Annual Undergrad Tuition & Fees (In-District): $2,745
Enrollment: 14,675 Coed
Affiliation or Control: Local IRS Status: 501(c)3
Highest Offering: Associate Degree
Program: Occupational; 2-Year Principally Bachelor's Creditable
Accreditation: NH, ACBSP, ACFEI, ADNUR, CAHIIM, COARC, CSHSE, DA, EMT, MAC

01 President ...... Mr. Randy SCHMAILZL
03 Executive Vice President ...... Mr. James GROTRIAN
05 Vice President Academic Affairs ...... Dr. Tom MCDONNELL
11 VP Technology/Administrative Svcs ...... Dr. Mary K. WISE
32 VP of Campuses/Student Affairs ...... Dr. Arthur RICH
28 Assoc Vice Pres Equity/Diversity ...... Dr. Cynthia GOOCH
15 Assoc Vice Pres of Human Resources ...... Ms. Maureen MOEGLIN
30 Assoc Vice Pres of Development ...... Ms. Pat CRISLER
20 Associate VP for Effect & Engag ...... Mr. William OWEN
84 Asst Vice Pres for Student Affairs ...... Ms. Marie VAZQUEZ
10 Executive College Business Officer ...... Mr. Dave KOEBEL
26 Exec Director of Public Affairs ...... Ms. Sheila O'CONNOR
18 Director Facilities Management ...... Mr. Bernard SEDLACEK
37 Director of Financial Aid ...... Ms. Wilma HJELLUM
96 Director Administrative Management ...... Mr. Richard HANNEMAN
19 Chief of Police/Dir Emergency Mgmt ...... Mr. David FRIEND
84 Dean of Enrollment Management ...... Ms. Ingrid BERLIN
27 Chief Information Officer ...... Mr. Mick GAHAN
06 Registrar ...... Ms. Albertha SCHMID
43 Dir Legal Services/General Counsel ...... Mr. Jim THIBODEAU
44 Director of Development ...... Ms. Jacqueline ALMQUIST
91 Director Administrative Computing ...... Ms. Jodie SNIDER
09 Senior Research Analyst ...... Ms. Denise JACOBSEN

Metropolitan Community College Elkhorn Valley Campus **(F)**
204th & Way Dodge Road, Omaha NE 68022
Telephone: (402) 289-1200 Identification: 770335
Accreditation: &NH

† Branch campus of Metropolitan Community College, Omaha, NE.

Metropolitan Community College South Omaha Campus **(G)**
2909 Edward Babe Gomez Avenue, Omaha NE 68107
Telephone: (402) 738-4500 Identification: 770336
Accreditation: &NH

† Branch campus of Metropolitan Community College, Omaha, NE.

Mid-Plains Community College (H)
601 W State Farm Road, North Platte NE 69101-9491
County: Lincoln FICE Identification: 002557
Unit ID: 181312
Telephone: (800) 658-4308 Carnegie Class: Assoc/Pub-R-M
FAX Number: (308) 535-3794 Calendar System: Semester
URL: www.mpcc.edu
Established: 1926 Annual Undergrad Tuition & Fees (In-District): $2,880
Enrollment: 2,143 Coed
Affiliation or Control: State/Local IRS Status: 501(c)3
Highest Offering: Associate Degree
Program: Occupational; 2-Year Principally Bachelor's Creditable; Technical Emphasis
Accreditation: NH, ADNUR, DA, EMT, MLTAD

01 President ...... Mr. Ryan PURDY
12 VP North Platte Community College ...... Dr. Jody TOMANEK
12 Vice Pres McCook Community College ...... Mr. Andrew LONG
10 Area Business Officer ...... Mr. Michael STEELE
05 Area VP for Academic Affairs ...... Dr. Jody TOMANEK
09 Area Dir Instl Effectiveness ...... Mr. Tad PFEIFER
32 Area Dean of Student Life ...... Dr. Brian OBERT
56 Area Director of Outreach ...... Ms. Gail KNOTT
36 Area Dean of Career Services ...... Mr. Bill EAKINS
84 Area Dean of Enrollment Management ...... Ms. Kelly RIPPEN
06 Area Registrar ...... Ms. Mari Jo WIDGER
26 Area Dir Public Inform/Marketing ...... Mr. Charles SALESTROM
15 Area Director of Human Resources ...... Ms. Rebecca WRAGE
13 Area Director Information Services ...... Mr. Tim HALL
37 Area Dir of Student Financial Aid ...... Ms. Erinn BRAUER

Midland University (I)
900 N Clarkson, Fremont NE 68025-4395
County: Dodge FICE Identification: 002553
Unit ID: 181330
Telephone: (402) 721-5480 Carnegie Class: Bac/Diverse
FAX Number: (402) 721-0250 Calendar System: 4/1/4
URL: www.midlandu.edu
Established: 1883 Annual Undergrad Tuition & Fees: $28,850
Enrollment: 1,362 Coed
Affiliation or Control: Evangelical Lutheran Church In America
IRS Status: 501(c)3
Highest Offering: Master's
Program: Occupational; Liberal Arts And General; Teacher Preparatory; Professional; Business Emphasis
Accreditation: NH, COARC, NUR

01 President ...... Ms. Jody HORNER
32 Vice Pres Student Affairs ...... Mr. Merritt NELSON
10 Vice Pres for Administration & CFO ...... Ms. Jodi BENJAMIN
30 Vice Pres for Development ...... Ms. Jessica JANSSEN
84 VP Admissions/Enrollment Management ...... Ms. Eliza FERZELY
15 Human Performance Director ...... Mr. Mark SNOW
26 Director of Communications ...... Mr. Nate NEUFIND
06 Registrar ...... Ms. Jenifer JOST
07 Director of Admissions ...... Mr. Nick BOONE
37 Director of Financial Aid ...... Mr. Doug WATSON
21 Controller ...... Ms. Denise PRATT
41 Athletic Director ...... Mr. Dave GILLESPIE
66 Director of Nursing ...... Ms. Linda QUINN
13 Chief Information Officer ...... Mr. Shane PERRIEN
18 Facilities Manager ...... Mr. Roger SONGSTER
44 Director of Annual Giving ...... Mr. Brad EBERSPACHER

Myotherapy Institute (J)
4001 Pioneer Woods Drive, Lincoln NE 68506-7547
County: Lancaster FICE Identification: 032793
Unit ID: 434432
Telephone: (402) 421-7410 Carnegie Class: Assoc/PrivFP
FAX Number: (402) 421-6736 Calendar System: Other
URL: www.myotherapy.edu
Established: 1992 Annual Undergrad Tuition & Fees: $16,800
Enrollment: 15 Coed
Affiliation or Control: Proprietary IRS Status: Proprietary
Highest Offering: Associate Degree
Program: Occupational
Accreditation: ACCSC

01 Director ...... Ms. Sue KOZISEK

National American University-Bellevue **(K)**
3604 Summit Plaza Drive, Bellevue NE 68123
Telephone: (402) 972-4250 Identification: 770406
Accreditation: &NH

† Branch campus of National American University, Rapid City, SD.

Nebraska Christian College (L)
12550 S 114th Street, Papillion NE 68046-4256
County: Sarpy FICE Identification: 012976
Unit ID: 181376
Telephone: (402) 935-9400 Carnegie Class: Spec/Faith
FAX Number: (402) 935-9500 Calendar System: Semester
URL: www.nechristian.edu
Established: 1945 Annual Undergrad Tuition & Fees: $22,900
Enrollment: 159 Coed
Affiliation or Control: Christian Churches And Churches of Christ
IRS Status: 501(c)3
Highest Offering: Baccalaureate
Program: Religious Emphasis
Accreditation: BI

01 President ...... Mr. Tony CLARK
05 Vice Pres Academics ...... Dr. Mark KRAUSE
26 Vice Pres Advancement ...... Mr. David MILLER
32 Dean of Students/Chief Stdnt Ofcr ...... Mr. Theo HUDALLA
07 Director of Admissions ...... Mrs. Kristin MILLER
08 Director of Library Services ...... Mr. Christopher KELLEHER
37 Financial Aid Officer ...... Mrs. Sarah NIGRO
04 Administrative Asst to President ...... Mrs. Laurie WILSON
06 Registrar ...... Dr. Mark HUDDLESTON
13 Chief Info Technology Officer (CIO) ...... Mrs. Susan SNYDER

Nebraska Indian Community College (M)
1111 Hwy 75 - PO Box 428, Macy NE 68039-0428
County: Thurston FICE Identification: 025508
Unit ID: 181419
Telephone: (402) 494-2311 Carnegie Class: Tribal
FAX Number: (402) 837-4183 Calendar System: Semester
URL: www.thenicc.edu
Established: 1973 Annual Undergrad Tuition & Fees: $4,080
Enrollment: 120 Coed
Affiliation or Control: Tribal Control IRS Status: Exempt
Highest Offering: Associate Degree
Program: Occupational; 2-Year Principally Bachelor's Creditable
Accreditation: NH

01 President ...... Dr. Michael OLTROGGE
05 Academic Dean ...... Don TORGERSON
32 Dean Student Services ...... Dawne PRICE
30 Director of Development ...... Mary JOHNSON
13 Chief Information Officer ...... Justin KOCIAN
06 Registrar ...... Annette LOCHE
15 Human Resource Director ...... Carlos VENABLE-RIDLEY

Nebraska Indian Community College-Santee **(N)**
415 North River Road, Santee NE 68760
Telephone: (402) 494-2311 Identification: 770339
Accreditation: &NH

† Branch campus of Nebraska Indian Community College, Macy, NE.

Nebraska Indian Community College-South Sioux City **(O)**
2605 1/2 Dakota Avenue, South Sioux City NE 68776
Telephone: (402) 494-2311 Identification: 770340
Accreditation: &NH

† Branch campus of Nebraska Indian Community College, Macy, NE.

Nebraska Methodist College (P)
720 N 87th Street, Omaha NE 68114-2852
County: Douglas FICE Identification: 006404
Unit ID: 181297
Telephone: (402) 354-7000 Carnegie Class: Spec/Health
FAX Number: (402) 354-7090 Calendar System: Semester
URL: www.methodistcollege.edu
Established: 1891 Annual Undergrad Tuition & Fees: $14,904
Enrollment: 996 Coed
Affiliation or Control: Independent Non-Profit IRS Status: 501(c)3
Highest Offering: Master's
Program: Professional; Nursing Emphasis
Accreditation: NH, COARC, DMS, MAC, NURSE, PTAA, RAD, SURGT

01 President ...... Dr. Dennis A. JOSLIN
05 Vice President Academic Affairs ...... Dr. Jody WOODWORTH
10 VP Bus Ops & Strategic Initiatives ...... Dr. Deborah CARLSON
84 VP Enrollment & Student Success ...... Dr. Brian SAJKO
66 Dean Nursing ...... Dr. Linda HUGHES
58 Program Director Master's Nursing ...... Dr. Linda FOLEY
66 Pgm Director Undergrad Nursing ...... Dr. Karen JOHNSON
88 Director of Special Pgms Nursing ...... Dr. Susie WARD
76 Dean Health Professions ...... Vacant
97 Dean General Education ...... Dr. Dean MANTERNACH

76 Pgm Director Phys Therapist Asst ... Ms. Shannon STRUBY
76 Program Director Respiratory Care ... Dr. John JAROSZ
88 Program Director Radiography ... Ms. Amy BOYD
88 Program Director Sonography ... Ms. Rebecca MATHIASEN
88 Pgm Director Surgical Technology ... Ms. Christy GRANT
08 Director of Library Services ... Ms. Beverly SEDLACEK
42 Dir Spiritual Dev/Campus Ministry ... Vacant
29 Alumni Engagement Director ... Ms. Angela HEESACKER-SMITH
07 Director Enrollment Services ... Ms. Megan MARYOTT
06 Director Registration & Records ... Ms. Melinda STONER
37 Director Financial Aid ... Ms. Penny JAMES
107 Exec Dir Professional Development ... Ms. Jillian PLYMESSER
88 Educational Compliance Officer ... Mr. Ryan PORTWOOD
04 Administrative Asst to President ... Ms. Cathy BECK
18 Chief Facilities/Physical Plant ... Ms. Pam EDGERTON
53 Director of Education ... Ms. Lisa NASSER

*Nebraska State College System (A)

1327 H Street, Suite 200, Lincoln NE 68508

County: Lancaster FICE Identification: 033441
Telephone: (402) 471-2505 Carnegie Class: N/A
FAX Number: (402) 471-2669
URL: www.nscs.edu

01 Chancellor ... Mr. Stan CARPENTER
43 General Counsel & VC for Emp Rel ... Ms. Kristin PETERSEN
10 Vice Chancellor Finance/Admin ... Ms. Carolyn MURPHY
32 VC Stdnt Affs/Mktg/Enrol/Pub Info ... Dr. Korinne TANDE
18 Vice Chanc Facilities & Info Tech ... Mr. Steve HOTOVY
05 VC Acad Planning/Partnerships ... Dr. Jodi KUPPER
11 Operations Director ... Ms. Becky KOHRS
88 Director of Systemwide Accounting ... Ms. Amy HOCK
13 System Data Analyst/Reports Develop ... Mr. Mike DUNKLE

*Chadron State College (B)

1000 Main Street, Chadron NE 69337-2690

County: Dawes FICE Identification: 002539
Unit ID: 180948
Telephone: (308) 432-6000 Carnegie Class: Bac/Diverse
FAX Number: (308) 432-6464 Calendar System: Semester
URL: www.csc.edu
Established: 1911 Annual Undergrad Tuition & Fees (In-State): $6,203
Enrollment: 3,033 Coed
Affiliation or Control: State IRS Status: 501(c)3
Highest Offering: Master's
Program: Liberal Arts And General; Teacher Preparatory; Professional
Accreditation: NH, ACBSP, SW, TED

02 President ... Dr. Randy RHINE
05 Vice President Academic Affairs ... Dr. Charles SNARE
11 Vice Pres Administration & Finance ... Mr. Dale E. GRANT
84 Vice Pres Enrollment Mgmt & Mktg ... Mr. Jon HANSEN
20 Assoc VP Teaching & Learning Tech ... Dr. Susan HINES
13 Chief Information Officer ... Ms. Ann M. BURK
58 Dean Graduate Studies/BEAMS ... Dr. Joel HYER
49 Dean Essential Studies/Liberal Art ... Dr. James MARGETTS
108 Dean Assessment & Accreditation ... Dr. James POWELL
10 Comptroller ... Ms. Kari GASWICK
09 Director Institutional Research ... Ms. Theresa R. DAWSON
102 Executive Director CS Foundation ... Ms. Connie A. RASMUSSEN
06 Director of Records ... Ms. Melissa MITCHELL
32 Sr Director Student Services ... Dr. Pat BEU
32 Sr Director Student Services ... Ms. Sherry L. DOUGLAS
07 Director of Admissions ... Ms. Lisa STEIN
15 Interim Director Human Resources ... Mr. Derby JOHNSON
39 Director of Housing ... Ms. Sherri J. SIMONS
41 Athletics Director ... Mr. Joel SMITH
36 Director of Internships/Career Svcs ... Ms. Deena KENNELL
21 Budget Director ... Ms. Melany HUGHES
27 Director College Relations ... Mr. Alex HELMBRECHT
18 Coordinator of Physical Facilities ... Mr. Blair BRENNAN
12 Director Extended Campus Sites ... Ms. Deann BAYNE

*Peru State College (C)

PO Box 10, Peru NE 68421-0010

County: Nemaha FICE Identification: 002559
Unit ID: 181534
Telephone: (402) 872-3815 Carnegie Class: Master's L
FAX Number: (402) 872-2375 Calendar System: Semester
URL: www.peru.edu
Established: 1867 Annual Undergrad Tuition & Fees (In-State): $6,397
Enrollment: 2,499 Coed
Affiliation or Control: State IRS Status: 501(c)3
Highest Offering: Master's
Program: Liberal Arts And General; Teacher Preparatory
Accreditation: NH, TED

02 President ... Dr. Daniel HANSON
05 Vice Pres Academic Affairs ... Dr. Tim BORCHERS
10 Vice Pres Administration & Finance ... Ms. Kathy CARROLL
32 VP Enrollment Mgmt/Student Services ... Dr. Michaela WILLIS
35 Dean of Student Life ... Mr. Jesse DORMAN
102 Exec Director PSC Foundations ... Mr. Todd SIMPSON
41 Director of Athletics ... Mr. Steve SCHNEIDER
26 Dir of Marketing & Communications ... Ms. Regan ANSON
06 Dir Student Records/Coll Registrar ... Ms. Dixie TETEN
37 Director of Financial Aid ... Vacant
08 Director of Library ... Ms. Veronica MCASEY
15 Director of Human Resources ... Ms. Eulanda CADE

18 Director Campus Services ... Ms. Jill MCCORMICK
21 Director of Business Services ... Ms. Kathy TYNON
07 Director of Admissions ... Mr. Heath CHRISTIANSEN
38 Licensed Student Counselor ... Ms. Jamie EBERLY

*Wayne State College (D)

1111 Main Street, Wayne NE 68787-1172

County: Wayne FICE Identification: 002566
Unit ID: 181783
Telephone: (402) 375-7000 Carnegie Class: Master's L
FAX Number: (402) 375-7204 Calendar System: Semester
URL: www.wsc.edu
Established: 1909 Annual Undergrad Tuition & Fees (In-State): $6,042
Enrollment: 3,470 Coed
Affiliation or Control: State IRS Status: 501(c)3
Highest Offering: Beyond Master's But Less Than Doctorate
Program: Liberal Arts And General; Teacher Preparatory; Professional
Accreditation: NH, ART, IACBE, MUS, TED

02 President ... Dr. Marysz RAMES
05 Vice President Academic Affairs ... Dr. Michael ANDERSON
10 Vice Pres Admin/Finance ... Ms. Angela FREDRICKSON
30 Vice Pres Institutional Advancement ... Ms. Phyllis CONNER
32 Vice President & Dean Students ... Dr. Jeffrey CARSTENS
37 Director Financial Aid ... Ms. Annette KAUS
07 Director of Admissions ... Mr. Kevin HALLE
38 Director of Counseling ... Ms. Lin BRUMMELS
39 Director of Residence Life ... Vacant
36 Director of Career Services ... Mr. Jason BARELMAN
13 Chief Information Officer ... Mr. John DUNNING
26 Director College Relations ... Mr. Jay COLLIER
41 Director of Athletics ... Mr. Mike POWICKI
18 Director of Facility Services ... Mr. Chad ALTWINE
08 Director of Library Services ... Mr. David GRABER
06 Registrar ... Ms. Cheri PARRAMORE
29 Dir Development & Alumni Relations ... Ms. Deb LUNDAHL
15 Director of Human Resources ... Ms. Candace TIMMERMAN
79 Dean School of Arts & Hum ... Mr. Steven ELLIOTT
50 Dean Sch of Business & Technology ... Dr. Vaughn BENSON
53 Dean Sch of Educ & Couns ... Dr. David HARYCKI
83 Dean Sch of Natural/Social Sci ... Dr. Tammy EVETOVICH
28 Director of Multicultural Affairs ... Dr. Leah KEINO
09 Research Analyst ... Ms. Jeannette BARRY
108 Director of Assessment ... Ms. Sue SYDOW
91 Director Administrative Computing ... Ms. Janell SCARDINO
44 Director Annual or Planned Giving ... Mr. Kevin ARMSTRONG

Nebraska Wesleyan University (E)

5000 St. Paul Avenue, Lincoln NE 68504-2794

County: Lancaster FICE Identification: 002555
Unit ID: 181446
Telephone: (402) 466-2371 Carnegie Class: Bac/A&S
FAX Number: (402) 465-2179 Calendar System: Semester
URL: www.nebrwesleyan.edu
Established: 1887 Annual Undergrad Tuition & Fees: $29,800
Enrollment: 2,083 Coed
Affiliation or Control: United Methodist IRS Status: 501(c)3
Highest Offering: Master's
Program: Liberal Arts And General
Accreditation: NH, ACBSP, CAATE, MUS, NUR, SW, TED

01 President ... Dr. Frederik OHLES
05 Provost ... Dr. Judy A. MUYSKENS
10 Vice Pres Finance/Administration ... Ms. Tish GADE-JONES
84 Vice President Enrollment Mgmt ... Mr. Bill MOTZER
30 Vice President Advancement ... Mr. John GREVING
58 Dean of University College ... Ms. Elizabeth M. WALLS
32 Dean of Students ... Mr. Peter ARMSTRONG
49 Dean College of Lib Arts & Sciences ... Dr. Sarah A. KELEN
88 Asst Provost Integr/Exper Learning ... Dr. Jeff A. ISAACSON
21 Asst VP & Controller ... Mr. Greg D. MASCHMAN
06 Vice Provost for Academic Systems ... Ms. Patty HALL
35 Associate Dean of Students ... Ms. Geri E. COTTER
15 Asst VP Human Resources ... Mrs. Nancy B. COOKSON
18 Asst VP Physical Plant ... Mr. Matthew T. KADAVY
07 Director of Admissions ... Mr. Gordie COFFIN
27 Director of Public Relations ... Ms. Sara M. OLSON
88 Director Student Success Retention ... Ms. Candice HOWELL
08 University Librarian ... Ms. Margaret L. EMONS
37 Director of Financial Aid ... Mr. Tom J. OCHSNER
29 Director of Alumni Relations ... Ms. Shelley MCHUGH
41 Athletic Director ... Dr. Ira A. ZEFF
13 Director of Computer Services ... Mr. Steven R. DOW
90 Director Instructional Technology ... Mr. Jay L. KAHLER
13 Director Administrative Systems ... Mr. Mark MURPHY
26 Director of Marketing ... Ms. Peggy S. HAIN
36 Director Career & Counseling Ctr ... Ms. Janelle S. ANDREINI
39 Director Residential Education ... Ms. Brandi SESTAK
104 Director of Global Engagement ... Ms. Sarah BARR
92 Director Wesleyan Honors Academy ... Dr. Marian BORGMANN-INGWERSEN
35 Dir Student Involvement & Ldrship ... Ms. Karri SANDERSON
102 Director of Foundation Relations ... Ms. Nancy WEHRBEIN
23 Director Student Health Services ... Ms. Nancy J. NEWMAN
42 University Minister ... Rev. Eduardo BOUSSON
04 Special Asst to President ... Ms. P. J. RABEL
44 Director Archway Fund ... Ms. Erika PASCHOLD
09 Assoc Director Inst Research ... Ms. Brooke GLENN
28 Asst Dean Multicultural Programs ... Mr. T. J. MCDOWELL, JR.
91 Director Administrative Computing ... Mr. Gredon TURNER

North Platte Community College-North Campus (F)

1101 Halligan Drive, North Platte NE 69101

Telephone: (308) 535-3600 Identification: 770338
Accreditation: &NH

† Branch campus of Mid-Plains Community College, North Platte, NE.

Northeast Community College (G)

801 E Benjamin, PO Box 469, Norfolk NE 68702-0469

County: Madison FICE Identification: 011667
Unit ID: 181491
Telephone: (402) 371-2020 Carnegie Class: Assoc/Pub-R-M
FAX Number: (402) 844-7400 Calendar System: Semester
URL: www.northeast.edu
Established: 1973 Annual Undergrad Tuition & Fees (In-District): $3,165
Enrollment: 5,061 Coed
Affiliation or Control: Local IRS Status: 501(c)3
Highest Offering: Associate Degree
Program: Occupational; 2-Year Principally Bachelor's Creditable; Technical Emphasis
Accreditation: NH, ADNUR, EMT, PTAA

01 President ... Dr. Michael R. CHIPPS
03 Executive Vice President ... Mrs. Mary J. HONKE
05 Vice President Educational Services ... Mr. John V. BLAYLOCK
10 Vice Pres of Administrative Svcs ... Ms. Lynne D. KOSKI
32 Vice President of Student Services ... Dr. Karen J. SEVERSON
13 Vice President of Technology ... Mr. Derek BIERMAN
88 Associate VP of Ctr for Enterprise ... Mr. Eric JOHNSON
30 Assoc VP of Devel/External Affairs ... Dr. Tracy L. KRUSE
15 Associate VP of Human Resources ... Mr. Craig GARRETT
75 Dean of Applied Technology ... Mr. Lyle J. KATHOL
47 Dean Ag/Health/Sciences ... Mrs. Corinne MORRIS
49 Dean Humanities/Arts/Social Sci ... Mrs. Faye KILDAY
50 Dean of Business/Math/Tech ... Dr. Wade HERLEY
76 Dean of Health/Wellness ... Dr. Michele GILL
11 Dean of Administrative Services ... Mrs. Coleen BRESSLER
21 Director of Business Services ... Mrs. Mary J. MEYER
44 Dean of Institutional Advancement . Ms. Michela KEELER-STROM
84 Dean of Enrollment Management ... Mrs. Amanda NIPP
12 South Sioux City College Ctr Dean ... Mrs. Pamela MILLER
18 Director of Physical Plant ... Mr. Brandon MCLEAN
06 Registrar ... Mrs. Kathy J. STOVER
37 Financial Aid Director ... Ms. Stacy DIECKMAN
36 Director of Career Services ... Mrs. Terri HEGGEMEYER
66 Director of Nursing Programs ... Mrs. Karen K. WEIDNER
21 Director of Accounting Services ... Mr. John ROBERTSON
16 Human Resources Coordinator ... Mrs. Jennifer HAPPOLD
96 Director of Purchasing ... Mrs. Nell VOTRUBA
41 Director of Athletics ... Mr. Jacob RIPPLE
39 Director Residence Life & Food Svcs ... Mr. Pete RIZZO
105 Director of Web System Services ... Mr. Mike AUTEN
08 Director of Library Services ... Mrs. Mary Louise FOSTER
26 Director of Public Relations ... Mr. James CURRY
40 College Store Manager ... Mrs. Julie CARLSON
35 Director of Student Conduct ... Mrs. Maureen BAKER
09 Director of Institutional Research ... Ms. Julie MELNICK
35 Student Activities Coordinator ... Ms. Carissa KOLLATH
27 Director of Marketing ... Ms. Jennifer GREVE
07 Director of Admissions ... Mr. Bradley RANSLEM
04 Administrative Asst to President ... Ms. Diane REIKOFSKI
28 Director of Diversity ... Mr. Ted MYERS
38 Director Student Counseling ... Ms. Stephanie BRUNDIECK

Omaha School of Massage and Healthcare of Herzing University (H)

9478 Park Drive, Omaha NE 68127

Telephone: (402) 331-3694 Identification: 770432
Accreditation: &NH

† Branch campus of Herzing University, Madison, WI.

Saint Gregory the Great Seminary (I)

800 Fletcher Road, Seward NE 68434-8145

County: Seward Identification: 667027
Telephone: (402) 643-4052 Carnegie Class: Not Classified
FAX Number: (402) 643-6964 Calendar System: Semester
URL: www.stgregoryseminary.edu
Established: 1998 Annual Undergrad Tuition & Fees: $9,500
Enrollment: 48 Male
Affiliation or Control: Roman Catholic IRS Status: 501(c)3
Highest Offering: Baccalaureate
Program: Liberal Arts And General; Religious Emphasis
Accreditation: NH

01 Rector/President ... Msgr. John T. FOLDA

Southeast Community College (J)

4771 West Scott Road, Beatrice NE 68310-7042

Telephone: (402) 228-3468 Identification: 770341
Accreditation: &NH

† Branch campus of Southeast Community College, Lincoln, NE.

Southeast Community College (A)

301 S 68 Street Place, Lincoln NE 68510-2449
County: Lancaster FICE Identification: 025083
Unit ID: 181640
Telephone: (402) 323-3400 Carnegie Class: Assoc/Pub-R-L
FAX Number: (402) 323-3420 Calendar System: Quarter
URL: www.southeast.edu
Established: 1973 Annual Undergrad Tuition & Fees (In-District): $2,778
Enrollment: 9,392 Coed
Affiliation or Control: State/Local IRS Status: 501(c)3
Highest Offering: Associate Degree
Program: Occupational; 2-Year Principally Bachelor's Creditable
Accreditation: NH, ACBSP, ACFEI, ADNUR, COARC, CSHSE, DA, DIETT, MAC, MLTAD, PNUR, POLYT, PTAA, RAD, SURGT

01 President .... Dr. Paul ILLICH
05 Vice President Instruction .... Dr. Dennis HEADRICK
22 Vice Pres Access/Equity/Diversity .... Mr. Jose SOTO
11 VP Administrative Svcs/Res Devel .... Ms. Amy G. JORGENS
12 VP Student Svcs/Campus Director .... Ms. Bev HARVEY
12 VP Technology/Campus Director .... Mr. Ed KOSTER
15 Vice Pres Human Resources .... Mr. Bruce TANGEMAN
12 Dean of Virtual Learning/Campus Dir .... Mr. Robert MORGAN
37 Director of Financial Aid .... Ms. Melissa TROYER
32 Dean Student Svcs/Dir Stdnt Support .... Dr. Thomas CARDWELL
84 Dean Student Svcs/Dir Enrollment .... Mr. Mike PEGRAM
26 Dir of Public Information/Marketing .... Mr. Stu OSTERTHUN
90 Information Services Manager .... Mr. Alan BRUNKOW
09 Director of Institutional Research .... Ms. Robin MOORE

Southeast Community College (B)

600 State Street, Milford NE 68405-8498
Telephone: (402) 761-2131 Identification: 770342
Accreditation: &NH

† Branch campus of Southeast Community College, Lincoln, NE.

Summit Christian College (C)

2025 21st Street, Gering NE 69341
County: Scotts Bluff Identification: 667209
Telephone: (308) 632-6933 Carnegie Class: Not Classified
FAX Number: (308) 632-8599 Calendar System: Semester
URL: www.summitcc.net
Established: 1951 Annual Undergrad Tuition & Fees: $6,200
Enrollment: 40 Coed
Affiliation or Control: Independent Non-Profit IRS Status: 501(c)3
Highest Offering: Baccalaureate
Program: Religious Emphasis
Accreditation: @BI

01 President .... David K. PARRISH
05 Academic Dean .... Scott GRIBBLE
06 Registrar .... Andi GRANT

Union College (D)

3800 S 48th, Lincoln NE 68506-4300
County: Lancaster FICE Identification: 002563
Unit ID: 181738
Telephone: (402) 486-2600 Carnegie Class: Bac/Diverse
FAX Number: (402) 486-2895 Calendar System: Semester
URL: www.ucollege.edu
Established: 1891 Annual Undergrad Tuition & Fees: $21,970
Enrollment: 886 Coed
Affiliation or Control: Seventh-day Adventist IRS Status: 501(c)3
Highest Offering: Master's
Program: 2-Year Principally Bachelor's Creditable; Liberal Arts And General; Teacher Preparatory; Professional
Accreditation: NH, ARCPA, NURSE, SW, TED

01 President .... Dr. Vinita SAUDER
05 Vice President for Academic Admin .... Dr. Malcolm RUSSELL
10 Vice President for Financial Admin .... Mr. Jeff LEEPER
32 Vice President Student Services .... Dr. Linda BECKER
30 Vice President for Advancement .... Ms. LuAnn DAVIS
84 Vice President Enrollment Services .... Ms. Nadine NELSON
42 Vice President for Spiritual Life .... Dr. Rich CARLSON
08 Library Director .... Ms. Sabrina RILEY
13 Director of Information Systems .... Mr. Richard HENRIQUES
33 Dean of Men .... Mr. Doug TALLMAN
06 Dir Records/Registrar .... Ms. Michelle YOUNKIN
26 Director of Public Relations .... Mr. Ryan TELLER
29 Director Alumni Relations .... Ms. Kenna Lee CARLSON
37 Director Student Financial Aid .... Ms. Taryn ROUSE
15 Director for Human Resources .... Mr. Jonathan SHIELDS
36 Career Center Coordinator .... Ms. Teresa EDGERTON

Universal College of Healing Arts (E)

8702 N 30th Street, Omaha NE 68112-1810
County: Douglas FICE Identification: 038214
Unit ID: 446598
Telephone: (402) 556-4456 Carnegie Class: Assoc/PrivFP
FAX Number: (402) 561-0635 Calendar System: Semester
URL: www.ucha.edu
Established: 1995 Annual Undergrad Tuition & Fees: $15,450
Enrollment: 14 Coed
Affiliation or Control: Proprietary IRS Status: Proprietary
Highest Offering: Associate Degree
Program: Occupational
Accreditation: ABHES

01 Director .... Ms. Paulette GENTHON

*University of Nebraska Central Administration (F)

3835 Holdrege, Lincoln NE 68583-0745
County: Lancaster FICE Identification: 008025
Unit ID: 181747
Telephone: (402) 472-2111 Carnegie Class: N/A
FAX Number: (402) 472-1237
URL: www.nebraska.edu

01 President .... Dr. Hank BOUNDS
05 Exec Vice President & Provost .... Dr. Susan M. FRITZ
10 Sr Vice Pres Business & Finance .... Mr. David LECHNER
43 Vice President & General Counsel .... Mr. Joel D. PEDERSEN
47 VP Agriculture/Natural Resources .... Dr. Ronnie GREEN
100 Chief of Staff .... Ms. Dara L. TROUTMAN
13 Chief Information Officer .... Mr. Walter G. WEIR
101 Corporation Secretary .... Ms. Carmen K. MAURER
86 Sr Assoc VP/Director Govt Relations .... Mr. Ron WITHEM
18 Asst VP/Dir Facility Plng/Mgmt .... Ms. Rebecca H. KOLLER
09 Asst VP/Dir Inst Research/Planning .... Dr. Kristin YATES
88 Asst VP P-16 Initiatives .... Dr. Gabrielle BANICK
88 Asst VP Global Strategy/Intl Init .... Vacant
26 Asst VP Univ Affs/Dir Comm & Mktg .... Ms. Jacqueline OSTROWICKI

*University of Nebraska at Kearney (G)

905 W 25th Street, Kearney NE 68849
County: Buffalo FICE Identification: 002551
Unit ID: 181215
Telephone: (308) 865-8208 Carnegie Class: Master's L
FAX Number: (308) 865-8665 Calendar System: Semester
URL: www.unk.edu
Established: 1903 Annual Undergrad Tuition & Fees (In-State): $6,724
Enrollment: 6,902 Coed
Affiliation or Control: State IRS Status: 501(c)3
Highest Offering: Beyond Master's But Less Than Doctorate
Program: Liberal Arts And General; Teacher Preparatory; Professional
Accreditation: NH, BUS, CAATE, CACREP, CIDA, MUS, NAIT, SP, SW, TED

02 Chancellor .... Dr. Douglas A. KRISTENSEN
05 Sr VC Academic & Student Affairs .... Dr. Charles J. BICAK
10 Vice Chanc Business & Finance .... Ms. Barbara L. JOHNSON
26 Asst VC Comm/Community Relations .... Ms. Kelly H. BARTLING
30 Vice President Development .... Mr. Lucas DART
13 Asst Vice Chanc Info Technology .... Ms. Debbie SCHROEDER
21 Asst Vice Chanc Business & Finance .... Ms. Jane SHELDON
81 Dean Natural/Social Science .... Dr. John C. LA DUKE
50 Dean Business/Technology .... Dr. Timothy J. BURKINK
53 Dean of Education .... Dr. Sheryl J. FEINSTEIN
57 Dean Fine Arts & Humanities .... Dr. William JURMA
20 Dean Graduate Studies & Research .... Dr. Kenya S. TAYLOR
32 Dean of Student Affairs .... Dr. Gilbert HINGA
04 Exec Assistant to the Chancellor .... Mr. Neal H. SCHNOOR
06 Registrar .... Ms. Kim SCHIPPOREIT
08 Dean of the Library .... Ms. Janet S. WILKE
36 Director Academic & Career Services .... Ms. Amy L. RUNDSTROM
07 Dir UG Recruitment/Admissions .... Mr. Dusty NEWTON
18 Dir Facilities Mgmt & Planning .... Mr. Lee MCQUEEN
19 Director Police & Parking Services .... Mr. James DAVIS
22 Dir Affirm Action/Equal Opportunity .... Ms. Mary J. CHINNOCK PETROSKI
09 Director Institutional Research .... Ms. Kathy LIVINGSTON
27 Dir News/Internal Commununication .... Mr. Todd GOTTULA
29 Director Alumni Services .... Mr. Lucas DART
88 Director Student Life .... Ms. Sharon PELC
23 Director Counseling & Health Care .... Ms. Wendy L. SCHARDT
39 Director Residence Life .... Mr. George HOLMAN
40 Director Bookstore .... Mr. Len J. FANGMEYER
41 Athletic Director .... Mr. Paul M. PLINSKE
21 Director Finance .... Mr. Larry RIESSLAND
108 Director Assessment .... Vacant
25 Director Sponsored Programs .... Mr. Richard A. MOCARSKI
104 Asst Vice Chanc for Intl Affairs .... Mr. Michael J. STOPFORD
21 Budget Director .... Ms. Jean MATTSON
96 Director Bus Svcs & Accts Payable .... Mr. Jonathan C. WATTS
37 Director Financial Aid .... Ms. Mary SOMMERS
93 Director Multicultural Affairs .... Mr. Juan GUZMAN
92 Director Honors Program .... Dr. John FALCONER
84 Assoc VC Acad Svcs/Enroll Mgmt .... Dr. Edgar (Ed) L. SCANTLING

*University of Nebraska - Lincoln (H)

14th and R Streets, Lincoln NE 68588-0002
County: Lancaster FICE Identification: 002565
Unit ID: 181464
Telephone: (402) 472-7211 Carnegie Class: RU/VH
FAX Number: (402) 472-2410 Calendar System: Semester
URL: www.unl.edu
Established: 1869 Annual Undergrad Tuition & Fees (In-State): $8,382
Enrollment: 25,006 Coed
Affiliation or Control: State IRS Status: 501(c)3
Highest Offering: Doctorate
Program: Liberal Arts And General; Teacher Preparatory; Professional
Accreditation: NH, ART, AUD, BUS, BUSA, #CAATE, CIDA, CLPSY, CONST, COPSY, CS, DANCE, DIETD, DIETI, ENG, IPSY, JOUR, LAW, LSAR, MFCD, MUS, PLNG, SCPSY, SP, TEAC, THEA

02 Chancellor .... Mr. Harvey PERLMAN
05 Int Sr Vice Chanc Academic Affairs .... Dr. Ronnie D. GREEN
10 Vice Chanc Business & Finance .... Ms. Christine JACKSON
32 Vice Chancellor Student Affairs .... Dr. Juan FRANCO
65 Vice Chanc Agric/Nat Resources .... Dr. Ronnie D. GREEN
46 VC Research & Economic Development .... Dr. Prem S. PAUL
13 VC Information Technology & CIO .... Mr. Mark ASKREN
04 Associate to Chancellor .... Mr. William NUNEZ
31 Asst to Chanc Community Relations .... Ms. Michelle WAITE
15 Asst Vice Chanc for Human Resources .... Mr. Bruce A. CURRIN
18 Executive Director .... Mr. Mark MILLER
07 Director Admissions .... Ms. Amber S. WILLIAMS
08 Dean University Libraries .... Dr. Nancy BUSCH
58 Dean Graduate Studies .... Dr. Lance C. PEREZ
49 Dean Arts & Sciences .... Dr. Joseph FRANCISCO
54 Dean Engineering .... Dr. Timothy WEI
61 Dean of Law .... Dr. Susan POSER
47 Dean Agric Scienc/Nat Resources .... Dr. Steven WALLER
50 Dean Business Administration .... Dr. Donde PLOWMAN
60 Dean Journ/Mass Communic .... Dr. Maria MARRON
53 Dean Education & Human Sciences .... Dr. Marjorie KOSTELNIK
48 Interim Dean College Architecture .... Dr. Kim L. WILSON
47 Dean Agricultural Research Division .... Dr. Archie CLUTTER
56 Dean & Dir Cooperative Extens .... Dr. Charles HIBBERD
93 Director Educ Access & TRIO Pgms .... Ms. Catherine YAMAMOTO
57 Dean Fine & Performing Arts .... Dr. Charles D. O'CONNOR
37 Director Scholarships/Financial Aid .... Mr. Craig D. MUNIER
09 Director Inst Research & Planning .... Dr. William J. NUNEZ
92 Director Honors Program .... Dr. Patrice BERGER
94 Director Women's Studies .... Dr. Marie-Chantal KALISA
06 University Registrar .... Dr. Richard MORRELL
36 Director Career Services Center .... Dr. Larry R. ROUTH
19 Chief University Police Services .... Mr. Owen YARDLEY
22 Director Instit Equity & Compliance .... Ms. Susan FOSTER
23 Director University Health Center .... Dr. James GUEST
39 Director Housing Office .... Ms. Susan M. GILDERSLEEVE
41 Director of Athletics .... Mr. Shawn EICHORST
55 Dir Distance Education Services .... Dr. Nancy ADEN-FOX
29 Exec Director Alumni Association .... Ms. Shelley ZABOROWSKI
26 Director University Communications .... Dr. Meg LAUERMAN
20 Associate Academic Officer .... Dr. Lance C. PEREZ
30 Chief Development .... Mr. Brian HASTINGS
38 Director Student Counseling .... Dr. Robert N. PORTNOY
84 Interim Dean Enrollment Management .... Dr. Amy GOODBURN
96 Director of Purchasing .... Mr. Gary L. KRAFT

*University of Nebraska Medical Center (I)

987020 Nebraska Medical Center, Omaha NE 68198-7020
County: Douglas FICE Identification: 006895
Unit ID: 181428
Telephone: (402) 559-4000 Carnegie Class: Spec/Med
FAX Number: (402) 559-4396 Calendar System: Semester
URL: www.unmc.edu
Established: 1869 Annual Undergrad Tuition & Fees (In-State): $9,441
Enrollment: 3,696 Coed
Affiliation or Control: State IRS Status: 501(c)3
Highest Offering: Doctorate
Program: Professional
Accreditation: NH, ARCPA, CYTO, DENT, DH, DIETI, DMS, MED, MT, NMT, NURSE, PERF, PH, PHAR, PTA, RAD, RADMAG, RTT

02 Chancellor .... Dr. Jeffery P. GOLD
05 Vice Chancellor Acad Affairs .... Dr. H. Dele O. DAVIES
10 Int Vice Chanc Business & Finance .... Ms. Deborah THOMAS
46 Vice Chancellor Research .... Dr. Jennifer LARSEN
86 Vice Chancellor External Affairs .... Mr. Robert BARTEE
20 Assoc Vice Chanc Academic Affairs .... Dr. James TURPEN
20 Asst Vice Chanc Acad Affairs .... Dr. Jilian ZHENG
20 Assoc Vice Chanc Acad Affs/Reg Comp .... Dr. Ernest D. PRENTICE
45 Assoc Vice Chanc Basic Sci Rsch .... Dr. Kenneth BAYLES
45 Assoc Vice Chancellor Clinical Rsch .... Dr. Christopher KRATOCHVIL
21 Sr Assoc Vice Chan Business/Finance .... Ms. Deborah THOMAS
13 Assoc Vice Chanc Bus Dev/CTO .... Dr. Rodney MARKIN
18 Asst Vice Chanc Facilities/Mgt/Plng .... Mr. Kenneth HANSEN
14 Asst Vice Chancellor ITS .... Ms. Yvette A. HOLLY
58 Dean Graduate Studies .... Dr. H. Dele O. DAVIES
52 Dean College of Dentistry .... Dr. Janet GUTHMILLER
63 Dean College of Medicine .... Dr. Bradley E. BRITIGAN
66 Dean College of Nursing .... Dr. Juliann SEBASTIAN
67 Dean College of Pharmacy .... Dr. Courtney FLETCHER
69 Dean College of Public Health .... Dr. Ali KHAN
76 Dean College of Allied Hlth Prof .... Dr. Kyle MEYER
88 Dir Eppley Cancer Research Inst .... Dr. Kenneth H. COWAN
88 Interim Director Munroe-Meyer Inst .... Dr. Wayne STUBERG
08 Director Library of Med .... Ms. Emily J. MCELROY
37 Dir Financial Aid Office .... Ms. Judith D. WALKER
26 Director of Public Relations .... Mr. William O'NEILL
15 Asst Vice Chanc for Human Resources .... Ms. Aileen WARREN
29 Director Alumni Affairs .... Ms. Roxana JOKELA
38 Director Student Counseling .... Dr. David S. CARVER
28 Director of Diversity .... Vacant
96 Director Procurement & Mtrls Mgt .... Mr. Jeffrey ELLIOTT
09 Director Institutional Research .... Ms. Jeanne FERBRACHE
19 Director Campus Security .... Mr. Gary SVANDA

*University of Nebraska at Omaha (A)

6001 Dodge Street, Omaha NE 68182-0001
County: Douglas FICE Identification: 002554
Unit ID: 181394
Telephone: (402) 554-2200 Carnegie Class: DRU
FAX Number: (402) 554-3555 Calendar System: Semester
URL: www.unomaha.edu
Established: 1908 Annual Undergrad Tuition & Fees (In-State): $6,898
Enrollment: 15,227 Coed
Affiliation or Control: State IRS Status: 501(c)3
Highest Offering: Doctorate
Program: Liberal Arts And General; Teacher Preparatory; Professional
Accreditation: NH, AAB, ART, BUS, BUSA, CAATE, CACREP, CS, MUS, #SP, SPAA, SW, TED

02 Chancellor .... Dr. John E. CHRISTENSEN
05 Sr Vice Chanc Acad/Student Affs .... Dr. Burton J. REED
10 Vice Chanc Business & Finance .... Mr. Bill CONLEY
04 Exec Assistant to the Chancellor .... Ms. Nancy CASTILOW
13 Assoc Vice Chanc Information Svcs .... Mr. John L. FIENE
21 Assoc Vice Chanc Business & Finance .... Mr. Joe HUEBNER
32 Assoc Vice Chanc Student Affairs .... Dr. Daniel SHIPP
84 Assoc Vice Chanc Enroll Mgmt Svcs .... Mr. Omar CORREA
58 Dean Graduate Studies .... Dr. Deb SMITH-HOWELL
57 Dean Fine Arts/Communication/Media .... Dr. Gail BAKER
53 Dean of Education .... Dr. Nancy EDICK
50 Dean of Business Administration .... Dr. Lou POL
49 Dean of Arts & Sciences .... Dr. David J. BOOCKER
82 Dean of International Studies/Pgms . Mr. Thomas E. GOUTTIERRE
72 Dean Info Science/Technology .... Dr. Hesham ALI
80 Dean Public Affairs/Community .... Dr. John R. BARTLE
62 Interim Dean of Library Services .... Mr. Michael LACROIX
09 Dir Institutional Effectiveness .... Dr. T. Hank ROBINSON
35 Chief Student Life Officer .... Ms. Rita HENRY
15 Director Human Resources .... Mr. Cecil HICKS, JR.
18 Director Facilities Mgmt/Planning .... Mr. John AMEND
06 Registrar .... Mr. Mark GOLDSBERRY
07 Director of Admissions .... Mr. Chris LIEWER
37 Director Financial Aid .... Mr. Marty HABROCK
88 Director Student Testing Center .... Ms. Marion FORTIN-WAVRA
41 Vice Chanc Athletic Leadership/Mgmt .... Mr. Trev ALBERTS
29 President/CEO Alumni Association .... Mr. Lee DENKER
26 Director University Communications .... Ms. Erin OWEN
96 Director of Purchasing .... Mr. Ken HULTMAN
40 Manager Book Store .... Vacant
19 Manager Campus Security .... Mr. Paul KOSEL

*University of Nebraska - Nebraska College of Technical Agriculture (B)

404 E 7th Street, Curtis NE 69025-9502
County: Frontier FICE Identification: 007358
Unit ID: 181765
Telephone: (308) 367-4124 Carnegie Class: Assoc/Pub2in4
FAX Number: (308) 367-5203 Calendar System: Semester
URL: www.ncta.unl.edu
Established: 1912 Annual Undergrad Tuition & Fees (In-State): $4,200
Enrollment: 350 Coed
Affiliation or Control: State IRS Status: 501(c)3
Highest Offering: Associate Degree
Program: Occupational; 2-Year Principally Bachelor's Creditable; Technical Emphasis
Accreditation: NH

02 Dean .... Dr. Ron ROSATI
03 Associate Dean .... Dr. Scott R. MICKELSEN
10 Business Manager .... Ms. Jan GILBERT

Western Nebraska Community College (C)

1601 E 27th Street, Scottsbluff NE 69361-1815
County: Scotts Bluff FICE Identification: 002560
Unit ID: 181817
Telephone: (308) 635-3606 Carnegie Class: Assoc/Pub-R-L
FAX Number: (308) 635-6100 Calendar System: Semester
URL: www.wncc.edu
Established: 1926 Annual Undergrad Tuition & Fees (In-District): $2,616
Enrollment: 1,836 Coed
Affiliation or Control: State/Local IRS Status: 501(c)3
Highest Offering: Associate Degree
Program: Occupational; 2-Year Principally Bachelor's Creditable
Accreditation: NH, CA, CAHIIM, PHLEB, PNUR

01 President .... Dr. Todd R. HOLCOMB
05 Vice President Educational Services .... Vacant
15 VP Human Resources/Inst Development .... Mr. David E. GROSHANS
32 Vice President Student Services .... Ms. Susan K. YOWELL
10 Vice Pres Administrative Services .... Mr. William D. KNAPPER
20 Interim Dean of Instruction .... Ms. Hallie FEIL
103 Dean of Workforce Development .... Mr. Jason L. STRATMAN
50 Dean Business & Individual Training .... Ms. Judith L. AMOO
35 Dean Student Services .... Dr. Michael HOUDYSHELL
12 Sidney Campus Director .... Ms. Paula J. ABBOTT
12 Ast Dn Instruct/Alliance Campus Dir .... Ms. Ellen M. DILLON
102 Foundation Executive Director .... Ms. Jennifer ROGERS
06 Registrar .... Mr. Roger S. HOVEY
37 Financial Aid Director .... Ms. Sheila R. JOHNS
26 Public Relations & Marketing Dir .... Ms. Allison JUDY
38 Counseling Director .... Mr. Norman J. STEPHENSON
62 Library Services Director .... Ms. Merrillene E. WOOD
21 Accounting Services Director .... Mr. David KOEHLER
41 Athletic Director .... Mr. Ryan C. BURGNER
51 Bus & Individual Training Director .... Ms. Lori S. STROMBERG
07 Admissions Director .... Ms. Gretchen K. FOSTER
39 Residence Life Director .... Mr. Norman COLEY
13 Information Technology Director .... Mr. Joe W. DEER
40 Bookstore Operations Director .... Mr. Rich RIDDICK
19 Safety/Environmental Mgmt Director .... Ms. Katrina TYLEE
09 Institutional Research Director .... Ms. Mary E. BARKELOO
88 Academic Testing & Tutoring Coord .... Ms. Tammie KLEICH
39 Student Life Assistant Director .... Ms. Megan WESCOAT
39 Student Life Assistant Director .... Ms. Molly A. BONUCHI
50 Division Chair Business .... Mr. Tom ROBINSON
83 Division Chair Social Sciences .... Ms. Hallie L. FEIL
79 Division Chair Language & Arts .... Ms. Jennifer L. PEDERSEN
75 Division Chair Career Tech Educ .... Mr. Jason STRATMAN
66 Nursing Education Director .... Ms. Rebecca KAUTZ
81 Math Coordinator .... Ms. Laurie ALKIRE
81 Sciences Coordinator .... Mr. David NASH
68 Health-Physical Education Coord .... Ms. Maria L. WINN-RATLIFF
88 Health Info Technology Program Dir .... Ms. Peg A. WOLFF
88 Academic Enrichment Coord-Language .... Ms. Amy WISNIEWSKI
29 Director Alumni Relations/Steward .... Ms. Jennifer R. SIBAL
88 Academic Enrichment Coord-Math .... Ms. Laurie A. ALKIRE
106 Instructional Tech Coordinator .... Ms. Heidi JACKSON

Western Nebraska Community College Alliance Campus (D)

1750 Sweetwater Avenue, Alliance NE 69301
Telephone: (308) 763-2000 Identification: 770343
Accreditation: &NH

† Branch campus of Western Nebraska Community College, Scottsbluff, NE.

Western Nebraska Community College Sidney Campus (E)

371 College Drive, Sidney NE 69162
Telephone: (308) 254-5450 Identification: 770344
Accreditation: &NH

† Branch campus of Western Nebraska Community College, Scottsbluff, NE.

Wright Career College (F)

3000 South 84th Street, Omaha NE 68124
Telephone: (913) 381-2577 Identification: 770739
Accreditation: ACICS

† Branch campus of Wright Career College, Overland Park, KS.

York College (G)

1125 E 8th Street, York NE 68467-2699
County: York FICE Identification: 002567
Unit ID: 181853
Telephone: (402) 363-5600 Carnegie Class: Bac/Diverse
FAX Number: (402) 363-5667 Calendar System: Semester
URL: www.york.edu
Established: 1890 Annual Undergrad Tuition & Fees: $17,200
Enrollment: 425 Coed
Affiliation or Control: Churches Of Christ IRS Status: 501(c)3
Highest Offering: Master's
Program: Liberal Arts And General; Business Emphasis
Accreditation: NH, TED

01 President .... Dr. Steven W. ECKMAN
05 Provost .... Dr. Shane MOUNTJOY
20 Academic Dean .... Dr. Tracey L. WYATT
10 Vice President Finance & Operations .... Mr. Todd SHELDON
30 Vice Pres Advancement .... Mr. Brent MAGNER
41 VP for Athletics and Enrollment .... Mr. Jared STARK
32 Dean of Student Development .... Mrs. Catherine SEUFFERLEIN
21 Business Manager .... Mr. Dan COLE
06 Registrar .... Dr. Tracey WYATT
35 Dean of Students .... Mr. Jeff FINCH
08 Director of Library .... Mrs. Ruth CARLOCK
26 Director of Publications .... Mr. Steddon L. SIKES
37 Financial Aid Director .... Mr. Brien ALLEY
40 Campus Store Manager .... Mrs. Janet RUSH
18 Supervisor Buildings & Grounds .... Mr. Bob GAVER
36 Director Student Placement .... Vacant
42 Campus Minister .... Vacant
50 Chair Business .... Dr. Mark MOORE
53 Chair Education .... Dr. Kirk MALLETTE
73 Chair Bible .... Dr. Frank E. WHEELER
88 Chair History .... Mr. Tim D. MCNEESE
50 Chair English .... Dr. Jennifer DUTCH
81 Chair Math/Sciences .... Dr. Alex WILLIAMS
57 Chair Performing Arts/Communication .... Dr. Clark A. ROUSH
29 Dir Alumni & Community Relations .... Mrs. Chrystal HOUSTON
04 Executive Asst to President .... Mrs. Gayle A. GOOD
44 Director Annual or Planned Giving .... Mr. Brent N. MAGNER
13 Chief Info Technology Officer (CIO) .... Mr. Joel COEHOORN
39 Director Student Housing .... Mr. Larry GOOD
106 Dir Online Education/E-learning .... Ms. Lisa MENKE

NEVADA

The Art Institute of Las Vegas (H)

2350 Corporate Circle, Henderson NV 89074-7737
Telephone: (702) 369-9944 FICE Identification: 030846
Accreditation: ACICS, ACFEI, CIDA

† Branch campus of The Art Institute of Phoenix, AZ.

Career College of Northern Nevada (I)

1421 Pullman Drive, Sparks NV 89434
County: Washoe FICE Identification: 026215
Unit ID: 181941
Telephone: (775) 856-2266 Carnegie Class: Assoc/PrivFP
FAX Number: (775) 856-0935 Calendar System: Quarter
URL: www.ccnn.edu
Established: 1984 Annual Undergrad Tuition & Fees: $25,225
Enrollment: 581 Coed
Affiliation or Control: Proprietary IRS Status: Proprietary
Highest Offering: Associate Degree
Program: Occupational
Accreditation: ACCSC

01 President .... Mr. L. Nathan N. CLARK

Carrington College - Las Vegas (J)

5740 S Eastern Avenue, Suite 140, Las Vegas NV 89119
Telephone: (702) 688-4300 Identification: 770742
Accreditation: &WJ, COARC, PTAA

† Regional accreditation is carried under the parent institution in Sacramento, CA.

Carrington College - Reno (K)

5580 Kietzke Lane, Reno NV 89511
Telephone: (775) 335-2900 Identification: 770743
Accreditation: &WJ, ADNUR

† Regional accreditation is carried under the parent institution in Sacramento, CA.

Chamberlain College of Nursing-Las Vegas (L)

9901 Covington Cross Dr, Las Vegas NV 89144
Telephone: (702) 786-1660 Identification: 770852
Accreditation: &NH, NURSE

† Branch campus of Chamberlain College of Nursing-Addison, Addison, IL.

Everest College (M)

170 North Stephanie Street, Henderson NV 89074
County: Clark FICE Identification: 022375
Unit ID: 182148
Telephone: (702) 567-1920 Carnegie Class: Assoc/PrivFP
FAX Number: (702) 566-9725 Calendar System: Semester
URL: www.everest.edu
Established: 2004 Annual Undergrad Tuition & Fees: $15,552
Enrollment: 800 Coed
Affiliation or Control: Proprietary IRS Status: Proprietary
Highest Offering: Associate Degree
Program: Occupational
Accreditation: ACICS, ADNUR

01 President .... Dr. Steven GUELL
03 Vice President .... Vacant

ITT Technical Institute (N)

168 N Gibson Road, Henderson NV 89014-6712
Telephone: (702) 558-5404 Identification: 666544
Accreditation: ACICS

† Branch campus of ITT Technical Institute, Indianapolis, IN.

ITT Technical Institute (O)

3825 West Cheyenne Avenue, Ste 600, North Las Vegas NV 89032
Telephone: (702) 240-0967 Identification: 770658
Accreditation: ACICS

† Branch campus of ITT Technical Institute, Indianapolis, IN.

Kaplan College (P)

3535 West Sahara Ave, Las Vegas NV 89102
County: Clark FICE Identification: 030432
Unit ID: 374875
Telephone: (702) 368-2338 Carnegie Class: Assoc/PrivFP
FAX Number: (702) 368-3853 Calendar System: Other
URL: www.kaplancollege.com
Established: 1991 Annual Undergrad Tuition & Fees: $15,648
Enrollment: 916 Coed
Affiliation or Control: Proprietary IRS Status: Proprietary
Highest Offering: Associate Degree
Program: Occupational; 2-Year Principally Bachelor's Creditable; Technical Emphasis

Accreditation: ACICS, CAHIIM, PNUR

01 Campus President .... Ms. Lisia MOORE
05 Director of Education .... Mr. Jeffrey FOUNTAIN
07 Director of Admissions .... Mr. Derrick PERRY
10 Director of Finance .... Ms. Carmen TORRES
67 Dept Chair Pharmacy Technician .... Mr. Mark BRUNTON
36 Director of Career Services .... Ms. Kristie CHILES
66 Director of Nursing/PN .... Ms. Julia MILLARD

Le Cordon Bleu College of Culinary Arts in Las Vegas (A)

1451 Center Crossing Road, Las Vegas NV 89144-7047
Telephone: (702) 365-7690 Identification: 666303
Accreditation: ACCSC, ACFEI, ACICS

† Branch campus of Le Cordon Bleu College of Culinary Arts, Scottsdale, AZ.

*Nevada System of Higher Education (B)

2601 Enterprise Road, Reno NV 89512-1666
County: Washoe FICE Identification: 008026
Unit ID: 182519
Telephone: (775) 784-4901 Carnegie Class: N/A
FAX Number: (775) 784-1127
URL: www.nevada.edu

01 Chancellor .... Mr. Daniel J. KLAICH
03 Executive Vice Chancellor .... Vacant
05 VC Academic & Student Affairs .... Ms. Crystal ABBA
10 Vice Chanc for Budget & Finance .... Mr. Larry EARDLEY
11 Vice Chanc for Finance & Admin .... Mr. Vic REDDING
101 Chief Exec Ofcr Board of Regents .... Vacant
43 Vice Chanc for Legal Affairs .... Ms. Brooke NIELSEN
86 VC Govt and Community Affairs .... Ms. Constance BROOKS
13 Vice Chanc for Info Tech .... Dr. Steven ZINK
88 Vice Chanc for Health Sci Sys .... Dr. Marcia TURNER

*College of Southern Nevada (C)

6375 W Charleston Boulevard, Las Vegas NV 89146-1139
County: Clark FICE Identification: 010362
Unit ID: 182005
Telephone: (702) 651-5000 Carnegie Class: Assoc/Pub4
FAX Number: (702) 651-4835 Calendar System: Semester
URL: www.csn.edu
Established: 1971 Annual Undergrad Tuition & Fees (In-State): $2,805
Enrollment: 38,000 Coed
Affiliation or Control: State IRS Status: 501(c)3
Highest Offering: Baccalaureate
Program: Occupational; 2-Year Principally Bachelor's Creditable
Accreditation: NW, ACBSP, ACFEI, ADNUR, CAHIIM, CEA, COARC, DA, DH, DMS, EMT, ENGT, #MAC, MLTAD, OPD, PNUR, PTAA, SURGT

02 President .... Dr. Michael D. RICHARDS
04 Exec Assistant to the President .... Ms. Annette LORD
45 Sr VP Strategic Initiatives .... Ms. Patricia A. CHARLTON
05 Interim Vice Pres Academic Affairs .... Dr. Hyla D. WINTERS
12 Campus Manager Charleston .... Dr. Joan MCGEE
12 Campus Manager Henderson .... Mr. Josh RUTER
20 Assoc VP Academic Affairs .... Dr. Hyla WINTERS
10 Vice President of Finance .... Ms. Mary Kaye BAILEY
18 Assoc VP Facilities/Oper/Maint .... Ms. Sherri PAYNE
43 Legal Counsel .... Mr. Richard HINCKLEY
06 Registrar .... Ms. Pat ZOZAYA
21 Exec Director Business Services .... Mr. Dan MORRIS
88 Sr Assoc VP Apprenticeship Program .... Mr. Dan GOUKER
32 Interim Director Student Services .... Mr. Ryan RISHLING
102 Exec Dir CSN Foundation .... Mr. Alan DISKIN
72 Dean Adv & Applied Technologies .... Dr. Michael SPANGLER
81 Dean Science & Mathematics .... Ms. Sally JOHNSTON
83 Dean Social Sciences & Education .... Dr. Charles OKEKE
88 Dean Arts & Letters .... Dr. Wendy WEINER
76 Dean Health Sciences .... Dr. Josh HAMILTON
50 Dean of Business .... Dr. Marcus JOHNSON
96 Associate VP of Purchasing .... Mr. Rolando MOSQUEDA
41 Director of Athletics .... Mr. L. Dexter IRVIN
26 Director of Communications .... Ms. Kathryn C. BREKKEN
88 Director of Budget Services .... Ms. Lisa BAKKE
09 Director of Institutional Research .... Mr. John BEARCE
62 Director Library Services .... Ms. Clarissa ERWIN
37 Asst Director Student Financial Aid .... Ms. Katharyn VAN DE CAR
19 Chief of Police .... Mr. Darryl CARABALLO
85 Int Dir International Student Ctr .... Mr. Lester TANAKA
13 Technology CIO .... Mr. Mugunth VAITHYLINGAM
15 Sr Director of Personnel Services .... Mr. John SCARBOROUGH
28 Executive Director of Diversity .... Ms. Maria MARINCH
106 Dir Online Education/E-learning .... Mr. Terry NORRIS
22 Dir Affirmative Action/EEO .... Vacant

*Great Basin College (D)

1500 College Parkway, Elko NV 89801-5032
County: Elko FICE Identification: 006977
Unit ID: 182306
Telephone: (775) 738-8493 Carnegie Class: Bac/Assoc
FAX Number: (775) 738-8771 Calendar System: Semester
URL: www.gbcnv.edu
Established: 1967 Annual Undergrad Tuition & Fees (In-State): $2,805
Enrollment: 3,081 Coed
Affiliation or Control: State IRS Status: 501(c)3
Highest Offering: Baccalaureate
Program: Occupational; 2-Year Principally Bachelor's Creditable
Accreditation: NW, ADNUR, CSHSE, NUR, RAD

02 President .... Dr. Mark CURTIS
32 Vice President Student Services .... Mrs. Lynn M. MAHLBERG
05 Vice President Academic Affairs .... Dr. Mike MCFARLANE
10 Vice President for Business Affairs .... Ms. Sonja SIBERT
106 Associate VP for Distance Education .... Ms. Lisa FRAZIER
04 Assistant to the President .... Ms. Mardell WILKINS
07 Director of Admissions .... Ms. Janice KING
09 Dir Institutional Rsrch/Effective .... Dr. Cathy FULKERSON
37 Dir Student Financial Svcs & VA .... Mr. Scott NIELSEN
84 Director Enrollment Management .... Ms. Julie BYRNES
75 Dean of Applied Science .... Mr. Bret MURPHY
76 Dir of Health Sciences & Human Svcs .... Dr. Amber DONNELLI
12 Director Ely Center .... Ms. Veronica NELSON
12 Director Winnemucca Center .... Ms. Lisa CAMPBELL
12 Manager Pahrump Valley Center .... Ms. Diane WRIGHTMAN
51 Director Continuing Education .... Mrs. Angie DEBRAGA
102 Director Foundation .... Mr. Gregory BRORBY
19 Director Safety and Security .... Ms. Patricia ANDERSON
25 Director Grants .... Ms. Jeannie BAILEY
43 General Counsel .... Mr. John ALBRECHT

*Nevada State College (E)

1125 Nevada State Drive, Henderson NV 89002-9455
County: Clark FICE Identification: 041143
Unit ID: 441900
Telephone: (702) 992-2000 Carnegie Class: Bac/Diverse
FAX Number: (702) 992-2226 Calendar System: Semester
URL: www.nsc.edu
Established: 2002 Annual Undergrad Tuition & Fees (In-District): $4,462
Enrollment: 3,549 Coed
Affiliation or Control: State/Local IRS Status: 501(c)3
Highest Offering: Baccalaureate
Program: Liberal Arts And General; Teacher Preparatory; Professional; Nursing Emphasis
Accreditation: NW, NURSE

02 President .... Mr. Bart PATTERSON
05 Provost .... Dr. Erika BECK
10 VP Finance and Business Operations .... Mr. Kevin BUTLER
26 VP for College Relations .... Dr. Spencer STEWART
06 Registrar .... Ms. Adelfa SULLIVAN
29 Exec Coordinator Alumni Relations .... Ms. Danielle JOHNSTON
30 Assoc Vice Pres Development .... Dr. Russell RAKER
100 Exec Assistant to the President .... Ms. Jennifer HAFT
15 Human Resources Director .... Ms. Cheri CANFIELD

*Truckee Meadows Community College (F)

7000 Dandini Boulevard, Reno NV 89512-3999
County: Washoe FICE Identification: 021077
Unit ID: 182500
Telephone: (775) 673-7000 Carnegie Class: Assoc/Pub-R-L
FAX Number: (775) 673-7108 Calendar System: Semester
URL: www.tmcc.edu
Established: 1971 Annual Undergrad Tuition & Fees (In-State): $2,925
Enrollment: 11,553 Coed
Affiliation or Control: State IRS Status: 501(c)3
Highest Offering: Associate Degree
Program: Occupational; 2-Year Principally Bachelor's Creditable
Accreditation: NW, ACFEI, ADNUR, DA, DH, DIETT, EMT

02 President .... Dr. Maria C. SHEEHAN
04 Executive Assistant to President .... Ms. Lisa D. FARMER
05 Vice President Academic Affairs .... Dr. Barbara BUCHANAN
10 Vice Pres Finance & Admin Services .... Dr. Rachel SOLEMSAAS
32 VP of Student Services .... Ms. Estela LEVARIO GUTIERREZ
81 Dean Division of Sciences .... Dr. Lance BOWEN
49 Dean Division of Liberal Arts .... Dr. Armida FRUZZETTI
50 Dean Division of Business .... Dr. Marie MURGOLO-POORE
72 Dean Division of Tech Sciences .... Mr. Jim NEW
20 Assoc Dean Office of the President .... Dr. Kyle DALPE
30 Exec Dir Institutional Advancement .... Vacant
07 Director Admissions & Records .... Mr. Andrew HUGHES
21 Program Director Accounting Svcs .... Mr. Rich WILLIAMS
37 Director Financial Aid .... Ms. Sharon WURM
88 Director Disability Resource Center .... Ms. Joan STEINMAN
15 Chief Human Resources Officer .... Ms. Michele MEADOR
18 Exec Director Facilities Services .... Mr. Dave ROBERTS
103 Dir Workforce Devel/Cont Education .... Ms. Deb O'GORMAN
38 Director Counseling .... Vacant
13 Interim Chief Info Tech Officer .... Mr. Thomas DOBBERT
19 Chief of Police/Campus Police .... Mr. Randy FLOCCHINI
09 Exec Dir Institutional Research .... Ms. Elena BUBNOVA
28 Dean of Equity & Inclusion .... Dr. Barbara WRIGHT-SANDERS
29 Alumni Coordinator .... Ms. Kate KIRKPATRICK
08 Head Librarian .... Ms. Shannon VAN KIRK

*University of Nevada, Las Vegas (G)

4505 S Maryland Parkway, Las Vegas NV 89154-1001
County: Clark FICE Identification: 002569
Unit ID: 182281
Telephone: (702) 895-3201 Carnegie Class: RU/H
FAX Number: (702) 895-1088 Calendar System: Semester
URL: www.unlv.edu
Established: 1957 Annual Undergrad Tuition & Fees (In-State): $6,710
Enrollment: 28,515 Coed
Affiliation or Control: State IRS Status: 501(c)3
Highest Offering: Doctorate
Program: Liberal Arts And General; Teacher Preparatory; Professional
Accreditation: NW, ART, BUS, BUSA, CAATE, CACREP, CIDA, CLPSY, CONST, CS, DENT, DIETD, DIETI, ENG, ENGR, LAW, LSAR, MFCD, MUS, NMT, NURSE, PH, PTA, RAD, SPAA, SW

02 President .... Dr. Len JESSUP
100 Chief of Staff .... Dr. Fred TREDUP
05 Acting Exec VP and Provost .... Mrs. Nancy B. RAPOPORT
10 Senior Vice Pres Finance & Business .... Mr. Gerry BOMOTTI
41 Director of Athletics .... Ms. Tina KUNZER-MURPHY
32 Vice President for Student Affairs .... Dr. Juanita FAIN
58 Int VP Research & Graduate Studies .... Dr. Thomas C. PIECHOTA
30 VP Advancement .... Dr. William BOLDT
86 VP Diversity & Govt Relations .... Mr. Luis VALERA
26 Sr Assoc VP Integrated Marketing .... Mr. Vince ALBERTA
43 General Counsel .... Mrs. Elda SIDHU
11 Assoc Vice Pres for Administration .... Dr. Mike SAUER
35 Assoc VP for Student Affairs .... Ms. Karen STRONG
29 Assoc VP Alumni Relations .... Mr. Jim RATIGAN
31 Assoc Vice Pres Community Relations .... Vacant
15 Chief Human Resources Officer .... Mr. Larry HAMILTON
87 Int Vice Prov Educational Outreach .... Dr. Margaret REES
13 Vice Provost Info Technology .... Dr. Lori TEMPLE
50 Dean Business .... Dr. Brent A. HATHAWAY
49 Dean Liberal Arts .... Dr. Chris HUDGINS
53 Dean of Education .... Dr. Kim K. METCALF
54 Dean of Engineering .... Dr. Rama VENKAT
63 Dean School of Medicine .... Dr. Barbara ATKINSON
52 Dean School of Dental Medicine .... Dr. Karen P. WEST
61 Dean School of Law .... Mr. Daniel W. HAMILTON
81 Dean of Sciences .... Dr. Timothy PORTER
88 Dean College of Hotel Admin .... Dr. Stowe SHOEMAKER
57 Interim Dean Fine Arts .... Dr. Helga WATKINS
08 Dean of Libraries .... Ms. Patricia IANNUZZI
88 Dean Urban Affairs .... Dr. Robert R. ULMER
92 Dean Honors College .... Dr. Marta MEANA
88 Dean Academic Success Ctr .... Dr. Ann MCDONOUGH
88 Dean Community Health Sciences . Dr. Shawn GERSTENBERGER
76 Dean Sch Allied Health Sciences .... Dr. Carolyn YUCHA
06 Registrar .... Ms. Katie HUMPHREYS
84 Assoc VP for Enrollment Management .... Dr. Michael L. SAUER
37 Dir Financial Aid & Scholarships .... Mr. Norm BEDFORD
26 Assoc VP Univ Communications .... Vacant
19 Director Public Safety .... Mr. Jose ELIQUE
09 Director Inst Analysis/Planning .... Mrs. Kari C. COBURN
39 Exec Dir Residential Life .... Mr. Richard CLARK
38 AVP Student Wellness .... Dr. Jamie DAVIDSON
23 Director Student Health .... Ms. Kathy A. UNDERWOOD
96 Director Purchasing .... Ms. Sharrie MAYDEN
85 Director Intl Students & Scholars .... Ms. Kristen YOUNG
25 Director Sponsored Programs .... Ms. Rochelle ATHEY
46 AVP for Research .... Dr. Stan SMITH
102 Sr Assoc VP & Exec Dir UNLV Found .... Ms. Nancy STROUSE
44 Assoc VP Development .... Mr. Scott ROBERTS

*University of Nevada, Reno (H)

1664 N. Virginia Street, Reno NV 89557
County: Washoe FICE Identification: 002568
Unit ID: 182290
Telephone: (775) 784-1110 Carnegie Class: RU/H
FAX Number: (775) 784-1300 Calendar System: Semester
URL: www.unr.edu
Established: 1874 Annual Undergrad Tuition & Fees (In-State): $6,872
Enrollment: 19,934 Coed
Affiliation or Control: State IRS Status: 501(c)3
Highest Offering: Doctorate
Program: Liberal Arts And General; Teacher Preparatory; Professional
Accreditation: NW, BUS, BUSA, CACREP, CEA, CLPSY, CS, DIETD, DIETI, ENG, JOUR, MED, MUS, NURSE, PH, SP, SW, TED

02 President .... Dr. Marc JOHNSON
05 Exec Vice Pres & Provost .... Dr. Kevin CARMAN
11 Vice Pres Administration & Finance .... Mr. Ronald M. ZUREK
63 VP Health Sci/Dean Sch of Medicine .... Dr. Thomas L. SCHWENK
30 Vice President Devel/Alumni Rels .... Mr. John CAROTHERS
32 Vice President for Student Services .... Dr. Shannon ELLIS
46 Vice President for Research .... Dr. Mridul GAUTAM
08 Dean of Libraries .... Dr. Kathlin D. RAY
20 Vice Prov Instr/Undergrad Programs .... Dr. Joseph CLINE
20 Vice Provost Faculty Affairs .... Dr. Stacy BURTON
58 Vice Provost/Dean Grad School .... Dr. David ZEH
51 Vice Provost for Extended Studies .... Dr. Fred B. HOLMAN
10 Assoc VP Business & Finance .... Mr. Thomas L. JUDY
84 Assoc VP Enrollment Services .... Dr. Melisa N. CHOROSZY
38 Assoc VP Student Success Services .... Dr. Jerry MARCZYNSKI
45 Asst VP Planning/Budget/Analysis .... Mr. Bruce L. SHIVELY
18 Asst Vice Pres Facilities Svcs .... Mr. Sean MCGOLDRICK
21 Controller .... Ms. Sheri MENDEZ
41 Director Athletics .... Mr. Doug KNUTH
96 Director Purchasing .... Mr. Garth KWIECHIEN
19 Director University Police Svcs .... Mr. Adam GARCIA
22 Dir Equal Opportunity & Title IX .... Ms. Denise CORDOVA
37 Director Student Financial Svcs .... Mr. Timothy WOLFF
39 Director Resident Life & Housing . Mr. Rodney L. AESCHLIMANN
23 Director Student Health Svcs .... Dr. Cheryl HUG-ENGLISH
09 Director Institutional Analysis .... Dr. Serge HERZOG
86 Spec Asst to Pres External Affairs .... Ms. Heidi GANSERT
65 Dir Mackay Sch Mines/Earth Science .... Dr. Russell FIELDS
66 Director of Nursing .... Dr. Patsy L. RUCHALA
57 Director School of the Arts .... Dr. Larry ENGSTROM

- 25 Director Sponsored Projects ... Ms. Charlene HART
- 40 Director Wolf Shop ... Mr. Steve DUBEY
- 49 Dean Liberal Arts ... Dr. Heather HARDY
- 47 Dean Agriculture/Biotech/Nat Res ... Dr. William PAYNE
- 50 Dean Business Admininistration ... Dr. Gregory MOSIER
- 53 Dean of Education ... Dr. Kenneth COLL
- 54 Dean Engineering ... Dr. Emmanuel MARAGAKIS
- 60 Dean School of Journalism ... Mr. Alan STAVITSKY
- 81 Dean College of Science ... Dr. Jeffrey S. THOMPSON
- 07 Director of Admissions ... Dr. Stephen MAPLES
- 29 Director Alumni Relations ... Ms. Amy CAROTHERS
- 06 Associate Registrar ... Ms. Heather TURK FIECOAT
- 26 Director of Communications ... Ms. Jane TORS

*Western Nevada College (A)

2201 W College Parkway, Carson City NV 89703-7316

County: Carson | FICE Identification: 010363 | Unit ID: 182564

Telephone: (775) 445-3000 | Carnegie Class: Assoc/Pub4

FAX Number: (775) 445-3051 | Calendar System: Semester

URL: www.wnc.edu

Established: 1971 | Annual Undergrad Tuition & Fees (In-State): $2,805

Enrollment: 4,032 | Coed

Affiliation or Control: State | IRS Status: 501(c)3

Highest Offering: Baccalaureate

Program: Occupational; 2-Year Principally Bachelor's Creditable

Accreditation: NW, ADNUR

- 02 President ... Mr. Chet BURTON
- 04 Assistant to the President ... Ms. Bonnie M. BERTOCCHI
- 05 Vice Pres Academic/Student Affairs ... Dr. Robert WYNEGAR
- 11 Vice Pres Admin/Legal Svcs ... Mr. Mark GHAN
- 20 Dean of Instruction ... Vacant
- 32 Dean Student Services ... Mr. John KINKELLA
- 10 Controller ... Ms. Coral LOPEZ
- 88 Director Child Development Center ... Ms. Andrea DORAN
- 38 Director of Counseling/Advising ... Ms. Piper MCCARTHHY
- 18 Director Facilities Mgmt/Planning ... Mr. Kevin GAFFNEY
- 37 Director Financial Aid ... Mr. John (JW) LAZZARI
- 26 Director Information & Marketing ... Ms. Anne P. HANSEN
- 08 Director Library & Media Services ... Mr. Kenneth A. SULLIVAN
- 06 Registrar/Director of Admissions ... Ms. Dianne HILLIARD
- 30 Director of Development ... Ms. Katie LEAO
- 09 Director of Institutional Research ... Ms. Cathy FULKERSON
- 13 Director of Computing Services ... Ms. Susan HOWLAND
- 21 Budget Officer ... Ms. Darla DODGE
- 15 Asst Director Human Resources ... Ms. Irene TUCKER
- 35 Student Life Coordinator ... Ms. Lilly LEON-VICKS
- 72 Academic Director Career & Tech Div ... Mr. Scott MORRISON
- 49 Academic Director Liberal Arts ... Dr. Georgia WHITE
- 66 Academic Dir Nursing/Allied Health ... Dr. Judith CORDIA
- 19 Director Security/Safety ... Mr. Jack PIIRAINEN
- 41 Athletic Director ... Mr. John KINKELLA

Northwest Career College (B)

7398 Smoke Ranch Road, Las Vegas NV 89128

County: Clark | FICE Identification: 038385 | Unit ID: 445948

Telephone: (702) 254-7577 | Carnegie Class: Not Classified

FAX Number: (702) 256-9181 | Calendar System: Other

URL: www.northwestcareercollege.edu

Established: 1997 | Annual Undergrad Tuition & Fees: $12,472

Enrollment: 189 | Coed

Affiliation or Control: Proprietary | IRS Status: Proprietary

Highest Offering: Associate Degree

Program: Occupational; 2-Year Principally Bachelor's Creditable; Technical Emphasis

Accreditation: ABHES

- 01 Director ... Dr. John KENNY
- 11 COO ... Patrick KENNY
- 10 CFO ... Stephanie KENNY
- 37 Director of Financial Aid ... Amy MORRIS
- 36 Director of Career Services ... Jilian LOPEZ
- 09 Director of Compliance ... Thomas KENNY
- 07 Director of Admissions ... Darlene CHIRICO
- 13 Director of Technology ... Michael KENNY
- 06 Registrar ... Xavier JOLLIFF

Pima Medical Institute-Las Vegas (C)

3333 E Flamingo Road, Las Vegas NV 89121-4329

Telephone: (702) 458-9650 | Identification: 666273

Accreditation: ABHES, COARC, PTAA, RAD

† Branch campus of Pima Medical Institute, Tucson, AZ.

Roseman University of Health Sciences (D)

11 Sunset Way, Henderson NV 89014-2333

County: Clark | FICE Identification: 040653 | Unit ID: 445735

Telephone: (702) 990-4433 | Carnegie Class: Spec/Health

FAX Number: (702) 990-4435 | Calendar System: Other

URL: www.roseman.edu

Established: 1999 | Annual Undergrad Tuition & Fees: $38,800

Enrollment: 1,444 | Coed

Affiliation or Control: Independent Non-Profit | IRS Status: 501(c)3

Highest Offering: Doctorate

Program: Professional

Accreditation: NW, DENT, IACBE, NUR, PHAR

- 01 President ... Dr. Renee COFFMAN
- 12 Chancellor Summerlin Campus ... Dr. Mark A. PENN
- 12 Chancellor Henderson Campus ... Dr. Eucharia E. NNADI
- 10 VP Business & Finance/Controller ... Mr. Ken WILKINS
- 18 VP of Facilities & Risk Management ... Mr. Terrell SPARKS
- 13 Vice President Info Technologies ... Vacant
- 03 Vice President Executive Affairs ... Dr. Charles F. LACY
- 26 Vice President Communications & PR ... Mr. Jason ROTH
- 09 VP Qual Assurance/Intercampus Cons ... Dr. Thomas METZGER
- 46 Assoc Dean for Research ... Dr. Ronald FISCUS
- 32 VP for Student Services ... Dr. Michael DEYOUNG
- 67 Dean College of Pharmacy ... Dr. Scott STOLTE
- 67 Campus Dean College of Pharmacy UT ... Dr. Larry FANNIN
- 66 Dean College of Nursing ... Dr. Mable H. SMITH
- 52 Dean College of Dental Medicine ... Dr. Frank LICARI
- 52 Dean College of Dental Medicine Hen ... Dr. Jaleh POURHAMIDI
- 50 Director MBA Program ... Dr. Okeleke NZEOGWU
- 05 Assoc Dean Acad Affs/Assessment ... Dr. Erik JORVIG
- 37 Director of Financial Aid ... Ms. Sally MICKELSON
- 51 Director of Continuing Education ... Dr. Katherine SMITH
- 52 Assoc Dean Academic Affairs Dental ... Dr. William CARROLL
- 52 Assoc Dean Clinical Affairs ... Dr. Kenneth KING
- 07 Assoc Dean Admissions/Student Svcs ... Dr. William HARMAN
- 15 Director of Human Resources ... Dr. G. Benjamin WILLS
- 62 Director of Library Services ... Ms. Karen CANEPI
- 44 Director of Development ... Ms. Brenda GRIEGO
- 06 Registrar/Director of Student Svcs ... Ms. Angela D. BIGBY
- 88 Marketing Director South Jordan ... Ms. Tracy HERNANDEZ
- 35 Dir of Admissions & Student Affairs ... Dr. Helen PARK

Sanford-Brown College (E)

2495 Village View Drive, Henderson NV 89074

Telephone: (702) 990-0150 | Identification: 770744

Accreditation: ACICS

† School is in teach-out plan.

Sierra Nevada College (F)

999 Tahoe Boulevard, Incline Village NV 89451-9500

County: Washoe | FICE Identification: 009192 | Unit ID: 182458

Telephone: (775) 831-1314 | Carnegie Class: Master's M

FAX Number: (775) 832-1696 | Calendar System: Semester

URL: www.sierranevada.edu

Established: 1969 | Annual Undergrad Tuition & Fees: $29,015

Enrollment: 1,037 | Coed

Affiliation or Control: Independent Non-Profit | IRS Status: 501(c)3

Highest Offering: Master's

Program: Liberal Arts And General

Accreditation: NW

- 00 Chairman Board of Trustees ... Dr. Atam LALCHANDANI
- 01 Interim President ... Ms. Shannon BEETS
- 05 Executive Vice President/Provost ... Ms. Shannon BEETS
- 30 Intermin Vice President Development ... Dr. Vance PETERSON
- 32 Dean of Students ... Mr. Will HOIDA
- 84 Dean Enrollment Services & Athletic ... Mr. Steve BERRY
- 20 Associate Provost ... Dr. Dan O'BRYAN
- 10 Chief Financial Officer ... Ms. Susan JOHNSON
- 37 Director of Financial Aid ... Ms. Nicole FERGUSON
- 26 Director of Marketing ... Ms. Sarah BERRY
- 09 Director of Institutional Resarch ... Ms. Annamarie JONES
- 18 Chief Facilities/Physical Plant ... Mr. Brian SCHULTES
- 08 Director of Library ... Dr. Elizabeth MARKLE
- 06 Registrar ... Ms. Rose WEHBY
- 53 Statewide Dir Teacher Education ... Ms. Beth TALIAFERRO
- 13 Director Information Technology ... Ms. Nicole FERGERSON
- 15 Human Resources Manager ... Ms. Veronica SHEARIN
- 21 Controller ... Ms. Lynda ODELL
- 04 Executive Asst to the President ... Ms. Kristine YOUNG

University of Phoenix Las Vegas Campus (G)

3755 Breakthrough Way, Las Vegas NV 89135-3047

Telephone: (702) 638-7279 | Identification: 770220

Accreditation: &NH, ACBSP

† Branch campus of University of Phoenix, Tempe, AZ.

NEW HAMPSHIRE

Antioch University New England (H)

40 Avon Street, Keene NH 03431-3516

Telephone: (800) 553-8920 | Identification: 666992

Accreditation: &NH, CACREP, CLPSY, MFCD

† Regional accreditation is carried under the parent institution in Yellow Springs, OH.

Colby-Sawyer College (I)

541 Main Street, New London NH 03257-7835

County: Merrimack | FICE Identification: 002572 | Unit ID: 182634

Telephone: (603) 526-3000 | Carnegie Class: Bac/Diverse

FAX Number: (603) 526-2135 | Calendar System: Semester

URL: www.colby-sawyer.edu

Established: 1837 | Annual Undergrad Tuition & Fees: $38,610

Enrollment: 1,369 | Coed

Affiliation or Control: Independent Non-Profit | IRS Status: 501(c)3

Highest Offering: Baccalaureate

Program: Liberal Arts And General; Teacher Preparatory

Accreditation: EH, CAATE, NURSE

- 01 President ... Mr. Thomas C. GALLIGAN
- 05 Academic Vice Pres/Dean of Faculty ... Dr. Deborah A. TAYLOR
- 15 Vice President for Human Resources ... Mr. Douglas G. ATKINS
- 10 Vice Pres for Finance & Treasurer ... Mr. Todd C. EMMONS
- 32 VP Stdnt Devel/Dean of Students ... Mr. David A. SAUERWEIN
- 30 Vice President Advancement ... Ms. Elizabeth A. CAHILL
- 84 Vice Pres Enrollment Management ... Mr. David L. PLACEY
- 101 Secretary of the College ... Ms. Linda J. VARNUM
- 100 Chief of Staff/Dir Strategic Plng ... Ms. Lisa F. TEDESCHI
- 21 Controller ... Ms. Karen I. BONEWALD
- 09 Director Institutional Research ... Dr. Yi NI
- 20 Academic Dean ... Dr. J Burton KIRKWOOD
- 35 Assoc Dean Stdnt/Dir Citizenship Ed ... Ms. Robin BURROUGHS-DAVIS
- 39 Director Residential Education ... Ms. Mary MCLAUGHLIN
- 37 Director of Financial Aid ... Mr. Beth W. RENZULLI
- 30 Director of Development ... Ms. Kathleen A. CARROLL
- 88 Senior Development Officer ... Mr. Glen R. KERKIAN
- 08 College Librarian ... Ms. Carrie THOMAS
- 06 Registrar ... Ms. Diane H. DRISCOLL
- 07 Director of Admission ... Ms. Anna G. MINER
- 13 Director Information Resources ... Mr. Kenneth G. KOCHIEN
- 41 Director of Athletics ... Mr. Bill FOTI
- 36 Director of Career Development ... Ms. Kathy J. TAYLOR
- 88 Asst Dir Acad Development Ctr ... Ms. Caren BALDWIN-DIMEO
- 44 Dir Annual Giving ... Mr. Christopher S. REED
- 29 Dir Alumni Relations ... Ms. Tracey M. AUSTIN
- 19 Director of Campus Safety ... Mr. Peter L. BERTHIAUME
- 40 Bookstore Manager ... Ms. Mairim KILMISTER
- 23 Dir of Baird Health & Counsel Ctr ... Ms. Pamela SPEAR
- 92 Coordinator of the Honors Program ... Ms. Ann Page STECKER

*Community College System of New Hampshire (J)

26 College Drive, Concord NH 03301-7407

County: Merrimack | Identification: 666462

Telephone: (603) 230-3500 | Carnegie Class: N/A

FAX Number: (603) 271-2725

URL: www.ccsnh.edu

- 01 Chancellor ... Dr. Ross GITTELL
- 03 Vice Chancellor ... Vacant
- 10 Assoc Vice Chanc Fin/Strategic Plng ... Kristyn VAN OSTERN
- 15 Assoc Vice Chanc Human Res Plng/Dev ... Richard COLADARCI
- 26 Director of Communications ... Shannon REID
- 13 Chief Info Technology Officer (CIO) ... Susan BROUILLET

*Great Bay Community College (K)

320 Corporate Drive, Portsmouth NH 03801-2879

County: Rockingham | FICE Identification: 002583 | Unit ID: 183150

Telephone: (603) 427-7600 | Carnegie Class: Assoc/Pub-R-M

FAX Number: (603) 334-6308 | Calendar System: Semester

URL: www.greatbay.edu

Established: 1945 | Annual Undergrad Tuition & Fees (In-State): $7,008

Enrollment: 2,079 | Coed

Affiliation or Control: State | IRS Status: 501(c)3

Highest Offering: Associate Degree

Program: Occupational; 2-Year Principally Bachelor's Creditable

Accreditation: EH, ACBSP, ADNUR, SURGT

- 02 President ... Mr. Wildolfo ARVELO
- 05 Vice President Academic Affairs ... Mr. Paul PETRITIS
- 32 Vice Pres Student Affairs ... Dr. Sarah BEDINGFIELD
- 06 Registrar ... Ms. Sandra HO
- 10 Chief Financial Officer ... Ms. Joanne BERRY
- 07 Director Admissions ... Ms. Carey WALKER

*Lakes Region Community College (L)

379 Belmont Road, Laconia NH 03246-1364

County: Belknap | FICE Identification: 007555 | Unit ID: 183123

Telephone: (603) 524-3207 | Carnegie Class: Assoc/Pub-R-S

FAX Number: (603) 527-2042 | Calendar System: Semester

URL: www.lrcc.edu

Established: 1967 | Annual Undergrad Tuition & Fees (In-District): $7,458

Enrollment: 1,575 | Coed

Affiliation or Control: State/Local | IRS Status: 501(c)3

Highest Offering: Associate Degree

Program: Occupational; 2-Year Principally Bachelor's Creditable

Accreditation: EH

- 02 President ... Dr. Scott KALICKI
- 05 VP of Academic & Community Affairs ... Vacant
- 32 VP of Student Services & Enrollment ... Dr. Larissa BAIA
- 10 Chief Financial Officer ... Mr. John HARRINGTON
- 04 Administrative Asst to President ... Mrs. Julia L. VELIE
- 06 Registrar ... Ms. Laura LEMIEN
- 07 Director of Admissions ... Mr. Wayne FRASER
- 37 Director Student Financial Aid ... Ms. Kristen PURRINGTON
- 26 Public Information Officer ... Mr. Max BROWN

*Manchester Community College (A)

1066 Front Street, Manchester NH 03102-8518
County: Hillsborough FICE Identification: 002582
Unit ID: 183132
Telephone: (603) 206-8000 Carnegie Class: Assoc/Pub-R-M
FAX Number: (603) 668-5354 Calendar System: Semester
URL: www.mccnh.edu
Established: 1945 Annual Undergrad Tuition & Fees (In-State): $6,440
Enrollment: 3,455 Coed
Affiliation or Control: State IRS Status: 501(c)3
Highest Offering: Associate Degree
Program: Occupational; 2-Year Principally Bachelor's Creditable
Accreditation: EH, ACBSP, ADNUR, MAC

02 President ... Dr. Susan D. HUARD
05 Vice President Academic Affairs ... Dr. John COOK
32 VP Students/Community Development ... Kim KEEGAN
20 Associate VP Academic Affairs ... Joan ACORACE
20 Associate VP of Academic Affairs ... Dr. Kate GUERDAT
32 Associate VP Student Services ... Jason AREY
07 Director of Admissions ... Miho BEAN
26 Director of Marketing ... Victoria JAFFE
37 Financial Aid Officer ... Stephanie J. WELDON
06 Registrar ... Evelyn R. PERRON
08 Interim Library Director ... Vandana DHAKAR
09 Director Institutional Research ... Dr. Jere TURNER
10 Business Affairs Officer ... Bettejean NEVEUX
22 Human Resources Officer ... Jeannette DIBELLA
40 Bookstore Manager ... Vacant
66 Nursing Director ... Charlene WOLFE-STEPRO
21 Accountant I ... Carol DESPATHY
13 Director Information Technology ... George WAGGONER
35 Director Student Life ... Aileen CLAY
88 Bursar ... Amy WHEELER
04 Administrative Asst to President ... Karen KEELER
103 Dir Workforce/Career Development ... Kathy DESROCHES
106 Dir Online Education/E-learning ... Brian CHICK
108 Director Institutional Assessment ... Dr. Kate GUERDAT
18 Chief Facilities/Physical Plant ... Joshua MURPHY
19 Director Security/Safety ... Jeff NYHAN
29 Director Alumni Relations ... Leslie PAUL

*Nashua Community College (B)

505 Amherst Street, Nashua NH 03063-1092
County: Hillsborough FICE Identification: 009236
Unit ID: 183141
Telephone: (603) 882-6923 Carnegie Class: Assoc/Pub-R-M
FAX Number: (603) 882-8690 Calendar System: Semester
URL: www.nashuacc.edu
Established: 1967 Annual Undergrad Tuition & Fees (In-State): $6,912
Enrollment: 2,184 Coed
Affiliation or Control: State IRS Status: 501(c)3
Highest Offering: Associate Degree
Program: Occupational; 2-Year Principally Bachelor's Creditable
Accreditation: EH, ACBSP, ADNUR, ENGT

02 President ... Ms. Lucille A. JORDAN
05 Vice Pres Academic Affairs ... Mr. William A. MCINTYRE
32 Vice Pres Student & Community Affs ... Ms. Lizbeth GONZALEZ
10 Chief Financial Officer ... Vacant
09 Assoc VP Inst Research/Acad Affs ... Mr. Phil FRANKLAND
06 Registrar-Nashua ... Ms. Jennifer LEITNER
37 Financial Aid Officer ... Ms. Ann EULE
15 Human Resources ... Ms. Catherine BARRY
18 Plant Maintenance Engineer ... Mr. Scott BIENVENUE
26 Director Marketing/Public Relations ... Mr. Barry MEEHAN

*NHTI-Concord's Community College (C)

31 College Drive, Concord NH 03301-7412
County: Merrimack FICE Identification: 002581
Unit ID: 183099
Telephone: (603) 271-6484 Carnegie Class: Assoc/Pub-R-M
FAX Number: (603) 230-9311 Calendar System: Semester
URL: www.nhti.edu
Established: 1965 Annual Undergrad Tuition & Fees (In-State): $6,660
Enrollment: 4,284 Coed
Affiliation or Control: State IRS Status: 501(c)3
Highest Offering: Associate Degree
Program: Occupational; 2-Year Principally Bachelor's Creditable
Accreditation: EH, ACBSP, ADNUR, DA, DH, DMS, EMT, ENGT, PNUR, RAD, RTT

02 President ... Dr. Susan DUNTON
32 VP Student Affairs ... Mr. Stephen P. CACCIA
35 Associate VP Student Affairs ... Dr. Charles LLOYD
05 Vice President Academic Affairs ... Dr. Pamela LANGLEY
20 Assoc Vice Pres of Academic Affairs ... Dr. Denis NORMANDIN
10 Chief Financial Officer ... Ms. Melanie KIRBY
08 Director Learning Resources ... Mr. Stephen AMBRA
07 Director of Admissions ... Vacant
06 Registrar ... Ms. Michele KARWOCKI
13 Director of Computer Services ... Mr. Thomas TOWLE
18 Director of Facilities Maintenance ... Mr. Michael THERRIEN
26 Director of Communications ... Mr. Alan BLAKE
36 Dir Residence Life/Career Counsel ... Ms. Trish LORING
38 Director Student Counseling ... Ms. Donna DOOLEY
37 Financial Aid Director ... Ms. Sheri GONTHIER
19 Chief of Campus Safety ... Ms. Anne L. BREEN
41 Athletic Director ... Mr. Paul HOGAN
15 Director Human Resources ... Ms. Alyssa LABELLE
28 Dir Cross-Cultural Education/ESOL ... Ms. Dawn HIGGINS
96 Director of Purchasing ... Ms. Barbara ANSTEY
21 Bursar ... Ms. Jessica BRYAN
105 Website Coordinator ... Ms. Christine METCALF
106 Dir Online Learning ... Ms. Trisha DIONNE

*River Valley Community College (D)

1 College Place, Claremont NH 03743-9707
County: Sullivan FICE Identification: 007560
Unit ID: 183114
Telephone: (603) 542-7744 Carnegie Class: Assoc/Pub-R-S
FAX Number: (603) 543-1844 Calendar System: Semester
URL: www.rivervalley.edu
Established: 1968 Annual Undergrad Tuition & Fees (In-State): $6,000
Enrollment: 1,007 Coed
Affiliation or Control: State IRS Status: 501(c)3
Highest Offering: Associate Degree
Program: Occupational; 2-Year Principally Bachelor's Creditable; Liberal Arts And General; Nursing Emphasis
Accreditation: EH, ACBSP, ADNUR, COARC, MAC, MLTAD, OTA, PTAA, RAD

02 President ... Dr. Alicia B. HARVEY-SMITH
05 Interim Vice Pres Academic Affairs ... Dr. Susan HENDERSON
32 Associate VP of Student Services ... Mrs. Kathleen ODELL-CARLSON
37 Financial Aid Officer ... Ms. Julia DOWER
06 Registrar ... Ms. Sharon GILBERT
10 Chief Business Affairs Officer ... Mrs. Cynthia LACASCE
26 Chief Public Relations/Marketing ... Mrs. Lynne BIRMINGHAM

*White Mountains Community College (E)

2020 Riverside Drive, Berlin NH 03570-3799
County: Coos FICE Identification: 005291
Unit ID: 183105
Telephone: (603) 752-1113 Carnegie Class: Assoc/Pub-R-S
FAX Number: (603) 752-6335 Calendar System: Semester
URL: www.wmcc.edu
Established: 1966 Annual Undergrad Tuition & Fees (In-State): $7,648
Enrollment: 1,205 Coed
Affiliation or Control: State IRS Status: 501(c)3
Highest Offering: Associate Degree
Program: Occupational; 2-Year Principally Bachelor's Creditable
Accreditation: EH, MAC

02 President ... Matthew WOOD
05 Vice Pres Academic Affairs ... Fran RANCOURT
32 Vice President Student Affairs ... Martha LAFLAMME
10 Chief Financial Officer ... Lynn MOORE
06 Registrar ... Laurie CARRIER
08 Director Learning Resources ... Meagan CARR
18 Chief Facilities/Physical Plant ... Stephen DEROSIER
13 Director Computer Center ... Jeffrey SCHALL
91 Director Administrative Computing ... Donald WEEKS
38 Director Student Counseling ... Vacant
22 Dir Affirmative Action/Equal Oppty ... Donna BRIERE
40 Director Bookstore ... Karen SEVIER
07 Director of Admissions ... Vacant
04 Administrative Asst to President ... Gretchen TAILLON
09 Director of Institutional Research ... Suzanne WASILESKI
37 Director Student Financial Aid ... Kathryn DUCHESNE

Daniel Webster College (F)

20 University Drive, Nashua NH 03063-1300
County: Hillsborough FICE Identification: 004731
Unit ID: 182661
Telephone: (603) 577-6000 Carnegie Class: Bac/Diverse
FAX Number: (603) 577-6001 Calendar System: Semester
URL: www.dwc.edu
Established: 1965 Annual Undergrad Tuition & Fees: $15,630
Enrollment: 757 Coed
Affiliation or Control: Proprietary IRS Status: Proprietary
Highest Offering: Master's
Program: Liberal Arts And General; Professional; Technical Emphasis
Accreditation: EH, ENG

01 President ... Dr. Michael E. DIFFILY
05 Provost ... Dr. Jeremy OWENS
10 Director of Finance & Operations ... Ms. Darla AMMIDOWN
09 Director of Institutional Research ... Ms. Heidi CROWELL
04 Exec Assistant to the President ... Mrs. Dee KOUMARIANOS
49 Dean Arts and Sciences ... Dr. Kathleen HIPP
88 Dean Aviation Sciences ... Mr. Glenn CARTER
20 Dean Academic Affairs Online ... Dr. Deborah JAMESON
50 Dean Business Management ... Dr. Deborah JAMESON
54 Dean Engnieering & Computer Sci ... Mr. Nicholas BERTOZZI
07 Manager of Recruitment ... Ms. Jennifer O'NEILL
08 Librarian ... Ms. Kristin HAYS
08 Librarian ... Ms. Elyse WOLF
06 Registrar ... Ms. Laura CLEAVES
32 Dean of Students ... Ms. Susan ELSASS
36 Director of Career Services ... Ms. Karen SOLIMINI
41 Director of Athletics ... Mr. Chris GILMORE
19 Director of Campus Safety ... Mr. Kevin MOORE
15 Human Resources Generalist ... Ms. Donna BAILEY

Dartmouth College (G)

Hanover NH 03755-4030
County: Grafton FICE Identification: 002573
Unit ID: 182670
Telephone: (603) 646-1110 Carnegie Class: RU/VH
FAX Number: N/A Calendar System: Quarter
URL: www.dartmouth.edu
Established: 1769 Annual Undergrad Tuition & Fees: $49,506
Enrollment: 6,298 Coed
Affiliation or Control: Independent Non-Profit IRS Status: 501(c)3
Highest Offering: Doctorate
Program: Liberal Arts And General; Professional
Accreditation: EH, BUS, ENG, IPSY, MED, PAST, PH

01 President ... Dr. Philip J. HANLON
03 Executive Vice President ... Mr. Richard G. MILLS
101 Secretary to Board of Trustees ... Ms. Marcia J. KELLY
05 Provost ... Dr. Carolyn M. DEVER
30 Sr Vice President for Advancement ... Mr. Robert W. LASHER
46 Vice Provost for Research ... Dr. Martin N. WYBOURNE
10 CFO and Vice Pres Finance ... Mr. Michael F. WAGNER
26 VP Communications ... Mr. Justin ANDERSON
28 Vice Pres for Inst Diversity/Equity ... Dr. Evelynn ELLIS
15 Chief Human Resources Officer ... Mr. Scot R. BEMIS
29 Vice President Alumni Relations ... Ms. Martha J. BEATTIE
63 Interim Dean Geisel Sch of Med ... Dr. Duane A. COMPTON
18 VP of Campus Services ... Ms. Lisa HOGARTY
43 General Counsel ... Mr. Robert B. DONIN
20 Dean of the College ... Dr. Rebecca E. BIRON
06 Registrar ... Ms. Meredith BRAZ
07 Dean Admiss/Finan Aid/Assoc Provost ... Ms. Maria LASKARIS
37 Director of Financial Aid ... Ms. Virginia S. HAZEN
13 VP for Information Technology ... Ms. Ellen J. WAITE-FRANZEN
08 Dean of Libraries/Librarian of Col ... Mr. Jeffrey L. HORRELL
49 Dean of Faculty of Arts & Sciences .. Dr. Michael MASTANDUNO
50 Dean of Amos Tuck School ... Dr. Matthew J. SLAUGHTER
54 Dean of the Thayer School ... Dr. Joseph HELBLE
58 Dean of Graduate Studies ... Dr. F. Jon KULL
102 Interim Dean of Tucker Foundation ... Ms. Theresa M. ELLIS
41 Director of Athletics ... Mr. Harry SHEEHY
88 Dir Risk/Internal Control Svcs ... Ms. Catherine LARK
23 Director of the Health Services ... Dr. Mark REED
36 Director Center for Prof Dev ... Mr. Roger W. WOOLSEY
25 Dir Office of Sponsored Projects ... Ms. Jill M. MORTALI
32 Vice Provost for Student Affairs ... Dr. Inge-Lise AMEER
19 Director Safety & Security ... Mr. Harry C. KINNE, III
09 Director of Institutional Research ... Ms. Alicia M. BETSINGER
38 Dir Counseling/Human Development ... Dr. Heather A. EARLE
22 Dir Equal Opportunity/Affirm Action ... Dr. Evelynn ELLIS
96 Director of Procurement ... Ms. Tammy L. MOFFATT
44 Chief Investment Officer ... Ms. Pamela L. PEEDIN

Franklin Pierce University (H)

40 University Drive, Rindge NH 03461-5046
County: Cheshire FICE Identification: 002575
Unit ID: 182795
Telephone: (603) 899-4000 Carnegie Class: Master's S
FAX Number: (603) 899-6448 Calendar System: Semester
URL: www.franklinpierce.edu
Established: 1962 Annual Undergrad Tuition & Fees: $33,320
Enrollment: 2,010 Coed
Affiliation or Control: Independent Non-Profit IRS Status: 501(c)3
Highest Offering: Doctorate
Program: Liberal Arts And General; Teacher Preparatory; Professional
Accreditation: EH, ARCPA, IACBE, NUR, PTA

01 President ... Mr. Andrew H. CARD
05 VP Academic Affairs/Provost ... Dr. Kim MOONEY
11 VP & COO ... Dr. Nathaniel PEIRCE
10 Vice Pres Finance & Administration ... Ms. Sandra QUAYE
32 Vice President for Student Affairs ... Dr. James P. EARLE
30 Vice Pres for Institutional Advance ... Ms. Lisa MURRAY
29 VP Alumni & Comm Rels ... Mr. Lawrence LEACH
84 Asst Vice Pres Enrollment Mgmt ... Ms. Linda QUIMBY
58 Dean Grad/Professional Studies ... Dr. Maria R. ANTOBELLO
35 Asst Dean Student Affairs ... Ms. Jill BASSETT
41 Athletic Director ... Mr. Bruce M. KIRSH
15 Director of Human Resources ... Ms. Janette T. MEREDITH
06 Registrar ... Ms. Tonya B. LABROSSE
08 Director of Library Resource Center ... Ms. Carissa DELIZIO
37 Asst Vice Pres Financial Services ... Mr. Kenneth FERREIRA
29 Director of Alumni & Parent Rel ... Ms. Julie ZAHN
12 Academic Dean Rindge Campus ... Dr. Kerry MCKEEVER
26 Dir of Marketing & Communication ... Mr. James WOLKEN
36 Director of Career Development ... Ms. Rosemary NICHOLS
20 Dir Center for Academic Excellence ... Dr. Karen J. BROWN
42 Chaplain ... Rev. Bill BEARDSLEE
19 Director Campus Safety ... Ms. Maureen STURGIS
39 Director Residential Life ... Ms. Kathleen DOUGHERTY
18 Chief Facilities/Physical Plant ... Mr. Doug LEAR
21 Accountant & Payroll Mgr ... Ms. Kathleen MAHONEY
96 Director of Purchasing ... Mr. Robert ST. JEAN
104 Director Study Abroad ... Ms. Patti VORFELD
13 Chief Info Technology Officer (CIO) ... Mr. Thomas MANLEY
04 Executive Asst to the President ... Ms. Ann M. GAGNON

MCPHS-Manchester Campus (I)

1260 Elm Street, Manchester NH 03101
Telephone: (603) 314-0210 Identification: 770113
Accreditation: &EH, ARCPA

† Branch campus of MCPHS University, Boston, MA.

Mount Washington College (A)

3 Sundial Avenue, Manchester NH 03103-7245
County: Hillsborough FICE Identification: 004729
Unit ID: 182865
Telephone: (603) 668-6660 Carnegie Class: Bac/Assoc
FAX Number: (603) 621-8994 Calendar System: Semester
URL: www.mountwashington.edu
Established: 1900 Annual Undergrad Tuition & Fees: $9,000
Enrollment: 1,511 Coed
Affiliation or Control: Proprietary IRS Status: Proprietary
Highest Offering: Baccalaureate
Program: Occupational; 2-Year Principally Bachelor's Creditable
Accreditation: EH, MAC, PTAA

01 President ....Dr. Francis X. MULGREW
05 Vice President Academic Affairs ....Dr. Jan WYATT
11 Vice President of Operations ....Ms. Maureen ZNOJ
03 Executive Director ....Ms. Tiffany DOHERTY
32 Dean of Student Services ....Vacant
10 Director of Finance ....Mr. David FAXON
37 Executive Director Financial Aid ....Ms. Elizabeth NILSSON
06 Registrar ....Ms. Susan PROVENCHER
08 Director of Library Services ....Vacant
36 Director of Career Services ....Ms. Heather LALLA
37 Financial Aid Officer ....Mr. Michael BEAN
04 Assistant to the President ....Mrs. Carol DEWALT

New England College (B)

98 Bridge Street, Henniker NH 03242-3244
County: Merrimack FICE Identification: 002579
Unit ID: 182980
Telephone: (603) 428-2211 Carnegie Class: Master's M
FAX Number: (603) 428-7230 Calendar System: Semester
URL: www.nec.edu
Established: 1946 Annual Undergrad Tuition & Fees: $33,966
Enrollment: 2,399 Coed
Affiliation or Control: Independent Non-Profit IRS Status: 501(c)3
Highest Offering: Doctorate
Program: Liberal Arts And General; Teacher Preparatory; Professional
Accreditation: EH

01 President ....Dr. Michele D. PERKINS
05 Provost ....Dr. Mark WATMAN
84 VP of Enrollment ....Mr. Brad POZNANSKI
10 Sr Vice President/CEO ....Dr. Paula A. AMATO
30 Vice Pres Advancement/Communication ....Ms. Morgan SMITH
04 Special Asst to President ....Ms. Tia HOOPER
08 Library Director ....Ms. Chelsea HANRAHAN
58 Dean Graduate School ....Dr. Nelly LEJTER
07 Director of Graduate Admission ....Ms. Meghan CADWALLADER
04 Admin Assistant to President ....Ms. Betsy MEDVETZ
13 Int Dir of Information Technology ....Ms. Paula AMATO
06 Registrar ....Mr. Frank L. HALL
37 Director Student Financial Svcs ....Ms. Kristen BLASE
21 Controller ....Mr. Steven LAVOIE
36 Director Career/Life Planning ....Mr. Gene DURKEE
30 Director of Development ....Ms. Meghan HALLOCK
26 Dir of Public Rels/Communications ....Mr. David DEZIEL
15 Human Resources Manager ....Vacant

New Hampshire Institute of Art (C)

148 Concord Street, Manchester NH 03104-4858
County: Hillsborough FICE Identification: 031823
Unit ID: 430810
Telephone: (603) 623-0313 Carnegie Class: Spec/Arts
FAX Number: (603) 641-1832 Calendar System: Semester
URL: www.nhia.edu
Established: 1898 Annual Undergrad Tuition & Fees: $23,410
Enrollment: 436 Coed
Affiliation or Control: Independent Non-Profit IRS Status: 501(c)3
Highest Offering: Master's
Program: Fine Arts Emphasis
Accreditation: EH, ART

01 President ....Mr. Kent DEVEREAUX
10 Vice President of Finance ....Ms. Leanna FLEMING
30 Vice President of Development ....Ms. Suzanne LENZ
84 Vice President of Enrollment ....Mr. Bob GIELOW
12 Sharon Arts Campus Director ....Ms. Camellia SOUSA
04 Executive Assistant to President ....Ms. Sara DADIAN PEREZ
05 Interim Dean of Undergrad Studies ....Mr. Patrick MCCAY
58 Dean of Graduate Studies ....Ms. Alison WILLIAMS
08 Library Director ....Ms. Betsy HOLMES
88 Director of Advising ....Ms. Tricia GIBBS
06 Registrar ....Ms. Karen GOSSELIN
20 Academic Affairs Administrator ....Ms. Rebecca DESROCHERS
88 Bursar ....Ms. Diane VESCI
32 Director of Student Affairs ....Vacant
37 Assistant Director Financial Aid ....Ms. Joan HANNAN
31 Community Education Director ....Mr. Chris ARCHER
15 Director of Human Resources ....Vacant
21 Accounting Manager ....Ms. Nancy JORDAN
18 Facilities Manager ....Mr. Paul GYMZIAK
13 Manager of Information Technologies ....Mr. John FALLAVOLLITA
88 IT Specialist ....Mr. Bob MASTERTON
38 Counselor ....Ms. Tanya POPOLOSKI
88 Academic Support Center Coordinator ....Ms. Liza OPPENHEIM

Northeast Catholic College (D)

511 Kearsarge Mountain Road, Warner NH 03278-4012
County: Merrimack FICE Identification: 022233
Unit ID: 182917
Telephone: (603) 456-2656 Carnegie Class: Bac/A&S
FAX Number: (603) 456-2660 Calendar System: Semester
URL: www.NortheastCatholic.edu
Established: 1973 Annual Undergrad Tuition & Fees: $21,200
Enrollment: 61 Coed
Affiliation or Control: Roman Catholic IRS Status: 501(c)3
Highest Offering: Baccalaureate
Program: Liberal Arts And General
Accreditation: @EH

01 President ....Dr. George A. HARNE
05 Academic Dean ....Dr. Mary K. MUMBACH
10 CFO ....Mr. Daniel PETERSON
32 Dean of Students ....Miss Katherine PAGOR
07 Director of Admissions ....Ms. Katie MOFFETT
37 Director Financial Aid/Librarian ....Mrs. Marie LASHER

Rivier University (E)

420 S Main Street, Nashua NH 03060-5086
County: Hillsborough FICE Identification: 002586
Unit ID: 183211
Telephone: (603) 888-1311 Carnegie Class: Master's L
FAX Number: (603) 897-8811 Calendar System: Semester
URL: www.rivier.edu
Established: 1933 Annual Undergrad Tuition & Fees: $28,800
Enrollment: 1,034 Coed
Affiliation or Control: Roman Catholic IRS Status: 501(c)3
Highest Offering: Doctorate
Program: Liberal Arts And General; Teacher Preparatory; Professional; Nursing Emphasis
Accreditation: EH, ADNUR, NUR

01 President ....Sr. Paula Marie BULEY
05 Vice President for Academic Affairs ....Dr. Douglas HOWARD
10 Vice Pres Finance & Administration ....Mr. Brent WINIGER
32 Vice President Student Affairs ....Mr. Kurt STIMELING
84 Vice Pres Enrollment Management ....Ms. Karen SCHEDIN
30 Vice Pres University Advancement ....Ms. Karen COOPER
35 Asst Vice Pres Student Affairs ....Ms. Paula RANDAZZA
13 Chief Information Officer ....Mr. H. William SCHLEIFER
21 Controller ....Ms. Jennifer YEOMANS
06 Registrar ....Mr. Kevin GATELY
08 Library Director ....Mr. Daniel SPEIDEL
36 Dir Career Development Center ....Ms. Marie SULLIVAN
37 Director Student Financial Aid ....Ms. Valerie PATNAUDE
15 Director Human Resources ....Ms. Diana STRANO
18 Director Facilities Management ....Mr. Richard PERRINE
14 Director Instructional Computing ....Sr. Martha VILLENEUVE
41 Athletic Director ....Ms. Joanne MERRILL
42 Chaplain Campus Ministry ....Bro. Paul DEMERS
28 Director Multicultural Affairs ....Ms. Sharron ROWLETT
29 Dir Alumni Relations/Special Events ....Ms. Mary BOLLINGER
26 Director Marketing/Communication ....Ms. Patricia GARRITY

Saint Anselm College (F)

100 Saint Anselm Drive, Manchester NH 03102-1310
County: Hillsborough FICE Identification: 002587
Unit ID: 183239
Telephone: (603) 641-7000 Carnegie Class: Bac/A&S
FAX Number: (603) 641-7116 Calendar System: Semester
URL: www.anselm.edu
Established: 1889 Annual Undergrad Tuition & Fees: $37,694
Enrollment: 1,968 Coed
Affiliation or Control: Roman Catholic IRS Status: 501(c)3
Highest Offering: Baccalaureate
Program: Liberal Arts And General; Teacher Preparatory
Accreditation: EH, NURSE

01 President ....Dr. Steven R. DISALVO
05 Vice Pres Academic Affairs ....Br. Isaac MURPHY, OSB
30 Vice President College Advancement ....Mr. James P. FLANAGAN
11 Vice President for Administration ....Ms. Patricia SHUSTER
32 Vice President Student Affairs ....Dr. Joseph M. HORTON
26 Exec Dir Col Comm & Mktg ....Ms. Michelle ADAMS
10 Chief Financial officer ....Dr. Harry E. DUMAY
06 Registrar ....Fr. Benet PHILLIPS
07 Dean of Admissions ....Mr. Eric NICHOLS
08 Librarian ....Mr. Charles M. GETCHELL, JR.
37 Director of Financial Aid ....Ms. Elizabeth KEUFFEL
35 Dean of Students ....Dr. Alicia A. FINN
36 Exec Dir Experiential Learning ....Vacant
20 Dean of Freshmen ....Dr. Anne E. HARRINGTON
66 Exec Director of Nursing ....Dr. Maureen A. O'REILLY
04 Assistant to the President ....Ms. Janet L. POIRIER
18 Director of Physical Plant ....Mr. Donald MOREAU
23 Director of Health Services ....Ms. Maura MARSHALL
29 Asst VP of Alum/Advanc Programming ....Ms. Patricia GUANCI-THERRIEN
41 Director of Athletics ....Mr. James HERLIHY
42 Director of Campus Ministry ....Ms. Susan S. GABERT
09 Director of Institutional Research ....Dr. Hui-Ling CHEN
13 Chief Information Officer ....Mr. Adam R. ALBINA
15 Director Human Resources ....Mr. David HARRINGTON
19 Director Security/Safety ....Mr. Donald DAVIDSON
53 Director Education Planning ....Dr. Laura WASIELEWSKI
28 Director Multicultural Center ....Ms. Oluyemi MAHONEY
39 Director Student Housing ....Ms. Susan WEINTRAUB
96 Director of Purchasing ....Mr. Jacques PLANTE
104 Assoc Dir Study Abroad ....Ms. Sarah GOOLKASIAN
25 Dir Sponsored Programs & Research ....Dr. William PLLOG
44 Asst VP Individual Giving ....Mr. John GENNETTI

St. Joseph School of Nursing (G)

5 Woodward Avenue, Nashua NH 03060
County: Hillsborough FICE Identification: 021404
Unit ID: 183248
Telephone: (603) 594-2567 Carnegie Class: Not Classified
FAX Number: (603) 578-5028 Calendar System: Semester
URL: www.sjson.edu
Established: 1964 Annual Undergrad Tuition & Fees: $29,150
Enrollment: 148 Coed
Affiliation or Control: Independent Non-Profit IRS Status: 501(c)3
Highest Offering: Associate Degree
Program: 2-Year Principally Bachelor's Creditable; Nursing Emphasis
Accreditation: ACCSC, ADNUR

01 Dean ....Vickie K. FIELER

Southern New Hampshire University (H)

2500 North River Road, Manchester NH 03106-1045
County: Hillsborough FICE Identification: 002580
Unit ID: 183026
Telephone: (603) 626-9100 Carnegie Class: Master's L
FAX Number: (603) 645-9665 Calendar System: Semester
URL: www.snhu.edu
Established: 1932 Annual Undergrad Tuition & Fees: $30,006
Enrollment: 43,743 Coed
Affiliation or Control: Independent Non-Profit IRS Status: 501(c)3
Highest Offering: Doctorate
Program: Liberal Arts And General; Teacher Preparatory; Professional; Business Emphasis
Accreditation: EH, ACBSP, NURSE, @TEAC

01 President ....Dr. Paul LEBLANC
04 Executive Assistant to President ....Ms. Lisa JENNINGS
100 Chief of Staff ....Mr. William ZEMP
05 Provost/Sr VP Academic Affairs ....Dr. Patricia LYNOTT
15 Sr VP Human Resources & Development ....Ms. Danielle STANTON
51 CEO College of Online & Cont Educ ....Mr. Stephen HODOWNES
88 Exec Director College for America ....Ms. Kris CLERKIN
10 Chief Financial Officer ....Mr. Joseph SERGI
13 Chief Information Officer ....Mr. Johnson AU-YEUNG
88 Chief Compliance Officer ....Ms. McCeil JOHNSON
43 General Counsel/Secretary to Board ....Ms. Yvette CLARK
30 VP Institutional Advancement ....Mr. Donald BREZINSKI
26 VP Marketing & Student Recruiting ....Mr. Gregg MAZZOLA
18 VP Facilities/Physical Plant ....Ms. Patricia WHITNEY
20 Assoc VP Academic Affairs ....Vacant
09 Assoc VP of Research & Planning ....Mr. Thomas F. BERALDI, JR.
104 Assoc VP of International Programs ....Mr. Geoff MOODY
37 Assoc VP Enrolled Student Services ....Ms. Kimberly REILLY
06 Assoc VP & Registrar ....Ms. Jennifer LIGENZA
49 Dean School of Arts & Sciences ....Dr. Karen ERICKSON
50 Dean School of Business ....Mr. William GILLETT
53 Dean School of Education ....Mr. Raymond MCNULTY
08 Dean of the Library ....Ms. Kathy GROWNEY
32 Dean of Students ....Ms. Heather LORENZ
20 Dean of Student Success ....Ms. Carey GLINES
19 Assoc Dean/Dir of Public Safety ....Mr. James WINN
35 Associate Dean of Students ....Mr. Marlin NABORS
27 Exec Director of Communications ....Ms. Libby MAY
07 Director of Freshman Admissions ....Ms. Bethany PERKINS
07 Director of Transfer Admissions ....Ms. Julie CALLAHAN
31 Dir Community Engaged Learning ....Ms. Elizabeth RICHARDS
28 Dir Cultural Outreach & Involvement ....Ms. Louisa MARTIN
29 Director of Alumni Relations ....Ms. Kristi DURETTE
26 Director Community Relations ....Ms. Helen DAVIES
23 Director Wellness Center ....Ms. Sheila LAMBERT
36 Exec Dir of Career Development Ctr ....Ms. Beth PRIETO
88 Exec Dir of the Student Center ....Dr. Scott TIERNO
39 Director of Residence Life ....Ms. Shannon BROWN
41 Director of Athletics ....Mr. Anthony FALLACARO
42 Director of Campus Ministry ....Rev. Bruce COLLARD
92 Director of Univ Honors Program ....Dr. Andrew MARTINO
85 Director of Intl Student Services ....Ms. Dawn SEDUTTO
96 Sr Dir of Procurement/Contracts ....Ms. Mary DUKAKIS
25 Director of Grants ....Ms. Audrey MCLAUGHLIN
14 Director of Computing Resources ....Mr. Daryl A. DREFFS
105 Director of Web Services ....Mr. Curtis KIMBALL
88 Director of Academic Advising ....Ms. Leah RICHARDS
88 Director of the Learning Center ....Ms. Lori DECONINCK
88 Director of Disability Services ....Ms. Hyla JAFFE
104 Director Study Abroad ....Mr. Stefano PARENTI
108 Director of Learning Assessment ....Dr. Randall CASE
90 Assoc Dir of Academic Computing ....Mr. Aaron FLINT
24 AV Services Manager ....Mr. Thomas HELM

The Thomas More College of Liberal Arts (I)

6 Manchester Street, Merrimack NH 03054-4805
County: Hillsborough FICE Identification: 030431
Unit ID: 183275
Telephone: (603) 880-8308 Carnegie Class: Bac/A&S

FAX Number: (603) 880-9280 Calendar System: Semester
URL: www.thomasmorecollege.edu
Established: 1978 Annual Undergrad Tuition & Fees: $20,400
Enrollment: 90 Coed
Affiliation or Control: Independent Non-Profit IRS Status: 501(c)3
Highest Offering: Baccalaureate
Program: Liberal Arts And General; Religious Emphasis
Accreditation: EH

01 President .... Dr. William E. FAHEY
30 Vice Pres Institutional Advancement .... Mr. Paul JACKSON
05 Academic Dean .... Dr. Walter THOMPSON
32 Dean of Students .... Mr. Denis KITZINGER
07 Director Admission/Inst Advancement .... Mr. Paul JACKSON
06 Registrar/Director of Business .... Ms. Pamela BERNSTEIN
35 Director of Student Life .... Dr. Sara KITZINGER
04 Executive Asst President's Office .... Ms. Valerie BURGESS

*University System of New Hampshire (A)

5 Chenell Drive, Suite 301, Concord NH 03301
County: Merrimack FICE Identification: 008027
Unit ID: 183327
Telephone: (603) 862-1800 Carnegie Class: N/A
FAX Number: (603) 862-0908
URL: usnh.edu

01 Chancellor .... Dr. Todd J. LEACH
03 Vice Chancellor & Treasurer .... Ms. Catherine A. PROVENCHER
43 General Counsel .... Mr. Ronald F. RODGERS
86 Assoc Vice Chanc Government Affs .... Vacant
05 Assoc Vice Chanc Academic & Student .... Vacant
09 Dir of Institutional Research .... Ms. Heidi HEDEGARD
15 Chief Human Resource Officer .... Mr. James MCGRAIL

*University of New Hampshire (B)

105 Main Street, Durham NH 03824
County: Strafford FICE Identification: 002589
Unit ID: 183044
Telephone: (603) 862-1234 Carnegie Class: RU/H
FAX Number: N/A Calendar System: Semester
URL: www.unh.edu
Established: 1866 Annual Undergrad Tuition & Fees (In-State): $16,986
Enrollment: 15,169 Coed
Affiliation or Control: State IRS Status: 501(c)3
Highest Offering: Doctorate
Program: Occupational; 2-Year Principally Bachelor's Creditable; Liberal Arts And General; Teacher Preparatory; Professional
Accreditation: EH, ACFEI, BUS, CAATE, CAEP, CARTE, CS, DIETD, DIETI, DIETT, ENG, ENGT, IPSY, LAW, MFCD, MT, MUS, NRPA, NURSE, OT, PH, SP, SW, TEAC

02 President .... Dr. Mark W. HUDDLESTON
100 Chief of Staff .... Ms. Megan W. DAVIS
05 Int Prov & VP Academic Affairs ... Dr. Palligarnai T. VASUDEVAN
10 VP Finance/Administration .... Mr. Chris D. CLEMENT
46 Sr Vice Provost Research .... Dr. Jane A. NISBET
26 Assoc VP Univ Communications .... Mr. Joel SELIGMAN
43 General Counsel .... Mr. Ronald F. RODGERS
88 Assoc Prov Academic Administration .... Ms. Leigh Anne MELANSON
28 Assoc VP Cmty/Equity/Diversity .... Ms. Jamie NOLAN
20 Int Sr Vice Prov Academic Affairs .... Dr. Mary RHIEL
15 Assoc VP/Chief HR Officer .... Ms. Kathleen A. NEILS
20 Asst Prov Acad Adm/MPA Program Dir .... Mr. James S. VARN
88 Sr VProv Engagement & Acad Outreach .... Dr. Julie E. WILLIAMS
21 Assoc VP for Finance .... Ms. Kerry SCALA
13 Asst VP Enterprise Computing .... Mr. William HALL
40 Manager of UNH Bookstore .... Ms. Karen MCLAUGHLIN
16 Asst VP Human Resources .... Ms. Sari M. BENNETT
21 Assoc VP Business Affairs .... Mr. David J. MAY
18 Assoc VP Facilities .... Mr. Paul D. CHAMBERLIN
32 Int Dean of Students .... Ms. Denise NELSON
35 Director Residential Life .... Mr. Scott CHESNEY
23 Director Health Services .... Dr. Kevin E. CHARLES
36 Assoc Prov Acad Achievement/Support .... Dr. Judith SPILLER
25 Dir Sponsored Programs .... Mr. Victor SOSA
30 VP Advancement .... Ms. Deborah DUTTON COX
47 Dean Life Sciences/Agriculture .... Dr. Jon M. WRAITH
49 Dean Liberal Arts .... Dr. Kenneth FULD
50 Dean Paul College of Business .... Dr. Deborah MERRILL-SANDS
58 Dean Graduate School .... Dr. Harry J. RICHARDS
76 Dean Health & Human Services .... Dr. Michael FERRARA
54 Dean Engineering/Physical Sciences .... Dr. Samuel MUKASA
12 Int Dean UNH at Manchester .... Dr. J. Michael HICKEY
08 Dean of the University Library .... Dr. Tara Lynn FULTON
56 Dean/Dir Cooperative Extension .... Dr. Ken LAVALLEY
88 Dir Thompson School Appl Science .... Dr. Regina A. SMICK-ATTISANO
22 Dir Affirmative Action & Equity ... Ms. Donna Marie SORRENTINO
07 Director Admissions .... Mr. Robert P H. MCGANN
06 Registrar .... Mr. Andrew COLBY
37 Dir Financial Aid .... Ms. Susan K. ALLEN
41 Dir Intercollegiate Athletics .... Mr. Martin SCARANO
38 Dir Counseling Center .... Dr. David CROSS
102 Dir Finance & Operations UNH Found .... Mr. Erik GROSS
39 Dir Housing/Conf Services .... Ms. Kathy IRLA-CHESNEY
19 Exec Dir Public Safety .... Chief Paul M. DEAN
85 Dir Intl Students & Scholars .... Ms. Leila L. PAJE-MANALO
42 University Chaplain .... Pastor Larry BRICKNER-WOOD
96 Dir Purchasing & Contract Svcs .... Ms. Denise M. SMITH
92 Dir Honors Program .... Dr. Jerry MARX
09 Dir Inst Research & Assessment .... Vacant
88 Dir Writing Program .... Dr. Edward A. MUELLER
104 Dir Center International Education .... Dr. Claire L. MALARTE-FELDMAN
94 Coord Women's Studies Program .... Dr. Marla B. BRETTSCHNEIDER
86 Asst Vice Pres Public Affairs .... Mr. Mica STARK
106 UNH Online Director .... Ms. Terri WINTERS
04 Administrative Asst to President .... Ms. Annie JONES

*Granite State College (C)

25 Hall Street, Concord NH 03301-7317
County: Merrimack FICE Identification: 031013
Unit ID: 183257
Telephone: (603) 228-3000 Carnegie Class: Bac/A&S
FAX Number: (603) 513-1389 Calendar System: Quarter
URL: www.granite.edu
Established: 1972 Annual Undergrad Tuition & Fees (In-State): $8,550
Enrollment: 2,206 Coed
Affiliation or Control: State IRS Status: 501(c)3
Highest Offering: Master's
Program: 2-Year Principally Bachelor's Creditable; Liberal Arts And General; Teacher Preparatory; Professional; Business Emphasis
Accreditation: EH, NURSE

02 President .... Dr. Mark RUBINSTEIN
05 Interim Provost/VP Academic Affairs .... Dr. Scott A. STANLEY
13 Chief Information Officer .... Mr. Kenneth WHITELAW
10 VP Finance/Technology/Infrastruct .... Ms. Lisa L. SHAWNEY
53 Dean of the School of Education .... Dr. Mary J. FORD
20 Interim Vice Provost .... Dr. Johnna A. HERRICK-PHELPS
84 VP of Enrollment Management .... Ms. Mary Beth LUFKIN
06 Registrar .... Ms. Kristin MULLANEY
24 Director of Educational Technology .... Ms. Reta CHAFFEE
14 Director Enterprise Infrastructure .... Mr. Charles LIPORTO
88 Asst VP of Enrollment Management .... Dr. Barbara LAYNE
15 VP of Student/Administrative Svcs .... Ms. Beth DOLAN
09 Director of Institutional Research .... Mr. Jim MILLER
18 Dir of Facilities/Safety/Sustain .... Mr. Peter CONKLIN
08 College Librarian/Senior Lecturer ..... Ms. Patricia ERWIN-PLOOG
21 Director of Financial Operations .... Mr. Steve PERROTTA
21 Bursar .... Ms. Jodi WOLBERT
04 Administrative Asst to President .... Ms. Lois E. MONETTE

*Keene State College (D)

229 Main Street, Keene NH 03435-0001
County: Cheshire FICE Identification: 002590
Unit ID: 183062
Telephone: (603) 352-1909 Carnegie Class: Master's S
FAX Number: (603) 358-2257 Calendar System: Semester
URL: www.keene.edu
Established: 1909 Annual Undergrad Tuition & Fees (In-State): $12,938
Enrollment: 4,957 Coed
Affiliation or Control: State IRS Status: 501(c)3
Highest Offering: Master's
Program: Liberal Arts And General; Teacher Preparatory; Professional
Accreditation: EH, CAATE, DIETD, DIETI, MUS, NURSE, TED

02 President .... Dr. Anne E. HUOT
05 Provost/VP Academic Affairs .... Dr. Walter ZAKAHI
32 VP Student Affairs & Enroll Mgmt .... Dr. Kemal ATKINS
10 VP Finance & Planning .... Dr. Jay V. KAHN
30 Vice President Advancement .... Ms. Maryann LINDBERG
100 Chief of Staff .... Ms. Patricia FRANCIS
04 Executive Asst to the President .... Vacant
35 Dean of Students .... Dr. Gail ZIMMERMAN
08 Dean of Library .... Dr. Celia E. RABINOWITZ
07 Director of Admissions .... Ms. Margaret RICHMOND
06 Registrar .... Mr. Thomas RICHARD
13 Chief Information Officer .... Ms. Laura SERAICHICK
44 Director of Development .... Mr. Ken GOEBEL
15 Human Resources Director .... Ms. Kim HARKNESS
26 Director of Marketing & Comm .... Ms. Kathleen WILLIAMS
37 Director Financial Aid .... Ms. Patricia A. BLODGETT
18 Director Physical Plant .... Mr. Frank MAZZOLA
39 Director of Residential Life .... Mr. Kent DRAKE-DEESE
09 Director of Institutional Research .... Dr. Cathryn TURRENTINE
29 Alumni & Parent Relations Director .... Ms. Patricia FARMER
38 Director Student Counseling .... Dr. Brian QUIGLEY
96 Purchasing Agent .... Mr. James DRAPER
81 Dean of Sciences .... Dr. Gordon LEVERSEE
58 Interim Dean Prof/Graduate Studies .... Dr. Wayne HARTZ
79 Dean Arts & Humanities .... Dr. Andrew HARRIS
28 Chief Officer Diversity/Multicult .... Dr. Dottie MORRIS

*Plymouth State University (E)

17 High Street, Plymouth NH 03264-1595
County: Grafton FICE Identification: 002591
Unit ID: 183080
Telephone: (603) 535-5000 Carnegie Class: Master's L
FAX Number: (603) 535-2654 Calendar System: Semester
URL: www.plymouth.edu
Established: 1871 Annual Undergrad Tuition & Fees (In-State): $13,128
Enrollment: 4,855 Coed
Affiliation or Control: State IRS Status: 501(c)3
Highest Offering: Doctorate
Program: Liberal Arts And General; Teacher Preparatory; Professional; Business Emphasis
Accreditation: EH, ACBSP, ART, CAATE, CACREP, NURSE, SW, TED

02 President .... Dr. Donald L. BIRX
05 Vice Pres Academic Affairs/Provost .... Dr. Julie N. BERNIER
10 VP for Finance & Administration .... Mr. Stephen TAKSAR
32 Vice Pres Enroll Mgmt/Student Affs .... Dr. James HUNDRIESER
20 VP for Undergraduate Studies .... Dr. David ZEHR
30 VP for University Advancement .... Ms. Paula L. HOBSON
20 Vice Provost Research & Engagement .... Dr. Thad GULDBRANDSEN
58 Dir Ofc of Graduate Stds/Col Dean .... Ms. Gail MEARS
13 AVP Info Tech Svcs/Chief Info Ofcr .. Mr. Richard G. GROSSMAN
84 Asst VP Enroll Mgmt/Dir Admissions ... Mr. Andrew B. PALUMBO
39 AVP Student Affairs - Res Life .... Mr. Frank L. COCCHIARELLA
88 AVP Student Affairs - HUB .... Ms. Terri L. POTTER
88 Exec Assc to Univ Pres/Comm Liaison .... Ms. Janet CAPAUL
35 Dean of Students .... Vacant
09 Dir Institutional Research/Assess .... Ms. Joyce LARSON
06 Registrar .... Vacant
08 Int Dean Library/Academic Support .... Ms. Elaine ALLARD
29 Director of Alumni Relations .... Mr. Rodney EKSTROM
37 Director of Financial Aid .... Ms. Crystal GAFF
15 Director of Human Resources .... Ms. Elaine DOELL
19 Chief of Campus Police .... Mr. Richard BAILEY
41 Athletic Director .... Mr. John P. CLARK
18 Director of Physical Plant .... Ms. Ellen SHIPPEE
38 Director of Counseling .... Dr. Michael L. FISCHLER
40 Bookstore Manager .... Mr. Steve RHEAUME
36 Career Services Manager .... Mr. James KURAS
96 Manager of Purchasing .... Ms. Heather HUCKINS

NEW JERSEY

Assumption College for Sisters (F)

200A Morris Avenue, Denville NJ 07834
County: Morris FICE Identification: 002595
Unit ID: 183600
Telephone: (973) 957-0188 Carnegie Class: Assoc/PrivNFP
FAX Number: (973) 957-0190 Calendar System: Semester
URL: www.acs350.org
Established: 1953 Annual Undergrad Tuition & Fees: $10,940
Enrollment: 39 Female
Affiliation or Control: Roman Catholic IRS Status: 501(c)3
Highest Offering: Associate Degree
Program: 2-Year Principally Bachelor's Creditable; Religious Emphasis
Accreditation: M

01 President/Chief of Development .... Sr. Joseph SPRING, SCC
05 Academic Dean .... Sr. Mary Catherine SLATTERY, SCC
10 Treasurer .... Mrs. Patricia MCGRADY
32 Chief Student Life Officer .... Sr. Marie Cecelia LANDIS, SCC
06 Registrar .... Mrs. Barbara KELLY-VERGONA

Atlantic Cape Community College (G)

5100 Black Horse Pike, Mays Landing NJ 08330-2699
County: Atlantic FICE Identification: 002596
Unit ID: 183655
Telephone: (609) 343-4900 Carnegie Class: Assoc/Pub-R-L
FAX Number: (609) 343-4917 Calendar System: Semester
URL: www.atlantic.edu
Established: 1964 Annual Undergrad Tuition & Fees (In-District): $4,266
Enrollment: 6,845 Coed
Affiliation or Control: State/Local IRS Status: 501(c)3
Highest Offering: Associate Degree
Program: Occupational; 2-Year Principally Bachelor's Creditable
Accreditation: M, ACFEI, ADNUR, SURGT

01 President .... Dr. Peter L. MORA
45 Vice President Planning/Research .... Dr. Richard PERNICIARO
15 Dean Human Resources & Compliance ... Ms. Eileen CURRISTINE
11 Dean Administration and Business .... Mr. August DAQUILA
100 Dean Res Dev/Pres & BOT Operations .... Ms. Jean MCALISTER
13 Dean Information Tech Services .... Mr. Douglas HEDGES
05 Vice President Academic Affairs .... Dr. Otto HERNANDEZ
10 Dean Finance .... Ms. Leslie JAMISON
32 Vice President Student Affairs .... Dr. Mitchell LEVY
84 Dean Enrollment Management .... Mr. Andre RICHBURG
08 Assoc Dean Academic Support Svcs .... Ms. Janet MARLER
49 Dean Liberal Studies .... Dr. Ronald MCARTHUR
88 Dean Academy of Culinary Arts .... Ms. Kelly MCCLAY
75 Dean Career Education .... Ms. Donna VASSALLO
51 Interim Associate Dean Cont Educ .... Ms. Esther GANDICA
81 Dean STEM .... Dr. Elmer GODENY
26 Director College Relations .... Mr. Michael BRUCKLER
38 Director Student Counseling .... Ms. Paula DAVIS
37 Director Financial Aid .... Ms. Linda DESANTIS
07 Director Admissions .... Ms. Kristin JACKSON
96 Director Business Services .... Ms. Dorie KEENER
102 Sr Director Res Dev/Alumni Outreach .... Ms. Maria KELLETT
09 Director Inst Research Plng/Assess .... Mr. Luis MONTEFUSCO
06 Registrar .... Ms. Heather PETERSON
35 Dir Student Dev & Judicial Officer .... Ms. Nancy PORFIDO
18 Director Facilities Management .... Mr. Russell WAUGH

Bais Medrash Toras Chesed (H)

910 Monmouth Avenue, Lakewood NJ 08701-1921
County: Ocean FICE Identification: 040813
Unit ID: 449658
Telephone: (732) 364-1220 Carnegie Class: Spec/Faith
FAX Number: (732) 886-2323 Calendar System: Semester

Established: 1999 Annual Undergrad Tuition & Fees: $9,100
Enrollment: 116 Male
Affiliation or Control: Independent Non-Profit IRS Status: 501(c)3
Highest Offering: Baccalaureate
Program: Professional
Accreditation: RABN

01 Dean .... Rabbi N. STEIN
37 Director of Financial Aid .... Mrs. H. WEISS
10 Bursar .... Rabbi M. GELFAND

Bais Medrash Zicron Meir (A)

1500 Vermont Ave, Lakewood NJ 08701
County: Ocean Identification: 667259
Telephone: (732) 370-1560 Carnegie Class: Not Classified
FAX Number: (732) 363-7864 Calendar System: Semester
Established: 2013 Annual Undergrad Tuition & Fees: $14,900
Enrollment: 38 Male
Affiliation or Control: Independent Non-Profit IRS Status: 501(c)3
Highest Offering: First Talmudic Degree
Program: Religious Emphasis
Accreditation: @RABN

01 CEO .... Zev MINTZ
10 CFO .... Nissim BASALA
37 Dir of Stdnt Financial Aid/Registr .... Shimshon AMSEL

Bergen Community College (B)

400 Paramus Road, Paramus NJ 07652-1595
County: Bergen FICE Identification: 004736
Unit ID: 183743
Telephone: (201) 447-7100 Carnegie Class: Assoc/Pub-S-SC
FAX Number: (201) 447-9042 Calendar System: Semester
URL: www.bergen.edu
Established: 1965 Annual Undergrad Tuition & Fees (In-District): $4,278
Enrollment: 15,651 Coed
Affiliation or Control: State/Local IRS Status: 501(c)3
Highest Offering: Associate Degree
Program: Occupational; 2-Year Principally Bachelor's Creditable
Accreditation: M, ADNUR, COARC, DH, DMS, MAC, RAD, RTT, SURGT

01 President .... Dr. B. Kaye WALTER
05 Vice President of Academic Affairs .... Dr. William MULLANEY
32 Vice President Student Services .... Dr. Naydeen GONZALEZ-DE JESUS
09 Vice Pres of Inst Effectiveness .... Dr. Yun KIM
50 Dean Business/Arts & Social Sci .... Dr. Carmen MARTINEZ-LOPEZ
79 Dean Humanities/English & Language .... Vacant
76 Dean Health Professions .... Dr. Susan BARNARD
81 Dean Science/Math & Technology .... Dr. Pascal J. RICATTO
51 Dean of Continuing Education .... Ms. Christine GILLESPIE
08 Dean Library Services .... Vacant
35 Dean of Student Affairs at Ciarco . Ms. Denise JERMAN LIGUORI
35 Dean of Student Support Services .... Ms. Jennifer REYES
15 Executive Director of Human Resourc .... Mr. James MILLER
18 Actg Mnging Director Physical Plant .... Mr. Samuel JOHN
19 VP Facil Opers/Plng & Pub Safety .... Mr. William CORCORAN
13 Executive Dir of Info Technolgy .... Ms. Sharyne MILLER
06 Mnging Dir Registration & Records .... Ms. Jacqueline OTTEY
88 Mnging Dir Community/Cultural Affs .... Mr. Peter LEDONNE
101 Exec Asst Board of Trustees/Pre .... Ms. Maria FERRARA
29 Managing Dir of Alumni Affairs .... Vacant
37 Mnging Dir Fin Ops/Stdnt Assistance .... Ms. Caroline OFODILE
102 Exec Dir Foundation/Development .... Vacant
25 Dir Grants Admin/Inst Effectiveness .... Dr. William YAKOWICZ
96 Director of Purchasing & Services .... Ms. Barbara HAMILTON-GOLDEN
26 Managing Dir of Public Relations .... Mr. Lawrence HLAVENKA
04 Exec Assistant to the President .... Dr. Ursula DANIELS

Berkeley College (C)

44 Rifle Camp Road, Woodland Park NJ 07424-3367
County: Passaic FICE Identification: 007502
Unit ID: 183789
Telephone: (973) 278-5400 Carnegie Class: Spec/Bus
FAX Number: (973) 278-0282 Calendar System: Quarter
URL: www.berkeleycollege.edu
Established: 1931 Annual Undergrad Tuition & Fees: $24,300
Enrollment: 3,659 Coed
Affiliation or Control: Proprietary IRS Status: Proprietary
Highest Offering: Master's
Program: Business Emphasis
Accreditation: M, MAC, SURGT

00 Chairman of the Board .... Mr. Kevin L. LUING
01 President .... Mr. Michael J. SMITH
04 Special Assistant to the President .... Dr. Rose Mary HEALY
04 Special Assistant to the President .... Ms. Katherine DELGADO
05 Provost .... Dr. Mary MCDONOUGH
84 SVP Enrollment Management .... Ms. Diane RECINOS
10 SVP Finance & Administration .... Mr. Robert HERZOG
45 VP Planning & Chief of Staff .... Vacant
43 VP & Chief Compliance Officer .... Mr. William BRANDT
26 Chief Marketing Officer .... Mr. William DIMASI
13 Chief Information Officer .... Mr. Leonard DE BOTTON
86 SVP Government Relations NJ .... Ms. Teri DUDA
86 VP Government Relations NY .... Mr. Gbubemi OKOTIEURO
88 VP Academic Advisement .... Ms. Liz BARRETT
08 VP Library Services .... Ms. Marlene DOTY
32 VP Student Development/Campus Life .... Dr. Dallas REED
36 VP Career Services .... Mr. Brian MAHER
07 VP Enrollment .... Vacant
37 VP Financial Aid .... Mr. Howard LESLIE
21 VP Budget & Student Accounts .... Ms. Eileen LOFTUS-BERLIN
85 VP International Division .... Ms. Cynthia C. MARCHESE
18 VP Operations .... Mr. Mark WAGENER
50 Dean School of Business .... Dr. Beth CASTIGLIA
76 Interim Dean School Health Studies ... Ms. Elizabeth FITZGERALD
49 Dean School of Liberal Arts .... Dr. Don KIEFFER
107 Dean School of Professional Studies .... Ms. Lenore MOLEE
20 Associate Provost Academic Affairs .... Dr. Judith KORNBERG
06 Associate Provost & Registrar .... Ms. Gail OKUN
106 Assistant Provost Online .... Ms. Carol SMITH
88 Dean Academic Support .... Dr. Gerald IACULLO
108 AVP Institutional Effectiveness .... Dr. Rachel FESTER
31 AVP Communications & Ext Relations .... Ms. Angela HARRINGTON
19 AVP Public Safety .... Mr. William ORTMAN
27 Director Media Relations .... Ms. Ilene GREENFIELD
41 Director Athletics .... Mr. Andrew DESTEPHANO
29 Director Alumni Relations .... Ms. Jennifer PORTER
09 Director of Institutional Research .... Ms. Rebecca J. DRENNEN

Beth Medrash Govoha (D)

617 Sixth Street, Lakewood NJ 08701-2797
County: Ocean FICE Identification: 007947
Unit ID: 183804
Telephone: (732) 367-1060 Carnegie Class: Spec/Faith
FAX Number: (732) 367-7487 Calendar System: Semester
URL: www.bmg.edu
Established: 1943 Annual Undergrad Tuition & Fees: $19,240
Enrollment: 6,721 Male
Affiliation or Control: Independent Non-Profit IRS Status: 501(c)3
Highest Offering: Beyond Master's But Less Than Doctorate
Program: Teacher Preparatory; Professional
Accreditation: RABN

01 President/Chief Executive Officer .... Rabbi Aaron KOTLER
05 Chairman Academic Council .... Rabbi A. Malkiel KOTLER
10 VP Finance/Technology Compliance .... Mr. Isaac LEVINE
43 VP Finance/Corporate/Legal Affairs .... Rabbi Eli KUPERMAN
11 Vice President Admin/Campus Life .... Rabbi Yitzchok S. KOTLER
33 Dean of Students .... Rabbi Mattisyahu SALOMON
58 Dean of Graduate Studies .... Rabbi Yisroel NEUMAN
30 Vice President of Fundraising .... Rabbi Mordechai HERSKOWITZ
88 Senior Executive Director .... Rabbi Yaakov APPLEGRAD
86 Director Government Affairs .... Mrs. Chanie JACOBOWITZ
06 Registrar .... Rabbi Jacob BURSZTYN
07 Director of Admissions .... Rabbi Avraham FEUER
08 Director Library/Research Programs .... Rabbi Benjamin SPIEGEL
36 Director of Field Services .... Rabbi Jacob SHULMAN
39 Director of Residence Halls .... Rabbi Avrohom COLMAN

Bloomfield College (E)

467 Franklin Street, Bloomfield NJ 07003-3425
County: Essex FICE Identification: 002597
Unit ID: 183822
Telephone: (973) 748-9000 Carnegie Class: Bac/A&S
FAX Number: (973) 743-3998 Calendar System: Semester
URL: www.bloomfield.edu
Established: 1868 Annual Undergrad Tuition & Fees: $27,800
Enrollment: 2,008 Coed
Affiliation or Control: Presbyterian Church (U.S.A.) IRS Status: 501(c)3
Highest Offering: Master's
Program: Liberal Arts And General; Teacher Preparatory; Professional
Accreditation: M, NURSE, TEAC

01 President .... Richard A. LEVAO
10 Vice Pres of Finance/Admin .... Howard BUXBAUM
04 Administrative Asst to President .... Christina NOLAN
05 Vice President Academic Affairs .... Tresmaine GRIMES
07 VP Enrollment Management/Admission .... Adam CASTRO
32 VP Student Affairs/Dean of Students .... Patrick J. LAMY
30 VP for Advancement .... Jacqueline BARTLEY
88 VP Inst Intl Training/Prof Studies .... Peter JEONG
21 AVP for Finance and Administration .... William A. MCDONALD
06 Registrar and Director of Advising .... Annette RAYMOND
09 Director Instnl Research/Assessment .... Eugene W. MULLER
20 Associate Dean for Faculty .... Carolyn I. SPIES
79 Chair Div of Humanities .... Angela CONRAD
83 Chair Div Social/Behavioral Science .... Daniel SKINNER
66 Chair Div of Nursing .... Neddie SERRA
81 Chair Div of Natural Science/Math .... Jim MURPHY
57 Chair Div Creative Arts Technology .... Nancy BACCI
50 Chair Div Accounting/Business/CIS .... Robert COLLMIER
53 Chair Div of Education .... Nora KRIEGER
88 Assoc Dean Inst Educ Support Svcs .... Leonard ROBERTS
08 Library Director .... Danilo H. FIGUEREDO
13 Director of Information Services .... Erzsebet FELSOVALYI
36 Director of Career Services .... Vacant
37 Director of Financial Aid .... Breanne SIMKIN
35 Associate Dean Student Development .... Rose MITCHELL
15 Assoc Director Human Resources .... Susan DACEY
18 Supervisor of Buildings & Grounds .... Jack V. MCGRANE
07 Coord Intl Admissions/Student Svcs .... Jamilah MOUDIAB
44 Dir Annual Fund/Alumni Innovation .... Vacant
38 Director Personal Counseling .... Nicole PALAGANO
26 Director Public Rels/Advancemnt Mkt .... Andrew MEES
42 Int Dir Spirtual Life/Col Chaplain .... Rev. Terri OFORI
88 Director Teacher Education .... Mary PORCELLI
41 Director of Athletics .... Sheila WOOTEN
88 Director Center Academic Develop .... Heather SHPIRO
19 Director of Security .... Jack CORTEZ
39 Director Res Educ & Housing .... Nicole FAISON
105 Webmaster .... Kyle RIVERS
24 Director of Media Center .... Barbara ISACSON
88 Director Office for Instnl Tech .... Yifeng BAI
40 Store Manager .... Roberta STEVENSON

Brookdale Community College (F)

Newman Springs Road, Lincroft NJ 07738-1597
County: Monmouth FICE Identification: 008404
Unit ID: 183859
Telephone: (732) 842-1900 Carnegie Class: Assoc/Pub-S-SC
FAX Number: (732) 224-2242 Calendar System: Other
URL: www.brookdalecc.edu
Established: 1967 Annual Undergrad Tuition & Fees (In-District): $4,566
Enrollment: 14,144 Coed
Affiliation or Control: State/Local IRS Status: 501(c)3
Highest Offering: Associate Degree
Program: Occupational; 2-Year Principally Bachelor's Creditable
Accreditation: M, ACFEI, ADNUR, CAHIIM, COARC, MLTAD, #RAD

01 President .... Dr. Maureen MURPHY
03 Executive Vice President .... Dr. Matthew REED
10 Vice Pres Finance/Operations .... Ms. Maureen LAWRENCE
04 Executive Assistant to President .... Ms. Louise M. HORGAN
46 Vice Pres Plng/Dev/Govt & Comm Rels .... Vacant
84 Dean Enrollment Dev/Student Affairs .... Dr. David STOUT
15 Dean Human Resources .... Ms. Patricia SENSI
08 Executive Director Library .... Dr. William BURNS
45 Dean Plng & Institutional Effective .... Dr. Nancy KEGELMAN
27 Dir Communications & Public Rels .... Ms. Avis MCMILLON
102 Exec Dir Foundation/Alumni Affs .... Mr. Timothy ZEISS
18 Exec Dir Facilities Plng/Engnrng .... Vacant
32 Dir Student Affairs/Support Svcs .... Dr. David STOUT
37 Director of Financial Aid .... Ms. Stephanie FITZSIMMONS
25 Director Grants & Institutional Dev ..... Ms. Laura V. QAISSAUNEE
38 Director Student Services .... Dr. Stephen A. CURTO
06 Registrar .... Ms. Kimberly HEUSER
09 Dir of Institutional Research/Evalu .... Dr. Laura LONGO
26 Dir of Marketing/Creative Services .... Ms. Laurie BENDER
96 Director Material & Printing Svcs .... Vacant
28 Mgr Diversity/Inclusion/Compliance .... Ms. Sondra CANNON

Brookdale Community College Western Monmouth Branch Campus (G)

3680 US Highway 9 South, Freehold NJ 07728
Telephone: (732) 780-0020 Identification: 770125
Accreditation: &M

† Branch campus of Brookdale Community College, Lincroft, NJ.

Caldwell University (H)

120 Bloomfield Avenue, Caldwell NJ 07006-5310
County: Essex FICE Identification: 002598
Unit ID: 183910
Telephone: (973) 618-3000 Carnegie Class: Master's M
FAX Number: (973) 618-3300 Calendar System: Semester
URL: www.caldwell.edu
Established: 1939 Annual Undergrad Tuition & Fees: $29,950
Enrollment: 2,182 Coed
Affiliation or Control: Roman Catholic IRS Status: 501(c)3
Highest Offering: Doctorate
Program: Liberal Arts And General; Teacher Preparatory
Accreditation: M, ACBSP, CACREP, NURSE, TEAC

01 President .... Dr. Nancy BLATTNER
05 Vice President for Academic Affairs .... Dr. Barbara CHESLER
10 Vice President for Finance & Admin .... Mr. Jack T. RAINEY
15 VP Institutional Effectiveness .... Mrs. Sheila N. O'ROURKE
32 Vice President for Student Affairs .... Sr. Kathleen TUITE
84 Vice President for Enrollment/Comm ..... Mr. Joseph J. POSILLICO
30 Vice Pres Development/Alumni Affs .... Mr. Kevin BOYLE
50 Associate Dean Business Division .... Dr. Bernard C. O'ROURKE
53 Associate Dean Education Division .... Dr. Joan MORIARTY
35 Director International Student Svcs .... Mr. Maulin JOSHI
44 Director Development .... Ms. Beth GORAB
29 Director of Gift Planning .... Ms. Kathleen BUSE
06 Registrar & Director Inst Research .... Mr. Ian K. WHITE
08 College Librarian .... Ms. Nancy BECKER
07 Asst Vice President Enrollment .... Mr. Stephen QUINN
58 Director Graduate Studies .... Ms. Vilma MUELLER
88 Assoc Dean External Partnerships .... Vacant
38 Director of Counseling .... Ms. Robin DAVENPORT
39 Director Residence Life .... Ms. Crystal LOPEZ
13 Exec Director Information Techn .... Mr. Donald O'HAGAN
36 Dir Career Plng & Development .... Ms. Geraldine PERRET
37 Director Financial Aid .... Ms. Eileen FELSKE
42 Chaplain .... Fr. Albert J. BERNER
41 Executive Director of Athletics .... Mr. Mark A. CORINO
88 Director Technical Support Services .... Vacant
26 Dir Media Relations and Advertising .... Ms. Colette LIDDY
19 Director Campus Safety .... Mr. Glenn GATES
91 Director Administrative Technology .... Mr. David BOHNY
16 Director of Human Resources .... Mrs. Michelle STAUSS
35 Director Student Engagement ...... Mr. Timothy KESSLER-CLEARY

20 Associate Academic Officer .... Dr. Victoria UKACHUKWU
106 Dir Online Education/E-learning .... Ms. Soheila KOBLER
108 Director Assessment .... Mrs. Susan HAYES

Camden County College (A)

PO Box 200, Blackwood NJ 08012-0200
County: Camden FICE Identification: 006865
Unit ID: 183938
Telephone: (856) 227-7200 Carnegie Class: Assoc/Pub-S-MC
FAX Number: (856) 374-4894 Calendar System: Semester
URL: www.camdencc.edu
Established: 1967 Annual Undergrad Tuition & Fees (In-District): $4,320
Enrollment: 12,051 Coed
Affiliation or Control: State/Local IRS Status: 501(c)3
Highest Offering: Associate Degree
Program: Occupational; 2-Year Principally Bachelor's Creditable
Accreditation: M, CAHIIM, DA, DH, DIETT, MLTAD, OPD

01 President .... Dr. Raymond YANNUZZI
03 Executive Vice President .... Mr. Donald BORDEN
05 Vice Pres Academic Affairs .... Dr. Margaret HAMILTON
30 VP for Institutional Advancement .... Mr. William THOMPSON
10 Vice Pres for Finance & Planning .... Ms. Helen ANTONAKAKIS
41 Athletic Director .... Mr. Peter DILORENZO
15 Executive Director Human Resources .... Ms. Rose COSTON-MCHUGH
26 Dean Communications/Enroll Dev .... Ms. Rosemary SCHAMP
21 Director Business Office .... Mr. Maris KUKAINIS
06 Dir Student System Records .... Ms. Bunny KOHL
08 Library Director .... Ms. Barbara LAYNOR
37 Director of Financial Aid .... Ms. Felicia BRYANT
36 Acting Director Testing .... Mr. Daniel MCMASTERS
09 Actg Dean Inst Research/Plng/ Grants .... Dr. Rebecca FIDLER-SHEPPARD
18 Exec Dir Safety and Facilities .... Mr. Edward CARNEY
84 Exec Dean Enrollment/Student Svcs .... Dr. James CANONICA
07 Dir Admissions/Registration Svcs .... Mr. Steve D'AMBROSIO
12 Exec Dean William G Rohrer Center ... Dr. Robert KACZOROWSKI
81 Dean of Math & Science .... Dr. Susan CHOI
66 Dean Nursing/Health Sci/Human Svcs .... Dr. Anne M. MCGINLEY
50 Dean Div Business/Comptr/Tech Stds .... Dr. Melvin ROBERTS
12 Exec Dean Camden City Campus .... Mr. Gary DIVENS

Camden County College Camden City Campus (B)

200 N Broadway, Camden NJ 08102-1185
Telephone: (856) 338-1817 Identification: 770126
Accreditation: &M

† Branch campus of Camden County College, Blackwood, NJ.

Centenary College (C)

400 Jefferson Street, Hackettstown NJ 07840-2100
County: Warren FICE Identification: 002599
Unit ID: 183974
Telephone: (908) 852-1400 Carnegie Class: Master's M
FAX Number: (908) 850-9508 Calendar System: Semester
URL: www.centenarycollege.edu
Established: 1867 Annual Undergrad Tuition & Fees: $30,942
Enrollment: 2,318 Coed
Affiliation or Control: Independent Non-Profit IRS Status: 501(c)3
Highest Offering: Master's
Program: Liberal Arts And General; Teacher Preparatory
Accreditation: M, IACBE, SW, TEAC

01 President .... Dr. Barbara-Jayne LEWTHWAITE
05 Provost & Chief Academic Officer .... Dr. James PATTERSON
10 Chief Operating Officer .... Mr. Roger ANDERSON
26 Sr VP College Relations .... Ms. Diane P. FINNAN
07 VP for Enrollment & Sch Prof Stds .... Dr. Dierdre LETSON
18 Assoc Vice Pres for Operations .... Mr. Todd MILLER
31 Dean Community & College Affairs .... Ms. Nancy PAFFENDORF
09 Dean of Inst Research/Assessment .... Mr. Robert MILLER
35 Sr Dir Student Engagement .... Ms. Tiffany KUSHNER
32 Dean of Students .... Ms. Kerry MULLINS
06 Registrar/Academic Dean .... Dr. Thomas BRUNNER
08 Director Taylor Memorial Library .... Mr. Timothy DOMICK
36 Director Career Development Center .... Mr. Joshua D. WALKER
15 Chief Human Resources Officer .... Ms. Virginia GALDIERI
41 Director of Athletics .... Ms. Billie Jo BLACKWELL
19 Director of Security .... Mr. Leonard CUNZ
38 Director of Counseling Center .... Ms. Lorna FARMER
29 Exec Dir of Alumni Engagement .... Ms. Deana CYNAR
13 Director Technology Services .... Mr. Matthew KELLY
40 Manager of the Bookstore .... Mr. Dave BOURDETTE

Chamberlain College of Nursing-North Brunswick (D)

630 US Highway One, North Brunswick NJ 08902
Telephone: (732) 875-1300 Identification: 770850
Accreditation: &NH, NURSE

† Branch campus of Chamberlain College of Nursing-Addison, Addison, IL.

The College of New Jersey (E)

2000 Pennington Road, Ewing NJ 08628-1104
County: Mercer FICE Identification: 002642
Unit ID: 187134
Telephone: (609) 771-1855 Carnegie Class: Master's L
FAX Number: (609) 637-5191 Calendar System: Semester
URL: www.tcnj.edu
Established: 1855 Annual Undergrad Tuition & Fees (In-State): $15,446
Enrollment: 7,409 Coed
Affiliation or Control: State IRS Status: 501(c)3
Highest Offering: Master's
Program: Liberal Arts And General; Teacher Preparatory; Professional
Accreditation: M, BUS, CACREP, CS, ENG, MUS, NURSE, TED

01 President .... Dr. R. Barbara GITENSTEIN
05 Provost/VP Academic Affairs .... Dr. Jacqueline TAYLOR
11 Vice Pres for Administration .... Mr. Curt HEURING
10 Treasurer .... Mr. Lloyd RICKETTS
43 General Counsel .... Mr. Thomas MAHONEY
30 Vice Pres Advancement .... Mr. John DONOHUE
32 Vice President Student Affairs .... Dr. Amy HECHT
15 Vice Pres Human Resources .... Dr. Gregory POGUE
84 Vice Pres Enrollment Management .... Ms. Lisa ANGELONI
100 Chief of Staff/Secy to Board .... Ms. Heather FEHN
18 Assoc VP Facilities & Admin Svcs .... Ms. Kathryn LEVERTON
44 Assoc Vice President of Development .... Mr. Charles WRIGHT
35 Asst VP for Student Affairs/Engage .... Ms. Elizabeth BAPASOLA
35 Asst Vice Pres Student Affairs .... Ms. Angela CHONG
26 Assoc VP for College Relations .... Ms. Stacy SCHUSTER
20 Vice Provost Grad/Profes/Cntng Educ .... Dr. Chandru RAJAM
57 Dean School of The Arts & Comm .... Dr. John LAUGHTON
50 Dean School of Business .... Dr. William KEEP
79 Int Dean Sch Humanities/Soc Sci .... Dr. John SISKO
53 Dean School of Education .... Dr. Jeffrey PASSE
54 Dean School of Engineering .... Dr. Steven SCHREINER
66 Dean Nursing/Health/Exercise Scienc .... Dr. Carole KENNER
81 Dean School of Science .... Dr. Jeffrey OSBORN
58 Dir Grad & Intersession Programs .... Dr. Susan HYDRO
21 Controller .... Ms. Catherine HECKMAN
37 Exec Dir of Student Fin Assistance .... Mr. Wil CASAINE
09 Asst Provost Ctr for Inst Effective .... Dr. Mosen AURYAN
41 Director of Athletics .... Dr. Sharon BEVERLY
29 Director Alumni Affairs .... Mr. John CASTALDO
102 Assoc VP Comm/Mktg/Brand Mgmt .... Mr. David MUHA
18 Director of Campus Construction .... Mr. William RUDEAU
23 Assoc Director for Health Services ...... Ms. Janice VERMEYCHUK
06 Exec Director Records/Registration .... Mr. Frank COOPER
19 Chief of Police/Dir Campus Police .... Chief John COLLINS
21 Exec Dir Procure/Fiscal Planning .... Mr. Mark MEHLER
28 Assoc VP/Chief Diversity Officer .... Ms. Kerry TILLETT
07 Director of Admissions .... Ms. Grecia MONTERO
36 Director Career Center .... Ms. Debra KELLY
96 Asst Director of Purchasing .... Ms. Kristine D'APOLITO

College of Saint Elizabeth (F)

2 Convent Road, Morristown NJ 07960-6989
County: Morris FICE Identification: 002600
Unit ID: 186618
Telephone: (973) 290-4000 Carnegie Class: Master's L
FAX Number: (973) 290-4488 Calendar System: Semester
URL: www.cse.edu
Established: 1899 Annual Undergrad Tuition & Fees: $31,679
Enrollment: 1,411 Coed
Affiliation or Control: Roman Catholic IRS Status: 501(c)3
Highest Offering: Doctorate
Program: Liberal Arts And General; Teacher Preparatory; Business Emphasis
Accreditation: M, DIETD, DIETI, NUR, TEAC

01 President .... Dr. Helen STREUBERT
05 VP for Academic Affairs .... Dr. Monique GUILLORY
32 VP Student Life .... Ms. Katherine BUCK
10 Interim VP Finance/Admin/Treasurer .... Mr. Neil BUCKLEY
30 Vice Pres Institutional Advancement .... Ms. Sally CLEARY
84 VP Enrollment Mangement .... Mr. Alexander SCOTT
21 Controller .... Vacant
07 Dean of Admission .... Ms. Donna TATARKA
32 Director of Student Services .... Ms. Jane BOURHILL
06 Registrar .... Ms. Susan ASTARITA
09 Director Institutional Research .... Dr. Louise MURRAY
08 Director of Library .... Ms. Amira UNVER
42 Campus Minister .... Ms. Abigail CIMORELLI
18 Director of Facilities & Security .... Mr. Frank A. NEGLIA
37 Director of Financial Aid .... Ms. Jacqueline WEISKOPFF
26 Director Marketing/Communications .... Ms. Maryann MATLOCK
22 Director EOF Program .... Mr. Clifford WOODWARD
36 Director Career Services .... Ms. Teri CORSO
38 Director of Counseling .... Ms. Zsuzsanna NAGY
88 Dir Volunteerism & Svc Learning .... Ms. Alaina TURSE
35 Director of Student Activities .... Vacant
41 Director of Athletics .... Ms. Juliene SIMPSON
44 Director of Annual Fund .... Ms. Tanya SORCE
24 Director Media Services .... Mr. Ronald LONEKER
29 Exec Director Alumni Relations .... Ms. Debbie MARTIN
15 Director Human Resources .... Mr. Anthony ROWE
85 Director Intl/Multicultural Affairs .... Ms. Lenee WOODSON
40 College Store Manager .... Ms. Amy HAUSMAN
102 Dir Corp Foundation/Corp Relations .... Ms. Janice HILL
105 Webmaster .... Mr. David B. RABINOWITZ
108 Asst Dean of Assessment .... Ms. Michele YURECKO
04 Administrative Asst to President .... Ms. MaryAnn RICCIOTTI
13 Chief Info Technology Officer .... Ms. Margie ROHR
28 Director of Diversity .... Ms. Trish FUENTES
50 Dean of Business .... Dr. Joseph CICCONE

County College of Morris (G)

214 Center Grove Road, Randolph NJ 07869-2086
County: Morris FICE Identification: 007729
Unit ID: 184180
Telephone: (973) 328-5000 Carnegie Class: Assoc/Pub-S-SC
FAX Number: (973) 328-1282 Calendar System: Semester
URL: www.ccm.edu
Established: 1965 Annual Undergrad Tuition & Fees (In-District): $4,570
Enrollment: 8,096 Coed
Affiliation or Control: State/Local IRS Status: 501(c)3
Highest Offering: Associate Degree
Program: Occupational; 2-Year Principally Bachelor's Creditable
Accreditation: M, ACBSP, ADNUR, COARC, ENGT, RAD

01 President .... Dr. Edward J. YAW
05 Vice President of Academic Affairs .... Dr. Dwight L. SMITH
10 Vice President of Business/Finance .... Ms. Karen VANDERHOOF
32 VP of Student Development .... Dr. Bette M. SIMMONS
30 Exec Dir Col Advancement/Planning .... Mr. Joseph VITALE
15 Dir Human Resources & Labor Rels .... Mr. Thomas BURK
09 Director Inst Research & Planning .... Ms. Phebe LACAY
21 Director Budget & Business Services .... Mr. John YOUNG
25 Director Resource Development .... Dr. Kevin KEEFE
07 Admissions Officer .... Mr. Eugene SOLTYS
37 Director Financial Aid .... Mr. Harvey WILLIS
06 Registrar .... Ms. Laura Lee BOWENS
26 Chief Public Relations Officer .... Ms. Kathleen BRUNET EAGAN
29 Director Alumni Office .... Ms. Barbara CAPSOURAS
13 Director Information Systems .... Mr. Roger FLAHIVE
08 Director of Library Services .... Ms. Heather CRAVEN
36 Director Career Svcs/Coop Education .... Ms. Denise SCHMIDT
38 Counseling Services Coordinator .... Ms. Janique CAFFIE
79 Dean Liberal Arts .... Mr. Keith SMITH
76 Dean Health/Natural Sciences .... Ms. Monica MARASKA
81 Dean Business/Math/Engr/Technology .... Mr. Patrick ENRIGHT
19 Director Security & Safety .... Mr. Harvey JACKSON
41 Director Athletics .... Mr. Jack SULLIVAN
23 Health Services Coordinator .... Ms. Elizabeth HOBAN
18 Director of Plant & Maintenance .... Mr. Joseph PONTURO
96 Director of Purchasing .... Ms. Joanne KEARNS
40 Bookstore Manager .... Vacant

Cumberland County College (H)

3322 College Drive, PO Box 1500, Vineland NJ 08362-1500
County: Cumberland FICE Identification: 002601
Unit ID: 184205
Telephone: (856) 691-8600 Carnegie Class: Assoc/Pub-R-M
FAX Number: (856) 690-0812 Calendar System: Semester
URL: www.cccnj.edu
Established: 1963 Annual Undergrad Tuition & Fees (In-District): $4,200
Enrollment: 3,844 Coed
Affiliation or Control: State/Local IRS Status: 501(c)3
Highest Offering: Associate Degree
Program: Occupational; 2-Year Principally Bachelor's Creditable
Accreditation: M, ADNUR, RAD

01 Interim President .... Dr. Shelly O. SCHNEIDER
05 VP Academic Affairs .... Dr. Jacqueline GALBIATI
10 Vice President Finance & Admin Svcs .... Dr. Mark D. HARRIS
30 Exec Dir Grant Develop/Trustee Rels .... Ms. Anne M. BERGAMO
21 Comptroller .... Ms. Sherri L. WELCH
07 Director of Admissions/Registration ... Ms. Anne M. DALY-EIMER
32 Sr Exec Dir Student Svcs .... Dr. Mary Ann WESTERFIELD
08 Director Library Services .... Ms. Patti A. SCHMID
20 Ex Dir Ctr for Acad & Student Succ .... Dr. Maud FRIED-GOODNIGHT
26 Director Comm/Marketing .... Mr. Keith WASSERMAN
29 Exec Dir Foundation & Alumni .... Ms. Sue A. PERRY
37 Director Student Financial Aid .... Mr. Maurice THOMAS
50 Dean Business/Educ/Soc Sci .... Dr. Lynn LICHTENBERGER
103 Exec Dir Workforce & Cmty Educ .... Vacant
81 Dean STEM/Health .... Dr. Godwin CHUNGAG
57 Dean Arts & Humanities .... Mr. James PICCONE
100 Assistant to the President .... Ms. Anne M. BERGAMO
15 Executive Director Human Resources .... Ms. Rosemarie FISCUS
72 Exec Dir IT Services .... Mr. Bernie CASTRO
18 Director Facilities & Grounds .... Mr. Brian EWAN
96 Purchasing Agent .... Ms. Cynthia OSTER
09 Exec Dir Assessment/Plng/Research .... Vacant

DeVry University - North Brunswick Campus (I)

630 US Highway One, North Brunswick NJ 08902-3362
Telephone: (732) 729-3960 FICE Identification: 009228
Accreditation: &NH, CAHIIM, ENGT, NDT

† Regional accreditation is carried under the parent institution in Downers Grove, IL.

Drew University (J)

36 Madison Avenue, Madison NJ 07940-1493
County: Morris FICE Identification: 002603
Unit ID: 184348
Telephone: (973) 408-3000 Carnegie Class: Bac/A&S
FAX Number: N/A Calendar System: 4/1/4
URL: www.drew.edu
Established: 1866 Annual Undergrad Tuition & Fees: $45,552
Enrollment: 2,113 Coed
Affiliation or Control: Independent Non-Profit IRS Status: 501(c)3

Highest Offering: Doctorate
Program: Liberal Arts And General; Professional
Accreditation: M, TEAC, THEOL

01 President Dr. MaryAnn BAENNINGER
05 Chief Academic Officer Dr. Christopher TAYLOR
30 Vice Pres Advanc/Alumni Affairs Dr. Kenneth ALEXO
10 Vice Pres Finance/Business Affairs Mr. Michael GROENER
49 Dean of College of Liberal Arts Dr. Christopher TAYLOR
73 Dean Theological School Dr. Javier VIERA
08 Interim Director of Libraries Dr. Linda CONNORS
32 Vice President Student Life Dr. Sara WALDRON
26 Chief Communications Officer Ms. Kira POPLOWSKI
15 Director of Human Resources Ms. Terri DEMAREST
22 Title IX Coordinator Ms. Rachel PEREIRA
90 Dir Instructional Technology Svcs Dr. Gamin BARTLE
21 Controller Ms. Renee LISCHIN
96 Asst Director Purchasing Ms. Marie ZACCAGNINI
18 Director Facilities Operations Mr. Michael KOPAS
37 Director Finan Assistance Ms. Colby MCCARTHY
19 Director Public Safety Mr. Robert LUCID
23 Director Health Services Ms. Joyce MAGLIONE
35 Director Student Activities Ms. Michelle BRISSON
38 Director Counseling Services Dr. Jim MANDALA
07 Director Theological Admissions Mr. Kevin D. MILLER
07 Director Graduate Admissions Ms. Corinn MCBRIDE
58 Dean of Casperson Sch Grad Stdy Dr. Robert READY
42 University Chaplain Rev. Tanya Lynn BENNETT
09 Dir Institutional Research Mr. Alex MCCLUNG
84 Director Enrollment Management Mr. Robert MASSA
41 Director Athletics Mr. Jason FEIN
06 Registrar Ms. Leslie SUTTON-SMITH
40 Manager Bookstore Ms. Liz GALLO
04 Administrative Asst to President Ms. Kathleen SUTHERLAND
100 Chief of Staff Ms. Marti WINER
104 Director Study Abroad Ms. Stacy FISCHER
105 Director Web Services Mr. Tryon EGGLESTON
13 Chief Info Technology Officer (CIO) Mr. E. Axel LARSSON
25 Chief Contracts/Grants Admin Ms. Linda DETITTA
29 Director Alumni Relations Mr. John HOLDEN
36 Director Student Placement Ms. Suzanne CERAVOLO
43 Dir Legal Services/General Counsel Mr. William BROWN

Eastern International College (A)

684 Newark Avenue, Jersey City NJ 07306
County: Hudson FICE Identification: 031226
Unit ID: 421878
Telephone: (201) 216-9901 Carnegie Class: Assoc/PrivFP
FAX Number: (201) 533-1027 Calendar System: Semester
URL: www.eicollege.edu
Established: 1990 Annual Undergrad Tuition & Fees: $17,650
Enrollment: 231 Coed
Affiliation or Control: Proprietary IRS Status: Proprietary
Highest Offering: Baccalaureate
Program: Occupational; 2-Year Principally Bachelor's Creditable; Technical Emphasis
Accreditation: ACCSC, DH

01 President Mr. Bashir MOHSEN
05 Vice President of Academic Affairs Dr. Mustafa MUSTAFA
06 Registrar Mrs. Soha ELSHICK
10 Chief Business Officer Ms. Karen LABUE
36 Director Student Placement Mr. John HUNTER
37 Director Student Financial Aid MS. Kinga GIZYNSKA
53 Dean of Education Mrs. Kimberly MCDONALD

Eastern International College- Belleville Campus (B)

251 Washington Avenue, Belleville NJ 07109
Telephone: (973) 751-9051 Identification: 770580
Accreditation: ACCSC

† Branch campus of Eastern International College, Jersey City, NJ.

Eastwick College (C)

250 Moore Street, Hackensack NJ 07601
County: Bergen Identification: 667131
Unit ID: 183488
Telephone: (201) 488-9400 Carnegie Class: Not Classified
FAX Number: (201) 488-1007 Calendar System: Quarter
URL: www.eastwick.edu
Established: 1985 Annual Undergrad Tuition & Fees: $22,777
Enrollment: 375 Coed
Affiliation or Control: Proprietary IRS Status: Proprietary
Highest Offering: Associate Degree
Program: Occupational
Accreditation: ACICS

01 President Thomas M. EASTWICK

Eastwick College (D)

103 Park Avenue, Nutley NJ 07110
County: Essex FICE Identification: 020923
Unit ID: 185721
Telephone: (973) 661-0600 Carnegie Class: Not Classified
FAX Number: (973) 661-2954 Calendar System: Quarter
URL: www.eastwick.edu
Established: 2014 Annual Undergrad Tuition & Fees: $15,413
Enrollment: 321 Coed
Affiliation or Control: Proprietary IRS Status: Proprietary
Highest Offering: Associate Degree
Program: Occupational
Accreditation: ACICS

01 President Thomas EASTWICK
11 Vice Pres of Operations Bhavna TAILOR
05 Dean of Academics Sameh FARAGALLA

Eastwick College (E)

10 South Franklin Turnpike, Ramsey NJ 07446
County: Bergen FICE Identification: 020537
Unit ID: 184959
Telephone: (201) 327-8877 Carnegie Class: Assoc/PrivFP
FAX Number: (201) 327-9054 Calendar System: Other
URL: www.eastwick.edu
Established: 1968 Annual Undergrad Tuition & Fees: $17,039
Enrollment: 865 Coed
Affiliation or Control: Proprietary IRS Status: Proprietary
Highest Offering: Associate Degree
Program: Occupational; 2-Year Principally Bachelor's Creditable; Nursing Emphasis
Accreditation: ACICS, CVT, OTA, SURGT

01 Corporate Systems Administrator Antonio JEREZ
03 Executive Vice President Rafael CASTILLA
05 Vice President Academic Affairs Joyce TRAINA
07 Vice President Admissions Vacant
32 Dean of Students Bobby DAVIES
37 Director of Financial Aid Christy DELAGUERRA

Essex County College (F)

303 University Avenue, Newark NJ 07102-1798
County: Essex FICE Identification: 007107
Unit ID: 184481
Telephone: (973) 877-3000 Carnegie Class: Assoc/Pub-U-MC
FAX Number: (973) 877-3044 Calendar System: Other
URL: www.essex.edu
Established: 1966 Annual Undergrad Tuition & Fees (In-District): $4,212
Enrollment: 11,468 Coed
Affiliation or Control: State/Local IRS Status: 501(c)3
Highest Offering: Associate Degree
Program: Occupational; 2-Year Principally Bachelor's Creditable
Accreditation: M, ACBSP, ADNUR, ENGT, OPD, PTAA, RAD

01 President Dr. Gale E. GIBSON
100 Exec Dir/Pres Initiatives Mr. Courtney INNISS
04 Exec Asst to the President Mrs. NaKesha DAVIS
05 VP & Chief Academic Ofcr Dr. S. Aisha STEPLIGHT JOHNSON
10 VP Administration & Finance Dr. Joyce W. HARLEY
21 Comptroller Mrs. Avril GEORGE-ROBINSON
15 VP Human Resources/Gen Counsel Ms. Rashidah HASAN
108 VP Planning Research & Assessment Dr. Douglas WALCERZ
13 Exec Dean/CIO Admin & Learning Tech Mr. Mohamed SEDDIKI
32 Acting Exec Dean Student Services Dr. Susan MULLIGAN
106 Assoc Dean Online Learning Resource Dr. Leigh BELLO-DECASTRO
25 Assoc Dir Grants Ms. Cynthia ROBERSON
09 Director Institutional Research Dr. Jinsoo PARK
88 Asst Dean Retention/Acad Advisement Ms. Marva MACK
51 Acting Dean Comm & Cont Educ/WEC Dr. Elvira VIEIRA
08 Director MLK Library Mrs. Gwendolyn SLATON
35 Assoc Dean Student Life/Development Ms. Patricia SLADE
18 Director Facilities Mgmt Mr. Jeff SHAPIRO
19 Director Public Safety Mr. Anthony CROMARTIE
26 Acting Dir Mktg & Communications Ms. Yla EASON
29 Resource Specialist Ms. Sybil BOST-WORMLEY
96 Director Purchasing Mrs. Marylyn RUTHERFORD
37 Director Financial Aid Mrs. Mildred COFER
06 Registrar/Asst Dean Stdnt Affairs Ms. Zewdnesh KASSA
21 Director Bursar's Office Ms. Darlene MILLER
36 Director Student Development Ms. Pamela MAYNARD
88 Director Child Development Center Ms. Deloris GRIMSLEY
41 Director Athletics Mr. Melvin KNIGHT
24 Director Media Prod Tech Mrs. Nadine ABRAM
88 Director College Information Ctr Mr. Ronald ROSS
00 President Emeritus Dr. A. Zachary YAMBA

Essex County College-West Essex Branch Campus (G)

730 West Bloomfield Avenue, West Caldwell NJ 07006
Telephone: (973) 877-6590 Identification: 770127
Accreditation: &M

† Branch campus of Essex County College, Newark, NJ.

Fairleigh Dickinson University (H)

1000 River Road, Teaneck NJ 07666-1996
County: Bergen FICE Identification: 002607
Unit ID: 184603
Telephone: (201) 692-2000 Carnegie Class: Master's L
FAX Number: N/A Calendar System: Semester
URL: www.fdu.edu
Established: 1942 Annual Undergrad Tuition & Fees: $35,880
Enrollment: 8,777 Coed
Affiliation or Control: Independent Non-Profit IRS Status: 501(c)3
Highest Offering: Doctorate
Program: Occupational; 2-Year Principally Bachelor's Creditable; Liberal Arts And General; Teacher Preparatory; Professional
Accreditation: M, BUS, CACREP, CLPSY, CS, ENG, ENGT, NURSE, @PHAR, TEAC

01 President Mr. Sheldon DRUCKER
43 University Counsel/Secretary Mr. John CODD
05 Univ Provost/VPAA Dr. Christopher CAPUANO
30 Sr Vice Pres University Advancement Mr. Richard REISS
03 Senior Vice President & CEO Vacant
10 Senior VP for Finance & COO Ms. Hania FERRARA
11 Vice President for Administration Mr. Richard A. FRICK
84 Vice Pres for Enrollment Management Vacant
13 VP/Chief Information Officer Mr. Neal M. STURM
26 Associate VP Communications Mr. Angelo CARFAGNA
15 Associate VP Human Resources Ms. Rose D'AMBROSIO
29 Director Alumni Affairs Mr. Okang MCBRIDE
12 Dean Petrocelli Col of Cont Stds Mr. Kenneth T. VEHRKENS
49 Dean Becton Col of Arts & Sci Dr. Geoffrey WEINMAN
50 Interim Dean College Business Admin Dr. James ALMEIDA
20 Dean University College Dr. Patti MILLS
32 Dean of Students-Teaneck Campus Ms. Michelle MCCROY-HEINS
32 Dean of Students-Madison Campus Dr. Jas VEREM
08 Assoc University Librarian-Florham Vacant
08 Associate University Librarian-Met Ms. Kathy STEIN-SMITH
51 Director Continuing Education Dr. Thomas SWANZEY
88 Dir Public Administration Institute Dr. William ROBERTS
38 Director Psychology Dr. Ronald DUMONT
21 Director Internal Audit Mr. Peter FORMAN
53 Director School of Education Dr. Vicki COHEN
66 Director Sch of Nurs/Allied Health Dr. Minerva GUTTMAN
41 Director of Athletics-Teaneck Mr. David LANGFORD
41 Director of Athletics-Madison Mr. William KLIKA
07 Univ Dir of Undergrad Admissions Mr. Andrew IPPOLITO
09 Director of Institutional Research Ms. Indira GOVINDAN
37 University Director Financial Aid Ms. Susan GROSS
19 Campus Dir Public Safety/F/M Campus Ms. Willie THORNTON
20 Provost Metropolitan Campus Dr. Joseph KIERNAN
12 Provost Florham/Madison Campus Dr. Peter WOOLLEY
19 Univ Dir Public Safety/T/H Campus Mr. David A. MILES
96 Director of Purchasing Ms. Juliette BROOKS

Felician College (I)

262 S Main Street, Lodi NJ 07644-2198
County: Bergen FICE Identification: 002610
Unit ID: 184612
Telephone: (201) 559-6000 Carnegie Class: Master's S
FAX Number: (201) 559-6188 Calendar System: Semester
URL: www.felician.edu
Established: 1942 Annual Undergrad Tuition & Fees: $31,775
Enrollment: 1,953 Coed
Affiliation or Control: Roman Catholic IRS Status: 501(c)3
Highest Offering: Doctorate
Program: Liberal Arts And General; Teacher Preparatory; Professional
Accreditation: M, IACBE, NURSE, TEAC

01 President Dr. Anne PRISCO
03 Senior Exec Vice President Vacant
05 Provost/Vice Pres Acad Affairs Dr. Edward OGLE
20 Asst VP Academic Support Services Dr. Ann V. GUILLORY
30 Vice Pres Institutional Advancement Mr. Edward EICHHORN
10 Interim Chief Financial Officer Mr. James F. GALBALLY, JR.
32 Vice President for Student Affairs Dr. James FITZPATRICK
11 VP Administration/Enrollment/Plng Ms. Francine ANDREA
04 Admin Assistant to the President Ms. Meggan O'NEILL
06 Registrar Ms. Priscilla KLYMENKO
07 Assoc Vice Pres Grad & Intl Enroll Mr. Michael SZAREK
07 Director Undergraduate Admissions Ms. Colleen FULLER
08 Director of the Library Mr. Paul GLASSMAN
09 Director Institutional Research Vacant
15 Director of Human Resources Ms. Virginia TOPOLSKI
88 Director Conferences and Event Plng Ms. Maria MALLIA
37 Director Student Financial Aid Ms. Cynthia MONTALVO
29 Director of Alumni Relations Ms. Patricia MALIZIA
42 Director Campus Ministry/Chaplain Fr. Richard KELLY
39 Director of Residence Life Ms. Laura PIEROTTI
36 Director of Career Counseling Ms. Melissa FAULKNER
13 Asst VP of Information Technology Mr. Christopher FINCH
24 Director A-V Center Mr. Anthony KLYMENKO
88 Assoc Director Center for Learning Mr. Hamdi SHAHIN
26 Dir Inst Marketing & Publications Ms. Barbara PURDUE-LYNCH
40 Manager College Bookstore Ms. Beth LIGNOWSKI
76 Dean School of Nursing Dr. Muriel SHORE
53 Dean School of Education Dr. Rose RUDNITSKI
49 Dean School of Arts/Science Dr. George E. ABAUNZA
50 Dean School of Business Dr. Beth CASTIGLIA
88 Dean Assessment/Fac Excellence Dr. Dolores HENCHY
88 Director EOF Program Ms. Dinelia GARDNER
104 Director Study Abroad Program Mr. Carlo COLECCHIA
85 Director of International Programs Ms. Corinne SPRING
23 Director Health Services Ms. Carolyn LEWIS
41 Director of Athletics Mr. Benjamin DINALLO, JR.
92 Director Honors Program Dr. Maria VECCHIO
91 Director Administrative Computing Mr. John PANNEGGIANTE

Georgian Court University (J)

900 Lakewood Avenue, Lakewood NJ 08701-2697
County: Ocean FICE Identification: 002608
Unit ID: 184773
Telephone: (732) 987-2200 Carnegie Class: Master's L
FAX Number: N/A Calendar System: Semester
URL: www.georgian.edu
Established: 1908 Annual Undergrad Tuition & Fees: $31,618
Enrollment: 2,308 Coed

Affiliation or Control: Roman Catholic IRS Status: 501(c)3
Highest Offering: Master's
Program: Liberal Arts And General; Teacher Preparatory; Professional
Accreditation: M, ACBSP, CACREP, NURSE, SW, TEAC

01 President ....Dr. Joseph R. MARBACH
05 Provost ....Dr. William BEHRE
10 Chief Financial Officer/VP Finance ....Mr. John SOMMER
30 Vice Pres Institutional Advancement ....Ms. Mellissia ZANJANI
20 Assoc Provost Academic Pgm Devel ....Dr. Michael GROSS
84 Interim VP of Enrollment Management ....Ms. Arlene CASH
32 Dean of Students ....Ms. Karen GOFF
42 Director of Campus Ministry ....Mr. Jeff SCHAFFER
41 Director Athletics/Recreation ....Ms. Laura LIESMAN
50 Dean School of Business ....Dr. Janice WARNER
53 Dean of School of Education ....Dr. Lynn DECAPUA
49 Dean School of Arts & Sciences ....Dr. Rita KIPP
09 Director of Institutional Research ....Mr. Wayne S. ARNDT
08 Int Director of Library Services ....Ms. Frances SCOTT
06 Registrar ....Ms. Christina REEVES
21 Controller ....Mrs. Maureen RYAN-HOFFMAN
15 Director of Human Resources ....Vacant
13 Chief Information Officer ....Mr. Steve CAROL
07 Director Undergraduate Admissions ....Ms. Tracey HOWARD-UBELHOER
37 Director of Student Accounts ....Ms. Linda PAGAN
26 Dir Public Rels/Col Communications ....Ms. Gail TOWNS
31 Dir Conferences & Special Events ....Ms. Mary E. CRANWELL
44 Dir Devel Alumni and Annual Giving ....Vacant
36 Director Career Development ....Ms. Kathleen BRADY
38 Director of Counseling ....Dr. Robin SOLBACH
23 Director of Health Services ....Ms. Cynthia MATTIA
22 Affirmative Action Officer ....Vacant
18 Director of Facilities ....Mr. Mark BIANCHI
19 Director of Security ....Mr. Thomas ZAMBRANO
09 Dir Ofc Assessment/Intl Research ....Ms. Elizabeth ANDERSON
07 Director Graduate Admissions ....Mr. Patrick GIVENS
39 Director of Residence Life ....Mr. Gary MILLER

Hudson County Community College (A)

70 Sip Avenue, Jersey City NJ 07306
County: Hudson FICE Identification: 012954
Unit ID: 184995
Telephone: (201) 714-7100 Carnegie Class: Assoc/Pub-U-SC
FAX Number: (201) 656-1799 Calendar System: Semester
URL: www.hccc.edu
Established: 1974 Annual Undergrad Tuition & Fees (In-District): $5,083
Enrollment: 9,203 Coed
Affiliation or Control: State/Local IRS Status: 501(c)3
Highest Offering: Associate Degree
Program: Occupational; 2-Year Principally Bachelor's Creditable
Accreditation: M, ACFEI

01 President ....Dr. Glen E. GABERT
05 Vice President Academic Affairs ....Dr. Eric FRIEDMAN
11 Vice President for Administration ....Mr. Thomas BRODOWSKI
30 VP Development/Asst to President ....Mr. Joseph SANSONE
32 VP North Hudson Ctr/Student Affairs ....Dr. Paula PANDO
88 Dean for Non Traditional Programs ....Ms. Ana CHAPMAN
09 Assoc Dean Institutional Rsrch/Plng ....Dr. Jerry TROMBELLA
84 Assoc Dean Enrollment Services ....Mr. Peter VIDA
50 Assoc Dean Business and Science ....Ms. Catherine SIRANGELO-ELBADAWY
37 Assoc Dean Student Financial Asst ....Ms. Pamela F. NORRIS-LITTLES
88 Assoc Dean ESL/Bilingual & Dev Educ ....Mr. Chris WAHL
06 Registrar ....Ms. Victoria ORELLANA
13 Chief Information Officer ....Ms. Pamela SCULLY
07 Director of Admissions ....Vacant
20 Dean of Arts and Sciences ....Mr. Chris WAHL
88 Director Testing & Assessment ....Ms. Darlery FRANCO
88 Director EOF ....Ms. Sabrina MAGLIULO
88 Executive Director Culinary Arts ....Mr. Paul DILLON
88 Ex Dir Ctr Bus/Industry/Cntrct Trng ....Ms. Ana CHAPMAN
45 Director Academic Foundations ....Ms. Elizabeth NESIUS
21 Controller ....Mr. Robert CRUZ
25 Director of Grants ....Mr. Ryan MARTIN
08 Librarian ....Ms. Carol VAN HOUTEN
35 Director Student Activities ....Mr. Michael REIMER
26 Director of Communications ....Ms. Jennifer CHRISTOPHER
29 Director Alumni Relations/Devel ....Mr. Joseph SANSONE
15 Executive Director Human Resources ....Ms. Vivyen RAY
38 Director Advisement & Counseling ....Mr. Michael REIMER
40 Manager HCCC Bookstore ....Ms. Tom COLBAN
96 Manager Purchasing ....Mr. Marvin SMITH
36 Coordinator Career & Transfer Svc ....Ms. Jennie NESENJUK
10 Chief Fiscal Officer ....Ms. Veronica ZEICHNER
19 Director Security/Safety ....Mr. Rafael NIVAR

ITT Technical Institute (B)

9000 Lincoln Drive E, Suite 100, Marlton NJ 08053
Telephone: (856) 396-3500 Identification: 770657
Accreditation: ACICS

† Branch campus of ITT Technical Institute, Indianapolis, IN.

Kean University (C)

1000 Morris Avenue, Union NJ 07083-0411
County: Union FICE Identification: 002622
Unit ID: 185262
Telephone: (908) 737-5326 Carnegie Class: Master's L
FAX Number: (908) 737-4636 Calendar System: Semester
URL: www.kean.edu
Established: 1855 Annual Undergrad Tuition & Fees (In-State): $11,580
Enrollment: 14,359 Coed
Affiliation or Control: State IRS Status: 501(c)3
Highest Offering: Doctorate
Program: Liberal Arts And General; Teacher Preparatory
Accreditation: M, ART, CAATE, CACREP, CIDA, MUS, NUR, OT, SP, SPAA, SW, TED, THEA

01 President ....Dr. Dawood FARAHI
10 Exec VP of Operations ....Mr. Philip CONNELLY
05 Provost/Vice Pres Academic Affairs ....Dr. Jeffrey TONEY
32 Vice President for Student Affairs ... Ms. Janice MURRAY-LAURY
30 VP Institutional Advancement ....Ms. Carla WILLIS
26 VP University Relations ....Ms. Susan KAYNE
101 Exec Asst Board/Exec Dir Media/Pub ....Ms. Audrey KELLY
43 Assoc VP/Chief University Counsel ....Ms. Geri BENEDETTO
88 Assoc VP for SIS & SP Counsel ....Ms. Felice VAZQUEZ
20 Assoc VP for Learning Support ....Dr. Sophia HOWLETT
12 Assoc VP/Dean Kean Ocean ....Dr. Stephen KUBOW
12 Assoc VPAA Kean Wenzhou ....Dr. Holger HENKE
84 Assoc VP Enrollment Management ....Ms. Marsha MCCARTHY
39 Asst VP Residential Stdnt Services ....Ms. Maximina RIVERA
18 Asst VP for Operations ....Ms. Phyllis DUKE
58 Dean Nathan Weiss Grad Col ....Dr. Jeffrey BECK
53 Dean Col Education ....Dr. Anthony PITTMAN
79 Dean Col Humanities/Social Sci ....Dr. Suzanne BOUSQUET
81 Dean Col Nat & Appl Hlth Sci ....Dr. George CHANG
50 Dean Col Business & Public Mgt ....Dr. Michael COOPER
57 Dean Col Visual & Performing Arts ....Vacant
48 Dean Michael Graves College ....Dr. David MOHNEY
06 Registrar ....Mr. Ken WOLPIN
07 Director for Undergrad Admissions ....Ms. Jennifer KANELLIS
37 Director Financial Aid ....Ms. Sherrell WATSON-HALL
106 Dir Online Learning ....Mr. Corey VIGDOR
15 Director Human Resources ....Mr. Faruque CHOWDHURY
13 Dir Office for Computer/Inform Svcs ....Mr. Anthony SANTORA
21 Dir General Accounting ....Mr. Mark ECKEL
08 Acting University Librarian ....Ms. Kimberly FRAONE
96 Director for Purchasing ....Mr. George THORN
22 Director Affirmative Action ....Dr. Charlie WILLIAMS
65 Director for Sustainability ....Dr. Feng QI
09 Director Institutional Research ....Dr. Shiji SHEN
108 Assoc Dir Accredit & Assessment ....Ms. Susan DEMATTEO
25 Director Research & Sponsored Pgms ....Ms. Susan GANNON
29 Director Alumni Relations ....Ms. Stella MAHER
38 Dir Counseling & Disability Servs ....Vacant
104 Dir Center International Studies ....Ms. Yaruby PETIT-FRERE
88 Veterans Affairs ....Ms. Lilliam BANNER
41 Director for Athletics ....Vacant
35 Dir Center for Leadership & Service ....Mr. Scott SNOWDEN
23 Director for Health Services ....Ms. Lori PURWIN
19 Acting Director of Campus Police ....Ms. Ana ZSAK
42 Chaplain for Campus Ministry ....Ms. Jackie OESMANN

Mercer County Community College (D)

1200 Old Trenton Road, PO Box 17202, Trenton NJ 08690-1099
County: Mercer FICE Identification: 004740
Unit ID: 185509
Telephone: (609) 586-4800 Carnegie Class: Assoc/Pub-R-L
FAX Number: (609) 570-3870 Calendar System: Semester
URL: www.mccc.edu
Established: 1966 Annual Undergrad Tuition & Fees (In-District): $4,452
Enrollment: 7,839 Coed
Affiliation or Control: State/Local IRS Status: 501(c)3
Highest Offering: Associate Degree
Program: Occupational; 2-Year Principally Bachelor's Creditable
Accreditation: M, AAB, ADNUR, FUSER, MLTAD, PTAA, RAD

01 President ....Dr. Jianping WANG
30 Vice President College Advancement ....Mr. Edward GWAZDA
05 Vice President Academic Affairs ....Dr. Eun-Woo CHANG
10 Interim VP for Admin & CBO ....Ms. Susan G. BOWEN
32 Exec Dean for Student Affairs ....Dr. Diane CAMPBELL
76 Actg Dean Sciences/Health Profess ....Dr. Linda SCHERR
49 Dean Liberal Arts ....Dr. Robin SCHORE
50 Dean Business and Technology ....Mr. Winston MADDOX
31 Asst Dean-JKC-Acad Pgm/Evening Svcs ....Vacant
13 Exec Dir for Info Technology Svcs ....Mr. Robert WALKER
21 Exec Dir of Finance ....Mr. Brian MCCLOSKEY
26 Dir Marketing/Public Information ....Ms. Lynn HOLL
15 Exec Dir for Compliance & Human Res ....Mr. Jose FERNANDEZ
06 Registrar ....Ms. Joan GUGGENHEIM
37 Director of Financial Aid ....Mr. Jason TAYLOR
09 Director Institutional Research ....Ms. Nina MAY
18 Chief Facilities/Physical Plant ....Mr. Bryon MARSHALL
96 Director of Purchasing ....Mr. Stephen GREGOROWICZ
07 Director of Admissions & Outreach ....Ms. Savita BAMBHROLIA
84 Director Enrollment Management ..Ms. Latonya ASHFORD-LIGON
08 Director of Library Services ....Ms. Pam PRICE
101 Secretary of the Institution/Board ....Ms. Diane BADESSA
103 Dean Workforce/Career Development ....Dr. Lynn COOPERSMITH
104 Director Study Abroad ....Prof. Andrea LYNCH
106 Dir Online Education/E-learning ....Vacant
25 Chief Contracts/Grants Admin ....Ms. Kay EATON
36 Director Student Placement ....Ms. Laurene JONES
41 Athletic Director ....Mr. John SIMONE
108 Acting Dean Inst Assessment ....Dr. Karen BEARCE
19 Director Security/Safety ....Mr. Bryon MARSHALL

Mesivta Keser Torah (E)

503 Eleventh Avenue, Belmar NJ 07719-2407
County: Monmouth FICE Identification: 041803
Unit ID: 461847
Telephone: (732) 367-4259 Carnegie Class: Not Classified
FAX Number: (732) 681-7171 Calendar System: Semester
Established: 1991 Annual Undergrad Tuition & Fees: $13,400
Enrollment: 45 Male
Affiliation or Control: Independent Non-Profit IRS Status: 501(c)3
Highest Offering: Baccalaureate
Program: Liberal Arts And General; Professional; Religious Emphasis
Accreditation: RABN

01 President ....Rabbi Dovid HEINEMANN

Middlesex County College (F)

2600 Woodbridge Avenue, Edison NJ 08818-3050
County: Middlesex FICE Identification: 002615
Unit ID: 185536
Telephone: (732) 548-6000 Carnegie Class: Assoc/Pub-S-SC
FAX Number: (732) 494-8244 Calendar System: Semester
URL: www.middlesexcc.edu
Established: 1964 Annual Undergrad Tuition & Fees (In-District): $4,215
Enrollment: 12,059 Coed
Affiliation or Control: State/Local IRS Status: 501(c)3
Highest Offering: Associate Degree
Program: Occupational; 2-Year Principally Bachelor's Creditable
Accreditation: M, ADNUR, DH, #DIETT, ENGT, MLTAD, RAD

01 President ....Dr. Joann LA PERLA-MORALES
05 VP Academic & Student Affairs ....Dr. Mark MCCORMICK
10 Vice Pres Finance & Administration ....Ms. Susan K. PERKINS
30 VP for Institutional Advancement ....Mr. Patrick MADAMA
32 Dean Student Affairs ....Ms. Marla BRINSON
84 Acting Dean Enrollment Management ....Ms. Aretha WATSON
107 Acting Dean Professional Studies ....Mr. Jeffrey HERRON
49 Dean Arts and Sciences ....Mr. David EDWARDS
51 Dean Continuing Education ....Dr. Roseann BUCCIARELLI
18 Exec Director Facilities Management ....Mr. Donald DROST
13 Exec Director Information Tech ....Mr. Bradley MORTON
21 Controller ....Ms. Lori PATTON
07 Acting Director of Admissions .Ms. Lisa RODRIGUEZ-GREGORY
06 Registrar ....Mr. Richard COLE
36 Director of Counseling/Career Svcs ....Dr. Fannie GORDON
37 Financial Aid Director ....Mr. Brian CLEMMONS
08 Director Learning Resources ....Mr. Mark THOMPSON
26 Chief Public Relations Officer ....Mr. Thomas PETERSON
96 Director of Purchasing ....Mr. David FRICKE

Monmouth University (G)

400 Cedar Avenue, West Long Branch NJ 07764-1898
County: Monmouth FICE Identification: 002616
Unit ID: 185572
Telephone: (732) 571-3400 Carnegie Class: Master's L
FAX Number: (732) 571-3629 Calendar System: Semester
URL: www.monmouth.edu
Established: 1933 Annual Undergrad Tuition & Fees: $33,728
Enrollment: 6,395 Coed
Affiliation or Control: Independent Non-Profit IRS Status: 501(c)3
Highest Offering: Doctorate
Program: 2-Year Principally Bachelor's Creditable; Liberal Arts And General; Teacher Preparatory; Professional
Accreditation: M, #ARCPA, BUS, CACREP, CS, ENG, NURSE, @SP, SW, TED

01 President ....Dr. Paul R. BROWN
04 Executive Assistant to President ....Ms. Annette GOUGH
101 Special Asst Board of Trustees ....Ms. Janet FELL
05 Provost/VP Academic Affairs ....Dr. Laura MORIARTY
20 Interim Vice Provost/Grad Studies ....Dr. Michael PALLADINO
20 Interim Vice Provost/Global Educ ....Dr. Rekha DATTA
20 Interim Vice Provost/Transform Lrng ....Dr. Kathryn KLOBY
20 Vice Provost/Plng & Dec Support ....Ms. Christine BENOL
20 Interim Vic Prov/Acad & Fac Affairs ....Dr. Datta V. NAIK
06 Registrar ....Mrs. Lynn REYNOLDS
49 Dean Sch Humanities/Social Science ....Dr. Kenneth WOMACK
50 Dean Leon Hess Business Sch ....Prof. Donald MOLIVER
53 Dean School of Education ....Dr. John HENNING
81 Co-Interim Dean Sch of Science ....Mr. John TIEDEMANN
81 Co-Interim Dean Sch of Science ....Dr. Catherine DUCKETT
66 Dean School of Nursing/Health Stds ....Dr. Janet MAHONEY
70 Dean School of Social Work ....Dr. Robin MAMA
92 Dean Honors College ....Dr. Kevin DOOLEY
08 University Librarian ....Vacant
10 Vice President Finance ....Mr. William G. CRAIG
21 Assoc VP for Finance/Budgets ....Mr. Jack GAVIN
96 Director of Purchasing ....Mr. Mark MIRANDA
43 Vice President & General Counsel ....Mr. John J. CHRISTOPHER
88 Dir of Compliance/Risk Mgr ....Mr. Michael WUNSCH
22 Dir Equity and Diversity ....Ms. Nina ANDERSON
11 Vice President Administrative Svcs ....Mrs. Patricia SWANNACK
18 Assoc VP Campus Plng/Construction ....Mr. Robert CORNERO
19 Director/Chief of Police ....Capt. William MCELRATH
15 Director of Human Resources ....Ms. Robyn SALVO
32 VP Student Life & Ldrshp Engagement ....Mrs. Mary Anne NAGY
35 Assoc VP for Student Life ....Mr. James PILLAR
35 Dir Student Activities/Student Ctr ....Ms. Amy BELLINA
27 Chief Univ Editor/Dir Exec Com ....Mr. Michael MAIDEN
30 Vice Pres External Affairs ....Mr. Jason KROLL
26 Assoc VP Univ Mktg/Communications ....Ms. Tara PETERS

29 Asst VP for University Engagement ....Ms. Yasmin NIELSEN
84 Vice Pres Enrollment Management ....Dr. Robert MC CAIG
37 Assoc VP/Director Financial Aid ....Ms. Claire ALASIO
07 Assoc VP for UG & GR Admission ...Ms. Lauren VENTO-CIFELLI
41 Vice Pres & Director of Athletics ....Dr. Marilyn MCNEIL
13 Vice Pres Information Management .....Dr. Edward CHRISTENSEN
97 Assoc Vice Prov/Acad Found/Gen Ed ....Dr. Judith NYE
09 Director of Institutional Research ....Dr. Eleanor SWANSON
38 Assoc Vice Provost/Student Success ....Dr. Mercy AZEKE
36 Assistant Dean for Career Services ....Mr. William HILL
86 Dir of Gov & Community Relations ....Mr. Paul DEMENT
25 Director of Grants & Contracts ....Mr. Tony LAZROE

Montclair State University (A)

1 Normal Avenue, Montclair NJ 07043-9987
County: Essex and Passaic FICE Identification: 002617
Unit ID: 185590
Telephone: (973) 655-4000 Carnegie Class: Master's L
FAX Number: N/A Calendar System: Semester
URL: www.montclair.edu
Established: 1908 Annual Undergrad Tuition & Fees (In-State): $11,772
Enrollment: 20,022 Coed
Affiliation or Control: State IRS Status: 501(c)3
Highest Offering: Doctorate
Program: Liberal Arts And General; Teacher Preparatory; Professional
Accreditation: M, ART, AUD, BUS, CAATE, CACREP, CS, DANCE, DIETD, DIETI, MUS, PH, SP, TED, THEA

01 President ....Dr. Susan A. COLE
05 Provost/Vice Pres Academic Affairs ......Dr. Willard P. GINGERICH
10 Vice Pres Finance & Treasurer ....Mr. Donald D. CIPULLO
32 Vice Pres Student Devel/Campus Life .Dr. Karen L. PENNINGTON
30 Vice Pres University Advancement ....Mr. John T. SHANNON
15 Vice Pres Human Resources ....Mr. Jerry M. CUTLER
18 Vice Pres Univ Facilities ....Mr. Gregory W. BRESSLER
13 Vice Pres Info Technology ....Dr. Candace C. FLEMING
88 Exec Director Enterprise Systems ....Mr. Samir BAKANE
43 University Counsel ....Mr. Mark FLEMING
86 Director Government Relations ....Ms. Shivaun P. GAINES
45 Exec Director Budget and Planning ....Mr. David JOSEPHSON
79 Dean Col Humanities & Soc Sciences ...Dr. Robert S. FRIEDMAN
81 Dean Col Science & Mathematics ....Dr. Robert S. PREZANT
53 Dean Col Educ & Human Services ....Dr. Tamara F. LUCAS
57 Dean Col of the Arts ....Dr. Daniel A. GURSKIS
50 Dean School of Business ....Dr. Alan G. CANT
08 Dean of Library Services ....Dr. Judith L. HUNT
58 Dean of Graduate School ....Dr. Joan C. FICKE
35 Dean of Students ....Ms. Marjorie COLEMAN-CARTER
20 Assoc Provost for Academic Affairs ....Dr. Frederick BONATO
108 Assoc Provost Acad Pgm/ Assessment ....Dr. Joanne F. COTE-BONANNO
20 Assoc Provost Undergrad Educ ....Dr. James D. GERMAN
91 Assoc VP Enterprise App Services ....Vacant
35 Assoc VP Student Dev/Campus Life ....Ms. Kathleen E. RAGAN
16 Assoc VP for Human Resources ....Mr. Gilbert RIVERA
16 Asst VP for HR Operations ....Ms. Catherine N. BONGO
88 Asst VP Talent Management ....Ms. Keesha CHAVIS
64 Director School of Music ....Dr. Robert CART
09 Director Institutional Research ....Dr. Steven L. JOHNSON
06 Acting Registrar ....Ms. Dianne RIVETTI
07 Director Undergraduate Admissions ....Mr. Jeffrey D. INDIVERI-GANT
26 Asst VP Marketing & Communication ....Vacant
31 Exec Director Community Relations ....Ms. Julie ADAMS
29 Asst VP Annual Giving & Alum Rels ....Ms. Jeanne MARANO
19 Chief of University Police ....Mr. Paul M. CELL
22 Dir EO/Affirmative Action/Diversity ....Ms. Barbara J. MILTON
38 Dir Counseling & Psych Services ....Dr. Jaclyn FRIEDMAN-LOMBARDO
39 Exec Director Residential Ed/Svcs ....Mr. John DELATE
40 Gen Manager University Bookstore ....Ms. Diane PELLEGRINO
41 Dir Intercollegiate Athletics ....Ms. Holly P. GERA
37 Director Financial Aid ....Mr. James T. ANDERSON
36 Exec Dir Ctr Career Svcs/Coop Educ ....Vacant
96 Dir Procurement/Fin Div Admin ....Ms. Nancy G. CARVER
88 Exec Director Center for Advising ....Ms. Michele CAMPAGNA
92 Director Honors Program ....Dr. Gregory L. WATERS
21 Asst VP for Finance & Controller ....Vacant
21 Director of Student Accounts ....Ms. Marion CAGGIANO
23 Director University Health Center ....Ms. Donna M. BARRY
104 Exec Director International Affairs ....Ms. Marina CUNNINGHAM
28 Director Equity & Diversity ....Vacant
25 Dir Research & Sponsored Programs ....Mr. Ted RUSSO
88 Asst Dean for Student Life ....Ms. Fatima DECARVALHO
105 Director Web Services ....Vacant
04 Exec Assistant to the President ....Ms. Phyllis L. WOOSTER
42 Chaplain ....Fr. James CHERN
88 Dir Construction Procurement ....Mr. Daniel ROCHE
88 Dir Tech Training and Integration ....Ms. Yanling SUN
88 Dir Environmental Health and Safety ....Dr. Amy FERDINAND
27 Director Media Relations ....Ms. Suzanne BRONSKI
100 Chief of Staff ....Mr. Keith BARRACK

New Brunswick Theological Seminary (B)

35 Seminary Place, New Brunswick NJ 08901
County: Middlesex FICE Identification: 002619
Unit ID: 185758
Telephone: (732) 247-5241 Carnegie Class: Spec/Faith
FAX Number: (732) 249-5412 Calendar System: Semester
URL: www.nbts.edu
Established: 1784 Annual Graduate Tuition & Fees: $13,390
Enrollment: 186 Coed
Affiliation or Control: Reformed Church In America IRS Status: 501(c)3
Highest Offering: Doctorate; No Undergraduates
Program: Professional; Religious Emphasis
Accreditation: THEOL

01 President ....Dr. Gregg A. MAST
04 Assistant to the President ....Ms. Yasha PEOPLE
05 Dean of the Seminary ....Dr. Willard W.C ASHLEY, SR.
10 Chief Financial Officer ....Mr. Kenneth TERMOTT
21 Accounting Manager ....Ms. Tara HAMILL
30 Director of Development ....Ms. Catherine PROCTOR
08 Director of the Library ....Vacant
06 Associate Dean & Registrar ....Ms. Sharon A. WATTS
32 Associate Dean of Student Services ....Ms. Joan MARSHALL
07 Admissions Committee Chair ....Dr. Beth L. TANNER
18 Facilities Manager ....Mr. Paul KUHN
13 Network Technician ....Mr. Thomas SCHLATTER
108 Director of Assessment ....Dr. Terry SMITH
36 Director of Field Education ....Dr. Faye TAYLOR

New Jersey City University (C)

2039 Kennedy Boulevard, Jersey City NJ 07305-1597
County: Hudson FICE Identification: 002613
Unit ID: 185129
Telephone: (201) 200-2000 Carnegie Class: Master's L
FAX Number: (201) 200-2352 Calendar System: Semester
URL: www.njcu.edu
Established: 1927 Annual Undergrad Tuition & Fees (In-State): $11,178
Enrollment: 8,136 Coed
Affiliation or Control: State IRS Status: 501(c)3
Highest Offering: Doctorate
Program: Liberal Arts And General; Teacher Preparatory; Professional
Accreditation: M, ACBSP, ART, CACREP, MUS, NUR, TEAC

01 President ....Dr. Sue HENDERSON
05 Provost/Sr VP Academic Affairs ....Dr. Daniel J. JULIUS
32 Vice Pres for Student Affairs ....Dr. Jimmy JUNG
10 Vice Pres Administration/Finance ....Dr. Aaron ASKA
30 VP University Advancement ....Mr. Daniel ELWELL
21 Controller ....Ms. Karen SURGENT
13 Assoc VP Computer Inform Systems ....Mr. Robert MCBRIDE
18 Assoc VP Facil/Construction Mgmt ....Mr. James ADAMS
07 Assoc VP Admissions/Enrollment Mgmt ....Vacant
15 Assoc VP Human Resources ....Mr. Hunt BARTINE
20 Associate Provost ....Dr. Deborah WOO
20 Assistant Provost ....Dr. Karen MORGAN
26 Asst VP Pub Info/Community Rel . Ms. Ellen WAYMAN-GORDON
14 Asst VP Information Technology ....Ms. Phyllis SZANI
30 Asst VP of Development ....Ms. Lori SUMMERS
88 Interim Asst VP Univ Advancement ....Mr. Michael PERNA
35 Asst Vice Pres Student Affairs ....Dr. Demond HARGROVE
20 Asst VP Academic Affairs ....Mr. Guillermo DEVEYGA
04 Executive Asst to the President ....Ms. Maria COBARRUBIAS
04 Executive Asst to the President ....Ms. Tamara CUNNINGHAM
49 Interim Dean Arts & Sciences ....Dr. Anne MABRY
53 Dean Education & Prof Studies ....Dr. Allan DE FINA
50 Dean School of Business ....Dr. Bernard MCSHERRY
35 Dean of Students ....Dr. Lyn HAMLIN
108 Director Institutional Effectivenes ....Dr. Sue GERBER
08 Director of Univ Library ....Mr. Frederick SMITH
06 Registrar ....Ms. Miriam LARIA
36 Director Career Planning/Placement ....Dr. Jennifer JONES
09 Director Institutional Research ....Vacant
16 Director Human Resources ....Mr. Robert PIASKOWSKY
19 Director Public Safety ....Vacant
41 Director Athletics/Recreation ....Ms. Alice DE FAZIO
22 Dir Affirmative Action/Equal Oppty ....Ms. Lisa NORCIA
29 Director Alumni Relations ....Ms. Jane MCCLELLAN
78 Director Cooperative Education ....Dr. Jennifer JONES
44 Director Annual Giving ....Vacant
38 Director Student Counseling ....Dr. Abisola GALLAGHER
96 Director of Purchasing ....Ms. Edie DELVECCHIO
43 General Counsel ....Mr. Alfred RAMEY
85 Foreign Student Advisor ....Mr. Craig KATZ
37 Director Student Financial Aid ....Mr. Frank CUOZZO
51 Director Prof & Lifelong Learning ....Dr. William BAJOR
88 Director of Leadership Gifts ....Vacant
88 Director Student Fin Svcs/Risk Mgr ....Mr. Peter LJUTIC

New Jersey Institute of Technology (D)

University Heights, Newark NJ 07102-1982
County: Essex FICE Identification: 002621
Unit ID: 185828
Telephone: (973) 596-3000 Carnegie Class: RU/H
FAX Number: (973) 642-4380 Calendar System: Semester
URL: www.njit.edu
Established: 1881 Annual Undergrad Tuition & Fees (In-State): $16,188
Enrollment: 10,646 Coed
Affiliation or Control: State IRS Status: 501(c)3
Highest Offering: Doctorate
Program: Professional
Accreditation: M, ART, BUS, CIDA, CS, ENG, ENGT, PH

01 President ....Dr. Joel S. BLOOM
05 Provost and Senior Executive VP ....Dr. Fadi P. DEEK
10 Senior Vice Pres Admin & Treasurer ....Mr. Henry A. MAUERMEYER
30 Vice Pres University Advancement ....Dr. Charles DEES
46 Sr VP Tech & Bus Dev/Pres NJII ....Dr. Donald H. SEBASTIAN
88 VP for Real Estate & Capital Dev ....Mr. Andrew P. CHRIST
15 Vice President Human Resources ....Ms. Kay CLARKE-TURNER
32 VP Academic Support & Stdnt Affairs ....Dr. Charles J. FEY
20 Vice Provost for Academic Affairs ....Dr. Basil BALTZIS
54 Dean Newark College of Engineering ....Dr. Moshe KAM
48 Dean of CoAD ....Mr. Urs P. GAUCHAT
49 Dean Col Sci/Liberal Arts ....Dr. Kevin D. BELFIELD
50 Dean School of Management ....Dr. Reggie J. CAUDILL
92 Dean A Dorman Honors College ....Dr. Katia PASSERINI
77 Dean College of Computing Science ....Dr. Marek E. RUSINKIEWICZ
88 Vice Provost for Research ....Dr. Atam P. DHAWAN
21 Assoc Vice Pres Finance & Controlle ....Mr. William GARCIA
18 Assoc VP Design & Construction ....Mr. Joseph F. TARTAGLIA
58 Assoc Provost Grad Studies ....Dr. Sotirios G. ZIAVRAS
13 Assoc Provost Information Svcs Tech ....Mr. David F. ULLMAN
45 Assoc VP for Business & Econ Devel ...Dr. Timothy V. FRANKLIN
51 Assoc VP Cont/Distance Education ....Dr. Gale T. SPAK
84 Assoc VP Enroll Mgmt & Acad ....Dr. Wendy LIN-COOK
44 Assoc VP for Development ....Ms. Jacqueline G. RHODES
88 Exec Dir Pre-College Program ....Dr. Jacqueline L. CUSACK
35 Assoc VP Stdnt Engag/Dean of Stdnts ....Dr. Laura VALENTE
89 Assoc Dean Ctr First Year Students ....Dr. Sharon E. MORGAN
26 Assoc VP Comm/Marketing & Branding ....Ms. Lauren D. UGORJI
29 Sr Exec Dir for Constituent Rels ....Mr. Michael A. WALL
04 Sr Assistant to President ....Ms. Mary Jane POHERO
36 Exec Director Career Devel Svcs ....Mr. Gregory MASS
27 Asst VP for Communications ....Dr. Denise ANDERSON
09 Director Inst Research/Planning ....Dr. Eugene P. DEESS
08 University Librarian ....Mr. Richard T. SWEENEY
06 Registrar ....Mr. Michael E. MAYSILLES
37 Dir Student Financial Aid Services ....Ms. Ivon NUNEZ
88 Executive Director EOP ....Mr. Laurence A. HOWELL
38 Dir Counseling & Psych Services ....Dr. Phyllis BOLLING
19 Chief of Police ....Mr. Joseph S. MARSWILLO
24 Dir Instructional Tech/Media Svcs ....Mr. William F. REYNOLDS
41 Asst VP & Dir Athletics/Phys Educ ....Mr. Leonard I. KAPLAN
85 Director International Students/Fac ....Mr. Jeffrey W. GRUNDY
88 Interim Director Campus Center ....Mr. Albert M. MARTINEZ
96 Director Purchasing/Office Services ....Ms. Eugenia REGENCIO
43 Office of General Counsel ....Ms. Holly C. STERN
100 Special Asst to Pres Pol/Gov Rels ....Ms. Angela R. GARRETSON
105 Director Web Services ....Mr. Aslam ERSAL
108 Director Academic Assessment ....Dr. Charles R. BROOKS
07 Dir of Univ Admissions ....Mr. Stephen M. ECK

Ocean County College (E)

PO Box 2001, Toms River NJ 08754-2001
County: Ocean FICE Identification: 002624
Unit ID: 185873
Telephone: (732) 255-0400 Carnegie Class: Assoc/Pub-S-SC
FAX Number: (732) 255-0444 Calendar System: Semester
URL: www.ocean.edu
Established: 1964 Annual Undergrad Tuition & Fees (In-District): $4,255
Enrollment: 9,296 Coed
Affiliation or Control: State/Local IRS Status: 501(c)3
Highest Offering: Associate Degree
Program: Occupational; 2-Year Principally Bachelor's Creditable
Accreditation: M, ADNUR, EMT

01 President ....Dr. Jon H. LARSON
10 Exec VP of Finance & Administration .....Ms. Sara WINCHESTER
32 VP Student Affairs ....Ms. Norma BETZ
05 VP of Academic Affairs ....Vacant
15 Asst VP Human Resources ....Vacant
20 Asst VP for Instructional Services ....Dr. Antoinette M. CLAY
18 Asst VP Facilities Mgmt/Constr ....Mr. Matthew KENNEDY
04 Senior Asst to the President ....Vacant
20 Assoc VP of Academic Affairs ....Dr. Lisa DIBISCEGLIE
57 Dean Language and the Arts ....Dr. Amy GILLEY
81 Dean Math/Science & Tech ....Mr. Paul SILBERQUIT
66 Dean of Nursing ....Ms. Teresa WALSH
83 Dean of Social Science ....Ms. Rosann BAR
106 Dean of Instructional Outreach ....Dr. Maysa HAYWARD
12 Director of Off-Campus Programs ....Ms. Sabrina MATHUES
102 Exec Dir OCC Foundation ....Ms. Heather BARBERI
106 Exec Director of e-Learning & CPE ....Ms. Patricia FENN
106 Executive Director of e-Learning ....Mr. Jeff S. HARMON
106 Dean of e-Learning Faculty ....Mr. Jack KELNHOFER
08 Director of Library Services ....Ms. Donna ROSINSKI-KAUS
13 Chief Information Officer ....Mr. Hatem AKL
37 Director of Financial Aid ....Ms. Eileen BUCKLE
06 Registrar ....Mr. Eric DANIELS
88 Dir of Academic Advising Services ....Ms. Anna REGAN
19 Director of College Security ....Mr. Robert KUMPF
26 Exec Director of College Relations ....Ms. Jan KIRSTEN
07 Director of Admissions ....Ms. Lisa KASPER
93 Director of EOF & OMS ....Ms. Laura RICKARDS
18 Director of Facilities ....Mr. James CALAMIA
41 Exec Director of Athletics ....Ms. Ilene COHEN
45 Exec Dir of Institutional Planning ....Ms. Alexa BESHARA
109 Director of Auxiliary Services ....Ms. Carol KAUNITZ
21 Controller ....Ms. Karen PAPAKONSTANTINOU
20 Dean of Academic Services ....Ms. Maureen REUSTLE
35 Director of Student Life ....Ms. Jennifer FAZIO
29 Director Alumni Relations ....Ms. Rebecca FEILER WHITE

Passaic County Community College (F)

1 College Boulevard, Paterson NJ 07509-1179
County: Passaic FICE Identification: 009994
Unit ID: 186034

Telephone: (973) 684-6868 Carnegie Class: Assoc/Pub-S-SC
FAX Number: (973) 684-5843 Calendar System: Semester
URL: www.pccc.edu
Established: 1968 Annual Undergrad Tuition & Fees (In-District): $4,433
Enrollment: 8,613 Coed
Affiliation or Control: State/Local IRS Status: 501(c)3
Highest Offering: Associate Degree
Program: Occupational; 2-Year Principally Bachelor's Creditable
Accreditation: M, ADNUR, CAHIIM, ENGT, RAD

01 President ... Dr. Steven ROSE
05 Vice Pres Academic/Student Affairs ... Dr. Jacqueline KINEAVY
10 Vice Pres Finance/Administration ... Mr. Steven HARDY
12 Vice Pres Passaic Academic Center . Ms. Josephine HERNANDEZ
13 Vice Pres Information Technology ... Mr. Robert MONDELLI
15 Vice Pres Human Resources ... Mr. Michael SILVESTRO
20 Dean Academic Affairs ... Dr. Bassel STASSIS
08 Associate Dean Learning Resources ... Mr. Greg FALLON
66 Assoc Dean Nurse Educ/Health Scis ... Ms. Donna STANKIEWICZ
88 Asst Dean for Testing & Tutoring ... Mr. Peter HYNES
09 Exec Dir Institutional Rsrch/Plng ... Mr. Justin HULL
88 Ex Dir Cultural Affs/The Poetry Ctr ... Ms. Maria GILLAN
30 Exec Dir of Institutional Devel ... Mr. Todd SORBER
84 Exec Dir of Enrollment Management ... Ms. Betsy MARINACE
18 Exec Dir Facilities Mgmt/Planning ... Mr. Brian EGAN
37 Director Financial Aid ... Mr. Eddie VIERA
06 Registrar ... Ms. Donna FISCHER
19 Director Security ... Mr. John MORGAN
35 Director Student Activities ... Ms. Maria MARTE
41 Athletic Director ... Mr. Wayne MARTIN
07 Director of Admissions ... Ms. Stephanie DECKER
29 Director Alumni Relations ... Mr. William MORRISON
32 Chief Student Life Officer ... Dr. Sharon GOLDSTEIN
36 Director Student Placement ... Vacant
26 Chief Public Relations Officer ... Ms. Betsy MARINACE
96 Director of Purchasing ... Mr. Michael D'AGATI
101 Dir Board Affairs/Asst to President ... Ms. Evelyn DEFEIS

Pillar College (A)

60 Park Place, Suite 701, Newark NJ 07102
County: Essex FICE Identification: 036663
Unit ID: 440794
Telephone: (973) 803-5000 Carnegie Class: Spec/Faith
FAX Number: (973) 242-3282 Calendar System: Semester
URL: www.pillar.edu
Established: 1908 Annual Undergrad Tuition & Fees: $19,440
Enrollment: 518 Coed
Affiliation or Control: Other IRS Status: 501(c)3
Highest Offering: Baccalaureate
Program: Liberal Arts And General; Teacher Preparatory; Professional; Religious Emphasis
Accreditation: M, BI

01 President ... Dr. David E. SCHROEDER
03 Provost ... Mr. Daniel W. WRIGHT
05 VP Academic Affairs ... Dr. Alford H. OTTLEY
11 VP Operations/Public Affairs ... Dr. Ralph T. GRANT
32 VP Student Life ... Ms. Linda SCHMITT
88 VP Institutional Outreach ... Ms. Keyla PAVIA
51 VP Strategic Alliances ... Dr. Wayne DYER
10 Assistant VP of Financial Services ... Mr. Joel DAVIS
20 Assistant VP of Academics ... Mrs. Amy HUBER
06 Registrar ... Mr. Brian SCHROEDER
37 Assistant Director of Financial Aid ... Ms. Eboni CRAWFORD
07 Director of Admissions ... Mr. Dominic DIGIOACCHINO
42 Coordinator of Spiritual Formation ... Mr. Nishanth THOMAS
04 Administrative Asst to President ... Ms. Ivette MUNIZ
08 Head Librarian ... Ms. Lorraine HODGES
26 Director of Marketing ... Mr. Kelvin THOMAS

Princeton Theological Seminary (B)

PO Box 821, Princeton NJ 08542-0803
County: Mercer FICE Identification: 002626
Unit ID: 186122
Telephone: (609) 921-8300 Carnegie Class: Spec/Faith
FAX Number: (609) 924-2973 Calendar System: Semester
URL: www.ptsem.edu
Established: 1812 Annual Graduate Tuition & Fees: $12,500
Enrollment: 523 Coed
Affiliation or Control: Presbyterian Church (U.S.A.) IRS Status: 501(c)3
Highest Offering: Doctorate; No Undergraduates
Program: Professional; Religious Emphasis
Accreditation: M, THEOL

01 President ... Dr. M. Craig BARNES
10 Sr Vice Pres/Chief Oper Ofcr/Treas ... Mr. John W. GILMORE
30 VP for Advancement ... Ms. Jaime ZAMPARELLI
26 VP for Communication & External Rel ... Dr. Shane A. BERG
05 Dean of Academic Affairs ... Dr. James F. KAY
32 Dean of Students Life ... Rev. John E. WHITE
45 Assoc Dean of Planning & Assessmen ... Dr. Shawn OLIVER
35 Assoc Dean Stdnt Life/Dir Sr Plcmnt .. RevDr. Catherine C. DAVIS
51 Assoc Dean of Continuing Educ ... Rev. Dayle G. ROUNDS
21 Assoc VP for Finance and Admin ... Mr. Kurt A. GABBARD
21 Controller ... Mr. James F. MORGAN
88 Director of Church Relations ... Rev. Larissa KWONG ABAZIA
06 Registrar ... Mr. David H. WALL
07 Director Admissions/Financial Aid ... Mr. Matthew R. SPINA
08 Chief Librarian ... Mr. Donald M. VORP
44 Director of Donor Relations ... Rev. J. Thomas CORT
15 Director of Human Resources ... Ms. Sandra J. MALEY
13 Chief Technology Officer ... Mr. William FRENCH
18 Director of Facilities ... Mr. German MARTINEZ
24 Director Educational Media ... Rev. Joicy BECKER-RICHARDS
39 Director of Housing/Auxiliary Svcs ... Mr. Stephen CARDONE
20 Assoc Dean for Academic Admin ... Dr. Rose Ellen DUNN
38 Director of Student Counseling ... Rev. Nancy L. SCHONGALLA-BOWMAN
42 Minister of the Chapel ... Rev. Janice S. AMMON
28 Director Multicultural Relations ... Rev. Victor ALOYO, JR.
04 Administrative Asst to President ... Mrs. Ellen L. MARTIN
37 Assoc Director Financial Aid ... Mr. Michael D. LIVIO

Princeton University (C)

Princeton NJ 08544-1098
County: Mercer FICE Identification: 002627
Unit ID: 186131
Telephone: (609) 258-3000 Carnegie Class: RU/VH
FAX Number: N/A Calendar System: Semester
URL: www.princeton.edu
Established: 1746 Annual Undergrad Tuition & Fees: $43,450
Enrollment: 8,088 Coed
Affiliation or Control: Independent Non-Profit IRS Status: 501(c)3
Highest Offering: Doctorate
Program: Liberal Arts And General; Teacher Preparatory; Professional
Accreditation: M, ENG, TEAC

01 President ... Cristopher L. EISGRUBER
03 Executive Vice President ... Treby WILLIAMS
05 Provost ... David S. LEE
04 Vice President & Secretary ... Robert K. DURKEE
10 Vice Pres for Finance & Treasurer ... Carolyn N. AINSLIE
30 Vice President for Development ... Elizabeth B. WOOD
26 Vice President for Public Affairs ... Robert K. DURKEE
32 Vice President of Campus Life ... Rochelle CALHOUN
18 Vice President for Facilities ... Michael E. MCKAY
13 Vice President Info Technology/CIO ... Jay DOMINICK
15 Vice President for Human Resources ... Lianne C. SULLIVAN-CROWLEY
11 VP for University Services ... Chad L. KLAUS
20 Vice Provost Academic Affairs ... Katherine ROHRER
22 Vice Provost Instl Equity/Diversity ... Michelle MINTER
09 Vice Provost Institutional Research ... Jed MARSH
25 Vice Prov Space Programming/Plan ... Paul LAMARCHE
21 Budget Dir/Vice Provost Finance ... Steven GILL
20 Vice Provost Intl Initiatives ... Anastasia T. VRACHNOS
26 Asst Vice President Communications ... Daniel A. DAY
29 Asst Vice President Alumni Affairs ... Margaret M. MILLER
44 Asst Vice President Annual Giving ... William M. HARDT
88 Asst VP for University Services ... Amy CAMPBELL
88 AVP Facilities Design/Construction ... Anne ST. MAURO
18 Asst Vice Pres University Services ... Andrew KANE
46 Chair Univ Rsrch Bd/Dean Research ... Pablo DEBENEDETTI
43 General Counsel ... Ramona E. ROMERO
88 President PRINCO ... Andrew K. GOLDEN
88 Dean of the Faculty ... Deborah PRENTICE
58 Dean of Graduate School ... Sanjeev KULKARNI
49 Dean of the College ... Jill S. DOLAN
54 Dean of School of Engineering ... H. Vincent POOR
82 Dean of WW Sch of Public/Intl Affs ... Cecilia ROUSE
48 Dean of School of Architecture ... Monica PONCE DE LEON
42 Dean of Religious Life ... Alison BODEN
35 Dean of Undergraduate Students ... Kathleen DEIGNAN
07 Dean of Admission ... Janet L. RAPELYE
17 Exec Director Health Services ... John KOLLIGIAN
08 University Librarian ... Karin TRAINER
06 Registrar ... Polly WINFREY GRIFFIN
37 Dir Undergraduate Financial Aid ... Robin A. MOSCATO
86 Director Government Affairs ... Joyce A. RECHTSCHAFFEN
31 Dir Community & Regional Affairs ... Kristin APPELGET
41 Director of Athletics ... Mollie D. MARCOUX
96 Director of Purchasing ... Donald E. WESTON, JR.
38 Dir of Counseling & Psych Services ... Anita MCLEAN
16 Director Human Resources ... Claire JACOBS ELSON
85 Director Davis International Center ... Jackie LEIGHTON
36 Executive Director Career Services ... Pulin SANGHVI
90 Assoc CIO/Dir Academic Services OIT ... Serge J. GOLDSTEIN
14 Assoc CIO/Dir Support Services OIT ... Steven M. SATHER
91 Dir Enterprise Infrastructure OIT ... Donna E. TATRO
105 Director of Web Communications ... Thomas J. BARTUS
88 Dir of Development Communications ... Ruth STEVENS
44 AVP for Development ... Kerstin LARSEN
104 Sr Asc Dn of Col/Dir Ofc Intl Pgms ... Nancy A. KANACH
39 Director Housing ... Andrew KANE
19 Executive Director Public Safety ... Paul OMINSKY

Rabbi Jacob Joseph School (D)

1 Plainfield Avenue, Edison NJ 08817-4494
County: Middlesex FICE Identification: 030775
Unit ID: 384421
Telephone: (732) 985-6533 Carnegie Class: Spec/Faith
FAX Number: (732) 985-6553 Calendar System: Semester
URL: www.jfgmc.org/rjjy/htm
Established: 1982 Annual Undergrad Tuition & Fees: $11,400
Enrollment: 84 Male
Affiliation or Control: Independent Non-Profit IRS Status: 501(c)3
Highest Offering: Baccalaureate
Program: Teacher Preparatory; Professional
Accreditation: @RABN

01 President ... Dr. Marvin SCHICK
03 Rosh Yeshiva ... Rabbi Yaakov BUSEL
05 Rosh Yeshiva ... Rabbi Joseph EICHENSTEIN
37 Financial Aid Director ... Rabbi Yitzchok WEINTRAUB

Rabbinical College of America (E)

226 Sussex Avenue, Morristown NJ 07960-3600
County: Morris FICE Identification: 008609
Unit ID: 186186
Telephone: (973) 267-9404 Carnegie Class: Spec/Faith
FAX Number: (973) 267-5208 Calendar System: Trimester
URL: www.rca.edu
Established: 1956 Annual Undergrad Tuition & Fees: $11,000
Enrollment: 209 Male
Affiliation or Control: Independent Non-Profit IRS Status: 501(c)3
Highest Offering: Baccalaureate
Program: Teacher Preparatory
Accreditation: RABN

00 Chairman of the Board ... David T. CHASE
01 Dean ... Rabbi Moshe HERSON
04 Admin Assistant to the Dean ... Rabbi Mendy HERSON
26 Public Relations Officer ... Rabbi Mendel SOLOMON
06 Registrar ... Mrs. Shoshana SOLOMON
88 Director New Direction Program ... Rabbi Zalman DUBINSKY
88 Merahel Advanced Talmud Program ... Rabbi Aharon GANCZ
10 Chief Business Officer ... Vacant
37 Director Student Financial Aid ... Rabbi Yisroel GOLDBERG
08 Chief Librarian ... Rabbi Sholom SPALTER
51 Dir Continuing Educ/Alumni Rels ... Rabbi Boruch HECHT
88 Director Semicha Program ... Rabbi Chaim SCHAPIRO
18 Director Building and Grounds ... Rabbi Hershel LIPSKIER

Ramapo College of New Jersey (F)

505 Ramapo Valley Road, Mahwah NJ 07430-1680
County: Bergen FICE Identification: 009344
Unit ID: 186201
Telephone: (201) 684-7500 Carnegie Class: Master's M
FAX Number: (201) 684-7508 Calendar System: Semester
URL: www.ramapo.edu
Established: 1969 Annual Undergrad Tuition & Fees (In-State): $13,698
Enrollment: 6,003 Coed
Affiliation or Control: State IRS Status: 501(c)3
Highest Offering: Master's
Program: Liberal Arts And General; Teacher Preparatory; Professional
Accreditation: M, BUS, NUR, SW, TEAC

01 President ... Dr. Peter P. MERCER
05 Provost/VP Academic Affairs ... Dr. Beth BARNETT
10 VP Administration & Finance ... Vacant
43 VP and General Counsel ... Mr. Michael A. TRIPODI
102 VP Inst Advance/Dir RC Foundation ... Ms. Cathleen DAVEY
84 Assoc VP of Enrollment Mgmt ... Mr. Christopher ROMANO
46 Chief Planning Officer ... Dr. Dorothy ECHOLS TOBE
100 Chief of Staff ... Ms. Brittany A. WILLIAMS-GOLDSTEIN
20 Vice Provost for Academic Affairs ... Dr. Eric DAFFRON
21 Assoc Vice Pres Admin/Finance ... Mr. Richard ROBERTS
13 Assoc VP/Chief Information Officer ... Mr. George TABBACK
86 Asst Vice Pres Government Rels ... Ms. Anna FARNESKI
105 Asst VP Mktg & Web Administrator ... Ms. Melissa HORVATH-PLYMAN
26 Asst VP of Comm & Public Relations ... Mr. Stephen HUDIK
08 College Librarian/Dean ... Ms. Elizabeth SIECKE
06 Registrar ... Ms. Michele DUNN
07 Director of Admissions ... Mr. Peter RICE
37 Director of Financial Aid ... Mr. F. Shawn O'NEILL
21 Controller ... Mr. Lawrence FERRIER
15 Director of Human Resources ... Mr. David VERNON
78 Dir Exper Learning/Career Svcs ... Ms. Beth RICCA
32 Dean of Students ... Ms. Melissa VAN DER WALL
41 Director of Athletics ... Mr. Charles J. GORDON
18 Director of Facilities ... Mr. Ronald MARTUCCI
19 Director Security & Safety ... Mr. Vincent MARKOWSKI
88 Director Educ Opportunity Program ... Mr. Lorne WEEMS
50 Dean Anisfield School of Business ... Dr. Lewis CHAKRIN
82 Dean Salameno Sch Amer Intl Studies ... Dr. Stephen RICE
57 Dean Sch of Contemporary Arts ... Mr. Steven PERRY
83 Dean Sch Soc Science & Human Svc ... Dr. Aaron R S. LORENZ
81 Dean Sch Theoretical/Applied Sci ... Dr. Edward SAIFF
53 Asst Dean for Teacher Education ... Dr. Rexton LYNN
38 Director Ctr for Health/Counseling ... Dr. Judith GREEN
29 Dir Alumni Relations/Dev Info Svcs ... Ms. Purvi PAREKH
24 Asst Manager Academic Media Svcs ... Mr. Michael SAVIANESO
04 Executive Assistant to President ... Vacant
23 Coordinator Health Services ... Ms. Debbie LUKACSKO
09 Director of Institutional Research ... Dr. Gurvinder KHANEJA
22 Dir Affirm Action/EEO & Acting DOS ... Ms. Melissa VAN DER WALL
40 Bookstore Manager ... Ms. Theresa KING
85 Exec Director of Intl Education ... Mr. Ben LEVY
36 Asst Dir Career Dev & Placement ... Ms. Debra STARK
96 Director of Purchasing ... Mr. Stephen SONDEY

Raritan Valley Community College (G)

118 Lamington Road, Branchburg NJ 08876
County: Somerset FICE Identification: 007731
Unit ID: 186645
Telephone: (908) 526-1200 Carnegie Class: Assoc/Pub-S-SC
FAX Number: (908) 526-0253 Calendar System: Semester
URL: www.raritanval.edu
Established: 1966 Annual Undergrad Tuition & Fees (In-District): $5,034

Enrollment: 8,214 Coed
Affiliation or Control: State/Local IRS Status: 501(c)3
Highest Offering: Associate Degree
Program: Occupational; 2-Year Principally Bachelor's Creditable
Accreditation: M, ADNUR, CAHIIM, MAC, OPD

01 President ....Dr. Michael MCDONOUGH
05 Sr Vice Pres Academic Affairs ....Vacant
10 Vice President Finance/Facilities ....Mr. John TROJAN
13 Vice Pres Technology/Assess/Plng ....Mr. Charles E. CHULVICK
15 VP Human Resources/Labor Relations ....Ms. Nancy MOORE
30 VP of Strategic Programs & Develop ....Ms. Jackie BELIN
20 Dean Academic Affairs ....Dr. Patrice MARKS
32 Dean Student Services ....Ms. Diane LEMCOE
85 Dean Multicultural Affairs ....Ms. Richeleen DASHIELD
18 Exec Director Facilities/Grounds ....Mr. Brian O'ROURKE
38 Dir of Student Advising & Couns ....Mr. Greg DESANCTIS
24 Director Media Relations ....Ms. Donna STOLZER
88 Conference Services Director ....Ms. Karen VAUGHAN
72 Executive Director Inst Technology ....Mr. Michael E. MACHNIK
102 Executive Director Foundation ....Ms. Ronnie WEYL
13 Information Technology Director ....Mr. Robert PESCINSKI
21 Controller/Exec Dir of Finance ....Ms. Violet J. WILLENSKY
57 Director of Theatre ....Mr. Alan C. LIDDELL
09 Dir of Inst Research/Assessment ....Mr. Faxian YANG
88 Director of Planetarium ....Ms. Amy GALLAGHER
88 Director of Child Care Center ....Ms. Cathy GRIFFIN
37 Director of Financial Aid ....Mr. Lenny MESONAS
08 Library Director ....Vacant
06 Registrar ....Mr. Dan PALUBNIAK
96 Executive Director Business Service ....Mr. Lester MILLER
35 Director of Student Life ....Mr. Russell BAREFOOT
36 Director Transfer/Career Services ....Mr. Paul MICHAUD
26 Executive Director Marketing ....Ms. Janet THOMPSON
07 Director of Admissions ....Ms. Jache WILLIAMS
103 Exec Dir Workforce Development ....Vacant
19 Director Security/Safety ....Mr. Robert SZKODNEY
41 Athletic Director ....Ms. Amanda DEMARTINO

Rider University (A)

2083 Lawrenceville Road, Lawrenceville NJ 08648-3099
County: Mercer FICE Identification: 002628
Unit ID: 186283
Telephone: (609) 896-5000 Carnegie Class: Master's L
FAX Number: (609) 896-8029 Calendar System: Semester
URL: www.rider.edu
Established: 1865 Annual Undergrad Tuition & Fees: $38,360
Enrollment: 5,326 Coed
Affiliation or Control: Independent Non-Profit IRS Status: 501(c)3
Highest Offering: Master's
Program: Liberal Arts And General; Teacher Preparatory; Professional
Accreditation: M, BUS, BUSA, CACREP, MUS, NURSE, TED

01 President ....Dr. Gregory DELL'OMO
05 Provost/Vice Pres Academic Affairs ....Dr. DonnaJean A. FREDEEN
10 Vice President Finance/Treasurer ....Ms. Julie A. KARNS
30 Vice Pres University Advancement ....Mr. Jonathan D. MEER
32 VP Student Affairs/Dean of Students ....Dr. Anthony CAMPBELL
84 Vice Pres Enrollment Management ....Mr. James P. O'HARA
13 Assoc VP Information Technology ....Ms. Carol S. KONDRACH
21 Associate Vice President/Controller ....Ms. Jennifer M. POTTER
09 Assoc Vice Pres Institutional Rsrch ....Mr. Ronald WALKER
18 AVP Facilities/Auxiliary Services ....Mr. Michael F. RECA
45 Associate Vice President Planning ....Ms. Debbie STASOLLA
26 Asst VP for Univ Comm/Marketing ....Mr. John G. LENOX
20 Associate Provost ....Dr. James O. CASTAGNERA
12 Dean Westminster ....Dr. Matthew R. SHAFTEL
07 Dean of Enrollment ....Ms. Susan C. CHRISTIAN
51 Dean College of Cont Studies ....Mr. Boris VILIC
49 Dean Liberal Arts & Science/Educ ....Dr. Pat MOSTO
53 Dean School of Education ....Dr. Sharon SHERMAN
50 Dean Business Administration ....Dr. Elad J. GRANOT
06 Registrar ....Ms. Susan A. STEFANICK
08 Dean of Library Services ....Mr. F. William CHICKERING
15 Dir Human Resources/Affirm Action ....Mr. Robert STOTO
19 Director of Public Safety ....Ms. Vickie L. WEAVER
29 Director of Alumni Relations ....Ms. Natalie M. POLLARD
41 Director of Athletics ....Mr. Donald P. HARNUM
37 Director Student Financial Svcs ....Mr. Drew C. AROMANDO
40 Manager College Store ....Mr. Joseph JUDGE
04 Executive Asst to the President ....Ms. Christine ZELENAK
27 Communications Director ....Ms. Aimee LABRIE
36 Director of Career Placement ....Vacant

Rowan College at Burlington County (B)

601 Pemberton-Browns Mills Road,
Pemberton NJ 08068-1599
County: Burlington FICE Identification: 007730
Unit ID: 183877
Telephone: (609) 894-9311 Carnegie Class: Assoc/Pub-S-MC
FAX Number: (609) 894-0183 Calendar System: Semester
URL: www.rcbc.edu
Established: 1966 Annual Undergrad Tuition & Fees (In-District): $4,065
Enrollment: 9,438 Coed
Affiliation or Control: State/Local IRS Status: 501(c)3
Highest Offering: Associate Degree
Program: Occupational; 2-Year Principally Bachelor's Creditable
Accreditation: M, ADNUR, CAHIIM, DH, DMS, ENGT, RAD

01 President ....Mr. Paul DRAYTON
04 Admin Asst to the President ....Ms. Lynne Marie DEVERICKS
05 Sr Vice Pres/Provost ....Dr. David SPANG
88 Interim VP Special Projects ....Dr. Beverly A. RICHARDSON
32 VP for Student Success ....Dr. Terrence HARDEE
84 Vice Pres Enrollment Mgmt ....Mr. Michael CIOCE
13 Chief Info Officer & Exec Dir Facil ....Mr. Mark MEARA
10 Chief Financial/Admin Officer ....Ms. Jaclyn ANGERMEIER
11 Chief Operations Officer ....Mr. Matthew FARR
102 Actg Exec Director Foundation ....Ms. Rebecca A. CORBIN
26 Exec Dir Marketing/Communications ....Mr. Greg VOLPE
09 Exec Dir of Inst Effect & Research ....Vacant
15 Exec Director of Human Resources ....Ms. Stacy JANKIEWICZ
49 Dean of Liberal Arts ....Dr. Nichole BENNETT-BEALER
81 Dean Science Math & Technology ....Dr. Anand RAMASWAMI
66 Assoc Dean of Nursing/Allied Health ....Dr. Sandra QUINN
06 Assoc Dean Admissions/ Registration ....Ms. Nyambura M. PHILLIPS
106 Assoc Dn Dist Educ/Integ Learn Res ....Mr. Martin A. HOFFMAN, SR.
88 Assoc Dean Educational Services ....Ms. Sharon ROGERS
35 Assoc Dean Student Act/Campus Pgms ....Ms. Catherine R. BRIGGS
20 Assoc Dean Acad Adv and Programs ....Ms. Tracey THOMAS
88 Assoc Dean of Client Services ....Mr. Roy MILLER
41 Director of Athletics ....Ms. Heather CONGER
36 Director of Career Services ....Ms. Roseanne BUCKLEY
88 Director of Culinary Arts ....Ms. Elizabeth M. DINICE
88 Director of EOF Program ....Ms. Edith CORBIN
88 Dir Bus Incub & Asst Dir Grants ....Ms. Barbara WITKOWSKI
25 Director of Grants ....Dr. Nicole SCOTT
88 Director of Military Ed & Vet Svcs ....Ms. Christine ULCH
19 Director of Public Safety ....Ms. Linda SCHMIDT
88 Director of Transfer ....Dr. Robert ARIOSTO

Rowan College at Gloucester County (C)

1400 Tanyard Road, Sewell NJ 08080-9518
County: Gloucester FICE Identification: 006901
Unit ID: 184791
Telephone: (856) 468-5000 Carnegie Class: Assoc/Pub-S-SC
FAX Number: N/A Calendar System: 4/1/4
URL: www.rcgc.edu
Established: 1966 Annual Undergrad Tuition & Fees (In-District): $4,125
Enrollment: 7,130 Coed
Affiliation or Control: State/Local IRS Status: 501(c)3
Highest Offering: Associate Degree
Program: Occupational; 2-Year Principally Bachelor's Creditable
Accreditation: M, ADNUR, DMS, NMT

01 President ....Dr. Frederick KEATING
05 VP Academic Services ....Dr. Linda HURLBURT
03 Vice President & COO ....Mr. Dominick BURZICHELLI
32 Vice President Student Svcs ....Ms. Judith ATKINSON
10 Exec Director Financial Services ....Mrs. Elizabeth HALL
15 Exec Director Human Resource ....Mrs. Marlene LOGLISCI
04 Sr Exec Assistant to the President ....Mrs. Karen SITARSKI
22 Exec Dir Diversity and Equity ....Mrs. Almarie JONES
09 Dean Inst Research & Assessment ....Ms. Karen DURKIN
13 Chief Information Officer ....Mr. Josh R. PIDDINGTON
66 Dean Nursing & Allied Health ....Dr. Susan HALL
49 Dean Liberal Arts ....Dr. Paul RUFINO
81 Dean STEM ....Dr. Brenden RICKARDS
20 Dean Academic Compliance ....Ms. Yvonne GREENBAUN
68 Dean Health/Physical Educ/Rec ....Mr. Ron CASE
88 Dean Public Safety & Security ....Mr. Fred H. MADDEN
50 Dean Business Studies ....Ms. Patricia CLAGHORN
07 Director Admissions/Registrar ....Ms. Sandra HOFFMAN
36 Director Advising ....Mr. Richard BROWN
35 Director Student Affairs ....Ms. Samantha VAN KOOY
08 Director Library Services ....Mrs. Jane S. CROCKER
102 Dir Foundation/Corporate Relations ....Mr. Ray PAGE
19 Director Security/Safety ....Mr. Joseph GETSINGER
26 Chief Public Relations/Marketing ....Ms. Eileen SHUTE
37 Exec Dir Financial Aid & Admission ....Mr. Michael CHANDO
96 Director of Purchasing ....Mr. Mark ZORZI

Rowan University (D)

201 Mullica Hill Road, Glassboro NJ 08028-1700
County: Gloucester FICE Identification: 002609
Unit ID: 184782
Telephone: (856) 256-4000 Carnegie Class: Master's L
FAX Number: (856) 256-4929 Calendar System: Semester
URL: www.rowan.edu
Established: 1923 Annual Undergrad Tuition & Fees (In-State): $12,864
Enrollment: 14,778 Coed
Affiliation or Control: State IRS Status: 501(c)3
Highest Offering: Doctorate
Program: Liberal Arts And General; Teacher Preparatory; Professional
Accreditation: M, ART, BUS, CAATE, CACREP, CS, ENG, #MED, MUS, NURSE, OSTEO, TED, THEA

01 President ....Dr. Ali A. HOUSHMAND
03 Executive VP ....Dr. Carl OXHOLM, III
05 Provost ....Dr. James NEWELL
10 Senior Vice Pres of Finance/CFO ....Mr. Joseph F. SCULLY
30 Senior VP University Advancement ....Mr. John ZABINSKI
32 VP Student Life/Dean of Students ....Mr. Richard JONES
86 Senior VP for Govt Rels/Gen Couns ....Mr. Steve WEINSTEIN
18 Senior VP for Facilities & Opers ....Mr. Donald MOORE
44 VP University Advancement ....Mr. Ronald J. TALLARIDA
20 VP Academic Affairs ....Dr. Roberta HARVEY
100 VP/Chief of Staff ....Mr. Robert ZAZZALI
46 VP Research ....Dr. Shreekanth MANDAYAM
13 VP Information Resources/CIO ....Dr. Mira LALOVIC-HAND
26 VP for University Relations ....Dr. Jose CARDONA
84 VP Strategic Enrollment Management ....Dr. Jeffrey HAND
88 Asst VP Campus Rec/Stdnt Ctr/CES ....Ms. Tina M. PINOCCI
19 Asst VP Public Safety/Emerg Mgmt ....Mr. Michael KANTNER
15 Asst VP Labor Relations ....Mr. Kenneth KUERZI
38 Sr Dir Counseling/Psych Services ....Dr. David RUBENSTEIN
91 Asst VP of EIS ....Mr. James HENDERSON
37 Interim Director of Financial Aid ....Ms. Sandra ROLLINS
06 Registrar ....Ms. Muriel FRIERSON
63 Dean of Cooper Medical School of RU ....Dr. Paul KATZ
08 Assoc Provost Library Info Services ....Mr. Scott MUIR
50 Dean Rohrer College of Business ....Dr. Susan LEHRMAN
81 Dean College of Science/Mathematics ....Dr. Karen MAGEE-SAUER
53 Dean of Education ....Dr. Monika SHEALEY
57 Dean of Performing Arts ....Dr. John R. PASTIN
58 VP Global Learning & Partnerships ....Dr. Horacio SOSA
54 Dean of Engineering ....Dr. Tony LOWMAN
60 Dean Communication & Creative Arts ....Dr. Lorin ARNOLD
83 Dean Humanities & Social Sciences ....Dr. Cindy VITTO
88 Dean School of Osteopathic Medicine ....Dr. Thomas CAVALIERI
88 AVP Global Learning & Partnerships ....Dr. Tyrone MCCOMBS
16 Assoc VP Employment/Labor Relations ....Ms. Eileen SCOTT
22 Asst VP for Equity and Diversity ....Dr. Johanna VELEZ-YELIN
41 Director of Athletics ....Mr. Dan GILMORE
88 Dir Distinguished Events/Spec Proj ....Ms. Kathy ROZANSKI
07 Director of Admissions ....Dr. Albert BETTS
36 Dir Career Management Center ....Vacant
96 Sr Dir Contracting & Procurement ....Ms. Christina BRASTETER
27 Asst VP University Relations ....Ms. Lori MARSHALL
105 Director University Web Services ....Ms. Jennifer BELL
85 Director International Center ....Mr. Timothy TORRE
28 Asst VP Acad Enrich/EOF/MAP Dir ....Dr. Penny MCPHERSON
04 Exec Asst to the President ....Dr. Joanne CONNOR

Rowan University at Camden (E)

200 North Broadway, Camden NJ 08102
Telephone: (856) 361-2900 Identification: 770132
Accreditation: &M

† Branch campus of Rowan University, Glassboro, NJ.

*Rutgers the State University of New Jersey Central Office (F)

83 Somerset Street, New Brunswick NJ 08901-1281
County: Middlesex FICE Identification: 002629
Unit ID: 186362
Telephone: (848) 445-4636 Carnegie Class: N/A
FAX Number: (732) 932-8060
URL: www.rutgers.edu

01 President ....Dr. Robert L. BARCHI
02 Chancellor Rutgers-New Brunswick ....Dr. Richard EDWARDS
11 Sr VP for Administration ....Mr. Bruce C. FEHN
05 Sr VP Academic Affairs ....Dr. Barbara A. LEE
102 Pres Rutgers Found/EVP Dev & Alum ....Mr. Nevin E. KESSLER
10 Senior VP for Finance & Admin ....Mr. John M. GOWER
21 Vice President Budgeting ....Dr. Nancy S. WINTERBAUER
13 Vice President Info Tech ....Mr. Donald E. SMITH
26 Vice President University Relations ....Ms. Kimberly M. MANNING
18 Vice Pres Univ Facil/Capital Plng ....Mr. Antonio CALCADO
88 Vice Chancellor Interprofess Ed ....Dr. Denise RODGERS
43 Interim Senior VP & General Counsel ....Ms. Monica C. BARRETT
30 Sr VP Campaign & Development Oper ....Ms. Julie SHADLE
04 Exec Assistant to the President ....Ms. Carol KONCSOL
20 VP Academic Affairs & Admin ....Dr. Karen R. STUBAUS
15 VP of Fac & Staff Resources ....Ms. Vivian FERNANDEZ
08 VP Info Services & Univ Librarian ....Ms. Krisellen MALONEY
101 Interim Secretary of the University ....Kimberlee M. PASTVA
19 Exec Director Police Services ....Kenneth B. COP
23 Exec Director Health Svcs ....Dr. Melodee S. LASKY
06 Executive University Registrar ....Mr. Kenneth J. IUSO
37 University Dir Financial Aid ....Ms. Jean MCDONALD-RASH
41 Director Intercollegiate Athletics ....Ms. Julie K. HERMANN
22 Assoc VP Labor Relations ....Mr. Harry M. AGNOSTAK
36 Director Career Services ....Ms. Jennifer BROYLES
09 Exec Dir Inst Research & Planning ....Dr. Robert J. HEFFERNAN
86 Senior VP External Affairs ....Mr. Peter J. MCDONOUGH, JR.
84 VP Enrollment Management ....Dr. Courtney MCANUFF
29 VP Alumni Relations ....Ms. Donna THORNTON
86 Asst VP Federal Relations ....Ms. Francine PFEIFFER
86 VP State Government Affairs ....Ms. Julane W. MILLER-ARMBRISTER
88 Assc VP Promtg Women Sci Eng Math ....Dr. Joan W. BENNETT
88 VP Health Science Partnerships ....Dr. Kenneth J. BRESLAUER
12 Chancellor New Brunswick ....Dr. Richard EDWARDS
12 Chancellor Rutgers-Camden ....Dr. Phoebe A. HADDON
12 Chancellor RU Newark ....Dr. Nancy E. CANTOR
88 Chancellor Biomed & Health Sci ....Dr. Brian L. STROM
88 Director Cancer Institute NJ ....Dr. Robert S. DIPAOLA
88 Senior VP Research & Econ Dev ....Dr. Christopher J. MOLLOY
88 VP Physical Sci & Eng Partnership ....Dr. Leonard C. FELDMAN
88 Sr Vice Chancellor Pub Affairs ....Dr. Peter T. ENGLOT
11 Vice Chancellor Admin & Finance ....Dr. Larry R. GAINES, JR.
20 Vice Chancellor Acad Pgms & Svcs ....Dr. John GUNKEL
88 University Controller ....Mr. Stephen J. DIPAOLO
21 VP Finance & Assoc Treasurer ....Ms. Delanie S. MOLER

88 VP International & Global Affairs .... Dr. Joanna REGULSKA
106 VP Cont Stdnt & Dist Educ .... Dr. Richard J. NOVAK
28 VP Intl Diversity & Inclusion .... Dr. Jorge R. SCHEMENT
88 Interim Sr VP/Chief Enterprise Risk .... Dr. Frances V. BOUCHOUX

*Rutgers the State University of New Jersey Camden Campus (A)

303 Cooper Street, Camden NJ 08102-1461

County: Camden FICE Identification: 004741
Unit ID: 186371
Telephone: (856) 225-6026 Carnegie Class: Master's M
FAX Number: (856) 225-6495 Calendar System: Semester
URL: www.camden.rutgers.edu
Established: 1927 Annual Undergrad Tuition & Fees (In-State): $14,000
Enrollment: 6,321 Coed
Affiliation or Control: State IRS Status: 501(c)3
Highest Offering: Doctorate
Program: Liberal Arts And General; Teacher Preparatory; Professional
Accreditation: &M, BUS, LAW, NURSE, PTA, SPAA, TEAC

02 Chancellor .... Dr. Phoebe A. HADDON
05 Provost .... Dr. Michael PALIS
11 Vice Chancellor Admin & Finance .... Dr. Larry R. GAINES, JR.
32 Assoc Chancellor Student Life .... Dr. Mary Beth B. DAISEY
20 Assoc Chancellor for UG Education .... Ms. Julie AMON
84 Assoc Chancellor Enroll Mgmt .... Dr. Craig WESTMAN
88 Asst Chancellor Civic Engage .... Ms. Nyemma WATSON
88 Director Economic Development .... Mr. Gregory GAMBLE
61 Acting Dean School of Law .... Dr. John F. OBERDIEK
58 Dean Grad School .... Dr. Kriste LINDENMEYER
50 Dean School of Business .... Dr. Jaishankar GANESH
49 Dean Fac Arts & Sci/Univ Col .... Dr. Kriste LINDENMEYER
66 Dean School of Nursing .... Dr. Joanne P. ROBINSON
26 Assoc Chancellor for Ext Relations .... Mr. Michael J. SEPANIC
06 Registrar .... Ms. Theresa R. CRISTOFARO
37 Director Financial Aid .... Ms. Linda J. TAYLOR-BURCH
10 Director Campus Financial Services .... Ms. Rosa M. RIVERA
19 Chief Campus Police .... Chief Guy M. STILL
29 Director Alumni Relations .... Mr. Scott D. OWENS
15 Human Resources Manager .... Mr. Gregory M. O'SHEA
18 Assoc Director Facilities Services .... Ms. Rona LEHTONEN
21 Business Manager FAS Camden .... Ms. Marlene DRUDING
41 Dir Athletics & Rec Services .... Mr. Jeffrey L. DEAN
36 Asst Dean Career Center .... Ms. Cheryl A. HALLMAN
38 Assoc Director Student Counseling .... Dr. N. Maria SERRA
30 Director of Development .... Ms. Akua ASIAMAH-ANDRADE
08 Director Paul Robeson Library .... Dr. Gary A. GOLDEN
23 Director Health Services .... Dr. N. Maria SERRA
39 Director Housing .... Mr. Brandon CHANDLER
87 Summer Coord/Sr Program Coordinator .... Dr. Paul C. BUTLER
46 Director Sponsored Research .... Ms. Carberta A. MORRISON
13 Director Information Technology .... Mr. Joseph R. SANDERS
30 Asst Chancellor Development .... Mr. Drew A. KAIDEN
07 Director of Admissions .... Ms. Victoria E. TOOMER
85 Asst Dean International Students .... Ms. Elizabeth A. ATKINS
35 Dean of Students .... Dr. Thomas J. DIVALERIO
96 Senior Buyer .... Mr. Christian AHA
100 Chief of Staff .... Dr. Loree D. JONES

† Regional accreditation is carried under Rutgers the State University of New Jersey New Brunswick.

*Rutgers the State University of New Jersey New Brunswick Campus (B)

85 Somerset Street, New Brunswick NJ 08901-1281

County: Middlesex FICE Identification: 006964
Unit ID: 186380
Telephone: (848) 932-4636 Carnegie Class: RU/VH
FAX Number: (732) 932-8060 Calendar System: Semester
URL: www.rutgers.edu
Established: 1766 Annual Undergrad Tuition & Fees (In-State): $14,131
Enrollment: 48,378 Coed
Affiliation or Control: State IRS Status: 501(c)3
Highest Offering: Doctorate
Program: 2-Year Principally Bachelor's Creditable; Liberal Arts And General; Teacher Preparatory; Professional
Accreditation: M, CACREP, CEA, CLPSY, DANCE, DIETD, ENG, LIB, LSAR, MUS, PH, PHAR, PLNG, SCPSY, SPAA, SW, TEAC

02 Chancellor NB Campus .... Dr. Richard EDWARDS
32 Vice Chancellor Student Affairs .... Ms. Felicia E. MCGINTY
10 Vice Chancellor Finance .... Ms. Mary Lou ORTIZ
05 Provost New Brunswick .... Dr. Lily Y. YOUNG
84 VP Enrollment Management .... Dr. Courtney O. MCANUFF
11 VP Acad Affairs & Administration .... Dr. Karen R. STUBAUS
28 VP Inst Diversity & Inclusion .... Dr. Jorge R. SCHEMENT
08 Interim VP Info Svcs/U Librarian .... Ms. Jeanne E. BOYLE
58 Dean Graduate School .... Dr. Jerome J. KUKOR
80 Dean EJB School Plng/Public Policy .... Dr. James W. HUGHES
81 Exec Dean Sch Enviro/Biological Sci .... Dr. Robert M. GOODMAN
12 Dean Douglass Residential College .... Dr. Jacquelyn S. LITT
12 Dean Livingston Campus .... Dr. Lea P. STEWART
12 Dean Busch Campus .... Dr. Thomas V. PAPATHOMAS
49 Executive Dean of SAS .... Dr. Peter MARCH
92 Honors College Admin Dean .... Dr. Paul GILMORE
12 Dean Cook Campus .... Dr. Barbara TURPIN
12 Dean Univ College Community .... Dr. Susan J. SCHURMAN
54 Dean School of Engineering .... Dr. Thomas N. FARRIS
67 Dean Ernest Mario Sch Pharm .... Dr. Joseph BARONE
57 Dean Mason Gross School of Art .... Dr. George B. STAUFFER
62 Dean Sch Communication & Info .... Dr. Jonathan POTTER
83 Dean Grad School Applied/Prof Psych ...... Dr. Stanley B. MESSER
53 Dean Grad School of Education .... Dr. Wanda J. BLANCHETT
66 Dean School of Nursing .... Dr. William L. HOLZEMER
70 Dean School of Social Work .... Dr. Cathryn C. POTTER
69 Interim Dean Sch Public Health .... Dr. George G. RHOADS
50 Dean Sch of Business Newark/NB .... Dr. Lei LEI
88 Dean Sch Mgmt Labor Relations .... Dr. James C. HAYTON
06 Executive University Registrar .... Mr. Kenneth J. IUSO
104 Director Rutgers Study Abroad .... Dr. Giorgio G. DIMAURO
07 Director Graduate Admissions .... Ms. Linda J. COSTA
37 University Dir Financial Aid .... Ms. Jean MCDONALD-RASH
36 Dir Career Dev/Placement Svcs .... Ms. Jennifer BROYLES
27 Deputy Chief Information Officer .... Ms. Bernice GINDER
09 Exec Dir Institutional Rsrch & Plng ...... Dr. Robert J. HEFFERNAN
39 Director Residence Life .... Mr. Michael TOLBERT
19 Exec Dir Police Services/Chief .... Mr. Kenneth B. COP
88 Dean College Avenue Campus .... Dr. Matthew K. MATSUDA
88 Director Rutgers China Office .... Dr. Jeff (Jianfeng) WANG

*Rutgers the State University of New Jersey Newark Campus (C)

249 University Avenue, Newark NJ 07102-1897

County: Essex FICE Identification: 002631
Unit ID: 186399
Telephone: (973) 353-5568 Carnegie Class: RU/H
FAX Number: (973) 353-1048 Calendar System: Semester
URL: www.newark.rutgers.edu
Established: 1892 Annual Undergrad Tuition & Fees (In-State): $13,597
Enrollment: 11,314 Coed
Affiliation or Control: State IRS Status: 501(c)3
Highest Offering: Doctorate
Program: Liberal Arts And General; Teacher Preparatory; Professional
Accreditation: &M, ANEST, BUS, LAW, NURSE, SPAA, SW, TEAC

02 Chancellor .... Dr. Nancy E. CANTOR
05 Provost & Sr Vice Chancellor .... Dr. Todd R. CLEAR
11 Exec Vice Chanc & Chief Oper Ofcr .... Dr. Shirley M. COLLADO
100 Vice Chancellor & Chief of Staff .... Dr. Peter T. ENGLOT
10 Vice Chancellor Admin & CFO .... Dr. Arcelio APONTE
86 Vice Chanc External & Govt Rels .... Dr. Marcia W. BROWN
15 Asst Vice Provost Human Resources .... Dr. Bil LEIPOLD
18 Assoc Vice Chancellor Facilities .... Dr. Christopher PYE
30 Vice Chancellor for Development .... Dr. Irene O'BRIEN
20 Vice Chancellor Acad Pgms & Svcs .... Dr. John GUNKEL
46 Vice Chancellor Research .... Dr. Nabil ADAM
84 Asst Chancellor for Enroll Managmnt .... Dr. Ben ROHDIN
45 Asst Provost for Budget .... Dr. Mary TAMASCO
32 Assoc Chancellor for Student Life .... Dr. Gerald MASSENBURG
31 Asst Chancellor Comm Partner .... Dr. Diane HILL
06 Registrar .... Dr. Marie DIAZ-TORRES
21 Exec Dir Business & Financial Svcs .... Dr. Sanjana RIMAL
13 Interim Dir Information Technology .... Mr. Galen J. WORK
07 Asst Prov & Dean of Admissions ... Ms. LaToya BATTLE-BROWN
19 Director Public Safety Newark .... Mr. Carmelo V. HUERTAS
27 Director of Communications .... Ms. Helen S. PAXTON
37 Director Financial Aid .... Ms. Natalie L. MORISSEAU
49 Dean Faculty Arts & Science .... Dr. Jan Ellen LEWIS
61 Acting Dean of School of Law .... Dr. Ronald K. CHEN, JR.
50 Dean Business Newark/New Bruns .... Dr. Lei LEI
66 Dean School of Nursing .... Dr. William L. HOLZEMER
88 Dean School Criminal Justice .... Dr. Shadd MARUNA
38 Director Student Counseling .... Dr. Anice THOMAS
96 Director of Purchasing & Admin Svc .... Mr. Alvin L. COOLEY
80 Dean Sch of Public Affairs & Admin .... Dr. Marc HOLZER
39 Director Housing & Residence Life .... Dr. Angelita BONILLA
23 Director Health Services .... Dr. Sandra SAMUELS
41 Director of Athletics & Recreation .... Mr. Mark GRIFFIN
82 Director of Global Affairs .... Dr. Jean-Marc COICAUD
58 Dean Graduate School Newark .... Dr. Kyle W. FARMBRY
87 Manager Summer Session .... Ms. Carmen L. PARDO
88 Assoc Dean/Dir Robeson Campus Ctr .... Dr. Clayton WALTON
28 Director Diverse Community Affairs .... Dr. Maren GREATHOUSE
04 Sr Exec Assoc to the Chancellor .... Ms. Sharon MACKLIN

† Regional accreditation is carried under Rutgers the State University of New Jersey New Brunswick.

*Rutgers Graduate School of Biomedical Sciences (D)

185 South Orange Avenue, MSB C-696, Newark NJ 07107-1709

Telephone: (973) 972-5332 FICE Identification: 011174
Accreditation: &M

† Branch campus of Rutgers the State University of New Jersey Central Office, New Brunswick, NJ.

*Rutgers-New Jersey Medical School (E)

185 S Orange Avenue, Newark NJ 07101-1709

Telephone: (973) 972-4538 FICE Identification: 002620
Accreditation: &M, MED

† Branch campus of Rutgers the State University of New Jersey Central Office, New Brunswick, NJ.

*Rutgers - Robert Wood Johnson Medical School (F)

675 Hoes Lane, Piscataway NJ 08854-5635

Telephone: (732) 235-6300 FICE Identification: 024549
Accreditation: &M, IPSY, MED, PAST

† Branch campus of Rutgers the State University of New Jersey Central Office, New Brunswick, NJ.

*Rutgers School of Dental Medicine (G)

110 Bergen Street, Room B-830, Newark NJ 07101-1709

Telephone: (973) 972-4633 FICE Identification: 024635
Accreditation: &M, DENT

† Branch campus of Rutgers the State University of New Jersey Central Office, New Brunswick, NJ.

*Rutgers School of Health Related Professions (H)

65 Bergen Street, Room 149, Newark NJ 07101-1709

Telephone: (973) 972-5454 FICE Identification: 020668
Accreditation: &M, ARCPA, CACREP, CAHIIM, COARC, CORE, CVT, CYTO, DA, DH, DIETC, DIETI, DMS, MT, #NMT, OTA, PHLEB, PTA

† Branch campus of Rutgers the State University of New Jersey Central Office, New Brunswick, NJ.

*Rutgers School of Nursing (I)

180 University Avenue, Newark NJ 07102

Telephone: (973) 353-5293 Identification: 666970
Accreditation: &M, MIDWF, NURSE

† Branch campus of Rutgers the State University of New Jersey Central Office, New Brunswick, NJ.

*Rutgers School of Public Health (J)

683 Hoes Lane West, Room 235, Piscataway NJ 08854-8021

Telephone: (732) 235-9700 Identification: 666991
Accreditation: &M, PH

† Branch campus of Rutgers the State University of New Jersey Central Office, New Brunswick, NJ.

Saint Peter's University (K)

2641 Kennedy Boulevard, Jersey City NJ 07306-5997

County: Hudson FICE Identification: 002638
Unit ID: 186432
Telephone: (201) 761-6000 Carnegie Class: Master's L
FAX Number: (201) 761-7801 Calendar System: Semester
URL: www.saintpeters.edu
Established: 1872 Annual Undergrad Tuition & Fees: $34,198
Enrollment: 3,302 Coed
Affiliation or Control: Roman Catholic IRS Status: 501(c)3
Highest Offering: Doctorate
Program: Liberal Arts And General; Teacher Preparatory; Professional
Accreditation: M, IACBE, NURSE

01 President .... Dr. Eugene J. CORNACCHIA
05 Provost/VP Academic Affairs .... Dr. Gerard P. O'SULLIVAN
10 Vice Pres of Finance & Business .... Mr. Denton L. STARGEL
30 Vice President Advancement .... Ms. Leah LETO
32 Assoc VP Student Life & Develop .... Ms. Carla THARP
42 Vice Pres for Mission & Ministry .... Fr. Michael L. BRADEN, SJ
84 VP Enrollment Mgmt & Marketing .... Mr. Jeffrey HANDLER
45 Spec Asst to President for Planning .... Dr. Virginia BENDER
51 Assoc Dean & Director of JC SPCS .... Ms. Elizabeth KANE
78 Exec Dir of Experiential Lrng .... Vacant
20 Associate Dean of Undergraduates .... Dr. Anna CICIRELLI
35 Dean of Students .... Mr. Anthony SKEVAKIS
26 Director University Communications .... Ms. Sarah MALINOWSKI-FERRARY
84 Director Enrollment/Research/Tech .... Mr. Ben SCHOLZ
07 Assoc VP and Dean of Admissions .... Ms. Elizabeth SULLIVAN
08 Director of the Libraries .... Mr. David HARDGROVE
37 Director of Student Fin Aid .... Ms. Jennifer RAGSDALE
06 Registrar .... Ms. Deborah EBBERT
13 Chief Information Officer .... Ms. Dale HOCHSTEIN
09 Director of Institutional Research .... Mr. Lamberto C. NIEVES
66 Dean of Nursing .... Dr. Lauren O'HARE
19 Director of Campus Safety .... Mr. Scott TORRE
15 Director of Human Resources .... Mr. Joseph A. DESCISCIO
29 Exec Director Alumni Engagement .... Ms. Gloria MERCURIO
30 Director of Gift/Planning .... Ms. Ana M. CRAVO
38 Director Personal Development .... Mr. Ron BECKER
39 Director of Residence Life .... Ms. Victoria FARRIS
41 Director of Athletics .... Mr. Joseph QUINLAN
42 Director of Campus Ministry .... Rev. Rocco DANZI, SJ
36 Director of Career Services .... Mr. Crescenzo FONZO
14 Director of Network Services .... Mr. Bert VABRE
85 Foreign Studies Adviser .... Mr. Tushar TRIVEDI
18 Manager of College Services .... Ms. Anna DE PAULA
102 Dir Foundation/Corporate Relations .... Vacant
104 Director Study Abroad .... Ms. Wendy GARAY
105 Director Web Services .... Vacant
50 Dean of Business .... Mr. Louis RUVOLO
53 Dean of Education .... Dr. Joseph DORIA

96 Director of Purchasing ... Mr. John MATTHEWS
04 Administrative Asst to President ... Ms. Janice P. VIZZACCHERO
101 Secretary of the Institution/Board ... Dr. Virginia A. BENDER

Saint Peter's University Englewood Cliffs Campus (A)

Hudson Terrace, Englewood Cliffs NJ 07632
Telephone: (201) 761-7480 Identification: 770133
Accreditation: &M

† Branch campus of Saint Peter's University, Jersey City, NJ.

Salem Community College (B)

460 Hollywood Avenue, Carneys Point NJ 08069-2799
County: Salem FICE Identification: 005461
Unit ID: 186469
Telephone: (856) 299-2100 Carnegie Class: Assoc/Pub-S-SC
FAX Number: (856) 351-2634 Calendar System: Semester
URL: www.salemcc.edu
Established: 1972 Annual Undergrad Tuition & Fees (In-District): $4,050
Enrollment: 1,108 Coed
Affiliation or Control: State/Local IRS Status: 501(c)3
Highest Offering: Associate Degree
Program: Occupational; 2-Year Principally Bachelor's Creditable
Accreditation: M, ADNUR

01 President ... Dr. Michael GORMAN
04 Admin Asst Office of the President ... Ms. Maria FANTINI
05 VP of Academic Affairs/CAO ... Dr. Eric PELLEGRINO
88 Manager of Academic Programs ... Ms. Amanda SORSHEK
07 Dean of Enrollment/Admissions ... Mr. Kevin CATALFAMO
09 Director Inst Rsrch/Planning/Devel ... Ms. Denise DERSCH
88 Dir of Institutional Effectiveness ... Mr. Marc ROY
10 Int Chief Financial/Business Ofcr ... Mr. Ketan GANDHI
21 Manager of Finance ... Ms. Catherine PRIEST
96 Manager of Purchasing ... Mr. Richard DAVIDSON
88 Accounts Manager ... Ms. Maureen DOUGHERTY
15 Director of Human Resources ... Ms. Caroline COULET DUGARD
19 Director of Security/Safety ... Mr. John MORRISON
20 Associate Dean of Academic Affairs ... Mr. John STEINER
88 Assistant Dean of Academic Affairs ... Mr. Kenneth ROBEL
30 Dir of Inst Advancement/Alumni ... Mr. William CLARK
37 Int Dir Student Financial Services ... Mr. Ronald BURKHARDT
66 Director of Nursing ... Mr. Charles MCGLADE
88 Director of Retention & Admissions ... Ms. Kelly MCSHAY
88 Director of Academic & Info Svcs ... Ms. Jennifer PIERCE
102 Chief Foundation Officer ... Ms. Ceil SMITH
103 Director of Workforce/Career Dev ... Ms. Mary Ellen HASSLER

Seton Hall University (C)

400 S Orange Avenue, South Orange NJ 07079-2697
County: Essex FICE Identification: 002632
Unit ID: 186584
Telephone: (973) 761-9000 Carnegie Class: DRU
FAX Number: N/A Calendar System: Semester
URL: www.shu.edu
Established: 1856 Annual Undergrad Tuition & Fees: $38,072
Enrollment: 9,627 Coed
Affiliation or Control: Roman Catholic IRS Status: 501(c)3
Highest Offering: Doctorate
Program: Liberal Arts And General; Teacher Preparatory; Professional
Accreditation: M, ARCPA, BUS, BUSA, CAATE, COPSY, HSA, LAW, MFCD, NURSE, OT, PTA, SP, SPAA, SW, TED, THEOL

01 President ... Dr. A. Gabriel ESTEBAN
05 Provost & Executive Vice President ... Dr. Larry A. ROBINSON
20 Senior Associate Provost ... Dr. Joan GUETTI
20 Associate Vice Provost ... Msgr. Robert COLEMAN
10 Vice Pres for Finance/CFO ... Mr. Stephen A. GRAHAM
11 Vice President for Administration ... Mr. Dennis J. GARBINI
43 Vice President & General Counsel ... Ms. Catherine A. KIERNAN
30 Vice Pres Univ Advancement ... Mr. David BOHAN
32 Vice President Student Affairs ... Dr. Tracy T. GOTTLIEB
84 Vice President of Enrollment Mgmt ... Dr. Alyssa MCCLOUD
42 Vice Pres for Mission & Ministry ... Msgr. C. Anthony ZICCARDI
15 Assoc Vice Pres Human Resources ... Mr. David K. MCNICHOL
29 Assoc VP Alumni/Government Rels ... Mr. Matthew BOROWICK
44 Assoc Vice Pres Univ Advance ... Mr. Joseph GUASCONI
26 Assoc VP Public Relations & Mktg ... Mr. Dan P. KALMANSON
18 Assoc VP for Facilities & Operation ... Mr. John SIGNORELLO
35 Asst VP Student Affs/Dir Pub Safety ... Mr. Patrick LINFANTE
31 Asc VP/Dean of Students/Cmty Dev ... Ms. Karen VAN NORMAN
88 Assoc Prov Finance/Administration ... Ms. Mary Ann HART
45 Assoc Provost/Dean Rsrch/Grad Stds ... Dr. Gregory A. BURTON
88 Assoc Provost for Academic Projects ... Mr. Erik LILLQUIST
49 Interim Dean of Arts & Sciences ... Dr. Chrysanthy GRIECO
50 Dean School of Business ... Dr. Joyce A. STRAWSER
66 Dean of Nursing ... Dr. Marie FOLEY
53 Dean College Education Svcs ... Dr. Grace MAY
73 Dean School of Theology ... Msgr. Joseph R. REILLY
63 Dean School of Health & Med Science ... Dr. Brian SHULMAN
82 Dean Diplomacy/Intl Relations ... Dr. Andrea BARTOLI
61 Dean of Law School ... Ms. Kathleen BOOZANG
08 Dean of University Libraries ... Dr. John E. BUSCHMAN
51 Dean Cont Educ/Professional Studies ... Vacant
88 Assoc Dean/Director of EOP ... Dr. Hasani CARTER
88 Assoc Dean/Exec Dir of Special Pgms ... Ms. Cassandra E. DAVIS
21 Director of Business Affairs ... Mr. Michael GARCIA
13 Chief Information Officer ... Dr. Stephen LANDRY
28 Director Compliance & Risk Mgmt ... Ms. Lori A. BROWN
37 Director for Financial Aid ... Ms. Javonda T. ASSANTE
39 Director of Housing/Residence Life ... Ms. Tara HART
06 University Registrar ... Ms. Mary Ellen FARRELL
07 Recruitment/Compensation Manager ... Ms. Jane JACOBS
36 Director of the Career Center ... Ms. Reesa GREENWALD
41 Dir Athletics/Recreational Services ... Mr. Patrick G. LYONS
18 Director of Physical Plant ... Mr. Steve KURTYKA
38 Director of Counseling ... Dr. Katherine EVANS
42 Director of Campus Ministry ... Rev. Robert P. MCLAUGHLIN
88 Minister to Priest Community ... Msgr. Robert M. COLEMAN
09 Dir Planning Inst Research & Asses ... Ms. Connie L. BEALE
07 Dir of Undergraduate Admissions ... Vacant
96 Director of Procurement ... Mr. Martin E. KOELLER
23 Director Health Services ... Ms. Mary Elizabeth COSTELLO
88 Director Core Curriculum ... Dr. Anthony C. SCIGLITANO, JR.
102 Dir Foundation/Corporate Relations ... Ms. Stephanie HAUGE
104 Director Study Abroad ... Ms. Maria BOUZAS
108 Director Institutional Assessment ... Kuldeep PUPPALA
88 Asst Provost for Academic Affairs ... Dr. Christopher CUCCIA
86 Director Government Relations ... Mr. Matthew BOROWICK

Stevens Institute of Technology (D)

Castle Point on Hudson, Hoboken NJ 07030-5991
County: Hudson FICE Identification: 002639
Unit ID: 186867
Telephone: (201) 216-5000 Carnegie Class: RU/H
FAX Number: (201) 216-8341 Calendar System: Semester
URL: www.stevens.edu
Established: 1870 Annual Undergrad Tuition & Fees: $45,540
Enrollment: 6,125 Coed
Affiliation or Control: Independent Non-Profit IRS Status: 501(c)3
Highest Offering: Doctorate
Program: Liberal Arts And General; Technical Emphasis
Accreditation: M, BUS, CS, ENG

01 President ... Dr. Nariman FARVARDIN
04 Exec Assistant to the President ... Ms. Diana COLOMBO
05 Provost/University Vice President ... Dr. George P. KORFIATIS
30 Vice Pres Development ... Mr. Brodie REMINGTON
10 Vice Pres for Finance/Treasurer ... Mr. Randy GREENE
07 VP Enrollment/Student Affairs ... Ms. Marybeth MURPHY
15 Vice President Human Resources ... Mr. Mark SAMOLEWICZ
43 Vice President General Counsel ... Ms. Kathy L. SCHULZ
13 VP for Information Technology & CIO ... Mr. David DODD
26 VP Communications & Marketing ... Mr. Edward STUKANE
18 VP for Facilities & Campus Opers ... Mr. Robert MAFFIA
32 Assistant VP Student Affairs ... Ms. Corlisse THOMAS
21 AVP for Financial Planning/Budget ... Mr. Justin OATES
20 Dean Undergraduate Academics ... Dr. Larry RUSS
35 Dean of Student Life ... Mr. Kenneth NILSEN
39 Dean of Residence Life ... Ms. Trina BALLANTYNE
20 Assoc Dean Undergraduate Academics ... Dr. Erol CESMEBASI
29 Exec Director Alumni Association ... Ms. Anita LANG
36 Director of Career Services ... Ms. Lynn INSLEY
19 Chief/Director of Security ... Mr. Timothy GRIFFIN
41 Athletic Director ... Mr. Russell ROGERS
85 Dir of Intl Student/Scholar Svcs ... Ms. Doris CLAUSEN
38 Director Student Counseling ... Ms. Jodi STREICH
40 Manager Campus Bookstore ... Ms. Teresa TRIDENTE
25 Director Sponsored Research ... Ms. Barbara DEHAVEN
58 Dean of Graduate Academics ... Dr. Charles SUFFEL
54 Dean School of Engineering & Scienc ... Dr. Michael S. BRUNO
72 Dean Howe Sch of Technology Mgmt ... Dr. Gregory PRASTACOS
49 Dean College of Arts & Letters ... Dr. Lisa DOLLING
88 Dean School of Systems & Enterprise ... Dr. Dinesh VERMA
09 Director of Institutional Research ... Vacant
100 Chief of Staff ... Ms. Elisabeth MCGRATH
28 Director of Diversity and Inclusion ... Ms. Susan METZ
88 Vice Provost Strategic Initiatives ... Mr. Ralph G. GIFFIN
20 Vice Provost Academics ... Dr. Constantin CHASSAPIS
46 Vice Provost of Research ... Dr. Mo DEHGHANI
06 Registrar ... Mr. Thomas CASTIGLIONE
08 Interim Director ... Ms. Linda BENINGHOVE
104 Director International Programs ... Ms. Susan RACHOUH
105 Director Web Services ... Mr. Aaron GARY
106 Assistant Dean Web Campus ... Mr. Robert ZOTTI
37 Director Student Financial Aid ... Ms. Susan GROSS
44 Director Annual Giving ... Ms. Melissa FUEST
96 Director of Procurement ... Mr. Jeff HADLEY

Stockton University (E)

101 Vera King Farris Drive, Galloway NJ 08205-9441
County: Atlantic FICE Identification: 009345
Unit ID: 186876
Telephone: (609) 652-1776 Carnegie Class: Master's M
FAX Number: (609) 652-0275 Calendar System: Semester
URL: www.stockton.edu
Established: 1969 Annual Undergrad Tuition & Fees (In-State): $12,820
Enrollment: 8,570 Coed
Affiliation or Control: State IRS Status: 501(c)3
Highest Offering: Doctorate
Program: Liberal Arts And General; Teacher Preparatory; Professional
Accreditation: M, NURSE, OT, PTA, @SP, SW, TEAC

01 Acting President ... Dr. Harvey KESSELMAN
05 Interim Provost/Exec VP Acad Affs ... Dr. Susan C. DAVENPORT
100 Chief of Staff ... Mr. Brian K. JACKSON
10 Vice Pres Administration & Finance ... Mr. Charles E. INGRAM
32 Vice President Student Affairs ... Dr. Thomasa GONZALEZ
20 Asst Provost Programs & Planning ... Dr. Carra HOOD
96 Director of Purchasing ... Ms. Margaret QUINN
13 Exec Dir Computer/Telecomm Services ... Mr. Robert R. HEINRICH
21 AVP Business Svcs/Chief Bdgt Ofcr ... Mr. James TIERNEY
18 Assoc VP Facilities/Construction ... Mr. Donald M. HUDSON
22 Chief Ofcr Inst Diversity/Equity ... Ms. Valerie HAYES
26 Chief Univ Relations/Marketing Ofcr ... Ms. Sharon SCHULMAN
30 Chief Dev Ofcr/Exec Dir Foundation ... Dr. Philip T. ELLMORE
84 Dean of Enrollment Management ... Mr. John IACOVELLI
07 Associate Dean of Admissions ... Ms. Alison HENRY
35 Dean of Students ... Dr. Pedro SANTANA
06 Assoc Dean Records/Registration ... Mr. Joseph LOSASSO
53 Dean School of Education ... Dr. Claudine KEENAN
97 Dean School of General Studies ... Dr. Robert S. GREGG
79 Dean School Arts & Humanities ... Dr. Lisa HONAKER
50 Dean School of Business ... Dr. Janet M. WAGNER
58 Dean School of Graduate Studies ... Vacant
81 Int Dean School of Natural Sci/Math ... Dr. Peter STRAUB
83 Dean Sch Social/Behavioral Sciences ... Dr. Cheryl KAUS
76 Dean School of Health Sciences ... Dr. Theresa BARTOLOTTA
15 Director Human Resource Management ... Mr. Thomas P. CHESTER
09 Director Institutional Research ... Dr. Xiangping KONG
08 Director of Library Services ... Mr. Joseph TOTH
88 Director South Regional ETTC ... Ms. Patricia WEEKS
37 Director of Financial Aid ... Ms. Jeanne LEWIS
19 Interim Chief of Police ... Ms. Cynthia Ann PARKER
88 Manager Performing Arts Center ... Ms. Suze DIPIETRO-STEWART
41 Dir of Athletics and Recreations ... Mr. Lonnie FOLKS
39 Director of Residential Life ... Dr. Denise O'NEILL
36 Director of Career Services ... Mr. Walter L. TARVER, III
43 General Counsel ... Mr. Michael ANGULO
38 Dir Counseling and Health Services ... Vacant
88 Dir Center for Academic Advising ... Dr. Peter HAGEN
21 Director Budget & Fiscal Planning ... Mr. Michael WOOD
29 Director Alumni Relations ... Ms. Sara FAUROT
44 Assoc Chf Devel Ofcr/Campaign Mgr ... Ms. Cindy CRAGER

Sussex County Community College (F)

One College Hill Road, Newton NJ 07860-1146
County: Sussex FICE Identification: 025688
Unit ID: 247603
Telephone: (973) 300-2100 Carnegie Class: Assoc/Pub-S-SC
FAX Number: (973) 579-9351 Calendar System: Semester
URL: www.sussex.edu
Established: 1982 Annual Undergrad Tuition & Fees (In-District): $6,000
Enrollment: 3,069 Coed
Affiliation or Control: State/Local IRS Status: 501(c)3
Highest Offering: Associate Degree
Program: Occupational; 2-Year Principally Bachelor's Creditable
Accreditation: M, MAC, SURGT

01 President ... Vacant
04 Asst to President/Board of Trustees ... Wendy FULLEM
05 VP of Academic and Student Affairs ... William WAITE
10 Exec VP of Finance and Operations ... Frank NOCELLA
32 VP Student Affairs ... Vacant
15 Exec Dir of Human Resources ... Michael GALLEGLY
26 Dir of Marketing/Public Info ... Kathleen PETERSON
30 VP Advancement & Foundation ... Karen DIMARIA
50 Dean of Business/Law/Math/Scienc ... Mary Ellen DONNER
49 Dean Lib Arts/Sol Sci/Educ ... Dr. Kathleen OKAY
24 Assoc Dean of Learning Resources ... Jan TENSEN
20 Asst Dean of Academic Affairs ... Vacant
41 Asst Dean of Athletics/Student Affs ... John KUNTZ
21 Director of Accounting ... Manal MESCHA
19 Dir Security & Campus Operations ... John SCULLY
13 Dir of Management Info Systems ... Craig MACKEY
88 Director of Bursar Office ... Catherine WINTERFIELD
106 Dir of Media Services/Distance Educ ... Tony SELIMO
08 Director of Library ... Stephanie COOPER
07 Director of Admissions ... Todd POLTERSDORF
37 Director of Financial Aid ... Diane PIENTA-LETTA
09 Dir of Inst Research & Assessment ... Cory HOMER
06 Registrar ... Solweig DIMINO

Talmudical Academy of New Jersey (G)

Route 524, Adelphia NJ 07710-9999
County: Monmouth FICE Identification: 011989
Unit ID: 186900
Telephone: (732) 431-1600 Carnegie Class: Spec/Faith
FAX Number: (732) 431-3951 Calendar System: Semester
Established: 1971 Annual Undergrad Tuition & Fees: $12,000
Enrollment: 64 Male
Affiliation or Control: Independent Non-Profit IRS Status: 501(c)3
Highest Offering: Baccalaureate
Program: Teacher Preparatory; Professional
Accreditation: RABN

01 President ... Mr. Charles SEMAH
05 Dean ... Rabbi Yeruchim SHAIN

Thomas Edison State College (H)

101 W State Street, Trenton NJ 08608-1176
County: Mercer FICE Identification: 021922
Unit ID: 187046
Telephone: (609) 984-1100 Carnegie Class: Master's S
FAX Number: (609) 292-9000 Calendar System: Other

URL: www.tesc.edu
Established: 1972 Annual Undergrad Tuition & Fees (In-State): $6,135
Enrollment: 18,684 Coed
Affiliation or Control: State IRS Status: 501(c)3
Highest Offering: Master's
Program: Liberal Arts And General; Professional
Accreditation: M, ENGT, NUR, NURSE, POLYT, TEAC

01 President .... Dr. George A. PRUITT
05 Vice President & Provost .... Mr. William J. SEATON
10 Vice Pres Administration & Finance ... Mr. Christopher STRINGER
26 Vice President Public Affairs .... Mr. John P. THURBER
31 Vice Pres Cmty & Govt Relations .... Ms. Robin WALTON
45 VP Institutional Planning/Research .... Mr. Dennis DEVERY
84 VP Enrollment Mgmt/Learner Services .... Dr. Mary Ellen CARO
58 Vice Prov Acad Admin/Dean Grad Pgms .... Dr. Henry VAN ZYL
51 Vice Prov/Dean Watson Sch Cont Stds .... Dr. Joseph YOUNGBLOOD
88 Vice Prov Ctr Assessment of Lrng .... Mr. Marc SINGER
88 Assoc VP Enrollment Management .... Ms. Sylvia HAMILTON
88 Assoc VP Military/Veteran Education .... Mr. Louis MARTINI
32 Assoc VP and Dean of Learner Svcs .... Dr. Raymond YOUNG
09 Assoc VP for Planning & Research .... Dr. Ann Marie SENIOR
27 Assoc VP/Director of Communications ..... Mr. Joseph GUZZARDO
88 Assoc Provost Learning Technology .... Mr. Matthew COOPER
21 Treasurer .... Mr. Stephen D. ALBANO
100 Chief of Staff .... Ms. Linda M. MEEHAN
27 Director Market Research/ Assessment .... Ms. Marie R. POWER-BARNES
43 General Counsel .... Ms. Barbara KLEVA
66 Dean School of Nursing .... Dr. Phyllis MARSHALL
49 Dean Heavin Sch of Arts & Sciences .... Dr. John WOZNICKI
50 Dean School of Business & Mgmt .... Dr. Michael WILLIAMS
06 Registrar .... Ms. Catharine PUNCHELLO-COBOS
72 Dean School of Applied Sci/Tech .... Dr. John AJE
21 Controller .... Ms. Michele EVANCHIK
13 Chief Information Officer .... Mr. Drew W. HOPKINS
07 Director Admissions .... Mr. David HOFTIEZER
29 Director of Alumni Affairs .... Ms. Roxanne GLOBIS
37 Director of Financial Aid .... Mr. James OWENS
18 Director Facilities & Operations .... Ms. Mary C. HACK
21 Admin of Student Fees & Revenues .... Mr. Philip SANDERS
30 Director of Development .... Ms. Misty ISAK
102 Director Corporate Relations .... Mr. Frederick BRAND
08 State Librarian .... Ms. Mary CHUTE
105 Director Website & Multimedia Produ .... Mr. Jeffery LUSHBAUGH
88 Director of Advancement Services .... Ms. Erica SPIZZIRRRI
44 Asc Dir Annual Fund/Donor Relations .... Ms. Jennifer GUERRERO
88 Executive Director Watson Institute .... Ms. Barbara JOHNSON
88 Dir Learning Outcomes Assessment ..... Ms. Cynthia MACMILLAN
88 ADA Coordinator .... Ms. Laura BRENNER-SCOTTI

Union County College (A)

1033 Springfield Avenue, Cranford NJ 07016-1598
County: Union FICE Identification: 002643
Unit ID: 187198
Telephone: (908) 709-7000 Carnegie Class: Assoc/Pub-S-MC
FAX Number: (908) 709-0527 Calendar System: Semester
URL: www.ucc.edu
Established: 1933 Annual Undergrad Tuition & Fees (In-District): $4,200
Enrollment: 11,781 Coed
Affiliation or Control: State/Local IRS Status: 501(c)3
Highest Offering: Associate Degree
Program: Occupational; 2-Year Principally Bachelor's Creditable
Accreditation: M, PNUR, PTAA

01 President .... Dr. Margaret M. MCMENAMIN
05 Vice President Academic Affairs .... Dr. Maris LOWN
10 Vice Pres Financial Affs/Treasurer .... Mr. Bernard LENIHAN
32 Vice President Student Development .... Ms. Helen BREWER
11 Vice Pres Administrative Services .... Dr. Stephen NACCO
12 Provost Elizabeth Campus .... Dr. Barbara GABA
12 Interim Dean Plainfield Campus .... Dr. Patricia CASTALDI
26 Exec Director College Relations .... Ms. Ellen DOTTO
13 Director of IT Operations .... Mr. Thomas CHERUBINO
06 Dir Admissions/Records/Registrar .... Ms. Nina HERNANDEZ
08 Director of Libraries .... Ms. Dena LEITER
38 Director of Counseling .... Ms. Heather KEITH
37 Director of Financial Aid .... Ms. Rebecca ROYAL
21 Director of Student Accounts .... Mr. Larry GOLDMAN
51 Dean Continuing Educ & Prof Educ .... Dr. Lisa HISCANO
108 Exec Dir of Institutional Research .... Ms. Elizabeth COONER
15 Director of Human Resources .... Mr. Michael ESNES
18 Director Facilities .... Mr. Henry KEY
45 Director of Grants .... Ms. Cheryl SHIBER
102 Exec Director Foundation .... Mr. Douglas ROUSE
20 Director Student Assessment Center .... Dr. Susan METTLEN
28 Director EOF .... Mr. Ruben MELENDEZ
41 Dean of College Life .... Ms. Tamalea SMITH
19 Director Public Safety .... Mr. Joseph HINES
27 Director Media Services .... Mr. Stephen KATO
88 Asst Dir Acad Learning Center .... Mr. Jose PAEZ-FIGUEROA
21 Controller .... Ms. Lynne WELCH
96 Director of Purchasing .... Ms. Sandra AULD
40 Manager Bookstore .... Ms. Christine SALZMAN
88 AVP/Dean of American Honors .... Dr. Negar FARAKISH

Union County College Elizabeth Campus (B)

40 W Jersey Street, Elizabeth NJ 07202-2314
Telephone: (908) 965-6000 Identification: 770134
Accreditation: &M, EMT

† Branch campus of Union County College, Cranford, NJ.

Union County College Plainfield Campus (C)

232 E 2nd Street, Plainfield NJ 07060
Telephone: (908) 412-3599 Identification: 770135
Accreditation: &M

† Branch campus of Union County College, Cranford, NJ.

Union County College Scotch Plains (D)

1776 Raritan Road, Scotch Plains NJ 07076
Telephone: (908) 889-2483 Identification: 770136
Accreditation: &M

† Branch campus of Union County College, Cranford, NJ.

University of Northern New Jersey (E)

20 Commerce Drive, Cranford NJ 07016
County: Union Identification: 667216
Telephone: (908) 300-5600 Carnegie Class: Not Classified
FAX Number: (908) 931-1993 Calendar System: Semester
URL: www.unnj.edu
Established: 2012 Annual Undergrad Tuition & Fees: $12,620
Enrollment: N/A Coed
Affiliation or Control: Independent Non-Profit IRS Status: 501(c)3
Highest Offering: Master's
Program: Business Emphasis
Accreditation: ACCSC, CEA

01 President .... Dr. Steven BRUNETTI

University of Phoenix Jersey City Campus (F)

100 Town Square Place, Jersey City NJ 07310-1756
Telephone: (201) 610-1408 Identification: 770218
Accreditation: &NH, ACBSP

† Branch campus of University of Phoenix, Tempe, AZ.

Warren County Community College (G)

475 Route 57 W, Washington NJ 07882-4343
County: Warren FICE Identification: 025039
Unit ID: 245625
Telephone: (908) 835-9222 Carnegie Class: Assoc/Pub-S-SC
FAX Number: (908) 689-9262 Calendar System: Semester
URL: www.warren.edu
Established: 1981 Annual Undergrad Tuition & Fees (In-District): $3,969
Enrollment: 2,555 Coed
Affiliation or Control: State/Local IRS Status: 501(c)3
Highest Offering: Associate Degree
Program: Occupational; 2-Year Principally Bachelor's Creditable
Accreditation: M, ADNUR, MAC

01 President .... Dr. William AUSTIN
10 Vice Pres Finance & Operations .... Ms. Barbara PRATT
51 Vice Pres Corporate/Continuing Educ .... Ms. Eve AZAR
11 Dean of Administration .... Mr. Dennis FLORENTINE
05 Acting VP of Academics .... Mr. Jeremy BEELER
37 Director of Financial Aid .... Ms. Debra WULFF
15 Director Human Resources .... Ms. Sharon HINTZ
32 Director Student Activities .... Ms. Rose LYNCH
21 Director Business Services .... Mr. Jay ALEXANDER

Westminster Choir College (H)

101 Walnut Lane, Princeton NJ 08540
Telephone: (609) 921-7100 Identification: 770128
Accreditation: &M

† Branch campus of Rider University, Lawrenceville, NJ.

William Paterson University of New Jersey (I)

300 Pompton Road, Wayne NJ 07470-2152
County: Passaic FICE Identification: 002625
Unit ID: 187444
Telephone: (973) 720-2000 Carnegie Class: Master's L
FAX Number: (973) 720-2399 Calendar System: Semester
URL: www.wpunj.edu
Established: 1855 Annual Undergrad Tuition & Fees (In-State): $12,365
Enrollment: 11,048 Coed
Affiliation or Control: State IRS Status: 501(c)3
Highest Offering: Doctorate
Program: Liberal Arts And General; Teacher Preparatory; Professional
Accreditation: M, ART, BUS, CAATE, CACREP, CS, MUS, NURSE, SP, TED

01 President .... Dr. Kathleen WALDRON
05 Senior Vice President/Provost .... Dr. Warren SANDMANN
100 Chf of Staff to Pres/Board of Trust .... Dr. Robert SEAL
10 Vice Pres Administration/Finance .... Mr. Stephen BOLYAI
30 Vice Pres Institutional Advancement .... Ms. Pamela FERGUSON
32 Vice President Student Development .... Dr. Miki CAMMARATA
84 VP of Enrollment Management .... Dr. Reginald ROSS
88 Assoc Provost Academic Development ..... Ms. Danielle LIAUTAUD
21 Assoc VP Finance Budget/Fiscal Plng .... Ms. Pamela WINSLOW
11 Assoc VP for Administration .... Mr. Richard STOMBER
26 Assoc VP Mkting & Public Relations .... Mr. Stuart GOLDSTEIN
15 Associate Vice Pres Human Resources .... Mr. John POLDING
08 Assoc VP Library Services/Info Tech .... Vacant
35 Associate VP for Campus Life .... Vacant
19 Dir Public Safety & Univ Police .... Mr. Robert FULLEMAN
35 Asst Vice Pres for Campus Life .... Mr. Francisco DIAZ
35 Assoc VP/Dean Student Development .... Dr. Glen SHERMAN
60 Dean Col Arts/Comm .... Mr. Daryl MOORE
53 Dean College of Education .... Dr. Candace BURNS
66 Dean College of Science & Health .... Dr. Kenneth WOLF
79 Dean Human & Social Science .... Dr. Kara M. RABBITT
50 Dean College of Business .... Dr. Siamack SHOJAI
08 Dean D & L Cheng Library .... Dr. Edward OWUSU-ANSAH
21 Assoc VP Finance & Comptroller .... Ms. Samantha GREEN
28 Dir Employment Equity & Diversity .... Ms. Michele JOHNSON
46 Exec Director Academic Development ... Ms. Janet DAVIS-DUKES
51 Exec Dir Cont Educ/Distance Lrng .... Dr. Bernadette TIERNAN
20 Associate Provost Academic Affairs .... Dr. Stephen HAHN
86 Assoc VP Govt & External Relations .... Mr. Patrick DEDEO
27 Director Public Information .... Ms. Mary Beth ZEMAN
29 Executive Director Alumni .... Ms. Janis SCHWARTZ
45 Director Inst Research & Assessment .... Dr. Jane ZEFF
13 Chief Information Officer .... Mr. Eric ROSENBERG
43 General Counsel .... Mr. Glenn JONES
16 Director of Human Resources ...... Ms. Denise ROBINSON-LEWIS
07 Director of Undergrad Admissions .... Mr. Rohan HOWELL
37 Director Financial Aid .... Mr. Michael CORSO
06 Registrar .... Ms. Nina TRELISKY
41 Director Athletics .... Ms. Sabrina GRANT
36 Director of Career Dev & Advisement ... Ms. Sharon ROSENGART
39 Director of Residence Life .... Mr. Joseph CAFFARELLI
23 Dir Counseling/Health & Wellness .... Dr. Eileen LUBECK
90 Director Instruction/Research Tech .... Dr. Sandra MILLER
09 Dir Institutional Research/Assess .... Dr. Jane ZEFF
40 Director Bookstore .... Mr. Scott DUNLAP
24 Head Audio Visual-Library .... Ms. Jane HUTCHISON
18 Director Capital Plng/Design/Constr .... Vacant
85 Director International Student Svcs .... Ms. Cinzia RICHARDSON
94 Director of Women's Center .... Ms. Librada SANCHEZ
96 Director of Purchasing .... Mr. Lirse JONES
89 Director of Freshmen Studies .... Dr. Kim DANIEL-ROBINSON
92 Interim Director of Honors College .... Dr. Barbara ANDREW

Yeshiva Gedolah Shaarei Schmuel (J)

511 Ocean Ave, Lakewood NJ 08701
County: Ocean Identification: 667260
Telephone: (732) 363-2164 Carnegie Class: Not Classified
FAX Number: (732) 364-3331 Calendar System: Other
Established: 2008 Annual Undergrad Tuition & Fees: $11,500
Enrollment: 56 Male
Affiliation or Control: Independent Non-Profit IRS Status: 501(c)3
Highest Offering: First Talmudic Degree
Program: Religious Emphasis
Accreditation: @RABN

Yeshiva Gedolah Zichron Leyma (K)

1000 Orchard Terrace, Linden NJ 07036
County: Union FICE Identification: 041924
Unit ID: 476692
Telephone: (908) 587-0502 Carnegie Class: Not Classified
FAX Number: N/A Calendar System: Semester
Established: 1999 Annual Undergrad Tuition & Fees: $11,500
Enrollment: 31 Male
Affiliation or Control: Independent Non-Profit IRS Status: 501(c)3
Highest Offering: First Talmudic Degree
Program: Professional
Accreditation: RABN

Yeshiva Toras Chaim (L)

999 Ridge Avenue, Lakewood NJ 08701-2120
County: Ocean FICE Identification: 041311
Unit ID: 451398
Telephone: (732) 414-2834 Carnegie Class: Spec/Faith
FAX Number: (732) 414-2838 Calendar System: Semester
Established: 2000 Annual Undergrad Tuition & Fees: $11,950
Enrollment: 215 Male
Affiliation or Control: Independent Non-Profit IRS Status: 501(c)3
Highest Offering: Baccalaureate
Program: Teacher Preparatory; Professional
Accreditation: RABN

05 Chief Academic Officer .... Rabbi Mendel SLOMOVITS
06 Registrar .... Mrs. Devoiry DURST
10 Bookkeeper .... Mrs. Ruth GROSSMAN

Yeshiva Yesodei Hatorah (M)

2 Yesodei Court, Lakewood NJ 08701
County: Ocean Identification: 667109
Unit ID: 481438
Telephone: (732) 370-3360 Carnegie Class: Not Classified
FAX Number: (732) 886-2659 Calendar System: Semester
Established: 1995 Annual Undergrad Tuition & Fees: $11,500
Enrollment: 72 Male
Affiliation or Control: Independent Non-Profit IRS Status: 501(c)3
Highest Offering: First Talmudic Degree
Program: Professional
Accreditation: RABN

05 Dean .... Rabbi Shaya TREFF
10 Chief Financial/Business Officer .... Rabbi Shaya UNGAR
20 Associate Academic Officer .... Rabbi Yisroel Meir TREFF

Yeshivas Be'er Yitzchok (A)

1391 North Avenue, Elizabeth NJ 07208-2480
County: Union FICE Identification: 041234
Unit ID: 451370
Telephone: (908) 354-6057 Carnegie Class: Spec/Faith
FAX Number: (908) 820-0431 Calendar System: Semester
Established: 1999 Annual Undergrad Tuition & Fees: $12,200
Enrollment: 58 Male
Affiliation or Control: Independent Non-Profit IRS Status: 501(c)3
Highest Offering: Baccalaureate
Program: Professional; Religious Emphasis
Accreditation: RABN

01 Chief Executive Officer .... Rabbi Avrohom SCHULMAN
37 Director of Student Financial Aid .... Chani MILLER
11 Chief of Administration .... Chani MILLER

NEW MEXICO

Brookline College (B)

4201 Central Avenue NW Ste J,
Albuquerque NM 87105-1649
Telephone: (505) 880-2877 Identification: 666724
Accreditation: ACICS, NUR

† Branch campus of Brookline College, Phoenix, AZ

Brown Mackie College - Albuquerque (C)

10500 Cooper Avenue NE, Albuquerque NM 87123
Telephone: (505) 559-5200 Identification: 770741
Accreditation: ACICS, OTA, SURGT, SURTEC

† Branch campus of The Art Institute of Phoenix, Phoenix, AZ.

Burrell College of Osteopathic Medicine (D)

3655 Research Dr., Genesis Bldg C,
Las Cruces NM 88003
County: Dona Ana Identification: 667248
Telephone: (575) 647-2266 Carnegie Class: Not Classified
FAX Number: (575) 647-2267 Calendar System: Semester
URL: www.bcomnm.org
Established: 2013 Annual Graduate Tuition & Fees: $46,650
Enrollment: N/A Coed
Affiliation or Control: Independent Non-Profit IRS Status: 501(c)3
Highest Offering: Doctorate; No Undergraduates
Program: Professional
Accreditation: @OSTEO

01 Dean .... George MYCHASKIW

Carrington College - Albuquerque (E)

1001 Menaul Boulevard NE, Albuquerque NM 87107-1642
Telephone: (505) 254-7777 Identification: 666014
Accreditation: &WJ, PTAA

† Regional accreditation is carried under the parent institution in Sacramento, CA.

Central New Mexico Community College (F)

525 Buena Vista, SE, Albuquerque NM 87106-4096
County: Bernalillo FICE Identification: 004742
Unit ID: 187532
Telephone: (505) 224-4412 Carnegie Class: Assoc/Pub-U-MC
FAX Number: (505) 224-4417 Calendar System: Semester
URL: www.cnm.edu
Established: 1965 Annual Undergrad Tuition & Fees (In-District): $1,920
Enrollment: 26,771 Coed
Affiliation or Control: State/Local IRS Status: 501(c)3
Highest Offering: Associate Degree
Program: 2-Year Principally Bachelor's Creditable
Accreditation: NH, ACBSP, ACFEI, ADNUR, CAHIIM, COARC, CONST, DA, DMS, EMT, MLTAD, PNUR, SURGT

01 President .... Dr. Katharine W. WINOGRAD
05 Vice President for Academic Affairs ... Dr. Sydney D. GUNTHORPE
35 Vice President for Student Services .... Mr. Phillip BUSTOS
10 Vice Pres for Finance & Operations ...... Mrs. Katherine ULIBARRI
84 Assoc Vice Pres Enrollment Mgmt .... Mr. Eugene PADILLA
08 Director Learning Resources ...... Ms. Poppy JOHNSON RENVALL
23 Director Student Health Center .... Ms. Marti BRITTENHAM
13 Director Info Technology Services .... Mr. Joe GIERI
103 Director Workforce Training Center .... Ms. Evelyn DOW
36 Director of Job Connection Center .... Ann Lyn HALL
30 Director of Development .... Ms. Roberta RICCI
07 Director Enrollment Services .... Mr. Glenn DAMIANI
26 Dir Marketing & Public Relations .... Mrs. Jennifer BROWER
27 Dir Communications & Media Relation .... Mr. Brad MOORE
37 Director Student Financial Aid .... Mr. Lee CARRILLO
15 Executive Director Human Resources .... Ms. Denise MONTOYA
81 Dean Sch of Math/Sci/Engr .... Mr. John CORNISH
50 Dean School of Bus/Info Technology .... Ms. Donna DILLER
72 Dean School of Applied Technologies .... Mr. John BRONISZ
97 Dean Sch of Adult & Gen Educ .... Ms. LouAnne LUNDGREN
83 Dean Comm/Humanities/Soc Sci .... Ms. Erica VOLKERS
76 Dean Health/Well/Pub Safety .... Ms. Tamra MASON
06 Registrar .... Ms. Yvonne MARTINEZ
18 Exec Dir Facilities/Physical Plant .... Mr. Luis CAMPOS
21 Comptroller .... Ms. Loretta MONTOYA
32 Dean of Student Services .... Mr. Rudy GARCIA
96 Director of Purchasing .... Ms. Wanda HELMS
19 Chief of Safety & Security .... Mr. John CORVINO
04 Administrative Asst to President .... Mrs. Diana CHAVEZ
09 Sr Dir Outcomes And Assessment .... Ms. Ursula WALN

Clovis Community College (G)

417 Schepps Boulevard, Clovis NM 88101-8381
County: Curry FICE Identification: 004743
Unit ID: 187639
Telephone: (575) 769-2811 Carnegie Class: Assoc/Pub-R-M
FAX Number: (575) 769-4190 Calendar System: Semester
URL: www.clovis.edu
Established: 1971 Annual Undergrad Tuition & Fees (In-State): $936
Enrollment: 3,750 Coed
Affiliation or Control: State IRS Status: 501(c)3
Highest Offering: Associate Degree
Program: Occupational; 2-Year Principally Bachelor's Creditable
Accreditation: NH, ADNUR, @PTAA, RAD

01 President .... Dr. Becky ROWLEY
03 Executive Vice President .... Dr. Robin JONES
10 Chief Financial Officer .... Mrs. Debbie ZURZOLO
05 Chief Academic Officer .... Dr. Robin JONES
13 Chief Information Officer .... Mr. Norman KIA
11 VP Administration/Govt Relations .... Mr. Tom DRAKE
21 Director of Business Affairs .... Ms. Jayne CRAIG
07 Dir Admissions/Records/Registrar .... Ms. Rosie CORRIE
37 Director of Financial Aid .... Ms. April CHAVEZ
08 Director Library/Learning Resources .... Ms. Kelly GRAY
32 Dir Center for Student Success .... Mrs. Mona Lee NORMAN-ARMSTRONG
38 Dir of Counseling/Testing/Advisemnt .... Mr. Marcus SMITH
15 Director of Human Resource Services .... Mrs. Rhonda JESKO
88 Director Small Business Development .... Mrs. Sandra TAYLOR-SAWYER
91 Director of Administrative Info Sys .... Ms. Teresa WHITEHEAD
56 Director Extended Learning .... Ms. Robin KUYKENDALL
36 Director Student Placement .... Vacant
30 Chief Development Officer .... Ms. Natalie DAGGETT
18 Director of Physical Plant .... Mr. Paul ARAGON
26 Director of Marketing/Cmty Rels .... Ms. Lisa SPENCER
76 Div Chair Allied Health Programs .... Ms. Shawna MCGILL
83 Div Chair Liberal Arts/Dev Studies .... Ms. Shelley DENTON
50 Div Chair of Business Admin & Tech . Mrs. Becky CARRUTHERS
81 Division Chair of Math/Science .... Mr. Todd KUYKENDALL

Dine College Shiprock Branch (H)

1228 Yucca St., PO Box 580, Shiprock NM 87420
Telephone: (505) 368-3500 Identification: 770007
Accreditation: &NH

† Branch campus of Dine College, Tsaile, AZ.

Eastern New Mexico University Main Campus (I)

1500 S Avenue K, Portales NM 88130-7400
County: Roosevelt FICE Identification: 002651
Unit ID: 187648
Telephone: (575) 562-1011 Carnegie Class: Master's S
FAX Number: (575) 562-2980 Calendar System: Semester
URL: www.enmu.edu
Established: 1927 Annual Undergrad Tuition & Fees (In-State): $5,410
Enrollment: 5,887 Coed
Affiliation or Control: State IRS Status: 501(c)3
Highest Offering: Master's
Program: Liberal Arts And General; Teacher Preparatory
Accreditation: NH, ACBSP, MUS, NUR, SP, SW, TED

01 President .... Dr. Steven GAMBLE
05 Vice President Academic Affairs .... Dr. Jamie LAURENZ
10 Vice President Business Affairs .... Mr. Scott SMART
32 Vice President for Student Affairs .... Dr. Jeff LONG
88 Vice President Academic Support .... Mr. Clark ELSWICK
88 Special Assistant to the President .... Ms. Ronnie BIRDSONG
45 Exec Dir Planning/Analysis/Inst Ren .... Dr. Patrice CALDWELL
20 Asst Vice Pres for Academic Affairs .... Dr. Renee NEELY
20 Asst Vice Pres Academic Affairs .... Dr. John MONTGOMERY
21 Comptroller .... Mrs. Carol FLETCHER
53 Dean Education/Technology .... Dr. Penny A. GARCIA
50 Dean Business .... Dr. Janet BUZZARD
57 Dean Fine Arts .... Dr. Joseph KLINE
49 Dean Liberal Arts & Science .... Dr. Mary AYALA
58 Dean Graduate School .... Dr. Linda WEEMS
22 Affirmative Action Officer .... Ms. Ashley KEEFER
08 Director of Library .... Ms. Melveta WALKER
06 Registrar .... Ms. Teresa BAKER-EVANS
37 Director Student Financial Aid .... Mr. Brent SMALL
07 Director Enrollment Services .... Mr. Cody SPITZ
30 Director Development .... Ms. Noelle BARTL
13 Dir Computing/Information Mgmt .... Mr. Clark ELSWICK
15 Director of Human Resources .... Mr. Benito GONZALES
88 Director of Broadcasting .... Mr. Duane RYAN
18 Director Physical Plant .... Mr. Ted FARES
41 Athletic Director .... Dr. Jeff GEISER
19 Chief of University Police .... Mr. Brad MAULDIN
36 Dir Counseling Ctr/Career Svcs .... Ms. Susan LARSEN
39 Director Student Housing .... Mr. Steven ESTOCK
09 Assoc Dir Institutional Research .... Mr. James ATKINSON
96 Director of Purchasing .... Mr. Brad KEMPER
27 Director of Publications .... Mr. John HOUSER
29 Coordinator of Alumni .... Mr. Robert GRAHAM
56 Dir of Distance Learning/Outreach .... Ms. Trish MAGUIRE
35 Director Campus Life .... Mr. Draco MILLER

Eastern New Mexico University-Roswell (J)

PO Box 6000, Roswell NM 88202-6000
County: Chaves FICE Identification: 002661
Unit ID: 187666
Telephone: (575) 624-7000 Carnegie Class: Assoc/Pub2in4
FAX Number: (575) 624-7342 Calendar System: Semester
URL: www.roswell.enmu.edu
Established: 1958 Annual Undergrad Tuition & Fees (In-State): $1,824
Enrollment: 3,303 Coed
Affiliation or Control: State IRS Status: 501(c)3
Highest Offering: Associate Degree
Program: Occupational; 2-Year Principally Bachelor's Creditable
Accreditation: NH, ADNUR, COARC, EMT, MAC, OTA

01 President .... Dr. John MADDEN
05 VP for Acacdemic Affairs .... Mr. Ken MAGUIRE
10 VP for Business Affairs .... Mr. Eric JOHNSTON-ORTIZ
32 VP for Student Affairs .... Mr. Mike MARTINEZ
21 Controller .... Ms. Karen FRANKLIN
35 Asst VP for Student Affairs .... Vacant
08 Director Learning Resource Center .... Mr. Rollah ASTON
37 Director Financial Aid .... Ms. Jessie SJUE
30 Director College Development .... Ms. Donna ORACION
07 Director Admissions and Records .... Ms. Linda NEEL
13 Director of Computer Services .... Vacant
15 Director of Human Resources .... Dr. Steve CHAMBERS
18 Director of Physical Plant .... Mr. Derek DUBIEL
19 Director of Security .... Mr. Robert NEWBERRY
96 Director of Purchasing .... Mr. Stephen WATTERS
09 Institutional Research Professional .... Ms. Rhonda CROCKER
04 Administrative Asst to President .... Ms. Lorinda WILKINS
49 Dean of Liberal Arts .... Ms. Joan ARNOLD
76 Dean of Health Services .... Ms. Susan GOLDEN
103 Dean of Career & Technical Educ .... Dr. Kenneth MAGUIRE

EC-Council University (K)

101C Sun Avenue NE, Albuquerque NM 87109
County: Bernalillo Identification: 667232
Telephone: (505) 922-2886 Carnegie Class: Not Classified
FAX Number: (505) 341-0050 Calendar System: Other
URL: www.eccuni.us
Established: 2003 Annual Graduate Tuition & Fees: $12,618
Enrollment: N/A Coed
Affiliation or Control: Proprietary IRS Status: Proprietary
Highest Offering: Master's; No Undergraduates
Program: Professional
Accreditation: DEAC

01 CEO/President .... Sanjay BAVISI
05 Dean .... Michael H. GOLDNER
20 Associate Dean .... Jessica KIMBROUGH
07 Director of Admissions/Registrar .... Deborah GEOFFRION

Institute of American Indian Arts (L)

83 Avan Nu Po Road, Santa Fe NM 87508-1300
County: Santa Fe FICE Identification: 021464
Unit ID: 187745
Telephone: (505) 424-2300 Carnegie Class: Tribal
FAX Number: (505) 424-4500 Calendar System: Semester
URL: www.iaia.edu
Established: 1962 Annual Undergrad Tuition & Fees: $4,220
Enrollment: 531 Coed
Affiliation or Control: Federal IRS Status: Exempt
Highest Offering: Master's
Program: Liberal Arts And General; Fine Arts Emphasis
Accreditation: NH, ART

01 President .... Dr. Robert MARTIN
05 Academic Dean .... Ms. Charlene TETERS
10 Chief Financial Officer .... Mr. Larry MIRABAL
32 Dean of Student Life .... Ms. Carmen HENAN
84 Chief Enroll and Retention Officer .... Ms. Nena ANAYA
30 Dir of Institutional Advancement .... Mr. Alex SHAPIRO
26 Dir of Marketing and Communication .... Mr. Eric DAVIS
88 Dir of Ctr for Lifelong Education .... Ms. Charlene CARR
88 Dir of IAIA Museum .... Ms. Patsy PHILLIPS
102 Dir of Sponsored Programs .... Ms. Laurie BRAYSHAW
09 Dir of Institutional Research .... Dr. William SAYRE

ITT Technical Institute (A)

5100 Masthead Street NE, Albuquerque NM 87109-4366
Telephone: (505) 828-1114 Identification: 666545
Accreditation: ACICS, CAHIIM

† Branch campus of ITT Technical Institute, Indianapolis, IN.

Luna Community College (B)

366 Luna Drive, Las Vegas NM 87701-1510
County: San Miguel FICE Identification: 009962
Unit ID: 363633
Telephone: (505) 454-2500 Carnegie Class: Assoc/Pub-R-M
FAX Number: (505) 454-2519 Calendar System: Semester
URL: www.luna.edu
Established: 1970 Annual Undergrad Tuition & Fees (In-District): $886
Enrollment: 1,440 Coed
Affiliation or Control: State/Local IRS Status: 501(c)3
Highest Offering: Associate Degree
Program: Occupational; Liberal Arts And General; Teacher Preparatory; Professional
Accreditation: NH, ACBSP, ADNUR, DA

01 President .... Dr. Pete CAMPOS
10 Vice President of Finance .... Ms. Donna FLORES-MEDINA
09 Exec Dir Inst Research/Development .... Dr. Peter MANTHEI
05 Vice Pres Academic/Student Affairs .... Dr. Vidal MARTINEZ
07 Director of Admissions .... Mr. Moses MARQUEZ
06 Registrar .... Mr. Johnathan ORTIZ
18 Director Physical Plant .... Mr. Ron GONZALES
37 Director Financial Aid .... Mr. Michael MONTOYA
15 Director Human Resources .... Ms. Carolyn CHAVEZ
30 Chief Development .... Ms. Mary WARD
13 Director of Computer Services .... Mr. Rick JARAMILLO

Mesalands Community College (C)

911 S 10th Street, Tucumcari NM 88401-3352
County: Quay FICE Identification: 032063
Unit ID: 188261
Telephone: (505) 461-4413 Carnegie Class: Assoc/Pub-R-S
FAX Number: (505) 461-1901 Calendar System: Semester
URL: www.mesalands.edu
Established: 1980 Annual Undergrad Tuition & Fees (In-District): $1,620
Enrollment: 771 Coed
Affiliation or Control: State/Local IRS Status: 501(c)3
Highest Offering: Associate Degree
Program: Occupational; 2-Year Principally Bachelor's Creditable
Accreditation: NH

01 President .... Dr. Thomas W. NEWSOM
04 Executive Asst to President .... Ms. Consuelo E. CHAVEZ
32 Vice President Student Affairs .... Dr. Aaron KENNEDY
05 Vice President of Academic Affairs .... Ms. Natalie GILLARD
10 Dir Business/Auxiliary Services .... Ms. Amanda HAMMER
37 Director Financial Aid .... Ms. Jessica ELEBARIO
26 Director Public Relations .... Ms. Kimberly HANNA
72 Director of NAWRTC .... Mr. Jim MORGAN
84 Director of Enrollment Management .... Ms. Amber MCCLURE
13 Director of Inst Technology .... Mr. James JONES
09 Dir Inst Research and Development .... Dr. Forrest KAATZ
15 Director of Human Resources .... Ms. Kacee BENFORD
20 Director of Academic Affairs .... Ms. Donna GARCIA
102 Foundation Chair .... Ms. Laurie BIDEGAIN
21 Business Manager .... Vacant
08 Library Director .... Mr. Todd MORRIS

National American University-Albuquerque (D)

4775 Indian School Road NE, Ste 200, Albuquerque NM 87110
Telephone: (505) 348-3700 Identification: 770407
Accreditation: &NH, MAC

† Branch campus of National American University, Rapid City, SD.

National American University-Albuquerque West (E)

10131 Coors Blvd NW, Suite I-01, Albuquerque NM 87114
Telephone: (505) 348-3750 Identification: 770408
Accreditation: &NH

† Branch campus of National American University, Rapid City, SD.

National College of Midwifery (F)

1041 Reed Street, Suite C, Taos NM 87571
County: Taos Identification: 666251
Telephone: (575) 758-8914 Carnegie Class: Not Classified
FAX Number: N/A Calendar System: Other
URL: www.midwiferycollege.edu
Established: 1989 Annual Undergrad Tuition & Fees: $5,000
Enrollment: 152 Coed
Affiliation or Control: Independent Non-Profit IRS Status: 501(c)3
Highest Offering: Doctorate
Program: Professional
Accreditation: MEAC

01 CEO/President .... Martha ANDREW
11 COO .... Anna KHAMSAMRAN
30 Chief Development Officer .... Cassaundra JAH
05 Chief Academic Officer .... Jessica FRECHETTE-GUTFREUN

Navajo Technical College (G)

PO Box 849, Crownpoint NM 87313-0849
County: McKinley FICE Identification: 023576
Unit ID: 187596
Telephone: (505) 786-4100 Carnegie Class: Tribal
FAX Number: (505) 786-5644 Calendar System: Semester
URL: www.navajotech.edu
Established: 1979 Annual Undergrad Tuition & Fees: $2,110
Enrollment: 2,075 Coed
Affiliation or Control: Tribal Control IRS Status: 501(c)3
Highest Offering: Baccalaureate
Program: Occupational; 2-Year Principally Bachelor's Creditable; Technical Emphasis
Accreditation: NH, ACFEI

01 President .... Dr. Elmer GUY
05 Provost .... Dr. Quintina DESCHENIE
32 Dean of Student Services .... Ms. Delores BECENTI
10 Chief Financial Officer .... Mr. Anthony W. MAJOR, JR.
06 Registrar/Director of Admissions .... Ms. Jerlynn HENRY
09 Data Assessment Director .... Ms. Shawnia GAMBLE
25 Contracts & Grant Officer .... Ms. Thomasina GREY
37 Student Financial Aid Officer .... Mr. Tyrrell HARDY
15 Human Resources Director .... Mr. Kenneth COOPER
18 Director of Operations .... Mr. Hank NEWMAN
20 Associate Academic Officer .... Dr. Casmir AGBARAJI
08 Head Librarian .... Mr. Darwin C. HENDERSON
04 Executive Assistant .... Ms. Tonilee BECENTI
13 IT Director .... Mr. Jason ARVISO
36 Job Placement Coordinator .... Mr. Wilson GILMORE
41 Athletic Director .... Mr. George LAFRANCE

† Tuition figure is for a student enrolled in a federally recognized Indian tribe.

New Mexico Highlands University (H)

PO Box 9000, Las Vegas NM 87701-9000
County: San Miguel FICE Identification: 002653
Unit ID: 187897
Telephone: (505) 425-7511 Carnegie Class: Master's L
FAX Number: N/A Calendar System: Semester
URL: www.nmhu.edu
Established: 1893 Annual Undergrad Tuition & Fees (In-State): $4,800
Enrollment: 3,560 Coed
Affiliation or Control: State IRS Status: 501(c)3
Highest Offering: Master's
Program: Liberal Arts And General; Teacher Preparatory; Professional
Accreditation: NH, ACBSP, CORE, NURSE, SW, TED

01 President .... Dr. Sam MINNER
05 VP for Academic Affairs .... Dr. Teresita AGUILAR
10 Interim VP Finance & Admin .... Mr. Max BACA
20 Associate VP of Academic Affairs .... Dr. Linda LAGRANGE
32 Dean of Students .... Dr. Fidel J. TRUJILLO
07 Registrar/Director of Admissions .... Mr. Michael RAINE
08 Library Director .... Mr. Ruben ARAGON
09 Dir Inst Effectiveness & Research .... Dr. Jean HILL
13 Director of Information Technology .... Vacant
15 Director Human Resources .... Ms. Donna CASTRO
18 Interim Dir of Facilities Mgmt .... Ms. Sylvia BACA
19 Chief Police/Security .... Mr. Donato SENA
21 Comptroller .... Mr. Jesus BAQUERA
26 Director of University Relations .... Mr. Sean WEAVER
29 Coordinator of Alumni Affairs .... Mr. James MANDARINO
30 Vice President for Advancement .... Vacant
36 Director of Career Services .... Mr. Ron GARCIA
37 Director of Financial Aid .... Ms. Eileen SEDILLO
40 Bookstore Manager .... Vacant
41 Athletic Director .... Vacant
49 Dean College of Arts & Sci .... Dr. Kenneth STOKES
50 Dean School of Business .... Dr. Sharles SWIM
70 Dean School of Social Work .... Dr. Andrew ISRAEL
53 Interim Dean School of Education .... Dr. Carolyn NEWMAN
96 Director of Purchasing .... Mr. Michael SAAVEDRA
04 Administrative Asst to President .... Ms. Carolina MARTINEZ
39 Director Student Housing .... Ms. Yvette WILKES

New Mexico Institute of Mining and Technology (I)

801 Leroy Place, Socorro NM 87801-4796
County: Socorro FICE Identification: 002654
Unit ID: 187967
Telephone: (575) 835-5434 Carnegie Class: Master's M
FAX Number: (575) 835-6329 Calendar System: Semester
URL: www.nmt.edu
Established: 1889 Annual Undergrad Tuition & Fees (In-State): $6,710
Enrollment: 2,127 Coed
Affiliation or Control: State IRS Status: 501(c)3
Highest Offering: Doctorate
Program: Professional; Technical Emphasis
Accreditation: NH, CS, ENG

01 President .... Dr. Daniel H. LOPEZ
10 Vice Pres Administration & Finance .... Mr. Lonnie G. MARQUEZ
05 Vice President Academic Affairs .... Dr. Warren OSTERGREN
32 VP Student & Univ Rels/Dean Stdnt .... Ms. Melissa JARAMILLO FLEMING
46 Vice Pres Research/Economic Devel .... Dr. Van D. ROMERO
20 Assoc Vice Pres Academic Affairs .... Dr. Mary DEZEMBER
45 Asst VP Research/Econ Development .... Mr. Richard CERVANTES
58 Dean of Graduate Studies .... Dr. Lorie LIEBROCK
08 Librarian .... Ms. Lisa BEINHOFF
15 Director of Human Resources .... Ms. Joann SALOME
06 Registrar .... Ms. Sara GRIJALVA
07 Director of Admission .... Mr. Anthony ORTIZ
37 Director of Financial Aid .... Ms. Marliss MONETTE
30 Director Office for Advancement .... Ms. Colleen GUENGERICH
22 Director Affirm Action & Compliance .... Mr. Randy SAAVEDRA
14 Director Computer Center .... Vacant
13 Director of Information Services .... Mr. Joseph FRANKLIN
65 Director Bur Geology & Mineral Res .... Dr. Matthew RHOADES
12 Director Petro Recovery Res Ctr .... Dr. Robert L. LEE
18 Director Facilities Management .... Ms. Yvonne MANZANO-BROWN
21 Director of Finance .... Ms. Arleen VALLES
31 Dir Community Education/Outreach .... Ms. Lillian ARMIJO
38 Dir Counseling/Disabilities Svcs .... Ms. Janet WARD
96 Chief Procurement Officer .... Ms. Kimela MILLER
09 Institutional Researcher .... Ms. Stephany MOORE

New Mexico Junior College (J)

1 Thunderbird Circle, Hobbs NM 88240-9123
County: Lea FICE Identification: 002655
Unit ID: 187903
Telephone: (575) 392-4510 Carnegie Class: Assoc/Pub-R-M
FAX Number: (575) 492-2732 Calendar System: Semester
URL: www.nmjc.edu
Established: 1965 Annual Undergrad Tuition & Fees (In-District): $1,248
Enrollment: 3,139 Coed
Affiliation or Control: Local IRS Status: 501(c)3
Highest Offering: Associate Degree
Program: Occupational; 2-Year Principally Bachelor's Creditable
Accreditation: NH, ADNUR

01 President .... Dr. Steve MCCLEERY
05 Vice President Instruction .... Dr. Dennis ATHERTON
10 Vice President Finance .... Dan HARDIN
32 Vice President Student Services .... Phillip ROYBAL
103 Vice President Training & Outreach .... Jeff MCCOOL
84 Dean Enrollment Management .... Dr. Michele CLINGMAN
13 Dir Computer Information System .... Bill KUNKO
26 Director of Communications .... Susan FINE
04 Executive Asst to the President .... Norma FAUGHT
37 Director Financial Aid .... Kerrie MITCHELL
09 Director of Inst Effectiveness .... Dr. Larry SANDERSON
66 Director of Nursing .... Delores THOMPSON
18 Chief Facilities/Physical Plant .... Dr. Charley CARROLL
81 Dean Business/Math & Sciences .... Kelly HOLLADAY
79 Dean Arts & Humanities .... Dianne MARQUEZ
40 Director of Bookstore Services .... Robert ADAMS
75 Dean of Public Safety .... Dr. August FONS
08 Director of Library Services .... James BRITSCH
96 Coordinator of Purchasing .... Regina CHOATE
41 Director of Athletics .... Jeremy CAPO
102 Acct/Controller-NMJC Foundation .... Christina KUNKO
11 Director of Administrative Services .... Bill MORRILL
88 Controller .... Joshua MORGAN
39 Director Student Housing .... Sandy HARDIN
88 Executive Director WHM/LCCHF .... Dr. Darrell BEAUCHAMP
88 Exec Dir NMJC Research Foundation .... Dale GANNAWAY
06 Associate Registrar .... Rebecca WHITLEY
19 Director of Public Safety .... Dennis KELLEY
106 Dean Distance Lrng & Prof Studies .... Dr. Steve HILL

New Mexico Military Institute (K)

101 W College, Roswell NM 88201-5173
County: Chaves FICE Identification: 002656
Unit ID: 187912
Telephone: (575) 622-6250 Carnegie Class: Assoc/Pub-Spec
FAX Number: (575) 624-8058 Calendar System: Semester
URL: www.nmmi.edu
Established: 1891 Annual Undergrad Tuition & Fees (In-State): $1,265
Enrollment: 457 Coed
Affiliation or Control: State IRS Status: 501(c)3
Highest Offering: Associate Degree
Program: 2-Year Principally Bachelor's Creditable
Accreditation: NH

01 Superintendent/President .... MGen. Jerry W. GRIZZLE
32 Commandant .... Vacant
100 Chief of Staff .... Col. David WEST
84 Vice Pres Enrollment/Marketing .... LtCol. Ira DAVIS
10 Chief Financial Officer .... Col. Judy SCHARMER
05 Dean .... BGen. Douglas J. MURRAY
21 Asst Chief Financial Officer .... Col. Charles HENDRICKSON
41 Athletic Director/Dir Physical Educ .... Col. Jose BARRON
30 Development and Advancement Officer .... Maj. Kris WARD
21 Internal Auditor .... Col. David GRAY
88 Professor of Military Science .... LtCol. Hubert STEPHENS
20 Vice Dean & High School Princ .... Col. George BRICK
15 Assistant Human Resources Director .... Ms. Carmen BELL
50 Assoc Dean Social Science/Business .... LtCol. Philip BACA
81 Assoc Dean Science/Mathematics .... Col. John R. MCVAY
79 Associate Dean Humanities .... Maj. Joel DYKSTRA
64 Director of Music .... LtCol. Stephen M. THORP

08 Director of the Library .... Col. Jerome J. KLOPFER
26 Marketing & Communication Director .... LtCol. Colleen COLE-VELASQUEZ
18 Chief Facilities/Physical Plant .... Mr. Kent TAYLOR
06 Registrar .... Maj. Chris WRIGHT
37 Director of Financial Aid .... Maj. Sonya F. RODRIGUEZ
88 Mil Services Academies Prep Dir .... LtCol. Jonathan GRAFF
19 Chief of Campus Police .... Mr. Jerrold LONOWSKI
38 Director of Cadet Counseling Center .... Maj. Chance MACE
29 Director Alumni Association .... LtCol. Danny ARMIJO
04 Administrative Asst to President .... Ms. Bernadette BEATTY
09 Director of Institutional Research .... Ms. Michele BATES
102 Dir Foundation/Corporate Relations .... Mr. Jimmy BARNES
13 Chief Info Technology Officer .... Mr. Duane ELMS

New Mexico State University Main Campus (A)

Box 30001, Las Cruces NM 88003-8001

County: Dona Ana FICE Identification: 002657
Unit ID: 188030
Telephone: (575) 646-2035 Carnegie Class: RU/H
FAX Number: (575) 646-6334 Calendar System: Semester
URL: www.nmsu.edu
Established: 1888 Annual Undergrad Tuition & Fees (In-State): $5,950
Enrollment: 15,829 Coed
Affiliation or Control: State IRS Status: 501(c)3
Highest Offering: Doctorate
Program: Liberal Arts And General; Teacher Preparatory; Professional
Accreditation: NH, BUS, BUSA, CAATE, CACREP, COPSY, DIETD, @DIETI, ENG, ENGT, MUS, NURSE, PH, SP, SPAA, SW, TED

01 President .... Dr. Garrey E. CARRUTHERS
05 Provost & Exec VP .... Dr. Dan HOWARD
10 Sr VP Administration/Finance .... Ms. Angela THRONEBERRY
30 VP Univ Advance/Pres NMSU Found ..... Ms. Cheryl HARRELSON
32 VP Student Affairs/Enroll Mgmt .... Dr. Bernadette MONTOYA
85 Assoc Provost Intl & Border Program .... Dr. Cornell MENKING
26 Assoc VP Univ Comm/Marketing .... Ms. Maureen HOWARD
21 Assoc VP Admin & Finance .... Ms. D'Anne STUART
15 Assoc VP Human Resources Svcs .... Dr. Andrew M. PENA
20 Assoc VP/Deputy Provost .... Dr. Greg FANT
09 Asst VP Institutional Analysis .... Ms. Judy BOSLAND
86 Asst VP Government Relations .... Mr. Ricardo REL
49 Dean College of Arts & Sciences .... Dr. Christa D. SLATON
50 Dean Business College .... Dr. James HOFFMAN
53 Dean College of Education .... Dr. Don POPE-DAVIS
54 Dean College of Engineering .... Dr. Ricardo JACQUEZ
58 Dean Graduate School .... Dr. Loui REYES
76 Int Dean Col Health & Social Svcs .... Dr. Donna WAGNER
35 Dean of Students .... Dr. Michael D. JASEK
13 Chief Information Officer .... Ms. Norma GRIJALVA
06 University Registrar .... Dr. Cassandra LACHICA-CHAVEZ
43 General Counsel .... Ms. Liz ELLIS
08 Dean University Library .... Dr. Elizabeth TITUS
29 AVP Alumni Engagement/Participation .... Ms. Tina BYFORD
25 Assoc Controller Sponsored Projects .... Ms. Norma NOEL
39 Director Student Housing .... Ms. Julie WEBER
23 Director Student Health Center .... Ms. Lori MCKEE
38 Director Counseling Center .... Dr. Karen D. SCHAEFER
41 Director Athletics .... Mr. Mario MOCCIA
36 Dir Placement/Career Services .... Dr. Anthony S. MARIN
96 Dir Purchasing/Materials Mgt .... Ms. Rennette APODACA
28 Dir Institutional Equity/EEO .... Mr. Gerard NEVAREZ
07 Interim Director Admissions .... Ms. Delia DELEON
18 Exec Dir Facilities/Services .... Mr. Timothy DOBSON
27 Dir of Marketilng/Creative Svcs .... Ms. Ellen J. CASTELLO

New Mexico State University at Alamogordo (B)

2400 N Scenic Drive, Alamogordo NM 88310-4239

County: Otero FICE Identification: 002658
Unit ID: 187994
Telephone: (575) 439-3600 Carnegie Class: Assoc/Pub2in4
FAX Number: (575) 439-3643 Calendar System: Semester
URL: www.nmsua.edu
Established: 1958 Annual Undergrad Tuition & Fees (In-State): $1,968
Enrollment: 2,095 Coed
Affiliation or Control: State IRS Status: 501(c)3
Highest Offering: Associate Degree
Program: Occupational; 2-Year Principally Bachelor's Creditable
Accreditation: NH

01 Interim President .... Dr. Ken VAN WINKLE
05 Vice President for Academic Affairs .... Dr. Mark CAL
32 Vice President for Student Services .... Mr. Juan B. GARCIA
10 Vice President for Business/Finance .... Mr. Antonio SALINAS
56 Assoc Vice Pres Extended Programs .... Mrs. Donna L. COOK
26 Marketing Director .... Vacant
13 Chief Info Technology Officer (CIO) .... Mr. David SANDERS
08 Librarian .... Dr. Sharon JENKINS
07 Director of Admissions/Registrar .... Mr. Jeremy PATTON
37 Director Student Financial Aid .... Dr. Vandeen MCKENZIE
09 Director of Institutional Research .... Mr. Greg HILLIS
36 Director Student Placement .... Mr. Juan B. GARCIA
15 Director Human Resources .... Mrs. Brenda W. GARCIA
18 Director Facilities/Physical Plant .... Ms. Nancy MONTGOMERY
38 Director Student Counseling .... Mr. Juan B. GARCIA
27 Dir of Marketing/Creative Svcs .... Vacant
96 Buyer Sr .... Mr. Lee M. KINNEY

04 Administrative Asst to President .... Ms. Mary FECHNER
106 Dir Online Education/E-learning .... Mrs. Sherrell WHEELER

New Mexico State University at Carlsbad (C)

1500 University Drive, Carlsbad NM 88220-3598

County: Eddy FICE Identification: 002659
Unit ID: 188003
Telephone: (575) 234-9200 Carnegie Class: Assoc/Pub2in4
FAX Number: (575) 885-4951 Calendar System: Semester
URL: www.carlsbad.nmsu.edu
Established: 1950 Annual Undergrad Tuition & Fees (In-State): $1,191
Enrollment: 1,852 Coed
Affiliation or Control: State IRS Status: 501(c)3
Highest Offering: Associate Degree
Program: Occupational; 2-Year Principally Bachelor's Creditable
Accreditation: NH, ADNUR

01 Campus President .... Dr. John GRATTON
05 Chief Academic Officer/Provost .... Dr. Andrew I. NWANNE
32 Vice Pres Student Services .... Mr. Michael J. CLEARY
10 VP Business & Finance .... Vacant
37 Director Financial Aid .... Ms. Diana CAMPOS
15 Human Resources Specialist .... Ms. Rebecca SILVA
26 Director Marketing & Publications .... Mr. Khushroo GHADIALI

New Mexico State University Dona Ana Community College (D)

Box 30001, MSC 3DA, Las Cruces NM 88003-8001

County: Dona Ana Identification: 666649
Unit ID: 187620
Telephone: (575) 527-7500 Carnegie Class: Assoc/Pub2in4
FAX Number: (575) 527-7515 Calendar System: Semester
URL: dacc.nmsu.edu
Established: 1973 Annual Undergrad Tuition & Fees (In-State): $1,632
Enrollment: 8,448 Coed
Affiliation or Control: State IRS Status: 501(c)3
Highest Offering: Associate Degree
Program: Occupational; 2-Year Principally Bachelor's Creditable
Accreditation: NH, ACBSP, ADNUR, COARC, DA, DH, DMS, EMT, IFSAC

01 President/CEO .... Dr. Renay M. SCOTT
05 VP for Academic Affairs .... Dr. Monica TORRES
10 VP for Business & Finance .... Ms. Kelly BROOKS
32 VP for Student Services .... Mr. Amadeo LEDESMA
20 Assoc VP for Academic Affairs .... Dr. John WALKER
50 Division Dean Business/Info Systems .... Ms. Lydia BAGWELL
97 Division Dean General Studies .... Dr. Bernard PINA
76 Div Dean Health/Public Services .... Mr. Douglas SCRIBNER
72 Division Dean Technical Studies .... Ms. Saundra CASTILLO
103 Exec Director Workforce Dev/Trng .... Mr. Fred OWENSKY
62 Director Library Services .... Ms. Tammy POWERS
36 Director of Career Services .... Ms. Rosa DE LA TORRE-BURMEISTER
09 Campus Inst Effectiveness/Plng Ofcr .... Dr. Fred LILLIBRIDGE
26 Dir Public Relations/Development .... Mr. Arthur BINDER
27 Director of Marketing/Publications .... Mr. John PAULMAN
31 Director Community Education .... Ms. Vickie GALINDO
40 Bookstore Manager .... Mr. Roman CORONADO
21 Manager Business Office .... Ms. Nancy RITTER
15 Human Resources Operation Manager .... Mr. Mack ADAMS
90 Director Computer Support .... Ms. Lori ALLEN
18 Manager Facilities Services .... Ms. Kathleen REDDINGTON
07 Director Admissions .... Ms. Geraldine MARTINEZ
37 Director Financial Aid .... Ms. Gladys CHAIREZ
28 Director Disabled Student Services .... Mr. Jesse HAAS

New Mexico State University Dona Ana Community College East Mesa Campus (E)

2800 N Sonoma Ranch Boulevard, Las Cruses NM 88011

Telephone: (575) 528-7250 Identification: 770346
Accreditation: &NH

† Branch campus of New Mexico State University Dona Ana Community College, Las Cruces, NM.

New Mexico State University Grants (F)

1500 Third Street, Grants NM 87020-2025

Telephone: (505) 287-6678 FICE Identification: 008854
Accreditation: &NH

† Regional accreditation is carried under the parent institution in Las Cruces, NM.

Northern New Mexico College (G)

921 N Paseo de Onate, Espanola NM 87532-2649

County: Rio Arriba FICE Identification: 020839
Unit ID: 188058
Telephone: (505) 747-2100 Carnegie Class: Bac/Assoc
FAX Number: (505) 747-2170 Calendar System: Semester
URL: www.nnmc.edu
Established: 1909 Annual Undergrad Tuition & Fees (In-State): $2,183
Enrollment: 1,348 Coed
Affiliation or Control: State IRS Status: 501(c)3
Highest Offering: Baccalaureate
Program: Occupational; 2-Year Principally Bachelor's Creditable; Liberal Arts And General; Teacher Preparatory

Accreditation: NH, ENGT, NURSE

01 President .... Dr. Nancy (Rusty) BARCELO
10 Vice Pres Finance & Administration .... Mr. Domingo SANCHEZ
30 Vice Pres Institutional Advancement .... Mr. Ricky SERNA
05 Provost/VP Academic Affairs .... Dr. Pedro L. MARTINEZ
32 Dean of Student Services .... Dr. Pedro MARTINEZ
12 Director El Rito Campus .... Vacant
06 Registrar .... Ms. Kathleen SENA
08 Head Librarian .... Ms. Amy ORTIZ
84 Director of Recruitment .... Mr. Frank ORONA
37 Director of Financial Aid .... Mr. Jacob PACHECO
13 Director of IT .... Mr. Jimi MONTOYA
15 Director of Human Resources .... Mr. Bernie PADILLA
18 Director of Facilities .... Mr. Andy ROMERO
09 Director of Inst Effectiveness .... Ms. Carmella MARTINEZ
21 Director of Business Operations .... Ms. Henrietta TRUJILLO
108 Dir Inst Advise/Coord Stdnt Advise .... Mr. Tobe BOTT-LYONS
41 Athletic Director/Coach .... Mr. Ryan CORDOVA
51 Coordinator Continuing Education .... Ms. Cecilia ROMERO
53 Dean College of Teacher Education .... Dr. Joaquin VILA
49 Dean College of Arts and Sciences .... Vacant

Pima Medical Institute-Albuquerque (H)

4400 Cutler Avenue NE, Albuquerque NM 87110-3935

Telephone: (505) 881-1234 FICE Identification: 036783
Accreditation: ABHES, COARC, DH, PTAA, RAD

† Branch campus of Pima Medical Institute-Tucson, Tucson, AZ.

Ruidoso Branch Community College (I)

709 Mechem Drive, Ruidoso NM 88345

Telephone: (575) 257-2120 Identification: 770345
Accreditation: &NH

† Branch campus of Eastern New Mexico University Main Campus, Portales, NM.

St. John's College (J)

1160 Camino de la Cruz Blanca, Santa Fe NM 87505-4599

County: Santa Fe FICE Identification: 002093
Unit ID: 245652
Telephone: (505) 984-6000 Carnegie Class: Master's S
FAX Number: (505) 984-6003 Calendar System: Semester
URL: www.sjc.edu
Established: 1964 Annual Undergrad Tuition & Fees: $47,826
Enrollment: 397 Coed
Affiliation or Control: Independent Non-Profit IRS Status: 501(c)3
Highest Offering: Master's
Program: Liberal Arts And General
Accreditation: NH

01 President .... Mr. Michael P. PETERS
05 Dean .... Mr. Ned WALPIN
30 Vice President for Advancement .... Ms. Victoria MORA
10 Treasurer .... Mr. Bryan VALENTINE
06 Registrar .... Mrs. Marline MARQUEZ-SCALLY
08 Library Director .... Ms. Jennifer SPRAGUE
07 Director of Admissions .... Mr. Larry CLENDENIN
58 Director of Graduate Institute .... Mr. David CARL
09 Director of Institutional Research .... Mr. Nick GIACONA
15 Director of Human Resources .... Mr. Aaron YOUNG
18 Chief Facilities/Physical Plant .... Mr. Pat HOLMAN
26 Dir of Communications/External Rels .... Mr. Gabe GOMEZ
29 Director of Alumni Relations .... Ms. Sarah PALACIOS
36 Director Student Placement .... Ms. Margaret ODELL
37 Director Student Financial Aid .... Mr. Mike RODRIQUEZ

† Affiliated with St. John's College, Maryland.

San Juan College (K)

4601 College Boulevard, Farmington NM 87402-4699

County: San Juan FICE Identification: 002660
Unit ID: 188100
Telephone: (505) 326-3311 Carnegie Class: Assoc/Pub-R-L
FAX Number: (505) 566-3385 Calendar System: Semester
URL: www.sanjuancollege.edu
Established: 1956 Annual Undergrad Tuition & Fees (In-District): $1,474
Enrollment: 9,906 Coed
Affiliation or Control: Local IRS Status: 501(c)3
Highest Offering: Associate Degree
Program: Occupational; 2-Year Principally Bachelor's Creditable
Accreditation: NH, ADNUR, CAHIIM, #COARC, DH, EMT, MLTAD, OTA, PTAA, SURGT

01 President .... Dr. Toni PENDERGRASS
05 Vice Pres for Learning .... Dr. Barbara AKE
10 Vice Pres Administrative Services .... Mr. Russell LITKE
32 Vice Pres for Student Services .... Mr. David EPPICH
04 Executive Asst to President .... Ms. Jeanne NOTSON
20 Assoc VP Learning/Strategic Init .... Ms. Lisa WILSON
102 Executive Director Foundation .... Ms. Gayle DEAN
31 Chief Community Relations Officer .... Ms. Nancy SHEPHERD
21 Controller .... Ms. Karen KING
26 Director Marketing/Public Relations .... Ms. Rhonda SCHAEFER
88 Dir Ctr for Student Engagement .... Dr. Michaele BRANDON
84 Sr Dir Enrollment Management .... Mr. Jon BETZ
50 Interim Dean Sch Business .... Mr. Jack KANT

79 Dean School of Humanities .... Mr. Allan NASS
76 Interim Dean Sch of Health Sciences .... Ms. Nisa BRUCE
65 Dean School of Energy .... Mr. Randy PACHECO
72 Dean School Trades & Technology .... Mr. Bill LEWIS
81 Int Dean Math/Science & Engineering .... Mr. Vernon WILLIE
22 Director Affirmative Action/EEO .... Ms. Stacey ALLEN
88 Director Native American Programs .... Ms. Michele PETERSON
08 Director Library Services .... Mr. Chris SCHIPPER
37 Director of Financial Aid .... Ms. Mindi-Kim SCHRUM
18 Interim Director Physical Plant .... Mr. Garry SMOTHERS
19 Director Security/Safety .... Mr. Kelly ANDERSON
35 Director Student Activities .... Ms. Marcia STERLING
96 Director Purchasing .... Mr. Frank COLE
38 Director Student Advising Center .... Ms. Christy FERRATO
74 Director Vet-Tech Program .... Dr. David WRIGHT
36 Dir Quality/Improve/Career Svcs Ctr .... Ms. Tonya NELSON
06 Registrar .... Ms. Sherri GAUGH
09 Int Dir of Institutional Research .... Mr. Ron JERNIGAN
15 Interim Director Human Resources .... Ms. Janet HEBBE
13 Chief Info Technology Officer (CIO) .... Ms. Shelley AMATOR

Santa Fe Community College (A)

6401 Richards Avenue, Santa Fe NM 87508-4887
County: Santa Fe FICE Identification: 022781
Unit ID: 188137
Telephone: (505) 428-1000 Carnegie Class: Assoc/Pub-R-L
FAX Number: (505) 428-1296 Calendar System: Semester
URL: www.sfcc.edu
Established: 1983 Annual Undergrad Tuition & Fees (In-State): $1,195
Enrollment: 6,497 Coed
Affiliation or Control: State IRS Status: 501(c)3
Highest Offering: Associate Degree
Program: Occupational; 2-Year Principally Bachelor's Creditable
Accreditation: NH, ADNUR, COARC, DA, MAC

01 President .... Mr. Randy W. GRISSOM
05 Vice Pres Academic Affairs .... Ms. Margaret PETERS
10 Vice Pres Finance .... Mr. Nick TELLES
09 VP Planning & Inst Effectiveness .... Mr. Yash MORIMOTO
32 Vice President Student Success .... Dr. Carmen GONZALES
21 Associate Vice President Finance .... Vacant
20 Assoc VP of Academic Support .... Ms. Jill DOUGLASS
84 Assoc VP Enrollment & Student Svcs .... Dr. Cheryl FIELDS
51 Director Cont Educ/Workforce Dev .... Mr. Gordon FLUKE
26 Exec Dir Marketing/Public Rels .... Ms. Janet WISE
102 Exec Dir SFCC Foundation .... Ms. Deborah BOLDT
06 Registrar .... Ms. Barbara TUCCI
13 Interim Chief Information Officer .... Mr. Jeremy LOVATO
37 Financial Aid Director .... Mr. Scott WHITAKER
66 Director of Nursing .... Vacant
08 Library Director .... Ms. Peg JOHNSON
15 Exec Director of Human Resources .... Mr. Daniel GUTIERREZ
88 Director Small Business Development .... Mr. Brian DUBOFF
18 Director of Plant Operations .... Mr. Henry MIGNARDOT
12 Director HEC .... Ms. Rebecca ESTRADA
49 Int Dean Liberal/Design/Media Arts .... Dr. Bernadette JACOBS
76 Dean Health & Fitness/Math/Sciences .... Dr. Jenny LANDEN
57 Int Dean School of Arts and Design .... Dr. Bernadette JACOBS
53 Int Dn Trds/Tech/Sustn Pro Stu/Educ . Dr. Camilla BUSTAMANTE
50 Dean Sch Business & Applied Tech .... Dr. Camilla BUSTAMANTE
101 Executive Asst to the President .... Ms. Barb MASCARENAS
96 Director of Purchasing .... Vacant
25 Chief Contracts/Grants Admin .... Ms. Ann BLACK

Santa Fe University of Art and Design (B)

1600 St. Michael's Drive, Santa Fe NM 87505-7634
County: Santa Fe FICE Identification: 002649
Unit ID: 188146
Telephone: (505) 473-6011 Carnegie Class: Spec/Arts
FAX Number: (505) 473-6127 Calendar System: Semester
URL: www.santafeuniversity.edu
Established: 1947 Annual Undergrad Tuition & Fees: $30,846
Enrollment: 954 Coed
Affiliation or Control: Proprietary IRS Status: Proprietary
Highest Offering: Master's
Program: Liberal Arts And General; Professional; Fine Arts Emphasis
Accreditation: NH

01 President .... Mr. Laurence A. HINZ
03 Interim Provost .... Ms. Debra TERVALA
32 Exec Dir Student Affairs/Operations .... Ms. Melissa LEWIS
35 Asst Dir Student Affs/Operations .... Mr. Jeremy HADLEY
07 Director of Enrollment .... Ms. Christine GUEVARA
10 Director of Finance .... Mr. Steven POSEY
18 Dir Facilities & Security .... Mr. Peter ROMERO
13 Dir Campus Technology Services .... Mr. Jeff PEARCE
37 Director of Financial Aid .... Ms. Celeste FRANKLIN
36 Director of Career Services .... Ms. Joanie SPAIN
15 Interim Director of Human Resources .... Ms. Susan WAUGH
06 Registrar .... Ms. Mary ANGELL
88 Executive Director of Marketing .... Ms. Betty CESARANO
88 Asst Marketing Manager .... Mr. Lauren LINSALATA
26 External & Public Relations Manager .... Ms. Lauren MCDANIEL

† Annual tuition for Graphic Design, Creative Writing, Digital Arts and Arts Management programs is $19,646.

Southwest Acupuncture College (C)

1622 Galisteo Street, Santa Fe NM 87505-6351
County: Santa Fe FICE Identification: 026220
Unit ID: 366605
Telephone: (505) 438-8884 Carnegie Class: Spec/Health
FAX Number: (505) 438-8883 Calendar System: Semester
URL: www.acupuncturecollege.edu
Established: 1980 Annual Undergrad Tuition & Fees: $17,170
Enrollment: 40 Coed
Affiliation or Control: Proprietary IRS Status: Proprietary
Highest Offering: Master's; No Lower Division
Program: Professional
Accreditation: ACUP

01 CEO .... Dr. Anthony ABBATE
03 Executive Director .... Dr. Skya ABBATE
10 Chief Fiscal Officer .... Mr. Charles ROUNTREE
12 Campus Director Santa Fe .... Ms. Latricia GONZALES-MCKOSKY
17 Clinical Director Santa Fe .... Dr. Melanie RICHARDSON
05 Academic Dean Santa Fe .... Ms. Annie SPARNO
37 Director of Financial Aid .... Ms. Angela ANAYA

Southwest Acupuncture College-Albuquerque (D)

7801 Academy Blvd N Town Bdg #1 NE,
Albuquerque NM 87109
Telephone: (505) 888-8898 Identification: 666666
Accreditation: ACUP

† Branch campus of Southwest Acupuncture College, Santa Fe, NM.

Southwest University of Visual Arts (E)

5000 Marble Avenue, NE, Albuquerque NM 87110-6344
Telephone: (505) 254-7575 Identification: 666524
Accreditation: &NH, CIDA

† Regional accreditation is carried under the parent institution in Tucson, AZ.

Southwestern College (F)

3960 San Filipe Road, Santa Fe NM 87507
County: Santa Fe FICE Identification: 030761
Unit ID: 188207
Telephone: (505) 471-5756 Carnegie Class: Assoc/PrivNFP4
FAX Number: (505) 471-4071 Calendar System: Quarter
URL: www.swc.edu
Established: 1979 Annual Graduate Tuition & Fees: $16,200
Enrollment: 162 Coed
Affiliation or Control: Independent Non-Profit IRS Status: 501(c)3
Highest Offering: Master's; No Undergraduates
Program: Professional
Accreditation: NH

01 President .... Dr. Jim NOLAN
03 Exec VP/Dir New Earth Institute SWC .... Ms. Katherine NINOS
05 Vice Pres Academic Affairs/Dean .... Dr. Ann FILEMYR
07 Director of Admissions .... Ms. Dru PHOENIX
06 Registrar .... Ms. Andrea PACHECO
10 Finance Manager .... Ms. Cheryl PAYSON
13 Chief Technology Officer .... Ms. Donna HARRINGTON

Southwestern Indian Polytechnic Institute (G)

9169 Coors Blvd., NW, Albuquerque NM 87120
County: Bernalillo FICE Identification: 025110
Unit ID: 188216
Telephone: (505) 346-2348 Carnegie Class: Tribal
FAX Number: (505) 346-2343 Calendar System: Trimester
URL: www.sipi.edu
Established: 1971 Annual Undergrad Tuition & Fees: $1,095
Enrollment: 481 Coed
Affiliation or Control: Federal IRS Status: 501(c)3
Highest Offering: Associate Degree
Program: Occupational; 2-Year Principally Bachelor's Creditable; Technical Emphasis
Accreditation: NH, OPD, OPLT

01 President .... Dr. Sherry ALLISON
10 Vice Pres College Operations .... Mr. Eric CHRISTENSEN
05 Vice President Academic Programs .... Ms. Valerie MONTOYA
39 Acting Director of Residential Life .... Ms. Bertha CURLEY
07 Director Admissions/Registrar .... Mr. Joseph CARPIO
09 Director of Institutional Research ...... Mr. Edward HUMMINGBIRD
15 Human Resources Specialist .... Ms. Dawn AMI
18 Acting Facilities Director .... Ms. Renee ALLEN
37 Director Student Financial Aid .... Mr. Joseph CARPIO

University of New Mexico Main Campus (H)

1 University of New Mexico, Albuquerque NM 87131-0001
County: Bernalillo FICE Identification: 002663
Unit ID: 187985
Telephone: (505) 277-0111 Carnegie Class: RU/VH
FAX Number: (505) 277-6019 Calendar System: Semester
URL: www.unm.edu
Established: 1889 Annual Undergrad Tuition & Fees (In-State): $6,664
Enrollment: 27,887 Coed
Affiliation or Control: State IRS Status: 501(c)3
Highest Offering: Doctorate
Program: Liberal Arts And General; Teacher Preparatory; Professional
Accreditation: NH, ARCPA, BUS, BUSA, CAATE, CACREP, CLPSY, CONST, CS, DANCE, DENT, DH, DIETD, DIETI, EMT, ENG, IPSY, JOUR, LAW, LSAR, MED, MIDWF, MT, MUS, NURSE, OT, PH, PHAR, PLNG, PTA, SP, SPAA, TED, THEA

01 President .... Dr. Robert G. FRANK
05 Provost/Exec VP Academic Affs .... Dr. Chaouki T. ABDALLAH
17 Chancellor of Health Sciences Ctr .... Dr. Paul B. ROTH
10 Exec Vice Pres Administration .... Dr. David W. HARRIS
100 Chief of Staff .... Dr. Amy WOHLERT
12 Special Asst for Branch Affairs .... Dr. Wynn M. GOERING
20 Sr Vice Provost Academic Affairs .... Carol PARKER
106 Vice Provost Extended Learning .... Dr. Monica OROZCO
46 Vice President Research .... Dr. Michael J. DOUGHER
25 AVP Research Administration .... Carlos ROMERO
20 Assoc Provost Faculty Development .... Dr. Virginia SCHARFF
20 Assoc Provost Curriculum .... Dr. Gregory HEILEMAN
32 Vice President Student Affairs .... Dr. Eliseo S. TORRES
28 Vice President Equity & Inclusion .... Dr. Josephine DE LEON
28 Vice Chancellor HSC Diversity ... Dr. Valerie ROMERO-LEGGOTT
84 AVP Enrollment Management .... Dr. Terry BABBITT
15 Vice President Human Resources .... Dorothy ANDERSON
41 Vice President for Athletics .... Paul R. KREBS
21 University Controller .... Elizabeth METZGER
13 Chief Information Officer .... Gilbert GONZALES
43 University Counsel .... Elsa KIRCHER COLE
29 AVP Alumni Relations .... Karen A. ABRAHAM
20 AVP Academic Administration .... Curtis R. PORTER
21 AVP Planning/Budget & Analysis .... Andrew CULLEN
35 AVP Student Life .... Dr. Walter C. MILLER
35 AVP Student Services .... Dr. Tim GUTIERREZ
50 Interim Dean ASM .... Dr. Craig WHITE
48 Dean Sch of Architecture & Planning .... Dr. Geraldine FORBES ISAIS
49 Dean College of Arts & Sciences .... Dr. Mark PECENY
53 Dean College of Education .... Dr. Hector OCHOA
54 Interim Dean School of Engineering .... Dr. Joseph CECCHI
57 Dean College of Fine Arts .... Dr. Kymberly PINDER
61 Dean School of Law .... David HERRING
63 Exec Vice Dean School of Medicine .... Dr. Martha MCGREW
66 Dean College of Nursing .... Dr. Nancy A. RIDENOUR
67 Dean College of Pharmacy .... Dr. Lynda S. WELAGE
80 Interim Dir School of Public Admin .... Dr. Mario RIVERA
92 Dean Honors & University Colleges .... Dr. Kate KRAUSE
58 Dean Office of Graduate Studies .... Dr. Julie COONROD
51 Assoc Dean Continuing Education .... Joseph MIERA
08 Dean University Libraries .... Dr. Richard CLEMENT
26 Chief Univ Marketing & Comm Officer .... Cinnamon BLAIR
27 HSC Exec Dir Comm & Marketing .... William O. SPARKS
27 Director University Communications .... Dianne ANDERSON
105 Mgr University Web Communications .... Matt CARTER
86 Interim Director Government Affairs .... Connie BEIMER
09 Director Institutional Analytics .... Paige D. BRIGGS
18 University Architect .... Amy COBURN
18 Director Physical Plant .... Jeff ZUMWALT
19 Chief of Police .... Kevin MCCABE
96 Chief Procurement Officer .... Bruce E. CHERRIN
23 Director Student Health Center .... Dr. Beverly KLOEPPEL
22 Intirim Dir Equal Opportunity .... Jeanne MARQUARDT
24 Dir New Media & Extended Learning .... Debby KNOTTS
35 Dean of Students .... Dr. Thomas AGUIRRE
07 Director Admissions and Recruitment .... Matt HULETT
06 Registrar .... Alex GONZALEZ
37 Director Student Financial Aid .... Brian MALONE
36 Director Career Services .... Jenna S. CRABB
39 Director Student Housing & Res Life .... Wayne SULLIVAN
40 Director Bookstore .... Carrie MITCHELL
108 Director of Assessment .... Neke MITCHELL
102 UNM Foundation President and CEO .... Henry NEMCIK
30 VP University Development .... Larry RYAN
30 VP Development Health Sciences Ctr .... Bill UHER
88 CEO UNM Hospital .... Steve MCKERNAN
04 Administrative Asst to President .... Mitch GARRITY
101 Secretary of the Institution/Board .... Mallory REVIERE

University of New Mexico-Gallup (I)

705 Gurley Avenue, Gallup NM 87301
Telephone: (505) 863-7500 FICE Identification: 006881
Accreditation: &NH, ADNUR, CAHIIM, DA, MLTAD

† Regional accreditation is carried under the parent institution in Albuquerque, NM.

University of New Mexico-Los Alamos (J)

4000 University Drive, Los Alamos NM 87544-2233
Telephone: (505) 662-5919 Identification: 666742
Accreditation: &NH

† Regional accreditation is carried under the parent institution in Albuquerque, NM.

University of New Mexico-Taos (K)

1157 Country Road 110, Ranchos de Taos NM 87557
Telephone: (575) 737-6200 Identification: 666743
Accreditation: &NH, ADNUR

† Regional accreditation is carried under the parent institution in Albuquerque, NM.

University of New Mexico-Valencia (A)

280 La Entrada Road, Los Lunas NM 87031-7633
Telephone: (505) 925-8500 Identification: 666741
Accreditation: &NH

† Regional accreditation is carried under the parent institution in Albuquerque, NM.

University of Phoenix New Mexico Campus (B)

5700 Pasadena Avenue, NE,
Albuquerque NM 87113-1570
Telephone: (505) 821-4800 Identification: 770219
Accreditation: &NH, ACBSP

† Branch campus of University of Phoenix, Tempe, AZ.

University of St. Francis (C)

1500 N. Renaissance Blvd, NE, Ste C,
Albuquerque NM 87107
Telephone: (505) 266-5565 Identification: 770099
Accreditation: &NH, ARCPA

† Branch campus of University of St. Francis, Joliet, IL.

University of the Southwest (D)

6610 Lovington Highway, Hobbs NM 88240-9129
County: Lea FICE Identification: 002650
Unit ID: 188182
Telephone: (575) 392-6561 Carnegie Class: Bac/Diverse
FAX Number: (575) 392-6006 Calendar System: Semester
URL: www.usw.edu
Established: 1962 Annual Undergrad Tuition & Fees: $12,528
Enrollment: 1,016 Coed
Affiliation or Control: Independent Non-Profit IRS Status: 501(c)3
Highest Offering: Master's
Program: Liberal Arts And General; Teacher Preparatory; Professional
Accreditation: NH

01 President .... Dr. Quint THURMAN
05 Provost .... Dr. Larry GUERRERO
10 VP for Financial Services/CFO .... Mr. Ronald MCBEE
32 VP for Enrollment Mgmt/Student Life .... Mrs. Michele GOAR
30 VP for Advancement .... Mr. William J. WEIDNER
18 Campus Steward .... Dr. David ARNOLD
20 Associate Provost .... Dr. Daniel CASTILLO
15 Asst VP HR & Regulatory Compliance .... Mrs. Veronica TORREZ
49 Dean School of Arts & Sciences .... Dr. Elyn PALMER
50 Dean School of Business .... Dr. Ryan TIPTON
53 Dean School of Education .... Dr. Mary R. HARRIS
08 Dean Library Services .... Mr. John MCCANCE
41 Director of Athletics .... Mr. William J. WEIDNER
42 Campus Minister .... Mr. Danny KIRKPATRICK
06 University Registrar .... Ms. Caitlin ODOM
37 Financial Aid Director .... Mrs. Dawny KRINGEL
26 Director Development & Marketing .... Ms. Laurie DEAN
88 Maintenance Supervisor .... Mr. Lonnie HARRISON
19 Director of Student Life .... Mrs. Nichole GREEN
07 Director of Admissions .... Ms. Sara DENNIS

Western New Mexico University (E)

PO Box 680, Silver City NM 88062-0680
County: Grant FICE Identification: 002664
Unit ID: 188304
Telephone: (505) 538-6011 Carnegie Class: Master's M
FAX Number: (505) 538-6364 Calendar System: Semester
URL: www.wnmu.edu
Established: 1893 Annual Undergrad Tuition & Fees (In-State): $5,705
Enrollment: 3,500 Coed
Affiliation or Control: State IRS Status: 501(c)3
Highest Offering: Beyond Master's But Less Than Doctorate
Program: Liberal Arts And General; Teacher Preparatory
Accreditation: NH, ACBSP, ADNUR, NURSE, #OT, #OTA, SW, TED

01 President .... Dr. Joseph SHEPARD
05 Provost/Vice Pres Academic Affairs .... Dr. Jack CROCKER
32 VP Student Affairs/Enrollment Mgmt .... Dr. Isaac BRUNDAGE
10 Vice President Business Affairs .... Dr. Brenda FINDLEY
30 VP External Affairs .... Dr. Magdaleno MANZANARES
20 Assoc Vice Pres Academic Affairs .... Dr. Linda HOY
06 Registrar .... Ms. Betsy MILLER
08 University Librarian .... Ms. Gilda BAEZA-ORTEGO
37 Director Student Financial Aid .... Ms. Onorina FRANCO
07 Interim Director Admissions .... Mr. Matthew LARA
09 Director of Institutional Research .... Mr. Paul LANDRUM
15 Director of Human Resources .... Vacant
18 Chief Facilities/Physical Plant .... Mr. Stan PENA
26 Chief Public Relations Officer .... Mr. Abe VILLARREAL
29 Int Director of Alumni Relations .... Ms. Cari LEMON
36 Career Services Coord .... Vacant
28 Dir Multi-Cultural Affs/Student Act .... Ms. Jessica MORALES
96 Director of Purchasing .... Ms. Amy BACA
100 Chief of Staff .... Ms. Julie MORALES
19 Director Security/Safety .... Mr. Eddie FLORES
41 Athletic Director .... Mr. Mark COLEMAN
50 Dean of College of Arts and Science .... Dr. Jose HERRERA
53 Interim Dean of Education .... Dr. Barbara TAYLOR

NEW YORK

Adelphi University (F)

1 South Avenue, PO Box 701,
Garden City NY 11530-0701
County: Nassau FICE Identification: 002666
Unit ID: 188429
Telephone: (516) 877-3000 Carnegie Class: DRU
FAX Number: (516) 877-3545 Calendar System: Semester
URL: www.adelphi.edu
Established: 1896 Annual Undergrad Tuition & Fees: $34,034
Enrollment: 7,610 Coed
Affiliation or Control: Independent Non-Profit IRS Status: 501(c)3
Highest Offering: Doctorate
Program: Liberal Arts And General; Teacher Preparatory; Professional
Accreditation: M, AUD, BUS, CLPSY, NURSE, SP, SW, TED

01 President .... Dr. Christine M. RIORDAN
03 Provost .... Dr. Gayle D. INSLER
05 Sr Assoc Provost for Acad Affairs .... Dr. Audrey S. BLUMBERG
20 Sr Assoc Provost for Acad Affairs .... Dr. Lester B. BALTIMORE
11 Assoc Provost for Administration .... Dr. Lawrence HOBBIE
28 Assoc Prov Fac Affairs & Diversity .... Dr. Perry GREENE
106 Assoc Provost Online Learning .... Dr. Laura MARTIN
84 VP Enroll Mgmt/Student Success .... Dr. Lauren MOUNTY
10 Senior Vice President & Treasurer .... Mr. Timothy P. BURTON
30 Vice Pres University Advancement .... Dr. Christian VAUPEL
26 Vice President for Communications .... Ms. Lori DUGGAN-GOLD
18 Asst to Pres Facilities Planning .... Mr. Bill PROTO
32 Assoc VP Enroll Mgt/Student Success .... Ms. Esther GOODCUFF
21 Assoc VP for Finance & Co-Treasurer .... Mr. Robert L. DECARLO
15 Assoc VP Human Resource/Labor Rel .... Ms. Lisa ARAUJO
49 Dean of Arts & Sciences .... Dr. Sam L. GROGG
53 Dean RS Ammon School of Education .... Dr. Jane ASHDOWN
66 Dean Col of Nursing & Public Hlth .... Dr. Patrick R. COONAN
70 Dean School of Social Work .... Dr. Andrew SAFYER
58 Dean Derner Inst Advanc Psych Std .... Dr. Jacques BARBER
50 Dean RB Willumstad Sch of Business .... Dr. Rajib N. SANYAL
92 Dean of Honors College .... Dr. Richard GARNER
88 Dean University Col/Adult Pgms .... Dr. Shawn O'RILEY
08 Dean University Libraries .... Mr. Brian LYM
35 Dean Student Affairs/Asst VP .... Mr. Jeffrey A. KESSLER
13 Chief Information Officer/CIO .... Mr. Jack CHEN
41 Director of Athletics .... Mr. Daniel MCCABE
56 Exec Dir Off-Campus Administration .... Mr. James MCGOWAN
19 Asst VP for Public Safety .... Mr. Eugene PALMA
18 Exec Dir Facilities/Physical Plant .... Mr. James KOSLOSKI
09 Exec Dir Research/Assessment/Plng .... Dr. Nava LERER
37 Asst VP Student Financial Aid .... Ms. Sheryl L. MIHOPULOS
07 Executive Director of Admissions .... Ms. Kristen CAPEZZA
36 Exec Dir Career Plng & Placement .... Mr. Thomas J. WARD
06 Registrar .... Ms. Jill GLATTER
104 Director International Education .... Ms. Shannon HARRISON
23 Director Health Services .... Ms. Jacqueline CARTABUKE
38 Director Student Counseling Center .... Dr. Carol A. LUCAS
39 Director Residential Life/Housing .... Mr. Guy SENEQUE
29 Exec Director Alumni Relations .... Ms. Polly SCHMITZ
88 Assoc Treasurer/Budget Director .... Mr. Michael J. MCLEOD
88 Director Business Affairs .... Mr. Russell A. PALMER
12 Director Manhattan Center .... Ms. June TRIZZINO-PECOR
12 Director Hudson Valley Center .... Ms. Eileen P. CHADWICK
96 Purchasing Manager .... Ms. Elizabeth F. KASH
108 Director Institutional Assessment .... Dr. Lori HOEFFNER

Albany College of Pharmacy and Health Sciences (G)

106 New Scotland Avenue, Albany NY 12208-3492
County: Albany FICE Identification: 002885
Unit ID: 188526
Telephone: (518) 694-7200 Carnegie Class: Spec/Health
FAX Number: (518) 694-7202 Calendar System: Semester
URL: www.acphs.edu
Established: 1881 Annual Undergrad Tuition & Fees: $30,300
Enrollment: 1,563 Coed
Affiliation or Control: Independent Non-Profit IRS Status: 501(c)3
Highest Offering: Doctorate
Program: Professional
Accreditation: M, CYTO, MT, PHAR

01 President .... Greg DEWEY
05 Provost .... Tarun PATEL
46 Vice Provost for Research .... Shaker MOUSA
88 Vice Provost Innovative Learning .... Vacant
49 Dean School of Arts and Sciences .... David CLARKE
67 Dean School of Pharmacy/Inst Effec .... Angela DOMINELLI
58 Dean School of Graduate Studies .... Martha HASS
12 Associate Dean for Vermont Campus .... Robert HAMILTON
32 Dean of Students .... Vacant
35 Associate Dean of Student Affairs .... Wendy NEIFELD WHEELER
43 General Counsel .... Vacant
10 VP of Finance .... Michele VIEN
30 VP of Institutional Advancement .... Vicki DILORENZO
84 VP of Enrollment Management .... Tiffany GUTIERREZ
13 Chief Technology Officer .... Pamela SMITH
11 AVP of Administrative Operations .... Packy MCGRAW
07 Director of Admissions .... Matthew STEVER
06 Registrar .... Jeff DUFOUR
08 Director of Library Services .... Sue IWANOWICZ
26 Exec Director of Marketing/Comm .... Gil CHORBAJIAN
41 Director of Athletics .... Katie BISHOP
15 Director of Human Resources .... Casey DIMARCO
09 Director of Prospect Research .... Deanna ENNELLO-BUTLER

Albany Law School (H)

80 New Scotland Avenue, Albany NY 12208-3494
County: Albany FICE Identification: 002886
Unit ID: 188535
Telephone: (518) 445-2311 Carnegie Class: Spec/Law
FAX Number: (518) 445-2315 Calendar System: Semester
URL: www.albanylaw.edu
Established: 1851 Annual Undergrad Tuition & Fees: $43,398
Enrollment: 479 Coed
Affiliation or Control: Independent Non-Profit IRS Status: 501(c)3
Highest Offering: First Professional Degree
Program: Professional
Accreditation: LAW

01 President & Dean .... Dean Alicia OUELLETTE
05 Assoc Dean Acad Affairs .... Dean Connie MAYER
10 Vice President Finance & Business .... Mr. Victor E. RAUSCHER
08 Director of Library .... Vacant
30 Interim Asst Dean Inst Advancement .... Ms. Anne Marie JUDGE
32 Associate Dean for Student Affairs .... Prof. Rosemary QUEENAN
06 Assistant Dean and Registrar .... Ms. Joanne FITZSIMMONS
36 Interim Asst Dean Career Center .... Ms. Joanne CASEY
26 Director Communications .... Mr. David SINGER
04 Executive Assistant to the Dean .... Ms. Barbara JORDAN-SMITH
07 Assistant Dean of Admissions .... Ms. Nadia CASTRIOTA
88 Director Clinical Program .... Prof. Sarah ROGERSON
13 Director Enterprise Tech Services .... Vacant
29 Director Alumni Affairs .... Ms. Tammy WEINMAN
15 Director Human Resources .... Ms. Sherri DONNELLY
37 Director Student Financial Aid .... Ms. Andrea WEDLER
18 Facilities Manager .... Mr. Brian LAPLANTE
36 Director of Career Services .... Vacant

Albany Medical College (I)

47 New Scotland Avenue, Mail #34,
Albany NY 12208-3479
County: Albany FICE Identification: 002887
Unit ID: 188580
Telephone: (518) 262-6008 Carnegie Class: Spec/Med
FAX Number: (518) 262-6515 Calendar System: Other
URL: www.amc.edu
Established: 1839 Annual Graduate Tuition & Fees: $56,874
Enrollment: 823 Coed
Affiliation or Control: Independent Non-Profit IRS Status: 501(c)3
Highest Offering: Doctorate; No Undergraduates
Program: Professional
Accreditation: M, ANEST, ARCPA, IPSY, MED, PAST

01 Dean/Exec VP Health Affairs .... Dr. Vincent P. VERDILE
10 EVP/Chief Financial Officer .... Mr. William HASSELBARTH
05 Vice Dean for Academic Admin .... Dr. Henry S. POHL
17 Vice Dean Clinical Affairs .... Dr. Ferdinand VENDITTI
32 Assoc Dean for Acad & Student Affs .... Dr. Elizabeth HIGGINS
63 Assoc Dean Graduate Medical Educ .... Dr. Joel BARTFIELD
90 Assoc Dean Info Resources & Tech .... Ms. Enid GEYER
88 Assoc Dean Medical Education .... Dr. Jonathan M. ROSEN
22 Assoc Dean Cmty Outreach/Medical Ed .... Ms. Ingrid M. ALLARD
08 Asc Dn Info Resrcs/Tech/Dir Library .... Ms. Enid GEYER
88 Asst Dean Medical Education .... Dr. Rebecca KELLER
58 Asst Dean for Graduate Studies .... Dr. Richard KELLER
06 Registrar .... Mr. Len SCHLEGEL
63 Director Graduate Medical Education .... Ms. Catherine RIDDLE
76 Director Physician Asst Program .... Mr. David IRVINE
07 Dir Admissions & Student Records .... Mr. Donald PRITCHETT
29 Executive Director Alumni Relations .... Ms. Maura MACK-HISGEN
26 Director Public Relations .... Mr. Jeffrey GORDON
30 Chief Development .... Ms. Terri OWENS
51 Director Cont Medical Education .... Ms. Jennifer PRICE
15 Director Human Resources .... Ms. Cathy HALAKAN
37 Director Student Financial Aid .... Ms. Ann LOUGHMAN
96 Director of Purchasing .... Ms. Ann CRISLIP
27 Marketing Specialist .... Ms. Nicolette VISCUSI

Alfred University (J)

One Saxon Drive, Alfred NY 14802-1205
County: Allegany FICE Identification: 002668
Unit ID: 188641
Telephone: (607) 871-2111 Carnegie Class: Master's L
FAX Number: (607) 871-2339 Calendar System: Semester
URL: www.alfred.edu
Established: 1836 Annual Undergrad Tuition & Fees: $30,200
Enrollment: 2,226 Coed
Affiliation or Control: Independent Non-Profit IRS Status: 501(c)3
Highest Offering: Doctorate
Program: Liberal Arts And General; Teacher Preparatory; Professional
Accreditation: M, ART, BUS, CAATE, CACREP, ENG, SCPSY, TEAC

01 President .... Dr. Charles M. EDMONDSON
05 Provost/VP for Academic Affairs .... Dr. Rick STEPHENS
10 VP for Business & Finance/Treasurer .... Ms. Giovina LLOYD
30 Acting VP for University Relations .... Mrs. Susan C. GOETSCHIUS
84 VP for Enrollment Management .... Mr. Earl E. PIERCE, JR.
32 VP for Student Affairs .... Mrs. Kathy WOUGHTER
57 Int Dean School of Art & Design .... Mr. Gerar EDIZEL

49 Dean Col of Lib Arts & Sciences .... Dr. Louis J. LICHTMAN
107 Dean College of Prof Studies .... Dr. Nancy EVANGELISTA
54 Dean School of Engineering .... Dr. Doreen EDWARDS
29 Exec Dir Annual Giv/Alum Relations ....Vacant
37 Director of Student Financial Aid ....Mr. Earl E. PIERCE, JR.
07 Director of Admissions .... Mr. Jamie MARCUS
06 Registrar ....Mr. Lawrence J. CASEY
19 Chief of Public Safety ....Mr. John M. DOUGHERTY
26 Acting Director of Communications ....Mrs. Deborah E. CLARK
39 Director of Residence Life ....Ms. Vicky GEBEL
13 Director Information Tech Svcs ....Mr. Gary O. ROBERTS
36 Director Career Development Ctr ....Mr. Mark MCFADDEN
41 Director of Athletics .... Mr. Paul VECCHIO
23 Dir Counseling & Wellness Center .... Dr. Stanley TAM
18 Director of Physical Plant ....Mr. Brian R. DODGE
08 Dir Herrick Lib/Dean of Libraries .... Mr. Stephen S. CRANDALL
08 Director of Scholes Library ....Mr. Mark SMITH
15 Director of Human Resources ....Mr. Mark A. GUINAN, JR.
21 Controller ....Ms. Jodi L. HOWE
92 Director of the Honors Program .... Dr. Gordan ATLAS
94 Coord of Women's Leadership Center ....Ms. Ana M. GAUTHIER
35 Director of Student Activities ....Mr. Daniel NAPOLITANO
43 Dir Capital Operations/Leg Affairs .. Mr. Michael A. NEIDERBACH
101 Secretary to the Corporation .... Ms. Mary C. MCALLISTER
104 Dir Intl Programs/Writing Ctr .... Dr. Vicky WESTACOTT
40 Bookstore Manager .... Mrs. Marcy K. BRADLEY
87 Dir of Summer/Parent Programs ....Mrs. Bonnie J. DUNGAN

AMDA College and Conservatory of the Performing Arts (A)

211 West 61st Street, New York NY 10023-7832

County: New York FICE Identification: 007572
Unit ID: 188854
Telephone: (212) 787-5300 Carnegie Class: Spec/Arts
FAX Number: (212) 247-0488 Calendar System: Semester
URL: www.amda.edu
Established: 1964 Annual Undergrad Tuition & Fees: $32,620
Enrollment: 1,735 Coed
Affiliation or Control: Independent Non-Profit IRS Status: 501(c)3
Highest Offering: Baccalaureate
Program: Liberal Arts And General; Fine Arts Emphasis
Accreditation: THEA

01 President/Artistic Director ....Mr. David MARTIN
03 President/Executive Director ....Ms. Jan MARTIN
32 Director of Student Affairs ....Mr. Robert MANGANARO
07 Director of Admissions ....Ms. Karen JACKSON
37 Assoc Dir Financial Aid/Cont Stdnt .... Ms. Darlene REYNOSO

American Academy of Dramatic Arts (B)

120 Madison Avenue, New York NY 10016-7089

County: New York FICE Identification: 007465
Unit ID: 188678
Telephone: (212) 686-9244 Carnegie Class: Assoc/PrivNFP
FAX Number: (212) 545-7934 Calendar System: Other
URL: www.aada.edu
Established: 1884 Annual Undergrad Tuition & Fees: $29,900
Enrollment: 271 Coed
Affiliation or Control: Independent Non-Profit IRS Status: 501(c)3
Highest Offering: Associate Degree
Program: Occupational; 2-Year Principally Bachelor's Creditable
Accreditation: M, THEA

01 President ....Ms. Susan ZECH
10 Chief Financial Officer ....Mr. John POLSKY
05 Director of Instruction ....Mr. Constantine SCOPAS
07 National Director of Admissions ....Mr. Steven HONG
27 Director of Marketing ....Mr. Lance STICKSEL
37 Director Financial Aid ....Mr. Roberto LOPEZ
08 Librarian ....Ms. Deborah PICONE
21 Controller ....Ms. Linda VIALA
11 Director of Operations ....Mr. Peter TUFEL
26 Director External Affairs ....Mrs. Elizabeth LAWSON
04 Assistant to the President .... Ms. Jackie REINKING

American Academy McAllister Institute of Funeral Service (C)

619 W 54th Street, 2nd Floor, New York NY 10019

County: New York FICE Identification: 010813
Unit ID: 188687
Telephone: (212) 757-1190 Carnegie Class: Assoc/PrivNFP
FAX Number: (212) 765-5923 Calendar System: Semester
URL: www.funeraleducation.org
Established: 1926 Annual Undergrad Tuition & Fees: $15,698
Enrollment: 418 Coed
Affiliation or Control: Independent Non-Profit IRS Status: 501(c)3
Highest Offering: Associate Degree
Program: Occupational
Accreditation: FUSER

01 President/CEO ....Ms. Meg DUNN
10 Bursar ....Mr. Jay TSO
37 Financial Aid Officer ....Ms. Natalie GIVAN
05 Director of Student Support ....Ms. Regina SMITH
69 Div Chair Public Health/Technical .... Dr. Elissa DEBENEDICTS
50 Division Chair Business/Law/Ethics ....Mr. Brian KASLER

06 Registrar ....Mr. Andre RAMPAUL
07 Director of Admissions ....Mr. Alan LOVEDER
08 Librarian ....Ms. Mary MOON
20 Academic Advisor .... Ms. Charlotte RERRICK
20 Academic Advisor ....Ms. Karen CARR
04 Exec Assistant to the President .... Ms. Stephanie HELSTON
43 Legal Counsel .... Mr. Charles MAURER

The Art Institute of New York City (D)

218-232 W. 40th Street, New York NY 10018

County: New York FICE Identification: 025256
Unit ID: 365055
Telephone: (212) 226-5500 Carnegie Class: Assoc/PrivFP
FAX Number: (212) 226-5644 Calendar System: Quarter
URL: www.ainyc.aii.edu
Established: 1980 Annual Undergrad Tuition & Fees: $24,470
Enrollment: 898 Coed
Affiliation or Control: Proprietary IRS Status: Proprietary
Highest Offering: Associate Degree
Program: 2-Year Principally Bachelor's Creditable; Fine Arts Emphasis
Accreditation: ACICS

† School is in teach-out plan.

ASA College (E)

81 Willoughby Street, Brooklyn NY 11201

County: Kings FICE Identification: 030955
Unit ID: 404994
Telephone: (718) 522-9073 Carnegie Class: Assoc/PrivFP
FAX Number: (718) 532-1433 Calendar System: Semester
URL: www.asa.edu
Established: 1985 Annual Undergrad Tuition & Fees: $14,600
Enrollment: 4,308 Coed
Affiliation or Control: Proprietary IRS Status: Proprietary
Highest Offering: Associate Degree
Program: Occupational; 2-Year Principally Bachelor's Creditable; Technical Emphasis
Accreditation: M, ACICS, #MAC

01 President ....Mr. Alex SHCHEGOL
05 Vice President Academic Affairs .... Ms. Shanthi KONKOTH
07 Vice President Marketing/Admissions .. Ms. Victoria KOSTYUKOV
36 Vice Pres Placement/Alumni Svcs ....Ms. Lesia WILLIS
86 Vice Pres Govt & Community Rels ....Mr. Roberto DUMAUAL
37 Vice President Financial Aid Svcs ....Ms. Victoriya SHTAMLER
06 Registrar ....Ms. Mariana ZINDER
08 Head Librarian ....Ms. Ann SWAIN
10 Chief Business Officer ....Mr. Jose VALENCIA
13 Chief Info Technology Officer (CIO) ....Mr. David ESTRIN
04 Administrative Asst to President ....Ms. Olga OBELOVA
09 Director of Institutional Research .... Ms. Anna BOUKHMAN
15 Director Personnel Services ....Ms. Alla SHCHEGOL
18 Chief Facilities/Physical Plant .... Mr. Walter KRUMER
32 Chief Student Affairs/Student Life .... Mr. Marcus BROWNE
41 Athletic Director ....Mr. Kenneth WILCOX
50 Dean of Business ....Dr. Edward KUFUOR

Bank Street College of Education (F)

610 W 112 Street, New York NY 10025-1898

County: New York FICE Identification: 002669
Unit ID: 189015
Telephone: (212) 875-4400 Carnegie Class: Spec/Other
FAX Number: (212) 875-4759 Calendar System: Semester
URL: www.bankstreet.edu
Established: 1916 Annual Graduate Tuition & Fees: $27,092
Enrollment: 747 Coed
Affiliation or Control: Independent Non-Profit IRS Status: 501(c)3
Highest Offering: Master's; No Undergraduates
Program: Teacher Preparatory; Professional
Accreditation: M, TED

01 President ....Shael P. SURANKSY
100 Chief of Staff ....Akilah ROSADO-MCQUEEN
10 Chief Financial Officer ....Marion KOWALSKI
11 Chief Operating Officer ....Justin TYACK
30 Vice Pres of Development ....Sonja CARTER
05 Dean of Innov/Policy & Research .... Josh THOMASES
58 Dean of the Graduate School ....Cecelia TRAUGH
88 Dean of Childrens Programs ....Alexis S. WRIGHT
11 Associate Dean Administration .... Barbara COLEMAN
20 Associate Dean Academic Affairs .... Diane NEWMAN
07 Director of Admissions ....Amy GREENSTEIN
06 Registrar ....Sandra SCLAFANI
37 Director Student Financial Aid ....Emmett COOPER
29 Director of Alumni Relations ....Linda REING
15 Chief Human Resources Officer ....Elyse MATTHEWS
13 Int Dir Information Technology .... David STURM
18 Director of Facilities .... Daniel BENCHIMOL
08 Director of Library Services ....Kristin FREDA
36 Director Student Placement ....Susan LEVINE
09 Director of Institutional Research ....Amy KLINE
19 Director Security/Safety .... Daniel BENCHIMOL

Bard College (G)

PO Box 5000, Annandale-On-Hudson NY 12504-5000

County: Dutchess FICE Identification: 002671
Unit ID: 189088
Telephone: (845) 758-6822 Carnegie Class: Bac/A&S
FAX Number: (845) 758-4294 Calendar System: Semester
URL: www.bard.edu
Established: 1860 Annual Undergrad Tuition & Fees: $50,136
Enrollment: 1,954 Coed
Affiliation or Control: Independent Non-Profit IRS Status: 501(c)3
Highest Offering: Doctorate
Program: Liberal Arts And General
Accreditation: M, TEAC

01 President ....Dr. Leon BOTSTEIN
03 Executive Vice President of College ....Dr. Dimitri B. PAPADIMITRIOU
100 Associate Vice President ....Mr. Taun TOAY
30 Vice Pres Alumni/ae Affairs/Devel ....Ms. Debra PEMSTEIN
10 VP for Admin & Finance/CFO ....Dr. James BRUDVIG
11 Vice President for Administration ....Ms. Coleen MURPHY ALEXANDER
05 Vice President/Dean of the College ....Ms. Rebecca THOMAS
32 VP Student Affairs/Dir Admissions ....Ms. Mary I. BACKLUND
20 VP Acad Affairs/Dir Civic Engagmt ....Dr. Jonathan BECKER
20 Associate VP for Academic Affairs ....Dr. David SHEIN
08 VP/Dean Info Svcs/Dir Libraries .... Mr. Jeffrey KATZ
19 Dean Campus Safety & Operations ....Ms. Gretchen PERRY
32 VP for Student Affairs ....Ms. Erin CANNAN
09 VP for Institutional Research ....Dr. Mark D. HALSEY
35 Dean of Student Affairs ....Ms. Bethany NOHLGREN
57 Dir Milton Avery Grad Sch of Arts .... Mr. Arthur GIBBONS
88 Dir Bard Grad Ctr Decorative Arts ....Dr. Susan WEBER
88 Exec Dir Ctr Curatorial Studies ....Mr. Tom ECCLES
88 Director of Institutional Support .... Ms. Karen UNGER
88 Director Ctr Environmental Policy ....Dr. Eban GOODSTEIN
37 Director Financial Aid .... Ms. Denise ACKERMAN
06 Registrar ....Mr. Peter GADSBY
26 Associate VP of Communications .... Mr. Mark PRIMOFF
15 Director of Human Resources ....Ms. Kimberly ALEXANDER
21 Associate VP for Finance ....Mr. Kevin PARKER
88 Director Inst Writing/Thinking .... Ms. Peg PEOPLES
18 Director of Buildings & Grounds .... Mr. Randy CLUM
13 Director Mgmt Info Systems .... Mr. Michael TOMPKINS
29 Director Alumni/ae Affairs ....Ms. Jane BRIEN
36 Director Career Development ....Ms. Elizabeth GIGLIO
19 Director Safety & Security ....Mr. Kenneth COOPER
09 Director of Institutional Research .... Mr. Joseph F. AHERN
24 Director of Audio/Video Services .... Mr. Paul LABARBERA
28 Director of Multicultural Affairs ....Dr. Ann SEATON
41 Director of Athletics ....Ms. Kristin E. HALL
40 Bookstore Manager ....Ms. Merry MEYER
23 Director Student Health Services .... Ms. Marsha DAVIS
38 Director Student Counseling ....Ms. Tamara TELBERG
96 Director of Purchasing ....Ms. Theresa VANETTEN

Bard High School Early College Manhattan (H)

525 East Houston Street, New York NY 10002

Telephone: (212) 995-8479 Identification: 770114
Accreditation: &EH

† Branch campus of Bard College at Simon's Rock, Great Barrington, MA.

Bard High School Early College Queens (I)

30-20 Thomson Avenue, Long Island City NY 11101

Telephone: (718) 361-3133 Identification: 770115
Accreditation: &EH

† Branch campus of Bard College at Simon's Rock, Great Barrington, MA.

Barnard College (J)

3009 Broadway, New York NY 10027-6598

County: New York FICE Identification: 002708
Unit ID: 189097
Telephone: (212) 854-5262 Carnegie Class: Bac/A&S
FAX Number: (212) 854-6220 Calendar System: Semester
URL: www.barnard.edu
Established: 1889 Annual Undergrad Tuition & Fees: $45,851
Enrollment: 2,573 Female
Affiliation or Control: Independent Non-Profit IRS Status: 501(c)3
Highest Offering: Baccalaureate
Program: Liberal Arts And General
Accreditation: M, DANCE, TEAC

01 President ....Debora L. SPAR
43 Chief of Staff to Pres/Gen Counsel ....Jomysha STEPHEN
05 Provost & Dean of Faculty ....Linda BELL
03 Chief Operating Officer ....Robert GOLDBERG
20 Dean of the College ....Avis HINKSON
30 Vice President for Development .... Bret SILVER
26 Vice Pres Comm/Counsel to Pres .... Joanne KWONG
10 Vice President for Finance ....Eileen M. DIBENEDETTO
11 Vice Pres Campus Services ....Gail BELTRONE
13 Vice Pres Information Technology ....Carol KATZMAN
15 Vice President of Human Resources ....Catherine GEDDIS
88 Dean of Studies .... Natalie FRIEDMAN
84 Dean of Enrollment Management .... Jennifer FONDILLER
06 Registrar ....Constance BROWN
37 Director of Financial Aid .... Nanette DILAURO
32 Associate Dean for Student Life ....Alina WONG
39 Assoc Dean Residential Life/Housing ....Ann AVERSA
23 Exec Director of Student Health Svc .... Mary Joan MURPHY
36 Director of Career Development ....Robert EARL
29 Exec Director of Alumnae Relations .... Caitlin TRAMEL
08 Dean of the Library ....Vacant
101 Secretary to the Board of Trustees .... Alyssa SCHIFFMAN

19 Director of Safety/Security ....Dianna PENNETTI
109 Director of Business Operations ....Douglas MAGET
18 Director Facilities Services ....Daniel DAVIS
09 Dir Institutional Research & Assess ....Rebecca FRIEDKIN

† Affiliated with Columbia University in the City of New York.

Be'er Yaakov Talmudic Seminary (A)

12 Jefferson Avenue, Spring Valley NY 10977
County: Rockland FICE Identification: 041928
Unit ID: 476717
Telephone: (845) 362-3053 Carnegie Class: Not Classified
FAX Number: (845) 406-9699 Calendar System: Semester
Established: 1995 Annual Undergrad Tuition & Fees: $8,740
Enrollment: 382 Male
Affiliation or Control: Independent Non-Profit IRS Status: 501(c)3
Highest Offering: First Talmudic Degree
Program: Professional
Accreditation: RABN

01 CEO ....Mr. Jacob UNGAR
05 Dean ....Rabbi Israel EISENBERGER
06 Registrar/Administrator ....Rabbi Yitzchok SOIFER
37 Financial Aid Administrator ....Mrs. Chana NOTIS
13 Chief Info Technology Officer ....Mr. Aron STERN

Beis Medrash Heichal Dovid (B)

211 Beach 17th Street, Far Rockaway NY 11691-4433
County: Queens FICE Identification: 037133
Unit ID: 444413
Telephone: (718) 868-2300 Carnegie Class: Spec/Faith
FAX Number: (718) 868-0517 Calendar System: Semester
Established: 1999 Annual Undergrad Tuition & Fees: $9,450
Enrollment: 94 Male
Affiliation or Control: Independent Non-Profit IRS Status: 501(c)3
Highest Offering: Second Talmudic Degree
Program: Teacher Preparatory; Professional
Accreditation: RABN

01 Dean ....Rabbi Yaakov BENDER
05 Rosh Yeshiva ....Rabbi Shlomo Avidgor ALTUSKY
37 Financial Aid Officer ....Rabbi Aaron STEINBERG

The Belanger School of Nursing (C)

650 McClellan Street, Schenectady NY 12304
County: Schenectady FICE Identification: 006448
Unit ID: 190956
Telephone: (518) 243-4471 Carnegie Class: Assoc/PrivNFP
FAX Number: (518) 243-4470 Calendar System: Other
URL: www.ellisbelangerschoolofnursing.org
Established: 1903 Annual Undergrad Tuition & Fees: $10,076
Enrollment: 127 Coed
Affiliation or Control: Independent Non-Profit IRS Status: 501(c)3
Highest Offering: Associate Degree
Program: 2-Year Principally Bachelor's Creditable; Nursing Emphasis
Accreditation: ADNUR

01 Director ....Dr. Marilyn STAPLETON
37 Director Student Financial Aid ....Mr. Michael DAGGETT

Berkeley College (D)

3 East 43rd Street, New York NY 10017-4604
County: New York FICE Identification: 007394
Unit ID: 189228
Telephone: (212) 986-4343 Carnegie Class: Spec/Bus
FAX Number: (212) 818-1169 Calendar System: Quarter
URL: www.berkeleycollege.edu
Established: 1931 Annual Undergrad Tuition & Fees: $24,300
Enrollment: 4,479 Coed
Affiliation or Control: Proprietary IRS Status: Proprietary
Highest Offering: Baccalaureate
Program: Business Emphasis
Accreditation: M

00 Chairman of the Board ....Mr. Kevin L. LUING
01 President ....Mr. Michael J. SMITH
04 Special Assistant to the President ....Dr. Rose Mary HEALY
04 Special Assistant to the President ....Ms. Katherine DELGADO
05 Provost ....Dr. Mary MCDONOUGH
84 SVP Enrollment Management ....Ms. Diane RECINOS
10 SVP Finance & Administration ....Mr. Robert HERZOG
45 VP Planning & Chief of Staff ....Vacant
43 VP & Chief Compliance Officer ....Mr. William BRANDT
26 Chief Marketing Officer ....Mr. William DIMASI
13 Chief Information Officer ....Mr. Leonard DE BOTTON
86 SVP Government Relations NJ ....Ms. Teri DUDA
86 VP Government Relations NY ....Mr. Gbubemi OKOTIEURO
20 VP Academic Advisement ....Ms. Liz BARRETT
08 VP Library Services ....Ms. Marlene DOTY
32 VP Student Development/Campus Life ....Dr. Dallas REED
36 VP Career Services ....Mr. Brian MAHER
07 VP Enrollment ....Vacant
37 VP Financial Aid ....Mr. Howard LESLIE
21 VP Budget & Student Accounts ....Ms. Eileen LOFTUS-BERLIN
85 VP International Division ....Ms. Cynthia C. MARCHESE
18 VP Operations ....Mr. Mark WAGENER
50 Dean School of Business ....Dr. Beth CASTIGLIA
76 Interim Dean School Health Studies ... Ms. Elizabeth FITZGERALD
49 Dean School of Liberal Arts ....Dr. Don KIEFFER
107 Dean School of Professional Studies ....Ms. Lenore MOLEE
20 Associate Provost Academic Affairs ....Dr. Judith KORNBERG
06 Associate Provost Registrar ....Ms. Gail OKUN
106 Assistant Provost Online ....Ms. Carol SMITH
88 Dean Academic Support ....Dr. Gerald IACULLO
108 AVP Institutional Effectiveness ....Dr. Rachel FESTER
31 AVP Communications & Ext Relations ....Ms. Angela HARRINGTON
19 AVP Public Safety ....Mr. William ORTMAN
27 Director Media Relations ....Ms. Ilene GREENFIELD
41 Director Athletics ....Mr. Andrew DESTEPHANO
29 Director Alumni Relations ....Ms. Jennifer PORTER
09 Director Institutional Research ....Ms. Rebecca J. DRENNEN

Bet Medrash Gadol Ateret Torah (E)

901 Quentin Road, Brooklyn NY 11223
County: Kings Identification: 667146
Telephone: (347) 394-1036 Carnegie Class: Not Classified
FAX Number: (347) 394-1096 Calendar System: Semester
Established: 1992 Annual Undergrad Tuition & Fees: $9,000
Enrollment: 112 Male
Affiliation or Control: Independent Non-Profit IRS Status: 501(c)3
Highest Offering: Second Talmudic Degree
Program: Teacher Preparatory; Professional
Accreditation: @RABN

01 President/CEO ....Rabbi Joseph HARARI-RAFUL
10 Chief Financial/Business Officer ....Irwin SHAMAH
06 Registrar ....Mrs. Ruchana MANSOUR
11 Chief of Operations/Administration ....Zev KLEINER

Beth Hamedrash Shaarei Yosher Institute (F)

4102-10 16th Avenue, Brooklyn NY 11204-1099
County: Kings FICE Identification: 011192
Unit ID: 189273
Telephone: (718) 854-2290 Carnegie Class: Spec/Faith
FAX Number: (718) 436-9045 Calendar System: Semester
Established: 1962 Annual Undergrad Tuition & Fees: $8,250
Enrollment: 44 Male
Affiliation or Control: Independent Non-Profit IRS Status: 501(c)3
Highest Offering: Second Talmudic Degree
Program: Teacher Preparatory; Professional; Religious Emphasis
Accreditation: RABN

05 Chief Academic Officer ....Rabbi Yosef ROSENBLUM
10 Chief Business Officer ....Rabbi Pinches KAFF
29 Director Alumni Association ....Rabbi Chaim ROSENBERG
15 Director Personnel Services ....Rabbi Mordechai MARGULIES
37 Director Student Financial Aid ....Rabbi Aaron ROTTENBERG
06 Registrar ....Rabbi Sol ROSENBERG

Beth Hatalmud Rabbinical College (G)

2127 82nd Street, Brooklyn NY 11214-2594
County: Kings FICE Identification: 011922
Unit ID: 189264
Telephone: (718) 259-2525 Carnegie Class: Spec/Faith
FAX Number: (718) 256-5592 Calendar System: Semester
Established: 1950 Annual Undergrad Tuition & Fees: $10,950
Enrollment: 29 Male
Affiliation or Control: Independent Non-Profit IRS Status: 501(c)3
Highest Offering: Second Talmudic Degree
Program: Teacher Preparatory; Professional; Religious Emphasis
Accreditation: RABN

01 President ....Rabbi Chaim STEFANSKY
10 Fiscal Officer ....Rabbi C. L. PERKOWSKI
08 Librarian ....Mr. Shimon HESS

Beth Medrash Meor Yitzchok (H)

65 Dykstra's Way East, Monsey NY 10952
County: Rockland Identification: 667111
Telephone: (845) 426-3488 Carnegie Class: Not Classified
FAX Number: (845) 425-5415 Calendar System: Semester
Established: 2007 Annual Undergrad Tuition & Fees: $8,000
Enrollment: 150 Male
Affiliation or Control: Independent Non-Profit IRS Status: 501(c)3
Highest Offering: First Talmudic Degree
Program: Professional
Accreditation: RABN

Bill and Sandra Pomeroy College of Nursing at Crouse Hospital (I)

736 Irving Avenue, Syracuse NY 13210
County: Onondaga FICE Identification: 006445
Unit ID: 190451
Telephone: (315) 470-7481 Carnegie Class: Assoc/PrivNFP
FAX Number: (315) 470-5774 Calendar System: Semester
URL: www.crouse.org/nursing
Established: 1913 Annual Undergrad Tuition & Fees: $11,627
Enrollment: 345 Coed
Affiliation or Control: Independent Non-Profit IRS Status: 501(c)3
Highest Offering: Associate Degree
Program: 2-Year Principally Bachelor's Creditable; Nursing Emphasis
Accreditation: ADNUR

01 Dean ....Rhonda READER
06 Registrar ....Cari MCLAUGHLIN
07 Director of Admissions ....Amy GRAHAM
08 Head Librarian ....Kristine DELANEY
37 Director Student Financial Aid ....Kenny KENDALL

Boricua College (J)

3755 Broadway, New York NY 10032-1599
County: New York FICE Identification: 013029
Unit ID: 189413
Telephone: (212) 694-1000 Carnegie Class: Bac/Diverse
FAX Number: (212) 694-1015 Calendar System: Semester
URL: www.boricuacollege.edu
Established: 1974 Annual Undergrad Tuition & Fees: $10,625
Enrollment: 1,163 Coed
Affiliation or Control: Independent Non-Profit IRS Status: 501(c)3
Highest Offering: Master's
Program: Liberal Arts And General; Professional
Accreditation: M, TEAC

01 President ....Dr. Victor G. ALICEA
04 Admin Assistant to the President ....Ms. Sandra BELLAMY
05 Sr VP/Dean Academic Affairs ....Dr. Maria MONTES-MORALES
20 Vice President and Dean ....Dr. Shivaji SENGUPTA
13 VP Information Tech/Facil Mgmt ....Mr. Irving RAMIREZ
20 VP/Academic Planning & Programming ....Dr. John GUZMAN
84 VP Enrollment & Management Bronx ....Mr. Abraham CRUZ
43 Legal Counsel ....Mr. Jorge BATISTA
10 Director Finance ....Mr. Elias OYOLA
07 Director Admissions Northside Ctr ....Mr. Ismael SANCHEZ
07 Director Admissions Graham ....Ms. Aurea MORALES
06 Director Registration & Assessment ....Ms. Beatriz AHORRIO
37 Director Financial Aid ....Ms. Rosalia CRUZ
15 Director Personnel/Human Resources ....Ms. Francia L. CASTRO
08 Director Library/Learning Resources ....Ms. Liza RIVERA
18 Director Environmental Services ....Mr. Elias RIVERA
41 Director of Athletics ....Vacant
30 Director of Development ....Vacant
20 Dean Academic Affairs Manhattan ....Mr. Moises PEREYRA
88 Dean of Generic Studies Bronx ....Mr. Jose Israel LOPEZ

Bramson ORT College (K)

69-30 Austin Street, Forest Hills NY 11375-4239
County: Queens FICE Identification: 021068
Unit ID: 189422
Telephone: (718) 261-5800 Carnegie Class: Assoc/PrivNFP
FAX Number: (718) 575-5119 Calendar System: Semester
URL: www.bramsonort.edu
Established: 1977 Annual Undergrad Tuition & Fees: $11,330
Enrollment: 555 Coed
Affiliation or Control: Independent Non-Profit IRS Status: 501(c)3
Highest Offering: Associate Degree
Program: Occupational; 2-Year Principally Bachelor's Creditable
Accreditation: #NY

01 President ....Mr. David KANANI
05 Dean of Academic Services ....Ms. Helen POLYNSKY
07 Recruitment/Admissions ....Ms. Susan MENTEL
08 Librarian ....Ms. Shelly SANTOS
21 Bursar ....Ms. Mazzie DOUSTAR
37 Financial Aid Coordinator ....Ms. Angelina MARRA
49 Arts/Science Coordinator ....Ms. Helen POLYNSKY
36 Job Development Advisor ....Ms. Angela NASIMOVA
50 Business Technology & Account Coord ....Ms. Shery DENG
88 Paralegal Program Coordinator ....Ms. Aisha CESAR
56 Computer Tech/Distance Learn Coord ....Mr. Damindra PERSAUD
56 Coordinator Extension Site ....Mr. Yair ROSENRAUCH
76 Medical Assistant Program Coord ....Dr. Emil ASDURIAN
96 Director of Purchasing ....Mr. Mark MIRENBERG
06 Registrar ....Ms. Aleksandra KAGAN
10 Controller ....Mr. Mark MIRENBERG
26 Dir Intergovermental Relations ....Mr. Eben BRONFMAN

Briarcliffe College (L)

1055 Stewart Avenue, Bethpage NY 11714-3545
County: Nassau FICE Identification: 020757
Unit ID: 189459
Telephone: (516) 918-3600 Carnegie Class: Bac/Assoc
FAX Number: (516) 470-6020 Calendar System: Semester
URL: www.briarcliffe.edu
Established: 1966 Annual Undergrad Tuition & Fees: $18,720
Enrollment: 1,742 Coed
Affiliation or Control: Proprietary IRS Status: Proprietary
Highest Offering: Baccalaureate
Program: Business Emphasis
Accreditation: M, DH

01 President ....Dr. George SANTIAGO, JR.
10 VP Finance & Oper/Chief Fin Ofcr ....Mr. Louis COMMISSO
07 Vice Pres Admissions ....Mr. C. Gabriel CASTANO
32 Vice President Student Affairs ....Ms. Kathy GENUA
05 Provost ....Dr. Hubert BENITEZ
35 Director of Student Management ....Ms. Georgette OSTROSKE
13 Director of Information Systems ....Mr. Hoober ZULUAGA
21 Business Office Manager ....Ms. Cindy ROYS
06 Registrar ....Ms. Christy LAW
36 Director of Career Services ....Mr. Tony EMERSON

41 Athletic Director ... Ms. Gina D'AMARO
08 Librarian ... Mr. Andrew GIBSON

Brooklyn Law School (A)

250 Joralemon Street, Brooklyn NY 11201-3798
County: Kings FICE Identification: 002677
Unit ID: 189501
Telephone: (718) 625-2200 Carnegie Class: Spec/Law
FAX Number: (718) 780-0393 Calendar System: Semester
URL: www.brooklaw.edu
Established: 1901 Annual Graduate Tuition & Fees: $46,176
Enrollment: 1,119 Coed
Affiliation or Control: Independent Non-Profit IRS Status: 501(c)3
Highest Offering: First Professional Degree; No Undergraduates
Program: Professional
Accreditation: LAW

01 Dean and President Emerita ... Dean Joan G. WEXLER
00 Chairman of the Board of Trustees ... Mr. Stuart SUBOTNICK
05 Dean ... Dean Nicholas W. ALLARD
20 Vice Dean of Academic Affairs ... Dean William ARAIZA
20 Assoc Dean for Profess Legal Educ ... Dean Stacy CAPLOW
20 Vice Dean ... Dean Suzanne DENNIS
32 Asst Dean of Student Affairs ... Dean Jennifer R. LANG
10 Chief Financial Officer ... Ms. Laurie H. NEWITZ
21 Treasurer ... Ms. Shoshanna M. CAMPBELL
07 Dean of Admissions & Financial Aid ... Dean Eulas BOYD
08 Director of Library & Assoc Prof ... Prof. Janet SINDER
30 Director of Development ... Ms. Ursula VESALA
29 Director of Alumni Relations .. Ms. Caitlin MONCK-MARCELLINO
36 Asst Dean of Career Development ... Ms. Karen EISEN
06 Registrar ... Mr. Christian BESTER
37 Director of Financial Aid ... Ms. Nancy L. ZAHZAM
26 Asst Dean of External Affairs ... Ms. Linda HARVEY
07 Director of Admissions ... Vacant
18 Facilities Manager Operations ... Mr. Salvatore DECANDIA
15 Human Resources Manager ... Ms. Christina WALLACE
13 Chief Info Technology Officer (CIO) ... Mr. Steven MARKS
19 Director of Public Safety ... Ms. Mercedes RAVELO
43 Gen Counsel/Chf Compliance Officer ... Ms. Stephanie VULLO

*Bryant & Stratton College System Office (B)

2410 N. Forest Road, Suite 101, Getzville NY 14068-1224
County: Erie Identification: 666828
Telephone: (716) 250-7500 Carnegie Class: N/A
FAX Number: (716) 250-7510
URL: www.bryantstratton.edu

01 President & CEO ... Dr. Francis J. FELSER
05 Vice Pres Chief Academic Officer ... Ms. Beth A. TARQUINO
10 VP/Chief Financial Ofcr/Treasurer ... Mr. David VADEN

*Bryant & Stratton College (C)

465 Main Street, Suite 400, Buffalo NY 14203-1795
County: Erie FICE Identification: 002678
Unit ID: 189583
Telephone: (716) 884-9120 Carnegie Class: Assoc/PrivFP4
FAX Number: (716) 884-0091 Calendar System: Semester
URL: www.bryantstratton.edu
Established: 1854 Annual Undergrad Tuition & Fees: $16,565
Enrollment: 800 Coed
Affiliation or Control: Proprietary IRS Status: Proprietary
Highest Offering: Baccalaureate
Program: 2-Year Principally Bachelor's Creditable; Business Emphasis
Accreditation: M, MAC

02 Campus Director ... Dr. Marvel E. ROSS-JONES
05 Dean of Instruction ... Dr. Adiam TSEGAI
07 Director of Admissions ... Mr. Phil J. STRUEBEL
36 Director of Career Services ... Ms. Diane WESTBROOK
10 WNY Business Office Director ... Ms. Kathleen OWCZARCZAK

*Bryant & Stratton College (D)

1259 Central Avenue, Albany NY 12205-5230
Telephone: (518) 437-1802 FICE Identification: 004749
Accreditation: &M, MAC

† Branch campus of Bryant & Stratton College, Buffalo, NY.

*Bryant & Stratton College (E)

854 Long Pond Road, Rochester NY 14612-3049
Telephone: (585) 720-0660 FICE Identification: 012470
Accreditation: &M, MAC

† Branch campus of Bryant & Stratton College, Buffalo, NY.

*Bryant & Stratton College (F)

953 James Street, Syracuse NY 13203-2502
Telephone: (315) 472-6603 FICE Identification: 008276
Accreditation: &M, MAC

† Branch campus of Bryant & Stratton College, Buffalo, NY.

Business Informatics Center, Inc. (G)

134 S Central Avenue, Valley Stream NY 11580-5418
County: Nassau FICE Identification: 025729
Unit ID: 189653
Telephone: (516) 561-0050 Carnegie Class: Assoc/PrivFP
FAX Number: (516) 561-0074 Calendar System: Quarter
URL: www.thecollegeforbusiness.com
Established: 1983 Annual Undergrad Tuition & Fees: $13,250
Enrollment: 24 Coed
Affiliation or Control: Proprietary IRS Status: Proprietary
Highest Offering: Associate Degree
Program: Occupational
Accreditation: ACCSC

01 President ... Ms. Constance BROWN
05 Academic Dean ... Dr. Eugene ALEXANDER
07 Admissions Director ... Mr. Ira WOLK
37 Financial Aid Director ... Mr. Salvatore FERRO

Canisius College (H)

2001 Main Street, Buffalo NY 14208-1098
County: Erie FICE Identification: 002681
Unit ID: 189705
Telephone: (716) 883-7000 Carnegie Class: Master's L
FAX Number: (716) 888-2525 Calendar System: Semester
URL: www.canisius.edu
Established: 1870 Annual Undergrad Tuition & Fees: $34,690
Enrollment: 4,181 Coed
Affiliation or Control: Roman Catholic IRS Status: 501(c)3
Highest Offering: Master's
Program: Liberal Arts And General; Teacher Preparatory; Professional; Business Emphasis
Accreditation: M, BUS, CAATE, CACREP, TED

01 President ... Mr. John J. HURLEY
05 VP Academic Affairs ... Dr. Margaret MCCARTHY
10 Vice President Business & Finance ... Mr. Marco F. BENEDETTI
32 VP Student Affs & Dean of Students ... Dr. Terri L. MANGIONE
30 VP Institutional Advancement ... Mr. William COLLINS, II
84 VP Enrollment Management ... Ms. Kathleen B. DAVIS
20 Assoc VP for Academic Affairs ... Dr. Margaret MCCARTHY
88 Asst VP/Dir Stdnt Rec & Fin Svcs ... Mr. Kevin M. SMITH
08 Director of Library ... Ms. Kristine E. KASBOHM
07 Director Undergrad Admissions ... Mrs. Mollie BALLARO
44 Director of Principal Gifts ... Mr. J. Patrick GREENWALD
21 Controller ... Mr. Ronald J. HABERER
49 Int Dean Col of Arts & Sciences ... Dr. Patricia E. ERICKSON
50 Dean School of Business ... Dr. Richard A. SHICK
37 Assoc Dir of Stdnt Records/Fin Svcs ... Ms. Mary A. KOEHNEKE
06 Registrar/Asst Dir Stdnt Rec & FA ... Ms. Deborah W. PROHN
26 Director of Public Relations ... Ms. Eileen C. HERBERT
15 Director of Human Resourses ... Ms. Deborah J. WINSLOW-SCHABER
88 Director of the Canisius Fund ... Ms. Erin HARTNETT
53 Assc Dean School Ed/Human Svcs .. Dr. Nancy A. WELLENZOHN
25 Director of Sponsored Programs ... Ms. Mary Ann LANGLOIS
18 Director Facilities Management ... Mr. Thomas E. CIMINELLI
19 Director of Public Safety ... Mr. H. Wilson JOHNSON
23 Director Student Health Center ... Ms. Patricia H. CREAHAN
38 Director Counseling Center ... Ms. Eileen A. NILAND
39 Assoc Dean of Stdnts/Dir Resid Life ... Mr. Matthew H. MULVILLE
104 Director Study Abroad ... Mr. Brian SMITH
40 Course Materials Manager/Bookstore ... Mr. Robert LINGLE
41 Director Athletics ... Mr. William J. MAHER
42 Director Campus Ministry ... Mr. Michael F. HAYES, JR.
88 Director of Creative Services ... Ms. Andalyn M. COURTNEY
90 Int Director of User Services ... Mr. Scott D. CLARK
94 Dir of Women's Business Center ... Ms. Sara L. VESCIO
92 Director of All College Honors Pgm ... Dr. Bruce J. DIERENFIELD
09 Director of Research & Inst Effect ... Dr. Matthew HERTZ
88 Director of Multi Cultural Programs ... Mr. Sababu C. NORRIS
13 Interim Chief Information Officer ... Mr. Lawrence DENI
14 Dir Computer Infrastructure/Opers ... Mr. Frank W. KIRSTEIN
24 Director Media Center ... Mr. Daniel J. DREW
96 Director of Purchasing ... Mr. Gary B. LEW
105 Web Development Specialist ... Mr. Kevin M. BLAKE
04 Assistant to the President ... Ms. Erica C. SAMMARCO
102 Asst Director Canisius Fund ... Ms. Emma PERROTT
91 Director Administrative Computing ... Mr. Robert SCHAEDEL

Cayuga Community College (I)

197 Franklin Street, Auburn NY 13021-3099
County: Cayuga FICE Identification: 002861
Unit ID: 189839
Telephone: (315) 255-1743 Carnegie Class: Assoc/Pub-S-SC
FAX Number: (315) 255-2117 Calendar System: Semester
URL: www.cayuga-cc.edu
Established: 1953 Annual Undergrad Tuition & Fees (In-District): $4,612
Enrollment: 4,290 Coed
Affiliation or Control: State/Local IRS Status: 501(c)3
Highest Offering: Associate Degree
Program: Occupational; 2-Year Principally Bachelor's Creditable
Accreditation: M, ADNUR

01 President ... Mr. Brian M. DURANT
04 Assistant to President/Board ... Ms. Carolyn L. GUARIGLIA
05 Provost/Vice Pres Academic Affairs ... Dr. Anne J. HERRON
32 Vice President Student Affairs ... Mr. Jeffrey E. ROSENTHAL
10 Vice Pres Administration/Treasurer ... Ms. Diane L. HUTCHINSON
102 Executive Director Foundation ... Mr. Jeffrey L. HOFFMAN
84 Dean Enrollment Management ... Ms. Cheryl A. LINDSAY
13 Dean Information Technology ... Mr. John KAFTAN
07 Director of Admissions ... Mr. Bruce M. BLODGETT
09 Director Institutional Research ... Ms. Carol E. RUNGE
41 Director Athletics ... Mr. Peter E. LIDDELL
15 Director HR & Affirmative Action ... Mr. Scott M. WHALEN
06 Registrar ... Mr. Michael A. PASTORE
35 Director Student Development ... Dr. Julie A. WHITE

Cazenovia College (J)

22 Sullivan Street, Cazenovia NY 13035
County: Madison FICE Identification: 002685
Unit ID: 189848
Telephone: (800) 654-3210 Carnegie Class: Bac/Diverse
FAX Number: (315) 655-4143 Calendar System: Semester
URL: www.cazenovia.edu
Established: 1824 Annual Undergrad Tuition & Fees: $31,754
Enrollment: 963 Coed
Affiliation or Control: Independent Non-Profit IRS Status: 501(c)3
Highest Offering: Baccalaureate
Program: Liberal Arts And General; Professional
Accreditation: M, IACBE, TEAC

01 President ... Vacant
11 Exec Vice Pres/COO/Sec of College ... Dr. Susan A. BERGER
05 VP Academic Affs/Dean of Faculty ... Dr. Sharon A. DETTMER
10 VP Financial Affs/Chief Fin Officer ... Mr. Mark H. EDWARDS
84 VP Enrol Mgmt/Dean Admiss/Fin Aid ... Vacant
30 VP for Institutional Advancement ... Ms. Carol SATCHWELL
32 Dean for Student Life ... Ms. Katie O'BRIEN
89 Dean First Year Program ... Mr. Jesse LOTT
08 Director of Library Services ... Ms. Heather C. WHALEN-SMITH
37 Assoc Dean Financial Aid/Registrar ... Ms. Christine MANDEL
26 Director Marketing/Communications ... Vacant
15 Director Human Resources ... Ms. Janice ROMAGNOLI
23 Director Health Services ... Dr. Susan A. BERGER
36 Dir Career/Extended Learning Svcs .. Ms. Christine RICHARDSON
41 Director Intercollegiate Athletics ... Mr. Michael BROOKS
13 Director of Technology Development ... Mr. David PALMER
06 Registrar ... Ms. Christine MANDEL
09 Dir Institutional Rsrch/Assessment ... Ms. Bridget MILLER
18 Dir of Physical Plant Operations ... Mr. Jeff SLOCUM
29 Director Alumni Relations ... Ms. Shari WHITAKER
38 Director of Counseling Services ... Dr. Todd SPANGLER
42 Chaplain ... Ms. Elizabeth BURLEW
07 Sr Assistant Director of Admissions ... Mr. Brett M. CARGUELLO

Central Yeshiva Beth Joseph (K)

1502 Avenue N, Brooklyn NY 11230
County: Kings Identification: 667157
Telephone: (718) 382-6003 Carnegie Class: Not Classified
FAX Number: (347) 702-4746 Calendar System: Semester
Established: 1942 Annual Undergrad Tuition & Fees: $14,000
Enrollment: 54 Male
Affiliation or Control: Independent Non-Profit IRS Status: 501(c)3
Highest Offering: First Talmudic Degree
Program: Professional
Accreditation: RABN

01 Chief Executive Officer ... Rabbi Mordechai JOFEN
37 Director Studen Financial Aid ... Rabbi Baruch MILLER
06 Registrar ... Rabbi Avraham JOFEN

Central Yeshiva Tomchei Tmimim Lubavitch America (L)

841-853 Ocean Parkway, Brooklyn NY 11230-2798
County: Kings FICE Identification: 004776
Unit ID: 189857
Telephone: (718) 434-0784 Carnegie Class: Spec/Faith
FAX Number: (718) 434-1519 Calendar System: Semester
Established: 1941 Annual Undergrad Tuition & Fees: $6,700
Enrollment: 613 Male
Affiliation or Control: Independent Non-Profit IRS Status: 501(c)3
Highest Offering: Second Talmudic Degree
Program: Teacher Preparatory; Professional; Music Emphasis
Accreditation: RABN

01 President ... Rabbi Shloime ZARCHI
05 Dean ... Rabbi Zalman LABKOWSKI
06 Registrar ... Rabbi Joseph WILMOWSKY
37 Financial Aid Director ... Rabbi Moshe M. GLUCKOWSKY
26 Director Public Relations ... Mr. Shaya BOYMELGREEN
10 Treasurer ... Rabbi Moshe BOGOMILSKY

Christ the King Seminary (M)

711 Knox Road, P.O. Box 607,
East Aurora NY 14052-0607
County: Erie FICE Identification: 002822
Unit ID: 189981
Telephone: (716) 652-8900 Carnegie Class: Spec/Faith
FAX Number: (716) 652-8903 Calendar System: Semester
URL: www.cks.edu
Established: 1974 Annual Graduate Tuition & Fees: $9,780
Enrollment: 101 Coed
Affiliation or Control: Roman Catholic IRS Status: 501(c)3
Highest Offering: Master's; No Undergraduates

Program: Religious Emphasis
Accreditation: M, THEOL

01 Rector/President ... Rev. Joseph C. GATTO
03 Vice Rector ... Rev. Gregory M. FAULHABER
05 Academic Dean ... Mr. Michael SHERRY
10 Comptroller ... Mrs. Nancy M. EHLERS
11 Chief of Operations ... Mr. Michael SHERRY
30 Director Institutional Advancement ... Mr. Richard SUCHAN
18 Director of Facilities ... Vacant
08 Library Director ... Ms. Teresa LUBIENECKI
38 Director of Ministry Development ... Mr. Douglas J. GEORGE
26 Chief Public Relations Officer ... Ms. Susan LANKES
06 Registrar ... Mr. Michael FAULHABER

Christie's Education, New York (A)

11 West 42nd Street, 8th Floor, New York NY 10036
County: New York FICE Identification: 036654
Unit ID: 475510
Telephone: (212) 355-1501 Carnegie Class: Not Classified
FAX Number: (212) 355-7370 Calendar System: Quarter
URL: www.christies.edu
Established: 1993 Annual Graduate Tuition & Fees: $53,529
Enrollment: 66 Coed
Affiliation or Control: Proprietary IRS Status: Proprietary
Highest Offering: Master's; No Undergraduates
Program: Professional; Fine Arts Emphasis
Accreditation: NY

01 Academic Director ... Dr. Veronique CHAGNON-BURKE
08 Learning Resources Manager ... Ms. Karen MAGUIRE
07 Recruitment and Admissions Officer ... Ms. Hilary SMITH
21 Admissions and Business Coordinator ... Ms. Amanda RAMBO
10 Business Manager ... Ms. Margaret CONKLIN
37 Academic/Financial Aid Administator ... Ms. Catherine WARDEN
11 Administrator ... Ms. Jillian SCOTT

*City University of New York (B)

205 E. 42nd Street, New York NY 10017
County: New York FICE Identification: 025061
Unit ID: 190035
Telephone: (646) 664-9100 Carnegie Class: N/A
FAX Number: (646) 664-3868
URL: www.cuny.edu

01 Chancellor ... Mr. James B. MILLIKEN
11 Exec Vice Chanc/Chief Oper Officer ... Mr. Allan H. DOBRIN
05 Interim Exec VC/University Provost ... Dr. Julia WRIGLEY
26 Sr Vice Chanc University Relations ... Mr. Jay HERSHENSON
43 Sr Vice Chancellor Legal Affairs ... Mr. Frederick P. SCHAFFER
10 Sr Vice Chancellor Budget/Finance ... Mr. Marc SHAW
18 Interim VC Facility Plng/Constr Mgt ... Ms. Judy BERGTRAUM
15 Vice Chanc for Human Resources Mgmt ... Ms. Gloriana WATERS
88 Vice Chancellor for Labor Relations ... Ms. Pamela S. SILVERBLATT
09 Vice Chancellor for Research ... Dr. Gillian SMALL
32 Vice Chancellor Student Affairs ... Dr. Frank SANCHEZ
13 Assoc VC/Chief Information Officer ... Mr. Brian COHEN
21 Vice Chancellor Budget/Finance ... Mr. Matthew SAPIENZA
100 Chief of Staff ... Ms. Doris L. SUAREZ
06 Registrar ... Ms. AnnaMarie J. BIANCO
27 Dir of Communications/Marketing ... Mr. Michael ARENA
84 Sr University Dean for Enrollment ... Mr. Robert A. PTACHIK
07 Director of Admissions ... Mr. Richard P. ALVAREZ

*Baruch College/City University of New York (C)

One Bernard Baruch Way, New York NY 10010-5526
County: New York FICE Identification: 007273
Unit ID: 190512
Telephone: (646) 312-1000 Carnegie Class: Master's L
FAX Number: N/A Calendar System: Semester
URL: www.baruch.cuny.edu
Established: 1968 Annual Undergrad Tuition & Fees (In-District): $6,330
Enrollment: 18,090 Coed
Affiliation or Control: State/Local IRS Status: 501(c)3
Highest Offering: Doctorate
Program: Liberal Arts And General; Professional; Business Emphasis
Accreditation: M, BUS, BUSA, HSA, SPAA

02 President ... Dr. Mitchel B. WALLERSTEIN
05 Provost/SVP Academic Affairs ... Dr. David CHRISTY
10 Vice Pres Administration/Finance ... Ms. Katharine COBB
84 Interim VP of Enrollment Mgmt ... Ms. Mary GORMAN
30 VP for College Advancement ... Mr. David SHANTON
50 VP & Dean Zicklin Sch Business ... Dr. Fenwick HUSS
18 Asst VP Campus Facilities ... Ms. Lisa EDWARDS
13 VP for Info Svcs/Dean of Library ... Mr. Arthur DOWNING
26 VP for Cmty/Ext Rels & Econ Dev ... Ms. Christina LATOUF
32 Asst Vice President Student Affairs ... Dr. Art KING
21 Asst Vice President Finance ... Ms. Mary FINNEN
102 President Baruch College Fund ... Mr. Joel J. COHEN
49 Interim Dean of the Weissman School ... Dr. Alison GRIFFITHS
20 Associate Provost ... Dr. Erec KOCH
20 Associate Provost ... Dr. Dennis SLAVIN
80 Dean School Public Affairs ... Dr. David BIRDSELL
43 Executive Legal Counsel ... Ms. Olga DAIS
58 Executive Officer Doctoral Program ... Dr. Joseph WEINTROP
100 Interim Chief of Staff ... Ms. Kenya N. LEE
25 Director of Sponsored Programs ... Mr. Dominic ESPOSITO
15 Exec Dir of Human Resources ... Ms. Monique GEORGE
36 Director Career Development Center ... Dr. Patricia IMBIMBO
90 Asst Dir Client Svcs/Fac Liais ... Mr. Frank WERBER
85 Director Intl Student Office ... Ms. Rosa KELLEY
19 Director Public Safety ... Mr. Henry J. MCLAUGHLIN
09 Dir Institutional Rsrch/Pgm Assess ... Mr. John CHOONOO
29 Director Alumni Relations ... Ms. Janet ROSSBACH
96 Director of Purchasing ... Dr. Diane OQUENDO
22 Chief Diversity Officer ... Ms. Kieran MORROW
41 Athletic Director ... Mr. Ray RANKIS
86 Dir of Govt and Community Relations ... Mr. Eric LUGO
06 Registrar ... Mr. Edward ADAMS
104 Director Study Abroad ... Dr. Richard MITTEN
37 Director of Financial Aid Services ... Ms. Elizabeth RIQUEZ
07 Dir of Undergraduate Admissions ... Ms. Marisa DELACRUZ

*City University of New York Borough of Manhattan Community College (D)

199 Chambers Street, New York NY 10007-1047
County: New York FICE Identification: 002691
Unit ID: 190521
Telephone: (212) 220-1230 Carnegie Class: Assoc/Pub-U-MC
FAX Number: (212) 220-1244 Calendar System: Semester
URL: www.bmcc.cuny.edu
Established: 1963 Annual Undergrad Tuition & Fees (In-District): $5,119
Enrollment: 26,606 Coed
Affiliation or Control: State/Local IRS Status: 501(c)3
Highest Offering: Associate Degree
Program: Occupational; 2-Year Principally Bachelor's Creditable
Accreditation: M, ADNUR, CAHIIM, COARC, EMT

02 President ... Dr. Antonio PEREZ
05 Provost/Senior VP Academic Affairs ... Dr. Karrin WILKS
11 Vice President Administration/Plng ... Mr. G. Scott ANDERSON
43 VP Legal Affs/Faculty & Staff Rels ... Mr. Robert DIAZ
32 Vice President of Student Affairs ... Dr. Marva CRAIG
30 Vice Pres of Development ... Ms. Doris HOLZ
10 Asst Vice Pres of Finance ... Ms. Elena SAMUELS
51 Dean Ctr for Cont Ed/Workforce Dev ... Dr. Sunil GUPTA
25 Dean Grants & Development ... Mr. John MONTANEZ
20 Dean for Instruction/Curriculum ... Dr. Erwin WONG
88 Assoc Dean Academic Support Svcs ... Dr. Michael GILLESPIE
37 Director Financial Aid ... Mr. Ralph W. BUXTON
15 Deputy Director Human Resources ... Ms. Gloria CHAO
07 Assoc Director of Admissions ... Ms. Antoinette MIDDLETON
84 Director Enrollment Management ... Dr. Eugenio BARRIOS
06 Senior Registrar ... Mr. Mohammad ALAM
08 Act Dir Learning Resource Center ... Mr. Gregory FARRELL
09 Dean Institutional Research ... Vacant
28 Chief Diversity Officer ... Ms. Iyana TITUS
18 Campus Facilities Officer ... Vacant
26 Public Relations Officer ... Mr. Manuel ROMERO
41 Director of Athletics ... Mr. Stephen KELLY
102 Dir Foundation/Corporate Relations ... Mr. Bryan HALLER
36 Act Dir Acad Advise/Transfer Ctr ... Ms. Carei THOMAS
38 Director Counseling Center ... Dr. Cicely Horsham BRATHWAITE
96 Director of Procurement ... Mr. Robert COX

*City University of New York Bronx Community College (E)

2155 University Avenue, Bronx NY 10453-2895
County: Bronx FICE Identification: 002692
Unit ID: 190530
Telephone: (718) 289-5100 Carnegie Class: Assoc/Pub-U-MC
FAX Number: (718) 289-6011 Calendar System: Semester
URL: www.bcc.cuny.edu
Established: 1957 Annual Undergrad Tuition & Fees (In-District): $5,205
Enrollment: 11,506 Coed
Affiliation or Control: State/Local IRS Status: 501(c)3
Highest Offering: Associate Degree
Program: Occupational; 2-Year Principally Bachelor's Creditable
Accreditation: M, ACBSP, ADNUR, ENGT, NMT, RAD

02 President ... Dr. Thomas A. ISEKENEGBE
05 VP of Academic Affairs & Provost ... Dr. Claudia V. SCHRADER
26 Government Rels and Ext Affairs Dir ... Mr. David W. LEVERS
04 Exec Asst to the Pres ... Ms. Carmen VÁSQUEZ
32 VP for Student Affairs ... Dr. Athos K. BREWER
30 VP for Strategic Initiatives ... Dr. Eddy BAYARDELLE
26 Asst VP Comm & Marketing ... Ms. Diane WEATHERS
84 Dean of Academic Services ... Mr. Bernard GANTT
11 AVP for Administrative Affairs ... Mr. David A. TAYLOR
44 Asst VP for Development ... Ms. Angela WAMBUGU COBB
103 Asst VP for Workforce Dev & Cont Ed ... Mr. Lawrence SHARPE
45 Dean for Research/Plng & Assessment ... Dr. Nancy RITZE
20 Assoc Dean AA for Curr & Fac Dev ... Dr. Alexander OTT
10 Dir for Financial & Bus Svcs ... Mr. Donovan THOMPSON
06 Registrar/Dir Enrollment ... Mr. Sanjay RAMDATH
13 Exec Dir of Information Technology ... Mr. Loïc AUDUSSEAU
37 Financial Aid Director ... Mr. Sinu JACOB
07 Admissions Officer ... Ms. Patricia A. RAMOS
15 Human Resources Director ... Mrs. Shelley LEVY
08 Chief Librarian ... Prof. Michael J. MILLER
19 Public Safety Director ... Mr. James VERDICCHIO
41 Student Athletics Manager ... Mr. Michael BELFIORE
18 Chief Super Phys Plant Svcs ... Mr. Wayne MURPHY
29 Alum Rel/Plan Giv/Indiv Donors Mgr ... Mr. Robert WHELAN
35 Assoc Dean Stdnt Engagement/Success ... Dr. Fenix ARIAS
88 Mgr of College Discovery ... Ms. Cynthia SUAREZ-ESPINAL
43 Executive Counsel & Labor Designee ... Ms. Karla R. WILLIAMS
96 Director of Purchasing ... Ms. Sharon LUCKIE
28 Chief Diversity/Affirm Act Ofcr ... Mrs. Jesenia MINIER-DELGADO
14 Deputy Chief Technology Officer ... Ms. Luisa MARTICH
108 Academic Assessment Manager ... Dr. Richard LAMANNA
20 Dean for Academic Affairs ... Vacant
90 Dir for Academic Comp Svcs Desk ... Ms. Wanda SANTIAGO
91 Manager of Admin Systems & Svcs ... Mr. Rolly WILTSHIRE
51 Mgr Continuing/Prof Education ... Mr. Wendell JOYNER
25 Dir of Grants Development ... Ms. Carin SAVAGE
22 Affirmative Action Specialist ... Mr. Raymond GONZALEZ
102 Dev Corp and Foundation Rel Mgmt ... Ms. Julia OLIVA
104 Dir Intl Educ and Study Aboard Pgm ... Ms. Marie LOURDES ELGIRUS
88 OIR Inst Research Specialist ... Mrs. Chelsea RAMOS
09 Director of Research & Testing ... Mr. Chris EFTHIMIOU
101 Conf Exec Assoc to the Pres ... Vacant
106 Dir IT Academic App/CTLT ... Mr. Mark LENNERTON
36 Dir Transfer and Job Placement ... Mr. Alán FUENTES

*City University of New York Brooklyn College (F)

2900 Bedford Avenue, Brooklyn NY 11210-2889
County: Kings FICE Identification: 002687
Unit ID: 190549
Telephone: (718) 951-5000 Carnegie Class: Master's L
FAX Number: N/A Calendar System: Semester
URL: www.brooklyn.cuny.edu
Established: 1930 Annual Undergrad Tuition & Fees (In-District): $6,835
Enrollment: 17,390 Coed
Affiliation or Control: State/Local IRS Status: 501(c)3
Highest Offering: Master's
Program: Liberal Arts And General; Teacher Preparatory; Professional
Accreditation: M, AUD, CACREP, DIETD, DIETI, PH, SP, TED

02 President ... Dr. Karen L. GOULD
05 Provost/Sr Vice Pres Acad Affairs ... Dr. William A. TRAMONTANO
10 Sr VP for Finance & Administration ... Mr. Joseph GIOVANNELLI
30 Vice Pres Institutional Advancement ... Dr. Andrew SILLEN
84 VP for Enrollment Management ... Dr. Stephen E. JOYNER
32 VP for Student Affairs ... Dr. Milga MORALES
26 AVP of Communications/Marketing ... Mr. Jason CAREY
100 Chief of Staff to President ... Ms. Nicole HAAS
20 Associate Provost for Faculty & Adm ... Dr. Matthew E. MOORE
20 Associate Provost for Acad Pgms ... Dr. Terence CHENG
21 AVP Budget & Planning & CFO ... Mr. Alan GILBERT
18 Asst VP Facilities Plng/Operations ... Mr. Francis X. FITZGERALD
13 Asst VP Info Technology Svcs/CIO ... Mr. Mark GOLD
15 Asst VP Human Resource Services ... Mr. Michael HEWITT
86 Exec Dir Govt & External Affairs ... Mr. Steven SCHECHTER
06 Registrar ... Mr. Richard FELTMAN
30 Assoc Exec Director of Development ... Ms. Beth F. LEVINE
22 Dir Diversity & Equity Programs ... Ms. Natalie L. MASON-KINSEY
43 Legal Counsel to the President ... Ms. Pamela POLLACK
29 Director Alumni Affairs ... Ms. Marla H. SCHREIBMAN
07 Dir Undergrad Admiss & Recruitment ... Ms. Penelope TERRY
19 Director Safety & Security ... Mr. Donald A. WENZ

*City University of New York The City College (G)

160 Convent Avenue, New York NY 10031-9198
County: New York FICE Identification: 002688
Unit ID: 190567
Telephone: (212) 650-7000 Carnegie Class: Master's L
FAX Number: (212) 650-7680 Calendar System: Semester
URL: www1.ccny.cuny.edu
Established: 1847 Annual Undergrad Tuition & Fees (In-District): $6,890
Enrollment: 15,745 Coed
Affiliation or Control: State/Local IRS Status: 501(c)3
Highest Offering: Doctorate
Program: Liberal Arts And General; Teacher Preparatory; Professional
Accreditation: M, ARCPA, CLPSY, CS, ENG, LSAR, #MED, TED

02 President ... Dr. Lisa STAIANO-COICO
05 Provost/Sr VP Academic Affairs ... Dr. Maurizio TREVISAN
26 Vice Pres Communication/Marketing ... Dr. Deidra W. HILL
30 VP Development/Inst Advancement ... Mr. Jeffrey MACHI
10 Vice Pres Finance & CFO ... Mr. Felix LAM
84 Asst Vice Pres Enrollment Mgmt ... Ms. Celia LLOYD
18 AVP Facilities Mgmt ... Mr. David ROBINSON
31 VP Governmental/Community Affairs ... Ms. Karen WITHERSPOON
32 Vice Pres for Student Affairs ... Ms. Juana REINA
13 AVP Information Technology/CIO ... Mr. Kenneth IHRER
100 Sr Advisor to Pres/Chief of Staff ... Ms. Deborah HARTNETT
63 Dean Sophie Davis Sch of BioMed Ed ... Dr. Maurizio TREVISAN
54 Dean of Engineering ... Dr. Gilda BARABINO
53 Dean of the School of Education ... Dr. Mary Erina DRISCOLL
47 Acting Dean School of Architecture ... Mr. Gordon GEBERT
88 Dean of CWE-Div of Interdiscip Stds ... Dr. Juan Carlos MERCADO
81 Dean of Science ... Dr. Tony LISS
83 Dean Sch Civic & Global Leadership ... Dr. Vincent BOUDREAU
79 Dean of Humanities & The Arts ... Dr. Eric WEITZ
04 Counsel to President ... Mr. Paul F. OCCHIOGROSSO
15 Asst Vice Pres of Human Resources ... Mr. John SIDERAKIS
29 Executive Director Alumni Affairs ... Mr. Donald K. JORDAN
35 Director Student Support Resources ... Ms. Teresa WALKER
06 Senior Registrar ... Mr. Daniel MATOS

35 Exec Dir of Student Affairs at CWE ....Ms. Sophia DEMETRIOU
08 Acting Chief Librarian .... Dr. Charles STEWART
46 Director Research Administration ....Dr. Alan SHIH
09 Director of Institutional Research ....Mr. Edward SILVERMAN
37 Director of Financial Aid ....Ms. Arshaw RAMKARAN
26 Assoc Director of Public Relations ....Mr. Sydney STEINHARDT
28 Chf Diversity Ofcr/Dean Faculty Rel ....Ms. Michele BAPTISTE
90 Dir Messaging/General Support Svcs ....Mr. Curtis RIAS
36 Director of Career Services ....Ms. Katie NAILLER
19 Exec Dir Public Safety/Security ....Mr. Pat MORENA
11 Administrative Superintendent ....Mr. Kyle MANLEY
24 Director of Instructional Media ....Mr. Nana ABEYIE
07 Director of Admissions ....Mr. Joseph FANTOZZI
38 Director Student Counseling ....Vacant
21 Director of Business & Finance ....Mr. Mario CRESCENZO
96 Director of Purchasing ....Mr. Mario CRESCENZO

*College of Staten Island CUNY (A)

2800 Victory Boulevard, Staten Island NY 10314-6600
County: Richmond FICE Identification: 002698
Unit ID: 190558
Telephone: (718) 982-2000 Carnegie Class: Master's L
FAX Number: N/A Calendar System: Semester
URL: www.csi.cuny.edu
Established: 1976 Annual Undergrad Tuition & Fees (In-District): $6,809
Enrollment: 14,344 Coed
Affiliation or Control: State/Local IRS Status: 501(c)3
Highest Offering: Doctorate
Program: 2-Year Principally Bachelor's Creditable; Liberal Arts And General; Teacher Preparatory; Professional
Accreditation: M, ADNUR, CS, ENG, ENGT, MT, NUR, PTA, SW, TED

02 President ....Dr. William J. FRITZ
05 Sr VP Acad Affairs/Provost ....Dr. Gary W. REICHARD
10 VP for Finance and Administration ....Mr. Ira PERSKY
32 VP Student & Enrollment Services ....Ms. Jennifer RUBAIN
30 VP Inst Advance/External Affairs ....Ms. Khatmeh OSSEIRAN-HANNA
13 VP Info Tech & Economic Devel ....Dr. Michael KRESS
21 AVP for Finance & Budget ....Vacant
100 Deputy to President/Chief of Staff ....Mr. Kenichi IWAMA
35 Asst VP for Student Affairs ....Dr. Christopher GIORDANO
18 AVP Campus Planning/Facilities Mgmt .Mr. Stephen J. BRENNAN
90 AVP Technology Systems .... Dr. Patricia KAHN
26 AVP Inst Advance/External Affairs ....Ms. Janine SCAFF
81 Acting Dean of Science & Tech ....Dr. Alfred LEVINE
79 Dean Humanities & Social Sci ....Dr. Nan M. SUSSMAN
08 Assoc Dean/Chief Librarian ....Dr. Wilma JONES
43 Special Counsel and Labor Designee .... Ms. Kathleen GALVEZ
28 Director of Diversity & Compliance .....Ms. Danielle E. DIMITROV
50 Dean of School of Business ....Dr. Susan L. HOLAK
76 Interim Dean School of Health Sci ....Dr. Maureen BECKER
53 Interim Dean School of Education ....Dr. Kenneth GOLD

*City University of New York Graduate Center (B)

365 Fifth Avenue, New York NY 10016-4309
County: New York FICE Identification: 004765
Unit ID: 190576
Telephone: (212) 817-7000 Carnegie Class: RU/VH
FAX Number: (212) 817-1624 Calendar System: Semester
URL: www.gc.cuny.edu
Established: 1961 Annual Undergrad Tuition & Fees (In-District): $9,060
Enrollment: 4,232 Coed
Affiliation or Control: State/Local IRS Status: 501(c)3
Highest Offering: Doctorate
Program: Professional
Accreditation: M, JOUR, PH, SCPSY

02 President ....Dr. Chase F. ROBINSON
05 Interim Provost/Sr VP ....Dr. Louise LENNIHAN
10 Sr VP Finance and Administration ....Dr. Sebastian T. PERSICO
20 Int Assoc Provost & Dean Acad Aff ....Dr. David OLAN
32 Vice President Student Affairs ......Mr. Matthew G. SCHOENGOOD
30 Vice Pres Institutional Advancement ....Mr. Jay GOLAN
13 VP Information Technology ....Mr. Robert D. CAMPBELL
21 Asst Vice President Finance ....Mr. Stuart B. SHOR
15 Asst VP for Faculty & Staff Rels ..Ms. Yosette JONES JOHNSON
46 Exec Dir Research & Sponsored Pgm ....Dr. Edith GONZALEZ
25 Director Sponsored Research ....Ms. Hilry FISHER
26 Exec Dir Communications/Marketing ....Ms. Jane E. TROMBLEY
08 Chief Librarian ....Ms. Polly THISTLETHWAITE
07 Director Admissions ....Mr. Les GRIBBEN
06 Dir Student Svcs/Senior Registrar ....Mr. Vincent J. DELUCA
37 Exc Dir Fellowships & Financial Aid ....Ms. Phyllis SCHULZ
09 Dir Institutional Research & Effect ....Vacant
88 Director Building Design/Exhibits ....Mr. Ray RING
28 Executive Officer Educ Opp/Div Pgm ....Dr. Herman BENNETT
85 Director International Students ....Mr. Douglas EWING
88 Dir Well Ctr/Psy Coun Svc/Adult Dev ....Dr. Robert HATCHER
23 Director Student Health Services ....Ms. Adraenne BOWE
22 Chief Diversity Officer ....Ms. Edith RIVERA
16 Exec Director of Human Resources ....Ms. Ella KISELYUK
18 Director Facilities/Campus Planning ....Mr. Michael BYERS
96 Director of Purchasing ....Mr. Ronald PAYNTER
35 Director Student Affairs ....Ms. Sharon LERNER
19 Exec Dir Security & Public Safety ....Mr. John FLAHERTY
04 Administrative Asst to President ....Ms. Alexandra ROBINSON
100 Chief of Staff ....Ms. Jane HERBERT
43 Legal Counsel ....Ms. Lynette M. PHILLIPS

*City University of New York Herbert H. Lehman College (C)

250 Bedford Park Boulevard W, Bronx NY 10468-1589
County: Bronx FICE Identification: 007022
Unit ID: 190637
Telephone: (718) 960-8000 Carnegie Class: Master's L
FAX Number: N/A Calendar System: Semester
URL: www.lehman.cuny.edu
Established: 1968 Annual Undergrad Tuition & Fees (In-District): $6,689
Enrollment: 12,398 Coed
Affiliation or Control: State/Local IRS Status: 501(c)3
Highest Offering: Master's
Program: Liberal Arts And General; Teacher Preparatory; Professional
Accreditation: M, CACREP, DIETD, DIETI, NURSE, PH, SP, SW, TED

02 President ....Dr. Ricardo R. FERNANDEZ
100 Chief of Staff/Chief Diversity Ofcr .... Ms. Dawn EWING-MORGAN
43 Sp Coun to Pres Legal Affs/Lab Rels ....Ms. Mary T. ROGAN
88 Dep to Pres/Educ Init & Spec Proj ....Ms. Sandra LERNER
05 Provost/SVP Academic Affairs .... Dr. Anny MORROBEL-SOSA
10 Vice Pres Administration/Finance ....Mr. Vincent W. CLARK
32 Vice President Student Affairs ....Mr. Jose MAGDALENO
30 Vice Pres Institutional Advancement ....Mr. Mario DELLAPINA
13 Vice Pres/Chief Info Officer ....Mr. Ronald BERGMANN
103 VP Workforce/Global Partnerships ....Dr. Marzie A. JAFARI
84 Assoc Provost/VP Enroll Mgmt ....Ms. Reine SARMIENTO
20 Vice Provost Academic Personnel ....Dr. Davina POROCK
20 Vice Provost Academic Programs ....Dr. Stefan BECKER
18 Asst VP Campus Planning/Facilities ....Ms. Rene M. ROTOLO
88 Exec Asst to Vice Pres Student Affs ....Mr. Vincent ZUCCHETTO
14 Asst VP Information Technology ....Mr. Ediltrudys RUIZ
79 Dean School of Arts/Humanities ....Dr. Deirdre PENNIPIECE
53 Dean School of Education ....Dr. Harriet FAYNE
83 Dean School of Nat & Soc Sci ....Dr. Gautam SEN
76 Dean Sch Heath Sci/Hum Svc & Nurs ....Dr. William LATIMER
35 Dean of Student Affairs ....Mr. John HOLLOWAY
21 Asst VP for Financial Operations ....Ms. Gina HARWOOD
08 Chief Librarian ....Dr. Kenneth SCHLESINGER
06 Senior Registrar ....Ms. Yvette ROSARIO
07 Director of Admissions ....Ms. Laurie AUSTIN
29 Director of Alumni Relations ....Ms. Maria-Cristina NEVADO
88 Director of the Art Gallery ....Ms. Susan HOELTZEL
36 Director Career Services ....Ms. Nancy A. CINTRON
38 Director Counseling Center ....Dr. Norma COFRESI
37 Director Financial Aid ....Mr. David MARTINEZ
89 Director Freshman Year Initiative ....Dr. Steven WYCKOFF
46 Dir Research & Sponsored Programs .... Ms. Saeedah HICKMAN
92 Director of Honors College Program .... Dr. Gary SCHWARTZ
15 Director of Human Resources ....Mr. Eric WASHINGTON
14 Director Info Tech Resources ....Vacant
09 Director of Institutional Research ....Dr. Susanne M. TUMELTY
38 Dir Instruct Support Services Pgm ....Ms. Althea FORDE
26 Dir Media Relations & Publications ....Mr. Joseph TIRELLA
88 Director Performing Arts Center ....Ms. Eva BORNSTEIN
19 Director of Public Safety ....Mr. Fausto RAMIREZ
96 Director of Purchasing ....Ms. Andrea PINNOCK
41 Athletic Director ....Dr. Martin ZWIREN
40 Bookstore Manager ....Ms. Maria VILLAGOMEZ

*Hostos Community College-City University of New York (D)

500 Grand Concourse, Bronx NY 10451-5323
County: Bronx FICE Identification: 008611
Unit ID: 190585
Telephone: (718) 518-4300 Carnegie Class: Assoc/Pub-U-MC
FAX Number: (718) 518-4294 Calendar System: Semester
URL: www.hostos.cuny.edu
Established: 1970 Annual Undergrad Tuition & Fees (In-District): $5,206
Enrollment: 6,985 Coed
Affiliation or Control: State/Local IRS Status: 501(c)3
Highest Offering: Associate Degree
Program: 2-Year Principally Bachelor's Creditable
Accreditation: M, DH, RAD

02 President ....Dr. David GOMEZ
05 Int Provost/VP for Academic Affairs ....Dr. Christine MANGINO
10 Senior Vice Pres for Admin/ Finance ....Ms. Esther RODRIGUEZ-CHARDAVOYNE
32 Vice Pres Student Development ....Mr. Nathaniel CRUZ
100 Deputy to President ....Ms. Dolly MARTINEZ
30 Vice Pres Institutional Advancement ....Ms. Ana M. CARRION-SILVA
103 VP for Cont Educ & Workforce Dev ....Dr. Carlos MOLINA
13 Asst Vice Pres Info Technology ....Mr. Varun SEHGAL
21 Budget Director ....Ms. Fanny DUMANCELA
18 Exec Dir Facil Plng Des Mgmt ....Ms. Elizabeth FRIEDMAN
04 Associate Dean for Community Rels ..Ms. Ana I. GARCIA-REYES
20 Asst Dean of Academic Affairs ....Mr. Felix CARDONA
35 Assistant Dean of Student Life ....Ms. Johanna GOMEZ
43 Executive Counsel & Labor Designee ....Mr. Eugene SOHN
26 Dir of Publications Development ....Vacant
38 Director of Counseling ....Ms. Linda ALEXANDER-WALLACE
15 College Personnel Officer ....Ms. Shirley SHEVACH
86 Director of Government Relations ....Mr. Joshua RIVERA
06 Registrar ....Ms. Nelida PASTORIZA
07 Director of Admissions ....Mr. Roland VELEZ
37 Director of Financial Aid ....Mr. Joseph ALICEA
19 Director of Campus Security ....Mr. Arnaldo BERNABE
25 Director Grants & Contracts ....Ms. Lourdes TORRES

09 Director Institutional Research ....Mr. Piotr KOCIK
08 Head Librarian ....Ms. Madeline FORD
22 Chief Diversity Officer ....Ms. Michele DICKINSON
29 Director Alumni Relations ....Ms. Nydia EDGECOMBE
36 Director Career Services ....Ms. Lisanette ROSARIO
35 Director Student Activities ....Mr. Jerry ROSA
96 Director of Purchasing ....Mr. Kevin CARMINE

*City University of New York Hunter College (E)

695 Park Avenue, New York NY 10065
County: New York FICE Identification: 002689
Unit ID: 190594
Telephone: (212) 772-4000 Carnegie Class: Master's L
FAX Number: N/A Calendar System: Semester
URL: www.hunter.cuny.edu
Established: 1870 Annual Undergrad Tuition & Fees (In-District): $6,780
Enrollment: 23,112 Coed
Affiliation or Control: State/Local IRS Status: 501(c)3
Highest Offering: Doctorate
Program: Liberal Arts And General; Teacher Preparatory; Professional
Accreditation: M, AUD, CACREP, CORE, CVT, DIETD, DIETI, ENGR, NURSE, PH, PLNG, PTA, SP, SW, TED

02 President ....Ms. Jennifer J. RAAB
100 Chief of Staff/Exec Asst to Pres ....Ms. Anne LYTLE
10 Vice Pres/Chief Operating Officer ....Mr. Giancarlo BONAGURA
05 Provost/Vice Pres Academic Affairs ....Mr. Lon KAUFMAN
32 VP Student Affs/Dean of Stdnts .... Ms. Eija AYRAVAINEN
43 Counsel to the President ....Ms. Laura HERTZOG
30 Asst VP Institutional Advancement ....Ms. Sara MEYERS
26 Asst VP & Dir Communication ....Mr. Christopher BROWNE
13 Asst Vice Pres Information Tech ....Mr. Mitch AHLBAUM
21 Executive Director Business Svcs ....Ms. Livia CANGEMI
21 Asst Vice Pres Business Services ....Mr. Carlos SERRANO
35 Asst Vice Pres of Student Affairs ....Ms. Madlyn STOKELY
18 Asst Vice Pres of Facilities ....Mr. James GLEBA
28 Dean Diversity and Compliance ....Mr. John ROSE
49 Dean School of Arts & Sciences ....Dr. Andrew POLSKY
70 Acting Dean School of Social Work ....Ms. Mary CAVANAUGH
53 Acting Dean School of Education ....Ms. Jennifer TUTEN
66 Dean School of Nursing ....Dr. Gail C. MCCAIN
08 Chief Librarian ....Mr. Daniel CHERUBIN
06 Registrar ....Ms. Marilyn DALY-WESTON
20 Asst Provost Assessment ....Dr. Edward BARBONI
09 Director of Institutional Research ....Ms. Joan LAMBE
15 Director of Human Resources ....Ms. Galia GALANSKY
35 Director Student Advising ....Mr. Bryan MAASJO
36 Director Student Placement ....Ms. Susan MCCARTY
37 Director Student Financial Aid ....Ms. Aristalia RODRIGUEZ
29 Director Alumni Relations ....Mr. Jorge DEJESUS
19 College Security Director ....Mr. Joseph FOELSCH
07 Director of Admissions ....Ms. Lori JANOWSKI
104 Director Study Abroad ....Ms. Elizabeth SACHS
108 Dir Institutional Assessment ....Dr. Meredith REITMAN
41 Athletic Director ....Ms. Terry WANSART
84 Dir Enrollment Mgmt/Recruit ....Ms. Sarah FARSAD

*City University of New York John Jay College of Criminal Justice (F)

524 West 59th Street, New York NY 10019-1093
County: New York FICE Identification: 002693
Unit ID: 190600
Telephone: (212) 237-8000 Carnegie Class: Master's L
FAX Number: (212) 237-8607 Calendar System: Semester
URL: www.jjay.cuny.edu
Established: 1964 Annual Undergrad Tuition & Fees (In-District): $6,810
Enrollment: 15,045 Coed
Affiliation or Control: State/Local IRS Status: 501(c)3
Highest Offering: Master's
Program: Liberal Arts And General; Professional
Accreditation: M, CLPSY, FEPAC, SPAA

02 President ....Mr. Jeremy TRAVIS
05 Prov/Sr Vice Pres Academic Affairs ....Dr. Jane BOWERS
11 Sr Vice Pres Administrative Affairs ....Mr. Robert PIGNATELLO
32 Vice Pres Student Affairs ....Ms. Lynette COOK-FRANCIS
30 Vice Pres Marketing/Dev ....Ms. Jayne ROSENGARTEN
84 Vice Pres Enrollment Management ....Dr. Robert TROY
45 Assoc Provost for Effect/Assessment ....Dr. James LLANA
04 Interim Exec Assoc to President ....Ms. Raeanne DAVIS
100 Chief of Staff ....Ms. Rulisa GALLOWAY-PERRY
58 Assoc Prov & Dean of Grad Studies ....Dr. Anne LOPES
46 Associate Provost/Dean of Research ....Dr. Anthony CARPI
32 Asst VP and Dean of Students ....Dr. Kenneth HOLMES
15 Executive Director Human Resources ....Mr. Kevin HAUSS
20 Assoc Prov & Dean of Undergrad Stds ....Dr. Scott STODDART
10 Exec Dir Financial/Business Svcs ....Ms. Patricia KETTERER
08 Chief Librarian ....Dr. Lawrence SULLIVAN
37 Director of Financial Aid ....Ms. Sylvia CRESPO-LOPEZ
44 Director of Development ....Ms. Kathryn COUSINS
35 Director Student Activities ....Ms. Danielle OFFICER
25 Director of Funded Research ....Ms. Susy MENDES
09 Director of Institutional Research ....Mr. Ricardo ANZALDUA
89 Director of First Year Experience ....Ms. Katalin SZUR
06 Interim Registrar ....Dr. Robert TROY
88 Director of CRJ Research & Eval ....Dr. Jeffrey BUTTS
07 Interim Director of Admissions ....Dr. Robert TROY
13 Chief Information Officer ....Mr. Joe LAUB

19 Director of Public Safety .... Mr. Kevin CASSIDY
90 Director Technology Services .... Vacant
24 Director of Media Services .... Mr. Paul BRENNER
27 Chief Communications Officer .... Ms. Rama SUDHAKAR
36 Director of Career Development Svcs .... Mr. Will SIMPKINS
38 Director of Counseling .... Dr. Gerard BRYANT
41 Athletic Director .... Ms. Carol KASHOW
21 Associate Business Officer .... Ms. Emily KARP
29 Director Alumni Relations .... Ms. Jerylle KEMP
96 Director of Purchasing .... Mr. Daniel DOLAN
04 Senior International Officer .... Ms. Mayra NIEVES
18 Director Facilities/Physical Plant .... Mr. Elmer PHELON
43 Assistant Vice President & Counsel .... Ms. Marjorie SINGER
86 Exec Dir of External Relations .... Ms. Mindy BOCKSTEIN
88 Director of Academic Advisement .... Dr. Sumaya VILLANUEVA
88 Int Dir of Accessibility Services .... Ms. Malanie CLARKE
104 Director Study Abroad .... Mr. Kenneth YANES
28 Director of Diversity .... Ms. Silvia MONTALBAN
39 Director Student Housing .... Ms. Jessica CARSON

† The Clinical Psychology PhD is awarded through the CUNY Graduate Center.

*City University of New York Kingsborough Community College (A)

2001 Oriental Boulevard, Brooklyn NY 11235-2333
County: Kings FICE Identification: 002694
Unit ID: 190619
Telephone: (718) 368-5109 Carnegie Class: Assoc/Pub-U-MC
FAX Number: (718) 368-5003 Calendar System: Other
URL: www.kbcc.cuny.edu
Established: 1963 Annual Undergrad Tuition & Fees (In-District): $5,200
Enrollment: 17,758 Coed
Affiliation or Control: State/Local IRS Status: 501(c)3
Highest Offering: Associate Degree
Program: Occupational; 2-Year Principally Bachelor's Creditable
Accreditation: M, #PTAA, SURGT

02 President .... Mr. Farley HERZEK
05 Vice Pres Academic Affs/Provost .... Dr. Stuart SUSS
10 Vice Pres Finance/Administration .... Vacant
100 Executive Chief of Staff .... Mr. Peter POBAT
32 Dean of Student Affairs .... Mr. Peter COHEN
51 Dean Continuing Educ/Dir Cmty Rels .... Ms. Christine BECKNER
35 Dean of Student Life .... Ms. Tasheka YOUNG
20 Vice Pres Academic Administration .... Vacant
84 Dean Enrollment Management .... Mr. Thomas FRIEBEL
09 Dean Inst Effective/Strategic Plng .... Dr. Richard FOX
30 Assoc Dean College Advancement .... Dr. Elizabeth BASILE
15 Director of Human Resources .... Ms. Micheline DRISCOLL
22 Dir Affirmative Action/EO Officer .... Mr. Angel RIVERA
19 Director of Security & Safety .... Mr. Tyrone FORTE
08 Chief Librarian .... Ms. Josephine MURPHY
06 Registrar .... Mr. Michael KLEIN
18 Campus Facilities Officer .... Mr. Anthony CORAZZA
37 Financial Aid Officer .... Mr. Wayne H. HAREWOOD
13 Chief Information Officer .... Mr. Asif HUSSAIN
36 Dir Career Couns/Placement/Transfer .... Mr. Brian MITRA
23 Director of Health Services .... Vacant
24 Director of Educational Media .... Mr. Michael ROSSON
41 Director of Athletics .... Mr. Domani THOMAS
26 Interim Director/Public Relations .... Ms. Dawn WALKER
96 Director of Purchasing .... Ms. Lyn RELAY
07 Director of Admissions .... Ms. Rosalie FAYAD
29 Director Alumni Relations .... Ms. Laura GLAZIER-SMITH
38 Director Student Counseling .... Ms. Dasha GORINSHTEYN
14 Assoc Director of Computer Center .... Vacant
21 Business Manager .... Mr. Anthony IMPERATO
88 Deputy Business Officer .... Mr. Bill CORRENTI

*La Guardia Community College/ City University of New York (B)

31-10 Thomson Avenue, Long Island City NY 11101-3083
County: Queens FICE Identification: 010051
Unit ID: 190628
Telephone: (718) 482-7200 Carnegie Class: Assoc/Pub-U-SC
FAX Number: (718) 609-2000 Calendar System: Semester
URL: www.lagcc.cuny.edu
Established: 1971 Annual Undergrad Tuition & Fees (In-District): $5,216
Enrollment: 19,770 Coed
Affiliation or Control: State/Local IRS Status: 501(c)3
Highest Offering: Associate Degree
Program: Occupational; 2-Year Principally Bachelor's Creditable
Accreditation: M, ADNUR, #DIETT, OTA, PTAA

02 President .... Dr. Gail O. MELLOW
05 Provost and Senior Vice President .... Dr. Paul ARCARIO
04 Executive Associate to President .... Ms. Rosemary TALMADGE
11 Vice President of Administration .... Mr. Shahir ERFAN
30 VP of Insitutional Advancement .... Ms. Susan LYDDON
13 Vice Pres Information Technology .... Mr. Henry SALTIEL
32 Vice President Student Affairs .... Dr. Michael BASTON
51 Vice Pres Adult/Continuing Educ .... Ms. Jane SCHULMAN
20 Assoc Dean for Academic Affairs .... Mr. Bret EYNON
84 Asst Dean Enrollment Services .... Ms. Nireata SEALS
18 Exec Dir Facilities Mgmt/Planning .... Mr. Kenneth CAMPANELLI
15 Exec Director of Human Resources .... Vacant
10 Exec Director Finance & Business .... Mr. Thomas HLADEK
86 Government Relations Manager .... Ms. Claudia CHAN
08 Chief Librarian .... Ms. Scott WHITE
06 Coordinator for Records Management .... Ms. Alexandra TORRES
37 Director Student Financial Services .... Ms. Gail BAKSH-JARRETT
36 Assoc Dean Acad & Career Develop .... Ms. Jane MACKILLOP
103 Asst Dean of Workforce Development .... Ms. Francesca FIORE
07 Director of Admissions .... Ms. LaVora DESVIGNE
26 Dir Marketing/Communications .... Mr. Charles ELIAS
43 Legal & Labor Relations Officer .. Ms. Jemma ROBAIN LACAILLE
22 Affirmative Action Specialist .... Vacant
09 Director of Institutional Research .... Mr. Nathan DICKMEYER
21 Associate Business Manager .... Ms. Carmen LUONG
36 Director Employment/Career Svc Ctr .... Ms. Claudia BALDONEDO
96 Director Procurement & Contracts .... Mr. Mitchell HENDERSON
20 Assoc Dean for Academic Affairs .... Ms. Ann FEIBEL
88 Asst Dean Ctr for Teaching & Lrng .... Mr. Howard WACH

*City University of New York Medgar Evers College (C)

1650 Bedford Avenue, Brooklyn NY 11225-2010
County: Kings FICE Identification: 010097
Unit ID: 190646
Telephone: (718) 270-4900 Carnegie Class: Bac/Assoc
FAX Number: (718) 270-5126 Calendar System: Semester
URL: www.mec.cuny.edu
Established: 1970 Annual Undergrad Tuition & Fees (In-District): $6,150
Enrollment: 6,000 Coed
Affiliation or Control: State/Local IRS Status: 501(c)3
Highest Offering: Baccalaureate
Program: Liberal Arts And General; Teacher Preparatory; Professional; Religious Emphasis
Accreditation: M, ACBSP, ADNUR, NUR, SW, TED

02 President .... Dr. Rudolph F. CREW
03 COO/Senior Vice President .... Mr. Jerald POSMAN
05 Provost/Senior Vice President .... Dr. Augustine OKERELE
10 VP Finance & Administration .... Ms. Jacqueline CLARK
32 VP of Student Affairs/Enroll Mgmt .... Dr. Evelyn CASTRO
51 Interim Dean Sch Prof & Comm Dev .... Dr. Simone RODRIGUEZ-DORESTANT
50 Dean of the School of Business .... Dr. Jo-Ann ROLLE
49 Interim Dean Sch of Lib Arts & Educ .... Dr. J. A. George IRISH
72 Dean School of Science/Health/Tech .... Dr. Mohsin PATWARY
100 Chief of Staff .... Vacant
21 Acting Comptroller .... Mr. Chi KOON
43 Counsel to President .... Mr. Gary JOHNSON
04 Exec Assistant to the President .... Mrs. Lisa ANDERSON
22 Director of Affirmative Action .... Ms. Sylvia KINARD
06 Registrar .... Ms. Tatiana MEJIC
27 Chief Information Officer .... Ms. Ediltrudy RUIZ
37 Director of Financial Aid .... Mr. Nigel THOMPSON
38 Director of Counseling .... Dr. JoAnn JOYNER-GRAHAM
19 Director of Security .... Mr. Victor STEVENS
41 Director of Athletics .... Ms. Renee BOSTIC
25 Grants Officer .... Mr. Chi KOON
89 Dir Freshman Year Program .... Dr. Janice ZUMMO
55 Director Evening/Weekend Programs .... Ms. Yvette WALL
36 Sr Director of Career Development .... Ms. Karen ABEL-BEY
30 Exec Director of Development .... Vacant
26 Asst VP of External Relations .... Ms. Jamilah FRASER
18 Supt of Buildings & Grounds .... Vacant
07 Director of Admissions .... Mrs. Shannon CLARKE-ANDERSON
29 Director of Alumni Relations .... Mrs. Tara REGIST-TOMLINSON
88 Exec Dir for Risk Mgmt & Int Con .... Vacant
96 Director of Purchasing .... Vacant
84 Director Enrollment Management .... Mr. Jeffrey SIGLER
09 Director of Institutional Research .... Dr. Eva CHAN
08 Chief Librarian .... Dr. David ORENSTEIN
66 Interim Chair Dept of Nursing .... Dr. Georgia MCDUFFIE
50 Chair Dept of Business Admin .... Ms. Evelyn MAGGIO
53 Chair Department of Education .... Dr. Sheilah PAUL
60 Interim Chair Dept of Mass Comm .... Dr. Clinton CRAWFORD
88 Chair Department Accounting .... Dr. Rosemary WILLIAMS
81 Chair Department of Mathematics .... Vacant
77 Chair Dept Physical/Computer Sci .... Dr. Wilbert HOPE
81 Chair Department of Biology .... Dr. Anthony UDEOGALANYA
83 Chair Dept of Social/Behavioral Sci .... Dr. Obasegun AWOLABI
88 Chair Department of Psychology .... Dr. Ethan GOLOGOR
88 Chair Dept of Public Administration .... Dr. Wallace FORD
13 Chair Computer Info Systems .... Dr. Adesina FADARIO
88 Chair Department Economics/Finance .... Dr. Emmanuel EGBE
88 Chair Department of English .... Ms. Brenda GREENE
88 Chair Dept of Philosophy & Religion .... Dr. Gary SEAY
88 Chair Dept of Foreign Languages .... Dr. Jesus BOTTARO
35 Director of Student Life .... Vacant
15 Executive Dir of Human Resources .... Ms. Tanya ISAACS
88 Acting Director of Bursar .... Ms. Sharon BARTELL
28 Chief Diversity Officer .... Dr. Sylvia G. KINARD
104 Director Study Abroad .... Mr. Eugene PURSOO
86 Director Government Relations .... Ms. Jennifer JAMES

*New York City College of Technology/City University of New York (D)

300 Jay Street, Brooklyn NY 11201-1909
County: Kings FICE Identification: 002696
Unit ID: 190655
Telephone: (718) 260-5000 Carnegie Class: Bac/Assoc
FAX Number: (718) 260-5198 Calendar System: Semester
URL: www.citytech.cuny.edu
Established: 1946 Annual Undergrad Tuition & Fees (In-District): $6,330
Enrollment: 17,374 Coed
Affiliation or Control: State/Local IRS Status: 501(c)3
Highest Offering: Baccalaureate
Program: Professional; Technical Emphasis
Accreditation: M, ADNUR, CSHSE, DH, DT, ENGT, NUR, OPD, RAD, TED

02 President .... Dr. Russell K. HOTZLER
05 Provost .... Dr. Bonne AUGUST
10 Vice Pres Finance/Administration .... Dr. Miguel CAIROL
84 VP Enrollment/Student Affairs .... Dr. Marcela ARMOZA
20 Associate Provost Academic Affairs .... Dr. Pamela BROWN
22 Counsel/Affirmative Action Officer .... Ms. Gilen CHAN
07 Director of Admissions .... Ms. Alexis CHACONIS
06 Registrar .... Ms. Tasha RHODES
37 Director of Financial Aid .... Ms. Sandra HIGGINS
08 Librarian .... Ms. Maura SMALE
13 Director of Computer Center .... Ms. Rita UDDIN
107 Int Dean of Professional Studies .... Mr. David SMITH
54 Interim Dean of Technology .... Mr. Kevin HOM
49 Dean of Arts & Science .... Vacant
51 Dean Continuing Education .... Dr. Carol SONNENBLICK
55 Director Evening Session .... Mr. James LAP
15 Director of Human Resources .... Ms. Sandra GORDON
25 Grants Officer .... Ms. Barbara BURKE
24 Director of Inst Tech/Media Svcs .... Ms. Karen LUNDSTREM
09 Director of Assessment .... Dr. Tammie CUMMING
26 Interim Exec Dir Public Relations .... Ms. Faith CORBETT
29 Director Alumni Relations .... Ms. Jessica MALAVEZ
36 Director Student Placement .... Mr. Adrian GRIFFIN
38 Director Student Counseling .... Ms. Cynthia BINK
96 Director of Purchasing .... Mr. Wayne ROBINSON
18 Chief Facilities/Physical Plant .... Mr. James VASQUEZ
30 Chief Development/Spec Asst to Pres .... Dr. Stephen SOIFFER
32 Administrator Student Affairs .... Vacant
21 Business Manager .... Mr. Wayne ROBINSON

*City University of New York Queens College (E)

65-30 Kissena Boulevard, Flushing NY 11367-1597
County: Queens FICE Identification: 002690
Unit ID: 190664
Telephone: (718) 997-5000 Carnegie Class: Master's L
FAX Number: (718) 997-5598 Calendar System: Semester
URL: www.qc.cuny.edu
Established: 1937 Annual Undergrad Tuition & Fees (In-District): $6,633
Enrollment: 19,310 Coed
Affiliation or Control: State/Local IRS Status: 501(c)3
Highest Offering: Master's
Program: Liberal Arts And General; Teacher Preparatory; Professional
Accreditation: M, AAFCS, CAEP, CLPSY, DIETD, DIETI, LAW, LIB, SP, TED

02 President .... Dr. Felix V. MATOS RODRIGUEZ
05 Provost .... Dr. Elizabeth HENDREY
10 Vice Pres Finance/Administration .... Mr. William KELLER
32 Vice President for Student Affairs .... Dr. Adam ROCKMAN
91 Asst Vice Pres Converging Tech .... Ms. Claudia COLBERT
20 Assoc Provost Academic Plng/Pgms .... Dr. Steven SCHWARZ
43 Asst Vice Pres for Labor Relations .... Ms. Meryl KAYNARD
27 Director of Communications .... Ms. Leanna YIP
21 Assistant VP Business Affairs .... Mr. Brian MURPHY
30 Asst VP Institutional Advancement .... Ms. Laurie DORF
88 Assistant Provost .... Dr. June BOBB
57 Dean Arts & Humanities .... Dr. William MCCLURE
81 Dean Math & Natural Sciences .... Dr. Robert ENGEL
53 Dean Education .... Dr. Craig MICHAELS
58 Dean of Research/Grad Studies .... Dr. Richard BODNAR
83 Dean Social Sciences .... Dr. Dean SAVAGE
15 Director Human Resources/Payroll .... Ms. Reinalda MEDINA
41 Assistant Vice President Athletics .... Ms. China JUDE
88 Director of Events .... Vacant
18 Asst VP Facilities .... Mr. Zeco KRCIC
07 Executive Director Admissions .... Mr. Vincent ANGRISANI
38 Dir of Counseling and Advisement .... Dr. Barbara MOORE
06 Director Registrar's Office .... Mr. Matthew CASANOVA
09 Director of Institutional Research .... Dr. Margaret MCAULIFFE
08 Chief Librarian .... Dr. Rolf SWENSEN
37 Director Financial Aid Services .... Ms. Rena SMITH-KIAWU
29 Manager Alumni Affairs .... Mr. Christopher GREAVES
19 Director Security/Safety .... Mr. Pedro PINEIRO
22 Dir Affirmative Action/Diversity .... Ms. Cynthia ROUNTREE
96 Director of Purchasing .... Mr. Surinder VIRK
86 Director Government Relations .... Mr. Jeffrey ROSENSTOCK
26 Director of Marketing .... Mr. Steve WHALEN
100 Chief of Staff .... Ms. Glenda GRACE

† The Clinical Psychology PhD is awarded through the CUNY Graduate Center.

*City University of New York Queensborough Community College (F)

222-05 56th Avenue, Bayside NY 11364-1497
County: Queens FICE Identification: 002697
Unit ID: 190673
Telephone: (718) 631-6262 Carnegie Class: Assoc/Pub-U-MC
FAX Number: N/A Calendar System: Semester
URL: www.qcc.cuny.edu
Established: 1958 Annual Undergrad Tuition & Fees (In-District): $4,800
Enrollment: 16,403 Coed
Affiliation or Control: State/Local IRS Status: 501(c)3
Highest Offering: Associate Degree
Program: Occupational; 2-Year Principally Bachelor's Creditable

Accreditation: M, ACBSP, ADNUR, ENGT

02 President .... Dr. Diane CALL
05 Provost/Vice Pres Academic Affairs .... Dr. Paul MARCHESE
10 Vice Pres Finance & Admin .... Mr. William FAULKNER
30 Vice Pres Institutional Advancement .... Ms. Rosemary S. ZINS
32 Vice President Student Affairs .... Mr. Michel HODGE
15 Dean Human Resource/Labor Rels .... Ms. Liza LARIOS
51 VP Continuing Ed/Workforce Dev .... Ms. Denise WARD
108 Int VP Strategic Plng/Assessment .... Dr. Karen B. STEELE
88 Dean Accred Assessment .... Dr. Arthur CORRADETTI
13 Chief Information Technology Ofcr .... Mr. George SHERMAN
08 Chief Librarian .... Ms. Jeanne GALVIN
06 Registrar .... Ms. Ann TULLIO
37 Financial Aid Exec Director .... Ms. Veronica LUKAS
07 Asst Dean Admissions & Recruitment .... Ms. Laura BRUNO
09 Director of Institutional Research .... Ms. Elisabeth LACKNER
16 Personnel Officer .... Ms. Ellen ADAMS
26 Exec Dir Communications/Marketing .... Mr. Stephen DI DIO
19 Director of Safety & Security .... Mr. Edward LOCKE
22 Chief Diversity Officer .... Ms. Josephine PANTALEO
04 Executive Assistant to President .... Ms. Millie CONTE
104 Dir Ctr for Intl Stds/Study Abroad .... Ms. Lampeto (Betty) EFTHYMIOU
90 Exec Dir Academic Computing Center .... Mr. Bruce NAPLES
18 Chief Admin Superintendent .... Mr. Joseph CARTOLANO
36 Director of Career Services .... Ms. Constance PELUSO
44 Development Officer .... Ms. Meghan GETTING-STRAESSER
21 Exec Dir Finance & Admin Services .... Mr. David WASSERMAN
45 Exec Dir Budget/Resource Planning .... Mr. Mark CARPENTIER
20 Dean for Academic Operations .... Mr. Glenn BURDI
35 Asst Dean of Student Development .... Dr. Brian KERR

*City University of New York Stella and Charles Guttman Community College (A)

50 West 40th Street, New York NY 10018
County: New York Identification: 667126
Unit ID: 475565
Telephone: (646) 313-8000 Carnegie Class: Not Classified
FAX Number: N/A Calendar System: Semester
URL: www.guttman.cuny.edu
Established: 2011 Annual Undergrad Tuition & Fees (In-District): $4,852
Enrollment: 691 Coed
Affiliation or Control: State/Local IRS Status: 501(c)3
Highest Offering: Associate Degree
Program: Occupational; 2-Year Principally Bachelor's Creditable
Accreditation: @M, NY

02 President .... Scott EVENBECK
05 Provost and Vice President .... Joan M. LUCARIELLO
10 Vice Pres Admin & Finance .... Mary COLEMAN
45 Dean Strategic Plng & Effectiveness .... Stuart COCHRAN
09 Director of Institutional Research .... Elisa HERTZ
100 Chief of Staff .... Linda MERIANS
13 Chief Info Technology Officer (CIO) .... John STROUD
15 Director Human Resources .... Nila BHAUMIK
18 Director Facilities Planning .... Shirley LAW
19 Director Public Safety .... Anastasia KOUTSIDIS
37 Director Student Financial Aid .... Vera SENESE
06 Registrar .... Cortes MARISOL
07 Director of Admissions .... So SOPHEA
86 Director Government Relations .... Manny LOPEZ

*City University of New York York College (B)

94-20 Guy Brewer Boulevard, Jamaica NY 11451-0001
County: Queens FICE Identification: 004759
Unit ID: 190691
Telephone: (718) 262-2000 Carnegie Class: Bac/Diverse
FAX Number: (718) 262-2730 Calendar System: Semester
URL: www.york.cuny.edu
Established: 1966 Annual Undergrad Tuition & Fees (In-District): $6,330
Enrollment: 8,520 Coed
Affiliation or Control: State/Local IRS Status: 501(c)3
Highest Offering: Master's
Program: Liberal Arts And General; Teacher Preparatory; Professional
Accreditation: M, ARCPA, MT, NUR, OT, SW, TED

02 President .... Dr. Marcia V. KEIZS
05 Provost/Sr VP for Academic Affs .... Dr. Panayiotis MELETIES
10 VP of Adm & Finance/COO .... Mr. Ronald C. THOMAS
32 Vice Pres for Student Development .... Vacant
100 Dean for the Executive Office .... Dr. William V. DINELLO
49 Dean School of Arts & Sciences .... Dr. Donna CHIRICO
83 Dean Sch of Health & Behavioral Sci .... Dr. Lynne CLARK
50 Dean Sch of Business & Info Systems .... Vacant
43 Labor & Legal Affairs .... Ms. Qiana WATSON
15 Assoc Exec Director HR .... Ms. Barbara MANUEL
13 Chief Information Officer .... Mr. Peter TIGHE
09 Director Institutional Research .... Dr. Aghajan MOHAMMADI
06 Registrar .... Ms. Sharon DAVIDSON
08 Chief Librarian .... Ms. Njoki KINYATTI
90 Director of Academic Computing .... Dr. Che-Tsao HUANG
86 Dir of Govt and Community Relations .... Mr. Earl G. SIMONS
19 Interim Director of Security .... Lt. Tamara BAILEY
37 Director of Financial Aid .... Ms. Beverly BROWN
18 Director Campus Planning .... Mr. Noel GAMBOA
35 Director Student Activites .... Dr. Jean PHELPS
36 Director Career Services .... Ms. Linda H. CHESNEY
25 Dir Research/Sponsored Programs .... Ms. Dawn HEWITT
38 Interim Director of Counseling .... Dr. Jayoung CHOI
41 Athletic Director .... Mr. Ronald ST. JOHN
04 Executive Asst to the President .... Ms. Sandra BELL ADAMS
07 Director of Admissions .... Dr. Latoro YATES
29 Director Alumni Relations .... Ms. Mondell SEALY
30 Chief Development/Advancement .... Ms. Dolores SWIRIN-YAO
28 Director of Diversity .... Ms. Gail MARSHALL
96 Director of Purchasing .... Ms. Rashmi MALESH

Clarkson University (C)

8 Clarkson Ave, Potsdam NY 13699
County: St. Lawrence FICE Identification: 002699
Unit ID: 190044
Telephone: (315) 268-6400 Carnegie Class: RU/H
FAX Number: (315) 268-7647 Calendar System: Semester
URL: www.clarkson.edu
Established: 1896 Annual Undergrad Tuition & Fees: $44,630
Enrollment: 3,873 Coed
Affiliation or Control: Independent Non-Profit IRS Status: 501(c)3
Highest Offering: Doctorate
Program: Liberal Arts And General; Professional; Technical Emphasis
Accreditation: M, ARCPA, BUS, ENG, PTA

01 President .... Dr. Anthony G. COLLINS
05 Senior Vice President & Provost .... Dr. Charles E. THORPE
26 Vice Pres External Relations .... Mrs. Kelly O. CHEZUM
32 Vice Pres Outreach & Stdnt Affairs .... Ms. Kathryn B. JOHNSON
30 Vice Pres Devel & Alumni Relations .... Mr. Patrick ROCHE
88 Assoc VP Student Success .... Mrs. Catherine MCNAMARA
10 Chief Financial Officer .... Mr. James D. FISH
13 Chief Information Officer .... Mr. Joshua A. FISKE
54 Dean of Engineering .... Dr. William JEMISON
50 Dean of Business .... Dr. Dayle M. SMITH
49 Dean of Arts & Sciences .... Dr. Peter TURNER
07 Dean of Admissions .... Mr. Brian T. GRANT
35 Dean of Students/Assoc VP Alumni .... Mr. Stephen NEWKOFSKY
15 Exec Director Human Resources .... Vacant
21 Controller .... Mrs. Donna MARTELL
41 Director Athletics & Recreation .... Mr. Steven J. YIANOUKOS
45 Director Budget & Planning .... Mrs. Allison S. ALDRICH
19 Director Campus Safety & Security .... Mr. David W. DELISLE
36 Director Career Center .... Mr. Jeffrey D. TAYLOR
102 Assoc Dir Corp & Foundation Rels .... Mrs. Elizabeth COLELLO
38 Exec Dir Counseling & Health Svcs .... Mr. James PITTMAN
18 Director Facilities & Services .... Mr. Ian HAZEN
37 Director Financial Aid .... Mrs. Pamela NICHOLS
92 Director Honors Program .... Mr. Jonathan D. GOSS
85 Director Intl Students & Scholars .... Mrs. Tess C. CASLER
08 Director Libraries .... Ms. Michelle L. YOUNG
96 Dir Payroll/Purchasing/Risk Mgmt .... Mr. George GIORDANO
46 Director Research & Tech Transfer .... Mr. Gregory C. SLACK
88 Director Student Administration .... Mrs. Suzanne E. DAVIS
23 Director Student Health Services .... Mrs. Susan KNOWLES
105 Director Web Development .... Mrs. Julie DAVIS
06 Registrar .... Mrs. Karen J. BURKUM
39 Assoc Dean for Residence Life .... Mr. Mark DERITIS
29 Assoc Director Alumni Relations .... Ms. Teresa PLANTY
09 Assoc Director Institutional Rsrch .... Mrs. Jenna STONE
84 Enrollment Officer .... Mr. Scott TOTH
25 Contract & Grant Administrator .... Ms. Anna Marie DAWLEY
106 Distance Learning Coordinator .... Mrs. Laura PERRY
40 Bookstore Manager .... Ms. Sara JOHNSON

Clinton Community College (D)

136 Clinton Point Drive, Plattsburgh NY 12901-9573
County: Clinton FICE Identification: 006787
Unit ID: 190053
Telephone: (518) 562-4200 Carnegie Class: Assoc/Pub-R-M
FAX Number: (518) 561-4890 Calendar System: Semester
URL: www.clinton.edu
Established: 1966 Annual Undergrad Tuition & Fees (In-District): $4,200
Enrollment: 1,890 Coed
Affiliation or Control: State/Local IRS Status: 501(c)3
Highest Offering: Associate Degree
Program: Occupational; 2-Year Principally Bachelor's Creditable
Accreditation: M, ADNUR, CSHSE

01 Interim President .... Mr. Frederick G. SMITH
05 Vice President for Academic Affairs .... Dr. Cheryl A. LESSER
10 Vice Pres for Admin/Business Affs .... Mrs. Lisa SHOVAN
32 Vice President for Student Affairs .... Mr. Edward KLEIN
30 Vice Pres InstitutionalAdvancement .... Mr. Steven G. FREDERICK
76 Dean Learning Resource Center .... Vacant
84 Assoc Dean Student Retention Svcs .... Vacant
09 Assoc Dean Inst Research/Planning .... Ms. Victoria DULEY
20 Assoc Dean of Academic Affairs .... Ms. Michele SNYDER
37 Interim Director of Financial Aid .... Ms. Mary LA PIERRE
07 Director Admissions .... Ms. Lauren CURRIE
06 Registrar .... Mr. Ronald SWEENEY
13 Mgmt Information Systems Director .... Mr. Rick BATCHELDER
15 Human Resource/Affirm Act Officer .... Vacant
26 Director of College Relations .... Vacant
18 Chief Facilities/Physical Plant .... Mr. John CONLEY

Cochran School of Nursing (E)

967 North Broadway, Yonkers NY 10701-1399
County: Westchester FICE Identification: 006443
Unit ID: 190071
Telephone: (914) 964-4282 Carnegie Class: Assoc/PrivNFP
FAX Number: (914) 964-4266 Calendar System: Semester
URL: www.cochranschoolofnursing.us
Established: 1894 Annual Undergrad Tuition & Fees: $12,032
Enrollment: 98 Coed
Affiliation or Control: Independent Non-Profit IRS Status: 501(c)3
Highest Offering: Associate Degree
Program: 2-Year Principally Bachelor's Creditable; Nursing Emphasis
Accreditation: ADNUR

01 Dean .... Dr. Ann Marie MCCALLISTER
08 Learning Resources Director .... Ms. Allyn KULK
06 Registrar .... Ms. Janee MCCOY
32 Dir Student Services/Finances .... Ms. Mirna PANTOJA

Cold Spring Harbor Laboratory/ Watson School of Biological Sciences (F)

PO Box 100, One Bungtown Road, Cold Spring Harbor NY 11724-0100
County: Suffolk FICE Identification: 034563
Unit ID: 436377
Telephone: (516) 367-6890 Carnegie Class: Not Classified
FAX Number: (516) 367-6919 Calendar System: Other
URL: www.cshl.edu
Established: 1890 Annual Graduate Tuition & Fees: N/A
Enrollment: 42 Coed
Affiliation or Control: Independent Non-Profit IRS Status: 501(c)3
Highest Offering: Doctorate; No Undergraduates
Program: Professional
Accreditation: NY

00 Chancellor Emeritis .... Dr. James D. WATSON
01 President .... Dr. Bruce STILLMAN
05 Dean .... Dr. Alexander GANN
20 Associate Dean .... Dr. Carrie COWAN

Colgate Rochester Crozer Divinity School (G)

1100 S Goodman Street, Rochester NY 14620-2589
County: Monroe FICE Identification: 002700
Unit ID: 190080
Telephone: (585) 271-1320 Carnegie Class: Spec/Faith
FAX Number: (585) 271-8013 Calendar System: Semester
URL: www.crcds.edu
Established: 1817 Annual Graduate Tuition & Fees: $10,770
Enrollment: 91 Coed
Affiliation or Control: Independent Non-Profit IRS Status: 501(c)3
Highest Offering: Doctorate; No Undergraduates
Program: Religious Emphasis
Accreditation: THEOL

01 President .... Dr. Marvin A. MCMICKLE
05 VP Academic Life & Dean of Faculty .... Prof. Stephanie L. SAUVE
10 Chief Financial Officer .... Mr. Gerald E. VANSTRYDONCK
84 Vice Pres of Enrollment Services .... Ms. Melissa MORRAL
30 VP Institutional Advancement .... Mr. W. Thomas MCDADE-CLAY
94 Dean of Women & Gender Studies .... Dr. Barbara MOORE
06 Registrar .... Ms. Andrea MASON
18 Director of Facilities .... Mr. Mark DEVINCENTIS
08 Director of Library Services .... Ms. Margaret A. NEAD
40 Director Bookstore .... Ms. Margaret A. NEAD
37 Director of Financial Aid .... Ms. Andrea MASON
26 Communications Coordinator .... Ms. Michele KAIDER-KOROL
07 Admissions Coordinator .... Ms. Polly BUSH
29 Director of Alumni Relations .... Mr. W. Thomas MCDADE-CLAY

Colgate University (H)

13 Oak Drive, Hamilton NY 13346-1386
County: Madison FICE Identification: 002701
Unit ID: 190099
Telephone: (315) 228-1000 Carnegie Class: Bac/A&S
FAX Number: (315) 228-7798 Calendar System: Semester
URL: www.colgate.edu
Established: 1819 Annual Undergrad Tuition & Fees: $49,970
Enrollment: 2,868 Coed
Affiliation or Control: Independent Non-Profit IRS Status: 501(c)3
Highest Offering: Master's
Program: Liberal Arts And General
Accreditation: M, TEAC

01 Interim President .... Jill HARSIN
101 VP/Sr Advisor/Sec Board of Trustees .... Robert L. TYBURSKI
05 Interim Dean of Faculty & Provost .... Constance HARSH
10 VP for Finance & Admin .... Brian HUTZLEY
26 AVP for Public Rels/Marketing .... Barbara BROOKS
30 Sr VP External Rels/Advancement .... Murray DECOCK
07 VP & Dean of Admiss/Financial Aid .... Gary L. ROSS
32 Vice Pres & Dean of the College .... Suzy NELSON
21 Associate Vice Pres/Controller .... Thomas O'NEILL
18 Assoc VP/Facilities & Cap Projects .... Annette ANGUEIRA
15 Assoc VP for Human Resources .... Lori CHLAD
20 Associate Dean of the Faculty .... Kenneth BELANGER
28 Assoc Provost Equity & Diversity .... Marilyn RUGG
06 Interim Registrar .... Tori CARHART
08 University Librarian .... Joanne SCHNEIDER
13 VP/Chief Information Officer .... Kevin LYNCH

29 AVP Inst Advancement/Alumni Affairs ... Tim MANSFIELD
37 Director of Financial Aid ... Marcelle TYBURSKI
109 AVP Cmty Affairs/Auxiliary Services ... Joanne BORFITZ
19 Director of Campus Safety ... William FERGUSON
36 AVP of Adv & Dir of Career Services ... Michael SCIOLA
41 VP & Director of Athletics ... Victoria CHUN
40 Dir Off-Campus Retail Operations ... Leslie PASCO
42 University Chaplain ... Mark SHINER
44 AVP Inst Advancement/Planned Giving ... Andrew CODDINGTON
38 Director Counseling/Psych Services ... Mark THOMPSON
96 Director of Purchasing ... Alan LEONARD
23 Director Student Health Services ... Merrill MILLER
94 Director Women's Studies ... Meika LOE
44 Director Annual Fund Operations ... Sara GROH
39 Director of Residential Housing ... Stacey MILLARD
09 Dir Institutional Planning/Research ... Brendt SIMPSON
04 Assistant to the President ... Claudia CARAHER
22 Dir EEO & Affirmative Action ... Tamala FLACK
102 Dir of Corp Foundation & Govt Rels ... Helen KEBABIAN
104 Int Director International Programs ... Carol DROGUS

College of Mount Saint Vincent (A)

6301 Riverdale Avenue, Riverdale NY 10471-1093
County: Bronx FICE Identification: 002703
Unit ID: 193399
Telephone: (718) 405-3200 Carnegie Class: Master's S
FAX Number: (718) 601-6392 Calendar System: Semester
URL: www.mountsaintvincent.edu
Established: 1847 Annual Undergrad Tuition & Fees: $31,290
Enrollment: 1,475 Coed
Affiliation or Control: Independent Non-Profit IRS Status: 501(c)3
Highest Offering: Master's
Program: Liberal Arts And General; Teacher Preparatory; Professional
Accreditation: M, ACBSP, NURSE, TEAC

01 President ... Dr. Charles L. FLYNN
05 Provost/Dean of Faculty ... Dr. Sarah STEVENSON
20 Dean Undergraduate College ... Dr. Patrick VALDEZ
07 Sr VP for Admission/External Rels ... Ms. Madeleine MELKONIAN
10 Executive VP/Treasurer ... Mr. Abed ELKESHK
11 VP for Operations ... Mr. Kevin DEGROAT
32 Dean of Students ... Ms. Kelli BODRATO
88 Executive Director/Mission ... Vacant
30 Assoc VP Institutional Advancement ... Sr. Kathleen TRACEY, SC
51 Dean School Professional/Cont Stds ... Dr. Mitchell SAKOFS
06 Registrar ... Mrs. Jeannette PICHARDO
08 Director of Library ... Mr. Sebastian DERRY
13 VP Information Technology/CIO ... Mr. Adam WICHERN
09 Director of Institutional Research ... Sr. Carol M. FINEGAN, SC
36 Director Internships/Career Devel ... Vacant
37 Director of Financial Aid ... Ms. Lorena MATOS
42 Dir Campus Ministry/Act Dir Mission ... Mr. Mathew SHIELDS
35 Dir of Student Affairs/Assoc Dean ... Dr. Gabrielle OCCHIOGROSSO
41 Acting Director Athletics & Recreat ... Mr. Barima YEBOAH
38 Director Counseling Services ... Ms. Vicki HALLAS
23 Director of Health Services ... Mrs. Eileen MCCABE
29 Dir Alumnae Relations/Annual Giving ... Mr. Michael QUINN
26 Assoc Director of College Relations ... Ms. Leah MUNCH
19 Dir Campus Safety/Security ... Mr. Paul RUNG
66 Director of Nursing ... Dr. Susan SALADINO
44 Assoc Dir Alumnae Resl/Annual Giv ... Mr. Michael SIN
15 Director of Human Resources ... Mr. Joseph BEHAN
21 Controller ... Mr. Ping XIE
04 Assistant to the President ... Ms. Catherine MCKENNA
18 Director of Facilities & Operations ... Mr. Ryan ANDERSON
07 Director of Admissions ... Ms. Jackie WILLIAMS
92 Director of Honors Program ... Dr. Heather ALUMBAUGH
97 Director of Core Curriculum ... Dr. Robert JACKLOSKY

The College of New Rochelle (B)

29 Castle Place, New Rochelle NY 10805-2338
County: Westchester FICE Identification: 002704
Unit ID: 193645
Telephone: (914) 654-5000 Carnegie Class: Master's L
FAX Number: (914) 654-5554 Calendar System: Semester
URL: www.cnr.edu
Established: 1904 Annual Undergrad Tuition & Fees: $33,600
Enrollment: 3,740 Coed
Affiliation or Control: Independent Non-Profit IRS Status: 501(c)3
Highest Offering: Master's
Program: Liberal Arts And General; Teacher Preparatory; Professional
Accreditation: M, NURSE, SW, TEAC

01 President ... Mrs. Judith A. HUNTINGTON
05 Sr Vice Pres Acad Affairs & Provost ... Dr. Dorothy A. ESCRIBANO
11 Senior VP for Strategic Initiatives ... Dr. Colette GEARY
10 Vice President Financial Affairs ... Dr. Betty ROBERTS
32 Vice President Student Services ... Ms. Elaine T. WHITE
84 VP for Enrollment Managment ... Mr. Kevin CAVANAGH
30 Vice President College Advancement ... Ms. Brenna S. MAYER
49 Dean School of Arts & Sciences ... Dr. Danielle WOZNIAK
58 Interim Dean of the Graduate School ... Dr. David DONNELLY
51 Dean School of New Resources ... Dr. Darryl JONES
66 Dean School of Nursing ... Dr. H. Michael DREHER
06 Registrar ... Ms. Tania QUINN
08 Dean of the Library ... Ms. Ana FONTOURA
37 Director of Financial Aid ... Ms. Anne C. PELAK
36 Interim Dir of Career Development ... Ms. Mariela TORRES
15 Director of Human Resources ... Ms. JoEllen L. VAVASOUR
18 Director of Facilities Management ... Mr. Fred SULLO
09 Director of Institutional Research ... Ms. Nancy KOTONIAS
21 Controller ... Mr. Keith BORGE
13 Chief Info Technology Officer (CIO) ... Mr. Warren ANDREWS
19 Director Security/Safety ... Mr. Rodney SAMUELS

The College of Saint Rose (C)

432 Western Avenue, Albany NY 12203-1490
County: Albany FICE Identification: 002705
Unit ID: 195234
Telephone: (518) 454-5111 Carnegie Class: Master's L
FAX Number: (518) 438-3293 Calendar System: Semester
URL: www.strose.edu
Established: 1920 Annual Undergrad Tuition & Fees: $29,826
Enrollment: 4,003 Coed
Affiliation or Control: Independent Non-Profit IRS Status: 501(c)3
Highest Offering: Master's
Program: Liberal Arts And General; Teacher Preparatory
Accreditation: M, ACBSP, ART, MUS, SP, SW, TED

01 President ... Dr. Carolyn J. STEFANCO
04 Assistant to President ... Ms. Debra LIBERATORE
05 Provost/VP Academic Affairs ... Dr. Hadi SALAVITABAR
10 Interim Chief Operating Officer ... Mr. Tom MAHER
32 Vice President Student Services ... Mr. Dennis MCDONALD
84 Vice Pres of Enroll Mgmt ... Mrs. Mary M. GRONDAHL
15 Assoc Vice Pres Human Res/Risk Mgt ... Mr. Jeffrey KNAPP
07 Asst VP of Undergrad Admissions ... Mr. Jeremy BOGAN
07 Asst VP of Graduate Admissions ... Ms. Susan PATTERSON
37 Asst VP of Financial Aid ... Mr. Steven W. DWIRE
26 VP of PR and Strategic Comm ... Mrs. Lisa HALEY-THOMSON
35 Asst VP Student Affairs ... Ms. Mary R. MCLAUGHLIN
18 AVP for Facilities ... Vacant
42 Dean of Spiritual Life ... Vacant
86 Exec Dir of Govt Community Affairs ... Mr. Michael D'ATTILIO
90 Exec Dir of Info Technology Service ... Mr. John ELLIS
29 Director Alumni Relations ... Ms. Lorrie PIZZOLA
30 Asst VP Institutional Advancement ... Ms. Lisa MCKENZIE
21 Assoc VP for Finance & Comptroller ... Ms. Debra Lee POLLEY
06 Registrar ... Ms. Judith KELLY
08 Director of Library ... Mr. Andrew URBANEK
39 Director Residence Life ... Ms. Jennifer RICHARDSON
36 Director Career Development Center ... Ms. Michelle OSBORNE
38 Clinical Dir Counseling/Psych Svcs ... Mr. Ronald J. HAMER
41 Director Athletics & Recreation ... Ms. Catherine A. HAKER
91 Director Administrative Info Sys ... Mr. William TRAVER
44 Director Annual Giving ... Mr. Jason MANNING
31 Director Community Services ... Mr. Kenneth SCOTT
42 Director of Campus Ministry ... Ms. Joan HORGAN
23 Director of Health Services ... Ms. Sandra FREHSE
19 Director of Safety/Security ... Mr. Steven STELLA
09 Exec Dir Budget & Inst Research ... Ms. Debra Lee POLLEY
28 Director of Diversity ... Ms. Shai BUTLER
38 Director of Advisement ... Dr. Kelly MEYER
88 Art Gallery Director ... Ms. Jeanne FLANAGAN
23 Director of Clinical Services ... Ms. Jacqueline KLEIN
96 Director Purchasing/Auxiliary Svcs ... Ms. Patricia BUCKLEY
27 Assoc Dir Media Relations ... Mr. Benjamin MARVIN
18 Dir of Facilities Planning & Mgmt ... Ms. Nancy MACDONALD
09 Director of Institutional Research ... Mrs. Lisa KEATING
40 Manager of Campus Store ... Mr. Chris WILSON
24 Dir of Computer/Media Services ... Mr. Michael STRATTON
04 Exec Admin Asst to the President ... Mrs. Julie KOCHAN

The College of Westchester (D)

PO Box 710, White Plains NY 10602-0710
County: Westchester FICE Identification: 005208
Unit ID: 197285
Telephone: (914) 948-4442 Carnegie Class: Assoc/PrivFP4
FAX Number: (914) 948-5441 Calendar System: Semester
URL: www.cw.edu
Established: 1915 Annual Undergrad Tuition & Fees: $22,350
Enrollment: 1,125 Coed
Affiliation or Control: Proprietary IRS Status: Proprietary
Highest Offering: Baccalaureate
Program: Business Emphasis
Accreditation: M

00 Chairman Emeritus ... Mr. Ernest H. SUTKOWSKI
01 President & CEO ... Mrs. Mary Beth DEL BALZO
03 Senior Executive VP & COO ... Vacant
05 Provost/VP Academic Affairs ... Dr. Warren ROSENBERG
88 Vice President Special Projects ... Mr. Dale T. SMITH
20 Dean Academic Services ... Ms. Daphne GALKIN
84 Sr Director Enrollment Management ... Mr. Matt CURTIS
36 Director of Career Services ... Ms. Joann SONDEY
88 Dir of Student Success/Retention ... Dr. Judith LILLESTON
37 Dir of Student Financial Services ... Mrs. Dianne PEPITONE

Columbia-Greene Community College (E)

4400 Route 23, Hudson NY 12534-9543
County: Columbia FICE Identification: 006789
Unit ID: 190169
Telephone: (518) 828-4181 Carnegie Class: Assoc/Pub-R-S
FAX Number: (518) 828-8543 Calendar System: Semester
URL: www.sunycgcc.edu
Established: 1966 Annual Undergrad Tuition & Fees (In-District): $4,552
Enrollment: 2,014 Coed
Affiliation or Control: State/Local IRS Status: 501(c)3
Highest Offering: Associate Degree
Program: Occupational; 2-Year Principally Bachelor's Creditable
Accreditation: M, ADNUR

01 President ... Mr. James R. CAMPION
05 VP & Dean of Academic Affairs ... Ms. Phyllis CARITO
10 Vice Pres & Dean of Administration ... Mr. A. Joseph MATTIES
32 VP/Dean of Students/Enrollment Mgmt ... Dr. Joseph WATSON
38 Counselor ... Ms. Diane JOHNSON
18 Director Building & Grounds ... Mr. James FOLZ
26 Director Public Information ... Mr. Allen KOVLER
37 Dir Stndt Fin Aid/Asst Dean Stdnts ... Mr. Joel PHELPS
21 Assistant Dean of Administration ... Ms. Dianne TOPPLE
06 Acting Registrar ... Ms. Gail SHADER
13 Director Information Systems ... Mr. Gino RIZZI
15 Director of Human Resources ... Ms. Melissa FANDOZZI
22 Affirmative Action Officer ... Ms. Melissa FANDOZZI
09 Director of Institutional Research ... Mr. Casey O'BRIEN
31 Director of Community Services ... Mr. Robert BODRATTI
41 Athletic Director ... Mr. Walter RICKARD
88 Director Academic Support Center ... Dr. Mary-Teresa HEATH
103 Director of Workforce Development ... Ms. Mary Alane WILTSE
07 Director of Admissions ... Mr. Josh HORN
30 Dir of Development & Alumni Svcs ... Ms. Joan KOWEEK
20 Assistant Dean of Academic Affairs ... Ms. Carol DOERFER
21 Bursar ... Ms. Christy DECKER
19 Director of Security ... Mr. John LEONE
96 Purchasing Officer ... Ms. Patricia DAY
62 Department Chair Library Services ... Ms. Geralynn DEMAREST
83 Div Chair Behavioral/Social Science ... Mr. Ted HILSCHER
81 Div Chair Math & Science ... Ms. Siri CARLISLE
57 Division Chair Arts & Humanities ... Mr. Michael ALLARD
66 Division Chair Nursing ... Ms. Dawn WRIGLEY
72 Division Co-Chair Technology ... Ms. Marcia FITZGERALD
72 Division Co-Chair Technology ... Ms. Susan ROBERTS

Columbia University in the City of New York (F)

615 West 131st Street, New York NY 10027-6902
County: New York FICE Identification: 002707
Unit ID: 190150
Telephone: (212) 854-1754 Carnegie Class: RU/VH
FAX Number: (212) 851-7022 Calendar System: Semester
URL: www.columbia.edu
Established: 1754 Annual Undergrad Tuition & Fees: $51,008
Enrollment: 27,589 Coed
Affiliation or Control: Independent Non-Profit IRS Status: 501(c)3
Highest Offering: Doctorate
Program: Liberal Arts And General; Professional
Accreditation: M, ANEST, BUS, CEA, DENT, ENG, HSA, IPSY, JOUR, LAW, MED, MIDWF, NURSE, OT, PH, PLNG, PTA, SPAA, SW

01 President ... Mr. Lee C. BOLLINGER
05 Provost ... Dr. John COATSWORTH
49 Exec Vice Pres Arts & Sciences ... Mr. David MADIGAN
76 Exec VP Health/Biomed Sciences ... Dr. Lee GOLDMAN
09 Exec Vice President Research ... Dr. G. Michael PURDY
86 Exec Vice Pres Govt & Cmty Affairs ... Ms. Maxine F. GRIFFITH
43 General Counsel ... Ms. Jane E. BOOTH
26 Exec Vice Pres Communications ... Mr. David M. STONE
101 Secretary of the University ... Mr. Jerome DAVIS
10 Exec Vice President for Finance ... Ms. Anne R. SULLIVAN
18 Exec Vice President Facilities ... Mr. David GREENBERG
88 Exec Vice President Global ... Mr. Safwan M. MASRI
30 Exec Vice Pres Development & Alumni ... Ms. Amelia J. ALVERSON
88 Special Advisor to the President ... Ms. Susan K. FEAGIN
32 Exec Vice President University Life ... Ms. Suzanne B. GOLDBERG
41 Athletic Director ... Mr. Peter E. PILLING
88 Ombuds Officer ... Ms. Joan WATERS
100 Chief of Staff to President ... Ms. Susan K. GLANCY
88 CEO IMC-Ofc of Univ Investments ... Mr. Nirmal P. NARVEKAR
20 Vice Provost Academic Programs ... Dr. Melissa D. BEGG
20 Vice Provost Faculty Affairs ... Mr. Christopher L. BROWN
88 Vice Provost for Academic Planning ... Dr. Andrew R. DAVIDSON
11 Vice Provost Administration ... Mr. Troy EGGERS
88 Vice Provost Teaching & Learning ... Soulaymane KACHANI
28 Vice Provost Diversity & Inclusion ... Dr. Dennis MITCHELL
08 Vice Provost & Univ Librarian ... Ms. Ann D. THORNTON
48 Dean Grad School Arch/Plng/Preserv ... Ms. Amale ANDRAOS
57 Dean School of the Arts ... Dr. Carol BECKER
58 Dean Grad School of Arts & Science ... Dr. Carlos J. ALONSO
50 Dean Graduate School of Business ... Dr. R. Glenn HUBBARD
49 Dean Columbia College ... Dr. James J. VALENTINI
51 Dean School Continuing Education ... Mr. Jason M. WINGARD
54 Dean Sch Engr/Applied Science ... Dr. Mary C. BOYCE
82 Dean School Intl/Public Affairs ... Ms. Merit E. JANOW
97 Dean School General Studies ... Dr. Peter AWN
60 Dean Graduate School Journalism ... Mr. Stephen W. COLL
61 Dean School of Law ... Ms. Gillian LESTER
70 Dean School of Social Work ... Dr. Jeanette C. TAKAMURA
63 Dean Faculty of Medicine ... Dr. Lee GOLDMAN
52 Dean Sch Dental & Oral Surgery ... Dr. Christian S. STOHLER
66 Dean School of Nursing ... Dr. Bobbie BERKOWITZ
69 Dean School of Public Health ... Dr. Linda P. FRIED
38 Exec Director Student Counseling ... Dr. Richard EICHLER
37 Assoc VP Student Financial Svcs ... Ms. Jane HOJAN-CLARK
06 Assoc Vice Pres & Registrar ... Mr. Barry S. KANE
07 Dean of Undergraduate Admissions ... Ms. Jessica MARINACCIO

† Parent institution of Barnard College and Teachers College, Columbia University.

Concordia College (A)

171 White Plains Road, Bronxville NY 10708-1923

County: Westchester — FICE Identification: 002709
Unit ID: 190248
Telephone: (914) 337-9300 — Carnegie Class: Bac/Diverse
FAX Number: (914) 395-4500 — Calendar System: Semester
URL: www.concordia-ny.edu
Established: 1881 — Annual Undergrad Tuition & Fees: $28,940
Enrollment: 1,037 — Coed
Affiliation or Control: Lutheran Church - Missouri Synod
IRS Status: 501(c)3
Highest Offering: Master's
Program: Liberal Arts And General; Teacher Preparatory; Professional
Accreditation: M, NURSE, SW, TED

01 President .... Dr. Viji D. GEORGE
10 Chief Financial Officer .... Mr. Theodore FRANCAVILLA
11 Vice Pres Administration .... Mr. Lloyd WARDLEY
30 Vice Pres Advancement .... Mr. James BUNN
43 Director of Legal Affairs .... Ms. Arlene TORRES
05 Provost .... Dr. Sherry J. FRASER
20 Vice Prov of Undergraduate Pgms .... Dr. Mandana NAKHAI
66 Dean of Nursing .... Dr. Kathleen FLAHERTY
88 Dean of Adult Education & Business .... Dr. William M. SALVA
42 Campus Chaplain .... Rev Dr. Joshua HOLLMANN
32 Dean of Students .... Mr. Michael KUSH
06 Registrar .... Mr. Mark E. BLANCO
08 Library Director .... Mr. William L. PERRENOD
38 Director of Counseling .... Ms. Marilyn AMES
41 Athletic Director .... Mr. Ivan MARQUEZ
23 Director Health Services .... Ms. Susan CRANE
37 Director Financial Aid .... Mr. Christopher D'AMBROSIO
18 Director Support Services .... Mr. Paul A. SCHULZ
26 Senior Director of Marketing .... Mr. North CALLAHAN
42 Director of Church Relations .... Ms. Kathy DRESSER
84 VP of Enrollment Management .... Mr. Donald VOS
31 Dir of Cmty Life & Judicial Affairs .... Vacant
92 Director of Honors Program .... Dr. Kate E. BEHR
15 Director of Human Resources .... Ms. Terry VIDAL
13 Director of Information Services .... Mr. Aaron J. MEYER
21 Business Manager .... Mr. Edward J. MCPARTLAN
44 Director of Development .... Vacant
35 Director of Student Success .... Ms. Johanna L. PERRY
36 Director of Student Placement .... Ms. Lois DIERLAM
88 Dean of Teacher Education .... Ms. Christine ROWE
85 Dir of Intl Stdtn Recruitment/Advis .... Ms. Claire ZHOU
29 Dir of Alumni Relations .... Mr. William DEITTE
104 Vice Prov Pgm Dev & Intl Education .... Dr. James BURKEE
09 Director of Institutional Research .... Ms. Kimberly GARGIULO
102 Dir Foundation/Corporate Relations .... Ms. Joyce KENNEDY
103 Dir Workforce/Career Development .... Ms. Laura GREVI
19 Manager of Campus Safety .... Mr. Stephen BONURA
106 Dir Online Education/E-learning .... Dr. Michael SCHLABRA
108 Director Institutional Assessment .... Ms. Kimberly GARGIULO

Cooper Union (B)

30 Cooper Square, New York NY 10003-7120

County: New York — FICE Identification: 002710
Unit ID: 190372
Telephone: (212) 353-4100 — Carnegie Class: Bac/Diverse
FAX Number: (212) 353-4244 — Calendar System: Semester
URL: www.cooper.edu
Established: 1859 — Annual Undergrad Tuition & Fees: $40,800
Enrollment: 949 — Coed
Affiliation or Control: Independent Non-Profit — IRS Status: 501(c)3
Highest Offering: Master's
Program: Liberal Arts And General; Professional
Accreditation: M, ART, ENG

01 President .... Jamshed BHARUCHA
10 Vice President Finance and Admin .... William MEA
26 Vice President of External Affairs .... Vacant
30 Acting VP of Development .... Chris CLOUD
100 Chf of Staff/Secy Board of Trustees .... Lawrence CACCIATORE
07 VP Enrollment Svcs/Dean Admissions .... Mitchell LIPTON
32 VP Student Affs/Community Relation .... Stephen BAKER
57 Dean of Art .... Saskia BOS
48 Acting Dean of Architecture .... Elizabeth O'DONNELL
79 Dean Humanities/Social Sciences .... William GERMANO
08 Acting Head Librarian .... Carol SALOMON
21 Dir Budget/Personnel/Inst Research .... Steven GLEIMER
44 Director of Institutional Giving .... Vacant
06 Registrar .... Vacant
46 Director of Research .... Vacant
26 Vice President of Communications .... Justin HARMON
13 Chief Technology Officer .... Robert P. HOPKINS
09 Director Assessment & Innovation .... Gerardo DEL CERRO
88 Director of Off Campus Programming .... Margaret MORTON
18 Director of Facilities Mgmt .... Carmelo PIZZUTO
51 Director of Continuing Education .... David GREENSTEIN
36 Director of Career Services .... Robert THILL
24 Director of Audiovisual/Media .... Paul TUMMOLO
35 Dean of Students .... Christopher CHAMBERLIN
91 Director of Administrative Database .... Sue MCCOY

† Every student receives a full-tuition scholarship.

Cornell University (C)

Day Hall Lobby, Ithaca NY 14850

County: Tompkins — FICE Identification: 002711
Unit ID: 190415
Telephone: (607) 255-2000 — Carnegie Class: RU/VH
FAX Number: (607) 255-5396 — Calendar System: Semester
URL: www.cornell.edu
Established: 1865 — Annual Undergrad Tuition & Fees: $49,116
Enrollment: 21,850 — Coed
Affiliation or Control: Independent Non-Profit — IRS Status: 501(c)3
Highest Offering: Doctorate
Program: Liberal Arts And General; Professional
Accreditation: M, BUS, CIDA, DIETD, DIETI, ENG, HSA, LAW, LSAR, PLNG, @TEAC, VET

01 President .... Elizabeth GARRETT
05 Provost .... Michael I. KOTLIKOFF
63 Prov Medical Affairs/Dean Med Col .... Laurie GLIMCHER
20 Sr Vice Provost Academic Affairs .... John A. SILICIANO
46 Senior Vice Provost Research .... Robert A. BUHRMAN
58 Senior Vice Prov & Dean Grad School .... Barbara A. KNUTH
88 Interim Vice Prov for Intl Affairs .... Laura M. SPITZ
88 Vice Provost .... Judith A. APPLETON
45 Vice Pres Planning & Budget .... Paul STREETER
30 Interim VP Alumni Affairs & Develop .... Jeffrey M. MCCARTHY
15 Vice President Human Resources .... Mary George G. OPPERMAN
32 VP Student & Campus Life .... Ryan T. LOMBARDI
26 Vice Pres for University Relations .... Joel M. MALINA
27 Vice President Univ Communications .... Tracy VOSBURGH
86 Associate VP for Govt Relations .... Charles KRUZANSKY
88 Vice Provost Cornell NYC Tech .... Daniel S. HUTTENLOCHER
43 University Counsel & Secretary Corp .... James J. MINGLE
10 VP Financial Affairs/CFO .... Joanne M. DESTEFANO
13 CIO and VP for Info Technology .... Thomas E. DODDS
18 Vice President Facilities/Services .... Kyu-Jung WHANG
84 Assoc Vice Provost Enrollment .... Jason LOCKE
21 University Controller .... Aimee L. TURNER
21 Assoc Vice President/Treasurer .... Harper WATTERS
21 University Auditor .... Glen C. MULLER
20 Dean of Faculty .... Joseph A. BURNS
47 Dean Col Agriculture/Life Sciences .... Kathryn J. BOOR
48 Dean College Arch/Art/Planning .... Kent KLEINMAN
49 Dean College Arts & Science .... Gretchen RITTER
54 Dean College of Engineering .... Lance R. COLLINS
88 Dean School Hotel Administration .... Michael D. JOHNSON
59 Dean College Human Ecology .... Alan D. MATHIOS
50 Dean Johnson Graduate School Mgmt .... Soumitra DUTTA
50 Dean Industrial/Labor Rels .... Kevin F. HALLOCK
61 Dean Law School .... Eduardo M. PEÑALVER
74 Dean College Veterinary Medicine .... Lorin D. WARNICK
77 Dean of Computing and Info Science .... Greg MORRISETT
51 Dean Cont Education/Summer Session .... Glenn C. ALTSCHULER
08 University Librarian .... Anne R. KENNEY
88 Director Africana Studies/Research .... Gerard L. ACHING
07 Dir Undergraduate Admissions .... Shawn FELTON
37 Director Financial Aid .... Susan HITCHCOCK
35 Dean of Students .... Kent L. HUBBELL
06 University Registrar .... Cassandra C. DEMBOSKY
41 Director Athletics/Physical Educ .... J. Andrew NOEL, JR.
36 Director of Cornell Career Services .... Rebecca M. SPARROW
22 Assoc VP Wrkfrce Dvrsty & Inclusion .... Lynette CHAPPELL-WILLIAMS
23 Assoc Vice Pres Campus Health .... Janet L. CORSON-RIKERT
93 Dean of Students .... Renee T. ALEXANDER
28 Assoc Vice Provost Acad Diversity .... Andrew T. MILLER
28 Assoc Vice Provost Facult Diversity .... Yael LEVITTE
42 Dir Cornell United Religious Works .... Kenneth I. CLARKE
25 Assoc Vice Pres Research Admin .... Catherine E. LONG
25 Sr Director Sponsored Fin Svcs .... Jeffrey A. SILBER
19 Chief Cornell Police .... Kathy R. ZONER
96 Sr Dir Procurement and Bus Svcs .... Thomas W. ROMANTIC
29 Assoc Vice Pres Alumni Affairs .... James A. MAZZA
09 Director Inst Research/Planning .... Marin E. CLARKBERG

† Parent institution of Weill Medical College of Cornell University.

Corning Community College (D)

One Academic Drive, Corning NY 14830-3297

County: Steuben — FICE Identification: 002863
Unit ID: 190442
Telephone: (607) 962-9011 — Carnegie Class: Assoc/Pub-R-M
FAX Number: (607) 962-9456 — Calendar System: Semester
URL: www.corning-cc.edu
Established: 1956 — Annual Undergrad Tuition & Fees (In-District): $4,930
Enrollment: 4,514 — Coed
Affiliation or Control: State/Local — IRS Status: 501(c)3
Highest Offering: Associate Degree
Program: Occupational; 2-Year Principally Bachelor's Creditable
Accreditation: M, ADNUR

01 President .... Dr. Katherine P. DOUGLAS
05 Vice President Academic Affairs .... Dr. Marian EBERLY
11 Vice President Administrative Svcs .... Mr. Thomas F. CARR
32 Vice Pres & Dean of Student Devel .... Ms. Joan BALLINGER
30 Exec Dir Institutional Advancement .... Mr. William LITTLE
08 Director Learning Resources Center .... Ms. Sarah WEISMAN
06 Registrar .... Ms. Karen BOULAS
07 Director of Admissions .... Ms. Karen BROWN
15 Director Human Resources .... Ms. Nannette NICHOLAS
10 Chief Business Officer .... Mr. Thomas F. CARR
18 Chief Facilities/Physical Plant .... Mr. Calvin WILLIAMS
37 Director Student Financial Aid .... Mrs. Barbara SNOW
09 Research Analyst .... Ms. Virginia RUDNICK

The Culinary Institute of America (E)

1946 Campus Drive, Hyde Park NY 12538-1499

County: Dutchess — FICE Identification: 007304
Unit ID: 190503
Telephone: (845) 905-4288 — Carnegie Class: Spec/Other
FAX Number: (845) 452-0165 — Calendar System: Semester
URL: www.ciachef.edu
Established: 1946 — Annual Undergrad Tuition & Fees: $29,250
Enrollment: 2,778 — Coed
Affiliation or Control: Independent Non-Profit — IRS Status: 501(c)3
Highest Offering: Baccalaureate
Program: Occupational; 2-Year Principally Bachelor's Creditable; Technical Emphasis
Accreditation: M

01 President .... Dr. Tim RYAN
10 Senior VP Finance/Administration .... Ms. Maria KRUPIN
30 VP Advancement & Business Develop .... Dr. Victor GIELISSE
05 Provost .... Mr. Mark ERICKSON
07 VP Admissions & Marketing .... Mr. Bruce HILLENBRAND
11 VP Administration & Shared Svcs .... Mr. Richard MIGNAULT
45 Vice President of Strategy .... Ms. Rose S. WANG
20 Vice Pres Academic Affairs .... Dr. Michael SPERLING
32 Assoc VP & Dean of Student Affairs .... Dr. Kathleen MERGET
35 Assoc Dean Student Activities .... Mr. David WHALEN
38 Director Counseling Services .... Dr. Daria PAPALIA
09 Director Assessment & Inst Research .... Ms. Elizabeth CARROLL
27 Director of Communications .... Mr. Stephen HENGST
23 Director Health Services .... Ms. Katherine MILLER
21 Director Finance & Accounting .... Mr. Steven STROM
96 Director Purchasing & Storeroom .... Mr. Brad MATTHEWS
88 Dir Student Financial & Reg Svcs .... Ms. Linda TERWILLIGER
18 Director Facilities .... Mr. Thomas M. HIRST
19 Director Safety .... Mr. William CAREY
37 Director Financial Aid .... Ms. Kathleen GAILOR
44 Senior Advancement Officer .... Ms. Denise ZANCHELLI
88 Dean Academic Support Services .... Ms. Carolyn TRAGNI
12 Assoc VP Branch Campuses .... Ms. Susan CUSSEN
88 Dean Culinary Arts .... Mr. Brendan WALSH
88 Dean Baking & Pastry Arts .... Mr. Thomas VACCARO
49 Dean of Liberal Arts & Business Mgt .... Vacant
108 Dir Inst Liaison & Accreditation .... Ms. Sharon ZRALY
06 Registrar .... Mr. Chester KOULIK
36 Director Career Services .... Ms. Theresa HOPKINS
08 Director Library & Information Sys .... Mr. Jon GRENNAN
13 Chief of Staff/CIO .... Mr. Rick TIETJEN
88 Director Compliance .... Ms. Maura KING
15 Director HR Administration .... Ms. Shaynan GARRIOCH
04 Administrative Asst to President .... Ms. Shannon CAMPER
102 Senior Advancement Officer .... Ms. Elly ERICKSON

Daemen College (F)

4380 Main Street, Amherst NY 14226-3592

County: Erie — FICE Identification: 002808
Unit ID: 190725
Telephone: (716) 839-3600 — Carnegie Class: Master's L
FAX Number: (716) 839-8516 — Calendar System: Semester
URL: www.daemen.edu
Established: 1947 — Annual Undergrad Tuition & Fees: $25,995
Enrollment: 2,720 — Coed
Affiliation or Control: Independent Non-Profit — IRS Status: 501(c)3
Highest Offering: Doctorate
Program: Liberal Arts And General; Teacher Preparatory; Professional
Accreditation: M, ARCPA, CAATE, IACBE, NUR, PTA, SW, TEAC

01 President .... Dr. Gary A. OLSON
05 Vice Pres Academic Affairs/Dean .... Dr. Michael S. BROGAN
10 VP for Business Affairs & Treasurer .... Mr. Richard G. SCHOTT
30 Vice Pres Institutional Advancement .... Dr. Richanne C. MANKEY
84 VP of Enrollment Management .... Dr. Patricia R. BROWN
32 VP Student Affairs/Dean of Students .... Dr. Greg J. NAYOR
20 Assoc VP Academic Affairs .... Dr. Kathleen C. BOONE
07 Dean of Admissions .... Mr. Frank S. WILLIAMS
21 Controller & Assistant Treasurer .... Ms. Lisa A. ARIDA
91 Director Information Resources Mgmt .... Mr. Brian J. WILKINS
13 Chief Information Technolog Officer .... Ms. Kelly DURAN
09 Director of Institutional Research .... Dr. Patricia L. BEAMAN
108 Assoc VP of Inst Effectivness .... Dr. Mimi H. STEADMAN
08 Director of RIC and Library Service .... Mr. Francis J. CAREY
06 Registrar .... Ms. Irene HOLOHAN-MOYER
88 Exec Dir for Academic Advisement .... Ms. Sabrina FENNELL
37 Director Financial Aid .... Mr. Jeffrey M. PAGANO
15 Director of Human Resources .... Mrs. Pamela R. NEUMANN
26 Dir of Institutional Communication .... Ms. Paula WITHERELL
44 Director of Annual Giving .... Mr. Justin JOHNSTON
78 Director of Career Services .... Dr. Maureen MILLANE
39 Dir of Housing & Residence Life .... Ms. Danielle WEAVER
35 Director of Student Activities .... Mr. Christopher P. MALIK
18 Director of Physical Plant .... Mr. Don PHILLIPS
19 Director Security & Fire Safety .... Mr. Kevin BAKER
42 Director Campus Ministry .... Rev. Cassandra L. SALTER-SMITH
41 Director of Athletics .... Ms. Bridget NILAND
96 Dir of Purchasing/Central Services .... Ms. Gwendolyn M. WALKER
92 Director of Honors Program .... Dr. Matthew WARD
29 Director Alumni Relations .... Ms. Katie M. GRAF
40 Bookstore Manager .... Ms. Jaclyn HERNE
88 Dir of New Program Development .... Ms. Susan M. MARCHIONE

Davis College (A)

400 Riverside Drive, Johnson City NY 13790-2714
County: Broome FICE Identification: 021691
Unit ID: 194569
Telephone: (607) 729-1581 Carnegie Class: Spec/Faith
FAX Number: (607) 729-2962 Calendar System: Semester
URL: www.davisny.edu
Established: 1900 Annual Undergrad Tuition & Fees: $12,915
Enrollment: 396 Coed
Affiliation or Control: Independent Non-Profit IRS Status: 501(c)3
Highest Offering: Baccalaureate
Program: Professional; Religious Emphasis
Accreditation: M, BI

01 Chief Executive Officer Dr. Dino J. PEDRONE
03 Provost Dr. Keith MARLETT
05 Academic Dean Dr. Gilbert A. PARKER
84 Enrollment Management Officer Mr. Rick CRAMER
32 Student Development Officer Mrs. Nichole POST
11 Operating Officer Vacant
10 Financial Officer Mr. Larry ELLIS
04 Assistant to the President Mr. Corey ADAMS
06 Registrar Mrs. Susan VANDEVENTER
08 Library Manager Mrs. Shelley BYRON
37 Director Financial Aid Mr. William REICHEL
88 Assistant to the Provost Miss Naomi SARAVANAPAVAN

Dominican College of Blauvelt (B)

470 Western Highway, Orangeburg NY 10962-1210
County: Rockland FICE Identification: 002713
Unit ID: 190761
Telephone: (845) 848-7800 Carnegie Class: Master's S
FAX Number: (845) 359-2313 Calendar System: Semester
URL: www.dc.edu
Established: 1952 Annual Undergrad Tuition & Fees: $26,450
Enrollment: 1,980 Coed
Affiliation or Control: Independent Non-Profit IRS Status: 501(c)3
Highest Offering: Doctorate
Program: Liberal Arts And General; Teacher Preparatory; Professional
Accreditation: M, CAATE, IACBE, NURSE, #OT, PTA, SW, TEAC

01 President Sr Dr. Mary Eileen O'BRIEN
00 Chancellor Sr. Kathleen SULLIVAN
05 Vice Pres/Dean Academic Affairs Dr. Thomas S. NOWAK
84 Vice Pres of Enrollment Management Mr. Brian FERNANDES
32 Dean of Students Mr. John BURKE
10 Director of Fiscal Affairs Mr. Anthony CIPOLLA
06 Registrar Ms. Mary MCFADDEN
07 Director of Admissions Mr. Daniel MENDOZA
08 Librarian Ms. Jennifer SHELTON
30 Director of Inst Advancement Ms. Dorothy FILORAMO
15 Director Human Resources Ms. Marybeth BRODERICK
26 Chief Public Relations Officer Mr. Brett BEKRITSKY
29 Director Alumni Relations Ms. Mary MCHUGH
35 Director Student Activities Ms. Katrina REDMOND
09 Inst Research/Plng/Assessment Ofcr Dr. Shao-Wei WU
37 Director Student Financial Aid Ms. Stacy SALINAS
36 Director Student Placement Ms. Evelyn FISKAA
38 Director Student Couseling Ms. Alise COHEN
21 Controller Ms. Joanne PORETTE
13 Director Information Technology Mr. Russell DIAZ
18 Chief Facilities/Physical Plant Mr. Michael DEMPSEY
20 Associate Academic Officer Ms. Ann VAVOLIZZA
39 Director Student Housing Mr. Ryan O'GORMAN
41 Athletic Director Mr. Joseph CLINTON
42 Director Campus Ministry Sr. Barbara MCENEANY
96 Director of Purchasing Ms. Amy BIANCO
28 Director of Diversity Vacant
19 Director of Security/Safety Mr. John LENNON
42 Chaplain Vacant
31 Dir Cmty Engagemt/Ldrship Develop Ms. Melissa GRAU

Dowling College (C)

Idle Hour Boulevard, Oakdale NY 11769-1999
County: Suffolk FICE Identification: 002667
Unit ID: 190770
Telephone: (631) 244-3000 Carnegie Class: Master's L
FAX Number: (631) 563-7831 Calendar System: Semester
URL: www.dowling.edu
Established: 1959 Annual Undergrad Tuition & Fees: $29,100
Enrollment: 2,024 Coed
Affiliation or Control: Independent Non-Profit IRS Status: 501(c)3
Highest Offering: Doctorate
Program: Liberal Arts And General; Teacher Preparatory; Professional
Accreditation: M, AAB, IACBE, TED

01 President Dr. Albert INSERRA
05 Provost Dr. Richard T. WILKENS
32 Dean of Student Affairs Mr. Thomas DALY
10 VP for Business & Finance Mr. Ralph CERULLO
41 VP of Athletics Ms. Melody COPE
21 Associate VP Business and Finance Ms. Jaclyn CARLO
84 Assistant VP Enrollment Services Mr. Jonathan WHITE
50 Dean School of Business Mr. Brucs HALLER
53 Dean School of Education Dr. Robert MANLEY
49 Dean School of Arts & Sciences Dr. Brian STIPELMAN
15 Exec Director Human Resources Ms. Anne DIMOLA
18 Exec Dir Safety/Facil/Compliance Mr. Robert CAMPBELL
06 Registrar Ms. Cathryn MOONEY
37 Director of Financial Svcs Ms. Carla GUEVARA
96 Director of Purchasing Mr. Michael KLOTZ
13 Dir of Information Technology Svcs Mr. Walter BENKA
108 Dean of Assessment Dr. Patrick JOHNSON

Dutchess Community College (D)

53 Pendell Road, Poughkeepsie NY 12601-1595
County: Dutchess FICE Identification: 002864
Unit ID: 190840
Telephone: (845) 431-8000 Carnegie Class: Assoc/Pub-R-L
FAX Number: (845) 431-8984 Calendar System: Semester
URL: www.sunydutchess.edu
Established: 1957 Annual Undergrad Tuition & Fees (In-District): $3,665
Enrollment: 9,904 Coed
Affiliation or Control: State/Local IRS Status: 501(c)3
Highest Offering: Associate Degree
Program: Occupational; 2-Year Principally Bachelor's Creditable; Business Emphasis
Accreditation: M, ADNUR, EMT, MLTAD

01 President Dr. Pamela R. EDINGTON
05 VP of Academic Affairs Dr. Ellen M. GAMBINO
32 VP & Dean of Student Services Dr. Carol STEVENS
10 VP & Dean of Administration Mr. William ANDERSON
20 Associate Dean of Academic Affairs Ms. Colleen TROGISCH
20 Associate Dean of Academic Affairs Mr. Michael BODEN
20 Associate Dean of Academic Affairs Dr. Holly MOLELLA
31 Dean Community Svcs/Special Pgms Ms. Virginia STOEFFEL
21 Associate Dean Administration Ms. Donna ROCAP
06 Interim Registrar Mr. William BENEDETTO
84 Associate Dean of Enrollment Mgmt Mr. Michael ROE
08 Director of the Library Ms. Cathy CARL
14 Director Information Systems Mr. Patrick GRIFFIN
30 Director Institutional Advancement Ms. Diana POLLARD
09 Director Planning/Inst Research Ms. Donna JOHNSON
24 Director Telecomm/Instructnl Media Vacant
37 Director Financial Aid Ms. Susan MEAD
36 Director Counseling/Career Svcs Mr. Michael BALABAN
15 Director Human Resources Mgmt Ms. Esther COURET
18 Assoc Dean of Admin Facilities Mgmt . Ms. Bridgette ANDERSON
19 Director Campus Security Mr. Ed COX
13 Assoc Dean Admin Info Technology Mr. Klaus GESSLER
88 Asst Director Systems Arch & Info Mr. Howard IGNAL
35 Director of Student Activities Mr. Michael WEIDA
26 Chief Public Relations Officer Ms. Judi STOKES
88 Assoc Dir Teaching Learning Center Ms. Chrisie MITCHELL
88 Director of Scheduling Ms. Virginia POZNACK
12 Director DCC South Branch Mr. Timothy DECKER
04 Assistant to the President Ms. AnneMarie ANDREWS
101 Secretary to the Board of Trustees Ms. Linda M. BEASIMER
22 Dir Affirmative Action/EEO Ms. Esther COURET
39 Director Residence Life Ms. Christina LANDETA

D'Youville College (E)

320 Porter Avenue, Buffalo NY 14201-1084
County: Erie FICE Identification: 002712
Unit ID: 190716
Telephone: (716) 829-8000 Carnegie Class: Master's L
FAX Number: (716) 829-7820 Calendar System: Semester
URL: www.dyc.edu
Established: 1908 Annual Undergrad Tuition & Fees: $23,900
Enrollment: 3,025 Coed
Affiliation or Control: Independent Non-Profit IRS Status: 501(c)3
Highest Offering: Doctorate
Program: Liberal Arts And General; Teacher Preparatory; Professional; Nursing Emphasis
Accreditation: M, CHIRO, ARCPA, DIETC, IACBE, NURSE, OT, PHAR, PTA

01 President Sr. Denise A. ROCHE, GNSH
05 Vice President for Academic Affairs Dr. Arup SEN
10 Vice President Financal Affairs Mr. John GARFOOT
32 VP Student Affairs & Enroll Mgmt Mr. Robert P. MURPHY
30 Vice Pres Institutional Advancement Ms. Kathleen CHRISTY
11 Associate Vice Pres of Operations Vacant
88 VP Admin Svcs & External Relations Dr. William MARIANI
06 Registrar Mr. Daryl SMITH
66 Dean School of Nursing Dr. Judith LEWIS
49 Dean Sch of Arts/Sciences & Educ Dr. Jason ADSIT
67 Dean School of Pharmacy Vacant
76 Dean School of Health Professions Vacant
88 Artistic Director Kavinoky Theater Mr. David LAMB
35 Associate VP for Student Affairs Mr. Jeffrey PLATT
35 Assistant VP for Student Affairs Mr. Anthony SPINA
21 Bursar Mrs. Lisa HIGGINS
21 Controller Ms. Laurie HALL
09 Dir Inst Rsrch & Assessment Support Mr. Mark ECKSTEIN
91 Director Administrative Computing Mr. Robert HALL
29 Director Alumni Relations Ms. Meg RITTLING
44 Director Annual Giving Mrs. Aimee PEARSON
41 Director Athletics Mr. Brian CAVANAUGH
42 Director Campus Ministry Fr. Patrick O'KEEFE
36 Director Career Services Center Ms. Christine DEMCIE
88 Director College Center Ms. Deborah E. OWENS
14 Director Computer & Network Svcs Ms. Mary SPENCE
102 Director Foundation Relations Mr. William P. MCKEEVER
25 Director Government Grants Mrs. Laurie Ann STAHL
23 Director Health Center Mrs. Nicole CONROE
15 Director Human Resources Ms. Linda MORETTI
85 Director International Stdnt Svcs Mrs. Laryssa PETRYSHYN
88 Director Learning Center Mrs. Christina SPINK-FORMANSKI
08 Director Library Services Mr. Rand BELLAVIA
44 Director Major & Planned Gifts Ms. Patricia VAN DYKE
28 Director Multicultural Affairs Mrs. Yolanda WOOD
38 Director Personal Counseling Ms. Kimberly ZITTEL
26 Director Public Relations Mr. D. John BRAY
19 Director of Security Mr. Jeremy SMITH
37 Director Student Financial Aid Mr. Matthew METZ
07 Director Undergraduate Admissions Dr. Steve SMITH
07 Director Graduate Admissions Mr. Mark PAVONE
07 Director Intl Admiss & Marketing Mr. Ronald DANNECKER
88 Director Veterans Affairs Office Mr. Benjamin RANDLE
13 Chief Information Officer Mr. Roozbeh TAVAKOLI
51 Director Prof Development Center Mrs. Catherine HUBER

Elim Bible Institute (F)

7245 College Street, Lima NY 14485
County: Livingston Identification: 667245
Telephone: (800) 670-3546 Carnegie Class: Not Classified
FAX Number: (585) 582-8130 Calendar System: Semester
URL: www.elim.edu
Established: 1924 Annual Undergrad Tuition & Fees: $7,880
Enrollment: N/A Coed
Affiliation or Control: Independent Non-Profit IRS Status: 501(c)3
Highest Offering: Associate Degree
Program: Religious Emphasis
Accreditation: @TRACS

01 President Mike CAVANAUGH

The Elmezzi Graduate School of Molecular Medicine (G)

350 Community Drive, Manhasset NY 11030-3828
County: Nassau Identification: 666671
Telephone: (516) 562-3405 Carnegie Class: Not Classified
FAX Number: (516) 562-1022 Calendar System: Other
URL: www.elmezzigraduateschool.org
Established: 1999 Annual Graduate Tuition & Fees: N/A
Enrollment: 8 Coed
Affiliation or Control: Independent Non-Profit IRS Status: 501(c)3
Highest Offering: Doctorate; No Undergraduates
Program: Professional; Technical Emphasis
Accreditation: NY

01 President Dr. Kevin J. TRACEY
05 Dean Dr. Bettie STEINBERG
20 Associate Dean Dr. Annette LEE
10 Chief Business Officer Ms. Cynthia HAHN
101 Secretary of the Institution/Board Mr. Laurence KRAEMER
11 Chief of Administration Ms. Emilia HRISTIS
19 Director Security/Safety Mr. Robert KIKEL
25 Director Contracts/Grants Admin Ms. Rita NIGRI

Elmira Business Institute (H)

Langdon Plaza, 303 N Main Street, Elmira NY 14901-3086
County: Chemung FICE Identification: 009043
Unit ID: 190974
Telephone: (888) 986-6561 Carnegie Class: Assoc/PrivFP
FAX Number: (607) 733-7178 Calendar System: Semester
URL: www.ebi-college.com
Established: 1858 Annual Undergrad Tuition & Fees: $19,400
Enrollment: 400 Coed
Affiliation or Control: Proprietary IRS Status: Proprietary
Highest Offering: Associate Degree
Program: Occupational; 2-Year Principally Bachelor's Creditable
Accreditation: ACICS, MAC

01 President Mr. Brad C. PHILLIPS
11 Vice President of Administration Mrs. Kathleen M. HAMILTON
05 Chief Academic Officer Vacant
32 Dean of Students Dr. Brian MCCONNELL
35 Director of Student Services Ms. Lindsay N. DULL
10 Corporate Accountant Ms. Erin MCCANN
07 Regional Director of Admissions Mr. Scott GALELEI
26 Regional Director of PR & Grad Svc Mr. Josh PATTON

Elmira Business Institute (I)

4100 Old Vestal Road, Vestal NY 13850
Telephone: (607) 729-8915 Identification: 770745
Accreditation: ACICS

† Branch campus of Elmira Business Institute, Elmira, NY.

Elmira College (J)

One Park Place, Elmira NY 14901-2099
County: Chemung FICE Identification: 002718
Unit ID: 190983
Telephone: (607) 735-1800 Carnegie Class: Bac/Diverse
FAX Number: (607) 735-1758 Calendar System: Other
URL: www.elmira.edu
Established: 1855 Annual Undergrad Tuition & Fees: $39,700
Enrollment: 1,482 Coed
Affiliation or Control: Independent Non-Profit IRS Status: 501(c)3
Highest Offering: Master's
Program: 2-Year Principally Bachelor's Creditable; Liberal Arts And General; Teacher Preparatory; Professional; Business Emphasis
Accreditation: M, NUR, TEAC

01 President Dr. Ronald O. CHAMPAGNE
10 Vice President & Treasurer Dr. Robert W. RUBLE
05 Academic Vice President Dr. Stephen F. COLEMAN
30 Vice Pres Institutional Advancement Dr. James T. BARRY
84 Vice Pres of Enrollment Management Mr. Christopher R. COONS
100 Vice President and Chief of Staff Mr. Michael B. ROGERS
41 Vice President of Athletics Ms. Patricia A. THOMPSON
32 Dean of Students Mr. Brandon T. DAWSON
51 Dean of Continuing Education Ms. Jeanne M. ESCHBACH
07 Dean of Admissions Mr. Brett C. MOORE
37 Dean of Financial Aid Ms. Kathleen L. COHEN
06 Registrar Mr. Michael HALPERIN
08 Dean of Library Ms. Elizabeth M. WAVLE-BROWN
36 Director of Career Services Mr. Michael D. BLASIC
50 Dept Chair of Business/Economics Prof. Philip M. HURDLE
57 Dept Chair of Creative Arts Prof. John J. KELLY
79 Dept Chair of Humanities Dr. Mitchell R. LEWIS
81 Dept Chair of Math/Natural Sciences Dr. Todd P. EGAN
83 Dept Chair of Soc/Behavior Science Dr. Jim TWOMBLY
107 Dept Chair of Professional Programs Dr. Linda PRATT
29 Director of Alumni Relations Ms. Ellen HIMMELREICH
66 Dean of Health Sciences Dr. Kathy T. LUCKE
18 Director of Facilities Management Ms. Tessa MOORE
105 Dir of Web Comm & Digital Media Ms. Kiersten RAY
39 Director of Residence Life Vacant
40 Dir of Bookstore & Special Projects Mrs. Shannon MOYLAN
15 Director of Human Resources Ms. Carey L. SENECA
09 Director of Institutional Research Ms. Karen L. JOHNSON
20 Assoc Dean Fac/Dir Acad Advising Dr. Charles W. LINDSAY
26 Exec Dir of Communications & Mktg Mr. Wade BENNETT
13 Chief Information Officer Mr. Brian CORNELL
19 Director of Campus Security Mr. Gary D. MILLER
44 Director of Annual Giving Mr. Kyle A. SMITH
102 Director of Grants Ms. Valerie R. ROSPLOCK
23 Dir of Health Services & Counseling Ms. Marjorie C. HITCHCOCK
04 Exec Assistant to the President Mrs. Mary C. BARRETT

Erie Community College (A)

121 Ellicott Street, Buffalo NY 14203-2698
County: Erie FICE Identification: 010684
Unit ID: 191083
Telephone: (716) 842-2770 Carnegie Class: Assoc/Pub-U-MC
FAX Number: (716) 851-1129 Calendar System: Semester
URL: www.ecc.edu
Established: 1971 Annual Undergrad Tuition & Fees (In-District): $5,183
Enrollment: 12,737 Coed
Affiliation or Control: State/Local IRS Status: 501(c)3
Highest Offering: Associate Degree
Program: Occupational; 2-Year Principally Bachelor's Creditable
Accreditation: M, ACFEI, ADNUR, CAHIIM, COARC, DH, DIETT, DT, EMT, ENGT, MAC, MLTAD, OPD, OTA, RTT

01 President Mr. Jack F. QUINN
11 Sr Vice Pres for Operations Mr. Michael PIETKIEWICZ
05 Exec Vice Pres Academic Affairs Mr. Richard C. WASHOUSKY
20 Associate Vice President Academics Dr. Edward J. HOLMES
88 Assoc VP Academic Transition Pgms Vacant
32 Exec Vice President Student Affairs Mr. Benjamin PACKER
35 Associate VP Student Services Dr. Marsha D. JACKSON
35 Dean of Students City Ms. Petrina HILL-CHEATOM
35 Dean of Students North Ms. Barbara M. RIEMAN
35 Dean of Students South Ms. Heather A. CRUZ
43 Exec Vice Pres Legal Affairs Ms. Kristin KLEIN-WHEATON
23 Associate Vice Pres Health Sciences Mr. Patrick J. WILES
13 Assoc Vice Pres/Chief Info Officer Mr. Joseph W. STEWART
14 Director of ERP Sys & Info Svcs Mr. David L. ARLINGTON
19 Assoc Vice President Security Vacant
102 Associate Vice Pres Foundation Mr. Jeffrey BAGEL
10 Chief Admin & Financial Officer Mr. William D. REUTER
109 Coordinator Institutional Services Mr. Joel J. DAMIANI
15 Human Resources Director Ms. Tracey CLEVELAND
16 Assistant Director Human Resources Ms. Maria CARROLL
103 Exec Dean Workforce Dev/Cmty Svcs Ms. Carrie W. KAHN
49 Asst Acad Dean Liberal Arts City Dr. Marcia A. GELLIN
49 Asst Acad Dean Liberal Arts North Ms. Mary A. BEARD
49 Asst Acad Dean Liberal Arts South Mr. Richard D. WOLCOTT
50 Asst Academic Dean Business Dr. Kenneth J. BARNES
56 Asst Acad Dean Distance Learning Ms. Martha J. DIXON
72 Assistant Academic Dean Technology Mr. Mark S. HOEBER
78 Coordinator Internships/Coop Ms. Margaret ARCADI
28 Director of Equity & Diversity Ms. Darley WILLIS
06 Director of Registration Mr. Paul A. LAMANA
06 Registrar City Ms. Rochelle WEBBER
06 Registrar South Ms. Cynthia LUDLOW
07 Director of Admissions Ms. Rahsanica HOWARD
84 Asst VP Enrollment Mgmt/Marketing Dr. Erik D'AQUINO
08 Librarian City Ms. Kathleen POWERS
08 Librarian North Mr. Matthew BEST
08 Librarian South Ms. Taheera SHAHEED-SONUBI
40 Bookstore Manager City Ms. Altricia GLISSON
40 Bookstore Manager North Ms. Teresa KALINOWSKI
88 Health Services Nurse City Ms. Frances WILLIAMS
88 Health Services Nurse North Ms. Rita A. BELZER
88 Health Services Nurse South Ms. Kelly ROCKWELL
36 Career Resource Center Director Mr. Michael M. GOLEBIEWSKI
36 Career Resource Center Coord City Ms. Katherine MARSHALL
36 Career Resource Center Coord North Mr. Joseph P. ABBARNO
26 Director of Public Relations Mr. Lance R. KONKLE
09 Director Institutional Research Ms. Marlene ARNO
45 Dir Assessment/Accreditation Vacant
27 Public Information Officer Mr. Michael FARRELL
41 Director of Athletics Mr. Peter J. JEREBKO
88 Assistant Director Athletics Mr. Steve L. MULLEN
18 Director Buildings & Grounds Mr. Anthony NESCI
37 Director of Financial Aid Mr. Scott WELTJEN
37 Financial Aid Coordinator City Ms. Charlotte M. COSTON
88 Financial Aid Asst Coordinator Ms. Robin FILIPPONE
21 Business Manager Mr. Paul F. DANIEU
24 Audio Visual Coordinator City Mr. Gregg S. FILIPPONE
24 Audio Visual Coordinator North Mr. Ryan NOGLE
24 Audio Visual Coordinator North Mr. Nicholas SONRICKER
24 Audio Visual Coordinator South Mr. David G. MALLORY
92 Coordinator Honors Program Vacant
88 Coordinator of Corporate Training Mr. John P. SLISZ
25 Grants Coordinator Mr. Michael J. BIGGANE
29 Director of Alumni Affairs Ms. Lindsey DOTSON
55 Asst Coordinator Evening Activities Vacant
04 Assistant to the President Mr. John FOLEY
85 Foreign Student Advisor Mr. John DANNA
88 Director of Student Access Dr. Marilou C. BLAIR
88 Advanced Studies Coordinator Ms. Deborah F. SCHMITT
88 Project Dir Transition Programs Ms. Joanne COLMERAUER

Excelsior College (B)

7 Columbia Circle, Albany NY 12203-5156
County: Albany FICE Identification: 002834
Unit ID: 196680
Telephone: (518) 464-8500 Carnegie Class: Master's M
FAX Number: (518) 464-8777 Calendar System: Other
URL: www.excelsior.edu
Established: 1971 Annual Undergrad Tuition & Fees: $38,825
Enrollment: 38,825 Coed
Affiliation or Control: Independent Non-Profit IRS Status: 501(c)3
Highest Offering: Master's
Program: Liberal Arts And General; Professional
Accreditation: M, ADNUR, ENGT, IACBE, NUR

01 President Dr. John F. EBERSOLE
100 Chief of Staff Dr. James BALDWIN
43 VP and General Counsel Mr. Joseph B. PORTER
84 VP Enrollment Management Mr. Craig MASLOWSKY
05 Chief Academic Officer/Provost Dr. Mary Beth HANNER
20 Vice Provost Dr. Patrick JONES
88 Associate Provost Dr. George TIMMONS
32 Assoc Provost Student & Fac Svcs Dr. Joan MIKALSON
88 Assistant Provost Ms. Emilsen HOLGUIN
13 VP Information Technology & CIO Dr. Wayne BROWN
15 Interim VP HR & Facilities Mr. James LETTKO
10 VP Finance & Administration Mr. John M. PONTIUS, JR.
30 VP Institutional Advancement Ms. Cathy KUSHNER
56 VP for Extended Education Ms. Chris MONTAGNINO
45 VP Strategy & IE Ms. Susan O'HERN
88 AVP for Analytics Dr. Lisa DANIELS
44 AVP Institutional Advancement Vacant
86 AVP for Government Relations Dr. Paul SHIFFMAN
43 Deputy Counsel Ms. Karen HALACO
88 AVP for Enrollment Management Mr. Thomas DALTON
21 AVP Budgets & Financial Analysis Mr. Todd S. THOMAS
13 AVP Information Technology Mr. Ronald MARZITELLI
16 AVP for Human Resources Ms. Anita BURNS
88 AVP Center for Military Ed Ms. Susan DEWAN
88 AVP COELAS Dr. Jennifer MCVAY-DYCHE
56 AVP Extended Education Dr. Susan KRYCZKA
88 AVP ESE Mr. Christopher GILMORE
21 Controller Ms. Hillary HARDING
49 Dean of Liberal Arts Dr. George TIMMONS
50 Dean of Business & Technology Dr. Karl LAWRENCE
66 Dean of Nursing Dr. Mary Lee POLLARD
76 Dean of Health Sciences Dr. Debbie SOPCZYK
97 Dean of Public Service Dr. Robert WATERS
88 Ombudsperson Ms. Kathy MORAN
88 Exec Director of CAPITAL Ms. Tina GRANT
88 Director Leadership Academy Dr. Murray BLOCK
108 Exec Director of IE Dr. Mohua BOSE
88 Exec Dir of Outreach Ms. Lynda HOLT
09 Exec Director of IR Dr. Nancy BECERRA-CORDOBA
06 Registrar Ms. Lori MORANO
07 Exec Director of Admissions Ms. Shannon EASTON
88 Exec Director of Outreach/Access Ms. Lisa LAVIGNA
88 Exec Dir Professional Dev Ms. Jennifer HUMMER
88 General Manager CEM Ms. Nurit SONNENSCHEIN
88 Exec Director of Marketing Ms. JoAnne LATHAM
30 Director of Development Ms. Marcy STRYKER
102 Director of Grants and Research Ms. Patricia CROOP
88 Director of Digital Engagement Mr. Donn AIKEN
88 Director of Technical Services Ms. Mare DONOHUE
88 Director of Business Intelligence Ms. Sophia BRAGA
88 Director of Applications Dev Mr. James SUN
88 Dir of Infrastructure and Security Mr. Scott GILREATH
88 Dir Enrollment Mgmt Ops Mr. Dan MERKT
88 Dir of Publications Ms. Maria SPARKS
29 Alumni Affairs Manager Ms. Renee KELLY
18 Chief Facilities/Physical Plant Mr. Robert RANALLI
88 Director of Hudson Whitman Press Ms. Susan PETRIE
88 Communications Manager Ms. Alicia JACOBS
88 PR Manager Mr. Michael LESCZINSKI
28 Diversity Coordinator Ms. Toby HAMLIN
88 Asst to Pres for Trustee Ms. Laurie KEENAN

Fashion Institute of Technology (C)

Seventh Avenue at 27 Street, New York NY 10001-5992
County: New York FICE Identification: 002866
Unit ID: 191126
Telephone: (212) 217-7999 Carnegie Class: Master's S
FAX Number: N/A Calendar System: Semester
URL: www.fitnyc.edu
Established: 1944 Annual Undergrad Tuition & Fees (In-District): $6,470
Enrollment: 9,764 Coed
Affiliation or Control: State/Local IRS Status: 501(c)3
Highest Offering: Master's
Program: 2-Year Principally Bachelor's Creditable; Professional
Accreditation: M, ART, CIDA

01 President Dr. Joyce F. BROWN
10 Treasurer/VP Finance/Administration Ms. Sherry F. BRABHAM
101 Secy of College/General Counsel Dr. Stephen TUTTLE
05 Vice President Academic Affairs Dr. Giacomo OLIVA
26 Vice Pres Comm/External Rels Ms. Loretta LAWRENCE KEANE
84 Acting VP Enrollment Mgmt/Student Dr. Kelly BRENNAN
84 Assistant VP Enrollment Services Vacant
15 Acting VP Human Res/Labor Rels Mr. Michael MOTTOLA
13 VP for Information Technology/CIO Mr. Gregg CHOTTINER
30 VP Develop & Exec Dir Mr. Robert FERGUSON
20 Assoc Vice Pres Academic Affairs Dr. Ronald MILON
88 Asst Vice Pres Human Res/Labor Rels Ms. Karen YUEN
21 Asst Vice Pres Finance Mr. Mark BLAIFEDER
21 Assistant VP of Administration Ms. Rebecca CORRADO
88 Asst VP Software Svcs/Info Access Mr. Van Buren WINSTON
27 Asst Vice Pres for Communications Ms. Carol LEVEN
04 Deputy to the President Ms. Shari PRUSSIN
20 Asst VP/Faculty & Academic Pgm Supp Dr. Yasemin JONES
32 Asst VP/Dean of Students Vacant
51 Dean Continuing & Prof Studies Vacant
57 Dean Art & Design Ms. Joanne ARBUCKLE
58 Dean School of Graduate Studies Dr. Mary DAVIS
49 Dean Liberal Arts Dr. Patrick KNISLEY
50 Dean Business & Technology Mr. Steven FRUMKIN
07 Dir of Admissions/Strat Recruiting Ms. Laura ARBOGAST DIMARCANTONIO
88 Director Special Events Ms. Vicki GURANOWSKI
11 Director Operational Services Mr. John WILSON
18 Executive Director of Facilities Mr. George JEFREMOW
22 Affirm Action Ofcr/Dir Compliance Ms. Griselda GONZALEZ
38 Director of the Counseling Center Ms. Terry GINDER
37 Director of Financial Aid Ms. Mina FRIEDMANN
08 Dir of the Gladys Marcus Library Mr. NJ BRADEEN
06 Director of Registration & Records Ms. Rita CAMMARATA
39 Director of Residental Life Ms. Ann Marie GRAPPO
36 Director Career & Internship Vacant
35 Director of Student Life Ms. Michelle VAN-ESS
23 Director of Health Services Ms. Anne MILLER
19 Director of Campus Safety Mr. Mario CABRERA
88 Director of The Museum at FIT Dr. Valerie STEELE
09 Asst Dean Inst Research & Effect Mr. Darrell GLENN
86 Dir Government/Community Relations Ms. Lisa WAGER
27 Exec Director of Public & Media Rel Ms. Cheri FEIN
104 Dean of International Programs Dr. Deirdre SATO
41 Director of Athletics & Recreation Ms. Kerri-Ann MCTIERNAN
96 Director of Budget Ms. Nancy SU
88 Dir of Education Opportunity Pgms Ms. Taur D. ORANGE
21 Controller/Assistant Treas Mr. John JOHNSTON
88 Int Dir Env Health/Sfty Compliance Mr. Paul DEBIASE
92 Coord Presidential Scholars Pgm Dr. Irene BUCHMAN
96 Director of Purchasing Vacant
105 Manager Digital Strategies Ms. Taryn REJHOLEC
55 Dir Evening/Weekend/Pre-College Ms. Michele NAGEL
29 Manager Alumni Engagement & Giving Vacant
102 Dir of Corporate & Foundation Rels Ms. Dirrane COVE
28 Chair of Diversity Council Ms. Griselda GONZALEZ
28 Chair of Diversity Council Mr. Michael COKKINOS

Fei Tian College (D)

140 Galley Hill Road, Cuddebackville NY 12729
County: Orange Identification: 667205
Telephone: (845) 672-0550 Carnegie Class: Not Classified
FAX Number: (845) 977-0481 Calendar System: Semester
URL: www.feitian.edu
Established: Annual Undergrad Tuition & Fees: $26,240
Enrollment: N/A Coed
Affiliation or Control: Independent Non-Profit IRS Status: 501(c)3
Highest Offering: Baccalaureate
Program: Liberal Arts And General; Fine Arts Emphasis
Accreditation: NY

01 President Ms. Vina LEE

Finger Lakes Community College (E)

3325 Marvin Sands Drive, Canandaigua NY 14424-8405
County: Ontario FICE Identification: 007532
Unit ID: 191199
Telephone: (585) 394-3522 Carnegie Class: Assoc/Pub-S-SC
FAX Number: (585) 394-5005 Calendar System: Semester
URL: www.flcc.edu
Established: 1965 Annual Undergrad Tuition & Fees (In-District): $5,154
Enrollment: 6,793 Coed
Affiliation or Control: State/Local IRS Status: 501(c)3
Highest Offering: Associate Degree
Program: Occupational; 2-Year Principally Bachelor's Creditable
Accreditation: M, ADNUR

01 President Dr. Barbara G. RISSER
05 Provost Ms. Kristen M. FRAGNOLI
10 Vice President of Admin/Treasurer Mr. James R. FISHER
84 Vice Pres Enrollment Management Ms. Carol S. URBAITIS

32 Assoc Vice Pres of Student Affairs .... Ms. Sarah E. WHIFFEN
20 Assoc VP Instruction & Assessment .... Dr. Karen TAYLOR
20 Assoc VP Academic Initiatives .... Mr. Jacob E. AMIDON
15 Director of Human Resources .... Ms. Grace H. LOOMIS
30 Chief Advancement Officer .... Mr. Joseph NAIRN
19 Dir of Campus Security Operations .... Mr. Jason R. MAITLAND
21 Controller .... Mr. Joseph L. DELFORTE
18 Director of Facilities & Grounds .... Ms. Catherine AHERN
07 Director of Admissions .... Ms. Bonnie B. RITTS
06 Registrar .... Mr. Michael FISHER
25 Director of Grants Development .... Ms. Karen A. VAN KEUREN
37 Director of Financial Aid .... Ms. Susan M. ROMANO
35 Director of Student Life .... Ms. Jennie ERDLE
13 Chief Information Officer .... Mr. John TAYLOR
38 Dir Educ Planning/Career Services ...... Ms. Corrine M. CANOUGH
36 Career Services Coordinator .... Ms. Tammie WOODY
08 Director Library Learning Resources .... Ms. Sarah MOON
26 Director of Marketing .... Ms. Heidi C. MARCIN
23 Director of Student Health Services .... Ms. Karen P Z. STEIN
24 Dir Instructional Technology .... Mr. Daniel P. FARSACI
09 Director Institutional Effectivenes .. Ms. Mary MCLEAN-SCANLON
29 Director of Alumni Relations .... Ms. Lisa L. SCOTT
96 Director of Business Services .... Ms. Andrea BARBER
72 Chair Science & Technology .... Dr. Melissa A. MILLER
50 Chair Business .... Ms. Mary M. WILSEY
65 Chair Environment Conservation Hort .... Ms. Ann B. SCHNELL
57 Chair Visual/Performing Arts .... Mr. Richard D. COOK
66 Chair Nursing .... Ms. Nancy E. CLARKSON
68 Chair Physical Education .... Mr. Dennis T. MOORE
81 Chair Computer Science .... Ms. April A. DEVAUX
79 Chair Humanities .... Mr. Jon A. PALZER
83 Chair Social Science .... Mr. Joshua W. HELLER
81 Chair Mathematics .... Ms. Theresa GAUTHIER

Finger Lakes Health College of Nursing (A)

196 North Street, Geneva NY 14456

County: Ontario — Identification: 667154 — Unit ID: 475422

Telephone: (315) 787-4005 — Carnegie Class: Not Classified

FAX Number: (313) 787-4770 — Calendar System: Semester

URL: www.flhealth.org/nursingeducation

Established: 2008 — Annual Undergrad Tuition & Fees: $11,190

Enrollment: 135 — Coed

Affiliation or Control: Independent Non-Profit — IRS Status: 501(c)3

Highest Offering: Associate Degree

Program: 2-Year Principally Bachelor's Creditable; Nursing Emphasis

Accreditation: **ADNUR**, SURTEC

01 Dean .... Victoria RECORD
32 Student Services Coordinator .... Ann DRAKE

Five Towns College (B)

305 North Service Road, Dix Hills NY 11746-6055

County: Suffolk — FICE Identification: 012561 — Unit ID: 191205

Telephone: (631) 656-2157 — Carnegie Class: Bac/Diverse

FAX Number: (631) 656-2172 — Calendar System: Semester

URL: www.ftc.edu

Established: 1972 — Annual Undergrad Tuition & Fees: $21,000

Enrollment: 687 — Coed

Affiliation or Control: Proprietary — IRS Status: Proprietary

Highest Offering: Doctorate

Program: 2-Year Principally Bachelor's Creditable; Liberal Arts And General; Teacher Preparatory; Professional; Music Emphasis

Accreditation: **M**, TED

01 Interim President .... Dr. Susan BARR
05 Interim Provost .... Ms. Carolann MILLER
10 Vice President of Finance .... Mr. Robert DANIELS
32 Dean of Students .... Dr. Jennifer ALBERT
06 Registrar .... Ms. Mara MALTZ
106 Director of Online Education .... Prof. Stephen GLEASON
37 Director of Financial Aid .... Mr. Jason LABONTE
08 Library Director .... Mr. John VANSTEEN
38 College Counselor .... Ms. Carolyn NEWMAN
64 Chair of Music Division .... Prof. Jeffrey LIPTON
50 Deputy Chair of Business Division .... Ms. Mary LOBIONDO
49 Chair of Liberal Arts Division .... Dr. Richard KELLEY
53 Chair of Education Division .... Mr. William FORTGANG
88 Chair of Film/Video .... Dr. Kathy CURTISS
88 Chair of Theatre Arts .... Mr. James BENEDUCE
36 Director Student Placement .... Ms. Krysti O'ROURKE
18 Chief Facilities/Physical Plant .... Mr. Mark SHAUGHNESSY
19 Director of Security .... Mr. Michael MORAN
39 Director of Residential Life .... Mr. Thomas O'BOYLE
07 Director of Admissions .... Ms. Ronnie MACDONALD

Fordham University (C)

441 East Fordham Road, Bronx NY 10458-9993

County: Bronx — FICE Identification: 002722 — Unit ID: 191241

Telephone: (718) 817-1000 — Carnegie Class: RU/H

FAX Number: (718) 817-4925 — Calendar System: Semester

URL: www.fordham.edu

Established: 1841 — Annual Undergrad Tuition & Fees: $46,120

Enrollment: 15,231 — Coed

Affiliation or Control: Independent Non-Profit — IRS Status: 501(c)3

Highest Offering: Doctorate

Program: Liberal Arts And General; Teacher Preparatory; Professional

Accreditation: **M**, BUS, CLPSY, COPSY, DANCE, LAW, SCPSY, SW, TED

01 President .... Rev. Joseph M. MCSHANE, SJ
04 Exec Assistant to the President .... Ms. Dorothy MARINUCCI
04 Assistant to the President .... Dr. Rosemary A. DEJULIO
05 Provost .... Dr. Stephen FREEDMAN
10 Sr VP & Chief Financial Officer .... Ms. Martha K. HIRST
21 Vice President for Finance .... Mr. Frank SIMIO
32 Vice President Student Affairs .... Mr. Jeffrey L. GRAY
13 VP for Information Technology .... Dr. Frank SIRIANNI
84 Vice President for Enrollment .... Dr. Peter A. STACE
12 Vice President for Lincoln Center .... Dr. Brian J. BYRNE
30 Vice President for Development .... Mr. Roger MILICI
88 Vice President for Mission/Ministry .... Msgr. Joseph G. QUINN
86 Vice President for Government Rels .... Mr. Thomas A. DUNNE
18 VP Facilities/Physical Plant .... Mr. Marc VALERA
11 Vice President for Administration .... Mr. Thomas A. DUNNE
20 Assoc Vice Pres Academic Affairs .... Dr. Benjamin CROOKER
20 Assoc Vice Pres Academic Affairs .... Dr. Ron JACOBSON
26 AVP Univ Marketing Communications ..... Ms. Catherine SPENCER
29 AVP/Director of Alumni Relations .... Mr. Michael GRIFFIN
07 Assoc Vice Pres Undgrad Enrollment .... Mr. John W. BUCKLEY
06 Asst Vice Pres Enrollment/Registrar .... Dr. Gene FEIN
37 Asst VP Student Financial Services .... Ms. Angela VAN DEKKER
86 Assoc Vice Pres for Government Rels .... Mr. Joseph P. MURIANA
101 Secretary of the University .... Ms. Margaret T. BALL
43 General Counsel .... Mr. Thomas E. DEJULIO
35 Dean of Students .... Mr. Christopher RODGERS
35 Dean of Student Services .... Mr. Gregory J. PAPPAS
12 Dean Fordham College at Rose Hill .... Dr. Maura B. MAST
58 Dean Graduate Arts & Science .... Dr. Eva BADOWSKA
73 Dean Graduate Religious Education .... Dr. C. Colt ANDERSON
50 Dean Gabelli Schools of Business .... Dr. Donna RAPACCIOLI
107 Dean Fordham Col of Prof Studies .... Dr. Isabel FRANK
12 Dean Fordham College Lincoln Center .... Rev. Robert GRIMES
53 Dean Graduate Education LC .... Dr. Virginia ROACH
61 Dean School of Law LC .... Mr. Matthew DILLER
70 Dean Graduate Social Service LC .... Dr. Debra MCPHEE
15 Exec Director of Human Resources .... Mr. Michael MINEO
09 Director Institutional Research .... Dr. Peter FEIGENBAUM
42 Executive Director Campus Ministry .... Rev. Jose-Luis SALAZAR, SJ
21 Controller .... Mr. Anthony GRONO
19 Director of Security .... Mr. John CARROLL
22 Administrative Policies Monitor .... Ms. Anastasia COLEMAN
46 Dir Research/Sponsored Programs .... Dr. Nancy BUSCH
08 Director of University Libraries .... Ms. Linda LOSCHIAVO
24 Director Media Center .... Mr. Jerry GREEN
23 Director of Health Center .... Ms. Kathleen MALARA
35 Assistant Dean of Students .... Ms. Alanna NOLAN
41 AVP of Athletic Alumni Relations ... Mr. Francis X. MCLAUGHLIN
96 Director of Procurement .... Mr. Frank A. DEORIO
38 Director of Psychological Svcs .... Dr. Jennifer NEUHOF
28 Director of Multicultural Programs .... Ms. Sofia BAUSTISTA PERTUZ
36 Director Career Services .... Ms. Stefany FATTOR

Fulton-Montgomery Community College (D)

2805 State Highway 67, Johnstown NY 12095-3790

County: Montgomery — FICE Identification: 002867 — Unit ID: 191302

Telephone: (518) 736-3622 — Carnegie Class: Assoc/Pub-R-M

FAX Number: (518) 762-4334 — Calendar System: Semester

URL: www.fmcc.edu

Established: 1963 — Annual Undergrad Tuition & Fees (In-District): $4,440

Enrollment: 2,589 — Coed

Affiliation or Control: State/Local — IRS Status: 501(c)3

Highest Offering: Associate Degree

Program: Occupational; 2-Year Principally Bachelor's Creditable

Accreditation: **M**, ADNUR, RAD

01 President .... Dr. Dustin SWANGER
05 Provost/Vice Pres Academic Affairs ... Dr. Greg TRUCKENMILLER
10 Vice Pres Finance & Administration .... Mr. David M. MORROW
32 Vice President of Student Affairs .... Ms. Jane KELLEY
20 Dean of Academic Affairs .... Ms. Diana PUTNAM
20 Assistant Dean of Academic Affairs .... Ms. Ronalyn WILSON
21 Director of Business Affairs .... Mr. Gregg WILBUR
13 Director of Information Technology .... Mr. Gregg ROTH
18 Director of Facilities .... Mr. Joshua FLEMMING
07 Director of Admissions .... Ms. Laura LAPORTE
06 Registrar .... Mr. Scott COLLINS
08 Librarian .... Ms. Mary DONOHUE
36 Director of Career Planning .... Ms. Andrea SCRIBNER
38 Director Advisement/Counseling/Test .... Ms. Mary-Jo FERRAUILO-DAVIS
30 Chief Development .... Ms. Lesley LANZI
09 Director of Institutional Research .... Mr. Eric KIMMELMAN
37 Coordinator Financial Aid .... Ms. Rebecca COZZOCREA
04 Administrative Asst to President .... Ms. Paula WEAVER
108 Director Institutional Assessment .... Ms. Jacqueline SNYDER
15 Director of Human Resources .... Mr. Jason RAUCH
19 Director of Public Safety .... Mr. Mark PIERCE
25 Director of Grants .... Ms. Jean KARUTIS
26 Coordinator Public Relations .... Ms. Amy RADIK
39 Director Student Housing .... Ms. Chrisitine SMITH
41 Athletic Director .... Mr. Kevin JONES
90 IT Infrastructure Administrator .... Mr. William BONNER
91 Associate Director of IT .... Mr. Paul PUTMAN

General Theological Seminary (E)

440 West 21st Street, New York NY 10011-2981

County: New York — FICE Identification: 002726 — Unit ID: 191320

Telephone: (212) 243-5150 — Carnegie Class: Spec/Faith

FAX Number: (212) 727-3907 — Calendar System: Semester

URL: www.gts.edu

Established: 1817 — Annual Graduate Tuition & Fees: $15,400

Enrollment: 76 — Coed

Affiliation or Control: Protestant Episcopal — IRS Status: 501(c)3

Highest Offering: Doctorate; No Undergraduates

Program: Professional; Religious Emphasis

Accreditation: **THEOL**

01 President and Dean .... Rev. Kurt DUNKLE
11 Vice President of Operations .... Mr. Anthony KHANI
30 VP for Institutional Advancement .... Ms. Donna ASHLEY
05 Academic Dean .... Vacant
08 Head Librarian .... Vacant
26 Director of Communications .... Mr. Chad RANCOURT
06 Registrar .... Vacant
04 Exec Asst to the President & Dean .... Ms. Kim ROBEY
15 Director of HR .... Ms. Trecia O'SULLIVAN
10 Controller .... Mr. Robert ELLIOT
30 Director of Development .... Mr. Jonathan SILVER

Genesee Community College (F)

One College Road, Batavia NY 14020-9704

County: Genesee — FICE Identification: 006782 — Unit ID: 191339

Telephone: (585) 343-0055 — Carnegie Class: Assoc/Pub-R-M

FAX Number: (585) 343-4541 — Calendar System: Semester

URL: www.genesee.edu

Established: 1966 — Annual Undergrad Tuition & Fees (In-District): $4,370

Enrollment: 6,883 — Coed

Affiliation or Control: State/Local — IRS Status: 501(c)3

Highest Offering: Associate Degree

Program: Occupational; 2-Year Principally Bachelor's Creditable

Accreditation: **M**, ADNUR, COARC, POLYT, PTAA

01 President .... Dr. James SUNSER
05 Provost/Exec VP Academic Affairs .... Dr. Kathleen SCHIEFEN
81 Dean Math/Science/Career Education .... Dr. Rafael ALICEA-MALDONADO
83 Dean Human Communication/Behavior .... Dr. Katharina E. KOVACH-ALLEN
56 Dean of Distributed Learning .... Mr. Craig LAMB
20 Asc Dean Accelerated Col Enrol Pgms ... Mr. Edward LEVINSTEIN
06 Registrar .... Mr. Terrence REDING
57 Director Fine & Performing Arts .... Ms. Maryanne ARENA
68 Director of Health and Phys Ed .... Ms. Rebecca DZIEKAN
45 Exec VP for Planning/Inst Effectiv .... Mr. William T. EMM
09 Assoc VP Inst Rsrch & Assessment .... Ms. Carol MARRIOTT
15 Assoc VP for Human Resources .... Ms. Gina WEAVER
25 Director of Grants Services .... Mr. James DONSBACH
103 Exec Dir for Workforce Development .... Mr. Reid SMALLEY
88 Director Business Skills Training .... Mr. John MCGOWAN
10 Vice Pres for Finance & Operations .... Mr. Kevin HAMILTON
21 Controller .... Ms. Kristin L. YUNKER
13 Director of Computer Services .... Ms. Cindy DELMAR
18 Director of Buildings & Grounds .... Mr. Timothy M. LANDERS
32 VP for Student & Enrollment Svcs .... Dr. Virginia TAYLOR
35 Assoc Dean for Student Development .... Ms. Margaret HEATER
35 Dean of Students .... Ms. Jennifer M. NEWELL
07 Director of Admissions .... Ms. Tanya LANE-MARTIN
37 Director of Financial Aid .... Mr. Joseph A. BAILEY
88 Director of Student Activities .... Mr. Clifford M. SCUTELLA
41 Director of Athletics .... Ms. Kristen SCHUTH
30 Director Devel & External Affairs .... Mr. Richard G. ENSMAN, JR.
90 Manager of Academic Computing .... Mrs. Mary Jane HEIDER

Globe Institute of Technology (G)

500 Seventh Avenue, New York NY 10018

County: New York — FICE Identification: 025408 — Unit ID: 188465

Telephone: (212) 349-4330 — Carnegie Class: Spec/Bus

FAX Number: (212) 302-9242 — Calendar System: Semester

URL: www.globe.edu

Established: 1985 — Annual Undergrad Tuition & Fees: $11,120

Enrollment: 490 — Coed

Affiliation or Control: Proprietary — IRS Status: Proprietary

Highest Offering: Baccalaureate

Program: Occupational

Accreditation: **NY**, MAAB

01 President .... Mr. Martin OLINER
05 Academic Dean .... Ms. Elena ESTRIN
11 Dean of Administrative Services .... Mr. Alex OLINER
32 Dean of Student Services .... Ms. Joelle BONNY
13 Director of Information Services .... Mr. Antonio SOLANO
14 Director of Information Technology ..... Mr. Jacob KUPERSHTEYN
07 Director of Admissions .... Mr. Sergey BEYDERMAN
37 Director of Financial Aid .... Ms. Tatiana NUSENBAUM
06 Director of Registrar Office .... Mr. Adrian TAHIRI
41 Athletic Director .... Mr. Cameron CHADWICK
38 Academic Adviser .... Ms. Nellie CHEN
08 Head Librarian .... Ms. Diana LEE

Hamilton College (A)

198 College Hill Road, Clinton NY 13323-1218
County: Oneida FICE Identification: 002728
Unit ID: 191515
Telephone: (315) 859-4011 Carnegie Class: Bac/A&S
FAX Number: (315) 859-4991 Calendar System: Semester
URL: www.hamilton.edu
Established: 1812 Annual Undergrad Tuition & Fees: $49,500
Enrollment: 1,896 Coed
Affiliation or Control: Independent Non-Profit IRS Status: 501(c)3
Highest Offering: Baccalaureate
Program: Liberal Arts And General
Accreditation: M

01 President .... Joan H. STEWART
05 VPAA/Dean of Faculty .... Patrick D. REYNOLDS
11 Vice Pres Administration/Finance .... Karen L. LEACH
30 Vice President Commun/Development .... Richard C. TANTILLO
13 Vice Pres Information Technology .... David L. SMALLEN
07 VP/Dean Admission & Financial Aid .... Monica C. INZER
32 Vice Pres/Dean of Students .... Nancy R. THOMPSON
20 Associate Dean of Faculty .... Margaret GENTRY
41 Athletic Director .... Jonathan T. HIND
39 Director Residential Life .... Travis R. HILL
10 Controller .... Shari K. WHITING
08 Dir of Library/Info Technology .... David L. SMALLEN
27 Director Strategic Communications .... Stacey J. HIMMELBERGER
37 Director of Financial Aid .... K. Cameron FEIST
36 Int Exec Director Career Center .... Richard TANTILLO
06 Registrar .... Kristin M. FRIEDEL
15 Director of Human Resources .... Stephen STEMKOSKI
23 Medical Dir Student Health Services .... Aimee PEARCE
18 Director Physical Plant .... Steven J. BELLONA
19 Director of Campus Safety .... Francis A. MANFREDO
38 Director Counseling/Psych Services .... David WALDEN
42 Newman Chaplain .... John CROGHAN
24 Director Audiovisual Services .... Timothy J. HICKS
09 Director of Institutional Research .... Gordon J. HEWITT
26 Exec Director of Communications .... Michael J. DEBRAGGIO
28 Chief Diversity Officer .... Vacant
29 Director Alumni Relations .... Sharon T. RIPPEY
96 Director of Purchasing .... Irene K. CORNISH
40 Manager College Store .... Jennifer PHILLIPS

Hartwick College (B)

One Hartwick Drive, Oneonta NY 13820-1790
County: Otsego FICE Identification: 002729
Unit ID: 191533
Telephone: (607) 431-4000 Carnegie Class: Bac/A&S
FAX Number: (607) 431-4206 Calendar System: 4/1/4
URL: www.hartwick.edu
Established: 1797 Annual Undergrad Tuition & Fees: $41,440
Enrollment: 1,540 Coed
Affiliation or Control: Independent Non-Profit IRS Status: 501(c)3
Highest Offering: Baccalaureate
Program: Liberal Arts And General; Professional
Accreditation: M, ART, MUS, NURSE, TEAC

01 President .... Dr. Margaret L. DRUGOVICH
05 Executive Vice President & Provost .... Dr. Michael TANNENBAUM
10 Vice President Finance/CFO .... Mr. George J. ELSBECK
30 Vice Pres Institutional Advancement .... Mr. Gregg FORTE
32 Vice President for Student Life .... Dr. Meg NOWAK
84 Vice Pres for Enrollment Management .... Ms. Karen MCGRATH
04 Exec Assistant to the President .... Vacant
15 Director Human Resources .... Ms. Suzanne JANITZ
39 Director Residence Life .... Mr. Zachary BROWN
06 Registrar .... Mr. Matthew SANFORD
20 Dean of Academic Affairs .... Vacant
37 Director of Financial Aid .... Ms. Melissa ALLEN
08 Director of Libraries .... Mr. F. Paul COLEMAN
85 Director International Pgms .... Dr. Godlove FONJWENG
13 Director Inst Info Systems Services .... Ms. Deb B. HILTS
91 Director Technologies Services .... Ms. Suzanne GAYNOR
18 Director of Facilities Services .... Mr. Joseph MACK
41 Director of Athletics .... Dr. Kimberly FIERKE
38 Director of Counseling Services .... Mr. Gary ROBINSON
23 Director of Student Health Center .... Ms. Elizabeth MORLEY
27 Exec Dir Marketing & Communications .... Ms. Susan SALTON
26 Sr Director of Donor & Alumni Aff .... Ms. Alicia FISH
07 Director Admissions .... Ms. Lisa STARKEY-WOODS
12 Director Pine Lake Campus .... Vacant
21 Director Financial Svcs/Controller .... Ms. Karen ZUILL
09 Director of Institutional Research .... Ms. Minghui WANG
29 Director of Alumni Engagement .... Mr. Duncan MACDONALD
19 Director of Campus Safety .... Mr. Thomas KELLY
40 Manager of B&N Bookstore .... Mr. Frank WERDANN
96 Manager of Purchasing .... Ms. Marilyn NIENART
44 Exec Director of Individual Giving .... Vacant
102 Dir Foundation/Corporate Relations .... Ms. Margaret ARTHURS
105 Director Web Services .... Ms. Stephanie BRUNETTA
108 Director Institutional Assessment .... Dr. Robert DRAKE

Hebrew Union College-Jewish Institute of Religion (C)

1 West 4th Street, New York NY 10012-1186
County: New York FICE Identification: 004054
Unit ID: 203067
Telephone: (212) 674-5300 Carnegie Class: Spec/Faith
FAX Number: (212) 388-1720 Calendar System: Semester
URL: www.huc.edu
Established: 1875 Annual Graduate Tuition & Fees: $24,000
Enrollment: 349 Coed
Affiliation or Control: Jewish IRS Status: 501(c)3
Highest Offering: Doctorate; No Undergraduates
Program: Professional; Religious Emphasis
Accreditation: M

01 President .... Rabbi Aaron PARKER
30 Vice President Inst Advancement .... Dr. Jane KARLIN
10 Chief Financial Officer .... Ms. Sandra M. MILLS
05 Vice Pres Academic Affairs/Provost .... Rabbi Michael MARMUR
101 Admin Exec to Board of Governors .... Ms. Sylvia POSNER
26 AVP National Dir Public Affs/Comm .... Ms. Jean B. ROSENSAFT
44 Natl Dir of Institutional Giving .... Dr. Andrew GRANT
08 Director of Libraries .... Dr. David GILNER
79 Director American Jewish Archives .... Dr. Gary ZOLA
09 Manager Institutional Research .... Mr. Bobby COVITZ
06 National Registrar .... Mr. Clyde PARRISH
13 Director of Information Systems .... Mr. John H. BRUGGEMAN
15 Director of Legal Affairs & HR .... Mr. Jeremy PERLIN
07 Director of Admissions .. Rabbi Rachel SABATH BEIT-HALACHMI
37 Director of Financial Aid .... Ms. Roseanne ACKERLEY

Helene Fuld College of Nursing (D)

24 East 120th Street, New York NY 10035
County: New York FICE Identification: 010153
Unit ID: 191597
Telephone: (212) 616-7200 Carnegie Class: Assoc/PrivNFP
FAX Number: (212) 616-7299 Calendar System: Quarter
URL: www.helenefuld.edu
Established: 1945 Annual Undergrad Tuition & Fees: $18,704
Enrollment: 444 Coed
Affiliation or Control: Independent Non-Profit IRS Status: 501(c)3
Highest Offering: Baccalaureate
Program: Occupational; 2-Year Principally Bachelor's Creditable; Nursing Emphasis
Accreditation: M, ADNUR, NURSE

01 President .... Dr. Wendy ROBINSON
05 Vice President for Academic Affairs .... Vacant
10 Head of Finance .... Mrs. Galina VILKINA
11 Director of Administration .... Ms. Celeste WALLIN
32 Director of Student Services .... Mrs. Sandra SENIOR
08 Director of Library & IT .... Mr. Indrajeet SINGH CHAUHAN
35 Assoc Director of Student Services .... Ms. Gladys PINEDA
26 Director of External Affairs .... Ms. Michelle HERNANDEZ
30 Development Officer .... Ms. Barbara PAXON
88 Director of BSN program .... Dr. Wendy ROBINSON
88 Director of Associate program .... Ms. Heather LASHLEY
37 Financial Aid Couselor .... Ms. Andrine THOMAS
15 Human Resources Generalist .... Ms. Kimberly LIPSCOMB
09 Institutional Researcher .... Mr. Robert RAWLINS
38 College Couselor .... Ms. Dana GOLIN
88 Executive Assistant .... Ms. Kadia DARBY
88 Information Technology/Library Asst .... Mr. Eickel ORTIZ
88 College Recruiter .... Ms. Alphonsa ITTOOP
29 Director Alumni Relations .... Ms. Barbara PAXTON

Herkimer County Community College (E)

100 Reservoir Road, Herkimer NY 13350-1598
County: Herkimer FICE Identification: 004788
Unit ID: 191612
Telephone: (315) 574-3997 Carnegie Class: Assoc/Pub-R-M
FAX Number: (315) 866-7253 Calendar System: Semester
URL: www.herkimer.edu
Established: 1966 Annual Undergrad Tuition & Fees (In-District): $4,590
Enrollment: 3,250 Coed
Affiliation or Control: State/Local IRS Status: 501(c)3
Highest Offering: Associate Degree
Program: Occupational; 2-Year Principally Bachelor's Creditable
Accreditation: M, EMT, PTAA

01 President .... Dr. Cathleen C. MCCOLGIN
10 Sr VP for Admin & Finance .... Mr. Nicholas LAINO
05 Provost .... Mr. Michael ORIOLO
32 Dean of Students .... Dr. Matthew HAWES
20 Associate Dean Academic Affairs BH .... Mr. Alan CRONAUER
13 Exec Director Information Services .... Mrs. AnneMarie AMBROSE
07 Director of Admissions .... Ms. Rebecca KOHLER
83 Assoc Dean Academic Affairs Soc Sci .... Dr. Robin VOETTERL RIECKER
20 Assoc Dean of Academic Affairs .... Mrs. Linda LAMB
15 Director of Human Resources .... Mr. James SALAMY
41 Director of Athletics .... Mr. Donald DUTCHER
08 Director of Library Services .... Mr. Alfred BEROWSKI
09 Director Institutional Research .... Ms. Karen AYOUCH
51 Director of Continuing Education .... Mr. Daniel SARGENT
18 Director Facilities Operations .... Mr. Robert WOUDENBERG
37 Director Student Financial Aid .... Mrs. Susan TRIPP
26 Director of Public Relations .... Ms. Rebecca RUFFING
06 Asst Dean of Academic Affairs .... Mr. Eric VERNOLD
36 Career Services Counselor .... Mrs. Suzanne PADDOCK
40 Bookstore Manager .... Ms. Krista MEZIK
96 Purchasing Agent .... Mr. Robert NEARY
102 Dir Foundation/Corporate Relations .... Mr. Robert FOWLER
19 Director of Campus Safety .... Mr. Timothy ROGERS

Hilbert College (F)

5200 S Park Avenue, Hamburg NY 14075-1597
County: Erie FICE Identification: 002735
Unit ID: 191621
Telephone: (716) 649-7900 Carnegie Class: Bac/Diverse
FAX Number: (716) 649-0702 Calendar System: Semester
URL: www.hilbert.edu
Established: 1957 Annual Undergrad Tuition & Fees: $20,650
Enrollment: 1,012 Coed
Affiliation or Control: Independent Non-Profit IRS Status: 501(c)3
Highest Offering: Master's
Program: Liberal Arts And General; Professional; Business Emphasis
Accreditation: M

01 President .... Dr. Cynthia A. ZANE
05 Provost/Vice Pres Academic Affairs . Dr. Christopher L. HOLOMAN
30 Int Vice Pres Inst Advancement .... Mr. Ted PIETRZAK
10 Vice President Business/Finance .... Mr. Richard J. PINKOWSKI, JR.
27 Vice President Information Services .... Mr. Michael MURRIN
84 Int VP Enrollment Mgmt/Retention .... Mr. Larry LESICK
88 Vice Prov for Student Engagement .... Ms. Denise HARRIS
32 VProv Leadership Dev/Dean of Stdnts .... Mr. James P. STURM
49 Chair Arts & Sciences .... Dr. Amy E. SMITH
26 Director Public Relations .... Mr. Matthew HEIDT
92 Director Honors Program .... Dr. Amy E. SMITH
39 Dir Residence Life/Judicial Affairs .... Mr. Jason LANKER
41 Athletic Director .... Mr. John CZARNECKI
19 Director Security/Safety .... Mr. Matthew SCHAMANN
29 Engagement Ofcr Alumni & Spec Event .... Ms. Stephanie KING
42 Dir Mission Intgrtn/Campus Ministry .... Mr. Jeffrey PAPIA
08 Director of McGrath Library .... Mr. Wilson PROUT
07 Director of Admissions .... Mr. Justin ROGERS
36 Director Placement/Career Services .... Ms. Katie MARTOCHE
37 Director Financial Aid .... Ms. Beverly CHUDY-SZCZUR
06 Director of Student Records .... Ms. Caprice ARABIA
38 Director Student Counseling .... Ms. Phyllis K. DEWEY
09 Director of Institutional Research .... Dr. Ron ESKEW
15 Director of Human Resources .... Ms. Maura FLYNN
28 Director of Multicultural Affairs . Ms. Tara JABBAAR-GYAMBRAH
35 Director of Student Activities .... Mr. Thomas VANE
96 Director of Purchasing .... Mr. Gary DILLSWORTH
21 Associate Business Officer .... Mr. Anthony WIERTEL
18 Chief Facilities/Physical Plant .... Mr. Gary DILLSWORTH
04 Administrative Asst to President .... Ms. Kathleen FAIRBANKS

Hobart and William Smith Colleges (G)

300 Pulteney Street, Geneva NY 14456-3397
County: Ontario FICE Identification: 002731
Unit ID: 191630
Telephone: (315) 781-3000 Carnegie Class: Bac/A&S
FAX Number: (315) 781-3654 Calendar System: Semester
URL: www.hws.edu
Established: 1822 Annual Undergrad Tuition & Fees: $48,586
Enrollment: 2,425 Coordinate
Affiliation or Control: Independent Non-Profit IRS Status: 501(c)3
Highest Offering: Master's
Program: Liberal Arts And General; Teacher Preparatory; Fine Arts Emphasis
Accreditation: M, TEAC

01 President .... Mr. Mark D. GEARAN
05 Provost and Dean of Faculty .... Dr. Titilayo UFOMATA
84 VP for Enrollment/Dean of Admission .... Mr. Robert MURPHY
32 Vice President for Student Affairs .... Mr. Robert FLOWERS
30 Vice President for Advancement .... Mr. Robert O'CONNOR
10 Vice President for Finance/CFO .... Ms. Carolee WHITE
13 VP for Strategic Initiatives/CIO .... Mr. Fred DAMIANO
15 Vice President for Human Resources .... Ms. Sandra BISSELL
26 Vice President for Communicatons .... Ms. Cathy WILLIAMS
33 Dean of Hobart College .... Dr. Eugen BAER
34 Dean of William Smith College .... Dr. Catherine GALLOUET
42 Chaplain .... Rev. D. Maurice CHARLES
100 Chief of Staff and Council .... Mr. Louis GUARD
04 Exec Assistant to the President .... Ms. Valerie VISTOCCO
20 Associate Dean of Faculty .... Dr. Dwayne LUCAS
20 Associate Provost .... Dr. Christine DE DENUS
88 Associate Dean 1st Yr Seminars .... Dr. Eric KLAUS
104 Associate Dean Global Education .... Dr. Thomas D'AGOSTINO
108 Assoc Dean Teach/Learn & Assessment .... Dr. Susan PLINER
48 Director Finger Lakes Institute .... Dr. Lisa CLECKNER
08 Director of the Library .... Mr. Vincent BOISSELLE
06 Registrar .... Mr. Peter SARRATORI
09 Assoc Dean Inst Research/Retent .... Mr. Don EMMONS
31 Dir Community Engagement .... Ms. Kathleen FLOWERS
88 Director Academic Opportunity Pgm .... Mr. James BURRUTO
37 Director of Financial Aid .... Ms. Beth NEPA
07 Director of Admissions .... Mr. John YOUNG
36 Director Center for Career Services .... Ms. Brandi FERRARA
35 Assistant VP for Student Affairs .... Dr. Montrose STREETER
41 Director of Hobart Athletics .... Mr. Michael HANNA
41 Director of William Smith Athletics .... Ms. Deborah STEWARD
38 Dir Counseling Ctr/Student Wellness .... Dr. Shelly LEAR
23 Coordinator Health Services/NP .... Ms. Betti GREEN
19 Director of Campus Safety .... Mr. Martin CORBETT
88 Director of Intercultural Affairs .... Dr. Alejandra MOLINA
85 Director of International Students .... Mr. David GAGE
44 Associate VP for Advancement .... Ms. Leila RICE
29 Assistant VP for Alumni Relations .... Mr. Jared WEEDEN

29 Assistant VP for Alumnae Relations .... Ms. Kathleen REGAN
102 Director Corp/Foundation Relations .... Ms. Martha BOND
88 Director Advancement Services .... Ms. Karen REUSCHER
21 Controller .... Mr. Michael PAPARO
88 Director Conferences/Events .... Ms. Erica COONEY-CONNOR
40 Director of the College Store .... Ms. Lucille SMART
16 Associate Director Human Resources .... Ms. Peggy FERRAN
88 Director of Communications .... Ms. Mary LECLAIR
88 Director of Publications .... Ms. Margaret KOWALIK
105 Director Web Development .... Mr. Michael DIMAURO
88 Director Athletic Communications .... Mr. Ken DEBOLT
88 Director Enterprise Solutions .... Mr. Jeremy TRUMBLE
88 Director Operations & Tech Services .... Ms. Kelly Anne MCLAUGHLIN
14 Dir Network/Systems Infrastructure .... Mr. Derek LUSTIG
106 Director of Digital Learning .... Ms. Juliet BOISSELLE
88 Associate Hobart Dean .... Mr. Chip CAPRARO
88 Assistant Hobart Dean .... Mr. David MAPSTONE
88 Associate William Smith Dean .... Ms. Lisa KAENZIG
88 Assistant William Smith Dean .... Ms. Valerie GUNTER
39 Director of Residential Education .... Mr. Brandon BARILE

Hofstra University (A)

Hempstead NY 11549-1000

County: Nassau — FICE Identification: 002732
Unit ID: 191649
Telephone: (516) 463-6600 — Carnegie Class: DRU
FAX Number: (516) 463-4848 — Calendar System: Semester
URL: www.hofstra.edu
Established: 1935 — Annual Undergrad Tuition & Fees: $40,460
Enrollment: 10,953 — Coed
Affiliation or Control: Independent Non-Profit — IRS Status: 501(c)3
Highest Offering: Doctorate
Program: Liberal Arts And General; Teacher Preparatory; Professional
Accreditation: M, ARCPA, AUD, BUS, BUSA, CAATE, CACREP, CLPSY, CORE, ENG, JOUR, LAW, MED, SCPSY, SP, TEAC

01 President .... Mr. Stuart RABINOWITZ
05 Provost/Sr VP for Academic Affairs .... Dr. Gail M. SIMMONS
45 Sr VP for Planning and Admin .... Ms. M. Patricia ADAMSKI
10 VP Financial Affairs/Treasurer .... Ms. Catherine HENNESSY
32 Vice President for Student Affairs .. Mr. W. Houston DOUGHARTY
30 Vice President for Development .... Mr. Alan J. KELLY
26 Vice President University Relations .... Ms. Melissa A. CONNOLLY
43 VP Legal Affairs & General Counsel .... Ms. Dolores FREDRICH
13 Vice Pres Information Technology ..... Mr. Robert W. JUCKIEWICZ
18 VP for Facilities and Operations .... Mr. Joseph BARKWILL
84 Vice Pres Enrollment Management .... Ms. Jessica L. EADS
86 Vice President Business Dev Ctr .... Mr. Richard V. GUARDINO
91 Asst VP for Information Technology ... Ms. Linda J. HANTZSCHEL
09 VP Inst Research/Admin Assess .... Dr. Stephanie BUSHEY
20 Vice Provost for Academic Affairs .... Dr. Cliff JERNIGAN
21 Assoc Provost Budget & Planning .... Mr. Richard M. APOLLO
25 Assoc Provost Rsrch/Sponsored Pgms .... Ms. Sofia KAKOULIDIS
07 VP Admissions & Financial Aid .... Ms. Jessica L. EADS
50 Acting Dean Zarb Sch of Business .... Dr. Herman A. BERLINER
54 Acting Dean School of Engineering .... Dr. Sina Y. RABBANY
60 Dean School of Communication .... Dr. Evan W. CORNOG
53 Dean School of Education .... Dr. Sean A. FANELLI
49 Dean College Liberal Arts/Science .... Dr. Bernard J. FIRESTONE
08 Acting Dean Library & Info Services .... Dr. Bernard J. FIRESTONE
88 Dean for University Advisement .... Ms. Anne M. MONGILLO
61 Dean of Maurice Deane School of Law .... Mr. Eric LANE
63 Dean Medical School .... Dr. Lawrence SMITH
66 Dean Sch/Grad Nursing & Health Prof .... Dr. Kathleen GALLO
35 Dean of Students .... Ms. Sofia B. PERTUZ
84 Asst Dean Law Sch Enrollment Mgmt .... Mr. John CHALMERS
29 Senior Director Alumni Affairs .... Ms. Amy R. REICH
39 Assoc Director Residential Programs .... Ms. Novia P. WHYTE
38 Dir Student Counseling Services .... Dr. John C. GUTHMAN
22 Equal Rights/Opportunity Ofcr .... Ms. Jennifer MONE
23 Director Health & Wellness Center .... Ms. Maureen B. HOUCK
41 Director Intercollegiate Athletics .... Mr. Jeffrey HATHAWAY
15 Director of Human Resources .... Ms. Evelyn V. MILLER-SUBER
90 Director Faculty Computing Services .... Ms. Judith L. TABRON
40 Manager Bookstore .... Mr. Steven BABBITT
19 Director Public Safety .... Ms. Karen O'CALLAGHAN
96 Director of Procurement Services .... Mr. John JAGARD
92 Dean Honors College .... Dr. Warren FRISINA
06 Registrar .... Ms. Lynne DOUGHERTY
04 Admin Assistant to the President .... Ms. Isabel D. FREY
37 Director Student Financial Aid .... Ms. Sandra MERVIUS

Holy Trinity Orthodox Seminary (B)

PO Box 36, Jordanville NY 13361-0036

County: Herkimer — FICE Identification: 002733
Unit ID: 191658
Telephone: (315) 858-0945 — Carnegie Class: Not Classified
FAX Number: (315) 858-0945 — Calendar System: Semester
URL: www.hts.edu
Established: 1948 — Annual Undergrad Tuition & Fees: $3,100
Enrollment: 25 — Male
Affiliation or Control: Russian Orthodox — IRS Status: 501(c)3
Highest Offering: Baccalaureate
Program: Professional; Religious Emphasis
Accreditation: NY

01 Rector and Dean .... V.Rev. Luke MURIANKA
06 Registrar .... Rev. Theophylact CLAPPER-DEWELL
32 Dean of Students .... Rev. Cyprian ALEXANDROU
04 Administrative Assistant .... RevDcn. Ephraim WILLMARTH

Houghton College (C)

One Willard Avenue, Houghton NY 14744-0128

County: Allegany — FICE Identification: 002734
Unit ID: 191676
Telephone: (585) 567-9200 — Carnegie Class: Bac/A&S
FAX Number: (585) 567-9572 — Calendar System: Semester
URL: www.houghton.edu
Established: 1883 — Annual Undergrad Tuition & Fees: $29,458
Enrollment: 1,103 — Coed
Affiliation or Control: Wesleyan Church — IRS Status: 501(c)3
Highest Offering: Master's
Program: Liberal Arts And General; Teacher Preparatory
Accreditation: M, MUS, TEAC

01 President .... Dr. Shirley A. MULLEN
05 Vice President for Academic Affairs .. Dr. Linda MILLS WOOLSEY
32 Vice President for Student Life .... Mr. Robert POOL
10 Vice President for Finance and Plng .... Mr. David SMITH
30 Vice President for Advancement .... Mr. Rick MELSON
84 Vice President for Enrollment .... Mr. Eric CURRIE
04 Dir of Operations Ofc of the Pres .... Ms. Cindy LASTORIA
06 Registrar .... Ms. Margery L. AVERY
37 Director of Financial Aid .... Ms. Marianne LOPER
08 Director of the Library .... Mr. David STEVICK
29 Dir Alumni & Community Relations .... Ms. Phyllis GAERTE
42 Dean of the Chapel .... Dr. Michael JORDAN
09 Assoc Dean Institutional Research .... Dr. John WISE
36 Director of VOCA .... Ms. Kim POOL
15 Director of Human Resources .... Mr. Dale F. WRIGHT
26 Dir Marketing & Communications .... Mr. Jeff BABBITT
13 Director of Technology .... Mr. Donald HAINGRAY
18 Director of Facilities .... Mr. Chad PLYMALE
19 Chief Security Officer .... Mr. Ray M. PARLETT
23 Director of Health Services .... Dr. David BRUBAKER
41 Executive Director of Athletics .... Mr. Harold W. LORD
21 Controller .... Mr. David M. MERCER
39 Director Residence Life .... Mr. Marc SMITHERS
38 Director Counseling Services .... Dr. William BURRICHTER
92 Director of Honors Program .... Dr. Benjamin LIPSCOMB

Hudson Valley Community College (D)

80 Vandenburgh Avenue, Troy NY 12180-6096

County: Rensselaer — FICE Identification: 002868
Unit ID: 191719
Telephone: (518) 629-4822 — Carnegie Class: Assoc/Pub-U-SC
FAX Number: (518) 629-4576 — Calendar System: Semester
URL: www.hvcc.edu
Established: 1953 — Annual Undergrad Tuition & Fees (In-District): $4,754
Enrollment: 12,252 — Coed
Affiliation or Control: State/Local — IRS Status: 501(c)3
Highest Offering: Associate Degree
Program: Occupational; 2-Year Principally Bachelor's Creditable
Accreditation: M, ADNUR, COARC, DH, DMS, EMT, ENGT, FUSER, POLYT

01 President .... Dr. Andrew J. MATONAK
14 VP Technology/Inst Assess/Planning .... Dr. Michael S. GREEN
04 Assistant to the President .... Ms. Suzanne K. KALKBRENNER
11 VP for Administration .... Mr. James J. LAGATTA
05 Vice President for Academic Affairs .... Dr. Carolyn G. CURTIS
32 VP Enroll Mgmt/Student Development .... Dr. Alexander J. POPOVICS
10 Vice President for Finance .... Mr. Joel R. FATATO
49 Dean Sch Liberal Arts .... Vacant
72 Dean Engr/Indus Tech/Business .... Mr. P. Phillip WHITE
107 Dean Cmty/Professional Pgms .... Ms. Christine A. HELWIG
76 Interim Dean Sch of Health Sciences .... Dr. Carol BOSCO
08 Director of Learning Resources Ctr .... Dr. David CLICKNER
07 Director of Admissions .... Ms. Mary Claire BAUER
06 Registrar .... Ms. Kathleen PETLEY
13 Interim Chief Information Officer .... Ms. Sarah GARRAND
18 Director Physical Plant .... Mr. Richard EDWARDS
38 Director Student Development .... Dr. Kathleen SWEENER
37 Director of Financial Aid .... Ms. Lisa VAN WIE
36 Dir Center For Careers/Employment .... Ms. Gayle HEALY
15 Director of Human Resources .... Mr. John TIBBETTS
19 Director of Public Safety .... Mr. Fred ALIBERTI
23 Coordinator Health Services .... Ms. Claudine POTVIN-GIORDANO
88 Director of Disability Resources .... Ms. Deanne MARTOCCI
09 Director Planning & Research .... Mr. James F. MACKLIN
35 Director of Student Life .... Mr. Louis COPLIN
85 International Student Advisor .... Dr. Jay DEITCHMAN
40 Director of Bookstore .... Mr. Stephen J. STEGMAN
41 Director of Athletics .... Ms. Kristan M. PELLETIER
72 Interim Asst to VP of Academics .... Dr. David C. CLICKNER
88 Assoc Dean Instruct SuppSvcs/Reten . Ms. Karen FERRER-MUNIZ
96 Dir Business Services/Purchasing .. Ms. Mary Ellen LAJEUNESSE
21 Comptroller .... Mr. John BRAUNGARD
26 Exec Dir Communications/Marketing .... Mr. Dennis KENNEDY
102 Interim Exec Director Foundation .... Ms. Regina LAGATTA
103 Assoc Dean Workforce Development . Mr. Richard E. BENNETT, II
25 Director of Grants .... Ms. Cheryl L. BEAUCHAMP
29 Dir Development & Alumni Relations .... Mr. Geoffrey N. MILLER
30 Director of Advancement Operations .... Ms. Kimberly G. BERRY
106 Director of Distance Learning .... Ms. Susan P. GALLAGHER
108 Dean Institutional Assessment .... Dr. Margaret GEEHAN

Icahn School of Medicine at Mount Sinai (E)

One Gustave L. Levy Place, New York NY 10029-6500

County: New York — FICE Identification: 007026
Unit ID: 193405
Telephone: (212) 241-6500 — Carnegie Class: Spec/Med
FAX Number: (212) 241-7146 — Calendar System: Other
URL: www.icahn.mssm.edu
Established: 1963 — Annual Graduate Tuition & Fees: $46,388
Enrollment: 1,074 — Coed
Affiliation or Control: Independent Non-Profit — IRS Status: 501(c)3
Highest Offering: Doctorate; No Undergraduates
Program: Professional; Technical Emphasis
Accreditation: M, DENT, IPSY, MED, PH

01 President & CEO .... Dr. Kenneth L. DAVIS
03 Exec Vice Pres/Dean Sch of Medicine .... Dr. Dennis S. CHARNEY
05 Dean for Medical Education .... Dr. David MULLER
11 Dean for Operations .... Mr. Jeffrey SILBERSTEIN

Iona College (F)

715 North Avenue, New Rochelle NY 10801-1890

County: Westchester — FICE Identification: 002737
Unit ID: 191931
Telephone: (914) 633-2000 — Carnegie Class: Master's L
FAX Number: (914) 633-2642 — Calendar System: Semester
URL: www.iona.edu
Established: 1940 — Annual Undergrad Tuition & Fees: $35,324
Enrollment: 3,909 — Coed
Affiliation or Control: Independent Non-Profit — IRS Status: 501(c)3
Highest Offering: Master's
Program: Liberal Arts And General; Teacher Preparatory; Professional
Accreditation: M, BUS, CS, JOUR, MFCD, @SP, SW, TED

01 President .... Dr. Joseph E. NYRE
05 Provost/Sr VP Academic Affairs .... Dr. Vincent CALLUZZO
10 Sr Vice President Finance & Admin .... Ms. Anne Marie SCHETTINI-LYNCH
30 Sr VP Advance/External Affairs .... Mr. Paul J. SUTERA
100 Sr Policy Advisor/Chief of Staff .... Ms. MaryEllen CALLAGHAN
84 VP Enrollment Management .... Ms. Mary Beth CAREY
13 Vice Provost Info Technology/CIO .... Ms. Joanne STEELE
32 Vice Provost Student Development .... Mr. Charles CARLSON
37 Asst VP Student Financial Services .... Ms. Eileen DOYLE
91 Asst Vice Provost for Info Tech .... Mr. Dimitris HALARIS
20 Assistant VP Academic Affairs .... Dr. Tresmaine GRIMES
35 Asst Vice Provost Student Devel .... Ms. Elizabeth OLIVIERI-LENAHAN
49 Dean School Arts & Sciences .... Dr. Sibdas GHOSH
50 Dean Hagan School of Business .... Vacant
43 General Counsel & Board Secretary .... Ms. Kathleen GILL
18 Director of Facilities Management .... Mr. Mark MURPHY
39 Director Residential Life .... Mr. Michael LABELLA
15 Director of Human Resources .... Ms. Tracey WILMOT
38 Director of Counseling Center .... Vacant
36 Director of Career Development .... Ms. F. Phyllis BLAKE
08 Director of Libraries .... Mr. Richard PALLADINO
42 Director of Campus Ministries .... Mr. Carl PROCARIO-FOLEY
06 Registrar .... Vacant
41 Director of Athletics .... Mr. Richard COLE, JR.
86 Director of Govt Relations/Grants .... Mr. Daniel KONOPKA
12 Co-Director of Rockland Campus .... Ms. Mary Beth CAREY
12 Co-Director of Rockland Campus .... Dr. Vincent CALLUZZO
09 Dir of Inst Effectiveness/Planning .... Mr. Jason DIFFENDERFER
21 Director of Business Services .... Ms. Joan CLARK
26 Director of Public Relations .... Ms. Dawn INSANALLI
19 Dir Campus Safety and Security .... Mr. Dominic LOCATELLI
23 Director of Health Services . Ms. Jacqueline AGNELLO-VAZQUEZ
44 Director of Annual Giving .... Ms. Kara BRENNAN
96 Purchasing Coordinator .... Ms. Kimberly MONTEMURRO
92 Director of Honors Program .... Dr. Kim PAFFENROTH
07 Director of Graduate Admissions .... Mr. Frank BOUGHNER
04 Administrative Asst to President .... Ms. Jennifer BAKER

Island Drafting and Technical Institute (G)

128 Broadway, Amityville NY 11701-2704

County: Suffolk — FICE Identification: 007375
Unit ID: 191959
Telephone: (631) 691-8733 — Carnegie Class: Assoc/PrivFP
FAX Number: (631) 691-8738 — Calendar System: Semester
URL: www.idti.edu
Established: 1957 — Annual Undergrad Tuition & Fees: $16,200
Enrollment: 126 — Coed
Affiliation or Control: Proprietary — IRS Status: Proprietary
Highest Offering: Associate Degree
Program: Occupational
Accreditation: ACCSC

01 President .... Mr. James G. DILIBERTO
03 Vice President .... Mr. John G. DILIBERTO

Ithaca College (H)

953 Danby Road, Ithaca NY 14850-7001

County: Tompkins — FICE Identification: 002739
Unit ID: 191968
Telephone: (607) 274-3011 — Carnegie Class: Master's L
FAX Number: N/A — Calendar System: Semester
URL: www.ithaca.edu
Established: 1892 — Annual Undergrad Tuition & Fees: $40,658
Enrollment: 6,587 — Coed
Affiliation or Control: Independent Non-Profit — IRS Status: 501(c)3
Highest Offering: Doctorate
Program: Liberal Arts And General; Teacher Preparatory; Professional

Accreditation: M, BUS, CAATE, MUS, NRPA, OT, PTA, SP, TED, THEA

01 President ... Dr. Thomas R. ROCHON
04 Exec Assistant to President ... Ms. Amanda L. LIPPINCOTT
05 Provost/Vice Pres Education Affairs ... Dr. Benjamin RIFKIN
10 VP of Finance & Administration ... Mr. Gerald HECTOR
43 Senior VP & General Counsel ... Ms. Nancy E. PRINGLE
84 Interim VP Enrollment Management ... Mr. Gerard TURBIDE
30 VP Institutional Advancement & Comm ... Mr. Christopher BIEHN
20 Asst Prov/Dean Interdis/Intl Stds ... Dr. Tanya R. SAUNDERS
26 Assoc VP Marketing/Communications ... Vacant
13 Assoc VP for Info Tech Svcs ... Mr. Keith MCINTOSH
15 Assoc VP for Human Resources ... Vacant
18 Assoc VP for Facilities Management ... Mr. Tim CAREY
32 Assoc Prov Diversity/Inclusion/Eng ... Dr. Roger RICHARDSON
20 Vice Provost ... Ms. Danette JOHNSON
58 Asst Provost Extended Studies ... Mr. Rob GEARHART
49 Interim Dean School Humanities/Sci ... Dr. Michael RICHARDSON
64 Dean of School of Music ... Dr. Karl PAULNACK
76 Dean Sch Health Sciences/Human Perf ... Ms. Linda PETROSINO
50 Dean School of Business ... Mr. Sean REID
60 Dean School of Communications ... Ms. Diane GAYESKI
29 Executive Director Alumni Relations ... Ms. Carrie BROWN
44 Executive Director of Development ... Vacant
06 Registrar ... Mr. Brian SCHOLTEN
22 Asst Counsel & Dir EO Compliance ... Vacant
09 Director Institutional Research ... Vacant
07 Director of Admission ... Ms. Nicole EVERSLEY BRADWELL
12 Director London Center ... Ms. Thorunn LONSDALE
36 Director Career Services ... Mr. John P. BRADAC
38 Director Counseling/Health/Wellness ... Dr. Deborah HARPER
37 Dir of Student Financial Services ... Mrs. Lisa HOSKEY
23 Director Health Center ... Vacant
39 Dir Res Life/Judicial Affairs ... Ms. Bonnie S. PRUNTY
08 College Librarian ... Ms. Lisabeth CHABOT
41 Dir Intercol Athletics/Rec Sports ... Ms. Susan BASSETT
21 Director of Budget ... Ms. Sally DIETZ
90 Dir Technology/Inst Support Svcs ... Vacant
91 Director Information Systems/Svcs ... Vacant
19 Director Public Safety ... Ms. Terri STEWART
27 Senior Assoc Dir for Campus Comm ... Mr. David C. MALEY
40 Manager of College Stores ... Mr. Rick WATSON
42 Coordinator of Chaplains ... Fr. Carsten P. MARTENSEN
89 Director of First Year Experience ... Ms. Erica SHOCKLEY
28 Director of Mulitcultural Affairs ... Ms. Malinda SMITH
85 Dir International Student Services ... Ms. Diana DIMITROVA
104 Director of Study Abroad ... Ms. Rachel CULLENEN
88 Dir Center for Faculty Excellence ... Mr. Wade PICKREN

ITT Technical Institute (A)

13 Airline Drive, Albany NY 12205-1003
Telephone: (518) 452-9300 Identification: 666138
Accreditation: ACICS

† Branch campus of ITT Technical Institute, Indianapolis, IN.

ITT Technical Institute (B)

2295 Millersport Hwy, PO Box 327, Getzville NY 14068
Telephone: (716) 689-2200 Identification: 666609
Accreditation: ACICS

† Branch campus of ITT Technical Institute, Indianapolis, IN.

ITT Technical Institute (C)

235 Greenfield Parkway, Liverpool NY 13088-6651
Telephone: (315) 461-8000 Identification: 666137
Accreditation: ACICS

† Branch campus of ITT Technical Institute, Indianapolis, IN.

Jamestown Business College (D)

7 Fairmount Avenue, Box 429, Jamestown NY 14702-0429
County: Chautauqua FICE Identification: 008495
Unit ID: 192004
Telephone: (716) 664-5100 Carnegie Class: Assoc/PrivFP4
FAX Number: (716) 664-3144 Calendar System: Quarter
URL: www.jamestownbusinesscollege.edu
Established: 1886 Annual Undergrad Tuition & Fees: $12,300
Enrollment: 318 Coed
Affiliation or Control: Proprietary IRS Status: Proprietary
Highest Offering: Baccalaureate
Program: Occupational; 2-Year Principally Bachelor's Creditable; Business Emphasis
Accreditation: M

01 President ... Mr. David CONKLIN
05 Dean ... Ms. Pamela REESE
32 VP Admin/Dean of Student Affairs ... Ms. Rosanne JOHANSON
06 Registrar & Assistant to the Dean ... Ms. Cynthia CARTWRIGHT
07 Director Admissions ... Ms. Brenda SALEMME
37 Director of Financial Aid ... Mrs. Diane STURZENBECKER
26 Director of Communications ... Ms. Jessica GOLLEY

Jamestown Community College (E)

525 Falconer Street, Jamestown NY 14701
County: Chautauqua FICE Identification: 002869
Unit ID: 191986
Telephone: (716) 338-1000 Carnegie Class: Assoc/Pub-R-M
FAX Number: (716) 338-1466 Calendar System: Semester
URL: www.sunyjcc.edu
Established: 1950 Annual Undergrad Tuition & Fees (In-District): $5,080
Enrollment: 5,065 Coed
Affiliation or Control: State/Local IRS Status: 501(c)3
Highest Offering: Associate Degree
Program: 2-Year Principally Bachelor's Creditable
Accreditation: M, ADNUR, OTA

01 President ... Dr. Cory L. DUCKWORTH
05 Vice Pres of Academic Affairs ... Dr. Marilyn A. ZAGORA
32 Vice Pres of Student Development ... Dr. Eileen J. GOODLING
84 Vice Pres Enrollment/Mktg/Comm ... Mr. Kirk YOUNG
12 VP of Catt County Campus/Cont Ed ... Mr. John J. SAYEGH
11 Int Vice Pres of Administration ... Mr. Michael MARTELLO
09 Dean Research & Planning ... Ms. Barbara RUSSELL
35 Dean Student Development ... Ms. Tammy SMITH
06 Registrar ... Mr. Kreig ELICKER
07 Director Admission ... Ms. Wendy PRESENT
26 Executive Director of Marketing ... Mr. Nelson J. GARIFI
08 Library Director ... Ms. Linda LARKIN
37 Exec Dir Student Finance/Records ... Ms. Laurie A. VORP
15 Exec Director Human Resources ... Ms. Susan BRONSTEIN
41 Athletic Director ... Mr. Keith MARTIN
43 Legal Counsel ... Mr. Stephen ABDELLA
18 Director Facilities/Physical Plant ... Mr. David JOHNSON

Jamestown Community College Cattaraugus County Campus (F)

260 North Union Street, PO Box 5901, Olean NY 14760-5901
Telephone: (716) 376-7500 Identification: 770138
Accreditation: &M

† Branch campus of Jamestown Community College, Jamestown, NY.

Jefferson Community College (G)

1220 Coffeen Street, Watertown NY 13601-1897
County: Jefferson FICE Identification: 002870
Unit ID: 192022
Telephone: (315) 786-2200 Carnegie Class: Assoc/Pub-R-M
FAX Number: (315) 786-0158 Calendar System: Semester
URL: www.sunyjefferson.edu
Established: 1961 Annual Undergrad Tuition & Fees (In-District): $4,547
Enrollment: 3,880 Coed
Affiliation or Control: State/Local IRS Status: 501(c)3
Highest Offering: Associate Degree
Program: Occupational; 2-Year Principally Bachelor's Creditable
Accreditation: M, ADNUR

01 President ... Dr. Carole A. MCCOY
05 Vice President Academic Affairs ... Mr. Thomas FINCH
10 Vice President Admin/Finance ... Mr. Daniel DUPEE
32 Vice Pres of Students/Enrollment ... Ms. Betsy S. PENROSE
49 Associate VP for Liberal Arts ... Dr. Marvin BLACHMAN
81 Associate VP for Math/Science ... Ms. Linda DITTRICH
20 Dean for Instructional Support ... Ms. Jerilyn FAIRMAN
51 Dean for Continuing Education ... Mr. Terrence HARRIS
32 Dean of Students ... Mr. Ronald C. SHIDEMANTLE
04 Assistant to the President ... Ms. Karen A. CARR
08 Library Director ... Ms. Connie HOLBERG
07 Director of Admissions ... Ms. Roseanne N. WEIR
37 Director Financial Aid ... Mr. James AMBROSE
06 Interim Registrar ... Ms. Deborah M. ELLIOTT
88 Director Small Business Center ... Mr. Eric F. CONSTANCE
09 Director of Institutional Research ... Ms. Mary A. PERRINE
18 Chief Facilities/Physical Plant ... Mr. Bruce ALEXANDER
29 Director Alumni Relations ... Ms. Edie ROGGIE
35 Director Student Devel/Activities ... Mr. Frank DOLDO
36 Director Student Placement ... Ms. Michele D. GEFELL
38 Director Student Counseling ... Mr. Matthew LAMBERT
26 Chief Public Relations Officer ... Ms. Karen J. FREEMAN
15 Exec Dir Finance/Human Resources ... Ms. Kerry A. YOUNG
30 College Development Officer ... Ms. Alicia M. DEWEY
31 Coordinator Community Services ... Ms. Andrea PEDRICK
13 Chief Information Officer ... Mr. James BUYEA
19 Director Security/Safety ... Mr. Wesley HISSONG
41 Athletic Director ... Mr. Jeffrey WILEY

Jewish Theological Seminary of America (H)

3080 Broadway, New York NY 10027-4649
County: New York FICE Identification: 002740
Unit ID: 192040
Telephone: (212) 678-8023 Carnegie Class: Spec/Faith
FAX Number: (212) 678-8947 Calendar System: Semester
URL: www.jtsa.edu
Established: 1886 Annual Undergrad Tuition & Fees: $20,340
Enrollment: 405 Coed
Affiliation or Control: Independent Non-Profit IRS Status: 501(c)3
Highest Offering: Doctorate
Program: Liberal Arts And General; Teacher Preparatory; Professional; Religious Emphasis
Accreditation: M, PAST

01 Chancellor ... Dr. Arnold M. EISEN
03 Exec VC/Chief Operating Officer ... Mr. Marc GARY
30 Vice Chanc/Chief Development Office ... Ms. Bonnie EPSTEIN
05 Provost ... Dr. Alan COOPER
10 Chief Financial Officer ... Mr. Fred SCHNUR
43 General Counsel ... Mr. Martin OPPENHEIMER
49 Dean List College Jewish Studies ... Dr. Shuly SCHWARTZ
53 Dean Davidson School of Education ... Dr. Bill ROBINSON
58 Dean The Graduate School ... Dr. Shuly SCHWARTZ
64 Director Miller Cantorial School ... Cantor Nancy ABRAMSON
73 Dean of Religious Leadership ... Rabbi Daniel NEVINS
32 Dean of Student Life ... Ms. Sara HOROWITZ
08 Librarian ... Dr. David KRAEMER
15 Director of Human Resources ... Ms. Diana TORRES-PETRILLI
18 Director of Operations ... Mr. James ESPOSITO
13 Director Information Technology ... Mr. Hal POLLENZ
26 Chief Communications Officer ... Ms. Elise DOWELL
06 Registrar/Director Financial Aid ... Ms. Linda LEVINE
39 Director of Residence Life ... Mr. Bradley MOOT
84 Director of Enrollment Management ... Ms. Melissa PRESENT
35 Director of Student Life ... Ms. Ruth DECALO
38 Director Student Counseling ... Dr. David DAVAR
29 Director of Alumni Affairs ... Mrs. Melissa FRIEDMAN
20 Associate Provost ... Dr. Stephen GARFINKEL
37 Director of Financial Aid ... Ms. Linda LEVINE
88 Director of Community Engagement ... Rabbi Julia ANDELMAN
04 Executive Asst to Chancellor ... Ms. Michelle GIOVANELLO
19 Director Security/Safety ... Chief Anthony VAUGHAN

The Juilliard School (I)

60 Lincoln Center Plaza, New York NY 10023-6588
County: New York FICE Identification: 002742
Unit ID: 192110
Telephone: (212) 799-5000 Carnegie Class: Spec/Arts
FAX Number: (212) 724-0263 Calendar System: Semester
URL: www.juilliard.edu
Established: 1905 Annual Undergrad Tuition & Fees: $38,190
Enrollment: 926 Coed
Affiliation or Control: Independent Non-Profit IRS Status: 501(c)3
Highest Offering: Doctorate
Program: Professional
Accreditation: M

01 President ... Dr. Joseph W. POLISI
05 Provost & Dean ... Mr. Ara GUZELIMIAN
10 Vice Pres/Chief Operating Officer ... Mr. Jon ROSENHEIN
30 Vice Pres for Dev/Public Affairs ... Ms. Elizabeth HURLEY
08 VP for Library/Info Resources ... Ms. Jane GOTTLIEB
18 Vice Pres for Facilities Management ... Mr. Joseph MASTRANGELO
21 Vice Pres for Finance & Controller ... Ms. Christine TODD
84 Vice Pres for Enroll Mgmt/Stdnt Dev ... Ms. Joan D. WARREN
88 Vice Pres for Global Initiatives ... Mr. Christopher MOSSEY
43 Vice President & General Counsel ... Mr. Maurice F. EDELSON
26 Associate VP for Communications ... Ms. Janet KESSIN
88 Assoc VP for Special Projects ... Ms. Tricia ROSS
32 Dean of Student Affairs ... Ms. Jennifer AWE
20 Associate Dean Academic Affairs ... Mr. Jose GARCIA-LEON
07 Associate Dean for Admissions ... Ms. Lee CIOPPA
64 Assoc Dean/Director Music Division ... Mr. Adam MEYER
64 Asst Dean/Dir of Chamber Music ... Ms. Barli NUGENT
35 Asst Dean for Student Affairs ... Ms. Sabrina TANBARA
57 Director Richard Rodgers Drama Div ... Mr. James HOUGHTON
57 Artistic Director of Dance Division ... Mr. Lawrence RHODES
88 Artistic Director of Vocal Arts ... Mr. Brian ZEGER
88 Artist in Residence/Artistic Advise ... Ms. Monica HUGGETT
88 Director of Historical Performance ... Mr. Robert MEALY
88 Artistic Dir Pre-College Division ... Ms. Yoheved KAPLINSKY
06 Registrar ... Ms. Katherine GERTSON
15 Director of Human Resources ... Ms. Caryn G. DOKTOR
38 Director of Counseling Services ... Mr. William BUSE
37 Director Student Financial Aid ... Ms. Tina GONZALEZ
88 Director of Juilliard Jazz ... Mr. Wynton MARSALIS
96 Director of Office Services ... Mr. Scott A. HOLDEN
36 Director Career Services ... Ms. Courtney BURTON
13 Chief Technology Officer ... Mr. Tunde GIWA

Kehilath Yakov Rabbinical Seminary (J)

638 Bedford Avenue, Brooklyn NY 11211-8007
County: Kings FICE Identification: 010549
Unit ID: 192165
Telephone: (718) 963-1212 Carnegie Class: Spec/Faith
FAX Number: (718) 387-8586 Calendar System: Semester
Established: 1948 Annual Undergrad Tuition & Fees: $9,900
Enrollment: 96 Male
Affiliation or Control: Independent Non-Profit IRS Status: 501(c)3
Highest Offering: First Talmudic Degree
Program: Teacher Preparatory; Professional
Accreditation: RABN

01 President ... Mr. Sandor SCHWARTZ

Keuka College (K)

141 Central Avenue, Keuka Park NY 14478
County: Yates FICE Identification: 002744
Unit ID: 192192
Telephone: (315) 279-5000 Carnegie Class: Master's S
FAX Number: (315) 279-5216 Calendar System: Semester
URL: www.keuka.edu
Established: 1890 Annual Undergrad Tuition & Fees: $28,917
Enrollment: 1,999 Coed
Affiliation or Control: Independent Non-Profit IRS Status: 501(c)3
Highest Offering: Master's
Program: Liberal Arts And General; Teacher Preparatory; Professional

Accreditation: M, IACBE, NURSE, OT, SW, TEAC

01 President .... Dr. Jorge L. DIAZ-HERRERA
05 Provost/VP for Academic Affairs .... Dr. Paul FORESTELL
10 VP for Finance/Administration .... Mr. Jerry HILLER
30 VP for Advancement/External Affs .... Ms. Amy STOREY
84 VP for Enroll Mgmt/Student Devel .... Mr. Mark PETRIE
20 Asc Vice Pres of Academic Programs .... Dr. Timothy SELLERS
36 Dean Student Engagement/Success .... Ms. Elizabeth LAMBERT
08 Director of Library .... Ms. Linda PARK
29 Exec Director of Alumni/Fam Rels .... Ms. Kathy WAYE
25 Exec Dir of Grants/Govt Rel/Comp .... Mr. Doug LIPPINCOTT
37 Director Financial Aid .... Ms. Jennifer BATES
108 Dir of Institutional Assessment .... Ms. Dorothy SCHRAMM
13 Chief Information Officer .... Ms. Andrea CAMPBELL
18 Director of Facilities .... Mr. Tony TUFANO
21 Controller .... Ms. Carol N. GROVER
19 Director of Campus Security .... Mr. James CUNNINGHAM
23 Coordinator of Health Services .... Ms. Cindy CHRISTIE
38 Director of Counseling Services .. Ms. Mary MARTINI-HAUSNER
32 AVP for Student Devel/Dean Stdnts .... Ms. Tracy MCFARLAND
07 Director of Admissions on Campus .... Ms. Megan RYAN
41 Director of Athletics .... Mr. David M. SWEET
107 AVP Center for Professional Studies .... Dr. Anne KILLEN
42 College Chaplain .... Mr. Eric DETAR
06 Registrar .... Mr. Carl DICKINSON
44 Sr Director of Advancement .... Ms. Ann TURNER
26 Dir of Marketing/Communications .... Mr. Pete BEKISZ
96 Purchasing Agent .... Ms. Audrey THORNTON
15 Director of Human Resources .... Ms. Michelle POLOWCHAK
76 Div Chair Occupational Therapy .... Dr. Victoria SMITH
83 Div Chair Basic Soc & Applied Sci .... Dr. Tom TREMER
50 Div Chair Business & Management .... Dr. Daniel ROBESON
53 Div Chair Ed & Dir Ed Grad Studies .... Dr. Pat PULVER
79 Div Chair Humanities/Fine Arts .... Dr. Jennie JOINER
81 Div Chair Natural Sciences/Math .... Dr. Michael KECK
66 Div Chair Nursing .... Dr. Deb GATES
70 Div Chair Social Work .... Ms. Stephanie CRAIG

The King's College (A)

56 Broadway, New York NY 10004-1613
County: New York FICE Identification: 040953
Unit ID: 454184
Telephone: (212) 659-7200 Carnegie Class: Bac/A&S
FAX Number: (212) 659-7210 Calendar System: Semester
URL: www.tkc.edu
Established: 1938 Annual Undergrad Tuition & Fees: $33,270
Enrollment: 473 Coed
Affiliation or Control: Independent Non-Profit IRS Status: 501(c)3
Highest Offering: Baccalaureate
Program: Liberal Arts And General; Business Emphasis
Accreditation: M

00 Chairman of the Board of Trustees .... Mr. William Lee HANLEY
01 President .... Dr. Gregory A. THORNBURY
07 Vice Pres Admissions/Advancement .... Dr. Kimberly THORNBURY
32 Vice President Student Development .... Mr. Eric BENNETT
05 Vice President for Academic Affairs .... Dr. Mark HIJLEH
35 Dean of Students .... Mr. David LEEDY
10 Vice President Finance/CFO .... Mr. Frank TORINO
21 Controller .... Ms. Judy BARRINGER
06 Registrar .... Ms. Leticia MOSQUEDA
37 Director of Financial Services .... Ms. Anna PETERS
04 Executive Asst to President .... Ms. Bre DUFFY
09 Director of Institutional Research .... Dr. Kimberly THORNBURY
11 Chief Administration Officer .... Mr. Kevin BROWN
15 Director Personnel Services .... Ms. Melody GARCIA
18 Chief Facilities/Physical Plant .... Mr. Rich SWITZER
26 Chief Public Relations Officer .... Ms. Natalie NAKAMURA
29 Acting Director of Alumni Relations .... Dr. Kimberly THORNBURY
36 Director Student Placement .... Ms. Michele DEKONTY
38 Director Student Counseling .... Ms. Stacy CHEN
84 Director Enrollment Management .... Mr. Luke SMITH
08 Head Librarian .... Ms. Christina ROGERS
39 Director Student Housing .... Mr. Nick SWEDICK
41 Athletic Director .... Mr. Sean HORAN

Le Moyne College (B)

1419 Salt Springs Road, Syracuse NY 13214-1301
County: Onondaga FICE Identification: 002748
Unit ID: 192323
Telephone: (315) 445-4100 Carnegie Class: Master's L
FAX Number: (315) 445-4540 Calendar System: Semester
URL: www.lemoyne.edu
Established: 1946 Annual Undergrad Tuition & Fees: $32,250
Enrollment: 3,148 Coed
Affiliation or Control: Independent Non-Profit IRS Status: 501(c)3
Highest Offering: Master's
Program: Liberal Arts And General; Teacher Preparatory; Professional; Business Emphasis
Accreditation: M, ARCPA, BUS, NURSE, TEAC

01 President .... Dr. Linda M. LEMURA
05 Interim Provost & VP Acad Affairs .... Dr. Thomas P. BROCKELMAN
84 Chief Enrollment Strategist .... Mr. Don SALEH
10 Senior VP Fin & Admin & Treasurer .... Mr. Roger W. STACKPOOLE
30 Vice Pres Inst Advancement .... Mr. Bill BROWER
32 Vice Pres Student Development .... Dr. Deborah M. CADY MELZER
88 Special Asst for Mission & Identity .... Rev. David C. MCCALLUM, SJ
88 Rector of the Jesuit Community .... Rev. John P. BUCKI, SJ
22 EEO/Affirmative Action Officer .... Mr. Tim BARRETT
49 Dean of Arts & Sciences .. Dr. Kathleen P. COSTELLO-SULLIVAN
50 Dean School of Business .... Mr. James E. JOSEPH
58 Dean of Graduate & Prof Studies .... Dr. Dennis R. DEPERRO
20 Assoc Provost .... Dr. Mary K. COLLINS
51 Director of Continuing Education .... Ms. Patricia J. BLISS
08 Director of the Library .... Dr. Robert C. JOHNSTON
07 Senior Director of Admission .... Ms. Mary CHANDLER
88 Sr Dir Enrollment Management .... Ms. Kristen P. TRAPASSO
88 Dir of Transfer Admission .... Mr. Scott SETEK
37 Int Asst VP for Enrollment Mngt .... Mr. William C. CHEETHAM
06 Registrar/Sr Director Enrollment .... Ms. Cynthia A. ALIBRANDI
21 Assoc VP for Finance & Controller .... Mr. Brian M. LOUCY
41 Asst VP & Director of Athletics .... Mr. Matthew D. BASSETT
18 Asst VP Facilities Mgmt & Planning .... Mr. Jed S. SCHNEIDER
15 Director of Human Resources .... Mr. Tim BARRETT
13 Acting Director of Info Technology .... Mr. Shaun C. BLACK
09 Director of Institutional Research .... Dr. Daniel L. SKIDMORE
40 Bookstore Manager .... Ms. Jessica L. MANNINO
26 Assoc VP for Marketing .... Mr. Peter S. KILLIAN
88 Director of Advancement Services .... Mr. Paul F. LYNCH
29 Director Alumni & Parent Programs ... Ms. Kimberly B. MCAULIFF
44 Dir of Annual Giving/Stewardship .... Ms. Katherine COGSWELL
88 Director of Communications .... Mr. Joseph B. DELLA POSTA
88 Senior Philanthropic Advisor .... Mr. Philip J. GEORGE
86 Director Govt/Foundation Relations .... Mr. Steven W. KULICK
88 Dean for Academic Advising .... Ms. Susan E. AMES
35 Asst Dean for Student Development .... Mr. Mark G. GODLESKI
88 Director Campus Life & Leadership .... Mr. John R. HALEY
42 Director of Campus Ministry .... Rev. John P. BUCKI, SJ
36 Director Career Advising/Devpment .... Ms. Patricia A. BEVANS
88 Dir Collegiate Sci Tech Entry Pgm .... Ms. Darshini ROOPNARINE
38 Director Health/Counseling Center .... Ms. Anne E. KEARNEY
88 Director of HEOP and AHANA .... Mr. Ted EMMANUEL
19 Director of Security .... Mr. Mark J. PETTERELLI
28 Asst to the Provost for Diversity ... Mr. Ludger VIEFHUES-BAILEY
04 Assistant to the President .... Ms. Carly J. COLBERT

LIM College (C)

12 E 53rd Street, New York NY 10022-5268
County: New York FICE Identification: 007466
Unit ID: 192271
Telephone: (212) 752-1530 Carnegie Class: Spec/Bus
FAX Number: (212) 832-6109 Calendar System: Semester
URL: www.limcollege.edu
Established: 1939 Annual Undergrad Tuition & Fees: $24,825
Enrollment: 1,689 Coed
Affiliation or Control: Proprietary IRS Status: Proprietary
Highest Offering: Master's
Program: Professional; Business Emphasis
Accreditation: M, ACBSP

01 President .... Elizabeth S. MARCUSE
03 Provost & Executive Vice President .... Christopher J. CYPHERS
10 Sr VP Finance and Operations/Treas .... Michael T. DONOHUE
00 President Emeritus .... Adrian G. MARCUSE
04 Special Assistant to the President .... Linda HARRIS PAOLILLO
88 Special Assistant to Provost & EVP .... Thomas MCDONALD
04 Assistant to the President .... Vacant
05 Dean of Academic Affairs .... Michael P. LONDRIGAN
58 Director of Graduate Studies .... Jacqueline M. JENKINS
20 Assoc Dean of Academic Affairs .... Patricia FITZMAURICE
08 Director of Library Services .... Lou ACIERNO
06 College Registrar .... Carolyn DISNEW
36 Sr Dir Exper Educ & Career Mgmt .... Susan BAUER
32 Vice Pres for Student Development .... Michael H. FERRY
35 Dean of Student Affairs .... Vacant
35 Assistant Dean of Student Life .... Christopher CONZEN
38 Sr Dir Counseling & Wellness Svcs .... Jodi N. LICHT
39 Dir of Housing & Residence Life .... Jennifer K. LUCIANO
07 Dean of Admissions .... Kristina ORTIZ
07 Director of Admissions Operations .... Tracy NILSEN
07 Associate Director of Admissions .... Vacant
88 Asst VP for Student Success .... William IMBRIALE
09 Director of Institutional Research .... Nikisha WILLIAMS
21 Accounting Manager .... Svetlana KANEVSKAYA
96 Purchasing Director .... Eric MARTIN
88 VP Student Finance/Chief Compl Ofcr .... Christopher E. BARTO
37 Sr Dir of Student Financial Svcs .... Vacant
30 VP for Institutional Advancement .... Gail NARDIN
88 VP for Strategic Initiatives .... Pamela LINTON
26 Director of Communications .... Meredith FINNIN
88 Director of College Marketing .... Laura CIOFFI
105 Web Application Developer .... Joshua J. HELLER
13 Chief Technology Officer .... Maurice MORENCY
14 Director of Information Technology .... Nelson LEON
90 Director of Instructional Tech .... Joseph THOMAS
15 Dir of HR & Title IX Coordinator .... Andrea L. GRANVILLE
18 Manager of Facilities .... Jonathan ABREU
108 VP for Planning & Assessment .... Jacqueline LEBLANC

Long Island Business Institute (D)

6500 Jericho Turnpike, Commack NY 11725
Telephone: (631) 499-7100 Identification: 770746
Accreditation: ACICS

† Branch campus of Long Island Business Institute, Flushing, NY.

Long Island Business Institute (E)

136-18 39th Avenue, Flushing NY 11354
County: Queens FICE Identification: 020937
Unit ID: 192509
Telephone: (718) 939-5100 Carnegie Class: Assoc/PrivFP
FAX Number: (718) 939-9235 Calendar System: Semester
URL: www.libi.edu
Established: 1968 Annual Undergrad Tuition & Fees: $14,769
Enrollment: 397 Coed
Affiliation or Control: Proprietary IRS Status: Proprietary
Highest Offering: Associate Degree
Program: Occupational; 2-Year Principally Bachelor's Creditable; Business Emphasis
Accreditation: ACICS

01 President .... Ms. Monica W. FOOTE
05 Provost .... Ms. Stacey JOHNSON
12 Asst Campus Program Director .... Mr. Jonathan ABAR
11 Dean of Administration .... Mr. Enos CHEUNG
37 Financial Aid Director .... Mr. Nazaret KIREGIAN
08 Librarian Commack Campus .... Ms. Terry CANAVAN
08 Librarian Flushing Campus .... Ms. Adrianna ARGUELLES

*Long Island University (F)

700 Northern Boulevard, Brookville NY 11548-1327
County: Nassau FICE Identification: 002751
Unit ID: 192457
Telephone: (516) 299-2501 Carnegie Class: N/A
FAX Number: N/A
URL: www.liu.edu

01 President .... Dr. Kimberly R. CLINE
11 COO & University Counsel .... Ms. Gale STEVENS HAYNES
30 Chief of Strategic Partnerships/Adv .... Mr. Michael GLICKMAN
05 Vice President Academic Affairs .... Dr. Jeffrey KANE
10 Vice President Finance & Treasurer ... Mr. Christopher N. FEVOLA
88 Sr Advisor & Treasurer Emerita .... Mrs. Mary M. LAI
20 Deputy VP Academic Affairs .... Dr. Lori KNAPP
13 VP for Information Technology & CIO .... Mr. George BAROUDI
21 Assoc Vice Pres/Controller .... Mr. Mark SCHMOTZER
37 Assoc VP Financial Svcs/Compliance .... Mr. David MAINENTI
21 Assoc VP Finance and Budget Dir .... Mr. Kirk LENGA
14 Deputy CIO Information Systems .... Mr. Gavi NARRA
88 Asst VP Instructional Innovation .... Mr. Paul RUSSO
18 Assoc VP for Capital Projects .... Mr. Peter TYMUS
108 Assoc VP for Inst Effectiveness .... Dr. Kathleen GILL
26 Dir Marketing/Advancement Ops .... Ms. Jennifer CARPENTER LOW
09 Exec Dir Institutional Research .... Mr. Claude CHEEK
84 Assoc Dean Enrollment/Registrar .... Ms. Beth WILKOW
15 Interim Exec Dir Human Resources .... Dr. Lee KELLY
25 Executive Director of Grants .... Mr. Alan EVELYN
102 Dir Foundation Relations .... Ms. Suzanne FARRELL
105 Assistant VP of Creative Services .... Mr. Stephen HAUSLER
62 Dean of University Libraries .... Ms. Valeda DENT
96 Dir Sourcing/Procurement Svcs .... Mr. Allan HOWELL

*LIU Post (G)

720 Northern Boulevard, Brookville NY 11548-1300
County: Nassau FICE Identification: 002754
Unit ID: 192448
Telephone: (516) 299-2900 Carnegie Class: Master's L
FAX Number: (516) 299-2137 Calendar System: Semester
URL: www.liu.edu/post
Established: 1954 Annual Undergrad Tuition & Fees: $35,546
Enrollment: 9,486 Coed
Affiliation or Control: Independent Non-Profit IRS Status: 501(c)3
Highest Offering: Doctorate
Program: Occupational; Liberal Arts And General; Teacher Preparatory; Professional
Accreditation: M, BUS, CACR

02 President .... Dr. Kimberly R. CLINE
100 Chief of Staff and Vice President .... Dr. Jackie NEALON
11 Exec Dir Operations/Partnerships .... Ms. Rita LANGDON
07 Dean of Admissions .... Vacant
37 Exec Dir of Student Financial Svcs .... Ms. Joanne GRAZIANO
13 Deputy Chief Information Officer .... Vacant
49 Acting Dean College Lib Arts Scienc .... Dr. Nicholas RAMER
66 Acting Dean Sch Health Prof/Nursing .... Dr. Stacy GROPACK
50 Dean College of Management .... Dr. Robert VALLI
57 Dean School Visual/Performing Arts .... Dr. Noel ZAHLER
53 Dean Col Education/Info/Tech .... Dr. Barbara GARII
51 Dir of Hutton House Continuing Ed .... Dr. Kay SATO
32 Dean of Students/LIU Promise .... Ms. Abagail VAN VLERAH
41 Director of Athletics .... Mr. Bryan COLLINS
35 Associate Dean of Students .... Mr. Adam GROHMAN
88 Director of Campus Life .... Mr. Michael BERTHEL
18 Director of Facilities .... Mr. William KIRKER
19 Director of Public Safety .... Mr. Paul RAPESS

**LIU Brentwood* (H)

Grant Campus, 1001 Crooked Hill Rd., Brentwood NY 11717
Telephone: (631) 287-8500 Identification: 666076
Accreditation: &M

† Branch campus of LIU Post, Brookville, NY.

* LIU Brooklyn (A)

1 University Plaza, Brooklyn NY 11201-5372
Telephone: (718) 488-1011 FICE Identification: 004779
Accreditation: &M, ARCPA, CAATE, CLPSY, COARC, DMS, NURSE, OT, PHAR, PTA, SP, SPAA, SURGT, SW, TEAC

† Branch campus of LIU Post, Brookville, NY.

* LIU Hudson at Rockland (B)

70 Route 340, Orangeburg NY 10962
Telephone: (845) 359-7200 Identification: 666077
Accreditation: &M

† Branch campus of LIU Post, Brookville, NY.

* LIU Hudson at Westchester (C)

735 Anderson Hill Road, Purchase NY 10577
Telephone: (914) 831-2700 Identification: 666078
Accreditation: &M, TEAC

† Branch campus of LIU Post, Brookville, NY.

* LIU Riverhead (D)

121 Speonk-Riverhead Road - LIU Bld, Riverhead NY 11901-3499
Telephone: (631) 287-8010 Identification: 666174
Accreditation: &M, TEAC

† Branch campus of LIU Post, Brookville, NY.

Louis V. Gerstner Jr. Graduate School of Biomedical Sciences, Memorial Sloan Kettering Cancer Center (E)

1275 York Avenue, P.O. Box 441, New York NY 10065
County: New York Identification: 666643
Unit ID: 458511
Telephone: (646) 888-6639 Carnegie Class: Not Classified
FAX Number: N/A Calendar System: Semester
URL: www.sloankettering.edu
Established: 2004 Annual Graduate Tuition & Fees: $37,279
Enrollment: 60 Coed
Affiliation or Control: Independent Non-Profit IRS Status: 501(c)3
Highest Offering: Doctorate; No Undergraduates
Program: Professional
Accreditation: NY

01 President .... Dr. Craig B. THOMPSON
05 Provost .... Dr. Joan MASSAGUE
20 Dean .... Dr. Kenneth J. MARIANS
88 Associate Dean .... Mrs. Linda BURNLEY
06 Registrar .... Miss Iwona ABRAMEK
08 Head Librarian .... Ms. Donna S. GIBSON

Machzikei Hadath Rabbinical College (F)

5407 16th Avenue, Brooklyn NY 11204-1805
County: Kings FICE Identification: 013026
Unit ID: 192624
Telephone: (718) 854-8777 Carnegie Class: Spec/Faith
FAX Number: (718) 851-1265 Calendar System: Semester
Established: 1956 Annual Undergrad Tuition & Fees: $11,050
Enrollment: 147 Male
Affiliation or Control: Independent Non-Profit IRS Status: 501(c)3
Highest Offering: First Talmudic Degree
Program: Teacher Preparatory
Accreditation: RABN

01 President .... Mr. Alexander SCHAECHTER

Mandl School (G)

254 W 54th Street, 9th Floor, New York NY 10019
County: New York FICE Identification: 007401
Unit ID: 192688
Telephone: (212) 247-3434 Carnegie Class: Assoc/PrivFP
FAX Number: (212) 247-3617 Calendar System: Semester
URL: www.mandl.edu
Established: 1924 Annual Undergrad Tuition & Fees: $13,200
Enrollment: 765 Coed
Affiliation or Control: Proprietary IRS Status: Proprietary
Highest Offering: Associate Degree
Program: Occupational; 2-Year Principally Bachelor's Creditable; Technical Emphasis
Accreditation: ABHES, #COARC, SURTEC

01 President .... Mr. Melvyn P. WEINER
05 Vice President of Academic Affairs .... Dr. Orsete DIAS
37 EVP/Director of Financial Aid .... Mr. Stuart WEINER
36 Vice President of Career Services .... Mr. James FLANAGAN
06 Dean of Records & Registration .... Mr. Marc WEINER
84 Director of Enrollment Management .... Ms. Randie SENSER
06 Registrar .... Ms. Manique HIGHSMITH
07 Director of Recruitment .... Ms. Racquel GARCIA
08 Head Librarian .... Ms. Clover STEELE
32 Assistant Dean Student Support Svcs .. Dr. Karlene RICHARDSON
10 Chief Business Officer .... Mrs. Nettie WEINER
100 Chief of Staff .... Ms. Maritza E. MERCADO

Manhattan College (H)

Manhattan College Parkway, Bronx NY 10471-4099
County: Bronx FICE Identification: 002758
Unit ID: 192703
Telephone: (718) 862-8000 Carnegie Class: Master's M
FAX Number: (718) 862-8014 Calendar System: Semester
URL: www.manhattan.edu
Established: 1853 Annual Undergrad Tuition & Fees: $38,900
Enrollment: 3,471 Coed
Affiliation or Control: Independent Non-Profit IRS Status: 501(c)3
Highest Offering: Master's
Program: Liberal Arts And General; Teacher Preparatory; Professional
Accreditation: M, BUS, ENG, TEAC

01 President .... Dr. Brennan O'DONNELL
05 Executive Vice President & Provost .... Dr. William CLYDE
10 VP for Finance & CFO .... Mr. Matthew S. MCMANNESS
32 Vice President Student Life .... Dr. Richard SATTERLEE
30 Vice President College Advancement .... Mr. Thomas MAURIELLO
15 Vice President for Human Resources .... Ms. Barbara A. FABE
18 Vice President for Facilities .... Mr. Andrew RYAN
84 Vice President Enrollment Mgmt .... Dr. William J. BISSET
88 Vice President for Mission .... Br. Jack CURRAN
20 Assoc Prov Res/Fac/Computer System .. Mr. Walter F. MATYSTIK
35 Assistant VP of Student Life .... Dr. Emmanuel AGO
35 Dean of Students .... Dr. Michael CAREY
06 Registrar .... Vacant
07 Director of Admissions .... Ms. Dana ROSE
08 Director of Libraries .... Dr. William WALTERS
13 Director of Information Tech Svcs .... Mr. Jake HOLMQUIST
19 Director of Public Safety .... Mr. Juan E. CEREZO
29 Director of Alumni Relations .... Mr. Thomas MCCARTHY
26 Director of Mktg & Communications .... Mrs. Lydia E. GRAY
36 Director Ctr Career Development .... Vacant
36 Director Ctr Career Development .... Ms. Rachel CIRELLI
38 Dir of Counseling & Health Services .... Dr. Terence HANNIGAN
39 Director of Residence Life .... Mr. Andrew WEINGARTEN
41 Director of Athletics .... Mr. Noah LEFEVRE
42 Director of Campus Ministry .... Ms. Lois HARR
44 Director of Development/Advancement .... Mr. Stephen WHITE
78 Director Academic Support Services .... Ms. Marilyn CARTER-STEVENS
40 Director of Campus Bookstore .... Mr. Henry CASTILLO
22 Dir of Personnel/Affirm Action Ofcr .... Ms. Vickie M. COWAN
09 Dir Inst Research/Assessment .... Dr. David MAHAN
21 Controller .... Mr. Dennis LONERGAN
21 Business Manager .... Mr. Kenneth WALDHOF
85 International Student Advisor .... Ms. Debra L. DAMICO
37 Director of Student Financial Svcs .... Vacant
49 Dean of Arts .... Dr. Keith BROWER
50 Dean of Business .... Dr. Salwa AMMAR
53 Dean of Education .... Dr. William J. MERRIMAN
54 Dean of Engineering .... Dr. Tim WARD
51 Exec Dir Sch Cont & Prof Studies .... Dr. Cheryl HARRISON
88 Director Ctr for Academic Success .... Ms. Marisa PASSAFIUME
81 Dean of Science .... Dr. Constantine THEODOSIOU
88 Dir of Specialized Resource Center .... Ms. Anne VACCARO
88 Dir Grad & Fellowship Advisement .... Dr. Rani R. ROY

Manhattan School of Music (I)

120 Claremont Avenue, New York NY 10027-4698
County: New York FICE Identification: 002759
Unit ID: 192712
Telephone: (212) 749-2802 Carnegie Class: Spec/Arts
FAX Number: (212) 749-5471 Calendar System: Semester
URL: www.msmnyc.edu
Established: 1917 Annual Undergrad Tuition & Fees: $42,600
Enrollment: 905 Coed
Affiliation or Control: Independent Non-Profit IRS Status: 501(c)3
Highest Offering: Doctorate
Program: Professional; Music Emphasis
Accreditation: M

01 President .... Dr. James GANDRE
05 Provost and Senior Vice President .... Dr. Marjorie MERRYMAN
10 VP for Business and Finance .... Mr. Gary MEYER
30 Vice President for Advancement .... Ms. Andrea T. SANSEVERINO GALAN
26 VP for Media and Communications .... Mr. Jeff BREITHAUPT
84 Dean of Enrollment .... Ms. Amy A. ANDERSON
32 Dean of Students .... Dr. Monica CHRISTENSEN
15 Sr Director Admin & Human Relations .... Ms. Carol MATOS
106 Dean of Dist Learning & Rec Arts .... Ms. Christianne ORTO
101 Liaison to the Board of Trustees .... Mr. Marc DAY
20 Assistant Dean of Academics .... Dr. Marjean OLSON
06 Registrar .... Mr. David MCDONAGH
13 Director of IT .... Vacant
14 Assistant IT Director .... Mr. Luis MOREL
37 Director of Financial Aid .... Mr. Adam GHILONI
35 Director of Student Life .... Ms. Melanie DORSEY
39 Director of Residence Life .... Mr. Jim LOVE
31 Director of Educational Outreach .... Ms. Rebecca CHARNOW
29 Alumni Manager .... Ms. Lauren FRANKOVICH
08 Director of Library Services .... Mr. Peter CALEB
102 Director of Foundation Relations .... Ms. Ronnie BORISKIN
40 Campus Store Manager .... Ms. Katherine COPLAND
85 Director Intl Student Services .... Mr. Michael LOCKHART
88 Dir Ctr for Music Entrepreneurship .... Dr. Angela BEECHING
88 Dean of Instrumental Performance .... Mr. David GEBER
21 Director of Accounting & Controller .... Ms. Susan FINK
18 Dir of Facilities & Campus Safety .... Mr. Luis PLAZA
07 Director of Admissions .... Ms. Christan CASSIDY
100 Chief of Staff .... Mr. Bryan GREANEY
19 Director Security/Safety .... Mr. Luis PLAZA

Manhattanville College (J)

2900 Purchase Street, Purchase NY 10577-2132
County: Westchester FICE Identification: 002760
Unit ID: 192749
Telephone: (914) 694-2200 Carnegie Class: Master's L
FAX Number: (914) 694-2386 Calendar System: Semester
URL: www.mville.edu
Established: 1841 Annual Undergrad Tuition & Fees: $36,220
Enrollment: 1,707 Coed
Affiliation or Control: Independent Non-Profit IRS Status: 501(c)3
Highest Offering: Doctorate
Program: Liberal Arts And General; Teacher Preparatory
Accreditation: M, IACBE, TED

01 President .... Mr. Jon C. STRAUSS
100 Chief of Staff .... Ms. Laura PROSTANO
04 Exec Admin Asst to the President .... Ms. Deborah A. FALLONE
05 Provost/VP of Academic Affairs .... Dr. Lisa DOLLING
10 VP Finance/Administration .... Ms. Marina VASARHELYI
84 Vice Pres Enrollment Management .... Mr. Nikhil KUMAR
30 Vice Pres Inst Advance/Alum Rels .... Ms. Teresa WEBER
11 Vice President of Operations .... Mr. Gregory PALMER
32 Int Vice Pres of Student Affairs .... Mr. John BALOG
58 Dean School of Business .... Dr. Anthony DAVIDSON
53 Dean School of Education .... Dr. Shelley WEPNER
26 Managing Dir Media/PR/Comm .... Ms. Jennifer JAMES PRYOR
06 Registrar .... Mr. Thomas MURASSO
85 Director of English Lang Institute .... Ms. Judith H. LEWIS
08 Director of the Library .... Mr. Jeff ROSEDALE
37 Director of Financial Aid .... Mr. Robert GILMORE
38 Director of Counseling Center .... Dr. Glenn POLLACK
35 Dean of Students .... Ms. Sharlise SMITH-RODRIGUEZ
41 Director of Athletics .... Mr. Keith LEVINTHAL
42 Int Catholic Chpln/Interfaith Coord .... Fr. Wil TYRRELL
36 Director Center for Career Devel .... Vacant
19 Director of Security .... Mr. Anthony HERRMANN
07 Director of Admissions .... Mr. Joseph COSENTINO
15 Director of Human Resources .... Mr. Don DEAN
35 Asst Director of Student Activities .... Mr. Andrew FULTON
96 Director of Purchasing .... Ms. Cheryl DOBSON
101 Secretary of the Board .... Ms. Laura PROSTANO
103 Dir Career Development .... Ms. Shannon HARGROVE
104 Director Study Abroad .... Mr. Wil TYRRELL
22 Dir Affirmative Action/EEO .... Mr. Donald DEAN
23 Director Health Center .... Ms. Kristen DONOHUE-GONZALES

Maria College of Albany (K)

700 New Scotland Avenue, Albany NY 12208-1798
County: Albany FICE Identification: 002763
Unit ID: 192785
Telephone: (518) 438-3111 Carnegie Class: Assoc/PrivNFP
FAX Number: (518) 438-7170 Calendar System: 4/1/4
URL: www.mariacollege.edu
Established: 1958 Annual Undergrad Tuition & Fees: $13,020
Enrollment: 886 Coed
Affiliation or Control: Independent Non-Profit IRS Status: 501(c)3
Highest Offering: Baccalaureate
Program: Liberal Arts And General
Accreditation: M, ADNUR, NUR, OTA

01 President .... Dr. Lea JOHNSON
05 Vice President for Academic Affairs .... Dr. John KOWAL
10 Chief Financial Officer .... Ms. Michele AURICCHIO
30 Director Development .... Ms. Helen ADAMS-KEANE
37 Director Financial Aid .... Ms. Donna MYERS
84 Dean of Enrollment Management .... Mr. Thomas D. IWANKOW
21 Director of Business Affairs .... Mrs. Frances BERNARD
06 Registrar .... Ms. Kari BENNETT
07 Director of Admissions .... Mr. John RAMOSKA
08 Director Library .... Vacant
32 Dean Student Svcs/Dir Counsel Ctr .... Ms. Deborah CORRIGAN
13 Director of Information Technology .... Mr. Mark HATLEE
18 Superintendent Physical Plant .... Mr. Andrew PEREZ
36 Director Career Services .... Mr. Andrew LEDOUX
26 Director Marketing/Communications .... Ms. Beth WALES
42 Campus Minister .... Mrs. Michelle THIVIERGE

Marist College (L)

3399 North Road, Poughkeepsie NY 12601-1387
County: Dutchess FICE Identification: 002765
Unit ID: 192819
Telephone: (845) 575-3000 Carnegie Class: Master's L
FAX Number: (845) 471-6213 Calendar System: Semester
URL: www.marist.edu
Established: 1929 Annual Undergrad Tuition & Fees: $33,250
Enrollment: 6,356 Coed
Affiliation or Control: Independent Non-Profit IRS Status: 501(c)3
Highest Offering: Master's
Program: Liberal Arts And General; Teacher Preparatory; Professional

Accreditation: M, BUS, CAATE, MT, SPAA, SW, TED

01 President Dr. Dennis J. MURRAY
03 Executive Vice President Dr. Geoffrey L. BRACKETT
05 Vice President for Academic Affairs Dr. Thomas S. WERMUTH
84 VP Admission & Enrollment Planning Mr. Sean P. KAYLOR
30 Vice President College Advancement Mr. Christopher M. DELGIORNO
13 VP Information Technology/CIO Mr. William T. THIRSK
32 VP/Dean of Student Affairs Mrs. Deborah A. DICAPRIO
10 Vice President Business Affairs/CFO Mr. John P. PECCHIA
20 Assoc VP/Dean Academic Affairs Dr. John RITSCHDORFF
07 Asst VP Enroll Mgmt/Dean UG Admiss Mr. Kenton W. RINEHART
35 Assoc Dean of Student Affairs Mr. Steve SANSOLA
29 Executive Director Alumni Relations Ms. Amy K. WOODS
09 Director Inst Research & Planning Dr. Judith STODDARD
20 Assoc Dean of Academic Affairs Mrs. Judith IVANKOVIC
37 Exec Dir Student Financial Services Mr. Joseph R. WEGLARZ
08 Director Library Vacant
90 Director Academic Technology Mr. Joshua D. BARON
18 Director of Physical Plant Mr. Justin BUTWELL
26 Chief Public Affairs Officer Mr. Gregory CANNON
15 Assoc VP for Human Resources Mrs. Deborah RAIKES-COLBERT
96 Director of Purchasing Mr. Stephen J. KOCHIS
36 Director Career Services Mr. Stephen W. COLE
19 Director of Safety & Security Mr. John T. GILDARD
39 Director of Housing & Resident Life Mrs. Sarah H. ENGLISH
41 Director of Athletics Mr. Timothy S. MURRAY
04 Executive Assitant to the President Ms. Eileen SICO
24 Director of Media & Instruct Tech Ms. Joey WALL
23 Director of Health Services Dr. Mary L. DUNNE
38 Director of Counseling Dr. Naomi A. FERLEGER
43 Director Campus Ministry Bro. Francis E. KELLY
44 Director of Annual Giving Ms. Jeanine M. THOMPSON

Marymount Manhattan College (A)

221 E 71st Street, New York NY 10021-4597
County: New York FICE Identification: 002769
Unit ID: 192864
Telephone: (212) 517-0400 Carnegie Class: Bac/A&S
FAX Number: (212) 517-0541 Calendar System: Semester
URL: www.mmm.edu
Established: 1936 Annual Undergrad Tuition & Fees: $28,700
Enrollment: 1,858 Coed
Affiliation or Control: Independent Non-Profit IRS Status: 501(c)3
Highest Offering: Baccalaureate
Program: Liberal Arts And General
Accreditation: M

01 President Dr. Kerry WALK
05 VP Acad Affairs/Dean of Faculty Dr. David PODELL
10 Exec Vice Pres Admin & Finance Mr. Paul CIRAULO
30 VP Institutional Advancement Ms. Marilyn L. WILKIE
32 VP Student Affairs Dr. Carol JACKSON
21 Associate Vice Pres & Controller Mr. Wayne SANTUCCI
07 Dean of Admissions Mr. James ROGERS
20 Associate Dean for Academic Affairs Dr. Kathleen LEBESCO
06 Registrar Ms. Regina CHAN
15 Director of Human Resources Ms. Bree BULLINGHAM
08 Librarian Mr. Brian ROCCO
13 Director Information Technology Ms. Patricia HANSEN
37 Director Student Financial Svcs Ms. Maria DEINNOCENTIIS
38 Dir Counseling & Psychological Svcs Dr. Paul GRAYSON
18 Director of Facilities Mr. Pete ROMAIN
36 Director Career Svcs & Internships Ms. Melissa BENCA
96 Director of Purchasing Ms. Maria MARZANO
88 Asst Controller Ms. Cassie GOULD
44 Director of Development Ms. Caitlin KIRKLIN
09 Assoc Dir Institutional Research Ms. Cheryl GOLDSTEIN
19 Director of Campus Safety Mr. Peter DECARO
26 Dir Public Relations/Marketing Ms. Stephanie POLICASTRO
28 Dean of Students/Diversity Officer Ms. Christine GREGORY
39 Director of Residence Life Ms. Emmalyn YAMRICK

Medaille College (B)

18 Agassiz Circle, Buffalo NY 14214-2695
County: Erie FICE Identification: 002777
Unit ID: 192925
Telephone: (716) 880-2000 Carnegie Class: Master's L
FAX Number: (716) 884-0291 Calendar System: Semester
URL: www.medaille.edu
Established: 1875 Annual Undergrad Tuition & Fees: $26,252
Enrollment: 2,136 Coed
Affiliation or Control: Independent Non-Profit IRS Status: 501(c)3
Highest Offering: Doctorate
Program: Liberal Arts And General; Teacher Preparatory
Accreditation: M, CACREP, CAHIIM, IACBE, TEAC

01 President Dr. Kenneth M. MACUR
05 Vice President Academic Affairs Dr. Norman R. MUIR
10 Vice President Business/Finance Mr. Matthew J. CARVER
30 Vice Pres for College Relations Mr. John P. CRAWFORD
07 VP Enroll Mgmt/Marketing/Admiss Mr. Christopher LARUSSO
20 Assoc Vice Pres Academic Affairs Dr. Sonja M. BROWN GIVENS
09 Asst Vice Pres Institutional Rsrch Mr. Patrick S. MCDONALD
32 Dean for Student Affairs Ms. Amy M. DEKAY
44 Dir of Major Gifts & Planned Giving Ms. Jeanine PURCELL
41 Athletic Director Ms. Amy DEKAY
36 Director Career Planning/Placement Ms. Carol CULLINAN
26 Chief Information Officer Mr. Robert D. CHYKA
06 Registrar Mrs. Kathleen LAZAR
08 Library Director Mr. Andrew YEAGER
37 Director Financial Aid Ms. Catherine BUZANSKI
15 Director of Human Resources Ms. Barbara J. BILOTTA
35 Director of Student Involvement Ms. Kayla A. BETACCHINI
38 Director Counseling Services Ms. Jeannine D. SUK
19 Director of Campus Public Safety Mr. Ronald J. CHRISTOPHER
29 Coordinator of Alumni Relations Mr. Nicholas J. KOZIOL
26 Director of Marketing Ms. Melissa D. HARRIS

Medaille College Rochester Branch Campus (C)

1880 S Winston Road, Rochester NY 14618
Telephone: (585) 272-0030 Identification: 770140
Accreditation: &M

† Branch campus of Medaille College, Buffalo, NY.

Memorial School of Nursing (D)

600 Northern Boulevard, Albany NY 12204-1004
County: Albany FICE Identification: 012203
Unit ID: 192961
Telephone: (518) 471-3260 Carnegie Class: Assoc/PrivNFP
FAX Number: (518) 447-3559 Calendar System: Semester
URL: www.nehealth.com
Established: Annual Undergrad Tuition & Fees: $11,287
Enrollment: 127 Coed
Affiliation or Control: Independent Non-Profit IRS Status: 501(c)3
Highest Offering: Associate Degree
Program: 2-Year Principally Bachelor's Creditable; Nursing Emphasis
Accreditation: NY, ADNUR

01 Director Ms. Mary-Jane S. ARALDI

Mercy College (E)

555 Broadway, Dobbs Ferry NY 10522-1189
County: Westchester FICE Identification: 002772
Unit ID: 193016
Telephone: (800) 637-2969 Carnegie Class: Master's L
FAX Number: (914) 674-5978 Calendar System: Semester
URL: www.mercy.edu
Established: 1950 Annual Undergrad Tuition & Fees: $18,076
Enrollment: 11,272 Coed
Affiliation or Control: Independent Non-Profit IRS Status: 501(c)3
Highest Offering: Doctorate
Program: 2-Year Principally Bachelor's Creditable; Liberal Arts And General; Teacher Preparatory; Professional
Accreditation: M, ARCPA, CAEP, NURSE, OT, OTA, PTA, SP, SW, TED

01 President Dr. Timothy HALL
05 Provost & Vice Pres Acad Affairs Dr. Concetta STEWART
20 Associate Provost for Acad Affairs Dr. Lucretia MANN
50 Dean School of Business Dr. Ed WEIS
53 Dean School of Education Dr. Alfred POSAMENTIER
83 Dean School Soc/Behavioral Sci Dr. Karol DEAN
76 Dean School Health/Natural Sci Dr. Joan TOGLIA
49 Dean School Liberal Arts Dr. Tamara JHASHI
15 Exec Dir of Human Resources/Safety Ms. Anne GILMARTIN
11 Chief Operating Officer Mr. Joseph SCHAEFER
84 Vice Pres for Enrollment Management Ms. Deirdre WHITMAN
10 VP & Chief Financial/Plng Officer Mr. Donald AUNGST
32 VP of Student Services Ms. Margaret MCGRAIL
35 Chief Student Affairs Officer Mr. William MARTINOV
30 Chief Advancement Officer Ms. Bernadette WADE
100 Chief of Staff Ms. Irene BUCKLEY
04 Staff Assistant Ms. Grace CREIGHTON
108 Director of Educational Assessment Ms. Victoria FERRARA
43 General Counsel Ms. Kristen BOWES
07 Executive Director of Admissions Ms. Tara FAY-REILLY
09 Dir Institutional Research/Planning Ms. Victoria TYLER
88 Exec Director External Affairs Mr. Andy PERSON
39 Assistant Dean of Student Affairs Ms. Patricia CHRISTIANO
35 Dean of Student Affairs Mr. Kevin JOYCE
13 Director of Information Technology Mr. Todd PRATTELLA
06 Exec Director of Sys Mgmt/Registrar Ms. Debra KENNEY
45 Asst VP of Inst Assess/Plng/Analy Ms. Jessica HABER
21 Director of Business Operations Ms. Felicia BRANDON
21 Controller Ms. Narda ROMERO
45 Director of Budgets & Planning Mr. Bernard COSTELLO
96 Director of Purchasing Ms. Patricia SABATINO
08 Director of Mercy College Libraries Mr. Mustafa SAKARYA
41 Director of Athletics Mr. Matt KILCULLEN
26 Director of Communications Ms. Jessica BAILY
29 Director of Alumni Relations Ms. Alexis MCGRATH
25 Dir Sponsored Programs Ms. Monique CAUBERE
104 Director Center Global Engagement Dr. Sheila GERSH
106 Director Online Learning Dr. Mary LOZINA
18 Executive Director of Facilities Mr. Tom SIMMONDS
19 Director Security/Safety Ms. Anne GILMARTIN
103 Senior Director of Career Services Ms. Jill HART
101 Secretary of the Institution/Board Ms. Irene BUCKLEY
105 Director Web Services Ms. Alexis D'AGOSTINO
37 Director Student Financial Aid Ms. Margaret MCGRAIL
44 Director Annual or Planned Giving Mr. Phil KEEFE

Mesivta of Eastern Parkway Rabbinical Seminary (F)

510 Dahill Road, Brooklyn NY 11218-5559
County: Kings FICE Identification: 009335
Unit ID: 193061
Telephone: (718) 438-1002 Carnegie Class: Spec/Faith
FAX Number: (718) 438-2591 Calendar System: Semester
Established: 1947 Annual Undergrad Tuition & Fees: $11,825
Enrollment: 32 Male
Affiliation or Control: Independent Non-Profit IRS Status: 501(c)3
Highest Offering: Second Talmudic Degree
Program: Teacher Preparatory; Professional
Accreditation: RABN

01 President Rabbi Issac HEIMOVITZ
32 Dean of Students Rabbi Shlomo Z. EPSTEIN
37 Director of Student Financial Aid Rabbi Ira LIBERMAN
46 Director of Research Rabbi Hersch BASCH
10 Chief Fiscal Officer Rabbi Joseph HALBERSTADT

Mesivta Tifereth Jerusalem of America (G)

145 E Broadway, New York NY 10002-6301
County: New York FICE Identification: 003974
Unit ID: 193070
Telephone: (212) 964-2830 Carnegie Class: Spec/Faith
FAX Number: (212) 349-5213 Calendar System: Semester
Established: 1907 Annual Undergrad Tuition & Fees: $13,750
Enrollment: 86 Male
Affiliation or Control: Independent Non-Profit IRS Status: 501(c)3
Highest Offering: Second Talmudic Degree
Program: Teacher Preparatory; Professional
Accreditation: RABN

01 President & Dean Faculties Rabbi David FEINSTEIN
06 Registrar Chana YAMPOLSKY

Mesivta Torah Vodaath Seminary (H)

425 E Ninth Street, Brooklyn NY 11218-5299
County: Kings FICE Identification: 007264
Unit ID: 193052
Telephone: (718) 941-8000 Carnegie Class: Spec/Faith
FAX Number: (718) 941-8032 Calendar System: Semester
Established: 1918 Annual Undergrad Tuition & Fees: $11,000
Enrollment: 279 Male
Affiliation or Control: Independent Non-Profit IRS Status: 501(c)3
Highest Offering: Second Talmudic Degree
Program: Teacher Preparatory; Professional
Accreditation: RABN

01 Dean Rabbi Yisroel BELSKY
03 Executive Director Rabbi Yitzchok GOTTDIENER
06 Registrar Rabbi Yaakov EHRENREICH
33 Dean of Men Rabbi Elya KATZ
31 Director Community Services Mr. Shraga WERNER

Metropolitan College of New York (I)

431 Canal Street, New York NY 10013-1919
County: New York FICE Identification: 009769
Unit ID: 190114
Telephone: (212) 343-1234 Carnegie Class: Master's L
FAX Number: (212) 343-7399 Calendar System: Semester
URL: www.metropolitan.edu
Established: 1964 Annual Undergrad Tuition & Fees: $18,030
Enrollment: 1,228 Coed
Affiliation or Control: Independent Non-Profit IRS Status: 501(c)3
Highest Offering: Master's
Program: Professional; Business Emphasis
Accreditation: M, ACBSP, TED

01 President Dr. Vinton THOMPSON
10 VP Finance & Admininstration/CFO Mr. Thomas BURKE
05 VP for Academic Affairs/CAO Dr. Daniel KATZ
07 Director of Admissions Mr. Stephen OSTENDORFF
58 Dean School Public Affairs & Admin Dr. Humphrey CROOKENDALE
50 AVP AA/Dean School for Business Dr. Tilokie DEPOO
88 Acting Dean ACSHSE Dr. Adele WEINER
32 Dean of Students Ms. Dona SOSA
37 Director of Financial Aid Ms. Andrea DAMAR
06 Registrar Ms. Noreen SMITH
08 Co-Director of Library Services Ms. Kate ADLER
08 Co-Director of Library Services Ms. Emma MOORE
09 Dir Institutional Rsrch/Assessment Mr. Anthony WILLIAMS
15 Director Human Resources Ms. Judith SANTIAGO
18 Chief Facilities/Physical Plant Ms. Mercedes MELENDEZ
30 Chief Development Officer Ms. Beth DUNPHE
26 Chief Public Relations Officer Ms. Tina GEORGIOU
13 Information Systems Manager Mr. Naftaly KLEINMAN
21 Bursar Mr. Taurean KENNEDY
88 Director Academic Support Services Ms. Parker PRACJEK
04 Exec Assistant to the President Ms. Isabel CABRERA

Mildred Elley (J)

855 Central Avenue, Albany NY 12206
County: Albany FICE Identification: 022195
Unit ID: 193201

Telephone: (518) 786-0855 Carnegie Class: Assoc/PrivFP
FAX Number: (518) 786-0890 Calendar System: Other
URL: www.mildred-elley.edu
Established: 1917 Annual Undergrad Tuition & Fees: $15,516
Enrollment: 705 Coed
Affiliation or Control: Proprietary IRS Status: Proprietary
Highest Offering: Associate Degree
Program: Occupational
Accreditation: ACICS

01 President .... Ms. Faith A. TAKES

Mildred Elley-New York City (A)

25 Broadway, 16th Floor, New York NY 10004
Telephone: (212) 380-9004 Identification: 770747
Accreditation: ACICS

† Branch campus of Mildred Elley, Albany, NY.

Mirrer Yeshiva Central Institute (B)

1795 Ocean Parkway, Brooklyn NY 11223-2010
County: Kings FICE Identification: 004798
Unit ID: 193247
Telephone: (718) 645-0536 Carnegie Class: Spec/Faith
FAX Number: (718) 645-9251 Calendar System: Semester
Established: 1947 Annual Undergrad Tuition & Fees: $6,650
Enrollment: 197 Male
Affiliation or Control: Independent Non-Profit IRS Status: 501(c)3
Highest Offering: Second Talmudic Degree
Program: Teacher Preparatory; Professional
Accreditation: RABN

00 Chancellor .... Rabbi Avrohom Yaakov NELKENBAUM
01 President and Dean .... Rabbi Osher KALMANOWITZ
05 Vice President & Dean .... Rabbi Osher BERENBAUM
33 Dean of Men .... Rabbi Esrael ERLANGER
03 Executive Director .... Rabbi Pinchas HECHT
06 Registrar-Administrator .... Mrs. Devorah BERENBAUM
08 Director of the Library .... Rabbi Jacob FELDMANN
38 Director of Guidance .... Rabbi Yisroel FISHMAN
37 Financial Aid Director .... Mrs. Rachel BERENBAUM

Mohawk Valley Community College (C)

1101 Floyd Avenue, Rome NY 13440
Telephone: (315) 339-3470 Identification: 770141
Accreditation: &M

† Branch campus of Mohawk Valley Community College, Utica, NY.

Mohawk Valley Community College (D)

1101 Sherman Drive, Utica NY 13501-5394
County: Oneida FICE Identification: 002871
Unit ID: 193283
Telephone: (315) 792-5400 Carnegie Class: Assoc/Pub-R-L
FAX Number: (315) 792-5666 Calendar System: Semester
URL: www.mvcc.edu
Established: 1946 Annual Undergrad Tuition & Fees (In-District): $4,636
Enrollment: 7,149 Coed
Affiliation or Control: State/Local IRS Status: 501(c)3
Highest Offering: Associate Degree
Program: Occupational; 2-Year Principally Bachelor's Creditable
Accreditation: M, ADNUR, CAHIIM, COARC, ENGT, SURTEC

01 President .... Dr. Randall J. VAN WAGONER
04 Assistant to the President .... Ms. Jill HEINTZ
88 Exec Dir Organizational Development .... Mr. David KATZ
09 Dir Institutional Research/Analysis .... Mr. Mark E. RADLOWSKI
05 Vice Pres Learning/Academic Affairs .... Dr. Maryrose EANNACE
20 Director of Academic Systems .... Mr. Richard PUCINE
79 Dean of Arts & Humanities .... Mr. Lewis KAHLER
88 Dean of Language & Learn Design .... Dr. Jennifer BOULANGER
76 Dean of Life & Health Sciences .... Dr. Kathleen LINAKER
81 Dean of STEM .... Dr. Seyed AKHAVI
50 Dean of Business/Soc Sci & Info Sci .... Ms. Marianne BUTTENSCHON
08 Director College Libraries .... Mr. Stephen FRISBEE
24 Dir of Educational Technologies .... Mr. James LYNCH
10 Vice Pres Administrative Services .... Mr. Thomas SQUIRES
32 VP Student Affairs .... Ms. Stephanie C. REYNOLDS
84 Assoc Dean Enrollment & Advisement .... Mrs. Jennifer DEWEERTH
36 Assoc Dean Development & Transition .... Mr. James MAIO
39 Assoc Dean Student & Residence Life .... Mr. Dennis GIBBONS
103 Assoc VP of Workforce Development .... Ms. Franca ARMSTRONG
30 Exec Dir Institutional Advancement .... Mr. Frank DUROSS
44 Dir of Donor & Resource Development .... Ms. Deanna FERRO
96 Coord Expend/Fixed Asset Procure .... Ms. Joyce PALMER
13 Exec Dir of Information Technology .... Mr. Paul KATCHMAR
31 Dir Ctr Community/Economic Dev .... Mr. William MCDONALD
15 Exec Director of Human Resources .... Mrs. Kimberly EVANS-DAME
26 Director Marketing/Communications .... Mr. Matthew SNYDER
07 Director of Admissions .... Mr. Daniel IANNO
37 Director of Financial Aid .... Mr. Michael PEDE
06 Dir of Student Records/Registrar .... Mrs. Rosemary V. SPETKA
18 Dir of Facilities and Operations .... Mr. Michael MCHARRIS
19 Exec Dir Public Safety & Emerg Mgmt .... Mr. David AMICO
21 Business Office Controller .... Mr. Brian MOLINARO
29 Coord Annual Funds/Alumni Relations .... Ms. Marie KOHL
41 Athletic Director .... Mr. Gary BROADHURST

Molloy College (E)

1000 Hempstead Avenue, PO Box 5002,
Rockville Centre NY 11571-5002
County: Nassau FICE Identification: 002775
Unit ID: 193292
Telephone: (516) 323-3000 Carnegie Class: Master's L
FAX Number: N/A Calendar System: 4/1/4
URL: www.molloy.edu
Established: 1955 Annual Undergrad Tuition & Fees: $26,980
Enrollment: 4,497 Coed
Affiliation or Control: Independent Non-Profit IRS Status: 501(c)3
Highest Offering: Doctorate
Program: Liberal Arts And General; Teacher Preparatory; Professional
Accreditation: M, COARC, CVT, MUS, NMT, NURSE, SP, SW, TED

01 President .... Dr. Drew BOGNER
05 VP Academic Affairs/Dean of Faculty .... Dr. Valerie COLLINS
10 Vice Pres for Finance & Treasurer .... Mr. Michael MC GOVERN
84 Vice Pres Enrollment Management .... Ms. Linda ALBANESE
30 Vice President for Advancement .... Mr. Edward J. THOMPSON
32 Vice President Student Affairs .... Mr. Robert HOULIHAN
45 VP Info Tech/Planning/Research .... Mr. Michael TORRES
88 VP for Mission Integration .... Sr. Dorothy FITZGIBBONS
42 Director of Campus Ministries .... Mr. Scott SALVATO
37 Director Student Financial Services .... Ms. Sharion SCOTT
36 Director of Career Development .... Ms. Mary BROSNAN
41 Director of Athletics .... Ms. Susan CASSIDY
07 Dean of Admissions .... Ms. Marguerite LANE
37 Director of Financial Aid .... Mrs. Ana C. LOCKWARD
21 Assistant Treasurer .... Ms. Barbara CALISSI
44 Executive Director for Development .... Ms. Catherine MUSCENTE
06 Registrar .... Ms. Susan FORTMAN
09 Dir of Institutional Effectiveness .... Ms. Christina D'AMATO
15 Director of Human Resources .... Ms. Lisa MILLER
18 Director of Facilities .... Mr. James MULTARI
26 Director Public Relations .... Mr. Ken YOUNG
96 Director Purchasing & Admin Service .... Ms. Lorraine JACKSON
35 Dean of Students .... Dr. Janine PAYTON
29 Alumni Relations Officer .... Ms. Mary Jane REILLY
19 Director of Public Safety .... Mr. Harry HERMAN
85 Director of International Education .... Ms. Kathleen REBA
105 Director Web Technologies .... Mr. Keith REDO
24 Director of Special Projects .... Mr. Nick SIMONE
20 Director Academic Support Services .... Ms. Nicolette CEO
13 Director of MIS & Operations .... Mr. Michael OLIVO
88 Director of Network Technology .... Mr. Sean LAURIE
08 Head Librarian .... Ms. Judith BRINK-DRESCHER
101 Secretary of the Institution/Board .... Ms. Diane K. FORNIERI

Monroe College (F)

2501 Jerome Avenue, Bronx NY 10468-5407
County: Bronx FICE Identification: 004799
Unit ID: 193308
Telephone: (718) 933-6700 Carnegie Class: Master's S
FAX Number: (718) 295-5861 Calendar System: Semester
URL: www.monroecollege.edu
Established: 1933 Annual Undergrad Tuition & Fees: $14,148
Enrollment: 7,203 Coed
Affiliation or Control: Proprietary IRS Status: Proprietary
Highest Offering: Master's
Program: Liberal Arts And General; Teacher Preparatory; Business Emphasis
Accreditation: M, ACBSP, ACFEI

01 President .... Stephen J. JEROME
03 Exec VP/Director of Branch Campus .... Marc M. JEROME
05 Vice President for Academics .... Dr. Karenann CARTY
11 Vice President Administration .... David DIMOND
10 Vice President for Finance .... Hiraim LAZAR
84 Vice Pres Enroll Mgmt/Campus Dean .... Anthony ALLEN
32 Vice President Student Affairs .... Roberta GREENBERG
58 Dean of Graduate Programs .... Alex CANALS
12 Assoc Vice Pres New Rochelle Camp .... Carol GENESE
86 Asst Vice Pres Governmental Affairs .... Dr. Donald E. SIMON
09 Dean Office of the Registrar/IR .... Dr. Edward S. SCHNEIDERMAN
55 Director of Evening Division .... Allen JENKINS
26 Director of Marketing .... Shane SEAMAN
06 Registrar .... Abigail THORPE
09 Dir Institutional Research .... Peter NWAKEZE
21 Bursar/Branch Campus .... Michael NIEDZWIECKI
21 Director Student Financial Services .... Daniel SHARON
35 Dean of Student Services - Branch .... Vacant
21 Bursar .... Villan CRUZ
35 Dean for Student Services .... Mark SONNENSTEIN
109 Director Auxilliary Services .... Nivia CAMARA
07 Dean of Admissions Branch .... Gersom LOPEZ
07 Vice President Admissions .... Craig PATRICK
37 Director Student Fin Aid Services .... Vacant
36 Exec Dir Ofc of Career Services .... Pamela DELLAPORTA
08 Director of Library Services .... Christine ARTIS
08 Director of Library Services/Branch .... Angela LAURETANO
39 Exec Director of Residential Life .... Mark GOODMAN
29 Director of Alumni Relations .... Leslie JEROME
13 Chief Info Technology Officer (CIO) .... Terrance MCGOWAN

Monroe Community College (G)

1000 E Henrietta Road, Rochester NY 14623-5780
County: Monroe FICE Identification: 002872
Unit ID: 193326
Telephone: (585) 292-2000 Carnegie Class: Assoc/Pub-U-MC
FAX Number: (585) 427-2749 Calendar System: Semester
URL: www.monroecc.edu
Established: 1961 Annual Undergrad Tuition & Fees (In-District): $3,800
Enrollment: 15,335 Coed
Affiliation or Control: State/Local IRS Status: 501(c)3
Highest Offering: Associate Degree
Program: Occupational; 2-Year Principally Bachelor's Creditable
Accreditation: M, ADNUR, CAHIIM, DA, DH, EMT, ENGT, MLTAD, RAD

01 President .... Dr. Anne M. KRESS
05 Provost & VP Academic Svcs .... Dr. Andrea C. WADE
32 Vice President Student Services .... Dr. Lloyd A. HOLMES
10 CFO and VP Administrative Svcs .... Mr. Hezekiah N. SIMMONS
103 VP Econ Dev/Workforce Svc .... Mr. Todd M. OLDHAM
102 Exec Director MCC Foundation .... Ms. Diane L. SHOGER
12 Exec Dean Damon City Campus .... Dr. Joel L. FRATER
26 Asst to the Pres Mktg & Comm Rels .... Ms. Cynthia L. COOPER
35 Asst Vice Pres Student Services .... Dr. Susan D. BAKER
88 Int Asst VP Educational Tech Svcs .... Mr. David J. LANE
18 Assistant Vice President Facilities .... Mr. Paul E. WURSTER
84 Asst Vice Pres Enrollment Mgmt .... Mr. Randyll BOWEN
88 Asst Vice Pres ETS .... Mr. Terrance KEYS
20 Asst Vice Pres Academic Services .... Ms. Kimberley COLLINS
20 Interim Dean Curriculum/Pgm Devel .... Ms. MaryJo A. WITZ
37 Director Financial Aid .... Mr. Jerome S. ST. CROIX
09 Director Institutional Research .... Mr. Angel E. ANDREU
08 Director ETS Libraries .... Mr. Mark F. MCBRIDE
36 Interim Director Career Center .... Ms. Michelle P. MAYO
21 Asst Vice President Admin Svcs .... Mr. Darrell K. JACHIM-MOORE
06 Director Registrar & Records .... Ms. Elizabeth R. RIPTON
30 Director of Development .... Mr. Mark J. PASTORELLA
38 Dir Counseling Center & Vet Svcs .... Ms. Peggy A. HARVEY-LEE
19 Director Public Safety .... Mr. Salvatore J. SIMONETTI
41 Director Athletics .... Mr. Dudley (Skip) L. BAILEY
25 Director Grants .... Ms. Patricia R. WILLIAMS
35 Director of Student Life .... Ms. Elizabeth J. STEWART
23 Director of Health Services .... Ms. Donna G. MUELLER
21 Controller .... Mr. Michael G. QUINN
79 Interim Dean Liberal Arts .... Ms. Nayda PARES-KANE
50 Dean Science/Health/Business .... Ms. Laurel T. SANGER
88 Dean Academic Foundations .... Ms. Catherine E. SMITH
19 Dean Public Safety Training Ctr .... Mr. Michael S. KARNES
32 Dean Student Services-DCC .... Dr. Ann V. TOPPING
35 Director Student Svcs-DCC .... Ms. Shelitha WILLIAMS
20 Interim Dean Acad Svcs DCC .... Dr. Kimberly MCKINSEY-MABRY
15 Asst to President HR/Affirm Act Ofc .... Ms. Melissa A. FINGAR
40 Manager Bookstore .... Ms. Carol M. MCKEOWN
88 Director Educ Opportunity Program .... Ms. Brenda A. SMITH
78 Director Adult/Experiential Lrng .... Mr. William D. SIGISMOND
43 Legal Counsel .... Vacant
88 Assoc Dir Master Scheduling .... Mr. Rick F. SADWICK
96 Director of Purchasing .... Mr. Patrick M. BATES
39 Director Housing/Residence Life .... Ms. Amy GREER
28 Chief Diversity Officer .... Dr. Lloyd A. HOLMES
04 Executive Asst to President .... Ms. Sheila M. STRONG
07 Director of Admissions .... Ms. Christine CASALINUOVO-ADAMS
101 Secy to the Board of Trustees/Pres .... Ms. Linda M. HALL
108 Asst Director Assess and Curriculum .... Mr. Michael A. HEEL
29 Coord Alumni & Annual Giving .... Ms. Karen A. SHAW
45 Director Planning .... Ms. Valarie L. AVALONE
90 Director Comm and Network Services .... Ms. Donna J. POGROSZEWSKI

Montefiore School of Nursing (H)

53 Valentine Avenue, Mount Vernon NY 10550
County: Westchester FICE Identification: 022178
Unit ID: 193380
Telephone: (914) 361-6221 Carnegie Class: Not Classified
FAX Number: (914) 665-7047 Calendar System: Semester
URL: www.montefiorehealthsystem.org
Established: 1901 Annual Undergrad Tuition & Fees: $11,430
Enrollment: 126 Coed
Affiliation or Control: Independent Non-Profit IRS Status: 501(c)3
Highest Offering: Associate Degree
Program: 2-Year Principally Bachelor's Creditable; Nursing Emphasis
Accreditation: ADNUR

01 Dean .... Rebecca GREER

Mount Saint Mary College (I)

330 Powell Avenue, Newburgh NY 12550-3412
County: Orange FICE Identification: 002778
Unit ID: 193353
Telephone: (845) 561-0800 Carnegie Class: Master's L
FAX Number: (845) 562-6762 Calendar System: Semester
URL: www.msmc.edu
Established: 1959 Annual Undergrad Tuition & Fees: $28,400
Enrollment: 2,025 Coed
Affiliation or Control: Independent Non-Profit IRS Status: 501(c)3
Highest Offering: Master's
Program: Liberal Arts And General; Teacher Preparatory; Professional; Nursing Emphasis
Accreditation: M, IACBE, NURSE, TED

01 President .... Dr. Anne CARSON DALY
05 Vice President Academic Affairs .... Dr. Ilona MCGUINESS
10 Vice Pres Finance & Admin/Treasurer .... Mrs. Nancy MAZZA
30 Vice Pres for College Advancement .... Mr. Joseph VALENTI
18 Vice Pres Facilities & Operations .... Mr. James RAIMO
07 Dean of Admissions .... Mrs. Elaine O'GRADY
32 Dean of Students .... Ms. Kelly YOUGH

38 Dir Counseling/Coord Prsns w/Disab .... Dr. Orin STRAUCHLER
20 Associate Dean for Academic Affairs .... Vacant
06 Registrar .... Mr. Carlos TONCHE, JR.
07 Director of Admissions .... Mrs. Nancy SCAFFIDI CLARKE
08 Director of the Library .... Mrs. Barbara W. PETRUZZELLI
37 Director of Financial Aid .... Ms. Barbara WINCHELL
09 Director of Planning and Research .... Mr. Ryan WILLIAMS
15 Director of Human Resources .... Mr. Lee ZAWISTOWSKI
42 Chaplain .... Fr. Francis AMODIO
35 Director of Student Activities .... Ms. Sandra HENDERSON
39 Exec Dir of Operations and Housing .... Mr. Michael O'KEEFE
29 Director of Alumni Affairs .... Ms. Michelle A. IACUESSA
41 Director of Athletics & Recreation .... Mr. Dan TWOMEY
36 Exec Director of the Career Center .... Mrs. Janet ZEMAN
13 Chief Information Officer .... Mr. Dennis RUSH
96 Purchasing Manager .... Mr. Brian MOORE
106 Exec Dir Curr & Instr Online Learn .... Vacant
39 Director of Residence Life .... Ms. Maxine MONROE
18 Director of Facilities .... Ms. Maryann PILON
26 Director of Marketing & Advertising .... Mr. Dean DIMARZO
04 Administrative Asst to President .... Ms. Barbara CONNOLLY
104 Director Study Abroad .... Ms. Emily MARMO
19 Director Security/Safety .... Mr. Patrick ARNOLD
44 Director Annual or Planned Giving .... Ms. Kathleen BARTON

Nassau Community College (A)

1 Education Drive, Garden City NY 11530-6793

County: Nassau
FICE Identification: 002873
Unit ID: 193478
Telephone: (516) 572-7501
Carnegie Class: Assoc/Pub-S-SC
FAX Number: (516) 572-7750
Calendar System: Semester
URL: www.ncc.edu
Established: 1959
Annual Undergrad Tuition & Fees (In-District): $4,534
Enrollment: 23,450
Coed
Affiliation or Control: State/Local
IRS Status: 501(c)3
Highest Offering: Associate Degree
Program: Occupational; 2-Year Principally Bachelor's Creditable
Accreditation: M, ADNUR, COARC, ENGT, FUSER, MLTAD, MUS, PTAA, RTT, SURGT

01 Acting President .... Dr. Kenneth K. SAUNDERS
03 Acting Executive Vice President .... Ms. Maria P. CONZATTI
05 Interim Vice Pres Academic Affairs .... Ms. Maria P. CONZATTI
11 Vice Pres Facilities Management .... Dr. Joseph V. MUSCARELLA
10 Vice President Finance .... Ms. Inna REZNIK
32 Vice Pres Academic/Student Svcs .... Ms. Maria P. CONZATTI
22 AVP Equity & Inclusion/AA Officer .... Mr. Craig J. WRIGHT
43 Spec Asst to Pres/College Counsel .... Ms. Donna M. HAUGEN
103 Asst Vice Pres Workforce Devel .... Dr. Janet CARUSO
21 Treasurer .... Ms. Lisa HAHN
13 Dean Management Info Svcs .... Vacant
18 Asst VP Maintenance/Operations .... Mr. Masoom ALI
15 Assoc Vice Pres Human Resources .... Ms. Dorlena DUNBAR
96 Director Procurement .... Mr. Phillip CAPPELLO
35 Dean of Students .... Ms. Charmian SMITH
09 Dean Institutional Effectiveness .... Dr. Dean KEVLIN
37 Dean Financial Aid .... Ms. Patricia NOREN
07 Dean of Admissions .... Mr. David FOLLICK
25 Resource Devel/Grants Fiscal Mgr .... Mr. Edmund KOEPPEL
86 General Counsel for Govt Relations .... Mr. Chuck CUTOLO
26 Director Marketing/Communications .... Ms. Alicia STEGER
08 Director of Library .... Ms. Nancy WILLIAMSON
41 Director Special Pgm Athletics/PED .... Mr. Michael C. PELLICCIA
06 Registrar .... Mr. Chester BARKAN
19 Director of Public Safety .... Mr. Martin RODDINI
23 Director Health Services .... Ms. Margaret MCGOVERN
36 Director of Placement Testing .... Ms. Noreen WADE
38 Dir Advisement/Special Programs .... Mr. John SPIEGEL
14 Chief Information Officer .... Mr. Richard LAWLESS
102 Exec Dir Nassau CC Foundation .... Ms. Joy DEDONATO
04 Administrative Asst to President .... Ms. Anne E. BRANDI

Nazareth College of Rochester (B)

4245 East Avenue, Rochester NY 14618-3790

County: Monroe
FICE Identification: 002779
Unit ID: 193584
Telephone: (585) 389-2525
Carnegie Class: Master's L
FAX Number: (585) 586-2452
Calendar System: Semester
URL: www.naz.edu
Established: 1924
Annual Undergrad Tuition & Fees: $31,520
Enrollment: 2,818
Coed
Affiliation or Control: Independent Non-Profit
IRS Status: 501(c)3
Highest Offering: Doctorate
Program: Liberal Arts And General; Teacher Preparatory; Professional
Accreditation: M, IACBE, MUS, NURSE, OT, PTA, SP, SW, TEAC

01 President .... Mr. Daan BRAVEMAN
04 Assistant to President .... Ms. Patricia GENTHNER
04 Executive Assistant to President .... Ms. Cathleen M. STEVENS
05 Vice President Academic Affairs .... Dr. Sara VARHUS
30 Vice Pres Institutional Advancement .... Ms. Kelly GAGAN
10 Vice President Finance & Treasurer .... Mr. Patrick RICHEY
32 Vice President Student Development .... Mr. Kevin WORTHEN
84 Vice Pres Enrollment Management .... Mr. Ian MORTIMER
29 Director of Alumni Relations .... Ms. Donna BORGUS
15 Assoc VP Human Resources .... Mrs. JoEllen PINKHAM
20 Asst VP Academic Affairs .... Vacant
06 Registrar .... Ms. Alison TEETER
37 Director Student Financial Aid .... Ms. Janice SCHEUTZOW
26 Director Marketing & Communications .... Ms. Elizabeth ZAPATA
13 Director Information Tech Svcs .... Ms. Karen KUPPINGER
08 Director of Library .... Ms. Catherine DOYLE
19 Director of Security .... Mr. Robert MALDONADO
39 Director of Campus Life .... Ms. Carey BACKMAN
41 Director of Athletics .... Mr. Peter G. BOTHNER
42 Director Center for Spirituality .... Ms. Lynne BOUCHER
36 Director of Career Services .... Mr. Michael D. KAHL
18 Director Buildings/Grounds .... Mr. Peter LANA
09 Director of Institutional Research .... Mr. Nicholas LAMENDOLA
23 Director of Health Services .... Ms. Donna WILLOME
20 Director of Academic Advisement .... Ms. Linda SEARING
88 Director of the Arts Center .... Ms. Susan C. LUSIGNAN
21 Bursar .... Mr. John GARBE
92 Director Honors Program .... Dr. Marjorie ROTH
49 Dean of Col of Arts and Sciences .... Dr. Diane OLIVER
76 Dean School of Health & Human Svcs .... Dr. Brigid NOONAN
53 Dean School of Education .... Dr. Craig HILL
88 Dean School of Management .... Mr. Gerard ZAPPIA
88 Exec Dir of Ctr International Educ .... Dr. Nevan FISHER
88 Dir of Center for Service Learning .... Dr. Brian BAILEY
89 Dir Stdnt Transition/First Year Ctr .... Mr. Thomas CHEW
96 Director of Purchasing .... Ms. Joanne FITZGERALD
88 Exec Dir Center 4 Civic Engagement .... Ms. Nuala BOYLE
07 Dir Graduate Admissions/Transer .... Ms. Judith G. BAKER

The New School (C)

66 W 12th Street, New York NY 10011-8603

County: New York
FICE Identification: 020662
Unit ID: 193654
Telephone: (212) 229-5600
Carnegie Class: DRU
FAX Number: N/A
Calendar System: Semester
URL: www.newschool.edu
Established: 1919
Annual Undergrad Tuition & Fees: $43,961
Enrollment: 10,477
Coed
Affiliation or Control: Independent Non-Profit
IRS Status: 501(c)3
Highest Offering: Doctorate
Program: 2-Year Principally Bachelor's Creditable; Liberal Arts And General; Professional
Accreditation: M, ART, CLPSY, SPAA

01 President .... Dr. David VAN ZANDT
04 Executive Assistant to President .... Ms. Lindsey WARFORD
05 Provost and Chief Academic Officer .... Mr. Tim MARSHALL
48 Exec Dean Parsons School for Design .... Mr. Joel TOWERS
88 Exec Dean School for Public Engage .... Dr. Mary WATSON
64 Exec Dean Perf Arts and Dean Mannes .... Mr. Richard KESSLER
83 Dean New School for Social Research .... Dr. William MILBERG
49 Dean Eugene Lang College .... Ms. Stephanie BROWNER
84 Chief Enrollment & Success Officer .... Mr. Donald RESNICK
30 Chief Development Officer .... Mr. Mark GIBBEL
26 Chief Marketing Officer .... Ms. Anne ADRIANCE
43 Chief Legal Officer & Sec of Corp .... Mr. Roy P. MOSKOWITZ
13 Sr VP & Chief Information Officer .... Mr. Anand PADMANABHAN
15 Sr VP for HR & Labor Relations .... Ms. Carol CANTRELL
10 VP Finance/Business & Treasurer .... Mr. Steve STABILE
32 Sr Vice President Student Services .... Ms. Linda REIMER
88 VP for Distributed & Global Ed .... Mr. Andy ATZERT
88 VP Design/Construction & Facilities .... Ms. Lia GARTNER
100 Chief of Staff .... Ms. Deborah BOGOSINA
20 Vice Provost Acad Planning Admin .... Ms. Pat BAXTER
20 Vice Provost Curr & Learning .... Ms. Lisa DEBENEDITTIS
07 VP Strat Enrollment Mgmt .... Dr. Carol KIM
88 VP for Student Success .... Ms. Michelle RELYEA
88 Assoc Dean/Dean Fashion .... Mr. Burak CAKMAK
88 Assoc Dean/Dean Milano School .... Ms. Michelle DEPASS
88 Assc Dn/Dean Art/Design Hist/Theory .... Dr. Sarah LAWRENCE
88 Assoc Dean/Dean Art/Media & Tech .... Ms. Anne GAINES
48 Assoc Dean/Dean Constructed Envir .... Mr. Brian MCGRATH
88 Assoc Dean/Dean Media Studies .... Dr. Anne BALSAMO
48 Assoc Dean/Dean Design Strategies .... Vacant
88 Assoc Dean/Dean Undergrad Stds .... Dr. Laura AURICCHIO
88 Assoc Dean/Dean School of Drama .... Mr. Pippin PARKER
64 Assoc Dean/Dean School of Jazz .... Mr. Martin MUELLER
20 Assoc Provost Faculty Affairs .... Dr. Eleni LITT
09 Assoc Provost Inst Rsrch/Effectiv .... Dr. Paula MAAS
108 Assoc Provost for Assessment .... Dr. Michaela ROME
46 Assoc Provost Research .... Dr. Michael SCHOBER
20 Assoc Provost Acad Budget & Plan .... Dr. Raymond BARCLAY
106 Assoc Provost Dist & Global Ed .... Ms. Cynthia LAWSON
27 Assoc VP Strategic Marketing .... Ms. Lisa PRESTON
35 Asst VP for Student & Campus Life .... Ms. Jennifer FRANCONE
21 Asst VP & Controller .... Ms. Natalie PRESSEY
21 Asst VP Budget & Planning .... Ms. Loretta FERRARI
06 University Registrar .... Mr. Larry FILLIAN
39 Asst VP Student Housing & Res Life .... Mr. Robert LUTOMSKI
16 Asst VP Human Resources .... Mr. Irwin KROOT
91 Asst VP Systems Network Security .... Mr. Chris BREZIL
90 Asst VP Academic Technology .... Ms. Lillian SARTORI
91 Asst VP Enterprise Applications .... Mr. Marcus LONGMUIR
102 Asst VP Development .... Ms. Marie-Noel APPEL
88 Asst VP Design & Constuction .... Ms. Marla APPELBAUM
88 Asst VP Capital Infrastructure .... Mr. Silviu HERSCHER
88 Asst VP Process Improvement .... Ms. Lisa BONNER
08 University Librarian .... Mr. Ed SCARCELLE
27 Director of Communications (PR) .... Ms. Josephine PARR
23 LCSW/Asst VP Student Health .... Ms. Tracy ROBIN
19 Director Security .... Mr. Thomas ILICETO
37 Director Financial Aid .... Ms. Lisa SHAHEEN
18 Director Facilities Management .... Mr. Thomas WHALEN
96 Sr Director of Business Operations .... Mr. Ed VERDI
85 Sr Dir International Student Svcs .... Ms. Monique N. NRI
38 Director Counseling Services .... Dr. Jerry FINKELSTEIN
36 Director of Career Success .... Ms. Kelly AHN
28 Director Social Justice Initiatives .... Ms. Gail DRAKES
28 Director Intercultural Support .... Ms. Keisha DAVENPORT-RAMIREZ
29 Director Alumni Engagement .... Ms. Amy GARAWITZ
88 Director Student Disability Svcs .... Mr. Jason LUCHS
25 Director Research Support .... Mr. Robert GUTIERREZ
24 Director Media Services .... Mr. Mark FITZPATRICK
41 Director Athletics and Recreation .... Ms. Diane YEE
44 Director Indivual Giving .... Mr. Jeff COTNOIR
101 Asst Secretary to the Corp .... Ms. Gayle BINNEY
20 Dep Provost & Sr VP Academic Affs .... Dr. Bryna SANGER
11 Chief Operating Officer .... Mr. Tokumbo SHOBOWALE

New York Academy of Art (D)

111 Franklin Street, New York NY 10013

County: New York
FICE Identification: 026001
Unit ID: 366368
Telephone: (212) 966-0300
Carnegie Class: Spec/Arts
FAX Number: N/A
Calendar System: Semester
URL: www.nyaa.edu
Established: 1982
Annual Graduate Tuition & Fees: $35,600
Enrollment: 108
Coed
Affiliation or Control: Independent Non-Profit
IRS Status: 501(c)3
Highest Offering: Master's; No Undergraduates
Program: Professional; Fine Arts Emphasis
Accreditation: @M, NY, ART

01 President .... Mr. David KRATZ
05 Dean of Academic Affairs .... Mr. Peter DRAKE
10 Chief Financial Officer .... Mr. Stephan KORSAKOV
100 Chief of Staff .... Mr. Harry MICHAS
11 Director of Operations .... Mr. Michael SMITH
07 Director of Admissions/Recruitment .... Mr. John GEORGES
06 Registrar/Dir of Student Services .... Ms. Katie HEMMER
08 Director of Libraries .... Ms. Holly FRISBEE
30 Development Director .... Ms. Lisa KIRK
26 Director of Public Relations .... Ms. Folake OLOGUNJA

New York Career Institute (E)

11 Park Place, 4th Floor, New York NY 10007

County: New York
FICE Identification: 021634
Unit ID: 195845
Telephone: (212) 962-0002
Carnegie Class: Assoc/PrivFP
FAX Number: (212) 385-7574
Calendar System: Trimester
URL: www.nyci.edu
Established: 1941
Annual Undergrad Tuition & Fees: $13,500
Enrollment: 550
Coed
Affiliation or Control: Proprietary
IRS Status: Proprietary
Highest Offering: Associate Degree
Program: Occupational; 2-Year Principally Bachelor's Creditable
Accreditation: NY

01 CEO .... Ivan LONDA
05 Chief Academic Officer .... Lisa Therese FOWLER
32 Director of Student Services .... Cindy MCMAHON
37 Director Financial Aid .... Brenda SORIANO

New York Chiropractic College (F)

2360 State Route 89, Seneca Falls NY 13148-0800

County: Seneca
FICE Identification: 012277
Unit ID: 193751
Telephone: (315) 568-3000
Carnegie Class: Spec/Health
FAX Number: (315) 568-3012
Calendar System: Trimester
URL: www.nycc.edu
Established: 1919
Annual Undergrad Tuition & Fees: $35,166
Enrollment: 965
Coed
Affiliation or Control: Independent Non-Profit
IRS Status: 501(c)3
Highest Offering: First Professional Degree
Program: Professional
Accreditation: M, ACUP, CHIRO

01 President .... Dr. Frank J. NICCHI
05 Exec Vice President & Provost .... Dr. Michael A. MESTAN
10 Vice Pres of Finance/Admin Svcs .... Mr. Sean ANGLIM
30 VP Inst Advance/Spec Asst to Pres .... Dr. David R. ODIORNE
84 Vice Pres Enrollment Management .... Ms. Magdalen KELLOGG
96 Assoc VP Admin Svcs/Dir Purchasing .... Mr. Richard B. WORDEN
20 Assoc VP Acad Affairs & Inst Effect .... Ms. Jennifer VONHAHMANN
13 Assoc VP Informational Tech .... Mr. Christophe MCQUEENEY
58 Dean Academic Programs & Services .... Dr. J. Nicolas POIRIER
88 Dean of Chiropractic .... Dr. Karen A. BOBAK
06 Registrar .... Mr. Kevin MCCARTHY
07 Director of Admissions .... Mr. Michael LYNCH
37 Director Financial Aid .... Mr. Darrin ROOKER
88 Director of Bachelor Prof Studies .... Dr. John DEMETROS
46 Dean of Research .... Dr. Jeanmarie R. BURKE
12 Depew Health Center Administrator .... Dr. Michael FLYNN
12 Levittown Health Ctr Chief of Staff .... Ms. Melissa MURPHY
17 Seneca Falls Hlth Ctr Chf of Staff .... Dr. Wendy L. MANERI
51 Dean Post Grad & Cont Educ .... Dr. Thomas VENTIMIGLIA
08 Director of the Library .... Ms. Bethyn BONI
38 Assoc Director Counseling Services .... Ms. Eve ABRAMS
88 Dir Academy Admc Excl Stdnt Success .... Mr. Peter THOMPSON
39 Secretary Housing .... Ms. Janette ELSTER
41 Dir Health & Fitness Education .... Mr. Rhett TICCONI
32 Director Student Life .... Ms. Holly Anne WAYE

36 Dir Ctr Career Dev Prof Success .... Ms. Susan D. PITTENGER
29 Director of Alumni Relations .... Ms. Diane ZINK
45 Director Accreditation .... Dr. Beth DONOHUE
09 Quality Engineer .... Ms. Patricia MERKLE
15 Human Resources Manager .... Ms. Christine MCDERMOTT
91 Information Tech Administrator .... Mr. Shane SHOWERS
19 Director Facilities/Security .... Mr. William WAYNE
40 Bookstore Manager .... Ms. Helen STUCK
58 Dir MS Clinical Anatomy Pgm .... Dr. Jennette BALL
76 Dir Applied Clinical Nutrition Pgm .... Dr. Peter NICKLESS
88 Dean of FL Sch Acup/Oriental Med .... Mr. Jason WRIGHT
88 Dir MS Diagnostic Imaging Program .... Dr. Chad WARSHEL
88 Dir Academy for Teaching Excellence .... Ms. Amy SIMOLO
12 Campus Health Ctr Chief of Staff .... Dr. Jonathon EGAN
12 Rochester Hlth Ctr Chf of Staff .... Dr. Wendy L. MANERI
90 Systems Administrator .... Ms. Shelly STUCK
24 Educational Tech Administrator .... Mr. Bernard CECCHINI
23 Int Executive Dir Health Centers .... Ms. Melissa MURPHY
21 Controller .... Ms. Karen QUEST
88 Dir MS Hum Anat Phys Instructn Pgm .... Dr. Robert A. CROCKER

New York College of Health Professions (A)

6801 Jericho Turnpike, Syosset NY 11791-4413
County: Nassau | FICE Identification: 025994
Unit ID: 418126
Telephone: (516) 364-0808 | Carnegie Class: Spec/Health
FAX Number: (516) 364-6645 | Calendar System: Trimester
URL: www.nycollege.edu
Established: 1981 | Annual Undergrad Tuition & Fees: $14,235
Enrollment: 735 | Coed
Affiliation or Control: Independent Non-Profit | IRS Status: 501(c)3
Highest Offering: Master's
Program: Professional; Technical Emphasis
Accreditation: NY, ACUP

01 President .... Ms. Lisa PAMINTUAN
04 Administrative Asst to President .... Ms. Anita HARIDAT
26 Sr VP Mktg/Comm/Business Oper .... Ms. Barbara CARVER
10 Chief Financial Officer .... Mr. Errol VIRASAWMI
63 Dean Grad Sch Oriental Medicine .... Dr. A. Li SONG
05 Dean of Academic Affairs .... Vacant
88 Chair of Massage Therapy .... Ms. Genevieve REITER
06 Assoc Registrar .... Mr. Kenneth REID
88 Senior Admissions Counselor .... Ms. Mary RODAS
07 Director of Admissions .... Vacant
08 Dir Library/Information Services .... Ms. Cynthia CAYEA
09 Director of Institutional Research .... Mr. Ross GRIFFITH
21 Bursar .... Ms. Jacqueline MCINTYRE
13 Manager Information Technology .... Mr. Brian ALVAREZ
32 Director of Student Services .... Mr. Kevin COURT
37 Associate Director of Financial Aid .... Mr. Bernard WALKER
88 Dean Sch of Massage Therapy NYC .... Vacant
88 Bursar .... Ms. Jacqueline MCINTYRE

New York College of Podiatric Medicine (B)

53 E 124th Street, New York NY 10035-1815
County: New York | FICE Identification: 002749
Unit ID: 194073
Telephone: (212) 410-8000 | Carnegie Class: Spec/Health
FAX Number: (212) 876-7670 | Calendar System: Semester
URL: www.nycpm.edu
Established: 1911 | Annual Undergrad Tuition & Fees: $31,870
Enrollment: 381 | Coed
Affiliation or Control: Independent Non-Profit | IRS Status: 501(c)3
Highest Offering: First Professional Degree
Program: Professional
Accreditation: POD

01 President .... Mr. Louis L. LEVINE
05 Vice Pres Academic Affairs/Dean .... Dr. Michael J. TREPAL
11 Chief Operating Ofcr/VP Admin .... Mr. Joel STURM
10 Chief Financial Officer .... Mr. Greg ONAIFO
13 Vice Pres Info Systems & Technology .... Vacant
63 VP Medical Education/Medical Dir .... Dr. Mark SWARTZ
30 VP of Development & Operations .... Mr. Desander MAS
32 Dean Student Affairs .... Dr. Laurence LOWY
20 Dean Clinical Educ/Dir Res Pgms .... Dr. Robert ECKLES
09 Dean Institutional Research .... Dr. Eileen CHUSID
07 Assoc Dean Admissions/Student Svcs .... Ms. Lisa LEE
26 Director Public Affairs/Development .... Mr. Roger GREENE
08 Director of Library .... Mr. Thomas WALKER
37 Director Financial Aid .... Ms. Eve TRAUBE
06 Registrar .... Ms. Kristy DIPALMA
19 Director Security/Safety .... Mr. James WARREN, JR.

New York College of Traditional Chinese Medicine (C)

200 Old Country Road, Suite 500, Mineola NY 11501-4204
County: Nassau | FICE Identification: 034433
Unit ID: 439783
Telephone: (516) 739-1545 | Carnegie Class: Spec/Health
FAX Number: (516) 873-9622 | Calendar System: Trimester
URL: www.nyctcm.edu
Established: 1996 | Annual Undergrad Tuition & Fees: $17,188
Enrollment: 164 | Coed
Affiliation or Control: Independent Non-Profit | IRS Status: 501(c)3
Highest Offering: Master's
Program: Professional
Accreditation: ACUP

01 President .... Dr. Yemeng CHEN
10 Administrative Dean .... Dr. James S. BARE
05 Academic Dean .... Dr. Sunny SHEN
07 Admissions Manager .... Ms. Vinglin BAI
23 Clinic Director .... Mr. Martin SILBER
88 Clinic Manager .... Ms. Yiping ZHAO
06 Records Manager .... Ms. Susan SU
37 Financial Aid/Admin Coordinator .... Ms. Elise MA
21 Financial Manager .... Ms. Lily ZOU
08 Operations Manager .... Ms. Ling Ling CHANG

The New York Conservatory for Dramatic Arts (D)

39 West 19th Street, New York NY 10011
County: New York | FICE Identification: 031207
Unit ID: 421841
Telephone: (212) 645-0030 | Carnegie Class: Not Classified
FAX Number: (212) 645-0039 | Calendar System: Semester
URL: www.sft.edu
Established: 1980 | Annual Undergrad Tuition & Fees: $31,200
Enrollment: 274 | Coed
Affiliation or Control: Proprietary | IRS Status: Proprietary
Highest Offering: Associate Degree
Program: Occupational; 2-Year Principally Bachelor's Creditable; Fine Arts Emphasis
Accreditation: THEA

00 Artistic Director .... Joan SEE
01 CEO .... David PALMER
05 Director of Education .... Richard OMAR
20 Assoc Director of Education .... Jay R. GOLDENBERG
06 Registrar .... Stefon SIMMONS
08 Head Librarian .... Martha REPETTO

New York Graduate School of Psychoanalysis (E)

16 West Tenth Street, New York NY 10011
Telephone: (212) 260-7050 | Identification: 770116
Accreditation: &EH

† Branch campus of Boston Graduate School of Psychoanalysis, Brookline, MA.

New York Institute of Technology (F)

Northern Boulevard, Old Westbury NY 11568-8000
County: Nassau | FICE Identification: 004804
Unit ID: 194091
Telephone: (516) 686-7516 | Carnegie Class: Master's L
FAX Number: (516) 686-7613 | Calendar System: Semester
URL: www.nyit.edu
Established: 1955 | Annual Undergrad Tuition & Fees: $32,300
Enrollment: 7,872 | Coed
Affiliation or Control: Independent Non-Profit | IRS Status: 501(c)3
Highest Offering: Doctorate
Program: Liberal Arts And General; Teacher Preparatory; Professional
Accreditation: M, ARCPA, BUS, CACREP, CIDA, ENG, ENGT, NURSE, OSTEO, OT, PTA, TED

01 President .... Dr. Edward GUILIANO
05 Provost/Vice Pres Academic Affairs .... Dr. Rahmat SHOURESHI
100 Chief of Staff .... Mr. Peter KINNEY
45 Vice Pres for Planning/Assessment .... Dr. Harriet ARNONE
30 Vice President for Development .... Mr. John ELIZANDRO
17 Vice President Health Affairs .... Dr. Barbara ROSS-LEE
32 VP Stdnt Affs/Chief Stdnt Affs Ofcr .... Dr. Patrick LOVE
13 Vice Pres of IT & Infrastructure .... Dr. Niyazi BODUR
84 Vice President Enrollment .... Mr. Ronald MAGGIORE
26 Vice Pres Comm & Mktg .... Ms. Nancy DONNER
10 CFO & Treasurer .... Mr. Leonard AUBREY
21 Controller .... Ms. Barbara HOLAHAN
43 General Counsel .... Ms. Catherine FLICKINGER
06 Registrar .... Ms. Kristen SMITH
76 Dean School of Health Professions .... Dr. Patricia CHUTE
48 Dean Sch Architecture & Design .... Ms. Judith DIMAIO
53 Dean School of Education .... Vacant
54 Dean School of Engr & Comp Sciences .... Dr. Nada ANID
49 Dean School Arts & Sciences .... Dr. Roger YU
50 Dean School of Management .... Dr. Jess BORONICO
108 Dean Operations/Assessments & Acc .... Dr. Patricia BURLAUD
35 Dean for Campus Life .... Ms. Francy MAGEE
36 Dean of Career Services .... Mr. John HYDE
75 Dean Voc Independence Program .... Dr. Ernst VANBERGEIJK
09 Director Inst Research & Assessment .... Mr. Michael LANE
07 Dean Admissions & Financial Aid .... Ms. Karen VAHEY
27 Director Publications & Advertising .... Ms. Susan WARNER
27 Director of Communications .... Ms. Bobbie DELL'AQUILO
29 Director of Alumni Relations .... Ms. Jennifer KELLY
18 Director of Facilities Operations .... Mr. William MARCHAND
37 Associate Dean of Financial Aid .... Ms. Rosemary FERRUCCI
19 Director Security .... Mr. Denis MCGUCKIN
41 Director Athletics & Recreation .... Mr. Duane BAILEY
25 Asst Provost Spnsrd Pgms & Research .... Dr. Allison ANDORS
13 Director Plng & Business Affairs .... Ms. Ajisa DERVISEVIC
96 Director Procurement Services .... Ms. Gina ARMS
88 Director of Internal Audit .... Ms. Rachel BERTHOUMIEUX
38 Director Counseling & Wellness Svcs .... Ms. Alice HERON-BURKE
88 Assistant Dean Academic Enrichment .... Ms. Monika SCHUEREN
15 Director of Human Resources .... Ms. Carol JABLONSKY
90 Director Client Services .... Ms. Laurie HARVEY
91 Director Systems & Network .... Mr. Brian MAROLDO
35 Assoc Dean Student Development .... Ms. Zennabelle SEWELL
88 Dir Events Planning & Hospitality .... Mr. Jerry LIMONCELLI
88 Vice President Med Affs/Global Hlth .... Dr. Jerry BALENTINE

New York Law School (G)

185 West Broadway, New York NY 10013-2959
County: New York | FICE Identification: 002783
Unit ID: 193821
Telephone: (212) 431-2100 | Carnegie Class: Spec/Law
FAX Number: (212) 965-8838 | Calendar System: Semester
URL: www.nyls.edu
Established: 1891 | Annual Graduate Tuition & Fees: $49,240
Enrollment: 968 | Coed
Affiliation or Control: Independent Non-Profit | IRS Status: 501(c)3
Highest Offering: Doctorate; No Undergraduates
Program: Professional
Accreditation: LAW

01 Dean and President .... Dean Anthony CROWELL
03 Executive VP & Chief Strategy Ofcr .... Ms. Carole POST
05 Assoc Dean Academic & Student Engag .... Dean William P. LAPIANA
10 Vice President for Finance & Admin .... Mr. Stuart KLEIN
45 Assoc Dean for Inst Accountability .... Dean Joan R. FISHMAN
26 Vice Pres Communications/Mktg .... Ms. Nancy J. GUIDA
08 Director of Law Library/Assoc Dean .... Prof. Camille BROUSSARD
84 Assoc Dean Admissions/Financial Aid .... Mr. Adam BARRETT
21 Asst VP Financial Planning & Mgmt .... Ms. Susan REDLER
18 Chief Maintenance/Operations/Secur .... Mr. Paul REPETTO
15 Asst Vice President Human Resources .... Ms. Jody PARIANTE
07 Asst Dean of Admissions & Finan Aid .... Ms. Ella Mae ESTRADA
21 Asst Vice Pres Business Operations .... Mr. George HAYES
09 Asst VP Institutional Research .... Dr. Joanne INGHAM
44 Assistant Vice Pres Development .... Ms. Anna FERBER
20 Assistant Dean Academic Affairs .... Ms. Victoria EASTUS
20 Asst Dean Academic Program Develop .... Ms. Erin BOND
06 Assistant Dean and Registrar .... Mr. Oral HOPE
58 Asst Dean for Graduate Education .... Ms. Hazel WEISER
13 Chief Information Officer .... Mr. Thomas SOCASH
32 Assistant Dean for Student Services .... Ms. Helena PRIGAL
36 Asst Dean for Career Planning .... Mr. Jeffery BECHERER
35 Sr Director of Student Life .... Ms. Sally HARDING
20 Assoc Director Academic Planning .... Ms. Kiera FLAD
20 Assoc Director Academic Planning .... Ms. Jaime LANGINESTRA
96 Purchasing Coordinator .... Mr. Norman DAWKINS
37 Director Student Financial Aid .... Ms. Jade KOLB
39 Director Student Housing .... Ms. Shani DARBY
30 Chief Development/Advancement .... Mr. Elliot BERGER
04 Administrativest to President .... Ms. MarySue DANIELS
104 Director Study Abroad .... Mr. Michael RHEE
105 Director Web Services .... Ms. Nancy GUIDA
28 Director of Diversity .... Ms. Deborah ARCHER
38 Director Student Counseling .... Ms. Helena PRIGAL
86 Director Government Relations .... Mr. Ariel DVORKIN

New York Medical College (H)

40 Sunshine Cottage Road, Valhalla NY 10595-1690
County: Westchester | FICE Identification: 002784
Unit ID: 193830
Telephone: (914) 594-4900 | Carnegie Class: Spec/Med
FAX Number: (914) 594-4145 | Calendar System: Other
URL: www.nymc.edu
Established: 1860 | Annual Graduate Tuition & Fees: $54,245
Enrollment: 1,427 | Coed
Affiliation or Control: Jewish | IRS Status: 501(c)3
Highest Offering: Doctorate; No Undergraduates
Program: Professional; Business Emphasis
Accreditation: M, DENT, MED, PAST, PH, PTA, SP

01 President .... Dr. Alan H. KADISH
03 Administrator .... Ms. Vilma BORDONARO
05 Vice Prov/Sr Assoc Dean Acad Admin .... Mr. William A. STEADMAN, II
17 CEO/Exec Dean/Chanc Health Affairs .... Dr. Edward C. HALPERIN
10 Sr VP/CFO/Vice Prov Admin & Finance .... Mr. Stephen PICCOLO, JR.
58 Dean Grad Sch Basic Medical Science .... Dr. Francis L. BELLONI
43 Vice President/General Counsel .... Mr. Waldemar A. COMAS
30 Vice President Univ Dev/Alumni Rels .... Ms. LArissa REECE
86 Vice President Government Affairs .... Dr. Robert W. AMLER
11 Vice President Operations .... Mr. Michael ROGOVIN
21 Assoc Vice Pres/Controller .... Mr. George NESTLER
43 Assoc Vice Pres Legal Affairs .... Ms. Dana LEE
20 Assoc Dean Academic Administration .... Mr. Randi D. SCHWARTZ
26 Director Communications .... Ms. Jennifer RIEKERT
13 Chief Information Officer .... Dr. Sandra SHIVERS
76 Dean Sch Health Sciences & Practice .... Dr. Robert W. AMLER
63 Vice Dean Grad Med Ed/Affiliations .... Dr. Richard G. MCCARRICK
09 Assoc Dean Research Administration .... Mr. Charles B. HATHAWAY
32 Sr Assoc Dean Student Affairs .... Dr. Gladys M. AYALA
37 Asc Dn Stdnt Affs/Dir Finan Plng .... Mr. Anthony M. SOZZO
07 Sr Associate Dean Admissions .... Dr. Fern R. JUSTER
51 Assoc Dean Continuing Med Education .... Dr. Joseph F. DURSI
08 Assoc Dean/Dir Health Sci Library .... Ms. Marie ASCHER
07 Director of Admissions .... Ms. Robin BAUM
06 University Registrar .... Ms. Jennifer SIMMONS

39	Director Student Housing	Ms. Katherine E. DILLON
18	Director Facilities Management	Mr. Michael J. SHALLO
19	Director of Security	Mr. William ALLISON
85	Intl Student/Scholar Advisor	Ms. Elizabeth WARD
51	Director of Continuing Medical Educ	Ms. Kathy J. KAVANAGH
23	Director Health Services	Dr. Joseph F. DURSI
38	Director Student Counseling	Dr. Mark SINGER
105	Director Web Services	Mr. Kevin R. CUMMINGS
40	Director Bookstore	Ms. Liz REYNOLDS
24	Head Educational Media	Mr. Michael COTTER
14	Coord of Instruct Computing Tech	Mr. Jason DI NARDI
04	Administrative Asst to President	Ms. Vera ROSARIO

New York School of Interior Design (A)

170 East 70th Street, New York NY 10021-5110

County: New York FICE Identification: 020690

Unit ID: 194116

Telephone: (212) 472-1500 Carnegie Class: Spec/Arts

FAX Number: (212) 472-3800 Calendar System: 4/1/4

URL: www.nysid.edu

Established: 1916 Annual Undergrad Tuition & Fees: $33,610

Enrollment: 539 Coed

Affiliation or Control: Independent Non-Profit IRS Status: 501(c)3

Highest Offering: Master's

Program: Professional

Accreditation: @M, ART, CIDA

01	President	Mr. David SPROULS
05	VP Academic Affairs/Dean	Dr. Ellen FISHER
10	VP for Finance & Administration	Ms. Jane CHEN
32	Dean of Students	Ms. Karen HIGGINBOTHAM
04	Assistant to the President	Ms. Jeanne KO
06	Registrar	Ms. Jennifer MELENDEZ
08	Director of the Library	Mr. Billy KWAN
07	Director of Admissions	Ms. Celeste COLLINS
37	Financial Aid Coordinator	Ms. Audrey ZAHOR
15	Director of Personnel Services	Ms. Yvonne MORAY
18	Chief Facilities/Physical Plant	Mr. Zeke KOLENOVIC
26	Director of External Relations	Ms. Samantha HOOVER
20	Associate Dean	Ms. Barbara LOWENTHAL
13	Dir Computing/Information Mgmt	Mr. Tomasz SOWINSKI
90	Director Academic Computing	Mr. Richard T. CLASS
38	Director Student Counseling	Dr. Penny MORGANSTEIN
09	Director of Institutional Research	Mr. Christopher VINGER
30	Director Development	Ms. Elizabeth GRAY KOGEN

New York Theological Seminary (B)

475 Riverside Drive, Suite 500, New York NY 10115-0083

County: New York FICE Identification: 002674

Unit ID: 193894

Telephone: (212) 870-1211 Carnegie Class: Not Classified

FAX Number: (212) 870-1236 Calendar System: Semester

URL: www.nyts.edu

Established: 1900 Annual Graduate Tuition & Fees: $17,850

Enrollment: 246 Coed

Affiliation or Control: Independent Non-Profit IRS Status: 501(c)3

Highest Offering: Doctorate; No Undergraduates

Program: Professional

Accreditation: THEOL

01	President	Dr. Dale T. IRVIN
30	VP Development/Inst Advancement	Dr. Courtney WILEY-HARRIS
05	Academic Dean	Dr. Kirkpatrick G. COHALL
10	Chief Financial Officer/Controller	Mr. Craig KING
08	Librarian	Dr. Jerry REISIG
06	Registrar	Ms. Lydia R. BUMGARDNER
37	Director Financial Aid	Ms. Tamisia WHITE
26	Coordinator Publications/Marketing	Ms. Cathy A. MORALES

New York University (C)

70 Washington Square S, New York NY 10012-1092

County: New York FICE Identification: 002785

Unit ID: 193900

Telephone: (212) 998-1212 Carnegie Class: RU/VH

FAX Number: N/A Calendar System: Semester

URL: www.nyu.edu

Established: 1831 Annual Undergrad Tuition & Fees: $47,750

Enrollment: 49,274 Coed

Affiliation or Control: Independent Non-Profit IRS Status: 501(c)3

Highest Offering: Doctorate

Program: Occupational; 2-Year Principally Bachelor's Creditable; Liberal Arts And General; Teacher Preparatory; Professional

Accreditation: M, BUS, COPSY, DENT, DH, DIETD, DIETI, ENG, HSA, IPSY, JOUR, LAW, MED, MIDWF, NURSE, OT, PH, PLNG, PTA, SP, SPAA, SURGT, SW, TEAC

01	President	Dr. John SEXTON
05	Provost	Dr. David MCLAUGHLIN
10	Executive VP for Finance/IT	Dr. Martin DORPH
11	Executive VP for Operations	Ms. Alison L. LEARY
17	Executive VP for Health	Dr. Robert BERNE
03	Deputy President	Ms. Diane YU
20	Deputy Provost & VC Europe	Dr. Katherine E. FLEMING
26	Sr VP for Univ Rels/Pub Affairs	Dr. Lynne BROWN
30	Sr VP Development/Alumni Relations	Ms. Debra A. LAMORTE
32	Sr Vice Pres for Student Affairs	Dr. Marc L. WAIS
43	General Counsel & Secretary	Mr. Terrance NOLAN
28	VProv Faculty/Arts/Human/Diversity	Dr. Ulrich C. BAER
46	Sr Vice Provost for Research	Dr. Paul M. HORN
03	Senior Presidential Fellow	Dr. Michael C. ALFANO
88	Sr VProv Global Fac Dev NYUAD/NYUSH	Dr. Ron ROBIN
20	Sr Vice Prov Undergrad Acad Affairs	Dr. Matthew S. SANTIROCCO
45	Vice Chancellor Strategic Planning	Dr. Richard FOLEY
35	VC Global Pgms/Univ Life at NYU	Dr. Linda G. MILLS
54	Exec VProv Engineering/Applied Sci	Dr. Katepalli R. SREENIVASAN
18	VP Construction Mgmt/Strategic Svcs	Mr. David ALONSO
26	Vice Pres for Public Affairs	Mr. John H. BECKMAN
45	VP Public Resource Admin & Develop	Dr. Richard N. BING
84	Vice Pres Enrollment	Mr. MJ KNOLL-FINN
88	VP Univ Enterprise Initiatives	Dr. Richard A. MATASAR
44	VP Development and Campaigns	Vacant
15	Vice Pres Human Resources	Mr. Andrew R. GORDON
13	VP for Global Technology & CGTO	Mr. Thomas DELANEY
86	VP Gov Affairs/Community Engagement	Dr. Alicia HURLEY
21	VP Budget & Planning	Mr. Anthony JIGA
88	VP of Global Campus Services	Dr. Robert KIVETZ
21	VP Finance Operations/Treasurer	Ms. Stephanie PIANKA
19	VP Global Campus Safety	Mr. Randy STEPHAN
105	VP Info Technology & CITO	Ms. Marilyn A. MCMILLAN
06	University Registrar	Ms. Elizabeth A. KIENLE-GRANZO
54	Vice Prov Science/Engineering Devel	Dr. Gerard A. BEN AROUS
45	VProv & Assoc VC Strategic Planning	Mr. Joseph P. JULIANO
88	Vice Prov Research/Faculty Affairs	Dr. C. Cybele RAVER
88	Vice Prov Global Stdnt Ldrshp Init	Ms. Melody C. BARNES
21	Assoc VP Finance & Technology	Mr. Chris TANG
27	Assoc VP for Marketing Comm	Ms. Deborah BRODERICK
29	Assoc VP for Alumni Relations	Mr. Brian PERILLO
88	Assoc VProv Rsrch Compliance/Admin	Dr. Martha L. DUNNE
96	Assoc VP Purchasing & Logistics	Vacant
88	Assoc VP Fac Housing/Resid Svcs	Ms. Karen GULINO
88	VP for Global Programs	Dr. Nancy J. MORRISON
20	Sr Assoc Prov/Chf of Staff to Prov	Dr. Carol K. MORROW
07	Asst VP for Undergrad Admissions	Mr. Shawn L. ABBOTT
20	Asst Provost Academic Pgm Review	Mr. Barnett W. HAMBERGER
31	Asst VP Cmty Outreach/Engagement	Mr. Allen M. MCFARLANE
21	Assoc Vice Pres/Controller	Ms. Kerri J. TRICARICO
41	Asst VP Stdnt Affairs/Dir Athletics	Mr. Christopher BLEDSOE
23	Assoc VP Stdnt Hlth/Exec Dir SHC	Dr. Carlo CIOTOLI
37	Asst VP Financial Aid	Ms. Lynn E. HIGINBOTHAM
102	Dir Office of Sponsored Programs	Ms. Nancy S. DANEAU
88	Asst VP Internal Audit	Jasmine DE NULLY
22	Exec Dir Ofc of Equal Opportunity	Ms. Mary SIGNOR
36	Asst VP Student Affairs	Ms. Trudy G. STEINFELD
08	Dean of Libraries	Ms. Carol A. MANDEL
38	Sr Director SHC	Ms. Patricia DELORENZO
39	Sr Director Housing Services	Mr. Neil S. HANRAHAN
50	Dean Business	Dr. Peter B. HENRY
53	Dean Education	Vacant
04	Counselor to the President	Mr. Norman DORSEN
104	Vice Chancellor for Global Programs	Linda MILLS
108	Director Institutional Assessment	Diana KARAFIN

Niagara County Community College (D)

3111 Saunders Settlement Road, Sanborn NY 14132-9460

County: Niagara FICE Identification: 002874

Unit ID: 193946

Telephone: (716) 614-6200 Carnegie Class: Assoc/Pub-S-SC

FAX Number: (716) 614-6700 Calendar System: Semester

URL: www.niagaracc.suny.edu

Established: 1962 Annual Undergrad Tuition & Fees (In-District): $4,274

Enrollment: 6,476 Coed

Affiliation or Control: State/Local IRS Status: 501(c)3

Highest Offering: Associate Degree

Program: Occupational; 2-Year Principally Bachelor's Creditable

Accreditation: M, ACFEI, ADNUR, MAC, PTAA, RAD, SURGT

01	President	Dr. James KLYCZEK
05	Vice President Academic Affairs	Dr. Luba CHLIWNIAK
103	Asst VP Workforce Development	Mr. Hal KINGSLEY
10	Vice President of Finance/Info Tech	Mr. William SCHICKLING
32	Vice President of Student Services	Mrs. Julia PITMAN
11	Vice President of Operations	Mr. Michael DOMBROWSKI
09	Director Planning and Research	Dr. Mary Jane FELDMAN
15	Interim Director of Human Resources	Mr. Donald ARMSTRONG
07	Director of Admissions	Ms. Kathy SAUNDERS
21	Director of Business Services	Ms. Theresa DIGREGORIO
04	Assistant to President	Ms. Barbara WALCK
06	Registrar	Ms. Julie SPEER
35	Director of Student Development	Mrs. Allison ARMUSEWICZ
30	Chief Development Officer	Ms. Deborah BREWER
37	Director of Financial Aid	Mr. James TRIMBOLI
26	Director Public Relations	Ms. Gina BEAM
18	Assistant Director of Facilities	Mr. Dennis GASBARRO
28	Interim Director of Diversity	Mr. Donald ARMSTRONG
08	Head Librarian	Ms. Nancy KENNEDY
105	Director Web Services	Mr. Cory WRIGHT
106	Dir Online Education/E-learning	Ms. Lisa DUBUC
13	Chief Info Technology Officer	Mr. Dennis MICHAELS
19	Director Security/Safety	Ms. Lisa BABCOCK
29	Director Alumni Relations	Ms. Denyel KOURY
39	Director Student Housing	Mr. Edward GONSER
41	Athletic Director	Mr. Robert MCKEOWN
91	Dir User & Administrative Tech	Ms. Cindy MACK

Niagara University (E)

Niagara University NY 14109-9999

County: Niagara FICE Identification: 002788

Unit ID: 193973

Telephone: (716) 285-1212 Carnegie Class: Master's L

FAX Number: (716) 286-8710 Calendar System: Semester

URL: www.niagara.edu

Established: 1856 Annual Undergrad Tuition & Fees: $29,900

Enrollment: 4,015 Coed

Affiliation or Control: Independent Non-Profit IRS Status: 501(c)3

Highest Offering: Doctorate

Program: Liberal Arts And General; Teacher Preparatory; Professional

Accreditation: M, BUS, NURSE, SW, TED

01	President	Rev. James MAHER, CM
03	Exec Vice President	Dr. Bonnie ROSE
05	Provost/VP for Academic Affairs	Dr. Timothy M. DOWNS
32	VP for Enrollment Management and St	Dr. Kevin HEARN
10	VP for Administration	Mr. Michael S. JASZKA
88	VP for International Relations	Dr. Hung P. LE
30	VP for Institutional Advancement	Vacant
42	VP Univ Mission and Ministry	Rev. Kevin CREAGH, CM
20	Assoc VP Acad Affs/Pgms & Policy	Dr. Thomas A. CHAMBERS
20	Assoc VP Operations & Outreach	Ms. Mary E. BORGOGNONI
26	Assoc VP of Comm/Public Relations	Mr. Thomas BURNS
44	Assoc VP for Institutional Advance	Mr. Benjamin D. MARCHIONE
88	Assistant VP Enrollment Management	Ms. Cathleen ANDERSON
45	Exec Dir Univ Planning & Assessment	Mr. Christopher R. SHEFFIELD
43	General Counsel	Ms. Stephanie A. COLE
35	Dean of Student Affairs	Ms. Carrie MCLAUGHLIN
49	Dean College of Arts & Science	Dr. Timothy IRELAND
50	Dean College Business Admin	Dr. Shawn p. DALY
53	Dean College of Education	Dr. Debra A. COLLEY
88	Dean Col Hospitality/Tourism Mgmt	Dr. Kurt A. STAHURA
09	Director Institutional Research	Dr. Vennessa L. WALKER
88	Facility Planner	Mr. Daniel MCMANN
07	Director of Admissions Operations	Mr. Harry S. GONG
07	Director of Admissions	Mr. Mark E. WOJNOWSKI
08	Director of Libraries	Mr. David SCHOEN
19	Director of Campus Safety	Mr. John F. BARKER
37	Director Student Financial Aid	Ms. Katie L. KOCSIS
39	Director of Residence Life	Mr. Jason JAKUBOWSKI
35	Director of Campus Activities	Mrs. Mati ORTIZ
29	Exec Director Alumni Engagement	Ms. Christine S. O'HARA
13	Director Information Technology	Mr. Richard P. KERNIN
57	Director of Art Museum	Ms. Kate KOPERSKI
15	Director of Human Resources	Ms. Donna MOSTILLER
23	Director of Health Services	Ms. Lori SOOS
41	Director of Athletics	Mr. Simon GRAY
18	Director of Facility Services	Mr. Daniel M. GUARIGLIA
88	Exec Dir Division of Academic Svcs	Ms. Antonia KNIGHT
88	Director of Academic Support	Mrs. Diane STOELTING
51	Dir Continuing/Community Education	Mr. Jon Jay STOCKSLADER
31	Dir Institute for Civic Engagement	Dr. David B. TAYLOR
88	Dir Rec & Intramurals/Kiernan Ctr	Mr. John K. SPANBAUER
38	Director Counseling Services	Ms. Monica ROMEO
21	Controller	Mr. Donald E. SMITH
96	Dir of Contract Services & Risk Mgt	Ms. Christy FERGUSON
88	Assoc Dean for Graduate Recruitment	Mr. Evan F. PIERCE
92	Honors Program Coordinator	Dr. Michael BARNWELL
85	Dir Multicultural & Intl Stdnt Affs	Vacant
06	University Registrar	Vacant
88	Director of Student Accounts	Ms. Martie HOWELL
25	Director Grants & Sponsored Program	Vacant
36	Director of Career Services	Mr. Robert P. SWANSON
88	Director of Academic Exploration	Ms. Stephanie CURRIE
104	Dir International Relations	Ms. Bernadette BRENNEN
31	Director of Learn and Serve	Ms. Fran BOLTZ
88	Veterans Services Coordinator	Mr. Robert HEALY
29	Assoc Dir Alumni & Volunteer Engmt	Mr. Howard M. MORGAN
44	Assoc Dir Leadership Giving	Ms. Jaclyn R. ROSSI
44	Director of Major Gifts	Mr. Wade S. HART
44	Director of Planned Giving	Ms. Leslie K. WISE
04	Administrative Asst to President	Ms. Jesenia RIVERA

North Country Community College (F)

23 Santanoni Avenue, PO Box 89, Saranac Lake NY 12983-0089

County: Essex FICE Identification: 007111

Unit ID: 194028

Telephone: (518) 891-2915 Carnegie Class: Assoc/Pub-R-S

FAX Number: (518) 891-2915 Calendar System: Semester

URL: www.nccc.edu

Established: 1967 Annual Undergrad Tuition & Fees (In-District): $5,258

Enrollment: 1,998 Coed

Affiliation or Control: State/Local IRS Status: 501(c)3

Highest Offering: Associate Degree

Program: Occupational; 2-Year Principally Bachelor's Creditable

Accreditation: M

01	President	Dr. Steve J. TYRELL
05	Int Vice Pres of Academic Affairs	Mr. Joe KEEGAN
10	Vice Pres for Administration/CFO	Dr. Sherry HAWN
07	Dean of Admissions	Mr. Christopher TACEA
06	Int Registrar/Records Officer	Ms. Shelly ST. LOUIS
09	Asst Dean Inst Research/Support	Mr. Scott HARWOOD
32	Director of Campus & Student Life	Mrs. Roberta KARP
29	Director Alumni Relations	Ms. Diana FORTUNE

Northeastern Seminary (A)

2265 Westside Drive, Rochester NY 14624-1932
County: Monroe FICE Identification: 034194
Unit ID: 439817
Telephone: (585) 594-6800 Carnegie Class: Spec/Faith
FAX Number: (585) 594-6801 Calendar System: Semester
URL: www.nes.edu
Established: 1998 Annual Graduate Tuition & Fees: $9,040
Enrollment: 154 Coed
Affiliation or Control: Independent Non-Profit IRS Status: 501(c)3
Highest Offering: Doctorate; No Undergraduates
Program: Professional; Religious Emphasis
Accreditation: M, NY, THEOL

01 President .... Dr. Deana L. PORTERFIELD
05 Academic Vice President and Dean .... Dr. Douglas CULLUM
03 Executive Vice President .... Dr. Samuel (Jack) CONNELL
26 AVP for Communications/Enrollment .... Ms. Lisa BENNETT
07 Director of Admissions .... Mr. Caleb MATTHEWS
04 Administrative Asst to President .... Mrs. Patti RADEL
06 Registrar .... Vacant
10 Chief Business Officer .... Mrs. Laurie LEO

† The Seminary is affiliated with Roberts Wesleyan College.

Nyack College (B)

1 South Boulevard, Nyack NY 10960-3698
County: Rockland FICE Identification: 002790
Unit ID: 194161
Telephone: (845) 675-4400 Carnegie Class: Master's L
FAX Number: (845) 358-1751 Calendar System: Semester
URL: www.nyack.edu
Established: 1882 Annual Undergrad Tuition & Fees: $24,300
Enrollment: 2,886 Coed
Affiliation or Control: The Christian And Missionary Alliance
IRS Status: 501(c)3
Highest Offering: Doctorate
Program: 2-Year Principally Bachelor's Creditable; Liberal Arts And General; Teacher Preparatory; Professional
Accreditation: M, MUS, NURSE, SW, TED, THEOL

01 President .... Dr. Michael G. SCALES
04 Assistant to the President .... Mrs. Carol Ann FREEMAN
10 Exec Vice President & Treasurer .... Mr. David C. JENNINGS
05 Provost/VP for Academic Affairs .... Dr. David F. TURK
84 Vice President for Enrollment .... Vacant
30 Vice President of Advancement .... Rev. Jeffery QUINN
20 Assistant Provost .... Dr. Bennett SCHEPENS
20 Assoc Dean Faculty Development .... Dr. Leonard KAGELER
73 Dean Seminary .... Dr. Ronald WALBORN
50 Dean School of Business & Ldrshp .... Dr. Anita UNDERWOOD
64 Dean School of Music .... Dr. Glenn KOPONEN
53 Dean School of Education .... Dr. JoAnn LOONEY
66 Dean School of Nursing .... Mrs. Elizabeth SIMON
49 Dean College of Arts & Sciences .... Dr. Fernando ARZOLA
08 Dean of Library Services .... Ms. Linda K. POSTON
89 Assoc Dean Student Success .... Dr. Gwen PARKER AMES
73 Assoc Dean Seminary (NYC) .... Dr. Luis CARLO
73 Asst Dean Seminary (Puerto Rico) .... Dr. Julio APONTE
32 Assoc Dean of Students .... Mrs. Wanda VELEZ
32 Assoc Dean of Students (NYC) .... Mr. Charles HAMMOND
06 Undergraduate Registrar .... Ms. Evangeline COUCHEY
06 Graduate Registrar .... Ms. Rebecca NOSS
07 Dir of Admissions Undergrad .... Mr. Dan BAILEY
07 Dir of Graduate Admissions .... Vacant
21 Assistant Treasurer .... Mrs. Dona P. SCHEPENS
37 Dir of Fin Svcs Undergrad .... Mr. Steve PHILLIPS
37 Dir of Fin Svcs Undergrad (NYC) .... Mr. Isaac FOSTER
31 Executive Director of Community Rel .... Mr. Earl MILLER
41 Director of Athletics .... Mr. Keith A. DAVIE
36 Director of Career Services .... Mrs. Tiffany AUSTIN
15 Director of Human Resources .... Mrs. Karen DAVIE
13 Director of Information Technology .... Mr. Kevin A. BUEL
09 Director of Institutional Research .... Mr. Greg BEEMAN
18 Director of Operations/Aramark .... Mr. Doug WALKER
26 Dir of Public & Media Relations .... Ms. Deborah WALKER
42 Director of Spiritual Formation .... Mrs. Wanda F. WALBORN
38 Director of Wellness Services .... Mrs. Drusila F. NIEVES
29 Coordinator of Alumni Services .... Mrs. Melissa HICKEY
105 Webmaster .... Mr. Joshua WAY

Nyack College Manhattan Center (C)

2 Washington Street, New York NY 10004
Telephone: (212) 625-0500 Identification: 770143
Accreditation: &M

† Branch campus of Nyack College, Nyack, NY.

Ohr Hameir Theological Seminary (D)

141 Furnace Woods Road,
Cortlandt Manor NY 10567-6112
County: Westchester FICE Identification: 011984
Unit ID: 194189
Telephone: (914) 736-1500 Carnegie Class: Spec/Faith
FAX Number: (914) 736-1055 Calendar System: Semester
Established: 1962 Annual Undergrad Tuition & Fees: $9,900
Enrollment: 96 Male
Affiliation or Control: Independent Non-Profit IRS Status: 501(c)3
Highest Offering: Second Talmudic Degree
Program: Teacher Preparatory; Professional
Accreditation: RABN

01 President .... Rabbi E. KANAREK
30 Chief Devel Ofcr/Dir Financial Aid .... Rabbi Jacob ROTHBERG
06 Registrar .... Rabbi Berel KANAREK

Ohr Somayach Tanenbaum Educational Center (E)

244 Route 306, Monsey NY 10952-0334
County: Rockland FICE Identification: 023201
Unit ID: 243805
Telephone: (845) 425-1370 Carnegie Class: Not Classified
FAX Number: (845) 425-8865 Calendar System: Trimester
URL: www.os.edu
Established: 1979 Annual Undergrad Tuition & Fees: $7,250
Enrollment: 50 Coordinate
Affiliation or Control: Independent Non-Profit IRS Status: 501(c)3
Highest Offering: First Professional Degree
Program: Professional
Accreditation: RABN

01 Director .... Rabbi Abraham BRAUN
05 Dean .... Rabbi Israel ROKOWSKY
06 Registrar .... Mrs. Miriam GROSSMAN
10 Chief Business Officer .... Rabbi Eli ROKOWSKY

Onondaga Community College (F)

4585 West Seneca Turnpike, Syracuse NY 13215-4585
County: Onondaga FICE Identification: 002875
Unit ID: 194222
Telephone: (315) 498-2622 Carnegie Class: Assoc/Pub-U-MC
FAX Number: (315) 492-9208 Calendar System: Semester
URL: www.sunyocc.edu
Established: 1962 Annual Undergrad Tuition & Fees (In-District): $5,337
Enrollment: 12,271 Coed
Affiliation or Control: State/Local IRS Status: 501(c)3
Highest Offering: Associate Degree
Program: Occupational; 2-Year Principally Bachelor's Creditable
Accreditation: M, ADNUR, CAHIIM, ENGT, PTAA, SURGT

01 President .... Dr. Casey CRABILL
05 Provost and SVP Educational Svcs .... Vacant
10 SVP College-affltd Ent & Asset Mgmt .... Mr. David W. MURPHY
05 VP Student Engmnt & Learning Supp .... Dr. Julie WHITE
03 VP College-affiliated Enterprises .... Mr. Seth TUCKER
03 VP College-affiliated Enterprises .... Ms. Anastasia URTZ
30 Vice President Development .... Ms. Lisa MOORE
15 VP HR & External Affairs .... Ms. Amy KREMENEK
09 VP Inst Planning/Assess/Research .... Dr. Agatha AWUAH
13 Chief Information Officer .... Ms. Andrea VENUTI
21 Chief Financial Officer .... Mr. Mark MANNING
20 AVP Student Engagement .... Ms. Rebecca HODA-KEARSE
20 Asst VP Academic & Support Svcs .... Ms. Kathleen D'APRIX
28 VP/Chief Diversity Officer .... Ms. Eunice WILLIAMS
18 VP Property Management .... Mr. John PADDOCK
84 AVP Enrollment Development .... Ms. Shannon PATRIE
37 Director Financial Aid .... Ms. Rebecca ROSE
41 Athletic Director .... Mr. Michael BORSZ
08 Chair Library .... Ms. Pauline SHOSTACK
38 Chair Counseling Department .... Mr. Timothy SINGER
19 VP Campus Safety & Security .... Vacant
88 Director Disability Services .... Ms. Nancy CARR
06 Director Registrar .... Ms. Tracey GREEN
21 Assistant Director Student Accounts .... Ms. Sally LUTON
96 Assistant VP Management Services .... Mr. Michael MCMULLEN
39 Exec Dir Housing & Campus Services .... Ms. Cathy DOTTERER
32 Coordinator Student Leadership Dev .... Ms. Sarah COLLINS
07 Associate VP Enrollment Management .... Mr. Denny NICHOLSON
88 Director Advising & Counseling .... Ms. Jeanine ECKENRODE
88 Director of Sustainability .... Mr. Sean VORMWALD
04 Assistant to the President .... Ms. Julie HART
103 AVP Economic & Workforce Dev .... Mr. Michael METZGAR
25 AVP Research & Grants .... Ms. Nicole SCHLATER
29 Assistant Director Alumni Comm .... Mr. Russ CORBIN
45 AVP Inst Effectiveness & Planning .... Ms. Wendy TARBY
88 AVP Advancement Communications .... Ms. Susan TORMEY
43 Interim General Counsel .... Dr. Kevin MOORE

Orange County Community College (G)

115 South Street, Middletown NY 10940-6437
County: Orange FICE Identification: 002876
Unit ID: 194240
Telephone: (845) 344-6222 Carnegie Class: Assoc/Pub-R-L
FAX Number: (845) 343-1228 Calendar System: Semester
URL: www.sunyorange.edu
Established: 1950 Annual Undergrad Tuition & Fees (In-District): $5,002
Enrollment: 6,951 Coed
Affiliation or Control: State/Local IRS Status: 501(c)3
Highest Offering: Associate Degree
Program: Occupational; 2-Year Principally Bachelor's Creditable; Business Emphasis
Accreditation: M, ACBSP, ADNUR, DH, MLTAD, OTA, PHLEB, PTAA

01 President .... Dr. Kristine M. YOUNG
05 Int Vice Pres Academic Affairs .... Ms. Stacey MOEGENBURG
32 Int Vice Pres Student Services .... Ms. Gerianne BRUSATI
10 Int VP Administration/Finance .... Ms. Jo Ann HAMBURG
30 Vice Pres Institutional Advancement .... Mr. Vinnie CAZZETTA
12 Vice President Newburgh Campus .... Ms. Mindy ROSS
13 Vice President & Chief Info Ofcr .... Mr. Jose BERNIER
20 Sr Assoc Vice Pres Academic Affairs .... Mr. Peter SOSCIA
84 Assoc VP for Enrollment Management .... Ms. Gerianne BRUSATI
76 Assoc VP Health Professions .... Mr. Michael GAWRONSKI, JR.
88 Assoc Vice Pres Resource Devel .... Mr. Russell HAMMOND
50 Assoc VP Business/Math/Sci/Tech .... Ms. Stacey MOEGENBURG
35 Assoc Vice Pres Stdnt Engagemt/Comp .... Ms. Madeline TORRES-DIAZ
15 Assoc Vice Pres Human Resources .... Ms. Wendy HOLMES
08 Director Learning Resource .... Ms. Susan PARRY
51 Dir Continuing/Professional Educ .... Mr. David KOHN
19 Director Campus Security/Safety .... Mr. John AHERNE
09 Inst Plng/Assessment/Research Ofcr .... Ms. Christine WORK
18 Director Administrative Services .... Mr. Michael WORDEN
37 Director of Financial Aid .... Mr. John IVANKOVIC
06 Registrar .... Mr. Neil FOLEY
26 Communications Officer .... Mr. Mike ALBRIGHT
38 Director Advising and Counseling .... Ms. Crystal SCHACHTER
07 Director of Admissions .... Mr. Maynard SCHMIDT
35 Director Student Activities .... Mr. Steve HARPST
37 Asst Director of Financial Aid .... Ms. Rosemary BARRETT

Orange County Community College Newburgh Branch Campus (H)

1 Washington Center, Newburgh NY 12550
Telephone: (845) 562-2454 Identification: 770144
Accreditation: &M

† Branch campus of Orange County Community College, Middletown, NY.

Pace University (I)

1 Pace Plaza, New York NY 10038-1598
County: New York FICE Identification: 002791
Unit ID: 194310
Telephone: (212) 346-1200 Carnegie Class: DRU
FAX Number: (212) 346-1933 Calendar System: Semester
URL: www.pace.edu
Established: 1906 Annual Undergrad Tuition & Fees: $39,697
Enrollment: 12,857 Coed
Affiliation or Control: Independent Non-Profit IRS Status: 501(c)3
Highest Offering: Doctorate
Program: Liberal Arts And General; Teacher Preparatory; Professional
Accreditation: M, ARCPA, BUS, BUSA, CS, IPSY, LAW, NURSE, PSPSY, TED

01 President .... Mr. Stephen J. FRIEDMAN
10 Exec Vice President/CFO .... Mr. Robert C. ALMON
05 Provost/Exec VP Academic Affairs .... Dr. Uday SUKHATME
11 Sr Vice Pres/Chief Admin Ofcr .... Mr. William MCGRATH
84 Vice Pres Enrollment/Placement .... Ms. Robina C. SCHEPP
30 VP Development/Alumni Relations .... Ms. Jennifer BERNSTEIN
13 Int VP Information Tech/CIO .... Mr. Christopher ELARDE
26 VP/Chief Marketing Ofcr Univ Rels .... Ms. Frederica N. WALD
15 Assoc Vice Pres Human Resources .... Mr. Matt RENNA
09 Asst Vice Pres Plng/Assess/Inst Res .... Ms. Barbara S. PENNIPEDE
86 Asst Vice Pres Govt/Community Rels .... Ms. Vanessa J. HERMAN
32 AVP Ofc Student Assistance .... Vacant
27 Assoc VP Marketing/Communications .... Mr. Peter R. SIKOWITZ
21 Asst Vice Pres Academic Finance .... Mr. Dominick BUMBACO
19 Associate VP General Services .... Mr. Frank MCDONALD
35 Assoc Vice Pres/Dean of Students .... Dr. Mark Allen POISEL
20 Assoc Provost for Academic Affairs .... Dr. Adelia WILLIAMS
50 Dean Lubin School of Business .... Mr. Neil S. BRAUN
49 Dean Dyson College Arts/Sci .... Dr. Nira HERRMANN
53 Dean School of Education .... Dr. Andrea M. SPENCER
76 Dean College Health Professions .... Dr. Harriet R. FELDMAN
77 Dean School of CSIS .... Dr. Amar GUPTA
32 Dean of Students New York .... Dr. Marijo RUSSELL O'GRADY
32 Dean of Students Westchester .... Dr. Lisa BARDILL MOSCARITOLO
61 Dean School of Law .... Mr. David YASSKY
06 Assoc VP Stdnt Svcs/Univ Registrar .... Mr. Steven L. JOHNSON
06 Graduate Registrar .... Ms. Margaret JONES
06 Registrar Pleasantville .... Ms. Annmarie MCGRAIL
06 Law School Registrar .... Ms. Nilda RODRIGUEZ
88 Associate University Registrar .... Ms. Barbara MCCARTHY
36 Exec Director Career Svcs/Coop Educ .... Ms. Jody QUEEN-HUBERT
88 Asst Director Adult Education NY .... Ms. Nicola FOSTER
21 Interim Comptroller .... Mr. William VOLL
44 Manager Annual Fund .... Ms. Nicole L. SOUZA
29 Director of Alumni Relations .... Ms. Sheri GIBSON
43 University Counsel .... Mr. Stephen BRODSKY
08 Associate Director Library .... Mr. Melvin ISAACSON
21 University Bursar .... Ms. Susan WEYGANT
37 Director Financial Aid .... Mr. Steven JOHNSON
07 Dir of Admissions NY/Westchester .... Ms. Joanna BRODA
45 Director Budget/Planning/Analysis .... Mr. Len CERTA
22 Affirmative Action Officer .... Ms. Arletha MILES
14 Univ Director Computer Systems .... Mr. Gerard TARPEY
24 Univ Director Educational Media Svc .... Mr. Frank MANNLE
84 Director Adult Enroll Svcs/New York .... Ms. Janet KIRTMAN
23 Assoc Director Health Care Unit .... Ms. Jamesetta NEWLAND
27 Director of Media Relations .... Mr. Christopher CORY
88 Director Pace Adult Resource Center .... Ms. Tamra PLOTNICK
35 Director of Student Devel New York .... Dr. David CLARK
38 Director Counseling Services .... Dr. Richard SHADICK
39 Director of Residential Life .... Mr. A. Patrick ROGER-GORDON
40 Executive Director Bookstore .... Ms. Mary LIETO
85 Assoc Dir Intl Pgms & Services .... Mr. Kraig WALKUP

96 Director of Purchasing - Contracts ....Ms. Alice SEIFERT
18 Director Facilities/Physical Plant ....Mr. Abdul JABAR
28 Director of Diversity ....Ms. Shanelle HENRY ROBINSON

Pacific College of Oriental Medicine (A)

110 William Street, 19th Floor, New York NY 10038
Telephone: (212) 982-3456 Identification: 666139
Accreditation: ACCSC, ACUP

† Branch campus of Pacific College of Oriental Medicine, San Diego CA.

Paul Smith's College (B)

PO Box 265, Paul Smiths NY 12970-0265
County: Franklin FICE Identification: 002795
Unit ID: 194392
Telephone: (518) 327-6000 Carnegie Class: Bac/Diverse
FAX Number: (518) 327-6060 Calendar System: Trimester
URL: www.paulsmiths.edu
Established: 1937 Annual Undergrad Tuition & Fees: $26,200
Enrollment: 886 Coed
Affiliation or Control: Independent Non-Profit IRS Status: 501(c)3
Highest Offering: Baccalaureate
Program: Technical Emphasis
Accreditation: M, ACFEI, ENGT

01 President ....Dr. Cathy S. DOVE
04 Assistant to the President ....Ms. Kathleen A. KECK
05 Provost ....Dr. Nicholas HUNT-BULL
10 Vice President Business/Finance ....Ms. Laura ROZELL
30 Vice President Inst Advancement ....Mr. F. Raymond AGNEW
84 Vice Pres Enrollment Management ....Mr. Peter BURNS
18 VP Facilities Mgmt/Capital Project ... Mr. Steven W. MCFARLAND
13 Director Information Services ....Mr. Jeffrey WALTON
29 Director of Alumni Relations ....Ms. Heather TUTTLE
38 Director of Student Development ....Ms. Ellen GOOCH
37 Director of Financial Aid ....Ms. Mary Ellen M. CHAMBERLAIN
23 Director of Health Services ....Ms. Reiko REXILIUS-TUTHILL
24 Director Education Support Services ....Mr. Neil SURPRENANT
26 Director of Communications ....Mr. Robert BENNETT
06 Registrar ....Ms. Kristin EATON
07 Director of Admissions ....Mr. Keith BRAUN
19 Lead Campus Safety Officer ....Mr. Phil FIACCO
09 Director Institutional Research ....Dr. Jeffrey WALTON
22 Director HEOP ....Ms. Kate MULLEN
41 Dir of Athletics/Physical Educ ....Mr. James TUCKER
21 Comptroller ....Ms. Laura ROZELL
32 VP Student Affairs/Campus Life ....Mr. Matthew SETON-SCHUR
40 Manager of College Store ....Ms. Diana L. LYNG-GLIDDI
15 Human Resources Director ....Ms. Sharon VAN AUKEN
96 Purchasing Coordinator ....Ms. Cynthia LEMERY
36 Career Coordinator ....Ms. Debra DUTCHER
49 Int Dean Comercial/Applied/Lib Arts ....Dr. Eric HOLMLUND
65 Int Dean Natural Res Mgmt/Ecology ....Dr. Dan KELTING

Phillips Beth Israel School of Nursing (C)

776 Sixth Avenue, 4th Floor, New York NY 10001-6354
County: New York FICE Identification: 006438
Unit ID: 189282
Telephone: (212) 614-6110 Carnegie Class: Assoc/PrivNFP
FAX Number: (212) 614-6109 Calendar System: Semester
URL: www.pbisn.edu
Established: 1904 Annual Undergrad Tuition & Fees: $40,195
Enrollment: 287 Coed
Affiliation or Control: Independent Non-Profit IRS Status: 501(c)3
Highest Offering: Baccalaureate
Program: Occupational; 2-Year Principally Bachelor's Creditable; Nursing Emphasis
Accreditation: NY, ADNUR

01 Dean ....Dr. Todd AMBROSIA
05 Assistant Dean ....Mrs. Bernice PASS-STERN
32 Director Student Services ....Ms. Linda FABRIZIO

Plaza College (D)

118-33 Queens Boulevard, Forest Hills NY 11375
County: Queens FICE Identification: 012358
Unit ID: 194499
Telephone: (718) 779-1430 Carnegie Class: Bac/Assoc
FAX Number: (718) 779-7423 Calendar System: Semester
URL: www.plazacollege.edu
Established: 1916 Annual Undergrad Tuition & Fees: $12,350
Enrollment: 757 Coed
Affiliation or Control: Proprietary IRS Status: Proprietary
Highest Offering: Baccalaureate
Program: Occupational; 2-Year Principally Bachelor's Creditable
Accreditation: M, MAC

01 President ....Charles E. CALLAHAN, SR.
03 Provost ....Charles E. CALLAHAN, III
10 Vice Pres of Financial Services ....Elizabeth K. CALLAHAN
11 Chief Operating Officer ....Charles E. CALLAHAN, IV
05 Academic Dean ....Marie DOLLA
06 Registrar ....Carol GARCIA
21 Comptroller ....Linda ROCKHILL
07 Dean of Admissions ....Vanessa LOPEZ
20 Dean Curriculum Development ....Marianne C. ZIPF
08 College Librarian ....Eva BABALIS
23 Director Health Services ....Candice CALLAHAN
37 Financial Aid Coord/Dir Fin Svcs ....Peggy CHUNG
29 Dean Student Activities ....Jonathan HOWLE
100 Chief of Staff/HR Officer/Placement ....Correne CAVALIERI
09 Assoc Dean Institutional Research ....Edward DEE
13 Director IT ....David COLUCCI
32 Dean of Students ....Dawn VETRANO
88 Director of ARC/Library ....Michelle RULLO
14 Manager Information Technology ....Norman ALVARADO
76 Program Director Medical Assisting ....Daryl ANDERSON
26 Director of Communications ....Brittany TRAVIS
38 Freshman Counseling ....Caroline CALLAHAN
103 Dir Career Services & Alumni Dev ....Anita LUCKETT

Pratt Institute (E)

200 Willoughby Avenue, Brooklyn NY 11205-3899
County: Kings FICE Identification: 002798
Unit ID: 194578
Telephone: (718) 636-3600 Carnegie Class: Master's L
FAX Number: (718) 636-3670 Calendar System: Semester
URL: www.pratt.edu
Established: 1887 Annual Undergrad Tuition & Fees: $46,586
Enrollment: 4,556 Coed
Affiliation or Control: Independent Non-Profit IRS Status: 501(c)3
Highest Offering: Master's
Program: 2-Year Principally Bachelor's Creditable; Liberal Arts And General; Teacher Preparatory; Professional
Accreditation: M, ART, CIDA, #LIB, PLNG, TEAC

01 President ....Dr. Thomas F. SCHUTTE
05 Provost ....Mr. Kirk PILLOW
32 Vice President for Student Life ....Dr. Helen MATUSOW-AYRES
10 Vice Pres Finance/Administration ....Ms. Cathleen KENNY
30 Interim Vice President Development ....Ms. Nancy WALKER
84 Vice President for Enrollment ....Ms. Judith AARON
11 Assistant to Pres Administration ....Ms. Josie CAPORUSCIO
06 Registrar ....Mr. Lisle HENDERSON
08 Director of the Library ....Mr. Russ ABELL
20 Associate Provost ....Dr. Marianthi ZIKOPOULOS
15 Director Human Resources ....Mr. Tom GREENE
51 Director Continuing Education ....Ms. Karen MILETSKY
21 Comptroller ....Ms. Sylvia ACUESTA
26 Executive Director Public Relations ....Ms. Mara MCGINNIS
29 Director Alumni Relations ....Mr. Michael SCLAFANI
36 Director of Career Services ....Ms. Rhonda SCHALLER
37 Director Student Financial Aid ....Mr. Nedzad GOGA
09 Exec Dir Institutional Research ....Mr. Vladimir BRILLER
07 Director of Undergraduate Admission ....Mr. William SWAN
96 Director of Purchasing ....Ms. Mitzi BRYAN
57 Dean of Art ....Mr. Gerry SNYDER
49 Dean Liberal Arts/Science ....Dr. Andrew BARNES
48 Dean School of Architecture ....Mr. Thomas HANRAHAN
62 Dean Information/Library Sci ....Dr. Tula GIANNINI
88 Dean of Design ....Ms. Anita COONEY
13 Chief Info Technology Officer (CIO) ....Mr. Joseph HEMWAY

Professional Business College (F)

408 Broadway, 2nd Floor, New York NY 10013
County: New York FICE Identification: 023065
Unit ID: 194611
Telephone: (212) 226-7300 Carnegie Class: Assoc/PrivNFP
FAX Number: (212) 431-8294 Calendar System: Semester
URL: www.pbcny.edu
Established: 2004 Annual Undergrad Tuition & Fees: $9,805
Enrollment: 884 Coed
Affiliation or Control: Independent Non-Profit IRS Status: 501(c)3
Highest Offering: Associate Degree
Program: Occupational; 2-Year Principally Bachelor's Creditable; Business Emphasis
Accreditation: ACICS

01 President ....Mr. Leon LEE
05 Academic Vice President ....Mr. Richard SLUSARCZYK
88 Chief Compliance Officer ....Mr. Nick POLISENO
36 Placement Director ....Ms. Judith RODRIGUEZ
06 Registrar ....Mr. Ken CHANG
08 Head Librarian ....Ms. Diane LEE
07 Admissions Director ....Mr. David WANG
37 Financial Aid Director ....Ms. Cheryl ZHANG
10 Director of Advising ....Ms. Taryn SHUHY

† School is in teach-out plan with Long Island Business Institute.

Rabbi Isaac Elchanan Theological Seminary (G)

2540 Amsterdam Avenue, New York NY 10033-9986
County: New York FICE Identification: 033104
Unit ID: 194727
Telephone: (212) 568-7300 Carnegie Class: Not Classified
FAX Number: (212) 568-7400 Calendar System: Semester
URL: riets.edu
Established: 1886 Annual Graduate Tuition & Fees: $15,250
Enrollment: 323 Male
Affiliation or Control: Jewish IRS Status: 501(c)3
Highest Offering: Beyond Master's But Less Than Doctorate; No Undergraduates
Program: Professional
Accreditation: NY

01 Dean of RIETS ....Rabbi Menachem PENNER

Rabbinical Academy Mesivta Rabbi Chaim Berlin (H)

1605 Coney Island Avenue, Brooklyn NY 11230-4715
County: Kings FICE Identification: 003976
Unit ID: 194657
Telephone: (718) 377-0777 Carnegie Class: Spec/Faith
FAX Number: (718) 338-5578 Calendar System: Semester
Established: 1939 Annual Undergrad Tuition & Fees: $12,250
Enrollment: 316 Male
Affiliation or Control: Independent Non-Profit IRS Status: 501(c)3
Highest Offering: Second Talmudic Degree
Program: Teacher Preparatory; Professional
Accreditation: RABN

01 Provost ....Rabbi Abraham H. FRUCHTHANDLER
05 President of the Faculty ....Rabbi Aaron M. SCHECHTER
03 Executive Director ....Rabbi Y. Mayer LASKER
29 Director of Alumni Association ....Mendel SCHECHTER
45 Chief Planning Officer ....Rabbi Tuvia M. OBERMEISTER
20 Associate Director ....Eli RABINOWITZ
37 Financial Aid Administrator ....Michael A. REISS

Rabbinical College Beth Shraga (I)

28 Saddle River Road, Monsey NY 10952-3035
County: Rockland FICE Identification: 010943
Unit ID: 194693
Telephone: (845) 356-1980 Carnegie Class: Spec/Faith
FAX Number: (845) 425-2604 Calendar System: Semester
Established: 1965 Annual Undergrad Tuition & Fees: $12,050
Enrollment: 42 Male
Affiliation or Control: Independent Non-Profit IRS Status: 501(c)3
Highest Offering: Second Talmudic Degree
Program: Teacher Preparatory; Professional
Accreditation: RABN

01 President ....Rabbi Emanuel SCHIFF

Rabbinical College Bobover Yeshiva B'nei Zion (J)

1577 48th Street, Brooklyn NY 11219-3293
County: Kings FICE Identification: 008614
Unit ID: 194666
Telephone: (718) 438-2018 Carnegie Class: Spec/Faith
FAX Number: (718) 871-9031 Calendar System: Semester
Established: 1947 Annual Undergrad Tuition & Fees: $7,750
Enrollment: 320 Male
Affiliation or Control: Independent Non-Profit IRS Status: 501(c)3
Highest Offering: Second Talmudic Degree
Program: Teacher Preparatory; Professional
Accreditation: RABN

01 President ....Rabbi Boruch Avrohom HOROWITZ

Rabbinical College Ch'san Sofer (K)

1876 50th Street, Brooklyn NY 11204-0304
County: Kings FICE Identification: 003977
Unit ID: 194675
Telephone: (718) 236-1171 Carnegie Class: Spec/Faith
FAX Number: (718) 236-1119 Calendar System: Semester
Established: 1940 Annual Undergrad Tuition & Fees: $8,500
Enrollment: 46 Male
Affiliation or Control: Independent Non-Profit IRS Status: 501(c)3
Highest Offering: Second Talmudic Degree
Program: Teacher Preparatory; Professional
Accreditation: RABN

01 Executive Vice President ....Rabbi D. EHRENFELD
05 Dean of the College ....Rabbi S. B. EHRENFELD
10 Treasurer ....Mr. Mordechai STUHL
06 Registrar ....Rabbi Meyer WEINBERGER

Rabbinical College of Long Island (L)

205 W Beech Street, Long Beach NY 11561-0630
County: Nassau FICE Identification: 010378
Unit ID: 194736
Telephone: (516) 255-4700 Carnegie Class: Spec/Faith
FAX Number: (516) 255-4701 Calendar System: Semester
Established: 1965 Annual Undergrad Tuition & Fees: $13,700
Enrollment: 115 Male
Affiliation or Control: Independent Non-Profit IRS Status: 501(c)3
Highest Offering: First Talmudic Degree
Program: Teacher Preparatory; Professional
Accreditation: RABN

01 President ....Rabbi Yitzchok FEIGELSTOCK
06 Registrar ....Rabbi Dovid N. ROTHSCHILD
32 Dean of Students ....Rabbi Yeruchem PITTER
07 Director of Admissions ....Rabbi Chaim HOBERMAN
37 Financial Aid Administrator ....Rabbi Shlomo TEICHMAN

Rabbinical College Ohr Shimon Yisroel (M)

215-217 Hewes Street, Brooklyn NY 11211-8102
County: Kings FICE Identification: 031292
Unit ID: 405854

Telephone: (718) 855-4092 Carnegie Class: Spec/Faith
FAX Number: (718) 855-8479 Calendar System: Semester
Established: Annual Undergrad Tuition & Fees: $11,500
Enrollment: 158 Male
Affiliation or Control: Independent Non-Profit IRS Status: 501(c)3
Highest Offering: First Talmudic Degree
Program: Professional
Accreditation: @RABN

01 President ....Rabbi Shulem WALTER

Rabbinical College Ohr Yisroel (A)

8800 Seaview Avenue, Brooklyn NY 11236

County: Kings Identification: 667145
Telephone: (718) 633-4715 Carnegie Class: Not Classified
FAX Number: (347) 702-5436 Calendar System: Semester
Established: 2009 Annual Undergrad Tuition & Fees: $9,000
Enrollment: 93 Male
Affiliation or Control: Independent Non-Profit IRS Status: 501(c)3
Highest Offering: First Talmudic Degree
Program: Teacher Preparatory; Professional
Accreditation: @RABN

01 President ....Rabbi Daniel GELDZAHLER

Rabbinical Seminary of America (B)

76-01 147th Street, Flushing NY 11367-3148

County: Queens FICE Identification: 003978
Unit ID: 194763
Telephone: (718) 268-4700 Carnegie Class: Spec/Faith
FAX Number: (718) 268-4684 Calendar System: Semester
Established: 1933 Annual Undergrad Tuition & Fees: $9,800
Enrollment: 507 Male
Affiliation or Control: Independent Non-Profit IRS Status: 501(c)3
Highest Offering: Second Talmudic Degree
Program: Teacher Preparatory; Professional
Accreditation: RABN

01 President ....Rabbi David HARRIS
01 President ....Rabbi Akiva GRUNBLATT
03 Executive Vice President ....Rabbi Hayim SCHWARTZ
11 Director of Operation ....Rabbi Meir GLAZER
06 Registrar ....Rabbi Abraham SEMMEL
30 Director Development ....Rabbi Yossi SINGER
37 Director of Financial Aid ....Mrs. Laya EISENSTEIN
18 Chief Physical Plant ....Mr. Eli TEIGMAN
88 Director of Special Projects ....Vacant
91 Director of Admin Computing ....Mr. Jonathan PLATOVSKY
39 Director Student Housing ....Rabbi Aryeh GOLDMAN
46 Director Research & Development ....Vacant
30 Director of Development ....Rabbi Moshe MARCOVICH

Relay Graduate School of Education (C)

40 West 20th Street, 7th Floor, New York NY 10011

County: New York Identification: 667117
Unit ID: 475033
Telephone: (212) 228-1888 Carnegie Class: Not Classified
FAX Number: (212) 228-1855 Calendar System: Other
URL: www.relayschool.org
Established: 2011 Annual Graduate Tuition & Fees: $17,500
Enrollment: 958 Coed
Affiliation or Control: Independent Non-Profit IRS Status: 501(c)3
Highest Offering: Master's; No Undergraduates
Program: Teacher Preparatory
Accreditation: M, TED

01 Co-Founder/President ....Mr. Norman ATKINS
05 Provost ....Dr. Brent MADDIN
10 Chief Financial Officer ....Ms. Piper EVANS
11 Chief Operating Officer ....Mr. Tim SAINTSING
13 Chief Technology Officer ....Mr. Rob UNDERWOOD
20 Dean ....Ms. Mayme HOSTELLER

Rensselaer Polytechnic Institute (D)

110 8th Street, Troy NY 12180-3590

County: Rensselaer FICE Identification: 002803
Unit ID: 194824
Telephone: (518) 276-6000 Carnegie Class: RU/VH
FAX Number: N/A Calendar System: Semester
URL: www.rpi.edu
Established: 1824 Annual Undergrad Tuition & Fees: $49,341
Enrollment: 6,835 Coed
Affiliation or Control: Independent Non-Profit IRS Status: 501(c)3
Highest Offering: Doctorate
Program: Liberal Arts And General; Professional
Accreditation: M, BUS, ENG

01 President ....Dr. Shirley Ann JACKSON
05 Provost ....Dr. Prabhat HAJELA
11 Vice President for Administration ....Mr. Claude ROUNDS
22 VP Strategic Comm/External Rels ....Vacant
10 Vice President for Finance/CFO ....Ms. Virginia GREGG
45 Vice Pres for Research ....Mr. Jonathan S. DORDICK
30 Vice Pres Institutional Advancement ....Mr. Graig R. EASTIN
32 Vice President Student Life ....Dr. Frank ROSS, III
15 Vice Pres Human Resources ....Mr. Curtis N. POWELL
13 Vice Pres for Info Services & CIO ....Mr. John E. KOLB
84 Vice Pres Enrollment Management ....Dr. Jonathan D. WEXLER
43 Secy of the Inst/General Counsel ....Mr. Charles F. CARLETTA
100 Chief of Staff ....Ms. Elisha MOZERSKY
21 Asst Vice Pres for Administration ....Mr. Paul MARTIN
26 Asst VP for Govt & Ext Relations ....Ms. Allison NEWMAN
29 Asst Vice Pres Alumni Relations ....Mr. Jeff SCHANZ
54 Dean School of Engineering ....Dr. Shekhar GARDE
81 Dean School of Science ....Dr. Curt BRENEMAN
79 Dean Sch of Humanities/Social Sci ....Dr. Mary SIMONI
50 Dean Lally School of Mgmt/Tech ....Dr. Thomas BEGLEY
48 Dean School of Architecture ....Mr. Evan DOUGLIS
20 Associate Dean for Information Tech ....Mr. David SPOONER
35 Dean of Students ....Mr. Mark SMITH
06 Dir Stdnt Records/Fin Svcs/Registr ....Ms. Sharon L. KUNKEL
37 Director Financial Aid ....Mr. Larry CHAMBERS
09 Director of Institutional Research ....Mr. Jack MAHONEY
08 Director of Libraries ....Vacant
25 Director Office Contracts & Grants ....Mr. Richard E. SCAMMELL
36 Director Career Development Center ....Mr. Thomas L. TARANTELLI
07 Director Undergrad Admissions ....Ms. Karen S. LONG
18 Director Physical Plant ....Mr. Mark FROST
86 Director of Federal Relations ....Ms. Deborah E. ALTENBURG
23 Director Student Health Center ....Dr. Leslie LAWRENCE
38 Director Student Counseling ....Dr. Benjamin MARTE
96 Manager Purchasing Systems ....Mr. Craig MCINTOSH

Richard Gilder Graduate School at the American Museum of Natural History (E)

Central Park West at 79th Street, New York NY 10024

County: New York Identification: 667003
Unit ID: 458548
Telephone: (212) 769-5055 Carnegie Class: Not Classified
FAX Number: (212) 769-5257 Calendar System: Other
URL: www.amnh.org/our-research/richard-gilder-graduate-school
Established: 2006 Annual Graduate Tuition & Fees: N/A
Enrollment: 17 Coed
Affiliation or Control: Independent Non-Profit IRS Status: 501(c)3
Highest Offering: Doctorate; No Undergraduates
Program: Professional
Accreditation: NY

01 Dean ....Dr. John J. FLYNN
10 Financial Administrator ....Jennifer BUTLER

Roberts Wesleyan College (F)

2301 Westside Drive, Rochester NY 14624-1997

County: Monroe FICE Identification: 002805
Unit ID: 194958
Telephone: (585) 594-6000 Carnegie Class: Master's L
FAX Number: (585) 594-6371 Calendar System: Semester
URL: www.roberts.edu
Established: 1866 Annual Undergrad Tuition & Fees: $28,630
Enrollment: 1,762 Coed
Affiliation or Control: Independent Non-Profit IRS Status: 501(c)3
Highest Offering: Master's
Program: Liberal Arts And General; Teacher Preparatory; Professional
Accreditation: M, ART, IACBE, MUS, NURSE, SW, TEAC

01 President ....Dr. Deana L. PORTERFIELD
05 Sr VP & Chief Academic Officer ....Dr. David BASINGER
03 Executive Vice President ....Dr. S. Jack CONNELL
10 Sr Vice President & Treasurer ....Ms. Laurie LEO
32 VP for Student Development ....Dr. Nelson W. HILL
11 Vice President for Administration ....Mrs. Ruth LOGAN
07 Assoc VP for UG Admissions ....Mr. JP ANDERSON
44 Assoc VP for Major Gifts ....Mr. Maurice (Max) MCGINNIS
26 AVP for Brand/Marketing Comm ....Ms. Donna MCLAREN
13 Assoc VP for Information Technology ....Mr. Pradeep SAXENA
40 Director of Bookstore Services ....Mr. Darren WALTON
41 Director of Athletics ....Mr. Robert SEGAVE
37 Director of Student Financial Svcs ....Mr. Stephen G. FIELD
09 Dir Institutional Research/Assess ....Dr. Paul W. KENNEDY
42 Chaplain ....Rev. Jonathan BRATT
06 Registrar ....Mrs. Lesa J. KOHR
08 Director of Library Services ....Mr. Alfred C. KROBER
102 Dir Foundation/Corporate Relations ....Mrs. Kelly E. SMITH
04 Administrative Asst to President ....Mrs. Patti RADEL
15 Director Personnel Services ....Mrs. Amy PORPILIA
18 Chief Facilities/Physical Plant ....Mr. T. Richard GREER
19 Director Security/Safety ....Mr. Rick BILLITIER
25 Chief Contracts/Grants Admin ....Mrs. Lisa TIFFIN
29 Director Alumni Relations ....Mr. Kirk KETTINGER

† Parent institution of Northeastern Seminary.

Rochester Institute of Technology (G)

1 Lomb Memorial Drive, Rochester NY 14623-5604

County: Monroe FICE Identification: 002806
Unit ID: 195003
Telephone: (585) 475-2411 Carnegie Class: Master's L
FAX Number: (585) 475-7049 Calendar System: Quarter
URL: www.rit.edu
Established: 1829 Annual Undergrad Tuition & Fees: $37,124
Enrollment: 18,063 Coed
Affiliation or Control: Independent Non-Profit IRS Status: 501(c)3
Highest Offering: Doctorate
Program: Liberal Arts And General; Teacher Preparatory; Professional; Technical Emphasis
Accreditation: M, ARCPA, ART, BUS, CIDA, CS, DIETD, DMS, ENG, ENGT, TEAC

01 President ....Dr. William W. DESTLER
05 Provost & Sr VP for Acad Affs ....Dr. Jeremy A. HAEFNER
100 Chief of Staff ....Mrs. Karen A. BARROWS
10 Sr Vice Pres Finance/Administration ....Dr. James H. WATTERS
84 Sr VP Enroll Mgmt/Career Svcs ....Dr. James G. MILLER
32 Sr Vice President Student Affairs ....Dr. Sandra S. JOHNSON
46 President NTID/RIT Vice Pres & Dean ....Dr. Gerard J. BUCKLEY
12 President RIT Dubai ....Dr. Yousef AL-ASSAF
30 VP for Development & Alumni Rels ....Dr. Lisa CAUDA
86 Vice President Govt/Cmty Relations ....Ms. Deborah M. STENDARDI
46 Vice President Research ....Dr. Ryne RAFFAELLE
28 VP for Diversity & Inclusion ....Dr. Kevin MCDONALD
12 VP AUK/Academic Dir RIT Pgms Kosovo ....Dr. Brian BOWEN
76 VP/Dean Coll Health Sciences/Tech ....Dr. Daniel B. ORNT
46 Senior Assoc Provost ....Dr. Christine M. LICATA
36 Assoc VP/Dir Coop Ed/Career Svcs ....Dr. Emanuel CONTOMANOLIS
26 Chief Communications Officer ....Mr. Robert FINNERTY
20 Asst Provost and Director CIMS ....Dr. Nabil NASR
08 Director of RIT Libraries ....Ms. Shirley BOWER
88 Assoc Provost Faculty Career Dev ....Dr. Lynn A. WILD
12 President-RIT Croatia ....Mr. Donald HUDSPETH
29 Assoc VP Alumni/Parent & Annual Giv ....Ms. Kimberly SLUSSER
21 Asst VP/Controller/Asst Treasurer ....Ms. Lyn KELLY
18 Asst VP Facilities Management Svs ....Mr. John MOORE
06 Asst VP/Registrar ....Mr. Joe LOFFREDO
07 Asst VP/Exec Dir of Admissions ....Dr. Daniel SHELLEY
37 Asst VP & Dir Fin Aid & Scholarship ....Ms. Verna J. HAZEN
88 Asst VP and Dir Grad/PT Enroll Svc ....Ms. Diane ELLISON
44 Asst VP for Campaigns & Const Dev ....Ms. Heather ENGEL
09 Asst VP Inst Rsrch/Policy Studies ....Dr. Joan E. GRAHAM
15 Asst VP/Director Human Resources ....Ms. Judy BENDER
44 Exec Dir Fund for RIT ....Ms. Marisa PSAILA
88 Assoc VP for Res Ed & Comm ....Dr. Dawn SOUFLERIS
35 Assoc VP Student Affairs & Comm Dev ....Dr. Heath BOICE-PARDEE
85 Director International Student Svcs ....Mr. Jeffrey W. COX
96 Exec Director Procurement Services ....Ms. Debra KUSSE
102 Sr Director Foundation Relations ....Ms. Bonnie BUTKUS
102 Exec Director Corporate Relations ....Mr. Paul HARRIS
101 Secretary of the Institute ....Mrs. Karen A. BARROWS
50 Dean of Business ....Dr. Jacqueline MOZRALL
54 Dean of Engineering ....Dr. Harvey J. PALMER
72 Dean Applied Science/Technology ....Dr. H. Fred WALKER
49 Dean of Liberal Arts ....Dr. James J. WINEBRAKE
81 Dean of Science ....Dr. Sophia MAGGELAKIS
57 Dean College Imaging Arts/Sci ....Ms. Lorraine JUSTICE
77 Int Dean Col Computer/Info Science ....Dr. Anne HAAKE
58 Dean Graduate Studies ....Dr. Hector FLORES
04 Exec Admin Asst to President ....Ms. Sonia RODRIGUEZ
11 Chief of Administration ....Ms. Karen A. BARROWS
13 Chief Info Technology Officer (CIO) ....Ms. Jeanne CASARES
41 Exec Dir Intercollegiate Athletics ....Mr. Louis SPIOTTI

Rockefeller University (H)

1230 York Avenue, New York NY 10065-6399

County: New York FICE Identification: 002807
Unit ID: 195049
Telephone: (212) 327-8000 Carnegie Class: RU/VH
FAX Number: (212) 327-8699 Calendar System: Other
URL: www.rockefeller.edu
Established: 1901 Annual Graduate Tuition & Fees: N/A
Enrollment: 209 Coed
Affiliation or Control: Independent Non-Profit IRS Status: 501(c)3
Highest Offering: Doctorate; No Undergraduates
Program: Professional
Accreditation: NY

01 President ....Dr. Marc TESSIER-LAVIGNE
43 Vice President & General Counsel ....Ms. Harriet RABB
05 Vice President Academic Affairs ....Mr. Michael W. YOUNG
10 Vice President Finance ....Mr. James H. LAPPLE
30 Sr Vice President Development ....Ms. Maren E. IMHOFF
17 Vice President for Medical Affairs ....Dr. Barry S. COLLER
20 Dean & Vice Pres of Educ Affairs ....Dr. Sidney STRICKLAND
100 Chief of Staff and Vice President ....Dr. Timothy O'CONNOR
15 Vice President Human Resources ....Ms. Virginia A. HUFFMAN
18 Assoc Vice Pres Plant Operations ....Mr. Alexander KOGAN
45 Assoc Vice Pres Plng & Constr ....Mr. George B. CANDLER
13 Chief Information Officer ....Mr. Anthony CARVALLOZA
25 Dir Pgm Dev & Sponsored Research ....Vacant
08 University Librarian ....Ms. Carol FELTES
19 Director Security ....Mr. James ROGERS

Rockland Community College (I)

145 College Road, Suffern NY 10901-3699

County: Rockland FICE Identification: 002877
Unit ID: 195058
Telephone: (845) 574-4000 Carnegie Class: Assoc/Pub-S-SC
FAX Number: (845) 574-4463 Calendar System: Semester
URL: www.sunyrockland.edu
Established: 1959 Annual Undergrad Tuition & Fees (In-District): $4,300
Enrollment: 7,593 Coed
Affiliation or Control: State/Local IRS Status: 501(c)3
Highest Offering: Associate Degree
Program: 2-Year Principally Bachelor's Creditable

Accreditation: M, ADNUR, OTA

01 President ... Dr. Cliff L. WOOD
10 VP Finance/Administration ... Dr. Nayyer HUSSAIN
05 Provost/VP Academic & Student Affs ... Dr. Susan DEER
21 Assoc VP Finance/Administration ... Mr. Joseph MARRA
88 AVP Academic/Community Partnershp ... Mr. Thomas DELLA TORRE
32 AVP Student Development ... Dr. James SIEGEL
84 AVP of Enrollment Management ... Ms. Dana STILLEY
37 Director Financial Aid ... Ms. Debra BOUABIDI
06 Registrar ... Ms. Robin CONKLIN
13 Director of Information Services ... Dr. Steven FERRES
08 Director of Library/Learning Res ... Vacant
18 Chief Facilities/Physical Plant ... Mr. Douglas SCHMIDT
28 Dir Equity/Compliance/Affirm Act ... Ms. Melissa ROY
09 Director of Institutional Research ... Dr. Jim ROBERTSON
20 Asst to Vice Pres Academic Affairs ... Ms. Patricia KOBES
26 Chief Public Relations Officer ... Ms. Tzipora REITMAN
04 Administrative Asst to President ... Mr. Ben NAYLOR
07 Director of Admissions ... Mr. Jude FLEURISMOND
101 Secretary of the Board ... Mr. Ben NAYLOR
106 Dir Online Education/E-learning ... Ms. Lilia JUELE
11 Chief of Administration ... Mr. Dennis CALLINAN
15 Director Human Resources ... Ms. Theresa MORGAN
19 Director Public Safety ... Mr. William MURPHY
25 Director of Grants ... Ms. Elizabeth KENDALL
41 Athletic Director ... Mr. Dan KEELEY
90 Director Academic Computing ... Ms. Lilia JUELE

The Sage Colleges (A)

65 First Street, Troy NY 12180-4199

County: Rensselaer — FICE Identification: 002810

Unit ID: 195128

Telephone: (518) 244-2000 — Carnegie Class: Master's L

FAX Number: (518) 244-2460 — Calendar System: Semester

URL: www.sage.edu

Established: 1916 — Annual Undergrad Tuition & Fees: $28,400

Enrollment: 2,885 — Coed

Affiliation or Control: Independent Non-Profit — IRS Status: 501(c)3

Highest Offering: Doctorate

Program: Liberal Arts And General; Teacher Preparatory; Professional

Accreditation: M, ART, DIETD, DIETI, IACBE, NURSE, OT, PTA, TED

01 President ... Dr. Susan C. SCRIMSHAW
05 Provost ... Dr. Susan W. BEATTY
30 VP for Institutional Advancement ... Ms. Melissa KOMORA
12 Dean Sage College of Albany ... Dr. Joanne CURRAN
12 Dean Russell Sage College ... Dr. Deborah LAWRENCE
51 Dean Professional & Continuing Ed ... Mr. Albert ORBINATI
10 VP for Finance & Treasurer ... Mr. Patrick JACOBSON-SCHULTE
84 VP Marketing/Enrollment Mgmt ... Dr. Daniel GREEN
32 Vice Pres for Campus Life ... Ms. Patricia CELLEMME
11 VP Administration & Planning ... Ms. Deirdre ZARRILLO
35 Assoc VP for Student Life-RSC ... Mr. Michael BAUMGARDNER
35 Assoc VP for Student Life-SCA ... Ms. Sharon MURRAY
76 Dean of Health Sciences ... Dr. Theresa HAND
06 Acting Registrar ... Ms. Patricia SCHUMANN
07 Senior Director of UG Admission ... Mr. Thomas BREEN
88 Assoc Dean School of Management ... Dr. Kimberly FREDERICKS
53 Dean School of Education ... Dr. Lori QUIGLEY
29 Dir of Alumni Relations SCA/SGS ... Ms. Rachel POMBO
29 Director Alumnae Relations RSC ... Ms. Joan CLIFFORD
07 Director of Graduate & Adult Admiss ... Ms. Wendy DIEFENDORF
37 Director of Financial Aid ... Ms. Kelley ROBINSON
38 Director Student Counseling ... Vacant
15 Director of Human Resources ... Ms. Carla MASTRIANO
09 Director of Institutional Research ... Ms. Lori PIZER
18 Director Facilities Management ... Mr. John ZAJACESKOWSKI
28 Dir Cultural Enrichment/Diversity ... Vacant
36 Associate Dean of Academic Advising ... Ms. Karen SCHELL
36 Associate Dean of Academic Advising ... Ms. Stacy GONZALEZ
26 Dir of Communications & Marketing ... Ms. Shannon BALLARD GORMAN
92 Interim Director of Honors Programs ... Dr. Andor SKOTNES
21 Director of Finance ... Ms. Kristina L. PRILL
96 Dir of Purchasing/Accts Payable ... Ms. Paula SELMER
04 Administrative Asst to President ... Ms. Rosemary L. GRIGNON
08 Head Librarian ... Ms. Lisa C. BRAINARD
105 Webmaster ... Mr. Kurt EYE
108 Director Institutional Assessment ... Dr. Donna HEALD
19 Director Security/Safety ... Mr. Robert GREBERT
39 Director of Residence Life ... Mr. Christopher OERTEL
41 Athletic Director ... Ms. Dani DREWS
44 Sr Director of Annual Giving ... Ms. Kathleen DANICA
86 Assoc Director Government Relations ... Mr. Nicholas DECAPRIO
91 Director of IT/Newwork Services ... Mr. John HARRIS
106 Dir Online Education/E-learning ... Mr. Albert ORBINATI

Saint Bernard's School of Theology & Ministry (B)

120 French Road, Rochester NY 14618-3822

County: Monroe — FICE Identification: 002815

Unit ID: 195155

Telephone: (585) 271-3657 — Carnegie Class: Spec/Faith

FAX Number: (585) 271-2045 — Calendar System: Semester

URL: www.stbernards.edu

Established: 1893 — Annual Graduate Tuition & Fees: $10,644

Enrollment: 95 — Coed

Affiliation or Control: Roman Catholic — IRS Status: 501(c)3

Highest Offering: Master's; No Undergraduates

Program: Professional

Accreditation: THEOL

01 President ... Rev. George P. HEYMAN
05 Academic Dean ... Dr. Devadasan N. PREMNATH
06 Registrar ... Ms. Ellen MORNINGSTAR
10 Controller ... Ms. Mary MUGGLETON
07 Admiss Director/Dir Stdnt Fin Aid ... Mr. Jonathan SCHOTT
51 Dir Certification/Professional Dev ... Rev. George HEYMAN
08 Librarian ... Ms. Katherine WAHL
30 Director of Advancement ... Vacant

St. Bonaventure University (C)

P.O. Box 2450, St. Bonaventure NY 14778

County: Cattaraugus — FICE Identification: 002817

Unit ID: 195164

Telephone: (716) 375-2000 — Carnegie Class: Master's L

FAX Number: N/A — Calendar System: Semester

URL: www.sbu.edu

Established: 1858 — Annual Undergrad Tuition & Fees: $31,389

Enrollment: 2,064 — Coed

Affiliation or Control: Roman Catholic — IRS Status: 501(c)3

Highest Offering: Master's

Program: Liberal Arts And General; Teacher Preparatory; Professional

Accreditation: M, BUS, CACREP, TED

01 President ... Dr. Margaret CARNEY, OSF
05 Provost and VP for Academic Affairs ... Dr. Joseph ZIMMER
32 Vice President for Student Affairs ... Mr. Richard C. TRIETLEY, JR.
10 Senior VP Finance & Administration ... Ms. Brenda L. MCGEE
26 Vice Pres University Relations ... Dr. Emily F. MORRIS
42 Exec Director of Faith Formation ... Fr. Francis J. DISPIGNO, OFM
88 Vice Pres for Franciscan Mission ... Vacant
30 Assoc VP Development ... Mr. Bernard VALENTO
57 Exec Dir of Q Arts Center ... Mr. Ludwig BRUNNER
20 Assoc Provost Academic Affairs ... Vacant
11 Director of Operations Ofc of Pres ... Mr. Thomas BUTTAFARRO, JR.
15 Director Human Resources ... Ms. Sharon BURKE
07 Director of Recruitment ... Ms. Monica EMERY
37 Director of Financial Aid ... Mr. Troy MARTIN
06 Registrar ... Ms. Debra LOVELESS
39 Exec Dir Res Living/Chief Judicial ... Ms. Nichole GONZALEZ
13 Exec Director Technology Services ... Dr. Michael HOFFMAN
08 Director of Friedsam Mem Library ... Mr. Paul J. SPAETH
38 Director Counseling ... Dr. Roger E. KEENER
41 Director of Athletics ... Mr. Tim KENNEY
09 Director of Inst Research ... Vacant
29 Director of Alumni Services ... Ms. Monica MATTIOLI
36 Director of Career Services ... Ms. Connie F. WHITCOMB
43 University Counsel ... Mr. Jeff REISNER
23 Director Wellness Center ... Dr. Roger E. KEENER
18 Director Physical Plant ... Mr. Philip G. WINGER
21 Controller ... Mrs. Nancy K. TAYLOR
19 Director of Safety and Security ... Mr. Gary SEGRUE
40 Manager Bookstore ... Ms. Annette DONAVON
44 Director Annual Giving Program ... Mr. Clarence PICARD
92 Director of Honors Program ... Dr. David HILMEY
96 Dir of Budget & Purchasing ... Ms. Lorraine SMITH
73 Dean SFS/Dir Franciscan Institute ... Fr. David COUTURIER, OFM
49 Dean School of Arts & Sci ... Dr. David DANAHAR
50 Dean School of Business ... Vacant
58 Assc Provost/Dean Sch Graduate Stds ... Vacant
53 Dean School of Education ... Dr. Nancy CASEY
60 Dean Jandoli Sch Journ/Mass Comm ... Dr. Pauline HOFFMANN
104 Director of International Studies ... Vacant
27 Dir Media Relations & Marketing ... Mr. Tom MISSEL

St. Elizabeth College of Nursing (D)

2215 Genesee Street, Utica NY 13501-5998

County: Oneida — FICE Identification: 006461

Unit ID: 195687

Telephone: (315) 798-8144 — Carnegie Class: Assoc/PrivNFP

FAX Number: (315) 798-8271 — Calendar System: Semester

URL: www.secon.edu

Established: 1904 — Annual Undergrad Tuition & Fees: $14,600

Enrollment: 209 — Coed

Affiliation or Control: Independent Non-Profit — IRS Status: 501(c)3

Highest Offering: Associate Degree

Program: 2-Year Principally Bachelor's Creditable; Nursing Emphasis

Accreditation: M, ADNUR

01 President ... Mrs. Varinya SHEPPARD
32 Dean of Students/Faculty Devel ... Ms. Christine MENARD
06 Registrar & Bursar ... Ms. Eileen MUHLIG
84 Enrollment Mgr/Dir of Financial Aid ... Ms. Sherry WOJNAS

St. Francis College (E)

180 Remsen Street, Brooklyn NY 11201-4398

County: Kings — FICE Identification: 002820

Unit ID: 195173

Telephone: (718) 522-2300 — Carnegie Class: Bac/Diverse

FAX Number: (718) 522-1274 — Calendar System: Semester

URL: www.sfc.edu

Established: 1859 — Annual Undergrad Tuition & Fees: $23,800

Enrollment: 2,749 — Coed

Affiliation or Control: Independent Non-Profit — IRS Status: 501(c)3

Highest Offering: Master's

Program: Liberal Arts And General; Teacher Preparatory; Technical Emphasis

Accreditation: M, NURSE, TEAC

01 President ... Mr. Brendan J. DUGAN
10 Exec Vice President for Finance ... Ms. June MCGRISKEN
05 Provost/Vice Pres for Academic Affs ... Dr. Timothy J. HOULIHAN
26 Vice Pres Govt/Community Relations ... Ms. Linda WERBEL DASHEFSKY
30 Vice President of Development ... Mr. Thomas FLOOD
84 Asst Vice Pres Enrollment Mgmt ... Mr. Joseph CUMMINGS
18 Asst Vice Pres Facilities Mgmt ... Mr. Kevin O'ROURKE
21 Asst Vice President for Finance ... Mr. John RAGNO
88 Dean Academic Program Development ... Dr. Allen BURDOWSKI
20 Asst Dean of Academic Affairs ... Dr. Michele HIRSCH
89 Asst Dean of Freshmen Studies ... Ms. Monica MICHALSKI
15 Exec Director Human Resources ... Mr. Richard GRASSO
13 Director of IT Operations ... Mr. Matthew HOGAN
06 Registrar ... Ms. Susan E. WEISMAN
32 Dean of Students ... Dr. Jose RODRIGUEZ
08 Director Library Services ... Dr. James SMITH
36 Director of Career Development ... Ms. Naomi KINLEY
29 Director of Alumni Relations ... Mr. Dennis MCDERMOTT
41 Director of Athletics ... Ms. Irma GARCIA
42 Director Campus Ministry ... Fr. Brian JORDAN
09 Director of Institutional Research ... Mr. Steven CATALANO
07 Senior Admissions Counselor ... Ms. Cortney ROBERT

St. John Fisher College (F)

3690 East Avenue, Rochester NY 14618-3597

County: Monroe — FICE Identification: 002821

Unit ID: 195720

Telephone: (585) 385-8000 — Carnegie Class: DRU

FAX Number: (585) 899-3870 — Calendar System: Semester

URL: www.sjfc.edu

Established: 1948 — Annual Undergrad Tuition & Fees: $30,690

Enrollment: 3,871 — Coed

Affiliation or Control: Independent Non-Profit — IRS Status: 501(c)3

Highest Offering: Doctorate

Program: Liberal Arts And General; Teacher Preparatory; Professional; Business Emphasis

Accreditation: M, BUS, CACREP, NURSE, PHAR, TED

01 President ... Dr. Gerard J. ROONEY
04 Exec Asst to Pres/Secy to Board ... Ms. Joan R. BENULIS
05 Interim Provost/Dean of College ... Dr. Ian C. NEWBOULD
84 VP Enrollment ... Mr. Jose J. PERALES
10 Vice President for Finance/CFO ... Ms. Jacqueline S. DISTEFANO
32 VP Student Affairs & Diversity ... Dr. Richard DEJESUS-RUEFF
49 Int VP Acad Affs/Dean Arts & Sci ... Dr. Theresa WESTBAY
50 Dean School of Business ... Dr. Raymond SHADY
53 Dean School of Education ... Dr. Michael WISCHNOWSKI
66 Dean School of Nursing ... Dr. Dianne C. COONEY MINER
67 Interim Dean School of Pharmacy ... Dr. Christine R. BIRNIE
28 Director Multicultural Affairs ... Mr. Yantee SLOBERT
06 Registrar ... Ms. Julia M. THOMAS
15 Interim Vice Pres Human Resources ... Ms. Jacqueline DISTEFANO
26 Director Marketing & Communications ... Ms. Kate M. TOROK
06 Associate Registrar ... Ms. Cheryl O. EVANS
08 Director of the Library ... Ms. Melissa JADLOS
13 Chief Information/Computing Officer ... Mr. Stacy S. SLOCUM
16 Director of Payroll & Benefits ... Ms. Mary R. POWLEY
29 Director Alumni Relations ... Mr. Christopher B. SULLIVAN
37 Director Student Financial Aid ... Mrs. Angela B. MONNAT
42 Director Campus Ministry ... Vacant
19 Director of Safety & Security ... Mr. David DICARO
41 Athletic Director ... Mr. Robert A. WARD
18 Director of Physical Plant ... Mr. Larry P. JACOBSON
21 Controller ... Ms. Linda M. STEINKIRCHNER
23 Director of Wellness Center ... Ms. Mary Lou D'AMICO
31 Director of Community Service ... Mrs. Sally J. VAUGHAN
07 Director of Freshman Admissions ... Ms. Stacy A. LEDERMANN
07 Dir of Transfer/Graduate Admissions ... Mr. Jose PERALES
09 Director of Institutional Research ... Ms. Elizabeth A. LACHANCE
35 Director Student Affairs ... Ms. Teah M. TERRANCE
36 Director Career Services ... Mr. Matt CARDIN
105 Webmaster ... Ms. Jody C. BENEDICT
108 Director Institutional Assessment ... Ms. Liz LACHANCE

St. John's University (G)

8000 Utopia Parkway, Queens NY 11439-0001

County: Queens — FICE Identification: 002823

Unit ID: 195809

Telephone: (718) 990-6161 — Carnegie Class: DRU

FAX Number: (718) 990-5723 — Calendar System: Semester

URL: www.stjohns.edu

Established: 1870 — Annual Undergrad Tuition & Fees: $38,680

Enrollment: 15,561 — Coed

Affiliation or Control: Roman Catholic — IRS Status: 501(c)3

Highest Offering: Doctorate

Program: Liberal Arts And General; Teacher Preparatory; Professional

Accreditation: M, ARCPA, ART, AUD, BUS, BUSA, CACREP, CLPSY, EMT, LAW, LIB, MT, PHAR, RAD, SCPSY, SP, TEAC

01 President ... Dr. Conrado M. GEMPESAW
03 Exec VP Mission ... Rev. Bernard M. TRACEY, CM
05 Provost ... Dr. Robert A. MANGIONE
15 Sr VP Human Res/Strategic Plan/IR ... Ms. Mary T. HARPER HAGAN
101 GenCouns/Univ Secy/Int Athletic Dir ... Mr. Joseph E. OLIVA
10 VP Business Affairs/CFO/Treasurer ... Ms. Sharon HEWITT WATKINS

20 VP Academic Support Services ... Dr. Andre A. MCKENZIE
31 VP Community Relations ... Mr. Joseph A. SCIAME
104 VP Global Programs ... Mr. Anthony R. PACHECO
13 VP Information Technology/CIO ... Mr. Joseph J. TUFANO
19 VP Public Safety ... Mr. Thomas J. LAWRENCE
32 VP Student Affairs ... Dr. Kathryn T. HUTCHINSON
30 Acting VP Institutional Advancement ... Mr. Edward M. KULL
20 Vice Provost ... Dr. Derek V. OWENS
84 Vice Provost & Chief Enroll Officer ... Mr. Jorge RODRIGUEZ
106 Vice Provost Digital Learning ... Dr. Elizabeth CIABOCCHI
58 Vice Provost Graduate Edu/Research ... Dr. Simon MOLLER
12 Vice Provost - SI ... Dr. James O'KEEFE
20 Assoc Provost Academic - SI ... Dr. Robert FANUZZI
49 Dean St John's College ... Dr. Jeffrey W. FAGEN
53 Dean The School of Education ... Dr. Michael SAMPSON
67 Dean Pharmacy/Health Sciences ... Dr. Russell J. DIGATE
50 Dean Tobin Colllege of Business ... Dr. Victoria L. SHOAF
107 Interim Dean College Prof Studies ... Mr. Jeffrey P. GROSSMANN
61 Dean School of Law ... Mr. Michael A. SIMONS
08 Dean University Libraries ... Ms. Theresa M. MAYLONE
21 Assoc VP Business Affairs ... Mr. Anthony MACALUSO
18 Assoc VP Campus Facilities/Services ... Mr. Brian BAUMER
35 Assoc VP & Dean of Students ... Dr. Daniel A. TRUJILLO
26 Assoc VP External Relations ... Mr. Dominic SCIANNA
91 Assoc VP Information Technology ... Ms. Maura A. WOODS
26 Assoc VP Marketing & Communications ... Ms. Caren BATZER
42 Assoc VP University Ministry ... Ms. Victoria R. SANTANGELO
20 Assoc Provost Administration ... Ms. Linda A. SHANNON
86 Asst VP Government Relations ... Mr. Brian BROWNE
20 Asst Provost Acad Res & Mmgt Plng ... Ms. Judy CHEN
06 University Registrar ... Ms. Joanne A. LLERANDI
36 Exec Director Career Center ... Ms. Denise C. HOPKINS
90 Exec Director User Services ... Mr. Kenneth J. MAHLMEISTER
88 Exec Director Vincentian Center ... Rev. Patrick J. GRIFFIN, CM
88 Director Ctr for Teaching/Learning ... Dr. Maura C. FLANNERY
105 Director Digital Communications ... Ms. Luci GERACI
25 Director Grants & Research ... Mr. Jared E. LITTMAN
92 Director Honors Program ... Dr. Robert J. FORMAN
16 Director Human Resources Svcs ... Ms. Cynthia F. SIMPSON
37 Director Int Financial Aid/Research ... Ms. Maryanne H. TWOMEY
88 Director Internal Audit ... Mr. Alex J. HOEHN
14 Director Network & Comm Services ... Ms. Anne L. ROCCO
44 Director Planned Giving ... Ms. Susan M. DAMIANI
96 Director Purchasing ... Mr. Jeffery I. WEISS
23 Director Queens Health Services ... Mrs. Pauline TUMMINO
39 Director Residence Life ... Mr. Eric M. FINKELSTEIN
56 Director Special Programs ... Mrs. Cecelia M. RUSSO
09 Acting Dir Institutional Research ... Ms. Christine M. GOODWIN
38 Assoc Director Counseling Center ... Ms. Dorothy M. SCHMITT
85 Asst Dir Int Students/Scholar Svcs ... Ms. Amy HARVEY
39 Asst Dean Std Life/Dir Res Life-SI ... Ms. Anilsa R. NUNEZ
37 Director Financial Aid - SI ... Ms. Nemaris C. RODRGUEZ
07 Sr Assoc Director Admissions - SI ... Mrs. Samantha R. WRIGHT
40 Manager of Bookstore ... Mrs. Denise SERVIDIO

Saint Joseph's College, New York (A)

245 Clinton Avenue, Brooklyn NY 11205-3688
County: Kings　FICE Identification: 002825
Unit ID: 195544
Telephone: (718) 940-5300　Carnegie Class: Master's M
FAX Number: (718) 636-7245　Calendar System: Semester
URL: www.sjcny.edu
Established: 1916　Annual Undergrad Tuition & Fees: $23,500
Enrollment: 1,356　Coed
Affiliation or Control: Independent Non-Profit　IRS Status: 501(c)3
Highest Offering: Master's
Program: Liberal Arts And General; Teacher Preparatory; Professional
Accreditation: M, ADNUR, NUR, TEAC

01 President ... Dr. Jack P. CALARESO
30 VP for Institutional Advancement ... Ms. Carrie BHADA
84 VP for Enrollment Management - BK ... Ms. Christine MURPHY
05 VP for Academic Affairs - BK ... Dr. Jill REHMANN
32 VP for Student Life - BK ... Ms. Sherrie VAN ARNAM
10 Chief Financial Officer ... Mr. John C. ROTH
13 VP IT and Chief Information Officer ... Ms. Michelle PAPAJOHN
06 College Registrar ... Mr. Robert PERGOLIS
08 Director of Library ... Dr. Elizabeth POLLICINO MURPHY
37 Director of Financial Aid ... Ms. Amy THOMPSON
36 Exec Director Career Development ... Ms. Ellen BURTI
41 AVP and Senior Athletics Director ... Ms. Shantey HILL
29 AVP Alumni Relations/Stewardship ... Ms. Mary Jo B. CHIARA
21 Controller ... Mr. Matthew BRELLIS
88 Director of Child Study Center ... Dr. Susan SHAPIRO
18 Director Physical Plant ... Mr. Alvin DORTA
15 Exec Director of Human Resources ... Ms. D'adra CRUMP
28 Coordinator of Diversity ... Ms. Christy BANKS
26 VP of Marketing and Communications ... Ms. Jessica MCALEER
88 Director of Public Affairs ... Mr. Michael BANACH
14 Exec Director Network Operations ... Mr. Ted DEC
90 Exec Director Client Services ... Ms. Lichele ABEAR
04 Executive Admin Asst to President ... Ms. Ann PAIVA
09 Director of Institutional Research ... Ms. Allison LIST
19 Director Security/Safety ... Mr. Michael MCGRANN

Saint Joseph's College, New York - Suffolk Campus (B)

155 W Roe Boulevard, Patchogue NY 11772-2399
Telephone: (631) 687-5100　FICE Identification: 029081
Accreditation: &M, NRPA

† Regional accreditation is carried under the parent institution in Brooklyn, NY.

St. Joseph's College of Nursing (C)

206 Prospect Avenue, Syracuse NY 13203-1806
County: Onondaga　FICE Identification: 006467
Unit ID: 195191
Telephone: (315) 448-5040　Carnegie Class: Assoc/PrivNFP
FAX Number: (315) 448-5745　Calendar System: Semester
URL: www.sjhcon.org
Established: 1898　Annual Undergrad Tuition & Fees: N/A
Enrollment: 317　Coed
Affiliation or Control: Independent Non-Profit　IRS Status: 501(c)3
Highest Offering: Associate Degree
Program: Occupational; 2-Year Principally Bachelor's Creditable; Nursing Emphasis
Accreditation: M

01 Dean ... Mrs. Marianne MARKOWITZ

Saint Joseph's Seminary (D)

Dunwoodie, #201 Seminary Avenue,
Yonkers NY 10704-1852
County: Westchester　FICE Identification: 002826
Unit ID: 195571
Telephone: (914) 968-6200　Carnegie Class: Spec/Faith
FAX Number: (914) 376-2019　Calendar System: Semester
URL: www.dunwoodie.edu
Established: 1896　Annual Graduate Tuition & Fees: $30,000
Enrollment: 180　Coed
Affiliation or Control: Roman Catholic　IRS Status: 501(c)3
Highest Offering: Master's; No Undergraduates
Program: Professional; Religious Emphasis
Accreditation: M, THEOL

01 Rector ... Msgr. Peter I. VACCARI
05 Academic Dean ... Rev. Kevin P. O'REILLY
32 Dean of Students/Admissions ... Rev. Nicholas A. ZIENTARSKI
08 Director Library Services ... Ms. Barbara CAREY
10 Director Finance ... Mr. Ronald TUTTLE
30 Director of Development ... Vacant
42 Director Campus Ministry ... Vacant
06 Registrar ... Ms. Kathleen M. RUSSELL
38 Director of Psychological Services ... Dr. Richard GALLAGHER
18 Director of Buildings & Grounds ... Mr. Joseph DI LELLO
26 Director of Communications ... Ms. Cynthia F. HARRISON
07 Director of Admissions ... Fr. Thomas BERG

St. Lawrence University (E)

23 Romoda Drive, Canton NY 13617-1423
County: St. Lawrence　FICE Identification: 002829
Unit ID: 195216
Telephone: (315) 229-5011　Carnegie Class: Bac/A&S
FAX Number: (315) 229-5502　Calendar System: Other
URL: www.stlawu.edu
Established: 1856　Annual Undergrad Tuition & Fees: $49,420
Enrollment: 2,419　Coed
Affiliation or Control: Independent Non-Profit　IRS Status: 501(c)3
Highest Offering: Master's
Program: Liberal Arts And General; Teacher Preparatory
Accreditation: M, TEAC

01 President ... Dr. William FOX
05 Vice Pres/Dean Academic Affairs ... Dr. Valerie D. LEHR
30 Vice Pres University Advancement ... Mr. Thomas PYNCHON
10 Vice President Finance & Treasurer ... Mr. Joseph MANORY
32 Vice Pres/Dean Student Life ... Dr. Joseph TOLLIVER
07 Vice Pres/Dean Admissions/Fin Aid ... Mr. Jeffrey RICKEY
31 VP for Employee/Community Relations ... Mrs. Lisa M. CANIA
21 Assoc Vice President for Finance ... Ms. Carol GABLE
89 Associate Dean of the First-Year ... Dr. Jennifer HANSEN
35 Associate Dean of Student Life ... Mr. Rance DAVIS
06 Registrar ... Ms. Lorie MACKENZIE
37 Director of Financial Aid ... Mrs. Patricia J B. FARMER
08 VP Libraries & Information Tech ... Mr. Justin SIPHER
36 Director of Career Planning ... Dr. Carol BATE
09 Director of Institutional Research ... Ms. Christine ZIMMERMAN
18 Chief Facilities/Physical Plant ... Mr. Daniel B. SEAMAN
20 Asst Dean of Academic Affairs ... Ms. Lorie MACKENZIE
29 Director Alumni Relations ... Ms. Kimberly HISSONG
35 Director Residence Life ... Mr. Christopher MARQUARDT
23 Director of Health & Counseling ... Ms. Pat ELLIS
84 Director Enrollment Management ... Mr. Jeffrey RICKEY
96 Director of Purchasing ... Ms. Ruta OZOLS
15 Director Personnel Services ... Mrs. Colleen MANLEY
38 Director Student Counseling ... Mr. Timothy CORBITT
26 Communications Coordinator ... Ms. Bev GAUTHIER

St. Paul's School of Nursing (F)

97-77 Queens Blvd, Rego Park NY 11374
County: Queens　FICE Identification: 012364
Unit ID: 189811
Telephone: (718) 357-0500　Carnegie Class: Assoc/PrivFP
FAX Number: (718) 357-4683　Calendar System: Semester
URL: www.stpaulsschoolofnursing.edu
Established: 1969　Annual Undergrad Tuition & Fees: $46,250
Enrollment: 490　Coed
Affiliation or Control: Proprietary　IRS Status: Proprietary
Highest Offering: Associate Degree
Program: Occupational; 2-Year Principally Bachelor's Creditable; Nursing Emphasis
Accreditation: ABHES

01 President ... Dr. Eric RICIOPPO
66 Regional Dean of Nursing Schools ... Genevieve M. JENSEN
37 Financial Aid Director ... Marlin FOKUSORGBOR
07 Asst Director of Admissions ... Nickeshia DURANT
08 Head Librarian ... Michelle BALSAN
10 Chief Financial/Business Officer ... Eric SEDA
06 Registrar ... Claudia MENJIVAR

Saint Paul's School of Nursing-Staten Island (G)

2 Teleport Dr Ste 203, Corp Comm 2,
Staten Island NY 10311
County: Richmond　FICE Identification: 009479
Unit ID: 195784
Telephone: (718) 818-6470　Carnegie Class: Assoc/PrivFP
FAX Number: (718) 818-6020　Calendar System: Semester
URL: www.stpaulsschoolofnursing.edu
Established: 1904　Annual Undergrad Tuition & Fees: $21,945
Enrollment: 694　Coed
Affiliation or Control: Proprietary　IRS Status: Proprietary
Highest Offering: Associate Degree
Program: Occupational; 2-Year Principally Bachelor's Creditable; Nursing Emphasis
Accreditation: ABHES

01 President ... Mr. Wynn BLANTON
05 Director of Education ... Dr. Ann LUBRANO
66 Dean of Nursing ... Ms. Elizabeth BRAUN
06 Registrar ... Ms. Nancy MULLER
10 Business Office Manager ... Ms. Olga FORINA
07 Director of Admissions ... Ms. Kimberly WEINSTEIN
32 Director of Career Services ... Ms. Lynn SALVAGE
37 Director of Financial Aid ... Ms. Nayamka WARD
88 LRC Manager ... Ms. Judy LEE

St. Thomas Aquinas College (H)

125 Route 340, Sparkill NY 10976-1050
County: Rockland　FICE Identification: 002832
Unit ID: 195243
Telephone: (845) 398-4000　Carnegie Class: Master's S
FAX Number: (845) 359-8136　Calendar System: 4/1/4
URL: www.stac.edu
Established: 1952　Annual Undergrad Tuition & Fees: $28,240
Enrollment: 1,950　Coed
Affiliation or Control: Independent Non-Profit　IRS Status: 501(c)3
Highest Offering: Master's
Program: Liberal Arts And General; Teacher Preparatory; Professional
Accreditation: M, IACBE, TED

01 President ... Dr. Margaret M. FITZPATRICK, SC
03 Senior Vice President ... Mr. Vincent CRAPANZANO
10 Vice Pres Administration & Finance ... Mr. Joseph DONINI
05 Provost/Vice Pres Academic Affairs ... Dr. Robert MURRAY
32 Vice Pres/Dean Student Development ... Dr. Kirk MANNING
30 Vice Pres Institutional Advancement ... Mr. Kevin DUIGNAN
15 Sr Exec Director Human Resources ... Ms. Patricia PACCHIANA
07 Director Admissions ... Ms. Samantha BAZILE
09 Dir Inst Research/Program Develop ... Dr. Renee QUINTYNE
21 Controller ... Ms. Jennifer MAZZA
44 Dir Annual Giving & Alumni Affairs ... Mrs. Joanne FAVATA
35 Director Student Activities ... Mr. Dave ENG
38 Director Student Counseling ... Dr. Louis MUGGEO
08 Librarian ... Mr. Kenneth DONOHUE
06 Registrar ... Mrs. Mildred ALEXIOU
36 Director Placement Services ... Mrs. Maureen MULHERN
37 Director Financial Aid ... Mrs. Jean Marie MOHR
13 Director of Computing Services ... Mr. Sunny ANTHWAL
18 Dir Facilities & Construction ... Mr. Patrick LAMBERT
26 Director Communications ... Mrs. Danielle KOBRYN
50 Dean School of Business ... Mr. Michael MURPHY
53 Dean School of Education ... Dr. Meenakshi GAJRIA
49 Dean School of Arts & Sciences ... Dr. Steven BURNS

Saint Vladimir's Orthodox Theological Seminary (I)

575 Scarsdale Road, Yonkers NY 10707
County: Westchester　FICE Identification: 002833
Unit ID: 195580
Telephone: (914) 961-8313　Carnegie Class: Spec/Faith
FAX Number: (914) 961-4507　Calendar System: Semester
URL: www.svots.edu
Established: 1938　Annual Graduate Tuition & Fees: $11,200
Enrollment: 88　Coed
Affiliation or Control: Independent Non-Profit　IRS Status: 501(c)3
Highest Offering: Doctorate; No Undergraduates
Program: Religious Emphasis
Accreditation: THEOL

01 Chancellor ... V.Rev. Chad HATFIELD
05 Dean ... V.Rev. John BEHR
10 Assoc Chanc for Finance ... Ms. Melanie RINGA
13 Assoc Chanc Tech/Dir Comp Systems ... Mr. Georgios KOKONAS
20 Assoc Dean Academic Affairs ... Dr. John BARNET
32 Assoc Dean for Student Affairs ... RevDr. David MEZYNSKI
06 Registrar ... Dr. John BARNET
08 Librarian ... Ms. Eleana SILK

35 Student Affairs Administrator Ms. Nina MATUSIAK
09 Dir Institutional Assessment Dr. Peter BOUTENEFF
07 Director Admissions/Financial Aid Pdn. Joseph MATUSIAK
30 Sr Advisor Advancement Mr. Ted BAZIL
40 Bookstore/Operations Manager Rev Dn. Gregory HATRAK

Salvation Army College for Officer Training (A)

201 Lafayette Avenue, Suffern NY 10901-4707

County: Rockland Identification: 666020
Telephone: (845) 368-7200 Carnegie Class: Not Classified
FAX Number: (845) 357-6644 Calendar System: Other
URL: www.use.salvationarmy.org
Established: 1905 Annual Undergrad Tuition & Fees: $1,070
Enrollment: 99 Coed
Affiliation or Control: Independent Non-Profit IRS Status: 501(c)3
Highest Offering: Associate Degree
Program: Professional
Accreditation: NY

01 Principal Col. Janet A. MUNN
03 Associate Principal Major William F. FURMAN
11 Asst Principal for Administration Capt. Cindy-Lou DRUMMOND
05 Director of Curriculum Major James H. GUEST
06 Registrar Ms. Allyssa COMPTON
09 Coord Inst Research/Accred Liaison Dr. Dennis VANDER WEELE
10 Chief Business Officer Major Ronald STARNES
15 Director Personnel Services Major Jongwoo KIM
20 Associate Academic Officer Major Lois A. GUEST
21 Associate Business Officer Mrs. Robin FRASER
32 Director Student Affairs Vacant

Samaritan Hospital School of Nursing (B)

1300 Massachusetts Avenue, Troy NY 12180

County: Rensselaer FICE Identification: 009248
Unit ID: 195289
Telephone: (518) 268-5010 Carnegie Class: Not Classified
FAX Number: (518) 268-5040 Calendar System: Semester
URL: www.nehealth.com
Established: 1903 Annual Undergrad Tuition & Fees: $11,359
Enrollment: 144 Coed
Affiliation or Control: Independent Non-Profit IRS Status: 501(c)3
Highest Offering: Associate Degree
Program: 2-Year Principally Bachelor's Creditable; Nursing Emphasis
Accreditation: NY

01 Director Ms. Susan BIRKHEAD

Sarah Lawrence College (C)

1 Meadway, Bronxville NY 10708-5999

County: Westchester FICE Identification: 002813
Unit ID: 195304
Telephone: (914) 337-0700 Carnegie Class: Bac/A&S
FAX Number: (914) 395-2668 Calendar System: Semester
URL: www.slc.edu
Established: 1926 Annual Undergrad Tuition & Fees: $51,030
Enrollment: 1,761 Coed
Affiliation or Control: Independent Non-Profit IRS Status: 501(c)3
Highest Offering: Master's
Program: Liberal Arts And General
Accreditation: M, TEAC

01 President Dr. Karen R. LAWRENCE
05 Dean of the College Dr. Kanwal SINGH
10 Vice Pres Finance/Operations Vacant
30 Vice President for Advancement Charles J. RASBERRY
26 Vice Pres Communication & Marketing Lyn CHAMBERLIN
11 Vice President for Administration Thomas L. BLUM
15 VP Human Resources/Legal Affairs Julie AUSTER
88 Assoc VP for Advancement Ellen REYNOLDS
20 Associate Dean of the College Cameron AFZAL
32 Dean of Studies & Student Life Vacant
22 Dean of Equity and Inclusion Dr. Allen GREEN
35 Dean of Student Affairs Dr. Paige CRANDALL
07 Dean of Enrollment Kevin MCKENNA
58 Dean Graduate/Professional Studies Dr. Judith BABBITTS
06 Registrar Daniel LICHT
08 Director of Libraries Bobbie SMOLOW
13 Chief Technology Officer Sean JAMESON
29 Director of Alumni Relations Cheryl CIPRO
36 Director Career Counseling Angela CHERUBINI
44 Individual Giving Officer Elizabeth CAFFERKEY
28 Director of Diversity Natalie GROSS
18 Asst Vice President of Facilities Maureen GALLAGHER
19 AVP of Public Safety/Purchasing Larry HOFFMAN
04 Executive Asst to President Rosemary DAHILL
100 Chief of Staff Thomas BLUM
104 Asst Dean Study Abroad Prema SAMUEL
37 Director Student Financial Aid Nick SALINAS

SBI Campus-An Affiliate of Sanford-Brown (D)

320 S Service Road, Melville NY 11747-3201

County: Suffolk FICE Identification: 011647
Unit ID: 192156
Telephone: (631) 370-3300 Carnegie Class: Assoc/PrivFP
FAX Number: (631) 293-5872 Calendar System: Quarter
URL: www.sbmelville.edu
Established: 2008 Annual Undergrad Tuition & Fees: $10,030
Enrollment: 240 Coed
Affiliation or Control: Proprietary IRS Status: Proprietary
Highest Offering: Associate Degree
Program: Occupational; 2-Year Principally Bachelor's Creditable
Accreditation: ACICS

01 President Mr. James SWIFT
05 Director of Education Dr. Bindu PILLAI
06 Registrar Ms. Andreia GONCALVES

† School is in teach-out plan through November 2016.

Schenectady County Community College (E)

78 Washington Avenue, Schenectady NY 12305

County: Schenectady FICE Identification: 006785
Unit ID: 195322
Telephone: (518) 381-1200 Carnegie Class: Assoc/Pub-U-SC
FAX Number: (518) 346-0379 Calendar System: Semester
URL: www.sunysccc.edu
Established: 1967 Annual Undergrad Tuition & Fees (In-District): $3,768
Enrollment: 6,497 Coed
Affiliation or Control: State/Local IRS Status: 501(c)3
Highest Offering: Associate Degree
Program: Occupational; 2-Year Principally Bachelor's Creditable
Accreditation: M, ACFEI, MUS

01 President Dr. Steady MOONO
05 Vice President of Academic Affairs Dr. Penny A. HAYNES
10 Vice President of Administration Mr. Charles J. RICHARDSON
32 Vice President Student Affairs Dr. Martha J. ASSELIN
37 Director of Financial Aid Ms. Cynthia ASTEMBORSKI-DECKER
20 Assistant VP Academic Affairs Dr. Carlos PENALOZA
11 Assoc VP for Business Development Ms. Susan BEAUDOIN
35 Asst Vice Pres of Student Affairs Mr. Stephen FRAGALE
108 Act Asst Dean for Assessment & Int Mr. Odo BUTLER
45 Asst Dean for Planning/Acct/Effect Mr. Darren JOHNSON
30 Int Exec Director of Development Ms. Susan FERRIS
06 Registrar Ms. Pamela ENSER
07 Dir Admiss/Matriculated Enrollment Mr. David G. SAMPSON
08 Director Library Services Ms. Lynne O. KING
90 Director of Academic Computing Vacant
18 Director of Facilities Mr. Alan J. YAUNEY
13 Chief Information Officer Mr. Antione HARRISON
44 Coordinator of Development Vacant
103 Actg Coord of Workforce Development Ms. Sarah WILSON-SPARROW
91 Manager of Administrative Computing Vacant
26 Public Rels/Publications Specialist Ms. Heather L. MEANEY
36 Director of Career & Transfer Svcs Mr. Robert FREDERICK
15 Human Resources Specialist Ms. Carianne TROTTA
88 Recruitment Specialist Ms. Sandra TROIANO
09 Coordinator Institutional Research Ms. Brandie DINGMAN
28 Dir Educ Opportunity Pgms/Access Ms. Angela WEST-DAVIS
21 Controller Ms. Aimee S. WARFIELD
100 Chief of Staff Ms. Paula OHLHOUS
27 Director of Communications Vacant

School of Visual Arts (F)

209 E 23rd Street, New York NY 10010-3994

County: New York FICE Identification: 007468
Unit ID: 197151
Telephone: (212) 592-2000 Carnegie Class: Spec/Arts
FAX Number: (212) 725-3587 Calendar System: Semester
URL: www.sva.edu
Established: 1947 Annual Undergrad Tuition & Fees: $33,560
Enrollment: 4,397 Coed
Affiliation or Control: Proprietary IRS Status: Proprietary
Highest Offering: Master's
Program: Music Emphasis
Accreditation: M, ART, CIDA, TED

00 Acting Chairman Milton GLASER
01 President David J. RHODES
03 Executive Vice President Anthony P. RHODES
05 Provost Jeffrey NESIN
10 Chief Financial Officer Gary SHILLET
32 Exec Dir of Student Affairs/Admiss Javier VEGA
26 Exec Director of External Relations Susan MODENSTEIN
13 Chief Information Officer Cosmin TOMESCU
06 Registrar Jason KOTH
07 Exec Director Admission Javier VEGA
35 Director of Student Affairs Bill MARTINO
08 Director Visual Arts Library Robert LOBE
37 Director Financial Aid William BERRIOS
36 Director Career Development Angie WOJAK
30 Assoc Dir Development/Alumni Affs Jane NUZZO
19 Director Security Nick AGJMURATI
15 Director of Human Resources Frank AGOSTA
09 Director of Institutional Research Jerold DAVIS
27 Director of Communications Jeffrey PERKINS

Sh'or Yoshuv Rabbinical College (G)

1 Cedar Lawn Avenue, Lawrence NY 11559-1714

County: Nassau FICE Identification: 025059
Unit ID: 195438
Telephone: (516) 239-9002 Carnegie Class: Spec/Faith
FAX Number: (516) 239-9003 Calendar System: Semester
URL: www.shoryoshuv.org
Established: 1963 Annual Undergrad Tuition & Fees: $9,000
Enrollment: 157 Male
Affiliation or Control: Independent Non-Profit IRS Status: 501(c)3
Highest Offering: Second Talmudic Degree
Program: Teacher Preparatory; Professional
Accreditation: RABN

01 Dean Rabbi Naftalie JAEGER
05 Director Rabbi Aaron KAGAN
32 Director of Student Affairs Rabbi Moshe GREENE
06 Registrar Mrs. Sheila FLEISCHER
37 Director SFA Rabbi Yosef ROSEN

Siena College (H)

515 Loudon Road, Loudonville NY 12211-1462

County: Albany FICE Identification: 002816
Unit ID: 195474
Telephone: (518) 783-2300 Carnegie Class: Bac/A&S
FAX Number: (518) 783-4293 Calendar System: Semester
URL: www.siena.edu
Established: 1937 Annual Undergrad Tuition & Fees: $33,165
Enrollment: 3,139 Coed
Affiliation or Control: Independent Non-Profit IRS Status: 501(c)3
Highest Offering: Master's
Program: Liberal Arts And General; Teacher Preparatory; Religious Emphasis
Accreditation: M, BUS, SW, TED

01 President Bro. F. Edward COUGHLIN, OFM
05 Vice President for Academic Affairs Dr. Margaret MADDEN
32 Vice President for Student Life Dr. Maryellen GILROY
10 Vice President for Finance & Admin Mr. Paul T. STEC
84 VP for Enrollment Management Mr. Ned J. JONES
30 VP for Development & External Affs Mr. David B. SMITH
100 VP & Chief of Staff Vacant
13 Chief Information Officer Mr. Mark A. BERMAN
49 Dean of Liberal Arts Vacant
50 Dean of Business Dr. Charles SEIFERT
81 Dean of Science Vacant
88 Assoc VP Stdnt Retention & Success Dr. Peter C. ELLARD
45 Assoc VP Acad Affs/Inst Effectivns Dr. Mary Lou D'ALLEGRO
15 Asst VP for Human Resources Ms. Cynthia B. KING-LEROY
07 Assoc VP Enrollment Management Vacant
21 Asst VP for Finance & Admin Ms. Mary C. STRUNK
18 Asst VP for Facilities Management Mr. Mark FROST
19 Asst VP Stdnt Aff/Dir Public Safety Mr. Michael PAPADOPOULOS
88 Assoc VP Acad Affs Mgmt/Compliance Vacant
06 Registrar Mr. James SERBALIK
37 Assoc Vice Pres Financial Aid Ms. Mary K. LAWYER
08 Dir of Library/Audio Visual Svcs Mr. Gary THOMPSON
92 Director of Honors Program Dr. Lois K. DALY
35 Dean of Students Mr. John R. FELIO
39 Director of Community Living Mr. Adam CASLER
41 VP & Director of Athletics Mr. John D'ARGENIO
36 Director of Career Center Ms. Debra DELBELSO
26 Deputy Chief Information Officer Ms. Mary W. PARLETT-SWEENEY
42 Chaplain of the College Fr. Lawrence ANDERSON, OFM
38 Director of Counseling Center Dr. Wally B. BZBELL
29 Director of Alumni Relations Ms. Mary Beth FINNERTY
09 Dir of Institutional Research Mr. Lee ALLARD
88 Dir of Risk Analysis/Project Mgmt Ms. Sandy SERBALIK
94 Dir Sr Thea Bowman Ctr for Women Dr. Shannon O'NEILL
23 Director of Health Services Ms. Carrie HOGAN
40 Bookstore Manager Mr. Richard IVES
44 Director of Development Mr. Brad R. BODMER
28 Dir of Damietta Cross-Cultural Ctr Ms. Christa J. GRANT
104 Director of Study Abroad/Intl Pgms Bro. Brian C. BELANGER, OFM
96 Dir of Auxiliary Svcs & Procurement Ms. Laura S. PARRY
09 Institutional Research Analyst Ms. Kai ZHOU
43 Legal Services/General Counsel Ms. Rose SEGGOS

Skidmore College (I)

815 N Broadway, Saratoga Springs NY 12866-1632

County: Saratoga FICE Identification: 002814
Unit ID: 195526
Telephone: (518) 580-5000 Carnegie Class: Bac/A&S
FAX Number: (518) 580-5936 Calendar System: Semester
URL: www.skidmore.edu
Established: 1911 Annual Undergrad Tuition & Fees: $48,970
Enrollment: 2,646 Coed
Affiliation or Control: Independent Non-Profit IRS Status: 501(c)3
Highest Offering: Master's
Program: Liberal Arts And General; Teacher Preparatory; Professional
Accreditation: M, ART, SW, TEAC

01 President Dr. Philip A. GLOTZBACH
05 VP Academic Affairs/Dean of Faculty Dr. Beau BRESLIN
10 Vice President Finance/Treasurer Mr. Michael D. WEST
30 Vice President for Advancement Mr. Michael T. CASEY
15 Assoc VP Fin & Admin/Dir of HR Ms. Barbara E. BECK
32 Dean of Students & VP Stdnt Affs Ms. W. Rochelle CALHOUN
07 VP & Dean of Admiss & Fin Aid Ms. Mary Lou W. BATES
71 Dean of Special Programs Mr. Paul CALHOUN
06 Registrar Mr. David DECONNO
20 Assoc Dean Acad Advis & VP Acad Aff Dr. Corey FREEMAN-GALLANT

28 Assoc Dean Personnel & Diversity .... Dr. Paty RUBIO
89 Dir of First Year Experience .... Ms. Janet CASEY
35 Assoc Dean Student Affairs .... Mr. David KARP
39 Int Director of Residential Life .... Ms. Ann Marie PRZYWARA
88 Assoc Dean of Student Affairs .... Ms. Susan LAYDEN
45 Exec Dir Pres Ofc/Coord Strat Init .... Dr. Joshua C. WOODFORK
26 Executive Director Communications .... Mr. Dan FORBUSH
09 Director of Institutional Research .... Mr. Joseph STANKOVICH
102 Dir Foundation & Corporate Rels .... Mr. Barry PRITZKER
46 Director of Sponsored Research .... Mr. Bill TOMLINSON
13 Dir Network & Technical Services .... Mr. Mark BAUER
105 Director Web Communications .... Mr. Andy CAMP
88 Director Institutes/Confs & Summer .... Ms. Sharon A. ARPEY
87 Director of Summer Acad Pgm & Resid .... Dr. Auden THOMAS
41 Assoc Dean Stdnt Affs/Athletic Dir .... Dr. Gail L. CUMMINGS-DANSON
88 Director for Intercultural Studies .... Dr. Kristie A. FORD
22 Asst Dir EEO & Workforce Diversity .... Mr. Herb CROSSMAN
91 Director IT-Enterprise Systems .... Mr. Jeffrey A. CLARK
104 Dir of Off-Campus Study & Exchanges .... Ms. Cori FILSON
31 Director of Community Relations .... Mr. Robert S. KIMMERLE
44 Senior Director Donor Relations .... Ms. Mary L. SOLOMONS
30 Director of Development .... Ms. Lori EASTMAN
29 Executive Dir Alumni Aff & Col Eve .... Mr. Michael SPOSILI
36 Director Career Development Center .... Ms. Kim CRABBE
37 Director of Financial Aid .... Ms. Beth POST-LUNDQUIST
38 Director Counseling Center .... Dr. Julia C. ROUTBORT
21 Director of Business Services .... Ms. Christine KACZMAREK
23 Director of Clinical Services .... Ms. Patricia BOSEN
18 Director of Facilities Services .... Mr. Daniel RODECKER
19 Director of Campus Safety .... Mr. Dennis S. CONWAY
08 College Librarian .... Ms. Marta BRUNNER
96 Director of Purchasing .... Mrs. Carol N. SCHNITZER
42 Dir of Religious & Spiritual Life .... Mr. Rick CHRISMAN
24 Director of Media Services .... Mr. T. Hunt CONARD
40 Director Skidmore Shop .... Mr. Jon NEIL
88 Special Assistant to the President .... Ms. Jeanne M. SISSON
101 Board Coordinator .... Ms. Susan W. KOPPI

Sotheby's Institute of Art (A)

570 Lexington Ave, 6th Floor, New York NY 10022

County: New York | Identification: 667007 | Unit ID: 481094

Telephone: (212) 517-3929 | Carnegie Class: Not Classified
FAX Number: (212) 517-6568 | Calendar System: Semester
URL: www.sothebysinstitute.com
Established: | Annual Graduate Tuition & Fees: $51,500
Enrollment: 153 | Coed
Affiliation or Control: Proprietary | IRS Status: Proprietary
Highest Offering: First Professional Degree; No Undergraduates
Program: Professional; Fine Arts Emphasis
Accreditation: ART

01 Director .... Ms. Lesley A. CADMAN
06 Registrar .... Ms. Tammy PARKS
07 Director of Admissions .... Ms. Melba REMICE
08 Head Librarian .... Ms. Erin ELLIOTT
10 Chief Business Officer .... Ms. Lilly KOGAN
15 Director Personnel Services .... Mrs. Barbara STRONGIN
32 Chief Student Affairs/Student Life .... Ms. Sara MOORE

*State University of New York System Office (B)

State University Plaza, Albany NY 12246-0001

County: Albany | FICE Identification: 008788 | Unit ID: 195827

Telephone: (518) 320-1100 | Carnegie Class: N/A
FAX Number: (518) 320-1561
URL: www.suny.edu

01 Chancellor .... Dr. Nancy L. ZIMPHER
03 Provost & Executive Vice Chancellor .... Dr. Alexander CARTWRIGHT
10 Vice Chancellor for Finance and CFO .. Ms. Eileen MCLOUGHLIN
05 Vice Provost & VC for Acad Affairs ... Dr. Elizabeth BRINGSJORD
43 VC for Legal Affairs & General Coun .... Mr. Joseph PORTER
26 Assoc VC Univ Rel & Chief of Staff . Ms. Stacey HENGSTERMAN
88 Assoc VC for External Affairs .... Ms. Jennifer LOTURCO
27 Assoc VC for Communications .... Mr. Sherman JEWETT
88 Sr VC for Cmty Col & Educ Pipeline .... Ms. Johanna DUNCAN-POITIER
11 Assistant VC for Operations .... Ms. Kellie J. DUPUIS
88 Faculty Council of Cmty Col Pres .... Ms. Tina GOOD
18 VC for Cap Facil/GM Constr Fund .... Mr. Robert HAELEN
88 University Faculty Senate President .... Mr. Peter KNUEPFER
20 Sr Assoc VC and Vice Prov Acad Affs .... Mr. Jason LANE
15 Vice Chancellor for Human Resources .... Mr. Curtis LLYOD
84 Assoc VC for Enrollment Management .... Mr. Paul MARTHERS

*University at Albany, SUNY (C)

1400 Washington Avenue, Albany NY 12222-1000

County: Albany | FICE Identification: 002835 | Unit ID: 196060

Telephone: (518) 442-3300 | Carnegie Class: RU/VH
FAX Number: N/A | Calendar System: Semester
URL: www.albany.edu
Established: 1844 | Annual Undergrad Tuition & Fees (In-State): $8,996
Enrollment: 17,338 | Coed
Affiliation or Control: State | IRS Status: 501(c)3
Highest Offering: Doctorate
Program: Liberal Arts And General; Teacher Preparatory; Professional
Accreditation: M, BUS, BUSA, CLPSY, COPSY, IPSY, LIB, PH, PLNG, SCPSY, SPAA, SW, TEAC

02 President .... Robert J. JONES
05 Sr VP for Academic Affs & Provost .... James R. STELLER
46 Vice President for Research .... James DIAS
10 Vice Pres Finance & Business .... James VAN BOORST
32 Vice President Student Success .... Christine A. BOUCHARD
30 VP Univ Dev & Exec Dir UA Found .... Fardin SANAI
26 VP Communications and Marketing .... Joseph A. BRENNAN
41 Director of Athletics .... Mark BENSON
21 Assoc Vice President & Controller .... Kevin WILCOX
35 Assoc Vice Pres for Student Success ...... Michael N. CHRISTAKIS
09 Provost & VP Institutional Research .... Bruce SZELEST
18 Associate VP Facilities .... John GIARRUSSO
20 Provost & Assoc VP Acad Affairs .... Robert K. ANDREA, JR.
28 Asst VP Diversity/Inclusion .... Tamra MINOR
84 AVP for Enrollment Management .... Robert K. ANDREA, JR.
97 Vice Prov Undergrad Educ/Dean Psych .... Jeanette ALTARRIBA
49 Dean of College of Arts & Sciences .... Edelgard WULFERT
53 Dean School of Education .... Robert BANGERT-DROWNS
50 Dean School of Business .... Donald S. SIEGEL
69 Dean School of Public Health .... Philip NASCA
61 Dean of Criminal Justice .... Alan J. LIZOTTE
80 Dean Rockefeller Col of Pub Affs .... David L. ROUSSEAU
70 Dean of School of Social Welfare .. Katharine H. BRIAR-LAWSON
77 Dean Col of Computing & Info .... Sue R. FAERMAN
58 Dean of Graduate Studies .... Kevin WILLIAMS
08 Dean/Director of Libraries .... Mary F. CASSERLY
13 Chief Information Officer .... Christine E. HAILE
06 Registrar .... Karen CHICO HURST
29 Exec Director Alumni Association .... Lee SERRAVILLO, JR.
90 Dir Academic Computing Center .... Felix WU
100 Chief of Staff .... Leanne WIRKKULA
20 Asst Vice Prov/Dir Advisement Ctr .... Suzanne K. FREED
43 Senior Counsel .... John H. REILLY
38 Director of Counseling Svcs .... Estela RIVERO
36 Director Career Services .... Philippe ABRAHAM
07 Director of Admissions .... Timothy LEE
105 Director Web Services .... Fred DOYLE

*State University of New York at Binghamton (D)

Vestal Parkway E, Box 6000, Binghamton NY 13902-6000

County: Broome | FICE Identification: 002836 | Unit ID: 196079

Telephone: (607) 777-2000 | Carnegie Class: RU/H
FAX Number: (607) 777-4000 | Calendar System: Semester
URL: www.binghamton.edu
Established: 1946 | Annual Undergrad Tuition & Fees (In-State): $9,044
Enrollment: 16,695 | Coed
Affiliation or Control: State | IRS Status: 501(c)3
Highest Offering: Doctorate
Program: Liberal Arts And General; Professional
Accreditation: M, BUS, CLPSY, CS, ENG, MUS, NURSE, SPAA, SW, TEAC

02 President .... Dr. Harvey G. STENGER, JR.
100 Chief of Staff .... Mr. Terrence KANE
05 Exec VP for Academic Affs/Provost .... Dr. Donald NIEMAN
10 Vice President Operations .... Ms. JoAnn NAVARRO
32 Vice Pres Student Affairs .... Mr. Brian T. ROSE
09 Vice President for Research .... Dr. Bahgat SAMMAKIA
104 Exec Vice Prov Intl Initiatives .... Dr. Hari SRIHARI
45 Senior Vice Provost .... Dr. Michael F. MCGOFF
84 Vice Prov Enrollment Management .... Vacant
58 Vice Prov/Dean of Graduate School .... Dr. Susan STREHLE
18 Assoc VP Facilities Management .... Mr. Lawrence J. ROMA
35 Dean of Students .... Dr. April THOMPSON
102 Exec Dir of Bing Foundation .... Ms. Sheila DOYLE
26 Assoc Vice Pres Univ Comm/Mktg .... Mr. Gregory DELVISCIO
27 Chief Information Officer .... Ms. Sharon PITT
04 Exec Assistant to the President .... Ms. Laura L. O'NEIL
15 Asst Vice Pres for Human Resources ...... Mr. Joseph P. SCHULTZ
07 Int Dir Undergraduate Admissions .... Mr. Randall EDOUARD
08 Dean of Libraries .... Dr. Curtis KENDRICK
85 Director Intl Students/Scholar Svcs ...... Ms. Patricia MARRAPESE
86 Director of State Relations .... Mr. Terrence KANE
37 Dir Financial Aid/Stdnt Records .... Mr. Dennis J. CHAVEZ
06 University Registrar .... Vacant
38 Director Health & Counseling .... Ms. Johann FIORE CONTE
36 Director Career Development Center .... Ms. Kelli SMITH
19 Director Public Safety .... Mr. Timothy FAUGHANAN
41 Director Athletics .... Mr. Patrick ELLIOTT
71 Director Educ Opportunities Prog .... Mr. Calvin GANTT
22 Dir Diversity/Equity & Inclusive .... Ms. Valerie J. HAMPTON
28 Director Multi-Cultural Res Ctr .... Ms. Nicole SIRJU-JOHNSON
92 Director Binghamton Univ Scholars .... Dr. William ZIEGLER
94 Exec Director of Women's Studies ...... Ms. Dara J. SILBERSTEIN
96 Director of Purchasing .... Mr. Kenneth G. WASKIE
09 Asst Provost Institutional Research .... Ms. Nasrin FATIMA
49 Dean Arts & Science Harpur Col .... Dr. Anne MCCALL
53 Interim Dean School of Education .... Dr. C. Beth BURCH
50 Dean School of Management .... Dr. Upinder S. DHILLON
54 Dn Watson Sch Engr/Applied Science .... Dr. Hari SRIHARI
66 Int Dean Decker School of Nursing .. Dr. Pamela STEWART FAHS
31 Dean Community & Public Affairs .... Dr. Laura BRONSTEIN
106 Dir Center for Innov/Cont Educ .... Mr. Thomas KOWALIK
29 Sr Director Alumni Relations .... Ms. Rose FRIERMAN
43 Campus Atty/General Counsel .... Ms. Barbara SCARLETT

*University at Buffalo-SUNY (E)

3435 Main Street, Buffalo NY 14214

County: Erie | FICE Identification: 002837 | Unit ID: 196088

Telephone: (716) 645-2000 | Carnegie Class: RU/VH
FAX Number: N/A | Calendar System: Semester
URL: www.buffalo.edu
Established: 1846 | Annual Undergrad Tuition & Fees (In-State): $9,381
Enrollment: 29,221 | Coed
Affiliation or Control: State | IRS Status: 501(c)3
Highest Offering: Doctorate
Program: Liberal Arts And General; Professional
Accreditation: M, ANEST, AUD, BUS, BUSA, CEA, CLPSY, CORE, DA, DENT, DIETI, ENG, IPSY, LAW, LIB, MED, MT, NMT, NURSE, OT, PH, PHAR, PLNG, PSPSY, PTA, SP, SW, TEAC

02 President .... Dr. Satish K. TRIPATHI
05 Provost/Exec VP Academic Affs .... Dr. Charles F. ZUKOSKI
10 Vice Pres Finance & Administration .... Ms. Laura E. HUBBARD
32 Vice President Student Affairs .... Mr. Dennis R. BLACK
17 Vice President Health Sciences .... Dr. Michael CAIN
30 Vice Pres Philanthropy & Alumni Eng .... Ms. Nancy L. WELLS
46 Vice President for Research/EcoDev ...... Dr. Venu GOVINDARAJU
84 Vice Provost of Enrollment .... Dr. Lee H. MELVIN
15 Asst VP Human Resources .... Ms. Susan KRZYSTOFIAK
58 Vice Provost Graduate Education .... Dr. Graham L. HAMMILL
20 Sr Vice Provost Acad Affairs .... Dr. A. Scott WEBER
20 Vice Provost for Faculty Affairs .... Prof. Robert GRANFIELD
104 Vice Provost for International Educ .... Dr. Stephen C. DUNNETT
45 Vice Provost Academic Plng & Budget .... Vacant
18 Assoc Vice Pres Univ Facilities .... Vacant
08 Assoc VP for Univ Libraries .... Mr. H. Austin BOOTH
13 VP & Chief Information Officer .... Mr. Brice BIBLE
37 Director Financial Aid .... Mr. John GOTTARDY
09 Assoc V Provost/Dir Inst Research .... Mr. Craig W. ABBEY
96 Asst Vice Pres Procurement Services .... Mr. Daniel VIVIAN
26 VP Univ Communications .... Ms. Nancy E. PATON
22 Vice Provost Equity & Inclusion .... Ms. Teresa A. MILLER
28 Dir Equity/Diversity/Inclusion .... Ms. Sharon E. NOLAN-WEISS
41 Director of Athletics .... Mr. Danny WHITE
91 Director Enterprise Application Svc .... Ms. Susan A. HUSTON
07 Director of UG Admissions .... Mr. Jose AVILES
19 Chief of Police .... Mr. Gerald W. SCHOENLE, JR.
39 Director of Campus Living .... Ms. Andrea COSTANTINO
38 Director of Counseling Services .... Dr. Sharon L. MITCHELL
23 Director Health Services .... Ms. Susan M. SNYDER
36 Director Career Services .... Ms. Arlene F. KAUKUS
85 Director Intl Students/Scholar Svc .... Ms. Ellen A. DUSSOURD
40 Director University Bookstores .... Mr. Gregory NEUMANN
92 Admin Dir Univ Honors College .... Ms. Krista L. HANYPSIAK
29 Sr Director Dev & Alumni Events .... Mr. Jay R. FRIEDMAN
27 Director of Marketing .... Mr. David WEDEKINDT
20 Dean of Undergraduate Educ .... Dr. Andrew M. STOTT
48 Dean School Arch & Planning .... Dr. Robert SHIBLEY
49 Dean College of Arts/Sciences .... Dr. Bruce PITMAN
52 Dean School Dental Medicine .... Vacant
53 Dean Graduate Sch of Education .... Dr. Jaekyung LEE
54 Dean School Engr/Applied Sci .... Dr. Liesl FOLKS
61 Interim Dean School of Law .... Prof. James A. GARDNER
50 Interim Dean School of Management .... Prof. Paul E. TESLUK
63 Dean School Medicine/Biomed Sci .... Dr. Michael E. CAIN
66 Dean School of Nursing .... Dr. Marsha L. LEWIS
67 Dean School Pharmacy/Pharm Sciences ... Dr. James O'DONNELL
76 Int Dean Sch Public Hlth/Hlth Prof .... Dr. Jean WACTAWSKI-WENDE
70 Dean School of Social Work .... Dr. Nancy J. SMYTH
06 Registrar .... Dr. Kara C. SAUNDERS

*State University of New York at Fredonia (F)

138 Fenton Hall, Fredonia NY 14063-1136

County: Chautauqua | FICE Identification: 002844 | Unit ID: 196158

Telephone: (716) 673-3111 | Carnegie Class: Master's M
FAX Number: N/A | Calendar System: Semester
URL: www.fredonia.edu
Established: 1826 | Annual Undergrad Tuition & Fees (In-State): $8,074
Enrollment: 5,214 | Coed
Affiliation or Control: State | IRS Status: 501(c)3
Highest Offering: Master's
Program: Liberal Arts And General; Teacher Preparatory; Professional
Accreditation: M, ART, MUS, SP, SW, TED, THEA

02 President .... Dr. Virginia S. HORVATH
05 Provost & VP for Acad Affairs .... Dr. Terry BROWN
10 VP for Finance and Administration .... Ms. Elizabeth PRAETORIUS
32 Vice President for Student Affairs .... Dr. David E. HERMAN
35 Assoc Vice Pres for Student Affairs .... Ms. Monica J. WHITE
30 Vice Pres University Advancement .... Dr. David M. TIFFANY
20 Assoc VP Curriculum/Assessment/Ac .... Dr. Lisa HUNTER
49 Dean College of Liberal Arts & Sci .... Dr. Roger A. BYRNE
88 VP Engagement & Economic Dev .... Dr. Kevin KEARNS
57 Dean College of Visual & Perf Arts .... Dr. Ralph BLASTING
58 Assoc Provost for Graduate Studies .... Dr. Judy HOROWITZ
50 Dean School of Business .... Dr. Russell P. BOISJOLY
53 Dean College of Education .... Dr. Christine E. GIVNER
102 Director Corp/Univ Advancement .... Dr. David M. TIFFANY
18 Director Facilities Services .... Mr. Kevin P. CLOOS
06 Registrar .... Mr. Scott D. SAUNDERS
07 Director of Admissions .... Mr. Cory M. BEZEK

37 Director Financial Aid .... Mr. Daniel M. TRAMUTA
08 Director Library Services .... Mr. Randolph Lee GADIKIAN
09 Dir Institutional Research/Planning .... Dr. Xiao Y. ZHANG
36 Director of Career Development .... Ms. Tracy COLLINGWOOD
84 Assoc Vice Pres for Enrollment Mgmt ... Mr. Daniel M. TRAMUTA
19 Chief University Police .... Ms. Ann K. BURNS
39 Director Residence Life .... Mrs. Kathy FORSTER
41 Athletic Director .... Mr. Gregory D. PRECHTL
23 Director of Health Services .... Ms. Deborah A. DIBBLE
38 Director Counseling Center .... Dr. Tracy L. STENGER
90 Academic Information Technology .... Mr. Stephen J. RIEKS
15 Director of Human Resources .... Mr. Michael D. DALEY
26 Director of Public Relations .... Mr. Michael BARONE
85 Director of Multicultural Affairs .... Ms. Jellema STEWART
92 Director of Honors Program .... Dr. David KINKELA
94 Coordinator of Women's Studies .... Mr. Jeffry J. IOVANNONE
96 Director of Purchasing .... Mrs. Shari K. MILLER
28 Chief Diversity Officer .... Dr. William BOERNER
29 Director Alumni Affairs .... Ms. Patricia A. FERALDI
04 Administrative Asst to President .... Mrs. Denise M. SZALKOWSKI

*State University of New York at New Paltz (A)

1 Hawk Drive, New Paltz NY 12561-2443
County: Ulster | FICE Identification: 002846
Unit ID: 196176
Telephone: (845) 257-7869 | Carnegie Class: Master's L
FAX Number: (845) 257-3009 | Calendar System: Semester
URL: www.newpaltz.edu
Established: 1823 | Annual Undergrad Tuition & Fees (In-State): $7,737
Enrollment: 7,692 | Coed
Affiliation or Control: State | IRS Status: 501(c)3
Highest Offering: Beyond Master's But Less Than Doctorate
Program: Liberal Arts And General; Teacher Preparatory; Professional
Accreditation: M, ART, BUS, ENG, MUS, SP, TED, THEA

02 President .... Dr. Donald P. CHRISTIAN
100 Chief of Staff/VP Communication .... Ms. Shelly A. WRIGHT
05 Interim Provost .... Dr. Stella DEEN
10 Vice Pres Administration & Finance .... Ms. Michele HALSTEAD
30 VP Development/Alumni Relations .... Ms. Erica MARKS
32 Student Affairs Vice President .... Dr. L. David ROONEY
84 Vice Pres Enrollment Management .... Mr. L. David EATON
58 Assoc Provost/Dean Graduate School .... Dr. Laurel GARRICK DUHANEY
13 Asst Vice Pres Tech/Info Systems .... Mr. Jonathan D. LEWIT
21 Asst Vice President Administration .... Ms. Julieta MAJAK
88 Asst VP Budget .... Ms. Julie WALSH
09 Asst VP Inst Research/Planning .... Ms. Lucy WALKER
18 Asst VP Facilities Management .... Mr. John SHUPE
53 Dean of Education .... Dr. Michael ROSENBERG
57 Dean Fine & Performing Arts .... Dr. Jennifer MOKREN
49 Dean Liberal Arts & Sciences .... Dr. Laura BARRETT
50 Dean School of Business .... Dr. Kristin BACKHAUS
54 Dean Science and Engineering .... Dr. Daniel FREEDMAN
07 Dean of Admissions .... Ms. Lisa JONES
08 Dean Sojourner Truth Library .... Mr. W. Mark COLVSON
86 Ex Dir Compliance/Camp Clm/Title IX .... Ms. Tanhena PACHECO DUNN
07 Asst Dean/Dir Freshmen Admissions .... Ms. Kimberly STRANO
15 Director Human Resources .... Ms. Dawn BLADES
37 Director of Financial Aid .... Ms. Maureen LOHAN-BREMER
06 Registrar .... Ms. Bernadette MORRIS
29 Director Alumni Relations .... Ms. Brenda DOW
38 Director Student Counseling .... Dr. Gweneth LLOYD
26 Media Relations Manager .... Ms. Melissa KACZMAREK
96 Director of Purchasing/Procurement .... Mr. David FARBANIEC
19 Director Security/Safety .... Mr. David DUGATKIN
41 Athletic Director .... Mr. Stuart ROBINSON

*State University of New York at Oneonta (B)

108 Ravine Parkway, Oneonta NY 13820-4015
County: Otsego | FICE Identification: 002847
Unit ID: 196185
Telephone: (607) 436-3500 | Carnegie Class: Master's S
FAX Number: N/A | Calendar System: Semester
URL: www.oneonta.edu
Established: 1889 | Annual Undergrad Tuition & Fees (In-State): $7,320
Enrollment: 6,101 | Coed
Affiliation or Control: State | IRS Status: 501(c)3
Highest Offering: Master's
Program: Liberal Arts And General; Teacher Preparatory; Professional
Accreditation: M, AAFCS, BUS, DIETD, DIETI, MUS, TED, THEA

02 President .... Dr. Nancy KLENIEWSKI
04 Senior Assistant to the President .... Ms. Colleen E. BRANNAN
05 Provost/Vice Pres Academic Affairs .... Vacant
10 Vice Pres Finance/Administration .... Mr. Todd D. FOREMAN
32 Vice President Student Development .. Dr. Franklin D. CHAMBERS
30 Vice President College Advancement .... Mr. Paul J. ADAMO
09 Assoc Prov Inst Assessment & Eff .... Dr. Wade THOMAS
20 Assoc Provost Academic Programs .... Dr. Eileen MORGAN-ZAYACHEK
83 Dean School of Arts and Humanities .... Dr. Joao SEDYCIAS
50 Dean School of Econ & Business .... Dr. David YEN
53 Dean School of Educ & Human Ecology .... Dr. Jan BOWERS
81 Dean School of Nat/Math Sciences .... Dr. Venkat SHARMA
83 Dean School of Social Science .... Dr. Susan TURELL
58 Director of Graduate Studies .... Mr. Patrick J. MENTE
84 Int Chief Enrollment Services Ofcr .... Dr. Mary BRUCK
35 Assoc Vice Pres Student Life .... Vacant
18 Assoc Vice Pres Facilities/Safety .... Mr. Thomas M. RATHBONE
19 Chief of Police .... Mr. Daniel P. CHAMBERS
15 Sr Exec Employee Services Officer .... Ms. Lisa M. WENCK
26 Director of Communications .... Mr. Hal S. LEGG
07 Director of Admissions .... Ms. Karen A. BROWN
29 Director of Alumni Affairs .... Ms. Laura MADELONE
88 Director Advancement Services .... Mr. Michael SULLIVAN
44 Director Fund for Oneonta .... Ms. Kim NOSTROM
41 Athletic Director .... Ms. Tracey M. RANIERI
21 Budget Control Officer/Budget Dir .... Ms. Julie ROSEBOOM
25 Director Business Services .... Ms. Betty M. TIRADO
36 Dir Career Dev/Student Emp Svcs .... Dr. Amy BENEDICT
13 Dir Computing Ctr/Chief Info Ofcr .... Dr. Karlis KAUGARS
90 Director IT Customer Support .... Mr. Steven J. MANISCALCO
38 Director Counseling Services .... Dr. Melissa A. FALLON
24 Director Creative Media Services .... Mr. David W. GEASEY
37 Director Financial Aid .... Mr. Bill GOODHUE
09 Dir Institutional Research .... Mr. Ernesto HENRIQUEZ
85 Director of International Education .... Dr. Vernon C. LARSON
89 Director Orientation/First Year Exp .... Ms. Monica C. GRAU
96 Procurement/Travel Office Manager .... Ms. Terri THOMAS
06 College Registrar .... Ms. Maureen P. ARTALE
39 Director Residential Community Life .... Ms. Michele LUETTGER
93 Director Special Programs/EOP .... Ms. Lynda D. BASSETTE
23 Int Dir Student Health Services .... Ms. Mary MANCUSO
28 Chief Diversity Officer .... Dr. Terrence MITCHELL
22 Affirmative Action Officer .... Mr. Andrew STAMMEL

*Stony Brook University (C)

310 Administration Building, Stony Brook NY 11794-0701
County: Suffolk | FICE Identification: 002838
Unit ID: 196097
Telephone: (631) 632-6265 | Carnegie Class: RU/VH
FAX Number: (631) 632-6621 | Calendar System: Semester
URL: www.stonybrook.edu
Established: 1957 | Annual Undergrad Tuition & Fees (In-State): $8,855
Enrollment: 24,607 | Coed
Affiliation or Control: State | IRS Status: 501(c)3
Highest Offering: Doctorate
Program: Liberal Arts And General; Teacher Preparatory; Professional
Accreditation: M, ARCPA, CAATE, CLPSY, COARC, COARCP, CS, DENT, DIETI, ENG, IPSY, JOUR, MED, MIDWF, MT, NURSE, OT, PCSAS, PH, POLYT, PTA, RADDOS, SW, TED

02 President .... Dr. Samuel L. STANLEY
05 Provost & Sr Vice Pres Acad Affairs .... Dr. Dennis N. ASSANIS
63 Sr VP HSC/Dean School of Medicine .... Dr. Kenneth KAUSHANSKY
46 Vice President Research .... Dr. David CONOVER
32 Vice President Student Affairs .... Dr. Peter M. BAIGENT
10 VP Finance .... Mr. Lyle GOMES
30 Sr VP University Advancement .... Mr. Dexter BAILEY
88 VP Econ Devel/Dean Engr/Applied Sci .... Dr. Yacov SHAMASH
100 Chief Deputy to President .... Ms. Judith GREIMAN
21 Associate VP for Budget .... Mr. Mark MACIULAITIS
11 Sr VP for Administration .... Vacant
26 VP Comm & Mktg/Chief Comm Officer ... Mr. Nicholas SCIBETTA
39 Asst Vice Pres Campus Residences .... Dr. Dallas BAUMAN
17 CEO University Hospital .... Dr. Reuven PASTERNAK
84 Assoc Prov Enrollment/Retent Mgmt .... Mr. Rodney MORRISON
13 Interim CIO .... Mr. Michael OSPITALE
45 Vice President Strategic Initiatves .... Dr. Matthew WHELAN
43 Senior Counsel in Charge .... Ms. Susan BLUM
49 Dean College Arts & Sciences .... Dr. Sacha KOPP
54 Dean Col of Engr & Applied Science .... Dr. Yacov SHAMASH
88 Dean School of Marine & Atmos Sci .... Dr. Minghua ZHANG
52 Int Dean School of Dental Medicine .... Dr. Mary R. TRUHLAR
68 Dean Div Physical Educ & Athletics .... Mr. Shawn R. HEILBRON
58 Dean Grad Sch & Sch of Prof Develop .... Dr. Charles TABER
76 Dean School Health Technology Mgmt .... Dr. Craig LEHMANN
35 Dean of Students .... Dr. Timothy ECKLUND
66 Dean School of Nursing .... Dr. Lee XIPPOLITOS
70 Dean School of Social Welfare .... Dr. Frances L. BRISBANE
08 Dean of Libraries .... Dr. Constantia CONSTANINOU
86 VP Government & Community Relations .... Vacant
88 Exec Dir LI State Vets Home .... Mr. Fred SGANGA
19 Chief of Police .... Mr. Robert LENAHAN
15 VP Human Resource Svcs .... Ms. Lynn JOHNSON
28 Dir Diversity/AA/Equal Employ Oppty .... Ms. Marjolie LEONARD
09 AVP Inst Rsrch/Plng/Effectiveness .... Dr. Braden J. HOSCH
85 Interim Dean International Programs .... Dr. Imin KAO
102 Exec Dir of Stony Brook Foundation .... Mr. Dexter A. BAILEY
29 Director Alumni Relations .... Mr. Matthew COLSON
23 Director University Health Services .... Dr. Rachel BERGESON
38 Int Dir Counseling/Psych Services .... Dr. Julian PESSIER
36 Director Career Placement Center .... Ms. Marianna SAVOCA
06 Registrar .... Ms. Diane BELLO
37 Financial Aid/Scholarships .... Ms. Jacqueline PASCARIELLO
50 Dean College of Business .... Dr. Manuel LONDON
27 University Media Relations Officer .... Ms. Lauren SHEPROW
96 Director of Purchasing/Procurement .... Mr. James FABIAN
60 Dean School of Journalism .... Mr. Howard SCHNEIDER
04 Executive Asst to President .... Ms. Carol LONDOIRO

*SUNY Downstate Medical Center (D)

450 Clarkson Avenue, Brooklyn NY 11203-2098
County: Kings | FICE Identification: 002839
Unit ID: 196255
Telephone: (718) 270-1000 | Carnegie Class: Spec/Med
FAX Number: (718) 270-4092 | Calendar System: Semester
URL: www.downstate.edu
Established: 1860 | Annual Undergrad Tuition & Fees (In-State): $6,780
Enrollment: 1,865 | Coed
Affiliation or Control: State | IRS Status: 501(c)3
Highest Offering: Doctorate
Program: Occupational; Professional
Accreditation: M, ANEST, ARCPA, DMS, MED, MIDWF, NURSE, OT, PH, PTA

02 President .... Dr. John F. WILLIAMS
10 Chief Financial Officer .... Ms. Melanie GEHEN
11 COO/Exec Vice Pres Administration .... Ms. Astra BAIN-DOWELL
63 Acting Dean Col of Medicine .... Dr. Pamela D. SASS
05 VP Acad Affs/SVP Inst Dev/Philthrpy .... Dr. JoAnn BRADLEY
32 Assoc VP Student Aff/Dean of Stdnts .... Dr. Jeffrey PUTMAN
30 AVP Institutional Advancement .... Ms. Ellen WATSON
13 Interim Chief Information Officer .... Mr. John DOOLEY
07 Director of Admissions .... Ms. Shushawana DEOLIVEIRA
06 Registrar .... Ms. Anne SHONBRUN
37 Director Student Financial Aid .... Mr. James NEWELL
26 Chief Public Relations Officer .... Ms. Ellen WATSON

*State University of New York Upstate Medical University (E)

750 E Adams Street, Syracuse NY 13210-2375
County: Onondaga | FICE Identification: 002840
Unit ID: 196307
Telephone: (315) 464-5540 | Carnegie Class: Spec/Med
FAX Number: (315) 464-8823 | Calendar System: Semester
URL: www.upstate.edu
Established: 1834 | Annual Undergrad Tuition & Fees (In-State): $6,966
Enrollment: 1,514 | Coed
Affiliation or Control: State | IRS Status: 501(c)3
Highest Offering: Doctorate
Program: Professional
Accreditation: M, ARCPA, COARC, DENT, DMOLS, IPSY, MED, MT, NURSE, PAST, PERF, PH, PTA, RAD, RTT

02 Interim President .... Dr. Gregory L. EASTWOOD
63 Dean College of Medicine .... Dr. David B. DUGGAN
17 CEO University Hospital .... Dr. John MCCABE
10 Vice President Finance & Management .... Mr. Eric SMITH
05 Vice President Academic Affairs .... Dr. Lynn CLEARY
46 Dean College Graduate Studies .... Dr. Mark SCHMITT
32 Dean Student Affairs .... Dr. Julie R. WHITE
102 Exec Director HSC Foundation .... Ms. Eileen PEZZI
66 Dean College of Nursing .... Dr. Joyce GRIFFIIN-SOBEL
76 Dean College Health Profession .... Dr. Hugh W. BONNER
06 Registrar/Dir Inst Research .... Ms. Jennifer MARTIN TSE
25 Vice President for Research .... Dr. Rosemary ROCHFORD
29 Director of Medical Alumni Affairs .... Mr. Paul W. NORCROSS
15 Assoc VP Human Resources .... Mr. Eric FROST
13 Chief Information Officer .... Ms. Teresa J. WAGNER
08 Director of Libraries .... Ms. Christina POPE
28 Dir Diversity & Affirmative Action .... Ms. Maxine THOMPSON
07 Assoc Dean Admissions/Financial Aid .... Ms. Jennifer C. WELCH
18 Chief Facilities/Physical Plant .... Mr. Bob LOTKOWICTZ
21 Assistant Vice President Finance .... Mr. David ANTHONY
37 Director Student Financial Aid .... Mr. Michael ALSHEIMER

*SUNY Broome Community College (F)

PO Box 1017, Binghamton NY 13902-1017
County: Broome | FICE Identification: 002862
Unit ID: 189547
Telephone: (607) 778-5000 | Carnegie Class: Assoc/Pub-R-L
FAX Number: (607) 778-5310 | Calendar System: Semester
URL: www.sunybroome.edu
Established: 1946 | Annual Undergrad Tuition & Fees (In-District): $4,224
Enrollment: 7,301 | Coed
Affiliation or Control: State/Local | IRS Status: 501(c)3
Highest Offering: Associate Degree
Program: Occupational; 2-Year Principally Bachelor's Creditable
Accreditation: M, ADNUR, CAHIIM, DH, ENGT, MAC, MLTAD, PTAA, RAD

01 President .... Dr. Kevin DRUMM
05 Exec VP/Chief Academic Officer .... Dr. Francis BATTISTI
11 Vice Pres Admin/Financial Affairs .... Ms. Regina LOSINGER
32 VP Student and Economic Development .... Ms. Debra MORELLO
10 Associate Vice Pres & Controller .... Ms. Jeanette TILLOTSON
50 Assoc VP & Dean Bus/Public Svcs .... Ms. Elizabeth MOLLEN
76 Assoc VP & Dean of Health Sciences .... Vacant
49 Assoc VP & Dean of Liberal Arts .... Dr. Michael KINNEY
51 Dir Continuing Educ & Workforce Dev .... Ms. Janet HERTZOG
81 Assoc Vice Pres & Dean STEM .... Dr. Kelli LIGEIKIS
35 Dean of Students .... Mr. Scott SCHUHERT
102 Executive Director BCC Foundation .. Ms. Catherine R. WILLIAMS
08 Director Learning Resource Center .... Ms. Robin PETRUS
07 Director of Admissions .... Ms. Jenae SCHMIDT-NORRIS
15 Human Resources Officer .... Ms. Lynn FEDORCHAK
06 Registrar .... Mr. Martin GUZZI
36 Director of Placement Services .... Mr. Lawrence T. TRUILLO
09 Dean Institutional Effectiveness .... Dr. Sesime ADANU
18 Campus Operations Director .... Mr. Phil TESTA
37 Director of Financial Aid .... Mr. Douglas S. LUKASIK
13 Dir Information Technology Services .... Mr. John PETKASH
23 Director of Health Services .... Mr. Joseph O'CONNOR
25 Director of Sponsored Programs .... Ms. Shelli CORDISCO
41 Director of Athletics .... Mr. Brett CARTER
19 Dir of Campus Safety & Security .... Mr. Joseph O'CONNOR
29 Director Alumni Affairs .... Ms. Natalie THOMPSON
40 Bookstore Manager .... Mr. Ryan SNYDER

88 Dir Educational Opportunity Pgm ... Ms. Claudia CLARKE
96 Director of Purchasing ... Mr. Randy CAMPBELL
26 Dir of Marketing/Communications ... Mr. Jesse WELLS
85 Ast Dir Intl Admiss/Intl Stdnt Stds ... Ms. Angela LAROSA
104 Coordinator Study Abroad Program ... Ms. Maria BASUALDO
38 Student Counseling ... Ms. Mary MCCARTHY
101 Secretary of the Institution/Board ... Ms. Patricia G. O'DAY
22 Dir Affirmative Action/EEO ... Ms. Paige SEDLACEK
39 Director Student Housing ... Vacant

*State University of New York, The College at Brockport (A)

350 New Campus Drive, Brockport NY 14420-2914
County: Monroe FICE Identification: 002841
Unit ID: 196121
Telephone: (585) 395-2211 Carnegie Class: Master's L
FAX Number: (585) 395-2401 Calendar System: Semester
URL: www.brockport.edu
Established: 1867 Annual Undergrad Tuition & Fees (In-State): $7,904
Enrollment: 8,106 Coed
Affiliation or Control: State IRS Status: 501(c)3
Highest Offering: Master's
Program: Liberal Arts And General; Teacher Preparatory; Professional
Accreditation: M, BUS, CAATE, CACREP, CS, DANCE, EXSC, NRPA, NURSE, SPAA, SW, TED, THEA

02 President ... Dr. Heidi R. MACPHERSON
05 Provost & VP Academic Affairs ... Dr. Mary Ellen ZUCKERMAN
10 VP Administration & Finance ... Dr. James A. WILLIS
32 VP Enrollment Mgmt/Student Affairs ... Dr. Kathryn WILSON
30 VP Advancement ... Mr. Michael ANDRIATCH
20 Vice Provost ... Dr. P. Michael FOX
58 Asst Provost Research/Dean Grad Sch ... Dr. James SPILLER
28 Interim Asst Provost for Diversity ... Dr. Faith PRATHER
84 Assoc VP Enroll Mgmt & Student Affs ... Dr. Leah A. BARRETT
18 Asst VP Facilities & Planning ... Mr. Robert HENRY
21 Asst VP Finance & Management ... Ms. Karen M. RIOTTO
88 Asst VP Enroll Mgmt ... Mr. Randall LANGSTON
13 Assoc Provost & CIO ... Mr. Jeff SMITH
49 Dean Arts/Humanities & Social Sci ... Dr. Darwin PRIOLEAU
50 Dean Business ... Dr. Daniel PETREE
53 Dean Education & Human Services ... Dr. Thomas J. HERNANDEZ
68 Dean Health & Human Performance ... Dr. Mark KITTLESON
81 Dean Science & Mathematics ... Dr. Jose MALIEKAL
13 Director of Info Tech System ... Mr. David R. STRASENBURGH
07 Int Dir of Undergrad Admissions ... Mr. Randall LANGSTON
56 Exec Dir Brockport Metro Center ... Vacant
44 Exec Dir Dev Comm & Campaign ... Ms. Darby KNOX
51 Exec Dir Continuing Professional Ed ... Ms. Kathleen H. GROVES
104 Exec Dir International Education ... Dr. Ralph R. TRECARTIN
26 Chief Communications Officer ... Mr. David MIHALYOV
37 Dir Financial Aid & Enrollment Svcs ... Mr. J. Scott ATKINSON
36 Director of Career Services ... Ms. Jill WESLEY
19 Chief of University Police ... Mr. Robert J. KEHOE
06 College Registrar ... Mr. Peter DOWE
15 Director of Human Resources ... Ms. Wendy CRANMER
22 Affirmative Action Officer ... Ms. Wendy CRANMER
23 Director Student Health/Counseling ... Ms. Elizabeth S. CARUSO
39 Dir Res Life/Learning Comm ... Dr. Sara KELLY
41 Director of Athletics ... Mr. Erick HART
25 Director of Grants Development ... Ms. Colleen DONALDSON
92 Director of Honors Program ... Dr. Donna M. KOWAL
09 Director of Inst Effectiveness ... Dr. Jeffrey T. LASHBROOK
96 Director of Procurement & Payment ... Mr. Mark W. STACY
94 Dir of Women and Gender Studies ... Dr. Barbara LESAVOY
29 Director Alumni Relations ... Mr. Kerry GOTHAM
04 Assistant to the President ... Ms. Julie A. PRUSS
08 Head Librarian ... Dr. Mary Jo ORZECH
108 Director Institutional Assessment ... Dr. Jeffrey LASHBROOK
86 Director Government Relations ... Mr. David MIHALYOV

*State University of New York College at Buffalo (B)

1300 Elmwood Avenue, Buffalo NY 14222-1091
County: Erie FICE Identification: 002842
Unit ID: 196130
Telephone: (716) 878-4000 Carnegie Class: Master's L
FAX Number: (716) 878-3039 Calendar System: Semester
URL: www.buffalostate.edu
Established: 1871 Annual Undergrad Tuition & Fees (In-State): $7,669
Enrollment: 11,083 Coed
Affiliation or Control: State IRS Status: 501(c)3
Highest Offering: Master's
Program: Liberal Arts And General; Teacher Preparatory; Professional
Accreditation: M, ART, #CIDA, DIETC, DIETD, ENGT, FEPAC, JOUR, MUS, NAIT, #SP, SW, TED, THEA

02 President ... Dr. Katherine S. CONWAY-TURNER
100 Chief of Staff/Secretary to Board ... Dr. Bonita R. DURAND
27 Asst to the Pres for Communications ... Vacant
05 Provost ... Dr. Melanie L. PERREAULT
10 Vice President Finance & Management ... Mr. Michael F. LEVINE
32 Vice President Student Affairs ... Dr. Hal D. PAYNE
30 Vice Pres Inst Advancement & Devel ... Dr. Susanne P. BAIR
28 Chief Diversity Officer ... Dr. Karen A. CLINTON JONES
13 Chief Information Officer ... Dr. David M. DEMERS
19 Chief University Police ... Mr. Peter M. CAREY
84 Associate Vice Pres Enrollment Mgmt ... Ms. Erin R. ALONZO
21 Assoc Vice President & Comptroller ... Mr. James A. THOR
88 AVP for Student Success ... Dr. Daniel C. VELEZ
15 Assoc VP Human Resource Management ... Ms. Susan J. EARSHEN
20 Special Adv to Provost for Educ ... Dr. John F. SISKAR
35 Assoc VP Student Affs/Dean of Stdnt ... Dr. Charles B. KENYON
14 Assoc Vice Pres Computing Services ... Ms. Judith B. BASINSKI
108 Assoc VP Curriculum/Assessment ... Dr. Rosalyn A. LINDNER
26 Assoc VP College Relations ... Mr. Timothy J. WALSH
08 Assoc VP ISAS ... Ms. Maryruth F. GLOGOWSKI
44 Assoc VP Development ... Ms. Mary E. DWYER
86 AVP Govt Relations/Alumni Director ... Mr. William J. BENFANTI
51 Assoc VP Continuing Prof Studies ... Dr. Margaret A. SHAW-BURNETT
20 Dean/AVP Ungrad & International Ed ... Dr. Scott L. JOHNSON
53 Dean School of Education ... Dr. Wendy A. PATERSON
49 Dean School of Arts & Humanities ... Mr. Benjamin C. CHRISTY
83 Dean Natural & Social Sciences ... Dr. Mark W. SEVERSON
107 Dean Professions ... Dr. James MAYROSE
58 Dean Graduate School ... Dr. Kevin J. RAILEY
88 Resident Manager Chartwells ... Mrs. Zena MAGGITTI
88 Exec Director Child Care Center ... Ms. Jennifer J. MINET
88 Director Liberty Partnership ... Ms. Patrice A. CATHEY
88 Director STEP ... Mr. Darryl CARTER
88 Director Upward Bound ... Mr. Donald A. PATTERSON
36 Director of Career Development ... Ms. Stephanie B. ZUCKERMAN-AVILES
27 Director Public Relations ... Mr. Jerod T. DAHLGREN
07 Director Admissions ... Dr. Carmela THOMPSON
06 Interim Registrar ... Ms. Cynthia M. FASLA
37 Director of Financial Aid ... Ms. Connie F. COOKE
39 Director Residence Life ... Mr. Michael A. HEFLIN
88 Director of Student Accounts ... Ms. Susan F. WRIGHT
38 Director Counseling Center ... Dr. Joan L. MCCOOL
41 Director Intercollegiate Athletics ... Mr. Jerry S. BOYES
39 Director of Housing ... Mr. Kris A. KAUFMAN
88 Director Orientation & New Student ... Mr. Robert W. MEAD-COLEGROVE
23 Director Student Health Center ... Dr. Theresa R. STEPHAN HAINS
35 Director Student Life ... Ms. Sarah M. YOUNG
85 Director Intl Student Affairs ... Dr. Jean F. GOUNARD
88 Director Accounts Payable & Travel ... Mr. Robert L. BAUMET
25 AVP for Sponsored Program Operation ... Mrs. Donna L. SCUTO
88 Director Special Events & Protocol ... Ms. Kathryn C. NEESON
18 Director Campus Services ... Mr. Terry M. HARDING
88 Director Events Management ... Mr. Thomas E. COATES
88 Director Budget & Internal Controls ... Ms. Rebecca J. SCHENK
09 Director Institutional Research ... Mr. Yves M. GACHETTE
29 Director of Alumni Affairs ... Ms. Mary-Jo JAGORD
88 Director Parking Services ... Ms. Jayme S. RITER
96 Asst to Comptroller for Procurement ... Mr. Steven M. OLSEN
40 Manager BSC Bookstore ... Ms. Lynn M. PUMA
88 Director Campbell Student Union ... Mrs. Sarah M. VELEZ
88 Director Disability Service ... Ms. Lisa T. MORRISON-FRONCKOWIAK
88 Director Judicial Affairs ... Dr. Latonia D. MARSH
88 Manager Design & Construction ... Mr. Steven E. SHAFFER

*State University of New York College at Cortland (C)

PO Box 2000, Cortland NY 13045-0900
County: Cortland FICE Identification: 002843
Unit ID: 196149
Telephone: (607) 753-2011 Carnegie Class: Master's L
FAX Number: (607) 753-5999 Calendar System: Semester
URL: www.cortland.edu
Established: 1868 Annual Undergrad Tuition & Fees (In-State): $8,050
Enrollment: 6,961 Coed
Affiliation or Control: State IRS Status: 501(c)3
Highest Offering: Master's
Program: Liberal Arts And General; Teacher Preparatory; Professional
Accreditation: M, CAATE, NRPA, @SP, TED

02 President ... Dr. Erik J. BITTERBAUM
05 Provost ... Dr. Mark PRUS
32 Vice Pres Student Affairs ... Mr. C. Gregory SHARER
30 Vice Pres Inst Advancement ... Mr. Peter PERKINS
10 Vice Pres for Finance & Admin ... Mr. David DURYEA
21 Assoc VP for Finance ... Ms. Mary K. MURPHY
13 Assoc Provost for Info Resources ... Ms. Amy BERG
18 Assoc VP Facilities Management ... Ms. Nasrin PARVIZI
20 Assoc Prov for Academic Affairs ... Dr. Carol VAN DER KARR
84 Asst Vice Pres Enrollment Mgmt ... Mr. Mark YACAVONE
27 Assoc Vice Pres Communications ... Mr. Gradin AVERY
04 Exec Assistant to the President ... Dr. Virginia LEVINE
09 Assoc Dir Inst Rsrch/Assessment ... Dr. Stephen CHEMSAK
08 Director of Libraries ... Ms. Gail WOOD
06 Registrar ... Mr. Thomas HANFORD
36 Director of Career Services ... Mr. John SHIRLEY
15 Asst VP Human Resources ... Ms. Joanne BARRY
29 Director Alumni Affairs ... Mr. Michael SGRO
38 Dir Counseling/Student Devel ... Dr. Carolyn BERSHAD
37 Dir of Student Financial Aid ... Ms. Karen GALLAGHER
19 Chief of University Police ... Mr. Steven DANGLER
91 Director Admin Computing Svcs ... Mr. Daniel SIDEBOTTOM
90 Director Campus Technology Services ... Ms. Lisa KAHLE
107 Dean Professional Studies ... Dr. John COTTONE
49 Dean Arts & Sciences ... Dr. Bruce MATTINGLY
26 Chief Public Relations Officer ... Mr. Frederic PIERCE
53 Dean of Education ... Dr. Andrea LACHANCE
93 Director Educational Oppty Program ... Dr. Lewis ROSENGARTEN
92 Director of Honors Program ... Dr. Lisi KRALL
94 Director of Women's Studies ... Dr. Caroline KALTEFLEITER
96 Director of Purchasing ... Mr. Samuel COLOMBO
22 Affirmative Action Officer ... Ms. Dawn NORCROSS
28 Dir Multicultural Life/Diversity ... Ms. Noelle PALEY
41 Athletic Director ... Mr. Mike URTZ
104 Director International Programs ... Dr. Mary SCHLARB
25 Asst VP Research & Sponsored Pgms ... Ms. Amy HENDERSON-HARR

*State University of New York College at Geneseo (D)

1 College Circle, Geneseo NY 14454-1401
County: Livingston FICE Identification: 002845
Unit ID: 196167
Telephone: (585) 245-5000 Carnegie Class: Master's S
FAX Number: (585) 245-5005 Calendar System: Semester
URL: www.geneseo.edu
Established: 1871 Annual Undergrad Tuition & Fees (In-State): $8,113
Enrollment: 5,658 Coed
Affiliation or Control: State IRS Status: 501(c)3
Highest Offering: Master's
Program: Liberal Arts And General; Teacher Preparatory; Professional
Accreditation: M, BUS, TED

02 President ... Dr. Denise A. BATTLES
05 Provost ... Dr. Carol S. LONG
20 Associate Provost ... Dr. David F. GORDON
20 Interim Associate Provost ... Dr. Kenneth KALLIO
11 Vice President Administration ... Dr. James B. MILROY
32 Vice Pres for Student & Campus Life ... Dr. Robert A. BONFIGLIO
30 Interim VP of College Advancement ... Mr. Jon HYSELL
84 Vice Pres Enrollment Mgmt ... Dr. Meaghan ARENA
10 Assoc VP Administration/Controller ... Mr. Brice M. WEIGMAN
26 Asst Vice Pres Communications ... Mr. Anthony T. HOPPA
86 Asst Prov of International Affairs ... Dr. Rebecca LEWIS
15 Asst Vice Pres Human Resources ... Ms. Julie A. BRIGGS
44 Asst VP for College Advancement ... Ms. Kim FABER
29 Director of Alumni & Parent Rels ... Ms. Ronna BOSKO
20 Dean of Curriculum & Academic Svcs ... Dr. Savitri V. IYER
35 Dean of Students ... Dr. Leonard SANCILIO
07 Interim Director of Admissions ... Mr. Kevin REED
08 Interim Library Director ... Ms. Katherine PITCHER
13 Director Computing/Info Technology ... Ms. Susan E. CHICHESTER
37 Director of Financial Aid ... Mr. Archie L. CURETON
25 Director of Sponsored Research ... Dr. Anne E. BALDWIN
09 Director of Institutional Research ... Dr. Julie M. RAO
06 Registrar ... Ms. Kimberley WILLIS
36 Director of Career Development ... Ms. Stacey WILEY
22 Affirmative Action Officer ... Ms. Adrienne COLLIER
88 Director of Multicultural Affairs ... Ms. Fatima R. JOHNSON
19 Chief of University Police ... Mr. Thomas KILCULLEN
18 Chief Facilities/Physical Plant ... Mr. George F. STOOKS
21 Dir of Budget & Financial Analysis ... Ms. Julie MORGAN
38 Clinical Dir Counseling Services ... Dr. Beth K. CHOLETTE
96 Director of Purchasing ... Ms. Rebecca E. ANCHOR
04 Administrative Asst to President ... Ms. Gayle DYCKMAN
100 Chief of Staff ... Dr. Becky L. GLASS
39 Dean Of Residential Living ... Dr. Celia A. EASTON
41 Dir of Intercollegiate Athletics ... Mr. Michael C. MOONEY
50 Dean of School of Business ... Dr. Denise ROTONDO
53 Dean of the School of Education ... Dr. Anjoo SIKKA
90 Asst Director & Manager Sys Net ... Mr. Kirk ANNE
91 Asst Director & Manager Info Sys ... Mr. Paul JACKSON

*State University of New York College at Old Westbury (E)

P.O. Box 210, 223 Store Hill Road, Old Westbury NY 11568-0210
County: Nassau FICE Identification: 007109
Unit ID: 196237
Telephone: (516) 876-3000 Carnegie Class: Bac/A&S
FAX Number: (516) 876-3209 Calendar System: Semester
URL: www.oldwestbury.edu
Established: 1965 Annual Undergrad Tuition & Fees (In-State): $7,643
Enrollment: 4,362 Coed
Affiliation or Control: State IRS Status: 501(c)3
Highest Offering: Master's
Program: Liberal Arts And General; Teacher Preparatory; Professional
Accreditation: M, TED

02 President ... Dr. Calvin O. BUTTS, III
03 Exec VP/Chief of Staff ... Ms. Mona G. RANKIN
05 Provost/Sr VP Academic Affairs ... Dr. Patrick O'SULLIVAN
84 VP for Enrollment Services ... Ms. Mary MARQUEZ BELL
32 VP for Student Affairs ... Dr. Wayne EDWARDS
10 Sr VP Div Business & Finance/CFO ... Mr. Len L. DAVIS
15 Asst to Pres for Admin/Dir HR ... Mr. William P. KIMMINS
30 Asst to President for Advancement ... Mr. Michael G. KINANE
21 Assoc VP Bus Affairs/Controller ... Mr. Pat LETTINI
21 Assoc VP of Business Compliance ... Mr. Arthur H. ANGST, JR.
20 Asst Vice Pres Academic Affairs ... Mr. Ronald J. WELTON
88 Asst VP SA/Acting Dean of Students ... Mr. Usama SHAIKH
49 Dean School of Arts & Sciences ... Dr. Barbara HILLERY
50 Dean School of Business ... Mr. Anthony BARBERA
53 Interim Dean School of Education ... Dr. Julio GONZALEZ
19 Chief of Police ... Mr. Michael C. YANNIELLO
26 Director Public & Media Relations ... Mr. Michael G. KINANE
13 Chief Information Officer ... Mr. Evan KOBOLAKIS
06 Registrar ... Ms. Patricia A. SMITH
96 Director of Purchasing ... Mr. Patrick ADAMS
89 Director First-Year Experience ... Dr. Laura M. ANKER

31 Director of Community Relations .... Ms. Carolyn BENNETT
38 Dir Counseling/Psych Wellness Svcs ....Dr. Trisha BILLARD
88 Environmental Health & Safety Ofcr ..Mr. Douglas BRODMERKEL
29 Director of Alumni Affairs .... Ms. Penny J. CHIN
92 Director Honors College .... Dr. Anthony L. DELUCA
88 Dir Commuter Program & Svcs .... Ms. Veronica GEROSIMO
88 Coordinator of Scholarships .... Ms. Pritpal KAINTH
09 Director of Institutional Research .... Ms. Sandra KAUFMANN
08 Library Director ....Mr. Stephen KIRKPATRICK
88 Director of Capital Planning ....Mr. Ray MAGGIORE
36 Career Plng & Development Director ....Ms. Jerilyn MARINAN
88 Dir Educational Opportunity Program ..Mr. Alonzo L. MCCOLLUM
18 Director of Facilities ....Mr. Timothy MCGARRY
35 Director of Student Activities ....Ms. Suzanne MCLOUGHLIN
23 Director of Student Health Services ....Ms. Susan R. MUNDY
25 Director of Sponsored Programs ....Mr. Thomas MURPHY
37 Director Financial Aid ....Ms. Mildred O'KEEFE
07 Director of Admissions ....Mr. Frank PIZZARDI
88 Dir Ofc of Student Conduct ....Mr. Brian SCHWIRZBIN
88 Dir New Student Orientation ....Ms. Jaclyn VENTO
41 Director of Athletics ....Ms. Lenore J. WALSH
109 Exec Mgr Auxil Svcs Corp ....Vacant

*State University of New York College at Oswego (A)

7060 State Route 104, Oswego NY 13126-3501

County: Oswego FICE Identification: 002848
Unit ID: 196194
Telephone: (315) 312-2500 Carnegie Class: Master's L
FAX Number: (315) 312-5799 Calendar System: Semester
URL: www.oswego.edu
Established: 1861 Annual Undergrad Tuition & Fees (In-State): $7,934
Enrollment: 8,034 Coed
Affiliation or Control: State IRS Status: 501(c)3
Highest Offering: Master's
Program: Liberal Arts And General; Teacher Preparatory; Professional
Accreditation: M, ART, BUS, MUS, TED, THEA

02 President ....Dr. Deborah F. STANLEY
05 VP Academic Affairs/Provost ....Dr. Lorrie A. CLEMO
10 Vice President Admin/Finance ....Mr. Nicholas A. LYONS
84 Vice Pres Student Affs/Enroll Mgmt .... Dr. Jerald WOOLFOLK
30 Vice Pres Devel/Alumni Relations ....Ms. Kerry DORSEY
100 Chief of Staff ....Ms. Kristi ECK
88 Dep to the Pres Ext Prtnr Econ Dev ...... Ms. Pamela CARACCIOLI
32 Assoc VP/Dean of Students Affs .... Dr. Jerri DRUMMOND
18 Asst VP for Facilities Services ....Mr. Mitch FIELDS
21 Actg Asst VP for Finance & Budget ....Ms. Vicki FURLONG
20 Associate Provost .... Dr. Rameen MOHAMMADI
04 Ex Asst to Pres/Int Affrm Act Ofcr .... Mr. Howard GORDON
26 Dir of Ofc of Communications/Mktg ....Ms. Julie H. BLISSERT
25 Dir Research/Sponsored Pgms .... Mr. William BOWERS
94 Director Gender & Women's Studies .... Dr. Mary MCCUNE
06 Registrar ....Mr. Jerret LEMAY
08 Director of Libraries ....Ms. Barbara SHAFFER
91 Assoc Dir Campus Tech Services ....Mr. Michael C. PISA
37 Director of Financial Aid ....Mr. Mark HUMBERT
09 Director Inst Research & Assessment ....Dr. Mehran NOJAN
36 Director Career Services ....Mr. Gary MORRIS
38 Director Counseling Services Center ....Dr. Maria GRIMSHAW-CLARK
15 Director Human Resources ....Ms. Amy PLOTNER
19 University Police Chief ....Mr. John ROSSI
23 Director of Student Health Center ....Ms. Elizabeth BURNS
11 Asst Provost for Operations ....Dr. Michael AMEIGH
28 Assoc Prov Multicltrl Pgms & Opps .... Ms. Catherine SANTOS
39 Dir Residence Life/Housing ....Dr. Richard KOLENDA
41 Director of Athletics ....Ms. Susan VISCOME
96 Director Purchasing ....Mr. Mark COLE
13 Chief Technology Officer ....Mr. Sean MORIARTY
29 Director Alumni Relations ....Ms. Laura KELLY
07 Director of Admissions ....Mr. Daniel GRIFFIN
40 College Store Manager ....Ms. Susan RABY
49 Dean Col Lib Arts & Science ....Dr. Adrienne MCCORMICK
53 Interim Dean School of Education ....Dr. Pamela MICHEL
58 Interim Dean Grad Studies ....Dr. Brad KORBESMEYER
50 Dean School of Business ....Dr. Richard J. SKOLNIK
51 Dean of Extended Learning ....Ms. Jill PIPPIN
88 Dean of Comm/Media & the Arts .... Dr. Julie PRETZAT
35 Asst VP Student Affairs ....Ms. Kathleen EVANS
109 Director of Auxiliary Services .... Mr. Michael FLAHERTY
44 Director Annual or Planned Giving ....Ms. Joy KNOPP

*State University of New York College at Plattsburgh (B)

101 Broad Street, Plattsburgh NY 12901-2637

County: Clinton FICE Identification: 002849
Unit ID: 196246
Telephone: (518) 564-2000 Carnegie Class: Master's L
FAX Number: (518) 564-7827 Calendar System: Semester
URL: www.plattsburgh.edu
Established: 1889 Annual Undergrad Tuition & Fees (In-State): $7,676
Enrollment: 5,968 Coed
Affiliation or Control: State IRS Status: 501(c)3
Highest Offering: Master's
Program: Liberal Arts And General; Teacher Preparatory; Professional
Accreditation: M, BUS, CACREP, DIETD, NURSE, SP, SW, TEAC

02 President .... Dr. John ETTLING
04 Exec Assistant to the President ....Mr. Keith D. TYO
05 Provost/Vice Pres Academic Affairs .... Dr. James LISZKA
10 Vice President for Administration ....Mr. John R. HOMBURGER
30 Vice Pres Institutional Advancement .... Ms. Anne W. HANSEN
32 Vice President for Student Affairs ....Mr. Bryan G. HARTMAN
49 Dean of Arts & Sciences .... Dr. Andrew S. BUCKSER
53 Dean Educ/Health/Human Services .... Dr. Michael D. MORGAN
50 Dean of Business/Economics .... Dr. Rowena ORTIZ-WALTERS
12 Dean Branch Campus at Queensbury ....Mr. Stephen DANNA
08 Dean Library/Info Services ....Ms. Holly B. HELLER-ROSS
22 Director of Affirmative Action ....Dr. Lynda J. AMES
88 Title IX Coordinator ....Ms. Butterfly L. BLAISE
07 Assoc VP Enroll Mgmt/Admissions ....Mr. Richard J. HIGGINS
20 Assistant Provost .... Ms. Diane K. MERKEL
21 Asst to Vice Pres Administration .... Mr. Sean B. DERMODY
15 Asst VP for Human Resources ....Ms. Susan T. WELCH
88 Asst VP for Institutional Advanc ....Mr. David P. GREGOIRE
06 Registrar ....Ms. Denise M. PHILO
11 Controller ....Ms. Diane A. WYAND
22 Budget Officer ....Mr. Clark M. FOSTER
19 Interim Chief University Police ....Mr. Jerry W. LOTTIE
109 Exec Dir College Auxiliary Services .... Mr. Wayne A. DUPREY
26 Exec Dir Marketing & Comm ....Mr. Kennith KNELLY
88 Director of Academic Advising ....Ms. Suzanne L. DALEY
29 Director of Alumni Relations ....Ms. Joanne E. NELSON
44 Director of Annual Giving ....Vacant
41 Director of Athletics ....Mr. Bruce W. DELVENTHAL
36 Director of Career Development Ctr .. Ms. Julia OVERTON-HEALY
40 Director of College Store .... Mr. Jerry L. DECELLE
30 Director of Development ....Ms. Faith M. LONG
18 Director of Facilities ....Mr. Kevin W. ROBERTS
37 Director of Financial Aid ....Mr. Todd A. MORAVEC
39 Director of Housing ....Mr. Stephen P. MATTHEWS
09 Dir of Institutional Effectiveness ....Mr. Robert M. KARP
28 Dir of Institutional Marketing ....Ms. Carla M. BEECHER
96 Director of Purchasing ....Mr. Joseph P. TESORIERE
46 Dir Sponsored Research/Programs .... Mr. Michael E. SIMPSON
88 Director of Student Conduct .... Mr. Larry K. ALLEN
23 Dir Ctr for Stdnt Hlth & Psych Svcs ......Dr. Kathleen M. CAMELO
91 Programming Manager .... Mr. Thomas J. HIGGINS

*State University of New York College at Potsdam (C)

44 Pierrepont Avenue, Potsdam NY 13676-2294

County: Saint Lawrence FICE Identification: 002850
Unit ID: 196200
Telephone: (315) 267-2000 Carnegie Class: Master's L
FAX Number: (315) 267-2496 Calendar System: Semester
URL: www.potsdam.edu
Established: 1816 Annual Undergrad Tuition & Fees (In-State): $7,893
Enrollment: 3,979 Coed
Affiliation or Control: State IRS Status: 501(c)3
Highest Offering: Master's
Program: Liberal Arts And General; Teacher Preparatory; Professional; Fine Arts Emphasis
Accreditation: M, IACBE, MUS, TED, THEA

02 President .... Dr. Kristin G. ESTERBERG
03 Executive Vice President ....Dr. Enrico A. MILLER
05 Provost ....Vacant
10 Vice President for Business Affairs .... Mr. Gerhard VOGGEL
32 Vice President for Student Affairs ....Vacant
30 Vice President College Advancement .... Ms. Vicki L. TEMPLETON-CORNELL
84 Assoc VP Enroll Mgmt/Inst Effect ....Vacant
04 Assistant to the President ....Ms. Carol M. ROURKE
20 Interim Associate Provost ....Dr. Jill R. PEARON
18 Asst Vice Pres for Facilities ....Mr. Anthony DITULLIO
88 Director of Special Programs .... Mr. Shailindar SINGH
27 Chief Information Officer ....Mr. Kyle BROWN
53 Dean Education & Prof Studies ....Vacant
49 Dean of Arts and Sciences ....Dr. Steven J. MARQUSEE
64 Dean of Music ....Dr. Michael R. SITTON
35 Dean of Students ....Mr. William G. MORRIS
88 Coordinator of Special Sessions .... Ms. Karla M. FENNELL
15 Asst VP for Human Resources .... Ms. Mary K. DOLAN
08 Director of Libraries .... Ms. Jenica P. ROGERS
06 Registrar ....Dr. Ramona M. RALSTON
07 Director of Admissions ....Mr. Thomas W. NESBITT
37 Interim Director of Financial Aid ....Ms. Susan E. GODREAU
36 Director of Career Planning ....Vacant
38 Director of Counseling Center ....Mrs. Gena C. NELSON
19 Chief of University Police ....Vacant
29 Director of Alumni Relations ....Ms. Mona O. VROMAN
31 Executive Dir of Auxiliary Corp ....Mr. Daniel J. HAYES
23 Director of Health Services ....Dr. Richard E. MOOSE
39 Director of Residence Life .... Mr. Eric D. DUCHSCHERER
40 Director of College Bookstore ....Mr. Lyndon J. LAKE
41 Athletic Director .... Mr. James A. ZALACCA
25 Director Research & Sponsored Pgms .... Dr. Nancy M. DODGE-REYOME
28 Director of Diversity Center ....Ms. Sheila M. MARSHALL
92 Director of Honors Program ....Dr. Thomas N. BAKER
94 Director of Women's Studies .Dr. Sharmain VAN BLOMMESTEIN
26 Asst VP Marketing/Communications ....Ms. Deborah L. DUDLEY
86 Community and Gov Rel Associate ....Mrs. Alexandra M. JACOBS-WILKE

*Purchase College, State University of New York (D)

735 Anderson Hill Road, Purchase NY 10577-1402

County: Westchester FICE Identification: 006791
Unit ID: 196219
Telephone: (914) 251-6000 Carnegie Class: Bac/A&S
FAX Number: (914) 251-6014 Calendar System: Semester
URL: www.purchase.edu
Established: 1967 Annual Undergrad Tuition & Fees (In-State): $8,267
Enrollment: 4,200 Coed
Affiliation or Control: State IRS Status: 501(c)3
Highest Offering: Master's
Program: Liberal Arts And General; Professional; Fine Arts Emphasis
Accreditation: M, ART

02 President ....Mr. Thomas J. SCHWARZ
19 Interim Chief of University Police ....Mr. Dayton TUCKER
10 CFO/VP Operations ....Ms. Judy NOLAN
05 Provost/VP Academic Affairs ....Dr. Barry PEARSON
32 Vice President Student Affairs ....Mr. Ernie PALMIERI
84 VP Enroll Mgmt/Integrated Mktg ....Mr. Dennis CRAIG
30 Vice Pres of Institutional Advance ....Ms. Jeannine STARR
57 Director Conservatory Theatre Arts ....Dr. Gregory TAYLOR
51 Int Exec Dir Liberal Stds/Cont Educ ....Ms. Kathleen CENG
81 Dean Sch Natural/Social Sciences .... Dr. Suzanne KESSLER
79 Chair School of Humanities ....Dr. Ross DALY
20 Associate Provost ....Dr. Peggy DECOOKE
88 Director Performing Arts Center .... Mr. Harry MCFADDEN
88 Director Neuberger Museum of Art ....Dr. Tracy FITZPATRICK
08 Director of the Library ....Mr. Patrick F. CALLAHAN
64 Director Conservatory of Music ....Dr. James UNDERCOFLER
57 Dean School of Arts ....Mr. Ravi RAJAN
13 Director Campus Technology Services ....Mr. Bill JUNOR
37 Director Student Financial Services ....Corey YORK
38 Director of Counseling Center ....Dr. Cathie CHESTER
36 Director Career Development ....Ms. Wendy MOROSOFF
15 Director of Human Resources ....Ms. Kathleen FARRELL
41 Athletic Director ....Mr. Chris BISIGNANO
39 Director Community Engagement ....Mr. Mario RAPETTI
96 Director of Purchasing ....Mr. Nikolaus LENTNER
06 Exec Dir Enroll Svcs/Assoc Dean Ac ....Ms. Patricia BICE
09 Director of Institutional Research ....Ms. Barbara MOORE
18 Dir Capital Facilities Planning .... Mr. Christopher GAVLICK
22 Affirmative Action Officer ....Mr. Joel AURE
88 Environmental Health/Safety Officer ....Mr. Edward MUSAL
44 Director Annual Giving ....Ms. Carla WEILAND-ZALEZNAK
26 Dir Communications/Creative Svcs ....Ms. Sandy DYLAK
86 Director of Govt Relations/Sp Proj .... Ms. Elizabeth C. ROBERTSON
04 Assistant to President ....Ms. Carrie K. BIANCHI
104 Director Study Abroad ....Ms. Suzanne NEARY

*State University of New York College of Agriculture and Technology at Cobleskill (E)

Route 7, Knapp Hall, Cobleskill NY 12043

County: Schoharie FICE Identification: 002856
Unit ID: 196033
Telephone: (518) 255-5011 Carnegie Class: Bac/Assoc
FAX Number: (518) 255-5333 Calendar System: Semester
URL: www.cobleskill.edu
Established: 1911 Annual Undergrad Tuition & Fees (In-State): $8,059
Enrollment: 2,535 Coed
Affiliation or Control: State IRS Status: 501(c)3
Highest Offering: Baccalaureate
Program: Occupational; 2-Year Principally Bachelor's Creditable; Liberal Arts And General; Technical Emphasis
Accreditation: M, ACFEI, EMT, HT

02 President ....Dr. Marion TERENZIO
05 Provost & Vice Pres Academic Affs .....Dr. Susan ZIMMERMANN
04 Assistant to President ....Ms. Amy HEALY
32 VP for Student Develop/Student Life .... Mr. Steven M. ACKERKNECHT
10 Vice Pres Business & Finance ....Ms. Carol BISHOP
11 Vice Pres Operations ....Ms. Bonnie MARTIN
30 Chief Advancement Officer ....Ms. Lois GOBLET
35 Asst VP for Student Affairs .... Mr. Edward ASSELIN
47 Dean Agriculture/Natural Res ....Mr. Timothy MOORE
49 Dean Liberal Arts & Sciences .... Dr. Jeffrey ANDERSON
08 Dean Library/Information Svcs ....Ms. Elizabeth ORGERON
27 Director of Communications ....Mr. James FELDMAN
88 Director Employee Relations ....Ms. Lynn BERGER
06 Registrar ....Ms. Christine JOHANNESEN
21 Chief Business Officer .... Ms. Carol VOSATKA
84 Chief Enrollment Officer ....Dr. Tara WINTER
29 Director Alumni Relations ....Mr. Matthew S. BARNEY
07 Director of Admissions ....Mr. Robert BLANCHET
39 Director of Residential Life ....Mr. Edward E. ASSELIN
36 Director of Student Success Ctr ....Ms. Donna PESTA
23 Co-Director Wellness Center ....Ms. Mary RADLIFF
23 Co-Director Wellness Center ....Ms. Lynn ONTL
37 Director of Financial Aid ....Ms. Louise BIRON
35 Director Student Life Center ....Mr. Jeffrey C. FOOTE
41 Director of Athletics ....Mr. Kevin MCCARTHY
13 Director Information Tech Services ....Mr. James DUTCHER
19 Chief University Police Dept ....Mr. Frank LAWRENCE
09 Director of Institutional Research ....Vacant
15 Human Resources Operations Manager ....Ms. Jan ELWELL

18 Director Facilities/Physical Plant ... Mr. Joseph BATCHELDER
40 Manager Bookstore ... Ms. Jeri USATCH
85 Director of International Programs ... Dr. Susan JAGENDORF
96 Director of Purchasing ... Ms. Laura GROSS
25 Dir of Grants and Sponsored Program ... Mr. Barry GELL
88 Director of EOP ... Mr. Derwin BENNETT
88 Dir of Student Accounts ... Ms. Sarah LEDERMANN
105 Webmaster ... Ms. Naomi MEKEEL
106 Dir Ctr for Ex in Learning & Teach ... Dr. Jiang TAN
108 Assessment Coordinator ... Ms. Dorothy WILCOX

*State University of New York College of Agriculture and Technology at Morrisville (A)

PO Box 901, Morrisville NY 13408-0901

County: Madison | FICE Identification: 002859
Unit ID: 196051
Telephone: (315) 684-6000 | Carnegie Class: Bac/Assoc
FAX Number: (315) 684-6116 | Calendar System: Semester
URL: www.morrisville.edu
Established: 1908 | Annual Undergrad Tuition & Fees (In-State): $8,001
Enrollment: 2,911 | Coed
Affiliation or Control: State | IRS Status: 501(c)3
Highest Offering: Baccalaureate
Program: Occupational; 2-Year Principally Bachelor's Creditable; Technical Emphasis
Accreditation: M, ACBSP, ADNUR, DIETT, ENGT

02 President ... Dr. David E. ROGERS
05 Interim Provost ... Dr. Michael A. CAPPETO
10 Vice Pres for Administration ... Ms. Mary Ellen BURDICK
32 Dean of Students ... Mr. Geoffrey S. ISABELLE
47 Dean School Agriculture & Business . Dr. Christopher L. NYBERG
83 Dean School Sci/Tech & Health ... Dr. Joseph H. BULARZIK
49 Dean School of Liberal Arts ... Dr. Paul F. GRIFFIN
97 Dean School of General Studies ... Ms. Jeannette H. EVANS
30 Exec Dir Inst Advancement & PR ... Ms. Sara A. WAY
26 Dir Public Relations/Govt Affairs ... Ms. Sara A. WAY
84 Asst VP Enrollment Management ... Ms. Leslie V. CROSLEY
37 Director of Financial Aid ... Ms. Dacia L. BANKS
08 Director of Library ... Ms. Christine A. RUDECOFF
38 Director Student Health Center ... Ms. Nancy S. ZLOMEK
15 Dir HR/Affirmative Action ... Ms. Sarah G. STEELE
29 Coordinator of Alumni Relations ... Ms. Kelly E. GARDNER
96 Project Mgr Planning & Procurement ... Vacant
27 Marketing Manager ... Ms. Amanda J. TARANTO
06 Registrar ... Ms. Marian D. WHITNEY
09 Director of Institutional Research ... Ms. Marian D. WHITNEY
108 Director Institutional Assessment ... Ms. Marian D. WHITNEY
13 Chief Info Technology Officer (CIO) ... Vacant
18 Chief Facilities/Physical Plant ... Mr. Mark P. GRISI
19 Director Security/Safety ... Mr. Enrico L. D'ALESSANDRO
22 Dir Affirmative Action/EEO ... Ms. Sarah G. STEELE
25 Grants Coordinator ... Ms. Lisa A. IANNELLO
36 Career Planning/Development Ofcr ... Ms. Barbara A. ROBACK
39 Director Student Housing ... Ms. Ursula M. HERZ
41 Athletic Director ... Mr. Gregory M. CARROLL
13 Asst Dir of Technology Services ... Mr. Jeff GAY

*State University of New York College of Environmental Science and Forestry (B)

1 Forestry Drive, Syracuse NY 13210-2778

County: Onondaga | FICE Identification: 002851
Unit ID: 196103
Telephone: (315) 470-6500 | Carnegie Class: DRU
FAX Number: (315) 470-6779 | Calendar System: Semester
URL: www.esf.edu
Established: 1911 | Annual Undergrad Tuition & Fees (In-State): $7,398
Enrollment: 2,200 | Coed
Affiliation or Control: State | IRS Status: 501(c)3
Highest Offering: Doctorate
Program: Liberal Arts And General
Accreditation: M, ENG, ENGT, LSAR

02 President ... Dr. Quentin D. WHEELER
05 Interim Provost/EVP Acad Affairs ... Dr. Valerie LUZADIS
11 Vice President for Administration ... Mr. Joseph RUFO
84 VP Enrollmt Mgt & Inst Research ... Dr. Robert C. FRENCH
86 VP for Govt & External Relations ... Dr. Maureen O. FELLOWS
30 Asst VP for Development ... Ms. Brenda T. GREENFIELD
100 Chief of Staff ... Mr. Mark LICHTENSTEIN
46 Vice Provost for Research ... Dr. Neil H. RINGLER
58 Assoc Prov & Dean Grad School ... Mr. Scott S. SHANNON
32 Dean for Student Affairs ... Dr. Anne E. LOMBARD
10 Director of Business Affairs ... Mr. David R. DZWONKOWSKI
13 Director of Information Technology ... Mr. Yuming TUNG
15 Director Human Resources ... Ms. Marcia A. BARBER
26 Director of Communications ... Mrs. Claire B. DUNN
19 Chief of University Police ... Mr. Scott M. BECKSTED
08 Director of College Libraries ... Mr. Stephen WEITER
07 Director of Admissions ... Mrs. Susan H. SANFORD
06 Registrar ... Ms. Leslie RUTKOWSI
37 Director of Financial Aid ... Mr. Mark J. HILL
29 Director of Alumni Affairs ... Ms. Debbie J. CAVINESS
28 Director of Multicultural Affairs ... Dr. Raydora S. DRUMMER FRANCIS
18 Chief Facilities/Physical Plant ... Mr. Gary S. PEDEN
36 Career Planning & Devel Officer ... Mr. John TURBEVILLE
35 Director Student Activities ... Mrs. Laura CRANDALL
51 Asst to President for Outreach ... Dr. Charles M. SPUCHES
04 Admin Asst to the President ... Ms. Ragan A. SQUIER
108 Associate Provost for Assessment ... Vacant

*State University of New York College of Optometry (C)

33 W 42nd Street, New York NY 10036-8003

County: New York | FICE Identification: 009929
Unit ID: 196228
Telephone: (212) 938-4000 | Carnegie Class: Spec/Health
FAX Number: (212) 938-5696 | Calendar System: Semester
URL: www.sunyopt.edu
Established: 1971 | Annual Graduate Tuition & Fees: $27,058
Enrollment: 363 | Coed
Affiliation or Control: State | IRS Status: 501(c)3
Highest Offering: Doctorate; No Undergraduates
Program: Professional
Accreditation: M, OPT, OPTR

02 President ... Dr. David A. HEATH
05 Dean/VP Academic Affairs ... Dr. David TROILO
10 VP For Administration and Finance ... Mr. David A. BOWERS
32 Vice Pres Student Affairs/Intl Pgms ... Dr. Jeffrey L. PHILPOTT
17 Vice Pres for Clinical Affairs ... Dr. Richard SODEN
30 Vice Pres Institutional Advancement ... Ms. Ann WARWICK
04 Assistant to the President ... Ms. Karen DEGAZON
09 Dir Institutional Research/Planning ... Dr. Steven SCHWARTZ
08 Director Library Services ... Ms. Elaine WELLS
15 Director of Human Resources ... Mr. Douglas SCHADING
37 Financial Aid Officer ... Mr. Vito CAVALLARO
06 Registrar ... Mrs. Jacqueline ESTEVEZ MARTINEZ
58 Assoc Dean Rsrch/Graduate Studies ... Dr. Stewart BLOOMFIELD
26 Director of Communications ... Mr. Greg HOULE
13 Chief Info Technology Officer (CIO) ... Mr. Robert PELLOT
84 Director Enrollment Management ... Dr. Guilherme ALBIERI
96 Director of Purchasing ... Mr. Roger CRUTTENDEN

*Alfred State College (D)

10 Upper College Drive, Alfred NY 14802-1196

County: Allegany | FICE Identification: 002854
Unit ID: 196006
Telephone: (607) 587-4010 | Carnegie Class: Bac/Assoc
FAX Number: N/A | Calendar System: Semester
URL: www.alfredstate.edu
Established: 1908 | Annual Undergrad Tuition & Fees (In-State): $8,057
Enrollment: 3,661 | Coed
Affiliation or Control: State | IRS Status: 501(c)3
Highest Offering: Baccalaureate
Program: 2-Year Principally Bachelor's Creditable; Nursing Emphasis
Accreditation: M, ADNUR, CAHIIM, CONST, ENGT, NURSE

02 President ... Dr. Irby (Skip) SULLIVAN
05 Vice Pres Academic Affairs ... Ms. Kristin POPPO
32 Vice President Student Affairs ... Mr. Gregory S. SAMMONS
11 Exec VP Administration/Enrollment ... Ms. Valerie NIXON
30 Sr Dir Institutional Advancement ... Ms. Danielle M. WHITE
20 Assoc Vice Pres Academic Affairs ... Mr. Charles V. NEAL
09 Institutional Research Analyst ... Mr. Daniel D. JARDINE
84 Assoc VP for Enrollment Mgmt ... Ms. Deborah J. GOODRICH
13 Director Computer Services ... Mr. Michael A. CASE
15 Director Human Res/Affirm Action ... Ms. Wendy DRESSER-RECKTENWALD
37 Sr Dir Student Financial Services ... Mrs. Jane A. GILLILAND
29 Director Alumni Relations ... Ms. Colleen ARGENTIERI
18 Director of Physical Plant ... Mr. Glenn R. BRUBAKER
14 Asst Director of Computing Services ... Mr. Carl H. RAHR, JR.
23 Sr Director Health Svcs/Wellness ... Ms. Hollie M. HALL
38 Director Learning Center ... Ms. Janette B. THOMAS
19 Lieutenant University Police ... Mr. Matthew D. HELLER
96 Director of Purchasing ... Mr. Glen E. CLINE
10 Controller ... Mr. Joseph T. GREENTHAL
36 Director of Career Services ... Ms. Elaine MORSMAN
49 Dean School of Arts & Sciences ... Dr. Robert CURRY
54 Dean School of Mgmt & Engr Tech ... Dr. John WILLIAMS
75 Dean Sch Applied Technology ... Mr. Craig CLARK

*SUNY Adirondack (E)

640 Bay Road, Queensbury NY 12804-1498

County: Warren | FICE Identification: 002860
Unit ID: 188438
Telephone: (518) 743-2200 | Carnegie Class: Assoc/Pub-R-M
FAX Number: (518) 745-1433 | Calendar System: Semester
URL: www.sunyacc.edu
Established: 1960 | Annual Undergrad Tuition & Fees (In-District): $4,238
Enrollment: 4,247 | Coed
Affiliation or Control: State/Local | IRS Status: 501(c)3
Highest Offering: Associate Degree
Program: Occupational; 2-Year Principally Bachelor's Creditable
Accreditation: M, ADNUR

02 President ... Dr. Kristine DUFFY
04 Assistant to the President ... Ms. Tressie LAFAY
05 Int Vice Pres Academic Affairs ... Mr. John JABLONSKI
10 Vice Pres Admin Services/Treasurer ... Ms. Ann Marie SOMMA
30 Exec Dir Dev/Alumni Rels/ACC Fndtn ... Ms. Rachael HUNSINGER PATTEN
20 Dean for Special Academic Svcs ... Ms. Diane WILDEY
32 Dean for Student Affairs ... Mr. Jason ENSER
26 Dean of Enrollment Mgt and Mktg ... Mr. Rob PALMIERI
09 Director of Inst Research/Planning ... Mr. David SMITH
13 Chief Information Officer ... Ms. Susan A. TRUMPICK
15 Director of Human Resources ... Ms. Mindy WILSON
51 Director of Cont & External Studies ... Mrs. Caelynn PRYLO
40 Director Bookstore ... Mr. Tom KENT
21 Director of Business Affairs ... Ms. Lisa DESTER
18 Director Facilities ... Mr. Anthony PALANGI
37 Director Student Financial Aid ... Ms. Maureen REILLY
06 Registrar ... Ms. Cindy ZIELASKOWSKI
84 Director of Enrollment Management ... Ms. Sarah J. LINEHAN
90 Director Academic Computer Services ... Ms. Roseann ANZALONE
08 Director of Library Services ... Ms. Teresa RONNING
35 Director of Student Activities ... Ms. Heather WHITNEY
41 Athletic Director ... Mr. John QUATTROCCHI
101 Secretary of the Institution/Board ... Ms. Kathy DRISLANE
102 Dir Foundation/Corporate Relations ... Ms. Rachael HUNSINGER PATTEN

*SUNY Canton-College of Technology (F)

34 Cornell Drive, Canton NY 13617-1098

County: Saint Lawrence | FICE Identification: 002855
Unit ID: 196015
Telephone: (315) 386-7011 | Carnegie Class: Bac/Assoc
FAX Number: (315) 386-7930 | Calendar System: Semester
URL: www.canton.edu
Established: 1906 | Annual Undergrad Tuition & Fees (In-State): $8,446
Enrollment: 3,178 | Coed
Affiliation or Control: State | IRS Status: 501(c)3
Highest Offering: Baccalaureate
Program: Occupational; 2-Year Principally Bachelor's Creditable; Technical Emphasis
Accreditation: M, ADNUR, DH, ENGT, FUSER, NUR, PTAA

02 President ... Dr. Zvi SZAFRAN
05 Provost ... Dr. Douglas SCHEIDT
11 Vice Pres for Administration ... Ms. Shawn MILLER
10 Chief Financial Officer ... Ms. Shawn MILLER
30 Acting Vice Pres for Advancement ... Mr. Keith R. ROSSER
32 Vice President for Student Affairs ... Ms. Courtney D. BISH
35 Dean of Students ... Ms. Courtney D. BISH
72 Int Dean Canino Sch Eng Tech ... Mr. Michael J. NEWTOWN
76 Dean Sch Sci/Health/Crim Justice ... Dr. Kenneth M. ERICKSON
50 Dean Sch Business/Liberal Arts ... Mr. Jondavid S. DELONG
88 Dean Acad Support Svcs/Instr Tech ... Dr. Molly A. MOTT
41 Director of Athletics ... Mr. Randy B. SIEMINSKI
100 Exec Dir for University Relations ... Ms. Lenore VANDERZEE
101 College Council Secretary ... Ms. Michaela J. YOUNG
04 Assistant to the President ... Ms. Michaela J. YOUNG
35 Director Student Activities ... Ms. Priscilla LEGGETTE
28 Director of Diversity ... Ms. Lashawanda T. INGRAM
96 Director of Purchasing ... Ms. Bethany A. MARTIN
37 Director of Financial Aid ... Ms. Kerrie L. COOPER
88 College Accountant ... Mr. Colin MACKEY
15 Director of Human Resources ... Mr. David M. ROURKE
36 Director of Career Services ... Ms. Julie PARKMAN
06 Registrar ... Ms. Memorie L. SHAMPINE
08 Director of Library Services ... Ms. Michelle L. CURRIER
18 Director of Physical Plant ... Mr. Patrick G. HANSS
18 Plant Superintendent ... Mr. Martin D. AVERY
19 Acting Chief of University Police ... Mr. Alan MULKIN
23 Director of Health Services ... Ms. Patricia A. TODD
26 Acting Dir Public Rels/Web Coord ... Mr. Travis SMITH
40 Manager Campus Store ... Mr. Corey JORDAN
39 Director of Residence Life ... Mr. John M. KENNEDY
09 Dir of Inst Research/Assessment ... Ms. Sarah E. TODD
13 Assistant VP IT/CIO ... Mr. Kyle BROWN
22 Director of Affirmative Action ... Ms. Amanda D. ROWLEY
29 Director of Alumni Affairs ... Ms. Peggy S. LEVATO
38 Director of Counseling ... Ms. Melinda A. MILLER
07 Director of Admissions ... Ms. Melissa EVANS
88 Director of Facilities ... Mr. Michael R. MCCORMICK
44 Director of Development ... Ms. Peggy S. LEVATO
90 Director of Academic Computing ... Ms. Theresa C. CORBINE
104 Coord Intl Student Initiatives ... Ms. Erin LASSIAL
103 Dir of Workforce Development ... Mr. Art GARNO
25 Grants Coordinator ... Ms. JoAnne M. FASSINGER
109 Exec Dir of College Association ... Mr. Michael J. PERRY

*State University of New York College of Technology at Delhi (G)

454 Delhi Drive, Delhi NY 13753-4454

County: Delaware | FICE Identification: 002857
Unit ID: 196024
Telephone: (607) 746-4000 | Carnegie Class: Bac/Assoc
FAX Number: (607) 746-4208 | Calendar System: Semester
URL: www.delhi.edu
Established: 1913 | Annual Undergrad Tuition & Fees (In-State): $8,195
Enrollment: 3,562 | Coed
Affiliation or Control: State | IRS Status: 501(c)3
Highest Offering: Master's
Program: Occupational; 2-Year Principally Bachelor's Creditable; Liberal Arts And General; Teacher Preparatory; Technical Emphasis
Accreditation: M, ACFEI, ADNUR, CONST, NUR

02 President ... Dr. Candace S. VANCKO

05 Provost .... Dr. John S. NADER
32 VP for Student Life .... Ms. Barbara E. JONES
10 VP for Business & Finance .... Ms. Carol M. BISHOP
11 VP for Operations .... Ms. Bonnie G. MARTIN
30 VP for College Relations & Advance .... Mr. Joel M. SMITH
36 Coordinator Career & Transfer Svcs .... Ms. Kristin A. DEFOREST
07 Director of Admissions .... Mr. Robert C. PIUROWSKI
13 Chief Information Officer .... Mr. Jonathan R. BRENNAN
19 Chief of University Police .... Mr. Martin A. PETTIT
39 Director of Residence Life .... Mr. John J. PADOVANI
08 Director of the Resnick Library .... Ms. Pamela J. PETERS
36 Dir Career & Business Development .... Ms. Glenda V. ROBERTS
88 Director of Resnick Learning Center .... Ms. Michele T. DEFREECE
18 Director of Physical Plant .... Mr. David A. LOVELAND
41 Director of Athletics .... Mr. Robert H. BACKUS
06 Registrar .... Ms. Nancy L. SMITH
37 Director of Financial Aid .... Ms. Nancy B. HUGHES
38 Director Counseling & Health Svcs .... Ms. Lori B. OSTERHOUDT
29 Alumni/Annual Giving Coordinator .... Ms. Lucinda C. BRYDON
21 Controller .... Ms. Amy L. BROWN
88 Communications & New Media Manager .... Ms. Kimberly M. MACLEOD
09 Director of Institutional Research .... Vacant
04 Administrative Asst to President .... Ms. Barbara KAPLAN
102 Exec Dir College Foundation .... Mr. Joel M. SMITH
15 Personnel Associate .... Ms. Jan A. ELWELL
22 Dir Affirmative Action & Empl Rels .... Ms. Lynn A. BERGER
25 Grants Specialist .... Ms. Ellen A. LIBERATORI
96 Assistant AP/Purchasing Manager .... Ms. Cheryl L. DIETZMAN

*State University of New York Empire State College (A)

2 Union Avenue, Saratoga Springs NY 12866-4390
County: Saratoga — FICE Identification: 010286
Unit ID: 196264
Telephone: (518) 587-2100 — Carnegie Class: Master's M
FAX Number: (518) 587-2886 — Calendar System: Other
URL: www.esc.edu
Established: 1971 — Annual Undergrad Tuition & Fees (In-State): $6,470
Enrollment: 11,952 — Coed
Affiliation or Control: State — IRS Status: 501(c)3
Highest Offering: Master's
Program: Liberal Arts And General; Professional
Accreditation: M, IACBE, NURSE, TEAC

02 President .... Dr. Merodie HANCOCK
100 Chief of Staff .... Mr. Michael MANCINI
05 Provost/Vice Pres AA .... Dr. Alfred NTOKO
10 Vice President for Administration .... Mr. Paul TUCCI
86 VP for Communications & Govt Rels .... Ms. Mary Caroline VAN DER VEER
30 VP of Advancement .... Mr. Walter WILLIAMS
13 Chief Information Officer .... Dr. Samuel CONN
09 VP for Decision Support .... Dr. Mitchell S. NESLER
20 Vice Provost Academic Services .... Dr. Marjorie W. LAVIN
12 Dean Central New York Center .... Dr. Nikki SHRIMPTON
12 Dean Genesee Valley Center .... Dr. Jonathan R. FRANZ
88 Dean HVA Center for Labor Studies .... Dr. Michael MERRILL
12 Dean Hudson Valley Center .... Dr. Gary LACY
12 Dean Long Island Center .... Dr. Michael SPITZER
12 Dean Metropolitan Center .... Dr. Cynthia L. WARD
12 Dean Niagara Frontier Center .... Dr. Nan M. DIBELLO
12 Dean Northeast Center .... Dr. Gerald F. LORENTZ
106 Int Dean Ctr for Distance Learning .... Dr. John MATHER
58 Dean School for Graduate Studies .... Dr. Tai ARNOLD
66 Dean School of Nursing .... Dr. Bridget NETTLETON
20 Vice Provost for Academic Affairs .... Dr. Thomas MACKEY
21 Asst Vice Pres for Adminstration .... Mr. Frederick BARTHELMAS
84 Asst VP Ctr Enroll Mgmt/Decis Sppt .... Ms. Anna MIARKA-GRZELAK
14 Dir Enterprise Sys/Infrastructure .... Mr. AJ LACOMBA
72 Dir of Library Information Services .... Ms. Suzanne HAYES
91 Director Admin Applications .... Mr. Mark CLAVERIE
88 Director Advancement Services .... Ms. Vicki SCHAAKE
29 Dir Alumni and Student Relations .... Ms. Maureen WINNEY
44 Director Annual Giving .... Ms. Diane THOMPSON
21 Director Business Affairs .... Ms. Becky PALMIERI
88 Director of Real Estate .... Mr. Jeffrey ELLENBOGEN
88 Dir Center for Mentoring & Learning .... Vacant
20 Dir Col Acad Sppt/H V Arsdale Labor .... Ms. Sophia MAVROGIANNIS
20 Dir Col Acad Sppt/Long Island Ctr .... Ms. Mildred VAN BERGEN
20 Dir Collegewide Academic Review .... Dr. Nan TRAVERS
32 Dir Collegewide Student Services .... Ms. Patricia MYERS
27 Director of Communications .... Mr. David HENAHAN
88 Director of Academic Development .... Mr. Brian GOODALE
88 Dir Environmental Sustainability .... Ms. Sadie ROSS
18 Senior Director of Operations .... Mr. Rick REIMANN
37 Director Financial Aid .... Ms. Kristina DELBRIDGE
30 Director of Development .... Mr. Toby TOBROCKE
25 Director of Sponsored Programs .... Vacant
15 Asst VP for Human Resources .... Ms. Mary Ellen R. KEENEY
88 Director Marketing .... Ms. Renelle SHAMPENY
88 Director Outcomes Asessment .... Vacant
88 Director Project Management .... Mr. Walter LEWIS
96 Director Procurement .... Mr. Charley SUMMERSELL
24 Director Publications .... Mr. Kirk STARCZEWSKI
19 Director of Safety & Security .... Mr. Mark JANKOWSKI
21 Director Student Accounts .... Ms. Pamela MALONE
88 Int Dir Veteran & Military Educ .... Ms. Desiree DRINDAK
26 Senior Director of Marketing .... Dr. John MCKENNA
22 Affirmative Action Officer .... Ms. Mary MORTON

06 Registrar .... Ms. Mary EDINBURGH
07 Director Admissions .... Ms. Jennifer D'AGOSTINO

*Farmingdale State College (B)

2350 Broadhollow Road, Farmingdale NY 11735-1021
County: Suffolk — FICE Identification: 002858
Unit ID: 196042
Telephone: (631) 420-2000 — Carnegie Class: Bac/Diverse
FAX Number: N/A — Calendar System: Semester
URL: www.farmingdale.edu
Established: 1912 — Annual Undergrad Tuition & Fees (In-State): $7,808
Enrollment: 8,474 — Coed
Affiliation or Control: State — IRS Status: 501(c)3
Highest Offering: Baccalaureate
Program: Liberal Arts And General; Professional; Technical Emphasis
Accreditation: M, DH, ENGT, MLTAD, MT, NAIT, PNUR

02 President .... Dr. Hubert KEEN
05 Provost/Vice Pres for Academic Affs .... Dr. Laura JOSEPH
10 Senior Vice President & CFO .... Mr. George P. LAROSA
32 Vice Pres Student Affairs .... Dr. Tom CORTI
84 VP Inst Advancement/Enrollment Mgmt .... Mr. Patrick CALABRIA
30 Chief Development Officer .... Dr. Henry SIKORSKI
20 Assistant VP Academic Affairs .... Dr. Marie HAYDEN-MILES
11 Asst Vice President Admin Services .... Vacant
35 Dean of Students .... Ms. Terry ESNES-JOHNSON
07 Dir Admissions/Enrollment Planning .... Mr. Jim HALL
19 Chief University Police .... Mr. Marvin J. FISCHER
18 Director of Physical Plant .... Mr. John S. DZINANKA
26 Sr Director of Communications .... Ms. Kathryn S. COLEY
06 Registrar .... Ms. Cindy MCCUE
08 Head Librarian .... Mr. Michael KNAUTH
15 Director Human Resources .... Ms. Marybeth INCANDELA
36 Director Career Development .... Ms. Dolores CIACCIO
37 Director Student Financial Services .... Ms. Diane KAZANECKI-KEMPTER
09 Institutional Research Associate .... Ms. Patricia LIND-GONZALEZ
23 Director Student Health Services .... Ms. Audrey KRAPF
41 Director Athletics .... Mr. Michael HARRINGTON
39 Director of Residence Life .... Ms. Andela JASUR
102 President Farmingdale Foundation .... Mr. Robert GODFREY
24 Director Media Resources .... Mr. Martin BRANDT
29 Director Alumni Relations .... Ms. Michelle JOHNSON
28 Director of Diversity .... Ms. Veronica HENRY
38 Director Student Success Center .... Ms. Marguerite FAGELLA-D'ALOSIO
40 Manager Bookstore .... Ms. Roberta MIRRO
21 Controller .... Mr. Richard HUME
96 Purchasing Associate .... Ms. Lisa BRUNS
75 Director LI Educ Oppty Center .... Mr. Brian MAHER
50 Dean School of Business .... Dr. Richard VOGEL
76 Dean School Health Sciences .... Dr. Denny RYMAN
49 Dean Sch of Arts & Sciences .... Dr. Lou REINISCH
54 Dean Sch Engineer Technology .... Dr. Kamal SHAHRABI
104 Director Study Abroad .... Ms. Jessica ZUNIGA
105 Director Web Services .... Ms. Sylvia NOVARRO-NICOSIA
53 Dean International Education .... Dr. Lorraine GREENWALD

*State University of New York Maritime College (C)

6 Pennyfield Avenue, Throggs Neck NY 10465-4198
County: Bronx — FICE Identification: 002853
Unit ID: 196291
Telephone: (718) 409-7200 — Carnegie Class: Bac/Diverse
FAX Number: (718) 409-7392 — Calendar System: Semester
URL: www.sunymaritime.edu
Established: 1874 — Annual Undergrad Tuition & Fees (In-State): $7,446
Enrollment: 1,799 — Coed
Affiliation or Control: State — IRS Status: 501(c)3
Highest Offering: Master's
Program: Liberal Arts And General; Professional
Accreditation: M, ENG

02 President .... RADM. Michael A. ALFULTIS
04 Executive Assistant to President .... Ms. Desiree MARTIN
05 Provost/Vice Pres Academic Affairs .... Dr. Timothy LYNCH
10 Vice Pres Finance/Admin .... Mr. Scott DIETERICH
26 Vice President University Relations .... Ms. Aimee BERNSTEIN
32 Commandant of Cadets/Master TSES .... CAPT. Richard S. SMITH
20 Academic Dean .... Dr. Gilbert TRAUB
100 Chief of Staff .... Capt. Mark WOOLLEY
07 Dean of Admissions .... Ms. Yamiley SAINTVIL
35 Assoc Provost/Dean of Students .... Dr. Irene R. DELGADO
21 Director of Business Affairs .... Mr. Keith MURPHY
26 Exec Director of External Affairs .... Ms. Mary MUECKE
15 Director Human Resources .... Ms. LuAnn AUGUSTINE-PLAISANCE
19 University Police Chief .... Mr. Myron PRYJMAK
84 Exec Dir Enroll Svcs/Financial Aid .... Mr. Paul BAMONTE
41 Director of Athletics .... Ms. Heather MACCULLOCH
06 Registrar .... Ms. Sarah GRADY
08 Library Director .... Mr. Shafeek FAZAL
88 Dean of Maritime Educ/Training .... CAPT. Ernest FINK

*SUNY Polytechnic Institute (D)

100 Seymour Road, Utica NY 13502
County: Oneida — FICE Identification: 011678
Unit ID: 196112
Telephone: (315) 792-7100 — Carnegie Class: Master's M
FAX Number: (315) 792-7222 — Calendar System: Semester
URL: www.sunyit.edu
Established: 1966 — Annual Undergrad Tuition & Fees (In-State): $7,759
Enrollment: 2,738 — Coed
Affiliation or Control: State — IRS Status: 501(c)3
Highest Offering: Master's
Program: Liberal Arts And General; Professional; Technical Emphasis
Accreditation: M, BUS, CAHIIM, ENGT, NURSE

02 President .... Dr. Alain KALOYEROS
03 Senior Vice President & COO .... Dr. Robert E. GEER
46 Executive VP of Innovation & Tech .... Dr. Michael LIEHR
04 Executive Assistant .... Ms. Erin COULTRY
101 Executive Assistant .... Ms. Laurie HARTMAN
05 Provost/Vice Pres Academic Affairs .... Dr. William DURGIN
84 VP for Enrollment Management .... Mr. Richard FULLER
26 VP for Strategic Communications .... Mr. Jerry GRETZINGER
30 VP for Advancement .... Mr. JP KIDWELL
15 Associate VP for Human Resources .... Ms. Rhonda HAINES
32 Vice President for Student Affairs .... Mr. Richard COLLIER
35 Assoc Provost for Student Affairs .... Ms. Marybeth LYONS
19 VP for Security & Safety Mgmt .... Mr. Tom LOUIS
49 Interim Dean Arts & Sciences .... Dr. Zora THOMOVA
76 Int Dean Health Sciences & Mgmt .... Dr. Robert YEH
54 Interim Dean Engineering .... Dr. Andrew WOLFE
72 Int Dean Engr & Tech Innovation .... Dr. Pradeep HALDER
81 Int Dean Nanoscale Science .... Dr. Alain DIEBOLD
46 Associate VP for Research .... Dr. John MARSH
18 Vice President of Facilities .... Mr. Jonathan HOLDER
25 Assoc VP of Sponsored Programs .... Ms. Christine WALLER
41 Director Athletics .... Mr. Kevin M. GRIMMER
10 Associate VP for Finance .... Mr. Scott BATEMAN
21 Associate VP of Business Affairs .... Ms. Susan HEAD
88 Director of Student Conduct .... Ms. Megan WYETT
36 Director Career Services .... Mr. Sim COVINGTON
38 Dir Counseling & Special Pgms .... Mr. David GARRETT
23 Director Health & Wellness Center .... Ms. Jo RUFFRAGE
09 Assistant VP Institutional Research .... Ms. Valerie FUSCO
39 Director of College Housing .... Mrs. Jennifer ADAMS
37 Director Student Financial Aid .... Ms. Melissa ROSE
06 Registrar .... Mrs. Meghan GETMAN
58 Coordinator Graduate Center .... Ms. Maryrose RAAB
102 Executive Director Foundation .... Mr. Nick GRIMMER
43 Associate Counsel .... Mr. Mark LEMIRE
88 VP Business Dev & Economic Outreach .... Mr. Michael FANCHER
108 Director Institutional Assessment .... Dr. Joanne JOSEPH
13 Chief Information Officer .... Mr. Andrew BELLINGER
07 Director of Admissions .... Ms. Gina LISCIO
08 Director of Library Services .... Mr. Shannon PRITTING

*Suffolk County Community College Central Administration (E)

533 College Road, Selden NY 11784-2899
County: Suffolk — Identification: 666658
Unit ID: 366395
Telephone: (631) 451-4000 — Carnegie Class: N/A
FAX Number: (631) 451-4715
URL: www.sunysuffolk.edu

01 President .... Dr. Shaun L. MCKAY
27 College Communications Director .... Mr. Drew BIONDO
43 College General Counsel .... Mr. Louis S. PETRIZZO
05 VP Academic Affairs .... Dr. Suzanne JOHNSON
10 VP Business Financial Affairs .... Ms. Gail VIZZINI
30 Vice Pres Institutional Advancement .... Ms. Mary Lou ARANEO
45 VP Planning/Inst Effectiveness .... Dr. Jeffrey M. PEDERSEN
20 Assoc VP Academic Affairs .... Dr. Maria DELONGORIA
32 VP of Student Affairs .... Dr. Christopher J. ADAMS
103 Assoc VP Workforce/Econ Development .... Mr. John LOMBARDO
15 Assistant VP Employee Resources .... Mr. Jeffrey L. TEMPERA
84 College Dean Enrollment Management .... Ms. Joanne E. BRAXTON
06 Assoc Dean Master Sched/Registrar .... Ms. Anna FLACK
35 Campus Assoc Dean Student Serv .... Mr. Charles BARTOLOTTA
37 College Director of Financial Aid .... Ms. Rose BANCROFT
28 Col Coord Multicultural Affairs .... Mr. James W. BANKS
100 Assistant to the President .... Ms. Sandra O'HARA
102 Exec Dir Development/Foundation .... Ms. Sylvia DIAZ
30 Col Assoc Dean Inst Advancement .... Mr. Andrew FAWCETT
104 Col Assoc Dean Spec Prog & Ext Part .... Ms. Iavoslava BABENCHUK
106 Assoc Dean Instructional Technology .... Mr. Troy J. HAHN
13 Assoc Dean Computer Info Systems .... Mr. Gary RIS
19 Director Security/Safety .... Mr. Baycan FIDELI
22 Affirmative Action Officer/Title IX .... Ms. Christina VARGAS
25 Chief Contracts/Grants Admin .... Mr. William T. TUCKER
26 Chief Public Relations/Marketing .... Ms. Mary M. FEDER
29 Director Alumni Relations .... Mr. Russell MALBROUGH
41 Athletic Director .... Mr. Kevin FOLEY
86 Col Director Legislative Affairs .... Mr. Benjamin ZWIRN
96 Director of Purchasing .... Vacant
36 Dir Career Services/Coop Educ .... Ms. Sylvia E. CAMACHO
04 Executive Asst to President .... Ms. Carol WICKLIFFE-CAMPBELL
18 Chief Facilities/Physical Plant .... Mr. Paul COOPER

*Suffolk County Community College Ammerman Campus (F)

533 College Road, Selden NY 11784-2899
County: Suffolk — FICE Identification: 002878
Unit ID: 195951
Telephone: (631) 451-4000 — Carnegie Class: Not Classified
FAX Number: (631) 451-4015 — Calendar System: Semester
URL: www.sunysuffolk.edu

Established: 1959 Annual Undergrad Tuition & Fees (In-District): $4,820
Enrollment: 26,908 Coed
Affiliation or Control: State/Local IRS Status: 501(c)3
Highest Offering: Associate Degree
Program: Occupational; 2-Year Principally Bachelor's Creditable; Business Emphasis
Accreditation: M, ADNUR, PNUR, PTAA

02 Executive Dean/Campus CEO ... Mr. P. Wesley LUNDBURG
05 VP Academic Affairs ... Dr. Suzanne JOHNSON
20 Assoc Dean Academic Affairs ... Dr. Sandra SPROWS
32 Assoc Dean of Student Services ... Mr. Charles BARTOLOTTA
37 Director of Financial Aid ... Ms. Nancy BREWER
07 Director of Admissions ... Ms. Katherine AGUIRRE
08 Head Librarian ... Ms. Susan LIEBERTHAL
13 Asst Dir of Application Development ... Mr. Christopher T. BLAKE
18 Chief Facilities/Physical Plant ... Mr. Edward BENZ
36 Dir Career Svcs/Cooperative Educ ... Ms. Sylvia E. CAMACHO
92 Coordinator Honors Program ... Mr. Albin COFONE
10 Director of Business Affairs ... Ms. Barbara HURST
90 ETU Coordinator ... Mr. Paul BASILEO
91 Data Control Supervisor ... Mr. Paul MATUS

* *Suffolk County Community College Eastern Campus* (A)

121 Speonk-Riverhead Road, Riverhead NY 11901-3499
Telephone: (631) 548-2500 FICE Identification: 004816
Accreditation: &M, DIETT

† Branch campus of Suffolk County Community College Ammerman Campus, Selden, NY.

* *Suffolk County Community College Grant Campus* (B)

1001 Crooked Hill Road, Brentwood NY 11717-1091
Telephone: (631) 851-6700 FICE Identification: 013204
Accreditation: &M, ADNUR, CAHIIM, OTA

† Branch campus of Suffolk County Community College Ammerman Campus, Selden, NY.

Sullivan County Community College (C)

112 College Road, Loch Sheldrake NY 12759-5721
County: Sullivan FICE Identification: 002879
Unit ID: 195988
Telephone: (845) 434-5750 Carnegie Class: Assoc/Pub-R-S
FAX Number: (845) 434-4806 Calendar System: Semester
URL: www.sullivan.suny.edu
Established: 1962 Annual Undergrad Tuition & Fees (In-District): $4,674
Enrollment: 1,647 Coed
Affiliation or Control: State/Local IRS Status: 501(c)3
Highest Offering: Associate Degree
Program: Occupational; 2-Year Principally Bachelor's Creditable
Accreditation: M, ACBSP, #COARC

01 President ... Dr. Karin M. HILGERSOM
05 Vice Pres Academic & Student Affs ... Dr. Robert SCHULTZ
30 Vice Pres for Advancement/Partners ... Ms. Cindy KASHAN
20 Asst VP Academic/Student Affairs ... Ms. Iman ELGINBEHI
32 Dean Student Services ... Ms. Sara THOMPSON-TWEEDY
45 Assoc VP for Planning/HR & Facilit ... Dr. Stephen MITCHELL
39 Asst Dean Student Life & Housing ... Vacant
31 Dir Spec Events/Campus Activities ... Ms. Hillary EGELAND
10 Chief Business Officer ... Ms. Susan HORTON
18 Chief Facilities/Physical Plant ... Mr. Tracy HALL
07 Director Admissions/Registration ... Ms. Sari ROSENHECK
21 Controller ... Ms. Susan HORTON
37 Director of Financial Aid ... Mr. James WINDERL
08 Director of Library Services ... Mr. Jon GRENNAN
35 Director Student Activities ... Ms. Adrianna MAYSON
41 Director of Athletics ... Mr. Chris DEPEW
15 Asst Director of Human Resources ... Ms. Stephanie SMART
09 Director Institutional Research ... Ms. Janet HALPRIN
38 Director Student Counseling ... Ms. Rose HANOFEE
96 Purchasing Agent ... Ms. Lorry IRWIN
13 Int Dir Campus Computer Services ... Ms. Cheryl WELSCH
06 Coord of Registration Services ... Mr. Frank SINIGAGLIA
26 Coord of Public & Alumni Relations ... Vacant
50 Chair Business/Information Tech ... Ms. Mary SUDOL
79 Chair Liberal Arts & Humanities ... Dr. Paul REIFENHEISER
88 Chair Sustainability ... Ms. Susan ROGERS
83 Chair Health/Social/Behavioral Sci ... Dr. Anita MCGLYNN
81 Chair Mathematics/Natural Sciences ... Ms. Debra LEWKIEWICZ
04 Exec Admin Assoc to President ... Ms. Linda ROFFEL
19 Director Security/Safety ... Mr. David SEIGERMAN

Swedish Institute--College of Health Sciences (D)

226 W 26th Street, New York NY 10001-6700
County: New York FICE Identification: 021700
Unit ID: 196389
Telephone: (212) 924-5900 Carnegie Class: Spec/Health
FAX Number: (212) 924-7600 Calendar System: Semester
URL: www.swedishinstitute.edu
Established: 1916 Annual Undergrad Tuition & Fees: $18,000
Enrollment: 680 Coed
Affiliation or Control: Proprietary IRS Status: Proprietary
Highest Offering: Master's
Program: Occupational; 2-Year Principally Bachelor's Creditable; Professional
Accreditation: ACCSC, ADNUR, SURGT

01 President ... Mr. Peter NEIGLER
03 Executive Vice President ... Ms. Stacey JAMESON
05 Director of Education ... Dr. Joseph BALATBAT
10 Chief Financial Officer ... Mr. Bill BERNARD
29 Dean of Alumni/Career Services ... Ms. Meg DARNELL
07 Director of Admissions ... Vacant
88 Dean for Massage Therapy ... Ms. Lucy LIBEN
13 Director of Information Technology ... Mr. Benn LI
32 Director of Student Services ... Vacant
26 Director of Public Relations ... Vacant
37 Financial Aid Director ... Mr. Alex ORMENO
08 Director of Library Services ... Ms. Jill GOLDSTEIN
06 Registrar ... Mr. Jeff NAMIAN
21 Bursar ... Ms. Beatriz ACEVEDO
51 Director of Continuing Education ... Ms. Tania OGULLUKIAN
40 Bookstore Manager ... Mr. Dan YUEN
36 Director Student Placement ... Mr. Richard GARDNER

Syracuse University Main Campus (E)

900 South Crouse Avenue, Syracuse NY 13244
County: Onondaga FICE Identification: 002882
Unit ID: 196413
Telephone: (315) 443-1870 Carnegie Class: RU/H
FAX Number: (315) 443-3503 Calendar System: Semester
URL: www.syr.edu
Established: 1870 Annual Undergrad Tuition & Fees: $43,318
Enrollment: 21,492 Coed
Affiliation or Control: Independent Non-Profit IRS Status: 501(c)3
Highest Offering: Doctorate
Program: Liberal Arts And General; Teacher Preparatory; Professional
Accreditation: M, ART, AUD, BUS, CACREP, CIDA, CLPSY, CS, DIETD, DIETI, ENG, JOUR, LAW, LIB, MFCD, MUS, PH, SCPSY, SP, SPAA, SW, TED

01 Chancellor & President ... Dr. Kent SYVERUD
05 Int Vice Chanc/Prov Academic Affs ... Dr. Elizabeth D. LIDDY
10 Executive Vice President & CFO ... Dr. Louis G. MARCOCCIA
43 Interim Sr VP University Counsel ... Mr. Daniel J. FRENCH
30 Chief Advancement Ofcr/Senior VP ... Mr. Matthew TER MOLEN
32 Sr Vice Pres/Dean Student Affairs ... Ms. Rebecca Reed KANTROWITZ
46 Vice Pres Research ... Dr. Gina LEE-GLAUSER
41 Interim Athletic Director ... Mr. Peter SALA
26 Sr Vice Pres Public Affairs ... Mr. Kevin C. QUINN
84 Sr Vice Pres Enrollment Management ... Mr. Christopher M. SEDORE
21 Comptroller ... Mr. David J. SMITH
104 Assoc Prov International Education ... Dr. Margaret R. HIMLEY
08 Dean of University Libraries ... Dr. David SEAMAN
15 Chief Human Resources Officer ... Dr. Andrew GORDON
20 Assoc Provost Academic Programs ... Ms. Andria COSTELLO STANIEC
48 Dean School of Architecture ... Dr. Michael A. SPEAKS
49 Dean College of Arts & Sciences ... Dr. Karin RUHLANDT
53 Dean School of Education ... Dr. Joanna O. MASINGILA
76 Dean Col of Sport & Human Dynamics ... Dr. Diane Lyden MURPHY
54 Dean Col Engreering & Computer Sci ... Dr. Laura J. STEINBERG
62 Interim Dean School of Info Studies ... Dr. Jeffrey M. STANTON
61 Int Dean College of Law ... Dr. William C. BANKS
50 Dean Whitman School of Management ... Dr. Kenneth A. KAVAJECZ
80 Dean Maxwell Sch of Citizenship ... Dr. James B. STEINBERG
60 Dean Newhouse School of Public Comm ... Ms. Lorraine BRANHAM
57 Dean Col Visual & Performing Arts ... Ms. Ann CLARKE
58 Dean Graduate Studies ... Dr. Ben R. WARE
51 Dean University College ... Ms. Bethaida GONZALEZ
101 Secretary Board of Trustees ... Ms. Lisa A. DOLAK
07 Dean of Admissions ... Dr. Maurice A. HARRIS

Talmudical Institute of Upstate New York (F)

769 Park Avenue, Rochester NY 14607-3046
County: Monroe FICE Identification: 025506
Unit ID: 196440
Telephone: (585) 473-2810 Carnegie Class: Spec/Faith
FAX Number: (585) 442-0417 Calendar System: Semester
Established: 1974 Annual Undergrad Tuition & Fees: $5,100
Enrollment: 21 Male
Affiliation or Control: Independent Non-Profit IRS Status: 501(c)3
Highest Offering: Second Talmudic Degree
Program: Professional
Accreditation: RABN

01 Dean ... Rabbi Menachem DAVIDOWITZ
03 Executive Vice President ... Rabbi Shlomo NOBLE

Talmudical Seminary of Bobov (G)

5120 New Utrecht Avenue, Brooklyn NY 11204-1108
County: Kings FICE Identification: 041155
Unit ID: 451404
Telephone: (718) 854-8700 Carnegie Class: Spec/Faith
FAX Number: (718) 854-8707 Calendar System: Semester
Established: 2005 Annual Undergrad Tuition & Fees: $7,600
Enrollment: 345 Male
Affiliation or Control: Independent Non-Profit IRS Status: 501(c)3
Highest Offering: First Talmudic Degree
Program: Teacher Preparatory; Professional; Religious Emphasis
Accreditation: RABN

01 Dean ... Rabbi Joshua RUBIN

Talmudical Seminary Oholei Torah (H)

667 Eastern Parkway, Brooklyn NY 11213-3397
County: Kings FICE Identification: 012011
Unit ID: 196431
Telephone: (718) 774-5050 Carnegie Class: Spec/Faith
FAX Number: (718) 778-0784 Calendar System: Semester
Established: 1956 Annual Undergrad Tuition & Fees: $9,300
Enrollment: 334 Male
Affiliation or Control: Independent Non-Profit IRS Status: 501(c)3
Highest Offering: First Talmudic Degree
Program: Teacher Preparatory
Accreditation: RABN

01 Chief Executive Officer ... Mendel MARSOW
05 Dean ... Elchonon LESCHES
10 Business Officer ... Gary SUSSKIND
37 Financial Aid Officer ... Sholom ROSENFELD

Teachers College, Columbia University (I)

525 West 120th Street, New York NY 10027
County: New York FICE Identification: 003979
Unit ID: 196468
Telephone: (212) 678-3000 Carnegie Class: RU/H
FAX Number: (212) 678-4048 Calendar System: Semester
URL: www.tc.columbia.edu
Established: 1887 Annual Graduate Tuition & Fees: $34,680
Enrollment: 4,945 Coed
Affiliation or Control: Independent Non-Profit IRS Status: 501(c)3
Highest Offering: Doctorate; No Undergraduates
Program: Teacher Preparatory; Professional
Accreditation: M, CLPSY, COPSY, DIETI, SCPSY, SP, TED

01 President ... Dr. Susan H. FUHRMAN
05 Provost & VP for Academic Affairs ... Dr. Thomas JAMES
100 Secretary to College/Chief of Staff ... Dr. Katie CONWAY
10 Vice Pres Finance & Administration ... Mr. Harvey SPECTOR
30 Vice Pres Devel/External Affairs ... Ms. Suzanne MURPHY
22 Vice Pres/Dir Diversity/Cmty Affs ... Ms. Janice S. ROBINSON
88 VP/Sch/Cmty Partnshp/Spec Advis ... Dr. Nancy STREIM
21 Assoc Vice Pres/Controller ... Mr. Henry PERKOWSKI
18 Asst VP Facilities ... Mr. Suzanne JABLONSKI
85 Assoc VP of International Affairs ... Dr. Thomas B. CORCORAN
84 Assoc Dean Enrollment/Student Svcs ... Dr. Thomas ROCK
06 Registrar ... Mr. Sam FUGAZZOTTO
13 Director Information Technology ... Ms. Ena HAINES
90 Director Academic Computing ... Mr. George SCHUESSLER
08 Library Director ... Dr. Gary NATRIELLO
09 Director of Institutional Studies ... Mr. Scott SCHNACKENBERG
36 Director Career Services/Stdnt Life ... Ms. Marianne TRAMELLI
15 Director Human Resources ... Mr. Randy GLAZER
19 Director Public Safety ... Mr. John DE ANGELIS
43 General Counsel ... Ms. Lori E. FOX
25 Director Grants & Contracts ... Mr. John L. HERNANDEZ
26 Exec Director of External Affairs ... Mr. Joe LEVINE
29 Sr Director Alumni Relations ... Ms. Rosella GARCIA
07 Director of Admissions ... Dr. Thomas ROCK
32 Dir Student Activities/Programs ... Ms. Maria HATAIER
11 Manager Administrative Services ... Ms. Patricia WALKER
37 Director Student Financial Aid ... Ms. Melanie WILLIAMS-BETHEA
39 Director of Residential Services ... Mr. Dewayne WHITE

† Affiliated with Columbia University in the City of New York.

Technical Career Institutes (J)

320 W 31st Street, New York NY 10001-2789
County: New York FICE Identification: 011031
Unit ID: 196477
Telephone: (212) 594-4000 Carnegie Class: Assoc/PrivFP
FAX Number: (212) 330-0898 Calendar System: Semester
URL: www.tcicollege.edu
Established: 1909 Annual Undergrad Tuition & Fees: $13,900
Enrollment: 2,762 Coed
Affiliation or Control: Proprietary IRS Status: Proprietary
Highest Offering: Associate Degree
Program: Occupational; 2-Year Principally Bachelor's Creditable; Technical Emphasis
Accreditation: M, NY, ENGT, OPD

00 Chief Executive Officer ... Dr. John MCGRATH
01 President ... Mr. William TALBOT
05 Provost & VP for Academic Affairs ... Dr. Peter SLATER
11 Exec Vice Pres Administration ... Mr. Felix PRETTO
84 Exec VP Enrollment Management ... Mr. Michael GALL
37 Vice President Financial Aid ... Ms. Cynthia FEKARIS
09 Vice Pres for Research and Planning ... Ms. Susanna KUNG
10 Chief Financial Officer ... Mr. Richard GOLDENBERG
07 Assoc Vice Pres for Admissions ... Ms. Iveth ZUNIGA
20 Dean of Academic Affairs ... Ms. Pansy JAMES
49 Dean of Arts & Sciences ... Dr. John LUUKKONEN
88 Dean of Facilities Technologies ... Ms. Regina CAHILL
50 Dean of Business and New Media Tech ... Ms. Clotilde DILLON

72 Dean of Technology .... Mr. Seyed AKHAVI
76 Dean of Health Sciences and Tech .... Dr. Michael MEIR

Tompkins Cortland Community College (A)

170 North Street, PO Box 139, Dryden NY 13053-8504
County: Tompkins FICE Identification: 006788
Unit ID: 196565
Telephone: (607) 844-8211 Carnegie Class: Assoc/Pub-R-M
FAX Number: (607) 844-9665 Calendar System: Semester
URL: www.TC3.edu
Established: 1968 Annual Undergrad Tuition & Fees (In-District): $5,491
Enrollment: 5,559 Coed
Affiliation or Control: State/Local IRS Status: 501(c)3
Highest Offering: Associate Degree
Program: Occupational; 2-Year Principally Bachelor's Creditable
Accreditation: M, ADNUR

01 President .... Dr. Carl E. HAYNES
03 Provost and VP of College .... Dr. John R. CONNERS
32 Dean of Student Life .... Ms. Amy TRUEMAN
05 Dean of Instruction .... Mr. Carl PENZIUL
08 Library Director .... Mr. Gregg KIEHL
84 Dean Operations & Enrollment Mgmt .... Ms. Blixy K. TAETZSCH
20 Assoc Dean Curriculum & Acad Record .... Ms. Jane F. HAMMOND
14 Director of Technology Support .... Mr. Brian ACKLEY
88 Dean Org Success & Learning .... Ms. Kathryn WUNDERLICH
09 Assoc Dean IR and Org Learning .... Dr. Kristine ALTUCHER
38 Coordinator/Counseling & Career Svc .... Ms. Meg GARVEY
37 Director of Financial Aid .... Ms. LaSonya GRIGGS
26 Dean of External Relations .... Dr. Bruce RYAN
15 Human Resources Administrator .... Ms. Sharon DOVI
07 Director of Admissions .... Mr. Sandy DRUMLUK
10 Director of Budget & Finance .... Ms. Susan DEWEY
13 Chief Information Officer .... Mr. Timothy DENSMORE
19 Director of Safety & Security .... Mr. J. Beau SAUL
41 Athletic Director .... Mr. Mick R. MCDANIEL
39 Director Residence Life .... Ms. Darese DOSKAL
36 Coordinator Counseling/Career Svcs .... Ms. Joan DONOVAN
18 Director of Facilities .... Mr. James TURNER
23 Director of Health Services .... Ms. Shari SHAPLEIGH
28 Director of Multicultural Services .... Mr. Seth THOMPSON
101 Asst to President/Clerk of Board .... Ms. Cathy NORTHROP

Torah Temimah Talmudical Seminary (B)

507 Ocean Parkway, Brooklyn NY 11218-5913
County: Kings FICE Identification: 021916
Unit ID: 196583
Telephone: (718) 853-8500 Carnegie Class: Spec/Faith
FAX Number: (718) 438-5779 Calendar System: Semester
Established: 1978 Annual Undergrad Tuition & Fees: $10,750
Enrollment: 98 Male
Affiliation or Control: Independent Non-Profit IRS Status: 501(c)3
Highest Offering: Second Talmudic Degree
Program: Teacher Preparatory; Professional
Accreditation: RABN

01 President & Dean .... Rabbi L. MARGULIES
03 Executive Director .... Rabbi L. MARGULIES
05 Chief Academic Officer .... Rabbi Lipa GELDWORTH
37 Financial Aid Administrator .... Mr. Mendel ROCHLITZ
38 Director of Guidance .... Rabbi Yirmiya GUGENHEIMER
11 Administrator .... Rabbi Yisroel KLEINMAN

Touro College (C)

500 7th Avenue, New York NY 10018
County: New York FICE Identification: 010142
Unit ID: 196592
Telephone: (646) 565-6000 Carnegie Class: Master's L
FAX Number: N/A Calendar System: Semester
URL: www.touro.edu
Established: 1970 Annual Undergrad Tuition & Fees: $16,500
Enrollment: 12,381 Coordinate
Affiliation or Control: Independent Non-Profit IRS Status: 501(c)3
Highest Offering: Doctorate
Program: Occupational; 2-Year Principally Bachelor's Creditable; Liberal Arts And General; Teacher Preparatory; Professional
Accreditation: M, ARCPA, LAW, NURSE, OSTEO, OT, OTA, PHAR, PTA, SP, SW, TEAC

01 President/Chief Executive Officer .... Dr. Alan KADISH
03 Executive Vice President .... Mr. David RAAB
03 Executive Vice President .... Mr. Moshe KRUPKA
10 Senior Vice President & CFO .... Mr. Melvin M. NESS
11 Sr Vice Pres/Chief Admin Officer .... Mr. Jeffrey ROSENGARDEN
30 Vice Pres Institutional Advancement .... Mr. Henry RUBIN
05 VP Undergrad Acad Affs/Dean of Fac .... Dr. Stanley L. BOYLAN
58 Vice Pres of Grad Studies .... Dr. Nadja GRAFF
45 VP Plng & Assessment/Dean of Stdnts .... Dr. Robert GOLDSCHMIDT
13 VP of Operations & Info Systems .... Dr. Franklin STEEN
84 VP Student Administrative Services .... Mr. Matthew BONILLA
53 Dean Grad School Education .... Dean Arnold SPINNER
56 Vice President Com Ed/Ex Dn NYSCAS .... Ms. Eva SPINELLI-SEXTER
106 VP Online Edu/Dean Women's Division .... Dr. Marian STOLTZ-LOIKE
09 Director Institutional Research .... Mr. Michael LIPKIN
43 Senior VP of Legal Affairs .... Mr. Michael NEWMAN
61 Dean Jacob D Fuchsberg Law Center .... Dr. Patricia SALKIN
63 Dean Col of Osteopathic Medicine .... Dr. Robert GOLDBERG
67 Dean College of Pharmacy .... Dr. Katherine KNAPP
70 Dean School of Social Work .... Dr. Steven HUBERMAN
76 Dean of School of Health Sciences .... Dr. Louis H. PRIMAVERA
58 Dean Grad School Jewish Studies .... Dr. Michael A. SHMIDMAN
90 Dn Grad Sch of Tech/Dir Acad Comp .... Dr. Issac HERSKOWITZ
12 Dean Lander College for Men .... Dr. Moshe Z. SOKOL
50 Acting Dean Grad School of Business .... Dr. Sabra BROCK
38 Dean of Advising & Counseling .... Dr. Avery HOROWITZ
51 Asst Dean School Lifelong Education .... Dr. Briendy STERN
06 University Registrar .... Ms. Lidia MEINDL
37 Int Dir Financial Aid/Compliance .... Ms. Margherite POWELL
08 Director of Libraries .... Ms. Bashe SIMON
07 Director of Admissions .... Mr. Arthur WIGFALL
76 Director Physician Asst Program .... Dr. Joseph TOMMASINO
75 Director of Occupational Therapy .... Dr. Stephanie DAPICE-WONG
76 Director of Physical Therapy .... Ms. Jill HORBACEWICZ
88 Pgm Dir Speech Lang Path/Grad Pgm .... Ms. Hindy LUBINSKY
44 Director Annual or Planned Giving .... Ms. Adrienne GRUSKIN
14 Director of OIT .... Mr. Len NIEBO
91 Chief Info Security Officer .... Ms. Patricia CIUFFO
19 Director of Security .... Ms. Lydia PEREZ
19 Dir of Emergency Preparedness .... Ms. Shoshana YEHUDAH
15 Director of Human Resources .... Ms. Roberta ROSENBLATT
96 Director of Purchasing .... Ms. Wanda HERNANDEZ
18 Dir of Facilities/Real Estate .... Mr. Kenneth DAVID
21 Controller .... Mr. Stuart LIPPMAN
26 Dir of Communication/External Rels .... Ms. Elisheva SCHLAM
29 Director Alumni Relations .... Vacant
36 Director Student Placement .... Mr. Stuart ANSEL
108 Director of Assessment & Evaluation .... Dr. Eric LINDEN
25 Director Office Sponsored Pgm .... Mr. Glenn DAVIS
04 Administrative Asst to President .... Ms. Elaine GOLDBERG
104 Director Study Abroad .... Dr. Chana SOSEVSKY
105 Director Web Services .... Ms. Lisa HALBERSTAM
41 Athletic Director .... Mr. Irv BADER
45 Director of Budget & Planning .... Mr. Adam D. HAMMERMAN

Touro College Bay Shore (D)

1700 Union Boulevard, Bay Shore NY 11706
Telephone: (631) 665-1600 Identification: 770145
Accreditation: &M, ARCPA, OT

† Branch campus of Touro College, New York, NY.

Touro College Flatbush (E)

1602 Avenue J, Brooklyn NY 11230
Telephone: (718) 252-7800 Identification: 770146
Accreditation: &M

† Branch campus of Touro College, New York, NY.

Touro Law School (F)

225 Eastview Drive, Central Islip NY 11722
Telephone: (631) 761-7000 Identification: 770148
Accreditation: &M

† Branch campus of Touro College, New York, NY.

Tri-State College of Acupuncture (G)

80 Eighth Avenue, #400, New York NY 10011-0890
County: New York FICE Identification: 025460
Unit ID: 130581
Telephone: (212) 242-2255 Carnegie Class: Spec/Health
FAX Number: (212) 242-2920 Calendar System: Semester
URL: www.tsca.edu
Established: 1982 Annual Graduate Tuition & Fees: $23,600
Enrollment: 125 Coed
Affiliation or Control: Proprietary IRS Status: Proprietary
Highest Offering: Master's; No Undergraduates
Program: Professional
Accreditation: ACUP

01 President .... Dr. Dennis MOSEMAN
06 Registrar .... Sandra TURNER

Trocaire College (H)

360 Choate Avenue, Buffalo NY 14220-2094
County: Erie FICE Identification: 002812
Unit ID: 196653
Telephone: (716) 826-1200 Carnegie Class: Assoc/PrivNFP
FAX Number: (716) 828-6107 Calendar System: Semester
URL: www.trocaire.edu
Established: 1958 Annual Undergrad Tuition & Fees: $17,540
Enrollment: 1,336 Coed
Affiliation or Control: Independent Non-Profit IRS Status: 501(c)3
Highest Offering: Baccalaureate
Program: Occupational; 2-Year Principally Bachelor's Creditable
Accreditation: M, ADNUR, CAHIIM, @DIETT, MAC, NUR, PHLEB, PNUR, RAD, SURGT

01 President .... Dr. Bassam M. DEEB
05 Vice President of Academic Affairs .... Dr. Richard T. LINN
10 VP for Finance .... Mr. John J. HUDACK
30 VP Development & Cmty Engagement .... Ms. Pamela WITTER
21 Associate VP for Finance .... Mr. Edward JOHNSON
32 Chief Student Affairs Officer .... Mr. Tony FUNIGIELLO
84 Chief Enrollment Officer .... Ms. Jacqueline MATHENY
66 Dean Catherine McAuley Sch of Nurs .... Dr. Carol FANUTTI
15 Exec Dir Human Resources .... Mrs. Rebecca BOYLE
35 Director of Student Life .... Ms. Joyce KAISER
13 Sr InformationTechnology Specialist .... Ms. Robin LOOMIS
105 Director Data Administration .... Ms. Michele PETERS
37 Director of Financial Aid .... Vacant
25 Director of Grants/Govt Relations .... Ms. Sandra MILLER
26 Director of Public Relations .... Ms. Emily Burns PERRYMAN
16 Payroll/Benefits/Human Res Coord .... Vacant
06 Registrar .... Mrs. Theresa HORNER
36 Director Career Center .... Mrs. Maureen PERNICK HUBER
42 Campus Minister .... Vacant
18 Facilities Director .... Mrs. Margaret ANDRZEJEWSKI
44 Director of Development .... Ms. Lindsey DOTSON
07 Dean of Admissions & Workforce Dev .... Mrs. Mollie A. BALLARO
38 Director Academic Support & Retent .... Ms. Kristin NESBITT
40 Manager Bookstore .... Ms. Debbie CAMMARATA
49 Dean of Arts/Sciences & Prof Stds .... Dr. Jennifer Higgins MCCORMICK
76 Dean Division of Health Prof .... Dr. Linda KERWIN
108 Director of Assessment & Research .... Dr. Nicole TOMASELLO
88 Director of Mission & Service .... Sr. Margaret Mary GORMAN

Ulster County Community College (I)

491 Cottekill Road, PO Box 557, Stone Ridge NY 12484
County: Ulster FICE Identification: 002880
Unit ID: 196699
Telephone: (845) 687-5000 Carnegie Class: Assoc/Pub-R-M
FAX Number: (845) 687-5083 Calendar System: Semester
URL: www.sunyulster.edu
Established: 1961 Annual Undergrad Tuition & Fees (In-District): $4,230
Enrollment: 3,664 Coed
Affiliation or Control: State/Local IRS Status: 501(c)3
Highest Offering: Associate Degree
Program: Occupational; 2-Year Principally Bachelor's Creditable
Accreditation: M, ADNUR

01 President .... Dr. Alan P. ROBERTS
84 Vice Pres & Dean Enrollment Mgmt .... Ms. Ann MARROTT
05 Dean of Academic Affairs .... Mr. Kevin STONER
51 Dean of Continuing & Prof Educ .... Mr. Christopher MARX
10 Dean of Admin/Chief Business Ofcr .... Vacant
30 Exec Dir of Inst Advance & Ext Rels .... Ms. Lorraine SALMON
04 Assistant to President .... Ms. Jennifer ZELL
08 Director of Library Services .... Ms. Kari MACK
37 Director of Financial Aid .... Mr. Christopher CHANG
06 Registrar .... Ms. Debra MILLER
41 Athletic Director .... Mr. Matthew BRENNIE
19 Director of Safety & Security .... Mr. Wayne FREER
07 Asst Dean Enrollment & Dir Admiss .... Mr. Matthew GREEN
26 Chief Public Relations Officer .... Ms. Ann MARROTT
36 Dir Student Place/Acad Support Svcs .... Ms. Jane KITHCART
32 Director Student Affairs .... Ms. Ann MARROTT
18 Director of Plant Operations .... Mr. Steven FREER
09 Director of Institutional Research .... Mr. Clarence (Hank) MILLER
103 Workforce Development .... Mr. Christopher MARX
15 Coordinator of Personnel Services .... Mrs. Debra DELANOY
21 Coordinator of Accounting .... Ms. Amy WINTERS
96 Coord Procurement/General Services .... Mr. Stephen GALLART

Unification Theological Seminary (J)

30 Seminary Drive, Barrytown NY 12507-5021
County: Dutchess FICE Identification: 032163
Unit ID: 246789
Telephone: (845) 752-3000 Carnegie Class: Spec/Faith
FAX Number: (845) 758-2156 Calendar System: Semester
URL: www.uts.edu
Established: 1975 Annual Undergrad Tuition & Fees: $11,360
Enrollment: 110 Coed
Affiliation or Control: Unification Church IRS Status: 501(c)3
Highest Offering: Doctorate
Program: Liberal Arts And General; Professional; Religious Emphasis
Accreditation: #M

01 President .... Dr. Hugh SPURGIN
05 Vice President for Academic Affairs .... Dr. Kathy WININGS
11 VP for Administration .... Dr. Michael MICKLER
88 Director of Field Education .... Dr. Jacob DAVID
10 Acting Director of Finances .... Mr. Steven JARES
06 Registrar .... Mrs. Ute DELANEY
08 Library Director .... Vacant
37 Student Financial Aid Director .... Mr. Henry CHRISTOPHER
18 Plant Director .... Mr. Carl VERDERBER
07 Director of Admissions .... Mr. Henry CHRISTOPHER
26 Director of Communications .... Mr. Doug BURTON
30 Dir for Development & Alumni Rels .... Mr. Robin GRAHAM

Union College (K)

807 Union Street, Schenectady NY 12308-3181
County: Schenectady FICE Identification: 002889
Unit ID: 196866
Telephone: (518) 388-6000 Carnegie Class: Bac/A&S
FAX Number: (518) 388-6800 Calendar System: Trimester
URL: www.union.edu
Established: 1795 Annual Undergrad Tuition & Fees: $49,542

Enrollment: 2,202 Coed
Affiliation or Control: Independent Non-Profit IRS Status: 501(c)3
Highest Offering: Baccalaureate
Program: Liberal Arts And General; Professional
Accreditation: M, ENG

01 President .... Dr. Stephen C. AINLAY
05 Dean Faculty/VP Academic Affs .... Dr. Therese A. MCCARTY
30 Vice President College Relations .... Ms. Terri A. CERVENY
10 Vice President for Finance & Admin .... Ms. Diane T. BLAKE
07 Vice President of Admissions/FA .... Mr. Matthew J. MALATESTA
100 Chief of Staff .... Dr. Robert D. KELLY
32 Vice President of Student Affairs .... Dr. Stephen C. LEAVITT
88 Dean of Studies .... Dr. Mark E. WUNDERLICH
13 Chief Information Officer .... Ms. Ellen Y. BORKOWSKI
06 Registrar .... Ms. Penelope S. ADEY
30 Sr Director of Development .... Mr. Dominick F. FAMULARE
08 College Librarian .... Ms. Frances J. MALOY
26 Director of Media and Public Rels .... Mr. Phillip J. WAJDA
37 Director of Financial Aid .... Ms. Linda M. PARKER
38 Director of Student Counseling .... Mr. Marcus S. HOTALING
36 Director of Career Center .... Mr. Robert C. SOULES
15 Director of Human Resources .... Mr. Eric NOLL
41 Director of Athletics .... Mr. James MCLAUGHLIN
22 Sr Director Campus Diversity/AA .... Dr. Gretchel L. HATHAWAY
19 Director Campus Safety .... Mr. Christopher HAYEN
39 Director Residence Life .... Ms. Molly MACELROY

† Tuition figure is a comprehensive fees figure.

Union Graduate College (A)

80 Nott Terrace, Schenectady NY 12308-3131
County: Schenectady FICE Identification: 038813
Unit ID: 446932
Telephone: (518) 631-9900 Carnegie Class: Master's M
FAX Number: (518) 631-9901 Calendar System: Trimester
URL: www.uniongraduatecollege.edu
Established: 2003 Annual Graduate Tuition & Fees: $2,828
Enrollment: 431 Coed
Affiliation or Control: Independent Non-Profit IRS Status: 501(c)3
Highest Offering: Master's; No Undergraduates
Program: Professional; Business Emphasis
Accreditation: M, BUS, HSA, TEAC

01 President .... Dr. Laura SCHWEITZER
10 Vice President of Finance/Operation .... Joseph MCDONALD
84 VP Enrollment Mgmt/Student Svcs .... Joanne FITZGERALD
30 VP Institutional Advancement .... Vacant
06 Registrar/Director of Admissions .... Rhonda SHEEHAN
50 Dean School of Management .... Bela MUSIT
54 Dean School of Engineering .... Bob KOZIK
53 Interim Dean School of Education .... Dr. Lynn GELZHEISER
88 Director Center for Bioethics .... Dr. Sean PHILPOTT
07 Director Student Recruitment .... Erin WHEELER
36 Coordinator of Career Services .... Jane FLEURY
09 Director Institutional Research .... Amy NEVIN
13 Director of Information Technology .... Robert KEENAN
37 Director Financial Aid .... Nikki GALLUCCI
106 Dir Online Education/E-learning .... Phylise BANNER

Union Theological Seminary (B)

3041 Broadway, New York NY 10027-5792
County: New York FICE Identification: 002890
Unit ID: 196884
Telephone: (212) 662-7100 Carnegie Class: Spec/Faith
FAX Number: (212) 280-1416 Calendar System: Semester
URL: www.utsnyc.edu
Established: 1836 Annual Graduate Tuition & Fees: $21,890
Enrollment: 233 Coed
Affiliation or Control: Independent Non-Profit IRS Status: 501(c)3
Highest Offering: Doctorate; No Undergraduates
Program: Religious Emphasis
Accreditation: M, THEOL

01 President .... Dr. Serene JONES
03 Executive Vice President .... Mr. Fred DAVIE
10 VP Finance & Operations .... Mr. Richard A. MADONNA, JR.
30 VP for Development .... Mr. Martin DUUS
05 Dean of Academic Affairs .... Dr. Mary BOYS
32 Associate Dean Student Affairs .... Ms. Yvette WILSON
08 Director Library .... Ms. Beth BIDLACK
06 Registrar/Asst Dir Financial Aid .... Mr. Rafael ORTIZ
18 Deputy Vice Pres Building/Grounds .... Mr. Michael MALONEY
39 Director Housing/Campus Services . Mr. Michael ORZECHOWSKI
07 Assoc Dean Admissions/Financial Aid .... Ms. Nichelle JENKINS

United Talmudical Seminary (C)

191 Rodney Street, Brooklyn NY 11211-7900
County: Kings FICE Identification: 011189
Unit ID: 197018
Telephone: (718) 963-9770 Carnegie Class: Spec/Faith
FAX Number: (718) 963-9775 Calendar System: Semester
Established: 1949 Annual Undergrad Tuition & Fees: $13,535
Enrollment: 2,102 Male
Affiliation or Control: Independent Non-Profit IRS Status: 501(c)3
Highest Offering: Second Talmudic Degree
Program: Teacher Preparatory; Professional; Religious Emphasis
Accreditation: RABN

01 Dean .... Rabbi Zalman TEITLBAUM
05 Assoc Dean Scholastic Services .... Rabbi Yeruchem DEUTSCH
37 Financial Aid Administrator .... Mr. Bernard KATZ
10 Business Officer .... Mr. Shia GREENFELD

University of Rochester (D)

500 Joseph C. Wilson Boulevard, Rochester NY 14627
County: Monroe FICE Identification: 002894
Unit ID: 195030
Telephone: (585) 275-2121 Carnegie Class: RU/VH
FAX Number: (585) 275-0359 Calendar System: Semester
URL: www.rochester.edu
Established: 1850 Annual Undergrad Tuition & Fees: $48,290
Enrollment: 11,060 Coed
Affiliation or Control: Independent Non-Profit IRS Status: 501(c)3
Highest Offering: Doctorate
Program: Liberal Arts And General; Teacher Preparatory; Professional
Accreditation: M, BUS, CACREP, CLPSY, DENT, ENG, IPSY, MED, MFCD, MUS, NURSE, PAST, PDPSY, PH, TED

01 President and CEO .... Mr. Joel SELIGMAN
05 Provost and Dean of AS&E Faculty .... Mr. Peter LENNIE
10 Sr VP Administration & Fin/CFO .... Mr. Ronald J. PAPROCKI
03 VP/University Dean .... Mr. Paul J. BURGETT
17 Sr VP Health Sciences/Med Ctr CEO .... Dr. Mark B. TAUBMAN
45 Sr VP for Institutional Resources .... Mr. Douglas PHILLIPS
30 Sr VP and Chief Advanc Officer .... Mr. Thomas FARRELL
43 VP and General Counsel .... Ms. Gail NORRIS
46 Sr VP for Research .... Mr. Rob CLARK
26 VP for Communications .... Ms. Elizabeth STAUDERMAN
13 VP and CIO for the University .... Mr. David E. LEWIS
29 Vice President Alumni Relations .... Vacant
15 Assoc VP Human Resources .... Mr. Tony KINSLOW
58 Vice Provost/Univ Dean Grad Studies .... Ms. Margaret KEARNEY
100 General Sect/Pres Chief of Staff .... Mr. Lamar R. MURPHY
28 Vice Provost Fac Devel & Diversity .... Dr. Vivian LEWIS
08 Dean River Campus Libraries .... Ms. Mary Ann MAVRINAC
88 Vice President/Laser Lab Director .... Mr. Robert L. MCCRORY
49 Dean of School of Arts & Sciences .... Ms. Gloria CULVER
54 Dean of Hajim Engineering School .... Mr. Rob CLARK
84 Dean AS&E Undergrad Admis & Fin Aid .... Mr. Jonathan BURDICK
21 Assoc VP for Budgets & Planning .... Ms. Holly CRAWFORD
32 Dean of Students Arts/Sci & Engr .... Mr. Matthew BURNS
63 Dean of School of Medicine & Dent .... Dr. Mark B. TAUBMAN
64 Dean of Eastman School of Music .... Mr. Jamal ROSSI
66 Dean of School of Nursing .... Ms. Kathy RIDEOUT
50 Dean of Simon Business School .... Mr. Andrew AINSLIE
53 Dean Warner Grad Sch Educ & Hum Dev .... Ms. Raffaella BORASI
89 Dean of Freshmen Arts/Sci & Engr .... Ms. Marcy KRAUS
88 Dean of Sophmores Arts/Sci & Engr .... Mr. Sean HANNA
37 Assoc Dean Enroll & Fin Aid A/S&E .... Vacant
35 Assoc Dean Students Arts/Sci & Engr .... Ms. Anne-Marie ALGIER
23 Strong Health Chief Medical Officer .... Dr. Raymond MAYEWSKI
52 Dir Eastman Institute Oral Health .... Dr. Eli ELIAV
25 Assoc VP Research & Project Admin .... Ms. Gunta LIDERS
18 Assoc VP Facilities & Services .... Mr. Bruce BASHWINER
86 Executive Director Govt Relations .... Mr. Peter J. ROBINSON
96 Assoc VP Purchasing & Supply .... Mr. Carl TIETJEN
04 Executive Asst to the President .... Ms. Susan NIGGLI
06 Registrar .... Ms. Nancy SPECHT
19 Director of Public Safety .... Mr. Mark T. FISCHER
57 Director Memorial Art Gallery .... Mr. Jonathan BINSTOCK
41 Director of Athletics & Recreation .... Mr. George VANDERZWAAG
39 Dir Res Life & Housing Services .... Ms. Laurel CONTOMANOLIS
36 Exec Dir Career & Internship Center .... Mr. Joe TESTANI
101 Administrator to Board of Trustees .... Ms. Jackie E. KING
79 Dean Humanities & Interdisc Studies .... Vacant
42 Director Religious & Spiritual Life .... Rev. Denise YARBROUGH

USC The Business College (E)

201 Bleecker Street, Utica NY 13501-2200
County: Oneida FICE Identification: 009077
Unit ID: 197081
Telephone: (315) 733-2307 Carnegie Class: Assoc/PrivFP
FAX Number: (315) 733-9281 Calendar System: Semester
URL: www.uscny.edu
Established: 1896 Annual Undergrad Tuition & Fees: $13,500
Enrollment: 282 Coed
Affiliation or Control: Proprietary IRS Status: Proprietary
Highest Offering: Associate Degree
Program: Occupational; 2-Year Principally Bachelor's Creditable; Business Emphasis
Accreditation: NY

01 President & Treasurer .... Mr. Philip M. WILLIAMS
05 Exec Vice President for Academics .... Dr. Mark MONTGOMERY
32 Exec Vice Pres Student Affairs .... Mr. Scott K. WILLIAMS
11 Exec Vice President Administration .... Mr. John L. CROSSLEY
103 VP Corp/Workforce Develop .... Mr. Donald G. REESE
10 Vice President of Finance .... Mr. Richard H. HILTON
43 General Counsel .... Mr. John H. STORY, JR.
12 Director Canastota Branch .... Mrs. Wendy M. CARY
06 Registrar/Bursar .... Mrs. Marian J. NIELSON
30 Director of Development .... Mr. John CROSSLEY
08 Head Librarian .... Ms. Anne K. NASSAR
37 Financial Aid Consultant .... Mr. Fred P. ZUCALLA
12 Director Oneonta Campus .... Ms. Deborah E. HADDOW
07 Director of Admissions .... Mr. Tom VERDOW
13 Director Information Technology .... Mr. Joseph M. CHEVRETTE, II
36 Dir of Career Svc/Human Resources .... Ms. Emily TRACY
18 Facilities Manager Physical Plant .... Mr. Dave DUTCHER

U.T.A. Mesivta of Kiryas Joel (F)

PO Box 2009, Monroe NY 10949-8509
County: Orange FICE Identification: 038023
Unit ID: 446604
Telephone: (845) 783-9901 Carnegie Class: Spec/Faith
FAX Number: (845) 782-3620 Calendar System: Semester
Established: 1999 Annual Undergrad Tuition & Fees: $9,000
Enrollment: 1,615 Male
Affiliation or Control: Independent Non-Profit IRS Status: 501(c)3
Highest Offering: First Talmudic Degree
Program: Teacher Preparatory; Professional
Accreditation: RABN

01 President .... Elias HOROWITZ
05 Rosh Yeshiva .... Rabbi Aharon TEITELBAUM
37 Financial Aid Director .... David SCHWARTZ

Utica College (G)

1600 Burrstone Road, Utica NY 13502-4892
County: Oneida FICE Identification: 002883
Unit ID: 197045
Telephone: (315) 792-3111 Carnegie Class: Master's M
FAX Number: (315) 792-3292 Calendar System: Semester
URL: www.utica.edu
Established: 1946 Annual Undergrad Tuition & Fees: $34,466
Enrollment: 4,249 Coed
Affiliation or Control: Independent Non-Profit IRS Status: 501(c)3
Highest Offering: Doctorate
Program: Liberal Arts And General; Teacher Preparatory; Professional
Accreditation: M, CONST, NURSE, OT, PTA, TEAC

01 President .... Dr. Todd S. HUTTON
05 Provost & Vice Pres Academic Aff .... Dr. Judith A. KIRKPATRICK
10 Vice Pres Financial Affs/Treasurer .... Ms. Tammara RAUB
32 Vice Pres Student Affairs .... Mr. Jeffrey GATES
04 Executive Assistant to President .... Ms. Kim D. LAMBERT
30 Senior VP & Chief Advanc Officer .... Ms. Laura CASAMENTO
84 Vice President for Enrollment Mgmt .... Mr. Jeffrey GATES
20 Associate Provost .... Dr. Robert M. HALLIDAY
26 Asst VP Marketing/Communication .... Mr. Kelly L. ADAMS
76 Dean for Health Professions/Educ .... Dr. Harry SLIFE
49 Dean for Arts & Sciences .... Dr. John H. JOHNSEN
50 Dean for Business & Justice Studies .... Mr. James NORRIE
53 Dean for Education .... Dr. Patrice HALLOCK
35 Dean of Students .... Ms. Alane P. VARGA
21 Director of Student Acct Operation .... Ms. Gail TUTTLE
29 Director Alumni & Parent Relations .... Mr. Mark C. KOVACS
36 Director Career Services .... Ms. Halina LOTYCZEWSKI
37 Exec Dir of Student Financial Svcs .... Ms. Laura BEDFORD
06 Registrar .... Mr. Craig DEWAN
44 Director of Development .... Mr. Athony VILLANTI
41 Director of Physical Educ/Athletics .... Mr. David FONTAINE
39 Director of Residence Life .... Mr. Scott NONEMAKER
13 Dir College Info & Application Svcs .... Mr. Scott HUMPHREY
15 Director of Human Resources .... Ms. Lisa GREEN
24 Dir Computer User Svcs .... Mr. Daniel SLOAN
31 Exec Dir Corp/Professional Pgms .... Ms. Joni L. PULLIAM
51 Director of Credit Programs .... Ms. Evelyn FAZEKAS
85 Dean of International Education .... Dr. Dorothy LEWIS
18 Director Facilities Management .... Mr. Donald L. HARTER
19 Director of Campus Safety .... Mr. Wayne SULLIVAN
92 Director Honors Program .... Dr. Lawrence DAY
28 Dir Office of Opportunity Programs .... Ms. Johnni F. MAHDI
96 Manager of Purchasing .... Ms. Bobbie H. SMOROL
09 Director of Institutional Research .... Mr. Matthew S. CARR
101 Secretary of the Institution/Board .... Ms. Jacqueline LYNCH
108 Director Institutional Assessment .... Ms. Marie MIKNAVICH
38 Director Student Counseling .... Dr. Michelle MORROW
07 Asst VP UG Admissions .... Ms. Donna SHAFFNER

† Utica College maintains an academic tie with Syracuse University that allows undergraduates to receive a Syracuse University degree.

Vassar College (H)

124 Raymond Avenue, Poughkeepsie NY 12604-0001
County: Dutchess FICE Identification: 002895
Unit ID: 197133
Telephone: (845) 437-7000 Carnegie Class: Bac/A&S
FAX Number: (845) 437-7187 Calendar System: Semester
URL: www.vassar.edu
Established: 1861 Annual Undergrad Tuition & Fees: $51,300
Enrollment: 2,386 Coed
Affiliation or Control: Independent Non-Profit IRS Status: 501(c)3
Highest Offering: Master's
Program: Liberal Arts And General
Accreditation: M, TEAC

01 President .... Dr. Catharine B. HILL
05 Dean of the Faculty .... Dr. Jonathan CHENETTE
20 Dean of the College .... Dr. Christopher ROELLKE
10 Vice President for Finance & Admin .... Mr. Robert WALTON
30 VP Alumnae/i Affairs/Development .... Ms. Catherine E. BAER
26 Vice Pres for Communications .... Ms. Susan DEKREY
13 Chief Information Officer .... Mr. Michael CATO
32 Dean of Students .... Dr. David H. BROWN
07 Dean Admission/Financial Aid .... Mr. Art D. RODRIGUEZ
49 Dean of Studies .... Dr. Benjamin LOTTO
20 Associate Dean College .... Mr. Edward L. PITTMAN
35 Assoc Dean Col/Dir Campus Activit .... Ms. Teresa QUINN

06 Registrar ... Ms. Colleen MALLET
08 Director of the Libraries ... Mr. Andrew ASHTON
37 Director of Financial Aid ... Ms. Jessica BERNIER
36 Director Career Development Center ... Ms. Stacy Lee SCHNEIDER BINGHAM
87 Director Conferences/Summer Pgms ... Ms. Katherine BUSH
39 Director Residential Life ... Mr. Luis INOA
09 Director of Institutional Research ... Mr. David DAVIS-VAN ATTA
15 Director Human Resources ... Ms. Ruth SPENCER
18 Exec Dir Buildings & Grounds ... Mr. Thomas ALLEN
38 Director of Psychological Services ... Dr. Wendy A. FREEDMAN
96 Director of Purchasing ... Ms. Rosaleen CARDILLO

Vaughn College of Aeronautics and Technology (A)

86-01 23rd Avenue, Flushing NY 11369
County: Queens FICE Identification: 002665
Unit ID: 188340
Telephone: (718) 429-6600 Carnegie Class: Bac/Assoc
FAX Number: (718) 429-0256 Calendar System: Semester
URL: www.vaughn.edu
Established: 1932 Annual Undergrad Tuition & Fees: $22,680
Enrollment: 1,614 Coed
Affiliation or Control: Independent Non-Profit IRS Status: 501(c)3
Highest Offering: Master's
Program: 2-Year Principally Bachelor's Creditable; Liberal Arts And General; Professional
Accreditation: M, ENG, ENGT, IACBE

01 President ... Dr. Sharon B. DEVIVO
05 Sr Vice Pres Academic/Student Affs ... Vacant
10 Vice Pres for Business & Finance ... Mr. Robert G. WALDMANN
84 Vice President Enrollment Services ... Mr. Ernie SHEPELSKY
11 Asst VP College Services/Human Res ... Ms. Mary DURKIN
20 Vice Pres of Academic Affairs ... Dr. Paul LAVERGNE
32 VP Student Affairs & Svcs ... Mr. Said LAMHAOUAR
35 Assoc VP/Dean Student Affairs ... Ms. Jerima DEWESE
88 VP Inst Rels/New Initiatives ... Mr. Vincent PAPANDREA
37 Director of Financial Aid ... Ms. Dorothy MARTIN
06 Registrar/Assoc VP Enrollment ... Mrs. Beatriz CRUZ
08 Librarian ... Ms. Joann JAYNE
102 Asst VP of Planning/Assessments ... Ms. Kalli KOUTSOUTIS
26 Director of Public Affairs ... Ms. Maureen KIGGINS
96 Coordinator of Purchasing ... Mr. Ernie MARSHALL
09 Asst Director of Inst Effectiveness ... Mr. Tipton RUSSELL
07 Acting Director of Admissions ... Mr. David SOOKDEO
18 Associate VP/College Services ... Mr. Michael DALY
38 Dir Student Counseling/Wellness ... Dr. Dinelly HOLDER
13 Asst Director Computer Operations ... Mr. Hamwant (Neil) SINGH
88 Vice Pres Training ... Mr. Domenic PROSCIA

Villa Maria College of Buffalo (B)

240 Pine Ridge Road, Buffalo NY 14225-3999
County: Erie FICE Identification: 002896
Unit ID: 197142
Telephone: (716) 896-0700 Carnegie Class: Assoc/PrivNFP4
FAX Number: (716) 896-0705 Calendar System: Semester
URL: www.villa.edu
Established: 1960 Annual Undergrad Tuition & Fees: $19,910
Enrollment: 477 Coed
Affiliation or Control: Independent Non-Profit IRS Status: 501(c)3
Highest Offering: Baccalaureate
Program: Liberal Arts And General; Fine Arts Emphasis
Accreditation: M, CIDA, MUS, PTAA

01 President ... Sr. Marcella Marie GARUS
05 Vice President for Academic Affairs ... Dr. Matthew GIORDANO
10 Vice President for Business Affairs ... Mr. Michael EADIE
30 Vice President for Development ... Mr. Thomas HONAN
32 VP for Enroll Mgmt & Student Svcs ... Mr. Brian EMERSON
06 Registrar ... Ms. Melany SHIELDS
07 Director of Admissions ... Mr. Kevin DONOVAN
08 Director of Library ... Ms. Lucy BUNGO
37 Director of Financial Aid ... Ms. Aimee MURCH
09 Director of Institutional Research ... Sr. Mary Albertine STACHOWSKI
38 Director Student Counseling ... Ms. Palma M. ZANGHI
13 Director of Computer Services ... Ms. Christine E. PALCZEWSKI
88 Systems Analyst ... Ms. Francis MONTGOMERY
18 Plant & Grounds Manager ... Mr. David WISNER
23 Director of Health Services ... Mrs. Minerva MONTIJO
25 Director of Grants ... Mrs. Mary ROBINSON
88 Instructional Design & Program Dev ... Dr. Ryan HARTNETT
36 Director of Career Services ... Ms. Blythe KACZMARCZYK
42 Director of Campus Ministry ... Ms. Joan MULLIN
85 Director of Foreign Students ... Ms. Palma ZANGHI
26 Coordinator of Communications ... Mr. Joseph DIDOMIZIO
35 Director of Student Life ... Vacant
88 Archivist ... Sr. Mary Mark JANIK
22 Affirmative Action Officer ... Ms. Diane M. HANDZLIK
29 Director of Alumni Relations ... Vacant
88 Director Student Success Center ... Ms. Agnes ZAK-MOSKAL
57 Art Department Chair ... Mr. Robert GRIZANTI
64 Music Department Chair ... Dr. Sylvia GRMELA
49 LiberalArts/Prof Studies Chair ... Ms. Joyce KESSEL
108 Director Institutional Assessment ... Dr. Janice HERCHMER
04 Administrative Asst to President ... Mrs. Kathy IVES
103 Dir Workforce/Career Development ... Dr. Ryan HARTNETT
41 Athletic Director ... Mr. Don SILVERI

Wagner College (C)

1 Campus Road, Staten Island NY 10301-4479
County: Richmond FICE Identification: 002899
Unit ID: 197197
Telephone: (718) 390-3100 Carnegie Class: Master's M
FAX Number: (718) 390-3467 Calendar System: Semester
URL: www.wagner.edu
Established: 1883 Annual Undergrad Tuition & Fees: $42,030
Enrollment: 1,808 Coed
Affiliation or Control: Independent Non-Profit IRS Status: 501(c)3
Highest Offering: Master's
Program: Liberal Arts And General; Teacher Preparatory; Professional
Accreditation: M, ACBSP, ARCPA, NUR, TED

01 President ... Dr. Richard GUARASCI
05 Provost/SVP Academic Affairs ... Dr. Lily D. MCNAIR
84 SVP for Enrollment ... Mr. Angelo G. ARAIMO
30 VP Instititutional Advancement ... Vacant
26 VP Administration ... Vacant
04 Assistant to the President ... Ms. Pat FITZPATRICK
32 VP and Dean of Campus Life ... Ms. Ruta SHAH-GORDON
10 CFO and VP for Finance & Business ... Mr. John CARRESCIA
108 Associate Provost for Assessment ... Dr. Anne LOVE
20 Vice Provost ... Dr. Jeffrey KRAUS
06 Interim Registrar ... Ms. Ann AYERS
13 Chief Information Officer ... Mr. Frank CAFASSO
42 Chaplain ... Rev. Martin MALZAHN
29 Director Alumni Relations ... Mr. Christopher FOURMAN
39 Director Housing ... Vacant
30 Director of Development ... Mr. Patrick MINSON
18 Director of Campus Operations ... Mr. Christian MILLER
41 Director of Athletics ... Mr. Walter HAMELINE
23 Assistant Dean Health & Wellness ... Ms. Kathleen OBERFELDT
19 Director of Public Safety ... Mr. Edwin MOSS
15 Director of Human Resources ... Vacant
37 Director of Financial Aid ... Ms. Theresa WEIMER
58 Coordinator of Graduate Studies ... Dr. Jeffrey KRAUS
07 Dean of Enrollment ... Mr. Robert HERR
88 Asst Dean of Enrollment ... Ms. Patricia CLANCY
35 Dean of Campus Life and Leadership ... Mr. Curtis WRIGHT
35 Dean of Campus Life and Engagement ... Dr. Sara KLEIN
36 Senior Assoc Dean & Director CACE ... Mr. Geoffrey HEMPILL
08 Head Librarian ... Ms. Dorothy DAVISON
100 Chief of Staff ... Vacant

Webb Institute (D)

298 Crescent Beach Road, Glen Cove NY 11542-1398
County: Nassau FICE Identification: 002900
Unit ID: 197221
Telephone: (516) 671-2213 Carnegie Class: Spec/Engg
FAX Number: (516) 674-9838 Calendar System: Semester
URL: www.webb.edu
Established: 1889 Annual Undergrad Tuition & Fees: $45,500
Enrollment: 89 Coed
Affiliation or Control: Independent Non-Profit IRS Status: 501(c)3
Highest Offering: Baccalaureate
Program: Professional; Technical Emphasis
Accreditation: M, ENG

01 President ... Mr. R. Keith MICHEL
05 Dean ... Prof. Matthew R. WERNER
20 Assistant Dean ... Prof. Richard C. HARRIS
08 Librarian ... Ms. Patricia M. PRESCOTT
30 Chief Development ... Mr. Anthony ZIC
10 Director of Financial Affairs ... Ms. Rhonda LIGHTCAP
09 Director of Institutional Research ... Prof. Richard A. ROYCE
32 Director of Student Affairs ... Ms. Katie BECKER
18 Director of Facilities ... Mr. John FERRANTE
84 Director of Enrollment Management ... Mr. William G. MURRAY
29 Director of Alumni Relations ... Ms. Gailmarie SUJECKI
26 Chief Public Relations Officer ... Ms. Kerri ALLEGRETTA
13 Director of Communications and IT ... Mr. Peter MILLER
06 Registrar ... Ms. Jocelyn M. WILSON
37 Director of Financial Aid ... Ms. Lauri D'AMBRA
04 Administrative Asst to President ... Ms. Gailmarie SUJECKI
15 Director Personnel Services ... Ms. Svetlana MILLER
07 Asst Dir Student Svcs/Admissions ... Ms. Katie BECKER

Weill Cornell Medical College (E)

1300 York Avenue, F-113, New York NY 10065-4805
Telephone: (212) 746-5900 FICE Identification: 004762
Accreditation: &M, ARCPA, DENT, IPSY, MED

† Regional accreditation is carried under the parent institution Cornell University, Ithaca, NY.

Wells College (F)

170 Main Street, Aurora NY 13026-0500
County: Cayuga FICE Identification: 002901
Unit ID: 197230
Telephone: (315) 364-3266 Carnegie Class: Bac/A&S
FAX Number: (315) 364-3227 Calendar System: Semester
URL: www.wells.edu
Established: 1868 Annual Undergrad Tuition & Fees: $37,500
Enrollment: 550 Coed
Affiliation or Control: Independent Non-Profit IRS Status: 501(c)3
Highest Offering: Baccalaureate
Program: Liberal Arts And General; Teacher Preparatory
Accreditation: M, TEAC

01 President ... Dr. Jonathan GIBRALTER
05 Provost and Dean of the College ... Dr. Cindy SPEAKER
11 Chief Operating Officer ... Mr. Terry NEWCOMB
10 Treasurer and Controller ... Ms. Melody PONZI
30 Vice President for Advancement ... Mr. Michael MCGREEVEY
32 Dean of Students ... Ms. Jennifer MICHAEL
07 Dir of Admissions/Financial Aid ... Ms. Susan SLOAN
06 Registrar ... Dr. Andre SIAMUNDELE
08 Library Director ... Vacant
37 Director Financial Aid ... Ms. Laura BURNS
44 Director of Annual Giving ... Ms. Pamela SHERADIN
26 Dir of Communications/Marketing ... Ms. Ann ROLLO
29 Director Alumni Relations ... Ms. Pamela SHERADIN
19 Director of Security ... Mr. Dennis FAIRCHILD
18 Dir of Facilities/Physical Plant ... Mr. Brian BROWN
15 Manager of Human Resources ... Ms. Kit VAN ORMAN

Westchester Community College (G)

75 Grasslands Road, Valhalla NY 10595-1636
County: Westchester FICE Identification: 002881
Unit ID: 197294
Telephone: (914) 606-6600 Carnegie Class: Assoc/Pub-S-SC
FAX Number: (914) 606-6780 Calendar System: Semester
URL: www.sunywcc.edu
Established: 1946 Annual Undergrad Tuition & Fees (In-District): $4,722
Enrollment: 13,916 Coed
Affiliation or Control: State/Local IRS Status: 501(c)3
Highest Offering: Associate Degree
Program: Occupational; 2-Year Principally Bachelor's Creditable
Accreditation: M, COARC, DIETT, RAD

01 President ... Dr. Belinda S. MILES
05 Acting VP Academic Affairs ... Dr. Peggy BRADFORD
32 Act VP Stdnt Access/Involve/Success ... Mr. Adam FRANK
10 Vice Pres Administrative Services ... Mr. Pat D'IMPERIO
102 VP Ext Affs/Exec Dir Found for WCC ... Mrs. Eve LARNER
51 VP & Dean Community/Adult/Cont Educ ... Ms. Teresita WISELL
81 Assoc Dean Math/Phys Engr/Tech ... Dr. Ted NYGREEN
76 Assoc Dean Natural/Health Sciences ... Mr. Michael OLIVETTE
83 Assoc Dean Bus/Behav/Soc Sci Svcs ... Mr. Jeffrey A. CONTE
79 Assoc Dean Arts/Humanities/Lrng Res .. Ms. Veronica DELCOURT
22 Associate Dean & Director of EOC ... Ms. Gina GAINES
35 Assoc Dean Student Personnel Svcs ... Ms. Ellen ZENDMAN
08 Asc Dn Lrng Res/Dist Lrng/Inst Tech ... Ms. Pamela POLLARD
26 Director of College/Cmty Relations ... Mr. Patrick HENNESSEY
06 Registrar ... Mr. John CAPOCCI
37 Dir of Student Financial Assistance ... Ms. Anita COOK
13 Vice President of IT ... Mr. Anthony SCORDINO
07 Director of Admissions ... Ms. Gloria LEON
38 Acting Director of Counseling ... Mr. Ruben BARATO
15 Director Human Resources ... Ms. Sabrina J. CHANDLER
88 Director Faculty Student Assoc ... Mr. David SKLAR
09 Director Inst Research & Planning ... Ms. Nancy M. DERIGGI
19 Director of Security ... Mr. Brian P. DOLANSKY
24 Director Media Services ... Mr. Gennaro MASELLI
41 Athletic Director ... Mr. Larry MASSARONI
21 Assoc Business Officer/Controller ... Ms. Dawn GILLIS
18 Director Physical Plant ... Mr. Robert CIRILLO
96 Deputy Purchasing Agent ... Mr. Richard CASHMAN
27 Publications Manager ... Mr. Craig FISCHER
23 Coordinator Student Health Services ... Ms. Janice GILROY
75 Coord of Transfer & Career Service ... Dr. Gwen D. ROUNDTREE
04 Administrative Asst to President ... Ms. Yolanda M. HOWELL
101 Secretary of the Institution/Board ... Ms. Yolanda M. HOWELL

Wood Tobé-Coburn School (H)

Eight E 40th Street, New York NY 10016
County: New York FICE Identification: 007405
Unit ID: 197522
Telephone: (212) 686-9040 Carnegie Class: Assoc/PrivFP
FAX Number: (212) 686-9171 Calendar System: Semester
URL: www.woodtobecoburn.edu
Established: 1879 Annual Undergrad Tuition & Fees: $16,860
Enrollment: 428 Coed
Affiliation or Control: Proprietary IRS Status: Proprietary
Highest Offering: Associate Degree
Program: Occupational; 2-Year Principally Bachelor's Creditable
Accreditation: NY, MAC

01 President ... Ms. Sandra GRUNINGER
05 Director of Education ... Ms. Carlene BLAKE-HUDSON
07 Director of Admissions ... Ms. Sandra ANDUJAR-WENDLAND
32 Student Services Director ... Ms. Celeste GRIFFITH
37 Financial Aid Administrator ... Ms. Celeste GRIFFITH
36 Placement Director ... Ms. Rhonda DOUGLAS CHARLES

Yeshiva Derech Chaim (I)

1573 39th Street, Brooklyn NY 11218-4413
County: Kings FICE Identification: 022651
Unit ID: 197647
Telephone: (718) 438-5476 Carnegie Class: Spec/Faith
FAX Number: (718) 435-9285 Calendar System: Semester
Established: 1975 Annual Undergrad Tuition & Fees: $11,300
Enrollment: 156 Male
Affiliation or Control: Independent Non-Profit IRS Status: 501(c)3
Highest Offering: Second Talmudic Degree
Program: Professional; Religious Emphasis

Accreditation: RABN

01 President .... Rabbi Chaim RENNERT
01 President .... Rabbi Yisroel PLUTCHOK

Yeshiva D'Monsey Rabbinical College (A)

2 Roman Boulevard, Monsey NY 10952-3106
County: Rockland　FICE Identification: 031473
Unit ID: 420325
Telephone: (845) 426-3276　Carnegie Class: Spec/Faith
FAX Number: (845) 352-1119　Calendar System: Semester
Established: 1984　Annual Undergrad Tuition & Fees: $5,900
Enrollment: 53　Male
Affiliation or Control: Independent Non-Profit　IRS Status: 501(c)3
Highest Offering: Second Talmudic Degree
Program: Teacher Preparatory; Professional
Accreditation: RABN

01 Rosh Yeshiva .... Rabbi Moishe GREEN
05 Rosh Yeshiva .... Rabbi Ruvain GREEN
37 Financial Aid Director .... Rabbi Aron BERGER

Yeshiva of Far Rockaway (B)

802 Hicksville Road, Far Rockaway NY 11691-5219
County: Queens　FICE Identification: 041196
Unit ID: 190752
Telephone: (718) 327-7600　Carnegie Class: Not Classified
FAX Number: (718) 327-1430　Calendar System: Semester
Established: 1969　Annual Undergrad Tuition & Fees: $10,500
Enrollment: 40　Male
Affiliation or Control: Independent Non-Profit　IRS Status: 501(c)3
Highest Offering: First Talmudic Degree
Program: Professional; Religious Emphasis
Accreditation: RABN

01 President .... Rabbi Yechiel I. PERR
03 Executive Director .... Rabbi Shayeh KOHN
32 Dean of Students .... Rabbi Dovid KLEINKAUFMAN
06 Registrar .... Mrs. Tamara MASLOW

Yeshiva Gedolah Imrei Yosef D'Spinka (C)

1466 56th Street, Brooklyn NY 11219-4696
County: Kings　FICE Identification: 030001
Unit ID: 375230
Telephone: (718) 851-8721　Carnegie Class: Spec/Faith
FAX Number: (718) 686-8849　Calendar System: Semester
Established: 1987　Annual Undergrad Tuition & Fees: $8,000
Enrollment: 122　Male
Affiliation or Control: Independent Non-Profit　IRS Status: 501(c)3
Highest Offering: First Talmudic Degree
Program: Teacher Preparatory; Religious Emphasis
Accreditation: @RABN

01 President .... Mordechai MAJEROWITZ

Yeshiva Gedolah Kesser Torah (D)

28 Cedar Lane, Monsey NY 10952
County: Rockland　Identification: 667112
Unit ID: 481410
Telephone: (845) 406-4308　Carnegie Class: Not Classified
FAX Number: (845) 406-4199　Calendar System: Semester
Established: 2004　Annual Undergrad Tuition & Fees: $9,300
Enrollment: 67　Male
Affiliation or Control: Independent Non-Profit　IRS Status: 501(c)3
Highest Offering: First Talmudic Degree
Program: Teacher Preparatory; Professional
Accreditation: RABN

00 CEO .... Rabbi David FISHMAN
01 President .... David BERNSTEIN

Yeshiva Gedolah Ohr Yisrael (E)

2899 Nostrand Avenue, Brooklyn NY 11229
County: Kings　Identification: 667077
Telephone: (718) 382-8702　Carnegie Class: Not Classified
FAX Number: (718) 382-8703　Calendar System: Semester
Established: 1999　Annual Undergrad Tuition & Fees: $6,750
Enrollment: 44　Male
Affiliation or Control: Independent Non-Profit　IRS Status: 501(c)3
Highest Offering: First Talmudic Degree
Program: Professional
Accreditation: RABN

01 Rosh Yeshiva .... Avraham ZUCKER
10 Treasurer .... Avi KAHN

Yeshiva Karlin Stolin Beth Aaron V'Israel Rabbinical Institute (F)

1818 54th Street, Brooklyn NY 11204-1545
County: Kings　FICE Identification: 025058
Unit ID: 197601
Telephone: (718) 232-7800　Carnegie Class: Spec/Faith
FAX Number: (718) 331-4833　Calendar System: Semester
Established: 1948　Annual Undergrad Tuition & Fees: $9,650
Enrollment: 125　Male
Affiliation or Control: Independent Non-Profit　IRS Status: 501(c)3
Highest Offering: Second Talmudic Degree
Program: Teacher Preparatory; Professional
Accreditation: RABN

01 Chief Executive Officer .... Rabbi Yochanan PILCHICK
05 Dean Theology/Chief Acad Officer .... Rabbi Chaim WOLPIN
06 Registrar .... Rabbi Aryeh WOLPIN
08 Librarian .... Rabbi Yochanan GOLDHABER
10 Fiscal Officer .... Rabbi Irving PERRES
37 Financial Aid Director .... Rabbi Tovia PILCHICK
33 Dean of Men .... Rabbi Gedelyah MACHLIS

Yeshiva and Kolel Bais Medrash Elyon (G)

73 Main Street, Monsey NY 10952-3013
County: Rockland　Identification: 666707
Unit ID: 245777
Telephone: (845) 356-7064　Carnegie Class: Spec/Faith
FAX Number: (845) 356-7065　Calendar System: Semester
Established: 1945　Annual Undergrad Tuition & Fees: $11,200
Enrollment: 116　Male
Affiliation or Control: Independent Non-Profit　IRS Status: 501(c)3
Highest Offering: Second Talmudic Degree
Program: Professional
Accreditation: @RABN

01 President .... Rabbi Yerachmiel CENSOR
05 Dean .... Rabbi Israel FALK

Yeshiva and Kollel Harbotzas Torah (H)

1049 E 15th Street, Brooklyn NY 11230-4462
County: Kings　FICE Identification: 023506
Unit ID: 245731
Telephone: (718) 692-0208　Carnegie Class: Spec/Faith
FAX Number: (718) 692-0363　Calendar System: Semester
Established: 1969　Annual Undergrad Tuition & Fees: $7,500
Enrollment: 53　Male
Affiliation or Control: Independent Non-Profit　IRS Status: 501(c)3
Highest Offering: Second Talmudic Degree
Program: Professional
Accreditation: @RABN

01 President .... Rabbi Y. BITTERSFELD

Yeshiva of Machzikai Hadas (I)

1301 47th Street, Brooklyn NY 11219
County: Kings　FICE Identification: 041381
Unit ID: 455257
Telephone: (718) 853-2442　Carnegie Class: Spec/Faith
FAX Number: (718) 853-2504　Calendar System: Semester
Established: 2001　Annual Undergrad Tuition & Fees: $7,800
Enrollment: 373　Male
Affiliation or Control: Independent Non-Profit　IRS Status: 501(c)3
Highest Offering: First Talmudic Degree
Program: Professional
Accreditation: RABN

01 Rosh Yeshiva .... Rabbi Yidel MONHEIT

Yeshiva Mikdash Melech (J)

1326 Ocean Parkway, Brooklyn NY 11230-5655
County: Kings　FICE Identification: 025068
Unit ID: 197610
Telephone: (718) 339-1090　Carnegie Class: Spec/Faith
FAX Number: (718) 998-9321　Calendar System: Semester
Established: 1972　Annual Undergrad Tuition & Fees: $8,100
Enrollment: 32　Male
Affiliation or Control: Independent Non-Profit　IRS Status: 501(c)3
Highest Offering: Second Talmudic Degree
Program: Teacher Preparatory; Professional; Religious Emphasis
Accreditation: RABN

01 Dean .... Rabbi Haim BENOLIEL
05 Dean of Faculty .... Rabbi David LOPIAN
06 Registrar .... Rabbi Josh SANANES
10 Chief Business Officer .... Rabbi Amram SANANES
11 Administrator .... Rabbi Abraham BENOLIEL

Yeshiva of Nitra Rabbinical College (K)

194 Division Avenue, Brooklyn NY 11211-7199
County: Kings　FICE Identification: 011670
Unit ID: 197674
Telephone: (718) 387-0422　Carnegie Class: Spec/Faith
FAX Number: (718) 387-9400　Calendar System: Semester
Established: 1946　Annual Undergrad Tuition & Fees: $8,200
Enrollment: 243　Male
Affiliation or Control: Independent Non-Profit　IRS Status: 501(c)3
Highest Offering: Second Talmudic Degree
Program: Professional
Accreditation: RABN

01 President .... Mr. Alfred SCHOENBERGER
03 Vice President .... Mr. Mendel KLEIN
05 Dean .... Rabbi Samuel D. UNGAR
11 Administrative Officer .... Mr. Ernest SCHWARTZ

Yeshiva Shaar HaTorah-Grodno (L)

83-96 117th Street, Kew Gardens NY 11415
County: Queens　FICE Identification: 021520
Unit ID: 197692
Telephone: (718) 846-1940　Carnegie Class: Spec/Faith
FAX Number: (718) 850-7916　Calendar System: Semester
Established: 1976　Annual Undergrad Tuition & Fees: $16,850
Enrollment: 56　Male
Affiliation or Control: Independent Non-Profit　IRS Status: 501(c)3
Highest Offering: Second Talmudic Degree
Program: Professional
Accreditation: RABN

01 Administrator .... Rabbi Yoel YANKELEWITZ

Yeshiva Shaarei Torah of Rockland (M)

91 W Carlton Road, Suffern NY 10901-4013
County: Rockland　FICE Identification: 034963
Unit ID: 441609
Telephone: (845) 352-3431　Carnegie Class: Spec/Faith
FAX Number: (845) 352-3433　Calendar System: Semester
Established: 1977　Annual Undergrad Tuition & Fees: $11,500
Enrollment: 98　Male
Affiliation or Control: Independent Non-Profit　IRS Status: 501(c)3
Highest Offering: First Talmudic Degree
Program: Professional; Religious Emphasis
Accreditation: RABN

01 President .... Rabbi Eli ABRAHAM
30 Chief Devel Officer/Financial Aid .... Mrs. Teri SCHILLER
06 Registrar .... Mr. Menachem FROMELL

Yeshiva Sholom Shachna (N)

401 Elmwood Avenue, Brooklyn NY 11230
County: Kings　Identification: 667147
Telephone: (718) 252-6333　Carnegie Class: Not Classified
FAX Number: (718) 338-2536　Calendar System: Semester
Established: 2005　Annual Undergrad Tuition & Fees: $9,400
Enrollment: 69　Male
Affiliation or Control: Independent Non-Profit　IRS Status: 501(c)3
Highest Offering: First Talmudic Degree
Program: Teacher Preparatory; Professional
Accreditation: @RABN

01 Chief Executive Officer .... Rabbi Meir Chaim GUTFREUND
10 Chief Financial/Business Officer .... Mrs. Dina GUTFREUND
05 Chief Academic Officer/Registrar .... Rabbi Simcha OLEN
37 Director Student Financial Aid .... Mrs. Yehudis KIRZNER

Yeshiva of the Telshe Alumni (O)

4904 Independence Avenue, Riverdale NY 10471
County: Bronx　FICE Identification: 025463
Unit ID: 431983
Telephone: (718) 601-3523　Carnegie Class: Spec/Faith
FAX Number: (718) 601-2141　Calendar System: Semester
Established: 1981　Annual Undergrad Tuition & Fees: $9,100
Enrollment: 116　Male
Affiliation or Control: Independent Non-Profit　IRS Status: 501(c)3
Highest Offering: First Talmudic Degree
Program: Teacher Preparatory; Professional
Accreditation: RABN

01 President .... Rabbi Avrohom AUSBAND
03 Executive Director .... Rabbi Noson JOSEPH
29 Director Alumni Relations .... Rabbi Moshe FERBER

Yeshiva University (P)

500 W 185th Street, New York NY 10033-3201
County: New York　FICE Identification: 002903
Unit ID: 197708
Telephone: (212) 960-5400　Carnegie Class: RU/VH
FAX Number: (212) 960-0055　Calendar System: Semester
URL: www.yu.edu
Established: 1886　Annual Undergrad Tuition & Fees: $39,530
Enrollment: 6,348　Coordinate
Affiliation or Control: Independent Non-Profit　IRS Status: 501(c)3
Highest Offering: Doctorate
Program: Liberal Arts And General; Professional
Accreditation: M, BUS, CLPSY, DENT, IPSY, LAW, MED, PSPSY, SW, TEAC

01 President .... Mr. Richard M. JOEL
05 Provost/Sr VP Academic Affairs .... Dr. Selma BOTMAN
100 Sr Vice Pres/Chief of Staff .... Mr. Josh JOSEPH
17 Vice President Medical Affairs .... Dr. Allen M. SPIEGEL
10 Vice Pres/Chief Financial Officer .... Mr. Jacob HARMAN
30 Vice Pres Institutional Advancement .... Mr. Seth MOSKOWITZ
11 Vice President University Affairs .... Dr. Herbert C. DOBRINSKY

13 VP Information Technology/CIO ... Mr. Marc MILSTEIN
43 VP Legal Affs/Secretary/Gen Counsel ... Mr. Andrew J. LAUER
32 Vice Pres Univ & Cmty Life ... Rabbi Kenneth BRANDER
26 Exec Dir Communications/Public Affs ... Dr. Paul OESTREICHER
18 Vice Pres Administrative Services ... Mr. Jeffrey ROSENGARTEN
04 Exec Assistant to President ... Ms. Linda DOS SANTOS
08 Dean of University Libraries ... Mrs. Pearl BERGER
35 Dean of Students ... Mr. David HIMBER
49 Dean Yeshiva College ... Dr. Barry EICHLER
49 Dn Undergrad Jewish Stds/Mazer Sch ... Rabbi Yona REISS
49 Dean Stern College for Women ... Dr. Karen BACON
50 Dean Sy Syms School of Business ... Dr. Moses PAVA
63 Dean Albert Einstein Col Medicine ... Dr. Allen M. SPIEGEL
58 Dean Ferkauf Graduate School Psych ... Dr. Lawrence J. SIEGEL
58 Dean Bernard Revel Graduate School ... Dr. David BERGER
58 Dean Azrieli Graduate Sch Jewish Ed ... Dr. David J. SCHNALL
70 Dean Wurzweiler School Social Work ... Dr. Carmen ORTIZ HENDRICKS
58 Director Sue Golding Grad Program ... Dr. Victoria FREEDMAN
84 Director Enrollment Management ... Ms. Diana BENMERGUI
37 Director of Student Finances ... Mr. Robert FRIEDMAN
07 Director Undergraduate Admissions ... Mr. Michael KRANZLER
29 Director University Alumni Affairs ... Ms. Barbara BIRCH
06 University Registrar ... Ms. Diana CHADI
09 Director of Institutional Research ... Dr. Ariel FISHMAN
96 Director of Purchasing ... Mr. Jack ZENCHECK
15 Chief Human Resources Officer ... Ms. Yvonne RAMIREZ
38 Director Student Counseling ... Dr. Chaim NISSEL

Yeshiva Zichron Aryeh (A)

1213 Bay 25th Street, Far Rockaway NY 11691
County: Queens Identification: 667110
Telephone: (516) 295-5700 Carnegie Class: Not Classified
FAX Number: (516) 295-5737 Calendar System: Semester
Established: 1992 Annual Undergrad Tuition & Fees: $8,250
Enrollment: 33 Male
Affiliation or Control: Independent Non-Profit IRS Status: 501(c)3
Highest Offering: Second Talmudic Degree
Program: Teacher Preparatory; Religious Emphasis
Accreditation: RABN

03 Executive Vice President ... Rabbi Shaya COHEN
06 Registrar ... Rabbi Yosef AMSTER
07 Dir of Admiss/Financial Aid Admin ... Rabbi Avraham BURGER
10 Controller ... Mr. Shmuel BURGER
18 Chief Facilities ... Mr. Danny SCHUSTER

Yeshivas Maharit Dsatmar (B)

475 County Rt. 105, Monroe NY 10950
County: Orange Identification: 667204
Telephone: (845) 782-1380 Carnegie Class: Not Classified
FAX Number: (845) 782-5169 Calendar System: Semester
Established: 2011 Annual Undergrad Tuition & Fees: $10,500
Enrollment: 102 Male
Affiliation or Control: Independent Non-Profit IRS Status: 501(c)3
Highest Offering: First Talmudic Degree
Program: Teacher Preparatory
Accreditation: RABN

01 CEO ... Abraham LIEBERMAN
06 Registrar ... Moses SCHWARTZ
37 Director of Financial Aid ... Joel BRAVER
21 Associate Business Officer ... Moses JACOBOWITZ

Yeshivas Novominsk (C)

1690 60th Street, Brooklyn NY 11204-2138
County: Kings FICE Identification: 031271
Unit ID: 405058
Telephone: (718) 438-2727 Carnegie Class: Spec/Faith
FAX Number: (718) 438-2472 Calendar System: Semester
Established: 1988 Annual Undergrad Tuition & Fees: $14,400
Enrollment: 129 Male
Affiliation or Control: Independent Non-Profit IRS Status: 501(c)3
Highest Offering: First Talmudic Degree
Program: Teacher Preparatory; Professional; Religious Emphasis
Accreditation: RABN

01 Administrative Director ... Rabbi Lipa BRENNAN
32 Dean of Students ... Rabbi Yaakov PERLOW
11 Administrator ... Rabbi Boruch TWERSKI

Yeshivath Viznitz (D)

PO Box 446, Monsey NY 10952-0446
County: Rockland FICE Identification: 013027
Unit ID: 197735
Telephone: (845) 731-3700 Carnegie Class: Spec/Faith
FAX Number: (845) 356-7359 Calendar System: Semester
Established: 1946 Annual Undergrad Tuition & Fees: $8,600
Enrollment: 642 Male
Affiliation or Control: Independent Non-Profit IRS Status: 501(c)3
Highest Offering: Second Talmudic Degree
Program: Teacher Preparatory; Professional
Accreditation: RABN

01 President ... Gershon NEIMAN
10 Chief Fiscal Officer ... Rabbi J. LURIA

Yeshivath Zichron Moshe (E)

PO Box 580, South Fallsburg NY 12779-0580
County: Sullivan FICE Identification: 011821
Unit ID: 197744
Telephone: (845) 434-5240 Carnegie Class: Spec/Faith
FAX Number: (845) 434-1009 Calendar System: Semester
Established: 1969 Annual Undergrad Tuition & Fees: $11,500
Enrollment: 194 Male
Affiliation or Control: Independent Non-Profit IRS Status: 501(c)3
Highest Offering: Second Talmudic Degree
Program: Professional
Accreditation: RABN

01 President ... Rabbi Ephraim Y. SHER
37 Director Student Financial Aid ... Rabbi Dov PERECMAN
06 Registrar ... Mrs. Miryom R. MILLER

NORTH CAROLINA

Apex School of Theology (F)

1701 T. W. Alexander Drive, Durham NC 27703-8024
County: Durham FICE Identification: 035134
Unit ID: 441511
Telephone: (919) 572-1625 Carnegie Class: Spec/Faith
FAX Number: (919) 572-1762 Calendar System: Other
URL: www.apexsot.edu
Established: 1995 Annual Undergrad Tuition & Fees: $6,300
Enrollment: 950 Coed
Affiliation or Control: Independent Non-Profit IRS Status: 501(c)3
Highest Offering: Doctorate
Program: Religious Emphasis
Accreditation: TRACS

01 President ... Dr. Joseph E. PERKINS
03 Executive Vice President ... Dr. Herbert R. DAVIS
05 Academic Dean/Graduate Dean ... Dr. Lafayette MAXWELL
06 Registrar ... Mr. Joseph A. PERKINS
08 Head Librarian ... Ms. Cynthia RUFFIN
10 Director of Finance ... Mrs. Carolyn PEEBLES
20 Undergraduate Dean ... Dr. Gladys LONG
88 Dean Master of Arts Christian Couns ... Dr. Tonya ARMSTRONG
73 Dean Doctor of Ministry ... Dr. Lafayette MAXWELL
32 Director Student Affairs ... Rev. George T. DANIELS
09 Dir of Institutional Effectiveness ... Dr. Henry D. WELLS, JR.
04 Executive Admin Asst to President ... Ms. Rolanda J. HOLLAND
07 Admissions Coordinator ... Ms. Sandra J. MANNING
13 Dir of Educational Technology ... Dr. Clarence BURKE
18 Chief Facilities/Physical Plant ... Mr. Anthony PATTERSON
26 Director of Recruiting ... Rev. M. Andrew DAVIS
37 Director Student Financial Aid ... Ms. Floya COTTEN-BROWN

The Art Institute of Charlotte (G)

2110 Water Ridge Parkway, Charlotte NC 28217-4536
Telephone: (704) 357-8020 FICE Identification: 021105
Accreditation: &SC, ACFEI

† Regional accreditation is carried under the parent institution in Savannah, GA.

The Art Institute of Raleigh-Durham (H)

410 Blackwell Street, Suite 200, Durham NC 27701
Telephone: (919) 317-3050 Identification: 770843
Accreditation: &SC, ACFEI

† Branch campus of South University, Savannah, GA.

Barton College (I)

704-A College Street, PO Box 5000, Wilson NC 27893
County: Wilson FICE Identification: 002908
Unit ID: 197911
Telephone: (252) 399-6300 Carnegie Class: Bac/Diverse
FAX Number: (252) 399-6571 Calendar System: Semester
URL: www.barton.edu
Established: 1902 Annual Undergrad Tuition & Fees: $27,941
Enrollment: 1,035 Coed
Affiliation or Control: Christian Church (Disciples Of Christ)
IRS Status: 501(c)3
Highest Offering: Master's
Program: Liberal Arts And General; Teacher Preparatory
Accreditation: SC, NURSE, SW, TED

01 President ... Dr. Douglas N. SEARCY
05 Vice President Academic Affairs ... Dr. Gary DAYNES
10 Vice Pres Finance & Aministration ... Mr. Kris LYNCH
30 Vice President Inst Advancement ... Ms. Jan MERIWETHER
32 Vice President Student Life ... Mr. George SOLAN
100 Senior Advisor to President ... Mrs. Carolyn HARMON
20 Associate Provost ... Dr. Jill FEGLEY
07 Asst VP of Admissions ... Ms. Amanda METTS
30 Asst VP for Development ... Mr. Tom MAZE
50 Dean School of Business ... Dr. Kevin RENSHLER
66 Dean School of Nursing ... Dr. Sharon SARVEY
53 Dean School of Education ... Dr. Jackie ENNIS
79 Dean School of Humanities ... Dr. James CLARK
81 Dean School of Sciences ... Dr. Kevin PENNINGTON
76 Dean Allied Health & Sport Studies ... Dr. Claudia DUNCAN
88 Dean School of Social Work ... Dr. Barbara CONKLIN
57 Dean Visual/Performing & Comm Arts ... Ms. Susan FECHO
41 Athletic Director ... Mr. Todd WILKINSON
09 Director of Institutional Research ... Dr. Jill FEGLEY
106 Dir Online Education/E-learning ... Ms. Lorraine RAPER
38 Asst Dean of Student Success ... Ms. Angie WALSTON
06 Registrar ... Ms. Sheila MILNE
21 Controller ... Mr. Larry GRIFFIN
37 Director Student Financial Aid ... Ms. Bridget ELLIS
26 Director of Public Relations ... Mrs. Kathy DAUGHETY
08 Director of the Library ... Mr. George LOVELAND
15 Director Human Resources ... Mrs. Linda TYSON
23 Director of Health Services ... Mrs. Amy BRIDGERS
29 Director of Alumni Affairs ... Ms. Summer BROCK
14 Director Technology ... Mr. Callie BISSETTE
13 Director of Information Technology ... Mrs. Susan WEEKLEY
35 Dean of Students ... Mr. Jared TICE
28 Director of Diversity and Inclusion ... Ms. Holly ZACHARIAS
18 Director of Physical Plant ... Mr. Sean WOODARD
42 Chaplain ... Rev. Jamie EUBANKS
40 Bookstore Manager ... Ms. Candice BARNES
04 Executive Asst to President ... Mrs. Sheila WILSON
39 Director of Housing/Res Life ... Mr. Joseph DLUGOS
43 Legal Counsel ... Mrs. Shannon RUSSELL

Belmont Abbey College (J)

100 Belmont Mount Holly Road, Belmont NC 28012-1802
County: Gaston FICE Identification: 002910
Unit ID: 197984
Telephone: (704) 461-6701 Carnegie Class: Bac/Diverse
FAX Number: (704) 461-6670 Calendar System: Semester
URL: belmontabbeycollege.edu/
Established: 1876 Annual Undergrad Tuition & Fees: $18,500
Enrollment: 1,488 Coed
Affiliation or Control: Roman Catholic IRS Status: 501(c)3
Highest Offering: Baccalaureate
Program: Liberal Arts And General; Teacher Preparatory
Accreditation: SC

01 President ... Dr. William K. THIERFELDER
10 Chief Financial Officer ... Mr. Allan MARK
05 VP for Academic Affairs ... Dr. David WILLIAMS
26 VP College Relations ... Mr. Gregory SWANSON
20 Assoc Dean for Academic Affairs ... Dr. Stephen SHIVONE
30 Director of Development ... Vacant
29 Alumni & Community Relations Dir ... Ms. Chris Goff PEELER
08 Director of the Library ... Mr. Donald BEAGLE
06 Registrar ... Ms. Margot RHOADES
09 Director of Institutional Research ... Ms. Sharell CANNADY
36 Director Career Counseling/Placemnt ... Ms. Stephannie MILES
27 Director Marketing ... Mr. Rolando RIVAS
37 Director of Financial Aid ... Mrs. Anne A. STEVENS
38 Wellness Center Counselor ... Mrs. Melanie ECKSTEIN
41 Athletic Director ... Mr. Stephen MISS
21 Staff Accountant ... Ms. Patti PIZZANO
19 Chief of Campus Police ... Mr. Mike WILLIAMS
42 Director of Campus Ministry ... Mr. Patrick FORD
15 Director of Human Resources ... Ms. Cheryl TROTTER
18 Chief Facilities/Physical Plant ... Mr. J. R. MARR
07 Executive Director of Admissions ... Ms. Nicole FOCARETO
13 Chief Info Technology Officer (CIO) ... Ms. Nancy OLIVER
32 Dean of Student Life ... Mr. Tom MACALESTER
04 Sr Executive Assistant ... Ms. Ashley MCCALLISTER

Bennett College (K)

900 E Washington Street, Greensboro NC 27401-3239
County: Guilford FICE Identification: 002911
Unit ID: 197993
Telephone: (336) 273-4431 Carnegie Class: Bac/A&S
FAX Number: (336) 370-8688 Calendar System: Semester
URL: www.bennett.edu
Established: 1873 Annual Undergrad Tuition & Fees: $17,130
Enrollment: 602 Female
Affiliation or Control: United Methodist IRS Status: 501(c)3
Highest Offering: Baccalaureate
Program: Liberal Arts And General; Teacher Preparatory; Business Emphasis
Accreditation: SC, SW, TED

01 President ... Dr. Rosalind FUSE-HALL
05 Interim Provost/Academic VP ... Dr. Michelle LINSTER
100 Chief of Staff ... Dr. Rolanda BURNEY
10 VP Business & Finance ... Mr. LeRoy SUMMERS
30 Interim Vice Pres Inst Advancement ... Ms. Audrey FRANKLIN
26 Dir Public Relations & Publication ... Ms. Wanda MOBLEY
09 Dir Institutional Effective/Rsrch ... Vacant
20 Assoc Provost of Academic Affairs ... Dr. Audrey WARD
84 VP Enrollment Mgmt ... Ms. Karen GREEN
06 Registrar ... Ms. Karen GREEN
08 Director of Holgate Library ... Ms. Joan WILLIAMS
07 Director of Admissions ... Vacant
37 Interim Director of Financial Aid ... Mr. Shawn GUY
29 Director Alumnae Affairs ... Ms. Audrey FRANKLIN
36 Director Career Services ... Mr. Darryl JOHNSON
38 Director of Counseling Services ... Ms. Robin CAMPBELL
23 Director of Health Services ... Vacant
15 Director of Human Resources ... Ms. Linda DIAMOND
42 Chaplain/Director Campus Ministry ... Rev Dr. Natalie MCLEAN
83 Int Chair Social Sci/Educ Div ... Dr. Henry JOHNSON
79 Int Chair Hum/Fine Arts Division ... Dr. Linda PARKER
81 Chair Natural & Behavioral Sciences ... Dr. Susan CURTIS

Brevard College (A)

One Brevard College Drive, Brevard NC 28712-3306
County: Transylvania | FICE Identification: 002912
Unit ID: 198066
Telephone: (828) 883-8292 | Carnegie Class: Bac/A&S
FAX Number: (828) 884-3790 | Calendar System: Semester
URL: www.brevard.edu
Established: 1853 | Annual Undergrad Tuition & Fees: $36,560
Enrollment: 705 | Coed
Affiliation or Control: United Methodist | IRS Status: 501(c)3
Highest Offering: Baccalaureate
Program: Liberal Arts And General
Accreditation: SC, MUS

01 President .... Dr. David C. JOYCE
05 VP Academic Affairs/Dean of Faculty .... Dr. Roy S. SHEFFIELD
10 Vice President for Business/Finance .... Ms. Deborah P. HALL
30 Vice Pres Institutional Advancement .... Ms. Susan L. COTHERN
07 Vice Pres Admissions/Financial Aid .... Mr. Ryan C. HOLT
04 Assistant to the President .... Mrs. Julie MCCAY
32 Dean of Students .... Mrs. Debora D'ANNA
13 Int Dir of Information Technology .... Mr. Jay TRUSSELL
06 Registrar .... Mrs. Amy HERTZ
37 Director of Financial Aid .... Mrs. Caron SURRETT
08 Director of Library .... Mr. Michael M. MCCABE
29 Director of Alumni Affairs .... Mrs. Rebecca GILL
19 Dir of Safety/Security/Risk Mgmt .... Mr. Stan JACOBSEN
41 Director of Athletics .... Mr. Juan MASCARO
18 Director of Facilities/Grounds .... Mr. James HARGIS
24 Director Academic Enrichment Ctr .... Ms. Shirley E. ARNOLD
36 Director of Career Exploration/Dev .... Ms. Nacole POTTS
92 Director of Honors Program .... Dr. Laura L. FRANKLIN
21 Controller .... Mr. Thomas Ove ANDERSEN
38 Assoc Dean/Dir of Counseling .... Ms. Deanne DASBURG
57 Chair Division of Fine Arts .... Dr. Laura FRANKLIN
79 Chair Division of Humanities .... Dr. Mary L. BRINGLE
83 Chair Div of Social Studies .... Dr. Helen C. GIFT
81 Chair Div Env Stds/Math/Nat Science .... Dr. Kenneth DUKE

Cabarrus College of Health Sciences (B)

401 Medical Park Drive, Concord NC 28025-3959
County: Cabarrus | FICE Identification: 006477
Unit ID: 198109
Telephone: (704) 403-1555 | Carnegie Class: Spec/Health
FAX Number: (704) 403-1764 | Calendar System: Semester
URL: www.cabarruscollege.edu
Established: 1942 | Annual Undergrad Tuition & Fees: $11,976
Enrollment: 448 | Coed
Affiliation or Control: Independent Non-Profit | IRS Status: 501(c)3
Highest Offering: Master's
Program: Occupational; 2-Year Principally Bachelor's Creditable; Nursing Emphasis
Accreditation: SC, ADNUR, MAC, NURSE, OTA, SURGT

01 Chancellor .... Dr. Dianne O. SNYDER
05 Provost .... Dr. Margaret B. PATCHETT
32 Dean of Student Aff/Enrollment Mgt .. Ms. Christine L. CORSELLO
10 Chief Financial Officer .... Mrs. Kim BRADSHAW
66 ADN Program Chair .... Mrs. Kim PLEMMONS
66 BSN Program Chair .... Mrs. Colleen BURGESS
88 OT Assistant Program Chair .... Ms. Nancy GREEN
88 Master OT Program Chair .... Dr. Carol FAIN
88 Medical Assisting Program Chair .... Ms. Rachel HOUSTON
88 Surgical Technology Program Chair .... Mrs. Michelle GAY
88 Medical Imagining Program Chair .... Mrs. Rhonda WEAVER
88 Associate in Science Program Chair .... Mrs. Zinat HASSANPOUR
88 Pharmacy Technology Program Chair .... Mrs. Annette SIMMONS
88 General Education Program Chair .... Mrs. Stacey WILSON
88 Coord Campus & Community Outreach .... Mrs. Cara LURSEN
26 Coord of Marketing & Graduate Educ .... Mrs. Melanie GASS
37 Director of Financial Aid .... Mrs. Valerie RICHARD
06 Dir Student Records & Info Mgmt .... Mr. Todd DEESE
07 Director of Recruitment & Retention .... Vacant
04 Administrative Asst to President .... Mrs. Donna HARLESS
08 Head Librarian .... Ms. Emily PATRIDGE

Campbell University (C)

PO Box 97, Buies Creek NC 27506-0097
County: Harnett | FICE Identification: 002913
Unit ID: 198136
Telephone: (910) 893-1200 | Carnegie Class: Master's L
FAX Number: (910) 893-1424 | Calendar System: Semester
URL: www.campbell.edu
Established: 1887 | Annual Undergrad Tuition & Fees: $28,820
Enrollment: 6,103 | Coed
Affiliation or Control: Baptist | IRS Status: 501(c)3
Highest Offering: Doctorate
Program: Liberal Arts And General; Teacher Preparatory; Professional
Accreditation: SC, ACBSP, ARCPA, CAATE, LAW, @OSTEO, PHAR, @PTA, SW, TED, THEOL

01 President .... Dr. J. Bradley CREED
05 Vice Pres Academic Affs & Provost .... Dr. Mark HAMMOND
10 Vice President Business/Treasurer .... Mr. Jim O. ROBERTS
30 Vice President for Advancement .... Mr. Britt DAVIS
32 Vice President for Student Life .... Dr. Dennis BAZEMORE
84 Vice Pres Enrollment Management .... Vacant
07 Asst Vice Pres of Admissions .... Mr. Jason HALL
49 Dean of College of Arts & Science .... Dr. Michael WELLS
61 Dean of the Law School .... Mr. J. Rich LEONARD
50 Dean Lundy-Fetterman Sch Business .... Mr. Keith FAULKNER
53 Dean School of Education .... Dr. Karen NERY
67 Acting VP of Health Sciences & Dean .... Dr. Michael ADAMS
63 Dean of Osteopathic Medical School .... Dr. John M. KAUFFMAN, JR.
35 Dean of Students .... Dr. Sherry L. DELLINGER
06 Registrar .... Mr. David MCGIRT
21 Assistant Treasurer .... Mr. Win QUAKENBUSH
29 Director of Alumni Relations .... Rev. Doug JONES
89 Director of Freshman Experience .... Dr. Jennifer A. LATINO
08 Dean of Library .... Mrs. Borree KWOK
37 Director of Financial Aid .... Ms. Mary KOSIN
13 Director of Computing Services .... Mr. Chris BUCKLEY
26 Director of Public Information .... Ms. Haven HOTTEL
15 Human Resources Director .... Mr. Bob COGSWELL
18 Chief Facilities/Physical Plant .... Mr. J. Scot PHILLIPS
38 Director Student Counseling .... Mrs. Laura RICH
96 Director of Purchasing .... Vacant
92 Director of Honors Program .... Dr. Ann ORTIZ
09 Director of Institutional Research .... Mrs. Maren HESS
106 Dean of Adult & Online Education .... Dr. John ROBERSON

Carolina Christian College (D)

PO Box 777, Winston-Salem NC 27102
County: Forsyth | FICE Identification: 035703
Unit ID: 199971
Telephone: (336) 744-0900 | Carnegie Class: Spec/Faith
FAX Number: (336) 744-0901 | Calendar System: Semester
URL: www.carolina.edu
Established: 1945 | Annual Undergrad Tuition & Fees: $9,000
Enrollment: 42 | Coed
Affiliation or Control: Independent Non-Profit | IRS Status: 501(c)3
Highest Offering: Master's
Program: Liberal Arts And General; Religious Emphasis
Accreditation: BI

01 President .... Ms. LaTanya V. LUCAS
05 VP of Academics .... Mrs. Derrick THORPE
32 Dean of Students .... Mr. Thayer TYSON
10 Chief Business Officer .... Ms. Della MURPHY
08 Library Director .... Ms. Laura RHODEN
37 Financial Aid Director .... Vacant
06 Registrar .... Vacant
26 Chief Public Relations Officer .... Mr. MacArthur DAVIS
09 Director of Institutional Research .... Vacant

Carolina College of Biblical Studies (E)

817 S. McPherson Church Road, Fayetteville NC 28303
County: Cumberland | FICE Identification: 041542
Unit ID: 461032
Telephone: (910) 323-5614 | Carnegie Class: Not Classified
FAX Number: (910) 323-0425 | Calendar System: Quarter
URL: www.ccbs.edu
Established: 1973 | Annual Undergrad Tuition & Fees: $4,725
Enrollment: 111 | Coed
Affiliation or Control: Non-denominational | IRS Status: 501(c)3
Highest Offering: Baccalaureate
Program: Religious Emphasis
Accreditation: BI

01 President .... Dr. Bill KORVER
05 Academic Dean .... Dr. Harry GHEE
30 Vice Pres Strategic Development .... Dr. Bill BOYD
06 Financial Aid Officer/Registrar .... Ms. Kathy SCHULTINGKEMPER
07 Admissions Director .... Ms. Marcia KORVER

Carolina Graduate School of Divinity (F)

2400 Old Chapman St., Greensboro NC 27403
County: Guilford | FICE Identification: 039395
Telephone: (336) 315-8660 | Carnegie Class: Not Classified
FAX Number: (336) 315-8660 | Calendar System: Semester
URL: www.carolinagrad.edu
Established: 2003 | Annual Graduate Tuition & Fees: $11,250
Enrollment: 55 | Coed
Affiliation or Control: Interdenominational | IRS Status: 501(c)3
Highest Offering: Doctorate; No Undergraduates
Program: Professional; Religious Emphasis
Accreditation: THEOL

01 President .... Dr. Frank P. SCURRY
05 Vice President for Academics .... Dr. Terry W. EDDINGER
32 Director of Student Life .... Dr. Darryl A. BODIE
06 Director of Student Records .... Mrs. Cindy H. BODIE
37 Director of Financial Aid .... Ms. Shirley P. CARTER
10 Business Manager .... Mrs. Rosalie CARR

Carolinas College of Health Sciences (G)

1200 Blythe Boulevard, Charlotte NC 28203
County: Mecklenburg | FICE Identification: 031042
Unit ID: 433174
Telephone: (704) 355-5043 | Carnegie Class: Assoc/Pub-Spec
FAX Number: (704) 355-9336 | Calendar System: Semester
URL: www.CarolinasCollege.edu
Established: 1990 | Annual Undergrad Tuition & Fees (In-District): $6,839
Enrollment: 494 | Coed
Affiliation or Control: State/Local | IRS Status: 501(c)3
Highest Offering: Associate Degree
Program: 2-Year Principally Bachelor's Creditable
Accreditation: SC, ADNUR, HT, MT, PHLEB, RAD, RTT, SURGT

01 President .... Dr. Ellen SHEPPARD
05 Provost .... Dr. Lori BEQUETTE
10 Dean of Business/Finance/Technology .... Ms. Kim BRADSHAW
32 Dean Student Svcs/Enrollment Mgmt .... Dr. T. Hampton HOPKINS
66 Dean of Nursing .... Dr. Deborah BLACKWELL
06 Registrar .... Ms. Sue ROUX
07 Admissions Coordinator .... Ms. Rhoda RILLORTA
37 Financial Aid Coordinator .... Ms. Jill POWELL
90 Instructional Tech Coordinator .... Mr. Larry TURNER
51 Director Continuing Education .... Ms. Susan THOMASSON
09 Director of Institutional Research .... Vacant
04 Administrative Asst to President .... Ms. Pat LEWIS
29 Director Alumni Relations .... Ms. Ruthie MIHAL

Catawba College (H)

2300 W Innes Street, Salisbury NC 28144-2488
County: Rowan | FICE Identification: 002914
Unit ID: 198215
Telephone: (704) 637-4111 | Carnegie Class: Bac/Diverse
FAX Number: (704) 637-4444 | Calendar System: Semester
URL: www.catawba.edu
Established: 1851 | Annual Undergrad Tuition & Fees: $28,730
Enrollment: 1,316 | Coed
Affiliation or Control: United Church Of Christ | IRS Status: 501(c)3
Highest Offering: Master's
Program: Liberal Arts And General; Teacher Preparatory
Accreditation: SC, CAATE, TED

01 President .... Mr. Brien LEWIS
03 Senior Vice President/Chaplain .... Dr. Kenneth W. CLAPP
05 Provost .... Dr. Michael BITZER
30 Vice President of Development .... Mr. Rex OTEY
84 Vice Pres of Enrollment Management .... Mrs. Cindy BARR
04 Assistant to President .... Mrs. Amy H. WILLIAMS
09 Dir Institutional Researh .... Mr. Timothy KENNEDY
10 Chief Financial Officer .... Mr. Nelson MURPHY
15 Chief Human Resources Officer .... Mr. Larry G. FARMER
26 Chief Public Relations Officer .... Mrs. Tonia BLACK-GOLD
32 Dean of Students .... Mr. G. Ben SMITH
39 Associate Dean of Residence Life .... Ms. Kara OSTLUND
08 Head Librarian .... Dr. Steve MCKINZIE
06 Registrar .... Ms. Carol GAMBLE
07 Sr Director of Admissions .... Ms. Elaine P. HOLDEN
37 Director of Financial Assistance .... Ms. Kelli HAND
36 Director of Placement .... Ms. Robin PERRY
88 Director Sports Info & Promotion .... Mr. Jim D. LEWIS
40 Director Bookstore .... Mrs. Stephanie TAYLOR
41 Athletic Director .... Mr. Larry W. LECKONBY
18 Chief Facilities/Physical Plant .... Vacant
29 Director Alumni Relations .... Ms. Margaret FAUST
38 Director Student Counseling .... Dr. Nancy ZIMMERMAN

Charlotte Christian College and Theological Seminary (I)

3117 Whting Avenue / PO Box 790106, Charlotte NC 28206-4910
County: Mecklenburg | FICE Identification: 038273
Unit ID: 444778
Telephone: (704) 334-6882 | Carnegie Class: Spec/Faith
FAX Number: (704) 334-6885 | Calendar System: Semester
URL: www.charlottechristian.edu
Established: 1996 | Annual Undergrad Tuition & Fees: $9,000
Enrollment: 128 | Coed
Affiliation or Control: Independent Non-Profit | IRS Status: 501(c)3
Highest Offering: Doctorate
Program: 2-Year Principally Bachelor's Creditable; Professional; Religious Emphasis
Accreditation: TRACS

01 President .... Dr. Eddie G. GRIGG
04 Executive Asst to the President .... Mr. Heith PICKLESIMER
05 Vice President of Academic Affairs .... Dr. James GIFFORD
32 Vice President of Student Affairs .... Vacant
30 Director of Advancement .... Vacant
06 Registrar/Dir International Student .... Ms. Anne WITT
08 Head Librarian .... Mr. Robert MCINNES
07 Director of Admissions .... Vacant
10 Chief Finance Officer .... Mr. Al WITT, JR.
37 Financial Aid Officer .... Mr. Kenneth ROACH
106 Dir Online Education/E-learning .... Vacant

Charlotte School of Law (J)

201 South College Street, Charlotte NC 28244
County: Mecklenburg | FICE Identification: 041435
Unit ID: 455169
Telephone: (704) 971-8500 | Carnegie Class: Spec/Law
FAX Number: (704) 971-8599 | Calendar System: Semester
URL: www.charlottelaw.edu
Established: 2008 | Annual Graduate Tuition & Fees: $41,348
Enrollment: 1,373 | Coed
Affiliation or Control: Proprietary | IRS Status: Proprietary

Highest Offering: First Professional Degree; No Undergraduates
Program: Professional
Accreditation: LAW

01 President ... Mr. Chidi OGENE
10 CFO ... Mr. Chris SCHMITZ
26 Dir Marketing & Admissions Outcomes ... Mr. Dallas BRAGG
13 Director of Information Technology ... Mr. Clark MACIAG
05 Dean ... Mr. Jay CONISON
20 Assoc Dean for Acad Svcs & Faculty ... Ms. Camille DAVIDSON
88 Assc Dean Practice Ready Education ... Mr. Jason HUBER
32 Assoc Dean of Student Engagement ... Mr. Michael FARLEY
20 Asst Dean for Academic Affairs ... Ms. Beth KOBACK
36 Director of Center for Prof Dev ... Ms. Aithyni RUCKER
08 Associate Dean for Library Services ... Ms. Katie BROWN
21 Assistant Dir of Fiscal Affairs ... Ms. Tamika JACKSON
88 Asst Dean for Academic Services ... Ms. Traci FLEURY
35 Asst Dean for Student Success ... Ms. Odessa ALM
18 Facilities Manager ... Mr. Jay BEAM
19 Director of Security ... Mr. William HARPER
06 Registrar ... Ms. Jessica PRIMERANO
07 Director of Admissions Operations ... Mr. Steve JONES

The Chef's Academy (A)

2001 Carrington Mill Boulevard, Morrisville NC 27560
Telephone: (919) 246-9394 Identification: 770101
Accreditation: ACICS

† Branch campus of Harrison College - Indianapolis Downtown Campus, Indianapolis, IN.

Chowan University (B)

One University Place, Murfreesboro NC 27855-1844
County: Hertford FICE Identification: 002916
Unit ID: 198303
Telephone: (252) 398-6500 Carnegie Class: Bac/Diverse
FAX Number: (252) 398-1190 Calendar System: Semester
URL: www.chowan.edu
Established: 1848 Annual Undergrad Tuition & Fees: $29,000
Enrollment: 1,430 Coed
Affiliation or Control: Baptist IRS Status: 501(c)3
Highest Offering: Master's
Program: Liberal Arts And General
Accreditation: SC, MUS, TED

01 President ... Dr. M. Chrisopher WHITE
05 Vice President Academic Affairs ... Dr. Danny B. MOORE
10 Vice President Business Affairs ... Mr. Donnie O. CLARY
32 Vice President Student Affairs ... Mr. P. Randy HARRELL
30 Vice President Advancement ... Mr. John TAYLOE
15 Vice President Human Resources ... Mr. John A. HINTON
07 Vice President Admissions ... Mr. P. Randy HARRELL
13 Exec Dir Info Tech/Network Svcs ... Mr. James R. HOWELL
06 Registrar ... Ms. Donna ROBBINS
26 Director of Public Relations ... Mr. Joshua BARKER
08 Head Librarian ... Mrs. Georgia E. WILLIAMS
37 Director of Financial Aid ... Mrs. Sharon ROSE
42 Campus Minister ... Ms. Mari E. WILES
18 Director Physical Plant ... Mr. Bob ROWE
19 Chief of Security ... Mr. Derek A. BURKE
35 Director Student Life ... Ms. Leah LAMBSON
38 Director Counseling/Career Services ... Vacant
39 Director Housing & Residence Life ... Mr. Brandon ZOCH
41 Athletics Director ... Mr. F. Ozzie MCFARLAND
09 Director Institutional Research ... Mr. Daniel MCCAMISH
88 Director Upward Bound ... Mr. E. Frank STEPHENSON
21 Director Business Services ... Mrs. Julie W. EMORY
29 Director Alumni Services ... Mrs. Kay M. THOMAS
49 Dean Liberal Arts ... Dr. John DILUSTRO
50 Dean Business ... Dr. Linda MILES
53 Dean Education ... Dr. Brenda S. TINKHAM
40 Bookstore Manager ... Vacant

Daoist Traditions College of Chinese Medical Arts (C)

382 Montford Ave, Asheville NC 28801
County: Buncombe FICE Identification: 041464
Unit ID: 455178
Telephone: (828) 225-3993 Carnegie Class: Not Classified
FAX Number: (828) 255-3306 Calendar System: Semester
URL: www.daoisttraditions.edu
Established: 2003 Annual Graduate Tuition & Fees: $17,750
Enrollment: 76 Coed
Affiliation or Control: Proprietary IRS Status: Proprietary
Highest Offering: Master's; No Undergraduates
Program: Professional
Accreditation: ACUP

01 President ... Dr. Mary Cissy MAJEBE

Davidson College (D)

PO Box 5000, Davidson NC 28035-5000
County: Mecklenburg FICE Identification: 002918
Unit ID: 198385
Telephone: (704) 894-2000 Carnegie Class: Bac/A&S
FAX Number: (704) 894-2005 Calendar System: Semester
URL: www.davidson.edu
Established: 1837 Annual Undergrad Tuition & Fees: $46,966
Enrollment: 1,770 Coed
Affiliation or Control: Presbyterian Church (U.S.A.) IRS Status: 501(c)3
Highest Offering: Baccalaureate
Program: Liberal Arts And General
Accreditation: SC

01 President ... Dr. Carol E. QUILLEN
05 Vice Pres Acad Affs/Dean of Faculty ... Dr. Wendy E. RAYMOND
26 Vice President College Relations ... Ms. Eileen M. KEELEY
10 Vice Pres Finance & Administration ... Mr. Edward A. KANIA
32 VP Student Life/Dean of Students ... Dr. Thomas C. SHANDLEY
07 VP & Dean Admissions/Financial Aid ... Mr. Christopher J. GRUBER
09 VP Planning/Institutional Research ... Ms. Linda M. LEFAUVE
27 Assoc VP Comm/Tech/Operations ... Ms. Cat S. NIEKRO
20 Assoc Dean Academic Administration ... Ms. Leslie M. MARSICANO
45 VP for Strategic Initiatives ... Dr. Patrick J. SELLERS
20 Assoc Dean Teaching/Lrng/Rsrch ... Dr. Verna M. CASE
06 Registrar ... Ms. Angela B. DEWBERRY
13 Exec Director Information Tecnology ... Vacant
37 Director Financial Aid ... Mr. David GELINAS
15 Director of Human Resources ... Dr. Kim BALL
41 Director of Athletics ... Mr. James E. MURPHY, III
08 Director of the Library ... Ms. Gillian (Jill) S. GREMMELS
29 Director Alumni Relations ... Ms. Marya L. HOWELL
21 Controller/Director Business Svcs ... Ms. Lori GASTON
18 Director Facilities & Engineering ... Mr. David M. HOLTHOUSER
19 Chief of Campus Police ... Mr. Todd D. SIGLER
36 Director Career Services ... Mr. Nathan J. ELTON
35 Director of College Union ... Mr. William H. BROWN
39 Dir Resid Life/Assoc Dean Students ... Mr. Jason S. SHAFFER
42 College Chaplain ... Dr. Robert C. SPACH
71 Dir Cntr for Interdisciplinary Stds ... Dr. Peter M. KRENTZ
82 Assoc Dean Int'l Programs/Studies ... Dr. M. Christopher ALEXANDER
25 Director of Grants & Contracts ... Dr. Mary W. MUCHANE
24 Director Instructional Support ... Ms. Diane S. STIRLING
38 Director Student Counseling Center ... Dr. Trish MURRAY
44 Director of Annual Giving ... Ms. Katharine H. ATKINS
96 Director of Purchasing ... Ms. Elizabeth S. CHRISTENBURY
40 College Store General Manager ... Mr. William T. REILLY

Duke University (E)

Durham NC 27706-8001
County: Durham FICE Identification: 002920
Unit ID: 198419
Telephone: (919) 684-8111 Carnegie Class: RU/VH
FAX Number: (919) 684-3200 Calendar System: Semester
URL: www.duke.edu
Established: 1838 Annual Undergrad Tuition & Fees: $63,273
Enrollment: 15,856 Coed
Affiliation or Control: Independent Non-Profit IRS Status: 501(c)3
Highest Offering: Doctorate
Program: Liberal Arts And General; Teacher Preparatory; Professional
Accreditation: SC, ANEST, ARCPA, BUS, CLPSY, @DIETI, ENG, IPSY, LAW, MED, NURSE, PA, PAST, PCSAS, PTA, TED, THEOL

01 President ... Richard H. BRODHEAD
05 Provost ... Sally KORNBLUTH
17 Chancellor for Health Affairs ... A. Eugene WASHINGTON
03 Exec Vice Pres for Administration ... Tallman TRASK, III
10 Vice President Financial Services ... Timothy WALSH
15 Vice President for Administration ... Kyle CAVANAUGH
07 Dean Undergraduate Admissions ... Christoph O. GUTTENTAG
21 Exec Vice Provost Finance & Admin ... James S. ROBERTS
13 Vice Prov Information Technology ... Tracy FUTHEY
88 Vice Provost Interdisciplin Studies ... Edward BALLEISEN
20 Vice Provost for Academic Affairs ... Keith WHITFIELD
88 Vice Prov Faculty Diversity & Dev ... Nancy ALLEN
88 Vice Provost for the Arts ... Scott A. LINDTORTH
46 Vice Provost for Research ... Lawrence CARIN
88 Vice Prov Innov/Entrepreneurship ... Eric TOONE
08 Librarian/Vice Prov Library Affairs ... Deborah JAKUBS
37 Asst Vice Provost/Dir Financial Aid ... Alison RABIL
65 Vice Provost Sch of the Environment ... Alan TOWNSEND
61 Dean of Law School ... David F. LEVI
63 Dn Sch Med/Sr Vice Chanc Acad Affs ... Nancy ANDREWS
50 Dean Fuqua School of Business ... William BOULDING
73 Dean of the Divinity School ... Richard HAYS
58 Dean Grad School/Vice Prov Grad Ed ... Paula D. MCCLAIN
49 Dean Faculty Arts/Science ... Valerie ASHBY
66 Dean School of Nursing ... Marion BROOME
54 Dean of Engineering ... Thomas KATSOULEAS
88 Director Duke University Press ... Stephen A. COHN
18 Vice President for Facilities ... John NOONAN
88 Vice Pres/Vice Prov Global Strategy ... Michael H. MERSON
06 Registrar ... Vacant
09 Director of Institutional Research ... David JAMIESON-DRAKE
04 Executive Asst to the President ... Lisa JORDAN
101 VP and University Secretary ... Richard RIDDELL
102 Asst VP Foundation Relations ... Beth EASTLICK
104 Director Study Abroad ... Amanda KELSOE
105 Senior Manager Web Services ... Ryn NASSER
22 Vice President Insitutional Equity ... Benjamin REESE, JR.
26 Chief Public Relations/Marketing ... Michael SCHOENFELD
29 Director Alumni Relations ... Sterly WILDER
30 Vice President Development ... Robert SHEPARD
32 Vice President Student Affairs ... Larry MONETA
36 Director Career Center ... William WRIGHT-SWADEL
38 Director Student Counseling ... Wanda COLLINS
39 Director Student Housing ... Rick JOHNSON
41 VP and Director Athletics ... Kevin WHITE
43 Vice President and General Counsel ... Pamela BERNARD
44 Asst VP Annual Giving ... Jennifer SPISAK-CAMERON
53 Vice Provost Undergraduate Educ ... Stephen NOWICKI
86 Assoc VP Federal Relations ... Christopher SIMMONS
96 Assoc VP Procurement ... Jane PLEASANTS

Elon University (F)

2700 Campus Box, Elon NC 27244-2010
County: Alamance FICE Identification: 002927
Unit ID: 198516
Telephone: (336) 278-2000 Carnegie Class: Master's S
FAX Number: N/A Calendar System: 4/1/4
URL: www.elon.edu
Established: 1889 Annual Undergrad Tuition & Fees: $32,172
Enrollment: 6,483 Coed
Affiliation or Control: Independent Non-Profit IRS Status: 501(c)3
Highest Offering: Doctorate
Program: Liberal Arts And General; Teacher Preparatory; Professional
Accreditation: SC, #ARCPA, BUS, JOUR, LAW, PTA, TED

01 President ... Dr. Leo M. LAMBERT
05 Provost/Exec VP Academic Affairs ... Dr. Steven D. HOUSE
100 Chief of Staff/Sec to the Board ... Mr. Jeff STEIN
07 VP of Admissions/Financial Planning ... Mr. Greg ZAISER
10 Senior VP for Business/Finance/Tech ... Mr. Gerald O. WHITTINGTON
30 Vice Pres Institutional Advancement ... Mr. James B. PIATT
32 Vice Pres/Dean of Student Life ... Dr. G. Smith JACKSON
26 Vice Pres University Communications ... Mr. Daniel J. ANDERSON
108 Associate Provost for Assessment ... Dr. Maurice LEVESQUE
20 Associate Provost for Academic Affs ... Vacant
20 Interim Assoc Provost for Inclusion ... Dr. Brooke BARNETT
88 Associate Provost for Faculty Affs ... Dr. Tim PEEPLES
21 Asst VP for Business and Finance ... Ms. Susan M. KIRKLAND
49 Interim Dean College of Arts & Sci ... Dr. Gabie SMITH
50 Dean Love School of Business ... Dr. Raghu TADEPALLI
60 Dean of School of Communications ... Dr. Paul F. PARSONS
53 Interim Dean of School of Education ... Dr. Deborah LONG
61 Dean of School of Law ... Mr. Luke BIERMAN
76 Dean of School of Health Sciences ... Dr. Elizabeth A. ROGERS
85 Dean of Global Studies ... Mr. Woody PELTON
35 Associate VP of Student Life ... Mrs. Jana Lynn F. PATTERSON
08 Dean and University Librarian ... Ms. Joan RUELLE
41 Director of Athletics ... Mr. Dave L. BLANK
06 Registrar ... Dr. Rodney PARKS
42 University Chaplain ... Dr. Janet FULLER
37 Director of Financial Planning ... Dr. M. Patrick MURPHY
29 Dir of Alumni Engagement ... Mr. Brian FEELEY
88 Assoc Dean of Academic Support ... Dr. Becky OLIVE-TAYLOR
36 Exec Director of Career Services ... Vacant
88 Dir of Planning/Design/Construction ... Mr. Brad D. MOORE
18 Assoc VP for Facilities Management ... Mr. Robert BUCHHOLZ
15 Director of Human Resources ... Vacant
109 Director of Auxiliary Services ... Vacant
19 Director of Campus Safety & Police ... Mr. Dennis FRANKS
23 Director of Health Services ... Dr. Ginette ARCHINAL
38 Director Counseling Services ... Mr. Bruce F. NELSON
11 Assistant VP for Admin Svcs ... Mr. Christopher D. FULKERSON
09 Exec Director Institutional Rsch ... Dr. Robert I. SPRINGER
13 Assistant VP for Technology and CIO ... Mr. Christopher C. WATERS
25 Director of Sponsored Programs ... Ms. Bonnie BRUNO
93 Dean of Multcultural Affairs ... Dr. Randy WILLIAMS
92 Director of Honors Program ... Dr. Tom MOULD
94 Director Women's Stds/Gender Stds ... Dr. Kim EPTING
96 Director of Purchasing ... Mr. Jeff HENDRICKS
88 Director of Sustainability ... Ms. Elaine DURR

Gardner-Webb University (G)

PO Box 897 (110 South Main Street), Boiling Springs NC 28017-0897
County: Cleveland FICE Identification: 002929
Unit ID: 198561
Telephone: (704) 406-2361 Carnegie Class: Master's L
FAX Number: (704) 406-4329 Calendar System: Semester
URL: www.gardner-webb.edu
Established: 1905 Annual Undergrad Tuition & Fees: $27,890
Enrollment: 4,470 Coed
Affiliation or Control: Baptist IRS Status: 501(c)3
Highest Offering: Doctorate
Program: 2-Year Principally Bachelor's Creditable; Liberal Arts And General; Teacher Preparatory; Professional
Accreditation: SC, ACBSP, ADNUR, #ARCPA, CAATE, CACREP, MUS, NUR, TED, THEOL

01 President ... Dr. A. Frank BONNER
05 Provost & Executive Vice President ... Dr. Benjamin C. LESLIE
04 Sr Assistant to the President ... Mrs. Glenda S. CROTTS
10 Vice President for Administration ... Mr. Mike W. HARDIN
26 VP for External Affairs ... Mr. H. Woodrow FISH
30 Vice President for Advancement ... Mr. Patrick W. WAGNER
32 Vice Pres Student Development ... Dr. Delores HUNT
84 Vice Pres Enroll Mgmt & Marketing ... Mr. David HAWSEY
41 Vice President for Athletics ... Mr. Chuck S. BURCH
09 VP Planning & Inst Effectiveness ... Dr. Jeffrey L. TUBBS
18 Assoc Vice Pres for Operations ... Mr. Wayne E. JOHNSON
91 Assoc VP for Technology Services ... Mr. Gregory G. HUMPHRIES
20 Assoc Provost Prof/Graduate Studies ... Dr. Franki BURCH
49 Assoc Provost for Arts & Sciences ... Dr. Earl LEININGER
21 Assoc VP for Business & Finance ... Ms. Robin G. HAMRICK

51 Asst Provost for Distance Education ....Dr. Bobbie COX
07 Assoc VP for Undergrad Admissions .....Ms. Gretchen G. TUCKER
37 Asst VP for Financial Planning ....Ms. Summer NANCE
06 Registrar ....Mrs. LouAnn P. SCATES
35 Assoc Provost Academic Development ....Dr. Doug BRYAN
19 Chief of University Police ....Mr. Barry JOHNSON
27 Assoc VP for Marketing/Comm ....Mr. Noel T. MANNING
08 Director of the Library ....Ms. Mary ROBY
38 Director of Counseling Services ....Ms. Cindy WALLACE
89 Director of Freshmen Programs ....Ms. Jessica HERRNDON
58 Dean of Graduate School ....Dr. Jeffrey ROGERS
73 Dean of Divinity School ....Dr. Robert W. CANOY
66 Dean of Nursing School ....Dr. Sharon STARR
50 Director of School Management ....Dr. Sue C. CAMP
92 Director of Honors Program ....Dr. Thomas H. JONES
88 Director Program for Blind/Deaf ....Mrs. Cheryl J. POTTER
21 Comptroller ....Ms. Haley KENDRICK
35 Director Student Activities ....Ms. Karissa L. WEIR
42 Minister to the University ....Dr. Tracy C. JESSUP
39 Director of Residence Life ....Mr. John R. JOHNSON, JR.
50 Dean of Business School ....Dr. Anthony I. NEGBENEBOR
15 Director Human Resources ....Mr. W. Scott WHITE
09 Director of Institutional Research ....Mr. Garry MCSWAIN
29 Director Alumni Relations ....Mrs. Leah CLEVENGER
44 Director of Annual Campaign ....Ms. Sara MCCALL
24 Asst Dir University Media Relations ....Ms. Kathy MARTIN
40 Bookstore Manager ....Ms. Cary CALDWELL
109 Director of Operations Support ....Mr. Brian SPEER

Grace College of Divinity (A)

5117 Cliffdale Road, Fayetteville NC 28314

County: Cumberland | FICE Identification: 041737
Unit ID: 461528
Telephone: (910) 221-2224 | Carnegie Class: Not Classified
FAX Number: (910) 221-2226 | Calendar System: Semester
URL: www.gcd.edu
Established: 2000 | Annual Undergrad Tuition & Fees: $5,100
Enrollment: 163 | Coed
Affiliation or Control: Other Protestant | IRS Status: 501(c)3
Highest Offering: Baccalaureate
Program: Religious Emphasis
Accreditation: **BI**

01 President ....Dr. Steven CROWTHER
11 Vice President of Administration ....Ms. Shaila BERMUDEZ
05 Academic Dean ....Mr. Ron MCBRIDE
84 Dean of Enrollment Management ....Mr. Jason CROWTHER
32 Dean of Students ....Mrs. Stefanie ERTEL
106 Dean of Online Education/E-Learning ....Mr. Tom JOHNSON
10 Chief Financial Officer ....Ms. Omayra COON
08 Librarian ....Mr. David ASPINALL
108 Director of Assessment & Planning ....Ms. Sharyn J. TEAGUE
06 Registrar ....Mr. Jacob SANCHEZ

Greensboro College (B)

815 W Market Street, Greensboro NC 27401-1875

County: Guilford | FICE Identification: 002930
Unit ID: 198598
Telephone: (336) 272-7102 | Carnegie Class: Bac/Diverse
FAX Number: (336) 217-6634 | Calendar System: Semester
URL: www.greensboro.edu
Established: 1838 | Annual Undergrad Tuition & Fees: $26,900
Enrollment: 907 | Coed
Affiliation or Control: United Methodist | IRS Status: 501(c)3
Highest Offering: Master's
Program: Liberal Arts And General; Teacher Preparatory
Accreditation: **SC**, ACBSP, CAATE, MUS, TED

01 President ....Dr. Lawrence D. CZARDA
04 Exec Asst to President/Clerk to BoT .... Ms. Susan J. BARRINGER
05 Senior VP Chief Academic Officer ....Dr. Paul L. LESLIE
11 Exec VP Chief Operating Officer ....Dr. Robin L. DANIEL
10 VP Chief Financial Officer ....Mr. Chris ELMORE
30 VP Chief Advancement Officer ....Ms. Michelle C. DAVIS
20 Assoc VP Academic Admin ....Ms. Martha M. BUNCH
20 Dean of the Faculty ....Dr. Richard A. MAYES
57 Dean School of Arts ....Dr. David SCHRAM
50 Dean School of Business ....Dr. William K. MACREYNOLDS
53 Dean School of Soc Sci & Education .... Dr. Rebecca BLOMGREN
79 Dean School of Humanities ....Dr. Daniel MALOTKY
81 Dean School of Science & Mathematic ..... Dr. Jessica G. SHARPE
07 Dean of Admissions ....Ms. Julianne SCHATZ
13 Information Technology Director ....Dr. Larry BURTON
37 Financial Aid Director ....Ms. Lindsay S. LATHEM
26 Communications Director ....Mr. Lex ALEXANDER
26 Marketing Director ....Ms. Kim THORE
06 Registrar ....Mr. Travis MICKEY
32 Dean of Students ....Mr. Matthew LONG
36 Career Services Director ....Vacant
108 Institutional Assessment Director ....Ms. Phyllis P. CHAMBERS
09 Institutional Research Director ....Ms. Phyllis P. CHAMBERS
88 Academic Success Director ....Ms. Tica D. GREEN
15 Human Resources Director ....Ms. Sonia HOFFMAN
18 Facilities Director ....Mr. Justin LISZKA
19 Security Director ....Mr. Calvin L. GILMORE
23 Student Health Director ....Ms. Lauren T. CHILDREY
38 Counseling Services Director ....Ms. Emily HOLMES
92 George Ctr/Honors Studies Director ....Mr. Neill CLEGG
44 Annual Giving Director ....Mr. Jayson JUDY
29 Alumni Engagement Director ....Vacant

08 Library Director ....Mr. Will RITTER
41 Athletic Director ....Mr. Bryan GALUSKI
42 Campus Chaplain ....Rev. Robert W. BREWER
40 Bookstore Manager ....Mr. Cliff BRALY, JR.
21 Controller ....Ms. Kristen TRASK

Guilford College (C)

5800 W Friendly Avenue, Greensboro NC 27410-4173

County: Guilford | FICE Identification: 002931
Unit ID: 198613
Telephone: (336) 316-2000 | Carnegie Class: Bac/A&S
FAX Number: (336) 316-2950 | Calendar System: Semester
URL: www.guilford.edu
Established: 1837 | Annual Undergrad Tuition & Fees: $34,090
Enrollment: 2,137 | Coed
Affiliation or Control: Friends | IRS Status: 501(c)3
Highest Offering: Baccalaureate
Program: Liberal Arts And General; Teacher Preparatory
Accreditation: **SC**, ACBSP

01 President ....Dr. Jane K. FERNANDES
05 Vice President & Academic Dean ....Dr. Beth RUSHING
04 Executive Assoc to the President ....Mrs. Joyce A. EATON
10 Interim Vice President Finance ....Mr. James WILSON
26 Vice President for Marketing ....Mr. Roger DEGERMAN
30 Vice Pres Institutional Advancement ....Mr. Michael J. POSTON
32 Vice President Student Affairs ....Dr. Todd A. CLARK
27 Assoc VP Communications & Marketing ....Mr. R. Ty BUCKNER
29 Assoc Vice Pres Alumni Relations .... Mr. Jerry W. HARRELSON
51 Asst Dean Continuing Education ....Mr. Martee HOLT
07 Vice President of Enrollment ....Dr. Arlene W. CASH
31 Asst Dean of Career/Community Lrng .... Mr. Alan C. MUELLER
20 Assistant Academic Dean ....Dr. Erin B. DELL
20 Assistant Academic Dean ....Dr. Barbara G. BOYETTE
37 Director Student Financial Svcs ....Vacant
06 Registrar ....Mrs. Norma L. MIDDLETON
08 Director of the Library ....Ms. Suzanne M. BARTELS
41 Director of Athletics ....Mr. Tom J. PALOMBO
19 Director of Public Safety ....Mr. Ron M. STOWE
15 Director Human Resources ....Mr. Rick WILLIAMS
09 Dir Institutional Research/Assess .... Ms. Stephanie HARGRAVE
90 Director Info Technology & Services ....Vacant
42 Campus Ministry Coordinator ....Rev. C. Wess DANIELS
38 Director Student Counseling ....Ms. Gaither M. TERRELL
92 Director Honors Program ....Dr. Heather HAYTON
89 Director of First Year Program ....Dr. Barbara G. BOYETTE
96 Director of Purchasing ....Ms. Tracy A. HALL
104 Director Study Abroad ....Dr. Jack ZERBE
25 Chief Contracts/Grants Admin ....Vacant

Heritage Bible College (D)

PO Box 1628, Dunn NC 28335-1628

County: Harnett | FICE Identification: 030893
Unit ID: 198677
Telephone: (910) 892-3178 | Carnegie Class: Spec/Faith
FAX Number: (910) 891-1809 | Calendar System: Semester
URL: www.heritagebiblecollege.edu
Established: 1971 | Annual Undergrad Tuition & Fees: $9,768
Enrollment: 69 | Coed
Affiliation or Control: Other | IRS Status: 501(c)3
Highest Offering: Baccalaureate
Program: Occupational; Religious Emphasis
Accreditation: **TRACS**

01 President ....Dr. Elvin BUTTS
05 Academic Dean ....Mr. Stephen RZONCA
32 Dean Student Services ....Mr. Randy BARKER
06 Registrar/Director of Financial Aid .. Ms. Kayla SUTTON-COLLIER
07 Admissions ....Ms. Kayla SUTTON-COLLIER
10 Business Administrator ....Ms. LeAnne PAGE
29 Director Alumni Rels/Inst Effectiv ....Miss Chrissy KRIEGBAUM
30 Director of Advancement ....Ms. Iris PRINCE
13 Chief Info Technology Officer (CIO) ....Mr. James SHEARON
26 Chief Public Relations/Marketing ....Ms. Iris PRINCE

High Point University (E)

One University Parkway, High Point NC 27268-0001

County: Guilford | FICE Identification: 002933
Unit ID: 198695
Telephone: (336) 841-9000 | Carnegie Class: Bac/Diverse
FAX Number: (336) 841-4599 | Calendar System: Semester
URL: www.highpoint.edu
Established: 1924 | Annual Undergrad Tuition & Fees: $32,430
Enrollment: 4,399 | Coed
Affiliation or Control: United Methodist | IRS Status: 501(c)3
Highest Offering: Doctorate
Program: Liberal Arts And General; Teacher Preparatory; Professional
Accreditation: **SC**, #ARCPA, CAATE, CIDA, TED

01 President ....Dr. Nido R. QUBEIN
05 Provost ....Dr. Dennis G. CARROLL
03 Executive Vice President ....Dr. Denny G. BOLTON
46 VP of Research and Planning ....Dr. Jeffrey M. ADAMS
84 VP of Enrollment ....Mr. Andy BILLS
26 VP of Communications ....Mr. Roger D. CLODFELTER, JR.
32 VP of Student Life ....Mrs. Gail C. TUTTLE
44 VP of Institutional Advancement .... Mr. Christopher H. DUDLEY
18 VP of Facilities & Auxiliary Ops ....Mr. Stephen L. POTTER

41 Athletic Director ....Mr. Dan HAUSER
07 Assoc VP of Graduate Admissions ....Mr. Andy MODLIN
07 Assoc VP of Undergrad Admissions ....Mr. Kerr C. RAMSAY
76 Dean of School of Health Sciences ....Dr. Daniel E. ERB
49 Dean of College of Arts & Science ......Dr. Carole B. STONEKING
57 Dean of School of Art and Design ....Dr. John C. TURPIN
50 Dean of School of Business ....Dr. James B. WEHRLEY
53 Dean of School of Education ....Dr. Mariann W. TILLERY
67 Dean of School of Pharmacy ....Dr. Ronald E. RAGAN
35 Dean of Students ....Dr. Paul KITTLE
20 Assistant Dean Academic Services ....Ms. Karen C. NAYLON
89 Assoc Dean of Freshman Success ....Dr. Beth HOLDER
08 Director of Library Services ....Mr. David L. BRYDEN
23 Medical Director ....Dr. Marnie S. MARLETTE
88 Bishop in Residence ....Bishop Thomas B. STOCKTON
19 Chief of Security ....Mr. Jeff A. KARPOVICH
06 Registrar ....Mr. Danny K. BROOKS
10 Chief Financial Officer ....Ms. Debi S. BUTT
13 Chief Information Officer ....Mr. John E. CHAMPION
29 Manager of Alumni Programs ....Ms. Emily M. SAUNDERS
37 Dir of Student Financial Planning ....Mr. Ronald ELMORE
25 Director of Sponsored Programs ....Mr. Timothy L. LINKER
15 Director of Human Resources ....Mrs. Kathy S. SMITH
88 Director of Student Accounts ....Ms. Janice A. FOLEY
38 Director of Student Counseling .... Ms. Lynda D. NOFFSINGER
88 Director of Interactive Media ....Ms. Hillary C. KOKAJKO
88 Director of University Events ....Ms. Melissa L. ANDERSON
108 Dir of Inst Research & Assessment ....Ms. Andrea KENNEDY
88 Director of Campus Enhancement ....Mr. Troy J. THOMPSON
88 Dir Athletic Facilities/Operations ....Mr. Sam PHIPPS
40 Manager Bookstore ....Mr. William HOLSTON
85 Director of International Students ....Ms. Marjorie R. CHURCH
36 Director of Career Services ....Ms. Bridget HOLCOMBE
104 Director of Study Abroad ....Ms. Heidi FISCHER
88 Director of Service Learning ....Dr. Joseph D. BLOSSER
88 Director of Undergraduate Research ....Dr. Joanne D. ALTMAN
27 Media Relations Coordinator ....Ms. Pamela J. HAYNES
04 Admin Assistant to President ....Ms. Judy K. RAY
88 Manager of University Mail Center ....Mr. Michael R. HALL

Hood Theological Seminary (F)

1810 Lutheran Synod Drive, Salisbury NC 28144-5768

County: Rowan | FICE Identification: 036633
Unit ID: 443076
Telephone: (704) 636-7611 | Carnegie Class: Spec/Faith
FAX Number: (704) 636-7699 | Calendar System: Semester
URL: www.hoodseminary.edu
Established: 1904 | Annual Undergrad Tuition & Fees: $13,500
Enrollment: 188 | Coed
Affiliation or Control: African Methodist Episcopal Zion Church
IRS Status: 501(c)3
Highest Offering: Doctorate
Program: Professional; Religious Emphasis
Accreditation: **THEOL**

01 President-Elect ....Dr. Vergel L. LATTIMORE
05 Academic Dean ....Dr. Trevor EPPEHIMER
32 Dean of Students .... Dr. Dora R. MBUWAYESANGO
10 Fiscal Officer ....Dr. Regina M. DANCY
30 Development Officer ....Mrs. Margaret KLUTTZ
06 Registrar ....Ms. Nancy BAKER

ITT Technical Institute (G)

5520 Dillard Drive, Suite 100, Cary NC 27518

Telephone: (919) 233-2520 | Identification: 666704
Accreditation: **ACICS**

† Branch campus of ITT Technical Institute, Indianapolis, IN.

ITT Technical Institute (H)

4135 Southstream Boulevard, Ste 200, Charlotte NC 28217-4555

Telephone: (704) 423-3100 | Identification: 666161
Accreditation: **ACICS**

† Branch campus of ITT Technical Institute, Indianapolis, IN.

ITT Technical Institute (I)

10926 David Taylor Drive, Suite 100, Charlotte NC 28262

Telephone: (704) 548-2300 | Identification: 666705
Accreditation: **ACICS**

† Branch campus of ITT Technical Institute, Indianapolis, IN.

ITT Technical Institute (J)

3518 Westgate Drive, Suite 150, Durham NC 27707

Telephone: (919) 401-1400 | Identification: 770656
Accreditation: **ACICS**

† Branch campus of ITT Technical Institute, Indianapolis, IN.

ITT Technical Institute (K)

4050 Piedmont Parkway, Suite 110, High Point NC 27265

Telephone: (336) 819-5900 | Identification: 666703
Accreditation: **ACICS**

† Branch campus of ITT Technical Institute, Indianapolis, IN.

Johnson & Wales University-Charlotte (A)

801 W Trade Street, Charlotte NC 28202-1122
Telephone: (980) 598-1000 Identification: 666375
Accreditation: &EH

† Regional accreditation is carried under the parent institution in Providence, RI.

Johnson C. Smith University (B)

100 Beatties Ford Road, Charlotte NC 28216-5398
County: Mecklenburg FICE Identification: 002936
Unit ID: 198756
Telephone: (704) 378-1000 Carnegie Class: Bac/A&S
FAX Number: (704) 372-1242 Calendar System: Semester
URL: www.jcsu.edu
Established: 1867 Annual Undergrad Tuition & Fees: $18,236
Enrollment: 1,400 Coed
Affiliation or Control: Independent Non-Profit IRS Status: 501(c)3
Highest Offering: Master's
Program: Liberal Arts And General
Accreditation: SC, SW

01 President .... Dr. Ronald L. CARTER
03 Exec Vice Pres/Chief Operating Ofcr .... Dr. Elfred A. PINKARD
10 Vice Pres for Finance .... Mr. Greg PETZKE
30 Vice President for Inst Advancement .... Ms. Joy PAIGE
86 VP Government Sponsored Pgms .... Dr. Diane BOWLES
15 Asst VP for Human Resources .... Ms. Latrelle P. MCALLISTER
18 Asst VP for Business Operations .... Mr. Anayo EZEIGBO
30 Asst VP for Institutional Advancmnt .... Vacant
05 Council of Deans Chair/Dean of STEM .... Dr. Magdy ATTIA
49 Dean of Arts and Letters .... Dr. Brian JONES
107 Dean of Professional Studies .... Dr. Helen CALDWELL
84 Dean of Enrollment Services .... Ms. Cathy HURD
32 Dean of Student Development .... Dr. Cathy JONES
51 Interim Co-Dean Biddle Institute .... Dr. Antonio HENLEY
51 Interim Co-Dean Metro College .... Dr. Laura MCLEAN
88 Dean of Academic Support Services .... Dr. Kelli RAINEY
08 Director of the Library .... Ms. Monika RHUE
07 Director of Admissions .... Mr. James BURRELL
13 Director Information Technology .... Mr. John NORRIS
31 Dir of App Leadership/Comm Dev .... Vacant
09 Dir Plng/Assess/Effect/Rsrch .... Mrs. Harriet HOBBS
26 Director of Comm and Marketing .... Ms. Sherri BELFIELD
29 Director Alumni Affairs .... Mr. Ron MATTHEWS
37 Director Financial Aid .... Vacant
38 Director Counseling .... Mr. Frederick MURPHY
19 Director of Campus Police .... Vacant
35 Director of Student Activities .... Mr. Aleczander WHITFIELD
41 Athletic Director .... Mr. Stephen JOYNER, SR.
06 Registrar .... Mrs. Keisha WILSON
85 Mgr Multi/International Student Aff .... Mr. Rixon CAMPBELL
44 Major Gift Officer .... Mr. Alvin AUSTIN
102 Director Foundations Rel/Priv Grant .... Vacant
96 Director of Procurement .... Ms. Angela MAULDIN
36 Director Career Services .... Mrs. Barbara WILKS
39 Director Residence Life .... Mr. Terry MCPHERSON
40 Manager of Bookstore .... Ms. Robin SORENSEN
16 Manager Risk Management .... Mrs. Debra HOLLIS
23 Health Center Coordinator .... Ms. Marian JONES

Kaplan College (C)

6070 East Independence Boulevard, Charlotte NC 28212
Telephone: (704) 567-3700 Identification: 770543
Accreditation: ACICS

† Branch campus of Kaplan College, Nashville, TN.

King's College (D)

322 Lamar Avenue, Charlotte NC 28204-2493
County: Mecklenburg FICE Identification: 002937
Unit ID: 382504
Telephone: (704) 372-0266 Carnegie Class: Assoc/PrivFP
FAX Number: (704) 348-2029 Calendar System: Semester
URL: www.kingscollegecharlotte.edu
Established: 1901 Annual Undergrad Tuition & Fees: $14,280
Enrollment: 397 Coed
Affiliation or Control: Proprietary IRS Status: Proprietary
Highest Offering: Associate Degree
Program: Occupational; 2-Year Principally Bachelor's Creditable
Accreditation: ACICS, MAC

01 School Director .... Mrs. Diane RYON
05 Chief Academic Officer .... Ms. Barbara ROCKECHARLIE

Laurel University (E)

1215 Eastchester Drive, High Point NC 27265-3115
County: Guilford FICE Identification: 002935
Unit ID: 198747
Telephone: (336) 887-3000 Carnegie Class: Spec/Faith
FAX Number: (336) 889-2261 Calendar System: Semester
URL: www.laureluniversity.edu
Established: 1903 Annual Undergrad Tuition & Fees: $12,300
Enrollment: 199 Coed
Affiliation or Control: Independent Non-Profit IRS Status: 501(c)3
Highest Offering: Doctorate
Program: Professional; Religious Emphasis
Accreditation: BI

01 President .... Dr. Stephen M. CONDON
10 Vice Pres for Finance & Instruction .... Mrs. Emily LITTLEFIELD
06 Registrar .... Mr. Greg WORKMAN
32 Director of Student Services .... Rev. Kim MILLER
37 Director of Financial Aid .... Ms. Kady HILL
09 Dir Institutional Effectiveness .... Mr. Brent STARLING
08 Director of Library Services .... Mrs. April LINDSEY
15 Director of Human Resources .... Mrs. Kathy CUTRELL
21 Exec Director of Business Services .... Mrs. Wendy KING
50 Int Dean School of Management .... Dr. Dennis RENFROE
29 Alumni Coordinator .... Ms. Kathy CUTRELL

Lees-McRae College (F)

191 Main Street, Banner Elk NC 28604-0128
County: Avery FICE Identification: 002939
Unit ID: 198808
Telephone: (828) 898-5241 Carnegie Class: Bac/Diverse
FAX Number: (828) 898-8814 Calendar System: Semester
URL: www.lmc.edu
Established: 1900 Annual Undergrad Tuition & Fees: $24,154
Enrollment: 940 Coed
Affiliation or Control: Presbyterian Church (U.S.A.) IRS Status: 501(c)3
Highest Offering: Baccalaureate
Program: Liberal Arts And General; Teacher Preparatory; Professional
Accreditation: SC, CAATE, NURSE, TEAC

01 President .... Dr. Barry M. BUXTON
04 Secretary to the President .... Ms. Darcy VASILAS
05 Provost & Dean of Faculty .... Dr. Todd LIDH
26 VP Enrollment Mgt/Communications .... Ms. Ginger HANSEN
10 VP Finance/Business Affairs .... Ms. Suzette FRONK
32 VP Stdnt Dev & Dean of Students .... Mr. Jon DRIGGERS
45 VP Strategic Planning/Effectiveness .... Mr. Blaine J. HANSEN
106 VP Extended Campus/Online Learning .... Dr. Bo BENNETT
30 VP Advancement .... Mr. Brent THOMAS
18 VP Facilities/Security .... Mr. Bill MCGOWAN
41 VP Athletics/Club Sports .... Mr. Craig MCPHAIL
20 Associate Provost .... Dr. Kacy CRABTREE
13 Director Technology .... Mr. Tom BURNE
08 Director Libraries .... Mr. Russell TAYLOR
66 Dean Nursing/Health Sciences .... Dr. Laura FERO
71 Chair Burton Center/Student Success .... Ms. Laura PADGETT
50 Interim Chair Business Admin .... Ms. Amy ANDERSON
53 Chair Education .... Dr. Robin BUCHANAN
57 Interim Chair Creative/Fine Arts .... Ms. Danielle CURTIS
79 Chair Humanities .... Dr. Ken CRAIG
81 Chair Science/Mathematics .... Dr. Gene SPEARS
83 Chair Social/Behavioral Sciences .... Dr. Sue HART
19 Director Security/Safety .... Mr. H.D STEWART
07 Director of Admissions .... Ms. Candace SILVER
06 Registrar .... Ms. Lynn HINSHAW
37 Director Financial Aid .... Ms. Cathy SHELL
15 Director Human Resources .... Mrs. Carolyn WARD
29 Director Giving/Alumni Relations .... Ms. Jillian ROSATO

Lenoir-Rhyne University (G)

625 7th Avenue NE, Hickory NC 28601-3984
County: Catawba FICE Identification: 002941
Unit ID: 198835
Telephone: (828) 328-1741 Carnegie Class: Bac/Diverse
FAX Number: (828) 328-7368 Calendar System: Semester
URL: www.lr.edu
Established: 1891 Annual Undergrad Tuition & Fees: $32,140
Enrollment: 2,143 Coed
Affiliation or Control: Evangelical Lutheran Church In America
IRS Status: 501(c)3
Highest Offering: Master's
Program: Liberal Arts And General; Teacher Preparatory; Professional
Accreditation: SC, ACBSP, CAATE, CACREP, @DIETI, NURSE, OT, TED, THEOL

01 President .... Dr. Wayne POWELL
05 Provost .... Dr. Larry HALL
10 Sr Vice President Finance/Admin .... Mr. Peter KENDALL
30 Vice Pres Institutional Advancement .... Dr. Drew VAN HORN
84 Vice President for Enrollment Mgmt .... Ms. Rachel NICHOLS
32 Asst Provost/Dean of Students .... Dr. Katie FISHER
104 Assoc Dean Global Learning .... Ms. Charlotte WILLIAMS
58 Dean Grad Studies/Lifelong Learning .... Dr. Amy WOOD
06 Registrar .... Mr. Stacey BRACKETT
08 Librarian .... Ms. Rita JOHNSON
15 Director of Human Resources .... Mr. Rick NICHOLS
40 Director of Bookstore .... Ms. Lucy MANZANARES
18 Director of Facilities/Plant .... Mr. Otis PITTS
41 Athletic Director .... Mr. Neill MCGEACHY
42 Campus Pastor .... Rev. Andrew WEISNER
19 Director of Security .... Mr. Norris YODER
92 Director of Honors Program .... Dr. Joshua RING
13 Chief Information Officer .... Mr. Ben TALLEY
26 Dir of Marketing/Communication .... Ms. Angela REITER
88 Director of Conferences & Events .... Ms. Janet MATTHEWS
29 Director of Alumni Relations .... Ms. Dana HAMILTON
07 Director of Enrollment Services .... Mr. Eric BRANDON
09 Director of Institutional Research .... Dr. Debra TEMPLETON
37 Director Student Financial Aid .... Mr. Nick JENKINS
38 Dir Student Counseling/Placement .... Ms. Jenny SMITH
88 Dir Liberal Arts/Visiting Writers .... Dr. Rand BRANDES
28 Director Multicultural Affairs .... Ms. Emma SELLERS
88 Dir of Deaf/Hard-of-Hearing Svcs .... Ms. Shawn FRANK
88 Institute on Obesity .... Ms. Kimberly PENNINGTON
65 Institute on Conservation .... Dr. John BRZORAD
85 Dir of International Programs .... Dr. Laura DOBSON
53 College of Education/Human Services .... Dr. Hank WEDDINGTON
76 College of Health Sciences .... Dr. Michael MCGEE
49 College of Arts & Sciences .... Dr. Dan KISER
81 Col of Professional/Math Studies .... Dr. Mary LESSER
04 Administrative Asst to President .... Ms. Sherry R. ERIKSON
36 Director Student Placement .... Ms. Katie WOHLMAN
39 Director Student Housing .... Mr. Jonathan RINK

Living Arts College @ School of Communication Arts (H)

3000 Wakefield Crossing Drive, Raleigh NC 27614-7076
County: Wake FICE Identification: 031090
Unit ID: 421832
Telephone: (919) 488-8500 Carnegie Class: Assoc/PrivFP
FAX Number: (919) 488-8490 Calendar System: Quarter
URL: www.living-arts-college.edu
Established: 1992 Annual Undergrad Tuition & Fees: $16,780
Enrollment: 413 Coed
Affiliation or Control: Proprietary IRS Status: Proprietary
Highest Offering: Baccalaureate
Program: Occupational; Technical Emphasis
Accreditation: ACICS, MAC

01 Director .... Ms. Debra A. HOOPER

Livingstone College (I)

701 W Monroe Street, Salisbury NC 28144-5298
County: Rowan FICE Identification: 002942
Unit ID: 198862
Telephone: (704) 216-6000 Carnegie Class: Bac/Diverse
FAX Number: (704) 216-6217 Calendar System: Semester
URL: www.livingstone.edu
Established: 1879 Annual Undergrad Tuition & Fees: $24,221
Enrollment: 1,301 Coed
Affiliation or Control: African Methodist Episcopal Zion Church
IRS Status: 501(c)3
Highest Offering: Baccalaureate
Program: Liberal Arts And General; Teacher Preparatory; Professional
Accreditation: SC, SW, TED

01 President .... Dr. Jimmy R. JENKINS, SR.
04 Exec Asst to the President .... Dr. State ALEXANDER
05 Vice Pres Academic Affairs .... Dr. Carolyn W. DUNCAN
10 Vice Pres Business & Finance/Ops .... Mr. Reginald DICKENS
32 Vice President Student Affairs .... Dr. Orlando LEWIS
30 Vice Pres Inst Advance/College Rels .... Dr. Herman FELTON
35 Assoc Vice Pres of Student Affairs .... Mr. Tony BALDWIN
20 Asst Vice Pres Academic Affairs .... Dr. Alexander ERWIN
38 Dean of Counseling Services .... Mrs. Elizabeth ALSTON-PINCKNEY
06 Registrar .... Mrs. Wendy JACKSON
08 Director Library Services .... Ms. Laura JOHNSON
26 Director of Public Relations .... Mr. State W. ALEXANDER
37 Director of Financial Aid .... Ms. Stephanie MCNEIL
36 Director of Career Services .... Ms. Sophia GAITHER
13 Director of Computer Info Systems .... Mr. Chong DAN
15 Director of Human Resources .... Mr. Mark SANDERS
29 Director Alumni Affairs .... Ms. Carmen C. WILDER
09 Director of Institutional Research .... Mr. Robert L. MCINNIS
84 Dir Enrollment Mgmt & Admissions .... Vacant
07 Director of Admissions .... Ms. Katrina JARRETT
40 Bookstore Director .... Mr. Keith ANDERSON
41 Athletic Director .... Mr. Andre SPRINGS
96 Director of Purchasing .... Ms. Debra WOOD
18 Director of Physical Plant .... Ms. Jean GRIFFIN
23 Health Services Manager .... Ms. Ethel PEEBLES

Louisburg College (J)

501 N. Main Street, Louisburg NC 27549-7705
County: Franklin FICE Identification: 002943
Unit ID: 198871
Telephone: (919) 496-2521 Carnegie Class: Assoc/PrivNFP
FAX Number: (919) 496-7141 Calendar System: Semester
URL: www.louisburg.edu
Established: 1787 Annual Undergrad Tuition & Fees: $17,346
Enrollment: 705 Coed
Affiliation or Control: United Methodist IRS Status: 501(c)3
Highest Offering: Associate Degree
Program: 2-Year Principally Bachelor's Creditable
Accreditation: SC

01 President .... Rev Dr. Mark D. LA BRANCHE
05 VP of Academic Life .... Dr. James C. ECK
11 VP of Administration/Inst Effect .... Vacant
30 Vice Pres Institutional Advancement .... Mr. Kurt CARLSON
32 Vice President of Student Life .... Mr. Jason E. MODLIN
10 Vice President of Finance .... Mr. Jonathan EHRLICH
84 Vice Pres of Enrollment Management .... Ms. Stephanie B. TOLBERT
29 Alumni Director .... Ms. Jamie PATRICK
06 Registrar/Dir of Inst Research .... Ms. Catherine ZIENCIK
08 Librarian .... Ms. Candace L. JONES
38 Director of Counseling Services .... Ms. Fonda PORTER
37 Director of Financial Aid .... Ms. Jessica ROBERSON
26 Director of College Communications .... Vacant
18 Chief Facilities/Physical Plant .... Mr. Nathan BIEGENZAHN

04 Administrative Asst to President .... Ms. Jennifer MITCHELL WHEELER
07 Director of Admissions .... Ms. Maura BUDUSKY
09 Director of Institutional Research .... Ms. Brittany HUNT
19 Director Security/Safety .... Ms. Vicki REID
39 Director Student Housing .... Mr. Christopher REID
41 Athletic Director .... Mr. Mike HOLLOMAN

Mars Hill University (A)

PO Box 370, Mars Hill NC 28754-0370

County: Madison | FICE Identification: 002944 | Unit ID: 198899

Telephone: (828) 689-1307 | Carnegie Class: Bac/Diverse
FAX Number: (828) 689-1478 | Calendar System: Semester
URL: www.mhu.edu
Established: 1856 | Annual Undergrad Tuition & Fees: $29,382
Enrollment: 1,435 | Coed
Affiliation or Control: Independent Non-Profit | IRS Status: 501(c)3
Highest Offering: Master's
Program: Liberal Arts And General; Teacher Preparatory; Professional
Accreditation: SC, CAATE, MUS, SW, TED, THEA

01 President .... Dr. Dan G. LUNSFORD
30 Vice President for Inst Advancement .... Mr. Harold (Bud) G. CHRISTMAN
05 Exec Vice Pres Acad & Student Affs .... Dr. John W. WELLS
10 Vice Pres for Finance .... Mr. Neil TILLEY
32 Asst Vice Pres for Student Life .... Ms. Laura WHITAKER-LEA
20 Asst Vice Pres for Academic Affairs .... Dr. Jason A. PIERCE
84 Asst Vice Pres for Enrollment Mgt .... Dr. Craig GOFORTH
06 Dean Academic Records/Registrar .... Ms. Edith L. WHITT
08 Director of Library Services .... Ms. Beverly ROBERTSON
26 Director of Communications .... Mr. Mike D. THORNHILL
42 Campus Chaplain .... Rev. Stephanie MCLESKEY
41 Director of Athletics .... Mr. David W. RIGGINS
37 Director of Financial Aid .... Ms. Nichole BUCKNER
29 Director of Alumni Relations .... Mr. John CHASTAIN
85 Director International Education .... Mr. Gordon HINNERS
09 Director Institutional Research .... Dr. Suzanne C. KLONIS
38 Director Student Counseling .... Ms. Cassandra PAVONE
15 Director of Human Resources .... Ms. Deana K. HOLLAND
13 Director Information Technology Svc .... Mr. Gerald D. BALL
18 Director of Facilities .... Mr. Donald EDWARDS
40 Director of Bookstore .... Mr. Darryl R. NORTON
51 Dean of Adult & Graduate Studies .... Ms. Marie NICHOLSON
97 Chair of General Studies .... Ms. Cathy L. ADKINS

Meredith College (B)

3800 Hillsborough Street, Raleigh NC 27607-5298

County: Wake | FICE Identification: 002945 | Unit ID: 198950

Telephone: (919) 760-8600 | Carnegie Class: Bac/Diverse
FAX Number: (919) 760-2828 | Calendar System: Semester
URL: www.meredith.edu
Established: 1891 | Annual Undergrad Tuition & Fees: $33,630
Enrollment: 1,885 | Female
Affiliation or Control: Independent Non-Profit | IRS Status: 501(c)3
Highest Offering: Master's
Program: Liberal Arts And General; Teacher Preparatory; Professional
Accreditation: SC, BUS, CIDA, DIETD, DIETI, MUS, SW, TED

01 President .... Dr. Jo ALLEN
05 Sr Vice Pres and Provost .... Dr. Matthew POSLUSNY
30 Vice Pres Institutional Advancement .... Dr. Charles (Lennie) BARTON
10 Vice Pres for Business & Finance .... Mr. Craig BARFIELD
32 Vice President for College Programs .... Dr. Jean JACKSON
84 Assoc Provost Enrollment Management .... Vacant
35 Dean of Students .... Ms. Ann C. GLEASON
58 Dean of Graduate Studies .... Vacant
06 Registrar .... Ms. Evie ODOM
09 Dir of Assessment & Inst Research .... Ms. Dianne RAUBENHEIMER
08 Director Library Info Services .... Ms. Laura DAVIDSON
07 Director of Admissions .... Ms. Shery BOYLES
37 Director of Financial Assistance .... Mr. Kevin MICHAELSEN
26 Executive Director of Marketing .... Ms. Kristi EAVES-MCLENNAN
35 Dir Student Activ/Leadership Devel .... Ms. Cheryl S. JENKINS
28 Dir Commuter Life/Diversity Pgms .... Ms. Tomecca SLOANE
36 Director of Career Planning .... Ms. Dana SUMNER
29 Dir of Alumnae & Parent Relations .... Ms. Hilary ALLEN
38 Director of Counseling Center .... Ms. Beth A. MEIER
39 Director Resident Life/Housing .... Ms. Heidi LECOUNT
20 Director of Academic Advising .... Ms. Amy HITLIN
31 Director Campus Events .... Mr. Bill BROWN
23 Director Health Services .... Ms. Sherri HENDERSON
42 Campus Minister .... Rev. Stacy PARDUE
13 Chief Information Officer .... Mr. Jeffrey HOWLETT
19 Chief Campus Police .... Mr. Al WHITE
15 Director of Human Resources .... Ms. Pamela DAVIS
18 Chief Facilities/Physical Plant .... Ms. Sharon CAMPBELL
21 Controller .... Ms. Lori DUKE

Methodist University (C)

5400 Ramsey Street, Fayetteville NC 28311-1498

County: Cumberland | FICE Identification: 002946 | Unit ID: 198969

Telephone: (910) 630-7000 | Carnegie Class: Bac/Diverse
FAX Number: (910) 630-7317 | Calendar System: Semester
URL: www.methodist.edu
Established: 1956 | Annual Undergrad Tuition & Fees: $30,530
Enrollment: 2,461 | Coed
Affiliation or Control: United Methodist | IRS Status: 501(c)3
Highest Offering: Master's
Program: Liberal Arts And General; Teacher Preparatory
Accreditation: SC, ACBSP, ARCPA, CAATE, NURSE, @PTA, SW

01 President .... Dr. Ben E. HANCOCK, JR.
05 Exec Vice Pres & Academic Dean .... Dr. Delmas S. CRISP, JR.
10 Vice President for Business Affairs .... Mr. Gene T. CLAYTON
32 Vice President for Student Affairs .... Mr. William WALKER
30 VP Univ Relations & Advancement .... Ms. Sandy AMMONS
09 VP Planning & Evaluation .... Dr. Donald L. LASSITER
20 Associate VP for Academic Affairs .... Ms. Jane W. GARDINER
35 Assoc Dean Student Services .... Mr. Todd D. HARRIS
84 Director Enrollment Management .... Mr. Rick D. LOWE
42 VP Campus Ministry/Cmty Engagement .... Rev. Kelli TAYLOR
26 Director of Public Relations .... Mrs. Sandy AMMONS
41 Director of Athletics .... Mr. Robert T. MCEVOY
29 Director of Alumni Affairs .... Ms. Lauren C. WIKE
07 Dean of Admissions .... Mr. Jamie W. LEGG
37 Director of Financial Aid .... Ms. Bonnie J. ADAMSON
06 Registrar .... Ms. Jasmin K. BROWN
08 Head Librarian .... Ms. Tracey PEARSON
104 Dir Intl Programs/Study Abroad .... Mr. Lyle SHEPPARD
19 Director Security/Safety .... Mr. James K. PHILLIPS
15 Director Personnel Services .... Mrs. Debra YEATTS
18 Chief Facilities/Physical Plant .... Mr. Thomas W. DAUGHTREY, III
21 Assoc VP Bus Affairs/Controller .... Ms. Dawn AUSBORN
36 Director Career Services .... Ms. Antoinette P. BELLAMY
38 Director Student Counseling .... Ms. Darlene HOPKINS
96 Director of Purchasing .... Ms. Deborah DEMBOSKY

Mid-Atlantic Christian University (D)

715 N Poindexter, Elizabeth City NC 27909-4054

County: Pasquotank | FICE Identification: 022809 | Unit ID: 199458

Telephone: (252) 334-2000 | Carnegie Class: Bac/Diverse
FAX Number: (252) 334-2071 | Calendar System: Semester
URL: www.macuniversity.edu
Established: 1948 | Annual Undergrad Tuition & Fees: $13,440
Enrollment: 172 | Coed
Affiliation or Control: Churches Of Christ | IRS Status: 501(c)3
Highest Offering: Baccalaureate
Program: Liberal Arts And General; Religious Emphasis
Accreditation: SC

01 President .... Dr. D. Clay PERKINS
05 Vice President Academic Affairs .... Dr. Kevin W. LARSEN
32 Vice President Student Services .... Dr. Ken S. GREENE
30 Vice President Institutional Advanc .... Mr. John MAURICE
09 Director of Institutional Research .... Dr. Kevin W. LARSEN
06 Registrar .... Miss Yolanda K. TESKE
08 Director of Library .... Mr. Ken D. GUNSELMAN
38 Counselor .... Mr. Donald W. MCKINNEY
37 Financial Aid Administrator .... Vacant
21 Assistant Vice President Finance .... Mrs. Carol M. STUART
42 Campus Minister .... Miss Andrea A. STRAWDERMAN
49 Chair of Arts and Sciences .... Dr. Robert W. SMITH
73 Chair of Biblical Studies .... Dr. Lee M. FIELDS
88 Chair of Christian Ministry .... Dr. Claudio F. DIVINO
88 Chair of Marketplace Ministry .... Mr. Donald W. MCKINNEY
35 Student Life Administrator .... Miss Andrea A. STRAWDERMAN
07 Director of Admissions .... Mr. Daniel C. SMITH

Miller-Motte College (E)

2205 Walnut Street, Cary NC 27518
Telephone: (919) 532-7171 | Identification: 770726
Accreditation: ACICS, MAC, SURGT

† Branch campus of Miller-Motte Technical College, Lynchburg, VA.

Miller-Motte College (F)

3725 Ramsey Street, Fayetteville NC 28311
Telephone: (910) 354-1900 | Identification: 770728
Accreditation: ACICS

† Branch campus of Miller-Motte Technical College, Lynchburg, VA.

Miller-Motte College (G)

1021 W.H. Smith Blvd, Suite 102, Greenville NC 27834
Telephone: (252) 215-2000 | Identification: 770730
Accreditation: ACICS

† Branch campus of Miller-Motte Technical College, Clarksville, TN.

Miller-Motte College (H)

1291 Hargett Street, Jacksonville NC 28540
Telephone: (910) 478-4300 | Identification: 770729
Accreditation: ACICS

† Branch campus of Miller-Motte Technical College, Lynchburg, VA.

Miller-Motte College (I)

3901 Capital Boulevard, Suite 151, Raleigh NC 27604
Telephone: (919) 723-2820 | Identification: 770727
Accreditation: ACICS, DA, MAC

† Branch campus of Miller-Motte Technical College, Lynchburg, VA.

Miller-Motte Technical College (J)

5000 Market Street, Wilmington NC 28405-3430
Telephone: (910) 392-4660 | FICE Identification: 030632
Accreditation: ACICS, DA, MAC, SURGT

† Branch campus of Miller-Motte Technical College, TN.

Montreat College (K)

PO Box 1267, 310 Gaither Circle, Montreat NC 28757-1267

County: Buncombe | FICE Identification: 002948 | Unit ID: 199032

Telephone: (828) 669-8012 | Carnegie Class: Master's S
FAX Number: (828) 669-9554 | Calendar System: Semester
URL: www.montreat.edu
Established: 1916 | Annual Undergrad Tuition & Fees: $33,866
Enrollment: 933 | Coed
Affiliation or Control: Non-denominational | IRS Status: 501(c)3
Highest Offering: Master's
Program: Liberal Arts And General
Accreditation: SC, IACBE, TED

01 President .... Dr. Paul J. MAURER
10 VP for Finance and Administration .... Mr. Jack HEINEN
30 VP of Advancement .... Mr. Alex MILLER
58 VP and Dean for Adult/Grad Studies .... Mrs. Susan DEWOODY
05 VP and Dean for Academic Affairs .... Dr. Greg KERR
84 VP for Enrollment and Management .... Ms. Kristin JANES
32 VP and Dean for Student Services .... Dr. Daniel BENNETT
88 Counselor to the President .... Mr. Joe KIRKLAND
26 Exec Dir Marketing/Communications .... Mrs. Annie CARLSON
09 Assoc Dean of Academics & Inst Eff .... Ms. Becky FRAWLEY
20 Associate Dean of Academic Affairs .... Mr. Tom OXENREIDER
41 Athletic Director .... Mr. Jose LARIOS
29 Director Alumni Relations .... Mr. David WALTERS
37 Director of Financial Aid .... Ms. Jill GABLE
38 Director of Counseling .... Mrs. Holleigh WOODWARD
88 Director for Advancement Services .... Mrs. Arla YEATMAN
08 Library Director .... Ms. Elizabeth R. PEARSON
21 Controller .... Mrs. Patti GUFFEY
04 Executive Assistant to President .... Ms. Hope DEIFELL
42 Dean of Spiritual Formation .... Rev. David TAYLOR
06 Registrar .... Ms. Keri BOER
40 Bookstore Manager .... Ms. Carly BRAENDEL
19 Chief of Campus Police .... Dr. N. Scott ADAMS
18 Chief Facilities/Physical Plant .... Mr. Jim LEENHOUTS

Native American Bible College (L)

PO Box 248, Shannon NC 28386

County: Robeson | Identification: 667092
Telephone: (910) 843-5304 | Carnegie Class: Not Classified
FAX Number: N/A | Calendar System: Semester
URL: nativeamericanbiblecollege.org
Established: 1968 | Annual Undergrad Tuition & Fees: $3,926
Enrollment: 30 | Coed
Affiliation or Control: Assemblies Of God Church | IRS Status: 501(c)3
Highest Offering: Baccalaureate
Program: Religious Emphasis
Accreditation: @BI

01 President .... James A. KEYS
05 Chief Academic Officer .... Dossie MORRIS WOOD, JR.
32 Chief Student Development Officer .... John DAVIS
84 Enrollment Director .... John WALKER, JR.
08 Chief Librarian .... T. Liisa KELLY
06 Director of Admissions/Registrar .... April LOCKLEAR

*North Carolina Community College System (M)

200 W Jones Street, 5001 MSC, Raleigh NC 27699-5001

County: Wake | FICE Identification: 033445 | Unit ID: 199166

Telephone: (919) 807-7100 | Carnegie Class: N/A
FAX Number: (919) 807-7166
URL: www.nccommunitycolleges.edu

01 President .... Dr. R. Scott RALLS
05 Senior VP Programs/Chief Acad Ofcr .... Dr. Lisa CHAPMAN
10 Exec VP Operation/Chief Fin Ofcr .... Ms. Jennifer HAYGOOD
13 SVP & Chief Technology Officer .... Dr. Saundra WILLIAMS
101 Director State Board Affairs .... Mr. Bryan JENKINS
04 Special Assistant to the President .... Ms. Pia MCKENZIE
46 VP Engagement/Strategic Innovation .... Ms. Linda WEINER

*Alamance Community College (N)

1247 Jimmie Kerr Road/PO Box 8000, Graham NC 27253-8000

County: Alamance | FICE Identification: 005463 | Unit ID: 199786

Telephone: (336) 578-2002 | Carnegie Class: Assoc/Pub-S-MC
FAX Number: (336) 578-1987 | Calendar System: Semester
URL: www.alamancecc.edu
Established: 1958 | Annual Undergrad Tuition & Fees (In-District): $1,758
Enrollment: 4,437 | Coed
Affiliation or Control: State/Local | IRS Status: 501(c)3
Highest Offering: Associate Degree
Program: Occupational; 2-Year Principally Bachelor's Creditable

Accreditation: SC, ACFEI, DA, MAC, MLTAD

02 President Dr. Algie C. GATEWOOD
05 Executive Vice President Mr. Scott QUEEN
10 VP Admin & Fiscal Svcs Ms. Cynthia COLLIE
30 VP Institutional Advancement Ms. Carolyn RHODE
49 VP of Instruction Ms. Catherine W. JOHNSON
20 VP Institutional Support Vacant
103 VP Workforce Development Mr. Gary SAUNDERS
32 VP Student Success Dr. Carol DISQUE
50 Dean Business/Arts & Sciences Ms. Sonya MCCOOK
72 Dean Industrial Technologies Mr. Wally M. SHEARIN
69 Dean Health & Public Svcs Vacant
21 Controller Mr. Matthew BANKO
06 Registrar Mr. Kenneth DOBBINS
11 Director Administrative Services Mr. Erik CONTI
15 Director Human Resources Ms. Lorri ALLISON
13 Director Information Services Mr. Winfield HENRY
08 Director Learning Resources Center Ms. Sheila STREET
26 Director Public Information/Mktg Mr. Edward WILLIAMS
56 Director Occupational Ext Program Mr. David PARKER
84 Director Enrollment Management Ms. Elizabeth BREHLER
37 Director Financial Aid Ms. Sabrina DEGAIN
36 Director Counseling & Career Svcs Ms. Ilona OWENS
38 Special Needs/Counseling Svcs Coord Ms. Monica ISBELL
88 Academic Support Specialist Ms. Jennifer BROWNELL
09 Institutional Researcher Dr. Jessica HARRELL

*Asheville - Buncombe Technical Community College (A)

340 Victoria Road, Asheville NC 28801-4897
County: Buncombe FICE Identification: 004033
Unit ID: 197887
Telephone: (828) 254-1921 Carnegie Class: Assoc/Pub-R-L
FAX Number: (828) 251-6355 Calendar System: Semester
URL: www.abtech.edu
Established: 1959 Annual Undergrad Tuition & Fees (In-District): $2,033
Enrollment: 7,507 Coed
Affiliation or Control: State/Local IRS Status: 501(c)3
Highest Offering: Associate Degree
Program: Occupational; 2-Year Principally Bachelor's Creditable
Accreditation: SC, ACFEI, DA, DH, DMS, EMT, MAC, MLTAD, PHLEB, RAD, SURGT

02 President Dr. Dennis KING
10 VP Business & Finance/CFO Ms. Rhonda DEVAN
13 Vice Pres Information Technology Mr. Brian WILLIS
05 VP Instructional Services Ms. Melissa QUINLEY
20 Associate VP Instructional Services Dr. Gene LOFLIN
32 VP Student Services Dr. Terry BRASIER
15 Vice President Human Resources & OD Ms. Kaye N. WAUGH
103 VP Econ Workforce Dev/Cont Educ Ms. Shelley WHITE
04 Executive Administrative Assistant Ms. Martha SHANKS
49 Dean Arts & Sciences Dr. Beth STEWART
50 Dean Business & Hospitality Educ Mr. RJ CORMAN
54 Dean Engineering & Applied Tech Mr. Vernon D. DAUGHERTY
91 Director Info Systems Technology Mr. David C. MCKINNEY
30 Exec Director/College Advancement Ms. Sue OLESIUK
35 Director Student Life/Development Ms. Michele HATHCOCK
61 Director Law Enforcement Academy Ms. Dianne L. DAVIS
21 Director Business Services Ms. Lisa EVANS
37 Director of Financial Aid Mr. Brian CLEMMONS
06 Registrar Ms. Katherine CAPPS
84 Director Enrollment Services Ms. Lisa F. BUSH
24 Director Library Services Vacant
12 Director Madison County Campus Ms. Sherri DAVIS
18 Director Plant Operations Mr. Benny R. SMITH
19 Chief of Police/Security Ms. Kara KELLER
31 Director Community Services Program Ms. Brinda W. CALDWELL
08 Librarian Ms. Margaret HIGGINS
09 Exec Director Research & Planning Mr. David B. WHITE
27 Exec Dir Community Rels/Marketing Ms. Kerri GLOVER
28 Director of Diversity Vacant
40 Bookstore Manager Mr. Kevin MILLS
96 Purchasing Agent Ms. Rebecca R. WATKINS
72 Dir Cust Rels/Technology Services Mr. Cris HARSHMAN

*Beaufort County Community College (B)

5337 US Hwy 264 East, Washington NC 27889-7889
County: Beaufort FICE Identification: 008558
Unit ID: 197966
Telephone: (252) 946-6194 Carnegie Class: Assoc/Pub-R-S
FAX Number: (252) 946-0271 Calendar System: Semester
URL: www.beaufortccc.edu
Established: 1967 Annual Undergrad Tuition & Fees (In-District): $2,368
Enrollment: 2,035 Coed
Affiliation or Control: State/Local IRS Status: 501(c)3
Highest Offering: Associate Degree
Program: Occupational; 2-Year Principally Bachelor's Creditable
Accreditation: SC, MLTAD

02 President Dr. Barbara TANSEY
05 VP of Academics Dr. Crystal ANGE
11 VP of Administrative Services Mr. Mark NELSON
32 VP of Student Services Mr. Rick ANDERSON
51 VP of Continuing Education Mrs. Stacey GERARD
45 VP of Research & Inst Effectiveness Dr. Jay SULLIVAN
26 Public Relations Coordinator Mr. David NORWOOD
88 Dir of Community Partnerships Mr. Clay CARTER
76 Dean Allied Health/Profess Services Mrs. Erica S. CARACOGLIA
49 Dean Arts & Sciences Mrs. Lisa HILL
50 Dean of Business & Industrial Tech Mr. Ben MORRIS
08 Dir Learning Resources Center Mrs. Penny SERMONS
88 Network Administrator Mr. Whiting TOLER
91 System Administrator Mr. Randy BURNETTE
15 Director of Human Resources Mrs. Emily WOOLARD
19 Chief of Campus Police Mr. Christopher HARRISON
88 Systems Administrator Assistant Mr. Brandon BUNCH
37 Director of Financial Aid Ms. Megan SOMMERS
06 Registrar Mrs. Camille RICHARDSON
07 Director of Admissions Mrs. Michele MAYO
103 Dir of Business & Industry Svcs Mr. Lentz STOWE
04 Administrative Asst to President Mrs. Jennie SINGLETON
96 Purchasing Coordinator Vacant
38 Director of Counseling Mrs. Kimberly JACKSON
102 Executive Dir of Foundation Ms. Serena SULLIVAN
105 Webmaster Mr. Keith SULLIVAN
18 Dir Campus Operations Mr. Wesley ADAMS
13 Director of Information Technology Mr. Arthur RICHARD
21 Director of Accounting Ms. Cecelia SCOTT

*Bladen Community College (C)

PO Box 266, Dublin NC 28332-0266
County: Bladen FICE Identification: 007987
Unit ID: 198011
Telephone: (910) 879-5500 Carnegie Class: Assoc/Pub-R-S
FAX Number: (910) 879-5564 Calendar System: Semester
URL: www.bladencc.edu
Established: 1967 Annual Undergrad Tuition & Fees (In-State): $2,397
Enrollment: 1,330 Coed
Affiliation or Control: State IRS Status: 501(c)3
Highest Offering: Associate Degree
Program: Occupational; 2-Year Principally Bachelor's Creditable; Technical Emphasis
Accreditation: SC

02 President Dr. William FINDT
04 Exec Admin Asst to the President Ms. Missi HESTER
05 Executive VP and Chief Acad Officer Mr. Jeffrey KORNEGAY
51 VP for Continuing Education Ms. Sondra GUYTON
20 Assoc VP for Academic Services Ms. Cynthia MCKOY
32 Vice President for Student Services Mr. Barry PRIEST
10 Vice President for Finance Mr. Jay STANLEY
88 Assoc VP for Program Services Mr. Lynn KING
21 Director of Budgeting Ms. Sheila DOCKERY
08 Director Student Resource Center Ms. Sherwin RICE
09 Dir Institutional Effect & Planning Ms. Twyla DAVIS
37 Director of Financial Aid Ms. Samantha BENSON
106 Director of Distance Learning Mr. Ray SHEPPARD
15 Human Resources Officer Ms. Tiina MUNDY
18 Director of Facilities Mr. Bradley TAYLOR
26 Public Information Specialist Ms. Cathy KINLAW
102 Foundation Specialist Ms. Linda BURNEY

*Blue Ridge Community College (D)

180 W Campus Drive, Flat Rock NC 28731-4728
County: Henderson FICE Identification: 009684
Unit ID: 198039
Telephone: (828) 694-1700 Carnegie Class: Assoc/Pub-R-M
FAX Number: (828) 694-1690 Calendar System: Semester
URL: www.blueridge.edu
Established: 1969 Annual Undergrad Tuition & Fees (In-District): $2,295
Enrollment: 2,215 Coed
Affiliation or Control: State/Local IRS Status: 501(c)3
Highest Offering: Associate Degree
Program: Occupational; 2-Year Principally Bachelor's Creditable
Accreditation: SC, EMT, SURGT

02 President Dr. Molly PARKHILL
05 VP for Instruction Dr. Alan H. STEPHENSON
32 VP for Student Services Ms. Marcia L. STONEMAN
13 VP for Technology-CIO Vacant
103 VP Workforce Dev/Cont Education Ms. Julie G. THOMPSON
10 AVP for Finance/CFO Ms. Carolyn W. ALLEY
11 Vice Pres Administration Dr. Chad MERRILL
49 Dean for Arts and Sciences Mr. David H. DAVIS
72 Dean for Applied Technology Mr. Chris ENGLISH
76 Dean for Allied Health Programs Ms. Rita D. CONNER
97 Dean for Basic Skills Mr. Rick MARSHALL
50 Dean for Business/Service Careers Ms. Kathy ALLEN
102 Executive Director Foundation Ms. Ann F. GREEN
44 Institutional Advance/Rsrch Coord Ms. Carol Ann LYDON
06 Registrar Ms. Kirsten H. BUNCH
08 Director for Library Services Ms. Susan D. WILLIAMS
37 Director Financial Aid Ms. Lisanne MASTERSON
38 Director for Counseling Vacant
14 Director Information Technologies Mr. Steve YOUNG
18 Director of Facilities Mr. Peter HEMANS
26 Dir of Marketing & Communications Ms. Lee Anna HANEY
35 Student Activities Coordinator Vacant
84 Director of Enrollment Management Ms. Cathy STEPHENSON
15 Director of Human Resources Mr. Tommy OAKMAN

*Brunswick Community College (E)

50 College Road, Bolivia NC 28422
County: Brunswick FICE Identification: 021707
Unit ID: 198084
Telephone: (910) 755-7300 Carnegie Class: Assoc/Pub-R-S
FAX Number: (910) 754-9609 Calendar System: Semester
URL: www.brunswickcc.edu
Established: 1979 Annual Undergrad Tuition & Fees (In-State): $2,404
Enrollment: 1,566 Coed
Affiliation or Control: State IRS Status: 501(c)3
Highest Offering: Associate Degree
Program: Occupational; 2-Year Principally Bachelor's Creditable; Professional; Business Emphasis
Accreditation: SC, CAHIIM, PHLEB

02 President Dr. Susanne H. ADAMS
05 VP Academic & Student Affairs Dr. Sharon THOMPSON
10 Vice President Budget and Finance Ms. Sheila GALLOWAY
32 Dean Student Services/Enroll Mgmt Vacant
11 Vice President Operations Mr. Donald BASSINGER
09 Director of Institutional Planning Mr. Michael COBB
08 Director Library Ms. Carmen BLANTON
06 Registrar Ms. Christine DYE
15 Director Human Resources Ms. Nicole WILLIAMS
19 Public Safety/Police Director Mr. Lindsay WALTON
18 Physical Plant Director Mr. Jack LUCIANO
102 Director Resource Development Ms. Elina DICOSTANZO
26 Director of Marketing & Public Info Ms. London SCHMIDT
37 Financial Aid/Veterans Affs Coord Ms. Tracy SOMERLAD
72 Dean Professional Technical Service Ms. Gina ROBINSON
49 Dean Arts & Sciences Dr. John GRAY
04 Administrative Asst to President Ms. Bea PALAZZI
13 Chief Info Technology Officer Mr. Ronnie BRYANT
41 Athletic Director Mr. Robert ALLEN

*Caldwell Community College and Technical Institute (F)

2855 Hickory Boulevard, Hudson NC 28638-1399
County: Caldwell FICE Identification: 004835
Unit ID: 198118
Telephone: (828) 726-2200 Carnegie Class: Assoc/Pub-R-M
FAX Number: (828) 726-2216 Calendar System: Semester
URL: www.cccti.edu
Established: 1964 Annual Undergrad Tuition & Fees (In-District): $2,638
Enrollment: 3,887 Coed
Affiliation or Control: State/Local IRS Status: 501(c)3
Highest Offering: Associate Degree
Program: Occupational; 2-Year Principally Bachelor's Creditable
Accreditation: SC, DMS, NMT, PTAA, RAD

02 President Dr. Kenneth A. BOHAM
03 Executive Vice President Dr. Mark POARCH
18 Director Facility Services Mr. Jeff HERMAN
32 Vice President Student Services Mrs. Dena HOLMAN
51 VP Continuing Educ/Workforce Dev Mrs. Elaine LOCKHART
12 Executive Director Watauga Campus Mr. Steve MELTON
05 Director Academic Support Vacant
84 Dir Enrollment Mgmt Services Mr. Dennis SEAGLE
08 Director Learning Resources Center Ms. Deborah JOYNER
37 Director Financial Aid/Veterans Aff Dr. Mark BARBER
36 Dir Career Planning/Job Placement Mr. Rick SHEW
15 Director Human Resources Mrs. Kathy SEITZ
26 Director Marketing & Communications Mrs. Sherry WILSON
10 Controller Mr. Scott ROGERS
09 Dir Inst Effectiveness/Researcg Mrs. Kim GANT
27 Public Relations Officer Mr. Edward TERRY
102 Director Foundation Office Ms. Marla CHRISTIE
28 Director of Diversity Vacant
38 Director Student Counseling Mr. Shannon BROWN
96 Director of Purchasing Mrs. Marcia POTTS
40 Manager Bookstore Mrs. Trina CURTIS
04 Executive Assistant Mrs. Donna CHURCH
19 Director Security/Safety Mr. Dennis HOPKINS
06 Registrar Mrs. Debra YOUNT
13 Chief Info Technology Officer (CIO) Ms. Susan WOOTEN

*Cape Fear Community College (G)

411 N Front Street, Wilmington NC 28401-3993
County: New Hanover FICE Identification: 005320
Unit ID: 198154
Telephone: (910) 362-7000 Carnegie Class: Assoc/Pub-R-L
FAX Number: (910) 763-2279 Calendar System: Semester
URL: www.cfcc.edu
Established: 1958 Annual Undergrad Tuition & Fees (In-District): $2,526
Enrollment: 9,062 Coed
Affiliation or Control: State/Local IRS Status: 501(c)3
Highest Offering: Associate Degree
Program: Occupational; 2-Year Principally Bachelor's Creditable
Accreditation: SC, ADNUR, DA, DH, DMS, OTA, PHLEB, RAD, SURGT

02 President Dr. Amanda LEE
05 Interim VP Instructional Service Mr. Robert PHILPOTT
10 Interim VP for Business & Inst Svcs Mr. Kennon BRIGGS
32 Interim VP for Student Services Mr. Patrick PITTMAN
09 VP for Inst Effectiveness/Planning Ms. Kim GANT
18 Director of Institutional Services Mr. Kenneth D. PEARCE
06 Registrar Mr. Phil FARINHOLT
102 VP for Institutional Advancement Ms. Margaret ROBISON
84 Director of Enrollment Management Ms. Linda KASYAN
08 Dean Learning Resources Center Ms. Catherine LEE
37 Interim Director of Financial Aid Ms. Rachel CAVANAUGH
36 Director of Career & Testing Mr. Patrick PITTMAN
26 Dir of Marketing & Public Relations Mr. David M. HARDIN
13 VP Info Technology Services Mr. Wellington DE SOUZA
15 Chief Human Resources Officer Ms. Elaine DOELL
41 Dir Student Activities/Athletics Mr. Robert MCGEE

96 Director of Purchasing & Inventory .... Mr. Wade QUINN
38 Director Student Counseling .... Ms. Jacqueline FOSTER
21 Controller .... Ms. Christina GREENE
28 Director of Diversity .... Mr. David HARDIN
07 Director of Admissions .... Ms. Linda KASYAN
44 Annual Giving Director .... Ms. Dana MCKOY
51 Dean of Continuing Education .... Ms. Melissa SINGLER
75 Dean Vocational/Technical Education .... Mr. Pat HOGAN
49 Dean Arts & Sciences .... Ms. Orangel J. DANIELS
105 Web Services Analyst .... Ms. Christina HEIKKILA
04 Exec Assistant to the President .... Ms. Michelle LEE
19 Director Security/Safety .... Chief Dan WILCOX
108 Director of Assessment & QEP .... Mr. Jason CHAFFIN

*Carteret Community College (A)

3505 Arendell Street, Morehead City NC 28557-2989
County: Carteret FICE Identification: 008081
Unit ID: 198206
Telephone: (252) 222-6000 Carnegie Class: Assoc/Pub-R-S
FAX Number: (252) 222-2514 Calendar System: Semester
URL: www.carteret.edu
Established: 1963 Annual Undergrad Tuition & Fees (In-District): $2,395
Enrollment: 1,480 Coed
Affiliation or Control: State/Local IRS Status: 501(c)3
Highest Offering: Associate Degree
Program: Occupational; 2-Year Principally Bachelor's Creditable
Accreditation: SC, ADNUR, COARC, MAC, RAD

02 President .... Dr. Kerry L. YOUNGBLOOD
05 VP for Instruction/Student Support .... Dr. Fran EMORY
10 VP Finance/Administrative Services .... Ms. Kary PORTER
31 Vice Pres Corporate & Community .... Mr. Perry L. HARKER
04 Executive Assistant to President .... Ms. Brenda REASH
08 Director LRC .... Ms. Elizabeth BAKER
32 Senior Director Student Services .... Ms. Robie MCFARLAND
35 Director of Student Success .... Mr. Rick HILL
13 Director Information Technology .... Mr. John GREEN
15 Director of Human Resources .... Ms. Barbara I. COOPER
30 Director of Advancement .... Mr. David NATEMAN
49 Dean Arts & Sciences .... Ms. Doree HILL
76 Div Director Health Sciences .... Ms. Laurie A. FRESHWATER
88 Dean of Applied Science .... Ms. Susan H. MCINTYRE
37 Financial Aid Officer .... Ms. Brenda J. LONG
06 Registrar .... Ms. Tammi COBLE
07 Admissions Officer .... Mr. Martin NICHOLS
09 Dir of Institutional Effectiveness .... Ms. Misty RASMUSSEN
18 Dir Operations/Facil Maintenance .... Mr. Steve SPARKS
26 Director of Public Affairs .... Ms. Alize PROISY
96 Purchasing/Accts Payable Manager .... Ms. Donna L. CUMBIE
106 Director Distance Learning .... Ms. Mary WALTON

*Catawba Valley Community College (B)

2550 Highway 70, SE, Hickory NC 28602-9699
County: Catawba FICE Identification: 005318
Unit ID: 198233
Telephone: (828) 327-7000 Carnegie Class: Assoc/Pub-R-M
FAX Number: (828) 327-7276 Calendar System: Semester
URL: www.cvcc.edu
Established: 1960 Annual Undergrad Tuition & Fees (In-District): $1,560
Enrollment: 4,700 Coed
Affiliation or Control: State/Local IRS Status: 501(c)3
Highest Offering: Associate Degree
Program: Occupational; 2-Year Principally Bachelor's Creditable
Accreditation: SC, ADNUR, CAHIIM, COARC, DH, EMT, IFSAC, NDT, POLYT, RAD, SURGT

02 President .... Dr. Garrett D. HINSHAW
05 Exec VP-Instruction .... Dr. Keith MACKIE
10 Sr VP Business Affairs-Operations .... Mr. Wes BUNCH
32 Dean of Student Access/Development .... Mrs. Cindy COULTER
15 Director Human Resources .... Mr. Mike KIDD
07 Director of Admissions/Records .... Ms. Kelly PLUMLEY
21 Controller .... Ms. Jennifer HAMM
37 Director Scholarships/Financial Aid .... Ms. RaChele SUMMERS
09 Ofc Accountability/Efficienc/Effect .... Mr. Kevin ROUSE
88 Director Industrial Training .... Ms. Crystal GLENN
88 Director Small Business Center .... Mr. Jeff NEUVILLE
50 Director Business/Technolgy Ext .... Ms. Susan KILLIAN
88 Director Hosiery Technology Center .... Mr. Daniel C. ST. LOUIS
13 Director Information Technologies .... Mr. Ken ELLIOTT
19 Director Campus Safety/Security .... Mr. Steve HUNT
31 Director Community Education .... Ms. Chanell MORELLO
36 Counselor/Job Placement Svcs Coord .... Ms. Teresa RAY
16 Coordinator Health/Human Services .... Ms. Robin ROSS
04 Administrative Asst to President .... Ms. Sherry WILLIAMS
29 Director Alumni Relations .... Ms. Mary REYNOLDS
41 Athletic Director .... Mr. Nick SCHROEDER

*Central Carolina Community College (C)

1105 Kelly Drive, Sanford NC 27330-9000
County: Lee FICE Identification: 005449
Unit ID: 198251
Telephone: (919) 775-5401 Carnegie Class: Assoc/Pub-R-M
FAX Number: (919) 718-7380 Calendar System: Semester
URL: www.cccc.edu
Established: 1958 Annual Undergrad Tuition & Fees (In-District): $2,268
Enrollment: 4,776 Coed
Affiliation or Control: State/Local IRS Status: 501(c)3
Highest Offering: Associate Degree
Program: Occupational; 2-Year Principally Bachelor's Creditable; Nursing Emphasis
Accreditation: SC, DA, DH, MAC, POLYT

02 President .... Dr. T. Eston MARCHANT
05 Vice President of Student Learning .... Dr. Brian MERRITT
11 Vice Pres of Administrative Svcs .... Mr. Philip PRICE
32 Vice President Student Services .... Mr. Ken R. HOYLE
51 VP Economic & Community Development .... Ms. Pamela SENEGAL
20 VP of Student Learning .... Mr. Mike BECK
26 Assoc VP of Marketing/HR .... Ms. Marcie DISHMAN
12 Provost Chatham Campus .... Mr. Mark HALL
12 Provost Harnett Campus .... Mr. William R. TYSON
08 Director of Library Services .... Ms. Tara GUTHRIE
15 Director of Human Resources .... Ms. Kimberly DELK
102 Exec Director of CCCC Foundation .... Ms. Emily HARE
06 Dean of Enrollment/Registrar .... Ms. Jamie CHILDRESS
07 Director of Admissions .... Ms. Jamee STIFFLER
37 Director Financial Aid .... Ms. Ann PEACOCK
96 Purchasing Director .... Mrs. Starlene JACKSON
18 Physical Plant Manager .... Mr. Ronnie MEASAMER
75 Dean Vocational/Technical Programs .... Dr. Stephan ATHANS
36 Dean of College & Career Readiness .... Ms. Dawn TUCKER
51 Assoc Provost Curriculum Admin .... Mr. John MATTHEWS
76 Dean of Health Sciences .... Ms. Lisa BAKER

*Central Piedmont Community College (D)

PO Box 35009, Charlotte NC 28235-5009
County: Mecklenburg FICE Identification: 002915
Unit ID: 198260
Telephone: (704) 330-2722 Carnegie Class: Assoc/Pub-U-MC
FAX Number: (704) 330-5045 Calendar System: Semester
URL: www.cpcc.edu
Established: 1963 Annual Undergrad Tuition & Fees (In-District): $2,664
Enrollment: 19,957 Coed
Affiliation or Control: State/Local IRS Status: 501(c)3
Highest Offering: Associate Degree
Program: Occupational; 2-Year Principally Bachelor's Creditable
Accreditation: SC, ACFEI, ADNUR, CAHIIM, COARC, CVT, CYTO, DA, DH, ENGT, MAC, MLTAD, OTA, PTAA, SURGT

02 President .... Dr. P. Anthony ZEISS
05 VP for Learning and Workforce Devel .... Mr. Richard ZOLLINGER
84 VP Enrollment & Student Services .... Dr. Marcia CONSTON
10 VP Finance/Administrative Services .... Mr. Michael MOSS
13 VP for Technology and CIO .... Mr. David KIM
30 VP for Inst Advancement .... Dr. Kevin MCCARTHY
04 Exec Assistant to the President .... Dr. Tracie CLARK
26 PIO & Asst to Pres Cmty Rels/Mktg .... Mr. Jeffrey LOWRANCE
103 Assoc VP Learning and Workforce Dev .... Dr. Deborah BOUTON
11 Assoc VP Financial Svcs .... Mr. Michael WHITEMAN
18 Assoc VP Facilities & Construction .... Ms. Vicki SAVILLE
09 Assoc VP Institutional Research .... Dr. Terri MANNING
88 Assoc VP Compliance and Audit .... Dr. Brenda LEONARD
15 Assoc VP of Human Resources .... Mr. Paul SANTOS
25 Assoc VP Government Rels & Grants .... Mr. Michael HORN
88 Assoc VP Services Corporation .... Ms. Quincy FOIL
35 Assoc VP Student Success .... Ms. Rita DAWKINS
12 Dean Levine Campus .... Dr. Edith MCELROY
12 Dean Merancas Campus .... Ms. Tamara WILLIAMS
12 Dean Central Campus .... Dr. Paul KOEHNKE
12 Dean Cato Campus .... Ms. Janet MALKEMES
12 Dean Harris Campus .... Ms. Mary VICKERS-KOCH
12 Dean Harper Campus .... Mr. Jay POTTER
54 Dean STEM-S .... Mr. Chris PAYNTER
88 Dean Retention Services .... Dr. Clint MCELROY
32 Dean Student Life/Service Learning .... Mr. Mark HELMS
84 Dean Enrollment Management .... Mr. Daniel MCEACHERN
08 Dean Libraries .... Ms. Gloria KELLEY
88 Dean College & Career Readiness .... Ms. Kathi MCLENDON
07 Dean Enrollment Services .... Ms. April JONES
106 Dean Profess Development/eLearning .... Ms. Karen MERRIMAN
88 Dir/Gen Station Manager WTVI PBS .... Ms. Amy BURKETT
22 Dir Affirmative Action/EEO .... Mr. Leon MATTHEWS

*Cleveland Community College (E)

137 S Post Road, Shelby NC 28152-6296
County: Cleveland FICE Identification: 008082
Unit ID: 198321
Telephone: (704) 669-6000 Carnegie Class: Assoc/Pub-R-M
FAX Number: (704) 669-4202 Calendar System: Semester
URL: www.clevelandcc.edu
Established: 1965 Annual Undergrad Tuition & Fees (In-District): $2,398
Enrollment: 2,990 Coed
Affiliation or Control: State/Local IRS Status: 501(c)3
Highest Offering: Associate Degree
Program: Occupational; 2-Year Principally Bachelor's Creditable
Accreditation: SC, RAD, SURGT

02 President .... Dr. L. Steve THORNBURG
05 Vice President of Academic Programs .... Dr. Becky SAIN
32 Vice President of Student Services .... Dr. Andy GARDNER
10 Senior VP Finance/Admin Svcs .... Mr. Tommy GREENE
20 EVP Instruction/Student Development .... Dr. Shannon KENNEDY
51 Vice Pres of Continuing Education .... Mr. Ken MOONEY
30 Sr Dean Devel/Governmental Rels .... Mr. Eddie HOLBROOK
84 Dean of Enrollment Management .... Vacant
102 Executive Director CCC Foundation .... Mr. U. L. PATTERSON, III
09 Dir Planning/Inst Effectiveness .... Mrs. Laura BOWEN
06 Registrar .... Vacant
88 Director CECHS Relations .... Ms. Nedra MADDOX
37 Financial Aid Coordinator .... Ms. Emily HURDT
08 Dean of Learning Resources .... Mrs. Barbara MCKIBBIN
96 Purchasing Officer .... Mrs. Kathy EVERETT
18 Director of Physical Plant .... Mr. Mark FOX
19 Director of Security .... Mr. Russell VOYLES
15 Human Resources & Safety Manager .... Mr. Allen KNICELEY
13 Chief Information Officer .... Mr. Howard ROBERTS
14 Network Administrator .... Mr. Robin DYER
24 Audiovisual Coordinator .... Mr. Rodger PERRY
26 Public Info/Marketing Coordinator .... Vacant
07 Admissions/Records Coordinator .... Ms. Emily AREY
49 Dean Arts & Sciences .... Mrs. Barbara ROMICH
50 Dean Business & Allied Health .... Dr. John LATTIMORE
75 Dean Vocational/Engrng/Public Svcs .... Mr. Michael MCSWAIN
88 Dean Learning Center .... Dr. Chris NANNEY

*Coastal Carolina Community College (F)

444 Western Boulevard, Jacksonville NC 28546-6816
County: Onslow FICE Identification: 005316
Unit ID: 198330
Telephone: (910) 455-1221 Carnegie Class: Assoc/Pub-R-M
FAX Number: (910) 455-7027 Calendar System: Semester
URL: www.coastalcarolina.edu
Established: 1963 Annual Undergrad Tuition & Fees (In-District): $2,624
Enrollment: 4,468 Coed
Affiliation or Control: State/Local IRS Status: 501(c)3
Highest Offering: Associate Degree
Program: Occupational; 2-Year Principally Bachelor's Creditable
Accreditation: SC, DA, DH, MLTAD, SURGT

02 President .... Dr. Ronald K. LINGLE
11 Executive Vice President .... Mr. David L. HEATHERLY
05 VP for Instruction .... Ms. Ginger TUTON
09 VP Inst Eff/Research/Innovation .... Ms. Sharon R. MCGINNIS
32 Division Chair for Student Services .... Dr. Donald R. HERRING
15 Personnel Officer .... Ms. Cindy B. WOOLRIDGE
26 Pub Info Ofcr/Ex Dir Col Foundation .... Ms. Krystal PHILLIPS
06 Dir Admin/Data Mgmt Svc/Registrar .... Ms. Sue FLAHARTY
18 Dir Physical Plant & Aux Services .... Ms. Carol PHILLIPS
37 Director for Financial Aid Services .... Ms. Tammy LYON
88 Director for Veterans Services .... Mr. Christopher P. SABIN
88 Director Economic Development .... Ms. Anne C. SHAW
84 Coordinator for Enrollment Services .... Mr. Timothy TOLFREE
04 Exec Assistant to the President .... Ms. Tonya L. MORTON

*College of the Albemarle (G)

1208 North Road Street, Elizabeth City NC 27906-2327
County: Pasquotank FICE Identification: 002917
Unit ID: 197814
Telephone: (252) 335-0821 Carnegie Class: Assoc/Pub-R-M
FAX Number: (252) 335-2011 Calendar System: Semester
URL: www.albemarle.edu
Established: 1960 Annual Undergrad Tuition & Fees (In-District): $2,415
Enrollment: 2,464 Coed
Affiliation or Control: State/Local IRS Status: 501(c)3
Highest Offering: Associate Degree
Program: Occupational; 2-Year Principally Bachelor's Creditable
Accreditation: SC, ADNUR, MAC, MLTAD, SURGT

02 President .... Dr. Kandi W. DEITEMEYER
10 Chief Financial Officer .... Mrs. Susan GENTRY
05 Vice President for Learning .... Dr. Evonne CARTER
32 VP for Student Suc & Enr Mgnt .... Ms. Lynn HURDLE-WINSLOW
12 Dean Dare County Campus .... Mr. Timothy SWEENEY
35 Assistant Dean SSEM .... Ms. Martha JOHNSON
30 Development Officer & External Affs .... Mrs. Lisa A. JOHNSON
07 Director Admissions & Testing .... Vacant
37 Director Admissions & Financial Aid .... Ms. Angela R. GODFREY-DAWSON
88 Director Student Life & Leadership .... Ms. Brooke DOVE
06 Registrar .... Ms. Andrea DANCE
88 Director Small Business Center .... Ms. Ginger H. O'NEAL
78 Work-Based Learning Liaison .... Mrs. Lynn JENNINGS
04 Exec Assistant to the President .... Mrs. Jenna HATFIELD
08 Director Library .... Vacant
12 Dean Edenton-Chowan Campus .... Mr. Charles PURSER
13 Director Mgmt Information Services .... Mr. Wayman WHITE
15 Director Human Resources .... Ms. Wendy W. BRICKHOUSE
18 Director Physical Facilities .... Mr. Patrick CUTHRELL
11 Chief Operations Officer .... Mr. Joseph TURNER
40 Administrative Services Manager .... Ms. Lisa JONES
36 Director Counseling & Career Devel .... Vacant
09 Director of Inst Effectiveness .... Ms. Pamela FEDERLINE
88 Coord Prison Education Programs .... Mr. Andre WILLIAMS
88 Coordinator Secondary Education .... Mr. Derek MEREDITH
49 Dean Arts and Sciences .... Mr. Dean ROUGHTON
50 Dean Business & Applied Tech .... Mrs. Michelle WATERS
76 Dean Health & Wellness .... Ms. Robin HARRIS
83 Department Chair Social Sciences .... Mr. Rodger ROSSMAN
60 Dept Chair English & Comm .... Mrs. Laura MORRISON
81 Dept Chair Math and Science .... Ms. Rhonda WATTS
75 Dept Chair Design Manuf & Ind Tech .... Mr. Charles PURSER
77 Dept Chair Bus & Computer Sys Tech .... Ms. Sharon BROWN
57 Department Chair Human & Fine Arts .... Ms. Gale FLAX
88 Department Chair Public Services .... Mrs. Robin ZINSMEISTER

19 Director Public Safety & Preparedns ....Mr. Dennis SMITH
88 Dir Basic Skills/Workforce Reading .... Mrs. Wanda FLETCHER

*Craven Community College (A)

800 College Court, New Bern NC 28562-4984

County: Craven FICE Identification: 006799
Unit ID: 198367
Telephone: (252) 638-7200 Carnegie Class: Assoc/Pub-R-M
FAX Number: (252) 638-4232 Calendar System: Semester
URL: www.cravencc.edu
Established: 1965 Annual Undergrad Tuition & Fees (In-District): $1,144
Enrollment: 3,955 Coed
Affiliation or Control: State/Local IRS Status: 501(c)3
Highest Offering: Associate Degree
Program: Occupational; 2-Year Principally Bachelor's Creditable
Accreditation: SC, ACBSP, CAHIIM, MAC, PTAA

02 President ....Dr. Ray STAATS
05 Exec VP Learning/Student Success ....Dr. Daryl MINUS
11 Vice Pres of Administrative Svcs ....Ms. Karla (Page) JONES-VARNELL
20 AVP Academic Affairs/Student Engage .... Ms. Kathleen GALLMAN
49 Dean Liberal Arts & Univ Transfer .... Ms. Betty K. HATCHER
36 Dean Career Programs ....Mr. James R. MILLARD
09 Exec Dir of Institutional Effective ....Ms. Mary C. CLARK
06 Registrar ....Mr. John A. FONVILLE
30 Exec Dir Institutional Advancement ....Ms. Judy EURICH
12 Dean Havelock-Cherry Point Campus ...... Mr. Walter CALABRESE
37 Director Financial Aid ....Ms. Kathryn M. BANKS
103 Dir Workforce Readiness & Spec Pgms ....Mr. Mark W. BEST
88 Director Basic Skills Programs ....Ms. Zeledith BLAKELY
08 Director Library Services ....Mrs. Catherine C. CAMPBELL
10 Exec Dir Financial Svcs/ Purchasing ....Mrs. Cynthia A. PATTERSON
88 Director TRIO Student Support Svcs .. Ms. Jennifer BUMGARNER
15 Exec Dir HR/Chief Diversity Officer ....Mrs. Vickie MOSELEY-JONES
103 Exec Dir Workforce Development ....Mr. Robin MATTHEWS
18 Director of Facilities ....Mr. John MELVILLE
13 Dean Technology Services/Facilities .... Ms. Bambi EDWARDS
96 Procurement & Fixed Assets Officer ....Mr. Hiram Todd MURPHREY
84 Exec Dir of Enrollment/Retention ....Ms. Zomar PETER
25 Dir Strategic Partnerships/Grants ....Ms. Monica MINUS
04 Exec Asst to Pres/Board of Trustees ....Ms. Cynthia ENSLEY
19 Dir of Security & Emergency Mgmt ....Mr. Paul DAMICO
103 AVP Workforce Solutions/Innovation .... Mr. Gery BOUCHER

*Davidson County Community College (B)

PO Box 1287, Lexington NC 27293-1287

County: Davidson FICE Identification: 002919
Unit ID: 198376
Telephone: (336) 249-8186 Carnegie Class: Assoc/Pub-S-SC
FAX Number: (336) 249-0379 Calendar System: Semester
URL: www.davidsonccc.edu
Established: 1958 Annual Undergrad Tuition & Fees (In-District): $1,846
Enrollment: 4,102 Coed
Affiliation or Control: State/Local IRS Status: 501(c)3
Highest Offering: Associate Degree
Program: Occupational; 2-Year Principally Bachelor's Creditable
Accreditation: SC, ADNUR, CAHIIM, MAC, MLTAD

02 President ....Dr. Mary E. RITTLING
05 VP Academic Programs & Services ....Ms. Jeannine H. WOODY
32 VP Student Affairs .... Dr. Rhonda Q. COATS
10 VP Financial/Administrative Svcs ....Dr. Rusty HUNT
102 VP Ext Affairs/Exec Dir Foundation ....Ms. Jenny M. VARNER
76 Dean Health/Wellness/Pub Safety ....Ms. Rose MCDANIEL
97 Dean Gen Studies & Acad Support .... Dr. Christy FORREST
50 Dean Business Engineering Technical ....Mr. Rodney JACKSON
12 Dean Davie Campus .... Ms. Teresa KINES
35 Dean Student Services ....Mr. Kevin LINEBERRY
21 Dean Financial/Admin Svcs .... Ms. Laura L. YARBROUGH
27 VP Student Success & Communications ... Ms. Susan BURLESON
26 Sen Dir Marketing & Communications ....Ms. Terri SMITH
06 Dir Student Records/Registration .... Mr. Bryan MCCULLOUGH
36 Director Career Development .... Mr. Charles MAYER
18 Director Physical Plant Services .... Mr. Keith RAKER
15 Director Personnel Services .... Ms. Denise BARNHARDT
04 Administrative Asst to President ....Ms. Carleen TERRELL
08 Head Librarian ....Mr. Jason SETZER
37 Director Student Financial Aid .... Ms. Lori BLEVINS
41 Athletic Director .... Mr. Kenneth KIRK

*Durham Technical Community College (C)

1637 Lawson Street, Durham NC 27703-5023

County: Durham FICE Identification: 005448
Unit ID: 198455
Telephone: (919) 536-7200 Carnegie Class: Assoc/Pub-U-SC
FAX Number: (919) 686-3601 Calendar System: Semester
URL: www.durhamtech.edu
Established: 1961 Annual Undergrad Tuition & Fees (In-District): $1,820
Enrollment: 5,606 Coed
Affiliation or Control: State/Local IRS Status: 501(c)3
Highest Offering: Associate Degree
Program: Occupational; 2-Year Principally Bachelor's Creditable
Accreditation: SC, ADNUR, CAHIIM, COARC, DT, EMT, MAC, OPD, OTA, PNUR, SURGT

02 President .... Dr. William G. INGRAM
30 Sr Vice Pres Institutional Advance ....Mr. Tom JAYNES
05 VP Stdnt Learning Instruc Svcs ....Vacant
10 VP Finance and Administration ....Mr. Matt WILLIAMS
51 VP Corp/Continuing Education ....Dr. Peter WOOLDRIDGE
32 VP Student Engage Dev Support ..... Dr. Christine KELLY KLEESE
04 Executive Secy to the President .... Ms. Gloria GAY
09 Director Institutional Research ....Dr. Teri L. KAASA
35 Dean Student Services .... Ms. Lisa INMAN
13 Executive Director Info Tech Svcs ....Mr. Patrick HINES
15 Director Human Resources .... Ms. Kathy MCKINLEY
08 Director Library & Media Services ....Ms. Irene H. LAUBE
37 Director Financial Aid ....Ms. Kevi DIXON
109 Director Auxiliary Services .... Ms. Yolanda V. MOORE-JONES
06 Director Student Records ....Vacant
84 Enrollment Counselor ....Dr. Johanna BROWN

*Edgecombe Community College (D)

2009 W Wilson Street, Tarboro NC 27886-9399

County: Edgecombe FICE Identification: 008855
Unit ID: 198491
Telephone: (252) 823-5166 Carnegie Class: Assoc/Pub-R-M
FAX Number: (252) 823-6817 Calendar System: Semester
URL: www.edgecombe.edu
Established: 1967 Annual Undergrad Tuition & Fees (In-District): $2,400
Enrollment: 2,642 Coed
Affiliation or Control: State/Local IRS Status: 501(c)3
Highest Offering: Associate Degree
Program: Occupational; 2-Year Principally Bachelor's Creditable
Accreditation: SC, ADNUR, CAHIIM, COARC, MAC, PNUR, RAD, SURGT

02 President ....Dr. Deborah L. LAMM
05 Vice President of Instruction ....Dr. John D. ENAMAIT
11 Vice Pres Administrative Services ....Mr. Charlie R. HARRELL
32 Vice President Student Services ....Mr. Michael J. JORDAN
20 Asc VP Instruct/Curriculum/Cont Ed ....Mr. Lynn CALE
84 Dean Enrollment Management ....Mr. Tony ROOK
35 Dean of Students ....Ms. Samanthia PHILLIPS
45 Director of Inst Effectiveness ....Ms. Sheila HOSKINS
26 Director of Public Information ....Ms. Mary T. BASS
08 Director of Library Services ....Ms. Deborah PARISHER
06 Registrar ....Ms. Cathy P. DUPREE
15 Director Personnel Services ....Ms. Susan BARKALOW
18 Chief Facilities/Physical Plant .... Mr. Freddy WHITLEY
37 Director Student Financial Aid ....Ms. Barbara MANNING
04 Administrative Asst to President ....Ms. Julie B. THOMAS
13 Chief Info Technology Officer ....Mr. Neil BAKER
43 Dir Legal Services/General Counsel ....Ms. Carmen NUNALEE

*Fayetteville Technical Community College (E)

PO Box 35236, 2201 Hull Road,
Fayetteville NC 28303-0236

County: Cumberland FICE Identification: 007640
Unit ID: 198534
Telephone: (910) 678-8400 Carnegie Class: Assoc/Pub-R-L
FAX Number: (910) 678-8269 Calendar System: Semester
URL: www.faytechcc.edu
Established: 1961 Annual Undergrad Tuition & Fees (In-State): $2,394
Enrollment: 12,364 Coed
Affiliation or Control: State IRS Status: 501(c)3
Highest Offering: Associate Degree
Program: Occupational; 2-Year Principally Bachelor's Creditable
Accreditation: SC, ADNUR, COARC, DA, DH, FUSER, NMT, PTAA, RAD, SURGT

02 President ....Dr. Larry KEEN
11 Vice Pres for Administrative Svcs ..Mr. Joseph W. LEVISTER, JR.
05 Sr Vice Pres Academic/Student Svcs .... Dr. David BRAND
15 VP Human Res/Inst Effect/Assessment .... Mr. Carl MITCHELL
10 Sr Vice Pres Business and Finance ....Mrs. Betty J. SMITH
26 Exec Dir Marketing/Public Relations .... Mr. Brent MICHAELS
72 Vice Pres Learning Technologies ....Mr. Bob J. ERVIN
51 Assoc Vice Pres for Continuing Educ ....Dr. Joe W. MULLIS
32 Assoc Vice Pres Student Services .... Dr. Rosemary KELLY
88 Assoc Vice Pres Curriculum Programs ....Mr. William (Bill) GRIFFIN
84 Dean Enrollment Mgmt/Financial Aid . Mr. Harper SHACKELFORD
06 Registrar ....Ms. Melissa A. JONES
21 Assoc Vice Pres Business & Finance ....Mrs. Robin DEAVER
07 Director of Admissions .... Dr. Louanna CASTLEMAN
13 Director Management Information Svc .... Mr. Roderick BROWER
12 Dean of Spring Lake Campus .... Ms. DeSandra WASHINGTON
18 Director of Facility Services .... Mr. Harold WYCKOFF
96 Procurement Manager Business/Financ .....Ms. Amy SAMPERTON
50 Dean of Business Programs ....Mrs. Cindy BURNS
49 Dean of Arts/Humanities .... Mr. Antonio JACKSON
76 Dean of Health Programs ....Mrs. Susan ELLIS
54 Dean Engr/Pub Svs/Applied Tech Pgms ....Mr. Daryle NOBLES
81 Interim Dean of Sciences .... Mr. Chris DIORIETES

*Forsyth Technical Community College (F)

2100 Silas Creek Parkway,
Winston-Salem NC 27103-5197

County: Forsyth FICE Identification: 005317
Unit ID: 198552
Telephone: (336) 723-0371 Carnegie Class: Assoc/Pub-U-SC
FAX Number: (336) 761-2399 Calendar System: Semester
URL: www.forsythtech.edu
Established: 1960 Annual Undergrad Tuition & Fees (In-State): $2,150
Enrollment: 9,213 Coed
Affiliation or Control: State IRS Status: 501(c)3
Highest Offering: Associate Degree
Program: Occupational; 2-Year Principally Bachelor's Creditable
Accreditation: SC, COARC, CVT, DA, DH, DMS, ENGT, MAC, NMT, RAD, RTT

02 President ....Dr. Gary M. GREEN
03 Executive Vice President ....Dr. Rachel M. DESMARAIS
05 Int Vice Pres Instructional Svcs ....Dr. Jewel B. CHERRY
13 Vice Pres of Planning & Info Svcs ....Vacant
32 Vice President Student Services ....Dr. Jewel B. CHERRY
30 VP Inst Advancement/Exec Dir Found .... Ms. Mamie M. SUTPHIN
10 Vice President Business Services ...... Ms. Wendy R. EMERSON
103 Vice Pres Economic & Workforce Dev ......Mr. Alan K. MURDOCK
100 Director Office of the President .... Ms. Sherri W. BOWEN
50 Dean Business Info Tech Div ....Ms. Pamela SHORTT
79 Dean of Humanities/Social Sci Div ....Vacant
81 Dean Math/Science & Technologies .... Mr. Michael V. AYERS
54 Dean of Engineering Tech Div .... Mr. Leonard R. KISER
17 Dean of Health Technologies ....Dr. Bonnie G. POPE
31 Dean Community/Economic Development ....Ms. Sharon D. ANDERSON
08 Dean Learning Resources ....Mr. J. Randel CANDELARIA
88 Dean Adult Literacy ....Mr. Michael E. HARRIS
66 Director Nursing .... Ms. Linda H. LATHAM
76 Director Imaging .... Ms. Tamara BECK
76 Director Health Services .... Ms. Jean E. MIDDLESWARTH
84 Dean Enrollment & Student Svcs ....Vacant
21 Dean Financial Services ....Ms. Melanie L. NUCKOLS
38 Dir Student Success Ctr/Counseling ....Mr. Joe E. MCINTOSH
15 Director Human Resources ....Mr. Gregory M. CHASE
09 Dir Institutional Effectiveness ....Ms. Dana L. DALTON
14 Director Information Systems ....Mr. Chris PEARCE
88 Dir Recruiting/Student Support Svcs .... Mr. Edwin B. WADDELL
37 Director Student Financial Services ....Mr. Ricky C. HODGES
06 Director Records/Registrar ....Ms. Gwen D. WHITAKER
07 Director of Admissions ....Ms. Jean M. GROOME
18 Director Physical Plant Services .... Mr. Scott BOOTH
19 Director Campus Police .... Mr. Renarde D. EARL
88 Director Small Business Center ....Mr. Allan YOUNGER
35 Director Student Activities ....Ms. Beverly N. LEWIS
96 Director Purchasing/Equipment .... Mr. Philip L. MCCLUNG
40 Director Auxiliary Svcs/Bookstore ....Mr. Brian A. HICKS
12 Director Grady Swisher Center ....Ms. Mary B. KING
12 Director Mazie Woodruff Center .... Mr. TerCraig D. EDWARDS
12 Director Northwest Forsyth Center ....Ms. Kristie F. HENDRIX
12 Sr Dir Off-Campus/Stokes Cty Op .... Ms. Ann B. WATTS
88 Dean Educational Partnerships ....Vacant
88 Dean Business and Industry ....Ms. Jennifer B. COULOMBE
88 Dean Health and Emergency Programs .... Mr. Wesley D. HUTCHINS
12 Dir Transportation Technology Ctr ....Mr. Forrest LINEBERRY
88 Dean Learning Technologies .... Mr. James COOK
44 Dir Major Gifts & Planned Giving ....Ms. Edyce ELWORTH
44 Dir Annual Giving & Special Events .... Ms. Angela BRYANT
04 Senior Administrative Associate ....Ms. Dawn P. MITCHELL
25 Director Grants and Contracts ....Mr. Mike MASSOGLIA

*Gaston College (G)

201 Highway 321 South, Dallas NC 28034-1499

County: Gaston FICE Identification: 002973
Unit ID: 198570
Telephone: (704) 922-6200 Carnegie Class: Assoc/Pub-S-SC
FAX Number: (704) 922-2323 Calendar System: Semester
URL: www.gaston.edu
Established: 1964 Annual Undergrad Tuition & Fees (In-District): $2,480
Enrollment: 5,244 Coed
Affiliation or Control: State/Local IRS Status: 501(c)3
Highest Offering: Associate Degree
Program: Occupational; 2-Year Principally Bachelor's Creditable
Accreditation: SC, ACBSP, ADNUR, DIETT, EMT, ENGT, IFSAC, MAC, PNUR

02 President ....Dr. Patricia A. SKINNER
10 VP Finance/Facilities/Operations .... Ms. Cynthia MCCRORY
21 Assoc VP Fin/Oper/Fac & Controller .... Mr. Bruce COLE
05 Vice President of Academic Affairs ....Dr. Don AMMONS
20 Associate VP Academic Affairs .... Dr. Dewey DELLINGER
32 VP Student Affairs/Enrollment Mgmt .... Dr. Silvia Patricia RIOS-HUSAIN
35 Assistant VP for Student Affairs ....Ms. Audrey SHERRILL
103 VP Economics & Workforce Develop .... Dr. Dennis MCELHOE
04 Exec Admin Assistant to the Pres .... Ms. Mary Ellen DILLON
09 Director Insti Effectiveness .... Dr. Rex CLAY
08 Director Libraries .... Dr. Harry COOKE
13 Chief Technology Services Officer .... Ms. Savonne MCNEILL
07 Dir of Enrollment Mgmt/Counseling .... Ms. Jennifer NICHOLS
06 Director of Registration/Records ....Ms. Alisa ROY
37 Director Financial Aid/Veteran Affs .... Mr. Everett JETER
19 Chief of Campus Police & Security .... Mr. Billy LYTTON
11 Chief Administrative Officer ....Mr. Todd BANEY
15 Mgr HR/Envir/Health/Safety/Prof Dev ....Ms. Carol DENTON
18 Director Facilities Management ....Vacant
26 Director of Marketing/PR ....Ms. Stephanie MICHAEL-PICKETT
30 Chief Development Officer .... Ms. Julia ALLEN
25 Chief Contracts/Grants Admin .... Mr. Luke UPCHURCH
96 Director Purchasing/Receiv/Shipping ....Mr. Chuck WRAY
40 Director Bookstore/Vending Services ....Mr. Charles WILSON
49 Dean of Liberal Arts & Science .... Ms. Heather WOODSON
72 Dean Engr/Industrial Technologies ....Mr. Virgil COX

66 Dean Health & Human Services ....Ms. Juanita GUNNELL
50 Dean Business & Information Tech ....Ms. Michelle BYRD
51 Dean Cont Educ and Public Safety ....Dr. Karen LESS
12 Dean Lincoln Campus ....Dr. John MCHUGH
12 Dean Kimbrell Campus/Textile Ctr ....Dr. Joe KEITH
78 Dir Educational Partnerships ....Ms. Kimberly WYONT
88 Dir Learn/Persist/Retent/Completion ....Mr. John ERICKSON
75 Director of Textile Technology Ctr ....Mr. Sam BUFF

*Guilford Technical Community College (A)

PO Box 309, Jamestown NC 27282-0309
County: Guilford   FICE Identification: 004838
Unit ID: 198622
Telephone: (336) 334-4822   Carnegie Class: Assoc/Pub-S-MC
FAX Number: (336) 454-2745   Calendar System: Semester
URL: www.gtcc.edu
Established: 1958   Annual Undergrad Tuition & Fees (In-State): $2,351
Enrollment: 12,438   Coed
Affiliation or Control: State   IRS Status: 501(c)3
Highest Offering: Associate Degree
Program: Occupational; 2-Year Principally Bachelor's Creditable; Technical Emphasis
Accreditation: SC, ACFEI, DA, DH, EMT, MAC, PTAA, RAD, SURGT

02 President ....Dr. Randy PARKER
03 Executive Vice President ....Mrs. Rae Marie SMITH
05 Vice President of Instruction ....Dr. Beth PITONZO
32 Vice Pres Student Support Services ....Dr. Quentin JOHNSON
11 Assoc Vice Pres Administrative Svcs ....Mr. Mitchell JOHNSON
10 Assoc VP of Business & Finance ....Ms. Nancy B. SOLLOSI
20 Assoc VP Student Support Services ....Dr. Alison WIERS
51 VP Corp & Continuing Educ ....Mr. Ralph SONEY
30 Exec Dir Institutional Advancement ....Mr. Alan PIKE
12 Dean Greensboro Campus ....Mr. Manuel DUDLEY
12 Dean High Point Campus ....Mr. Mark HARRIS
50 Dir Business & Industry Training ....Mr. Stephen CASTELLOE
30 Director of Development ....Mr. Harry STILLERMAN
15 Director of Human Resources ....Ms. Gwendolyn BURSTON
13 Chief Information Officer ....Mr. Rob RAMEY
18 Director of Construction ....Mr. Charles YOUNG
09 Director of Institutional Research ....Ms. Sherry DOWNING
07 Director of Admissions ....Mr. Jesse CROSS
35 Director of Student Life ....Ms. Berri V. CROSS
37 Director Financial Aid ....Ms. Lisa A. KORETOFF
19 Chief of Campus Police ....Mr. James PHILLIPS
06 Registrar ....Vacant
21 Controller ....Ms. Angela M. CARTER
40 Bookstore Manager ....Mr. Shawn G. DEE
36 Coordinator Career Services ....Mr. Daniel J. GRIGG
38 Director Counseling & Assessment ....Ms. Angela LEAK
29 Asst Director of Development ....Ms. Nancy GRIFFIN CALKINS
08 Dir of Library Services ....Ms. Monica YOUNG
41 Athletic Director ....Mr. Kirk CHANDLER
96 Director of Purchasing ....Mr. Michael STOUT

*Halifax Community College (B)

PO Drawer 809, Weldon NC 27890-0809
County: Halifax   FICE Identification: 007986
Unit ID: 198640
Telephone: (252) 536-4221   Carnegie Class: Assoc/Pub-R-S
FAX Number: (252) 536-4144   Calendar System: Semester
URL: www.halifaxcc.edu
Established: 1967   Annual Undergrad Tuition & Fees (In-District): $1,213
Enrollment: 1,356   Coed
Affiliation or Control: State/Local   IRS Status: 501(c)3
Highest Offering: Associate Degree
Program: Occupational; 2-Year Principally Bachelor's Creditable; Technical Emphasis
Accreditation: SC, DH, MLTAD, PHLEB

02 President ....Dr. Ervin V. GRIFFIN, SR.
04 Exec Assistant to the President ....Ms. Kimberly J. MACK
05 Vice Pres Academic Affairs ....Dr. Deryl FULMER
10 Vice President Admin Services ....Ms. Debra SMITH
30 Vice Pres Institutional Advancement ....Dr. Dianne RHOADES
32 Dean Student Svcs & Enrollment Mgmt ....Dr. Barbara BRADLEY-HASTY
20 Dean of Curriculum Programs ....Ms. B. T. BROWN
06 Registrar ....Ms. Dawn VELIKY
07 Director of Admissions ....Mr. James Bernard WASHINGTON
08 Director Learning Resources ....Mr. Marc FINNEY
09 Dir of Institutional Effectiveness ....Dr. Adriane LECHE
26 Dir Public Relations & Marketing ....Vacant
40 Bookstore Manager ....Mrs. Doris GARNER
38 Director Counseling Services ....Ms. Teresa MAYLE
18 Facilities/Physical Plant ....Ms. Debra SMITH
36 Coord of Testing & Job Placement ....Ms. Angela RANDOLPH
37 Director of Financial Aid ....Mrs. Tara KEETER
96 Purchasing Agent ....Ms. Darlene PERRY
15 Personnel Officer ....Mrs. Margaret MURGA
13 Computer Network Manager ....Mr. Jerry THOMPSON
49 Div Chair Arts & Sciences/Business ....Mr. Calvin STANSBURY
76 Div Chair Health Sciences & Humanit ....Mr. Michael EARL
75 Div Chair Vocation/Industrial Tech ....Mr. Hunter TAYLOR
106 Dir Online Education/E-learning ....Mrs. Beth GRAY-ROBERTSON
19 Director Security/Safety ....Mr. Emmett SMITH
25 Chief Contracts/Grants Admin ....Mr. Daniel LOVETT
44 Director Annual or Planned Giving ....Dr. Dianne BARNES-RHOADES

*Haywood Community College (C)

185 Freedlander Drive, Clyde NC 28721-9453
County: Haywood   FICE Identification: 008083
Unit ID: 198668
Telephone: (828) 627-2821   Carnegie Class: Assoc/Pub-R-M
FAX Number: (828) 627-3606   Calendar System: Semester
URL: www.haywood.edu
Established: 1965   Annual Undergrad Tuition & Fees (In-State): $2,409
Enrollment: 2,012   Coed
Affiliation or Control: State   IRS Status: 501(c)3
Highest Offering: Associate Degree
Program: Occupational; 2-Year Principally Bachelor's Creditable; Technical Emphasis
Accreditation: SC, MAC

02 President ....Dr. Barbara PARKER
05 Vice President of Instruction ....Mrs. Wendy HINES
32 Vice President Student Services ....Dr. Laura LEATHERWOOD
10 Vice President Business Operations ....Mrs. Karen DENNEY
18 Director of Campus Development ....Mr. Brek LANNING
30 Int Dir Institutional Advancement ....Dr. Laura LEATHERWOOD
26 Director Marketing & Communications ....Mr. Aaron MABRY
15 Director of Human Resources ....Mrs. Marsha STINES
84 Director of Enrollment Management ....Mrs. Jennifer HERRERA
37 Director of Financial Aid ....Mrs. Tracy RAPP
36 Career Devel Specialist/Recruiter ....Ms. Sharon CHILDERS
09 Exec Dir Research & Inst Support ....Dr. Marlowe MAGER
103 Dean of Workforce Dev/Cont Educ ....Mr. Doug BURCHFIELD

*Isothermal Community College (D)

PO Box 804, Spindale NC 28160-0804
County: Rutherford   FICE Identification: 002934
Unit ID: 198710
Telephone: (828) 286-3636   Carnegie Class: Assoc/Pub-R-M
FAX Number: (828) 286-1120   Calendar System: Semester
URL: www.isothermal.edu
Established: 1964   Annual Undergrad Tuition & Fees (In-District): $2,565
Enrollment: 2,141   Coed
Affiliation or Control: State/Local   IRS Status: 501(c)3
Highest Offering: Associate Degree
Program: Occupational; 2-Year Principally Bachelor's Creditable
Accreditation: SC

02 President ....Mr. Walter H. DALTON
11 Vice Pres Administrative Services ....Mr. Stephen MATHENY
05 Executive Vice President ....Dr. Kim GOLD
103 Vice Pres Cmty/Workforce Educ ....Mr. Thad HARRILL
30 VP for Institutional Advancement ....Mr. Thad HARRILL
32 Dean of Student Affairs ....Dr. Karen JONES
50 Dean of Business Sciences ....Ms. Kim ALEXANDER
49 Dean of Arts & Sciences ....Dr. Kathy ACKERMAN
75 Dean of Applied Science & Engr ....Mr. Joe LOONEY
51 Dean of Continuing Education ....Mrs. Donna HOOD
12 Director of Polk Campus ....Mrs. Kate BARKSCHAT
20 Director Academic Development ....Mrs. Debbie PUETT
08 Director Library Services ....Mr. Charles WIGGINS
10 Controller ....Mrs. Amy M. PENSON
37 Financial Aid Officer ....Mrs. Karen HARRIS
26 Dir Marketing/Community Relations ....Mr. Mike GAVIN
18 Dir Plant Operations/Maintenance ....Mr. Rick EDWARDS
38 Director of Retention & Support ....Mrs. Kimberly SNYDER
84 Director of Enrollment Management ....Ms. Alice MCCLUNEY
06 Registrar ....Ms. Kelly METCALF
96 Director of Purchasing ....Ms. Trish HUNTSINGER
13 Director of Information Technology ....Mr. Robby WALTERS
40 Bookstore Manager ....Mrs. Danielle ALEY
04 Administrative Asst to President ....Mrs. DeeDee BARNARD

*James Sprunt Community College (E)

PO Box 398, Kenansville NC 28349-0398
County: Duplin   FICE Identification: 007687
Unit ID: 198729
Telephone: (910) 296-2400   Carnegie Class: Assoc/Pub-R-S
FAX Number: (910) 296-1636   Calendar System: Semester
URL: www.jamessprunt.edu
Established: 1964   Annual Undergrad Tuition & Fees (In-State): $2,500
Enrollment: 1,213   Coed
Affiliation or Control: State   IRS Status: 501(c)3
Highest Offering: Associate Degree
Program: Occupational; 2-Year Principally Bachelor's Creditable; Technical Emphasis
Accreditation: SC, MAC

02 Chief Executive Officer/President ....Dr. Lawrence L. ROUSE
05 VP of Curriculum Services ....Ms. June DAVIS
51 VP of Continuing Education ....Vacant
10 VP of Admin & Fiscal Services ....Mr. John HARDISON
32 VP of Student Services ....Vacant
30 VP Col Advance/Inst Effectiveness ....Mr. Jimmy T. TATE
06 Registrar ....Ms. Patricia NORRIS
07 Admissions Specialist ....Ms. Wanda EDWARDS
37 Director Financial Aid/Vet Affairs ....Ms. Tracy WARD
38 Director of Student Counseling ....Ms. Amber FERRELL
08 Director Library Services ....Vacant
15 Dir Human Resources/Campus Safety ....Ms. Debbie MARTIN
97 Director of General Education ....Mr. Andy CAVENAUGH
09 Dir Research/Plng/Instl Effective ....Mr. William (Bill) CANUETTE, JR.

26 Dir of Public Info/Print Media ....Vacant
18 Chief Facilities/Physical Plant ....Mr. Arthur KORNEGAY
96 Director of Purchasing ....Ms. Toni HENDERSON
55 Instr/Coord Evening/Weekend Svcs ....Mr. James THOMAS
13 Chief Info Technology Officer (CIO) ....Ms. Gail HENRY
19 Director Security/Safety ....Mr. Kevin HORNADAY

*Johnston Community College (F)

PO Box 2350, 245 College Road, Smithfield NC 27577-2350
County: Johnston   FICE Identification: 009336
Unit ID: 198774
Telephone: (919) 934-3051   Carnegie Class: Assoc/Pub-S-SC
FAX Number: (919) 209-2142   Calendar System: Semester
URL: www.johnstoncc.edu
Established: 1969   Annual Undergrad Tuition & Fees (In-District): $2,401
Enrollment: 5,051   Coed
Affiliation or Control: State/Local   IRS Status: 501(c)3
Highest Offering: Associate Degree
Program: Occupational; 2-Year Principally Bachelor's Creditable
Accreditation: SC, DMS, MAC, NMT, RAD

02 President ....Dr. David N. JOHNSON
10 VP Admin/Fiscal and Personnel Svcs ....Mr. Michael CROSS
05 Vice Pres of Instruction ....Mrs. Dee Dee D. DAUGHTRY
32 Vice Pres of Student Services ....Dr. Pamela J. HARRELL
30 VP Institutional Effectiveness ....Mrs. Dale A. O'NEILL
09 Dir of Research and IE ....Dr. Terri S. LEE
102 Executive Director of Foundation ....Ms. Twyla C. WELLS
13 Executive Director Info Technology ....Mr. Hal MURY
08 Library Administrator ....Ms. Jaxie BRYAN
105 Internet Info Systems Coordinator ....Ms. Lisa H. MCLAURIN
06 Registrar ....Ms. Deena H. HENRY
37 Director Financial Aid ....Mrs. Betty C. WOODALL
109 Assoc VP of Auxiliary Enterprises ....Mr. Ken H. MITCHELL
15 Director of Human Resources ....Ms. Bernadette CARTER-DOVE
07 Dir of Enrollment & Student Success ....Mrs. Megan L. SHANER
103 Dean of Economic and Community Dev ....Mrs. Joy T. CALLAHAN
76 Dean Health/Wellness & Human Svcs ....Dr. Linda D. SMITH
49 Dean Arts/Sciences & Learning Res ....Mrs. Dawn S. DIXON
71 Dean of Found Studies and Acad Supp ....Dr. Pam J. EARP
26 Media Relations & Pub Info Officer ....Mrs. Traci D. ASHLEY
18 Maintenance Director ....Mr. Michael MASSEY
96 Purchasing and Equipment Director ....Mr. Doug PATE

*Lenoir Community College (G)

231 Highway 58 South, Kinston NC 28502-0188
County: Lenoir   FICE Identification: 002940
Unit ID: 198817
Telephone: (252) 527-6223   Carnegie Class: Assoc/Pub-R-M
FAX Number: (252) 233-6879   Calendar System: Semester
URL: www.lenoircc.edu
Established: 1958   Annual Undergrad Tuition & Fees (In-District): $2,424
Enrollment: 3,090   Coed
Affiliation or Control: State/Local   IRS Status: 501(c)3
Highest Offering: Associate Degree
Program: Occupational; 2-Year Principally Bachelor's Creditable
Accreditation: SC, ACFEI, EMT, MAC, POLYT, RAD, SURGT

02 President ....Dr. Brantley BRILEY
51 VP Continuing Education ....Dr. Jay CARRAWAY
11 Senior VP Administrative Services ....Ms. Deborah SUTTON
05 VP Academic & Student Services ....Dr. Deborah GRIMES
10 Chief Financial Officer ....Ms. Deborah S. SUTTON
06 Registrar ....Ms. Shelia WIGGINS
84 Director Enrollment Mgmt/Admissions ....Vacant
32 Dean of Student Services ....Dr. John Paul BLACK
37 Director of Student Financial Aid ....Mr. J. D. GIBBS
13 Chief Information Officer ....Mr. Lee WETHERINGTON
09 Director Inst Effectiveness ....Mrs. Jo WILSON
15 Director Human Resources ....Mrs. Tasha JOHNSON
18 Director of Maintenance ....Mr. Reed LOVICK
41 Athletic Director ....Mrs. Shelly BARNES
21 Director of Financial Services ....Ms. Jessica MCMAHON
96 Purchasing Agent ....Ms. Rhonda DEAVER
26 Director of Mktg/Recruiting/Comm ....Mrs. Richy HUNEYCUTT
30 Director Institutional Advancement ....Mrs. Jeanne KENNEDY
103 Director Work-Based Lrng/Job Devel ....Mrs. Frances GASKINS
08 Director of Learning Resources ....Mr. Rich GARAFOLO
50 Dean of Business/Industrial/Technol ....Mr. Gary CLEMENTS
49 Dean of Arts & Sciences ....Mr. Levey BROWN
76 Dean of Health Sciences & Nursing ....Dr. Alexis WELCH
89 Director of Freshman Studies ....Vacant
92 Dean/Director of Honors Program ....Dr. John Paul BLACK
94 Dean/Director of Women's Studies ....Dr. Deborah GRIMES
35 Director Student Activities ....Mrs. Shelly BARNES

*Martin Community College (H)

1161 Kehukee Park Road, Williamston NC 27892-9988
County: Martin   FICE Identification: 007988
Unit ID: 198905
Telephone: (252) 792-1521   Carnegie Class: Assoc/Pub-R-S
FAX Number: (252) 792-0826   Calendar System: Semester
URL: www.martincc.edu
Established: 1967   Annual Undergrad Tuition & Fees (In-State): $1,836
Enrollment: 654   Coed
Affiliation or Control: State   IRS Status: 501(c)3
Highest Offering: Associate Degree
Program: Occupational; 2-Year Principally Bachelor's Creditable

Accreditation: SC, DA, MAC, PTAA

02 President ....Dr. Ann BRITT
05 Dean Academic Affairs/Student Svcs ....Dr. Jennifer BURRUSS
11 Dean of Administrative Services ....Mr. Steve TAYLOR
10 Business Services Director ....Ms. Cynthia JERNIGAN
20 Assoc Dean Acad Affs/Student Svcs ....Dr. Brian BUSCH
04 Asst to Pres for Business/Industry ....Mr. Billy BARBER
37 Financial Aid Director ....Vacant
38 Counselor and Admissions ....Ms. Crystal PUGH
06 Registrar ....Vacant
51 Exec Dir Continuing Education ....Mr. AJ TYSON
13 Systems Administrator ....Ms. Donna ROGERS
18 Director of Facilities ....Mr. Walter WHEELER
15 Human Resource Director ....Mr. Harland FRYE
14 Telecommunication/Network Manager ....Mr. Elijah T. FREEMAN
09 Director of Institutional Research ....Vacant
96 Director of Purchasing ....Ms. Jennifer CHERRY
12 Director of Bertie Campus ....Mr. Norman CHERRY
08 Library Director ....Ms. Mary Anne CAUDLE
101 Exec Asst to President and BOT ....Ms. Kismet MATTHEWS
13 Director of IT ....Mr. Jeff PICKERING
26 Dir Public Affairs/Inst Advancement ....Ms. Judy JENNETTE

*Mayland Community College (A)

PO Box 547, Spruce Pine NC 28777-0547

County: Avery FICE Identification: 011197
Unit ID: 198914
Telephone: (828) 765-7351 Carnegie Class: Assoc/Pub-R-S
FAX Number: (828) 765-0728 Calendar System: Semester
URL: www.mayland.edu
Established: 1971 Annual Undergrad Tuition & Fees (In-District): $2,449
Enrollment: 1,098 Coed
Affiliation or Control: State/Local IRS Status: 501(c)3
Highest Offering: Associate Degree
Program: Occupational; 2-Year Principally Bachelor's Creditable; Technical Emphasis
Accreditation: SC, MAC

02 President ....Dr. John C. BOYD
04 Assistant to the President ....Ms. Brooke BURLESON
05 Vice Pres Instructional Services ....Vacant
10 Vice President Administrative Svcs ....Mr. Gerald HYDE
103 Vice Pres Economic/Workforce Devel ....Mrs. Rita EARLEY
32 Dean of Students ....Ms. Michelle MUSICH
76 Dean of Health Sciences Programs ....Mrs. Kim BURR
49 Acting Dean of Arts & Sciences ....Ms. Liz SILVERS
72 Dean of Career Technologies ....Ms. Brenda MCFEE
08 Director Learning Resources Center ....Mr. Jon WILMESHERR
09 Director Institutional Effectivness ....Mrs. Liz SILVERS
06 Registrar ....Mrs. Jill MCNABB
88 Dean of Basic Skills Programs ....Mr. Steve GUNTER
12 Dean Avery County EWD ....Mrs. Melissa C. PHILLIPS
12 Dean Mitchell County EWD ....Mr. Chris HELMS
12 Dean Yancey County EWD ....Dr. Monica S. CARPENTER
37 Director Student Financial Aid ....Mrs. Cassie FORBES
18 Director Facilities/Physical Plant ....Mr. Lee WHITTINGTON
13 Dir Management Information Systems ....Mr. Tommy R. LEDFORD
15 Director Personnel Services ....Mr. Judy MCCLURE
26 Chief Public Relations Officer ....Mrs. Beth MORRIS
96 Coordinator of Purchasing/Equipment ....Mr. Sam PRESNELL

*McDowell Technical Community College (B)

54 College Drive, Marion NC 28752-8728

County: McDowell FICE Identification: 008085
Unit ID: 198923
Telephone: (828) 652-6021 Carnegie Class: Assoc/Pub-R-S
FAX Number: (828) 652-1014 Calendar System: Semester
URL: www.mcdowelltech.edu
Established: 1964 Annual Undergrad Tuition & Fees (In-District): $2,288
Enrollment: 1,056 Coed
Affiliation or Control: State/Local IRS Status: 501(c)3
Highest Offering: Associate Degree
Program: Occupational; 2-Year Principally Bachelor's Creditable
Accreditation: SC, CAHIIM

02 President ....Dr. Bryan W. WILSON
05 Vice President for Learning ....Dr. John GOSSETT
10 Vice Pres Finance/Administration ....Mr. Ryan GARRISON
20 Dean Academic Programs ....Dr. James BENTON
09 Director of Inst Effectiveness ....Mr. Ladelle HARMON
26 Director of External Relations ....Mr. Michael K. LAVENDER
13 Director of Technology/Info Systems ....Mr. Elmer R. MACOPSON
08 Director of Library Services ....Ms. Sharon P. SMITH
88 Director of Correctional Programs ....Mr. Frank D. SILVER
88 Director of Industrial Training ....Mr. Eddie SHUFORD
76 Director of Health Sciences ....Mrs. Penny CROSS
06 Registrar ....Ms. Kelly HAMLIN
37 Dir Student Financial Aid/Counselor ......Ms. Kim M. LEDBETTER
36 Director of Student Enrichment Ctr ....Mrs. Donna SHORT
88 Dir College/Career Readiness ....Mrs. Teresa VALENTINO
88 Counselor/VA Director ....Mrs. Donna SHORT
51 Director of Continuing Education ....Mr. Brad LEDBETTER
88 Director Basic Law Enforcement Trng ....Mr. Stacy BUFF
07 Director of Admissions ....Mr. Wingate CAIN
15 Director of Human Resources Devel .....Mrs. Mary L. LEDBETTER
30 Resource Development ....Ms. Susan BERLEY
106 Coordinator of Distance Education ....Mrs. Joan WEILER
18 Coord Maintenance/Custodial Svcs ....Mr. Carl COSTNER
88 Coord of Small Business Center ....Mr. H. Dean KANIPE
04 Exec Assistant to the President ....Mrs. Rhonda SILVER

*Mitchell Community College (C)

500 W Broad Street, Statesville NC 28677-5293

County: Iredell FICE Identification: 002947
Unit ID: 198987
Telephone: (704) 878-3200 Carnegie Class: Assoc/Pub-R-M
FAX Number: (704) 878-0872 Calendar System: Semester
URL: www.mitchellcc.edu
Established: 1852 Annual Undergrad Tuition & Fees (In-State): $2,404
Enrollment: 3,106 Coed
Affiliation or Control: State IRS Status: 501(c)3
Highest Offering: Associate Degree
Program: Occupational; 2-Year Principally Bachelor's Creditable
Accreditation: SC, ADNUR, MAC

02 President ....Dr. Tim BREWER
05 Vice President of Instruction ....Dr. Camille REESE
10 Vice Pres of Finance/Administration ....Mr. John WILKINSON
103 Vice Pres Workforce Development/CEC ....Ms. Carol JOHNSON
32 Vice Pres Student Services ....Mr. Dan MANNING
09 Director of Research & Planning ....Ms. Eva EISNAUGLE
08 Director of Learning Resources ....Ms. Vicki CALDWELL
37 Director of Financial Aid ....Ms. Candace COOPER
18 Exec Dir Facilities/Auxiliary Svcs ....Mr. Gary JOHNSON
26 Public Relations/Marketing ....Ms. Megan SUBER
30 Dir Development/College Relations ....Ms. Celeste GRUNER

*Montgomery Community College (D)

1011 Page Street, Troy NC 27371-0787

County: Montgomery FICE Identification: 008087
Unit ID: 199023
Telephone: (910) 576-6222 Carnegie Class: Assoc/Pub-R-S
FAX Number: (910) 576-2176 Calendar System: Semester
URL: www.montgomery.edu
Established: 1967 Annual Undergrad Tuition & Fees (In-District): $2,409
Enrollment: 863 Coed
Affiliation or Control: State/Local IRS Status: 501(c)3
Highest Offering: Associate Degree
Program: Occupational; 2-Year Principally Bachelor's Creditable
Accreditation: SC, CSHSE, DA, MAC

02 President ....Dr. Chad A. BLEDSOE
05 VP of Instruction/Continuing Ed ....Randy GUNTER
11 VP of Administrative Services ....Jeanette MCBRIDE
32 VP of Student Services ....Beth SMITH
51 Dean of Continuing Education ....Robin COATES
102 Executive Director Foundation/Grant ....Gay ROATCH
26 Public Information Officer ....Michele HAYWOOD
09 Dir Institutional Effectiveness ....Carol HOLTON
13 Dir of Information Technology ....Mitch WALKER
04 Assistant to the President ....Korrie ERVIN
38 Counseling Services ....Natalie WINFREE
07 Admissions Officer ....Karen FRYE
37 Director of Financial Aid ....Doni S. CODY
15 Coordinator Of Human Resources ....Melisa BOND
10 Accountant ....Cathy BIBY
18 Director of Facilities ....Wanda FRICK
35 Student Activities Coordinator ....Riley BEAMAN

*Nash Community College (E)

522 N Old Carriage Road, Rocky Mount NC 27804-0488

County: Nash FICE Identification: 008557
Unit ID: 199087
Telephone: (252) 443-4011 Carnegie Class: Assoc/Pub-R-M
FAX Number: (252) 451-8201 Calendar System: Semester
URL: www.nashcc.edu
Established: 1967 Annual Undergrad Tuition & Fees (In-District): $2,200
Enrollment: 3,500 Coed
Affiliation or Control: State/Local IRS Status: 501(c)3
Highest Offering: Associate Degree
Program: Occupational; 2-Year Principally Bachelor's Creditable; Business Emphasis
Accreditation: SC, MAC, PHLEB, PTAA

02 President ....Dr. William S. CARVER, II
05 Vice President for Instruction ....Dr. Trent L. MOHRBUTTER
10 Executive Vice President and CFO ....Ms. Annette H. DISHNER
30 Assoc VP Institutional Advancement ....Ms. Pat E. DANIELS
88 Dean of Transfer ....Ms. Deana GUIDO
88 Director Small Business Center ....Mr. Fred BROOKS
86 Assoc VP Community & Govt Affairs ....Dr. Keith SMITH
32 VP Student & Enrollment Svcs ....Mr. Larry K. MITCHELL
20 Assoc VP Curriculum ....Mr. Mike LATHAM
09 Assoc Dean Institutional Effective ....Ms. Farley PHILLIPS
13 Chief Information Officer ....Mr. Jonathan VESTER
07 Director of Admissions ....Ms. Stephanie BROWN
06 Registrar ....Ms. Kathy S. ADCOX
37 Director of Financial Aid ....Ms. Tammy LESTER
15 Director Human Resources ....Ms. Michelle NOYES
04 Administrative Asst to President ....Ms. Faye CAHOON
24 Dir Instructional Publ/Printing ....Mr. James M. QUIGLEY
18 Director of Facilities ....Mr. C. Ted KENNEDY
26 Sr Dir Marketing/Communication ....Ms. Kelley DEAL

*Pamlico Community College (F)

PO Box 185, Grantsboro NC 28529-0185

County: Pamlico FICE Identification: 007031
Unit ID: 199263
Telephone: (252) 249-1851 Carnegie Class: Assoc/Pub-R-S
FAX Number: (252) 249-2377 Calendar System: Semester
URL: www.pamlicocc.edu
Established: 1962 Annual Undergrad Tuition & Fees (In-District): $2,203
Enrollment: 410 Coed
Affiliation or Control: State/Local IRS Status: 501(c)3
Highest Offering: Associate Degree
Program: Occupational; 2-Year Principally Bachelor's Creditable; Technical Emphasis
Accreditation: SC, MAC, NDT

02 President ....Dr. Cleve H. COX
11 Vice Pres Administrative Svcs ....Mr. James CURRY
05 Vice Pres Instructional Svcs ....Dr. Maria FRASER-MOLINA
32 Vice Pres of Student Services ....Mr. Jamie GIBBS
09 Director of Institutional Research ....Ms. Brandi MCCULLOUGH
06 Registrar ....Ms. Tammy SPAIN
37 Director of Financial Aid ....Ms. Melissa WHITMAN
10 Controller ....Ms. Sherry RABY
26 Director of Public Affairs ....Mr. Ben CASEY

*Piedmont Community College (G)

1715 College Dr, Roxboro NC 27573-1197

County: Person FICE Identification: 009646
Unit ID: 199324
Telephone: (336) 599-1181 Carnegie Class: Assoc/Pub-R-M
FAX Number: (336) 597-3817 Calendar System: Semester
URL: www.piedmontcc.edu
Established: 1970 Annual Undergrad Tuition & Fees (In-District): $1,209
Enrollment: 1,468 Coed
Affiliation or Control: State/Local IRS Status: 501(c)3
Highest Offering: Associate Degree
Program: Occupational; 2-Year Principally Bachelor's Creditable; Technical Emphasis
Accreditation: SC, EMT, MAC

02 President ....Dr. Walter C. BARTLETT
05 Vice Pres Instruction/Student Devel ....Dr. Joyce B. JOHNSON
31 Vice Pres Continuing Education ....Dr. Doris W. CARVER
11 Vice Pres Administrative Services ....Mr. Richard B. SELF
12 Provost Caswell County Campus ....Ms. Shelly T. STONE
106 Spec Asst to VP for Distance Learn ....Dr. Elizabeth M. MOORE
71 Dean Accelerated & Innovative Lrng ....Dr. Michelle L. AHERON
51 Dean Adult Basic Skills ....Ms. Debra B. HARLOW
103 Dean Corp and Occup Training ....Mr. Bradley K. JORDAN
76 Dean Health Sciences and Human Svcs ....Ms. Alisa L. MONTGOMERY
79 Dean Humanities and Social Sciences ....Mr. Wayne L. COHAN
08 Dean LRC ....Mr. Lionel PARKER
81 Dean Math/Sci and Director QEP ....Ms. Lisa K. COOLEY
75 Dean Technical/Occupational Pgms ....Mr. Walter L. MONTGOMERY
103 Dean Workforce Development ....Ms. Nicole M. DUNEVANT
32 Interim Dean Student Development ....Mr. Richard L. PROCTOR
84 Director Enrollment Management ....Mr. Eugene W. RITTER
06 Registrar ....Ms. Susan L. GREINER
37 Dir Financial Aid/Veterans Affairs ....Ms. Paulita N. WILLIAMS
18 Director Buildings and Grounds ....Mr. Bruce T. CHISHOLM
25 Director Grants ....Mr. Ricky FARMER
15 Director Personnel/Payroll ....Ms. Pamela C. HOBBS
102 Director PCC Foundation ....Ms. Pamela F. BRADSHER
26 Director Public Information ....Ms. Elizabeth R. TOWNSEND
09 Dir Research/Inst Effectiveness ....Dr. Jeff PATON
13 Chief Information Officer ....Mr. Vernon T. BROWN, SR.
19 Deputy Director College Safety ....Mr. Adam W. IRBY
29 Fin Coord Foundation/Alumni Rels ....Ms. Patricia I. CLAYTON
96 Purchasing/Accountant ....Ms. Sharon L. KERR
40 Manager Bookstore ....Ms. Tammy H. MORRIS
04 Administrative Asst to President ....Ms. Cindy W. FOX

*Pitt Community College (H)

PO Drawer 7007, Greenville NC 27835-7007

County: Pitt FICE Identification: 004062
Unit ID: 199333
Telephone: (252) 493-7200 Carnegie Class: Assoc/Pub-R-L
FAX Number: (252) 321-4458 Calendar System: Semester
URL: www.pittcc.edu
Established: 1961 Annual Undergrad Tuition & Fees (In-State): $2,294
Enrollment: 8,962 Coed
Affiliation or Control: State IRS Status: 501(c)3
Highest Offering: Associate Degree
Program: Occupational; 2-Year Principally Bachelor's Creditable
Accreditation: SC, ADNUR, CAHIIM, COARC, CSHSE, DMS, MAC, OTA, POLYT, RAD, RADDOS, RTT

02 President ....Dr. Dennis MASSEY
05 Vice President Academic Affairs ....Dr. Thomas GOULD
11 Vice Pres Administrative Services ....Mr. Rick OWENS
32 Vice President Student Development ....Dr. Donald R. SPELL
30 Vice Pres Institutional Advancement ....Mrs. Susan Q. NOBLES
20 Asst Vice Pres Academic Affairs ....Ms. Lori PREAST
13 AVP Information Technology/Services ....Mr. Ernest SIMONS
10 Chief Financial Officer ....Mr. Ricky BROWN
04 Administrative Asst to President ....Mrs. Kathy M. CARNES

31 Dean Economic & Cmty Development .... Vacant
08 Director Library .... Mr. Xudong JIN
09 Dean of Planning & Research .... Vacant
46 Resource Development Director .... Vacant
15 Director of Human Resources .... Mr. Michael SHREVES
91 Director of Admin Computing .... Mrs. Janet MINTERN
06 Registrar .... Ms. Angela CLINE
38 Director of Counseling .... Dr. Kimberly WILLIAMSON
88 Director Basic Skills Program .... Vacant
18 Director of Facilities .... Mr. Timothy STRICKLAND
103 Director of JobLink Career Center .... Vacant
84 Dean Student Svcs/Enrollment Mgmt .... Ms. Joanne T. CERES
41 Athletic Director .... Mr. William BAILEY
29 Director of Alumni Relations .... Mrs. Ashley SMITH
36 Director of Student Placement .... Ms. Sharon CERES
96 Director of Purchasing .... Vacant
19 Chief Public Safety/Campus Police .... Mr. Jay SHINGLETON
88 Director Business & Industry Svcs .... Mrs. Mary PARAMORE
104 Director Study Abroad .... Mrs. Darlene SMITH-WORTHINGTON
09 Director Planning & Analysis .... Dr. Brian MILLER
37 Director Financial Aid .... Mrs. Lisa M. REICHSTEIN
40 Manager of College Store .... Vacant
106 Coord Instructional Tech/Dist Ed .... Mr. Mike CLENDENEN
55 Coord/Counselor Evening Programs .... Mr. Kendrick PRICE
50 Division Dean of Business .... Ms. Katherine CLYDE
76 Division Dean Health Sciences .... Ms. Donna V. NEAL
49 Division Dean of Art & Sciences ... Dr. Stephanie MANLEY-ROOK
75 Div Dean Construct/Indus Tech .... Mr. Mark FAITHFUL
61 Div Dean Legal Sci/Public Svc .... Dr. Dan MAYO

*Randolph Community College (A)

629 Industrial Park Avenue, Asheboro NC 27205
County: Randolph FICE Identification: 005447
Unit ID: 199421
Telephone: (336) 633-0200 Carnegie Class: Assoc/Pub-S-SC
FAX Number: (336) 629-4695 Calendar System: Semester
URL: www.randolph.edu
Established: 1962 Annual Undergrad Tuition & Fees (In-District): $2,392
Enrollment: 2,771 Coed
Affiliation or Control: State/Local IRS Status: 501(c)3
Highest Offering: Associate Degree
Program: Occupational; 2-Year Principally Bachelor's Creditable; Technical Emphasis
Accreditation: SC, ADNUR, RAD

02 President .... Dr. Robert S. SHACKLEFORD, JR.
10 Vice Pres Administrative Services .... Ms. Daffie H. GARRIS
05 Vice Pres Instructional Services .... Ms. Anne B. HOCKETT
32 Vice President Student Services .... Mr. James W. KELLEY
51 VP Workforce Development/Cont Educ .... Mr. Elbert J. LASSITER
30 Assoc VP Institutional Advancement .... Ms. Shelley W. GREENE
62 Dean Library Services .... Ms. Deborah S. LUCK
12 Director Archdale Center .... Vacant
21 Dir Financial Svcs/Controller .... Ms. Susan I. RICE
26 Director Marketing .... Mr. Kris N. JULIAN
18 Director Facilities Operations .... Ms. Cindi J. GOODWIN
13 Director Information Tech Svcs .... Ms. Tara A. WILLIAMS
09 Director Planning & Assessment .... Ms. Karen R. RITTER
15 Director of Human Resources .... Ms. Nancy BULLINS
37 Director Student Support Services .... Mr. Chad WILLIAMS
06 Director Enrollment Mgmt/Registrar .... Ms. Brandi F. HAGERMAN
106 Director Distance Education .... Mr. Devin A. SOVA
88 Director of ABE and AHS .... Vacant
88 Director ESTC .... Mr. Paul G. GOINS
96 Purchasing Agent .... Ms. Sharon P. REYNOLDS
27 Asst Dir Public Information .... Ms. Cathy D. HEFFERIN
04 Exec Asst to Pres/Board of Trustees .. Ms. Heather O. CLOUSTON
102 Dir Foundation/Corporate Relations .... Ms. Lorie L. MCCROSKEY
19 Director Security/Safety .... Mr. Robert A. GRAVES

*Richmond Community College (B)

Box 1189, Hamlet NC 28345-1189
County: Richmond FICE Identification: 005464
Unit ID: 199449
Telephone: (910) 410-1700 Carnegie Class: Assoc/Pub-R-S
FAX Number: (910) 582-7028 Calendar System: Semester
URL: www.richmondcc.edu
Established: 1964 Annual Undergrad Tuition & Fees (In-District): $2,382
Enrollment: 2,531 Coed
Affiliation or Control: State/Local IRS Status: 501(c)3
Highest Offering: Associate Degree
Program: Occupational; 2-Year Principally Bachelor's Creditable; Technical Emphasis
Accreditation: SC, MAC

02 President .... Dr. W. Dale MCINNIS
32 Vice President for Student Services .... Ms. Sharon GOODMAN
05 Vice President for Instruction/CAO .... Mr. Kevin PARSONS
10 Executive VP/VP Admin Svcs/CFO .... Mr. Brent BARBEE
103 VP for Workforce & Economic Develop .... Mr. Robbie TAYLOR
08 Dean of Learning Resources .... Ms. Carolyn BITTLE
88 Director of Basic Skills .... Ms. Sherry BYRD
108 Dean of Inst Effectiveness & Improv .. Ms. Sheri DUNN-RAMSAY
06 Registrar .... Ms. Lori GRAHAM
09 Director of Institutional Research .... Ms. Chihoko TERRY
15 Director of Human Resources .... Ms. Gaye CLARK
26 Director of Marketing & Communic .... Ms. Wylie BELL
21 Controller .... Ms. Debbie CASHWELL
37 Director Student Financial Aid .... Mr. Jon CARTER
96 Purchasing Officer .... Mr. Martin BRIDGES

18 Director of Facility Services .... Mr. Scotty MABE
38 Director Student Counseling .... Mr. Chris GARDNER
04 Executive Asst to President .... Ms. Teena PARSONS

*Roanoke-Chowan Community College (C)

109 Community College Road, Ahoskie NC 27910
County: Hertford FICE Identification: 008613
Unit ID: 199467
Telephone: (252) 862-1200 Carnegie Class: Assoc/Pub-R-S
FAX Number: (252) 862-1358 Calendar System: Semester
URL: www.roanokechowan.edu
Established: 1967 Annual Undergrad Tuition & Fees (In-District): $2,405
Enrollment: 1,007 Coed
Affiliation or Control: State/Local IRS Status: 501(c)3
Highest Offering: Associate Degree
Program: Occupational; 2-Year Principally Bachelor's Creditable
Accreditation: SC

02 President .... Dr. Michael A. ELAM
05 Dean of Curriculum Programs/CAO .... Dr. Pocahantas JONES
103 Sr Dean Workforce/Student Devel .... Ms. Myra POOLE
88 Dean Basic Skills .... Mrs. Michelle MEISCHEID
32 Dean of Student Services .... Mrs. Wendy VANN
10 Controller .... Ms. Sheena SUGGS
08 Dean Learning Res/Info Systems .... Mrs. Monique MITCHELL
18 Director Facilities .... Mr. Charles STRICKLAND
38 Director Student Counseling .... Ms. Sandra COPELAND
106 Director Distance Learning .... Vacant
37 Director Financial Aid .... Mrs. Crystal HARRIS
09 Coord Compliance & Data Resources .. Mr. Juan E. VAUGHAN, II
84 Director Enrollment Svcs/Curric Reg .... Mrs. Amy F. WIGGINS
35 Director Student Support Services .... Ms. Lorraine C. MITCHELL
15 Director Human Resources .... Ms. Kathleen TOURE
06 Registrar .... Ms. Shirley GAY

*Robeson Community College (D)

PO Box 1420, Lumberton NC 28359-1420
County: Robeson FICE Identification: 008612
Unit ID: 199476
Telephone: (910) 272-3700 Carnegie Class: Assoc/Pub-R-M
FAX Number: (910) 272-3328 Calendar System: Semester
URL: www.robeson.edu
Established: 1965 Annual Undergrad Tuition & Fees (In-District): $2,257
Enrollment: 1,988 Coed
Affiliation or Control: State/Local IRS Status: 501(c)3
Highest Offering: Associate Degree
Program: Occupational; 2-Year Principally Bachelor's Creditable
Accreditation: SC, COARC, RAD, SURGT

02 President .... Dr. Pamela HILBERT
05 Int VP Instruction/Sppt Svcs/CAO .... Mr. Bill MAUNEY
51 Vice Pres Adult & Continuing Educ .... Mr. R. Channing JONES
10 Vice President Business Services .... Mrs. Tami B. GEORGE
11 VP for Institutional Services .... Mr. Alphonzo MCRAE
55 Asst VP Public Svc/Appl Tech Pgms ... Mr. William L. LOCKLEAR
88 Asst VP Univ Transfer/Bus/Hlth Pgms .... Ms. Sheila A. REGAN
32 Asst Vice Pres Student Services .... Mr. Billy L. MAUNEY
13 Asst VP/Chief Information Officer .... Mr. Dustin LONG
07 Director of Admissions/Enroll Svcs .... Mr. Ronnie LOCKLEAR
22 Director Affirm Action/Equal Oppty .... Mr. Alphonzo MCRAE
08 Director of Learning Resource Svcs .... Mrs. Maryellen O'BRIEN
38 Director Counseling & Testing .... Mr. Danford F. GROVES
06 Dir Records/Registration/Registrar .... Mrs. Beth CARMICAL
37 Financial Aid Director .... Ms. Teresa TUBBS
25 Director of Grants and Sponsored .... Mrs. Lisa O. HUNT
18 Chief Facilities/Physical Plant .... Mr. Alphonzo MCRAE
102 Director Foundation/Development .... Ms. Rebekah R. LOWRY
29 Director Alumni Relations .... Ms. Rebekah LOWRY
84 Director Enrollment Management .... Mrs. Beth CARMICAL
36 Counseling & Career Services .... Ms. Bonita BELL
15 Personnel Services Specialist .... Ms. Pam ROMANO
96 Purchasing Officer .... Mr. Jason O. LEVISTER

*Rockingham Community College (E)

PO Box 38, Wentworth NC 27375-0038
County: Rockingham FICE Identification: 002958
Unit ID: 199485
Telephone: (336) 342-4261 Carnegie Class: Assoc/Pub-R-M
FAX Number: (336) 349-9986 Calendar System: Semester
URL: www.rockinghamcc.edu
Established: 1963 Annual Undergrad Tuition & Fees (In-District): $2,304
Enrollment: 2,013 Coed
Affiliation or Control: State/Local IRS Status: 501(c)3
Highest Offering: Associate Degree
Program: Occupational; 2-Year Principally Bachelor's Creditable
Accreditation: SC, COARC, PHLEB, SURGT

02 President .... Dr. Mark O. KINLAW
05 Vice President for Academic Affairs .... Ms. Suzanne Y. ROHRBAUGH
11 VP of Administrative Services .... Mr. Steven W. WOODRUFF
32 Vice Pres for Student Development .. Dr. Robert S. LOWDERMILK
88 Assoc VP Administrative Services .... Dr. E. Anthony GUNN
103 Dean of Workforce Development .... Ms. Laura F. COFFEE
49 Dean of Arts & Sciences .... Ms. Celeste H. ALLIS
76 Dean of Health & Public Safety .... Dr. Kimberly M. CLARK
88 Assoc Dean Learning Resources .... Ms. Kimberly SHIREMAN

45 Assoc VP Inst Effectiveness .... Mr. Kevin OSBORNE
06 Registrar .... Ms. Carla MOORE
08 Director Library/Archivist .... Ms. Mary GOMEZ
30 Director Development/Foundation .... Ms. Gaye B. CLIFTON
13 Dir Technology Support Services .... Ms. Gretchen PARRISH
37 Director of Financial Aid .... Ms. Sarah EVANS
84 Director of Enrollment Services .... Mr. Derick SATTERFIELD
35 Director Student Life .... Mr. Stewart MCCLINTOCK
40 Bookstore Manager .... Ms. Della J. GASTON
15 Director Human Resources .... Ms. Joy G. CHAPPELL
26 Director Public Information .... Ms. Kim A. PRYOR
96 Director of Purchasing .... Mr. John PARRISH

*Rowan-Cabarrus Community College (F)

1333 Jake Alexander Blvd., South, Salisbury NC 28145
County: Rowan FICE Identification: 005754
Unit ID: 199494
Telephone: (704) 216-7222 Carnegie Class: Assoc/Pub-S-MC
FAX Number: N/A Calendar System: Semester
URL: www.rccc.edu
Established: 1963 Annual Undergrad Tuition & Fees (In-State): $2,304
Enrollment: 6,352 Coed
Affiliation or Control: State IRS Status: 501(c)3
Highest Offering: Associate Degree
Program: Occupational; 2-Year Principally Bachelor's Creditable
Accreditation: SC, ADNUR, DA, PNUR, RAD

02 President .... Dr. Carol SPALDING
05 Academic Vice President .... Dr. Michael D. QUILLEN
10 Chief Financial Officer .... Ms. Janet SPRIGGS
84 Vice President Student Services .... Ms. Gaye MCCONNELL
51 Vice President of Corp & Cont Educ .... Mr. Craig LAMB
13 Chief Information Officer .... Mr. Kenneth G. INGLE, III
15 CO Human Resour & Org Effectiveness .... Ms. Tina HAYNES
18 Chief Facilities Officer .... Mr. Jonathan CHAMBERLIN
102 CO Governance/Foundation & Pub Rels .... Ms. Carla HOWELL
20 Assoc Academic Vice President .... Mr. Angelo MARKANTONAKIS
21 Assoc VP & Controller .... Ms. Kizzy LEA
32 Assoc VP Student Services .... Mr. Mark EBERSOLE
103 Assoc VP Corporate & Con Ed .... Mrs. Ann MORRIS
76 Dean Health Programs .... Mrs. Wendy BARNHARDT
50 Dean Science Bus Math & Info Tech . Ms. Carol SCHERCZINGER
49 Dean Liberal Arts & General Educ .... Dr. Carolyn HOLBERT
71 Dean Public Services .... Mr. Spencer RUMMAGE
54 Dean Engineering & Bus Technologies .... Mr. Van MADRAY
106 Dean Eductional Resource Services .... Ms. Debra NEESMITH
71 Dean Special Programs .... Ms. Claudia SWICEGOOD
72 Assoc Dean Information Technology .... Mr. Ian STEVENS
49 Assoc Dean Lib Arts & Gen Educ .... Ms. Betty STACK
88 Exec Dir Pre-College Studies .... Mr. Gary CONNOR
08 Director Learning Resource Ctr .... Mr. Rodney LIPPARD
25 Director Grants Development .... Ms. Rebecca HOOKS
37 Director Fin Aid & VA Benefit .... Mrs. Lisa LEDBETTER
96 Director of Purchasing .... Ms. Kathy PIPER
07 Director Admissions & Recruitment .... Ms. Dina HARKEY
06 Director Registration & Records .... Mrs. Joan CREEGER
35 Director Student Life & Leadership .... Ms. Natasha LIPSCOMB
38 Director Counseling and Career Svs .... Ms. Misty MOLER
16 Director of Human Resources .... Mrs. Nekita EUBANKS
09 Dir Research/Plng/Inst Effectiv .... Ms. Christine PROMIN
19 Director of Campus Security .... Mr. Tim BOST
102 Director RCCC Foundation .... Mr. Marty RICHARDS
26 Dir College Relations Mktg & Comm .... Ms. Paula DIBLEY

*Sampson Community College (G)

PO Box 318, Clinton NC 28329-0318
County: Sampson FICE Identification: 007892
Unit ID: 199625
Telephone: (910) 592-8081 Carnegie Class: Assoc/Pub-R-S
FAX Number: (910) 592-8048 Calendar System: Semester
URL: www.sampsoncc.edu
Established: 1967 Annual Undergrad Tuition & Fees (In-District): $2,381
Enrollment: 1,551 Coed
Affiliation or Control: State/Local IRS Status: 501(c)3
Highest Offering: Associate Degree
Program: Occupational; 2-Year Principally Bachelor's Creditable
Accreditation: SC, ADNUR, PNUR

02 President .... Dr. Paul C. HUTCHINS
05 Vice Pres Academic Affairs/Admin .... Dr. William STARLING
10 Vice Pres Finance/Auxiliary Svcs .... Mrs. Virginia S. LUCAS
32 Dean of Student Services .... Ms. Amy NOEL
51 Dean of Continuing Education .... Mrs. Ann BUTLER
07 Director of Admissions .... Ms. Blair HAIRR
06 Registrar .... Mrs. Delsey BREWINGTON
26 Public Information Office .... Mr. Dan GRUBB
37 Asst Director Financial Aid .... Ms. Maureen POWELL
08 Director Library Services .... Vacant
102 Foundation Director .... Mrs. Lisa TURLINGTON
15 Personnel Officer .... Mrs. Frankie K. SUTTER

*Sandhills Community College (H)

3395 Airport Road, Pinehurst NC 28374-8283
County: Moore FICE Identification: 002961
Unit ID: 199634
Telephone: (910) 692-6185 Carnegie Class: Assoc/Pub-R-M
FAX Number: (910) 695-1823 Calendar System: Semester
URL: www.sandhills.edu
Established: 1963 Annual Undergrad Tuition & Fees (In-State): $2,385

Enrollment: 4,158 Coed
Affiliation or Control: State IRS Status: 501(c)3
Highest Offering: Associate Degree
Program: Occupational; 2-Year Principally Bachelor's Creditable
Accreditation: SC, COARC, MLTAD, POLYT, RAD, SURGT

02 President ... Dr. John R. DEMPSEY
03 Exec Vice President ... Ms. Brenda JACKSON
05 VP of Academic Affairs ... Dr. Rebecca ROUSH
32 VP of Student Services ... Mrs. Kellie SHOEMAKE
51 VP of Continuing Education ... Ms. Andi KORTE
35 Dean of Student LIfe ... Mr. David FARMER
04 Exec Assistant to the President ... Ms. Heather LYONS
10 Chief Financial Officer ... Ms. Elizabeth THOMAS
20 Dean of Instruction ... Ms. Linda CHANDLER
09 Dean of Institutional Plng/Rsrch ... Dr. Kristie SULLIVAN
102 Exec Director of SCC Foundation ... Ms. Germaine ELKINS
08 Dean of Learning Resources ... Dr. John STACEY
06 Director of Records & Registration ... Ms. Jean BLUE
37 Financial Aid Officer ... Ms. Lindsey FARMER
106 Director of Distance Learning ... Ms. Wendy KAUFFMAN
13 Director of Information Services ... Mr. Brad ROBBINS
19 Director of Security/Safety ... Mr. Dwight THREET
18 Physical Plant Manager ... Mr. Doug SMITH
15 Director Human Resources ... Ms. Wendy B. DODSON
21 Dir Finance & Student Accounts ... Mr. Joseph BROWN
26 Director of Marketing and PR ... Ms. Karen MANNING
40 Bookstore Manager ... Ms. Sandra DALES
07 Director of Admissions ... Ms. Cary GREENE

*South Piedmont Community College (A)

PO Box 126, Polkton NC 28135-0126
County: Anson/Union FICE Identification: 007985
Unit ID: 197850
Telephone: (704) 272-5300 Carnegie Class: Assoc/Pub-R-M
FAX Number: (704) 272-5350 Calendar System: Semester
URL: www.spcc.edu
Established: 1999 Annual Undergrad Tuition & Fees (In-District): $1,873
Enrollment: 2,658 Coed
Affiliation or Control: State/Local IRS Status: 501(c)3
Highest Offering: Associate Degree
Program: Occupational; 2-Year Principally Bachelor's Creditable; Business Emphasis
Accreditation: SC, DMS, MAC

02 President ... Dr. Stanley M. SIDOR
03 Exec Vice President ... Mr. John DEVITTO
10 VP Finance/Administrative Svcs/CFO ... Ms. Michelle BROCK
05 Int Vice Pres Academic Affairs ... Ms. Joyce LONG
32 Vice Pres Student Services ... Mrs. Elaine CLODFELTER
51 Vice Pres Career Devel/Cont Educ ... Mr. Dan MERLE
30 VP Inst Advancement/SPCC Foundation ... Ms. Hayne WHITE
04 Exec Assistant to President ... Ms. Nanci OSVAI
15 Assoc VP Human Res/Payroll/Org Dev ... Ms. Susan R. FLAKE
21 Asst Vice Pres Finance/Admin Svcs ... Mr. Richard ASHLEY
13 Asst VP Information Tech Svcs/CIO .. Mr. Dan DOMBCHEWSKYJ
18 Asst VP of Facilities ... Mr. William M. TRUETT
108 Assoc VP Planning/IE ... Ms. Jill MILLARD
49 Dean School of Arts & Science ... Mr. Carl BISHOP
76 Dean Allied Health ... Ms. Alice BRADLEY
66 Interim Dean Nursing ... Ms. Alice BRADLEY
72 Dean Applied Science & Technology ... Dr. Maria LANDER
84 Dean of Enrollment Services ... Mr. John RATLIFF
35 Dean of Student Development ... Ms. Makena STEWART
06 Registrar ... Ms. Cathy HORNE
102 Executive Director SPCC Foundation ... Ms. Laura BYRD
08 Director Library Services ... Mr. Grant LEFOE
88 Director of Basic Skills ... Ms. Denise WILSON
16 Director Human Resources ... Ms. Linda KAPPAUF
107 Director Professional Programs ... Ms. Geri DUNCAN
38 Director of Counseling ... Vacant
36 Director of Advising/QEP ... Dr. Malinda DANIEL
35 Director Student Engagement ... Mr. Michael MAFFUCCI
44 Development Officer ... Ms. Gina RHODES
25 Dir Corporate/Community Development ... Mr. Scott COLLIER
26 Dir Marketing/Public Inform Ofcr ... Mr. Michael MCALLISTER
09 Dir Institutional Research/Effect ... Ms. Marci JACKSON

*Southeastern Community College (B)

4564 Chadbourn Highway, PO Box 151,
Whiteville NC 28472-0151
County: Columbus FICE Identification: 002964
Unit ID: 199722
Telephone: (910) 642-7141 Carnegie Class: Assoc/Pub-R-M
FAX Number: (910) 642-5658 Calendar System: Semester
URL: www.sccnc.edu
Established: 1964 Annual Undergrad Tuition & Fees (In-State): $2,457
Enrollment: 1,348 Coed
Affiliation or Control: State IRS Status: 501(c)3
Highest Offering: Associate Degree
Program: Occupational; 2-Year Principally Bachelor's Creditable; Nursing Emphasis
Accreditation: SC, MLTAD, PHLEB

02 President ... Dr. Kathy MATLOCK
10 Vice President Administrative Svcs ... Ms. Betty Jo RAMSEY
05 Acting Vice Pres Academic Affairs ... Ms. Lauren G. COLE
103 VP Workforce & Cmty Development ... Ms. Beverlee S. NANCE
30 Exec Dean Institutional Advancement ... Ms. Sue W. HAWKS
32 Exec Dean Student Services ... Ms. Sylvia COX
76 Dean Allied Hlth/Sci/Fine Arts/Math ... Dr. James HUTCHERSON
103 Dean of Workforce & Comm Dev ... Ms. Teresa TRIPLETT
08 Librarian ... Ms. Kay HOUSER
15 Human Resources Director ... Mr. Bill MAULTSBY
21 Controller/Operations/Finance ... Ms. Donna TURBEVILLE
26 Director Marketing & Outreach ... Ms. Liz MCLEAN
13 Director of Information Technology ... Mr. Jason STRICKLAND
51 Director of Continuing Education ... Ms. Mary Ruth EDWARDS
37 Director of Financial Aid ... Mr. Justin CRISTELLO
06 Dir of Student Records/Registrar ... Ms. Sylvia MCQUEEN
36 Director of Counseling ... Ms. Julia ROBERTS
09 Research & Reporting Coordinator ... Mr. Don WHITE

*Southwestern Community College (C)

447 College Drive, Sylva NC 28779-8581
County: Jackson FICE Identification: 008466
Unit ID: 199731
Telephone: (828) 339-4000 Carnegie Class: Assoc/Pub-R-M
FAX Number: (828) 586-3129 Calendar System: Semester
URL: www.southwesterncc.edu
Established: 1964 Annual Undergrad Tuition & Fees (In-District): $2,100
Enrollment: 2,603 Coed
Affiliation or Control: State/Local IRS Status: 501(c)3
Highest Offering: Associate Degree
Program: Occupational; 2-Year Principally Bachelor's Creditable
Accreditation: SC, CAHIIM, COARC, DMS, EMT, MAC, MLTAD, PHLEB, PTAA, RAD

02 President ... Dr. Don L. TOMAS
05 Exec VP Instructional/Student Svcs ... Dr. Thom R. BROOKS
10 VP for Financial & Admin Services ... Mr. Clifford STALTER
13 VP Information Technology ... Mr. Scott BAKER
30 Exec Dir Institutional Development ... Ms. Lynda W. PARLETT
103 Dean of Workforce/Economic Devel ... Ms. Sonja HAYNES
12 Dean Macon Campus ... Dr. Cheryl DAVIDS
32 Dean of Students ... Ms. Cheryl CONTINO-CONNER
06 Registrar ... Ms. Christy DEAVER
08 Director of Learning Resources ... Mrs. Dianne LINDGREN
09 Director Inst Research & Planning ... Mr. Jonathan E. DEAN
37 Director of Financial Aid ... Ms. Melody L. LAWRENCE
26 Director of Public Relations ... Mr. Tyler GOODE
102 Director of SCC Foundation ... Mr. Brett WOODS
84 Director of Enrollment Management ... Mr. Martin AUCOIN

*Stanly Community College (D)

141 College Drive, Albemarle NC 28001-7458
County: Stanly FICE Identification: 011194
Unit ID: 199740
Telephone: (704) 982-0121 Carnegie Class: Assoc/Pub-R-M
FAX Number: (704) 982-0819 Calendar System: Semester
URL: www.stanly.edu
Established: 1971 Annual Undergrad Tuition & Fees (In-District): $2,523
Enrollment: 2,745 Coed
Affiliation or Control: State/Local IRS Status: 501(c)3
Highest Offering: Associate Degree
Program: Occupational; 2-Year Principally Bachelor's Creditable
Accreditation: SC, COARC, MAC, MLTAD

02 President ... Dr. Brenda KAYS
05 Exec VP of Educational Services ... Mrs. Robin MCCREE
32 Exec VP Student/Academic Affairs ... Ms. Robin MCCREE
10 VP Administrative Services/CFO ... Mrs. Becky WALL
76 Assoc VP Health & Public Svcs ... Dr. Tammy CRUMP
50 Assoc VP Business & Technology ... Mrs. Merlin AMIRTHARAJ
51 VP Organizational Growth/Dev/Effect ... Ms. Lois SMITH
04 Exec Aide to Pres/Governmental Affs ... Mrs. Ashley SMITH
37 Dean Financial Aid Management ... Ms. Petra FIELDS
84 Dean of Enrollment Management ... Mr. Patrick HOLYFIED
36 Asst Dean Students/Career Placement ... Mr. Marcus PRYOR
06 Dir Registration/Stdnt Information ... Ms. Michelle POPLIN
26 Director Marketing & Communication ... Mrs. Michelle PEIFER
07 Director of Admissions ... Ms. Jeania MARTIN
21 Controller ... Mrs. Debra HARWOOD
18 Director of Facilities Services ... Mr. Blake BOSTIC
102 Exec Director of SCC Foundation ... Ms. Christy BOGLE
15 Human Resources Officer ... Vacant
08 Director Library Services ... Mrs. Erin ALLEN
24 Media Specialist Services ... Mr. Mark SAMPLE
96 Purchasing Agent ... Mrs. Shelley OSBORNE

*Surry Community College (E)

630 S Main Street, Dobson NC 27017-0304
County: Surry FICE Identification: 002970
Unit ID: 199768
Telephone: (336) 386-8121 Carnegie Class: Assoc/Pub-R-M
FAX Number: (336) 386-8951 Calendar System: Semester
URL: www.surry.edu
Established: 1964 Annual Undergrad Tuition & Fees (In-State): $2,410
Enrollment: 3,346 Coed
Affiliation or Control: State IRS Status: 501(c)3
Highest Offering: Associate Degree
Program: Occupational; 2-Year Principally Bachelor's Creditable; Business Emphasis
Accreditation: SC, MAC, PTAA

02 President ... Dr. David R. SHOCKLEY
05 Vice Pres Curriculum Programs ... Dr. Jami WOODS
10 Vice President for Finance ... Mr. Tony L. MARTIN
32 Vice Pres Student Services ... Mr. Randy LEDFORD
45 Vice Pres Institutional Effective ... Dr. Anne R. HENNIS
51 VP Corporate & Cont Education ... Dr. George O. SAPPENFIELD
13 Vice President Technology Services ... Dr. Candace HOLDER
15 Director Personnel Services ... Ms. Melonie WEATHERS
18 Chief Facilities/Physical Plant ... Mr. Randy ROGERS
19 Director Security/Safety ... Mr. Marty SHROPSHIRE
26 Chief Public Relations/Marketing ... Ms. Julie PHARR
41 Athletic Director ... Mr. Mark TUCKER

*Tri-County Community College (F)

21 Campus Circle, Murphy NC 28906-7919
County: Cherokee FICE Identification: 009430
Unit ID: 199795
Telephone: (828) 837-6810 Carnegie Class: Assoc/Pub-R-S
FAX Number: (828) 837-0028 Calendar System: Semester
URL: www.tricountycc.edu
Established: 1964 Annual Undergrad Tuition & Fees (In-State): $236,2.5
Enrollment: 1,294 Coed
Affiliation or Control: State IRS Status: 501(c)3
Highest Offering: Associate Degree
Program: Occupational; 2-Year Principally Bachelor's Creditable; Technical Emphasis
Accreditation: SC, #MAC

02 President ... Dr. Donna TIPTON-ROGERS
09 VP Instruction/Institution Effect ... Dr. Steve WOOD
13 Dir of Computing & Information Mgt ... Mr. Jason OUTEN
88 Coordinator Recruitment/Retention ... Ms. Samantha MAJOR
103 Dir of Economic & Workforce Develop ... Mr. Paul WORLEY
45 VP College & Community Initiatives ... Mr. Bo GRAY
12 Asst to Pres Graham Cty Operations ... Ms. Charlene WOOD
88 Dean Research & Planning/EC Liaison ... Dr. Jason CHAMBERS
10 VP for Business & Finance ... Mr. Bill VESPASIAN
15 Director of Human Resources ... Ms. Sallie BAKER
91 Systems Administrator/Data Base Mgr ... Mr. Randy GUYETTE
08 Dean Learning Resources ... Ms. Linda KRESSAL
106 Learning Mgt Systems Administrator ... Mr. Cody ANDERSON
30 Coordinator Institutional Advancemt ... Mr. Roarke ARROWOOD
06 Registrar Curriculum ... Ms. Holly HYDE
37 Director of Financial Aid ... Ms. Diane OWL
96 Purchasing Agent ... Ms. Judy OWENBY
84 Director of Enrollment Management ... Ms. Lee BEAL
18 Coordinator of Facility Services ... Mr. Tim NICHOLSON

*Vance-Granville Community College (G)

PO Box 917, Henderson NC 27536-0917
County: Vance FICE Identification: 009903
Unit ID: 199838
Telephone: (252) 492-2061 Carnegie Class: Assoc/Pub-R-M
FAX Number: (252) 430-0460 Calendar System: Semester
URL: www.vgcc.edu
Established: 1969 Annual Undergrad Tuition & Fees (In-State): $1,826
Enrollment: 3,618 Coed
Affiliation or Control: State Related IRS Status: 501(c)3
Highest Offering: Associate Degree
Program: Occupational; 2-Year Principally Bachelor's Creditable
Accreditation: SC, CSHSE, MAC, RAD

02 President ... Dr. Stelfanie WILLIAMS
05 Vice Pres of Acad & Stdnt Affairs ... Dr. Angela BALLENTINE
10 Vice Pres for Finance & Operations ... Mr. Steve GRAHAM
09 VP of Institutional Research & Tech ... Dr. Kenneth A. LEWIS, JR.
26 VP of Employee & Public Relations . Ms. Stacey CARTER-COLEY
12 Dean South Campus ... Ms. Cecilia B. WHEELER
12 Dean Franklin County Campus ... Ms. Bobbie Jo C. MAY
12 Dean Warren County Campus ... Mr. Lyndon HALL
08 Director Learning Resources Center ... Ms. Elaine STEM
06 Registrar ... Ms. Kathy KTUL
15 Director of Human Resources ... Ms. Audrey PARKER
37 Director of Financial Aid ... Ms. Kali BROWN
18 Director of Plant Operations ... Mr. Jack PUCKETT
27 Director of Communications ... Mr. James EDWARDS
38 Dir of Student Success ... Ms. Amy O'GEARY
07 Director of Admissions & Records ... Ms. Tonya WADDLE
09 Director of Planning & Research ... Vacant
40 Bookstore Manager ... Ms. Sandra NEWTON

*Wake Technical Community College (H)

9101 Fayetteville Road, Raleigh NC 27603-5696
County: Wake FICE Identification: 004844
Unit ID: 199856
Telephone: (919) 866-5000 Carnegie Class: Assoc/Pub-U-MC
FAX Number: (919) 779-3360 Calendar System: Semester
URL: www.waketech.edu
Established: 1958 Annual Undergrad Tuition & Fees (In-District): $1,020
Enrollment: 21,296 Coed
Affiliation or Control: State/Local IRS Status: 501(c)3
Highest Offering: Associate Degree
Program: Occupational; 2-Year Principally Bachelor's Creditable
Accreditation: SC, ACFEI, ADNUR, ADNUR, DA, DH, MAC, MLTAD, PHLEB, RAD, SURGT

02 President Dr. Stephen C. SCOTT
03 Executive Vice President Mrs. Gayle GREENE
102 EVP Foundation/College Dev & Comm Mr. O. Mort CONGLETON
43 General Counsel/VP Legal Services Clay T. HINES
05 SVP Curriculum Education Svcs Mr. Bryan K. RYAN
32 SVP Enrollment & Student Services Mrs. Rita H. JERMAN
103 VP Workforce Continuing Education Mr. Anthony CAISON
10 SVP of Financial & Business Svcs Mr. Arthur W. ANDREWS
18 Facility Engineering Officer Mr. Wendell B. GOODWIN
26 VP Communications/Public Relations Mrs. Laurie C. CLOWERS
20 AVP Arts and Sciences Ms. Tonya FORBES
20 AVP Career Programs Ms. Sandra DIETRICH
84 AVP Enrollment Services Mr. John W. SAPARILAS
15 AVP Human Res and Title IX Coord Ms. Benita I. CLARK
19 Chief of Police Mr. Michael A. PENRY
21 AVP Accounting Officer Ms. Marla L. TART
10 AVP Business Services Mrs. Debra S. WALLACE
46 Dean IE/Accreditation & Research Dr. John B. BOONE
30 Sr Dir Foundation Rels/Admin Mrs. Stephanie S. LAKE
25 Dean Sponsored Programs Mr. Richard W. SULLINS
06 Senior Associate Registrar for Spec Ms. Salanna D. HOLMES
06 Dean Records & Reg/Registrar CE Ms. Karen R. HOLDING-JORDAN
35 Dean Student Dev/Stdnt Conduct Ofcr Mr. Mark T. GIBSON
72 Dean Educ Svcs & Technology Mr. Ray L. TIMS
37 Dean Financial Aid/Veterans Affairs Mrs. Regina M. HUGGINS
35 Sr Dean Strat Innovations Sp Proj Mrs. Karen B. PHINAZEE
88 Dean BioNetwork Capstone Center Ms. Ana M. MCCLANAHAN
20 AVP Student Services Mr. Kevin A. BROWN
07 Dean Admissions/Outreach Services Ms. Susan R. BLOOMFIELD
08 Interim Dean Library Services Ms. Julia MIELISH
12 Campus Dean Public Safety Ed Campus Ms. Angela J. MIZELLE
27 Dir Communications Ops/Brand Mgmt Mrs. Francie W. SANDERSON
36 Assoc Dean Career & Empl Resources Mrs. Lynn E. KAVCSAK
76 Dean Health Sciences Campus Dr. Molly CURRY
81 Dean Mathematics/Sciences Div Ms. Sharon L. WELKER
79 Dean Arts/Humanities/Soc Sci Div Dr. Rebecca NEAGLE
50 Dean Business & Public Svcs Tech Mr. Walter MARTIN
75 Dean Applied Engr & Technologies Ms. Patricia A. GODIN
88 Sr Dean Instructional Support Mr. James A. ROBERSON
55 Director Career Dev & Pers Enrich Mr. Larry M. BUIE
77 Dean Computer Technologies Ms. Angela L. BEQUETTE
88 AVP CE Open Enrollment Mrs. Monica P. GEMPERLEIN

*Wayne Community College (A)

3000 Wayne Memorial Drive Box 8002,
Goldsboro NC 27533-8002

County: Wayne | FICE Identification: 002980
Unit ID: 199892
Telephone: (919) 735-5151 | Carnegie Class: Assoc/Pub-R-M
FAX Number: (919) 736-9425 | Calendar System: Semester
URL: www.waynecc.edu
Established: 1957 | Annual Undergrad Tuition & Fees (In-District): $2,396
Enrollment: 3,351 | Coed
Affiliation or Control: State/Local | IRS Status: 501(c)3
Highest Offering: Associate Degree
Program: Occupational; 2-Year Principally Bachelor's Creditable
Accreditation: SC, ADNUR, DA, DH, MAC, PNUR

02 President Dr. Kay H. ALBERTSON
05 VP Academic and Student Services Mr. Gene SMITH
10 Chief Financial Officer Mrs. Joy KORNEGAY
11 Vice Pres Administrative Services Mr. Don MAGOON
45 VP Inst Effectiveness/Innovation Dr. Tracey IVEY
32 AVP Academic and Student Services Ms. Joanna MORRISETTE
51 AVP Continuing Education Services Ms. Renita DAWSON
15 AVP Human Res/Safety/Compliance Mr. Charles GAYLOR, IV
72 Division Head Applied Technologies Mr. Ernie WHITE
49 Division Head Arts & Sciences Dr. Tracey IVEY
50 Div Head Business & Computer Tech Mrs. Beth HOOKS
76 Division Head Allied Health Mrs. Pattie PFEIFFER
88 Division Head Public Safety Ms. Beverly DEANS
62 Head Librarian Dr. Aletha ANDREW
12 Coordinator Seymour Johnson AFB Mrs. Dori FRASER
92 Honors Program Coordinator Mr. Brandon JENKINS
106 Distance Education Specialist Mr. Randall SHEARON
105 Coord Educ Tech Services/Webmaster Mr. Brent HOOD
13 Director Information Systems Ms. Katherine JONES
18 Facility Operations Supt Mr. Edward E. FARRIS
19 Campus Police & Security Chief Willie L. BRINSON
40 Director Bookstore Mrs. Trellie HERRING
88 Ex Dir Wayne Bus/Indus Ctr & WORKS Mrs. Diane IVEY
07 Director Admissions & Records Ms. Jennifer MAYO
37 Director Student Financial Aid Mrs. Brenda D. MERCER
84 Dir Student Devel/Enrollment Mgmt Ms. Joanna MORRISETTE
36 Coord Coop Ed and Career Services Mrs. Lorie WALLER
78 Director Cooperative Programs Ms. Lorie WALLER
35 Student Activities Coordinator Ms. Paige HAM
96 Accountant/Equipment Coordinator Mr. Mark R. JOHNSON
102 Executive Director of Foundation Mr. Jack KANNAN
26 Public Information Officer Ms. Tara HUMPHRIES
16 Director Human Resources Mrs. Ina R. RAWLINSON
55 Evening Coord/Security Services Mr. James BYNUM

*Western Piedmont Community College (B)

1001 Burkemont Avenue, Morganton NC 28655-4504

County: Burke | FICE Identification: 002982
Unit ID: 199908
Telephone: (828) 438-6000 | Carnegie Class: Assoc/Pub-R-M
FAX Number: (828) 438-6015 | Calendar System: Semester
URL: www.wpcc.edu
Established: 1964 | Annual Undergrad Tuition & Fees (In-State): $2,416
Enrollment: 2,056 | Coed
Affiliation or Control: State | IRS Status: 501(c)3
Highest Offering: Associate Degree
Program: Occupational; 2-Year Principally Bachelor's Creditable; Business Emphasis
Accreditation: SC, ADNUR, DA, MAC, MLTAD

02 President Dr. Michael HELMICK
05 Vice Pres Academic Affairs Ms. Rhia M. CRAWFORD
10 VP Admin Svcs/Chief Financial Ofcr Ms. Sandra K. HOILMAN
32 Vice President Student Development Mr. Atticus J. SIMPSON
51 Dean of Continuing Education Mr. Lee KISER
35 Dean of Student Services Ms. Susan WILLIAMS
08 Library Director Ms. Nancy DANIEL
54 Dean Science/Engineering/Math Mr. Michael DANIELS
79 Dean Humanities/Social Sciences Mrs. Mary C. SAFFORD
76 Dean Health Sciences Ms. Ann Marie MCNEELY
50 Dean Business & Public Services Mrs. Leslie MCKESSON
21 Controller Mr. Michael BINGHAM
06 Director Records & Registration Mrs. Joan P. HOGAN
15 Director Human Resources Ms. Lisa H. SESSIONS
84 Director Enrollment Management Mrs. Jennifer PROPST
37 Director Student Financial Aid Ms. Dori BARRON
13 Director Management Info Systems Ms. Nancy E. NORRIS
09 Director of Planning & Research Mr. William L. LEFEVERS
96 Director of Purchasing Ms. Linda CARSWELL
18 Director of Maintenance Vacant
04 Exec Admin Asst to President Ms. Kathy F. DURHAM

*Wilkes Community College (C)

1328 S Collegiate Drive, Wilkesboro NC 28697-0120

County: Wilkes | FICE Identification: 002983
Unit ID: 199926
Telephone: (336) 838-6100 | Carnegie Class: Assoc/Pub-R-M
FAX Number: (336) 903-3219 | Calendar System: Semester
URL: www.wilkescc.edu
Established: 1965 | Annual Undergrad Tuition & Fees (In-State): $3,594
Enrollment: 2,730 | Coed
Affiliation or Control: State | IRS Status: 501(c)3
Highest Offering: Associate Degree
Program: Occupational; 2-Year Principally Bachelor's Creditable; Technical Emphasis
Accreditation: SC, COARC, DA, MAC, RAD

02 President Dr. Jeff A. COX
05 Sr VP of Instruction Vacant
10 Senior VP of Administration Mr. D. Morgan FRANCIS, JR.
20 VP of Instr Support/Student Svcs Ms. Kim E. FAW
103 VP Adv Industrial & Workforce Dev Dr. John HAUSER
13 Assoc VP Information Technology Mr. Mike WINGLER
12 Assoc VP Ashe Campus Mr. Christopher D. ROBINSON
12 Director Alleghany Center Ms. Jayne PHIPPS-BOGER
09 Inst Effectiveness Exec Director Mr. J. Kelly PIPES, III
50 Dean Business/Public Svc Tech Div Mrs. Robin PHILLIPS-HAUSER
76 Dean Health Sciences Division Mr. Billy WOODS
49 Dean Arts & Sciences Division Ms. Blair M. HANCOCK
18 Exec Director/Facilities Services Mr. Ronald DOLLYHITE
30 Exec Director/Endowment Ms. Allison PHILLIPS
15 Director of Human Resources Mr. Tracy D. MCENTIRE
06 Registrar Ms. Melonie KILBY
07 Director of Admissions Mr. Scott JOHNSON
37 Director of Financial Aid Ms. Vickie G. CALL
38 Director Counseling & Career Svcs Dr. Lynda K. BLACK
32 Director Enrollment Mgmt/Stdnt Life Mr. Curt MILLER
08 Director Learning Resources Ms. Christy EARP
38 Director Student Support Services Mr. John CANTY
40 Bookstore Manager Ms. Holly EDWARDS
26 PIO & Relations Officer Ms. Amber HERMAN
19 Safety & Security Manager Mr. Jamie MCGUIRE
04 Administrative Asst to President Ms. Angela BOND
96 Director of Purchasing Ms. Kim BARFIELD

*Wilson Community College (D)

PO Box 4305, Wilson NC 27893-0305

County: Wilson | FICE Identification: 004845
Unit ID: 199953
Telephone: (252) 291-1195 | Carnegie Class: Assoc/Pub-R-M
FAX Number: (252) 243-7148 | Calendar System: Semester
URL: www.wilsoncc.edu
Established: 1958 | Annual Undergrad Tuition & Fees (In-State): $2,757
Enrollment: 2,715 | Coed
Affiliation or Control: State | IRS Status: 501(c)3
Highest Offering: Associate Degree
Program: Occupational; 2-Year Principally Bachelor's Creditable
Accreditation: SC, SURGT

02 President Dr. Rusty STEPHENS
05 Vice Pres Instruction/Student Devel Dr. Denise L. SESSOMS
10 Vice Pres for Finance & Admin Svcs Mr. Hadie C. HORNE
09 Assoc VP Institutional Effective Vacant
51 Dean of Cont Educ/Ind Tech/Sust Mr. Robert D. HOLSTEN
32 Dean of Student Development Mr. Don L. BOYETTE
76 Dean of Allied Health & Sciences Ms. Glenda P. BONDURANT
50 Dean Business/Applied Tech/Ed Part Mr. Wes HILL
15 Director of Human Resources Ms. Kathy WILLIAMSON
08 Head Librarian Mr. Gerry J. O'NEILL
21 Controller Ms. Jessica S. JONES
06 Registrar Ms. Jennifer DAVIS
07 Assoc Dean of Enrollment Ms. Sandra LACKNER
18 Director of Facilities Mr. Ray OWEN
37 Dir of Financial Aid/Vet Affairs Ms. Lisa SHEARIN
30 Director of Institutional Advance Ms. Renee WATKEVICH
13 Director of IT Ms. Molly ARMSTRONG
96 Purchasing & Capital Projects Mgr Ms. Donna A. TURNER
40 Bookstore Manager Ms. Kaschia SPELLS

North Carolina Wesleyan College (E)

3400 N Wesleyan Boulevard,
Rocky Mount NC 27804-8630

County: Nash | FICE Identification: 002951
Unit ID: 199209
Telephone: (252) 985-5100 | Carnegie Class: Bac/Diverse
FAX Number: (252) 985-5231 | Calendar System: 4/1/4
URL: www.ncwc.edu
Established: 1956 | Annual Undergrad Tuition & Fees: $28,000
Enrollment: 1,872 | Coed
Affiliation or Control: United Methodist | IRS Status: 501(c)3
Highest Offering: Baccalaureate
Program: Liberal Arts And General; Teacher Preparatory
Accreditation: SC, TED

01 President Dr. Dewey CLARK
05 Provost/Sr VP Academic Affairs Dr. Michael B. BROWN
10 Vice President of Finance Mr. Jason EDWARDS
30 Vice President of Development Mr. Michael PRATT
84 Vice President of Enrollment Mrs. Judy ROLLINS
32 VP Student Affairs/Dean of Students Mr. Edward NAYLOR
09 Chief Planning & Research Officer Dr. Larry H. KELLEY
06 Registrar Mrs. Candace CASHWELL
08 Director of Library Mrs. Kathy WINSLOW
26 Director of Communications Mrs. Susan BEST
23 Director Health Services Ms. Jessica BRYS-WILSON
36 Director Internship & Career Center Ms. Tiffany ALEXANDER
19 Director of Campus Security Vacant
41 Director of Athletics Mr. John THOMPSON
29 Director Alumni Rels/Annual Fund Vacant
21 Controller Vacant
37 Director of Financial Aid Ms. Leah HILL
15 Director of Human Resources Mr. Darrell S. WHITLEY
18 Director of Facilities Mr. Raymond THOMPSON
07 Assistant Director of Admissions Mr. Ben LILLEY
38 Director Student Counseling Vacant
40 Manager College Store Ms. Rachel T. DIX
20 Associate Academic Officer Dr. Molly WYATT
108 Director Institutional Assessment Dr. Larry H. KELLEY
13 Chief Info Technology Officer (CIO) Mr. Nhan NGUYEN
39 Director Student Housing Ms. Jesse LANGLEY
50 Chair Business Dr. Jackie LEWIS

Pfeiffer University (F)

48380 US Highway 52 N / PO Box 960,
Misenheimer NC 28109-0960

County: Stanly | FICE Identification: 002955
Unit ID: 199306
Telephone: (704) 463-1360 | Carnegie Class: Master's L
FAX Number: (704) 463-1363 | Calendar System: Semester
URL: www.pfeiffer.edu
Established: 1885 | Annual Undergrad Tuition & Fees: $26,292
Enrollment: 1,784 | Coed
Affiliation or Control: United Methodist | IRS Status: 501(c)3
Highest Offering: Master's
Program: Liberal Arts And General; Teacher Preparatory; Professional
Accreditation: SC, MFCD, MUS, NURSE, TED

01 President Dr. Colleen PERRY KEITH
04 Executive Assistant to President Ms. Teena P. MAULDIN
11 Chief Operations Officer Vacant
10 Vice President for Finance/CFO Mr. Jeffrey B. PLYLER
05 Provost/VP Academic Affairs Dr. Tracy Y. ESPY
32 VP for Student Devel/Dn of Students Dr. Russell SHARPLES
30 Vice Pres for Advancement Mr. John LELFER
84 Vice Pres for Enrollment Mr. David BOISVERT
41 Vice Pres Athletics Mr. Bob REASSO
06 Registrar Ms. Lourdes SILVA
84 Director of Enrollment Operations Mr. Michael UTSMAN
15 Director of Human Resources Ms. Kathy ODELL
09 Exec Director IR/Plng & Research Ms. Mary Ellen GOLDSTEIN
26 Director Inst Communications Ms. Susan G. MESSINA
38 Int Director Counseling Mr. Tony OETTINGER
08 Director of the Library Ms. Lara LITTLE
37 Director of Financial Aid Ms. Amy BROWN
13 Director Information Technology Mr. William SEWARD, II
07 Director of Undergrad Admissions Ms. Emily CARELLA
20 Dir of Academic Support Services Dr. Jim E. GULLEDGE
19 Dir of Campus Safety & Security Mr. Erik MCGINNIS
23 Director of Health Services Vacant
18 Director of Facilities Ms. Sharon K. BARD
42 Minister to the University Rev. Dana MCKIM
36 Director of Career Development Mr. Jay LAURENS
39 Dir of Residence Life Ms. Regina SIMMONS
58 Director of MCE Program Rev. Kathleen KILBOURNE
31 Director of Community Relations Ms. Carol MAY
29 Director of Alumni Affairs Ms. Amy BUNTING
12 Director of Triangle Campus Vacant
39 Asst Director of Residence Life Mr. Jill ROGERS
40 Bookstore Manager Ms. Dechelle ELLIS
104 Coord of Intl Studies/Study Abroad Ms. Rebecca HRACZO

50	Int Dean Division of Business	Dr. Dawn LUCAS
53	Dean Division of Education	Dr. Dawn LUCAS
79	Dean Division of Humanities	Dr. David HECKEL
49	Dean Division of Liberal Arts	Dr. Marilyn SUTTON-HAYWOOD
83	Dean Div of Social & Behav Sciences	Dr. Donald POE, JR.
51	Dean of Cont Ed & Adult Prof Stds	Dr. Paulita BROOKER
76	Dean Div of Applied Health Science	Ms. Vernease MILLER

Piedmont International University (A)

420 S Broad Street, Winston-Salem NC 27101-5197
County: Forsyth FICE Identification: 002956
Unit ID: 199315
Telephone: (336) 725-8344 Carnegie Class: Spec/Faith
FAX Number: (336) 725-5522 Calendar System: Semester
URL: www.piedmontu.edu
Established: 1945 Annual Undergrad Tuition & Fees: $9,580
Enrollment: 388 Coed
Affiliation or Control: Independent Non-Profit IRS Status: 501(c)3
Highest Offering: Doctorate
Program: 2-Year Principally Bachelor's Creditable; Liberal Arts And General; Teacher Preparatory; Professional; Religious Emphasis
Accreditation: TRACS

00	Chancellor	Dr. Howard L. WILBURN
01	President	Dr. Charles W. PETITT
05	Provost	Dr. Beth D. ASHBURN
11	Vice President of Operations	Mr. Chris RONK
30	Vice Pres of Advancement	Dr. Barkev TRACHIAN
06	Registrar	Mr. Jeremy PATTISALL
08	Librarian	Dr. Catherine CHATMON
32	Director of Student Services	Mr. Paul SMELTZER
34	Dean of Women	Mrs. Rebecca BOTTOMS
42	Director of Church Relations	Mr. Tony WILSON

Queens University of Charlotte (B)

1900 Selwyn Avenue, Charlotte NC 28274-0001
County: Mecklenburg FICE Identification: 002957
Unit ID: 199412
Telephone: (704) 337-2200 Carnegie Class: Master's M
FAX Number: (704) 337-2517 Calendar System: Semester
URL: www.queens.edu
Established: 1857 Annual Undergrad Tuition & Fees: $31,360
Enrollment: 2,248 Coed
Affiliation or Control: Presbyterian Church (U.S.A.) IRS Status: 501(c)3
Highest Offering: Master's
Program: Liberal Arts And General; Teacher Preparatory; Professional
Accreditation: SC, ADNUR, BUS, MUS, NURSE, TED

01	President	Dr. Pamela L. DAVIES
05	VP Academic Affairs & Provost	Dr. Lynn MORTON
30	VP University Advancement	Mr. James BULLOCK
84	VP Enrollment Management	Dr. Brian RALPH
26	VP Marketing & Community Relations	Mrs. Rebecca ANDERSON
45	VP Campus Planning and Services	Mr. Bill NICHOLS
10	CFO & VP for Administration	Mr. Matthew PACKEY
49	Dean Col Arts & Sci & Cato Sch Educ	Dr. Alexa ROYDEN
50	Dean of McColl School of Business	Dr. Richard MATHIEU
60	Dean Knight School of Communication	Dr. Eric FREEDMAN
76	Dean Blair College of Health	Dr. Tama MORRIS
20	Assoc Provost/Dean Univ Programs	Dr. Sarah FATHERLY
06	Registrar	Ms. Linda FLEISCHMAN
15	Director of Human Resources	Ms. Teri ORSINI, SPHR

Reformed Theological Seminary (C)

2101 Carmel Road, Charlotte NC 28226-6399
Telephone: (704) 366-5066 Identification: 666785
Accreditation: &SC, THEOL

† Regional accreditation is carried under the parent institution in Jackson, MS.

St. Andrews University (D)

1700 Dogwood Mile, Laurinburg NC 28352-5598
Telephone: (910) 277-5000 FICE Identification: 002967
Accreditation: &SC

† Regional accreditation is carried under the parent institution, Webber International University, Babson Park, FL.

Saint Augustine's University (E)

1315 Oakwood Avenue, Raleigh NC 27610-2298
County: Wake FICE Identification: 002968
Unit ID: 199582
Telephone: (919) 516-4000 Carnegie Class: Bac/Diverse
FAX Number: (919) 828-0817 Calendar System: Semester
URL: www.st-aug.edu
Established: 1867 Annual Undergrad Tuition & Fees: $17,890
Enrollment: 1,016 Coed
Affiliation or Control: Protestant Episcopal IRS Status: 501(c)3
Highest Offering: Baccalaureate
Program: Liberal Arts And General; Teacher Preparatory
Accreditation: SC

01	President	Dr. Everett B. WARD
04	Exec Assistant to the President	Mrs. Gloria T. ROWLAND
11	VP for Inst Adv & Chief Oper Ofcr	Dr. Steven E. HAIRSTON
05	Provost and VP of Academic Affairs	Dr. Yvonne COSTON
10	VP for Business & Finance	Ms. Angela N. HAYNES
32	VP Enrollment Mgmt & Student Svcs	Dr. Ronald H. BROWN
26	VP Marketing & Communications Ofcr	Mrs. Shelley M. WILLINGHAM-HINTON
09	Assoc Provost/Inst Eff & Planning	Dr. Orlando E. HANKINS
21	Asst VP/Comptroller	Ms. Pamela E. TWITTY
20	Associate Provost	Dr. Linda H. CURTIS
15	Acting Director Human Resources	Ms. Lottie FERRELL
89	Dean of First Year Experience	Mr. Paul A. NORMAN
34	Dean of Women/Director Student Act	Ms. Ann BROWN
42	Chaplain	Rev. Nita BYRD
13	Chief Information Officer	Mr. Harod C. DEMBY
41	Director Athletics	Mr. George D. WILLIAMS
06	Registrar	Ms. Carla WASHINGTON
50	Dean Business/Mgmt & Technology	Vacant
83	Dean Social and Behavioral Sciences	Dr. Zaphon WILSON
81	Dean Sciences/Math/Public Health	Dr. Mark A. MELTON
49	Dean Liberal Arts & Educ	Dr. Lynne T. JEFFERSON
97	Executive Director General College	Dr. Sevealyn V. SMITH
07	Dean of Enrollment	Mr. Jorge E. SOUSA
37	Director Financial Aid/Scholarships	Ms. Nadine Y. FORD
08	Director of Library Service	Ms. Tiawanna S. NEVELS
36	Interim Director Career Services	Ms. Tasha A. ANDREWS
19	Chief of Police	Mr. George H. BOYKIN, III
18	Director Physical Plant	Mr. Hector F. GALLEGO
29	Director Alumni Affairs	Ms. Sheryl H. XIMINES
24	Executive Director of Facilities	Mr. Brian R. FLOYD

Salem College (F)

601 South Church Street, Winston-Salem NC 27101
County: Forsyth FICE Identification: 002960
Unit ID: 199607
Telephone: (336) 721-2600 Carnegie Class: Bac/A&S
FAX Number: (336) 917-5339 Calendar System: 4/1/4
URL: www.salem.edu
Established: 1772 Annual Undergrad Tuition & Fees: $25,870
Enrollment: 1,118 Female
Affiliation or Control: Moravian Church IRS Status: 501(c)3
Highest Offering: Master's
Program: Liberal Arts And General; Teacher Preparatory; Professional
Accreditation: SC, MUS, TED

01	President	Dr. D. E. Lorraine STERRITT
05	VP Acad & Stdnt Affs/Dn of College	Dr. Susan CALOVINI
30	VP for Institutional Advancement	Vacant
07	Dean Admissions & Financial Aid	Ms. Katherine K. WATTS
32	Dean of Students	Ms. Krispin W. BARR
58	Dean of Graduate Studies	Dr. Sheryl LONG
51	Dean of Continuing Studies	Dr. Sydney RICHARDSON
20	Dean Undergraduate Studies	Dr. Richard VINSON
11	Director of Administration	Ms. Anna GALLIMORE
08	Librarian	Ms. Elizabeth NOVICKI
44	Director Annual Giving	Vacant
13	Director Information Technology	Mr. Paul BENNINGER
15	Director of Payroll & Benefits	Ms. Cheryl HAMILTON
10	Chief Financial Officer	Mr. Derek BRYAN
38	Director Counseling Services	Mr. Jack LOCICERO
37	Director Student Financial Aid	Mr. Paul COSCIA
27	Director of Communications	Vacant
26	Assistant Director Public Relations	Ms. Hannah CALLAWAY
36	Director Career Devel/Internships	Ms. Monica BOYD
06	Registrar/Dir Inst Research	Ms. Jeannette RORK
18	Chief Facilities/Physical Plant	Mr. George MORALES
29	Director Alumnae Relations	Ms. Jenny STOKES
21	Accounts Receivable Manager	Ms. Nikki BROCK
21	Accounts Payable Manager	Ms. Judy SIGMON
19	Coordinator Institutional Services	Mr. Tommy WILLIAMSON

Shaw University (G)

118 E South Street, Raleigh NC 27601
County: Wake FICE Identification: 002962
Unit ID: 199643
Telephone: (919) 546-8300 Carnegie Class: Bac/Diverse
FAX Number: (919) 546-8301 Calendar System: Semester
URL: www.shawu.edu
Established: 1865 Annual Undergrad Tuition & Fees: $16,480
Enrollment: 1,802 Coed
Affiliation or Control: Baptist IRS Status: 501(c)3
Highest Offering: Master's
Program: Liberal Arts And General
Accreditation: SC, #CAATE, KIN, SW, TED, THEOL

01	President	Dr. Tashni-Ann DUBROY
05	Vice Pres for Academic Affairs	Dr. Patrena BENTON
10	Int Vice Pres for Finance & Admin	Dr. Ronald DOWDY
30	Vice Pres Institutional Advancement	Ms. Clarenda STANLEY-ANDERSON
32	Vice Pres for Student Affairs	Dr. Stanley ELLIOTT
84	Chief Enrollment Management Officer	Mr. Anthony BROOKS
20	Assoc VP for Academic Affairs	Dr. Renata DUSENBURY
21	Assoc VP for Finance & Admin	Ms. Gwen WEBB
35	Assoc VP for Student Affairs	Dr. Keith POWELL
25	Spec Asst/Dir of Special Programs	Ms. Paula 'Tendai' JOHNSON
88	Project Asst Process Optimization	Ms. Melissa ADRANGNA
49	Dean Col of Arts and Sciences	Dr. Paulette DILLARD
58	Int Dean Col of Grad/Prof Studies	Dr. James MCCALLUM
73	Int Dean Shaw Univ Divinity School	Dr. David FORBES
15	Director of Human Resources	Ms. Diane CRAWFORD
84	Director or Financial Aid	Ms. Rochelle KING
07	Director of Admissions/Recruitment	Ms. Stacey SOWELL
06	Registrar	Ms. Jody HAMILTON-DAVIS
26	Dir of Public Relations & Marketing	Ms. Odessa HINES
08	Director of Library Services	Ms. Carolyn PETERSON
45	Dir of Stratetic Planning/Inst Res	Dr. Cecil MCMANUS
41	Director of Athletics	Dr. Alfonza CARTER
38	Director of Counseling Center	Ms. Jerelene CARVER
88	Director of Judicial Affairs	Ms. Agnes BAXTER
36	Dir Experential Lrng/Career Devel	Ms. Nikesha ROLLACK
50	Chair Dept Business/Public Admin	Dr. Mma KALU
53	Chair Dept Education	Dr. Paula MOTEN-TOLSON
81	Chair Dept Natural Science/Math	Dr. Doreen CUNNINGHAM
76	Chair Dept Allied Health	Dr. James MCCALLUM
79	Chair Dept Humanities	Dr. Desire' BALOUBI
60	Chair Dept Mass Comm	Dr. Cassandra MITCHELL
57	Chair Dept Visual/Performing Arts	Mr. George HATCHER
83	Int Chair Dept Social Sciences	Dr. Beau NILES
77	Int Chair Dept Computer Info Sci	Dr. Lloyd WILLIAMS
88	Chair Dept Religion/Philosophy	Dr. James KIRKLEY
70	Int Chair Dept Social Work	Dr. Manina MCNEILL
19	Chief of Campus Police & Security	Mr. Wayne JOINER
18	Facility Manager	Mr. Cleon PIERCE

Shepherds Theological Seminary (H)

6051 Tryon Road, Cary NC 27518-9316
County: Wake FICE Identification: 041730
Unit ID: 461485
Telephone: (919) 573-5350 Carnegie Class: Not Classified
FAX Number: (919) 573-1438 Calendar System: Semester
URL: www.shepherds.edu
Established: 2003 Annual Graduate Tuition & Fees: $6,620
Enrollment: 79 Coed
Affiliation or Control: Independent Non-Profit IRS Status: 501(c)3
Highest Offering: Master's; No Undergraduates
Program: Professional; Religious Emphasis
Accreditation: @THEOL, TRACS

01	President	Dr. Stephen DAVEY
05	Provost/Dean	Dr. Larry PETTEGREW
20	Vice President of Academic Affairs	Mr. Edward HERRELKO
30	Vice President of Advancement	Dr. Alan POTTER
10	Chief Financial Officer	Mr. Ewart HODGINS
07	Director of Recruitment	Dr. Douglas BOOKMAN
18	Chief Facilities/Physical Plant	Dr. Samuel WINCHESTER
06	Registrar/Financial Aid Officer	Mrs. Lucy BURGGRAFF

South College-Asheville (I)

140 Sweeten Creek Road, Asheville NC 28803
County: Buncombe FICE Identification: 010264
Unit ID: 198242
Telephone: (828) 398-2500 Carnegie Class: Assoc/PrivFP4
FAX Number: (828) 277-6151 Calendar System: Quarter
URL: www.southcollegenc.edu
Established: 1905 Annual Undergrad Tuition & Fees: $19,000
Enrollment: 283 Coed
Affiliation or Control: Proprietary IRS Status: Proprietary
Highest Offering: Baccalaureate
Program: Occupational; 2-Year Principally Bachelor's Creditable; Nursing Emphasis
Accreditation: ACICS, MAC, OTA, PTAA, RAD, SURGT

00	President/Owner	Mr. Stephen A. SOUTH
01	Executive Director	Mr. Nick G. SOUTH
05	Dean Academic Affairs	Dr. Vickie SAMUELS
32	Director of Student Services	Mr. Charlie MILLING
10	Business Manager	Ms. Christine CHANCEY
07	Admissions Director	Ms. Wendy REWERTS
37	Financial Aid Officer	Ms. Ronda BLACKMAN
08	Head Info Resorces Specialist	Ms. Marissa DEZIEL
06	Registrar	Ms. Anne MOSS

South University (J)

3975 Premier Drive, High Point NC 27265
Telephone: (336) 812-7200 Identification: 770915
Accreditation: &SC, ACBSP, NURSE, @PTAA

† Branch campus of South University, Savannah, GA.

Southeastern Baptist Theological Seminary (K)

Box 1889, Wake Forest NC 27588-1889
County: Wake FICE Identification: 002963
Unit ID: 199759
Telephone: (919) 761-2100 Carnegie Class: Not Classified
FAX Number: N/A Calendar System: Semester
URL: www.sebts.edu
Established: 1950 Annual Undergrad Tuition & Fees: $8,124
Enrollment: 2,645 Coed
Affiliation or Control: Southern Baptist IRS Status: 501(c)3
Highest Offering: Doctorate
Program: 2-Year Principally Bachelor's Creditable; Liberal Arts And General; Professional; Religious Emphasis
Accreditation: SC, THEOL

01	President	Dr. Daniel L. AKIN
05	Provost/Dean of Faculty	Dr. Bruce R. ASHFORD
10	Executive VP for Operations	Mr. Ryan HUTCHINSON

06 Registrar ..... Mr. Cody OLDARCE
07 Director of Admissions ..... Mr. Larry LYON
09 Asst VP Institutional Effectiveness ..... Dr. Keith WHITFIELD
29 Director of Alumni Development ..... Mr. Jonathan SIX
30 Vice Pres Institutional Advancement ..... Mr. Art RAINER
37 Director of Financial Aid ..... Dr. Don ALLARD
04 Administrative Asst to President ..... Mrs. Kim HUMPHREY
08 Head Librarian ..... Mr. Jason FOWLER
106 Dir Online Education ..... Mr. Jerry LASSETTER
108 Coord Institutional Research ..... Mr. Andrew J. SPENCER
13 Director of Information Technology ..... Mr. Wayne JENKS
15 Director Human Resources ..... Mrs. Dawn SATTERWHITE
28 Spec Asst Pres for Diversity ..... Mr. Walter STRICKLAND
39 Director Student Housing ..... Mr. Doug NALLEY
43 General Counsel ..... Mr. George HARVEY
44 Director of Financial Development ..... Mr. Daniel PALMER

Southern Evangelical Seminary (A)

3000 Tilley Morris Road, Matthews NC 28105-8635
County: Union FICE Identification: 036115
Unit ID: 438522
Telephone: (704) 847-5600 Carnegie Class: Not Classified
FAX Number: (704) 845-1747 Calendar System: Semester
URL: www.ses.edu
Established: 1992 Annual Undergrad Tuition & Fees: $6,058
Enrollment: 230 Coed
Affiliation or Control: Independent Non-Profit IRS Status: 501(c)3
Highest Offering: Doctorate
Program: Professional; Religious Emphasis
Accreditation: TRACS

01 President & COO ..... Dr. Richard D. LAND
05 Academic Dean ..... Dr. J. Thomas RIDGES
07 Director of Admissions ..... Ms. Dianna NEWMAN
10 Business Manager ..... Mr. Christian DRAKE
08 Librarian ..... Mr. Ronald I. JORDAHL
06 Registrar ..... Dr. Douglas E. POTTER
32 Director Student Services ..... Mrs. Jill JOYNER
13 Dir of Information Technology ..... Mr. Timothy BURKETT
26 Dir Communications/Special Events ..... Mr. Eric T. GUSTAFSON
04 Executive Asst to President ..... Mrs. Christina S. WOODSIDE
33 Dean of Men ..... Dr. Brian HUFFLING
88 Director Missions ..... Mr. Adam TUCKER
106 Dir Online Education/E-learning ..... Mr. Jeff LENHART
30 Dir of Institutional Advancement ..... Mr. Robert ANDREWS
12 Director of Bible College ..... Dr. Floyd ELMORE

University of Mount Olive (B)

634 Henderson Street, Mount Olive NC 28365-1263
County: Wayne FICE Identification: 002949
Unit ID: 199069
Telephone: (919) 658-2502 Carnegie Class: Bac/Diverse
FAX Number: (919) 658-7180 Calendar System: Semester
URL: www.umo.edu
Established: 1951 Annual Undergrad Tuition & Fees: $18,400
Enrollment: 3,456 Coed
Affiliation or Control: Original Free Will Baptist Church IRS Status: 501(c)3
Highest Offering: Master's
Program: Liberal Arts And General
Accreditation: SC, ACBSP, NURSE

01 President ..... Dr. Philip P. KERSTETTER
03 Executive Vice President ..... Dr. Carol G. CARRERE
05 VP for Academic Affairs ..... Dr. Kenneth D. HINES
10 VP for Finance & Administration ..... Mr. John KUNST
84 VP for Enrollment ..... Dr. Barbara R. KORNEGAY
32 VP for Student Affairs ..... Mr. Dan SULLIVAN
30 VP for Institutional Advancement ..... Dr. James WILLIAMS
20 AVP Acad Affairs/Dean Grad Studies ..... Dr. David DOMMER
49 Dean School of Arts and Sciences ..... Dr. Burt LEWIS
50 Dean Tillman School of Business ..... Dr. Bankole OLATOSI
56 Dean of Extended Education ..... Ms. Lisa M. NUESELL
88 Dean of the Chapel ..... Dr. John BLACKWELL
08 Director of Library Services ..... Ms. Pamela R. WOOD
12 Director of UMO New Bern ..... Mr. Luis MIRANDA
12 Director of UMO Jacksonville ..... Mr. Oscar RODRIGUEZ
12 Director of UMO Goldsboro ..... Mr. John KLEMMER
12 Director of UMO Evening College ..... Dr. John P. RUTTER
12 Director of UMO Wilmington ..... Dr. Marna R. MCMURRY
12 Director UMO Research Triangle Park ..... Dr. Nicole CHILDS
09 Director Inst Research & Planning ..... Dr. Juliane SANTIAGO
108 Director of Assessment ..... Vacant
07 Director of Admissions ..... Mr. Timothy E. WOODARD
06 Registrar ..... Mr. David L. BOURGEOIS
35 Director of Campus Life ..... Ms. Nicole L. GARRETT
36 Director of Career Center ..... Vacant
39 Director of Housing/Resident Life ..... Vacant
19 Director Security/Safety ..... Capt. William JOHNSON
26 Director of Public Relations ..... Ms. Rhonda E. JESSUP
102 Dir Foundations & Sponsored Program ..... Ms. Kari SANDER
29 Director of Alumni Relations ..... Ms. Tiffany S. MCPHERSON FIELDS
44 Director of Annual Fund ..... Ms. Melinda HOLLAND
37 Director of Financial Aid ..... Ms. Katrina K. LEE
15 Director of Human Resources ..... Ms. Cordelia A. WILCOX
23 Student Health Services ..... Ms. Joanne L. MORGAN
42 Campus Chaplain ..... Ms. Carla WILLIAMSON
04 Assistant to the President ..... Ms. Katherine B. GARDNER
18 Superintendent Building & Grounds ..... Mr. Jeff D. BROGDEN
41 Athletics Director ..... Mr. Jeffrey M. EISEN

13 Director Technology Support ..... Mr. Robert R. PRUETT
88 Director Technology Services ..... Mr. Kenneth M. DAVIS, JR.
92 Director Honors Program ..... Dr. Norman CRUMPACKER
40 Bookstore Manager ..... Ms. Mee So YIM

*University of North Carolina General Administration (C)

Box 2688, 910 Raleigh Road, Chapel Hill NC 27515-2688
County: Orange FICE Identification: 002971
Unit ID: 199175
Telephone: (919) 962-1000 Carnegie Class: N/A
FAX Number: (919) 962-2751
URL: www.northcarolina.edu

01 President ..... Mr. Thomas W. ROSS
100 Chief of Staff ..... Mr. Kevin FITZGERALD
05 Sr Vice Pres Academic Affairs ..... Dr. Junius GONZALES
10 Vice President for Finance ..... Mr. Charles E. PERUSSE
88 VP Academic & University Programs ..... Dr. Alisa CHAPMAN
13 Vice Pres Information Resources/CIO ..... Mr. John LEYDON
43 VP Legal Affs/General Counsel ..... Mr. Thomas SHANAHAN
46 VP Research/Graduate Education ..... Dr. Christopher BROWN
101 Secretary of the University ..... Ms. Ann LEMMON
86 Vice President for Govt Relations ..... Mr. Drew MORETZ
86 Vice President for Federal Rels ..... Ms. Kimrey RHINEHARDT
26 Vice President for Communications ..... Ms. Joni WORTHINGTON
15 Vice Pres for Human Resources ..... Mr. William FLEMING
88 VP for Intl/Community/Econ Engagmnt ..... Mr. Leslie BONEY

*Appalachian State University (D)

287 Rivers Street, Boone NC 28608-0001
County: Watauga FICE Identification: 002906
Unit ID: 197869
Telephone: (828) 262-2000 Carnegie Class: Master's L
FAX Number: (828) 262-2347 Calendar System: Semester
URL: www.appstate.edu
Established: 1899 Annual Undergrad Tuition & Fees (In-State): $7,117
Enrollment: 18,026 Coed
Affiliation or Control: State IRS Status: 501(c)3
Highest Offering: Doctorate
Program: Liberal Arts And General; Teacher Preparatory; Professional
Accreditation: SC, AAFCS, ART, BUS, CAATE, CACREP, CIDA, CS, DANCE, DIETD, DIETI, IPSY, MFCD, MUS, NRPA, NURSE, SP, SPAA, SW, TED, THEA

02 Chancellor ..... Dr. Sheri N. EVERTS
100 Vice Chanc/Int Chief of Staff ..... Dr. Randy EDWARDS
05 Provost/Exec Vice Chancellor ..... Dr. Darrell P. KRUGER
10 Vice Chanc Business Affairs ..... Mr. Greg M. LOVINS
32 Vice Chanc Student Development ..... Ms. Cindy A. WALLACE
30 Vice Chanc Univ Advancement ..... Mrs. Susan H. PETTYJOHN
20 Vice Provost for Undergrad Educ ..... Dr. Mike W. MAYFIELD
46 Vice Provost for Research ..... Dr. Alan UTTER
26 Sr Assc VC Advance/Chief Comm Ofcr ..... Mr. Hank T. FOREMAN
84 Assoc VC for Enrollment Services ..... Mrs. Susan DAVIES
22 AVC Equity/Diversity/Compliance ..... Ms. Bindu K. JAYNE
29 Exec Director of Alumni Affairs ..... Mr. Patrick K. SETZER
43 General Counsel ..... Mr. Dayton T. COLE
13 Chief Information Officer ..... Mrs. Cathy J. BATES
06 University Registrar ..... Ms. Debbie RACE
38 Dir Counseling/Psychological Svcs ..... Dr. Dan L. JONES
37 Director of Financial Aid ..... Ms. Lori A. TOWNSEND
15 Director of Human Resources ..... Mr. Mark BACHMEIER
09 Int Director Inst Research/Planning ..... Mrs. Heather H. LANGDON
51 Exec Director of Distance Education ..... Dr. Terry RAWLS
41 Director of Athletics ..... Mr. Douglas P. GILLIN
49 Dean for College of Arts & Sciences ..... Dr. Anthony G. CALAMAI
50 Dean for College of Business ..... Dr. Heather NORRIS
53 Int Dean for College of Education ..... Dr. Robin GROCE
57 Dean for College Fine/Applied Arts ..... Dr. Glenda J. TREADAWAY
64 Dean for the School of Music ..... Dr. William L. PELTO
58 Dean of Research/Graduate Studies ..... Dr. Max C. POOLE
08 Dean of Libraries ..... Ms. Joyce L. OGBURN
18 Director of the Physical Plant ..... Mr. Mike J. O'CONNOR
21 Budget Director ..... Mr. Ken W. SMITH
35 Dean of Students/Assoc VC Stdnt Dev ..... Mr. J.J BROWN
96 Director of Materials Management ..... Mr. Dwayne E. ODVODY
28 Dir Multicultural Student Devel ..... Ms. Traci D. ROYSTER

*East Carolina University (E)

1000 East Fifth Street, Greenville NC 27858-4353
County: Pitt FICE Identification: 002923
Unit ID: 198464
Telephone: (252) 328-6212 Carnegie Class: DRU
FAX Number: (252) 328-4155 Calendar System: Semester
URL: www.ecu.edu
Established: 1907 Annual Undergrad Tuition & Fees (In-State): $6,407
Enrollment: 27,511 Coed
Affiliation or Control: State IRS Status: 501(c)3
Highest Offering: Doctorate
Program: Liberal Arts And General; Teacher Preparatory; Professional
Accreditation: SC, AAFCS, ANEST, ARCPA, ART, AUD, BUS, CAATE, CACREP, CAHIIM, CARTE, CEA, CIDA, CLPSY, CONST, CORE, DENT, DIETD, DIETI, ENG, LIB, MED, MFCD, MIDWF, MT, MUS, NAIT, NRPA, NURSE, OT, PH, PLNG, PTA, SCPSY, SP, SPAA, SW, TED, THEA

02 Chancellor ..... Dr. Steve BALLARD
100 Chief of Staff ..... Mr. Chris LOCKLEAR
05 Provost & Sr VC Academic Affairs ..... Dr. Ron MITCHELSON
32 Vice Chancellor for Student Affairs ..... Dr. Virginia HARDY
17 Vice Chanc Health Sciences ..... Dr. Phyllis N. HORNS
10 Vice Chanc Administration & Finance ..... Dr. Frederick NISWANDER
30 Int Vice Chanc Univ Advancement ..... Mr. Christopher DYBA
46 Int VC Research/Graduate Studies ..... Dr. Michael VAN SCOTT
29 Assoc VC for Alumni Relations ..... Mrs. Marcy ROMARY
39 Assoc VC Camp Liv/Dining ..... Mr. William L. MCCARTNEY, JR.
38 Assoc Vice Chanc & Dean of Stdnts ..... Dr. Lynn M. ROEDER
35 Assoc Dean of Students ..... Dr. Lathan E. TURNER
22 Assoc Provost Equity/Diversity ..... Ms. Lakesha ALSTON FORBES
43 Vice Chancellor for Legal Affairs ..... Ms. Donna G. PAYNE
09 Associate Provost IPAR ..... Dr. Ying ZHOU
41 Athletic Director ..... Mr. Jeff COMPHER
13 CIO and Assoc Vice Chanc ITCS ..... Mr. Don SWEET
15 Assoc Vice Chanc Human Resources ..... Ms. Melissa BARD
18 Assoc VC for Campus Opers ..... Mr. William BAGNELL
21 Assoc VC for Business Services ..... Mr. A. Scott BUCK
88 Assoc VC Environ Health & Safety ..... Mr. Bill KOCH
82 Assoc VC of International Affairs ..... Dr. Jim GEHLHAR
88 Assoc VC for Emerging Acad Init ..... Dr. Elmer POE
20 Int Dir Acad Pgm Planning & Develop ..... Ms. Rita REAVES
88 Asst VC Recreational/Wellness Svcs ..... Ms. Nancy MIZE
84 Assoc Provost for Enrollment Svcs ..... Dr. John FLETCHER
26 Ex Dir Communication/Pub Affs/Mktg ..... Ms. Mary C. SHULKEN
07 Director of Admissions ..... Dr. Dave MEREDITH
06 Registrar ..... Ms. Angela R. ANDERSON
08 Director JY Joyner Library ..... Ms. Jan LEWIS
88 Int Dir Health Sciences Library ..... Dr. Gregory L. HASSLER
101 Asst Secretary to Board of Trustees ..... Dr. Steve DUNCAN
37 Director of Financial Aid ..... Ms. Julie POORMAN
19 Director/Chief of Police ..... Mr. Gerald LEWIS
51 Director of Continuing Studies ..... Dr. F. Clayton SESSOMS
27 Director of University Marketing ..... Mr. Clint BAILEY
27 Director of Publications ..... Mr. Jimmy ROSTAR
88 Director of Military Programs ..... Dr. Steve DUNCAN
96 Director of Purchasing ..... Mr. Kevin CARRAWAY
36 Director Career Center ..... Ms. Karen S. THOMPSON
88 Director of Internal Audit ..... Ms. Stacie TRONTO
21 Associate VC for Financial Services ..... Ms. Anne JENKINS
49 Dean College of Arts & Sciences ..... Dr. William DOWNS
76 Dean Sch Allied Health Sciences ..... Dr. Stephen W. THOMAS
68 Dean Col Health/Human Performance ..... Dr. Glen G. GILBERT
59 Dean College of Human Ecology ..... Dr. Judy SIGUAW
66 Dean College of Nursing ..... Dr. Sylvia BROWN
50 Dean College of Business ..... Dr. Stanley G. EAKINS
57 Dean Col Fine Arts/Comm ..... Dr. Christopher BUDDO
53 Dean College of Education ..... Dr. Linda PATRIARCA
72 Dean Col of Engineering and Tech ..... Dr. David WHITE
58 Dean Graduate School ..... Dr. Paul GEMPERLINE
92 Dean Honors College ..... Dr. Marianna WALKER
63 Dean Brody School of Medicine ..... Dr. Paul R G. CUNNINGHAM
52 Dean School of Dental Medicine ..... Dr. Gregory CHADWICK
04 Assistant to Chancellor ..... Ms. Christy DANIELS
25 Dir of Grants and Contracts ..... Ms. Kathleen HALL
86 Director of Strategic Initiatives ..... Ms. Michelle BROOKS
102 President/CEO ECU Foundation ..... Mr. Bill CLARK
54 Chairperson Engineering ..... Dr. Hayden GRIFFIN

*Elizabeth City State University (F)

1704 Weeksville Road, Elizabeth City NC 27909-7806
County: Pasquotank FICE Identification: 002926
Unit ID: 198507
Telephone: (252) 335-3400 Carnegie Class: Bac/Diverse
FAX Number: (252) 335-3731 Calendar System: Semester
URL: www.ecsu.edu
Established: 1891 Annual Undergrad Tuition & Fees (In-State): $6,822
Enrollment: 1,867 Coed
Affiliation or Control: State IRS Status: 501(c)3
Highest Offering: Master's
Program: Liberal Arts And General; Teacher Preparatory; Fine Arts Emphasis
Accreditation: SC, BUS, MUS, NAIT, SW, TED

02 Chancellor ..... Dr. Stacey F. JONES
05 VC Academic Affairs ..... Dr. Vann NEWKIRK
20 Interim Assoc VC Academic Affairs ..... Dr. Harry BASS
10 Interim VC for Bus & Fin/Dir Budget ..... Mr. Joshua LASSITER
30 Interim VC for Institutional Advanc ..... Ms. Ralisha MERCER
43 General Counsel ..... Mr. Alyn GOODSON
32 Interim VC for Student Affairs ..... Mrs. Deborah G. BRANCH
13 Chief Information Officer ..... Mr. Suresh MARUGAN
15 Director Human Resources ..... Mr. Rafeal BONES
41 Athletic Director ..... Mr. Derrick JOHNSON
84 Asst VC Enrollment Mgmt ..... Mr. Andre FARLEY
09 Int Dir Institutional Effectiveness ..... Mr. Brian JORDAN
06 Interim Registrar ..... Ms. Althea L. RIDDICK
35 Asst VC/Dean of Students ..... Mr. Kelvin BROWN
08 Director of Library Services ..... Dr. Juanita MIDGETTE
07 Director of Admissions ..... Vacant
38 Dir Counsel/Test Student Affairs ..... Ms. Felicia BROWN
36 Director of Career Services ..... Ms. Makitta WHITEHURST-MCLEAN
37 Director Student Financial Aid ..... Ms. Jill GABLE
29 Director of Alumni Relations ..... Ms. Barbara B. SUTTON
18 Director of Facilities/Planning ..... Mr. Charles HALL
26 Director Univ Relation/Marketing ..... Dr. Linita SHANNON
87 Director of Summer School ..... Mr. Derrick WILKINS
92 Director of Honors Program ..... Dr. Kenneth JONES
96 Director of Purchasing ..... Ms. Rachel HAINES
58 Director of Graduate Education ..... Dr. Harry BASS
04 Administrative Asst to President ..... Ms. Lucretia BANKS
101 Secretary of the Institution/Board ..... Ms. Gwendolyn SANDERS

104 Director Study Abroad ... Dr. Glen BOWMAN
105 Director Web Services ... Ms. Dana COBB
106 Dir Online Education/E-learning ... Dr. Kim STEVENSON
100 Chief of Staff ... Ms. Theresa TIBBS
19 Director Security/Safety ... Mr. John MANLEY
39 Interim Director Student Housing ... Ms. Sabrina WILLIAMS
86 Director Government Relations ... Mrs. Kathryn UNDERWOOD

*Fayetteville State University (A)

1200 Murchison Road, Fayetteville NC 28301-4298
County: Cumberland FICE Identification: 002928
Unit ID: 198543
Telephone: (910) 672-1111 Carnegie Class: Master's M
FAX Number: (910) 672-1769 Calendar System: Semester
URL: www.uncfsu.edu
Established: 1867 Annual Undergrad Tuition & Fees (In-State): $6,869
Enrollment: 5,899 Coed
Affiliation or Control: State IRS Status: 501(c)3
Highest Offering: Doctorate
Program: Liberal Arts And General; Teacher Preparatory
Accreditation: SC, ART, BUS, CS, MUS, NURSE, SW, TED

02 Chancellor ... Dr. James A. ANDERSON
100 Vice Chancellor and Chief of Staff ... Dr. Thomas CONWAY
05 Provost & Vice Chanc Academic Affs ... Dr. Jon YOUNG
10 Vice Chancellor Business/Finance ... Mr. Kenneth CRAIG
32 Vice Chancellor Student Affairs ... Dr. Janice HAYNIE
30 Vice Chancellor Inst Advancement ... Mr. Getchel CALDWELL
13 Vice Chanc Info Technology/CIO ... Mr. Arasu GANESAN
44 Asst Vice Chanc for Advancement ... Ms. Mary H. BAILEY
35 Assoc Vice Chanc Student Affairs ... Dr. Juanette COUNCIL
18 Assoc Vice Chanc Facilities Mgmt ... Mr. Rudolph CARDENAS
21 Asst VC Business/Financ/Controller .. Ms. Christine M. JUMALON
15 Assoc Vice Chanc Human Resources . Ms. Denise BROWN-HART
85 Asst VC Acad Affs/Interntl Studies ... Dr. Chen YUNKAI
88 Senior Assoc Vice Chancellor ... Dr. Perry A. MASSEY
45 Assoc VC Pgms/Plng/Assessment ... Vacant
84 Assoc VC for Enrollment Management ... Vacant
36 Director Career Svcs & Bus Mgr SA ... Vacant
92 Acting Program Director Honors ... Dr. Erin WHITE
06 Registrar ... Ms. Sarah BAKER
29 Director of Alumni Affairs ... Ms. YaKima RHINEHART
26 Director Public Relations ... Mr. Jeff WOMBLE
08 Director of Library Services ... Mr. Bobby C. WYNN
07 Director of Admissions ... Ms. Ulisa BOWLES
90 Director of IT Operations ... Ms. Michelle WHITAKER
09 Director Institutional Research ... Mr. Ivan WALKER
39 Director of Residence Life ... Mr. Greg MOYD
37 Director Student Financial Aid ... Ms. Kamesia EWING
43 General Counsel ... Mrs. Wanda LESSANE JENKINS
41 Athletic Director ... Dr. Edward MCLEAN
96 Director of Purchasing ... Ms. Willie MCINTYRE
38 Dir Center Personal Development ... Mr. Fred SAPP
28 Director of Diversity ... Vacant
88 Dean University College ... Dr. John I. BROOKS
66 Department Chair Nursing ... Dr. Afua ARHIN
50 Dean School Business/Economics ... Dr. Assad TAVAKOLI
53 Dean School of Education ... Dr. Marion GILLIS-OLION
58 Dean Graduate Studies ... Vacant
49 Dean College of Arts and Sciences ... Dr. David BARLOW
101 Secretary of Univ/Board Liaison ... Ms. Suzetta M. PERKINS
19 Asst VC Police & Public Safety ... Mr. Charles F. KIMBLE
04 Administrative Asst to President ... Mrs. Ann ZOMERFELD
86 Director Government Relations ... Mr. Wesley FOUNTAIN

*North Carolina Agricultural and Technical State University (B)

1601 E Market Street, Greensboro NC 27411-0001
County: Guilford FICE Identification: 002905
Unit ID: 199102
Telephone: (336) 334-7500 Carnegie Class: DRU
FAX Number: (336) 334-7136 Calendar System: Semester
URL: www.ncat.edu
Established: 1891 Annual Undergrad Tuition & Fees (In-State): $7,699
Enrollment: 10,725 Coed
Affiliation or Control: State IRS Status: 501(c)3
Highest Offering: Doctorate
Program: Liberal Arts And General; Teacher Preparatory; Professional
Accreditation: SC, AAFCS, BUS, BUSA, CACREP, CONST, CORE, CS, #DIETD, ENG, JOUR, LSAR, MUS, NAIT, NUR, SW, TED, THEA

02 Chancellor ... Dr. Harold L. MARTIN, SR.
05 Provost/Vice Chanc Academic Affairs ... Dr. Joe B. WHITEHEAD, JR.
10 Vice Chanc Business & Finance ... Mr. Robert POMPEY, JR.
100 Chief of Staff ... Ms. Nicole PRIDE
46 Vice Chanc Research/Economic Dev ... Dr. Barry L. BURKS
32 Vice Chancellor of Student Affairs ... Dr. Melody C. PIERCE
15 Interim VC for Human Resources ... Dr. Ericka M. SMITH
13 Vice Chanc Info Tech Services/CIO ... Dr. Darryl D. MCGRAW
43 General Counsel for Legal Affairs ... Dr. J. Charles WALDRUP
20 Vice Prov for Acad Affs/UG Programs ... Dr. G. Scott JENKINS
26 Assoc Vice Chanc for Univ Relations ... Ms. Nanyamka A. FARRELLY
45 Asst VC for Budget & Planning ... Vacant
88 Vice Prov Rsrch Grad Pgm/Extnd Lrng ... Dr. Sanjiv SARIN
18 Asst VC for Bus/Finance/Facilities .. Mr. Andrew M. PERKINS, JR.
19 Asst VC Police/Public Safety ... Mr. Glen C. NEWELL
08 Dean of Library Services ... Ms. Vicki COLEMAN
47 Int Dean Agric/Environmental Sci ... Dr. Shirley HYMON-PARKER
49 Dean Arts & Sciences ... Dr. Goldie S. BYRD
53 Int Dean School of Education ... Dr. Anthony GRAHAM
54 Dean of Engineering ... Dr. Robin N. COGER
58 Dean of Graduate School ... Dr. Sanjiv SARIN
66 Dean of Nursing ... Dr. Inez TUCK
50 Dean of Business & Economics ... Dr. Beryl MCEWEN
72 Dean School of Technology ... Dr. Benjamin O. UWAKWEH
88 Dean Joint Sch Nanoscience/Nanoengr ... Dr. James G. RYAN
09 Asst VC for Inst Research/Planning ... Vacant
06 Interim University Registrar ... Dr. Dawn FORBES MURPHY
07 Interim AVC for Enroll Mgt ... Ms. Cheryl POLLARD-BURNS
37 Director Financial Aid ... Mrs. Sherri M. AVENT
36 Director Career Services ... Ms. Joyce P. EDWARDS
91 Asst VC for Info Syst/Data Ctr Ops ... Vacant
29 Assoc VC for Alumni Affairs ... Ms. Rosetta L. CLAY
85 Dir International Student Affairs ... Ms. Loreatha D. GRAVES
88 Dir Multicultural Student Center ... Mr. Gerald SPATES
41 Director of Athletics ... Mr. Earl M. HILTON, III
39 Dir Student Housing/Residence Life ... Ms. Linda D. INMAN
23 Interim Dir Student Health Services ... Ms. Bettye J. YOUNG-STEWART
38 Director of Counseling Service ... Dr. Vivian D. BARNETTE
25 Director of Contracts/Grants ... Ms. Natalie TEAGLE
92 Director of Honors Program ... Dr. Michael CUNDALL, JR.
96 Interim Director of Purchasing ... Ms. Martinique WILLIAMS
27 Director of Media Relations ... Vacant
40 Manager of Bookstore ... Ms. Catrina JACKSON
102 Dir Foundation/Corporate Relations ... Mr. Stephone WHITE
103 Dir Workforce/Career Development ... Dr. Eric M. GLADNEY
104 Asst Director for Study Abroad ... Mr. Christopher M. BROWN
106 Dir of ITS/Distance Education ... Dr. Tracie O. LEWIS
108 AVC Institutional Research ... Dr. William B. ZHANG
22 Dir Affirmative Action/EEO ... Ms. Linda MANGUM
44 Director of Annual Giving ... Ms. Carletta SIMMONS
86 Director External Affairs ... Mr. Michael A. BROWN, II

*North Carolina Central University (C)

1801 Fayetteville Street, Durham NC 27707-3129
County: Durham FICE Identification: 002950
Unit ID: 199157
Telephone: (919) 530-6100 Carnegie Class: Master's L
FAX Number: (919) 530-5014 Calendar System: Semester
URL: www.nccu.edu
Established: 1910 Annual Undergrad Tuition & Fees (In-State): $9,396
Enrollment: 8,155 Coed
Affiliation or Control: State IRS Status: 501(c)3
Highest Offering: Doctorate
Program: Liberal Arts And General; Teacher Preparatory; Professional
Accreditation: SC, BUS, CAATE, CACREP, DIETD, DIETI, LAW, LIB, NRPA, NUR, SP, SW, TED, THEA

02 Chancellor ... Dr. Debra SAUNDERS-WHITE
05 Provost/VC Academic Affairs ... Dr. Johnson AKINLEYE
100 Chief of Staff ... Mr. Wendell F. PHILLIPS
43 General Counsel ... Ms. Melissa JACKSON HOLLOWAY
46 Interim VC Res/Economic Devel ... Dr. Undi N. HOFFLER
11 Vice Chanc Admin & Finance ... Mr. Benjamin DURANT
32 Vice Chancellor Student Affairs ... Dr. Miron P. BILLINGSLEY
30 Vice Chanc Inst Advancement ... Dr. Harriet F. DAVIS
20 Assoc Provost for Academic Programs ... Dr. Tau KADHI
10 Assoc VC Administration/ Finance ... Ms. Yolanda E. BANKS-DEAVER
20 Interim Assoc VC Faculty Develop ... Dr. Yolanda B. ANDERSON
15 Chief Human Resources Officer ... Mr. Linc BUTLER
88 Assoc VC Innovat/Engaged & Global ... Dr. Ontario S. WOODEN
88 Director Student Union ... Dr. Toya CORBETT
45 Director Strategic Planning ... Mr. Johnnie SOUTHERLAND
35 Dir Student Rights/Responsibilities ... Mr. Gary L. BROWN
13 Chief Information Officer ... Ms. Leah KRAUS
07 Director Undgraduate Admissions ... Dr. Nicole GIBBS
31 Director of External Affairs ... Ms. Pamela THORPE-YOUNG
88 Dir JLC Biomed/Biotech Rsrch Inst ... Vacant
88 Interim Dir Bio Rsch Inst/Tech Ent ... Ms. Anita L. JACKSON
44 Director Annual Giving ... Ms. Quanda BAKER
06 Registrar ... Dr. Jerome GOODWIN
91 Interim Dir Enterprise Info System ... Ms. Billie HANES
29 Director of Alumni Relations ... Ms. Chatonda COVINGTON
26 Assoc VC for Public Relations ... Ms. Ayana D. HERNANDEZ
37 Director of Financial Aid ... Ms. Sharon J. OLIVER
08 Director Library Services ... Dr. Theodosia T. SHIELDS
19 Interim Chief of University Police ... Mr. Willie BELL, JR.
88 Assoc Dean Univ Clge/Acad Advising ... Dr. Jennifer SCHUM
88 Director Art Museum ... Dr. Kenneth G. RODGERS
18 Director Facilities Services ... Mr. Phillip POWELL
39 Director Residential Life ... Mr. Ronnie DAVIS
41 Director Athletics ... Dr. Ingrid L. WICKER-MCCREE
09 Interim VC Inst Research/Eval/Plng ... Dr. Jeanette BARKER
96 Interim Director of Purchasing ... Ms. Constance G. MALLETTE
92 Director of Honors Program ... Dr. Ansel E. BROWN
38 Exec Director of Counseling Center . Dr. Ruth GILLIAM PHILLIPS
22 Director of EEO & Employee Relation .. Ms. Sylvia C. ANDERSON
84 Assoc VC Enrollment Management ... Dr. Monica T. LEACH
21 Dir Auxiliaries/Business Services ... Mr. Timothy J. MOORE
40 Manager Bookstore ... Ms. Stephanie L. GETCHELL
58 Dean Sch Grad Stds/Asc VC Grad Rsch ... Dr. Jaleh REZAIE
61 Dean of the Law School ... Ms. Phyliss V. CRAIG-TAYLOR
62 Dean School of Library/Info Science ... Dr. Irene OWENS
50 Interim Dean School of Business ... Dr. Wanda LESTER
88 Dean of University College ... Dr. Ontario S. WOODEN
49 Dean College of Arts and Sciences ... Dr. Carlton E. WILSON
83 Dean College Behavioral/Social Scis ... Dr. Debra O. PARKER
53 Interim Dean School of Education ... Dr. Audrey W. BEARD
04 Administrative Asst to Chancellor ... Ms. Zelda STANFIELD
101 Secretary of the Board of Trustees ... Mr. Wendell F. PHILLIPS
102 Executive Director NCCU Foundation ... Mr. Ernest JENKINS
104 Asst Director International Affairs ... Dr. Olivia JONES
105 Director Web Services ... Mr. Damond NOLLAN
106 Director Division Extended Studies ... Ms. Kimberly C. PHIFER-MCGHEE
108 Director of Assessment ... Ms. Tia M. DOXEY
25 Director Contracts/Grants Admin ... Ms. Denise Y. WYNN
36 Director Career Services ... Ms. Donna Y. HEMBRICK

*North Carolina State University (D)

20 Watauga Club Drive, Raleigh NC 27695-0001
County: Wake FICE Identification: 002972
Unit ID: 199193
Telephone: (919) 515-2191 Carnegie Class: RU/VH
FAX Number: (919) 515-7740 Calendar System: Semester
URL: www.ncsu.edu
Established: 1887 Annual Undergrad Tuition & Fees (In-State): $8,580
Enrollment: 33,989 Coed
Affiliation or Control: State IRS Status: 501(c)3
Highest Offering: Doctorate
Program: Occupational; Liberal Arts And General; Teacher Preparatory; Professional; Technical Emphasis
Accreditation: SC, ART, BUS, BUSA, CACREP, CS, ENG, LSAR, NRPA, SCPSY, SPAA, SW, TED, VET

02 Chancellor ... Dr. William Randy WOODSON
05 Provost/Exec Vice Chancellor ... Dr. Warwick A. ARDEN
43 Vice Chanc & General Counsel ... Ms. Eileen GOLDGEIER
10 Vice Chanc Finance & Business ... Mr. Charles D. LEFFLER
46 Vice Chanc Research & Innovation ... Dr. Alan REBAR
32 Vice Chan/Dean Div Acad & Stdnt Aff ... Dr. Michael D. MULLEN
30 Vice Chanc Univ Advancement ... Mr. Brian C. SISCHO
13 Vice Chanc Information Technology ... Dr. Marc I. HOIT
101 Secretary of the University ... Ms. P. J. TEAL
26 Asst to Chanc External Affairs ... Mr. Kevin HOWELL
88 Sr Vice Provost for Acad Strategy ... Dr. Duane K. LARICK
106 Sr Vice Prov Acad Outreach/Entrepre ... Dr. Thomas K. MILLER
08 Vice Provost/Director of Libraries ... Ms. Susan K. NUTTER
22 Int VP Inst Equity & Diversity ... Ms. Amy CIRCOSTA
21 Assoc Vice Chanc Finance/Res Mgt ... Mr. Stephen W. KETO
18 Assoc Vice Chanc Facilities ... Mr. Steve A. ARNDT
39 Vice Provost for Residential Life ... Dr. Timothy R. LUCKADOO
29 Assoc Vice Chanc Alumni Relations ... Mr. Benny SUGGS
15 Assoc Vice Chanc Human Resources ... Ms. Barbara L. CARROLL
19 Director Public Safety ... Mr. Jack W. MOORMAN
09 Sr Vice Prov Inst Rsrch & Planning ... Ms. Mary K. LELIK
07 Director Undergrad Admissions ... Mr. Thomas H. GRIFFIN
06 Registrar & Vice Provost ... Dr. Louis D. HUNT
25 Director Contracts & Grants ... Ms. Julie A. BRASFIELD
27 Director News Services ... Mr. Fred W. HARTMAN
37 Director of Financial Aid ... Ms. Krista R. DOMNICK
38 Director of Counseling Center ... Dr. Monica OSBURN
41 Director Athletics ... Ms. Deborah YOW
84 Asst Director of Enrollment Plng ... Mr. Trey STANDISH
21 Treasurer ... Ms. Mary T. PELOQUIN-DODD
88 Director of Materials Management ... Mrs. Sharon LOOSMAN
79 Dean Humanities/Social Sciences ... Dr. Jeffery P. BRADEN
48 Dean of Design ... Dr. Marvin J. MALECHA
54 Dean of Engineering ... Dr. Louis A. MARTIN-VEGA
47 Dean Agriculture/Life Sciences ... Dr. Richard H. LINTON
65 Dean of Natural Resources ... Dr. Mary WATZIN
53 Interim Dean of Education ... Dr. Mary Ann DANOWITZ
50 Dean of Management ... Dr. Ira R. WEISS
81 Dean College of Sciences ... Dr. Daniel L. SOLOMON
88 Interim Dean of Textiles ... Dr. David HINKS
74 Dean of Veterinary Medicine ... Dr. D. Paul LUNN
58 Dean of Graduate School ... Dr. Maureen G. GRASSO

*University of North Carolina at Asheville (E)

1 University Heights, Asheville NC 28804-8503
County: Buncombe FICE Identification: 002907
Unit ID: 199111
Telephone: (828) 251-6600 Carnegie Class: Bac/A&S
FAX Number: (828) 251-6495 Calendar System: Semester
URL: www.unca.edu
Established: 1927 Annual Undergrad Tuition & Fees (In-State): $6,604
Enrollment: 3,845 Coed
Affiliation or Control: State IRS Status: 501(c)3
Highest Offering: Master's
Program: Liberal Arts And General; Teacher Preparatory
Accreditation: SC, BUS, ENG, TED

02 Chancellor ... Ms. Mary K. GRANT
100 Chief of Staff ... Vacant
05 Provost/VC Academic Affairs ... Dr. Joseph URGO
10 Vice Chancellor Finance/Operations ... Mr. John PIERCE
30 Vice Chancellor Advancement ... Ms. Elizabeth BAGWELL
32 Vice Chanc for Student Affairs ... Dr. Bill HAGGARD
41 Director of Athletics ... Ms. Janet R. CONE
43 University General Counsel ... Ms. Heather PARLIER
15 Dir HR/Affirmative Act ... Ms. Nicole NORIAN
09 Director of Institutional Research ... Dr. Archer R. GRAVELY
20 Asst Provost Academic Admin ... Ms. Patricia MCCLELLAN
81 Dean Natural Science ... Dr. Keith KRUMPE
79 Dean Humanities ... Dr. Gwen ASHBURN
83 Dean Social Science ... Dr. Jeff KONZ
88 Dean University Programs ... Dr. Edward J. KATZ

08 University Librarian Ms. Leah DUNN
13 Chief Information Officer Mr. Jeff BROWN
07 Sr Dir Admissions/Financial Aid Ms. Shannon EARLE
25 Director Contracts & Grants Dr. Gerard VOOS
06 Associate Registrar Ms. Alicia SHOPE
21 Assoc Vice Chancellor of Finance Ms. Suzanne BRYSON
21 Controller Ms. Mary HALL
19 Director of Public Safety Mr. Eric BOYCE
96 Senior Buyer Mr. Joel KNISLEY
26 Assoc VC Communication & Mktg Mr. Luke BUKOSKI
27 Asst Director News Services Mr. Steve PLEVER
23 Dir Student Health/Counseling Mr. John CUTSPEC
39 Director Residential Education Ms. Melanie FOX
39 Director Housing Operations Mr. Vollie BARNWELL
36 Director of Career Center Ms. Marlane MOWITZ
35 Dean of Students Ms. Jackie MCHARGUE
04 Exec Asst to Chancellor Ms. Chelsey BURKE

*University of North Carolina at Chapel Hill (A)

Chapel Hill NC 27599-0001
County: Orange
FICE Identification: 002974
Unit ID: 199120
Telephone: (919) 962-2211
Carnegie Class: RU/VH
FAX Number: (919) 962-5604
Calendar System: Semester
URL: www.unc.edu
Established: 1789
Annual Undergrad Tuition & Fees (In-State): $8,562
Enrollment: 29,135
Coed
Affiliation or Control: State
IRS Status: 501(c)3
Highest Offering: Doctorate
Program: Occupational; Liberal Arts And General; Teacher Preparatory; Professional
Accreditation: #SC, ACAE, AUD, BUS, CAATE, CACREP, CLPSY, CORE, DA, DENT, DH, DIETC, DMOLS, HSA, IPSY, JOUR, LAW, LIB, MED, MT, NMT, NUR, NURSE, OT, PAST, PH, PHAR, PLNG, PTA, RAD, RADDOS, RTT, SCPSY, SP, SPAA, SW, TED

02 Chancellor Dr. Carol L. FOLT
05 Exec Vice Provost/Chief Intl Ofcr Dr. Ronald STRAUSS
10 Vice Chancellor Finance & Admin Mr. Matthew W. FAJACK
32 Vice Chancellor Student Affairs Mr. Winston B. CRISP
13 VC Info Technology/Chief Info Ofcr Mr. Chris KIELT
46 Vice Chancellor for Research Dr. Barbara ENTWISLE
26 Assoc Vice Chanc Univ Relations Vacant
90 Asst VC Rsch Computing/Learng Tech Dr. Michael BARKER
08 Assoc Prov/University Librarian Ms. Sarah MICHALAK
21 Vice Prov Finance & Acad Planning Dr. Dwayne PINKNEY
20 Vice Provost Academic Initiatives Dr. Carol TRESOLINI
18 Assoc Vice Chanc Facilities Plng Mr. Bruce L. RUNBERG
31 Director Community Relations Ms. Linda DOUGLAS
28 Vice Prov Diversity/Multicultural Dr. Taffye B. CLAYTON
11 Provost Administration Dr. Lynn E. WILLIFORD
39 Dir Housing & Residential Education Vacant
41 Director of Athletics Mr. Lawrence (Bubba) R. CUNNINGHAM
06 Asst Prov/University Registrar Mr. Christopher DERICKSON
07 Vice Prov Enrollment & Ugrad Admiss Dr. Stephen M. FARMER
29 Pres/Director General Alumni Assoc Mr. Douglas S. DIBBERT
37 Assoc Prov/Dir Scholar/Student Aid Ms. Shirley A. ORT
36 Director University Career Services Mr. Ray ANGLE
38 Dir Counseling & Psychological Svcs Dr. Allen H. O'BARR
44 Director of Annual Giving Ms. Rebecca BRAMLETT
19 Dir Public Safety/Chief of Police Chief Jeff B. MCCRACKEN
51 Director Center for Cont Education Mr. Rob BRUCE
27 Director University Relations Mr. Mike MCFARLAND
96 Director Procurement Services Ms. Martha PENDERGRASS
35 Assoc Vice Chanc Student Affairs Dr. Bettina SHUFORD
87 Dean of the Summer School Ms. Jan YOPP
49 Dean College Arts & Sciences Dr. Karen GIL
61 Dean School of Law Mr. John C. BOGER
17 V Chanc Med Affs/CEO UNC HlthCare Dr. William L. ROPER
52 Dean School of Dentistry Dr. Jane WEINTRAUB
58 Dean of Graduate School Dr. Steven W. MATSON
50 Dean Kenan-Flagler Business School Vacant
70 Dean School of Social Work Dr. Jack M. RICHMAN
67 Dean School of Pharmacy Dr. Robert A. BLOUIN
60 Dean School of Journalism/Mass Comm Ms. Susan R. KING
62 Dean School of Info/Library Science Dr. Gary MARCHIONINI
69 Dean School of Public Health Dr. Barbara K. RIMER
53 Dean School of Education Dr. Bill MCDIARMID
80 Dean School of Government Dr. Michael R. SMITH
23 Exec Dir Campus Health Services Dr. Mary COVINGTON
92 Associate Dean for Honors Dr. James L. LELOUDIS

*University of North Carolina at Charlotte (B)

9201 University City Boulevard, Charlotte NC 28223-0001
County: Mecklenburg
FICE Identification: 002975
Unit ID: 199139
Telephone: (704) 687-8622
Carnegie Class: DRU
FAX Number: N/A
Calendar System: Semester
URL: www.uncc.edu
Established: 1946
Annual Undergrad Tuition & Fees (In-State): $6,532
Enrollment: 27,238
Coed
Affiliation or Control: State
IRS Status: 501(c)3
Highest Offering: Doctorate
Program: Liberal Arts And General; Teacher Preparatory; Professional
Accreditation: SC, ANEST, BUS, BUSA, CAATE, CACREP, CLPSY, ENG, ENGT, EXSC, HSA, IPSY, MUS, NURSE, PH, POLYT, SPAA, SW, TED

02 Chancellor Dr. Philip L. DUBOIS
100 Chief of Staff Ms. Krista L. NEWKIRK
05 Provost/Vice Chanc Acad Affairs Dr. Joan F. LORDEN
20 Senior Associate Provost Dr. Jay RAJA
20 Assoc Provost Academic Services Dr. Cynthia WOLF JOHNSON
88 Assoc Provost Metro Studies/Ext Pgm Dr. Owen J. FURUSETH
10 Vice Chancellor Business Affairs Ms. Elizabeth A. HARDIN
30 Vice Chancellor Univ Advancement Mr. Niles F. SORENSEN
86 Spec Asst for Constituent Relations Ms. Betty DOSTER
32 Vice Chancellor Student Affairs Dr. Arthur R. JACKSON
46 Vice Chanc Research/Econ Dev Dr. Robert W. WILHELM
13 Vice Chanc Info Tech Svcs/CIO Dr. Michael CARLIN
18 Assoc Vice Chanc Facilities Mgmt Mr. Philip M. JONES, JR.
08 Dean Atkins Library Dr. Anne C. MOORE
88 Assoc Prov Budget & Personnel Ms. Lori MCMAHON
82 Asst Provost for Intl Programs Mr. Joel A. GALLEGOS
88 Assistant Provost Dr. Leslie ZENK
26 Exec Dir Univ Communications Mr. Stephen P. WARD
87 Int Dir Summer Pgms/Dist Ed Ms. Shanna COLES
51 Dir Continuing Education Ms. Lesley NICHOLS
27 Director of Public Relations Mr. John D. BLAND
31 Director Community Affairs Ms. Jeanette SIMS
39 Assoc Vice Chanc/Dir Residence Life Ms. Jacklyn A. SIMPSON
21 Assoc Vice Chancellor for Finance Mr. Paul FORTE
21 Assoc Vice Chanc Business Svcs Mr. Keith N. WASSUM
58 Assoc Provost/Dean Graduate School Dr. Thomas L. REYNOLDS
84 Assoc Provost for Enrollment Mgmt Ms. Tina M. MCENTIRE
43 General Counsel Mr. David E. BROOME, JR.
07 Director Undergraduate Admissions Ms. Claire J. KIRBY
35 Dean of Students/Assoc VC Stdnt Aff Ms. Christine REED DAVIS
37 Director of Financial Aid Mr. Bruce BLACKMON
38 Assoc VC Health Programs & Services Dr. David B. SPANO
36 Director University Career Center Dr. Patrick MADSEN
40 Bookstore and Licensing Mgr Mr. Greg MCCAMBRIDGE
29 Exec Director Alumni Affairs Ms. Jenny JONES
88 Assoc VC Risk Mgmt/Safety/Security Mr. Henry D. JAMES
19 Chief/Dir Police & Public Safety Mr. Jeffrey A. BAKER
09 Asst Provost Institutional Reseach Mr. Stephen A. COPPOLA
41 Director of Athletics Ms. Judy W. ROSE
96 Director of Purchasing Mr. Randy DUNCAN
93 Dir Multicultural Academic Services Dr. Sam T. LOPEZ
23 Admin Director Student Health Svcs Mr. David ROUSMANIERE
15 Assoc Vice Chanc HumanRes/Aff Act Mr. Gary W. STINNETT
16 Exec Dir HR/EPA/Emp Rel/Complianc Ms. Jeanne L. MADORIN
85 Dir Intl Student/Scholar Svcs Mr. Tarek A. ELSHAYEB
104 Director Study Abroad Mr. Brad SEKULICH
48 Dean College of Arts/Architecture Mr. Kenneth A. LAMBLA
50 Dean College of Business Dr. Steven H. OTT
54 Dean College of Engineering Dr. Robert E. JOHNSON
53 Dean College of Education Dr. Ellen C. MCINTYRE
49 Dean Col of Liberal Arts & Sciences Dr. Nancy A. GUTIERREZ
88 Dean College Health & Human Svcs Dr. Nancy FEY-YENSAN
72 Dean College Computing/Informatics Dr. Yi DENG
97 Dean University College Dr. John SMAIL
92 Exec Director of Honors College Dr. Malin PEREIRA
06 University Registrar Mr. Christopher B. KNAUER
44 Director of Planning Giving Mr. John W. CULLUM
44 Director of Annual Giving Ms. Stacie G. YOUNG
04 Executive Asst to President Ms. Shari DUNN
108 Exec Dir Assessment & Accreditation Dr. Christine ROBINSON
25 Exec Dir Contracts/Grants Admin Mr. Lou HARRELL
28 Director Faculty Affairs/Diversity Dr. Yvette HUET

*University of North Carolina at Greensboro (C)

PO Box 26170,1000 Spring Garden St, Greensboro NC 27402-6170
County: Guilford
FICE Identification: 002976
Unit ID: 199148
Telephone: (336) 334-5000
Carnegie Class: RU/H
FAX Number: (336) 256-0408
Calendar System: Semester
URL: www.uncg.edu
Established: 1891
Annual Undergrad Tuition & Fees (In-State): $6,733
Enrollment: 18,647
Coed
Affiliation or Control: State
IRS Status: 501(c)3
Highest Offering: Doctorate
Program: Liberal Arts And General; Teacher Preparatory; Professional
Accreditation: SC, ANEST, BUS, BUSA, CAATE, CACREP, CIDA, CLPSY, CS, DANCE, DIETD, DIETI, LIB, MUS, NRPA, NUR, NURSE, PH, SP, SPAA, SW, TED, THEA

02 Acting Chancellor Dr. Dana L. DUNN
100 Chief of Staff Ms. Bonita J. BROWN
05 Provost Exc VC for Academic Affairs Dr. Dana L. DUNN
10 Vice Chancellor Business Affairs Mr. Charles A. MAIMONE
11 Vice Chanc Info Tech Services Dr. James H. CLOTFELTER
32 Vice Chanc for Student Affairs Dr. Cheryl M. CALLAHAN
30 VC University Advancement Ms. Janis I. ZINK
88 Assoc VC for Central Dev Programs Ms. Judy PIPER
43 Interim University Counsel Dr. Elizabeth C. BUNTING
20 Vice Provost Dr. Alan J. BOYETTE
97 Coordinator of Undergrad Studies Dr. Ben RAMSEY
46 Vice Chanc Research & Econ Devel Dr. Terri L. SHELTON
104 Assoc Provost Intl Programs Dr. Penelope J. PYNES
84 Assoc Provost Enrollment Mgmt Dr. Bryan J. TERRY
15 Assoc VC Human Resource Services Vacant
21 Associate VC Financial Services Mr. Steven W. RHEW
18 Associate Vice Chanc for Facilities Mr. Jorge QUINTAL
88 Associate VC for Campus Enterprises Mr. Michael T. BYERS
09 Director of Institutional Research Dr. Sarah D. CARRIGAN
26 Vice Chanc University Relations Mr. James L. THORNTON
35 Associate VC for Student Affairs Dr. Jim S. SETTLE
91 Assoc VC for Admin Systems Ms. Laura R. YOUNG
88 Asst VC for Foundation Finance Ms. Jill HILLYER
58 Dean of Graduate School Dr. William R. WIENER
49 Dean of Arts & Sciences Dr. Timothy D. JOHNSTON
50 Dean of Business & Economics Dr. McRae BANKS
53 Dean of Education Dr. Karen WIXSON
68 Dean of Health & Human Sciences Dr. Celia R. HOOPER
64 Dean of Music/Theatre & Dance Dr. Peter ALEXANDER
66 Dean of Nursing Dr. Robin E. REMSBURG
08 Dean of University Libraries Ms. Rosann V. BAZIJIAN
06 University Registrar Ms. Deb B. HURLEY
108 Dir Assessment and Accreditation Dr. Jodi E. PETTAZZONI
07 Director of Admissions Vacant
29 Dir Alumni Affairs & Annual Giving Ms. Mary G. LANDERS
88 Director of Campus Recreation Ms. Jill BEVILLE
23 Director Student Health Services Dr. Tresa M. SAXTON
36 Director Career Services Center Mr. Patrick O. MADSEN
51 Int Dean Division of Continual Lrng Dr. James M. EDDY
25 Dir Contracts and Grants Mr. William D. WALTERS
37 Director of Financial Aid Ms. Deborah TOLLEFSON
39 Director Housing & Residence Life Mr. Timothy JOHNSON
41 Director Intercollegiate Athletics Ms. Kim RECORD
88 Dir New Stdnt/Spartan Fam Programs Dr. Kim SOUSA-PEOPLES
19 Assoc VC for Safety and Risk Mgmt Mr. Rollin DONELSON
28 Director Intercultural Engagement Ms. Audrey O. LUCAS
96 Dir Purchasing and Materials Mgmt Mr. Trace LITTLE
40 University Bookstore Manager Mr. Brad LIGHT

*University of North Carolina at Pembroke (D)

One University Drive, PO Box 1510, Pembroke NC 28372-1510
County: Robeson
FICE Identification: 002954
Unit ID: 199281
Telephone: (910) 521-6000
Carnegie Class: Master's M
FAX Number: (910) 521-6176
Calendar System: Semester
URL: www.uncp.edu
Established: 1887
Annual Undergrad Tuition & Fees (In-State): $5,534
Enrollment: 6,269
Coed
Affiliation or Control: State
IRS Status: 501(c)3
Highest Offering: Master's
Program: Liberal Arts And General; Teacher Preparatory
Accreditation: SC, ART, BUS, CAATE, CACREP, MUS, NURSE, SW, TED

02 Chancellor Dr. Kyle R. CARTER
05 Interim Provost/VC Academic Affairs Dr. Zoe W. LOCKLEAR
10 Vice Chanc Finance & Administration Dr. Richard E. COSENTINO
32 Vice Chanc Student Affairs Dr. John R. JONES
30 Vice Chancellor for Advancement Ms. Wendy LOWERY
84 Assoc Vice Chanc Enrollment Dr. Melissa SCHAUB
26 Special Asst for Constituent Rels Dr. Glen G. BURNETTE, JR.
100 Chief of Staff Mr. Daniel KENNEY
20 Assoc Vice Chanc Planning and Acred Dr. Elizabeth NORMANDY
35 Assoc Vice Chanc Student Affairs Dr. Lisa SCHAEFFER
13 Assoc VC Information Resources/CIO Ms. Nancy CROUCH
85 Director of International Pgms Ms. Jessica HALL
43 General Counsel Mr. Joshua MALCOLM
39 Dir Housing and Resident Life Mr. R. Preston SWINEY
49 Interim Dean of Arts & Sciences Dr. Meredith STORMS
08 Dean of Library Services Ms. Susan WHITT
58 Dean of Grad Studies & Research Dr. Rebecca BULLARD-DILLARD
92 Dean of Honors College Dr. Mark MILEWICZ
53 Interim Dean of School of Education Dr. Karen STANLEY
50 Interim Dean of School of Business Dr. John PARNELL
29 Director Alumni Relations Ms. Morgan HUNT
09 Asst VC Inst Research Dr. Chunmei YAO
36 Director Career Services Center Dr. Karen PRUETT
38 Director Counseling/Testing Center Dr. Mary-Jeanne RALEIGH
06 Interim Registrar Ms. Natricia DRAKE
37 Director Financial Aid Ms. Jenelle HANDCOX
96 Director of Business Services Ms. Denise CARROLL
15 Director of Human Resources Ms. Angela REVELS-BULLARD
44 Assistant Director of Annual Fund Ms. Chris DAVIS
25 Dir Ofc of Sponsored Rsrch & Pgms Dr. Chantal A. RIVERA
88 Director Public Administration Pgm Dr. Michael PENNINGTON
27 Public Communications Specialist Mr. Scott BIGELOW
21 Asst Vice Chancellor for Finance Mr. Carlton SPELLMAN
40 Director of Bookstore Ms. Karen SWINEY
88 Sports Information Director Mr. Todd ANDERSON
07 Director of Admissions Ms. Lela CLARK
18 Director of Physical Plant Mr. Larry FREEMAN
28 Dir Multicultural/Minority Affairs Mr. Robert L. CANIDA, II
88 Dir Fac Plng/Construction/Univ Engr Mr. Michael CLARK
88 Dir Ctr for Academic Excellence Mr. Derek OXENDINE
88 Internal Auditor Ms. Kelley R. HORTON
41 Director of Athletics Mr. Dick CHRISTY
88 Faculty Senate Chair Dr. Scott HICKS
23 Director of Student Health Services Ms. Cora BULLARD
46 Asst to the Chancellor-Rsrch/Comm Ms. Lisa CANADA
04 Executive Asst to the Chancellor Ms. Marla LOCKLEAR
88 Director of Disability Support Svcs Mr. Jim KESSLER
104 Director Study Abroad Dr. Laura DOBSON
106 Dir Online Education/E-learning Dr. Charles TITA
19 Director Security/Safety Mr. McDuffie CUMMINGS, JR.

*University of North Carolina Wilmington (A)

601 S College Road, Wilmington NC 28403-5931
County: New Hanover FICE Identification: 002984
Unit ID: 199218
Telephone: (910) 962-3030 Carnegie Class: Master's L
FAX Number: (910) 962-4050 Calendar System: Semester
URL: www.uncw.edu
Established: 1947 Annual Undergrad Tuition & Fees (In-State): $6,647
Enrollment: 14,611 Coed
Affiliation or Control: State IRS Status: 501(c)3
Highest Offering: Doctorate
Program: Liberal Arts And General; Teacher Preparatory; Professional
Accreditation: SC, BUS, CAATE, CEA, CS, MUS, NURSE, SPAA, SW, TED

02 Chancellor ... Dr. Jose V. SARTARELLI
05 Provost/Vice Chanc Academic Affairs ... Dr. Marilyn SHEERER
10 Vice Chancellor Business Affairs ... Dr. Rick WHITFIELD
32 Vice Chanc for Student Affairs ... Ms. Patricia L. LEONARD
30 Vice Chanc University Advancement ... Mr. Eddie STUART
21 Sr Assoc Vice Chanc Finance ... Mr. Rick N. WHITFIELD
44 Assoc Vice Chanc Univ Advancement ... Ms. Christy WARD
20 Vice Provost Academic Affairs ... Dr. Stephen L. MCFARLAND
21 Assoc Vice Chanc Business Services ... Ms. Sharon H. BOYD
21 Assoc VC Business Affs/Facilities ... Mr. Mark D. MORGAN
28 Chief Diversity Officer ... Dr. Kent GUION
26 Exec Dir of University Relations ... Ms. Janine IAMUNNO
09 Assoc Dir Inst Research/Assesment ... Ms. Steffaney COHEN
35 Assoc VC/Dean of Students ... Dr. Michael A. WALKER
84 Assoc Provost for Enrollment Mgmt ... Dr. Terrence M. CURRAN
85 Asst Provost International Programs ... Dr. Raymond BURT
15 Assoc VC for Human Resources ... Dr. Rosalynn MARTIN
100 Chief of Staff ... Vacant
06 Registrar ... Mr. Jonathan REECE
08 University Librarian ... Ms. Sarah WATSTEIN
37 Director Fin Aid/Veterans Svcs ... Dr. Ixchel BAKER-TATE
18 Director of Physical Plant ... Mr. Thomas A. FRESHWATER
19 Director Envir Health & Safety ... Mr. Stanley H. HARTS
23 Dir Student Health/Wellness Center ... Ms. Katrin WESNER
109 Director of Auxiliary Services ... Mr. Brian DAILEY
41 Director of Athletics ... Mr. Jimmy BASS
36 Director Career Services ... Mr. Thomas D. RAKES
29 Director of Alumni Relations ... Mrs. Lindsay LEROY
96 Director of Purchasing ... Ms. Mary E. FORSYTHE
38 Director Student Counseling Center ... Dr. Lynne REEDER
40 Manager Bookstore ... Mrs. Stephanie BIRNBAUM
49 Dean Col Arts & Sciences ... Dr. Aswani VOLETY
50 Dean Cameron School of Business ... Dr. Robert BURRUS
53 Dean Watson School of Education ... Dr. Van O. DEMPSEY
66 Interim Director School of Nursing ... Dr. Carol HEINRICH
58 Assoc Prov/Dean of Graduate School ... Dr. Ron VETTER
76 Dean Col Health & Human Svcs ... Dr. Charles HARDY

*University of North Carolina School of the Arts (B)

1533 S Main Street, Winston-Salem NC 27127-2738
County: Forsyth FICE Identification: 003981
Unit ID: 199184
Telephone: (336) 770-3399 Carnegie Class: Spec/Arts
FAX Number: (336) 770-3375 Calendar System: Semester
URL: www.uncsa.edu
Established: 1963 Annual Undergrad Tuition & Fees (In-State): $8,637
Enrollment: 958 Coed
Affiliation or Control: State IRS Status: 501(c)3
Highest Offering: Master's
Program: Fine Arts Emphasis
Accreditation: SC

02 Chancellor ... Mr. Lindsay BIERMAN
05 Provost ... Dr. David NELSON
10 Senior Director of Business Affairs ... Ms. Carin IOANNOU
11 Chief Operating Officer ... Mr. George BURNETTE
18 Assoc VC Facilities/Services ... Mr. Chrispher BOYD
09 Director of Institutional Research ... Dr. Xiaoyun YANG
07 Director of Admissions ... Ms. Sheeler LAWSON
08 Librarian ... Ms. Vicki WEAVIL
26 Director of Communications ... Ms. Marla CARPENTER
06 Registrar ... Ms. Erin MORIN
15 Director Human Resources ... Mr. James LUCAS
37 Director Financial Aid ... Mrs. Jane KAMIAB
49 Dean of Liberal Arts & Grad Studies ... Mr. Dean WILCOX
64 Dean School of Music ... Dr. Wade WEAST
57 Dean School of Dance ... Ms. Susan JAFFE
88 Int Dean Sch of Design/Production ... Ms. Jamie CALL-BLANKINSHIP
88 Dean School of Drama ... Mr. Carl FORSMAN
13 Chief Information Officer ... Ms. Lisa HARDEN SMITH
19 Chief of Police ... Mr. Gregory HARRIS
38 Dir of Counseling & Testing Svcs ... Dr. Thomas MURRAY
20 Vice Provost & Dean Acad Affairs ... Dr. David ENGLISH
30 Chief Advancement Officer ... Mr. Edward LEWIS
29 Director of Alumni Affairs ... Mr. Jonas SILVER
32 Vice Provost & Dean Student Affairs ... Mr. Ward CALDWELL
96 Director of Purchasing ... Mr. Allen CARNES
88 Dir Ctr for Design Innovation ... Dr. Pamela JENNINGS
88 Ex Dir Kenan Inst for the Arts ... Corey MADDEN
88 Dean School of Filmmaking ... Ms. Susan RUSKIN
88 Director of Student Engagement ... Mr. Steve GALLAGHER
87 Dir Educ Outreach & Summer Programs ... Ms. Suzanna WATKINS
39 Assistant Dean & Dir of RLPH ... Mr. Joseph RICK
23 Interim Dir of Health Services ... Mr. Joseph RICK
36 Dir Outreach & Career Services ... Mr. Joseph MOUNT
100 Chief of Staff ... Mr. James DECRISTO
43 General Counsel ... Mr. David HARRISON
102 Foundation Executive Dir ... Ms. Cindy LIBERTY
24 Director of Digitial Media ... Ms. Claire MACHAMER

*Western Carolina University (C)

65 West University Way, HFR 501, Cullowhee NC 28723-9646
County: Jackson FICE Identification: 002981
Unit ID: 200004
Telephone: (828) 227-7211 Carnegie Class: Master's L
FAX Number: (828) 227-7202 Calendar System: Semester
URL: www.wcu.edu
Established: 1889 Annual Undergrad Tuition & Fees (In-State): $8,139
Enrollment: 10,382 Coed
Affiliation or Control: State IRS Status: 501(c)3
Highest Offering: Doctorate
Program: Liberal Arts And General; Teacher Preparatory; Professional
Accreditation: SC, ANEST, ART, BUS, CAATE, CACREP, CARTE, CIDA, CONST, DIETD, DIETI, EMT, ENG, ENGT, MUS, NURSE, PTA, SP, SPAA, SW, TED, THEA

02 Chancellor ... Dr. David O. BELCHER
05 Provost ... Dr. Alison MORRISON-SHETLAR
10 Vice Chanc Admin & Finance ... Mr. Mike BYERS
32 Vice Chancellor/Student Affairs ... Dr. H. Samuel MILLER
35 Asst Vice Chanc Student Affairs ... Mrs. Jane ADAMS-DUNFORD
35 Asst Vice Chanc Student Success ... Dr. Lowell K. DAVIS
35 Asst Vice Chanc/Student Affairs ... Ms. Kellie MONTEITH
30 Assoc Vice Chancellor Development ... Mr. Jim MILLER
44 Assoc Provost Academic Affairs ... Dr. Brandon SCHWAB
20 Assoc Provost Undergraduate Studies ... Dr. Carol BURTON
18 Assoc VC for Facilities Management ... Mr. Joe WALKER
100 Chief of Staff ... Dr. Melissa WARGO
04 Assistant to the Chancellor ... Ms. Terry WELCH
43 Legal Counsel ... Ms. Mary Ann LOCHNER
38 Director of Counseling Services ... Dr. Kimberly GORMAN
06 Registrar ... Mr. Larry HAMMER
07 Director of Student Recruitment ... Mr. Phil CAULEY
09 Asst Vice Chancellor of OIPE ... Mr. Tim METZ
37 Director of Financial Aid ... Ms. Trina ORR
15 Assoc VC of Human Resources ... Mr. Cory CAUSBY
13 Chief Information Officer ... Mr. Craig FOWLER
29 Director of Alumni Affairs ... Mr. Marty RAMSEY
08 Dean of Library Services ... Dr. Farzaneh RAZZAGHI
19 Director University Police ... Mr. Earnest HUDSON
88 Int Director Education Outreach ... Dr. Susan FOUTS
31 Director Campus Services ... Mr. Bryant BARNETT
41 Athletic Director ... Mr. Randy EATON
23 Director University Health Services ... Ms. Pamela BUCHANAN
28 Int Director Intercultural Affairs ... Mr. Brandon TIGUE
96 Director of Purchasing ... Ms. Cindy NICHOLSON
40 Director Book & Supply Store ... Ms. Pamela DEGRAFFENREID
88 Director of Orientation ... Ms. Tammy HASKETT
38 Acting Director of Advising Center ... Ms. Kim CHERRY-BECK
36 Director of Career Services ... Ms. Theresa CRUZ PAUL
26 Sr Director Comm & Public Relations ... Mr. Bill STUDENC
57 Dean of Fine & Performing Arts ... Mr. George H. BROWN
58 Interim Dean Grad School & Research ... Dr. Brian KLOEPPEL
49 Dean Arts & Sciences ... Dr. Richard STARNES
72 Dean Kimmel School Constr Mgmt/Tech ... Dr. Jeffrey RAY
50 Dean College of Business ... Dr. Darrell PARKER
53 Dean Educ & Allied Professions ... Dr. Dale CARPENTER
76 Dean Health & Human Sciences ... Dr. Douglas R. KESKULA
92 Dean of Honors College ... Dr. Jill GRANGER
88 Director of Marketing ... Ms. Robin C. OLIVER
86 Director of External Relations ... Ms. Meredith WHITFIELD
25 Director of Sponsored Research ... Ms. Andrea MOSHIER
39 Director of Residence Life ... Ms. Mistie BIBBEE

*Winston-Salem State University (D)

601 MLK Jr. Drive, 200 Blair Hall, Winston-Salem NC 27110-0001
County: Forsyth FICE Identification: 002986
Unit ID: 199999
Telephone: (336) 750-2000 Carnegie Class: Master's M
FAX Number: (336) 750-2049 Calendar System: Semester
URL: www.wssu.edu
Established: 1892 Annual Undergrad Tuition & Fees (In-State): $5,708
Enrollment: 5,220 Coed
Affiliation or Control: State IRS Status: 501(c)3
Highest Offering: Doctorate
Program: Liberal Arts And General; Teacher Preparatory; Professional
Accreditation: SC, BUS, CORE, CS, MT, MUS, NRPA, NURSE, OT, PTA, SW, TED

02 Chancellor ... Dr. Elwood L. ROBINSON
05 Provost/VC Academic Affairs ... Dr. Brenda ALLEN
32 Vice Chancellor Student Affairs ... Dr. Trae COTTON
09 Associate Provost ... Dr. Carolynn BERRY
45 Asst Prov Administration/Plng ... Mrs. Letitia C. WALL
10 Int Vice Chanc Finance & Admin ... Dr. Randy W. MILLS
30 Vice Chanc University Advance ... Mrs. Michelle COOK
18 Assoc Vice Chanc Facilities Mgmt ... Mr. Owen J. COOKS
13 Assoc Prov/Chief Information Ofcr ... Dr. Derrick MURRAY
87 Dir Summer Sessions ... Mr. W. Kenneth BULLS
88 Director Internal Audit/Compliance ... Ms. Shannon B. HENRY
19 Chief of Campus Police ... Mrs. Patricia D. NORRIS
08 Interim Librarian ... Dr. Lizzie REEDER
39 Director Hous/Residence Life ... Mrs. Abeer MUSTAFA
37 Director of Financial Aid ... Mr. Robert MUHAMMED
15 Asst Vice Chanc Human Resources ... Mr. Lester ARNOLD
36 Asst Director of Career Services ... Ms. LaMonica SLOAN
26 Director Marketing/Communications ... Ms. Sigrid HALL
27 Director Public Relations ... Mr. Aaron SINGLETON
88 Dir Enrollment Communications ... Ms. Cathy HOOTS
29 Director of Alumni Affairs ... Mr. Gregory G. HAIRSTON
44 Director Annual Fund ... Mrs. Kimberly REESE
35 Assoc Director Student Activities ... Ms. Heather DAVIS
23 Int Dir of Student Health Center ... Dr. Philadelphia ANTHONY
41 Athletic Director ... Mrs. Tonia WALKER
101 Asst to the Chancellor/Sec of Univ ... Mrs. RaVonda DALTON-RANN
07 Director of Admissions ... Vacant
43 General Legal Counsel ... Mrs. Camille KLUTTZ-LEACH
96 Director Purchasing ... Mr. Alan IRELAND
90 Director Academic Computer Center ... Mr. Cuthrell JOHNSON
88 Dean University College LLL ... Dr. Doria K. STITTS
49 Dean College Arts/Sci/Business/Educ ... Dr. Corey D. WALKER
76 Dean School of Health Sciences ... Dr. Peggy VALENTINE
92 Int Director of Honors College ... Dr. Soncerey L. MONTGOMERY
88 Director of Title III ... Dr. Everette L. WITHERSPOON
06 Registrar ... Ms. Sharon STODDARD
108 Director Institutional Assessment . Dr. Becky MUSSAT-WHITLOW
22 Dir Affirmative Action/EEO ... Mrs. Sylvia RAMOS

University of Phoenix Charlotte Campus (E)

3800 Arco Corporate Drive, Charlotte NC 28273-3409
Telephone: (704) 504-5409 Identification: 770216
Accreditation: &NH, ACBSP

† Branch campus of University of Phoenix, Tempe, AZ.

Virginia College (F)

3740 South Holden Road, Greensboro NC 27406
Telephone: (336) 398-5400 Identification: 770619
Accreditation: ACICS, MAAB

† Branch campus of Virginia College, Birmingham, AL.

Wake Forest University (G)

1834 Wake Forest Road, Winston-Salem NC 27109-8758
County: Forsyth FICE Identification: 002978
Unit ID: 199847
Telephone: (336) 758-5000 Carnegie Class: RU/H
FAX Number: (336) 758-6074 Calendar System: Semester
URL: www.wfu.edu
Established: 1834 Annual Undergrad Tuition & Fees: $47,120
Enrollment: 7,788 Coed
Affiliation or Control: Independent Non-Profit IRS Status: 501(c)3
Highest Offering: Doctorate
Program: Liberal Arts And General; Teacher Preparatory; Professional
Accreditation: SC, ANEST, ARCPA, BUS, BUSA, CACREP, DENT, LAW, MED, TED, THEOL

01 President ... Dr. Nathan O. HATCH
43 VP Gen Counsel/Sec Board of Trust ... Mr. J. Reid MORGAN
03 Sr Vice Pres/Chief Financial Ofcr ... Mr. B. Hofler MILAM
05 Provost ... Mr. Rogan KERSH
10 Exec VP Finance/Admin/Chf Oper Ofcr ... Vacant
17 Sr Vice Pres Health Affairs ... Vacant
11 Vice President for Administration ... Vacant
30 Vice Pres University Advancement ... Mr. Mark A. PETERSEN
32 Vice Pres Campus Life ... Dr. Penny RUE
88 Vice Pres/Chief Investment Officer ... Mr. James J. DUNN
20 Assoc Provost Academic Initiatives ... Vacant
100 Chief of Staff ... Ms. Mary E. PUGEL
35 Assoc VP/Dean of Student Services ... Mr. Adam GOLDSTEIN
44 Ast VP/Dir Parent/Donor Relations ... Ms. Minta A. MCNALLY
30 Asst VP/Director of Development ... Mr. Robert T. BAKER
13 CIO/Assoc Provost for Tech/IS ... Mr. Mur MUCHANE
46 Assoc Provost for Research ... Dr. S. Bruce KING
49 Dean of the College ... Dr. Michele K. GILLESPIE
63 Dean School Med/Int Health Sci Pres ... Dr. Edward ABRAHAM
61 Dean School of Law ... Mr. Suzanne REYNOLDS
50 Dean of Business ... Mr. Charles IACOVOU
73 Dean of Divinity ... Dr. Gail R. O'DAY
09 Dir Inst Research/Academic Admin ... Mr. Phil HANDWERK
08 Dir of the Z Smith Reynolds Library ... Dr. Lynn SUTTON
85 Director of International Studies ... Mr. Steven DUKE
07 Director of Admissions ... Ms. Martha B. ALLMAN
37 Director of Financial Aid ... Mr. William T. WELLS
36 VP/Office of Personal & Career Dev ... Mr. Andy CHAN
06 Registrar ... Mr. Harold PACE
41 Director of Athletics ... Mr. Ronald D. WELLMAN
15 Chief Human Resources Officer ... Ms. Carmen I. CANALES
18 Director Facilities Management ... Mr. John SHENETTE
38 Dir University Counseling Center ... Dr. Marianne A. SCHUBERT
84 Director Enrollment Management ... Vacant
23 Director Student Health Service ... Dr. Cecil D. PRICE
39 Exec Dir of Residential Services ... Vacant
42 Chaplain ... Rev. Timothy L. AUMAN
19 Chief University Police ... Ms. Regina G. LAWSON
22 EEO Mgr/Diversity & Compliance Dir ... Ms. Angela CULLER
94 Director Women's & Gender Studies ... Dr. Wanda BALZANO
26 Chief Public Relations Officer ... Mr. Brett EATON
28 Director of Diversity & Inclusion ... Dr. Barbee OAKES

Warren Wilson College (A)

PO Box 9000, Asheville NC 28815-9000
County: Buncombe FICE Identification: 002979
Unit ID: 199865
Telephone: (828) 298-3325 Carnegie Class: Bac/A&S
FAX Number: (828) 771-7097 Calendar System: Semester
URL: www.warren-wilson.edu
Established: 1894 Annual Undergrad Tuition & Fees: $30,462
Enrollment: 893 Coed
Affiliation or Control: Presbyterian Church (U.S.A.) IRS Status: 501(c)3
Highest Offering: Master's
Program: Liberal Arts And General; Teacher Preparatory
Accreditation: SC, SW

01 President .... Dr. Steven L. SOLNICK
05 VP Academic Affairs/Dean of College .... Dr. Paula K. GARRETT
10 VP for Administration/CFO .... Ms. Stehanie OWENS
30 Vice Pres for Advancement .... Ms. K. Johnson BOWLES
84 VP Enrollment Management .... Ms. Janelle HOLMBOE
32 Dean of Students .... Mr. Paul PERRINE
88 Dean of Work .... Mr. Ian ROBERTSON
88 Dean of Service .... Ms. Cathy KRAMER
06 Registrar .... Miss Christa L. BRIDGMAN
09 Director Institutional Research .... Ms. Allyson HETTRICK
37 Assoc Director Financial Aid .... Ms. Eleanor WILL
21 Controller .... Ms. Mary DAVIS
29 Director Alumni Relations .... Mr. Rodney LYTLE
26 Director of Media Relations .... Mr. Benjamin J. ANDERSON
31 Director Community Relations .... Ms. Ally WILSON
20 Director Academic Support Service .... Ms. Lyn O'HARE
88 Director of Service Leaning .... Ms. Brooke MILLSAPS
35 Director of Student Activities .... Mr. Daniel SEEGER
38 Director of Counseling .... Mr. Arthur SHUSTER
36 Director Career Services .... Ms. Wendy SELIGMANN
42 Dir of Spiritual Life & Chaplain .... Rev. Brian AMMONS
41 Athletic Director .... Ms. Stacey ENOS
91 Dir Admin Data Processing .... Ms. Omega HODGES
15 Director Human Resources .... Ms. Gail BAYLOR
18 Acting Dir Facil Mgmt/Tech Svcs .... Ms. Deborah ANSTROM
19 Director Public Safety .... Mr. Terry PAYNE
88 Int Dir Environment Leadership Ctr .... Mr. Stan CROSS
88 Director Swannanoa Gathering .... Mr. Jim MAGILL
104 Director of International Programs .... Ms. Naomi OTTERNESS
28 Inclusion/Diversity/Equity Director .... Mr. Obie FORD, III
96 Director of Purchasing .... Ms. Deborah ANSTROM
13 Manager Computing Services .... Mr. David HARPER

William Peace University (B)

15 E Peace Street, Raleigh NC 27604-1194
County: Wake FICE Identification: 002953
Unit ID: 199272
Telephone: (919) 508-2000 Carnegie Class: Bac/A&S
FAX Number: (919) 508-2326 Calendar System: Semester
URL: www.peace.edu
Established: 1857 Annual Undergrad Tuition & Fees: $25,850
Enrollment: 1,077 Coed
Affiliation or Control: Presbyterian Church (U.S.A.) IRS Status: 501(c)3
Highest Offering: Baccalaureate
Program: Liberal Arts And General
Accreditation: SC

01 President .... Dr. Debra M. TOWNSLEY
04 Executive Secretary to President .... Ms. Patricia L. LUKASZEWSKI
05 Vice President for Academic Affairs .... Vacant
32 Vice President for Student Services .... Mr. Frank RIZZO
30 Vice President for Engagement .... Ms. Julie E. RICCIARDI
06 Registrar .... Ms. Sharon KISSICK
09 Director of Institutional Research .... Ms. Ying LIU
10 Vice Pres Finance & Administration .... Mr. George A. YEARWOOD
84 Vice Pres Enrollment Mgmt/Admission .... Mr. Justin G. ROY
15 Assoc Vice Pres for Human Resources .... Ms. Amber M. KIMBALL
45 Vice Pres for Strategic Initiatives .... Ms. Laurie MCCULLOUGH
18 Asst VP for Buildings and Grounds .... Mr. John B. CRANHAM
37 Director of Financial Aid .... Ms. Michelle DAY
41 Director of Athletics .... Mr. P. Kelly JOHNSON, JR.
26 VP for Communications and Marketing .... Mr. Justin G. ROY

Wingate University (C)

220 N. Camden Street, Wingate NC 28174-0157
County: Union FICE Identification: 002985
Unit ID: 199962
Telephone: (704) 233-8000 Carnegie Class: Master's S
FAX Number: (704) 233-8014 Calendar System: Semester
URL: www.wingate.edu
Established: 1896 Annual Undergrad Tuition & Fees: $27,930
Enrollment: 3,034 Coed
Affiliation or Control: Southern Baptist IRS Status: 501(c)3
Highest Offering: Doctorate
Program: Liberal Arts And General; Teacher Preparatory; Professional; Business Emphasis
Accreditation: SC, ACBSP, ARCPA, CAATE, MUS, NUR, PHAR, @PTA, TED

01 President .... Dr. T. Rhett BROWN
05 Senior VP Academic Affairs .... Dr. Martha S. ASTI
10 VP Business/Chief Financial Ofcr .... Mr. William H. DURHAM
30 Vice President Resource Development .... Mr. E. Vincent TILSON
41 Vice Pres & Director of Athletics .... Mr. R. Stephen POSTON
32 VP for Student Life/Enrollment Mgmt .... Dr. Heather C. MILLER
58 VP for Grad & Prof Programs .... Dr. Robert B. SUPERNAW
11 VP for Buriness Operations .... Mr. Scott E. HUNSUCKER
23 Asst VP for Health Sciences Div .... Mr. Roy Lee RAGSDALE, JR.
58 Asst VP Grad & Prof Programs .... Mr. Cameron JACKSON
32 Dean of Student Affairs .... Mrs. Glenda H. BEBBER
49 Dean School Arts & Sciences .... Dr. H. Donald MERRILL
50 Interim Dean School of Business .... Dr. Peter FRANK
53 Dean School of Education .... Dr. Sarah H. BURNS
08 Director of Library .... Mrs. Amee M. ODOM
35 Director of Involvement .... Ms. Brandy SHOTT
30 Director of Development .... Vacant
09 Director Inst Research/Registrar .... Mrs. Nicci C. BROWN
37 Director Student Financial Planning .... Ms. Teresa G. WILLIAMS
26 Dir of Marketing/Communications .... Mr. Jeffrey ATKINSON
91 Director Administrative Computing .... Mr. Timothy D. HERRIN
29 Director of Alumni Development .... Mrs. Suzanne B. PHILEMON
42 Minstr to Stdnts/Asst Dn Stdnt Affs .... Rev. A. Dane JORDAN
40 Director of Campus Store .... Mrs. Sherri SHANK
19 Campus Safety Chief .... Mr. Mike EASLEY
44 Director of Annual Giving .... Ms. Candice KANE
44 Dir of Major Gifts & Planned Giving .... Mr. J. Theodore JOHNSON
27 Asst Dir Marketing & Communications .... Vacant
38 Director of Counseling Services .... Ms. Lori HINNANT
13 Director of Information Technology .... Ms. Jeanette K. BUJAK
36 Dir of Internships and Career Svcs .... Ms. Sharon ROBINSON
15 Human Resources Coordinator .... Mrs. Lisa B. RAGSDALE
39 Dir Resid Life/Asst Dn Stdnt Affs .... Mr. Michael REYNOLDS
35 Dir of Retention/Asst Dn Stdnt Affs .... Ms. Kristin WHARTON
06 Registrar .... Mrs. Nicci C. BROWN
07 Director of Admissions .... Mr. Gabe HOLLINGSWORTH
100 Chief of Staff .... Dr. Heather C. MILLER
04 Executive Assistant to President .... Ms. Tammy T. BRITT

NORTH DAKOTA

Cankdeska Cikana Community College (D)

PO Box 269, 214 First Avenue, Fort Totten ND 58335-0269
County: Benson FICE Identification: 022365
Unit ID: 200208
Telephone: (701) 766-4415 Carnegie Class: Tribal
FAX Number: (701) 766-4077 Calendar System: Semester
URL: www.littlehoop.edu
Established: 1974 Annual Undergrad Tuition & Fees: $3,300
Enrollment: 185 Coed
Affiliation or Control: Independent Non-Profit IRS Status: 501(c)3
Highest Offering: Associate Degree
Program: Occupational; 2-Year Principally Bachelor's Creditable
Accreditation: NH

01 President .... Dr. Cynthia A. LINDQUIST
05 Academic Dean .... Mrs. Teresa HARDING
10 Vice President for Finance .... Mrs. Chelly VEER
32 Vice Pres Student Services .... Mrs. Erica CAVANAUGH
06 Registrar .... Mr. Ermen BROWN, JR.

Ft. Berthold Community College (E)

PO Box 490, New Town ND 58763-0490
County: Mountrail FICE Identification: 025537
Unit ID: 200086
Telephone: (701) 627-4738 Carnegie Class: Tribal
FAX Number: (701) 627-3609 Calendar System: Semester
URL: www.fortbertholdcc.edu
Established: 1973 Annual Undergrad Tuition & Fees: $4,210
Enrollment: 158 Coed
Affiliation or Control: Independent Non-Profit IRS Status: 501(c)3
Highest Offering: Baccalaureate
Program: Occupational; 2-Year Principally Bachelor's Creditable
Accreditation: NH

01 President .... Dr. Twila BAKER-DEMARAY
05 Vice President of Academics .... Dr. Waylon BAKER
32 Vice Pres Student Services .... Dr. Constance FRANKBERRY
10 Chief Finance Ofcr/VP Support Svcs .... Mr. Philip LEWIS
37 Financial Aid Assistant .... Hadley OLSON
06 Registrar .... Mr. Garrett TITUS
08 Director Library Services .... Ms. Amy SOLIS
38 Guidance Counselor .... Ms. Colette KEITH
40 Bookstore Manager .... Ms. Iona LITTLE WHITEMAN

*North Dakota University System Office (F)

600 E Boulevard Avenue, Dept 215, Bismarck ND 58505-0230
County: Burleigh FICE Identification: 033434
Telephone: (701) 328-2960 Carnegie Class: N/A
FAX Number: (701) 328-2961
URL: www.ndus.edu

01 Interim Chancellor .... Larry C. SKOGEN
05 Interim Vice Chanc Acad/Stdnt Affs .... Sonia S. COWEN
10 Vice Chanc Administrative Affairs .... Laura GLATT
45 VC of Strategic Engagement .... Linda DONLIN
13 VC for IT & Institutional Research .... Lisa FELDNER
37 Director Financial Aid .... Brenda ZASTOUPIL
20 Dir Acad Pgm Rsrch & Accreditation .... Richard M. ROTHAUS
88 Dir State Approving Agency .... Rhonda SCHAUER
21 Director of Finance .... Cathy MCDONALD
88 Research Analyst .... Jennifer WEBER
100 Chief of Staff/NDUS Ethics Officer .... Murray SAGSVEEN
26 Dir of Communications & Media Rels .... Billie Jo LORIUS
88 Director Financial Reporting .... Robin PUTNAM
106 Exec Dir Acad Tech/Dist Ed & K-12 .... Tanya SPILOVOY
88 Dir Student Entry Trans & Retention .... Lisa JOHNSON
32 Director of Student Affairs .... Becky LAMBOLEY
18 Director Facility Planning .... Rick TONDER

*University of North Dakota (G)

264 Centennial Drive, Grand Forks ND 58202
County: Grand Forks FICE Identification: 003005
Unit ID: 200280
Telephone: (701) 777-2011 Carnegie Class: RU/H
FAX Number: (701) 777-2696 Calendar System: Semester
URL: www.und.edu
Established: 1883 Annual Undergrad Tuition & Fees (In-State): $7,965
Enrollment: 14,906 Coed
Affiliation or Control: State IRS Status: 501(c)3
Highest Offering: Doctorate
Program: Liberal Arts And General; Teacher Preparatory; Professional
Accreditation: NH, AAB, ANEST, ARCPA, ART, BUS, CAATE, CLPSY, COPSY, CS, CYTO, DIETC, ENG, HT, IPSY, LAW, MED, MT, MUS, NAIT, NURSE, OT, PTA, SP, SPAA, SW, TED, THEA

02 President .... Dr. Robert O. KELLEY
29 CEO Alumni Assoc & Foundation .... Ms. Deanna CARLSON ZINK
05 Vice Pres Academic Affairs/Provost .... Dr. Thomas DILORENZO
10 Vice President Operations/Finance .... Ms. Alice BREKKE
32 Vice Pres Student Affairs .... Dr. Lori REESOR
17 Vice President Health Affairs .... Dr. Joshua WYNNE
46 Int VP Research/Economic Devel .... Dr. Barry MILAVETZ
26 VP for University & Public Affairs .... Ms. Susan WALTON
27 Exec Assoc VP University Rels .... Mr. Peter B. JOHNSON
30 Chief Development Officer .... Mr. Dan MUUS
35 Associate VP & Dean of Students .... Dr. Cara HALGREN
21 Assoc VP Finance/Operations .... Ms. Karla MONGEON-STEWART
21 Assoc VP Finance/Operations .... Vacant
45 Assoc Vice Pres Research/Econ Dev .... Dr. Barry MILAVETZ
88 Assoc VP Research/Capacity Building .... Dr. Mark HOFFMANN
25 AVP Intellectual Prop Comm/Econ Dev .... Mr. Michael MOORE
88 Assoc VP for Health & Wellness .... Dr. Laurie BETTING
25 AVP Res & Econ Dev/Grants/Contracts .... Mr. David O. SCHMIDT
20 Asst VP Student Academic Services .... Ms. Lisa BURGER
07 Asst VP Enrollment Services .... Mr. Sol JENSEN
88 Vice Prov & Chief Strategy Officer .... Dr. Joshua RIEDY
20 Assoc VP for Academic Affairs .... Dr. Steven LIGHT
28 Assoc VP Diversity & Inclusion .... Ms. Sandra MITCHELL
27 Dir Branding & Campus Client Svcs .... Ms. Susan CARAHER
08 Dean of Libraries & Info Res .... Vacant
06 Registrar .... Dr. Suzanne ANDERSON
15 Dir Human Resources/Payroll Svcs .... Ms. Patricia HANSON
19 AVP Public Safety/Police Chief .... Mr. Eric PLUMMER
38 Director Counseling Center .... Dr. Kenneth CARLSON
36 Director Career Services .... Ms. Ilene ODEGARD
20 Director Instructional Development .... Dr. Anne KELSCH
22 Director EEO/Affirmative Action .... Ms. Donna SMITH
37 Director Student Financial Aid .... Ms. Janelle KILGORE
39 Exec Director Housing & Dining .... Ms. Connie FRAZIER
23 Director of Student Health .... Ms. Michelle D. ESLINGER-SCHNEIDER
43 General Counsel .... Ms. Julie EVANS
41 Director Athletics .... Mr. Brian FAISON
18 AVP for Facilities Management .... Mr. Dave CHAKRABORTY
85 Director International Programs .... Mr. Ray LAGASSE
21 Controller .... Ms. Sharon LOILAND
88 Director Judicial Affs/Crisis Pgm .... Mr. Alex POKORNAWSKI
09 Director of Institutional Research .... Ms. Carmen WILLIAMS
94 Director Women's Center .... Ms. Kay MENDICK
96 Director Purchasing .... Ms. Jana THOMPSON
92 Director Honors Program .... Dr. Sally PYLE
28 Dir Multicultural Student Services .... Dr. Malika CARTER
21 Budget Manager .... Ms. Cindy FETSCH
40 Manager University Bookstore .... Ms. Marie MACK
49 Dean of Arts & Sciences .... Dr. Debbie STORRS
58 Int Dean School of Graduate Studies .... Dr. Wayne SWISHER
61 Dean School of Law .... Ms. Kathryn RAND
66 Dean Col Nursing/Profess Discip .... Dr. Gayle ROUX
50 Dean Business/Public Administration .... Dr. Margaret WILLIAMS
54 Dean College of Engr/Mines .... Dr. Hesham EL-REWINI
53 Dean Col Education/Human Devel .... Dr. Robert HILL
88 Dean of Aerospace Sciences .... Dr. Bruce SMITH
63 Dean Sch Medicine/Health Science .... Dr. Joshua WYNNE
88 Dir American Indian Student Svcs .... Dr. Leigh JEANOTTE
35 Asst Dean Stdnt Involvement/Ldrshp .... Dr. Cassie GERHARDT
88 Int Director Memorial Union .... Dr. Cassie GERHARDT
88 Director Wellness Center .... Ms. Jenn PUHL WINKLER
88 Dir Health & Wellness Promotions .... Ms. Jane CROEKER
88 Director Dining Services .... Mr. Orlynn ROSAASEN
88 Dir Children's Learning Center .... Ms. Dawnita NILLES
88 Dir Student Affairs Technology .... Ms. Michelle RAKOCZY
88 Dir Disability Svcs for Students .... Ms. Debrah GLENNEN
88 Director TRIO Programs .... Mr. Derek SPORBERT
27 Director Student Affairs Marketing .... Ms. Sarah NISSEN
88 Dir One Stop Student Serv .... Mr. Joshua LINDENBERG
07 Director Admissions .... Mr. Jason TRAINER

*Dickinson State University (H)

291 Campus Drive, Dickinson ND 58601-4896
County: Stark FICE Identification: 002989
Unit ID: 200059

Telephone: (701) 483-2507 Carnegie Class: Bac/Diverse
FAX Number: (701) 483-2006 Calendar System: Semester
URL: www.dickinsonstate.edu
Established: 1918 Annual Undergrad Tuition & Fees (In-State): $6,172
Enrollment: 1,479 Coed
Affiliation or Control: State IRS Status: 501(c)3
Highest Offering: Baccalaureate
Program: Liberal Arts And General; Teacher Preparatory
Accreditation: NH, IACBE, MUS, NUR, PNUR, TED

02 President .... Dr. D.C COSTON
05 Provost/Vice Pres Academic Affairs .... Dr. Cynthia PEMBERTON
10 VP for Finance & Administration .... Mr. Mark LOWE
32 VP for Student Affairs & Enrollment .... Ms. Melanie TUCKER
49 Dean of Arts & Sciences .... Dr. Kenneth HAUGHT
53 Dean of Educ/Business/Applied Sci .... Dr. Dawn OLSON
102 Exec Dir Alumni Assoc/Foundation .... Vacant
84 Exec Dir Enrollment & Communication .... Ms. Marie MOE
41 Director of Intercollege Athletics .... Mr. Tim DANIEL
88 Strom Ctr for Entrpshp & Ino .... Ms. Ray Ann KILEN
56 Asst Director of Extended Learning .... Mr. Anthony WILLER
12 Asst Director of DSU Bismarck .... Vacant
06 Director of Academic Records .... Ms. Kathy MEYER
08 Director of Library Services .... Ms. Mary SHEAHAN
13 Director of Information Technology .... Mr. Todd HAUF
37 Director of Financial Aid .... Ms. Sandy L. KLEIN
88 Asst Director Academic Success Ctr .... Ms. Jennifer WITHERS
88 Director of Food Service .... Mr. Jason BENSON
40 Manager University Store .... Ms. Loretta A. HEIDT
21 Controller .... Ms. Janet REISENAUER
36 Director of Career Services .... Vacant
09 Coordinator of Institutional Rsrch .... Dr. Chris P. BELCHER
85 Associate Dir International Program .... Ms. Perzen POLISHWALLA
39 Housing Coordinator .... Ms. Jenna WILLIAMSON
15 Coordinator of Human Resources .... Ms. Gail EBELTOFT
04 Administrative Asst to President .... Ms. Kari HANSTAD
18 Chief Facilities/Physical Plant .... Mr. Mick RIESINGER
19 Director Security/Safety .... Mr. Jack SCHULZ
22 Dir Affirmative Action/EEO .... Dr. Christopher BELCHER
26 Chief Public Relations/Marketing .... Vacant

*Mayville State University (A)

330 3rd Street, NE, Mayville ND 58257-1299
County: Traill FICE Identification: 002993
Unit ID: 200226
Telephone: (701) 788-2301 Carnegie Class: Bac/Diverse
FAX Number: (701) 788-4748 Calendar System: Semester
URL: www.mayvillestate.edu
Established: 1889 Annual Undergrad Tuition & Fees (In-State): $6,380
Enrollment: 1,081 Coed
Affiliation or Control: State IRS Status: 501(c)3
Highest Offering: Baccalaureate
Program: 2-Year Principally Bachelor's Creditable; Liberal Arts And General; Teacher Preparatory; Business Emphasis
Accreditation: NH, TED

02 President .... Dr. Gary D. HAGEN
04 Exec Assistant to the President .... Ms. Mary L. TRUDEAU
05 Vice President for Academic Affairs .... Dr. Keith A. STENEHJEM
10 Vice President for Business Affairs .... Mr. Steven P. BENSEN
32 VP for Student Affairs/Inst Rsrch .. Dr. Raymond H. GERSZEWSKI
41 Athletic Director .... Mr. Mike K. MOORE
102 Executive Foundation Director .... Mr. John J. KLOCKE
26 Chief Public Relations Officer .... Ms. Beth I. SWENSON
07 Director of Admissions & Ext Lrng .... Ms. Misti L. WUORI
06 Registrar .... Ms. Pamela K. BRAATEN
37 Director of Financial Aid .... Ms. Shirley M. HANSON
84 Director of Enrollment Services .... Mr. James R. MOROWSKI
08 Director of Library Services .... Ms. Kelly J. KORNKVEN
35 Director of Student Life .... Mr. Matthew M. NELSON
40 Director of Bookstore .... Ms. Pam B. SOHOLT
18 Director of Physical Plant .... Mr. Dan P. LORENZ
18 Director of Facilities Services .... Mr. Bob J. KOZOJED
15 Director of Human Resources .... Mr. Noah M. FISCHER
13 Director of Information Technology .... Mr. Patrick W. STEELE
14 Director of Computer Center .... Mr. Shawn D. OGBURN
21 Controller .... Ms. Laura M. NELSON
38 Director of Counseling .... Ms. Kristi L. LENTZ
88 Director Student Success/Disability .... Ms. Katie J. RICHARDS
108 Director of Academic Assessment .... Dr. Mark E. SKEAN
25 Director of Grants Office .... Ms. Allison JOHNSON
28 Director of Diversity .... Vacant
36 Dir Career Services & Internships .... Mr. Jay A. HENRICKSON

*Minot State University (B)

500 University Avenue W, Minot ND 58707-0001
County: Ward FICE Identification: 002994
Unit ID: 200253
Telephone: (701) 858-3000 Carnegie Class: Master's M
FAX Number: (701) 839-6933 Calendar System: Semester
URL: www.minotstateu.edu
Established: 1913 Annual Undergrad Tuition & Fees (In-State): $6,391
Enrollment: 3,410 Coed
Affiliation or Control: State IRS Status: 501(c)3
Highest Offering: Beyond Master's But Less Than Doctorate
Program: Liberal Arts And General; Teacher Preparatory; Professional; Business Emphasis
Accreditation: NH, CAATE, IACBE, MUS, NUR, SP, SW, TED

02 President .... Dr. Steven SHIRLEY
05 VP for Academic Affairs .... Dr. Lenore KOCZON
10 Vice President for Finance/Admin .... Mr. Brian FOISY
30 Vice President for Advancement .... Mr. Marv SEMRAU
32 Vice President for Student Affairs .... Mr. Kevin HARMON
21 AVP Business Services/Controller .... Ms. Jonelle WATSON
07 Admissions .... Ms. Katie TYLER
18 Facilities Management .... Mr. Brian SMITH
06 Registrar .... Ms. Rebecca PORTER
08 Director of the Library .... Mr. Stephen BANISTER
35 Director of Student Life .... Ms. Lisa ERIKSMOEN
37 Director of Financial Aid .... Ms. Laurie WEBER
58 Asst Dean of Graduate School .... Dr. Lorraine WILLOUGHBY
50 Dean College of Business .... Dr. Jacek MROZIK
49 Dean College Arts & Science .... Dr. Conrad DAVIDSON
53 Dean Col Education/Health Sci .... Dr. Cheryl NILSEN
51 Dean Continuing Education .... Dr. Kristin WARMOTH
29 Director Alumni Relations .... Ms. Janna MCKECHNIE
13 Director Computer Services .... Mr. George WITHUS
40 Director Bookstore .... Ms. Gerri KUNA
41 Athletic Director .... Mr. Rick HEDBERG
26 Director of Public Information .... Ms. Alysia HUCK
15 Director of Human Resources .... Mr. Wesley MATTHEWS
12 Dean of Dakota College at Bottineau .... Vacant
36 Director of Campus Career Services .... Ms. Lynda BERTSCH
25 Grants & Contracts Accountant .... Ms. Sheila LATHAM
09 Director of Institutional Research .... Ms. Cari OLSON
04 Administrative Asst to President .... Ms. Deb WENTZ
39 Director Student Housing .... Mr. Devin MCCALL
27 Director of Marketing .... Ms. Teresa LOFTESNES
104 Director International Programs .... Ms. Libby CLAERBOUT
19 Director Security/Safety .... Mr. Gary ORLUCK

*North Dakota State University Main Campus (C)

P.O. Box 6050, Fargo ND 58108-6050
County: Cass FICE Identification: 002997
Unit ID: 200332
Telephone: (701) 231-8011 Carnegie Class: RU/VH
FAX Number: (701) 231-8722 Calendar System: Semester
URL: www.ndsu.edu
Established: 1890 Annual Undergrad Tuition & Fees (In-State): $7,978
Enrollment: 14,747 Coed
Affiliation or Control: State IRS Status: 501(c)3
Highest Offering: Doctorate
Program: Liberal Arts And General; Teacher Preparatory; Professional
Accreditation: NH, ART, BUS, CAATE, CACREP, CIDA, COARC, CONST, DIETC, DIETD, ENG, EXSC, LSAR, MFCD, MUS, NURSE, PHAR, TED, THEA

02 President .... Dr. Dean BRESCIANI
05 Provost/Vice Pres Academic Affairs .... Dr. Beth INGRAM
10 Vice President Business & Finance .... Mr. Bruce BOLLINGER
32 Vice President for Student Affairs .... Dr. Timothy ALVAREZ
46 Vice Pres Research Crea Act & Tech .... Dr. Kelly RUSCH
88 Vice President Ag/Univ Extension .... Dr. Ken GRAFTON
30 Int Pres/CEO Dev/Fdn/Alum Assn .... Mr. Keith BJERKE
13 VP Information Technology .... Mr. Marc WALLMAN
22 VP Equity/Diversity/Global Outreach .... Mrs. Eveadean MYERS
84 Dean of Enrollment Management .... Ms. Laura OSTER-AALAND
88 Assoc VP Sponsored Programs Admin .... Ms. Valrey V. KETTNER
06 University Registrar .... Ms. Rhonda KITCH
88 Director Student Affairs Admin Sys .... Mr. Viet DOAN
08 Dean of Libraries .... Ms. Bridget BURKE
35 Dean Student Life .... Ms. Janna M. STOSKOPF
51 Int Dir Distance/Continuing Ed .... Mr. Paul KELTER
37 Director Student Financial Services .... Mr. Jeff JACOBS
36 Director Career Center .... Ms. Jill J. WILKEY
26 Communication Coordinator .... Ms. Ann ROBINSON-PAUL
88 Assoc VP University Relations .... Ms. Laura MCDANIEL
56 Director Extension Service .... Mr. Chris BOERBOOM
50 Interim Dean Business .... Dr. Jane SCHUH
54 Dean Engineering/Architecture .... Dr. Gary R. SMITH
59 Dean Human Development & Education .... Dr. Virginia L. CLARK JOHNSON
49 Dean Arts/Humanities/Social Science .... Dr. Kent SANDSTROM
81 Dean of Science & Math .... Dr. Scott WOOD
67 Dean of Pharmacy/Nursing/Allied Sci .... Dr. Charles D. PETERSON
58 Dean Graduate School .... Dr. David A. WITTROCK
89 Assoc Dean University Studies .... Dr. Carolyn A. SCHNELL
21 Director of Budget .... Ms. Cynthia ROTT
25 Manager Grant & Contract Acctng .... Ms. Karen HENDRICKSON
18 Director Facilities Management .... Mr. Mike ELLINGSON
19 Dir of Univ Police/Safety Officer .... Mr. Mike BORR
38 Director Counseling/Disability Svcs .... Dr. William BURNS
23 Director Wellness Center .... Mr. Jobey LICHTBLAU
39 Director of Residence Life .... Mr. Rian NOSTRUM
40 Director Bookstore .... Ms. Carol J. MILLER
41 Director of Athletics .... Mr. Matt LARSEN
57 Director Fine Arts .... Dr. E. John MILLER
09 Int Dir Inst Research/Analysis .... Ms. Emily BERG
96 Director of Purchasing .... Ms. Stacey O. WINTER
07 Interim Director of Admissions .... Ms. Merideth SHERLIN
04 Executive Asst to President .... Ms. Barb PEDERSON
108 Dir Accred/Assessment/Acad Advising .... Dr. Larry PETERSON
15 Director HR/Payroll .... Ms. Colette ERICKSON

*Valley City State University (D)

101 College Street, SW, Valley City ND 58072-4098
County: Barnes FICE Identification: 003008
Unit ID: 200572
Telephone: (701) 845-7122 Carnegie Class: Bac/Diverse
FAX Number: (701) 845-7104 Calendar System: Semester
URL: www.vcsu.edu
Established: 1889 Annual Undergrad Tuition & Fees (In-State): $6,798
Enrollment: 1,378 Coed
Affiliation or Control: State IRS Status: 501(c)3
Highest Offering: Master's
Program: Liberal Arts And General; Teacher Preparatory
Accreditation: NH, MUS, TED

02 President .... Dr. Tisa MASON
10 Vice President Business Affairs .... Mr. Doug DAWES
32 Vice President Student Affairs .... Vacant
53 Dean Sch of Educ/Graduate Stds .... Dr. Gary THOMPSON
08 Library Director .... Ms. Donna JAMES
05 Director Student Academic Services .... Mr. John ANDRICK
37 Director Student Financial Aid .... Ms. Betty A. SCHUMACHER
36 Director Career Services .... Ms. Marcia J. FOSS
13 Chief Information Officer .... Mr. Joseph TYKWINSKI
41 Athletic Director .... Mr. Jack DENHOLM
84 Director of Enrollment Services .... Ms. Charlene STENSON
30 Director of University Advancement .... Mr. Larry J. ROBINSON
18 Director of Facilities Services .... Mr. Ron POMMERER
15 Director of Human Resources .... Ms. Jennifer LARSON
44 Asst Dir Univ Advance/Alumni Rels .... Ms. Kim HESCH
38 Director of Student Counseling .... Ms. Erin KLINGENBERG
26 Director Marketing/Communications .... Mr. Greg VANNEY
40 Director Bookstore .... Mr. Todd ROGELSTAD
06 Registrar .... Ms. Jody KLIER
09 Dir Institutional Rsch/Assessment .... Mr. Gregory CARLSON
28 Dir of Diversity & Stdnt Success .... Dr. Nadja JOHNSON

*Bismarck State College (E)

PO Box 5587, Bismarck ND 58506-5587
County: Burleigh FICE Identification: 002988
Unit ID: 200022
Telephone: (701) 224-5400 Carnegie Class: Assoc/Pub4
FAX Number: (701) 224-5550 Calendar System: Semester
URL: bismarckstate.edu
Established: 1939 Annual Undergrad Tuition & Fees (In-State): $3,843
Enrollment: 4,002 Coed
Affiliation or Control: State IRS Status: 501(c)3
Highest Offering: Baccalaureate
Program: Occupational; 2-Year Principally Bachelor's Creditable; Liberal Arts And General
Accreditation: NH, EMT, ENGT, MLTAD, PHLEB, SURGT

02 President .... Dr. Larry C. SKOGEN
03 Executive Vice President .... Mr. Dave CLARK
05 Provost/VP Academic Affairs .... Dr. Drake CARTER
30 VP College Advance/Exec Dir Found .... Mr. Gordy BINEK
88 VP National Energy Ctr of Excellenc .... Ms. Kari KNUDSON
32 Associate VP for Student Affairs .... Dr. Donna FISHBECK
10 Assoc VP Finance/Operations .... Ms. Tamara BARBER
88 Assoc VP Nat Energy Ctr of Excell .... Mr. Bruce EMMIL
51 Assoc VP Cont Educ/Training & Innov .... Ms. Carla HIXSON
20 Dean of Academic Affairs .... Mr. Dan LEINGANG
15 Chief Human Resources Officer .... Ms. Rita LINDGREN
13 Chief Information Officer .... Mr. Elmer WEIGEL
09 Chief Inst Effect/Strat Plan Office .... Dr. Stacie IKEN
106 Chief Dist Learning/Military Affair .... Mr. Lane HUBER
18 Chief Buildings/Grounds Officer .... Mr. Don ROETHLER
08 Director of Library Services .... Ms. Marlene ANDERSON
26 Director of College Relations .... Ms. Marnie PIEHL
41 Director of Athletics .... Mr. Buster GILLISS
37 Director of Financial Aid .... Mr. Scott LINGEN
07 Dir Admissions/Enrollment Services .... Ms. Karen ERICKSON
88 Dir Great Plains Energy Corridor .... Ms. Emily MCKAY
35 Director Student & Residence Life .... Ms. Heather SHEEHAN
06 Director Academic Records/Registrar .... Mr. Tom LENO
36 Dir Couseling and Advising Services .... Mr. Jay MEIER
88 Program Manager NECE .... Mr. Dan SCHMIDT
88 Project Manager NECE .... Mr. Zachery ALLEN
88 Program Manager NECE .... Mr. Ryan CAYA
88 Training & Program Manager NECE .... Ms. Alicia UHDE
88 Program Manager NECE .... Mr. Kyren MILLER
46 Resource Development Manager .... Ms. Janet DIXON
44 Development Manager .... Vacant
29 Alumni Coordinator .... Ms. Rita NODLAND
40 Bookstore Manager/Purchasing Coord .... Ms. Debra SANDNESS
04 Executive Assistant to President .... Ms. Debbie VAN BERKOM
19 Campus Safety & Security Manager .... Mr. Duane JOHNSON

*Dakota College at Bottineau (F)

105 Simrall Boulevard, Bottineau ND 58318-1198
County: Bottineau FICE Identification: 002995
Unit ID: 200314
Telephone: (701) 228-2277 Carnegie Class: Assoc/Pub2in4
FAX Number: (701) 228-5468 Calendar System: Semester
URL: www.dakotacollege.edu
Established: 1906 Annual Undergrad Tuition & Fees (In-State): $4,181
Enrollment: 753 Coed
Affiliation or Control: State IRS Status: 501(c)3
Highest Offering: Associate Degree
Program: Occupational; 2-Year Principally Bachelor's Creditable
Accreditation: NH

02 Campus Dean .... Dr. Ken GROSZ
10 Director of Business Affairs .... Ms. Laura PFEIFER
32 Assoc Dean for Student Affairs .... Mr. Dan DAVIS
05 Assoc Dean for Academic Affairs .... Mr. Larry BROOKS
08 Librarian .... Ms. Hattie ALBERTSON
07 Director of Admissions .... Vacant

06 Registrar ... Mr. Dan DAVIS
37 Director Financial Aid ... Ms. Valerie HEILMAN
41 Athletic Director ... Mr. Brandon COLVIN
29 Director Alumni Relations ... Ms. Courtney VANDAL
39 Housing Director ... Ms. Michelle DAVIS
28 Director of Diversity ... Mr. Marcus JOHNSON
40 Bookstore Manager ... Ms. Janeen POLLMAN
18 Chief Facilities/Physical Plant ... Mr. Darrell WATERS
38 Director Student Counseling ... Ms. Corey GORDER

*Lake Region State College (A)

1801 College Drive N, Devils Lake ND 58301-1598

County: Ramsey | FICE Identification: 002991
Unit ID: 200192
Telephone: (701) 662-1600 | Carnegie Class: Assoc/Pub-R-M
FAX Number: (701) 662-1570 | Calendar System: Semester
URL: www.lrsc.edu
Established: 1941 | Annual Undergrad Tuition & Fees (In-State): $4,138
Enrollment: 1,989 | Coed
Affiliation or Control: State | IRS Status: 501(c)3
Highest Offering: Associate Degree
Program: Occupational; 2-Year Principally Bachelor's Creditable
Accreditation: NH

02 President ... Dr. Douglas D. DARLING
05 VP Academic/Student Affairs ... Mr. Lloyd HALVORSON
10 VP Administrative Affairs ... Mr. Corry G. KENNER
12 Director of Branch Campus ... Mr. John COWGER
30 Vice Pres Advancment/Foundation ... Ms. Laurel GOULDING
84 Director of Enrollment Management ... Ms. Stephanie SHOCK
37 Dir Student Finan Aid/Placemnt Svcs ... Ms. Katie NETTELL
88 Director Food Service ... Ms. Rosalie SEIBEL
18 Superintendent Buildings/Grounds ... Mr. Chad ESTENSON
08 Librarian ... Ms. Celeste ERTELT
41 Director Athletics ... Mr. Daniel MERTENS
13 Chief Information Officer ... Ms. Toofawn SIMHAI
15 Human Relations Risk Management ... Mrs. Sandi LILLEHAUGEN
40 Director of Bookstore ... Ms. Melissa STOTTS
06 Registrar ... Mr. Daniel JOHNSON
26 Director of Public Relations/Mktg ... Ms. Erin WOOD
31 Director Community Education ... Ms. Edith ARMEY
09 Director of Institutional Research ... Ms. Brandi NELSON
28 Director of Diversity ... Mrs. Kristi HERNANDEZ
38 Director Counseling Services ... Ms. Brigitte FRESCHETTE
07 Director of Admissions ... Ms. Stephanie SHOCK
21 Controller ... Ms. Joann KITCHENS
04 Administrative Asst to President ... Ms. Bobbi J. LUNDAY
29 Director Alumni Relations ... Mrs. Laurel GOULDING
39 Director Student Housing ... Dr. Randall FIXEN

*North Dakota State College of Science (B)

800 N Sixth Street, Wahpeton ND 58076-0002

County: Richland | FICE Identification: 002996
Unit ID: 200305
Telephone: (800) 342-4325 | Carnegie Class: Assoc/Pub-R-M
FAX Number: (701) 671-2145 | Calendar System: Semester
URL: www.ndscs.edu
Established: 1903 | Annual Undergrad Tuition & Fees (In-State): $4,571
Enrollment: 3,033 | Coed
Affiliation or Control: State | IRS Status: 501(c)3
Highest Offering: Associate Degree
Program: Occupational; 2-Year Principally Bachelor's Creditable
Accreditation: NH, CAHIIM, DA, DH, EMT, OTA, PNUR

02 President ... Dr. John RICHMAN
05 VP Academic & Student Affairs ... Mr. Harvey LINK
10 Vice Pres Administrative Affairs ... Mr. Dennis GLADEN
09 AVP Stdt Success/Inst Effectiveness ... Mrs. Jane VANGSNESS FRISCH
32 Assoc Vice Pres Acad/Student Affs ... Dr. Philip PARNELL
37 Director Financial Aid ... Mrs. Shelley BLOME
08 Director Library ... Ms. Tina GRENIER
26 Dir Marketing/Communications/PR ... Mrs. Barbara SPAETH-BAUM
29 Int Exec Dir of Alumni Foundation ... Mrs. Kim NELSON
41 Athletic Director ... Mr. Stuart ENGEN
15 Int Exec Dir Human Resources ... Mr. Dennis GLADEN
18 Director Facilities/Physical Plant ... Mr. Dallas FOSSUM
20 Academic Services Director ... Ms. Maria KADUC
39 Director of Residence Life ... Mrs. Melissa JOHNSON
07 Director of Admissions & Records ... Mrs. Barb MUND
21 Business Manager ... Mr. Keith JOHNSON
24 Instructional Technology Coord ... Mr. Tom HICKMAN
06 Asst Director Admissions & Records ... Mr. Justin GRAMS
38 Counseling Center ... Mr. Vince PLUMMER
49 Dean Arts Sciences/Business ... Mr. Ken KOMPELIEN
72 Dean Technology/Services Division ... Mrs. Barbara BANG
64 Director of Music ... Ms. Laurie LEKANG
56 Dean of Extended Learning ... Mrs. Patricia SCHROM
88 Dean of College Outreach ... Mrs. Patricia KLINE

*Williston State College (C)

1410 University Avenue, Williston ND 58801-1326

County: Williams | FICE Identification: 003007
Unit ID: 200341
Telephone: (701) 774-4200 | Carnegie Class: Assoc/Pub-R-S
FAX Number: (701) 774-4211 | Calendar System: Semester
URL: www.willistonstate.edu
Established: 1961 | Annual Undergrad Tuition & Fees (In-State): $4,445
Enrollment: 883 | Coed
Affiliation or Control: State | IRS Status: 501(c)3
Highest Offering: Associate Degree
Program: Occupational; 2-Year Principally Bachelor's Creditable
Accreditation: NH

02 President ... Dr. Raymond NADOLNY
05 Vice President Academic Affairs ... Dr. John MILLER
26 VP College Advancement ... Vacant
32 Vice President Student Affairs ... Kaylyn BONDY
10 Chief Financial Officer ... Laurie FURUSETH
103 CEO of Workforce Education Train ... Deanette PIESIK
21 Director for Financial Services ... Cynthia PROM

Rasmussen College - Bismarck (D)

1701 East Century Avenue, Bismarck ND 58503

Telephone: (701) 530-9600 | Identification: 666301
Accreditation: &NH, MAAB

† Regional accreditation carried under the parent institution in Saint Cloud, MN. The tuition figure is an average, actual tuition may vary.

Rasmussen College - Fargo/Moorhead (E)

4012 19th Avenue, SW, Fargo ND 58103-7196

Telephone: (701) 277-3889 | FICE Identification: 004846
Accreditation: &NH

† Regional accredtiation is carried under parent institution in Saint Cloud, MN. The tuition figure is an average, actual tuition may vary.

Sitting Bull College (F)

9299 Highway 24, Fort Yates ND 58538-9706

County: Sioux | FICE Identification: 021882
Unit ID: 200466
Telephone: (701) 854-8000 | Carnegie Class: Tribal
FAX Number: (701) 854-8197 | Calendar System: Semester
URL: www.sittingbull.edu
Established: 1971 | Annual Undergrad Tuition & Fees: $3,910
Enrollment: 290 | Coed
Affiliation or Control: Tribal Control | IRS Status: 501(c)3
Highest Offering: Master's
Program: Occupational; 2-Year Principally Bachelor's Creditable
Accreditation: NH

01 President ... Dr. Laurel VERMILLION
05 Vice President of Academic Affairs ... Dr. Koreen RESSLER
37 Director Financial Student Aid ... Ms. Donna SEABOY
06 Registrar ... Ms. Melody AZURE
08 Head Librarian ... Mr. Mark HOLMAN
40 Director of Bookstore ... Mrs. Tracy MAHER

Trinity Bible College (G)

50 S 6th Avenue, Ellendale ND 58436-7150

County: Dickey | FICE Identification: 012059
Unit ID: 200484
Telephone: (701) 349-3621 | Carnegie Class: Spec/Faith
FAX Number: (701) 349-5443 | Calendar System: Semester
URL: www.trinitybiblecollege.edu
Established: 1948 | Annual Undergrad Tuition & Fees: $15,506
Enrollment: 230 | Coed
Affiliation or Control: Assemblies Of God Church | IRS Status: 501(c)3
Highest Offering: Master's
Program: 2-Year Principally Bachelor's Creditable; Liberal Arts And General; Teacher Preparatory; Professional; Religious Emphasis
Accreditation: BI

01 President ... Dr. Paul ALEXANDER
05 Vice President of Academic Affairs ... Dr. Stephen CHANDLER
10 Vice President of Administration ... Rev. Winston TITUS
32 Vice President of Student Life ... Rev. Ian O'BRIEN
30 Vice President of Advancement ... Mr. Dan KUNO
58 Director of Graduate School ... Dr. Carol ALEXANDER
06 Academic Registrar ... Mrs. Luanne CHANDLER
35 Associate VP of Student Affairs ... Mrs. Kate BOMMARITO
08 Librarian ... Mrs. Phyllis KUNO
106 Director of Distance Education ... Mr. Daryel ERICKSON
37 Director Student Financial Aid ... Mrs. Mary Ann WHITMAN
13 Director of Computer Services ... Mr. Matthew JOHNSON
108 Director Institutional Assessment ... Mr. Scott TOWNSEND
18 Chief Facilities/Physical Plant ... Mr. Anthony NUBILE
41 Athletic Director ... Mr. Dustin MORGAN
29 Director Alumni Relations ... Mr. Dan KUNO

Turtle Mountain Community College (H)

Box 340, Belcourt ND 58316-0340

County: Rolette | FICE Identification: 023011
Unit ID: 200527
Telephone: (701) 477-7862 | Carnegie Class: Tribal
FAX Number: (701) 477-7870 | Calendar System: Semester
URL: www.tm.edu
Established: 1972 | Annual Undergrad Tuition & Fees: $1,125
Enrollment: 520 | Coed
Affiliation or Control: Independent Non-Profit | IRS Status: 501(c)3
Highest Offering: Baccalaureate
Program: Occupational; 2-Year Principally Bachelor's Creditable; Technical Emphasis
Accreditation: NH, MLTAD, PHLEB

01 President ... Jim L. DAVIS
05 Academic Dean/Dean of Student Affs ... Kellie HALL
37 Director Financial Aid ... Wanda LADUCER
10 Comptroller ... Tracy AZURE
75 Director Vocational/Education ... Sheila TROTTIER
06 Registrar ... Angel GLADUE
36 Career Ladder Coordinator ... Vacant
31 Dir of Community/Adult Education ... Sandra LAROCQUE
07 Director of Admissions ... Joni LAFONTAINE
15 Director Personnel Services ... Holly CAHILL
37 Financial Aid Officer ... Alexsis MARCELLAIS
40 Director of Bookstore ... Laisee ALLERY
18 Chief Facilities/Physical Plant ... Wesley DAVIS
30 Chief Development ... Dave RIPLEY
13 Chief Informational Officer ... Vacant
32 Student Support Services Coord ... Steve DECOTEAU
04 Administrative Asst to President ... Judy A. BELGARDE
101 Secretary of the Institution/Board ... Jackie DE LOS SANTOS
38 Director Student Counseling ... Tammy MORIN
41 Athletic Director ... Ray PARISIEN
09 Director of Institutional Research ... Terri MARTIN-PARISIEN
19 Director Security/Safety ... Wesley DAVIS

United Tribes Technical College (I)

3315 University Drive, Bismarck ND 58504-7596

County: Burleigh | FICE Identification: 022429
Unit ID: 200554
Telephone: (701) 255-3285 | Carnegie Class: Tribal
FAX Number: (701) 530-0605 | Calendar System: Semester
URL: www.uttc.edu
Established: 1969 | Annual Undergrad Tuition & Fees: $5,770
Enrollment: 383 | Coed
Affiliation or Control: Independent Non-Profit | IRS Status: 501(c)3
Highest Offering: Baccalaureate
Program: Occupational; 2-Year Principally Bachelor's Creditable
Accreditation: NH, PNUR

01 President ... Dr. Leander MCDONALD
05 Vice Pres Academic Affairs ... Dr. Lisa AZURE
32 Vice Pres Student Services ... Vacant
11 Vice Pres Campus Services ... Dr. William GOURNEAU
10 Finance Director ... Mrs. Katina DECOTEAU
07 Director of Admissions ... Mr. Donovan LAMBERT
06 Registrar ... Mr. Charles GITTER
15 Director Human Resources ... Mr. Wes LONGFEATHER
84 Director Enrollment Management ... Vacant
41 Athletic Director ... Mr. Hunter BERG
13 Director of IT/Jenzabar Coordinator ... Vacant
19 Director of Safety and Security ... Mr. Joely HEAVY RUNNER
04 Exec Assistant to the President ... Mrs. Charisse FANDRICH
08 Librarian ... Mrs. Charlene WEIS
30 Resources Director ... Mrs. Larretta HALL
37 Director Student Financial Aid ... Mr. Scott SKARRO

University of Jamestown (J)

6000 College Lane, Jamestown ND 58405-0001

County: Stutsman | FICE Identification: 002990
Unit ID: 200156
Telephone: (701) 252-3467 | Carnegie Class: Bac/Diverse
FAX Number: (701) 253-4318 | Calendar System: Semester
URL: www.uj.edu
Established: 1883 | Annual Undergrad Tuition & Fees: $26,730
Enrollment: 963 | Coed
Affiliation or Control: Presbyterian Church (U.S.A.) | IRS Status: 501(c)3
Highest Offering: Doctorate
Program: Liberal Arts And General; Teacher Preparatory; Professional
Accreditation: NH, IACBE, NUR, @PTA

01 President ... Dr. Robert S. BADAL
05 Vice Pres/Dean Academic Affairs ... Dr. Paul OLSON
32 Dean of Students ... Mr. Gary VAN ZINDEREN
11 VP Planning/Administrative Services ... Mr. Thomas R. HECK
03 Executive Vice President ... Ms. Polly J. PETERSON
84 Vice President of Enrollment Mgmt ... Mr. Scott GOPLIN
26 VP for Marketing/Public Relations ... Ms. Tena LAWRENCE
101 Asst to Pres/Secy to Bd of Trustees ... Ms. Erin KLEIN
06 Registrar ... Mr. Michael P. WOODLEY
37 Director of Financial Aid ... Ms. Judy HAGER
08 Librarian ... Mrs. Phyllis K. BRATTON
36 Director Experiential Education ... Vacant
27 Director Information Office ... Ms. Donna SCHMITZ
41 Athletic Director ... Mr. Sean JOHNSON
13 Director Computer Center ... Mr. Tim KACHEL
18 Chief Facilities/Physical Plant ... Mr. Mark KOEPKE
105 Director Web Services ... Vacant
19 Director Security/Safety ... Dr. Peter GROFF
22 Dir Affirmative Action/EEO ... Ms. Becky KNODEL
39 Director Student Housing ... Ms. Jenna BREHM

University of Mary (K)

7500 University Drive, Bismarck ND 58504-9652

County: Burleigh | FICE Identification: 002992
Unit ID: 200217
Telephone: (701) 255-7500 | Carnegie Class: Master's L
FAX Number: (701) 255-7687 | Calendar System: Other
URL: www.umary.edu
Established: 1959 | Annual Undergrad Tuition & Fees: $16,500
Enrollment: 2,809 | Coed
Affiliation or Control: Roman Catholic | IRS Status: 501(c)3
Highest Offering: Doctorate

Program: Liberal Arts And General; Professional
Accreditation: NH, CAATE, COARC, EXSC, IACBE, MUS, NURSE, OT, PTA, SW

01 President ....Msgr. James P. SHEA
03 Executive Vice President ....Mr. Gregory A. VETTER
05 Vice President for Academic Affairs ....Dr. Diane FLADELAND
10 Vice President Financial Affairs ....Mrs. Mary B. HAGER
32 Vice President Student Development ....Dr. Timothy SEAWORTH
30 Vice President Mission Advancement ....Mr. Patrick D. O'MEARA
26 Vice President for Public Affairs ....Mr. Jerome J. RICHTER
06 Registrar ....Mr. Rod SCHEETT
08 Librarian ....Mrs. Cheryl BAILEY
37 Director of Financial Aid ....Mrs. Janell D. THOMAS
07 Director of Admissions ....Mr. Michael MCMAHON
09 Director of Institutional Research ....Mr. Scott J. STAUDINGER
15 Director Human Resources ....Vacant
20 Associate Academic Officer ....Dr. Kimberly MCDOWALL-LONG
18 Chief Facilities/Physical Plant ....Mr. Mark R. STEPHENS

OHIO

AIC College of Design (A)

1171 East Kemper Road, Cincinnati OH 45246-3322
County: Hamilton FICE Identification: 021286
Unit ID: 200624
Telephone: (513) 751-1206 Carnegie Class: Assoc/PrivFP
FAX Number: (513) 751-1209 Calendar System: Semester
URL: www.aic-arts.edu
Established: 1976 Annual Undergrad Tuition & Fees: $23,000
Enrollment: 100 Coed
Affiliation or Control: Proprietary IRS Status: Proprietary
Highest Offering: Baccalaureate
Program: Occupational; 2-Year Principally Bachelor's Creditable; Liberal Arts And General; Fine Arts Emphasis
Accreditation: ACCSC

00 CEO ....Ms. Marion K. ALLMAN
01 President ....Mr. Sean M. MENDELL
07 Director of Admissions ....Ms. Cyndi MENDELL
08 Head Librarian ....Ms. Donna WAKEFIELD
10 Chief Business Officer ....Ms. Laura LEWIS
36 Director Student Placement ....Mr. Dennis GATES
37 Director Student Financial Aid ....Ms. Rita SCHRAND

Allegheny Wesleyan College (B)

2161 Woodsdale Road, Salem OH 44460-8920
County: Columbiana FICE Identification: 034573
Unit ID: 200873
Telephone: (330) 337-6403 Carnegie Class: Spec/Faith
FAX Number: (424) 228-3006 Calendar System: Semester
URL: www.awc.edu
Established: 1956 Annual Undergrad Tuition & Fees: $8,800
Enrollment: 71 Coed
Affiliation or Control: Wesleyan Church IRS Status: 501(c)3
Highest Offering: Baccalaureate
Program: Professional; Religious Emphasis
Accreditation: BI

01 President ....Rev. Daniel R. HARDY, SR.
05 Academic Dean ....Dr. Tony BUCHANAN
10 Business Manager ....Mr. Troy MUIR
32 Dean of Students ....Rev. Timothy FORRIDER
26 Director of Public Relations ....Mr. Tom SANDERS
06 Registrar & Director Admissions ....Mrs. Jeanne ZVARITCH
08 Head Librarian ....Mrs. Alice WEINGARD
37 Financial Aid Administrator ....Mrs. Esther PHELPS
09 Dir of Institutional Effectiveness ....Mrs. Jeanne ZVARITCH
40 Bookstore Manager ....Rev. Daniel R. HARDY
33 Dean of Men ....Rev. Timothy FORRIDER
34 Dean of Women ....Mrs. Holly FORRIDER
07 Director of Admissions ....Mrs. Jeanne ZVARITCH
18 Chief Facilities/Physical Plant ....Mr. Darrin PATTERSON
21 Associate Business Officer ....Mrs. Linda SAY
29 Director Alumni Relations ....Rev. Rocky NEWMAN
35 Director Student Affairs ....Rev. Timothy FORRIDER
38 Director Student Counseling ....Mrs. Kimberly FORD

American Institute of Alternative Medicine (C)

6685 Doubletree Avenue, Columbus OH 43229-1113
County: Franklin FICE Identification: 035344
Unit ID: 441636
Telephone: (614) 825-6255 Carnegie Class: Not Classified
FAX Number: (614) 825-6279 Calendar System: Quarter
URL: www.aiam.edu
Established: 1994 Annual Undergrad Tuition & Fees: $33,880
Enrollment: 315 Coed
Affiliation or Control: Proprietary IRS Status: Proprietary
Highest Offering: Master's
Program: 2-Year Principally Bachelor's Creditable; Professional; Nursing Emphasis
Accreditation: ACCSC, ACUP

01 Campus President ....Mark SULLIVAN
05 Academic Dean ....Dr. Elaine HIATT
32 Dir of Student & Graduate Services ....Linda FLEMING-WILLIS
06 Registrar ....Emily MINNEMA
37 Financial Aid Officer ....Ulrike ROSSER
07 Clinic/Outside Admissions Coord ....Laurel TAYLOR

American National University (D)

4736 Dressler Road NW, Canton OH 44718
Telephone: (330) 492-5300 Identification: 770698
Accreditation: ACICS

† Branch campus of American National University, Salem, VA.

American National University (E)

6871 Steger Drive, Cincinnati OH 45237
Telephone: (513) 761-1291 Identification: 770699
Accreditation: ACICS, MAC, SURGT

† Branch campus of American National University, Salem, VA.

American National University (F)

5665 Forest Hills Boulevard, Columbus OH 43231
Telephone: (614) 212-2800 Identification: 770700
Accreditation: ACICS, CAHIIM, MAC

† Branch campus of American National University, Salem, VA.

American National University (G)

1837 Woodman Center Drive, Kettering OH 45420
Telephone: (937) 299-9450 Identification: 770697
Accreditation: ACICS, CAHIIM, MAC, SURGT

† Branch campus of American National University, Salem, VA.

American National University (H)

3855 Fishcreek Road, Stow OH 44224
Telephone: (330) 676-1351 Identification: 770702
Accreditation: ACICS, MAC, SURGT

† Branch campus of American National University, Salem, VA.

American National University (I)

27557 Chardon Road, Willoughby Hills OH 44092
Telephone: (440) 944-0825 Identification: 770703
Accreditation: ACICS, MAC

† Branch campus of American National University, Salem, VA.

American National University (J)

3487 Belmont Avenue, Youngstown OH 44505
Telephone: (330) 759-0205 Identification: 770701
Accreditation: ACICS, CAHIIM, MAC, SURGT

† Branch campus of American National University, Salem, VA.

Antioch College (K)

One Morgan Place, Yellow Springs OH 45387
County: Greene Identification: 667214
Unit ID: 483018
Telephone: (937) 767-1286 Carnegie Class: Not Classified
FAX Number: N/A Calendar System: Quarter
URL: www.antiochcollege.org
Established: 1853 Annual Undergrad Tuition & Fees: $34,004
Enrollment: 238 Coed
Affiliation or Control: Independent Non-Profit IRS Status: 501(c)3
Highest Offering: Baccalaureate
Program: Liberal Arts And General
Accreditation: @NH

01 President ....Mr. Mark ROOSEVELT
05 Vice Pres Academic Affairs ....Ms. Lori COLLINS-HALL
10 Vice Pres for Finance & Opers ....Ms. Andi ADKINS
26 Vice Pres External Relations ....Ms. Jennifer JOLLS
07 Dean of Admissions ....Mr. Micah CANAL

*Antioch University (L)

900 Dayton Street, Yellow Springs OH 45387-1635
County: Greene FICE Identification: 003010
Unit ID: 442392
Telephone: (937) 769-1351 Carnegie Class: N/A
FAX Number: (937) 769-1350
URL: www.antioch.edu

01 Chancellor ....Ms. Felice NUDELMAN
10 Vice Chancellor/CFO ....Mr. Tim JORDAN
05 Vice Chancellor Academic Affairs ....Dr. Iris WEISMAN
13 Chief Operations Officer ....Dr. Bob DEWITT
15 Chief Human Resources Officer ....Ms. Suzette CASTONGUAY
27 Chief Communications Officer ....Mr. Matt COOKSON
91 Dir Administrative Info Systems ....Ms. Candice SANTELL
04 Executive Asst to the Chancellor ....Ms. Michelle WARD
06 Registrar ....Ms. Maureen HEACOCK
08 Head Librarian ....Mr. Steve SHAW
43 Vice Chancellor/General Counsel ....Mr. William GROVES
30 Vice Chancellor/Inst Advancement ....Mr. Tim FORBESS
101 Secretary to the Board ....Ms. Leslie JOHNSON

† Parent institution of Antioch University Midwest in OH; Antioch University Seattle in WA; Antioch University New England in NH; and Antioch University Los Angeles and Antioch University Santa Barbara in CA.

*Antioch University Midwest (M)

900 Dayton Street, Yellow Springs OH 45387-1745
County: Greene Identification: 666811
Unit ID: 245892
Telephone: (937) 769-1800 Carnegie Class: Master's M
FAX Number: (937) 769-1805 Calendar System: Semester
URL: midwest.antioch.edu/
Established: 1988 Annual Undergrad Tuition & Fees: $13,043
Enrollment: 247 Coed
Affiliation or Control: Independent Non-Profit IRS Status: 501(c)3
Highest Offering: Doctorate
Program: Liberal Arts And General; Teacher Preparatory; Professional; Business Emphasis
Accreditation: NH, TED

02 President ....Dr. Karen SCHUSTER WEBB
05 Chief Academic Officer ....Dr. Marian GLANCY
10 Regional CFO ....Ms. Barbara STEWART
04 Executive Assistant to President ....Ms. Jennifer MAYNARD
84 Enrollment Services Director ....Mr. Arlyn LOVE
37 Assoc Director Financial Aid ....Ms. Tina BUNCH
27 Campus Marketing Manager ....Ms. Kelly LEFF
15 Director Personnel Services ....Ms. Suzette CASTONGUAY
21 Associate Business Officer ....Mr. Kyle FUCHS
62 Library Director ....Dr. Stephen SHAW
06 Registrar ....Dr. Maureen HEACOCK
18 Director Facility Management ....Mr. Ray SIMONELLI
30 Manager Institutional Advancement ....Ms. Rosemary NAULTY
53 Dir Div of Education ....Dr. Michele NOBEL
43 Dir Legal Services/General Counsel ....Mr. William GROVES
101 Secretary of the Institution/Board ....Ms. Jennifer MAYNARD
09 Institutional Research Analyst ....Ms. Sarah WALLIS
19 Director Security/Safety ....Mr. Ray SIMONELLI

Antonelli College (N)

124 E Seventh Street, Cincinnati OH 45202-2592
County: Hamilton FICE Identification: 012891
Unit ID: 201016
Telephone: (800) 505-4338 Carnegie Class: Assoc/PrivFP
FAX Number: (513) 241-9396 Calendar System: Semester
URL: www.antonellicollege.edu
Established: 1947 Annual Undergrad Tuition & Fees: $15,980
Enrollment: 182 Coed
Affiliation or Control: Proprietary IRS Status: Proprietary
Highest Offering: Associate Degree
Program: Occupational
Accreditation: ACCSC

01 Campus President ....Ms. Leah ELKINS
05 Director Of Education ....Ms. Andrea MILLETTE
32 Associate Campus Director ....Mr. Corey BJARNSON
06 Registrar ....Ms. Tashena REED
36 Career Services Coordinator ....Ms. Charlene SMITH

Art Academy of Cincinnati (O)

1212 Jackson Street, Cincinnati OH 45202-7106
County: Hamilton FICE Identification: 003011
Unit ID: 201061
Telephone: (513) 562-6262 Carnegie Class: Spec/Arts
FAX Number: (513) 562-8778 Calendar System: Semester
URL: www.artacademy.edu
Established: 1869 Annual Undergrad Tuition & Fees: $26,908
Enrollment: 196 Coed
Affiliation or Control: Independent Non-Profit IRS Status: 501(c)3
Highest Offering: Master's
Program: Professional; Fine Arts Emphasis
Accreditation: NH, ART

01 President ....Mr. John M. SULLIVAN
05 VP for Academic Affairs/CAO ....Mr. Kimberly G. KRAUSE
10 VP for Finance & Operations/CFO ....Mr. Thomas J. PACK
30 VP of Institutional Advancement ....Ms. Joan KAUP
07 Director of Admissions ....Mr. Joseph FISHER
37 Director of Financial Aid ....Ms. Kristina KILLEN
06 Registrar ....Ms. Sue HUTCHENS
21 Director of Finance ....Ms. Jean SPOHR
18 Director of Facilities and Security ....Mr. Jack HENNEN
32 Director of Student Services ....Mr. Galen CRAWFORD
04 Executive Assistant to President ....Ms. Katie E. DREYER
105 Digital Media Specialist ....Mr. Jimmy BAKER
13 Lead Systems Engineer ....Mr. Kyle GRIZZELL
26 Marketing/Communications Specialist ....Ms. Amanda PARKER-WOLERY

The Art Institute of Ohio-Cincinnati (P)

8845 Governors Hill Drive, Cincinnati OH 45249
Telephone: (513) 833-2400 Identification: 666693
Accreditation: &NH, ACFEI

† Regional accreditation is carried under the parent institution The Illinois Institute of Art, Chicago, IL.

Ashland University (A)

401 College Avenue, Ashland OH 44805
County: Ashland   FICE Identification: 003012
Unit ID: 201104
Telephone: (800) 882-1548   Carnegie Class: DRU
FAX Number: N/A   Calendar System: Semester
URL: www.ashland.edu
Established: 1878   Annual Undergrad Tuition & Fees: $20,242
Enrollment: 5,737   Coed
Affiliation or Control: Brethren Church   IRS Status: 501(c)3
Highest Offering: Doctorate
Program: 2-Year Principally Bachelor's Creditable; Liberal Arts And General; Teacher Preparatory; Professional
Accreditation: NH, ACBSP, CAATE, CACREP, CEA, DIETD, MUS, NURSE, SW, TED, THEOL

01 President .... Dr. Carlos CAMPO
88 President Theological Seminary .... Dr. John C. SHULTZ
05 Interim Provost .... Dr. Douglas FIORE
32 Vice President Student Affairs .... Dr. Hannah CLAYBORNE
30 Vice Pres Development & Inst Advanc ... Mrs. Margaret POMFRET
18 Vice Pres Facilities/Mgmt & Plng .... Mr. Rick M. EWING, II
10 Vice President for Finance & Admin .... Dr. Stephen STORCK
13 Exec Director of IT .... Mr. Bob MATNEY
42 Director of Religious Life .... Mr. Jason BARNHART
06 Registrar .... Mrs. Vicki G. YOHO
37 Director Student Financial Aid .... Mr. Stephen C. HOWELL
29 Director Alumni/Parent Relations .... Mr. Jeff ALIX
15 Director of Human Resources/Legal .... Mr. Joshua A. HUGHES
36 Executive Director Career Services .... Ms. Karen HAGANS
26 Director of Public Relations .... Mr. Steven M. HANNAN
41 Director of Athletics .... Mr. Albert KING
88 Exec Dir Ashbrook Ctr .... Mr. Roger BECKETT
09 Director Inst Research & Assessment .... Mr. Eric A. SPONSELLER
07 Director of Admissions .... Mr. W.C VANCE
49 Dean College of Arts & Sciences .... Dr. Dawn WEBER
73 Dean Theological Seminary .... Dr. Paul CHILCOTE
50 Dean College Business/Econ .... Dr. Jeffery RUSSELL
53 Interim Dean College of Education .... Dr. Linda K. BILLMAN
66 Dean Col Nursing & Health Sci .... Dr. Faye GRUND
51 Dir Founders School of Cont Educ .... Dr. Eugene LINTON
28 Dir Multicultural Stdnt Svcs & Stds .... Mr. Jonathan E. LOCUST, JR.
19 Director Security/Safety .... Mr. David B. MCLAUGHLIN
38 Director of Counseling .... Dr. Oscar MCKNIGHT
44 Director Planned Giving .... Mr. Joseph MACEDO
03 Executive Vice President .... Dr. Scott D. VAN LOO

Athenaeum of Ohio (B)

6616 Beechmont Avenue, Cincinnati OH 45230-5900
County: Hamilton   FICE Identification: 003013
Unit ID: 201140
Telephone: (513) 231-2223   Carnegie Class: Spec/Faith
FAX Number: (513) 231-3254   Calendar System: Semester
URL: www.athenaeum.edu
Established: 1829   Annual Graduate Tuition & Fees: $20,750
Enrollment: 235   Coed
Affiliation or Control: Roman Catholic   IRS Status: 501(c)3
Highest Offering: Master's; No Undergraduates
Program: Professional; Religious Emphasis
Accreditation: NH, THEOL

01 President & Rector .... Rev. Benedict O'CINNSEALAIGH
10 Vice President for Finance .... Mr. Dennis K. EAGAN
30 Vice President for Advancement .... Vacant
05 Dean of Athenaeum .... Rev. Earl K. FERNANDES
08 Librarian .... Mrs. Connie SONG
06 Registrar .... Mr. Michael E. SWEENEY
42 Dir Lay Pastoral Ministry Program .... Dr. Susan MCGURGAN
108 Director of Assessment .... Dr. Tobias NATHE

Aultman College of Nursing and Health Sciences (C)

2600 Sixth Street SW, Canton OH 44710-1799
County: Stark   FICE Identification: 006487
Unit ID: 201177
Telephone: (330) 363-6347   Carnegie Class: Assoc/PrivNFP
FAX Number: (330) 580-6654   Calendar System: Semester
URL: www.aultmancollege.edu
Established: 2004   Annual Undergrad Tuition & Fees: $18,828
Enrollment: 358   Coed
Affiliation or Control: Independent Non-Profit   IRS Status: 501(c)3
Highest Offering: Baccalaureate
Program: 2-Year Principally Bachelor's Creditable; Nursing Emphasis
Accreditation: NH, ADNUR, RAD

01 President .... Ms. Rebecca R. CROWL
10 VP Business & Student Affairs .... Ms. Jeannine SHAMBAUGH
05 Vice President Academic Affairs .... Dr. Jean PADDOCK
09 Director IE and Compliance .... Ms. Lyn SABINO

Baldwin Wallace University (D)

275 Eastland Road, Berea OH 44017-2088
County: Cuyahoga   FICE Identification: 003014
Unit ID: 201195
Telephone: (440) 826-2900   Carnegie Class: Master's L
FAX Number: (440) 826-2329   Calendar System: Semester
URL: www.bw.edu/
Established: 1845   Annual Undergrad Tuition & Fees: $29,908
Enrollment: 3,987   Coed
Affiliation or Control: United Methodist   IRS Status: 501(c)3
Highest Offering: Master's
Program: Liberal Arts And General; Teacher Preparatory; Professional
Accreditation: NH, #ARCPA, CAATE, MUS, NURSE, @SP, TED

01 President .... Dr. Robert C. HELMER
03 Senior Vice President .... Mr. Richard L. FLETCHER
05 Provost .... Dr. Stephen D. STAHL
10 Vice President for Finance & Admin .... Mr. William M. RENIFF
32 VP Student Affairs/Dean of Students .... Dr. Trina DOBBERSTEIN
84 Vice Pres of Enrollment Management .... Mr. Scott SCHULZ
26 Asst VP/Director College Relations .... Vacant
20 Associate Provost .... Dr. Guy E. FARISH
35 Director of Student Success .... Mr. Marc ADKINS
51 Director of Adult Learning .... Ms. Nancy JIROUSEK
08 Director of Ritter Library .... Mr. John DIGENNARO
13 Chief Information Officer .... Mr. Greg G. FLANIK
44 Director Annual Giving .... Ms. Aimee BELL
29 Director Alumni Relations .... Mr. Terry J. KURTZ
30 Senior Advancement Officer .... Ms. Deborah S. MILLER
37 Director of Financial Aid .... Dr. George ROLLESTON
15 Asst VP for Human Resources .... Mr. Sam RAMIREZ
38 Director of Counseling Services .... Ms. Joy D. WYATT
36 Director of Academic Advising .... Ms. Margaret STINER
06 Registrar .... Ms. Linda L. YOUNG
07 Interim Dir Undergraduate Admission .... Ms. Winifred W. GERHARDT
88 Dir of Adult/Cont Educ Admission .... Ms. Winifred GERHARDT
18 Director of Buildings & Grounds .... Mr. William KERBUSCH
88 Director of Intercultural Education .... Dr. Judith B. KRUTKY
96 Director of Purchasing .... Ms. Karen STENGER
28 Director Campus Diversity Affairs .... Mr. Charles HARKNESS
04 Administrative Asst to President .... Ms. Kimberlee A. KUHAJDA
09 Director of Institutional Research .... Ms. Susan T. WARNER
104 Director Study Abroad .... Ms. Christy L. SHREFLER
39 Director Student Housing .... Mr. Robin W. GAGNOW

Beckfield College (E)

225 Pictoria Drive Suite 200, Cincinnati OH 45246
Telephone: (513) 671-1920   Identification: 666673
Accreditation: ACICS

† Branch campus of Beckfield College, Florence, KY.

Belmont College (F)

68094 Hammond Road, Saint Clairsville OH 43950-9766
County: Belmont   FICE Identification: 009941
Unit ID: 201283
Telephone: (740) 695-9500   Carnegie Class: Assoc/Pub-R-M
FAX Number: (740) 695-2247   Calendar System: Semester
URL: www.belmontcollege.edu
Established: 1969   Annual Undergrad Tuition & Fees (In-State): $4,409
Enrollment: 1,000   Coed
Affiliation or Control: State   IRS Status: 501(c)3
Highest Offering: Associate Degree
Program: Occupational; 2-Year Principally Bachelor's Creditable; Technical Emphasis
Accreditation: NH, MAC

01 President .... Dr. Paul GASPARRO
05 VP of Learning & Student Success .... Dr. Rebecca KURTZ
11 Vice Pres of Administrative Affairs .. Mr. John S. KOUCOUMARIS
32 Dean of Student Services .... Mr. Tim HOUSTON
18 Director of Facilities Management .... Mr. Steve MORGAN
06 Registrar .... Ms. Jennifer NIPPERT
15 Vice President of HR & Org Dev .... Mr. Matt KENDALL
37 Assoc Dean of Financial Aid .... Ms. Alicia FREY
88 Dir Teaching and Learning .... Mrs. Amy LEONI
36 Transfer/Articulat/Academic Advisor .... Ms. Jane BLACK
13 Exec Dir of Information Services .... Mr. Troy CALDWELL
30 Vice President of Advancement & Mkt .... Mr. RJ KONKOLESKI
04 Asst to President .... Ms. Kristy KOSKY
19 Director Security/Safety .... Mr. Glenn TRUDO
26 Public Relations Coordinator .... Ms. Julie MAMIE

Bexley Seabury (G)

583 Sheridan Avenue, Columbus OH 43209
County: Franklin   FICE Identification: 037473
Unit ID: 443702
Telephone: (614) 231-3095   Carnegie Class: Spec/Faith
FAX Number: (614) 231-3236   Calendar System: Semester
URL: www.bexleyseabury.edu
Established: 1824   Annual Graduate Tuition & Fees: $14,890
Enrollment: 12   Coed
Affiliation or Control: Independent Non-Profit   IRS Status: 501(c)3
Highest Offering: Master's; No Undergraduates
Program: Religious Emphasis
Accreditation: THEOL

01 President .... Rev. Roger A. FERLO
05 VP Academic Affairs/Academic Dean .Rev. Thomas C. FERGUSON
10 Director of Finance .... Mr. Robert DOAK

Bluffton University (H)

1 University Drive, Bluffton OH 45817-2104
County: Allen   FICE Identification: 003016
Unit ID: 201371
Telephone: (419) 358-3000   Carnegie Class: Bac/Diverse
FAX Number: (419) 358-3323   Calendar System: Semester
URL: www.bluffton.edu
Established: 1899   Annual Undergrad Tuition & Fees: $29,718
Enrollment: 1,094   Coed
Affiliation or Control: Mennonite Church   IRS Status: 501(c)3
Highest Offering: Master's
Program: Liberal Arts And General; Teacher Preparatory; Business Emphasis
Accreditation: NH, DIETD, MUS, SW, TED

01 President .... Dr. James M. HARDER
10 Vice President for Fiscal Affairs .... Mr. Kevin A. NICKEL
30 Vice President for Inst Advancement .... Dr. Hans HOUSHOWER
05 Vice Pres & Dean Academic Affairs .... Dr. Sally W. SOMMER
84 VP for Enrollment Management/Mktg .... Mr. Ronald HEADINGS
32 VP for Student Life/Dean of Stdnts .... Dr. Julie DEGRAW
21 Chief Business Officer .... Mr. Richard LICHTLE
08 Director of Libraries .... Ms. Mary Jean JOHNSON
06 Registrar .... Ms. Iris NEUFELD
26 Chief Public Relations Officer .... Mrs. Robin BOWLUS
29 Dir of Alumni Relations/Annual Giv .... Mrs. Julia SZABO
07 Director of UG Admissions .... Mr. Derek STEMEN
18 Director Building/Grounds .... Mr. Mustaq AHMED
15 Director Human Resources .... Mr. Scott A. SHARIK
04 Administrative Asst to President .... Ms. Sally L. SIFERD
13 Chief Info Technology Officer (CIO) .... Ms. Deb TURNER
36 Director Student Placement .... Ms. Shari AYERS
38 Director Student Counseling .... Ms. Rae STATON
39 Director Student Housing .... Mr. Caleb FARMER
41 Athletic Director .... Mr. Phillip TALAVINIA
44 Director Annual or Planned Giving .... Ms. Julia SZABO
105 Director Web Services .... Ms. Sara KISSEBERTH
37 Director of Financial Aid .... Mr. Christopher FOWLER

Bowling Green State University (I)

220 McFall Center, Bowling Green OH 43403-0001
County: Wood   FICE Identification: 003018
Unit ID: 201441
Telephone: (419) 372-2211   Carnegie Class: RU/H
FAX Number: (419) 372-8446   Calendar System: Semester
URL: www.bgsu.edu
Established: 1910   Annual Undergrad Tuition & Fees (In-State): $10,606
Enrollment: 18,856   Coed
Affiliation or Control: State   IRS Status: 501(c)3
Highest Offering: Doctorate
Program: 2-Year Principally Bachelor's Creditable; Liberal Arts And General; Teacher Preparatory; Professional
Accreditation: NH, ART, BUS, BUSA, CAATE, CACREP, CLPSY, CONST, DIETD, DIETI, EXSC, IPSY, JOUR, MT, MUS, NAIT, NRPA, NURSE, PH, SP, SPAA, SW, TED, THEA

01 President .... Dr. Mary Ellen MAZEY
05 Sr VP Academic Affairs/Provost .... Dr. Rodney K. ROGERS
10 CFO/VP Finance & Admin .... Ms. Sherideen S. STOLL
100 Chief of Staff .... Ms. Lisa C. MATTIACE
32 Vice President Student Affairs .... Dr. Sidney CHILDS
04 Asst to President .... Ms. Laurel E. ZAWODNY
30 VP Univ Advancement .... Mr. Shea MCGREW
84 VP Strategic Enrollment Planning .... Ms. Cecilia CASTELLANO
20 Vice Provost Undergraduate Educ .... Dr. John FISCHER
35 Dean of Students .... Ms. Jodi WEBB
11 Assoc VP for Campus Operations .... Mr. Bruce MEYER
26 Chief Marketing & Comm Officer .... Mr. David KIELMEYER
29 Director Alumni Affairs .... Ms. Becky KOCHER
46 VP Research & Econ Dev .... Dr. Michael Y. OGAWA
41 Asst VP Student Affs/Dir Rec Sports .... Dr. Stephen KAMPF
41 Director of Athletics .... Mr. Chris KINGSTON
15 Chief Human Resources Officer .... Ms. Viva MCCARVER
39 Director of Residence Life .... Ms. Sarah WATERS
88 VP Capital Planning & Design .... Mr. Steve P. KRAKOFF
13 Chief Information Officer .... Mr. John M. ELLINGER
43 General Counsel .... Mr. Sean P. FITZGERALD
22 Director Equity & Diversity .... Ms. Barbara WADDELL
58 Dean Graduate College .... Dr. Michael OGAWA
49 Dean College Arts/Sciences .... Dr. Raymond CRAIG
50 Dean College Business Admin .... Mr. Raymond BRAUN
51 Exec Director University Outreach .... Dr. Marcia SALAZAR-VALENTINE
53 Dean College Educ/Human Development .... Dr. Brad COLWELL
12 Interim Dean Firelands College .... Dr. Andrew KURTZ
69 Dean College Hlth/Human Svcs .... Dr. Marie HUFF
08 Dean University Libraries .... Ms. Sara BUSHONG
64 Dean College of Musical Arts .... Dr. Jeffrey A. SHOWELL
72 Dean College of TAAE .... Dr. Venu DASIGI
57 Director of School of Art .... Dr. Katerina R. RAY
60 Dir Sch of Media & Communication .... Dr. Laura STAFFORD
88 Dir Sch Human Move/Sport/ Leisure .... Dr. Stephen J. LANGENDORGER
88 Dir Sch Family & Consumer Sciences .... Dr. Deborah G. WOOLDRIDGE
53 Dir Sch Educ Fnds/Leadership/Policy .... Dr. Sherri HORNER
53 Dir Sch of Teaching and Learning .... Dr. Dawn SHINEW
92 Dean Honors College .... Dr. Simon MORGAN-RUSSELL
106 Exec Director On-line Programs .... Dr. Marcia SALAZAR-VALENTINE
85 Exec Dir International Student Svcs .... Dr. Marcia SALAZAR-VALENTINE
21 Exec Dir of Business Operations .... Mr. Bradley K. LEIGH
07 Interim Director Admissions .... Ms. Cecilia CASTELLANO
21 Dir Budgeting & Resource Planning .... Mr. Geofrey L. TRACY
09 Director of Institutional Research .... Vacant

06 University Registrar ....Mr. Christopher P. COX
40 Director Bookstore ....Mr. Jeffrey D. NELSON
19 Director Public Safety ....Ms. Monica M. MOLL
36 Director Career Center ....Mr. Jeff JACKSON
23 Exec Director Center for Health ....Mr. Richard G. SIPP
38 Director Counseling Center ....Dr. Garrett GILMER
37 Interim Dir Student Financial Aid ....Ms. Tina COULTER
88 Interim Dir Student Scholarships ....Mr. Jerry AMELING
23 Asst Director Center for Health ....Ms. Marlene REYNOLDS
44 Director of Annual Giving ....Ms. Shannon SPENCER
101 Secretary to the Board ....Dr. Patrick PAUKEN
88 Co-Gen Manager WBGU Public Media ......Mr. Anthony E. SHORT
88 Co-Gen Manager WBGU Public Media ....Ms. Tina L. SIMON
35 Director TRIO Collegiate Services ....Mr. Sidney CHILDS
21 Internal Auditing & Adv Svcs ....Mr. James LAMBERT
88 Director Women's Center ....Dr. Mary M. KRUEGER
88 Assoc Director Disability Services ....Ms. Peggy DENNIS
88 Dir President's Leadership Acad ....Dr. Julie A. SNYDER
88 Director Dining Services ....Mr. Michael L. PAULUS
96 Director of Business Operations ....Mr. Andrew D. GRANT
88 Director Student Employment ....Ms. Dawn CHONG
88 Director Learning Commons ....Mr. Mark NELSON
88 Director Advising Services ....Mr. Dermot M. FORDE
88 Asst VP Non-Trad & Transfer Svcs ....Dr. Barbara L. HENRY
20 Vice Provost Academic Operations ....Dr. Joseph FRIZADO
65 Dir Sch Earth/Environ & Society ....Dr. Charles ONASCH

Bowling Green State University Firelands College (A)

One University Drive, Huron OH 44839-9719
Telephone: (419) 433-5560 FICE Identification: 007856
Accreditation: &NH, CAHIIM, COARC, DMS

† Regional accreditation is carried under the parent institution in Bowling Green, OH.

Bradford School (B)

2469 Stelzer Road, Columbus OH 43219-3129
County: Franklin FICE Identification: 004853
Unit ID: 202161
Telephone: (614) 416-6200 Carnegie Class: Assoc/PrivFP
FAX Number: (614) 416-6210 Calendar System: Semester
URL: www.bradfordschoolcolumbus.edu
Established: 1985 Annual Undergrad Tuition & Fees: $13,980
Enrollment: 450 Coed
Affiliation or Control: Proprietary IRS Status: Proprietary
Highest Offering: Associate Degree
Program: Occupational
Accreditation: ACICS, ACFEI, MAC, PTAA

01 President ....Mr. Dennis BARTELS
05 Director of Education ....Ms. Beth WOOD
07 Director of Admissions ....Ms. Raeann LEE

Brown Mackie College-Akron (C)

755 White Pond Drive, Suite 101, Akron OH 44320-4221
Telephone: (330) 869-3600 Identification: 666470
Accreditation: ACICS, OTA

† Branch campus of Brown Mackie College-Cincinnati, Cincinnati, OH.

Brown Mackie College-Cincinnati (D)

1011 Glendale-Milford Road, Cincinnati OH 45215-1107
Telephone: (513) 771-2424 FICE Identification: 005127
Accreditation: ACICS

† Branch campus of The Art Institute of Phoenix, Phoenix, AZ.

Brown Mackie College-Findlay (E)

1700 Fostoria Avenue, Suite 100, Findlay OH 45840-6857
Telephone: (419) 423-2211 FICE Identification: 026162
Accreditation: ACICS, OTA, SURTEC

† Branch campus of The Art Institute of Phoenix, Phoenix, AZ.

Brown Mackie College-North Canton (F)

4300 Munson Street, NW, Canton OH 44718-3674
Telephone: (330) 494-1214 FICE Identification: 030778
Accreditation: ACICS, SURTEC

† Branch campus of Brown Mackie College-Tucson, Tucson, AZ.

Bryant & Stratton College (G)

12955 Snow Road, Parma OH 44130-1013
Telephone: (216) 265-3151 FICE Identification: 022744
Accreditation: &M, MAC

† Regional accreditation is carried under the parent institution (corporate office) in Buffalo, NY.

Capital University (H)

1 College and Main Street, Columbus OH 43209-2394
County: Franklin FICE Identification: 003023
Unit ID: 201548
Telephone: (614) 236-6011 Carnegie Class: Master's M
FAX Number: (614) 236-6820 Calendar System: Semester
URL: www.capital.edu
Established: 1850 Annual Undergrad Tuition & Fees: $32,830
Enrollment: 3,494 Coed
Affiliation or Control: Evangelical Lutheran Church In America
IRS Status: 501(c)3
Highest Offering: First Professional Degree
Program: Liberal Arts And General; Teacher Preparatory; Professional
Accreditation: NH, ACBSP, CAATE, LAW, MUS, NURSE, SW, TED

01 President ....Dr. Denvy A. BOWMAN
05 Vice Pres Academic/Student Affairs ....Dr. Richard M. ASHBROOK
10 Vice President Business & Finance ....Dr. Michael D. HORAN
20 Dean of Studies ....Dr. Jody FOURNIER
30 Interim Vice Pres Advancement ....Ms. Jennifer PATTERSON
84 Interim VP Enrollment Services ....Dr. Amy ADAMS
21 Director Business Services ....Ms. Mary Ellen BORCHERS
44 Asst Vice President Major Gifts ....Ms. April NOVOTNY
43 University Counsel ....Dr. Tanya J. POTEET
20 Assoc VP/Provost Academic Affairs ....Dr. Terry D. LAHM
101 Dir Pres Ofc/Liaison to Board Trust ....Ms. Nona S. MCGUIRE
27 Dir Communications/Media Relations .. Ms. D. Nichole JOHNSON
26 Director Public Relations ....Ms. Denise RUSSELL
09 Director of Institutional Research ....Dr. Larry T. HUNTER
06 Registrar ....Mr. Brent KOERBER
37 Director of Financial Aid ....Ms. Susan E. KANNENWISCHER
07 Director of Admissions ....Ms. Amanda SOHL
29 Director Alumni/Parent Relations ....Ms. Diane LOESER
36 Director of Career Services ....Mr. Eric R. ANDERSON
08 University Librarian/Director IMC ....Vacant
88 Academic Service Coordinator ....Mr. Bruce EPPS
41 Athletic Director ....Dr. Steve BRUNING
13 Int Director Information Technology ....Mr. Jeff GUILER
85 Director Intl Education & ESL Pgm ....Ms. Jennifer ADAMS
32 Director Student Engagement ....Ms. Deanna WAGNER
18 Director Facilities Management ....Ms. Beth Anne CARMAN
15 Director of Human Resources ....Ms. Theresa FELDMEIER
38 Dir Univ Counseling/Health Svcs ....Dr. Cathy MCDANIELS WILSON
28 Dir Diversity and Inclusion ....Mr. Almar WALTERS
92 Honors Program ....Dr. Stephanie Gray WILSON
40 Manager Bookstore ....Mr. Joseph AMBUSKE
42 Dean of the Chapel ....Mr. Gary SANDBERG
61 Interim Dean of Law School ....Ms. Rachel JANUTIS
49 Dean of the College ....Dr. Cedric ADDERLEY
64 Assoc Dean of the College ....Dr. Lynn ROSEBERRY
66 Assoc Dean of the College ....Dr. Jens HEMMINGSEN
100 Chief of Staff ....Ms. Nona S. MCGUIRE
102 Dir Foundation/Corporate Relations ....Ms. Ashley STRIGLE

Capital University Law School (I)

303 East Broad Street, Columbus OH 43215
Telephone: (614) 236-6500 Identification: 770347
Accreditation: &NH

† Branch campus of Capital University, Columbus, OH.

Case Western Reserve University (J)

10900 Euclid Avenue, Cleveland OH 44106-7001
County: Cuyahoga FICE Identification: 003024
Unit ID: 201645
Telephone: (216) 368-2000 Carnegie Class: RU/VH
FAX Number: N/A Calendar System: Semester
URL: www.case.edu
Established: 1826 Annual Undergrad Tuition & Fees: $44,200
Enrollment: 10,771 Coed
Affiliation or Control: Independent Non-Profit IRS Status: 501(c)3
Highest Offering: Doctorate
Program: Liberal Arts And General; Professional
Accreditation: NH, AA, ANEST, BUS, BUSA, CLPSY, CS, DENT, DIETD, DIETI, ENG, LAW, MED, MIDWF, MUS, NUR, NURSE, PH, SP, SW, TEAC

01 President ....Ms. Barbara R. SNYDER
05 Provost/Executive Vice President ....Dr. William A. BAESLACK, III
20 Deputy Provost/VP Academic Affairs ....Dr. Lynn T. SINGER
10 Senior Vice Pres for Finance & CFO ....Mr. John F. SIDERAS
11 Senior Vice Pres for Administration ....Mr. John D. WHEELER
30 Sr VP for Univ Rels & Development ....Mr. Bruce A. LOESSIN
17 Sr Vice President Medical Affairs ....Dr. Pamela B. DAVIS
46 Vice President for Research ....Vacant
13 VP for Information Services/CIO ....Ms. Sue B. WORKMAN
32 Vice President for Student Affairs ....Mr. Louis W. STARK
18 VP Campus Planning/Facilities Mgmt .....Mr. Stephen CAMPBELL
15 Vice President for Human Resources ....Ms. Carolyn GREGORY
43 Sr Vice Pres/Gen Counsel/Secretary ....Ms. Elizabeth KEEFER
19 Vice President for Campus Services .....Mr. Richard J. JAMIESON
26 Vice Pres for University Relations ....Ms. Lara A. KALAFATIS
86 Assoc VP Govt/Foundation Relations ....Dr. Julie M. REHM
86 Exec Director Government Relations ....Ms. Jennifer RUGGLES
31 Sr Director Local Govt and Comm Rel ....Ms. Latisha JAMES
45 Vice Pres for University Planning ....Ms. Christine A. ASH
84 Vice Pres for Enrollment Management . Mr. Richard W. BISCHOFF
28 VP Inclusion/Diversity/Equal Opptny ....Dr. Marilyn S. MOBLEY
30 Vice Pres Development ....Ms. Chris SHERIDAN
88 Treasurer ....Mr. Robert C. BROWN
88 Chief Investment Officer ....Ms. Sally STALEY
20 Vice Provost Undergrad Education ....Dr. Donald L. FEKE
88 Assoc Prov for International Affs ....Mr. David FLESHLER
88 Dean of Undergraduate Studies ....Mr. Jeffrey WOLCOWITZ
21 Interim Controller ....Ms. Patricia L. KOST
06 Registrar ....Ms. Amy S. HAMMETT
37 Director of Financial Aid ....Ms. Venus PULIAFICO
07 Director Undergraduate Admissions ....Mr. Robert R. MCCULLOUGH
08 University Librarian ....Mr. Arnold HIRSHON
36 Director Career Center ....Dr. Thomas MATTHEWS
85 Dir International Student Svcs ....Ms. Marielena MAGGIO
38 Director University Counseling Svcs ....Dr. James E. SELLERS
09 Director of Institutional Research ....Ms. Jean E. GUBBINS
96 Int Dir Procurement/Distrib Svcs ....Ms. Mandy CARTE
41 Athletic Director ....Ms. Amy BACKUS
61 Interim Co-Dean of Law ....Mr. Michael P. SCHARF
61 Interim Co-Dean of Law ....Ms. Jessica W. BERG
49 Dean of Arts & Sciences ....Dr. Cyrus C. TAYLOR
63 Dean of Medicine ....Dr. Pamela B. DAVIS
66 Dean of Nursing ....Dr. Mary E. KERR
52 Dean of Dental Medicine ....Dr. Kenneth B. CHANCE
50 Dean of Management ....Dr. Robert E. WIDING, II
70 Dean Applied Social Science ....Dr. Grover C. GILMORE
54 Dean of Engineering ....Dr. Jeffrey DUERK
58 Dean of Graduate Studies ....Dr. Charles E. ROZEK
04 Executive Asst to President ....Ms. Jane M. VONDRAK
102 Senior Exec Director Corporate Rels .....Ms. Anne M. BORCHERT

Cedarville University (K)

251 N Main Street, Cedarville OH 45314-0601
County: Greene FICE Identification: 003025
Unit ID: 201654
Telephone: (937) 766-2211 Carnegie Class: Bac/Diverse
FAX Number: (937) 766-2760 Calendar System: Semester
URL: www.cedarville.edu
Established: 1887 Annual Undergrad Tuition & Fees: $27,206
Enrollment: 3,585 Coed
Affiliation or Control: Baptist IRS Status: 501(c)3
Highest Offering: Doctorate
Program: Liberal Arts And General; Teacher Preparatory; Professional
Accreditation: NH, ACBSP, CAATE, CS, ENG, MUS, NURSE, @PHAR, SW, TED

01 President ....Dr. Jerry T. WHITE
05 Int Vice President for Academics ....LtGen. Loren RENO, RET.
10 Vice President for Business ....Mr. Christopher SOHN
30 Int Vice President for Advancement ....Mr. David C. BARTLETT
32 VP Stdt Life/Christian Ministries ....Mr. Jon WOOD
84 Vice Pres Enrollment Mgmt/Marketing ....Dr. Janice SUPPLEE
43 General Counsel ....Mr. John HART
11 Assoc VP for Operations ....Mr. Rodney JOHNSON
06 University Registrar ....Mrs. Frances CAMPBELL
15 Assoc VP of Human Resources ....Mrs. Lydia GADDIS
13 Assoc VP Information Technology/CIO ....Dr. David L. ROTMAN
69 Dean of Undergraduate Programs ....Dr. Pamela D. JOHNSON
58 Dean of Graduate Programs ....Dr. Mark MCCLAIN
08 Dean of Library Services ....Mr. Lynn A. BROCK
67 Dean School of Pharmacy ....Dr. Marc SWEENEY
34 Assoc Dean Women ....Miss Rebecca STOWERS
35 Associate Dean Campus Life ....Mr. Brad D. SMITH
37 Executive Director of Financial Aid ....Mr. Kim JENERETTE
38 Director of Counseling Services ....Miss Mindy MAY
29 Director of Alumni Relations ....Mr. Jeff BESTE
36 Director Career Services ....Mr. Jeff REEP
92 Director Honors Program ....Dr. Thomas MACH
96 Director of Purchasing/Inventory ....Mr. Tim P. JOHNSON
04 Executive Asst to the President ....Mr. Zach BOWDEN
41 Athletic Director ....Dr. Alan GEIST
26 Exec Director of Public Relations ....Mr. Mark WEINSTEIN
19 Director of Campus Safety ....Mr. Douglas W. CHISHOLM
40 Manager of Retail Services ....Mrs. Tammy L. SLONE

Central Ohio Technical College (L)

1179 University Drive, Newark OH 43055-1767
County: Licking FICE Identification: 011046
Unit ID: 201672
Telephone: (740) 366-1351 Carnegie Class: Assoc/Pub-S-SC
FAX Number: (740) 366-5047 Calendar System: Semester
URL: www.cotc.edu
Established: 1971 Annual Undergrad Tuition & Fees (In-State): $4,296
Enrollment: 3,537 Coed
Affiliation or Control: State IRS Status: 501(c)3
Highest Offering: Associate Degree
Program: Occupational; 2-Year Principally Bachelor's Creditable; Technical Emphasis
Accreditation: NH, ADNUR, DMS, EMT, RAD, SURGT

01 President ....Dr. Bonnie L. COE
10 Vice President Business & Finance ....Mr. David BRILLHART
32 Director of Student Life ....Ms. Holly MASON
15 VP for Instnl Planning & HR Develop .... Ms. Jacqueline PARRILL
08 Director of Library ....Vacant
06 Records Manager/Registrar ....Ms. Veronica RINE
84 Director of Enrollment Management ....Mr. Brad PULCINI
26 Director Marketing/Public Relations ....Vacant
37 Director Financial Aid/Veteran Affs ....Ms. Faith PHILLIPS
19 Director Public Safety ....Mr. Denny HOLLERN
29 Dir Alumni Rels/Development Officer ....Mr. Matthew KELLY
35 Asst Director of Student Affairs ....Vacant
13 Chief Information Officer ....Mr. Howard IMHOF
38 Program Mgr Learn Asst Ctr Disabled ....Ms. Connie ZANG
05 Director of Academic Operations ....Mr. Chad WEIRICK
96 Manager of Purchasing ....Ms. Kimberley SIBERT
18 Manager Facilities ....Mr. Brian BOEHMER
51 Coord of Community Svc/Learning ....Ms. Vorley TAYLOR
36 Dir Career Dev & Experiential Lrng ....Mr. Derek THATCHER
04 Assistant to the President ....Ms. Jan TOMLINSON

09 Director of Institutional Research .... Vacant
50 Dean for Business/Engineering/IT .... Mr. Ron SCOZZARI
07 Gateway Manager/Admission .... Mr. Dustin DUNLAVY
101 Secretary of the Institution/Board .... Ms. Jan TOMLINSON
103 Manager Workforce Development .... Ms. Vicki MAPLE

Central Ohio Technical College Coshocton Campus (A)

200 North Whitewoman Street, Coshocton OH 43812
Telephone: (740) 622-1408 Identification: 770348
Accreditation: &NH

† Branch campus of Central Ohio Technical College, Newark, OH.

Central Ohio Technical College Knox Campus (B)

236 South Main Street, Mount Vernon OH 43050
Telephone: (740) 392-2526 Identification: 770350
Accreditation: &NH

† Branch campus of Central Ohio Technical College, Newark, OH.

Central Ohio Technical College Pataskala Campus (C)

8660 East Broad Street, Reynoldsburg OH 43068
Telephone: (740) 755-7090 Identification: 770351
Accreditation: &NH

† Branch campus of Central Ohio Technical College, Newark, OH.

Central State University (D)

PO Box 1004, 1400 Brush Row Road,
Wilberforce OH 45384-1004
County: Greene FICE Identification: 003026
Unit ID: 201690
Telephone: (937) 376-6332 Carnegie Class: Bac/Diverse
FAX Number: (937) 376-6138 Calendar System: Semester
URL: www.centralstate.edu
Established: 1887 Annual Undergrad Tuition & Fees (In-State): $6,246
Enrollment: 1,751 Coed
Affiliation or Control: State IRS Status: 501(c)3
Highest Offering: Master's
Program: Liberal Arts And General; Teacher Preparatory; Business Emphasis
Accreditation: NH, ART, ENG, MUS, @SW, TED

01 President .... Dr. Cynthia JACKSON-HAMMOND
04 Exec Asst to the President .... Mrs. Wendy HAYES
05 Provost/VP Academic Affairs .... Dr. Charles WESLEY FORD
10 Vice President Admin & Finance .... Mrs. Daarel BURNETTE
30 Vice Pres Institutional Advancement .... Mr. Anthony FAIRBANKS
11 Asst VP Administration & Finance .... Vacant
32 Vice President Student Affairs .... Ms. Stephanie KRAH
13 Vice Pres/Chief Information Officer .... Mr. Keith MATTHEWS
20 Assoc Vice Pres Academic Affairs .... Dr. Lovette CHINWAH
06 University Registrar .... Mrs. LaTonya BRANHAM
07 Asst Director of Admissions .... Vacant
08 Director of Hallie Q Brown Library .... Ms. Carolin STERLING
89 Assoc Dean of University College .... Dr. Dwedor FORD
12 Dean CSU Dayton Campus .... Dr. Lovette CHINWAH
09 Director Assessment/Inst Research .... Mr. Mohammad ALI
19 Chief of Police .... Capt. Mark MACHAN
26 Director Public Relations .... Dr. Edwina BLACKWELL-CLARK
23 Medical Director .... Dr. Karen MATHEWS
29 Director Alumni Relations .... Mr. Keith PERKINS
36 Director Career Services .... Ms. Karla HARPER
37 Director Student Financial Aid .... Ms. Sonia SLOMBIA
39 Director Residence Life .... Mr. Dillon BECKFORD
41 Athletic Director .... Mr. Jahan CULBREATH
42 Director Campus Ministry .... Rev. Kima CUNNINGHAM
46 Director Sponsored Pgms/Research .... Mr. Morakinyo KUTI
49 Dean Coll Humanities/Arts & Sci .... Dr. James SMITH
50 Dean College of Business .... Dr. Fidelis M. IKEM
53 Dean College of Education .... Dr. Charles HODGE
15 Director of Human Resources .... Ms. Kimberly MANIGAULT
21 Director Business Svcs/Capital Dev .... Ms. Cynthia MICHAEL
25 Director Grants Accounting .... Vacant
92 Director Honors Program .... Dr. Geoffrey J. GIDDINGS
21 Controller .... Vacant
21 Exec Dir of Fiscal Affairs .... Mr. Curtis PETTIS
38 Director Student Counseling .... Mr. NseAbasi EKPO
88 Budget Director .... Ms. Sheila BROWN
84 Enrollment Specialist .... Mr. William RANDOLPH

Chamberlain College of Nursing-Cleveland (E)

6700 Euclid Avenue, Suite 201, Cleveland OH 44103
Telephone: (216) 361-6005 Identification: 770505
Accreditation: &NH, NURSE

† Branch campus of Chamberlain College of Nursing-Addison, Addison, IL.

Chamberlain College of Nursing-Columbus Campus (F)

1350 Alum Creek Drive, Columbus OH 43209
Telephone: (614) 252-8890 Identification: 770499
Accreditation: &NH, ADNUR, NURSE

† Branch campus of Chamberlain College of Nursing-Addison, Addison, IL.

Chatfield College (G)

20918 State Route 251, Saint Martin OH 45118-9059
County: Brown FICE Identification: 010880
Unit ID: 201751
Telephone: (513) 875-3344 Carnegie Class: Assoc/PrivNFP
FAX Number: (513) 875-3912 Calendar System: Semester
URL: www.chatfield.edu
Established: 1971 Annual Undergrad Tuition & Fees: $9,645
Enrollment: 408 Coed
Affiliation or Control: Independent Non-Profit IRS Status: 501(c)3
Highest Offering: Associate Degree
Program: 2-Year Principally Bachelor's Creditable; Fine Arts Emphasis
Accreditation: NH

01 President .... Mr. John P. TAFARO
03 Vice President/CEO .... Mr. Robert ELMORE
05 Chief Academic Officer/Dean .... Mr. Alan D. SIMMONS
10 Director of Finance .... Ms. Mary R. JACOBS
30 Director of Advancement .... Mr. James LUDWIG
07 Director of Admissions .... Mr. John PENROSE
20 Associate Dean/Site Director .... Ms. Wanda HILL
20 Associate Dean/Site Director .... Sr. Patricia HOMAN
26 Director of Marketing Communication .... Ms. Pamela SPENCER
04 Administrative Asst to President .... Ms. Cheryl A. KERN
06 Registrar .... Mr. Frank CHAPIN
08 Head Librarian .... Ms. Dolores BERISH
13 Chief Info Technology Officer .... Mr. Nathan SCHULER
18 Chief Facilities/Physical Plant .... Mr. Bradley JONES
29 Director Alumni Relations .... Mr. James LUDWIG
37 Director Student Financial Aid .... Ms. Dawn HUNDLEY
09 Inst Research/Assessment .... Ms. Mary Fran HEINSCH
101 Secretary of the Institution/Board .... Ms. Cheryl A. KERN
28 Director of Diversity .... Mr. Alan D. SIMMONS
44 Director Annual or Planned Giving .... Mr. James P. LUDWIG

The Christ College of Nursing and Health Sciences (H)

2139 Auburn Avenue, Cincinnati OH 45219
County: Hamilton FICE Identification: 006489
Unit ID: 201821
Telephone: (513) 585-2401 Carnegie Class: Assoc/PrivNFP
FAX Number: (513) 585-3540 Calendar System: Semester
URL: www.thechristcollege.edu
Established: 2006 Annual Undergrad Tuition & Fees: $37,800
Enrollment: 712 Coed
Affiliation or Control: Independent Non-Profit IRS Status: 501(c)3
Highest Offering: Baccalaureate
Program: Nursing Emphasis
Accreditation: NH, ADNUR, NURSE

01 President .... Dr. W. Gary PACK
05 Dean of Academics .... Dr. Kelly M. SIMMONS
20 Dean of Academic Support Services . Dr. Meghan E. HOLLOWELL
11 Dean of Operations/Presidential Lia .... Ms. Carolyn A. HUNTER
84 Dean of Enrollment Management .... Mr. Bradley A. JACKSON
04 Assistant to the President .... Ms. Cheryl A. BOONE

Cincinnati Christian University (I)

2700 Glenway Avenue, Cincinnati OH 45204-3200
County: Hamilton FICE Identification: 003029
Unit ID: 201858
Telephone: (513) 244-8100 Carnegie Class: Spec/Faith
FAX Number: (513) 244-8140 Calendar System: Semester
URL: www.ccuniversity.edu
Established: 1924 Annual Undergrad Tuition & Fees: $16,216
Enrollment: 844 Coed
Affiliation or Control: Christian Churches And Churches of Christ
IRS Status: 501(c)3
Highest Offering: First Professional Degree
Program: 2-Year Principally Bachelor's Creditable; Liberal Arts And General; Teacher Preparatory; Professional; Religious Emphasis
Accreditation: NH, BI, CACREP, MUS, TEAC, THEOL

01 President .... Mr. Ken A. TRACY
05 Chief Academic Officer .... Dr. Tom THATCHER
10 Director of Financial Services .... Mr. Randy KOEHLER
30 Dir of Advancement & Development .... Dr. Steve CARR
20 Dean of Seminary .... Dr. David RAY
51 Dir of College of Adult Learning .... Mr. Byron WILLIAMS
84 Director of CAL Enrollment .... Dr. Rhansyl HARRIS
73 Dean of Russell School of Ministry .... Dr. Mike SHANNON
49 Dean Biblical Studies/Arts & Sci .... Mr. Paul FRISKNEY
83 Dean Education/Behavioral Sciences .... Dr. Marlene ESTENSON
50 Dean of School of Business .... Dr. Aaron BURGESS
108 Dean of Institutional Effectiveness .... Dr. Sara FUDGE
20 Director of Faculty Development .... Dr. James A. SMITH
21 Bursar .... Mrs. Linda WAUGH
06 Registrar .... Mr. Don A. THOMASON
08 Director of Libraries .... Mr. James H. LLOYD
32 Director of Student Life .... Mrs. Kristin MERRILL
33 Dean of Men/Campus Minister .... Mr. Dan BURTON
37 Associate Director of Financial Aid .... Ms. Marcella FARMER
07 Director of Admissions .... Ms. Carrie BOULDIN
106 Director of Online Learning .... Mrs. Kate HILL
29 Manager of Alumni Relations .... Mrs. Shelley WEISS
41 Director of Athletics .... Ms. Beth ROGERS
18 Director of Operations .... Mr. Josh MASON
15 Director of Human Resources .... Mrs. Nancy HARTMAN
13 Director of Information Technology .... Mr. James MCINTYRE
19 Director of Security .... Mr. Dan JACKSON
40 Manager of Bookstore .... Ms. Beth ROGERS
07 Director of Graduate Admissions .... Mr. Alex EDDY
04 Exec Assistant to the President .... Mrs. Wendy SPALDING
104 Director Study Abroad .... Mr. Steve SKAGGS
26 Dir of Marketing & Communications .... Vacant
89 First Year Programs Coordinator .... Ms. Kaci DURHAM
44 Director Annual or Planned Giving .... Mr. Dick DEVINE

Cincinnati College of Mortuary Science (J)

645 W North Bend Road, Cincinnati OH 45224-1462
County: Hamilton FICE Identification: 010906
Unit ID: 201867
Telephone: (513) 761-2020 Carnegie Class: Spec/Other
FAX Number: (513) 761-3333 Calendar System: Semester
URL: www.ccms.edu
Established: 1882 Annual Undergrad Tuition & Fees: $20,750
Enrollment: 115 Coed
Affiliation or Control: Independent Non-Profit IRS Status: 501(c)3
Highest Offering: Baccalaureate
Program: Occupational
Accreditation: NH, FUSER

01 President .... Mr. Gene KRAMER
07 Admissions/Registrar .... Ms. Blanche KABENGELE
37 Financial Aid Director .... Mr. Russ ROMANDINI

Cincinnati State Technical and Community College (K)

3520 Central Parkway, Cincinnati OH 45223-2690
County: Hamilton FICE Identification: 010345
Unit ID: 201928
Telephone: (513) 569-1500 Carnegie Class: Assoc/Pub-U-SC
FAX Number: (513) 569-1495 Calendar System: Other
URL: www.cincinnatistate.edu
Established: 1966 Annual Undergrad Tuition & Fees (In-State): $3,825
Enrollment: 10,707 Coed
Affiliation or Control: State IRS Status: 501(c)3
Highest Offering: Associate Degree
Program: Occupational; 2-Year Principally Bachelor's Creditable; Business Emphasis
Accreditation: NH, ACFEI, ADNUR, CAHIIM, COARC, CONST, DIETT, DMS, ENGT, IFSAC, MAC, MLTAD, OTA, SURGT

01 President .... Dr. O'dell OWENS
03 Executive Vice President .... Ms. Carla CHANCE
05 Academic Vice President .... Dr. Monica POSEY
13 Vice President for Technology .... Dr. David HICKEY
10 Vice President Finance/Treasurer .... Mr. Michael GEOGHEGAN
26 Vice Pres Marketing/Communications .... Ms. Jean MANNING
103 Vice Pres Workforce Development Ctr .... Dr. Dennis ULRICH
72 Dean of Engineering Technology .... Mr. Doug BOWLING
50 Dean of Business Technologies .... Dr. Nick NISSLEY
76 Dean Health/Public Safety .... Dr. Jean CHAPPELL
81 Dean Humanities/Sciences .... Ms. Robbin HOOPES
84 Dean Enrollment/Student Development .... Dr. Wendy BOLT
06 Registrar .... Vacant
08 Library Director .... Mrs. Cindy SEFTON
41 Dir Athletics/Student Activities .... Mr. Tom HATHAWAY
18 Director of Facilities .... Mr. Rob EPLING
09 Director of Institutional Research .... Ms. Anne FOSTER
07 Director of Admissions .... Ms. Gabriele BOECKERMANN
15 Director of Human Resources .... Ms. Lisa EVANS
32 Chief Student Life Officer .... Vacant
30 Chief of Development .... Mr. Elliott RUTHER
35 Director of Student Affairs .... Mrs. Sharon DAVIS
96 Director of Purchasing .... Mr. Jeffrey COOK
92 Coordinator Honors Program .... Dr. Andrea LESLIE
86 Director of Government Affairs .... Ms. Nan KOHNEN-CAHALL
04 Executive Administrative Associate .... Mrs. Michelle GRIFFIN-DONALDSON
19 Director of Public Safety .... Mr. Michael WYLIE
37 Director of Financial Aid .... Mrs. La Saundra CRAIG
101 Secretary to the Board of Trustees .... Mrs. Nancy STUBBEMAN
88 Director of Student Success .... Mr. Martino HARMON
25 Contract Administrator .... Mrs. Ann JAMES

Clark State Community College (L)

570 E Leffel Lane, PO Box 570,
Springfield OH 45501-0570
County: Clark FICE Identification: 004852
Unit ID: 201973
Telephone: (937) 325-0691 Carnegie Class: Assoc/Pub-U-SC
FAX Number: (937) 328-6142 Calendar System: Quarter
URL: www.clarkstate.edu
Established: 1966 Annual Undergrad Tuition & Fees (In-State): $3,359
Enrollment: 5,969 Coed
Affiliation or Control: State IRS Status: 501(c)3
Highest Offering: Associate Degree
Program: Occupational; 2-Year Principally Bachelor's Creditable
Accreditation: NH, ADNUR, MAC, MLTAD, PTAA

01 President .... Dr. Jo A. BLONDIN
05 Provost/Vice Pres Academic Affairs .... Dr. Amit SINGH
10 Vice President Business Affairs .... Joseph R. JACKSON

30 Vice President of Advancement ....Kristin J. CULP
21 Controller ....Dixie A. DEPEW
32 Dean Student Support Services ....Dr. Edward J. BUSHER
08 Director Library Services ....Beth DEGER
84 Dean Enrollment Services ....Nina WILEY
49 Dean Arts & Sciences/Public Svcs ....Martha CRAWMER
50 Dean Business/Applied Technologies .... Aimee BELANGER-HAAS
76 Dean Health and Human Services ....Kathleen J. WILCOX
37 Financial Aid Director ....Kathy A. KLAY
06 Registrar ....Diane SEAMAN
31 Director of Community Outreach ....Corey HOLLIDAY
13 Director Information Technology ....Matt FRANZ
45 Dir of Inst Research and Planning ....Cynthia APPLIN
15 Director of Human Resources ....Marvin NEPHEW
57 Exec Dir Performing Arts Center ....Adele ADKINS
18 Dir Facilities/Oper/Maintenance ....Randall CONOVER
41 Dir Athletics/Act & Evening Svcs ....Kenneth LAAKE
103 Director Workforce Development ....Duane HODGE
09 Institutional Research Technician ....Kelly NERIANI
04 Assistant to the President ....Mellanie TOLES
26 Marketing Manager ....Laurie MEANS

Clark State Community College Greene Center (A)

3775 Pentagon Boulevard, Beavercreek OH 45431
Telephone: (937) 429-8819 Identification: 770352
Accreditation: &NH

† Branch campus of Clark State Community College, Springfield, OH.

Cleveland Institute of Art (B)

11601 Euclid Avenue, Cleveland OH 44106-1710
County: Cuyahoga FICE Identification: 003982
Unit ID: 202046
Telephone: (216) 421-7000 Carnegie Class: Spec/Arts
FAX Number: (216) 421-7438 Calendar System: Semester
URL: www.cia.edu
Established: 1882 Annual Undergrad Tuition & Fees: $38,487
Enrollment: 560 Coed
Affiliation or Control: Independent Non-Profit IRS Status: 501(c)3
Highest Offering: Baccalaureate
Program: Professional; Fine Arts Emphasis
Accreditation: NH, ART

01 President & CEO ....Mr. Grafton J. NUNES
05 VP Faculty Affairs & CAO ....Mr. Chris WHITTEY
30 Vice Pres Inst Advancement ....Ms. Amy E. RAUFMAN
10 Vice President Business Affairs/CFO ....Mrs. Almut ZVOSEC
26 Vice President Mktg & Communication ....Mr. Mark INGLIS
84 VP Enrollment/Financial Aid ....Mr. Robert BORDEN
37 Asst Director of Financial Aid ....Ms. Delores HALL
06 Registrar ....Mrs. Karen HUDY
08 Library Director ....Ms. Cristine ROM
07 Assoc Director of Admissions ....Mr. Tom GREEN
13 Vice President Support Service ....Mr. Mat FELTHOUSEN
29 Director Annual Giving/Alumni Rels ....Ms. Liz HUFF
20 Director of Academic Services ....Ms. Anne GATES
44 Dir Leadership/Planned Giving ....Ms. Sarah OTT-HANSEN
15 Exec Dir of HR & Inclusion ....Mr. Raymond SCRAGG
32 Dean of Student Affairs ....Ms. Nancy NEVILLE
37 Director of Financial Aid ....Mr. Martin CARNEY
27 Director of Mktg & Communications ....Ms. Ann MCGUIRE
57 Art Director ....Mr. Richard SARIAN
21 Assoc VP of Business Affairs ....Ms. Julie MELVIN
25 Director of Grants/Special Projects ....Ms. Jennifer GRASSO

Cleveland Institute of Music (C)

11021 East Boulevard, Cleveland OH 44106-1776
County: Cuyahoga FICE Identification: 003031
Unit ID: 202073
Telephone: (216) 791-5000 Carnegie Class: Spec/Arts
FAX Number: (216) 791-3063 Calendar System: Semester
URL: www.cim.edu
Established: 1920 Annual Undergrad Tuition & Fees: $45,700
Enrollment: 450 Coed
Affiliation or Control: Independent Non-Profit IRS Status: 501(c)3
Highest Offering: Doctorate
Program: Professional; Music Emphasis
Accreditation: NH, MUS

01 President/CEO ....Mr. Joel SMIRNOFF
03 Vice President/COO/Asst Treasurer ....Mr. Eric BOWER
30 VP for Institutional Advancement ....Ms. Karin STONE
05 Associate Dean of Conservatory ....Ms. Joyce GRIGGS
26 Director Marketing & Communications ....Ms. Susan ILER
13 Director Systems Management ....Mr. Daniel BETTING
07 Director Admission & Enrollment Mgt ....Ms. Lynn JOHNSON
32 Associate Dean of Student Affairs ....Mr. David GILSON
37 Director Financial Aid ....Ms. Kristine GRIPP
10 Chief Financial Officer ....Ms. Kristen KOLLAR
06 Registrar ....Mrs. Hallie MOORE
15 Director Human Resources ....Mrs. Megan SWERBINSKY
08 Director of the Library ....Ms. Jean TOOMBS
88 Director of Concerts & Events ....Ms. Lori WRIGHT
40 Bookstore Manager ....Ms. Antoinette MILLER
106 Director of Distance Learning ....Mr. Gregory HOWE
04 Executive Admin Asst to President ....Ms. Nancy SNELL

Cleveland State University (D)

2121 Euclid Avenue, Cleveland OH 44115-2214
County: Cuyahoga FICE Identification: 003032
Unit ID: 202134
Telephone: (216) 687-2000 Carnegie Class: RU/H
FAX Number: (216) 687-9366 Calendar System: Semester
URL: www.csuohio.edu
Established: 1964 Annual Undergrad Tuition & Fees (In-State): $9,636
Enrollment: 17,345 Coed
Affiliation or Control: State IRS Status: 501(c)3
Highest Offering: Doctorate
Program: Liberal Arts And General; Teacher Preparatory; Professional
Accreditation: NH, ARCPA, BUS, BUSA, CACREP, CEA, COPSY, ENG, ENGT, LAW, MUS, NURSE, OT, PH, PLNG, PTA, SP, SPAA, SW, TED

01 President ....Dr. Ronald M. BERKMAN
100 Chief of Staff ....Mr. James BENNETT
05 Interim Provost ....Dr. Jianping ZHU
10 VP Business Affairs ....Ms. Stephanie MCHENRY
84 VP Enrollment Services ....Dr. Cindy SKARUPPA
46 VP Research ....Dr. Jerzy SAWICKI
31 VP University Engagement ....Dr. Byron WHITE
30 VP Univ Advancement/Exec Dir Found ....Ms. Berinthia LEVINE
20 Vice Provost for Academic Planning ....Dr. Teresa LAGRANGE
32 VP Student Affairs ....Dr. Ernest YARBROUGH
26 Assoc VP University Mktg ....Mr. Robert SPADEMAN
15 Asst VP Human Resources ....Mr. Jesse DRUCKER
88 Assoc VP Student Affairs ....Ms. Clare RAHM
21 Controller/Asst VP Finance ....Ms. Kathleen MURPHY
49 Dean Col Liberal Arts/Soc Sci ....Dr. Gregory M. SADLEK
81 Dean College of Science ....Dr. Meredith R. BOND
50 Interim Dean College of Business ....Dr. Richard REED
53 Dean College Education & Human Svcs ....Dr. Sajit ZACHARIAH
54 Dean Fenn College of Engineering ....Dr. Anette KARLSSON
58 Interim Dean College Grad Studies ....Dr. Donna SCHULTHEISS
61 Dean of College of Law ....Mr. Craig BOISE
80 Interim Dean College Urban Affairs ....Dr. Robert GLEESON
92 Dean Honors College ....Dr. Elizabeth LEHFELDT
43 General Counsel ....Ms. Sonali B. WILSON
86 Sr Advisor to Pres Government Rels ....Dr. William NAPIER
08 Director of Libraries ....Dr. Glenda THORNTON
22 Dir Office of Institutional Equity ....Ms. Yulanda MCCARTY-HARRIS
07 Director Undergraduate Admissions ....Ms. Lee FURBECK
09 Director Institutional Research ....Mr. Tom GEAGHAN
85 Director International Programs ....Mr. Harlan SMITH
36 Director Talent Development Career ....Ms. Mitzi VAZQUEZ-LONG
38 Director Counseling Center ....Dr. Katharine HAHN
19 Assoc VP Administration/Operations ....Dr. Joseph HAN
37 Director Student Financial Aid ....Ms. Rachel SCHMIDT
06 Asst Vice President/Registrar ....Ms. Janet STIMPLE
41 Director of Athletics ....Mr. John PARRY
29 Director Alumni Affairs ....Mr. Brian BREITHOLZ
18 Director Facilities Management ....Mr. Shehadeh ABDELKARIM
96 Director of Purchasing ....Ms. Laurie MCCOMBS
92 Director Honors Program ....Dr. Peter MEIKSINS
28 Chief Diversity Officer ....Dr. Byron WHITE
04 Administrative Asst to President ....Ms. Shane CONNOR
13 Chief Info Technology Officer (CIO) ....Mr. William WILSON

The College of Wooster (E)

1189 Beall Avenue, Wooster OH 44691-2363
County: Wayne FICE Identification: 003037
Unit ID: 206589
Telephone: (330) 263-2000 Carnegie Class: Bac/A&S
FAX Number: (330) 263-2427 Calendar System: Semester
URL: www.wooster.edu
Established: 1866 Annual Undergrad Tuition & Fees: $44,520
Enrollment: 2,024 Coed
Affiliation or Control: Independent Non-Profit IRS Status: 501(c)3
Highest Offering: Baccalaureate
Program: Liberal Arts And General; Teacher Preparatory
Accreditation: NH, MUS, TED

01 President ....Dr. Grant H. CORNWELL
05 Provost ....Dr. Carolyn NEWTON
10 Vice Pres Finance/Bus/Treasurer ....Ms. Dee MCCORMICK
30 Vice President for Development ....Ms. Laurie HOUCK
84 Vice Pres Enrollment/College Rels ....Dr. Scott FRIEDHOFF
04 Administrative Asst to President ....Mrs. Lynette ARNER
26 Assoc VP College Rels & Marketing ....Mr. John HOPKINS
109 Assoc VP Facilities & Auxiliaries ....Ms. Jacqueline MIDDLETON
20 Dean Curriculum/Academic Engagement ....Dr. Henry B. KREUZMAN
20 Dean for Faculty Development ....Dr. Heather M. FITZGIBBON
07 Dean of Admissions ....Ms. Jennifer D. WINGE
32 Senior Associate Dean of Students ....Ms. Carolyn BUXTON
35 Assoc Dean of Students ....Ms. Robyn LADITKA
85 Dir Office of Intl Student Affairs ....Mr. Yorgun MARCEL
09 Chief Information Planning Officer ....Dr. Ellen FALDUTO
06 Registrar ....Ms. Suzanne BATES
08 Director of Libraries ....Mr. Mark A. CHRISTEL
37 Director of Financial Aid ....Mr. Joseph WINGE
27 Director Office Public Information ....Mr. John FINN
29 Dir of Alumni Rels & Wooster Fund ....Ms. Heidi A. MCCORMICK
36 Director Career Services ....Ms. Lisa KASTOR
41 Dir Phys Educ/Athletics/Recreat ....Dr. Keith BECKETT
18 Director Physical Plant Operations ....Mr. Doug LADITKA
19 Director Security/Protective Svcs ....Mr. Steven GLICK
15 Director of Human Resources ....Ms. Marcia BEASLEY
42 Camp Chaplain/Dir Intfth Camp Mins ....Rev. Linda MORGAN-CLEMENT
101 Secretary of College/Chief Staff ....Ms. Angela JOHNSTON

Columbus College of Art & Design (F)

60 Cleveland Avenue, Columbus OH 43215-1758
County: Franklin FICE Identification: 003039
Unit ID: 202170
Telephone: (614) 224-9101 Carnegie Class: Spec/Arts
FAX Number: (614) 222-4040 Calendar System: Semester
URL: www.ccad.edu
Established: 1879 Annual Undergrad Tuition & Fees: $30,840
Enrollment: 1,249 Coed
Affiliation or Control: Independent Non-Profit IRS Status: 501(c)3
Highest Offering: Master's
Program: Professional; Fine Arts Emphasis
Accreditation: NH, ART, CIDA

01 Interim President ....Mr. Kevin J. CONLON
04 Exec Assistant to the President ....Ms. Sheri LUCAS
05 Provost ....Mr. Kevin J. CONLON
10 Senior Vice President/CFO ....Mr. Jeffrey A. FISHER
30 Vice President for Advancement ....Ms. Lindsey DUNLEAVY
26 Assoc VP Communications & Marketing ....Vacant
07 Assoc VP for Enrollment Operations ....Mr. Densil R. PORTEOUS
32 Vice President for Student Affairs ....Mr. Dwayne TODD
60 Dean School of Design Arts ....Mr. Tom GATTIS
57 Dean School of Studio Arts ....Ms. Julie TAGGART
58 Director Graduate Studies ....Mr. Ric PETRY
06 Registrar ....Ms. Michele KIBLER
13 Chief Information Officer ....Mr. Jeffrey BROTHERTON
15 Director of Human Resources ....Ms. Barbara DAVIS
08 Director of Library Services ....Ms. Leslie JANKOWSKI NIEMCZURA
19 Director of Safety & Security ....Mr. Wallace TANKSLEY
18 Director of Facilities ....Mr. Joseph SPYBEY
38 Director of Counseling & Wellness ....Ms. Erin VLACH
37 Director Student Financial Aid ....Ms. Anna M. SCHOFIELD
36 Director Career Resources ....Ms. Tiffany SPERRING
21 Controller ....Mr. Roger ESCOLAS
35 Dir of Student Involvement ....Ms. Heather BRAY
51 Dir Continuing/Professional Study ....Ms. Dorothy KEIL
39 Director of Residence Life ....Mr. Mickey HART
88 Director of Special Projects ....Mr. Dave STOCKWELL
40 Supply Store Manager ....Mr. Danny HINTY

Columbus State Community College (G)

Box 1609, Columbus OH 43216-1609
County: Franklin FICE Identification: 006867
Unit ID: 202222
Telephone: (614) 287-5353 Carnegie Class: Assoc/Pub-U-SC
FAX Number: (614) 287-5113 Calendar System: Semester
URL: www.cscc.edu
Established: 1963 Annual Undergrad Tuition & Fees (In-State): $4,078
Enrollment: 23,858 Coed
Affiliation or Control: State IRS Status: 501(c)3
Highest Offering: Associate Degree
Program: Occupational; 2-Year Principally Bachelor's Creditable
Accreditation: NH, ACBSP, ACFEI, ADNUR, CAHIIM, COARC, CONST, CSHSE, DH, DIETT, EMT, ENGT, MAC, MLTAD, PHLEB, RAD, SURGT

01 President ....Dr. David T. HARRISON
05 Senior Vice Pres Academic Affairs ....Dr. John COOLEY
10 Sr Vice President & CFO ....Ms. Theresa GEHR
26 Vice Pres Marketing/Communications ....Mr. Allen KRAUS
13 Vice Pres Information Technology ....Ms. Carol THOMAS
43 Vice President and General Counsel ....Ms. Kimberly HALL
32 Vice Pres Enroll Mgmt/Student Svcs ....Dr. Diane WALLESER
84 Dean of Enrollment Services ....Dr. Martin MALIWESKY
12 Dean of Delaware Campus ....Vacant
49 Dean of Arts & Sciences ....Dr. Allysen TODD
76 Dean Health and Human Services ....Dr. Thomas HABEGGER
50 Dean Business & Engineering Tech ....Mr. Angelo FROLE
35 Dean Student Life ....Ms. Renee HILL
102 Executive Director Foundation ....Ms. Pamela BISHOP
88 Director IT Budget/Planning ....Mr. Etienne MARTIN
21 Director Business/College Services ....Ms. Aletha SHIPLEY
06 Director of Records & Registration ....Dr. Regina RANDALL
37 Director Financial Aid ....Mr. David METZ
19 Chief of Police ....Chief Sean ASBURY
18 Director of Facilities Management ....Mr. Mark FRENCH
28 Dir of Global Diversity/Inclusion ....Mr. Brett WELSH
09 Dir Institutional Effectiveness ....Ms. Jennifer ANDERSON
08 Director Library ....Mr. Bruce MASSIS
07 Director of Admissions ....Ms. Gina GILES-HISER
40 Director of Operations/Bookstore ....Ms. Stacy MULINEX
96 Director Procurement/College Svcs ....Mr. Bradley FARMER
14 Director IT Technical Services ....Mr. James BEIDLER

Columbus State Community College-Delaware (H)

5100 Cornerstone Drive, Delaware OH 43015
Telephone: (740) 203-8000 Identification: 770353
Accreditation: &NH

† Branch campus of Columbus State Community College, Columbus, OH.

Cuyahoga Community College (A)

700 Carnegie Avenue, Cleveland OH 44115-2878

County: Cuyahoga FICE Identification: 003040
Unit ID: 202356
Telephone: (216) 987-4000 Carnegie Class: Assoc/Pub-U-MC
FAX Number: (216) 566-5977 Calendar System: Semester
URL: www.tri-c.edu
Established: 1963 Annual Undergrad Tuition & Fees (In-District): $3,136
Enrollment: 27,104 Coed
Affiliation or Control: State/Local IRS Status: 501(c)3
Highest Offering: Associate Degree
Program: Occupational; 2-Year Principally Bachelor's Creditable; Business Emphasis
Accreditation: NH, ACFEI, ADNUR, ARCPA, CAHIIM, COARC, DH, DIETT, DMS, EMT, ENGT, MAC, MLTAD, NDT, NMT, OTA, POLYT, PTAA, RAD, SURGT

01 President .... Dr. Alex JOHNSON
05 Interim Provost/EVP .... Dr. Craig FOLTIN
11 Exec Vice Pres Admin and Finance .... Dr. Craig FOLTIN
103 Exec Vice Pres Workforce & Econ Dev .... Mr. William GARY
12 Campus President/VP East Campus .... Dr. J. Michael THOMSON
12 Corporate College President .... Mr. Robert PETERSON
12 Campus President/VP Metro Campus .... Dr. Michael SCHOOP
12 Campus President/VP WestshoreCampus .... Dr. Terri POPE
12 Interim Campus Pres West Campus .. Dr. Janice TAYLOR HEARD
10 Vice Pres Finance & Business Svcs .... Mr. Mike ABOUSERHAL
15 Vice Pres/Chief Human Res Officer .... Ms. Judith MCMULLEN
30 Vice Pres Development Office .... Ms. Gloria MOOSMANN
27 Vice Pres/Chief Information Officer .... Mr. Gerard HOURIGAN
09 Vice Pres Evidence & Inquiry .... Dr. Jennifer SPIELVOGEL
86 Vice Pres Govt Affair/Comm Outreach .... Ms. Claire ROSACCO
84 Vice President Access & Completion .... Dr. Karen MILLER
26 Vice Pres Integrated Communications .... Mr. David HOOVLER
43 Vice Pres Legal Svcs/Gen Counsel .... Ms. Renee RICHARD
20 Vice Pres Learning & Engagement .... Ms. Lisa WILLIAMS
17 VP Health Care Educ Initiatives .... Ms. Patricia REID
19 Vice Pres Public Safety & Security .... Chief Clayton HARRIS
18 Vice President Ops & Mfg .... Ms. Alicia BOOKER
32 Assoc VP Access & Comm Engagement ... Dr. JaNice MARSHALL
88 Exec Dir Access Learning & Success .... Ms. Sandra MCKNIGHT
88 Exec Dir Business Continuity .... Mr. Marvin RICHARDS
88 Exec Director Media Engineering .... Mr. Robert BRYAN
13 Exec Director EIS .... Mr. Jon DOLINAR
07 Executive Director Enrollment Opers .... Ms. Angela JOHNSON
88 Exec Director Plant Operations .... Mr. Blair BOSWORTH
88 Exec Dir Veteran Services/Programs .... Mr. Richard DE CHANT
88 Exec Dir College Svcs & Retail .... Mr. Chris MOIR
88 Exec Dir College Pathway Programs .... Mr. Kenneth HALE
96 Executive Dir Supplier Managed Svcs .... Ms. Cynthia LEITSON
88 Exec Dir/GM Hospitality Mgmt .... Mr. Brandt EVANS
88 Exec Dir Organizational Development .... Mr. Barry ROYKO
20 Dean Learning & Engagement East .... Dr. John W. MARR, JR.
20 Dean Learning & Engagement West .. Dr. Janice TAYLOR HEARD
20 Dean Learning & Engagement Metro .... Mr. Lindsay ENGLISH
20 Dean Lrng & Engagement Westshore .... Mr. Robert SEARSON
35 Dean Access & Completion Metro .... Ms. Denise MCCORY
35 Dean Access & Completion West .... Ms. Diana DEL ROSARIO
35 Dean Access & Completion East .... Dr. Mel A. MAY
35 Dean Access & Completion Westshore .... Dr. Ann PROUDFIT
66 Dean Nursing .... Dr. Vivian M. YATES
88 Assoc Dean Creative Arts Metro .... Ms. Amy PARKS
76 Assoc Dean Health Careers & Science .... Ms. Barbara MIKUSZEWSKI
76 Assoc Dean Health Careers & Science .... Ms. Lisa DIONISI
81 Interim Assoc Dean Math West .... Mr. Paul ROKICKY
83 Assoc Dean Social Sciences West .... Vacant
49 Assoc Dean Liberal Arts East .... Dr. William CUNION
49 Assoc Dean Liberal Arts Metro ...... Dr. Jocelyn LADNER-MATHIS
49 Assoc Dean Liberal Arts West .... Ms. Delia BOBER
50 Assoc Dean Bus/Math & Tech Metro .... Dr. Pamela ELLISON
50 Assoc Dean Bus/Math & Tech East .... Dr. Lorraine HARTLEY
72 Assoc Dean Bus IT Applied Tech West .... Mr. Scott HALM
54 Assoc Dean Engineering Metro .... Dr. Lam WONG
88 Interim Assoc Dean Hospitality Mgmt .... Dr. John MARR
76 Assoc Dean Health Careers West .... Mr. David FRAZEE
66 Assoc Dean Nursing Metro .... Ms. Irene MEYER
100 Chief of Staff/Exec Asst to Pres .... Ms. Ronna MCNAIR
23 Dir Healthcare Industry Solutions .... Dr. John SCHMIDT
28 Director of Diversity & Inclusion .... Dr. Deborale RICHARDSON-PHILLIPS
37 District Dir Student Financial Aid .... Ms. Kimberly NASH-YORE
29 Director Alumni Relations .... Mr. John NOLAN
105 Director Info Technology Svcs .... Mr. Dana WALTERS
108 Director Institutional Research .... Mr. G. Rob STUART
38 Assistant Dean Counseling-Metro .... Mrs. Ralonda ELLIS-HILL
38 Assistant Dean Counseling-East .... Ms. Johanna BACIK
38 Assistant Dean Counseling-West .... Mr. Marcos RIVERA
04 Admin Associate to President .... Ms. Barbara BELL
102 Exec Dir Foundation/Corporate Rel .... Ms. Kate MCDADE
41 Athletic Director West .... Mr. Mark RODRIGUEZ
41 Athletic Director East .... Ms. Rita MCKINLEY
41 Athletic Director Metro .... Ms. Jennifer ELLIS

Cuyahoga Community College Eastern Campus (B)

4250 Richmond Road, Highland Hills OH 44122

Telephone: (800) 954-8742 Identification: 770355
Accreditation: &NH

† Branch campus of Cuyahoga Community College, Cleveland, OH.

Cuyahoga Community College Metropolitan Campus (C)

2900 Community College Avenue, Cleveland OH 44115

Telephone: (800) 954-8742 Identification: 770354
Accreditation: &NH, PHLEB

† Branch campus of Cuyahoga Community College, Cleveland, OH.

Cuyahoga Community College Western Campus (D)

11000 Pleasant Valley Road, Parma OH 44130

Telephone: (800) 954-8742 Identification: 770356
Accreditation: &NH

† Branch campus of Cuyahoga Community College, Cleveland, OH.

Cuyahoga Community College Westshore (E)

31001 Clemens Road, Westlake OH 44145

Telephone: (800) 954-8742 Identification: 770357
Accreditation: &NH

† Branch campus of Cuyahoga Community College, Cleveland, OH.

Davis College (F)

4747 Monroe Street, Toledo OH 43623-4389

County: Lucas FICE Identification: 004855
Unit ID: 202435
Telephone: (419) 473-2700 Carnegie Class: Assoc/PrivFP
FAX Number: (419) 473-2472 Calendar System: Quarter
URL: www.daviscollege.edu
Established: 1858 Annual Undergrad Tuition & Fees: $13,650
Enrollment: 193 Coed
Affiliation or Control: Proprietary IRS Status: Proprietary
Highest Offering: Associate Degree
Program: Occupational; 2-Year Principally Bachelor's Creditable; Business Emphasis
Accreditation: NH, MAC

01 President .... Diane BRUNNER
32 VP of Student & Academic Services .... Mary RYAN BULONE
06 Registrar .... Marilyn BOVIA
37 Director Student Financial Aid .... Melissa DODSWORTH
07 Director of Admissions .... Dana STERN
36 Director of Student Placement .... Nick NIGRO
04 Assistant to the President .... Jane MULLIKIN
30 VP of Institutional Advancement .... Tim BRUNNER
18 Chief Facilities/Physical Plant .... Greg RIPPKE
08 Librarian .... Peggy PETERSON-SENIUK
13 Director of Information Technology .... Brian FROST
108 Director Institutional Assessment .... Vacant
50 Program Director Business & IT .... Mary DELOE
57 Program Director Design .... Janet WEBER
97 Program Director General Education .... Jane PFEIFER
76 Prog Director Admin & Allied Health .... Terry DIPPMAN

The Defiance College (G)

701 N Clinton Street, Defiance OH 43512-1695

County: Defiance FICE Identification: 003041
Unit ID: 202514
Telephone: (419) 784-4010 Carnegie Class: Bac/Diverse
FAX Number: (419) 784-0426 Calendar System: Semester
URL: www.defiance.edu
Established: 1850 Annual Undergrad Tuition & Fees: $31,082
Enrollment: 937 Coed
Affiliation or Control: United Church Of Christ IRS Status: 501(c)3
Highest Offering: Master's
Program: Liberal Arts And General; Teacher Preparatory
Accreditation: NH, CAATE, IACBE, NURSE, SW, TED

01 Interim President .... Mr. Edward R. BUHL
05 Interim VP for Academic Affairs .... Dr. Timothy RICKABAUGH
30 Vice Pres Institutional Advancement .... Dr. Kenneth WETSTEIN
10 Vice Pres for Finance & Management .... Mrs. Lois N. MCCULLOUGH
32 Dean of Students .... Mrs. Lisa MARSALEK
84 Vice Pres for Enrollment Management .... Mr. Michael SUZO
88 Dean McMaster Sch Adv Hum .... Mrs. Mary Ann STUDER
07 Director of Admissions .... Mr. Brad HARSHA
15 Director of Human Resources .... Ms. Mary E. BURKHOLDER
29 Director Alumni and Parent Relation .... Mrs. Lorie RATH
08 Dir of Library and Instr Resource .... Mrs. Michelle BLANK
26 Director Public Relations/Marketing .... Mrs. Kathy M. PUNCHES
13 Director of Computer Services .... Mr. Jeremy KENNEDY
06 Registrar .... Mrs. Mariah ORZOLEK
36 Director of Career Development .... Vacant
37 Director of Financial Aid .... Mrs. Amy FRANCIS
41 Athletic Director .... Mr. Rudy YOVICH
42 Campus Minister/Church Relations .... Rev. Janice L. BECHTEL
28 Director Intercultural Relations .... Ms. Mercedes CLAY
39 Director of Residence Life .... Mrs. Jennifer WALTERS
18 Director of Physical Plant .... Mr. James CORESSEL
21 Director of Accounting .... Mrs. Kristine BOLAND

Denison University (H)

100 W College Street, Granville OH 43023-1359

County: Licking FICE Identification: 003042
Unit ID: 202523
Telephone: (740) 587-0810 Carnegie Class: Bac/A&S
FAX Number: (740) 587-6417 Calendar System: Semester
URL: www.denison.edu
Established: 1831 Annual Undergrad Tuition & Fees: $47,290
Enrollment: 2,151 Coed
Affiliation or Control: Independent Non-Profit IRS Status: 501(c)3
Highest Offering: Baccalaureate
Program: Liberal Arts And General
Accreditation: NH, CAATE

01 President .... Dr. Adam S. WEINBERG
05 Provost .... Dr. Kimberly A. COPLIN
20 Associate Provost Faculty Affairs .... Dr. Catherine L. DOLLARD
20 Associate Provost Academic Admin .... Dr. James R. PLETCHER
28 Associate Provost Diversity .... Dr. Alison P. WILLIAMS
10 VP Finance & Management .... Mr. David A. ENGLISH
30 VP Institutional Advancement .... Ms. Julia BEYER HOUPT
32 VP Student Development .... Dr. Laurel B. KENNEDY
84 VP Enrollment Management .... Vacant
07 Director of Admissions .... Mr. Michael S. HILLS
89 Dean of First-Year Students .... Dr. Mark MOLLER
35 Dean of Students .... Mr. William A. FOX
06 Registrar .... Ms. Yadigar COLLINS
08 Director of Libraries .... Ms. BethAnn ZAMBELLA
37 Dir of Financial Aid & Student Empl .... Ms. Laura E. MEEK
13 Dir Information Technology Services .... Ms. Dena L. SPERANZA
15 Director of Human Resources .... Mr. Jim ABLES
18 Director of Facilities Services .... Mr. Arthur J. CHONKO
19 Director of Campus Safety .... Mr. Daniel HECT
26 Dir of Univ Communications .... Mr. Jack HIRE
88 Dir of Strategic Communications .... Ms. Barbara STAMBAUGH
29 Director of Alumni Relations .... Mr. Steven R. CRAWFORD
36 Dir Career Exploration & Dev .... Mr. Richard T. BERMAN
38 Dir of Health & Counseling Svc .... Ms. Amanda L. LEFELD
42 Chaplain/Director of Religious Life .... Rev. Mark ORTEN
100 Special Asst to Pres/Chief of Staff .... Dr. Joyce MEREDITH
93 Dir Multicultural Stdnt Affs/Ast Dn .... Mr. Erik S. FARLEY
11 Director of Administrative Services .... Ms. Jenna MCDEVITT
09 Director of Institutional Research .... Dr. Todd M. JAMISON
41 Director of Athletics .... Ms. Nan CARNEY-DEBORD
88 Chief Investment Officer .... Ms. Adele N. GORRILLA
04 Sr Executive Asst to President .... Ms. Trish RUESS
102 Dir Foundation/Corporate Relations .... Ms. Anne M. STENGLE
104 Interim Director Study Abroad .... Dr. Sue F. DAVIS
39 Director Student Housing .... Ms. Kristan R. HAUSMAN
44 Assoc VP Inst Advancement .... Mr. Greg R. BADER

DeVry University - Columbus Campus (I)

1350 Alum Creek Drive, Columbus OH 43209-2705

Telephone: (614) 253-7291 FICE Identification: 003099
Accreditation: &NH, CAHIIM, ENGT

† Regional accreditation is carried under the parent institution in Downers Grove, IL.

Eastern Gateway Community College - Jefferson County Campus (J)

4000 Sunset Boulevard, Steubenville OH 43952-3594

County: Jefferson FICE Identification: 007275
Unit ID: 203331
Telephone: (740) 264-5591 Carnegie Class: Assoc/Pub-R-M
FAX Number: (740) 264-1338 Calendar System: Semester
URL: www.egcc.edu
Established: 1966 Annual Undergrad Tuition & Fees (In-District): $3,330
Enrollment: 3,182 Coed
Affiliation or Control: State/Local IRS Status: 501(c)3
Highest Offering: Associate Degree
Program: Occupational; 2-Year Principally Bachelor's Creditable; Technical Emphasis
Accreditation: NH, CAHIIM, COARC, DA, MAC, MLTAD, RAD

01 President .... Dr. Jimmie D. BRUCE
05 Exec Vice Pres Academic/Stdnt Affs .... Dr. James BABER
10 Vice Pres Business Services/Treas .... Mr. James J. MCGRAIL, III
11 Vice Pres Administrative Services .... Ms. Sherri VANTASSEL
46 Vice Pres Strategic Initiatives .... Vacant
84 Dean Enrollment Management .... Ms. Patty J. STURCH
76 Dean Health & Biological Sciences .... Dr. Robin FLOHR
81 Dean Student Learning/Humanities .... Ms. Christina WANAT
32 Dean TRIO/Student Svcs & Retention .... Dr. Dorothy COLLINS
50 Dean Business/Engineering & Info .... Mr. Jerry KLINESMITH
21 Controller .... Ms. Joanna FLANIGAN
07 Director of Admissions .... Vacant
26 Dir Public Information/Web Coord .... Vacant
37 Director Student Info/Financial Aid .... Ms. Kelly WILSON
103 Workforce/Community Outreach Coord .... Mr. Jerry KLINESMITH
13 Int Director Technology Services .... Mr. David SMITH
36 Director Career Services/Alumni .... Vacant
40 Director of Bookstore .... Mrs. Judith LUDE
21 Director Student Billing/Payroll .... Ms. Tonya LOGAN
18 Director Building & Grounds .... Mr. Julius J. DZIEWATKOSKI
08 Int Dean/Library Services .... Mrs. Lois T. REKOWSKI
06 Registrar .... Ms. Patty J. STURCH
29 Director of Alumni Relations .... Vacant

Edison State Community College (K)

1973 Edison Drive, Piqua OH 45356-9239

County: Miami FICE Identification: 012750
Unit ID: 202648
Telephone: (937) 778-8600 Carnegie Class: Assoc/Pub-S-SC

FAX Number: (937) 778-1920 Calendar System: Semester
URL: www.edisonohio.edu
Established: 1973 Annual Undergrad Tuition & Fees (In-State): $4,219
Enrollment: 3,042 Coed
Affiliation or Control: State IRS Status: 501(c)3
Highest Offering: Associate Degree
Program: Occupational; 2-Year Principally Bachelor's Creditable
Accreditation: NH, ADNUR, MAC, MLTAD, PHLEB, PTAA

01 President .... Dr. Doreen LARSON
04 Executive Asst to the President .... Ms. Heather LANHAM
05 Sr VP of Academic Affairs .... Dr. Patricia A. ROSS
10 VP of Administration & Finance .... Mr. John W. SHISHOFF
30 VP for Institutional Advancement .... Ms. Kimberly HORTON
15 VP of Strategic Human Resources .... Mrs. Linda M. PELTIER
32 Vice President of Student Affairs .... Mr. Scott M. BURNAM
13 Chief Information Officer .... Mr. Harry LAWHORN
35 Director of Student Services .... Ms. Teresa ROTH
49 Dean of Arts and Science .... Ms. Naomi LOUIS
50 Dean of Business/IT & Engineering .... Ms. Shirley MOORE
66 Dean of Nursing & Health Sciences .... Ms. Gwendolyn A. STEVENSON
09 Director of Institutional Research .... Ms. Rebecca P. TELFORD
88 Director of Student Success .... Ms. Pamela GIBELLINO
21 Controller .... Mr. Thomas FRYMAN
41 Director Athletics & Student Life .... Mr. Nathan COLE
37 Director of Financial Aid .... Ms. Kathi S. RICHARDS
26 Dir of Marketing & Communications .... Mr. Bruce MCKENZIE
84 Enrollment Manager .... Ms. Stacey BEAN
06 Registrar .... Ms. Mary BORNHORST
08 Director of the Library .... Ms. Nancy MADDEN
18 Dir of Physical Plant/Facilities .... Mr. Douglas RIEHLE

Edison State Community College Darke County Campus (A)

601 Wagner Avenue, Greenville OH 45331
Telephone: (937) 548-5546 Identification: 770358
Accreditation: &NH

† Branch campus of Edison State Community College, Piqua, OH.

ETI Technical College of Niles (B)

2076-86 Youngstown-Warren Road, Niles OH 44446-4398
County: Trumbull FICE Identification: 030790
Unit ID: 200590
Telephone: (330) 652-9919 Carnegie Class: Assoc/PrivFP
FAX Number: (330) 652-4399 Calendar System: Semester
URL: www.eticollege.edu
Established: 1989 Annual Undergrad Tuition & Fees: $8,920
Enrollment: 170 Coed
Affiliation or Control: Proprietary IRS Status: Proprietary
Highest Offering: Associate Degree
Program: Occupational; 2-Year Principally Bachelor's Creditable
Accreditation: ACCSC

01 Director .... Mrs. Renee ZUZOLO
07 Director of Admissions .... Mrs. Diane MARSTELLER
37 Director Financial Aid .... Ms. Kay MADIGAN

Fortis College (C)

555 E Alex-Bell Road, Centerville OH 45459-6120
County: Montgomery FICE Identification: 021907
Unit ID: 205179
Telephone: (937) 433-3410 Carnegie Class: Assoc/PrivFP
FAX Number: (937) 435-6516 Calendar System: Semester
URL: www.fortiscollege.edu
Established: 1970 Annual Undergrad Tuition & Fees: $17,201
Enrollment: 1,645 Coed
Affiliation or Control: Proprietary IRS Status: Proprietary
Highest Offering: Baccalaureate
Program: Occupational; 2-Year Principally Bachelor's Creditable
Accreditation: ACCSC, ADNUR, EMT, MAC, NURSE

01 President .... Richard MALLOW
05 VP/Chief Academic Officer .... Diana LAWRENCE
09 Dir Inst Effectiveness/Compliance .... Mimi SUMMER
20 Director Education .... Diana LAWRENCE
07 Director Admissions .... Mike MONTGOMERY
37 Director Financial Aid .... Rachel KARMON

Fortis College (D)

2545 Bailey Road, Cuyahoga Falls OH 44221-2949
County: Summit FICE Identification: 009412
Unit ID: 204307
Telephone: (330) 923-9959 Carnegie Class: Assoc/PrivFP
FAX Number: (330) 923-0886 Calendar System: Other
URL: www.fortis.edu
Established: 1922 Annual Undergrad Tuition & Fees: $13,533
Enrollment: 526 Coed
Affiliation or Control: Proprietary IRS Status: Proprietary
Highest Offering: Associate Degree
Program: Occupational
Accreditation: ACCSC, DA

01 Director .... Ms. Carson BURKE

Fortis College (E)

653 Enterprise Parkway, Ravenna OH 44266-8058
Telephone: (330) 297-7319 FICE Identification: 023036
Accreditation: ACICS, CAHIIM

† Branch campus of Fortis College, Norfolk, VA.

Fortis College (F)

4151 Executive Parkway, Suite 120,
Westerville OH 43081-3860
County: Franklin Identification: 666602
Unit ID: 450058
Telephone: (614) 882-2551 Carnegie Class: Assoc/PrivFP
FAX Number: (614) 882-2914 Calendar System: Other
URL: www.fortis.edu
Established: 2010 Annual Undergrad Tuition & Fees: $14,641
Enrollment: 694 Coed
Affiliation or Control: Proprietary IRS Status: Proprietary
Highest Offering: Associate Degree
Program: Occupational; 2-Year Principally Bachelor's Creditable; Music Emphasis
Accreditation: ABHES, RAD, SURGT, SURTEC

01 President .... Mr. Peter MARTINELLO

Franciscan University of Steubenville (G)

1235 University Boulevard, Steubenville OH 43952-1763
County: Jefferson FICE Identification: 003036
Unit ID: 205957
Telephone: (740) 283-3771 Carnegie Class: Master's M
FAX Number: (740) 283-6472 Calendar System: Semester
URL: www.franciscan.edu
Established: 1946 Annual Undergrad Tuition & Fees: $24,780
Enrollment: 2,714 Coed
Affiliation or Control: Roman Catholic IRS Status: 501(c)3
Highest Offering: Master's
Program: Liberal Arts And General; Religious Emphasis
Accreditation: NH, CACREP, NUR, SW, TED

01 President .... Rev. Sean SHERIDAN, TOR
00 Chancellor .... Rev. Terence HENRY, TOR
03 Executive Vice President .... Vacant
88 Vice Pres of Pastoral Care & Evange .... Rev. Nathan MALAVOLTI, TOR
10 VP of Finance & Admin Operations .... Mr. David M. SKIVIAT
05 Vice President of Academic Affairs .... Dr. Daniel KEMPTON
30 Vice President of Advancement .... Mr. Michael HERNON
31 Vice Pres of Community Relations .... Vacant
46 Vice Pres for Mission Effectiveness .... Vacant
15 Vice Pres of Human Resources .... Mr. Brenan PERGI
32 Vice President of Student Life .... Mr. David A. SCHMIESING
84 Vice Pres of Enrollment Management .... Mr. Joel S. RECZNIK
88 Religious Administrator .... Rev. Terence HENRY, TOR
42 University Chaplain .... Rev. Dominic SCOTTO, TOR
20 Dir of Advising & Acad Operations .... Ms. Ann DULANY
13 Exec Dir of Information Technology .... Mr. Kevin G. SEBOLT
35 Asst Vice Pres of Student Life .... Ms. Catherine J. HECK
08 Director of Library .... Mr. William JAKUB
88 Exec Director Christian Outreach .... Mr. Mark JOSEPH
44 Director of Planned Giving .... Dr. Mark E. RECZNIK
30 Director of Development .... Mr. Mark NEHRBAS
29 Director of Alumni Relations .... Mr. Timothy J. DELANEY
26 Director of Public Relations .... Miss Lisa M. FERGUSON
07 Director of Admissions .... Mrs. Margaret WEBER
07 Director of Graduate Enrollment .... Mr. Mark T. MCGUIRE
06 Registrar .... Mr. Cody SCHMITZ
84 Exec Dir of Enrollment Services .... Mr. John L. HERRMANN
09 Director of Institutional Research .... Dcn. Mark A. ERSTE, SR.
21 Controller .... Mr. John A. STEITZ
96 Director of Business Services .... Ms. Marlene K. TERPENNING
40 Bookstore Manager .... Mr. John RECZNIK
91 Director of Administrative Systems .... Mrs. Pam SHANE
16 Director of Human Resources .... Vacant
18 Director Physical Plant Services .... Mr. Joseph P. MCGURN
88 Director of Missionary Outreach .... Mr. Rhett YOUNG
88 Director of Chapel Ministries .... Mr. Robert PALLADINO
88 Director of JCW Center/Planning .... Mrs. Kathy L. MATTIOLI
104 Director of Study Abroad .... Mr. Mark HANRAHAN
38 Director of Counseling .... Mr. Joseph A. LOIZZO
41 Director of Athletics .... Mr. Christopher L. LEDYARD
36 Director Career Planning/Placement .... Mrs. Nancy S. RONEVICH
73 Director MA Theology Program .... Dr. Michael SIRILLA
50 Director MBA Program .... Mr. Joseph ZORIC
83 Director MA Counseling Program .... Dr. Christin JUNGERS
53 Director MS Education Program .... Dr. Mark FURDA
88 Director MA Philosophy Program .... Dr. John CROSBY
90 Coord Academic Computer Services .... Ms. Sandy M. RADVANSKY
28 Director of Diversity .... Vacant
66 Director MS Nursing .... Dr. Carolyn MILLER
19 Director Security/Safety .... Mr. Michael CONN
106 Dir Online Education/E-learning .... Dr. Cory MALONEY
108 Director Institutional Assessment .... Vacant

Franklin University (H)

201 S Grant Avenue, Columbus OH 43215-5399
County: Franklin FICE Identification: 003046
Unit ID: 202806
Telephone: (614) 797-4700 Carnegie Class: Spec/Bus
FAX Number: N/A Calendar System: Trimester
URL: www.franklin.edu
Established: 1902 Annual Undergrad Tuition & Fees: $14,520
Enrollment: 5,737 Coed
Affiliation or Control: Independent Non-Profit IRS Status: 501(c)3
Highest Offering: Master's
Program: Professional; Business Emphasis
Accreditation: NH, IACBE, NURSE

01 President .... Dr. David R. DECKER
11 Sr VP Adminstration/Chief of Staff .... Ms. Christi L. CABUNGCAL
05 Provost/Sr VP for Academic Affairs .... Dr. Christopher L. WASHINGTON
12 Director Indianapolis Location .... Vacant
07 VP Enrollment & Student Affairs .... Ms. Linda M. STEELE
30 Vice Pres University Advancement .... Ms. Bonnie SMITH QUIST
15 VP of Human Resources & Campus Svcs .... Ms. Christi CABUNGCAL
09 VP Accred/Institutional Effective .... Dr. Pamela SHAY
22 VP Planning & University Services .... Ms. Evelyn LEVINO
20 Associate Provost Academic Quality .... Dr. Karen MINER ROMANOFF
04 Executive Assistant to President .... Ms. Bonnie MCCANN
32 Dean of Students .... Vacant
108 Dean/Exec Dir of AIE .... Mr. Wayne C. MILLER
10 Chief Financial Officer .... Mr. Marvin BRISKEY
13 Chief Information Officer .... Mr. Rick SUNDERMAN
20 Dir of Academic Support Services .... Ms. Susanne SMITH
06 Registrar .... Mr. Frank YANCHAK
08 Director of Library Services .... Vacant
37 Director of Financial Aid .... Ms. Goldie LANGLEY
46 Director of Strategic Relations .... Ms. Jody NOREEN
35 Dir Student Development .... Ms. Wendi ROBINSON
88 VP Franklin Learning Systems .... Mr. Patrick BENNETT
84 Exec Director of Marketing & Enroll .... Mr. Scott BOOTH
12 Exec Dir Domestic Expan/Reg Cmps .... Mr. Bill CHAN
18 Director of Facilities .... Mr. Carl BROWN
26 Director of Public Relations .... Ms. Sherry MERCURIO
29 Director of Alumni Engagement & Dev .. Mr. Kevin GREENWOOD
96 Director of Purchasing .... Mr. Bob DONAHUE
28 Director of Benefits .... Ms. Brenda LISTON
24 Director of Student Learning Center .... Mr. Christopher FIELDS
88 Director of Teaching Effectiveness .... Dr. Fawn WINTERWOOD
49 Dean Arts/Science & Technology .... Dr. Keith GROFF
50 Dean College of Business .... Dr. Tom SEILER
69 Dean College of Health & Public Adm .... Dr. Leslie KING
88 Dean Global Programs .... Dr. Godfrey MENDES
16 Director of Human Resources .... Ms. Randi QUINN
88 Director of Accounting .... Mr. Jeffrey GERBERRY
88 Exec Dir of Financial Services .... Mr. Randolph SNYDER

Galen College of Nursing (I)

100 E Business Way, Suite 200, Cincinnati OH 45241
Telephone: (513) 475-3600 Identification: 770537
Accreditation: &SC

† Branch campus of Galen College of Nursing, Louisville, KY.

Gallipolis Career College (J)

1176 Jackson Pike, Suite 312, Gallipolis OH 45631-2600
County: Gallia FICE Identification: 030079
Unit ID: 205513
Telephone: (740) 446-4367 Carnegie Class: Assoc/PrivFP
FAX Number: (740) 446-4124 Calendar System: Quarter
URL: www.gallipoliscareercollege.edu
Established: 1962 Annual Undergrad Tuition & Fees: $12,050
Enrollment: 96 Coed
Affiliation or Control: Proprietary IRS Status: Proprietary
Highest Offering: Associate Degree
Program: 2-Year Principally Bachelor's Creditable; Business Emphasis
Accreditation: ACICS

01 President .... Mr. Robert L. SHIREY, JR.
05 Director of Education .... Mr. Danny DOUGHERTY
07 Director of Admissions .... Mr. Bo SHIREY, III
10 Director of Finance .... Mrs. Jeanette SHIREY
37 Director Student Financial Aid .... Ms. Christina SHOCKEY

God's Bible School and College (K)

1810 Young Street, Cincinnati OH 45202-6838
County: Hamilton FICE Identification: 022205
Unit ID: 202903
Telephone: (513) 721-7944 Carnegie Class: Spec/Faith
FAX Number: (513) 763-6649 Calendar System: Semester
URL: www.gbs.edu
Established: 1900 Annual Undergrad Tuition & Fees: $6,840
Enrollment: 301 Coed
Affiliation or Control: Interdenominational IRS Status: 501(c)3
Highest Offering: Master's
Program: Religious Emphasis
Accreditation: NH, BI

01 President .... Dr. Michael R. AVERY
05 Vice President Academic Affairs .... Dr. Aaron PROFITT
32 Vice President Student Development .... Mr. Richard MILES
30 Director Institutional Advancement .... Mrs. Faith AVERY
06 Registrar .... Mr. Christopher LAMBETH
08 Head Librarian .... Mr. Joshua AVERY
10 Director of Finance .... Mr. David FREDERICK

11 Campus Administrator .... Mr. Richard MILES
26 Director of Public Relations .... Mr. Don DAVISON
13 Coordinator Information Services .... Mr. Steve HARMS
07 Student Recruiter .... Mr. Kent STETLER
37 Financial Aid Coordinator .... Ms. Sharree POUZAR
84 Director Enrollment Services .... Mr. Nathan DAHLER

Good Samaritan College of Nursing and Health Science (A)

375 Dixmyth Avenue, Cincinnati OH 45220-2489
County: Hamilton FICE Identification: 006494
Unit ID: 202912
Telephone: (513) 862-2743 Carnegie Class: Assoc/PrivNFP
FAX Number: (513) 862-3572 Calendar System: Semester
URL: www.gscollege.edu
Established: 2001 Annual Undergrad Tuition & Fees: $15,054
Enrollment: 353 Coed
Affiliation or Control: Independent Non-Profit IRS Status: 501(c)3
Highest Offering: Baccalaureate
Program: 2-Year Principally Bachelor's Creditable; Professional; Nursing Emphasis
Accreditation: NH, ADNUR, NUR

01 President .... Mr. Morris COHEN
05 Dean of Academic Affairs .... Ms. Patricia MCMAHON
32 Dean of Students/Alumni .... Ms. Mary Jo KATHMAN
09 Dir of Inst Assessment/Planning .... Dr. Terri PULLEN
84 Dean of Enrollment Management .... Dr. Linda HAYES

Harrison College-Columbus Ohio Campus (B)

3880 Jackpot Road, Grove City OH 43123
Telephone: (614) 539-8800 Identification: 770748
Accreditation: ACICS, MAC

† Branch campus of Harrison College - Indianapolis Downtown Campus, Indianapolis, IN.

Heidelberg University (C)

310 E Market Street, Tiffin OH 44883-2462
County: Seneca FICE Identification: 003048
Unit ID: 203085
Telephone: (419) 448-2000 Carnegie Class: Master's S
FAX Number: (419) 448-2124 Calendar System: Semester
URL: www.heidelberg.edu
Established: 1850 Annual Undergrad Tuition & Fees: $27,900
Enrollment: 1,493 Coed
Affiliation or Control: United Church Of Christ IRS Status: 501(c)3
Highest Offering: Master's
Program: Liberal Arts And General; Teacher Preparatory
Accreditation: NH, CAATE, CACREP, MUS, TED

01 President .... Dr. Robert HUNTINGTON
05 VP for Academic Affairs & Provost .... Dr. Beth SCHWARTZ
10 VP for Admin & Business Affairs .... Mr. John WILKIN
84 VP for Enrollment Mgmt .... Mr. Doug KELLAR
30 VP Inst Advancement & Univ Relation .... Ms. Connie L. HARRIS
20 Assoc VP Acad Affs/Dean Undergr Fac .... Dr. Vicki OHL
44 Exec Dir for Development .... Ms. Ashley HELMSTETTER
13 Assoc VP for Information Resources .... Mr. Kurt HUENEMANN
18 Assoc VP for Facilities & Engrng .... Mr. Rodney MORRISON
50 Dean of the School of Business .... Dr. Haseeb AHMED
06 Registrar .... Ms. Cindy SUTER
88 Director MA in Counseling Pgm .... Dr. Jo-Ann SANDERS
53 Director of School of Education .... Dr. Robert SWANSON
64 Director of School of Music .... Dr. John OWEN
92 Assoc Dean for Honors Program .... Dr. Doug COLLAR
104 Director Intl Affairs & Studies .... Ms. Julie ARNOLD
36 Asst Dean Stdnt Affs for Stdnt Succ .... Dr. Kristen LINDSAY
58 Dir Graduate Studies in Business .... Mr. Allen UNDERWOOD
88 Assoc Dean of Advising & Assessment .... Dr. Ellen NAGY
08 Director of Library .... Dr. Nainsi HOUSTON
41 Athletic Director .... Mr. Matt PALM
21 Business Officer .... Ms. Barb GABEL
37 Director Student Financial Aid .... Mrs. Juli WEININGER
30 Director of Development .... Mr. Lee MARTIN
32 Dean of Student Affairs .... Mr. Dustin BRENTLINGER
39 Asst Dn Stdnt Affs for Campus Life .... Mr. Mark ZENO
88 Dir Student Engagement .... Vacant
15 Director of Human Resources .... Ms. Margaret RUDOLPH
21 Controller .... Ms. Kelly WARNKE
04 Exec Assistant to President .... Ms. Monica VERHOFF
40 Director of University Bookstore .... Ms. Gail ROBERTS
42 Director of Campus Ministry .... Rev. Paul STARK
105 Assoc Director Web Services .... Mr. Dustin SMITH
19 Director Security/Safety .... Mr. Jeff RHOADES

Herzing University-Akron (D)

1600 S Arlington Street, Suite 100, Akron OH 44306-3958
Telephone: (330) 724-1600 FICE Identification: 020695
Accreditation: &NH, ADNUR, DA, MAC, MLTAD

† Regional accreditation is carried under the parent institution in Madison, WI.

Herzing University Toledo Campus (E)

5212 Hill Avenue, Toledo OH 43615
Telephone: (419) 776-0030 Identification: 770434
Accreditation: &NH, MAAB, SURTEC

† Branch campus of Herzing University, Madison, WI.

Hiram College (F)

Box 67, Hiram OH 44234-0067
County: Portage FICE Identification: 003049
Unit ID: 203128
Telephone: (330) 569-3211 Carnegie Class: Bac/A&S
FAX Number: (330) 569-5494 Calendar System: Other
URL: www.hiram.edu
Established: 1850 Annual Undergrad Tuition & Fees: $31,530
Enrollment: 1,259 Coed
Affiliation or Control: Independent Non-Profit IRS Status: 501(c)3
Highest Offering: Master's
Program: Liberal Arts And General; Teacher Preparatory
Accreditation: NH, MUS, NURSE, TED

01 President .... Dr. Lori E. VARLOTTA
05 Vice President & Dean of College .... Dr. Robert HAAK
10 Vice President Business & Finance .... Mr. Stephen W. JONES
30 Vice Pres Development & Alumni Rels .... Mr. Patrick S. ROBERTS
32 Vice President & Dean of Students .... Ms. Elizabeth M. OKUMA
07 VP of Enrollment .... Ms. Lindajean H. WESTERN
20 Associate Dean of the College .... Ms. Ellen L. WALKER
107 Director Professional/Grad Studies .... Ms. Jennifer L. MILLER
06 Registrar .... Ms. Lisa N. DELANEY
08 Head Librarian .... Mr. David D. EVERETT
29 Director Alumni Relations .... Mr. John B. COYNE
37 Director Student Financial Services .... Ms. Andrea L. CAPUTO
36 Director of Career Services .... Ms. Heather M. BALAS
13 Director of Computer Center .... Mr. Frank J. VENTURA
09 Director of Institutional Research .... Ms. Maria A. O'CONNOR
41 Director of Athletics .... Ms. Ellen E. DEMPSEY
15 Director of Human Resources .... Ms. Lynn M. KOSTRAB
18 Director of the Physical Plant .... Mr. Sam V. MORGANO
21 Controller/Director of Accounting .... Ms. Susan A. BOYLE
35 Director of Student Involvement .... Ms. Alexandra K. ULBRICHT
38 Director Student Counseling .... Dr. Kevin P. FEISTHAMEL
28 Director Ethnic Diversity Affairs .... Ms. Detra E. WEST
96 Director of Purchasing .... Ms. Martha A. SCHETTLER
26 Chief Public Relations/Marketing .... Ms. Cristine D. BOYD
04 Administrative Asst to President .... Mr. Phil J. EAVES
102 Dir Foundation/Corporate Relations .... Ms. Christine KOHLS
104 Director Study Abroad .... Ms. Kimberly S. MICK
19 Director Security/Safety .... Mr. Steve J. CHAPMAN
39 Director Student Housing .... Mr. Mike F. CORR

Hocking College (G)

3301 Hocking Parkway, Nelsonville OH 45764-9704
County: Athens FICE Identification: 007598
Unit ID: 203155
Telephone: (740) 753-3591 Carnegie Class: Assoc/Pub-R-L
FAX Number: (740) 753-7039 Calendar System: Semester
URL: www.hocking.edu
Established: 1968 Annual Undergrad Tuition & Fees (In-State): $4,390
Enrollment: 3,474 Coed
Affiliation or Control: State IRS Status: 501(c)3
Highest Offering: Associate Degree
Program: Occupational; 2-Year Principally Bachelor's Creditable; Technical Emphasis
Accreditation: NH, ACBSP, ACFEI, ADNUR, CAHIIM, MAC, PNUR, #PTAA

01 President .... Dr. Betty YOUNG
10 Vice President & Treasurer .... Ms. Gina FETTY
05 Provost/VP Acad & Student Affairs .... Vacant
11 Vice Pres Administrative Services .... Dr. Myriah DAVIS
15 VP Human Resources/Gen Counsel .... Ms. Nicolette DIOGUARDI
20 Assoc VP Acad/Student Affairs .... Mr. Joe WAKEMAN
04 Executive Assistant to President .... Ms. Nancy VANDEMAN
20 Dean of Reg Campuses/Industry Tech .... Mr. Neil HINTON
66 Dean School of Health & Nursing .... Ms. Tammy KEITH
13 Chief Technology Officer .... Mr. Ben DALTON
37 Exec Director Financial Aid .... Ms. Deneene MERCHANT
19 Director Public Safety Services .... Mr. Scott MONG
08 Dir Learning Resource Ctr/Librarian .... Mr. Jeff GRAFFIUS
26 Exec Dir Marketing/Public Relations .... Mr. Michael BROWN
19 Director Campus Safety .... Mr. Al MATTHEWS
06 Registrar .... Ms. Judy BOWIE
18 Director Building/Grounds .... Mr. Andrew FREEMAN
29 Dir Alumni Relations/Foundation .... Ms. Libby VILLAVICENCIO
09 Director of Institutional Research .... Ms. Kensey LOVE
21 Controller/Assistant Treasurer .... Mrs. Anna JOHNSON
101 Secretary of the Institution/Board .... Ms. Jestinah MCDONALD
28 Director of Diversity .... Mr. George PETROVAY
38 Director Student Counseling .... Mr. Roger BUCK

Hocking College Perry Campus (H)

5454 State Route 37, New Lexington OH 43764
Telephone: (740) 342-3337 Identification: 770359
Accreditation: &NH

† Branch campus of Hocking College, Nelsonville, OH.

Hondros College (I)

1810 Successful Drive, Fairborn OH 45324
Telephone: (937) 879-1940 Identification: 770751
Accreditation: ACICS

† Branch campus of Hondros College, Westerville, OH.

Hondros College (J)

4100 Rockside Road, Second Floor, Independence OH 44131
Telephone: (216) 524-1143 Identification: 770750
Accreditation: ACICS

† Branch campus of Hondros College, Westerville, OH.

Hondros College (K)

7600 Tyler's Place Boulevard, West Chester OH 45069
Telephone: (513) 508-3005 Identification: 770749
Accreditation: ACICS

† Branch campus of Hondros College, Westerville, OH.

Hondros College (L)

4140 Executive Parkway, Westerville OH 43081-3855
County: Franklin FICE Identification: 040743
Unit ID: 203386
Telephone: (614) 508-7277 Carnegie Class: Assoc/PrivFP
FAX Number: (614) 508-7280 Calendar System: Quarter
URL: www.hondros.edu
Established: 1981 Annual Undergrad Tuition & Fees: $22,114
Enrollment: 1,924 Coed
Affiliation or Control: Proprietary IRS Status: Proprietary
Highest Offering: Baccalaureate
Program: Occupational; 2-Year Principally Bachelor's Creditable; Nursing Emphasis
Accreditation: ACICS, NURSE

01 CEO .... Mr. Harry T. WILKINS
66 President Nursing Programs .... Ms. Carol THOMAS
07 Director of Admission .... Ms. Tenique DENNIS
06 Registrar .... Ms. Danielle ANDREWS

International College of Broadcasting (M)

6 S Smithville Road, Dayton OH 45431-1898
County: Montgomery FICE Identification: 013132
Unit ID: 203289
Telephone: (937) 258-8251 Carnegie Class: Assoc/PrivFP
FAX Number: (937) 258-8714 Calendar System: Semester
URL: www.icb.edu
Established: 1968 Annual Undergrad Tuition & Fees: $14,950
Enrollment: 96 Coed
Affiliation or Control: Proprietary IRS Status: Proprietary
Highest Offering: Associate Degree
Program: Occupational; Technical Emphasis
Accreditation: ACCSC

01 President .... J. Michael LEMASTER
05 School Director .... Eric CLARK

ITT Technical Institute (N)

3428 W Market Street, Akron OH 44333
Telephone: (330) 865-8600 Identification: 770660
Accreditation: ACICS

† Branch campus of ITT Technical Institute, Indianapolis, IN.

ITT Technical Institute (O)

4717 Hilton Corporate Drive, Columbus OH 43232
Telephone: (614) 868-2000 Identification: 666706
Accreditation: ACICS

† Branch campus of ITT Technical Institute, Indianapolis, IN.

ITT Technical Institute (P)

3325 Stop 8 Road, Dayton OH 45414-3425
Telephone: (937) 264-7700 FICE Identification: 009088
Accreditation: ACICS

† Branch campus of ITT Technical Institute, Indianapolis, IN.

ITT Technical Institute (Q)

3781 Park Mill Run Drive, Hilliard OH 43026-8110
Telephone: (614) 771-4888 Identification: 666318
Accreditation: ACICS

† Branch campus of ITT Technical Institute, Indianapolis, IN.

ITT Technical Institute (R)

1656 Henthorne Boulevard, Suite B, Maumee OH 43537-3920
Telephone: (419) 861-6500 Identification: 666160
Accreditation: ACICS

† Branch campus of ITT Technical Institute, Indianapolis, IN.

ITT Technical Institute (S)

4750 Wesley Avenue, Norwood OH 45212-2244
Telephone: (513) 531-8300 Identification: 666546

Accreditation: ACICS

† Branch campus of ITT Technical Institute, Indianapolis, IN.

ITT Technical Institute (A)

14955 Sprague Road, Strongsville OH 44136-1758
Telephone: (440) 234-9091 Identification: 666547
Accreditation: ACICS

† Branch campus of ITT Technical Institute, Indianapolis, IN.

ITT Technical Institute (B)

24865 Emery Road, Warrensville Heights OH 44128
Telephone: (216) 896-6500 Identification: 666379
Accreditation: ACICS

† Branch campus of ITT Technical Institute, Indianapolis, IN.

ITT Technical Institute (C)

7116 Office Park Drive, West Chester OH 45069
Telephone: (513) 644-0600 Identification: 770659
Accreditation: ACICS

† Branch campus of ITT Technical Institute, Indianapolis, IN.

ITT Technical Institute (D)

1030 N Meridian Road, Youngstown OH 44509-4098
Telephone: (330) 270-1600 FICE Identification: 009837
Accreditation: ACICS

† Branch campus of ITT Technical Institute, Indianapolis, IN.

James A. Rhodes State College (E)

4240 Campus Drive, Lima OH 45804-3597
County: Allen FICE Identification: 010027
Unit ID: 203678
Telephone: (419) 995-8200 Carnegie Class: Assoc/Pub-R-M
FAX Number: (419) 221-0450 Calendar System: Semester
URL: www.rhodesstate.edu
Established: 1971 Annual Undergrad Tuition & Fees (In-State): $4,045
Enrollment: 3,657 Coed
Affiliation or Control: State IRS Status: 501(c)3
Highest Offering: Associate Degree
Program: Occupational; 2-Year Principally Bachelor's Creditable
Accreditation: NH, ACBSP, ADNUR, COARC, COARCP, CSHSE, DH, ENGT, MAC, OTA, PTAA, RAD

01 President .... Dr. Debra L. MCCURDY
10 Vice President Business & Treasurer .... Vacant
05 VP Academic Affairs .... Dr. Richard WOODFIELD
32 Vice President Student Affairs .... Dr. Cynthia E. SPIERS
35 Associate Dean for Student Services .... Ms. Judi MAZZARELLLI
30 Executive Director of Development .... Mr. Kevin L. REEKS
20 Associate VP of Academic Affairs .... Dr. Antoinette BALDIN
07 Director of Admissions .... Ms. Traci R. COX
37 Director Student Financial Aid .... Ms. Cathy L. KOHLI
09 Director Institutional Research .... Vacant
36 Director of Career Services .... Ms. Krista RICHARDSON
08 Head Librarian .... Ms. Tina SCHNEIDER
103 Exec Dir for Workforce & Econ Dev .... Dr. Matthew J. KINKLEY
15 Director Human Resources .... Mr. Ray BURTON
50 Dean Div Business & Public Services .... Mr. Roger YOUNG
54 Dean Business/Tech & Public Svcs .... Mr. Ken BAKER
49 Dean Division of Arts & Sciences .... Mr. William C. WELLS
66 Dean Division of Nursing .... Ms. Carol SCHMIDT
76 Dean Div of AH/Sciences .... Ms. Tish HATFIELD
45 Vice President Inst Effect/Planning .... Ms. Becky BURRELL
18 Chief Facilities/Physical Plant .... Vacant
21 Assoc VP Fin/Controller/Asst Treas .... Ms. Beverly REX-COOK
26 Asst Dir Mktg & College Relations .... Vacant
06 Registrar .... Dr. Rose REINHART
38 Director Advising & Counseling .... Mr. Chris JEBSEN

John Carroll University (F)

1 John Carroll Boulevard,
University Heights OH 44118-4581
County: Cuyahoga FICE Identification: 003050
Unit ID: 203368
Telephone: (216) 397-1886 Carnegie Class: Master's L
FAX Number: (216) 397-4256 Calendar System: Semester
URL: www.jcu.edu
Established: 1886 Annual Undergrad Tuition & Fees: $37,180
Enrollment: 3,700 Coed
Affiliation or Control: Roman Catholic IRS Status: 501(c)3
Highest Offering: Beyond Master's But Less Than Doctorate
Program: Liberal Arts And General; Teacher Preparatory; Professional
Accreditation: NH, BUS, BUSA, CACREP, TED

01 President .... Rev. Robert L. NIEHOFF, SJ
88 Title IX Coordinator .... Ms. Kendra E. SVILAR
04 Assistant to the President .... Ms. Lisa DEBICK
11 Vice President for Administration .... Mr. Richard F. MAUSSER
88 Asst to Pres External Affairs .... Mr. James P. CROSBY
43 General Counsel .... Ms. Colleen TREML
88 VP for Univ Mission & Identity .... Dr. Edward J. PECK
05 Provost & Academic Vice President .... Dr. Jeanne COLLERAN
30 Vice President for Univ Advancement .... Ms. Doreen K. RILEY
84 Vice President for Enrollment .... Mr. Brian G. WILLIAMS
10 Chief Financial Officer .... Vacant
32 Vice President for Student Affairs .... Dr. Mark D. MCCARTHY
20 Assoc Academic Vice President .... Dr. James H. KRUKONES
21 Dir Academic Budget .... Mr. David W. WONG
09 Assoc Provost for Accred & IE .... Dr. Nicholas SANTILLI
108 Dir Office of Academic Assessment .... Dr. Robert (Todd) BRUCE
49 Dean College of Arts & Sciences .... Dr. Margaret FARRAR
50 Dean Boler School of Business .... Dr. Alan MICIAK
79 Assoc Dean Humanities/GR Programs .... Dr. Anne KUGLER
81 Assoc Dean Science and Health .... Dr. Graciela LACUEVA
83 Assoc Dean Soc Sci/Global/Ed .... Dr. Pamela MASON
35 Dean of Students .... Dr. Sherri A. CRAHEN
13 Chief Information Officer .... Mr. Michael J. BESTUL
18 Assoc Vice Pres for Facilities .... Ms. Carol P. DIETZ
26 Interim Exec Dir of Communications .... Ms. Tonya STRONG CHARLES
15 Asst Vice Pres Human Resources .... Mr. Alex J. TEODOSIO
08 Director of the Library .... Ms. Michelle MILLET
86 Assoc VP & Dir of Govt & Cmty Rels .... Ms. Dora J. PRUCE
36 Interim Dir Ctr for Career Svcs .... Dr. Cynthia D. MARCO SCANLON
28 Asst Prov Diversity & Inclus Excel .... Dr. Terry L. MILLS
22 Affirmative Action Officer/EEO .... Dr. James H. KRUKONES
06 Registrar .... Ms. Martha C. MONDELLO-HENDREN
21 Controller .... Mr. John P. CLIFFORD
88 Bursar & Dir of Student Accounts .... Ms. Diane M. WARD
39 Director of Residence Life .... Ms. Lisa M. BROWN
92 Director Honors Program .... Vacant
07 Executive Director of Enrollment .... Mr. Steven P. VITATOE
88 Sr Dir Major Gifts/Liaison to A&S .... Ms. Mary RYCYNA
14 Associate CIO .... Mr. James A. BURKE
37 Director of Financial Aid .... Ms. Claudia A. WENZEL
88 Director Budget/Financial Analysis .... Ms. Jennifer A. DILLON
31 Dir Ctr Service and Social Action .... Ms. Katherine FEELY, SND
42 Director of Campus Ministry .... Mr. John B. SCARANO
38 Director Univ Counseling Center .... Vacant
23 Director Student Health Center .... Ms. Janet M. KREVH
41 Sr Director Athletics & Recreation .... Ms. Laurie J. MASSA
29 Director Alumni Relations .... Mr. David A. VITATOE
44 Sr Director Philanthropic Relations .... Mr. Peter R. BERNARDO
102 Dir Corporate Giving/Liaison Bus .... Ms. Christina BEG
102 Director Foundation Relations/Grant .... Ms. Pamela L. GEORGE
96 Director Purchasing & Aux Services .... Mr. Andrew F. FRONCZEK
25 Director Sponsored Research .... Ms. Catherine T. ANSON
19 Director Campus Safety Services .... Mr. Timothy J. PEPPARD
91 Dir Enterprise Applications .... Mr. John M. SULLY
88 Exec Dir Mktg/Creative Svcs .... Mr. Michael J. RICHWALSKY
88 Center Digital Media Fac Liaison .... Dr. Jay TARBY

Kaplan College (G)

2800 East River Road, Dayton OH 45439
County: Montgomery FICE Identification: 020520
Unit ID: 204626
Telephone: (937) 294-6155 Carnegie Class: Assoc/PrivFP
FAX Number: (937) 294-2259 Calendar System: Quarter
URL: dayton.kaplancollege.com
Established: 1971 Annual Undergrad Tuition & Fees: $15,195
Enrollment: 317 Coed
Affiliation or Control: Proprietary IRS Status: Proprietary
Highest Offering: Associate Degree
Program: Occupational; Technical Emphasis
Accreditation: ACICS, MAC

01 President .... Mr. Greg SHIELDS
05 Director of Education .... Ms. Melissa CURRY

Kent State University Main Campus (H)

PO Box 5190, Kent OH 44242-0001
County: Portage FICE Identification: 003051
Unit ID: 203517
Telephone: (330) 672-3000 Carnegie Class: RU/H
FAX Number: (330) 672-2190 Calendar System: Semester
URL: www.kent.edu
Established: 1910 Annual Undergrad Tuition & Fees (In-State): $10,012
Enrollment: 29,477 Coed
Affiliation or Control: State IRS Status: 501(c)3
Highest Offering: Doctorate
Program: Liberal Arts And General; Teacher Preparatory; Professional
Accreditation: NH, AAB, ART, AUD, BUS, BUSA, CAATE, CACREP, CIDA, CLPSY, CORE, DANCE, DIETD, DIETI, EXSC, JOUR, LIB, MUS, NAIT, NRPA, NURSE, POD, SCPSY, SP, SPAA, TED, THEA

01 President .... Dr. Beverly J. WARREN
05 Provost/Sr VP Academic Affairs .... Dr. Todd DIACON
10 Vice Pres Finance & Administration .... Mr. Gregg S. FLOYD
15 Interim Vice Pres Human Resources .... Mr. Willis WALKER
30 Vice Pres Institutional Advancement .... Mr. Jeff L. MCLAIN
32 Int Vice Pres Student Affairs .... Dr. Shay DAVIS LITTLE
26 Vice Pres Univ Relations .... Ms. Iris E. HARVEY
46 Vice President Research .... Dr. Paul E. DICORLETO
13 Vice Pres Information Services/CIO .... Mr. Edward G. MAHON
22 VP Diversity/Equity/Inclusion .... Dr. Alfreda BROWN
20 Dean Undergraduate Studies .... Ms. Eboni PRINGLE
35 Student Ombuds .... Dr. Jennifer KULICS
45 Sr Assoc Provost .... Dr. Melody TANKERSLEY
20 Assoc Provost Faculty Affairs .... Ms. Sue AVERILL
84 Sr Assoc Vice Pres Enrollment Svcs .... Mr. David GARCIA
29 Asst Vice Pres Alumni Affairs .... Mrs. Lori RANDORF
07 Director of Admissions .... Ms. Nancy J. DELLAVECCHIA
16 Human Resources Director-CPM .... Mr. David DIXON
06 Registrar .... Ms. Gail REBETA
43 Vice Pres University Counsel .... Mr. Willis WALKER
100 Sec Bd Trustees/Chief of Staff .... Ms. Charlene K. REED
41 Director Intercollegiate Athletics .... Mr. Joel NIELSON
22 Director of Compliance & Benefits .... Ms. Loretta SHIELDS
37 Director Student Financial Aid .... Mr. Mark EVANS
19 Director of Public Safety .... Mr. John PEACH
12 Assoc Provost/Dean Trumbull Campus .... Dr. Wanda THOMAS
96 Director of Procurement .... Mr. Timothy J. KONCZAL
49 Interim Dean Arts & Sciences .... Dr. James BLANK
50 Dean of Business Administration .... Dr. Deborah F. SPAKE
53 Dean of Education .... Dr. Daniel F. MAHONY
57 Dean of the Arts .... Dr. John CRAWFORD
66 Dean College of Nursing .... Dr. Barbara BROOME
51 Exec Director Continuing Studies .... Ms. Deborah C. HUNTSMAN
92 Dean Honors College .... Dr. Donald F. PALMER
08 Dean Library & Media Services .... Dr. James BRACKEN
48 Dean Architect/Environ Design .... Mr. Douglas STEIDL
60 Dean Col of Comm & Information .... Dr. Christine M. ANDERSON
72 Interim Dean Applied Engr/Sust/Tech .... Dr. Robert G. SINES
58 Dean of Graduate Studies .... Vacant
88 Dean College of Podiatric Medicine .... Dr. Allan BOIKE
20 Sr Assoc Dean-CPM .... Dr. Vincent J. HEATHERINGTON
21 Sr Business Manager .... Mr. Mark M. MATEJCIK
08 Librarian-CPM .... Mrs. Donna M. PERZEKI
18 Director of Operations-CPM .... Mr. Dan RIDGWAY
84 Director of Enrollment Mgmt-CPM .... Vacant

Kent State University at Ashtabula (I)

3300 Lake Road W, Ashtabula OH 44004-2299
Telephone: (440) 964-3322 FICE Identification: 003052
Accreditation: &NH, ADNUR, COARC, OTA, PTAA, RAD

† Regional accreditation is carried under the parent institution in Kent, OH.

Kent State University East Liverpool Campus (J)

400 E Fourth Street, East Liverpool OH 43920-3497
Telephone: (330) 385-3805 FICE Identification: 003056
Accreditation: &NH, ADNUR, OTA, PTAA

† Regional accreditation is carried under the parent institution in Kent, OH.

Kent State University Geauga Campus (K)

14111 Claridon-Troy Road,
Burton Township OH 44021-9500
Telephone: (440) 834-4187 FICE Identification: 003059
Accreditation: &NH

† Regional accreditation is carried under the parent institution in Kent, OH.

Kent State University Salem Campus (L)

2491 State Road 45 South, Salem OH 44460-9412
Telephone: (330) 332-0361 FICE Identification: 003061
Accreditation: &NH, RAD, RTT

† Regional accreditation is carried under the parent institution in Kent, OH.

Kent State University Stark Campus (M)

6000 Frank Avenue NW, North Canton OH 44720-9988
Telephone: (330) 499-9600 FICE Identification: 003054
Accreditation: &NH

† Regional accreditation is carried under the parent institution in Kent, OH.

Kent State University Trumbull Campus (N)

4314 Mahoning Avenue, NW, Warren OH 44483-1998
Telephone: (330) 847-0571 FICE Identification: 003064
Accreditation: &NH

† Regional accreditation is carried under the parent institution in Kent, OH.

Kent State University Tuscarawas Campus (O)

330 University Drive, NE,
New Philadelphia OH 44663-9403
Telephone: (330) 339-3391 FICE Identification: 003062
Accreditation: &NH, ADNUR, ENGT

† Regional accreditation is carried under the parent institution in Kent, OH.

Kenyon College (P)

106 College-Park Street, Gambier OH 43022-9623
County: Knox FICE Identification: 003065
Unit ID: 203535
Telephone: (740) 427-5000 Carnegie Class: Bac/A&S
FAX Number: (740) 427-3077 Calendar System: Semester
URL: www.kenyon.edu
Established: 1824 Annual Undergrad Tuition & Fees: $49,140
Enrollment: 1,656 Coed
Affiliation or Control: Independent Non-Profit IRS Status: 501(c)3
Highest Offering: Baccalaureate
Program: Liberal Arts And General
Accreditation: NH

01 President .... Dr. Sean DECATUR
05 Provost .... Dr. Joe L. KLESNER
30 Vice President College Relations .... Ms. Heidi H. MCCRORY
10 Vice President for Finance .... Mr. Todd E. BURSON
08 Vice Pres Library & Info Svcs .... Mr. Ronald K. GRIGGS
100 Chief of Staff .... Ms. Susan MORSE
21 Assoc Vice President for Finance .... Vacant
44 Assoc VP College Relations .... Mr. Kyle W. HENDERSON
32 Dean of Students .... Dr. Henry P. TOUTAIN
07 Dean of Admissions/Fin Aid .... Ms. Diane ANCI
20 Associate Provost .... Dr. Brad HARTLAUB
20 Associate Provost .... Dr. Ivonne GARCIA
08 Director of Information Resources .... Mr. Joseph M. MURPHY
06 Registrar/Dean Academic Support .... Ms. Ellen K. HARBOURT
26 Director of Public Affairs .... Mr. Mark ELLIS
13 Director Systems Design/Consulting .... Vacant
29 Dir Alumni/Parent Rels .... Mr. Scott R. BAKER
37 Director of Financial Aid .... Mr. Craig A. DAUGHERTY
38 Director of Counseling Services .... Dr. Patrick K. GILLIGAN
15 Director of Human Resources .... Ms. Jennifer G. CABRAL
42 Director of Religious/Spiritual .... Rabbi Marc BRAGIN
21 Chief Business Officer .... Mr. Mark KOHLMAN
22 Civil Rights/Title IX Coordinator .... Ms. Andrea GOLDBLUM
19 Director of Campus Safety .... Mr. Robert D. HOOPER
09 Director of Institutional Research .... Ms. Erika M. FARFAN
21 Manager of Business Services .... Mr. Frederick S. LINGER
28 Director of Multicultural Affairs .... Mr. A. Chris KENNERLY
101 Director of Board Relations .... Ms. Kathryn LAKE

Kettering College (A)

3737 Southern Boulevard, Kettering OH 45429-1299
County: Montgomery FICE Identification: 007035
Unit ID: 203544
Telephone: (937) 395-8601 Carnegie Class: Spec/Health
FAX Number: (937) 395-8106 Calendar System: Semester
URL: www.kc.edu
Established: 1967 Annual Undergrad Tuition & Fees: $13,680
Enrollment: 760 Coed
Affiliation or Control: Seventh-day Adventist IRS Status: 501(c)3
Highest Offering: Doctorate
Program: Occupational; 2-Year Principally Bachelor's Creditable; Professional; Nursing Emphasis
Accreditation: NH, ADNUR, ARCPA, COARC, DMS, NUR, PAST, RAD

00 Chairman of the Board .... Dr. Roy CHEW
01 President .... Dr. Nate BRANDSTATER
15 Vice President Human Resources .... Mr. Timothy DUTTON
05 Dean for Academic Affairs .... Dr. Ruth ABBOTT
102 President Foundation .... Dr. Martin CLARK
84 Dean Enrollment Mgmt/Student Affs .... Mr. Victor BROWN
10 Chief Business Officer .... Vacant
06 Registrar .... Mrs. Robin VANDERBILT
88 Dean Assessment & Learning Support .... Ms. Sue DALTON
37 Director Student Financial Aid .... Mrs. Kim SNELL
40 Manager Bookstore .... Mrs. Stella FREEMAN
42 Chaplain Director Campus Ministry .... Mr. Clive WILSON
32 Director Student Life .... Mr. Kris HARTER
26 Public Relations Officer .... Ms. Jessica BEANS
08 Director of Library .... Mr. John KISSINGER
29 Director Alumni Relations .... Mrs. Amy ORTIZ-MORETTA
07 Director of Admissions .... Mrs. Becky MCDONALD
13 Senior Information Officer .... Mr. Jim NESBIT

Lake Erie College (B)

391 W Washington Street, Painesville OH 44077-3389
County: Lake FICE Identification: 003066
Unit ID: 203580
Telephone: (440) 375-7000 Carnegie Class: Master's S
FAX Number: (440) 375-7005 Calendar System: Semester
URL: www.lec.edu
Established: 1856 Annual Undergrad Tuition & Fees: $29,162
Enrollment: 1,035 Coed
Affiliation or Control: Independent Non-Profit IRS Status: 501(c)3
Highest Offering: Master's
Program: Liberal Arts And General; Teacher Preparatory; Professional; Business Emphasis
Accreditation: NH, #ARCPA, IACBE, TEAC

01 Interim President .... Dana DENNIS
05 Vice Pres for Academic Affairs/CAO .... Bryan DEPOY
10 Vice Pres Administration & Finance .... Brian DIRK
30 VP for Institutional Advancement .... Scott EVANS
20 Assoc VP for Academic Admin .... Dr. Jennifer COLLIS
53 Dean School of Educ & Prof Studies .... Dr. Dale SHEPTAK
50 Dean School of Business .... Dr. Robert TREBAR
88 Dean School of Equine Studies .... Dr. Pam HESS
88 Dean School of Arts/Human & SS .... Dr. Tom DAVIS
81 Interim Dean Sch of Nat Sci & Math .... Dr. Jonathan TEDESCO
06 Registrar .... Barbara ARILSON
107 Director Prof Development .... Lisa STRAUSBAUGH
58 Director Parker MBA Program .... Donna BARES
88 Director Physician Assistant Pgm .... Joe WEBER
36 Director Career Services .... Sarah KOSTIHA
13 Director of Information Technology .... Brad LUHTA
38 Director Student Counseling Center .... Dr. John SPIESMAN
37 Director Financial Aid .... Tricia PANGONIS
15 Director Human Resources .... Andrea MYERS
32 VP Student Affairs .... Billie DUNN
84 VP Enrollment Management .... Steve LAZOWSKI
18 Director Physical Plant .... Herb DILL
29 Director Alumni & Community Rels .... Debra REMINGTON
41 Director Athletics .... Reid GUARNIERI
08 Director Lincoln Library .... Christopher BENNETT
19 Director Security .... Richard KLINE
39 Director Residence Life .... Megan MCKENNA
40 Bookstore Manager .... Natalie SCALA
04 Executive Asst to President & BOD .... Julie HERBERT
26 Director of Public Relations/Mktg .... Ruta GREINER
44 Director of Development .... Pamela PALERMO

Lakeland Community College (C)

7700 Clocktower Drive, Kirtland OH 44094-5198
County: Lake FICE Identification: 006804
Unit ID: 203599
Telephone: (440) 525-7000 Carnegie Class: Assoc/Pub-S-SC
FAX Number: (440) 525-7651 Calendar System: Semester
URL: www.lakelandcc.edu
Established: 1967 Annual Undergrad Tuition & Fees (In-District): $3,217
Enrollment: 8,277 Coed
Affiliation or Control: State/Local IRS Status: 501(c)3
Highest Offering: Associate Degree
Program: Occupational; 2-Year Principally Bachelor's Creditable
Accreditation: NH, ADNUR, CAHIIM, COARC, DH, ENGT, HT, IFSAC, MAC, MLTAD, RAD, SURGT

01 President .... Dr. Morris W. BEVERAGE, JR.
05 Interim Exec VP & Provost .... Dr. Morrs BEVERAGE
10 Sr Vice Pres Admin Svcs/Treasurer .... Mr. Michael E. MAYHER
100 Chief of Staff/Sr VP Inst Effectiv .... Ms. Catherine BUSH
26 Chief Commun Ofcr/VP College Rels .... Ms. Dawn M. PLANTE
20 Assoc Provost Teach & Learn .... Dr. Deborah L. HARDY
84 Assoc Provost for Enrollment Mgmt .... Mr. William KRAUS
20 Assoc VP Student Development .... Mr. Richard J. NOVOTNY
81 Dean of Arts and Sciences .... Dr. Steven OLUIC
76 Dean of Health Technologies .... Dr. Deborah L. HARDY
50 Dean of Applied Studies .... Ms. Laura BARNARD
88 Chief Academic Technologies Officer .... Mr. William KNAPP
21 Assoc VP Bus Svcs/Deputy Treasurer .... Mr. Brian COOK
13 Dir Administrative Technologies .... Mr. Rick PENNY
21 Controller .... Vacant
15 Director Human Resources .... Ms. Cathy BUSH
18 Director for Facilities Management .... Mr. Bert DIEHL
19 Chief of Police/Director of Safety .... Mr. Gerald JENKINS
07 Director for Admissions/Registrar .... Ms. Tracey L. COOPER
37 Dir Financial Aid/Enroll Support .... Ms. Melissa A. AMSPAUGH
32 Director of Student Activities .... Mr. Mario PETITTI
30 Dir Development/Alumni Relations .... Dr. Robert CAHEN
96 Director of Purchasing .... Mr. Tom A. KIRCHNER
09 Director of Institutional Research .... Mrs. Lisa DURST

Lakewood College (D)

2231 North Taylor Road, Cleveland Heights OH 44112
County: Cuyahoga Identification: 666715
Telephone: (800) 517-0857 Carnegie Class: Not Classified
FAX Number: (216) 803-9899 Calendar System: Other
URL: www.lakewoodcollege.edu
Established: 1998 Annual Undergrad Tuition & Fees: $4,950
Enrollment: N/A Coed
Affiliation or Control: Independent Non-Profit IRS Status: 501(c)3
Highest Offering: Associate Degree
Program: Occupational
Accreditation: DEAC

01 CEO and Founder .... Ms. Tanya HAGGINS
11 Vice President of Operations .... Ms. Aleia EVANS
10 Vice President of Administration .... Ms. Summer HAGGINS
30 Vice President of Business Develop .... Mr. Isaac HAGGINS

Lorain County Community College (E)

1005 N Abbe Road, Elyria OH 44035-1691
County: Lorain FICE Identification: 003068
Unit ID: 203748
Telephone: (440) 365-5222 Carnegie Class: Assoc/Pub-U-SC
FAX Number: (440) 365-6519 Calendar System: Semester
URL: www.lorainccc.edu
Established: 1963 Annual Undergrad Tuition & Fees (In-District): $3,771
Enrollment: 11,542 Coed
Affiliation or Control: State/Local IRS Status: 501(c)3
Highest Offering: Associate Degree
Program: Occupational; 2-Year Principally Bachelor's Creditable
Accreditation: NH, ADNUR, ART, DH, DMS, EMT, ENGT, MAC, MLTAD, OTA, PHLEB, PNUR, PTAA, RAD, SURGT

01 President .... Dr. Roy A. CHURCH
46 VP Strategic & Institutional Devel .... Ms. Tracy A. GREEN
05 Provost/VP for Acad & Student Svcs .... Dr. Marcia J. BALLINGER
10 Vice President Admin Svcs/Treasurer .... Mr. David CUMMINS
88 Assoc Prov University Partnership .... Dr. John R. CROOKS
08 Int Dean Library/Instruction Media .... Ms. Susan PAUL
84 Dean Enroll Svcs/Fin Aid/Registrar .... Ms. Stephanie SUTTON
09 Dean Rsch/Inst Effect/Public Svcs .... Ms. Shara DAVIS
13 Director Information Systems .... Mr. Lou KOMPARE
15 Director Human Resources/Campus Sec .... Mr. Keith BROWN
88 Dir Entrepreneurship Innov Inst .... Ms. Terri B. SANDU
18 Director of Physical Plant .... Mr. Robert FLYER
51 Director Public Services .... Ms. Shara DAVIS
57 Dir Stocker Humanit/Fine Arts Ctr .... Ms. Janet HERMAN-BARLOW
96 Dir Purchasing/Facilities Planning .... Ms. Laura K. CARISSIMI
54 Dean Engineering & Information Tech .... Ms. Kelly ZELESNIK
76 Int Dean Allied Health & Nursing .... Ms. Hope MOON
79 Dean Arts/Humanities .... Dr. Robert A. BECKSTROM
81 Dean Science/Math .... Dr. Rosa HAINAJ
83 Int Dean Social Science/Human Svc .... Dr. Jonathan N. DRYDEN

Lourdes University (F)

6832 Convent Boulevard, Sylvania OH 43560-2898
County: Lucas FICE Identification: 003069
Unit ID: 203757
Telephone: (419) 885-3211 Carnegie Class: Master's S
FAX Number: (419) 882-3987 Calendar System: Semester
URL: www.lourdes.edu
Established: 1958 Annual Undergrad Tuition & Fees: $18,970
Enrollment: 1,780 Coed
Affiliation or Control: Roman Catholic IRS Status: 501(c)3
Highest Offering: Master's
Program: Liberal Arts And General; Professional
Accreditation: NH, ANEST, IACBE, NURSE, SW, TEAC

01 President .... Dr. David J. LIVINGSTON
00 President Emerita .... Sr. Ann Francis KLIMKOWSKI
05 Provost .... Dr. Geoffrey J. GRUBB
32 Vice Pres for Student Life .... Ms. Roseann GILL-JACOBSON
10 Vice Pres Finance & Administration .... Dr. Robert ROOD
42 Vice Pres for Mission & Ministry .... Sr. Ann Carmen BARONE, OSF
30 Vice President for Inst Advancement .... Ms. Mary ARQUETTE
84 Vice President of Enrollment .... Dr. Dean LUDWIG
45 Asst Vice Pres for Inst Planning .... Ms. Michelle RABLE
49 Dean College of Arts & Sciences .... Dr. Holly L. BAUMGARTNER
53 Int Dean Col Education/Human Svcs .... Dr. Christine KNAGGS
66 Dean College of Nursing .... Dr. Judy DIDION
50 Dean College Business & Leadership .... Ryan BUTT
58 Dean of Graduate School .... Sr. Shannon SCHREIN, OSF
35 Director of Title III & Retention .... Ms. Rachel DUFF-ANDERSON
37 Dir of Student Financial Services .... Ms. Deb LAJEUNESSE
26 Director of University Relations .... Ms. Helene SHEETS
08 Director of Library Services .... Sr. Sandra RUTKOWSKI
06 Registrar .... Ms. Michelle A. RABLE
13 Director of Information Technology .... Mr. Scott CROW
15 Director of Human Resources .... Mr. Scott SIMON
85 Director Foreign Students .... Vacant
36 Director of Career Counseling .... Ms. Andrea DOMACHOWSKI
11 Director of Administrative Systems .... Ms. Laurie ORZECHOWSKI
21 Director of Finance .... Mr. Jeffrey GANUES
88 Director Academic Advising .... Dr. Robert DETWILER
44 Dir Development/Annual Fund Officer .... Mr. Michael GEORGE
18 Director of Facilities & Grounds .... Mr. Michael CRAVENS
07 Director of Admissions .... Mr. Shawn BUSSELL
07 Director of Graduate Admissions .... Ms. Tara HANNA
88 Dir Campus Ministry/Svc Learning .... Sr. Barbara VANO
29 Alumni Relations Officer .... Ms. Oriana RIFE
40 Manager of Bookstore .... Ms. Ann MORRIS

Malone University (G)

2600 Cleveland Avenue NW, Canton OH 44709-3897
County: Stark FICE Identification: 003072
Unit ID: 203775
Telephone: (330) 471-8100 Carnegie Class: Master's M
FAX Number: (330) 471-8478 Calendar System: Semester
URL: www.malone.edu
Established: 1892 Annual Undergrad Tuition & Fees: $27,960
Enrollment: 1,980 Coed
Affiliation or Control: Friends IRS Status: 501(c)3
Highest Offering: Master's
Program: Liberal Arts And General; Teacher Preparatory; Professional
Accreditation: NH, ACBSP, CACREP, MUS, NURSE, SW, TED

01 President .... Dr. David A. KING
10 Vice President for Finance/CFO .... Mrs. Joy E. BRATHWAITE
05 Interim Provost .... Dr. D. Nathan PHINNEY
32 Vice Pres for Student Development .... Dr. Christopher T. ABRAMS
30 Vice Pres for Univ Advancement .... Mr. Stephen T. WEINGART
26 Vice Pres for Marketing & Comm .... Mr. Timothy A. BRYAN
49 Int Dean Col of Theol/Arts & Sci .... Dr. James H. BROWNLEE
53 Dean Sch of Education & Human Devel .... Dr. Rhoda C. SOMMERS
66 Dean Sch of Nursing & Health Sci .... Dr. Debra A. LEE
50 Actg Dean Sch of Business & Ldrshp .... Dr. D. Nathan PHINNEY
21 Finance Manager .... Mr. Tracy L. MILLER
06 Registrar .... Mr. Gary L. PHELPS
07 Director of Admissions .... Mrs. Linda A. KURTZ HOFFMAN
29 Dir of Alumni & Parent Relations .... Mrs. Deborah M. ROBINSON
44 Director of Annual Giving .... Mrs. Paula M. CALHOUN
108 Dir Inst Effectiveness/Assessment .... Dr. Charles R. LARTEY
37 Director of Financial Aid .... Mrs. Pamela S. PUSTAY
15 Director of Human Resources .... Mr. Michael J. FAIRLESS
41 Athletic Director .... Mr. Charles R. GRIMES
08 Director of Library .... Ms. Rebecca L. FORT
106 Dir Online Education/E-learning .... Mr. John W. KOSHMIDER, III
93 Director of Multicultural Services .... Mrs. Brenda D. STEVENS
104 Dir Ctr/Cross-Cultural Engagement .... Mr. Ryan J. DONALD
19 Director Security/Safety .... Mr. David W. BURNIP
24 Support and Infrastructure Manager .... Mr. M. Adam KLEMANN
90 Senior Systems Engineer .... Mr. Alexander YU
42 University Pastor .... Vacant
105 Content Mgr for Publications/Web .... Mrs. Amber L. BALASH
40 Bookstore Manager .... Mrs. Kathy L. SECREST
04 Exec Asst to Pres/Asst to Board .... Mrs. Teresa L. PITTINGER
09 Assistant to the Provost .... Ms. Karen R. WARNER

92 Director of Honors Programs ....Dr. Diane M. CHAMBERS
89 Dir of the College Experience Pgm ....Dr. Marcia K. EVERETT
38 Director of Counseling Center ....Mr. Timothy T. MORBER
23 Health Center Nurse ....Mrs. Janet A. PERKO

Marietta College (A)

215 Fifth Street, Marietta OH 45750-4033
County: Washington FICE Identification: 003073
Unit ID: 203845
Telephone: (740) 376-4000 Carnegie Class: Bac/Diverse
FAX Number: (740) 376-4896 Calendar System: Semester
URL: www.marietta.edu
Established: 1835 Annual Undergrad Tuition & Fees: $34,300
Enrollment: 1,500 Coed
Affiliation or Control: Independent Non-Profit IRS Status: 501(c)3
Highest Offering: Master's
Program: Liberal Arts And General; Teacher Preparatory; Professional
Accreditation: NH, ARCPA, CAATE, ENG, MUS, TED

01 President ....Dr. Joseph W. BRUNO
05 Provost/Dean of Faculty ....Dr. Janet L. BLAND
10 Vice President for Admin & Finance ....Mr. Daniel C. BRYANT
30 Interim VP for College Advancement ...Ms. Angela B. ANDERSON
32 VP Student Life/Chf Diversity Ofcr ....Dr. Richard K. DANFORD
84 VP for Enrollment Management ....Mr. Ron K. PATTERSON
29 Assoc VP Alumni/College Relations ....Vacant
88 Dean McDonough Ctr for Leadership ....Dr. Gamaliel (Gama) PERRUCI
101 Secretary Board of Trustees ....Mr. William H. DONNELLY
08 Director of Library ....Dr. N. Douglas ANDERSON
21 Controller ....Mr. Dan HUNGERFORD
37 Director Student Financial Services ....Ms. Emily G. SCHUCK
18 Director of Physical Plant ....Mr. Fred R. SMITH
38 Director of Counseling Services ....Vacant
06 Registrar ....Ms. Tina K. PERDUE
15 Director of Human Resources ....Ms. Debra C. EVANS
19 Chief of Campus Police ....Mr. James S. WEAVER
26 Executive Dir of College Relations ....Mr. Thomas D. PERRY
09 Director of Institutional Research ...Dr. Gregory J. DELEMEESTER
36 Career Center Director ....Ms. B. Hilles HUGHES
41 Director of Athletics ....Mr. Larry R. HISER
13 Director of Information Technology ....Mr. Aaron COWDERY
63 PA Program Director ....Ms. Miranda COLLINS
104 Director of Education Abroad ....Ms. Christy BURKE
105 Director of Web Services ....Mr. Christopher G. LAW
25 Grants Officer ....Ms. Elizabeth B. MCNALLY
51 Continuing Education ....Ms. Tina K. PERDUE
35 Dean of Students ....Vacant

Marion Technical College (B)

1467 Mount Vernon Avenue, Marion OH 43302-5694
County: Marion FICE Identification: 010736
Unit ID: 203881
Telephone: (740) 389-4636 Carnegie Class: Assoc/Pub-R-M
FAX Number: (740) 389-6136 Calendar System: Semester
URL: www.mtc.edu
Established: 1971 Annual Undergrad Tuition & Fees (In-State): $4,383
Enrollment: 2,471 Coed
Affiliation or Control: State IRS Status: 501(c)3
Highest Offering: Associate Degree
Program: Occupational; 2-Year Principally Bachelor's Creditable
Accreditation: NH, ADNUR, CAHIIM, DMS, MAC, MLTAD, OTA, PTAA, RAD

01 Interim President ....Dr. John S. ERWIN
05 Chief Academic Officer ....Dr. Vicky WOOD
32 VP of Student Svcs & Inst Advance ....Vacant
84 Dean of Enrollment Services ....Mr. Joel O. LILES
06 Registrar ....Mr. Jim LAVERY
13 Director of Information Systems ....Ms. Joanna DUVALL
26 Director of Public Relations ....Ms. Nikki WORKMAN
66 Director of Nursing Technology ....Ms. Cynthia HARTMAN
103 Director Ctr Workforce Development ....Ms. Tami GALLOWAY
15 Director Human Resources ....Ms. Brenda FEASEL
88 Dir Physical Therapist Asst Pgm ....Mr. Chad HENSEL
88 Dir Occupational Therapy ....Mr. Chad SCHNEIDER
04 Assistant to Pres for Research/Plng ....Ms. Teresa PARKER
18 Coord Facil Improvements/Operations ....Ms. Leeann GRAU
37 Coordinator Student Financial Aid ....Ms. Deb LANGDON
54 Director of Engineering Technology ....Mr. Matthew FARSON
50 Dean of Business/Information Tech ....Ms. Debbie STARK
49 Dean of Arts and Sciences ....Ms. Lillie KIRSCH
76 Dean of Allied Health ....Mr. Chris GASE
10 Chief Financial Officer ....Mr. Jeff NUTTER
108 Dean Institutional Effectiveness ....Dr. Bob HAAS

Mercy College of Ohio (C)

2221 Madison Avenue, Toledo OH 43604
County: Lucas FICE Identification: 030970
Unit ID: 203960
Telephone: (419) 251-1313 Carnegie Class: Spec/Health
FAX Number: (419) 251-1570 Calendar System: Semester
URL: www.mercycollege.edu
Established: 1993 Annual Undergrad Tuition & Fees: $12,555
Enrollment: 1,193 Coed
Affiliation or Control: Roman Catholic IRS Status: 501(c)3
Highest Offering: Baccalaureate
Program: Occupational; 2-Year Principally Bachelor's Creditable; Professional; Nursing Emphasis
Accreditation: NH, ADNUR, CAHIIM, CVT, EMT, NUR, NURSE, POLYT, RAD

01 President ....Dr. Susan WAJERT
05 Int VP Acad Affs/Dean of Faculty ....Ms. Patricia REID
11 Vice Pres Administrative Services ....Mr. James L. HARTER
66 Dean Nursing ....Dr. Susan BERNHEISEL
81 Dean Scimatics Division ....Dr. Barbara STOOS
76 Dean Allied Health/Dist Educ ....Mr. Christopher GIBBONS
88 Dean of Innovative/Trans Educ ....Ms. Cheryl NUTTER
32 Dean Student Affairs/Placement ....Ms. Jennifer PIZIO
10 Director College Finances/Res Plng ..Ms. Joan M. RUTHERFORD
30 Director College Advancement ....Mr. Michael WHALEN
84 VP of Strategic Plng & Enroll Mgmt ....Ms. Lori EDGEWORTH
08 Director Library/Resource Services ....Ms. Deborah JOHNSON
09 Dir Inst Research/Registrar ....Ms. Heather HOPPE
37 Financial Aid Director ....Ms. Julie LESLIE
26 Director of Communications ....Ms. Denise HUDGIN
42 Dir Campus Ministry/Coord Ser Learn ....Sr. Sally BOHNETT
21 Business Officer ....Ms. Diane RAHN
15 Director Personnel Services ....Ms. Joan BUNCH
18 Chief Facilities/Physical Plant ....Mr. James HARTER
29 Director Alumni Relations ....Sr. Barbara DAVIS
38 Director Student Counseling ....Ms. Lisa SANCRANT
36 Director of Career & Prof Develop ....Ms. Megan GRAY
106 Int Dir Online Education/E-learning ....Ms. Christina SIEGFRIED
28 Director of Diversity ....Dr. Shelly MCCOY GRISSOM

Methodist Theological School in Ohio (D)

3081 Columbus Pike, Delaware OH 43015-3211
County: Delaware FICE Identification: 003075
Unit ID: 203997
Telephone: (740) 363-1146 Carnegie Class: Spec/Faith
FAX Number: (740) 362-3135 Calendar System: 4/1/4
URL: www.mtso.edu
Established: 1958 Annual Graduate Tuition & Fees: $19,370
Enrollment: 194 Coed
Affiliation or Control: United Methodist IRS Status: 501(c)3
Highest Offering: Doctorate; No Undergraduates
Program: Professional; Religious Emphasis
Accreditation: NH, THEOL

01 President ....Rev. Jay A. RUNDELL
05 Dean and VP for Academic Affairs ....Dr. Lisa WITHROW
30 VP of Institutional Advancement ....Ms. April CASPERSON
04 Executive Asst to the President ....Ms. Leigh PRECISE
26 Director of Communications ....Mr. Danny RUSSELL
07 Director of Admissions ....Rev. Benjamin HALL
06 Registrar ....Ms. Sue LAMPHERE
08 Director of the Library ....Mr. Paul BURNAM
10 Controller ....Rev. Jim SUMMERS
18 Facilities Manager ....Mr. Keith HUFFMAN
32 Director of Student Services ....Ms. Kristin FROMENTO
13 Director Information Technology ....Mr. Matthew REHM
37 Director of Financial Aid ....Ms. Molly HOFFMAN
44 Director of Annual Giving ....Rev. Claudine LEARY

Miami-Jacobs Career College (E)

150 E Gay Street, 1st Floor, Columbus OH 43215-3227
Telephone: (614) 221-7770 Identification: 666465
Accreditation: ACICS, MAC

† Branch campus of McCann School of Business & Technology, Pottsville, PA.

Miami-Jacobs Career College (F)

110 N Patterson Boulevard, Dayton OH 45402-1771
Telephone: (937) 222-7337 FICE Identification: 003076
Accreditation: ACICS, MAC, #SURGT

† Branch campus of McCann School of Business & Technology, Pottsville, PA.

Miami-Jacobs Career College (G)

6400 Rockside Road, Independence OH 44131
Telephone: (216) 834-1400 FICE Identification: 021521
Accreditation: ACICS

† Branch campus of McCann School of Business & Technology, Pottsville, PA.

Miami-Jacobs Career College (H)

2 Crowne Point Court, Suite 100, Sharonville OH 45241
Telephone: (513) 693-4400 Identification: 770755
Accreditation: ACICS

† Branch campus of McCann School of Business & Technology, Pottsville, PA.

Miami-Jacobs Career College (I)

875 Central Avenue, Springboro OH 45066
Telephone: (937) 746-1830 Identification: 770757
Accreditation: ACICS, DA

† Branch campus of McCann School of Business & Technology, Pottsville, PA.

Miami-Jacobs Career College (J)

865 West Market Street, Troy OH 45373
Telephone: (937) 332-8585 Identification: 770756
Accreditation: ACICS

† Branch campus of McCann School of Business & Technology, Pottsville, PA.

Miami University (K)

501 E High Street, Oxford OH 45056-1846
County: Butler FICE Identification: 003077
Unit ID: 204024
Telephone: (513) 529-1809 Carnegie Class: RU/H
FAX Number: (513) 529-3841 Calendar System: Semester
URL: www.miamioh.edu
Established: 1809 Annual Undergrad Tuition & Fees (In-State): $13,532
Enrollment: 24,066 Coed
Affiliation or Control: State IRS Status: 501(c)3
Highest Offering: Doctorate
Program: Liberal Arts And General; Teacher Preparatory; Professional
Accreditation: NH, ART, BUS, BUSA, CAATE, CIDA, CLPSY, CS, DIETD, ENG, ENGT, IPSY, MUS, NURSE, SP, SW, TED, THEA

01 President ....Dr. David HODGE
05 Provost ....Dr. Phyllis CALLAHAN
10 VP Finance & Bus Svcs/Treasurer ....Dr. David CREAMER
32 Vice President Student Affairs ....Dr. Jayne E. BROWNELL
30 VP University Advancement ....Mr. Tom HERBERT
13 VP Information Technology ....Mr. J. Peter NATALE
15 Ast Prov Personnel/Dir Acad Per Svc ....Dr. Janet L. COX
21 Assoc VP Finance/Business Svcs ....Dr. David A. ELLIS
20 Assoc Provost for Undergrad Studies ....Dr. Carolyn A. HAYNES
35 Dean of Students ....Dr. Michael A. CURME
26 Assoc VP Comm/Marketing ....Ms. Deedie Kay DOWDLE
18 Assoc VP Facilities Planning & Op ....Mr. Cody J. POWELL
84 VP Enrollment Management ....Mr. Michael S. KABBAZ
28 Assoc VP Inst Diversity ....Dr. Ronald B. SCOTT
29 Asst Vice Pres Alumni Relations ....Mr. Raymond F. MOCK
27 Director Institutional Relations ....Mr. Randi Malcolm THOMAS
27 Assoc Dir Univ Communications ....Ms. Claire M. WAGNER
100 Secy Board/Exec Asst to President ....Mr. Ted O. PICKERILL
49 Dean College Arts & Science ....Dr. Christopher A. MAKAROFF, JR.
53 Dean Education/Health & Society ....Dr. Michael DANTLEY
50 Dean Farmer Sch of Business ....Dr. Matthew B. MYERS
57 Dean College of Creative Arts ....Dr. Elizabeth R. MULLENIX
54 Dean College of Engr & Computing ....Dr. Marek DOLLAR
08 Dean University Libraries ....Mr. Jerome CONLEY
58 Dean Graduate School ....Dr. James T. ORIS
107 Dean College of Prof Studies/App Sc ....Dr. G. Michael PRATT
07 Director of Admissions ....Ms. Susan SCHAURER
88 Asst Provost Global Initiatives ....Ms. Cheryl D. YOUNG
108 Univ Dir Ctr for Teaching Excellenc ....Dr. Rose Marie WARD
88 Univ Dir Liberal Educ/Assessment ....Dr. Richard TAYLOR
92 Univ Dir Honors & Scholars Program ....Dr. Linda MARCHANT
16 Int Assoc VP Human Resources ....Ms. Kate STOSS
88 Dir Center American/World Cultures ....Dr. Mary Jane BERMAN
23 Medical Director Student Health Svc ....Dr. Gregory CALKINS
104 Director Intl Education Services ....Dr. David KEITGES
06 University Registrar ....Mr. David M. SAUTER
36 Director Career Services ....Mr. Michael GOLDMAN
38 Director Student Counseling Service ....Dr. Kip C. ALISHIO
09 Director Institutional Research ....Ms. Denise A. KRALLMAN
19 Chief of Police/Dir Public Safety ....Mr. John MCCANDLESS
96 Sr Director Purchasing/Central Svcs ....Mr. William G. SHAWVER
43 University General Counsel ....Ms. Robin L. PARKER
22 Director Equity & Equal Opportunity ....Ms. Kenya D. ASH
41 Director Intercollegiate Athletics ....Mr. David A. SAYLER
17 Asst VP Student Health & Wellness ....Ms. Gail A. WALENGA
04 Assistant to the President ....Ms. Deborah P. MASON
106 Asst Provost for E-learning ....Dr. Beth RUBIN
37 Director Student Financial Aid ....Mr. Brent L. SHOCK
102 Dir Corporate/Found Relations ....Mr. Whitney RILEY
109 Assoc VP Auxiliaries ....Mrs. Kim K. KINSEL
44 Sr Director Annual Giving ....Ms. Emily BERRY
45 Assoc VP Budgeting & Analysis ....Dr. David A. ELLIS
105 Univ Web Content Manager ....Ms. Jeri MOORE
25 Dir Research & Sponsored Pgms ....Ms. Anne P. SCHAUER
39 Int Dir Residential Services ....Ms. Stacy GEORGE

Miami University Hamilton Campus (L)

1601 University Boulevard, Hamilton OH 45011-3399
Telephone: (513) 785-3000 FICE Identification: 003079
Accreditation: &NH

† Regional accreditation is carried under the parent institution in Oxford, OH.

Miami University Middletown (M)

4200 E University Boulevard, Middletown OH 45042-3497
Telephone: (513) 727-3200 FICE Identification: 003080
Accreditation: &NH

† Regional accreditation is carried under the parent institution in Oxford, OH.

Mount Carmel College of Nursing (N)

127 S Davis Avenue, Columbus OH 43222-1504
County: Franklin FICE Identification: 030719
Unit ID: 204176

Telephone: (614) 234-5800 Carnegie Class: Spec/Health
FAX Number: (614) 234-2875 Calendar System: Semester
URL: www.mccn.edu
Established: 1990 Annual Undergrad Tuition & Fees: $12,425
Enrollment: 1,084 Coed
Affiliation or Control: Roman Catholic IRS Status: 501(c)3
Highest Offering: Doctorate
Program: Professional; Nursing Emphasis
Accreditation: NH, NURSE

01 President ... Dr. Christine A. WYND
05 Interim Academic Dean ... Dr. Tara SPALLA
66 Assoc Dean Undergrad Nursing Pgm ... Dr. Barbara BARTA
58 Associate Dean Graduate Nursing Pgm ... Dr. Angela PHILLIPS
106 Associate Dean Distance Education ... Dr. Tara SPALLA
06 Director of Records & Registration ... Ms. Karen L. GREENE
10 Director Business Affairs ... Ms. Kathy SMITH
07 Director Recruitment & Admissions ... Ms. Kim CAMPBELL
13 Systems Administrator ... Mr. Tim TABOL
37 Director Financial Aid ... Ms. Mary CANNON
32 Director Student Life ... Ms. Colleen CIPRIANI
28 Director Diversity/Comm Initiative ... Ms. Kathlynne D. ESPY
04 CON Administrator ... Ms. Robin L. SHOCKLEY
29 Director Alumni Relations ... Ms. Debbie DUNN BOGGS
26 Dir Marketing/College Relations .. Ms. Robin HUTCHINSON BELL
08 Regional Director Library Services ... Mr. Stevo ROKSANDIC

Mount St. Joseph University (A)

5701 Delhi Road, Cincinnati OH 45233-1670
County: Hamilton FICE Identification: 003033
Unit ID: 204200
Telephone: (513) 244-4200 Carnegie Class: Master's M
FAX Number: (513) 244-4654 Calendar System: Semester
URL: www.msj.edu
Established: 1920 Annual Undergrad Tuition & Fees: $27,500
Enrollment: 2,219 Coed
Affiliation or Control: Roman Catholic IRS Status: 501(c)3
Highest Offering: Doctorate
Program: Liberal Arts And General; Teacher Preparatory; Professional
Accreditation: NH, CAATE, MUS, NURSE, PTA, SW, TEAC

01 Interim President ... Dr. Joel THIERSTEIN
30 Vice Pres Institutional Advancement ... Vacant
84 Vice Pres Enrollment Management ... Mr. William MINOR
05 Interim Provost ... Dr. Diana DAVIS
10 Chief Financial Officer ... Ms. Anne Marie WAGNER
43 Chief Compliance and Risk Officer ... Ms. Linda PANZECA
20 Associate Academic Dean ... Ms. Maggie DAVIS
15 Director of Human Resources ... Ms. Ashley TERRELL
32 Dean of Students ... Ms. Janet COX
06 Registrar ... Ms. Irene RICHARDSON
29 Director of Alumni Relations ... Ms. Gina BATH
37 Director Student Admin Services ... Ms. Kathy KELLY
36 Director Career/Experi Educ ... Ms. Linda POHLGEERS
102 Director Corporate & Found Rels ... Ms. Linda B. LIEBAU
18 Director Buildings & Grounds ... Mr. Michael DITTMER
09 Director Institutional Rsrch ... Mr. Fred OKANDA
07 Director of Admission ... Ms. Peggy MINNICH
21 Controller Fiscal Operations ... Ms. Patricia HASSEL
38 Director Wellness Center ... Ms. Patsy SCHWAIGER
08 Director Library ... Mr. Paul JENKINS
13 Director Instructional Technology ... Ms. Kim HUNTER
19 Director of Campus Police ... Mr. John KRAFT
41 Director of Athletics ... Mr. Steve RADCLIFFE
88 Director Learning Center ... Ms. Meghann LITTRELL
42 Director of Campus Ministry ... Sr. Nancy BRAMLAGE, SC
44 Director of Development ... Ms. Lisa ODENBECK
40 Manager of Bookstore ... Ms. Lori HATTENDORF
76 Dean Div of Health Sciences ... Dr. Darla VALE
79 Dean of Div of Arts & Hum ... Dr. Michael SONTAG
50 Dean of Business ... Dr. Jamal RASHED
53 Interim Dean of Education ... Dr. Darla VALE
83 Interim Dean Behav/Natural Sci ... Dr. Michael SONTAG
26 Director of Marketing ... Ms. Kathleen LUNDRIGAN
91 Director Administrative Computing ... Mr. Dan LUKAC
105 Webmaster ... Ms. Carolyn BOLAND
88 Director Individual & Campaign Giv ... Mr. Joe CORNELY
88 Exec Dir Ethical Leadership Devel ... Dr. Tim BRYANT
44 Coord Annual Giv & Young Alum Pgm ... Mr. Mark OSBORNE
23 Coordinator Health Services ... Ms. Amy DEMKO
39 Coordinator of Residence Life ... Mr. Warren GROVE
04 Admin Asst to the President ... Ms. Tina MERSMANN
108 Academic Assessment Coordinator ... Dr. Mary Kay FLEMING
28 Director of Diversity ... Dr. Terri HURDLE

Mount Vernon Nazarene University (B)

800 Martinsburg Road, Mount Vernon OH 43050-9500
County: Knox FICE Identification: 007085
Unit ID: 204194
Telephone: (740) 392-6868 Carnegie Class: Master's M
FAX Number: (740) 397-2769 Calendar System: 4/1/4
URL: www.mvnu.edu
Established: 1968 Annual Undergrad Tuition & Fees: $25,498
Enrollment: 2,143 Coed
Affiliation or Control: Church Of The Nazarene IRS Status: 501(c)3
Highest Offering: Master's
Program: Liberal Arts And General; Teacher Preparatory
Accreditation: NH, ACBSP, MUS, NURSE, SW, TED

01 President/CEO ... Dr. Henry W. SPAULDING, II
10 Vice Pres for Finance/CFO ... Dr. Robert P. HAMILL
05 Vice Pres for Academic Affairs/CAO ... Dr. B.Barnett COCHRAN
84 Vice President for GPS & Enrollment ... Dr. Brock SCHROEDER
32 Interim Student Life Administrator ... Mr. Joe NOONEN
32 Vice President Student Life ... Vacant
42 University Chaplain ... Rev. Joe NOONEN
26 VP for University Relations ... Rev. Scott PETERSON
30 Managing Dir of Advancement ... Mrs. Laura M. SHORT
21 Director of Business Services ... Mr. Steven JENKINS
07 Asst VP for Traditional Admission ... Mr. James SMITH
58 Asst VP for Grad & Prof Operations ... Mr. Kevin CHANEY
06 University Registrar ... Mr. Mel SEVERNS
15 Director of Human Resources ... Mr. Alan SHAFFER
38 Director Counseling and Wellness ... Dr. Eric BROWNING
13 Director of Information Tech ... Mr. John WALCHLE
19 Director of Campus Safety ... Mr. Denny TAYLOR
29 Director of Alumni Relations ... Mr. Travis KELLER
40 Director of the Bookstore ... Mrs. Gina A. BLANCHARD
41 Athletic Director ... Mr. Keith VEALE
27 Coord Communications & Pub Rels ... Vacant
53 Dir Teacher Education/Certification ... Dr. Sharon METCALFE
37 Dir of Student Fin Services ... Mr. Jared SPONSELLER
18 Director of Facilities Management ... Mr. Dennis D. TAYLOR
21 Controller ... Ms. Debra DEVORE
35 Director of Campus Life ... Ms. Rochel FURNISS
39 Director of Residence Life ... Vacant
28 Director Intercultural Affairs ... Mr. James M. SINGLETARY
108 Director Assessment & Reporting ... Mrs. Kathy GRIFFITH
04 Assistant to President ... Mrs. Pamela K. SNOW

Muskingum University (C)

163 Stormont Street, New Concord OH 43762-1199
County: Muskingum FICE Identification: 003084
Unit ID: 204264
Telephone: (740) 826-8211 Carnegie Class: Master's M
FAX Number: (740) 826-8404 Calendar System: Semester
URL: www.muskingum.edu
Established: 1837 Annual Undergrad Tuition & Fees: $25,776
Enrollment: 2,074 Coed
Affiliation or Control: Presbyterian Church (U.S.A.) IRS Status: 501(c)3
Highest Offering: Beyond Master's But Less Than Doctorate
Program: Liberal Arts And General; Teacher Preparatory
Accreditation: NH, ENG, MUS, NURSE, TED

01 President ... Dr. Anne C. STEELE
05 Vice President Academic Affairs ... Dr. James E. CALLAGHAN
10 Vice President Business & Finance ... Mr. James R. WILSON
30 Vice President of Inst Advancement ... Ms. Kathy A. BONAVIST
32 Dean of Student Life ... Mrs. Janet A. HEETER-BASS
84 Dean Enrollment/Dir Financial Aid ... Mr. Jeff W. ZELLERS
20 Associate Academic Dean ... Vacant
08 Director of Library ... Dr. Sheila J. ELLENBERGER
06 Registrar ... Mr. Daniel B. WILSON
36 Assistant Director Career Services ... Mrs. Jacquelyn L. VASCURA
13 Director of Computing Services ... Mr. Ryan D. HARVEY
26 Director Public Relations ... Ms. Janice L. TUCKER-MCCLOUD
29 Director Alumni Relations ... Ms. Jennifer L. BRONNER
07 Director of Admissions ... Mrs. Beth A. DALONZO
19 Director of Public Safety ... Mr. Danny E. VINCENT
42 College Minister ... Rev. William E. MULLINS
18 Supt of Building & Grounds ... Mr. Kevin J. WAGNER
41 Director of Athletics ... Mr. Larry L. SHANK
21 Associate Business Officer ... Mr. Philip E. LAUBE
35 Director of Student Affairs ... Ms. Susan H. WARYCK
37 Director of Student Financial Aid ... Mrs. Beth A. DALONZO
38 Director of Student Counseling ... Mrs. Tracy F. BUGGLIN
40 Manager of Bookstore ... Ms. Jessica MILLER
15 Coordinator of Human Resources ... Ms. Kathy J. MOORE

National Institute of Massotherapy (D)

3681 Manchester Road, Suite 304, Akron OH 44319
County: Summit FICE Identification: 034684
Unit ID: 412003
Telephone: (330) 867-1996 Carnegie Class: Assoc/PrivFP
FAX Number: (330) 867-6422 Calendar System: Other
URL: www.nim.edu
Established: 1991 Annual Undergrad Tuition & Fees: $16,992
Enrollment: 40 Coed
Affiliation or Control: Proprietary IRS Status: Proprietary
Highest Offering: Associate Degree
Program: Occupational; 2-Year Principally Bachelor's Creditable; Technical Emphasis
Accreditation: CNCE

01 President ... Mr. Stephen PERKINSON
32 Dean of Students ... Ms. Ewa PERKINSON
37 Director Financial Aid ... Mr. Dan BILICH

North Central State College (E)

2441 Kenwood Circle, Mansfield OH 44906
County: Richland FICE Identification: 005313
Unit ID: 204422
Telephone: (419) 755-4800 Carnegie Class: Assoc/Pub-R-M
FAX Number: (419) 755-4750 Calendar System: Semester
URL: www.ncstatecollege.edu
Established: 1961 Annual Undergrad Tuition & Fees (In-State): $3,661
Enrollment: 2,926 Coed
Affiliation or Control: State IRS Status: 501(c)3
Highest Offering: Associate Degree
Program: Occupational; 2-Year Principally Bachelor's Creditable
Accreditation: NH, ACBSP, ADNUR, COARC, OTA, PTAA, RAD

01 President ... Dr. Dorey DIAB
04 Exec Assistant to the President ... Mr. Stephen R. WILLIAMS
10 VP Business Services ... Mr. Koffi AKAKPO
05 Vice President Academic Services ... Dr. Karen A. REED
26 Chief Public Affairs Officer ... Mr. Keith STONER
32 Dean of Student Services ... Dr. Jane BIRKHOLZ
15 Director of Human Resources ... Mr. R. Douglas HANUSCIN
37 Director of Financial Aid ... Mr. James PHINNEY
08 Head Librarian ... Ms. Pamela BENJAMIN
22 Counselor/Coord Disability Services ... Ms. Michelle MCGREGOR
49 Dean of Lib Arts/Ed/Prof & Pub Svcs ... Mr. Gregory BUSCH
88 Asst Dean Liberal Arts ... Ms. Deborah HYSELL
53 Asst Dean Education/Prof/Pub Svcs ... Mr. Craig ALI
50 Dean of Business Ind & Technology ... Dr. Gregory TIMBERLAKE
88 Asst Dean Business Ind & Technology ... Mr. Daniel WAGNER
76 Dean Health & Public Services ... Mr. James L. HULL
66 Asst Dean Health Sci/Dir Nursing ... Ms. Kelly GRAY
13 Interim Director IT ... Mr. Major PRICE, JR.
06 Registrar ... Mr. Mark J. MONNES
18 Chief Facilities/Physical Plant ... Mr. Dean SCHAAD
96 Purchasing Specialist ... Ms. Renee NUSSBAUM
102 Foundation Director ... Mr. Scott HEIMANN
09 Director of Institutional Research ... Mr. Thomas M. PRENDERGAST
84 Dir of Student Success & Retention ... Mr. Troy SHUTLER
85 Director of Title III ... Ms. Beverly WALKER
88 Phi Theta Kappa Advisor ... Ms. Barb KEENER
40 Campus Bookstore Manager ... Ms. Carla BUTDORFF
21 Controller ... Ms. Lori MCKEE
105 Web Master ... Mr. Mark HUPP
88 Director of Tech Prep ... Mr. Tom KLUDING
51 Continuing Education Director ... Ms. Gina KAMWITHI
35 Coord Student Life Activities ... Ms. Elise RIGGLE
41 Coord Recreation/Intra Sports ... Mr. Mike LACROIX
29 Coord of Alumni/Employer Relations ... Ms. Mary J. RODRIGUEZ
36 Coordinator of Career Development ... Mr. Troy SHUTLER
07 Dir of Admissions/Recruitment ... Mr. Thomas MANSPERGER

Northeast Ohio Medical University (F)

4209 State Route 44, PO Box 95,
Rootstown OH 44272-0095
County: Portage FICE Identification: 024544
Unit ID: 204477
Telephone: (330) 325-2511 Carnegie Class: Spec/Med
FAX Number: (330) 325-7943 Calendar System: Other
URL: www.neomed.edu
Established: 1973 Annual Graduate Tuition & Fees: $37,943
Enrollment: 897 Coed
Affiliation or Control: State IRS Status: 501(c)3
Highest Offering: First Professional Degree; No Undergraduates
Program: Professional
Accreditation: NH, MED, PH, PHAR

01 President ... Dr. Jay A. GERSHEN
100 Chief of Staff ... Mr. Sergio A. GARCIA
28 VP Diversity/Equity and Inclusion ... Mr. Sergio A. GARCIA
10 VP Administration/Finance ... Mr. John W. WRAY
05 VP for Academic Affairs ... Dr. Charles T. TAYLOR
17 VP Health Affairs & Cmty Health ... Dr. Jeffrey L. SUSMAN
30 VP Advancement ... Mr. Daniel S. BLAIN
46 VP Research ... Dr. Walter E. HORTON, JR.
67 Dean College of Pharmacy ... Dr. Charles T. TAYLOR
63 Dean College of Medicine ... Dr. Jeffrey L. SUSMAN
58 Dean College of Graduate Studies ... Dr. Walter E. HORTON, JR.
43 General Counsel ... Ms. Maria R. SCHIMER
32 Chief Student Affairs Officer ... Ms. Sandra M. EMERICK
88 Exec Dir Interprofess Education ... Ms. Holly A. GERZINA
84 Exec Dir Enrollment Services ... Ms. Heidi L. TERRY
88 Executive Director Research ... Ms. Elizabeth W. CLINE
88 Exec Dir Academic Services ... Ms. Penny R. SMITH
09 Exec Dir Institutional Research ... Dr. Margarita D. KOKINOVA
26 Director Public Relations ... Mr. Roderick L. INGRAM, SR.
109 Dir Operations & Auxiliary Services ... Mr. Chris J. METTEE
96 Accounting Purchasing Controller ... Ms. Kathy L. CHUDAKOFF
13 Director Information Technology ... Mr. Ronald L. MCGRADY
24 Dir Academic Technology Services ... Mr. Rey T. NOTARESCHI
86 Dir Government Relations/Sec BOT ... Mr. Richard W. LEWIS
88 Director Comparative Medicine Unit ... Dr. Stanley D. DANNEMILLER
18 Director Campus Operations ... Mr. Blaine M. WYCKOFF
15 Director Human Resources ... Ms. Barbara A. TOBIAS
35 Dir Career Development & Advising ... Ms. Anita R. POKORNY
36 Director Academic Support ... Vacant
40 Supervisor Bookstore ... Ms. Christine L. KOVACICH
19 Director Public Safety/Police Chief ... Ms. Kali A. MEONSKE
04 Exec Assistant to the President ... Ms. Michelle M. MULHERN
11 Chief Operating Officer ... Ms. Carrie L. BAST
38 Director Student Counseling ... Ms. Theresa C. NOVAK
06 Registrar ... Ms. Mary Beth SEITH
06 Assoc Dir Enrollment Svcs & Registr ... Mr. Michael A. KEMPE
29 Director Alumni Relations ... Mr. Craig S. EYNON

Northwest State Community College (G)

22-600 State Route 34, Archbold OH 43502-9542
County: Henry FICE Identification: 008677
Unit ID: 204440
Telephone: (419) 267-5511 Carnegie Class: Assoc/Pub-R-M
FAX Number: (419) 267-3688 Calendar System: Semester
URL: www.northweststate.edu

Established: 1968 Annual Undergrad Tuition & Fees (In-State): $5,000
Enrollment: 4,669 Coed
Affiliation or Control: State IRS Status: 501(c)3
Highest Offering: Associate Degree
Program: Occupational; 2-Year Principally Bachelor's Creditable
Accreditation: NH, ACBSP, ADNUR, MAC

01 President ....Dr. Thomas L. STUCKEY
05 VP for Academics ....Dr. Cindy KRUEGER
30 VP for Institutional Advancement ....Ms. Mari YODER
88 VP for Innovation ....Mr. Todd HERNANDEZ
32 Dean of Student Services ....Mr. Michael BLACK
50 Dean of Business Technologies ....Dr. Michael WOLFE
69 Dean of Allied Health & Public Svcs ....Mrs. Lori ROBISON
49 Dean of Arts & Science ....Ms. Lana SNIDER
66 Dean of Nursing ....Mrs. Lori BIRD
06 Registrar ....Ms. Connie KLINGSHIRN
08 Director of Student Resources ....Vacant
18 Director of Plant Operations ....Mr. Timothy NELSON
15 Human Resource Officer ....Ms. Kathy SOARDS
21 Director of Business Services ....Ms. Lynn SPEISER
07 Director of Admissions ....Ms. Amanda POTTS
10 Chief Fiscal Officer ....Ms. Kathy SOARDS
44 Chief Development ....Ms. Robbin WILCOX
37 Director Student Financial Aid ....Ms. Amber YOCOM
35 Coordinator Student Activities ....Vacant
26 Coordinator Communications ....Ms. Dawn HAUTER
40 Bookstore Manager ....Mr. Kemp STAPLETON

Notre Dame College (A)

4545 College Road, South Euclid OH 44121-4293
County: Cuyahoga FICE Identification: 003085
Unit ID: 204468
Telephone: (216) 381-1680 Carnegie Class: Bac/Diverse
FAX Number: (216) 381-3802 Calendar System: Semester
URL: www.notredamecollege.edu
Established: 1922 Annual Undergrad Tuition & Fees: $26,844
Enrollment: 2,281 Coed
Affiliation or Control: Roman Catholic IRS Status: 501(c)3
Highest Offering: Master's
Program: Liberal Arts And General; Teacher Preparatory
Accreditation: NH, NURSE, TED

01 President ....Mr. Thomas KRUCZEK
05 Int Vice Pres Student/Academic Affs ....Dr. John GALOVIC
10 Sr Vice Pres Finance/Administration ....Mr. John TORTELLI
45 Vice Pres for Assessment Planning ....Vacant
30 Director of Development ....Ms. Maureen ISCHAY
31 Vice Pres for Board/Community Rels ....Ms. Karen L. POELKING
20 Assoc Dean of Academic Affairs ....Vacant
66 Nursing Division Chair ....Dr. Patrice MCCARTHY
53 Education Division Chair ....Dr. Yvonne ALLEN
81 Math & Science Division Chair ....Dr. Sharon BALCHAK
50 Business Division Chair ....Mr. Vince PALOMBO
57 Fine Arts Division Chair ....Ms. Lynn ZIMMERMAN
26 Director of Public Relations ....Vacant
84 Dean of Enrollment ....Ms. Beth FORD
07 Director of Admissions ....Mr. David HILBORN
88 Director of the Finn Center (Adult) ....Ms. Mary Ann SCHNEIDER
32 Dean for Student Affairs ....Mr. Karl RISHE
06 Registrar ....Ms. Jameka WINDHAM
37 Dir Student Financial Assistance ....Ms. Mary MCCRYSTAL
88 Director of Student Accounts ....Mr. Jason LAPINSKI
19 Director Security/Safety ....Mr. Jeff SCOTT
18 Director Physical Plant ....Mr. Tom MEEKS
13 Director Information Technology ....Mr. Michael KIEC
15 Director Personnel Services ....Ms. Susan ANDERSON
08 Director of Library ....Ms. Karen ZOLLER
42 Director Ctr Campus Theol/Ministry ....Mr. Ted STEINER
78 Director Coop Educ & Career Devel ....Ms. Kimberly LANE
38 Director of Counseling Center ....Ms. Susan LIPIEC
39 Director of Residence Life ....Ms. Tera JOHNSON
29 Dir Alumni Rels/Asc Dir Development ....Mrs. Mary Elizabeth COTLEUR
04 Admin Assistant to the President ....Ms. April KENNEDY
14 Chief Information Officer ....Ms. Deborah SHEREN
26 Chief Communications Officer ....Mr. Brian JOHNSTON
106 Online Education/E-learning ....Ms. Mary Ann SCHNEIDER

Oberlin College (B)

173 West Lorain Street, Oberlin OH 44074-1057
County: Lorain FICE Identification: 003086
Unit ID: 204501
Telephone: (440) 775-8121 Carnegie Class: Bac/A&S
FAX Number: (440) 775-8886 Calendar System: 4/1/4
URL: www.oberlin.edu
Established: 1833 Annual Undergrad Tuition & Fees: $50,356
Enrollment: 2,978 Coed
Affiliation or Control: Independent Non-Profit IRS Status: 501(c)3
Highest Offering: Master's
Program: Liberal Arts And General; Professional
Accreditation: NH, MUS

01 President ....Mr. Marvin KRISLOV
10 Vice President for Finance ....Dr. Michael FRANDSEN
30 VP Development/Alumni Affair ....Mr. William BARLOW
26 Vice President College Relations ....Mr. Ben JONES
49 Dean of Arts & Sciences ....Dr. Timothy ELGREN
64 Dean Conservatory Music ....Ms. Andrea KALYN
32 Dean of Student Life ....Dr. Eric ESTES
45 VP for Strategic Initiatives ....Dr. Kathryn STUART
07 Dean Admissions/Financial Aid ....Mrs. Debra J. CHERMONTE
43 VP/General Counsel and Secretary ....Ms. Sandhya SUBRAMANIAN
86 Spec Asst Community/Govt Relations ....Ms. Tita REED
21 Assoc Vice Pres Finance/Controller ....Mr. Mark R. BATES
29 Exec Director Alumni Assoc ....Ms. Danielle YOUNG
05 Dean of Studies ....Dr. Joyce BABYAK
88 Sr Assoc Dean of College Arts & Sci ....Dr. Steve WOJTAL
88 Assoc Dean of College of Arts & Sci ....Dr. Pablo MITCHELL
13 Chief Tech Ofcr/Dir Computing Ctr ....Dr. John E. BUCHER
08 Interim Director of Libraries ....Dr. Alan BOYD
07 Director Admissions Conservatory ....Mr. Michael C. MANDEREN
38 Director of Counseling Center ....Mr. John HARSHBARGER
57 Director of Allen Art Museums ....Dr. Andria DERSTINE
06 Registrar ....Ms. Elizabeth CLERKIN
37 Director of Financial Aid ....Mr. Robert A. REDDY, JR.
09 Director of Institutional Research ....Mr. Ross PEACOCK
18 Asst VP for Facilities ....Mr. Tom PICCORELLI
36 Director Career Devel/Placement ....Vacant
42 Director Religious and Spiritual Li ....Rev. David F. DORSEY
39 Dir Residential/Dining Services ....Mr. Adrian BATISTA
41 Director of Physical Educ/Athletics ....Ms. Natalie WINKELFOOS
19 Director of Safety & Security ....Ms. Marjorie BURTON
28 Director Multicultural Affairs ....Vacant
96 Director of Purchasing ....Mr. James S. KLAIBER
15 Chief Human Resources Officer ....Mr. Joseph VITALE, JR.
04 Administrative Asst to President ....Mrs. Jennifer S. BRADFIELD
104 Assoc Dean & Dir of Intl Studies ....Ms. Ellen SAYLES
100 Chief of Staff ....Ms. Jane MATHISON
102 Exec Dir Office of Foundations ....Ms. Pamela SNYDER
44 Sr Philanthropic Advisor ....Ms. Catherine GLETHEROW

Ohio Business College (C)

4525 Trueman Boulevard, Hilliard OH 43026
Telephone: (614) 891-5030 FICE Identification: 030658
Accreditation: ACICS, #MAC

† Branch campus of Ohio Business College, Lorain Branch, Sheffield Village, OH.

Ohio Business College (D)

5202 Timber Commons Drive, Sandusky OH 44870-5894
Telephone: (419) 627-8345 Identification: 666467
Accreditation: ACICS

† Branch campus of Ohio Business College, Sheffield Village, OH.

Ohio Business College, Lorain Branch (E)

5095 Waterford Drive, Sheffield Village OH 44035-0701
County: Lorain FICE Identification: 021585
Unit ID: 203720
Telephone: (440) 934-3101 Carnegie Class: Assoc/PrivFP
FAX Number: (440) 934-3105 Calendar System: Quarter
URL: www.ohiobusinesscollege.edu
Established: 1903 Annual Undergrad Tuition & Fees: $14,500
Enrollment: 375 Coed
Affiliation or Control: Proprietary IRS Status: Proprietary
Highest Offering: Associate Degree
Program: Occupational; 2-Year Principally Bachelor's Creditable
Accreditation: ACICS, MAC

01 Executive Director ....Mrs. Rosanne CATELLA
07 Admissions Director ....Mrs. Rosemerry NICKELS
10 Financial Manager ....Mrs. Christine TODD
36 Career Services ....Ms. Cheryl JANKOWSKI

Ohio Christian University (F)

1476 Lancaster Pike, Circleville OH 43113-0458
County: Pickaway FICE Identification: 003030
Unit ID: 201964
Telephone: (740) 474-8896 Carnegie Class: Bac/Diverse
FAX Number: (740) 477-7755 Calendar System: Semester
URL: www.ohiochristian.edu
Established: 1948 Annual Undergrad Tuition & Fees: $17,490
Enrollment: 4,058 Coed
Affiliation or Control: Other Protestant IRS Status: 501(c)3
Highest Offering: Master's
Program: 2-Year Principally Bachelor's Creditable; Liberal Arts And General; Teacher Preparatory; Professional; Religious Emphasis
Accreditation: NH, BI, TEAC

01 President ....Dr. Mark A. SMITH
05 Provost ....Dr. Hank KELLY
10 Vice President of Finance ....Mr. Robert HARTMAN
30 Vice President for Advancement ....Mr. Mark TAYLOR
32 Vice President Student Development ....Dr. Rick CHRISTMAN
11 Vice President of Operations ....Mr. Mike FRACASSA
13 Vice President for IT ....Mr. Ryan WHISLER
09 Asst VP for Institutional Research ....Dr. Cynthia TWEEDELL
06 Registrar ....Dr. Rodney SONES
84 Vice President of Enrollment ....Mr. Michael EGENREIDER
55 VP College of Adult & Graduate Stds ....Dr. Bradford SAMPLE
84 VP of AGS Enrollment Mgmt ....Ms. Sylvia LACASCHI-DECKER
35 Asst VP of Student Developement ....Ms. Rebecca WAKEMAN
08 Director of Library Services ....Mrs. Barbara MEISTER
37 Director Student Financial Services ....Mr. Wes BROTHERS
41 Athletic Director ....Mr. Ben BELLEMAN
29 Alumni Relations Coordinator ....Mr. Jonathan FALKS
50 Dean/Director of Business ....Dr. David GARRISSON
50 Director of Business AGS ....Dr. Debra GRIMM
53 Director of Education ....Dr. Valerie WILSON
04 Administrative Asst to President ....Mrs. Ronda BALDWIN
07 Director of Admissions ....Mr. Kevin EDWARDS

Ohio College of Massotherapy (G)

225 Heritage Woods Drive, Akron OH 44321-1363
County: Summit FICE Identification: 031163
Unit ID: 204592
Telephone: (330) 665-1084 Carnegie Class: Assoc/PrivNFP
FAX Number: (330) 319-7733 Calendar System: Semester
URL: www.ocm.edu
Established: 1973 Annual Undergrad Tuition & Fees: $16,333
Enrollment: 72 Coed
Affiliation or Control: Proprietary IRS Status: Proprietary
Highest Offering: Associate Degree
Program: 2-Year Principally Bachelor's Creditable; Technical Emphasis
Accreditation: ACCSC

01 President ....Mr. Jeffrey S. MORROW
11 Director of Administration ....Mrs. Debra M. SMITH

Ohio Dominican University (H)

1216 Sunbury Road, Columbus OH 43219-2099
County: Franklin FICE Identification: 003035
Unit ID: 204617
Telephone: (614) 251-4500 Carnegie Class: Master's L
FAX Number: (614) 251-4634 Calendar System: Semester
URL: www.ohiodominican.edu
Established: 1911 Annual Undergrad Tuition & Fees: $29,690
Enrollment: 2,707 Coed
Affiliation or Control: Roman Catholic IRS Status: 501(c)3
Highest Offering: Master's
Program: Liberal Arts And General; Teacher Preparatory; Professional
Accreditation: NH, ACBSP, #ARCPA, SW, TED

01 President ....Dr. Peter CIMBOLIC
05 Vice President Academic Affairs ....Dr. Theresa HOLLERAN
32 Vice Pres Stdnt Dev/Dean Retention ....Dr. James A. CARIDI
10 Vice Pres Finance & Admin/CFO ....Mr. Clair KNAPP
30 Vice President for Advancement ....Mr. Douglas STEIN
26 Vice Pres Marketing & Public Rels ....Mr. Mark COOPER
04 Executive Asst to the President ....Ms. Amy THOMAS
35 Asst Vice Pres Student Development ....Ms. Sharon REED
20 Assoc Vice Pres Academic Affairs ....Dr. Linda WOLF
58 Dean Graduate/Professional Studies ....Vacant
51 Exec Dir of Adult/Continuing Educ ....Ms. Karen GRAY
09 Dir of Inst Research/Assessment ....Dr. Linda WOLF
06 Registrar ....Ms. Christine GROVES
07 Director of Admissions ....Mr. Kevin BRINKMAN
08 Director of the Library ....Ms. Michelle SARFF
37 Director of Financial Aid ....Ms. Laura MEEK
36 Director Career Services ....Ms. Mandy POWELL
38 Director of Counseling Services ....Mr. Michael LEWIS
85 Director of International Education ....Ms. Deanna SHINE
42 Director of Campus Ministry ....Rev. Thomas BLAU
13 Chief Information Officer ....Mr. Fred LASSITER
15 Director of Human Resources ....Ms. Krystina LAMB
18 Director of Physical Facilities ....Mr. Darrel PLUMLEE
29 Dir of Alumni Rels/Annual Giving ....Ms. Christie FLOOD-WEINER
39 Director of Resident Life ....Ms. Kerry SOLLER
41 Athletic Director ....Mr. Jeff BLAIR
24 Dir Center for Instruct Technology ....Vacant
96 Director of Purchasing ....Sr. Margaret WALSH
19 Director of Safety & Security ....Ms. Lisa SPRAGUE
92 Director of Honors Program ....Mr. John MARAZITA

Ohio Northern University (I)

525 S Main Street, Ada OH 45810-1599
County: Hardin FICE Identification: 003089
Unit ID: 204635
Telephone: (419) 772-2000 Carnegie Class: Bac/Diverse
FAX Number: (419) 772-1932 Calendar System: Semester
URL: www.onu.edu
Established: 1871 Annual Undergrad Tuition & Fees: $28,810
Enrollment: 3,695 Coed
Affiliation or Control: United Methodist IRS Status: 501(c)3
Highest Offering: First Professional Degree
Program: Liberal Arts And General; Teacher Preparatory; Professional
Accreditation: NH, BUS, CAATE, CS, ENG, EXSC, LAW, MT, MUS, NAIT, NURSE, PHAR, TED

01 President ....Dr. Daniel A. DIBIASIO
05 Provost/Vice Pres Academic Affairs ....Dr. David C. CRAGO
10 Vice President Financial Affairs ....Mr. William H. BALLARD
30 Vice Pres of University Advancement ....Ms. Shannon SPENCER
84 Vice Pres Enrollment Management ....Dr. William T. EIOLA
32 VP Student Affairs/Dean of Students ....Dr. Adriane THOMPSON-BRADSHAW
49 Dean of Arts & Sciences ....Dr. Catherine ALBRECHT
54 Dean of Engineering ....Dr. Eric T. BAUMGARTNER
67 Dean of Pharmacy ....Dr. Steven J. MARTIN
50 Dean Business Administration ....Dr. James W. FENTON
61 Dean of Law ....Mr. Richard C. BALES
30 Senior Director of Development ....Mr. Scott D. WILLS
08 Director of Heterick Library ....Ms. Kathleen BARIL

39 Dir of Res Life/Int Dir Career Svcs ....Mr. Justin COURTNEY
38 Director of Counseling ....Dr. Michael SCHAFER
29 Int Director of Alumni Relations .Mrs. Annmarie BAUMGARTNER
08 Law Librarian ....Dr. Nancy A. ARMSTRONG
42 University Chaplain ....Dr Rev. David MACDONALD
18 Director of Physical Plant ....Mr. Marc STALEY
13 Director of Technology ....Mr. Jeff RIEMAN
09 Director of Institutional Research ....Dr. Omer MINHAS
15 Director of Human Resources ....Ms. Tonya PAUL
20 Associate Academic Officer ....Dr. Juliet K. HURTIG
37 Director of Student Financial Aid ....Mrs. Melanie WEAVER
92 Director of Honors Program ....Dr. Patrick T. CROSKERY
21 Controller ....Mr. Mark RUSSELL
26 Dir of Communications & Marketing ....Mrs. Amy PRIGGE
07 Director of Admissions ....Ms. Deborah MILLER
06 Registrar ....Ms. Melanie HOUGH
28 Director Multicultural Development ....Ms. LaShonda GURLEY
41 Athletic Director ....Mr. Thomas SIMMONS
44 Director of Annual Giving ....Ms. Kelly ANDERSON
96 Manager of Purchasing ....Ms. Vicki J. NIESE
04 Executive Assistant to President ....Ms. Ann DONNELLY HAMILTON
101 Secretary of the Institution/ Board ....Ms. Sharon A. STECHSCHULTE
19 Director Security/Safety ....Mr. George SLEESMAN
25 Chief Contracts/Grants Admin ....Ms. Beckie WATERCUTTER

The Ohio State University Main Campus (A)

281 W. Lane Ave., Columbus OH 43210-1358
County: Franklin — FICE Identification: 003090
Unit ID: 204796
Telephone: (614) 292-6446 — Carnegie Class: RU/VH
FAX Number: (614) 292-9180 — Calendar System: Semester
URL: www.osu.edu
Established: 1870 — Annual Undergrad Tuition & Fees (In-State): $10,037
Enrollment: 58,322 — Coed
Affiliation or Control: State — IRS Status: 501(c)3
Highest Offering: Doctorate
Program: Liberal Arts And General; Teacher Preparatory; Professional
Accreditation: NH, ACAE, ART, AUD, BUS, BUSA, CAATE, CAHIIM, CIDA, CLPSY, COARC, CONST, CS, DANCE, DENT, DH, DIETC, DIETD, DIETI, DMS, ENG, HSA, IPSY, LAW, LSAR, MED, #MFCD, MIDWF, MT, MUS, NMT, NURSE, OPT, OPTR, OT, PCSAS, PH, PHAR, PLNG, PTA, RTT, SP, SPAA, SW, TED, THEA, VET

01 President ....Dr. Michael DRAKE
05 Executive Vice Pres/Provost ....Dr. Joseph E. STEINMETZ
10 Senior VP Business & Finance/CFO ....Mr. Geoffrey CHATAS
43 Sr VP & General Counsel ....Mr. Christopher M. CULLEY
32 Vice President for Student Life ......Dr. Javaune ADAMS-GASTON
20 Vice Provost for Academic Planning ....Mr. Michael J. BOEHM
26 VP University Communications ....Ms. Ann HAMILTON
15 Sr VP Talent/Cult & Human Resources ..Ms. Andraea DOUGLASS
46 Vice Pres for Research ....Dr. Caroline WHITACRE
86 Vice Pres of Govt Affairs ....Mr. Blake THOMPSON
23 Sr Exec Vice Pres Health Sci ....Dr. Sheldon M. RETCHIN
47 Vice Pres Ag Admin & Dean FAES ....Dr. Bruce MCPHERON
30 Sr VP for Advance/Pres OSU Found ....Mr. Michael EICHER
28 Vice Prov Diversity & Inclusion ....Dr. Sharon DAVIES
20 Vice Provost UG Stds & Dean UG Ed ......Dr. Wayne E. CARLSON
58 Int Vice Provost/Dean Grad School ....Dr. Scott HERNESS
41 Vice President/Director Athletics ....Mr. Gene SMITH
44 Vice President of Development ....Mr. David RIPPLE
18 Assoc VP Facilities Op/Dev ....Ms. Mary L. READEY
07 Assoc VP Enrol Svcs & Dir of Admiss ....Mr. Vern GRANGER
13 Vice President and CIO ....Mr. Michael HOFHERR
08 Director of Libraries ....Ms. Carol P. DIEDRCHS
101 Secretary Board of Trustees ....Mr. Blake THOMPSON
17 COO Medical Center ....Dr. Peter E. GEIER
85 Vice Prov Global Strat/Intl Affs ....Dr. William I. BRUSTEIN
90 Exec Dir Ohio Supercompufr Ctr ....Mr. Pankaj SHAW
29 Int Pres & CEO OSU Alumni Assoc ....Mr. Andy GURD
12 Exec Dean of Reg Campuses ....Dr. William L. MACDONALD
49 Vice Prov & Exec Dean Arts & Sci ....Dr. David C. MANDERSCHEID
50 Dean Fisher Col of Business ....Dr. Anil K. MAKHIJA
52 Dean College of Dentistry ....Dr. Patrick M. LLOYD
53 Dean College of Educ & Hum Ecology ....Dr. Cheryl L. ACHTERBERG
54 Dean College of Engineering ....Dr. David B. WILLIAMS
61 Dean College of Law ....Dr. Alan C. MICHAELS
63 Dean College of Medicine ....Dr. E. Christopher ELLISON
88 Dean College of Optometry ....Dr. Karla S. ZADNIK
67 Dean College of Pharmacy ....Dr. Henry J. MANN
69 Dean College of Public Health ....Dr. William J. MARTIN
70 Dean College of Social Work ....Dr. Tom GREGOIRE
74 Dean Col Veterinary Medicine ....Dr. Lonnie KING
66 Dean College of Nursing ....Dr. Bernadette MELNYK
84 VP Strategic Enrollment Planning ....Mr. Dolan EVANOVICH
09 Asst VP Inst Research/Planning ....Ms. Julie CARPENTER-HUBIN
37 Exec Dir Student Financial Aid ....Ms. Diane CORBETT
06 University Registrar ....Mr. Brad MYERS
88 Director of OES Analysis & Reportng ...Ms. Gail C. STEPHENOFF
35 Sr Assoc VP Student Life ....Dr. Gretchen METZELAARS
96 Director of Purchasing ....Mr. Russell CHUNG
11 Sr Vice Pres Admin & Planning ....Mr. Jay D. KASEY
40 General Manager OSU Bookstores ....Ms. Kathy SMITH
19 Asst VP Public Safety ....Mr. Vernon L. BAISDEN
39 Director Housing Administration .Ms. Toni GREENSLADE-SMITH
88 Dean JG College of Public Affairs ....Dr. Trevor L. BROWN

The Ohio State University Agricultural Technical Institute (B)

1328 Dover Road, Wooster OH 44691-4000
County: Wayne — FICE Identification: 010687
Unit ID: 204662
Telephone: (330) 264-3911 — Carnegie Class: Assoc/Pub2in4
FAX Number: (330) 287-1333 — Calendar System: Semester
URL: ati.osu.edu/
Established: 1971 — Annual Undergrad Tuition & Fees (In-State): $6,744
Enrollment: 702 — Coed
Affiliation or Control: State — IRS Status: 501(c)3
Highest Offering: Associate Degree
Program: Occupational; 2-Year Principally Bachelor's Creditable
Accreditation: NH

01 Interim Director ....Dr. Jim KINDER
05 Assoc Director Academic Affairs ....Ms. Jeanne OSBORNE
26 Mrktng & Communications Coordinator ...Ms. Frances P. WHITED
03 Assistant Director ....Dr. Rhonda BILLMAN
37 Coordinator Student Financial Aid ....Ms. Barbara LAMOREAUX
07 Manager of Enrollment ....Mr. David DIETRICH
10 Business Manager ....Ms. Lisa SIIMPSON
32 Coordinator Student Programs ....Ms. Kathy E. MAKSYMICZ
40 Bookstore Manager ....Ms. Patricia A. PAXTON
08 ATI Head Librarian ....Ms. Kathy YODER
19 Police Seargent ....Mr. Chad K. STANTON
13 Systems Manager ....Mr. Rick L. MITCHELL
50 Director Business Trng & Educ Svcs .....Ms. Kimberly J. SAYERS
39 Housing Coordinator ....Mr. Michael STEINER
88 Licensed Psych/Disability Svcs ....Dr. Jaqueline BELANGER
88 Program Director Program EXCEL ....Ms. Dee Dee SNYDER
06 Academic Records Manager ....Ms. Peggy E. LAMBERT
35 Coordinator Student Services ....Ms. Ruth MONTZ

The Ohio State University at Lima Campus (C)

4240 Campus Drive, Lima OH 45804-3597
Telephone: (419) 995-8600 — FICE Identification: 003092
Accreditation: &NH

† Regional accreditation is carried under the parent institution in Columbus, OH.

The Ohio State University Mansfield Campus (D)

1760 University Drive, Mansfield OH 44906-1599
Telephone: (419) 755-4011 — FICE Identification: 003093
Accreditation: &NH

† Regional accreditation is carried under the parent institution in Columbus, OH.

The Ohio State University at Marion (E)

1465 Mount Vernon Avenue, Marion OH 43302-5628
Telephone: (740) 389-6786 — FICE Identification: 003094
Accreditation: &NH

† Regional accreditation is carried under the parent institution in Columbus, OH.

The Ohio State University Newark Campus (F)

1179 University Drive, Newark OH 43055-9990
Telephone: (740) 366-3321 — FICE Identification: 003095
Accreditation: &NH

† Regional accreditation is carried under the parent institution in Columbus, OH.

Ohio Technical College (G)

1374 E 51st Street, Cleveland OH 44103-1269
County: Cuyahoga — FICE Identification: 011745
Unit ID: 204608
Telephone: (216) 881-1700 — Carnegie Class: Assoc/PrivFP
FAX Number: (216) 881-9145 — Calendar System: Quarter
URL: www.ohiotech.edu
Established: 1969 — Annual Undergrad Tuition & Fees: $27,300
Enrollment: 1,375 — Coed
Affiliation or Control: Proprietary — IRS Status: Proprietary
Highest Offering: Associate Degree
Program: Occupational; Technical Emphasis
Accreditation: ACCSC

84 Director of Enrollment Management ....Mr. Tom KING
07 Assistant Director of Admissions ....Ms. Rachele E. STECK

Ohio University Main Campus (H)

1 Ohio University, Athens OH 45701-2979
County: Athens — FICE Identification: 003100
Unit ID: 204857
Telephone: (740) 593-1000 — Carnegie Class: RU/H
FAX Number: N/A — Calendar System: Semester
URL: www.ohio.edu
Established: 1804 — Annual Undergrad Tuition & Fees (In-State): $11,548
Enrollment: 39,201 — Coed
Affiliation or Control: State — IRS Status: 501(c)3
Highest Offering: Doctorate
Program: Liberal Arts And General; Teacher Preparatory; Professional
Accreditation: NH, AAFCS, ADNUR, #ARCPA, AUD, BUS, BUSA, CAATE, CACREP, CIDA, CLPSY, CORE, CS, DANCE, DIETD, ENG, FEPAC, JOUR, MUS, NAIT, NRPA, NURSE, OSTEO, PH, PTA, SP, SW, TED, THEA

01 President ....Dr. Roderick J. MCDAVIS
100 Chief of Staff President's Ofc ....Ms. Jennifer KIRKSEY
05 Executive Vice President & Provost ....Dr. Pam BENOIT
10 VP for Finance & Administration ....Mr. Stephen T. GOLDING
32 Interim VP for Student Affairs ....Dr. Jenny HALL-JONES
30 VP Univ Advance/Pres/CEO OU Fdn ....Mr. Bryan BENCHOFF
13 Chief Information Officer ....Mr. Craig BANTZ
46 VP Research & Dean Grad College ....Dr. Joseph SHIELDS
84 Vice Provost Enrollment Management ....Mr. Craig CORNELL
43 General Counsel ....Mr. John J. BIANCAMANO
26 Exec Dir Comm/Marketing ....Ms. Renea MORRIS
88 Vice Provost/Dean Univ College ....Dr. Elizabeth SAYRS
21 Sr Assoc Vice Pres Finance/Admin ....Ms. Deborah SHAFFER
49 Dean College of Arts & Sciences ....Dr. Robert FRANK
50 Dean College of Business ....Dr. Hugh SHERMAN
60 Dean Scripps Col Communication ....Dr. Scott TITSWORTH
53 Dean Patton College of Education ....Dr. Renee A. MIDDLETON
54 Dean Russ Col Engineering/Tech ....Dr. Dennis IRWIN
57 Dean College of Fine Arts ....Dr. Margaret KENNEDY-DYGAS
69 Dean Col Health/Human Services ....Dr. Randy LEITE
92 Dean Honors Tutorial College ....Dr. Jeremy WEBSTER
63 Dean Heritage Col Osteopathic Med ....Dr. Kenneth JOHNSON
62 Dean University Libraries ....Mr. Scott H. SEAMAN
35 Dean of Students ....Dr. Jenny HALL-JONES
12 Exec Dean Regional Campuses ....Dr. William WILLAN
12 Dean Eastern Campus ....Dr. Paul ABRAHAM
12 Dean Southern Campus ....Dr. Nicole PENNINGTON
12 Dean Chillicothe Campus ....Dr. Martin TUCK
12 Dean Lancaster Campus ....Dr. James SMITH
12 Dean Zanesville Campus ....Dr. Jenifer CUSHMAN
20 Associate Provost Academic Affairs ....Dr. Howard DEWALD
58 Director Graduate Student Services ....Dr. Katherine TADLOCK
88 Vice Provost Global Affairs ....Dr. Lorna Jean EDMONDS
28 Vice Prov Diversity & Inclusion ....Dr. Shari CLARKE
09 Assoc Prov Inst Rsrch/Effectiveness ....Dr. Barbara WHARTON
41 Director of Athletics ....Mr. Jim SCHAUS
06 University Registrar ....Mrs. Debra M. BENTON
15 Chief Human Resources Officer ....Ms. Colleen BENDEL
29 Asst Vice Pres Alumni Relations ....Ms. Jennifer NEUBAUER
36 Asst Dean for Career Services ....Mr. Imants JAUNARAJS
07 Asst Vice Provost/Dir Ungrad Admiss ..Ms. Candace BOENINGER
38 Director Counseling Services ....Dr. Alfred B. WEINER
44 Exec Dir of Develop Planned Giving ....Ms. Kelli KOTOWSKI
37 Director Student Financial Aid ....Ms. Valerie MILLER
23 Medical Dir of Campus Care ....Dr. John J. KEMERER
106 Vice Provost for eLearning/Str Prtn ....Dr. Deb GEARHART
96 Director of Procurement Services ....Ms. Laura NOWICKI
19 Chief of Police/Dir Campus Safety ....Mr. Andrew POWERS
85 Assoc Dir Intl Students/Fac Svcs ....Dr. Krista MCCALLUM-BEATTY
39 Exec Director of Residential Hous ....Mr. Peter TRENTACOSTE
109 Asst Vice Pres Auxiliary Services ....Ms. Christine SHEETS
25 Asst VP Res & Sponsored Programs ....Mr. Shane L. GILKEY
24 Media Library Manager ....Ms. Robin KRIVESTI
88 Bursar ....Ms. Sherry DOWNS
101 Secretary to Board of Trustees ....Dr. David MOORE
11 Sr Assoc VP of Tech/Admin Svcs ....Mr. Joseph LALLEY
86 Director of Government Relations ....Mr. Eric BURCHARD

Ohio University Chillicothe Campus (I)

PO Box 629, 101 University Drive, Chillicothe OH 45601-0629
Telephone: (740) 774-7200 — FICE Identification: 003102
Accreditation: &NH

† Regional accreditation is carried under the parent institution in Athens, OH.

Ohio University Eastern Campus (J)

45425 National Road, Saint Clairsville OH 43950-9724
Telephone: (740) 695-1720 — FICE Identification: 003101
Accreditation: &NH

† Regional accreditation is carried under the parent institution in Athens, OH.

Ohio University Lancaster Campus (K)

1570 Granville Pike, Lancaster OH 43130-1097
Telephone: (740) 654-6711 — FICE Identification: 003104
Accreditation: &NH, MAC

† Regional accreditation is carried under the parent institution in Athens, OH.

Ohio University Southern Campus (L)

1804 Liberty Avenue, Ironton OH 45638-2279
Telephone: (740) 533-4600 — Identification: 666000
Accreditation: &NH

† Regional accreditation is carried under the parent institution in Athens, OH.

Ohio University Zanesville Branch (M)

1425 Newark Road, Zanesville OH 43701-2695
Telephone: (740) 453-0762 — FICE Identification: 003108
Accreditation: &NH

† Regional accreditation is carried under the parent institution in Athens, OH.

Ohio Valley College of Technology (A)

15258 State Route 170, East Liverpool OH 43920
County: Columbiana FICE Identification: 023014
Unit ID: 204884
Telephone: (330) 385-1070 Carnegie Class: Assoc/PrivFP
FAX Number: (330) 385-4606 Calendar System: Semester
URL: www.ovct.edu
Established: 1886 Annual Undergrad Tuition & Fees: $11,180
Enrollment: 198 Coed
Affiliation or Control: Proprietary IRS Status: Proprietary
Highest Offering: Associate Degree
Program: Occupational; Nursing Emphasis
Accreditation: ACICS, MAC

01 President .... Mr. Scott S. ROGERS
05 Director of Academic Operations ..... Ms. Angel BROCK-MURPHY
37 Director of Financial Aid .... Ms. Rebecca STECKMAN

Ohio Wesleyan University (B)

61 S Sandusky Street, Delaware OH 43015-2398
County: Delaware FICE Identification: 003109
Unit ID: 204909
Telephone: (740) 368-2000 Carnegie Class: Bac/A&S
FAX Number: (740) 368-3299 Calendar System: Semester
URL: www.owu.edu
Established: 1842 Annual Undergrad Tuition & Fees: $43,230
Enrollment: 1,723 Coed
Affiliation or Control: United Methodist IRS Status: 501(c)3
Highest Offering: Baccalaureate
Program: Liberal Arts And General
Accreditation: NH, MUS, TED

01 President .... Dr. Rockwell F. JONES
05 Provost .... Dr. Charles L. STINEMETZ
10 VP for Finance/Admin/Treasurer .... Mr. Dan J. HITCHELL
26 VP for University Advancement .... Ms. Colleen C. GARLAND
84 Vice President for Enrollment .... Ms. Susan R. DILENO
32 Vice President for Student Affairs .... Dr. Craig E. ULLOM
30 Asst VP for University Advancement .... Ms. Jodi L. BOPP
20 Dean of Academic Affairs .... Dr. Martin J. EISENBERG
09 Assoc Provost for Inst Research .... Dr. Dale E. SWARTZENTRUBER
108 Asst Provost Assmt/Accreditation .... Dr. Barbara S. ANDERECK
37 Director Student Financial Aid .... Mr. Kevin F. PASKVAN
36 Director of Career Services .... Ms. Leslie J. MELTON
08 Chief Info Officer/Dir of Libraries .... Ms. Cathi A. CARDWELL
06 Registrar .... Ms. Shelly A. MCMAHON
14 Director of Computer Center .... Mr. Harold D. WIEBE
13 Exec Director Information Tech .... Mr. Brian A. RELLINGER
19 Director of Public Safety .... Mr. Robert A. WOOD
29 Director Alumni Relations .... Ms. Brenda E. DEWITT
26 Director Marketing/Communications .... Mr. Will E. KOPP
85 Director International Student Svcs .... Mr. Darrell J. ALBON
18 Director Physical Plant .... Mr. Peter K. SCHANTZ
15 Interim Director Human Resources .... Mr. John A. SANDERS
31 Director Community Svc Learning .... Ms. Sally S. LEBER
04 Asst to President/Board Secy .... Ms. Lisa D. JACKSON
23 Director Wellness Center .... Ms. Marsha A. TILDEN
35 Dean of Students .... Dr. Kimberlie L. GOLDSBERRY
39 Director Residential Life .... Ms. Wendy L. PIPER
41 Director of Athletics .... Mr. Roger D. INGLES
42 Chaplain .... Rev. Jon R. POWERS
89 Dean First Year Students .... Vacant
92 Honors Program Director .... Dr. Amy MCCLURE
93 Dir Multicultural Student Affairs .... Ms. Terree L. STEVENSON
102 Dir Foundation/Corp/Govt Relations .... Ms. Karen CROSMAN
07 Associate Director of Admissions .... Ms. Alisha M. COUCH
40 Bookstore Manager .... Mr. Kevin U. STITH
38 Coord Counseling/Mental Health Svcs .... Dr. Doug L. BENNETT
96 Purchasing Coordinator .... Ms. Melanie T. KALB

Otterbein University (C)

1 South Grove Street, Westerville OH 43081-2006
County: Franklin FICE Identification: 003110
Unit ID: 204936
Telephone: (614) 890-3000 Carnegie Class: Master's M
FAX Number: (614) 823-3114 Calendar System: Semester
URL: www.otterbein.edu
Established: 1847 Annual Undergrad Tuition & Fees: $31,424
Enrollment: 2,792 Coed
Affiliation or Control: United Methodist IRS Status: 501(c)3
Highest Offering: Doctorate
Program: Liberal Arts And General; Teacher Preparatory; Professional
Accreditation: NH, ANEST, CAATE, MUS, NURSE, TED, THEA

01 President .... Dr. Kathy A. KRENDL
100 Chief of Staff .... Ms. Kristine ROBBINS
05 Provost/VPAA .... Dr. Miguel MARTINEZ-SAENZ
32 Vice President Student Affairs .... Mr. Robert M. GATTI
10 Vice President for Business Affairs .... Mrs. Rebecca D. VAZQUEZ-SKILLINGS
30 VP Institutional Advancement .... Vacant
84 Vice President for Enrollment .... Mr. Jefferson BLACKBURN-SMITH
20 Assoc VP AA/Dean Academic Services .... Dr. Wendy SHERMAN-HECKLER
91 Exec Director of Information Tech .... Mr. Dave BENDER
08 Director of the Library .... Ms. Tiffany LIPSTREU
06 Registrar .... Mr. Donald W. FOSTER
26 Exec Dir Marketing/Communications .... Mrs. Jennifer PEARCE
36 Director Career Planning/Placement .... Mr. Ryan BRECHBILL
37 Director of Financial Aid .... Mr. Thomas V. YARNELL
41 Athletic Director .... Ms. Dawn STEWART
42 Chaplain .... Dr. Judy GUION-UTSLER
51 Assoc Dean Adult & Transfer Office .... Vacant
107 Dean School of Prof Studies .... Dr. Barbara H. SCHAFFNER
49 Dean School of Arts/Sciences .... Dr. Paul EISENSTEIN
85 Exec Director Intl Programs .... Vacant
07 Director of Admissions .... Mr. Ben SHOEMAKER
15 Director Human Resources .... Mr. Scott FITZGERALD
18 Director/Physical Plant .... Mr. David D. BELL
29 Director Alumni Relations .... Ms. Rebecca F. SMITH
28 Director of Diversity .... Dr. Lisa PATTERSON
96 Director of Purchasing .... Mr. Steven H. ROSENBERGER
21 Inst Rsrch Spec/Financial Analyst .... Mr. Christopher A. HAYTER
09 Director of Institutional Research .... Dr. Sean M. MCLAUGHLIN
19 Director of Security .... Mr. Larry BANASZAK
04 Executive Assistant to President .... Mrs. Sarah HICKEY
39 Director Student Housing .... Ms. Tracy BENNER
38 Director Student Counseling .... Dr. Kathleen RYAN
44 Director Annual or Planned Giving .... Mr. Matthew D'OYLY

Owens Community College (D)

30335 Oregon, PO Box 10000, Toledo OH 43699-1947
County: Wood FICE Identification: 005753
Unit ID: 204945
Telephone: (567) 661-7000 Carnegie Class: Assoc/Pub-U-MC
FAX Number: N/A Calendar System: Semester
URL: www.owens.edu
Established: 1965 Annual Undergrad Tuition & Fees (In-State): $3,745
Enrollment: 12,577 Coed
Affiliation or Control: State IRS Status: 501(c)3
Highest Offering: Associate Degree
Program: Occupational; 2-Year Principally Bachelor's Creditable; Technical Emphasis
Accreditation: NH, ACBSP, ACFEI, ADNUR, CAHIIM, DH, DIETT, DMS, EMT, MAC, NAIT, OTA, PTAA, RAD, RADMAG, SURGT

01 President .... Dr. Mike BOWER
101 Secretary to the Board of Trustees .... Ms. Patricia JEZAK
04 Executive Assistant to President .... Ms. Vicki DUPKE
05 Vice President Academic Affairs .... Dr. Steve ROBINSON
10 Treasurer .... Ms. Laurie SABIN
15 VP Human Resources .... Mr. Jack WITT
84 VP Enroll Mgmt/Student Svcs/Mktg .... Dr. Betsy JOHNSON
108 Assoc Vice Pres Inst Effectiveness .... Vacant
20 Assoc VP Academic Services .... Ms. Denise SMITH
103 Executive Dir Wrkfrce/Comm Service .... Dr. Brian PASKVAN
12 Associate VP Findlay Campus .... Dr. Melissa GREEN
21 Controller .... Ms. Pam BECK
13 Chief Information Officer .... Dr. Connie SCHAFFER
19 Chief of Police .... Mr. John BETORI
37 Director Financial Aid .... Ms. Andrea MORROW
18 Executive Director Operations .... Mr. Michael MCDONALD
09 Inst Research Associate .... Ms. Debra RATHKE
81 Interim Dean School of STEM .... Mr. Glenn RETTIG
66 Dean School of Nursing/Health Prof .... Ms. Dawn WETMORE
50 Dean School Business/Info/Publc Svc .... Dr. Ann THEIS
57 Dean School of Liberal Arts .... Ms. Michele JOHNSON
62 Dean Library .... Mr. Tom SINK
106 Director eLearning .... Mr. Mark KARAMOL
43 In-House Legal Counsel .... Dr. Natalie JACKSON
22 Equal Opp/Inclusiveness Officer .... Ms. Lisa DUBOSE
06 Interim Registrar .... Mr. David SHAFFER
86 Exec Dir Govt/Comm Relations .... Ms. Jennifer FEHNRICH
29 Director Alumni Affairs .... Ms. Laura MOORE
32 Director Student Life .... Vacant
109 Manager Auxiliary Services .... Mr. David WAHR
85 Director International Programs .... Ms. Annette SWANSON
41 Director Athletics .... Vacant

Owens Community College Findlay Campus (E)

3200 Bright Road, Findlay OH 45840
Telephone: (567) 429-3500 Identification: 770360
Accreditation: &NH

† Branch campus of Owens Community College, Toledo, OH.

Payne Theological Seminary (F)

PO Box 474, Wilberforce OH 45384-0474
County: Greene FICE Identification: 010017
Unit ID: 204990
Telephone: (937) 376-2946 Carnegie Class: Spec/Faith
FAX Number: (937) 376-3330 Calendar System: 4/1/4
URL: www.payne.edu
Established: 1844 Annual Graduate Tuition & Fees: $11,450
Enrollment: 125 Coed
Affiliation or Control: African Methodist Episcopal IRS Status: 501(c)3
Highest Offering: Master's; No Undergraduates
Program: Professional; Business Emphasis
Accreditation: THEOL

01 Interim President .... Dr. Michael BROWN
05 Academic Dean .... Dr. Michael BROWN
30 Director of Development .... Rev. Jules DUNHAM HOWIE
10 Finance Director .... Mr. Alan COSTNER
37 Financial Aid Officer .... Ms. Pat COPELY
08 Director of Library Services .... Ms. Shanee Yvette MURRAIN

Pontifical College Josephinum (G)

7625 N High Street, Columbus OH 43235-1498
County: Franklin FICE Identification: 003113
Unit ID: 205027
Telephone: (614) 885-5585 Carnegie Class: Spec/Faith
FAX Number: (614) 885-2307 Calendar System: Semester
URL: www.pcj.edu
Established: 1888 Annual Undergrad Tuition & Fees: $30,948
Enrollment: 212 Male
Affiliation or Control: Roman Catholic IRS Status: 501(c)3
Highest Offering: Beyond Master's But Less Than Doctorate
Program: Liberal Arts And General; Professional; Religious Emphasis
Accreditation: NH, THEOL

01 Rector/President .... R.Msgr. Christopher J. SCHRECK
10 VP for Administration/Treasurer .... Mr. John O. ERWIN
05 Vice Rector School of Theology .... Rev. Walter R. OXLEY
30 Vice President for Advancement .... Rev. John A. ALLEN
49 Vice Rector College Liberal Arts .... Rev. John ROZEMBAJGIER
73 Academic Dean School of Theology .... Dr. Perry J. CAHALL
20 Academic Dean College Liberal Arts .... Dr. David J. DE LEONARDIS
06 Registrar .... Mr. Samuel J. DEAN
08 Librarian .... Mr. Peter G. VERACKA
33 Dean of Community Life .... Rev. Walter R. OXLEY
33 Dean of Community Life .... Rev. Raymond ENZWEILER
07 Director of Admissions .... Rev. Joseph A. MURPHY
37 Financial Aid Director .... Mrs. Marky LEICHTNAM
108 Dir of Inst Plng/Assessment/Accred .... Mr. Eric S. GRAFF
26 Director of Communications .... Ms. Carolyn DINOVO

PowerSport Institute (H)

21210 Emery Road, North Randall OH 44128
Telephone: (216) 587-5000 Identification: 770582
Accreditation: ACCSC

† Branch campus of Ohio Technical College, Cleveland, OH.

Professional Skills Institute (I)

1505 Holland Road, Maumee OH 43537
County: Lucas FICE Identification: 023377
Unit ID: 205054
Telephone: (419) 720-6670 Carnegie Class: Assoc/PrivFP
FAX Number: (419) 720-6674 Calendar System: Quarter
URL: www.proskills.edu
Established: 1984 Annual Undergrad Tuition & Fees: $16,361
Enrollment: 286 Coed
Affiliation or Control: Proprietary IRS Status: Proprietary
Highest Offering: Associate Degree
Program: Occupational; 2-Year Principally Bachelor's Creditable; Nursing Emphasis
Accreditation: ABHES, PTAA

01 CEO .... Mr. Daniel FINCH
07 Admissions Coordinator .... Mr. Tony DICKENS

Rabbinical College of Telshe (J)

28400 Euclid Avenue, Wickliffe OH 44092-2584
County: Lake FICE Identification: 003115
Unit ID: 205124
Telephone: (440) 943-5300 Carnegie Class: Spec/Faith
FAX Number: (440) 943-5303 Calendar System: Quarter
Established: 1941 Annual Undergrad Tuition & Fees: $10,200
Enrollment: 90 Male
Affiliation or Control: Independent Non-Profit IRS Status: 501(c)3
Highest Offering: Doctorate
Program: Teacher Preparatory; Professional
Accreditation: RABN

01 President .... Rabbi David GOLDBERG
06 Registrar .... Rabbi Abraham MATITIA

Remington College Cleveland Campus (K)

14445 Broadway Avenue, Cleveland OH 44125-1900
County: Cuyahoga FICE Identification: 007777
Unit ID: 375416
Telephone: (216) 475-7520 Carnegie Class: Assoc/PrivFP
FAX Number: (216) 475-6055 Calendar System: Other
URL: www.remingtoncollege.edu
Established: 1990 Annual Undergrad Tuition & Fees: $19,181
Enrollment: 510 Coed
Affiliation or Control: Independent Non-Profit IRS Status: 501(c)3
Highest Offering: Associate Degree
Program: Occupational
Accreditation: ACCSC, PTAA

01 Campus President .... Mr. Todd ZVAIGZNE

Rosedale Bible College (L)

2270 Rosedale Road, Irwin OH 43029-9517
County: Madison FICE Identification: 034253
Unit ID: 439899
Telephone: (740) 857-1311 Carnegie Class: Assoc/PrivNFP
FAX Number: (877) 857-1312 Calendar System: Semester
URL: www.rosedale.edu

Established: 1952 Annual Undergrad Tuition & Fees: $8,311
Enrollment: 58 Coed
Affiliation or Control: Mennonite Church IRS Status: 501(c)3
Highest Offering: Associate Degree
Program: 2-Year Principally Bachelor's Creditable; Religious Emphasis
Accreditation: BI

01 President .... Mr. Jonathan SHOWALTER
05 Academic Dean .... Mr. Phil WEBER
32 Dean of Students .... Mr. Matthew SHOWALTER
84 Director of Enrollment Services .... Mr. Darnell BRENNEMAN
08 Director of Library Services .... Mr. Reuben SAIRS
06 Registrar .... Ms. Bethany GEIB
10 Chief Financial Officer .... Mr. Lynford SCHROCK
26 Chief Public Relations Officer .... Mr. Kenneth MILLER
04 Administrative Asst to President .... Mrs. Twila WEBER
18 Chief Facilities/Physical Plant .... Mr. David TROYER
37 Director Student Financial Aid .... Mr. Darnell BRENNEMAN

Saint Mary Seminary and Graduate School of Theology (A)

28700 Euclid Avenue, Wickliffe OH 44092-2585
County: Lake FICE Identification: 004061
Unit ID: 205319
Telephone: (440) 943-7600 Carnegie Class: Not Classified
FAX Number: (440) 943-7577 Calendar System: Semester
URL: www.stmarysem.edu
Established: 1848 Annual Graduate Tuition & Fees: $10,120
Enrollment: 132 Coed
Affiliation or Control: Roman Catholic IRS Status: 501(c)3
Highest Offering: Doctorate; No Undergraduates
Program: Professional; Religious Emphasis
Accreditation: NH, THEOL

01 President/Rector .... Rev. Mark A. LATCOVICH
03 Vice President/Vice Rector .... Rev. Gerald J. BEDAR
05 Academic Dean .... Sr. Mary MCCORMICK, OSU
33 Student Dean .... Rev. Michael G. WOOST
42 Spiritual Director .... Rev. Mark HOLLIS
06 Registrar/Assistant Dean .... Sr. Brendon ZAJAC, SND
08 Librarian .... Mr. Alan K. ROME
10 Treasurer .... Mr. Philip GUBAN
04 Administrative Asst to President .... Ms. Kathryn C. SIMMONS
90 Director Academic Computing .... Sr. Brendon ZAJAC
18 Chief Facilities/Physical Plant .... Mr. Philip GUBAN
108 Director Institutional Assessment .... Dr. Edward KACZUK
13 Chief Info Technology Officer (CIO) .... Mr. Alan K. ROME
19 Director Security/Safety .... Mr. Philip GUBAN

School of Advertising Art (B)

1725 E David Road, Dayton OH 45440-1612
County: Montgomery FICE Identification: 025530
Unit ID: 205391
Telephone: (877) 300-9866 Carnegie Class: Assoc/PrivFP
FAX Number: (937) 294-5869 Calendar System: Semester
URL: www.saa.edu
Established: 1983 Annual Undergrad Tuition & Fees: $27427.16
Enrollment: 139 Coed
Affiliation or Control: Proprietary IRS Status: Proprietary
Highest Offering: Associate Degree
Program: Occupational; 2-Year Principally Bachelor's Creditable; Technical Emphasis
Accreditation: ACCSC

01 Owner/President/Creative Director .... Ms. Jessica BARRY
03 Vice President .... Mr. Matt FLICK
06 Vice President/HR/Registrar .... Mr. Nathan SUMMERS
05 Director of Education .... Ms. Karen ABNEY KORN
36 Director of Career Services .... Ms. Roxann PATRICK
37 Director of Financial Aid .... Ms. Tracy GARDNER
26 Director of Communications .... Ms. Betsy WOODS
07 Asst Admissions Director .... Ms. Mariesa BLOOM

Shawnee State University (C)

940 Second Street, Portsmouth OH 45662-4344
County: Scioto FICE Identification: 009942
Unit ID: 205443
Telephone: (740) 351-3205 Carnegie Class: Bac/A&S
FAX Number: (740) 351-3470 Calendar System: Semester
URL: www.shawnee.edu
Established: 1975 Annual Undergrad Tuition & Fees (In-State): $8,795
Enrollment: 4,230 Coed
Affiliation or Control: State IRS Status: 501(c)3
Highest Offering: Master's
Program: Occupational; Liberal Arts And General; Teacher Preparatory
Accreditation: NH, ADNUR, CAATE, COARC, DH, EMT, MLTAD, NUR, OT, OTA, PTAA, RAD, TED

01 President .... Dr. Rick KURTZ
05 Provost/VP Academic Affairs .... Dr. Alan WALKER
10 Vice President for Finance & Admin .... Dr. Elinda BOYLES
32 Vice President for Student Affairs .... Mr. Robert TRUSZ
43 General Counsel/Asst to the Pres .... Ms. Cheryl HACKER
84 Assoc Vice Pres Enrollment Mgmt .... Mr. Robert TRUSZ
20 Associate Provost .... Dr. Becky THIEL
26 Director Communications .... Ms. Elizabeth BLEVINS
107 Dean Professional Studies .... Dr. Paul MADDEN
49 Dean College Arts & Sciences .... Dr. Jeffery BAUER
08 Interim Director Library .... Dr. Alan WALKER
13 Director Univ Information Systems .... Mr. Charles WARNER
30 Executive Director of Development .... Mr. Eric BRAUN
07 Interim Director of Admission .... Mr. Rick MERB
06 Registrar .... Mr. Mark MOORE
15 Director of Human Resources/Payroll .... Mr. Dave ZINDER
41 Athletic Director .... Mr. Jeff HAMILTON
37 Director of Financial Aid .... Dr. Nicole NEAL
36 Asst Director Career Development .... Ms. Nikki KARABINIS
38 Director of Counseling & Psych Svcs .... Dr. Michael HUGHES
21 Assoc VP for Finance & Admin .... Ms. Joanne CHARLES
88 Dean University College .... Dr. Brenda HAAS
86 Special Asst to Pres for Govt Rels .... Mr. Eric BRAUN
85 Interim Dir for International Pgms .... Mr. Ryan WARNER
96 Dir of Procurement Services .... Ms. Pat CARSON
18 Director of Facilities .... Mr. Butch KOTCAMP
97 Director General Education Program .... Dr. Phil BLAU
09 Dir of Institutional Effectiveness .... Mr. Christopher SHAFFER
21 Controller .... Mr. Greg BALLENGEE
35 Dean of Students .... Ms. Marcie SIMMS
19 Chief of Police .... Mr. David THOROUGHMAN

Sinclair Community College (D)

444 W Third Street, Dayton OH 45402-1460
County: Montgomery FICE Identification: 003119
Unit ID: 205470
Telephone: (937) 512-3000 Carnegie Class: Assoc/Pub-U-SC
FAX Number: (937) 512-4596 Calendar System: Semester
URL: www.sinclair.edu
Established: 1887 Annual Undergrad Tuition & Fees (In-District): $2,971
Enrollment: 21,476 Coed
Affiliation or Control: State/Local IRS Status: 501(c)3
Highest Offering: Associate Degree
Program: Occupational; 2-Year Principally Bachelor's Creditable
Accreditation: NH, ACBSP, ACFEI, ADNUR, ART, CAHIIM, COARC, CSHSE, DH, DIETT, EMT, ENGT, MAC, MUS, OTA, PTAA, RAD, SURGT, THEA

00 President Emeritus .... Dr. Ned J. SIFFERLEN
01 President .... Dr. Steven L. JOHNSON
05 Provost .... Dr. Dave COLLINS
20 Associate Provost Stdnt Completion .... Dr. Kathleen CLEARY
103 VP for Workforce Development .... Ms. Deb NORRIS
100 Chief of Staff .... Mr. Mitchell BAILEY
30 VP for Advancement .... Ms. Madeline ISELI
10 Sr VP and CFO .... Mr. Jeff BOUDOURIS
21 VP for Business Operations .... Dr. Ty STONE
88 VP for School & Community Partners .... Dr. Annesa CHEEK
45 VP for Organizational Development .... Dr. Mary GAIER
84 VP Enroll Mgmt & Student Affairs .... Dr. Anthony CRUZ
12 VP for Regional Centers .... Dr. Scott MARKLAND
81 Dean of Science/Math/Engineering .... Mr. Anthony PONDER
76 Dean Health Sciences .... Ms. Rena SHUCHAT
105 Dean Distance Learning/Inst Support .... Dr. Nancy THIBEAULT
20 Associate Provost .... Dr. Lori ZAKEL
50 Dean Business & Public Services .... Dr. Sue MERRELL
26 Director of Public Affairs .... Mr. Adam MURKA
83 Dean Arts/Commun & Social Science .... Ms. Shari RETHMAN
13 Chief Information Officer .... Mr. Scott MCCOLLUM
43 General Counsel .... Ms. Lauren ROSS
06 Registrar .... Ms. Tina HUMMONS
37 Director Financial Aid .... Mr. Matthew MOORE
104 Director International Education .... Ms. Deborah GAVLIK
88 Chief Academic Advising Officer .... Mr. Andy RUNYAN

South University (E)

4743 Richmond Road, Cleveland OH 44128
Telephone: (216) 755-5000 Identification: 770916
Accreditation: &SC, ACBSP, NURSE, PTAA

† Branch campus of South University, Savannah, GA.

Southern State Community College (F)

100 Hobart Drive, Hillsboro OH 45133-9488
County: Highland FICE Identification: 012870
Unit ID: 205966
Telephone: (937) 393-3431 Carnegie Class: Assoc/Pub-R-M
FAX Number: (937) 393-9370 Calendar System: Semester
URL: www.sscc.edu
Established: 1975 Annual Undergrad Tuition & Fees (In-State): $4,186
Enrollment: 2,456 Coed
Affiliation or Control: State IRS Status: 501(c)3
Highest Offering: Associate Degree
Program: Occupational; 2-Year Principally Bachelor's Creditable
Accreditation: NH, ADNUR, MAC

01 President .... Dr. Kevin S. BOYS
05 Vice President Academic Affairs .... Dr. Ryan MCCALL
10 Vice President Business & Finance .... Mr. James E. BUCK
32 Vice Pres Student Svcs/Enroll Mgmt .... Mr. James BLAND
30 Vice Pres Inst Advancement .... Dr. Nicole ROADES
12 Director of Fayette Campus .... Dr. Jessica WISE
12 Director of South Campus .... Dr. Peggy CHALKER
103 Dean Workforce Dev/Community Svcs .... Mr. John JOY
15 Director of Human Resources .... Ms. Mindy MARKEY-GRABILL
88 Dean of Adult Opportunity Center .... Ms. Karyn EVANS
102 Executive Director Foundation .... Vacant
91 Computer System/Communication Mgr .... Ms. Shirley A. CORNWELL
26 Director of Public Relations .... Ms. Kris CROSS
06 Registrar .... Ms. Amanda THOMPSON
66 Director of Nursing .... Dr. Julianne KREBS
08 Librarian .... Vacant
37 Director Financial Aid .... Ms. Linda MYERS
07 Director of Admissions .... Ms. Lisa HORD
41 Athletic Director .... Mr. Matt WELLS
40 Bookstore Manager .... Ms. Jessica STEADMAN
13 Director Information Tech .... Mr. Dennis R. GRIFFITH
36 Director of Recruitment .... Vacant
04 Executive Asst to President .... Ms. Robin THOLEN

† Enrollment figure emcompasses all 4 campuses.

Southern State Community College Brown County Campus (G)

351 Brooks-Malott Rd, Mt Orab OH 45154
Telephone: (937) 444-7722 Identification: 770361
Accreditation: &NH

† Branch campus of Southern State Community College, Hillsboro, OH.

Southern State Community College Fayette Campus (H)

1270 US Route 62 SW,
Washington Court House OH 43160
Telephone: (740) 333-5115 Identification: 770362
Accreditation: &NH, COARC

† Branch campus of Southern State Community College, Hillsboro, OH.

Southern State Community College North Campus (I)

1850 Davids Drive, Wilmington OH 45177
Telephone: (937) 382-6645 Identification: 770363
Accreditation: &NH

† Branch campus of Southern State Community College, Hillsboro, OH.

Stark State College (J)

6200 Frank Avenue, NW, North Canton OH 44720-7299
County: Stark FICE Identification: 010881
Unit ID: 205841
Telephone: (330) 494-6170 Carnegie Class: Assoc/Pub-R-L
FAX Number: (330) 497-6313 Calendar System: Semester
URL: www.starkstate.edu
Established: 1960 Annual Undergrad Tuition & Fees (In-District): $4,753
Enrollment: 14,123 Coed
Affiliation or Control: State/Local IRS Status: 501(c)3
Highest Offering: Associate Degree
Program: Occupational; 2-Year Principally Bachelor's Creditable; Technical Emphasis
Accreditation: NH, ACBSP, ADNUR, CAHIIM, COARC, DH, @DIETT, ENGT, MAC, MLTAD, OTA, PTAA

01 President .... Dr. Para M. JONES
05 Provost and Chief Academic Officer .... Dr. Lada GIBSON-SHREVE
10 VP for Business and Finance .... Mr. Thomas A. CHIAPPINI
11 VP for EM/SS and Administration .... Mr. Michael DRONEY
46 VP/Spec Asst to Prov-Strateg Init .... Mrs. Cheryl RICE
15 Director of Human Resources .... Ms. Melissa A. GLANZ
53 Dean Ed/Liberal Arts/Math/Science .... Mr. Andrew STEPHAN
76 Dean Health and Human Services .... Mr. Dan MCDERMOTT
21 Controller .... Mr. Scott ANDREANI
13 Director Computer Services .... Vacant
36 Director of Career Development .... Ms. Kristin HANNON
37 Dean Financial Aid and Registration .... Ms. Amy WELTY
18 Director of Physical Plant and Cons .... Mr. Steve SPRADLING
40 Bookstore Manager .... Ms. Kathryn FEICHTER
06 Registrar .... Ms. Pam ARRINGTON
26 Director Marketing & Communications .... Ms. Marisa ROHN
21 Director of Budget .... Mr. Bruce WYDER
09 Director of Institutional Research .... Mr. Peter TRUMPOWER
54 Dean Eng Tech/Info Tech .... Mr. Don BALL
106 Director eStarkState .... Ms. Linda MOROSKO
08 Head Librarian .... Ms. Marcia ADDISON
04 Exec Admin Asst to President .... Ms. Catherine D. SPINO
102 Exec Dir Advancement/SSC Foundation .... Ms. Joanne L. EBERHART
103 Exec Dir Workforce and Econ Devel .... Dr. Daryl REVOLDT

Stautzenberger College (K)

8001 Katherine Boulevard, Brecksville OH 44141
Telephone: (440) 838-1999 Identification: 770760
Accreditation: ACICS

† Branch campus of Stautzenberger College, Maumee, OH.

Stautzenberger College (L)

1796 Indian Wood Circle, Maumee OH 43537-4007
County: Lucas FICE Identification: 004866
Unit ID: 205887
Telephone: (419) 866-0261 Carnegie Class: Assoc/PrivFP
FAX Number: (419) 867-9821 Calendar System: Quarter
URL: www.sctoday.edu
Established: 1926 Annual Undergrad Tuition & Fees: $11,870
Enrollment: 708 Coed
Affiliation or Control: Proprietary IRS Status: Proprietary

Highest Offering: Associate Degree
Program: Occupational; 2-Year Principally Bachelor's Creditable; Technical Emphasis
Accreditation: **ACICS**, MAC

01 Campus President .... Mr. Steven R. ALLEN
03 Vice President .... Mr. Brian E. NIEDZWIECKI
07 Director of Admissions .... Ms. Amanda L. BOYD
05 Dean of Academics .... Ms. Susan M. LIPPENS
37 Financial Aid Director .... Mrs. Mari L. HUFFMAN
36 Career Services Director .... Mr. Robert A. GARVER
06 Registrar .... Ms. Patricia A. PENTEK
08 Head Librarian .... Ms. Lori VAN LIERE

Terra State Community College (A)

2830 Napoleon Road, Fremont OH 43420-9670
County: Sandusky FICE Identification: 008278
Unit ID: 206011
Telephone: (419) 334-8400 Carnegie Class: Assoc/Pub-R-M
FAX Number: (419) 334-3719 Calendar System: Semester
URL: www.terra.edu
Established: 1968 Annual Undergrad Tuition & Fees (In-State): $4,282
Enrollment: 2,540 Coed
Affiliation or Control: State IRS Status: 501(c)3
Highest Offering: Associate Degree
Program: Occupational; 2-Year Principally Bachelor's Creditable; Technical Emphasis
Accreditation: **NH**, ADNUR, CAHIIM, PTAA

01 President .... Dr. Jerome WEBSTER
10 VP for Financial Affairs .... Mr. Randy MCCULLOUGH
26 Dir Mktg Public Relations .... Ms. Mary E. MCCUE
30 VP Inst Advancement .... Dr. Cory STINE
05 Vice President Academic Affairs .... Dr. Cindy KRUEGER
15 Director of Human Resources .... Ms. Nanci KOSANKA
21 Controller .... Mr. Jack FATICA
54 Dean Engineering Technology/Math .... Mr. Andrew G. CARROLL
09 Dean Planning & Inst Effect .... Dr. Michael C. KAPPER
50 Dean Business/Communication/Arts .... Ms. Jolene MEYERS
66 Dean Allied Health/Nursing/Science .... Ms. Amy ANWAY
84 Dean of Enrollment Services .... Mr. Heath MARTIN
09 Registrar .... Mr. Eric J. STEINBERGER
37 Director Financial Aid .... Ms. Marla MOHR
18 Director Facilities/Plant Ops .... Ms. Elaine ROSENGARTEN
19 Director Campus Safety/Evening Svcs .... Mr. Jeffery HUFFMAN
21 Director of Finance .... Ms. Renee D. BROWN
88 Director of Global Studies .... Dr. Julianna G. BORDERS
13 Manager Information Technology .... Mr. Wayne YERDON
08 Acquisition Librarian .... Ms. Clare KEATING

Tiffin University (B)

155 Miami Street, Tiffin OH 44883-2161
County: Seneca FICE Identification: 003121
Unit ID: 206048
Telephone: (419) 447-6442 Carnegie Class: Master's L
FAX Number: (419) 443-5022 Calendar System: Semester
URL: www.tiffin.edu
Established: 1888 Annual Undergrad Tuition & Fees: $22,140
Enrollment: 4,282 Coed
Affiliation or Control: Independent Non-Profit IRS Status: 501(c)3
Highest Offering: Master's
Program: Liberal Arts And General; Professional
Accreditation: **NH**, ACBSP

01 President .... Dr. Curtis B. CHARLES
05 Vice President for Academic Affairs .... Dr. Lillian SCHUMACHER
30 Vice Pres Development/Pub Affairs .... Mr. Ron SCHUMACHER
10 Vice Pres Finance/Administration .... Mr. Leon WYDEN
15 VP Human Resources/Campus Services .... Ms. Lori HALL
84 Vice Pres Enrollment Management .... Mr. Jeremy MARINIS
58 Asst Vice Pres Academic Affairs .... Dr. Virginia ARP
88 Exec Dir Academic Support Programs .... Ms. Annette STAUNTON
04 Exec Assistant to the President .... Ms. Nancy GILBERT
32 Dean of Students .... Mr. Mike HERDLICK
13 Chief Information Officer .... Mr. Scott FERGUSON
07 Director Undergrad Admissions .... Ms. Sarah JOHNSON
26 Exec Dir Media Rels/Publications .... Ms. Lisa WILLIAMS
38 Dir of Undergrad Academic Advising .... Ms. Judith GARDNER
06 Registrar .... Ms. Missy WEININGER
41 Director Athletics .... Mr. Lonny ALLEN
21 Controller .... Mr. Robert WATSON
08 Head Librarian .... Ms. Frances FLEET
20 Asst Vice Pres for Academic Affairs .... Dr. Teresa SHAFER
29 Director Alumni Relations .... Ms. Vickie GALASKA
36 Director of Career Development .... Ms. Celinda SCHERGER
18 Director of Facilities .... Mr. Harold KINN
22 Equal Opportunity Officer .... Ms. Lori HALL
39 Director of Residence Life .... Ms. Mandi HUMMEL
44 Director of Annual Fund .... Mr. Joe BORICH
28 Asst VP for Diversity & Equity .... Dr. Sharon PERRY-NAUSE
37 Director Student Financial Aid .... Ms. Andrea FABER
49 Dean of Arts & Sciences .... Dr. Joyce HALL-YATES
50 Interim Dean of Business .... Dr. Terry SULLIVAN
88 Dean Criminal Justice/Social Sci .... Dr. Gordon CREWS

Tri-State Bible College (C)

506 Margaret Street, PO Box 445,
South Point OH 45680-8402
County: Lawrence FICE Identification: 034754
Unit ID: 206154
Telephone: (740) 377-2520 Carnegie Class: Spec/Faith
FAX Number: (740) 377-0001 Calendar System: Semester
URL: www.tsbc.edu
Established: 1970 Annual Undergrad Tuition & Fees: $7,800
Enrollment: 67 Coed
Affiliation or Control: Independent Non-Profit IRS Status: 501(c)3
Highest Offering: Baccalaureate
Program: 2-Year Principally Bachelor's Creditable; Professional; Religious Emphasis
Accreditation: **BI**

00 Chancellor .... Dr. Clifford L. MARQUARDT
01 President .... Dr. Jack R. FINCH
05 Vice President Academic Affairs .... Mr. John DUNCAN
10 Vice President Finance .... Mr. Brian TRIPPETT
11 Vice President Administrative Affs .... Ms. Roberta (Bobby) MERCER
32 Vice Pres Student Affairs .... Mr. Leroy FULFORD

Trinity Lutheran Seminary (D)

2199 E Main Street, Columbus OH 43209-2334
County: Franklin FICE Identification: 003044
Unit ID: 206215
Telephone: (614) 235-4136 Carnegie Class: Spec/Faith
FAX Number: (614) 238-0263 Calendar System: Semester
URL: www.TLSohio.edu
Established: 1830 Annual Graduate Tuition & Fees: $15,900
Enrollment: 111 Coed
Affiliation or Control: Evangelical Lutheran Church In America
IRS Status: 501(c)3
Highest Offering: Doctorate; No Undergraduates
Program: Professional; Religious Emphasis
Accreditation: **NH**, THEOL

01 President .... Rev. Robert C. BARGER
30 Vice President for Advancement .... Mr. Bradley A. GEE
11 Vice President for Operations .... Mr. Ronald W. BENEDICK
05 Academic Dean .... Dr. Brad A. BINAU
20 Associate Academic Dean .... Dr. Diane J. HYMANS
88 Dean of Leadership Formation .... Rev. Emlyn A. OTT
07 Director of Admissions .... Mr. Seth BRIDGER
06 Registrar .... Mr. Lee RICHARDS
08 Director Hamma Library .... Mr. Ray A. OLSON
26 Director Communications/Marketing .... Ms. Margaret L. FARNHAM
37 Director Financial Aid .... Mrs. Melissa CURTIS POWELL
88 Director Contextual Education .... Sr. Becky SWANSON
88 Director MA in Church Music Program .... Ms. May L. SCHWARZ
58 Director Graduate Studies .... Dr. Walter F. TAYLOR, JR.
88 Director MACE/MAYFM Programs .... Dr. Diane J. HYMANS
10 Controller .... Mrs. Patricia A. FORK
18 Director Facilities Management .... Ms. Laura K. STARKEY

Trumbull Business College (E)

3200 Ridge Road, Warren OH 44484-3272
County: Trumbull FICE Identification: 020543
Unit ID: 206224
Telephone: (330) 369-3200 Carnegie Class: Assoc/PrivFP
FAX Number: (330) 369-6792 Calendar System: Quarter
URL: www.trumbull.edu
Established: 1972 Annual Undergrad Tuition & Fees: $13,376
Enrollment: 192 Coed
Affiliation or Control: Proprietary IRS Status: Proprietary
Highest Offering: Associate Degree
Program: Occupational
Accreditation: **ACICS**

01 President .... Mr. Dennis J. GRIFFITH
37 Director of Financial Aid .... Ms. Florence HENNING
36 Director of Student Placement .... Ms. Kimberly STRANIAK
12 Director of Branch Campus .... Ms. Kimberly STRANIAK
06 Registrar .... Ms. Teresa SHAMBACH

Union Institute & University (F)

440 E McMillan Street, Cincinnati OH 45206-1947
County: Hamilton FICE Identification: 010923
Unit ID: 206279
Telephone: (513) 861-6400 Carnegie Class: DRU
FAX Number: (513) 861-0779 Calendar System: Semester
URL: www.myunion.edu
Established: 1964 Annual Undergrad Tuition & Fees: $11,760
Enrollment: 1,480 Coed
Affiliation or Control: Independent Non-Profit IRS Status: 501(c)3
Highest Offering: Doctorate
Program: Liberal Arts And General; Professional
Accreditation: **NH**, ISW

01 President .... Dr. Roger H. SUBLETT
05 VP Academic Affairs .... Dr. Nelson SOTO
04 Executive Assistant to President .... Ms. Carolyn KRAUSE
10 Chief Fiscal Officer .... Mr. Tom CUNNINGHAM
15 Vice President Human Resources .... Ms. Deborah EAMOE
84 VP Enrollment Management .... Vacant
30 Vice President Advancement .... Ms. Carolyn KRAUSE
46 Assoc VP Inst Effectiveness .... Dr. Elizabeth PRUDEN
88 Assoc VP Special Projects .... Dr. James ROCHELEAU
58 Assoc VP Grad Programs .... Dr. Arlene SACKS
58 Dean PsyD Program .... Dr. William LAX
06 Registrar .... Ms. Lew Rita MOORE
09 Director Institutional Research .... Ms. Linda C. VAN VOLKENBURGH
13 Director Information Technology .... Dr. Bob COTTER
18 Director Facilities Management .... Mr. Ken LAMB
12 Regional Dean Florida Center .... Dr. David GEORGE
12 Regional Dean LA Center .... Dr. Elizabeth PASTORRES-PALFFY
12 National Dean Undergrad Programs .... Dr. Peter CACCAVERI
12 Regional Dean Sacramento Center .... Dr. Neal MEIER
08 Library Director .... Mr. Matthew PAPPATHAN
37 Director Financial Aid .... Mr. Edward WALTON
29 Director Alumni Relations .... Dr. Neal MEIER
32 Director Student Success .... Dr. Jay KEEHN
106 Dir Center for Teaching & Learning .... Dr. Bob COTTER

United Theological Seminary (G)

4501 Denlinger Road, Dayton OH 45426-2308
County: Montgomery FICE Identification: 003122
Unit ID: 206288
Telephone: (937) 529-2201 Carnegie Class: Spec/Faith
FAX Number: (866) 433-8235 Calendar System: Semester
URL: www.united.edu
Established: 1871 Annual Graduate Tuition & Fees: $15,685
Enrollment: 561 Coed
Affiliation or Control: United Methodist IRS Status: 501(c)3
Highest Offering: Doctorate; No Undergraduates
Program: Professional; Religious Emphasis
Accreditation: **NH**, THEOL

01 President & CEO .... Dr. Wendy J. DEICHMANN
05 Vice Pres Academic Affairs & Dean .... Dr. David WATSON
10 Vice Pres Finance/Treasurer .... Mr. Ronald KUKER
88 VP Afric Amer/Multicult Church Rels .... Dr. Harold HUDSON
101 Sr Asst to the President/Corp Secy .... Ms. JoAnn WAGNER
20 Assoc Dean Academic Affairs .... Dr. Vivian JOHNSON
06 Registrar .... Ms. Karolyn ELLINGSON
13 Director of Information Technology .... Mr. Rick MOHR
106 Dir Distance Learning/Educ Tech .... Ms. Phyllis ENNIST
08 Librarian .... Ms. Sarah D. BROOKS BLAIR
42 Director of Contextual Ministries .... Rev. Gary EUBANK
26 Director of Communications .... Ms. JoAnn WAGNER
37 Director Financial Aid .... Ms. Marcia BYRD
29 Coordinator of Alumni/ae Relations .... Rev. Tesia MALLORY
18 Facility Manager .... Mr. Roger BOWYER
108 Chf Strategy/Admin/Assessment Ofcr .... Ms. Karen E. PAYNE
84 Senior Dir Enrollment Mgmt .... Ms. Monique TREMAINE
36 Director of Student Success .... Rev. R. Dean BLIMLINE
30 Sr Dir of Development Operations .... Ms. Calle PICARDO

The University of Akron, Main Campus (H)

302 Buchtel Common, Akron OH 44325
County: Summit FICE Identification: 003123
Unit ID: 200800
Telephone: (330) 972-7111 Carnegie Class: RU/H
FAX Number: (330) 972-6990 Calendar System: Semester
URL: www.uakron.edu
Established: 1870 Annual Undergrad Tuition & Fees (In-State): $11,215
Enrollment: 26,000 Coed
Affiliation or Control: State IRS Status: 501(c)3
Highest Offering: Doctorate
Program: 2-Year Principally Bachelor's Creditable; Liberal Arts And General; Teacher Preparatory; Professional
Accreditation: **NH**, ACBSP, ANEST, ART, AUD, BUS, BUSA, CAATE, CACREP, CIDA, COARC, COPSY, DANCE, DIETC, DIETD, ENG, ENGR, ENGT, IFSAC, IPSY, LAW, MAC, MFCD, MUS, NURSE, PH, SP, SURGT, SW, TED

01 President .... Dr. Scott L. SCARBOROUGH
05 Senior Vice President & Provost .... Dr. Mike SHERMAN
58 Vice Pres Research/Dean of Grad Sch .... Vacant
10 VP Finance & Administration/CFO .... Mr. Nathan J. MORTIMER
43 Vice President & General Counsel .... Mr. Ted A. MALLO
30 Vice Pres of Advancement .... Mr. Lawrence J. BURNS
13 Chief Information Officer .... Mr. Godfrey OVWIGHO
18 Vice Pres Capital Plng/Facil Mgmt .... Mr. Ted CURTIS
88 Assistant Secretary of the BOT .... Mr. Ted A. MALLO
100 Vice President/Chief of Staff .... Vacant
101 Secretary Board of Trustees .... Mr. Paul A. HEROLD
32 Interim Assoc Dean of Students .... Mr. Mike STRONG
44 Assoc Vice Pres Development .... Mr. Timothy R. DUFORE
88 Special Assistant to the President .... Mr. Paul A. HEROLD
88 Director of Presidential Communicat .... Mr. David NYPAVER
21 Assc VP Treasury/Financial Planning .... Mr. Brian E. DAVIS
46 Assoc Vice President for Research .... Mr. Kenneth G. PRESTON
46 Assoc Vice President for Research .... Mr. Wayne H. WATKINS
88 Assoc VP Strategic Init & Engage .... Mrs. Holly HARRIS BANE
22 Assoc VP Inclusion & Equity .... Mr. Lee A. GILL
27 Assoc Vice Pres/Chief Comm Officer .... Vacant
15 Assoc VP Talent Dev/Human Resources .... Mr. Bill J. VIAU
26 Assoc VP/Chief Marketing Officer .... Mr. Wayne R. HILL
35 Assoc VP for Student Services .... Vacant
88 Assoc VP for Student Success .... Dr. Stacey MOORE
19 Ast VP Camp Safety/Chf Univ Police .... Major Jim P. WEBER
43 Asst VP & Assoc General Counsel .... Mr. Sidney C. FOSTER, JR.
29 Asst VP Alumni/College Cen Programs .... Mrs. Kimberly K. COLE
06 Registrar .... Mr. Ronald L. BOWMAN, JR.
07 Director of Admissions .... Ms. Diane R. RAYBUCK
09 Director Institutional Research .... Ms. Sabrina L. ANDREWS
14 Director Technology Transfer .... Mr. Kenneth G. PRESTON
08 Interim Dean University Libraries .... Mrs. Phyllis G. O'CONNOR
49 Dean Buchtel College of Arts & Sci .... Dr. Chand MIDHA
54 Interim Dean College of Engineering .... Mr. Mario R. GARZIA
53 Interim Dean College of Education .... Dr. Susan G. CLARK

50	Dean College of Business Admin	Dr. Ravi KROVI
76	Dean College Health Professions	Dr. David GORDON
72	Dean Col of Appl Sci & Tech	Dr. Todd A. RICKEL
61	Dean School of Law	Mr. Matthew J. WILSON
54	Dean of Polymer Science/Engineering	Dr. Eric J. AMIS
12	Interim Dean Wayne College	Dr. Daniel B. DECKLER
37	Director Student Financial Aid	Mrs. Jennifer E. HARPHAM
96	Director of Purchasing	Mr. Andrew W. ROTH
88	Senior Director Integrated Comm	Mr. Robert KROPFF
105	Director of Web Services	Mr. Eric W. KRIEDER
92	Dean Honors College	Dr. Lakeesha K. RANSOM
88	Director UA Adult Focus	Mrs. Laura H. CONLEY
41	Director Athletics	Mr. Lawrence R. WILLIAMS
36	Ex Dir Counseling/Test/Career Ctr	Dr. Juanita K. MARTIN
39	Asst VP & Chief Housing Officer	Mr. John A. MESSINA
25	Asst VP Office Research Admin	Ms. Katie WATKINS-WENDELL
85	Int Director International Programs	Mrs. Holly B. HARRISBANE
23	Director Health Services	Ms. Alma E. OLSON
88	Dir Alumni Rels & Stdnt Engagement	Dr. Matthew P. AKERS
88	Asst VP Computer Operations	Mrs. Deborah WHITE
88	Director of Media Relations	Mr. Dan MINNICH
28	Assoc VP/Chief Diversity Officer	Dr. Lee A. GILL
102	Asst VP Corp Fund Relations	Mrs. Ellen PERDUYN
84	Assoc VP Enrollment Management	Ms. Lauri S. THORPE

The University of Akron-Wayne College (A)

1901 Smucker Road, Orrville OH 44667-9758

County: Wayne | FICE Identification: 010818 | Unit ID: 200846

Telephone: (330) 683-2010 | Carnegie Class: Assoc/Pub2in4

FAX Number: (330) 684-8989 | Calendar System: Semester

URL: www.wayne.uakron.edu

Established: 1972 | Annual Undergrad Tuition & Fees (In-State): $6,200

Enrollment: 2,161 | Coed

Affiliation or Control: State | IRS Status: 501(c)3

Highest Offering: Associate Degree

Program: Occupational; 2-Year Principally Bachelor's Creditable

Accreditation: NH

01	Interim Dean	Dr. Dan DECKLER
04	Senior Administrative Assistant	Ms. Ann MARTIN
05	Associate Dean of Instruction	Vacant
10	Sr Dir Business Operations/Finance	Mrs. Tamara A. LOWE
32	Sr Dir Student Life/Enroll Mgmt	Mr. Gordon K. HOLLY
18	Chief Facilities/Physical Plant	Mr. Shon ENOS
26	Chief Public Relations Officer	Mrs. Debby MUNIAK
08	Director Library Services	Mrs. Maureen T. LERCH
06	Registrar/Manager Student Services	Mrs. Barb CAILLET
07	Director of Admissions	Mrs. Alicia BROADUS
09	Director of Institutional Research	Mr. William CLARK
15	Director Personnel Services	Ms. Kathy BATCHELDER
20	Associate Academic Officer	Mr. Garth D. SCHOFFMAN
30	Director of Development	Mr. Kevin E. ENGLE
35	Student Activities Coordinator	Ms. Jackie E. ASHBAUGH
36	Coord Career and Assessment Svcs	Ms. Carol J. PLEUSS
37	Manager Student Svcs/Financial Aid	Mrs. Barb CAILLET
38	Coordinator of Academic Advising	Ms. Wendy CUNDIFF
96	Assistant Director Business/Finance	Ms. Amy M. HAYNES
13	Manager Technical Support Services	Ms. Cher DEEDS
19	University Police	Lt. Chad CUNNINGHAM
40	Director Bookstore	Ms. Pat PAXTON
41	Athletic Director	Mr. Dave RUBENS

University of Cincinnati Main Campus (B)

2624 Clifton Avenue, Cincinnati OH 45221-0001

County: Hamilton | FICE Identification: 003125 | Unit ID: 201885

Telephone: (513) 556-6000 | Carnegie Class: RU/VH

FAX Number: (513) 556-3237 | Calendar System: Quarter

URL: www.uc.edu

Established: 1819 | Annual Undergrad Tuition & Fees (In-State): $10,784

Enrollment: 43,691 | Coed

Affiliation or Control: State | IRS Status: 501(c)3

Highest Offering: Doctorate

Program: 2-Year Principally Bachelor's Creditable; Liberal Arts And General; Teacher Preparatory; Professional

Accreditation: NH, ANEST, ART, AUD, BUS, CAATE, CACREP, CAEP, CAHIIM, CIDA, CLPSY, CONST, CS, DANCE, DENT, DIETC, DIETD, ENG, ENGR, ENGT, LAW, MED, MIDWF, MT, MUS, NMT, NURSE, PH, PHAR, PLNG, PTA, PTAA, SP, SURGA, SW, TED, THEA

01	President	Dr. Santa J. ONO
05	Sr VP/Provost Academic Affairs	Dr. Beverly DAVENPORT
11	Sr VP for Administration & Finance	Mr. Robert AMBACH
03	Executive VP	Dr. Ryan HAYS
46	Vice President for Research	Dr. William S. BALL
63	Dean Medicine/Sr VP Health Affairs	Dr. Williams S. BALL
30	VP Development/Alumni Rels	Mr. Rod M. GRABOWSKI
86	Vice Pres Govt Rels/University Comm	Mr. Gregory J. VEHR
32	Vice Pres Student Affairs & Svcs	Ms. Debra S. MERCHANT
10	Vice President for Finance	Mr. Patrick A. KOWALSKI
13	VP & CIO for Information Technology	Dr. Nelson C. VINCENT
20	Sr Vice Provost Academic Affairs	Dr. Eileen L. STREMPEL
43	General Counsel	Ms. Kenya D. MANN FAULKNER
15	Chief Human Resources Officer	Ms. Tamie L. GRUNOW
84	Sr Assoc Vice President Enrollment	Dr. Caroline B. MILLER
21	Assoc VP Community Development	Mr. Gerald A. SIEGERT
26	Director Media Relations	Ms. MB REILLY
07	Assoc Vice Pres for Admissions	Dr. Thomas CANEPA
44	Assoc Vice Pres for Principal Gifts	Mr. E.R. (Jay) BROWNING
76	Dean Allied Health Sciences	Dr. Tina WHALEN
49	Dean Arts & Sciences	Dr. Kenneth PETREN
50	Dean Business Administration	Dr. David M. SZYMANSKI
64	Dean College Conservatory of Music	Mr. Peter LANDGREN
48	Dean Design/Architecture/Art & Plng	Dr. Robert PROBST
53	Dean Education/Crim Justice & HS	Dr. Lawrence J. JOHNSON
54	Dean Engineering & Applied Sci	Dr. Teik C. LIM
61	Dean Law	Dr. Jennifer S. BARD
66	Dean Nursing	Dr. Greer L. GLAZER
67	Dean Pharmacy	Dr. Neil J. MACKINNON
70	Director School Social Work	Mr. James CLARK
08	Dean Library	Mr. Xuemao WANG
29	VP Alumni Affairs	Ms. Jennifer HEISEY
28	Chief Diversity Officer	Dr. Bleuzette MARSHALL
41	Director Athletics	Mr. Michael BOHN
40	Director Bookstore	Ms. Linda K. GINDELE
36	Director Career Development	Ms. Kathleen GRANT
38	Director Counseling Center	Dr. Tow Y. YAU
22	Director Equal Opportunity	Vacant
39	Asst VP Housing/Food Service	Mr. Todd DUNCAN
37	Director Student Financial Aid	Mr. Randy ULSES
09	Director Institutional Research	Mrs. Suzana H. LUZURIAGA
19	Director Public Safety	Mr. Jason J. GOODRICH
06	Registrar	Dr. Douglas BURGESS
96	Assoc VP Purchasing	Mr. Thomas B. GUERIN
45	Co-Dir Institute for Policy Rsrch	Dr. Eric RADEMACHER
45	Co-Dir Institute for Policy Rsrch	Dr. Kimberly DOWNING
104	Vice Provost International Programs	Dr. Raj MEHTA
18	Chief Facilities/Physical Plant	Mr. Rick WIGGINS
101	Secretary of the Institution/Board	Ms. Nicole BLOUNT
102	Dir Foundation/Corporate Relations	Mr. Tom I. SEDDON
105	Asst VP Digital Comm	Ms. Nicola ZIADY
25	Assoc VP Sponsored Research	Ms. Deborah J. GALLOWAY
90	Director Academic Computing	Mr. Christopher J. EDWARDS
04	Administrative Asst to President	Mr. Lawrence P. LAMPE
100	Chief of Staff	Dr. Ryan HAYS

University of Cincinnati-Blue Ash College (C)

9555 Plainfield Road, Blue Ash OH 45236-1096

County: Hamilton | FICE Identification: 004868 | Unit ID: 201955

Telephone: (513) 745-5600 | Carnegie Class: Assoc/Pub2in4

FAX Number: (513) 745-5780 | Calendar System: Semester

URL: www.ucblueash.edu

Established: 1967 | Annual Undergrad Tuition & Fees (In-State): $6,010

Enrollment: 5,024 | Coed

Affiliation or Control: State | IRS Status: 501(c)3

Highest Offering: Baccalaureate

Program: Occupational; 2-Year Principally Bachelor's Creditable

Accreditation: NH, ADNUR, ART, DH, EMT, MAC

01	Dean	Dr. Cady SHORT-THOMPSON
05	Assoc Dean Academic Affairs	Dr. Marlene R. MINER
10	Director of Business Affairs	Mr. Marc WATSON
20	Asst Dean Academic Affairs	Mr. Gregory METZ
18	Int Director Facilities/Events	Mr. Tom CRUSE
13	Director Information Technology	Mr. Dale HOFSTETTER
84	Director Enrollment Services	Mr. Christopher POWERS
09	Director Institutional Research	Ms. Sandra PARKER
30	Director of Development	Ms. Meredith DELANEY
08	Library Director	Ms. Heather MALONEY
26	Director of Communication	Mr. Peter GEMMER
32	Director of Student Life	Mr. Marcus LANGFORD

University of Cincinnati-Clermont College (D)

4200 Clermont College Drive, Batavia OH 45103-1785

County: Clermont | FICE Identification: 010805 | Unit ID: 201946

Telephone: (513) 732-5200 | Carnegie Class: Assoc/Pub2in4

FAX Number: (513) 732-5275 | Calendar System: Quarter

URL: www.ucclermont.edu

Established: 1972 | Annual Undergrad Tuition & Fees (In-State): $5,316

Enrollment: 3,246 | Coed

Affiliation or Control: State | IRS Status: 501(c)3

Highest Offering: Baccalaureate

Program: Occupational; 2-Year Principally Bachelor's Creditable; Technical Emphasis

Accreditation: NH, CAHIIM, COARC, MAC, SURGT

01	Dean	Dr. Jeffrey C. BAUER
05	Int Assoc Dean Academic Affairs	Ms. Kim JACOBS-BECK
20	Sr Assistant Dean Academic Affairs	Ms. Mary F. STEARNS
08	Director Library	Ms. Katie FORHAN-MULCAHY
24	Dir Learning Center	Ms. Amy ABAFO
09	Director of Institutional Research	Ms. Susan RILEY
10	Director Business Affairs	Ms. Maria KERI
32	Sr Dir Retention & Student Success	Ms. Jennifer RADT
07	Sr Director Recruitment	Mr. John STILES
06	Asst Dir Registration & Scheduling	Ms. Kristine LOUGHRAN
88	Director Disability Services	Vacant
35	Director of Student Life	Ms. Kimberly ELLISON
41	Program Coord/Athletic Director	Mr. Brian SULLIVAN
18	Asst Dean Facilities & Tech Svcs	Mr. Stephen W. YOUNG
30	Director of Development	Ms. Dana PARKER
26	Asst Dean Communications & Mktg	Ms. Mae HANNA

University of Dayton (E)

300 College Park, Dayton OH 45469-0001

County: Montgomery | FICE Identification: 003127 | Unit ID: 202480

Telephone: (937) 229-1000 | Carnegie Class: RU/H

FAX Number: (937) 229-4000 | Calendar System: Semester

URL: www.udayton.edu

Established: 1850 | Annual Undergrad Tuition & Fees: $39,090

Enrollment: 11,368 | Coed

Affiliation or Control: Roman Catholic | IRS Status: 501(c)3

Highest Offering: Doctorate

Program: Liberal Arts And General; Teacher Preparatory; Professional

Accreditation: NH, #ARCPA, ART, BUS, BUSA, CACREP, DIETD, ENG, ENGT, LAW, MUS, PTA, SPAA, TED

01	President	Dr. Daniel J. CURRAN
05	Interim Provost	Dr. Paul H. BENSON
32	VP Student Development	Mr. William M. FISCHER
10	VP Finance & Admin Services	Mr. Andrew E. HORNER
30	VP Univ Advancement	Mr. David L. HARPER
41	VP/Director of Athletics	Mr. Timothy J. WABLER
15	Interim VP Human Resources	Mr. Troy W. WASHINGTON
84	Interim VP for Enrollment Mgmt	Dr. Jason K. REINOEHL
46	Int VP of Research/Exec Dir UDRI	Dr. John E. LELAND
44	Sr Development Officer	Mr. James F. BROTHERS
42	Director Campus Ministry	Ms. Crystal C. SULLIVAN
88	VP for Mission and Rector	Rev. James F. FITZ, SM
31	Interim Dir Ctr for Ldrshp in Cmty	Mr. Donald A. VERMILLION
20	Assoc Provost Faculty & Admin Affs	Dr. Carolyn ROECKER-PHELPS
88	Asc Prov Lrng Spprt/Dir Rch Tch Ctr	Dr. Deborah J. BICKFORD
90	Assoc Prov/Chief Information Ofcr	Dr. Thomas D. SKILL
06	Registrar	Mr. Thomas J. WESTENDORF
07	Asst VP/Dean of Admission	Mr. Robert F. DURKLE
19	Director Public Safety	Mr. Bruce E. BURT
09	Director Institutional Studies	Ms. Susan K. SEXTON
21	Comptroller	Ms. Angela K. BUECHELE
88	Assoc VP/Dean of Students	Ms. Christine M. SCHRAMM
36	Director Career Services	Mr. Jason C. ECKERT
38	Asst VP Student Dev/Dir Counseling	Dr. Steven D. MUELLER
18	VP for Facilities/Campus Opers	Ms. Beth H. KEYES
23	Medical Director Univ Health Ctr	Dr. Mary P. BUCHWALDER
62	Dean University Libraries	Ms. Kathleen M. WEBB
49	Dean College A&S	Dr. Jason L. PIERCE
61	Dean School of Law	Mr. Andrew L. STRAUSS
50	Dean Sch of Business Admin	Dr. Paul M. BOBROWSKI
58	Assoc Prov Graduate Acad Affairs	Dr. Paul M. VANDERBURGH
53	Dean School of Educ & Allied Prof	Dr. Kevin R. KELLY
54	Dean School of Engineering	Dr. Eddy M. ROJAS
29	Sr Development Officer	Mr. Todd W. IMWALLE
35	Dir Student Life & Kennedy Union	Ms. Amy L. LOPEZ-MATTHEWS
37	Dean of Admission/Dir of Fin Aid	Ms. Kathy M. HARMON
39	Asst Dean Students & Dir Res Life	Mr. Steven T. HERNDON
40	Manager UD Bookstore	Ms. Julie M. BANKS
43	Univ Counsel/Dir Legal Affairs	Ms. Mary A. RECKER
96	Dir Univ Purchases/Business Service	Mr. Ken R. SOUCY
92	Dir University Honors/Scholars Pgm	Dr. David W. DARROW
94	Women's and Gender Studies Program	Dr. Rebecca S. WHISNANT
22	Dir Affirmative Action & Compliance	Ms. Patricia BERNAL-OLSON
86	Government/Regional Relations Dir	Mr. S. Ted BUCARO
28	Exe Dir Inst Diversity & Inclusion	Vacant
27	Dir Marketing & Creative Services	Ms. Kim B. LALLY

The University of Findlay (F)

1000 North Main Street, Findlay OH 45840-3653

County: Hancock | FICE Identification: 003045 | Unit ID: 202763

Telephone: (419) 422-8313 | Carnegie Class: Master's L

FAX Number: (419) 434-4822 | Calendar System: Semester

URL: www.findlay.edu

Established: 1882 | Annual Undergrad Tuition & Fees: $31,508

Enrollment: 5,166 | Coed

Affiliation or Control: Church Of God | IRS Status: 501(c)3

Highest Offering: Doctorate

Program: Occupational; Liberal Arts And General; Teacher Preparatory; Professional

Accreditation: NH, ACBSP, ARCPA, CAATE, CEA, ENGR, NMT, OT, PHAR, PTA, SW, TED

01	President	Dr. Katherine R. FELL
05	Vice President for Academic Affairs	Dr. Darin FIELDS
10	Vice President for Business Affairs	Mr. Martin L. TERRY
84	Vice President Enrollment Mgmt	Ms. Rebecca A. BUTLER
20	Assoc VPAA/Inst Effectiveness	Dr. John OSAE-KWAPONG
30	Vice Pres University Advancement	Dr. Marcia SLOAN LATTA
32	Vice President for Student Affairs	Mr. David W. EMSWELLER
04	Assistant to the President	Ms. Liz DITTO
81	Dean College of Sciences	Dr. Jeffrey FRYE
50	Interim Dean College of Business	Dr. E. Kevin RENSHLER
49	Dean College of Liberal Art	Dr. Ronald TULLEY
76	Dean College of Health Professions	Dr. Andrea KOEPKE
67	Dean College of Pharmacy	Dr. Debra PARKER
53	Dean College of Education	Dr. Julie MCINTOSH
18	Director of Physical Plant	Mr. Myreon K. COBB
09	Director of Institutional Research	Mr. Tony G. GOEDDE
06	Registrar	Mr. Tony G. GOEDDE
41	Athletic Director	Ms. Brandi LAURITA

08 Director of Shafer Library .... Mr. Andrew WHITIS
37 Director of Financial Aid .... Mr. Edward R. RECKER
13 Chief Information Officer .... Dr. Raymond MCCANDLESS
29 Director of Alumni Affairs .... Ms. Deanna SPRAW
26 Dir Public Relations/Media Rels .... Ms. Rebecca JENKINS
36 Director of Career Placement .... Mr. Bradley C. HAMMER
15 Director of Human Resources .... Mr. Robert LINK
23 Director of Health Services .... Ms. Julie R. YINGLING
38 Director Counseling Services .... Ms. Karyn J. WESTRICK
40 Manager of Bookstore .... Mr. Jay CANTERBURY
42 Director Christian Ministries .... Rev. William D. MILLER
19 Interim Director of Security/Safety .... Mr. Steven BAUM
21 Business Manager .... Mr. Robert LINK
28 Asst Dean International Education .... Mr. Christopher SIPPEL
85 Interim Dir Intl Student Adm & Svcs .... Mr. R. Craig HAINES
101 Secretary to the Board of Trustees .... Ms. C. Sue PIRSCHEL
25 Grants Manager .... Ms. Tricia VALASEK
07 Director of Admissions .... Mr. Christopher HARRIS
21 Associate Business Officer .... Mr. Dane ERFORD
22 Director Affirmative Action/Equal .... Mr. Robert LINK
35 Asst Dean of Students .... Mr. Brian TREECE
39 Director Student Housing .... Ms. Rachel WALTER
44 Director Annual Giving .... Mr. Todd LACOMBA

University of Mount Union (A)

1972 Clark Avenue, Alliance OH 44601-3993
County: Stark | FICE Identification: 003083
Unit ID: 204185
Telephone: (330) 821-5320 | Carnegie Class: Bac/Diverse
FAX Number: (330) 823-3457 | Calendar System: Semester
URL: www.mountunion.edu
Established: 1846 | Annual Undergrad Tuition & Fees: $28,550
Enrollment: 2,262 | Coed
Affiliation or Control: United Methodist | IRS Status: 501(c)3
Highest Offering: Master's
Program: Liberal Arts And General; Teacher Preparatory
Accreditation: NH, ARCPA, CAATE, MUS, TED

01 President .... Dr. W. R. MERRIMAN
05 Vice Pres Acad Affs/Dean of Univ .... Dr. Patricia H. DRAVES
10 Vice Pres Business Affs/Treasurer ... Mr. Patrick D. HEDDLESTON
30 Vice President Univ Advancement .... Mr. Gregory KING
32 Vice Pres Student Affs/Dean Stdnts .... Mr. John FRAZIER
84 Vice President for Enrollment Mgmt .... Ms. Amy A. TOMKO
26 Vice President for Marketing .... Ms. Melissa GARDNER
08 Librarian .... Mr. Robert R. GARLAND
06 Registrar .... Ms. Wendy LEWIS
29 Exec Dir Alumni Relations/MU Fund .... Ms. Anne GRAFFICE
07 Director of Admissions .... Ms. Jessie CANAVAN
44 Director Annual Fund .... Ms. Elizabeth JOHNSON
44 Director of Planned Giving .... Ms. Sherrie WALLACE
13 Director Computer Information Sys .... Ms. Tina STUCHELL
88 Director of Advance for Major Gifts .... Mr. Don MONTGOMERY
09 Director Assesment/Program Develop .... Dr. Fang DU
29 Director Alumni/College Activities .... Ms. Tiffany HOGYA
85 Director Center for Global Educ .... Dr. Jennifer HALL
18 Director of Physical Plant .... Mr. Blaine D. LEWIS
15 Director of Human Resources .... Ms. Pamela NEWBOLD
39 Director of Housing .... Ms. Michelle GAFFNEY
42 Chaplain .... Rev. Martha D. CASHBURLESS
36 Director of Career Services .... Ms. Jessica CUNION
37 Director of Student Financial Svcs .... Ms. Emily MATTISON
40 Manager of College Bookstore .... Ms. Aimee SCHULLER
41 Athletic Director .... Mr. Larry T. KEHRES
04 Exec Assistant to the President .... Ms. Audra YOUNGEN
21 Assoc VP for Business Affairs .... Mr. Ronald CROWL
20 Associate Academic Officer .... Dr. Raymond POSEY
35 Associate Dean of Students .... Ms. Michelle GAFFNEY
96 Purchasing Agent .... Mr. Shawn BAGLEY

University of Northwestern Ohio (B)

1441 N Cable Road, Lima OH 45805-1498
County: Allen | FICE Identification: 004861
Unit ID: 204486
Telephone: (419) 227-3141 | Carnegie Class: Assoc/PrivNFP4
FAX Number: (419) 229-6926 | Calendar System: Quarter
URL: www.unoh.edu
Established: 1920 | Annual Undergrad Tuition & Fees: $9,725
Enrollment: 4,111 | Coed
Affiliation or Control: Independent Non-Profit | IRS Status: 501(c)3
Highest Offering: Master's
Program: 2-Year Principally Bachelor's Creditable; Business Emphasis
Accreditation: NH, ACBSP, MAC

01 President .... Dr. Jeffrey A. JARVIS
05 Vice Provost/Dean Col Business .... Dr. Dean HOBLER
10 Vice President Finance .... Mrs. Marcia EICKHOLT
84 Vice Pres Enrollment Management .... Mr. Ricky MORRISON
18 Vice Pres of Property Management .... Mr. Don RICKER
26 VP Public Rels/Mktg/Special Events .... Mrs. Cheryl STEINWEDEL
30 Vice President Development .... Mr. Steve FARMER
32 Vice President Campus Life .... Mr. Bob FRICKE
15 Exec Director of Human Resources .... Ms. Geri MORRIS
21 Controller .... Mr. James S. BRONDER
37 Director of Financial Aid .... Mr. Wendell SCHICK
04 Executive Assistant to President .... Mrs. Jennifer BENDELE
72 Dean College of Technologies .... Mr. Andy O'NEAL

University of Phoenix Cleveland Main Campus (C)

3401 Enterprise Parkway, Suite 115,
Beachwood OH 44122-7343
Telephone: (216) 378-0473 | Identification: 770238
Accreditation: &NH, ACBSP

† No longer accepting campus-based students.

University of Rio Grande (D)

218 N College Avenue, PO BOX 500,
Rio Grande OH 45674-3100
County: Gallia | FICE Identification: 003116
Unit ID: 205203
Telephone: (740) 245-5353 | Carnegie Class: Master's M
FAX Number: (740) 245-5266 | Calendar System: Semester
URL: www.rio.edu
Established: 1876 | Annual Undergrad Tuition & Fees: $23,260
Enrollment: 2,202 | Coed
Affiliation or Control: Independent Non-Profit | IRS Status: 501(c)3
Highest Offering: Master's
Program: 2-Year Principally Bachelor's Creditable; Liberal Arts And General; Teacher Preparatory; Professional
Accreditation: NH, ADNUR, COARC, DMS, IACBE, NUR, RAD, SW, TED

01 President .... Dr. Michelle R. JOHNSTON
05 Provost/VP of Academic Affairs .... Dr. Richard SAX
30 Exec VP & VP for Inst Advancement .... Mr. Paul D. HARRISON
10 Chief Financial Officer .... Mr. Tim PRUETT
11 Vice President for Administration .... Mrs. Rebecca LONG
15 Director of Human Resources .... Mr. Chris NOURSE
88 Chief Compliance Officer .... Mr. Russell HENCHEY
49 Dean Col of Arts & Sciences .... Dr. David LAWRENCE
76 Dean College Prof/Tech Studies .... Dr. Donna MITCHELL
84 Dean of Enrollment Mgmt/Registrar .... Mr. Mark ABELL
07 Actg Director Admissions .... Ms. Kristie RUSSELL
44 Director of Development .... Mrs. Kara WILLIS
32 Dean of Students .... Mr. Aaron QUINN
41 Athletics Director .... Mr. Jeff LANHAM
08 Int Director of the Library .... Ms. Amy R. WILSON
14 Dir Campus Computing & Networking .... Mr. Kingsley MEYER
13 MIS Director .... Dr. Steve COX
29 Director of Alumni Relations .... Mrs. Annette P. WARD
04 Exec Assistant to the President .... Mrs. Lori TAYLOR

University of Toledo (E)

2801 W Bancroft, Toledo OH 43606-3390
County: Lucas | FICE Identification: 003131
Unit ID: 206084
Telephone: (419) 530-4636 | Carnegie Class: RU/H
FAX Number: (419) 530-4984 | Calendar System: Semester
URL: www.utoledo.edu
Established: 1872 | Annual Undergrad Tuition & Fees (In-State): $9,242
Enrollment: 20,626 | Coed
Affiliation or Control: State | IRS Status: 501(c)3
Highest Offering: Doctorate
Program: Liberal Arts And General; Teacher Preparatory; Professional
Accreditation: NH, ARCPA, ART, BUS, BUSA, CAATE, CACREP, CAHIIM, CLPSY, COARC, CS, DENT, ENG, ENGR, ENGT, LAW, MED, MT, MUS, NRPA, NURSE, OT, PH, PHAR, PTA, SP, SPAA, SW, TED

01 President .... Dr. Sharon L. GABER
05 Int EVP Academic Affairs/Provost .... Mr. John A. BARRETT, JR.
17 CEO Univ of Toledo Medical Center .... Mr. David R. MORLOCK
10 Int Exec VP Finance & Admin .... Mr. Thomas BIGGS
43 Vice President/General Counsel .... Mr. Peter J. PAPADIMOS
32 Sr VP for Student Affairs .... Dr. Kaye PATTEN-WALLACE
30 Vice President for Advancement .... Mr. Samuel MCCRIMMON
86 Vice President Government Relations .... Dr. Frank J. CALZONETTI
46 Vice President Research .... Dr. William S. MESSER
11 Vice President Corporate Relations .... Mr. Charles LEHNERT
13 Vice President CIO/CTO .... Mr. William MCCREARY
41 Vice Pres and Director of Athletics .... Mr. Michael E. O'BRIEN
09 Exec Dir Inst Research .... Mr. Ying LIU
06 Interim University Registrar .... Ms. Julie R. QUIÑONEZ
58 Dean College of Graduate Studies .... Dr. Patricia R. KOMUNIECKI
50 Dean Business & Innovation .... Dr. Gary INSCH
88 Dean Communication and the Arts .... Ms. Debra DAVIS
53 Int Dean J Herb College of Ed .... Dr. Virginia KEIL
54 Dean Engineering .... Dr. Nagi NAGANATHAN
76 Dean Health Sciences .... Dr. Christopher INGERSOLL
83 Dean Languages/Lit & Soc Sciences .... Dr. Jamie BARLOWE
61 Dean Law .... Mr. Ben BARROSS
63 Exec VP for Clin Aff Dean COMLS .... Dr. Christopher COOPER
81 Dean Natural Sciences & Mathematics .... Dr. Karen BJORKMAN
66 Int Dean Nursing .... Dr. Kelly PHILLIPS
67 Dean Pharmacy & Pharm Sciences .... Dr. Johnnie EARLY
83 Dean Social Justice/Human Svcs .... Dr. Thomas GUTTERIDGE
88 Dean Adult & Lifelong Learning .... Dr. Dennis LETTMAN
92 Int Dean Jesup Scott Honors College .... Mr. Kelly MOORE
88 Acting Dean YouCollege .... Ms. Julie FISCHER-KINNEY
35 Dean of Students .... Ms. Tamika MITCHELL
39 AVP Residence Life .... Ms. Virginia SPEIGHT
37 AVP Financial Aid/Enrollment Svcs .... Mr. Stephen SCHISSLER
15 Sr Director Faculty Labor Relations .... Mr. Kevin WEST
102 President Foundation .... Ms. Brenda LEE
29 Assoc Vice Pres Alumni Relations .... Mr. Daniel J. SAEVIG
36 Dir Exp Lrng and Career Svcs .... Ms. Shelly DROUILLARD
85 Asst Provost Ctr for Intl Studies .... Mr. Sammy SPANN
21 Director Internal Audit .... Mr. David CUTRI
19 Chief of Police .... Mr. Jeff NEWTON
101 Secretary to Brd of Trustees .... Ms. Joan STASA
40 General Manager Bookstore SU .... Ms. Colleen STRAYER
100 Chief of Staff .... Mr. Matt J. SCHROEDER
18 AVP Facilities/Physical Plant .... Mr. Jason TOTH

Urbana University (F)

579 College Way, Urbana OH 43078-2091
County: Champaign | FICE Identification: 003133
Unit ID: 206330
Telephone: (937) 484-1400 | Carnegie Class: Bac/Diverse
FAX Number: (937) 484-1322 | Calendar System: Semester
URL: www.urbana.edu
Established: 1850 | Annual Undergrad Tuition & Fees: $22,012
Enrollment: 1,922 | Coed
Affiliation or Control: Independent Non-Profit | IRS Status: 501(c)3
Highest Offering: Master's
Program: Liberal Arts And General; Teacher Preparatory
Accreditation: #NH, #IACBE, NURSE

01 President .... Dr. George LUCAS, JR.
05 Vice President for Academic Affairs .... Dr. Shah HASAN
30 Vice Pres Inst Advancement & Alumni .... Mrs. Jan HILLMAN
10 Vice President/CFO .... Vacant
44 Exec Director of Development .... Mr. David ORMSBEE
06 Registrar .... Mr. Frank YANCHAK
37 Director of Financial Aid .... Mr. Samuel SELVAGE
09 Dean of Institutional Research .... Dr. Denise BOLDMAN
08 Director Library Services .... Mrs. Julie MCDANIEL
39 Director of Residence Life .... Mr. Mitch JOSEPH
13 Director Computer Center .... Mrs. Monica KRAMER
32 Dean of Students .... Mr. John GORE
15 Director of Human Resources .... Vacant
07 Director of Admissions .... Mr. Donnell WIGGINS
19 Campus Safety Officer .... Mr. David FLEECE
26 Dir Communications/Govt Relations .... Ms. Cherie MOORE
41 Athletic Director .... Mr. Larry COX
40 Bookstore Manager .... Ms. Karen ENGLE

Ursuline College (G)

2550 Lander Road, Cleveland OH 44124-4398
County: Cuyahoga | FICE Identification: 003134
Unit ID: 206349
Telephone: (440) 449-4200 | Carnegie Class: Master's S
FAX Number: (440) 646-8318 | Calendar System: Semester
URL: www.ursuline.edu
Established: 1871 | Annual Undergrad Tuition & Fees: $28,230
Enrollment: 1,236 | Female
Affiliation or Control: Roman Catholic | IRS Status: 501(c)3
Highest Offering: Doctorate
Program: Liberal Arts And General; Teacher Preparatory; Professional; Technical Emphasis
Accreditation: NH, CAEP, IACBE, NURSE, SW, TED

01 President .... Sr. Christine DEVINNE
05 Interim Vice Pres Academic Affairs .... Dr. Elizabeth KAVRAN
10 Vice Pres & Chief Financial Officer .... Mr. David STEINER
30 Vice Pres Institutional Advancement .... Mr. Kevin GLADSTONE
18 Vice Pres of Facility Management .... Ms. June GRACYK
32 Vice President of Student Affairs .... Ms. Deanne HURLEY
84 Vice Pres of Enrollment Management .... Ms. Deanne HURLEY
58 Dean of Graduate Studies .... Dr. Gina MESSINA-DYSERT
49 Interim Dean of Arts & Sciences .... Ms. Sarah PRESTON
66 Dean Division of Nursing .... Dr. Patricia SHARPNACK
88 Exec Director Accelerated Program .... Ms. JoAnne MAZUR
08 Director of Library .... Ms. Betsey BELKIN
06 Registrar .... Ms. Leah SULLIVAN
21 Accounting Manager .... Mr. Timothy REARDON
44 Director of Development .... Dr. Patrick RILEY
07 Director of Admissions .... Ms. Carolyn NOLL SORG
37 Director of Financial Aid .... Ms. Mary Lynn PERRI
29 Dir Alumae Relations/Dev Specialist .... Ms. Tiffany MUSHRUSH-MENTZER
26 Dir of Marketing/Communications .... Ms. Angela DELPRETE
38 Director Counseling & Career Svcs .... Ms. Geraldine M. JENKINS
15 Director of Personnel .... Ms. Kelli KNAUS
13 Dir of Computer Information Svcs .... Mr. Tim FARRIS
09 Director of Institutional Research .... Vacant
102 Dir of Corp & Foundation Relations .... Vacant
39 Director of Residence Life .... Ms. Gina DEMART-KRAUS
42 Director Campus Ministry .... Ms. Joann PIOTRKOWSKI
28 Asst Dean of Inclusion .... Ms. Tina ROAN
93 Director of Wellness Program .... Vacant
24 Library Electronic & Media Services .... Ms. Suzanna SCHROEDER-GREEN
40 Manager Bookstore .... Ms. Casey DUNN
41 Athletic Director .... Ms. Cynthia MCKNIGHT
43 Dir Legal Services/General Counsel .... Mr. Terry BILLUPS

Valor Christian College (H)

PO Box 800, Columbus OH 43216
County: Franklin | Identification: 667093
Telephone: (614) 837-4088 | Carnegie Class: Not Classified
FAX Number: (614) 837-6904 | Calendar System: Semester
URL: www.valorcollege.com
Established: 1990 | Annual Undergrad Tuition & Fees: $4,107
Enrollment: 225 | Coed
Affiliation or Control: Independent Non-Profit | IRS Status: 501(c)3
Highest Offering: Associate Degree

Program: Religious Emphasis
Accreditation: @BI

01 President ... Jimmy DUPREE
05 Vice Pres Academic Affairs ... Randy TURPIN
32 Dean of Students ... Edward RAMIREZ
84 Director of Enrollment Management ... Sean SAMS
35 Director of Student Life ... Ashton PARSLEY
04 Admin Asst to Pres/Office Mgr ... Debbie BARANICH
37 Director of Financial Aid ... Dana MEJIA

Vatterott College-Cleveland (A)

5025 E Royalton Road,
Broadview Heights OH 44147-3502
Telephone: (440) 526-1660 Identification: 666156
Accreditation: ACCSC, MAAB

† Branch campus of Vatterott College-North Park, Berkeley, MO.

Virginia Marti College of Art & Design (B)

11724 Detroit Avenue, Lakewood OH 44107-3002
County: Cuyahoga FICE Identification: 012896
Unit ID: 206394
Telephone: (216) 221-8584 Carnegie Class: Assoc/PrivFP
FAX Number: (216) 221-2311 Calendar System: Quarter
URL: www.vmcad.edu
Established: 1966 Annual Undergrad Tuition & Fees: $17,459
Enrollment: 175 Coed
Affiliation or Control: Proprietary IRS Status: Proprietary
Highest Offering: Associate Degree
Program: Occupational; 2-Year Principally Bachelor's Creditable; Technical Emphasis
Accreditation: ACCSC

01 Director of Operations ... Mr. Dennis MARTI
11 Assistant Director ... Vacant
05 Director of Education ... Mr. Joseph GUSTIN
37 Financial Aid Administrator ... Ms. Martha SNODGRASS
06 Registrar ... Mrs. Lisa ALESSANDRO
07 Director of Admissions ... Mr. Quinn E. MARTI
36 Director of Career Services ... Ms. Diane NAHRA

Walsh University (C)

2020 East Maple Street, North Canton OH 44720
County: Stark FICE Identification: 003135
Unit ID: 206437
Telephone: (330) 490-7090 Carnegie Class: Master's M
FAX Number: (330) 499-7165 Calendar System: Semester
URL: www.walsh.edu
Established: 1958 Annual Undergrad Tuition & Fees: $27,710
Enrollment: 2,919 Coed
Affiliation or Control: Roman Catholic IRS Status: 501(c)3
Highest Offering: Doctorate
Program: Liberal Arts And General; Teacher Preparatory; Professional
Accreditation: NH, CACREP, NURSE, PTA, TED

01 President ... Mr. Richard JUSSEAUME
03 Provost ... Dr. Laurence BOVE
10 Vice Pres Finance/Business Affairs ... Ms. Shelley BROWN
32 VP Student Affairs/Dean of Students ... Ms. Amy MALASKA
05 Vice Pres Academic Affairs ... Dr. Douglas PALMER
30 Vice Pres of Advancement/Univ Rels ... Mr. Eric BELDEN
84 Vice Pres of Enrollment Management ... Ms. Alejandra SOSA PIERONI
41 Vice Pres for Athletics ... Mr. Dale S. HOWARD
88 VP Acad Proj/Coord Cultural Events ... Ms. Nancy BLACKFORD
26 VP for Marketing/Communications ... Ms. Teresa GRIFFIN
13 VP of Administration/CIO ... Mr. Brian GREENWELL
20 Dean for Academic Services ... Dr. Cynthia STAUDT
09 Dean Inst Effectiveness/Lib Svcs ... Mr. Daniel S. SUVAK
18 Director of Facilities & Grounds ... Mr. John SCHISSLER
91 Database Administrator ... Ms. Hope STANCIU
22 Director of Compliance ... Mr. Jason FAUTAS
36 Director of Career Services ... Mr. Andy WEYAND
42 Chaplain ... Fr. Thomas CEBULA
38 Director Counseling Services ... Ms. Frances MORROW
42 Director of Campus Ministry ... Mr. Miguel CHAVEZ
31 Dir Campus & Community Programs ... Ms. Jacqueline M. MANSER
37 Director Financial Aid ... Mrs. Holly VAN GILDER
15 Director of Human Resources ... Mr. Frank MCKNIGHT
29 Director of Alumni Relations ... Ms. Sarah TRESCOTT
25 Director of Grants ... Ms. Rachel HAMMEL
19 Chief of Campus Police ... Mr. Louis DARROW
08 Director of Library Services ... Ms. Heidi BEKE-HARRIGAN
17 Chair Division of Health Services ... Dr. Pamela RITZLINE
49 Dean School of Arts & Sciences ... Dr. Ute LAHAIE
66 Dean Byers School of Nursing ... Dr. Linda LINC
73 Chair Div of Philosophy/Theology ... Dr. Bradley BEACH
81 Chair Division of Math & Sciences ... Dr. Michael DUNPHY
83 Chair Div of Social/Behavioral Sci ... Dr. Penny BOVE
92 Director Honors Program ... Dr. Koop BERRY

Washington State Community College (D)

710 Colegate Drive, Marietta OH 45750-9225
County: Washington FICE Identification: 010453
Unit ID: 206446
Telephone: (740) 374-8716 Carnegie Class: Assoc/Pub-R-M
FAX Number: (740) 374-9562 Calendar System: Semester
URL: www.wscc.edu
Established: 1971 Annual Undergrad Tuition & Fees (In-State): $4,450
Enrollment: 1,623 Coed
Affiliation or Control: State IRS Status: 501(c)3
Highest Offering: Associate Degree
Program: Occupational; 2-Year Principally Bachelor's Creditable; Technical Emphasis
Accreditation: NH, COARC, MLTAD, PTAA

01 President ... Dr. Bradley J. EBERSOLE
10 VP of Finance and Operations/Treas ... Mr. Jess N. RAINES
84 VP of Enrollment & Student Success ... Ms. Amanda K. HERB
05 Vice President for Academic Affairs ... Dr. Mark NUTTER
27 Chief Information Officer ... Mr. Jason G. DIXON
15 Executive Director Human Resources ... Mr. Jeff FARLEY
102 Exec Dir Foundation & Grants Dev ... Mr. Gary L. WILLIAMS
76 Dean of Health Sciences ... Dr. Dixie VAUGHAN
49 Interim Dean of Arts and Sciences ... Dr. Mark NUTTER
50 Dean of Bus/Engr/Industrial Tech ... Ms. Brenda L. KORNMILLER
36 Director of Advising & Transfer ... Ms. Heather SAILING
06 Registrar ... Ms. Terry SEEBER
07 Interim Director of Admissions ... Ms. Carrie THRASH
26 Dir of Marketing & Communications ... Vacant
37 Director of Financial Aid ... Ms. Shannon VENEZIA
08 Director Library Services ... Ms. Mary Lou MOEGLING
40 Bookstore Operations Director ... Ms. Jennifer L. DAVIS
37 Assistant Director of Financial Aid ... Ms. Reba BARTRUG
88 Director of College Access and ETS ... Ms. Donna MUNTZ

Wilberforce University (E)

PO Box 1001, Wilberforce OH 45384-1001
County: Greene FICE Identification: 003141
Unit ID: 206491
Telephone: (937) 376-2911 Carnegie Class: Bac/Diverse
FAX Number: (937) 376-2627 Calendar System: Semester
URL: www.wilberforce.edu
Established: 1856 Annual Undergrad Tuition & Fees: $19,706
Enrollment: 387 Coed
Affiliation or Control: African Methodist Episcopal IRS Status: 501(c)3
Highest Offering: Master's
Program: Liberal Arts And General; Fine Arts Emphasis
Accreditation: NH, CORE

01 President ... Dr. Algenia FREEMAN
05 Provost ... Dr. Quentin JOHNSON
03 Executive Vice President ... Dr. Carols CLARK
20 Vice Pres Academic Affairs ... Dr. Emeka MORAH
10 VP of Administration and Finance ... Mr. William WOODSON
30 VP of Institutional Advancement ... Mr. Jeff SELLERS
84 VP Enroll Mgt Exc Adm Student Svcs ... Mr. Antonio BOYLE
45 VP Institutional Effec/Rsrch/Plng ... Dr. D.R BUFFINGER
32 VP Student Svcs/Dean of Students ... Rev. John E. FREEMAN
43 General Counsel ... Vacant
58 AVP Academic Affairs/Dean Grad Sch ... Dr. Robin MOORE-COOPER
29 AVP Development/Dir Alumni Affairs ... Ms. Carole BERNARDINO
11 AVP Admin and Finance/Controller ... Mr. Kevin HOWARD
35 AVP Student Services ... Mr. Dana MERCK
19 Campus Police Chief ... Chief James BERRY
37 AVP Admissions and Financial Aid ... Ms. Terry JEFFRIES
26 AVP Public Relations ... Ms. Danene YOUNG
13 Deputy Director of IT ... Mr. Mayhew CUTHBERTSON
15 Senior Director of Human Resources ... Ms. Anita GOMEZ
107 Dean of Professional Studies ... Dr. Freddie JORDAN
49 Dean of Arts & Sciences ... Dr. Eugenia SHITTU
06 Registrar ... Mrs. Gail D. LASH
25 Director Title III/Sponsored Pgms ... Ms. Lisa TURNER
88 Director of CLIMB Program ... Ms. Toni PRESTON
41 Dir Corp Relations/Athletics Dir ... Mr. Leon KERRY
39 Director of Residence Life ... Ms. Kinya MCBETH
08 Chief Librarian ... Ms. Jacqueline BROWN
21 Assistant Bursar ... Ms. Debra OLIVER

Wilmington College (F)

1870 Quaker Way, Wilmington OH 45177-2499
County: Clinton FICE Identification: 003142
Unit ID: 206507
Telephone: (937) 382-6661 Carnegie Class: Bac/Diverse
FAX Number: (937) 383-8574 Calendar System: Semester
URL: www.wilmington.edu
Established: 1870 Annual Undergrad Tuition & Fees: $24,500
Enrollment: 1,093 Coed
Affiliation or Control: Friends IRS Status: 501(c)3
Highest Offering: Master's
Program: Liberal Arts And General; Teacher Preparatory
Accreditation: NH, CAATE, TEAC

01 President ... Dr. James M. REYNOLDS
04 Assistant to the President ... Mrs. Leslie A. NICHOLS
05 Vice President Academic Affairs ... Dr. Erika A. GOODWIN
10 Vice President Business/Finance ... Mr. Bradley J. MITCHELL
30 Vice President College Advancement ... Mr. Matt WAHRHAFTIG
84 Vice President Enrollment Mgmt ... Mr. Dennis KELLY
88 Vice President External Programs ... Ms. Sylvia STEVENS
32 Vice President Student Affairs ... Ms. Sigrid B. SOLOMON
41 Vice President Athletic Admin ... Dr. Terry A. RUPERT
20 Assoc Vice Pres Academic Affairs ... Dr. Mei Mei BURR
35 Assoc Vice Pres Student Affairs ... Mr. Kenneth A. LYDY
26 Director of Public Relations ... Mr. Randall F. SARVIS
06 Registrar/Asst Dean Acad Affairs ... Ms. Karen M. GARMAN
08 Director of Watson Library ... Vacant
15 Director of Human Resources ... Ms. Libby HAYES
36 Director of Career Services ... Ms. Tammy FRASER
18 Director of Physical Plant ... Mr. Terry L. JOHNSON
29 Dir Alumni and Parent Relations ... Ms. Kathy L. MILAM
37 Director Student One Stop Center ... Ms. Cheryl LOUALLEN
07 Director of Admission ... Ms. Tina M. GARLAND
09 Dir of Institutional Effectiveness ... Ms. Katie BONTRAGER
28 Director of Multicultural Affairs ... Ms. Bennyce HAMILTON
96 Purchasing Manager ... Ms. Laura BAESSLER

Wilmington College Blue Ash Branch (G)

9987 Carver Road, Blue Ash OH 45242
Telephone: (513) 793-1337 Identification: 770364
Accreditation: &NH

† Branch campus of Wilmington College, Wilmington, OH.

Winebrenner Theological Seminary (H)

950 N Main Street, Findlay OH 45840-3652
County: Hancock FICE Identification: 004060
Unit ID: 206516
Telephone: (419) 434-4200 Carnegie Class: Spec/Faith
FAX Number: (419) 434-4267 Calendar System: Trimester
URL: www.winebrenner.edu
Established: 1942 Annual Graduate Tuition & Fees: $15,426
Enrollment: 64 Coed
Affiliation or Control: Independent Non-Profit IRS Status: 501(c)3
Highest Offering: Doctorate; No Undergraduates
Program: Professional; Religious Emphasis
Accreditation: #NH, THEOL

01 President/CEO ... Dr. David E. DRAPER
30 VP of Institutional Advancement ... Mr. Jim ALLEN
05 VP of Academic Advancement ... Rev. Joel COCKLIN
07 Regional Coordinator Admiss/Devel ... Mr. Jim WILDER
08 Director of Library Services ... Mrs. Margaret HIRSCHY
06 Registrar ... Mrs. Shari BRANDEBERRY
04 Assistant to the President ... Ms. Marilynn C. DUNN

Wittenberg University (I)

PO Box 720, Springfield OH 45501-0720
County: Clark FICE Identification: 003143
Unit ID: 206525
Telephone: (937) 327-6231 Carnegie Class: Bac/A&S
FAX Number: (937) 327-6340 Calendar System: Semester
URL: www.wittenberg.edu
Established: 1845 Annual Undergrad Tuition & Fees: $38,030
Enrollment: 1,929 Coed
Affiliation or Control: Evangelical Lutheran Church In America
IRS Status: 501(c)3
Highest Offering: Master's
Program: Liberal Arts And General; Teacher Preparatory
Accreditation: NH, MUS, TED

01 President ... Dr. Laurie M. JOYNER
05 Interim Provost ... Dr. Mary Jo ZEMBAR
10 Int Chief Financial Officer ... Mr. Randal FREEBOURN
32 Vice Pres Stdnt Devel/Dean Students ... Ms. Casey GILL
46 Vice Pres Strategic Initiatives ... Dr. Ty BUCKMAN
20 Assistant Provost Academic Svcs ... Ms. Mary Jo ZEMBAR
31 Dean School Community Education ... Dr. Thomas T. TAYLOR
35 Dean of Students ... Ms. Casey GILL
88 Assoc Dean of Students ... Mr. Jonathan DURAJ
85 Director International Education ... Ms. JoAnn BENNETT
42 Pastor to the University ... Rev. Rachel SANDUM TUNE
08 Director of the Library ... Mr. Douglas K. LEHMAN
13 Chief Information Officer ... Mr. Richard MICKOOL
26 Chief Marketing & Communications Of ... Vacant
31 Director Community Service ... Ms. Kristen L. COLLIER
06 Registrar ... Mr. Jack M. CAMPBELL
41 Director Athletics/Recreation ... Mr. Gary WILLIAMS
58 Director Graduate Studies in Educ ... Dr. Roberta LINDNER
94 Director of Women's Studies ... Dr. Heather H. WRIGHT
09 Asst Provost Inst Research ... Dr. Darby L. HILLER-FREUND
29 Director of Alumni Relations ... Ms. Linda M. BEALS
27 Dir of News Services/Sports Info ... Mr. Ryan S. MAURER
105 Webmaster ... Vacant
39 Associate Dean for Residence Life ... Mr. Mark B. DEVILBISS
38 Director Student Counseling ... Ms. Linda M. LAUFFENBURGER
88 Director of Greek Life ... Ms. Carol NICKOSON
28 Director Multicultural Stdnt Pgms ... Mr. John YOUNG
07 Exec Director of Admission ... Ms. Karen HUNT
37 Director of Financial Aid ... Mr. Jonathan RANDY GREEN
21 Director Budget ... Ms. Deborah S. DEWITT
18 Asst VP Plant/Safety & Environment ... Mr. Michael BRADY
15 Director Human Resources ... Mr. Kevin EVANS
19 Chief of Police ... Mr. Jim HUTCHINS
40 Manager of Bookstore ... Ms. Amy DALTON

Wright State University Lake Campus (J)

7600 Lake Campus Drive, Celina OH 45822-2952
Telephone: (419) 586-0300 FICE Identification: 009169
Accreditation: &NH

† Regional accreditation is carried under the parent institution in Dayton, OH.

Wright State University Main Campus (A)

3640 Colonel Glenn Highway, Dayton OH 45435-0001
County: Greene FICE Identification: 003078
Unit ID: 206604
Telephone: (937) 775-3333 Carnegie Class: RU/H
FAX Number: (937) 775-3301 Calendar System: Semester
URL: www.wright.edu
Established: 1964 Annual Undergrad Tuition & Fees (In-State): $8,730
Enrollment: 17,779 Coed
Affiliation or Control: State IRS Status: 501(c)3
Highest Offering: Doctorate
Program: Liberal Arts And General; Teacher Preparatory; Professional
Accreditation: NH, BUS, BUSA, CAATE, CACREP, CEA, CLPSY, CORE, CS, ENG, EXSC, IPSY, MED, MT, MUS, NURSE, PH, SPAA, SW, TED

01 President .... Dr. David R. HOPKINS
05 Provost .... Dr. S. NARAYANAN
10 Vice Pres Business and Finance .... Dr. Mark M. POLATAJKO
32 Vice President Student Affairs .... Dr. Dan ABRAHAMOWICZ
46 Vice Pres Research/Graduate Studies .... Dr. Robert FYFFE
30 Vice President Univ Advancement .... Ms. Rebecca S. COLE
84 Vice Pres Enrollment Management .... Ms. Mary Ellen ASHLEY
20 VP Instruction & Curriculum .... Dr. Thomas A. SUDKAMP
58 Dean Sch Graduate Studies .... Dr. Robert FYFFE
45 Exec Vice President for Planning .... Dr. Robert J. SWEENEY
08 Interim University Librarian .... Mrs. Sheila G. SHELLABARGER
26 Executive Director of Marketing .... Ms. Denise ROBINOW
15 Assoc Vice Pres for Human Resources .... Ms. Shari MICKEY-BOGGS
18 Assoc VP Facilities Mgmt & Svcs .... Mr. Dan PAPAY
35 Associate Vice Pres Student Affairs .... Ms. Katherine W. MORRIS
50 Dean Raj Soin College of Business .... Dr. Joanne LI
53 Dean Education/Human Services .... Dr. Charlotte HARRIS
54 Dean Engineering/Computer Science .... Dr. Nathan W. KLINGBEIL
12 Dean WSU Lake Campus .... Dr. Jay ALBAYYARI
49 Dean Liberal Arts .... Dr. Kristin SOBOLIK
66 Dean College of Nursing & Health .... Dr. Rosalie O'DELL MAINOUS
63 Dean Boonshaft School of Medicine .... Dr. Margaret DUNN
83 Interim Dean Sch of Prof Psychology .... Dr. LaPearl Logan WINFREY
81 Dean Science/Mathematics .... Dr. Yi LI
06 Registrar .... Ms. Amanda STEELE-MIDDLETON
07 AVP Undergraduate Admissions .... Ms. Cathleen M. DAVIS
13 Chief Information Officer .... Mr. Craig WOOLLEY
46 Asst VP Research/Sponsored Pgms .... Ms. Ellen REINSCH FRIESE
36 Director Career Services .... Ms. Cheryl STUART
37 Director of Financial Aid .... Ms. Amy BARNHART
38 Director Counsel/Wellness Svcs .... Dr. Robert A. RANDO
29 Exec Dir Alumni Relations .... Mr. Gregory SCHARER
22 Director Equity and Inclusion .... Mr. Matt BOAZ
31 Assoc Director Event Svcs .... Vacant
88 Director Disability Services .... Mr. Tom WEBB
86 Assoc VP Public Affairs .... Mr. Robert E. HICKEY, JR.
41 Director of Athletics .... Mr. Bob GRANT
43 General Counsel .... Ms. Gwen M. MATTISON
40 Store Manager .... Ms. Jennifer L. GEBHART
85 Director Intl Student/Scholar Svcs .... Mr. Steven J. LYONS
39 Director Residence Services .... Mr. Daniel BERTSOS
19 Chief Police Department .... Mr. David A. FINNIE
96 Dir Strategic Procurement & Contr .... Vacant
92 Director Honors Program .... Dr. Susan CARRAFIELLO
94 Director Womens Studies Program .... Dr. Hope JENNINGS
09 Asst VP Institutional Research .... Mr. Craig THIS
28 VP Multicultural Affairs & Comm Eng .... Dr. Kimberly BARRETT
04 Executive Asst to President .... Ms. Teresa M. BEDWELL
102 CFO WSU Foundation .... Mr. Robert BATSON
44 Director Annual or Planned Giving .... Ms. Jennifer M. FOSTER

Xavier University (B)

3800 Victory Parkway, Cincinnati OH 45207-1096
County: Hamilton FICE Identification: 003144
Unit ID: 206622
Telephone: (513) 745-3000 Carnegie Class: Master's L
FAX Number: (513) 745-4223 Calendar System: Semester
URL: www.xavier.edu
Established: 1831 Annual Undergrad Tuition & Fees: $35,080
Enrollment: 6,538 Coed
Affiliation or Control: Roman Catholic IRS Status: 501(c)3
Highest Offering: Doctorate
Program: Liberal Arts And General; Teacher Preparatory; Professional
Accreditation: NH, BUS, CAATE, CACREP, CEA, CLPSY, HSA, MACTE, MUS, NURSE, OT, RAD, SW, TEAC

01 President .... Rev. Michael J. GRAHAM, SJ
11 Administrative Vice President .... Dr. John F. KUCIA
05 Provost & Chief Academic Officer .... Dr. Scott CHADWICK
10 Sr VP Financial Administration/CFO .... Ms. Maribeth AMYOT
26 Vice Pres for University Relations .... Mr. Gary R. MASSA
88 Asst to Pres for Mission & Identity .... Dr. Debra MOONEY
13 Assoc Provost Info Technologies/CIO .... Ms. Annette MARKSBERRY
84 Vice Pres for Enrollment Management .... Mr. Terry RICHARDS
28 Chief Diversity/Inclusion Officer .... Vacant
26 Director Strategic Communications .... Ms. Kelly LEON
30 Assoc VP for University Relations .... Ms. Susan ABEL
32 Assoc Provost for Student Affairs .... Mr. David J. JOHNSON
18 Vice President for Facilities .... Mr. Robert M. SHEERAN
41 Director Athletics .... Mr. Greg CHRISTOPHER
15 Assoc Vice Pres for Human Resources .... Mrs. Connie PERME
07 Dean Undergraduate Admission .... Mr. Aaron MEIS
44 Exec Dir Gifts & Estate Planning .... Mr. Mark MCLAUGHLIN
42 Dir Center for Mission/Identity .... Mr. Joseph SHADLE
06 Registrar .... Dr. Andrea WAWRZUSIN
85 Exec Dir Center for Intl Education .... Ms. Lea MINNITI
105 Exec Dir Ofc University Commun .... Mr. Doug RUSCHMAN
39 Senior Director of Residence Life .... Ms. Lori A. LAMBERT
40 Director of Bookstore .... Mr. Michael HUBBARD
86 Dir of Comm & Government Relations .... Dr. Eugene L. BEAUPRE'
83 Dean Col Social Sci/Health/Educ .... Dr. Paul GORE
36 Senior Director Student Involvement .... Ms. Leah BUSAM
23 Director for Health Services .... Ms. Mary ROSENFELDT
49 Dean College Arts & Sciences .... Dr. Janice B. WALKER
19 Director of Campus Police/Security .... Mr. Michael COUCH
37 Dir of Financial Aid/Scholarships .... Mr. Aaron MEIS
43 General Counsel/Sec of the Board .... Mr. Joseph H. FELDHAUS
29 Dir Alumni Rels/Ex Dir Athletic Dev .... Mr. Brian MALEY
09 Dir Office Institutional Research .... Vacant
50 Int Dean Williams Col of Business .... Dr. R. Stafford JOHNSON
51 Director Weekend Degree Program .... Ms. Patricia MEYER
96 Dir of Purchasing & Supply Mngt .... Mr. John MERCER

Youngstown State University (C)

One University Plaza, Youngstown OH 44555-0001
County: Mahoning FICE Identification: 003145
Unit ID: 206695
Telephone: (330) 941-3001 Carnegie Class: Master's L
FAX Number: (330) 941-7169 Calendar System: Semester
URL: www.ysu.edu
Established: 1908 Annual Undergrad Tuition & Fees (In-State): $8,087
Enrollment: 12,551 Coed
Affiliation or Control: State IRS Status: 501(c)3
Highest Offering: Doctorate
Program: Occupational; Liberal Arts And General; Teacher Preparatory; Professional; Technical Emphasis
Accreditation: NH, AAFCS, ANEST, ART, BUS, CACREP, COARC, COARCP, DH, DIETC, DIETD, DIETT, EMT, ENG, ENGT, MAC, MLTAD, MUS, NUR, PH, PTA, SW, TED, THEA

01 President .... Mr. James P. TRESSEL
05 Provost & VP for Academic Affairs .... Dr. Martin ABRAHAM
10 Vice Pres Finance & Business Op .... Mr. Neal P. MCNALLY
26 Assoc VP for University Relations .... Mrs. Shannon TIRONE
32 Assoc VP for Student Experience .... Dr. Eddie HOWARD, JR.
84 Assoc Vice Pres Enrollment Mgmt .... Mr. Gary D. SWEGAN
43 Vice President and General Counsel .... Ms. Holly A. JACOBS
49 Int Dean Liberal Arts/Soc Science .... Dr. Jane KESTNER
50 Dean of Business Administration .... Dr. Betty Jo LICATA
53 Dean of Education .... Dr. Charles HOWELL
81 Int Dean of Science/Tech/Eng/Math .... Dr. W. Gregg STURRUS
57 Dean Creative Arts & Communication .... Dr. Michael R. CRIST
76 Dean Health & Human Services .... Dr. Joseph L. MOSCA
58 Dean College of Graduate Studies .... Dr. Salvatore A. SANDERS
45 Assoc Provost Acad Pgms/Planning .... Dr. Kevin BALL
20 Senior Associate Provost .... Dr. Teri RILEY
15 Chief Human Resources Officer .... Mr. Kevin W. REYNOLDS
13 Director Computer Services .... Mr. Richard J. MARSICO
41 Exec Director of Athletics .... Mr. Ronald A. STROLLO
35 Assoc VP for Student Success .... Dr. Michael REAGLE
08 Manager Library Operations .... Ms. Anna TORRES
88 Director Special Projects .... Mr. Jack FAHEY
29 Dir University Events & Protocol .... Ms. Jacquelyn LEVISEUR
28 Ex Director Multicultural Affairs .... Dr. Sylvia J. IMLER
07 Director Undergrad Recruit/Admiss .... Ms. Sue E. DAVIS
06 Registrar .... Ms. Jeanne HERMAN
19 Chief of University Police .... Mr. John BESHARA
18 Executive Director Facilities .... Mr. John P. HYDEN
21 Director Student Accts/Receivables .... Ms. Gloria KOBUS
23 Dir Environ/Occup Health & Safety .... Mr. Daniel SAHLI
37 Director Financial/Scholarships .... Ms. Elaine RUSE
21 Director General Accounting .... Ms. Katrena J. DAVIDSON
21 Cash Management Officer .... Mr. David EDWARDS
25 Director Grants & Sponsored Pgms .... Mr. Edward ORONA
39 Director Housing Services .... Ms. Danielle MEYER
85 Director International Studies .... Mr. Jef C. DAVIS
30 Director of Development .... Ms. Catherine CALA
28 Director Student Diversity Programs .... Mr. William J. BLAKE
88 Dir Assoc Degree/Tech Prep Pgms .... Ms. Arlene FLOYD
40 Director of Bookstore .... Mr. Charles A. SABATINO
88 Director Support Services .... Mr. Danny J. O'CONNELL
88 Dir Electronic Maintenance Svcs .... Mr. Michael REPETSKI
90 Director Media/Acad Computing .... Mr. Michael S. HRISHENKO
92 Director Univ Scholars/Honors Pgm .... Dr. Ronald SHAKLEE
96 Director Procurement Services .... Mr. William WHEELOCK
91 Manager IT Operations .... Mr. Troy CROSS
35 Dir Campus Rec/Intramural Sports .... Ms. Joy POLKABLA-BYERS
88 Director WYSU-FM .... Mr. Gary SEXTON
04 Exec Administrator to President .... Ms. Cynthia M. BELL
106 Dir Online Education/E-learning .... Ms. Millie RODRIGUEZ
86 Director Government Relations .... Dr. William C. BINNING

Zane State College (D)

9900 Brick Church Road, Cambridge OH 43725
Telephone: (740) 432-6568 Identification: 770365
Accreditation: &NH

† Branch campus of Zane State College, Zanesville, OH.

Zane State College (E)

1555 Newark Road, Zanesville OH 43701-2626
County: Muskingum FICE Identification: 008133
Unit ID: 204255
Telephone: (740) 454-2501 Carnegie Class: Assoc/Pub-R-M
FAX Number: (740) 454-0035 Calendar System: Semester
URL: www.zanestate.edu
Established: 1969 Annual Undergrad Tuition & Fees (In-State): $4,560
Enrollment: 3,969 Coed
Affiliation or Control: State IRS Status: 501(c)3
Highest Offering: Associate Degree
Program: 2-Year Principally Bachelor's Creditable; Technical Emphasis
Accreditation: NH, ACBSP, ACFEI, CAHIIM, ENGT, MAC, MLTAD, OTA, PTAA, RAD

01 President .... Dr. Chad M. BROWN
102 Exec Dir Inst Advancemnt/Foundation .... Vacant
05 Provost/Executive Vice President .... Dr. Richard WOODFIELD
10 Vice Pres for Business Services .... Ms. Terri M. BALDWIN
32 Vice Pres for Student Success .... Dr. Tricia LEGGETT
54 Acad Dean Business & Engineering .... Mr. Randy WHARTON
12 Exec Dean Cambridge Campus .... Mr. Mike WITSON
15 Vice President for Admin & CHRO .... Dr. James KEMPER
13 Exec Chief Info Officer .... Dr. Terry HERMAN
08 Library Director .... Vacant
09 Dir of Inst Effectiveness & Plng .... Dr. Tricia LEGGETT
25 Director of Grants & Contracts .... Mr. Matthew RIDDLE
07 Director of Admissions .... Vacant
37 Director Student Financial Aid .... Ms. Amanda B. REISINGER
36 Director Career/Employment Services .... Ms. Jamie K. CLARK
26 Director Marketing & Communications .... Mr. Nick WELCH
49 Dean of Arts & Sciences .... Ms. Rebecca R. AMENT
38 Dir of One Stop .... Ms. Jamie K. CLARK
21 Controller .... Ms. Tammy S. HUFFMAN
40 Director of Bookstore Operations .... Ms. Linda D. METZ
19 Director of Safety and Security .... Ms. Bethany HAYES
76 Dean of Educ Hlth & Hum Svcs .... Vacant
06 Asst Dean Curriculum/Registrar .... Ms. Theresa KOLK-CONNER
18 Director Facilities Management .... Mr. Joseph KEATING
28 Multicultural Outreach Coordinator .... Ms. Keisha NORRIS
04 Administrative Asst to President .... Mrs. Julie A. MACLAINE

OKLAHOMA

Bacone College (F)

2299 Old Bacone Road, Muskogee OK 74403-1568
County: Muskogee FICE Identification: 003147
Unit ID: 206817
Telephone: (918) 683-4581 Carnegie Class: Bac/Assoc
FAX Number: (918) 781-7422 Calendar System: Semester
URL: www.bacone.edu
Established: 1880 Annual Undergrad Tuition & Fees: $14,500
Enrollment: 968 Coed
Affiliation or Control: American Baptist IRS Status: 501(c)3
Highest Offering: Baccalaureate
Program: 2-Year Principally Bachelor's Creditable; Liberal Arts And General; Teacher Preparatory
Accreditation: NH, IACBE, NUR, NURSE, RAD

01 President .... Mr. Franklin K. WILLIS
05 Exec Vice Pres & Dean of Faculty .... Dr. Robert K. BROWN
88 Director Center for American Indian .... Dr. Patricia J. KING
30 Exec Director of Development .... Ms. Kimberlie GILLILAND
84 Director of Enrollment Management .... Mr. Kindle HOLDERBY
42 VP Christian Ministry .... Rev Dr. Leroy THOMPSON
10 VP Finance .... Mr. Mustafa YUNDEM
32 Director of Student Life/Housing .... Mr. Kindle HOLDERBY
06 Registrar .... Mrs. Virginia THOMPSON
40 Bookstore Manager .... Ms. Dawn OSBORNE
41 Asst VP Athletics .... Mr. Alan FOSTER
37 Asst Director Financial Aid .... Ms. Misty OLESON
15 Asst Director Human Resources .... Ms. Jeanetta RAINWATER
18 Chief Facilities/Physical Plant .... Vacant
29 Director Alumni Relations .... Vacant
07 Director of Admissions .... Mr. John NORWOOD
108 Coord Institutional Assessment Data .... Ms. Linda MILAM
21 Controller .... Vacant
36 Director of Career Services .... Vacant
08 Dir Betts Library/Head Librarian .... Ms. Faye DAVIS
13 Director of Network Systems .... Mr. Chris EHLERS
04 Assistant to President .... Ms. Marcia TAYLOR
19 Chief of Campus Police .... Mr. Brad BEESLEY

Brown Mackie College-Oklahoma City (G)

7101 Northwest Expy, Suite 800, Oklahoma City OK 73132
Telephone: (405) 261-8000 Identification: 770252
Accreditation: &NH, OTA

† Branch campus of Brown Mackie College-Salina, Salina, KS.

Brown Mackie College-Tulsa (H)

4608 South Garnett Road, Ste. 110, Tulsa OK 74146
Telephone: (918) 628-3700 Identification: 666783
Accreditation: ACICS, OTA, SURGT, SURTEC

† Branch campus of Brown Mackie College, South Bend, IN.

Cameron University (A)

2800 W Gore Boulevard, Lawton OK 73505-6377

County: Comanche FICE Identification: 003150
Unit ID: 206914
Telephone: (580) 581-2200 Carnegie Class: Master's S
FAX Number: (580) 581-2867 Calendar System: Semester
URL: www.cameron.edu
Established: 1908 Annual Undergrad Tuition & Fees (In-State): $5,580
Enrollment: 5,537 Coed
Affiliation or Control: State IRS Status: 501(c)3
Highest Offering: Master's
Program: Liberal Arts And General; Teacher Preparatory
Accreditation: NH, ACBSP, MUS, TED

01 President ..... Dr. John M. MCARTHUR
05 Vice President for Academic Affairs .. Dr. Ronna J. VANDERSLICE
10 Vice Pres for Business & Finance ..... Ms. Ninette CARTER
30 Vice Pres University Advancement ... Mr. Albert D. JOHNSON, JR.
84 VP for Enroll Mgmt & Stdnt Success ..... Mr. Jon HORINEK
20 Assoc Vice Pres Academic Affairs ..... Dr. Sylvia BURGESS
20 Asst Vice Pres Academic Affairs ..... Dr. Margery KINGSLEY
50 Dean School of Business ..... Dr. John CAMEY
79 Dean School of Liberal Arts ..... Dr. Von E. UNDERWOOD
53 Dean Sch of Educ/Behav Science ..... Dr. Lisa HUFFMAN
81 Dean School Science/Tech ..... Dr. Terry CONLEY
12 Director Duncan Campus ..... Ms. Susan CAMP
21 Controller ..... Ms. Ninette CARTER
104 Director Academic Enrichment ..... Dr. Anton WOHLERS
26 Senior Director of Public Affairs ..... Vacant
08 Director Library ..... Dr. Sheridan YOUNG
29 Director Develop & Alumni Relations .. Ms. Maurissa BUCHWALD
41 Director Athletic Administration ..... Mr. Jim C. JACKSON
07 Director of Admissions ..... Ms. Zoe W. DURANT
06 Registrar ..... Mrs. Linda PHILLIPS
09 Dir Inst Rsrch/Assess/Accountabity ..... Dr. Karla OTY
37 Director of Financial Assistance ..... Mr. Donald HALL
13 Director Information Tech Services ..... Ms. Debbie GOODE
15 Director of Human Resources ..... Vacant
38 Director of Student Development ..... Dr. Jennifer PRUCHNICKI
32 Dean of Students ..... Mr. Zeak NAIFEH
19 Director Public Safety ..... Mr. John DEBOARD
18 Director Physical Facilities ..... Mr. Robert HANEFIELD
96 Purchasing Agent ..... Mr. Richard MCCOMAS
22 EEO Officer/Title IX Coordinator ..... Mr. Thomas RUSSELL

Career Point College (B)

3138 South Garnett Road, Tulsa OK 74146-1933
Telephone: (918) 627-8074 Identification: 770761
Accreditation: ACICS

† Branch campus of Career Point College, San Antonio, TX.

Carl Albert State College (C)

1507 S McKenna, Poteau OK 74953-5208

County: Le Flore FICE Identification: 003176
Unit ID: 206923
Telephone: (918) 647-1200 Carnegie Class: Assoc/Pub-R-M
FAX Number: (918) 647-1201 Calendar System: Semester
URL: www.carlalbert.edu
Established: 1933 Annual Undergrad Tuition & Fees (In-State): $3,182
Enrollment: 2,241 Coed
Affiliation or Control: State IRS Status: 501(c)3
Highest Offering: Associate Degree
Program: Occupational; 2-Year Principally Bachelor's Creditable
Accreditation: NH, ACBSP, ADNUR, PTAA, RAD

01 President ..... Mr. Garry M. IVEY
32 Vice President for Student Affairs ..... Vacant
05 Vice President of Academic Affairs ..... Dr. Jason MORRISON
10 Vice Pres for Business Operations ..... Mr. Tony CROUCH
35 Assoc Vice Pres Student Life ..... Mr. Randy GRAVES
84 Assoc Vice Pres for Enrollment Mgmt ..... Mr. Jay FALKNER
13 Information Technology Director ..... Mr. Michael MARTIN
04 Assistant to the President ..... Vacant
26 Public Relations Director ..... Ms. Judi WHITE
06 Registrar/Director Admissions ..... Ms. Dee Ann DICKERSON
37 Director of Financial Aid ..... Ms. Robin BENSON
86 Director Federal Programs ..... Ms. Michelle WHITE
18 Director of Physical Plant ..... Mr. Chuck LEWIS
15 Director Personnel Services ..... Ms. Vicki HILL
21 Business Office Manager ..... Ms. Rena BROOKS
108 Instutional Effectiveness Officer ..... Dr. Kathy HARRELL

Carl Albert State College (D)

1601 S. Opdyke Street, Sallisaw OK 74955
Telephone: (918) 776-0001 Identification: 770366
Accreditation: &NH

† Branch campus of Carl Albert State College, Poteau, OK.

Clary Sage College (E)

3131 South Sheridan Road, Tulsa OK 74145-1102
Telephone: (918) 298-8200 Identification: 666368
Accreditation: ACICS

† Branch campus of Community Care College, Tulsa, OK.

College of the Muscogee Nation (F)

PO Box 917, 2170 Raven Circle, Okmulgee OK 74447

County: Okmulgee Identification: 667122
Unit ID: 480967
Telephone: (918) 549-2800 Carnegie Class: Not Classified
FAX Number: (918) 549-2880 Calendar System: Semester
URL: www.mvsktc.org
Established: 1994 Annual Undergrad Tuition & Fees: $3,516
Enrollment: 204 Coed
Affiliation or Control: Tribal Control IRS Status: 501(c)3
Highest Offering: Associate Degree
Program: Occupational
Accreditation: @NH

01 President ..... Mr. Robert BIBLE

Comanche Nation College (G)

1608 SW 9th Street, Lawton OK 73501

County: Comanche Identification: 667123
Telephone: (580) 591-0203 Carnegie Class: Not Classified
FAX Number: (580) 591-0643 Calendar System: Semester
URL: www.cnc.cc.ok.us
Established: 2002 Annual Undergrad Tuition & Fees: $5,280
Enrollment: 50 Coed
Affiliation or Control: Tribal Control IRS Status: 501(c)3
Highest Offering: Associate Degree
Program: Occupational
Accreditation: @NH

01 President ..... Dr. Rafe Edward TRICKEY
05 Vice Pres Student/Academic Affairs ..... Johnny POOLAW
06 Registrar ..... Sarah GODSAVE
108 Dir Institutional Effectiveness ..... Dr. Kurtis KOLL

Community Care College (H)

4242 S Sheridan Road, Tulsa OK 74145-1119

County: Tulsa FICE Identification: 033674
Unit ID: 439570
Telephone: (918) 610-0027 Carnegie Class: Assoc/PrivFP
FAX Number: (918) 610-0029 Calendar System: Other
URL: www.communitycarecollege.edu
Established: 1995 Annual Undergrad Tuition & Fees: $15,490
Enrollment: 889 Coed
Affiliation or Control: Independent Non-Profit IRS Status: 501(c)3
Highest Offering: Associate Degree
Program: Occupational; 2-Year Principally Bachelor's Creditable; Technical Emphasis
Accreditation: ACICS, MAAB, SURGT

00 CEO ..... Ms. Teresa L. KNOX
01 President ..... Dr. Kevin L. KIRK

Connors State College (I)

700 College Road, Warner OK 74469-9700

County: Muskogee FICE Identification: 003153
Unit ID: 206996
Telephone: (918) 463-2931 Carnegie Class: Assoc/Pub-R-M
FAX Number: (918) 463-2233 Calendar System: Semester
URL: www.connorsstate.edu
Established: 1908 Annual Undergrad Tuition & Fees (In-State): $3,797
Enrollment: 2,278 Coed
Affiliation or Control: State IRS Status: 501(c)3
Highest Offering: Associate Degree
Program: Occupational; 2-Year Principally Bachelor's Creditable
Accreditation: NH, ADNUR

01 President ..... Dr. Tim W. FALTYN
05 Sr VP for Acad/Student Affairs ..... Dr. Ron RAMMING
10 VP for Fiscal Services ..... Mr. Mike LEWIS
21 Assoc VP for Fiscal Services ..... Ms. Kim RYALS
30 Exec Dir Development Foundation ..... Dr. Ryan BLANTON
37 Director of Financial Aid ..... Mr. Baxter STEWART
08 Director of Learning Center ..... Vacant
13 Director of Information Technology ..... Mr. Heath HODGES
06 Registrar ..... Ms. Kwanna KING
07 Director of Recruitment ..... Ms. Logan KNAPPER
26 Director of Public Information ..... Ms. Ami MADDOCKS
15 Director of Human Resources ..... Mr. Nate WALKER
09 Director of Institutional Research ..... Mr. Heath HODGES
41 Athletic Director ..... Mr. Bill MUSE
32 Director of Campus Life ..... Mr. Mike JACKSON
19 Chief of Police ..... Mr. James MENDENHALL
04 Executive Asst to the President ..... Ms. Cindy ANDERSON
04 Executive Asst to the President ..... Ms. Jody BUTLER
108 Asst VP Acad/Stdt Affrs/ Assessment ..... Ms. Julie DINGER-BLANTON
20 Asst VP Acad/Stdt Affs/Acad Support ..... Ms. Robin O'QUINN

Connors State College Muskogee Port Branch Campus (J)

2501 N 41st Street East, Muskogee OK 74403
Telephone: (918) 687-6747 Identification: 770367
Accreditation: &NH

† Branch campus of Connors State College, Warner, OK.

East Central University (K)

1100 E 14th Street, Ada OK 74820-6899

County: Pontotoc FICE Identification: 003154
Unit ID: 207041
Telephone: (580) 332-8000 Carnegie Class: Master's L
FAX Number: (580) 332-1623 Calendar System: Semester
URL: www.ecok.edu
Established: 1909 Annual Undergrad Tuition & Fees (In-State): $5,873
Enrollment: 4,428 Coed
Affiliation or Control: State IRS Status: 501(c)3
Highest Offering: Master's
Program: Liberal Arts And General; Teacher Preparatory; Professional
Accreditation: NH, ACBSP, CAATE, CACREP, CORE, MUS, NUR, SW, TED

01 President ..... Dr. John R. HARGRAVE
05 Provost/Vice Pres Academic Affairs ..... Dr. Katricia PIERSON
32 Vice President Student Development ..... Dr. Gerald FORBES
10 Exec VP Administration/Finance ..... Ms. Jessica BOLES
53 Dean of Education ..... Dr. Brenda WALLING
50 Dean of Business ..... Mr. Wendell GODWIN
51 Director Continuing Education ..... Dr. G. Richard WETHERILL
35 AVP for Stdnt Devel/Dean of Stdnts ..... Dr. Boomer APPLEMAN
37 Director of Financial Aid ..... Ms. Becky ISAACS
09 Director of Institutional Research ..... Dr. Sheilynda STEWART
08 Librarian ..... Dr. Adrianna LANCASTER
06 Registrar ..... Ms. Adeidre SIMMONS
13 Director Computer Center ..... Mr. Jeremy BENNETT
41 Athletic Director ..... Mr. Jeff WILLIAMS
15 Director of Human Resources ..... Mr. Lynn LOFTIN
19 Chief of Police ..... Mr. Henry MILLER
18 Director Facilities Management ..... Mr. Darryl OVERSTREET
26 Dir of Marketing & Communication ..... Ms. Amy FORD
29 Director Alumni Relations ..... Ms. Katie WELLINGTON
84 Director Enrollment Management ..... Mr. B. J ECHARD
96 Director of Purchasing ..... Ms. Jo Ann JOHNSON

Eastern Oklahoma State College (L)

1301 W Main Street, Wilburton OK 74578-4999

County: Latimer FICE Identification: 003155
Unit ID: 207050
Telephone: (918) 465-2361 Carnegie Class: Assoc/Pub-R-S
FAX Number: (918) 465-2431 Calendar System: Semester
URL: www.eosc.edu
Established: 1909 Annual Undergrad Tuition & Fees (In-State): $3,947
Enrollment: 1,673 Coed
Affiliation or Control: State IRS Status: 501(c)3
Highest Offering: Associate Degree
Program: Occupational; 2-Year Principally Bachelor's Creditable
Accreditation: NH, ADNUR, MLTAD

01 President ..... Dr. Stephen E. SMITH
05 Vice President of Academic Affairs ..... Dr. Karen D. HARRISON
10 Vice Pres of Business Affairs ..... Ms. La Donna HOWELL
32 Vice Pres for Student Affairs ..... Dr. Steve G. GLAZIER
12 Director of McAlester Campus ..... Ms. Ann BROOKS
35 Dean of Students/Athletic Director ..... Mr. Greg WARREN
30 Exec Dir Development/Alumni Rels ..... Mrs. Treva KENNEDY
26 Dir Marketing/Comminucations ..... Mrs. Trish MCBEATH
09 Director of Institutional Research ..... Dr. Janet WANSICK
20 Associate Academic Officer ..... Dr. Janet WANSICK
84 Dir Enrollment Mgmt/Financial Aid ..... Dr. Steve GLAZIER
13 Chief Technical Officer ..... Mr. Jeff WEEMS
08 Director Library & Media Services ..... Ms. Maria MARTINEZ
15 Director Human Resources ..... Mrs. Joyce BILLS
06 Registrar ..... Mrs. Jennifer LABOR
18 Chief Facilities/Physical Plant ..... Mr. Rich LYNES
44 Dir of Institutional Advancement ..... Ms. Treva KENNEDY
37 Financial Aid Director ..... Ms. Mimi KELLEY

Eastern Oklahoma State College McAlester Campus (M)

1802 E College Avenue, McAlester OK 74501
Telephone: (918) 426-5272 Identification: 770368
Accreditation: &NH

† Branch campus of Eastern Oklahoma State College, Wilburton, OK.

Family of Faith College (N)

PO Box 1805, Shawnee OK 74802-1805

County: Pottawatomie FICE Identification: 036763
Unit ID: 443058
Telephone: (405) 273-5331 Carnegie Class: Spec/Faith
FAX Number: (405) 273-8535 Calendar System: Semester
URL: www.familyoffaithcollege.edu
Established: 1992 Annual Undergrad Tuition & Fees: $6,000
Enrollment: 24 Coed
Affiliation or Control: Independent Non-Profit IRS Status: 501(c)3
Highest Offering: Baccalaureate
Program: Professional; Religious Emphasis
Accreditation: BI

01 President ..... Dr. Samuel W. MATTHEWS
05 Vice President Academic Affairs ..... Mrs. Elaine W. PHILLIPS
10 Actg Vice Pres Operations/Finance ..... Mr. Daniel MATTHEWS
32 Vice Pres Student Affs/Dir Fin Aid ..... Mrs. Dara GILLIAM
46 Director of Resource Development ..... Vacant
42 Director of Spiritual Life ..... Mr. Daniel J. MATTHEWS

108 Dir of Accreditation/Assessment ....Mrs. Elaine W. PHILLIPS
104 Director of International Studies ....Mrs. Dara GILLIAM

Heritage College (A)

7100 I-35 Services Road, Suite 7118,
Oklahoma City OK 73149-2740
County: Oklahoma FICE Identification: 031151
Unit ID: 410070
Telephone: (405) 631-3399 Carnegie Class: Assoc/PrivFP
FAX Number: (405) 631-6711 Calendar System: Quarter
URL: www.heritage-education.com
Established: 2002 Annual Undergrad Tuition & Fees: $24,550
Enrollment: 715 Coed
Affiliation or Control: Proprietary IRS Status: Proprietary
Highest Offering: Associate Degree
Program: Occupational
Accreditation: ABHES, SURTEC

01 Director ....Ms. Andrea RILEY

Hillsdale Free Will Baptist College (B)

PO Box 7208, Moore OK 73153-1208
County: Cleveland FICE Identification: 010266
Unit ID: 207157
Telephone: (405) 912-9000 Carnegie Class: Spec/Faith
FAX Number: (405) 912-9050 Calendar System: Semester
URL: www.hc.edu
Established: 1959 Annual Undergrad Tuition & Fees: $14,800
Enrollment: 283 Coed
Affiliation or Control: Free Will Baptist IRS Status: 501(c)3
Highest Offering: Master's
Program: Liberal Arts And General; Teacher Preparatory; Religious Emphasis
Accreditation: TRACS

01 President ....Dr. Timothy W. EATON
05 Chief Academic Officer ....Dr. Mark H. BRAISHER
10 Chief Business Officer ....Ms. Pat MILLER
30 Director Institutional Advancement ....Mr. Bob THOMPSON
07 Admissions Coordinator ....Ms. Lyndsey BRAISHER
37 Financial Aid Coordinator ....Ms. Denise CONKLIN
08 LRC Director ....Ms. Nancy J. DRAPER
13 Director of MIS ....Mr. Quentin C. LOOP
06 Registrar ....Ms. Patti ASHBY
58 Dean of Graduate Studies ....Dr. Mark H. BRAISHER
39 Resident Life Coordinator ....Mr. Sam CRILLY
41 Athletic Director ....Ms. Autumn DRAKE
32 Dean of Students ....Ms. Jody BLACKWELL
40 Bookstore Manager ....Mr. Lee BAUDER
106 Director of Online Learning ....Dr. Paulette JONES

ITT Technical Institute (C)

1900 NW Expressway, Suite 305R,
Oklahoma City OK 73118
Telephone: (405) 810-4100 Identification: 666159
Accreditation: ACICS

† Branch campus of ITT Technical Institute, Indianapolis, IN.

ITT Technical Institute (D)

4500 S. 129th East Avenue, Ste. 152, Tulsa OK 74134
Telephone: (918) 615-3900 Identification: 666147
Accreditation: ACICS

† Branch campus of ITT Technical Institute, Indianapolis, IN.

Langston University (E)

PO Box 1500, Langston OK 73050
County: Logan FICE Identification: 003157
Unit ID: 207209
Telephone: (405) 466-2231 Carnegie Class: Master's S
FAX Number: N/A Calendar System: Semester
URL: www.langston.edu
Established: 1897 Annual Undergrad Tuition & Fees (In-State): $13,840
Enrollment: 2,455 Coed
Affiliation or Control: State IRS Status: 501(c)3
Highest Offering: Doctorate
Program: Liberal Arts And General; Teacher Preparatory; Professional
Accreditation: NH, ACBSP, CORE, NUR, PTA, TED

01 President ....Dr. Kent J. SMITH, JR.
05 Vice President Academic Affairs ....Dr. Clyde MONTGOMERY
10 VP Fiscal/Admin Affairs ....Dr. Sharron T. BURNETT
32 VP Student Affairs ....Dr. Raphael X. MOFFETT
30 Interim VP Inst Develop/Advance ....Dr. Sharron T. BURNETT
100 Chief of Staff ....Ms. Theresa D. GRAVES
13 Chief Information Officer ....Mr. Pritchard MONCRIFFE
20 Assoc VP Academic Affairs LU/ OKC ....Mrs. Alice STRONG-SIMMONS
20 COO/Assoc VP Academic Affs LU/ Tulsa ....Dr. Bruce W. MCGOWAN
21 Asst VP of Fiscal Affairs ....Ms. Debra G. MASTERS
35 Dean of Students ....Dr. Natasha M. STEPHENS
29 Director Alumni Affairs ....Mrs. Vonnie W. ROBERTS
36 Dir Assessment/Career Placement ....Mr. James A. WALLACE
26 Director Public Relations ....Mrs. Koshia SILVER
07 Director of Admissions ....Mr. Jeremy LANE
37 Director Financial Aid ....Ms. Shelia R. MCGILL
15 Director of Human Resources ....Mrs. Cynthia S. BUCKLEY
18 Director Facilities/Physical Plant ....Mr. Ruben D. OLIVER
38 Dir Professional Counseling Center ..Dr. Jeffrey W. MARTINDALE
09 Director Inst Research & Planning ....Dr. Carol S. CAWYER
08 Director of Libraries ....Ms. Bettye R. BLACK
06 Registrar ....Mrs. Kathy SIMMONS
41 Athletic Director ....Mrs. Donnita ROGERS
21 Comptroller ....Ms. Helen S. RAMBO
58 Director of Graduate Programs ....Dr. Alex O. LEWIS
19 Chief of Police ....Mr. Frank ATKINSON
96 Director of Purchasing ....Mrs. Deirdra M. STEVENSON
49 Dean School of Arts & Sciences ....Dr. Clarence A. HEDGE
50 Acting Dean School of Business ....Dr. Gregory N. PRICE
46 Dean School Agric/Applied Science ....Dr. Marvin BURNS
66 Dean School of Nursing/Hlth Profess ....Dr. Cynthia HUDSON
53 Dean School of Education/Behav Sci ....Dr. Ruth R. JACKSON
92 Dean Honors Program ....Vacant
88 Dean School of Physical Therapy ....Dr. Aliya CHAUDRY
88 Director Entrepreneurial Studies ..... Dr. Sharron HUNTER-RAINEY
84 Int Exec Director Enrollment Mgmt ......Mr. Chauncey J. JACKSON

Langston University Oklahoma City Campus (F)

4205 N Lincoln, Oklahoma City OK 73105
Telephone: (405) 962-1620 Identification: 770370
Accreditation: &NH

† Branch campus of Langston University, Langston, OK.

Langston University Tulsa Campus (G)

914 North Greenwood, Tulsa OK 74106
Telephone: (918) 877-8100 Identification: 770371
Accreditation: &NH

† Branch campus of Langston University, Langston, OK.

McCurtain County Higher Education Center (H)

2805 NE Lincoln Road, Idabel OK 74745
Telephone: (580) 286-9431 Identification: 770369
Accreditation: &NH

† Branch campus of Eastern Oklahoma State College, Wilburton, OK.

Mid-America Christian University (I)

3500 SW 119th Street, Oklahoma City OK 73170-4500
County: Cleveland FICE Identification: 006942
Unit ID: 245953
Telephone: (405) 691-3800 Carnegie Class: Bac/Diverse
FAX Number: (405) 692-3165 Calendar System: Semester
URL: www.macu.edu
Established: 1953 Annual Undergrad Tuition & Fees: $16,798
Enrollment: 2,688 Coed
Affiliation or Control: Church Of God IRS Status: 501(c)3
Highest Offering: Master's
Program: Liberal Arts And General; Teacher Preparatory; Religious Emphasis
Accreditation: NH

01 President ....Dr. John D. FOZARD
05 Vice Pres for Academic Affairs ....Dr. Sharon LEASE
30 Vice Pres Strategic Initiatives ....Mr. Eric JOSEPH
84 VP Student Engagement/Success ....Mrs. Jessica RIMMER
26 Vice Pres Strategic Initiatives ....Mr. Eric JOSEPH
88 Dean Academic Scholarship ....Dr. Shirley RODDY
13 Chief Information Officer ....Mr. Jody ALLEN
15 Chief Administration Officer (HR) ....Mr. Owen SEVIER
20 Exec Dir Academic Assessment/Accred ....Mr. Saeed SARANI
42 Exec Director of Church Relations ....Rev. Morgan ALSIP
06 Registrar ....Ms. Stephanie DAVIDSON
37 Director Student Financial Services ....Mrs. Christina PADILLA
07 Director of Admissions ....Mr. Mike WILKINSON
18 Director of Facilities ....Ms. Connie GALL
29 Director Alumni Relations ....Vacant

Murray State College (J)

One Murray Campus, Tishomingo OK 73460-3130
County: Johnston FICE Identification: 003158
Unit ID: 207236
Telephone: (580) 371-2371 Carnegie Class: Assoc/Pub-R-M
FAX Number: (580) 371-9844 Calendar System: Semester
URL: www.mscok.edu
Established: 1908 Annual Undergrad Tuition & Fees (In-State): $4,148
Enrollment: 2,473 Coed
Affiliation or Control: State IRS Status: 501(c)3
Highest Offering: Associate Degree
Program: Occupational; 2-Year Principally Bachelor's Creditable
Accreditation: NH, ADNUR, OTA, PTAA

01 President ....Ms. Joy MCDANIEL
04 Exec Assistant to President/Board ....Mrs. Malynda COBB
10 VP Finance/Administration/CFO ....Mr. Dennis WESTMAN
05 Vice Pres for Academic Affairs ....Dr. Roger STACY
32 Vice Pres for Student Affairs ....Ms. Michaelle GRAY
20 AVP Learing and Student Success ....Ms. Becky HENTHORN
18 Exec Director Campus Facilities ....Mr. Sam HOLT
102 Exec Director MSC Foundation ....Dr. Brenda STACY
84 Exec Dir Enrollment Services ....ms. Marilyn SCHWARZ
37 Director Financial Aid ....Ms. Machelle ELLIS
08 Director of Library ....Ms. Mary RIXEN
74 Veterinary Tech Program Director ....Dr. Carey FLOYD
66 Director of Nursing ....Ms. Robin COPPEDGE
88 Director of Academic Advisement ....Ms. Amanda BALDRIDGE
07 Registrar ....Ms. Pam WARD
15 Director of Human Resources ....Ms. Misty TREAS
35 Director Student Support Services ....Ms. Linda TAYLOR
26 Public Information Officer ....Ms. Erin KNIGHT
21 Comptroller ....Ms. Sherry GRAY-DEVINE

National American University-Tulsa (K)

8040 S Sheridan Road, Tulsa OK 74133
Telephone: (918) 879-8400 Identification: 770409
Accreditation: &NH

† Branch campus of National American University, Rapid City, SD.

Northeastern Oklahoma Agricultural and Mechanical College (L)

200 I Street, NE, Miami OK 74354-6434
County: Ottawa FICE Identification: 003160
Unit ID: 207290
Telephone: (918) 542-8441 Carnegie Class: Assoc/Pub-R-M
FAX Number: (918) 542-9759 Calendar System: Semester
URL: www.neo.edu
Established: 1919 Annual Undergrad Tuition & Fees (In-State): $3,833
Enrollment: 2,216 Coed
Affiliation or Control: State IRS Status: 501(c)3
Highest Offering: Associate Degree
Program: Occupational; 2-Year Principally Bachelor's Creditable
Accreditation: NH, ADNUR, MLTAD, PTAA

01 President ....Dr. Jeffery L. HALE
05 Vice President Academic Affairs ....Dr. Bethene FAHNESTOCK
10 Vice President for Fiscal Affairs ....Mr. Mark RASOR
32 VP Student Affairs/Enrollment Svcs ....Mrs. Amy ISHMAEL
20 Asst VP for Academic Affairs ....Vacant
37 Director of Financial Aid ....Mr. David FISHER
26 Chief Public Relations Officer ....Mrs. Katie DEWEY
15 Director Human Resources ....Mr. Steve BEARDEN
18 Director Facilities/Physical Plant ....Mr. Steve GRIMES
13 Coord InstructionalTechnology ....Mr. Matt WESTPHAL
30 Dir Devel/Alumni Rels/Foundation ....Ms. Jennifer HESSEE
38 Director Academic Advising Center ....Mrs. Rachel LLOYD
41 Athletic Director ....Mr. Dale PATTERSON
88 Economic Development Coordinator ....Vacant
105 Webmaster ....Mr. David FRAZIER
06 Registrar ....Mrs. Melanie STEGEMAN
21 Asst Vice Pres for Fiscal Affairs ....Mr. Michael ALLGOOD
40 Bookstore Manager ....Mrs. Kathryn VANOVER
36 Dir Ctr for Academic Success & Adv ....Ms. Rachel LLOYD
08 Director Library Services ....Ms. Sloane BROWN
47 Department Chair Agriculture ....Mr. Tyler DEWEY
83 Department Chair Social Science ....Dr. Jeff BIRDSONG
57 Dept Chair Commun/Performing Arts ....Mr. Steve MCCURLEY
81 Dept Chair Mathematics/Science ....Dr. Mark GRIGSBY
66 Dept Chr Nursing/Allied Hlth/Phy Ed ....Mrs. Deborah MORGAN
50 Dept Chair Business and Technology ....Mrs. Pat CREECH
04 Administrative Asst to President ....Mrs. Peggy L. RHINE
19 Director Security/Safety ....Mr. Mark WALL
39 Director Student Housing ....Mr. Jim ROWLAND
90 Dir Academic/Admin Computing ....Ms. Kimberly BUNCH
96 Coord of Purchasing ....Ms. Kendra CUMMINS

Northeastern State University (M)

600 N Grand Avenue, Tahlequah OK 74464-2399
County: Cherokee FICE Identification: 003161
Unit ID: 207263
Telephone: (918) 456-5511 Carnegie Class: Master's L
FAX Number: (918) 458-2015 Calendar System: Semester
URL: www.nsuok.edu
Established: 1909 Annual Undergrad Tuition & Fees (In-State): $5,547
Enrollment: 8,310 Coed
Affiliation or Control: State IRS Status: 501(c)3
Highest Offering: First Professional Degree
Program: Liberal Arts And General; Teacher Preparatory; Professional; Business Emphasis
Accreditation: NH, ACBSP, CACREP, DIETD, MT, MUS, NUR, OPT, OPTR, SP, SW, TED

01 President ....Dr. Steve TURNER
05 Provost & Vice Pres Academic Affs ....Dr. Mark ARANT
11 Vice President for Administration ....Dr. Aaron CHRISTOPHER
86 Dir Community/Government Relations ....Mr. Jerry COOK
26 VP University Relations ....Mr. Ben HARDCASTLE
32 Int Vice President Student Affairs ....Dr. Jerrid FREEMAN
58 Asst VP Acad Affs/Research ....Dr. Tom JACKSON
30 Asst VP Educ Foundation Leadership ....Dr. Pam FLY
12 Dean Broken Arrow Campus ....Vacant
12 Dean Muskogee Campus ....Dr. Tim MCELROY
49 Dean College of Liberal Arts ....Dr. Phillip BRIDGMON
50 Dean College of Business/Technology ....Dr. Roger COLLIER
53 Dean College of Education ....Dr. Debbie LANDRY
81 Dean Science & Health Professions ....Dr. Pamela HATHORN
88 Dean Optometry ....Dr. Douglas PENISTEN

10 Asst Vice Pres Business Finance Ms. Sue CATRON
08 Exec Director of NSU Libraries Mr. Steven EDSCORN
21 Director of Budget Ms. Christy LANDSAW
30 Director of Development Ms. Peggy GLENN-SUMMITT
15 Director of Human Resources Ms. Alisa HAMETT
37 Director Student Financial Services Dr. Teri COCHRAN
06 Assc Registrar/Veterans Coordinator Ms. Janet KELLEY
07 Director Admissions/Recruitment Ms. Jennifer MCCLENDON
84 Int Exec Dir Enrollment Management Mr. Jerrett PHILLIPS
18 Assistant VP Facilities Mr. Jonathan ASBILL
41 Director of Athletics Mr. Tony DUCKWORTH
27 Director of Communications Mrs. Susan SMEDLEY
19 Director of Campus Police Ms. Patti BUHL
29 Director Alumni Services Mr. Daniel JOHNSON
07 Asst Director of Admission/Rec Ms. Damita CUNNINGHAM
06 Registrar Dr. Julie SAWYER
109 Director of Auxiliary Services Mr. Chris ADNEY
39 Director of Housing Vacant
38 Director Student Counseling Ms. Sheila SELF
96 Purchasing Agent Mr. Thad TURMAN
44 Stewards/Annual Giving Coordinator Ms. Cami HIGHERS
04 Administrative Asst to President Ms. Robin HUTCHINS
13 Chief Info Technology Officer (CIO) Dr. Richard REIF

Northeastern State University (A)

3100 East New Orleans St, Broken Arrow OK 74014
Telephone: (918) 449-6000 Identification: 770372
Accreditation: &NH

† Branch campus of Northeastern State University, Tahlequah, OK.

Northeastern State University at Muskogee (B)

2400 W Shawnee, Muskogee OK 74401
Telephone: (918) 683-0040 Identification: 770373
Accreditation: &NH

† Branch campus of Northeastern State University, Tahlequah, OK.

Northern Oklahoma College (C)

PO Box 2300, Enid OK 73702
Telephone: (580) 242-6300 Identification: 770374
Accreditation: &NH

† Branch campus of Northern Oklahoma College, Tonkawa, OK.

Northern Oklahoma College (D)

PO Box 1869, Stillwater OK 74076
Telephone: (405) 744-2246 Identification: 770375
Accreditation: &NH

† Branch campus of Northern Oklahoma College, Tonkawa, OK.

Northern Oklahoma College (E)

1220 E Grand Avenue, PO Box 310,
Tonkawa OK 74653-0310
County: Kay FICE Identification: 003162
Unit ID: 207281
Telephone: (580) 628-6200 Carnegie Class: Assoc/Pub-R-M
FAX Number: (580) 628-6209 Calendar System: Semester
URL: www.noc.edu
Established: 1901 Annual Undergrad Tuition & Fees (In-State): $3,454
Enrollment: 4,756 Coed
Affiliation or Control: State IRS Status: 501(c)3
Highest Offering: Associate Degree
Program: Occupational; 2-Year Principally Bachelor's Creditable
Accreditation: NH, ACBSP, ADNUR, COARC

01 President Dr. Cheryl EVANS
05 Vice President for Academic Affairs Dr. Pam STINSON
10 Vice President Financial Affairs Mrs. Anita SIMPSON
12 Vice President for NOC Enid Dr. Ed VINEYARD
12 Vice President for NOC Stillwater Dr. Shannon CUNNINGHAM
32 Vice President for Student Affairs Mr. Jason JOHNSON
30 Vice President for Devel/Cmty Rels Mrs. Sheri SNYDER
13 Director Information Technology Mr. Michael MACHIA
15 Director Human Resources Ms. Shannon CRANFORD
20 Dean of Academic Instruction Vacant
84 Vice Pres Enroll Mgmt/Registrar Dr. Rick EDGINGTON
08 Director of Library Services Mr. Benjamin HAINLINE
18 Assoc Vice Pres of Physical Plant Mr. Larry DYE
41 Athletic Director Mr. Jeremy HISE
37 Director Student Financial Aid Ms. Holly LEE
40 Manager Student Bookstore Mrs. Jimilea JANSSON

Northwestern Oklahoma State University (F)

709 Oklahoma Boulevard, Alva OK 73717-2799
County: Woods FICE Identification: 003163
Unit ID: 207306
Telephone: (580) 327-1700 Carnegie Class: Master's S
FAX Number: (580) 327-1881 Calendar System: Semester
URL: www.nwosu.edu
Established: 1897 Annual Undergrad Tuition & Fees (In-State): $6,090
Enrollment: 2,171 Coed
Affiliation or Control: State IRS Status: 501(c)3
Highest Offering: Master's
Program: Liberal Arts And General; Teacher Preparatory; Professional
Accreditation: NH, ACBSP, NUR, SW, TED

01 President Dr. Janet L. CUNNINGHAM
05 Exec Vice Pres/Chief Acad Affairs Dr. Steven L. LOHMANN
10 Vice President for Administration Dr. David M. PECHA
26 Assoc VP for University Relations Mr. Steven J. VALENCIA
32 Dean of Student Affairs Mr. Calleb N. MOSBURG
41 Athletic Director Mr. Andrew V. CARTER
06 Registrar Mrs. Sheri K. LAHR
37 Director Financial Aid Ms. Rita J. CASTLEBERRY
21 Bursar Mrs. Fawn M. KINGCADE
07 Director of Recruitment Ms. Paige L. FISCHER
18 Chief Facilities/Physical Plant Mr. Jim DETGEN
15 Human Resource Director Mrs. Tami L. COOPER
39 Director of Students/Housing Mr. Shane C. HANSEN
29 Director Alumni Relations Mr. John W. ALLEN
38 Director of Student Life/Counselor Mrs. Kaylyn L. HANSEN
58 Assoc Dean of Graduate Studies Dr. Shawn P. HOLLIDAY
08 Director of Libraries Mrs. Susan K. JEFFRIES
09 Institutional Research Specialist Ms. Kylea C. AMERIN

Northwestern Oklahoma State University (G)

2929 E Randolph, Enid OK 73701
Telephone: (580) 237-0334 Identification: 770376
Accreditation: &NH

† Branch campus of Northwestern Oklahoma State University, Alva, OK.

Northwestern Oklahoma State University (H)

2007 34th Street, Woodward OK 73801
Telephone: (580) 256-0049 Identification: 770377
Accreditation: &NH

† Branch campus of Northwestern Oklahoma State University, Alva, OK.

Oklahoma Baptist University (I)

500 W University, Shawnee OK 74804-2590
County: Pottawatomie FICE Identification: 003164
Unit ID: 207403
Telephone: (405) 585-4000 Carnegie Class: Bac/Diverse
FAX Number: N/A Calendar System: Semester
URL: www.okbu.edu
Established: 1910 Annual Undergrad Tuition & Fees: $30,780
Enrollment: 1,979 Coed
Affiliation or Control: Southern Baptist IRS Status: 501(c)3
Highest Offering: Master's
Program: Liberal Arts And General; Teacher Preparatory; Professional
Accreditation: NH, ACBSP, MUS, NURSE, TED

01 President Dr. David W. WHITLOCK
05 Provost/Exec Vice Pres Campus Life Dr. Robert S. NORMAN
10 Exec VP Business Affs/Admin Svcs Mr. Randy L. SMITH
30 Vice Pres University Advancement Mr. Will SMALLWOOD
42 Dean of Spiritual Life Mr. Dale M. GRIFFIN
26 Assoc VP Marketing & Communication Mrs. Paula GOWER
79 Assc Provost/Dn Humanities/Soc Sci Dr. Pam ROBINSON
13 Asst Vice Pres Info Sys/Services Mr. Gary NICKERSON
08 VP Information Int/Dean Library Svc Mr. Paul ROBERTS
32 Dean of Students Mr. Brandon SKAGGS
29 Exec Director OBU Alumni Assn Mrs. Lori R. HAGANS
11 Director of Executive Offices Mrs. Tonia KELLOGG
37 Director Student Financial Services Mrs. Jonna G. RANEY
12 Director Geiger Center Mrs. Cynthia K. GATES
06 Dir Academic Records/Registrar Ms. Marcia MCQUERRY
20 Academic Director/Asst Registrar Mrs. Teri F. WALKER
21 Asst VP Finance/Admin Svcs Mrs. Lauri A. FLUKE
21 Controller Mr. Steven FLOYD
15 Director of Human Resources Mr. Mike JOHNSON
35 Director of Campus Services Mr. Larry A. WALKER
19 Chief of University Police Mr. David SHANNON
41 Athletic Director Mr. Robert DAVENPORT
18 Dir Facilities Mgt & Services Mr. George HAINES
96 Director of Purchasing Mr. Larry WALKER
84 Assoc VP for Enrollment Management Mr. Bruce PERKINS
58 Dean College of Grad & Prof Stds Dr. Rhonda RICHARDS
36 Director of Career Development Ms. Marissa LIGHTSEY
57 Dean of Fine Arts Dr. Ken GABRIELSE
81 Dean College of Math and Science Dr. Debbie BOSCH
73 Dean School Christian Service Vacant
50 Dean School of Business Dr. David C. HOUGHTON
66 Dean School of Nursing Mrs. Lepaine MCHENRY
108 Director of Assessment Vacant
07 Director of Admissions Vacant
04 Administrative Asst to President Ms. Nancy DEICHMAN
39 Director Student Housing Mr. Michael BURNS

Oklahoma Christian University (J)

PO Box 11000, Oklahoma City OK 73136-1100
County: Oklahoma FICE Identification: 003165
Unit ID: 207324
Telephone: (405) 425-5000 Carnegie Class: Master's M
FAX Number: (405) 425-5090 Calendar System: Semester
URL: www.oc.edu
Established: 1950 Annual Undergrad Tuition & Fees: $19,890
Enrollment: 2,479 Coed
Affiliation or Control: Independent Non-Profit IRS Status: 501(c)3
Highest Offering: Master's
Program: Liberal Arts And General; Teacher Preparatory; Professional
Accreditation: NH, ACBSP, CIDA, ENG, MUS, NURSE, TED

01 President Mr. John DESTEIGUER
03 Executive Vice President Dr. William GOAD
05 Vice Pres for Academic Affairs Dr. Scott LAMASCUS
11 Exec Dir of University Services Mr. Kinney BRYANT
10 Vice President for Finance Vacant
26 Vice Pres for Marketing Mrs. Risa FORRESTER
29 Exec Dir for Alumni Relations Mr. Bob LASHLEY
44 Vice Pres Estate/Planned Giving Mr. Stephen ECK
32 Vice Pres and Dean of Student Life Mr. Neil ARTER
35 Assoc Dean of Students Mr. Jeff BENNETT
84 Vice President for Admissions Mrs. Risa FORRESTER
13 Vice President for Information Tech Mr. John HERMES
43 Vice President & General Counsel Mr. Stephen ECK
30 Vice President for Advancement Mr. Kent ALLEN
50 Dean Col of Business Administration Dr. Jeff SIMMONS
73 Dean College of Biblical Studies Dr. Charles RIX
49 Dean College of Liberal Arts Dr. David LOWRY
54 Dean Col of Engineering & Comp Sci Dr. Byron NEWBERRY
81 Dean Col of Nat & Health Sciences Dr. Jeff MCCORMACK
06 Registrar Dr. Stephanie BAIRD
08 Library Director Mrs. Tamie L. WILLIS
19 Chief of Police Dept Vacant
41 Athletic Director Mr. Curtis JANZ
18 Director of Physical Plant Services Mr. Cary FALLING
27 Director Communications Marketing Mr. Wes MCKINZIE
37 Exec Dir Financial Svcs & Budgets Mr. Clint LARUE
104 Director of International Programs Mr. John OSBORNE
15 Vice Pres and Chief HR Officer Mr. Terry WINN
31 Director of Church Relations Vacant
42 Dean for Spiritual Life Mr. Jeff MCMILLON
89 Dir of Freshman Experience Mrs. Amy ROBERTS
88 Director of Creative Services Mr. Judson COPELAND
40 Manager of Bookstore Mr. Doug RICHARDSON
21 Controller Mr. Chad ROBERTSON
07 Director of Admissions Mr. Michael MITCHELL
36 Director of Career Services Mrs. Candace OWENS
85 International Student Adviser Mrs. Joslyn HILL
38 Director of Counseling Services Mr. Sheldon ADKINS
35 Director of Student Services Mrs. Amy JANZEN
28 Multicultural & Service Learning Mr. Gary JONES
04 Administrative Asst to President Mrs. Brooke TALLON
09 Institutional Effectiveness Analyst Mr. Phil DREW
39 Director Student Housing Mr. Curtis SMITH

Oklahoma City Community College (K)

7777 S May Avenue, Oklahoma City OK 73159-4444
County: Oklahoma FICE Identification: 010391
Unit ID: 207449
Telephone: (405) 682-1611 Carnegie Class: Assoc/Pub-U-SC
FAX Number: (405) 682-7585 Calendar System: Other
URL: www.occc.edu
Established: 1972 Annual Undergrad Tuition & Fees (In-District): $3,390
Enrollment: 13,471 Coed
Affiliation or Control: State/Local IRS Status: 501(c)3
Highest Offering: Associate Degree
Program: Occupational; 2-Year Principally Bachelor's Creditable
Accreditation: NH, ACBSP, ADNUR, EMT, OTA, PTAA

01 President Dr. Jerry L. STEWARD
04 Exec Assistant to the President Ms. Gina QUINN
101 Exec Asst to the Board of Regents Ms. Paige LANDRETH
03 Acting Executive Vice President Mr. Steven BLOOMBERG
05 Acting VP for Academic Affairs Dr. Anne DECLOUETTF
30 Exec Director Inst Advancement Mr. Lealon TAYLOR
43 General Counsel Dr. Nancy GERRITY
45 Executive Dir Planning & Research Mr. Stu HARVEY
84 Acting VP Enrollment/Student Svcs Dr. Lisa FISHER
10 Chief Financial Officer Dr. John BOYD
31 Acting VP Community Development Mr. Lemuel BARDEGUEZ
15 Vice Pres Human Resources Dr. Angie CHRISTOPHER
13 VP for Info/Instructional Tech Svcs Mr. David ANDERSON
11 VP for Administrative Services Dr. Marlene SHUGART
20 Associate VP Academic Affairs Mr. Greg GARDNER
32 Assoc VP Enrollment/Student Svcs Dr. Liz LARGENT
49 Dean of Arts Ms. Ruth CHARNAY
79 Dean of English/Humanities Ms. Kim JAMESON
76 Dean of Health Professions Mr. Thomas KRAFT
50 Interim Dean of Business Mr. Greg GARDNER
81 Dean Math/Engineering/Phys Science Dr. Max SIMMONS
83 Dean of Social Sciences Dr. Susan TABOR
88 Dean Chemistry/Biological Sciences Dr. Sonya WILLIAMS
77 Dean of Information Technology Mr. Thomas ASHBY
44 Director of Development Ms. Jennifer HARRISON
26 Dir of Marketing & Public Relations Mr. Cordell JORDAN
25 Director of Grants & Contracts Mr. Joe SWALWELL
09 Dir Institutional Effectiveness Dr. Janet PERRY
37 Director of Student Financial Aid Ms. Sonya GORE
35 Director of Student Life Ms. Erin LOGAN
88 Dir Child Development/Lab School Dr. Mary MCCOY
106 Director of E-Student Services Ms. E.J WARREN
21 Director of Financial Accounting Ms. Brenda CARPENTER
21 Dir of Budgeting/Fiscal Planning Mr. David CHURCHILL
19 Chief of Police Mr. James FITZPATRICK
21 Bursar Ms. Cynthia GARY
18 Director of Facilities Management Mr. Chris SNOW
40 Director of Bookstore Ms. Brenda REINKE
88 Dir Emergency Planning/Risk Mgmt Dr. Marlene SHUGART
96 Director of Purchasing Mr. Craig SISCO
88 Director of Cultural Programs Mr. Lemuel BARDEGUEZ
88 Acting Dir Recreation and Fitness Mr. Michael SHUGART

31 Dir Community Outreach & Education .... Ms. Jessica MARTINEZ-BROOKS
103 Director Career Transitions Program .... Ms. Lisa BROWN
88 Director of Prof Development Inst .... Mr. John CLAYBON
16 Dir Employment & Employee Relations .... Dr. Jana LEGAKO
16 Dir of Compensation & HR Systems ....Mr. Larry ROBERTSON
22 Director of Equal Opportunity ....Dr. Regina SWITZER
14 Dir Enterprise Resource Planning ....Ms. Connie DRUMMOND
14 Dir Info Technology Infrastructure ....Mr. Rob GREGGS
14 Dir of Info Systems and Services .... Mr. Tim WHISENHUNT
84 Dir of Student Academic Success .... Ms. Darby JOHNSEN
08 Director of Library Services .... Ms. Barbara KING
88 Dir of Curriculum and Assessment ....Ms. Catherine KINYON
88 Director Cooperative Alliances ....Ms. Alexa MASHLAN
90 Dir of Cntr for Learning/Teaching ....Dr. Glenne WHISENHUNT
88 Dir of Testing and Assessment Svcs ....Ms. Linda LITTLE
07 Dir of Recruitment & Admissions .Ms. Mary BODINE AL-SHARIF
88 Director of Academic Advising ....Ms. Tamara MADDEN
06 Registrar .... Mr. Alan STRINGFELLOW

Oklahoma City University (A)

2501 N Blackwelder, Oklahoma City OK 73106-1493
County: Oklahoma FICE Identification: 003166
Unit ID: 207458
Telephone: (405) 208-5000 Carnegie Class: Master's L
FAX Number: (405) 208-5916 Calendar System: Semester
URL: www.okcu.edu
Established: 1904 Annual Undergrad Tuition & Fees: $30,726
Enrollment: 3,072 Coed
Affiliation or Control: United Methodist IRS Status: 501(c)3
Highest Offering: First Professional Degree
Program: Liberal Arts And General; Teacher Preparatory; Professional
Accreditation: NH, BUS, LAW, MACTE, MUS, NUR, TED

01 President ....Mr. Robert H. HENRY
05 Provost/Vice Pres Academic Affairs ....Dr. Susan C. BARBER
30 Vice Pres University Advancement ....Mr. Marty O'GWYNN
26 Vice Pres Univ/Church Relations ....Rev. Charles NEFF
10 Chief Financial Officer ....Ms. Donna S. NANCE
32 Acting VP for Student Affairs ....Dr. Liz DONNELLY
84 Asst VP/Dean Enrollment Services ....Mr. Kevin WINDHOLZ
35 Dean of Students ....Dr. Liz DONNELLY
06 Registrar .... Mr. Charles MONNOT
09 Director of Institutional Research ....Dr. Kelly MEREDITH
08 Director Dulaney-Browne Library ....Dr. Victoria SWINNEY
37 Director of Financial Aid ....Ms. Denise FLIS
27 Director of Communications ....Ms. Sandy PANTLIK
15 Chief Human Resources Officer .... Ms. Joey CROSLIN
92 Director of Honors Program ....Dr. Karen YOUMANS
07 Director of Undergrad Admissions ....Ms. Michelle COOK
18 Chief Facilities/Physical Plant ....Mr. Mark CLOUSE
29 Director Alumni Relations ....Mr. Cary PIRRONG
36 Director of Career Services ....Ms. Amelia HURT
49 Dean College of Arts & Sciences ....Dr. Mark Y. DAVIES
50 Dean School of Business ....Dr. Steve AGEE
61 Dean School of Law ....Dr. Valerie COUCH
64 Dean School of Music ....Mr. Mark PARKER
66 Dean of School of Nursing ....Dr. Lois SALMERON
73 Dean School of Religion ....Dr. Mark DAVIES
88 Dean School of Amer Dance/Arts Mgt ....Mr. John BEDFORD
100 Chief of Staff ....Mr. Craig KNUTSON
88 Associate Dean School of Theatre ....Mr. Brian PARSONS
104 Director Study Abroad .... Ms. Mary BENNER
108 Director Institutional Assessment .... Dr. Jo Lynn DIGRANES
13 Chief Info Officer (CIO) ....Mr. Gerry HUNT
19 Chief of Police ....Mr. Bradd BROWN
38 Director University Counseling ....Ms. Brandi GIBSON
39 Director University Housing ....Mr. Ade OKEDIJI
41 Director of Athletics ....Mr. Jim ABBOTT
43 University General Counsel .... Ms. Mary JENKINS
44 Assistant Director Annual Giving ....Ms. Carrie SAUER
106 Instructional Technologist ....Ms. Amanda DILLS

Oklahoma Panhandle State University (B)

Box 430, Goodwell OK 73939-0430
County: Texas FICE Identification: 003174
Unit ID: 207351
Telephone: (580) 349-2611 Carnegie Class: Bac/Diverse
FAX Number: (580) 349-2302 Calendar System: Semester
URL: www.opsu.edu
Established: 1909 Annual Undergrad Tuition & Fees (In-State): $6,820
Enrollment: 1,308 Coed
Affiliation or Control: State IRS Status: 501(c)3
Highest Offering: Baccalaureate
Program: Liberal Arts And General
Accreditation: NH, NUR, TED

01 President ....Dr. David A. BRYANT
05 Vice Pres Academic Affairs/Outreach ....Dr. Wayne MANNING
10 Vice Pres Business & Fiscal Affairs ....Mr. Benny DAIN
47 Dean Agriculture ....Dr. Peter CAMFIELD
50 Dean Business & Technology ....Ms. Diane MURPHEY
53 Dean Education ....Dr. R. Wayne STEWART
57 Dean Liberal Arts ....Dr. Sara RICHTER
66 Dean Science/Mathematics/Nursing ....Dr. Justin COLLINS
32 Dean of Student Affairs ....Ms. Jessica LOFLAND
06 Registrar/Director of Admissions ....Mr. Bobby JENKINS
37 Director Student Financial Aid ....Ms. Lori FERGUSON
09 Director Institutional Research ....Mr. Nick TUTTLE
13 Director of Technology ....Mr. Howard HENDERSON
15 Director Personnel Services ....Ms. Dana COLLINS
08 Director of Library ....Ms. Alton (Tony) HARDMAN
21 Comptroller ....Ms. Elizabeth MCMURPHY
38 Director Counseling/Career Services .... Ms. Deanna Rene RAMON
26 Campus Communications Director ....Ms. Danae MOORE
41 Athletic Officer ....Dr. R. Wayne STEWART
40 Bookstore Manager ....Ms. Mandy BATENHORST
18 Director Physical Plant ....Mr. Bob SCOTT
29 Director Alumni Relations ....Mr. Nick TUTTLE
96 Director of Purchasing ....Ms. Elizabeth MCMURPHY

Oklahoma State University (C)

Stillwater OK 74078
County: Payne FICE Identification: 003170
Unit ID: 207388
Telephone: (405) 744-5000 Carnegie Class: RU/H
FAX Number: N/A Calendar System: Semester
URL: osu.okstate.edu/
Established: 1890 Annual Undergrad Tuition & Fees (In-State): $7,778
Enrollment: 25,854 Coed
Affiliation or Control: State IRS Status: 501(c)3
Highest Offering: Doctorate
Program: Liberal Arts And General; Teacher Preparatory; Professional
Accreditation: NH, AAB, BUS, BUSA, CAATE, CACREP, CARTE, CIDA, CLPSY, COPSY, DIETD, DIETI, ENG, ENGT, JOUR, LSAR, MFCD, MUS, NRPA, SCPSY, SP, TED, THEA, VET

01 President ....Dr. V. Burns HARGIS
04 Exec Assistant to the President ....Ms. Deborah LANE
05 Provost & Sr Vice President ....Dr. Gary SANDEFUR
10 Vice Pres Administration & Finance .Mr. Joseph B. WEAVER, JR.
03 Sr Vice President & General Counsel .... Mr. Gary C. CLARK
32 Vice President Student Affairs ....Dr. Lee E. BIRD
46 Vice President for Research ....Dr. Kenneth SEWELL
28 Assoc VP Institutional Diversity ....Dr. Jason KIRKSEY
47 VP/Dean/Director Ag Sci & Nat Res ....Dr. Thomas COON
41 Vice President Athletic Programs ....Mr. Mike HOLDER
20 Assoc Provost/Assoc VP Undergrad Ed ....Dr. Pamela FRY
21 Assoc Vice President & Controller ....Ms. Kathy ELLIOTT
15 Asst Vice Pres Human Resources ....Ms. Jamie A. PAYNE
102 President & CEO OSU Foundation ....Mr. Kirk JEWELL
29 President & CEO OSU Alumni Assoc ......Mr. Chris BATCHELDER
88 President OSU Research Foundation ....Dr. David WAITS
54 Dean Engineering ....Dr. Paul J. TIKALSKY
49 Dean Arts & Sciences .... Dr. Bret DANILOWICZ
50 Dean Spears School of Business ....Dr. Ken EASTMAN
53 Interim Dean Education ....Dr. C. Robert DAVIS
59 Dean Human Sciences ....Dr. Stephan M. WILSON
74 Dean Veterinary Medicine ....Dr. Jean E. SANDER
58 Assoc Provost/Dean Graduate College ....Dr. Sheryl TUCKER
08 Dean Library ....Dr. Sheila G. JOHNSON
23 Director University Health Services ....Mr. Christopher BARLOW
27 Director Communication Services ....Mr. Gary SHUTT
26 Vice Pres Enroll Mgmt/Univ Mktg ....Mr. Kyle WRAY
07 Director Undergraduate Admissions .... Ms. Christine CRENSHAW
13 Chief Information Officer .... Ms. Darlene HIGHTOWER
43 Board of Regents General Counsel ....Mr. Steve STEPHENS
06 Registrar ....Dr. K. Celeste TABER
39 Interim Director University Housing ....Ms. Tanya MASSEY
38 Director University Counseling Svcs ....Dr. Suzanne M. BURKS
37 Director Scholarships/Financial Aid ....Mr. Chad BLEW
92 Dean Honors College ....Dr. Keith GARBUTT
36 Director Career Services ....Dr. Pam EHLERS
19 Chief Public Safety Officer ....Mr. Michael ROBINSON
25 Dir Grants/Contracts/Financial Admn ....Dr. Robert DIXON
22 Director EEO/Title IX/ADA ....Dr. Rosalyn GREEN
24 Asst Prov/Dir Inst Tch/Lrng Excel ....Dr. Christine ORMSBEE
09 Assoc VP/Dir Inst Res/Info Mgmt ....Dr. Christie HAWKINS
96 Chief Procurement Officer ....Mr. Scott SCHLOTTHAUER
18 Chief Facilities Officer ....Mr. Richard KRYSIAK
88 Asst VP/Director Student Union ....Mr. Mitch KILCREASE
40 Asst Dir Student Union Bookstore ....Mr. Lance HINKLE
85 Manager Intl Students & Scholars ....Mr. Tim T. HUFF
108 Director Univ Assessment & Testing ....Dr. Sarah GORDON

Oklahoma State University Center for Health Sciences College of Osteopathic Medicine (D)

1111 W 17th Street, Tulsa OK 74107-1898
Telephone: (918) 582-1972 FICE Identification: 011282
Accreditation: &NH, FEPAC, OSTEO

† Regional accreditation is carried under the parent institution in Stillwater, OK.

Oklahoma State University Institute of Technology-Okmulgee (E)

1801 E Fourth Street, Okmulgee OK 74447-3901
County: Okmulgee FICE Identification: 003172
Unit ID: 207564
Telephone: (918) 293-4678 Carnegie Class: Assoc/Pub4
FAX Number: (918) 293-4644 Calendar System: Trimester
URL: www.osuit.edu
Established: 1946 Annual Undergrad Tuition & Fees (In-State): $4,605
Enrollment: 3,379 Coed
Affiliation or Control: State IRS Status: 501(c)3
Highest Offering: Baccalaureate
Program: Occupational; 2-Year Principally Bachelor's Creditable; Technical Emphasis
Accreditation: NH, ADNUR, ENGT

01 President ....Dr. Bill PATH
03 Executive Vice President .... Ms. Anita GORDY-WATKINGS
10 VP Fiscal Services ....Mr. Jim SMITH
05 VP Academic Affairs ....Dr. Scott NEWMAN
32 VP Student Services ....Dr. Ina AGNEW
66 Nursing & Health Sciences ....Ms. Jana MARTIN
49 Arts & Sciences ....Dr. Mark ALLEN
72 Automotive Technologies ....Mr. Bill VOORHEES
72 Construction Technologies ....Mr. Steve OLMSTEAD
88 Culinary Arts ....Mr. Rene JUNGO
54 Engineering Technologies ....Dr. Abul HASAN
88 Heavy Equipment & Vehicle Institute ....Mr. Roy ACHEMIRE
77 Information Technologies ....Mr. Randy RITCHEY
75 Watchmaking ....Mr. Jason CHAMPION
57 Visual Communications ....Mr. James MCCULLOUGH
37 Dir Student Financial Services ....Ms. Diana SANDERS
13 Dir Computer Information Systems ....Mr. Kevin HULETT
06 Registrar ....Ms. Crystal BOWLES
07 Director of Admissions & Records ..Ms. Chenoa WORTHINGTON
106 Director of Distance Learning ....Ms. Kari HENRY HULETT
103 Exec Dir Econ Dev & Training Ctr ....Ms. Sheryl HALE
15 Director of Human Resources ....Ms. Paula NORTH
09 Director of Institutional Research ....Ms. Michelle CANAN
18 Dir Physical Plant Services ....Mr. Mark PITCHER
35 Dean of Students ....Mr. Devin DEBOCK
109 Dir Student Union & Auxiliary Svcs ....Mr. James BYRD
35 Director of Student Life ....Mr. Bruce FORCE
39 Director of Residential Life ....Mr. Bo HUDSON
08 Director of Library ....Ms. Jenny DUNCAN
96 Director of Purchasing ....Mrs. Chandra MILLER
12 Dir MAIP-Pryor Campus ....Mr. Scott FRY
38 Counselor ....Ms. Kathy AVERY
40 Manager Bookstore ....Ms. Barbara WRIGHT
26 Director of Marketing ....Ms. Shari ERWIN
19 Campus Police Chief ....Mr. Matt WOOLIVER
04 Admin Asst to President ....Ms. Claudette BUTCHER
88 Dir Tutoring Ctr/Acad Accommodation .... Mr. Chad SPURLOCK
25 Director of Grants ....Ms. Jennifer MENZ PAYTON

Oklahoma State University - Oklahoma City (F)

900 N Portland Ave, Oklahoma City OK 73107-6195
County: Oklahoma FICE Identification: 009647
Unit ID: 207397
Telephone: (405) 947-4421 Carnegie Class: Assoc/Pub4
FAX Number: (405) 945-3289 Calendar System: Semester
URL: www.osuokc.edu
Established: 1961 Annual Undergrad Tuition & Fees (In-State): $3,536
Enrollment: 6,712 Coed
Affiliation or Control: State IRS Status: 501(c)3
Highest Offering: Baccalaureate
Program: Occupational; 2-Year Principally Bachelor's Creditable; Technical Emphasis
Accreditation: NH, ADNUR, DIETT, DMS, EMT

01 President ....Ms. Natalie SHIRLEY
05 Vice President Academic Affairs ....Dr. Joey FRONHEISER
10 Vice President Budget & Finance ....Ms. Ronda REECE
32 Vice President Student Services ....Mr. Brad WILLIAMS
50 Vice Pres for Business and Industry ....Ms. Robin ROBERTS KRIEGER
20 Associate VP Academic Affairs ....Mr. Tracy EDWARDS
84 Director Enrollment Management ....Mr. Kyle WILLIAMS
30 Associate Dir Development OSU-OKC ....Mr. Donovan WOODS
11 Vice Pres of Operations ....Mr. Mike WIDELL
08 Director Library Services ....Ms. Elaine REGIER
37 Director Financial Aid ....Ms. Bessie CARTER
15 Director Human Resources ....Ms. Melissa HERREN
18 Dir of Building Maint/Energy Mgr ....Mr. Mickey FULLER
26 Marketing/Communications ....Mr. Brad WILLIAMS
07 Assistant Director of Admissions ....Mr. Jason ROCKWELL
29 Director Alumni Relations ....Dr. JoElla FLINTON
96 Director of Purchasing ....Ms. Sharon FITZPATRICK
06 Registrar ....Ms. Lyndsay PITTMAN
25 Sr Dir Institutional Grants ....Ms. Amber COLE
19 Director Security/Safety ....Mr. Sam COX

Oklahoma State University - Tulsa (G)

700 N Greenwood Avenue, Tulsa OK 74106-0702
Telephone: (918) 594-8000 Identification: 666053
Accreditation: &NH

† Regional accreditation is carried under the parent institution in Stillwater, OK.

Oklahoma Technical College (H)

4444 South Sheridan, Tulsa OK 74145-1122
Telephone: (918) 895-7500 Identification: 666718
Accreditation: ACICS

† Branch campus of Community Care College, Tulsa, OK.

Oklahoma Wesleyan University (I)

2201 Silver Lake Road, Bartlesville OK 74006-6299
County: Washington FICE Identification: 003151
Unit ID: 206835
Telephone: (918) 333-6151 Carnegie Class: Bac/Diverse
FAX Number: (918) 335-6228 Calendar System: Semester
URL: www.okwu.edu

Established: 1910 Annual Undergrad Tuition & Fees: $24,808
Enrollment: 1,399 Coed
Affiliation or Control: Wesleyan Church IRS Status: 501(c)3
Highest Offering: Master's
Program: 2-Year Principally Bachelor's Creditable; Liberal Arts And General; Teacher Preparatory; Professional
Accreditation: NH, IACBE, NURSE, TED

01 President ... Dr. Everett G. PIPER
05 Provost/Exec VP for Acad Affairs ... Dr. Robert HERRON
07 Executive Vice President ... Mr. John MEANS
10 Vice President for Business Affairs ... Mrs. Andrea ZEPEDA
32 Vice President for Student Life ... Mr. Kyle WHITE
20 Assoc VP for Academic Affairs ... Dr. Mark WEETER
42 Assoc VP for Student Dev ... Rev. Ben ROTZ
07 Assoc VP for Admissions ... Mrs. Samantha PETERSON
53 Dean of School of Education ... Dr. Jeffrey KEENEY
73 Dean of School of Religion & Phil ... Dr. Mark WEETER
49 Dean of School of Arts & Sciences ... Dr. Gentry SUTTON
50 Dean of School of Business ... Dr. Brian EPPERSON
66 Dean School of Nursing ... Mrs. Jessica JOHNSON
106 Director of Online Learning ... Dr. Bryan EASLEY
108 Dir Academic Effectiveness ... Mrs. Elizabeth SMITH
21 Director of Accounting ... Mrs. Margaret FRIEND
06 Registrar ... Mr. Jeff LEBERT
13 Director of Computer Services ... Mr. Eric GOINGS
08 Head Librarian ... Mr. Gavin WOLTJERS
37 Director of Financial Aid ... Mrs. Kandi MOLDER
88 Exec Dir Oper Innovation ... Ms. Julia CROUCH
41 Athletic Director ... Mr. Mark MOLDER
29 Director of University Relations ... Mrs. Marci PIPER
15 Human Resources Administrator ... Mrs. Jessica MORROW
04 Executive Assistant to President ... Mrs. Kathy LINDQUIST
39 Dir of Residential Life ... Mr. Chris BREILAND
34 Women's RD/Campus Care ... Mrs. Whitney BREILAND
88 FYE/SYE Director ... Mr. Aaron BUNKER
23 Director Student Health ... Mrs. Debra COOK
18 Director of Buildings and Grounds ... Mr. Dalton HIGGINS
19 Dir of Security/Educ Counselor ... Mr. Stevan DJUKIC
101 Secretary of the Institution/Board ... Mr. Francisco GONZALEZ
40 Bookstore Manager ... Mrs. Melissa HECK

Oklahoma Wesleyan University (A)

10810 E 45th Street, Tulsa OK 74146
Telephone: (918) 728-6143 Identification: 770378
Accreditation: &NH

† Branch campus of Oklahoma Wesleyan University, Bartlesville, OK.

Oral Roberts University (B)

7777 S Lewis Avenue, Tulsa OK 74171-0003
County: Tulsa FICE Identification: 003985
Unit ID: 207582
Telephone: (918) 495-6161 Carnegie Class: Master's S
FAX Number: (918) 495-6033 Calendar System: Semester
URL: www.oru.edu
Established: 1965 Annual Undergrad Tuition & Fees: $24,792
Enrollment: 3,481 Coed
Affiliation or Control: Independent Non-Profit IRS Status: 501(c)3
Highest Offering: Doctorate
Program: Liberal Arts And General; Teacher Preparatory; Professional; Religious Emphasis
Accreditation: NH, ACBSP, ENG, MUS, NURSE, SW, TED, THEOL

01 President ... Dr. William M. WILSON
05 Provost ... Dr. Kathaleen REID-MARTINEZ
10 EVP and Chief Financial Officer ... Mr. Neal STENZEL
11 EVP and Chief Operations Officer ... Mr. Tim PHILLEY
30 EVP for University Advancement ... Mrs. Laura BISHOP
84 VP for Enrollment Management ... Dr. Nancy BRAINARD
43 VP and General Counsel ... Mr. Terry KOLLMORGEN
32 Vice President Student Life ... Dr. Dan GUAJARDO
13 Chief Information Officer ... Mr. Michael MATHEWS
21 Controller ... Ms. Michelle MCMILLAN
42 Dean of Spiritual Formation ... Dr. Clarence BOYD
08 Dean Learning Resources ... Dr. William JERNIGAN
54 Dean Col of Science & Engineering ... Dr. Kenneth WEED
49 Dean Col of Arts & Cultural Studies ... Dr. Mark HALL
73 Dean College Theology/Ministry ... Dr. Thomson MATHEW
50 Dean College of Business ... Dr. Julie HUNTLEY
66 Dean & Chairman College of Nursing ... Dr. Kenda JEZEK
53 Dean College of Education ... Dr. Kim BOYD
33 Dean of Men ... Mr. Matthew OLSEN
34 Dean of Women ... Ms. Lori COOK
09 Director of Institutional Research ... Dr. Cal EASTERLING
41 Director for Athletics ... Mr. Mike CARTER
25 Director of Sponsored Programs ... Ms. Kim FALCON
38 Director of Student Counseling ... Ms. Michelle TAYLOR
89 Director of Freshmen Studies ... Mr. Tom BELLATTI
92 Director of Honors Program ... Dr. John KORSTAD
88 Director Student Accounts ... Ms. Karen JOHNSON
96 Director of Purchasing ... Mr. Mark PEPIN
06 Registrar ... Mr. David FULMER
07 Director of Admissions ... Vacant
37 Director of Financial Aid ... Mr. William WOMACK
29 Director of Alumni Relations ... Mr. Robert BEARD
19 Director of Security/Safety ... Mr. Jerry ISAACS
15 Director Human Resources/Risk Mgmt ... Dr. Karen ADAMS
36 Director of Student Placement ... Ms. Julie HEADLEY
26 Director of Public Relations ... Mr. Jeremy BURTON
04 Administrative Asst to President ... Mrs. Lois NEWMAN
101 Secretary of the Institution/Board ... Ms. Marian BAUMGARDNER

Phillips Theological Seminary (C)

901 N Mingo Road, Tulsa OK 74116-5612
County: Tulsa FICE Identification: 025602
Unit ID: 414966
Telephone: (918) 610-8303 Carnegie Class: Spec/Faith
FAX Number: (918) 610-8404 Calendar System: Semester
URL: www.ptstulsa.edu
Established: 1907 Annual Graduate Tuition & Fees: $10,080
Enrollment: 110 Coed
Affiliation or Control: Christian Church (Disciples Of Christ)
IRS Status: 501(c)3
Highest Offering: Doctorate; No Undergraduates
Program: Professional; Religious Emphasis
Accreditation: NH, THEOL

01 President ... Gary PELUSO-VERDEND
51 Special Assistant to the President ... John M. IMBLER
05 Vice Pres Academic Affairs & Dean ... Nancy Claire PITTMAN
10 Chief Financial Ofcr/VP Admin ... Lora CONGER
108 Assoc Dean Assessment and Faculty ... Joseph A. BESSLER
07 Assoc Dean Admissions/Student Svcs ... Belva Brown JORDAN
20 Assoc Dn Contextual Ed/Church Rels ... John THOMAS, JR.
88 Director Doctor of Ministry Program ... Kathleen D. MCCALLIE
07 Director Admissions/Student Svcs ... Judy DEERE
37 Financial Aid Director ... Katrina MORRISON
08 Director of Library ... Sandy SHAPOVAL
44 Director of Planned Giving ... Virginia WALKER
29 Director of Alumni Relations ... Geoffrey BREWSTER
44 Annual Fund Program Director ... Malisa PIERCE
26 Director of Seminary Relations ... Kurt GWARTNEY
06 Registrar ... Toni WINE IMBLER
15 Human Resources Manager ... Gwen DERRICK
04 Executive Assistant to President ... Mary E. MCGILVRAY

Platt College (D)

201 N Eastern Avenue, Moore OK 73160
Telephone: (405) 912-3260 Identification: 770585
Accreditation: ACCSC, ACFEI, COARC

† Branch campus of Platt College, Tulsa, OK.

Platt College (E)

2727 W Memorial Road, Oklahoma City OK 73134
Telephone: (405) 749-2433 Identification: 770584
Accreditation: ACCSC, MLTAD

† Branch campus of Platt College, Tulsa, OK.

Platt College (F)

3801 S Sheridan, Tulsa OK 74145-1132
County: Tulsa FICE Identification: 023068
Unit ID: 245962
Telephone: (918) 663-9000 Carnegie Class: Assoc/PrivFP
FAX Number: (918) 622-1240 Calendar System: Other
URL: www.plattcolleges.edu
Established: 1979 Annual Undergrad Tuition & Fees: $34,020
Enrollment: 276 Coed
Affiliation or Control: Proprietary IRS Status: Proprietary
Highest Offering: Baccalaureate
Program: Occupational
Accreditation: ACCSC, ACFEI, MLTAD

01 President ... Mr. Mike A. PUGLIESE
05 Director of Campus ... Mr. Mike ROANE
07 Director of Admission & Marketing ... Mr. Joe LOCKWOOD

Platt College-OKC Central (G)

309 South Ann Arbor Avenue, Oklahoma City OK 73128-1112
Telephone: (405) 946-7799 Identification: 666341
Accreditation: ACCSC, ACFEI, SURGT

† Branch campus of Platt College, Tulsa, OK.

Redlands Community College (H)

1300 S Country Club Road, El Reno OK 73036-5304
County: Canadian FICE Identification: 003156
Unit ID: 207069
Telephone: (405) 262-2552 Carnegie Class: Assoc/Pub-S-SC
FAX Number: (405) 422-1200 Calendar System: Semester
URL: www.redlandscc.edu
Established: 1938 Annual Undergrad Tuition & Fees (In-District): $3,882
Enrollment: 2,604 Coed
Affiliation or Control: State/Local IRS Status: 501(c)3
Highest Offering: Associate Degree
Program: Occupational; 2-Year Principally Bachelor's Creditable
Accreditation: NH, ADNUR, EMT

01 President ... Mr. Jack BRYANT
05 Provost & VP for Academic Affairs ... Dr. John DELEON
10 Vice Pres Finance/Campus Services ... Ms. Jena MARR
32 Dean of Student Services ... Mr. Matt NEWGENT
46 Assoc VP Communications/Research ... Dr. Amanda EVERT
18 Director Physical Plant ... Mr. Richard BUCHHOLZ
66 Director Nursing/Allied Health ... Mrs. Cathie SALES
72 Dir Liberal Studies/Mgmt Science ... Dr. Laura GRUNTMEIR
81 Dir Math/Science/Developmental Stds ... Ms. Barbara KNOP-COX
08 Director Learning Resource Center ... Mrs. Christine DETTLAFF
06 Registrar/Director Student Records ... Mr. Dennis HARRIS
37 Director Financial Aid ... Ms. Paris PRZEKURAT
41 Athletic Director ... Mr. Matt NEWGENT
13 Director Administrative Computing ... Mr. Troy MILLIGAN
22 Director of Upward Bound ... Mrs. Linda MCDOWN
09 Director of Institutional Research ... Mr. Troy MILLIGAN
84 Dean of Enrollment Management ... Mrs. Tricia HOBSON
21 Associate Business Officer ... Mrs. Maxine CALVERT
36 Coordinator Career Services ... Ms. Jacki HERREL
15 Coordinator Personnel/Payroll ... Mrs. Kim ANDRADE
26 Coordinator Public Information ... Mrs. Carlee JONES
29 Coord Alumni Rels/Alternative Educ ... Mrs. Jill WORTHINGTON
39 Coordinator of Resident Life ... Ms. Margie MOORE

Rogers State University (I)

1701 W Will Rogers Boulevard, Claremore OK 74017-3252
County: Rogers FICE Identification: 003168
Unit ID: 207661
Telephone: (918) 343-7777 Carnegie Class: Bac/Assoc
FAX Number: (918) 343-7898 Calendar System: Semester
URL: www.rsu.edu
Established: 1909 Annual Undergrad Tuition & Fees (In-State): $6,009
Enrollment: 4,043 Coed
Affiliation or Control: State IRS Status: 501(c)3
Highest Offering: Master's
Program: 2-Year Principally Bachelor's Creditable; Liberal Arts And General; Business Emphasis
Accreditation: NH, ADNUR, EMT, NUR

01 President ... Dr. Larry RICE
05 Vice President for Academic Affairs ... Dr. Richard BECK
10 Exec VP for Admin & Finance ... Mr. Tom VOLTURO
30 Vice President for Development ... Dr. Maynard PHILLIPS
32 Vice Pres for Student Affairs ... Dr. Brent MARSH
09 Asst VP Accountability & Academics ... Dr. Mary MILLIKIN
21 Comptroller/Asst Vice Pres Bus Affs ... Mr. Mark MEADORS
12 Director Pryor Campus ... Ms. Sherry ALEXANDER
12 Provost Bartlesville Campus ... Mr. Bill BEIERSCHMITT
50 Dean School of Business & Tech ... Dr. Susan WILLIS
83 Dean School of Liberal Arts ... Dr. Frank ELWELL
81 Dean Sch of Math/Sci/Hlth Sci ... Dr. Keith MARTIN
35 Director of Student Development ... Ms. Katy LAUNIUS
08 Director of the Library ... Mr. J. Alan LAWLESS
07 Director of Admissions ... Ms. Joy Lin HALL
06 Registrar ... Vacant
29 Director of Alumni ... Ms. Katelyn TITTLE
04 Exec Assistant to the President ... Ms. Rhonda SPURLOCK
18 Director Physical Plant ... Vacant
19 Director Campus Police ... Mr. Gary BOERGERMANN
26 Director Public Relations ... Mr. David HAMBY
37 Director of Financial Aid ... Ms. Kelly HICKS
91 Director Administrative Computing ... Ms. Cathy BURNS
13 Director Information Technology ... Mr. Brian REEVES
15 Director Employment & Benefits ... Ms. Kristi MALLETT
41 Director of Athletics ... Mr. Ryan ERWIN
39 Director Residential Life ... Ms. Kyla SHORT
23 Director Student Health Clinic ... Ms. Lisa MARTIN
25 Director Research & Special Program ... Mr. Daniel MARANGONI

Rogers State University-Bartlesville (J)

401 South Dewey Avenue, Bartlesville OK 74003
Telephone: (918) 338-8000 Identification: 770379
Accreditation: &NH

† Branch campus of Rogers State University, Claremore, OK.

Rogers State University-Pryor (K)

2155 Highway 69A, Pryor Creek OK 74361
Telephone: (918) 825-6117 Identification: 770380
Accreditation: &NH

† Branch campus of Rogers State University, Claremore, OK.

Rose State College (L)

6420 SE 15th, Midwest City OK 73110-2799
County: Oklahoma FICE Identification: 009185
Unit ID: 207670
Telephone: (405) 733-7311 Carnegie Class: Assoc/Pub-S-SC
FAX Number: (405) 733-7399 Calendar System: Semester
URL: www.rose.edu
Established: 1970 Annual Undergrad Tuition & Fees (In-District): $3,375
Enrollment: 8,452 Coed
Affiliation or Control: State/Local IRS Status: 501(c)3
Highest Offering: Associate Degree
Program: Occupational; 2-Year Principally Bachelor's Creditable
Accreditation: NH, ADNUR, CAHIIM, COARC, DA, DH, MLTAD, RAD

01 President ... Dr. Jeanie WEBB
05 Vice President for Academic Affairs ... Dr. Frances HENDRIX
10 Exec Vice President and CFO ... Dr. Kent LASHLEY
32 VP for Student Affairs & Marketing ... Ms. Tamara PRATT
13 Vice President for Info Technology ... Mr. John PRIMO
103 Vice President for Workforce Devel ... Mr. Stan GREIL
20 Associate VP Academic Affairs ... Dr. Jeff CALDWELL

102 Exec Dir Foundation & Resource Dev ... Ms. Cindy MIKEMAN
15 Exec Dir Human Res/Affirm Act Ofcr ... Ms. Kim DELK
06 Registrar/Dir Admissions & Records ... Ms. Mechelle AITSON-ROESSLER
37 Director Financial Aid ... Mr. Steve DAFFER
26 Director Marketing ... Ms. Ali SEXTON
31 Assoc VP Workforce and Comm Dev ... Dr. Bret WOOD
18 Director Operations ... Mr. Ardie RODGERS
41 Dir Health & Wellness Activities ... Mr. Chris LELAND
09 Assoc VP Inst Effectiveness ... Ms. Isabelle BILLEN
21 Director of Finance ... Mr. Raymond BLANKE
36 Director Spec Svcs/Student Outreach ... Dr. Joanne STAFFORD
25 Dir Grants and Contracts ... Dr. Alan NEITZEL
08 Dean Learning Resources Center ... Mr. Chris MEYER
50 Dean Business & Info Tech Division ... Dr. Mark TIPPIN
54 Dean Engineering & Science Division ... Dr. Wayne JONES
79 Dean Humanities Division ... Ms. Claudia BUCKMASTER
76 Dean Health Sciences Division ... Mr. Dan POINTS
83 Dean Social Sciences Division ... Dr. Juanita ORTIZ

St. Gregory's University (A)

1900 W MacArthur, Shawnee OK 74804-2499
County: Pottawatomie | FICE Identification: 003183
Unit ID: 207689
Telephone: (405) 878-5100 | Carnegie Class: Bac/Diverse
FAX Number: (405) 878-5198 | Calendar System: Semester
URL: www.stgregorys.edu
Established: 1875 | Annual Undergrad Tuition & Fees: $20,280
Enrollment: 649 | Coed
Affiliation or Control: Roman Catholic | IRS Status: 501(c)3
Highest Offering: Master's
Program: Liberal Arts And General; Technical Emphasis
Accreditation: NH

01 President ... Mr. Gregory MAIN
03 Vice President for Operations ... Mr. Harley W. LINGERFELT
05 Provost ... Dr. Richard L. MCDOWELL
26 Vice Pres Marketing & Development ... Ms. Becky M. BEAUCHAMP
10 Chief Financial Officer ... Mr. Joe M. FLECKINGER
88 VP for Mission & Identity ... Rev. Nicholas AST
84 Vice Pres for Enrollment Management ... Vacant
51 Director Continuing Studies ... Dr. Ron DIGGS
83 Academic Dean ... Dr. Ron H. FAULK
32 Interim Dean of Student Life ... Rev. Simeon SPITZ
06 Registrar ... Mrs. Ramah NATION
08 Library Director ... Mrs. Anita SEMTNER
26 Director of Marketing ... Mrs. Amber THEINERT
37 Director of Student Financial Aid ... Ms. Marcia MATHEWS
41 Athletic Director ... Mr. John MARTIN
85 Director of International Office ... Vacant
15 Interim Director of Human Resources ... Mrs. Sherri CONASTER
18 Director Facilities/Physical Plant ... Mr. Mark SAUNDERS
13 Director of Information Systems ... Mr. Douglas D. MCCULLAR
07 Director of CAS Admissions ... Mr. Sean BROWN
07 Director of CCS Admissions ... Mrs. Danielle MALONE
29 Director Alumni Relations ... Mrs. Ashley ANDERSON

St. Gregory's University Tulsa Campus (B)

5801 E 41st Street, Suite 900, Tulsa OK 74135
Telephone: (405) 878-5200 | Identification: 770381
Accreditation: &NH

† Branch campus of St. Gregory's University, Shawnee, OK.

Seminole State College (C)

PO Box 351, Seminole OK 74818-0351
County: Seminole | FICE Identification: 003178
Unit ID: 207740
Telephone: (405) 382-9950 | Carnegie Class: Assoc/Pub-R-M
FAX Number: (405) 382-3122 | Calendar System: Semester
URL: www.sscok.edu
Established: 1931 | Annual Undergrad Tuition & Fees (In-District): $3,809
Enrollment: 1,900 | Coed
Affiliation or Control: State/Local | IRS Status: 501(c)3
Highest Offering: Associate Degree
Program: Occupational; 2-Year Principally Bachelor's Creditable
Accreditation: NH, ADNUR, MLTAD, PHLEB

01 President ... Dr. Jim W. UTTERBACK
05 Vice President Academic Affairs ... Dr. Tom MILLS
10 Vice President Fiscal Affairs ... Mrs. Katherine BENTON
30 Exec VP Institutional Advancement ... Ms. Lana REYNOLDS
32 Vice President of Student Affairs ... Dr. Mark AMES
13 Director Mgmt Information Systems ... Mr. Marc HUNTER
66 Director of Nursing ... Mrs. Donna CHAMBERS
06 Registrar ... Mrs. Corey QUIETT
15 Director Personnel Services ... Mrs. Courtney JONES
18 Chief Facilities/Physical Plant ... Mr. Braden BROWN
26 Coordinator of Media Relations ... Ms. Kristin DUNN
04 Administrative Asst to President ... Ms. Mechell DOWNEY
22 Dir Affirmative Action/EEO ... Mr. Dan FACTOR
38 Director Student Counseling ... Mr. Justin STREATER

Southeastern Oklahoma State University (D)

1405 N 4th Avenue, Durant OK 74701-3330
County: Bryan | FICE Identification: 003179
Unit ID: 207847
Telephone: (580) 745-2000 | Carnegie Class: Master's M
FAX Number: N/A | Calendar System: Semester
URL: www.se.edu
Established: 1909 | Annual Undergrad Tuition & Fees (In-State): $6,163
Enrollment: 4,698 | Coed
Affiliation or Control: State | IRS Status: 501(c)3
Highest Offering: Master's
Program: Liberal Arts And General; Teacher Preparatory; Professional
Accreditation: NH, AAB, BUS, CACREP, MUS, TED

01 President ... Mr. Sean BURRAGE
05 Vice Pres Acad Affairs ... Dr. Douglas MCMILLAN
10 Vice President Business Affairs ... Mr. Ross WALKUP
32 Vice President Student Affairs ... Ms. Sharon ROBINSON
20 Asst VP Academic Affs/Instruction ... Dr. Bryon CLARK
20 Executive Dean of Academic Affairs ... Dr. Lucretia SCOUFOS
07 Assoc Dean Admissions/Registrar ... Ms. Kristie LUKE
88 Assoc Dean Academic Services ... Mr. Tim BOATMUN
13 Exec Dir of Information Technology ... Mr. Dan MOORE
30 Vice President of Univ Advancement ... Mr. Kyle STAFFORD
37 Director Student Financial Aid ... Mr. Tony LEHRLING
36 Director of Career Management Ctr ... Mr. Scott HENSLEY
08 Library Director ... Ms. Sharon MORRISON
51 Director Continuing Education ... Mr. Scott HENSLEY
41 Director of Athletics ... Mr. Keith BAXTER
26 Dir Univ Comm/Spec Asst Pres ... Mr. Alan BURTON
21 Director Finance/Controller ... Ms. Kay Lynn ROBERTS
18 Director Facilities/Physical Plant ... Mr. Eddie HARBIN
28 Special Asst to the Pres/Diversity ... Dr. Claire STUBBLEFIELD
96 Purchasing Agent ... Mrs. Carol COATS
40 Book Store Manager ... Ms. Jackie CODNER
29 Director Alumni Relations ... Ms. Stephanie SHADE-DAVISON
106 Dir Online Education/E-learning ... Ms. Christala SMITH
19 Director Security/Safety ... Mr. Stacy BALLEW
22 Dir Affirmative Action/EEO ... Dr. Claire STUBBLEFIELD
39 Director Student Housing ... Dr. Kelly D'ARCY
35 Dean of Student Life ... Ms. Liz MCCRAW

Southern Nazarene University (E)

6729 NW 39 Expressway, Bethany OK 73008-2694
County: Oklahoma | FICE Identification: 003149
Unit ID: 206862
Telephone: (405) 789-6400 | Carnegie Class: Master's L
FAX Number: (405) 491-6381 | Calendar System: Semester
URL: www.snu.edu
Established: 1899 | Annual Undergrad Tuition & Fees: $23,000
Enrollment: 2,163 | Coed
Affiliation or Control: Church Of The Nazarene | IRS Status: 501(c)3
Highest Offering: Master's
Program: Liberal Arts And General; Teacher Preparatory; Professional; Business Emphasis
Accreditation: NH, ACBSP, CAATE, MUS, NURSE, TED

01 President ... Dr. Loren P. GRESHAM
05 Vice Pres Academic Affairs ... Dr. Melany KYZER
10 Vice President Financial Affairs ... Dr. Scott STRAWN
30 VP of Univ Advance & Church Rels ... Dr. Terry TOLER
32 Vice President Student Development ... Dr. Mike REDWINE
42 University Pastor ... Dr. Blair SPINDLE
84 Vice Pres of Enrollment Management ... Dr. Linda CANTWELL
20 Dean College of Humanities ... Dr. Steve BETTS
81 Dean College of Sci & Health ... Dr. Mark WINSLOW
06 Registrar ... Mr. Charles CHITWOOD
37 Director Student Financial Aid ... Ms. Diana LEE
35 Director Student Affairs ... Mrs. Marian REDWINE
38 Director Student Counseling ... Mrs. Kimberly CAMPBELL
36 Director Career Planning/Placement ... Mrs. Angela RHODES
08 Director Learning Resources Center ... Prof. Katie KING
29 Director Alumni Relations ... Vacant
13 Director Information Technology ... Vacant
88 Director Academic Services ... Mr. Wes LEE
09 Director Institutional Research ... Dr. Randy ZABEL
58 Dean Col of Grad & Prof Study ... Dr. Davis BERRYMAN
66 Director of Nursing ... Dr. Katie SIGLER
15 Director Human Resources ... Mr. Chris PETERSON
18 Director of Physical Plant ... Mr. Ron LESTER
24 Director Network ... Mrs. Chichi FREELANDER
26 Director Communications & Marketing ... Mrs. Eunice TRENT
40 Bookstore Manager ... Mr. Reggie COLEMAN
41 Athletic Director ... Mr. Bobby MARTIN
88 Dean College of Teach & Learn ... Dr. Dennis WILLIAMS
04 Administrative Asst to President ... Mrs. Rita MCCLAIN
19 Director Security/Safety ... Mr. Glen HOLCOMB
25 Chief Contracts/Grants Admin ... Dr. Gwen HACKLER
39 Director Student Housing ... Mrs. Stacey CLOWERS
44 Director Annual or Planned Giving ... Mr. Todd BRANT

Southwestern Christian University (F)

PO Box 340, 7210 NW 39th Expressway, Bethany OK 73008-0340
County: Oklahoma | FICE Identification: 003180
Unit ID: 207856
Telephone: (405) 789-7661 | Carnegie Class: Bac/Diverse
FAX Number: (405) 495-0078 | Calendar System: Semester
URL: www.swcu.edu
Established: 1946 | Annual Undergrad Tuition & Fees: $15,710
Enrollment: 813 | Coed
Affiliation or Control: Pentecostal Holiness Church | IRS Status: 501(c)3
Highest Offering: Master's
Program: Liberal Arts And General
Accreditation: NH

01 President ... Dr. Reggies WENYIKA
05 Provost & VP Academic Affairs ... Dr. Connie SJORBERG
10 Vice President for Fiscal Affairs ... Mr. Wallace O. HAMILTON
32 Vice President for Student Life ... Mr. Brad DAVIS
41 Vice President of Athletics ... Mr. Mark ARTHUR
37 Director of Financial Aid ... Mrs. Kellye JOHNSON
07 Director of Admissions & Enrollment ... Ms. Rita PALMER
08 Director of Library Services ... Vacant
06 Registrar ... Mrs. Sherri HENDRIX
107 Dean of Professional Studies & Grad ... Dr. Adrian HINKLE
49 Dean of Arts & Sciences ... Vacant
18 Director of Plant/Property Mgmt ... Mr. Greg DAVALT
26 Director of Sports Information/PR ... Mr. Matthew STEPHENS
13 Director of Information Technology ... Mr. Daniel DRESSLER
106 Dean of Online Educ/Adult Studies ... Dr. Julian COWART
108 Dean of Institutional Effectiveness ... Dr. Dana OWENS-DELONG
15 Director of Employee Relations ... Ms. Shawna SALKIL
30 Chief Development Officer ... Mr. Joe BLACKWELL
84 Director Enrollment Management ... Mr. Kyron SMOOT

Southwestern Oklahoma State University (G)

100 Campus Drive, Weatherford OK 73096-3098
County: Custer | FICE Identification: 003181
Unit ID: 207865
Telephone: (580) 772-6611 | Carnegie Class: Master's M
FAX Number: (580) 774-3795 | Calendar System: Semester
URL: www.swosu.edu
Established: 1901 | Annual Undergrad Tuition & Fees (In-State): $5,820
Enrollment: 4,994 | Coed
Affiliation or Control: State | IRS Status: 501(c)3
Highest Offering: First Professional Degree
Program: Liberal Arts And General; Teacher Preparatory; Professional
Accreditation: NH, CAATE, CAHIIM, ENGT, IACBE, MUS, NAIT, NUR, OTA, PHAR, PTAA, TED

01 President ... Dr. Randy L. BEUTLER
10 Exec Vice Pres Business and Finance ... Mr. Thomas W. FAGAN
05 VP for Academic Affairs/Provost ... Dr. James D. SOUTH
32 VP Student Affairs/Assoc Provost ... Dr. Ruth BOYD
20 Assoc Provost Acad Affairs ... Dr. Monica VARNER
26 VP for Marketing/Public Relations ... Mr. Brian D. ADLER
30 Asst to Pres for Inst Advancement ... Ms. Lynne F. THURMAN
96 Dir Business Affairs/Comptroller ... Ms. Brenda K. BURGESS
35 Dean of Students/Dir Student Act ... Ms. Cynthia R. DOUGHERTY
13 Dir Information Technology Services ... Ms. Karen KLEIN
06 Registrar ... Mr. Shamus MOORE
08 Library Director ... Mr. Jason M. DUPREE
37 Director Student Financial Services ... Mr. Jerome L. WICHERT
15 Dir Human Resources/Affirm Action ... Mr. David MISAK
84 Dir Enrollment Mgmt/Career Svcs ... Mr. Todd T. BOYD
41 Athletic Director ... Mr. Todd A. THURMAN
06 Registrar Sayre Campus ... Ms. Terry L. BILLEY
37 Dir Financial Svcs/Sayre Campus ... Mr. Ron KISTLER
38 Director Counseling Services ... Ms. Kim K. LIEBSCHER
18 Director Physical Plant ... Mr. Rick SKINNER
57 Manager Fine Arts Center ... Mr. Kyle J. BARTEL
36 Career Services Coordinator ... Ms. Savannath SCHONES
58 Dean College of Prof/Grad Studies ... Dr. Ken G. ROSE
49 Actg Dean College of Arts/Sciences ... Dr. Peter GRANT
67 Dean College of Pharmacy ... Dr. Dennis F. THOMPSON
12 Dean College of Assoc/Applied Prog ... Ms. Sherron K. MANNING
76 Associate Dean Sch of Allied Health ... Vacant
53 Assoc Dean Sch of Behavioral Sci ... Dr. L. Chad KINDER
50 Assoc Dean School of Business/Tech ... Dr. Patsy PARKER
66 Associate Dean School of Nursing ... Dr. Barbara A. PATTERSON

† Campus at Sayre offers a two-year degree and is regionally accredited (NH) under parent institution.

Southwestern Oklahoma State University-Sayre (H)

409 E Mississippi, Sayre OK 73662
Telephone: (580) 928-5533 | Identification: 770382
Accreditation: &NH, MLTAB, RAD

† Branch campus of Southwestern Oklahoma State University, Weatherford, OK.

Spartan College of Aeronautics and Technology (I)

8820 E Pine Street, Tulsa OK 74115
County: Tulsa | FICE Identification: 007678
Unit ID: 207254
Telephone: (918) 836-6886 | Carnegie Class: Spec/Tech
FAX Number: (918) 831-5287 | Calendar System: Other
URL: www.spartan.edu
Established: 1928 | Annual Undergrad Tuition & Fees: $16,395
Enrollment: 849 | Coed
Affiliation or Control: Proprietary | IRS Status: Proprietary
Highest Offering: Baccalaureate
Program: Occupational; 2-Year Principally Bachelor's Creditable; Technical Emphasis
Accreditation: ACCSC

00 CEO ... Mr. Peter H. HARRIS
10 CFO/Vice President Finance ... Mr. Jason LICAR
01 President ... Mr. Ryan GOERTZEN
11 Vice President Administration ... Mr. Dean RILING

Tulsa Community College (A)

6111 E Skelly Drive, Tulsa OK 74135-6198

County: Tulsa
FICE Identification: 009763
Unit ID: 207935
Telephone: (918) 595-7000
Carnegie Class: Assoc/Pub-U-MC
FAX Number: (918) 595-7910
Calendar System: Semester
URL: www.tulsacc.edu
Established: 1968
Annual Undergrad Tuition & Fees (In-State): $2,729
Enrollment: 17,861
Coed
Affiliation or Control: State
IRS Status: 501(c)3
Highest Offering: Associate Degree
Program: Occupational; 2-Year Principally Bachelor's Creditable
Accreditation: NH, ADNUR, CAHIIM, COARC, CVT, DH, MAC, MLTAD, OTA, PHLEB, PTAA, RAD

01 President/CEO .... Dr. Leigh GOODSON
100 Special Assistant to the President .... Dr. Bill IVEY
05 Sr VP and Chief Academic Officer .... Dr. Cynthia HESS
10 Chief Financial Officer .... Mr. Shane NETHERTON
26 Vice President External Affairs .... Ms. Lauren F. BROOKEY
11 Vice President Administration .... Mr. Sean A. WEINS
32 Assoc Vice Pres Student Affairs .... Dr. Jan L. CLAYTON
108 Assoc Vice Pres Inst Effectiveness .... Dr. Kevin DAVID
15 Assoc Vice Pres Human Resources .... Ms. Patricia L. FISCHER
12 Provost Southeast Campus .... Dr. Brett S. CAMPBELL
12 Provost Northeast Campus .... Dr. John GIBSON
12 Provost Metro Campus .... Dr. Greg STONE
12 Provost West Campus .... Dr. Peggy D. DYER
12 Dean Community Campuses .... Dr. Paul WILLYARD
08 Dean Libraries .... Ms. Paula SETTOON
28 Dean of Diversity/Civic Engagement .... Vacant
51 Dean Corporate/Continuing Educ .... Mr. Anthony BRETTI
84 Dean Enrollment Management .... Ms. Traci HECK
18 Director Physical Facilities .... Mr. Steven COX
37 Director Financial Aid .... Ms. Karen JEFFERS
96 Dir Purch & Inventory Control .... Mr. Bill CREECH
09 Dir Institutional Research/Assess .... Dr. Jennifer IVIE
19 Director Campus Police .... Mr. Gene WIDEMAN
27 Dir Communications/Production .... Ms. Susie A. BROWN
21 Director Administrative Services .... Dr. Frederick D. ARTIS
92 Director of Honors Program .... Ms. Susan ONEAL
30 Director Development .... Ms. Eileen KENNEY
25 Director Sponsored Programs .... Ms. Julie HALL
104 Director Global Learning .... Dr. Douglas PRICE
105 Director Web Services .... Ms. Kimberly WEBBER
106 Director Online Learning .... Mr. Randy G. DOMINGUEZ

Tulsa Community College Metro Campus (B)

909 South Boston Avenue, Tulsa OK 74119

Telephone: (918) 595-7224
Identification: 770383
Accreditation: &NH

† Branch campus of Tulsa Community College, Tulsa, OK.

Tulsa Community College Northeast Campus (C)

3727 East Apache Street, Tulsa OK 74115

Telephone: (918) 595-7524
Identification: 770384
Accreditation: &NH

† Branch campus of Tulsa Community College, Tulsa, OK.

Tulsa Community College Southeast Campus (D)

10300 East 81st Street, Tulsa OK 74133

Telephone: (918) 595-7724
Identification: 770385
Accreditation: &NH

† Branch campus of Tulsa Community College, Tulsa, OK.

Tulsa Community College West Campus (E)

7505 W 41st Street South, Tulsa OK 74102

Telephone: (918) 595-8100
Identification: 770386
Accreditation: &NH

† Branch campus of Tulsa Community College, Tulsa, OK.

Tulsa Welding School (F)

2545 E 11th Street, Tulsa OK 74104-3909

County: Tulsa
FICE Identification: 009618
Unit ID: 207962
Telephone: (918) 587-6789
Carnegie Class: Assoc/PrivFP
FAX Number: (918) 587-8170
Calendar System: Other
URL: www.weldingschool.com
Established: 1949
Annual Undergrad Tuition & Fees: $19,405
Enrollment: 1,220
Coed
Affiliation or Control: Proprietary
IRS Status: Proprietary
Highest Offering: Associate Degree
Program: Occupational
Accreditation: ACCSC

01 Campus President .... Mr. Mark STAATS
05 Academic Dean .... Mr. Brian SEITZ
07 Senior Director of Admissions .... Mr. Joe MCKINNEY
37 Director of Financial Aid .... Mrs. Teresa FRANKLIN
36 Regional Director of Career Service .... Mr. Charles HARBIN

University of Central Oklahoma (G)

100 N University Drive, Edmond OK 73034-5209

County: Oklahoma
FICE Identification: 003152
Unit ID: 206941
Telephone: (405) 974-2000
Carnegie Class: Master's L
FAX Number: (405) 359-5841
Calendar System: Semester
URL: www.uco.edu
Established: 1890
Annual Undergrad Tuition & Fees (In-State): $5,812
Enrollment: 16,840
Coed
Affiliation or Control: State
IRS Status: 501(c)3
Highest Offering: Master's
Program: Liberal Arts And General; Teacher Preparatory; Professional
Accreditation: NH, ACBSP, ART, CAATE, CIDA, CS, DIETD, DIETI, ENG, EXSC, FUSER, MUS, NUR, SP, TED

01 President .... Dr. Don BETZ
03 Vice President of Administration .... Dr. Don CHRUSCIEL
05 Provost/Vice Pres Academic Affairs .... Dr. John BARTHELL
32 Vice President Student Affairs .... Dr. Myron POPE
13 Vice President Information Tech .... Dr. Cynthia ROLFE
26 Vice Pres University Relations .... Mr. Charlie JOHNSON
88 Vice Pres Public Affairs .... Dr. Mark KINDERS
102 Vice Pres Development/Foundation .... Mrs. Anne HOLZBERLEIN
11 Assoc VP Planning & Budget .... Ms. Patti NEUHOLD
06 Associate Vice President/Registrar .... Dr. Adam JOHNSON
20 Assoc VP Academic Affairs .... Dr. Charlotte SIMMONS
20 Assoc VP Inst Effectiveness .... Dr. Gary STEWARD
10 Asst VP Financial Operations .... Ms. Lisa HARPER
18 Asst Vice Pres Facilities Mgt .... Mr. Mark RODOLF
35 Asst Vice Pres Student Affairs .... Mr. Cole STANLEY
23 Asst VP Wellness/Sports .... Mr. Mark HERRIN
21 Asst VP Business Enterprises .... Mr. Kevin FREEMAN
88 Operations Manager Student Affairs .... Ms. Amy ROGALSKY
41 Athletic Director .... Mr. Joe MULLER
09 Exec Dir Institutional Research .... Ms. Cindy BOLING
08 Exec Director University Libraries .... Dr. Habib TABATABAI
37 Director Student Financial Services .... Ms. Susan PRATER
29 Director Alumni Relations .... Vacant
85 Exec Dir Global Affairs .... Dr. Dennis DUNHAM
39 Exec Dir Business Enterprises .... Dr. Josh OVEROCKER
19 Exec Dir Public Safety/Trans .... Mr. Jeff HARP
15 Asst VP Human Resources .... Ms. Diane FEINBERG
88 Exec Director Leadership Central .... Dr. Jarrett JOBE
07 Dir of Undergraduate Admissions .... Mr. Dallas CALDWELL
28 Director of Diversity & Inclusion .... Ms. MeShawn CONLEY
96 Director of Purchasing .... Mr. David YOUNG
43 Senior Legal Counsel .... Dr. Brad MORELLI
50 Dean of Business Administration .... Dr. Mickey HEPNER
53 Dean College Education .... Dr. James MACHELL
49 int Dean College of Liberal Arts .... Dr. Joan LUXENBURG
81 Int Dean College Math/Science .... Dr. Wei CHEN
58 Dean Graduate Studies .... Dr. Richard BERNARD
57 Dean College Fine Arts & Design .... Dr. Pamela WASHINGTON

University of Oklahoma Health Sciences Center (H)

1000 Stanton L. Young Boulevard, Oklahoma City OK 73117

Telephone: (405) 271-4000
FICE Identification: 005889
Accreditation: &NH, #ARCPA, AUD, DENT, DH, DIETC, DIETD, DIETI, DMS, ENGR, HSA, IPSY, MED, NMT, NUR, NURSE, OT, PDPSY, PH, PHAR, PTA, RAD, RADDOS, RTT, SP

† Regional accreditation is carried under the parent institution in Norman, OK.

University of Oklahoma Norman Campus (I)

660 Parrington Oval, Norman OK 73019-3070

County: Cleveland
FICE Identification: 003184
Unit ID: 207500
Telephone: (405) 325-0311
Carnegie Class: RU/VH
FAX Number: (405) 325-7605
Calendar System: Semester
URL: www.ou.edu
Established: 1890
Annual Undergrad Tuition & Fees (In-State): $7,782
Enrollment: 27,278
Coed
Affiliation or Control: State
IRS Status: 501(c)3
Highest Offering: Doctorate
Program: Liberal Arts And General; Teacher Preparatory; Professional
Accreditation: NH, AAB, BUS, BUSA, CIDA, CONST, COPSY, CS, ENG, JOUR, LAW, LIB, LSAR, MUS, PLNG, SW, TED, THEA

01 President .... Mr. David L. BOREN
10 VP Administration & Finance .... Mr. Nicholas S. HATHAWAY
101 VP Univ Gov/Exec Secy Bd of Regents .... Dr. Chris A. PURCELL
05 Senior Vice President/Provost .... Dr. Kyle HARPER
43 VP of Univ/General Counsel .... Mr. Anil V. GOLLAHALLI
32 Vice President for Student Affairs .... Mr. Clarke A. STROUD
30 Vice Pres for University Devel .... Mr. Jim HALL, III
51 VP Univ Outreach/Dn Col Lib Std .... Dr. James P. PAPPAS
58 Dean Grad College .... Dr. T. H. Lee WILLIAMS
46 Vice President for Research .... Dr. Kelvin K. DROEGEMEIER
26 Vice President for Public Affairs .... Ms. Catherine F. BISHOP
13 Assoc VP/Chief Information Ofcr .... Ms. Loretta M. EARLY
86 Vice Pres for Governmental Relation .... Mr. W. Scott MASON, IV
20 Associate Provost/Dir of Acad Integ .... Dr. Gregory M. HEISER
20 Acting Assoc Prov for Acad Advising .... Michele E. NABONNE
09 Assoc Provost/Dir Inst Research .... Ms. Susannah B. LIVINGOOD
06 Registrar/VP Enroll/Stdnt Fin Svcs .... Mr. Matthew W. HAMILTON
35 AVP/Director Student Life .... Ms. Kristen N. PARTRIDGE
21 Assoc VP Administration & Finance .... Mr. B. Burr MILLSAP
21 Assoc VP Admin & Finance .... Mr. Chris KUWITZKY
29 Assoc VP Alum & Dev/Ex Dir Alum Asn .... Mr. Jean Paul AUDAS
18 Director Facilities Management .... Mr. Brian F. ELLIS
39 Director of Housing & Food Services .... Mr. David L. ANNIS
41 Director of Athletics .... Mr. Joseph R. CASTIGLIONE
21 Controller .... Ms. Terri B. PINKSTON
23 AVP/Director Goddard Health Center .... Dr. William R. WAYNE
36 Director Career Services .... Ms. Robin E. HUSTON
19 Chief of Police .... Ms. Elizabeth G. WOOLLEN
15 AVP/Director of Human Resources .... Mr. Les J. HOVEN
22 Equal Opportunity Officer .... Mr. Bobby J. MASON
07 Director of Admissions/Recruitment .... Mr. Jeffrey J. BLAHNIK
25 Assoc VP for Research Services .... Ms. Andrea D. DEATON
85 Dir Intl Student Services .... Ms. Robyn D. ROJAS
104 Director Education Abroad .... Ms. Laura R. BRUNSON
37 Director of Financial Aid .... Ms. Caryn L. PACHECO
48 Dean College of Architecture .... Dr. Charles W. GRAHAM
49 Dean College Arts & Sciences .... Dr. Kelly R. DAMPHOUSSE
53 Dean Jeannine Rainbolt Col of Educ .... Dr. Gregg A. GARN
54 Dean College of Engineering .... Dr. Thomas L. LANDERS
57 Int Dn Weitzenhoffer Col Fine Arts .... Ms. Mary Margaret HOLT
61 VP/Dean College of Law .... Mr. Joseph HARROZ, JR.
62 Dean University Libraries .... Mr. Richard E. LUCE
65 VP/Dn Col Atmospheric/Geographic Sc .... Dr. Berrien MOORE, III
50 Dean Price Col of Business .... Mr. Daniel W. PULLIN
92 Dean McClendon Honors College .... Dr. David H. RAY
60 Int Dn Gaylord Col Journ/Mass Comm .... Mr. Ed KELLEY
89 Dean University College .... Dr. Nicole J. CAMPBELL
65 Dean Mewborne Col of Earth & Energy .... Dr. J. Michael STICE
82 Dean Col Intl Studies .... Dr. Suzette R. GRILLOT
88 VP for the University Community .... Mr. Jabar SHUMATE
84 AVP/Enrollment/Student Finan Svcs .... Mr. Bradley T. BURNETT

† Tuition is based on 30 credit hour per year.

University of Oklahoma Schusterman Center (J)

4502 E 41st Street, Tulsa OK 74135-2512

Telephone: (918) 660-3000
Identification: 770387
Accreditation: &NH, ARCPA, OT

† Branch campus of University of Oklahoma Norman Campus, Norman, OK.

University of Phoenix Oklahoma City Campus (K)

3 Broadway Exec Pk, 6501 N Broadway, Oklahoma City OK 73116-8244

Telephone: (405) 842-8007
Identification: 770221
Accreditation: &NH, ACBSP

† No longer accepting campus-based students.

University of Science and Arts of Oklahoma (L)

1727 W Alabama, Chickasha OK 73018-5322

County: Grady
FICE Identification: 003167
Unit ID: 207722
Telephone: (405) 224-3140
Carnegie Class: Bac/A&S
FAX Number: (405) 574-1220
Calendar System: Trimester
URL: www.usao.edu
Established: 1908
Annual Undergrad Tuition & Fees (In-State): $6,570
Enrollment: 904
Coed
Affiliation or Control: State
IRS Status: 501(c)3
Highest Offering: Baccalaureate
Program: Liberal Arts And General; Teacher Preparatory
Accreditation: NH, MUS, TED

01 President .... Dr. John H. FEAVER
05 VP for Academic Affairs .... Dr. Krista MAXSON
10 Vice Pres for Business & Finance .... Mr. Mike D. COPONITI
84 Vice Pres for Enrollment Management .... Ms. Monica TREVINO
30 Vice Pres University Advancement .... Dr. Michael NEALEIGH
13 VP for Information Services & Tech .... Ms. Lynn BOYCE
06 Registrar/Dir of Enrollment/Records .... Ms. Chelsea PHILLIPS
08 Director of Nash Library .... Ms. Kelly BROWN
37 Director of Financial Aid .... Ms. Laura I. COPONITI
32 Dean of Students/Dir Student Svcs .... Ms. Nancy HUGHES
26 Director Media/Community Relations .... Ms. Kelly ARNOLD
29 Director of Alumni Development .... Mr. Eric FEUERBORN
18 Director of Physical Plant .... Mr. Mike COPONITI
14 Director of Data Processing .... Ms. Lynn BOYCE
09 Director of Institutional Research .... Mr. George GUAJARDO
15 Director Personnel Services .... Mr. Mike COPONITI
07 Acting Director of Admissions .... Ms. Monica TREVINO
38 Director Student Counseling .... Ms. Misty STEELE
49 Chair Div of Arts & Humanities .... Dr. Stephen WEBER
50 Chair Div of Business & Social Sci .... Dr. James WELCH
53 Chair Division of Education .... Dr. Vicki FERGUSON
81 Chair Div of Science/Physical Educ .... Dr. J.C SANDERS
88 Chair Interdisciplinary Studies .... Dr. Jennifer LONG
19 Director Security/Safety .... Mr. Chris BASCO
41 Athletic Director .... Mr. Brisco MCPHERSON

University of Tulsa (M)

800 S Tucker, Tulsa OK 74104

County: Tulsa
FICE Identification: 003185
Unit ID: 207971
Telephone: (918) 631-2000
Carnegie Class: DRU

FAX Number: (918) 631-2033 Calendar System: Semester
URL: www.utulsa.edu
Established: 1894 Annual Undergrad Tuition & Fees: $39,571
Enrollment: 4,682 Coed
Affiliation or Control: Independent Non-Profit IRS Status: 501(c)3
Highest Offering: Doctorate
Program: Liberal Arts And General; Teacher Preparatory; Professional
Accreditation: NH, BUS, CAATE, CLPSY, CS, ENG, LAW, MUS, NUR, SP, TEAC

01 President ... Dr. Steadman UPHAM
10 Exec Vice President & Treasurer ... Mr. Kevan C. BUCK
05 Provost/Vice Pres Academic Affairs ... Dr. Roger N. BLAIS
45 Vice Pres Institutional Advancement ... Dr. Kayla ACEBO
84 VP Enrollment & Stdnt Svcs ... Mr. Earl JOHNSON
41 VP & Athletic Director ... Dr. Derrick GRAGG
13 VP Info Services & CIO ... Mr. Richard KEARNS
88 VP Museum Affs/Dir Helmerich Center ... Dr. Duane KING
86 VP Public Affairs/COO Gilcrease ... Ms. Susan NEAL
108 Sr Vice Provost & Assoc VP ... Ms. Winona M. TANAKA
46 Vice Prov Research/Dean Grad School ... Dr. Janet A. HAGGERTY
28 VP Diversity & Engagement ... Ms. Jacqueline H. CALDWELL
104 Vice Provost Global Education ... Dr. Cheryl MATHERLY
09 Assoc VP Institutional Research ... Mr. John BURY
42 University Chaplain ... Dr. Jeffrey FRANCIS
49 Dean Arts & Sciences ... Dr. Kalpana MISRA
50 Dean Business Administration ... Dr. A. Gale SULLENBERGER
54 Dean Engineering/Natural Sciences ... Dr. James R. SOREM, JR.
61 Dean Law ... Ms. Lyn ENTZEROTH
08 RM & Ida McFarlin Dean of Library ... Mr. Adrian W. ALEXANDER
30 Assoc VP Institutional Advancement ... Ms. Amy ENGLAND
06 Registrar ... Ms. Ginna V. LANGSTON
15 Associate VP Human Resources ... Mr. Wayne PAULISON
22 Dir Acad Support/504 Coordinator ... Dr. Tawny TAYLOR
18 Assoc VP Operations/Physical Plant ... Mr. Robert SHIPLEY
21 Assoc VP & Controller ... Mr. Michael D. THESENVITZ
07 Assoc VP Enrollment Dean Admission ... Ms. Barbara ADKINS
32 Assoc VP Enrollment Dean Students ... Ms. Yolanda D. TAYLOR
39 Assoc VP Director Housing ... Ms. Melissa H. FRANCE
85 Dean International Students ... Ms. Pamela A. SMITH
51 Dean Lifelong Learning ... Dr. J. Phillip APPLEGATE
62 Assoc Dean McFarlin Library ... Ms. Francine J. FISK
23 Director Health Center ... Ms. Stephanie FELL
38 Director Counseling & Psych Svcs ... Dr. Thomas J. BRIAN
19 Director Campus Security ... Mr. Joseph F. TIMMONS
29 Exec Director Alumni Relations ... Ms. Amy M. FREIBERGER
36 Director Career Services ... Ms. Shelly HOLLY
37 Director Student Financial Svcs ... Ms. Vicki A. HENDRICKSON
96 Director Purchasing ... Mr. Jerry R. HOLLOWAY
90 Dir Academic Tech Services ... Ms. Janet CAIRNS
91 Dir ERP Operations ... Mr. Martin PAGE
31 Assoc Dean Community Relations ... Mr. Michael MILLS
26 Dir Marketing & Communications ... Ms. Mona CHAMBERLIN
105 Exec Dir Digital Communication ... Mr. Matt CASTEEL
101 Secretary Board of Trustees ... Ms. June E. BROWN
04 Sr Admin Associate to President ... Ms. Susan LAYMAN

Vatterott College-Oklahoma City (A)

5537 NW Expressway, Warr Acres OK 73132-5230
Telephone: (405) 945-0088 Identification: 666061
Accreditation: ACCSC

† Branch campus of Vatterott College, Quincy, IL.

Vatterott College-Tulsa (B)

4343 S 118th E Avenue, Ste A, Tulsa OK 74146-4406
Telephone: (918) 835-8288 Identification: 666102
Accreditation: ACCSC

† Branch campus of Vatterott College-NorthPark, Berkeley, MO.

Virginia College (C)

5124 South Peoria Avenue, Tulsa OK 74105
Telephone: (918) 960-5400 Identification: 770825
Accreditation: ACICS

† Branch campus of Virginia College, Birmingham, AL.

Western Oklahoma State College (D)

2801 N Main Street, Altus OK 73521-1397
County: Jackson FICE Identification: 003146
Unit ID: 208035
Telephone: (580) 477-2000 Carnegie Class: Assoc/Pub-R-M
FAX Number: (580) 477-7777 Calendar System: Semester
URL: www.wosc.edu
Established: 1926 Annual Undergrad Tuition & Fees (In-State): $3,280
Enrollment: 1,460 Coed
Affiliation or Control: State IRS Status: 501(c)3
Highest Offering: Associate Degree
Program: Occupational; 2-Year Principally Bachelor's Creditable
Accreditation: NH, ADNUR, RAD

01 President ... Dr. Phil BIRDINE
04 Admin Secretary to the President ... Ms. Briar JENKINS
05 VP for Academic & Student Supp Svcs ... Ms. Lisa GREENLEE
10 Vice President for Business Affairs ... Ms. Tricia LATHAM
49 Dean Arts & Sciences ... Ms. Jeri DULANEY
32 Vice Pres Student Support Services ... Mr. Chad WIGINTON
72 Dean of Technical Education ... Ms. Chrystal OVERTON
09 Dir of Institutional Effectiveness ... Mr. Justin SMITH
13 Chief Info Technology Officer ... Mr. Steve PRATER
26 Dir Public Information/Marketing ... Ms. Judith NORTON
07 Director of Admissions & Registrar ... Ms. Lana SCOTT
37 Director of Student Financial Aid ... Ms. Myrna J. CROSS
29 Dir Development/Alumni Relations ... Ms. Lora Lea PICKERING
41 Director Athletics ... Mr. Bob PEARSON
62 Director of Learning Resources ... Ms. Suzanne ROOKER
15 Director Personnel Services ... Ms. April NELSON
18 Director Physical Plant ... Mr. Doyle JENCKS
40 Bookstore Manager ... Ms. Kass DEWEESE
38 Counselor ... Ms. April DILL
81 Science Instructor ... Mr. Don SCROGGINS
88 History Instructor ... Mr. Mickey GRAHAM

Wright Career College (E)

2219 W 1240 Service Road, Suite 124,
Oklahoma City OK 73159
Telephone: (405) 681-2300 Identification: 770763
Accreditation: ACICS

† Branch campus of Wright Career College, Overland Park, KS.

Wright Career College (F)

4908 S Sheridan Road, Tulsa OK 74135
Telephone: (918) 628-7700 Identification: 770762
Accreditation: ACICS

† Branch campus of Wright Career College, Overland Park, KS.

OREGON

American College of Healthcare Sciences (G)

5940 SW Hood Avenue, Portland OR 97239-3719
County: Multnomah FICE Identification: 041944
Unit ID: 443599
Telephone: (503) 244-0726 Carnegie Class: Not Classified
FAX Number: (503) 244-0727 Calendar System: Semester
URL: www.achs.edu
Established: 1978 Annual Undergrad Tuition & Fees: $10,560
Enrollment: 603 Coed
Affiliation or Control: Proprietary IRS Status: Proprietary
Highest Offering: Master's
Program: Occupational; 2-Year Principally Bachelor's Creditable; Professional
Accreditation: DEAC

01 President/CEO ... Dorene PETERSEN
11 Chief Operating Officer ... Tracey ABELL
09 Chief Institutional Ofcr/Compliance ... Erika YIGZAW
10 Chief Financial Officer ... Debbie PARIGIAN
32 Dean of Students ... Heather BALEY
07 Dean of Admissions ... Amy SWINEHART
06 Registrar ... Jennifer MORRISON
26 Chief Marketing Officer ... Kate HARMON

The Art Institute of Portland (H)

1122 NW Davis Street, Portland OR 97209-2911
County: Multnomah FICE Identification: 007819
Unit ID: 208239
Telephone: (503) 228-6528 Carnegie Class: Spec/Arts
FAX Number: (503) 228-4227 Calendar System: Quarter
URL: www.artinstitutes.edu/portland
Established: 1963 Annual Undergrad Tuition & Fees: $18,000
Enrollment: 1,111 Coed
Affiliation or Control: Proprietary IRS Status: Proprietary
Highest Offering: Baccalaureate
Program: Occupational; Liberal Arts And General
Accreditation: NW, CIDA

01 President ... Dr. Gregg CROWE
05 Dean of Academic Affairs ... Dr. Anthony PIRES
32 Dean of Student Affairs ... Mr. Jason CLARY
06 Registrar ... Ms. Yvonne PETERSON
07 Director of Admission ... Ms. Christi CALZEY
08 Head Librarian ... Ms. Jennifer COX
37 Financial Aid Director ... Ms. Lauren PATTERSON

† Granted candidacy at the Master's level.

Birthingway College of Midwifery (I)

12113 SE Foster Road, Portland OR 97266-4042
County: Multnomah FICE Identification: 036683
Unit ID: 442949
Telephone: (503) 760-3131 Carnegie Class: Spec/Health
FAX Number: (503) 760-3332 Calendar System: Quarter
URL: www.birthingway.edu
Established: 1993 Annual Undergrad Tuition & Fees: $20,449
Enrollment: 76 Coed
Affiliation or Control: Independent Non-Profit IRS Status: 501(c)3
Highest Offering: Baccalaureate
Program: 2-Year Principally Bachelor's Creditable; Professional
Accreditation: MEAC

01 President ... Ms. Holly SCHOLLES
03 Faculty Coordinator ... Ms. Nancy LONGATAN
05 Academic Coordinator ... Ms. Nichole REDING
10 Finance Coordinator ... Ms. Elizabeth BRAGG
37 Financial Aid Officer ... Ms. Stacey MAURER
06 Registrar ... Ms. Dawn BAKER
88 Midwifery Program Coordinator ... Ms. Rhonda RAY
88 Lactation Program Coordinator ... Ms. Stacey MARSHALL
88 Administrative Programs Coordinator ... Ms. Amari FAUNA
08 Head Librarian ... Ms. Kathryn CONSTANT

Blue Mountain Community College (J)

PO Box 100, Pendleton OR 97801-0100
County: Umatilla/Morrow/Baker FICE Identification: 003186
Unit ID: 208275
Telephone: (541) 276-1260 Carnegie Class: Assoc/Pub-R-M
FAX Number: (541) 278-5886 Calendar System: Quarter
URL: www.bluecc.edu
Established: 1962 Annual Undergrad Tuition & Fees (In-District): $4,982
Enrollment: 1,868 Coed
Affiliation or Control: State/Local IRS Status: 501(c)3
Highest Offering: Associate Degree
Program: Occupational; 2-Year Principally Bachelor's Creditable; Business Emphasis
Accreditation: NW, DA

01 President ... Ms. Camille PREUS
05 Vice President of Instruction ... Mr. Jim WHITTAKER
32 Vice Pres Student Affairs ... Ms. Diane DREBIN
88 Vice Pres of Economic Development ... Mr. Art HILL
15 Assoc Vice Pres Human Resources ... Ms. Tammie PARKER
08 Director of Library & Media Svcs ... Ms. Jacqueline RAY
07 Registrar/Dir of Enrollment Svcs ... Ms. Theresa BOSWORTH
102 Director Foundation ... Ms. Margaret GIANOTTI
29 Director Alumni Relations ... Vacant
25 Director of Grants ... Vacant
37 Director of Student Financial Aid ... Ms. Yadira GONZALEZ
04 Administrative Asst to President ... Ms. Shannon FRANKLIN
10 AVP Finance & Business Operations ... Ms. Celeste INSKO
106 Dir Online Education/E-learning ... Mr. Bruce KAUSS
13 Chief Info Technology Officer (CIO) ... Mr. Brad HOLDEN
38 Director Student Counseling ... Ms. Cindy WOMACK
41 Athletic Director ... Mr. Brett BRYAN

Central Oregon Community College (K)

2600 NW College Way, Bend OR 97701-5998
County: Deschutes FICE Identification: 003188
Unit ID: 208318
Telephone: (541) 383-7700 Carnegie Class: Assoc/Pub-R-M
FAX Number: (541) 383-7506 Calendar System: Quarter
URL: www.cocc.edu
Established: 1949 Annual Undergrad Tuition & Fees (In-District): $3,393
Enrollment: 6,312 Coed
Affiliation or Control: Local IRS Status: 501(c)3
Highest Offering: Associate Degree
Program: Occupational; 2-Year Principally Bachelor's Creditable
Accreditation: NW, ACFEI, CAHIIM, COMTA, DA, EMT, IACBE, MAC

01 President ... Dr. Shirley I. METCALF
05 Vice President for Instruction ... Vacant
11 Vice Pres for Administration ... Mr. Matthew J. MCCOY
10 Chief Financial Officer ... Mr. Kevin KIMBALL
51 Dean of Extended Learning ... Mr. Jerry SCHULZ
20 Instructional Dean ... Dr. Michael FISHER
20 Instructional Dean ... Mr. Chad HARRIS
20 Instructional Dean ... Ms. Jennifer NEWBY
84 Dean of Student/Enrollment Svcs ... Ms. Alicia MOORE
07 Director of Admissions & Records ... Ms. Courtney WHETSTINE
08 Director of Library Services ... Dr. Tina HOVEKAMP
26 Director College Relations ... Mr. Ronald S. PARADIS
13 Director Information Technology ... Mr. Dan CECCHINI
18 Director Campus Services ... Mr. Joe VIOLA
15 Director Human Resources ... Ms. Sally SORENSON
22 Affirmative Action Officer ... Mrs. Dianne CAPPOZZOLA
37 Director Student Financial Aid ... Mr. Kevin MULTOP
28 Dir of Multicultural Activities ... Ms. Karen ROTH
32 Director of Student Life ... Mr. Gordon PRICE
09 Dir Institutional Effectiveness ... Ms. Brynn PIERCE
21 Assoc Chief Financial Officer ... Mr. David DONA
38 Director Student Counseling ... Ms. Vickery VILES
96 Director of Purchasing ... Ms. Julie MOSIER
40 Bookstore Director ... Ms. Lori A. WILLIS
36 Coordinator of Career Services ... Ms. Vickery VILES
19 Director Security/Safety ... Mr. Seth ELLIOTT
25 Chief Contracts/Grants Admin ... Mrs. Sharla ANDRESEN
39 Director Student Housing ... Mr. Paul WHEELER
102 Director Foundation ... Mr. Jim WEAVER
51 Director of Continuing Education ... Ms. Glenda LANTIS

Chemeketa Community College (L)

PO Box 14007, Salem OR 97309-7070
County: Marion FICE Identification: 003218
Unit ID: 208390
Telephone: (503) 399-5000 Carnegie Class: Assoc/Pub-R-L
FAX Number: (503) 399-5214 Calendar System: Quarter
URL: www.chemeketa.edu
Established: 1962 Annual Undergrad Tuition & Fees (In-District): $4,230
Enrollment: 11,101 Coed
Affiliation or Control: Local IRS Status: 501(c)3
Highest Offering: Associate Degree

Program: Occupational; 2-Year Principally Bachelor's Creditable
Accreditation: NW, ADNUR, DA, EMT, IFSAC

01 President/Chief Executive Officer ... Ms. Julie HUCKESTEIN
05 VP/Chief Academic Officer ... Mr. Jim EUSTROM
12 Campus President Yamhill Valley ... Mr. Jim EUSTROM
20 Exec Dean Career/Tech Education ... Mr. Johnny MACK
32 Exec Dean Student Dev/Learning Res ... Dr. Claire OLIVEROS
88 Exec Dean Acad Progress/Reg Ed Svcs ... Dr. Susan MURRAY
68 Dean Life Science ... Mr. Marshall ROACHE
79 Dean Humanities & Communications ... Mr. Don BRASE
66 Dean Dental Asst/Med Asst/Nursing ... Ms. Sandi KELLOGG
37 Dean Financial Aid/Enrollment Svcs ... Ms. Kathy CAMPBELL
38 Dean Counseling/Career Services ... Dr. Sue ORCHARD
72 Dean Applied Technologies ... Mr. Glen MILLER
81 Dean Math/Science/Technologies ... Mr. Michael MILHAUSEN
83 Dean Early Chld/Hum Svc/Soc Sci/Ed ... Ms. R. TAYLOR
84 Dean Marketing/Student Recruitment ... Mr. Greg HARRIS
45 Dean Curriculum Resource Center ... Dr. Deborah SIPE
65 Director Agricultural Sciences ... Mr. Joel KEEBLER
30 VP Governance & Administration ... Mr. Andrew BONE
08 Director Learning Resource Center ... Ms. Natalie BEACH
88 Director Enterprise Services ... Mr. Brian RADER
10 Director Business Services ... Ms. Miriam ROZIN
18 Director Facilities & Operations ... Mr. Phil WRIGHT
15 Director Human Resources ... Ms. Alice SPRAGUE
19 Director Public Safety ... Mr. Bill KOHLMEYER
109 Director Auxiliary Services ... Ms. Meredith SCHREIBER
41 Athletic Director ... Ms. Cassie BELMODIS
50 Dir Chemeketa Ctr for Bus/Industry ... Ms. Diane MCLARAN
88 Coordinator Prof Tech Educ ... Mr. Ed WOODS
28 Diversity & Equity Officer ... Ms. Linda HERRERA
35 Director Student Life/Retention ... Mr. Manuel GUERRA
07 Registrar/Director of Admissions ... Ms. Melissa FREY
96 Director of Procurement ... Vacant
26 Assoc VP/Chief Information Officer ... Mr. Tim ROGERS
102 Executive Director Foundation ... Ms. Nancy DUNCAN
25 Grants Coordinator ... Ms. Peggy GREENE
09 Coord of Institutional Research ... Mr. Fauzi NAAS

Clackamas Community College (A)

19600 Molalla Avenue, Oregon City OR 97045-7998
County: Clackamas FICE Identification: 004878
Unit ID: 208406
Telephone: (503) 594-6000 Carnegie Class: Assoc/Pub-S-MC
FAX Number: N/A Calendar System: Quarter
URL: www.clackamas.edu
Established: 1966 Annual Undergrad Tuition & Fees (In-District): $4,133
Enrollment: 7,302 Coed
Affiliation or Control: Local IRS Status: 501(c)3
Highest Offering: Associate Degree
Program: Occupational; 2-Year Principally Bachelor's Creditable
Accreditation: NW, CA, MAC

01 President ... Dr. Joanne TRUESDELL
05 VP Instruct & Stdnt Svcs/Provost ... Dr. David PLOTKIN
11 Vice Pres College Services ... Mr. Jim HUCKESTEIN
04 Executive Asst to the President ... Ms. Denice BAILEY
30 Assoc VP Govt/Cmty/Bus ... Ms. Shelly PARINI
102 Executive Director Foundation ... Mr. Greg FITZGERALD
26 Public Information Officer ... Ms. Janet PAULSON
88 Dean Acad Found/Connections Div ... Mr. Phillip KING
06 Registrar ... Mr. Chris SWEET
32 Assoc Dean Acad Found/Connect Div ... Ms. Tara SPREHE
13 Dean/CIO Information Technology ... Mr. Dion BAIRD
49 Dean Arts & Sciences ... Ms. Sue GOFF
46 Dean Curriculum/Planning/Research ... Mr. Steffen MOLLER
72 Dean Tech/Hlth Occup/Workforce Div ... Ms. Cynthia RISAN
15 Dean Human Resources ... Ms. Patricia ANDERSON WIECK
88 Director Educational Partnerships ... Ms. Cyndi ANDREWS
10 Director Business Services ... Ms. Chris ROBUCK
11 Dean Campus Services ... Mr. Bob COCHRAN
18 Director Campus Services ... Mr. Lloyd HELM
41 Director Athletics/Health/PE ... Mr. Jim MARTINEAU

Clatsop Community College (B)

1651 Lexington Avenue, Astoria OR 97103
County: Clatsop FICE Identification: 003189
Unit ID: 208415
Telephone: (503) 325-0910 Carnegie Class: Assoc/Pub-R-M
FAX Number: (503) 325-5738 Calendar System: Quarter
URL: www.clatsopcc.edu
Established: 1958 Annual Undergrad Tuition & Fees (In-District): $4,022
Enrollment: 867 Coed
Affiliation or Control: State/Local IRS Status: 501(c)3
Highest Offering: Associate Degree
Program: Occupational; 2-Year Principally Bachelor's Creditable
Accreditation: NW

01 Interim President ... Mr. Gerald HAMILTON
05 VP Academic & Student Affairs ... Dr. Donna LARSON
10 Vice President Finance & Operations ... Ms. JoAnn ZAHN
84 Dean Students & Enrollment Mngt ... Dr. Chris OUSLEY
06 Registrar ... Dr. Chris OUSLEY
26 Chief Public Rels Officer/Marketing ... Ms. Patricia WARREN
78 Dir Co-op Educ & Special Project ... Ms. Christine RIEHL
51 Director Distance Education ... Mrs. Kirsten HORNING
15 Director Personnel Services ... Ms. Leslie LIPE
37 Director Student Financial Aid ... Mr. Lloyd MUELLER
09 Director of Institutional Research ... Mr. Tom GILL
18 Chief Facilities/Physical Plant ... Mr. Greg DORCHEUS
21 Associate Business Officer ... Ms. Margaret ANTILLA
29 Director of Alumni Relations/Devel ... Ms. Patricia WARREN
04 Administrative Asst to President ... Ms. Stephanie DORCHEUS

Columbia Gorge Community College (C)

400 East Scenic Drive, The Dalles OR 97058
County: Wasco FICE Identification: 041519
Unit ID: 420556
Telephone: (541) 506-6000 Carnegie Class: Assoc/Pub-R-S
FAX Number: N/A Calendar System: Quarter
URL: www.cgcc.edu
Established: 1977 Annual Undergrad Tuition & Fees (In-District): $4,545
Enrollment: 991 Coed
Affiliation or Control: State/Local IRS Status: 501(c)3
Highest Offering: Associate Degree
Program: 2-Year Principally Bachelor's Creditable
Accreditation: NW, MAC

01 President ... Dr. Frank TODA
05 Chief Academic/Student Affairs Ofcr ... Lori UFFORD
10 Chief Financial Officer ... Will NORRIS
11 Chief Operating Officer ... Robb VAN CLEAVE
30 Chief Inst Advancement Officer ... Dan SPATZ
13 Chief Technology/Planning Officer ... Bill BOHN
101 Dir of Board/Executive Services ... Tria BULLARD
06 Registrar ... Dawn SALLEE-JUSTESEN
07 Director of Admissions ... Vacant
08 Director of Library Services ... John SCHOPPERT
09 Institutional Researcher ... Matt BYRNE
15 Director Personnel Services ... Vacant
18 Director of Facilities Services ... Jim AUSTIN
37 Director Financial Aid ... Sara VIEMEISTER

Concorde Career College (D)

1425 NE Irving Street, Suite 300, Portland OR 97232
County: Multnomah FICE Identification: 008887
Unit ID: 208479
Telephone: (503) 281-4181 Carnegie Class: Assoc/PrivFP
FAX Number: (503) 281-6739 Calendar System: Other
URL: www.concorde.edu/campus/portland
Established: 1996 Annual Undergrad Tuition & Fees: $14,495
Enrollment: 804 Coed
Affiliation or Control: Proprietary IRS Status: Proprietary
Highest Offering: Associate Degree
Program: Occupational
Accreditation: ACCSC, COARC, MAC, SURGT

01 Campus President ... Kim IERIEN

Concordia University (E)

2811 NE Holman Ave, Portland OR 97211-6099
County: Multnomah FICE Identification: 003191
Unit ID: 208488
Telephone: (503) 288-9371 Carnegie Class: Master's L
FAX Number: (503) 280-8518 Calendar System: Semester
URL: www.cu-portland.edu
Established: 1905 Annual Undergrad Tuition & Fees: $27,900
Enrollment: 7,000 Coed
Affiliation or Control: Lutheran Church - Missouri Synod
IRS Status: 501(c)3
Highest Offering: Doctorate
Program: Liberal Arts And General; Teacher Preparatory
Accreditation: NW, ACBSP, #LAW, NURSE, SW

01 President ... Dr. Charles E. SCHLIMPERT
26 Exec Vice Pres External Affairs ... Dr. Gary WITHERS
102 Exec Vice Pres Strategic Planning ... Mr. Johnnie DRIESSNER
05 Provost/Chief Academic Officer ... Dr. Mark E. WAHLERS
10 Chief Financial Officer ... Mr. Dennis J. STOECKLIN
11 Chief Operating Officer ... Ms. Jilma MENESES
32 VP Student Svcs/Enrollment Mgmt ... Dr. Glenn C. SMITH
04 Executive Administrator ... Ms. Brenna THOMAS
30 Chief Development Officer ... Mr. Kevin MATHENY
06 Registrar ... Ms. Danielle AMBROISE
07 Vice President Enrollment ... Ms. Bobi SWAN
09 Director of Institutional Research ... Mr. Ron FONGER
15 Director of Human Resources ... Ms. Andrea STEN
18 Chief Facilities/Physical Plant ... Mr. Doug MEYER
20 Associate Academic Officer ... Vacant
88 Chief Public Relations Officer ... Ms. Madeline TURNOCK
29 Director Alumni & Parent Engagement ... Ms. Becky SPRECHER
35 Dean of Students ... Mr. Steve DEKLOTZ
08 Librarian ... Mr. Brent MAI
37 Senior Director of Financial Aid ... Mr. Robert CLARKE
41 Athletic Director ... Dr. Matthew ENGLISH
38 Director Student Counseling ... Ms. Jaklin PEAKE
85 Director of International Studies ... Ms. Linda ROUNTREE
42 Campus Pastor ... Rev. Greg FAIROW
13 Chief Information Officer ... Dr. Joe MANNION
50 Dean School of Management ... Dr. Candace PETERSON
53 Interim Dean College of Education ... Dr. Sheryl REINISCH
49 Dean Theol Studies/Arts/Sciences ... Dr. David KLUTH
76 Dean Col of Health/Human Service ... Dr. Sarah SWEITZER
61 Dean School of Law ... Ms. Cathy SILAK
19 Director Security/Safety ... Mr. Todd TAYLOR

Corban University (F)

5000 Deer Park Drive SE, Salem OR 97317
County: Marion FICE Identification: 001339
Unit ID: 210331
Telephone: (503) 581-8600 Carnegie Class: Bac/Diverse
FAX Number: (503) 585-4316 Calendar System: Semester
URL: www.corban.edu
Established: 1935 Annual Undergrad Tuition & Fees: $28,640
Enrollment: 1,125 Coed
Affiliation or Control: Independent Non-Profit IRS Status: 501(c)3
Highest Offering: Master's
Program: Liberal Arts And General; Teacher Preparatory; Professional
Accreditation: NW

01 President ... Dr. Sheldon NORD
05 Provost/Executive Vice President ... Dr. Matthew LUCAS
10 Vice President For Business ... Mr. Kevin BRUBAKER
32 Vice President For Student Life ... Dr. Brenda ROTH
26 Vice President for Marketing ... Mr. J. Steven HUNT
30 Vice President for Advancement ... Mr. Bill PUGH
84 Vice Pres for Enrollment Management ... Vacant
35 Dean of Students ... Mr. Nathan GEER
11 Campus Administrator ... Dr. Leroy GOERTZEN
53 Dean of Global Initiatives ... Dr. Janine ALLEN
51 Dean of Adult Degree Programs ... Mrs. Pam TESCHNER
50 Dean of Business ... Mr. P. Griffith LINDELL
91 Chief Information Systems Officer ... Mr. Brian SCHMIDT
18 Director of Campus Care ... Mr. Paul EHENGER
06 Assoc Provost/Enrollment Management ... Dr. Chris VETTER
08 Librarian ... Mr. Garrett TROTT
07 Director of Admissions ... Ms. Heidi STOWMAN
39 Director of Community Life ... Mr. Eugene EDWARDS
42 Dean of Ministries ... Dr. Gregory TRULL
41 Athletic Director ... Mr. Greg EIDE
36 Director of Student Support ... Mr. Daren MILIONIS
37 Director of Financial Aid ... Mrs. Ellen ZARFAS
29 Director of Alumni Services ... Vacant
21 Associate Business Officer ... Mr. Brian ELLIOTT
40 Bookstore Manager ... Mr. Larry HULTBERG

Eastern Oregon University (G)

One University Boulevard, La Grande OR 97850-2807
County: Union FICE Identification: 003193
Unit ID: 208646
Telephone: (541) 962-3672 Carnegie Class: Master's S
FAX Number: (541) 962-3493 Calendar System: Quarter
URL: www.eou.edu
Established: 1929 Annual Undergrad Tuition & Fees (In-State): $7,758
Enrollment: 3,653 Coed
Affiliation or Control: State IRS Status: 501(c)3
Highest Offering: Master's
Program: Liberal Arts And General; Teacher Preparatory; Professional
Accreditation: NW, IACBE

01 President ... Mr. Thomas INSKO
05 Int Provost/Sr VP Academic Affairs ... Dr. Sarah WITTE
32 Vice President for Student Services ... Mr. Xavier ROMANO
10 Vice President Finance & Admin ... Ms. Lara MOORE
30 Vice Pres UA ... Mr. Tim SEYDEL
49 Int Dean College Arts & Science ... Dr. Regina BRAKER
50 Int Dean College of Business & Educ ... Dr. Dan MIELKE
37 Director of Financial Aid ... Ms. Lara MOORE
08 Director of Pierce Library ... Ms. Karen CLAY
07 Director of Admissions ... Ms. Gina GALAVIZ
06 Registrar ... Vacant
15 Director of Human Resources ... Ms. Cheryl MARTIN
29 Dir of Alumni Relations ... Ms. Jessie BRETT
41 Director of Athletics ... Ms. Anji WEISSENFLUH
39 Director of Residence Life ... Mr. Jeremy JONES
18 Director of Facilities & Planning ... Mr. David LAGESON
38 Director Counseling Center ... Dr. Marianne WEAVER
04 Exec Assistant to the President ... Ms. Heather CASHELL
21 Director of Business Affairs ... Ms. Cora BEACH
20 Int Vice Provost Academic Affairs ... Dr. Donald WOLFF
88 Learning Center Operations Manager ... Ms. Kathryn SHORTS
35 Director of Student Relations ... Ms. Colleen DUNNE-CASCIO
19 Campus Security/Public Safety Ofcr ... Mr. Bill BENSON

Everest College (H)

600 SW 10th Avenue, Suite 400, Portland OR 97205-2793
County: Multnomah FICE Identification: 009079
Unit ID: 210359
Telephone: (503) 222-3225 Carnegie Class: Assoc/PrivFP
FAX Number: (503) 228-6926 Calendar System: Quarter
URL: www.everest-college.com
Established: 1955 Annual Undergrad Tuition & Fees: $14,400
Enrollment: 161 Coed
Affiliation or Control: Proprietary IRS Status: Proprietary
Highest Offering: Associate Degree
Program: Occupational; 2-Year Principally Bachelor's Creditable
Accreditation: ACICS, #MAC

01 President ... Ms. Siri DIXON
05 Academic Dean ... Ms. Sara DAVENPORT
07 Director of Admissions ... Ms. Suzanne SALEH
06 Registrar ... Mrs. Renee HATFIELD
37 Director Student Financial Aid ... Ms. Nicole TONE
36 Director of Student Placement ... Mr. Randy BEAMER

George Fox University (A)

414 N Meridian, Newberg OR 97132-2697
County: Yamhill FICE Identification: 003194
Unit ID: 208822
Telephone: (503) 538-8383 Carnegie Class: Master's L
FAX Number: (503) 554-3834 Calendar System: Semester
URL: www.georgefox.edu
Established: 1891 Annual Undergrad Tuition & Fees: $31,866
Enrollment: 3,786 Coed
Affiliation or Control: Friends IRS Status: 501(c)3
Highest Offering: Doctorate
Program: Liberal Arts And General; Teacher Preparatory; Business Emphasis
Accreditation: NW, ACBSP, CAATE, CACREP, CLPSY, ENG, MUS, NURSE, PTA, SW, TED, THEOL

01 President ... Dr. Robin E. BAKER
03 Vice President/Dean of Seminary ... Dr. Charles J. CONNIRY, JR.
05 Provost ... Dr. Linda SAMEK
10 Exec VP Finance/Business Operations ... Mr. Ted ALLEN
30 Vice President Advancement ... Dr. Lynn ANDREWS
32 Vice President Student Life ... Dr. Bradley A. LAU
26 Exec VP Marketing/Enrollment Svcs ... Mr. Robert K. WESTERVELT
04 Executive Assistant to President ... Ms. Missy D. TERRY
28 AVP Intercultural Engagement ... Dr. Rebecca HERNANDEZ
21 Asst VP of Finance/Controller ... Ms. Cris BANTON
08 Dean of Libraries ... Mr. Merrill L. JOHNSON
07 Director of Undergrad Admissions ... Ms. Lindsay KNOX
06 Registrar ... Ms. Melissa THOMAS
29 Director University Events ... Ms. Jill DOWNING
36 Dir of Career Services/IDEA Center ... Ms. Deb MUMM-HILL
18 Director of Plant Services ... Mr. Clyde G. THOMAS
37 Director of Financial Aid ... Mr. James OSHIRO
96 Director Purchasing/Admin Services ... Vacant
41 Director of Athletics ... Mr. Craig B. TAYLOR
105 Director of Web Development ... Mr. Peter CRACKENBERG
15 Director Human Resources ... Ms. Peggy L. KILBURG
42 Univ Pastor/Dean of Spiritual Life ... Ms. Jamie NOLING-AUTH
27 Dir Pub Info/Mrkting/Communications ... Mr. Rob FELTON
13 Chief Information Officer ... Mr. Tim GOODFELLOW
19 Director Security Services ... Mr. Ed GIEROK
35 Dean Stdnt Svcs/Dir Hlth/Counseling ... Dr. William C. BUHROW
49 Dean School of Arts & Sciences ... Ms. Laura HARTLEY
83 Dean Sch Behavioral/Health Sci ... Dr. James E. FOSTER
53 Dean School of Education ... Dr. Scot HEADLEY
50 Dean School of Business ... Dr. Christopher MEADE

Gutenberg College (B)

1883 University Street, Eugene OR 97403-1368
County: Lane FICE Identification: 039324
Unit ID: 420510
Telephone: (541) 683-5141 Carnegie Class: Not Classified
FAX Number: (541) 683-6997 Calendar System: Quarter
URL: www.gutenberg.edu
Established: 1994 Annual Undergrad Tuition & Fees: $12,650
Enrollment: 18 Coed
Affiliation or Control: Independent Non-Profit IRS Status: 501(c)3
Highest Offering: Baccalaureate
Program: Liberal Arts And General; Religious Emphasis
Accreditation: TRACS

01 President ... David CRABTREE
03 Vice President ... Richard BOOSTER
05 Dean ... Thomas DEWBERRY
07 Admissions Director ... Tim MCINTOSH
06 Registrar ... Chris SWANSON

ITT Technical Institute (C)

9500 NE Cascades Parkway, Portland OR 97220
Telephone: (503) 255-6500 FICE Identification: 011852
Accreditation: ACICS

† Branch campus of ITT Technical Institute, Indianapolis, IN.

ITT Technical Institute (D)

4825 Commercial Street SE, Ste 100,
Salem OR 97302-2177
Telephone: (503) 576-2300 Identification: 770637
Accreditation: ACICS

† Branch campus of ITT Technical Institute, Indianapolis, IN.

Klamath Community College (E)

7390 S 6th Street, Klamath Falls OR 97603-7121
County: Klamath FICE Identification: 034283
Unit ID: 428392
Telephone: (541) 882-3521 Carnegie Class: Assoc/Pub-R-S
FAX Number: (541) 885-7758 Calendar System: Quarter
URL: www.klamathcc.edu
Established: 1996 Annual Undergrad Tuition & Fees (In-District): $4,590
Enrollment: 1,343 Coed
Affiliation or Control: State/Local IRS Status: 501(c)3
Highest Offering: Associate Degree
Program: Occupational; 2-Year Principally Bachelor's Creditable
Accreditation: NW

01 President ... Dr. Roberto GUTIERREZ
11 Int Vice Pres Administrative Svcs ... Ms. Allison BRYSON
05 Vice Pres Academic Affairs ... Ms. Jamie JENNINGS
88 Vice Pres of External Programs ... Ms. Julie MURRAY-JENSEN
32 Vice President Student Services ... Mr. David MINGER
15 VP Human Res/Instl Effectiveness ... Ms. Frances KELLY
20 Dean of Instruction ... Mr. James JANSON
102 Exec Director of Foundation KCC ... Dr. Steven MENESES
13 Director Information Services ... Mr. Paul BREEDLOVE
06 Registrar ... Mr. John DUARTE
26 Chief Public Information Officer ... Mr. Ryan BROWN
18 Facilities Director ... Mr. Mike HOMFELDT
10 Senior Accountant ... Mr. Jack NOWAK
37 Financial Aid Director ... Ms. Allison BRYSON

Lane Community College (F)

4000 E 30th Avenue, Eugene OR 97405-0640
County: Lane FICE Identification: 003196
Unit ID: 209038
Telephone: (541) 463-3000 Carnegie Class: Assoc/Pub-R-L
FAX Number: (541) 463-5201 Calendar System: Quarter
URL: www.lanecc.edu
Established: 1964 Annual Undergrad Tuition & Fees (In-District): $4,047
Enrollment: 9,400 Coed
Affiliation or Control: Local IRS Status: 501(c)3
Highest Offering: Associate Degree
Program: Occupational; 2-Year Principally Bachelor's Creditable
Accreditation: NW, ACFEI, COARC, DA, DH, EMT, MAC, PTAA

01 President ... Dr. Mary SPILDE
05 Int Exec Vice President/CAO ... Ms. Dawn DEWOLF
11 Vice President College Operations ... Mr. Brian KELLY
20 Exec Dean Academic/Student Affairs ... Ms. Kerry LEVETT
20 Exec Dean Academic Affs/Career Tech ... Ms. Mary Jeanne KUHART
20 Exec Dean Academic Affs/Transfer ... Mr. Maurice HARRINGTON
32 Div Dean Student Life/Leadership ... Dr. Barbara DELANSKY
68 Div Dean Health/Physical Education ... Mr. Chris HAWKIN
28 Interim Chief Diversity Officer ... Dr. Donna KOECHIG
13 Chief Information Officer ... Mr. Bill SCHUETZ
10 Chief Financial Officer ... Mr. Greg HOLMES
35 Executive Dean/Student Affairs ... Ms. Helen GARRETT
15 Chief Human Resources Officer ... Mr. Dennis CARR
09 Dir Inst Research/Assess/Planning ... Dr. Craig TAYLOR
18 Interim Director Facilities & PM ... Mr. Todd SMITH
19 Director Public Safety ... Mr. Jace SMITH
08 Interim Library Director ... Ms. Marika PINEDA
38 Dir Counseling/Student Placement ... Mr. Jerry DELEON
37 Director of Financial Aid ... Ms. Helen FAITH
96 Director of Finance/Purchasing ... Vacant
26 Public Information Officer ... Ms. Joan ASCHIM
102 Foundation Director ... Ms. Wendy JETT

Le Cordon Bleu College of Culinary Arts in Portland (G)

600 SW 10th Avenue, Suite 500, Portland OR 97205-2793
County: Multnomah FICE Identification: 030226
Unit ID: 375841
Telephone: (503) 223-2245 Carnegie Class: Assoc/PrivFP
FAX Number: (503) 223-0126 Calendar System: Other
URL: www.chefs.edu/portland
Established: 1983 Annual Undergrad Tuition & Fees: $13,361
Enrollment: 452 Coed
Affiliation or Control: Proprietary IRS Status: Proprietary
Highest Offering: Associate Degree
Program: Occupational
Accreditation: ACICS, ACFEI

01 Campus President/CAO ... Brian WILLIAMS
05 Campus Director ... Adam THOMPSON
07 Director of Admissions ... Richard BUNCH, III
32 Director Student Services ... Marsha PARMER
10 Business Operations Manager ... Lizza NOVO
06 Associate Registrar ... John ELIASSEN

Lewis and Clark College (H)

0615 SW Palatine Hill, Portland OR 97219-7899
County: Multnomah FICE Identification: 003197
Unit ID: 209056
Telephone: (503) 768-7000 Carnegie Class: Bac/A&S
FAX Number: (503) 768-7055 Calendar System: Semester
URL: www.lclark.edu
Established: 1867 Annual Undergrad Tuition & Fees: $45,104
Enrollment: 3,504 Coed
Affiliation or Control: Independent Non-Profit IRS Status: 501(c)3
Highest Offering: Doctorate
Program: Liberal Arts And General; Professional
Accreditation: NW, CACREP, LAW, MFCD, TED

01 President ... Dr. Barry GLASSNER
03 Vice President & Provost ... Dr. Jane M. ATKINSON
43 VP General Counsel/Secy of College ... Mr. David ELLIS
53 Dean Grad Sch Education/Counseling ... Dr. Scott FLETCHER
49 Dean College of Arts & Sciences ... Dr. Catherine KODAT
61 Dean of the Law School ... Ms. Jennifer JOHNSON
10 Vice Pres Business/Finance/Treas ... Mr. Carl VANCE
30 Vice Pres Institutional Advancement ... Mr. Hal ABRAMS
32 Dean of Students ... Dr. Anna GONZALEZ
09 Assoc Provost Research & Planning ... Dr. Mark FIGUEROA
26 Exec Dir of Public Affairs & Comm ... Mr. Joe BECKER
07 Dean for Enrollment & Communication ... Ms. Lisa MEYER
21 Associate Vice Pres for Finance/Con ... Mr. George BATTISTEL
13 Assoc Vice Pres & Chief Info Ofcr ... Mr. Adam BUCHWALD
15 Assoc VP/Director Human Resources ... Mr. Isaac DIXON
18 Assoc Vice Pres Facilities ... Mr. Michel GEORGE
49 Assoc Dean College of Arts/Science ... Dr. John KRUSSEL
49 Assoc Dean College of Arts/Science ... Dr. Gary REINESS
06 Registrar College of Arts/Sciences ... Ms. Judy FINCH
06 Registrar Law School ... Mr. Seneca GRAY
06 Registrar Graduate School ... Ms. River MONTIJO
37 Director of Financial Aid ... Ms. Anastacia DILLON
08 Director of Watzek Library ... Mr. Mark DAHL
35 Assoc Dean of Student Engagement ... Ms. Cathy BUSHA
85 Assoc Dean Intl Stdnts & Scholars ... Mr. Brian WHITE
44 Assoc VP & Director of Development ... Mr. Aaron WHITEFORD
29 Senior Director Alumni/Parent Pgms ... Mr. Andrew MCPHEETERS
19 Director of Campus Safety ... Mr. Timothy O'DWYER
42 Dean of Religious & Spiritual Life ... Dr. Mark DUNTLEY
41 Director of Athletics ... Ms. Shana LEVINE
39 Director of Housing & Orientation ... Ms. Sandi BOTTEMILLER
24 Director of IT Ops/Instr Media Svc ... Mr. Patrick RYALL
17 Assoc Dean Stdnt Health & Wellness ... Dr. John HANCOCK
04 Executive Asst Board Relations ... Ms. Tina BLACKWELL
04 Special Assistant to the President ... Ms. Annette LANIER
102 Dir Corporate/Foundation Relations ... Mr. Erik FAST
104 Dir Overseas & Off-Campus Programs ... Mr. Larry MEYERS

Linfield College (I)

900 SE Baker Street, McMinnville OR 97128-6894
County: Yamhill FICE Identification: 003198
Unit ID: 209065
Telephone: (503) 883-2200 Carnegie Class: Bac/A&S
FAX Number: (503) 883-2472 Calendar System: 4/1/4
URL: www.linfield.edu
Established: 1858 Annual Undergrad Tuition & Fees: $38,654
Enrollment: 2,466 Coed
Affiliation or Control: American Baptist IRS Status: 501(c)3
Highest Offering: Baccalaureate
Program: Liberal Arts And General; Teacher Preparatory; Professional
Accreditation: NW, CAATE, MUS, NURSE

01 President ... Dr. Thomas HELLIE
05 Vice Pres Acad Affs/Dean of Faculty ... Ms. Susan AGRE-KIPPENHAN
10 Vice Pres Finance/Admin/CFO ... Ms. Mary Ann RODRIGUEZ
26 Vice Pres Institutional Advancement ... Mr. David OSTRANDER
84 Vice Pres for Enrollment Management ... Mr. Daniel PRESTON
32 VP Student Svcs/Dean of Students ... Ms. Susan HOPP
43 Vice President & General Counsel ... Mr. John MCKEEGAN
66 Dean of Nursing ... Dr. Mallie KOZY
20 Associate Dean of Faculty ... Dr. J. Christopher GAISER
35 Associate Dean of Students ... Mr. Jeff MACKAY
15 Interim Director of Human Resources ... Ms. Betty HENNINGER
18 Director Facilities & Auxiliary Svc ... Ms. Allison HORN
28 Director Multicultural Programs ... Mr. Jason RODRIQUEZ
06 Registrar ... Ms. Diane CRABTREE
07 Director of Admission ... Ms. Lisa KNODLE-BRAGIEL
08 Library Director ... Ms. Susan BARNES WHYTE
09 Director of Institutional Research ... Ms. Jennifer BALLARD
37 Director of Financial Aid ... Ms. Keri BURKE
13 Chief Technology Officer ... Ms. Virginia TOMLINSON
91 Assoc Director Integrated Tech Svcs ... Mr. Michael BLANCO
105 Webmaster ... Mr. Jonathan PIERCE
85 Director of International Programs ... Dr. Shaik ISMAIL
51 Director of Continuing Education ... Dr. Laura BRENER
19 Director of Security ... Mr. Ronald NOBLE
38 Director of Counseling Services ... Ms. Patricia HADDELAND
26 Director of Public Relations ... Ms. Mardi MILEHAM
44 Director of Annual Giving ... Ms. Lisa GOODWIN
44 Director of Philanthropic Planning ... Mr. Craig HAISCH
102 Dir Corp & Foundation Relations ... Ms. Catherine JARMIN MILLER
29 Director of Alumni/Parent Relations ... Ms. Debbie HARMON
36 Director Career & Development ... Mr. Michael HAMPTON
42 Chaplain ... Dr. David MASSEY
41 Athletic Director ... Mr. Scott CARNAHAN
40 Bookstore Manager ... Mr. Chad COTTRILL
04 Exec Assistant to the President ... Ms. Jolene SMITH

Linn-Benton Community College (J)

6500 Pacific Boulevard, SW, Albany OR 97321-3774
County: Linn FICE Identification: 006938
Unit ID: 209074
Telephone: (541) 917-4999 Carnegie Class: Assoc/Pub-R-L
FAX Number: (541) 917-4445 Calendar System: Quarter
URL: www.linnbenton.edu
Established: 1966 Annual Undergrad Tuition & Fees (In-District): $3,045
Enrollment: 5,314 Coed
Affiliation or Control: State/Local IRS Status: 501(c)3
Highest Offering: Associate Degree
Program: Occupational; 2-Year Principally Bachelor's Creditable; Business Emphasis
Accreditation: NW, DA, MAC, OTA, POLYT

01 President ... Dr. Gregory J. HAMANN
05 Vice Pres Academic Affs/Wrkfce Dev ... Ms. Ann BUCHELE
10 Vice Pres Finance & Operations ... Mr. Dave HENDERSON
32 Vice President Student Affairs ... Dr. Bruce CLEMETSEN
35 Assoc Dean Student Affairs ... Ms. Lynne COX

12 Regional Director Linn County .... Mr. Gary PRICE
12 Regional Director Benton County .... Mr. Jeff DAVIS
15 Dir Human Resources/Affirm Act Ofcr .... Mr. Scott ROLEN
41 Director of Athletics .... Mr. Randy FALK
81 Dean Science/Engr & Tech .... Mr. Andrew FELDMAN
49 Dean Arts/Soc Sci/Humanities Div .... Ms. Katie WINDER
20 Dean Instruction .... Ms. Sally WIDENMANN
30 Exec Dir Institutional Advancement .... Mr. Dale STOWELL

Marylhurst University (A)

PO Box 261, 17600 Pacific Highway,
Marylhurst OR 97036-0261

County: Clackamas | FICE Identification: 003199
Unit ID: 209108
Telephone: (503) 636-8141 | Carnegie Class: Master's L
FAX Number: (503) 636-9526 | Calendar System: Quarter
URL: www.marylhurst.edu
Established: 1893 | Annual Undergrad Tuition & Fees: $20,835
Enrollment: 1,215 | Coed
Affiliation or Control: Independent Non-Profit | IRS Status: 501(c)3
Highest Offering: Master's
Program: Liberal Arts And General
Accreditation: NW, CIDA, IACBE, MUS

01 President .... Dr. Melody ROSE
10 Interim VP Finance & Campus Service .... Ms. Debra MEYERS
30 Vice Pres Institutional Advancement .... Ms. Nicola SYSYN
84 VP Enrollment Mgmt .... Ms. Beth WOODWARD
04 Chief Assistant to the President .... Mr. Rod JOHNSON
07 Director of Admissions .... Mr. Ryan CLARK
06 Registrar .... Ms. Gwen HYATT
08 University Librarian .... Ms. Nancy HOOVER
26 Director Marketing & Communications .... Ms. Simona BOUCEK
37 Director of Financial Aid .... Ms. Tracy REISINGER
88 Director Art Therapy Graduate Pgm .... Ms. Christine TURNER
72 Director Center for Learning Tech .... Mr. Nathan PHILLIPS
13 Director of Infrastructure Services .... Mr. Keelan CLEARY
18 Director of Facilities .... Mr. Mark STRULOEFF
49 Chair Sci/Religion/Interdisc Stds .... Dr. Jan DABROWSKI
88 Chair Art/Music/Creative Therapies .... Dr. Laura BEER
64 Director of Choral Activities .... Dr. Justin SMITH
57 Art Dept/Dir Interior Design Dept .... Ms. Nancy HISS
73 Religious Studies & Philosophy .... Dr. Jeroid ROUSSELL
88 Interdisciplinary Studies .... Mr. Simeon DREYFUSS
79 Chrpsn Culture & Media .... Dr. David DENNY
81 Science & Math .... Mr. Greg DARDIS
83 Chairperson Human Sciences .... Dr. Jennifer SASSER
88 Real Estate Studies .... Mr. Sunny LISTON
88 Chrpsn English Literature/Writing .... Dr. Meg ROLAND
60 Communication Studies .... Vacant
50 Acting Director of Business .... Mr. Paul VENTURA
88 Chair Food Systems & Society .... Dr. Patricia ALLEN

Mount Angel Seminary (B)

1 Abbey Drive, St. Benedict OR 97373-0505

County: Marion | FICE Identification: 003203
Unit ID: 209241
Telephone: (503) 845-3951 | Carnegie Class: Spec/Faith
FAX Number: (503) 845-3128 | Calendar System: Semester
URL: www.mountangelabbey.org
Established: 1887 | Annual Undergrad Tuition & Fees: $31,598
Enrollment: 159 | Coed
Affiliation or Control: Roman Catholic | IRS Status: 501(c)3
Highest Offering: Master's
Program: Liberal Arts And General; Professional; Religious Emphasis
Accreditation: NW, THEOL

01 President/Rector .... Msgr. Joseph V. BETSCHART
05 Vice President/Academic Dean .... Dr. Owen CUMMINGS
03 VP of Admin/Dir Pastoral Formation .... Rev. Stephen CLOVIS
08 Librarian .... Ms. Victoria ERTELT
10 Business Manager .... Fr. Martin GRASSEL, OSB
06 Registrar & Student Financial Aid .... Ms. Marina KEYS
32 Dean of Students Theology .... Abbot Peter EBERLE, OSB
32 Dean of Students College .... Rev. Terrence TOMPKINS
20 Academic Dean College .... Dr. Creighton LINDSAY
85 Director of Foreign Students .... Ms. Tamara SWANSON-ORR
07 Director of Admissions .... Fr. Ralph RECKER, OSB
04 Admin Assistant to the President .... Mrs. Carol MARTIN
13 Director of Information Technology .... Vacant
40 Director of Bookstore .... Mrs. Beth WELLS
20 Academic Dean Theology .... Dr. Seymour HOUSE
29 Director Alumni Relations .... Ms. Jeanne HOBSON

Mt. Hood Community College (C)

26000 SE Stark, Gresham OR 97030-3300

County: Multnomah | FICE Identification: 003204
Unit ID: 209250
Telephone: (503) 491-6422 | Carnegie Class: Assoc/Pub-S-SC
FAX Number: (503) 491-7389 | Calendar System: Quarter
URL: www.mhcc.edu
Established: 1965 | Annual Undergrad Tuition & Fees (In-District): $4,601
Enrollment: 9,450 | Coed
Affiliation or Control: Local | IRS Status: 501(c)3
Highest Offering: Associate Degree
Program: Occupational; 2-Year Principally Bachelor's Creditable
Accreditation: NW, COARC, DH, FUSER, PTAA, SURGT

01 President .... Dr. Debra DERR
11 VP of Administrative Services .... Mr. Richard DOUGHTY
05 Vice Pres Instruction/Student Dev .... Ms. Christie PLINSKI
32 Executive Dean Success Services .... Vacant
15 Director Human Resources .... Ms. Gale BLESSING
88 Dir Child Dev/Family Support Pgms .... Ms. Jean WAGNER
18 Director Facilities Management .... Mr. Charles GEORGE
10 Director of Finance .... Ms. Jennifer DEMENT
09 Director of Institutional Research .... Mr. Sergey SHEPELOV
37 Director Student Financial Aid .... Ms. Christi HART
07 Director of Admissions .... Mr. John HAMBLIN
13 Chief Information Officer .... Ms. Linda VIGESAA
28 Director of Diversity .... Mr. David SUSSMAN
29 Exec Dir Foundation/Alumni Rels .... Mr. Al SIGALA
76 Dean Allied Health & Nursing .... Ms. Janie GRIFFIN
81 Dean Perf/Visual Arts/Integ Media .... Ms. Janet MCINTYRE
79 Dean Humanities .... Ms. Sara RIVARA
72 Dean Sciences .... Dr. Steve GOLDSMITH
50 Dean Business and Info Systems .... Mr. Rod BARKER
103 Exec Dean WF Dev & Industrial Tech .... Mr. Jarrod HOGUE
26 Chief Public Relations Officer .... Mr. Bruce BATTLE
84 Director Enrollment Management .... Mr. John HAMBLIN

Multnomah University (D)

8435 NE Glisan Street, Portland OR 97220-5898

County: Multnomah | FICE Identification: 003206
Unit ID: 209287
Telephone: (503) 255-0332 | Carnegie Class: Spec/Faith
FAX Number: (503) 254-1268 | Calendar System: Semester
URL: www.multnomah.edu
Established: 1936 | Annual Undergrad Tuition & Fees: $22,760
Enrollment: 728 | Coed
Affiliation or Control: Independent Non-Profit | IRS Status: 501(c)3
Highest Offering: Doctorate
Program: Teacher Preparatory; Professional; Religious Emphasis
Accreditation: NW, BI, THEOL

01 President .... Dr. G. Craig WILLIFORD
05 Chief Academic Officer/Provost .... Dr. Wayne G. STRICKLAND
84 VP Enrollment Management .... Ms. Gina BERQUIST
10 CFO and VP Administration .... Mr. W. Chandler WILSON
49 Dean School of Arts and Sciences .... Dr. Daniel SCALBERG
73 Dean School of Bible & Theology .... Dr. Roy ANDREWS
107 Dean Adult & Professional Studies .... Dr. Steve HOLLER
32 Director/Dean of Students .... Ms. Kim STAVE
35 Associate Dean of Students .... Mr. Richard WARD
35 Associate Dean of Students .... Dr. Karen FANCHER
12 Executive Director of MU Reno .... Mr. John MCKENDRICKS
108 Dir of Institutional Effectiveness .... Dr. David FUNK
06 Registrar .... Ms. Amy M. STEPHENS
21 Controller .... Mrs. Debbie WHITEHEAD
08 Librarian .... Dr. Philip M. JOHNSON
37 Director Student Financial Aid .... Vacant
36 Seminary Director of Placement .... Dr. Roger TRAUTMANN
13 Director Information Technology .... Mrs. Brenda GIBSON
15 Director of Human Resources .... Ms. Tracy L. MORESCHI
41 Athletic Director .... Ms. Lois VOS
26 Director of Marketing .... Mr. Tom MORLAN
07 Director of Admissions .... Vacant
18 Director of Campus Facilities .... Mr. Eric LINMAN
29 Director Alumni Relations .... Mrs. Michelle UNDERWOOD
04 Assistant to the President .... Mrs. Denise STONE
19 Director of Campus Safety .... Mr. Josh HARPER
38 Director Student Counseling .... Ms. Lisa WOLD
39 Assistant Director of Housing .... Mrs. Christy MARTIN
106 Dir Online Education/E-learning .... Mr. Robert MCDOLE
30 Vice President of Advancement .... Mr. Steve CUMMINGS
50 Dean of Business .... Mr. Lee SELLERS
53 Dean of Education .... Ms. Susan BOE

National American University-Tigard (E)

1333 SW 68th Parkway, Tigard OR 97223

Telephone: (503) 403-3500 | Identification: 770410
Accreditation: &NH

† Branch campus of National American University, Rapid City, SD.

National College of Natural Medicine (F)

049 SW Porter Street, Portland OR 97201-4878

County: Multnomah | FICE Identification: 025340
Unit ID: 209296
Telephone: (503) 552-1555 | Carnegie Class: Spec/Health
FAX Number: (503) 499-0022 | Calendar System: Quarter
URL: www.ncnm.edu
Established: 1956 | Annual Graduate Tuition & Fees: $28,560
Enrollment: 704 | Coed
Affiliation or Control: Independent Non-Profit | IRS Status: 501(c)3
Highest Offering: Doctorate; No Undergraduates
Program: Professional
Accreditation: NW, ACUP, NATUR

01 President .... Dr. David J. SCHLEICH
05 Provost/VP Academic .... Dr. Andrea SMITH
10 Chief Financial Officer/VP Finance .... Mr. Gerald BORES
30 VP of Advancement .... Ms. Susan HUNTER
26 VP of Marketing & Communications .... Dr. Sandra SNYDER
04 Executive Asst to the President .... Ms. Colleen CORDER
09 Dir of Inst Research & Compliance .... Ms. Laurie MCGRATH
63 Dean of Naturopathic Medicine .... Dr. Melanie HENRIKSEN
63 Dean Classical Chinese Medicine .... Dr. Laurie REGAN
46 Dean of Research & Graduate Studies .... Dr. Heather ZWICKEY
23 Dean of Clinics .... Dr. Regina DEHEN
32 Dean of Student Affairs .... Ms. Cheryl MILLER
06 Registrar .... Ms. Kelly GAREY
07 Director of Admissions .... Mr. Brandon HAMILTON
37 Director of Financial Aid .... Ms. Laurie RADFORD
27 Director PR & Communications .... Ms. Marilynn CONSIDINE
15 Director Human Resources .... Ms. Kathy STANFORD
13 Director IT .... Mr. Steve FONG
18 Director Campus Development .... Mr. Keith NORTH
20 Dir Curriculum/Faculty Developmnt .... Dr. Denise DALLMANN
08 College Librarian .... Ms. Noelle STELLO
109 Director Ancillary Services .... Ms. Nicole WRIGHT
19 Chief Campus Security .... Mr. Spencer BRAZES
20 Assoc Dean Academic Progress .... Dr. Catherine DOWNEY
29 Alumni Officer .... Mr. Bill TRIBE
38 Director Student Counseling .... Dr. Adrienne WOLMARK
36 Manager Career Services .... Ms. Tafflyn WILLIAMS-THOMAS
51 Director Continuing Education .... Dr. Audra MEHAN
35 Director Student Life & Inclusion .... Ms. Morgan CHICARELLI
105 Webmaster .... Ms. Ellen YARNELL
28 Mgr Intercultural Support & Engmnt . Ms. Ayasha SHAMSUD-DIN

National College of Technical Instruction-College of Emergency Services (G)

9800 SE McBrod Ave, Ste 200, Milwaukie OR 97222

County: Clackamas | Identification: 667128
Telephone: (971) 236-9231 | Carnegie Class: Not Classified
FAX Number: (971) 653-9239 | Calendar System: Semester
URL: www.ncti.edu
Established: 1995 | Annual Undergrad Tuition & Fees: $10,900
Enrollment: 60 | Coed
Affiliation or Control: Proprietary | IRS Status: Proprietary
Highest Offering: Associate Degree
Program: Occupational
Accreditation: ABHES, EMT

01 Program Director .... Mr. William PHRASHER

New Hope Christian College (H)

2155 Bailey Hill Road, Eugene OR 97405-1194

County: Lane | FICE Identification: 021597
Unit ID: 208725
Telephone: (541) 485-1780 | Carnegie Class: Spec/Faith
FAX Number: (541) 343-5801 | Calendar System: Semester
URL: www.newhope.edu
Established: 1925 | Annual Undergrad Tuition & Fees: $24,430
Enrollment: 163 | Coed
Affiliation or Control: Other | IRS Status: 501(c)3
Highest Offering: Baccalaureate
Program: Religious Emphasis
Accreditation: BI

00 Chancellor .... Mr. Wayne CORDEIRO
01 President/Dir College Advancement .... Dr. Guy S. HIGASHI
04 Executive Assistant to President .... Mrs. Lori HIGASHI
05 Academic Dean .... Dr. Mark L. KELLEY
32 Dean of Student Services .... Mr. Gary MATSDORF
29 Director of Alumni Relations .... Ms. Karen BOBST
10 Business Administrator .... Dale SORENSEN
06 Registrar .... Ms. Mary Ellen PEREIRA
07 Enrollment Management .... Ms. Crystie RIOS
37 Director of Financial Aid .... Mr. Casey CRAIGIE
08 Head Librarian .... Ms. Janet L. KELLEY
38 Director of Christian Counseling .... Ms. Fay DEMEYER

Northwest Christian University (I)

828 E. 11th Ave., Eugene OR 97401-3745

County: Lane | FICE Identification: 003208
Unit ID: 209409
Telephone: (541) 343-1641 | Carnegie Class: Bac/Diverse
FAX Number: (541) 343-9159 | Calendar System: Semester
URL: www.nwcu.edu
Established: 1895 | Annual Undergrad Tuition & Fees: $27,100
Enrollment: 705 | Coed
Affiliation or Control: Christian Church (Disciples Of Christ)
IRS Status: 501(c)3
Highest Offering: Master's
Program: 2-Year Principally Bachelor's Creditable; Liberal Arts And General; Teacher Preparatory; Religious Emphasis
Accreditation: NW, IACBE

01 President .... Dr. Joseph WOMACK
05 VP Academic Affairs/Dean of Faculty .... Dr. Dennis LINDSAY
10 Vice Pres Finance/Administration .... Mr. Gene DE YOUNG
30 Vice President Advancement .... Mr. Greg STRAUSBAUGH
32 VP Student Development/Enrollment .... Mr. Michael FULLER
26 Director University Relations .... Ms. Jeannine JONES
39 Dir Residence Life & Student Svcs .... Mr. Greg BROCK
08 Director Kellenberger Library .... Mr. Steve SILVER
06 Registrar .... Mr. Aaron PRUITT
42 Campus Pastor Dir Church Relations .... Mr. Troy DEAN
37 Director Financial Aid .... Ms. Jocelyn HUBBS
07 Executive Director Admissions .... Ms. Kacie GERDRUM

35 Director Student Programs ..... Ms. Princess FOX
18 Plant Manager ..... Mr. Oskar BUCHER
41 Athletic Director ..... Mr. Corey R. ANDERSON
36 Dir Academic Svc & Career Develop ..... Ms. Angela DOTY
04 Exec Administrative Assistant ..... Ms. Carla AYDELOTT
44 Major Gifts Officer ..... Ms. Glenda GORDON
108 Director of Assessment ..... Mr. Brian MILLS
29 Alumni Relations/Event Coordinator ..... Ms. Heather HECKER
88 Asst Dean Adult Studies ..... Ms. Melanie TOWNE
88 Asst Dean Business ..... Mr. Pete DIFFENDERFER
88 Interim Chair Educ & Counseling ..... Mr. Gene JAMES
88 Director Ctr Leadership Ethics ..... Mr. Keith POTTER

Oregon College of Art and Craft (A)

8245 SW Barnes Road, Portland OR 97225-6349
County: Washington FICE Identification: 030073
Unit ID: 209533
Telephone: (503) 297-5554 Carnegie Class: Spec/Arts
FAX Number: (503) 297-3155 Calendar System: Semester
URL: www.ocac.edu
Established: 1907 Annual Undergrad Tuition & Fees: $29,580
Enrollment: 155 Coed
Affiliation or Control: Independent Non-Profit IRS Status: 501(c)3
Highest Offering: Baccalaureate
Program: Fine Arts Emphasis
Accreditation: NW, ART

01 President ..... Ms. Denise MULLEN
10 Chief Financial Officer ..... Mr. Michael LAMMERS
05 Dean of Academic Affairs ..... Ms. Jiseon LEE ISBARA
30 Chief Advanc/Marketing & CP Officer ..... Ms. Roma PEYSER
07 Chief Enroll Officer/Dir of Admiss ..... Ms. Anne BOERNER
06 Registrar ..... Ms. Anna VARGAS
08 Head of Library Services ..... Ms. Elsa LOFTIS
32 Coordinator of Student Services ..... Vacant
31 Community Programs Coordinator ..... Ms. Katie WISDOM WEINSTEIN
37 Director of Financial Aid ..... Ms. Linda ANDERSON
29 Dir of Exhibitions/Alumni Affairs ..... Mr. Arthur DEBOW
04 Exec Assistant to the President ..... Ms. Kris KEBISEK

† Granted candidacy at the Master's level.

Oregon College of Oriental Medicine (B)

75 NW Couch Street, Portland OR 97209-4018
County: Multnomah FICE Identification: 026037
Unit ID: 369659
Telephone: (503) 253-3443 Carnegie Class: Spec/Health
FAX Number: (503) 253-2701 Calendar System: Quarter
URL: www.ocom.edu
Established: 1983 Annual Graduate Tuition & Fees: $25,616
Enrollment: 272 Coed
Affiliation or Control: Independent Non-Profit IRS Status: 501(c)3
Highest Offering: Doctorate; No Undergraduates
Program: Professional
Accreditation: ACUP

01 President ..... Dr. Deborah HOWE
05 Vice President for Academic Affairs ..... Dr. Tim CHAPMAN
10 Vice President for Finance ..... Susan SLOAN
11 Vice President of Operations ..... Chris CHIACCHIERINI
32 Dean of Academic & Student Affairs ..... Carol TAUB
88 Dean of Doctoral Studies ..... Dr. Beth BURCH
46 Associate Dean of Research ..... Dr. Deborah ACKERMAN
17 Dean of Clinical Education ..... Dr. Martin KIDWELL
30 Development Officer ..... Glenn FEE
09 Planning & Inst Assessment Officer ..... Shelley STUMP
15 Director of Human Resources ..... Helen SMITH
26 Director of Community Relations ..... Gretchen HORTON
06 Registrar ..... Carol ACHESON

Oregon Culinary Institute (C)

1701 SW Jefferson Street, Portland OR 97201-2571
Telephone: (503) 961-6200 Identification: 666177
Accreditation: ACICS

† Branch campus of Pioneer Pacific College, Wilsonville, OR.

Oregon Health & Science University (D)

3181 SW Sam Jackson Park Road, Portland OR 97239-3098
County: Multnomah FICE Identification: 004882
Unit ID: 209490
Telephone: (503) 494-8311 Carnegie Class: Spec/Med
FAX Number: (503) 494-5738 Calendar System: Quarter
URL: www.ohsu.edu
Established: 1974 Annual Undergrad Tuition & Fees (In-State): $17,895
Enrollment: 2,861 Coed
Affiliation or Control: State IRS Status: 501(c)3
Highest Offering: Doctorate
Program: Professional
Accreditation: NW, ANEST, ARCPA, CAHIIM, DENT, DIETI, EMT, IPSY, MED, MIDWF, MT, NURSE, PH, RTT

01 President ..... Dr. Joseph E. ROBERTSON
03 Executive Vice Provost ..... Dr. David W. ROBINSON
05 Provost Education & Research ..... Dr. Jeanette MLADENOVIC
18 Assoc VP Facilities/Physical Plant ..... Mr. Scott PAGE
84 Assoc Vice Prov Enroll Management ..... Ms. Cherie HONNELL
63 Dean School of Medicine ..... Dr. Mark RICHARDSON
52 Dean School of Dentistry ..... Dr. Phillip T. MARUCHA
66 Dean School of Nursing ..... Dr. Susan BAKEWELL-SACHS
06 Registrar ..... Mrs. Mickie BUSH
17 Director University Hospital ..... Mr. Peter RAPP
88 Director Vollum Inst Adv Biomed Res ..... Dr. Richard H. GOODMAN
15 Director of Human Resources ..... Mr. Dan FORBES
08 Director Health Sciences Libraries ..... Mr. Chris SHAFFER
46 Director of Research Services ..... Dr. Daniel DORSA
26 Director Corporate Communications ..... Ms. Lora L. CUYKENDALL
88 Director Child Devel/Rehab Center ..... Dr. Brian ROGERS
37 Director Student Financial Aid ..... Ms. Rachel DURBIN
28 Director of Diversity ..... Ms. Leslie GARCIA

Oregon Institute of Technology (E)

3201 Campus Drive, Klamath Falls OR 97601-8801
County: Klamath FICE Identification: 003211
Unit ID: 209506
Telephone: (541) 885-1000 Carnegie Class: Bac/Diverse
FAX Number: (541) 885-1101 Calendar System: Quarter
URL: www.oit.edu
Established: 1947 Annual Undergrad Tuition & Fees (In-State): $8,839
Enrollment: 4,273 Coed
Affiliation or Control: State IRS Status: 501(c)3
Highest Offering: Master's
Program: Liberal Arts And General; Technical Emphasis
Accreditation: NW, COARC, DH, ENG, ENGR, ENGT, IACBE, MT, POLYT

01 President ..... Dr. Christopher MAPLES
05 Provost/Vice Pres Academic Affairs ..... Mr. Bradley BURDA
10 VP Finance/Administration ..... Ms. Mary Ann ZEMKE
32 VP Student Affairs/Dean of Students ..... Dr. Erin FOLEY
35 Dean of Students ..... Dr. Erin FOLEY
37 Director of Financial Aid ..... Ms. Tracey A. LEHMAN
15 Director of Human Resources ..... Mr. Ron MCCUTCHEON
07 Director of Admissions ..... Mr. Carl THOMAS
06 Registrar ..... Ms. Wendy IVIE
21 Director of Business Affairs ..... Ms. Michelle MEYER
13 Assoc VP/Chief Information Officer ..... Mr. Paul ROWAN
23 Director Student Health Services ..... Mrs. Gaylyn MAURER
18 Director Facilities Services ..... Vacant
41 Athletic Director ..... Mr. Michael J. SCHELL
35 Director Campus Life ..... Mr. Joseph MAURER
36 Director of Career Services ..... Vacant
09 Director of Institutional Research ..... Vacant
30 Assoc VP Devel/Alumni Relations ..... Mrs. Tracy RICKETTS

Oregon State University (F)

Corvallis OR 97331-8507
County: Benton FICE Identification: 003210
Unit ID: 209542
Telephone: (541) 737-0123 Carnegie Class: RU/VH
FAX Number: N/A Calendar System: Quarter
URL: www.oregonstate.edu
Established: 1868 Annual Undergrad Tuition & Fees (In-State): $10,008
Enrollment: 28,886 Coed
Affiliation or Control: State IRS Status: 501(c)3
Highest Offering: Doctorate
Program: Liberal Arts And General; Teacher Preparatory; Professional
Accreditation: NW, BUS, BUSA, CAATE, CACREP, CEA, CONST, CS, DIETD, DIETI, ENG, ENGR, IPSY, PH, PHAR, SPAA, TED, VET

01 President ..... Dr. Edward J. RAY
05 Provost/Executive Vice President ..... Dr. Sabah U. RANDHAWA
10 Vice Pres Finance/Administration ..... Mr. Glenn FORD
30 Vice Pres University Advancement ..... Mr. Steve CLARK
46 Interim Vice President for Research ..... Ms. Cynthia SAGERS
20 Vice Prov Academic Affs/Intl Pgms ..... Dr. Rebecca WARNER
13 Vice Prov for Information Svcs/CIO ..... Ms. Lois BROOKS
32 Vice Prov for Student Affairs ..... Dr. Susie BRUBAKER-COLE
56 Vice Prov Univ Outreach/Engagement ..... Dr. Scott REED
12 V Prov/Campus Ex Ofcr OSU-Cascades ..... Dr. Rebecca JOHNSON
84 Asst Provost Enrollment Management ..... Ms. Kate M. PETERSON
102 President & CEO OSU Foundation ..... Mr. Mike GOODWIN
47 Dean of Agricultural Sciences ..... Dr. Dan ARP
50 Dean of Business ..... Dr. Ilene K. KLEINSORGE
54 Dean of Engineering ..... Dr. Scott ASHFORD
65 Dean of Forestry ..... Dr. Thomas MANESS
68 Dean of Health & Human Sciences ..... Dr. Tammy BRAY
49 Interim Dean of Liberal Arts ..... Dr. Larry RODGERS
88 Dean of Oceanic & Atmos Science ..... Dr. Mark R. ABBOTT
67 Dean of Pharmacy ..... Dr. Mark ZABRISKIE
81 Dean of Science ..... Dr. Sastry PANTULA
74 Interim Dean of Veterinary Medicine ..... Dr. Susan TORNQUIST
51 Assoc Provost Extended Campus ..... Dr. David A. KING
58 Dean of Graduate School ..... Dr. Brenda MCCOMB
35 Interim Dean of Student Life ..... Ms. Tracy BENTLEY-TOWNLIN
92 Dean University Honors College ..... Dr. Toni DOOLEN
53 Dean of Education ..... Dr. Larry FLICK
08 University Librarian ..... Ms. Faye CHADWELL
22 Director Equity and Inclusion ..... Mr. Angelo GOMEZ
43 General Counsel ..... Ms. Becca GOSE
41 Director Intecollegiate Athletics ..... Vacant
36 Director of Career Services ..... Mr. Douglas COCHRAN
37 Dir of Financial Aid/Scholarship ..... Mr. Doug SEVERS
31 Director Memorial Union ..... Mr. Michael HENTHORNE
23 Int Dir Student Health Services ..... Dr. Jeff MULL
38 Dir Univ Counseling/Psych Svcs ..... Dr. Jackie ALVAREZ
39 Director Univ Housing/Dining Svcs ..... Mr. Dan LARSON
06 Registrar ..... Ms. Rebecca MATHERN
07 Director of Admissions ..... Mr. Noah BUCKLEY
24 Director Media & Outreach Services ..... Mr. John GREYDANUS
14 Dir of Enterprise Computing Service ..... Mr. Kent KUO
21 AVP Finance & Administration ..... Mr. Mike GREEN
15 Director of Human Resources ..... Mr. David BLAKE
18 Director Facility Services ..... Mr. Dave BLAKE
19 Director Public Safety ..... Mr. Denson CHATFIELD
29 Exec Dir of Alumni Association ..... Ms. Kathy BICKEL
86 Director Government Relations ..... Mr. Jock S. MILLS
44 Director of Annual Giving ..... Ms. Lacie LA RUE
27 Dir News/Comm Svcs/Asst Vice Pres ..... Ms. Annie HECK
26 Director of University Marketing ..... Ms. Melody K. OLDFIELD
105 Asst Director Web Communications ..... Mr. David A. BAKER
20 Dir Academic Planning/Assessment ..... Mr. Gary BEACH
28 Director of Equity and Inclusion ..... Mr. Angelo GOMEZ
09 Director of Institutional Research ..... Mr. Salvador CASTILLO
40 General Mgr & CEO OSU Bookstores ..... Mr. Steve E. ECKRICH
96 Manager Procurement/Contract Svcs ..... Ms. Kelly L. KOZISEK

Pacific Bible College (G)

409 N. Front Street, Medford OR 97501
County: Jackson Identification: 667252
Telephone: (541) 776-9942 Carnegie Class: Not Classified
FAX Number: N/A Calendar System: Semester
URL: www.pacficbible.com
Established: 1991 Annual Undergrad Tuition & Fees: $4,800
Enrollment: 47 Coed
Affiliation or Control: Non-denominational IRS Status: 501(c)3
Highest Offering: Associate Degree
Program: Religious Emphasis
Accreditation: @BI

01 President ..... Mr. Mike ROBINSON
11 Vice President Administration ..... Mr. Dennis ALLEN

Pacific Northwest College of Art (H)

511 NW Broadway, Portland OR 97209-3023
County: Multnomah FICE Identification: 003207
Unit ID: 209603
Telephone: (503) 226-4391 Carnegie Class: Spec/Arts
FAX Number: (503) 226-3587 Calendar System: Semester
URL: www.pnca.edu
Established: 1909 Annual Undergrad Tuition & Fees: $31,500
Enrollment: 519 Coed
Affiliation or Control: Independent Non-Profit IRS Status: 501(c)3
Highest Offering: Master's
Program: Fine Arts Emphasis
Accreditation: NW, ART

01 President ..... Dr. Thomas MANLEY
05 Dean of Academic Affairs ..... Ms. Tracey COCKRELL
10 Chief Financial Officer/HR Director ..... Ms. Nancy BARROWS
84 Vice Pres Enrollment Services ..... Mr. Kavin BUCK
04 Executive Administrative Assistant ..... Ms. Elizabeth CAMPBELL
51 Director of Continuing Education ..... Mr. Patrick FORSTER
37 Director Financial Aid ..... Ms. Heidi LOCKE
26 Director of Communications ..... Ms. Gillian FLOREN
06 Registrar ..... Ms. Jenifer DE KALB
08 Director of Library Services ..... Mr. Dan MCCLURE
07 Director of Admissions ..... Ms. D. Jean HESTER
15 HR Director ..... Mr. Sean WOODARD
100 Chief of Staff ..... Ms. Gillian FLOREN
09 Dir of Institutional Research ..... Mr. Gus BAUM
18 Chief Facilities/Physical Plant ..... Mr. Dave NEESON
19 Director Security/Safety ..... Mr. Joel SMITH
32 Assistant Dir of Student Services ..... Ms. Rachael ALLEN
39 Assoc Director of Residence Life ..... Mr. Jordan BERMINGHAM
45 Major Gifts Officer ..... Ms. Sharon JOHNSON

Pacific University (I)

2043 College Way, Forest Grove OR 97116-1797
County: Washington FICE Identification: 003212
Unit ID: 209612
Telephone: (503) 357-6151 Carnegie Class: Master's L
FAX Number: (503) 352-2242 Calendar System: Semester
URL: www.pacificu.edu
Established: 1849 Annual Undergrad Tuition & Fees: $39,858
Enrollment: 3,712 Coed
Affiliation or Control: Independent Non-Profit IRS Status: 501(c)3
Highest Offering: Doctorate
Program: Liberal Arts And General; Teacher Preparatory; Professional
Accreditation: NW, ARCPA, @AUD, CAATE, CLPSY, DH, IPSY, MUS, OPT, OPTR, OT, PHAR, PTA, @SP, SW, TED

01 President ..... Dr. Lesley M. HALLICK
05 Vice Pres Academic Affairs/Provost ..... Dr. John MILLER
10 Vice Pres Finance & Administration ..... Mr. Mike MALLERY
30 Vice Pres University Advancement ..... Ms. Cassie WARMAN
32 Vice Pres Enrollment/Student Affs ..... Dr. Mark ANKENY
35 Assoc Vice Pres Student Affairs ..... Mr. Will PERKINS
21 Assistant Vice Pres for Finance ..... Mr. William RAY
26 Assoc VP for University Relations ..... Ms. Jan STRICKLIN
18 Director of Facilities ..... Ms. Cindy SCHUPPERT
07 Executive Director of Admissions ..... Ms. Karen DUNSTON

06 Registrar .... Ms. Anne HERMAN
37 Director Financial Aid .... Ms. Leslie LIMPER
13 Chief Information Officer .... Mr. James FLEMING
88 Director of Conference Services .... Ms. Lois HORNBERGER
88 Director University Events .... Ms. Paula THATCHER
76 Exec Dean Col of Health Professions .. Dr. Ann BARR-GILLESPIE
49 Dean of Arts & Sciences .... Dr. Lisa CARSTENS
63 Dean of Optometry .... Dr. Jennifer COYLE
67 Dean of Pharmacy .... Dr. Reza KARIMIGEVARI
53 Dean College of Education .... Dr. Leif GUSTAVSON
83 Dean Sch Professional Psychology .... Dr. Christiane BREMS
41 Athletic Director .... Mr. Kenneth SCHUMANN
76 Director School Physical Therapy .... Dr. Richard RUTT
76 Dir School Occupational Therapy .... Dr. Gregory WINTZ
15 Director of Human Resources .... Mr. Kris KOSIK
23 Director of Health Services .... Ms. Kathryn L. EISENBARTH
88 Acad Coord/English Language Inst .... Ms. Monique GRINDELL
44 Director of Annual Giving .... Ms. Kristin STORFA
07 Exec Director of Grad/Prof Admiss .... Mr. Jon-Erik LARSEN
76 Interim Dir Physician Asst Studies .... Dr. Mary VON
29 Director Alumni Relations .... Ms. Martha CALUS-MCLAIN
88 Dir External Relations Optometry .... Ms. Jeanne OLIVER
08 Library Director .... Ms. Marita KUNKEL
88 Senior Editor/Writer .... Ms. Jenni LUCKETT
32 Dir Univ Center/Student Activities .... Mr. Steve KLEIN
36 Director Career Development .... Mr. Brian O'DRISCOLL
52 Program Director-Dental .... Ms. Lisa ROWLEY
40 Manager Bookstore .... Ms. Stacie BLANKENHORN
38 Director Counseling Center .... Ms. Robin KEILLOR
09 Director of Institutional Research .... Mr. William O'SHEA
04 Executive Asst to President .... Ms. Sue WEINBENDER
100 Chief of Staff .... Ms. Mic HOWE
28 Director of Diversity .... Mr. Alfonso LOPEZ-VASQUEZ
43 Dir Legal Services/General Counsel .... Mr. Scott SHUMAN

Pioneer Pacific College (A)

27501 SW Parkway Avenue, Wilsonville OR 97070-9296
County: Clackamas | FICE Identification: 023301
Unit ID: 210076
Telephone: (503) 682-3903 | Carnegie Class: Assoc/PrivFP4
FAX Number: (503) 682-1514 | Calendar System: Other
URL: www.pioneerpacific.edu
Established: 1981 | Annual Undergrad Tuition & Fees: $15,000
Enrollment: 1,195 | Coed
Affiliation or Control: Proprietary | IRS Status: Proprietary
Highest Offering: Baccalaureate
Program: Occupational
Accreditation: ACICS

01 President .... Mr. Don MOUTOS
05 Vice President of Academic Affairs .... Mr. Fred OSBORN
21 Controller .... Ms. Wendy HUTCHISONS

Pioneer Pacific College-Eugene Branch (B)

3800 Sports way, Springfield OR 97447
Telephone: (541) 684-4644 | Identification: 770764
Accreditation: ACICS

† Branch campus of Pioneer Pacific College, Wilsonville, OR.

Portland Community College (C)

PO Box 19000, Portland OR 97280-0990
County: Multnomah | FICE Identification: 003213
Unit ID: 209746
Telephone: (971) 722-6111 | Carnegie Class: Assoc/Pub-U-MC
FAX Number: (971) 722-4960 | Calendar System: Quarter
URL: www.pcc.edu/
Established: 1961 | Annual Undergrad Tuition & Fees (In-District): $3,127
Enrollment: 30,929 | Coed
Affiliation or Control: Local | IRS Status: 501(c)3
Highest Offering: Associate Degree
Program: Occupational; 2-Year Principally Bachelor's Creditable
Accreditation: NW, ADNUR, CAHIIM, DA, DH, DT, EMT, IFSAC, MAC, MLTAD, RAD

01 Interim President .... Ms. Sylvia J. KELLEY
100 Chief of Staff .... Dr. Traci FORDHAM
05 VP Academic & Student Affairs .... Dr. Christine CHAIRSELL
11 Vice Pres Finance/Administration .... Mr. Jim LANGSTRAAT
10 Assoc VP Financial Services .... Mr. Jim LANGSTRAAT
13 Assoc VP Information Tech Svcs .... Ms. Leslie RIESTER
44 Assoc VP College Advancement .... Mr. Robert A. WAGNER
12 Campus President Sylvania .... Dr. Lisa AVERY
12 Campus President Cascade .... Dr. Karin EDWARDS
12 Campus President Rock Creek .... Dr. Sandra FOWLER-HILL
12 Campus President Extended Lrng .... Dr. Jessica HOWARD
20 Int Dean Instruction Sylvania .... Ms. Loretta GOLDY
20 Dean Instruction Cascade Campus .... Mr. Kurt SIMONDS
20 Int Dean Instr Rock Creek Campus .... Dr. Cheryl SCOTT
20 Dean Instr Ext Learning Campus .... Dr. Craig KOLINS
32 Dean Student Dev Sylvania Campus .... Ms. Heather LANG
32 Dean Stdnt Dev Rock Creek Campus .... Ms. Narce RODRIGUEZ
32 Dean Student Dev Cascade Campus .... Dr. Linda REISSER
35 Interim Dean Student Affairs .... Ms. Tammy N. BILLICK
15 Director Human Resources .... Ms. Lisa BLEDSOE
18 Director Facilities Management .... Mr. Keith GREGORY
08 Director Libraries .... Dr. Donna REED
09 Dir Institutional Effectiveness .... Ms. Laura MASSEY
19 Director Public Safety .... Mr. Ken GOODWIN

37 Director Financial Aid .... Mr. Bert LOGAN
22 Director Affirmative Action .... Ms. Kim BAKER-FLOWERS
30 Director of Development .... Ms. Kim KONO
84 Dir of Enrollment Services .... Ms. Shasta BUCHANAN

Portland State University (D)

PO Box 751, Portland OR 97207-0751
County: Multnomah | FICE Identification: 003216
Unit ID: 209807
Telephone: (503) 725-3000 | Carnegie Class: RU/H
FAX Number: (503) 725-4882 | Calendar System: Quarter
URL: www.pdx.edu
Established: 1946 | Annual Undergrad Tuition & Fees (In-State): $8,118
Enrollment: 28,931 | Coed
Affiliation or Control: State | IRS Status: 501(c)3
Highest Offering: Doctorate
Program: Liberal Arts And General; Teacher Preparatory; Professional
Accreditation: NW, BUS, BUSA, CACREP, CEA, CORE, CS, ENG, HSA, MUS, PH, PLNG, SP, SPAA, SW, TED, THEA

01 President .... Dr. Wim WIEWEL
43 General Counsel .... Mr. David REESE
05 Provost & VP Academic Affairs .... Dr. Sona ANDREWS
10 Vice President Finance/Admin .... Dr. Kevin REYNOLDS
102 CEO PSU Foundation .... Ms. Francoise AYLMER
100 Chief of Staff & VP Public Affairs .... Ms. Lois DAVIS
32 VP Enroll Mgmt & Student Affairs .... Dr. John FRAIRE
46 VP Rsrch & Strategic Partnerships .... Dr. Jonathan FINK
45 Vice Prov Academic/Fiscal Planning .... Mr. Scott MARSHALL
20 Vice Provost Acad Pers Ldrshp & Dev .... Dr. Shelly CHABON
21 Assoc VP Budget & Finance .... Mr. Alan FINN
15 Assc VP HR & Univ Policy/Practice .... Ms. Shana SECHRIST
36 Assoc VP Academic/Career Services .... Mr. Dan FORTMILLER
84 Assoc VP Enrollment Management .... Ms. Cindy SKARUPPA
22 Int Chief Diversity Officer .... Dr. Charles LOPEZ
26 Assoc VP Communications .... Mr. Christopher BRODERICK
09 Director Inst Research/Planning .... Dr. Kathi A. KETCHESON
19 Director Campus Public Safety .... Mr. Phil ZERZAN
13 AVP Strategic Plng/Prtnrshps/Tech .... Mr. Erin FLYNN
08 Dean University Librarian .... Dr. Marilyn MOODY
41 Athletics Director .... Mr. Mark ROUNTREE
88 Vice Prov Acad Innov/Stdnt Success .... Mr. Sukhwant S. JHAJ
49 Dean of CLAS .... Dr. Karen MARRONGELLE
50 Dean of SBA .... Dr. Daniel CONNELLY
53 Dean Graduate Sch of Education .... Dr. Randy HITZ
54 Dean Col Engr/Computer Science .... Dr. Ren Jeng SU
57 Dean College of the Arts .... Dr. Robert BUCKER
70 Dean School of Social Work .... Dr. Laura NISSEN
80 Dean College Urban/Public Affairs .... Dr. Stephen PERCY
35 Dean Student Life .... Ms. Michele TOPPE
13 AVP/Chief Information Officer .... Mr. Kirk KELLY
88 Dir Diversity & Mult Student Svcs .... Ms. Cece RIDDER
06 Registrar .... Ms. Cindy BACCAR
86 Dir Local & Fed Govt Relations .... Ms. Mary MOLLER
86 Dir State Govt Relations .... Ms. Debbie KORESKI
23 Exec Dir Stdnt Health & Counseling .... Dr. Dana TASSON
58 AVP & Dean Graduate Studies .... Ms. Margaret EVERETT
44 PSUF VP Develop & Chief Dev Officer .... Ms. Kristin COPPOLA
28 Exec Dir Diversity & Inclusion .... Mr. Chas LOPEZ
88 AVP Research .... Mr. Mark SYTSMA
21 Exec Dir Financial Svcs & Contr .... Vacant

Reed College (E)

3203 SE Woodstock Boulevard, Portland OR 97202-8199
County: Multnomah | FICE Identification: 003217
Unit ID: 209922
Telephone: (503) 771-1112 | Carnegie Class: Bac/A&S
FAX Number: (503) 777-7769 | Calendar System: Semester
URL: www.reed.edu
Established: 1908 | Annual Undergrad Tuition & Fees: $49,940
Enrollment: 1,355 | Coed
Affiliation or Control: Independent Non-Profit | IRS Status: 501(c)3
Highest Offering: Master's
Program: Liberal Arts And General
Accreditation: NW

01 President .... Mr. John KROGER
05 Dean of the Faculty .... Dr. Nigel J. NICHOLSON
26 Vice President College Relations .... Dr. Hugh E. PORTER
10 Vice President & Treasurer .... Ms. Lorraine ARVIN
32 Vice President for Student Services .... Dr. Michael BRODY
04 Exec Asst to the President .... Ms. Dawn G. THOMPSON
28 Dean for Institutional Diversity .... Dr. Mary B. JAMES
35 Dean of Students .... Mr. Bruce SMITH
23 Director Health & Counseling .... Ms. Kathryn A. SMITH
07 Vice Pres/Dean Admission & Fin Aid .... Mr. Milyon TRULOVE
06 Registrar .... Ms. Nora MCLAUGHLIN
08 College Librarian .... Ms. Dena HUTTO
30 Director of Development .... Ms. Jan KURTZ
37 Director of Financial Aid .... Vacant
09 Director of Institutional Research .... Mr. Mike TAMADA
26 Exec Dir Comm & Public Affairs .... Ms. Mandy HEATON
29 Director of Alumni Relations .... Mr. Michael J. TESKEY
13 Chief Information Officer .... Dr. Martin D. RINGLE
105 Director of Web Support Services .... Ms. Marianne M. COLGROVE
91 Director Administrative Computing .... Mr. Gabriel LEAVITT
21 Controller .... Ms. Tracy L. FRANTEL
15 Director of Human Resources .... Ms. Michelle VALINTIS
44 Dir Annual Fund & Special Gifts .... Ms. Mary M. ASKELSON
102 Dir Corporate/Foundation Support .... Ms. Diane B. GUMZ

104 Director International Programs .... Dr. Paul D. DEYOUNG
36 Dean of Stdnts/Dir Life Beyond Reed .... Ms. Alice HARRA
88 Director of Special Programs .... Ms. Barbara A. AMEN
18 Director Facilities Operations .... Mr. Townsend ANGELL
19 Director Community Safety .... Mr. Gary GRANGER
68 Director of Physical Education .... Mr. Michael LOMBARDO
40 Manager of the Bookstore .... Mr. Ueli STADLER

Rogue Community College (F)

3345 Redwood Highway, Grants Pass OR 97527-9298
County: Josephine | FICE Identification: 010182
Unit ID: 209940
Telephone: (541) 956-7500 | Carnegie Class: Assoc/Pub-R-L
FAX Number: (541) 471-3591 | Calendar System: Quarter
URL: www.roguecc.edu
Established: 1970 | Annual Undergrad Tuition & Fees (In-District): $4,005
Enrollment: 1,418 | Coed
Affiliation or Control: Local | IRS Status: 501(c)3
Highest Offering: Associate Degree
Program: Occupational; 2-Year Principally Bachelor's Creditable; Technical Emphasis
Accreditation: NW, EMT

01 President .... Dr. Peter ANGSTADT
05 VP of Instruction/CAO .... Mr. Kirk GIBSON
13 VP of College Services/CIO .... Mr. Curtis SOMMERFELD
32 Vice President Student Services .... Ms. Kori EBENHACK-BIEBER
103 Dean School of Workforce/Col Prep .... Ms. Theresa RIVENES
72 Dean School of Arts and Technology .... Mr. Kevin HOFF
76 Dean School of Health/Public Svcs .... Ms. Genna SOUTHWORTH
88 Director SBDC .... Mr. Ronald GOSS
81 Dean School of Science and Tech .... Mr. Steve SCHILLING
08 Head Librarian .... Mr. Robert FELTHOUSEN
102 Executive Director Foundation .... Ms. Judith BASKER
15 Director of Human Resources .... Ms. Sara MOYE
24 Director Instructional Media .... Mr. Josh OGLE
109 Director Auxiliary Services .... Ms. Laura HAGA-DUFFY
26 Dir Marketing & Recruitment .... Mr. Grant WALKER
37 Director Student Financial Aid .... Ms. Anna MANLEY
13 Director I/T Network & User Support .... Mr. Mike MCCLURE
105 Director Internet & Telephone Svcs .... Ms. Susie ASHBRIDGE
71 Director TRiO-EOC .... Mr. Jason FIANO
71 Director TRiO-SSS .... Ms. Colletta YOUNG
51 Apprenticeship Coordinator .... Ms. Cathy PIERSON
96 Contract and Procurment Manager .... Ms. Jodie FULTON
25 Grants and Planning Coordinator .... Ms. Mary O'KIEF
91 Director of IT Programming .... Vacant
18 Director of Facilities/Operations .... Mr. Grant LAGORIO
20 Director of Curriculum/Scheduling .... Ms. Laura BENNETT
31 Director of WF Training & Cmty Educ .... Mr. Bill JIRON
88 Director of Adult Basic Skills .... Ms. Laurie RYDELL
88 Director of Student Programs .... Ms. Rene MCKENZIE
88 Accreditation Liaison Officer .... Ms. Denise SWAFFORD
06 Director Enrollment Services .... Mr. John DUARTE
04 Asst to President and Board .... Ms. Denise NELSON
35 Dean of Students .... Mr. Roger FRIESEN
10 Chief Financial Officer .... Ms. Lisa STANTON
41 Athletic Director .... Ms. Kori EBENHACK-BIEBER

Southern Oregon University (G)

1250 Siskiyou Boulevard, Ashland OR 97520-5001
County: Jackson | FICE Identification: 003219
Unit ID: 210146
Telephone: (541) 552-7672 | Carnegie Class: Master's L
FAX Number: (541) 552-6329 | Calendar System: Quarter
URL: www.sou.edu
Established: 1872 | Annual Undergrad Tuition & Fees (In-State): $8,010
Enrollment: 5,954 | Coed
Affiliation or Control: State | IRS Status: 501(c)3
Highest Offering: Master's
Program: Liberal Arts And General; Teacher Preparatory; Professional
Accreditation: NW, ACBSP, CACREP, MUS

02 Interim President .... Dr. Roy H. SAIGO
05 Int Prov/VP Acad & Student Affairs .... Dr. Susan WALSH
10 VP for Finance & Administration .... Mr. Craig MORRIS
30 Int Vice President Development .... Ms. Janet FRATELLA
15 Director for Human Resource Svcs .... Vacant
100 Chief of Staff/Dir Governmt Rels .... Ms. Liz SHELBY
84 Assoc VP Enrollment & Retention .... Ms. Lisa GARCIA-HANSON
26 Ex Dir Interactive Mktg/Media Rels .... Ms. Nicolle ALEMAN
18 Dir for Facilities Mgmt & Planning .... Mr. Drew GILLILAND
58 Assoc Provost/Director Grad Stds .... Dr. Jody WATERS
21 Director of Business Services .... Mr. Steve LARVICK
08 University Librarian .... Mr. Jeffrey GAYTON
32 Director for Student Life .... Ms. Jennifer FOUNTAIN
51 Exec Dir Division of Continuing Edu .... Ms. Jeanne STALLMAN
19 Co-Director of Campus Public Safety .... Mr. Frederick CREEK
19 Co-Director of Campus Public Safety .... Mr. Randall SCHOEN
13 Director of Information Technology .... Mr. Brad CHRIST
29 Director of Alumni Affairs .... Mr. Mike BEAGLE
21 Assoc Director of Business Services .... Ms. Debbie MICHAELS
106 Director of Distance Education .... Dr. Vicki SUTER
88 Director of Schneider Museum of Art .... Ms. Erika LEPPMANN
88 Dir of Accelerated Baccalureate Pgm .... Mr. Curt BACON
28 Director of Diversity and Inclusion .... Ms. Marjorie TRUEBLOOD-GAMBLE
44 Annual Fund Coordinator .... Ms. Chava FLORENDO
57 Director Performing Arts .... Dr. David HUMPHREY
83 Director Social Sciences .... Dr. Dan DENEUI

97 Director Undergraduate Studies Dr. Lee AYERS
81 Director STEM Dr. Sherry ETTLICH
50 Director Business Comm & Environmt Dr. Greg JONES
79 Director Humanities & Culture Dr. Scott REX
88 Director Educ Health & Leadership Dr. John KING
06 Registrar Dr. Matt STILLMAN
07 Director of Admissions Ms. Kelly MOUTSATSON
37 Director of Financial Aid Ms. Patricia MCAULEY
09 Director of Institutional Research Mr. Chris STANEK
25 Chief Contracts/Grants Admin Ms. Joanne PRESTON
41 Athletic Director Mr. Matt SAYRE

Southwestern Oregon Community College (A)

1988 Newmark Avenue, Coos Bay OR 97420-2911
County: Coos FICE Identification: 003220
Unit ID: 210155
Telephone: (541) 888-2525 Carnegie Class: Assoc/Pub-R-M
FAX Number: (541) 888-7285 Calendar System: Quarter
URL: www.socc.edu
Established: 1961 Annual Undergrad Tuition & Fees (In-District): $5,655
Enrollment: 2,315 Coed
Affiliation or Control: Local IRS Status: 501(c)3
Highest Offering: Associate Degree
Program: Occupational; 2-Year Principally Bachelor's Creditable
Accreditation: NW, ACFEI, EMT

01 President Dr. Patty SCOTT
11 VP Administrative Services Mr. Eric STASAK
05 VP Instructional Services Dr. Ross TOMLIN
12 Dean Curry County Ms. Janet PRETTI
72 Dean of Career and Technical Educ Ms. Cody YEAGER
56 Dean of Extended Learning Ms. Karen DOMINE
32 Dean of Student Services Mr. Tim DAILEY
84 Exec Director Enrollment Management Mr. Tom NICHOLLS
13 Director Integrated Technology Mr. Rocky LAVOIE
88 Exec Director OCCI (Culinary) Mr. Shawn HANLIN
20 Associate Dean of LDC & Devel Ed Mr. Rod KELLER
41 Director Athletics Dr. Mike HERBERT
07 Director of Admissions Mr. Tom NICHOLLS
19 Director Campus Safety Mr. Joe THOMAS
30 Dir College Advancement/Alumni Rels Ms. Elise HAMNER
18 Director Facilities Services Ms. Emerald BRUNETT
06 Registrar Ms. Shawn LIGGETT
37 Director Financial Aid Ms. Avena SINGH
15 Exec Director Human Resources Dr. Jan BAXTER
08 Director Learning Resources Vacant
66 Director Nursing Ms. Susan WALKER
39 Director Residence Life Mr. Jeff WHITEY
88 Director SOCC Business Dev Center Ms. Arlene SOTO
38 Director Student Support Srvcs Ms. Michele BENOIT
40 Manager Bookstore Ms. Shawna STEPHENS
09 Institutional Researcher Ms. Robin BUNNELL
35 Coordinator Student Life and Events Mr. Nathan HELLAND
04 Exec Asst to the Pres/Board of Educ Ms. Deb NICHOLLS
10 Chief Business Officer Ms. Kathy DIXON
22 Dir Affirmative Action/EEO Mr. Eric STASAK
26 Chief Public Relations/Marketing Ms. Anne MATTHEWS

Sumner College (B)

15115 SW Sequoia Parkway, Ste 200,
Tigard OR 97224-7157
County: Multnomah FICE Identification: 021049
Unit ID: 208512
Telephone: (503) 223-5100 Carnegie Class: Not Classified
FAX Number: (503) 952-0010 Calendar System: Other
URL: www.sumnercollege.edu
Established: 1974 Annual Undergrad Tuition & Fees: $27,290
Enrollment: 262 Coed
Affiliation or Control: Proprietary IRS Status: Proprietary
Highest Offering: Associate Degree
Program: Occupational
Accreditation: ACICS

01 President Joanna S. RUSSELL

Tillamook Bay Community College (C)

4301 3rd Street, Tillamook OR 97141
County: Tillamook Identification: 666647
Unit ID: 420723
Telephone: (503) 842-8222 Carnegie Class: Assoc/Pub-R-S
FAX Number: (503) 842-8336 Calendar System: Quarter
URL: www.tillamookbay.cc
Established: 1981 Annual Undergrad Tuition & Fees (In-District): $4,680
Enrollment: 473 Coed
Affiliation or Control: State/Local IRS Status: 501(c)3
Highest Offering: Associate Degree
Program: 2-Year Principally Bachelor's Creditable
Accreditation: NW

01 President Dr. Constance C. GREEN
05 Chief Academic Officer Dr. Ann HOVEY
10 Comptroller/Budget Officer Ms. Kyra WILLIAMS
30 Chief Development Mrs. Heidi LUQUETTE
32 Dir Student Services & Registrar Ms. Michele BURTON
15 Dir Human Resources/Facilities Mr. Pat RYAN
09 Coordinator Institutional Research Ms. Cindy ROWE

Treasure Valley Community College (D)

650 College Boulevard, Ontario OR 97914-3423
County: Malheur FICE Identification: 003221
Unit ID: 210234
Telephone: (541) 881-8822 Carnegie Class: Assoc/Pub-R-M
FAX Number: (541) 881-5525 Calendar System: Quarter
URL: www.tvcc.cc
Established: 1961 Annual Undergrad Tuition & Fees (In-District): $5,424
Enrollment: 2,396 Coed
Affiliation or Control: Local IRS Status: 501(c)3
Highest Offering: Associate Degree
Program: Occupational; 2-Year Principally Bachelor's Creditable
Accreditation: NW, ADNUR, PNUR

01 President Ms. Dana YOUNG
05 Vice President of Academic Affairs Dr. Rachel ANDERSON
11 Vice Pres Administrative Services Mr. Randy R. GRIFFIN
08 Librarian Mr. Dennis GILL
32 Vice President Student Services Dr. Paul KRAFT
37 Financial Aid Director Mr. Keith RAAB
13 Director Data Processing Mr. Scott CARPENTER
07 Director of Admissions Ms. Stephanie OESTER
15 Director of Human Resources Mr. Doug HAMMAN
51 Director of Continuing Education Ms. Andrea TESTI
18 Dir of Housing/Building & Grounds Mr. Bernie BABCOCK
10 Comptroller Mr. Jonathan GILLEN
35 Director of Student Activities Mr. Justin CORE
41 Athletic Director Mr. Ed ARONSON
88 Corrections Education Director Mr. Eddie ALVES
06 Registrar Dr. Paul KRAFT
09 Director of Institutional Research Dr. Michelle LANDA
28 Director of Diversity Dr. Paul KRAFT
30 Chief Development Ms. Cathy YASUDA
40 Bookstore Manager Mr. Kjetil ROM
04 Executive Asst to President Ms. Gina ROPER
29 Director Alumni Relations Ms. Abby LEE

Umpqua Community College (E)

1140 Umpqua College Road, Roseburg OR 97470
County: Douglas FICE Identification: 003222
Unit ID: 210270
Telephone: (541) 440-4600 Carnegie Class: Assoc/Pub-R-M
FAX Number: (541) 440-4637 Calendar System: Quarter
URL: www.umpqua.edu
Established: 1964 Annual Undergrad Tuition & Fees (In-District): $4,011
Enrollment: 2,045 Coed
Affiliation or Control: Local IRS Status: 501(c)3
Highest Offering: Associate Degree
Program: Occupational; 2-Year Principally Bachelor's Creditable
Accreditation: NW, ADNUR, EMT

01 Interim President Dr. Rita CAVIN
05 Vice President for Instruction Dr. Roxanne KELLY
10 Chief Financial Officer Ms. Rebecca REDELL
32 Vice President Student Services Ms. Joyce COLEMAN
84 Director Enrollment Management Mr. David FARRINGTON
38 Director of Advising & Counseling Ms. Mandie PRITCHARD
37 Director of Financial Aid Ms. Michelle BERGMANN
13 Director Instructional Technology Vacant
08 Director of Library Services Ms. Carol MCGEEHON
103 Director of Community/Workforce Ms. Robynne VAN WINKLE
09 Director Inst Research/Assess/Plng Mr. Dan YODER
15 Director of Human Resources Ms. Lynn JOHNSON

University of Oregon (F)

1585 E. 13th Avenue, Eugene OR 97403
County: Lane FICE Identification: 003223
Unit ID: 209551
Telephone: (541) 346-1000 Carnegie Class: RU/VH
FAX Number: (541) 346-3017 Calendar System: Quarter
URL: www.uoregon.edu
Established: 1876 Annual Undergrad Tuition & Fees (In-State): $10,289
Enrollment: 24,181 Coed
Affiliation or Control: State IRS Status: 501(c)3
Highest Offering: Doctorate
Program: Liberal Arts And General; Professional
Accreditation: NW, ART, BUS, BUSA, CAATE, CEA, CIDA, CLPSY, COPSY, CSHSE, IPSY, JOUR, LAW, LSAR, MFCD, MUS, PCSAS, PLNG, SCPSY, SP, SPAA

01 President Mr. Michael H. SCHILL
100 Senior Advisor/Chief of Staff Mr. Greg J. STRIPP
05 Senior Vice President & Provost Dr. Scott L. COLTRANE
10 VP Finance & Admin & CFO Ms. Jamie H. MOFFITT
32 Vice President for Student Life Dr. Robin H. HOLMES
30 Vice Pres University Advancement Mr. Michael C. ANDREASEN
46 VP Research/Dean Graduate School Vacant
20 Vice Provost Undergraduate Studies Dr. Lisa FREINKEL
28 Vice Pres Inst Equity/Diversity Dr. Yvette M. ALEX-ASSENSOH
13 Vice Prov Information Services/CIO Dr. Melissa Z. WOO
85 Vice Provost International Affairs Dr. Dennis C. GALVAN
86 Assoc Vice Pres Federal Affairs Ms. Betsy A. BOYD
29 AVP Alumni Affairs/Exec Dir UOAA Mr. Paul J. CLIFFORD
43 Actg General Counsel to University Mr. Doug Y. PARK
102 Chief Investment Officer Foundation Mr. Jay NAMYET
06 University Registrar Ms. Susan M. EVELAND
07 Director of Admissions Mr. Jim H. RAWLINS
08 Philip H Knight Dean of Libraries Dr. Adriene I. LIM
21 Dir Business Affairs and Controller Mr. Kelly B. WOLF
37 Director Student Financial Aid Mr. Jim J. BROOKS
36 Director of Career Center Dr. Daniel PASCOE AGUILAR
15 Chief Human Resources Officer Ms. Nancy E. RESNICK
18 Assoc VP Campus Operations Mr. George E. HECHT
22 Director Affirmative Action Ms. Penny J. DAUGHERTY
41 Director Intercollegiate Athletics Mr. Rob A. MULLENS
56 Executive Dir UO Academic Extension Ms. Sandra K. GLADNEY
49 Int Dean College Arts & Sciences Dr. W. Andrew MARCUS
48 Actg Dean Architecture/Allied Arts Mr. Brook W. MULLER
50 Dean College of Business Dr. Cornelis A. DE KLUYVER
53 Dean College of Education Dr. Randy W. KAMPHAUS
60 Actg Dean School of Journ & Comm Ms. Julianne H. NEWTON
58 Dean of Graduate School Dr. Scott L. PRATT
61 Dean School of Law Mr. Michael L. MOFFITT
64 Dean School of Music & Dance Dr. Brad FOLEY
92 Dean Clark Honors College Dr. Terry L. HUNT
09 Director of Institutional Research Dr. JP MONROE
35 Associate VP for Student Life Mr. Michael E. EYSTER
38 Dir Counseling & Testing Center Dr. Shelly K. KERR
84 VP for Enrollment Management Mr. Roger J. THOMPSON
96 Dir Purchasing & Contracting Svcs Ms. Catherine D. SUSMAN
101 Secretary of the Institution/Board Ms. Angela WILHELMS
19 Chief of Police Ms. Carolyn G. MCDERMED
26 Assoc VP Comm Mktg & Brand Mgt Mr. Tim R. CLEVENGER
39 Director Student Housing Mr. Michael M. GRIFFEL
44 Director Annual Giving Program Mr. Rick F. ERICSON
45 Vice Provost Budget & Planning Dr. Brad SHELTON
90 Director Academic Technology Ms. Helen Y. CHU

University of Phoenix Oregon Campus (G)

13221 SW 68th Parkway, Tigard OR 97223-8328
Telephone: (503) 403-2900 Identification: 770222
Accreditation: &NH, ACBSP

† No longer accepting campus-based students.

University of Portland (H)

5000 N Willamette Boulevard, Portland OR 97203-5798
County: Multnomah FICE Identification: 003224
Unit ID: 209825
Telephone: (503) 943-8000 Carnegie Class: Master's L
FAX Number: (503) 943-7491 Calendar System: Semester
URL: www.up.edu
Established: 1901 Annual Undergrad Tuition & Fees: $40,080
Enrollment: 4,169 Coed
Affiliation or Control: Independent Non-Profit IRS Status: 501(c)3
Highest Offering: Doctorate
Program: Liberal Arts And General; Teacher Preparatory; Professional
Accreditation: NW, BUS, CS, ENG, MUS, NURSE, SW, TED, THEA

01 President Rev. Mark L. POORMAN, CSC
05 Provost Dr. Thomas G. GREENE
03 Executive Vice President Vacant
26 Vice Pres for University Relations Ms. Laurie C. KELLEY
11 Vice Pres for University Operations Mr. James B. RAVELLI
10 Vice Pres for Financial Affairs Mr. Alan P. TIMMINS
32 Vice President for Student Affairs Rev. Gerard J. OLINGER, CSC
43 Gen Couns & Specia Asst to the Pres Ms. Danielle E. HERMANNY
35 Assoc VP for Student Development Rev. John J. DONATO, CSC
07 Dean of Admissions Mr. Jason S. MCDONALD
21 Controller Mr. Eric C. BARGER
06 Registrar Ms. Roberta D. LINDAHL
30 Sr Assoc Vice President Development Mr. Bryce B. STRANG
36 Director Career Services Ms. Amy CAVANAUGH
15 Assoc VP for Human Resources Ms. Bryn M. SOPKO
37 Director Student Financial Aid Ms. Janet K. TURNER
27 Director of Marketing Ms. Rachel E. BARRY-ARQUIT
49 Dean of Arts & Sciences Dr. Michael F. ANDREWS
50 Dean of the Business School Dr. Robin D. ANDERSON
66 Dean of Nursing Dr. Joane T. MOCERI
54 Dean of Engineering Dr. Sharon A. JONES
53 Dean of Education Dr. John L. WATZKE
23 Director University Health Services Vacant
19 Director of Public Safety Mr. Gerald A. GREGG
29 Director Alumni Relations Mr. Craig SWINYARD
39 Director Residence Life Mr. Christopher HAUG
41 Athletic Director Mr. Scott LEYKAM
42 Director Campus Ministry Rev. James T. GALLAGHER, CSC
102 Director Foundation Development Vacant
18 Director Facilities Planning Constr Mr. Paul J. LUTY
18 Director Physical Plant Mr. Andre HUTCHINSON
40 Director Bookstore Ms. Erin L. BRIGHT
88 Director University Events Mr. William O. REED
09 Director of Institutional Research Ms. Karen K. NELSON
35 Director Student Activities Mr. Jeromy A. KOFFLER
04 Administrative Asst to President Ms. Kathy M. SIMEK

University of Western States (I)

2900 NE 132nd Avenue, Portland OR 97230-3099
County: Multnomah FICE Identification: 012309
Unit ID: 210438
Telephone: (503) 256-3180 Carnegie Class: Spec/Health
FAX Number: (503) 251-5723 Calendar System: Quarter
URL: www.uws.edu
Established: 1904 Annual Undergrad Tuition & Fees: $29,701
Enrollment: 759 Coed
Affiliation or Control: Independent Non-Profit IRS Status: 501(c)3
Highest Offering: Doctorate

Program: Professional
Accreditation: NW, CHIRO, COMTA

01 President Dr. Joseph BRIMHALL
10 VP for Finance Administration Mr. Eric BLUMENTHAL
05 Provost Dr. Will EVANS
88 Special Assistant to the President Dr. Patrick BROWNE
23 Vice President of Clinic Affairs Dr. Joseph PFEIFER
108 VP Institutional Effectiveness Dr. Laura LAMM
86 Assoc VP for Community Relations Ms. Rosalia MESSINA
100 Chief of Staff Ms. Catherine HOOPER
46 Assoc Vice President of Research Dr. Mitch HAAS
23 Assoc VP of Clinical Internships Dr. Stanley EWALD
13 Director of Information Technology Mr. Erick RUIZ
84 Dean of Enrollment & Student Svcs Dr. Tim FOLEY
26 Dir of PR/Marketing/Communications Ms. Megan NUGENT
15 Director Human Resources Ms. Kathleen CANNON
06 Registrar Ms. Michelle DODGE
08 University Librarian Ms. Janet TAPPER
07 Director of Admissions Ms. Mary STAFFORD
18 Director Campus Facilities Mr. Todd BENSON
37 Director Financial Aid Mr. Peter GROSS

Warner Pacific College (A)

2219 SE 68th Avenue, Portland OR 97215
County: Multnomah FICE Identification: 003225
Unit ID: 210304
Telephone: (503) 517-1000 Carnegie Class: Bac/Diverse
FAX Number: (503) 517-1350 Calendar System: Semester
URL: www.warnerpacific.edu
Established: 1937 Annual Undergrad Tuition & Fees: $20,800
Enrollment: 1,287 Coed
Affiliation or Control: Church Of God IRS Status: 501(c)3
Highest Offering: Master's
Program: 2-Year Principally Bachelor's Creditable; Liberal Arts And General; Teacher Preparatory; Professional
Accreditation: NW, @SW

01 President Dr. Andrea P. COOK
05 Vice Pres Acad Affs/Dean of Faculty Dr. Reginald NICHOLS
10 Vice Pres of Operations Mr. Steve STENBERG
30 Vice President for Inst Advancement Mr. Aaron MCMURRAY
32 Vice President for Community Life Dr. Daymond GLENN
20 Assoc VP for Acad Affairs/Dean ADP Dr. Lori K. JASS
84 VP for Enrollment and Marketing Mr. Dale SEIPP
37 Dir of Student Financial Services Mrs. Cindy POLLARD
07 Director of Admissions Mr. Geraldo CIFUENTES
41 Director of Athletics Vacant
08 Director of Library Services Ms. Mari BETTINESKI
06 Registrar Ms. Victoria CUMINGS
13 Director of Information Technology Ms. Linda RUDAWITZ
29 Director of Alumni/Church Relations Ms. Serena CLINE
88 Dir of Contextualized Ministries Dr. Jess BIELMAN
42 Associate Dir Campus Ministries Ms. Michelle LANG
39 Dir of Res Life & Judicial Affairs Mr. Jared VALENTINE
18 Director of Facilities Mr. Dean JENKS
15 Dir of Human Resources/Prof Devel Mrs. Bev FITTS
09 Dir of Institutional Effectiveness Dr. Warren J. BEAMAN
40 Director Bookstore Mrs. Mimi FONSECA
26 Marketing/College Relations Ms. Melody BURTON
38 Director Student Counseling Dr. Carol DELLOLIVER
21 Associate Business Officer Mr. Nathan DUNBAR
36 Director of Academic Success Mr. Rod JOHANSON

Western Oregon University (B)

345 N Monmouth Avenue, Monmouth OR 97361-1394
County: Polk FICE Identification: 003209
Unit ID: 210429
Telephone: (503) 838-8000 Carnegie Class: Master's M
FAX Number: (503) 838-8474 Calendar System: Quarter
URL: www.wou.edu
Established: 1856 Annual Undergrad Tuition & Fees (In-State): $9,369
Enrollment: 6,063 Coed
Affiliation or Control: State IRS Status: 501(c)3
Highest Offering: Beyond Master's But Less Than Doctorate
Program: Liberal Arts And General; Teacher Preparatory
Accreditation: NW, CORE, MUS, TED

01 President Dr. Rex FULLER
03 Vice President & General Counsel Mr. Ryan HAGEMANN
05 Provost/Vice Pres Academic Affairs Dr. Stephen SCHECK
32 Vice President Student Affairs Dr. Gary DUKES
10 Vice Pres Finance & Administration Mr. Eric YAHNKE
35 Dean of Students Ms. Tina M. FUCHS
49 Dean Col Liberal Arts & Sciences Dr. Susanne MONAHAN
53 Dean College of Education Dr. Mark GIROD
20 Associate Provost Mr. David MCDONALD
56 Director Division Extended Progams Mr. Dan CLARK
06 Registrar Vacant
30 Director of Development Mr. Tommy LOVE
08 Dean Hamersly Library Dr. Allen MCKIEL
13 Director University Computing Svcs Mr. William KERNAN
15 Director Human Resources Ms. Judy J. VANDERBURG
18 Director Physical Plant Mr. Tom NEAL
19 Director University Public Safety Ms. Rebecca CHILES
23 Dir Student Health/Counseling Ctr Mr. Jaime SILVA
26 Dir Public Relations/Communications Ms. Denise VISUANO
32 Dir Student Leadership & Activities Mr. Paul MOSER
37 Director Financial Aid Ms. Kella HELYER
41 Athletic Director Ms. Barbara DEARING
46 Dir of Teaching Research Institute Dr. Ella TAYLOR

85 Dir Intl Students/Scholars Affairs Mr. Neng YANG
88 Dir Multicultural Student Svcs/Pgms Ms. Anna HERNANDEZ-HUNTER
22 Director AAEO Ms. Judy J. VANDERBURG
29 Dir Leadership Giving/Athletic Dev Mr. Michael FEULING
25 Project & Contract Officer Mr. Stan HAGEN
04 Executive Asst to President Mrs. LouAnn VICKERS
21 Director of Business Services Mr. Darin SILBERNAGEL

Western Seminary (C)

5511 SE Hawthorne Boulevard, Portland OR 97215-3399
County: Multnomah FICE Identification: 007178
Unit ID: 210368
Telephone: (503) 517-1800 Carnegie Class: Spec/Faith
FAX Number: (503) 517-1801 Calendar System: Semester
URL: www.westernseminary.edu
Established: 1927 Annual Graduate Tuition & Fees: $13,200
Enrollment: 743 Coed
Affiliation or Control: Independent Non-Profit IRS Status: 501(c)3
Highest Offering: Doctorate; No Undergraduates
Program: Professional; Religious Emphasis
Accreditation: NW, CACREP, THEOL

01 President Dr. Randal R. ROBERTS
10 Administrative Vice President/CFO Mr. Steve MANSDOERFER
05 Academic Dean Dr. Rob WIGGINS
88 VP of Educ Innovation/Global Outrea Andy PETERSON
30 VP for Advancement/Dir Alumni Rels Mr. Greg MOON
20 Associate Academic Dean Vacant
06 Dean Student Devel/Registrar Dr. Reid KISLING
21 Controller Ms. Patricia A. PRICHARD
32 Dean of Students Mr. Andy PELOQUIN
36 Director of Student Placement Dr. Larry MCCRACKEN
13 Director of Information Services Mr. Doug MABRY
37 Financial Aid Director Ms. Shelle RIEHL
56 Asst Director of Distance Education Mr. Jon RAIBLEY
88 Assistant Registrar Ms. Sandy FOSTER
15 Human Resources Director Ms. Julia EIDENBERG
08 Library Director Dr. Robert A. KRUPP
84 Director Enrollment Services/Mktg Mr. P.J OSWALD
18 Chief Facilities/Physical Plant Mr. Cliff STEIN
106 Director of Distance Education Mr. James STEWART
07 Director of Admissions Mr. Demetrius ROGERS

Willamette University (D)

900 State Street, Salem OR 97301-3930
County: Marion FICE Identification: 003227
Unit ID: 210401
Telephone: (503) 370-6300 Carnegie Class: Bac/A&S
FAX Number: (503) 370-6148 Calendar System: Semester
URL: www.willamette.edu
Established: 1842 Annual Undergrad Tuition & Fees: $45,617
Enrollment: 2,668 Coed
Affiliation or Control: Independent Non-Profit IRS Status: 501(c)3
Highest Offering: Doctorate
Program: Liberal Arts And General; Professional
Accreditation: NW, BUS, CEA, LAW, MUS, SPAA

01 President Dr. Stephen THORSETT
10 Senior VP Finance & Adminsitration Ms. Monica RIMAI
30 Vice President for Advancement Mr. Dennis BERGVALL
07 Vice President Enrollment Mr. Michael BESEDA
13 Vice President Integrated Tech Dr. John D. BALLING
18 VP Capital Planning & Facilities Mr. James R. BAUER
32 Dean of Campus Life Dr. David A. DOUGLASS
49 Dean of Liberal Arts Dr. Marlene MOORE
61 Dean of Law Mr. Curtis BRIDGEMAN
50 Dean Graduate School Management Ms. Debra RINGOLD
42 Chaplain Dr. Karen WOOD
23 Director of Bishop Wellness Center Ms. Margaret TROUT
88 Director Center Dispute Resolution Dr. Richard BIRKE
91 Director Administrative Computing Mr. Harvey J. PRUDHOMME
37 Director Student Financial Aid Ms. Patricia K. HOBAN
09 Director of Institutional Research Dr. Michael J. MOON
06 University Registrar Ms. Laura JACOBS ANDERSON
08 University Librarian Ms. Deborah B. DANCIK
21 Controller Mr. Kenneth PIFER
40 Bookstore Director Mr. Donald C. BECKMAN
104 Director of International Education Mr. Kris LOU
41 Athletic Director Ms. Valerie A. CLEARY
29 Assistant VP Alumni Relations Mr. James LIPPINCOTT
44 Senior Director Gift Planning & Dev Ms. Lori L. HOBY
15 Director of Human Resources Mr. Keith GRIMM
35 Director of Student Activities Ms. Lisa C. HOLLIDAY
36 Director Career Services Dr. Gerald B. HOUSER
28 Director of Multicultural Affairs Mr. Gordon K. TOYAMA
18 Manager Operations/Energy Mr. Gary GRIMM
96 Purchasing Coordinator Ms. Kindra K. JORDAY
26 Int Director Marketing Communic Mr. Adam TORGERSON

PENNSYLVANIA

Albright College (E)

13th & Bern Streets, PO Box 15234,
Reading PA 19612-5234
County: Berks FICE Identification: 003229
Unit ID: 210571
Telephone: (610) 921-2381 Carnegie Class: Bac/A&S
FAX Number: (610) 921-7530 Calendar System: 4/1/4
URL: www.albright.edu
Established: 1856 Annual Undergrad Tuition & Fees: $39,850
Enrollment: 2,393 Coed
Affiliation or Control: United Methodist IRS Status: 501(c)3
Highest Offering: Master's
Program: Liberal Arts And General; Teacher Preparatory; Professional
Accreditation: M

01 President Dr. Lex O. MCMILLAN, III
05 Int Provost & VP Academic Affairs Dr. Joseph M. THOMAS
10 Vice President Finance & Admin Mr. Gregory L. FULMER
30 Vice President Advancement Ms. Deborah M. MCCREERY
84 VP Enrollment Mgt/Dean Admission Mr. Gregory E. EICHHORN
32 VP Student Affairs/Dean of Students Dr. Gina-Lyn CRANCE
26 Assoc VP College Relations/Mktg Mr. Thomas W. DURSO
13 Chief Technology Officer Ms. Rashmi RADHAKRISHNAN
04 Executive Assistant to President Mrs. Kathy L. CAFONCELLI
20 Interim Dean for Academic Affairs Dr. Devon MASON
08 Library Director Ms. Rosemary L. DEEGAN
44 Asst VP for Development Mr. Jud CHRIFIELD
14 Director of Core Technologies Mr. Hoerr U. JASON
21 Controller Mr. Rick W. MELCHER
37 Director of Financial Aid Mr. Christopher HANLON
58 Coordinator of Graduate Program Dr. Joseph YARWORTH
35 Assistant Dean of Students Ms. Amanda HANINCIK
06 Registrar Mr. David C. BALLABAN
36 Director Career Development Center Ms. Karen V. EVANS
39 Director of Residential Life Mr. Timothy R. MORAN
38 Director of Counseling Center Dr. Brenda J. INGRAM-WALLACE
29 Dir of Alumni Relations Mrs. Karen MORAN
18 Director Facilities/Operations/Svcs Mr. Timothy RISSEL
41 Co-Athletic Director Mr. Richard E. FERRY
41 Co-Athletic Director Ms. Janice J. LUCK
19 Director of Safety & Security Mr. Michael L. GROSS
40 Book Store Manager Ms. Coreen MCCAFFERTY
23 Director of Gable Health Center Ms. Samantha WESNER
42 Chaplain Rev. Paul E. CLARK
22 Affirmative Action Coord/Dir HR Ms. Kimberly A. HUBRIC
85 Asst Dir Multi-Ethnic Student Affs Ms. Tiffany CLAYTON
88 Dir of Accelerated Degree Pgm Mr. Kevin EZZELL
09 Director of Institutional Research Mr. Jack LAFAYETTE
35 Director of Student Involvement Mr. Bradley A. SMITH
25 Director of Grants Vacant
92 Director Honors Program Dr. Julia F. HEBERLE
07 Director of Admission Ms. Jennifer WILLIAMSON
88 Director of Conferences Ms. Lois A. KUBINAK

Allegheny College (F)

520 N Main Street, Meadville PA 16335-3902
County: Crawford FICE Identification: 003230
Unit ID: 210669
Telephone: (814) 332-3100 Carnegie Class: Bac/A&S
FAX Number: (814) 332-2796 Calendar System: Semester
URL: www.allegheny.edu
Established: 1815 Annual Undergrad Tuition & Fees: $42,470
Enrollment: 2,023 Coed
Affiliation or Control: United Methodist IRS Status: 501(c)3
Highest Offering: Baccalaureate
Program: Liberal Arts And General
Accreditation: M

01 President Dr. James H. MULLEN
03 Exec Vice President and COO Dr. Susan STUEBNER
30 Vice Pres Devel & Alumni Affairs Ms. Marjorie S. KLEIN
84 VP Enrollment/College Relations Dr. Brian F. DALTON
04 Assistant to the President Ms. Pamela S. HIGHAM
28 AVP for Diversity & Org Development Dr. Andrea DIAZ
10 Sr Assoc Vice President of Finance Vacant
45 Assoc Vice Pres for Advancement Mr. Bruce WHITEHAIR
29 AVP Development & Alumni Affairs Mr. Philip R. FOXMAN
26 Assoc VP Marketing/Communications Vacant
05 Provost & Dean of the College Dr. Ronald B. COLE
32 Interim Dean of Students Ms. Jacquelyn KONDROT
28 Associate Dean of the College Dr. Armenta HINTON
20 Associate Provost Dr. Terry BENSEL
37 Director Financial Aid Mr. Jonathan BOLERATZ
108 VP for Info Svcs & Assessment Dr. Richard A. HOLMGREN
06 Registrar Dr. Ann D. SHEFFIELD
08 Director of the Library Ms. Linda G. BILLS
15 Director of Human Resources Ms. Patricia A. FERREY
19 Director Campus Safety & Security Dr. Jeffrey A. SCHNEIDER
44 Director of Annual Giving Ms. Sara PINEO
18 Director Physical Plant Mr. Cliff K. WILLIS
91 Associate Director of Info Tech Svc Mr. Richard A. METZGER
41 Director of Athletics Ms. Portia HOEG
31 Director of Civic Engagement Dr. David RONCOLATO
13 Dir Tech Computer & Networking Svcs Mr. Tim W. HUNTER
100 Chief of Staff Ms. Gillian F. FORD
38 Director of Counseling Center Ms. Yvonne M. EATON-STULL
102 AVP of Development Dr. Ann H. ARESON
09 Director of Institutional Research Ms. Marian D. SHERWOOD
36 Director Career Education Mr. James FITCH
35 Interim Associate Dean of Students Ms. Gretchen A. BECK
21 CFO & Treasurer Ms. Linda S. WETSELL
42 Chaplain Dr. Jane Ellen NICKELL
88 Dir Center Political Participation Dr. Brian HARWARD
88 Director of Disability Services Mr. John J. MANGINE
57 Art Director Ms. Penny M. DREXEL
07 Sr Asst Director of Admissions Mr. Jason ANDRACKI
40 Manager of Bookstore Mr. Peter M. LEBAR
96 Purchasing & Student Services Coord Ms. Kathleen M. CONAWAY
88 Int Assoc Dir Student Involvement Ms. Jayne PISKORIK

Allegany College of Maryland Bedford County Campus (A)

18 North River Lane, Everett PA 15337-1410
Telephone: (814) 652-9528 Identification: 770124
Accreditation: &M

† Branch campus of Allegany College of Maryland, Cumberland, MD.

Allegany College of Maryland Somerset County Campus (B)

6022 Glades Pike, Suite 100, Somerset PA 15501-4300
Telephone: (814) 445-9848 Identification: 770123
Accreditation: &M

† Branch campus of Allegany College of Maryland, Cumberland, MD.

Alvernia University (C)

400 Saint Bernardine Street, Reading PA 19607-1799
County: Berks FICE Identification: 003233
Unit ID: 210775
Telephone: (610) 796-8200 Carnegie Class: Master's M
FAX Number: (610) 777-6632 Calendar System: Semester
URL: www.alvernia.edu
Established: 1958 Annual Undergrad Tuition & Fees: $33,010
Enrollment: 2,917 Coed
Affiliation or Control: Roman Catholic IRS Status: 501(c)3
Highest Offering: Doctorate
Program: Liberal Arts And General; Teacher Preparatory; Professional
Accreditation: M, ACBSP, CAATE, NURSE, OT, @PTA, SW

01 President .... Dr. Thomas F. FLYNN
05 Provost .... Dr. Shirley J. WILLIAMS
10 VP for Finance & Administration .... Mr. Douglas F. SMITH
30 Vice Pres for Advancement .... Ms. Laramie JUNG
32 Vice Pres Univ Life/Dean of Stdnts .. Dr. Joseph J. CICALA, RSM
84 Vice Pres for Enrollment Management .... Mr. John R. MCCLOSKEY, JR.
42 Asst to the President For Mission .... Sr. Roberta MCKELVIE, OSF
26 VP Mktg & Comms/Chief PR Ofcr .... Mr. Brad DREXLER
35 Director of Student Activities .... Ms. Abby SWATCHICK
39 Director Residence Life .... Ms. Karolina DREHER
06 Registrar .... Ms. Beki STEIN
21 Controller .... Mr. Larry SHAUB
29 Assoc VP of Advancement .... Mr. Thomas MINICK
92 Director Honors Program .... Dr. Victoria WILLIAMS
41 Director Athletics & Recreation .... Mr. Bill STILES
07 Dean of UG Admissions .... Ms. Rebecca FINNKENNEY
09 Director of Institutional Research .... Dr. Evelina PANAYOTOVA
15 Director Human Resources .... Ms. Laurel CLINE
18 Dir of Facilities Planning .... Mr. David REPPERT
36 Director of Career Services .... Mrs. Megan ADUKAITIS
27 Dir of Marketing/Communications .... Ms. Amy MUSIC
37 Dir of Student Financial Planning .... Ms. Christine SAADI
96 Procurement Manager .... Ms. Cynthia URICK
28 Dir of Multicultural Initiatives .... Ms. Wanda COPELAND
21 Director of Student Billing .... Ms. Gwynne KOLODZIEJSKI
31 Dir Ctr for Community Engagement .... Mr. Jay WORRALL
58 Dean of Graduate & Cont Studies .... Ms. Daria LATORRE
49 Dean of Arts & Sciences .... Dr. Beth ARACENA
76 Dean of Professional Programs .... Ms. Karen S. THACKER
04 Assistant to the President .... Ms. Karen SCHRODER
13 Chief Info Technology Officer (CIO) .... Ms. Robin ALLEN
19 Director of Public Safety .... Mr. Edward HEIM

The American College of Financial Services (D)

270 S Bryn Mawr Avenue, Bryn Mawr PA 19010-2196
County: Delaware FICE Identification: 033173
Unit ID: 210809
Telephone: (610) 526-1000 Carnegie Class: Spec/Bus
FAX Number: (610) 526-1310 Calendar System: Quarter
URL: www.theamericancollege.edu
Established: 1927 Annual Graduate Tuition & Fees: $5,040
Enrollment: 20,911 Coed
Affiliation or Control: Independent Non-Profit IRS Status: 501(c)3
Highest Offering: Doctorate; No Undergraduates
Program: Professional; Business Emphasis
Accreditation: M

01 President & CEO .... Dr. Robert R. JOHNSON
03 Executive Vice President .... Mr. Keith E. HICKERSON
05 Vice Pres Academic Affairs & Dean .... Dr. Walter J. WOERHEIDE
30 Sr Vice President Advancement .... Mr. Charles CRONIN
04 Assistant to the President .... Ms. Mary C. VARNER
10 Chief Financial Officer .... Mr. Neal R. FEGELY
26 Chief Marketing Officer .... Mr. Jack HONDROS
13 Chief Technology Officer .... Mr. Ed M. MCEVOY
108 AVP Institutional Assessment .... Mr. Thomas ARMINGTON
21 Asst Dean Business Affairs .... Ms. Sophia DUFFY
15 Vice Pres Human Resources .... Ms. Debra GLENN
06 Registrar .... Ms. Antoinette CHRISTALDI
08 Librarian .... Mr. John H. WHITHAM
88 Director Exam Systems .... Ms. Diane M. HAMMONDS

Antonelli Institute (E)

300 Montgomery Avenue, Erdenheim PA 19038-8242
County: Montgomery FICE Identification: 007430
Unit ID: 210890
Telephone: (215) 836-2222 Carnegie Class: Assoc/PrivFP
FAX Number: (215) 836-2794 Calendar System: Semester
URL: www.antonelli.edu
Established: 1938 Annual Undergrad Tuition & Fees: $19,830
Enrollment: 188 Coed
Affiliation or Control: Proprietary IRS Status: Proprietary
Highest Offering: Associate Degree
Program: Occupational
Accreditation: ACCSC

01 President .... Dr. John D. HAYDEN
05 Director of Education/Student Svcs .... Ms. Trish FLEMING
37 Financial Aid Officer .... Ms. Stephanie SHOWALTER

Arcadia University (F)

450 S Easton Road, Glenside PA 19038-3295
County: Montgomery FICE Identification: 003235
Unit ID: 211088
Telephone: (215) 572-2900 Carnegie Class: Master's L
FAX Number: (215) 572-0240 Calendar System: Semester
URL: www.arcadia.edu
Established: 1853 Annual Undergrad Tuition & Fees: $39,560
Enrollment: 3,939 Coed
Affiliation or Control: Independent Non-Profit IRS Status: 501(c)3
Highest Offering: Doctorate
Program: Liberal Arts And General; Teacher Preparatory; Professional
Accreditation: M, ACBSP, ARCPA, ART, FEPAC, PH, PTA

01 President .... Dr. Nicolette D. CHRISTENSEN
05 Provost & VP Academic Affairs .... Dr. Barbara F. NODINE
84 VP Enrollment Management .... Mr. Mark LAPREZIOSA
10 VP Finance & Administration .... Mr. Len SIPPEL
26 VP University Relations .... Dr. Matthew GOLDEN
43 General Counsel .... Mr. Michael KOROLISHIN
13 Chief Information Officer .... Vacant
30 VP University Advancement .... Ms. Mary MCRAE
88 VP/Exec Dir Col of Global Studies .... Ms. Lorna STERN
32 Dean of Students .... Mr. Andrew GORETSKY
18 Assoc VP Facilities/Capital Plng .... Mr. Thomas J. MACCHI
21 Assoc VP Finance & COO TCGS .... Ms. Colleen BURKE
15 Assoc VP Human Resources .... Ms. Rhonda HOSPEDALES
88 Assoc Prov Acad Personnel & Mgmt .... Dr. Thomas EGAN
06 Registrar .... Mr. William ELNICK
06 Associate Registrar .... Mrs. Nicole M. ZUCKER
49 Dean College of Arts & Sciences .... Dr. John R. HOFFMAN
76 Dean College of Health Sciences .... Dr. Rebecca L. CRAIK
51 Interim Dean School of Cont Stds .... Dr. Michael DRYER
50 Dean School of Global Business .... Dr. Alla WILSON
58 Dean Graduate & Undergrad Studies .... Ms. Nancy ROSOFF
82 Dean International Affairs .... Dr. Warren HAFFAR
53 Dean School of Education .... Dr. Graciela SLESARANSKY-POE
88 Assoc Prov Acad Improvement & Innov .... Dr. John A. NOAKES
28 Assoc Dean Institutional Diversity .... Ms. Judith DALTON
35 Assoc Dean of Students .... Ms. Dian TAYLOR-ALLEYNE
20 Assoc Dean Undergraduate Studies .... Mr. Bruce KELLER
88 Asst Dean Graduate Studies .... Ms. Mary Kate MCNULTY
37 Exec Dir Federal Aid Pgms & FA .... Ms. Elizabeth RIHL-LEWINSKY
13 Deputy CIO Operations & Plans .... Mr. Eric MCCLOY
88 Director Administrative Services .... Ms. Mimi BASSETTI
29 Director Alumni Relations .... Mr. Jeffery SPENCE
88 Director University Art Gallery .... Mr. Richard TORCHIA
41 Director Athletics & Recreation .... Mr. Brian GRANATA
88 Director Campus Visits and EM .... Ms. Kathleen BEARDSLEY
36 Director Career Education .... Mr. Mark GRESS, JR.
38 Director Counseling Services .... Ms. Amy HENNING
88 Director EM & Financial Aid .... Ms. Holly R. KIRKPATRICK
91 Director Enterprise Applications .... Mr. Scott GRABUS
25 Director Sponsored Research & Pgms .... Ms. Nataliia SHABLIA
09 Director Institutional Research .... Mr. Will PADDOCK
88 Director of Academic Administration .... Ms. Kristin O. JUDGE
88 Assoc Dean Instr Tech & Lib Res .... Dr. Jeanne BUCKLEY
96 Purchasing Coordinator .... Ms. Jennifer SUDLOW
88 Payroll Manager .... Ms. Sharon ANTHONY
19 Director of Public Safety .... Ms. Joanna GALLAGHER
39 Asst Dean of Students .... Ms. Catherine MATTINGLY
88 Title IX Coordinator .... Ms. Nora NELLE
04 Executive Asst to President .... Ms. Allison GOETZ
104 Assoc Dean International Affairs .... Ms. Janice FINN

Art Institute of Philadelphia (G)

1622 Chestnut Street, Philadelphia PA 19103-5198
County: Philadelphia FICE Identification: 008350
Unit ID: 210942
Telephone: (215) 567-7080 Carnegie Class: Spec/Arts
FAX Number: (215) 405-6398 Calendar System: Quarter
URL: www.artinstitutes.edu/philadelphia
Established: 1971 Annual Undergrad Tuition & Fees: $17,920
Enrollment: 1,953 Coed
Affiliation or Control: Proprietary IRS Status: Proprietary
Highest Offering: Baccalaureate
Program: Occupational
Accreditation: M, ACFEI, CIDA

01 Interim President .... Mr. Joseph GIANNATTASIO
05 Dean of Academic Affairs .... Dr. Harry COSTIGAN
10 Regional Director of Finance .... Mr. Norman BEASLEY
07 Director of Admissions .... Ms. Amanda HOSKING
36 Director of Career Services .... Ms. Kimberly BURNS
20 Assoc Dean of Academic Affairs .... Mr. Harry COSTIGAN
32 Dean of Students .... Mr. John ROBINSON
37 Director Student Financial Services .... Ms. Fatisha STRICKLAND
06 Registrar .... Ms. Adriane MEDFORD
08 Library Director .... Ms. Marie DENNIS
38 Counselor/Disability Coordinator .... Ms. Lisa STANKIEWICZ
40 Manager Supply Store .... Ms. Sharon MASULLO

Art Institute of Pittsburgh (H)

420 Boulevard of the Allies, Pittsburgh PA 15219-1301
County: Allegheny FICE Identification: 007470
Unit ID: 210960
Telephone: (412) 263-6600 Carnegie Class: Spec/Arts
FAX Number: (412) 263-3715 Calendar System: Quarter
URL: www.artinstitutes.edu/pittsburgh
Established: 1921 Annual Undergrad Tuition & Fees: $21,915
Enrollment: 10,000 Coed
Affiliation or Control: Proprietary IRS Status: Proprietary
Highest Offering: Baccalaureate
Program: Occupational; Fine Arts Emphasis
Accreditation: M, ACFEI, CIDA

01 President .... Mr. George W. SEBOLT
10 Vice Pres/Dir Admin/Financial Svcs .... Mr. Kevin KOLESZAR
05 VP/Dean Academic Affairs .... Mr. Daniel GARLAND
32 Vice Pres/Director Student Affairs .... Ms. Nadine W. JOSEPHS
36 VP/Director Career Services .... Ms. Dana MELVIN
07 Director of Admissions .... Ms. Kimbra BROWNING
37 Director Student Financial Aid .... Ms. Lara HEMWALL
15 Director Human Resources .... Ms. Bobbi Jo GRAHAM
97 Director General Education .... Ms. Katie TALERICO
105 Dir Graphic/Dig Design/Web Design .... Vacant
72 Director of Technology .... Mr. Ryan SLATER
88 Dir Indust Dsgn Tech/Entertnmt Dsgn .... Ms. Kelly SPEWOCK
88 Dir Media Animation/Game Design .... Mr. Hans WESTMAN
88 Director of Photography .... Mr. Andrew ENGLISH
06 Registrar .... Ms. Diane E. CARNEY
84 Enrollment Management Supervisor .... Ms. Lara HEMWALL
88 Director Culinary .... Mr. Shawn CULP
88 Dir Fashion/Retail Mktng/Fashn Dsgn .... Ms. Stephanie TAYLOR
88 Dir Video Production/Visual Effects .... Mr. Andres TAPIA URZUA
88 College Affiliate/HS Articulation .... Mr. Daniel GARLAND
29 Director Alumni Relations .... Ms. Janey CINK

The Art Institute of York - Pennsylvania (I)

1409 Williams Road, York PA 17402-9012
County: York FICE Identification: 025578
Unit ID: 210906
Telephone: (717) 755-2300 Carnegie Class: Assoc/PrivFP
FAX Number: (717) 757-5552 Calendar System: Other
URL: www.artinstitutes.edu/york
Established: 1952 Annual Undergrad Tuition & Fees: $17,344
Enrollment: 369 Coed
Affiliation or Control: Proprietary IRS Status: Proprietary
Highest Offering: Baccalaureate
Program: Liberal Arts And General; Professional
Accreditation: ACICS

01 President .... Mr. Tim HOWARD
05 Dean of Academic Affairs .... Ms. Marla PRICE

Berks Technical Institute (J)

2205 Ridgewood Road, Wyomissing PA 19610-1168
County: Berks FICE Identification: 022539
Unit ID: 213534
Telephone: (610) 372-1722 Carnegie Class: Assoc/PrivFP
FAX Number: (610) 376-4684 Calendar System: Other
URL: www.berks.edu
Established: 1974 Annual Undergrad Tuition & Fees: $10,120
Enrollment: 985 Coed
Affiliation or Control: Proprietary IRS Status: Proprietary
Highest Offering: Associate Degree
Program: Occupational; Technical Emphasis
Accreditation: ACICS, MAC

01 Campus Director .... Mr. Joseph F. REICHARD
05 Dean .... Mr. Elizabeth VLASTOS

Biblical Theological Seminary (K)

200 N Main Street, Hatfield PA 19440-2499
County: Montgomery FICE Identification: 023230
Unit ID: 211130
Telephone: (215) 368-5000 Carnegie Class: Spec/Faith
FAX Number: (215) 368-2301 Calendar System: Trimester
URL: www.biblical.edu
Established: 1971 Annual Graduate Tuition & Fees: $14,667
Enrollment: 290 Coed
Affiliation or Control: Independent Non-Profit IRS Status: 501(c)3
Highest Offering: Doctorate; No Undergraduates
Program: Professional; Religious Emphasis
Accreditation: M, THEOL

01 President .... Dr. Frank JAMES, III
32 VP for Student Advancement .... Mrs. Pamela J. SMITH
30 Director of Development .... Mr. Thom SKINNER
05 Academic Dean .... Dr. R. Todd MANGUM

10 Chief Financial Planner .... Mr. David VIEHMAN
108 Director of Inst Assessment .... Dr. Susan DISSTON
88 Director of DMin Program .... Dr. Kyuboem LEE
88 Director of Urban Initiatives .... Dr. Dan WILLIAMS
20 Director of Academic Services .... Mr. Rick HOUSEKNECHT
13 Director of Information Technology .... Mr. Kelly PFLEIGER
18 Director of Physical Plant .... Mr. Anthony W. PLETSCHER

Bidwell Training Center (A)

1815 Metropolitan Street, Pittsburgh PA 15233-2200

County: Allegheny | FICE Identification: 031015
Unit ID: 211149
Telephone: (412) 323-4000 | Carnegie Class: Assoc/PrivNFP
FAX Number: (412) 325-7378 | Calendar System: Semester
URL: www.bidwell-training.org
Established: 1968 | Annual Undergrad Tuition & Fees: $14,000
Enrollment: 150 | Coed
Affiliation or Control: Independent Non-Profit | IRS Status: 501(c)3
Highest Offering: Associate Degree
Program: Occupational
Accreditation: **ACCSC**

01 Exec Director/Sr Vice President .... Ms. Valerie NJIE
11 Senior Director/Operations .... Mr. Ken HUSELTON

Bradford School (B)

125 W Station Square Dr, Ste 129,
Pittsburgh PA 15219-2602

County: Allegheny | FICE Identification: 009721
Unit ID: 211200
Telephone: (412) 391-6710 | Carnegie Class: Assoc/PrivFP
FAX Number: (412) 471-6714 | Calendar System: Semester
URL: www.bradfordpittsburgh.edu
Established: 1968 | Annual Undergrad Tuition & Fees: $15,300
Enrollment: 413 | Coed
Affiliation or Control: Proprietary | IRS Status: Proprietary
Highest Offering: Associate Degree
Program: Occupational; Business Emphasis
Accreditation: **ACICS**, DA, MAC

01 President .... Mr. Vincent S. GRAZIANO

Bryn Athyn College of the New Church (C)

PO Box 717, Bryn Athyn PA 19009-0717

County: Montgomery | FICE Identification: 003228
Unit ID: 210492
Telephone: (267) 502-2400 | Carnegie Class: Bac/A&S
FAX Number: (215) 938-2658 | Calendar System: Trimester
URL: www.brynathyn.edu
Established: 1876 | Annual Undergrad Tuition & Fees: $19,353
Enrollment: 281 | Coed
Affiliation or Control: Church of New Jerusalem | IRS Status: 501(c)3
Highest Offering: Master's
Program: Liberal Arts And General; Teacher Preparatory; Professional
Accreditation: **M**

01 President .... Mr. Brian BLAIR
10 Chief Finance Officer .... Mr. Daniel T. ALLEN
05 Dean of Academic Affairs .... Dr. Allen BEDFORD
73 Dean of Theological School .... Rev. Andrew M T. DIBB
32 Dean of Student Affairs .... Ms. Kiri ROGERS
07 Director of Admissions .... Ms. Stephanie WALKER
08 Director of Swedenborg Library .... Mrs. Carroll C. ODHNER
41 Director of Athletics .... Mr. Matthew KENNEDY
13 Director of Information Technology .... Ms. Lelia HOWARD
15 Director of Human Resources .... Ms. T. Muriel BRISBON
19 Director of Security & Safety .... Mr. R. Scott COOPER
42 Chaplain .... Rev. Thane GLENN
04 Administrative Asst to President .... Mrs. Aurelle GENZLINGER
30 Chief Development/Advancement .... Mrs. Jessica CARSWELL
09 Director of Institutional Research .... Ms. Karin SMITH
37 Director of Financial Aid .... Mr. Brian KEISTER

Bryn Mawr College (D)

101 N Merion Avenue, Bryn Mawr PA 19010-2899

County: Montgomery | FICE Identification: 003237
Unit ID: 211273
Telephone: (610) 526-5000 | Carnegie Class: Bac/A&S
FAX Number: (610) 526-7450 | Calendar System: Semester
URL: www.brynmawr.edu
Established: 1885 | Annual Undergrad Tuition & Fees: $47,140
Enrollment: 1,709 | Female
Affiliation or Control: Independent Non-Profit | IRS Status: 501(c)3
Highest Offering: Doctorate
Program: Liberal Arts And General
Accreditation: **M**, SW

01 President .... Kimberly CASSIDY
05 Provost .... Mary J. OSIRIM
49 Interim Dean Undergraduate College .... Judith BALTHAZAR
11 Chief Administrative Officer .... Jerry A. BERENSON
10 Chief Financial Officer .... Kari FAZIO
30 Chief Development Officer .... Bob MILLER
07 Chief Enrollment Officer .... Pelema I. MORRICE
08 Director Libraries/Chief Info Ofcr .... Gina SIESING
58 Dean of Graduate Studies .... Sharon BURGMAYER
28 Asst Dean/Dir Intercultural Affairs .... Vanessa CHRISTMAN
06 Registrar .... Kirsten O'BEIRNE
37 Director of Financial Aid .... Ethel M. DESMARAIS
19 Director of Public Safety .... Tom KING
29 Exec Director Alumnae Association .... Wendy M. GREENFIELD
68 Director of Athletics & Physical Ed .... Kathleen TIERNEY
21 Controller .... Ms. Betsy STEWART
09 Director of Institutional Research .... Richard BARRY
18 Chief Facilities/Physical Plant .... Glenn R. SMITH

Bucknell University (E)

1 Dent Drive, Lewisburg PA 17837

County: Union | FICE Identification: 003238
Unit ID: 211291
Telephone: (570) 577-2000 | Carnegie Class: Bac/A&S
FAX Number: (570) 577-3760 | Calendar System: Semester
URL: www.bucknell.edu
Established: 1846 | Annual Undergrad Tuition & Fees: $50,152
Enrollment: 3,624 | Coed
Affiliation or Control: Independent Non-Profit | IRS Status: 501(c)3
Highest Offering: Master's
Program: Liberal Arts And General; Teacher Preparatory; Professional
Accreditation: **M**, BUS, CS, ENG, MUS

01 President .... Dr. John C. BRAVMAN
05 Provost .... Dr. Barbara ALTMAN
10 VP Finance & Administration .... Mr. David J. SURGALA
30 VP Development & Alumni Rels .... Dr. Scott G. ROSEVEAR
43 General Counsel .... Ms. Amy C. FOERSTER
84 VP Enrollment Management .... Mr. William T. CONLEY
41 Director Athletics & Recreation .... Mr. John P. HARDT
13 VP Library & Information Technology .... Mr. Param S. BEDI
26 VP Communications & Cmty Rels .... Vacant
88 Chief Investment Officer .... Mr. Christopher D. BROWN
49 Dean of Arts & Sciences .... Dr. George C. SHIELDS
54 Dean of Engineering .... Dr. Keith W. BUFFINTON
15 Assoc VP Human Resources .... Mr. Pierre D. JOANIS
32 Acting Dean of Students .... Ms. Amy A. BADAL
21 Associate VP Finance .... Mr. Dennis W. SWANK
21 Treasurer and Controller .... Mr. Michael S. COVER
29 Assoc VP Development & Alumni Rels .... Ms. Kathleen GRAHAM
06 AProv/Regis/Dn Grad Std & Summ Sess .... Dr. Robert M. MIDKIFF, JR.
20 Assoc Provost .... Dr. Karen M. MORIN
50 Director School of Management .... Dr. Michael E. JOHNSON-CRAMER
18 Associate VP Facilities .... Mr. Dennis W. HAWLEY
45 Director Business Planning .... Mr. Edward J. LOFTUS
28 Assoc Provost for Diversity .... Ms. Bridget M. NEWELL
04 Dir President Ofc & Univ Secretary .... Ms. Carol M. KENNEDY
46 Assistant Provost for Research .... Vacant
88 Director of Internal Audit .... Mr. Robert L. HOSTER
88 Interim Exec Dir Leadership Gifts .... Mr. J. Mark ELLIOTT
29 Exec Dir Alumni Relations .... Mr. Joshua L. GRILL
88 Exec Dir Advancement Services .... Ms. Cindy BELKNAP
44 Executive Director of Annual Fund .... Ms. Lucille M. TARIN
102 Dir Corporate & Foundation Rels .... Mr. David M. FOREMAN
88 Director Parents Fund .... Ms. Ann L. DISTEFANO
44 Director of Gift Planning .... Ms. Melissa M. DIEHL
14 Asst Chief Information Officer .... Mr. Mark E. YERGER
14 Asst Chief Technology Officer .... Mr. J. Christopher WEBER
88 Chief Information Officer .... Mr. Eric J. SMITH
27 Asst VP of Communications .... Mr. Andrew H. HIRSCH
88 Dir of Construction & Design .... Mr. James D. HOSTETLER
88 Dir of Facility Services .... Mr. Michael J. PATTERSON
84 Asst VP Enroll Mgmt/Dir Partnerships .... Mr. Mark D. DAVIES
07 Dean of Admissions .... Mr. Robert G. SPRINGALL
37 Director Financial Aid .... Ms. Andrea C. LEITHNER STAUFFER
88 Exec Dir BU Ctr Sustain/Environ .... Mr. Peter R. WILSHUSEN
38 Dir Counseling/Student Development .... Dr. Linda L. LOCHER
88 Dir of Investments .... Mr. John R. LUTHI
36 Exec Director Career Services .... Ms. Pamela G. KEISER
16 Dir of Recruitment & Compensation .... Ms. Marcia J. COONEY
16 Director of HRIS & Benefits .... Ms. Cindy L. BILGER
09 Asst Provost Inst Research/Assess .... Mr. Kevork T. HORISSIAN
109 Director of Business Services .... Ms. Lori J. WILSON
88 Exec Dir Events Management Office .... Ms. Dana M. MIMS
88 Assoc Controller Financial Services .... Mr. Ronald E. STAUFFER, II
88 Assoc Controller Accounting Svcs .... Mr. William D. GEORGE
88 Asst Controller .... Ms. Michelle M. HENDRICKS
104 Dir Global & Off-Campus Education .... Mr. Stephen K. APPIAH-PADI
88 Dir Risk Management & Insurance .... Mr. Clint D. WEVODAU
19 Chief of Public Safety .... Mr. Stephen J. BARILAR
35 Associate Dean of Students .... Ms. Kari M. CONRAD
35 Associate Dean of Students .... Mr. Daniel C. REMLEY
88 Exec Dir Weis Center Perform Arts .... Ms. Kathryn L. MAGUET
88 Title IX Coordinator Clery Act Comp .... Ms. Barbara G. MARTIN
88 Dir of Instructional Technology .... Mr. Matthew K. GARDZINA
88 Dir Advancement Campaign Mgmt .... Ms. Barbara A. HARTMAN
88 Dir Dev Research & Prospect Mgmt .... Ms. Cynthia D. JANESCH
42 University Chaplain .... Mr. John P. COLATCH
88 Dir Publications/Print & Mail .... Ms. Lisa D. HOOVER
105 Interim Dir Digital Communications .... Mr. Ryan LEBRETON
88 Dir Provost Business Operations .... Ms. Pamela A. BENFER
88 Director of Disbursement Services .... Mr. Jody D. GRAYBILL
105 Dir University Marketing & Web .... Ms. Molly E. O'BRIEN-FOELSCH
88 Dir Small Business Development Ctr .... Mr. Steven V. STUMBRIS
88 Dir Card Svcs & Student Transit .... Mr. Glenn R. FISHER
88 Dir of Civic Engagement .... Ms. Janice R. BUTLER
96 Director of Procurement Services .... Mr. Donald A. KRECH
88 Dir Financial Information Systems .... Ms. Pamela K. NOONE
88 Dir of Disability Services .... Ms. Heather L. FOWLER
85 Dir International Student Services .... Ms. Jennifer E. FIGUEROA
88 Director Office of LGBTQ Resources .... Mr. William K. MCCOY
88 Director of Women's Resource Center .... Ms. Tracy E. RUSSELL
92 Honors Council Chair .... Dr. Erin L. JABLONSKI
88 Director of Writing Center .... Ms. Deirdre M. O'CONNOR
88 Director of Events .... Ms. Patricia M. RINGKAMP
39 Dir of Housing Services .... Mr. Stephen J. APANEL

Bucks County Community College (F)

275 Swamp Road, Newtown PA 18940-4106

County: Bucks | FICE Identification: 003239
Unit ID: 211307
Telephone: (215) 968-8000 | Carnegie Class: Assoc/Pub-S-MC
FAX Number: (215) 968-8129 | Calendar System: Semester
URL: www.bucks.edu
Established: 1964 | Annual Undergrad Tuition & Fees (In-District): $4,178
Enrollment: 9,388 | Coed
Affiliation or Control: Local | IRS Status: 501(c)3
Highest Offering: Associate Degree
Program: Occupational; 2-Year Principally Bachelor's Creditable
Accreditation: **M**, ACBSP, ADNUR, ART, MUS, RAD

01 President .... Dr. Stephanie SHANBLATT
05 Provost .... Dr. Clayton RAILEY
10 VP for Administrative Affairs & CFO .... Mr. Dennis W. MATTHEWS
32 VP Student Affairs/Dean of Students .... Ms. Barbara H. YETMAN
13 Vice Pres/Chief Info Technology .... Dr. Andrew LAWLOR
20 Assoc Provost Academic Svcs .... Ms. Catherine C. MCELROY
88 Assoc Provost Learning Resources .... Dr. Maureen MCCREADIE
84 Dean Enrollment Services .... Dr. Eric HILTON
38 Dean Advising & Student Planning .... Ms. Christine HAGEDORN
102 Exec Director Foundation .... Mr. Tobias BRUHN
21 Exec Dir Budget & Internal Audit .... Ms. Loren HERBERT
09 Exec Dir Inst Research & Assessment .... Vacant
12 Exec Dir Upper Bucks Campus .... Dr. Rodney H. ALTEMOSE
88 Exec Dir Public Safety Training .... Mr. Rob FREESE
103 Exec Dir Workforce Development .... Ms. Lauren LOEFFLER
18 Exec Director Physical Plant .... Mr. Martin SNYDER
26 Exec Dir Marketing/Public Relations .... Ms. Marta KAUFMANN
04 Exec Assistant to President .... Ms. Kathleen C. FEDORKO
15 Exec Director Human Resources .... Ms. Tracey DONALDSON
96 Director of Purchasing .... Mr. James F. LOUGHERY
106 Director Online Learning .... Ms. Georglyn L. DAVIDSON
37 Director Financial Aid .... Ms. Donna M. WILKOSKI
36 Director Career Services .... Ms. Sharon STEPHENS
35 Director Student Life & Athletics .... Mr. Matt J. CIPRIANO
19 Director of Security/Safety .... Mr. Dennis MCCAULEY
08 Director Library Services .... Ms. Linda MCCANN
20 Executive Assistant to Provost .... Dr. Charlie GROTH
07 Director of Admissions .... Ms. Marlene T. BARLOW
06 Director Registration .... Mr. Robert MALEY
29 Alumni Relations Manager .... Ms. Jackie GEAR
68 Dean Kinesiology & Sport Studies .... Dr. Priscilla RICE
81 Dean STEM .... Ms. Lisa ANGELO
50 Dean Business Studies .... Ms. Tracy TIMBY
57 Dean Arts .... Mr. John MATHEWS
88 Int Dean Language & Literature .... Dr. Kelly KELLEWAY
83 Int Dean Social & Behavioral Sci .... Mr. Jason TOTTEN
107 Dean Professional Studies .... Dr. Maria TOTH

Butler County Community College (G)

107 College Drive, Butler PA 16002

County: Butler | FICE Identification: 003240
Unit ID: 211343
Telephone: (724) 287-8711 | Carnegie Class: Assoc/Pub-S-SC
FAX Number: (724) 285-6047 | Calendar System: Semester
URL: www.bc3.edu
Established: 1965 | Annual Undergrad Tuition & Fees (In-District): $3,984
Enrollment: 3,606 | Coed
Affiliation or Control: Local | IRS Status: 501(c)3
Highest Offering: Associate Degree
Program: Occupational; 2-Year Principally Bachelor's Creditable
Accreditation: **M**, ACBSP, ADNUR, MAC, PTAA

01 President .... Dr. Nicholas C. NEUPAUER
05 Interim VP for Academic Affairs .... Dr. Bruce RUSSELL
11 VP for Administration & Finance .... Mr. James A. HRABOSKY
32 VP Student Affairs/Enrollment Mgt .... Dr. G. Case WILLOUGHBY
51 VP Continuing Ed Off-Campus Centers .... Mr. William T. O'BRIEN
10 Chief Business Officer .... Mr. Wm. Jake FRIEL
50 Interim Dean of Business .... Ms. Ann MCCANDLESS
83 Dean of Social Science/Humanities .... Mr. William L. MILLER
66 Dean of Nursing/Allied Health .... Dr. Patricia MIHALCIN
72 Interim Dean of Nat Science/Tech .... Mr. Matt KOVAC
106 Dean of Education Technology .... Ms. Ann MCCANDLESS
08 Dean of Library Services .... Mr. Stephen M. JOSEPH
35 Dean of Students .... Mr. Joshua NOVAK
103 Exec Dir Workforce Dev Training .... Dr. Stephen R. CATT
15 Exec Director Human Resources .... Ms. Linda M. DODD
26 Exec Director of Comm & Mktg .... Ms. Susan J. CHANGNON
51 Director Adult/Continuing Education .... Mr. Paul M. LUCAS
06 Director of Records & Registration .... Ms. Amy DOUBLE PIGNATORE
13 Dir Telecommunications & MIS .... Ms. Kathleen C. SOMMERS
32 Director of Student Life .... Mr. Rob A. SNYDER
09 Dir Instl Research/Strategic Plng .... Ms. Sharla M. ANKE
18 Exec Director of Operations .... Mr. Brian R. OPITZ

07 Director of Admissions ... Mr. Robert MORRIS
12 Director of BC3 @ Lawrence Crossing ... Ms. Diane M. DECARBO
12 Director of BC3 @ Cranberry ... Mr. Alex J. GLADIS
12 Director of BC3 @ LindenPointe ... Mr. John P. SUESSER
12 Director of BC3 @ Brockway ... Ms. Jill MARTIN-REND
37 Financial Aid Director ... Ms. Julianne E. LOUTTIT
41 Athletic Director ... Mr. Rob A. SNYDER
50 Director of Business/Industry Trng ... Ms. Lisa M. CAMPBELL
38 Director Student Counseling ... Vacant
29 Director Alumni Relations ... Ms. Michelle E. JAMIESON
30 Exec Director of Advancement ... Ms. Ruth PURCELL
19 Exec Dir of Campus Police/Security ... Mr. Patrick W. MASSARO
88 Director of Cultural Center ... Mr. Lawrence E. STOCK
88 Director of Children's Center ... Ms. Judith A. ZUZACK
88 Associate Director Admissions ... Mr. Sean M. CARROLL
40 Bookstore Manager ... Ms. Donna L. PALLONE
96 Director of Purchasing ... Ms. Nicole BARNES

Byzantine Catholic Seminary of SS. Cyril and Methodius (A)

3605 Perrysville Avenue, Pittsburgh PA 15214-2229
County: Allegheny FICE Identification: 041180
Unit ID: 444103
Telephone: (412) 321-8383 Carnegie Class: Spec/Faith
FAX Number: (412) 321-9936 Calendar System: Semester
URL: www.bcs.edu
Established: 1950 Annual Graduate Tuition & Fees: $24,946
Enrollment: 12 Coed
Affiliation or Control: Other IRS Status: 501(c)3
Highest Offering: Master's; No Undergraduates
Program: Liberal Arts And General; Religious Emphasis
Accreditation: THEOL

01 Rector ... Rev. Robert M. PIPTA
05 Academic Dean ... Rev. Christiaan KAPPES
06 Registrar ... Ms. Carol PRZYBOROKI

Cabrini College (B)

610 King of Prussia Road, Radnor PA 19087-3698
County: Delaware FICE Identification: 003241
Unit ID: 211352
Telephone: (610) 902-8100 Carnegie Class: Master's L
FAX Number: (610) 902-8309 Calendar System: Semester
URL: www.cabrini.edu
Established: 1957 Annual Undergrad Tuition & Fees: $29,842
Enrollment: 2,156 Coed
Affiliation or Control: Roman Catholic IRS Status: 501(c)3
Highest Offering: Doctorate
Program: Liberal Arts And General
Accreditation: M, SW

01 President ... Dr. Donald TAYLOR
05 Provost/VP Academic Affairs ... Dr. Jeffrey GINGERICH
10 VP Finance & Treasurer ... Mr. Eric OLSON
30 VP Institutional Advancement ... Ms. Christen WILSON
32 VP of Student Life ... Dr. Christine LYSIONEK
84 VP of Enrollment Management ... Mr. Robert REESE
20 Dean for Academic Affairs ... Dr. Mary HARRIS
35 Dean of Students ... Mr. George STROUD
53 Dean of Education ... Dr. Beverly BRYDE
04 Assistant to the President ... Ms. Joan KLECKNER
06 Registrar ... Ms. M. Frances HARKNESS
08 Library Director ... Dr. Roberta JACQUET
13 Interim Dir Info Tech & Resources ... Mr. Chris SHIELDS
19 Director of Public Safety ... Mr. Creig DOYLE
18 Director of Facilities ... Ms. Dawn BARNETT
29 Dir of Alumni Engagement and Giving ... Ms. Rachel MCCARTER
37 Director of Financial Aid ... Ms. Elizabeth GINGERICH
36 Dir of Career & Professional Dev ... Ms. Nancy HUTCHISON
41 Director of Athletics & Recreation ... Mr. Bradley KOCH
15 Director of Human Resources ... Ms. Susan ROHANNA
21 Controller ... Ms. Diane SCUTTI
24 Coord of Education Resources Center ... Ms. Mary BUDZILOWICZ
40 Bookstore Manager ... Mr. Bill BRIDDES
105 Digital Designer ... Mr. Matthew HOLMES
09 Director of Institutional Research ... Ms. Lisa PLUMMER
35 Dir Student Engagement & Leadership ... Ms. Anne FILIPPONE
92 Co-Director of the Honors Program ... Dr. Paul WRIGHT
92 Co-Director of the Honors Program ... Dr. Leonard PRIMIANO
28 Dir Student Diversity Initiatives ... Ms. Stephanie REED
38 Director Counseling/Psych Service ... Dr. Sara MAGGITTI
39 Director of Residence Life ... Ms. Sue KRAMER
07 Director of Admissions ... Ms. Shannon ZOTTOLA
101 Exec Governance Admin Sec Board ... Mrs. Nancy OLLINGER
102 Dir Sponsored Pgms & Foundation Rel ... Ms. Jean JACOBSON
108 Asst to Provost Assess/Accred ... Dr. Maliha ZAMAN
88 Creative Director ... Ms. Heidi HABEL
44 Director Annual Giving ... Mr. William GUSLER

Cairn University (C)

200 Manor Avenue, Langhorne Manor PA 19047-2990
County: Bucks FICE Identification: 003351
Unit ID: 215114
Telephone: (215) 752-5800 Carnegie Class: Master's S
FAX Number: (215) 702-4341 Calendar System: Semester
URL: www.cairn.edu
Established: 1913 Annual Undergrad Tuition & Fees: $23,920
Enrollment: 1,027 Coed
Affiliation or Control: Independent Non-Profit IRS Status: 501(c)3
Highest Offering: Master's
Program: Liberal Arts And General; Teacher Preparatory; Professional
Accreditation: M, BI, IACBE, MUS, SW

01 President ... Dr. Todd J. WILLIAMS
05 Provost ... Dr. Brian G. TOEWS
32 Sr VP Student Affairs ... Mr. J. Scott CAWOOD
10 Sr VP Finance & Administration ... Mr. Jan M. HAAS
30 Sr VP Univ Advancement ... Mr. Russell T. NIXON
26 Sr VP Marketing & Enrollment ... Mr. Paul NEAL
15 VP Human Resources ... Ms. Mary BOYER
108 Vice Provost ... Dr. Jean MINTO
06 Registrar ... Dr. Steven SCHLENKER
08 Dean Educational Resources ... Dr. Timothy K. HUI
35 Dean Student Life ... Mr. Tom SHERF
73 Dean School of Divinity ... Dr. Jonathan L. MASTER
49 Dean School of Liberal Arts & Sci ... Dr. Brenda MELLEN
50 Dean School of Business ... Mr. Yunn K. KANG
53 Dean School of Education ... Ms. Paula GOSSARD
64 Dean School of Music ... Dr. Benjamin HARDING
70 Dean School of Social Work ... Dr. Llloyd GESTOSO
84 Exec Director Enrollment Mgmt ... Mr. David URBAN
07 Director Admissions ... Ms. Rebecca LIPPERT
29 Director Alumni Relations ... Mr. Nathan WAMBOLD
18 Director Campus Services ... Mr. Robert WATSON
40 Campus Store Manager ... Ms. Emily MAYER
36 Director Career Center ... Ms. Teri T. CANTANIO
37 Director Financial Aid ... Mr. Stephen CASSEL
23 Director Health Services ... Ms. Alison KIKENDALL
09 Director Institutional Research ... Dr. Lynn WALLACE
39 Director Resident Life ... Mr. Evan CURRY
19 Director Safety & Security ... Mr. Chris LLOYD
38 Director Student Counseling ... Mr. Baron KING
13 Director Technology Services ... Mr. Curt D. WINTERS
106 Dir Online Education/E-learning ... Mr. Sali KACELI
11 Controller ... Mr. Jeff EUBANK
21 Asst Director Business Services ... Dr. Andrew HUI
04 Administrative Asst to President ... Ms. Lori MILLER
41 Athletic Director ... Ms. Laura BEHNKE

Cambria-Rowe Business College (D)

422 S 13th Street, Indiana PA 15701-2804
Telephone: (724) 463-0222 Identification: 666476
Accreditation: ACICS

† Branch campus of Cambria-Rowe Business College, Johnstown, PA.

Cambria-Rowe Business College (E)

221 Central Avenue, Johnstown PA 15902-2494
County: Cambria FICE Identification: 004889
Unit ID: 211398
Telephone: (814) 536-5168 Carnegie Class: Assoc/PrivFP
FAX Number: (814) 536-5160 Calendar System: Quarter
URL: www.crbc.net
Established: 1891 Annual Undergrad Tuition & Fees: $14,560
Enrollment: 144 Coed
Affiliation or Control: Proprietary IRS Status: Proprietary
Highest Offering: Associate Degree
Program: Occupational; 2-Year Principally Bachelor's Creditable; Business Emphasis
Accreditation: ACICS

01 President ... Mr. William COWARD
03 CEO ... Mr. Michael ARTIM
88 Director of Compliance ... Mr. Jeffrey ALLEN
05 Director of Curriculum ... Dr. Jonathan WOLF
12 Campus Director ... Mrs. Amy HORWATH
37 Director of Financial Aid Services ... Mrs. Linda WESS
10 Staff Accountant ... Mrs. Stacey THOMAS

Career Training Academy (F)

4314 Old William Penn Hwy, Ste 103,
Monroeville PA 15146-1455
Telephone: (412) 372-3900 Identification: 666051
Accreditation: ACCSC

† Branch campus of Career Training Academy, New Kensington, PA.

Career Training Academy (G)

950 Fifth Avenue, New Kensington PA 15068-6308
County: Westmoreland FICE Identification: 026095
Unit ID: 210951
Telephone: (724) 337-1000 Carnegie Class: Assoc/PrivFP
FAX Number: (724) 335-7140 Calendar System: Other
URL: www.careerta.edu
Established: 1986 Annual Undergrad Tuition & Fees: $10,549
Enrollment: 171 Coed
Affiliation or Control: Proprietary IRS Status: Proprietary
Highest Offering: Associate Degree
Program: Occupational; 2-Year Principally Bachelor's Creditable; Technical Emphasis
Accreditation: ACCSC

01 Campus Director ... Mr. Michael DISCELLO

Career Training Academy (H)

1014 West View Park Drive, Pittsburgh PA 15229
Telephone: (412) 367-4000 Identification: 666100
Accreditation: ACCSC

† Branch campus of Career Training Academy, New Kensington, PA.

Carlow University (I)

3333 Fifth Avenue, Pittsburgh PA 15213-3165
County: Allegheny FICE Identification: 003303
Unit ID: 211431
Telephone: (800) 333-2275 Carnegie Class: Master's M
FAX Number: (412) 578-6668 Calendar System: Semester
URL: www.carlow.edu
Established: 1929 Annual Undergrad Tuition & Fees: $26,832
Enrollment: 2,213 Coed
Affiliation or Control: Roman Catholic IRS Status: 501(c)3
Highest Offering: Doctorate
Program: Liberal Arts And General; Teacher Preparatory; Professional; Nursing Emphasis
Accreditation: M, #COARC, COPSY, NURSE, SW

01 President ... Dr. Suzanne K. MELLON
05 Interim Provost/VP Academic Affairs ... Deanne H. D'EMILIO
10 CFO/VP Finance and Operations ... Mr. Patrick J. CUNNINGHAM
30 VP Advancement ... Dr. Derek M. WESLEY
84 VP Enrollment Management ... Ms. Carol A. DESCAK
13 Chief Information Officer ... Mr. Jeffrey P. DEVLIN
26 VP Communications & External Rels ... Vacant
88 Special Asst to Pres/Mercy Heritage ... Sr. Sheila A. CARNEY
32 VP Student Engagement ... Dr. Jennifer A. CARLO
09 AVP Inst Rsrch/Effect & Planning ... Ms. Anne M. CANDREVA
04 Asst to the President ... Ms. Barbara L. GILLES
15 Director Human Resources ... Ms. Andra M. TOKARSKY
42 Campus Minister ... Ms. Siobhan K. DEWITT
06 Registrar ... Mr. Jason KRALL
88 Exec Dir & Principal Campus School ... Ms. Michelle A. PEDUTO
07 Director Undergraduate Admissions ... Ms. Wivinia A. WINSTEL
36 Director Career Development ... Ms. Erin R. BRIDGEN
58 Dir Student Accounts ... Mr. James V. SHANKEL
08 Director Library Services ... Vacant
85 Coordinator Center for Global Lrng ... Mr. Benjamin J. PILCHER
35 Director Campus Life ... Mr. Christopher M. MEANER
39 Asst Director Campus Life ... Vacant
23 Director Health Services ... Ms. Mary Frances REIDELL
41 Director Athletics ... Mr. George S. SLIMAN
88 Director Wellness & Fitness Svcs ... Ms. Julie M. GAUL
28 Director Diversity Initiative ... Ms. Barbara G. JOHNSON
21 Controller and Assoc VP of Finance ... Ms. Dorothy M. ANTONUCCI
18 Director Facilities ... Mr. Timothy D. CARNEY
19 Chief of Police ... Mr. Sean D. JOHNSON
37 Director Financial Aid ... Ms. Natalie L. WILSON
44 Exec Director Philanthropy ... Ms. Anita S. DACAL
29 Director Alumni Relations ... Ms. Rose M. WOOLLEY
44 Senior Director Philanthropy ... Ms. Marcia M. WALLANDER
102 Director of Corp & Found Relations ... Ms. Marjorie P. BERNARD
27 Director Media & Public Rels ... Mr. Andrew G. WILSON
105 Director Web Communications ... Ms. Lindsay M. O'LEARY
108 Director of Assessment ... Mr. August C. DELBERT

Carnegie Mellon University (J)

5000 Forbes Avenue, Pittsburgh PA 15213-3890
County: Allegheny FICE Identification: 003242
Unit ID: 211440
Telephone: (412) 268-2000 Carnegie Class: RU/VH
FAX Number: (412) 268-2330 Calendar System: Semester
URL: www.cmu.edu
Established: 1900 Annual Undergrad Tuition & Fees: $50,410
Enrollment: 13,285 Coed
Affiliation or Control: Independent Non-Profit IRS Status: 501(c)3
Highest Offering: Doctorate
Program: Liberal Arts And General; Teacher Preparatory; Professional
Accreditation: M, BUS, ENG, MUS, SPAA

01 President ... Dr. Subra SURESH
05 Provost ... Dr. Farnam JAHANIAN
10 Vice President and CFO ... Dr. Amir RAHNAMAY-AZAR
30 Interim VP for Univ Advancement ... Ms. Pamela EAGER
46 Vice President of Research ... Vacant
43 Vice President/General Counsel ... Ms. Mary Jo DIVELY
26 VP Marketing & Communications ... Mr. Steven KLOEHN
101 Secretary Board of Trustees ... Ms. Cheryl M. HAYS
04 Exec Asst to President ... Ms. Caryn MAKER
20 Vice Provost for Education ... Dr. Amy L. BURKERT
11 Vice President for Campus Affairs ... Dr. Michael C. MURPHY
13 Vice Provost for Comp Svcs/CIO ... Mr. Steven K. HUTH
15 Interim VP HR & Chief HR Officer ... Mr. Dan MCNULTY
29 Exec Dir Alumni Relations ... Ms. Nancy MERRITT
18 Asc VP Campus Design/Facility Devel ... Mr. Ralph R. HORGAN
26 Acting Exec Dir For Media Relations ... Mr. Kenneth WALTERS
28 Asst Vice Pres for Diversity & EOS ... Mr. Everett L. TADAMY
41 Dir Athletics & Physical Ed ... Mr. Josh CENTOR
19 Director Security/Chief Univ Police ... Mr. Thomas A. OGDEN
32 AVP & Dean Student Affairs ... Ms. Gina CASALEGNO
84 AVP & Dir of Enrollment Services ... Ms. Lisa M. KRIEG
14 Director Software Engr Inst ... Dr. Paul D. NIELSEN
07 Director of Admission ... Mr. Michael STEIDEL
08 Dean of University Libraries ... Mr. Keith WEBSTER
96 Director of Procurement ... Mr. Shawn G. FRONZAGLIA
06 Registrar ... Mr. John R. PAPINCHAK
09 Director of Institutional Research ... Ms. Janel SUTKUS
36 Assoc Dean for Career/Prof Dev ... Mr. Kevin MONAHAN
38 Dir Counseling & Psychological Svcs ... Dr. Kurt KUMLER
54 Dean Carnegie Inst of Technology ... Dr. James GARRETT
57 Dean College Fine Arts ... Dr. Dan J. MARTIN
49 Dean Dietrich College ... Dr. Richard SCHEINES

50 Dean Tepper School of Business ... Dr. Robert DAMMON
81 Dean Mellon College of Science ... Dr. Frederick J. GILMAN
80 Dean Heinz Sch Publ Policy/Mgmt ... Dr. Ramayya KRISHNAN
77 Dean School of Computer Science ... Dr. Andrew MOORE
35 Asst Dean of Student Affairs ... Ms. Anne WITCHNER
100 Director Office of President ... Ms. Cathy LIGHT
102 Dir Foundation Relations ... Ms. Lauren WARD
104 Director Study Abroad ... Ms. Linda GENTILE
25 Chief Contracts/Grants Admin ... Mr. Matthew D'EMILIO
37 Director Student Financial Aid ... Ms. Linda ANDERSON
39 Director Housing Services ... Mr. Thomas COOLEY
44 Director Annual or Planned Giving ... Ms. Pamela EAGER
86 Director Government Relations ... Mr. Timothy MCNULTY

Cedar Crest College (A)

100 College Drive, Allentown PA 18104-6196
County: Lehigh FICE Identification: 003243
Unit ID: 211468
Telephone: (610) 437-4471 Carnegie Class: Bac/Diverse
FAX Number: (610) 437-5955 Calendar System: Semester
URL: www.cedarcrest.edu
Established: 1867 Annual Undergrad Tuition & Fees: $34,546
Enrollment: 1,531 Female
Affiliation or Control: Non-denominational IRS Status: 501(c)3
Highest Offering: Master's
Program: Liberal Arts And General; Teacher Preparatory; Professional
Accreditation: M, ACBSP, DIETD, DIETI, FEPAC, NUR, SW

01 President ... Ms. Carmen T. AMBAR
05 Provost ... Dr. Elizabeth MEADE
10 Chief Financial Officer ... Ms. Audra J. KAHR
30 VP of Development/Alumnae Relation ... Ms. Susan ARNOLD
32 Dean of Student Affairs/VP of Adm ... Ms. Mary-Alice OZECHOSKI
06 Registrar ... Ms. Janet BAKER
29 Exec Director for Alumnae Affairs ... Mrs. Susan S. COX
19 Chief of Campus Safety and Security ... Mr. Mark VITALOS
18 Director of Facilities ... Mr. Matthew YENCHA
08 Library Director ... Ms. Mary Beth FREEH
91 Director Administrative Technology ... Mrs. Kathleen CUNNINGHAM
09 Dir of Institutional Research ... Ms. Lyn WILLIAMS
04 Assistant to the President ... Ms. Meghan GRADY
37 Dir Student Financial Services ... Ms. Valerie KREISER
22 Director Health/Counseling Services ... Ms. Nancy ROBERTS
26 Chief Marketing Officer ... Mr. Gaetan GIANNINI
96 Purchasing Coordinator ... Ms. Karen KHATTARI
40 Manager Bookstore ... Ms. Maureen YOACHIM

Central Penn College (B)

College Hill Road, Summerdale PA 17093-0309
County: Cumberland FICE Identification: 004890
Unit ID: 211477
Telephone: (800) 759-2727 Carnegie Class: Bac/Diverse
FAX Number: (717) 732-5254 Calendar System: Quarter
URL: www.centralpenn.edu
Established: 1881 Annual Undergrad Tuition & Fees: $28,868
Enrollment: 1,330 Coed
Affiliation or Control: Proprietary IRS Status: Proprietary
Highest Offering: Master's
Program: Occupational; 2-Year Principally Bachelor's Creditable; Professional; Business Emphasis
Accreditation: M, MAC, OTA, PTAA

01 President ... Dr. Karen SCOLFORO
03 Provost ... Vacant
07 Vice President Enrollment ... Ms. Stacey OBI
10 Chief Financial Officer ... Mr. Richard VARMECKY
29 Director Alumni Relations ... Mr. Matt LANE
06 Director Records & Registration ... Mr. Jen CORRELL
88 Director of Compliance ... Ms. Kathy ANDERSEN
18 Facilities Director ... Mr. Rodney GROFF
09 Institutional Research Director ... Col. Wilbur E. GRAY
26 Marketing Services Manager ... Mrs. Mary E. WETZEL
37 Financial Aid Director ... Ms. Kathy J. SHEPARD
41 Athletic Director ... Mr. Ed LIESCH
36 Career Services Coordinator ... Mr. Steven HASSINGER
15 Director Personnel Services ... Ms. Maggie LEBO
39 Director Student Housing ... Ms. Megan PETERSON

Chatham University (C)

Woodland Road, Pittsburgh PA 15232-2826
County: Allegheny FICE Identification: 003244
Unit ID: 211556
Telephone: (412) 365-1100 Carnegie Class: Master's L
FAX Number: (412) 365-1505 Calendar System: Other
URL: www.chatham.edu
Established: 1869 Annual Undergrad Tuition & Fees: $33,429
Enrollment: 2,134 Coed
Affiliation or Control: Independent Non-Profit IRS Status: 501(c)3
Highest Offering: Doctorate
Program: Liberal Arts And General; Teacher Preparatory; Professional
Accreditation: M, ARCPA, CIDA, COPSY, IACBE, LSAR, NURSE, OT, PTA, SW

01 President ... Dr. Esther L. BARAZZONE
10 Vice Pres Finance/Administration ... Mr. Walter B. FOWLER
05 Vice President Academic Affairs ... Dr. Jenna TEMPLETON
84 Vice Pres Enrollment Management ... Ms. Amy BECHER
32 VP Student Affairs/Dean of Stdnts ... Dr. Zauyah WAITE
26 Vice Pres for Mktg & Communications ... Mr. Bill CAMPBELL
30 Vice Pres University Advancement ... Vacant
51 Dean Continuing/Prof Studies ... Vacant
88 Dean Falk School Sustainability ... Dr. Peter WALKER
21 Asst VP Finance/Administration ... Ms. Jennifer LUNDY
45 VP of Planning/Sec to the Board ... Mr. Sean COLEMAN
09 Director of Institutional Research ... Dr. Robert ZHANG
06 Registrar ... Ms. Maria KRONISER
37 Director of Financial Aid ... Ms. Jennifer A. BURNS
08 Director of Library ... Ms. Jill AUSEL
29 Director Alumnae Affairs ... Ms. Cori BEGG
44 Director of Annual Giving ... Mr. Dominick OLIVER
102 Director of Foundation/Corp Support ... Ms. Amy BALDONIERI
15 Director of Human Resources ... Mr. Frank M. GRECO
18 Director of Facilities Management ... Mr. Robert R. DUBRAY
19 Director of Safety & Security ... Mr. Don AUBRECHT
41 Director of Athletics ... Vacant
36 Asst Dean for Career Development ... Mr. Sean MCGREEVEY
38 Director of Student Counseling ... Dr. Elsa M. ARCE
35 Dir Student Affs/Residence Life ... Ms. Heather BLACK
49 Dean School Arts/Science/Business ... Dr. Darlene MOTTLEY
76 Dean School of Health Sciences ... Dr. Patricia DOWNEY

Chestnut Hill College (D)

9601 Germantown Avenue, Philadelphia PA 19118-2693
County: Philadelphia FICE Identification: 003245
Unit ID: 211583
Telephone: (215) 248-7000 Carnegie Class: Master's L
FAX Number: (215) 248-7155 Calendar System: Semester
URL: www.chc.edu
Established: 1924 Annual Undergrad Tuition & Fees: $33,235
Enrollment: 2,063 Coed
Affiliation or Control: Roman Catholic IRS Status: 501(c)3
Highest Offering: Doctorate
Program: Liberal Arts And General; Teacher Preparatory
Accreditation: M, CLPSY, MACTE

01 President ... Sr. Carol Jean VALE, SSJ
05 Vice Pres for Academic Affairs ... Dr. Wolfgang NATTER
10 Sr Vice Pres for Financial Affairs ... Ms. Lauri STRIMKOVSKY
30 Vice President for Inst Advancement ... Mr. Kenneth HICKS
32 Vice President for Student Life ... Dr. Lynn ORTALE
11 Asst to Pres for Administration ... Sr. Kathryn MILLER, SSJ
42 Asst to Pres for Mission & Ministry ... Sr. Roseann QUINN, SSJ
58 Dean School of Graduate Studies ... Dr. Barbara HOGAN
97 Dean School of Undergrad Studies ... Sr. Cecelia CAVANAUGH, SSJ
51 Dean of Continuing Studies ... Dr. Elaine GREEN
08 Dean Library/Information Resources ... Sr. Mary Josephine LARKIN, SSJ
07 Vice President for Admissions ... Ms. Jodie KING
20 Assoc Dir Student Success ... Ms. Clare DOYLE
06 Registrar ... Mr. Michael REIG
35 Director of Student Activities ... Ms. Emily SCHADEMAN
38 Director Counseling Center ... Sr. Sheila KENNEDY, SSJ
85 Foreign Student Advisor ... Ms. Trachanda BROWN
28 Dir Cultural Diversity Initiatives ... Vacant
92 Director of Honors Programs ... Vacant
23 Director Health Services ... Ms. Shannon ROBERTS
36 Director of Career Services ... Ms. Nancy DACHILLE
07 Dir Admission/Sch Graduate Studies ... Ms. Jayne MASHETT
07 Director Accelerated Admissions ... Sr. Mary Esther LEE, SSJ
21 Controller ... Ms. Ellen MCGUINN
37 Director Financial Aid ... Ms. Sarah FEVIG
09 Director of Institutional Research ... Sr. Patricia O'DONNELL, SSJ
102 Dir Corporate/Found/Govt Relations ... Ms. Carol PATE
29 Director of Alumnae/i Affairs ... Ms. Catherine QUINN
41 Director of Athletics ... Ms. Lynn TUBMAN
15 Director Human Resources ... Ms. Sharon DOUGHERTY
19 Dir Security/Safety/Bldgs/Grounds ... Ms. Polly TETI
18 Director of Physical Plant ... Mr. Mark MCGRATH
91 Administrative Software Manager ... Ms. Darlene BROWN
26 Director of Communications ... Ms. Kathleen SPIGELMYER
40 Manager of Campus Store ... Vacant

The Commonwealth Medical College (E)

525 Pine Street, Scranton PA 18509
County: Lackawanna FICE Identification: 041672
Unit ID: 456542
Telephone: (570) 504-7000 Carnegie Class: Assoc/PrivNFP4
FAX Number: (570) 504-7289 Calendar System: Semester
URL: www.tcmc.edu
Established: 2009 Annual Graduate Tuition & Fees: $44,040
Enrollment: 405 Coed
Affiliation or Control: Independent Non-Profit IRS Status: 501(c)3
Highest Offering: Doctorate; No Undergraduates
Program: Professional
Accreditation: M, MED

01 President and Dean ... Dr. Steven J. SCHEINMAN
10 VP for Finance & Admin/CFO ... Ms. Anna RUSNAK NOON
30 VP Institutional Advancement ... Ms. Marise GAROFALO
31 VP Cmty & Government Relations ... Ms. Ida L. CASTRO
05 VP Acad & Clin Affairs/Vice Dean ... Dr. William IOBST
45 VP Strategic Initiatives/Planning ... Mr. V. Scott KOERWER
32 Assoc Dean Student Affs/ Admissions ... Ms. Linda BERARDI-DEMO
88 Assoc Dean of Fac Affairs/Fac Devel ... Ms. Andrea DIMATTIA
15 Assoc VP & Chief HR Officer ... Mr. Joseph CORTESE
21 Dir Budgeting & Financial Services ... Mr. Sam DIAZ
13 Sr Director of Technology ... Mr. Jay FORTIN
35 Director of Student Affairs ... Ms. Julia KOLCHARNO
06 Registrar ... Mr. Edward LAHART
37 Director of Financial Aid ... Ms. Ellen MCGUIRE
09 Dir Alumni Relations/Annual Giving ... Ms. Chris CARROLL

Commonwealth Technical Institute at the Hiram G. Andrews Center (F)

727 Goucher Street, Johnstown PA 15905-3092
County: Cambria FICE Identification: 025366
Unit ID: 212975
Telephone: (814) 255-8200 Carnegie Class: Assoc/PrivNFP
FAX Number: (814) 255-5709 Calendar System: Semester
URL: www.hgac.org
Established: 1959 Annual Undergrad Tuition & Fees: $33,456
Enrollment: 207 Coed
Affiliation or Control: Proprietary IRS Status: Proprietary
Highest Offering: Associate Degree
Program: Occupational; 2-Year Principally Bachelor's Creditable; Technical Emphasis
Accreditation: ACCSC

01 President ... Vacant
03 Executive Vice President ... Jill MORICONI
05 Director of Education ... Karen BILCHAK
07 Director of Admissions ... Jason GIES
32 Chief Student Life Officer ... Stacie ANDREWS
37 Director Student Financial Aid ... Vacant

Community College of Allegheny County (G)

800 Allegheny Avenue, Pittsburgh PA 15233-1895
County: Allegheny FICE Identification: 003231
Unit ID: 210605
Telephone: (412) 323-2323 Carnegie Class: Assoc/Pub-U-MC
FAX Number: (412) 237-4420 Calendar System: Semester
URL: www.ccac.edu
Established: 1966 Annual Undergrad Tuition & Fees (In-District): $3,821
Enrollment: 17,170 Coed
Affiliation or Control: State/Local IRS Status: 501(c)3
Highest Offering: Associate Degree
Program: 2-Year Principally Bachelor's Creditable
Accreditation: M, ADNUR, CA, CAHIIM, COARC, DIETT, DMS, EMT, MAC, MLTAD, NMT, OTA, PTAA, RAD, RTT, SURGT

01 President ... Dr. Quintin B. BULLOCK
05 Executive Vice President/Provost ... Dr. Stewart BLACKLAW
10 Vice President ... Ms. Joyce BRECKENRIDGE
12 Campus President Allegheny ... Dr. Donna IMHOFF
12 Campus President Boyce ... Hon. Charles MARTONI
12 Campus President North ... Dr. Gretchen SAWICKI
12 Campus President South ... Dr. Charlene NEWKIRK
86 Executive Director Govt Affairs ... Ms. Nancilee BURZACHECHI
103 VP Workforce Development ... Ms. Theresa BRYANT
15 VP Human Resources ... Ms. Kimberly MANIGAULT
102 CEO Educational Foundation ... Ms. Rose Ann DICOLA
13 CIO ... Mr. Ibrahim GARBIOGLU
06 Registrar ... Dr. Diane JACOBS
51 Dir Center Professional Dev ... Mr. Reginald OVERTON
45 Exec Dir of Strategic Planning ... Mr. Kevin SMAY
18 Director of Facilities Management ... Mr. James MESSER
21 Controller ... Mr. Paul SWEARENGIN
25 Director Contracts & Grants ... Dr. Carol YOANNONE
96 Director Purchasing/Contracts Admin ... Mr. Mike CVETIC
28 Special Asst to Pres for Diversity ... Mr. Clyde PICKETT
100 Assistant to the President ... Ms. Bonita L. RICHARDSON
22 Human Resources Generalist ... Mr. Paul SCHWARZMILLER
29 Dir Alumni Affairs ... Mr. Rocco PALELLA
26 Executive Director Public Relations ... Ms. Elizabeth JOHNSTON
43 Vice President and Genetal Counsel ... Mr. Anthony DITOMASSO

Community College of Allegheny County Boyce Campus (H)

595 Beatty Road, Monroeville PA 15146-1348
Telephone: (724) 325-6614 Identification: 770150
Accreditation: &M

† Branch campus of Community College of Allegheny County, Pittsburgh, PA.

Community College of Allegheny County North Campus (I)

8701 Perry Highway, Pittsburgh PA 15237-5353
Telephone: (412) 366-7000 Identification: 770151
Accreditation: &M

† Branch campus of Community College of Allegheny County, Pittsburgh, PA.

Community College of Allegheny County South Campus (J)

1750 Clairton Road, West Mifflin PA 15122-3029
Telephone: (412) 469-1100 Identification: 770152
Accreditation: &M

† Branch campus of Community College of Allegheny County, Pittsburgh, PA.

Community College of Beaver County (A)

1 Campus Drive, Monaca PA 15061-2588

County: Beaver FICE Identification: 006807
Unit ID: 211079

Telephone: (724) 480-2222 Carnegie Class: Assoc/Pub-S-SC
FAX Number: (724) 480-3573 Calendar System: Semester
URL: www.ccbc.edu
Established: 1966 Annual Undergrad Tuition & Fees (In-District): $5,380
Enrollment: 2,289 Coed
Affiliation or Control: State/Local IRS Status: 501(c)3
Highest Offering: Associate Degree
Program: Occupational; 2-Year Principally Bachelor's Creditable; Liberal Arts And General
Accreditation: M, ADNUR, PHLEB

01 President ... Dr. Christopher M. REBER
05 Provost ... Mrs. Melissa D. DENARDO
10 Vice President Finance & Operations ... Mr. Scott MONIT
15 Vice Pres Human Resources ... Vacant
26 Exec Dir Mktg/Comm Rel & Advance ... Ms. Leslie A. TENNANT
13 Vice Pres Information Technology ... Mr. Walter P. LUKHAUP
38 Dean Student Services & Enrollment ... Ms. Janice M. KAMINSKI
84 Director of Enrollment Services ... Ms. Angela M. VEDRO
103 Dean Workforce Dev/Continuing Educ ... Mr. John S. GOBERISH
09 Exec Dir Research & Engagement ... Mr. Brian J. HAYDEN
37 Director Student Financial Svcs ... Ms. Janet DAVIDSON
04 Admin Assistant to President ... Mrs. Leanne CONDRON
76 Dean Health Sciences ... Dr. Shelly MOORE
49 Dean Business/Arts/Science & Tech ... Dr. John HIGGS
88 Dean Aviation Sciences ... Mr. William PINTER
41 Athletic Director ... Mr. John ASHAOLU

Community College of Philadelphia (B)

1700 Spring Garden Street, Philadelphia PA 19130-3991

County: Philadelphia FICE Identification: 003249
Unit ID: 215239

Telephone: (215) 751-8000 Carnegie Class: Assoc/Pub-U-SC
FAX Number: (215) 751-8762 Calendar System: Semester
URL: www.ccp.edu
Established: 1965 Annual Undergrad Tuition & Fees (In-District): $4,440
Enrollment: 19,119 Coed
Affiliation or Control: State/Local IRS Status: 501(c)3
Highest Offering: Associate Degree
Program: Occupational; 2-Year Principally Bachelor's Creditable
Accreditation: M, ADNUR, COARC, DH, MLTAD, PHLEB, RAD

01 President ... Dr. Donald GENERALS
10 Vice President Business & Finance ... Mr. Jacob EAPEN
05 Vice President Academic Affairs ... Dr. Judith GAY
30 Vice Pres Institutional Advancement ... Mr. Gregory MURPHY
32 Vice President Student Affairs ... Dr. Samuel HIRSCH
86 Vice Pres Marketing/Government Rels ... Ms. Lynette BROWN-SOW
43 General Counsel/VP Human Resources ... Vacant
13 Chief Information Officer ... Ms. Jody BAUER
35 Dean of Students ... Dr. Donovan MCCARGO
84 Dean Div of Enrollment Services ... Dr. Warren HILTON
49 Dean Liberal Studies ... Dr. Sharon THOMPSON
51 Dean Div Adult/Community Education ... Dr. David E. THOMAS
72 Div Dean of Business/Technology ... Vacant
09 Director Institutional Research ... Dr. Dawn SINNOT
06 Director Stdnt Records/Registration ... Ms. Bonnie HARRINGTON
18 Chief Facilities/Physical Plant ... Mr. Harry MOORE
28 Affirmative Action Director ... Mr. Simon BROWN
07 Director of Recruitment/Admissions ... Ms. Jeri DRAPER
37 Director Financial Aid ... Mr. Gim LIM
96 Director of Purchasing ... Ms. Marsia HENLEY
38 Dept Head Student Counseling ... Mr. Todd JONES
36 Coord Career Info/Placement Svcs ... Ms. Tarsha SCOVENS
29 Coord Alumni Rels/Annual Giving ... Ms. Lyvette BROOKS
25 Coord Grants/Prospect Research ... Ms. Anne GRECO

Consolidated School of Business (C)

2124 Ambassador Circle, Lancaster PA 17603-2389

County: Lancaster FICE Identification: 030299
Unit ID: 260354

Telephone: (717) 394-6211 Carnegie Class: Assoc/PrivFP
FAX Number: (717) 394-6213 Calendar System: Other
URL: www.csb.edu
Established: 1981 Annual Undergrad Tuition & Fees: $28,200
Enrollment: 99 Coed
Affiliation or Control: Proprietary IRS Status: Proprietary
Highest Offering: Associate Degree
Program: Occupational
Accreditation: ACICS

01 CEO/President ... Mr. Robert L. SAFRAN
11 Vice President for Administration ... Mr. William HOYT
10 Vice President for Finance ... Mr. Craig D. ELLIS
05 School Director ... Dr. Andrea STEPHENSON
37 Financial Aid Director ... Ms. Gail DOUGHERTY
36 Placement Director ... Ms. Kelly SWIGERT
13 Data Systems Director ... Mr. Gholamereza SALARI
21 Bursar ... Mrs. Diane GRANT

Consolidated School of Business (D)

1605 Clugston Road, York PA 17404-1798

County: York FICE Identification: 022896
Unit ID: 211820

Telephone: (717) 764-9550 Carnegie Class: Assoc/PrivFP
FAX Number: (717) 764-9469 Calendar System: Other
URL: www.csb.edu
Established: 1981 Annual Undergrad Tuition & Fees: $14,450
Enrollment: 102 Coed
Affiliation or Control: Proprietary IRS Status: Proprietary
Highest Offering: Associate Degree
Program: Occupational
Accreditation: ACICS

01 CEO/President ... Mr. Robert L. SAFRAN
10 Vice President of Finance ... Mr. Craig D. ELLIS
11 Vice President of Administration ... Mr. Bill HOYT
37 Financial Aid Director ... Mrs. Gail E. DOUGHERTY
32 School Director ... Ms. Jennifer HATCH

Curtis Institute of Music (E)

1726 Locust Street, Philadelphia PA 19103-6187

County: Philadelphia FICE Identification: 003251
Unit ID: 211893

Telephone: (215) 893-5252 Carnegie Class: Spec/Arts
FAX Number: (215) 893-9065 Calendar System: Semester
URL: www.curtis.edu
Established: 1924 Annual Undergrad Tuition & Fees: $2,525
Enrollment: 176 Coed
Affiliation or Control: Independent Non-Profit IRS Status: 501(c)3
Highest Offering: Master's
Program: Professional; Music Emphasis
Accreditation: M, MUS

01 President & Chief Executive Officer ... Mr. Roberto DIAZ
10 Sr VP Admin/Chief Financial Officer ... Mr. Raul GARCIA
30 Sr VP Advancement ... Ms. Kristin B. LODEN
05 Dean of Faculty/Students ... Mr. Paul BRYAN
06 Registrar ... Ms. Makiko FREEMAN
07 Admissions Officer ... Mr. Christopher HODGES
08 Dir Music Library Info Resources ... Ms. Michelle OSWELL

Dean Institute of Technology (F)

1501 W Liberty Avenue, Pittsburgh PA 15226-1197

County: Allegheny FICE Identification: 009186
Unit ID: 211909

Telephone: (412) 531-4433 Carnegie Class: Assoc/PrivFP
FAX Number: (412) 531-4435 Calendar System: Quarter
URL: www.deantech.edu
Established: 1947 Annual Undergrad Tuition & Fees: $15,270
Enrollment: 169 Coed
Affiliation or Control: Proprietary IRS Status: Proprietary
Highest Offering: Associate Degree
Program: Occupational; Technical Emphasis
Accreditation: ACCSC

01 President/Director ... Mr. James S. DEAN
05 Director of Education/Asst Director ... Mr. Richard D. ALI
07 Director of Admissions ... Mr. Nicholas D. ALI
37 Director Student Financial Aid ... Ms. Valerie L. VELTRI
36 Placement Director ... Ms. Valerie A. HAGEDORN
26 Director Information Office ... Mr. Stephen FALAVOLITO

Delaware County Community College (G)

901 S Media Line Road, Media PA 19063-1094

County: Delaware FICE Identification: 007110
Unit ID: 211927

Telephone: (610) 359-5000 Carnegie Class: Assoc/Pub-S-SC
FAX Number: (610) 359-5343 Calendar System: Semester
URL: www.dccc.edu
Established: 1967 Annual Undergrad Tuition & Fees (In-District): $6,305
Enrollment: 12,459 Coed
Affiliation or Control: State/Local IRS Status: 501(c)3
Highest Offering: Associate Degree
Program: Occupational; 2-Year Principally Bachelor's Creditable
Accreditation: M, ADNUR, COARC, EMT, MAC, SURGT

01 President ... Dr. Jerome S. PARKER
10 Vice Pres Administration/Treasurer ... Mr. John A. GLAVIN, JR.
05 Acting Provost ... Dr. Eric WELLINGTON
30 Vice President for Advancement ... Ms. Kathleen A. BRESLIN
12 Vice Provost & Vice Pres Chester Co ... Dr. Mary Jo BOYER
15 Vice President of Human Resources ... Ms. Connie L. MCCALLA
84 Vice President of Enrollment Mgmt ... Ms. Frances M. CUBBERLEY
13 VP & CIO Information Technology ... Mr. George J. SULLIVAN
32 Vice Provost Student/Instr Support ... Dr. Grant S. SNYDER
96 Assoc VP Admin & Facilities Plng ... Mr. Jeffrey S. BAUN
88 Director Learning Centers ... Ms. Dawn M. MOSCARIELLO
88 Director Municipal Police Academy ... Mr. William DAVIS
106 Director Distance Learning Services ... Mr. Alexander PLUCHUTA
37 Director of Financial Aid ... Mr. Raymond L. TOOLE
07 Dir Admissions/Enrollment Services ... Ms. Hope L. DIEHL
36 Director Career/Counseling Center ... Ms. Christine M. DOYLE
06 Registrar ... Mr. Thomas W. LUGG
09 Assoc Vice Prov Inst Effectiveness ... Dr. Christopher TOKPAH
21 Associate VP Finance ... Mr. William J. MARKLE
103 Director Workforce Entry Center ... Ms. Susan E. BOND
85 Director International Student Svs ... Ms. Lydia J. DELL'OSA
16 Director Human Resources ... Mr. Christopher M. DICKERMAN
14 Assoc CIO OIT/Technical Services ... Ms. Bianca VALENTE
91 Director Admin Computing ... Mr. Bob HARDCASTLE
29 Director Alumni Programs ... Mr. Douglas J. FERGUSON
25 Director Grants Management ... Ms. Susan M. SHISLER-RAPP
31 Director Community Education ... Ms. Nan L. SMITH
35 Director Campus Life ... Ms. Amy WILLIAMS-GAUDIOSO
19 Director Safety & Security ... Mr. Raymond VISCUSI
88 Dir Dual Enrollment HS Initiatives ... Ms. Katherine DIAMOND-ROTHSTEIN
12 Director Southeast & UD Centers ... Ms. Jane SCHURMAN
89 Director First Year Experiences ... Dr. Kendrick MICKENS
88 Director Assessment Center ... Ms. Carol MULLIN
96 Director Purchasing ... Ms. Jenny M. RARIG
18 Dir Plant Oper/Construction Svcs ... Mr. Tony DELUCA
103 Dean Workforce Dev & Cmty Educ ... Ms. Karen KOZACHYN
72 Dean Tech/Engineering & Math ... Dr. John R. AGAR
88 Acting Dean Learning Support Svcs ... Ms. Dolores E. MARTINO
50 Dean Business & Social Science ... Dr. Marian MCGORRY
79 Dean Comm/Arts & Humanities ... Dr. Robert KLEINSCHMIDT
76 Interim Dean Health/Nursing/EMS .. Dr. Sharvette LAW-PHILMON
40 Manager Bookstore ... Mr. Kris STACHOWIAK

Delaware Valley University (H)

700 E Butler Avenue, Doylestown PA 18901-2697

County: Bucks FICE Identification: 003252
Unit ID: 211981

Telephone: (215) 345-1500 Carnegie Class: Bac/Diverse
FAX Number: (215) 345-5277 Calendar System: Semester
URL: www.delval.edu
Established: 1896 Annual Undergrad Tuition & Fees: $35,256
Enrollment: 1,788 Coed
Affiliation or Control: Independent Non-Profit IRS Status: 501(c)3
Highest Offering: Doctorate
Program: 2-Year Principally Bachelor's Creditable; Liberal Arts And General; Professional; Business Emphasis
Accreditation: M

01 President ... Dr. Joseph S. BROSNAN
04 Exec Assistant to the President ... Ms. Angela T. RECKNER
05 VP Acad Affairs/Dean of the Faculty ... Dr. Bashar W. HANNA
32 VP Student Affairs/Dean of Students ... Dr. April VARI
10 VP for Finance & Administration ... Mr. Arthur GLASS
30 Vice President for Inst Advancement ... Mr. Joseph ERCKERT
09 AVP Rsrch/Plng/Accr & Dir I&R ... Ms. Deborah DAILEY
84 VP for Enrollment Mgmt ... Mr. Arthur GOON
81 Dean of Life & Physical Sciences ... Dr. Benjamin RUSILOSKI
47 Interim Dean of Agric & Environ Sci ... Dr. Christopher TIPPING
50 Dean of Business & Humanities ... Dr. Kim LONG
58 Interim Dean of Grad/Prof & Entr ... Dr. James MORYAN
06 Registrar ... Mr. James SLIZEWSKI
41 Athletic Director ... Mr. Steve CANTRELL
26 Chief Marketing Officer ... Ms. Laurie WARD
07 Director of Admissions ... Mr. Dwayne WALKER
36 Exec Dir Ctr for Student Prof Dev ... Dr. Benjamin RUSILOSKI
08 Librarian ... Mr. Peter A. KUPERSMITH
37 Director Student Financial Aid ... Mrs. Joan HOCK
58 Director Graduate & Prof Studies ... Ms. Yolonda UDVARDY
38 Director Counseling/Learn Support ... Ms. Sharon DONNELLY
23 Director Health Services ... Ms. Miriam TORRES
13 Director of Media Services ... Mr. James LINDEN
39 Director of Residence Life ... Mr. Derek SMITH
19 Director Security/Public Safety ... Vacant
15 Director Human Resources ... Ms. Barbara HLADIK
18 Director Physical Plant ... Mr. Joseph GUCKAVAN
44 Director Annual Fund ... Ms. Jennifer ROCK
96 Director of Purchasing ... Mr. William LYLE
101 Secretary of the Institution/Board ... Ms. Nancy SCHUYLER
102 Dir Foundation/Corporate Relations ... Ms. Wendy CONNUCK
103 Dir Workforce/Career Development ... Ms. Deanna PARKTON
104 Director Study Abroad ... Mr. Matthew KAMINSKI-LUCAS
106 Dir Online Education/E-learning ... Ms. Cynthia RENNER
29 Director Alumni Engagement ... Ms. Lynn CARROLL

DeSales University (I)

2755 Station Avenue, Center Valley PA 18034-9568

County: Lehigh FICE Identification: 003986
Unit ID: 210739

Telephone: (610) 282-1100 Carnegie Class: Master's L
FAX Number: (610) 282-2254 Calendar System: Semester
URL: www.desales.edu
Established: 1965 Annual Undergrad Tuition & Fees: $33,350
Enrollment: 3,188 Coed
Affiliation or Control: Roman Catholic IRS Status: 501(c)3
Highest Offering: Doctorate
Program: Liberal Arts And General; Teacher Preparatory; Professional
Accreditation: M, ACBSP, ARCPA, NUR, @PTA

01 President ... Dr. Bernard F. O'CONNOR, OSFS
04 Admin Assistant to the President ... Ms. Mary A. GOTZON
05 Provost/Vice Pres Academic Affairs ... Dr. Karen WALTON
06 Registrar ... Mr. Thomas MANTONI
08 Librarian ... Ms. Deborah MALONE
51 Dean of Lifelong Learning ... Ms. Deborah BOOROS
88 Dean of Undergraduate Education ... Dr. Robert BLUMENSTEIN
36 Director Career Svcs & Internships ... Ms. Kristin EICHOLTZ
30 Vice Pres Institutional Advancement ... Mr. Thomas L. CAMPBELL

86 Director of Government Relations ... Dr. Bernard F. O'CONNOR, OSFS
102 Director Corp/Foundation Relations ... Mrs. Kathy DIAMANDOPOULOS
26 Executive Director of Communication ... Mr. Thomas MCNAMARA
44 Executive Dir of Annual Giving ... Ms. Lina BARBIERI
29 Director of Alumni Relations ... Ms. Nicole GINGRICH
10 VP for Admin/Finance & Campus Env ... Mr. Robert J. SNYDER
45 Assoc VP for Admin & Planning ... Mr. Peter RAUTZHAN
21 Director of Finance/Treasurer ... Mr. Michael SWEETANA
19 Chief of Police ... Chief Steven MARSHALL
09 Director of Institutional Research ... Vacant
88 Assoc VP of Campus Environment ... Mr. Marc ALBANESE
18 Director of Facilities ... Mr. Jim MOLCHANY
40 Campus Store Manager ... Ms. Catherine WONG
15 Director of Human Resources ... Mrs. Margie GRANDINETTI
16 Employment Benefits Coordinator ... Vacant
13 Director of Information Technology ... Ms. Patricia CLAY
32 Vice President Student Life ... Dr. Gerard JOYCE
84 Dean of Enrollment Mgmt ... Mrs. Mary BIRKHEAD
35 Dean of Students ... Mrs. Linda ZERBE
39 Director of Residence Life ... Ms. Melinda QUINONES
07 Director of Admissions ... Mr. Derrick WETZEL
37 Director of Student Financial Aid ... Mrs. Joyce FARMER
42 Chaplain ... Fr. Timothy MCINTIRE, OSFS
38 Director of Counseling Center ... Ms. Wendy KRISAK
41 Athletic Director ... Mr. Scott COVAL
28 Director Multicultural/Intl Affairs ... Vacant
58 Dean of Graduate Education ... Dr. Peter LEONARD, OSFS
96 Campus Environment/Dir Purchasing ... Mr. Michael DUFFY
103 Dir Workforce/Career Development ... Vacant
104 Director Study Abroad ... Mr. Brian MACDONALD
50 Dean of Business ... Mr. Christopher R. COCOZZA
53 Dean of Education ... Dr. Judith RANCE-RONEY

DeVry University - Fort Washington Campus (A)

1140 Virginia Drive, Fort Washington PA 19034-3204
Telephone: (215) 591-5700 Identification: 666218
Accreditation: &NH, CAHIIM, ENGT

† Regional accreditation is carried under the parent institution in Downers Grove, IL.

Dickinson College (B)

Box 1773, College & Louther Street, Carlisle PA 17013-2896
County: Cumberland FICE Identification: 003253
Unit ID: 212009
Telephone: (717) 243-5121 Carnegie Class: Bac/A&S
FAX Number: N/A Calendar System: Semester
URL: www.dickinson.edu
Established: 1783 Annual Undergrad Tuition & Fees: $49,464
Enrollment: 2,364 Coed
Affiliation or Control: Independent Non-Profit IRS Status: 501(c)3
Highest Offering: Baccalaureate
Program: Liberal Arts And General; Teacher Preparatory
Accreditation: M

01 President ... Dr. Nancy A. ROSEMAN
05 Provost and Dean of the College ... Dr. Neil B. WEISSMAN
84 VP Enrollment Marketing and Comm ... Dr. Stefanie D. NILES
10 VP Finance & Administration ... Dr. Bronté JONES
30 VP College Advancement ... Ms. Marsha M. RAY
32 VP Student Life ... Ms. Joyce A. BYLANDER
13 VP & Chief Information Officer ... Mr. Robert E. RENAUD
07 Dean of Admissions ... Ms. Catherine M. DAVENPORT
15 Assoc VP Human Resource Services ... Vacant
43 General Counsel ... Ms. Dana E. SCADUTO
101 Chief of Staff/Secretary of College ... Ms. Karen N. FARYNIAK
18 Assoc VP Sustain & Facilities Plng ... Mr. Kenneth E. SHULTES
20 Sr Assoc Provost Academic Affairs ... Dr. Robert P. WINSTON
20 Sr Assoc Provost Academic Affairs ... Dr. Brenda K. BRETZ
44 Assoc VP College Advance ... Mr. Brian G. FALCK
21 Assoc VP Aux Svcs & Budget Mgt ... Mr. Stephen C. HIETSCH
26 Exec Dir Marketing & Communications ... Ms. Connie MCNAMARA
06 Registrar ... Ms. Karen A. WEIKEL
41 Director Athletics ... Mr. Joe GIUNTA
09 Director Institutional Research ... Mr. Jason E. RIVERA
37 Director of Financial Aid ... Mr. Richard A. HECKMAN
104 Exec Dir Ctr Global Stdy & Engagmnt ... Mr. Michael D. MONAHAN
36 Dean Career Dev/Asst VP Student Dev ... Mr. Philip JONES
94 Professor American Studies ... Dr. Sharon J. O'BRIEN
88 Executive Director Wellness Center ... Dr. Alecia D. SUNDSMO
35 Assoc VP Stdnt Ldrshp/Campus Engage ... Ms. Rebecca J. HAMMELL
90 Director Academic Computing ... Ms. Patricia A. PEHLMAN
88 Director of Media Relations ... Ms. Christine M. DUGAN
29 Asst VP Engagement/Annual Fund ... Ms. Coco MINARDI
08 Director Library Services ... Ms. Eleanor MITCHELL
40 Dir College Bookstore/Central Svcs ... Mr. David A. NELSON
19 Asst VP Compliance/Campus Safety ... Ms. Dolores A. DANSER
91 Assoc VP Enterprise Systems ... Ms. Jill M. FORRESTER
102 Dir Academic & Foundation Relations ... Ms. Cheryl E. KREMER
39 Assoc Dean Stdnts/Dir Res Life ... Ms. Angie HARRIS
102 Executive Director Donor Relations ... Ms. Tara C. RENAULT
105 Director Online Marketing ... Ms. Sarah M. SHERIFF
42 Director Cmty Svcs/Religious Life ... Rev. Donna D. HUGHES
100 Asst Chief of Staff ... Ms. Ashley M. PERZYNA
88 VP Institutional Initiatives ... Mr. Michael E. REED

Dickinson Law (C)

150 South College Street, Carlisle PA 17013-2861
Telephone: (717) 240-5000 FICE Identification: 003254
Accreditation: &M, LAW

† Part of Penn State University. Regional accreditation is carried under the parent institution in University Park, PA.

Douglas Education Center (D)

130 Seventh Street, Monessen PA 15062-1097
County: Westmoreland FICE Identification: 020683
Unit ID: 212045
Telephone: (724) 684-3684 Carnegie Class: Assoc/PrivFP
FAX Number: (724) 684-7463 Calendar System: Semester
URL: www.dec.edu
Established: 1904 Annual Undergrad Tuition & Fees: $17,596
Enrollment: 272 Coed
Affiliation or Control: Proprietary IRS Status: Proprietary
Highest Offering: Associate Degree
Program: Occupational; 2-Year Principally Bachelor's Creditable; Fine Arts Emphasis
Accreditation: ACICS

01 President ... Mr. Jeffrey D. IMBRESCIA
05 Vice President of Academic Affairs ... Ms. Patricia A. DECONCILIS
10 Chief Financial Officer ... Mr. Jay B. CLAYTON
20 Director of Academic Progress ... Ms. Susan F. ROUNDTREE
20 Academic Affairs Coordinator ... Ms. N. Renee MCDOWELL
07 Director of Admissions ... Mr. Tony BAEZ MILAN
37 Director of Financial Aid ... Ms. Amanda PHILLIPS
26 Chief Marketing Officer ... Mr. Kevin G. FEAR
88 Cosmetology Supervisor ... Ms. Carrie HOLMAN
36 Director of Career Services ... Mrs. Donna STAIRS
27 Public Relations Coordinator ... Ms. Courtney LAMANNA
13 Information Technology Manager ... Mr. John SECHRIST

Drexel University (E)

3141 Chestnut Street, Philadelphia PA 19104-2875
County: Philadelphia FICE Identification: 003256
Unit ID: 212054
Telephone: (215) 895-2000 Carnegie Class: RU/H
FAX Number: (215) 895-1414 Calendar System: Quarter
URL: www.drexel.edu
Established: 1891 Annual Undergrad Tuition & Fees: $48,756
Enrollment: 26,359 Coed
Affiliation or Control: Independent Non-Profit IRS Status: 501(c)3
Highest Offering: Doctorate
Program: Liberal Arts And General; Professional
Accreditation: M, ANEST, ARCPA, ART, BUS, CEA, CIDA, CLPSY, CONST, CS, DENT, DIETD, ENG, ENGT, HT, LAW, LIB, MED, MFCD, NURSE, PA, PH, PTA, RAD

01 President ... Mr. John A. FRY
05 Provost/Sr VP Academic Affairs ... Dr. Brian BLAKE
30 Interim SVP Inst Advancement ... Mr. David UNRUH
10 Sr Vice Pres Finance/Treasurer/CFO ... Mrs. Helen Y. BOWMAN
32 Sr VP Admin Services/Student Life ... Mr. James R. TUCKER
84 SVP Enrollment Mgmt/Student Success ... Dr. Randall C. DEIKE
26 Sr VP University Communications ... Ms. Lori DOYLE
11 Sr Vice Provost Budget Plng/Admin ... Dr. Janice BIROS
43 Sr VP & General Counsel ... Mr. Michael J. EXLER
03 Sr VP & Executive Director ... Mr. Brian KEECH
20 Sr Vice Provost Academic Affairs ... Dr. N. John DINARDO
13 Vice Pres Info Resources/Technology ... Mr. Ken BLACKNEY
88 Vice President Internal Audit ... Mr. James SEAMAN
21 Vice Pres & Assoc Treasurer ... Mr. Jeffrey A. EBERLY
86 VP Govt & Community Relations ... Mr. David E. WILSON
100 VP & Exec Dir Office of President ... Dr. Rosalind REMER
07 Vice Pres/Dean of Admissions ... Mr. Christopher FERGUSON
100 Senior VP President's Office ... Mr. Keith ORRIS
46 Interim Vice Provost of Research ... Dr. Aleister SAUNDERS
09 Vice Provost Institutional Research ... Dr. Mark FREEMAN
88 Vice Provost Partnerships ... Dr. Lucy E. KERMAN
18 Vice Pres Univ Facilities ... Dr. Robert FRANCIS
15 Vice President Human Resources ... Mr. Louis BELLARDINE
88 Assoc Vice President & Comptroller ... Ms. Patricia J. RUSSO
108 Associate Vice Provost Assessment ... Mr. Stephen DIPIETRO
49 Dean College Arts & Sciences ... Dr. Donna MURASKO
50 Dean LeBow College of Business ... Dr. Francis LINNEHAN
54 Dean College of Engineering ... Dr. Joseph B. HUGHES
107 Exec Dir Goodwin Col of Prof Stds ... Dr. Timothy GILRAIN
77 Dean Col of Computing & Informatics ... Dr. Spiros MANCORIDIS
92 Dean of Pennoni Honors College ... Dr. Paula COHEN
62 Dean of Libraries ... Dr. Danuta NITECKI
88 Dean of Close School ... Dr. Donna DECAROLIS
58 Exec Vice Prov Center Grad Studies ... Dr. James HERBERT
61 Dean Drexel School of Law ... Mr. Roger J. DENNIS
60 Dean Col of Media Arts & Design ... Mr. Allen SABINSON
17 Sr VP & Dean College of Medicine ... Dr. Daniel SCHIDLOW
66 Dean College of Nursing/Health Prof ... Dr. Gloria DONNELLY
69 Dean Sch of Public Health ... Dr. Ana V. DIEZ ROUX
88 Pres & CEO Acad of Natural Sciences ... Mr. George W. GEPHART, JR.
88 Int Dean School Biomed Engineering ... Dr. Kenneth BARBIE
19 Interim VP Public Safety ... Ms. Eileen BEHR
88 Senior Assoc Vice President ... Ms. Rita LARUE
25 Assoc Vice Provost for Research ... Ms. Patricia RUSSO
41 Athletic Director ... Dr. Eric A. ZILLMER
45 Interim AVP Financial Planning ... Ms. Maribeth SCHNELLER
90 Assoc VP Info Resources & Tech ... Ms. Kathryn MATUCH
29 Associate VP Alumni Relations ... Ms. Cristina A. GESO
102 Assoc VP Corporate/Foundation Rels ... Dr. Anika K. WARREN
35 AVP and Dean of Student Life ... Mr. Subir SAHU
44 Assoc VP Planned Giving ... Mr. David J. TOLL
36 Vice Prov Career Development Ctr ... Mr. Peter FRANKS
22 Asst Vice Pres Equality & Diversity ... Ms. Michele ROVINSKY
88 Asst Vice Pres Recruitment ... Dr. Lois (Casey) TURNER
35 Assoc Dean of Students ... Dr. Rebecca L. WEIDENSAUL
23 Assoc Dean Counseling and Health ... Dr. Annette MOLYNEUX
06 Registrar ... Mr. Joseph J. SALOMONE
24 Director Instructional Media Svcs ... Mr. Christopher GIBSON
38 Assoc Director of Counseling ... Dr. Amy HENNING
39 Exec Director University Housing ... Mr. Christopher HEASLEY
104 Asst Vice Provost Study Abroad ... Ms. Daniela ASCARELLI
04 Executive Admin President's Office ... Ms. Kaitlyn BOYLE
40 Manager Bookstore ... Mr. John RORER
106 President Drexel e-Learning ... Dr. Susan C. ALDRIDGE
88 Ombuds ... Dr. David FLOOD
88 Vice Provost Strategic Dev & Init ... Dr. Janet FLEETWOOD
85 Vice Provost Global Initatives ... Dr. Julie MOSTOV
37 Director Student Financial Aid ... Ms. Elaine VARAS
53 Dean School of Education ... Dr. Nancy B. SONGER

DuBois Business College (F)

One Beaver Drive, DuBois PA 15801-2401
County: Clearfield FICE Identification: 004893
Unit ID: 212072
Telephone: (814) 371-6920 Carnegie Class: Assoc/PrivFP
FAX Number: (814) 371-3974 Calendar System: Quarter
URL: www.dbcollege.edu
Established: 1885 Annual Undergrad Tuition & Fees: $11,875
Enrollment: 185 Coed
Affiliation or Control: Proprietary IRS Status: Proprietary
Highest Offering: Associate Degree
Program: Occupational
Accreditation: ACICS

01 President and Director ... Ms. Jackie D. SYKTICH
05 Academic Dean ... Ms. Mary O. JONES
37 Financial Aid Director ... Ms. Karen S. ALDERTON
07 Director of Admissions ... Ms. Terry L. KHOURY
36 Career Services ... Ms. Barbara M. MARTINI
12 Director Huntingdon Campus ... Mrs. Susan RAMEY
12 Director Oil City Campus ... Mrs. Terry KHOURY

DuBois Business College (G)

1001 Moore Street, Huntingdon PA 16652-1800
Telephone: (814) 641-0440 Identification: 666479
Accreditation: ACICS

† Branch campus of DuBois Business College, DuBois, PA.

DuBois Business College (H)

701 E Third Street, Oil City PA 16301-2407
Telephone: (814) 677-1322 Identification: 666480
Accreditation: ACICS

† Branch campus of DuBois Business College, DuBois, PA.

Duquesne University (I)

600 Forbes Avenue, Pittsburgh PA 15282-0001
County: Allegheny FICE Identification: 003258
Unit ID: 212106
Telephone: (412) 396-6000 Carnegie Class: RU/H
FAX Number: (412) 396-4186 Calendar System: Semester
URL: www.duq.edu
Established: 1878 Annual Undergrad Tuition & Fees: $33,778
Enrollment: 9,757 Coed
Affiliation or Control: Roman Catholic IRS Status: 501(c)3
Highest Offering: Doctorate
Program: Liberal Arts And General; Teacher Preparatory; Professional
Accreditation: M, ARCPA, BUS, CAATE, CACREP, CEA, CLPSY, FEPAC, LAW, MUS, NURSE, OT, PHAR, PTA, SCPSY, SP, TED

01 President ... Dr. Charles J. DOUGHERTY
04 Assistant to President ... Ms. Mary F. MCINTYRE
05 Provost/Academic Vice President ... Dr. Timothy R. AUSTIN
10 Vice President Management Business ... Mr. David R. BEAUPRE
32 Vice Pres for Student Life ... Dr. Douglas FRIZZELL
30 VP for University Advancement ... Mr. John J. PLANTE
88 Vice President Mission & Identity ... Rev. Raymond FRENCH, CSSP
43 VP Legal Affairs & General Counsel ... Ms. Madelyn REILLY
20 Assoc Academic Vice Pres Research ... Dr. Alan W. SEADLER
20 Assoc Academic Vice President ... Dr. Jeffrey A. MILLER
21 Assoc Vice Pres Financial Affairs ... Dr. Matthew FRIST
13 Executive Director CTS ... Vacant
109 Director Auxiliary Services ... Mr. Scott RICHARDS
85 Exec Director Intl Programs ... Dr. Roberta C. ARONSON
84 Assoc Vice Pres Enrollment Mgmt ... Mr. Paul-James CUKANNA
06 Registrar ... Ms. Kim HOERITZ
08 Librarian ... Ms. Diana SASSO
29 Director Alumni Relations ... Ms. Sarah SPERRY
35 Director Student Affairs ... Vacant
09 Director of Institutional Research ... Mr. Matthew NORTH
37 Director Financial Aid ... Mr. Richard C. ESPOSITO
15 Director of Human Resource Mgmt ... Vacant

19 Director of Security .... Mr. Thomas HART
88 Dir Environmental Health/Safety .... Ms. Paula D. SWEITZER
18 Director of Facilities Management .... Mr. Rodney W. DOBISH
36 Director of Career Services .... Ms. Nicole FELDHUES
41 Director of Athletics .... Vacant
26 Assoc Vice Pres of Public Affairs .... Ms. Bridget M. FARE
22 Director of Anti-discricrimination .... Mr. Sean F. WEAVER
23 Director Health Service .... Ms. Dessa MRVOS
38 Director Univ Counseling Center .... Dr. Ian C. EDWARDS
39 Director Residence Life .... Mrs. Sharon G. OELSCHLAGER
42 Director Campus Ministry .... Rev. Daniel WALSH, CSSP
28 Director of Multicultural Affairs .... Mr. Jeff MALLORY
50 Dean Business & Administration .... Dr. Dean B. MCFARLIN
66 Dean of Nursing .... Dr. Mary Ellen S. GLASGOW
67 Dean of Pharmacy .... Dr. J. Douglas BRICKER
64 Dean of Music .... Dr. Seth BECKMAN
53 Dean of Education .... Dr. Olga M. WELCH
76 Dean of Health Sciences .... Dr. Gregory H. FRAZER
61 Dean of Law .... Mr. Ken GORMLEY
49 Dean of Liberal Arts/Graduate .... Dr. James SWINDAL
65 Dean of Natural/Environment Sci .... Dr. Philip P. REEDER
40 Bookstore Manager .... Mr. John KACHUR
07 Director of Admissions .... Ms. Debra A. ZUGATES
86 Director Government Relations .... Ms. Mary Ellen SOLOMON
102 Dir Foundation/Corporate Relations .... Ms. Mary Beth FORD
106 Dir Online Education/E-learning .... Dr. Michael W. BRIDGES

Eastern University (A)

1300 Eagle Road, Saint Davids PA 19087-3696
County: Delaware FICE Identification: 003259
Unit ID: 212133
Telephone: (610) 341-5800 Carnegie Class: Master's L
FAX Number: (610) 341-1377 Calendar System: Semester
URL: www.eastern.edu
Established: 1925 Annual Undergrad Tuition & Fees: $30,590
Enrollment: 3,762 Coed
Affiliation or Control: American Baptist IRS Status: 501(c)3
Highest Offering: Doctorate
Program: Liberal Arts And General; Teacher Preparatory; Professional
Accreditation: M, CAATE, EXSC, NURSE, SW

01 President .... Dr. Robert DUFFETT
73 Dean of the Seminary .... Vacant
10 Vice Pres for Finance/Operations .... Mr. J. Pernell JONES
21 Associate VP Finance .... Ms. Polly BEROL
03 Executive Vice President .... Dr. M. Thomas RIDINGTON
05 Provost .... Dr. R. Keith IDDINGS
06 Registrar .... Ms. Sara ROCHE
32 Vice Pres for Student Development .... Dr. Bettie Ann BRIGHAM
45 Vice Pres Inst Plng Research Assess .... Dr. Christine P. MAHAN
30 Vice President Advancement .... Ms. Lisa TITUS
84 Vice Pres Enrollment Mgmt .... Dr. Kenton SPARKS
07 Exec Director Enrollment (CAS) .... Mr. Michael DZIEDZIAK
07 Exec Dir Enrollment (CCGPS) .... Mr. Casey MALONE
07 Director Admissions Palmer Sem .... Ms. Tiffany MURPHY
07 Director Admissions Esperanza .... Ms. Silvia ROJAS-HAYES
15 Senior Director of Human Resources .... Ms. Kacey BERNARD
04 Exec Asst to the President .... Ms. Heather NORCINI
35 Dean of Students .... Mr. Daryl HAWKINS
12 Dean Esperanza College .... Dr. Elizabeth CONDE-FRAZIER
49 Dean Arts and Sciences .... Dr. John PAULEY, II
58 Executive Dean Grad/Prof Studies .... Vacant
50 Dean College of Business .... Dr. Douglas CLARK
53 Assoc Dean Education .... Dr. Harry GUTELIUS
66 Chair Department of Nursing .... Dr. Dianne DELONG
18 Exec Director Campus Services .... Mr. Jeffrey GROMIS
105 Dir Web and User Services .... Mr. Mark HOFFMAN
09 Director Institutional Research .... Mr. Thomas A. DAHLSTROM
108 Director of Assessment .... Dr. Eilen MCGOVERN
26 Director of Communications .... Ms. Denise MCMILLAN
88 Senior Director Student Accounts .... Ms. Lisa WELLER
08 Library Director .... Mr. James L. SAUER
42 University Chaplain .... Rev Dr. Joseph B. MODICA
42 Seminary Chaplain .... Rev Dr. Willette BURGIE-BRYANT
37 Director of Financial Aid .... Ms. Christal JENNINGS
13 Interim Exec Director Tech Services .... Mr. Philip MUGRIDGE
36 Director of Talent & Career Dev .... Ms. Sarah TODD
29 Dir Alumni/Parent Relations .... Ms. Mary GARDNER
25 Dir Foundations/Grants/Govt Rel .... Ms. Ingrid COOPER
41 Director of Athletics .... Vacant
19 Director of Campus Security .... Mr. Jim MAGEE
88 Director of Conferences .... Ms. Meggin CAPERS
38 Dir Counseling/Academic Support .... Dr. Lisa M. HEMLICK
23 Director University Health Center .... Ms. Janet TOPPER
96 Manager of Purchasing .... Ms. Patricia G. ROOT
85 Dir Intl Student & Scholar Services .... Vacant
39 Coordinator of Housing .... Mr. Anthony HARRIS
40 Bookstore Manager .... Ms. Helen RICOTTA
88 Chair Urban Studies .... Dr. Kimberlee JOHNSON
28 Asst Dean Stdnts for Multicultural .... Ms. Jacqueline IRVING
89 Director Advising/1st Yr Programs .... Ms. Amy PEREZ
92 Dean Templeton Honors College .... Dr. Jonathan YONAN
84 Director of Enroll Oper CCGPS .... Ms. Jacqueline FRANKEAS
109 Director Auxiliary Services .... Mr. Byron MCMILLAN
104 Director Study Abroad .... Ms. Lori BRISTOL
88 Dir Faculty Development .... Dr. Michael THOMAS

† Parent institution of Palmer Theological Seminary.

Elizabethtown College (B)

1 Alpha Drive, Elizabethtown PA 17022-2298
County: Lancaster FICE Identification: 003262
Unit ID: 212197
Telephone: (717) 361-1000 Carnegie Class: Bac/Diverse
FAX Number: (717) 361-1207 Calendar System: Semester
URL: www.etown.edu
Established: 1899 Annual Undergrad Tuition & Fees: $39,920
Enrollment: 1,822 Coed
Affiliation or Control: Church Of The Brethren IRS Status: 501(c)3
Highest Offering: Master's
Program: Liberal Arts And General; Teacher Preparatory; Professional
Accreditation: M, ACBSP, ENG, MUS, OT, SW

01 President .... Dr. Carl J. STRIKWERDA
05 Provost & Sr Vice President .... Dr. Susan TRAVERSO
10 Vice Pres Administration/Finance .... Mr. Robert M. WALLET
30 Vice President Advancement/Cmty Rel .... Mr. David C. BEIDLEMAN
84 Vice Pres Enrollment Mgmt .... Mr. Paul CRAMER
32 Dean of Students .... Ms. Marianne CALENDA
20 Dean of Faculty .... Dr. Fletcher MCCLELLAN
51 Dean Ctr Continuing Educ/Dist Lrng .... Mr. John KOKOLUS
07 Director Admissions .... Ms. Lauren C. DEIBLER
35 Asst Dean of Students & Dir of CSS .... Ms. Stephanie A. RANKIN
26 Exec Dir Marketing/ Communications .... Ms. Elizabeth A. BRAUNGARD
13 Exec Director Information/Tech Svcs .... Mr. Ronald P. HEASLEY
102 Exec Dir Foundation/Govt Relations .... Ms. Lesley M. FINNEY
46 Director Research & Planning .... Dr. Richard BASOM
37 Director of Financial Aid .... Ms. Elizabeth K. MCCLOUD
08 Director The High Library .... Ms. Sarah PENNIMAN
29 Director Alumni Devel & Programs .... Mr. Mark A. CLAPPER
19 Director of Campus Security .... Mr. Andrew L. POWELL
41 Director of Athletics .... Ms. Nancy J. LATIMORE
42 Chaplain of the College .... Dr. Tracy SADD

Erie Institute of Technology (C)

940 Millcreek Mall, Erie PA 16565-1002
County: Erie FICE Identification: 022039
Unit ID: 212434
Telephone: (814) 868-9900 Carnegie Class: Assoc/PrivFP
FAX Number: (814) 868-9977 Calendar System: Semester
URL: www.erieit.edu
Established: 1958 Annual Undergrad Tuition & Fees: $18,400
Enrollment: 232 Coed
Affiliation or Control: Proprietary IRS Status: Proprietary
Highest Offering: Associate Degree
Program: Occupational; Technical Emphasis
Accreditation: ACCSC

01 Director .... Mr. Paul FITZGERALD
05 Director of Education .... Ms. Kate HUSHON
37 Financial Aid Officer .... Ms. Kelly SCHULTZ
07 Admissions Director .... Ms. Barb BOLT
36 Placement Director .... Mr. David THORNBURG

Esperanza College (D)

4261 North 5th Street, Philadelphia PA 19140
Telephone: (215) 324-0746 Identification: 770153
Accreditation: &M

† Branch campus of Eastern University, Saint Davids, PA.

Evangelical Theological Seminary (E)

121 S College Street, Myerstown PA 17067-1222
County: Lebanon FICE Identification: 003263
Unit ID: 212443
Telephone: (717) 866-5775 Carnegie Class: Spec/Faith
FAX Number: (717) 866-4667 Calendar System: 4/1/4
URL: www.evangelical.edu
Established: 1953 Annual Graduate Tuition & Fees: $11,500
Enrollment: 123 Coed
Affiliation or Control: Evangelical Congregational Church
IRS Status: 501(c)3
Highest Offering: Master's; No Undergraduates
Program: Professional; Religious Emphasis
Accreditation: M, MFCD, THEOL

01 President .... Dr. Anthony L. BLAIR
30 Vice Pres Institutional Advancement .... Rev. Ann E. STEEL
10 Vice President Finance & Operations .... Mr. Kevin C. HENRY
26 VP of Marketing/Communications .... Mr. George DAVIS
05 Dean of Academic Programs .... Dr. Laurie A. MELLINGER
08 Head Librarian .... Dr. Mark DRAPER
18 Director of Buildings & Grounds .... Mr. William J. ROBERTSON
88 Database Manager .... Mrs. Marsha A. CONLEY
06 Registrar/Financial Aid Admin .... Mr. Ellis I. KIRK

Everest Institute (F)

100 Forbes Avenue, Suite 1200,
Pittsburgh PA 15222-3618
County: Allegheny FICE Identification: 007091
Unit ID: 212090
Telephone: (412) 261-4520 Carnegie Class: Assoc/PrivFP
FAX Number: (412) 261-4546 Calendar System: Quarter
URL: www.everest.edu
Established: 1840 Annual Undergrad Tuition & Fees: $13,500
Enrollment: 526 Coed
Affiliation or Control: Proprietary IRS Status: Proprietary
Highest Offering: Associate Degree
Program: Occupational; 2-Year Principally Bachelor's Creditable; Business Emphasis
Accreditation: ACICS, MAC

01 President .... Mr. Steven NELSON
05 Academic Dean .... Ms. Jennifer RICHMOND
07 Director of Admissions .... Ms. Lynn FISCHER
36 Director of Career Services .... Mr. George MORE
37 Director of Student Finance .... Mrs. Sarah SOLDINGER

† School is in teach-out plan.

Fortis Institute (G)

5757 West Ridge Road, Erie PA 16506-1013
County: Erie FICE Identification: 030108
Unit ID: 216418
Telephone: (814) 838-7673 Carnegie Class: Assoc/PrivFP
FAX Number: (814) 838-8642 Calendar System: Quarter
URL: www.fortis.edu
Established: 1984 Annual Undergrad Tuition & Fees: $13,766
Enrollment: 652 Coed
Affiliation or Control: Proprietary IRS Status: Proprietary
Highest Offering: Associate Degree
Program: Occupational; 2-Year Principally Bachelor's Creditable
Accreditation: ACICS, DH, EMT

01 President .... Mr. Peter CORREA
05 Director of Education .... Ms. Amy THOMPSON SMITH
10 Business Officer .... Ms. Shelley FAYTAK
07 Admissions .... Mr. Michael MURRAY
06 Registrar .... Ms. Margo DEVERS
37 Financial Aid .... Mr. James DINEEN
36 Placement .... Ms. Wendy FUGATE

Fortis Institute (H)

166 Slocum Street, Forty Fort PA 18704-2347
County: Luzerne FICE Identification: 030115
Unit ID: 249609
Telephone: (570) 288-8400 Carnegie Class: Assoc/PrivFP
FAX Number: (570) 287-7936 Calendar System: Other
URL: www.fortis.edu
Established: 1984 Annual Undergrad Tuition & Fees: $15,214
Enrollment: 186 Coed
Affiliation or Control: Proprietary IRS Status: Proprietary
Highest Offering: Associate Degree
Program: Occupational
Accreditation: ACCSC

01 Campus President .... Ruth BRUMAGIN
05 Director of Education .... Ruth BRUMAGIN
07 Director of Admissions .... Jane AUSTIN

Fortis Institute (I)

517 Ash Street, Scranton PA 18509
County: Lackawanna FICE Identification: 030116
Unit ID: 385503
Telephone: (570) 558-1818 Carnegie Class: Assoc/PrivFP
FAX Number: (570) 342-4537 Calendar System: Other
URL: www.fortis.edu/scranton-pennsylvania.php
Established: 1986 Annual Undergrad Tuition & Fees: N/A
Enrollment: 385 Coed
Affiliation or Control: Proprietary IRS Status: Proprietary
Highest Offering: Associate Degree
Program: Occupational; Nursing Emphasis
Accreditation: ACCSC, DH

01 Campus President .... Ms. Madeline LEVY CRUZ
06 Registrar .... Mr. Jacy HOBBS
07 Director of Admissions .... Mr. Timothy PARSONS
36 Director Student Placement .... Ms. Erica MAHONEY
37 Director Student Financial Aid .... Ms. Stacie TAROLI

† Tuition varies by degree program.

Franklin & Marshall College (J)

PO Box 3003, Lancaster PA 17604-3003
County: Lancaster FICE Identification: 003265
Unit ID: 212577
Telephone: (717) 291-3911 Carnegie Class: Bac/A&S
FAX Number: (717) 291-4183 Calendar System: Semester
URL: www.fandm.edu
Established: 1787 Annual Undergrad Tuition & Fees: $50,300
Enrollment: 2,209 Coed
Affiliation or Control: Independent Non-Profit IRS Status: 501(c)3
Highest Offering: Baccalaureate
Program: Liberal Arts And General
Accreditation: M

01 President .... Dr. Daniel R. PORTERFIELD
10 Vice Pres for Finance and Treasurer .... Mr. David R. PROULX
30 Vice Pres for College Advancement .... Mr. Matthew EYNON
84 VP Dean of Admission/Financial Aid .... Mr. Eric G. MAGUIRE
26 Vice Pres for College Communication .... Mr. Kevin BURKE
05 Provost/Dean of Faculty .... Dr. Joel MARTIN
20 Dean of the College .... Ms. Margaret HAZELETT
88 Assoc Dean of Col & Dir Klehr Ctr .... Dr. Ralph TABER
21 Assoc Vice President for Finance .... Ms. Wendy S. STARNER
11 Associate VP for Administration .... Mr. Barry BOSLEY
44 Associate VP of Advancement .... Mr. Patrick BURKE
45 Sr Asc Dean Fac/VP Plng & Inst Res .... Dr. Alan S. CANIGLIA

100 VP Strat Initiatives/Chief of Staff ... Dr. Samuel HOUSER
08 College Librarian ... Mr. Scott VINE
44 Major Gifts Officer ... Ms. Catherine T. FERRY
85 Assoc Dean International Programs ... Ms. Sue MENNICKE
20 Associate Dean of Faculty ... Dr. Ken KREBS
20 Associate Dean of Faculty ... Dr. Kimberly ARMSTRONG
32 Associate Dean of Students ... Dr. Marion A. COLEMAN
88 Associate Dean/House Dean ... Dr. Roger A. GODIN
88 Associate Dean/House Dean ... Ms. Katharine J. SNIDER
88 Associate Dean/House Dean ... Dr. Suzanna L. RICHTER
88 Associate Dean/House Dean ... Dr. Beth PROFFITT
88 Associate Dean/House Dean ... Dr. Amy R. MORENO
21 Controller ... Ms. Kathryn ELLIEHAUSEN-SLOBOZIEN
15 Director Human Resources ... Ms. Laura FIORE
18 Associate VP/Facilities Management ... Mr. Mike WETZEL
19 Director Public Safety ... Mr. William MCHALE, JR.
23 Director Health Services ... Dr. Amy A. MYERS
13 Assoc VP/Chief Information Officer ... Ms. Carrie RAMPP
37 Director Financial Aid ... Mr. Clarke C. PAINE
38 Clinical Dir Counseling Services ... Dr. Christine G. CONWAY
90 Dir Instructional & Emerg Technol ... Mr. Teb LOCKE
09 Director of Institutional Research ... Dr. Alan CANIGLIA
06 Registrar & Assoc Director Inst Res ... Ms. Christine D. ALEXANDER
29 Executive Dir of Alumni Relations ... Ms. Mary MAZZUCA
07 Director of Admission ... Ms. Julie A. KERICH
41 Athletic Director ... Ms. Patricia EPPS
43 General Counsel ... Mr. Pierce BULLER

Gannon University (A)

University Square, Erie PA 16541-0001

County: Erie FICE Identification: 003266
Unit ID: 212601
Telephone: (814) 871-7000 Carnegie Class: Master's L
FAX Number: (814) 871-7338 Calendar System: Other
URL: www.gannon.edu
Established: 1925 Annual Undergrad Tuition & Fees: $28,590
Enrollment: 4,410 Coed
Affiliation or Control: Roman Catholic IRS Status: 501(c)3
Highest Offering: Doctorate
Program: Liberal Arts And General; Teacher Preparatory; Professional
Accreditation: M, ACBSP, ANEST, ARCPA, CACREP, COARC, COARCP, CS, ENG, NURSE, OT, PTA, RAD, SW

01 President ... Dr. Keith TAYLOR
05 Provost/VP Academic Affairs ... Dr. Carolynn B. MASTERS
10 Vice President Finance/Admin ... Mrs. Linda L. WAGNER
30 Vice Pres University Advancement ... Mr. Jack SIMS
88 Assoc Vice President for Mission ... Rev. Michael KESICKI
84 Vice President for Enrollment ... Mr. William EDMONDSON
32 VP Student Development & Engagement ... Mr. Brian NICHOLS
04 Assistant to the President ... Mrs. Darlene A. THEISEN
79 Dean Col Humanities/Educ/Soc Sci ... Dr. Linda FLEMING
54 Dean College Engineering/Business ... Dr. William L. SCHELLER
76 Dean Morosky Col Health Profess/Sci ... Dr. Steven A. MAURO
49 Director of Liberal Studies ... Dr. Penny L. SMITH
08 Director Nash Library ... Mr. Ken BRUNDAGE
37 Director of Financial Aid ... Ms. Sharon A. KRAHE
06 Registrar ... Ms. Marilyn A. MOORE
36 Dir Career Develop/Employment Svcs ... Mr. James M. FINEGAN
39 Director of Residence Life ... Ms. Denise GOLDEN
23 Head Nurse ... Vacant
88 Dir Student Organiz/Leadership Dev ... Ms. Beth Ann SCHICK
44 Director Development ... Ms. Cathy FRESCH
26 Dir Marketing & Communications ... Ms. Melanie A. WHALEY
102 Dir of Research/Foundation Rels ... Ms. Anita L. MILLER
21 Controller ... Mr. Jeffrey S. TAYLOR
45 Director of Budgeting ... Ms. Mary Kathleen LEONARD
15 Director of Human Resources ... Mr. Robert J. CLINE
41 Director of Athletics ... Ms. Lisa GODDARD MCGUIRK
19 Director Campus Police & Safety ... Mr. Ted MARNEN
13 Director of Computing/Telecomm ... Mr. Mark JORDANO
42 University Chaplain ... Vacant
07 Director of Admissions ... Mr. Thomas P. CAMILLO
09 Director of Institutional Research ... Ms. Margaret JAMES
18 Chief Facilities/Physical Plant ... Mr. Gary G. GARNIC
27 Chief Media Relations Officer ... Vacant
38 Director Student Counseling ... Mr. James M. FINEGAN
86 Dir Community/Government Relations ... Ms. Erika A. RAMALHO
96 Director of Purchasing ... Mr. Andrew TEETS
40 Bookstore Manager ... Ms. Amber COOK

Geneva College (B)

3200 College Avenue, Beaver Falls PA 15010-3557

County: Beaver FICE Identification: 003267
Unit ID: 212656
Telephone: (724) 846-5100 Carnegie Class: Bac/Diverse
FAX Number: (724) 847-6687 Calendar System: Semester
URL: www.geneva.edu
Established: 1848 Annual Undergrad Tuition & Fees: $25,680
Enrollment: 1,717 Coed
Affiliation or Control: Reformed Presbyterian Church IRS Status: 501(c)3
Highest Offering: Master's
Program: Liberal Arts And General; Teacher Preparatory; Professional
Accreditation: M, ACBSP, CACREP, ENG

01 President ... Dr. William J. EDGAR
03 Executive Vice President ... Mr. Larry K. GRIFFITH
05 Chief Academic Officer ... Dr. Melinda R. STEPHENS
30 Vice Pres of Advancement ... Dr. Jeffrey A. JONES
10 Assoc Vice Pres & Controller ... Mr. Stephen C. ROSS
15 Assoc Vice Pres & Director of HR ... Mr. Timothy R. BAIRD
32 Dean of Students ... Mr. Brian C. JENSEN
20 Dean of Undergraduate Programs ... Dr. Melinda R. STEPHENS
84 Assoc VP for Enrollment ... Mr. David B. LAYTON
35 Director of Student Programs ... Mr. Ryan J. HOLT
58 Dean Grad/Adult & Online Programs ... Mr. John D. GALLO
06 Registrar ... Mrs. Jennifer L. CARTER
37 Director of Financial Aid ... Mr. Steven K. BELL
08 Librarian ... Dr. John G. DONCEVIC
26 Director Public Relations ... Mrs. Cheryl L. JOHNSTON
29 Director of Alumni Relations ... Ms. Laura A. DEPIETRO
88 Assoc Dir Parent & Church Relations ... Vacant
13 CIO & AVP Information Technology ... Mr. Scott F. BARNES
41 Director of Athletics ... Mr. Van G. ZANIC
18 Director of Physical Plant ... Mr. Robert M. SKOFF
36 Director of Career Development ... Mrs. Joy E. DOYLE
85 International Admissions Counselor ... Ms. Jillian MOOMAW
88 Director International Student Svcs ... Vacant
40 Campus Store Manager ... Ms. Rachael E. VAN DERVEER
19 Director of Security ... Mr. Dennis E. DAMAZO
44 Director of Planned Giving ... Mrs. Wendy B. SMITH
93 Dir Multiethnic Student Services ... Vacant
92 Director Honors Program ... Vacant
39 Director of Residence Life ... Mr. Neil A. BEST
23 Health Services Director ... Mrs. Connie I. ERWIN
96 Director of Purchasing ... Mrs. Nancy D. GRAHAM
21 Accounting and Payroll Manager ... Ms. Ruth Ann HARTZEL
38 ACCESS Director ... Mr. Thomas C. PYLE
04 Administrative Asst to President ... Miss Barbara J. MCKENZIE
09 Director of Institutional Research ... Mr. Jordan BOUSCHER
50 Business Dept Chair ... Dr. Gordon RICHARDS
53 Education Dept Chair ... Mrs. Adel G. AIKEN
54 Engineering Dept Chair ... Dr. James S. GIDLEY
90 Director of Technology Services ... Dr. Joseph D. HINES
07 Assoc Director of Admissions ... Mr. Joel A. BRUBAKER
104 Dir Crossroads/Ctr Special Progrm ... Dr. Jeffrey S. COLE
105 Online Marketing/Webmaster ... Mr. Michael W. DUNCAN
28 Dir of Multicultural Student Svcs ... Vacant

Gettysburg College (C)

300 N Washington Street, Gettysburg PA 17325-1486

County: Adams FICE Identification: 003268
Unit ID: 212674
Telephone: (717) 337-6000 Carnegie Class: Bac/A&S
FAX Number: (717) 337-6008 Calendar System: Semester
URL: www.gettysburg.edu
Established: 1832 Annual Undergrad Tuition & Fees: $49,140
Enrollment: 2,600 Coed
Affiliation or Control: Evangelical Lutheran Church In America
IRS Status: 501(c)3
Highest Offering: Baccalaureate
Program: Liberal Arts And General
Accreditation: M, MUS

01 President ... Dr. Janet MORGAN RIGGS
03 Executive Vice President ... Ms. Jane D. NORTH
05 Provost ... Dr. Christopher ZAPPE
30 Vice Pres Dev & Alumni/Parent Rels ... Mr. Robert KALLIN
10 Vice President Finance/Treasurer ... Mr. Daniel T. KONSTALID
32 Vice President for College Life ... Dr. Julie L. RAMSEY
84 Vice Pres Enrollment/Education Svcs ... Ms. Barbara B. FRITZE
13 Vice President Information Tech ... Dr. Rod TOSTEN
45 Assoc Provost for Planning ... Mrs. Rhonda GOOD
28 Chief Diversity Officer ... Ms. Jeanne ARNOLD
20 Assoc Provost for Faculty Dev ... Mr. Robert E. BOHRER
21 Associate Vice President/Treasurer ... Mr. Christopher DELANEY
26 Exec Dir of Comm & Marketing ... Mr. Paul W. REDFERN
35 Associate Dean of College Life ... Mr. James P. DUFFY
44 Associate Vice Pres for Development ... Ms. Susan PYRON
93 Dean Intercultural Resource Ctr ... Mr. H. Pete CURRY, JR.
06 Registrar ... Mr. Brian REESE
37 Director of Financial Aid ... Ms. Christina L. GORMLEY
07 Director Admissions ... Ms. Gail M. SWEEZEY
42 Chaplain ... Rev. Joseph A. DONNELLA, II
09 Director for Institutional Analysis ... Ms. Suhua DONG
38 Exec Dir of Health & Counseling ... Ms. Kathy BRADLEY
36 Exec Director of Career Services ... Ms. Kathleen L. WILLIAMS
08 Dean of the Library ... Ms. Robin WAGNER
29 Exec Director of Alumni Relations ... Mr. Joe LYNCH
41 Asst VP for Athletics ... Mr. David W. WRIGHT
19 Exec Dir of Campus Safety/Security ... Mr. William J. LAFFERTY
18 Director Facilities Planning & Mgmt ... Mr. James BIESECKER
21 Dir of Financial Svs/Controller ... Ms. Sharon S. DAYHOFF
80 Director Center for Public Service ... Ms. Gretchen NATTER
39 Director Residence Life ... Ms. Danielle PHILLIPS
20 Dean of Academic Advising ... Ms. Gail Ann RICKERT
23 Director Health Services ... Ms. Susan S. REYNOLDS
35 Director Student Activities ... Mr. Joseph GURRERI
40 Director of College Bookstore ... Mr. Michael J. KOTLINSKI
94 Dir Women's Center ... Ms. Jennifer Q. MCCARY
96 Asst Director of Procurement ... Ms. Patricia K. VERDEROSA
15 Co-Director Human Resources ... Ms. Jennifer R. LUCAS
15 Co-Director Human Resources ... Ms. Regina Z. CAMPO
25 Asst Dir of Found/Govt Grants ... Ms. Laura RUNYAN
86 Assoc VP for Govt & Comm Rels ... Ms. Patricia A. LAWSON
104 Director of Off-Campus Studies ... Ms. Rebecca A. BERGREN
04 Administrative Asst to President ... Ms. Pamela EISENHART
109 Dir of Auxiliary/Life Sfty Manger ... Mr. Peter C. NORTH

Gratz College (D)

7605 Old York Road, Melrose Park PA 19027-3010

County: Montgomery FICE Identification: 004058
Unit ID: 212771
Telephone: (215) 635-7300 Carnegie Class: Master's L
FAX Number: (215) 635-1046 Calendar System: Trimester
URL: www.gratz.edu
Established: 1895 Annual Undergrad Tuition & Fees: $24,230
Enrollment: 662 Coed
Affiliation or Control: Independent Non-Profit IRS Status: 501(c)3
Highest Offering: Doctorate
Program: Liberal Arts And General; Teacher Preparatory; Professional
Accreditation: M

01 President ... Ms. Joy W. GOLDSTEIN
05 Dean and Vice Pres for Acad Affairs ... Dr. Rosalie GUZOFSKY
26 Chief Public Relations Officer ... Ms. Dodi KLIMOFF
08 Librarian ... Ms. Nancy NITZBERG
10 Director of Finance ... Mr. Michael FOLENSBEE
06 Director of Student Records ... Ms. Lovisa WOODSON
15 Director Personnel Services ... Ms. Yaffa HOWARD
30 Dir of Institutional Advancement ... Ms. Beth SCHONBERGER
09 Director of Institutional Research ... Vacant
07 Director Admissions ... Ms. Ann SABOL
88 Dir Jewish Community High Sch ... Rabbi Erin HIRSH
37 Student Financial Services Advisor ... Ms. Michelle TAYLOR
105 Director Web Services ... Ms. Rose ACTOR-ENGEL
106 Dir Online Education/E-learning ... Ms. Deborah ARON
13 Chief Info Technology Officer ... Ms. Suzette MARTINEZ-QUILES
53 Director of Jewish Education Prog ... Dr. Saul WACHS
03 Executive Vice President ... Dr. Rosalie GUZOFSKY
18 Chief Facilities/Physical Plant ... Ernest COLLINS
04 Administrative Asst to President ... Ms. Dodi KLIMOFF

Great Lakes Institute of Technology (E)

5100 Peach Street, Erie PA 16509

County: Erie FICE Identification: 021122
Unit ID: 213181
Telephone: (814) 864-6666 Carnegie Class: Not Classified
FAX Number: (814) 868-1717 Calendar System: Other
URL: www.glit.edu
Established: 1965 Annual Undergrad Tuition & Fees: $16,023
Enrollment: 427 Coed
Affiliation or Control: Proprietary IRS Status: Proprietary
Highest Offering: Associate Degree
Program: Occupational; 2-Year Principally Bachelor's Creditable
Accreditation: ACCSC, DMS, SURGT

01 Executive Director ... Tony PICCIRILLO
07 Director of Admissions ... Barbara BOLT
37 Director Student Financial Aid ... Kelly KEENER
05 Director of Education ... Vickie CLEMENTS

Grove City College (F)

100 Campus Drive, Grove City PA 16127-2104

County: Mercer FICE Identification: 003269
Unit ID: 212805
Telephone: (724) 458-2000 Carnegie Class: Bac/A&S
FAX Number: (724) 458-2190 Calendar System: Semester
URL: www.gcc.edu
Established: 1876 Annual Undergrad Tuition & Fees: $16,154
Enrollment: 2,472 Coed
Affiliation or Control: Presbyterian IRS Status: 501(c)3
Highest Offering: Baccalaureate
Program: Liberal Arts And General; Teacher Preparatory; Professional
Accreditation: M, ACBSP, ENG, EXSC

01 President ... Mr. Paul J. MCNULTY
05 Provost & VP for Academic Affairs ... Dr. Robert J. GRAHAM
10 Vice Pres for Financial Affairs ... Mr. Roger K. TOWLE
32 Vice Pres For Student Life/Learning ... Mr. Larry E. HARDESTY
30 Vice President for Inst Advancement ... Mr. Jeffrey D. PROKOVICH
11 Vice President for Operations ... Mr. James M. LOPRESTI
13 Vice Pres/Chief Information Officer ... Dr. Vincent F. DISTASI
84 VP of Enrollment Svcs & Registrar ... Dr. John G. INMAN
04 Assistant to the President ... Ms. Betty L. TALLERICO
49 Dean of School of Arts/Letters ... Dr. David J. AYERS
81 Dean of School of Sci/Engr/Math ... Dr. Stacy G. BIRMINGHAM
35 Assistant Dean of Students ... Mr. John M. COYNE
15 Dir of HR & Business Operations ... Mrs. Marci K. WAGNER
07 Director of Admissions ... Mrs. Sarah E. GIBBS
88 Admn Dir For Ctr For Vision/Values ... Mr. Lee S. WISHING, III
36 Director of Career Services ... Dr. James T. THRASHER
08 Librarian ... Mrs. Barbra M. MUNNELL
37 Director of Financial Aid ... Mr. Thomas G. BALL
88 Dir Std Rec/Club Sports/Frat Life ... Mr. Andrew A. TONCIC, JR.
35 Director Stdnt Activities/Programs ... Mr. T. Scott GORDON
19 Director of Campus Safety ... Mr. Seth J. VAN TIL
23 Director of Health & Wellness Ctr ... Mrs. Amy E. PAGANO
40 Bookstore Manager ... Mrs. Carrie J. GAULT
41 Athletic Director ... Vacant
42 Dean of the Chapel ... Rev. F. Stanley KEEHLWETTER
29 Sr Dir Alumni & College Relations ... Ms. Melissa A. MACLEOD
38 Director of College Counseling ... Dr. Suzanne N. HOUK
39 Director of Residence Life ... Vacant

Gwynedd Mercy University (A)

1325 Sumneytown Pike, PO Box 901,
Gwynedd Valley PA 19437-0901

County: Montgomery FICE Identification: 003270
Unit ID: 212832
Telephone: (215) 646-7300 Carnegie Class: Master's M
FAX Number: (215) 641-5596 Calendar System: Semester
URL: www.gmercyu.edu
Established: 1948 Annual Undergrad Tuition & Fees: $31,510
Enrollment: 2,477 Coed
Affiliation or Control: Roman Catholic IRS Status: 501(c)3
Highest Offering: Doctorate
Program: Occupational; Liberal Arts And General; Teacher Preparatory; Nursing Emphasis
Accreditation: M, ADNUR, COARC, IACBE, NUR, RTT

01 President .... Dr. Kathleen C. OWENS
05 VP Academic Affairs .... Dr. Frank E. SCULLY, JR.
10 Vice President Finance & Admin .... Mr. Kevin O'FLAHERTY
30 Vice Pres Institutional Advancement .... Mr. Gerald MCLAUGHLIN
27 Chief Communications Officer .... Ms. Kelly STATMORE
84 Vice Pres for Enrollment & SS .... Dr. Cheryl L. HORSEY
101 Secretary of the Institution/Board .... Ms. Barbara MCHALE
108 AVP for Assessment & Compliance .... Dr. Dawn HAYWARD
06 Registrar .... Ms. Joanna VACCHIANO
08 Director of Library .... Mr. Daniel SCHABERT
37 Director of Student Financial Aid .... Ms. Elizabeth HOWARD
13 Chief Information Officer .... Dr. Karl HORVATH
88 Dean of Students .... Dr. Carol GRUBER
29 Director Alumni Relations .... Ms. Gianna QUINN
32 Director Student Activities ... Ms. Rouseline EMMANUEL-FRENEL
09 Director of Institutional Research .... Dr. Jing GAO
15 Director Human Resources .... Ms. Donna HAWKINS
18 Director of Physical Plant .... Mr. Kevin WALDRON
21 Controller .... Ms. Jennifer GINNETTI
38 Director Counseling .... Dr. Kristin OLSON
07 Director of Undergrad Admissions .... Ms. Michele DIEHL
96 Director of Purchasing/Payables .... Ms. Joyce SCHARLE
102 Dir Foundation/Corporate Relations .... Ms. Bernadette WALSH
19 Director Campus Safety/Security .... Mr. James MCNESBY
41 Athletic Director .... Mr. Keith MONDILLO

Gwynedd Mercy University at East Norriton (B)

480 East Germantown Pike, East Norriton PA 19401
Telephone: (215) 643-8458 Identification: 770155
Accreditation: &M

† Tuition varies by degree program. Additional sites include Gwynedd Mercy University Philadelphia and Gwynedd Mercy University Bensalem.

Harcum College (C)

750 Montgomery Avenue, Bryn Mawr PA 19010-3476
County: Montgomery FICE Identification: 003272
Unit ID: 212869
Telephone: (610) 525-4100 Carnegie Class: Assoc/PrivNFP
FAX Number: (610) 526-6009 Calendar System: Semester
URL: www.harcum.edu
Established: 1915 Annual Undergrad Tuition & Fees: $21,900
Enrollment: 1,591 Coed
Affiliation or Control: Independent Non-Profit IRS Status: 501(c)3
Highest Offering: Associate Degree
Program: Occupational; 2-Year Principally Bachelor's Creditable; Technical Emphasis
Accreditation: M, ADNUR, DA, DH, HT, MLTAD, OTA, PTAA, RAD

01 President .... Dr. Jon Jay DETEMPLE
05 VP of Academic & Legal Affairs .... Ms. Julia INGERSOLL
10 Vice Pres of Finance & Operations .... Ms. Patricia BENSON
32 Dean of Student Life .... Mr. Urick LEWIS
07 Exec Dir Enrollment Management .... Ms. Rachel BOWEN
30 VP of College Advancement .... Dr. Susan BARRETT
20 Asst VP Academic Support Services .... Ms. Koyuki YIP
51 Exec Dir of Partnership Sites .... Ms. Evelyn SANTANA
18 Facilities Manager .... Mr. Nikolay KARPALO
15 Exec Dir of Human Resources .... Ms. Claudine VITA
06 Registrar .... Ms. Madeleine V. WRIGHTSON
08 Director of Library Services .... Ms. Katie MCGOWAN
85 Director of International Programs .... Mr. Daniel STABB
26 Director of Communic & Mktg .... Ms. Gale MARTIN
29 Director of Alumni Relations .... Ms. Melissa SAMANGO
38 Director of Counseling Services .... Ms. Kathy ANTHONY
36 Dir of Career & Transfer Services .... Ms. Danyele DOVE
37 Director of Financial Aid .... Ms. Melissa WALSH
39 Director of Residence Life .... Mr. Jameel TUCKER
35 Director of Campus Activities .... Ms. Laurie PLAZA
21 Director of Business Services .... Mr. Stephen KLEPONIS
19 Director of Campus Safety .... Mr. Rick SANFILIPPO
41 Director of Athletics .... Mr. Drew KELLY
04 Executive Assistant to President .... Ms. Margaret WALLACE
102 Director of Foundations & Gifts .... Vacant
13 Director of IT Services .... Mr. Joseph DONAHUE

Harrisburg Area Community College (D)

1 HACC Drive, Harrisburg PA 17110-2999
County: Dauphin FICE Identification: 003273
Unit ID: 212878
Telephone: (717) 780-2300 Carnegie Class: Assoc/Pub-U-MC
FAX Number: (717) 780-2551 Calendar System: Semester
URL: www.hacc.edu
Established: 1964 Annual Undergrad Tuition & Fees (In-District): $4,812
Enrollment: 20,230 Coed
Affiliation or Control: State/Local IRS Status: 501(c)3
Highest Offering: Associate Degree
Program: Occupational; 2-Year Principally Bachelor's Creditable
Accreditation: M, ACBSP, ACFEI, ADNUR, ART, COARC, CSHSE, CVT, DA, DH, DMS, EMT, MAC, MLTAD, PNUR, RAD, SURGT

01 President/CEO .... Dr. John J. SYGIELSKI
05 Provost/VP Academic Affairs .... Dr. Cynthia A. DOHERTY
32 VP Student Affairs/Enrollment Mgmt .... Dr. Rob R. STEINMETZ
10 VP Finance/College .... Mr. John M. EBERLY
30 VP College Advancement .... Dr. Linnie S. CARTER
20 Assoc Provost Academic Affairs .... Dr. Kathleen T. DOHERTY
103 Assoc Provost Workforce Development .... Mr. Victor RODGERS
15 Chief HR Officer .... Ms. Aimee B. BROUGH
12 Campus VP Lancaster/Lebanon .... Mr. Victor E. RAMOS
12 Exec Dir Lebanon Campus .... Ms. Laurie A. BOWERSOX
12 Campus VP Gettysburg .... Ms. Shannon S. HARVEY
12 Interim Campus VP York .... Dr. Marjorie A. MATTIS
106 Exec Dir Virtual Learning Outreach .... Ms. Amy S. WITHROW
08 Executive Director HACC Libraries .... Ms. Beth A. EVITTS
35 Dean Student/Acad Success .... Ms. Christine M. NOWIK
06 Registrar .... Ms. Genita D. MANGUM
26 Chief Information Officer .... Mr. Robert H. MESSNER
96 Director Procurement .... Ms. Monique Y. BAYLOR
19 Director Safety and Security .... Mr. Ivan A. QUINONES
29 Director Alumni Relations .... Ms. Maureen G. HOEPFER
40 Director College Bookstores .... Mr. Kyle J. DIBRITO
21 Controller .... Mr. Matthew R. SHADE
104 Director Global Education .... Ms. Christine M. NOWIK
09 Dir Institutional Effectiveness .... Mr. Lynold K. MCGHEE
37 Director Financial Aid .... Ms. Leanne C. FRECH
07 Interim Dean Student Aff/Enroll Mgt .... Ms. Jennifer PRICE
12 Campus VP Harrisburg Campus .... Dr. Irvin T. CLARK
102 Executive Director HACC Foundation .... Dr. Linnie S. CARTER
100 Chief of Staff .... Dr. Oren YAGIL

Harrisburg Area Community College Gettysburg Campus (E)

731 Old Harrisburg Road, Gettysburg PA 17325
Telephone: (717) 337-3855 Identification: 770156
Accreditation: &M

† Branch campus of Harrisburg Area Community College, Harrisburg, PA.

Harrisburg Area Community College Lancaster Campus (F)

1641 Old Philadelphia Pike, Lancaster PA 17602
Telephone: (717) 293-5000 Identification: 770157
Accreditation: &M

† Branch campus of Harrisburg Area Community College, Harrisburg, PA.

Harrisburg Area Community College Lebanon Campus (G)

735 Cumberland Street, Lebanon PA 17042
Telephone: (717) 270-4222 Identification: 770158
Accreditation: &M

† Branch campus of Harrisburg Area Community College, Harrisburg, PA.

Harrisburg Area Community College York Campus (H)

2010 Pennsylvania Avenue, York PA 17404
Telephone: (717) 718-0328 Identification: 770159
Accreditation: &M

† Branch campus of Harrisburg Area Community College, Harrisburg, PA.

Harrisburg University of Science and Technology (I)

326 Market Street, Harrisburg PA 17101-2116
County: Dauphin FICE Identification: 039483
Unit ID: 446640
Telephone: (717) 901-5100 Carnegie Class: Bac/A&S
FAX Number: (717) 901-3152 Calendar System: Trimester
URL: www.harrisburgu.edu
Established: 2001 Annual Undergrad Tuition & Fees: $23,900
Enrollment: 892 Coed
Affiliation or Control: Independent Non-Profit IRS Status: 501(c)3
Highest Offering: Master's
Program: Professional; Technical Emphasis
Accreditation: #M

01 President .... Dr. Eric D. DARR
05 Provost/Chief Academic Officer .... Dr. Bili S. MATTES
10 Vice Pres Finance & Chief Fin Ofcr .... Mr. Duane F. MAUN
103 VP Strategic Workforce Devel .... Ms. Kelly POWELL LOGAN
26 Assoc VP Comm/Marketing/Alum Rels .... Mr. Steven M. INFANTI
88 Assoc VP for University Centers .... Mr. Dale HAMBY
15 Dir Human Resources/Administration .... Vacant
13 Director of Technology Services .... Mr. Alex C. PITZNER
09 Director Compliance & Research .... Mr. Keith A. GREEN
30 Director of Advancement .... Ms. Amy SCHREIBER
37 Director Financial Aid .... Mr. Vincent P. FRANK
06 Director Records & Registration .... Ms. Jeanne A. WAGNER
84 Director Enrollment Mgmt/Admissions .... Mr. Timothy DAWSON
08 University Librarian .... Mr. David RUNYON
32 Asst Director of Student Affairs .... Ms. Kimberly BOWMAN

Haverford College (J)

370 Lancaster Avenue, Haverford PA 19041-1392
County: Delaware & Montgomery FICE Identification: 003274
Unit ID: 212911
Telephone: (610) 896-1000 Carnegie Class: Bac/A&S
FAX Number: (610) 896-4202 Calendar System: Semester
URL: www.haverford.edu
Established: 1833 Annual Undergrad Tuition & Fees: $49,098
Enrollment: 1,194 Coed
Affiliation or Control: Independent Non-Profit IRS Status: 501(c)3
Highest Offering: Master's
Program: Liberal Arts And General
Accreditation: M

01 President .... Dr. Kimberly BENSTON
05 Provost .... Dr. Frances BLASE
10 Vice Pres Finance & Administration .... Mitchell L. WEIN
30 VP of Advancement .... Ann W. FIGUEREDO
20 Dean of the College .... Dr. Martha DENNEY
07 Dean of Admission .... Jess LORD
85 Dean of Intl Academic Programs .... Dr. Donna MANCINI
89 Dean of Freshmen Students .... Michael MARTINEZ
21 Asst VP for Budgeting and Finance .... Michael CASEL
88 Assistant VP of Inst Advancement .... Diane WILDER
100 Chief of Staff .... Dr. Jesse LYTLE
41 Director of Athletics .... Wendall SMITH
26 VP College Communications .... Chris MILLS
09 Director of Institutional Research .... Catherine FENNELL
08 Librarian .... Dr. Terry SNYDER
15 Director of Human Resources .... Vacant
21 Controller & Assistant Treasurer .... Michael GAVANUS
96 Director of Purchasing .... Nikoletta MILLAS
18 Director of Physical Plant .... Donald CAMPBELL
19 Director of Safety & Security .... Thomas KING
88 Director Conferences/Dir Campus Ctr .... Geoffey LABE
88 Director of Dining Services .... Bernie CHUNG
40 Bookstore Manager .... Lydia WHITELAW
39 Director of Student Housing .... Marianne SMITH
34 Director of Women's Center .... Mary Louise ALLEN
23 Director of Health Services .... Catherine SHARBAUGH
38 Director Counseling/Disability Svcs .... Dr. Philip ROSENBAUM
36 Dean for Career and Prof Develop .... Kelly CLEARY
06 Registrar .... James KEANE
37 Director of Financial Aid .... David HOY
29 Director of Alumni & Parent Rels .... Lauren NASH
44 Director of Individual Giving .... Deborah STRECKER
88 Director of Gift Planning .... Steven KAVANAUGH
102 Dir Foundation/Corporate Relations .... Dr. John MOSTELLER
28 Director of Multicultural Affairs .... Dr. Theresa TENSUAN
32 Coordinator of Student Activities .... Lilly LAVNER
13 Chief Information Officer .... Vacant

Holy Family University (K)

9801 Frankford Avenue, Philadelphia PA 19114-2009
County: Philadelphia FICE Identification: 003275
Unit ID: 212984
Telephone: (215) 637-7700 Carnegie Class: Master's L
FAX Number: (215) 637-3787 Calendar System: Semester
URL: www.holyfamily.edu
Established: 1954 Annual Undergrad Tuition & Fees: $29,168
Enrollment: 2,623 Coed
Affiliation or Control: Roman Catholic IRS Status: 501(c)3
Highest Offering: Doctorate
Program: Liberal Arts And General; Teacher Preparatory; Professional; Nursing Emphasis
Accreditation: M, ACBSP, IFSAC, NURSE, RAD, @TEAC

01 President .... Sr. Maureen MCGARRITY
10 Vice Pres Finance & Administration .... Mr. James TRUSDELL
30 Vice Pres Mission .... Ms. Margaret S. KELLY
13 Vice Pres Information Technology .... Mr. Mark GALGANO
32 Vice President for Student Life .... Sr. Marcella BINKOWSKI
30 Vice Pres for Development .... Mr. Robert WETZEL
84 VP for Enrollment Services .... Ms. Beth TERELL
06 Assoc VP Academic Svcs/Registrar .... Ms. Ann Marie VICKERY
45 Assoc VP for Planning & Pgm Dev .... Ms. Karen GALARDI
37 Director of Student Financial Aid .... Mrs. Janice HETRICK
21 Associate VP/Controller & Treas .... Ms. Judy KLEIN
15 Interim Director of Human Resources .... Ms. Rachel SALLEY
08 Director of Library Services .... Ms. Shannon BROWN
36 Director of the Career Center .... Mr. Donald BROM
26 Dir Marketing/Communications .... Ms. Heather DOTCHEL
38 Director Counseling Center .... Ms. Tara GUTGESELL
42 Chaplain/Campus Minister .... Rev. James MACNEW
07 Executive Director of Admissions .... Ms. Lauren CAMPBELL
41 Assoc VP/Dir Athletics .... Mrs. Sandra MICHAEL
53 Dean of the School of Education .... Dr. Kevin ZOOK
66 Dean Sch Nursing/Allied Health Prof .... Dr. Cynthia RUSSELL
49 Dean of School of Arts & Sciences .... Dr. Shelly ROBBINS
50 Dean of School of Business Admin .... Dr. J. Barry DICKINSON
29 Director Alumni & Parent Giving .... Ms. Kathy WARCHOL
09 Dir of Inst Research & Assessment .... Mr. Chad L. MAY
18 Director of Campus Operations & Fac .... Vacant
96 Director of Purchasing .... Mrs. Marie MELNICK
28 Coordinator Diversity .... Dr. Gloria KERSEY-MATUSIAK

39 Director of Residence Life .... Mr. Brett BUCKRIDGE
102 Dir Foundation/Corporate Relations .... Mrs. Suzanne LEWIS

Hussian School of Art (A)

111 S Independence Mall East, #300,
Philadelphia PA 19106-2521
County: Philadelphia | FICE Identification: 007469
Unit ID: 212993
Telephone: (215) 574-9600 | Carnegie Class: Assoc/PrivFP
FAX Number: (215) 574-9800 | Calendar System: Semester
URL: www.hussianart.edu
Established: 1946 | Annual Undergrad Tuition & Fees: $18,200
Enrollment: 79 | Coed
Affiliation or Control: Proprietary | IRS Status: Proprietary
Highest Offering: Baccalaureate
Program: Occupational; Fine Arts Emphasis
Accreditation: ACCSC

01 President .... Ms. Melissa MORGAN
03 Vice President .... Vacant
06 Dir of Student Services/Registrar .... Ms. Maureen P. FLANAGAN
37 Director Financial Aid .... Ms. Susan J. COHEN
07 Admissions Representative .... Mr. Mark CERNERO
10 Director of Finance .... Mr. Eric STRUBEL
11 Administrative Coordinator .... Ms. Jodi BRABAZON

Immaculata University (B)

1145 King Road, Immaculata PA 19345-0654
County: Chester | FICE Identification: 003276
Unit ID: 213011
Telephone: (610) 647-4400 | Carnegie Class: DRU
FAX Number: (610) 251-1668 | Calendar System: Semester
URL: www.immaculata.edu
Established: 1920 | Annual Undergrad Tuition & Fees: $33,280
Enrollment: 3,299 | Coed
Affiliation or Control: Roman Catholic | IRS Status: 501(c)3
Highest Offering: Doctorate
Program: Liberal Arts And General; Teacher Preparatory; Professional
Accreditation: M, ACBSP, CAATE, CLPSY, DIETD, DIETI, IPSY, MUS, NURSE

01 President .... Sr. R. Patricia FADDEN
05 Vice President Academic Affairs .... Sr. Ann HEATH
10 Vice Pres Finance/Administration .... Ms. Jenni SAUER
30 Vice Pres University Advancement .... Mr. Kevin QUINN
32 Vice Pres Student Develoopment .... Dr. John STAFFORD
26 Int VP of Univ Communications .... Mr. Kevin QUINN
20 Assistant VP of Academic Affairs .... Vacant
06 Registrar .... Ms. Janice BATES
09 Dir Inst Res/Planning/Effectiveness .... Dr. Erin EBERSOLE
08 Executive Director of Library .... Dr. Jeffrey ROLLISON
37 Director Student Financial Aid .... Mr. Robert FOREST
44 Director Planned Giving .... Sr. Rita O'LEARY
91 Director Administrative Computing .... Mr. Grant DAVIS
27 Executive Director Communications .... Vacant
29 Director Alumni Relations .... Ms. Karen MATWEYCHUK
36 Director Career Development .... Ms. Diane MASSEY
41 Athletic Director .... Ms. Patricia CANTERINO
85 International Student Advisor .... Sr. Catarin CONJAR
90 Director Academic Technology .... Ms. Sharon AINSLEY
42 Chaplain .... Vacant
58 Dean Graduate Division .... Dr. Thomas O'BRIEN
34 Dean College of Undergrad Studies .... Sr. Joseph CARTER
51 Dean College of Lifelong Learning .... Dr. Angela TEKELY
19 Director Campus Safety .... Mr. Dennis DOUGHERTY
15 Director of Personnel Services .... Vacant
18 Director of Administrative Services .... Mr. Dennis SHORES
44 Director of the Annual Fund .... Ms. Melissa HENRY
42 Exec Dir of Mission and Ministry .... Sr. Cathy NALLY
07 Exec Director of Admissions .... Dr. Nicola DIFRONZO-HEITZER
20 Dean of Academic Affairs .... Ms. Mary Kate BOLAND
38 Director Counseling Services .... Dr. Jamie HAGENBAUGH
102 Dir Foundation/Corporate Relations .... Vacant
13 Chief Info Technology Officer (CIO) .... Mr. Mike SALEM
39 Director Student Housing .... Ms. Rhonda FIORESI
04 Administrative Asst to President .... Ms. Leslie BOKOSKI
104 Director Study Abroad .... Sr. Elaine GLANZ
106 Dir Online Education/E-learning .... Mr. Dean JULIAN
84 Senior Enrollment Counselor .... Mr. Dan BERADI

International Institute for Restorative Practices (C)

P.O. Box 229, Bethlehem PA 18016-0229
County: Northampton | FICE Identification: 042061
Unit ID: 448691
Telephone: (610) 807-9221 | Carnegie Class: Assoc/PrivNFP4
FAX Number: (610) 807-0423 | Calendar System: Trimester
URL: www.iirp.edu
Established: 2005 | Annual Graduate Tuition & Fees: $19,110
Enrollment: 50 | Coed
Affiliation or Control: Independent Non-Profit | IRS Status: 501(c)3
Highest Offering: Master's; No Undergraduates
Program: Professional
Accreditation: M

01 President .... Dr. John BAILIE
05 Vice President for Academic Affairs .... Dr. Patrick MCDONOUGH
11 Vice President for Administration .... Ms. Judy B. HAPP
06 Registrar .... Ms. Jamie KAINTZ
10 Director of Finance .... Ms. Robin TURNER-TOLLEY

ITT Technical Institute (D)

1000 Meade Street, Dunmore PA 18512-3195
Telephone: (570) 330-0600 | Identification: 666150
Accreditation: ACICS

† Branch campus of ITT Technical Institute, Indianapolis, IN.

ITT Technical Institute (E)

449 Eisenhower Blvd., Suite 100,
Harrisburg PA 17111-2302
Telephone: (717) 565-1700 | Identification: 666548
Accreditation: ACICS

† Branch campus of ITT Technical Institute, Indianapolis, IN.

ITT Technical Institute (F)

311 Veteran's Highway, Suite 100E, Levittown PA 19056
Telephone: (215) 702-6300 | Identification: 667161
Accreditation: ACICS

† Branch Campus of ITT Technical Institute, Indianapolis, IN.

ITT Technical Institute (G)

5460 Campbells Run Road, Pittsburgh PA 15205
Telephone: (412) 446-2900 | Identification: 666483
Accreditation: ACICS

† Branch campus of ITT Technical Institute, Indianapolis, IN.

ITT Technical Institute (H)

220 W Germantown Pike, Suilte 100,
Plymouth Meeting PA 19462
Telephone: (610) 832-3400 | Identification: 667162
Accreditation: ACICS

† Branch Campus of ITT Technical Institute, Indianapolis, IN.

ITT Technical Institute (I)

100 Pittsburgh Mills Cir, Ste 100, Tarentum PA 15084
Telephone: (724) 274-1400 | Identification: 666482
Accreditation: ACICS

† Branch campus of ITT Technical Institute, Indianapolis, IN.

JNA Institute of Culinary Arts (J)

1212 S Broad Street, Philadelphia PA 19146-3119
County: Philadelphia | FICE Identification: 031033
Unit ID: 419341
Telephone: (215) 468-8800 | Carnegie Class: Assoc/PrivFP
FAX Number: (215) 468-8838 | Calendar System: Quarter
URL: www.culinaryarts.edu
Established: 1988 | Annual Undergrad Tuition & Fees: $25,300
Enrollment: 31 | Coed
Affiliation or Control: Proprietary | IRS Status: Proprietary
Highest Offering: Associate Degree
Program: Occupational; 2-Year Principally Bachelor's Creditable; Technical Emphasis
Accreditation: ACCSC

01 Director .... Mr. Joseph DIGIRONIMO
07 Director of Admission .... Ms. Cheryl FREEDMAN

Johnson College (K)

3427 North Main Avenue, Scranton PA 18508-1495
County: Lackawanna | FICE Identification: 021142
Unit ID: 213233
Telephone: (570) 342-6404 | Carnegie Class: Assoc/PrivNFP
FAX Number: (570) 348-2181 | Calendar System: Semester
URL: www.johnson.edu
Established: 1912 | Annual Undergrad Tuition & Fees: $17,684
Enrollment: 455 | Coed
Affiliation or Control: Independent Non-Profit | IRS Status: 501(c)3
Highest Offering: Associate Degree
Program: 2-Year Principally Bachelor's Creditable; Technical Emphasis
Accreditation: ACCSC, @PTAA, RAD

01 President & CEO .... Dr. Ann L. PIPINSKI
05 Chief Academic Officer .... Mr. Dominick A. CARACHILO
84 Vice Pres of Enrollment Services .... Ms. Melissa IDE
10 Chief Financial Officer .... Mr. Jeffrey NOVAK
06 Associate Registrar .... Mr. Joshua HAWKINS
30 Sr VP of Institutional Advancement .... Ms. Katie LEONARD
09 Dir of Program & Research .... Ms. Shirley HELBING

Juniata College (L)

1700 Moore Street, Huntingdon PA 16652-2119
County: Huntingdon | FICE Identification: 003279
Unit ID: 213251
Telephone: (814) 641-3000 | Carnegie Class: Bac/A&S
FAX Number: (814) 641-3199 | Calendar System: Semester
URL: www.juniata.edu
Established: 1876 | Annual Undergrad Tuition & Fees: $51,740
Enrollment: 1,600 | Coed
Affiliation or Control: Independent Non-Profit | IRS Status: 501(c)3
Highest Offering: Master's
Program: Liberal Arts And General; Teacher Preparatory
Accreditation: M, SW

01 President .... Dr. James A. TROHA
05 Provost .... Dr. Lauren BOWEN
84 Exec VP Enrollment and Retention .... Mr. Fumio SUGIHARA
10 Vice President Finance/Operations .... Mr. Robert E. YELNOSKY
26 Vice President Advancement/Mkt .... Mr. Gabriel WELSCH
13 Asst VP/Chief Information Officer .... Ms. Anne WOOD
27 Exec Director of Marketing .... Ms. Rosann BROWN
07 Dean of Enrollment .... Ms. Michelle M. BARTOL
85 Dean of International Education .... Ms. Kati R. CSOMAN
06 Registrar .... Ms. Athena D. FREDERICK
36 Director Career Services .... Dr. Darwin V. KYSOR
37 Enrollment Mgr/Dir Student Fin Plng .... Mr. Shane D. HIMES
08 Library Director .... Mr. John W. MUMFORD
91 Director Admin Information Svcs .... Ms. Barbara J. HUGHES
15 Director of Human Resources .... Ms. Gail L. ULRICH
32 Interim Dean of Students .... Mr. Daniel J. COOK-HUFFMAN
09 Dir Institutional Planning/Research .... Ms. Carlee K. RANALLI
18 Director of Facilities Services .... Mr. Tristan S. DEL GIUDICE
19 Director Public Safety .... Mr. Jesse W. LEONARD
41 Athletic Director .... Mr. Greg M. CURLEY
90 Dir Technology Solutions Center .... Mr. Joel C. PHEASANT
21 Bursar .... Ms. Lauren A. PEROW
21 Budget Director .... Ms. Susan F. SHONTZ
21 Controller .... Ms. Karla D. WISER
44 Director of Major Gifts .... Mr. Joseph M. SCIALABBA
35 Interim Assistant Dean of Students .... Ms. Ellen CAMPBELL
42 College Chaplain .... Mr. Lowell D. WITKOVSKY
20 Director of Academic Support Svcs .... Ms. Sarah M. CLARKSON
88 Director of Student Activities .... Ms. Jessica MUMFORD
88 Director of Conferences & Events .... Ms. Lorri P. SHIDELER
07 Senior Associate Dean of Admission .... Ms. Terri L. BOLLMAN-DALANSKY
38 College Counselor .... Ms. Kerry HARPER
28 Asst to Pres Diversity & Inclusion .... Ms. Rosalie M. RODRIGUEZ
29 Director Alumni Relations .... Mr. David D. MEADOWS
39 Director of Residential Life .... Mr. John D. CUTRIGHT
04 Executive Asst to President .... Mrs. Bethany D. SHEFFIELD

Kaplan Career Institute (M)

5650 Derry Street, Harrisburg PA 17111-4112
County: Dauphin | FICE Identification: 004910
Unit ID: 251075
Telephone: (717) 564-4112 | Carnegie Class: Assoc/PrivFP
FAX Number: (717) 564-3779 | Calendar System: Quarter
URL: www.kci-harrisburg.com
Established: 1918 | Annual Undergrad Tuition & Fees: $14,585
Enrollment: 217 | Coed
Affiliation or Control: Proprietary | IRS Status: Proprietary
Highest Offering: Associate Degree
Program: Occupational
Accreditation: ACICS, MAC

01 Executive Director .... Susan LYNCH
07 Director Admissions .... Eric SNYDER
36 Director Student Placement .... Jennifer RIORDAN
05 Director of Education .... Jennifer PIPER
37 Director Student Financial Aid .... Sarah BROOKER

Kaplan Career Institute (N)

177 Franklin Mills Boulevard, Philadelphia PA 19154-3140
County: Bucks | FICE Identification: 022898
Unit ID: 211617
Telephone: (215) 612-6600 | Carnegie Class: Assoc/PrivFP
FAX Number: (215) 612-6695 | Calendar System: Quarter
URL: www.chitraining.com
Established: 1982 | Annual Undergrad Tuition & Fees: $15,585
Enrollment: 640 | Coed
Affiliation or Control: Proprietary | IRS Status: Proprietary
Highest Offering: Associate Degree
Program: Occupational
Accreditation: ACICS, COARC

01 President .... Ms. Karen SPRINGER
07 Director of Admissions .... Mr. Dan WATKINS
05 Education Department Head .... Mrs. Dorothy MCCADEN
36 Director of Placement .... Ms. Cheryl BRAIDES
37 Director Financial Aid .... Ms. Nina BALAGOUR

Kaplan Career Institute (O)

3010 Market Street, Philadelphia PA 19104
Telephone: (215) 594-4000 | Identification: 770766
Accreditation: ACICS

† Branch campus of Kaplan Career Institute, Harrisburg, PA.

Kaplan Career Institute/Broomall Campus (P)

1991 Sproul Road, Suite 42, Broomall PA 19008-3516
County: Delaware | FICE Identification: 007781
Unit ID: 215646
Telephone: (610) 353-7630 | Carnegie Class: Assoc/PrivFP
FAX Number: (610) 359-1370 | Calendar System: Quarter
URL: broomall.kaplancareerinstitute.com
Established: 1958 | Annual Undergrad Tuition & Fees: $18,965
Enrollment: 300 | Coed

Affiliation or Control: Proprietary IRS Status: Proprietary
Highest Offering: Associate Degree
Program: Occupational; 2-Year Principally Bachelor's Creditable; Technical Emphasis
Accreditation: ACICS

01 President ... Mr. William SCHNELL
05 Director of Education ... Ms. Amy BERRIOS
36 Placement Director ... Mr. James LINCKE
07 Director of Admissions ... Vacant

Kaplan Career Institute - ICM Campus (A)

933 Penn Avenue, Pittsburgh PA 15222-3802
County: Allegheny FICE Identification: 007436
Unit ID: 213002
Telephone: (412) 338-4770 Carnegie Class: Assoc/PrivFP
FAX Number: (412) 261-0998 Calendar System: Quarter
URL: www.kcipittsburgh.com
Established: 1963 Annual Undergrad Tuition & Fees: $17,800
Enrollment: 444 Coed
Affiliation or Control: Proprietary IRS Status: Proprietary
Highest Offering: Associate Degree
Program: Occupational; 2-Year Principally Bachelor's Creditable; Technical Emphasis
Accreditation: ACICS, MAC, OTA

01 President ... Mr. Hunter H. HOPKINS
05 Director of Education ... Vacant
37 Director of Financial Aid ... Mr. Chris FOX
07 Director of Admissions ... Mr. Justin PAPARIELLA
36 Director of Career Services ... Ms. Jennifer KELLY

Keystone College (B)

One College Green, P.O. Box 50,
La Plume PA 18440-0200
County: Lackawanna FICE Identification: 003280
Unit ID: 213303
Telephone: (570) 945-8000 Carnegie Class: Bac/Diverse
FAX Number: (570) 945-8962 Calendar System: Semester
URL: www.keystone.edu
Established: 1868 Annual Undergrad Tuition & Fees: $24,300
Enrollment: 1,484 Coed
Affiliation or Control: Independent Non-Profit IRS Status: 501(c)3
Highest Offering: Baccalaureate
Program: Liberal Arts And General
Accreditation: M, IACBE

01 President ... Dr. David L. COPPOLA
03 Executive Vice President ... Dr. Marie GEORGE
05 Vice President for Academic Affairs ... Dr. Karen YARRISH
10 Vice Pres Finance & Administration ... Mr. Kevin WILSON
30 Vice President for Advancement ... Ms. Charlotte RAVAIOLI
84 Dean of Enrollment ... Ms. Kara STONE
32 Interim Dean of Student Life ... Ms. Nicole LANGAN
08 Director Miller Library ... Ms. Mari FLYNN
07 Director of Admissions ... Ms. Jennifer SEKOL
06 Registrar ... Ms. Kate OWENS
37 Dir Financial Assistance & Planning ... Ms. Delaina JAYNE
13 Director Information Technology ... Mr. Charles L. PROTHERO
15 Director of Human Resources ... Ms. Alberta GRUSHINSKI
26 Senior Director College Relations ... Mr. Fran CALPIN
29 Director of Alumni Outreach ... Ms. Mariellen WALSH
36 Director Career Development ... Ms. Kourtney SHICK COWENS
09 Director Institutional Research ... Mr. Curtis BAUMAN
41 Director of Athletics ... Dr. Matthew GRIMALDI

Keystone Technical Institute (C)

2301 Academy Drive, Harrisburg PA 17112-1012
County: Dauphin FICE Identification: 022342
Unit ID: 210483
Telephone: (717) 545-4747 Carnegie Class: Assoc/PrivFP
FAX Number: (717) 901-9090 Calendar System: Semester
URL: www.kti.edu
Established: 1980 Annual Undergrad Tuition & Fees: $13,772
Enrollment: 250 Coed
Affiliation or Control: Proprietary IRS Status: Proprietary
Highest Offering: Associate Degree
Program: Occupational; 2-Year Principally Bachelor's Creditable; Technical Emphasis
Accreditation: ACCSC, ACFEI, MAC

01 President ... Mr. David W. SNYDER
03 Vice President ... Mrs. Andrea SNYDER
05 Dean of Education ... Mr. Jason KARMANN
07 Admissions Officer ... Ms. Donna STIRBER-GAMELIN
10 Chief Business Officer ... Mr. Dennis FIELDS
37 Director Student Financial Aid ... Ms. Tracy STEWART

King's College (D)

133 N River Street, Wilkes-Barre PA 18711-0801
County: Luzerne FICE Identification: 003282
Unit ID: 213321
Telephone: (570) 208-5900 Carnegie Class: Master's S
FAX Number: (570) 825-9049 Calendar System: Semester
URL: www.kings.edu
Established: 1946 Annual Undergrad Tuition & Fees: $33,090
Enrollment: 2,308 Coed
Affiliation or Control: Roman Catholic IRS Status: 501(c)3
Highest Offering: Master's
Program: Liberal Arts And General; Teacher Preparatory; Professional; Business Emphasis
Accreditation: M, ARCPA, BUS, CAATE, TED

01 President ... Rev. John RYAN, CSC
05 Vice President for Academic Affairs ... Dr. Joseph EVAN
10 Vice President for Business Affairs ... Mr. John LOYACK
30 Vice President for Inst Advancement ... Mr. Frederick PETTIT
32 Vice President for Student Affairs .. Ms. Janet E. MERCINCAVAGE
84 Vice President for Enrollment Mgmt ... Mr. Corry UNIS
04 Exec Assistant to the President ... Mrs. Anne NOONE
13 Exec Dir Info & Tech Svc Div ... Mr. Paul J. MORAN
08 Director of Library ... Dr. Terrence F. MECH
88 Assoc VP Stdnt Success & Retention ... Ms. Teresa M. PECK
35 Assoc Vice Pres Student Affairs ... Mr. Robert B. MCGONIGLE
07 Director of Admissions ... Mr. James ANDERSON
50 Dean Wm G McGowan Sch Business ... Dr. Barry WILLIAMS
06 Registrar ... Mr. Daniel T. CEBRICK
37 Director of Financial Aid ... Ms. Donna CERZA
42 Chaplain/Director Campus Ministry ... Rev. Thomas LOONEY, CSC
36 Director Career Planning & Placemnt ... Mr. Christopher SUTZKO
15 Director of Human Resources ... Ms. Lita PIEKARA
26 Director of Public Relations ... Mr. John MCANDREW
29 Director of Alumni Relations ... Ms. Patrice PERSICO
18 Executive Director of Facilities ... Mr. Thomas BUTCHKO
19 Director of Security/Safety ... Mr. Gerard DESSOYE
41 Dir of Intercollegiate Athletics ... Ms. Cheryl J. ISH
21 Associate VP/Controller & CAO ... Mr. Thomas GRABER
39 Director of Residence Life ... Ms. Megan SELLICK
58 Dean of Graduate Programs ... Vacant
09 Director of Institutional Research ... Ms. Marian K. PALMERI
28 Director of College Diversity ... Vacant
90 Managing Dir of User Services ... Mr. Raymond G. PRYOR
91 Managing Director for MIS ... Mr. William M. CORCORAN
44 Dir Major Gifts & Planned Giving ... Mr. William LYNN

La Roche College (E)

9000 Babcock Boulevard, Pittsburgh PA 15237-5898
County: Allegheny FICE Identification: 003987
Unit ID: 213358
Telephone: (412) 367-9300 Carnegie Class: Bac/Diverse
FAX Number: (412) 536-1062 Calendar System: Semester
URL: www.laroche.edu
Established: 1963 Annual Undergrad Tuition & Fees: $25,500
Enrollment: 1,412 Coed
Affiliation or Control: Roman Catholic IRS Status: 501(c)3
Highest Offering: Master's
Program: Liberal Arts And General; Professional
Accreditation: M, ACBSP, ADNUR, ANEST, ART, CIDA, NUR

01 President ... Sr. Candace INTROCASO, CDP
04 Admin Asst to the President ... Ms. Karen P. WILLOUGHBY
05 Vice President Academic Affairs ... Dr. Howard J. ISHIYAMA
84 VP for Enrollment Mgmt & Mktg ... Mr. William H. FIRMAN, JR.
10 VP for Business & Finance ... Mr. Robert VOGEL
32 Vice Pres Student Life/Dean Stdnts ... Ms. Colleen RUEFLE
30 VP for Institutional Advancement ... Mr. Michael ANDREOLA
20 Assoc VP Academic Affairs ... Dr. Rosemary MCCARTHY
20 Assoc Vice Pres Academic Affairs ... Dr. Thomas G. SCHAEFER
36 Assoc Dean Academic/Student Support ... Ms. Marie DEEM
35 Director of Student Development ... Mr. David DAY
83 Div Chair Natural & Behavioral Sci ... Dr. Rebecca BOZYM
79 Div Chair Humanities ... Sr. Michele BISBEY, CDP
50 Div Co-Chair Business ... Dr. Lynn ARCHER
50 Div Co-Chair Business ... Ms. Shelia MUELLER
57 Div Chair Design ... Ms. Lisa KAMPHAUS
53 Div Co-Chair Education & Nursing ... Dr. Kathryn SILVIS
53 Div Co-Chair Education & Nursing ... Dr. Terri LIBERTO
06 Registrar ... Ms. Joan CUTONE
08 Director Library/Learning Center ... Ms. Laverne COLLINS
07 Director of Admissions ... Mr. Terrance KIZINA
26 Director of Mktg & Media Relations ... Mr. Brady BUTLER
37 Director of Financial Aid ... Ms. Sharon PLATT
41 Director of Athletics ... Mr. Jim TINKEY
42 Director of Mission & Ministry ... Sr. Elena ALMENDAREZ
07 Director Grad Studies/Adult Ed ... Ms. Hope SCHIFFGENS
39 Director Residence Life ... Mr. Christopher WILLIS
13 Director Information Technology ... Ms. Terri BALLARD
85 Director International Student Svcs ... Dr. Natasha GARRETT
29 Director Alumni Relations ... Ms. Gina MILLER
21 Director of Finance ... Ms. Cathleen JACOBS
09 Director of Institutional Research ... Ms. Patricia A. CONNOLLY
18 Director of Facilities Management ... Mr. J.R YOUNG
38 Director Counseling Services ... Ms. Lori AREND
19 Director Public Safety ... Mr. David HILKE
15 Assoc VP of Human Resources ... Ms. Eileen PETRONE
40 Bookstore Manager ... Mr. Tim JONES
88 Director of Student Accounts ... Ms. Danya TINKEY
101 Secretary of the Institution/Board ... Ms. Kathy KOZDEMBA
104 Coordinator Study Abroad ... Ms. Nicole GABLE
44 Director Annual or Planned Giving ... Mr. Craig BRUNO
86 Director Government Relations ... Mr. Michael ANDREOLA

La Salle University (F)

1900 W Olney Avenue, Philadelphia PA 19141-1199
County: Philadelphia FICE Identification: 003287
Unit ID: 213367
Telephone: (215) 951-1000 Carnegie Class: Master's L
FAX Number: N/A Calendar System: Semester
URL: www.lasalle.edu
Established: 1863 Annual Undergrad Tuition & Fees: $41,100
Enrollment: 6,242 Coed
Affiliation or Control: Roman Catholic IRS Status: 501(c)3
Highest Offering: Doctorate
Program: 2-Year Principally Bachelor's Creditable; Liberal Arts And General; Professional
Accreditation: M, ANEST, BUS, CACREP, CLPSY, DIETC, DIETD, MFCD, NURSE, SP, SW

01 President ... Dr. Colleen M. HANYCZ
05 Int Provost/VP Academic Affairs ... Dr. Brian A. GOLDSTEIN
04 Exec Assistant to the President ... Dr. Alice L. HOERSCH
04 Exec Assistant to the President ... Bro. Joseph WILLARD
30 VP University Advancement ... Mr. R. Brian ELDERTON
84 Asst VP Enrollment Services ... Ms. Kathryn PAYNE
10 VP Finance and Admin and Treasurer ... Mr. Matthew MCMANNESS
32 VP Student Affairs/Dean of Students ... Dr. James E. MOORE
20 Assistant Provost ... Bro. John MCGOLDRICK
49 Dean School of Arts & Sciences ... Dr. Thomas A. KEAGY
50 Dean School of Business Admin ... Dr. Gary A. GIAMARTINO
51 Dean Col of Professional/Cont Stds ... Dr. Joseph Y. UGRAS
66 Dean School of Nursing/Health Sci ... Dr. Brian GOLDSTEIN
22 Asst VP Admin/Plng/Affirm Action ... Ms. Rose Lee PAULINE
26 Asst VP Mktg & Communication ... Ms. Karen MULDOON GEUS
29 Asst VP Alumni Relations ... Mr. Trey P. ULRICH
86 Asst VP Government Affairs ... Mr. Edward A. TURZANSKI
21 Asst VP Finance & Asst Treasurer ... Ms. Rebecca L. HORVATH
88 Director Advancement Services ... Ms. Elizabeth LOCHNER
88 Director Economic Development ... Mr. William J. DEVITO
82 Dir Grad Ctr/East Eur Studies ... Dr. Luis GOMEZ
77 Director Grad Computer Info Science ... Ms. Margaret MCCOEY
53 Director Grad Education Program ... Dr. Greer RICHARDSON
83 Dir Grad Counseling & Family Therap ... Dr. Donna A. TONREY
73 Director Grad Pgms of Theology ... Fr. Francis J. BERNA
60 Dir Grad Prof Communication ... Dr. Pamela LANNUTTI
66 Director Undergraduate Nursing ... Vacant
66 Dir Grad Nursing RN-MSN Pgm ... Dr. Patricia DILLON
69 Dir Master Public Health Program ... Dr. Holly M. HARNER
88 Dir Grad Econ Crime Forensics ... Ms. Margaret MCCOEY
88 Dir Grad Pgm Human Capital Develop ... Ms. Kathleen BAGNELL FINNEGAN
58 Dir Grad Pgms Nonprofit Leadership ... Dr. Laura OTTEN
25 Director Grants/Research ... Dr. Fred J. FOLEY
35 Senior Assoc Dean of Students ... Mr. Alan B. WENDALL
35 Associate Dean of Students ... Dr. Lane B. NEUBAUER
35 Associate Dean of Students ... Ms. Anna M. ALLEN
51 Asst Dean Prof/Continuing Studies ... Ms. Elizabeth A. HEENAN
42 Director Univ Ministry & Service ... Bro. Robert J. KINZLER
92 Dir University Honors Program ... Dr. Richard A. NIGRO
13 Chief Information Officer ... Mr. Edward NICKERSON
08 Director of the Library ... Mr. John S. BAKY
18 Asst VP Facilities Mgmt/Capital Dev ... Mr. Robert C. KROH, JR.
19 Asst VP for Safety & Security ... Mr. Arthur GROVER
15 Asst VP for Human Resources ... Dr. Margurete WALSH
41 Athletic Director ... Dr. Thomas BRENNAN
44 Director of Major Gifts ... Bro. Charles E. GRESH
102 Director of The La Salle Fund ... Ms. Helene HOLMES BACZKOWSKI
30 Dir of Prospect Development ... Ms. Sarah PARNUM CADBURY
36 Director of Career Services ... Mr. Louis A. LAMORTE, JR.
36 Exec Dir Career & Employ Svcs ... Mr. Steve MCGONIGLE
07 Executive Director of Admission ... Mr. James C. PLUNKETT
37 Director Financial Aid ... Mr. Joseph ALAIMO
06 Registrar ... Ms. Jean W. LANDIS
09 Dir Inst Research & Asst Provost ... Dr. Michael J. ROSZKOWSKI
88 Dir Doctorate in Psych Program ... Dr. Randy FINGERHUT
88 Dir Graduate English Studies ... Dr. Stephen P. SMITH
88 Grad Director Instr Tech Mgt ... Dr. Bobbe G. BAGGIO
88 Director Part-time MBA Program ... Ms. Denise SAURENNANN
88 Director Full-time MBA Program ... Ms. Elizabeth A. SCOFIELD
40 Manager Campus Store ... Mr. Mark ALLAN
28 Multicultural Education Coordinator ... Ms. Cherlyn L. RUSH
105 Director of Web Communication ... Mr. Gregory FALA
88 Dir Doctor of Nursing Practice Pgm ... Dr. Patricia BICKNELL
88 Director Graduate History ... Dr. George B. STOW
58 Assoc Provost for Graduate Studies .. Dr. Margaret M. MCMANUS
88 Dir Grad Prof Clinical Counseling ... Dr. John J. ROONEY
88 Dir Hispanic Inst & Bilingual Stds ... Dr. Carmen LAMAS

Lackawanna College (G)

501 Vine Street, Scranton PA 18509-3206
County: Lackawanna FICE Identification: 003283
Unit ID: 213376
Telephone: (570) 961-7810 Carnegie Class: Assoc/PrivNFP
FAX Number: (570) 961-7858 Calendar System: 4/1/4
URL: www.lackawanna.edu
Established: 1894 Annual Undergrad Tuition & Fees: $13,400
Enrollment: 1,435 Coed
Affiliation or Control: Independent Non-Profit IRS Status: 501(c)3
Highest Offering: Associate Degree
Program: Occupational; 2-Year Principally Bachelor's Creditable; Business Emphasis
Accreditation: M, DMS, PTAA, SURGT

01 President ... Mr. Mark VOLK
03 Exec Vice President/CAO ... Dr. Jill MURRAY
10 Vice Pres Finance/Administration ... Ms. Alycia SCHWARTZ
05 Vice President Academic Affairs ... Dr. Erica PRICCI
32 VP for Student Affairs ... Mrs. Suellen MUSEWICZ
35 Dean of Students ... Mr. Dan LAMAGNA
84 VP for Enrollment Management ... Mr. Brian COSTANZO
20 Dean of Faculty ... Mrs. Suzanne CERCONE

29 Director Alumni Relations .... Vacant
09 Director Institutional Research .... Dr. Rachel FRANCIS
88 Dir Programming & Special Events .... Mr. Jim CULLEN
31 Director of External Relations .... Ms. Wendy HINTON
51 Director of Continuing Education .... Mrs. Anita COLA
41 Director of Athletics .... Mrs. Kim MECCA
88 Director of Advising & Transfer Svc . Mrs. Barbara NOWOGORSKI
06 Registrar .... Mrs. Theresa SCOPELLITI
19 Director of Public Safety .... Mr. Gary SHOENER
12 Director of Hazleton Center .... Mr. Joseph SCARCELLA
12 Director of Center Operations .... Mr. Jeffery GREGORY
12 Exec Director School of PNGT .... Mr. Richard MARQUARDT
91 Director Admin Computing Svcs .... Vacant
08 Library Director .... Mrs. Mary Beth ROCHE
102 Director of Grant Support Services .... Ms. Michelle WILLIAMS
39 Director Housing & Residence Life .... Mr. Stephen DUDA
15 Director of Human Resources .... Mrs. Sharon EBERT
18 Director of Facilities .... Mr. Derek GREGORY
37 Director of Financial Aid .... Mr. Matthew PETERS
12 Director Towanda Center .... Ms. Kim MAPES
13 Director of MIS .... Mrs. Melanie KOWALSKI
35 Director of Student Life .... Ms. Karen LEGGE
88 Director of Health Club Facilities .... Mr. Joseph LUCIANO
07 Asst Director of Admissions .... Vacant
88 Service Learning Coordinator .... Ms. Jo-Ann ORCUTT

Lafayette College (A)

730 High Street, Easton PA 18042-1798
County: Northampton FICE Identification: 003284
Unit ID: 213385
Telephone: (610) 330-5000 Carnegie Class: Bac/A&S
FAX Number: (610) 330-5127 Calendar System: Semester
URL: www.lafayette.edu
Established: 1826 Annual Undergrad Tuition & Fees: $47,010
Enrollment: 2,465 Coed
Affiliation or Control: Independent Non-Profit IRS Status: 501(c)3
Highest Offering: Baccalaureate
Program: Liberal Arts And General; Professional
Accreditation: M, CS, ENG

01 President .... Dr. Alison R. BYERLY
05 Provost .... Dr. S. Abu Turab RIZVI
30 Vice Pres Dev/College Relations .... Ms. Kimberly SPANG
32 VP Campus Life .... Dr. Annette DIORIO
15 Vice President Human Resources ..... Ms. Leslie F. MUHLFELDER
26 VP Marketing & Communications .... Mr. Michael D. KISER
13 VP and Chief Information Officer .... Mr. John L. O'KEEFE
10 VP Finance & Administration .... Mr. Roger DEMARESKI
54 Director of Engineering .... Dr. Scott R. HUMMEL
04 Executive Assistant .... Dr. James F. KRIVOSKI
84 Vice Pres for Enrollment Management .... Mr. Gregory MACDONALD
20 Dean Advising & Co-Curricular Pgms ..... Ms. Erica D'AGOSTINO
08 Dean of Libraries .... Mr. Neil J. MCELROY
35 Dean of Students .... Dr. Paul J. MCLOUGHLIN, II
07 Dean of Admissions .... Mr. Matthew HYDE
37 Director of Student Financial Aid .... Ms. Ashley BIANCHI
09 Director of Institutional Research .... Dr. James P. SCHAFFER
06 Registrar .... Mr. Francis A. BENGINIA
41 Director of Athletics .... Dr. Bruce E. MCCUTCHEON
36 Int Exec Director Career Services .... Ms. Nanette COOLEY
23 Director Health Services .... Dr. Jeffrey E. GOLDSTEIN
38 Director Counseling Center .... Dr. Karen J. FORBES
19 Director of Public Safety .... Mr. Robert SABATTIS
18 Dir Physical Planning & Plant Oper .... Mr. Bruce S. FERRETTI
29 Executive Director Alumni Relations .... Ms. Rachel NELSON MOELLER
16 Director Employment .... Ms. Lisa Youngkin REX
96 Manager of Procurement .... Ms. Linda L. JROSKI
88 Title IX Coordinator .... Ms. Amy A. O'NEILL
20 Dean of the Faculty .... Dr. Robin C. RINEHART
21 Chief Investment Officer .... Mr. Joseph S. BOHRER

Lake Erie College of Osteopathic Medicine (B)

1858 W Grandview Boulevard, Erie PA 16509-1025
County: Erie FICE Identification: 030908
Unit ID: 407629
Telephone: (814) 866-6641 Carnegie Class: Spec/Med
FAX Number: (814) 866-8123 Calendar System: Semester
URL: www.lecom.edu
Established: 1993 Annual Graduate Tuition & Fees: $31,495
Enrollment: 3,776 Coed
Affiliation or Control: Independent Non-Profit IRS Status: 501(c)3
Highest Offering: First Professional Degree; No Undergraduates
Program: Professional
Accreditation: M, OSTEO, PHAR

01 President/CEO .... Dr. John M. FERRETTI
05 Provost/Sr Vice Pres/Dean Acad Affs .... Dr. Silvia M. FERRETTI
10 Vice Pres of Fiscal Affairs/CFO .... Mr. Richard P. OLINGER
20 VP Acad Affs/Dn LECOM Sch Pharmacy .... Dr. Hershey BELL
12 Vice Pres for LECOM at Seton Hill .... Dr. Irving FREEMAN
52 Dean School of Dental Medicine .... Dr. Anton GOTLIEB
58 Asst Dean Students/Grad Studies .... Dr. Mark KAUFFMAN
20 Assoc Dean Acad Affairs Bradenton .... Dr. Robert GEORGE
63 Assoc Dean Clinical Educ Bradenton ..... Dr. Anthony J. FERRETTI
63 Assoc Dean of Preclinical Educ .... Dr. Christine KELL
63 Asst Dean of Clinical Education .... Dr. Regan SHABLOSKI
63 Asst Dean Preclinical Ed Bradenton .... Dr. Mark COTY
63 Asst Dean Preclinical Ed Erie .... Dr. Jon KALMEY
63 Asst Dean of Biomed Sci .... Dr. Randy KULESZA
20 Asst Dean Acad Affairs Bradenton .... Dr. Ronald BEREZNIAK
67 Assoc Dean of Accelerated Pathway .... Dr. Rachel OGDEN
67 Assoc Dean for Traditional Pathway .... Dr. Julie WILKINSON
67 Assistant Dean for Assessment .... Dr. Nina PAVULURI
52 Asst Dean Preclinial Dental .... Dr. Mark ROMER
88 Asst Dean Clinical Dental Med .... Dr. Francis CURD
32 Director of Student Affairs .... Dr. David FRIED
09 Inst Dir Plng/Assess/Accred/Rsrch .... Dr. Mathew BATEMAN
26 Inst Dir Communications/Marketing .... Mr. Pierre A. BELLICINI
08 Inst Dir of Learning Resources .... Mr. Dan WELCH
13 Director of Information Technology .... Mr. Randy HARRIS
46 Director of Research .... Dr. Bertalan DUDAS
15 Inst Dir of Human Resources .... Mr. Aaron SUSMARSKI
19 Inst Dir of Security .... Mr. George HOOKER
38 Director Behavioral Health .... Dr. Richard HAHN
88 Inst Dir of Faculty Development .... Dr. Mark TERRELL
27 Asst Dir Communications/Marketing .... Vacant
18 Building Operations Supervisor .... Mr. Brian KING
37 Inst Director of Financial Aid .... Ms. Bonnie CRILLEY
06 Registrar .... Mr. Jeremy SIVILLO
07 Admissions Coordinator .... Ms. Amy W. ROWE
40 Bookstore Manager .... Ms. Naz KROL

Lancaster Bible College (C)

901 Eden Road, Lancaster PA 17601-5036
County: Lancaster FICE Identification: 003285
Unit ID: 213400
Telephone: (717) 569-7071 Carnegie Class: Spec/Faith
FAX Number: (717) 560-8260 Calendar System: Semester
URL: www.lbc.edu
Established: 1933 Annual Undergrad Tuition & Fees: $19,980
Enrollment: 1,398 Coed
Affiliation or Control: Independent Non-Profit IRS Status: 501(c)3
Highest Offering: Doctorate
Program: Teacher Preparatory; Professional; Religious Emphasis
Accreditation: M, BI, @SW

01 President .... Dr. Peter W. TEAGUE
04 Assistant to the President .... Mrs. Judith M. HECKAMAN
03 Executive Vice President .... Mr. John ZESWITZ
05 Provost .... Dr. Philip E. DEARBORN
84 VP for Student Experience .... Mr. Josh BEERS
30 VP of Advancement .... Vacant
13 Vice President Information Systems .... Mr. Vince JOHNSON
10 VP of Finance .... Mr. Matthew MASON
09 AVP of Institutional Effectiveness .... Dr. Dale MORT
20 VP of Strategic Initiatives .... Vacant
06 Registrar .... Mr. Jeffrey HOOVER
32 Dean of Students .... Mr. Robert MCMICHAEL
38 Director of Student Development .... Mr. Scott BOYER
08 Director of Library Services .... Mr. Clint BANZ
37 Director of Financial Aid .... Mrs. Karen L. FOX
21 Controller .... Mr. Lonnie MARTIN
18 Director of Plant Operations .... Vacant
23 Director of Health Services .... Mrs. Mary Lou JOLINE
29 Dir of Alumni & Career Services .... Vacant
41 Athletic Director .... Mr. Peter BEERS
15 Director of People Development & HR .... Mrs. Paula POOLE
07 Director of Admissions .... Mr. David BURGE
19 Director Security/Safety .... Mr. Robert WEGMAN

Lancaster County Career and Technology Center (D)

1730 Hans Herr Drive, Willow Street PA 17584
County: Lancaster FICE Identification: 023108
Unit ID: 418533
Telephone: (717) 464-7050 Carnegie Class: Not Classified
FAX Number: (717) 464-9518 Calendar System: Semester
URL: lcctc.org
Established: 1970 Annual Undergrad Tuition & Fees (In-District): $12,098
Enrollment: 462 Coed
Affiliation or Control: State/Local IRS Status: 501(c)3
Highest Offering: Associate Degree
Program: Occupational; 2-Year Principally Bachelor's Creditable
Accreditation: COE

01 Executive Director .... David WARREN

Lancaster Theological Seminary (E)

555 W James Street, Lancaster PA 17603-2812
County: Lancaster FICE Identification: 003286
Unit ID: 213446
Telephone: (717) 393-0654 Carnegie Class: Spec/Faith
FAX Number: (717) 393-4254 Calendar System: Semester
URL: www.lancasterseminary.edu
Established: 1825 Annual Graduate Tuition & Fees: $17,050
Enrollment: 118 Coed
Affiliation or Control: United Church Of Christ IRS Status: 501(c)3
Highest Offering: Doctorate; No Undergraduates
Program: Professional; Religious Emphasis
Accreditation: M, THEOL

01 President .... Dr. Carol E. LYTCH
10 Vice President Business & Finance ..... Ms. Elizabeth P. BENNETT
05 Vice Pres Academic Affairs & Dean .... Dr. David M. MELLOTT
07 Director of Admissions .... Rev. Ruth-Aimée BELONNI-ROSARIO
08 Seminary Librarian .... Mrs. Myka K. STEPHENS
06 Registrar .... Mrs. Teresa BENNEIAN
29 Director Alumni Relations .... Rev. Paul EYER
13 Director Computing/Information Mgmt ..... Mr. Augustine APPREY
30 Vice President Advancement .... Ms. Crystal MILLS
04 Exec Assistant to the President .... Ms. Carter FARMER

Lansdale School of Business (F)

290 Wissahickon Ave, North Wales PA 19454-4114
County: Montgomery FICE Identification: 007779
Unit ID: 213473
Telephone: (215) 699-5700 Carnegie Class: Assoc/PrivFP
FAX Number: (215) 699-8770 Calendar System: Semester
URL: www.LSB.edu
Established: 1918 Annual Undergrad Tuition & Fees: $11,830
Enrollment: 389 Coed
Affiliation or Control: Proprietary IRS Status: Proprietary
Highest Offering: Associate Degree
Program: Occupational; 2-Year Principally Bachelor's Creditable; Business Emphasis
Accreditation: ACICS

01 President .... Mr. Marlon D. KELLER
03 Executive Director .... Mrs. Marianne H. JOHNSON
05 Academic Dean .... Mr. David P. HEFFLEY
32 Student Services Coordinator .... Ms. Debora GAHMAN
08 Librarian .... Mrs. Marie B. WALCROFT
10 Director of Student Finance .... Mr. Robert RUSSO
36 Career Services Coordinator .... Ms. Jodi L. TASHMAN

Laurel Business Institute (G)

11 East Penn Street, Uniontown PA 15401-3453
County: Fayette FICE Identification: 025462
Unit ID: 250027
Telephone: (724) 439-4900 Carnegie Class: Assoc/PrivFP
FAX Number: (724) 439-3607 Calendar System: Semester
URL: www.laurel.edu
Established: 1985 Annual Undergrad Tuition & Fees: $12,591
Enrollment: 200 Coed
Affiliation or Control: Proprietary IRS Status: Proprietary
Highest Offering: Associate Degree
Program: Occupational; Technical Emphasis
Accreditation: ACICS, COARC, MLTAD

01 President .... Mrs. Nancy M. DECKER
05 Executive Director .... Mrs. Bonnie MARSH
10 Vice President of Finance .... Ms. Vicki M. JOLLIFFE
15 Vice President of Human Resources ..... Mr. Chuck SANTORE, JR.
12 Campus Director .... Mrs. Bonnie Jean MARSH
13 Network Administrator .... Mrs. JoAnna MEESE
37 Director of Financial Aid .... Ms. Stephanie M. MIGYANKO
07 Director of Admission/Marketing .... Mr. Douglas S. DECKER

Laurel Technical Institute (H)

200 Sterling Avenue, Sharon PA 16146
County: Mercer FICE Identification: 020925
Unit ID: 215992
Telephone: (724) 983-0700 Carnegie Class: Assoc/PrivFP
FAX Number: (724) 983-8355 Calendar System: Semester
URL: www.laurel.edu
Established: 1925 Annual Undergrad Tuition & Fees: $9,694
Enrollment: 157 Coed
Affiliation or Control: Proprietary IRS Status: Proprietary
Highest Offering: Associate Degree
Program: Occupational; 2-Year Principally Bachelor's Creditable
Accreditation: ACICS, COARC, MLTAD

01 President .... Ms. Nancy DECKER
05 Director .... Mr. Douglas DECKER
07 Director of Admission .... Ms. Maria CLYDE

Lebanon Valley College (I)

101 N College Avenue, Annville PA 17003-1400
County: Lebanon FICE Identification: 003288
Unit ID: 213507
Telephone: (717) 867-6161 Carnegie Class: Bac/Diverse
FAX Number: (717) 867-6124 Calendar System: Semester
URL: www.lvc.edu
Established: 1866 Annual Undergrad Tuition & Fees: $39,030
Enrollment: 1,901 Coed
Affiliation or Control: United Methodist IRS Status: 501(c)3
Highest Offering: Doctorate
Program: Liberal Arts And General; Teacher Preparatory; Professional
Accreditation: M, ACBSP, MUS, PTA

01 President .... Dr. Lewis E. THAYNE
05 Vice Pres Acad Affs/Dean of Faculty .... Dr. Michael R. GREEN
30 Vice President of Advancement .... Mr. Daniel HELWIG
10 Vice Pres Finance/Administration .... Mr. Shawn P. CURTIN
84 Vice President of Enrollment .... Mr. Edwin R. WRIGHT
32 VP Student Affairs/Dean of Students . Mr. Gregory H. KRIKORIAN
101 Spec Asst to Pres/Secy of College .... Mr. Steven P. O'DAY
26 Exec Dir Marketing/Communications .... Mr. Martin J. PARKES
13 Director of Information Technology .... Mr. David W. SHAPIRO
15 Director of HR/Title IX Coordinator .... Mrs. Ann C. HAYES
20 Associate Dean of Academic Affairs .... Dr. Ann E. DAMIANO

88 Assoc Vice Pres of Advancement .. Mr. Francis G. SCHODOWSKI
09 Director of Institutional Research ... Ms. Jessica L. ICKES
58 Assoc Dean of Grad Stds/Cont Educ ... Dr. Gregory A. BUCKLEY
06 Registrar ... Mr. Jeremy A. MAISTO
41 Director of Athletics ... Mr. Richard L. BEARD
88 Dir of Financial Planning/Analysis ... Mrs. Eleanor M. LEWIS
21 Controller ... Mr. Gabriel PAZ
37 Director of Financial Aid ... Mrs. Kendra M. FEIGERT
36 Director of Career Development ... Ms. Sharon M. GIVLER
28 Director of Multicultural Affairs ... Ms. Venus RICKS
19 Director of Public Safety ... Mr. Brent OBERHOLTZER
104 Director of Study Abroad ... Mrs. Jill T. RUSSELL
39 Director of Residential Life ... Dr. Michael R. DIESNER
38 Director of Disability Services ... Ms. Dawn R. SHOWERS
50 Director of the MBA Program ... Dr. David M. SETLEY
107 Director of Professional Studies ... Ms. Beth E. ROMANSKI
08 Director of the Bishop Library ... Ms. Sarah E. GREENE
105 Director of Communications ... Mrs. Jasmine A. BUCHER
102 Director of Development ... Mrs. Jamie N. CECIL
18 Sr Director Facilities Management ... Mr. Donald SANTOSTEFANO
35 Assoc Dean Student Affairs ... Dr. Robert L. MIKUS
42 Chaplain ... Rev. Paul FULLMER
07 Sr Assoc Director of Admission ... Mrs. Susan S. JONES
44 Director of Annual Giving ... Mrs. Danielle VIGILANTE-WEBB
27 Dir Editorial Standards/Brand Msgng ... Dr. Thomas M. HANRAHAN
91 Dir Enterprise Information Systems ... Mr. Robert J. DILLANE
90 Director Technology/User Support ... Mr. Michael C. ZEIGLER
24 Director of Audiovisual Technology ... Mr. Andrew S. GREENE
38 Director of Counseling ... Dr. Stephanie A. FALK
88 Director of Student Activities ... Mrs. Jennifer M. EVANS
23 Director of Health Services ... Ms. Valerie G. ANGELI
88 Assistant Controller ... Mr. Todd M. LATSHAW

Lehigh Carbon Community College (A)

4525 Education Park Drive, Schnecksville PA 18078-2598
County: Lehigh FICE Identification: 006810
Unit ID: 213525
Telephone: (610) 799-2121 Carnegie Class: Assoc/Pub-S-SC
FAX Number: (610) 799-1527 Calendar System: Semester
URL: www.lccc.edu
Established: 1966 Annual Undergrad Tuition & Fees (In-District): $3,800
Enrollment: 6,779 Coed
Affiliation or Control: Local IRS Status: 501(c)3
Highest Offering: Associate Degree
Program: Occupational; 2-Year Principally Bachelor's Creditable
Accreditation: M, ACBSP, ADNUR, CAHIIM, CSHSE, MAC, OTA, PNUR, PTAA

01 President ... Dr. Ann D. BIEBER
05 VP Academic/Student Development ... Dr. Thomas W. MEYER
10 VP Finance & Admin Svcs ... Mr. Brian KAHLER
84 VP Enrollment Management ... Ms. Cindy M. HANEY
04 Exec Asst to President and Board ... Mrs. Cindy L. BROOKS
32 Dean of Student Development ... Ms. Peggy M. HEIM
62 Dean Library & Ed Support Services ... Dr. Richard W. WILT
20 Dean of Academic Services ... Dr. Barry L. SPRIGGS
13 Exec Dir Information Technology ... Mr. Ervin J. MEASE
106 Assoc Dean Distance Education ... Mr. Dominic CHRISTISON
20 Assoc Academic Dean ... Dr. Andra M. BASU
20 Assoc Academic Dean ... Ms. Larissa M. VERTA
103 Exec Dir Workforce/Community Ed ... Ms. Terri K. KEEFE
26 Exec Dir College Relations ... Ms. Linda BAKER
09 Assoc Dean Inst Research & Effectiv ... Dr. Glynis A. DANIELS
45 Assoc Dean Planning & Assessment ... Dr. Cecelia A. CONNELLY-WEIDA
21 Dir Budgets & Purchasing ... Ms. Shannon HELMER
102 Executive Director Foundation ... Mr. Timothy J. HERRLINGER
38 Dir Advising ... Ms. Susan J. FREAD
07 Dir Recruitment & Admissions ... Mr. Louis L. HEGYES
88 Dir Application Services ... Mr. Robert F. GARVEY
36 Dir Career Development ... Ms. Christina L. MOYER
88 Assoc Dean Prof Accred/Curriculum ... Mr. Scott W. AQUILA
88 Dir High School Connections ... Ms. Jennifer K. AQUILA
15 Dir HR/Title IX/Equity Coord ... Ms. Donna M. WILLIAMS
88 Dir Infrastructure Svcs/Client Sol ... Mr. Frank D. MROZ
88 Dir Fac Dev/Student Retention ... Ms. Cheryl A. DOLL
103 Dir Workforce Training ... Mr. Thomas A. BUX
66 Director Nursing Programs ... Ms. Barbara H. LUPOLE
35 Dir Student Life ... Ms. Gene F. EDEN
14 Dir IT Support Services ... Mr. George C. HEGEDUS
18 Dir Facilities Management ... Mr. Carl S. PECKITT, JR.
37 Dir of Financial Aid ... Ms. Marian L. SNYDER
25 Dir Academic Grants ... Ms. Linda L. MESICS
41 Director Athletics ... Mr. Andrew JOHNSON
88 Dir Early Learning Center ... Ms. Mary G. SALINGER
12 Dir of Community Outreach/Strategic ... Dr. David LAPINSKY
88 Dir of Literacy and Job Training ... Ms. Mary KOVALCHICK
88 Dir Audits & Reporting ... Ms. Stefanie E. NESTER
25 Dir Institutional Advance Grants ... Mr. Thomas J. MULDERICK
74 Co-Dir Veterinary Tech Program ... Ms. Lisa A. MARTINI-JOHNSON
27 Dir Marketing and Publications ... Ms. Holly YACYNYCH
06 Dir Registration/Student Records ... Ms. Sandra L. MOSSER
40 Bookstore Manager ... Ms. Jennifer L. ERB
88 Assoc Dean Student Success ... Mr. Brian C. DELONG
19 Dir Public Safety ... Vacant
88 Dir Student Accounts ... Ms. Stacey A. BETZ

Lehigh University (B)

27 Memorial Drive W, Bethlehem PA 18015-3094
County: Northampton FICE Identification: 003289
Unit ID: 213543
Telephone: (610) 758-3000 Carnegie Class: RU/H
FAX Number: (610) 691-5420 Calendar System: Semester
URL: www.lehigh.edu
Established: 1865 Annual Undergrad Tuition & Fees: $58,510
Enrollment: 7,119 Coed
Affiliation or Control: Independent Non-Profit IRS Status: 501(c)3
Highest Offering: Doctorate
Program: Liberal Arts And General; Teacher Preparatory; Professional
Accreditation: M, BUS, BUSA, COPSY, CS, ENG, SCPSY, THEA

01 President ... Dr. John D. SIMON
05 Provost & VP for Academic Affairs ... Dr. Patrick V. FARRELL
10 Vice Pres Finance & Administration ... Ms. Patricia A. JOHNSON
88 VP for International Affairs ... Dr. Mohamed S. EL-AASSER
30 Vice President Advancement ... Mr. Joseph P. KENDER, JR.
46 VP & Assoc Prov Research/Graduate ... Dr. Alan J. SNYDER
26 VP Communications & Public Affairs ... Mr. Frederick J. MCGRAIL
88 Chief Investment Officer ... Mr. Peter M. GILBERT
09 Vice Provost Institutional Research ... Dr. J. Gary LUTZ
32 Vice Provost Student Affairs ... Dr. John W. SMEATON
13 Vice Provost Library & Tech Svcs ... Dr. Bruce M. TAGGART
86 Assoc VP for Govt Relations ... Mr. William D. MICHALERYA
21 Assoc VP Finance/Asst Secy Board ... Ms. Denise M. BLEW
15 Assoc VP for Human Resource ... Mr. Chris HALLADAY
18 Assoc Vice Pres Facilities Services ... Vacant
20 Deputy Provost Academic Affairs ... Ms. Jennifer M. JENSEN
35 Assoc Vice Provost Dean of Students ... Ms. Sharon K. BASSO
29 Interim Asst VP of Alumni Relations ... Ms. Lori B. KENNEDY
31 Asst VP Community & Regional Affs ... Mr. Dale A. KOCHARD
54 Interim Dean Engr & Applied Science ... Dr. John P. COULTER
49 Dean Arts & Sciences ... Dr. Donald E. HALL
50 Dean of Business/Economics ... Dr. Georgette C. PHILLIPS
53 Dean of Education ... Dr. Gary M. SASSO
07 Dean of Admissions/Financial Aid ... Mr. J. Leon WASHINGTON
41 Murray H Goodman Dean of Athletics ... Mr. Joseph D. STERRETT
06 Registrar ... Mr. Emil A. GNASSO
37 Director Financial Aid ... Ms. Jennifer L. MERTZ
106 Director Distance Education ... Ms. Margaret A. PORTZ
36 Director Career Services ... Ms. Lori B. KENNEDY
23 Director Health Center ... Dr. Susan C. KITEI
39 Director Residential Services ... Mr. Ozzie BREINER
40 Director Bookstore ... Mr. Brian ADLER
19 Chief University Police ... Mr. Edward K. SHUPP
38 Director of Counseling Services ... Dr. Ian T. BIRKY
42 Chaplain ... Rev. Lloyd H. STEFFEN
43 General Counsel ... Mr. Frank A. ROTH
21 Director of Budget ... Mr. Stephen J. GUTTMAN
28 Vice Provost for Academic Diversity ... Mr. Henry U. ODI
96 Manager Strategic Sourcing ... Ms. Jane ALTEMOSE
84 Director Enrollment Management ... Ms. Jennifer E. O'BRIEN-KNOTTS
100 Chief of Staff ... Mr. Erik J. WALKER

Lincoln Technical Institute (C)

5151 Tilghman Street, Allentown PA 18104-3298
County: Lehigh FICE Identification: 007759
Unit ID: 213570
Telephone: (610) 398-5300 Carnegie Class: Assoc/PrivFP
FAX Number: (610) 395-2706 Calendar System: Semester
URL: www.lincolnedu.com
Established: 1946 Annual Undergrad Tuition & Fees: $16,200
Enrollment: 540 Coed
Affiliation or Control: Proprietary IRS Status: Proprietary
Highest Offering: Associate Degree
Program: Occupational
Accreditation: ACCSC

01 Campus President ... Mrs. Lisa M. KUNTZ
05 Director of Education ... Ms. Anne CONNELY
11 Director of Administration ... Mrs. Angela REPPERT
37 Financial Aid Manager ... Ms. Erica BRANDI
07 Director of Admissions ... Mr. Vincent SALVANTORIELLO
36 Director of Career Services ... Mrs. Charmain BRODY

Lincoln Technical Institute (D)

9191 Torresdale Avenue, Philadelphia PA 19136-1595
County: Philadelphia FICE Identification: 007832
Unit ID: 213589
Telephone: (215) 335-0800 Carnegie Class: Assoc/PrivFP
FAX Number: (215) 335-1443 Calendar System: Other
URL: www.lincolntech.com
Established: 1946 Annual Undergrad Tuition & Fees: $35,899
Enrollment: 264 Coed
Affiliation or Control: Proprietary IRS Status: Proprietary
Highest Offering: Associate Degree
Program: Occupational; Technical Emphasis
Accreditation: ACCSC

01 Campus President ... Mr. John WILLIE
07 Dir Admiss High School/Adult Educ ... Ms. Nicole ZUCCHERI
32 Student Services Coordinator ... Ms. Tijania GOODWIN
05 Director of Education ... Mr. Michael CONCILIO
11 Director Administration ... Ms. Gina ALTSHULER
36 Director of Career Services ... Ms. TaJuan BUSH

Lincoln University (E)

PO Box 179, 1570 Baltimore Pike,
Lincoln University PA 19352-0999
County: Chester FICE Identification: 003290
Unit ID: 213598
Telephone: (484) 365-8000 Carnegie Class: Master's L
FAX Number: (484) 365-7316 Calendar System: Semester
URL: www.lincoln.edu
Established: 1854 Annual Undergrad Tuition & Fees (In-State): $11,860
Enrollment: 1,819 Coed
Affiliation or Control: State Related IRS Status: 501(c)3
Highest Offering: Master's
Program: Liberal Arts And General
Accreditation: M

01 Interim President ... Dr. Richard GREEN
30 Interim VP for Institutional Advanc ... Mr. Peter CAPUTO
100 Chief of Staf/Mgr Board of Trustees ... Ms. Diane M. BROWN
05 Interim VP for Academic Affairs ... Dr. Denise WILBUR
10 Vice Pres Fiscal Affairs/Treasurer ... Mr. Charles GRADOWSKI
32 Vice Pres for Student Affairs ... Dr. Juliana M. MOSLEY
13 Asst VP for Information Technology ... Mr. Andre WARNER
43 General Counsel ... Dr. Valerie HARRISON
09 Int Director Institutional Research ... Ms. Roxanne FOSTER
108 Dir of Assessment & Accreditation ... Ms. Gloria OIKELOME
39 Dean Students and Campus Life ... Dr. Lenetta LEE
84 Assoc VP of Enrollment Management ... Ms. Kimberly TAYLOR-BENNS
08 Interim Director of Library ... Mr. Neal CARLSON
26 Assoc VP External Relations/Mktg ... Ms. Maureen STOKES
27 Director of Communications ... Mr. Eric C. WEBB
29 Interim Dir of Alumni Relations ... Ms. Takeyah YOUNG
06 Registrar ... Ms. Catherine RUTLEDGE
30 Director Development & Major Gifts ... Vacant
102 Dir Foundation/Corporate Relations ... Vacant
36 Director Counseling/Career Svcs Ctr ... Mr. Ralph SIMPSON
41 Director of Athletics ... Dr. Darryl POPE
42 Chaplain ... Mr. Frederick FAISON
21 Controller ... Mr. Joseph JOHNSON
18 Interim Director Physical Plant ... Ms. Kelli GODDARD-SOBERS
85 Director International Services ... Ms. Constance L. LUNDY
23 Director Health Services ... Ms. Velva GREENE-RAINEY
58 Dir Graduate Student Svcs/Admission ... Ms. Jernice LEA
35 Director of Student Life & Develop ... Ms. Ihsan R. MUJAHID
37 Director Financial Aid ... Ms. Kim ANDERSON
96 Director of Purchasing ... Ms. Sue REED
81 Int Dean College of Science & Tech ... Dr. Derrick SWINTON
83 Dean Col Professional/Grad/Ext Stds ... Dr. Patricia A. JOSEPH
79 Dean Col of Arts/Humanities/Soc Sci ... Dr. Cheryl Renee GOOCH

Lutheran Theological Seminary at Gettysburg (F)

61 Seminary Ridge, Gettysburg PA 17325-1795
County: Adams FICE Identification: 003291
Unit ID: 213631
Telephone: (717) 334-6286 Carnegie Class: Spec/Faith
FAX Number: (717) 334-3469 Calendar System: 4/1/4
URL: www.ltsg.edu
Established: 1826 Annual Graduate Tuition & Fees: $16,000
Enrollment: 166 Coed
Affiliation or Control: Evangelical Lutheran Church In America
IRS Status: 501(c)3
Highest Offering: Doctorate; No Undergraduates
Program: Professional; Religious Emphasis
Accreditation: M, THEOL

01 President ... Rev. Michael L. COOPER-WHITE
30 Chief Advancement Officer ... Rev. Glenn LUDWIG
10 Chief Financial Officer ... Mrs. Jennifer BYERS
05 Dean of the Seminary ... Dr. Kristin LARGEN
08 Library Director and Archivist ... Dr. Briant BOHLEKE
06 Registrar ... Dr. Marty STEVENS
26 Exec Asst to Pres for Comm/Plng ... Rev. John R. SPANGLER
91 Director of Info Systems/Ed Tech ... Mr. Donald L. REDMAN
15 Asst to the Pres/Personnel Officer ... Mrs. Elizabeth A. MEIGHAN
07 Director of Admissions ... Rev. Lauren MURATORE

Lutheran Theological Seminary at Philadelphia (G)

7301 Germantown Avenue, Philadelphia PA 19119-1794
County: Philadelphia FICE Identification: 003292
Unit ID: 213640
Telephone: (215) 248-4616 Carnegie Class: Spec/Faith
FAX Number: (215) 248-4577 Calendar System: Other
URL: www.ltsp.edu
Established: 1864 Annual Graduate Tuition & Fees: $15,900
Enrollment: 223 Coed
Affiliation or Control: Evangelical Lutheran Church In America
IRS Status: 501(c)3
Highest Offering: Doctorate; No Undergraduates
Program: Professional; Religious Emphasis
Accreditation: M, THEOL

01 President ... Dr. David J. LOSE
05 Dean ... Dr. J. Jayakiran SEBASTIAN
10 Chief Financial Officer ... Mr. John HEIDGERD
30 Vice President of Advancement ... Dr. Dennis TROTTER
58 Director of Graduate Studies ... Dr. J. Jayakiran SEBASTIAN
08 Director of the Library ... Dr. Karl KRUEGER
88 Vice President for Student Vocation ... Rev. Christina JOHNSTEN
21 Director of Finance ... Ms. Mariam NOWAR
15 Human Resources ... Ms. Yvonne CURTIS
32 Director of Student Services ... Rev. Heidi RODRICK-SCHNAATH
06 Registrar ... Ms. Rene DIEMER

37 Financial Aid Associate .... Mrs. Susan KOWALSKI
19 Director of Security/Safety .... Mr. Vincent FERGUSON
13 Director of Information and LDL .... Mr. Kyle BARGER
26 Director of Communications .... Ms. Merri BROWN
42 Chaplain .... Dr. Michael KRENTZ
108 VP Planning/Assessment and Admin .... Dr. David GRAFTON
04 Executive Assistant to President .... Ms. Diana DOWNEY
18 Director of Operations .... Mr. Craig EISENHARD
44 Director of Donor Services .... Ms. Kathie AFFLERBACH
07 Director of Admissions .... Mr. Matthew O'REAR
88 Director of Contextual Education .... Dr. Charles LEONARD
88 Director of Urban Theological Inst .... Dr. Quintin ROBERTSON

Luzerne County Community College (A)

1333 S Prospect Street, Nanticoke PA 18634-3899

County: Luzerne | FICE Identification: 006811 | Unit ID: 213659
Telephone: (570) 740-0200 | Carnegie Class: Assoc/Pub-S-SC
FAX Number: (570) 740-0386 | Calendar System: Semester
URL: www.luzerne.edu
Established: 1966 | Annual Undergrad Tuition & Fees (In-District): $4,590
Enrollment: 6,049 | Coed
Affiliation or Control: Local | IRS Status: 501(c)3
Highest Offering: Associate Degree
Program: Occupational; 2-Year Principally Bachelor's Creditable
Accreditation: M, ACBSP, ADNUR, COARC, DA, DH, EMT, SURGT

01 President .... Mr. Thomas P. LEARY
04 Spec Ast to Pres Policy/Staff Devel .... Ms. Laura KATRENICZ
05 Vice Pres Academic Affairs/Provost .... Dr. Dana CLARK
32 Dean Enrollment Mgmt/Student Dev .... Ms. Rosana REYES
103 VP Workforce/Community Development .... Ms. Susan SPRY
15 Dean Human Resources .... Mr. John SEDLAK
66 Dean of Nursing/Health Sciences .... Ms. Deborah VILEGI PAYNE
50 Dean of Business/Technologies .... Ms. Bonita MOYER
49 Dean of Arts & Sciences .... Vacant
10 Dean Finance .... Mr. Joseph GASPER
13 Chief Technology Office .... Mr. Don NELSON
07 Assistant Director Admissions .... Mr. Ed HENNIGAN
37 Director of Student Financial Aid .... Mr. Mark CARPENTIER
08 Director of Library Services .... Mrs. Mia W. BASSHAM
38 Dir Counseling/Stdnt Support Svcs .... Mrs. Linda WALTERS
35 Dir Student Life/Athletics .... Ms. Mary SULLIVAN
09 Director Inst Research/Planning .... Ms. Graceann PLATUKUS
36 Director Career Services .... Ms. Mary GHILANI
18 Director of Physical Plant .... Mr. Keith GRAHAM
30 Exec Dir of Institutional Advance .... Ms. Sandra NICHOLAS
84 Director Enrollment Management .... Mr. Jim DOMZALSKI
26 Chief Public Relations Officer .... Ms. Lisa NELSON
29 Director Alumni Relations .... Ms. Bonnie LAUER
96 Director of Purchasing .... Mr. Len OLZINSKI
28 Diversity Coordinator .... Ms. Judi MYERS
19 Director of Safety/Security .... Mr. William BARRETT

Lycoming College (B)

700 College Place, Williamsport PA 17701-5192

County: Lycoming | FICE Identification: 003293 | Unit ID: 213668
Telephone: (570) 321-4000 | Carnegie Class: Bac/A&S
FAX Number: (570) 321-4337 | Calendar System: Semester
URL: www.lycoming.edu
Established: 1812 | Annual Undergrad Tuition & Fees: $35,900
Enrollment: 1,357 | Coed
Affiliation or Control: United Methodist | IRS Status: 501(c)3
Highest Offering: Baccalaureate
Program: Liberal Arts And General; Fine Arts Emphasis
Accreditation: M

01 President .... Dr. Kent C. TRACHTE
05 Provost and Dean of the College .... Dr. Philip W. SPRUNGER
10 VP for Finance and Admin/Treasurer .... Mr. Jeffrey L. BENNETT
30 Vice President for Advancement .... Mr. Charles W. EDMONDS
84 VP for Enrollment Management .... Mr. Michael J. KONOPSKI
21 Controller .... Ms. Dawn HENDRICKS
32 Vice President for Student Life .... Dr. Daniel P. MILLER
44 Associate VP for Development .... Ms. Loni KLINE
89 Dean for First Year Students .... Mr. Andrew W. KILPATRICK
08 Director of Snowden Library .... Ms. Alison GREGORY
06 Registrar .... Ms. Whitney A. MERINAR
26 Exec Dir Marketing & Communications .... Mr. James R. RABY
37 Director of Financial Aid .... Mr. James LAKIS
13 Chief Information Officer .... Mr. Robert L. DUNKLEBERGER
36 Director of Career Services .... Ms. MaryJo CAMPANA
29 Director Alumni Relations .... Ms. Amy S. REYES
44 Planned Giving Officer .... Ms. Karen M. SHEAFFER
19 Director of Safety & Security .... Mr. Donald TROUTMAN
35 Director of Student Programs .... Mr. Lawrence P. MANNOLINI, III
39 Director Residence Life .... Ms. Kate HEISER
41 Director of Athletics .... Mr. Michael CLARK
30 Senior Major Gift Officer .... Mr. Gregory J. BELL
44 Director of Annual Giving .... Ms. Erin MILLER
42 Campus Minister .... Rev. Jeffrey L. LECRONE
15 Director of Human Resources .... Ms. Jackie BILGER
18 Chief Facilities/Physical Plant .... Mr. F. Douglas KUNTZ
23 Director of Health Services .... Ms. Sondra L. STIPCAK
38 Director Student Counseling .... Mr. Townsend VELKOFF
40 Campus Store Manager .... Ms. Patricia E. BAUSINGER
92 Lycoming Scholars .... Dr. Cullen J. CHANDLER
94 Women's Studies .... Dr. Kerry RICHMOND

16 Human Resources Coordinator .... Mrs. Cathleen A. LUTZ
04 Assistant to the President .... Ms. Diane CARL
09 Director of Institutional Research .... Dr. Chiaki KOTORI
108 Associate Provost .... Dr. Eileen PELUSO
90 Dir Academic Computing/End User Svc .... Mr. Steve CARAVAGGIO
91 Director Administrative Computing .... Ms. Janet PAYNE
07 Director of Admissions .... Mr. Jason R. MORAN
102 Foundations Relations Officer .... Ms. Melanie TAORMINA
104 Coordinator of Study Abroad .... Mr. Philip WITHERUP

Manor College (C)

700 Fox Chase Road, Jenkintown PA 19046-3399

County: Montgomery | FICE Identification: 003294 | Unit ID: 213774
Telephone: (215) 885-2360 | Carnegie Class: Assoc/PrivNFP
FAX Number: (215) 576-6564 | Calendar System: Semester
URL: www.manor.edu
Established: 1947 | Annual Undergrad Tuition & Fees: $16,550
Enrollment: 860 | Coed
Affiliation or Control: Independent Non-Profit | IRS Status: 501(c)3
Highest Offering: Associate Degree
Program: Occupational; 2-Year Principally Bachelor's Creditable
Accreditation: M, ACBSP, DA, DH

01 President .... Vacant
04 Exec Secretary to the President .... Ms. Barbara J. OZER
05 Exec VP/Dean of Academic Affairs .... Ms. Sally P. MYDLOWEC
06 Registrar .... Ms. Dianne I. SARIDAKIS
10 Director Finance & Physical Plant .... Mr. John W. WINICKI
13 Director Information Technology .... Mr. Paul VAN RIJN
15 Human Resource Generalist .... Ms. Brittney RICHARDSON
18 Director Finance & Physical Plant .... Mr. John W. WINICKI
19 Assistant Director Security .... Ofcr. John MADSEN
30 Dir Development & Alum Relations .... Ms. Marialice F. STANZESKI
26 Director Marketing Communications .... Mr. Steven D. GREENBAUM
32 Director of Student Activities .... Ms. Allison C. MOOTZ
36 Career & Transfer Coord/Counseling .... Ms. Christine KREWSON
37 Director Financial Aid .... Mr. Chris T. HARTMAN
38 Director Counseling .... Ms. Christine B. PRINCE
39 Residence Hall Coordinator .... Ms. Elizabeth MACNEILL
41 Director Athletics .... Mr. Robert F. REEVES
45 Chairperson LRP .... Sr. Monica LESNICK, OSBM
53 Lib Arts Chair/Dir Early Child Ed .... Ms. Cherie L. CROSBY
08 Head Librarian .... Ms. Donna GUERIN
09 Director of Institutional Research .... Mr. John T. KREBS
84 Director Enrollment Management .... Ms. Claire GOWEN

Marywood University (D)

2300 Adams Avenue, Scranton PA 18509-1598

County: Lackawanna | FICE Identification: 003296 | Unit ID: 213826
Telephone: (570) 348-6211 | Carnegie Class: Master's L
FAX Number: (570) 961-4769 | Calendar System: Semester
URL: www.marywood.edu
Established: 1915 | Annual Undergrad Tuition & Fees: $32,692
Enrollment: 3,091 | Coed
Affiliation or Control: Roman Catholic | IRS Status: 501(c)3
Highest Offering: Doctorate
Program: Liberal Arts And General; Teacher Preparatory; Professional
Accreditation: M, ACBSP, ARCPA, ART, CAATE, CACREP, CLPSY, DIETC, DIETD, DIETI, MUS, NUR, NURSE, SP, SW, TED

01 President .... Sr. Anne MUNLEY
05 Vice Pres Academic Affairs .... Dr. Alan M. LEVINE
10 VP Business Affairs/Treasurer .... Mr. Joseph X. GARVEY, JR.
30 Vice Pres University Advancement .... Ms. Renee G. ZEHEL
84 VP Enrollment Svcs/Student Success .... Ms. Ann BOLAND-CHASE
101 Secretary Univ & General Counsel .... Atty. Mary T. GARDIER PATERSON
15 Assoc Vice Pres for Human Resources .... Dr. Patricia E. DUNLEAVY
26 Assoc VP Marketing/Communication .... Mr. Peter KILCULLEN
18 Asst VP for Buildings & Grounds .... Mrs. Wendy YANKELITIS
32 Asst VP for Student Life .... Dr. Amy PACIEJ-WOODRUFF
49 Dn Munley College Liberal Arts/Sci .... Dr. Frances M. ZAUHAR
53 Int Dean Reap College Ed/Human Dev .... Dr. Teresa A. PETERS
76 Dean Col of Health/Human Svcs .... Dr. Mark E. RODGERS
88 Dn Col of Creative/Performing Arts .... Mr. Collier B. PARKER
48 Dean School of Architecture .... Mr. James SULLIVAN
90 Director User Support Services .... Dr. Michael MIRABITO
70 Director School of Social Work .... Dr. Diane W. KELLER
08 Director of Library Services .... Mr. David G. SCHAPPERT
06 Registrar .... Ms. Rosemary BURGER
07 Dir of University Admissions .... Mr. Christian M. DIGREGORIO
21 Controller/Asst Treasurer .... Mr. Patrick E. CASTELLANI
21 Asst Controller .... Ms. Melissa A. SADDLEMIRE
13 Director of Enterprise Systems .... Mr. Michael P. GIBBONS
88 Asst Director Buildings & Grounds .... Mr. Myron MARCINEK
37 Director of Financial Aid .... Ms. Barbara L. SCHMITT
102 Corporate Foundation Relations Ofcr .... Ms. Tina L. MCGOVERN
44 Director of Planned Giving .... Ms. Elizabeth A. CONNERY
27 Public Relations Director .... Ms. Juneann GRECO
42 Chaplain/Asst Dir Campus Ministry .... Rev. Joseph P. ELSTON
39 Sr Dir Student Conduct/Res Life .... Mr. Ross NOVAK
41 Director Athletics/Recreation .... Dr. Mary Jo GUNNING
36 Director of Career Services .... Dr. Carole R. GUSTITUS
42 Director of Campus Ministry .... Sr. Catherine LUXNER
88 Resident District Manager .... Mr. Thomas K. NOTCHICK
13 Chief Information Officer .... Mr. Anthony SPINILLO

19 Chief Campus Safety .... Mr. Michael J. FINEGAN
23 Director of Student Health Services .... Ms. Linda MCDADE
38 Director Counseling & Student Devel .... Dr. Robert S. SHAW
40 Bookstore Manager .... Ms. Joan DIEHL
104 Assoc Dir International Affairs .... Vacant
14 Director of Operations .... Mr. John B. PORTER
44 Dir Advanc Svc/Scholarships/Steward .... Mr. Steven A. GREEN
29 Director of Alumni Engagement .... Ms. Ann L. WILLIAMS
35 Dir of Student Act/Leadership Devel .... Ms. Callie FRIELER
28 Director of Diversity .... Dr. Lia Richards PALMITER
88 Director Human Physiology Lab .... Vacant
09 Sr Director Institutional Research .... Dr. Ellen BOYLAN
45 Assoc VP Plng/Inst Effectiveness .... Dr. Kathleen O. RUTHKOSKY
90 Asst Director of User Support .... Ms. Katherine P. LEWIS

McCann School of Business & Technology (E)

2200 North Irving Street, Allentown PA 18109

Telephone: (484) 223-4601 | Identification: 770768
Accreditation: ACICS, MAC, MLTAD, SURGT

† Branch campus of McCann School of Business & Technology, Pottsville, PA.

McCann School of Business & Technology (F)

346 York Road, Carlisle PA 17013

Telephone: (714) 218-3400 | Identification: 770767
Accreditation: ACICS, SURGT

† Branch campus of McCann School of Business & Technology, Pottsville, PA.

McCann School of Business & Technology (G)

2227 Scranton Carbondale Highway, Dickson City PA 18519

Telephone: (570) 969-4330 | Identification: 770769
Accreditation: ACICS, MAC

† Branch campus of McCann School of Business & Technology, Pottsville, PA.

McCann School of Business & Technology (H)

370 Maplewood Drive, Humbolt Ind Pk, Hazleton PA 18202-9790

Telephone: (570) 454-6172 | Identification: 666484
Accreditation: ACICS, MAC, SURGT

† Branch campus of McCann School of Business & Technology, Pottsville, PA.

McCann School of Business & Technology (I)

2650 Woodglen Road, Pottsville PA 17901-1335

County: Schuylkill | FICE Identification: 004898 | Unit ID: 438212
Telephone: (570) 622-7622 | Carnegie Class: Assoc/PrivFP
FAX Number: (570) 622-7770 | Calendar System: Quarter
URL: www.mccann.edu
Established: 1897 | Annual Undergrad Tuition & Fees: $9,820
Enrollment: 3,346 | Coed
Affiliation or Control: Proprietary | IRS Status: Proprietary
Highest Offering: Associate Degree
Program: Occupational
Accreditation: ACICS, MAC, MLTAD

01 Director Pottsville Campus .... Ms. Shannon BRENNAN
05 Director of Education .... Ms. MaryLou ORAM
36 Director of Career Services .... Ms. Michelle SCRIBBICK

McCann School of Business & Technology (J)

1147 N Fourth Street, Sunbury PA 17801-3413

Telephone: (570) 286-3058 | Identification: 666485
Accreditation: ACICS, MAC, MLTAD, SURGT

† Branch campus of McCann School of Business & Technology, Pottsville, PA.

McCann School of Business & Technology (K)

264 Highland Park Boulevard, Wilkes Barre PA 18702

Telephone: (570) 235-2200 | Identification: 770770
Accreditation: ACICS

† Branch campus of McCann School of Business & Technology, Pottsville, PA.

Mercyhurst University (L)

501 E 38th Street, Erie PA 16546-0001

County: Erie | FICE Identification: 003297 | Unit ID: 213987
Telephone: (814) 824-2000 | Carnegie Class: Master's S
FAX Number: (814) 824-2438 | Calendar System: 4/1/4
URL: www.mercyhurst.edu
Established: 1926 | Annual Undergrad Tuition & Fees: $33,314
Enrollment: 3,938 | Coed
Affiliation or Control: Roman Catholic | IRS Status: 501(c)3
Highest Offering: Doctorate
Program: Occupational; 2-Year Principally Bachelor's Creditable; Liberal Arts And General; Teacher Preparatory; Professional

Accreditation: M, ADNUR, #ARCPA, CAATE, DANCE, IACBE, MUS, OTA, PTAA, SW

01 President .... Mr. Michael T. VICTOR
05 Provost & VP Academic Affairs .... Dr. David DAUSEY
10 Vice Pres Finance & Administration .... Hoa NGUYEN
12 Exec VP Mercyhurst - NE .... Dr. Gary BROWN
30 Vice Pres University Development .... Dr. David RUBINO
32 Vice Pres of Student Life .... Dr. Laura ZIRKEL
13 Chief Information Officer .... Ms. Jeanette BRITT
18 Director Facilities/Physical Plant .... Mr. Kenneth STEPHERSON
38 Director Student Counseling Service .... Ms. Judy SMITH
07 Interim Director of Admissions .... Mr. Christian BEYER
06 Registrar .... Sr. Patricia WHALEN
08 Dir Univ Libraries/Online Learning .... Ms. Darci JONES
39 Dir Residential Life/Stdnt Conduct .... Ms. Alice AGNEW
19 Director of Public Safety Programs .... Mr. Robert KUHN
29 Dir Alumni Rels & Annual Giving .... Ms. Tamara WALTERS
42 Director of Campus Ministry .... Fr. James PISZKER
37 Director of Student Financial Svcs .... Ms. Carrie NEWMAN
41 Director of Athletics .... Mr. Joseph KIMBALL
09 Director of Institutional Research .... Mrs. Sheila W. RICHTER
15 Director Human Resources .... Mr. Jim TOMETSKO
28 Director Multicultural Affairs .... Ms. Petrina MARRERO

Mercyhurst University Northeast (A)

16 W Division Street, North East PA 16428
Telephone: (814) 725-6100 Identification: 770161
Accreditation: &M, COARC, MLTAD

† Branch campus of Mercyhurst University, Erie, PA.

Messiah College (B)

One College Avenue, Mechanicsburg PA 17055
County: Cumberland FICE Identification: 003298
Unit ID: 213996
Telephone: (717) 766-2511 Carnegie Class: Bac/Diverse
FAX Number: (717) 691-6025 Calendar System: Semester
URL: www.messiah.edu
Established: 1909 Annual Undergrad Tuition & Fees: $32,240
Enrollment: 2,789 Coed
Affiliation or Control: Interdenominational IRS Status: 501(c)3
Highest Offering: Doctorate
Program: Liberal Arts And General; Teacher Preparatory; Professional
Accreditation: M, ACBSP, ART, CAATE, CACREP, DIETD, @DIETI, ENG, MUS, NURSE, SW, THEA

01 President .... Dr. Kim S. PHIPPS
05 Provost .... Dr. Randall G. BASINGER
30 Vice President for Advancement .... Mr. Barry G. GOODLING
84 Vice Pres for Enrollment Management .... Mr. John A. CHOPKA
10 Vice Pres for Finance & Planning .... Mr. David S. WALKER
15 VP for Human Res & Compliance .... Ms. Amanda A. COFFEY
13 VP Info Technology/Assoc Provost .... Dr. William G. STRAUSBAUGH
11 Vice President for Operations .... Mrs. Kathrynne G. SHAFER
32 Vice Provost & Dean of Students .... Dr. Kristin M. HANSEN-KIEFFER
58 Int Asst Prov Grad & Nontrad Pgms .... Dr. Robert PEPPER
57 Dean School of the Arts .... Dr. Richard E. ROBERSON
53 Dean Sch Bus/Educ/Soc Sci .... Dr. Carolyn MAURER
79 Dean School of Humanities .... Dr. Peter K. POWERS
81 Int Dean School of Sci/Engr/Health .... Dr. Angela HARE
35 Associate Dean of Students .... Mr. Douglas M. WOOD
88 Dir of Intercultural Office .... Mrs. Faith MINNICH KJESBO
88 Dir Stdnt Involvemnt Leadership Pgm .... Mr. Kevin J. VILLEGAS
07 Director of Admissions .... Mrs. Dana J. BRITTON
37 Director of Financial Aid .... Mr. Gregory L. GEARHART
39 Asst Dir of Residence Life/Housing .... Mrs. Rhonda KING
21 Dir Financial Operations/Controller .... Mrs. Christine HARTMAN
06 Registrar .... Mr. James J. SOTHERDEN
08 Director of the Murray Library .... Mr. Jonathan D. LAUER
91 Director Information Services .... Mr. John P. LUFT
90 Dir Learning Technology Services .... Mrs. Susan K. SHANNON
09 Director of Institutional Research .... Ms. Laura M. MILLER
42 College Pastor .... Dr. Donald OPITZ
30 Director of Development .... Dr. Jon C. STUCKEY
26 Exec Dir Marketing & Communications .... Mrs. Carla E. GROSS
29 Director Alumni & Parent Relations .... Mr. Jay W. MCCLYMONT
44 Director of Annual Giving .... Ms. Beth TROTT CLARK
38 Director of the Engle Center .... Mrs. Eleanor M. ADDLEMAN
23 Coordinator of Health Services .... Mrs. Michelle LUCAS
41 Director of Athletics .... Mr. Jack T. COLE
92 Dir of the College Honors Program .... Dr. Dean C. CURRY
18 Director of Facility Services .... Mr. Bradley A. MARKLEY
36 Director of Career Development .... Mrs. Christina R. HANSON
40 Campus Store Manager .... Ms. Candice TRITLE
19 Director Safety/Dispatch Services .... Ms. Cindy L. BURGER
04 Executive Asst to President .... Ms. Melissa COHEN
96 Purchasing Manager .... Mrs. Daisy ANDERSON

Metropolitan Career Center Computer Technology Institute (C)

100 S Broad Street, Suite 830, Philadelphia PA 19110-1018
County: Philadelphia FICE Identification: 031091
Unit ID: 214023
Telephone: (215) 568-9215 Carnegie Class: Assoc/PrivNFP
FAX Number: (215) 568-3511 Calendar System: Semester
URL: www.cti-careers.org
Established: 1974 Annual Undergrad Tuition & Fees: $24,194
Enrollment: 31 Coed
Affiliation or Control: Independent Non-Profit IRS Status: 501(c)3
Highest Offering: Associate Degree
Program: Occupational; 2-Year Principally Bachelor's Creditable; Technical Emphasis
Accreditation: ACCSC

01 President .... Dr. Richard COHEN
03 Executive Director .... Ms. Wendy-Anne ROBERTS-JOHNSON
10 Controller .... Mr. Timothy DONOHUE
05 Director of Education .... Mr. Paul BOYLE
37 Financial Aid Director .... Ms. Madeline SARGENT
07 Admissions Representative .... Ms. Marie HICKS
36 Relationship Manager .... Ms. Christina HARRIS

Misericordia University (D)

301 Lake Street, Dallas PA 18612-1098
County: Luzerne FICE Identification: 003247
Unit ID: 214069
Telephone: (570) 674-6400 Carnegie Class: Master's M
FAX Number: (570) 675-2441 Calendar System: Semester
URL: www.misericordia.edu
Established: 1924 Annual Undergrad Tuition & Fees: $28,294
Enrollment: 2,371 Coed
Affiliation or Control: Roman Catholic IRS Status: 501(c)3
Highest Offering: Doctorate
Program: Liberal Arts And General; Teacher Preparatory; Professional
Accreditation: M, #ARCPA, DMS, IACBE, NURSE, OT, PTA, RAD, SP, SW

01 President .... Dr. Thomas J. BOTZMAN
10 Vice Pres Finance & Administration .... Mr. Eric NELSON
05 Vice President Academic Affairs .... Dr. Charles J. BRODY
30 VP of Institutional Advancement .... Ms. Susan M. HELWIG
88 Vice Pres of Mission Integration .... Sr. Jean MESSAROS
45 VP of Planning/External Rel .... Dr. Barbara SAMUEL LOFTUS
32 Vice President of Student Life .... Ms. Kathleen FOLEY
21 Controller .... Mr. Ronald S. HROMISIN
06 Registrar .... Mr. Joseph REDINGTON
84 Director Enrollment Management .... Ms. Jane F. DESSOYE
29 Director Alumni Relations .... Ms. Denise MISCAVAGE
08 Librarian .... Ms. Jennifer LUKSA
04 Exec Assistant to the President .... Ms. Michelle DONATO
96 Director of Purchasing .... Mr. Thomas F. KANE
38 Exec Dir Learning Resource Ctr .... Ms. Jennifer RANDALL
42 Director Campus Ministry .... Ms. Christine SOMERS
41 Director of Athletics .... Mr. David MARTIN
39 Director of Residents .... Ms. Donna ELLIS
13 Director of Management Info Systems .... Mr. Joseph J. MACK
14 Director of Information Technology .... Mr. Val APANOVICH
35 Director of Student Life .... Ms. Darcy BRODMERKEL
36 Dir Insalaco Ctr Career Development .... Ms. Bernadette RUSHMER
102 Dir Foundation/Government Relations .... Mr. Larry PELLEGRINI
51 Director of Adult Education .... Mr. Paul NARDONE
15 Director of Human Resources .... Ms. Pamela PARSNIK
07 Director of Admissions .... Mr. Glenn BOZINSKI
26 Dir of Public Relations/Marketing .... Mr. James ROBERTS
37 Director of Financial Aid .... Ms. Susan FRONZONI
28 Director of Multicultural Initiativ .... Dr. Scott RICHARDSON
19 Assoc Director Security/Safety .... Mr. Robert ZAVADA
18 Director of Facilities .... Mr. Paul MURPHY
09 Asst Dir of Institutional Research .... Ms. Sharon HUDAK
90 Manager of User Services .... Mr. David A. JOHNDROW
101 Secretary of the Institution/Board .... Ms. Carol FAHNESTOCK

Montgomery County Community College (E)

340 Dekalb Pike, Blue Bell PA 19422-1400
County: Montgomery FICE Identification: 004452
Unit ID: 214111
Telephone: (215) 641-6300 Carnegie Class: Assoc/Pub-S-MC
FAX Number: (215) 461-1460 Calendar System: Semester
URL: www.mc3.edu
Established: 1964 Annual Undergrad Tuition & Fees (In-District): $4,920
Enrollment: 13,100 Coed
Affiliation or Control: State/Local IRS Status: 501(c)3
Highest Offering: Associate Degree
Program: Occupational; 2-Year Principally Bachelor's Creditable
Accreditation: M, ADNUR, CSHSE, DH, IFSAC, MAC, MLTAD, PHLEB, RAD, SURGT

01 Interim President .... Dr. James LINKSZ
04 Exec Assistant to the President .... Mr. Joshua SCHWARTZ
101 Exec Asst to the Board of Trustees .... Ms. Deborah ROGERS
12 VP of the West Campus .... Vacant
13 VP for Information Technology .... Ms. Celeste M. SCHWARTZ
10 VP for Finance & Administration .... Vacant
26 Vice Pres of Devel & External Rels .... Ms. Arline STEPHAN
84 VP for Student Affairs & Enrol Mgt .... Dr. Kathrine SWANSON
05 VP for Academic Affairs & Provost .... Dr. Victoria BASTECKI-PEREZ
06 Registrar .... Ms. Sherry PHILLIPS
15 Executive Director Human Resources .... Ms. Diane O'CONNOR
21 Controller .... Ms. Kathleen MCGIRR
44 Dir of Annual Giving & Adv Services .... Vacant
19 Director of Campus Safety .... Mr. Joseph MCGURIMAN
37 Director of Financial Aid .... Ms. Tracey RICHARDS
09 Director of Institutional Research .... Mr. Leon HILL
28 Dir Equity & Diversity Initiatives .... Ms. Rose MAKOFSKE
29 Director of Major Gifts and Alumni .... Ms. Stephanie WITTIG
27 Director Media/Public Relations .... Ms. Alana MAUGER
103 Dean Workforce Development & CE .... Ms. Suzanne HOLLOMAN
86 Exec Dir of Govt Relations .... Ms. Margaret LEE-CLARK
41 Dir of Athletics & Campus Rec .... Mr. Bruce BACH
44 Sr Dir of Major and Planned Gifts .... Ms. Leslie BLUESTONE

Montgomery County Community College West Campus (F)

101 College Drive, Pottstown PA 19464
Telephone: (610) 718-1800 Identification: 770162
Accreditation: &M

† Branch campus of Montgomery County Community College, Blue Bell, PA.

Moore College of Art and Design (G)

20th and The Parkway, Philadelphia PA 19103-1179
County: Philadelphia FICE Identification: 003300
Unit ID: 214148
Telephone: (215) 965-4000 Carnegie Class: Spec/Arts
FAX Number: (215) 568-8017 Calendar System: Semester
URL: www.moore.edu
Established: 1848 Annual Undergrad Tuition & Fees: $36,828
Enrollment: 432 Female
Affiliation or Control: Independent Non-Profit IRS Status: 501(c)3
Highest Offering: Master's
Program: Fine Arts Emphasis
Accreditation: M, ART, CIDA

01 President .... Ms. Cecelia FITZGIBBON
10 Vice Pres Finance & Administration .... Mr. William L. HILL, II
05 Interim Academic Dean .... Ms. Claudine THOMAS
32 Dean of Students .... Ms. Ruth ROBBINS
20 Assoc Dean Educational Support Svcs .... Vacant
39 Director Residence Life/Housing .... Mr. Matthew POINT
88 Executive Director of Galleries .... Ms. Kaytie JOHNSON
51 Director of Continuing Education .... Ms. Judith WOODWORTH
26 Dir of Marketing/Communications .... Mr. Roy A. WILBUR
30 Assoc Director of Development .... Ms. Andrea SILVA
29 Dir Alumnae Affairs/Annual Fund .... Ms. Kathryn MYERS
08 Library Director .... Ms. Sharon WATSON-MAURO
07 Exec Director of Admissions .... Ms. Elizabeth MATHIS
37 Director of Financial Aid .... Ms. Laverne GLENN
06 Registrar .... Ms. Alyssa TRUSZKOWSKI
18 Director of Operations .... Mr. Kenneth M. FERRETTI
15 Director Human Resources .... Ms. Rachel PHILLIPS
36 Director Career Center .... Ms. Belena CHAPP
58 Director of Graduate Studies .... Ms. Michelle GARRIGAN-DURANT
38 Director Student Counseling .... Ms. Ruth R. GAYLE
90 Academic Computing Manager .... Mr. Dennis DAWTON

Moravian College (H)

1200 Main St., Bethlehem PA 18018-6650
County: Northampton FICE Identification: 003301
Unit ID: 214157
Telephone: (610) 861-1300 Carnegie Class: Bac/A&S
FAX Number: (610) 625-7918 Calendar System: Semester
URL: www.moravian.edu
Established: 1742 Annual Undergrad Tuition & Fees: $38,132
Enrollment: 1,930 Coed
Affiliation or Control: Moravian Church IRS Status: 501(c)3
Highest Offering: Master's
Program: Liberal Arts And General; Teacher Preparatory; Professional; Nursing Emphasis
Accreditation: M, MUS, NURSE, THEOL

01 President .... Dr. Bryon L. GRIGSBY
05 Provost .... Dr. Cynthia KOSSO
10 Vice President Finance & Admin .... Mr. Mark F. REED
30 Vice Pres Institutional Advancement .... Mr. Gary CARNEY
32 Vice President Student Affairs .... Dr. Nicole L. LOYD
73 Vice Pres/Dean of the Seminary .... Dr. Frank CROUCH
84 Vice President for Enrollment .... Mr. Steven SOBA
13 Chief Information Officer .... Mr. Scott HUGHES
09 Chief Research Officer .... Ms. Carole A. REESE
15 Chief Human Resources Officer .... Mr. Jon B. CONRAD
35 Dean of Students .... Dr. Nicole L. LOYD
36 Assoc Dean of Stdnts/Dir Career Dev .... Ms. Amy SAUL
20 Dean of Curriculum .... Dr. Carol TRAUPMAN-CARR
28 Assoc Dean Intercultural Advance .... Mr. Chris HUNT
39 Asst Dean for Residence Life .... Ms. Liz YATES
59 Asst Dean of Continuing/Graduate .... Ms. LaKeisha THORPE
88 Asst Dean for Academic Advising .... Dr. James SKALNIK
21 Treasurer .... Ms. Anne M. REID
88 Bursar .... Ms. Susan O'HARE
06 Institutional Registrar .... Ms. Alexandra SMITH
88 Director of Event Management .... Mrs. Ann E. CLAUSSEN
21 Dir Business/Financial Operations .... Ms. Amy JOHNSON
24 Dir Academic & Disability Support .... Ms. Laurie ROTH
44 Director of Leadership Giving .... Ms. Bertie KNISELY
18 Dir Facilities Mgt Plng/Construct .... Mr. Douglas J. PLOTTS
19 Director of Campus Safety .... Mr. George BOKSAN
26 Director of Marketing and Commun .... Mr. Michael P. WILSON
08 Library Director .... Ms. Janet OHLES
37 Director of Financial Aid .... Vacant
38 Director of Counseling .... Dr. Ronald J. KLINE
58 Dean Continuing/Graduate Studies .... Vacant
40 Bookstore Manager .... Ms. Kari JACKSON
41 Director of Athletics .... Vacant
42 College Chaplain .... Rev. Jennika BORGER

88 Director of the Payne Gallery .... Dr. Diane RADYCKI
88 Asst to Pres Projects & Board Suppt .... Ms. Deborah L. EVANS
23 Nurse Coordinator .... Ms. Stella GORDON
104 Director of International Studies .... Mr. Kerry SETHI
24 Media Center Manager .... Mr. Craig UNDERWOOD
04 Executive Secretary to President .... Ms. Deborah HINKEL
07 Executive Director of Admissions .... Mr. Scott DAMS

Moravian Theological Seminary (A)

60 W. Locust St., Bethlehem PA 18018
Telephone: (610) 861-1516 Identification: 770163
Accreditation: &M

† Branch campus of Moravian College, Bethlehem, PA.

Mount Aloysius College (B)

7373 Admiral Peary Highway, Cresson PA 16630-1999
County: Cambria FICE Identification: 003302
Unit ID: 214166
Telephone: (814) 886-6300 Carnegie Class: Bac/Assoc
FAX Number: (814) 886-2978 Calendar System: Semester
URL: www.mtaloy.edu
Established: 1853 Annual Undergrad Tuition & Fees: $21,360
Enrollment: 1,893 Coed
Affiliation or Control: Independent Non-Profit IRS Status: 501(c)3
Highest Offering: Master's
Program: Occupational; 2-Year Principally Bachelor's Creditable; Liberal Arts And General
Accreditation: M, ADNUR, DMS, MAC, MLTAD, NUR, PTAA, SURGT

01 President .... Dr. Thomas P. FOLEY
05 Sr VP Academic Affs/Dean of Faculty .... Dr. Stephen PUGLIESE
11 Sr VP Administrative Services .... Ms. Suzanne P. CAMPBELL
32 VP Student Affs/Dean Students .... Dr. Jane M. GRASSADONIA
84 VP Enrollment Mgmt/Dean Admissions .... Mr. Francis C. CROUSE, JR.
07 Director of Freshmen Admissions .... Mr. Andrew D. CLOUSE
07 Director of Transfer Admissions .... Mr. Richard MISHLER
30 VP Institutional Advancement .... Ms. Jennifer DUBUQUE
10 Controller/CFO .... Ms. Donna K. YODER
06 Registrar .... Dr. Christopher M. LOVETT
08 Director of Library .... Dr. Michael JONES
37 Director of Financial Aid .... Ms. Stacy L. SCHENK
15 Director of Human Resources .... Ms. Tonia J. GORDON
26 Director of Communications .... Mr. John COYLE
13 Director of Information Technology .... Mr. Rich J. SHEA
23 Director of Health Services .... Ms. Shannon D. GROVE
40 Director of Bookstore .... Ms. Christine M. CLINTON
41 Director of Athletics .... Mr. Ryan M. SMITH
19 Director of Safety & Security .... Mr. William H. TREXLER
18 Director of Physical Plant .... Mr. Gerald RUBRITZ
09 Institutional Researcher .... Mr. Bryan J. PEARSON
36 Career Development Coordinator .... Ms. Kristy MAGEE
38 Dir Student Counseling/Disabilities .... Ms. Marisa L. EVANS
39 Director of Residence Life .... Ms. Christina KOREN
42 Director Campus Ministry .... Ms. Andrea T. CECILLI
44 Manager of Annual Giving .... Ms. Sally GORDON
04 Administrative Asst to President .... Ms. Carla NELEN

Muhlenberg College (C)

2400 West Chew Street, Allentown PA 18104-5586
County: Lehigh FICE Identification: 003304
Unit ID: 214175
Telephone: (484) 664-3100 Carnegie Class: Bac/A&S
FAX Number: (484) 664-3234 Calendar System: Semester
URL: www.muhlenberg.edu
Established: 1848 Annual Undergrad Tuition & Fees: $45,875
Enrollment: 2,440 Coed
Affiliation or Control: Evangelical Lutheran Church In America
IRS Status: 501(c)3
Highest Offering: Baccalaureate
Program: Liberal Arts And General; Teacher Preparatory
Accreditation: M

01 President .... Mr. John I. WILLIAMS, JR.
05 Provost .... Dr. John G. RAMSAY
10 Treasurer & Vice Pres for Finance .... Mr. Kent DYER
26 Vice President of Public Relations .... Mr. Michael S. BRUCKNER
30 VP Development & Alumni Relations .... Ms. Rebekkah L. BROWN
15 Vice President of Human Resources .... Ms. Anne SPECK
04 Exec Assistant to the President .... Mr. Ken BUTLER
102 Asst VP Corporate/Found & Govt Rels .... Ms. Deborah J. KIPP
32 Dean of Students .... Ms. Karen GREEN
88 Dean of College for Academic Life .... Dr. Michael HUBER
20 Assoc Dean Institutional Assessment .... Dr. Kathleen E. HARRING
86 Assoc Dean International Programs .... Dr. Donna M. KISH-GOODLING
37 Associate Dean Financial Aid .... Mr. Gregory S. MITTON
88 Asst Dean Acad Res/Disability Svcs .... Mr. David HALLOWELL
29 Alumni Relations Director .... Ms. Natalie HAND
55 Dean Wescoe Sch Muhlenberg College .... Ms. Jane E. HUDAK
07 Dean Admissions/Financial Aid .... Mr. Christopher HOOKER-HARING
08 Director of Trexler Library .... Ms. Tina L. HERTEL
06 Registrar .... Ms. Deborah TAMTE-HORAN
13 Director Information Technology .... Mr. Harry E. MILLER
19 Director of Campus Safety/Security .... Mr. Brian FIDATI
39 Director of Residence Life .... Ms. Janette SCHUMACHER
36 Director of the Career Center .... Ms. Alana M. ALBUS

21 Assistant Treasurer .... Mr. Jason FEIERTAG
23 Director of Student Health Services .... Ms. Brynnmarie DORSEY
38 Director Counseling Services .... Ms. Anita KELLY
42 Chaplain .... Rev. Callista S. ISABELLE
09 Director of Institutional Research .... Ms. Nicole HAMMEL
18 Chief Facilities/Physical Plant .... Mr. Michael H. BREWER
96 Director of Purchasing .... Ms. Elizabeth M. LEES
40 Bookstore Manager .... Ms. Karen R. NORMANN

Neumann University (D)

One Neumann Drive, Aston PA 19014-1298
County: Delaware FICE Identification: 003988
Unit ID: 214272
Telephone: (610) 459-0905 Carnegie Class: Master's M
FAX Number: (610) 459-1370 Calendar System: Semester
URL: www.neumann.edu
Established: 1965 Annual Undergrad Tuition & Fees: $26,918
Enrollment: 3,047 Coed
Affiliation or Control: Roman Catholic IRS Status: 501(c)3
Highest Offering: Doctorate
Program: Liberal Arts And General; Teacher Preparatory; Professional
Accreditation: M, ACBSP, CAATE, CACREP, MT, NUR, PTA

01 President .... Dr. Rosalie M. MIRENDA
05 Vice President Academic Affairs .... Dr. Lawrence DIPAOLO
43 Vice President and General Counsel .... Mr. Jonathan PERI
10 Vice Pres Finance/Administration .... Mr. Joseph GORMAN
42 Vice President Mission/Ministry .... Sr. Marguerite O'BEIRNE, OSF
30 Vice Pres Inst Advance/Univ Rels .... Mr. Henry A. SUMNER
84 Vice Pres Student Affairs .... Dr. Dianna C. DALE
15 Vice President HR & Risk Management .... Mr. David W. BROWNLEE
49 Dean Division of Arts & Science .... Dr. Alfred G. MUELLER, II
50 Dean Div of Bus/Info Mgmt .... Dr. Lawrence E. BURGEE
53 Dean Div of Educ/Human Svcs .... Dr. Barbara HANES
51 Dean of Cont Adult/Prof Stds .... Dr. Robert D. BUNNELL
66 Dean Div Nursing/Health Sciences .... Dr. Kathleen HOOVER
04 Assistant to President .... Ms. Danielle WAGNER
06 Registrar .... Mr. Joel A. NATALE
18 Facilities Director .... Mr. William LEONARD
19 Director Safety & Security .... Mr. Leon FRANCIS
08 Director Library .... Ms. Tiffany MCGREGOR
26 Exec Director Mktg/Communications .... Mr. Stephen BELL
09 Director Institutional Research .... Ms. Melissa THORPE
42 Chaplain .... Rev. Philip J. LOWE, OFM
44 Director Annual Giving/Prospect Mgt .... Ms. Christina FARRELL
29 Dir Alumni Rels/Special Programs .... Ms. Judi STANAITIS
88 Director Inst Gifts/Donor Rels .... Ms. Josephina E. BANNER
38 Director Counseling .... Mr. Fritz HAAS
39 Director Residence Life .... Mr. Michael WEBSTER
13 Exec Director University Computing .... Mr. David O'LEARY
24 Director Academic Resource Center .... Ms. Theresa HUKE
41 Director Athletics .... Mr. Chuck SACK
36 Dir Career & Personal Development .... Ms. Mary MCCAFFREY
88 Director of Academic Advising .... Mr. Michael MULLEN
88 Director Child Development Center .... Ms. Mary Ann MELISI
21 Controller .... Mr. John YOUHOUSE
37 Director Financial Assistance .... Ms. Andrea DEL VACCHIO
23 Director Health Services .... Ms. Janet GEDDIS
96 Director of Purchasing .... Ms. Elena BARRAR
88 Director Physical Therapy Program .... Dr. Robert POST
07 Director of Admissions .... Mr. Christopher MAYERSKI
88 Dir Ctr for Sprt/Spir/Char Dev .... Ms. Lee M. DELLEMONACHE
90 Director Instructional Technology .... Mr. Scott BEADENKOPF
88 Director Conference/Scheduling Svcs .... Ms. Melissa HAINES
40 Director University Bookstore .... Ms. Natalie VAN WYK
108 Associate VP for Assessmen/Learning .... Dr. Janet THIEL, OSF
88 Director Development Education .... Ms. Lori BLOUNT
104 Coord International Studies Educ .... Ms. Jen MINTZER
88 Director of Retention .... Ms. Coleen NEDBALSKI
105 Director Web Services .... Ms. Lisa CADORETTE
106 Dir Online Education/E-learning .... Dr. Jilian DONNELLY
109 Dean of Enrollment Management .... Mr. Eric SZENTESY
88 Program Director Athletic Training .... Dr. Hubert LEE

New Castle School of Trades (E)

4117 Pulaski Road, New Castle PA 16101
County: Lawrence FICE Identification: 007780
Unit ID: 214290
Telephone: (724) 964-8811 Carnegie Class: Assoc/PrivFP
FAX Number: (724) 202-6147 Calendar System: Other
URL: www.ncstrades.edu
Established: 1945 Annual Undergrad Tuition & Fees: $12,750
Enrollment: 825 Coed
Affiliation or Control: Proprietary IRS Status: Proprietary
Highest Offering: Associate Degree
Program: Occupational; 2-Year Principally Bachelor's Creditable; Technical Emphasis
Accreditation: ACCSC

01 Director .... Mr. Jim BUTTERMORE
05 Director of Education .... Mr. Tony GIOVANNELLI
07 Director of Admissions .... Mr. Joe BLAZAK
88 Veteran Affairs Director .... Mr. Jim CATHELINE
10 Fiscal Director .... Mrs. JoAnn MELNIK
36 Director Student Placement .... Ms. Carrie KRAYNAK
37 Director Student Financial Aid .... Miss Trudy SOTTER

Northampton Community College (F)

3835 Green Pond Road, Bethlehem PA 18020-7599
County: Northampton FICE Identification: 007191
Unit ID: 214379
Telephone: (610) 861-5300 Carnegie Class: Assoc/Pub-S-MC
FAX Number: (610) 861-5070 Calendar System: Semester
URL: www.northampton.edu
Established: 1966 Annual Undergrad Tuition & Fees (In-District): $3,990
Enrollment: 10,531 Coed
Affiliation or Control: State/Local IRS Status: 170(c)1
Highest Offering: Associate Degree
Program: Occupational; 2-Year Principally Bachelor's Creditable
Accreditation: M, ACBSP, ADNUR, DH, DMS, FUSER, PNUR, RAD

01 President .... Dr. Mark H. ERICKSON
05 Int Vice President Academic Affairs .... Dr. Carolyn BORTZ
11 Vice Pres Administrative Affairs .... Ms. Helene M. WHITAKER
10 Vice President Finance & Operations .... Mr. James F. DUNLEAVY
30 Vice Pres Institutional Advancement .... Ms. Sharon BEALES
32 Vice President Student Affairs .... Dr. Susan SALVADOR
31 Vice President Community Education .... Dr. Paul E. PIERPOINT
12 Dean Monroe Campus .... Dr. Matthew J. CONNELL
79 Dean Humanities & Social Sciences .... Dr. Christine PENSE
53 Dean Education/Academic Success .... Dr. Elizabeth BUGAIGHIS
50 Interim Dean Business & Technology .... Ms. Denise FRANCOIS-SEENY
76 Dean Allied Health & Sciences .... Vacant
13 Dean & Chief Information Officer .... Dr. Deborah BURAK
26 Director Public Info/Community Rels .... Ms. Heidi BUTLER
06 Registrar .... Ms. Kara HOWE
07 Director Admissions .... Mr. James MCCARTHY
37 Director Financial Aid .... Ms. Cynthia L. KING
45 Dir Plng/Assessment/Instl Effective .... Dr. E. Jill HIRT
15 Director of Human Resources .... Ms. Kathy SIEGFRIED
09 Director of Institutional Research .... Ms. Kathy KAPCSOS
18 Director Buildings & Grounds .... Mr. Mark K. CULP
29 Dir Alumni Engagement/Annual Fund .... Ms. Rebecca WALZ
36 Director Career Services .... Ms. Karen VERES
35 Dean of Students .... Ms. Gloria LOPEZ
84 Senior Assoc Dir of Enrollment Svcs .... Ms. Mary S. MANCINO

Northampton Community College Monroe County Branch Campus (G)

205 Old Mill Road, Tannersville PA 18372
Telephone: (570) 620-9221 Identification: 770164
Accreditation: &M

† Branch campus of Northampton Community College, Bethlehem, PA.

Orleans Technical College (H)

2770 Red Lion Road, Philadelphia PA 19114-1014
County: Philadelphia FICE Identification: 021830
Unit ID: 214528
Telephone: (215) 728-4700 Carnegie Class: Assoc/PrivNFP
FAX Number: (215) 745-1689 Calendar System: Semester
URL: www.orleanstech.edu
Established: 1974 Annual Undergrad Tuition & Fees: $13,104
Enrollment: 332 Coed
Affiliation or Control: Independent Non-Profit IRS Status: Exempt
Highest Offering: Associate Degree
Program: Occupational; 2-Year Principally Bachelor's Creditable; Technical Emphasis
Accreditation: ACCSC

01 Campus President .... Ms. Jayne SINIARI
72 Technology Program Director .... Mr. Bruce WARTMAN
05 Director of Academic Affairs .... Ms. Anna BOGDANOV
11 Associate Director .... Mr. William LYNCH
07 Director of Admissions .... Ms. Debbie BELLO
18 Facilities Manager .... Mr. Chris TYSON
36 Director Student Placement .... Ms. Tawana SKIPPER
37 Director Student Financial Aid .... Ms. Latanya BYRD

Palmer Theological Seminary of Eastern University (I)

588 North Gulph Road, King of Prussia PA 19406
County: Montgomery FICE Identification: 003260
Unit ID: 212124
Telephone: (610) 896-5000 Carnegie Class: Not Classified
FAX Number: (610) 649-3834 Calendar System: 4/1/4
URL: www.palmerseminary.edu
Established: 1925 Annual Graduate Tuition & Fees: $24,500
Enrollment: 438 Coed
Affiliation or Control: American Baptist IRS Status: 501(c)3
Highest Offering: Doctorate; No Undergraduates
Program: Professional
Accreditation: THEOL

01 University President .... Dr. Robert G. DUFFETT
05 Int Dean Palmer Seminary .... Dr. R. Keith IDDINGS
10 Chief Operating Officer .... Mr. Anup KAPUR
04 President's Assistant .... Ms. Ruth E. MCFARLAND
20 Associate Dean .... Dr. Colleen DIRADDO
15 Director of Human Resources .... Ms. Kacey BERNARD
29 Director Alumni & Church Relations .... Ms. Mary GARDNER
42 Dir Stdnt Form/Seminary Chaplain .... Rev. Willette A. BURGIE-BRYANT

88 Director D Min Marriage & Family .... Dr. Peter SCHRECK
08 Director University Libraries .... Mr. James SAUER
09 Director of Institutional Research .... Dr. Thomas DAHLSTROM
06 Associate Registrar .... Mr. Craig MILLER
07 Director Admissions .... Ms. Tiffany S. MURPHY
26 Director Communications .... Ms. Kristyn KOMARNICKI
18 Manager Plant Operations .... Vacant
24 Educational Technologist .... Ms. Masego KEBAETSE

† Affiliated with Eastern University, Saint Davids, PA.

Peirce College (A)

1420 Pine Street, Philadelphia PA 19102-4699
County: Philadelphia FICE Identification: 003309
Unit ID: 214883
Telephone: (215) 545-6400 Carnegie Class: Bac/Diverse
FAX Number: (215) 670-9366 Calendar System: Semester
URL: www.peirce.edu
Established: 1865 Annual Undergrad Tuition & Fees: $17,680
Enrollment: 1,833 Coed
Affiliation or Control: Independent Non-Profit IRS Status: 501(c)3
Highest Offering: Master's
Program: Occupational; Business Emphasis
Accreditation: M, ACBSP, CAHIIM

01 President & CEO .... Mr. James J. MERGIOTTI
10 VP Finance/Administration .... Ms. Elizabeth M. KNAPP
05 VP Academic Advancement .... Dr. Rita J. TOLIVER-ROBERTS
30 VP Institutional Advancement .... Ms. Uva C. COLES
26 VP Marketing & Admissions .... Ms. Lisa PARIS
32 VP Student Services .... Mr. Brad K. HODGE
15 VP Human Resources .... Ms. Harriet S. GOLEN
108 Asst VP Institutional Assessment .... Ms. Debra S. SCHRAMMEL
13 Chief Information Officer .... Mr. James T. BURNS
109 Chief Auxiliary Services Officer .... Mr. Vito R. CHIMENTI
20 Assoc Dean Academic Ops/Faculty Sup .... Mr. Jon LENROW
21 Controller .... Vacant

Penn Commercial Business/ Technical School (B)

242 Oak Spring Road, Washington PA 15301-6822
County: Washington FICE Identification: 004902
Unit ID: 214892
Telephone: (724) 222-5330 Carnegie Class: Assoc/PrivFP
FAX Number: (724) 222-4722 Calendar System: Quarter
URL: www.penncommercial.edu
Established: 1929 Annual Undergrad Tuition & Fees: $19,500
Enrollment: 410 Coed
Affiliation or Control: Proprietary IRS Status: Proprietary
Highest Offering: Associate Degree
Program: Occupational; Technical Emphasis
Accreditation: ACICS, #MAC

01 Director .... Mr. Robert S. BAZANT
11 Vice President of Operations .... Ms. Marianne ALBERT
04 Assistant to the President .... Ms. Barbara KENNEDY
07 Director of Admissions .... Mrs. Darlene GIBSON
32 Director of Student Affairs .... Ms. Betty SHINGLE
37 Director of Financial Aid .... Ms. Cyndi GALLOWAY
88 Director of Education .... Mrs. Kristin WISSINGER
05 Director of Academic Affairs .... Ms. Sandy PHILLIPS
09 Dir of Reports & Statistics .... Mrs. Melissa PAPSON
36 Director of Career Services .... Mrs. Kristin WISSINGER

Penn State University Park (C)

201 Old Main, University Park PA 16802-1503
County: Centre FICE Identification: 003329
Unit ID: 214777
Telephone: (814) 865-4700 Carnegie Class: RU/VH
FAX Number: (814) 863-7590 Calendar System: Semester
URL: www.psu.edu
Established: 1855 Annual Undergrad Tuition & Fees (In-State): $17,514
Enrollment: 46,502 Coed
Affiliation or Control: State Related IRS Status: 501(c)3
Highest Offering: Doctorate
Program: Occupational; 2-Year Principally Bachelor's Creditable; Liberal Arts And General; Teacher Preparatory; Professional
Accreditation: M, ADNUR, ART, BUS, CACREP, CEA, CLPSY, COPSY, CORE, DIETD, DIETI, ENG, FEPAC, HSA, IPSY, JOUR, LAW, LSAR, MUS, NURSE, SCPSY, SP, TED, THEA

01 President .... Dr. Eric J. BARRON
05 Executive Vice President & Provost .... Dr. Nicholas P. JONES
46 Vice President Research .... Dr. Neil A. SHARKEY
32 Vice President Student Affairs .... Dr. Damon R. SIMS
26 Vice Pres Strategic Communications .... Mr. Lawrence H. LOKMAN
30 Sr Vice Pres Devel/Alumni Relations .... Mr. Rodney P. KIRSCH
10 Sr Vice Pres Finance & Bus/Treas .... Mr. David J. GRAY
106 VP Outreach/Vice Prov Online Educ .... Dr. Craig D. WEIDEMANN
11 Vice President for Administration .... Dr. Thomas G. POOLE
104 Vice Provost for Global Programs .... Dr. Michael A. ADEWUMI
43 Vice President & General Counsel .... Dr. Stephen S. DUNHAM
49 Vice Pres & Dean Undergrad Educ ...... Dr. Robert N. PANGBORN
20 Vice Provost Academic Affairs .... Dr. Blannie E. BOWEN
28 Interim Vice Provost Educ Equity .... Dr. Marcus A. WHITEHURST
12 Vice Pres Commonwealth Campuses .... Dr. Madlyn L. HANES
13 Vice Provost Information Technology ... Mr. Kevin M. MOROONEY
108 Interim Exec Dir Plng/Inst Assessmt .... Dr. Betty J. HARPER
22 Vice Provost for Affirmative Action . Dr. Kenneth F. LEHRMAN, III
45 University Budget Officer .... Ms. Rachel E. SMITH
21 Assoc Vice Pres Finance/Corp Cont ..... Mr. Joseph J. DONCSECZ
21 Assoc Vice Pres Finance/Business .... Mr. Daniel W. SIEMINSKI
15 Vice President Human Resources .... Ms. Susan M. BASSO
18 Assoc Vice President Physical Plant .... Mr. H. Ford STRYKER
21 Assoc Vice Pres Aux & Business Svcs .... Ms. Gail A. HURLEY
106 Associate Vice Prov Online Programs .... Dr. Renata S. ENGEL
27 Director News/Media Relations .... Ms. Lisa M. POWERS
39 Asst Vice President HFS & Res Life .... Ms. Diane L. ANDREWS
37 Asst VP UG Ed/Exec Dir Stdnt Aid .... Ms. Anna M. GRISWOLD
29 Assoc VP/Exec Dir Alumni Assoc .... Vacant
21 Exec Director Investment Management .... Mr. David E. BRANIGAN
07 Exec Director Undergrad Admissions .... Mr. Clark V. BRIGGER
38 Sr Director Counseling/Psych Svcs ..... Dr. Dennis E. HEITZMANN
41 Athletic Director .... Dr. A. Sandy BARBOUR
86 Vice President for Govt Affairs .... Mr. Michael J. DIRAIMO
06 University Registrar .... Mr. Robert A. KUBAT
36 Senior Director Career Services .... Dr. Robert M. ORNDORFF
17 Sr Vice Pres Hlth Affs/CEO & Dean ...... Dr. A. Craig HILLEMEIER
08 Dean Univ Libraries/Scholar Comm .... Ms. Barbara I. DEWEY
47 Dean Agricultural Sciences .... Dr. Richard T. ROUSH
48 Dean Arts & Architecture .... Dr. Barbara O. KORNER
50 Dean Business .... Dr. Charles H. WHITEMAN
60 Dean Communications .... Dr. Marie HARDIN
65 Dean Earth & Mineral Sciences .. Dr. William E. EASTERLING, III
53 Dean Education .... Dr. David H. MONK
54 Dean Engineering .... Dr. Amr S. ELNASHAI
58 V Prov Grad Educ/Dean Grad School .... Dr. Regina VASILATOS-YOUNKEN
76 Dean Health & Human Development .... Dr. Ann C. CROUTER
66 Dean School of Nursing .... Dr. Paula F. MILONE-NUZZO
56 Assoc Dean Dir Cooperative Exten .... Dr. Dennis D. CALVIN
83 Dean Liberal Arts .... Dr. Susan WELCH
81 Dean Science .... Dr. Douglas R. CAVENER
72 Dean Info Sciences/Technology .... Dr. Andrew L. SEARS
92 Dean Honors College .... Dr. Christian M. BRADY
61 Interim Dean School of Law .... Dr. James W. HOUCK
63 Dean College of Medicine .... Dr. A. Craig HILLEMEIER
75 Chief Penn College of Technology .... Dr. Davie J. GILMOUR
44 Executive Director Annual Giving .... Ms. Ann LEHMAN
25 Assoc Vice President for Research .... Dr. John W. HANOLD
19 Actg Vice Pres Police/Public Safety .... Mr. Tyrone A. PARHAM
23 Director University Health Services .... Vacant
96 Director Procurement Services .... Ms. Joyce A. HANEY
31 Director Campus & Comm Affairs .... Ms. Barbara ETTARO
102 Exec Dir Corp/Foundation Relations .... Mr. Mark S. ARMAGOST
04 Exec Admin Assistant to President .... Ms. Carmella MULROY-DEGENHART
40 General Manager Bookstore .... Mr. Steve J. FALKE
25 Contract Coordinator .... Ms. Cristene N. BOOB
16 Senior Director Employee Relations .... Mr. Robert L. MANEY
21 Director of Internal Audit .... Mr. Daniel P. HEIST

† The legal name of Penn State and all its campuses is The Pennsylvania State University. For communication purposes, the name is shortened to Penn State followed by the name of the campus.

Penn State Abington (D)

1600 Woodland Road, Abington PA 19001-3918
Telephone: (215) 881-7300 FICE Identification: 003342
Accreditation: &M

† Regional accreditation is carried under the parent institution in University Park, PA.

Penn State Altoona (E)

3000 Ivyside Park, Altoona PA 16601-3777
Telephone: (814) 949-5000 FICE Identification: 003331
Accreditation: &M, ENGT

† Regional accreditation is carried under the parent institution in University Park, PA.

Penn State Beaver (F)

100 University Drive, Monaca PA 15061-2764
Telephone: (724) 773-3800 FICE Identification: 003332
Accreditation: &M

† Regional accreditation is carried under the parent institution in University Park, PA.

Penn State Berks (G)

Tulpehocken Road, PO Box 7009, Reading PA 19610-6009
Telephone: (610) 396-6000 FICE Identification: 003334
Accreditation: &M, ENGT, OTA

† Regional accreditation is carried under the parent institution in University Park, PA.

Penn State Brandywine (H)

25 Yearsley Mill Road, Media PA 19063-5522
Telephone: (610) 892-1200 FICE Identification: 006922
Accreditation: &M

† Regional accreditation is carried under the parent institution in University Park, PA.

Penn State DuBois (I)

One College Place, DuBois PA 15801-2549
Telephone: (814) 375-4700 FICE Identification: 003335
Accreditation: &M, ENGT, OTA, @PTAA

† Regional accreditation is carried under the parent institution in University Park, PA.

Penn State Erie, The Behrend College (J)

4701 College Drive, Erie PA 16563-0001
Telephone: (814) 898-6000 FICE Identification: 003333
Accreditation: &M, BUS, ENG, ENGT

† Regional accreditation is carried under the parent institution in University Park, PA.

Penn State Fayette, The Eberly Campus (K)

2201 University Drive, Lemont Furnace PA 15456-1025
Telephone: (724) 430-4100 FICE Identification: 003336
Accreditation: &M, ENGT, PTAA

† Regional accreditation is carried under the parent institution in University Park, PA.

Penn State Great Valley School of Graduate Professional Studies (L)

30 E Swedesford Road, Malvern PA 19355-1488
Telephone: (610) 648-3200 FICE Identification: 003348
Accreditation: &M, BUS

† Regional accreditation is carried under the parent institution in University Park, PA.

Penn State Greater Allegheny (M)

4000 University Drive, McKeesport PA 15132-7644
Telephone: (412) 675-9000 FICE Identification: 003339
Accreditation: &M

† Regional accreditation is carried under the parent institution in University Park, PA.

Penn State Harrisburg (N)

777 West Harrisburg Pike, Middletown PA 17057-4846
Telephone: (717) 948-6250 FICE Identification: 006814
Accreditation: &M, BUS, ENG, ENGT, SPAA, TED

† Regional accreditation is carried under the parent institution in University Park, PA.

Penn State Hazleton (O)

76 University Drive, Hazleton PA 18202-8025
Telephone: (570) 450-3000 FICE Identification: 003338
Accreditation: &M, MLTAD, PTAA

† Regional accreditation is carried under the parent institution in University Park, PA.

Penn State Lehigh Valley (P)

2809 Saucon Valley Road, Center Valley PA 18034-8447
Telephone: (610) 285-5000 FICE Identification: 003330
Accreditation: &M

† Regional accreditation is carried under the parent institution in University Park, PA.

Penn State Milton S. Hershey Medical Center College of Medicine (Q)

500 University Drive, Hershey PA 17033-2360
Telephone: (717) 531-8563 FICE Identification: 006813
Accreditation: &M, #ARCPA, IPSY, MED, PAST, PH

† Regional accreditation is carried under the parent institution in University Park, PA.

Penn State Mont Alto (R)

One Campus Drive, Mont Alto PA 17237-9700
Telephone: (717) 749-6000 FICE Identification: 003340
Accreditation: &M, OTA, PTAA

† Regional accreditation is carried under the parent institution in University Park, PA.

Penn State New Kensington (S)

3550 Seventh Street Road, New Kensington PA 15068-1765
Telephone: (724) 334-5466 FICE Identification: 003341
Accreditation: &M, ENGT, RAD

† Regional accreditation is carried under the parent institution in University Park, PA.

Penn State Schuylkill (A)

200 University Drive, Schuylkill Haven PA 17972-2202
Telephone: (570) 385-6000 FICE Identification: 003343
Accreditation: &M, RAD

† Regional accreditation is carried under the parent institution in University Park, PA.

Penn State Shenango (B)

147 Shenango Avenue, Sharon PA 16146-1537
Telephone: (724) 983-2803 FICE Identification: 003345
Accreditation: &M, OTA, PTAA

† Regional accreditation is carried under the parent institution in University Park, PA.

Penn State Wilkes-Barre (C)

Old Route 115, PO Box PSU, Lehman PA 18627-0217
Telephone: (570) 675-2171 FICE Identification: 003346
Accreditation: &M, ENG, ENGT

† Regional accreditation is carried under the parent institution in University Park, PA.

Penn State Worthington-Scranton (D)

120 Ridge View Drive, Dunmore PA 18512-1602
Telephone: (570) 963-2500 FICE Identification: 003344
Accreditation: &M

† Regional accreditation is carried under the parent institution in University Park, PA.

Penn State York (E)

1031 Edgecomb Avenue, York PA 17403-3326
Telephone: (717) 771-4000 FICE Identification: 003347
Accreditation: &M, ENGT

† Regional accreditation is carried under the parent institution in University Park, PA.

Pennco Tech (F)

3815 Otter Street, Bristol PA 19007-3696
County: Bucks FICE Identification: 009449
Unit ID: 214944
Telephone: (215) 785-0111 Carnegie Class: Assoc/PrivFP
FAX Number: (215) 785-1945 Calendar System: Other
URL: www.penncotech.edu
Established: 1973 Annual Undergrad Tuition & Fees: $21,095
Enrollment: 500 Coed
Affiliation or Control: Proprietary IRS Status: Proprietary
Highest Offering: Associate Degree
Program: Occupational; Technical Emphasis
Accreditation: ACCSC

01 CEO .... Michael S. HOBYAK
03 School Director .... Scott SIMPSON
05 Director of Education .... Steve CAIMI
07 Director of Admissions .... Dave TRIMBLE
06 Registrar .... Sondra KOOB
32 Director Student Services .... Hakien COLES
37 Director Student Financial Aid .... Keena FITZHUGH
36 Director Student Placement .... Teresa SCHEERER

Pennsylvania Academy of the Fine Arts (G)

128 N Broad St, Philadelphia PA 19102-1424
County: Philadelphia FICE Identification: 021073
Unit ID: 214971
Telephone: (215) 972-7600 Carnegie Class: Spec/Arts
FAX Number: (215) 569-0153 Calendar System: Semester
URL: www.pafa.edu
Established: 1805 Annual Undergrad Tuition & Fees: $32,960
Enrollment: 292 Coed
Affiliation or Control: Independent Non-Profit IRS Status: 501(c)3
Highest Offering: Master's
Program: Liberal Arts And General; Professional; Fine Arts Emphasis
Accreditation: M, ART

01 President & CEO .... Dr. David R. BRIGHAM
30 Exec Vice President Development .... Ms. Melissa D. KAISER
26 Exec Vice President of Marketing .... Ms. Heike RASS
10 Chief Financial Officer .... Mr. Anthony DECOCINIS
84 Dean of Enrollment .... Mr. André S F. VAN DE PUTTE
57 Dean of the School of Fine Arts .... Mr. Clint A. JUKKALA
32 Dean of Students .... Ms. Anne K. STASSEN
37 Director of Financial Aid .... Ms. Dana MOORE
36 Director of Career Services .... Mr. Gregory MARTINO
08 Director of Library Services .... Mr. Brian DUFFY
06 Registrar .... Mr. Peter MEDWICK
18 Director of Facilities Management .... Mr. Ed POLETTI
19 Director of Security and Safety .... Mr. Jimmie GREENO
13 Director of Information Technology .... Mr. Kevin MARTIN
05 Director of Academic Affairs .... Mr. Nathanael T. BROUHARD
04 Exec Assistant to President and CEO .... Ms. Sheryl KESSLER

Pennsylvania College of Art & Design (H)

204 N Prince Street, Box 59, Lancaster PA 17608-0059
County: Lancaster FICE Identification: 022699
Unit ID: 215053
Telephone: (717) 396-7833 Carnegie Class: Spec/Arts
FAX Number: (717) 396-1339 Calendar System: Semester
URL: www.pcad.edu
Established: 1982 Annual Undergrad Tuition & Fees: $22,800
Enrollment: 200 Coed
Affiliation or Control: Independent Non-Profit IRS Status: 501(c)3
Highest Offering: Baccalaureate
Program: Professional; Fine Arts Emphasis
Accreditation: M, ART

01 President .... Ms. Mary Colleen HEIL
05 Academic Dean .... Mr. Marc TORICK
32 Dean of Student Services .... Ms. Jessica EDONICK
26 Director of Communications .... Ms. Kathleen TROY SMYSER
10 VP for Finance & Operations .... Ms. Patricia ERNST
07 Dir of Admiss/Mktg & Recruitment .... Ms. Natalie LASCEK-SPEAKMAN
84 Director of Enrollment Planning .... Ms. Barbara ELLIOTT
37 Director Financial Aid .... Mr. J. David HERSHEY
08 Library Director .... Ms. Karen HUTCHISON
30 Director of Development .... Ms. Megan GALLAGHER
51 Director of Continuing Education .... Mr. Nick MOHLER
18 Director of Facilities .... Mr. Dan FREILER
06 Registrar .... Vacant
13 Director of Information Technology .... Mr. Derrick GUTIERREZ

Pennsylvania College of Health Sciences (I)

410 N Lime Street, Lancaster PA 17602-2337
County: Lancaster FICE Identification: 009863
Unit ID: 442356
Telephone: (717) 544-4912 Carnegie Class: Assoc/PrivNFP
FAX Number: (717) 544-5970 Calendar System: Semester
URL: www.pacollege.edu
Established: 1903 Annual Undergrad Tuition & Fees: $15,960
Enrollment: 1,447 Coed
Affiliation or Control: Independent Non-Profit IRS Status: 501(c)3
Highest Offering: Master's
Program: 2-Year Principally Bachelor's Creditable; Nursing Emphasis
Accreditation: M, ADNUR, COARC, CVT, DMS, EMT, MT, NMT, NURSE, RAD, SURGT

01 President .... Dr. Mary Grace SIMCOX
05 Vice Pres of Academic Affairs .... Dr. Penni LONGENECKER
10 Vice President of Finance & Admin .... Mr. Thomas HULSTINE
30 Vice President of Advancement .... Ms. Ellen WILEY
84 VP of Strategic Enrollment Mgmt .... Ms. Anne HAMILL

Pennsylvania College of Technology (J)

One College Avenue, Williamsport PA 17701-5799
County: Lycoming FICE Identification: 003395
Unit ID: 366252
Telephone: (570) 326-3761 Carnegie Class: Bac/Assoc
FAX Number: (570) 327-4503 Calendar System: Semester
URL: www.pct.edu
Established: 1941 Annual Undergrad Tuition & Fees (In-State): $15,810
Enrollment: 5,623 Coed
Affiliation or Control: State IRS Status: 501(c)3
Highest Offering: Baccalaureate
Program: Occupational; 2-Year Principally Bachelor's Creditable; Technical Emphasis
Accreditation: M, ACBSP, ACFEI, ADNUR, ARCPA, CAHIIM, CONST, CSHSE, DH, EMT, ENGT, NAIT, NUR, OTA, PNUR, RAD, SURGT

01 President .... Dr. Davie Jane GILMOUR
05 VP for Academic Affairs/Provost .... Dr. Paul L. STARKEY
108 VP Assessment/Research/Planning .... Vacant
10 VP for Finance/CFO .... Ms. Suzanne T. STOPPER
30 Vice Pres Institutional Advancement .... Ms. Debra M. MILLER
13 Vice Pres for Info Tech/CIO .... Mr. Michael M. CUNNINGHAM
22 VP Human Resources/Employees/EEO .... Vacant
15 VP for College Services .... Mr. R. David KAY
84 VP Enrollment Mgmt & Assoc Provost .... Ms. Carolyn R. STRICKLAND
20 Director for Academic Services .... Ms. Wendy A. MILLER
20 Associate VP for Instruction .... Mr. Tom F. GREGORY
04 Administrative Asst to President .... Mrs. Valerie A. BAIER
32 Chief Student Affairs Officer .... Mr. Elliott STRICKLAND, JR.
103 VP for Workforce Development .... Dr. Tracy L. BRUNDAGE
76 Dean of Health Sciences .... Dr. Edward A. HENNINGER
88 Dean Construction & Design Tech .... Mr. Marc E. BRIDGENS
54 Dean Industrial/Comp/Engineering .... Mr. Dave R. COTNER
81 Dean of Sciences/Human/Visual Comm .... Dr. Michael J. REED
88 Dean Transportation/Natl Resources .... Mr. Brett A. REASNER
50 Dean of Business/Hospitality .... Dr. Gerri F. LUKE
37 Assoc Dean of Admissions & Fin Aid .... Mr. Dennis L. CORRELL
102 Exec Dir of Penn College Foundation .... Mr. Robert C. DIETRICH
08 Director of the Madigan Library .... Ms. Tracey AMEY
56 Director Instructional Technology .... Mr. Walter J. SHULTZ, JR.
18 Director of Facilities Operations .... Mr. Don J. LUKE
09 Exec Dir Assessment/Research/Plng .... Mr. Brian L. CYGAN
06 Registrar .... Mr. Dennis L. DUNKLEBERGER
38 Director of Advisement Center .... Vacant
36 Dir Counsel/Career & Disability Svc .... Dr. Jennifer MCLEAN
39 Dir Residence Life/Judicial Affairs .... Mr. Jon D. WESCOTT
19 Chief of Police .... Mr. Chris E. MILLER
26 VP Public Relations & Marketing .... Mr. Joseph S. YODER
35 Director Student Activities .... Mrs. Kimberly R. CASSEL
29 Director Alumni Relations .... Dr. Tammy M. RICH
44 Director of Corporate Relations .... Ms. Elizabeth A. BIDDLE
88 Director Children Learning Center .... Ms. Barbara J. ALBERT
40 Director of College Store .... Mr. Matthew P. BRANCA
41 Director of Athletics .... Mr. Scott E. KENNELL
90 Director Network Services .... Mr. Mike E. RAE
91 Director Administrative Info Sys .... Mr. Randall L. MONROE
23 Director College Health Services .... Mr. Carl L. SHANER
28 Assoc Dir Student Act/Diversity .... Ms. Sara H. OUSBY
88 Coordinator of Disability Services .... Ms. Kay E. DUNKLEBERGER
85 International Programs Specialist .... Ms. Shanin L. DOUGHERTY
96 Director/Procurement Services .... Ms. Karen P. FESSLER
07 Director of Admissions .... Mr. Joseph J. BALDUINO
89 Dean Acad Svcs/First Year Programs .... Mr. Paul R. WATSON, II

† Affiliate of Pennsylvania State University.

Pennsylvania Highlands Community College (K)

101 Community College Way, Johnstown PA 15904-2949
County: Cambria FICE Identification: 031804
Unit ID: 414911
Telephone: (814) 262-6400 Carnegie Class: Assoc/Pub-R-M
FAX Number: (814) 269-9700 Calendar System: Semester
URL: www.pennhighlands.edu
Established: 1994 Annual Undergrad Tuition & Fees (In-District): $4,536
Enrollment: 2,493 Coed
Affiliation or Control: State/Local IRS Status: 501(c)3
Highest Offering: Associate Degree
Program: Occupational; 2-Year Principally Bachelor's Creditable
Accreditation: M

01 President .... Dr. Walter J. ASONEVICH
05 VP Academic Affairs/Student Svcs .... Dr. Edward NICHOLS
10 Vice Pres Finance & Admin Services .... Lorraine DONAHUE
102 AVP for External Relations .... Trish CORLE
20 Dean of Faculty .... Erica REIGHARD
84 Dean Enrollment Services/Registrar .... Michelle STUMPF
08 Assoc Dean for Learning Resources .... Dr. Barbara ZABOROWSKI
09 Assoc Dean Inst Research/Assessment .... Gary BOAST
88 Assoc Dean Curriculum/Adult Educca .... Cynthia MCCABE
103 Assoc Dean Career Svcs/Workforce Ed .... Larry BRUGH
07 Director of Admissions .... Jeffrey MAUL
15 Director of Human Resources .... April RENZI
21 Director of Finance/Admin Services .... Christopher PRIBULSKY
37 Director Student Financial Aid .... Brenda COUGHENOUR
26 Director of Marketing .... Raymond WEIBLE, JR.
32 Director of Student Activities .... Suzanne BRUGH
18 Director of Facilities Operation .... Reb BROWNLEE
13 Director of IT .... Danielle GERKO
19 Director of Security & Safety .... Cregg DIBERT
04 Exec Asst to the President's Office .... Michelle MAKSYMIK

Pennsylvania Institute of Health and Technology (L)

PO Box 278, Mount Braddock PA 15465-0278
Telephone: (724) 437-4600 Identification: 666035
Accreditation: ACICS

† Branch campus of West Virginia Junior College, Morgantown, WV.

Pennsylvania Institute of Technology (M)

800 Manchester Avenue, Media PA 19063-4098
County: Delaware FICE Identification: 010998
Unit ID: 214582
Telephone: (610) 892-1500 Carnegie Class: Assoc/PrivNFP
FAX Number: (610) 892-1510 Calendar System: Semester
URL: www.pit.edu
Established: 1953 Annual Undergrad Tuition & Fees: $12,750
Enrollment: 661 Coed
Affiliation or Control: Independent Non-Profit IRS Status: 501(c)3
Highest Offering: Associate Degree
Program: Occupational; 2-Year Principally Bachelor's Creditable; Technical Emphasis
Accreditation: M, PTAA

01 President .... Mr. Walter R. GARRISON
11 Chief Operating Officer .... Ms. Jayne B. GARRISON
05 Dean of Academic Affairs .... Dr. Robert E. HANCOX
32 Dean Student Services .... Dr. Dona M. FABRIZIO
20 Asst Dean of Academic Affairs .... Ms. Rachelle CHAYKIN
13 Chief Information Officer .... Mr. Jack BACON
10 Chief Financial Officer .... Ms. Annamarie CASSIDY
06 Dir of Inst Research/Registrar .... Mr. Craig M. JACOBS
08 Director of the Library .... Ms. Lynea ANDERMAN
18 Director of Facilities .... Mr. Frederick FIVECOAT
36 Dir Career Placement/Transfer .... Ms. Heather DI LALLA
37 Financial Aid Director .... Ms. Laura BLOMGREN
84 Director Enrollment Management .... Mr. Jack BACON

*Pennsylvania State System of Higher Education, Office of the Chancellor (A)

Dixon University Ctr, 2986 N 2nd St,
Harrisburg PA 17110-1201
County: Dauphin FICE Identification: 029371
Unit ID: 214661
Telephone: (717) 720-4000 Carnegie Class: N/A
FAX Number: (717) 720-4011
URL: www.passhe.edu

01 Chancellor .... Mr. Frank T. BROGAN
03 Executive Vice Chancellor .... Dr. Peter H. GARLAND
10 Vice Chancellor Admin/Finance .... Mr. James S. DILLON
21 Assoc Vice Chancellor Admin/Finance .... Ms. Lois M. JOHNSON
18 Asst Vice Chancellor Facilities .... Mr. Steven DUPES
05 Sr Assoc Vice Chanc A/S Affairs .... Dr. Kathleen HOWLEY
43 Chief Legal Counsel .... Mr. Andrew LEHMAN
100 Chief of Staff .... Mr. Randy GOIN, JR.

*Bloomsburg University of Pennsylvania (B)

400 E Second Street, Bloomsburg PA 17815-1399
County: Columbia FICE Identification: 003315
Unit ID: 211158
Telephone: (570) 389-4000 Carnegie Class: Master's L
FAX Number: (570) 389-3700 Calendar System: Semester
URL: www.bloomu.edu
Established: 1839 Annual Undergrad Tuition & Fees (In-State): $9,326
Enrollment: 9,998 Coed
Affiliation or Control: State IRS Status: 501(c)3
Highest Offering: Doctorate
Program: Liberal Arts And General; Teacher Preparatory; Professional
Accreditation: M, ANEST, ART, AUD, BUS, CAATE, CS, ENGT, EXSC, MUS, NURSE, SP, SW, TED, THEA

02 President .... Dr. David L. SOLTZ
05 Sr VP/Provost Academic Affairs .... Dr. Ira BLAKE
10 Vice Pres Finance/Administration .... Mr. John F. LOONAN
32 Vice Pres Student Affairs .... Dr. Dionne D. SOMERVILLE
30 Vice Pres University Advancement .... Mr. Erik EVANS
84 VP Strategic Enrol Mgt/Dean Ext Pgm .... Mr. Thomas FLETCHER
22 Deputy to Pres for Equity .... Dr. Robert WISLOCK
04 Exec Asst to the President .... Ms. Brenda CROMLEY
58 Assoc VP/Dean Grad Studies .... Dr. Robert GATES
13 Assoc VP Technology & Library Serv .... Mr. Wayne C. MOHR
18 Asst VP for Facilities Management .... Mr. Eric NESS
21 Asst VP Finance/Budget & Bus Svcs .... Ms. Claudia THRUSH
35 Asst VP Student Affairs .... Mr. Thomas KRESCH
26 Asst VP External Relations .... Mr. Jim HOLLISTER
27 AVP Marketing/Communications .... Ms. Rosalee RUSH
29 AVP Alumni/Professional Engagement .... Ms. Lynda MICHAELS
49 Dean College of Liberal Arts .... Dr. James BROWN
50 Dean College of Business .... Dr. Jeffrey KRUG
81 Dean College of Science/Tech .... Dr. Robert S. ARONSTAM
53 Dean College of Education .... Dr. Elizabeth MAUCH
88 Assoc Dean Acad Achievement .... Vacant
15 Director Human Resources/Labor Rel .... Mr. Jerry REED
46 Interim Dir Research/Sponsored Pgms .... Dr. John M. HRANITZ
06 Registrar .... Mr. Joseph KISSELL
07 Interim Director of Admissions .... Mr. Christopher LAPOS
36 Director Career Development .... Mr. Christopher KELLER
38 Director of Counsel & Human Devel .... Dr. William R. HARRAR
37 Interim Director Financial Aid .... Ms. Amanda KISHBAUGH
90 Manager Technology Support Services .... Mr. David S. CELLI
40 Manager University Store .... Ms. Nancy KELLER
41 Director of Athletics .... Mr. Michael S. MCFARLAND
85 Director International Educ Svcs .... Dr. Madhav P. SHARMA
42 Director Protestant Campus Ministry .... Rev. Jill YOUNG
42 Director Catholic Campus Ministry .... Fr. David HERESHKO
19 Dir Univ Safety & Police .... Mr. Tom PHILLIPS
92 Director University Honors Program .... Dr. Stephen KOKOSKA
96 Director of Purchasing & Operations .... Mr. Jeffrey MANDEL
08 Director Library Services .... Ms. Charlotte DROLL
91 Dir Applications Develop/Operations .... Mr. James C. GESSNER
09 Director of Institutional Research .... Ms. Karen L. SLUSSER
108 AVP Planning & Assessment .... Dr. Sheila Dove JONES
104 Director Global & Multicultural Ed .... Vacant
102 Exec Dir BU Foundation .... Mr. Jerome DVORAK

*California University of Pennsylvania (C)

250 University Avenue, California PA 15419-1394
County: Washington FICE Identification: 003316
Unit ID: 211361
Telephone: (724) 938-4000 Carnegie Class: Master's L
FAX Number: (724) 938-4138 Calendar System: Semester
URL: www.calu.edu
Established: 1852 Annual Undergrad Tuition & Fees (In-State): $9,556
Enrollment: 7,978 Coed
Affiliation or Control: State IRS Status: 501(c)3
Highest Offering: Master's
Program: 2-Year Principally Bachelor's Creditable; Liberal Arts And General; Teacher Preparatory; Professional
Accreditation: M, ART, CAATE, CACREP, CS, ENGT, NAIT, NRPA, NURSE, PTAA, SP, SW, TED, THEA

02 Acting President .... Ms. Geraldine JONES
05 Provost/Vice Pres Academic Affairs .... Dr. Bruce BARNHART
10 Interim VP Administration & Finance .... Mr. Robert THORN
09 Director Institutional Research .... Dr. Wei ZHOU
58 Dean of Graduate Studies .... Dr. Stan KOMACEK
20 Assoc Provost/Student Retent Ofcr .... Dr. Dan M. ENGSTROM
30 Assoc Vice Pres for Development .... Mr. Mitch KOZIKOWSKI
72 Actg Dean of Science/Technology .... Dr. John A. KALLIS
49 Interim Dean of Liberal Arts .... Dr. Mohamed YAMBA
53 Act Dean Col Education/Human Svcs .... Dr. Kevin A. KOURY
62 Dean of Library Services .... Mr. Douglas HOOVER
07 Dean of Admissions .... Dr. William A. EDMONDS
37 Director of Financial Aid .... Mrs. Jill FERNANDES
37 Sr Assoc Director of Financial Aid .... Mr. Jeff DERUBBO
06 Registrar .... Ms. Heidi WILLIAMS
36 Director of Career Services .... Ms. Rhonda GIFFORD
92 Director Honors Program .... Mr. Mark AUNE
29 Director of Alumni Relations .... Ms. Leslie FLEENOR
44 Director of Planned Giving .... Mr. Gordon CORE
38 Assoc VP Student Development & Svcs .... Dr. Timothy SUSICK
13 Assoc VP for University Technology .... Mr. Brian KRAUS
39 Director of University Housing .... Ms. Jackie THORN
94 Director Women's Studies .... Dr. Marta MCCLINTOCK
85 International Student Advisor .... Mr. John WATKINS
41 Athletic Director .... Dr. Karen HJERPE
15 Interim Director of Personnel .... Mr. Eric GUISER
22 Director of Social Equity .... Dr. John BURNETT
19 Chief of Police .... Mr. Ed MCSHEFFERY
18 Director of Physical Plant .... Mr. Michael PEPLINSKI
26 Director of Communications & PR .... Mrs. Christine KINDL
27 Director of Publications .... Mr. Greg SOFRANKO
40 Book Store Manager .... Mr. Greg KARAFA
96 Director of Purchasing .... Ms. Joyce SHEPPICK

*Cheyney University of Pennsylvania (D)

1837 University Circle PO Box 200,
Cheyney PA 19319-0200
County: Delaware FICE Identification: 003317
Unit ID: 211608
Telephone: (610) 399-2000 Carnegie Class: Master's S
FAX Number: (610) 399-2415 Calendar System: Semester
URL: www.cheyney.edu
Established: 1837 Annual Undergrad Tuition & Fees (In-State): $9,344
Enrollment: 1,022 Coed
Affiliation or Control: State IRS Status: 501(c)3
Highest Offering: Master's
Program: Liberal Arts And General
Accreditation: M

02 Interim President .... Dr. Frank POGUE
100 Chief of Staff/Deputy to President .... Ms. Sheilah VANCE
05 Provost/VP Academic Affairs .... Dr. Phyllis DAWKINS
10 Vice Pres Finance & Administration .... Mr. Al SKUDZINSKAS
30 Int Vice Pres Inst Advancement .... Dr. John L. GRAHAM
32 Int VP Student Affairs/Student Life .... Dr. J. Michael HARPE
84 Assoc VP Enrollment Management .... Dr. Deborah BOWLES
25 Asst Vice Pres Sponsored Programs .... Mr. Lawrence GREEN
21 Asst VP of Finance/Controller .... Ms. Layna HOLMES-BUTLER
49 Dean of Faculty & Academic Schools .... Dr. Donna PARKER
38 Chairperson Guidance & Counseling .... Ms. Jolly RAMAKRISHNAN
06 Registrar .... Ms. Brenda SHIELDS
37 Director Financial Aid .... Ms. Shaunda LANE SAMPSON
13 Director of Technology .... Mr. Rich HUG
09 Director Institutional Research .... Dr. Sesime ADANU
15 Director Human Resources .... Ms. Jo-Anne HARRIS
18 Facilities Manager .... Mr. Charlie BERKHEIMER
19 Director Public Safety .... Mr. Lawrence RICHARDS
36 Director Career Services .... Vacant
41 Athletic Director .... Mr. Ruffin BELL
17 College Physician .... Dr. Pamela HADLEY
43 University Legal Counsel .... Ms. Jacqualine BARNETT
35 Director Student Affairs .... Ms. Sharon THORN
25 Contract Compliance Officer .... Mr. Michael FLANAGAN
29 Director Alumni Relations .... Mr. Gregory BENJAMIN
39 Manager Housing Ops/Auxiliary Svcs .... Ms. Elizabeth BURTON
103 Dir Economic/Workforce Devel .... Ms. Sharon CANNON
24 Director Telecommunications .... Mr. Phil PAGLIARO
88 Bursar .... Ms. Lauronda FLETCHER
92 Dean of Keystone Honors Academy .... Dr. Tara KENT

*Clarion University of Pennsylvania (E)

840 Wood Street, Clarion PA 16214-1232
County: Clarion FICE Identification: 003318
Unit ID: 211644
Telephone: (814) 393-2000 Carnegie Class: Master's L
FAX Number: (814) 393-1826 Calendar System: Semester
URL: www.clarion.edu
Established: 1867 Annual Undergrad Tuition & Fees (In-State): $9,912
Enrollment: 5,712 Coed
Affiliation or Control: State IRS Status: 501(c)3
Highest Offering: Master's
Program: 2-Year Principally Bachelor's Creditable; Liberal Arts And General; Teacher Preparatory; Professional
Accreditation: M, ART, BUS, CORE, CSHSE, LIB, NUR, SP, TED

02 President .... Dr. Karen M. WHITNEY
05 Provost/Academic Vice President .... Dr. Ronald NOWACZYK
32 Vice Pres Student & University Affs .... Dr. Susanne FENSKE
10 Vice Pres Finance/Administration .... Mr. Len CULLO
102 Chief Exec Officer Foundation .... Mr. Michael R. KEEFER
30 Vice President Univ Advancement .... Mr. James GEIGER
21 Assoc VP for Finance/Administration .... Mr. Timothy P. FOGARTY
22 Asst to President for Social Equity .... Dr. Jocelind E. GANT
12 Executive Dean Venango College .... Dr. Roxanne GONZALES
84 Dean of Enrollment Management .... Dr. David BEHRS
08 Dean of Libraries .... Dr. Terry S. LATOUR
49 Dean of Arts & Sciences .... Dr. Todd PFANNESTIEL
50 Dean of Business Administration .... Dr. Philip FRESE
76 Director School of Health Sciences .... Dr. Susan MULLER
09 Director Info Mgmt & Inst Research .... Vacant
06 Registrar .... Ms. Lisa L. HEPLER
21 Comptroller .... Ms. Tamara B. VARSEK
13 Assoc VP for Information Technology .... Mr. Samuel T. PULEIO
46 Director Faculty Research .... Ms. Kristen GEIGER
26 Dir of Marketing & Communications .... Mr. David LOVE
37 Director of Student Financial Svs .... Ms. Ragan GRIFFIN
18 Director of Facilities Mgmt & Plng .... Vacant
29 Director of Alumni Relations .... Ms. Laura C. KING
36 Director Career Services .... Mr. William BAILEY
39 Director of Residence Life .... Ms. Michelle L. KEALEY
19 Director of Public Safety .... Mr. Jason HENDERSHOT
41 Athletic Director .... Mr. David J. KATIS
96 Director of Purchasing .... Mr. Rein A. POLD

*East Stroudsburg University of Pennsylvania (F)

200 Prospect Street, East Stroudsburg PA 18301-2999
County: Monroe FICE Identification: 003320
Unit ID: 212115
Telephone: (570) 422-3211 Carnegie Class: Master's L
FAX Number: (570) 422-3777 Calendar System: Semester
URL: www.esu.edu
Established: 1893 Annual Undergrad Tuition & Fees (In-State): $9,684
Enrollment: 6,485 Coed
Affiliation or Control: State IRS Status: 501(c)3
Highest Offering: Master's
Program: Liberal Arts And General; Teacher Preparatory; Professional
Accreditation: M, CAATE, CS, EXSC, NRPA, NUR, PH, SP, SW, TED

02 President .... Dr. Marcia G. WELSH
05 Provost & Vice Pres Academic Affair .... Ms. Joanne Z. BRUNO
32 Vice President Student Affairs .... Dr. Doreen TOBIN
10 Vice Pres Administration & Finance .... Mr. Kenneth A. LONG
46 Vice Pres Research & Econ Dev .. Ms. Mary Frances POSTUPACK
84 Vice Pres Enrollment Management .... Mr. David BOUSQUET
58 Dean of Graduate College .... Vacant
49 Dean of Arts & Sciences .... Dr. Peter HAWKES
76 Dean of Health Sciences .... Dr. Alberto CARDELLE
53 Interim Dean of Education .... Dr. Terry BARRY
50 Dean of Business & Management .... Vacant
08 Dean of Library & Univ Collections .... Vacant
20 Assoc Provost & Dean Univ College .... Dr. Thomas TAUER
35 Asst Vice President Student Affairs .... Mr. Michael SACHS
100 Chief of Staff .... Mr. Miguel BARBOSA
88 Asst Vice Pres Instruct Supp & Outr .... Mr. Michael SOUTHWELL
07 Director of Admissions .... Mr. Jeff JONES
06 Registrar/Dir Enrollment Services .... Ms. Kizzy MORRIS
37 Sr Assoc Dir Financial Aid .... Ms. Phyllis SWINSON
36 Director of Career Services .... Ms. Daria WIELEBINSKI
38 Director Counseling Center .... Dr. John A. ABBRUZZESE
41 Director Intercollegiate Athletics .... Dr. Thomas GIOGLIO
39 Director of Residence Life .... Mr. Robert M. MOSES
88 Dir of Student Activity Association .... Mr. Joe AKOB
21 Controller .... Ms. Donna R. BULZONI
13 Chief Information Officer .... Mr. Robert D'AVERSA
15 Director of Human Resources .... Ms. Teresa FRITSCHE
18 Director Facilities Management .... Mr. Syed S. ZAIDI
96 Director of Procurement/Contracting .... Ms. Patricia REICH
29 Director of Alumni Engagement .... Mr. Leon S. JOHN, JR.
26 Director University Relations .... Dr. Brenda FRIDAY
09 Int Dir Inst Research & Assessment .... Dr. Tami SELBY

*Edinboro University (G)

219 Meadville Street, Edinboro PA 16444-0001
County: Erie FICE Identification: 003321
Unit ID: 212160
Telephone: (814) 732-2000 Carnegie Class: Master's L
FAX Number: (814) 732-2880 Calendar System: Semester
URL: www.edinboro.edu
Established: 1857 Annual Undergrad Tuition & Fees (In-State): $9,536
Enrollment: 6,837 Coed
Affiliation or Control: State IRS Status: 501(c)3
Highest Offering: Doctorate
Program: Occupational; 2-Year Principally Bachelor's Creditable; Liberal Arts And General; Teacher Preparatory; Professional
Accreditation: M, ART, ACBSP, CACREP, CORE, CS, MUS, NUR, NURSE, SP, SW, TED

02 President .... Dr. Julie E. WOLLMAN
05 Provost/VP Academic Affairs .... Dr. Michael HANNAN
10 VP Finance & Administration .... Mr. Guilbert BROWN
32 Vice President for Student Affairs .... Dr. Kahan SABLO
30 Vice Pres University Advancement .... Ms. Tina MENGINE
15 Assoc VP Human Res/Fac Rels .... Mr. Sid BOOKER
08 Vice President University Libraries .... Dr. Donald H. DILMORE
07 Asst VP for Enrollment Services .... Mr. Christopher LARUSSO
09 Dir Inst Research & Assessment .... Mr. Matthew CETTIN
20 Sr Exec Associate to the Provost .... Ms. Judy KUBEJA

18 Int Dir Facilities Management/Plng .... Mr. Michael HILBERT
27 Director of Communications .... Mr. Jeffrey HILEMAN
26 Director of Marketing .... Mr. William BERGER
37 Int Director of Financial Aid .... Ms. Kelly VITELLI
92 Director Honors Program .... Dr. Jean JONES
22 Dir of Social Equity/Ombudsperson .... Ms. Valerie O. HAYES
79 Int Dn Col Arts/Humanities/Soc Sci .... Dr. Scott MILLER
81 Dean Col Science & Health Prof .... Dr. Nathan RITCHEY
58 Dean of Graduate Studies/Research .... Dr. Alan BIEL
53 Dean School of Education .... Dr. Alan BIEL
50 Dean School of Business .... Dr. Scott MILLER
06 Registrar .... Mr. Tim W. PILEWSKI
36 Dir Office of Career Development .... Dr. Jody GALLAGHER
29 Dir Alumni Relations/Fund Devel .... Mr. Jon PULICE
41 Athletic Director .... Mr. Bruce BAUMGARTNER
38 Dir Counseling/Psychological Svcs .... Dr. Michael BUCELL
19 Chief of Police .... Ms. Angela VINCENT
39 Dir Ofc Students with Disabilities .... Ms. Kim KENNEDY
12 Dir & Outreach Coord EUP in Erie .... Ms. Janet L. BOWKER
23 Medical Dir Student Health Services .... Dr. Ronald C. MARTIN
109 Director Auxiliary Operations .... Mr. Paul B. KIGHTLINGER
85 Dir International Student Services .... Ms. Linda KIGHTLINGER
25 Int Dir Grant & Sponsored Programs .... Ms. Kristina HUBER
14 Dir Networks & Telecommunications .... Ms. Karen MURDZAK
90 Dir Desktop Systems/Learning Tech .... Mr. Dennis J. BRADLEY
13 Director Enterprise Systems .... Ms. Sallie A. TERPACK
96 Director Purchasing & Contract .... Ms. Darla SPAID
102 Director of Major Gifts .... Ms. Julie A. CHACONA
44 Dir of Annual Fund/Steward/Ombuds .... Ms. Marilyn GOELLNER
88 Director of Budget and Payroll .... Ms. Theresa VILLELLA
21 Controller .... Mr. Wayne T. OCHS
88 Bursar .... Mr. Mark MATLOCK
35 Dir Campus Life/Leadership Dev .... Ms. Michelle BARBICH
17 Director of Health & Wellness Ctr .... Ms. Darla ELDER
106 Manager of Online Programs .... Dr. James BOULDER
24 Learning Technology Svcs Manager .... Mr. Randall MCCASLIN
88 Coordinator Non-Credit Programs .... Ms. Beth ZEWE

*Indiana University of Pennsylvania (A)

1011 South Drive, Indiana PA 15705-0001

County: Indiana FICE Identification: 003277
Unit ID: 213020

Telephone: (724) 357-2100 Carnegie Class: DRU
FAX Number: (724) 357-6213 Calendar System: Semester
URL: www.iup.edu
Established: 1875 Annual Undergrad Tuition & Fees (In-State): $9,936
Enrollment: 14,369 Coed
Affiliation or Control: State IRS Status: 501(c)3
Highest Offering: Doctorate
Program: Liberal Arts And General; Teacher Preparatory; Professional
Accreditation: M, ACFEI, ART, BUS, CAATE, CACREP, CLPSY, COARC, CS, DIETD, DIETI, ENGR, EXSC, MUS, NURSE, PLNG, SP, TED, THEA

02 President .... Dr. Michael DRISCOLL
05 Provost & VP Academic Affairs .... Dr. Timothy S. MOERLAND
11 Vice Pres Administration/Finance .... Dr. Cornelius WOOTEN
32 Vice President Student Affairs .... Dr. Rhonda H. LUCKEY
30 Vice Pres University Advancement .... Mr. William SPEIDEL, III
20 Assoc VP Academic Administration .... Dr. John N. KILMARX
58 Dean Graduate Studies & Research .... Dr. Randy MARTIN
15 Assoc Vice Pres Human Resources .... Mr. Craig BICKLEY
79 Dean College Humanities & Soc Sci .... Dr. Yaw A. ASAMOAH
50 Dean Eberly Col Bus/Inform Tech .... Dr. Robert C. CAMP
20 Assoc Provost for Acad Pgms & Plng .... Vacant
53 Dean College Educ/Educ Tech .... Dr. Lara LUETKEHANS
81 Dean Col Natural Science & Math .... Dr. Deanne SNAVELY
57 Dean College of Fine Arts .... Mr. Michael J. HOOD
66 Dean College Health & Human Svcs .... Dr. Mark E. CORREIA
84 VP Enrollment Mgmt & Communications .... Mr. James BEGANY
08 Dean of Libraries .... Dr. Luis GONZALEZ
06 Registrar .... Mr. Robert SIMON
38 Counseling Center .... Dr. Patti SHAFFER
13 Chief Information Officer .... Mr. Bill BALINT
09 Inst Research Planning & Assessment .... Mrs. Barbe MOORE
14 Exec Dir of Technology Services Ctr .... Mr. Todd CUNNINGHAM
28 Dir Social Equity/Civic Engagement .... Mr. Pablo MENDOZA
19 Director of Public Safety .... Mr. Douglas CAMPBELL
36 Director Career Development Ctr .... Ms. Tammy MANKO
29 Exec Director Alumni Association .... Mrs. Mary Jo LYTTLE
44 Director Annual Giving .... Ms. Emily SMELTZ
85 Asst VP Intl Education & Global .... Ms. Michele PETRUCCI
46 Assistant Dean for Research .... Dr. Hilliary CREELY
39 Exec Director Housing/Resid Living .... Mr. Michael LEMASTERS
40 Bookstore Director .... Mr. Tim SHARBAUGH
41 Director Athletics .... Mr. Steve ROACH
23 Director Health Services .... Ms. Melissa DICK
12 Dean Northpointe Campus .... Mr. Richard MUTH
12 Dean Punxsutawney Campus .... Dr. Terry APPOLONIA
43 Staff Attorney .... Ms. Suzanne WILLIAMSON
26 Exec Dir Commun & Media Relations .... Ms. Michelle FRYLING
96 Director of Purchasing .... Vacant
10 Assoc Vice President for Finance .... Mrs. Susanna C. SINK
04 Exec Assistant to the President .... Ms. Robin GORMAN
37 Director of Financial Aid .... Ms. Stacy HOPKINS
23 Exec Dir Health & Well-Being .... Ms. Malinda LEVIS
88 Dir Admin Services Culinary Arts .... Ms. Enid RESENIC
07 Director of Admissions .... Ms. Stacy HOPKINS
105 Director Web Services .... Mr. Michael POWERS
18 Chief Facilities/Physical Plant .... Mr. R. Michael BROWN

*Kutztown University of Pennsylvania (B)

15200 Kutztown Road, Kutztown PA 19530-0730

County: Berks FICE Identification: 003322
Unit ID: 213349

Telephone: (610) 683-4000 Carnegie Class: Master's L
FAX Number: (610) 683-4693 Calendar System: Semester
URL: www.kutztown.edu
Established: 1866 Annual Undergrad Tuition & Fees (In-State): $9,099
Enrollment: 9,218 Coed
Affiliation or Control: State IRS Status: 501(c)3
Highest Offering: Doctorate
Program: Liberal Arts And General; Teacher Preparatory; Professional
Accreditation: M, ART, BUS, MUS, SW, TED

02 Acting President .... Dr. Carlos VARGAS-ABURTO
05 Acting VP Academic & Stdnt Affairs .... Dr. James E. MACKIN
10 VP Administration & Finance .... Mr. Gerald L. SILBERMAN
22 Assoc Vice Pres Equity & Compliance .... Mr. Jesus PENA
102 Executive Director KU Foundation .... Ms. Tracey THOMPSON
30 Assoc Vice Pres Comm/Mktg & Ext Aff .... Mr. John C. GREEN
20 Vice Provost Academic Affairs .... Dr. Carole WELLS
21 Asst Vice Pres Admin & Finance .... Mr. Brent PENNY
32 Assoc Provost/Dean of Students .... Mr. Robert WATROUS
13 Asst Vice Pres/Info Technology .... Mr. Mitchell FREED
15 Executive Director Human Resources .... Ms. Sharon M. PICUS
18 Asst Vice President for Facilities .... Mr. Robert J. GRIMM
27 AVP Commmunications/Marketing .... Mr. John GREEN
88 Dean College Visual/Performing Arts .... Dr. William J. MOWDER
49 Dean College Liberal Arts/Sci .... Dr. Anne E. ZAYAITZ
50 Dean College of Business .... Dr. William DEMPSEY
53 Dean College Education .... Dr. Darrell GARBER
62 Director of Library Services .... Ms. Martha STEVENSON
26 Director of University Relations .... Mr. Matthew SANTOS
09 Director Institutional Research .... Ms. Natalie SNOW
06 Registrar .... Ms. Michelle HUGHES
37 Director of Financial Aid .... Mr. Bernard L. MCCREE
39 Director Housing/Residential Svcs .... Mr. Kent R. DAHLQUIST
41 Director of Athletics .... Mr. Gregory BAMBERGER
38 Director Counseling & Psych Svcs .... Dr. Lisa COULTER
96 Purchasing Manager .... Ms. Barbara REITZ
07 Director of Admissions .... Ms. Nancy WUNDERLY
19 Acting Chief of Police .... Mr. John DILLON
36 Director Career/Community Services .... Ms. Kerri GARDI
29 Director Dev & Alumni Engagement .... Mr. Alex OGEKA
04 Executive Asst to President .... Ms. Toyia HEYWARD
108 Asst Vice Provost/Assessment .... Mr. Ernest CLARY

*Lock Haven University (C)

401 N Fairview Street, Lock Haven PA 17745-2390

County: Clinton FICE Identification: 003323
Unit ID: 213613

Telephone: (570) 484-2001 Carnegie Class: Master's S
FAX Number: (570) 484-2432 Calendar System: Semester
URL: www.lhup.edu
Established: 1870 Annual Undergrad Tuition & Fees (In-State): $9,665
Enrollment: 4,917 Coed
Affiliation or Control: State IRS Status: 170(c)1
Highest Offering: Master's
Program: Liberal Arts And General; Teacher Preparatory; Professional
Accreditation: M, ACBSP, ADNUR, ARCPA, CAATE, NRPA, NUR, SW, TED

02 President .... Dr. Michael FIORENTINO, JR.
05 Provost/Vice Pres Academic Affs .... Dr. Donna WILSON
10 Vice Pres Finance & Administraton .... Mr. William HANELLY
32 Assoc Provost for Student Affairs .... Dr. Dwayne ALLISON
84 Assoc Provost for Enrollment Mgmt .... Ms. Tyana LANGE
49 Dean of Liberal Arts & Education .... Dr. Susan RIMBY
83 Dean Natural/Behavioral/Health Sci .... Dr. Scott CARNICOM
50 Dean Business/Info Sys/Human Svcs .... Dr. Stephen NEUN
12 Director Clearfield Branch Campus .... Dr. William CURLEY
85 Director of International Studies .... Ms. Rosana CAMPBELL
09 Director Institutional Research .... Mr. Mike ABPLANALP
15 Associate VP of Human Resources .... Ms. Deana HILL
07 Director of Admissions .... Ms. Donna TATARKA
06 Registrar .... Mrs. Jill MITCHLEY
22 Dir Affirm Action/Equal Opportunity .... Ms. Jamie PENN
37 Director of Financial Aid .... Mr. Robert FRYER
36 Director of Career Services .... Ms. Joan C. WELKER
26 Vice President for University Rels .... Mr. Rodney JENKINS
19 Director of Public Safety .... Mr. Paul ALTIERI
18 Director of Facilities .... Mr. Keith ROUSH
41 Director of Athletics .... Vacant
66 Director of Nursing Program .... Ms. Kimberly OWENS
38 Director of Counseling .... Dr. Dan E. TESS
90 Dir Computing/Instructional Tech .... Mr. Donald W. PATTERSON
88 Director of Physician Asst Program .... Mr. Walt EISENHAUER
92 Director Honors Program .... Dr. Jacqueline WHITLING
94 Director Women's Studies .... Dr. Kimberly ALEXANDER
93 Director Minority Students .... Mr. Kenneth L. HALL
40 Manager University Bookstore .... Mr. James KOWNACKI
29 Director Alumni Relations .... Ms. Tammy RICH
102 Dir Foundation/Corporate Relations .... Mr. Troy MILLER
103 Dir Workforce Development & CE .... Ms. Shannon TYSON

*Mansfield University of Pennsylvania (D)

Academy Street, Mansfield PA 16933-1697

County: Tioga FICE Identification: 003324
Unit ID: 213783

Telephone: (570) 662-4000 Carnegie Class: Master's M
FAX Number: (570) 662-4995 Calendar System: Semester
URL: www.mansfield.edu
Established: 1857 Annual Undergrad Tuition & Fees (In-State): $9,600
Enrollment: 2,900 Coed
Affiliation or Control: State IRS Status: 501(c)3
Highest Offering: Master's
Program: Liberal Arts And General; Teacher Preparatory
Accreditation: M, COARC, DIETD, MUS, NUR, RAD, SW, TED

02 President .... Gen. Francis L. HENDRICKS
10 Vice Pres Finance/Administration .... Mr. John ADAMS
30 Vice Pres for Univ Advancement .... Vacant
32 Vice President of Student Affairs .... Dr. Christopher BRIDGES
39 Assoc Vice Pres Stdnt Affairs & Aux .... Mr. Chuck COLBY
05 Provost/Sr Vice Pres Acad Affs .... Dr. Steven SICONOLFI
20 Assoc Provost/Dean of Faculty .... Vacant
15 Exec Dir Employee & Leadership Svcs .... Ms. Dia M. CARLETON
08 Director Library/Info Resource Svcs .... Mr. Scott R. DIMARCO
18 Assoc Vice Pres F&A (Facilities) .... Vacant
84 Exec Director Enrollment Management .... Vacant
26 Director Public Rels/Publications .... Mr. Dennis R. MILLER
37 Director of Student Financial Aid .... Mr. Charles SCHEETZ
19 Director University Police & Safety .... Ms. Christine SHEGAN
41 Director of Athletics .... Vacant
85 Social Equity/Multicultural Affairs .... Mr. Alan ZELLNER
25 Director of Grants Development .... Vacant
09 Dir Institutional Rsrch/Assess Data .... Dr. John COSGROVE
29 Director of Alumni Relations .... Vacant
06 Registrar .... Ms. Lori CASS
38 Director Counseling Center .... Ms. Jolene MEISNER
07 Dir of Admissions Tactical/Enroll .... Ms. Rachel GREEN
88 Director of Marketing .... Ms. Casey WOOD
13 Chief Info Technology Officer (CIO) .... Mr. Michael THARP

*Millersville University of Pennsylvania (E)

PO Box 1002, Millersville PA 17551-0302

County: Lancaster FICE Identification: 003325
Unit ID: 214041

Telephone: (717) 872-3024 Carnegie Class: Master's L
FAX Number: (717) 872-3968 Calendar System: 4/1/4
URL: www.millersville.edu
Established: 1855 Annual Undergrad Tuition & Fees (In-State): $10,268
Enrollment: 8,500 Coed
Affiliation or Control: State IRS Status: 501(c)3
Highest Offering: Doctorate
Program: Liberal Arts And General; Teacher Preparatory; Professional
Accreditation: M, ACBSP, ART, COARC, CS, ENGR, MUS, NAIT, NUR, SW, TED

02 President .... Dr. John M. ANDERSON
05 Vice Pres Academic Affs/Provost .... Dr. Vilas A. PRABHU
10 Vice Pres Finance & Administration .... Mr. Roger BRUSZEWSKI
30 Vice Pres for Advancement .... Dr. Aminta HAWKINS BREAUX
32 VP Student Affs & Enrollment Mgmt .... Mr. Brian HAZLETT
22 Int Dir Diversity & Social Justice .... Ms. Janice BECHTEL
20 Associate Provost Academic Admin .... Dr. Jeffrey R. ADAMS
20 Asst VP for Student Success and Ret .... Dr. Minor (Will) REDMOND
108 Asst VP Inst Assessment & Planning .... Dr. Lisa R. SHIBLEY
21 Assoc Vice Pres Finance/Admin .... Ms. Nancy PRUSKOWSKI
39 Assoc Vice President .... Ms. Michelle PEREZ
15 Exec Director of Human Resources .... Mrs. Melanie A. DESANTIS
37 Asst VP Enrollment Mgmt/Dir Fin Aid .... Mr. Dwight G. HORSEY
35 Assoc VP/Dean of Students .... Mr. Thomas J. RICHARDSON
88 Corporate Gift Officer .... Mr. Gregory FREEDLAND
18 Asst VP Facilities .... Mr. Thomas A. WALTZ, JR.
53 Dean of Education .... Dr. George DRAKE
79 Dean Humanities/Social Sciences .... Dr. Diane UMBLE
81 Dean of Science & Mathematics .... Dr. Michael JACKSON
58 Dean Graduate Studies .... Dr. Victor DESANTIS
06 Registrar .... Ms. Alison HUTCHINSON
07 Director of Admissions .... Ms. Katy FERRIER
36 Assoc Director Career Management .... Ms. Margo J. SASSAMAN
38 Director Counseling/Human Devel .... Dr. Kelsey K. BACKELS
19 Chief of University Police .... Mr. Peter J. ANDERS
23 Medical Director .... Dr. Susan F. NORTHWALL
41 Interim Dir of Intercollegiate Ath .... Dr. Anthony GRANT
40 Manager University Bookstore .... Ms. Audrey HERR
42 Campus Minister .... Mrs. Kirstin SHROM-RHOADS
42 Campus Minister .... Mr. Duane METZLER
30 AVP Advancement & Dir External Rels .... Mr. Steven A. DIGUISEPPE
44 Assoc VP for Advancement .... Ms. Alice MCMURRY
09 Director Institutional Research .... Mr. Joseph E. REVELT
88 Senior Major Gift Officer .... Ms. Martha P. MACADAM
102 Dir Sponsored Pgms & Research Admin .... Dr. Rene MUNOZ
96 Director of Purchasing/Campus Svcs .... Mr. David C. ERRICKSON
12 Director of Visual & Perform Arts .... Ms. Laura KENDALL
26 Director of Communications .... Ms. Janet KACSKOS

*Shippensburg University of Pennsylvania (F)

1871 Old Main Drive, Shippensburg PA 17257-2200

County: Cumberland FICE Identification: 003326
Unit ID: 216010

Telephone: (717) 477-7447 Carnegie Class: Master's L
FAX Number: (717) 477-1273 Calendar System: Semester
URL: www.ship.edu
Established: 1871 Annual Undergrad Tuition & Fees (In-State): $9,774
Enrollment: 7,355 Coed

Affiliation or Control: State IRS Status: 501(c)3
Highest Offering: Doctorate
Program: Liberal Arts And General; Teacher Preparatory; Professional; Fine Arts Emphasis
Accreditation: M, BUS, CACREP, CS, JOUR, SW, TED

02 President ... Dr. George F. HARPSTER
03 Exec VP Ext & University Relations ... Vacant
05 Provost & Sr VP Academic Affairs ... Dr. Barbara G. LYMAN
10 Vice Pres Administration/Finance ... Vacant
15 Assoc VP for Human Resources ... Dr. David TOPPER
21 Assoc VP & Chief Financial Officer ... Ms. Melinda D. FAWKS
102 Pres Shippensburg Univ Foundation ... Mr. John CLINTON
32 VP for Student Affairs ... Dr. Roger L. SERR
13 VP for Technology & Library Service ... Dr. Rick RUTH
20 Assoc Provost/Dean of Graduate ... Dr. Tracy A. SCHOOLCRAFT
20 Assoc Provost/Dean of Acad Outreach ... Dr. Christina SAX
20 Assoc VP for Enrollment Management .. Dr. William E. SOMMERS
07 Dean of Admissions ... Mr. Angelo C. LEE
35 Dean of Students ... Dr. David L. LOVETT
06 Registrar ... Ms. Cathy J. SPRENGER
36 Director Career Development ... Ms. Victoria KERR BUCHBAUER
37 Director Financial Aid ... Dr. Sandra TARBOX
29 Exec Dir University/AlumniRelations ... Dr. Tim EBERSOLE
26 Director Publications & Advertising ... Ms. Laura LUDLAM
88 Exec Dir Univ Communications/Mrktg ... Dr. Peter GIGLIOTTI
08 Dean Library & Multi-Media Services ... Dr. Dennis MATHES
22 Director Social Equity ... Mr. Cecil E. HOWARD
88 Director Womens Center ... Ms. Stephanie ERDICE
09 Director Inst Research & Planning ... Mr. Mark PILGRIM
25 Dir Sponsored Pgms/Inst Public Svc . Mr. Christopher WONDERS
38 Director Counseling Services ... Dr. Philip W. HENRY
88 Director of Conferences ... Mr. Randy HAMMOND
53 Dean College Education & Human Svcs .. Dr. James R. JOHNSON
49 Dean College Arts & Science ... Dr. James MIKE
50 Dean College of Business ... Dr. John KOOTI
88 Dean Academic Engagement & Student ... Dr. Sarah STOKELY
18 Chief Facilities/Physical Plant ... Mr. Lance BRYSON
96 Director of Purchasing/Contracting ... Ms. Deborah MARTIN
19 Director Public Safety ... Ms. Cytha D. GRISSOM
41 Athletic Director ... Mr. Jeff A. MICHAELS
04 Exec Asst to the President ... Ms. Robin MAUN
101 Secretary of the Institution/Board ... Ms. Robin MAUN
104 Director Study Abroad ... Ms. Mary BURNETT
39 Director Student Housing ... Mr. Barry MCCLANAHAN

*Slippery Rock University of Pennsylvania (A)

1 Morrow Way, Slippery Rock PA 16057-1326
County: Butler FICE Identification: 003327
Unit ID: 216038
Telephone: (724) 738-9000 Carnegie Class: Master's L
FAX Number: (724) 738-2169 Calendar System: Semester
URL: www.sru.edu
Established: 1889 Annual Undergrad Tuition & Fees (In-State): $9,675
Enrollment: 8,495 Coed
Affiliation or Control: State IRS Status: 501(c)3
Highest Offering: Doctorate
Program: Liberal Arts And General; Professional
Accreditation: M, ART, ACBSP, CAATE, CACREP, CARTE, CS, DANCE, EXSC, MUS, NRPA, NUR, PTA, SW, TED, THEA

02 President ... Dr. Cheryl NORTON
05 Provost/Vice Pres Acad & Stdnt Affs ... Dr. Philip WAY
10 Vice Pres Finance/Administration ... Dr. Amir MOHAMMADI
30 Vice President for Univ Advancement ... Vacant
21 Asst Vice Pres for Finance ... Ms. Molly MERCER
18 Asst Vice Pres for Facilities/Plng ... Mr. Scott ALBERT
23 Exec Dir Student Health & Wellness ... Dr. John S. BONANDO
32 Exec Dir for Student Services ... Ms. Debra PINCEK
35 Exec Dir for Student Development ... Mr. Brad KOVALESKI
15 Asst Vice Pres Human Resources ... Ms. Lynne M. MOTYL
28 Asst VP Diversity & Equal Oppty ... Ms. Holly M. MCCOY
100 Chief of Staff ... Ms. Tina L. MOSER
84 Assoc Provost Enrollment Services ... Dr. Amanda A. YALE
13 Assoc Provost Info Technology ... Dr. John ZIEGLER
102 Exec Director Univ Foundation ... Dr. Edward R. BUCHA
26 Exec Director Public Relations ... Ms. Rita E. ABENT
37 Director Student Financial Aid ... Ms. Michelle JACKSON
19 Director Public Safety ... Mr. Paul NOVAK
19 Director University Police ... Mr. Michael SIMMONS
09 Assoc Prov Inst Rsrch/Acad Fin Mgmt ... Ms. Carrie J. BIRCKBICHLER
08 Director of Library Services ... Mr. Philip J. TRAMDACK
14 Director of Info & Adm Tech Svcs ... Mr. Henry MAGUSIAK
06 Director Acad Records/Summer School ... Mr. Eliott G. BAKER
07 Director Undergraduate Admissions ... Mr. Michael MAY
23 Director Health Services ... Ms. Kristina BENKESER
36 Associate Director Career Services ... Mr. John F. SNYDER
29 Director Alumni Affairs ... Ms. Kelly BAILEY
76 Dean Col Health Environment/Sci ... Dr. Susan E. HANNAM
07 Director Graduate Admissions ... Ms. Brandi WEBER-MORTIMER
41 Athletic Director ... Mr. Paul A. LUEKEN
39 Director Housing/Residence Life ... Mr. Patrick T. BESWICK
85 Director International Services ... Ms. Pamela J. FRIGOT
25 Director Grants & Sponsored Rsrch . Ms. Nancy L. CRUIKSHANK
38 Director of Student Counseling ... Dr. Chris CUBERO
93 Director of Minority Students ... Ms. Corinne J. GIBSON
96 Director of Purchasing ... Mr. Mark S. COMBINE
88 Interim Assoc Provost Trans Exper ... Dr. Bradley WILSON
57 Dean Col Liberal Arts ... Dr. Eva TSUQUIASHI-DADDESIO
50 Dean Col Business ... Dr. Lawrence SHAO
53 Dean College of Education ... Dr. Keith DILS
88 Assoc Provost Student Success ... Dr. Warren ANDERSON

*West Chester University of Pennsylvania (B)

University & High Street, West Chester PA 19383-0001
County: Chester FICE Identification: 003328
Unit ID: 216764
Telephone: (610) 436-1000 Carnegie Class: Master's L
FAX Number: (610) 436-3115 Calendar System: Semester
URL: www.wcupa.edu
Established: 1871 Annual Undergrad Tuition & Fees (In-State): $9,461
Enrollment: 16,086 Coed
Affiliation or Control: State IRS Status: 501(c)3
Highest Offering: Doctorate
Program: Liberal Arts And General; Teacher Preparatory; Professional
Accreditation: M, ART, BUS, CAATE, CACREP, COARC, CS, DIETD, EXSC, FEPAC, MUS, NURSE, #PH, SP, SPAA, SW, TED, THEA

02 President ... Dr. Greg R. WEISENSTEIN
100 COS and Exec Deputy to President ... Dr. John VILLELLA
04 Sr Assoc to the President ... Ms. Rebecca HOOK
22 Director Social Equity ... Ms. Lynn KLINGENSMITH
05 Int Provost & VP for Acad Affairs .... Dr. R. Lorraine BERNOTSKY
11 Vice President Admin/Finance ... Mr. Mark P. MIXNER
13 Interim Exec Dir Info Services ... Mr. J.T SINGH
30 Vice President Advancement ... Dr. Mark G. PAVLOVICH
12 VP for External Operations ... Dr. Christopher M. FIORENTINO
32 VP Student Affs/Dean of Students ... Dr. Matthew M. BRICKETTO
88 Assoc VP/Planning and Acad Admin ... Dr. Vernon HARPER
58 Int Assoc Prov & Dean Grad Studies ... Dr. Jeffery OSGOOD
07 Director Admissions ... Ms. Marsha L. HAUG
53 Dean College Education ... Dr. Kenneth D. WITMER
50 Dean College of BPA ... Dr. Michelle PATRICK
49 Dean College Arts/Sciences ... Dr. Lori A. VERMEULEN
76 Dean College Health Science ... Dr. Linda ADAMS
64 Dean College Visual/Performing Arts ... Dr. Timothy V. BLAIR
25 Assoc VP Sponsored Research ... Dr. Gautam PILLAY
23 Interim Dir Health Center ... Ms. Robyn SPRAGINS
15 Assoc Vice Pres Human Resources ... Mr. Michael T. MALOY
35 Asst Vice Pres Student Affairs ... Ms. Sara HINKLE
35 Asst Vice Pres Student Affairs ... Dr. Thomas J. PURCE
10 Asst VP Finance/Business Svcs ... Ms. Bernadette HINKLE
84 Asst Prov & Asst VP Enrollment Mgmt . Mr. Joseph SANTIVASCI
85 Interim Dir International Programs ... Dr. Peter LOEDEL
102 Exec Director WCU Foundation ... Mr. Richard T. PRZYWARA
18 Director of Plant Operations ... Mr. Greg CUPRAK
18 Exec Dir Facilities Design/Const ... Mr. Patrick BRUNNER
18 Assoc VP for Facilities ... Mr. Jim LEWIS
88 Dir Facilities Finance/Support Svcs ... Ms. Susan MILLER
21 Dir Accounting/Financial Reporting ... Mr. Kevin MCCADDEN
09 AVP Institutional Research ... Ms. Lisa YANNICK
21 Bursar/Director Student Finan Svcs ... Mr. Daniel PAULETTI
88 Director Budget ... Ms. Eileen MATES
26 Executive Director Communications ... Ms. Pamela SHERIDAN
88 Director Publications/Printing Svcs ... Mr. Matthew BORN
31 Director Cultural/Community Affairs ... Mr. John RHEIN
88 Director Conference Services ... Ms. Mary Beth KURIMAY
08 Director Library Services ... Mr. Richard SWAIN
88 Director Teacher Education Center ... Dr. James B. PRICE
36 Director Career Devel Center ... Ms. Rebecca ROSS
88 Int Dir Acad Development Pgm ... Ms. Marie BRUNNER
88 Dir Learning Asst/Resource ... Ms. Gerardina MARTIN
37 Director Financial Aid ... Mr. Dana C. PARKER
38 Director Counseling Center ... Dr. Julie PERONE
29 Director Alumni Relations ... Ms. Debbie NAUGHTON
41 Director Athletics ... Dr. Edward M. MATEJKOVIC
88 Director Sports Information ... Mr. James ZUHLKE
28 Director Multicultural Affairs ... Mr. Jerome HUTSON
88 Director Women's Center ... Ms. Alicia HAHN-MURPHY
19 Director Public Safety ... Mr. Michael D. BICKING
96 Director Business Services ... Ms. Marianne PEFFALL
88 Dir Environmental Health/Safety ... Ms. Gail FELLOWS
88 Director Network & Telecom ... Mr. Joseph SINCAVAGE
91 Dir Administrative Computing Systms ... Mr. Patrick LENZI
88 Dir IT Strategic Sourcing/Planning ... Ms. Chaw-ye CHANG
105 Director Content and Web Svcs ... Ms. Kimberly SLATTERY
90 Spec Asst to VP Information Svcs ... Dr. James FABREY
88 Director New Student Programs ... Mr. Jared BROWN
88 Asst Dean Student Dev & Involvmnt ... Mr. Peter GALLOWAY
39 Director Residence Life ... Ms. Marion MCKINNEY
88 Dir Judicial Affairs/Student Assist ... Ms. Christina BRENNER
88 Director Campus Recreation ... Dr. Stephen GAMBINO
88 Dir Student Leadership/Involve ... Mr. Charles WARNER
109 Director Sykes Student Union ... Mr. David TIMMANN
88 Dir Fraternity & Sorority Life ... Ms. Cara JENKINS
88 Dir Service Lrng & Volunteer Pgm ... Ms. Jodi ROTH
88 Int Dir Acad Dvlpmt Pgm/Act 101 Pgm .... Dr. Francis ATUAHENE
88 Dir Pre-major Academic Advising ... Dr. Joanne CONLON
92 Director Honors College ... Dr. Kevin DEAN
104 Asst VP for International Programs ... Dr. Peter LOEDEL
106 Exec Director Distance Education ... Dr. Rui LI
88 Exec Dir Student Service Inc ... Ms. Donna SNYDER
40 Student Svcs Inc Bookstore Manager ..... Mr. Stephen MANNELLA

*Lock Haven University Clearfield Branch Campus (C)

201 University Drive, Clearfield PA 16830
Telephone: (814) 768-3405 Identification: 770186
Accreditation: &M

† Branch campus of Lock Haven University, Lock Haven, PA.

*Venango College of Clarion University (D)

1801 W First Street, Oil City PA 16301-3297
Telephone: (814) 676-6591 FICE Identification: 003319
Accreditation: &M, ADNUR, COARC, NAIT, NUR

† Branch campus of Clarion University of Pennsylvania, Clarion, PA.

Philadelphia College of Osteopathic Medicine (E)

4170 City Avenue, Philadelphia PA 19131-1694
County: Philadelphia FICE Identification: 003352
Unit ID: 215123
Telephone: (215) 871-6100 Carnegie Class: Spec/Med
FAX Number: (215) 871-6719 Calendar System: Trimester
URL: www.pcom.edu
Established: 1899 Annual Graduate Tuition & Fees: $41,017
Enrollment: 2,806 Coed
Affiliation or Control: Independent Non-Profit IRS Status: 501(c)3
Highest Offering: Doctorate; No Undergraduates
Program: Professional
Accreditation: M, ARCPA, CLPSY, IPSY, OSTEO

01 President & CEO ... Dr. Jay S. FELDSTEIN
05 Provost/Senior VP Acad Affairs/Dean ... Dr. Kenneth J. VEIT
10 Vice Pres Finance/Treasurer/CFO ... Mr. Peter DOULIS
58 Vice Pres Grad Pgms/Academic Plng ... Dr. Robert G. CUZZOLINO
63 Dean Osteopathic Med Pgm-GA Campus ... Dr. William CRAVER, III
67 Dean School of Pharmacy ... Dr. Mark P. OKAMOTO
17 Vice Dean Osteopathic Clinical Educ ... Dr. Richard A. PASCUCCI
20 Asst Dean Graduate Medical Educ ... Dr. David KUO
20 Asst Dean Clinical Education ... Dr. Paula GREGORY
88 Asst Dean Clinical Education ... Dr. Joseph KACZMARCZYK
35 Asst Dean Pharmacy Student Affairs ... Dr. Michael LEE
20 Asst Dean Curriculum ... Dr. Kerin FRESA
20 Asst Dean Curriculum ... Dr. Bonnie BUXTON
12 Chief Campus Officer-Georgia Campus ... Mr. Bryan GINN
46 Chief Science Officer ... Dr. Kenneth SLAVIK
32 Chief Student Affair Officer ... Dr. Tina WOODRUFF
26 Chief Marketing/Communications Ofcr ... Ms. Wendy W. ROMANO
37 Chief Student Financial Aid Officer ... Mr. Michael WISNIEWSKI
15 Chief Human Resources Officer ... Mr. Edward J. POTTS
07 Chief Admissions Officer ... Ms. Deborah A. BENVENGER
28 Chief Diversity Officer ... Dr. Lisa M. MCBRIDE
13 Chief Technology Officer ... Mr. James A. WILLIAMS
88 Chief Compliance Officer ... Dr. Allan MCLEOD
88 Chief Risk Management Officer ... Ms. Laura G. BELL
18 Chief Facilities/Plant Operations ... Mr. Frank H. WINDLE
30 Chief Advancement Officer ... Ms. Carri COLLINS
08 Chair of Library/Exec Director ... Ms. Stephanie FERRETTI
06 Registrar ... Ms. Deborah A. CASTELLANO
96 Director of Purchasing ... Ms. Natalie COOPER

Philadelphia University (F)

4201 Henry Avenue, Philadelphia PA 19144
County: Philadelphia FICE Identification: 003354
Unit ID: 215099
Telephone: (215) 951-2700 Carnegie Class: Master's L
FAX Number: (215) 951-2615 Calendar System: Semester
URL: www.philau.edu
Established: 1884 Annual Undergrad Tuition & Fees: $35,230
Enrollment: 3,762 Coed
Affiliation or Control: Independent Non-Profit IRS Status: 501(c)3
Highest Offering: Doctorate
Program: Professional
Accreditation: M, ACBSP, ARCPA, ART, CIDA, ENG, LSAR, MIDWF, OT, OTA

01 President ... Dr. Stephen SPINELLI, JR.
11 VP for Administration/COO ... Dr. Geoffrey CROMARTY
10 Chief Financial Officer/Treasurer ... Mr. James P. HARTMAN
05 Provost ... Dr. Randy SWEARER
30 VP Development & Alumni Relations ... Mr. Jesse SHAFER
26 Vice Pres Marketing/Public Rels ... Ms. Patricia M. BALDRIDGE
13 Vice President/CIO ... Mr. Jeff CEPULL
18 Asst Vice Pres for Operations ... Mr. J. Thomas BECKER
15 Asst Vice Pres Human Resources ... Ms. Katherine FLANNERY
84 Dean of Enrollment Management ... Ms. Christine GREB
32 Dean of Students ... Dr. Mark GOVONI
48 Exec Dean College of Architecture .... Dr. Barbara KLINKHAMMER
81 Exec Dean Col Science & Health ... Dr. Mike DRYER
54 Exec Dean Col Design Engr/Comm ... Dr. Ron KANDER
50 Dean School of Business Admin ... Dr. Sue LEHRMAN
58 Director Acad Pgm Continuing Stds ... Ms. Susan CALDER
08 Director of Library Services ... Ms. Karen ALBERT
38 Director Advising/Counseling ... Dr. Patricia THATCHER
41 Athletic Director ... Mr. Thomas R. SHIRLEY, JR.
29 Director Alumni Relations ... Ms. Elona LAKURIQI
36 Director of Career Services ... Ms. Tracy DEPEDRO
40 Director College Store ... Ms. Shirley A. LANDIS
37 Director Financial Aid ... Ms. Lisa J. COOPER
23 Director Health Services ... Ms. Kirstin PATRAGNONI-SAUTER
06 Registrar ... Ms. Julia AGGREH
39 Director of Residence Life Educ ... Vacant
19 Director Safety & Security ... Mr. Jeffrey BAIRD
35 Director Student Activities ... Mr. Timothy J. BUTLER
09 Director of Institutional Research ... Mr. Mark PALLADINO
07 Director of Admissions ... Mr. Greg POTTS

Pittsburgh Career Institute (A)

421 Seventh Avenue, Pittsburgh PA 15219-1907

County: Allegheny
FICE Identification: 022023
Unit ID: 216782
Telephone: (412) 281-2600
Carnegie Class: Assoc/PrivFP
FAX Number: (412) 227-0807
Calendar System: Other
URL: www.pci.edu
Established: 2014
Annual Undergrad Tuition & Fees: $17,547
Enrollment: 114
Coed
Affiliation or Control: Proprietary
IRS Status: Proprietary
Highest Offering: Associate Degree
Program: Occupational
Accreditation: ACICS, COARC, DMS

01 Campus President .... Patti L. YAKSHE

Pittsburgh Institute of Aeronautics (B)

5 Allegheny County Airport, West Mifflin PA 15122-2674

County: Allegheny
FICE Identification: 005310
Unit ID: 215381
Telephone: (412) 346-2100
Carnegie Class: Assoc/PrivNFP
FAX Number: (412) 466-0513
Calendar System: Quarter
URL: www.pia.edu
Established: 1929
Annual Undergrad Tuition & Fees: $19,125
Enrollment: 382
Coed
Affiliation or Control: Independent Non-Profit
IRS Status: 501(c)3
Highest Offering: Associate Degree
Program: Occupational; 2-Year Principally Bachelor's Creditable; Technical Emphasis
Accreditation: ACCSC

01 President/CFO .... Mr. John GRAHAM, III
03 Executive Vice President/Director .... Ms. Suzanne MARKLE
05 Director of Compliance .... Mr. Jason MONGAN
07 Director of Admissions .... Mr. Steven SABOLD

Pittsburgh Institute of Mortuary Science (C)

5808 Baum Boulevard, Pittsburgh PA 15206-3706

County: Allegheny
FICE Identification: 010814
Unit ID: 215390
Telephone: (412) 362-8500
Carnegie Class: Assoc/PrivNFP
FAX Number: (412) 362-1684
Calendar System: Trimester
URL: www.pims.edu
Established: 1939
Annual Undergrad Tuition & Fees: $17,400
Enrollment: 292
Coed
Affiliation or Control: Independent Non-Profit
IRS Status: 501(c)3
Highest Offering: Associate Degree
Program: Occupational; 2-Year Principally Bachelor's Creditable
Accreditation: FUSER

01 President & CEO .... Eugene C. OGRODNIK
06 Registrar .... Karen S. ROCCO

Pittsburgh Technical Institute (D)

1111 McKee Road, Oakdale PA 15071-3205

County: Allegheny
FICE Identification: 007437
Unit ID: 215415
Telephone: (412) 809-5100
Carnegie Class: Assoc/PrivFP
FAX Number: (412) 809-5320
Calendar System: Quarter
URL: www.pti.edu
Established: 1946
Annual Undergrad Tuition & Fees: $16,285
Enrollment: 2,045
Coed
Affiliation or Control: Proprietary
IRS Status: Proprietary
Highest Offering: Associate Degree
Program: Occupational; 2-Year Principally Bachelor's Creditable; Technical Emphasis
Accreditation: M, MAC, PNUR, SURGT

01 President .... Mr. Gregory DEFEO
03 Executive Vice President .... Mr. George PRY
05 Sr Vice Pres Academic Affairs .... Mr. Mark SCOTT
10 Sr Vice Pres Financial Affairs .... Mr. Terry FARRELL
26 Vice President of Marketing .... Mr. Bart LEVITT
10 Vice President of Business Affairs .... Mr. Chuck CUBELIC
21 Vice President Financial Services .... Mrs. Connie FRIEDBERG
32 Vice President Student Services .... Mr. Keith MERLINO
20 Vice President Education .... Ms. Eileen STEFFAN
30 Vice President of Inst Advancement .... Mrs. Ruth DELACH
09 Vice Pres of Strategic Initiatives .... Mr. Jeff BELSKY
43 General Counsel .... Mr. William KIEFER
06 Registrar .... Mrs. Patricia TARVIN
36 Director of Career Services .... Mrs. Josephine SMITH
26 Director of Public Relations .... Mrs. Linda ALLAN
15 Director of Human Resources .... Ms. Nancy SHEPPARD
13 IT Department Director .... Mr. Bill SHOWERS
19 Director of Public Safety .... Dr. James LAURIA
39 Director of Resident Life .... Ms. Gloria RITCHIE
88 Director of Compliance .... Ms. Melissa BROWN
40 Campus Store Manager .... Mrs. Cynthia KLEIN
29 Alumni Coordinator .... Mrs. Christine IOLI
105 Web Marketing Coordinator .... Mr. Tom ESTLACK
18 Director of Facilities Services .... Mr. Tom VUCELICH
37 Director Student Financial Aid .... Ms. Denise FISHER

Pittsburgh Theological Seminary (E)

616 N. Highland Avenue, Pittsburgh PA 15206-2596

County: Allegheny
FICE Identification: 003356
Unit ID: 215424
Telephone: (412) 362-5610
Carnegie Class: Spec/Faith
FAX Number: (412) 363-3260
Calendar System: Quarter
URL: www.pts.edu
Established: 1794
Annual Graduate Tuition & Fees: $11,520
Enrollment: 215
Coed
Affiliation or Control: Presbyterian Church (U.S.A.)
IRS Status: 501(c)3
Highest Offering: Doctorate; No Undergraduates
Program: Professional; Religious Emphasis
Accreditation: M, THEOL

01 President .... Dr. David V. ESTERLINE
05 VP Academic Affs/Dean of Faculty .... Dr. Byron H. JACKSON
30 VP Strategic Advance/Mktg .... Mr. Thomas J. PAPPALARDO
32 VP Student Svcs/Dean of Students .... Mr. John WELCH
45 VP Planning/Inst Effectiveness .... Dr. James DOWNEY
10 Vice Pres Finance & Administration .... Ms. Ann GETKIN
06 Registrar .... Ms. Anne B. MALONE
08 Interim Director of the Library .... Ms. Darlene VEGHTS
88 Director of Field Education .... Dr. Carolyn J. JONES
29 Director of Alumni/ae Services .... Ms. Carolyn CRANSTON
88 Director Doctor of Ministry Program .... Dr. Susan KENDALL
51 Director Continuing Education .... Dr. Helen BLIER
37 Director of Financial Aid .... Ms. Cheryl DEPAOLIS
84 Director of Enrollment Mgmt .... Rev. Derek DAVENPORT

Point Park University (F)

201 Wood Street, Pittsburgh PA 15222-1984

County: Allegheny
FICE Identification: 003357
Unit ID: 215442
Telephone: (412) 391-4100
Carnegie Class: Master's L
FAX Number: (412) 392-3998
Calendar System: Semester
URL: www.pointpark.edu
Established: 1960
Annual Undergrad Tuition & Fees: $27,746
Enrollment: 3,737
Coed
Affiliation or Control: Independent Non-Profit
IRS Status: 501(c)3
Highest Offering: Doctorate
Program: Liberal Arts And General; Teacher Preparatory; Professional
Accreditation: M, DANCE, ENGT, IACBE

01 President .... Dr. Paul HENNIGAN
05 Sr VP Academic and Student Affairs .... Dr. Karen MCINTYRE
10 Sr VP Finance and Operations .... Ms. Bridget MANCOSH
43 Sr VP and General Counsel .... Ms. Amy Elizabeth MCCALL
26 VP of External Affairs .... Ms. Mariann K. GEYER
84 Vice Pres Enrollment Management .... Mr. Gary BRACKEN
30 Vice Pres Development/Alumni Rels .... Ms. Sharon M. NAVONEY
88 Vice Pres for Special Campaigns .... Mr. Rick HASKINS
18 Vice President of Operations .... Mr. Christopher J. HILL
07 Asst Vice Pres for Admissions .... Ms. Trudy WILLIAMS
96 Asst VP Procurement/Business Svcs .... Ms. Ruth RAULUK
20 Asst VP Academic/Student Affairs .... Mr. Fredrick JOHNSON
19 AVP Public Safety/Chief Police .... Mr. Jeffrey D. BESONG
09 AVP Institutional Research .... Mr. Christopher E. CHONCEK
15 AVP Human Resources .... Mr. Guy CATANIA
21 AVP of Finance .... Mr. Jim HARDT
32 Dean of Student Affairs .... Mr. Keith PAYLO
53 Chair Education .... Dr. Darlene MARNICH
79 Actg Chair Humanities/Human Science .... Mr. William PURCELL
88 Chair of Faculty .... Dr. Heather STARR FIEDLER
54 Act Chair Natural Science/Engr Tech .... Dr. Mark FARRELL
88 Chair Criminal Justice/Intell Stds .... Mr. Greg ROGERS
88 Chair Management .... Ms. Margaret GILFILLAN
88 Chair Theatre .... Ms. Sheila MCKENNA
88 Chair Dance .... Ms. Susan STOWE
88 Chair Cinema .... Mr. Nelson CHIPMAN
49 Actg Dean School Arts and Sciences .... Dr. Robert FESSLER
60 Dean School of Communication .... Dr. Thom BAGGERMAN
50 Dean School of Business .... Vacant
04 Exec Assistant to the President .... Ms. Nina CAMPBELL
06 University Registrar .... Ms. Jennifer FEDELE
08 Director/Librarian/Academic Svcs .... Ms. Liz EVANS
27 Mng Dir Marketing/Public Relations .... Mr. Louis CORSARO
39 Director of Campus Life .... Ms. Janet D. EVANS
07 Director of Admissions .... Ms. Joell MINFORD
41 Director of Athletics .... Mr. Dan SWALGA
54 Dir of Sciences/Engineering Mgmt .... Dr. John KUDLAC
88 Dir Conference & Event Services .... Ms. Terri SNOE
38 Student Counseling .... Ms. Patti SCHWARTZ

Prism Career Institute-Upper Darby Campus (G)

6800 Market Street, Upper Darby PA 19082-1926

County: Delaware
FICE Identification: 023013
Unit ID: 215433
Telephone: (610) 789-6700
Carnegie Class: Assoc/PrivFP
FAX Number: (610) 789-5208
Calendar System: Semester
URL: www.prismcareerinstitute.edu
Established: 1981
Annual Undergrad Tuition & Fees: $11,500
Enrollment: 543
Coed
Affiliation or Control: Proprietary
IRS Status: Proprietary
Highest Offering: Associate Degree
Program: Occupational
Accreditation: ACCSC

01 Campus Director .... Mr. Jeffery MANN
05 Director of Education .... Ms. Donna ZARVATANY
07 Director of Admissions .... Mr. Bobby FISHER

† School is in teach-out plan and is closing December 31, 2015.

Reading Area Community College (H)

PO Box 1706, Reading PA 19603-1706

County: Berks
FICE Identification: 010388
Unit ID: 215585
Telephone: (610) 372-4721
Carnegie Class: Assoc/Pub-R-M
FAX Number: (610) 372-4264
Calendar System: Semester
URL: www.racc.edu
Established: 1971
Annual Undergrad Tuition & Fees (In-District): $5,130
Enrollment: 4,198
Coed
Affiliation or Control: State/Local
IRS Status: 501(c)3
Highest Offering: Associate Degree
Program: Occupational; 2-Year Principally Bachelor's Creditable
Accreditation: M, ADNUR, COARC, MLTAD, PNUR

01 President .... Dr. Anna D. WEITZ
05 Sr VP of Academic Affairs/Provost .... Dr. Susan D. LOONEY
10 Sr VP Fin & Admin Svcs/Treasurer .... Mr. Kenneth DEARSTYNE
103 VP Workforce Dev/Community Educ .... Vacant
30 VP External Aff/Exec Dir Foundation .... Mr. Michael NAGEL
32 Dean of Student Affairs .... Ms. Maria MITCHELL
21 Assoc VP for Bus Svcs/Controller .... Ms. Dolores PETERSON
62 Asst Dean Library Svcs/Learning Res .... Ms. Mary Ellen HECKMAN
15 Director Human Resources .... Mr. Scott HEFFELFINGER
26 Director Marketing/Communications .... Ms. Melissa KUSHNER
13 Director Information Technology .... Mr. Chet WINTERS
09 Dir of Asessment/Research/Planning .... Ms. Mary FLAGG
37 Director Financial Aid/Registrar .... Mr. Benjamin ROSENBERGER
57 Dir of Miller Center for the Arts .... Ms. Cathleen STEPHEN
25 Dir Grant Dev/Mgmt/Title IX Coord .... Ms. Patricia HELFENSTEIN
96 Purchasing Manager .... Mr. Michael HODOWANEC
19 Director of Safety & Security .... Mr. James SURGEONER
35 Coordinator of Student Activities .... Ms. Sue GELSINGER
04 Sr Admin Asst to the President .... Ms. Sandra STRAUSE
50 Asst Dean of Business Division .... Ms. Linda BELL
76 Asst Dean of Health Professions .... Dr. Amelia CAPOTOSTA
79 Acting Assistant Dean of Humanities .... Dr. Joanne GABEL
81 Asst Dean of Science/Math .... Dr. Steve WALLER
83 Asst Dean of Social Sci/Human Svcs .... Ms. Cynthia SEAMAN
07 Admissions Manager .... Ms. Georgene ZIELINSKI

Reconstructionist Rabbinical College (I)

1299 Church Road, Wyncote PA 19095-1898

County: Montgomery
FICE Identification: 022734
Unit ID: 215619
Telephone: (215) 576-0800
Carnegie Class: Spec/Faith
FAX Number: (215) 576-6143
Calendar System: Semester
URL: www.rrc.edu
Established: 1968
Annual Graduate Tuition & Fees: $21,000
Enrollment: 45
Coed
Affiliation or Control: Jewish
IRS Status: 501(c)3
Highest Offering: Doctorate; No Undergraduates
Program: Professional
Accreditation: M

01 President .... Rabbi Deborah WAXMAN
05 Vice Pres Academic Affairs .... Dr. Elsie STERN
11 Vice President Administration .... Mrs. Jennifer S. ABRAHAM
31 Int VP Community Engagement .... Rabbi David TEUTSCH
45 VP Strategic Advancement .... Dr. Josh PESKIN
32 VP Student Development .... Rabbi Amber POWERS
30 Asst Vice Pres Development .... Ms. Barbara G. LISSY
10 Controller .... Ms. Lisa COHEN
20 Dean Academic Administration .... Ms. Barbara HIRSH
08 Director of the Library .... Ms. Deborah STERN

Reformed Episcopal Seminary (J)

826 Second Avenue, Blue Bell PA 19422-1257

County: Montgomery
Identification: 667050
Unit ID: 216348
Telephone: (610) 292-9852
Carnegie Class: Not Classified
FAX Number: (610) 292-9853
Calendar System: Quarter
URL: www.reseminary.edu
Established: 1887
Annual Graduate Tuition & Fees: $6,880
Enrollment: N/A
Coed
Affiliation or Control: Reformed Episcopal Church
IRS Status: 501(c)3
Highest Offering: Master's; No Undergraduates
Program: Professional; Religious Emphasis
Accreditation: THEOL

01 Chancellor and President .... Rt Rev. David L. HICKS
05 Dean .... Rev Dr. Jonathan S. RICHES
08 Librarian .... Rev. Russell BUCHANAN
07 Director of Admissions & Recruiting .... Mr. David A. FRANCE
06 Assistant Registrar and Bookkeeper .... Rev. Peter GEROMEL
90 Director Information & Technology .... Mr. Gregory R. WRIGHT
18 Maintenance/Grounds Supervisor .... Mr. Shawn RILEY

Reformed Presbyterian Theological Seminary (K)

7418 Penn Avenue, Pittsburgh PA 15208-2594

County: Allegheny
FICE Identification: 003358
Unit ID: 215628

Telephone: (412) 731-6000 Carnegie Class: Spec/Faith
FAX Number: (412) 731-4834 Calendar System: Quarter
URL: www.rpts.edu
Established: 1810 Annual Graduate Tuition & Fees: $11,520
Enrollment: 82 Coed
Affiliation or Control: Reformed Presbyterian Church IRS Status: 501(c)3
Highest Offering: Doctorate; No Undergraduates
Program: Professional; Religious Emphasis
Accreditation: THEOL

01	President	Dr. Jerry F. O'NEILL
05	Dean of the Faculty	Mr. Barry YORK
06	Registrar/Head Librarian	Mr. Thomas G. REID, JR.
40	Bookstore Manager	Mrs. Vicki SMITH
10	Treasurer	Mr. James MCFARLAND
07	Director of Admissions	Mr. Mark SAMPSON
37	Director of Financial Aid	Mrs. Sharon SAMPSON
30	Director of Development	Mr. Mark SAMPSON
04	Administrative Asst to President	Mrs. Vicki SMITH

The Restaurant School at Walnut Hill College (A)

4207 Walnut Street, Philadelphia PA 19104-3518
County: Philadelphia FICE Identification: 021928
Unit ID: 215637
Telephone: (215) 222-4200 Carnegie Class: Spec/Other
FAX Number: (215) 222-4219 Calendar System: Other
URL: www.walnuthillcollege.edu
Established: 1974 Annual Undergrad Tuition & Fees: $23,550
Enrollment: 396 Coed
Affiliation or Control: Proprietary IRS Status: Proprietary
Highest Offering: Baccalaureate
Program: 2-Year Principally Bachelor's Creditable
Accreditation: ACCSC

01	President	Mr. Daniel LIBERATOSCIOLI
03	Executive Vice President	Mr. Karl D. BECKER
11	Vice President Administrative Svcs	Ms. Peggy LIBERATOSCIOLI
10	Vice President of Operations	Mr. Dennis LIBERATI
88	Vice Pres/Actg Dir of Culinary Arts	Chef Tom DELCAMP
05	Chief Academic Officer	Mr. David MORROW
07	Director of Admissions	Vacant
21	Chief Business Officer	Mr. Chris MOLZ
32	Chf Student Life Ofcr/Stdnt Plcmnt	Ms. Meghan BICKEL
51	Director Continuing Education	Ms. Jocelyn WOOD
50	Director School of Management	Mr. David MORROW

Robert Morris University (B)

6001 University Boulevard,
Moon Township PA 15108-1189
County: Allegheny FICE Identification: 003359
Unit ID: 215655
Telephone: (412) 397-6400 Carnegie Class: Master's L
FAX Number: (412) 397-5958 Calendar System: Semester
URL: www.rmu.edu
Established: 1921 Annual Undergrad Tuition & Fees: $27,194
Enrollment: 5,555 Coed
Affiliation or Control: Independent Non-Profit IRS Status: 501(c)3
Highest Offering: Doctorate
Program: Teacher Preparatory; Professional; Business Emphasis
Accreditation: M, BUS, CS, ENG, NMT, NURSE

01	President	Dr. Gregory G. DELL'OMO
10	Sr Vice Pres for Business Affairs	Mr. Dan W. KIENER
05	Provost/Sr VP Academic Affairs	Mr. David L. JAMISON
30	Sr VP Institutional Advancement	Mr. Jay T. CARSON
43	Vice President & General Counsel	Ms. Renee T. CAVALOVITCH
21	Vice President Financial Operations	Mr. Jeffrey A. LISTWAK
15	Vice President of Human Resources	Mr. Peter K. FAIX
106	Vice President & Sr Vice Provost	Dr. Derya A. JACOBS
84	VP Enrollment Management	Ms. Wendy C. BECKEMEYER
32	Vice President for Student Life	Mr. John MICHALENKO
30	Vice President for Development	Ms. Kimberley A. HAMMER
13	Vice Pres Information Technology	Ms. Ellen G. WIECKOWSKI
18	Vice Pres for Facilities	Mr. Perry F. ROOFNER
26	Vice Pres Public Rels/Marketing	Mr. Kyle FISHER
20	Vice Provost for Academic Affairs	Dr. Lawrence A. TOMEI
46	Vice Pres & Senior Vice Provost	Dr. Derya JACOBS
09	Vice Provost	Dr. David R. MAJKA
60	Dean School Comm/Info Systems	Dr. Barbara J. LEVINE
50	Dean School of Business	Dr. John M. BEEHLER
54	Dean School of Engr/Math/Science	Dr. Maria V. KALEVITCH
53	Dean Sch Education/Social Sciences	Dr. Mary Ann RAFOTH
66	Dean School Nursing/Health	Dr. Valerie M. HOWARD
88	Dir Univ Sponsorships/Athletic Fund	Mr. Matthew B. MILLET
07	Dean of Admissions	Ms. Kellie L. LAURENZI
88	Exec Dir Bayer Ctr Nonprofit Mgmt	Ms. Peggy M. OUTON
35	Assistant Dean of Students	Mrs. Maureen H. KEEFER
41	Director of Athletics	Dr. Craig S. COLEMAN
08	Director University Library	Dr. Timothy M. SCHLAK
21	Chief Accounting Officer/Controller	Ms. Melissa A. MICCO
06	Registrar/Exec Dir of Academic Svcs	Mr. Frank E. PERRY
19	Director Public Safety	Mr. Randy L. MINK
36	Director Career Center	Ms. Kishma DECASTRO-SALLIS
39	Director Residence Life	Mrs. Anne L. LAHODA
38	Director Center for Student Success	Ms. Cassandra L. ODEN
28	Chief Diversity/Inclusion Officer	Dr. Yasmin S. PUROHIT
27	Senior Director Public Relations	Mr. Jonathan POTTS
109	Senior Director Business Operations	Mr. Neal F. BINSTOCK
37	Director Student Financial Aid	Ms. Stephanie N. HENDERSHOT
29	Dir Development/Alumni Relations	Mr. Warner O. JOHNSON
96	Asst Dir Business Operations	Ms. Beth A. BAIC

Rosedale Technical Institute (C)

215 Beecham Drive, Suite 2, Pittsburgh PA 15205-9791
County: Allegheny FICE Identification: 012050
Unit ID: 215682
Telephone: (412) 521-6200 Carnegie Class: Assoc/PrivNFP
FAX Number: (412) 521-2520 Calendar System: Semester
URL: www.rosedaletech.org
Established: 1949 Annual Undergrad Tuition & Fees: $14,380
Enrollment: 446 Coed
Affiliation or Control: Independent Non-Profit IRS Status: 501(c)3
Highest Offering: Associate Degree
Program: Occupational; 2-Year Principally Bachelor's Creditable; Technical Emphasis
Accreditation: ACCSC

01	President	Dennis F. WILKE
05	Director of Education	Kara CHAN
07	Director of Admissions	Debbie BIER

Rosemont College (D)

1400 Montgomery Avenue, Rosemont PA 19010-1699
County: Montgomery FICE Identification: 003360
Unit ID: 215691
Telephone: (610) 527-0200 Carnegie Class: Master's M
FAX Number: (610) 527-0341 Calendar System: Semester
URL: www.rosemont.edu
Established: 1921 Annual Undergrad Tuition & Fees: $32,780
Enrollment: 890 Coed
Affiliation or Control: Roman Catholic IRS Status: 501(c)3
Highest Offering: Master's
Program: Liberal Arts And General; Teacher Preparatory
Accreditation: M

01	President	Dr. Sharon LATCHAW HIRSH
05	Provost/VP Academic/Student Affairs	Dr. B. Christopher DOUGHERTY
10	VP for Finance & Administration	Dr. Randy ELDRIDGE
37	Dir Enrollment Svcs/Fin Compliance	Ms. Deborah CAWLEY
30	Vice Pres College Relations	Ms. Christyn MORAN
32	Dean of Students	Mr. Troy CHIDDICK
84	Vice President for Enrollment Mgmt	Mr. Dennis J. MURPHY
88	Vice President for Mission	Sr. Jeanne Marie HATCH, SHCJ
08	Exec Director of Library Services	Mrs. Catherine FENNELL
58	Dean Schools Graduate/Prof Studies	Dr. Dennis R. DOUGHERTY
20	Academic Dean Undergrad College	Mrs. Paulette HUTCHINSON
29	Director of Alumni Relations	Mr. Kevin GARY
26	Managing Director of Communications	Ms. Roberta PERRY
06	Registrar/Dir of Inst Research	Mr. Joseph T. ROGERS
41	Director of Athletics	Ms. Lynn S. ROTHENHOEFER
15	Asst VP Human Resources	Ms. Jane FEDEROWICZ
42	Director of Campus Ministry	Mr. Jay VERZOSA
40	Store Manager Campus Bookstore	Ms. Amy LAWSON
18	Director of Operations	Mr. Raymond A. BROWN
38	Director Student Counseling	Ms. Bonnie MARSHALL
39	Director of Res Life/Asst Dean	Ms. Dianne VILLAR
19	Director of Public Safety	Mr. Chuck LORENZ
21	Controller	Ms. Faith BYRNE
07	Associate Director of Admissions	Ms. Bettsy THOMMEN

Saint Charles Borromeo Seminary (E)

100 E Wynnewood Road, Wynnewood PA 19096-3099
County: Montgomery FICE Identification: 003364
Unit ID: 216047
Telephone: (610) 667-3394 Carnegie Class: Spec/Faith
FAX Number: (610) 667-7635 Calendar System: Semester
URL: www.scs.edu
Established: 1832 Annual Undergrad Tuition & Fees: $22,000
Enrollment: 239 Male
Affiliation or Control: Roman Catholic IRS Status: 501(c)3
Highest Offering: Master's
Program: Liberal Arts And General; Professional; Religious Emphasis
Accreditation: M, THEOL

01	Rector & President	M.Rev. Timothy C. SENIOR
03	Vice Rector of the College	Rev. Joseph SHENOSKY
10	Vice Pres of Finance & Operations	Vacant
73	Academic Dean Theology Division	Rev. Robert A. PESARCHICK
49	Academic Dean College Division	Mr. James F. GROWDON
73	Director of Religious Studies	Mr. Jared HASELBARTH
33	Dean of Men College Division	Rev. Sean BRANSFIELD
33	Dean of Men Theol/Dir of Liturgy	Rev. Patrick J. WELSH
06	Registrar	Sr. Gilmary KAY
08	Director of Library Services	Mrs. Cait KOKOLUS
42	Director Spiritual Formation Col	Fr. Herb SPERGER
42	Director Spiritual Formation Theol	Fr. Ned SHLESINGER
88	Director Pastoral/Apostolic Form	Rev. Joseph T. SHENOSKY
64	Director of Music	Vacant
21	Director of Financial Services	Ms. Mary D. D'URSO
37	Director Student Financial Aid	Ms. Nora DOWNEY
19	Director of Safety and Security	Mr. Nicholas MANCINI

Saint Francis University (F)

PO Box 600, Loretto PA 15940-0600
County: Cambria FICE Identification: 003366
Unit ID: 215743
Telephone: (814) 472-3000 Carnegie Class: Master's L
FAX Number: (814) 472-3003 Calendar System: Semester
URL: www.francis.edu
Established: 1847 Annual Undergrad Tuition & Fees: $32,178
Enrollment: 2,380 Coed
Affiliation or Control: Roman Catholic IRS Status: 501(c)3
Highest Offering: Doctorate
Program: Liberal Arts And General; Teacher Preparatory; Professional
Accreditation: M, ARCPA, ENG, EXSC, IACBE, NURSE, OT, PTA, SW, @TEAC

01	President	Rev. Malachi VAN TASSELL, TOR
05	Provost	Dr. Wayne POWEL
10	Vice President for Finance	Mr. Jeffrey SAVINO
32	Vice Pres for Student Development	Dr. Frank MONTECALVO
42	Director of Mission Integration	Rev. Joseph LEHMAN
45	Vice Pres for Strategic Initiatives	Ms. Patricia SEROTKIN
30	Vice President for Advancement	Mr. Robert CRUSCIEL
84	Vice Pres for Enrollment Management	Ms. Erin E. MCCLOSKEY
08	Dean of Library Services	Ms. Sandra A. BALOUGH
97	Assoc Dean of General Education	Ms. Martha O'BRIEN
06	Registrar	Dr. Stephen R. ROMBOUTS
09	Director of Institutional Research	Ms. Kate DEATER
37	Financial Aid Director	Mr. Jamie KOSH
26	Director Marketing & Public Affairs	Ms. Marie YOUNG
44	Director of Development	Ms. Marie B. MELUSKY
38	Director of Counseling Center	Mr. David P. WILSON
13	Director Computer Services	Mr. George F. PYO
29	Director of Alumni Relations	Ms. Anita M. BAUMANN
51	Director Continuing Education	Ms. Julie BARRIS
18	Director of Physical Plant	Mr. Doug EPPLEY
21	Controller	Mr. Thomas R. FRITZ
41	Director of Athletics	Mr. Bob S. KRIMMEL
88	Dir Small Business Devel Center	Mr. Edward R. HUTTENHOWER
19	Director Security & Safety	Mr. Donald MILES
39	Director of Residence Life	Mr. Donald MILES
42	Director of Campus Ministry	Rev. John Mark KLAUS
88	Dir Center for Academic Success	Ms. Renee BERNARD
35	Dir of Student Engagement	Mr. Bobby ANDERSON
15	Director of Human Resources	Ms. Marian BENDER
28	Director of Multicultural Affairs	Ms. Lynne BANKS
96	Director of Purchasing	Mr. William AGOSTA
20	Associate Provost	Dr. Peter R. SKONER
40	Manager of Bookstore	Ms. Barbara SHINGLE

Saint Joseph's University (G)

5600 City Avenue, Philadelphia PA 19131-1376
County: Philadelphia FICE Identification: 003367
Unit ID: 215770
Telephone: (610) 660-1000 Carnegie Class: Master's L
FAX Number: (610) 660-3300 Calendar System: Semester
URL: www.sju.edu
Established: 1851 Annual Undergrad Tuition & Fees: $42,180
Enrollment: 8,974 Coed
Affiliation or Control: Roman Catholic IRS Status: 501(c)3
Highest Offering: Doctorate
Program: Liberal Arts And General; Teacher Preparatory; Professional
Accreditation: M, BUS, BUSA, CS

01	President	Dr. Mark C. REED
05	Interim Provost	Dr. Rosalind REICHARD
03	Senior Vice President	Mr. John W. SMITHSON
88	Associate Provost for Mission	Dr. E. Springs STEELE
32	VP Student Life/Assoc Provost	Dr. Cary M. ANDERSON
11	Vice Pres Administrative Services	Mr. Kevin W. ROBINSON
30	VP University Advancement	Mr. Martin F. FARRELL
26	Vice President External Affairs	Ms. Joan F. CHRESTAY
10	Vice President Financial Affairs	Vacant
15	VP Human Resources	Ms. Sharon O'GRADY EISENMANN
26	VP Marketing & Communications	Mr. Joseph M. LUNARDI
39	VP Campus Life	Dr. John A. JEFFERY
43	General Counsel	Ms. Marianne SCHIMELFINIG
100	Assistant Vice President	Ms. Sarah F. QUINN
20	Associate Provost Faculty Support	Dr. Paul ASPAN
49	Interim Dean Col Arts & Sciences	Dr. Richard A. WARREN
50	Dean Haub School of Business	Dr. Joseph A. DIANGELO, JR.
41	Vice Pres/Director Athletics	Mr. Dominick J. DIJULIA
58	Exec Dir Graduate A&S	Dr. Elisabeth M. WOODWARD
84	Int Assoc Provost Enrollment Mgt	Mr. Robert J. MCBRIDE
06	University Registrar	Mr. Scott J. SPENCER
08	Director Drexel Library	Ms. Anne Z. KRAKOW
21	Assoc VP Fin Planning & Analysis	Ms. Stephanie PRICKEN
21	Assoc VP & Controller	Mr. Joseph CASSIDY
86	Asst VP Govt & Community Rels	Mr. Wadell RIDLEY, JR.
35	Asst VP Student Educ Support Svcs	Dr. Kimberly M. ALLEN-STUCK
29	Asst Vice Pres Alumni Relations	Mr. Thomas MONAGHAN
13	Chief Information Officer	Mr. Francis J. DISANTI
88	Asst Provost for Operations	Ms. Dawn M. BURDSALL
88	Asst VP Student Development	Dr. Mary Elaine PERRY
24	Exec Dir Acad Tech/Dist Learning	Dr. David LEES
07	Asst Prov Undergrad Admiss/Enroll	Ms. Maureen MATHIS
42	Director Campus Ministry	Mr. Thomas J. SHEIBLEY
36	Exec Director Career Dev Center	Ms. Trish SHAFER
38	Director Counseling/Pers Dev Ctr	Dr. Gregory NICHOLLS
18	Director Facilities Management	Mr. Kevin M. KANE
37	Dir Student Records/Financial Svcs	Ms. Eileen TUCKER
28	Director of Inclusion and Diversity	Ms. Monica M. SMITH
19	Director Public Safety & Security	Mr. John GALLAGHER
96	Director Purchasing	Mr. William O. ANDERSON
23	Director Student Health Service	Ms. Laura HURST
35	Dir Student Leadership/Activities	Dr. Beth HAGOVSKY
09	Asst Prov Inst Effectiveness/Rsrch	Ms. Wenjun CHI

04 Executive Asst to President ....Ms. Helene TAYLOR
102 Dir Foundation/Corporate Relations .... Ms. Georgette HAMATY
104 Director International Programs ....Mr. Thomas L. KESARIS
25 Director Academic Research Svcs .... Mr. Thomas J. KAEO
44 Director Planned Giving ....Ms. Anat BECKER

St. Tikhon's Orthodox Theological Seminary (A)

PO Box 130, South Canaan PA 18459-0130
County: Wayne FICE Identification: 039193
Unit ID: 216180
Telephone: (570) 561-1818 Carnegie Class: Not Classified
FAX Number: N/A Calendar System: Semester
URL: www.stots.edu
Established: 1938 Annual Undergrad Tuition & Fees: $7,500
Enrollment: 32 Coed
Affiliation or Control: Other IRS Status: 501(c)3
Highest Offering: First Professional Degree
Program: Professional; Religious Emphasis
Accreditation: THEOL

01 President ....Metr. Tikhon MOLLARD
03 Rector .... Abp. Michael DAHULICH
05 Dean/COO .... V.Rev. Steven A. VOYTOVICH
04 Administrative Asst to Dean/COO ....Ms. Teresa VAUX-MICHEL
06 Registrar ....Prof. Sergei D. ARHIPOV
09 Director of Institutional Research ....Dr. Paul J. WITEK
10 Chief Financial Officer ....V.Rev. Dennis SWENCKI
30 Chief Development/Advancement .... Mr. Seraphim DANCKAERT

Saint Vincent College (B)

300 Fraser Purchase Road, Latrobe PA 15650-2690
County: Westmoreland FICE Identification: 003368
Unit ID: 215798
Telephone: (724) 805-2500 Carnegie Class: Bac/A&S
FAX Number: (724) 805-2019 Calendar System: Semester
URL: www.stvincent.edu
Established: 1846 Annual Undergrad Tuition & Fees: $32,392
Enrollment: 1,829 Coed
Affiliation or Control: Roman Catholic IRS Status: 501(c)3
Highest Offering: Doctorate
Program: Liberal Arts And General; Professional
Accreditation: M, ACBSP

01 President ....Br. Norman W. HIPPS, OSB
03 Executive Vice President .... Rev. Paul TAYLOR, OSB
05 VP Academic Affairs ....Dr. John SMETANKA
10 VP/Chief Finance/Admin Officer ....Mr. Richard WILLIAMS
32 VP Student Affairs ....Ms. Mary COLLINS
26 VP Marketing and Communication ....Ms. Suzanne ENGLISH
07 Dean of Admissions ....Mr. Stephen NEITZ
13 Chief Information Officer ....Mr. Peter E. MAHONEY
20 Dean of Studies ....Ms. Alice J. KAYLOR
50 Dean McKenna Sch Bus/Econ/Govt ....Dr. Gary QUINLIVAN
60 Dean Sch Soc Sci/Communication/Educ ....Dr. MaryBeth SPORE
79 Dean Humanities & Fine Arts ....Rev. Rene KOLLAR, OSB
81 Dean Science/Math & Computing ....Dr. Stephen M. JODIS
06 Registrar ....Ms. Celine R. BRUDNOK
08 Librarian ....Bro. David KELLY, OSB
29 Director of Alumni Affairs .... Mr. Michael GERDICH
26 Director of Public Relations ....Mr. Donald A. ORLANDO
36 Director Career Services ....Ms. Courtney BAUM
15 Director of Human Resources ....Ms. Judith MAHER
42 Director of Campus Ministry ....Rev. Killian LOCH, OSB
23 Director Wellness Center ....Ms. Gretchen FLOCK
19 Director Public Safety ....Mr. Steve BROWN
41 Athletic Director ....Rev. Myron KIRSCH, OSB
39 Director Resident Life ....Mr. Robert BAUM
96 Dir of Purchasing/Chief Fire Dept ....Mr. Terry NOEL
09 Director of Institutional Research ....Ms. Julia CAVALLO
18 Director of Facility Management .... Mr. Larry HENDRICK
40 Manager Book Center ....Rev. Anthony GROSSI, OSB
88 Exec Dir Fred Rogers Center ....Mr. Rick FERNANDES
58 Coord of Graduate Studies .... Ms. Amanda GUNTHER
04 Administrative Asst to President ....Ms. Patricia OWENS
104 Director Study Abroad ....Ms. Sara HART
37 Director Student Financial Aid .... Ms. Mary GAZAL
102 Dir Fdn/Gov/Corporate Relations ....Ms. Christine FOSCHIA
43 Dir Legal Services/General Counsel ....Mr. Bruce ANTKOWIAK

Saint Vincent Seminary (C)

300 Fraser Purchase Road, Latrobe PA 15650-2690
County: Westmoreland Identification: 666018
Unit ID: 215813
Telephone: (724) 805-2592 Carnegie Class: Spec/Faith
FAX Number: (724) 532-5052 Calendar System: Semester
URL: www.saintvincentseminary.edu
Established: 1846 Annual Undergrad Tuition & Fees: $26,092
Enrollment: 54 Coed
Affiliation or Control: Roman Catholic IRS Status: 501(c)3
Highest Offering: Master's
Program: Religious Emphasis
Accreditation: THEOL

01 Rector ....V.Rev. Edward M. MAZICH, OSB
88 Director of Spiritual Formation ......Rev. Jeremiah N. LANGE, OSB
05 Academic Dean ....Rev. Patrick T. CRONAUER, OSB
20 Director of Human Formation ..Rev. John-Mary TOMPKINS, OSB
03 Vice-Rector ....Rev. John-Mary TOMPKINS, OSB
42 Director of Liturgy ....Rev. Cyprian G. CONSTANTINE, OSB
88 Director of Pastoral Formation ....Rev. Nathan MUNSCH, OSB
88 Director of Pastoral Formation ..Rev. Thomas More SIKORA, OSB

Salus University (D)

8360 Old York Road, Elkins Park PA 19027-1516
County: Philadelphia FICE Identification: 003311
Unit ID: 214564
Telephone: (215) 780-1400 Carnegie Class: Spec/Health
FAX Number: (215) 780-1325 Calendar System: Quarter
URL: www.salus.edu
Established: 1919 Annual Undergrad Tuition & Fees: $37,805
Enrollment: 1,470 Coed
Affiliation or Control: Independent Non-Profit IRS Status: 501(c)3
Highest Offering: Doctorate
Program: Professional
Accreditation: M, #ARCPA, AUD, OPT, OPTR, OT, SP

01 President ....Dr. Michael H. MITTLEMAN
05 Vice President Faculty Affairs ....Dr. Janice SCHARRE
10 Vice Pres Finance/Business Affairs ....Mr. Donald KATES
17 Vice Pres Clinical Services ....Dr. John GAAL
45 Vice President for Inst Planning .... Dr. Lawrence MCCLURE
32 Dean Student Affairs ....Dr. James CALDWELL
20 Exec Assistant to the Provost ....Ms. Karen BOYKIN
09 Asst Dir Research Admin ....Ms. Lydia PARKE
06 Registrar ....Ms. Shannon BOSS
13 Chief Information Officer .... Mr. William BRICHTA
38 Director Personal/Prof Development .... Dr. James CALDWELL
37 Assoc Dean Student Financial Affs ..... Dr. H. Lawrence MCCLURE
18 Director Physical Plant .... Mr. Richard ECHEVARRI
30 Director of Development .... Ms. Lynne CORBOY
26 Director Publications/Communication ....Ms. Alexis ABATE
29 Director Alumni Relations/Giving .... Ms. Jamie LEMISCH
51 Coord Continuing/Post-Graduate Educ ....Mrs. Melissa PADILLA
58 Chairperson Graduate Studies ....Vacant
40 Bookstore Manager .... Mr. Joe NOCE
24 Director Instructional Media ....Mr. Glenn ROEDEL
36 Director Student Placement .... Ms. Janice MIGNOGNA
84 Director Enrollment Management .... Dr. Jim CALDWELL
88 Exec Dir Inst Visually Impaired .... Dr. Audrey SMITH
08 Head Librarian .... Ms. Marietta DOOLEY
19 Director of Security .... Mr. Wayne PANCZA
15 Dir Human Res/Affirm Action/Facil .... Ms. Maura KEENAN
96 Director of Purchasing ....Ms. Lydia FRIEL

Seton Hill University (E)

Seton Hill Drive, Greensburg PA 15601-1599
County: Westmoreland FICE Identification: 003362
Unit ID: 215947
Telephone: (724) 834-2200 Carnegie Class: Bac/Diverse
FAX Number: (724) 830-4611 Calendar System: Semester
URL: www.setonhill.edu
Established: 1883 Annual Undergrad Tuition & Fees: $31,420
Enrollment: 2,883 Coed
Affiliation or Control: Roman Catholic IRS Status: 501(c)3
Highest Offering: Master's
Program: Liberal Arts And General; Teacher Preparatory; Professional
Accreditation: M, ARCPA, DENT, DIETC, IACBE, #MFCD, MUS, SW

01 President ....Dr. Mary FINGER
32 VP Mission/Identity .... Sr. Lois SCULCO, SC
05 Provost & Dean of the Faculty ....Dr. Mary Ann GAWELEK
10 Vice Pres Finance & Business ....Mr. David MYRON
11 Vice Pres Administration/Registrar ....Mrs. Barbara C. HINKLE
44 Vice Pres Institutional Advancement ......Ms. Christine MUESELER
13 Chief Information Officer ....Ms. Melissa ALSING
84 Vice Pres Enrollment Management .... Mr. Brett FRESHOUR
21 Controller ....Mr. Paul EDSALL
35 Dean of Student Services ....Dr. Charmaine R. STRONG
07 Director Admissions ....Ms. Ashley JOSAY ZULLO
08 Director of Library ....Mr. David STANLEY
30 Director Development ....Ms. Molly ROBB SHIMKO
29 Director of Alumni Relations ....Ms. Mary COX
37 Director of Financial Aid .... Ms. Tracey DE BAEZ SNYDER
36 Director of Career Development .... Ms. Renee STAREK
15 Director Personnel Services ....Mrs. Darlene SAUERS
18 Director Facilities .... Mr. Bill VOKES
41 Executive Athletic Director ....Mr. Chris SNYDER
42 Director Campus Ministry ....Sr. Maureen O'BRIEN
88 Dir Natl Educ Ctr Women in Business .... Mrs. Jayne HUSTON
04 Assistant to the President ....Mrs. Carol BILLMAN
06 Registrar ....Ms. Barbara HINKLE
38 Director Student Counseling .... Ms. Teresa BASSI-COOK
09 Director of Institutional Research ....Mrs. Edith COOK
26 Chief Public Relations Officer .... Ms. Jennifer REEGER
96 Director of Purchasing .... Mr. Charles O'NEILL
19 Director Security/Safety .... Mr. Gerald STOFKO
22 Dir Affirmative Action/EEO .... Ms. Darlene SAUERS
25 Chief Contracts/Grants Admin ....Vacant
39 Director Student Housing ....Mrs. Robin ANKE
86 Director Government Relations ....Mrs. Carol BILLMAN

South Hills School of Business and Technology (F)

508 58th Street, Altoona PA 16602
Telephone: (814) 944-6134 Identification: 770772
Accreditation: ACICS, CAHIIM, MAAB

† Branch campus of South Hills School of Business and Technology, State College, PA.

South Hills School of Business and Technology (G)

480 Waupelani Drive, State College PA 16801-4516
County: Centre FICE Identification: 013263
Unit ID: 216083
Telephone: (814) 234-7755 Carnegie Class: Assoc/PrivFP
FAX Number: (814) 234-0926 Calendar System: Quarter
URL: www.southhills.edu
Established: 1970 Annual Undergrad Tuition & Fees: $16,521
Enrollment: 630 Coed
Affiliation or Control: Proprietary IRS Status: Proprietary
Highest Offering: Associate Degree
Program: Occupational
Accreditation: ACICS, CAHIIM, DMS, MAAB

01 President & Owner .... Mrs. Maralyn MAZZA
05 Director ....Mr. Mark MAGGS

Summit University of Pennsylvania (H)

538 Venard Road, Clarks Summit PA 18411-1297
County: Lackawanna FICE Identification: 002670
Unit ID: 211024
Telephone: (570) 586-2400 Carnegie Class: Spec/Faith
FAX Number: (570) 586-1753 Calendar System: Semester
URL: www.summitu.edu
Established: 1932 Annual Undergrad Tuition & Fees: $21,850
Enrollment: 836 Coed
Affiliation or Control: Baptist IRS Status: 501(c)3
Highest Offering: Doctorate
Program: Teacher Preparatory; Professional; Religious Emphasis
Accreditation: M, BI

01 President ....Dr. James R. LYTLE
05 Vice President of Academics ....Dr. William J. HIGLEY
10 Vice President Business/Finance ....Vacant
30 Vice Pres Inst Advancement ....Vacant
27 VP Communications/External Rels ....Mr. Mel WALKER
20 Seminary Dean .... Dr. Michael STALLARD
32 Vice Pres Student Development ....Mr. Roddy HANNAH
33 Associate Dean of Men ....Mr. Ted BOYKIN
34 Assoc Dean/Dir Women Ministries ....Mrs. Faye MOORE
04 President's Executive Assistant .... Dr. Lee KLIEWER
06 Exec Dir for Admin Svcs/Registrar ....Mr. Allen R. DREYER
08 Librarian ....Mr. Jeremy MCGINNISS
09 Dir Inst Research/Strategic Plng .... Dr. Barry C. SMITH
37 Director of Financial Aid ....Mr. Steve BROWN
26 Exec Dir Communications/Marketing .... Ms. Dena CAMBRA
19 Director Safety/Security ....Mr. Ken MORRIS
84 Exec Dir for Enrollment Management ....Mr. Drew WHIPPLE
18 Chief Facilities/Physical Plant .... Mr. Wayne STEVENS
13 Manager of Information/Technology ....Mr. Douglas HEITNER
73 Dean School of Bible and Theology ....Dr. David A. LACKEY
53 Dean of School of Education ....Dr. Ritch KELLEY
49 Dean of School of Arts & Sciences .... Dr. Janet K. HICKS
15 Director Personnel Services .... Mrs. Renelle THEODORE
29 Coordinator Alumni Relations ....Ms. Michelle HAMMAKER
36 Vice Pres Student Development ....Mr. Roddy HANNAH

Susquehanna University (I)

514 University Avenue, Selinsgrove PA 17870-1025
County: Snyder FICE Identification: 003369
Unit ID: 216278
Telephone: (570) 374-0101 Carnegie Class: Bac/A&S
FAX Number: (570) 372-4040 Calendar System: Semester
URL: www.susqu.edu
Established: 1858 Annual Undergrad Tuition & Fees: $42,040
Enrollment: 2,093 Coed
Affiliation or Control: Evangelical Lutheran Church In America
IRS Status: 501(c)3
Highest Offering: Baccalaureate
Program: Liberal Arts And General; Teacher Preparatory
Accreditation: M, BUS, MUS

01 President ....Dr. L. Jay LEMONS
100 VP & Chief of Staff ....Dr. Philip E. WINGER
05 Co-COO/Provost/Dean of Faculty ....Dr. Linda A. MCMILLIN
10 Co-COO & VP for Finance & Admin ....Mr. Michael COYNE
26 Vice President for Univ Relations .... Mr. Ronald A. COHEN
84 VP for Enrollment & Marketing ....Ms. Madeleine E. RHYNEER
32 VP Student Engagement & Success .... Ms. Lisa M. SCOTT
20 Assoc Provost/Dean A&S ....Dr. Valerie G. MARTIN
50 Dean Weis School of Business ....Dr. Marsha KELLIHER
27 Chief Communications Officer ....Ms. Angie BURROWS
30 Asst Vice President Gift Planning ....Mr. Doug SEABERG
04 Assistant to the President ....Ms. Joann B. MIERES
04 Senior Admin Asst to the President .... Ms. Sharon POPE
38 Asst Dean & Director of Counseling .... Dr. Stacey PEARSON-WHARTON
89 Asst Dean/First Year Programs ....Vacant
28 Dir Center for Diversity & Soc Just ....Ms. Dena SALERNO
07 Director of Admissions ....Vacant
08 Director of the Library ....Ms. Katherine FURLONG
37 Director of Financial Aid .... Ms. Erin M. WOLFE
06 Registrar ....Ms. Alison A. RICHARD
42 University Chaplain ....Rev. Scott M. KERSHNER
13 Chief Information Officer ....Mr. Mark D. HUBER

41 Director of Athletics ... Dr. Pamela SAMUELSON
18 Director of Facilities Management ... Mr. Chris C. BAILEY
36 Asst Provost Post-Graduate Outcomes .. Ms. Michaeline SHUMAN
88 Director of Event Management ... Ms. Brenda MULL
29 Asst VP Alumni/Parent & Donor ... Ms. Becky DEITRICK
09 Dir Institute Research/Asst Provost ... Dr. Colleen FLEWELLING
102 Dir Corp/Found Supprt/Asst Provost ... Vacant
104 Dean of Global Programs ... Dr. Scott MANNING
15 Director Human Resources ... Ms. Jennifer BUCHER
19 Asst VP Stdnt Life/Dir Pub Safety ... Vacant
44 Director of the Annual Fund ... Vacant
92 Director of Honors Program ... Dr. Dave RAMSARAN

Swarthmore College (A)

500 College Avenue, Swarthmore PA 19081-1390
County: Delaware — FICE Identification: 003370
Unit ID: 216287
Telephone: (610) 328-8000 — Carnegie Class: Bac/A&S
FAX Number: (610) 328-8673 — Calendar System: Semester
URL: www.swarthmore.edu
Established: 1864 — Annual Undergrad Tuition & Fees: $47,000
Enrollment: 1,542 — Coed
Affiliation or Control: Independent Non-Profit — IRS Status: 501(c)3
Highest Offering: Baccalaureate
Program: Liberal Arts And General
Accreditation: M, ENG

01 President ... Valerie A. SMITH
05 Provost ... Thomas STEPHENSON
10 Vice President Finance & Admin ... Gregory N. BROWN
30 Vice President Alumni/Development ... Karl CLAUSS
04 Sp Asst/Col & Comm Relations ... Maurice G. ELDRIDGE
18 Vice Pres Facilities & Services ... C. Stuart HAIN
15 Vice Pres for Human Resources ... Pamela PRESCOD-CAESAR
26 VP/Communications & Secretary/Col ... Nancy NICELY
07 Vice Pres & Dean of Admissions ... Jim BOCK
21 Asst Vice Pres Finance & Controller ... Eileen E. PETULA
32 Dean of Students ... H. Elizabeth BRAUN
28 Assoc Dean of Diversity/Inclusion ... Vacant
06 Registrar ... Martin O. WARNER
08 College Librarian ... Peggy SEIDEN
09 Director Institutional Research ... Robin H. SHORES
29 Director of Alumni Relations ... Lisa LEE
37 Director of Financial Aid ... Varo L. DUFFINS
36 Director Career Services ... Nancy BURKETT
19 Director of Public Safety ... Michael HILL
88 Asst VP Risk Mgmt/Legal Affairs ... Sharmaine LAMAR
23 Director Worth Health Center ... Alice HOLLAND
38 Director Psychological Services ... David RAMIREZ
41 Director Physical Educ/Athletics ... Adam HERTZ
44 Director Annual and Parent Giving ... Lisa SHAFER
13 Chief Info Technology Officer ... Joel COOPER
35 Director Student Activities ... Michael ELIAS
104 Director Off-Campus Study ... Pat MARTIN
39 Asst Dir Residential Communities ... Isaiah THOMAS

Talmudical Yeshiva of Philadelphia (B)

6063 Drexel Road, Philadelphia PA 19131-1296
County: Philadelphia — FICE Identification: 012523
Unit ID: 216311
Telephone: (215) 473-1212 — Carnegie Class: Spec/Faith
FAX Number: (215) 477-5065 — Calendar System: Semester
Established: 1953 — Annual Undergrad Tuition & Fees: $8,650
Enrollment: 121 — Male
Affiliation or Control: Independent Non-Profit — IRS Status: 501(c)3
Highest Offering: Second Talmudic Degree
Program: Teacher Preparatory; Professional; Religious Emphasis
Accreditation: RABN

05 Dean ... Rabbi Shmuel KAMENETSKY
05 Dean ... Rabbi Yehuda SVEI
05 Dean ... Rabbi Sholom KAMENETSKY

Temple University (C)

1801 N. Broad Street, Philadelphia PA 19122-6072
County: Philadelphia — FICE Identification: 003371
Unit ID: 216339
Telephone: (215) 204-7000 — Carnegie Class: RU/H
FAX Number: (215) 204-5694 — Calendar System: Semester
URL: www.temple.edu
Established: 1884 — Annual Undergrad Tuition & Fees (In-State): $14,406
Enrollment: 37,788 — Coed
Affiliation or Control: State Related — IRS Status: 501(c)3
Highest Offering: Doctorate
Program: Liberal Arts And General; Teacher Preparatory; Professional
Accreditation: M, ART, BUS, CAATE, CAHIIM, CARTE, CLPSY, DANCE, DENT, ENG, ENGT, HSA, IPSY, JOUR, LAW, LSAR, MED, MUS, NRPA, NURSE, OT, PH, PHAR, PLNG, POD, PTA, SCPSY, SP, SW, TEAC, THEA

01 President ... Dr. Neil D. THEOBALD
03 Vice President ... Mr. William T. BERGMAN, JR.
05 Provost/Sr VP Academic Affairs ... Dr. Hai-Lung DAI
43 University Counsel/Univ Secretary ... Mr. Michael B. GEBHARDT
32 VP for Student Affairs ... Dr. Theresa A. POWELL
13 Interim VP Computer/CIO ... Ms. Barbara A. DOLHANSKY
17 Sr EVP Health Sci/CEO Health System ... Dr. Larry R. KAISER
03 Sr Vice Provost Strategic Init/Comm ... Dr. Elizabeth LEEBRON TUTELMAN
10 VP/CFO & Treasurer ... Mr. Kenneth H. KAISER
86 Sr VP Govt/Community/Public Affs ... Mr. Kenneth LAWERENCE, JR.
26 VP Strategic Mktg & Communications ... Ms. Karen B. CLARKE
35 Assoc VP/Dean of Students ... Dr. Stephanie IVES
30 VP Institutional Advancement ... Mr. James DICKER
46 Vice Provost Research ... Dr. Michele M. MASUCCI
18 Sr VP Construction & Facilities ... Mr. James CREEDON
21 Assoc VP Finance ... Mr. William J. WILKINSON
39 Assoc VP Student Affairs/Housing ... Mr. Michael D. SCALES
15 Assoc VP Human Resources ... Ms. Sharon I. BOYLE
21 Assoc VP/Controller ... Mr. Frank P. ANNUNZIATO
88 Assoc VP Business Services ... Mr. Richard RUMER
22 Int Assoc VP Inst Diversity ... Dr. Tiffenia D. ARCHIE
11 Asst VP Administration/Planning ... Ms. Kathryn P. D'ANGELO
88 Vice Provost for Faculty Affairs ... Dr. Kevin J. DELANEY
84 Senior Vice Provost Enrollment ... Mr. William N. BLACK
20 Sr Vice Provost Undergrad Studies ... Dr. Peter JONES
20 Vice Prov Acad Affs/Assessment/IR ... Dr. Jodi LEVINE LAUFGRABEN
08 Dean for University Libraries ... Mr. Joseph LUCIA
06 Registrar ... Mr. Bhavesh BAMBHROLIA
41 VP/Athletic Director ... Mr. Kevin G. CLARK
38 Director Tuttleman Counseling Svcs ... Dr. John L. DIMINO
36 Sr Director Career Services ... Ms. Rosalie SHEMMER
09 Director IR/Assessment ... Ms. Sally M. FRAZEE
88 Sr Vice Provost International Affs ... Dr. Hai-Lung DAI
88 Asst VP International Student Svcs ... Ms. Brooke WALKER
88 Asst VP International Affairs ... Ms. Denise A. CONNERTY
23 Assoc Director Health Services ... Dr. Mark DENYS
37 Director Student Financial Services ... Mr. Craig FENNELL
88 Vice Provost University College ... Dr. Vicki Lewis MCGARVEY
96 Director of Purchasing ... Ms. Theresa E. BURT
88 Assistant VP/Bursar ... Mr. David R. GLEZERMAN
97 Director General Education ... Dr. Istvan L. VARKONYI
12 Exec Dir Ambler/Ctr City Campuses ... Mr. William PARSHALL
88 Assoc Dir Adult & Veteran Recruit ... Ms. Laura S. REDDICK
40 Bookstore Manager ... Mr. Jim HANLEY
49 Interim Dean Liberal Arts ... Dr. William STULL
53 Dean of Education ... Dr. Greg ANDERSON
61 Dean Law School ... Dr. Joanne A. EPPS
64 Dean Center for the Arts ... Dr. Robert STROKER
50 Dean Business/Management ... Dr. Moshe PORAT
52 Dean of Dentistry ... Dr. Amid ISMAIL
63 Dean of Medicine ... Dr. Larry KAISER
67 Dean of Pharmacy ... Dr. Peter H. DOUKAS
54 Dean Engineering ... Dr. Keya SADEGHIPOUR
88 Dean Podiatric Medicine ... Dr. John A. MATTIACCI
72 Dean Science & Technology ... Dr. Michael KLEIN
60 Dean Media & Communication ... Mr. David BOARDMAN
76 Dean Health Prof & Social Work ... Dr. Laura SIMINOFF
88 Dean of Tourism/Hospitality Mgmt ... Dr. Moshe PORAT
88 Interim Dean Environmental Design ... Dr. William STULL
88 Dean Temple Japan ... Dr. Bruce STRONACH
88 Dean Temple Rome ... Dr. Hilary L. LINK

Thaddeus Stevens College of Technology (D)

750 E King Street, Lancaster PA 17602-3198
County: Lancaster — FICE Identification: 007912
Unit ID: 216296
Telephone: (717) 299-7730 — Carnegie Class: Assoc/Pub-R-S
FAX Number: (717) 299-7748 — Calendar System: Semester
URL: www.stevenscollege.edu
Established: 1905 — Annual Undergrad Tuition & Fees (In-State): $7,475
Enrollment: 913 — Coed
Affiliation or Control: State — IRS Status: 501(c)3
Highest Offering: Associate Degree
Program: Occupational; 2-Year Principally Bachelor's Creditable
Accreditation: M

01 President ... Dr. William E. GRISCOM
05 Vice President Academic Affairs ... Dr. Robert K. NYE
10 Vice President Finance and Admin ... Mrs. Betty TOMPOS
32 Director for Student Services ... Mr. Christopher METZLER
84 Dir Enrollment Services/Admissions ... Dr. Erin NELSEN
08 Learning Resources Center Director .... Ms. Sharon MCILHENNEY
108 Director Assessment/Accountability ... Ms. Cheryl LUTZ
15 Director of Personnel Services ... Ms. Sue EMSWILER
26 Dir of Marketing/Public Information ... Mr. Chad BAKER
38 Director of Student Counseling ... Ms. Debra SCHUCH
28 Director Multicultural Affairs ... Mr. Paul CULBRETH
29 Alumni Foundation Exec Director ... Mr. Alex MUNRO
37 Director Financial Aid/Registrar ... Mr. Michael DEGROFT
41 Athletic Director ... Mr. Christopher METZLER
30 Director of Development ... Mr. Allen TATE
36 Director of Career Services ... Ms. Laurie GROVE
39 Director Residence Life ... Mr. Jason KUNTZ
18 Facilities Maintenance Manager ... Mr. Gene DUNCAN, JR.

† Qualified individuals are eligible for full scholarships based on family/financial status.

Thiel College (E)

75 College Avenue, Greenville PA 16125-2181
County: Mercer — FICE Identification: 003376
Unit ID: 216357
Telephone: (724) 589-2000 — Carnegie Class: Bac/Diverse
FAX Number: (724) 589-2850 — Calendar System: Semester
URL: www.thiel.edu
Established: 1866 — Annual Undergrad Tuition & Fees: $29,168
Enrollment: 1,057 — Coed
Affiliation or Control: Evangelical Lutheran Church In America — IRS Status: 501(c)3
Highest Offering: Baccalaureate
Program: Liberal Arts And General; Teacher Preparatory
Accreditation: M

01 President ... Dr. Troy D. VAN AKEN
05 VP Academic Affairs/Dean of College ... Dr. Lynn FRANKEN
30 Vice President College Advancement ... Mrs. Theresa LAW
10 Vice President Finance/Management ... Mr. Robert SCHMOLL
13 Chief Information Officer ... Mr. Kurt ASHLEY
04 Administrative Asst to President ... Mrs. Linda NOCHTA
32 VP of Student Life ... Mr. Michael MCKINNEY
84 VP Enrollment Management ... Vacant
20 Assoc Academic Dean/Prof of Psych ... Dr. Jennifer S. GRIFFIN
26 Dir Communications/Marketing ... Mr. Jonathan L. SHEARER
41 Director of Athletics ... Mr. Jack LEIPHEIMER
44 Dir of Special & Planned Giving ... Mr. Mario MARINI
44 Exec Dir of the Capital Campaign ... Ms. Roberta LEONARD
29 Director of Alumni Relations ... Mr. Kraig SMITH
44 Director Annual Giving ... Mrs. Leta JEFFERS
18 Director of Facilities ... Mr. Michael SHULTZ
08 Director Library ... Mr. Allen MORRILL
15 Director Human Resources ... Mrs. Jennifer CLARK
36 Assoc Dean of Career Development ... Mr. Martin BLACK
19 Chief of Police/Dir Public Safety ... Mr. Eric ALLEN
06 Registrar ... Ms. Denise UREY
35 Assoc Dean of Students ... Mrs. Bobbi MUTINELLI
42 Campus Pastor ... Rev. Jayne M. THOMPSON
07 Assoc Director Admissions ... Mrs. Sonya L. LAPIKAS
37 Exec Director Financial Aid ... Ms. Cynthia H. FARRELL
23 Director Student Health Services ... Ms. Christine CIANCI

Thomas Jefferson University (F)

11th and Walnut Streets, Philadelphia PA 19107-5083
County: Philadelphia — FICE Identification: 012393
Unit ID: 216366
Telephone: (215) 955-6000 — Carnegie Class: Spec/Med
FAX Number: (215) 955-3739 — Calendar System: Quarter
URL: www.jefferson.edu
Established: 1824 — Annual Undergrad Tuition & Fees: $35,301
Enrollment: 3,651 — Coed
Affiliation or Control: Independent Non-Profit — IRS Status: 501(c)3
Highest Offering: Doctorate
Program: Liberal Arts And General; Professional
Accreditation: M, ANEST, #ARCPA, CYTO, DENT, DMS, MED, MFCD, MT, NMT, NURSE, OT, PAST, PH, PHAR, PTA, RAD, RADDOS, RADMAG, RTT

01 President & CEO ... Dr. Stephen K. KLASKO
03 Sr Executive VP & CAO ... Ms. Kathleen GALLAGHER
05 Provost ... Dr. Mark L. TYKOCINSKI
26 Senior VP Univ Marketing/Relations ... Ms. Lee LANDAU
10 Sr Vice President for Finance ... Mr. Kirk GORMAN
30 Sr VP Institutional Advancement ... Dr. Elizabeth DALE
43 Sr VP & University Counsel ... Ms. Cristina G. CAVALIERI
46 Vice President for Research ... Vacant
18 Sr Vice Pres for Facilities Mgmt ... Mr. Ronald E. BOWLAN
15 SVP Human Resources ... Vacant
58 Dean Jeff Grad Sch of Biomed Sci ... Dr. Gerald GRUNWALD
20 Vice Provost Academic Affairs ... Dr. Peter MILLER
63 Dean Jefferson Medicial College ... Dr. Mark L. TYKOCINSKI
66 Dean Jefferson School of Nursing ... Dr. Beth Ann SWAN
67 Dean Jefferson School of Pharmacy ... Dr. Rebecca FINLEY
76 Dean Jefferson Sch Hlth Professions ... Dr. Janice P. BURKE
69 Dean Jefferson Sch of Pop Health ... Dr. David NASH
32 Dean of Student & Admissions SKMC ... Dr. Clara A. CALLAHAN
07 Director of Admissions ... Dr. Elizabeth BROOKS
06 University Registrar ... Dr. Raelynn COOTER
29 Exec Director of Alumni Assoc JMC ... Vacant
08 University Librarian ... Mr. Anthony FRISBY
23 Medical Director Univ Health Svcs ... Dr. Ellen M. O'CONNOR
24 Director Medical Media Services ... Mr. Pejman MAKARECHI
35 Assoc VP Student Affairs ... Vacant
39 Manager Housing/Residence Life ... Ms. Laurie YUNKE
37 Univ Director Student Financial Aid ... Ms. Susan MCFADDEN
40 Director Bookstore ... Ms. Patricia HAAS
91 Chief Information Officer ... Mr. Praveen CHOPRA
19 Director of Security ... Mr. Joseph BYHAM
85 Dir International Exchange Services ... Ms. Janice M. BOGEN
07 Dir Admission/Recruitment/Grad Stds ... Mr. Marc STEARNS
28 Assoc Dean Diversity/Minority Affs ... Dr. Bernard LOPEZ
96 Director of Purchasing ... Mr. Robert C. BURKHOLDER
35 Associate Provost Student Affairs ... Dr. Charles A. POHL
04 Executive Associate to President ... Ms. Grace L. HARDESKI
09 Director of Institutional Research ... Dr. Carolyn GIORDANO
101 Secretary of the Institution/Board ... Ms. Michele R. DOUGHERTY
102 Dir Foundation/Corporate Relations ... Ms. Molly GERBER
103 Dir Workforce/Career Development ... Ms. Jennifer M. GRONSKY
105 Director Web Services ... Ms. Chris MCNAMEE-SMITH
25 Chief Contracts/Grants Admin ... Mr. Brian N. SQUILLA
36 Director Student Placement ... Ms. Jennifer FOGERTY
38 Director Student Counseling ... Dr. Deanna NOBLEZA
44 Director Annual or Planned Giving ... Mr. Frederick RUCCIUS
45 Chief Institutional Planning ... Mr. John EKARIUS
84 Director Enrollment Management ... Ms. Erin M. FINN
86 Director Government Relations ... Mr. Hugh J. LAVERY
90 Director Academic Computing ... Mr. Kenneth M. OEFFLER
106 Dir Online Education/E-learning ... Dr. Anthony FRISBY
22 Dir Affirmative Action/EEO ... Mr. Joseph HILL

Triangle Tech (A)

191 Performance Road, Sunbury PA 17801

Telephone: (570) 988-0700 Identification: 770586

Accreditation: ACCSC

† Branch campus of Triangle Tech, Dubois, Falls Creek, PA.

Triangle Tech, Bethlehem (B)

3184 Airport Road, Bethlehem PA 18017

Telephone: (610) 691-1300 Identification: 770587

Accreditation: ACCSC

† Branch campus of Triangle Tech, Greensburg, Greensburg, PA.

Triangle Tech, Dubois (C)

225 Tannery Row Rd, Falls Creek PA 15840

County: Clearfield FICE Identification: 021744

Unit ID: 216454

Telephone: (814) 371-2090 Carnegie Class: Assoc/PrivFP

FAX Number: (814) 371-9227 Calendar System: Semester

URL: www.triangle-tech.edu

Established: 1982 Annual Undergrad Tuition & Fees: $16,216

Enrollment: 148 Coed

Affiliation or Control: Proprietary IRS Status: Proprietary

Highest Offering: Associate Degree

Program: Occupational; 2-Year Principally Bachelor's Creditable; Technical Emphasis

Accreditation: ACCSC

01 Director .... Mrs. Stephanie A. CRAIG
03 Assistant Director .... Mr. Steve CURLL
05 Academic Affairs Advisor .... Mrs. Joan HOCKMAN
07 Admiss/Recruiting/Training Coord .... Mrs. Peggy SHILK
07 Admiss/Recruiting/Training Coord .... Mrs. Joy BURKE
36 Career Advisor .... Mr. Jarred HETRICK
37 Financial Aid Administrator .... Ms. Michelle L. JASHINSKI

Triangle Tech, Erie (D)

2000 Liberty Street, Erie PA 16502-2594

County: Erie FICE Identification: 020902

Unit ID: 216427

Telephone: (814) 453-6016 Carnegie Class: Assoc/PrivFP

FAX Number: (814) 454-2818 Calendar System: Semester

URL: www.triangle-tech.edu

Established: 1976 Annual Undergrad Tuition & Fees: $16,449

Enrollment: 46 Coed

Affiliation or Control: Proprietary IRS Status: Proprietary

Highest Offering: Associate Degree

Program: Occupational; Technical Emphasis

Accreditation: ACCSC

00 CEO .... Mr. James R. AGRAS
01 Campus Director .... Mr. Ken ADAMS
03 Executive Vice President .... Mr. Rudy K. AGRAS
07 Vice President of Admissions .... Vacant

Triangle Tech, Greensburg (E)

222 E Pittsburgh Street, Suite A,
Greensburg PA 15601-3304

County: Westmoreland FICE Identification: 021290

Unit ID: 216445

Telephone: (724) 832-1050 Carnegie Class: Assoc/PrivFP

FAX Number: (724) 834-0325 Calendar System: Semester

URL: www.triangle-tech.edu

Established: 1944 Annual Undergrad Tuition & Fees: $16,500

Enrollment: 186 Coed

Affiliation or Control: Proprietary IRS Status: Proprietary

Highest Offering: Associate Degree

Program: Occupational; 2-Year Principally Bachelor's Creditable; Technical Emphasis

Accreditation: ACCSC

00 Chairman/CEO .... James R. AGRAS
01 President .... Timothy J. MCMAHON
05 Dir School Compliance/Operations .... Deborah G. HEPBURN
12 Director of Branch Campus/CEO .... Paul BEADLE

Triangle Tech, Pittsburgh (F)

1940 Perrysville Avenue, Pittsburgh PA 15214-3897

County: Allegheny FICE Identification: 007839

Unit ID: 216436

Telephone: (412) 359-1000 Carnegie Class: Assoc/PrivFP

FAX Number: (412) 359-1012 Calendar System: Semester

URL: www.triangle-tech.edu

Established: 1944 Annual Undergrad Tuition & Fees: $16,590

Enrollment: 226 Coed

Affiliation or Control: Proprietary IRS Status: Proprietary

Highest Offering: Associate Degree

Program: Occupational; 2-Year Principally Bachelor's Creditable; Technical Emphasis

Accreditation: ACCSC

00 Chairman/CEO .... James R. AGRAS
01 President .... Timothy J. MCMAHON
07 Director of Admissions .... Jason VALLOZZI
05 Senior Director .... Deborah G. HEPBURN
12 School Director .... Ken ADAMS

Trinity Episcopal School for Ministry (G)

311 11th Street, Ambridge PA 15003-2397

County: Beaver FICE Identification: 022993

Unit ID: 216463

Telephone: (724) 266-3838 Carnegie Class: Spec/Faith

FAX Number: (724) 266-4617 Calendar System: Semester

URL: www.tsm.edu

Established: 1976 Annual Graduate Tuition & Fees: $12,270

Enrollment: 201 Coed

Affiliation or Control: Protestant Episcopal IRS Status: 501(c)3

Highest Offering: Doctorate; No Undergraduates

Program: Professional; Religious Emphasis

Accreditation: THEOL

01 Dean/President .... V.Rev. Justyn TERRY
05 Academic Dean .... Rev Dr. Mark STEVENSON
30 Dean Advancement/Dir DMin Degree .... Rev Dr. H. Lawrence THOMPSON, III
32 Dean of Students .... Mr. Geoffrey MACKEY
06 Registrar/Financial Aid Director .... Ms. Stacey WILLIARD
07 Director of Admissions .... Rev. Aidan SMITH
08 Library Director .... Ms. Susanah HANSON
11 Dean of Administration .... Mrs. Karen GETZ
44 Director of Development .... Mr. Jerry MOTE
04 Administrative Asst to President .... Ms. Megan CAREY
26 Chief Public Relations/Marketing .... Rev. Christopher M. KLUKAS

The University of the Arts (H)

320 S Broad Street, Philadelphia PA 19102-4944

County: Philadelphia FICE Identification: 003350

Unit ID: 215105

Telephone: (215) 717-6000 Carnegie Class: Spec/Arts

FAX Number: (215) 717-6045 Calendar System: Semester

URL: www.uarts.edu

Established: 1876 Annual Undergrad Tuition & Fees: $38,410

Enrollment: 1,894 Coed

Affiliation or Control: Independent Non-Profit IRS Status: 501(c)3

Highest Offering: Master's

Program: Liberal Arts And General; Teacher Preparatory; Fine Arts Emphasis

Accreditation: M, ART, MUS

01 President .... Vacant
05 Interim Provost .... Dr. Stephen TARANTAL
30 Vice Pres Advancement .... Ms. Josephine BURRI
04 Exec Assistant to the President .... Ms. Megan STORTI
10 Vice Pres Finance/Administration .... Mr. Stephen LIGHTCAP
13 Vice Pres Technology & Info Svcs .... Mr. Thomas CARNWATH
84 VP Enroll Mgmt/Retention/Stdnt Affs .... Mr. Rick LONGO
06 Registrar .... Ms. Margaret KIP
84 AVP Enroll/Dir Stdnt Financial Svcs .... Mr. Michael LIGHT

University of Pennsylvania (I)

1 College Hall, Room 100, Philadelphia PA 19104-6830

County: Philadelphia FICE Identification: 003378

Unit ID: 215062

Telephone: (215) 898-5000 Carnegie Class: RU/VH

FAX Number: (215) 898-5756 Calendar System: Semester

URL: www.upenn.edu

Established: 1740 Annual Undergrad Tuition & Fees: $49,536

Enrollment: 24,806 Coed

Affiliation or Control: Independent Non-Profit IRS Status: 501(c)3

Highest Offering: Doctorate

Program: Liberal Arts And General; Teacher Preparatory; Professional

Accreditation: M, ANEST, BUS, CEA, CLPSY, CS, DENT, ENG, IPSY, LAW, LSAR, MED, MIDWF, NURSE, PAST, PCSAS, PH, PLNG, SW, VET

01 President .... Dr. Amy GUTMANN
03 Executive Vice President .... Mr. Craig CARNAROLI
05 Provost .... Dr. Vincent PRICE
06 Deputy Registrar .... Ms. Janet M. ANSERT
07 Dean of Admissions .... Mr. Eric J. FURDA
32 Vice Provost University Life .... Dr. Valarie S. MCCOULLUM
10 Vice Pres Finance & Treasurer .... Mr. Stephen D. GOLDING
18 Vice Pres Facil/Real Est Svcs .... Ms. Anne PAPAGEORGE
17 CEO Univ of PA Health System .... Dr. Ralph W. MULLER
08 Vice Provost/Dir of Libraries .... Mr. Harry C. ROGERS
13 Vice Pres Info Technology/CIO .... Mr. Thomas H. MURPHY
100 Vice Pres & Chief of Staff .... Mr. Gregory S. ROST
88 Vice Pres Institutional Affairs .... Ms. Joann MITCHELL
30 Vice Pres Dev/Alumni Relations .... Mr. John H. ZELLER
15 Vice Pres Human Resources .... Dr. John J. HEUER
86 Vice Pres Govt & Comm Relations .... Mr. Jeffrey COOPER
19 Vice President Public Safety .... Ms. Maureen RUSH
26 Vice Pres for Univ Communications .... Mr. Stephen J. MACCARTHY
88 Vice Pres Business Services .... Ms. Marie D. WITT
45 Vice Pres Budget Mgmt Analysis .... Ms. Bonnie C. GIBSON
43 Senior Vice Pres/General Counsel .... Ms. Wendy S. WHITE
101 VP & Secretary of the University .... Ms. Leslie L. KRUHLY
20 Vice Provost for Education .... Dr. Beth A. WINKELSTEIN
20 Vice Provost Faculty Affairs .... Dr. Anita L. ALLEN
29 Asst Vice Pres Alumni Relations .... Mr. Fredrick H. WAMPLER
88 Vice Provost for Research .... Dr. Dawn A. BONNELL
88 Assoc Vice Pres Rsrch Svcs .... Ms. Elizabeth D. PELOSO
14 Assoc Vice Pres Networking/Telecom .... Vacant
88 Assoc VP Audit Compl & Privacy .... Ms. Mary Lee BROWN
31 Assoc VP/Dir Ctr Cmty Partnerships .... Dr. Ira HARKAVY
28 Assoc Vice Prov Equity & Access .... Rev. William GIPSON
21 Comptroller .... Mr. John F. HORN
63 Exec Vice Pres/Dean Sch of Medicine .... Dr. J. L. JAMESON
49 Dean School Arts & Sciences .... Dr. Steven J. FLUHARTY
54 Dean School of Engr/Applied Science .... Dr. Eduardo D. GLANDT
66 Dean School of Nursing .... Dr. Antonia VILLARRUEL
50 Dean Wharton School .... Dr. Geoffrey GARRETT
60 Dean Annenberg Sch Communications .... Dr. Michael X. DELLI CARPINI
52 Dean School of Dental Medicine .... Dr. Denis F. KINANE
57 Dean PennDesign .... Ms. Marilyn J. TAYLOR
53 Dean Graduate School Education .... Dr. Pam GROSSMAN
61 Dean School of Law .... Dr. Theodore W. RUGER
70 Dean School Social Policy/Practice .... Dr. John L. JACKSON
74 Dean School of Veterinary Medicine .... Dr. Joan C. HENDRICKS
107 Vice Dean Liberal & Prof Studies .... Ms. Nora E. LEWIS
35 Assoc VP Student Services .... Ms. Michelle H. BROWN-NEVERS
09 Assoc VP & Sr Adv to Pres .... Ms. Stacey J. LOPEZ
85 Dir Intl Student & Scholar Svcs .... Dr. Rodolfo R. ALTAMIRANO
36 Dir of Career Services .... Ms. Patricia L. ROSE
37 Dir Student Financial Aid .... Mr. Joel B. CARSTENS
35 Assoc Vice Prov for Student Affairs .... Mr. Hikaru KOZUMA
38 Dir Counseling/Psych Services .... Dr. William B. ALEXANDER
102 Exec Dir Corp Rels/Int Dir Fnd Rels .... Vacant
22 Exec Dir Affirm Action & Equal Op .... Mr. Sam B. STARKS
23 Dep Dir Student Health Services .... Dr. SallyAnn M. BOWMAN
88 Mgng Dir Annenberg Cr/Penn Presents .... Dr. Michael J. ROSE
88 Exec Dir Morris Arboretum .... Mr. Paul W. MEYER
88 Dir Institute of Contempory Art .... Ms. Amy SADAO
88 Dir Museum of Archlgy/Anthrplgy .... Mr. Julian F. SIGGERS
88 Director Research Services .... Ms. Heather G. LEWIS
41 Dir Intercollegiate Athletics .... Ms. M. Grace CALHOUN
24 IT Director .... Mr. James F. JOHNSON
91 IT Exec Dir Admin Info Tech .... Ms. Jeanne F. CURTIS
39 Exec Dir Col Houses & Acad Svcs .... Mr. Martin REDMAN
42 University Chaplain .... Rev. Charles L. HOWARD
104 Dir Study Abroad .... Ms. Barbara C. GORKA
106 Online Learning Director .... Ms. Jacqueline P. CANDIDO
04 Administrative Asst to President .... Ms. Jodi SARKISIAN
105 Dir Web Strategy & Visual Comm .... Mr. Steven MINICOLA
44 Exec Dir Gift Plng/Assoc Gen Couns .... Ms. Marcie L. MERZ
96 Director of Purchasing .... Mr. Mark MILLS

University of Phoenix Philadelphia Campus (J)

30 South 17th Street, 2nd Floor, Philadelphia PA 19103

Telephone: (267) 234-2000 Identification: 770933

Accreditation: &NH, ACBSP

† Branch campus of University of Phoenix, Tempe, AZ.

University of Pittsburgh (K)

4200 Fifth Avenue, Pittsburgh PA 15260-3583

County: Allegheny FICE Identification: 003379

Unit ID: 215293

Telephone: (412) 624-4141 Carnegie Class: RU/VH

FAX Number: N/A Calendar System: Semester

URL: www.pitt.edu

Established: 1787 Annual Undergrad Tuition & Fees (In-State): $18,192

Enrollment: 28,617 Coed

Affiliation or Control: State Related IRS Status: 501(c)3

Highest Offering: Doctorate

Program: Occupational; Liberal Arts And General; Teacher Preparatory; Professional

Accreditation: M, ANEST, ARCPA, AUD, BUS, CAATE, CAHIIM, CEA, CLPSY, CORE, DENT, DH, DIETC, DIETD, EMT, ENG, HSA, HT, IPSY, LAW, LIB, MED, NURSE, OPE, OT, PCSAS, PERF, PH, PHAR, PTA, SP, SPAA, SW, @TEAC, THEA

01 Chancellor and Chief Exec Officer .... Dr. Patrick GALLAGHER
05 Sr Vice Chancellor & Provost .... Dr. Patricia E. BEESON
63 Sr VC Health Sci/Dean Sch of Med .... Dr. Arthur S. LEVINE
101 Secy of Board of Trustees .... Vacant
10 Senior Vice Chancellor and CFO .... Mr. Arthur G. RAMICONE
30 Vice Chancellor Inst Advancement .... Mr. Albert J. NOVAK, JR.
43 Sr Vice Chanc & Chief Legal Officer .... Ms. Geovette WASHINGTON
26 Vice Chancellor Communications .... Mr. Kenneth P. SERVICE
100 Sr VC for Engmnt and Chief of Staff .... Dr. Kathy HUMPHREY
86 Vice Chanc Community and Gov Rel .... Mr. Paul A. SUPOWITZ
15 Assoc Vice Chanc Human Resources .... Mr. Ronald W. FRISCH
27 Director University News .... Ms. Cara MASSET
20 Vice Provost Undergraduate Studies .... Dr. Juan J. MAFREDI
58 Vice Provost Graduate Studies .... Dr. Alberta M. SBRAGIA
45 Vice Prov Acad Plng/Resource Mgmt .... Dr. David N. DEJONG
46 Vice Provost for Research .... Dr. Mark S. REDFERN
29 Assoc Vice Chanc Alumni Relations .... Mr. Jeffery T. GLEIM
39 Associate Vice Chancellor Business .... Mr. James V. EARLE
06 University Registrar .... Ms. Patti J. MATHAY
41 Athletic Director .... Mr. Scott BARNES
07 Chief Enrollment Officer .... Mr. Marc L. HARDING
32 Int Vice Prov & Dean of Students .... Mr. Kenyon R. BONNER
49 Dean Deitrich Sch Arts & Sci/CGS .... Dr. N. John COOPER
92 Dean University Honors College .... Dr. Edward M. STRICKER
50 Dean Jos M Katz Gr Sch Bus .... Dr. Arjang A. ASSAD
53 Dean of School of Education .... Dr. Alan M. LESGOLD
54 Dean Swanson School of Engineering .... Dr. Gerald D. HOLDER

61 Dean of School of Law .... Mr. William M. CARTER
80 Dean Grad Sch Public/Intl Affs .... Dr. John T. KEELER
70 Dean School of Social Work .... Dr. Larry E. DAVIS
62 Dean School Information Sciences .... Dr. Ronald L. LARSEN
52 Dean School of Dental Medicine .... Dr. Thomas W. BRAUN
66 Dean of School of Nursing .... Dr. Jacqueline DUNBAR-JACOB
67 Dean School of Pharmacy .... Dr. Patricia D. KROBOTH
69 Dean Grad School Public Health .... Dr. Donald S. BURKE
76 Dean School Health & Rehab Science .... Vacant
12 President Johnstown Campus .... Dr. Jem M. SPECTAR
12 President Greensburg Campus .... Dr. Sharon P. SMITH
12 President Bradford and Titusville .... Dr. Livingston ALEXANDER
40 Director Book Centers .... Ms. Debra R. FYOCK
24 Dir Ctr Instruct Dev/Distance Educ .... Ms. Cynthia GOLDEN
13 Dir Computer Svcs/Systems Devel .... Ms. Jinx P. WALTON
85 Interim Dir International Services .... Ms. Genevieve COOK
09 Director Institutional Research .... Mr. Robert D. GOGA
21 Director Internal Audit .... Mr. John P. ELLIOTT
36 Dir Career Dev/St Empl/Place Asst .... Ms. Cheryl S. FINLAY
25 Director Research .... Mr. Allen A. DIPALMA
38 Assoc Director of Counseling Center .... Dr. Lisa MACCARELLI
08 Director Univ Library System .... Vacant
19 Chief University Police .... Mr. James K. LOFTUS
23 Director Student Health Svcs .... Ms. Marian VANEK
96 Manager Purchasing Services .... Mr. Thomas E. YOUNGS, JR.
44 Sr Exec Director Planned Giving .... Mr. Walter E. BROWN, JR.
102 Exec Dir Corp & Found Relations .... Mr. Andrew B. KOVALCIK
04 Exec Asst to the Chancellor .... Ms. Mary Jo RACE
104 Director Study Abroad .... Mr. Jeffrey R. WHITEHEAD
106 Dir Online Programs .... Ms. Lorna R. KEARNS
37 Director Financial Aid .... Dr. Randall MCCREADY
28 Vice Chanc Diversity & Inclusion .... Ms. Pamela W. CONNELLY
88 Vice Chanc Economic Partnerships .... Ms. Rebecca BAGLEY

University of Pittsburgh at Bradford (A)

300 Campus Drive, Bradford PA 16701-2812
Telephone: (814) 362-7500 FICE Identification: 003380
Accreditation: &M, ADNUR, CAATE, NUR

† Regional accreditation is carried under the parent institution in Pittsburgh, PA.

University of Pittsburgh at Greensburg (B)

150 Finoli Drive, Greensburg PA 15601-5898
Telephone: (724) 837-7040 FICE Identification: 003381
Accreditation: &M

† Regional accreditation is carried under the parent institution in Pittsburgh, PA.

University of Pittsburgh at Johnstown (C)

450 Schoolhouse Road, Johnstown PA 15904-2990
Telephone: (814) 269-7000 FICE Identification: 003382
Accreditation: &M, COARC, ENGT, SURGT

† Regional accreditation is carried under the parent institution in Pittsburgh, PA.

University of Pittsburgh at Titusville (D)

504 E Main, Titusville PA 16354-2097
Telephone: (814) 827-4400 FICE Identification: 003383
Accreditation: &M, ADNUR, PTAA

† Regional accreditation is carried under the parent institution in Pittsburgh, PA.

University of the Sciences in Philadelphia (E)

600 S 43rd Street, Philadelphia PA 19104-4495
County: Philadelphia FICE Identification: 003353
Unit ID: 215132
Telephone: (215) 596-8800 Carnegie Class: Spec/Health
FAX Number: (215) 895-1100 Calendar System: Semester
URL: www.usciences.edu
Established: 1821 Annual Undergrad Tuition & Fees: $37,446
Enrollment: 2,748 Coed
Affiliation or Control: Independent Non-Profit IRS Status: 501(c)3
Highest Offering: Doctorate
Program: Professional
Accreditation: M, ACBSP, #ARCPA, OT, PHAR, PTA

01 President .... Dr. Kathleen MAYES
05 Provost .... Vacant
10 VP Finance and Administration .... Mr. John VITALI
30 VP for Institutional Advancement .... Vacant
86 Director Govt and Cmty Affairs .... Ms. Mary Kate MCGINTY
26 Director Marketing/ Communications .... Mr. Michael SCHWARTZMAN
102 Dir of Corporate & Foundation Rels .... Ms. Rebecca POWERS
13 Exec Dir Information Technology .... Mr. John MASCIANTONIO
13 Associate Provost/CIO .... Dr. Mark NESTOR
37 Director of Financial Aid .... Ms. Paula LEHRBERGER
06 Registrar .... Ms. Therese ANDERSON
29 Director of Alumni Relations .... Mr. Casey RYAN
08 Director of Library Services .... Mr. Charles MYERS
32 Dean of Students .... Dr. William J. CUNNINGHAM
67 Dean of Pharmacy .... Dr. Lisa LAWSON
49 Dean Misher College Arts & Sci .... Dr. Suzanne K. MURPHY
76 Dean Samson College of Health Sci .... Dr. Laurie SHERWEN
88 Dean of Mayes College .... Dr. Andrew PETERSON
15 Exec Director Human Resources .... Mr. Diedrick GRAHAM
19 Director Public Safety .... Ms. Kim C. CARTER
41 Athletic Director .... Dr. Mark CASERIO
88 Director of Student Engagement .... Mr. Ross RADISH
35 Director of Student Life .... Ms. Susanne E. FERRIN
39 Associate Director of Student Life .... Mr. Jay TIFONE
85 Director of Multicultural Affairs .... Mr. Walter PERRY
09 Director of Institutional Research .... Dr. Dale TRUSHEIM
21 Controller/Asst VP Finance .... Ms. Brigid K. ISACKMAN
36 Director Career Services .... Ms. Kimberly BRYANT
38 Assoc Director Student Counseling .... Dr. Karen LEVINSON
96 Manager University Purchasing .... Mr. Vincent HORN
88 Associate Provost Academic Affairs .... Dr. John CONNORS
88 Director Academic Advising .... Mr. Joseph CANADAY
18 Director of Facilities .... Mr. Dan SEVERINO
04 Executive Asst to President .... Ms. Beth PILIPZECK
104 Director Study Abroad .... Mr. James YARRISH
106 Director Academic Technology .... Dr. Rodney B. MURRAY
84 Director Enrollment Management .... Mr. Peter NACY

The University of Scranton (F)

800 Linden St, Scranton PA 18510-4622
County: Lackawanna FICE Identification: 003384
Unit ID: 215929
Telephone: (570) 941-7400 Carnegie Class: Master's L
FAX Number: (570) 941-6369 Calendar System: Semester
URL: www.scranton.edu
Established: 1888 Annual Undergrad Tuition & Fees: $40,644
Enrollment: 5,589 Coed
Affiliation or Control: Roman Catholic IRS Status: 501(c)3
Highest Offering: Doctorate
Program: Liberal Arts And General; Teacher Preparatory; Professional
Accreditation: M, ANEST, BUS, CACREP, CORE, CS, CSHSE, ENG, HSA, NURSE, OT, PTA, TEAC, TED

01 President .... Rev. Kevin P. QUINN, SJ
05 Sr VP Academic Affairs & Provost .... Dr. Donald R. BOOMGAARDEN
10 Sr VP Finance & Administration .... Mr. Edward J. STEINMETZ, JR.
30 VP for University Advancement .... Mr. Gary R. OLSEN
26 VP Enroll Mgmt/External Affairs .... Mr. Gerald C. ZABOSKI
21 Asst VP Budget/Financial Planning .... Mr. Patrick R. DONOHUE
13 Assoc Vice President Info Tech/CIO .... Ms. Robyn L. DICKINSON
15 Assoc Vice Pres Human Resources .... Ms. Patricia L. TETREAULT
42 Interim Dir of Campus Ministry .... Rev. Richard G. MALLOY, SJ
43 General Counsel .... Mr. Robert B. FARRELL
100 Chief of Staff .... Mr. Robert W. DAVIS, JR.
49 Dean Arts & Sciences .... Dr. Brian P. CONNIFF
50 Dean Kania School Management .... Dr. Michael O. MENSAH
107 Dean Panuska Col of Prof Studies .... Dr. Debra A. PELLEGRINO
08 Dean of the Library/Info Fluency .... Mr. Charles E. KRATZ, JR.
51 Asst Dir for OL/Off Campus-Programs .... Mrs. Lisa M. LOBASSO
32 Vice Prov Std Formation/Campus Life .... Dr. Anitra M. MCSHEA
20 Assoc Provost for Academic Affairs .... Dr. Joseph H. DREISBACH
108 Int Assoc Prov Inst Effectiveness .... Dr. Patricia HARRINGTON
07 Assoc VP Admiss & Undergrad Enroll .... Mr. Joseph M. ROBACK
07 Asst VP Admissions & Enrollment .... Ms. Mary Kay ASTON
18 Assoc VP Facilities Operations .... Mr. James DEVERS
29 Assoc VP for Ann Fund & Alum Rel .... Ms. Melissa D. STARACE
06 Registrar .... Ms. Helen H. STAGER
37 Director of Financial Aid .... Mr. William R. BURKE
36 Director of Career Services .... Mrs. Constance F. MCDONNELL
28 Director of Equity/Diversity Office .... Ms. Jennifer LAPORTA
09 Director of Institutional Research .... Ms. Valerie A. TAYLOR
38 Director of Counseling Center .... Mr. Thomas P. SMITH
96 Director of Purchasing .... Mr. Gary S. ZAMPANO

University of Valley Forge (G)

1401 Charlestown Road, Phoenixville PA 19460-2399
County: Chester FICE Identification: 003306
Unit ID: 216542
Telephone: (610) 935-0450 Carnegie Class: Bac/Diverse
FAX Number: (610) 935-9353 Calendar System: Semester
URL: www.valleyforge.edu
Established: 1939 Annual Undergrad Tuition & Fees: $20,294
Enrollment: 931 Coed
Affiliation or Control: Assemblies Of God Church IRS Status: 501(c)3
Highest Offering: Master's
Program: Occupational; 2-Year Principally Bachelor's Creditable; Liberal Arts And General; Teacher Preparatory; Professional; Religious Emphasis
Accreditation: M, SW

01 President .... Dr. Donald G. MEYER
03 Executive VP & VP of Development .... Dr. Daniel W. MORTENSEN
05 VP of Academic Affairs .... Dr. Kevin E. BEERY
10 VP of Finance .... Mr. Jonathan CAPECI
32 VP of Student Life .... Rev. Jennifer D. GALE
20 Associate Dean .... Rev. Stuart P. ROSS
21 Controller .... Mrs. Myra D. OCASIO
84 Exec Director Enrollment Management .... Mrs. Evie MEYER
49 Arts & Sciences Dept Chair .... Mrs. Laura BROOKINS
83 Behavioral Sciences Dept Chair .... Mr. Kenneth LANG
50 Business Dept Chair .... Dr. William CLARKSON
73 Church Ministry Dept Chair .... Dr. Jerome DOUGLAS
73 Deaf Pastoral Minstries Dept Chair .... Dr. JoAnn SMITH
72 Digital Media/Commun Dept Chair .... Mr. Leone BILOTTA
53 Education Dept Chair .... Dr. A. Glenn MCCLURE
88 Intercultural Studies Dept Chair .... Rev. David KIM
64 Music Dept Chair .... Dr. William DESANTO
88 Director of Accounting .... Mrs. Betty SMITH
07 Director of Admissions .... Rev. Joseph OCASIO
30 Coordinator of Development .... Mrs. Darlene GRUBER
41 Director of Athletics .... Mr. Jon MACK
36 Director Career Services .... Rev. Amy THURSTON
37 Director of Financial Aid .... Mrs. Linda STEIN
15 Director Human Resources .... Mrs. Veronica BIRD
13 Director of Information Technology .... Mr. Brian SWOMLEY
105 Web Master .... Mr. Steve THURSTON
08 Librarian/Dir Storms Research Ctr .... Mrs. Deborah HIRNEISEN
26 Director of Marketing .... Mrs. Michelle MALONEY
06 Registrar .... Dr. Troy GEARHART
23 Nurse .... Mrs. Lauren BORN
35 Campus Director .... Rev. Wendy BEERY
35 Campus Director .... Vacant
39 Residence Director .... Mrs. Katharyn MCLELLAN
39 Residence Director .... Mr. Yung Won PARK

Ursinus College (H)

PO Box 1000, 601 East Main Street, Collegeville PA 19426-1000
County: Montgomery FICE Identification: 003385
Unit ID: 216524
Telephone: (610) 409-3000 Carnegie Class: Bac/A&S
FAX Number: (610) 489-0627 Calendar System: Semester
URL: www.ursinus.edu
Established: 1869 Annual Undergrad Tuition & Fees: $47,500
Enrollment: 1,645 Coed
Affiliation or Control: Independent Non-Profit IRS Status: 501(c)3
Highest Offering: Baccalaureate
Program: Liberal Arts And General
Accreditation: M

01 President .... Dr. Brock BLOMBERG
05 Dean & Exec VP Acad Affairs .... Dr. Lucien T. WINEGAR
10 Vice Pres Finance & Administration .... Mr. Jonathan C. IVEC
30 Senior Vice Pres for Advancement .... Ms. Jill A. MARSTELLER
84 Interim Vice Pres for Enrollment .... Ms. Kathryn BAUGHER
32 Vice Pres of Student Affairs/Dean .... Ms. Deborah O. NOLAN
21 Associate Vice Pres/Controller .... Mr. James MORETTI
07 Director of Admissions .... Ms. Dana MATASSINO
44 Exec Director of Planned Giving .... Mr. Mark P. GADSON
08 Special Library Collections .... Mr. Charles JAMISON
36 Director of Career Services .... Mrs. Carla M. RINDE
18 Director of Physical Facilities .... Mr. Jason VAN BUREN
41 Director of Athletics .... Mrs. Laura MOLIKEN
26 Chief Communications Officer .... Mr. Thomas YENCHO
37 Director Student Financial Services .... Mrs. Suzanne SPARROW
06 Registrar .... Ms. Barbara A. BORIS
29 Director of Alumni Relations .... Ms. Pamela PANARELLA
20 Associate Dean of the College .... Dr. Jay MILLER
15 Director Human Resources .... Ms. Kelley WILLIAMS
09 Director of Institutional Research .... Ms. Annemarie BARTLETT
102 Dir Foundation/Corporate Relations .... Mr. Edmond CLARKE
13 Chief Info Technology Officer (CIO) .... Mr. Eugene SPENCER
28 Coord of Diversity/Inclusion .... Mr. Terrence WILLIAMS
04 Executive Asst to President .... Ms. Teri A. LOBO

Valley Forge Military College (I)

1001 Eagle Road, Wayne PA 19087-3695
County: Delaware FICE Identification: 003386
Unit ID: 216551
Telephone: (610) 989-1451 Carnegie Class: Not Classified
FAX Number: (610) 975-9642 Calendar System: Semester
URL: www.vfmac.edu
Established: 1935 Annual Undergrad Tuition & Fees: $44,675
Enrollment: 340 Coed
Affiliation or Control: Independent Non-Profit IRS Status: 501(c)3
Highest Offering: Associate Degree
Program: 2-Year Principally Bachelor's Creditable
Accreditation: M

01 President Military Academy/College .... Dr. Stacey R. SAUCHUK
05 Head of School - Academy .... Ms. Sandra YOUNG
10 Chief Financial Officer/COO .... Mr. Vincent VUONO
30 Vice Pres Institutional Advancement .... Mr. Douglas HASBROUCK
18 Director of Facilities .... Mr. Bryan K. GEILING
07 Director College Admissions .... Ms. Kristen ROSE
08 Director of Library Services .... LTC. Jean L. SMITH
15 Director of Human Resources .... Ms. Marianne MEADE
13 Director Information Technology .... Mr. Michael BROCK
41 Director of Athletics .... Mr. Richard CASEY
32 Dean Student Services .... Maj. Robert WOOD
09 Institutional Research Analyst .... Miss Kristen A. GREENER
06 Assistant Dean/Registrar .... Mrs. Maureen MALONE
88 Transfer Advisor .... Ms. Joann MCCRACKEN

Vet Tech Institute (J)

125 Seventh Street, Pittsburgh PA 15222-3400
County: Allegheny FICE Identification: 008568
Unit ID: 213914
Telephone: (412) 391-7021 Carnegie Class: Assoc/PrivFP
FAX Number: (412) 232-4348 Calendar System: Semester
URL: www.vettechinstitute.edu
Established: 1958 Annual Undergrad Tuition & Fees: $14,860
Enrollment: 361 Coed
Affiliation or Control: Proprietary IRS Status: Proprietary
Highest Offering: Associate Degree
Program: Occupational; Technical Emphasis

Accreditation: ACCSC

01 Director ... Jackie FLYNN

Villanova University (A)

800 Lancaster Avenue, Villanova PA 19085-1699
County: Delaware FICE Identification: 003388
Unit ID: 216597
Telephone: (610) 519-4500 Carnegie Class: Master's L
FAX Number: (610) 519-5000 Calendar System: Semester
URL: www.villanova.edu
Established: 1842 Annual Undergrad Tuition & Fees: $46,966
Enrollment: 10,544 Coed
Affiliation or Control: Roman Catholic IRS Status: 501(c)3
Highest Offering: Doctorate
Program: Liberal Arts And General; Teacher Preparatory; Professional
Accreditation: M, ANEST, BUS, BUSA, CACREP, CS, ENG, LAW, NURSE, SPAA

01 President ... Rev. Peter M. DONOHUE, OSA
43 Vice President & General Counsel ... Ms. Debra FICKLER
05 Provost ... Dr. Patrick G. MAGGITTI
30 Sr Vice Pres University Advancement ... Mr. Michael O'NEILL
10 Exec VP Administration/Finance ... Mr. Kenneth G. VALOSKY
13 Vice Pres/Chief Information Officer ... Mr. Stephen FUGALE
32 Vice President for Student Life ... Rev. John P. STACK, OSA
26 Vice Pres University Communication ... Ms. Ann DIEBOLD
42 Vice Pres for Mission & Ministry ... Dr. Barbara E. WALL
20 Assoc Vice Pres Academic Affairs ... Dr. Craig WHEELAND
35 Assoc Vice Pres for Student Life ... Ms. Kathleen J. BYRNES
15 AVP Human Res/Affirm Action Ofcr ... Ms. Ellen KRUTZ
109 Assoc Vice Pres for Auxiliary Svcs ... Mr. Frederick C. SIEBER
29 Assoc Vice Pres Alumni Relations ... Mr. George R. KOLB
46 AVP Research/Graduate Programs ... Dr. Alfonso ORTEGA
51 Asst Vice Pres for Academic Affairs ... Dr. Robert D. STOKES
28 Asst VP Multicultural Affairs ... Dr. Teresa A. NANCE
84 Dean Enrollment Management ... Mr. Stephen R. MERRITT
09 Exec Dir Planning/Inst Research ... Dr. James F. TRAINER
18 Vice Pres Facilities Management ... Mr. Robert MORRO
88 Assoc Dean Enrol Mgt For Stdnt Info . Ms. Catherine H. CONNOR
07 Director University Admission ... Mr. Michael M. GAYNOR
08 Interim Director of Falvey Library ... Ms. Millicent GASKELL
35 Dean of Students ... Mr. Paul F. PUGH
49 Int Dean Liberal Arts & Sciences ... Dr. Adele LINDENMEYR
50 Int Dean Villanova Sch of Business ... Dr. Daniel WRIGHT
58 Int Dean Graduate Studies LA&S ... Dr. Christine PALUS
61 Dean School of Law ... Mr. John GOTANDA
66 Dean of Nursing ... Dr. M. Louise FITZPATRICK
54 Dean of Engineering ... Dr. Gary A. GABRIELE
88 Dir Ctr Spirituality/Discernment ... Ms. Linda JACZYNSKI
88 Dir Ctr Service/Social Justice ... Ms. Irene KING
88 Director Center for Worship ... Rev. Joseph MOSTARDI, OSA
88 Dir Ctr Grad Pastoral Ministry Educ ... Ms. Joyce ZAVARICH
107 Dean Col of Professional Studies ... Dr. Deborah J. TYKSINSKI
55 Dir Part Time Stds/Summer Sessions ... Ms. Mary BUSTAMANTE
85 Dir International & Human Services ... Mr. Stephen T. MCWILLIAMS
37 Director Financial Assistance ... Ms. Bonnie Lee BEHM
19 Director of Public Safety ... Mr. David TEDJESKE
36 Director Career Services ... Ms. Nancy J. DUDAK
92 Director of the Honors Program ... Dr. Thomas W. SMITH
38 Director of Univ Counseling Center ... Dr. Joan G. WHITNEY
94 Co-Dir Women's Studies Programming ... Dr. Lisa SEWELL
94 Co-Dir Women's Studies Academics ... Dr. Jean LUTES
39 Director Office of Residence Life ... Mr. Thomas DE MARCO
96 Director of Procurement ... Mr. John R. DURHAM
27 Director of Media Relations ... Mr. Jonathan GUST
41 Director of Athletics ... Mr. Vincent P. NICASTRO
23 Director Student Health Center ... Dr. Mary MCGONIGLE
23 Medical Director Student Health Ctr ... Dr. Brian BULLOCK
06 Registrar ... Ms. Pamela BRAXTON
22 Asc Dir Center Multicultural Affs ... Ms. Linda COLEMAN
04 Special Asst to President/Ext Rels ... Rev. George F. RILEY, OSA
88 University Compliance Officer ... Ms. Leyda L. BENITEZ

Washington & Jefferson College (B)

60 S Lincoln Street, Washington PA 15301-4801
County: Washington FICE Identification: 003389
Unit ID: 216667
Telephone: (724) 503-1001 Carnegie Class: Bac/A&S
FAX Number: (724) 223-6534 Calendar System: 4/1/4
URL: www.washjeff.edu
Established: 1781 Annual Undergrad Tuition & Fees: $43,226
Enrollment: 1,362 Coed
Affiliation or Control: Independent Non-Profit IRS Status: 501(c)3
Highest Offering: Master's
Program: Liberal Arts And General; Teacher Preparatory
Accreditation: M

01 President ... Dr. Tori HARING-SMITH
05 VP Academic Affairs/Dean of Faculty ... Dr. John E. ZIMMERMAN
10 CFO/VP Business/Finance ... Mr. Dennis MCMASTER
30 VP Development/Alumni Relations ... Mr. Michael P. GRZESIAK
84 Vice President for Enrollment ... Mr. Robert J. GOULD
21 Assoc VP for Business & Finance ... Mr. Thomas SZEJKO
32 VP and Dean of Student Life ... Ms. Eva CHATTERJEE-SUTTON
44 Dir of Campaigns & Advancement Oper ... Ms. Lori DOUGHERTY
20 Associate Dean of the Faculty ... Dr. Charles HANNON
58 Assoc Dean Grad/Continuing Studies ... Dr. Michael SHAUGHNESSY
28 Asst Dean Stdnt Life/Dir Diver Pgm ... Ms. Ketwana SCHOOS
20 Asst Dean for Academic Affairs ... Dr. Steven MALINAK
18 Dir of Campus Operations & Planning ... Mr. Jim MILLER
26 Dir Comm/Special Asst to President ... Ms. Karen OOSTERHOUS
06 Registrar ... Ms. Leslie MAXIN
29 Assoc VP Alumni Relations & Dev ... Ms. Michele HUFNAGEL
07 Director of Admission ... Mr. Robert ADKINS
37 Director Financial Aid ... Ms. Michelle ANDERSON
13 Dir of Information/Technology Svcs ... Mr. Daniel FAULK
15 Director Human Resources ... Mr. Robert ALLISON
19 Director Protection Services ... Mr. Robert COCCO
36 Director Career Services ... Ms. Roberta CROSS
40 Bookstore Manager ... Ms. Cynthia BRICELAND
41 Director of Athletics ... Mr. Scott MCGUINNESS
08 Director of Library Services ... Ms. Alexis RITTENBERGER
102 Foundation & Corp Relations Officer ... Ms. Julie THROCKMORTON
91 Assoc Director for Admin Computing ... Mr. Michael A. TIMKO
104 Director of Study Abroad ... Ms. Sara KOCHUBA
108 Dir of Assessment & Inst Research ... Ms. Lindsey GUINN
88 Director of Academic Advising ... Ms. Elizabeth MCCLINTOCK
88 Director Conferences and Events ... Ms. Maureen VALENTINE
38 Director of Counseling Services ... Ms. Lisa HAMILTON
39 Director of Residence Life ... Mr. Tyler KOWCHECK

Waynesburg University (C)

51 W College Street, Waynesburg PA 15370-1222
County: Greene FICE Identification: 003391
Unit ID: 216694
Telephone: (724) 627-8191 Carnegie Class: Master's L
FAX Number: N/A Calendar System: Semester
URL: www.waynesburg.edu
Established: 1849 Annual Undergrad Tuition & Fees: $21,620
Enrollment: 2,039 Coed
Affiliation or Control: Presbyterian Church (U.S.A.) IRS Status: 501(c)3
Highest Offering: Doctorate
Program: Liberal Arts And General; Teacher Preparatory; Professional
Accreditation: M, CAATE, CACREP, NURSE

00 Chancellor ... Dr. Timothy R. THYREEN
01 President ... Mr. Doug LEE
05 Vice Pres Academic Affairs/Provost ... Dr. Jaqueline CORE
10 Chief Financial Officer ... Mr. John OLON
32 VP of Student Services ... Mrs. Mary CUMMINGS
06 Registrar ... Mrs. Vicki WILSON
41 Athletic Director ... Mr. Larry MARSHALL
13 Interim Dir Information Technology ... Mr. William DUMIRE
08 Director Eberly Library ... Mr. Rea REDD
26 Communication Specialist ... Ms. Ashley WISE
36 Director of Placement ... Mrs. Marie E. COFFMAN
38 Student Counselor ... Mrs. Jane S. OWEN
21 Business Ofc Supervisor/Controller ... Mr. Dave MARTIN
23 Director of Health Services ... Ms. Jennifer SHIRING
15 Director Human Resources ... Mr. Tom HELMICK
37 Director Student Financial Aid ... Mr. Matthew STOKAN

Westminster College (D)

319 South Market Street, New Wilmington PA 16172-0001
County: Lawrence FICE Identification: 003392
Unit ID: 216807
Telephone: (724) 946-8761 Carnegie Class: Bac/A&S
FAX Number: (724) 946-7132 Calendar System: Semester
URL: www.westminster.edu
Established: 1852 Annual Undergrad Tuition & Fees: $34,105
Enrollment: 1,426 Coed
Affiliation or Control: Presbyterian Church (U.S.A.) IRS Status: 501(c)3
Highest Offering: Master's
Program: Liberal Arts And General; Teacher Preparatory
Accreditation: M, MUS

01 President ... Dr. Richard H. DORMAN
05 Vice Pres Academic Affs/Dean of Col ... Dr. Jane M. WOOD
30 VP Inst Advancement/Chief Dev Ofcr ... Mr. Matthew P. STINSON
10 Vice Pres Finance/Mgmt Services ... Mr. Kenneth J. ROMIG
06 Registrar ... Mr. Scott D. WIGNALL
07 Vice President for Enrollment ... Dr. Thomas H. STEIN
42 Dean of the Chapel ... Rev. James R. MOHR
32 VP Student Affairs/Dean of Students ... Dr. Neal A. EDMAN
35 Assoc Dean of Student Affairs ... Ms. Gina M. VANCE
37 Director Student Financial Aid ... Ms. Cheryl GERBER
08 Int Assoc Dean Library/Info Service ... Ms. Erin T. SMITH
36 Director of Career Center ... Ms. Kathryn K. DEMEDAL
29 Director of Alumni Relations ... Ms. Kara H. MONTGOMERY
26 Sr Dir Marketing/Communications ... Mr. Richard A. SHERLOCK
20 Assoc Dean Academic Affairs ... Dr. Jamie G. MCMINN
58 Dir Graduate School/Adult Studies ... Dr. Robert L. ZORN
41 Athletic Director ... Mr. James E. DAFLER
18 Director of Physical Plant ... Mr. Ronald J. PENNINGTON
21 Business Manager ... Ms. Janet M. SMITH
19 Director of Public Safety ... Mr. James D. WALKER
09 Director of Institutional Research ... Dr. Jamie G. MCMINN
23 Director Health Services ... Ms. Melissa M. BARON
40 Bookstore Manager ... Ms. Kay A. GALANSKI
21 Controller ... Ms. Christine A. MILLER
15 Director of Human Resources ... Ms. Kimberlee K. CHRISTOFFERSON
38 Counselor ... Ms. Barbara I. QUINCY
28 Director of Diversity Services ... Ms. Jeannette HUBBARD

Westminster Theological Seminary (E)

2960 Church Road, Glenside PA 19038
County: Montgomery FICE Identification: 003393
Unit ID: 216816
Telephone: (215) 887-5511 Carnegie Class: Spec/Faith
FAX Number: (215) 887-5404 Calendar System: Semester
URL: www.wts.edu
Established: 1929 Annual Graduate Tuition & Fees: $13,500
Enrollment: 560 Coed
Affiliation or Control: Independent Non-Profit IRS Status: 501(c)3
Highest Offering: Doctorate; No Undergraduates
Program: Professional; Religious Emphasis
Accreditation: M, THEOL

01 President ... Dr. Peter A. LILLBACK
05 Provost/Executive Vice President ... Dr. Jeffrey K. JUE
30 Vice Pres Development/Gen Counsel ... Mr. James M. SWEET
32 VP for Campus Life/Dean of Students ... Mr. Steven J. CARTER
44 Vice Pres Advancement Operations ... Mr. Chun LAI
10 Chief Financial Officer ... Mr. Mark R. WILSON
20 Associate Dean for Academic Affairs ... Ms. Rebecca M. LIPPERT
06 Registrar ... Ms. Melinda E. DUGAN
07 Director of Admissions ... Mr. Jonathan M. BRACK
08 Director of Library Services ... Mr. Alexander (Sandy) FINLAYSON
73 Director DMin/Supervised Ministry ... Mr. Timothy Z. WITMER
40 Director Bookstore ... Mr. Chun LAI
37 Financial Aid Officer ... Ms. Fiona E. DAVENPORT
13 Information Systems Director ... Mr. Cris R. SIMPSON
18 Physical Plant Manager ... Mr. Richard W. MAIENSHEIN
04 Administrative Asst to President ... Ms. Abigail DAISE

Westmoreland County Community College (F)

145 Pavilion Lane, Youngwood PA 15697-1895
County: Westmoreland FICE Identification: 010176
Unit ID: 216825
Telephone: (724) 925-4000 Carnegie Class: Assoc/Pub-S-SC
FAX Number: (724) 925-1150 Calendar System: Semester
URL: www.wccc.edu
Established: 1970 Annual Undergrad Tuition & Fees (In-District): $4,830
Enrollment: 5,638 Coed
Affiliation or Control: Local IRS Status: 501(c)3
Highest Offering: Associate Degree
Program: Occupational; 2-Year Principally Bachelor's Creditable
Accreditation: M, ACFEI, ADNUR, DA, DH, DMS, MAC

01 President ... Dr. Tuesday STANLEY
05 Vice Pres Acad Affs/Stdnt Svcs ... Dr. Kristy BISHOP
11 Vice Pres Administrative Services ... Vacant
51 VP Cont Educ/Workforce & Cmty Devel ... Dr. Patrick E. GERITY
20 Assoc VP Academic Affairs ... Dr. Donna CARUTHERS
10 Chief Business Officer ... Vacant
25 Director of Grants ... Ms. Debra J. WILLIAMS
15 Director Human Resources ... Ms. Lauren M. FARRELL
106 Dir Distance Edu/Learning Resources ... Ms. Annette BOYER
77 Dean Computer Tech/Business ... Mr. Edwin C. NELSON
76 Dean Health Profess/Biology ... Dr. Kathleen A. MALLOY
103 Dean Workforce Development ... Mr. Frank J. KORDALSKI
79 Dean Public Svc/Human/Soc Science ... Dr. Andrew BARNETTE
32 Dean of Students ... Ms. Diane D. HIGHTOWER
84 Director Enrollment Management ... Vacant
102 Exec Director Education Foundation ... Ms. Debra D. WOODS
37 Director Financial Aid ... Ms. Sheila NELSON-HENSLEY
18 Director Facilities ... Vacant
21 Controller ... Mr. Timothy W. STAHL
13 Director Information Technology ... Vacant
109 Director College Services ... Mr. Ronald A. KRIVDA
26 Director Public Relations ... Ms. Anna Marie PALATELLA
07 Director Admissions ... Ms. Janice T. GRABOWSKI
41 Director Student Life/Athletics ... Mr. Richard G. HOLLER
09 Dir Institutional Research/Data Svc ... Vacant
96 Director of Purchasing ... Mr. James LUTZ
36 Coord Student Placement/Coop Ed ... Ms. Cheryl A. NOEL

Widener University (G)

One University Place, Chester PA 19013-5792
County: Delaware FICE Identification: 003313
Unit ID: 216852
Telephone: (610) 499-4000 Carnegie Class: DRU
FAX Number: (610) 876-9751 Calendar System: Semester
URL: www.widener.edu
Established: 1821 Annual Undergrad Tuition & Fees: $41,224
Enrollment: 5,985 Coed
Affiliation or Control: Independent Non-Profit IRS Status: 501(c)3
Highest Offering: Doctorate
Program: Liberal Arts And General; Teacher Preparatory; Professional
Accreditation: M, BUS, CLPSY, ENG, HSA, IPSY, LAW, NURSE, PTA, SW, TED

01 Interim President ... Dr. Stephen C. WILHITE
05 Interim Sr Vice President/Provost ... Dr. Jerry M. GREINER
10 Sr Vice Pres Administration/Finance ... Mr. Joseph J. BAKER
30 Vice Pres University Advancement ... Ms. Linda S. DURANT
13 Chief Information Officer ... Mr. Peter D. SHOUDY
21 Associate VP & Controller ... Ms. Catherine MCGEEHAN
11 Associate VP of Administration ... Mr. George E. HASSEL
26 Asst Vice Pres University Relations ... Ms. Lou Anne BULIK
18 Director of Operations ... Mr. Carl G. PIERCE
58 Assoc Provost Grad Studies ... Dr. Penelope S. GREENBERG
20 Associate Provost Undergraduate ... Dr. Geraldine A. BLOEMKER
32 Assoc Provost/Dean of Students ... Dr. Denise D. GIFFORD
54 Dean School of Engineering ... Dr. Fred A. AKL
49 Dean College Arts & Sciences ... Dr. Sharon M. MEAGHER
50 Dean School of Business Admin ... Vacant

66 Dean School of Nursing ....Dr. Laura C. DZUREC
51 Dean Sch of Educ/Innov/Cont Studies ....Dr. Shawn M. FITZGERALD
88 Dean Sch Human Svc Professions ....Dr. Paula SILVER
21 Bursar ....Ms. Diana BARRACLOUGH
08 Librarian ....Dr. Robert E. DANFORD
37 Exec Dir Student Financial Services ....Mr. Thomas K. MALLOY
06 Director of Records/Registration ....Ms. Kristen CHANDO
29 Director of Alumni Engagement ....Ms. Tina A. PHILLIPS
09 Dir of Inst Res & Effectiveness ....Dr. Stephen W. THORPE
36 Placement Director ....Ms. Jan MOPPERT
41 Director of Athletics ....Mr. Jack L. SHAFER
85 Director International Student Svcs ....Ms. Kandy TURNER
19 Director of Campus Safety ....Mr. Patrick SULLIVAN
23 Director of Health Services ....Ms. Lynn A. NELSON-RUSSOM
24 Head of Multimedia/Classroom Spprt ....Mr. Eric WOEBKENBERG
40 Manager Campus Bookstore ....Vacant
91 Director Information Systems ....Mrs. Linda TAYLOR
88 Director Technical Resources ....Mr. Perry M. DRAYFAHL
15 Director of Human Resources ....Ms. Beth GLASSMAN
96 Director of Purchasing ....Ms. Michelle SHELTON
89 Dir Student Success/Retention ....Mr. Timothy J. CAIRY
97 Dir Honors Program in General Educ ....Dr. Ilene LIEBERMAN
94 Director of Women's Studies ....Dr. Annalisa CASTALDO
86 Director Government Relations ....Ms. Julie DIETRICH

† See Delaware listing of Widener University School of Law.

Widener University Commonwealth Law School (A)

3800 Vartan Way, PO Box 69380,
Harrisburg PA 17106-9380
Telephone: (717) 541-3900 Identification: 667244
Accreditation: &M, LAW

† Branch campus of Widener University, Chester, PA.

Wilkes University (B)

84 W South Street, Wilkes-Barre PA 18766-0001
County: Luzerne FICE Identification: 003394
Unit ID: 216931
Telephone: (570) 408-5000 Carnegie Class: Master's L
FAX Number: (570) 408-2934 Calendar System: Semester
URL: www.wilkes.edu
Established: 1933 Annual Undergrad Tuition & Fees: $32,356
Enrollment: 4,562 Coed
Affiliation or Control: Independent Non-Profit IRS Status: 501(c)3
Highest Offering: Doctorate
Program: Liberal Arts And General; Teacher Preparatory; Professional
Accreditation: M, ACBSP, CEA, ENG, NURSE, PHAR

01 President ....Dr. Patrick F. LEAHY
05 Provost & Sr Vice President ....Dr. Anne SKLEDER
30 Vice Pres University Advancement ....Mr. Michael WOOD
10 Vice President & General Counsel ....Mr. Loren D. PRESCOTT
21 Controller ....Ms. Janet KOBYLSKI
84 Vice President Enrollment Services ....Ms. Melanie WADE
32 Vice President Student Affairs ....Dr. Paul S. ADAMS
15 Chief Human Resource Officer ....Mr. Joseph HOUSENICK
35 Dean of Students ....Mr. Mark R. ALLEN
88 Associate Dean Student Affairs ....Vacant
54 Dean of Science & Engineering ....Dr. William HUDSON
49 Dean College Arts & Humanities ....Dr. Paul RIGGS
67 Dean Nesbitt Col Pharmacy ....Dr. Bernard GRAHAM
88 VP of Strategic Initiatives ....Dr. Michael SPEZIALE
50 Dean Sidhu School of Business ....Dr. Jeffrey ALVES
62 Dean Library ....Mr. John STACHACZ
09 Exec Director Info/Analysis/Plng ....Mr. Brian BOGERT
29 Director Alumni Relations ....Ms. Bridget GIUANTA
41 Director of Athletics ....Ms. Addy MALATESTA
23 Director Health Services ....Ms. Diane E. O'BRIEN
36 Director Career Services ....Mrs. Carol A. BOSACK-KOSEK
39 Director Residence Life ....Ms. Elizabeth ROVEDA
58 Director Graduate Teach Education ....Ms. Grace SURDOVEL
06 Registrar ....Mrs. Susan A. HRITZAK
37 Interim Director of Financial Aid ....Ms. Delaina JAYNE
26 Assoc VP Marketing Communications ....Mr. Jack A. CHIELLI
18 Director Facilities Services ....Mr. Charles CARY
07 Director of Admissions ....Mr. Alex SPERRAZZA
28 Exec Director of Diversity ....Ms. Georgia COSTALAS
96 Dir Procurement & Financial Svcs ....Ms. Alicia BOND
25 Director of Sponsored Programs ....Ms. Amanda MODROVSKY
27 Director of Marketing ....Mrs. Kim D. BOWER SPENCE
04 Assistant to the President ....Ms. Dawn LEAS

Williamson Free School of Mechanical Trades (C)

106 S New Middletown Road, Media PA 19063-5299
County: Delaware FICE Identification: 041238
Unit ID: 216940
Telephone: (610) 566-1776 Carnegie Class: Not Classified
FAX Number: (610) 566-6502 Calendar System: Semester
URL: www.williamson.edu
Established: 1888 Annual Undergrad Tuition & Fees: N/A
Enrollment: 275 Male
Affiliation or Control: Independent Non-Profit IRS Status: 501(c)3
Highest Offering: Associate Degree
Program: Occupational
Accreditation: ACCSC

01 President ....Mr. Michael J. ROUNDS
10 Exec Vice President and CEO ....Mr. Gregory L. LINDEMUTH
05 Vice President of Education & CAO ....Mr. Thomas E. WISNESKI
30 Vice President of Inst Advancement ....Vacant
32 Dean of Students ....Mr. Thomas J. MOFFITT
84 Director of Enrollments ....Mr. Jason C. MERILLAT
41 Director of Athletics ....Mr. Dale H. PLUMMER
42 Chaplain/Counselor ....Rev. Mark A. SPECHT
06 Registrar ....Ms. Anne M. HAYES
36 Director of Placement ....Ms. Margaret T. KINGHAM
26 Director of Public Relations ....Mr. Carl A. VAIRO

Wilson College (D)

1015 Philadelphia Avenue, Chambersburg PA 17201-1285
County: Franklin FICE Identification: 003396
Unit ID: 217013
Telephone: (717) 262-4141 Carnegie Class: Bac/Diverse
FAX Number: (717) 264-1578 Calendar System: 4/1/4
URL: www.wilson.edu
Established: 1869 Annual Undergrad Tuition & Fees: $24,392
Enrollment: 759 Coed
Affiliation or Control: Presbyterian Church (U.S.A.) IRS Status: 501(c)3
Highest Offering: Master's
Program: Liberal Arts And General; Teacher Preparatory
Accreditation: M

01 President ....Dr. Barbara K. MISTICK
05 VP for Academic Affairs/Dean of Fac ....Dr. Elissa HEIL
30 VP for Institutional Advancement ....Ms. Camilla B. RAWLEIGH
10 Vice Pres Finance & Administration ....Mr. Brian ECKER
84 Vice President for Enrollment ....Ms. Mary Ann NASO
32 Vice President for Student Dev/Dean ....Dr. Mary Beth WILLIAMS
26 VP for Marketing and Communications ....Mr. Brian SPEER
100 Chief of Staff ....Ms. Melissa J. IMES
06 Registrar ....Ms. Jean B. HOOVER
37 Dean of Financial Aid ....Ms. Linda D. BRITTAIN
09 Asst Dean IR and Assesment ....Vacant
08 Director of Library ....Ms. Kathleen MURPHY
18 Director of Physical Plant ....Mr. Jack KELLY
27 Manager of Media Relations ....Ms. Cathy MENTZER
40 College Store Coordinator ....Ms. Robin HERRING
41 Athletic Director ....Ms. Lori FREY
51 Director of Conferences ....Mr. Joel PAGLIARO
29 Director of Alumnae Programs ....Ms. Marybeth FAMULARE
44 Director of Annual Fund ....Ms. Carolyn WOODS
15 Director Human Resources ....Vacant
20 Assoc Dean of Academic Advising ....Dr. Deborah AUSTIN
21 Assoc VP for Finance/Admin ....Ms. Lori TOSTEN
36 Director of Career Development ....Ms. Linda A. BOECKMAN
38 Director of Student Counseling ....Ms. Cindy SHOEMAKER
88 Director of Women With Children Pgm ....Ms. Katherine KOUGH
37 Coordinator of Financial Aid ....Ms. Christine KNOUSE
28 Coordinator of Diversity ....Vacant
42 Chaplain ....Rev. Emily MORGAN
39 Director of Residence Life ....Ms. Sherri SADOWSKI
102 Dir Foundation/Corporate Relations ....Ms. Margaret LIGHT
07 Director of Admissions ....Ms. Patty BEIDE

Won Institute of Graduate Studies (E)

137 S Easton Road, Glenside PA 19038
County: Montgomery FICE Identification: 039493
Unit ID: 442064
Telephone: (215) 884-8942 Carnegie Class: Spec/Health
FAX Number: (215) 884-9002 Calendar System: Trimester
URL: www.woninstitute.edu
Established: 2002 Annual Graduate Tuition & Fees: $19,143
Enrollment: 88 Coed
Affiliation or Control: Independent Non-Profit IRS Status: 501(c)3
Highest Offering: Master's; No Undergraduates
Program: Professional
Accreditation: M, ACUP

01 President ....Dr. Bokin KIM
11 Chief Administrative Officer ....Ms. Colleen O'CONNELL
10 Chief Financial Officer ....Mr. Walter SINGER
05 Chief Academic Officer ....Ms. Gloria NOUEL
06 Registrar ....Ms. Annie MAHONEY
08 Librarian ....Mrs. Sandy HOSTETTER
85 International Student Advisor ....Rev. Hojin PARK
13 Chief Info Technology Officer (CIO) ....Ms. Elizabeth REED
26 Chief Public Relations/Marketing ....Mr. Zach BREMMER

WyoTech-Blairsville (F)

500 Innovation Drive, Blairsville PA 15717-8060
Telephone: (724) 459-9500 Identification: 666305
Accreditation: ACCSC

† Branch campus of Wyoming Technical Institute, Laramie, WY.

Yeshiva Beth Moshe (G)

930 Hickory Street, Scranton PA 18505-2196
County: Lackawanna FICE Identification: 013134
Unit ID: 217040
Telephone: (570) 346-1747 Carnegie Class: Spec/Faith
FAX Number: (570) 346-2251 Calendar System: Semester
Established: 1965 Annual Undergrad Tuition & Fees: $8,800
Enrollment: 56 Male
Affiliation or Control: Independent Non-Profit IRS Status: 501(c)3
Highest Offering: Second Talmudic Degree
Program: Teacher Preparatory; Professional; Religious Emphasis
Accreditation: RABN

01 Chief Executive Officer ....Rabbi Yaakov SCHNAIDMAN
03 Executive Director ....Rabbi Avraham PRESSMAN

York College of Pennsylvania (H)

Country Club Road, York PA 17403-3651
County: York FICE Identification: 003399
Unit ID: 217059
Telephone: (717) 846-7788 Carnegie Class: Master's S
FAX Number: (717) 849-1607 Calendar System: Semester
URL: www.ycp.edu
Established: 1787 Annual Undergrad Tuition & Fees: $18,240
Enrollment: 5,062 Coed
Affiliation or Control: Independent Non-Profit IRS Status: 501(c)3
Highest Offering: Doctorate
Program: Liberal Arts And General; Teacher Preparatory; Professional
Accreditation: M, ACBSP, ANEST, COARC, CS, ENG, MUS, NRPA, NURSE

01 President ....Dr. Pamela J. GUNTER-SMITH
05 Dean of Academic Affairs ....Dr. TJ ARANT
10 Chief Financial Officer ....Mr. Matthew SMITH
20 Assoc Dean Academic Affairs ....Dr. Carl SEAQUIST
20 Dean of Academic Services ....Dr. Deborah D. RICKER
32 Dean of Student Affairs ....Mr. Joseph F. MERKLE
18 Dean of Campus Operations ....Dr. Kenneth M. MARTIN
44 Dean of College Advancement ....Vacant
41 Asst Dean Athletics & Recreation ....Mr. Paul SAIKIA
84 Dean Enrollment Management ....Dr. Janine BECKER
26 Asst Dean Institutional Advancement ....Ms. Mary E. DOLHEIMER
30 Asst Dean Development ....Mr. Zane GIZZI
07 Director of Admissions ....Vacant
06 Registrar ....Ms. Rebecca C. LINK
08 Librarian ....Vacant
37 Director of Financial Aid ....Mr. Calvin H. WILLIAMS
13 Assoc Dean Information Technology ....Vacant
29 Director Alumni Relations ....Mrs. Kristin SCHAB
36 Asst Dean Career Development ....Ms. Beverly A. EVANS
06 Assoc Registrar/Director of Records ....Mr. William BENTON
19 Director of Public Safety ....Mr. Edward C. BRUDER
39 Director of Residence Life ....Mr. Robbie BACON
31 Director Community Education ....Mr. Leroy M. KEENEY
15 Director Human Resources ....Mrs. Vicki L. STEWART
38 Director Counseling Services ....Mr. Darrell WILT
91 Dir Administrative Computer Center ....Mr. Brian K. SMELTZER
23 Director Health Services ....Mrs. Amy DOWNS
40 Director Bookstore ....Mrs. Lynn P. FERRO
88 Director Campus & Special Events ....Ms. Sherry HEFLIN
102 Dir Corporate/Foundation/Govt Rels ....Mr. Jeffrey VERMEULEN
27 College Editor ....Mrs. Gail HUGANIR
42 Coordinator Religious Activities ....Mrs. Louise WORLEY
31 Dean Ctr for Community Engagement ....Dr. Dominic F. DELLICARPINI
09 Director of Institutional Research ....Ms. Sarah GALLIMORE
35 Asst Dean Student Affairs ....Dr. Darrien DAVENPORT
24 Dir Center for Teaching & Learning ....Mrs. Cindy CRIMMINS
44 Sr Dir Principal & Planned Gifts ....Mr. Mark RANK
04 Executive Asst to President ....Mrs. Cynthia E. REISINGER

YTI Career Institute (I)

2900 Fairway Drive, Altoona PA 16602
County: Blair FICE Identification: 030819
Unit ID: 375939
Telephone: (814) 944-5643 Carnegie Class: Not Classified
FAX Number: (814) 944-5309 Calendar System: Quarter
URL: www.yti.edu
Established: 2006 Annual Undergrad Tuition & Fees: N/A
Enrollment: 334 Coed
Affiliation or Control: Proprietary IRS Status: Proprietary
Highest Offering: Associate Degree
Program: Occupational
Accreditation: ACCSC, #COARC, MAC

01 Campus President ....Ms. Natalie LOMBARDO
05 Director of Education ....Mr. Jack MARQUIS

YTI Career Institute (J)

3050 Hempland Road, Lancaster PA 17601
Telephone: (717) 295-1100 Identification: 770588
Accreditation: ACCSC, CAHIIM, MAC

† Branch campus of YTI Career Institute, York, PA.

YTI Career Institute (K)

1405 Williams Road, York PA 17402-9017
County: York FICE Identification: 021274
Unit ID: 217077
Telephone: (717) 757-1100 Carnegie Class: Assoc/PrivFP
FAX Number: (717) 757-4964 Calendar System: Quarter
URL: www.yti.edu
Established: 1967 Annual Undergrad Tuition & Fees: $33,140
Enrollment: 1,677 Coed
Affiliation or Control: Proprietary IRS Status: Proprietary
Highest Offering: Associate Degree
Program: Occupational
Accreditation: ACCSC, ACFEI, MAC

01 Chairman and CEO ... Mr. Timothy FOSTER
12 President - York ... Ms. Adrienne SCOTT
12 President - Lancaster ... Mr. Michael MARINO
12 President - Altoona ... Mrs. Natalie LOMBARDO
12 President - MTC ... Mr. Michael MARINO
05 Sr VP Education & Regulatory ... Ms. Eva STEIN
10 CFO ... Mr. Andrew EMMERLING
13 Director of Technology ... Vacant

RHODE ISLAND

Brown University (A)

Providence RI 02912
County: Providence FICE Identification: 003401
Unit ID: 217156
Telephone: (401) 863-1000 Carnegie Class: RU/VH
FAX Number: (401) 863-3700 Calendar System: Semester
URL: www.brown.edu
Established: 1764 Annual Undergrad Tuition & Fees: $49,346
Enrollment: 9,181 Coed
Affiliation or Control: Independent Non-Profit IRS Status: 501(c)3
Highest Offering: Doctorate
Program: Liberal Arts And General; Professional
Accreditation: EH, ENG, IPSY, MED, PDPSY, PH

01 President ... Christina H. PAXSON
05 Provost ... Richard M. LOCKE
30 Sr Vice Pres for Univ Advancement ... Patricia WATSON
102 Exec Vice Pres Planning & Policy ... Russell C. CAREY
10 Exec VP Finance/Administration ... Barbara D. CHERNOW
26 VP for Communications ... Cass CLIATT
43 Vice President/General Counsel ... Beverly E. LEDBETTER
13 Vice Pres Computing/Info Services ... Ravindra PENDSE
29 Vice President Alumni Relations ... Todd G. ANDREWS
18 Vice Pres for Facilities Management ... Stephen M. MAIORISI
46 Vice President for Research ... David SAVITZ
15 Vice Pres for Human Resources ... Karen DAVIS
32 Vice Pres Campus Life/Student Svcs ... Margaret M. KLAWUNN
20 Deputy Provost ... Joseph S. MEISEL
28 Assoc Provost Acad Devel/Diversity ... Liza CARIAGA-LO
63 Dean Medicine & Biological Sciences ... Jack ELIAS
58 Dean of Graduate School ... Peter M. WEBER
20 Dean of the Faculty ... Kevin MCLAUGHLIN
20 Dean of the College ... Maud MANDEL
07 Dean of Admission ... James S. MILLER
31 Director State/Community Relations ... Albert A. DAHLBERG
08 University Librarian ... Harriette HEMMASI
21 University Controller/Assistant VP ... Donald S. SCHANCK
41 Director of Athletics ... Jack HAYES
06 Registrar ... Robert F. FITZGERALD
37 Director of Financial Aid ... James TILTON
19 Dir Public Safety/Chief of Police ... Mark J. PORTER
38 Director Psychological Services ... Sherri NELSON
09 Director of Institutional Research ... Katharine T. BARNES
96 Director of Procurement ... Jeanne HEBERT

Bryant University (B)

1150 Douglas Pike, Smithfield RI 02917-1291
County: Providence FICE Identification: 003402
Unit ID: 217165
Telephone: (401) 232-6000 Carnegie Class: Master's M
FAX Number: (401) 232-6319 Calendar System: Semester
URL: www.bryant.edu
Established: 1863 Annual Undergrad Tuition & Fees: $39,421
Enrollment: 3,462 Coed
Affiliation or Control: Independent Non-Profit IRS Status: 501(c)3
Highest Offering: Beyond Master's But Less Than Doctorate
Program: Liberal Arts And General; Business Emphasis
Accreditation: EH, #ARCPA, BUS

00 Chairman Board of Trustees ... Mr. Michael FISHER
01 President ... Mr. Ronald K. MACHTLEY
04 Exec Asst to the President ... Mr. James PATTI
05 Provost ... Mr. Glenn SULMASY
32 VP & Dean Student Affairs ... Dr. John SADDLEMIRE
82 VP International Affairs ... Dr. Hong YANG
10 VP Business Affairs ... Mr. Barry F. MORRISON
30 VP University Advancement ... Mr. David WEGRZYN
13 VP Information Services/CIO ... Mr. Chuck LOCURTO
15 Assoc VP Human Resources ... Ms. Linda S. LULLI
18 Asst VP Campus Management ... Mr. Brian J. BRITTON
21 Asst VP Business & Controller ... Mr. Farokh BHADA
49 Dean College of Arts & Sciences ... Dr. Wendy SAMTER
50 Int Dean College of Business ... Dr. V. K. UNNI
58 Asst Dean Graduate School ... Mr. Richard CHENEY
84 VP Enrollment Management ... Ms. Michelle CLOUTIER
51 Dir Exec Development Center ... Ms. Annette CERILLI
88 Exec Dir Inst for Family Enterprise ... Dr. William T. O'HARA
88 Dir RI Export Assistance Center ... Mr. Raymond FOGARTY
89 Dir Academic Center for Excellence ... Dr. Laurie L. HAZARD
20 Asst VP Teaching and Learning ... Vacant
06 Registrar ... Ms. Susan MCLACKEN
20 Asst to VP Academic Affairs ... Ms. Elizabeth A. POWERS
35 Assoc Dean of Students ... Mr. Robert E. SLOSS
39 Assoc Dean Residence Life ... Mr. John DENIO
35 Assoc Dean Student Life ... Ms. Judy KAWAMOTO
88 Dir Bryant Center Operations ... Mr. Richard DANKEL
36 Dir Career Services ... Ms. Barbara FINEMAN
42 Chaplain Campus Ministry ... Rev. Philip DEVENS
38 Dir Counseling Services ... Mr. William PHILLIPS
23 Dir Health Services ... Ms. Susan CURRAN
28 Dir Intercultural Center ... Dr. Mailee KUE
19 Dir Public Safety ... Mr. Stephen BANNON
31 Dir Student Involvement Center ... Mr. John LINDSAY
88 Interim Dir Women's Center ... Ms. Kristin BIGGINS
07 Dir Transfer Admission ... Ms. Brenda DORAN
07 Sr Assoc Dir Mulitcult Admission ... Ms. Priscilla ALICEA
07 Assoc Dir International Admission ... Mr. John ERIKSEN
37 Dir Financial Aid ... Mr. John B. CANNING
88 Dir Conferences & Special Events ... Ms. Sheila GUAY
96 Dir Purchasing & Support Services ... Ms. Paulette RATTIGAN
44 Exec Dir Development ... Ms. Robin MAREK
29 Dir Alumni Relations ... Ms. Robin T. WARDE
90 Dir Acad Computing & Media Svcs ... Mr. Phillip LOMBARDI
91 Dir Admin Systems ... Ms. Christine BIGWOOD
14 Dir Computer & Telecomm Svcs ... Mr. Richard SIEDZIK
08 Dir Library Services ... Ms. Mary F. MORONEY
16 Assoc Dir Human Resources ... Ms. Catherine CURRIE
41 Dir Athletics ... Mr. Bill SMITH
09 Dir Planning & Inst Research ... Mr. Robert JONES
88 Exec Dir US-China Institute ... Dr. Hong YANG
40 Manager Bookstore ... Mr. Stanley STOWIK
26 Chief Public Relations/Marketing ... Ms. Elizabeth O'NEILL
104 Director Study Abroad ... Ms. Cyndi LEWIS

Community College of Rhode Island (C)

400 East Avenue, Warwick RI 02886-1807
County: Kent FICE Identification: 003408
Unit ID: 217475
Telephone: (401) 825-1000 Carnegie Class: Assoc/Pub-U-MC
FAX Number: (401) 825-2365 Calendar System: Semester
URL: www.ccri.edu
Established: 1964 Annual Undergrad Tuition & Fees (In-State): $4,226
Enrollment: 17,553 Coed
Affiliation or Control: State IRS Status: 501(c)3
Highest Offering: Associate Degree
Program: Occupational; 2-Year Principally Bachelor's Creditable
Accreditation: EH, ACBSP, ADNUR, COARC, COMTA, DA, DH, DMS, HT, MLTAD, MUS, OTA, PNUR, PTAA, RAD

01 President ... Mr. Ray M. DI PASQUALE
05 Vice President for Academic Affairs ... Dr. Gregory A. LAMONTAGNE
10 Vice President for Business Affairs ... Mr. David B. PATTEN
30 Vice Pres Institutional Advancement ... Vacant
32 Assoc VP for Student Services ... Dr. Ronald L. SCHERTZ
84 Int Dean of Enrollment Services ... Mr. Joel A. FRIEDMAN
11 Interim Director of Administration ... Mr. Kenneth F. MCCABE
49 Dean Arts/Humanities/Soc Sciences ... Vacant
66 Dean of Nursing/Allied Health ... Vacant
50 Dean Business/Science/Technology ... Dr. Peter N. WOODBERRY
51 Assoc Vice President of CWCE ... Ms. Robin Ann SMITH
08 Dean of Learning Resources ... Ms. Ruth D. SULLIVAN
35 Dean of Students ... Mr. Michael J. CUNNINGHAM, II
21 Controller ... Ms. Sharon A. PICARD
35 Assoc Dean Student Life/Svc Lrng ... Dr. Rebecca H. YOUNT
15 Director of Human Resources ... Ms. Sheri L. NORTON
13 Interim Chief Information Officer ... Mr. William R. FERLAND
19 Director of Safety & Security ... Mr. Dale R. WETHERELL
26 Director Marketing & Communications ... Mr. Richard H. COREN
41 Director of Athletics ... Mr. Joseph PAVONE
09 Director Inst Research/Planning ... Dr. William LEBLANC
21 Bursar ... Mr. Dennis J. GRASSINI
88 Director Access to Opportunity ... Ms. Tracy KARASINSKI
40 Director Bookstore Operations ... Ms. Colleen D. TURCOTTE
29 Director of Alumni Affairs ... Ms. Marisa ALBINI
18 Int Chief Facilities/Physical Plant ... Mr. David A. SNOW
96 Director of Purchasing ... Ms. Lisa M. CONSIVINE-FONTES
21 Business Manager ... Ms. Ruth A. BARRINGTON
36 Coordinator Career Services ... Ms. Camille NUMRICH
37 Director of Financial Aid ... Mr. Joel A. FRIEDMAN

Johnson & Wales University (D)

8 Abbott Park Place, Providence RI 02903-3703
County: Providence FICE Identification: 003404
Unit ID: 217235
Telephone: (401) 598-1000 Carnegie Class: Master's L
FAX Number: (401) 598-2880 Calendar System: Quarter
URL: www.jwu.edu
Established: 1914 Annual Undergrad Tuition & Fees: $28,539
Enrollment: 9,955 Coed
Affiliation or Control: Independent Non-Profit IRS Status: 501(c)3
Highest Offering: Doctorate
Program: Occupational; 2-Year Principally Bachelor's Creditable; Teacher Preparatory; Professional
Accreditation: EH, #ARCPA, DIETD

00 Chairman of the Board ... Mr. Guy B. SNOWDEN
01 Chancellor ... Mr. John J. BOWEN
12 Providence Campus President/COO ... Ms. Mim L. RUNEY
32 Vice President of Student Affairs ... Mr. Ronald MARTEL
05 University Provost ... Mr. Thomas L. DWYER
30 Exec Dir of University Advancement ... Ms. Page C. SCIOTTO
85 Senior VP of Special Projects ... Mr. Kenneth R. LEVY
10 Treasurer and CFO ... Mr. Joseph J. GREENE
43 Sr VP and General Counsel ... Mr. Wayne M. KEZIRIAN
36 VP of Experiential Ed & Career Svc ... Ms. Maureen DUMAS
84 Sr VP of Enrollment Management ... Mr. Kenneth F. DISAIA
15 Vice President of Human Resources ... Ms. Diane D'AMBRA
50 Dean of College of Mgmt ... Mr. Michael PETRILLOSE
49 Dean of Arts & Sciences ... Ms. Angela RENAUD
54 Dean of the School of Engr & Design ... Mr. Frank TWEEDIE
88 Dean of Culinary Education ... Mr. Peter LEHMULLER
109 Vice President of Auxiliary Service ... Mr. Michael DOWNING
18 Vice President of Facilities Mgmt ... Mr. Christopher PLACCO
13 Chief Information Officer ... Ms. Marianne DORAN COLLINS
11 Senior Vice Pres of Administration ... Ms. Marie BERNARDO-SOUSA
100 Chief of Staff & Corp Secretary ... Ms. Emily GILCREAST
96 Director of Procurement ... Mr. Michael GILLARDI
36 Director of Ext Educ & Career Svcs ... Ms. Sheri ISPIR
09 Director of Institutional Research ... Mr. George REZENDES
19 Exec Dir of Campus Safety/Security ... Major Michael P. QUINN
21 University Budget Director ... Ms. Eileen T. HASKINS
88 University Dean of Culinary Educ ... Mr. Karl J. GUGGENMOS
88 Director of Student Communications ... Ms. Kristine E. MCNAMARA
88 Dean of Academic Program Develop ... Mr. Paul J. MCVETY
106 Dean School Online & Cont Educ ... Ms. Cynthia L. PARKER

New England Institute of Technology (E)

One New England Tech Blvd., East Greenwich RI 02818
County: Kent FICE Identification: 007845
Unit ID: 217305
Telephone: (800) 736-7744 Carnegie Class: Bac/Assoc
FAX Number: (401) 886-0859 Calendar System: Quarter
URL: www.neit.edu
Established: 1940 Annual Undergrad Tuition & Fees: $23,031
Enrollment: 2,922 Coed
Affiliation or Control: Independent Non-Profit IRS Status: 501(c)3
Highest Offering: Master's
Program: 2-Year Principally Bachelor's Creditable; Technical Emphasis
Accreditation: EH, ADNUR, #COARC, ENGT, NUR, OT, OTA, PTAA, SURGT

01 President ... Mr. Richard I. GOUSE
03 Executive Vice President ... Mr. Seth KURN
05 Senior Vice President and Provost ... Dr. Douglas H. SHERMAN
10 Sr VP Financial Affs & Endowment ... Ms. Cheryl C. CONNORS
32 Vice Pres Student Support Services ... Ms. Catherine B. KENNEDY
21 VP of Finance & Business Admin ... Mr. Robert R. THEROUX
20 Associate Provost ... Dr. Henry YOUNG
07 Director of Admissions ... Mr. Michael CARUSO
37 Director Financial Aid ... Ms. Anna KELLY
08 Director Library ... Ms. Susan WARTHMAN
36 Director of Career Services ... Ms. Patricia BLAKEMORE
109 Director Auxiliary Services ... Mr. Patrick TRACEY
06 Registrar ... Ms. Doreen LASIEWSKI
35 Director Student Affairs ... Ms. Lee PEEBLES
30 Dir of Development & Alumni Rels ... Ms. Joan SEGERSON
09 Director of Institutional Research ... Dr. Henry YOUNG
106 Dir Online Education/E-learning ... Mr. Larry BOUTHILLIER
13 Chief Info Technology Officer (CIO) ... Mr. Jacques LAFLAMME
18 Chief Facilities/Physical Plant ... Mr. Patrick TRACEY
26 Chief Public Relations/Marketing ... Mr. Steven H. KITCHIN
84 Director Enrollment Management ... Ms. Kathleen EHLERS
103 Dir Workforce/Career Development ... Mr. Steven H. KITCHIN
19 Director Security/Safety ... Mr. Robert WARREN

Providence College (F)

1 Cunningham Square, Providence RI 02918-0001
County: Providence FICE Identification: 003406
Unit ID: 217402
Telephone: (401) 865-1000 Carnegie Class: Master's L
FAX Number: (401) 865-2057 Calendar System: Semester
URL: www.providence.edu
Established: 1917 Annual Undergrad Tuition & Fees: $44,520
Enrollment: 4,687 Coed
Affiliation or Control: Roman Catholic IRS Status: 501(c)3
Highest Offering: Master's
Program: Liberal Arts And General; Teacher Preparatory
Accreditation: EH, BUS, MUS, SW

01 President ... Rev. Brian J. SHANLEY, OP
03 Executive Vice President/Treasurer ... Rev. Kenneth R. SICARD, OP
04 Asst to Pres & Exec Vice President ... Ms. Ann MANCHESTER-MOLAK
05 Sr VP Academic Affairs/Provost ... Dr. Hugh F. LENA, III
10 Sr VP for Finance & Business/CFO ... Mr. John M. SWEENEY
30 Sr VP for Institutional Advancement ... Mr. Gregory T. WALDRON
32 Vice Pres Student Affairs Admin ... Ms. Kristine C. GOODWIN
43 Vice President/General Counsel ... Ms. Marifrances MCGINN
42 Vice Pres for Mission & Ministry ... Rev. R. Gabriel PIVARNIK, OP
21 Assoc VP for Finance/Asst Treasurer ... Ms. Jacqueline M. WHITE
35 Assoc VP for Student Affairs ... Dr. Steven A. SEARS
20 Assoc VP for Academic Affairs ... Dr. Brian J. BARTOLINI
41 Assoc VP for Athletics/Athletic Dir ... Mr. Robert G. DRISCOLL
15 Assoc Vice Pres for Human Resources ... Ms. Kathleen M. ALVINO
28 Assoc VP/Chief Diversity Officer ... Mr. Rafael A. ZAPATA
26 Ast VP for Public Affairs/Cmty Rels ... Mr. Steven J. MAURANO
20 Asst Vice Pres for Academic Affairs ... Mr. Charles J. HABERLE
21 Asst Vice Pres for Business Svcs ... Mr. Warren S. GRAY
29 Asst Vice Pres for Alumni Relations ... Mr. Robert FERREIRA
44 Asst Vice Pres for Development ... Ms. Lynne FRASER
45 Asst VP Capital Projects & Fac Plng ... Mr. Mark F. RAPOZA
58 Dean of Undergrad & Grad Studies ... Rev. Mark D. NOWEL, OP
49 Dean School of Arts & Sciences ... Dr. Sheila A. LIOTTA
107 Dean School of Professional Studies ... Dr. Brian M. MCCADDEN

07 Assoc VP Admissions/Financial Aid ... Mr. Raul A. FONTS
50 Dean School of Business ... Dr. Sylvia MAXFIELD
51 Dean School of Continuing Education ... Dr. Janet L. CASTLEMAN
39 Asst Dean of Students ... Ms. Tiffany D. GAFFNEY
84 Dean of Enrollment Services ... Ms. Yvonne D. ARRUDA
104 Dean of International Studies ... Mr. Adrian G. BEAULIEU
35 Director of Student Activities ... Ms. Sharon L. HAY
84 Associate Dean of Enrollment Svcs ... Ms. Ann E. BARONE
37 Exec Director of Financial Aid ... Ms. Sandra J. OLIVEIRA
19 Exec Director Safety & Security ... Mr. John J. LEYDEN
88 Asst VP Integrated Learning & Admin ... Ms. Patricia A. GOFF
18 Exec Director of Physical Plant ... Mr. William J. HARTIGAN
08 Director of Library ... Dr. Donald R. BAILEY
09 Director of Institutional Research ... Ms. Melanie R. SULLIVAN
88 Director of Telecommunications ... Mr. Carmine R. PISCOPO
92 Program Dir Liberal Arts Honors ... Dr. Stephen J. LYNCH
96 Director Central Purch/Receiving ... Mr. Mark S. MCGOVERN
88 Director of Academic Svcs/Wrt Ctr ... Mr. Bryan D. MARINELLI
38 Exec Director Personal Counseling ... Dr. James F. CAMPBELL
13 Chief Info Technology Officer (CIO) ... Vacant

Rhode Island College (A)

600 Mount Pleasant Avenue, Providence RI 02908-1991
County: Providence FICE Identification: 003407
Unit ID: 217420
Telephone: (401) 456-8000 Carnegie Class: Master's L
FAX Number: (401) 456-8379 Calendar System: Semester
URL: www.ric.edu
Established: 1854 Annual Undergrad Tuition & Fees (In-State): $8,197
Enrollment: 8,641 Coed
Affiliation or Control: State IRS Status: 501(c)3
Highest Offering: Doctorate
Program: Liberal Arts And General; Teacher Preparatory; Professional
Accreditation: EH, ART, MUS, NURSE, SW, TED

01 President ... Dr. Nancy CARRIUOLO
05 Vice President Academic Affairs ... Dr. Ronald E. PITT
10 Vice Pres Administration & Finance ... Ms. Lysa D. TEAL
32 Int Vice President Student Affairs ... Dr. Scott KANE
30 Int VP College Advance & Ext Rels ... Mr. Clark GREENE
107 Assoc VP Prof Studies & Cont Ed ... Ms. Jennifer GIROUX
20 Asst VP Acad Affairs & Dir Enr Mgt ... Dr. Holly L. SHADOIAN
21 Asst Vice Pres Finance/Controller ... Vacant
13 Asst VP Information Services ... Ms. Pamela CHRISTMAN
44 Assc VP for Develop & External Affs ... Mr. Edwin R. PACHECO
15 Director of Human Resources ... Ms. Maggie SULLIVAN
49 Dean Faculty Arts & Sciences ... Dr. Earl L. SIMSON
53 Dean Sch Education & Human Dev ... Dr. Donald C. HALQUIST
66 Dean School of Nursing ... Dr. Jane WILLIAMS
50 Dean School of Management ... Dr. David M. BLANCHETTE
70 Dean School of Social Work ... Dr. Roberta S. PEARLMUTTER
58 Int Dean of Graduate Studies ... Dr. Leslie SCHUSTER
08 Int Director of the Library ... Ms. Tovah REIS
35 Dean of Students ... Vacant
100 Coordinator of President's Staff ... Mr. Paul BROOKS
26 Dir of Communications & Marketing ... Ms. Laura HART
105 Director Web Services ... Ms. Karen M. RUBINO
07 Director of Admissions ... Mr. John MCLAUGHLIN
06 Director of Records ... Vacant
37 Director Student Financial Aid ... Mr. James T. HANBURY
25 Director of Research & Grants ... Ms. Lisa SMOLSKI
18 Director Facilities & Operations ... Mr. John PARAS
90 Director User Support Services ... Vacant
91 Director MIS ... Dr. Bin YU
14 Director Network/Telecommunications ... Mr. Henk E. SONDER
19 Director of Security ... Mr. Frederick W. GHIO
09 Dir Inst Research/Planning ... Dr. Christopher P. HOURIGAN
96 Director of Purchasing ... Ms. Jessica L. SILVA
41 Dir of Athletics & AVP for Admin ... Mr. Donald E. TENCHER
39 Director Residential Life/Housing ... Ms. Teresa L. BROWN
36 Director Career Development Center ... Vacant
23 Director College Health Services ... Ms. Lynn A. WACHTEL
38 Director Counseling Center ... Dr. Thomas J. LAVIN
29 Director Alumni Affairs ... Ms. Suzanna ALBA
40 Bookstore Manager ... Mr. Steven PLATT
104 Director of Study Abroad ... Dr. Olga JUZYN
88 Director of Budget ... Mr. Robert EATON
102 Int Director RIC Foundation ... Mr. Clark GREENE
28 Director of Diversity ... Ms. Antoinette GOMES

Rhode Island School of Design (B)

2 College Street, Providence RI 02903-2784
County: Providence FICE Identification: 003409
Unit ID: 217493
Telephone: (401) 454-6100 Carnegie Class: Spec/Arts
FAX Number: (401) 454-6320 Calendar System: 4/1/4
URL: www.risd.edu
Established: 1877 Annual Undergrad Tuition & Fees: $45,840
Enrollment: 2,449 Coed
Affiliation or Control: Independent Non-Profit IRS Status: 501(c)3
Highest Offering: Master's
Program: Liberal Arts And General; Professional; Fine Arts Emphasis
Accreditation: EH, ART, LSAR

01 President ... Ms. Rosanne SOMERSON
04 Executive Assistant to President ... Ms. Jessica HODGDEN
05 Provost ... Mr. Pradeep SHARMA
11 Chief Operating Officer ... Ms. Jean EDDY
30 Vice Pres Institutional Engagement ... Vacant
15 Vice Pres Human Resources ... Ms. Candace BAER
26 Exec Dir Marketing & Communications ... Ms. Kerci M. STROUD
88 Director RISD Museum of Art ... Mr. John W. SMITH
100 AVP Plng & Eff/Chief of Staff ... Ms. Mara HERMANO
10 Chief Financial Officer ... Mr. Samuel SOLOMON
20 Vice Provost Acad Affairs ... Ms. Carol STROHECKER
48 Dean Architecture & Design ... Ms. Nancy SKOLOS
57 Dean of Fine Arts ... Ms. Sheri WILLS
58 Dean of Graduate Studies ... Ms. Patricia PHILLIPS
89 Dean of Foundation Studies ... Ms. Joanne STRYKER
49 Dean of Liberal Arts ... Dr. Daniel CAVICCHI
51 Exec Dir Continuing Education ... Mr. Gregory J. VICTORY
08 Director Library Services ... Ms. Carol S. TERRY
84 Assoc VP Enrollment ... Mr. Edward NEWHALL, JR.
13 CIO ... Mr. Richard MICKOOL
18 Assoc VP Facilities & EHS ... Mr. Jack SILVA
32 Dean of Students ... Ms. Margaret BALCH
105 Sr Dir Digital Media Communication ... Mr. Brian CLARK
43 General Counsel ... Mr. Steven MCDONALD
31 Director of Media Relations ... Ms. Jaime MARLAND
19 Director Public Safety ... Mr. Normand GAMACHE
09 Director Institutional Research ... Ms. Jennifer DUNSEATH
45 Director Budget ... Mr. Robert HANKE
86 Director Government Relations ... Ms. Babette ALLINA
29 Director of Alumni Relations ... Ms. Christina HARTLEY
88 Exec Dir Dev/Strategic Initiatives ... Vacant
44 Director Annual Fund ... Ms. Sarah SLIGO
06 Registrar ... Mr. Steven BERENBACK
96 Director Procurement Services ... Vacant
14 Director Network Services ... Mr. Steven BOUDREAU
27 Director Editorial Services/Media ... Ms. Liisa SILANDER
23 Director Health Services ... Vacant
39 Director of Residence Life ... Mr. Kevin FORTI
38 Dir Student Development/Counseling ... Vacant
07 Asst VP for Enrollment Services ... Mr. Anthony GALLONIO
40 Director RISD Store ... Ms. Tila ADAMS
28 Dir Intercultural Stdnt Engagement ... Mr. Anthony JOHNSON
104 Director RISD Global ... Ms. Gwen FARRELLY
109 Dir of Auxiliary Services ... Ms. Ginnie DUNLEAVY

Roger Williams University (C)

One Old Ferry Road, Bristol RI 02809-2921
County: Bristol FICE Identification: 003410
Unit ID: 217518
Telephone: (401) 253-1040 Carnegie Class: Master's S
FAX Number: N/A Calendar System: Semester
URL: www.rwu.edu
Established: 1956 Annual Undergrad Tuition & Fees: $31,750
Enrollment: 4,884 Coed
Affiliation or Control: Independent Non-Profit IRS Status: 501(c)3
Highest Offering: First Professional Degree
Program: Liberal Arts And General; Teacher Preparatory; Professional
Accreditation: EH, BUS, CONST, EMT, ENG, LAW

01 President ... Dr. Donald J. FARISH
05 Provost/Sr VP Academic Affairs ... Dr. Andrew A. WORKMAN
10 EVP Finance/Administration ... Mr. Jerome WILLIAMS
43 Sr VP Legal Affs/General Counsel ... Mr. Robert H. AVERY
100 Chief of Staff ... Mr. Richard HALE
26 Vice Pres Marketing/Communications ... Ms. Judith CONNERY
84 VP Enrollment Management ... Ms. Catherine C. CAPOLUPO
21 VP for Accounting/Treasury Mgmt ... Mr. David GILMORE
32 Vice President for Student Life ... Mr. John J. KING
30 VP Institutional Advancement ... Ms. Lisa RAIOLA
45 VP University Outreach/Engagement ... Mr. Peter B. WILBUR
08 Associate Dean University Library ... Ms. Betsy P. LEARNED
35 Dean of Students ... Dr. Kathleen N. MCMAHON
88 Asst VP Enrollment Management ... Ms. Tracy M. DACOSTA
28 Assoc Dean/Dir Intercultural Center ... Vacant
61 Dean RWU School of Law ... Mr. Michael J. YELNOSKY
48 Dean Sch Arch/Art & Hist Preserv ... Mr. Stephen E. WHITE
50 Dean Gabelli School of Business ... Dr. Susan MCTIERNAN
54 Dean Sch Engrng/Comput/Constr Mgmt ... Dr. Robert A. POTTER
61 Dean School of Justice Studies ... Dr. Stephanie PICOLO MANZI
20 Vice Provost Academic Affairs ... Dr. Robert A. COLE
51 Dir Cont Studies/Grad Admiss ... Ms. Jamie GRENON
49 Dean Feinstein Col Arts & Sciences ... Dr. Robert EISINGER
07 Dir Admissions Operations/Outreach ... Ms. Amanda MARSILI
96 Director of Purchasing ... Mr. Thomas KANE
29 Assoc Dean/Dir of Conferences ... Ms. Allison CHASE PADULA
06 Registrar ... Ms. Joan ROMANO
19 Director of Public Safety ... Mr. Steven MELARAGNO
41 Director of Athletics ... Mr. Dave KEMMY
18 Director of Facilities Management ... Mr. John TAMEO
36 Director of Career Center ... Vacant
38 Director Counseling & Student Devel ... Dr. James A. AZAR
23 Director Health Services ... Ms. Anne M. ANDRADE
39 Director of Housing ... Mr. Anthony MONTEFUSCO
46 Director of Prospect Research ... Ms. Nancy L. RAMOS
39 Director Residence Life/Women's Ctr ... Ms. Jennifer STANLEY
09 Director Institutional Research ... Vacant
27 Director of Marketing ... Ms. Lori COCHRANE
40 Manager Bookstore ... Vacant

Salve Regina University (D)

100 Ochre Point Avenue, Newport RI 02840-4192
County: Newport FICE Identification: 003411
Unit ID: 217536
Telephone: (401) 847-6650 Carnegie Class: Master's M
FAX Number: (401) 341-2925 Calendar System: Semester
URL: www.salve.edu
Established: 1947 Annual Undergrad Tuition & Fees: $37,090
Enrollment: 2,739 Coed
Affiliation or Control: Roman Catholic IRS Status: 501(c)3
Highest Offering: Doctorate
Program: Liberal Arts And General; Teacher Preparatory; Professional
Accreditation: EH, ART, CORE, IACBE, NURSE, SW

01 President ... Dr. Jane GERETY, RSM
05 Vice President Academic Affairs ... Dr. Scott ZEMAN
32 Vice President Student Affairs ... Dr. Barbara LOMONACO
30 VP University Rels/Advancement ... Mr. Michael L. SEMENZA
10 Vice President Administration & CFO ... Mr. William B. HALL
84 Vice President Enrollment Services ... Mr. James FOWLER
88 Vice Pres Mission Integration ... Dr. Leona MISTO, RSM
26 Assoc Vice Pres Univ Rels/CCO ... Ms. Kristine HENDRICKSON
21 Assoc Vice Pres Finance/ Controller ... Mr. Michael N. GRANDCHAMP
13 Sr Director Info Technology/CIO ... Mr. Glenn CLARK
15 Director Human Resources ... Ms. Cynthia DONNELLY
20 Associate Provost ... Dr. Donna M. COOK
09 Asst VP for Research & Compliance ... Dr. Frederick C. PROMADES
07 Dean of Undergraduate Admissions ... Ms. Colleen EMERSON
35 Interim Dean of Students ... Mr. J. Malcolm SMITH
49 Dean of Art & Sciences ... Dr. Laura L. O'TOOLE
107 Dean of Professional Studies ... Dr. Traci WARRINGTON
06 Registrar ... Ms. Louise MONAST
37 Director of Financial Aid ... Ms. Ann MCDERMOTT
29 Assoc Director Alumni & Parent Pgms ... Mr. John RISTAINO
41 Actg Athletic Director ... Ms. Kelly SCAFARIELLO
08 Director of Library Services ... Ms. Kathleen BOYD
39 Assoc Dean Students/Dir Campus Life ... Dr. Gerry WILLIS
90 Director Academic Computing ... Mr. Brian A. MCDONNELL
18 Director of Facilities ... Mr. Eric MILNER
19 Director of Security/Safety ... Mr. Michael CARUOLO
40 Director of Bookstore ... Mr. Michael LEDDY
44 Sr Dir Advancement Operations/ Pgms ... Ms. Victoria DUCLOS-BARRETT
23 Director of Health Services ... Ms. Cathy VOLTAS
35 Director of Student Activities ... Ms. Chiquita BAYLOR
36 Director of Career Development ... Mr. Michael WISNEWSKI
96 Director of Purchasing ... Ms. Francine MONFETTE
104 Director of International Programs ... Ms. Erin FITZGERALD
38 Dir of Student Counseling Services ... Mr. David DAWSON

University of Rhode Island (E)

Kingston RI 02881-0806
County: Washington FICE Identification: 003414
Unit ID: 217484
Telephone: (401) 874-1000 Carnegie Class: RU/H
FAX Number: (401) 874-7149 Calendar System: Semester
URL: www.uri.edu
Established: 1892 Annual Undergrad Tuition & Fees (In-State): $12,862
Enrollment: 16,795 Coed
Affiliation or Control: State IRS Status: 501(c)3
Highest Offering: Doctorate
Program: Liberal Arts And General; Teacher Preparatory; Professional
Accreditation: EH, BUS, BUSA, CLPSY, CYTO, DIETD, DIETI, ENG, LIB, LSAR, MFCD, MUS, NURSE, PHAR, PTA, SCPSY, SP, TED

01 President ... Dr. David M. DOOLEY
100 Chief of Staff ... Ms. Michelle CURRERI
05 Provost/Vice Pres Academic Affairs ... Dr. Donald H. DEHAYES
46 Vice Pres Research/Economic Devel ... Dr. Gerald SONNENFELD
88 Assoc VP Res/Int Prop Mgmt/Comm ... Mr. Michael KATZ
88 Dir Univ Res External Relations ... Ms. Melissa MCCARTHY
88 Dir Research Development ... Ms. Karen MARKIN
25 Director Sponsored Projects ... Ms. Winfred NWANGWU
88 Dir Research Integrity ... Mr. Theodore A. MYATT
29 Exec Dir Alumni Relations/Secy Assn ... Ms. Michele NOTA
86 Dir Legislative and Govt Rels ... Ms. Kelly MAHONEY
26 Exec Dir Cmty & Community Rels ... Ms. Linda A. ACCIARDO
88 Dir Publications and Creative Svcs ... Vacant
10 Vice Pres for Admin & Finance ... Dr. Christina VALENTINO
21 Dir Budget & Financial Planning ... Ms. Linda BARRETT
21 Controller ... Ms. Sharon B. BELL
15 Asst Vice Pres Human Resource Admin ... Ms. Anne Marie COLEMAN
16 Director Personnel Services ... Ms. Laura KENERSON
18 Asst Vice Pres Business Services ... Mr. J. Vernon WYMAN
19 Int Director Public Safety ... Mr. Stephen N. BAKER
12 Dir W.A. Jones Campus ... Ms. Maria DISANO
88 Dir RI Transportation Center ... Dr. Deborah ROSEN
88 Dir Capital Projects ... Mr. Paul DEPACE
88 Dir Campus Planning and Design ... Mr. Christopher MCMAHAN
88 Dir Facility Services ... Mr. Jerome SIDIO
88 Dir Property & Support Svc ... Mr. Bill MATTESON
96 Director Purchasing & Univ Stores ... Ms. Betty GIL
28 Assoc VP Comm/Equity/Diversity ... Ms. Naomi THOMPSON
43 General Counsel ... Mr. Louis J. SACCOCCIO
32 Vice President Student Affairs ... Dr. Thomas R. DOUGAN
109 Dir Dining Services/Auxiliary ... Mr. Steven MELLO
41 Director of Athletics ... Mr. Thorr D. BJORN
103 Dir Career and Experiential Edu ... Ms. Kim STACK
38 Director Counseling Center ... Dr. Robert SAMUELS
88 Dir Recreational Services ... Ms. Jodi HAWKINS
35 Asst VP Stdnt Affs & Dean of Stdnts ... Dr. Mary J. GONZALES
88 Dir Special Pgms/Talent Devel ... Mr. Gerald WILLIAMS
88 Mgr Conf & Spec Pgm Dev ... Mr. Joseph PITTLE
35 Asst VP Student Affs & Dir HRL ... Mr. John SEARS
39 Interim Dir Housing & Res Life ... Dr. Jeffrey PLOUFFE
23 Director Health Services ... Ms. Ellen REYNOLD
40 Administrator Bookstore ... Mr. Paul WHITNEY
88 Spec Asst to the Prov for Acad Plng ... Ms. Ann M. MORRISSEY

88 Vice Prov Acad Finance/Personnel ....Dr. Clifford H. KATZ
09 Director of Institutional Research ....Vacant
84 Vice Provost Enrollment Management .... Mr. Dean LIBUTTI
07 Dean of Admissions ....Ms. Cynthia L. BONN
06 Dir Enrollment Services ....Dr. Carnell JONES
101 Vice Provost Faculty Affairs ....Dr. Laura BEAUVAIS
13 Chief Information Officer ....Mr. Garrett A. BOZYLINSKY
90 Dir Media & Technology Services .... Mr. David S. PORTER
91 Dir University Computing Systems .... Mr. Charlie SCHIFINO
51 V Prov Urban Pgms/Dn Col Cont Educ ....Dr. John H. MCCRAY, JR.
49 Dean of Arts & Sciences ....Dr. Winifred E. BROWNELL
50 Dean Business Administration .... Dr. Maling EBRAHIMPOUR
54 Dean of Engineering ....Dr. Raymond M. WRIGHT
88 Dean Univ Col & Spec Acad Pgms .... Dr. Jayne E. RICHMOND
58 Dean of Graduate School ....Dr. Nasser H. ZAWIA
66 Interim Dean of Nursing ....Dr. Mary SULLIVAN
67 Interim Dean of Pharmacy ....Dr. Paul LARRAT
69 Int Dean Human Sciences & Services .. Dr. Lori CICCOMASCOLO
53 Director School of Education ....Dr. David BYRD
88 Dean Grad School Oceanography .... Dr. Bruce CORLISS
88 Dean of Environment & Life Sciences ....Dr. John KIRBY
08 Dean University Libraries ....Mr. Karim BOUGHIDA
22 Director Affirm Act/Equal Oppty/Div .... Ms. Roxanne GOMES
37 Sr Assoc Dir Enrol Svcs/Fin Aid .... Mr. Paul LANGHAMMER
92 Director Honors Program ....Dr. Lynne DERBYSHIRE
102 President URI Foundation ....Mr. James HOPKINS
85 Dir Intl Students and Scholars .... Dr. Dania BRANDFORD-CALVO
106 Dir Learning/Assessment & Online ....Dr. Diane GOLDSMITH
94 Dir Gender and Women Studies .... Dr. Rosaria PISA
105 Manager Web Services ....Ms. Lisa CHEN
30 Dir Advancement Services ....Mr. John PELTIER
44 Director Annual or Planned Giving .... Ms. Bernadine SADWIN

University of Rhode Island Feinstein Providence Campus (A)

80 Washington Street, Providence RI 02903
Telephone: (401) 277-5000 Identification: 770118
Accreditation: &EH

† Branch campus of University of Rhode Island, Kingston, RI.

University of Rhode Island Narragansett Bay Campus (B)

215 South Ferry Road, Narragansett RI 02882-1197
Telephone: (401) 874-6222 Identification: 770129
Accreditation: &EH

† Branch campus of University of Rhode Island, Kingston, RI.

SOUTH CAROLINA

Aiken Technical College (C)

PO Drawer 696, Aiken SC 29802-0696
County: Aiken FICE Identification: 010056
Unit ID: 217615
Telephone: (803) 508-7263 Carnegie Class: Assoc/Pub-R-M
FAX Number: (803) 593-6641 Calendar System: Semester
URL: www.atc.edu
Established: 1972 Annual Undergrad Tuition & Fees (In-District): $4,262
Enrollment: 2,350 Coed
Affiliation or Control: State/Local IRS Status: 501(c)3
Highest Offering: Associate Degree
Program: Occupational; 2-Year Principally Bachelor's Creditable; Technical Emphasis
Accreditation: SC, ACBSP, ADNUR, DA, MAC, RAD, SURGT

01 President ....Dr. Susan A. WINSOR
04 Executive Assistant to President ....Ms. Jill UHLER
30 Director Foundation & Alumni .... Ms. Mary COMMONS
05 Vice President Education & Training .... Dr. Gemma FROCK
76 Dean of Health Sciences ....Dr. Hermecender WALTON
72 Dean of Technical Education ....Dr. Joy WATSON
97 Dean of General Education ....Fr. Frederick ROGERS
51 Dean Business/Computer Technolog .... Dr. Steven SIMMONS
10 Vice Pres Administrative Services ....Mr. Andy JORDAN
37 Director of Financial Aid ....Ms. Sue SIMS
13 Director of Info Systems Mgmt .... Mr. Walter BUSBEE
15 Director of Human Resources ....Ms. Sylvia BYRD
21 Director of Financial Accounting ....Mr. Don TRUE
96 Director of Purchasing .... Ms. Toni MARSHALL
18 Campus Engineer .... Mr. Mike DUNCAN
84 Vice President Enrollment Mgmt ....Mr. Bryan NEWTON
07 Director of Intake Services ....Mrs. Jessica MOON
06 Registrar ....Mrs. Dawn BUTTS
32 Dean of Enrollment Services .... Dr. Vinson BURDETTE
38 Director Counseling/Disabilities ....Mr. Rich WELDON
88 Manager Mktg & Student Experience ....Ms. Anna DOLIANITIS

Allen University (D)

1530 Harden Street, Columbia SC 29204-1085
County: Richland FICE Identification: 003417
Unit ID: 217624
Telephone: (803) 376-5700 Carnegie Class: Bac/A&S
FAX Number: N/A Calendar System: Semester
URL: www.allenuniversity.edu
Established: 1870 Annual Undergrad Tuition & Fees: $12,740
Enrollment: 644 Coed
Affiliation or Control: African Methodist Episcopal IRS Status: 501(c)3
Highest Offering: Baccalaureate
Program: Liberal Arts And General; Business Emphasis
Accreditation: SC

01 Interim President ....Dr. Lady June COLE
05 VP Academic/Student Affairs .... Dr. Charlene SPEAREN
84 VP Enrollment Mgmt .... Mrs. Marilyn DEBERRY
10 Chief Finanical Officer ....Ms. Ruby FIELDING
21 Assoc Vice Pres Fiscal Affairs ....Vacant
88 Executive Director of Tiltle III ....Mr. William ROBINSON
07 Interim Director of Admissions ....Mr. Adam DILLIHAY
15 Exec Dir Human Resources & Admin ....Mrs. Paige MOORE
26 Executive Director Marketing .... Dr. Flavia ELDEMIRE
18 Facilities/Physical Plant ....Mr. Timothy TAYLOR
23 Health Services ....Ms. Leslie BASTON
29 Director of Alumni Relations ....Mr. Gaurachandra GARRETT
37 Director of Student Financial Aid ....Ms. Sherri JEFFERSON
38 Director Counseling Services ....Vacant
04 Exec Assistant to President .... Ms. Geraldine LIVINGSTON
08 Head Librarian ....Ms. Carol BOWERS
19 Director Security/Safety ....Chief Kelvin DAVIS
41 Athletic Director ....Mr. Chad WASHINGTON

Anderson University (E)

316 Boulevard, Anderson SC 29621-4035
County: Anderson FICE Identification: 003418
Unit ID: 217633
Telephone: (864) 231-2000 Carnegie Class: Bac/Diverse
FAX Number: (864) 231-2004 Calendar System: Semester
URL: www.andersonuniversity.edu
Established: 1911 Annual Undergrad Tuition & Fees: $24,860
Enrollment: 3,112 Coed
Affiliation or Control: Other IRS Status: 501(c)3
Highest Offering: Doctorate
Program: Liberal Arts And General; Teacher Preparatory; Professional
Accreditation: SC, ACBSP, ART, MUS, NURSE, TED

01 President ....Dr. Evans P. WHITAKER
05 Provost ....Dr. Timothy L. SMITH
10 VP for Finance and Operations ....Dr. Danny M. PARKER
30 VP for Development ....Mr. James W. LANDRITH
84 VP for Enrollment Mgt & Marketing .... Mr. D. Omar RASHED
42 VP for Christian Life ....Dr. J. Robert CLINE
32 VP for Student Development .... Dr. James A. FEREIRA
13 Chief Information Officer ....Mr. Peter B. HARVIN
28 VP for Presidential Affairs ....Dr. Beverly R. MCADAMS
44 VP for Principal Gifts ....Mr. Dean WOODS
18 Assoc VP for Facil & Procurement ....Mr. Dane S. SLAUGHTER
06 Dean of Enrollment Svcs & Registrar ....Mrs. Carol A. PARKER
20 Vice Provost ....Mrs. Susan B. WOOTEN
07 Dean of Admissions ....Ms. Pam ROSS
41 Director of Athletics ....Mr. Bill J. D'ANDREA
32 Dean of Student Life ....Mr. Jonathan GROPP
08 Director of Library Services ....Mr. Kent A. MILLWOOD
09 Director of External Reporting ....Mr. Daryl A. IVERSON
37 Director of Financial Aid Planning ....Ms. Allison SULLIVAN
26 Director Marketing & Communications ....Mr. Barry D. RAY
38 Director of Counseling Services ....Ms. Erin C. MAURER
29 Director of Alumni Relations ....Vacant
36 Director Career Services ....Ms. Kelly A. BELL
23 Director Health Services ....Mrs. Deb A. TAYLOR
88 Dir of The Ctr for Student Success ....Ms. L. Dianne KING
15 Director of Human Resources ....Mrs. Rose Mariee ALLISON
39 Assoc Dean of Residence Life ....Ms. Melissa JONES
21 Controller ....Ms. Kristie C. COLE
35 Director of Student Activities ....Ms. Sara MUDD
04 Exec Assistant to the President ....Mrs. Diane SUTHERLAND
104 Director of International Programs ....Dr. Ann-Margaret J. THEMISTOCLEOUS
19 Director of Campus Safety ....Mr. James KINES

Benedict College (F)

Harden and Bland Streets, Columbia SC 29204-1086
County: Richland FICE Identification: 003420
Unit ID: 217721
Telephone: (803) 253-5000 Carnegie Class: Bac/Diverse
FAX Number: (803) 253-5059 Calendar System: Semester
URL: www.benedict.edu
Established: 1870 Annual Undergrad Tuition & Fees: $18,286
Enrollment: 2,450 Coed
Affiliation or Control: Independent Non-Profit IRS Status: 501(c)3
Highest Offering: Baccalaureate
Program: Liberal Arts And General; Teacher Preparatory
Accreditation: SC, ACBSP, ART, NRPA, SW, TED

01 President ....Dr. David H. SWINTON
05 Senior Vice Pres Academic Affairs ....Dr. Janeen WITTY
03 Executive Vice President ....Dr. Ruby W. WATTS
10 Vice President Business/Finance .... Ms. Brenda WALKER
32 Vice President Student Affairs ....Mr. Gary E. KNIGHT
30 Vice Pres Institutional Advancement .... Mrs. Barbara C. MOORE
20 Assoc Vice Pres Academic Affairs ....Dr. George A. DEVLIN
21 Asst VP for Business & Finance ....Ms. Jackie BROWN
26 Asst VP for Comm & Marketing ....Ms. Kymm HUNTER
07 Asst VP for Admissions/Student Mktg ...Mrs. Phyllis THOMPSON
29 Assistant VP for Alumni Relations ....Mrs. Ada A. BELTON
13 Dir Information Technology ....Mr. Dave MEDEIROS
27 Chief Information Officer ....Mr. Dan MURPHY
15 Director of Human Resources ....Mrs. Betty A. JENKINS
06 Registrar/Director Student Records ....Mrs. Wanda A. SCOTT-KINNEY

41 Athletics Director ....Mr. Willie WASHINGTON
38 Director Service Learning & Leaders ......Ms. Tondaleya JACKSON
42 Dir Campus Ministry/Dean of Chapel ....Mr. Thomas DAVIS
19 Director Campus Safety ....Mr. Haywood M. BAZEMORE
36 Director Career Services ....Ms. Karen W. RUTHERFORD
37 Director Financial Aid ....Ms. Sul BLACK
19 Director Physical Plant ....Ms. Chonte' MARTIN
08 Director of Library ....Mrs. Darlene ZINNERMAN-BETHEA
09 Director Institutional Research ....Mr. Jesse BELLINGER
108 Director Institutional Assessment ....Vacant
25 Coordinator Title III ....Mrs. Doris W. JOHNSON
96 Manager Procurement Services .... Ms. Sharling THOMPSON
49 Dean Sch Human/Arts/Soc Sci ....Dr. Charles AUSTIN
50 Dean School of Business/Econ ....Mr. Gerald SMALLS
88 Dean School of Health Human Service ....Dr. Tanya BRICE
53 Dean School of Education .... Dr. Damara HIGHTOWER
72 Dean Sch Science/Tech/Engrng/ Math ....Dr. Samir S. RAYCHOUDHURY
92 Dean School of Honors .... Dr. Warren ROBINSON
57 Chair Fine Arts ....Ms. Gina MOORE
50 Chair Business Admin/Mgmt/Mktg .... Dr. Tracy H. DUNN
88 Chair Education and Family Studies ....Dr. Tracy MIDDLETON
70 Int Chair Social Work ....Mrs. Brenda CLARK
88 Chair English/Foreign Language Dept .... Dr. Herman HOWARD
88 Chair Bio/Chem/Enviroment Hlth Sci .... Dr. Helene TAMBOUE
81 Chair Math/Computer Science ....Ms. Fereshtah ZAHED
54 Chair Physics/Engineering ....Dr. Fouzi H. ARAMMASH
88 Int Chair Economics/Finance/Acctg .... Dr. Syed MAHDI

Bob Jones University (G)

1700 Wade Hampton Boulevard, Greenville SC 29614-0001
County: Greenville FICE Identification: 003421
Unit ID: 217749
Telephone: (864) 242-5100 Carnegie Class: Spec/Faith
FAX Number: (864) 235-6661 Calendar System: Semester
URL: www.bju.edu
Established: 1927 Annual Undergrad Tuition & Fees: $14,900
Enrollment: 3,108 Coed
Affiliation or Control: Proprietary IRS Status: Proprietary
Highest Offering: Doctorate
Program: Liberal Arts And General
Accreditation: TRACS, ENG

00 Chancellor ....Dr. Bob JONES, III
01 President ....Dr. Stephen D. PETTIT
05 Exec Vice Pres for Academic Affairs ....Dr. Gary M. WEIER
11 Executive Vice Pres for Operations ......Mr. Marshall E. FRANKLIN
30 VP Advancement & Alumni Relations .....Mr. John D. MATTHEWS
42 VP for Ministerial Advancement ....Dr. Samuel E. HORN
27 Chief Communication Officer .... Ms. Carol A. KEIRSTEAD
20 Vice Provost/Chief Admin Officer ....Dr. David A. FISHER
10 Chief Financial Officer ....Mr. Kennie M. STILL
32 Dean of Students/Chief SLO ....Dr. Eric D. NEWTON
26 Chief Publication Officer ....Mr. Bill APELIAN
15 Chief Human Resources Officer .... Mr. Kevin TAYLOR
18 Chief Facilities Management Officer ....Mr. Steve L. HENSLEY
13 Chief Information Officer ....Mr. Marvin P. REEM
84 Chief Enrollment Officer ....Vacant
49 Dean College of Arts and Science ....Dr. Renae WENTWORTH
73 Dean School of Religion & Seminary ....Dr. Samuel E. HORN
57 Dean Sch Fine Arts & Communication .....Dr. Darren P. LAWSON
53 Dean School of Education ....Dr. Brian A. CARRUTHERS
50 Dean School of Business ....Mr. Mike BUITER
73 Assoc Dean School of Religiion ....Dr. Royce B. SHORT
73 Assoc Dean Seminary/GrdSch Religion ...Dr. Stephen J. HANKINS
06 Registrar ....Dr. Daniel SMITH
33 Dean of Men ....Mr. Jonathan G. DAULTON
34 Dean of Women ....Ms. Deneen LAWSON
07 Director of Admission ....Mr. Gary A. DEEDRICK
88 Director of Ministry Training ....Dr. Nathan CROCKETT
41 Athletic Director ....Mr. Neal RING
37 Director of Financial Aid ....Mr. Kevin DELP
08 Libraries Manager ....Mr. Van CARPENTER
09 Sr Dir Planning/Rsrch/Assessment ....Rev. Phil GERARD

Brown Mackie College-Greenville (H)

75 Beattie Place, Ste. 100, Greenville SC 29601-2155
Telephone: (864) 239-5301 Identification: 666781
Accreditation: ACICS, OTA, SURGT

† Branch campus of Brown Mackie College, Tucson, AZ.

Central Carolina Technical College (I)

506 N Guignard Drive, Sumter SC 29150-2499
County: Sumter FICE Identification: 003995
Unit ID: 218858
Telephone: (803) 778-1961 Carnegie Class: Assoc/Pub-R-M
FAX Number: (803) 778-7880 Calendar System: Semester
URL: www.cctech.edu
Established: 1962 Annual Undergrad Tuition & Fees (In-State): $3,960
Enrollment: 3,970 Coed
Affiliation or Control: State IRS Status: 501(c)3
Highest Offering: Associate Degree
Program: Occupational; 2-Year Principally Bachelor's Creditable; Technical Emphasis
Accreditation: SC, ADNUR, MAC, PNUR, SURGT

01 President ....Dr. Tim HARDEE

05 Vice Pres Academics Mr. David WATSON
11 VP for Administration & Planning Mrs. Ann A. COOPER
10 Vice President for Business Affairs Ms. Terry L. BOOTH
32 Vice President for Student Affairs Ms. Lisa BRACKEN
04 Assistant to the President Ms. Diana REARDON
51 Director Cont Educ/Workforce Devel Ms. Elizabeth WILLIAMS
08 Dean of Learning Resources Ms. Nancy BISHOP
102 Director Foundation Ms. Meree MCALISTER
26 Director Public Relations Ms. Becky RICKENBAKER
15 Director of Personnel Mrs. Ronalda S. STOVER
13 Director Information Systems Dr. Vicky G. HOOKS
06 Registrar Ms. Henrietta SCOTT
37 Director Student Financial Aid Ms. Tiffany WILSON
09 Dir Research/Institutional Effect Mr. Bryan MAY
07 Director of Admissions & Counseling Mrs. Barbara WRIGHT
54 Dean of Industrial and Engineering Mr. Brent RUSSELL
76 Dean of Health Sciences Ms. Miriam LANEY
53 Dean of General Education Mr. Myles WILLIAMS

Charleston School of Law (A)

81 Mary Street, PO Box 535, Charleston SC 29402
County: Charleston FICE Identification: 040963
Unit ID: 451510
Telephone: (843) 329-1000 Carnegie Class: Spec/Law
FAX Number: (843) 720-7899 Calendar System: Semester
URL: www.charlestonlaw.edu
Established: 2003 Annual Graduate Tuition & Fees: $40,116
Enrollment: 454 Coed
Affiliation or Control: Proprietary IRS Status: Proprietary
Highest Offering: First Professional Degree; No Undergraduates
Program: Professional
Accreditation: LAW

01 Interim President Mr. Joseph D. HARBAUGH
05 Dean Mr. Andrew L. ABRAMS
20 Associate Dean Academic Affairs Ms. Margaret M. LAWTON
07 Associate Dean Admissions Mr. John S. BENFIELD
32 Assoc Dean of Students Mr. Brett BARKER
13 Assoc Dean of Info Services Ms. Lisa SMITH-BUTLER
10 Chief Financial Officer Ms. Wende WOOD
06 Registrar Ms. Jennifer SUMMERS

Charleston Southern University (B)

PO Box 118087, Charleston SC 29423-8087
County: Charleston FICE Identification: 003419
Unit ID: 217688
Telephone: (843) 863-7000 Carnegie Class: Master's M
FAX Number: (843) 863-8074 Calendar System: Semester
URL: www.csuniv.edu
Established: 1964 Annual Undergrad Tuition & Fees: $23,400
Enrollment: 3,417 Coed
Affiliation or Control: Southern Baptist IRS Status: 501(c)3
Highest Offering: Master's
Program: Liberal Arts And General; Teacher Preparatory; Professional
Accreditation: SC, CAATE, CS, IACBE, MUS, NUR, TED

01 President Dr. Jairy C. HUNTER, JR.
05 Vice President Academic Affairs Dr. Jacqueline FISH
10 Vice President for Business Affairs Mr. Luke BLACKMON
04 Exec Assistant to the President Mrs. Faye WOOD
84 Vice Pres Enrollment Management Mrs. Debbie WILLIAMSON
26 Vice Pres Advancement & Marketing Mr. David BAGGS
88 Asst to the VP for Retention Dr. Scott YARBROUGH
30 Executive Director of Development Mr. Bill WARD
32 Dean of Students Mr. Clark CARTER
91 Director of Administrative Services Mr. Shannon PHILLIPS
08 Director of the Library Mrs. Sandra HUGHES
06 Registrar Mrs. Amanda SISSION
29 Director of BUC Club Ms. Cathryn BRODERHAUSEN
21 Associate Business Officer Mrs. Janet MIMS
27 Director of Integrated Marketing Mr. John STRUBEL
09 Dir of Institutional Effectiveness Mr. Jeffrey BABETZ
58 Director MBA Program Dr. Darin GERDES
41 Athletic Director Mr. Hank SMALL
42 Director Campus Ministry Mr. Jon DAVIS
19 Director Security Mr. John WILSON
90 Director Computing & Info Science Mr. James ROBERTS
18 Director Physical & Auxiliary Svcs Mr. Nick CIMORELLI
29 Director of Alumni Relations Mrs. Rebecca POISION
07 Director of Admission Mr. James M. RHOTON
15 Director of Personnel Services Mrs. Lindsey WALKE
36 Director Career Planning Mrs. Hester YOUNG
38 Director Student Counseling Ms. Joanne JEMSEK
96 Director of Purchasing Mrs. Nicole WALLENFELSZ
37 Director Student Financial Aid Mrs. Teri KARGES
39 Director Residence Life Mr. Tyler DAVIS
50 Dean of Business Dr. John B. DUNCAN
58 Dean Education Dr. George METZ
83 Dean Humanities/Social Sciences Dr. Keith CALLIS
81 Dean Science & Mathematics Dr. Jeryl JOHNSON
66 Dean of Nursing Dr. Andreea TOADER
53 Dean of Education Dr. George METZ
76 Dean College of Health Sci Vacant
107 College of Adult Professional Stds Vacant

The Citadel, The Military College of South Carolina (C)

171 Moultrie Street, Charleston SC 29409-0001
County: Charleston FICE Identification: 003423
Unit ID: 217864
Telephone: (843) 225-3294 Carnegie Class: Master's L
FAX Number: (843) 953-5287 Calendar System: Semester
URL: www.citadel.edu
Established: 1842 Annual Undergrad Tuition & Fees (In-State): $11,364
Enrollment: 3,592 Coed
Affiliation or Control: State IRS Status: 501(c)3
Highest Offering: Beyond Master's But Less Than Doctorate
Program: Liberal Arts And General; Teacher Preparatory; Professional
Accreditation: SC, BUS, CACREP, CAEP, CS, ENG, TED

01 President LtGen. John W. ROSA
05 Provost/Dean of College BGen. Connie L. BOOK
11 Vice Pres for Operations Col. Thomas G. PHILIPKOSKY
10 Vice President of Finance Col. Joseph GARCIA
32 Commandant of Cadets Capt. Eugene PALUSO
26 Vice President for Comm & Marketing LtCol. W. Brett ASHWORTH
41 Director Intercollegiate Athletics Mr. James E. SENTER
30 VP Inst Advanc/Citadel Fndtn Ex Dir Mr. Jay DOWD
04 Executive Assistant to President Capt. Taylor SKARDON
18 Assoc VP/Facilities & Engr Col. Ben WHAM
43 General Counsel Mr. Mark C. BRANDENBURG
20 Assoc Provost Academic Affairs Col. Mark A. BEBENSEE
20 Assoc Prov Plng/Assess/Evaluation Col. Tara F. HORNOR
58 Assoc Provost/Citadel Graduate Col. Bob H. MCNAMARA
07 Director of Admissions LtCol. John W. POWELL, JR.
06 Registrar LtCol. Sylvia L. NESMITH
21 Treasurer Capt. F. Ward LOGAN
29 Director Alumni Affairs/Placement Col. J. Laurence HUTTO
08 Director of Library LtCol. David S. GOBLE
13 Int Dir Info Technology Services Mr. Jeff WELLS
37 Director Financial Aid/ Scholarships LtCol. Henry M. FULLER, JR.
15 Director of Human Resources Maj. Leah S. SCHONFELD
36 Director of Career Services Mr. Brent A. STEWART
38 Director of Student Counseling Dr. Suzanne BUFANO
09 Institutional Research Director Ms. Lisa L. PACE
19 Director Security/Safety Col. William A. FLETCHER
23 College Physician Dr. Carey M. CAPELL
40 Director of the Cadet Store Mr. Kenneth A. WOODRUFF
42 Chaplain/Dir Religious Activities LtCol. Joel C. HARRIS
92 Director Honors Program Col. Jack W. RHODES
86 Director Govt & Community Affairs Col. Cardon B. CRAWFORD
96 Director of Purchasing LtCol. James P. DE LUCA
28 Chief Diversity Officer Ms. Shawn EDWARDS
50 Dean of the School of Bus Admin Col. William N. TRUMBULL
53 Dean of the School of Education Col. Larry DANIEL
54 Dean of the School of Engineering Col. Ronald W. WELCH
81 Dean of the School of Science/ Math Col. Lok C. LEW YAN VOON
79 Dean Sch Humanities/Social Sciences Col. Winifred B. MOORE
101 Spec Asst to President/Brd Matters Ms. Patricia M. KINARD
85 Director Multicultural Affairs LtCol. Robert P. PICKERING
16 Human Resources Deputy Director Mr. Wesley S. SAMS
25 Grants Writer Ms. Sylvia R. WILLIAMS

Claflin University (D)

400 Magnolia Street, Orangeburg SC 29115-4477
County: Orangeburg FICE Identification: 003424
Unit ID: 217873
Telephone: (803) 535-5000 Carnegie Class: Bac/A&S
FAX Number: (803) 531-2860 Calendar System: Semester
URL: www.claflin.edu
Established: 1869 Annual Undergrad Tuition & Fees: $15,520
Enrollment: 1,866 Coed
Affiliation or Control: United Methodist IRS Status: 501(c)3
Highest Offering: Master's
Program: Liberal Arts And General
Accreditation: SC, ACBSP, MUS, TED

01 President Dr. Henry N. TISDALE
11 Vice President for Administration Mr. Drexel B. BALL
05 Provost/Chief Academic Officer Dr. Karl S. WRIGHT
10 Vice President for Fiscal Affairs Mrs. Tijuana R. HUDSON
30 Vice Pres Institutional Advancement Rev. Whittaker V. MIDDLETON
32 Vice Pres Student Devel & Services Dr. Leroy A. DURANT
45 VP Plng/Assessment/Information Svcs Dr. Zia HASAN
20 Vice Provost for Academic Programs Dr. Angela W. PETERS
26 Interim Assistant VP Communications Ms. Charlene D. SLAUGHTER
35 Asst VP Student Devel & Services Mr. Devin L. RANDOLPH
07 Director of Admissions Mr. Michael ZEIGLER
79 Dean Sch Humanities & Soc Science Dr. Donald G. PACE
50 Dean School of Business Dr. Charles RICHARDSON, JR.
53 Dean School of Education Dr. Valerie E. HARRISON
81 Dean Sch Natural Sciences & Math Dr. Verlie A. TISDALE
13 Asst VP Information Tech Svcs Mr. James E. BRENN
51 Exec Dir for Prof & Cont Studies Dr. Cindye T. RICHBURG
08 Library Director Ms. Marilyn Y. GIBBS
37 Director of Financial Aid Ms. Terria C. WILLIAMS
36 Director of Career Development Mrs. Carolyn R. SNELL
41 Athletic Director Dr. Jerome H. FITCH
15 Director of Human Resources Ms. Shirley A. BIGGS
06 Registrar Mrs. Roe B. HUNT
29 Director Alumni Affairs/Annual Fund Mr. Allen M. JACKSON
19 Chief of Campus Public Safety Mr. Steven A. PEARSON
109 Director of Auxiliary Services Mr. Rodeny B. HUDSON
25 Director of Sponsored Programs Ms. Veronica GOODMAN
09 Dir of Institutional Effectiveness Mrs. Bridget DEWEES
04 Executive Admin Asst to President Ms. Melvenia WILLIAMS

Clemson University (E)

201 Sikes Hall, Clemson SC 29634-0001
County: Pickens FICE Identification: 003425
Unit ID: 217882
Telephone: (864) 656-3311 Carnegie Class: RU/H
FAX Number: (864) 656-4040 Calendar System: Semester
URL: www.clemson.edu
Established: 1889 Annual Undergrad Tuition & Fees (In-State): $13,882
Enrollment: 32,800 Coed
Affiliation or Control: State IRS Status: 501(c)3
Highest Offering: Doctorate
Program: Liberal Arts And General; Teacher Preparatory; Professional
Accreditation: SC, ART, BUS, BUSA, CACREP, CONST, CS, CVT, DIETD, ENG, ENGR, IPSY, LSAR, NRPA, NURSE, PLNG, TED

01 President Dr. James P. CLEMENTS
05 Provost Dr. Robert H. JONES
43 General Counsel Mr. W.C. (Chip) HOOD
20 Assoc Provost for Faculty Develop Dr. Nadim M. AZIZ
10 Chief Financial Officer Mr. Brett A. DALTON
32 Interim VP Student Affairs Dr. Almeda JACKS
101 Executive Secretary to the Board Ms. Angie LEIDINGER
30 Vice President for Advancement Mr. A. Neill CAMERON, JR.
103 Vice Pres Public Svc Dr. George R. ASKEW
46 Vice President for Research Dr. Larry DOOLEY
88 Vice President for Economic Develop Dr. John M. BALLATO
13 Vice Prov Computer/Info Technology Mr. James R. BOTTUM
88 Vice Provost for International Affs Ms. Sharon NAGY
29 Chief Alumni Officer Mr. Brian J. O'ROURKE
18 Chief Facilities Officer Mr. Robert J. WELLS, JR.
35 Associate VP/Dean of Students Dr. Joy S. SMITH
88 Associate Provost for Faculty Devel Dr. Nadim AZIZ
27 Chief Public Affairs Officer Ms. Catherine T. SAMS
08 Dean of Libraries Ms. Mary M. FARRELL
07 Director of Admissions Mr. Robert S. BARKLEY
06 Interim Registrar Mrs. Debra SPARACINO
37 Director of Financial Aid Mr. Chuck KNEPFLE
36 Director of Career Center Mr. Burton O'NEIL
38 Director Counseling/Psych Services Dr. Raquel J. CONTRERAS
47 Dean Col Agric/Forestry/Life Sci Dr. Thomas R. SCOTT
58 Dean Graduate School/Vice Provost Vacant
48 Dean Col Arch/Arts/Humanities Dr. Richard E. GOODSTEIN
54 Dean Col Engr/Sciences Dr. Anand GRAMOPADHYE
50 Int Dn Col Business/Behavioral Sci Dr. Charles K. WATT
53 Dean Col Health/Educ/Human Dev Vacant
09 Director Institutional Research Dr. S. Wickes WESTCOTT, III
39 Executive Director of Housing Ms. Verna G. HOWELL
41 Director of Athletics Mr. Dan RADAKOVICH
44 Director of Estate & Planned Giving Ms. Jovanna J. KING
22 Director Access & Equity Mr. Byron A. WILEY
23 Director Student Health Services Mr. George W. CLAY
15 Chief Human Resources Ms. Michelle PIEKUTOWSKI
91 Executive Director Enterprise Appl Mr. Barrett KENDJORIA
25 Director Sponsored Programs Ms. Sheila T. LISCHWE
19 Director Law Enforcement & Safety Chief Johnson LINK
96 Director of Purchasing Mr. Michael NEBESKY
04 Asst to the President/Vice Prov Ms. Debra JACKSON
88 Dir Teaching Effectiveness & Innova Ms. Linda TILSON
88 Director of Bridge to Clemson Pgm Ms. Susan WHORTON
106 Director of Online Education Mr. DeWitt SALLEY, JR.
87 Director of Summer School Mr. Blake SNIDER
104 Director Study Abroad Dr. Uttiyo RAYCHAUDHURI
108 Director Institutional Assessment Dr. David K. KNOX
26 Director of Marketing Svcs Ms. Susan SCHIFF
100 Chief of Staff Mr. Max ALLEN

Clinton College (F)

1029 Crawford Road, Rock Hill SC 29730-5152
County: York FICE Identification: 004923
Unit ID: 217891
Telephone: (803) 327-7402 Carnegie Class: Assoc/PrivNFP
FAX Number: (803) 327-3261 Calendar System: Semester
URL: www.clintoncollege.edu
Established: 1894 Annual Undergrad Tuition & Fees: $16,802
Enrollment: 191 Coed
Affiliation or Control: African Methodist Episcopal Zion Church
IRS Status: 501(c)3
Highest Offering: Baccalaureate
Program: Liberal Arts And General
Accreditation: TRACS

01 President Dr. Elaine J. COPELAND
04 Assistant to the President Ms. Cheryl A. WEBB
05 VP for Academic Affairs/Dean Ms. Janis S. PENDLETON
30 Director for Development Mr. Raymond CORLEY
32 VP for Student Affairs Dr. Robert M. COPELAND, JR.
10 VP of Business & Finance Ms. Archinya INGRAM
09 VP for Institutional Effectiveness Ms. Judith COWAN
06 Registrar Mrs. Altavese HUNT-ALLEN
37 Financial Aid Ms. Pamela WHITE
08 Librarian Ms. Minora HICKS
41 Athletic Director Mr. Roderick WOODS
18 Director Facilities/Bldgs/Grounds Rev. Lloyd SNIPES
07 Admissions Ms. Kim SHEPARD
35 Coord Student Support Services Ms. Shawntae BURTON

Coastal Carolina University (G)

PO Box 261954, Conway SC 29528-6054
County: Horry FICE Identification: 003451
Unit ID: 218724
Telephone: (843) 347-3161 Carnegie Class: Master's S

FAX Number: (843) 349-2990 Calendar System: Semester
URL: www.coastal.edu
Established: 1954 Annual Undergrad Tuition & Fees (In-State): $10,220
Enrollment: 9,976 Coed
Affiliation or Control: State IRS Status: 501(c)3
Highest Offering: Doctorate
Program: Liberal Arts And General
Accreditation: SC, ART, BUS, CS, MUS, NUR, TED, THEA

01 President ....Dr. David A. DECENZO
05 Provost/Exec VP Acad/Student Affs ....Dr. J. Ralph BYINGTON
10 Vice Pres Finance/Administration ....Ms. Staci A. BOWIE
30 Vice Pres Philanthropy ....Mr. Mark ROACH
32 VP Student Life & Campus Engagement ....Dr. Deborah CONNER
88 VP Stdnt Rights & Responsibilities ....Mr. Travis E. OVERTON
26 Vice Pres Univ Communications ....Mr. William PLATE
50 Dean Business Administration ....Dr. Barbara RITTER
53 Dean of Education ....Dr. Edward JADALLAH
79 Dean of Humanities & Fine Arts ....Dr. Daniel ENNIS
81 Dean of Science ....Dr. Michael H. ROBERTS
08 Dean Library Services ....Dr. Barbara BURD
13 Chief Information & Technology Ofcr ....Mr. Abdallah HADDAD
20 Assoc Provost Admin/Academic ....Ms. Sallie CLARKSON
108 Assoc Prov Assessment/Accreditation ....Dr. John P. BEARD
58 Assoc Provost/Dir Graduate Studies ....Dr. James O. LUKEN
09 Exec Dir of Inst Rsrch/Assessment ....Ms. Christine L. MEE
06 University Registrar ....Mr. Daniel M. LAWLESS
19 Director Public Safety ....Mr. David ROPER
21 Controller ....Ms. Lori CHURCH
28 Dir Multicultural Student Services ....Ms. Patricia SINGLETON-YOUNG
41 Director of Athletics ....Mr. Matthew L. HOGUE
38 Director of Counseling Services ....Dr. Jennie M. CASSIDY
85 Director of International Programs ....Mr. Geoffrey J. PARSONS
39 Director of Housing/Residence Life ....Mr. Steve HARRISON
37 Dir Financial Aid & Scholarship ....Ms. Wendy WATTS
92 Director Honors Program ....Dr. Michael RUSE
36 Director Career Services ....Dr. Tom WOODLE
96 Dir Procurement/Business Services ....Mr. Dean P. HUDSON
18 Interim Director of Facilities ....Mr. T. Rein MUNGO
27 Chief Public Relations Officer ....Ms. Martha S. HUNN
29 Director Alumni Relations ....Ms. Jean Ann BRAKEFIELD
104 Assoc Provost Global Initiatives . Dr. Darla J. DOMKE-DAMONTE
07 Asst Provost Admiss & Merit Award . Ms. Amanda E. CRADDOCK
15 Director Human Resources/EEO Office . Ms. Kimberly SHERFESEE
43 Dir Legal Services/General Counsel .... Mr. Timothy E. MEACHAM
90 Director Academic Computing ....Mr. Fadi N. BAROODY

Coker College (A)

300 E College Avenue, Hartsville SC 29550-3797
County: Darlington FICE Identification: 003427
Unit ID: 217907
Telephone: (843) 383-8000 Carnegie Class: Bac/Diverse
FAX Number: (843) 383-8048 Calendar System: Semester
URL: www.coker.edu
Established: 1908 Annual Undergrad Tuition & Fees: $26,568
Enrollment: 1,219 Coed
Affiliation or Control: Independent Non-Profit IRS Status: 501(c)3
Highest Offering: Master's
Program: Liberal Arts And General; Teacher Preparatory
Accreditation: SC, ART, MUS, SW, TED

01 President ....Dr. Robert L. WYATT
101 Secretary of the College ....Ms. Barbara STEADMAN
05 Provost & Dean of the College ....Dr. Tracy PARKINSON
88 VP for Student Experience ....Ms. Patricia MEINHOLD
10 EVP Administration & Legal Counsel ....Mr. Tony FLOYD
78 Asst Dean/Dir CTR Engaged Learning ....Ms. Darlene SMALL
26 VP Institutional Identity & IT ....Mr. R. Kyle SAVERANCE
32 Dean of Students ....Ms. Whitney WATTS
41 VP Athletics & Athletic Facilities ....Dr. Lynn GRIFFIN
20 VP Acad Affairs/Dean of Faculty ....Dr. Will CARSWELL
07 Assoc VP for Enrollment Management ....Mr. Adam CONNOLLY
11 VP for Administration ....Ms. Brianna DOUGLAS
06 Dir Academic Records/Inst Research ....Ms. Marcy KERSHNER
18 Director of Facilities ....Vacant
21 Director of Accounting & Reporting ....Mrs. Robin A. PERDUE
37 Director of Financial Aid ....Mrs. Betty B. WILLIAMS
44 Director of Annual Gifts & Plan Giv ....Ms. Johnna SHIRLEY
29 Director of Alumni Affairs & Spec ....Ms. Tiletha LANE
35 Dir Student Activities/Leadership ....Mr. Tyler MICEK
07 Director of Admissions ....Mr. Jeremy NERE
08 Director of Library ....Ms. Alexa BARTEL
19 Director of Campus Safety ....Mr. Michael WILLIAMSON

College of Charleston (B)

66 George Street, Charleston SC 29424-0100
County: Charleston FICE Identification: 003428
Unit ID: 217819
Telephone: (843) 953-5507 Carnegie Class: Master's M
FAX Number: (843) 953-5811 Calendar System: Semester
URL: www.cofc.edu
Established: 1770 Annual Undergrad Tuition & Fees (In-State): $10,900
Enrollment: 11,456 Coed
Affiliation or Control: State IRS Status: 501(c)3
Highest Offering: Master's
Program: Liberal Arts And General
Accreditation: SC, BUS, BUSA, CAATE, CS, MUS, SPAA, TED, THEA

01 President ....Mr. Glenn F. MCCONNELL
101 VP Col Evnts/Sec Brd Trustees ....Ms. Elizabeth W. KASSEBAUM
10 Exec VP Business Affairs ....Mr. Steven C. OSBORNE
11 VP for Admin & Planning ....Mr. Paul D. PATRICK
100 Sr Exec Admin for the Pres ....Ms. Debbie HAMMOND
26 Dir of College Mktg & Comm ....Mr. Mark E. BERRY
30 Exec VP Institutional Advancement ....Mr. George P. WATT, JR.
32 Interim Exec VP Student Affairs ....Dr. Jeri O. CABOT
05 Interim Provost Exec VP Admin ....Dr. Brian MCGEE
43 General Counsel ....Ms. Angela MULLHOLLAND
20 Associate Provost ....Dr. Consuela FRANCIS
19 Chief of Police/Dir Public Saf ....Chief Robert S. REESE
20 Associate Provost ....Dr. Deanna M. CAVENY-NOECKER
20 Associate Vice Pres ....Dr. Lynne E. FORD
104 Assoc Provost for Intl Education ....Dr. Andrew M. SOBIESUO
13 Senior VP/Chief Information Officer ....Dr. Robert E. CAPE
30 Senior VP Economic Development ....Mr. Robert W. MARLOWE
18 VP Facilities Planning ....Ms. Monica R. SCOTT
21 VP Fiscal Services ....Ms. Priscilla D. BURBAGE
21 Dir of Financial Srvcs ....Ms. Debra B. ALDERMAN
109 Director of Bus and Aux Svcs ....Ms. Janet J. BREWTON
96 Procurement Director ....Ms. Wendy E. WILLIAMS
30 Vice President Development ....Mr. Christopher TOBIN
15 VP of Human Resources ....Mr. Edward POPE
16 Dir of Hum Rel & Min Affairs ....Ms. Kimberly A. GERTNER
84 Assoc Vice Pres Enrollment Planning ....Mr. Donald C. BURKARD
09 Assoc VP Institutional Research ....Dr. James T. POSEY
28 Associate VP Diversity ....Dr. John BELLO-OGUNU
88 Asst VP New Student Programs ....Ms. Melinda MILEY
06 Interim Registrar ....Ms. Mary BERGSTROM
21 Controller ....Ms. Dawn E. WILLAN
21 Treasurer ....Mr. David G. KATZ
58 Dean Graduate School ....Dr. Amy T. MCCANDLESS
58 Associate Dean ....Mr. David W. OWENS
57 Dean School of the Arts ....Ms. Valerie B. MORRIS
50 Dean School of Business ....Dr. Alan T. SHAO
53 Dean School of Education ....Dr. Frances C. WELCH
82 Dean School of Languages ....Dr. Antonio D. TILLIS
81 Dean School of Science & Math ....Dr. Michael AUERBACH
79 Dean Sch of Humanitites/Social Sci ....Dr. Jerold L. HALE
107 Dean College of Charleston North ....Dr. Godfrey GIBBISON
51 Director CCEPD ....Dr. Alice M. HAMILTON
92 Dean Honors College ....Dr. Trisha H. FOLDS-BENNETT
41 Director Athletics ....Mr. Joe HULL, JR.
25 Director Research and Grants ....Ms. Susan A. RIVALEAU
37 Dir Financial Asst/Veteran Affairs ....Mr. Donald R. GRIGGS
07 Exec Dir of Admissions ....Ms. Suzette STILLE
88 Dir Center for Academic Advising ....Ms. Karen HAUSCHILD
88 Dir Center for Student Learning ....Ms. Melissa M. THOMAS
108 Dir Academic Assessment & Planning ....Dr. Karin ROOF
88 Director Strategic Initiatives ....Ms. Denise MITCHELL
88 Dir Ctr for Disabilities Services ....Ms. Deborah F. MIHAL
35 Director Student Life ....Ms. Susan PAYMENT
36 Director Career Services ....Mr. Denny D. CIGANOVIC
38 Dir Counseling & Substance Abuse ....Mr. Frank C. BUDD
23 Director Health Services ....Ms. Jane RENO-MUNRO
39 Director Residence Life ....Ms. Melantha ARDREY
19 Dir of Fire and Life Safety ....Mr. Richard N. KRANTZ
88 Dir Enviro Health and Safety ....Mr. Randy L. BEAVER
21 Associate Vice President ....Mr. Samuel B. JONES
28 Associate Vice President Diversity ....Dr. John O. BELO-OGUNU
88 Director of ECDC ....Candace L. JARUSZEWICZ
88 AVP Student Affairs Dir HSLC ....K.M DUNCAN
88 Director of Sustainability ....P.B FISHER
88 Director Avery Research Cntr ....Patricia WILLIAMS LESSANE
31 Sr Dir of Community Relations ....Evelyn H. NADEL
88 Dir Undergrad Acad Svcs ....Michelle G. FUTRELL

Columbia College (C)

1301 Columbia College Drive, Columbia SC 29203-5998
County: Richland FICE Identification: 003430
Unit ID: 217934
Telephone: (803) 786-3178 Carnegie Class: Master's M
FAX Number: (803) 786-3752 Calendar System: Semester
URL: www.columbiasc.edu
Established: 1854 Annual Undergrad Tuition & Fees: $28,100
Enrollment: 1,218 Female
Affiliation or Control: United Methodist IRS Status: 501(c)3
Highest Offering: Master's
Program: Liberal Arts And General; Teacher Preparatory
Accreditation: SC, ART, DANCE, MUS, SW, TED

01 President ....Ms. Elizabeth A. DINNDORF
05 Provost/VP for Academic Affairs ....Dr. Laurie B. HOPKINS
10 Vice President for Finance ....Mr. John C. SIRCY
84 Vice Pres for Enrollment Management ....Mr. Ken HUUS
88 Ex Dir Inst Lship & Prof Excellenc ....Ms. Chris LACOLA
30 VP for Advancement ....Ms. Amy S. LANIER
32 Dean Student Affairs ....Ms. LaNae R. BRIGGS
29 Exec Director of Alumnae Relations ....Ms. Carla L. MOORE
06 Registrar/Dir Institutional Rsrch ....Dr. Scott A. SMITH
08 Director of Library ....Ms. Jane TUTTLE
19 Chief of Police ....Chief Howard M. COOK
37 Director of Financial Aid ....Ms. Donna QUICK
36 Director of Ctr for Career Coaching ....Ms. Kenetta PIERCE
13 Dir of Info Technology Services ....Mr. Floyd STAYNER
18 Director of Facilities Management ....Mr. Chad BOUFFIOU
26 Exec Director Mktg & Communications ....Ms. Tracy BENDER
41 Director of Athletics ....Ms. Kellyanne STUBBLEFIELD
40 Director Bookstore ....Mr. Chris FREEMAN
38 Director Counseling Services ....Ms. Mimi MERIWETHER
04 Executive Assistant to President ....Ms. Joye G. HIPP
07 Director of Admissions ....Ms. Julie A. KING
92 Director Honors Program/Faculty Dev ....Dr. John ZUBIZARRETA

Columbia International University (D)

PO Box 3122, Columbia SC 29230-3122
County: Richland FICE Identification: 003429
Unit ID: 217925
Telephone: (803) 754-4100 Carnegie Class: Master's S
FAX Number: (803) 786-4209 Calendar System: Semester
URL: www.ciu.edu
Established: 1923 Annual Undergrad Tuition & Fees: $27,960
Enrollment: 1,103 Coed
Affiliation or Control: Independent Non-Profit IRS Status: 501(c)3
Highest Offering: Doctorate
Program: Liberal Arts And General; Professional
Accreditation: SC, BI, THEOL

01 President ....Dr. William H. JONES
00 Chancellor ....Dr. George W. MURRAY
05 Senior Vice President/Provost ....Dr. Jim LANPHER
11 Sr Vice Pres of Operations ....Mr. D. Keith MARION
30 Sr VP of Institutional Advancement ....Mr. Jeff WHEELER
27 VP Communications ....Vacant
73 Dean Seminary & School of Ministry ....Dr. John HARVEY
49 Dean College of Arts and Sciences ....Dr. Bryan BEYER
53 Dean College of Education ....Dr. Connie MITCHELL
88 Dean College of Counseling ....Dr. Harvey PAYNE
104 Dean College Intercultural Studies ....Dr. Michael BARNETT
09 Dir Institutional Research/Assess ....Dr. Ben BRYAN
56 Director of CEID ....Mr. Rob MCDOLE
08 Director of Library ....Ms. Stephanie SOLOMON
06 University Registrar ....Mrs. Jennifer BOOTH
15 Director Human Resources ....Mr. Donald E. JONES
29 Int Director of Alumni ....Mrs. Diane MULL
32 Dean of Students ....Mr. Rick SWIFT
07 Director University Admissions ....Vacant
13 Corporate IT Coordinator ....Mr. Tirrell HOWELL
18 Director Physical Plant ....Mr. Dave MAGNUSON
40 Director of Business Services ....Mr. Roger L. TILTON
10 Chief Financial Officer ....Mr. Keith STOKELD
30 Director Development ....Mr. Frank BEDELL
37 Director Financial Aid ....Mrs. Patty HIX
88 General Mgr WMHK/WRCM Radio ....Mr. Joseph PAULO
36 Director Student Placement ....Mrs. Stephanie BRYANT
04 Administrative Asst to President ....Ms. Cheryl BRANNAN
19 Director Security/Safety ....Mr. Bob REGISTER
41 Athletic Director ....Mrs. Kim ABBOTT

Converse College (E)

580 E Main, Spartanburg SC 29302-0006
County: Spartanburg FICE Identification: 003431
Unit ID: 217961
Telephone: (864) 596-9000 Carnegie Class: Master's M
FAX Number: (864) 596-9158 Calendar System: 4/1/4
URL: www.converse.edu
Established: 1889 Annual Undergrad Tuition & Fees: $16,500
Enrollment: 1,389 Female
Affiliation or Control: Independent Non-Profit IRS Status: 501(c)3
Highest Offering: Beyond Master's But Less Than Doctorate
Program: Liberal Arts And General; Teacher Preparatory; Professional; Business Emphasis
Accreditation: SC, ART, CIDA, MFCD, MUS, TED

01 President ....Dr. Elizabeth A. FLEMING
05 Provost ....Dr. Jeffrey H. BARKER
10 Vice Pres Finance/Administration ....Ms. Robin LESLIE
30 VP External Affairs/Univ Relations ....Mrs. Charlotte VERREAULT
79 Dean Humanities/Sciences/Education ....Mrs. Ann PLETCHER
57 Dean School of the Arts ....Dr. Boone HOPKINS
32 Dean of Community Life ....Ms. Rhonda MINGO
08 Librarian ....Mr. Wade WOODWARD
37 Director of Financial Planning ....Mrs. Nancy GARMROTH
06 Registrar ....Mrs. Mary L. BROWN
15 Human Resources Director ....Ms. Dennis HUGHES
13 Chief Information Officer ....Mr. Zach CORBITT
36 Dean of Professional Development ....Ms. Witney FISHER
26 Director of Media/Communications ....Mrs. Beth LANCASTER
04 Assistant to the President ....Mrs. Stacey BREWER
38 Director of Counseling Services ....Mrs. Bethany GARR
09 Director Institutional Research ....Dr. Yongmei LI
07 Assoc Vice Pres of Enrollment Mgmt ....Mr. Trevor PITTMAN
18 Chief Facilities/Physical Plant ....Mr. Hayden HUTCHINGS
109 Facilities Planner ....Mr. Rick JOLLEY

Denmark Technical College (F)

PO Box 327, Denmark SC 29042-0327
County: Bamberg FICE Identification: 005363
Unit ID: 217989
Telephone: (803) 793-5176 Carnegie Class: Assoc/Pub-R-S
FAX Number: (803) 793-5942 Calendar System: Semester
URL: www.denmarktech.edu
Established: 1948 Annual Undergrad Tuition & Fees (In-State): $2,734
Enrollment: 1,603 Coed
Affiliation or Control: State IRS Status: 501(c)3
Highest Offering: Associate Degree
Program: Occupational; 2-Year Principally Bachelor's Creditable
Accreditation: SC, ACBSP, ENGT

01 President ....Dr. Leonard MCINTYRE
100 Executive Director to the President ....Dr. Lamin DRAMMEH
05 VP for Academic Affairs ....Dr. Valerie FIELDS

09 VP for Inst Research/Plng/Dev .... Dr. Ashok KABISATPATHY
10 Interim VP for Fiscal Affairs .... Mr. Clarence BONNETTE
84 VP for Enrollment Management .... Mr. Marcus CORBETT
15 Director of Human Resources .... Ms. Alfredia BOYD
32 Interim VP for Student Services .... Mrs. Avis GATHERS
08 Dean of Learning Resources Ctr .... Mrs. Carolyn FORTSON
13 Director of Information Technology .... Mr. Derrick STEWARD
19 Chief of Public Safety .... Mr. Elton SHULER
25 Director of Grants & Contracts .... Mrs. Teresa MACK
36 Director Career Plng/Placement .... Vacant
37 Director of Financial Aid .... Mrs. Laura FOGLE
40 Dean of Public Service .... Mrs. Bijayalaxmi KABISATPATHY
49 Acting Dean of Arts & Sciences .... Mrs. Shannon WILLIAMS
54 Dean of Industrial/Related Tech .... Dr. Ambrish LAVANIA
50 Dean Business/Computer/Related Tech .... Mrs. Tia WRIGHT-RICHARDS
60 Dean of Transitional Studies .... Dr. Tasha LOUIS-NANCE
07 Director of Recruitment .... Ms. Margaree BONNETTE
103 AVP Economic/Workforce Development .... Mr. Stephen MASON
39 Director Student Housing .... Ms. Charlene DICKERSON

Edward Via College of Osteopathic Medicine-Carolinas Campus (A)

350 Howard Street, Sparntanburg SC 29303
Telephone: (864) 327-9800 Identification: 770941
Accreditation: OSTEO

† Branch campus of Edward Via College of Osteopathic Medicine, Blacksburg, VA.

Erskine College (B)

PO Box 338, 2 Washington Street, Due West SC 29639-0338
County: Abbeville FICE Identification: 003432
Unit ID: 217998
Telephone: (864) 379-2131 Carnegie Class: Bac/A&S
FAX Number: (864) 379-2167 Calendar System: 4/1/4
URL: www.erskine.edu
Established: 1837 Annual Undergrad Tuition & Fees: $33,315
Enrollment: 593 Coed
Affiliation or Control: Other IRS Status: 501(c)3
Highest Offering: Doctorate
Program: Liberal Arts And General; Professional
Accreditation: #SC, CAATE, TED, THEOL

01 President .... Dr. Paul D. KOOISTRA
05 Sr VP of Academic Affairs .... Dr. N. Bradley CHRISTIE
10 Sr VP for Finance & Operations .... Mr. Gregory W. HASELDEN
32 Vice President Student Services .... Vacant
30 Vice President for Advancement .... Mr. David EARLE
06 Registrar .... Mrs. Tracy M. SPIRES
37 Director of Student Financial Aid .... Mrs. A. Michelle LODATO
13 Director of Information Technology ...... Mr. Robert S. CLARKE, III
09 Director of Institutional Research .... Mr. Buck F. BROWN, JR.
41 VP for Athletics .... Mr. Mark L. PEELER
42 RUF Campus Minister .... Mr. Paul G. PATRICK
21 Controller .... Mr. Christian M. HABEGER
15 Director Human Resources .... Mrs. Barbara PECK
19 Chief of Erskine Police .... Mr. Charles R. ESTEP
35 Assoc Dean of Students .... Vacant
36 Coordinator for Student Transitions .... Mr. Trent D. PAYNE
26 Vice President for Communications .... Mr. Cliff L. SMITH
29 Director of Alumni Affairs .... Mr. William L. FERGUSON
73 Vice Pres Theological Seminary .... Dr. Christopher H. WISDOM
04 Administrative Asst to President .... Mrs. Dena S. HODGE
07 Director of Admissions .... Ms. Tobe R. FRIERSON
105 Director of Comm Technology .... Mr. Brian K. SMITH
108 Assoc Dean of Inst Effectiveness ..... Mr. John F. KENNERLY, JR.
39 Coord Residential Lrng & Develop .... Vacant

Florence - Darlington Technical College (C)

PO Box 100548, Florence SC 29502-0548
County: Florence FICE Identification: 003990
Unit ID: 218025
Telephone: (843) 661-8324 Carnegie Class: Assoc/Pub-R-M
FAX Number: (843) 661-8011 Calendar System: Semester
URL: www.fdtc.edu
Established: 1964 Annual Undergrad Tuition & Fees (In-District): $4,890
Enrollment: 6,215 Coed
Affiliation or Control: State/Local IRS Status: 501(c)3
Highest Offering: Associate Degree
Program: Occupational; 2-Year Principally Bachelor's Creditable
Accreditation: SC, ACBSP, ADNUR, CAHIIM, COARC, CSHSE, DA, DH, MLTAD, RAD, SURGT

01 President .... Dr. Ben P. DILLARD, III
05 Vice President Academic Affairs .... Dr. Suresh TIWARI
32 Vice Pres Student Svcs/Enroll Mgmt .... Dr. Shelley FORTIN
30 Vice Pres Institutional Advancement .... Ms. Jill LEWIS
26 Vice Pres Marketing/Public Affs .... Mr. Edward BETHEA
10 Assoc Vice Pres Business Office .... Ms. Connie MORRIS
76 Assoc VP Allied Health .... Dr. Maureen DEVER-BUMBA
13 Assoc Vice Pres Info Tech/CIO .... Mr. Tyron JONES
15 Assoc VP Internal Relations/EEO .... Ms. Terry DINGLE
09 Director Institutional Research .... Ms. Melissa MILLER
06 Registrar .... Vacant
37 Director Financial Aid .... Mr. Joseph DURANT

Forrest College (D)

601 E River Street, Anderson SC 29624-2405
County: Anderson FICE Identification: 004924
Unit ID: 218043
Telephone: (864) 225-7653 Carnegie Class: Assoc/PrivFP
FAX Number: (864) 261-7471 Calendar System: 4/1/4
URL: www.forrestcollege.edu
Established: 1946 Annual Undergrad Tuition & Fees: $9,420
Enrollment: 100 Coed
Affiliation or Control: Proprietary IRS Status: Proprietary
Highest Offering: Associate Degree
Program: Occupational; 2-Year Principally Bachelor's Creditable
Accreditation: ACICS, #MAC

00 Chairman Board of Directors .... Dr. John RE
01 Acting President .... Dr. Cosmo J. RE
05 Academic Dean .... June STEWART
11 Administrative Dean .... Scott PETERSON
101 Secy/Treasurer Board of Directors .... Charles PALMER
06 Registrar .... Chris HRENKO
08 Librarian .... Brandy ROSCOE
76 Medical Assisting Program Coord .... Alica SWANEY
07 Admissions Rep .... Janie TURMON
07 Admissions Rep .... Veronica WRIGHT
07 Admissions Rep .... Candace BENTLEY
37 Financial Aid Officer .... Kathryn MONTGOMERY

Francis Marion University (E)

PO Box 100547, Florence SC 29501-0547
County: Florence FICE Identification: 009226
Unit ID: 218061
Telephone: (843) 661-1362 Carnegie Class: Master's S
FAX Number: (843) 661-1202 Calendar System: Semester
URL: www.fmarion.edu
Established: 1970 Annual Undergrad Tuition & Fees (In-State): $10,100
Enrollment: 3,440 Coed
Affiliation or Control: State IRS Status: Exempt
Highest Offering: Master's
Program: Liberal Arts And General; Teacher Preparatory; Professional
Accreditation: SC, ART, BUS, NUR, TED, THEA

01 President .... Dr. Luther F. CARTER
05 Provost/Dean Col of Liberal Arts .... Dr. Richard N. CHAPMAN
10 Vice President Business Affairs .... Mr. John J. KISPERT
11 Vice President Administration .... Dr. Charlene WAGES
30 Vice President Devel/Exec Dir .... Mr. Darryl BRIDGES
26 VP Public & Community Affairs .... Mr. Tucker MITCHELL
32 Vice President for Student Affairs .... Mrs. Teresa RAMEY
84 Assoc Provost For Academic Affiars .... Dr. Peter KING
21 Asst Vice Pres for Accounting .... Mr. M. Augustus MCDILL
88 Asst Vice Pres Financial Services .... Mr. Thomas WELCH
50 Dean School of Business .... Dr. Barry O'BRIEN
53 Dean School of Educaion .... Dr. Shirley BAUSMITH
08 Dean of the Library .... Mrs. Joyce M. DURANT
20 Associate Provost .... Dr. Alissa WARTERS
37 Financial Assistance Director .... Ms. Kimberly M. ELLISOR
41 Athletic Director .... Mr. Murray G. HARTZLER
06 Registrar .... Ms. Dollie NEWHOUSE
38 Director Counseling and Testing .... Dr. Rebecca L. LAWSON
18 Director of Facilities Management .... Mr. Ralph U. DAVIS
36 Director Career Development .... Dr. Ronald E. MILLER, JR.
07 Director of Admissions .... Mrs. Perry T. WILSON
35 Asst Dean of Students .... Ms. R. Daphne CARTER
29 Director of Alumni Affairs .... Mr. Julian M. YOUNG
96 Director of Purchasing .... Mr. Eric L. GARRIS
92 Director of Honors Program .... Dr. Pamela A. ROOKS
13 Chief Information Officer .... Mr. John DIXON
04 Administrative Asst to President .... Mrs. Kim DAVIS
105 Media Production/Web Design Coord .... Mr. Larry B. FALCK
19 Chief of Campus Police .... Mr. Donald R. TARBELL
39 Director Student Housing .... Mrs. Cheryl R. TUTTLE
43 Dir Legal Services/General Counsel ... Mr. Jonathan P. EDWARDS

Furman University (F)

3300 Poinsett Highway, Greenville SC 29613-0001
County: Greenville FICE Identification: 003434
Unit ID: 218070
Telephone: (864) 294-2000 Carnegie Class: Bac/A&S
FAX Number: (864) 294-3001 Calendar System: Semester
URL: www.furman.edu
Established: 1826 Annual Undergrad Tuition & Fees: $45,632
Enrollment: 2,973 Coed
Affiliation or Control: Independent Non-Profit IRS Status: 501(c)3
Highest Offering: Master's
Program: Liberal Arts And General
Accreditation: SC, MUS, TED

01 President .... Dr. Elizabeth DAVIS
05 VP Academic Affairs & Dean .... Dr. John S. BECKFORD
10 VP for Finance & Administration .... Ms. Mary Lou MERKT
07 Vice President for Enrollment .... Mr. Michael HENDRICKS
32 Vice President for Student Life .... Ms. Connie L. CARSON
30 Vice President for Development .... Mr. Michael D. GATCHELL
26 VP Marketing/Public Relations .... Mr. Mark L. KELLY
20 Sr Associate Academic Dean .... Dr. Marianne PIERCE
20 Associate Academic Dean .... Dr. Paula S. GABBERT
06 University Registrar .... Mr. Brad E. BARRON
58 Director Graduate Studies .... Dr. Troy M. TERRY
08 Director Libraries .... Dr. Janis M. BANDELIN
19 Chief of Police .... Mr. Tom SACCENTI
108 Asst Vice President Assessment .... Dr. David EUBANKS
09 Director Inst Assessment & Research .... Mr. Donald E. PIERCE
37 Assoc Vice Pres of Financial Aid .... Mr. Forrest M. STUART
29 Director of Alumni Association .... Mr. Mike WILSON
07 Assoc Vice President of Admissions .... Mr. Brad POCHARD
44 Director of Annual Giving .... Mr. John KEMP
44 Director of Planned Giving .... Mr. Steve PERRY
25 Grants Administrator .... Ms. Judith J. ROMANO
28 Director of Multicultural Affairs .... Vacant
94 Dir Women's/Gender/Sexuality Study .... Dr. Karni BHATI
15 Interim Asst VP Human Resources/AAO .... Mr. Robert BIERLY
13 Chief Information Officer .... Mr. Fred MILLER
85 Asst Dean Intl Educ/Study Away .... Vacant
36 Director Career Services .... Dr. John D. BARKER
109 Auxil Services Director .... Ms. Rebecca VUKSTA
18 Asst VP for Facilities Services .... Mr. Jeff P. REDDERSON
51 Director Continuing Education .... Dr. Brad BECHTOLD
41 VP & Director of Athletics .... Dr. Gary E. CLARK
46 Director UG Research & Internships .... Dr. Tim G. FEHLER
88 Director CTL .... Dr. Jane LOVE
17 Director Student Health Services .... Dr. Paul V. CATALANA
38 Director Counseling Center .... Dr. Stephen DAWES
39 Director University Housing .... Mr. Ronald C. THOMPSON
88 Director Disability Services .... Vacant
42 Chaplain .... Dr. Vaughn CROWETIPTON
40 Director Bookstore .... Ms. K. C ROBINSON
04 Assistant to President .... Ms. Cindy ALEXANDER
21 Assoc VP Finance Budget Director .... Ms. Amy BLACKWELL
96 Director of Purchasing .... Ms. Lishan YAU
35 Director Student Activities .... Ms. Jessica BERKEY
104 Director Study Abroad .... Vacant
43 Dir Legal Services/General Counsel ... Ms. Angela F. LITTLEJOHN

Golf Academy of America (G)

1900 Mr. Joe White Ave., Myrtle Beach SC 29577
Telephone: (800) 342-7342 Identification: 666490
Accreditation: ACICS

† Branch campus of Virginia College, Birmingham, AL.

Greenville Technical College (H)

PO Box 5616, Greenville SC 29606-5616
County: Greenville FICE Identification: 003991
Unit ID: 218113
Telephone: (864) 250-8000 Carnegie Class: Assoc/Pub-U-MC
FAX Number: (864) 250-8507 Calendar System: Semester
URL: www.gvltec.edu
Established: 1962 Annual Undergrad Tuition & Fees (In-State): $2,052
Enrollment: 12,592 Coed
Affiliation or Control: State IRS Status: 501(c)3
Highest Offering: Associate Degree
Program: Occupational; 2-Year Principally Bachelor's Creditable; Technical Emphasis
Accreditation: SC, ACBSP, ACFEI, ADNUR, CAHIIM, COARC, DA, DH, DMS, EMT, ENGT, MAC, MLTAD, OTA, PTAA, RAD, SURGT

01 President .... Dr. Keith MILLER
05 Vice President for Academic Affairs .... Dr. Lenna YOUNG
10 Vice President for Finance .... Mrs. Jacqueline R. DIMAGGIO
32 Vice President Student Services .... Dr. Matteel JONES
51 Vice Pres Corp & Economic Devel .... Mrs. Cynthia G. EASON
45 VP Institutional Effectiveness .... Mrs. Lauren SIMER

Horry-Georgetown Technical College (I)

2050 Highway 501 E, Conway SC 29526-9521
County: Horry FICE Identification: 004925
Unit ID: 218140
Telephone: (843) 347-3186 Carnegie Class: Assoc/Pub-R-M
FAX Number: (843) 347-4207 Calendar System: Semester
URL: www.hgtc.edu
Established: 1966 Annual Undergrad Tuition & Fees (In-District): $3,960
Enrollment: 7,331 Coed
Affiliation or Control: State/Local IRS Status: 501(c)3
Highest Offering: Associate Degree
Program: 2-Year Principally Bachelor's Creditable; Technical Emphasis
Accreditation: SC, ACBSP, ACFEI, ADNUR, DA, DH, DMS, EMT, PNUR, PTAA, RAD, SURGT

01 President .... Mr. Neyle WILSON
05 Senior VP .... Dr. Marilyn FORE
10 Vice President for Business/Finance .... Mr. Harold HAWLEY
13 VP for Tech/Institutional Planning .... Mr. Ralph SELANDER
103 VP Wrkfc Dev/Prov GS/Georgetwn Camp . Mr. Gregory MITCHELL
84 AVP Enrollment Dev/Registration .... Mr. George SWINDOLL
32 Asc VP Student Affs/Campus Life .... Dr. Melissa BATTEN
20 AVP Acad Affs/Dean Academic Support .... Dr. Becky BOONE
20 AVP Acad Affs/Dn Univ Paral/Engr .... Dr. Shirley BUTLER
20 AVP Acad Affs/Dn Nur/Health Science .... Dr. Christy CIMINERI
15 AVP Human Res/Employee Relations .... Ms. Jacqueline BARRETT
08 AVP/Dn Library/Learning Resources .... Ms. Peggy SAYLOR
20 AVP Acad Affs/Dn Bus/Dental .... Dr. Philip RENDER
21 AVP/Controller .... Ms. Ellen BLACK
84 AVP Student Enrollment Services .... Ms. Cynthia JOHNSTON
26 Dir Public Relations/Marketing .... Ms. Mary EADDY
18 Superintendent Bulidings & Grounds .... Mr. Kevin BROWN
37 Dir of Financial Aid/Veterans Affs .... Ms. Susan THOMPSON
07 Dir Stdnt Recruitment/Admissions .... Ms. Thyssene FREDERICK

36 Career Resource Ctr Coordinator .... Ms. April GARNER
09 Dir Institutional Rsrch/Assessment .... Ms. Lori HEAFNER
96 Procurement Manager .... Ms. Dianna CECALA
105 Web Services Coordinator .... Ms. Melissa MONOLO
19 Director Security/Safety .... Mr. Barry MARSH

ITT Technical Institute (A)

1628 Browning Road, Suite 180, Columbia SC 29210
Telephone: (803) 216-6000 Identification: 666162
Accreditation: ACICS

† Branch campus of ITT Technical Institute, Indianapolis, IN.

ITT Technical Institute (B)

6 Independence Pointe, Greenville SC 29615-4506
Telephone: (864) 288-0777 Identification: 666549
Accreditation: ACICS

† Branch campus of ITT Technical Institute, Indianapolis, IN.

ITT Technical Institute (C)

9654 N Kings Highway, Suite 101, Myrtle Beach SC 29752
Telephone: (843) 497-7820 Identification: 770661
Accreditation: ACICS

† Branch campus of ITT Technical Institute, Indianapolis, IN.

ITT Technical Institute (D)

2431 W Aviation Avenue, North Charleston SC 29406
Telephone: (843) 745-5700 Identification: 770662
Accreditation: ACICS

† Branch campus of ITT Technical Institute, Indianapolis, IN.

Lander University (E)

320 Stanley Avenue, Greenwood SC 29649-2099
County: Greenwood FICE Identification: 003435
Unit ID: 218229
Telephone: (864) 388-8000 Carnegie Class: Bac/Diverse
FAX Number: (864) 388-8890 Calendar System: Semester
URL: www.lander.edu
Established: 1872 Annual Undergrad Tuition & Fees (In-State): $10,752
Enrollment: 2,787 Coed
Affiliation or Control: State IRS Status: 501(c)3
Highest Offering: Master's
Program: Liberal Arts And General; Teacher Preparatory; Professional; Business Emphasis
Accreditation: SC, ART, BUS, CAATE, MACTE, MUS, NURSE, TED

01 President .... Dr. Richard E. COSENTINO
05 Provost/Vice Pres Academic Affairs .... Dr. David MASH
10 Vice Pres Business/Administration .... Mr. Gary MCCOMBS
32 Vice President for Student Affairs ...... Mr. H. Randall BOUKNIGHT
30 Vice President for Univ Advancement .... Mr. Ralph PATTERSON
86 VP for Governmental Relations .... Mr. Adam TAYLOR
84 Dean of Enrollment Services .... Mrs. Jennifer M. MATHIS
08 Librarian .... Ms. Lisa WIECKI
38 Director Counseling .... Ms. Debra J. FRANKS
41 Vice President/Athletic Director .... Mr. Jefferson J. MAY
15 Director Human Resources .... Ms. Jeannie MCCALLUM
19 Director University Police .... Mr. Eddie BRIGGS
26 Director of Public Information .... Mrs. Megan PRICE
37 Director of Financial Aid .... Mr. Fred HARDIN
36 Director of Career Services .... Mrs. Amanda MORGAN
21 Controller .... Mr. Tom COVAR
40 Dir Bookstore/Procurement/Print Svc .... Mrs. Mary W. MCDANIEL
13 Dir Office Inform Tech Services .... Ms. Robin P. LAWRENCE
07 Director of Admissions .... Mrs. Jennifer M. MATHIS
18 Director Physical Plant/Engr Svcs .... Mr. Jeff S. BEAVER
06 Registrar .... Ms. Kelly PROCTOR
29 Director Alumni Relations .... Ms. Myra GREENE
09 Director of Institutional Research .... Mr. Mac KIRKPATRICK

Limestone College (F)

1115 College Drive, Gaffney SC 29340-3799
County: Cherokee FICE Identification: 003436
Unit ID: 218238
Telephone: (864) 489-7151 Carnegie Class: Bac/Diverse
FAX Number: (864) 487-8706 Calendar System: Semester
URL: www.limestone.edu
Established: 1845 Annual Undergrad Tuition & Fees: $23,900
Enrollment: 3,214 Coed
Affiliation or Control: Independent Non-Profit IRS Status: 501(c)3
Highest Offering: Master's
Program: Liberal Arts And General; Teacher Preparatory; Professional
Accreditation: SC, CAATE, MUS, SW, TED

01 President .... Dr. Walt R. GRIFFIN
05 Exec Vice Pres/VP Academic Affairs .... Dr. Karen W. GAINEY
10 Vice President Financial Affairs .... Mr. David S. RILLING
30 VP Institutional Advancement .... Ms. Kelly T. CURTIS
84 Vice President Enrollment Services . Mr. Christopher N. PHENICIE
32 Vice President Student Services .... Mr. Robert A. OVERTON
13 Vice Pres Information Technology .... Mr. C. R. HORTON
41 Vice Pres Intercollegiate Athletics .... Mr. Michael H. CERINO
14 Assoc VP Information Technology .... Mr. C. Adam LONG
20 Assoc Vice Pres Academic Affairs .... Dr. Mark A. REGER
45 Assoc Vice Pres Planning/Assessment ...... Dr. Bonnie M. WRIGHT
88 Dean of Academic Support .... Dr. Charles J. CUNNING
106 Dean of Extended Campus Program .... Dr. Mark A. REGER
04 Administrative Asst to President .... Mrs. Nani Lou S. COOPER
56 Dir Extended Campus Classroom Pgm .... Mrs. Donna HUDSON
06 Registrar .... Ms. Pennie D. HUGHES
37 Director Financial Aid .... Mr. Bobby T. GREER
44 Director of Development .... Vacant
08 Director Library .... Ms. Lizah ISMAIL
26 Director Communications .... Mr. Charles W. WYATT
35 Director Student Services .... Ms. Jessica D. GOINS
36 Director Career Services .... Ms. Ileka L. LEAKS
90 Director of Server Services .... Dr. Scott D. BERRY
18 Director Physical Plant .... Mr. Logan RICHARDSON
92 Director Academic Honors Program .... Ms. Carol TAYLOR
83 Assoc Dean/Director Social Work .... Mr. Jackie A. PUCKETT
19 Chief of Campus Security .... Mr. Richard E. SIMMONS
21 Controller .... Mr. L. Wayde DAWSON
23 Campus Nurse .... Mrs. Sandy B. GREEN
44 Director Advancement Services .... Mrs. Brandi P. HARTMAN
20 Director of Academic Advising .... Ms. Pennie D. HUGHES
29 Director Alumni Programs .... Ms. Mandy C. HOYLE
88 Dir Christian Ed/Leadership Program ...... Rev. J. Ron SINGLETON
88 Director of Food Services .... Mr. Joe FIELDS
42 College Chaplain .... Rev. J. Ron SINGLETON
88 Dir Accessibility Services/PALS .... Ms. Andrea ALLISON
15 Dir Human Resources/AAEEO Officer ...... Ms. Brenda F. WATKINS
50 Director of MBA Program .... Mr. Brandon J. GIBSON
88 Sr Assoc Athletics Dir Compliance .... Mr. Dennis L. BLOOMER
88 Asst Athletics Dir for Media Rels .... Mr. Ernest G. MEYERS
88 Asst Athletics Dir Sports Perform .... Mr. Curtis S. LAMB
88 Assc Dir Extend Campus Internet Pgm .... Mrs. Katie P. JONES
88 Director Extended Internet Program .... Dr. Barry W. SHREVE
07 Assoc Director of Admissions .... Mr. Travis MCDOWELL
40 Campus Store Manager .... Mrs. Patti H. MCCRAW
38 College Counselor .... Mrs. Mary B. CAMPBELL
107 Chair Div of Professional Studies .... Dr. Paul R. LEFRANCOIS
88 Chair Div of Natural Sciences .... Mr. Brian F. AMELING
49 Chair Div of Arts & Letters .... Dr. Gena E. POOVEY
83 Chair Div Social & Behav Sciences .... Dr. Betsy A. WITT
53 Chair Div Educ/Phys Ed/Teacher Educ .... Dr. Shelly A. MEYERS

Medical University of South Carolina (G)

179 Ashley Avenue, Charleston SC 29425
County: Charleston FICE Identification: 003438
Unit ID: 218335
Telephone: (843) 792-2300 Carnegie Class: Spec/Med
FAX Number: N/A Calendar System: Semester
URL: www.musc.edu
Established: 1824 Annual Undergrad Tuition & Fees (In-State): N/A
Enrollment: 2,900 Coed
Affiliation or Control: State IRS Status: Exempt
Highest Offering: Doctorate
Program: Professional
Accreditation: SC, ANEST, ARCPA, DENT, DIETI, HSA, HT, IPSY, MED, NURSE, OT, PERF, PHAR, PTA

01 President .... Dr. David J. COLE
100 Chief of Staff .... Dr. Sabra C. SLAUGHTER
05 VP Academic Affairs & Provost .... Dr. Mark S. SOTHMANN
17 Interim Dean Col of Medicine .... Dr. Deborah DEAS
10 Exec Vice President Finance & Admin .... Ms. Lisa P. MONTGOMERY
30 Vice President Development .... Mr. William J. FISHER
17 VP Clinical Operations .... Dr. Patrick J. CAWLEY
13 VP Information Technology/CIO .... Vacant
20 Assoc Prov Education/Student Life .... Dr. Darlene L. SHAW
46 Interim Associate Provost Research .... Dr. Kathleen T. BRADY
52 Dean of Dental Medicine .... Dr. John J. SANDERS
76 Dean of Health Professions .... Dr. Lisa SALADIN
58 Dean of Graduate Studies .... Dr. Paula TRAKTMAN
66 Dean of Nursing .... Dr. Gail W. STUART
67 Int Campus Dean SC Col of Pharmacy .... Dr. Philip D. HALL
88 Exec Dir SC Area Hlth Ed Consortium .... Dr. David R. GARR
08 Director of Libraries .... Dr. Shannon JONES
84 Director Enrollment Management .... Mr. George W. OHLANDT
28 Exec Director Student Programs .... Dr. Willette S. BURNHAM
43 General Counsel .... Ms. Annette R. DRACHMAN
26 Director Public Relations .... Dr. Sarah KING
22 Dir Affirm Act/Equal Opportunity ...... Mr. Wallace T. BONAPARTE
07 Director of Admissions .... Ms. Lyla HUDSON
18 Chief Facilities/Physical Plant .... Mr. Greg WEIGLE
06 Registrar .... Ms. Sandra L. MORRIS
15 Director Personnel Services .... Ms. Susan H. CARULLO
09 Dir Inst Research/Resources .... Dr. Andrew GELASCO
38 Director Student Counseling .... Dr. Alice Q. LIBET
29 Director Alumni Affairs .... Ms. Sallie HUTTON
37 Director Student Financial Aid .... Mr. Joseph M. DURANT
96 Director of Purchasing .... Ms. Betty SANDIFER

† Tuition varies by degree program.

Midlands Technical College (H)

PO Box 2408, Columbia SC 29202-2408
County: Richland FICE Identification: 003993
Unit ID: 218353
Telephone: (803) 738-8324 Carnegie Class: Assoc/Pub-U-MC
FAX Number: (803) 738-7784 Calendar System: Semester
URL: www.midlandstech.edu
Established: 1974 Annual Undergrad Tuition & Fees (In-District): $4,516
Enrollment: 11,424 Coed
Affiliation or Control: State/Local IRS Status: 501(c)3
Highest Offering: Associate Degree
Program: Occupational; 2-Year Principally Bachelor's Creditable
Accreditation: SC, ACBSP, ADNUR, CAHIIM, COARC, DA, DH, ENGT, MAC, MLTAD, NMT, PNUR, PTAA, RAD, SURGT

01 President .... Dr. Ronald RHAMES
05 Vice President Academic Affairs .... Dr. Ronald DRAYTON
10 Interim VP for Business Affairs .... Mrs. Debbie WALKER
32 Vice Pres Student Development Svcs .... Ms. Sandi OLIVER
30 VP for Institutional Support .... Ms. Starnell BATES
51 VP Economic Devel & Continuing Educ .... Dr. Barrie KIRK
43 General Counsel .... Ms. Crystal ROOKARD
06 Registrar .... Ms. Susan HOUCK
13 Director Information Resource Mgmt .... Mr. Tony HOUGH
37 Director of Student Financial Aid .... Mrs. Angela WILLIAMS
84 Director of Enrollment Services .... Ms. Sylvia LITTLEJOHN
26 Director of Public Affairs .... Mr. Todd GAVIN
44 Interim Associate VP of Development .... Mr. Jack HOEKSTRA
15 Human Resourse Director .... Mrs. Mary Beth LAMPE
07 Director of Admissions .... Mr. Derrah CASSIDY

Miller-Motte Technical College (I)

2451 Highway 501 East, Conway SC 29526
Telephone: (843) 591-1101 Identification: 770778
Accreditation: ACICS

† Branch campus of Miller-Motte Technical College, Lynchburg, VA.

Miller-Motte Technical College (J)

8085 Rivers Avenue, Suite E, North Charleston SC 29406
Telephone: (843) 574-0101 Identification: 666256
Accreditation: ACICS, MAC, SURGT

† Branch campus of Miller-Motte Technical College, Clarksville, TN.

Morris College (K)

100 W College Street, Sumter SC 29150-3599
County: Sumter FICE Identification: 003439
Unit ID: 218399
Telephone: (803) 934-3200 Carnegie Class: Bac/Diverse
FAX Number: (803) 773-3687 Calendar System: Semester
URL: www.morris.edu
Established: 1908 Annual Undergrad Tuition & Fees: $12,649
Enrollment: 802 Coed
Affiliation or Control: Baptist IRS Status: 501(c)3
Highest Offering: Baccalaureate
Program: Liberal Arts And General; Teacher Preparatory
Accreditation: SC, ACBSP, TED

01 President .... Dr. Luns C. RICHARDSON
05 Academic Dean .... Dr. Leroy STAGGERS
10 Director of Business Affairs .... Mr. Robert EAVES
86 Director Planning/Govt Relations .... Mrs. Dorothy S. CHEAGLE
32 Dean Student Affairs .... Dr. Juana DAVIS-FREEMAN
15 Personnel Officer .... Mr. Roy GRAHAM
42 College Minister .... Dr. Charles M. PEE
07 Director Admissions & Records .... Ms. Deborah C. CALHOUN
08 Director Learning Resources Ctr .... Mrs. Janet S. CLAYTON
37 Director of Financial Aid .... Mrs. Sandra S. GIBSON
13 Director MIS/Computer Center .... Vacant
36 Director Career Services Center .. Dr. Gloria SEABROOK WRIGHT
108 Director of Assessment .... Dr. Lewis P. GRAHAM, JR.
29 Alumni Affairs Officer .... Mrs. Altoya A. FELDER-DEAS
38 Director Counseling & Testing Ctr .... Dr. Quanda D. SIMS
39 Director Residential Life .... Mrs. Venessa F. JEFFERSON
23 Director of Health Services .... Mrs. Johnell ROGERS
41 Director of Athletics .... Mr. Clarence M. HOUCK
26 Director Public Relations .... Mrs. Nicole W. LYNCH
30 Director Inst Advanc/Church Rels .... Rev. Melvin MACK
96 Director of Purchasing .... Mr. Robert EAVES
89 Acting Director of Freshmen Studies .... Mr. Robert ZALIMAS
92 Director of Honors Program .... Dr. Joseph K. POPOOLA
06 Registrar .... Ms. Deborah C. CALHOUN
18 Chief Facilities/Physical Plant .... Mr. Roy GRAHAM
20 Associate Academic Officer .... Dr. Kay M. RHOADS
21 Associate Business Officer .... Mrs. Bernice IRBY
40 Bookstore Manager .... Ms. Jeanette MOSES-HOLMES
35 Coordinator Student Activities .... Mr. Alston FREEMAN
19 Coordinator Campus Safety Services .... Ms. Lucille W. WILLIAMS
09 Director of Institutional Research .... Ms. Dorothy S. CHEAGLE

Newberry College (L)

2100 College, Newberry SC 29108-2126
County: Newberry FICE Identification: 003440
Unit ID: 218414
Telephone: (800) 845-4955 Carnegie Class: Bac/Diverse
FAX Number: (803) 321-5627 Calendar System: Semester
URL: www.newberry.edu
Established: 1856 Annual Undergrad Tuition & Fees: $25,000
Enrollment: 1,093 Coed
Affiliation or Control: Evangelical Lutheran Church In America
IRS Status: 501(c)3
Highest Offering: Baccalaureate
Program: Liberal Arts And General; Teacher Preparatory
Accreditation: SC, MUS, NURSE, TED

01 President ... Dr. Maurice W. SCHERRENS
05 VP Academic Affairs & Dean ... Dr. Timothy G. ELSTON
10 VP for Admin Affairs & CFO ... Ms. Kathy WORSTER
30 VP for Institutional Advancement ... Mr. Scott JOYNER
84 Dean of Enrollment Management ... Ms. Delsie PHILLIPS
32 Dean of Student Affairs ... Ms. Jane WILLIS
41 Director of Athletics ... Mr. Matt FINLEY
15 Director of Human Resources ... Mrs. Peggy SHULER
09 Dir Institutional Effectiveness ... Dr. Sid PARRISH
06 Registrar ... Mrs. Carol A. BICKLEY
29 Assoc Dir of Alumni Relations ... Mr. Jeff WICKER
08 Librarian ... Ms. Nancy ROSENWALD
18 Director of Facilities ... Mr. Fred ERRIGO
42 Chaplain ... Rev. Ernie WORMAN
21 Director of Accounting ... Mrs. Landee BUZHARDT
38 Dir Health & Counselling Services ... Mrs. Martha DORRELL
37 Director of Financial Aid ... Mrs. Danielle BELL
26 Director of Marketing & PR ... Ms. Jill JOHNSON
07 Director of Admissions ... Mr. Joel VANDER HORST
19 Director Security/Safety ... Mr. Paul WHITMAN

North Greenville University (A)

PO Box 1892, Tigerville SC 29688-1892
County: Greenville FICE Identification: 003441
Unit ID: 218441
Telephone: (864) 977-7000 Carnegie Class: Bac/Diverse
FAX Number: (864) 977-7021 Calendar System: Semester
URL: www.ngu.edu
Established: 1892 Annual Undergrad Tuition & Fees: $16,290
Enrollment: 2,581 Coed
Affiliation or Control: Southern Baptist IRS Status: 501(c)3
Highest Offering: Doctorate
Program: Liberal Arts And General; Religious Emphasis
Accreditation: **SC**, MUS, TED

01 Interim President/CEO ... Dr. Randall J. PANNELL
04 Admin Assistant for President ... Ms. Elise STYLES
05 Vice President Academics ... Dr. Randall PANNELL
32 Vice President Student Services ... Dr. Tony BEAM
20 Asst VP Acads/Dean Communication ... Dr. Linwood HAGIN
58 Vice President Graduate Studies ... Dr. J. Samuel ISGETT
10 Vice President Business Affairs ... Ms. Michelle L. SABOU
07 VP Enrollment Services ... Ms. Keli SEWELL
30 Vice President Advancement ... Vacant
88 Vice President Church Relations ... Rev. Mayson EASTERLING
42 Vice President Campus Ministries ... Dr. Steve CROUSE
102 VP Corp Found Giving/Crusader Club ... Vacant
35 Director Student Services ... Mr. Billy WATSON
09 Director of Institutional Research ... Dr. George A. HOPSON, JR.
06 Registrar ... Ms. Pam FARMER
18 Director of University Properties ... Mr. Larry MATHIS
41 Athletic Director ... Ms. Jan MCDONALD
34 Director Residential Living Women ... Ms. Lorry GREEN
33 Director Residential Living Men ... Mr. Dillon KEY
08 Director of Hester Library ... Ms. Carla MCMAHAN
19 Director Campus Security ... Mr. Rick MORRIS
88 Dean of Graduate Academic Services ... Mrs. Tawana SCOTT
26 Director Public Rels/Stewardship ... Mr. LaVerne B. HOWELL
29 Dir Alumni Affairs/Planned Giving ... Mrs. Julie STYLES
15 Human Resource Manager ... Mrs. Beth HOUCK
40 Bookstore Manager ... Mrs. Cindy COWAN
38 Personal Counselor Men ... Mr. Steve BIELBY
38 Personal Counselor Women ... Mrs. Sue SUOMI
36 Career Services Coordinator ... Mr. Joshua PUTNAM
23 Director Health Services ... Ms. Kathy BAILEY
30 Executive Director Development ... Rev. Joe F. HAYES
44 Director of Development ... Mr. Jason ROSS
13 Asst VP Information Tech Services ... Mr. Paul GARRETT
37 Director Financial Planning ... Mr. Michael JORDAN
53 Dean Education ... Dr. Constance WRIGHT
79 Dean Humanities ... Dr. H. Paul THOMPSON
57 Dean Fine Arts ... Dr. Jacquelyn H. GRIFFIN
81 Dean Science & Mathematics ... Dr. Tom ALLEN
73 Dean Christian Studies ... Dr. Walter JOHNSON
50 Dean Business & Sport Professions ... Dr. Ralph JOHNSON
88 Asst VP for Online Education ... Dr. Lena MASLENNIKOVA

Northeastern Technical College (B)

1201 Chesterfield Hwy, Cheraw SC 29520
County: Chesterfield FICE Identification: 007602
Unit ID: 217837
Telephone: (843) 921-6900 Carnegie Class: Assoc/Pub-R-S
FAX Number: (843) 537-6148 Calendar System: Semester
URL: www.netc.edu
Established: 1969 Annual Undergrad Tuition & Fees (In-State): $7,200
Enrollment: 1,089 Coed
Affiliation or Control: State IRS Status: 501(c)3
Highest Offering: Associate Degree
Program: Occupational; 2-Year Principally Bachelor's Creditable
Accreditation: **SC**

01 President ... Dr. Ron BARTLEY
05 Vice Pres Instruction/Student Svcs ... Dr. Forest MAHAN
10 Vice Pres Administration & Finance ... Mrs. Debbie Q. CHEEK
30 Director for Inst Advancement ... Mrs. Erin FANN
15 Director for Human Resources ... Mrs. Donna CHAVIS
06 Coordinator for Student Records ... Ms. Anne JONES
26 Coordinator for Public Relations ... Ms. Shannon JUSTICE
84 Director of Enrollment Management ... Ms. Danielle PACE

Orangeburg-Calhoun Technical College (C)

3250 Saint Matthews Road, Orangeburg SC 29118-8299
County: Orangeburg FICE Identification: 006815
Unit ID: 218487
Telephone: (803) 536-0311 Carnegie Class: Assoc/Pub-R-M
FAX Number: (803) 535-1388 Calendar System: Semester
URL: www.octech.edu
Established: 1966 Annual Undergrad Tuition & Fees (In-State): $4,970
Enrollment: 3,060 Coed
Affiliation or Control: State IRS Status: 501(c)3
Highest Offering: Associate Degree
Program: Occupational; 2-Year Principally Bachelor's Creditable
Accreditation: **SC**, ACBSP, ADNUR, COARC, ENGT, MAC, PNUR, PTAA, RAD

01 President ... Dr. Walt TOBIN, JR.
05 Vice Pres Academic Affairs ... Mrs. Donna ELMORE
10 Vice President Business Affairs ... Mr. Kim HUFF
32 Vice President of Student Services ... Mrs. Sandra S. DAVIS
11 Assoc VP of Administration ... Mr. Mike HAMMOND
36 Assoc VP Corp Trng/Econ Develop ... Mrs. Sandra MOORE
06 Registrar ... Ms. Amy OTT
30 Dean Development/Marketing ... Ms. Faith MCCURRY
46 Dean Planning/Research/Development ... Ms. Faith MCCURRY
13 Director Information Technology ... Mr. Gary A. FOLEY
62 Dean Learning Resource Center ... Mrs. Harris MURRAY
18 Chief Facilities/Physical Plant ... Mr. James S. BRYANT, III
37 Director Student Financial Aid ... Ms. Bichevia GREEN
08 Director Library Services ... Mrs. Harris MURRAY
07 Director of Admissions ... Vacant
19 Chief of Safety/Security ... Mr. Douglas STOKES
09 Dir Acad Spprt/Institutional Effect ... Mr. Cleveland WILSON
15 Human Resource Director ... Ms. Marie HOWELL
96 Procurement Manager ... Mrs. Scarlet GEDDINGS
84 Enrollment/Records Mgmt Specialist ... Ms. Phylllis STOUDENMIRE

Piedmont Technical College (D)

620 N. Emerald Road, Greenwood SC 29646
County: Greenwood FICE Identification: 003992
Unit ID: 218520
Telephone: (864) 941-8324 Carnegie Class: Assoc/Pub-R-M
FAX Number: (864) 941-8555 Calendar System: Semester
URL: www.ptc.edu
Established: 1966 Annual Undergrad Tuition & Fees (In-District): $3,908
Enrollment: 5,694 Coed
Affiliation or Control: State/Local IRS Status: 501(c)3
Highest Offering: Associate Degree
Program: Occupational; 2-Year Principally Bachelor's Creditable
Accreditation: **SC**, ADNUR, COARC, CVT, ENGT, FUSER, MAC, RAD, SURGT

01 President ... Dr. L. Rayburn BROOKS
10 Vice Pres Business & Finance ... Ms. K. Paige CHILDS
05 Vice President Academic Affairs ... Dr. Jack BAGWELL
32 Vice Pres Student Development ... Vacant
51 Assoc Vice Pres Cont Educ/Econ Dev ... Mr. Rusty DENNING
24 Assoc VP Instructional Technology ... Dr. Joel GRIFFIN
108 Assoc VP Institutional Assessment ... Ms. Donna FOSTER
84 Assoc VP Enrollment Mgmt/Comm ... Mr. Joshua BLACK
12 Dean County Centers ... Dr. Jennifer WILBANKS
76 Dean Health Sciences ... Mr. Jerry ALEWINE
54 Int Dean Engr/Indust Technologies ... Mr. David KIBLER
66 Dean Nursing ... Ms. Tara HARRIS
35 Dean Student Services ... Mr. J. Andrew OMUNDSON
07 Dean of Admissions ... Ms. Renae FRAZIER
09 Director of Inst Effectiveness ... Ms. Zeolean F. KINARD
26 Director Marketing/Public Relations ... Mr. Russell MARTIN
88 Director College Outreach ... Mr. Steve B. COLEMAN
18 Director Facilities/Management ... Mr. Chad TEAGUE
102 Foundation Exec Dir/Alumni Affairs ... Ms. Fran K. WILEY
08 Head Librarian ... Mr. Daniel MEREDITH
19 Director Campus Police/Security ... Mr. Terry LEDFORD
36 Assoc Dean Student Services ... Mr. David R. ROSENBAUM
37 Director of Financial Aid ... Ms. Missy PERRY
06 Registrar ... Ms. Tamatha SELLS
21 Controller ... Ms. Paige CHILDS
15 Director Human Resources ... Ms. Alesia BROWN
21 Manager Business Office ... Ms. Crystal PITTMAN

Presbyterian College (E)

503 S Broad Street, Clinton SC 29325-2865
County: Laurens FICE Identification: 003445
Unit ID: 218539
Telephone: (864) 833-2820 Carnegie Class: Bac/A&S
FAX Number: (864) 833-8481 Calendar System: Semester
URL: www.presby.edu
Established: 1880 Annual Undergrad Tuition & Fees: $36,060
Enrollment: 1,460 Coed
Affiliation or Control: Presbyterian Church (U.S.A.) IRS Status: 501(c)3
Highest Offering: Doctorate
Program: Liberal Arts And General; Teacher Preparatory; Professional; Business Emphasis
Accreditation: **SC**, MUS, PHAR, TED

01 President ... Dr. Claude C. LILLY
101 Executive Asst to the President ... Ms. Christie L. MUELLER
04 Sr Admin Asst to the President ... Ms. Jenny G. BOGAN
84 Dean of Enrollment Management ... Mr. Brian J. FORTMAN
07 Associate Dean of Admissions ... Mr. Mark O. FOX, II
05 Provost ... Dr. Donald R. RABER, II
20 Dean of Academic Programs ... Vacant
09 Director of Institutional Research ... Dr. Norman B. BRYAN, JR.
08 Director of Thomason Library ... Mr. David W. CHATHAM
24 Director of Media Services ... Mr. Douglas J. WALLACE
104 Director of International Programs ... Mr. Viet X. HA
85 Asst Dir of International Programs ... Ms. Elizabeth M. DILLE
06 Registrar & Director of Records ... Ms. Kendra B. WOODSON
67 Dean School of Pharmacy ... Dr. L. Clifton FUHRMAN, JR.
07 Dir of Admissions Pharmacy School ... Ms. Katherine J. KANE
10 VP Finance/Administration ... Ms. Susan A. MADDUX
21 Controller ... Ms. Dawn W. DURHAM
18 Exec Director of Campus Services ... Mr. Mark L. OSINGA
37 Director of Financial Aid ... Ms. Linda J. MCANNALLY
13 Director of Information Technology ... Mr. H William ROACH
90 Academic Computing Services Coord ... Dr. Robert W. HOWILER
91 Desktop Support/Aux Systems Sr Tech ... Ms. Nellie R. SHELTON
40 Sodexo General Manager ... Mr. Jason T. KOENIG
32 VP for Campus Life/Dean of Students ... Dr. Joy S. SMITH
39 Assoc Dean Students/Residence Life ... Mr. Andrew T. PETERSON
36 Assoc Dean Students/Career Dev ... Vacant
42 Director of Campus Ministries ... Ms. Rachel E. PARSONS-WELLS
19 Director of Safety & Risk Mgmt ... Mr. Lawrence P. MULHALL
38 Director Counseling Services ... Ms. Susan C. GENTRY-WRIGHT
28 Asst Dir of Multicultural Programs ... Ms. Lashawna A. WRIGHT
30 VP for Advancement/Mktg/PR/Comms ... Mr. Grady B. JONES
44 Director of Annual Fund ... Mr. Alex K. SCULL
88 Director of Athletic Major Gifts ... Mr. R. Matthew CAIN
29 Director Alumni Relations ... Ms. Leni N. PATTERSON
105 Webmaster ... Vacant
41 Director of Athletics ... Mr. Brian P. REESE
15 VP of Human Resources ... Ms. Barbara H. FAYAD

Professional Golfers Career College (F)

4454 Bluffton Pk Crescent, Ste 200, Bluffton SC 29910
Telephone: (843) 759-9611 Identification: 770779
Accreditation: **ACICS**

† Branch campus of Professional Golfers Career College, Temecula, CA.

Sherman College of Chiropractic (G)

PO Box 1452, Spartanburg SC 29304-1452
County: Spartanburg FICE Identification: 020637
Unit ID: 218751
Telephone: (864) 578-8770 Carnegie Class: Spec/Health
FAX Number: (864) 599-4860 Calendar System: Quarter
URL: www.sherman.edu
Established: 1973 Annual Graduate Tuition & Fees: $30,160
Enrollment: 346 Coed
Affiliation or Control: Independent Non-Profit IRS Status: 501(c)3
Highest Offering: Doctorate; No Undergraduates
Program: Professional; Technical Emphasis
Accreditation: **SC**, CHIRO

01 President ... Dr. Edwin CORDERO
03 Executive Vice President ... Dr. Neil COHEN
05 Provost/Vice Pres for AA ... Dr. Robert IRWIN
84 Sr Director for Enrollment Services ... Mrs. Kristy SHEPHERD
10 Vice Pres for Business & Finance ... Mrs. Karen CANUP
32 Dean of Student Affairs ... Mrs. LaShanda HUTTO-HARRIS
29 Dir Alumni Rels/Instl Advancement ... Ms. Marggi ROLDAN
06 Registrar ... Ms. Melody SABIN
08 Librarian ... Mrs. Crissy LEWIS
37 Director of Financial Aid ... Mrs. Tina CASEY-CORREA
45 Dir Institutional Effectiveness ... Mrs. Crissy LEWIS
04 Administrative Asst to President ... Ms. Roberta THOMAS
26 Director of Public Relations ... Ms. Karen RHODES

South Carolina State University (H)

300 College Street, NE, Orangeburg SC 29117-0001
County: Orangeburg FICE Identification: 003446
Unit ID: 218733
Telephone: (803) 536-7000 Carnegie Class: DRU
FAX Number: (803) 533-3622 Calendar System: Semester
URL: www.scsu.edu
Established: 1896 Annual Undergrad Tuition & Fees (In-State): $10,088
Enrollment: 3,331 Coed
Affiliation or Control: State IRS Status: 501(c)3
Highest Offering: Doctorate
Program: Liberal Arts And General; Teacher Preparatory; Professional; Business Emphasis
Accreditation: **#SC**, AAFCS, ART, BUS, CACREP, CORE, CS, #DIETD, ENG, ENGT, MUS, SP, SW, TED

01 Acting President ... Dr. W. Franklin EVANS
04 Exec Asst to the President ... Ms. Shondra N. ABRAHAM
05 Acting Provost ... Dr. Learie B. LUKE
10 Int Vice Pres for Finance/Mgmt ... Mr. Edward PATRICK
32 Vice Pres for Student Affairs ... Dr. Tamara J. HUGHES
30 Vice Pres Inst Advancement ... Vacant
46 VP Research/Economic Development ... Mr. Delbert T. FOSTER
11 Interim VP of Administration ... Dr. Rita J. TEAL
43 General Counsel ... Mr. Craig E. BURGESS
20 Associate Provost ... Vacant
26 VP External Affairs/Communications ... Ms. Sonja A. BENNETT-BELLAMY
84 VP Enrollment Management ... Ms. Betty R. BOATWRIGHT
46 Int Assoc Provost/Sponsored Program ... Mr. Elbert R. MALONE

72 Dean Col Sci/Math/Engineering Tech Dr. Kenneth LEWIS
53 Int Dn Col Educ/Humanities/Soc Sci Dr. Albert G. HAYWARD
58 Int Dean Col of Graduate Studies Dr. Frederick M G. EVANS
50 Interim Dean School of Business Dr. Barbara L. ADAMS
08 Dean Library & Information Services Ms. Adrienne C. WEBBER
88 Interim Dir Stdnt Success Retent Ms. Sandra E. SCOTT
06 Registrar Ms. Ann BELTON
07 Asst Dir Admissions/Recruitment Ms. LaSandra ROBINSON
13 Dir Univ Computing/Info Tech Svcs Dr. James L. MYERS
37 Director of Financial Aid Mrs. C. C JACKSON
38 Director Counseling/Student Dev Dr. Cherilyn Y. TAYLOR-MINNIEFIELD
21 Controller Ms. Teare BREWINGTON
09 Exec Dir Institutional Research Dr. Rita TEAL
26 Director of Public Relations Mrs. Elizabeth MOSELY-HAWKINS
36 Int Director of Career Placement Mr. Joseph THOMAS
15 Director Human Resource Mgmt Vacant
41 Director Athletics Mr. Paul BRYANT
18 Director of Facilities Mgmt Mr. Ken DAVIS
96 Director Procurement Services Ms. Jessica FAVOR
39 Director of Residential Life Dr. Kelvin RACHELL
19 Interim Chief of Campus Police Mr. Mernard CLARKSON
92 Interim Dean Honors College Dr. Harriet A. ROLAND
88 Interim Director Sports Information Mr. Kendrick D. LEWIS
35 Asst Director of Student Life Ms. Cammy D. GRATE
88 Director of Internal Audit Ms. Evelyn ANDERSON
25 Dir Grants & Contract Ms. Gwendolyn F. MITCHELL
88 Director of Title III Ms. Gloria D. PYLES
88 Director of Staff Development Ms. Patricia GIBSON-HAIGLER
28 Director of Multicultural Affairs Ms. Carolyn G. FREE
88 Station Manager WSSB-FM Mr. Carlito D. A'SEE
88 Athletics Compliance Coordinator Mr. Eric M. SEIFARTH
101 Secretary/Board of Trustees Ms. Eartha J. MOSLEY
104 Dir International/National Exchange Dr. Learie LUKE
105 Web Services Mr. Jason BARR
29 Director Alumni Relations Ms. Iva GARDNER
54 Dean of Engineering Dr. Kenneth LEWIS

South University Columbia Campus (A)

9 Science Court, Columbia SC 29203-6400
Telephone: (803) 799-9082 FICE Identification: 004922
Accreditation: &SC, ACBSP, CACREP, MAC, NURSE, PHAR

† Regional accreditation is carried under the parent institution in Savannah, GA.

Southern Wesleyan University (B)

907 Wesleyan Drive, PO Box 1020,
Central SC 29630-1020
County: Pickens FICE Identification: 003422
Unit ID: 217776
Telephone: (864) 644-5000 Carnegie Class: Master's L
FAX Number: (864) 644-5900 Calendar System: Semester
URL: www.swu.edu
Established: 1906 Annual Undergrad Tuition & Fees: $23,020
Enrollment: 1,778 Coed
Affiliation or Control: Wesleyan Church IRS Status: 501(c)3
Highest Offering: Master's
Program: 2-Year Principally Bachelor's Creditable; Liberal Arts And General; Teacher Preparatory; Professional
Accreditation: SC, MUS, TED

01 President Dr. Todd S. VOSS
05 Provost Dr. Tonya STRICKLAND
10 VP for Finance & Auxiliary Services Mr. Mark T. REEVES
13 Director Information Technology Mr. Mike PREUSZ
37 Director of Financial Aid Mrs. Melanie GILLESPIE
18 Director of Physical Plant Mr. Jonathan CATRON
09 Assoc VP for Planning & Assessment Dr. Corey AMAKER
06 Registrar Ms. Janet HARTSOE
08 Int Director of Library Services Mrs. Shannon BROOKS
84 VP for Enrollment Management Mr. Chad PETERS
07 Dir of Admissions & Enrollment Mgmt Mr. David SLABAUGH
32 Vice President for Student Life Dr. W. Joseph BROCKINTON
42 AVP Spiritual Life/Univ Chaplain Rev. Ken DILL
30 Vice President for Development Dr. Lisa MCWHERTER
29 Exec Dir of Alumni/Constituent Rels Mrs. Joy L. BRYANT
15 Director of Human Resources Mrs. Dana L. FROST
04 Administrative Asst to President Mrs. Andrea PILGRIM
106 Dir Online Education/E-learning Mr. Tyler WATTS
38 Director Student Counseling Ms. Monica PEREZ
41 Athletic Director Mr. Chris WILLIAMS
50 Dean of the School of Business Dr. Jeannie TRUDEL
53 Dean of the School of Education Dr. Sandra MCLENDON

Spartanburg Community College (C)

107 Community College Drive, Spartanburg SC 29303
County: Spartanburg FICE Identification: 003994
Unit ID: 218830
Telephone: (864) 592-4600 Carnegie Class: Assoc/Pub-U-SC
FAX Number: (864) 592-4642 Calendar System: Semester
URL: www.sccsc.edu
Established: 1963 Annual Undergrad Tuition & Fees (In-State): $4,192
Enrollment: 5,495 Coed
Affiliation or Control: State IRS Status: 501(c)3
Highest Offering: Associate Degree
Program: Occupational; 2-Year Principally Bachelor's Creditable
Accreditation: SC, ACBSP, ACFEI, ADNUR, COARC, DA, ENGT, MAC, MLTAD, RAD, SURGT

01 President Mr. Henry C. GILES, JR.
05 Sr Vice President Academic Affairs Dr. Cheryl COX
10 Vice Pres for Business Affairs Mr. Ray SWITZER
102 Exec Dir Advancement/SCC Foundation Mr. Samuel S. HOOK
32 Vice President for Student Affairs Mr. Ron JACKSON
12 Asc Vice Pres Enroll Mgt/Retention Mrs. Lynn F. DALE
20 Assoc Vice Pres of Instruction Vacant
51 Exec Asst to Pres/Dir Economic Dev Mr. Michael P. FORRESTER
12 Executive Director Cherokee Campus Mr. Daryl SMITH
12 Exec Director Tyger River Campus Dr. Anya SEBASTIEN
12 Exec Director Downtown Campus Mrs. Judy SIEG
12 Site Coord Union County Campus Mrs. Kathy LANCASTER
108 Director Eval/Accreditation/Plng Mr. Jay JACKSON
88 Dean of CCE Mr. Robert LESLIE
08 Dean of Learning Resources Mr. Mark ROSEVEARE
76 Dean Health & Human Services Dr. Berta HOPKINS
49 Dean of Arts & Sciences Mrs. Kem HARVEY
07 Director of Admissions Ms. Alison CANN
15 Director of Human Resources Mr. Rick TEAL
13 Director Information Technologies Mr. Peter C. GALLEN
09 Director of Institutional Research Mr. Jack R. BOURGEOIS
26 Chief Public Relations Officer Mrs. Cheri A. HUCKS
88 Director of Instructional Support Mr. Jason FORD
29 Director Alumni Relations Vacant
38 Director Student Counseling Vacant
14 Director Computer Center Mrs. Tina S. REID
18 Chief Facilities/Physical Plant Mr. Gladden SMOKE
19 Director Security/Safety Mr. Andre KERR
96 Director of Procurement Vacant
06 Registrar Ms. Celia N. BAUSS
21 Business Manager Mr. Cecil L. HUTCHERSON
21 Director of Finance Mrs. Mary FUHRMAN
37 Director of Financial Aid Mr. Jeffery BOYLE
106 Dir Online Education/E-learning Mr. Neil GRIFFIN
25 Chief Contracts/Grants Admin Mrs. Elena RUSH
54 Dean of Engineering Mr. Jeff HUNT
04 Administrative Asst to President Ms. Betty HALL
36 Director Student Placement Ms. Jennifer LITTLE

Spartanburg Methodist College (D)

1000 Powell Mill Road, Spartanburg SC 29301-5899
County: Spartanburg FICE Identification: 003447
Unit ID: 218821
Telephone: (864) 587-4000 Carnegie Class: Assoc/PrivNFP
FAX Number: (864) 587-4355 Calendar System: Semester
URL: www.smcsc.edu
Established: 1911 Annual Undergrad Tuition & Fees: $16,820
Enrollment: 793 Coed
Affiliation or Control: United Methodist IRS Status: 501(c)3
Highest Offering: Associate Degree
Program: 2-Year Principally Bachelor's Creditable
Accreditation: SC

01 President Dr. Colleen P. KEITH
05 Vice President for Academic Affairs Dr. Anita K. BOWLES
10 Vice President for Business Affairs Mr. Eric MCDONALD
84 Vice Pres for Enrollment Management Mr. Daniel L. PHILBECK
30 Vice Pres Institutional Advancement Mr. Bob FUZY
32 Dean of Students Mr. Ron LAFFITTE
06 Registrar Ms. Jill R. JOHNSON
08 Library Director Mrs. Erin WASHINGTON
04 Admin Assistant to the President Mrs. Cheryl SOMERSET
13 Exec Dir Information Technology Mr. Trey ARRINGTON
26 Director of Public Information Mrs. Yvonne HARPER
44 Director of Development Mr. Don TATE
37 Director of Financial Aid Ms. Kendra STRANGE
38 Director of Student Counseling Mr. Pete AYLOR
42 Chaplain/Director of Church Rels Rev. Candice Y. SLOAN
41 Athletic Director Mr. Tim WALLACE
18 Director Facilities Management Mr. Marty WOODS
29 Director of Alumni Relations Mrs. Leah L. PRUITT
15 Dir of Human Resources/Budget Mrs. Jeanette R. DUNN
35 Director of Student Support Svcs Ms. Sharon PORTER
44 Director of Church Funding Rev. Michael E. BOWERS
19 Chief of Campus Safety Ms. Teresa D. FERGUSON
84 Exec Director of Enrollment Mr. Wells SHEPARD
09 Director of Assessment Activities Mr. Robert W. ISENHOWER

Technical College of the Lowcountry (E)

921 S Ribaut Road, PO Box 1288,
Beaufort SC 29901-1288
County: Beaufort FICE Identification: 009910
Unit ID: 217712
Telephone: (843) 525-8211 Carnegie Class: Assoc/Pub-R-M
FAX Number: (843) 525-8330 Calendar System: Semester
URL: www.tcl.edu
Established: 1969 Annual Undergrad Tuition & Fees (In-State): $5,100
Enrollment: 2,529 Coed
Affiliation or Control: State IRS Status: 501(c)3
Highest Offering: Associate Degree
Program: Occupational; 2-Year Principally Bachelor's Creditable
Accreditation: SC, ACBSP, ADNUR, COMTA, PNUR, PTAA, RAD, SURGT

01 President Dr. Richard J. GOUGH
11 Vice Pres Administrative Services Mr. Hayes WISER
05 Vice President for Academic Affairs Dr. Gina MOUNFIELD
26 VP Marketing/Enrollment Management Ms. Nancy WEBER
32 Vice President for Student Affairs Ms. Nancy WEBER
35 Dean of Students Mr. Rodney ADAMS

09 Director for Research/Planning Ms. Camille MYERS
15 Human Resources Director Ms. Sonya LYTTLE
20 Director for Learning Resources Ms. Cindy HALSEY
50 Div Dean Business Technologies Dr. Kenneth FLICK
49 Div Dean Arts & Sciences Dr. Wesla FLETCHER
76 Division Dean Health Sciences Mr. Glenn LEVICKI
13 Director of Information Technology Mr. Floyd HENDERSON
37 Director Financial Aid Ms. Cleo MARTIN
30 Director of Inst Advancement Ms. Mary Lee CARNS
27 Director Public Relations Ms. Leigh COPELAND
40 Bookstore Director Ms. Louise RENNIX
18 Director of Facility Management Mr. Larry BECKLER
38 Campus Life Manager Ms. Mackenzie MCGREW
96 Director of Purchasing Ms. Carol MACK
06 Registrar Dr. Debralee MCCLELLAN
36 Career & Transfer Services Manager Ms. Melanie GALLION

Tri-County Technical College (F)

PO Box 587, Pendleton SC 29670-0587
County: Anderson FICE Identification: 004926
Unit ID: 218885
Telephone: (864) 646-8361 Carnegie Class: Assoc/Pub-S-SC
FAX Number: (864) 646-1895 Calendar System: Semester
URL: www.tctc.edu
Established: 1962 Annual Undergrad Tuition & Fees (In-District): $4,959
Enrollment: 6,553 Coed
Affiliation or Control: State/Local IRS Status: 501(c)3
Highest Offering: Associate Degree
Program: Occupational; 2-Year Principally Bachelor's Creditable
Accreditation: SC, ACBSP, ADNUR, DA, MAC, MLTAD, PNUR, SURGT

01 President Dr. Ronnie L. BOOTH
05 Senior Vice President Mr. Galen DEHAY
10 Vice Pres Business Affairs Mr. Gregg STAPLETON
102 Executive Director Foundation Mr. Grayson KELLY
20 AVP Instruction & Effectiveness Vacant
51 Dean of Continuing Education Mr. Rick COTHRAN
84 Dean of Transition to College Ms. Jenni CREAMER
32 Dean of Student Development Mr. Dan HOLLAND
49 Dean Arts & Sciences Division Dr. Alfred WHEELER
72 Dean Engineering Technology Div Dr. Dan AVERETTE
50 Dean Business/Human Services Div Mrs. Jackie BLAKLEY
76 Dean Health Education Division Dr. Lynn LEWIS
08 Head Librarian Ms. Marla ROBERSON
37 Student Financial Aid Director Mrs. Sarah DOWD
13 CIO/Information Technology Dir Mr. Matthew EDWARDS
26 Dir Public Relations/Communication Mrs. Rebecca W. EIDSON
30 Director of Development Mrs. Courtney WHITE
44 Director of Annual Giving Mrs. Tammy FISK
15 Asst VP Human Resources Mrs. Sharon COLCOLOUGH
07 Director of Admissions Vacant
06 Registrar Mr. Scott HARVEY
09 Director of Institutional Research Mr. Chris MARINO
18 Chief Facilities/Physical Plant Mr. Ken KOPERA
21 Director of Fiscal Affairs Mrs. Cara HAMILTON
96 Director of Purchasing Ms. Kristal DOHERTY
38 Director of Student Life/Counseling Ms. Croslena JOHNSON
04 Administrative Asst to President Mrs. Kathy BRANT
19 Director Security/Safety Mr. Jonathan FINCH
25 Chief Contracts/Grants Admin Ms. Laneika MUSALINI
86 Dir Econ Dev/Government Relations Mr. Dan COOPER
109 Chief Auxilary Services Officer Mr. Kevin STEELE

Trident Technical College (G)

PO Box 118067, Charleston SC 29423-8067
County: Charleston FICE Identification: 004920
Unit ID: 218894
Telephone: (843) 574-6111 Carnegie Class: Assoc/Pub-U-MC
FAX Number: (843) 574-6541 Calendar System: Semester
URL: www.tridenttech.edu
Established: 1964 Annual Undergrad Tuition & Fees (In-District): $4,070
Enrollment: 16,136 Coed
Affiliation or Control: State/Local IRS Status: 501(c)3
Highest Offering: Associate Degree
Program: Occupational; 2-Year Principally Bachelor's Creditable
Accreditation: SC, ACBSP, ACFEI, ADNUR, COARC, CSHSE, DA, DH, EMT, MAC, MLTAD, OTA, PNUR, PTAA, RAD

01 President Dr. Mary THORNLEY
10 Vice Pres Finance & Administration Mr. Scott POELKER
05 Vice President Academic Affairs Dr. Patricia ROBERTSON
32 Vice President Student Services Dr. Patrice MITCHELL
30 Vice President Advancement Ms. Meg HOWLE
51 Vice Pres Continuing Educ/Econ Dev Mr. Robert WALKER
13 Vice Pres Information Technology Mr. Bernie STRAUB
45 Assoc VP Planning/Accreditation Ms. Cathy ALMQUIST
20 Asst Vice Pres Academic Programs Ms. Susan NORTON
51 Asst Vice Pres Continuing Education Ms. Yvonne BROWN
72 Asst Vice Pres Info Technology Vacant
35 Asst Vice Pres for Student Svcs Ms. Lynne ANKERSEN
20 Asst Vice President Instruction Mr. Eddie SIMMONS
15 Director Human Resources Ms. DeVetta HUGHES
96 Dir Procurement/Risk Management Ms. Carol BELCHER
40 Dir Auxiliary Enterprises/Bookstore Ms. Jloundia PINCKNEY
18 Director Facilities Mr. Eric HAMILTON
21 Director Finance Ms. Melody TAYLOR
26 Director Marketing Ms. Tina AHLEMANN
27 Director Public Info Mr. David HANSEN
88 Director High School Programs Ms. Melissa STOWASSER
30 Associate VP Development Ms. Kimberley STURGEON

14 Dir Information Technology Training ... Mr. Joseph GIBSON
36 Director Career Employment Services ... Mr. Brian ALMQUIST
81 Dean Science & Mathematics ... Mr. Bill LANDRY
79 Dean Humanities & Social Sciences ... Dr. Tim BROWN
88 Dean The Learning Center ... Mr. David HARRIS
50 Dean Business Technology ... Ms. Connie JOLLY
76 Dean Allied Health Sciences ... Vacant
57 Dean Film Media and Visual Arts ... Ms. Pat FOX
54 Dean Industrial/Engineering Tech ... Ms. Christine LANG
88 Dean Culinary Inst of Charleston ... Mr. Mike SABOE
61 Dean Law-Related Studies ... Mr. John UNGARO
66 Dean Nursing ... Ms. Marilyn BRADY
38 Dean Student Development ... Ms. Pamela BROWN
88 Dean Comm/Family/Child Studies ... Ms. Stephany HEWITT
84 Dean Enrollment Management ... Mr. John JAMROGOWICZ
75 Dean Aeronautical Studies ... Dr. Barry FRANCO
12 Dean Berkeley Campus ... Ms. Karen WRIGHTEN
12 Dean Mount Pleasant Campus ... Mr. Michael PATTERSON
12 Dean Palmer Campus ... Dr. Louester ROBINSON
19 Director Public Safety ... Mr. Lawrence SAVIDGE
06 Registrar ... Ms. Pamela DROSTE
07 Director of Admissions ... Ms. Clara MARTIN
09 Director of Institutional Research ... Mr. James GREEN
37 Director Student Financial Aid ... Ms. Charlotte SORG

University of Phoenix Columbia SC Campus (A)

1001 Pinnacle Point Drive, Columbia SC 29223-5727
Telephone: (803) 699-5096 Identification: 770223
Accreditation: &NH, ACBSP

† No longer accepting campus-based students.

University of South Carolina Columbia (B)

Columbia SC 29208-0001
County: Richland FICE Identification: 003448
Unit ID: 218663
Telephone: (803) 777-7000 Carnegie Class: RU/VH
FAX Number: (803) 777-0101 Calendar System: Semester
URL: www.sc.edu
Established: 1801 Annual Undergrad Tuition & Fees (In-State): $11,482
Enrollment: 32,971 Coed
Affiliation or Control: State IRS Status: 501(c)3
Highest Offering: Doctorate
Program: Liberal Arts And General; Teacher Preparatory; Professional
Accreditation: SC, ANEST, ART, BUS, BUSA, CAATE, CACREP, CEA, CLPSY, CORE, CS, DANCE, ENG, HSA, IPSY, JOUR, LAW, LIB, MED, MUS, NURSE, PH, PHAR, PTA, SCPSY, SP, SPAA, SW, TED, THEA

01 President ... Dr. Harris PASTIDES
03 Vice President & CIO ... Dr. William F. HOGUE
05 Interim Exec VP Acad Affair/ Provost ... Dr. Helen I. DOERPINGHAUS
10 Vice President Finance & Planning ... Mr. Edward I. WALTON
32 VP Student Affairs/VProv Acad Suppt ... Dr. Dennis A. PRUITT
15 Vice President Human Resources ... Mr. Christopher D. BYRD
30 VP Development & Alumni Relations ... Ms. Jancy HOUCK
12 VP/Exec Vice Chanc Palmetto College ... Dr. Chris P. PLYLER
46 Vice President for Research ... Dr. Prakash NAGARKATTI
26 Director Comm & Marketing/CCO ... Mr. Wesley HICKMAN
101 Secretary to Board of Trustees ... Ms. Amy E. STONE
58 Sr Vice Prov & Dean Graduate School ... Dr. Lacy K. FORD
85 Vice Provost & Dir Intl Affairs ... Dr. Allen MILLER
84 Asst Vice Provost Enrollment Mgmt ... Mr. Scott VERZYL
08 Dean of University Libraries ... Dr. Tom MCNALLY
43 Gen Counsel & Exec Dir Compliance ... Mr. Walter H. PARHAM
09 Exec Dir Inst Research & Assessment ... Mr. Donald MILES
18 VP for Facilities & Transportation ... Mr. Derrick E. HUGGINS
27 Assoc Director Creative Services ... Mr. Bob WERTZ
19 Assoc VP & Chief of Police ... Mr. Christopher L. WUCHENICH
37 Dir Student Fin Aid & Scholarship ... Dr. Edgar MILLER
36 Director Career Center ... Mr. Thomas HALASZ
06 University Registrar ... Mr. Aaron C. MARTERER
22 Exec Asst to Pres Equal Oppty Pgm ... Mr. Bobby D. GIST
21 CFO & VP for Finance ... Mrs. Leslie G. BRUNELLI
07 Director of Admissions ... Dr. Mary WAGNER
39 Director Housing/Business Opers ... Mr. Parker LEAKE
38 Exec Director Student Health Svcs ... Dr. Deborah C. BECK
41 Athletic Director ... Mr. Ray TANNER
35 Assoc VP for Student Life ... Mr. Jerry T. BREWER
27 Director News & Internal Relations ... Mr. Wesley T. HICKMAN
96 Director of Purchasing ... Mrs. Venis MANIGO
29 Exec Director Alumni Association ... Mr. Jack CLAYPOOLE
49 VP & Dean Col of Arts and Sciences ... Dr. Mary Anne FITZPATRICK
88 Dean Hospitality/Retail/Sport Mgt ... Mr. Brian MIHALIK
50 Dean Moore School of Business ... Dr. Peter J. BREWS
53 Dean College of Education ... Dr. Lemuel WATSON
54 Dean Col Engineering & Computing ... Dr. Anthony P. AMBLER
69 Dean Arnold School of Public Health ... Dr. G. Thomas CHANDLER
60 Dn College of Mass Comm/Infor Stdys ... Mr. Charles BIERBAUER
61 Dean School of Law ... Dr. Robert M. WILCOX
63 Int Dean School of Medicine ... Dr. Caughman TAYLOR
63 Dean Greenville School of Medicine ... Dr. Jerry R. YOUKEY
64 Dean School of Music ... Dr. Tayloe HARDING
66 Dean College of Nursing ... Jeannette ANDREWS
67 Interim Exec Dean Col of Pharmacy ... Dr. Randall C. ROWEN
70 Dean College of Social Work ... Dr. Anna M. SCHEYETTE
92 Dir Fellowships & Scholar Programs ... Ms. Novella BESKID
88 Director of Academic Programs ... Dr. Kristia H. FINNIGAN
88 Executive Director USC Connect ... Dr. Irma J. VANSCOY

University of South Carolina Aiken (C)

471 University Parkway, Aiken SC 29801-6399
County: Aiken FICE Identification: 003449
Unit ID: 218645
Telephone: (803) 648-6851 Carnegie Class: Bac/Diverse
FAX Number: (803) 641-3362 Calendar System: Semester
URL: www.usca.edu
Established: 1961 Annual Undergrad Tuition & Fees (In-State): $9,828
Enrollment: 3,444 Coed
Affiliation or Control: State IRS Status: 501(c)3
Highest Offering: Master's
Program: Liberal Arts And General; Teacher Preparatory
Accreditation: SC, BUS, MUS, NURSE, TED

01 Chancellor ... Dr. Sandra JORDAN
05 Exec Vice Chanc Academic Affairs ... Dr. Jeffrey M. PRIEST
30 Vice Chanc Advance & External Rels ... Ms. Mary DRISCOLL
32 Vice Chancellor Student Life & Svcs ... Dr. Deborah KLADIVKO
13 Vice Chancellor Information Tech ... Mr. Ernest PRINGLE
10 Vice Chanc Business and Finance ... Mr. Joe SOBIERALSKI
20 Vice Chanc Academic Affairs ... Mr. Blanche PREMO-HOPKINS
84 Assoc Vice Chanc Enrollment Svcs ... Mr. Daniel J. ROBB
18 Asst Chanc Facilities Management ... Vacant
79 Col Coord Humanitie & Soc Science ... Dr. Tom MACK
83 College Coordinator Sciences ... Dr. Edward CALLEN
50 Dean School of Business Admin ... Dr. Michael FEKULA
53 Dean of the School of Education ... Dr. Wendy SCHWEDER
66 Dean of the School of Nursing ... Dr. L. Julia BALL
88 Dir Academic Success Center ... Dr. Stacie WILLIAMS
09 Dir Institutional Effectiveness ... Dr. Lloyd A. DAWE
08 Interim Library Director ... Ms. Natalia BOWDOIN
88 Dir Ruth Patrick Sci Ed Center ... Ms. Deborah MCMURTRIE
25 Dir Sponsored Research ... Dr. Bill PIRKLE
40 Dir Bookstore ... Ms. Heidi DIFRANCO
88 Dir Campus Support Services ... Mr. Jeff JENIK
88 Dir Children's Center ... Ms. Lynn WILLIAMS
88 Dir Convocation Center ... Mr. Josh SMALL
88 Dir Dining Services ... Mr. Brent WUSTMAN
12 Exec Dir of Etherredge Center ... Mr. Jack BENJAMIN
21 Controller ... Mr. Kevin CRAWFORD
15 Dir Human Resources & Affirm Action ... Ms. Maria CHANDLER
17 Dir Wellness Center ... Ms. Mila PADGETT
07 Dir of Admissions ... Mr. Andrew HENDRIX
58 Coord Citizenshp Residenc Grad Stds ... Ms. Karen MORRIS
36 Dir of Career Services ... Mr. Corey FERALDI
37 Director Financial Aid ... Linda A. HIGGINS
06 Registrar ... Ms. Vivian D. GRICE
14 Director of Client Services ... Mr. Chris SPIRES
90 Dir Communications & Hardware ... Mr. Bob WIESNER
105 Director Network Systems ... Ms. Joann WILLIAMSON
41 Dir of Athletics ... Mr. Douglas R. WARRICK, JR.
38 Dir Counseling & Disablilities ... Ms. Cynthia B. GELINAS
23 Dir Student Health Center ... Ms. Cynthia B. GELINAS
39 Director of Housing ... Mr. Deri WILLS
28 Dir Global Stds/Multicult Engagemnt ... Mr. Mutombo KABASELE
35 Asst Vice Chanc Student Life ... Mr. Ahmed SAMAHA
19 Chief of Police ... Mr. Kevin LILES
29 Dir Alumni Rels/Community Partner ... Mr. Randy DUCKETT
51 Dir Conferences & Continuing Ed .. Ms. Mary Anne CAVANAUGH
44 Director of Major Gifts ... Ms. Linda EVANS
26 Dir Marketing & Community Relations ... Ms. Patti MCGRATH
105 Coord Web Comm & Social Media ... Ms. Lauren COULS
88 Director Instructional Svcs ... Mr. Keith PIERCE

University of South Carolina Beaufort (D)

1 University Boulevard, Bluffton SC 29909-6085
County: Beaufort FICE Identification: 003450
Unit ID: 218654
Telephone: (843) 208-8000 Carnegie Class: Bac/Diverse
FAX Number: (843) 208-8299 Calendar System: Semester
URL: www.uscb.edu
Established: 1959 Annual Undergrad Tuition & Fees (In-State): $9,798
Enrollment: 1,794 Coed
Affiliation or Control: State IRS Status: 501(c)3
Highest Offering: Baccalaureate
Program: Liberal Arts And General; Teacher Preparatory; Professional
Accreditation: SC, NURSE, TED

01 Chancellor ... Dr. Jane UPSHAW
32 Vice Chanc for Student Development ... Dr. Douglas OBLANDER
10 Vice Chancellor Finance/Operations ... Mr. Earle HOLLEY
26 Vice Chanc University Advancement ... Dr. Lynn MCGEE
18 Director of Facilities ... Mr. Mike PARROTT
13 Chief Information Officer ... Mr. Eddie KING
08 Interim Dir & Acquisitins Librarian ... Ms. Geni FLOWERS
06 Registrar ... Dr. James TISDALE
84 Assoc VP Enrollment Mgmt ... Vacant
37 Director of Financial Aid ... Ms. Patricia GREENE
30 Director of Development ... Ms. Colleen CALLAHAN
09 Dir Inst Effectiveness/Research ... Ms. Jodi HERRIN
19 Director Public Safety ... Dr. Henry GARBADE
35 Director of Student Life ... Ms. Kate TORBORG
15 Director of Human Resources ... Dr. Sue GOLABEK

University of South Carolina Lancaster (E)

PO Box 889, Lancaster SC 29721-0889
Telephone: (803) 313-7000 FICE Identification: 003453
Accreditation: &SC, ACBSP, ADNUR, PNUR

† Regional accreditation is carried under University of South Carolina - Columbia.

University of South Carolina Salkehatchie (F)

PO Box 617, Allendale SC 29810-0617
County: Allendale FICE Identification: 003454
Unit ID: 218681
Telephone: (803) 584-3446 Carnegie Class: Assoc/Pub2in4
FAX Number: (803) 584-5038 Calendar System: Semester
URL: uscsalkehatchie.sc.edu
Established: 1965 Annual Undergrad Tuition & Fees (In-State): $6,878
Enrollment: 1,076 Coed
Affiliation or Control: State IRS Status: 501(c)3
Highest Offering: Associate Degree
Program: 2-Year Principally Bachelor's Creditable
Accreditation: &SC

01 Dean ... Dr. Ann C. CARMICHAEL
05 Interim Academic Dean ... Dr. Aaron ARD
32 Asc Dean Student Svcs/Dir Athletics ... Ms. Jane T. BREWER
08 Head Librarian ... Mr. Daniel JOHNSON
10 Director Budget & Finance ... Mr. Jeff IRWIN
37 Director Financial Aid ... Ms. Julie HADWIN
18 Dir Facilities/Safety/HR Director ... Dr. William A. SANDIFER
40 Bookstore Manager ... Mr. Lamar HEWETT
15 Director of Human Resources ... Dr. William A. SANDIFER
07 Director of Admissions ... Ms. Carmen BROWN
30 Chief Development ... Dr. Ann C. CARMICHAEL
84 Director Enrollment Mgmt Svcs ... Mr. Mike SMITH
88 Director Leadership Center ... Ms. Ann RICE
88 Dir Ctr Leadership Development ... Mr. Warren CHAVOUS
88 Sports Information Director ... Mr. Trent KINARD

† Regional accreditation is carried under University of South Carolina - Columbia.

University of South Carolina School of Medicine Greenville (G)

607 Grove Road, Greenville SC 29605
County: Greenville Identification: 667114
Telephone: (864) 455-7992 Carnegie Class: Not Classified
FAX Number: (864) 455-8404 Calendar System: Semester
URL: greenvillemed.sc.edu
Established: 2010 Annual Graduate Tuition & Fees: $38,514
Enrollment: 188 Coed
Affiliation or Control: State IRS Status: 501(c)3
Highest Offering: Doctorate; No Undergraduates
Program: Professional
Accreditation: #MED

01 Dean ... Dr. Jerry R. YOUKEY
05 Sr Assoc Dean Acad Affs/Diversity ... Dr. Spence TAYLOR
20 Assoc Dean for Faculty Affairs ... Dr. Robert BEST
32 Assoc Dean Student Affairs/Admiss ... Dr. James BUGGY
53 Assoc Dean for Education ... Dr. Lynn CRESPO
07 Asst Dean for Admissions ... Dr. Paul CATALANA
10 Chief Business Officer ... Derek PAYNE
06 Registrar & Financial Aid Director ... Casey WILEY
30 Director of Development ... Susan WARD
15 HR Manager ... Claire GREGG
13 Director of IT and Facility ... Ron KNAPPENBERGER

University of South Carolina Sumter (H)

200 Miller Road, Sumter SC 29150-2498
County: Sumter FICE Identification: 003426
Unit ID: 218690
Telephone: (803) 775-8727 Carnegie Class: Assoc/Pub2in4
FAX Number: (803) 775-2180 Calendar System: Semester
URL: www.uscsumter.edu
Established: 1966 Annual Undergrad Tuition & Fees (In-State): $6,878
Enrollment: 879 Coed
Affiliation or Control: State IRS Status: 501(c)3
Highest Offering: Associate Degree
Program: 2-Year Principally Bachelor's Creditable
Accreditation: &SC

01 Associate Dean ... Mr. Lynwood WATTS
10 Assoc Dean for Admin/Financial Svcs ... Mr. Bruce K. BLUMBERG
09 Institutional Research Analyst ... Mr. Chuck W. WRIGHT
08 Head Librarian ... Ms. Sharon H. CHAPMAN
07 Director of Admissions ... Mr. Keith E. BRITTON
51 Director of Continuing Education ... Ms. Susan S. BRABHAM
26 Dir of Public Relations/Marketing ... Ms. Misty HATFIELD
40 Bookstore Manager ... Ms. Julie MCCOY
15 Human Resources Officer ... Ms. Marchetta L. WILLIAMS
88 Director Opportunity Scholars ... Ms. Lisa ROSDAIL
18 Superintendent Buildings & Grounds ... Mr. Jeff LINGEFELT

† Regional accreditation is carried under University of South Carolina - Columbia.

University of South Carolina Union (I)

PO Drawer 729, Union SC 29379-0729
County: Union FICE Identification: 004927
Unit ID: 218706
Telephone: (864) 429-8728 Carnegie Class: Assoc/Pub2in4
FAX Number: (864) 427-3682 Calendar System: Semester
URL: uscunion.sc.edu
Established: 1965 Annual Undergrad Tuition & Fees (In-State): $6,878

Enrollment: 679 Coed
Affiliation or Control: State IRS Status: 501(c)3
Highest Offering: Associate Degree
Program: Occupational; 2-Year Principally Bachelor's Creditable
Accreditation: &SC

01 Dean ... Dr. Alice TAYLOR-COLBERT
05 Associate Dean Acad Affairs ... Dr. Stephen LOWE
84 Director Enrollment Manager ... Mr. M. Bradley GREER
37 Director Financial Aid ... Mr. Robert HOLCOMBE
15 Human Resources ... Ms. Susan P. JETT
40 Administration Bookstore ... Ms. Tanja BLACK
13 Director of Information Technology ... Mr. Wesley C. BELK
30 Director of Marketing & Development ... Ms. Annie SMITH
08 Library Manager ... Ms. Sharon L. RUPP
88 TRIO Admin & Opp Scholars Pgms ... Ms. Alice HOOPER

† Regional accreditation is carried under University of South Carolina - Columbia.

University of South Carolina Upstate (A)

800 University Way, Spartanburg SC 29303-4996
County: Spartanburg FICE Identification: 006951
Unit ID: 218742
Telephone: (864) 503-5000 Carnegie Class: Bac/Diverse
FAX Number: (864) 503-5375 Calendar System: Semester
URL: www.uscupstate.edu
Established: 1967 Annual Undergrad Tuition & Fees (In-State): $10,648
Enrollment: 5,397 Coed
Affiliation or Control: State IRS Status: 501(c)3
Highest Offering: Master's
Program: Liberal Arts And General; Teacher Preparatory
Accreditation: SC, ART, BUS, CAHIIM, CS, ENGT, NURSE, TED

01 Chancellor ... Dr. Thomas MOORE
05 Sr Vice Chanc for Acad Affair ... Dr. John MASTERSON
13 Interim Vice Chanc Information Tech ... Mr. Chris HANKE
10 Vice Chanc Admin & Business Affs ... Ms. Sheryl TURNER-WATTS
30 V Chanc Advancement Upstate Found ... Mr. Michael E. IRVIN
09 VC Planning/IR/Metro Studies ... Ms. Kathleen BRADY
13 Vice Chanc Info Tech & Svcs ... Ms. Jeanne SKUL
12 Dir Acad Engagement Greenville Ctr ... Dr. Judith PRINCE
20 Assoc VC Academic Affairs ... Mr. Clif FLYNN
32 Dean of Students ... Mrs. Laura PUCKETT-BOLER
06 Registrar ... Ms. Mary David FOX
84 Asst Vice Chanc Enrollment Services ... Ms. Donette STEWART
38 Director Counseling Services ... Ms. Frances L. JARRATT
08 Dean Library ... Ms. Frieda M. DAVISON
37 Asst Director Financial Aid ... Ms. Bonnie C. CARSON
49 Dean Arts & Sciences ... Dr. Dirk SCHLINGMANN
50 Dean Johnson Col Business & Econ ... Dr. Frank RUDISILL
53 Dean Education ... Dr. Lee HURREN
66 Dean Nursing ... Dr. Katharine GIBB
58 Director Graduate Education ... Dr. Tina HERZBERG
29 Director of Alumni Relations ... Ms. Charlianne NESTLEN
102 Director Dev & Found Scholarships ... Mrs. Bea W. SMITH
40 Director Bookstore ... Mr. Jerry CARROLL
41 Athletic Director ... Mr. Lee FOWLER
18 Director Custodial Services ... Mr. Paul SCHMIDT
19 Dir Public Safety & Chief of Police ... Mr. Klay PETERSON
35 Director Student Life ... Ms. Khrystal SMITH
39 Dir Housing Residential Life ... Ms. Mandy WHITTEN
23 Director Health Services ... Ms. Lou Anne WEBER
88 Exec Dir Univ Boards & Public Affs ... Mr. John F. PERRY
09 Dir Inst Effectiveness & Compliance ... Mr. Brian MALLORY
88 Dir for Fitness and Campus Rec ... Mr. Mark RITTER
88 Dir Disability Services ... Ms. Margaret CAMP
51 Dir Continuing Education ... Dr. Faruk TANYEL
21 Dir Budget Resource Planning ... Ms. Connie HOLLOMAN
22 Dir Equal Opp & Employee Relations ... Ms. Sharon WOODS
88 Dir Intl Studies & Language Svcs ... Dr. Deryle HOPE
88 Dir Sponsored Awards ... Ms. Elaine MARSHALL
106 Dir Distance Education ... Dr. David MCCURRY
92 Dir Honors Program ... Dr. Cathy CANINO
88 Dir Ctr Teaching Excellence ... Dr. June CARTER

Virginia College (B)

7201 Two Notch Road, Columbia SC 29223
Telephone: (803) 509-7100 Identification: 770829
Accreditation: ACICS, MAAB, SURGT

† Branch campus of Virginia College, Birmingham, AL.

Virginia College (C)

2400 David H. McLeod Blvd, Suite F, Florence SC 29501
Telephone: (843) 407-2200 Identification: 770832
Accreditation: ACICS, MAAB

† Branch campus of Virginia College, Birmingham, AL.

Virginia College (D)

78 Global Drive, Greenville SC 29607
Telephone: (864) 679-4900 Identification: 770838
Accreditation: ACICS, ACFEI, MAAB, SURGT

† Branch campus of Virginia College, Birmingham, AL.

Virginia College (E)

6185 Rivers Avenue, North Charleston SC 29406-4999
Telephone: (843) 614-4300 Identification: 770830
Accreditation: ACICS, MAAB, SURGT

† Branch campus of Virginia College, Birmingham, AL.

Virginia College (F)

8150 Warren H. Abernathy Highway, Spartanburg SC 29301-2450
Telephone: (864) 504-3200 Identification: 770831
Accreditation: ACICS, MAAB

† Branch campus of Virginia College, Birmingham, AL.

Voorhees College (G)

PO Box 678, Denmark SC 29042-0678
County: Bamberg FICE Identification: 003455
Unit ID: 218919
Telephone: (803) 780-1234 Carnegie Class: Bac/Diverse
FAX Number: (803) 780-1015 Calendar System: Semester
URL: www.voorhees.edu
Established: 1897 Annual Undergrad Tuition & Fees: $12,630
Enrollment: 468 Coed
Affiliation or Control: Protestant Episcopal IRS Status: 501(c)3
Highest Offering: Baccalaureate
Program: Liberal Arts And General; Fine Arts Emphasis
Accreditation: SC, ACBSP

01 President ... Dr. Cleveland L. SELLERS, JR.
05 Ex Vice Pres Academic/Student Affs ... Dr. Pamela WILSON
10 VP Fiscal/Admin Affairs/CFO ... Mrs. V. Diane O'BERRY
30 Vice Pres Institutional Advancement ... Mr. Marcus BURGESS
45 VP Planning & Information Mgmt ... Mr. Samuel BLACKWELL
44 AVP Institutional Advancement ... Mrs. Teesa BRUNSON
20 AVP Academic Affairs/Registrar ... Mrs. Melika JACKSON
21 AVP Fiscal Affairs/Admin Affairs ... Mr. Augusta KITCHEN
32 Director of Student Engagement ... Mr. Benjamin O. WATSON
08 Library Director ... Dr. Marie MARTIN
18 Director of Physical Plant ... Mr. Eddie PATTERSON
29 Director Alumni Affairs ... Mrs. Dorothy PATTERSON
36 Director Career Planning & Outreach ... Mr. Gerald DEVAUGHN
42 Chaplain ... Rev. James YARSIAH
41 Director of Athletics ... Mr. Willie JEFFERSON
19 Director of Safety/Security ... Mr. James WELDON
23 Director of Health Services ... Ms. Kimberly SOLOMON
07 Director of Admissions ... Mrs. Diondra SMALLS
15 Director of Human Resources ... Mrs. Constance COLTER-BRABHAM
13 Chief Technology Officer ... Mr. Timothy KENTOPP
40 Bookstore Manager ... Mrs. Shanda RUFFIN
04 Exec Assistant to the President ... Ms. Lakya RICE
50 Division Chair Business ... Dr. Victor OYINBO
81 Div Chair Natural Sciences/Math ... Dr. Doris WARD

Williamsburg Technical College (H)

601 Martin Luther King, Jr. Avenue, Kingstree SC 29556-4103
County: Williamsburg FICE Identification: 009322
Unit ID: 218955
Telephone: (843) 355-4110 Carnegie Class: Assoc/Pub-R-S
FAX Number: (843) 355-4296 Calendar System: Semester
URL: www.wiltech.edu
Established: 1969 Annual Undergrad Tuition & Fees (In-District): $3,756
Enrollment: 717 Coed
Affiliation or Control: State/Local IRS Status: 501(c)3
Highest Offering: Associate Degree
Program: Occupational; 2-Year Principally Bachelor's Creditable
Accreditation: SC, ACBSP

01 President ... Dr. Patricia A. LEE
05 Vice Pres for Academic Affairs ... Dr. Clifton R. ELLIOTT
10 Vice Pres for Business Affairs ... Ms. Melissa A. COKER
32 Vice Pres for Student Affairs ... Dr. Leron PETERKIN
46 Dir Planning/Research/Grants ... Mr. Andrew MULLER
08 Library Director ... Ms. Caren AGATA
07 Admissions Counselor ... Ms. Cheryl DUBOSE
30 Director of Development/Public Rels ... Mrs. Mona B. DUKES
37 Financial Aid Officer ... Mrs. Jean BOOS
09 Research/Systems Analyst ... Mr. T. Kent COKER
06 Director Enrollment and Record Svcs ... Dr. Alexis WRIGHT-DUBOSE
18 Director of Facilities Maintenance ... Mr. Tyrone THOMAS
15 Director Human Resources ... Mrs. Jennifer STRONG
26 Dir Development & Public Relations ... Mrs. Mona B. DUKES
103 Dir Cont Education/Workforce Dev ... Mr. James BOSTIC

Winthrop University (I)

Oakland Avenue, Rock Hill SC 29733-0001
County: York FICE Identification: 003456
Unit ID: 218964
Telephone: (803) 323-2211 Carnegie Class: Master's L
FAX Number: (803) 323-3001 Calendar System: Semester
URL: www.winthrop.edu
Established: 1886 Annual Undergrad Tuition & Fees (In-State): $14,156
Enrollment: 6,024 Coed
Affiliation or Control: State IRS Status: 501(c)3
Highest Offering: Beyond Master's But Less Than Doctorate
Program: Liberal Arts And General; Teacher Preparatory; Professional
Accreditation: SC, ART, BUS, CAATE, CACREP, CIDA, CS, DANCE, DIETD, DIETI, JOUR, MUS, SW, TED, THEA

01 President ... Dr. Daniel F. MAHONY
05 Provost/Vice Pres Academic Affairs ... Dr. Debra C. BOYD
10 Vice President Finance & Business ... Mr. J. P. MCKEE
30 Vice Pres Institutional Advancement ... Dr. William D. NICHOLSON, II
32 Vice President of Student Life ... Dr. Frank P. ARDAIOLO
84 VP Access & Enrollment Management ... Mr. Eduardo PRIETO
100 Chief of Staff ... Dr. Kimberly A. FAUST
26 Sr Counsel to Pres Public Affairs ... Dr. Jeffrey PEREZ
19 Asst VP/Chief Campus Police ... Chief Frank J. ZEBEDIS
20 Asst VP Acad Affs/Dir GLI ... Dr. Meg WEBBER
88 Asst VP Curriculum/Program Support ... Mr. Tim DRUEKE
21 Associate VP Finance/Business ... Ms. Amanda F. MAGHSOUD
18 Assoc VP Facilities Management ... Mr. Walter A. HARDIN
15 Associate VP Human Resources ... Ms. Lisa COWART
88 Assoc VP Institutional Advancement ... Mr. Ken SHEETZ
88 Assoc VP Acad Affs/Accred/Accntblty ... Ms. Karen JONES
27 Assoc VP/Exec Dir University Rels ... Ms. Ellen M. WILDER-BYRD
04 Asst to Pres University Events ... Ms. DeeAnna BROOKS
58 Dean of Graduate School ... Dr. Jack DEROCHI
49 Dean College Arts & Science ... Dr. Karen M. KEDROWSKI
50 Dean Col of Business Administration ... Dr. Roger D. WEIKLE
53 Dean College of Education ... Dr. Jennie RAKESTRAW
64 Dean College of Visual/Perf ... Dr. David WOHL
08 Dean Library Services ... Dr. Mark Y. HERRING
88 Dean University College ... Dr. Gloria JONES
35 Dean of Students ... Ms. Bethany MARLOWE
41 Athletic Director ... Mr. Thomas N. HICKMAN
25 Director Sponsored Pgms/Research ... Ms. Teresa R. JUSTICE
90 Director Technology Services ... Mr. Patrice BRUNEAU
06 Registrar ... Ms. Gina G. JONES
07 Director of Admissions ... Ms. Deborah G. BARBER
37 Director of Financial Aid ... Ms. Michelle HARE
38 Director Health/Counseling ... Ms. Jackie CONCODORA
39 Asst VP for Student Life ... Ms. Cynthia A. CASSENS
36 Director Career Development/Svcs ... Ms. Ellin MCDONOUGH
96 Director Procurement/Risk Mgmt ... Mr. Bob REID
53 Director Teaching/Learning Ctr ... Dr. John BIRD
23 Dir Health/Counseling Services ... Ms. Jackie CONCODORA
85 Director-International Center ... Dr. Leigh POOLE
44 Exec Dir Alumni Rel/Annl Givng ... Ms. Lori TUTTLE
88 Director Advancement Services ... Mr. Ryan SHEEHAN
105 Director Web Development ... Ms. Kimberly BYRD
106 Director of Online Learning ... Dr. Kimarie WHETSTONE

Wofford College (J)

429 N Church Street, Spartanburg SC 29303-3663
County: Spartanburg FICE Identification: 003457
Unit ID: 218973
Telephone: (864) 597-4000 Carnegie Class: Bac/A&S
FAX Number: (864) 597-4018 Calendar System: 4/1/4
URL: www.wofford.edu
Established: 1854 Annual Undergrad Tuition & Fees: $38,705
Enrollment: 1,643 Coed
Affiliation or Control: United Methodist IRS Status: 501(c)3
Highest Offering: Baccalaureate
Program: Liberal Arts And General
Accreditation: SC

01 President ... Dr. Nayef H. SAMHAT
10 Chief Financial Officer ... Ms. Barbie F. JEFFERSON
05 Provost ... Dr. Dennis M. WISEMAN
30 Sr VP Development/College Relations ... Dr. David S. WOOD
11 Sr Vice Pres for Administration ... Mr. David M. BEACHAM
32 Vice President Student Affairs ... Ms. Roberta H. BIGGER
13 VP for Information Technology ... Mr. Jason H. WOMICK
84 Vice President for Enrollment ... Mr. Brand R. STILLE
26 VP for Marketing and Communications ... Ms. Annie S. MITCHELL
18 Assoc VP Facilities/Cap Projects ... Mr. Jason H. BURR
21 AVP for Finance and Controller ... Mr. Chris L. GARDNER
08 Dean of Library ... Mr. Kevin J. REYNOLDS
82 Dean of International Programs ... Ms. Amy E. LANCASTER
23 Assoc Dean Students/Dir Health Svcs ... Ms. Beth D. WALLACE
04 Exec Assistant to the President ... Ms. Lisa P. BARNETT
41 Director of Athletics ... Mr. Richard A. JOHNSON
06 College Registrar ... Ms. Jennifer R. ALLISON
42 Chaplain ... Dr. Ronald R. ROBINSON
15 Human Resources Director ... Ms. Carole B. LISTER

York Technical College (K)

452 S Anderson Road, Rock Hill SC 29730-3395
County: York FICE Identification: 003996
Unit ID: 218991
Telephone: (803) 327-8000 Carnegie Class: Assoc/Pub-S-SC
FAX Number: (803) 327-8059 Calendar System: Semester
URL: www.yorktech.edu
Established: 1964 Annual Undergrad Tuition & Fees (In-State): $4,404
Enrollment: 5,061 Coed
Affiliation or Control: State IRS Status: 501(c)3
Highest Offering: Associate Degree
Program: Occupational; 2-Year Principally Bachelor's Creditable
Accreditation: SC, ACBSP, ADNUR, DA, DH, ENGT, MLTAD, PNUR, RAD, SURGT

01 President ... Dr. Greg F. RUTHERFORD
05 Exec Vice Pres Acad/Student Affs ... Vacant

10 VP Business Services Dr. Marc TARPLEE
32 Assoc VP Academic/Student Affairs Ms. Bridgett GOLMAN
30 Vice President for Advancement Ms. Melanie E. JONES
50 Assoc VP Business/Computer/AA/AS Ms. Yolanda WILSON
76 Assoc VP Health & Human Services Ms. Linda WEAVER-GRIGGS
54 Assoc VP Industry/Engineering Tech Dr. Sidney VALENTINE
103 Interim AVP Economic/Workforce Dev Dr. Sidney VALENTINE
08 Librarian Ms. Erinnae BAKER
84 Dean of Enrollment Services Ms. Monique PERRY
35 Dean for Student Engagement Mr. James B. ROBSON
88 Dean Center for Teaching/Learning Ms. Kathy L. HOELLEN
71 ReadySC Area Director Ms. Marianne BORDERS
09 Director of Institutional Research Ms. Mary Beth SCHWARTZ
15 Director of Human Resources Ms. Edwina ROSEBORO-BARNES
37 Director Student Financial Aid Ms. Elizabeth J. ROLLINS
13 Information Services Director Mr. Richard PARTRIDGE
18 Facilities Management Director Mr. Robert L. BROWN
45 Director of Planning Mrs. Jacquelyn H. NESBITT
06 Registrar Mrs. Tanisha LATIMER-DAVIS
26 Director of Strategic Communication Ms. Sasha TROSH

SOUTH DAKOTA

Augustana University (A)

2001 S Summit, Sioux Falls SD 57197-0001

County: Minnehaha FICE Identification: 003458
Unit ID: 219000
Telephone: (605) 274-0770 Carnegie Class: Bac/Diverse
FAX Number: (605) 274-5299 Calendar System: 4/1/4
URL: www.augie.edu
Established: 1860 Annual Undergrad Tuition & Fees: $30,090
Enrollment: 1,671 Coed
Affiliation or Control: Evangelical Lutheran Church In America
IRS Status: 501(c)3
Highest Offering: Master's
Program: Liberal Arts And General; Teacher Preparatory; Professional
Accreditation: NH, CAATE, MUS, NURSE, TED

01 President Mr. Robert C. OLIVER
05 Sr Vice Pres Academic Affairs Dr. Susan S. HASSELER
32 Vice President Student Services Dr. James B. BIES
10 Vice Pres Finance/Administration Mr. Thomas MEYER
30 Vice President for Advancement Mr. Robert PRELOGER
07 Vice President for Admission Ms. Nancy DAVIDSON
11 Assoc VP Admin/Chief Info Officer Mr. Daniel D. DRENKOW
21 Assoc Vice President for Finance Ms. Carol SPILLUM
20 Assoc VP for Academic Affairs Dr. Mitchell G. KINSINGER
51 Assoc VP of Grad and Cont Educ Dr. Jerry JORGENSEN
35 Asst Dean of Students & Dir of Div Mr. Mark BLACKBURN
15 Director of Human Resources Ms. Deanna VERSTEEG
37 Director of Financial Aid Ms. Brenda MURTHA
08 Director of Library Ms. Ronelle THOMPSON
36 Director Career Center Ms. Sandi VIETOR
13 Director Mgmt Information Systems Ms. Debra FREDERICK
18 Chief Facilities/Physical Plant Mr. Frank HUGHES
29 Director of Alumni Relations Ms. Mary TOSO
41 Athletic Director Mr. Slade LARSCHEID
06 Registrar/Asst Dean of Instr Data Ms. Joni KRUEGER
36 Exec Director of Career/Success Ctr Ms. Billie STREUFERT
88 Dir of Student Acad Support Service Ms. Susan BIES
104 Director of International Prgrams Mr. Donn GRINNAGER
108 Director of Assessment Dr. David SORENSON
19 Director of Campus Safety Mr. Rick TUPPER
09 Director of Institutional Research Vacant

Colorado Technical University (B)

3901 W 59th Street, Sioux Falls SD 57108-2272
Telephone: (605) 361-0200 Identification: 666731
Accreditation: &NH

† Regional accreditation is carried under the parent institution in Colorado Springs, CO. School is in teach-out plan, closing September 2016.

Dakota Wesleyan University (C)

1200 W University, Mitchell SD 57301-4398
County: Davison FICE Identification: 003461
Unit ID: 219091
Telephone: (605) 995-2600 Carnegie Class: Bac/Diverse
FAX Number: (605) 995-2699 Calendar System: Semester
URL: www.dwu.edu
Established: 1885 Annual Undergrad Tuition & Fees: $24,550
Enrollment: 816 Coed
Affiliation or Control: United Methodist IRS Status: 501(c)3
Highest Offering: Master's
Program: Liberal Arts And General; Teacher Preparatory
Accreditation: NH, ADNUR, CAATE, NURSE

01 President Dr. Amy C. NOVAK
05 Provost Dr. Rochelle VON EYE
10 Executive Vice President Ms. Theresa KRIESE
26 Vice Pres of University Relations Ms. Lori ESSIG
06 Registrar Ms. Karen KNOELL
08 Chief Info Ofcr/Dir Lrng Resources Mr. Kevin KENKEL
88 Dir Kelley Ctr for Entrepreneurship Dr. Ryan VAN ZEE
88 Executive Director McGovern Center Ms. Alisha VINCENT
81 Dean Col Health/Fitness & Science Dr. Mike CATALANO
79 Dean College Arts & Humanities Dr. Vince REDDER
30 VP for Institutional Advancement Ms. Kitty ALLEN
29 Director of Alumni Relations Ms. Jackie WENTWORTH
37 Director of Financial Aid Ms. Mary ALEXANDER
13 Director of Information Technology Mr. Matt MOORE
15 Director of Human Resources Ms. Janet HAYEN
42 Campus Pastor Rev. Eric VAN METER
41 Athletic Director Mr. Curt HART
18 Director of Physical Plant Mr. Louis SCHOENFELDER
32 Director of Student Life Ms. Diana GOLDAMMER
35 Director Student Support Services Ms. Kate MILLER
07 Dean of Admissions Ms. Fredel THOMAS
38 Student Support Services Counselor Ms. Linda CIMPL
40 Director of University Services Ms. Lori SOLBERG
88 Dean Col Ldrshp & Pub Service Dr. W. Jesse WEINS
88 Associate Dean of Digital Learning Dr. Derek DRIEDGER

Globe University (D)

5101 South Broadband Lane, Sioux Falls SD 57108
Telephone: (605) 977-0705 Identification: 770780
Accreditation: ACICS, MAAB

† Branch campus of Globe University, Woodbury, MN.

John Witherspoon College (E)

4021 Range Road, Rapid City SD 57702
County: Pennington Identification: 667246
Telephone: (605) 342-0317 Carnegie Class: Not Classified
FAX Number: N/A Calendar System: Semester
URL: www.johnwitherspooncollege.org
Established: 2004 Annual Undergrad Tuition & Fees: $6,000
Enrollment: N/A Coed
Affiliation or Control: Independent Non-Profit IRS Status: 501(c)3
Highest Offering: Baccalaureate
Program: Religious Emphasis
Accreditation: @TRACS

01 President C. Richard WELLS

Kilian Community College (F)

300 E 6th Street, Sioux Falls SD 57103-7020
County: Minnehaha FICE Identification: 021446
Unit ID: 219055
Telephone: (605) 221-3100 Carnegie Class: Assoc/PrivNFP
FAX Number: (605) 336-2606 Calendar System: Trimester
URL: www.kilian.edu
Established: 1976 Annual Undergrad Tuition & Fees: $11,088
Enrollment: 224 Coed
Affiliation or Control: Independent Non-Profit IRS Status: 501(c)3
Highest Offering: Associate Degree
Program: 2-Year Principally Bachelor's Creditable; Business Emphasis
Accreditation: NH

01 President Mr. Mark MILLAGE
05 Dean for Academic Services Ms. Janet GARCIA
11 Dean of Institutional Services Vacant
37 Financial Aid Director Ms. Mary KLOCKMAN
06 Academic Dean/Registrar Ms. Janet K. GARCIA
88 Director Student Success Center Ms. Rose TOERING
07 Director of Admissions Ms. Wendy THORSON
30 Director of Development Ms. Wendy MCDONNEL
04 Assistant to the President Ms. Joyce HUBREGTSE
18 Chief Facilities/Physical Plant Mr. Herb ROE
49 Instruction Liberal Arts Division Ms. Cheryl J. HARTMAN
50 Instruction Business Division Ms. Wendy JANSEN

Lake Area Technical Institute (G)

1201 Arrow Avenue, PO Box 730,
Watertown SD 57201-2869
County: Codington FICE Identification: 005309
Unit ID: 219143
Telephone: (605) 882-5284 Carnegie Class: Assoc/Pub-R-S
FAX Number: (605) 882-6299 Calendar System: Semester
URL: www.lakeareatech.edu
Established: 1965 Annual Undergrad Tuition & Fees (In-District): $5,230
Enrollment: 1,726 Coed
Affiliation or Control: Local IRS Status: 501(c)3
Highest Offering: Associate Degree
Program: Occupational; 2-Year Principally Bachelor's Creditable; Technical Emphasis
Accreditation: NH, DA, EMT, MAC, MLTAD, OTA, PNUR, PTAA

01 President Mr. Michael D. CARTNEY
03 Executive Vice President Ms. Diane STILES
84 Director of Enrollment Mr. Eric SCHULTZ
05 Dean of Instruction Ms. Kim BELLUM
26 Chief Public Relations Officer Ms. LuAnn STRAIT
31 Business/Industry Coordinator Mr. Steven HAUCK
32 Student Services Coordinator Mr. Shane ORTMEIER
37 Financial Aid Coordinator Ms. Marlene SEEKLANDER
38 Academic Counselor Ms. Megan HOWARD

Mitchell Technical Institute (H)

1800 E Spruce, Mitchell SD 57301-2002
County: Davison FICE Identification: 008284
Unit ID: 219189
Telephone: (605) 995-3025 Carnegie Class: Assoc/Pub-R-S
FAX Number: (605) 995-3083 Calendar System: Semester
URL: www.mitchelltech.edu
Established: 1968 Annual Undergrad Tuition & Fees (In-District): $5,500
Enrollment: 1,245 Coed
Affiliation or Control: Local IRS Status: 501(c)3
Highest Offering: Associate Degree
Program: Occupational; 2-Year Principally Bachelor's Creditable; Technical Emphasis
Accreditation: NH, ACFEI, MAC, MLTAD, RAD, RTT

01 President Mr. Mark WILSON
03 Executive Vice President Ms. Vicki WIESE
05 Vice President for Academic Affairs Ms. Vicki WIESE
10 Vice Pres for Admin Svcs/CFO Ms. Stephanie KAUL
13 Vice President for Technology Mr. Dan MUCK
88 Vice Pres for Industrial Relations Mr. Mark GERHARDT
88 Director of Secondary Relations Mr. Scott FOSSUM
06 Registrar Ms. Janet GREENWAY
37 Director Student Financial Aid Ms. Morgan HUBER
07 Director of Admissions Mr. Clayton DEUTER
38 Learning Services Coordinator Vacant
09 Institutional Research Coordinator Ms. Marla SMITH
20 Director of Curriculum Ms. Carol GRODE-HANKS
26 Director of Marketing Ms. Julie BROOKBANK
102 Foundation Director Ms. Heather LENTZ
88 Retention Coordinator Ms. Sarah DUFF
36 Employment Coordinator Ms. Elizabeth KITCHENS

Mount Marty College (I)

1105 W 8th, Yankton SD 57078-3724
County: Yankton FICE Identification: 003465
Unit ID: 219198
Telephone: (605) 668-1011 Carnegie Class: Bac/Diverse
FAX Number: (605) 668-1607 Calendar System: Semester
URL: www.mtmc.edu
Established: 1936 Annual Undergrad Tuition & Fees: $24,306
Enrollment: 1,236 Coed
Affiliation or Control: Roman Catholic IRS Status: 501(c)3
Highest Offering: Master's
Program: Liberal Arts And General; Teacher Preparatory; Professional; Nursing Emphasis
Accreditation: NH, ANEST, CACREP, NURSE

01 President Mr. Marcus LONG
04 Asst to the Pres/Asst Sec to Board Ms. Carla ENG
05 Interim VP for Academic Affairs Ms. Celia MINER
10 VP for Finance Ms. Tabitha LIKNESS
32 VP of Student Affairs Ms. Sarah CARDA
07 VP for Admissions Ms. Paula TACKE
30 Chief Advancement Officer Ms. Barb REZAC
11 Chief Operations Officer Mr. Greg HEINE
09 Director of Institutional Research Ms. Kristen WELKER
66 Director of Nurse Anesthesia Dr. Mary Anne KROGH
42 Director of Campus Ministry Sr. Maribeth WENTZLAFF
12 Int Director of Watertown Location Dr. Linda SCHURMANN
37 Director Student Financial Aid Mr. Ken KOCER
06 Registrar Ms. Jonna SUPURGECI
13 Director Information Support Svcs Mr. Paul LAMMERS
08 Director of Library Ms. Sandra BROWN
40 Dir Bookstore/Central Scheduling Ms. Mary ABBOTT
36 Dir Career Planning/Disability Svcs Ms. Tracy TAYLOR
41 Athletic Director Mr. Chuck IVERSON
15 Human Resources Specialist Ms. Julie DATHER
27 Director of Media Relations Ms. Kristi TACKE
44 Director of Annual/Planned Giving Ms. Shannon VIERECK
19 Director Security/Safety Ms. Sonja OLSON
29 Director Alumni Relations Mr. David DICKES

National American University (J)

5301 S Highway 16, Rapid City SD 57701-8932
County: Pennington FICE Identification: 004057
Unit ID: 219204
Telephone: (605) 394-4800 Carnegie Class: Master's S
FAX Number: (605) 721-5241 Calendar System: Quarter
URL: www.national.edu
Established: 1941 Annual Undergrad Tuition & Fees: $13,287
Enrollment: 1,479 Coed
Affiliation or Control: Proprietary IRS Status: Proprietary
Highest Offering: Doctorate
Program: Occupational; Professional
Accreditation: NH, CAHIIM, IACBE, MAC, NURSE

01 University President Dr. Jerry L. GALLENTINE
11 COO Dr. Ronald SHAPE

National American University-Sioux Falls (K)

5801 S Corporate Place, Sioux Falls SD 57108
Telephone: (605) 336-5430 Identification: 770388
Accreditation: &NH

† Branch campus of National American University, Rapid City, SD.

Oglala Lakota College (L)

Box 490, Kyle SD 57752-0490
County: Shannon FICE Identification: 014659
Unit ID: 219277
Telephone: (605) 455-6000 Carnegie Class: Tribal
FAX Number: (605) 455-2787 Calendar System: Semester
URL: www.olc.edu
Established: 1971 Annual Undergrad Tuition & Fees: $2,580
Enrollment: 1,423 Coed

Affiliation or Control: Tribal Control IRS Status: 501(c)3
Highest Offering: Master's
Program: Liberal Arts And General
Accreditation: NH, SW

01 President .... Mr. Thomas H. SHORTBULL
05 Vice President for Instruction .... Dr. Dawn FRANK
10 Vice President for Business .... Ms. Julie JOHNSON
06 Registrar .... Ms. Leslie MESTETH
08 Director Learning Resources .... Ms. Michelle MAY
15 Personnel Director .... Ms. Faith RICHARDS
37 Financial Aid Director .... Ms. Billi HORNBECK
84 Director Enrollment Management .... Mt. Adetokunbo OREDEIN
07 Director of Admissions .... Ms. Leslie MESTETH
09 Director of Institutional Research .... Ms. Dawn FRANK
96 Assoc Business Ofcr/Dir Purchasing .... Ms. Arlis POURIER
29 Director Alumni Relations .... Ms. Marilyn POURIER
89 Director of Freshman Studies .... Ms. Thedna ZIMIGA
13 MIS Director .... Mr. Cliff DELONG
32 Director Student Affairs .... Mr. Wayne WESTON
30 Inst Development Coordinator .... Ms. Marilyn POURIER
51 Community/Cont Education Coord .... Ms. Kateri MONTILEAUX
88 Applied Science Department Chair .... Mr. David WHITE BULL
81 Math & Science Department Chair .... Ms. Karla WITT
49 Art & History Department Chair .... Ms. Kim BETTELYOUN
53 Education Department Chair .... Mr. Thomas RAYMOND
66 Nursing Department Chair .... Ms. Michelle BRUNS
83 Human Services Department Chair .... Ms. Kathryn KIDD
88 LAKOTA Studies Department Chair .... Ms. Karen LONE HILL
18 Chief Facilities/Physical Plant .... Mr. Leonard FERGUSON

Presentation College (A)

1500 N Main Street, Aberdeen SD 57401-1280
County: Brown FICE Identification: 003467
Unit ID: 219295
Telephone: (605) 225-1634 Carnegie Class: Bac/Diverse
FAX Number: (605) 229-8330 Calendar System: Semester
URL: www.presentation.edu
Established: 1951 Annual Undergrad Tuition & Fees: $17,990
Enrollment: 597 Coed
Affiliation or Control: Roman Catholic IRS Status: 501(c)3
Highest Offering: Baccalaureate
Program: Occupational; Professional; Nursing Emphasis
Accreditation: NH, ADNUR, IACBE, MAC, NUR, RAD, SURGT, SW

01 President .... Dr. Margaret HUBER
05 Vice Pres for Academics .... Dr. Michelle METZINGER
10 Vice Pres for Finance .... Ms. Cathy HALL
84 Vice Pres for Enrollment .... Mr. Michael MATTISON
32 Vice Pres for Student Services .... Mr. Bob SCHUCHARDT
30 Vice President for Advancement .... Ms. Cynthia WHITNEY
88 Executive Director for Mission .... Sr. Pam DONELAN
06 Registrar .... Vacant
37 Director Student Financial Aid .... Ms. Maureen SCHUCHARDT
108 Assessment Coordinator .... Dr. Nancy VANDER HOEK
15 Director of Human Resources .... Mr. Jason PETTIGREW
04 Administrative Asst to President .... Ms. Stacy BAUER
26 Dir of Marketing/Public Relations .... Mr. Tim BECKHAM

Sinte Gleska University (B)

PO Box 105, Mission SD 57555-0105
County: Todd FICE Identification: 021437
Unit ID: 219374
Telephone: (605) 856-5880 Carnegie Class: Tribal
FAX Number: (605) 856-5401 Calendar System: Semester
URL: www.sintegleska.edu
Established: 1970 Annual Undergrad Tuition & Fees: $3,154
Enrollment: 641 Coed
Affiliation or Control: Independent Non-Profit IRS Status: 501(c)3
Highest Offering: Master's
Program: Liberal Arts And General; Teacher Preparatory; Professional
Accreditation: #NH

01 President .... Mr. Lionel BORDEAUX
05 Vice Pres Academic Affairs .... Ms. Cheryl MEDEARIS
32 Vice Pres Student Services .... Mr. Mike BENGE
06 Registrar .... Mr. Harvey HERMAN
10 VP Finance/Resource Devel .... Ms. Georgia HACKETT
31 VP Community Education .... Ms. Sherry RED OWL
08 Int Library Director .... Ms. Diana DILLION
20 Chief Finance Officer .... Ms. Sarah AROBBA
37 Director Financial Aid .... Mr. William HAY
55 Director Adult Education .... Mr. James SHERMAN, III
15 Director Personnel .... Mr. Mark BORDEAUX

Sioux Falls Seminary (C)

2100 S Summit Ave, Sioux Falls SD 57105-2729
County: Minnehaha FICE Identification: 004056
Unit ID: 219240
Telephone: (605) 336-6588 Carnegie Class: Spec/Faith
FAX Number: (605) 335-9090 Calendar System: 4/1/4
URL: www.sfseminary.edu
Established: 1858 Annual Graduate Tuition & Fees: $15,974
Enrollment: 195 Coed
Affiliation or Control: North American Baptist IRS Status: 501(c)3
Highest Offering: Doctorate; No Undergraduates
Program: Professional; Religious Emphasis
Accreditation: #NH, THEOL

01 President .... Mr. Gregory J. HENSON
05 Chief Academic Officer & Dean .... Dr. Larry W. CALDWELL
10 Chief Financial Officer .... Mr. Nathan M. HELLING
84 Director of Enrollment Management .... Mr. Dustin J. BROUWER
37 Assoc Dir of Enrollment & Fin Aid .... Ms. Tracy A. JONES
26 Director of Integrated Marketing .... Ms. Shanda L. STRICHERZ
29 Dir of Church & Alumni Relations .... Dr. Randall C. TSCHETTER
21 Office Manager .... Ms. Sheryl L. SLETTEN
58 Director of Doctoral Studies .... Dr. Gary E. STRICKLAND
83 Director of Counseling Programs .... Ms. Gretchen L. HARTMANN

Sisseton-Wahpeton College (D)

PO Box 689, Sisseton SD 57262-0689
County: Roberts FICE Identification: 022773
Unit ID: 219408
Telephone: (605) 698-3966 Carnegie Class: Tribal
FAX Number: (605) 698-3132 Calendar System: Semester
URL: www.swc.tc
Established: 1979 Annual Undergrad Tuition & Fees (In-District): $4,410
Enrollment: 165 Coed
Affiliation or Control: Local IRS Status: 501(c)3
Highest Offering: Associate Degree
Program: Occupational; 2-Year Principally Bachelor's Creditable
Accreditation: NH

01 President .... Dr. Harvey DUMARCE
05 Vice President of Academic Affairs .... Dr. Jeanette GRAVDAHL
10 Chief Financial Officer .... Ms. Tanya LAFROMEOISE
37 Financial Aid Officer .... Ms. Janel MANY LIGHTNINGS
07 Director of Admissions/Registrar .... Mrs. Darlene REDDAY
66 Director Nursing .... Ms. Sandra REDDAY
29 Alumni Director .... Mr. Tyler BIRNEY
18 Director Facilities .... Mr. Darrick REDWING

*South Dakota State Board of Regents System Office (E)

306 E Capitol Avenue, Suite 200, Pierre SD 57501-2545
County: Hughes FICE Identification: 033438
Telephone: (605) 773-3455 Carnegie Class: N/A
FAX Number: (605) 773-5320
URL: www.sdbor.edu

01 Executive Director & CEO .... Dr. Mike RUSH
10 System VP Finance & Administration .... Dr. Monte KRAMER
05 System VP Academic Affairs .... Dr. Paul TURMAN
46 Asst System VP Research & Econ Dev .... Mr. Nathan LUKKES
43 General Counsel .... Dr. James F. SHEKLETON
15 Director of Human Resources .... Ms. Barbara BASEL
26 Director of Communications .... Dr. Janelle TOMAN
32 Director of Student Affairs .... Ms. Molly WEISGRAM
09 Director of Institutional Research .... Dr. Daniel PALMER
13 System CIO .... Mr. David HANSEN
20 Associate Academic Officer .... Dr. Jay PERRY

*The University of South Dakota (F)

414 E Clark, Vermillion SD 57069-2390
County: Clay FICE Identification: 003474
Unit ID: 219471
Telephone: (605) 677-5011 Carnegie Class: RU/H
FAX Number: (605) 677-5073 Calendar System: Semester
URL: www.usd.edu
Established: 1862 Annual Undergrad Tuition & Fees (In-State): $8,039
Enrollment: 10,061 Coed
Affiliation or Control: State IRS Status: 501(c)3
Highest Offering: Doctorate
Program: Liberal Arts And General; Teacher Preparatory; Professional
Accreditation: NH, ADNUR, ARCPA, ART, AUD, BUS, CACREP, CLPSY, DH, #JOUR, LAW, MED, MUS, NURSE, OT, PTA, SP, SPAA, SW, TED, THEA

02 President .... Mr. James W. ABBOTT
05 Provost/VP Academic Affairs .... Dr. James D. MORAN, III
17 Vice President Health Affairs .... Dr. Mary DEKKER NETTLEMAN
10 Vice Pres Finance - CFO .... Ms. Sheila GESTRING
46 Interim Vice President for Research .... Dr. Mary BERRY
26 VP of Marketing/Enrollment Svcs .... Mr. Scott POHLSON
11 Vice Pres Administration & ITS .... Ms. Roberta S. AMBUR
20 Assoc Vice Pres Academic Affairs .... Vacant
28 Associate VP of Diversity .... Dr. Jesus TREVINO
08 Dean of Libraries .... Mr. Daniel R. DAILY
32 VP Student Svcs & Dean of Students .... Dr. Kimberly GRIEVE
29 Exec Dir Alumni Association .... Ms. Kersten JOHNSON
96 Director of Purchasing .... Mr. Darby GANSCHOW
15 Vice President Human Resources .... Mr. E. Lee FELDER, JR.
22 Affirmative Action Officer .... Ms. Roberta H. HAKL
18 Asst VP Facilities Management .... Mr. Bob OEHLER
37 Director of Financial Aid .... Ms. Julie H. PIER
09 Director of Institutional Research .... Vacant
36 Dir Ctr for Academic & Career Plng .... Mr. Steve WARD
06 Registrar .... Ms. Jennifer M. THOMPSON
41 Athletic Director .... Mr. David HERBSTER
38 Director Student Counseling .... Vacant
19 Director Public Safety .... Mr. Peter E. JENSEN
84 Dean of Enrollment .... Mr. Mark PETTY
49 Dean College Arts & Sciences .... Dr. Matthew C. MOEN
50 Dean School of Business .... Dr. A. R VENKATACHALAM
51 Assoc Prov/Dn Grad Sch/Div Cont Edu .... Dr. Michael CARD
53 Interim Dean School of Education .... Dr. Hee-Sook CHOI
57 Dean College Fine Arts .... Dr. Larry SCHOU
63 Dean Sanford School of Medicine .... Dr. Mary DEKKER NETTLEMAN
61 Dean School of Law .... Mr. Thomas GEU

*Black Hills State University (G)

1200 University Street, Spearfish SD 57799-9500
County: Lawrence FICE Identification: 003459
Unit ID: 219046
Telephone: (605) 642-6111 Carnegie Class: Master's S
FAX Number: (605) 642-6763 Calendar System: Semester
URL: www.bhsu.edu
Established: 1883 Annual Undergrad Tuition & Fees (In-State): $8,004
Enrollment: 4,489 Coed
Affiliation or Control: State IRS Status: 501(c)3
Highest Offering: Master's
Program: 2-Year Principally Bachelor's Creditable; Liberal Arts And General; Teacher Preparatory
Accreditation: NH, BUS, MUS, TED

02 President .... Dr. Tom JACKSON, JR.
05 Provost/Vice Pres Academic Affairs .... Dr. Rodney CUSTER
10 Vice President Finance/Admin .... Ms. Kathy J. JOHNSON
30 Vice Pres University Advancement .... Mr. Steve L. MEEKER
32 Vice President for Student Life .... Dr. Lois FLAGSTAD
26 Director Univ & Community Relations .... Ms. Corinne HANSEN
13 Chief Info Technology Officer .... Dr. Warren WILSON
37 Director Student Financial Aid .... Ms. Deb HENRIKSEN
38 Director Counseling Center .... Dr. James FLEMING
39 Director Residence Life .... Dr. Michael L. ISAACSON
35 Director Student Services .... Dr. Jane KLUG
15 Director of Human Resources .... Mr. Nick OAKS
06 Registrar .... Ms. April M. MEEKER
07 Director of Admissions .... Ms. Beth OAKS
21 Director of Business Services .... Mr. Rob HOUDEK
18 Director Facilities/Physical Plant .... Mr. Randy CULVER
29 Director Alumni Relations .... Mr. Tom WHEATON
09 Director of Institutional Research .... Mr. Maxwell KWENDA
08 Director Library Operations .... Mr. Scott AHOLA
104 Director International Studies .... Dr. James FLEMING
30 Director of Development .... Ms. Shauna JUNEK
19 Director Security/Safety .... Mr. Philip PESHECK
40 Director University Bookstore .... Mr. Michael JASTORFF
41 Director of Athletics .... Mr. Jhett ALBERS
13 Director Network & Computer Svcs .... Mr. Fred NELSON
49 Dean College of Liberal Arts .... Dr. David WOLFF
50 Dean Col of Business & Natural Sci .... Dr. Priscilla ROMKEMA
53 Dean Col of Educ & Behavioral Sci .... Dr. Patricia SIMPSON
36 Career Development Specialist .... Ms. Sara ELIAS
04 Administrative Asst to President .... Ms. Judy A. BAUER
25 Chief Contracts/Grants Admin .... Mr. William KELLY

*Dakota State University (H)

820 N Washington Avenue, Madison SD 57042-1799
County: Lake FICE Identification: 003463
Unit ID: 219082
Telephone: (605) 256-5111 Carnegie Class: Master's S
FAX Number: (605) 256-5316 Calendar System: Semester
URL: www.dsu.edu
Established: 1881 Annual Undergrad Tuition & Fees (In-State): $7,974
Enrollment: 3,047 Coed
Affiliation or Control: State IRS Status: 501(c)3
Highest Offering: Doctorate
Program: 2-Year Principally Bachelor's Creditable; Liberal Arts And General; Teacher Preparatory; Professional; Technical Emphasis
Accreditation: NH, ACBSP, CAHIIM, COARC, TED

02 President .... Dr. José -Marie GRIFFITHS
05 Vice Pres for Academic Affairs .... Dr. Judith L. DITTMAN
10 Vice Pres for Business & Admin Svcs .... Mr. Stacy L. KRUSEMARK
32 Vice Pres/Dean Student Affairs .... Mr. Marcus GARSTECKI
50 Dean Col Business/Info Systems .... Vacant
53 Dean College of Education .... Dr. Gale WIEDOW
49 Dean College of Arts and Sciences .... Dr. Benjamin F. JONES
58 Dean of Graduate Studies/Research .... Dr. Omar F. EL-GAYAR
102 Exec Director DSU Foundation .... Vacant
41 Director of Athletics .... Mr. Jeff L. DITTMAN
36 Asst VP Stdnt Affs/Dir Career Svcs .... Dr. Marie A. LOHSANDT
08 Director of Library .... Ms. Ethelle S. BEAN
13 Director of Computing Services .... Mr. David B. OVERBY
29 Director of Alumni .... Ms. Jona M. SCHMIDT
18 Director of Physical Plant .... Vacant
06 Registrar .... Ms. Kathryn CALLIES
37 Director Financial Aid .... Ms. Denise R. GRAYSON
38 Asst Dean for Student Development .... Mr. O. Keith BUNDY
39 Dir of Student Union/Residence Life .... Mr. Steven J. BARTEL
35 Director of Student Activities .... Ms. Amanda L. PARPART
04 Admin Assistant to the President .... Vacant
15 Director Human Resources .... Ms. Maria D. HARDER
56 Director Extended Programs .... Ms. Sarah RASMUSSEN
84 Assoc VP of Enrollment Mgmt .... Ms. Amy S. CRISSINGER
09 Director of Assessment .... Dr. Jay KAHL
21 Comptroller .... Ms. Amy L. DOCKENDORF
25 Dir of Ctr for Adv of HIT .... Mr. Dan FRIEDRICH
85 International Programs Director .... Ms. Jacy FRY
40 Director of Bookstore .... Ms. Heather GILLESPIE
25 Director of Budget & Grants Admin .... Ms. Sara HARE
25 Director of Sponsored Programs .... Ms. Kacie M. FODNESS
28 Diversity Coordinator .... Vacant
26 Assoc Director of Marketing .... Ms. Erica CLEMENTS

*Northern State University (A)

1200 S Jay Street, Aberdeen SD 57401-7198
County: Brown FICE Identification: 003466
Unit ID: 219259
Telephone: (605) 626-3011 Carnegie Class: Bac/Diverse
FAX Number: (605) 626-3022 Calendar System: Semester
URL: www.northern.edu
Established: 1901 Annual Undergrad Tuition & Fees (In-State): $7,887
Enrollment: 3,580 Coed
Affiliation or Control: State IRS Status: 501(c)3
Highest Offering: Master's
Program: Liberal Arts And General; Teacher Preparatory; Business Emphasis
Accreditation: NH, ART, MUS, TED

02 President .... Dr. James M. SMITH
05 Vice Pres Academic Affs/Provost .... Dr. Alan LAFAVE
10 Vice Pres Finance/Administration .... Ms. Veronica PAULSON
32 Vice President for Student Affairs .... Ms. JoEllen LINDNER
20 Associate VPAA .... Dr. Joelle LIEN
13 Chief Information Tech Officer .... Ms. Debbi BUMPOUS
44 Director of Annual Funds .... Vacant
102 President/CEO of Foundation .... Mr. Todd JORDRE
06 Registrar .... Ms. Peggy HALLSTROM
84 Exec Dir of Enrollment Management .... Ms. JoEllen LINDNER
07 Director of Admissions .... Vacant
08 Director of Library .... Mr. Robert RUSSELL
38 Director of Counseling Center .... Vacant
09 Institutional Research Officer .... Ms. Heather SCOTT
25 Director Grants Sponsored Research .... Ms. Karen MARCHANT
37 Director of Financial Aid .... Ms. Sharon KIENOW
39 Director of Residence Life .... Mr. Martin SABOLO
21 Controller .... Ms. Kay FREDRICK
15 Director of Human Resources .... Ms. Susan BOSTIAN
26 Director of University Relations .... Mr. Gregory SMITH
43 General Counsel .... Mr. John MEYER
18 Director of Facilities Management .... Mr. Monte MEHLHOFF
49 Dean College of Arts & Science .... Dr. Celestino MENDEZ
50 Dean School of Business .... Dr. Willard BROUCEK
53 Dean School of Education .... Dr. Kelly DUNCAN
57 Interim Dean School of Fine Arts .... Dr. William WIELAND
58 Director of Graduate Studies .... Dr. Joelle LIEN
56 Director of Extended Studies .... Mr. Ronald BROWNIE
41 Director of Athletics .... Mr. Joshua MOON
40 Director of Bookstore .... Ms. Beth RASMUSSON
96 Director of Purchasing .... Mr. Earl WEISENBURGER
92 Director of Honors Program .... Dr. Erin FOUBERG
71 Director of Special Initiatives .... Dr. Connie RUHL-SMITH
28 Interim Multicultural Advisor .... Ms. Sarah BOTKIN
35 Director of Student Activities .... Ms. Sarah BOTKIN
04 Administrative Asst to President .... Ms. Lisa GROTE
104 Study Abroad Coordinator .... Ms. Elizabeth HANNUM
106 Dir Online Education/E-learning .... Mr. Ronald BROWNIE
108 Director Institutional Assessment .... Ms. Heather SCOTT
22 Dir Affirmative Action/EEO .... Ms. Susan BOSTIAN
36 Director Student Placement .... Ms. Britt LORENZ

*South Dakota School of Mines and Technology (B)

501 E Saint Joseph, Rapid City SD 57701-3995
County: Pennington FICE Identification: 003470
Unit ID: 219347
Telephone: (605) 394-2511 Carnegie Class: Spec/Engg
FAX Number: (605) 394-6131 Calendar System: Semester
URL: www.sdsmt.edu
Established: 1885 Annual Undergrad Tuition & Fees (In-State): $11,170
Enrollment: 2,798 Coed
Affiliation or Control: State IRS Status: 501(c)3
Highest Offering: Doctorate
Program: Professional; Technical Emphasis
Accreditation: NH, CS, ENG

02 President .... Dr. Heather WILSON
05 Interim Provost/VP Academic Affs .... Dr. Richard SINDEN
10 Vice Pres Finance/Administration .... Mr. Stephen MALOTT
46 Vice President of Research .... Dr. Jan A. PUSZYNSKI
32 VP Student Affs/Dean of Students .... Dr. Patricia G. MAHON
30 VP University Relations .... Vacant
15 Vice President Human Resources .... Ms. Kelli R. SHUMAN
20 Associate Provost Academic Affairs .... Dr. Kathryn E. ALLEY
84 Assoc Provost for Enrollment Mgmt .... Dr. Michael C. GUNN
96 Purchasing Manager .... Ms. Barbara MUSTARD
07 Asst VP for Enrl Mgmt/Dir of Adm .... Mrs. Molly E. MOORE
29 Director of Alumni Association .... Mr. Timothy J. VOTTERO
90 Director Information Tech Svcs .... Mr. Bryan J. SCHUMACHER
08 Director Devereaux Library .... Ms. Patricia M. ANDERSEN
36 Director Career Services .... Dr. Darrell R. SAWYER
37 Director of Financial Aid .... Mr. David W. MARTIN
88 Dir Inst Atmospheric Sciences .... Dr. Andrew G. DETWILER
41 Director of Athletics .... Mr. Joel LEUKEN
102 President SDSM&T Foundation .... Mr. Michael M. SELZER
18 Director of Facilities Services .... Ms. Jerilyn C. ROBERTS
11 Director of Administrative Services .... Mr. Terry H. GRANT
39 Dir Residence Life/Student Conduct .... Dr. Daniel SEPION
85 Director Ivanhoe International Ctr .... Ms. Susan R. AADLAND
58 Dean of Graduate Education .... Dr. Douglas WELLS
38 Director Student Counseling Svcs .... Vacant
84 Registrar and Dir Academic Services .... Ms. Carla TIU
09 Director of Retention & Testing .... Vacant
06 Registration Officer .... Mrs. Diana O'TOOLE

40 Manager College Bookstore .... Mr. Marlin L. KINZER
35 Student Activities Coordinator .... Mr. Michael KEEGAN
26 Dir of Marketing & Communications .... Mr. Jon MICHAELS

*South Dakota State University (C)

Brookings SD 57007-2298
County: Brookings FICE Identification: 003471
Unit ID: 219356
Telephone: (605) 688-4151 Carnegie Class: RU/H
FAX Number: (605) 688-5822 Calendar System: Semester
URL: www.sdstate.edu
Established: 1881 Annual Undergrad Tuition & Fees (In-State): $8,172
Enrollment: 12,557 Coed
Affiliation or Control: State IRS Status: 501(c)3
Highest Offering: Doctorate
Program: Liberal Arts And General; Teacher Preparatory; Professional
Accreditation: NH, AAB, CAATE, CACREP, CIDA, CONST, CORE, CS, DIETD, @DIETI, ENG, EXSC, JOUR, MT, MUS, NURSE, PHAR, TED

02 President .... Dr. David L. CHICOINE
05 Provost/Vice Pres Academic Affairs .... Dr. Laurie NICHOLS
32 Vice President Student Affairs .... Vacant
45 VP for Research/Economic Dev .... Dr. Kevin KEPHART
13 VP for Tech/Security .... Dr. Michael ADELAINE
10 Vice Pres Finance & Business/CFO ... Mr. Wesley G. TSCHETTER
20 Assoc Vice Pres for Academic Affs .... Dr. Mary Kay HELLING
18 Asst Vice Pres Facilities Services .... Mr. Dean KATTELMANN
88 Asst VP AA Intl Affairs/Outreach .... Dr. Kathleen FAIRFAX
15 Asst Vice Pres Human Resources .... Mr. Marc SERRETT
04 Executive Asst to the President .... Mr. Robert OTTERSON
08 Dean of the Library .... Dr. Kristi TORNQUIST
97 Dean of University College .... Dr. Keith CORBETT
07 Director of Admissions .... Ms. Tracy WELSH
06 Registrar .... Dr. Aaron AURE
38 Director Wellness .... Mr. Jeffrey HUSKEY
37 Financial Aid Officer .... Ms. Carolyn HALGERSON
102 President & CEO of Foundation .... Mr. Steve ERPENBACH
29 President & CEO Alumni Affairs .... Ms. Andi FOUBERG
14 Director Admin Information Svcs .... Mr. William (Joe) MOORE
19 Chief Security/Safety .... Mr. Tim HEATON
39 Director of Residential Life .... Mr. Jeffrey HALE
40 Director of Bookstore .... Mr. Derek PETERSON
41 Director of Athletics .... Mr. Justin SELL
28 Dir of Diversity/Equal Opportunity .... Vacant
56 Assoc Director of Extension .... Dr. Karla TRAUTMAN
26 Dir Marketing & Communications .... Mr. Michael LOCKREM
96 Purchasing Director .... Ms. Vicki SOREN
43 University Legal Counsel .... Dr. Tracy GREENE
25 Director of Grants/Contracts .... Ms. Jackie NELSON
24 Mgr Instructional Design Services .... Dr. Shouhong ZHANG
85 Mgr International Students/Scholars .... Mr. Greg WYMER
47 Dean Agriculture/Biological Sci .... Dr. Barry DUNN
49 Dean of Arts & Sciences .... Dr. Dennis PAPINI
54 Dean of Engineering .... Dr. Lewis BROWN
53 Dean Education & Human Science .... Dr. Jill THORNGREN
66 Dean of Nursing .... Dr. Nancy FAHRENWALD
67 Dean of Pharmacy .... Dr. Dennis HEDGE
58 Dean of Graduate School .... Dr. Kinchel DOERNER
92 Dean Honors College .... Dr. Timothy NICHOLS
51 Dean Continuing & Extended Educ .... Vacant
09 Coordinator Institutional Research .... Ms. Jennifer VANDER WAL

Southeast Technical Institute (D)

2320 N Career Avenue, Sioux Falls SD 57107-1302
County: Minnehaha FICE Identification: 007764
Unit ID: 219426
Telephone: (605) 367-7624 Carnegie Class: Assoc/Pub-R-M
FAX Number: (605) 367-8305 Calendar System: Semester
URL: www.southeasttech.edu
Established: 1968 Annual Undergrad Tuition & Fees (In-District): $4,728
Enrollment: 2,332 Coed
Affiliation or Control: Local IRS Status: 501(c)3
Highest Offering: Associate Degree
Program: Occupational; Technical Emphasis
Accreditation: NH, ADNUR, CVT, DMS, NDT, NMT, SURGT

01 President .... Mr. Jeffrey R. HOLCOMB
05 Vice President of Academics .... Mr. James JACOBSEN
10 Vice President Finance & Operations .... Mr. Richard KLUIN
32 Vice Pres Student Affs/Inst Rsrch .... Mr. Tracy NOLDNER
35 Director of Students .... Mr. Jim ROKUSEK
50 Training Solutions Institute .... Mr. Lon HIRD
06 Registrar .... Ms. Kristie VORTHERMS
15 Human Resources Specialist .... Ms. Kathy STRUCK
20 Director of Academic Support .... Dr. Craig PETERS
26 Marketing Coordinator .... Ms. Margaret PENNOCK
37 Financial Aid Director .... Ms. Lynette GRABOWSKA
102 Foundation Associate .... Ms. Nancee STURDEVANT
21 Business Manager .... Mr. James WESTCOTT
38 Student Personal Counselor .... Ms. Nicole MCMILLIN

University of Sioux Falls (E)

1101 W 22nd Street, Sioux Falls SD 57105-1699
County: Minnehaha FICE Identification: 003469
Unit ID: 219383
Telephone: (605) 331-5000 Carnegie Class: Bac/Diverse
FAX Number: (605) 331-6615 Calendar System: 4/1/4
URL: www.usiouxfalls.edu
Established: 1883 Annual Undergrad Tuition & Fees: $26,240
Enrollment: 1,419 Coed

Affiliation or Control: American Baptist IRS Status: 501(c)3
Highest Offering: Beyond Master's But Less Than Doctorate
Program: Liberal Arts And General; Teacher Preparatory; Professional
Accreditation: NH, IACBE, NURSE, SW, TED

01 President .... Dr. Mark BENEDETTO
04 Exec Assistant to the President .... Ms. Karen BANGASSER
05 Provost/Vice Pres Academic Affairs .... Dr. Brett BRADFIELD
10 VP for Business and Finance .... Ms. Marsha DENNISTON
30 VP for Institutional Advancement .... Dr. Bruce BLUMER
44 VP for Principal Gifts .... Mr. Jon HIATT
15 VP of Human Resources .... Ms. Julie GEDNALSKE
32 Dean of Students .... Mr. Corey ROSS
13 VP Information Technology .... Mr. William BARTELL
26 VP for Marketing and Grants .... Ms. Megan FISCHER
42 Dean of the Chapel .... Rev. Dennis L. THUM
06 Registrar .... Ms. Anna HECKENLAIBLE
21 Controller .... Ms. Susan THIE
37 Director of Financial Aid .... Ms. Karrie MORGAN
07 Director of Admissions .... Ms. Aimee VANDER FEEN
08 Director of Library Services .... Ms. Rachel CROWLEY
18 Director of Facilities Services .... Ms. Traci LINDSTEN
41 Director of Intercollegiate Ath .... Mr. Josh SNYDER
88 Director of Degree Comp Program .... Ms. LuAnn GROSSMAN
19 Director of Campus Safety .... Mr. Kevin GREBIN
29 Director Annual Giving & Alumni Rel .... Mr. Cody SCHREIBER
104 Director of International Education .... Mr. Randy NELSON
106 Director of Online Education .... Ms. Veda IVERSON
40 Bookstore Manager .... Ms. Jennifer KNUTSON
50 Dean School of Bus & Entrep Ldrshp .... Dr. Deb HERB-SEPICH
53 Chair Fredrikson School of Educ .... Ms. Julie MCAREAVEY
57 Chair Visual & Performing Arts .... Mr. Jonathan NEIDERHISER
81 Chair of Natural Sciences .... Dr. William SOEFFING
79 Chair of Humanities .... Ms. Nicholle SCHUELKE
66 Director of School of Nursing .... Ms. Jessica CHERENEGAR
83 Chair of Social Sciences .... Ms. Beth O'TOOLE

Western Dakota Technical Institute (F)

800 Mickelson Drive, Rapid City SD 57703-4018
County: Pennington FICE Identification: 010170
Unit ID: 219480
Telephone: (605) 394-4034 Carnegie Class: Assoc/Pub-R-S
FAX Number: (605) 394-1789 Calendar System: Semester
URL: www.wdt.edu
Established: 1968 Annual Undergrad Tuition & Fees (In-District): $5,960
Enrollment: 840 Coed
Affiliation or Control: Local IRS Status: 501(c)3
Highest Offering: Associate Degree
Program: Occupational; 2-Year Principally Bachelor's Creditable
Accreditation: NH, SURGT

01 President .... Dr. Ann BOLMAN
05 Dean of Academics .... Ms. Kelly OEHLERKING
10 Dean of Fiscal Operations .... Ms. Heidi ANDERSON
30 Dean of Accreditation & Advancement .... Mr. Stephen BUCHHOLZ
20 Associate Dean of Academics .... Ms. Jennifer SEALS
37 Manager of Financial Aid .... Ms. Starla RUSSELL
15 Human Resources Manager .... Ms. Theresa SCHARN
07 Admissions Director .... Ms. Jill ELDER

TENNESSEE

American Baptist College (G)

1800 Baptist World Center Drive, Nashville TN 37207
County: Davidson FICE Identification: 010460
Unit ID: 219505
Telephone: (615) 256-1463 Carnegie Class: Spec/Faith
FAX Number: (615) 226-7855 Calendar System: Semester
URL: www.abcnash.edu
Established: 1924 Annual Undergrad Tuition & Fees: $9,447
Enrollment: 157 Coed
Affiliation or Control: Baptist IRS Status: 501(c)3
Highest Offering: Baccalaureate
Program: Occupational; Liberal Arts And General; Religious Emphasis
Accreditation: BI

01 President .... Dr. Forrest E. HARRIS, SR.
03 Executive Vice President .... Atty. Richard JACKSON
05 Vice President Academic Affairs .... Dr. Renita WEEMS
06 Registrar .... Ms. Pamela TABOR
10 Chief Financial Officer .... Ms. Clara A. WILLIAMS
11 Chief of Campus Operations .... Mr. Martin ESPINOSA
08 Director Library Services .... Ms. Nicole WHITE
04 Executive Assistant to President .... Ms. Mary CARPENTER
32 Dir of Student Success Services .... Ms. LaShante WALKER
09 Director of Institutional Research .... Dr. Regina PRUDE
07 Dir Admissions/Public Relations .... Ms. Dee BOMER

American National University (H)

1328 Highway 11 W, Bristol TN 37620-8530
Telephone: (423) 878-4440 Identification: 666500
Accreditation: ACICS, MAC

† Branch campus of American National University, Salem, VA.

American National University (I)

8415 Kingston Pike, Knoxville TN 37919
Telephone: (865) 539-2011 Identification: 770786

Accreditation: ACICS, MAC

† Branch campus of American National University, Salem, VA.

Aquinas College (A)

4210 Harding Pike, Nashville TN 37205-2005
County: Davidson FICE Identification: 003477
Unit ID: 219578
Telephone: (615) 297-7545 Carnegie Class: Bac/Assoc
FAX Number: (615) 279-3898 Calendar System: Semester
URL: www.aquinascollege.edu
Established: 1961 Annual Undergrad Tuition & Fees: $20,800
Enrollment: 474 Coed
Affiliation or Control: Roman Catholic IRS Status: 501(c)3
Highest Offering: Master's
Program: 2-Year Principally Bachelor's Creditable; Liberal Arts And General; Teacher Preparatory; Nursing Emphasis
Accreditation: SC, ADNUR, NUR

01 President ... Sr. Mary Sarah GALBRAITH, OP
10 Vice Pres of Finance & Admin ... Mr. Steve MCGRORY
05 Provost and Vice Pres for Academics ... Sr. Mary BENDYNA, OP
30 Vice Pres for Advancement ... Mr. Andrew SHAFER
32 Vice Pres for Student Life ... Sr. Mary Cecilia GOODRUM, OP
20 Associate Provost ... Dr. William SMART
26 Dir of Communications/Marketing ... Mr. Paul DOWNEY
07 Director of Admissions ... Ms. Connie HANSOM
06 Registrar ... Ms. Michele PRIDDY
08 Librarian ... Mr. Mark HALL
30 Director of Development ... Mr. Tom COSTA
40 Bookstore Manager ... Mr. Alan BRADLEY
66 Dean School of Nursing ... Bro. Ignatius PERKINS, OP
66 Director of ASN Nursing Program ... Mrs. Margaret DANIEL
53 Dean School of Education ... Sr. Mary Anne ZUBERBUELER, OP
37 Director of Financial Aid ... Ms. Cynthia PIANA
21 Business Manager ... Ms. Deb WELSH
35 Director of Student Affairs ... Vacant
09 Director of Institutional Research ... Dr. William SMART
29 Director of Alumni Relations ... Ms. Rachel HUDSON
18 Chief of Facilities/Physical Plant ... Mr. John WALL
88 Director of Student Learning Svcs ... Mrs. Suzette TELLI
88 Director of Catechetics ... Sr. Mary Rose BINGHAM, OP
49 Dean School of Arts and Sciences ... Dr. Aaron URBANCZYK
50 Dean School of Business ... Dr. Daniel DONNELLY
88 Dir Center for Catholic Education ... Sr. Elizabeth Anne ALLEN, OP
19 Director Security/Safety ... Mr. Alan BRADLEY
39 Director Student Housing ... Ms. Marisa QUINN
84 Director Enrollment Management ... Mr. Jesse FORTNEY
91 Director Administrative Computing ... Mr. Ron HAZEN
04 Administrative Asst to President ... Mrs. Brenda L. KINCAID
101 Secretary of the Institution/ Board ... Sr. Mary Agnes GREIFFENDORF, OP
104 Director Study Abroad ... Ms. Maria KOSHUTE
36 Career Services Coordinator ... Ms. Cathy HENDON

Argosy University, Nashville (B)

100 Centerview Drive, Suite 225,
Nashville TN 37214-3438
Telephone: (615) 525-2800 Identification: 666668
Accreditation: &WC

† Regional accreditation is carried under the parent institution in Orange, CA.

Baptist College of Health Sciences (C)

1003 Monroe Avenue, Memphis TN 38104-3199
County: Shelby FICE Identification: 034403
Unit ID: 219639
Telephone: (901) 575-2247 Carnegie Class: Spec/Health
FAX Number: (901) 572-2461 Calendar System: Trimester
URL: www.bchs.edu
Established: 1994 Annual Undergrad Tuition & Fees: $12,090
Enrollment: 1,170 Coed
Affiliation or Control: Independent Non-Profit IRS Status: 501(c)3
Highest Offering: Baccalaureate
Program: Occupational; Professional
Accreditation: SC, COARC, DMS, NMT, NURSE, RAD, RTT

01 President ... Dr. Betty S. MCGARVEY
10 Vice President Financial & Business ... Ms. Leanne SMITH
11 Vice President Admin Svcs/HR ... Dr. Adonna CALDWELL
05 Chief Academic Officer/Provost ... Dr. Loredana C. HAEGER
97 Dean General Educ & Health Studies ... Dr. Barry SCHULTZ
66 Dean Nursing ... Dr. Anne M. PLUMB
76 Dean Allied Health ... Dr. Carol WARREN
32 Dean Student Services ... Ms. Nancy REED
06 Registrar ... Ms. Denise BOWMAN
07 Director of Admissions ... Ms. Lissa MORGAN
09 Dir of Institutional Effectiveness ... Dr. Mitzi C. ROBERTS
29 Director Alumni Relations ... Ms. Megan M. BURSI
35 Director Student Services & Housing ... Mr. Jeremy WILKES
37 Director Financial Aid ... Ms. April TYSON
84 Dean Enrollment Management ... Dr. Arnold ARREDONDO
04 Administrative Asst to President ... Ms. Joyce J. PERKINS

Belmont University (D)

1900 Belmont Boulevard, Nashville TN 37212-3757
County: Davidson FICE Identification: 003479
Unit ID: 219709
Telephone: (615) 460-6000 Carnegie Class: Master's L
FAX Number: (615) 460-6446 Calendar System: Semester
URL: www.belmont.edu
Established: 1890 Annual Undergrad Tuition & Fees: $30,000
Enrollment: 7,244 Coed
Affiliation or Control: Christian Churches And Churches of Christ
IRS Status: 501(c)3
Highest Offering: Doctorate
Program: Liberal Arts And General; Teacher Preparatory; Professional
Accreditation: SC, ART, BUS, BUSA, ENGT, #LAW, MUS, NURSE, OT, PHAR, PTA, SW, TED, THEA

01 President ... Dr. Robert C. FISHER
05 Provost ... Dr. Thomas D. BURNS
07 Director of University Admissions ... Ms. Brooke DAILEY
11 Vice Pres for Admin & Univ Counsel ... Dr. Jason ROGERS
30 VP for Institutional Effectiveness ... Dr. Paula GILL
30 VP for Develop & External Relations ... Dr. Perry MOULDS
10 Vice President Finance & Operations ... Mr. Steven T. LASLEY
100 Vice President/Chief of Staff ... Dr. Susan H. WEST
42 Vice Pres Spiritual Development ... Dr. Todd LAKE
20 Assoc Provost for Academic Affairs ... Dr. Beverly SCHNELLER
32 Assoc Provost/Dean of Students ... Dr. Jeffery BURGIN
84 Assoc Provost/Dean Enrollment Svcs ... Dr. David MEE
09 Assoc Provost/Assess/Inst Research ... Dr. Tracy ROKAS
88 Assoc Provost ISGE ... Dr. Mimi BARNARD
50 Dean College of Business ... Dr. Patrick RAINES
88 Dean College Visual/Performing Arts ... Dr. Cynthia A. CURTIS
49 Dean Col of Lib Arts & Soc Sci ... Dr. Bryce SULLIVAN
81 Dean Col of Sciences & Mathematics ... Dr. Thomas SPENCE
76 Dean Col Health Sciences/Nursing ... Dr. Cathy TAYLOR
73 Dean of Col Theol & Christian Min ... Dr. Darrell GWALTNEY
61 Dean College of Law ... Dr. Alberto GONZALES
35 Asst Dean of Students ... Dr. Molly ZLOCK
35 Asst Dean of Students ... Ms. Angie BRYANT
85 Director of International Education ... Ms. Katherine SKINNER
15 Director of Human Resources ... Mrs. Sally MCKAY
37 Director of Financial Aid ... Mrs. Patricia SMEDLEY
29 Director of Alumni Relations ... Ms. Debbie COPPINGER
18 Director of Facilities Management ... Mr. Henry LACHER
19 Chief of Campus Security ... Mr. Pat CUNNINGHAM
90 Director Technology Services ... Mr. Randall REYNOLDS
06 University Registrar ... Mr. Steven REED
08 Director of Library Services ... Dr. Ernest W. HEARD, JR.
41 Athletic Director ... Mr. Michael D. STRICKLAND
40 Manager Bookstore ... Mrs. Catherine MURPHY
36 Dir Career & Professional Develop ... Mrs. Patricia JACOBS
26 Director of Communications ... Mr. Greg S. PILLON
38 Director Student Counseling ... Ms. Peg LEONARD-MARTIN
104 Director Study Abroad ... Ms. Shelley JEWELL
39 Assistant Dean of Students ... Mr. Anthony DONOVAN
43 Dir Legal Services/General Counsel ... Dr. Jason ROGERS

Bethel University (E)

325 Cherry Avenue, McKenzie TN 38201-1705
County: Carroll FICE Identification: 003480
Unit ID: 219718
Telephone: (731) 352-4000 Carnegie Class: Master's M
FAX Number: (731) 352-4069 Calendar System: Semester
URL: www.bethelu.edu
Established: 1842 Annual Undergrad Tuition & Fees: $15,714
Enrollment: 6,228 Coed
Affiliation or Control: Cumberland Presbyterian IRS Status: 501(c)3
Highest Offering: Master's
Program: 2-Year Principally Bachelor's Creditable; Liberal Arts And General; Teacher Preparatory; Professional; Business Emphasis
Accreditation: SC, ARCPA, CAATE, NURSE

01 President ... Mr. Walter BUTLER
05 Chief Academic Officer ... Dr. Phyllis CAMPBELL
49 VP College of Arts and Sciences ... Ms. Nancy BEAN
88 VP College of Public Service ... Mr. Roland COLSON
107 VP College of Prof Studies ... Ms. Kelly SANDERS-KELLEY
06 University Registrar ... Ms. Becky HAMES
10 Business Manager ... Mr. David HUSS
84 Dean of Enrollment CLA ... Mrs. Tina HODGES
30 Vice President for Development ... Dr. Dale HENRY
32 Dean of Student Development ... Mr. James STEWART
37 Director of Financial Aid ... Ms. Janie BURNS
26 Director of Public Relations ... Ms. Jennifer GLASS
38 Director Student Counseling ... Mrs. Sandy LOUDEN
42 Chaplain ... Rev. Anne HAMES
08 Library Director ... Ms. Jill WHITFILL
15 Human Resource Director ... Ms. Carolyn FLOOD
41 Athletic Director ... Mr. Dale KELLEY
09 Director of Institutional Effective ... Dr. Lisa NORRIS
29 Director Alumni Relations ... Mrs. Myra CARLOCK
76 Director of Col of Health Sciences ... Dr. Joe HAMES
88 Dir Sch of Conflict Resolution ... Mr. Clay PHILLIPS
07 Assoc Dean of Enrollment Services ... Ms. Kim HOUSTON
18 Chief Facilities/Physical Plant ... Mr. Randy TANAKA
35 Director Student Affairs ... Mr. James STEWART

Bryan College (F)

721 Bryan Drive, Dayton TN 37321-6275
County: Rhea FICE Identification: 003536
Unit ID: 219790
Telephone: (423) 775-2041 Carnegie Class: Bac/Diverse
FAX Number: (423) 775-7330 Calendar System: Semester
URL: www.bryan.edu
Established: 1930 Annual Undergrad Tuition & Fees: $23,300
Enrollment: 1,259 Coed
Affiliation or Control: Independent Non-Profit IRS Status: 501(c)3
Highest Offering: Master's
Program: Liberal Arts And General; Teacher Preparatory
Accreditation: SC, IACBE

01 President ... Dr. Stephen D. LIVESAY
04 Exec Assistant to the President ... Ms. Margaret A. LEGG
05 Academic Vice President ... Dr. Kevin L. CLAUSON
10 VP of Finance and Enrollment ... Mr. Rick J. TAPHORN
30 Vice Pres of College Advancement ... Vacant
32 VP Student Services/Ministries ... Mr. Timothy J. HOSTETLER
13 Vice Pres Information Systems ... Vacant
58 Dean Sch of Adult & Graduate Stds ... Dr. Paul RICKERT
35 Dean of Students ... Mr. Bruce MORGAN
37 Director of Financial Aid ... Mr. David L. HAGGARD
13 Director of Information Systems ... Mr. James SULLIVAN
06 Registrar ... Ms. Janet M. PIATT
08 Director of Library Sciences ... Dr. Gary N. FITSIMMONS
15 Director Personnel Services ... Mrs. Angie C. PRICE
41 Athletic Director ... Mr. Taylor HASTY
18 Director of Physical Plant ... Mr. David MORGAN
29 Director of Alumni Affairs ... Mrs. Paulakay HALL
07 Director of Admissions ... Mr. Joshua HOOD
88 Accreditation Liaison ... Mr. Samuel YOUNGS

Carson-Newman University (G)

1646 Russell Avenue, PO Box 557,
Jefferson City TN 37760-2204
County: Jefferson FICE Identification: 003481
Unit ID: 219806
Telephone: (865) 471-2000 Carnegie Class: Bac/Diverse
FAX Number: (865) 471-3502 Calendar System: Semester
URL: www.cn.edu
Established: 1851 Annual Undergrad Tuition & Fees: $25,360
Enrollment: 2,362 Coed
Affiliation or Control: Southern Baptist IRS Status: 501(c)3
Highest Offering: Doctorate
Program: Liberal Arts And General; Teacher Preparatory; Professional
Accreditation: SC, AAFCS, ART, CACREP, DIETD, MUS, NURSE, TED

01 President ... Dr. J. Randall O'BRIEN
05 Vice Pres Academic Affairs/Provost ... Dr. Paul PERCY
30 Vice President for Advancement ... Ms. Valerie I. DAY
32 Vice President Student Affairs ... Dr. Ross BRUMMETT
35 Dean of Student Affairs ... Mrs. Shelley BALL
08 Dean of Library Services ... Mr. Bruce KOCOUR
26 Exec Dir University Relations ... Mrs. Mary LEIDIG
37 Director Financial Aid ... Mrs. Danette SEALE
38 Director Counseling Services ... Mrs. Jennifer CATLETT
13 Chief Information Officer/IT ... Mrs. Valerie STEPHENS
18 Chief Facilities/Physical Plant ... Mr. Ondes WEBSTER
84 Dean of Enrollment Management ... Mr. Aaron PORTER
92 Director of Honors Program ... Dr. Brian AUSTIN
15 Director of Human Resources ... Mr. Jimmy WYATT
41 Athletic Director ... Mr. Allen MORGAN
10 Chief Financial/Business Officer ... Mrs. Martha CHAMBERS
85 Dean of Global Education ... Dr. Regina SULLIVAN
06 Registrar ... Mrs. Sheryl GRAY

Chattanooga College (H)

248 Northgate Mall Drive, Suite 130,
Chattanooga TN 37415
County: Hamilton FICE Identification: 022042
Unit ID: 220118
Telephone: (423) 624-0077 Carnegie Class: Assoc/PrivFP
FAX Number: (423) 624-1575 Calendar System: Quarter
URL: www.chattanoogacollege.edu
Established: 1968 Annual Undergrad Tuition & Fees: $10,087
Enrollment: 347 Coed
Affiliation or Control: Proprietary IRS Status: Proprietary
Highest Offering: Associate Degree
Program: Occupational
Accreditation: ACCSC

01 President ... Mr. William G. FAOUR
03 Vice President ... Mr. Toney C. MCFADDEN
37 Director Financial Aid ... Mrs. Evelyn DAVIS

Christian Brothers University (I)

650 East Parkway S, Memphis TN 38104-5581
County: Shelby FICE Identification: 003482
Unit ID: 219833
Telephone: (901) 321-3000 Carnegie Class: Master's M
FAX Number: (901) 321-3494 Calendar System: Semester
URL: www.cbu.edu
Established: 1871 Annual Undergrad Tuition & Fees: $29,316
Enrollment: 1,670 Coed
Affiliation or Control: Roman Catholic IRS Status: 501(c)3
Highest Offering: Master's
Program: Liberal Arts And General; Teacher Preparatory; Professional
Accreditation: SC, #ARCPA, ENG, NURSE, TED

01 President ... Dr. John SMARRELLI, JR.
05 Interim VP Academics & Student Life ... Dr. Paul HAUGHT
10 CFO & VP Administration ... Ms. Carolyn HEAD
30 Vice Pres Institutional Advancement ... Mr. Steve CRISMAN
84 VP for Enrollment Management ... Dr. Anne KENWORTHY
32 Dean of Students ... Ms. Karen CONWAY
13 Dean Information Technology ... Mr. David PALMER

06 Registrar ... Mrs. Melody L. NABORS
36 Director Career Center ... Mrs. Amy WARE
08 Director of Plough Library ... Ms. Kay CUNNINGHAM
07 Director of Admissions ... Ms. Kristi FORMAN
38 Director of Counseling ... Mrs. Sadie LISENBY
37 Director Financial Resources ... Mr. John LEWIS
09 Dir Inst Research/Effectiveness ... Ms. Melissa S. HANSON
39 Director Residence Life ... Mr. Alton WADE
35 Associate VP for Student Life ... Dr. Timothy DOYLE
42 Director of Ministry and Mission ... Br. Dominic EHRMANTRAUT
92 Director Honors Program ... Dr. Tracie L. BURKE
41 Athletic Director ... Mr. Brian SUMMERS
44 Director Development ... Mr. Stephen KIRKPATRICK
29 Director Alumni ... Mr. Terez WILSON
21 Controller ... Mr. Thomas COCHRAN
15 Director of Personnel ... Mr. Greg ELLER
18 Chief Facility/Physical Plant ... Mr. Philip R. YELVINGTON
19 Director of Security ... Mr. John D. LOTRIONTE
40 Director Bookstore ... Ms. Shannon DAVIS
50 Dean School of Business ... Dr. Jack HARGETT
54 Dean School of Engineering ... Dr. Pong MALASRI
49 Interim Dean School of Arts ... Dr. Scott GEIS
81 Dean School of Science ... Dr. Johnny B. HOLMES
107 Dir Graduate/Professional Stds Pgms ... Ms. Toni ROSS
58 Director Graduate Education Program ... Dr. Samantha ALPERIN
58 Director MBA Program ... Dr. Scott LAWYER
66 Director Nursing Program ... Dr. Margaret I. VEESER
88 Director Physician Assistant Stds ... Mr. Mark J. SCOTT
04 Senior Executive Asst to President ... Mrs. Donna M. FREEMAN
104 Director Study Abroad ... Dr. Emily FORSDICK
25 Chief Contracts/Grants Admin ... Mr. Robert ARNOLD
101 Secretary of the Institution/Board ... Ms. Melanie BREMER

Concorde Career College (A)

5100 Poplar Avenue, Suite 132, Memphis TN 38137-0132
County: Shelby — FICE Identification: 021571
Unit ID: 219903
Telephone: (901) 761-9494 — Carnegie Class: Assoc/PrivFP
FAX Number: (901) 761-3293 — Calendar System: Semester
URL: www.concorde.edu
Established: 1967 — Annual Undergrad Tuition & Fees: $8,227
Enrollment: 1,166 — Coed
Affiliation or Control: Proprietary — IRS Status: Proprietary
Highest Offering: Associate Degree
Program: Occupational; 2-Year Principally Bachelor's Creditable
Accreditation: COE, COARC, DA, DH, OTA, POLYT, PTAA, RAD, SURGT

01 Campus President ... Mrs. Lori SPENCER
11 Regional Vice President Operations ... Mr. Tommy STEWART

The Crown College of the Bible (B)

2307 W. Beaver Creek Drive, Powell TN 37849
County: Knox — Identification: 667141
Telephone: (865) 938-8186 — Carnegie Class: Not Classified
FAX Number: (865) 938-8188 — Calendar System: Semester
URL: thecrowncollege.com
Established: 1991 — Annual Undergrad Tuition & Fees: N/A
Enrollment: 3,800 — Coed
Affiliation or Control: Baptist — IRS Status: 501(c)3
Highest Offering: Master's
Program: Religious Emphasis
Accreditation: @TRACS

01 Founder & President ... Clarence SEXTON
05 Vice President of Academics ... Tim TOMLINSON

Cumberland University (C)

1 Cumberland Square, Lebanon TN 37087-3554
County: Wilson — FICE Identification: 003485
Unit ID: 219949
Telephone: (615) 547-1290 — Carnegie Class: Master's M
FAX Number: (615) 444-2569 — Calendar System: Semester
URL: www.cumberland.edu
Established: 1842 — Annual Undergrad Tuition & Fees: $21,310
Enrollment: 1,481 — Coed
Affiliation or Control: Independent Non-Profit — IRS Status: 501(c)3
Highest Offering: Master's
Program: Liberal Arts And General; Teacher Preparatory; Professional; Nursing Emphasis
Accreditation: SC, ACBSP, CAATE, NUR, NURSE, TED

01 President ... Dr. Paul STUMB
03 Executive Vice President ... Mr. Eddie PAWLAWSKI
05 Vice President for Academic Affairs ... Dr. William MCKEE
10 Vice President of Finance ... Ms. Judy G. JORDAN
30 Vice President of Advancement ... Mr. Rusty RICHARDSON
18 Vice Pres Facilities/IT ... Mr. Joe GRAY
32 AVP/Dean of Students ... Ms. Stephanie WALKER
66 Dean Nursing and Health Sciences ... Dr. Carol Anne BACH
100 Executive Coordinator to President ... Ms. Leslie STEELE
44 Exec Dir Development/Alumni Rels ... Mr. Jonathan HAWKINS
106 Dir Online Professional Studies ... Mr. Eddie PAWLAWSKI
08 Director Library Services ... Ms. Eloise HITCHCOCK
84 Exec Director Enrollment Services ... Ms. Beatrice LACHANCE
41 Athletic Director ... Mr. Ron PAVAN
06 Registrar ... Ms. Tammi PAVAN
15 Director Human Resources ... Ms. Annie BUTLER
13 Director of Information Technology ... Mr. William LAMBERT
09 Director of Institutional Research ... Mr. Larry F. VAUGHAN
26 Exec Director Communications ... Mr. Phillip CARTER
36 Dir of Career Services/Internships ... Mrs. Ronie MCPEAK

Daymar Institute (D)

2961 Trenton Road, Clarksville TN 37040-6718
Telephone: (931) 552-7600 — Identification: 666492
Accreditation: ACICS, PTAA

† Branch campus of Daymart Institute, Nashville, TN.

Daymar Institute (E)

415 Golden Bear Court, Murfreesboro TN 37128-5508
Telephone: (615) 217-9347 — Identification: 666392
Accreditation: ACICS

† Branch campus of Daymar Institute, Nashville, TN.

Daymar Institute (F)

340 Plus Park Boulevard, Nashville TN 37217-1056
County: Davidson — FICE Identification: 004934
Unit ID: 220002
Telephone: (615) 361-7555 — Carnegie Class: Assoc/PrivFP
FAX Number: (615) 367-2736 — Calendar System: Quarter
URL: www.daymarinstitute.edu
Established: 1884 — Annual Undergrad Tuition & Fees: $17,000
Enrollment: 89 — Coed
Affiliation or Control: Proprietary — IRS Status: Proprietary
Highest Offering: Baccalaureate
Program: Technical Emphasis
Accreditation: ACICS

01 President ... Mr. Mark A. GABIS
12 Campus Director ... Ms. Shauna MCCOY
05 Campus Dean ... Ms. Laurna TAYLOR
07 Director of Admissions ... Ms. Lynn SANDERS
10 Director of Financial Services ... Ms. Denise JERNIEAN
36 Director of Career Services ... Ms. Angela PEARROW
06 Registrar ... Mr. Ryan PALOMBO

Fisk University (G)

1000 17th Avenue N, Nashville TN 37208-3051
County: Davidson — FICE Identification: 003490
Unit ID: 220181
Telephone: (615) 329-8500 — Carnegie Class: Bac/A&S
FAX Number: N/A — Calendar System: Semester
URL: www.fisk.edu
Established: 1866 — Annual Undergrad Tuition & Fees: $19,624
Enrollment: 773 — Coed
Affiliation or Control: Independent Non-Profit — IRS Status: 501(c)3
Highest Offering: Master's
Program: Liberal Arts And General; Teacher Preparatory
Accreditation: SC, ACBSP, MUS

01 Interim President ... Mr. Frank L. SIMS
05 VP of Academic Affairs & Provost ... Dr. Rodney S. HANLEY
10 Vice President for Finance and CFO ... Ms. Sydney R. LEO
04 Exec Assistant to the President ... Mrs. Sherri B. RUCKER
30 Vice President of Inst Advancement ... Mrs. Edwina H. HAMBY
09 AVP for Inst Effectiveness Accredit ... Dr. Jason R. CURRY
32 VP of Student Engagement & Enroll ... Mr. Anthony E. JONES
20 Vice Provost Academic Initiatives ... Dr. Arnold BURGER
13 Infrastructure Manager ... Mr. Drew JENKINS
29 Exec Director of Alumni Affairs ... Mrs. Adrienne LATHAM
07 Dean of Recruitment & Admission ... Ms. Loretta MCDONALD
37 Director of Financial Aid ... Mr. Letherio ZEIGLER
06 Registrar ... Ms. Fantina CARTER
08 University Librarian ... Dr. Jessie C. SMITH
81 Dean Sch Natural Science/Math/Bus ... Dr. Lee LIMBIRD
79 Dean School Humanities/Social Sci ... Dr. Reavis MITCHELL
41 Dir of Athletics & Intramural Pgms ... Dr. Larry GLOVER
42 Dean of the Chapel ... Dr. Jason CURRY
25 Dir Sponsored Research & Programs ... Ms. Amelia HUNTER
44 Director of Planned Giving ... Ms. Sheila SMITH
18 Director of Facilities ... Mr. Norman RAPP
19 Chief/Director of Campus Safety ... Mr. Mickey WEST
96 Director of Purchasing ... Vacant
36 Director Career Development . Ms. Tashaye BYRDSONG-WOODS
38 Coordinator of Student Counseling ... Dr. Sheila PETERS
15 Director of Human Resources ... Dr. JaCenda DAVIDSON
21 Comptroller ... Mr. Warren IRONS
102 Dir Foundation/Corporate Relations ... Mr. Van PINNOCK
105 Webmaster ... Mr. George DOTSON
39 Director Student Housing ... Dr. Christopher DUKE
43 Dir Legal Services/General Counsel ... Ms. Stacey GARRETT

Fortis Institute (H)

1025 Highway 111, Cookeville TN 38501-4305
County: Putnam — FICE Identification: 023263
Unit ID: 418870
Telephone: (931) 526-3660 — Carnegie Class: Assoc/PrivFP
FAX Number: (931) 372-2603 — Calendar System: Quarter
URL: www.fortis.edu/cookeville-tennessee.php
Established: 1970 — Annual Undergrad Tuition & Fees: $15,525
Enrollment: 218 — Coed
Affiliation or Control: Proprietary — IRS Status: Proprietary
Highest Offering: Associate Degree
Program: Occupational; 2-Year Principally Bachelor's Creditable; Technical Emphasis
Accreditation: COE, MLTAD, RAD, SURGT

06 Registrar ... Ms. Wendy BANDY
07 Director of Admissions ... Mr. Brett TADLOCK
10 Chief Business Officer ... Ms. Melissa LEWIS
36 Director Student Placement ... Ms. Cindy GARRISON
37 Director Student Financial Aid ... Ms. Lisa WALLING

Fortis Institute-Nashville (I)

3354 Perimeter Hill Drive, Nashville TN 37211
Telephone: (615) 320-5917 — Identification: 770509
Accreditation: ABHES, CVT, MLTAD, RAD, SURGT, SURTEC

† Branch campus of Fortis Institute, Baton Rouge, LA.

Fountainhead College of Technology (J)

10208 Technology Drive, Knoxville TN 37932
County: Knox — FICE Identification: 007439
Unit ID: 221795
Telephone: (865) 688-9422 — Carnegie Class: Spec/Tech
FAX Number: (865) 688-2419 — Calendar System: Semester
URL: www.fountainheadcollege.edu
Established: 1947 — Annual Undergrad Tuition & Fees: $14,750
Enrollment: 123 — Coed
Affiliation or Control: Proprietary — IRS Status: Proprietary
Highest Offering: Baccalaureate
Program: Occupational; 2-Year Principally Bachelor's Creditable; Technical Emphasis
Accreditation: ACCSC

01 President ... Mr. Richard W. RACKLEY

Freed-Hardeman University (K)

158 E Main, Henderson TN 38340-2398
County: Chester — FICE Identification: 003492
Unit ID: 220215
Telephone: (731) 989-6000 — Carnegie Class: Master's M
FAX Number: N/A — Calendar System: Semester
URL: www.fhu.edu
Established: 1869 — Annual Undergrad Tuition & Fees: $21,500
Enrollment: 1,846 — Coed
Affiliation or Control: Churches Of Christ — IRS Status: 501(c)3
Highest Offering: Doctorate
Program: Liberal Arts And General; Teacher Preparatory
Accreditation: SC, ACBSP, NURSE, SW, TED, @THEOL

01 President ... Dr. Joe WILEY
04 Executive Assistant to President ... Mrs. Donna STEELE
10 Exec VP and CFO ... Dr. Dwayne WILSON
30 VP for Univ Advancement ... Mr. Dave CLOUSE
05 Provost and VP Academics ... Dr. Charles VIRES
88 VP for Spiritual Development ... Dr. Samuel JONES
32 VP Student Services ... Dr. Wayne SCOTT
84 VP for Enrollment Management ... Dr. Matt VEGA
20 Associate VP for Academics ... Dr. Vicki JOHNSON
41 Director of Athletics ... Mr. Michael MCCUTCHEN
29 Director of Alumni Relations ... Mr. Ryan MALECHA
07 Director of Admissions ... Mr. Joseph ASKEW
35 Dean of Students ... Mr. Stuart VARNER
35 Dean of Student Life ... Mr. Tony ALLEN
06 Registrar ... Mr. Jared GOTT
37 Director Student Financial Services ... Mrs. Summer JUDD
40 University Book Store Manager ... Ms. Katie NIXON
08 Library Director ... Mr. Wade OSBURN
70 Director of Social Work Program ... Mrs. Nadine MCNEAL
24 A-V Supervisor ... Mrs. Gail NASH
21 Controller ... Mr. Barry V. SMITH
45 Director of Instnl Effectiveness ... Dr. Jason BRASHIER
09 Director of Institutional Research ... Mr. Micah SMITH
15 Human Resources Coordinator ... Mr. Jay SATTERFIELD
18 Director of Facilities ... Mr. Jeff BARKMAN
26 Director Marketing & Univ Relations ... Vacant
73 Dean College of Biblical Studies ... Dr. Billy R. SMITH
50 Dean College of Business ... Mr. Mark STEINER
53 Dean College of Educ & Behav Sci ... Dr. Sharen CYPRESS
49 Dean College of Arts & Sciences ... Dr. LeAnn SELF-DAVIS
92 Dean of Honors College ... Dr. Jenny JOHNSON
23 Campus Physician ... Vacant
104 Dir of International Studies ... Dr. Jenny JOHNSON
38 Director of Counseling ... Mrs. Nicole YOUNG
36 Director of Univ Career Center ... Mr. Jim BROWN
96 Purchasing Coordinator ... Mr. Chris CURRY

Harding School of Theology (L)

1000 Cherry Road, Memphis TN 38117-5499
Telephone: (901) 761-1350 — FICE Identification: 004081
Accreditation: &NH, THEOL

† Regional accreditation is carried under Harding University, Searcy, AR.

Hiwassee College (M)

225 Hiwassee College Drive, Madisonville TN 37354
County: Monroe — FICE Identification: 003494
Unit ID: 220312
Telephone: (423) 442-2001 — Carnegie Class: Assoc/PrivNFP
FAX Number: (423) 420-1929 — Calendar System: Semester
URL: www.hiwassee.edu
Established: 1850 — Annual Undergrad Tuition & Fees: $14,918

Enrollment: 422 Coed
Affiliation or Control: United Methodist IRS Status: 501(c)3
Highest Offering: Baccalaureate
Program: Liberal Arts And General
Accreditation: TRACS, DH

01 President .... Dr. Robin J. TRICOLI
05 Vice President/Academic Dean .... Dr. Alan JACKSON
10 VP Business Affairs & Treasurer .... Mr. David WATTS
37 Director of Financial Aid .... Mr. John CAGLE
06 Registrar .... Jane DYE

Huntington College of Health Sciences (A)

117 Legacy View Way, Knoxville TN 37918
County: Knox Identification: 666971
Unit ID: 371274
Telephone: (800) 290-4226 Carnegie Class: Not Classified
FAX Number: (865) 524-8339 Calendar System: Semester
URL: www.hchs.edu
Established: 1985 Annual Undergrad Tuition & Fees: $6,000
Enrollment: 275 Coed
Affiliation or Control: Proprietary IRS Status: Proprietary
Highest Offering: Doctorate
Program: Occupational
Accreditation: DEAC

01 Chief Executive Officer .... Dr. Art PRESSER
05 Dean of Academics .... Mr. Gene BRUNO
10 Director of Finance .... Mr. Robert SCHMAEF
11 Senior Vice President .... Ms. Jennifer GREEN
07 Director of Admissions .... Ms. Kim GALYON

ITT Technical Institute (B)

5600 Brainerd Road, Suite G-1, Chattanooga TN 37411
Telephone: (423) 510-6800 Identification: 666708
Accreditation: ACICS

† Branch campus of ITT Technical Institute, Indianapolis, IN.

ITT Technical Institute (C)

7260 Goodlett Farms Parkway, Cordova TN 38016-4908
Telephone: (901) 381-0200 Identification: 666550
Accreditation: ACICS

† Branch campus of ITT Technical Institute, Indianapolis, IN.

ITT Technical Institute (D)

4721 Lake Park Drive, Suite 100, Johnson City TN 37615
Telephone: (423) 952-4400 Identification: 770663
Accreditation: ACICS

† Branch campus of ITT Technical Institute, Indianapolis, IN.

ITT Technical Institute (E)

9123 Executive Park Drive, Knoxville TN 37923
Telephone: (865) 342-2300 FICE Identification: 030734
Accreditation: ACICS

† Branch campus of ITT Technical Institute, Indianapolis, IN.

ITT Technical Institute (F)

2845 Elm Hill Pike, Nashville TN 37214-3717
Telephone: (615) 889-8700 FICE Identification: 023598
Accreditation: ACICS

† Branch campus of ITT Technical Institute, Indianapolis, IN.

John A. Gupton College (G)

1616 Church Street, Nashville TN 37203-2920
County: Davidson FICE Identification: 008859
Unit ID: 220464
Telephone: (615) 327-3927 Carnegie Class: Assoc/PrivNFP
FAX Number: (615) 321-4518 Calendar System: Semester
URL: www.guptoncollege.edu
Established: 1946 Annual Undergrad Tuition & Fees: $9,920
Enrollment: 129 Coed
Affiliation or Control: Independent Non-Profit IRS Status: 501(c)3
Highest Offering: Associate Degree
Program: Occupational; 2-Year Principally Bachelor's Creditable
Accreditation: SC, FUSER

01 President .... Mr. B. Steven SPANN
08 Library Director .... Mr. William P. BRUCE
06 Registrar .... Ms. Lisa MOFFITT
07 Director of Admissionss .... Ms. Terri PURCELL

Johnson University (H)

7900 Johnson Drive, Knoxville TN 37998-0001
County: Knox FICE Identification: 003495
Unit ID: 220473
Telephone: (865) 573-4517 Carnegie Class: Spec/Faith
FAX Number: (865) 251-2337 Calendar System: Semester
URL: www.johnsonu.edu
Established: 1893 Annual Undergrad Tuition & Fees: $12,650
Enrollment: 1,124 Coed
Affiliation or Control: Christian Churches And Churches of Christ
IRS Status: 501(c)3
Highest Offering: Doctorate
Program: Occupational; 2-Year Principally Bachelor's Creditable; Liberal Arts And General; Teacher Preparatory; Professional; Religious Emphasis
Accreditation: SC, BI

01 President .... Dr. Gary E. WEEDMAN
10 VP for Finance .... Cindy BARNARD
11 VP for Administration .... Cliff MCCARTNEY
09 VP for Institutional Effectiveness .... Dr. Mark PIERCE
05 VP for Academic Affairs/Provost .... Dr. Thomas SMITH
84 VP for Enrollment Services .... Dr. Tim WINGFIELD
30 VP for Advancement .... Philip EUBANKS
32 VP for Student Services .... David LEGG
06 Asst Provost for Academic Records .... Cindy LEWIS
88 Assoc Provost for Accreditation .... Dr. Greg LINTON
106 Assoc Provost for Online Education .... Dr. John KETCHEN
42 Dean of the Chapel .... Bill WOLF
08 Head Librarian .... Carrie Beth LOWE
15 Director Human Resources .... Ruthanne BEAM
18 Director of Plant Services .... Ben LUTZ, JR.
26 Director of Public Relations .... Kevin O'BRIEN
07 Director of Graduate Admissions .... Stacy ABERNATHY
88 Director of Program Administration .... Joy WINGFIELD
37 Assoc Dean/Director Financial Aid .... Larry RECTOR
13 IT Manager .... Matt TURNER
41 Athletic Director .... Ken UNDERWOOD

Kaplan College (I)

750 Envious Lane, Nashville TN 37217-1342
County: Davidson FICE Identification: 023262
Unit ID: 246202
Telephone: (615) 279-8300 Carnegie Class: Assoc/PrivFP
FAX Number: (615) 297-6678 Calendar System: Other
URL: www.kci-nashville.com
Established: 1981 Annual Undergrad Tuition & Fees: $15,577
Enrollment: 369 Coed
Affiliation or Control: Proprietary IRS Status: Proprietary
Highest Offering: Associate Degree
Program: Occupational
Accreditation: ACICS, DA

01 Executive Director .... Ms. Haley JOHNSON

King University (J)

1350 King College Road, Bristol TN 37620-2699
County: Sullivan FICE Identification: 003496
Unit ID: 220516
Telephone: (423) 968-4861 Carnegie Class: Master's M
FAX Number: (423) 968-4456 Calendar System: Other
URL: www.king.edu
Established: 1867 Annual Undergrad Tuition & Fees: $26,480
Enrollment: 2,897 Coed
Affiliation or Control: Presbyterian Church (U.S.A.) IRS Status: 501(c)3
Highest Offering: Doctorate
Program: Liberal Arts And General; Teacher Preparatory; Professional; Nursing Emphasis
Accreditation: SC, CAATE, NURSE

01 Interim President .... Dr. Richard A. RAY
05 Vice Pres Acad Affairs/Acad Dean .... Dr. Matthew ROBERTS
10 Vice President Finance/Operations .... Mr. James P. DONAHUE
32 Vice President for Student Affairs .... Dr. Robert A. LITTLETON
84 Assoc VP of Enrollment Mgmt .... Mr. Micah R. CREWS
26 Vice Pres Marketing .... Mrs. A. LeAnn HUGHES
08 Dean of Library Services .... Ms. Erika BRAMMER
35 Assoc VP/Dean of Student Success .... Mr. Matthew S. PELTIER
04 Executive Assistant to President .... Mrs. Gerri S. BROCKWELL
06 Registrar/Dir Regist & Records .... Mrs. Jessica SWINEY
30 Chief Development Officer .... Mr. John W. KING
09 Director of Institutional Research .... Mr. J. Kevin DEFORD
30 Director of Development .... Mrs. Denise ASBURY
42 Chaplain .... Dr. Brian ALDERMAN
21 Director of Business Operations .... Mr. Thomas R. LARSON
36 Director of Career Development .... Ms. Donna H. FELTY
41 Athletic Director .... Mr. J. David HICKS
38 Director of Counseling .... Mr. Charles S. THOMPSON
88 Sports Information Director .... Mr. Travis L. CHELL
40 Bookstore Manager .... Ms. Susan D. MARSHALL
37 Director Student Financial Aid .... Mr. Richard BRAND
18 Chief Facilities/Physical Plant .... Mr. Todd THOMAS
92 Director of Honors Program .... Dr. Craig STREETMAN
27 Director Marketing & Communications .... Ms. Sarah CLEVINGER
27 Assoc Director of Communication .... Mrs. Laura K. BOGGAN

Lane College (K)

545 Lane Avenue, Jackson TN 38301-4598
County: Madison FICE Identification: 003499
Unit ID: 220598
Telephone: (731) 426-7500 Carnegie Class: Bac/A&S
FAX Number: (731) 427-3987 Calendar System: Semester
URL: www.lanecollege.edu
Established: 1882 Annual Undergrad Tuition & Fees: $9,780
Enrollment: 1,262 Coed
Affiliation or Control: Christian Methodist Episcopal IRS Status: 501(c)3
Highest Offering: Baccalaureate
Program: Liberal Arts And General
Accreditation: SC, @TEAC

01 President .... Dr. Logan C. HAMPTON
03 Executive Vice President .... Dr. Moses GOLDMON
05 Int Vice President Academic Affairs .... Dr. Michelle CURTAIN
10 Vice President Business & Finance .... Mr. Melvin R. HAMLETT
32 Vice President Student Affairs .... Ms. Sherrill B. SCOTT
30 Vice Pres Inst Advance/Dir Alum Aff .... Mr. Richard H. DONNELL
04 Exec Assistant to the President .... Ms. Darlette C. SAMUELS
18 Chief Facilities/Physical Plant .... Mr. Michael BATES
26 Chief Public Relations Officer .... Ms. Darlette C. SAMUELS
09 Director Institutional Research .... Ms. Charlise ANDERSON
08 Librarian .... Ms. Lan WANG
07 Director of Admissions .... Ms. Evelyn BROWN
06 Registrar .... Mr. Terry W. BLACKMON
37 Director of Financial Aid .... Mr. Tony CALHOUN
20 Director Academic Assessment .... Dr. Juanita MORRIS
84 Director Enrollment Management .... Dr. Monica CLAYBORNE-SCOTT
89 Director of Freshman Studies .... Vacant
96 Director of Purchasing .... Ms. Troneka DUNLAP
36 Director Placement Services .... Ms. Virginia S. CRUMP
13 Assoc VP Information Technology ... Mr. Earnest L. MITCHELL, III
15 Director of Personnel .... Ms. Juanita MARSHALL
19 Director Security .... Mr. Ernest BOYD
40 Director Bookstore .... Mr. Jeremy MORRIS
19 Director of Safety .... Ms. Aleshia COX-THOMPSON
20 Associate Academic Officer .... Vacant
21 Associate Business Officer .... Mr. Duan ROBINSON
41 Director of Athletics .... Ms. Penny MINTER
29 Director Alumni Relations .... Ms. Tori HALIBURTON
35 Dean of Students .... Mr. William SMITH
27 Chief Information Officer .... Vacant
38 Director Student Counseling .... Dr. April SMITH

L'Ecole Culinaire Memphis (L)

1245 North Germantown Parkway, Cordova TN 38016
Telephone: (901) 754-7115 Identification: 770841
Accreditation: ACCSC

† Branch campus of Vatterott College-Des Moines, Des Moines, IA.

Lee University (M)

1120 N Ocoee Street, Cleveland TN 37320-3450
County: Bradley FICE Identification: 003500
Unit ID: 220613
Telephone: (423) 614-8100 Carnegie Class: Master's M
FAX Number: (423) 614-8083 Calendar System: Semester
URL: www.leeuniversity.edu
Established: 1918 Annual Undergrad Tuition & Fees: $15,000
Enrollment: 5,097 Coed
Affiliation or Control: Church Of God IRS Status: 501(c)3
Highest Offering: Beyond Master's But Less Than Doctorate
Program: Liberal Arts And General; Teacher Preparatory
Accreditation: SC, ACBSP, CAATE, MUS, TED

01 President .... Dr. C. Paul CONN
04 Executive Assistant to President .... Mrs. Stephanie TAYLOR
10 Vice President Business & Finance .... Mr. Chris CONINE
05 Vice President for Academic Affairs .... Dr. Deborah MURRAY
84 Vice President for Enrollment .... Mr. Phil COOK
26 VP for University Relations .... Dr. Jerome HAMMOND
32 VP for Student Development .... Mr. Mike HAYES
13 VP for Information Services .... Dr. Jayson VAN HOOK
21 Comptroller .... Mr. Duane PACE
37 Director of Financial Aid .... Mrs. Marian DILL
35 Dean of Students .... Mr. Alan MCCLUNG
15 Director of Human Resources .... Mrs. Ann MCELRATH
14 Director of IT Operations .... Mr. Chris GOLDEN
14 Director of IT Systems .... Mr. Nate TUCKER
29 Director of Alumni Relations .... Mrs. Patti CAWOOD
39 Director of Residential Life .... Ms. Tracey CARLSON
06 Registrar .... Ms. Cathy THOMPSOM
21 Bursar .... Ms. Kristy HARNER
08 Librarian .... Dr. Louis MORGAN
42 Director of Campus Ministries .... Rev. Jimmy HARPER
25 Director of Grants .... Mrs. Vanessa HAMMOND
19 Director of Campus Safety .... Mr. Matt BRINKMAN
23 Director of Health Services .... Mr. Mickey MOORE
27 Director of Public Information .... Mr. Brian CONN
73 Dean School of Religion .... Dr. Terry CROSS
49 Dean College of Arts & Sciences .... Dr. Matthew MELTON
53 Dean College of Education .... Dr. William ESTES
64 Dean School of Music .... Dr. William GREEN
66 Dean School of Nursing .... Dr. Sara CAMPBELL
51 Exec Dir of Div of Adult Learning .... Dr. Joshua BLACK
07 Director of Graduate Enrollment .... Ms. Vicki GLASSCOCK
38 Director Counseling & Testing .... Dr. David QUAGLIANA
18 Director of Physical Plant .... Mr. Larry BERRY
41 Athletic Director .... Mr. Larry CARPENTER
104 Director of Global Perspectives .... Mrs. Angeline MCMULLIN
36 Director of Calling and Career .... Vacant
07 Director of Admissions .... Mr. Darren ECHOLS
09 Director of Institutional Research .... Dr. Stacey TUCKER

LeMoyne-Owen College (N)

807 Walker Avenue, Memphis TN 38126-6595
County: Shelby FICE Identification: 003501
Unit ID: 220604
Telephone: (901) 435-1000 Carnegie Class: Bac/Diverse
FAX Number: (901) 435-1699 Calendar System: Semester
URL: www.loc.edu

Established: 1862 Annual Undergrad Tuition & Fees: $10,680
Enrollment: 1,006 Coed
Affiliation or Control: Multiple Protestant Denominations IRS Status: 501(c)3
Highest Offering: Baccalaureate
Program: Liberal Arts And General; Teacher Preparatory
Accreditation: SC, TED

01 President .... Mr. Johnnie B. WATSON
05 VP/Chief Academic Officer .... Dr. Cheryl GOLDEN
10 Chief Financial Officer .... Mr. Jim DUGGER
88 Director Title III Administration .... Ms. Shirley HILL
32 Dean of Students .... Ms. Edythe COBB
30 Exec Dir Institutional Advancement .... Mr. Roger BROWN
84 Exec Dir Strategic Enrollment Mgmt .... Dr. Delphia HARRIS
15 Director of Human Resources .... Mr. Michael WASHINGTON
08 Librarian .... Ms. Annette BERHE
37 Director Student Financial Services .... Ms. Phyllis TORRY
06 Registrar .... Mr. Addie HARVEY
36 Director Career Services/Placement .... Dr. Denita HEDGEMAN
29 Director of Alumni Relations .... Ms. Frankie JEFFRIES
13 Director Information Technology .... Mr. Robert MOORE
21 Controller .... Ms. Colleen GIBSON
09 Director Institutional Research .... Mr. Reoungeneria MCFARLAND
92 Director Dubois Honors Program .... Mr. Dorsey PATTERSON
35 Director Student Activities .... Ms. Felecia FOSTER
50 Chair Div Business & Econ Devel .... Dr. Katherine CAUSEY
53 Chair Education Division .... Dr. Ralph CALHOUN
57 Chair Div Fine Arts & Humanities .... Mr. Claybourne FOSTER
65 Chair Div Natural & Math Science .... Dr. Sherry PAINTER
83 Chair Div Social & Behavioral Sci .... Mr. Michael ROBINSON
38 Director Student Counseling .... Mr. Tony WHITSON
26 Dir Public Relations & Marketing .... Ms. Daphne J. THOMAS
41 Director of Athletics .... Mr. Clint JACKSON
11 Director Administrative Services .... Mr. Jesse CHATMAN
88 Exec Director Engaged Student Learn .... Dr. Linda WHITE
07 Director of Admissions .... Mr. Samuel KING
04 Administrative Asst to President .... Ms. Velma GRAY
18 Chief Facilities/Physical Plant .... Mr. Anthony COWAN
39 Director Student Housing .... Ms. Carolyn BISHOP

Lincoln College of Technology Nashville (A)

1524 Gallatin Road, Nashville TN 37206-3298
County: Davidson FICE Identification: 007440
Unit ID: 221148
Telephone: (615) 226-3990 Carnegie Class: Assoc/PrivFP
FAX Number: (615) 262-8466 Calendar System: Other
URL: www.lincolncollegeoftechnology.com
Established: 1919 Annual Undergrad Tuition & Fees: $28,067
Enrollment: 2,834 Coed
Affiliation or Control: Proprietary IRS Status: Proprietary
Highest Offering: Associate Degree
Program: Occupational; Technical Emphasis
Accreditation: ACCSC

01 President .... Mr. Jim COAKLEY
05 Academic Dean .... Ms. Jackie RODDY
07 Vice President of Admissions .... Mr. Shayne PULVER
37 Director of Financial Aid .... Mr. Chris BIDDLE
06 Registrar .... Mr. Gary WHITE

Lincoln Memorial University (B)

6965 Cumberland Gap Parkway, Harrogate TN 37752-1901
County: Claiborne FICE Identification: 003502
Unit ID: 220631
Telephone: (423) 869-3611 Carnegie Class: Master's L
FAX Number: (423) 869-6250 Calendar System: Semester
URL: www.lmunet.edu
Established: 1897 Annual Undergrad Tuition & Fees: $20,546
Enrollment: 3,735 Coed
Affiliation or Control: Independent Non-Profit IRS Status: 501(c)3
Highest Offering: Doctorate
Program: 2-Year Principally Bachelor's Creditable; Liberal Arts And General; Teacher Preparatory; Professional
Accreditation: SC, ACBSP, ADNUR, ANEST, ARCPA, CAATE, CACREP, CEA, #LAW, MT, NUR, OSTEO, SW, TED, @VET

01 President .... Dr. B. James DAWSON
11 VP for Administration .... Ms. Lisa B. COX
30 VP University Advancement .... Ms. Cynthia L. WHITT
05 Provost/Vice Pres for Acad Affairs .... Dr. Clayton HESS
10 Vice President of Finance .... Ms. Christy GRAHAM
61 Interim VP/Dean School of Law .... Mr. Matthew LYON
84 VP Pres Student Enrollment Svcs .... Dr. James (Chip) WEISGERBER
53 Dean of School of Education .... Dr. Michael CLYBURN
81 Dean of Mathematics & Sciences .... Dr. Amiel JARSTFER
66 Dean School of Nursing .... Dr. Mary Anne MODRCIN
50 Dean School of Business .... Dr. James HURLEY
32 Dean of Students .... Vacant
04 Exec Assistant to the President .... Mrs. Janet SMITH
37 Executive Director of Financial Aid .... Ms. Tammy TOMFOHRDE
09 Director of Institutional Research .... Mr. John MOORE
41 Athletic Director .... Vacant
18 Director Properties/Physical Plant .... Mr. Rodney COCHRAN
15 Director of Human Resources .... Ms. Libby KING
96 Director Purchasing .... Ms. Pat TENNYSON
06 Registrar .... Ms. Helen BAILEY
42 University Chaplain .... Vacant
43 Legal Counsel .... Mr. Mark CUSHING
13 Chief Information Officer .... Mr. Jason MCCONNELL
26 Senior Director of Marketing .... Mrs. Kate M. REAGAN
29 Director Alumni Services .... Vacant
40 Bookstore Manager .... Mr. Nathan ADKINS
49 Dean of Arts/Humanities/Social Sci .... Dr. Martin SELLERS
108 Director of Assessment .... Dr. Travis WRIGHT

Lipscomb University (C)

One University Park Dr., Nashville TN 37204-3951
County: Davidson FICE Identification: 003486
Unit ID: 219976
Telephone: (615) 966-1000 Carnegie Class: Master's L
FAX Number: (615) 966-1798 Calendar System: Semester
URL: www.lipscomb.edu
Established: 1891 Annual Undergrad Tuition & Fees: $28,614
Enrollment: 4,489 Coed
Affiliation or Control: Churches Of Christ IRS Status: 501(c)3
Highest Offering: Doctorate
Program: Liberal Arts And General; Teacher Preparatory; Professional
Accreditation: SC, ACBSP, CACREP, DIETD, DIETI, ENG, MUS, NUR, PHAR, SW, TED, THEOL

01 President .... Dr. L. Randolph LOWRY, III
05 Provost .... Dr. W. Craig BLEDSOE
32 Senior VP Student Life .... Dr. Scott MCDOWELL
10 Senior VP Finance & Administration .... Mr. Danny TAYLOR
53 Int VP & Dean Col of Education .... Dr. Deborah BOYD
88 VP University Relations .... Mr. Walt LEAVER
29 VP Development & Alumni Relations .... Vacant
84 VP Enrollment Management .... Mr. Rick HOLAWAY
86 VP External Affairs .... Dr. John LOWRY
26 Sr VP Communications & Marketing .... Ms. Deby K. SAMUELS
42 Vice President for Church Services .... Dr. Scott SAGER
13 Vice President Info Technology/CIO .... Mr. Mike GREEN
20 Vice Prov Acad Admin & Fin Affairs .... Dr. Susan C. GALBREATH
100 Senior Advisor to the President .... Dr. Jim THOMAS
43 General Counsel .... Dr. David WILSON
30 Senior Development Counsel .... Mr. Dale ARMSTRONG
41 Director of Athletics .... Mr. Philip HUTCHESON
20 Associate Provost Academic Support .... Mr. Steve PREWITT
58 Vice Provost for Grad Studies .... Dr. Randy BOULDIN
88 Assoc Prov for Inst Effectiveness .... Dr. Elaine GRIFFIN
88 Assoc Provost Sponsored Programs .... Vacant
79 Dean College of Arts & Sciences .... Dr. Norma BURGESS
73 Dean College of Bible & Ministry .... Dr. C. Leonard ALLEN
50 Int Dean College of Business .... Dr. Ray ELDRIDGE
81 Dean College of Engineering .... Dr. Justin MYRICK
67 Dean College of Pharmacy .... Dr. Roger DAVIS
107 Int Dean College of Prof Studies .... Dr. Nina MOREL
55 Dean School of Computing/Technology .... Dr. Fortune MHLANGA
66 Exec Assoc Dean Sch of Nursing .... Dr. Beth YOUNGBLOOD
35 Dean of Student Life .... Dr. Sam SMITH
21 Associate VP Finance .... Mr. Darrell DUNCAN
102 Assoc VP Donor Rel & Stewardship .... Mr. David ENGLAND
44 Asst VP Annual Giving & Advanc Svcs .... Mrs. Carrie THOMPSON
06 Registrar .... Ms. Teresa WILLIAMS
37 Director of Financial Aid .... Ms. Tiffany SUMMERS
08 Director of Library Services .... Ms. Sandra PARHAM
19 Dir of Campus Security & Safety .... Mr. Darrin BELLOWS
36 Director of Career Development Ctr .... Mrs. Monica WENTWORTH
88 Senior Director of Student Success .... Dr. Brian MAST
88 Director of Student Advocacy .... Ms. Carla BROOKINS
55 Int Dean Adult Degree Program .... Dr. Nina MOREL
73 Assoc Dir Hazelip Sch of Theology .... Dr. Mark BLACK
88 Dir of Grad Exercise & Nutrit Sci .... Dr. Karen ROBICHAUD
83 Chair Grad Studies in Psychology .... Dr. Shanna RAY
88 Managing Dir Inst for ConflictMgmt .... Dr. Steve JOINER
88 Dir Inst for Christian Spirituality .... Dr. Kris MILLER
88 Dir Inst for Law Justice & Society .... Dr. Randy SPIVEY
88 Found Dir Inst for Civic Leadership .... Ms. Linda SCHACHT
88 Found Dir Inst for Sustain Practice .... Mr. Dodd GALBREATH
88 Director of Global Learning .... Mr. Michael WINEGEART
38 Director Counseling Center .... Dr. Frank SCOTT
88 Senior Campus Minister .... Mr. Steve DAVIDSON
28 Asst Dean Intercultural Development .... Ms. Lisa STEELE
09 Director of Institutional Research .... Mr. Matt REHBEIN
15 Director Human Resources .... Mr. Stan LOWERY
18 Director of Campus Plant .... Mr. Jeff WILSON
96 Director of Procurment .... Ms. Deidra PIATT
105 Director of Information Security .... Mr. Dave WAGNER

Martin Methodist College (D)

433 W Madison Street, Pulaski TN 38478-2799
County: Giles FICE Identification: 003504
Unit ID: 220701
Telephone: (931) 363-9800 Carnegie Class: Bac/Diverse
FAX Number: (931) 363-9818 Calendar System: Semester
URL: www.martinmethodist.edu
Established: 1870 Annual Undergrad Tuition & Fees: $21,850
Enrollment: 1,018 Coed
Affiliation or Control: United Methodist IRS Status: 501(c)3
Highest Offering: Master's
Program: Liberal Arts And General
Accreditation: SC, NURSE

01 President .... Dr. Ted R. BROWN
05 Vice President of Academic Affairs .... Dr. Judy B. CHEATHAM
10 VP for Finance & Administration .... Mr. David J. STEPHENS
32 VP Campus Life/Enrollment Mgmt .... Mr. Robby C. SHELTON
30 Vice Pres for College Advancement .... Mr. David JONES
06 Registrar .... Mrs. Casey CAPPS
41 Athletic Director .... Mr. Jeff N. BAIN
42 Chaplain .... Rev. Laura KIRKPATRICK
08 Librarian .... Mr. Richard MADDEN
40 Director of Bookstore .... Mrs. Margaret W. JACKSON
29 Alumni Affairs Director .... Mrs. Edna LUNA
04 Assistant to the President .... Mrs. Kim W. HARRISON
84 VP for Campus Life/Enrollment .... Mr. Robby SHELTON
15 Director Personnel Services .... Mr. James R. HLUBB
21 Controller .... Ms. Rhonda CLINARD
37 Director Student Financial Aid .... Mrs. Emma HLUBB
18 Chief Facilities/Physical Plant .... Mr. Fred HYDE
26 Director of Public Relations .... Mr. Grant VOSBURGH
38 Dir Student Counseling/Career/Svcs .... Ms. Doris F. WOSSUM
85 Director Foreign Students .... Mrs. Robin HOOD
13 Director of Technology .... Mr. Edward MARTIN
09 Director of Institutional Research .... Dr. Dennis HASKINS
11 Chief of Administration .... Ms. Mae SANDERS
19 Director Security/Safety .... Mr. Dean GLOSSUP

Maryville College (E)

502 E Lamar Alexander Parkway, Maryville TN 37804-5907
County: Blount FICE Identification: 003505
Unit ID: 220710
Telephone: (865) 981-8000 Carnegie Class: Bac/A&S
FAX Number: (865) 981-8010 Calendar System: Semester
URL: www.maryvillecollege.edu
Established: 1819 Annual Undergrad Tuition & Fees: $32,104
Enrollment: 1,213 Coed
Affiliation or Control: Presbyterian Church (U.S.A.) IRS Status: 501(c)3
Highest Offering: Baccalaureate
Program: Liberal Arts And General; Teacher Preparatory; Professional
Accreditation: SC, MUS

01 President .... Dr. William T. BOGART
04 Assistant to President .... Ms. Laura M. CASE
05 Vice President & Dean of College .... Dr. Barbara WELLS
10 VP of Finance & Administration .... Mr. Jeffery S. INGLE
32 Vice President & Dean of Students .... Ms. Vandy KEMP
84 Vice President for Enrollment .... Dr. Dolph HENRY
30 VP for Institutional Advancement .... Ms. Suzy BOOKER
09 Associate Dean & Dir of IR .... Dr. Martha P. CRAIG
07 Director of Admissions .... Ms. Cyndi SWEET
35 Assistant Dean of Students .... Ms. Allison NORRIS
21 Controller .... Ms. Julie RAMSEY
39 Director Campus Life .... Ms. Kristin GOURLEY
26 Exec Dir for Mktg & Communications .... Ms. Karen ELDRIDGE
85 Director of International Education .... Ms. Kirsten SHEPPARD
06 Registrar .... Ms. Kathi WILSON
13 Director of Information Technology .... Mr. John BERRY
88 Director of Learning Services .... Ms. Kim D. OCHSENBEIN
90 Dir of Instructional Technology .... Dr. Steven JAMES
36 Director of the Career Center .... Ms. Christy MCDONALD
37 Director of Financial Aid .... Ms. Melena VERITY
41 Athletic Director .... Ms. Kandis SCHRAM
08 Director of the Library .... Ms. Angela QUICK
18 Director of Physical Plant .... Mr. Andy K. MCCALL
42 Campus Minister .... Rev. Anne MCKEE
15 Director of Human Resources .... Ms. Keri LANAGAN
38 Director of Counseling .... Mr. Bruce HOLT
88 Director of Development .... Mr. Eric BELLAH
44 Director of Maryville Fund .... Dr. Louis DIEZ
29 Dir of Alumni Affairs & Stewardship .... Ms. Angela MILLER
22 Director of Multicultural Affairs .... Mr. Larry ERVIN
88 Dir New Opportunity Sch for Women .... Ms. Linda EULAND
88 Director of the Maryville Symposium .... Dr. Ronald WELLS
40 Bookstore Manager .... Mr. Jeff HUFFMAN
88 Gen Mgr Clayton Center for the Arts .... Mr. Blake SMITH
19 Director of Safety & Security .... Mr. Jack PIEPENBRING

Meharry Medical College (F)

1005 Dr. D. B. Todd Jr. Boulevard, Nashville TN 37208-3501
County: Davidson FICE Identification: 003506
Unit ID: 220792
Telephone: (615) 327-6111 Carnegie Class: Spec/Med
FAX Number: (615) 327-6540 Calendar System: Semester
URL: www.mmc.edu
Established: 1876 Annual Graduate Tuition & Fees: $45,580
Enrollment: 803 Coed
Affiliation or Control: Independent Non-Profit IRS Status: 501(c)3
Highest Offering: Doctorate; No Undergraduates
Program: Professional
Accreditation: SC, DENT, MED, PH

01 President/Chief Executive Ofcr .... Dr. James E.K HILDRETH
63 Sr VP Health/Dean Sch of Medicine .... Dr. Marquetta FAULKNER
32 Int Assoc Dean Student/Academic Aff .... Dr. Mildred D. COLLINS
30 Sr VP Institutional Advancement .... Mr. Robert S. POOLE
10 Senior Vice President & CFO .... Mrs. LaMel BANDY-NEAL
35 Sr VP Student & Faculty Affairs .... Dr. A. Dexter SAMUELS
45 Vice President for Research .... Dr. Russell POLAND
31 Int Asst VP External Affairs .... Mr. Lawrence HALL, JR.
13 Assoc VP Information Technology .... Mr. Andrew JACKSON
15 Assoc Vice Pres Human Resources .... Mr. Mark SMITH
26 SVP Marketing/Communications .... Ms. Janet CALDWELL

21 Assoc Vice Pres Financial Systems .... Mr. Larry HOLDEN
46 Assoc VP for Research-Grants Mgmt .... Vacant
44 Assoc VP Development .... Mrs. Linda WITT
25 Asst Vice Pres Grants & Contracts .... Mr. George WILLIAMS
43 SVP General Counsel/Corp Sec/Sr VP .... Mrs. Ivanetta DAVIS-SAMUELS
58 Dean Graduate Studies and Research .... Dr. Maria DE FATIMA LIMA
51 Director Lifelong Learning .... Dr. Allyson FLEMING
76 Dean Allied Health Professions .... Vacant
52 Dean School of Dentistry .... Dr. Cherae FARMER-DIXON
29 Executive Director Alumni Affairs .... Dr. Henry MOSES
07 Int Dir Admissions & Recruitment .... Dr. Allyson F. FLEMING
08 Director of Library .... Dr. Fatima MNCUBE-BARNES
19 Director Campus Safety & Security .... Ms. Theresa MCKINNON
37 Director Student Financial Aid .... Ms. Barbara THARPE
09 Director Institutional Research .... Dr. Chau-Kuang CHEN
100 Chief of Staff .... Mrs. Sandra ANDERSON-WILLIAMS
18 Director Facilities .... Mr. George N. KELLY
38 Director Counseling Center .... Ms. Sharda D. MISHRA
06 Registrar .... Ms. Sonja COGGINS VIENTOS
45 Dir Inst Effectiveness & Planning .... Dr. Juanita BUFORD

Memphis College of Art (A)

1930 Poplar Avenue, Memphis TN 38104

County: Shelby | FICE Identification: 003507 | Unit ID: 220808
Telephone: (901) 272-5100 | Carnegie Class: Spec/Arts
FAX Number: (901) 272-5104 | Calendar System: Semester
URL: www.mca.edu
Established: 1936 | Annual Undergrad Tuition & Fees: $28,870
Enrollment: 435 | Coed
Affiliation or Control: Independent Non-Profit | IRS Status: 501(c)3
Highest Offering: Master's
Program: Professional; Fine Arts Emphasis
Accreditation: SC, ART

01 President .... Dr. Ronald L. JONES
05 Dean & VP Academic Affairs .... Mr. Remy MILLER
10 VP Operation/Chf Financial Ofcr .... Mr. George NINAN
30 Vice President College Advancement .... Ms. Laura HINE
32 Vice President Student Affairs .... Ms. Susan S. MILLER
26 Vice Pres Communications/Mrktng .... Ms. Carrie CORBETT
21 Assoc Vice Pres Finance & Admin .... Mr. Jonathan WELDEN
08 Librarian .... Mr. Derrick CASEY
04 Assistant to President .... Ms. Anne BALLAM
07 Dean of Admissions .... Ms. Annette JAMES-MOORE
35 Director Student Life .... Ms. Ashley WALKER
37 Director Financial Aid .... Mr. Aaron WHITE
06 Registrar .... Mr. Sean SCOTT
36 Director Career Services .... Ms. Carrie Allison BROOKS
19 Director Campus Security .... Mr. Mark KIMBALL
109 Business Office Manager .... Ms. Heather RAGLAND
31 Director Community Education .... Ms. Cecelia PALAZOLA

Memphis Theological Seminary (B)

168 East Parkway S at Union, Memphis TN 38104-4395

County: Shelby | FICE Identification: 010529 | Unit ID: 220871
Telephone: (901) 458-8232 | Carnegie Class: Spec/Faith
FAX Number: (901) 452-4051 | Calendar System: Semester
URL: www.memphisseminary.edu
Established: 1852 | Annual Graduate Tuition & Fees: $15,652
Enrollment: 286 | Coed
Affiliation or Control: Cumberland Presbyterian | IRS Status: 501(c)3
Highest Offering: Doctorate; No Undergraduates
Program: Professional; Religious Emphasis
Accreditation: SC, THEOL

01 President .... Dr. Daniel J. EARHEART-BROWN
05 Vice President Academic Affs & Dean .... Dr. Robert S. WOOD
30 Vice President of Advancement .... Dr. Keith GASKIN
08 Librarian .... Ms. Jane K. WILLIAMSON
51 Assoc Dean Continuing Education .... Mr. Pete GATHJE
10 Vice President of Operations/ CFO .... Mrs. Cassandra F. PRICE-PERRY
32 Director of Student Services .... Dr. Barry L. ANDERSON
108 Assoc Dean Inst Effectiveness .... Dr. Gail ROBINSON
06 Dir Acad Rec/Regist & Accreditation .... Dr. Gail D. ROBINSON
26 Communications Coordinator .... Mr. Baxter BUCK

Mid-America Baptist Theological Seminary (C)

2095 Appling Road, Cordova TN 38016-4911

County: Shelby | FICE Identification: 029172 | Unit ID: 220914
Telephone: (901) 751-8453 | Carnegie Class: Not Classified
FAX Number: (901) 751-8454 | Calendar System: Semester
URL: www.mabts.edu
Established: 1972 | Annual Undergrad Tuition & Fees: $6,290
Enrollment: 411 | Coed
Affiliation or Control: Independent Non-Profit | IRS Status: 501(c)3
Highest Offering: Doctorate
Program: 2-Year Principally Bachelor's Creditable; Teacher Preparatory; Professional
Accreditation: SC

01 President .... Dr. Michael R. SPRADLIN
03 Executive Vice President .... Dr. Bradley THOMPSON
05 Academic Vice President .... Dr. Timothy SEAL
10 Vice Pres for Finance & Operations .... Mr. Randy REDD
30 Chief Development Officer .... Mr. Duffy GUYTON
20 Dean of Masters & Associate Pgm .... Dr. Kirk KILPATRICK
12 Director NE Branch .... Dr. Michael HAGGARD
06 Registrar .... Mrs. Rose MINK
08 Director of Library Services .... Mr. Terrence BROWN
42 Director of Practical Missions .... Dr. Kirk KILPATRICK
07 Director of Admissions .... Dr. Tanner HICKMAN
04 Admin Assistant to the President .... Mrs. Maria WOOTEN
18 Supt of Buildings & Grounds .... Mr. Gene APPLEBURY
40 Manager Bookstore .... Mr. David FOUST

Mid-South Christian College (D)

PO Box 181056, Memphis TN 38181

County: Shelby | Identification: 667046
Telephone: (901) 375-4400 | Carnegie Class: Not Classified
FAX Number: (901) 375-4085 | Calendar System: Semester
URL: www.midsouthcc.org
Established: 1959 | Annual Undergrad Tuition & Fees: $6,188
Enrollment: 21 | Coed
Affiliation or Control: Independent Non-Profit | IRS Status: 501(c)3
Highest Offering: Baccalaureate
Program: Religious Emphasis
Accreditation: BI

01 President .... Mr. Larry GRIFFIN
05 Academic Dean .... Dr. Robert GRIFFIN
32 Director of Student Services .... Mr. Brent LINN
30 Chief Development Officer .... Mr. John BLIFFEN
04 Administrative Asst to President .... Mrs. Jane GIBSON
06 Registrar .... Mr. Keith GRAHAM
08 Head Librarian .... Mrs. Judi HOMAN
10 Chief Business Officer .... Mrs. Renae MASK
37 Director Student Financial Aid .... Mrs. Mary JACKSON

Middle Tennessee School of Anesthesia (E)

PO Box 417, 315 Hospital Drive, Madison TN 37116-6414

County: Davidson | FICE Identification: 007783 | Unit ID: 220996
Telephone: (615) 868-6503 | Carnegie Class: Spec/Health
FAX Number: (615) 868-9885 | Calendar System: Quarter
URL: www.mtsa.edu
Established: 1950 | Annual Graduate Tuition & Fees: $33,100
Enrollment: 198 | Coed
Affiliation or Control: Independent Non-Profit | IRS Status: 501(c)3
Highest Offering: Doctorate; No Undergraduates
Program: Professional; Nursing Emphasis
Accreditation: SC, ANEST

01 President .... Dr. Kenneth L. SCHWAB
05 Dean/Program Administrator .... Dr. Christopher P. HULIN
10 VP for Finance & Administration .... Sam L. MINTEN
30 VP for Advancement & Alumni .... James B. CLOSSER
20 Assistant Program Administrator .... Dr. Rachel M. BROWN
88 Dir of Inst Effectiveness & LR .... Dr. Amy C. GIDEON
07 Coordinator of Admissions .... Pam NIMMO

Miller-Motte Technical College (F)

6397 Lee Highway, Suite 100, Chattanooga TN 37421

Telephone: (423) 510-9675 | Identification: 770781
Accreditation: ACICS, MAC, SURGT

† Branch campus of Miller-Motte Technical College, Clarksville, TN.

Miller-Motte Technical College (G)

1820 Business Park Drive, Clarksville TN 37040-6023

County: Montgomery | FICE Identification: 026142 | Unit ID: 382771
Telephone: (931) 553-0071 | Carnegie Class: Assoc/PrivFP
FAX Number: (931) 552-2916 | Calendar System: Quarter
URL: www.miller-motte.edu
Established: 1916 | Annual Undergrad Tuition & Fees: $9,900
Enrollment: 404 | Coed
Affiliation or Control: Proprietary | IRS Status: Proprietary
Highest Offering: Associate Degree
Program: Occupational; Technical Emphasis
Accreditation: ACICS, #COARC, MAC, POLYT, SURGT

01 Campus Director .... Ms. Kala FIELDER
05 Director of Education .... Ms. Shannon MANZELLA
37 Financial Aid Director .... Ms. Debbie STRATMAN
36 Director of Career Development .... Mr. John MCCASLIN
07 Director of Admissions .... Ms. Gail MASSEY

Miller-Motte Technical College (H)

1515 North Gallatin Pike, Madison TN 37115

Telephone: (615) 859-8090 | Identification: 770782
Accreditation: ACICS

† Branch campus of Miller-Motte Technical College, Clarksville, TN.

Milligan College (I)

2010 Milligan College PO Box 500, Milligan College TN 37682-4000

County: Carter | FICE Identification: 003511 | Unit ID: 221014
Telephone: (423) 461-8700 | Carnegie Class: Bac/Diverse
FAX Number: (423) 461-8755 | Calendar System: Semester
URL: www.milligan.edu
Established: 1866 | Annual Undergrad Tuition & Fees: $29,830
Enrollment: 1,177 | Coed
Affiliation or Control: Independent Non-Profit | IRS Status: 501(c)3
Highest Offering: Doctorate
Program: Liberal Arts And General; Teacher Preparatory; Professional
Accreditation: SC, NURSE, OT, TED, THEOL

01 President .... Dr. William B. GREER
05 Vice Pres Academic Affairs/Dean .... Dr. Garland YOUNG
32 Vice Pres Athletics & Student Dev .... Mr. Mark FOX
30 Vice Pres Institutional Advancement .... Mr. Jack SIMPSON
84 Vice Pres Enrollment Management .... Dr. Lee FIERBAUGH
10 Vice Pres Business & Finance .... Mrs. Jacqui STEADMAN
06 Registrar .... Mrs. Sue SKIDMORE
07 Director of Admissions .... Ms. Kristin WRIGHT
08 Director of Library Services .... Mr. Gary DAUGHT
35 Director of Student Activities .... Mr. Jason ONKS
29 Director of Alumni Relations .... Ms. Theresa GARBE
15 Director Personnel Services .... Ms. Linda LAWSON
09 Director of Institutional Research .... Ms. Cindy WYMER
37 Coordinator of Financial Aid .... Ms. Diane KEASLING
26 Director of Church Relations .... Mrs. Phyllis FOX
36 Director Student Placement .... Ms. Beth ANDERSON
18 Service Manager Facilities .... Mr. Ken BROYLES
28 Director of Diversity .... Mr. Jeff SMITH
27 Dir of Public Relations/Marketing .... Ms. Chandrea SHELL

National College (J)

5760 Stage Road, Bartlett TN 38134

Telephone: (901) 213-1681 | Identification: 770783
Accreditation: ACICS, MAC

† Branch campus of National College, Nashville, TN.

National College (K)

900 Madison Square, Madison TN 37115

Telephone: (615) 612-3015 | Identification: 770784
Accreditation: ACICS, CAHIIM, MAC

† Branch campus of National College, Nashville, TN.

National College (L)

2526 Thousand Oaks Cove, Memphis TN 38118

Telephone: (901) 363-9046 | Identification: 770785
Accreditation: ACICS, CAHIIM, MAC

† Branch campus of National College, Nashville, TN.

National College (M)

1638 Bell Road, Nashville TN 37211

County: Davidson | FICE Identification: 004617 | Unit ID: 388043
Telephone: (615) 333-3344 | Carnegie Class: Assoc/PrivFP
FAX Number: (615) 333-3429 | Calendar System: Quarter
URL: www.national-college.edu
Established: 1991 | Annual Undergrad Tuition & Fees: $11,555
Enrollment: 517 | Coed
Affiliation or Control: Proprietary | IRS Status: Proprietary
Highest Offering: Baccalaureate
Program: Occupational
Accreditation: ACICS, MAC

01 Director .... Mr. Mark LIVERMAN

North Central Institute (N)

168 Jack Miller Boulevard, Clarksville TN 37042-4810

County: Montgomery | FICE Identification: 030791 | Unit ID: 418889
Telephone: (931) 431-9700 | Carnegie Class: Assoc/PrivFP
FAX Number: (931) 431-9771 | Calendar System: Semester
URL: www.nci.edu
Established: 1988 | Annual Undergrad Tuition & Fees: $16,352
Enrollment: 372 | Coed
Affiliation or Control: Proprietary | IRS Status: Proprietary
Highest Offering: Associate Degree
Program: Occupational; 2-Year Principally Bachelor's Creditable; Technical Emphasis
Accreditation: COE

01 President .... Ms. Tamela K. TALIENTO

Nossi College of Art (O)

590 Cheron Road, Nashville TN 37115

County: Davidson | FICE Identification: 025782 | Unit ID: 368452
Telephone: (615) 514-2787 | Carnegie Class: Spec/Arts
FAX Number: (615) 514-2788 | Calendar System: Trimester
URL: www.nossi.edu

Established: 1973 Annual Undergrad Tuition & Fees: $17,700
Enrollment: 295 Coed
Affiliation or Control: Proprietary IRS Status: Proprietary
Highest Offering: Baccalaureate
Program: Occupational; Technical Emphasis
Accreditation: ACCSC

01 President ....Ms. Nossi VATANDOOST
03 Executive Vice President ....Mr. Cyrus VATANDOOST
07 Admissions Director ....Ms. Mary ALEXANDER
37 Financial Aid Director ....Ms. Mary KIDD
06 Registrar ....Mrs. Mindy GILBERT
08 Head Librarian ....Mrs. Kolleen LONGMIRE
26 Chief Public Relations/Marketing ....Mrs. Libby LUFF
10 Business Office Manager ....Mrs. Kristi BINKLEY

O'More College of Design (A)

423 S Margin Street, Franklin TN 37064
County: Williamson FICE Identification: 021064
Unit ID: 221254
Telephone: (615) 794-4254 Carnegie Class: Spec/Arts
FAX Number: (615) 790-1662 Calendar System: Semester
URL: www.omorecollege.edu
Established: 1970 Annual Undergrad Tuition & Fees: $28,260
Enrollment: 175 Coed
Affiliation or Control: Independent Non-Profit IRS Status: 501(c)3
Highest Offering: Baccalaureate
Program: Occupational; Liberal Arts And General; Fine Arts Emphasis
Accreditation: ACCSC, CIDA

01 President ....Dr. David ROSEN
05 Provost ....Ms. Lisa HENLINE
30 Director of Development & Marketing ....Ms. Amy SHELTON
10 Chief Business Officer ....Ms. Teresa CORLEY
19 Director of Security ....Mr. DeWayne PULLIAM
07 Director of Admissions ....Ms. Lisa SMITH
08 Librarian and Bookstore Manager ....Ms. Nicole FOX
88 Dean Fashion ....Ms. Jamie ATLAS
88 Dean Interior Design ....Ms. Kelly GORE
88 Dean Interior Design ....Ms. Rebecca ANDREWS
11 Chief Administrative Officer ....Ms. Jamie SHAFFER
18 Director of Facilities ....Mr. Kirk MANGRUM
06 Registrar ....Ms. Anita WHITE
32 Director of Student Services ....Mr. Alan CORRY
37 Director of Financial Aid ....Ms. Lea VOIGT
88 Assistant Director of Admissions ....Ms. Tori BAGSBY
88 Dean Visual Design ....Mr. Shane PRINE

Oxford Graduate School (B)

500 Oxford Drive, Dayton TN 37321-6736
County: Rhea FICE Identification: 038403
Unit ID: 461120
Telephone: (423) 775-6596 Carnegie Class: Not Classified
FAX Number: (423) 775-6599 Calendar System: Trimester
URL: www.ogs.edu
Established: 1981 Annual Graduate Tuition & Fees: $31,500
Enrollment: 95 Coed
Affiliation or Control: Independent Non-Profit IRS Status: 501(c)3
Highest Offering: Doctorate; No Undergraduates
Program: Professional
Accreditation: TRACS

01 President ....Dr. Kimberly GEIGER
00 Chancellor ....Dr. Rollin VAN BROEKHOVEN
05 Dean of Faculty ....Dr. Robert ANDREWS
11 Vice President of Administration ....Dr. Paul LAWHORN
07 Director of Admissions & Phys Opers ....Ms. Gwen BOLLANT
108 Institutional Assessment Officer ....Dr. Joshua REICHARD
10 Business Officer ....Ms. Sharlene DANIEL
29 Director Alumni Relations ....Dr. Bonnie LIBHART
42 Chaplain ....Dr. David WARD

Pentecostal Theological Seminary (C)

900 Walker Street, NE, Cleveland TN 37311
County: Bradley FICE Identification: 021883
Unit ID: 219842
Telephone: (423) 478-1131 Carnegie Class: Spec/Faith
FAX Number: (423) 478-7711 Calendar System: 4/1/4
URL: www.ptseminary.edu
Established: 1975 Annual Graduate Tuition & Fees: $8,527
Enrollment: 235 Coed
Affiliation or Control: Church Of God IRS Status: 501(c)3
Highest Offering: Doctorate; No Undergraduates
Program: Professional
Accreditation: SC, THEOL

01 President ....Dr. R. Lamar VEST
05 VP for Academics ....Dr. Sang-Ehil HAN
42 VP for Inst Effect/Accreditation ....Dr. Oliver L. MCMAHAN
10 Director for Finance ....Mr. Robert E. BUXTON
30 VP for Institutional Advancement ....Rev. Ken R. DAVIS
04 Exec Assistant to the President ....Mrs. Teresa GILBERT
84 Director of Enrollment ....Dr. Welton WRISTON
06 Director of Acad Records/Registrar ....Ms. Anita F. BLEVINS
15 Director of Administrative Services ....Mrs. Alanna L. HENRY
18 Dir of Facilities/Support Services ....Mr. Phillip WOODS
29 Dir Donor and Alumni Relations ....Mrs. Joylita TERPSTRA
32 Director of Student Services ....Dr. Angela MCCAIN-WALTRIP
37 Director of Financial Aid ....Mrs. Robin SLUDER
38 Director of Counseling/Testing ....Dr. Douglas SLOCUMB
07 Director of Admissions ....Ms. Regina TOWLES WILHELM

Remington College (D)

2710 Nonconnah Boulevard, Memphis TN 38132-2110
Telephone: (901) 345-1000 Identification: 666062
Accreditation: ACCSC

† Branch campus of Remington College, Mobile, AL.

Remington College (E)

441 Donelson Pike, Suite 150, Nashville TN 37214-3558
Telephone: (615) 889-5520 Identification: 666307
Accreditation: ACCSC, DH

† Branch campus of Remington College, Mobile, AL.

Rhodes College (F)

2000 North Parkway, Memphis TN 38112-1690
County: Shelby FICE Identification: 003519
Unit ID: 221351
Telephone: (901) 843-3000 Carnegie Class: Bac/A&S
FAX Number: N/A Calendar System: Semester
URL: www.rhodes.edu
Established: 1848 Annual Undergrad Tuition & Fees: $43,224
Enrollment: 2,054 Coed
Affiliation or Control: Presbyterian Church (U.S.A.) IRS Status: 501(c)3
Highest Offering: Master's
Program: Liberal Arts And General
Accreditation: SC, MUS

01 President ....Dr. William E. TROUTT
05 Interim Dean of Academic Affairs ....Dr. Milton MORELAND
10 VP for Finance & Business Affairs ....Mr. J. Allen BOONE
13 Vice Pres for Information Services .Dr. Robert M. JOHNSON, JR.
30 Vice President for Development ....Ms. Jennifer G. WADE
84 Vice Pres Enrollment/Communications ....Mr. Carey THOMPSON
32 Dean of Students ....Ms. Carol E. CASEY
35 Associate Dean of Students ....Ms. Kathleen LAAKSO
20 Assoc Dean of Academic Affairs ....Dr. Brian W. SHAFFER
20 Assoc Dean of Academic Affairs ....Dr. Michelle MATTSON
20 Assoc Dean of Academic Affairs ....Dr. Anita A. DAVIS
06 Registrar ....Ms. DeAnna ADAMS
37 Director of Financial Aid ....Mr. Michael MORGAN
08 Librarian ....Ms. Darlene D. BROOKS
21 Comptroller ....Mr. Kyle WEBB
29 Director of Alumni Relations ....Mr. Warren A. RICHEY
15 Director of Human Resources ....Ms. Claire R. SHAPIRO
14 Director of Info Tech Services ....Mr. Richard TRENTHEM
19 Director of Campus Safety ....Mr. Ike SLOAS
41 Director of Athletics ....Mr. Michael T. CLARY
36 Director of Career Services ....Ms. Sandra G. TRACY
38 Director of Counseling Services ....Mr. Robert B. DOVE
18 Director of Physical Plant ....Mr. Brian E. FOSHEE
44 Director of Planned Giving ....Mr. Jim DUNCAN
26 Director of Communications ....Mr. Ken WOODMANSEE
09 Director of Institutional Research .Ms. Dawn CLEMENT CORNIES
04 Exec Assistant to the President ....Ms. Melody H. RICHEY

Richmont Graduate University (G)

1815 McCallie Avenue, Chattanooga TN 37404
County: Hamilton FICE Identification: 033554
Unit ID: 441104
Telephone: (423) 266-4574 Carnegie Class: Spec/Health
FAX Number: (423) 265-7375 Calendar System: Semester
URL: www.richmont.edu
Established: 1933 Annual Graduate Tuition & Fees: $13,200
Enrollment: 285 Coed
Affiliation or Control: Independent Non-Profit IRS Status: 501(c)3
Highest Offering: Master's; No Undergraduates
Program: Professional
Accreditation: SC

01 President ....Mr. Bob RODGERS, JR.
32 Dean of Students ....Dr. Amanda BLACKBURN
05 Academic Dean ....Dr. Keny FELIX
73 Dean School of Ministry ....Dr. Michael STEWART
10 VP of Finance ....Mr. Tim MCPHERSON
04 Assistant to the President ....Ms. Jennifer COOPER

SAE Institute Nashville (H)

7 Music Circle North, Nashville TN 37203
County: Davidson FICE Identification: 038303
Unit ID: 446525
Telephone: (615) 244-5848 Carnegie Class: Not Classified
FAX Number: (615) 244-3192 Calendar System: Semester
URL: nashville.sae.edu
Established: Annual Undergrad Tuition & Fees: $17,750
Enrollment: 143 Coed
Affiliation or Control: Proprietary IRS Status: Proprietary
Highest Offering: Associate Degree
Program: 2-Year Principally Bachelor's Creditable; Music Emphasis
Accreditation: ACCSC

01 Director ....Lynn DORTON

Sewanee: The University of the South (I)

735 University Avenue, Sewanee TN 37383-1000
County: Franklin FICE Identification: 003534
Unit ID: 221519
Telephone: (931) 598-1000 Carnegie Class: Bac/A&S
FAX Number: (931) 598-1145 Calendar System: Semester
URL: www.sewanee.edu
Established: 1857 Annual Undergrad Tuition & Fees: $38,700
Enrollment: 1,714 Coed
Affiliation or Control: Protestant Episcopal IRS Status: 501(c)3
Highest Offering: Doctorate
Program: Liberal Arts And General; Professional
Accreditation: SC, THEOL

01 Vice Chancellor & President ....Dr. John M. MCCARDELL, JR.
05 Executive Vice President & Provost ....Dr. John R. SWALLOW
30 Vice President for Advancement ....Mr. Jay FISHER
10 Vice President for Admin Svcs ....Mr. Frank GLADU
45 Vice Provost for Planning and Admin ....Dr. Nancy BERNER
13 Assoc Provost Info Tech/Librarian ....Dr. Vicki G. SELLS
49 Dean College of Arts & Sciences ....Dr. Terry L. PAPILLON
73 Dean School of Theology ....Rt Rev. J Neil ALEXANDER
32 Dean of Students ....Dr. Marichal GENTRY
09 Asst Dir of Inst Research ....Ms. Sarah STAPLETON
06 Assistant Provost for Academic Svcs ....Mr. Paul G. WILEY
07 Dean of Admission & Financial Aid .Ms. Lee Ann M. BACKLUND
37 Assoc Dean Student Financial Aid ....Ms. Beth CRAGAR
20 Associate Dean for Academic Affairs ....Dr. Alex M. BRUCE
26 Exec Dir Marketing/Communications ....Mr. Parker OLIVER
15 Director of Human Resources ....Ms. Mary WILSON
41 Director of Athletics ....Mr. Mark F. WEBB
29 Director of Alumni Relations ....Ms. Susan S. ASKEW
36 Director of Career Services ....Ms. Kim D. HEITZENRATER
38 Director of Wellness Center ....Dr. Nicole NOFFSINGER-FRAZIER
93 Director of Minority Affairs ....Mr. Eric V. BENJAMIN
18 Director of Physical Plant Services ....Mr. Michael D. GARDNER
43 University Legal Counsel ....Ms. Donna L. PIERCE
19 Chief of Police ....Ms. Marie ELDRIDGE
21 Treasurer ....Dr. Douglass WILLIAMS
23 Director of Univ Health Services ....Ms. Karen THARP
24 Director of Media Services ....Mr. Larry E. WOOD
42 University Chaplain & Dean ....VRev. Thomas E. MACFIE

South College (J)

3904 Lonas Drive, Knoxville TN 37909-3323
County: Knox FICE Identification: 004938
Unit ID: 220552
Telephone: (865) 251-1800 Carnegie Class: Bac/Assoc
FAX Number: (865) 584-7335 Calendar System: Quarter
URL: www.southcollegetn.edu
Established: 1882 Annual Undergrad Tuition & Fees: $19,425
Enrollment: 1,200 Coed
Affiliation or Control: Proprietary IRS Status: Proprietary
Highest Offering: Doctorate
Program: Occupational; 2-Year Principally Bachelor's Creditable; Teacher Preparatory; Professional
Accreditation: SC, ARCPA, DMS, MAC, NMT, NUR, PHAR, @PTA, PTAA, RAD

01 President ....Mr. Stephen A. SOUTH
05 Executive VP and Provost ....Dr. Kim B. HALL
11 VP Admin & Regulatory Compliance ....Mr. Steve WOODFORD
13 VP Information Tech/Facilities ....Mr. Ron HALL
84 VP Enrollment Management ....Mr. Walter HOSEA
10 Chief Financial Officer ....Mr. Brad ADAMS
36 Career Services Coordinator ....Mr. Gary TAYLOR
06 Registrar ....Ms. Kim WOOD
37 Director of Financial Aid ....Mr. Larry BROADWATER
08 Head Librarian ....Ms. Mary MCHUGH
72 Director Instructional Technology ....Ms. Jennifer GLAAB
07 Director for Admissions ....Ms. Carrie MAJOR
108 Director of Inst Effectiveness ....Dr. Lisa SATTERFIELD

Southern Adventist University (K)

Box 370, 5010 University Drive,
Collegedale TN 37315-0370
County: Hamilton FICE Identification: 003518
Unit ID: 221661
Telephone: (423) 236-2000 Carnegie Class: Bac/Diverse
FAX Number: (423) 236-1000 Calendar System: Semester
URL: www.southern.edu
Established: 1892 Annual Undergrad Tuition & Fees: $20,690
Enrollment: 3,174 Coed
Affiliation or Control: Seventh-day Adventist IRS Status: 501(c)3
Highest Offering: Doctorate
Program: Liberal Arts And General; Teacher Preparatory
Accreditation: SC, ADNUR, CACREP, CS, IACBE, MUS, NUR, SW, TED

01 President ....Dr. Gordon BIETZ
05 Vice Pres Academic Administration ....Dr. Robert YOUNG
10 Vice President Financial Admin ....Mr. Tom VERRILL
32 Vice President Student Services ....Mr. Dennis NEGRON
45 Director Strategic Initiatives ....Mrs. Barb EDENS
30 Vice President Advancement ....Vacant
84 Vice Pres Enrollment Management ....Mr. Marc A. GRUNDY
20 Associate VP Academic Admin ....Dr. Volker HENNING
21 Associate VP Financial Admin ....Mr. Marty HAMILTON
13 Assoc VP Information Systems ....Mr. Gary SEWELL

09 Director Inst Research/Planning ... Dr. Hollis JAMES
08 Director of Libraries ... Mr. Daniel MAXWELL
06 Director Records & Advisement ... Mrs. Joni I. ZIER
15 Director Human Resources ... Mrs. Brenda FLORES-LOPEZ
26 Director Marketing Univ Relation ... Ms. Ingrid SKANTZ
29 Director Alumni Relations ... Ms. Evonne CROOK
38 Director Student Success Center ... Dr. Jim WAMPLER
33 Dean of Men ... Mr. Dwight E. MAGERS
34 Dean of Women ... Ms. Lisa HALL
50 Dean School of Business/Mgmt ... Dr. Mark HYDER
53 Dean School of Education/Psych ... Dr. John MCCOY
57 Dean School of Visual Art/Design ... Mr. Randy CRAVEN
60 Dean School of Journalism/Comm ... Dr. Linda CRUMLEY
64 Dean School of Music ... Dr. Scott BALL
66 Dean School of Nursing ... Dr. Barbara JAMES
68 Dean Sch of Phys Ed/Health/Wellness ... Dr. Robert BENGE
73 Dean School of Religion ... Dr. Greg KING
77 Dean School of Computing ... Dr. Rick HALTERMAN
70 Dean Social Work/Family Studies ... Dr. Kristie WILDER
72 Chair Technology ... Dr. Mark HYDER
81 Chair Mathematics ... Dr. Kevin BROWN
76 Chair Biology/Allied Health ... Dr. Keith SNYDER
88 Chair Chemistry ... Dr. Rhonda J. SCOTT
88 Chair English ... Dr. Keely TARY
88 Chair History & Political Studies ... Dr. Lisa C. DILLER
88 Chair Modern Languages ... Vacant
88 Chair Physics ... Dr. Chris HANSEN
18 Director Plant Services ... Mr. Eric SCHOONARD
35 Director Student Affairs & Life Act ... Ms. Kari SHULTZ
37 Director Student Finance ... Mrs. Paula WALTERS
96 Director of Purchasing Services ... Mr. Russell ORRISON
04 Administrative Asst to President ... Mrs. Joylynn SCOTT

Southern College of Optometry (A)

1245 Madison Avenue, Memphis TN 38104-2222
County: Shelby FICE Identification: 003517
Unit ID: 221670
Telephone: (901) 722-3200 Carnegie Class: Spec/Health
FAX Number: (901) 722-3279 Calendar System: Trimester
URL: www.sco.edu
Established: 1932 Annual Graduate Tuition & Fees: $20,136
Enrollment: 527 Coed
Affiliation or Control: Independent Non-Profit IRS Status: 501(c)3
Highest Offering: Doctorate; No Undergraduates
Program: Professional
Accreditation: SC, OPT, OPTR

01 Interim President ... Dr. Lewis REICH
04 Executive Admin Assistant to Pres ... Ms. Sandra S. STEPHENS
05 Interim VP for Academic Affairs ... Dr. John B. CAMPBELL
30 Vice President for Inst Advancement ... Dr. Kristin K. ANDERSON
102 Dir of Corp & Foundation Relations ... Ms. Christine M. WEINREICH
10 Vice President for Finance & Admin ... Mr. David L. WEST
13 Director of Information Services ... Mr. Dean SWICK
18 Director of Physical Plant ... Mr. Danny ANDERSON
17 Vice Pres for Clinical Programs ... Dr. James E. VENABLE
23 Director of Clinic Operations ... Mr. Gary SNUFFIN
06 Vice President for Student Services ... Mr. Joseph H. HAUSER
07 Dir of Admissions/Enrollment Svcs . Mr. Michael N. ROBERTSON
07 Director of Student Recruitment ... Ms. Sunnie EWING
08 Director of Library ... Ms. Leslie HOLLAND
26 Dir of Communications/Media Svcs ... Mr. Jim HOLLIFIELD
15 Vice President for Human Resources ... Ms. Ann Z. FIELDS
37 Director of Financial Aid ... Ms. Cindy GARNER
09 Director of Institutional Research ... Dr. Michael CHRISTENSEN
108 Director Institutional Assessment ... Ms. Pamela MOSS
19 Director Security/Safety ... Mr. Ken COBLE

*Tennessee Board of Regents Office (B)

1415 Murfreesboro Road, Nashville TN 37217-2833
County: Davidson FICE Identification: 029031
Unit ID: 409379
Telephone: (615) 366-4400 Carnegie Class: N/A
FAX Number: (615) 366-3922
URL: www.tbr.edu

01 Chancellor ... Mr. John G. MORGAN
05 Vice Chanc Academic Affairs ... Dr. Tristan DENLEY
10 Vice Chanc Business & Finance ... Mr. Dale SIMS
11 Vice Chanc Admin & Fac Mgmt ... Mr. David B. GREGORY
12 VC TN Colleges of Applied Tech ... Mr. James KING
13 Vice Chanc Information Systems ... Mr. Tom DANFORD
88 Vice Chanc for Community Colleges ... Dr. Warren NICHOLS
43 General Counsel ... Ms. Mary MOODY
09 Asst Vice Chanc Research/Assess ... Mr. Greg SCHUTZ
20 Assoc Vice Chanc Academic Affairs ... Vacant
20 Assoc Vice Chance Academic Affairs ... Dr. Pamela KNOX
21 Assistant Vice Chancellor Business ... Vacant
15 Asst Vice Chanc for Human Resources ... Ms. April PRESTON
21 Assistant Vice Chancellor Business ... Ms. Renee STEWART
88 Exec Dir of Operations for ROCC ... Dr. Patrick WILSON
26 Director of Communications ... Ms. Monica GREPPIN-WATTS

*Austin Peay State University (C)

601 College Street, Clarksville TN 37044-0002
County: Montgomery FICE Identification: 003478
Unit ID: 219602
Telephone: (931) 221-7011 Carnegie Class: Master's L
FAX Number: (931) 221-7475 Calendar System: Semester
URL: www.apsu.edu
Established: 1927 Annual Undergrad Tuition & Fees (In-State): $7,501
Enrollment: 10,111 Coed
Affiliation or Control: State IRS Status: 501(c)3
Highest Offering: Beyond Master's But Less Than Doctorate
Program: Liberal Arts And General; Teacher Preparatory; Professional; Fine Arts Emphasis
Accreditation: SC, ART, ENGT, MT, MUS, NUR, RAD, SW, TED

02 President ... Dr. Alisa WHITE
04 Exec Asst to the President ... Ms. Carol D. CLARK
05 Provost/VP Academic Affairs ... Dr. Rex GANDY
10 Vice President for Finance & Admin ... Mr. Mitch ROBINSON
43 University Attorney ... Ms. Stephanie REEVERS
32 VP for Student Affairs ... Dr. Sherryl BYRD
46 VP Advancement/Comm/Strategic Init ... Mr. Derek VAN DER MERWE
21 Asst Vice Pres for Finance ... Mr. Timothy HURST
20 Int Asst Provost/VP Acad Affairs ... Ms. Lori BUCHANAN
84 Assoc Provost for Enrollment Mgmt ... Dr. Beverly BOGGS
30 Exec Director Univ Advancement ... Vacant
31 Dir Community/Business Rels ... Ms. Carol CLARK
26 Exec Dir Marketing/Public Rels ... Mr. Bill PERSINGER
12 Exec Dir APSU Fort Campbell ... Dr. William COX
29 Director of Alumni Relations ... Ms. Nicole PETERSON
21 Director Budgets ... Ms. Sonja STEWART
08 Director Library ... Mr. Joe WEBER
13 Interim Director of Info Technology ... Mr. Austin SIDERS
09 Dir Inst Research & Effectiveness ... Ms. Melissa HUNTER
07 Director of Admissions ... Ms. Amy CORLEW
06 Registrar ... Ms. Telaina WRIGLEY
18 Director of Plant Administration ... Mr. Thomas HUTCHINS
45 Dir Facilities Planning & Projects ... Mr. Marc BRUNNER
41 Athletics Director ... Mr. Ryan IVEY
27 Director of Athletic Information ... Mr. Brad J. KIRTLEY
37 Director of Student Financial Aid ... Ms. Donna PRICE
88 Dir Ctr for Teaching & Learning ... Ms. Loretta GRIFFY
38 Dir of Student Counseling Services ... Dr. Jeff RUTTER
35 Dean of Students ... Mr. Gregory SINGLETON
88 Dir African Amer Cultural Ctr ... Mr. Henderson HILL
15 Asst VP & Chief HR Officer ... Mr. Michael HAMLET
16 Director of Human Resources ... Ms. Fonda FIELDS
19 Director Public Safety ... Mr. Michael KASITZ
39 Director Housing/Resident Life ... Mr. F. Joe MILLS
21 Director Internal Audit ... Ms. Jacqueline STRUCKMEYER
25 Exec Dir Research & Sponsored Pgms ... Mr. Andrew SHEPARD-SMITH
96 Director of Purchasing ... Ms. Judy BLAIN
22 Dir Equal Opport & Affirm Action ... Ms. Sheila M. BRYANT
36 Director of Career Services ... Ms. Amanda WALKER
49 Dean College Arts & Letters ... Dr. Dixie WEBB
81 Dean Col Science & Math ... Dr. Jaime TAYLOR
83 Dean Col Behav Health Science ... Dr. David DENTON
58 Interim Dean Coll Graduate Studies ... Dr. Mike GOTCHER
51 Exec Dir Extended & Distance Educ ... Mr. Dana WILLETT
104 Director of Study Abroad ... Ms. Marissa CHANDLER
50 Dean of Business ... Dr. William RUPP
53 Dean of Education ... Dr. Carlette HARDIN

*East Tennessee State University (D)

1276 Gilbreath Drive, Johnson City TN 37614-1700
County: Washington FICE Identification: 003487
Unit ID: 220075
Telephone: (423) 439-1000 Carnegie Class: DRU
FAX Number: (423) 439-5770 Calendar System: Semester
URL: www.etsu.edu
Established: 1911 Annual Undergrad Tuition & Fees (In-State): $8,153
Enrollment: 14,046 Coed
Affiliation or Control: State IRS Status: 501(c)3
Highest Offering: Doctorate
Program: Occupational; Liberal Arts And General; Teacher Preparatory; Professional; Business Emphasis
Accreditation: SC, ART, #AUD, BUS, BUSA, CACREP, CLPSY, COARC, CS, DH, DIETD, DIETI, ENGR, ENGT, MED, MUS, NURSE, PH, PHAR, PTA, RAD, SP, SW, TED, THEA

02 President ... Dr. Brian E. NOLAND
100 Chief of Staff/Assoc VP Health Affs ... Dr. Jane M. JONES
100 Chief of Staff External Operations ... Mr. Jeremy B. ROSS
05 Provost/Vice Pres Academic Affairs ... Dr. Bert C. BACH
10 Vice Pres Finance & Administration ... Dr. David D. COLLINS
17 Vice President Health Affairs ... Dr. Wilsie S. BISHOP
30 VP University Advancement ... Ms. Pamela S. RITTER
41 Athletic Director ... Dr. Richard L. SANDER
28 Spec Asst to Pres Equity/Diversity ... Ms. Mary V. JORDAN
88 Director of Internal Audit ... Ms. Rebecca B. LEWIS
43 University Counsel ... Mr. Edward J. KELLY
26 Exec Director of Univ Relations ... Mr. Joseph E. SMITH
84 Vice Provost Enrollment Services ... Dr. Ramona A. WILLIAMS
51 Dean Cont Studies & Acad Outreach ... Dr. Richard E. OSBORN
46 Vice Prov Research/Sponsored Pgms ... Dr. William R. DUNCAN
32 Vice Pres Student Affairs ... Dr. Joe H. SHERLIN
20 Vice Provost Academic Affairs ... Dr. M. Marshall GRUBE
20 VProv Ugrad Ed/Dir Plan & Analysis .. Dr. William G. KIRKWOOD
18 Assoc VP for Facilities Management ... Mr. William B. RASNICK, JR.
35 Dean of Students ... Dr. Jeffery S. HOWARD
13 CIO/Sr Vice Provost for ITS ... Dr. Karen D. KING
96 Assoc VP Procurement/Contract Svcs ... Dr. Katherine M. KELLEY
21 Sr Assoc VP Finance & Admin ... Dr. B. J. KING
44 Assoc VP Univ Adv/Planned Giving ... Mr. Jeffrey W. ANDERSON
29 Assoc VP Univ Adv/Exec Dir Alumni ... Dr. Robert M. PLUMMER
09 Director of Institutional Research ... Dr. Michael B. HOFF
86 Exec Asst to Pres Cmty & Govt Rels ... Ms. Bridget R. BAIRD
49 Dean College Arts & Science ... Dr. Gordon K. ANDERSON
50 Dean College of Business/Technology ... Dr. Dennis R. DEPEW
76 Dean College of Clin/Rehab Sci ... Dr. Donald A. SAMPLES
53 Dean College of Education ... Dr. Terence HICKS
92 Interim Dean Honors College ... Dr. Judith B. SLAGLE
63 Dean College of Medicine ... Dr. Robert T. MEANS, JR.
67 Dean College of Pharmacy ... Dr. Larry D. CALHOUN
66 Dean College of Nursing ... Dr. Wendy M. NEHRING
69 Dean College of Public Health ... Dr. Randolph F. WYKOFF
58 Dean School of Graduate Studies ... Dr. Cecilia A. MCINTOSH
08 Dean of Libraries ... Ms. Patricia R. VAN ZANDT
06 University Registrar ... Ms. Sheryl L. BURNETTE
07 Director of Admissions ... Mr. Brian L. HENLEY
36 Director University Career Services ... Dr. David E. MAGEE, JR.
38 Director Counseling Center ... Dr. Steve D. BROWN
37 Director of Financial Aid ... Ms. Margaret L. MILLER
92 Director University Honors Program ... Dr. Joy E. WACHS
39 Director Student Housing ... Dr. Bonnie L. BURCHETT
85 Dir International Programs/Services ... Dr. Maria D. COSTA
93 Multicultural Director ... Ms. Laura C. TERRY
19 Director Public Safety ... Chief Jack R. COTREL
25 Director of Sponsored Programs ... Dr. Louise C. NUTTLE
87 Director Summer & Winter Sessions ... Dr. Sarah E. HARKNESS
94 Director of Women's Studies ... Dr. Phyllis A. THOMPSON
105 Web Manager ... Ms. Michaele D. LAWS
15 Dir Empl Relations/Compensation/Dev ... Ms. Diana D. MCCLAY
16 Director Benefits/Retirement/HRIS ... Ms. Tammy S. HAMM
108 Dir Institutional Effectiveness ... Dr. Cheri CLAVIER

*Middle Tennessee State University (E)

1301 E Main Street, Murfreesboro TN 37132-0001
County: Rutherford FICE Identification: 003510
Unit ID: 220978
Telephone: (615) 898-2300 Carnegie Class: DRU
FAX Number: (615) 898-5538 Calendar System: Semester
URL: www.mtsu.edu
Established: 1911 Annual Undergrad Tuition & Fees (In-State): $8,404
Enrollment: 22,729 Coed
Affiliation or Control: State IRS Status: 501(c)3
Highest Offering: Doctorate
Program: Liberal Arts And General; Teacher Preparatory
Accreditation: SC, AAB, AAFCS, ART, BUS, BUSA, CAATE, CACREP, CIDA, CS, DIETD, ENGT, JOUR, MUS, NAIT, NRPA, NURSE, SW, TED, THEA

02 President ... Dr. Sidney A. MCPHEE
03 University Provost ... Dr. Brad N. BARTEL
10 Senior Vice Pres Business & Finance ... Dr. John W. COTHERN
30 Vice President Devel/Univ Relations ... Mr. William J. BALES
32 VP Stdnt Affs/V Prov Enroll Mgmt ... Dr. Debra K. SELLS
13 VP Info Tech/Chief Info Officer ... Mr. Bruce PETRYSHAK
05 Vice Prov for Academic Affairs ... Dr. John O. OMACHONU
58 Vice Provost Rsrch/Dean Grad Stds ... Dr. Jackie ELLER
88 Vice Provost for Student Success ... Dr. Richard SLUDER
43 Univ Counsel & Asst to the Pres ... Ms. Heidi ZIMMERMAN
04 Exec Assistant to the President ... Ms. Kimberly S. EDGAR
22 Exec Dir Institutional Equity/Com ... Ms. Barbara L. PATTON
31 Community Engagement/Asst to Pres ... Dr. Gloria L. BONNER
07 Assoc Vice Prov Admis & Enroll Svcs .. Dr. Laurie B. WITHEROW
14 Assoc Vice Pres Info Technology ... Mr. Tom WALLACE
21 Assoc Vice Pres Business Office ... Mr. Alan THOMAS
35 Assoc Vice Pres/Dean Student Life ... Ms. Sarah SUDAK
26 Assoc Vice Pres Mktg/Communications ... Mr. Andrew OPPMANN
15 Asst Vice Pres Human Resource Svcs ... Ms. Kathy I. MUSSELMAN
18 Asst Vice Pres Facilities Services ... Mr. Joe WHITEFIELD
11 Asst Vice Pres Admin/Business Svcs ... Ms. Kathryn CRISP
91 Asst Vice Pres Entrprse Rsrce Plng ... Mrs. Lisa C. ROGERS
90 Asst Vice Pres Acad & Instruct Tech ... Ms. Barbara J. DRAUDE
81 Dean Col Basic/Applied Science ... Dr. Robert U. FISCHER, JR.
83 Dean College Behavioral & Hlth Sci ... Dr. Harold D. WHITESIDE
60 Dean College Mass Communication ... Dr. Ken A. PAULSON
50 Dean College of Business ... Dr. David J. URBAN
53 Dean College of Education ... Dr. Lana C. SEIVERS
49 Dean College of Liberal Arts ... Dr. Mark E. BYRNES
51 Dean University College ... Dr. Mike A. BOYLE
92 Dean University Honors College ... Dr. John R. VILE
08 Dean University Library ... Ms. Bonnie J. ALLEN
09 Asst Vice Provost for IEPR ... Mr. Chris BREWER
36 Dir Career & Employment Center ... Mr. Bill FLETCHER
88 Asst Vice Prov Student Success ... Mr. Vincent WINDROW
37 Dir of Financial Aid & Scholarship ... Mr. Stephen F. WHITE
25 Dir Research Services ... Mr. Jeffry PORTER
29 Director Alumni Relations ... Ms. Ginger C. FREEMAN
40 Director Bookstore ... Mr. Jeff WHITWELL
24 Manager Center for Educational Med ... Mr. Anthony TATE
38 Director Counseling Services ... Dr. Jane TIPPS
44 Director Development Office ... Vacant
06 Director Enrollment Technical Sys ... Ms. Teresa W. THOMAS
27 Director News & Media Relations ... Mr. Jimmy W. HART
41 Director of Athletics ... Mr. Chris J. MASSARO
23 Director of Health Services ... Mr. Richard L. CHAPMAN
94 Director Women's and Gender Studies ... Dr. Ida F. LEGGETT
06 Registrar ... Ms. Ann S. REAVES
19 Chief of Police/Dir Public Safety ... Mr. Carl S. PEASTER

*Tennessee State University (F)

3500 John A Merritt Boulevard, Nashville TN 37209-1561
County: Davidson FICE Identification: 003522
Unit ID: 221838
Telephone: (615) 963-5000 Carnegie Class: DRU
FAX Number: (615) 963-7412 Calendar System: Semester

URL: www.tnstate.edu
Established: 1912 Annual Undergrad Tuition & Fees (In-State): $6,930
Enrollment: 9,027 Coed
Affiliation or Control: State IRS Status: 501(c)3
Highest Offering: Doctorate
Program: Occupational; Liberal Arts And General; Teacher Preparatory; Professional
Accreditation: **SC**, AAFCS, ADNUR, ART, BUS, CAHIIM, COARC, COPSY, CS, DH, DIETD, ENG, MUS, NAIT, NUR, OT, PH, PTA, SP, SPAA, SW, TED

02 President .... Dr. Glenda GLOVER
05 Vice President Academic Affairs .... Dr. Mark G. HARDY
04 Senior Office Assistant .... Ms. Zanetta GOUCH
10 VP Business & Finance .... Mrs. Cynthia BROOKS
32 Assoc VP Student Affairs .... Dr. Michael FREEMAN
30 VP Institutional Advancement .... Ms. Robin WATSON
41 Athletic Director .... Mrs. Teresa LAWRENCE-PHILLIPS
43 University Legal Counsel .... Mr. Laurence PENDLETON
84 Assoc Provost Enrollment Mgmt .... Dr. John OADE
20 Assoc VP Academic Affairs .... Dr. Patricia CROOK
20 Assoc VP Academic Affairs Ext Ed .... Dr. Evelyn NETTLES
15 Assoc VP/Dir Human Resources .... Ms. Linda C. SPEARS
21 Assoc VP Finance/Accounting .... Mr. Robert HUGHES
18 Assoc VP Facilities/Physical Plant .... Mr. Ronnie BROOKS
11 AVP Administrative Affairs .... Ms. Michelle VIERA
88 Asst VP Budget/Travel .... Mr. Bradley WHITE
09 Dir Inst Effectiveness & Research ..... Dr. G. Pamela BURCH-SIMS
28 Dir Equity Diversity & Compliance .... Ms. Tiffa COX
37 Director Financial Aid .... Ms. Amy B. WOOD
06 Registrar .... Mrs. Thelria HARDAWAY
26 Director Media Relations .... Mr. Richard DELAHAYA
19 Chief TSU Police Department .... Mr. Richard BRIGGANCE
08 Dean Libraries & Media Centers .... Dr. Murle KENERSON
49 Int Dean College of Liberal Arts .... Dr. Gloria C. JOHNSON
50 Dean College of Business .... Dr. Millicent LOWNES-JACKSON
53 Dean College of Education .... Dr. Kimberly KING-JUPITER
54 Dean College of Engr/Tech/Comp Sci ..... Dr. S. Keith HARGROVE
47 Dn Agriculture/Human & Natural Sci .... Dr. Chandra REDDY
76 Dean Col Health Sciences .... Dr. Stephanie BAILEY

*Tennessee Technological University (A)

1000 N Dixie Avenue, Cookeville TN 38505-0001
County: Putnam FICE Identification: 003523
Unit ID: 221847
Telephone: (931) 372-3101 Carnegie Class: Master's L
FAX Number: (931) 372-3898 Calendar System: Semester
URL: www.tntech.edu
Established: 1915 Annual Undergrad Tuition & Fees (In-State): $8,011
Enrollment: 11,339 Coed
Affiliation or Control: State IRS Status: 501(c)3
Highest Offering: Doctorate
Program: Liberal Arts And General; Teacher Preparatory; Professional
Accreditation: **SC**, AAFCS, ART, BUS, BUSA, CACREP, CS, DIETD, EMT, ENG, MUS, NAIT, NURSE, TED

02 President .... Dr. Philip B. OLDHAM
05 Provost/Vice President Acad Affairs .... Dr. Bahman GHORASHI
10 Vice Pres Planning & Finance .... Dr. Claire STINSON
32 Vice President Student Affairs .... Mr. Marc BURNETT
35 Asst VP Student Affairs .... Mr. Ed BOUCHER
46 VP Research & Economic Development .... Dr. Bharat SONI
86 Director Government Relations .... Dr. Terry SALTSMAN
46 Assoc VP for Research .... Dr. Francis O. OTUONYE
30 Vice President Univ Advancement .... Dr. Kevin BRASWELL
20 Sr Assoc VP Academic Affairs .... Dr. Mark STEPHENS
20 Assoc Provost/Vice Pres Acad Affs .... Dr. Xiaoming (Sharon) HUO
13 Interim CIO Info Tech Svcs .... Dr. Terry SALTSMAN
37 Director Financial Aid .... Mr. Lester MCKENZIE
08 Director Library & Learning Assist .... Dr. Doug BATES
09 Director Institutional Research .... Dr. Glenn W. JAMES
45 Director of Institutional Planning .... Dr. Claire STINSON
15 Assoc VP Human Resources .... Dr. Leslie CRICKENBERGER
19 Director of University Police .... Mr. Tony NELSON
39 Director of Housing .... Mr. Charles MACKE
41 Director of Athletics .... Mr. Mark WILSON
18 Assoc VP Physical Plant .... Mr. Jack BUTLER
38 Director Counseling Center .... Ms. Patricia SMITH
23 Director of Health Svcs .... Ms. Leigh A. RAY
36 Director Career Services .... Ms. Lynn HALEY
26 Assoc VP Communications & Mkting .... Ms. Karen LYKINS
85 Director International Education .... Mr. Charles WILKERSON
06 Interim Dir Records & Registrar .... Ms. Brandi HILL
92 Director Honors Program .... Dr. Rita BARNES
93 Asst VP Multicultural Affairs .... Dr. Robert OWENS
96 Director of Purchasing .... Ms. Judy M. HULL
21 Associate VP Business .... Mr. Jeff YOUNG
43 Director University Counsel .... Ms. Kae CARPENTER
29 Director Alumni Relations .... Ms. Tracey DUNCAN
88 Director of Internal Audit .... Ms. Deanna METTS
28 Dir of AA & Employee Relations .... Ms. Elizabeth GAYS
07 Director of Admissions .... Vacant
19 Dir Envir Health & Safety .... Mr. James COBB
84 Assoc VP Enr Mgmt & Student Success .... Dr. Robert HODUM
49 Dean of Arts & Sciences .... Dr. Paul SEMMES
54 Dean of Engineering .... Dr. Joseph RENCIS
47 Dean Agric & Human Ecology .... Dr. Liz MULLENS
50 Dean of Business Admin .... Dr. Thomas PAYNE
53 Dean College of Education .... Dr. Jennifer SHANK
66 Dean School of Nursing .... Dr. Huey-Ming TZENG
88 Int Dean Interdisciplinary Studies .... Dr. Melissa GEIST

58 Assoc Dean of Graduate Studies .... Dr. Alice CAMUTI
04 Administrative Asst to President .... Ms. Terri TAYLOR
105 Director Web Services .... Mr. David WILLIS
108 Director Institutional Assessment .... Dr. Theresa ENNIS
44 Director Annual or Planned Giving .... Mr. Tracy RUSSELL
90 Director Academic Computing .... Dr. Annette LITTRELL
91 Director Administrative Computing .... Mr. Rick CUMBY

*The University of Memphis (B)

Memphis TN 38152
County: Shelby FICE Identification: 003509
Unit ID: 220862
Telephone: (901) 678-2000 Carnegie Class: RU/H
FAX Number: N/A Calendar System: Semester
URL: www.memphis.edu
Established: 1912 Annual Undergrad Tuition & Fees (In-State): $8,619
Enrollment: 21,059 Coed
Affiliation or Control: State IRS Status: 501(c)3
Highest Offering: Doctorate
Program: Liberal Arts And General; Teacher Preparatory; Professional
Accreditation: **SC**, ART, AUD, BUS, BUSA, CACREP, CIDA, CLPSY, COPSY, CORE, CS, DIETD, DIETI, ENG, ENGT, HSA, IPSY, JOUR, LAW, MUS, NURSE, PH, PLNG, SCPSY, SP, SPAA, SW, TED, THEA

02 President .... Dr. M. David RUDD
05 Provost .... Dr. Karen WEDDLE-WEST
10 Vice President Business & Finance .... Mr. David G. ZETTERGREN
30 Assoc Vice Pres for Development .... Mr. Bobby A. PRINCE
32 Vice President Student Affairs .... Dr. Rosie P. BINGHAM
26 Interim VP External Relations .... Ms. Tammy HEDGES
46 Int Vice President for Research .... Dr. Andrew W. MEYERS
41 Director of Athletics .... Mr. Tom BOWEN
43 University Counsel .... Ms. Melanie MURRY
13 CIO/Vice Provost for Info Tech .... Dr. Ellen WATSON
84 Int Vice Provost Enrollment Svcs .... Mr. Steve MCKELLIPS
58 Int Vice Prov/Dean Graduate School .... Dr. Jasbir DHALIWAL
21 Assistant Vice President Finance .... Ms. Jeannie SMITH
15 Asst Vice Pres Human Resources .... Ms. Maria ALAM
08 Dean U of M Libraries .... Dr. Sylverna V. FORD
09 Director Institutional Research .... Dr. Gary L. DONHARDT
36 Director Career & Employment Svcs .... Ms. Alisha D. ROSE
06 Registrar .... Ms. Donna S. VAN CANNEYT
37 Director of Student Aid .... Mr. Richard RITZMAN
96 Director of Purchasing .... Ms. Canty ROBBINS
29 Executive Director Alumni Assn .... Ms. Tammy L. HEDGES
92 Director University Honors Program .... Dr. Melinda L. JONES
07 Director of Admissions .... Mr. Stephen MCKELLIPS
28 Director of Diversity Initiatives .... Dr. Karen WEDDLE-WEST
88 Dn Communication Sciences Disorders .... Dr. Maurice I. MENDEL
49 Dean of Arts & Sciences .... Dr. Thomas J. NENON
50 Dean Business & Economics .... Dr. Rajiv GROVER
53 Int Dean of Educ Health/Human Sci .... Dr. Ernest A. RAKOW
54 Dean of Engineering .... Dr. Richard J. SWEIGARD
55 Dean University College .... Dr. Dan L. LATTIMORE
57 Dean Communication & Fine Arts .... Dr. Richard R. RANTA
61 Dean School of Law .... Mr. Peter V. LETSOU
66 Dean School of Nursing .... Dr. Lin ZHAN
69 Dean School of Public Health .... Dr. Lisa M. KLESGES
76 Exec Dean of Health Sciences .... Dr. Donald I. WAGNER

*Chattanooga State Community College (C)

4501 Amnicola Highway, Chattanooga TN 37406-1097
County: Hamilton FICE Identification: 003998
Unit ID: 219824
Telephone: (423) 697-4400 Carnegie Class: Assoc/Pub-R-L
FAX Number: N/A Calendar System: Semester
URL: www.chattanoogastate.edu
Established: 1965 Annual Undergrad Tuition & Fees (In-State): $3,973
Enrollment: 9,332 Coed
Affiliation or Control: State IRS Status: 501(c)3
Highest Offering: Associate Degree
Program: Occupational; 2-Year Principally Bachelor's Creditable
Accreditation: **SC**, ACBSP, ADNUR, CAHIIM, COARC, DA, DH, DMS, EMT, ENGR, ENGT, MAC, NMT, PTAA, RAD, RTT, SURGT

02 President .... Dr. Flora TYDINGS
04 Special Assistant to the President .... Mr. Joe HELSETH
26 Vice President IE/IR & Marketing .... Ms. Eva LEWIS
05 Provost/Vice Pres Academic Affairs ..... Dr. Kimberly MCCORMICK
10 Exec Vice Pres Business & Finance .... Ms. Tammy SWENSON
32 Vice President Student Services .... Ms. Debbie ADAMS
31 Vice President Economic & Comm Dev .... Vacant
13 Vice President Technology .... Dr. James BARROTT
44 Assoc Vice Pres Fund Development .... Ms. Nancy PATTERSON
20 Assoc Vice Pres Academic Affairs .... Vacant
21 Asst Vice Pres Business & Finance .... Ms. Susan JOSEPH
35 Asst Vice Pres Student Affairs .... Mr. Brad MCCORMICK
18 Asst VP Plant Operations/Facil Plng .... Mr. Steve HUSKINS
56 Asst VP Distributed Education .... Ms. Judy LOWE
25 Asst VP Grants/Contracts/Stdnt Acct .... Ms. Debbie MAILEN
51 Dir/Mgr Continuing Education .... Ms. Ju-Hsin LUSK
09 Director Institutional Research .... Ms. Bonnie RIGGS
27 Director Marketing .... Ms. Patty BROWN
15 Director Human Resources .... Vacant
36 Director Career Services/Counseling .... Ms. Sheila ALBRITTON
37 Director Student Financial Aid .... Ms. Julae GROSZ
07 Director of Admissions/Records .... Ms. Gail CAMPBELL
28 Director Diversity .... Ms. Mary KNAFF
41 Athletic Director .... Vacant

08 Dean Library Services .... Ms. Susan JENNINGS
76 Dean Allied Health & Nursing .... Dr. Mark KNUTSEN
79 Dean Humanities & Fine Arts .... Mr. Darrin HASSEVOORT
83 Interim Dean Social/Behavioral Scie .... Mr. John HAWORTH
81 Dean Math & Sciences .... Dr. Mosunmola GEORGE-TAYLOR
50 Dean Business/Info Tech .... Mr. Barry JENNISON
32 Dean Student Life/Judicial Affairs .... Ms. Sandy RUTTER
75 Dean Tennessee Technology Center .... Dr. Mike RICKETTS
54 Dean Engineering Technology .... Mr. Tim MCGHEE
84 Dir of Enrollment Services Center .... Ms. Kisha CALDWELL
22 Dir Affirmative Action/EEO .... Mr. Jerome GOBER

*Cleveland State Community College (D)

PO Box 3570, Cleveland TN 37320-3570
County: Bradley FICE Identification: 003999
Unit ID: 219879
Telephone: (423) 472-7141 Carnegie Class: Assoc/Pub-R-M
FAX Number: (423) 478-6255 Calendar System: Semester
URL: www.clevelandstatecc.edu
Established: 1967 Annual Undergrad Tuition & Fees (In-State): $2,064
Enrollment: 3,750 Coed
Affiliation or Control: State IRS Status: 501(c)3
Highest Offering: Associate Degree
Program: Occupational; 2-Year Principally Bachelor's Creditable
Accreditation: **SC**, ACBSP, ADNUR, MAC, NAIT

02 President .... Dr. William SEYMOUR
05 Vice President for Academic Affairs .... Dr. Denise KING
32 Vice President for Student Services .... Dr. Michael STOKES
10 Vice President Admin & Finance .... Dr. Thomas WRIGHT
09 Director of Institutional Research .... Mrs. Marcia O'CONNOR
37 Director of Financial Aid .... Mrs. Jamie HAMBY
30 Dir of Institutional Advancement .... Vacant
26 Director Marketing & Promotions .... Mr. Tony BARTOLO
06 Asst Dir Enrollment Svcs/Registrar .... Mrs. Gail GREENWOOD
15 Director of Human Resources .... Ms. Joan BATES
08 Director of the Library .... Ms. Sarah COPELAND
13 Director of College Computing .... Mr. Chris MOWERY
19 Coordinator Campus Security .... Mr. Mike HODGES
50 Dean of Business & Technology .... Ms. Susan WEBB-CURTIS
66 Dean of Health & Wellness .... Mrs. Nancy LABINE
79 Dean Humanities/Social Sciences .... Dr. Robert BRANDON
81 Dean of Math/Science .... Dr. Mitchell RHEA
38 Dir Student Development/ACCESS Ctr .... Mr. Mark WILSON
103 Dir Workforce Development .... Mr. Rick CREASY
18 Director of Plant Operations .... Mr. Guy DAVIS
21 Business Manager .... Ms. Alisha FOX
84 Director of Enrollment Services .... Mr. Jason SEWELL
07 Asst Director of Admissions .... Ms. Suzanne BAYNE
41 Athletic Director .... Mr. Mike POLICASTRO

*Columbia State Community College (E)

1665 Hampshire Pike, Columbia TN 38401-5653
County: Maury FICE Identification: 003483
Unit ID: 219888
Telephone: (931) 540-2722 Carnegie Class: Assoc/Pub-R-M
FAX Number: (931) 540-2535 Calendar System: Semester
URL: www.columbiastate.edu
Established: 1966 Annual Undergrad Tuition & Fees (In-State): $3,929
Enrollment: 5,117 Coed
Affiliation or Control: State IRS Status: 501(c)3
Highest Offering: Associate Degree
Program: Occupational; 2-Year Principally Bachelor's Creditable
Accreditation: **SC**, ACBSP, ADNUR, COARC, EMT, RAD

02 President .... Dr. Janet F. SMITH
05 Executive Vice President/Provost .... Dr. Margaret D. SMITH
10 Vice Pres Financial/Admin Services .... Mr. Kenneth R. HORNER
30 Executive for Advancement .... Ms. Bethany LAY
20 Assoc VP Faculty/Curric & Programs .... Ms. Joni L. LENIG
32 Assoc VP Student Services .... Ms. Cecelia JOHNSON
13 Assoc VP Info Technology .... Dr. Emily SICIENSKY
21 Assoc VP Business Services .... Ms. Elaine CURTIS
26 Dir Public Rels & Marketing .... Ms. Amy SPEARS-BOYD
28 Asst to Pres for Access & Diversity .... Dr. Christa S. MARTIN
06 Director Records .... Ms. Sharon G. BOWEN
15 Director Human Resources .... Ms. Christie MILLER
08 Director Library .... Ms. Kathy BREEDEN
38 Coord Counseling & Student Succ Svc .... Vacant
09 Dir Inst Effectiveness & Planning .... Ms. Tammy BORREN
37 Director Financial Aid .... Ms. Cherry JOHNSON
41 Interim Director Athletics .... Mr. Johnny LITTRELL
18 Director Facility Services & Safety .... Mr. Tim HALLMARK
56 Dean Extended Svcs & Will Campus .... Dr. Shanna JACKSON
35 Director Student Success Counseling .... Ms. Connie GALLON
96 Coordinator Purchasing .... Mr. Jon ARNOLD
84 Chief Enrollment Svcs Officer .... Ms. Jill RILEY
103 Dir Workforce/Career Development .... Ms. Terri KINLOCH
104 Director Study Abroad .... Ms. Ana BASOA-MCMILLAN
106 Dir Online Education/E-learning .... Dr. Marilia GERGES
108 Director Institutional Assessment .... Mr. Rion MCDONALD
19 Director Security/Safety .... Mr. Randy CARROLL

*Dyersburg State Community College (F)

1510 Lake Road, Dyersburg TN 38024-2450
County: Dyer FICE Identification: 006835
Unit ID: 220057

Telephone: (731) 286-3200 Carnegie Class: Assoc/Pub-R-M
FAX Number: (731) 286-3333 Calendar System: Semester
URL: www.dscc.edu
Established: 1967 Annual Undergrad Tuition & Fees (In-State): $4,127
Enrollment: 2,847 Coed
Affiliation or Control: State IRS Status: 501(c)3
Highest Offering: Associate Degree
Program: Occupational; 2-Year Principally Bachelor's Creditable
Accreditation: SC, ACBSP, ADNUR, CAHIIM, EMT

02 President ....Dr. Karen A. BOWYER
05 Vice President for the College ....Dr. Teri MADDOX
10 Vice President Finance/Admin Svcs ....Mr. Lowell (Bud) HOFFMANN
30 Vice Pres Institutional Advancement ....Vacant
13 Vice President Technology ....Ms. Diane CAMPER
32 Dean of Student Services ....Ms. Larenda FULTZ
08 Dean Learning Resources Center ....Ms. Susan CHARLEY
37 Director of Financial Aid ....Mrs. Sandra ROCKETT
09 Director of Institutional Research ..Ms. Youlanda JONES-WILCOX
15 Director Human Resources ....Ms. Sheilah GILLAHAN
103 Director of Workforce Development ....Ms. Margaret PRATER
29 Director of Alumni Relations ....Ms. Amy FINCH
38 Academic/Career Counselor ....Ms. Sherry BAKER
41 Director of Athletics ....Mr. Alan BARNETT
18 Director of Physical Plant ....Mr. Kent JETTON
07 Director of Admissions ....Ms. Donna NEBLETT
06 Director of Records ....Ms. Patricia WALKER
26 Director of Public Information ....Ms. Amy FINCH
96 Director of Purchasing ....Ms. Amy WATTS
21 Business & Student Fin Svcs Manager ....Ms. Donna MEALER
49 Dean Arts & Sciences ....Mr. James BARHAM
72 Dean Business/Tech/Allied Health ....Ms. Julie FRAZIER
66 Int Dean Nursing/Allied Health Div ....Ms. Amy JOHNSON
51 Dean of Continuing Education ....Ms. Youlanda JONES-WILCOX

*Jackson State Community College (A)

2046 North Parkway, Jackson TN 38301-3797
County: Madison FICE Identification: 004937
Unit ID: 220400
Telephone: (731) 424-3520 Carnegie Class: Assoc/Pub-R-M
FAX Number: (731) 425-2647 Calendar System: Semester
URL: www.jscc.edu
Established: 1965 Annual Undergrad Tuition & Fees (In-State): $4,113
Enrollment: 4,924 Coed
Affiliation or Control: State IRS Status: 501(c)3
Highest Offering: Associate Degree
Program: Occupational; 2-Year Principally Bachelor's Creditable
Accreditation: SC, ACBSP, ADNUR, COARC, EMT, MLTAD, NAIT, PTAA, RAD

02 President ....Dr. Bruce BLANDING
05 VP of Academic Affairs ....Dr. Larry BAILEY
10 Vice Pres of Finance & Admin Affs ....Mr. Horace W. CHASE
30 Dir of Development/Alumni Relations ....Ms. Dee HENDERSON
32 VP of Student Services ....Mr. Bobby SMITH
30 VP of Institutional Advancement ....Vacant
88 Internal Auditor ....Mrs. Angela P. BROWN
15 Dir Human Resources/Affirm Action ....Mrs. Amy WEST
09 Dir Inst Research & Accountability ....Vacant
31 Dir of Lifetime Learning ....Ms. Leah GRAY
13 Director of Information Technology ....Ms. Dana NAILS
21 Director of Business Services ....Mr. Tim DELLINGER
18 Director of Physical Plant ....Mr. Gerald BATCHELOR
96 Director of Purchasing ....Mr. Robert D. HEMRICK
12 Director Lexington Campus ....Ms. Sandy STANFILL
12 Director Savannah Campus ....Mrs. Meda FALLS
12 Director Humboldt Campus ....Ms. Lisa BARKER
88 Director of HS Initiatives ....Mrs. Andrea WINCHESTER
26 Coordinator of PR and Marketing ....Vacant
37 Director Student Financial Aid ....Ms. Dewana LATIMER
07 Director of Admissions and Records ....Ms. Robin MAREK
08 Head Librarian ....Mr. Scott COHEN
19 Director Security/Safety ....Mr. Darron BILLINGS

*Motlow State Community College (B)

PO Box 8500, Lynchburg TN 37352-8500
County: Moore FICE Identification: 006836
Unit ID: 221096
Telephone: (931) 393-1500 Carnegie Class: Assoc/Pub-R-M
FAX Number: (931) 393-1681 Calendar System: Semester
URL: www.mscc.edu
Established: 1969 Annual Undergrad Tuition & Fees (In-State): $3,949
Enrollment: 4,790 Coed
Affiliation or Control: State IRS Status: 501(c)3
Highest Offering: Associate Degree
Program: Occupational; 2-Year Principally Bachelor's Creditable
Accreditation: SC, ACBSP, ADNUR

02 President ....Dr. Anthony KINKEL
05 VP for Academic Affairs ....Dr. Cynthia KELLEY
10 Vice Pres for Business Affairs ....Ms. Hilda TUNSTILL
13 VP for Technology & Admin Services ....Ms. Cynthia LOGAN
20 Asst Vice Pres for Academic Affair ....Dr. Scott COOK
32 VP for Student Affairs ....Mr. Jerry TUNSTILL
18 Director of Facilities ....Mr. Brian GAFFORD
14 Director of Technical Operations ....Mr. Matt HULVEY
31 Director Student & Campus Relations ....Ms. Brenda CANNON
35 Asst Vice President Student Affairs ....Ms. Regina BURDEN
08 Director of Libraries ....Mr. Stuart GAETJENS
37 Executive Director of Financial Aid ....Mr. Joe MYERS
38 Director of Disability & Testing ....Ms. Sonya HOOD
07 Director of Admissions & Records ....Ms. Greer ALSUP
66 Interim Director of Nursing ....Ms. Pat HENDRIX
41 Director of Athletics ....Ms. Tori RABY-GENTRY
09 Dir of Research/Planning & Comm ....Ms. Sylvia COLLINS
90 Director Center for Academic Tech ....Dr. Shelly MCCOY
12 Director McMinnville Center ....Ms. Melody EDMONDS
12 Director Fayetteville Center ....Ms. Laura MONKS
12 Director Smyrna Site ....Ms. Cheryl HYLAND
36 Dir of Career Placement & Extended ....Mr. Tom DILLINGHAM
15 Director of Human Resources ....Ms. Laura JENT
96 Director of Purchasing ....Ms. Sandy SCHAFFER
04 Admin Assistant to the President ....Ms. Christy GLENN

*Nashville State Community College (C)

120 White Bridge Road, Nashville TN 37209-4515
County: Davidson FICE Identification: 008145
Unit ID: 221184
Telephone: (615) 353-3333 Carnegie Class: Assoc/Pub-U-MC
FAX Number: (615) 353-3713 Calendar System: Semester
URL: www.nscc.edu
Established: 1969 Annual Undergrad Tuition & Fees (In-State): $3,998
Enrollment: 10,044 Coed
Affiliation or Control: State IRS Status: 501(c)3
Highest Offering: Associate Degree
Program: Occupational; 2-Year Principally Bachelor's Creditable; Business Emphasis
Accreditation: SC, ACBSP, ACFEI, ADNUR, NAIT, OTA, SURGT

02 President ....Dr. George H. VAN ALLEN
05 Vice President of Academic Affairs ....Dr. Ronald DAVIS
10 Vice Pres Finance & Administration ....Mrs. Mary M. CROSS
09 VP of Institutional Effectiveness ....Dr. Flora R. SETAYESH
45 Assoc VP Planning/Assessment ....Mr. Ted M. WASHINGTON
30 Exec Dir of Devel/Dir Public Affs ....Mr. Keith D. FERGUSON
32 Dean of Students ....Dr. Carol J. MARTIN-OSORIO
21 Internal Auditor ....Mrs. Patricia A. FELLER
06 Registrar ....Mr. Lance L. WOODARD
07 Director of Admissions ....Mrs. Laura P. MORAN
13 Director of Computer Services ....Mr. Paul A. KAMINSKY
19 Director of Safety and Security ....Mr. Derrek G. SHEUCRAFT
37 Director of Financial Aid ....Mr. James J. MORAN
15 Dir Human Res/Affirm Act/Diversity ....Ms. Lori B. MADDOX
18 Director of Operations/Maintenance ....Mr. Jim T. DAWSON
103 Dir Workforce and Community Dev ....Ms. Gail G. PHILLIPS
26 Manager of Publications ....Ms. Ellen L. ZINK
106 Director of Online Learning ....Vacant
83 Dean of Social and Life Sciences ....Dr. Julie E. WILLIAMS
72 Dean of Comp/Eng Technologies ....Dr. Reginald J. GARDNER
81 Dean Math & Natural Sciences ....Dr. Sarah E. ROBERTS
79 Dean English/Humanities & Arts ....Dr. Patricia J. ARMSTRONG
62 Dean Lrng Resources & Distance Educ ....Dr. Faye M. JONES
50 Dean Business & Applied Arts ....Ms. Karen L. STEVENSON
96 Director of Purchasing ....Ms. Jo SMITH
66 Director of Nursing ....Dr. Cynthia G. WALLER
04 Administrative Asst to President ....Mrs. Judy I. COOK

*Northeast State Community College (D)

PO Box 246, 2425 Highway 75, Blountville TN 37617-0246
County: Sullivan FICE Identification: 005378
Unit ID: 221908
Telephone: (423) 323-3191 Carnegie Class: Assoc/Pub-R-M
FAX Number: (423) 279-7636 Calendar System: Semester
URL: www.northeaststate.edu
Established: 1965 Annual Undergrad Tuition & Fees (In-State): $3,924
Enrollment: 5,865 Coed
Affiliation or Control: State IRS Status: 501(c)3
Highest Offering: Associate Degree
Program: Occupational; 2-Year Principally Bachelor's Creditable
Accreditation: SC, ACBSP, ADNUR, CVT, DA, EMT, MLTAD, NAIT, SURGT

02 President ....Dr. Janice H. GILLIAM
04 Exec Assistant to the President ....Ms. Cindy S. CHRISTIAN
05 Vice Pres Academic Affairs ....Dr. Allana R. HAMILTON
10 Chief Financial Officer ....Dr. Steven CAMPBELL
11 Vice Pres Administrative Svcs ....Mr. Fred LEWIS
32 Vice President Student Affairs ....Mr. Matt DELOZIER
12 VP for Northeast State at Kingsport ....Mr. Jeff D. MCCORD
56 Asst VP Evening/Distance Educ ....Dr. Pashia HOGAN
20 Asst Vice Pres Academic Affairs ....Mr. Don COLEMAN
06 Registrar/Admissions & Records ....Ms. Deidra CLOSE
15 Director Human Resources ....Ms. Tyro COPAS
31 Director Community Relations ....Mr. Robert CARPENTER
26 Director of Marketing ....Ms. Amanda ADAMS
09 Institutional Effectiveness Officer ....Dr. Susan E. GRAYBEAL
08 Dean Library ....Vacant
79 Dean Humanities ....Mr. William WILSON
81 Dean Math ....Ms. Malissa TRENT
76 Dean Health Related Profession ....Ms. Connie MARSHALL
72 Dean Advance Technologies ....Mr. Sam S. ROWELL
83 Dean Behavior/Social Sciences ....Dr. Xiaoping WANG
81 Dean Science ....Dr. Carolyn MCCRACKEN
50 Dean Business Technologies ....Mr. Danny L. LAWSON
66 Dean Nursing ....Dr. Melessia D. WEBB
84 Dean of Enrollment Management ....Ms. Jennifer STARLING
07 VA Admissions/Records Tech Clerk ....Mr. John ADCOX

*Pellissippi State Community College (E)

PO Box 22990, Knoxville TN 37933-0990
County: Knox FICE Identification: 012693
Unit ID: 221643
Telephone: (865) 694-6400 Carnegie Class: Assoc/Pub-U-MC
FAX Number: (865) 539-7240 Calendar System: Semester
URL: www.pstcc.edu
Established: 1974 Annual Undergrad Tuition & Fees (In-State): $3,987
Enrollment: 10,099 Coed
Affiliation or Control: State IRS Status: 501(c)3
Highest Offering: Associate Degree
Program: Occupational; 2-Year Principally Bachelor's Creditable
Accreditation: SC, ACBSP, ACFEI, ADNUR, NAIT

02 President ....Dr. L. Anthony WISE
05 Vice President of Academic Affairs ....Dr. Ted A. LEWIS
13 Vice President Information Services ....Ms. Audrey J. WILLIAMS
10 Vice President Business & Finance ....Mr. Ronald L. KESTERSON
30 VP College Advancement/Exec Dir Fdn ....Ms. Peggy M. WILSON
32 Vice President of Student Affairs ....Dr. Rebecca L. ASHFORD
103 Exec Dir Business/Workforce Dev ....Ms. Teri T. BRAHAMS
12 Campus Dean Blount County Programs ....Ms. Holly L. BURKETT
12 Campus Dean Strawberry Pl Program ....Dr. Mike NORTH
12 Campus Dean Magnolia Ave Programs ..Ms. Rosalyn P. TILLMAN
12 Campus Dean Division Street Program ....Ms. Esther L. DYER
35 Asst Vice President/Dean of Student ....Ms. Mary C. BLEDSOE
21 Asst VP Business Services ....Ms. Renee MOORE
20 Asst VP of Academic Affairs ....Vacant
84 Asst VP Enrollment Services ....Ms. Leigh A. TOUZEAU
22 Exec Director Equity & Compliance ....Dr. Patrick SHIPWASH
35 Dir of Student Life & Recreation ....Ms. Kim THOMAS-LARUE
36 Director of Placement ....Ms. Carolyn N. CARSON
88 Director of Disability Services ....Ms. Ann E. SATKOWIAK
38 Director Counseling Department ....Dr. Elizabeth E. FIRESTONE
26 Director Marketing & Communications ....Ms. Julia H. WOOD
06 Registrar ....Ms. Melanie PARADISE
08 Director of Library Services ....Mr. J. Peter NERZAK
24 Interim Dir Educ Technology Svcs ....Mr. Brandon BALLENTINE
37 Director of Financial Aid ....Mr. Dick SMELSER
09 Dir Inst Effective/Assess/Planning ....Ms. Nancy A. RAMSEY
18 Director of Facilities ....Ms. Regina MCNEW
19 Director Safety/Security ....Mr. Fred BREINER
21 Director/Budget & Payroll ....Ms. Nancy DONAHUE
96 Director of Purchasing ....Mr. John S. CLARK
15 Director Human Resources ....Ms. Carole GARY
25 Interim Driector/Grant Development ....Mr. David CAZALET
104 Exec Dir TnCIS/International Educ ....Ms. Tracey BRADLEY
44 Director Major Gift Development ....Ms. Marilyn RODDY
44 Director of Annual & Planned Giving ..Ms. Aneisa L. MCDONALD
29 Dir Cmty Outreach/Donor Engagement ....Ms. Patricia T. MYERS
91 Dir Applications Programming Sup ....Mr. James (Dean) COPPLE
07 Director of Admissions & Com Ctr ....Ms. Heather HATFIELD
28 Director of Access & Diversity ....Ms. Gayle E. WOOD
88 Director of Academic Testing ....Ms. Joan NEWMAN
88 Dir Curriculum & New Programs ....Ms. Judy GOSCH
88 Director of Advising ....Ms. Rachael C. CRAGLE
88 Dir Academic Support Programs ....Ms. Marilyn A. HARPER
88 Bursar ....Ms. Mandy BENTZ
88 Director of Internal Audit ....Ms. Suzanne WALKER
88 Director of QEP ....Ms. Kellie TOON
88 Director of New Student Orientation ....Ms. Rebecca MILAM
88 Director TRIO Student Support Svcs ....Dr. Mark S. COTTER

*Roane State Community College (F)

276 Patton Lane, Harriman TN 37748-5011
County: Roane FICE Identification: 009914
Unit ID: 221397
Telephone: (865) 354-3000 Carnegie Class: Assoc/Pub-R-M
FAX Number: (865) 882-4585 Calendar System: Semester
URL: www.roanestate.edu
Established: 1971 Annual Undergrad Tuition & Fees (In-State): $4,389
Enrollment: 5,832 Coed
Affiliation or Control: State IRS Status: 501(c)3
Highest Offering: Associate Degree
Program: Occupational; 2-Year Principally Bachelor's Creditable
Accreditation: SC, ACBSP, ADNUR, CAHIIM, COARC, COMTA, DH, EMT, OPD, OTA, POLYT, PTAA, RAD

02 President ....Dr. Chris WHALEY
05 Vice Pres for Student Learning ....Dr. Diane WARD
10 Exec Vice Pres Business & Finance ....Mr. Danny C. GIBBS
103 VP Workforce Develop/Student Affs ....Ms. Teresa S. DUNCAN
30 VP Inst Advancement & Cmty Rels ....Ms. Melinda HILLMAN
21 Asst VP Fiscal/Auxiliary Services ....Ms. Jamie WILMOTH
13 Asst Vice Pres of Info Technology ....Mr. Timothy D. CARROLL
09 Asst VP Institutional Research ....Ms. Karen L. BRUNNER
22 Coordinator Affirmative Action ....Mr. Odell FEARN
08 Director of Library Services ....Mr. Robert M. BENSON
06 Director of Records & Registration ....Ms. Brenda RECTOR
18 Director Physical Plant & Expo Ctr ....Mr. Stan R. STARKEY
29 Director Alumni Relations ....Ms. Tamsin MILLER
96 Director of Purchasing ....Mrs. Dana PRESLEY
36 Workforce Placement & Job Placement ....Ms. Kim HARRIS
04 Executive Assistant to President ....Mrs. Pam WOODY
19 Director Security/Safety ....Mr. Thomas STUFANO
26 Chief Public Relations/Marketing ....Mr. Owen DRISKILL
41 Athletic Director ....Mr. Randy NESBIT

*Southwest Tennessee Community College (A)

PO Box 780, Memphis TN 38101-0780
County: Shelby FICE Identification: 010439
Unit ID: 221485
Telephone: (901) 333-5020 Carnegie Class: Assoc/Pub-U-MC
FAX Number: (901) 333-5024 Calendar System: Semester
URL: www.southwest.tn.edu
Established: 2000 Annual Undergrad Tuition & Fees (In-State): $3,963
Enrollment: 10,227 Coed
Affiliation or Control: State IRS Status: 501(c)3
Highest Offering: Associate Degree
Program: Occupational; 2-Year Principally Bachelor's Creditable
Accreditation: SC, ACBSP, ACFEI, ADNUR, #DIETT, EMT, ENGT, MLTAD, PHLEB, PTAA, RAD

02 President .... Dr. Tracy D. HALL
04 Assistant to the President .... Ms. Veronica RELIFORD-THOMAS
05 Provost/Executive Vice President .... Ms. Barbara ROSEBOROUGH
41 Athletic Director .... Mr. Sherman D. GREER
30 Vice Pres Institutional Advancement .... Ms. Karen F. NIPPERT
10 Vice Pres Finance & Admin Services .... Mr. Ronald G. PARR
32 Vice Pres Student Svcs/Enroll Mgmt .... Dr. Dwayne SCOTT
84 Exec Director Enrollment Management .... Ms. Thalia WILSON
26 Exec Director of Comm & Marketing .... Mr. Robert G. MILLER
15 Exec Director Hum Res/Affirm Action .... Mr. Tracy HORTON
06 Registrar .... Ms. Barbara WELLS
18 Director Physical Plant .... Vacant
96 Director of Purchasing .... Mr. Charles FENNELL
37 Dir Student Financial Aid .... Ms. Lechelle DAVENPORT
09 Institutional Research Analyst .... Mr. Donald C. MYERS

*Volunteer State Community College (B)

1480 Nashville Pike, Gallatin TN 37066-3188
County: Sumner FICE Identification: 009912
Unit ID: 222053
Telephone: (615) 452-8600 Carnegie Class: Assoc/Pub-S-SC
FAX Number: (615) 230-3577 Calendar System: Semester
URL: www.volstate.edu
Established: 1970 Annual Undergrad Tuition & Fees (In-State): $3,607
Enrollment: 7,664 Coed
Affiliation or Control: State IRS Status: 501(c)3
Highest Offering: Associate Degree
Program: Occupational; 2-Year Principally Bachelor's Creditable
Accreditation: SC, ACBSP, CAHIIM, COARC, DA, DMS, EMT, MLTAD, POLYT, PTAA, RAD

02 President .... Dr. Jerry FAULKNER
04 Exec Assistant to the President .... Dr. Lauren K. COLLIER
05 Vice President Academic Affairs .... Dr. George PIMENTEL
10 Vice President Business & Finance .... Ms. Beth COOKSEY
32 Vice President Student Services .... Ms. Patty T. POWELL
30 Vice Pres for Resource Development .... Ms. Karen MITCHELL
45 Vice Pres Inst Planning/Research .... Ms. Jane MCGUIRE
20 Asst VP of Academic Affairs .... Dr. Michael TORRENCE
21 Asst Vice Pres Business & Finance .... Ms. Renee AUSTIN
35 Asst VP Student Svcs/Enrollment Mgt .... Ms. Emily SHORT
51 Asst VP/Dean Continuing Education .... Mrs. Hilary B. MARABETI
76 Dean of Health .... Mr. Elvis BRANDON
79 Dean Humanities .... Dr. Alycia EHLERT
53 Dean Social Science/Education .... Ms. Phyllis FOLEY
81 Dean Math & Science .... Vacant
50 Interim Dean of Business .... Dr. Rob MORRIS
88 Director of Development Studies Pgm .... Ms. Kay DAYTON
15 Dir Personnel/Affirm Act/Human Res .... Ms. Lori CUTRELL
08 Director Library Services .... Ms. Sarah SMITH
07 Dir Admissions & College Registrar .... Mr. Tim AMYX
13 Director Information Technology .... Mr. Kevin BLANKENSHIP
37 Director Student Financial Aid .... Mrs. Sue H. PEDIGO
26 Director Public Relations .... Mrs. Tami WALLACE
18 Senior Director Physical Plant .... Mr. William NEWMAN
19 Chief Security & Safety .... Mr. William D. ROGAN
41 Director of Athletics .... Mr. Bobby HUDSON
106 Director Distance Learning .... Ms. Rhonda GREGORY
88 Special Adult Programs/ADA Director .... Ms. Kathy SOWELL
55 Director of Evening Services .... Ms. Brenda BUFFINGTON
09 Director of Institutional Research .... Mrs. Ann Marie CALDERON
96 Director Purchasing .... Mr. Terry MCGOVERN
24 Director Media Services .... Mr. Terry HEINEN
88 Director Retention Support Services .... Ms. Heather HARPER
36 Director of Career Placement .... Dr. Rick PARRENT
38 Director Counseling & Testing .... Mr. Terry BUBB
28 Director Student Life & Diversity .... Mr. Kenny YARBROUGH
88 Dir Health Sciences Ctr of Emphasis .... Ms. Terri CRUTCHER
44 Director of Development .... Ms. Debra DAUGHERTY
06 Registrar .... Mr. Tim AMYX
84 Director Enrollment Management .... Ms. Emily SHORT

*Walters State Community College (C)

500 S Davy Crockett Parkway, Morristown TN 37813-6899
County: Hamblen FICE Identification: 008863
Unit ID: 222062
Telephone: (423) 585-2600 Carnegie Class: Assoc/Pub-R-L
FAX Number: (423) 585-6853 Calendar System: Semester
URL: www.ws.edu
Established: 1969 Annual Undergrad Tuition & Fees (In-State): $3,936
Enrollment: 6,339 Coed
Affiliation or Control: State IRS Status: 501(c)3
Highest Offering: Associate Degree
Program: Occupational; 2-Year Principally Bachelor's Creditable
Accreditation: SC, ACBSP, ACFEI, ADNUR, CAHIIM, COARC, EMT, NAIT, PTAA

02 President .... Dr. Wade B. MCCAMEY
04 Exec Director to the President .... Ms. Brenda L. SMALL
05 Vice President Academic Affairs .... Dr. Lori CAMPBELL
10 Vice President Business Affairs .... Dr. Rosemary JACKSON
32 Vice President Student Affairs .... Dr. Foster CHASON
30 Vice Pres for College Advancement .... Dr. Mark HURST
45 VP for Planning/Research/Assessment .... Dr. Debbie L. MCCARTER
20 Asst Vice Pres for Academic Affairs .... Ms. Linda ROBERTS
35 Asst Vice Pres Student Affairs .... Mr. Michael A. CAMPBELL
18 Ast Vice Pres Facilities Management .... Mr. Max E. WILLIAMS
21 Asst Vice Pres Business Affairs .... Mr. Roger D. BEVERLY
28 Spec Asst to Pres for Diversity .... Ms. W. Ann BOWEN
08 Dean of Library .... Dr. Jamie POSEY
31 Dean/Dir Cmty & Economic Devel .... Dr. Joseph L. COMBS
19 Dean of Public Safety Division .... Mr. Thomas STRANGE
17 Dean Health Programs .... Ms. Marty K. RUCKER
12 Dean Greenville/Greene Co Center .... Ms. Drucilla W. MILLER
12 Dean Sevier County Campus .... Dr. Jama SUTTON
83 Dean of Behavioral/Social Sciences .... Dr. Marilyn R. BOWERS
50 Dean of Business .... Dr. Amy ROSS
79 Dean of Humanities .... Ms. Carla TODARO
81 Dean of Mathematics .... Dr. John P. LAPRISE
49 Dean of Natural Science .... Dr. Jeffrey T. HORNER
75 Dean of Technical Education .... Mr. Thomas R. SEWELL
06 Dean Student Info System/Records .... Ms. Linda MASON
103 Dean Ctr for Workforce Development .... Dr. Nancy B. BROWN
37 Dean of Financial Aid .... Ms. Terri STANSBERRY
38 Exec Director Counseling/Testing .... Dr. Andy HALL
15 Exec Dir of Human Resources .... Ms. Tammy GOODE
26 Vice President Public Information .... Mr. James B. PECTOL
13 Exec Director for Information .... Mr. Joe E. SARGENT
41 Director of Athletics .... Dr. Foster CHASON
07 Director of Admissions .... Ms. Avery SWINSON
19 Chief of Campus Police .... Ms. Sarah ROSE
89 Director Freshmen Studies .... Dr. Marilyn R. BOWERS
36 Director Student Placement .... Dr. Andy HALL
92 Director Honors Program .... Ms. Janice M. DONAHUE
96 Director of Purchasing .... Ms. Jerri L. HAMER
105 Director of Network Services .... Mr. Bill R. MOREFIELD
29 Coordinator of Alumni Relations .... Ms. Wanda HARRELL
84 Director Enrollment Development .... Ms. Avery SWINSON
93 Coord Minority Student Recruit .... Ms. Roxanne BOWEN
108 Exec Dir of Planning & Assessment .... Dr. Deanna GARMAN

Tennessee Wesleyan College (D)

204 East College St., Athens TN 37303
County: McMinn FICE Identification: 003525
Unit ID: 221731
Telephone: (423) 745-7504 Carnegie Class: Bac/Diverse
FAX Number: (423) 744-9968 Calendar System: Semester
URL: www.twcnet.edu
Established: 1857 Annual Undergrad Tuition & Fees: $22,000
Enrollment: 1,011 Coed
Affiliation or Control: United Methodist IRS Status: 501(c)3
Highest Offering: Master's
Program: Liberal Arts And General; Teacher Preparatory; Professional
Accreditation: SC, NURSE

01 President .... Dr. Harley KNOWLES
05 Vice President for Academic Affairs .... Dr. Kim E. SPEZIO
10 Vice Pres Financial/Business Affs .... Ms. Gail HARRIS
32 Vice President for Student Life .... Dr. Scott MASHBURN
84 Asst Vice President for Enrollment .... Ms. Jessica EDWARDS
09 VP Institutional Effectiveness .... Mrs. Traci N. WILLIAMS
04 Admin Assistant to President .... Mrs. Gail ROGERS
08 Assoc Dean of Library Svcs .... Mrs. Sandra CLARIDAY
06 Registrar .... Mrs. Julie MCCASLIN
37 Director of Financial Aid .... Mrs. Lacey WEESE
29 Director of Alumni Relations .... Vacant
41 Athletic Director .... Mr. Donny MAYFIELD
15 Human Resources Director .... Mrs. Melody LANTZ
18 Chief of Facilities/Physical Plant .... Mr. Mike INGRAM
26 Director Public Relations .... Ms. Bridgette RAPER
35 Director of Student Activities .... Ms. Kerrie LYNN
13 Exec Director of Information Tech .... Mr. Brandon LAMBDIN

Trevecca Nazarene University (E)

333 Murfreesboro Road, Nashville TN 37210-2877
County: Davidson FICE Identification: 003526
Unit ID: 221892
Telephone: (615) 248-1200 Carnegie Class: DRU
FAX Number: (615) 248-7728 Calendar System: Semester
URL: www.trevecca.edu
Established: 1901 Annual Undergrad Tuition & Fees: $23,248
Enrollment: 2,606 Coed
Affiliation or Control: Church Of The Nazarene IRS Status: 501(c)3
Highest Offering: Doctorate
Program: 2-Year Principally Bachelor's Creditable; Liberal Arts And General; Teacher Preparatory; Professional
Accreditation: SC, ARCPA, CACREP, MUS, NURSE, SW, TED

01 President .... Dr. Dan BOONE
05 University Provost .... Dr. Stephen M. PUSEY
10 Exec Vice Pres Finance & Admin .... Mr. David CALDWELL
26 Vice President External Relations .... Mrs. Peggy J. COONING
51 Assoc Provost Graduate-Cont Stds .... Dr. Tim EADES
20 Assoc Vice Pres Academic Services .... Dr. Tom MIDDENDORF
20 Assoc Vice Pres Academic Programs .... Dr. Jim HIATT
32 Assoc Provost/Dean of Student Dev .... Mr. Stephen A. HARRIS
84 Assoc Provost/Dean of Enroll Mgmt .... Ms. Holly WHITBY
73 Dean School of Theol/Christian Min .... Dr. Timothy M. GREEN
50 Dean of Business and Technology .... Dr. Jim HIATT
35 Assoc Dean Student Community Life .... Mr. Matt SPRAKER
39 Asc Dean Students Residential Life .... Mrs. Ronda LILIENTHAL
53 Dean of the School of Education .... Dr. Suzann HARRIS
49 Dean of School of Arts & Science .... Dr. Lena WELCH
13 Chief Information Officer/ITS .... Mr. Jeff TURNER
08 Director Library Services .... Mrs. Ruth KINNERSLEY
09 Director Institutional Research .... Ms. Donna K. TUDOR
06 Registrar .... Mrs. Becky NIECE
19 Director of Security .... Mr. Norm ROBINSON
07 Director of Admissions .... Ms. Melinda MILLER
41 Athletic Director .... Mr. Mark ELLIOTT
88 Director Ctr/Ldrshp Calling Service .... Ms. Michelle GAERTNER
36 Director Counseling Services .... Dr. Sara HOPKINS
88 Coordinator of Sophomore Year Pgm .... Ms. Jennifer NEELY
88 Coordinator of Senior Year Programs .... Ms. Nicole RABALAIS
106 Director Online Learning .... Ms. LaMetrius DANIELS
21 Director of Financial Services .... Mr. Chuck SEAMAN
15 Director Human Resources .... Mr. Steve SEXTON
37 Director of Financial Aid .... Mr. Eddie WHITE
76 Director Physician Asst Pgm .... Mr. Bret REEVES
18 Director Plant Operations .... Mr. Glen LINTHICUM
44 Director Annual-Corp Giving .... Ms. Rebekah MEADOWS
29 Director of Alumni Services .... Mr. Michael JOHNSON
26 Director of Public Relations .... Mrs. Jan GREATHOUSE
88 Director of Marketing & Comm .... Mr. Matthew TOY

Tusculum College (F)

60 Shiloh Road, Greeneville TN 37743-9997
County: Greene FICE Identification: 003527
Unit ID: 221953
Telephone: (423) 636-7300 Carnegie Class: Master's S
FAX Number: (423) 638-7166 Calendar System: Other
URL: www.tusculum.edu
Established: 1794 Annual Undergrad Tuition & Fees: $22,670
Enrollment: 1,921 Coed
Affiliation or Control: Presbyterian Church (U.S.A.) IRS Status: 501(c)3
Highest Offering: Master's
Program: Liberal Arts And General; Teacher Preparatory; Professional
Accreditation: SC, CAATE

01 President .... Dr. Nancy B. MOODY
05 VP Academic Affairs .... Dr. Ron MAY
30 VP Institutional Advancement .... Ms. Heather PATCHETT
10 Vice Pres/Chief Financial Officer .... Mr. Steve GEHRET
84 VP for Enrollment Management .... Ms. LeAnn HUGHES
20 Asst VP for Academic Affairs .... Dr. Lisa JOHNSON
32 Dean of Students .... Dr. David MCMAHAN
35 Associate Dean of Students .... Ms. Jonita ASHLEY-PAULEY
06 Registrar .... Ms. Bobbie CLARKSTON
21 Controller .... Ms. Tracey JULIAN
07 Director of Operations/Admissions .... Ms. Melissa RIPLEY
45 Asst to Pres Inst Plng/Effectivenes .... Dr. Carl LARSEN
15 Director Human Resources .... Ms. Mary SONNER
36 Director Career Counseling .... Ms. Robin LAY
08 Librarian .... Mr. Myron J. SMITH, JR.
42 College Minister .... Mr. Mark STOKES
37 Director of Financial Aid .... Ms. Karen SARTAIN
41 Athletic Director .... Mr. Frankie DEBUSK
26 Director of Communications .... Ms. Suzanne RICHEY
13 Director of Information Systems .... Dr. Blair HENLEY
18 Director Facilities Management .... Mr. David MARTIN
92 Director of Honors Program .... Dr. Tom HARLOW
40 Bookstore Manager .... Mr. Cliff HOY
19 Director of Campus Safety .... Mr. Jonathan GRESHAM
49 Dean School of Arts and Sciences .... Mr. Wayne THOMAS
50 Dean School of Business .... Dr. Michael DILLON
53 Dean School of Education .... Dr. Paul FOX
66 Dean School of Nursing .... Dr. Lois EWEN

Union University (G)

1050 Union University Drive, Jackson TN 38305-3697
County: Madison FICE Identification: 003528
Unit ID: 221971
Telephone: (731) 668-1818 Carnegie Class: Master's L
FAX Number: (731) 661-5175 Calendar System: 4/1/4
URL: www.uu.edu
Established: 1823 Annual Undergrad Tuition & Fees: $29,190
Enrollment: 4,018 Coed
Affiliation or Control: Southern Baptist IRS Status: 501(c)3
Highest Offering: Doctorate
Program: Liberal Arts And General
Accreditation: SC, ANEST, ART, BUS, CAATE, ENG, MUS, NURSE, PHAR, SW, TED

01 President .... Dr. Samuel (Dub) W. OLIVER
05 Provost/VP Academic Affairs .... Dr. C. Ben MITCHELL
10 Sr Vice Pres Business Services .... Mr. Gary L. CARTER
30 Vice Pres Institutional Advancement .... Dr. Bob AGEE
84 Vice Pres Enrollment Services .... Mr. Dan GRIFFIN
32 Dean of Students .... Dr. Bryan CARRIER
26 Vice Pres for University Ministries .... Dr. Todd BRADY
108 Vice Pres Institutional Assessment .... Dr. Jimmy H. DAVIS
04 Exec Assistant to the President .... Mrs. Gaye CHRISTY
21 Assoc Vice Pres Business Svcs .... Mr. Robert SIMPSON

08 Assoc VP Academic Res/Dir Library ... Ms. Anna B. MORGAN
27 Assoc VP University Communications ... Mr. Tim ELLSWORTH
90 Assoc VP Information Technology ... Mr. James AVERY
15 Assoc VP Business Svcs/Human Res ... Mr. John CARBONELL
07 Asst VP for Undergraduate Admiss ... Mr. Robbie GRAVES
37 Director Student Financial Planning ... Mr. John WINDHAM
49 Dean College Arts & Sciences ... Dr. John NETLAND
50 Interim Dean School of Business ... Dr. Bill NANCE
66 Acting Dean School of Nursing ... Dr. Carol KELLIM
53 Exec Dean Col Educ/Human Studies ... Dr. Tom ROSEBROUGH
88 Dean Sch of Theology Missions ... Dr. Nathan FINN
67 Dean School of Pharmacy ... Dr. Sheila MITCHELL
91 Assoc Dir Information Technology ... Miss Karen MCWHERTER
36 Asst Dean Students/Dir Career Svcs ... Mrs. Jackie TAYLOR
29 Director of Alumni Relations ... Mr. Josh CLARKE
13 Director of Data Management ... Mr. David PORTER
06 Registrar ... Mrs. Susan HOPPER
19 Director of Security/Safety ... Mr. Chris MCDANIEL
41 Director of Athletics ... Mr. Tommy SADLER
18 Chief Facilities/Physical Plant ... Mr. David MCBRIDE

University of Phoenix Memphis Campus (A)

65 Germantown Court, Cordova TN 38018-7290
Telephone: (901) 751-1086 Identification: 770224
Accreditation: &NH, ACBSP

† No longer accepting campus-based students.

University of Phoenix Nashville Campus (B)

616 Marriott Drive, Nashville TN 37214-5048
Telephone: (615) 872-0188 Identification: 770225
Accreditation: &NH, ACBSP

† No longer accepting campus-based students.

*University of Tennessee System Office (C)

800 Andy Holt Tower, Knoxville TN 37996-0180
County: Knox FICE Identification: 008051
Unit ID: 221722
Telephone: (865) 974-1000 Carnegie Class: N/A
FAX Number: (865) 974-3753
URL: www.tennessee.edu

01 President ... Dr. Joe DIPIETRO
03 Executive Vice President ... Dr. David E. MILLHORN
05 VP Academic Affairs/Student Success ... Dr. Katherine N. HIGH
30 CEO UT Found/VP Develop & Alumni ... Mr. Ricky N. MCCURRY
86 VP for Government Rels/Advocacy ... Mr. Anthony HAYNES
45 Vice President for Research ... Dr. David E. MILLHORN
10 Treasurer & CIO/CFO ... Mr. Charles (Butch) M. PECCOLO, JR.
43 VP/General Counsel/Secretary ... Ms. Catherine S. MIZELL
15 Vice President for Human Resources ... Ms. Linda HENDRICKS HARIG
86 Int Vice Pres Inst for Public Svc ... Dr. Herb BYRD
04 Exec Assistant to the President ... Mr. Keith CARVER
21 Exec Dir Auditing/Consulting Svcs ... Ms. Sandy JANSEN
29 Exec Dir UT Natl Alumni Assn ... Mr. Lofton K. STUART
26 VP Communications & Marketing ... Dr. Tonjanita JOHNSON

*University of Tennessee, Knoxville (D)

1331 Circle Park, Andy Holt Tower,
Knoxville TN 37996-0184
County: Knox FICE Identification: 003530
Unit ID: 221759
Telephone: (865) 974-1000 Carnegie Class: RU/VH
FAX Number: (865) 974-1182 Calendar System: Semester
URL: www.utk.edu
Established: 1794 Annual Undergrad Tuition & Fees (In-State): $12,436
Enrollment: 30,856 Coed
Affiliation or Control: State IRS Status: 501(c)3
Highest Offering: Doctorate
Program: Liberal Arts And General; Teacher Preparatory; Professional
Accreditation: SC, ANEST, ART, AUD, BUS, BUSA, CACREP, CIDA, CLPSY, COPSY, #CORE, CS, DENT, DIETD, DIETI, ENG, IPSY, JOUR, LAW, LIB, LSAR, MT, MUS, NRPA, NURSE, PAST, PH, RAD, SCPSY, SP, SW, TED, THEA, VET

02 Chancellor ... Dr. Jimmy G. CHEEK
100 Chancellor's Executive Assistant ... Mr. Russ SWAFFORD
05 Provost/Senior VC for Acad Affairs ... Dr. Susan D. MARTIN
32 Vice Chancellor for Student Life ... Dr. Vincent CARILLI
46 Vice Chancellor Research/Engagement ... Dr. Taylor EIGHMY
10 Vice Chanc Finance & Administration ... Mr. Chris CIMINO
26 Vice Chanc for Communications ... Ms. Margie NICHOLS
30 Vice Chanc Development/Alumni Affs ... Mr. Scott RABENOLD
20 Vice Provost for Academic Affairs ... Ms. Sally J. MCMILLAN
20 Vice Provost Academic Operations ... Vacant
58 Vice Provost/Dean Graduate School ... Dr. Carolyn R. HODGES
46 Ast VC Student Life/Dean of Student ... Dr. Melissa SHIVERS
39 Asst VC/Exec Dir Univ Housing ... Dr. Frank CUEVAS
51 Asst Provost Univ Outrch/Cont Educ ... Dr. Norvel BURKETT
07 Asst Provost Enrollment Svcs ... Mr. Richard L. BAYER
18 Assoc Vice Chanc Facilities Svcs ... Mr. Dave IRVIN
41 Vice Chancellor/Dir Athletics ... Mr. Dave HART
28 Assoc Vice Chanc Equity & Diversity ... Ms. Jennifer RICHTER
37 Director of Financial Aid ... Mr. Jeffrey G. GERKIN
09 Dir Inst Research/Assessmt ... Ms. Denise GARDNER
38 Director of Student Counseling ... Dr. Victor BARR
06 Registrar ... Ms. Monique W. ANDERSON
27 Director of Marketing ... Ms. Caitlin MCCLEARY
47 Dean Ag Sciences/Natural Resources ... Dr. Caula BEYL
48 Dean of Architecture and Design ... Dr. Scott POOLE
50 Dean Business Administration ... Dr. Steve MANGUM
60 Dean Communication/Information ... Dr. Michael WIRTH
53 Dean Educ/Health/Human Sciences ... Dr. Robert RIDER
54 Dean of Engineering ... Dr. Wayne DAVIS
61 Dean of Law ... Prof. Melanie WILSON
49 Dean of Arts & Sciences ... Dr. Theresa LEE
66 Dean of Nursing ... Dr. Victoria NIEDERHAUSER
70 Dean of Social Work ... Dr. Karen SOWERS
74 Dean of Veterinary Medicine ... Dr. James P. THOMPSON
47 Dean of Agricultural Extension Svc ... Dr. Tim L. CROSS
08 Dean of Libraries ... Dr. Steve SMITH

*University of Tennessee at Chattanooga (E)

615 McCallie Avenue, Chattanooga TN 37403-2504
County: Hamilton FICE Identification: 003529
Unit ID: 221740
Telephone: (423) 425-4111 Carnegie Class: Master's L
FAX Number: (423) 425-2200 Calendar System: Semester
URL: www.utc.edu
Established: 1886 Annual Undergrad Tuition & Fees (In-State): $8,382
Enrollment: 11,670 Coed
Affiliation or Control: State IRS Status: 501(c)3
Highest Offering: Doctorate
Program: Liberal Arts And General; Teacher Preparatory; Professional
Accreditation: SC, ANEST, ART, BUS, BUSA, CAATE, CACREP, CIDA, CS, DIETD, ENG, ENGT, JOUR, MUS, NURSE, PTA, SPAA, SW, TED, THEA

02 Chancellor ... Dr. Steven ANGLE
05 Provost & Sr Vice Chancellor ... Dr. Jerald AINSWORTH
30 Vice Chanc University Advancement ... Dr. Bryan ROWLAND
10 Exec Vice Chanc Fin/Operations & IT ... Dr. Richard BROWN
46 Vice Chancellor for Research ... Dr. Joanne ROMAGNI
32 Vice Chanc Student Development ... Dr. John DELANEY
20 Assoc Provost for Academic Affairs ... Dr. Jocelyn SANDERS
21 Assoc Vice Chanc Business/Fin Affs ... Ms. Vanasia Conley PARKS
26 Assoc VC University Relations ... Mr. Chuck CANTRELL
18 Asst VC Operations/Fac Plng & Mgt ... Mr. Tom M. ELLIS
91 Assoc VC & CIO ... Mr. Tom HOOVER
35 Asst VC Student Development ... Dr. Dee Dee ANDERSON
108 Assoc Provost SLO/Assess & Accred ... Dr. David RAUSCH
100 Chief of Staff ... Ms. Terry DENNISTON
08 Dean of Lupton Library ... Ms. Theresa LIEDTKA
88 Assoc Dean of Student Life ... Mr. Jim HICKS
84 Asst Provost Enrollment Services ... Mr. Yancy FREEMAN
06 Director of Records and Registrar ... Ms. Linda ORTH
13 Director of Information Systems ... Vacant
09 Dir of Planning/Eval/Inst Research ... Dr. Karen ADSIT
36 Int Dir Placemt/Student Employment ... Mrs. Donna COOPER
15 Director of Human Resources ... Mr. Dan WEBB
38 Director of Counseling ... Dr. Nancy BADGER
37 Interim Director of Financial Aid ... Ms. Jennifer BUCKLES
41 Vice Chanc & Dir of Athletics ... Mr. David BLACKBURN
58 Dean of the Graduate School ... Dr. Joanne ROMAGNI
49 Dean of Arts & Sciences ... Dr. Jeff ELWELL
50 Dean of Business Administration ... Dr. Robert DOOLEY
53 Dean of Health/Educ/Prof Studies ... Dr. Valerie RUTLEDGE
54 Int Dean Engineering/Comp Science ... Dr. Neslihan ALP
66 Director of Nursing ... Dr. Chris SMITH
22 Director of Equity & Diversity ... Dr. Bryan SAMUEL
78 Director of Cooperative Education ... Vacant
25 Director of Sponsored Programs ... Ms. Meredith PERRY
29 Director of Alumni Affairs ... Ms. Jayne HOLDER
96 Mgr of Business Svcs (Purchasing) ... Mr. Charles SCOTT
19 Chief of Police ... Mr. Robert RATCHFORD
39 Director Student Housing ... Ms. Valara SAMPLE
92 Dean Honors College ... Dr. Linda FROST
88 Director of Community Partnerships ... Ms. Ann YOACHIM

*University of Tennessee at Martin (F)

554 University Street, Martin TN 38238-0001
County: Weakley FICE Identification: 003531
Unit ID: 221768
Telephone: (731) 881-7000 Carnegie Class: Master's M
FAX Number: (731) 881-7019 Calendar System: Semester
URL: www.utm.edu
Established: 1900 Annual Undergrad Tuition & Fees (In-State): $8,327
Enrollment: 7,042 Coed
Affiliation or Control: State IRS Status: 501(c)3
Highest Offering: Master's
Program: Liberal Arts And General; Teacher Preparatory; Professional
Accreditation: SC, AAFCS, BUS, DIETD, DIETI, ENG, JOUR, MUS, NUR, SW, TED

02 Interim Chancellor ... Dr. Robert M. SMITH
05 Provost & Vice Chanc for Acad Affs ... Dr. E. Jerald OGG
10 Int Vice Chanc for Finance & Admin ... Ms. Nancy J. YARBROUGH
32 Vice Chancellor for Student Affairs ... Dr. Margaret Y. TOSTON
30 Vice Chancellor for Univ Advancemnt ... Mr. Andrew A. WILSON
20 Assoc Vice Chanc for Academic Affr ... Dr. Victoria S. SENG
13 Interim Chief Information Officer ... Mr. Terry W. LEWIS
21 Dir of Budget & Mgmt Reporting ... Ms. Petra R. MCPHEARSON
35 Asst Vice Chanc for Student Affairs ... Mr. John ABEL
44 Asst VChanc Devel & Planned Giving ... Ms. Jeanna C. SWAFFORD
04 Exec Assistant to the Chancellor ... Ms. Edie B. GIBSON
29 Asst Vice Chanc for Alumni Rels ... Mr. Charley T. DEAL
06 Dir of Acad Records & Registrar ... Ms. Brandy D. CARTMELL
28 Equity & Diversity Officer AA/EEO ... Dr. Gail M. STEPHENS
15 Director of Human Resources ... Mr. James (Phillip) BRIGHT
09 Int Dir Institutional Research ... Dr. Desiree A. MCCULLOUGH
41 Director Intercollegiate Athletics ... Mr. Julio A. FREIRE
08 Director of Library ... Dr. Charles A. JULIAN
18 Director of Physical Plant Opers ... Mr. Tim J. NIPP
19 Director of Public Safety ... Mr. Scott D. ROBBINS
96 Purchasing Agent ... Ms. Lori A. DONAVANT
38 Dir Student Health & Counseling Svc ... Ms. Shannon DEAL
39 Director of Student Housing ... Vacant
26 Director of University Relations ... Mr. Robert (Bud) D. GRIMES
85 Dir Tenn Intensive English Pgm ... Ms. Amy E. FENNING
47 Dean Col Agri & App Sciences ... Dr. Todd A. WINTERS
50 Dean Col Business & Global Affairs ... Dr. Ross N. DICKENS
53 Dean Col Educ/Health/Behav Sci ... Ms. Cynthia L. WEST
79 Dean Col Humanities/Fine Arts ... Dr. Lynn M. ALEXANDER
54 Dean Col Engr & Natural Sci ... Dr. Richard J. HELGESON
105 Director Web Services ... Mr. Brian C. INGRAM
106 Dir Online Education/E-learning ... Dr. Tommy CATES
25 Chief Contracts/Grants Admin ... Dr. Joan K. WEST

University of Tennessee Health Science Center (G)

920 Madison Ave, Memphis TN 38163-0002
County: Shelby FICE Identification: 006725
Unit ID: 221704
Telephone: (901) 448-5500 Carnegie Class: Not Classified
FAX Number: (901) 448-7750 Calendar System: Semester
URL: www.uthsc.edu
Established: 1911 Annual Undergrad Tuition & Fees (In-State): $10,374
Enrollment: 2,976 Coed
Affiliation or Control: State IRS Status: 501(c)3
Highest Offering: Doctorate
Program: Professional
Accreditation: SC, ANEST, #ARCPA, CAHIIM, CYTO, DENT, DH, HT, IPSY, MED, MT, NURSE, OT, PHAR, PTA

01 Chancellor ... Dr. Steve J. SCHWAB
03 Executive Vice Chancellor/COO ... Dr. Kennard D. BROWN
52 Dean Dentistry ... Dr. Timothy L. HOTTEL
58 Dean Graduate Health Sciences ... Dr. Donald B. THOMASON
76 Dean Health Professions ... Dr. Noma B. ANDERSON
63 Executive Dean Medicine ... Dr. David M. STERN
63 Dean Medicine Chattanooga ... Dr. David C. SEABERG
63 Dean Medicine Knoxville ... Dr. James J. NEUTENS
66 Interim Dean Nursing ... Dr. Wendy M. LIKES
67 Dean Pharmacy ... Dr. Marie A. CHISHOLM- BURNS
05 VC Academic/Faculty/Student Affs ... Dr. Cheryl R. SCHEID
10 Vice Chancellor Finance/Operations ... Mr. Anthony A. FERRARA
13 VC Information Technology Services ... Dr. Jan VAN DER AA
46 Interim VC Research ... Dr. Lawrence M. PFEFFER
30 VC Development and Alumni Affairs ... Dr. Randy L. FARMER
06 Registrar ... Dr. Darla M. KEEL
07 Director of Admissions ... Mr. William CARTER
37 Director of Financial Aid ... Mr. Samuel MATHENY
08 Director Library ... Dr. Tom SINGARELLA

Vanderbilt University (H)

2305 West End Avenue, Nashville TN 37203
County: Davidson FICE Identification: 003535
Unit ID: 221999
Telephone: (615) 322-7311 Carnegie Class: RU/VH
FAX Number: (615) 343-7765 Calendar System: Semester
URL: www.vanderbilt.edu
Established: 1873 Annual Undergrad Tuition & Fees: $44,712
Enrollment: 12,686 Coed
Affiliation or Control: Independent Non-Profit IRS Status: 501(c)3
Highest Offering: Doctorate
Program: Liberal Arts And General; Teacher Preparatory; Professional
Accreditation: SC, AUD, BUS, CACREP, CLPSY, CS, DENT, DIETI, DMS, ENG, IPSY, LAW, MED, MIDWF, MT, MUS, NDT, NMT, NUR, PERF, PH, SP, TED, THEOL

01 Chancellor ... Dr. Nicholas ZEPPOS
05 Provost/Vice Chancellor ... Dr. Susan R. WENTE
17 Vice Chanc Hlth Affs/Dean Med Sch ... Dr. Jeffrey R. BALSER
10 Vice Chancellor Finance/CFO ... Mr. Brett SWEET
11 Vice Chanc Administration ... Mr. Eric KOPSTAIN
30 Vice Chanc Dev & Alumni Relations ... Ms. Susie STALCUP
13 Vice Chanc for Investments and CIO ... Mr. Anders W. HALL
15 Assoc VC/Chief Human Resource Ofcr ... Ms. Traci NORDBERG
26 VC Univ Affairs and Athletics ... Dr. David WILLIAMS
20 Assoc Vice Chanc Academic Affairs ... Ms. Susan HART
18 Deputy VC Facilities & Environment ... Mr. Judson NEWBERN
27 Vice Chancellor for Public Affairs ... Ms. Beth FORTUNE
09 Exec Dir Institutional Research ... Dr. Roberta BELL
20 Vice Provost Learning & Res Affairs ... Ms. Cynthia J. CYRUS
88 Vice Prov Acad & Strat Affairs ... Dr. John G. GEER
58 Vice Prov Research/Dean Grad Sch ... Dr. Dennis G. HALL
08 Interim Dean of Libraries ... Mr. Joseph D. COMBS
27 Dean of Student Publicats/Comm ... Mr. F. Clark WILLIAMS
21 Asst V Chanc for Finance/Controller ... Ms. Dalana ROBERTSON
06 Registrar ... Mr. Bart P. QUINET
84 Vice Provost Univ Enrollment Affs ... Dr. Douglas CHRISTIANSEN
07 Dir Undergraduate Admissions ... Mr. John GAINES
37 Director Student Financial Aid ... Mr. Brent B. TENER
38 Director Psych Counseling Center ... Dr. Catherine FUCHS
36 Dir Center for Student Prof Devel ... Ms. Cynthia FUNK

25 Assoc Director Contract Mgmt ... Mr. Jeff NEWMAN
14 Vice Chancellor Information Tech ... Mr. John M. LUTZ
32 Dean of Students/Assoc Provost ... Mr. Mark BANDAS
106 Assoc Provost for Digital Learning ... Dr. John M. SLOOP
49 Dean College of Arts and Science ... Dr. Lauren BENTON
54 Dean School of Engineering ... Dr. Philippe M. FAUCHET
66 Dean School of Nursing ... Dr. Linda NORMAN
53 Dean Education & Human Development ... Dr. Camilla P. BENBOW
64 Dean Blair School of Music ... Dr. Mark WAIT
73 Dean of the Divinity School ... Dr. Emilie M. TOWNES
61 Dean of the School of Law ... Dr. Chris GUTHRIE
50 Dean Owen Grad School of Mgmt ... Dr. James BRADFORD
88 Dean of the Ingram Commons ... Dr. Vanessa BEASLEY
42 Associate Chaplain ... Rev. Gretchen PERSON
19 Chief of Police/Asst Vice Chanc ... Mr. August J. WASHINGTON
22 Dir EO/AA & Disability Svcs ... Ms. Anita JENIOUS
23 Assoc Dean Student Health/Wellness ... Dr. Keith G. MEADOR
41 Dir Sport Operations/Asst Vice Chan ... Mr. Brockton WILLIAMS
104 Director Global Support Services ... Ms. Kathryn HOFELDT
39 Sr Director Housing Operations ... Mr. James S. KRAMKA
43 Vice Chancellor/General Counsel ... Ms. Audrey J. ANDERSON
44 Asst Vice Chancellor Annual Giving ... Mr. Kyle D. MCGOWAN
86 Asst Vice Chanc Federal Relations ... Ms. Christina D. WEST

Vatterot Career College (A)

6991 Appling Farms Parkway, Memphis TN 38133
Telephone: (901) 372-2399 Identification: 770592
Accreditation: ACCSC

† Branch campus of Vatterott College-Des Moines, Des Moines, IA.

Vatterott College-Memphis (B)

2655 Dividend Drive, Memphis TN 38132-1713
Telephone: (901) 761-5730 Identification: 666308
Accreditation: ACCSC

† Branch campus of Vatterott College-NorthPark, Berkeley, MO.

Virginia College School of Business and Health (C)

721 Eastgate Loop, Chattanooga TN 37411-5600
Telephone: (423) 893-2000 Identification: 666136
Accreditation: ACICS, ACFEI, MAAB

† Branch campus of Virginia College, Birmingham, AL.

Virginia College School of Business and Health (D)

5003 North Broadway Street, Knoxville TN 37918
Telephone: (865) 745-4500 Identification: 770828
Accreditation: ACICS, MAAB

† Branch campus of Virginia College, Birmingham, AL.

Visible Music College (E)

200 Madison Avenue, Memphis TN 38103
County: Shelby FICE Identification: 039823
Unit ID: 449764
Telephone: (901) 381-3939 Carnegie Class: Spec/Arts
FAX Number: (901) 377-0544 Calendar System: Semester
URL: www.visible.edu
Established: 2000 Annual Undergrad Tuition & Fees: $24,500
Enrollment: 130 Coed
Affiliation or Control: Independent Non-Profit IRS Status: 501(c)3
Highest Offering: Baccalaureate
Program: Professional; Music Emphasis
Accreditation: TRACS

01 President ... Dr. Ken STEORTS
05 Vice President of Academics ... Dr. Corey LATTA
32 Director of Students ... JD WILSON
30 Vice President of Advancement ... Geordy WELLS
10 Vice President of Business ... Ben RAWLEY
07 Director of Admissions ... Susan HARRIS
37 Director of Financial Aid ... Cynthia BROWN
06 Registrar ... Scott LENCKE
21 Business Office Manager ... Toni MELTON
18 Operations Manager ... Matt BROWN
84 Director Enrollment Management ... Brian DUFFY

Watkins College of Art, Design & Film (F)

2298 Rosa L. Parks Boulevard, Nashville TN 37228-1306
County: Davidson FICE Identification: 030888
Unit ID: 392840
Telephone: (615) 383-4848 Carnegie Class: Spec/Arts
FAX Number: (615) 383-4849 Calendar System: Semester
URL: www.watkins.edu
Established: 1885 Annual Undergrad Tuition & Fees: $23,100
Enrollment: 304 Coed
Affiliation or Control: Independent Non-Profit IRS Status: 501(c)3
Highest Offering: Baccalaureate
Program: Fine Arts Emphasis
Accreditation: SC, ART, CIDA

01 President ... Ms. Ellen MEYER
30 Vice Pres Institutional Advancement ... Ms. Hilrie BROWN
05 Vice President for Academic Affairs ... Ms. Joy MCKENZIE
10 Vice Pres Finance and Operations ... Ms. Mary Ellen LOTHAMER
07 Director Admissions ... Ms. Linda SCHWAB
26 Director External Relations ... Ms. Caroline DAVIS
06 Registrar ... Ms. Tracie JOHNSON
37 Director Financial Aid ... Ms. Regina GILBERT
08 Library Director ... Ms. Lisa WILLIAMS
13 Director Information Technology ... Mr. Chris MCQUISTION
18 Director of Facilities ... Mr. Martin DILLINGHAM
88 Chair Film School ... Mr. Richard GERSHMAN
57 Chair Fine Art Department ... Ms. Kristi HARGROVE
88 Chair Graphic Design Department ... Mr. Dan BRAWNER
88 Chair Interior Design Department ... Ms. Cheryl GULLEY
88 Chair Photography Department ... Ms. Robin PARIS
97 Director General Education ... Ms. Cary Beth MILLER
51 Director Community Education ... Ms. Mary Beth HARDING
32 Director Student Life ... Ms. Samantha BRZOZOWSKI

Welch College (G)

3606 West End Avenue, Nashville TN 37205-2498
County: Davidson FICE Identification: 030018
Unit ID: 220206
Telephone: (615) 844-5000 Carnegie Class: Bac/Diverse
FAX Number: (615) 844-5004 Calendar System: Semester
URL: www.welch.edu
Established: 1942 Annual Undergrad Tuition & Fees: $17,398
Enrollment: 329 Coed
Affiliation or Control: Free Will Baptist IRS Status: 501(c)3
Highest Offering: Baccalaureate
Program: Liberal Arts And General; Teacher Preparatory; Religious Emphasis
Accreditation: SC, BI

01 President ... Dr. J. Matthew PINSON
05 Provost ... Dr. Paul G. KETTEMAN
10 Vice President Financial Affairs ... Mr. Craig MAHLER
45 Dir Institutional Planning/Assess ... Dr. Kevin HESTER
30 Vice Pres Institutional Advancement ... Mr. David WILLIFORD
88 Vice President for Church Relations ... Mr. Gary FRY
32 VP Student Svcs/Dean of Students ... Dr. Jon FORLINES
34 Dean of Women ... Mrs. Susan FORLINES
21 Staff Accountant ... Mrs. Leigh Ann SMITH
08 Librarian ... Mrs. Carol REID
18 Director of Plant Operations ... Mr. Sandy GOODFELLOW
84 Dir of Enrollment Services ... Mrs. Debbie MOUSER
106 Dir of Online and Adult Studies ... Mr. Allan CROWSON
09 Director of Institutional Research ... Mr. Wayne SPRUILL
41 Athletic Director ... Mr. Gary TURNER
04 Exec Assistant to the President ... Mrs. Martha FLETCHER
06 Registrar ... Mr. Matthew BRACEY
37 Student Financial Aid Coordinator ... Mrs. Angie EDGMON
44 Director of the Annual Fund ... Mr. Mike EDWARDS

Williamson College (H)

274 Mallory Station Road, Franklin TN 37067
County: Williamson FICE Identification: 035135
Unit ID: 443340
Telephone: (615) 771-7821 Carnegie Class: Spec/Faith
FAX Number: (615) 771-7810 Calendar System: Semester
URL: www.williamsoncc.edu
Established: 1996 Annual Undergrad Tuition & Fees: $10,375
Enrollment: 82 Coed
Affiliation or Control: Non-denominational IRS Status: 501(c)3
Highest Offering: Baccalaureate
Program: Professional; Religious Emphasis
Accreditation: BI

01 President ... Dr. Ed SMITH
05 Vice Pres Academic Affairs ... Dr. Todd BRADLEY
88 Dean Emeritus ... Dr. Sharon LANDER
11 Vice President for Operations ... Ms. Susan MAYS
06 Registrar/Dir Instl Effectiveness ... Ms. Karen HUDSON
37 Director Financial Aid ... Ms. Jennifer SPEER
08 Librarian ... Ms. Elizabeth HUTCHISON
04 Executive Team Coordinator ... Ms. Laura FLOWERS

TEXAS

Abilene Christian University (I)

ACU Box 29100, Abilene TX 79699-9100
County: Taylor FICE Identification: 003537
Unit ID: 222178
Telephone: (325) 674-2000 Carnegie Class: Master's L
FAX Number: (325) 674-2202 Calendar System: Semester
URL: www.acu.edu
Established: 1906 Annual Undergrad Tuition & Fees: $30,830
Enrollment: 4,427 Coed
Affiliation or Control: Churches Of Christ IRS Status: 501(c)3
Highest Offering: Doctorate
Program: Liberal Arts And General; Teacher Preparatory; Professional
Accreditation: SC, BUS, CIDA, DIETD, @DIETI, JOUR, MFCD, MUS, NURSE, SP, SW, TEAC, THEOL

01 President ... Dr. Phil SCHUBERT
100 Senior Advisor to the President ... Ms. Suzanne ALLMON
03 Executive Vice President ... Dr. Allison GARRETT
03 Vice President of the University ... Dr. Gary D. MCCALEB
05 Provost ... Dr. Robert RHODES
05 Exec VP Academic Affairs-Dallas ... Dr. Jay GOIN
30 VP for Advancement ... Mr. Jim ORR
32 VP for Student Life ... Mr. Chris RILEY
10 VP & Chief Financial Officer ... Mr. Steven HOLLEY
20 VP Academic Affairs-Dallas ... Dr. Stephen JOHNSON
88 Chief Investment Ofcr/Pres ACIMCO ... Mr. Jack W. RICH
43 Vice President & General Counsel ... Mr. Slade SULLIVAN
00 Chancellor ... Dr. Royce MONEY
88 Exec Assistant to the Chancellor ... Mr. Jim HOLMANS
102 Vice Chancellor/Pres ACU Foundation ... Mr. Dan T. GARRETT
20 Vice Provost ... Dr. Susan LEWIS
84 Asst VP Enrollment-Dallas ... Ms. Jessica MANNING
49 Dean College of Arts & Sciences ... Dr. Greg STRAUGHN
73 Dean College of Biblical Studies ... Dr. Ken R. CUKROWSKI
50 Dean College of Business Admin ... Dr. Rick S. LYTLE
53 Dean College of Educ & Human Svcs ... Dr. Donnie SNIDER
92 Dean Honors College ... Dr. Jason MORRIS
58 Int Dean Graduate School ... Dr. Donnie SNIDER
66 Dean School of Nursing ... Dr. Becky HAMMACK
08 Dean Library/Educational Technology ... Dr. John WEAVER
104 Director of the Ctr Intl Educ ... Dr. Stephen SHEWMAKER
106 Managing Director Online Programs ... Mr. Corey PATTERSON
35 Dean of Students ... Mr. Mark LEWIS
36 Director Career Center ... Mrs. Jill FORTSON
06 Registrar/Int Dir General Education ... Dr. Eric GUMM
84 Chief Enroll Ofcr/Dir Stdnt Fin Svc ... Mr. Kevin CAMPBELL
26 Chief Marketing Officer ... Mr. Jason GROVES
39 Director Residence Life ... Dr. Bob STRADER
38 Director Univ Counseling Center ... Mr. Steve ROWLANDS
88 Dir Center for Christian Service ... Ms. Jan MEYER
11 VP of Operations ... Mr. Kevin J. ROBERTS
18 Exec Dir Facilities/Campus Develop ... Mr. Corey RUFF
13 Exec Dir of Information Technology ... Mrs. Kay REEVES
24 Exec Dir Adams Ctr Teaching/Lrng ... Dr. Jennifer SHEWMAKER
29 Dir of Alumni Rels & Annual Project ... Mr. Craig FISHER
19 Chief of Police ... Mr. Jimmy ELLISON
44 Director of Major Gifts ... Mr. Don GARRETT
41 Director of Athletics ... Mr. Lee DE LEON
15 Director of Human Resources ... Mrs. Wendy JONES
88 Director of Faculty Enrichment ... Dr. Laura CARROLL
09 Asst Provost & SACS COC Liaison ... Dr. Tom A. MILHOLLAND
96 Director of Procurement ... Ms. Sandy HALL
40 Chief Business Services Officer ... Mr. Anthony T. WILLIAMS
101 Secretary to the Board of Trustees ... Mr. Slade SULLIVAN
04 Exec Assistant Office of President ... Mrs. Stephanie A. WOODLEE
46 Director Research/Sponsored Progams ... Dr. Megan ROTH
58 Dean College Grad/Professional Stds ... Dr. Jamie GOFF

*Alamo Community College District Central Office (J)

201 W. Sheridan, San Antonio TX 78204-1429
County: Bexar FICE Identification: 003607
Unit ID: 222497
Telephone: (210) 485-0020 Carnegie Class: N/A
FAX Number: (210) 486-9166
URL: www.alamo.edu

01 Chancellor ... Dr. Bruce LESLIE
05 Vice Chanc for Academic Success ... Dr. Jo-Carol FABIANKE
11 Vice Chanc for Finance & Admin ... Ms. Diane E. SNYDER
32 Vice Chancellor for Student Success ... Dr. Adelina SILVA
103 Vice Chanc Economic/Workforce Devel ... Dr. Federico ZARAGOZA
44 VC Plng/Performance/Inform/Systems ... Dr. Thomas CLEARY
15 Assoc Vice Chanc Human Resources . Ms. Linda BOYER-OWENS
26 Assoc Vice Chanc Communications ... Mr. Leo ZUNIGA
18 Assoc Vice Chanc Facilities ... Mr. John STRYBOS
10 Assoc VC Finance & Fiscal Services ... Ms. Pamela ANSBOURY
04 Deputy to the Chancellor ... Ms. Michelle PERALES
30 Exec Director Inst Advancement ... Mr. Jim ESKIN
21 Director of Internal Audit ... Mr. Matthew MILLS
96 Director Acquisitions & Admin Svcs ... Mr. Gary O'BAR
19 Chief Department of Public Safety ... Mr. Don ADAMS
21 Comptroller ... Ms. Gettie MORENO
12 President Northwest Vista College ... Dr. Ric BASER
12 President San Antonio College ... Dr. Robert VELA
12 President St Philip's College ... Dr. Adena WILLIAMS LOSTON
12 President Palo Alto College ... Dr. Michael FLORES
12 Pres Northeast Lakeview College ... Mr. Craig FOLLINS
37 Director Student Financial Aid ... Mr. Harold WHITIS
43 Dir Legal Services/General Counsel ... Mr. Ross LAUGHEAD
09 Dist Dir Inst Rsch/Effect/Planning ... Mr. Velda VILLARREAL

*Northwest Vista College (K)

3535 N Ellison Drive, San Antonio TX 78251-4217
County: Bexar FICE Identification: 033723
Unit ID: 420398
Telephone: (210) 486-4000 Carnegie Class: Assoc/Pub-U-MC
FAX Number: (210) 486-9105 Calendar System: Semester
URL: www.alamo.edu/nvc
Established: 1995 Annual Undergrad Tuition & Fees (In-District): $2,142
Enrollment: 15,965 Coed
Affiliation or Control: Local IRS Status: 501(c)3
Highest Offering: Associate Degree
Program: 2-Year Principally Bachelor's Creditable
Accreditation: SC

02 President ... Dr. Ric N. BASER
03 Vice President for College Services ... Mrs. Erin L. SHERMAN
05 Vice President for Academic Success ... Vacant

32 Vice President of Student Success ....Mrs. Deborah GAITAN
30 Director Institutional Advancement ....Mrs. Lynne DEAN
08 Learning Resources Chair .... Ms. Judy MCMILLAN
35 Dean of Student Success ....Mrs. Jennifer COMEDY-HOLMES
26 Dir of Public Relations & Marketing ....Mrs. Renata SERAFIN
13 Director Info/Communications Tech .... Mr. Felix SALINAS
37 Associate Director of Financial Aid ....Mrs. Rosalinda ENCINA
10 Assistant Bursar ....Mrs. Jennifer ORTIZ
15 Sr Human Resources Generalist ....Mrs. Jessica SACAL-TRENT
45 Director of Resources & College Dev ....Mr. Carlos AGUIRRE
18 Superintendent NVC ....Mr. Bernie ZERTUCHE
103 Dean of Workforce Development .... Mr. Patrick FONTENOT
49 Dean of Arts and Sciences .... Dr. Amy WHITWORTH
09 Director of Institutional Research .... Dr. Eliza HERNANDEZ
84 Director of Enrollment Management .... Mrs. Robin SANDBERG
07 Associate Director of Admissions ....Mrs. Yvonne GUERRA
04 Executive Assistant to President ....Mrs. Lydia BEAVER

*Palo Alto College (A)

1400 W Villaret Boulevard, San Antonio TX 78224-2499

County: Bexar FICE Identification: 023413
Unit ID: 246354
Telephone: (210) 486-3000 Carnegie Class: Assoc/Pub-U-MC
FAX Number: (210) 921-5005 Calendar System: Semester
URL: www.alamo.edu
Established: 1985 Annual Undergrad Tuition & Fees (In-District): $2,088
Enrollment: 8,376 Coed
Affiliation or Control: Local IRS Status: 501(c)3
Highest Offering: Associate Degree
Program: Occupational; 2-Year Principally Bachelor's Creditable
Accreditation: SC

02 President ....Dr. Michael FLORES
05 Vice President Academic Success .... Ms. Elizabeth TANNER
10 Vice Pres College Services .... Dr. Beatriz JOSEPH
32 Vice President Student Success ....Vacant
49 Dean Arts & Sciences ....Dr. Mary Ellen JACOBS
72 Dean Career/Technical Education ....Vacant
08 Dean of Learning Resources ....Ms. Tina MESA
35 Int Dean of Student Success .....Ms. Katherine BEAUMONT DOSS
26 Director of Public Relations .... Mr. Jerry ARELLANO
21 Bursar ....Mr. Daniel ROCHA
84 Director of Enrollment Management ....Ms. Elizabeth AGUILAR-VILLARUAL
37 Director Student Financial Services .... Ms. Shirley LEIJA
41 Athletic Director ....Mr. Adrian MONTOYA
18 Chief Facilities/Physical Plant ....Mr. Sergio RIVERA
38 Director Student Counseling .... Dr. Yolanda REYNA
29 Director Alumni Relations ....Ms. Danielle ESPINOZA
09 Dir Inst Rsrch/Plng/Effectiveness ....Vacant
30 Chief Development ....Ms. Christina ALDRETE
06 Chief Records Officer ....Ms. Diane BURRESS

*St. Philip's College (B)

1801 Martin Luther King, San Antonio TX 78203-2098

County: Bexar FICE Identification: 003608
Unit ID: 227854
Telephone: (210) 486-2000 Carnegie Class: Assoc/Pub-U-MC
FAX Number: N/A Calendar System: Semester
URL: www.alamo.edu/spc/
Established: 1898 Annual Undergrad Tuition & Fees (In-District): $2,088
Enrollment: 10,514 Coed
Affiliation or Control: Local IRS Status: 501(c)3
Highest Offering: Associate Degree
Program: Occupational; 2-Year Principally Bachelor's Creditable
Accreditation: SC, ACFEI, CAHIIM, COARC, HT, MLTAD, OTA, PTAA, RAD, SURGT

02 President ....Dr. Adena WILLIAMS LOSTON
05 Vice Pres of Academic Success .... Ms. Maureen CARTLEDGE
32 Int Vice Pres of Student Success .... Mr. George JOHNSON
11 Vice President for College Svcs ....Ms. Lacy HAMPTON
12 Int Dean of Southwest Campus .... Dr. Josha SCOTT
35 Dean Student Success .... Dr. Paul MACHEN
08 Dean Interdisciplinary Programs ....Dr. Natasha SCHMITTOU
75 Dean Applied Science & Tech .... Mr. Christopher BEARDSALL
49 Int Dean Arts & Science .... Mr. Randall DAWSON
76 Dean of Health Sciences .... Ms. Rose SPRUILL
51 Dean of Workforce Dev/Continuing Ed ....Mr. Art HALL
37 Asst Director of Financial Aid ....Ms. Grace ZAPATA
45 Director Planning & Research .... Dr. Maria HINOJOSA
10 Assistant Bursar ....Ms. Sophia GONZALEZ
26 Dir Community & Public Relations ....Ms. Tracy ROSS-GARCIA
30 Director Institutional Advancement .... Dr. Sharon CROCKETT-RAY
72 Director Instructional Technology ....Mr. John ORONA
18 Chief Facilities/Physical Plant .... Ms. Bertha NORWOOD
29 Director Alumni Relations .... Dr. Sharon CROCKETT-RAY
84 Director Enrollment Management .... Ms. Beautrice BUTLER
96 Chief Budget Manager ....Mr. Paul BORREGO

*San Antonio College (C)

1300 San Pedro Avenue, San Antonio TX 78212-4299

County: Bexar FICE Identification: 009163
Unit ID: 227924
Telephone: (210) 486-0000 Carnegie Class: Assoc/Pub-U-MC
FAX Number: N/A Calendar System: Semester
URL: www.alamo.edu/sac
Established: 1925 Annual Undergrad Tuition & Fees (In-District): $2,088
Enrollment: 21,280 Coed
Affiliation or Control: Local IRS Status: 501(c)3
Highest Offering: Associate Degree
Program: Occupational; 2-Year Principally Bachelor's Creditable
Accreditation: SC, ADNUR, CEA, DA, EMT, FUSER, MAC

02 President ....Dr. Robert H. VELA
05 Int Vice Pres Stdnt/Acad Success ....Dr. Lisa ALCORTA
11 Vice President of College Services ....Mr. David E. MRIZEK
32 Int Dean of Student Success ....Ms. Emma MENDIOLA
72 Dean Professional & Tech Educ ....Ms. Vernell E. WALKER
49 Dean of Arts & Sciences .... Dr. Conrad KRUEGER
51 Dean Cont Educ/Training Network ....Mr. Tim ROCKEY
08 Dean of Learning Resources ....Dr. Alice JOHNSON
88 Dean of Performance Excellence ....Dr. David WOOD
84 Director of Enrollment Services .... Mr. J. Martin ORTEGA
35 Dir Student Success/Activities .... Mr. Richard FARIAS
85 Coordinator International Students .... Ms. Martha BUCHANAN
26 Director Public Relations .... Ms. Vanessa TORRES
45 Director Resource & College Devel .... Ms. Susan B. ESPINOZA
18 Chief Facilities/Physical Plant ....Mr. David ORTEGA
23 Director Health Services .... Ms. Paula DAGGETT
37 Coordinator of Financial Aid ....Mr. Tom CAMPOS
29 Coordinator of Alumni and Friends ....Vacant

Alvin Community College (D)

3110 Mustang Road, Alvin TX 77511-4898

County: Brazoria FICE Identification: 003539
Unit ID: 222567
Telephone: (281) 756-3500 Carnegie Class: Assoc/Pub-R-L
FAX Number: (281) 756-3854 Calendar System: Semester
URL: www.alvincollege.edu
Established: 1948 Annual Undergrad Tuition & Fees (In-District): $1,534
Enrollment: 4,938 Coed
Affiliation or Control: Local IRS Status: 501(c)3
Highest Offering: Associate Degree
Program: Occupational; 2-Year Principally Bachelor's Creditable
Accreditation: SC, ADNUR, COARC, DMS, NDT, POLYT

01 President ....Dr. Christal M. ALBRECHT
05 Vice President Instruction ....Dr. Cynthia GRIFFITH
10 VP Financial/Admin Services .... Mr. Karl STAGER
32 VP Student Services ....Ms. Marilyn DEMENT
20 Dean of Academic Programs .... Dr. Drew NELSON
75 Dean Technical Programs .... Dr. John BETHSCHEIDER
51 Dean/Exec Dir Cont Ed/Wkforce Devel .... Mr. Jim SIMPSON
06 Registrar ....Ms. Irene M. ROBINSON
08 Director Library Services .... Mr. Tom BATES
21 Director Fiscal Affairs/Controller .... Ms. Deborah KRAFT
13 Director Information Technology .... Mr. Jeff CERNOCH
37 Dir Student Financial Aid Placement .... Ms. Dora SIMS
45 Dir Institutional Effectiveness ....Mr. Patrick SANGER
15 Exec Director Human Resources .... Ms. Karen EDWARDS
18 Director Physical Plant ....Mr. Mark PUTNAM
29 Director Alumni Relations .... Ms. Wendy DEL BELLO
07 Dir Admissions/Acad Advising Svcs .. Ms. Stephanie STOCKSTILL
09 Director of Inst Effective/Research ....Mr. Patrick SANGER
30 Chief Development .... Ms. Wendy DEL BELLO
26 Chief Public Relations Officer .... Ms. Wendy DEL BELLO
88 Assistant Director Fiscal Affairs ....Ms. Laurel JOSEPH
35 Coordinator Student Activities .... Ms. Amanda SMITHSON
04 Administrative Asst to President ....Ms. Tammy GIFFROW
19 Director Security/Safety ....Mr. Howard I. HAMRICK

Amarillo College (E)

PO Box 447, Amarillo TX 79178-0001

County: Potter FICE Identification: 003540
Unit ID: 222576
Telephone: (806) 371-5000 Carnegie Class: Assoc/Pub-R-L
FAX Number: (806) 371-5370 Calendar System: Semester
URL: www.actx.edu
Established: 1929 Annual Undergrad Tuition & Fees (In-District): $2,010
Enrollment: 10,325 Coed
Affiliation or Control: State/Local IRS Status: 501(c)3
Highest Offering: Associate Degree
Program: Occupational; 2-Year Principally Bachelor's Creditable
Accreditation: SC, ADNUR, COARC, DH, EMT, FUSER, MLTAD, MUS, NMT, OTA, PTAA, RAD, RTT, SURGT

01 President ....Dr. Russell LOWERY-HART
05 VP of Academic Affairs .... Dr. Deborah L. VESS
10 VP of Business Affairs ....Mr. Terry BERG
51 Dean of Continuing Education ....Vacant
32 VP of Student Affairs ....Mr. Robert C. AUSTIN
13 VP for Information Technology ....Mr. Lee M. COLAW
102 Dir AC Foundation/Development ....Mrs. Kathleen B. DOWDY
76 Director Ctr Cont Health Care Educ ..Mrs. Kimberly A. CROWLEY
18 Director Physical Plant .... Mr. Bruce COTGREAVE
37 Director Financial Aid ....Ms. Kelly PRATER
08 Director AC Library Network ....Mr. Mark HANNA
06 Registrar ....Mrs. Diane BRICE
27 VP of Communication/Mktg ....Mrs. Ellen R. GREEN
15 VP for Employee and Org Dev ....Ms. Lyndy D. FORRESTER
19 Chief of Police .... Mr. Steve L. CHANCE
26 Dir Foundation Mktg/Special Events .. Mrs. Tracy D. DOUGHERTY
09 Director of Institutional Research ....Ms. Melanie CASTRO
35 Assoc VP of Student Affairs .... Mrs. April L. SESSLER
38 Director Advising & Counseling .... Mr. Jason A. NORMAN
88 Director Amarillo Museum of Art ....Mrs. Kim B. MAHAN
88 Director Criminal Justice Program ....Ms. Toni GRAY
96 Director of Purchasing .... Mrs. Vickie SHELTON
66 Dean of Nursing ....Dr. Richard L. PULLEN

49 Dean of Liberal Arts ....Dr. Daniel W. FERGUSON
81 Dean of STEM ....Vacant
76 Dean of Health Sciences ....Mr. Mark E. ROWH
72 Dean of Technical Education ....Vacant
88 Dean of Academic Success ....Dr. Tamara T. CLUNIS
100 Chief of Staff ....Ms. Cara J. CROWLEY
84 Recruitment Spec/Enrollment Mgmt ....Mr. Richie GARZA

Amberton University (F)

1700 Eastgate Drive, Garland TX 75041

County: Dallas FICE Identification: 022594
Unit ID: 222628
Telephone: (972) 279-6511 Carnegie Class: Master's L
FAX Number: (972) 279-9773 Calendar System: Quarter
URL: www.amberton.edu
Established: 1971 Annual Undergrad Tuition & Fees: $6,000
Enrollment: 1,381 Coed
Affiliation or Control: Independent Non-Profit IRS Status: 501(c)3
Highest Offering: Master's
Program: Professional; Business Emphasis
Accreditation: SC

01 President .... Dr. Melinda REAGAN
05 Academic Dean .... Dr. Jonathan SCHULTZ
30 Dean Univ Advance/VP Strategic Svcs ....Dr. Jo Lynn LOYD
10 Chief Business Officer ....Mr. Brent BRADSHAW
06 Registrar ....Ms. Marge MASSEY
32 Interim Director Student Services .... Ms. Heather MILLER
84 Director for Recruiting ....Mr. Glenn SORRELLS
08 Head Librarian ....Ms. Judy GIBSON
29 Dir Alumni Relations & Inst Rsch ....Dr. Jo Lynn LOYD
07 Director of Admissions .... Dr. Don HEBBARD

American College of Acupuncture and Oriental Medicine (G)

9100 Park West Drive, Houston TX 77063-4104

County: Harris FICE Identification: 031533
Unit ID: 429085
Telephone: (713) 780-9777 Carnegie Class: Spec/Health
FAX Number: (713) 781-5781 Calendar System: Trimester
URL: www.acaom.edu
Established: 1991 Annual Graduate Tuition & Fees: $14,850
Enrollment: 136 Coed
Affiliation or Control: Proprietary IRS Status: Proprietary
Highest Offering: Doctorate; No Undergraduates
Program: Professional
Accreditation: SC, ACUP

01 President ....Dr. John Paul LIANG
11 Vice President of Operations .... Ms. Angel GUINARA
05 Dean of Academic Affairs .... Dr. Wen HUANG
20 Dean of Clinical Training ....Dr. Baisong ZHONG
06 Registrar ....Ms. Vicki ROSSMAN
09 Dir Inst Research/Effectiveness ....Mr. Michael Dale STAFFORD
37 Financial Aid Ofcr/Inst Compliance ....Ms. Theresa LIGON

American InterContinental University-Houston Campus (H)

9999 Richmond Avenue, Houston TX 77042-4516

Telephone: (832) 201-3600 Identification: 666335
Accreditation: &NH, ACBSP

† Regional accreditation is carried under the parent institution in Hoffman Estates, IL.

Angelina College (I)

PO Box 1768, Lufkin TX 75902-1768

County: Angelina FICE Identification: 006661
Unit ID: 222822
Telephone: (936) 639-1301 Carnegie Class: Assoc/Pub-R-M
FAX Number: (936) 639-4299 Calendar System: Semester
URL: www.angelina.edu
Established: 1966 Annual Undergrad Tuition & Fees (In-District): $2,280
Enrollment: 5,160 Coed
Affiliation or Control: State/Local IRS Status: 501(c)3
Highest Offering: Associate Degree
Program: Occupational; 2-Year Principally Bachelor's Creditable
Accreditation: SC, COARC, DMS, RAD, SURGT

01 President .... Dr. Michael SIMON
05 Vice President/Dean of Instruction ....Dr. Patricia M. MCKENZIE
10 Vice President Business Services ....Mr. Joe MADDEN
31 Vice Pres of Community Services ....Mr. Tim DITORO
32 Dean of Student Services .... Mr. Steve HUDMAN
13 Dir Management Information Systems ....Mr. Kenneth STREET
37 Director Student Financial Aid ....Mrs. Sue JONES
18 Chief Facilities/Physical Plant ....Mr. Steve CAPPS
09 Coord Inst Effectiveness & QEP .... Dr. Monica PETERS
26 Coordinator Marketing/Development ....Mr. Gary STALLARD
15 Coord of Human Resources ....Mrs. Tifini WHIDDON
06 Registrar & Records Coordinator ....Mrs. Sandra COX
38 Assoc Dean Academic Support Svcs ....Ms. Sellestine HUNT

AOMA Graduate School of Integrative Medicine (A)

4701 West Gate Boulevard, Austin TX 78745
County: Travis FICE Identification: 031564
Unit ID: 429094
Telephone: (512) 454-1188 Carnegie Class: Spec/Health
FAX Number: (512) 454-7001 Calendar System: Quarter
URL: www.aoma.edu
Established: 1993 Annual Graduate Tuition & Fees: $15,705
Enrollment: 196 Coed
Affiliation or Control: Proprietary IRS Status: Proprietary
Highest Offering: Doctorate; No Undergraduates
Program: Professional
Accreditation: SC, ACUP

01 President ... Dr. William R. MORRIS
05 Vice President of Faculty ... Dr. Qianzhi WU
10 VP Finance and Operations ... Ms. Donna HURTA
32 Dean of Students ... Mr. Robert LAGUNA
45 Program and Research Director ... Dr. John FINNELL
88 Program Director ... Ms. Lesley HAMILTON
08 Head Librarian ... Mr. David YORK
07 Dir Admissions ... Mr. Greg GREEN
06 Registrar ... Ms. Kristen BORTHWICK
58 Dean of Academics ... Dr. Yuxin HE
88 Director of Herbal Studies ... Dr. Dongxin MA
88 Director Acupuncture ... Dr. Zheng ZENG
23 Clinic Business Director ... Ms. Stephanee OWENBY
18 Facilities Coordinator ... Vacant
20 Academic Advisor ... Mr. Robert LAGUNA
26 Dir of Mktg/Community Relations ... Ms. Sarah BENTLEY
81 Director of Biomedical Sciences ... Dr. Raja MANDYAM
37 Director Student Financial Aid ... Ms. Estella SEARS
13 Director of Information Technology ... Mr. Mario CASTILLO
09 Dir Inst Effectiveness/Cont Educ ... Ms. Cara EDMOND

Argosy University, Dallas (B)

5001 Lyndon B. Johnson Freeway,
Farmers Branch TX 75244
Telephone: (214) 890-9900 Identification: 666181
Accreditation: &WC, HT, MLTAD

† Regional accreditation is carried under the parent institution in Orange, CA.

Arlington Baptist College (C)

3001 W Division, Arlington TX 76012-3497
County: Tarrant FICE Identification: 020814
Unit ID: 222877
Telephone: (817) 461-8741 Carnegie Class: Spec/Faith
FAX Number: (817) 274-1138 Calendar System: Semester
URL: www.arlingtonbaptistcollege.edu
Established: 1939 Annual Undergrad Tuition & Fees: $11,000
Enrollment: 248 Coed
Affiliation or Control: Baptist IRS Status: 501(c)3
Highest Offering: Master's
Program: Teacher Preparatory; Professional; Religious Emphasis
Accreditation: BI

01 President ... Dr. D. L MOODY
05 Academic Dean ... Ms. Janie TAYLOR
32 Dean of Students ... Mr. Richard KOONS
10 Business Manager/Dir Financial Aid ... Mr. David INGRAM
06 Registrar ... Ms. Janie TAYLOR
08 Head Librarian ... Vacant
18 Director Physical Plant ... Mr. Stan SPENCE
40 Director Bookstore ... Mrs. Vickie BRYANT
30 Director Institutional Advancement ... Mrs. Kim MARVIN
41 Athletic Director ... Mr. Cliff MCDANIEL
106 Dir Online Education/E-learning ... Dr. Carl JOHNSON
37 Director Student Financial Aid ... Mrs. Cindy TREAT

Art Institute of Dallas (D)

8080 Park Lane, Suite 100, Dallas TX 75231-5993
Telephone: (214) 692-8080 FICE Identification: 025396
Accreditation: &SC, ACFEI, CIDA

† Regional accreditation is carried under the parent institution, South University, Savannah, GA.

The Art Institute of Fort Worth (E)

7000 Calmont Ave, Ste 150, Fort Worth TX 76116
Telephone: (817) 210-0808 Identification: 770918
Accreditation: &SC

† Branch campus of South University, Savannah, GA.

The Art Institute of Houston (F)

4140 Southwest Freeway, Houston TX 77027
County: Harris FICE Identification: 021171
Unit ID: 222938
Telephone: (713) 623-2040 Carnegie Class: Spec/Arts
FAX Number: (713) 966-2700 Calendar System: Quarter
URL: www.aih.aii.edu
Established: 1978 Annual Undergrad Tuition & Fees: $29,880
Enrollment: 1,544 Coed
Affiliation or Control: Proprietary IRS Status: Proprietary
Highest Offering: Baccalaureate
Program: Occupational; Technical Emphasis
Accreditation: SC, ACFEI, CIDA

01 President ... Susanne BEHRENS
05 Dean of Academic Affairs ... Dr. Gary EATON
32 Dean of Student Affairs ... Daryl CONTE
10 Director of Accounting ... Trena DEAN
07 Senior Director of Admissions ... Jane CHASTANT
15 Human Resources Generalist ... Elizabeth WHITTINGTON
36 Director of Career Services ... Mary Kate ROBINSON
37 Dir of Student Financial Services ... Shanika GEORGE
06 Registrar ... Grace JACKSON

Austin College (G)

900 N Grand Avenue, Sherman TX 75090-4400
County: Grayson FICE Identification: 003543
Unit ID: 222983
Telephone: (903) 813-2000 Carnegie Class: Bac/A&S
FAX Number: (903) 813-3199 Calendar System: 4/1/4
URL: www.austincollege.edu
Established: 1849 Annual Undergrad Tuition & Fees: $36,230
Enrollment: 1,301 Coed
Affiliation or Control: Presbyterian Church (U.S.A.) IRS Status: 501(c)3
Highest Offering: Master's
Program: Liberal Arts And General; Teacher Preparatory
Accreditation: SC

01 President ... Dr. Marjorie HASS
05 VP Academic Affairs/Dean of Faculty ... Dr. Sheila A. PINERES
32 Vice Pres Student Affairs/Athletics ... Mr. Timothy P. MILLERICK
30 Vice Pres Institutional Advancement ... Mr. Brooks A. HULL
10 Vice President for Business Affairs ... Ms. Heidi B. ELLIS
84 Vice President for Inst Enrollment ... Ms. Nan M. DAVIS
21 Assoc VP Business Affairs ... Ms. Rana ASKINS
07 Asst VP Institutional Enrollment ... Mr. Matthew KROV
44 Sr Assoc VP for Inst Advancement ... Ms. Cary E. WACKER
29 AVP Inst Adv/Exec Dir Alumni Rels ... Ms. Paula JONSE
37 AVP/Exec Director Financial Aid ... Ms. Laurie COULTER
88 Exec Dir Admission ... Ms. Amanda KISSELLE
42 Chaplain/Dir of Church Relations ... Dr. John D. WILLIAMS
35 Dean of Student Life ... Mr. Michael DEEN
06 Registrar ... Dr. Dawn REMMERS
08 College Librarian/Library Director ... Mr. John R. WEST
79 Dean of Humanities ... Dr. Max GROBER
81 Dean of Sciences ... Dr. Steve GOLDSMITH
83 Dean of Social Sciences ... Dr. David GRIFFITH
15 Director of Human Resources ... Mr. Keith L. LAREY
36 Director Career Services ... Ms. Margie A. NORMAN
13 Interim Exec Director IT ... Mr. Charles CURTIS
58 Director of Graduate Program ... Dr. Julia SHAHID
104 Study Abroad Coordinator ... Ms. Jade FERNBERG
26 Director of Public Affairs ... Dr. Lynn Z. WOMBLE
19 Chief of Police ... Mr. James PERRY
40 Manager of Campus Store ... Mr. Kenton BEAL
27 Sr Dir Editorial Communications ... Ms. Vickie S. KIRBY
18 Exec Director of Facilities ... Mr. John L. JENNINGS
96 Purchasing Representative ... Ms. Debra REED
102 Dir Corp & Foundation Reltns ... Ms. Britanny DEREBERY
41 Athletic Director ... Mr. David NORMAN

Austin Community College District (H)

5930 Middle Fiskville Road, Austin TX 78752-4390
County: Travis FICE Identification: 012015
Unit ID: 222992
Telephone: (512) 223-7000 Carnegie Class: Assoc/Pub-U-MC
FAX Number: (512) 223-7185 Calendar System: Semester
URL: www.austincc.edu
Established: 1972 Annual Undergrad Tuition & Fees (In-District): $2,550
Enrollment: 41,350 Coed
Affiliation or Control: State/Local IRS Status: 501(c)3
Highest Offering: Associate Degree
Program: Occupational; 2-Year Principally Bachelor's Creditable
Accreditation: SC, ACBSP, ACFEI, ADNUR, CAHIIM, DH, DMS, EMT, MLTAD, OTA, PHLEB, PNUR, PTAA, RAD, SURGT

01 President/CEO ... Dr. Richard M. RHODES
03 Provost/Exec Vice Pres ... Dr. Charles COOK
10 Exec VP Finance & Administration ... Dr. Ben B. FERRELL
05 VP Instruction ... Mr. Michael T. MIDGLEY
32 VP Student Services ... Dr. Virginia FRAIRE
15 VP Human Resources ... Ms. Geraldine TUCKER
09 VP Effectiveness & Accountability ... Ms. Soon O. MERZ
20 AVP College Access Programs ... Dr. Stephanie HAWLEY
13 AVP Information Technology ... Mr. Stanley T. GUNN
21 VP Finance & Budget ... Mr. Neil W. VICKERS
35 AVP Student Success ... Dr. Richard R. ARMENTA
04 VP External Affairs ... Dr. Molly Beth MALCOLM
25 AVP Planning/Develop & Evaluation ... Dr. Mary E. HARRIS
18 Exec Dir Facilities & Construction ... Mr. William S. MULLANE
26 Exec Dir Public Info & College Mktg ... Ms. Brette E. LEA
102 Executive Director ACC Foundation ... Ms. Stephanie C. DEMPSEY
06 Registrar ... Ms. Glynis MILLER
07 Executive Director of Admissions ... Ms. Linda KLUCK
08 Dean Library Services ... Dr. Julie TODARO
19 Chief of Police ... Mr. Lynn DIXON
37 Executive Director Financial Aid ... Ms. Teresita BAZAN
96 Director of Purchasing ... Mr. Anthony OWENS
29 Director Alumni Relations ... Ms. Mary Ann CICALA

Austin Graduate School of Theology (I)

7640 Guadalupe Street, Austin TX 78752
County: Travis FICE Identification: 023628
Unit ID: 247825
Telephone: (512) 476-2772 Carnegie Class: Spec/Faith
FAX Number: (512) 476-3919 Calendar System: Semester
URL: www.austingrad.edu
Established: 1976 Annual Undergrad Tuition & Fees: $8,750
Enrollment: 52 Coed
Affiliation or Control: Independent Non-Profit IRS Status: 501(c)3
Highest Offering: Master's
Program: Liberal Arts And General; Professional; Religious Emphasis
Accreditation: SC

01 President ... Dr. Stanley G. REID
37 Vice President/Dir Financial Aid ... Mr. Dave ARTHUR
07 Director Recruiting & Admissions ... Mrs. Lauren PORTER
30 Director of Development ... Mr. Neil HANEY

Austin Presbyterian Theological Seminary (J)

100 E 27th Street, Austin TX 78705-5797
County: Travis FICE Identification: 003544
Unit ID: 223001
Telephone: (512) 472-6736 Carnegie Class: Spec/Faith
FAX Number: (512) 479-0738 Calendar System: Semester
URL: www.austinseminary.edu
Established: 1902 Annual Graduate Tuition & Fees: $11,755
Enrollment: 145 Coed
Affiliation or Control: Presbyterian Church (U.S.A.) IRS Status: 501(c)3
Highest Offering: Doctorate; No Undergraduates
Program: Professional; Religious Emphasis
Accreditation: SC, THEOL

01 President ... Rev. Theodore J. WARDLAW
05 Academic Dean ... Dr. David H. JENSEN
10 Vice Pres Finance/Administration ... Ms. Karen MONTGOMERY
30 Vice Pres Institutional Advancement ... Ms. Donna SCOTT
32 Vice Pres Student Affairs/Vocation ... Rev. Jackie SAXON
07 Vice President for Admissions ... Rev. John H. BARDEN
51 VP Education Beyond the Walls ... Ms. Melissa WIGINTON
29 Director Alumni & Church Relations ... Rev. Lemuel GARCIA-ANOYO
08 Director of the Stitt Library ... Dr. Timothy LINCOLN
06 Asst Dean Academic Affs/Registrar ... Ms. Jacqueline D. HEFLEY
37 Director of Financial Aid ... Ms. Glenna BALCH

Baptist Health System School of Health Professions (K)

8400 Datapoint Drive, San Antonio TX 78229
County: Bexar FICE Identification: 006606
Unit ID: 223083
Telephone: (210) 297-9636 Carnegie Class: Assoc/PrivFP
FAX Number: (210) 297-0075 Calendar System: Semester
URL: www.bshp.edu
Established: 1903 Annual Undergrad Tuition & Fees: N/A
Enrollment: 625 Coed
Affiliation or Control: Proprietary IRS Status: Proprietary
Highest Offering: Baccalaureate
Program: Occupational; 2-Year Principally Bachelor's Creditable; Nursing Emphasis
Accreditation: ABHES, ADNUR, NUR, RAD, SURGT, SURTEC

01 President ... Dr. Marion JEWEL
04 Administrative Asst to President ... Diane TYLER
07 Director of Admissions ... Jillian DENMAN
08 Director of Library ... Leslie BEALE
05 Director of Gen Educ and Online ... Lucinda FLORES
10 Director of Finance ... Priti LAXMI
37 Director of Student Financial Aid ... Patrick REYNA
13 Director of Information Systems ... Nancy ORTIZ
06 Registrar ... Christopher ESPINOZA

† Tuition varies by degree program.

Baptist Hospitals of Southeast Texas School of Radiologic Technology (L)

3030 Fannin Ste A, Beaumont TX 77704
County: Jefferson Identification: 667153
Telephone: (409) 212-5724 Carnegie Class: Not Classified
FAX Number: N/A Calendar System: Semester
URL: www.bhset.net
Established: 1952 Annual Undergrad Tuition & Fees: $6,000
Enrollment: 11 Coed
Affiliation or Control: Independent Non-Profit IRS Status: 501(c)3
Highest Offering: Associate Degree
Program: Occupational; 2-Year Principally Bachelor's Creditable; Technical Emphasis
Accreditation: RAD

01 Program Director ... Deborah SMITH
11 Chief of Administration ... David PARMER

Baptist Missionary Association Theological Seminary (A)

P.O. Box 670, 1530 East Pine Street, Jacksonville TX 75766-5407
County: Cherokee FICE Identification: 023312
Unit ID: 223117
Telephone: (903) 586-2501 Carnegie Class: Spec/Faith
FAX Number: (903) 586-0378 Calendar System: Semester
URL: www.bmats.edu
Established: 1957 Annual Undergrad Tuition & Fees: $5,200
Enrollment: 137 Coed
Affiliation or Control: Baptist IRS Status: 501(c)3
Highest Offering: Master's
Program: Professional; Religious Emphasis
Accreditation: SC, THEOL

01 President .... Dr. Charley HOLMES
05 Dean-Registrar .... Dr. Philip ATTEBERY
04 Administrative Asst to President .... Mrs. Carol SHINE
09 Director of Institutional Research .... Dr. James BLAYLOCK
32 Director of Student Services .... Dr. Ronnie JOHNSON

Baptist University of the Americas (B)

8019 S Pan Am Expressway, San Antonio TX 78224-1336
County: Bexar FICE Identification: 037333
Unit ID: 444398
Telephone: (210) 924-4338 Carnegie Class: Spec/Faith
FAX Number: (210) 924-0888 Calendar System: Semester
URL: www.bua.edu
Established: 1947 Annual Undergrad Tuition & Fees: $7,500
Enrollment: 168 Coed
Affiliation or Control: Baptist IRS Status: 501(c)3
Highest Offering: Baccalaureate
Program: 2-Year Principally Bachelor's Creditable; Liberal Arts And General; Professional; Religious Emphasis
Accreditation: BI

01 President .... Mr. Rene MACIEL
10 Vice Pres for Admin and Finance .... Mr. Barry TYLER
30 Vice Pres for Development .... Mr. Teo CISNEROS
05 Vice Pres for Academic Affairs .... Dr. Marconi MONTEIRO
32 Vice Pres for Student Svcs/Enroll .... Ms. Mary RANJEL
88 Vice Pres for Ext Affairs/Dean BBI .... Dr. Moises RODRIGUEZ
06 Registrar .... Mr. Isaac ORTIZ
37 Financial Aid Administrator .... Mrs. Araceli ACOSTA

Baylor College of Medicine (C)

One Baylor Plaza, Houston TX 77030-3411
County: Harris FICE Identification: 004949
Unit ID: 223223
Telephone: (713) 798-4951 Carnegie Class: Spec/Med
FAX Number: (713) 798-3692 Calendar System: Quarter
URL: www.bcm.edu
Established: 1900 Annual Graduate Tuition & Fees: $20,481
Enrollment: 1,584 Coed
Affiliation or Control: Independent Non-Profit IRS Status: 501(c)3
Highest Offering: Doctorate; No Undergraduates
Program: Professional
Accreditation: SC, ANEST, ARCPA, IPSY, #MED, OPE

00 Chancellor .... Dr. Bobby R. ALFORD
01 President and CEO .... Dr. Paul KLOTMAN
05 Provost/SVP Acad & Faculty Affairs .... Dr. Alicia MONROE
88 Dean Natl Sch Tropical Medicine .... Dr. Peter J. HOTEZ
17 Vice Pres/Chief Medical Officer .... Dr. Steve SIGWORTH
10 Chief Business Officer .... Mrs. Kimberly C. DAVID
30 Vice Pres Philanthropy .... Ms. Kristi SHERWOOD COOPER
43 Sr Vice Pres/General Counsel .... Mr. Robert F. CORRIGAN, JR.
26 VP Public Affairs .... Ms. Claire M. BASSETT
15 Vice President Human Resources .... Mr. Dane FRIEND
46 Sr Vice President for Research .... Dr. Adam KUSPA
13 VP/Information Technology .... Dr. Alexander IZAGUIRRE
86 Vice Pres Government Relations .... Mr. Tom KLEINWORTH
63 Dean of Medical Education .... Dr. Jennifer CHRISTNER
58 Dean Grad School of Biomed Sciences .... Dr. Deborah JOHNSON
76 Dean School Allied Health Programs .... Dr. J. David HOLCOMB
88 Senior Associate Dean .... Dr. James L. PHILLIPS
07 Associate Dean Admissions .... Dr. Karen E. JOHNSON
63 Sr VP/Dean of Medical Education .... Dr. C. Michael FORDIS, JR.
20 Interim Sr Assoc Dean Med Education .... Dr. Mary L. BRANDT
63 Sr Assoc Dean Grad Medical Educ .... Dr. Linda ANDREWS
88 Associate Dean Res Assurances .... Dr. Stacey L. BERG
88 Sr Assoc Dean Graduate Education .... Dr. Barbara R. SLAUGHTER
88 Asst Dean Graduate Medical Educ .... Dr. Jacqueline LEVESQUE
88 Assistant Dean for Admissions .... Dr. Jesus G. VALLEJO
35 Assistant Dean Student Affairs .... Dr. Toi B. HARRIS
88 Assoc Dean Medical Education .... Dr. Jerry C. GOODMAN
21 Controller .... Mr. Douglas R. SPADE
37 Director Student Financial Planning .... Ms. Hilda DELEON
32 Director of Student Affairs .... Mr. John RAPP
88 Director Environmental Safety .... Mr. Paul MURACA
23 Director Occupational Medicine .... Dr. James E. KELAHER
29 Director Alumni Affairs .... Mr. Alexander M. HOPKINS
19 Exec Director of Security .... Mr. John A. ROBERSON
96 Director Supply Chain Management .... Vacant
28 Sr Assoc Dean Diversity Council .... Dr. Barbara R. SLAUGHTER
06 Registrar .... Ms. Latoya R. WHITAKER

Baylor University (D)

One Bear Place #97096, Waco TX 76798-7096
County: McLennan FICE Identification: 003545
Unit ID: 223232
Telephone: (254) 710-1011 Carnegie Class: RU/H
FAX Number: (254) 710-3557 Calendar System: Semester
URL: www.baylor.edu
Established: 1845 Annual Undergrad Tuition & Fees: $40,198
Enrollment: 16,263 Coed
Affiliation or Control: Baptist IRS Status: 501(c)3
Highest Offering: Doctorate
Program: Liberal Arts And General; Teacher Preparatory; Professional
Accreditation: SC, AAFCS, BUS, BUSA, CAATE, CIDA, CLPSY, CS, DIETD, DIETI, ENG, HSA, JOUR, LAW, MIDWF, MUS, NURSE, PAST, PH, PTA, SP, SW, TED, THEA, THEOL

01 President & Chancellor .... Judge Kenneth W. STARR
05 Exec Vice President & Provost .... Dr. Edwin TREVATHAN
100 Chief of Staff to the President .... Mrs. Tommye Lou DAVIS
10 Senior VP for Operations & CFO .... Dr. Reagan RAMSOWER
30 Sr VP for Univ Dev/Strategic Initia .... Vacant
32 Vice President Student Life .... Dr. Kevin JACKSON
26 Vice President Marketing & Comm .... Mr. John BARRY
13 VP for IT & Dean of Libraries .... Ms. Pattie ORR
31 Vice Pres Constituent Engagement .... Ms. Tommye Lou DAVIS
43 General Counsel .... Mr. Charles D. BECKENHAUER
41 Director of Athletics .... Mr. Ian J. MCCAW
88 VP for Governance/Risk & Compliance .... Dr. Juan ALEJANDRO
09 Director Inst Research/Testing .... Dr. Kathleen MORLEY
84 Assoc VP for Summer & Strat Initiat .... Mrs. Diana M. RAMEY
21 Assoc VP Financial Svcs & Treasurer .... Mr. Bob C. SPENCE
21 Assoc VP Oper Plng & Budget Dir .... Mr. Wilson E. MCGREGOR
18 VP for Operations & Facilities Mgmt .... Mr. Brian W. NICHOLSON
15 Assoc Vice Pres Human Resources .... Mrs. Cheryl GOCHIS
91 Assoc VP Info Sys/Svcs & Dpty CIO .... Mrs. Becky L. KING
08 Assoc Dean of the Libraries .... Mr. Jeffrey STEELY
35 Associate Vice Pres Student Life .... Dr. Martha Lou SCOTT
06 Registrar .... Mr. Jonathan C. HELM
88 Assoc VP Strategic Initiatives .... Mr. Chris KRAUSE
90 Assoc Vice Pres Electronic Library .... Mr. Timothy M. LOGAN
108 Vice Provost Inst Effectiveness .... Dr. Michael MATIER
97 Vice Provost Undergrad Education .... Dr. Wesley NULL
20 Vice Prov/Academic Affs & Policy .... Dr. James BENNIGHOFF
46 Vice Provost for Research .... Dr. Truell HYDE
07 Asst VP of Undergrad Enrollment .... Ms. Jennifer CARRON
88 Asst Vice President & Controller .... Ms. Susan ANZ
88 Asst VP Stdnt Fin Svcs & Strat Plng .... Mrs. Jackie DIAZ
88 Chief Investment Officer .... Mr. R. Brian WEBB
19 Chief of Police .... Mr. Brad WIGTIL
93 Director Multiculture Affairs .... Mrs. Pearlie BEVERLY
20 Director Academic Support Programs .... Ms. Sally E. FIRMIN
23 Medical Director Health Center .... Dr. Sharon STERN
36 Exec Dr Career & Professional Dev .... Dr. Marjorie N. ELLIS
25 Director Sponsored Programs .... Ms. Lisa H. MCKETHAN
38 Director Counseling Svcs .... Dr. James G. MARSH
40 Director Baylor Bookstore .... Mr. Paul BEAULIEU
86 Director Governmental Relations .... Ms. Rochonda FARMER-NEAL
96 Director Procurement Services .... Mr. Tom HOFFMEYER
31 Director Community Relations .... Ms. Jana HIXSON
49 Dean College of Arts/Sciences .... Dr. Lee C. NORDT
50 Dean School of Business .... Dr. Terry S. MANESS
53 Dean School of Education .... Dr. Michael MCLENDON
61 Dean School of Law .... Mr. Bradley J B. TOBEN
64 Dean School of Music .... Dr. Gary MORTENSON
66 Dean School of Nursing .... Dr. Shelley F. CONROY
58 Dean Graduate School .... Dr. Larry LYON
73 Dean Truett Theological Sem .... Dr. Todd STILL
54 Dean Engineering & Computer Science .... Dr. Dennis O'NEAL
92 Dean Honors College .... Dr. Thomas S. HIBBS
85 Vice Provost for Global Engagement .... Dr. Jeffrey HAMILTON
35 Dean Student Development .... Dr. Elizabeth PALACIOS
39 Dean Student Learning & Engagement .... Dr. Jeff DOYLE
42 University Chaplain .... Dr. Burt BURLESON
88 Assoc Dean Student Conduct Admin .... Ms. Bethany J. MCCRAW
37 Asst VP for Stdnt Financial Aid .... Ms. Lyn KINSON
88 Assoc VP Public Safety & Security .... Mr. Mark CHILDERS

B.H. Carroll Theological Institute (E)

301 South Center Street, Suite 100, Arlington TX 76010-7140
County: Tarrant Identification: 667089
Telephone: (817) 274-4284 Carnegie Class: Not Classified
FAX Number: (817) 274-2226 Calendar System: Semester
URL: www.bhcarroll.edu
Established: 2004 Annual Graduate Tuition & Fees: $4,300
Enrollment: 302 Coed
Affiliation or Control: Southern Baptist IRS Status: 501(c)3
Highest Offering: Doctorate; No Undergraduates
Program: Religious Emphasis
Accreditation: BI, @THEOL

01 President .... Dr. C. Gene WILKES
10 CFO/Director Business Affairs .... Dr. Bruce MUSKRAT
06 Registrar .... Dr. Stan MOORE
07 Director of Admissions .... Ms. Meredith CHACIN
08 Dir Library & Information Services .... Mr. Don DAY
09 Dir of Institutional Effectiveness .... Ms. Amanda CRANE

Blinn College (F)

902 College Avenue, Brenham TX 77833-4098
County: Washington FICE Identification: 003549
Unit ID: 223427
Telephone: (979) 830-4000 Carnegie Class: Assoc/Pub-R-L
FAX Number: (979) 830-4030 Calendar System: Semester
URL: www.blinn.edu
Established: 1883 Annual Undergrad Tuition & Fees (In-District): $2,256
Enrollment: 18,769 Coed
Affiliation or Control: State/Local IRS Status: 501(c)3
Highest Offering: Associate Degree
Program: Occupational; 2-Year Principally Bachelor's Creditable
Accreditation: SC, ADNUR, DH, EMT, IFSAC, PTAA, RAD

01 District President/CEO .... Dr. Mary HENSLEY
32 Vice Pres Student Services .... Dr. Dennis CROWSON
10 CFO/Sr VP Finance/Admin Svcs .... Ms. Kelli SHOMAKER
05 Vice Pres Instruction .... Vacant
12 President Brazos Cty Campuses .... Ms. Sylvia MCMULLEN
86 Assoc VP Government & Public Affair .... Ms. Cathy BOEKER
20 Dean Academic Affairs .... Dr. John BEAVER
09 Dean Inst Effectiveness/Enroll Mgt .... Mr. Joe BAUMANN
06 Dean Admissions/Records/Regstrar .... Ms. Andrea LINER
88 Judicial Officer .... Vacant
35 Dean of Student Success .... Mr. Jeremy THOMAS
11 Spec Asst to Pres Brazos County .... Mr. Ted HAJOVSKY
102 Executive Director Foundation .... Ms. Susan MYERS
18 Exec Dir Facilities/Planning/Constr .... Mr. Richard O'MALLEY
12 Director Schulenburg Campus .... Ms. Rebecca GARLICK
12 Director Sealy Campus .... Ms. Lisa CATON
72 Dean Technical/Prof Programs .... Ms. Megan COSTANZA
88 Director Disability Services (Bre) .... Ms. Patricia MORAN
88 Dir Disability Services (Bryan) .... Ms. Brenda JONES-WILKINS
04 Admin Asst to District President .... Ms. Becky KREBS
21 Director Accounting .... Mr. Thomas BRAZZEL
08 Dean Library Services .... Ms. Linda FLYNN
38 Director of Counseling .... Mr. Robert LOVELIDGE
13 Dir Administrative Computing Svcs .... Ms. Christine WIED
37 Director Financial Aid .... Mr. Brent WILLIFORD
15 Director Human Resources .... Ms. Marie KIRBY
41 Athletic Dir/Mens Head Bsktbl Coach .... Mr. Scott SCHUMACHER
19 Chief College Police Department .... Mr. Craig WIESEPAPE
96 Director Purchasing/Transportation .... Mr. Ross SCHROEDER
07 Director Admissions & Records .... Ms. Kristi URBAN
27 Dir Prospective Student Relations .... Ms. Jennifer BYNUM
26 Dir Marketing/Media Relations .... Mr. Jeff TILLEY
35 Dir of Student Leadership/Activites .... Mr. Mordecai BROWNLEE
39 Housing Director .... Mr. James REED
27 Asst Dir Marketing/Media Relations .... Mr. Richard BRAY
88 Coord Student Center/Campus .... Ms. Sheri RICH

Brazosport College (G)

500 College Drive, Lake Jackson TX 77566-3199
County: Brazoria FICE Identification: 007287
Unit ID: 223506
Telephone: (979) 230-3000 Carnegie Class: Assoc/Pub4
FAX Number: (979) 230-3443 Calendar System: Semester
URL: www.brazosport.edu
Established: 1968 Annual Undergrad Tuition & Fees (In-District): $2,505
Enrollment: 6,300 Coed
Affiliation or Control: Local IRS Status: 501(c)3
Highest Offering: Baccalaureate
Program: Occupational; 2-Year Principally Bachelor's Creditable
Accreditation: SC, EMT

01 President .... Dr. Millicent M. VALEK
05 VP Academic & Sutdent Affairs .... Dr. Lynda VILLANUEVA
31 VP Industry & Community Resources .... Ms. Anne BARTLETT
30 VP College Advancement .... Ms. Serena ANDREWS
10 VP Administrative Services & CFO .... Mr. Fred SCOTT
15 VP Human Resources .... Mr. Marshall CAMPBELL
32 Dean of Student Services .... Ms. Jo GREATHOUSE
09 Director Institutional Research .... Mr. Scott FURTWENGLER
07 Director Admissions/Registrar .... Ms. Priscilla SANCHEZ
38 Director Student Counseling .... Mr. Arnold RAMIREZ
21 Internal Auditor .... Ms. Cynthia STRADER
26 Director Marketing & Communications .... Mr. Kyle SMITH
13 Director Information Technology .... Mr. Ron PARKER
37 Director of Financial Aid .... Ms. Kay WRIGHT
08 Director Library Services .... Ms. Cassie BRUNER
24 Director Learning Services .... Mr. Terry COMINGORE
19 Director College Services .... Mr. Gary DICKS
18 Director Facility Services .... Mr. Frank HICKL
76 Director Health Professions & ADN .... Dr. Susan MCCORMICK
88 Director Small Business Dev Center .... Dr. Janice GOINES
51 Director Community Education .... Ms. Catherine HANSON
88 Director Children's Center .... Ms. Julie LITTLEFIELD
25 Director Grant Administration .... Ms. Rebecca SHAWVER
109 Director Business Services .... Ms. Ginger WOOSTER

Brite Divinity School (H)

2925 Princeton Street, Fort Worth TX 76129-0001
County: Tarrant Identification: 666228
Unit ID: 450304
Telephone: (817) 257-7575 Carnegie Class: Spec/Faith
FAX Number: (817) 257-6932 Calendar System: Semester
URL: www.brite.tcu.edu
Established: 1873 Annual Graduate Tuition & Fees: $18,720
Enrollment: 198 Coed
Affiliation or Control: Independent Non-Profit IRS Status: 501(c)3
Highest Offering: Doctorate; No Undergraduates

Program: Professional; Religious Emphasis
Accreditation: SC, THEOL

01 President & Chief Executive Officer ....Dr. D. Newell WILLIAMS
10 Vice President Business/Finance ....Ms. Michele G. SMITH
07 Director of Admission ....Dr. Valerie FORSTMAN

Brown Mackie College - Dallas/Ft. Worth (A)

2200 North Hwy 121, Suite 250, Bedford TX 76021
Telephone: (817) 799-0500 Identification: 770798
Accreditation: ACICS, SURTEC

† Branch campus of The Art Institute of Phoenix, Phoenix, AZ.

Brown Mackie College - San Antonio (B)

4715 Fredericksburg Road, Suite 100,
San Antonio TX 78229
Telephone: (877) 460-1714 Identification: 770799
Accreditation: ACICS, SURTEC

† Branch campus of The Art Institute of Phoenix, Phoenix, AZ.

Career Point College (C)

4522 Fredericksburg Rd, Suite A-18,
San Antonio TX 78201
County: Bexar FICE Identification: 025911
Unit ID: 224439
Telephone: (210) 732-3000 Carnegie Class: Assoc/PrivFP
FAX Number: (210) 734-9225 Calendar System: Other
URL: www.careerpointcollege.edu
Established: 1921 Annual Undergrad Tuition & Fees: $24,982
Enrollment: 1,208 Coed
Affiliation or Control: Proprietary IRS Status: Proprietary
Highest Offering: Baccalaureate
Program: Occupational; 2-Year Principally Bachelor's Creditable
Accreditation: ACICS

01 Director .... Ms. Debbie ROBBINS

Center for Advanced Legal Studies (D)

800 W Sam Houston Pkwy, S Suite 100,
Houston TX 77042
County: Harris FICE Identification: 026047
Unit ID: 379782
Telephone: (713) 529-2778 Carnegie Class: Assoc/PrivFP4
FAX Number: (713) 523-2715 Calendar System: Other
URL: www.paralegal.edu
Established: 1987 Annual Undergrad Tuition & Fees: $7,695
Enrollment: 170 Coed
Affiliation or Control: Proprietary IRS Status: Proprietary
Highest Offering: Associate Degree
Program: Occupational; Technical Emphasis
Accreditation: COE

01 President/CEO .... Mr. Doyle HAPPE

Central Texas College (E)

PO Box 1800, Killeen TX 76540-9990
County: Bell FICE Identification: 004003
Unit ID: 223816
Telephone: (254) 526-7161 Carnegie Class: Assoc/Pub-Spec
FAX Number: (254) 526-0817 Calendar System: Semester
URL: www.ctcd.edu
Established: 1965 Annual Undergrad Tuition & Fees (In-District): $1,824
Enrollment: 23,686 Coed
Affiliation or Control: Local IRS Status: 501(c)3
Highest Offering: Associate Degree
Program: Occupational; 2-Year Principally Bachelor's Creditable
Accreditation: SC, ADNUR, EMT, MLTAD

01 Chancellor ....Vacant
03 Deputy Chanc Resource Management ....Ms. Michele CARTER
88 President International/Navy Op .... Mr. Jim YEONOPOLUS
88 President DL/TX Campus Op ....Dr. Ralph FORD
05 Deputy Chanc Educ Pgm/Supp Svcs .... Dr. Dana WATSON
12 Dean Ft Hood/Service Area Campus .... Dr. Tina ADY
12 Dean Central Campus .... Ms. Janice ANDERSON
32 Dean Student Services ....Dr. Johnelle WELSH
08 Dean Library Services ....Ms. Deba SWAN
38 Director Guidance/Counseling .... Ms. Jennilee WILLIAMS
06 Associate Dean Admin/Reg/Records ......Mr. Stephen O'DONOVAN
10 Comptroller ....Mr. Bob LIBERTY
15 Director Human Resource Mgmt ....Ms. Holly JORDAN
106 Director Distance Education/Ed Tech ....Ms. Sharon DAVIS
18 Director Facilities Management ....Mr. Mark HARMSEN
21 Director Business Services ....Ms. Carol GRAY
30 Director College Development ....Ms. Amy BAWCOM
09 Director Institutional Effectivenes ....Ms. Quevarra MOTEN
13 Director Information Technology ....Vacant
07 Director Admissions/Recruitment .... Ms. Shannon BRALLEY
88 Director Testing ....Ms. JoAnna JOHNSON
85 Director International Student Svcs .... Ms. Rosemary YARGICI
88 Director Disability Support Svcs .... Ms. Sharon FREDERICK
88 Director Substance Abuse Resource . Dr. Gerald MAHONE-LEIWS
36 Director Career Planning/Placement ....Ms. Elaine RILEY
26 Dir Community Relations/Marketing ....Ms. Barbara MERLO
88 Liaison Military Programs ....Ms. Diana CASTILLO
19 Chief Police/Security Services ....Ms. Mary WHEELER
40 Manager Bookstore ....Ms. Callie LATIMER
37 Director Student Financial Aid ....Ms. Annabelle SMITH
96 Director of Purchasing ....Ms. Carol GRAY
04 Administrative Asst to President ....Ms. Debra HAVENS
43 Dir Legal Services/General Counsel ....Ms. Deborah SHIBLEY
86 Director Government Relations ....Mr. Brian SUNSHINE

Chamberlain College of Nursing-Houston (F)

11025 Equity Drive, Houston TX 77041
Telephone: (713) 277-9800 Identification: 770500
Accreditation: &NH, NURSE

† Branch campus of Chamberlain College of Nursing-Addison, Addison, IL.

Chamberlain College of Nursing-Irving (G)

4800 Regent Blvd, Ste 200, Irving TX 75063
Telephone: (469) 706-6705 Identification: 770853
Accreditation: &NH, NURSE

† Branch campus of Chamberlain College of Nursing-Addison, Addison, IL.

Chamberlain College of Nursing-Pearland Campus (H)

12000 Shadow Creek Pkwy, Pearland TX 77584
Telephone: (832) 664-7000 Identification: 770934
Accreditation: &NH, NURSE

† Branch campus of Chamberlain College of Nursing-Addison, Addison, IL.

Cisco College (I)

101 College Heights, Cisco TX 76437-1900
County: Eastland FICE Identification: 003553
Unit ID: 223898
Telephone: (254) 442-5000 Carnegie Class: Assoc/Pub-R-M
FAX Number: (254) 442-5100 Calendar System: Semester
URL: www.cisco.edu
Established: 1940 Annual Undergrad Tuition & Fees (In-State): $2,790
Enrollment: 3,608 Coed
Affiliation or Control: State IRS Status: 501(c)3
Highest Offering: Associate Degree
Program: Occupational; 2-Year Principally Bachelor's Creditable
Accreditation: SC, COARC, MAC, SURGT

01 President ....Mr. Bobby SMITH
05 Vice Pres of Instruction ....Mr. Randy GOLSON
32 Vice President for Student Services ....Dr. Jerry DODSON
13 Exec Dir of Information Technology ....Mr. Steve POWELL
09 Exec Dir of Institutional Research ....Mr. Joe CARTER
12 Provost Abilene Education Center ....Dr. Carol DUPREE
84 Dean of Enrollment Services .... Mr. Olin O. ODOM, III
38 Dean of Counseling .... Mr. Randy LEATH
30 Director of Development ....Ms. Martha MONTGOMERY
37 Director of Financial Aid ....Ms. Dianne PHARR
15 Director Human Resources ....Ms. Pamela PAGE
35 Director New Student Services ....Ms. Shae WHITE
08 Director of Library Services ....Ms. Makenzie BINGHAM
19 Director Campus Safety ....Mr. Brad TEAFF
07 Director of Admissions ....Ms. Shirley DOVE

Clarendon College (J)

PO Box 968, Clarendon TX 79226-0968
County: Donley FICE Identification: 003554
Unit ID: 223922
Telephone: (806) 874-3571 Carnegie Class: Assoc/Pub-R-S
FAX Number: (806) 874-3201 Calendar System: Semester
URL: www.clarendoncollege.edu
Established: 1898 Annual Undergrad Tuition & Fees (In-District): $3,030
Enrollment: 1,216 Coed
Affiliation or Control: State/Local IRS Status: 501(c)3
Highest Offering: Associate Degree
Program: Occupational; 2-Year Principally Bachelor's Creditable
Accreditation: SC

01 President ....Dr. Robert RIZA
05 Interim Vice Pres of Instruction .... Dr. Roger SCHUSTEREIT
32 Vice Pres of Student Services .... Mr. Tex BUCKHAULTS
08 Librarian ....Ms. Pamela REED
37 Director of Financial Aid .... Ms. Susan RUSSELL
06 Registrar ....Ms. Brandi HAVENS
81 Division Chair Science/Health ....Mrs. Scarlet ESTLACK
49 Division Chair Liberal Arts ....Mr. Brian FULLER
09 Director of Institutional Research .... Dr. Robert TAYLOR

Coastal Bend College (K)

3800 Charco Road, Beeville TX 78102-2197
County: Bee FICE Identification: 003546
Unit ID: 223320
Telephone: (361) 358-2838 Carnegie Class: Assoc/Pub-R-M
FAX Number: (361) 358-3971 Calendar System: Semester
URL: www.coastalbend.edu
Established: 1965 Annual Undergrad Tuition & Fees (In-District): $2,752
Enrollment: 3,810 Coed
Affiliation or Control: State/Local IRS Status: 501(c)3
Highest Offering: Associate Degree
Program: Occupational; 2-Year Principally Bachelor's Creditable; Technical Emphasis
Accreditation: SC, DH, RAD

01 President ....Dr. Beatriz T. ESPINOZA
05 Dean of Academics .... Mr. Mark SECORD
32 Dean of Student Services .... Dr. Michael CHAVEZ
07 Director of Admissions/Registrar ....Ms. Tammy ADAMS
30 Dir Institutional Advancement/PR ....Ms. Monica CRUZ
25 Director of Grants/Special Projects .... Dr. Michael CHAVEZ
37 Director of Financial Aid ....Ms. Nora MORALES
12 Director of Alice Campus .... Ms. Dee Dee ARISMENDEZ
12 Director of Kingsville Campus ....Ms. Amanda BARRERA
09 Institutional Research Director ....Dr. Shannon LANE
08 Director Library Services ....Vacant
15 Personnel Director ....Ms. Denice HADWIN
18 Chief Facilities/Physical Plant ....Mr. Jacinto (JC) COLMENERO
26 Chief Public Relations Officer ....Ms. Monica CRUZ
04 Administrative Asst to President ....Ms. Daria HEIL

College of Biblical Studies-Houston (L)

7000 Regency Square Boulevard, Houston TX 77036-3298
County: Harris FICE Identification: 034224
Unit ID: 388520
Telephone: (713) 785-5995 Carnegie Class: Spec/Faith
FAX Number: (713) 785-5998 Calendar System: Semester
URL: www.cbshouston.edu
Established: 1976 Annual Undergrad Tuition & Fees: $6,946
Enrollment: 496 Coed
Affiliation or Control: Independent Non-Profit IRS Status: 501(c)3
Highest Offering: Baccalaureate
Program: Religious Emphasis
Accreditation: SC, BI

01 President ....Dr. Bill BLOCKER
04 Exec Administrative Assistant ....Mrs. Vicki PATTERSON
05 VP Academic Affairs/Acad Dean ....Mr. Joseph D. PARLE
10 VP Finance & Business Affairs ....Mr. Richard CAMPBELL
32 VP for Inst Effect & Student Affs ....Mr. Paul KEITH
08 Director of Library Services ....Mr. Artis LOVELADY, III
09 Dir Inst Effect and Accreditation ....Dr. Bryce F. HANTLA
06 Registrar ....Mr. Chad KNIFFEN
21 Director Accounting ....Mrs. Shaffer GAYLA
37 Director Student Financial Aid ....Ms. Roshanna HARDISON
40 Director Bookstore ....Mr. Terry BRYAN
26 Director of Marketing and PR ....Ms. Melinda MERILLAT
07 Director of Admissions ....Ms. Maggie RODRIGUEZ
106 Assoc Dean Dist Education ....Mr. Shane BOOTHE

The College of Health Care Professions (M)

6505 Airport Blvd, Suite 102, Austin TX 78752
County: Travis FICE Identification: 034263
Unit ID: 437635
Telephone: (512) 892-2835 Carnegie Class: Not Classified
FAX Number: (512) 892-6643 Calendar System: Other
URL: www.chcp.edu
Established: Annual Undergrad Tuition & Fees: $17,000
Enrollment: 260 Coed
Affiliation or Control: Proprietary IRS Status: Proprietary
Highest Offering: Associate Degree
Program: Occupational
Accreditation: ABHES

01 Director ....Ms. Sara RAMBIKUR

The College of Health Care Professions (N)

240 Northwest Mall, Houston TX 77092
County: Harris FICE Identification: 031281
Unit ID: 392257
Telephone: (713) 425-3100 Carnegie Class: Assoc/PrivFP
FAX Number: (713) 425-3192 Calendar System: Other
URL: www.chcp.edu
Established: 1988 Annual Undergrad Tuition & Fees: $17,000
Enrollment: 1,172 Coed
Affiliation or Control: Proprietary IRS Status: Proprietary
Highest Offering: Associate Degree
Program: Occupational; 2-Year Principally Bachelor's Creditable
Accreditation: ABHES, SURGT, SURTEC

01 Campus President ....Terri LOWERY

The College of Health Care Professions-Dallas (O)

8390 Lyndon B. Johnson Fwy, Ste 300, Dallas TX 75243
Telephone: (214) 420-3400 Identification: 770531
Accreditation: ABHES

† Branch campus of The College of Health Care Professions, Austin, TX.

The College of Health Care Professions-Fort Worth (A)

4248 North Freeway, Fort Worth TX 76137
Telephone: (817) 632-5900 Identification: 770532
Accreditation: ABHES

† Branch campus of The College of Health Care Professions, Houston, TX.

College of the Mainland (B)

1200 Amburn Road, Texas City TX 77591-2499
County: Galveston FICE Identification: 007096
Unit ID: 226408
Telephone: (409) 933-8271 Carnegie Class: Assoc/Pub-R-M
FAX Number: (409) 933-8010 Calendar System: Semester
URL: www.com.edu
Established: 1966 Annual Undergrad Tuition & Fees (In-District): $1,773
Enrollment: 3,858 Coed
Affiliation or Control: Local IRS Status: 501(c)3
Highest Offering: Associate Degree
Program: Occupational; 2-Year Principally Bachelor's Creditable
Accreditation: SC, ADNUR, CAHIIM, EMT, MAC

01 President ....Dr. Beth LEWIS
05 Vice President for Instruction ....Dr. Pam MILLSAP
10 Vice President for Fiscal Affairs ....Dr. Clen BURTON
32 Vice President for Student Servies ....Dr. Vicki STANFIELD
20 Dean Gen Education Programs ....Dr. Pam MILLSAP
35 Assoc VP Student Success & Conduct ....Ms. Kris KIMBARK
06 Assoc VP for Enrollment/Registrar ....Mrs. Kelly MUSICK
18 Assoc VP Facility Services ....Mr. Charles KING
08 Director Library Services ....Ms. Kathryn PARK
13 Chief Information Officer ....Mr. James TAGLIARENI
37 Director of Student Financial Svcs ....Mr. Carl GORDON
28 Director of Diversity & Equity ....Ms. Lonica BUSH
96 Director of Purchasing ....Ms. Sonja BLINKA
09 Research Specialist ....Ms. Cheryl YOUNG

Collin County Community College District (C)

3452 Spur 399, McKinney TX 75069
County: Collin FICE Identification: 023614
Unit ID: 247834
Telephone: (972) 758-3800 Carnegie Class: Assoc/Pub-S-MC
FAX Number: (972) 758-3807 Calendar System: Semester
URL: www.collin.edu
Established: 1985 Annual Undergrad Tuition & Fees (In-District): $1,174
Enrollment: 27,991 Coed
Affiliation or Control: State/Local IRS Status: 501(c)3
Highest Offering: Associate Degree
Program: Occupational; 2-Year Principally Bachelor's Creditable
Accreditation: SC, ACFEI, ADNUR, CAHIIM, COARC, DH, EMT, POLYT, SURGT

01 District President ....Dr. H. Neil MATKIN
05 Dist Sr VP Acad Affairs & Stdnt Dev ....Dr. Colleen A. SMITH
10 Dist VP Admin Services & CFO ....Mr. Ralph G. HALL
15 Dist VP Org & Systems Effectiveness ..Ms. Kimberly K. DAVISON
32 VP Student Development ....Dr. Barbara MONEY
26 VP PR & College Development ....Ms. Lisa R. VASQUEZ
20 VP Academic & Workforce Dev ....Dr. Dani R. DAY
12 VP/Provost Spring Creek Campus ....Dr. Mary S. MCRAE
12 VP/Provost Preston Ridge Campus ....Dr. Brenda K. KIHL
12 VP/Provost Central Park Campus ....Dr. Sherry L. SCHUMANN
106 Assoc VP Academic Outreach ....Mr. Joe R. BUTLER
51 Assoc VP Cont Educ/Workforce Dev ....Mr. Stephen R. HARDY
09 Assoc VP Institutional Research ....Dr. Thomas K. MARTIN
21 Assoc VP Fin Svcs & Reporting ....Ms. Barbara A. JINDRA
21 Assoc VP Controller/Stdnt Fin Svcs ....Ms. Julie M. BRADLEY
16 Assoc VP HR & Compliance ....Ms. Norma L. ALLEN
50 Dean Business & Computer Systems ....Mr. William J. BLITT
88 Dean Developmental Education ....Mr. James N. BARKO
57 Dean Fine Arts ....Ms. Gaye M. COOKSEY
76 Dean Health Sci/Emergency Svcs ....Dr. Abe JOHNSON
66 Dean Nursing ....Ms. Donna M. HATCH
20 Dean Acad Affairs Central Park ....Ms. Brenda C. CARTER
79 Dean Comm/Hum/Soc Sci Preston Ridge ....Ms. Wendy A. GUNDERSON
81 Dean STEM Preston Ridge ....Mr. Jon H. HARDESTY
79 Dean Comm & Hum Spring Creek ....Dr. Donald L. WEASENFORTH
81 Dean Math & Nat Sci Spring Creek ....Dr. L. Cameron NEAL, JR.
83 Dean Soc & Behav Sci Spring Creek ....Mr. Gary B. HODGE
84 Dean Enrollment & Student Success ....Dr. Alicia L. HUPPE
35 Dean Student Dev Central Park ....Mr. Douglas G. WILLIS
35 Dean Student Dev Preston Ridge ....Ms. Stephanie MEINHARDT
35 Dean Student Dev Spring Creek ....Mr. Terrence P. BRENNAN
88 Assoc Dean Hlth Sci/Emerg Svcs ....Mr. Raul J. MARTINEZ
38 Assoc Dean Counseling/Career Svcs ....Dr. Linda R. QUALIA
06 Registrar/Dir of Admissions ....Mr. Todd E. FIELDS
13 Chief Information Systems Officer ....Mr. David R. HOYT
18 Dist Dir Safety/Secur/Facil/Const ....Mr. Ed C. LEATHERS
08 Exec Dir Central Park Library ....Dr. Greg G. REID
08 Exec Dir Preston Ridge Library ....Mr. John C. MULLIN
08 Exec Dir Spring Creek Library ....Ms. Linda A. KYPRIOS
102 Exec Dir Foundation/Development ....Ms. Amy M. EVANS
41 Athletic Director ....Dr. Sherry L. SCHUMANN
96 Director of Purchasing ....Ms. Cynthia L. WHITE
37 Dir Financial Aid/Vets Affairs ....Mr. Alan D. PIXLEY
109 Dir Auxiliary Services ....Ms. Amanda L. MUNROE
85 International Student Coordinator ....Ms. Rebecca C. CROWELL

Commonwealth Institute of Funeral Service (D)

415 Barren Springs, Houston TX 77090-5913
County: Harris FICE Identification: 003556
Unit ID: 366261
Telephone: (281) 873-0262 Carnegie Class: Assoc/PrivNFP
FAX Number: (281) 873-5232 Calendar System: Quarter
URL: www.commonwealth.edu
Established: 1936 Annual Undergrad Tuition & Fees: $10,904
Enrollment: 228 Coed
Affiliation or Control: Independent Non-Profit IRS Status: 501(c)3
Highest Offering: Associate Degree
Program: Occupational
Accreditation: FUSER

01 President/CEO ....Mr. Jason C. ALTIERI
10 Vice President/Treasurer ....Mr. W. Blair WALTRIP
05 Chief Academic Officer ....Mr. Stuart MOEN
20 Associate Academic Officer ....Mr. Christopher LAYTON
37 Director Student Financial Aid ....Ms. Jessika JENKINS
06 Registrar ....Ms. Patricia MORENO
08 Head Librarian ....Ms. Melissa DAVI

Concorde Career College (E)

12606 Greenville Avenue, Suite 130, Dallas TX 75243
Telephone: (469) 221-3411 Identification: 770593
Accreditation: ACCSC, #COARC, DH, PTAA, SURGT

† Branch campus of Concorde Career College, Aurora, CO.

Concorde Career College (F)

4803 NW Loop 410, Suite 200, San Antonio TX 78229
Telephone: (210) 428-2000 Identification: 770594
Accreditation: ACCSC, #COARC, DH, PTAA, SURGT

† Branch campus of Concorde Career College, Kansas City, MO.

Concorde Career Institute (G)

3015 West I20, Grand Prairie TX 75052
County: Tarrant FICE Identification: 035423
Unit ID: 441742
Telephone: (469) 348-2500 Carnegie Class: Not Classified
FAX Number: (469) 348-2580 Calendar System: Semester
URL: www.concorde.edu
Established: 1991 Annual Undergrad Tuition & Fees: $27,128
Enrollment: 987 Coed
Affiliation or Control: Proprietary IRS Status: Proprietary
Highest Offering: Associate Degree
Program: Occupational
Accreditation: ACCSC, NDT, POLYT, SURGT

01 Campus President ....Mr. Mike LOVEJOY

Concordia University Texas (H)

11400 Concordia University Drive, Austin TX 78726
County: Travis FICE Identification: 003557
Unit ID: 224004
Telephone: (512) 313-3000 Carnegie Class: Master's L
FAX Number: (512) 313-3339 Calendar System: Semester
URL: www.concordia.edu
Established: 1926 Annual Undergrad Tuition & Fees: $27,600
Enrollment: 2,504 Coed
Affiliation or Control: Lutheran Church - Missouri Synod
IRS Status: 501(c)3
Highest Offering: Master's
Program: Liberal Arts And General; Teacher Preparatory; Professional
Accreditation: SC, IACBE, NURSE

01 President/CEO ....Dr. Donald CHRISTIAN
04 Executive Asst to Pres/CEO ....Ms. Kathy ARNOLD
88 Pres Amb for Mission ....Rev. Gerald KIESCHNICK
42 Int Dir Campus Spiritual Life ....Dr. Jacob YOUMANS
18 Assoc VP Facilities Svcs ....Mr. Dan GREGORY
13 Chief Information Officer ....Vacant
45 Chief Strategy Officer ....Dr. Shane SOKOLL
14 Director of Information Systems ....Vacant
90 Director Academic Computing ....Mr. Joel RAHN
19 Chief of Police ....Mr. H.E JENKINS
10 VP of Administration/CFO ....Mr. Brad JOHNSTON
21 Assoc VP of Finance ....Ms. Sarah LOGHIN
40 Bookstore Manager ....Ms. Jessica BRIGHT
15 Assoc VP Human Resources ....Ms. LaDonna WERNLI
05 Provost/CAO ....Dr. Erik ANKERBERG
50 Dean College of Business ....Dr. Lynette GILLIS
58 Director MBA Graduate Program ....Dr. Elise BRAZIER
53 Dean College of Education ....Dr. Gayle GROTJAN
58 Director MED Graduate Program ....Dr. Chris WINKLER
49 Dean College of Liberal Arts ....Dr. Carl TROVALL
81 Dean College of Science ....Dr. Janet WHITSON
66 Director Nursing Program ....Dr. Kathy LAUCHNER
12 Center Dean Austin ....Dr. DeEadra ALBERT-GREEN
12 Center Dean Dallas/Ft Worth ....Dr. Rebecca BURTON
12 Center Dean San Antonio ....Dr. Mary DARDEN
106 Center Dean Online ....Alex HERRON
08 Director of Library Services ....Ms. Mikail MCINTOSH-DOTY
09 Director of Institutional Research ....Vacant
30 VP External Relations ....Ms. Beth ATHERTON
26 Assoc VP External Relations ....Mr. James CANDIDO
29 Dir Donor & Alumni Relations ....Mr. Jeff FROSCH
102 Director Corporate Relations ....Ms. Meredith ALLEN
84 Director of Recruitment ....Ms. Brooke JOEKEL
03 Exec VP & Chief Mission Officer ....Dr. Kristi KIRK
88 Assoc VP Enrollment & Programs ....Ms. Tammy STEWART
06 Registrar ....Ms. Connie BERAN
37 Director Student Financial Services ....Mr. Russell JEFFREY
07 Assoc VP of Admissions ....Ms. Kristin COULTER
32 Dean of Students ....Dr. Elizabeth MEDINA
38 Director Student Success Center ....Ms. Ruth COOPER
36 Director Career Center ....Ms. Randa SCOTT
39 Director of Residential Life ....Ms. Sarah EBERLE
41 Athletic Director ....Mr. Stan BONEWITZ

Criswell College (I)

4010 Gaston Avenue, Dallas TX 75246-1537
County: Dallas FICE Identification: 041218
Unit ID: 224208
Telephone: (214) 821-5433 Carnegie Class: Not Classified
FAX Number: (214) 370-0497 Calendar System: Semester
URL: www.criswell.edu
Established: 1970 Annual Undergrad Tuition & Fees: $8,230
Enrollment: 343 Coed
Affiliation or Control: Independent Non-Profit IRS Status: 501(c)3
Highest Offering: Master's
Program: Religious Emphasis
Accreditation: SC

01 President ....Barry CREAMER
05 Vice President Academic Affairs ....Joseph WOODDELL
10 Chief Business Officer ....Kevin STILLEY
84 Assoc Vice Pres Enrollment Services ....Russell MARRIOTT
30 Director of Development ....Mike GOFF

Culinary Institute LeNotre (J)

7070 Allensby Street, Houston TX 77022-4322
County: Harris FICE Identification: 037233
Unit ID: 444565
Telephone: (713) 692-0077 Carnegie Class: Assoc/PrivFP
FAX Number: (713) 692-7399 Calendar System: Other
URL: www.culinaryinstitute.edu
Established: 1998 Annual Undergrad Tuition & Fees: $23,664
Enrollment: 430 Coed
Affiliation or Control: Proprietary IRS Status: Proprietary
Highest Offering: Associate Degree
Program: Occupational; 2-Year Principally Bachelor's Creditable
Accreditation: ACCSC, ACFEI

01 School Director ....Mark STROEH

Culinary Institute of America San Antonio (K)

312 Pearl Parkway, Bldg 3, San Antonio TX 78215
Telephone: (210) 554-6400 Identification: 770131
Accreditation: &M

† Branch campus of The Culinary Institute of America, Hyde Park, NY.

Dallas Baptist University (L)

3000 Mountain Creek Parkway, Dallas TX 75211-9299
County: Dallas FICE Identification: 003560
Unit ID: 224226
Telephone: (214) 333-7100 Carnegie Class: Master's L
FAX Number: (214) 333-5447 Calendar System: 4/1/4
URL: www.dbu.edu
Established: 1898 Annual Undergrad Tuition & Fees: $24,890
Enrollment: 5,445 Coed
Affiliation or Control: Baptist IRS Status: 501(c)3
Highest Offering: Doctorate
Program: 2-Year Principally Bachelor's Creditable; Liberal Arts And General; Teacher Preparatory; Professional
Accreditation: SC, ACBSP, MUS

01 Chancellor ....Dr. Gary COOK
04 Asst to Chancellor/Dir Gift Acctng ....Mr. Mitch BENNETT
13 VP for InformationTechnology ....Dr. Matt MURRAH
10 Vice President Financial Affairs ....Mr. Eric BRUNTMYER
30 VP Advancement & Graduate Affairs ....Dr. Cory HINES
58 Vice Pres/Dean Cook School of Ldshp ....Dr. Adam WRIGHT
11 Vice Pres for Admin Affairs ....Mr. Jonathan TEAT
26 Vice Pres for Communications ....Dr. Blake KILLINGSWORTH
106 VP Intl Affairs/Dean Online Educ ....Mr. Randy BYERS
32 Dean of Students and Spiritual Life ....Mr. Jay HARLEY
35 Associate Dean of Students ....Dr. Heather HADLOCK
05 Provost ....Dr. Denny DOWD
20 Associate Provost ....Mrs. Deemie NAUGLE
20 Asst Provost/Director Hybrid Educ ....Dr. Mark HALE
20 Academic Dean ....Dr. Gail LINAM
50 Dean College of Business ....Dr. Dale SIMS
81 Dean College Natural Science & Math ....Dr. Dionisio FLEITAS
53 Dean College of Education ....Dr. Neil DUGGER
57 Dean College of Fine Arts ....Mr. Ron BOWLES
73 Dean College of Christian Faith ....Dr. Steve MULLEN
79 Dean Col Humanities/Social Sciences ....Dr. Rob SULLIVAN
88 Dean College Professional Studies ....Dr. Donovan FREDRICKSEN
55 Director of Weekend College ....Ms. Joyce WALLACE

58 Director of Graduate Programs .... Mrs. Kit MONTGOMERY
06 Registrar .... Mrs. Linda RONEY
84 Asst Vice Pres for Enrollment Svcs .... Mr. Jason WILLIAMS
07 Director of Undergrad Admissions .... Mr. Bobby SOTO
37 Asst VP for Financial Aid .... Mr. Lee FERGUSON
15 Director of Human Resources .... Mrs. Tamy ROGERS
08 Director of Library .... Ms. Debra COLLINS
41 Director of Athletics .... Mr. Connor SMITH
19 Chief of University Police .... Mr. Gary LINDSEY
19 Director of Campus Security .... Mr. Donald KABETZKE
85 Dir Intl Admissions & Immigration .... Mr. Timothy WATTS
85 Director of Intl Student Services .... Ms. Susie LAMBRIGHT
38 Director Counseling Services .... Dr. Joan DAVIS
29 Asst VP Advanc/Dir Alumni Relations .... Mr. Andrew BRISCOE
36 Director of Career Services .... Ms. Marion HILL
39 Director of Residence Life .... Mrs. Kelly ANDERSON
42 Dir Intercessory Prayer Ministry .... Ms. Cyndi PETTIT
88 Academic Projects Administrator .... Ms. Lou ESPARZA
43 General Counsel .... Mr. Dan MALONE
21 Controller .... Mrs. Mendi MCMAHAN
27 Director of Marketing .... Mrs. Layna EVANS
24 Director of Media Services .... Mr. Jonathan HOOVER
09 Coord Institutional Effectiveness .... Mrs. Carol REID
09 Coord of Institutional Research .... Mrs. Pam NEUMANN
40 Manager Bookstore .... Mr. Jason SMITH

Dallas Christian College (A)

2700 Christian Parkway, Dallas TX 75234-7299

County: Dallas FICE Identification: 006941
Unit ID: 224244

Telephone: (972) 241-3371 Carnegie Class: Spec/Faith
FAX Number: (972) 241-8021 Calendar System: 4/1/4
URL: www.dallas.edu
Established: 1950 Annual Undergrad Tuition & Fees: $15,492
Enrollment: 309 Coed
Affiliation or Control: Christian Churches And Churches of Christ
IRS Status: 501(c)3
Highest Offering: Baccalaureate
Program: Occupational; 2-Year Principally Bachelor's Creditable; Teacher Preparatory; Professional; Religious Emphasis
Accreditation: BI

01 President .... Dr. Brian D. SMITH
05 Vice President for Academic Affairs .... Dr. Perry STEPP
84 Vice Pres Enrollment Management .... Mr. Matthew MEEKS
30 Vice President Advancement .... Mr. Mark WORLEY
10 Vice President for Business .... Ms. Andrea SHORT
09 Dir Institutional Effectiveness .... Mr. Bruce LONG
06 Registrar .... Mrs. Crystal LAIDACKER
37 Director of Financial Aid .... Ms. Dana MINGO
07 Director of Admissions .... Mr. Matthew MEEKS
18 Director of Facilities .... Mr. Gary ADAMS

*Dallas County Community College District Office (B)

1601 South Lamar Street, Dallas TX 75215

County: Dallas FICE Identification: 009331
Unit ID: 224253

Telephone: (214) 378-1601 Carnegie Class: N/A
FAX Number: (214) 378-1810
URL: www.dcccd.edu

01 Chancellor .... Dr. Joe L. MAY
10 Exec Vice Chanc Business Affairs .... Mr. Ed DESPLAS
05 Exec Dist Dir WF Educ & Compliance .... Mr. Don PERRY
18 Asc Vice Chanc Facil Mgmt/Architect .... Mr. Clyde PORTER
43 District Legal Counsel .... Mr. Robert WENDLAND
86 Vice Chanc Public & Govt Affairs .... Mr. Justin H. LONON
102 Assoc Vice Chanc Foundation .... Mrs. Pyeper WILKINS
101 Executive Director Board Relations .... Mrs. Susan HALL
30 Sr Exec Development & Foundation .... Ms. Mary BRUMBACH
96 Director of Purchasing .... Mr. Steve PARK
62 Director of Technical Services .... Mr. John CRISWELL

*Brookhaven College (C)

3939 Valley View, Dallas TX 75244-4997

County: Dallas FICE Identification: 021002
Unit ID: 223524

Telephone: (972) 860-4700 Carnegie Class: Assoc/Pub-U-MC
FAX Number: (972) 860-4897 Calendar System: Semester
URL: www.brookhavencollege.edu
Established: 1978 Annual Undergrad Tuition & Fees (In-District): $1,770
Enrollment: 12,403 Coed
Affiliation or Control: State/Local IRS Status: 501(c)3
Highest Offering: Associate Degree
Program: Occupational; 2-Year Principally Bachelor's Creditable
Accreditation: SC, ADNUR, ART, EMT, RAD

02 President .... Dr. Thom D. CHESNEY
05 Vice President of Academic Affairs .... Mr. Donald SMITH
10 Vice President of Business Services .... Mr. George HERRING
32 Vice Pres Student Dev/Enroll Mgmt .... Mr. Oscar LOPEZ
04 Exec Assistant to President .... Ms. Edna LOVE
50 Exec Dean Business Studies .... Mr. Sandy WYCHE
36 Assoc VP Career & Program Resources .... Mrs. Marilyn K. KOLESAR-LYNCH
103 Assoc VP Workforce/Continuing Educ .... Mr. Vernon L. HAWKINS
30 Assoc Vice Pres Development .... Ms. Marilyn K. LYNCH
45 Exec Dean Educational Resources .... Ms. Sarah FERGUSON
57 Exec Dean Fine Arts/Phys Ed .... Mr. Rick MAXWELL
81 Exec Dean Science/Math .... Dr. Kathryn WETZEL
23 Exec Dean of Health/Human Svcs .... Dr. Juanita FLINT
09 AVP Plng/Rsrch/Inst Effectiveness .... Dr. Michael DENNEHY
13 Director Information Technology .... Mr. Michael DEASON
83 Exec Dean Social Sci/Distance Lrng .... Mr. Sam GOVEA
26 Executive Dean Communications .... Mrs. Kendra VAGLIENTI
88 Exec Dean Stdnt Success/Enroll Svcs .... Ms. Brenda DALTON
27 Asst Dir Marketing & Public Info .... Mrs. Meridith DANFORTH
07 Director of Admissions/Registrar .... Ms. Thoa Hoang VO
41 Director of Athletics .... Ms. Lynne LEVESQUE
21 Director of Business Office .... Ms. Willadean MARTIN
36 Director Career Services .... Ms. Dominica MCCARTHY
88 Dir Brookhaven Geotech Institute .... Ms. Melanie GAMBLE
18 Director of Facilities .... Mr. Tommy GALLEGOS
15 Exec Dir of Human Resources .... Ms. Terri EDRICH
20 Assoc Instructional Dean .... Mr. Grant SISK
35 Dir Office of Student Life .... Mr. Brian BORSKI
19 Captain of College Police .... Mr. John KLINGENSMITH
23 Nurse Health Services .... Ms. Mildred KELLEY
04 Assistant to President .... Ms. Carrie SCHWEITZER
88 Exec Dean Educational Partnerships .... Ms. Doris ROUSEY
88 Exec Dean World Languages .... Mr. Grant SISK

*Cedar Valley College (D)

3030 N Dallas Avenue, Lancaster TX 75134-3799

County: Dallas FICE Identification: 003561
Unit ID: 223773

Telephone: (972) 860-8201 Carnegie Class: Assoc/Pub-U-MC
FAX Number: (972) 682-7075 Calendar System: Semester
URL: www.cedarvalleycollege.edu
Established: 1974 Annual Undergrad Tuition & Fees (In-District): $1,416
Enrollment: 6,759 Coed
Affiliation or Control: State/Local IRS Status: 501(c)3
Highest Offering: Associate Degree
Program: Occupational; 2-Year Principally Bachelor's Creditable; Business Emphasis
Accreditation: SC

02 President .... Dr. Jennifer L. WIMBISH
05 Vice President for Instruction .... Ms. Audra BARRETT
32 Vice Pres Student Svcs/Enroll Mgmt .... Ms. Anna MAYS
10 Vice President Business Services .... Mr. Huan LUONG
81 Director Dean Math/Science/Health .... Mr. Eddy RAWLINSON
09 Dir Inst Research/Effectiveness .... Dr. Joseph PAUL
49 Division Dean Liberal Arts .... Dr. Elsie BURNETT
50 Div Dean Bus/Science/Technology .... Dr. Ruben JOHNSON
20 Dean Instructional SupportDist Ed .... Mrs. Lisa NIGHTINGALE
51 Executive Dean Cmty & Resource Dev .... Mrs. Patricia DAVIS
08 Assoc Dean Educ Resource/ Librarian .... Ms. Vidya KRISHNASWAMY
07 Director of Admissions .... Ms. Linda OSAGIE
18 Director Facilities Management .... Mrs. Cindy A. ROGERS
26 Dir Marketing & Public Relations .... Mr. Henry MARTINEZ
15 Director Human Resources .... Dr. Anthony WADE
37 Director of Financial Aid .... Ms. Cathryn ADAMS
88 Director of Upward Bound .... Ms. Olivia GUERRA
88 Director of Independent Study .... Ms. Rosalyn WALKER
35 Coordinator Office Student Life .... Ms. Myioshi U. HOLMES
36 Senior Placement Coordinator .... Ms. Lathera ADDISON
06 Registrar .... Ms. Linda OSAGIE
29 Director Alumni Relations .... Ms. Patricia DAVIS
38 Director Student Counseling .... Ms. Jarlene DECAY
84 Director Enrollment Management .... Ms. Anna MAYS
96 Director of Purchasing .... Ms. Susan PIERCE

*Eastfield College (E)

3737 Motley Drive, Mesquite TX 75150-2099

County: Dallas FICE Identification: 008510
Unit ID: 224572

Telephone: (972) 860-7100 Carnegie Class: Assoc/Pub-U-MC
FAX Number: (972) 860-8373 Calendar System: Semester
URL: www.eastfieldcollege.edu
Established: 1970 Annual Undergrad Tuition & Fees (In-District): $1,770
Enrollment: 15,113 Coed
Affiliation or Control: State/Local IRS Status: 170(c)1
Highest Offering: Associate Degree
Program: Occupational; 2-Year Principally Bachelor's Creditable
Accreditation: SC

02 President .... Dr. Jean L. CONWAY
05 Exec VP Academic Affairs .... Mr. Michael J. GUTIERREZ
45 Int VP Organizational Development .... Mr. Larry L. WILSON
10 VP Business Services .... Dr. Adrian H. DOUGLAS
32 Exec Dean Student Development ..... Mr. Paul M. GOERTEMILLER
26 Assistant to the President .... Ms. Sharon L. COOK
15 Executive Director Human Resources .... Vacant
12 Exec Dir Pleasant Grove Campus .... Mr. Javier E. OLGUIN
04 Admin Assistant to the President .... Ms. Gloria M. JOHNSON
09 Director Institutional Research .... Mr. Ricardo RODRIGUEZ
57 Executive Dean Arts & Communication .... Ms. Rachel B. WOLF
72 Int Executive Dean Career Tech .... Mr. Johnnie O. BELLAMY
81 Executive Dean STEM .... Dr. Gretchen K. RIEHL
83 Executive Dean Social Sciences .... Dr. Michael D. WALKER
103 Director Workforce Devel .... Mrs. Christa K. JONES
51 Exec Dean Workforce/Corp/Cont Educ .... Mr. Roy L. BOND
08 Dean Educational Resources .... Ms. Karla J. GREER
07 Executive Dean Student Enrollment .... Ms. Kimberly M. LOWRY
84 Exec Dean Stdnt Engagemt/ Retention .... Ms. Courtney CARTER-HARBOUR
37 Director Financial Aid .... Vacant
41 Director Intercollegiate Athletics .... Mr. Anthony S. FLETCHER
23 Director Health Center .... Mrs. Cynthia S. TAYLOR
38 Professional Counselor .... Mr. Jeff QUAN
88 Director Disability Services .... Ms. Bobbi L. WHITE
21 Financial Manager .... Ms. Heidi M. BASSETT
21 Asst Director Business Operations .... Ms. Linda S. ZABOJNIK
18 Director Facilities Services .... Mr. Michael BRANTLEY
90 Interim Dean Information Tech .... Mr. Jack O. THIEHOFF
91 Manager Administrative Computing .... Ms. Dana R. HASKINS
46 Dean Resource Development ..... Dr. Tricia THOMAS-ANDERSON
19 Director College Police .... Chief Michael D. HORAK
20 Associate Dean of Educational Res ..... Ms. Lucinda A. GONZALES
35 Associate Dean Student Support .... Mr. Nathaniel A. SIMPSON
25 Director of Grants .... Ms. Ashley L. BAKER
26 Director Marketing/Educ Partnership .... Ms. Donielle R. JOHNSON

*El Centro College (F)

801 Main Street, Dallas TX 75202-3604

County: Dallas FICE Identification: 004453
Unit ID: 224615

Telephone: (214) 860-2000 Carnegie Class: Assoc/Pub-U-MC
FAX Number: (214) 860-2335 Calendar System: Semester
URL: www.elcentrocollege.edu
Established: 1966 Annual Undergrad Tuition & Fees (In-District): $2,124
Enrollment: 10,424 Coed
Affiliation or Control: State/Local IRS Status: 501(c)3
Highest Offering: Associate Degree
Program: Occupational; 2-Year Principally Bachelor's Creditable
Accreditation: SC, ACFEI, ADNUR, COARC, CVT, DMS, MAC, MLTAD, PNUR, RAD, SURGT

02 President .... Dr. Jose ADAMES
05 VP Academic Affairs .... Ms. Sondra G. FLEMMING
32 VP of Student Svcs & Enrollment .... Dr. Chemene L. CRAWFORD
10 VP Business Services .... Mr. David A. BROWNING
44 Assoc VP of Development .... Ms. Lenora REECE
50 Exec Dean Bus/Pub Svc/Info Tech .... Mr. Howard H. FINNEY
60 Exec Dean Communications/Math .... Ms. Lisa M. THERIOT
49 Exec Dean Arts & Sciences .... Dr. Charles MORRIS
76 Exec Dean Health Occ/Legal Studies .... Dr. Mary L. MCPHERSON
103 Exec Dean Workforce/Cont Educ .... Ms. Jennie POLLARD
108 Dean Curriculum Assessment .... Ms. Karen MONGO
09 Dean Institutional Effectiveness .... Ms. Teresa S. ISBELL
08 Asst Dean Educational Resources .... Dr. Norman HOWDEN
07 Assoc Dean Admissions/Registrar .... Ms. Rebecca J. GARZA
35 Assoc Dean Student Services .... Ms. Karen STILLS
12 Interim Exec Director West Campus .... Mr. Ivan MARTINEZ
15 Exec Director Human Resources .... Ms. Dawn M. SEGROVES
19 College Director College Police .... Mr. Joseph HANNIGAN
26 Col Dir Marketing/Communications .... Ms. Priscilla A. STALEY
18 Col Dir Facilities Services .... Mr. Jeremy MCCLELLAND
21 Int College Dir Business Operation ...... Ms. Keisha FARRINGTON
88 Assoc Dean Stdnt Recruit/Outreach .... Mr. Monty E. FRANCIS
37 Dir Student Financial Aid .... Ms. Pam A. LUCAS
35 Assoc Dean Student Programs .... Ms. Shanee' S. MOORE
13 Director Information Technology .... Mr. Michael C. JOHNSON
85 Coordinator International Center .... Mr. Robert G. REYES
36 Pgm Svcs Coord Career Services .... Ms. Christol JOHNSON
40 Manager Bookstore .... Mr. Richard SCHLEIFFER

*Mountain View College (G)

4849 W Illinois, Dallas TX 75211-6599

County: Dallas FICE Identification: 008503
Unit ID: 226930

Telephone: (214) 860-8680 Carnegie Class: Assoc/Pub-U-MC
FAX Number: (214) 860-8521 Calendar System: Semester
URL: www.mountainviewcollege.edu
Established: 1970 Annual Undergrad Tuition & Fees (In-District): $1,665
Enrollment: 8,903 Coed
Affiliation or Control: State/Local IRS Status: 501(c)3
Highest Offering: Associate Degree
Program: Occupational; 2-Year Principally Bachelor's Creditable
Accreditation: SC

02 President .... Dr. Robert GARZA
05 Vice President of Instruction .... Vacant
32 VP Student Svcs/Enrollment Mgmt .... Dr. Leonard GARRETT
10 Vice President of Business Services .... Dr. Sharon DAVIS
84 Exec Dean Student Support Svcs .... Mr. Matthew SANCHEZ
90 Exec Dean Curriculum & Instruction .... Dr. Karen VALENCIA
45 Dean Education Center/Dir Title V .... Vacant
06 Assoc Dean Student Support Svcs .... Ms. Glenda GARRETT
18 Director Facilities Services .... Mr. Allan KNOTT
09 Dir of Planning/Research & IE .... Ms. Iva BERGERON
37 Director Financial Aid .... Ms. Bianca MATLOCK
35 Director of Student Life .... Ms. Cathy EDWARDS
103 Exec Dean of Workforce/Cont Educ .... Ms. Pat WEBB
26 Director Public Info/Marketing .... Vacant
21 Director of Business Operations .... Mr. Jose RODRIGUEZ
07 Asst Director of Admissions .... Mr. Kenne EVANS
38 Director of Advising .... Vacant
15 Director Human Resources .... Mr. Willie NEAL
36 Director Career Development .... Ms. Regina GARNER
45 Dean Resource Development .... Ms. Heather A. MARSH
04 Administrative Asst to President .... Ms. Brenda EPPERSON
08 Head Librarian .... Ms. Jean BAKER
19 Director Security/Safety .... Mr. Marvis MOSLEY
41 Athletic Director .... Mr. Keith MCKINNON

*North Lake College (A)

5001 N MacArthur Boulevard, Irving TX 75038-3899
County: Dallas FICE Identification: 020774
Unit ID: 227191
Telephone: (972) 273-3000 Carnegie Class: Assoc/Pub-U-MC
FAX Number: (972) 273-3014 Calendar System: Semester
URL: www.dcccd.edu
Established: 1977 Annual Undergrad Tuition & Fees (In-District): $885
Enrollment: 10,998 Coed
Affiliation or Control: State/Local IRS Status: 501(c)3
Highest Offering: Associate Degree
Program: Occupational; 2-Year Principally Bachelor's Creditable; Technical Emphasis
Accreditation: SC, CONST

02 President ... Ms. Christa SLEJKO
05 Vice President Academic Affairs ... Dr. Martha HUGHES
103 VP Workforce Education ... Dr. Paul KELEMEN
10 Interim Vice Pres Business Services ... Dr. Eddie TEALER
45 Vice Pres Planning & Development ... Ms. Candace CASTILLO
84 VP Stdnt Svcs/Enrollment Mgmt ... Ms. Mary CIMINELLI
88 Director of Learning Resources ... Mr. Kent SEAVER
07 Director Admissions & Registration ... Ms. Francyenne MAYNARD
26 Director Marketing & Public Info ... Ms. Gina FEDERER
12 Ex Director North and South Campus ... Mr. Arthur JAMES
08 Head Librarian ... Dr. Enrique CHAMBERLAIN
18 Director Facilities Services ... Mr. John WATSON
19 Director Campus Police ... Vacant
88 Int Director of Decision Support ... Ms. Peggy SINDELAR
15 Director Human Resources ... Ms. Ella BARBER
21 Director Business Operations ... Ms. Elsy CARRANZA
32 Dir Student Programs/Resources ... Ms. Beth NIKOPOULOS
103 Director Workforce Dev/CE ... Vacant
38 Dir Acad Advising Career Edu Pl ... Ms. DeAira HOLLOWAY
83 Executive Dean Liberal Arts ... Dr. Shawnda FLOYD
81 Exec Dean Math/Science ... Dr. Marilyn MAYS
50 Exe Dean Arts/Bus/Sports Sci Tech ... Dr. David EVANS
12 Exec Dean West Campus ... Mr. Mike COOLEY

*Richland College (B)

12800 Abrams Road, Dallas TX 75243-2199
County: Dallas FICE Identification: 008504
Unit ID: 227766
Telephone: (972) 238-6194 Carnegie Class: Assoc/Pub-U-MC
FAX Number: (972) 238-6978 Calendar System: Semester
URL: www.rlc.dcccd.edu
Established: 1972 Annual Undergrad Tuition & Fees (In-District): $1,416
Enrollment: 19,664 Coed
Affiliation or Control: State/Local IRS Status: 501(c)3
Highest Offering: Associate Degree
Program: Occupational; 2-Year Principally Bachelor's Creditable
Accreditation: SC, MAC

02 President ... Dr. Kathryn K. EGGLESTON
04 Dean/Exec Assistant to President ... Ms. Janet C. JAMES
05 VP Teaching & Learning ... Dr. Zarina BLANKENBAKER
32 VP for Student Development ... Dr. Tony E. SUMMERS
10 VP for Business Services ... Mr. Ron M. CLARK
84 Assoc VP Enrollment/Supt RCHS ... Ms. Donna WALKER
50 Exec Dean Sch of Engr/Business/Tech ... Ms. Martha A. HOGAN
79 Exec Dean Human/Fine & Perf Arts ... Ms. Diane HILBERT
81 Exec Dean of Math/Science/Hlth Prof ... Dr. Raymond P. CANHAM
09 Exec Dean Plng/Rsrch/Inst Effect ... Ms. Fonda L. VERA
60 Exec Dean World Lang/Cultures/Comm ... Ms. Susan E. BARKLEY
88 Exec Dean Lrng Enrich & Acad Dev ... Ms. Mary K. DARIN
06 Registrar ... Vacant
41 Director Athletic Programs ... Mr. Guy SIMMONS
35 Director of Student Life ... Mr. Carter BEDFORD
08 Director of Library Services ... Ms. Lennijo HENDERSON
26 Dir College Comm and Marketing ... Ms. Whitney ROSENBALM
18 Director of Facilities Services ... Mr. Kenneth DUNSON
15 Executive Director Human Resources ... Vacant
19 Chief of College Police ... Mr. Robert D. BAKER
88 Principal Richland Collegiate HS ... Mr. Craig HINKLE

Dallas Institute of Funeral Service (C)

3909 S Buckner Boulevard, Dallas TX 75227-4314
County: Dallas FICE Identification: 010761
Unit ID: 224271
Telephone: (214) 388-5466 Carnegie Class: Assoc/PrivNFP
FAX Number: (214) 388-0316 Calendar System: Quarter
URL: www.dallasinstitute.edu
Established: 1945 Annual Undergrad Tuition & Fees: $18,500
Enrollment: 130 Coed
Affiliation or Control: Independent Non-Profit IRS Status: 501(c)3
Highest Offering: Associate Degree
Program: Occupational; 2-Year Principally Bachelor's Creditable; Technical Emphasis
Accreditation: FUSER

01 President ... Mr. James M. SHOEMAKE

Dallas Nursing Institute (D)

12170 North Abrams Road, Suite 125, Dallas TX 75243
County: Dallas FICE Identification: 034165
Unit ID: 437732
Telephone: (469) 941-8300 Carnegie Class: Not Classified
FAX Number: (214) 593-0975 Calendar System: Semester
URL: www.dni.edu
Established: 1991 Annual Undergrad Tuition & Fees: $27,300
Enrollment: 160 Coed
Affiliation or Control: Proprietary IRS Status: Proprietary
Highest Offering: Associate Degree
Program: Occupational
Accreditation: ABHES

01 Executive Director ... Dr. Patricia PERRYMAN

Dallas Theological Seminary (E)

3909 Swiss Avenue, Dallas TX 75204-6493
County: Dallas FICE Identification: 003562
Unit ID: 224305
Telephone: (214) 887-5000 Carnegie Class: Spec/Faith
FAX Number: (214) 887-5532 Calendar System: Semester
URL: www.dts.edu
Established: 1924 Annual Graduate Tuition & Fees: $15,320
Enrollment: 2,134 Coed
Affiliation or Control: Independent Non-Profit IRS Status: 501(c)3
Highest Offering: Doctorate; No Undergraduates
Program: Professional; Religious Emphasis
Accreditation: SC, THEOL

01 President ... Dr. Mark L. BAILEY
05 Vice Pres Academic Affs/Acad Dean ... Dr. Mark M. YARBROUGH
32 VP Dean Stdnt Svcs/Dean of Students ... Dr. Robert J. GARIPPA
10 Vice President Business & Finance ... Mr. Dale C. LARSON
30 Vice President for Advancement ... Ms. Kimberly B. TILL
11 Vice President Campus Operations ... Mr. Robert F. RIGGS
26 Exec Dir Communications/Ed Tech ... Mr. John C. DYER
102 President Dallas Sem Foundation ... Mr. Stephen M. GOLDING
108 Dean of Assessment ... Dr. Eugene W. POND
20 Dean of Academic Administration ... Dr. James H. THAMES
12 Dean of DTS Houston ... Dr. Bruce W. FONG
58 Director of PhD Studies ... Dr. Richard A. TAYLOR
58 Director of DMin Studies ... Dr. D. Scott BARFOOT
09 Dir of Institutional Effectiveness ... Dr. Eugene W. POND
06 Registrar ... Mr. Billy R. TODD, JR.
88 Actg Exec Dir of Leadership Center ... Dr. Bill HENDRICKS
88 Exec Dir of Cultural Engagement ... Dr. Darrell L. BOCK
07 Acting Director of Admissions ... Dr. Gregory A. HATTEBERG
08 Library Director ... Mr. Marvin T. HUNN, II
29 Dean of Enrollment/Alumni Services ... Mr. Gregory A. HATTEBERG
36 Director of Placement ... Dr. Paul E. PETTIT
24 Director of Audio/Visual Support ... Mr. James W. HOOVER
42 Chaplain ... Vacant
34 Adviser to Women Students ... Ms. Lynn Etta G. MANNING
93 Adviser to African-American Studnts ... Dr. Terrance S. WOODSON
13 Director of Information Technology ... Mr. Richard D. BLAKE
19 Chief of Campus Police ... Mr. John S. BLOOM
39 Director of Housing & Food Services ... Mr. Drew H. WILLIAMS
106 Dir Online and External Studies ... Mr. Robert M. ABEGG
88 Director of Online Chinese Studies ... Dr. Samuel CHIA
38 Director of Counseling Services ... Dr. Kelly CHEATHAM
21 Controller ... Ms. Patricia MAYABB
40 Bookstore Manager ... Mr. Kevin D. STERN
85 International Student Adviser ... Ms. Rachel O'BRIEN
04 Administrative Asst to President ... Ms. Michelle B. SCHIWIETZ
15 Director Personnel Services ... Ms. Karen G. HOLDER
44 Director Annual or Planned Giving ... Ms. Kimberley B. TILL
91 Director Administrative Computing ... Mr. Kevin B. COX
105 Director Web Services ... Mr. John C. DYER
37 Director Student Financial Aid ... Ms. Karen G. HOLDER

Del Mar College (F)

101 Baldwin Blvd., Corpus Christi TX 78404-3897
County: Nueces FICE Identification: 003563
Unit ID: 224350
Telephone: (361) 698-1200 Carnegie Class: Assoc/Pub-R-L
FAX Number: (361) 698-1559 Calendar System: Semester
URL: www.delmar.edu
Established: 1935 Annual Undergrad Tuition & Fees (In-District): $2,914
Enrollment: 10,439 Coed
Affiliation or Control: Local IRS Status: 501(c)3
Highest Offering: Associate Degree
Program: Occupational; 2-Year Principally Bachelor's Creditable
Accreditation: SC, ACFEI, ADNUR, ART, CAHIIM, COARC, DA, DH, DMS, MLTAD, MUS, NMT, OTA, PTAA, RAD, SURGT, THEA

01 President ... Dr. Mark ESCAMILLA
05 Int Provost/VP Instruc/Stdnt Svcs ... Ms. Lenora KEAS
10 CFO & VP of Operations ... Dr. Lee SLOAN
103 VP Workforce Dev/Strategic Init ... Ms. Lenora KEAS
26 Exec Dir Community & Legal Rels ... Ms. Claudia JACKSON
30 Exec Director of Development ... Ms. Mary MCQUEEN
07 Dean Student Outreach & Enroll Svcs ... Mr. Gilbert BECERRA
35 Dean Student Engagement & Retention ... Ms. Cheryl GARNER
49 Dean Division Arts & Sciences ... Dr. Jonda HALCOMB
50 Interim Dean Business/Prof/Tech Ed ... Dr. David ARREGUIN
15 Exec Director HR & Administration ... Ms. Tammy MCDONALD
21 Comptroller ... Mr. John J. JOHNSON
96 Director of Purchasing/Business Svc ... Mr. David DAVILA
13 Chief Information Officer ... Mr. August ALFONSO
19 Dir Environ/Health/Safety/Risk Mgmt ... Mr. Kelly L. WHITE
37 Director of Financial Aid ... Ms. Nancy M. BRISENO
06 Registrar ... Vacant
32 Dir Student Leadership/Campus Life ... Ms. Beverly CAGE
88 Director of Accounting ... Ms. Cathy WEST
88 Dir of Financial Services/Bursar ... Ms. D'Ann POLAND
08 Director of Libraries ... Vacant
09 Director of Institutional Research ... Mr. Sushil PALLEMONI
16 Director of Human Resources ... Mr. Jerry W. HENRY

DeVry University - Houston Campus (G)

11125 Equity Drive, Houston TX 77041-8217
Telephone: (713) 973-3000 Identification: 666219
Accreditation: &NH, CAHIIM, ENGT

† Regional accreditation is carried under the parent institution in Downers Grove, IL.

DeVry University - Irving Campus (H)

4800 Regent Boulevard, Ste 200, Irving TX 75063-2439
Telephone: (972) 929-6777 FICE Identification: 010139
Accreditation: &NH, CAHIIM, ENGT

† Regional accreditation is carried under the parent institution in Downers Grove, IL.

East Texas Baptist University (I)

One Tiger Drive, Marshall TX 75670-1498
County: Harrison FICE Identification: 003564
Unit ID: 224527
Telephone: (903) 935-7963 Carnegie Class: Bac/Diverse
FAX Number: (903) 938-1705 Calendar System: Semester
URL: www.etbu.edu
Established: 1912 Annual Undergrad Tuition & Fees: $24,218
Enrollment: 1,211 Coed
Affiliation or Control: Southern Baptist IRS Status: 501(c)3
Highest Offering: Master's
Program: Liberal Arts And General
Accreditation: SC, CAATE, MUS, NURSE

01 President ... Dr. J. Blair BLACKBURN
100 Executive Assistant to President ... Mr. Kevin CAFFEY
05 Provost ... Dr. Lawrence E. RESSLER
20 Vice Pres Academic & Grad Programs ... Dr. Thomas SANDERS
30 Vice Pres University Advancement ... Dr. Catherine CRAWFORD
42 Vice Pres Spiritual Development ... Dr. Scott BRYANT
10 Vice Pres Administration & Finance ... Mr. Ned CALVERT
32 Vice President for Student Affairs ... Dr. Xavier WHITAKER
84 Vice Pres for Enrollment Mgmt/Mktg ... Mr. Vince BLANKENSHIP
35 Dean of Students ... Mr. Tyler SELLERS
09 Dean Acad Services & Inst Research ... Mrs. Karen WILEY
07 Director of Admissions ... Vacant
13 Director of Inst Technology ... Mr. Barry HALE
06 University Registrar ... Mr. Chris WOOD
29 Director of Alumni Relations ... Mrs. Allison PETEET
107 Dean School of Professional Studies ... Dr. Rebekah GRIGSBY
08 Director of Library ... Ms. Cynthia PETERSON
26 Director of Public Relations ... Mr. Mike MIDKIFF
37 Director of Financial Aid ... Mr. Tommy YOUNG
41 Director of Athletics ... Mr. Kent REEVES
88 Director Baptist Student Ministry ... Mr. Mark YATES
40 Director of Bookstore ... Ms. Karan SUSTAIRE
44 Director of Alumni Development ... Mr. Paul TAPP
18 Director of Physical Facilities ... Mr. Eric WILBURN
88 Director Rec & Athletic Facilities ... Mr. Randy PRINGLE
35 Asst Dean Student Affairs Operation ... Mr. Blair PREVOST
88 Director Great Commission Center ... Dr. Lisa SEELEY
53 Dean School of Education ... Vacant
88 Dean School of Christian Studies ... Dr. John HARRIS
83 Dean School of Nat/Soc Sciences ... Dr. Lynn NEW
50 Dean School of Business ... Dr. Scott RAY
79 Dean School of Humanities ... Dr. Jerry SUMMERS
85 Director of International Education ... Mr. Alan HUESING
21 Director of Financial Services ... Mr. Richard HUTSELL
88 Director of Student Success ... Mrs. Kelley PAUL
57 Dean School of Comm & Perf Arts ... Dr. Tom WEBSTER
102 Assoc VP for University Advancement ... Dr. Dane FOWLKES
88 Director of Leadership Development ... Dr. Emily PREVOST

El Paso Community College (J)

9050 Viscount Boulevard, El Paso TX 79925
County: El Paso FICE Identification: 010387
Unit ID: 224642
Telephone: (915) 831-3722 Carnegie Class: Assoc/Pub-U-MC
FAX Number: (915) 831-6507 Calendar System: Semester
URL: www.epcc.edu
Established: 1969 Annual Undergrad Tuition & Fees (In-District): $3,100
Enrollment: 28,280 Coed
Affiliation or Control: Local IRS Status: 501(c)3
Highest Offering: Associate Degree
Program: Occupational; 2-Year Principally Bachelor's Creditable
Accreditation: SC, ADNUR, CAHIIM, #COARC, DA, DH, DMS, EMT, MAC, MLTAD, PTAA, RAD, SURGT

01 President ... Dr. William SERRATA
05 Vice President Instruction ... Mr. Steve SMITH
10 Vice Pres Admin & Fin Operations ... Vacant
13 Vice Pres Information Tech/CIO ... Dr. Jenny GIRON
32 Vice President Student Services ... Ms. Linda GONZALEZ
10 Interim VP of Admin & Fin Op/CFO ... Ms. Josette SHAUGHNESSY
88 Assoc VP Employee Relations ... Ms. Nancy N. NELSON
26 Dir Marketing & Community Rels ... Ms. Joyce CORDELL
12 Dean Instruct Programs-MDP Campus ... Dr. Julie PENLEY

76 Dean Health Career/TechEd/Math/Sci ... Dr. Paula MITCHELL
60 Dean Arts/Comm/Career/TechEd/SoSci ... Dr. Eileen CONKLIN
83 Dean Arts/Comm & Soc Sci ... Ms. Janet EVELER
79 Dean ESL Reading Social Science ... Ms. Susana RODARTE
81 Dean Arch/Arts/Math/Science ... Ms. Toni BADILLO
57 Dean Comm/Performing Arts ... Mr. Claude MATHIS
53 Dean Education/Career/Tech Pgms ... Dr. Jaime D. FARIAS
66 Dean Nursing ... Ms. Paula G. MEAGHER
12 Dean Instructional Pgms-NW Campus ... Dr. Lydia TENA
81 Int Dean Math/Sci/Career Tech Ed ... Mr. Ernest R. WEBB, II
37 Exec Director Student Fin Aid ... Mr. Raul H. LERMA
45 Director Inst Effectiveness ... Dr. Ron STROUD
08 Director Library Technical Services ... Mr. Luis CHAPARRO
21 Comptroller ... Mr. Fernando FLORES
36 Director Career Services ... Ms. Carla CARDOZA
18 Executive Director Physical Plant ... Mr. Richard L. LOBATO
19 Chief of Police ... Chief Jose L. RAMIREZ
15 Exec Dir Human Resources ... Ms. Elizabeth OLGUIN-RYAN
07 Exec Director Admissions/Registrar ... Vacant
96 Dir Purchasing & Contract Mgmt ... Mr. Ruben C. GALLARDO
09 Director Institutional Research ... Dr. Carol KAY
88 Director Human Resources Devel ... Mr. Alex HERNANDEZ
31 Director Inst & Community Planning ... Ms. Dolores GROSS
21 Director Budget ... Ms. Laura TELLEZ
88 Director Workplace Literacy Pgm ... Mrs. Sara MARTINEZ
85 Director International Education ... Dr. Miguel A. MARTINEZ-LASSO
102 Exec Dir Foundation/Development ... Vacant
88 Dir Ctr for Students w/Disabilities ... Ms. Janet M. LOCKHART
88 Director Recruitment/School Rels ... Ms. Nita CORRAL-NAVA
88 Exec Dir Outreach Transition Svcs ... Vacant
25 Director Grants Management ... Mr. Alfred C. LAWRENCE
103 Director Workforce Development ... Ms. Luz E. TABOADA
106 Director Distance Education ... Mr. Robert P. JONES
88 Director Student Success ... Vacant
88 Dir Law Enforcement Trng Academy ... Mr. Barry J. BOGLE
28 Director of Diversity Programs ... Mrs. Olga CHAVEZ
41 Athletic Director ... Mr. Felix HINOJOSA

Everest College (A)

300 Six Flags Drive, Suite 100, Arlington TX 76011
Telephone: (817) 652-7790 Identification: 770788
Accreditation: ACICS

† Branch campus of Everest College, Springfield, MO.

Everest College (B)

6080 N Central Expressway, Dallas TX 75206-5202
Telephone: (214) 234-4850 Identification: 666254
Accreditation: ACICS

† Branch campus of Everest College, Portland, OR.

Everest College (C)

4200 South Freeway, Suite 1940, Fort Worth TX 76115
Telephone: (817) 566-7700 Identification: 770790
Accreditation: ACICS

† Branch campus of Everest College, Colorado Springs, CO.

Fortis Institute (D)

401 East Palace Pkwy Ste 100, Grand Prairie TX 75050
Telephone: (972) 375-0006 Identification: 770937
Accreditation: ABHES, RAD, SURGT, SURTEC

† Branch campus of Fortis Institute, Baton Rouge, LA.

Frank Phillips College (E)

PO Box 5118, Borger TX 79008-5118
County: Hutchinson FICE Identification: 003568
Unit ID: 224891
Telephone: (806) 457-4200 Carnegie Class: Assoc/Pub-R-S
FAX Number: (806) 457-4224 Calendar System: Semester
URL: www.fpctx.edu
Established: 1948 Annual Undergrad Tuition & Fees (In-District): $2,800
Enrollment: 1,348 Coed
Affiliation or Control: Local IRS Status: 501(c)3
Highest Offering: Associate Degree
Program: Occupational; 2-Year Principally Bachelor's Creditable
Accreditation: SC

01 President ... Dr. Jud HICKS
11 Vice Pres Administrative Services ... Dr. Jud HICKS
05 Vice President of Academic Affairs ... Dr. Shannon CARROLL
12 VP for Extended Services ... Dr. Lew HUNNICUTT
08 Director of the Library ... Mr. Jason PRICE
18 Director Physical Plant ... Ms. Regina HANEY
26 Col Advancement/Community Rels Ofcr ... Ms. Lydia RINEHART
103 Dean of Career & Technical Educ ... Mr. David CARR
37 Dir Student Financial Services ... Ms. Beverly FIELDS
38 Director Student Counseling/Testing ... Ms. Deborah JOHNSON
07 Director Admissions & Records ... Ms. Michele STEVENS
56 Director of Extended Education ... Vacant
10 Director of Accounting ... Ms. Bridey MCCORMACK

Galen College of Nursing (F)

7411 John Smith Drive, Suite 300, San Antonio TX 78229
Telephone: (210) 733-3056 Identification: 770538
Accreditation: &SC

† Branch campus of Galen College of Nursing, Louisville, KY.

Galveston College (G)

4015 Avenue Q, Galveston TX 77550-7496
County: Galveston FICE Identification: 004972
Unit ID: 224961
Telephone: (409) 944-4242 Carnegie Class: Assoc/Pub-R-M
FAX Number: (409) 944-1500 Calendar System: Semester
URL: www.gc.edu
Established: 1966 Annual Undergrad Tuition & Fees (In-District): $1,558
Enrollment: 2,048 Coed
Affiliation or Control: State/Local IRS Status: 501(c)3
Highest Offering: Associate Degree
Program: Occupational; 2-Year Principally Bachelor's Creditable; Business Emphasis
Accreditation: SC, ADNUR, EMT, NMT, RAD, RTT

01 President ... Dr. Myles SHELTON
05 Vice President of Instruction ... Dr. Cissy MATTHEWS
11 VP for Administration/Finance ... Ms. Pamela LEE
30 VP Community Engagement/Spec Proj ... Dr. Gaynelle H. HAYES
32 Actg VP of Student Svcs/Dir Fin Aid ... Mr. Ron C. CRUMEDY
75 Dean of Tech & Prof Education ... Ms. Vera LEWIS-JASPER
30 Dir of Development/GC Foundation ... Ms. Maria TRIPOVICH
10 Director of Business Services ... Mr. M. Jeff ENGBROCK
13 Dir of Information Technology ... Mr. Kelly KLIMPT
26 Director of Public Affairs ... Mr. Joseph E. HUFF, III
15 Dir Human Resources/Risk Management ... Dr. Mary Jan LANTZ
41 Athletic Director/Head Coach ... Mr. Ken DELCAMBRE
07 Director Admissions/Registrar ... Mr. Scott BRANUM
66 Director of Nursing ... Dr. Sandra BRANNAN
09 Director Inst Effectiveness/Rsrch ... Dr. Larry ROOT
18 Director of Facilities/Security ... Mr. Tim W. SETZER
62 Dir of Library/Learning Resources ... Dr. Alan M. UYEHARA
04 Executive Assistant ... Ms. Carla D. BIGGERS

Golf Academy of America (H)

1861 Valley View Lane, Suite 100,
Farmers Branch TX 75234
Telephone: (972) 763-8100 Identification: 770621
Accreditation: ACICS

† Branch campus of Virginia College, Birmingham, AL.

Grace School of Theology (I)

PO Box 7477, The Woodlands TX 77387
County: Montgomery Identification: 667100
Telephone: (877) 476-8674 Carnegie Class: Not Classified
FAX Number: (281) 602-8009 Calendar System: Semester
URL: www.gsot.edu
Established: 2002 Annual Undergrad Tuition & Fees: $4,754
Enrollment: 153 Coed
Affiliation or Control: Independent Non-Profit IRS Status: 501(c)3
Highest Offering: Doctorate
Program: Religious Emphasis
Accreditation: TRACS

01 President ... Dr. Dave ANDERSON
43 Exec Vice President/General Counsel ... Mr. Tom KRUPPSTADT

Graduate Institute of Applied Linguistics (J)

7500 W Camp Wisdom Road, Dallas TX 75236-5629
County: Dallas FICE Identification: 038513
Telephone: (972) 708-7340 Carnegie Class: Not Classified
FAX Number: (972) 708-7292 Calendar System: Other
URL: www.gial.edu
Established: 1999 Annual Undergrad Tuition & Fees: $15,000
Enrollment: 105 Coed
Affiliation or Control: Independent Non-Profit IRS Status: 501(c)3
Highest Offering: Master's
Program: Professional; Religious Emphasis
Accreditation: SC

01 President ... Dr. David A. ROSS
05 Dean of Academic Affairs ... Dr. Doug TIFFIN
10 Vice President of Finance ... Mr. Rod JENKINS
11 Vice President of Operations ... Mr. David HARRELL
32 Dean of Students ... Ms. Katie M. HOOGERHEIDE
06 Registrar ... Mrs. Lynne M. LAMIMAN
07 Director of Admissions ... Mrs. Maggie A. JOHNSON
08 Librarian ... Ms. Ferne L. WEIMER
30 Director of Development ... Ms. Judy POLLOCK
09 Director of Inst Research/Svcs ... Mr. Richard E. LYNCH
13 Director of Computing Services ... Mr. Chuck WALEK
21 Business Manager ... Mr. Paul W. SETTER
37 Financial Aid Administrator ... Ms. Margaret JOHNSON
88 Veterans' Officer ... Mrs. Mary Sue TIFFIN
42 Chaplain ... Mr. Victor JACKSON
29 Alumni Correspondent ... Mrs. Allison PYLE
04 Administrative Asst to President ... Ms. Gail DYKSTRA

Grayson College (K)

6101 Grayson Drive, Denison TX 75020-8299
County: Grayson FICE Identification: 003570
Unit ID: 225070
Telephone: (903) 465-6030 Carnegie Class: Assoc/Pub-R-M
FAX Number: (903) 463-5284 Calendar System: Semester
URL: www.grayson.edu
Established: 1963 Annual Undergrad Tuition & Fees (In-District): $1,632
Enrollment: 4,636 Coed
Affiliation or Control: State/Local IRS Status: 501(c)3
Highest Offering: Associate Degree
Program: Occupational; 2-Year Principally Bachelor's Creditable
Accreditation: SC, ADNUR, DA, EMT, MLTAD

01 President ... Dr. Jeremy P. MCMILLEN
05 Vice Pres Academic/Student Affs ... Dr. Regina ORGAN
10 Vice President of Business Services ... Mr. Giles BROWN
13 VP Info Technology/Dir of Library ... Mr. Gary PAIKOWSKI
102 Exec Dir Grayson College Foundation ... Mr. Randy TRUXAL
07 Director of Admissions/Registrar ... Mrs. Christy KLEMIUK
37 Director of Financial Aid ... Ms. Donna KING
14 Director of Network Services ... Mr. Mike BROWN
19 Int Director Campus Police ... Mr. Kirk ROBERTS
26 Dir Marketing/Public Information ... Mrs. Shelle R. CASSELL
21 Director of Fiscal Services ... Mr. Danny HYATT
41 Athletic Director ... Mr. Mike MCBRAYER
40 Bookstore Manager ... Ms. Brenda FOX

Hallmark University (L)

10401 IH-10 W, San Antonio TX 78230-1737
County: Bexar FICE Identification: 010509
Unit ID: 225201
Telephone: (210) 690-9000 Carnegie Class: Assoc/PrivFP
FAX Number: (210) 697-8225 Calendar System: Other
URL: www.hallmarkuniversity.edu
Established: 1969 Annual Undergrad Tuition & Fees: $32,880
Enrollment: 792 Coed
Affiliation or Control: Independent Non-Profit IRS Status: 501(c)3
Highest Offering: Master's
Program: Occupational; Professional; Technical Emphasis
Accreditation: ACCSC, MAC

01 CEO ... Mr. Joseph B. FISHER
12 University President ... Mr. Brent FESSLER
11 Sr Vice President of Operations ... Mr. Donald GREGSON
05 Dean of Academics ... Dr. Darla KENWARD
106 Dean of Curriculum/Faculty Develop ... Vacant
20 Chief of Academics/Faculty Develop ... Mr. William CASTEEL
26 VP Public/Media Engagement ... Ms. Sonia ROSS
06 Registrar ... Ms. Racquel SULLEMUN
36 Director Student Placement ... Ms. Evonn SHORT
37 Director Student Financial Aid ... Ms. Grace CALIXTO

Hardin-Simmons University (M)

2200 Hickory, Abilene TX 79698-0001
County: Taylor FICE Identification: 003571
Unit ID: 225247
Telephone: (325) 670-1000 Carnegie Class: Master's M
FAX Number: (325) 670-1267 Calendar System: Semester
URL: www.hsutx.edu
Established: 1891 Annual Undergrad Tuition & Fees: $24,500
Enrollment: 2,084 Coed
Affiliation or Control: Baptist IRS Status: 501(c)3
Highest Offering: Doctorate
Program: Liberal Arts And General; Teacher Preparatory; Professional
Accreditation: SC, ACBSP, CAATE, MUS, NURSE, PTA, SW, THEOL

01 President ... Dr. Lanny HALL
05 Provost & Chief Academic Officer ... Dr. Thomas V. BRISCO
10 VP for Finance & Management ... Mrs. Brenda ALEXANDER
30 VP for Institutional Advancement ... Mr. Mike HAMMACK
32 Vice Pres for Student Life ... Dr. Dave ROZEBOOM
84 VP for Enrollment Management ... Mrs. Vicki HOUSE
07 Assoc VP for Enrollment Svcs ... Mr. Jim JONES
53 Dean Irvin School of Education ... Dr. Pamela K. WILLIFORD
49 Dean College of Liberal Arts ... Dr. Alan STAFFORD
50 Dean Kelley College of Business ... Mr. Michael MONHOLLON
64 Dean College of Fine Arts ... Dr. Robert TUCKER
73 Dean Logsdon School of Theology ... Dr. Don WILLIFORD
58 Dean of Graduate Studies ... Dr. Nancy KUCINSKI
66 Dean School of Nursing ... Dr. Nina OUIMETTE
81 Dean School Sciences/Mathematics ... Dr. Christopher L. MCNAIR
13 Assoc Vice Pres Technical Services ... Mr. Travis P. SEEKINS
21 Asst VP For Finance/Controller ... Mrs. Jessica GARCIA
38 Assoc VP Academic Advising/Retent ... Mrs. Gracie CARROLL
08 Dean/Dir of University Libraries ... Mrs. Elizabeth J. WORLEY
09 Director of Institutional Research ... Mrs. Lori BLAKE
06 Registrar ... Mrs. Kacey HIGGINS
35 Dean of Students ... Mr. Brian DAWSON
29 Director of Alumni Relations ... Mrs. Britt E. JONES
19 Chief of Police ... Mr. Frank LOZA
23 University Nurse ... Mrs. Sue A. BIGGS
42 Chaplain ... Dr. Kelly PIGOTT
39 Director of Residence Life ... Mr. Johnathan YORKOWITZ
15 Director of Human Resources ... Mr. John SNAPP
27 Dir of Univ Communications ... Mr. James STONE
37 Dir Student Fin Aid & Scholarships ... Mrs. Bridget MOORE
18 Facilities Services Director ... Mr. Tim MCCARRY
41 Athletic Director ... Mr. John M. NEESE
85 Director of International Studies ... Dr. Allan J. LANDWER
26 Public Relations Director ... Mrs. Cheryl SAWYERS
93 Coordinator of Minority Studies ... Dr. Joe H. ALCORTA
28 Coord of Student Diversity Programs ... Dr. Kelvin J. KELLEY

Hill College (A)

112 Lamar Drive, Hillsboro TX 76645-2711

County: Hill
FICE Identification: 003573
Unit ID: 225371
Telephone: (254) 659-7500
Carnegie Class: Assoc/Pub-R-M
FAX Number: (254) 582-7591
Calendar System: Semester
URL: www.hillcollege.edu
Established: 1923
Annual Undergrad Tuition & Fees (In-District): $1,922
Enrollment: 4,022
Coed
Affiliation or Control: Local
IRS Status: 501(c)3
Highest Offering: Associate Degree
Program: Occupational; 2-Year Principally Bachelor's Creditable
Accreditation: SC, EMT

01 President Dr. Pamela BOEHM
04 Executive Asst to the President Ms. Vonnie MORPHEW
05 Vice President Instruction Mr. Rex PARCELLS
25 Vice President External Affairs Ms. Jessyca BROWN
10 Vice Pres Administrative Services Mr. Billy D. CURBO
32 Vice President Student Services Ms. Lizza TRENKLE
13 Vice Pres Information Technology Mrs. Jessie WHITE
84 Executive Dean Enrollment Services Vacant
09 Dean Inst Research/Effectiveness Dr. Teri WALKER
21 Dean Financial Services Mrs. Debbie GERIK
08 Librarian - Hill Campus Mr. Joseph SHAUGHNESSY
08 Librarian - Cleburne Campus Mr. Kevin HENARD
15 Executive Director Human Resources Dr. Heather KISSACK
12 Exec Dir JCC/Dean of Students Mr. Bill GILKER
41 Athletic Director Mr. Paul BROWN
26 Director of Marketing & Public Rels Mr. Jim DALGLISH
06 Dir Student Records & Registration Ms. Sherry DAVIS
37 Director of Financial Aid Vacant
18 Facilities Coordinator Ms. Wendie HERNANDEZ
29 Director Alumni Relations Vacant

Houston Baptist University (B)

7502 Fondren Road, Houston TX 77074-3298

County: Harris
FICE Identification: 003576
Unit ID: 225399
Telephone: (281) 649-3000
Carnegie Class: Master's M
FAX Number: (281) 649-3012
Calendar System: Semester
URL: www.hbu.edu
Established: 1960
Annual Undergrad Tuition & Fees: $29,800
Enrollment: 3,128
Coed
Affiliation or Control: Southern Baptist
IRS Status: 501(c)3
Highest Offering: Master's
Program: Liberal Arts And General; Teacher Preparatory; Professional
Accreditation: SC, NUR

01 President Dr. Robert B. SLOAN, JR.
05 Interim Provost Dr. Cynthia SIMPSON
10 Vice President Financial Operations Ms. Sandra N. MOONEY
30 Vice President for Advancement Mr. Tommy BAMBRICK
26 Vice Pres University Relations Mrs. Sharon E. SAUNDERS
84 Vice Pres Enrollment Management Mr. James STEEN
20 Associate Provost Ms. Ritamarie TAUER
20 Associate Provost Dr. Matt BOYLESTON
21 Planning & Budget Director Mr. Michael DEI
79 Dean College Arts & Humanities Dr. Chris HAMMONS
50 Dean School of Business Dr. Michael WEEKS
81 Dean College of Science & Math Dr. Doris C. WARREN
92 Director Honors College Dr. Gary HARTENBURG
53 Interim Dean School of Education Dr. Carol MCGAUGHEY
57 Dean School of Fine Arts Dr. Jason LESTER
66 Dean Sch Nursing & Allied Hlth Dr. Renae SCHUMANN
41 Athletic Director Mr. Steve C. MONIACI
06 University Registrar Ms. Erinn HUGHES
40 Director of University Store Mr. Anthony MARTIN
07 Director of Admissions Mr. Eduardo BORGES
08 Director of Libraries Ms. Ann NOBLE
42 University Minister Vacant
21 Assoc VP Financial Operations Ms. Loree WATSON
29 Dir of Alumni Relations & Advance Ms. Amy YOUNGBLOOD
39 Director Housing Operations Vacant
13 Chief Information Officer (IT) Mr. Glen JOHNSON
19 Chief of Police Mr. Charles RAGAIN
09 Dir Inst Research & Effectiveness Mr. Todd COCKRELL
32 Vice President Student Life Mr. Whittington GOODWIN
88 SACS Liaison Ms. Ritamarie TAUER
04 Admin Asst to the President Mrs. Karen FRANCIES
15 Director of Human Resources Mrs. Jennifer BOHRNSTEDT
18 Dir of Maintenance & Operations Mr. Gary DYKE
36 Dir of Career & Calling Ms. Colette CROSS
37 Sr Dir Financial Aid & Scholarships Ms. Veronica GABBARD
96 Cost Control Analyst Ms. Jody WILDING-FARRELL
100 Chief of Staff Mrs. Sharon SAUNDERS
102 Dir Foundation/Denominat Relations Mr. Rick OGDEN
105 Director Web Services Mr. Alan PRESLEY

Houston Community College (C)

3100 Main Street, Houston TX 77002

County: Harris
FICE Identification: 010633
Unit ID: 225423
Telephone: (713) 718-2000
Carnegie Class: Assoc/Pub-U-MC
FAX Number: N/A
Calendar System: Semester
URL: www.hccs.edu
Established: 1971
Annual Undergrad Tuition & Fees (In-State): $816
Enrollment: 61,956
Coed
Affiliation or Control: State
IRS Status: 501(c)3
Highest Offering: Associate Degree
Program: Occupational; 2-Year Principally Bachelor's Creditable
Accreditation: SC, CAHIIM, COARC, DA, DH, DMS, EMT, ENGT, HT, MAC, MLTAD, NMT, OTA, PTAA, RAD, SURGT

01 Chancellor Dr. Cesar MALDONADO
100 Chief of Staff Ms. Shantay GRAYS
43 Associate General Counsel Ms. Destinee WAITERS
05 Vice Chancellor of Academic Affairs Dr. Charles M. COOK
10 Vice Chancellor Finance & Planning Ms. Teri ZAMORA
32 Vice Chancellor Student Success Dr. Diana PINO
13 Vice Chancellor Information Tech Dr. William E. CARTER
45 VC Planning and Inst Effectiveness Vacant
20 Assoc VC of Academic Instruction Dr. Steve LEVEY
18 Chief Facilities Officer Mr. Winston DAHSE
15 Chief Human Resource Officer Ms. Janet MAY
22 Director EEO/Compliance Mr. David CROSS
21 Controller Dr. Karla BENDER
21 Treasurer Mr. Ron E. DEFALCO
26 Director Communication Services Ms. Frederica GUTHRIE
76 Dean Health Science Programs Dr. Michael EDWARDS
66 Department Chair Vocational Nursing Ms. Deborah SIMMONS-JOHNSON
07 Director of Admissions & Registrar Ms. Mary LEMBURG
09 Exec Dir of Inst Research & Innov Dr. Martha OBURN
46 Director of Resource Development Vacant
102 Executive Director Foundation Ms. Carmetha WILLIAMS
12 President-Northeast College Dr. Margaret FORD FISHER
12 President-Southwest College Dr. Fena GARZA
12 President-Central College Dr. William HARMON
12 President-Southeast College Dr. Irene PORCARELLO
12 President-Northwest College Dr. Zachary HODGES
12 President-Coleman College Dr. Betty K. YOUNG
85 Int Dir International Initiatives Mr. Ricardo SOLIS
29 Alumni Relations Officer Ms. Andrea STOLLER
96 Ex Dir Purchasing/Procurement Oper Mr. Rogelio ANASAGASTI
35 Director Student/Financial Services Mr. Hernando BALDONADO
37 Ex Director Student Financial Aid Ms. JoEllen SOUCIER
88 Director Internal Auditing Ms. Belinda BROCKMAN
06 Registrar Ms. Mary LEMBURG

Houston Graduate School of Theology (D)

4300-C West Bellfort, Houston TX 77035

County: Harris
FICE Identification: 023202
Unit ID: 246345
Telephone: (713) 942-9505
Carnegie Class: Spec/Faith
FAX Number: (713) 942-9506
Calendar System: Semester
URL: www.hgst.edu
Established: 1983
Annual Graduate Tuition & Fees: $9,215
Enrollment: 167
Coed
Affiliation or Control: Independent Non-Profit
IRS Status: 501(c)3
Highest Offering: Doctorate; No Undergraduates
Program: Professional; Religious Emphasis
Accreditation: THEOL

01 President Dr. James H. FURR
05 Provost/Chief Academic Officer Dr. Kent EATON
20 Assoc Acad Dean/Dir DMin Program Dr. Becky L. TOWNE
10 Chief Financial Officer Vacant
07 Dir of Admissions/Recruiting Ms. Gloria FIKES
06 Registrar Ms. Laura HAMILTON
08 Director of Library Services Ms. Janet KENNARD

Howard College (E)

1001 Birdwell Lane, Big Spring TX 79720-3799

County: Howard
FICE Identification: 003574
Unit ID: 225520
Telephone: (432) 264-5000
Carnegie Class: Assoc/Pub-R-M
FAX Number: (432) 264-5082
Calendar System: Semester
URL: www.howardcollege.edu
Established: 1945
Annual Undergrad Tuition & Fees (In-District): $2,542
Enrollment: 3,920
Coed
Affiliation or Control: State/Local
IRS Status: 501(c)3
Highest Offering: Associate Degree
Program: Occupational; 2-Year Principally Bachelor's Creditable
Accreditation: SC, ADNUR, COARC, DH, EMT, RAD, SURGT

01 President Dr. Cheryl T. SPARKS
05 Vice President Academic Affairs Dr. Amy BURCHETT
20 Dean Academic Affairs SWCID Mr. Danny CAMPBELL
32 Dean Student Affairs SWCID Ms. Nancy BONURA
12 Executive Dean San Angelo Ms. Jamie RAINEY
12 Executive Dean Big Spring Area Dr. Kinsey HANSEN
10 Chief Business Officer Mr. Steve SMITH
18 Chief Facilities Operations Officer Mr. John PARSONS
10 Chief Financial Officer Ms. Brenda CLAXTON
08 Dean of Libararies Mr. Luis KINCADE
13 Dean Information Technology Mr. Eric HANSEN
106 Director eLearning Services Ms. Kym CLARK
37 Dean Financial Aid Ms. Candice DRAPER
26 Director Effectiveness/Information Ms. Cindy SMITH
41 Athletic Director Mr. Britt SMITH
103 Dean Career Technical Education Ms. Gayla WILLIAMS
15 Director Human Resources/Payroll Ms. Rhonda KERNICK
20 Dean Teaching and Learning Ms. Pam CALLAN
06 Dean Student Affairs/Registrar Mrs. Liz ADAMSON
88 Director Campus Programming Ms. Carlea ULRICH
21 Director Student Accounting Ms. Margaret CERVANTES
30 Director Institutional Advancement Mrs. Jan FORESYTH
76 Dean Health Professions Ms. Luci GABEHART
09 Research and Reporting Official Ms. Rebecca VILLANUEVA
21 Director Financial Accounting Ms. Jeannie CARROLL
04 Executive Asst to the President Ms. Julie BAILEY

Howard Payne University (F)

1000 Fisk Street, Brownwood TX 76801-2794

County: Brown
FICE Identification: 003575
Unit ID: 225548
Telephone: (325) 646-2502
Carnegie Class: Bac/Diverse
FAX Number: (325) 649-8975
Calendar System: Semester
URL: www.hputx.edu
Established: 1889
Annual Undergrad Tuition & Fees: $25,600
Enrollment: 1,137
Coed
Affiliation or Control: Baptist
IRS Status: 501(c)3
Highest Offering: Master's
Program: Liberal Arts And General; Teacher Preparatory
Accreditation: SC, CAATE, IACBE, MUS, SW

01 President Dr. William N. ELLIS
05 Provost/Chief Academic Officer Dr. Mark TEW
10 Int Chief Financial Officer Mr. Bill FISHBACK
32 Vice Pres Stdnt Life/Dean Stdnts Dr. Magen BUNYARD
44 Vice President Development Mr. Randy YEAKLEY
84 Assoc VP for Enrollment Management Mr. Kevin KIRK
15 Asst VP for Bus & Hum Resources Mr. Bill FISHBACK
18 AVP Facilities/Planning Mr. Terry PRITCHETT
06 Registrar Mrs. Lana WAGNER
37 Director Financial Aid Mrs. Glenda HUFF
07 Director of Admission Mrs. P.J GRAMLING
36 Dir Academic Testing/Career Svcs Ms. Wendy MCNEELEY
26 Director of Publications Mr. Kyle C. MIZE
09 Director Institutional Research Mrs. Shannon TURNER
41 Athletic Director Mr. Mike JONES
91 Database Administrator Mr. Randy GINTHER
90 Computer Network Administrator Mr. Russell EZZELL
29 Coordinator of Alumni Relations Mr. Stephen SULLIVAN
88 Special Events Coordinator Ms. Kathy JAMES
04 Executive Assistant to President Ms. Tammy LOWREY
38 University Counselor Dr. Athena BEAN
56 Dean Extended Education Dr. Robert BICKNELL
08 Dean of Libraries Mrs. Alexia RIGGS
81 Dean School of Science & Math Dr. Pam BRYANT
50 Dean School of Business Vacant
53 Dean School of Ecucation Dr. Mike ROSATO
64 Dean School of Music & Fine Arts Dr. Richard FIESE
73 Dean School of Christian Studies Dr. Donnie AUVENSHINE
79 Dean School of Humanities Dr. Justin MURPHY

Huston-Tillotson University (G)

900 Chicon Street, Austin TX 78702-2795

County: Travis
FICE Identification: 003577
Unit ID: 225575
Telephone: (512) 505-3000
Carnegie Class: Bac/A&S
FAX Number: (512) 505-3190
Calendar System: Semester
URL: www.htu.edu
Established: 1875
Annual Undergrad Tuition & Fees: $14,346
Enrollment: 1,031
Coed
Affiliation or Control: Multiple Protestant Denominations
IRS Status: 501(c)3
Highest Offering: Baccalaureate
Program: Liberal Arts And General
Accreditation: SC, ACBSP

01 President & CEO Dr. Colette PIERCE BURNETTE
04 Executive Assistant to President Dr. Terry S. SMITH
05 Int Prov/VP Academic & Stdnt Affs Dr. Archibald W. VANDERPUYE
32 Dean of Student Affairs Dr. LaTanya LOWERY
44 VP for Institutional Advancement Vacant
10 VP for Administration & Finance Mrs. Valerie D. HILL
08 Director Library & Media Services Ms. Patricia A. WILKINS
36 Director Career & Grad Development Mr. Paul LEVERINGTON
41 Director of Athletics Ms. Ellen J. MCEWEN
84 Dean of the University College Dr. Jeffrey G. WILSON
06 University Registrar Mrs. Earnestine J. STRICKLAND
25 Dir Sponsored PRGs/Title III Coord Ms. Rhonda M. MOSES
09 Exec Dir Inst Plng/Research/Assess Ms. Jaya K. SONI
13 Dir Information Technology Mr. Mario A. LEAL
26 Director University Relations Mrs. Linda Y. JACKSON
18 Director of Facilities Mr. William S. GRIMES
30 Director of Development Vacant
29 Director of Alumni Affairs Mrs. Bridgett C. LEE
35 Director of Campus Life Dr. Kyle N. BOONE
88 Dir of Ctr for Academic Excellence Ms. Ericka D. JONES
15 Director of Human Resources Ms. Joy S. KING
38 Dir Counseling & Consultation Ctr Ms. Barbara L. FOUNTAIN
42 University Chaplain Rev. Donald E. BREWINGTON
07 Director of Admission Mr. Dwayne R. SHORTER
49 Interim Dean of Arts & Sciences Dr. Rosalee R. MARTIN
50 Actg Dean of Business & Technology Dr. Steven EDMOND
37 Int Director Student Financial Aid Ms. Sheila BROWN
88 Director of Disability Services Ms. Barbara L. FOUNTAIN
23 University Nurse Ms. Ebony S. BEST

International Business College (H)

5700 Cromo Drive, El Paso TX 79912

County: El Paso
FICE Identification: 009082
Unit ID: 225779
Telephone: (915) 842-0422
Carnegie Class: Assoc/PrivFP
FAX Number: (915) 584-5325
Calendar System: Other
URL: www.icbelpaso.edu

Established: 1898 Annual Undergrad Tuition & Fees: $23,000
Enrollment: 72 Coed
Affiliation or Control: Proprietary IRS Status: Proprietary
Highest Offering: Associate Degree
Program: Occupational; 2-Year Principally Bachelor's Creditable
Accreditation: ACICS

00 CEO .... Lee CHAYES
01 President .... Rebecca CANCHOLA

International Business College-East Campus (A)
1155 North Zaragosa Road, El Paso TX 79907
Telephone: (915) 859-0422 Identification: 770622
Accreditation: ACICS

† Branch campus of International Business College, El Paso, TX.

ITT Technical Institute (B)
551 Ryan Plaza Drive, Arlington TX 76011-3919
Telephone: (817) 794-5100 FICE Identification: 023286
Accreditation: ACICS

† Branch campus of ITT Technical Institute, Indianapolis, IN.

ITT Technical Institute (C)
6330 Highway 290 E, Suite 150, Austin TX 78723-1035
Telephone: (512) 467-6800 Identification: 666551
Accreditation: ACICS

† Branch campus of ITT Technical Institute, Indianapolis, IN.

ITT Technical Institute (D)
921 West Belt Line Road, Suite 181, Desoto TX 75115
Telephone: (972) 274-8600 Identification: 770633
Accreditation: ACICS

† Branch campus of ITT Technical Institute, Indianapolis, IN.

ITT Technical Institute (E)
2950 South Gessner, Houston TX 77063-3751
Telephone: (713) 952-2294 FICE Identification: 023287
Accreditation: ACICS

† Branch campus of ITT Technical Institute, Indianapolis, IN.

ITT Technical Institute (F)
15651 North Freeway, Houston TX 77090-5903
Telephone: (281) 873-0512 Identification: 666554
Accreditation: ACICS

† Branch campus of ITT Technical Institute, Indianapolis, IN.

ITT Technical Institute (G)
2101 Waterview Parkway, Richardson TX 75080-2208
Telephone: (972) 690-9100 Identification: 666327
Accreditation: ACICS

† Branch campus of ITT Technical Institute, Indianapolis, IN.

ITT Technical Institute (H)
5700 Northwest Parkway, San Antonio TX 78249-3303
Telephone: (210) 694-4612 FICE Identification: 030714
Accreditation: ACICS

† Branch campus of ITT Technical Institute, Indianapolis, IN.

ITT Technical Institute (I)
2895 NE Loop 410, San Antonio TX 78218
Telephone: (210) 651-8500 Identification: 770635
Accreditation: ACICS

† Branch campus of ITT Technical Institute, Indianapolis, IN.

ITT Technical Institute (J)
1001 Magnolia Avenue, Webster TX 77598-5418
Telephone: (281) 316-4700 Identification: 666552
Accreditation: ACICS

† Branch campus of ITT Technical Institute, Indianapolis, IN.

Jacksonville College (K)
105 B. J. Albritton Drive, Jacksonville TX 75766-4759
County: Cherokee FICE Identification: 003579
Unit ID: 225876
Telephone: (903) 586-2518 Carnegie Class: Assoc/PrivNFP
FAX Number: (903) 586-0743 Calendar System: Semester
URL: www.jacksonville-college.edu
Established: 1899 Annual Undergrad Tuition & Fees: $8,170
Enrollment: 564 Coed
Affiliation or Control: Baptist IRS Status: 501(c)3
Highest Offering: Associate Degree
Program: 2-Year Principally Bachelor's Creditable
Accreditation: SC

01 President .... Dr. Mike SMITH
05 Academic Dean/Registrar .... Mr. Lynn NABI
32 Dean of Students .... Mrs. Kaley DEAN
10 Business Officer .... Mrs. Ann CUMBEE
41 Athletic Director .... Mr. Lynn NABI
06 Registrar .... Ms. Jodye HERRING
07 Director of Admissions .... Mrs. Sandra CLAY
18 Chief Facilities/Physical Plant .... Mr. Dan SHOFFNER
26 Chief Public Relations Officer .... Dr. David HEFLIN
29 Director of Alumni Relations .... Mrs. Neatha CAGLE
30 Chief Development Officer .... Mr. Buddy AULTMAN
37 Director Student Financial Aid .... Mr. Paul GALYEAN

Jarvis Christian College (L)
Highway 80 E., PR 7631, Hawkins TX 75765-1470
County: Wood FICE Identification: 003637
Unit ID: 225885
Telephone: (903) 730-4890 Carnegie Class: Bac/Diverse
FAX Number: (903) 769-4842 Calendar System: Semester
URL: www.jarvis.edu
Established: 1912 Annual Undergrad Tuition & Fees: $11,720
Enrollment: 763 Coed
Affiliation or Control: Christian Church (Disciples Of Christ)
IRS Status: 501(c)3
Highest Offering: Baccalaureate
Program: Liberal Arts And General; Teacher Preparatory
Accreditation: SC, ACBSP

01 President .... Dr. Lester C. NEWMAN
05 Provost/Vice Pres Academic Affairs .... Dr. Glenell PRUITT
10 Vice Pres Administration & Finance .... Mr. Dexter ODOM
32 Vice President Student Affairs .... Dr. Marcus CHANAY
30 VP Institutional Advancement/Devel .... Ms. Sunya YOUNG
45 Vice Pres for Inst Effectiveness .... Dr. William SMIALEK
13 Director Information Technology .... Mr. Quinton LATIN
06 Registrar .... Ms. Adrian WYATT
39 Director of Housing .... Mr. Cory GIPSON
29 Director of Alumni Affairs .... Mr. William HAMPTON
07 Dir Admissions & Enrollment Svcs .... Mr. Brandon BYRD
26 Director Public Relations/Publicity .... Vacant
04 Exec Asst to the President .... Mrs. Cynthia HOLLMAN-STANCIL
08 Head Librarian .... Mr. Rodney ATKINS
38 Director Career Services .... Mr. Chestley TALLEY
37 Director of Financial Aid .... Ms. Gail JOHNSON
41 Athletic Director .... Vacant
42 College Pastor .... Mr. Olin FREGIA
15 Dir Human Resources .... Dr. Daphne SINGLETON
09 Dir Institutional Research .... Ms. Celestine KEMAH
108 Dir Assessment .... Dr. Belinda PRIHODA
18 Chief Facilities/Physical Plant .... Mr. Willie SANDIFER
53 Dean of Education .... Dr. Jan DUNCAN

Kaplan College (M)
2241 South Watson Road, Arlington TX 76010
Telephone: (972) 623-4700 Identification: 770544
Accreditation: ACICS

† Branch campus of Kaplan College, Dallas, TX.

Kaplan College (N)
6115 Eastex Freeway, Suite A-142, Beaumont TX 77706
Telephone: (409) 833-2722 Identification: 770545
Accreditation: ACICS

† Branch campus of Kaplan College, San Antonio, TX.

Kaplan College (O)
1900 North Expressway, Brownsville TX 78521
Telephone: (956) 547-8200 Identification: 770595
Accreditation: ACICS

† Branch campus of Kaplan College, El Paso, TX.

Kaplan College (P)
1620 S Padre Island Drive, Ste 600,
Corpus Christi TX 78416
Telephone: (361) 852-2900 Identification: 770597
Accreditation: ACICS

† Branch campus of Kaplan College, San Antonio, TX.

Kaplan College (Q)
12005 Ford Road, Suite 100, Dallas TX 75234
County: Dallas FICE Identification: 032723
Unit ID: 382896
Telephone: (972) 385-1446 Carnegie Class: Assoc/PrivFP
FAX Number: (972) 385-0641 Calendar System: Other
URL: dallas.kaplancollege.com
Established: Annual Undergrad Tuition & Fees: $15,000
Enrollment: 302 Coed
Affiliation or Control: Proprietary IRS Status: Proprietary
Highest Offering: Associate Degree
Program: Occupational; Technical Emphasis
Accreditation: ACICS, PTAA

01 Executive Director .... Ms. Michelle OWENS

Kaplan College (R)
8360 Burnham Road, Ste 100, El Paso TX 79907
County: El Paso FICE Identification: 025919
Unit ID: 246266
Telephone: (915) 595-1935 Carnegie Class: Not Classified
FAX Number: (915) 595-6619 Calendar System: Other
URL: www.kaplan.edu
Established: Annual Undergrad Tuition & Fees: $15,200
Enrollment: 576 Coed
Affiliation or Control: Proprietary IRS Status: Proprietary
Highest Offering: Associate Degree
Program: Occupational
Accreditation: ACICS, MAC

01 President .... Ms. Dawn MICHELLE
05 Director of Education .... Ms. Ramona GARCIA

Kaplan College (S)
2001 Beach Street, Suite 201, Fort Worth TX 76103
Telephone: (817) 413-2000 Identification: 770598
Accreditation: ACICS

† Branch campus of Kaplan College, San Antonio, TX.

Kaplan College (T)
6410 McPherson, Laredo TX 78041
Telephone: (956) 717-5909 Identification: 770546
Accreditation: ACICS

† Branch campus of Kaplan College, San Antonio, TX.

Kaplan College (U)
1421 9th Street, Lubbock TX 79401
Telephone: (806) 765-7051 Identification: 770547
Accreditation: ACICS

† Branch campus of Kaplan College, San Antonio, TX.

Kaplan College (V)
1500 S Jackson Road, McAllen TX 78503
Telephone: (956) 630-1499 Identification: 770596
Accreditation: ACICS

† Branch campus of Kaplan College, San Antonio, TX.

Kaplan College (W)
7142 San Pedro Avenue, Suite 100,
San Antonio TX 78216
County: Bexar FICE Identification: 009466
Unit ID: 364955
Telephone: (210) 733-0777 Carnegie Class: Assoc/PrivFP
FAX Number: (210) 340-6603 Calendar System: Other
URL: nsan-antonio.kaplancollege.com
Established: Annual Undergrad Tuition & Fees: $15,879
Enrollment: 574 Coed
Affiliation or Control: Proprietary IRS Status: Proprietary
Highest Offering: Associate Degree
Program: Occupational; 2-Year Principally Bachelor's Creditable; Technical Emphasis
Accreditation: ACICS, MAC

01 Executive Director .... Rene CANDELARIA

Kaplan College (X)
6441 NW Loop 410, San Antonio TX 78238
County: Bexar FICE Identification: 031158
Unit ID: 431886
Telephone: (210) 308-8584 Carnegie Class: Not Classified
FAX Number: (210) 308-8985 Calendar System: Other
URL: www.kaplancollege.com
Established: Annual Undergrad Tuition & Fees: $16,200
Enrollment: 556 Coed
Affiliation or Control: Proprietary IRS Status: Proprietary
Highest Offering: Associate Degree
Program: Occupational
Accreditation: ACICS, CAHIIM

01 President .... Ms. Liza CANCHOLA

KD Conservatory College of Film and Dramatic Arts (Y)
2600 N Stemmons Fwy, Suite 117, Dallas TX 75207-2111
County: Dallas FICE Identification: 023182
Unit ID: 225991
Telephone: (214) 638-0484 Carnegie Class: Assoc/PrivFP
FAX Number: (214) 630-5140 Calendar System: Semester
URL: www.kdstudio.com
Established: 1979 Annual Undergrad Tuition & Fees: $13,396
Enrollment: 150 Coed
Affiliation or Control: Proprietary IRS Status: Proprietary
Highest Offering: Associate Degree
Program: 2-Year Principally Bachelor's Creditable; Fine Arts Emphasis
Accreditation: THEA

00 Chief Executive Officer .... Ms. Kathy TYNER
01 President .... Mr. Gary TYNER, JR.
05 Director/CAO .... Mr. T. A TAYLOR
88 Program Chair - MT .... Mr. Michael SERRECCHIA
88 Program Chair - Film Program .... Mr. Dennis BISHOP
11 Head of Operations .... Mr. Kaleb WADE
32 Head of Student Services .... Ms. Ashlyn NICHOLS
37 Student Financial Aid .... Ms. Linda CRAFT
08 Chief Library Officer .... Ms. Judith HEAD

Kilgore College (A)

1100 Broadway, Kilgore TX 75662-3299
County: Gregg FICE Identification: 003580
Unit ID: 226019
Telephone: (903) 984-8531 Carnegie Class: Assoc/Pub-R-M
FAX Number: (903) 983-8600 Calendar System: Semester
URL: www.kilgore.edu
Established: 1935 Annual Undergrad Tuition & Fees (In-District): $1,464
Enrollment: 5,768 Coed
Affiliation or Control: Local IRS Status: 501(c)3
Highest Offering: Associate Degree
Program: Occupational; 2-Year Principally Bachelor's Creditable
Accreditation: SC, ADNUR, PTAA, SURGT

01 President .... Dr. William M. HOLDA
05 Vice President of Instruction .... Dr. Michael H. TURPIN
11 Vice Pres Administrative Services .... Mr. Duane MCNANEY
32 Vice President Student Development .... Dr. Mike JENKINS
09 Vice Pres Institutional Planning .... Mrs. Staci MARTIN
57 Div Dean Liberal & Fine Arts .... Mrs. Becky JOHNSON
81 Div Dean Science/Math/Health Sci .... Mrs. Louise WILEY
50 Div Dean Business/Tech/Lang Devel/ .... Mr. Randy LEWELLEN
88 Div Dean of Public Services .... Mr. Randy LEWELLEN
75 Dir of Adult Voc Educ .... Ms. Martha WOODRUFF
12 Div Dean of Longview Center .... Dr. Julie H. FOWLER
06 Registrar .... Mr. Chris GORE
15 Director of Human Resources .... Mr. Tony JOHNSON
13 Director of Information Technology .... Mr. John COLVILLE
08 Director Library .... Ms. Kathy FAIR
40 Manager of Bookstore .... Mr. Corrie THIBODEAUX
18 Director Physical Plant .... Vacant
19 Chief of Police .... Chief Heath CARIKER
84 Dir of Marketing & Enrollment Mgmt .... Mr. Trey HATTAWAY
04 Assistant to the President .... Mrs. Nancy LAW
30 Director of Development .... Mrs. Leah GORMAN
37 Financial Aid Officer .... Mrs. Annette MORGAN
85 International Student Advisor .... Ms. Estonia GRAVES
26 Coordinator of Public & Sports Info .... Mr. Chris CRADDOCK
09 Coord of Institutional Research .... Ms. Robin HUSKEY
36 Coordinator of Career Services .... Ms. Patty BELL
29 Coordinator of Alumni Relations .... Mrs. Paula JAMERSON
38 Coordinator of Counseling .... Mrs. Pam GATTON
96 Purchasing Agent .... Ms. Tammie PASCOE
39 Director of Residential Life .... Mr. Edward WILLIAMS
07 Director of Admissions .... Mr. Chris GORE
106 Dir Online Education/E-learning .... Ms. Charleen WORSHAM

The King's University (B)

2121 E. Southlake Boulevard, South Lake TX 76092-6507
County: Tarrant FICE Identification: 035163
Unit ID: 439701
Telephone: (817) 552-3700 Carnegie Class: Spec/Faith
FAX Number: (818) 779-8241 Calendar System: Quarter
URL: tku.edu/
Established: 1997 Annual Undergrad Tuition & Fees: $12,390
Enrollment: 692 Coed
Affiliation or Control: Independent Non-Profit IRS Status: 501(c)3
Highest Offering: Doctorate
Program: Professional; Religious Emphasis
Accreditation: BI, TRACS

01 President .... Dr. John SPURLING
05 Vice Pres Academic Affairs .... Dr. Pete SANCHEZ
11 Vice Pres Operations/Support Svcs .... Mr. Tom MCCLAIN
32 Vice Pres Student Development .... Dr. David COLE
10 Director of Finance .... Ms. Ashley GREEN
106 Dean/Administrator Online Education .... Prof. Donald C. BRUBAKER
09 Dir Institutional Effectiveness .... Dr. Bobbi STRINGER
35 Dean of Student Life .... Mr. Shawn BRANN
07 Director of Admissions .... Mr. Tyler MAXEY
06 Student Recruitment Manager .... Ms. Angela TRANEL
37 Director Financial Aid .... Ms. Jackie WADLEIGH
08 Director of Library Services .... Mr. Tracey R. LANE
30 Chief Development .... Mr. Lee S. MIMMS
13 Director Computing & Info Mgmt ... Mr. Edmond M. MUGWANYA
21 Student Accounts Officer .... Ms. June M. HADLEY
90 Dir Acad Computing/Dir Student Affs .... Prof. Donald C. BRUBAKER
29 Director Alumni Relations .... Ms. Maureen A. BRODERSON
96 Director of Purchasing .... Mr. Bob CARON
28 Director of Diversity .... Dr. Michael J. GREGG
102 Dir Foundation/Corporate Relations .... Mr. Lee S. MIMMS
26 Dir of Marketing/Communications .... Ms. Jovan OVERSHOWN

Laredo Community College (C)

West End Washington Street, Laredo TX 78040-4395
County: Webb FICE Identification: 003582
Unit ID: 226134
Telephone: (956) 722-0521 Carnegie Class: Assoc/Pub-R-L
FAX Number: (956) 721-5381 Calendar System: Semester
URL: www.laredo.edu
Established: 1946 Annual Undergrad Tuition & Fees (In-District): $5,040
Enrollment: 8,307 Coed
Affiliation or Control: Local IRS Status: 501(c)3
Highest Offering: Associate Degree
Program: Occupational; 2-Year Principally Bachelor's Creditable; Technical Emphasis
Accreditation: SC, ADNUR, OTA, PTAA, RAD

01 President .... Dr. Juan L. MALDONADO
05 VP Instruction & Student Services .... Dr. Vincent R. SOLIS
13 Information Technology Officer .... Mr. Luciano RAMON
25 Vice President for Resource Develop .... Dr. Nora R. GARZA
26 Communications & IE Officer .... Ms. Deirdre REYNA
10 Comptroller .... Mr. Cesar E. VELA, JR.
89 Dean of College Readiness .... Ms. Marissa GUERRERO-LONGORIA
76 Dean of Health Sciences .... Mr. J. Alfredo INIGUEZ-JIMENEZ
35 Dean of Student Affairs .... Ms. Raquel A. PENA
84 Dean of Enrollment & Reg Services .... Ms. Priscilla G. MEDINA
09 Dir Institutional Research & Plng .... Mrs. Maria Luisa RAMIREZ
08 Director of Library .... Ms. Rachel C. BOHMFALK
18 Director Physical Plant .... Mr. Jerome ROSALES
27 Dir Marketing/Public Relations .... Mr. Esteban TREVINO, JR.
37 Director of Financial Aid .... Mr. Steven AGUILAR
51 Dir of Adult & Continuing Education .... Ms. Sandra L. CORTEZ
41 Athletic Director .... Mr. Troy G. VAN BRUNT
06 Registrar .... Ms. Olga D. RUBIO
15 Director of Human Resources .... Ms. Veronica CARDENAS
102 Dir Donor Relations & Spec Proj .... Vacant
38 Director of Student Success Ctr .... Mr. Carmelino CASTILLO, JR.
96 Director of Purchasing .... Mr. George M. AYALA
19 Chief of Campus Police .... Mr. Ray CORTEZ
23 Director of Health Services .... Ms. Melissa GARCIA
20 Assoc VP for Instruction .... Dr. Federico SOLIS, JR.
32 Assoc VP for Student Services .... Mr. Robert L. OCHOA
49 Dean of Arts & Sciences .... Ms. Marisela RODRIGUEZ

Le Cordon Bleu College of Culinary Arts in Austin (D)

3110 Esperanza Crossing Suite 100, Austin TX 78758
County: Travis FICE Identification: 025693
Unit ID: 364973
Telephone: (512) 837-2665 Carnegie Class: Assoc/PrivFP
FAX Number: (512) 977-9753 Calendar System: Other
URL: www.chefs.edu/austin
Established: 1981 Annual Undergrad Tuition & Fees: $13,390
Enrollment: 643 Coed
Affiliation or Control: Proprietary IRS Status: Proprietary
Highest Offering: Associate Degree
Program: Occupational; Technical Emphasis
Accreditation: ACICS, ACFEI

01 President .... Steve SMITH

Le Cordon Bleu College of Culinary Arts in Dallas (E)

11830 Webb Chapel Road, Suite 1200, Dallas TX 75234
Telephone: (214) 647-8505 Identification: 666728
Accreditation: ACICS, ACFEI

† Branch campus of Le Cordon Bleu College of Culinary Arts, Austin, TX.

Lee College (F)

511 S Whiting, PO Box 818, Baytown TX 77522-0818
County: Harris FICE Identification: 003583
Unit ID: 226204
Telephone: (281) 427-5611 Carnegie Class: Assoc/Pub-S-MC
FAX Number: (281) 425-6555 Calendar System: Semester
URL: www.lee.edu
Established: 1934 Annual Undergrad Tuition & Fees (In-District): $1,518
Enrollment: 6,481 Coed
Affiliation or Control: State/Local IRS Status: 501(c)3
Highest Offering: Associate Degree
Program: Occupational; 2-Year Principally Bachelor's Creditable; Technical Emphasis
Accreditation: SC, ADNUR, CAHIIM

01 President .... Dr. Dennis BROWN
100 Senior Assistant to the President .... Ms. Leslie D. GALLAGHER
101 Senior Assistant to the President .... Ms. Leslie D. GALLAGHER
10 VP Finance & Administration .... Mr. Steve EVANS
05 VP Instruction .... Dr. Cathy KEMPER
32 VP Student Affairs .... Dr. Donnetta SUCHON
103 VP Student Success/Workforce & RD .... Dr. Christina PONCE
12 Dean of Huntsville Center at TDCJ .... Ms. Donna P. ZUNIGA
09 Exec Dir Institutional Research .... Dr. Michael K. FLEMING
13 Chief Information Officer .... Dr. Carolyn A. LIGHTFOOT
103 Exec Dir of Workforce & Comm Ed .... Ms. Debi JORDAN
06 Registrar .... Mr. Scott BENNETT
15 Director Human Resources .... Ms. Amanda SUMMERS
26 Director Marketing & Public Affairs .... Vacant
31 Director of Community Education .. Ms. Kimberlee WHITTINGTON
37 Director Financial Aid .... Ms. Sharon STEELE
102 Director of Foundation & Donor Dev .... Ms. Pam WARFORD
96 Director Purchasing .... Mr. Mike SPARKES

LeTourneau University (G)

PO Box 7001, 2100 S Mobberly Ave, Longview TX 75607-7001
County: Gregg FICE Identification: 003584
Unit ID: 226231
Telephone: (903) 233-3000 Carnegie Class: Master's M
FAX Number: (903) 233-3101 Calendar System: Semester
URL: www.letu.edu
Established: 1946 Annual Undergrad Tuition & Fees: $27,380
Enrollment: 2,432 Coed
Affiliation or Control: Independent Non-Profit IRS Status: 501(c)3
Highest Offering: Master's
Program: Liberal Arts And General; Teacher Preparatory; Professional
Accreditation: SC, ENG, ENGT, IACBE

01 President .... Dr. Dale A. LUNSFORD
05 Provost & Executive Vice President .... Dr. Philip COYLE
30 Int Executive Director Development .... Mr. Steve SHARPE
10 VP Finance/Administration .... Mr. Mike HOOD
32 Dean of Students .... Ms. Kristy MORGAN
84 VP Enrollment Services .... Dr. Terry CRUSE
20 Assoc VP Provost Office .... Dr. Steven D. MASON
26 Associate VP-Global Enrollment Svcs .... Mr. Christopher W. FONTAINE
18 Asst VP of Facilities Services .... Mr. Ben HAYWOOD
53 Interim Dean School of Education .... Dr. Darla BAGGETT
50 Dean School of Business .... Dr. Ron SONES
54 Dean Sch Engineering & Engr Tech .... Dr. Ronald DELAP
49 Dean School of Arts & Sciences .... Dr. Larry FRAZIER
88 Dean School of Aeronautical Science .... Mr. Fred L. RITCHEY
35 Assoc Dean Student Life .... Vacant
08 Director Learning Resource Center .... Mrs. Colleen HALUPA
41 Director of Athletics .... Ms. Terri DEIKE
46 Director Office of Sponsored Pgms .... Mr. Paul R. BOGGS
106 Director Distance Learning .... Ms. Colleen HALUPA
13 Dean CITL/Chief Information Officer .... Mr. Matthew HENRY
15 Director of Human Resources .... Mr. Sam PALOMARIA
23 Director Health Services .... Mrs. Jerrie REYNOLDS
42 University Chaplain .... Dr. Harold F. CARL
19 Chief of Police .... Vacant
36 Director of Career Services .... Mrs. Deena SHELTON
06 University Registrar .... Ms. Kathy MAJZNER
07 Director of Admissions .... Mr. Michael VANBROCKLIN
29 Director of Alumni & Parent Rels .... Ms. Jamie DEYOUNG
27 Director of University Relations .... Ms. Janet RAGLAND
27 Director Marketing & Communication .... Ms. Kate GRONEWALD
44 Dir of Gift Planning and Endowed .... Mr. Bryan E. BENSON
88 Dir Curriculum/Academic Resources .... Mrs. Colleen HALUPA
21 Controller .... Ms. Vikki KEILERS
09 Asst VP for Quality Assurance .... Dr. Pamela JOHNSON
88 Development Officer .... Mr. Stephen SHARPE
96 Purchasing Agent .... Mrs. Jana CAMPBELL
88 Executive Dir Ctr for Faith & Work .... Mr. Bill PEEL
04 Administrative Asst to President .... Mrs. Denise BAILEY
84 Exec Dir of Enrollment Services .... Mr. Carl ARNOLD
28 Director of Diversity .... Mr. Carlton MITCHELL
37 Director Student Financial Aid .... Ms. Tracy WATKINS
38 Dir Ctr Student Counselng/Psych .... Mrs. Judi COYLE
20 Associate Provost-Quality Assurance .... Mrs. Stephanie KIRSCHMANN
104 Chief Global Initatives Officer .... Dr. Kelly LIEBENGOOD
58 VP Online & Global Enrollment .... Dr. Robert HUDSON
83 Dean Psychology & Counseling .... Dr. Melanie ROUDKOVSKI
26 VP Marketing & Communications .... Mr. Don EGLE
73 Dean School of Theology/Vocation .... Dr. Aaron KUECKER

Lincoln College of Technology (H)

2915 Alouette Drive, Grand Prairie TX 75052
County: Tarrant FICE Identification: 008353
Unit ID: 226277
Telephone: (972) 660-5701 Carnegie Class: Assoc/PrivFP
FAX Number: (972) 660-6148 Calendar System: Other
URL: www.lincolntech.com
Established: Annual Undergrad Tuition & Fees: $24,800
Enrollment: 947 Coed
Affiliation or Control: Proprietary IRS Status: Proprietary
Highest Offering: Associate Degree
Program: Occupational
Accreditation: ACCSC

01 Executive Director .... Mr. Cory HUGHES

Lone Star College System (I)

5000 Research Forest Drive, The Woodlands TX 77381-4356
County: Harris FICE Identification: 011145
Unit ID: 227182
Telephone: (832) 813-6500 Carnegie Class: Assoc/Pub-S-MC
FAX Number: N/A Calendar System: Semester
URL: www.lonestar.edu
Established: 1972 Annual Undergrad Tuition & Fees (In-District): $1,864
Enrollment: 82,818 Coed
Affiliation or Control: State/Local IRS Status: 501(c)3
Highest Offering: Associate Degree
Program: Occupational; 2-Year Principally Bachelor's Creditable
Accreditation: SC, ADNUR, CAHIIM, CEA, COARC, DH, DMS, EMT, MAC, MUS, OTA, PTAA, RAD, SURGT

01 Chancellor .... Dr. Stephen HEAD
03 Executive Vice Chancellor .... Dr. Austin LANE
05 Vice Chanc Academic Affairs .... Vacant
10 Vice Chanc for Admin & Finance .... Ms. Cynthia GILLIAM
13 Vice Chanc/Chief Info Officer .... Mr. Link ALANDER
26 Vice Chancellor External Affairs .... Mr. Ray LAUGHTER
32 AVC Student Success .... Mr. Wendell WILLIAMS
43 General Counsel .... Mr. Mario CASTILLO
103 Vice Chanc Workforce Econ Dev .... Dr. Melissa GONZALEZ
100 Chief of Staff/Board Liaison .... Ms. Helen CLOUGHERTY
12 President of LSC-Kingwood .... Dr. Katherine PERSSON
12 President of LSC-Tomball .... Dr. Lee Ann NUTT
12 President of LSC-North Harris .... Dr. Gerald NAPOLES
12 President of LSC-Montgomery .... Dr. Rebecca RILEY
12 President of LSC-CyFair .... Vacant
12 President of LSC-University Park .... Mr. Shah ARDALAN
27 AVC Marketing & Comm .... Ms. Laura MORRIS
18 Chief Fac/Construction Officer .... Mr. Jimmy MARTIN
15 Exec Dir HR Services .... Vacant
105 Director Portal Services .... Mr. Harry KHEHRA
88 Director Compliance & Training .... Mr. Norman SIEVERT
20 AVC Academic Affairs & EMI .... Vacant
21 AVC Admin & Finance .... Ms. Tammy CORTES
21 Associate CFO .... Ms. Carin HUTCHINS
21 AVC Accounting .... Ms. Diane NOVAK
106 AVC LSC-Online .... Ms. Wendi PRATER
09 AVC Research & Institute .... Dr. Christopher TKACH
14 AVC Office Tech Services .... Mr. Mario BERRY
08 Director Library/LSC-Kingwood .... Mr. Anthony MCMILLIAN
08 Director Library/LSC-Tomball .... Ms. Pamela SHAFER
08 Director Library/LSC-North Harris .... Ms. Pradeep LELE
08 Director Library/LSC-Cy Fair .... Mr. Michael STAFFORD
08 Director Library/LSC-Montgomery .... Dr. Janice PEYTON
08 Director Library/LSC-Univ Park .... Ms. Shannon HAUSINGER
37 Exec Dir Financial Aid .... Ms. Donna KING
21 Exec Director Internal Audit .... Ms. Leticia CHARBONNEAU
19 Chief of Police/Dir Pub Safety .... Vacant
96 Director of Purchasing .... Mr. William DODD
04 Executive Asst to Chancellor .... Ms. Elva BORSCH
30 Chief Advancement Officer .... Ms. Leah GOSS
29 Director of Constituent Engagement .... Ms. Susan SUMMERS

Lubbock Christian University (A)

5601 19th Street, Lubbock TX 79407-2099
County: Lubbock FICE Identification: 003586
Unit ID: 226383
Telephone: (806) 796-8800 Carnegie Class: Master's S
FAX Number: (806) 720-7255 Calendar System: Semester
URL: www.lcu.edu
Established: 1957 Annual Undergrad Tuition & Fees: $20,320
Enrollment: 1,902 Coed
Affiliation or Control: Churches Of Christ IRS Status: 501(c)3
Highest Offering: Master's
Program: Liberal Arts And General; Teacher Preparatory; Professional
Accreditation: SC, NUR, SW, @THEOL

01 President .... Mr. L. Timothy PERRIN
03 Executive Vice President .... Dr. Brian STARR
05 Provost & Chief Academic Officer .... Dr. Rodney B. BLACKWOOD
43 General Counsel .... Mrs. Monica BARNARD
26 Vice Pres University Advancement .... Mr. Raymond RICHARDSON
10 Vice Pres for Financial Services .... Mr. Rory WAIDE
13 Vice President for Technology .... Dr. Karl MAHAN
107 Dean Col of Professional Studies .... Dr. Toby ROGERS
49 Dean College Liberal Arts/Education .... Dr. Susan BLASSINGAME
73 Dean Col Biblical Stds/Behavior Sci .... Dr. Jesse LONG
09 Asst VP for Instl Effectiveness .... Mr. Randy SELLERS
41 Athletic Director .... Mr. Paul HISE
06 Registrar .... Mrs. Janice STONE
37 Director of Financial Assistance .... Mrs. Amy HARDESTY
32 Dean of Students .... Mr. Josh STEPHENS
08 Director of Library Services .... Ms. Paula GANNAWAY
18 Director of Campus Facilities .... Mr. Mike SELLECK
38 Director Student Counseling .... Ms. Janelle M. BUCHANAN
92 Director of Honors Program .... Dr. Stacy PATTY
23 Director of Medical Clinic .... Dr. Jeff SMITH
13 Director of Technology Services .... Mr. Robert SMITH
88 Director of Disability Services .... Vacant
39 Director of Residental Life .... Mrs. Sunny PARK
07 Director of Admissions .... Mr. Charlie WEBB
15 Human Resources Director .... Mrs. Brenda LOWE
29 Director Alumni Relations .... Mrs. Sheila DYE
19 Director of Security .... Mr. Michael SMITH
40 Bookstore Manager .... Mrs. Denise MCNEILL
04 Administrative Asst to President .... Ms. Rhonda SHOOTER
101 Secretary of the Institution/Board .... Ms. Page PRATHER
84 Director Enrollment Management .... Mr. Mondy BREWER

Lutheran Seminary Program of the Southwest (B)

PO Box 4790, Austin TX 78765
Telephone: (512) 477-2666 Identification: 770081
Accreditation: &NH

† Branch campus of Lutheran School of Theology at Chicago, Chicago, IL.

McLennan Community College (C)

1400 College Drive, Waco TX 76708-1498
County: McLennan FICE Identification: 003590
Unit ID: 226578
Telephone: (254) 299-8000 Carnegie Class: Assoc/Pub-R-L
FAX Number: (254) 299-8654 Calendar System: Semester
URL: www.mclennan.edu
Established: 1965 Annual Undergrad Tuition & Fees (In-District): $3,450
Enrollment: 8,329 Coed
Affiliation or Control: State/Local IRS Status: 501(c)3
Highest Offering: Associate Degree
Program: Occupational; 2-Year Principally Bachelor's Creditable; Nursing Emphasis
Accreditation: SC, ADNUR, CAHIIM, COARC, MAC, MLTAD, PTAA, RAD, SURGT

01 President .... Dr. Johnette MCKOWN
10 Vice Pres Finance & Administration .... Mr. Gene GOOCH
05 Vice President Instruction .... Dr. Donald BALMOS
46 Vice President Program Development .... Mr. Al POLLARD
32 Vice President Student Success .... Dr. Drew CANHAM
09 Vice Pres Research/Effectiveness .... Dr. Phil RHODES
102 Exec Director MCC Foundation .... Mr. Harry HARELIK
11 Director Administrative Services .... Ms. Lori SOUTHERN
37 Director Financial Aid .... Mr. James KUBACAK
26 Director Marketing & Communication .... Ms. Lisa WILHELMI
41 Director Athletics .... Mrs. Shawn TROCHIM
06 Director Records & Registration .... Mr. Herman V. TUCKER
07 Director Admissions & Recruitment .... Mrs. Karen CLARK
08 Director Library Services .... Mr. Daniel MARTINSEN
15 Director Human Resources .... Ms. Missy KITTNER
18 Director Physical Plant .... Mrs. Dianne E. FEYERHERM
21 Director Financial Services .... Mrs. Terry LECHLER
76 Dean Health Professions .... Ms. Glynnis GAINES
49 Dean Arts & Sciences .... Dr. Fred HILLS
51 Dean Continuing Education .... Mr. Frank GRAVES

McMurry University (D)

1400 Sayles Boulevard, Abilene TX 79697-0002
County: Taylor FICE Identification: 003591
Unit ID: 226587
Telephone: (325) 793-3800 Carnegie Class: Bac/Diverse
FAX Number: (325) 793-6800 Calendar System: Semester
URL: www.mcm.edu
Established: 1923 Annual Undergrad Tuition & Fees: $25,588
Enrollment: 1,007 Coed
Affiliation or Control: United Methodist IRS Status: 501(c)3
Highest Offering: Master's
Program: Liberal Arts And General; Teacher Preparatory
Accreditation: SC, NURSE

01 President .... Dr. Sandra HARPER
05 Vice President for Academic Affairs .... Dr. James HUNT
10 Vice Pres for Financial Affairs .... Mrs. Lisa L. WILLIAMS
30 Vice Pres Institutional Advancement .... Ms. Debra HULSE
11 Vice Pres for Info & Support Svcs .... Mr. Brad POORMAN
84 Vice Pres for Enrollment Management .... Mr. David HERINGER
105 Webmaster .... Mr. Jim QUINNETT
14 Director of Customer Services .... Mr. Freddie FAMBLE, JR.
13 Director of Administrative Systems .... Ms. Kathy DENSLOW
06 Registrar .... Mrs. Carolyn A. CALVERT
08 Director Jay-Rollins Library .... Ms. Terry YOUNG
32 Dean of Student Affairs .... Ms. Vanessa ROBERTS-BRYAN
66 Dean School of Nursing .... Dr. Nina OUIMETTE
35 Director of Student Activities .... Ms. Megan BALDREE
37 Director of Financial Aid .... Ms. Lori HERRICK
21 Controller .... Vacant
15 Director of Human Resources .... Ms. Lecia HUGHES
108 Dir of Institutional Effectiveness .... Dr. Thomas BENOIT
09 Director of Institutional Research .... Ms. Terry NIXON
26 AVP of Marketing & Communications .... Mr. Daniel MANSON
29 Director Alumni/Church Relations .... Ms. Suzann COUTS
38 Director Counseling & Career Svcs .... Mr. James GREER
41 Director of Athletics .... Mr. Sam FERGUSON
42 Dir of Religious Life/Univ Chaplain .... Rev. Jeff LUST
19 Director of Campus Security .... Mr. Mark R. ODOM
23 Director of Health Services .... Ms. Ronda HOELSCHER
39 Director of Residence Life .... Vacant
102 Executive Director Donor Relations .... Ms. Nancy SMITH
92 Director Honors Program .... Dr. Philip LE MASTERS
106 Director of Online Education .... Vacant

Messenger College (E)

400 S. Industrial Boulevard, Euless TX 76040
County: Tarrant FICE Identification: 030926
Unit ID: 417752
Telephone: (817) 554-5950 Carnegie Class: Spec/Faith
FAX Number: (817) 391-4003 Calendar System: Semester
URL: www.messengercollege.edu
Established: 1987 Annual Undergrad Tuition & Fees: $8,760
Enrollment: 168 Coed
Affiliation or Control: Pentecostal Church of God IRS Status: 501(c)3
Highest Offering: Baccalaureate
Program: 2-Year Principally Bachelor's Creditable; Liberal Arts And General; Religious Emphasis
Accreditation: TRACS

01 President .... Rev. Daniel P. DAVIS
04 Administrative Asst to President .... Sharon TOW
05 Chief Academic Officer .... Gwen MINOR
07 Director of Admissions/Registrar .... Carrie UNDERWOOD
08 Head Librarian .... Mary THOMASON
10 Chief Business Officer .... Angela HEPPNER
32 Chief Student Affairs/Student Life .... Rhonda DAVIS
37 Director Student Financial Aid .... Diana SPEEGLE

Midland College (F)

3600 N Garfield, Midland TX 79705-6397
County: Midland FICE Identification: 009797
Unit ID: 226806
Telephone: (432) 685-4500 Carnegie Class: Assoc/Pub4
FAX Number: (432) 685-4714 Calendar System: Semester
URL: www.midland.edu
Established: 1969 Annual Undergrad Tuition & Fees (In-District): $2,970
Enrollment: 4,618 Coed
Affiliation or Control: Local IRS Status: 501(c)3
Highest Offering: Baccalaureate
Program: Occupational; 2-Year Principally Bachelor's Creditable
Accreditation: SC, CAHIIM, COARC, DMS, EMT

01 President .... Dr. Steve THOMAS
03 Executive Vice President .... Dr. Richard C. JOLLY
88 Special Advisor to President .... Dr. Deana SAVAGE
10 Vice Pres Administrative Services .... Mr. Rick BENDER
32 Vice President Student Services .... Ms. Rita Nell DIFFIE
13 Vice Pres Info Tech/Facilities .... Mr. Dennis SEVER
101 Asst to President/Sec to Board .... Mrs. Bahola EDWARDS
106 Dean of Distance Learning/Cont Educ .... Mr. Dale BEIKIRCH
57 Dean of Fine Arts/Communication .... Mr. William FEELER
72 Dean of Applied Technology .... Mr. Curt PERVIER
76 Dean of Health Sciences .... Ms. Carmen EDWARDS
81 Dean of Math/Natural Sciences .... Dr. Margaret WADE
83 Dean Adult/Developmental Education .... Dr. Lynda WEBB
30 Exec Dir Inst Advancement/Col Fndn .... Ms. Kathy FLETCHER
06 Registrar .... Mrs. Angela BALCH
08 Head Librarian .... Mr. John DEATS
15 Director of Human Services .... Mrs. Natasha MORGAN
18 Director Physical Plant .... Mr. Ken RILEY
19 Chief of Police .... Mr. Richard MCKEE
26 Dean of Public Information .... Ms. Rebecca BELL
35 Student Life Director .... Ms. Tana BAKER
41 Athletic Director .... Mr. Forrest ALLEN
09 Dir Institutional Effect/Planning .... Mr. Thomas CORLL
37 Director Student Financial Aid .... Ms. Yolanda RAMOS
96 Purchasing Director .... Ms. Barbara FENNELL
84 Dean of Enrollment Management .... Ms. Liz ZENTENO
07 Director of Admissions/Recruitment .... Mr. Jeremy MARTINEZ

Midwestern State University (G)

3410 Taft Boulevard, Wichita Falls TX 76308-2095
County: Wichita FICE Identification: 003592
Unit ID: 226833
Telephone: (940) 397-4000 Carnegie Class: Master's M
FAX Number: (940) 397-4042 Calendar System: Semester
URL: www.mwsu.edu
Established: 1922 Annual Undergrad Tuition & Fees (In-State): $8,004
Enrollment: 5,874 Coed
Affiliation or Control: State IRS Status: 501(c)3
Highest Offering: Master's
Program: Liberal Arts And General; Teacher Preparatory; Professional
Accreditation: SC, ART, BUS, CAATE, COARC, DH, ENG, MUS, NURSE, RAD, SW, TED, THEA

01 President .... Dr. Suzanne SHIPLEY
05 Provost .... Dr. Betty STEWART
46 VP Inst Effectiveness .... Dr. Robert E. CLARK
10 VP Business Affairs & Finance .... Dr. Marilyn FOWLE
30 VP Univ Advncmnt & Stdnt Affairs .... Dr. Howard M. FARRELL
32 VP Student Affairs/Enrollment Mgmt .... Dr. Keith LAMB
18 Assoc VP Facilities Services .... Mr. Kyle OWEN
35 Assoc VP Student Affairs/Enrol Mgmt .... Mr. Matthew PARK
13 Chief Information Systems .... Mr. Randy KIRKPATRICK
06 Registrar .... Ms. Darla INGLISH
08 University Librarian .... Dr. Clara LATHAM
37 Director of Student Financial Aid .... Ms. Kathy PENNARTZ-BROWNING
38 Director of Counseling Center .... Dr. Pam MIDGETT
51 Director of Extended Education .... Dr. Pamela MORGAN
07 Director of Admissions .... Ms. Gayonne BEAVERS
19 Chief of Police .... Mr. Dan WILLIAMS
26 Director Public Info/Marketing .... Ms. Julie GAYNOR
30 Dir Donor Services and Scholarships .... Ms. Laura PETERSON
36 Director Career Management Center .... Mr. Dirk WELCH
41 Director of Athletics .... Mr. Charles CARR
15 Director of Human Resources .... Ms. Dawn FISHER
09 Director Inst Research & Planning .... Mr. Mark MCCLENDON
21 Controller .... Mr. Chris STOVALL
23 Director Vinson Health Center .... Dr. Keith WILLIAMSON
20 Associate VP Academic Affairs .... Vacant
50 Dean College Business Admin .... Dr. Terry PATTON
53 Dean College of Education .... Dr. Matthew CAPPS
57 Dean College of Fine Arts .... Dr. Martin CAMACHO
76 Dean Col Health Sci/Human Svcs .... Dr. James JOHNSTON
79 Dean College Humanities/Social Sci .... Dr. Samuel E. WATSON, III
81 Dean College of Science & Math .... Vacant
86 Director Board & Govt Relations .... Ms. Deborah L. BARROW
29 Director of Alumni Relations .... Ms. Leslee PONDER
88 Director of Academic Success Center .... Ms. Naoma CLARK
105 Webmaster .... Mr. Jonathan SHIREY
96 Director of Purchasing .... Mr. Stephen SHELLEY
88 Dir Disability Support Services .... Ms. Debra HIGGINBOTHAM
39 Director Housing & Residence Life .... Vacant
30 Director University Development .... Mr. Steve SHIPP
85 Director of International Education .... Vacant
88 Director Testing Center .... Ms. Lynn DUCIOAME
88 Director International Services .... Dr. Randy GLEAN

88 Director Budget & Management ... Ms. Valarie MAXWELL
88 Director Museum ... Dr. Francine CARRARO
88 Director Student Support Services ... Ms. Lisa ESTRADA-HAMBY
88 Campus Postal Supervisor ... Mr. Jon LANE
92 Coordinator Honors Program ... Mrs. Juliana LEHMAN-FELTS
43 Dir Legal Services/General Counsel ... Mr. Barry MACHA

National American University-Austin (A)

13801 Burnet Road, Suite 300, Austin TX 78727
Telephone: (512) 651-4700 Identification: 770411
Accreditation: &NH, MAC

† Branch campus of National American University, Rapid City, SD.

National American University-Georgetown (B)

1015 W University Avenue, Suite 700, Georgetown TX 78628
Telephone: (512) 942-6750 Identification: 770413
Accreditation: &NH

† Branch campus of National American University, Rapid City, SD.

National American University Harold D. Buckingham Graduate School (C)

6838 Austin Center Blvd, Ste 270, Austin TX 78731
Telephone: (512) 813-2300 Identification: 770931
Accreditation: &NH

† Branch campus of National American University, Rapid City, SD.

National American University-Houston (D)

11511 Katy Freeway Ste 200, Houston TX 77079
Telephone: (832) 619-7300 Identification: 770930
Accreditation: &NH

† Branch campus of National American University, Rapid City, SD.

National American University-Lewisville (E)

475 State Hwy 121 Bypass #150, Lewisville TX 75067
Telephone: (972) 829-2150 Identification: 770415
Accreditation: &NH

† Branch campus of National American University, Rapid City, SD.

National American University-Mesquite (F)

18600 LBJ Freeway, Mesquite TX 75150
Telephone: (972) 773-8800 Identification: 770416
Accreditation: &NH

† Branch campus of National American University, Rapid City, SD.

National American University-Richardson (G)

300 N Coit Road, Suite 225, Richardson TX 75080
Telephone: (972) 773-8650 Identification: 770414
Accreditation: &NH

† Branch campus of National American University, Rapid City, SD.

National American University-South Austin (H)

6800 Westgate Boulevard, #102, Austin TX 78945
Telephone: (512) 651-4750 Identification: 770412
Accreditation: &NH

† Branch campus of National American University, Rapid City, SD.

Navarro College (I)

3200 W Seventh Avenue, Corsicana TX 75110-4899
County: Navarro FICE Identification: 003593
Unit ID: 227146
Telephone: (903) 874-6501 Carnegie Class: Assoc/Pub-R-L
FAX Number: (903) 874-4636 Calendar System: Semester
URL: www.navarrocollege.edu
Established: 1946 Annual Undergrad Tuition & Fees (In-District): $1,786
Enrollment: 9,999 Coed
Affiliation or Control: Local IRS Status: 501(c)3
Highest Offering: Associate Degree
Program: Occupational; 2-Year Principally Bachelor's Creditable
Accreditation: SC, ADNUR, EMT, MLTAD, OTA, @PTAA

01 District President ... Dr. Barbara KAVALIER
12 President Ellis Co Campuses ... Dr. Kenneth MARTIN
05 Exec Vice President Academic Affs ... Dr. Harold HOUSLEY
10 Vice President Finance & Admin ... Mr. James JONES
30 Vice Pres Opers/Advance & Tech ... Dr. Bruce TABOR
32 Vice President Student Services ... Ms. Maryann HAILEY
84 VP Access & Accountability ... Mr. T. Dewayne GRAGG
15 Assoc VP Human Resources ... Ms. Marcy BALLEW
12 VP Ellis County Campus (Midlothian) ... Dr. Alex KAJSTURA
26 Exec Dir of Mktg/Public Information ... Ms. Meredith CHASE
41 Athletic Director ... Mr. Roark MONTGOMERY
20 Exec Dean of Academic Studies ... Ms. Carol HANES
50 Exec Dean Business/Workforce Educ ... Ms. Judy CUTTING
106 Dean of Online Instruction ... Mr. Matthew MILLER
76 Dean of Health Professions ... Mr. Guy FEATHERSTON
12 Dean of Navarro College South ... Dr. Joel MICHAELIS
21 Comptroller ... Ms. Aaron YORK-LANGSTON
103 Dean of Workforce & Cont Educ ... Ms. Kristin WALKER
08 Dean of Libraries ... Mr. Tim KEVIL
06 Registrar ... Mr. David EDWARDS
18 Exec Director of Facilities ... Mr. Karl HUMPHRIES
13 Interim CIO ... Mr. Jeff GAMBLIN
37 Director Student Financial Aid ... Ms. Kristal NICHOLSON
39 Director of Residence Life ... Mr. Charles BETTS
104 Director of International Programs ... Ms. Elizabeth PILLANS
88 Campus Dean Waxahachie Acad Svcs ... Ms. Terry GIBSON
49 Dean of Sciences/Kinesiology ... Mr. Terry PETERMAN
108 Dean of Institutional Effectiveness ... Ms. Sina RUIZ
71 Assoc Dean of External Programs ... Ms. Sheri SHORT
35 Dean of Student Guidance ... Dr. Audrey WILLIAMS
92 Dean of Academic Support Programs ... Dr. Jill BAKER

North American University (J)

3203 North Sam Houston Pkwy West, Houston TX 77038
County: Harris FICE Identification: 041795
Unit ID: 461795
Telephone: (832) 230-5555 Carnegie Class: Not Classified
FAX Number: (832) 230-5546 Calendar System: Semester
URL: www.na.edu
Established: 2010 Annual Undergrad Tuition & Fees: $11,900
Enrollment: 477 Coed
Affiliation or Control: Non-denominational IRS Status: 501(c)3
Highest Offering: Master's
Program: Professional
Accreditation: ACICS

01 President & Professor ... Dr. Reg R. PECEN
05 Vice Pres Academic Affairs-Provost ... Dr. John C. TOPUZ
11 Vice Pres Administrative Affairs ... Dr. Can DOGAN
04 Administrative Asst to President ... Marizela LUPIC
06 Registrar ... Antera SHARP
07 Director of Admissions ... Shawn WASHINGTON
08 Head Librarian ... Stacey NGUYEN
106 Dir Online Education/E-learning ... Mustafa MALDAR
13 Chief Info Technology Officer (CIO) ... Khudoyor S. ORTIKOV
32 Chief Student Affairs/Student Life ... Osman KANLIOGLU
37 Director Student Financial Aid ... Amy GIAP

North Central Texas College (K)

1525 W. California Street, Gainesville TX 76240-4699
County: Cooke FICE Identification: 003558
Unit ID: 224110
Telephone: (940) 668-7731 Carnegie Class: Assoc/Pub-R-L
FAX Number: (940) 668-6049 Calendar System: Semester
URL: www.nctc.edu
Established: 1924 Annual Undergrad Tuition & Fees (In-District): $1,680
Enrollment: 10,169 Coed
Affiliation or Control: State/Local IRS Status: 501(c)3
Highest Offering: Associate Degree
Program: Occupational; 2-Year Principally Bachelor's Creditable
Accreditation: SC, ADNUR, EMT, SURGT

01 President ... Dr. Brent WALLACE
05 Vice President of Instruction ... Dr. Andrew FISHER
32 Vice President of Student Services ... Dr. Billy ROESSLER
10 Vice President Financial Services ... Dr. Janie NEIGHBORS
30 Vice Pres Institutional Advancement ... Ms. Debbie SHARP
15 Assoc Vice Pres Human Resources ... Mr. Bill WINANS
18 Associate VP of Campus Operations ... Mr. Robbie BAUGH
103 Associate VP Academic Partnerships ... Dr. Emily KLEMENT
13 Chief Information Officer ... Ms. Denise CASON
108 Sr Dir Assessment & Strategic Plng ... Mr. David BROWN
06 Registrar/Director of Admissions ... Ms. Melinda CARROLL
08 Director of Libraries ... Ms. Diane ROETHER
37 Financial Aid Director ... Ms. Ashley TATUM
38 Director Advisement ... Ms. Tracey FLENIKEN
26 Dir Marketing and Public Relations ... Mrs. Dianne WALTERSCHEID
41 Athletic Director ... Mr. Van HEDRICK
35 Director of Student Life ... Ms. Daisy GARCIA
76 Dean of Health Science ... Mrs. Gie ARCHER
72 Dean of Instruction Gainesville ... Mrs. Debbie HUFFMAN
49 Dean of Instruction Corinth ... Dr. Larry GILBERT
49 Dean of Instruction Flower Mound ... Mrs. Sara ALFORD
19 Police Chief ... Mr. James FITCH
35 Dean of Students ... Dr. Rodney LIPSCOMB
12 Dean of Denton County Campuses ... Mr. Roy CULBERSON
12 Director of Flower Mound Campus ... Ms. Jessica DEROCHE
12 Director of Bowie Campus ... Dr. Jose DASILVA
12 Director of Graham Campus ... Ms. Kim BIRDWELL

Northeast Texas Community College (L)

PO Box 1307, Mount Pleasant TX 75456-1307
County: Titus FICE Identification: 023154
Unit ID: 227225
Telephone: (903) 434-8100 Carnegie Class: Assoc/Pub-R-M
FAX Number: (903) 572-6712 Calendar System: Semester
URL: www.ntcc.edu
Established: 1984 Annual Undergrad Tuition & Fees (In-District): $2,014
Enrollment: 3,193 Coed
Affiliation or Control: Local IRS Status: 501(c)3
Highest Offering: Associate Degree
Program: Occupational; 2-Year Principally Bachelor's Creditable; Teacher Preparatory
Accreditation: SC, MAC, MLTAD, PTAA

01 President ... Dr. Brad W. JOHNSON
04 Executive Asst to the President ... Ms. Pat L. TALLANT
05 Executive Vice Pres for Instruction ... Dr. Ron CLINTON
11 Vice Pres Administrative Services ... Ms. Beth THOMPSON
30 Vice Pres Institutional Advancement ... Dr. Jonathan W. MCCULLOUGH
32 VP for Student & Outreach Services ... Dr. Johnny MOORE
103 Assoc VP for Workforce Development ... Dr. Kevin ROSE
37 Dean Enroll/Dir Student Fin Assist ... Ms. Kim LAWRENCE
76 Dean of Allied Health Professions ... Dr. Shannon COX-KELLEY
84 Associate Dean of Outreach Services ... Ms. Melody HENRY
18 Director of Plant Services ... Mr. Tim JOHNSTON
08 Director Learning Resource Center ... Mr. Ron BOWDEN
91 Director of Computer Services ... Mr. Kenneth GOODSON
26 Director Marketing/Public Relations ... Ms. Jodi WEBER
06 Registrar ... Ms. Betsy GOODING
15 Director Human Resources ... Ms. Amy ADKINS
10 Controller ... Ms. Jaci M. MERRITT
09 Dir Institutional Effectiveness ... Ms. Toni LABEFF
88 Advisor/Retention Specialist ... Mr. John COLEMAN
36 Career Development/Advisor ... Ms. Lynda WATSON

Northwood University (M)

1114 West FM 1382, Cedar Hill TX 75104
Telephone: (972) 293-5400 Identification: 770280
Accreditation: &NH, ACBSP

† Branch campus of Northwood University, Midland, MI.

Oblate School of Theology (N)

285 Oblate Drive, San Antonio TX 78216-6693
County: Bexar FICE Identification: 003595
Unit ID: 227289
Telephone: (210) 341-1366 Carnegie Class: Spec/Faith
FAX Number: (210) 341-4519 Calendar System: Semester
URL: www.ost.edu
Established: 1903 Annual Graduate Tuition & Fees: $14,735
Enrollment: 158 Coed
Affiliation or Control: Roman Catholic IRS Status: 501(c)3
Highest Offering: Doctorate; No Undergraduates
Program: Professional; Religious Emphasis
Accreditation: SC, PAST, THEOL

01 President ... Rev. Ronald ROLHEISER
05 Vice Pres Academic Affairs/Dean ... Dr. Scott WOODWARD
10 Vice Pres Finance/Human Resources ... Mr. Rene ESPINOSA
11 Vice Pres Administrative Affairs ... Rev. David KALERT
30 Vice Pres Institutional Advancement ... Mrs. Lea KOCHANEK
20 Associate Dean ... Sr. Linda GIBLER
51 Assoc Dean of Continuing Educ ... Mrs. Rose MARDEN
88 Director Oblate Renewal Center ... Mr. Brian WALLACE
18 Director of Physical Plant ... Mr. Morris LIM
08 Director of the Library ... Ms. Maria GARCIA
06 Registrar & Director of Admissions ... Mr. Mario PORTER
88 Director Lay Ministry Institute ... Mrs. Bonnie ABADIE
88 Director Ministry to Ministers Pgm ... Rev. Vincent LOUWAGIE
09 Dir Instl Research/Plng/Assessment ... Rev. David KALERT
88 Director DMin Program ... Rev. Wayne CAVALIER
88 Director PhD Program ... Rev. John MARKEY
26 Director of Communations ... Mr. Michael PARKER

Odessa College (O)

201 W University Boulevard, Odessa TX 79764-7127
County: Ector FICE Identification: 003596
Unit ID: 227304
Telephone: (432) 335-6400 Carnegie Class: Assoc/Pub-R-M
FAX Number: (432) 335-6860 Calendar System: Semester
URL: www.odessa.edu
Established: 1946 Annual Undergrad Tuition & Fees (In-District): $2,580
Enrollment: 5,476 Coed
Affiliation or Control: Local IRS Status: 501(c)3
Highest Offering: Associate Degree
Program: Occupational; 2-Year Principally Bachelor's Creditable
Accreditation: SC, ADNUR, EMT, MUS, PTAA, RAD

01 President ... Dr. Gregory D. WILLIAMS
05 Vice President for Instruction ... Ms. Valorie JONES
10 Vice President Business Affairs ... Ms. Virginia E. CHISUM
32 VP Student Svcs/Enrollment Mgmt ... Ms. Kimberly MCKAY
13 Vice President for Information Tech ... Mr. Shawn SHREVES
09 VP for Institutional Effectiveness ... Dr. Donald WOOD
30 Exec Director for Advancement ... Mr. Jeffrey MEYERS
11 Exec Dir of Administration & HR ... Mr. Ken ZARTNER
75 Exec Dean Career/Tech & Wrkforce Ed ... Vacant
49 Dean of Arts & Sciences ... Dr. Eric YEAGER
84 Exec Director Enrollment Services ... Mr. Louis GONZALES
06 Registrar ... Ms. Karen DOUGHTY
41 Director Intercollegiate Athletics ... Mr. Wayne BAKER
37 Director Student Financial Svcs ... Ms. Dee NESMITH
18 Director Facilities & Construction ... Mr. Bryan HEIFNER
26 Exec Director of Marketing ... Mr. Frank RICH
38 Exec Director Student Completion ... Ms. Kristi CLEMMER
96 Dir of Purchasing/Business Services ... Ms. Cindy CURNUTT

Our Lady of the Lake University (P)

411 SW 24th Street, San Antonio TX 78207-4689
County: Bexar FICE Identification: 003598
Unit ID: 227331

Telephone: (210) 434-6711 Carnegie Class: DRU
FAX Number: (210) 431-3928 Calendar System: Semester
URL: www.ollusa.edu
Established: 1895 Annual Undergrad Tuition & Fees: $25,300
Enrollment: 3,173 Coed
Affiliation or Control: Roman Catholic IRS Status: 501(c)3
Highest Offering: Doctorate
Program: Liberal Arts And General; Teacher Preparatory
Accreditation: **SC**, ACBSP, COPSY, MFCD, SP, SW

01 President ... Sr. Jane Ann SLATER
11 Chief Operating Officer ... Dr. Dwayne BANKS
05 Vice President for Academic Affairs ... Dr. Marcheta EVANS
32 Vice President of Student Life ... Mr. Jack L. HANK
10 Vice President Finance & Facilities ... Mr. Allen R. KLAUS
30 Vice Pres Institutional Advancement ... Mr. Daniel YOXALL
84 Vice Pres of Enrollment Management ... Ms. Mary SCOTKA
26 Vice Pres Communications/Marketing ... Mr. Daniel YOXALL
42 Vice President of Mission/Ministry ... Ms. Gloria URRABAZO
13 Chief Technology Officer ... Mr. Joseph G. DECK
108 Asst VP for I/E & Accreditation ... Ms. Kara LARKAN-SKINNER
18 Director Physical Plant ... Mr. Darrell R. GLASSCOCK
15 Director Human Resources ... Mr. Phillip VARGAS
06 Registrar ... Ms. Betty GALVAN
14 Director Network & Telecomm ... Mr. David LYTLE
19 Chief of Police/Dir Campus Safety ... Mr. David JUAREZ
39 Director Residence Life ... Mr. Mark R. CENTER
36 Director Career Counsel/Placement ... Mr. Andres JAIME
38 Director of Counseling Services ... Dr. Rosa ESPINOSA
23 Director Student Health Services ... Ms. Julie STUCKEY
40 Director Bookstore ... Mr. Edward CROCE
102 Corporate Relations Officer ... Ms. Roxanne SANCHEZ
46 Director of Advancement Services ... Mr. John SANCHEZ
44 Dir of Stewardship/Constituent Rels ... Ms. Debora GUZMAN
37 Director of Financial Aid ... Ms. Esmarelda FLORES
09 Dir Institutional Research ... Ms. Frances FREY
07 Asst Dir of Undergrad Admissions ... Ms. Shannon TIJERINA

Panola College (A)

1109 West Panola Street, Carthage TX 75633-2397
County: Panola FICE Identification: 003600
Unit ID: 227386
Telephone: (903) 693-2000 Carnegie Class: Assoc/Pub-R-M
FAX Number: (903) 693-1167 Calendar System: Semester
URL: www.panola.edu
Established: 1947 Annual Undergrad Tuition & Fees (In-District): $1,608
Enrollment: 2,579 Coed
Affiliation or Control: Local IRS Status: 501(c)3
Highest Offering: Associate Degree
Program: Occupational; 2-Year Principally Bachelor's Creditable
Accreditation: **SC**, ADNUR, CAHIIM, EMT, MLTAD, OTA

01 President ... Dr. Gregory S. POWELL
05 Vice President of Instruction ... Dr. Joe SHANNON
32 Vice President of Student Services ... Mr. Don CLINTON
10 Vice President of Fiscal Services ... Mr. Steve WILLIAMS
76 Dean of Health Sciences ... Dr. Barbara CORDELL
08 Director of Library ... Mrs. Cristie FERGUSON
07 Director of Admissions/Registrar ... Mr. Jeremy DORMAN
103 Dir of Workforce & Economic Devel ... Mrs. Whitney EDENS
30 Dir Institutional Advancement ... Mrs. Jessica PACE
09 Director of Institutional Research ... Mrs. Christine BLAIR
106 Dir Distance Education/Webmaster ... Mrs. Teresa BROOKS
12 Director of Shelby County Operation ... Mrs. Natalie OSWALT
12 Director of Marshall Operations ... Mrs. Laura WOOD
13 Computer Services Director ... Mr. Allen WEST
11 Director of Administrative Services ... Mr. Mike EDENS
19 Campus Police Chief ... Mr. Ernie DAVIS
37 Director Student Financial Aid ... Mrs. Denise WELCH
27 Marketing Coordinator ... Ms. Teresa BEASLEY

Paris Junior College (B)

2400 Clarksville Street, Paris TX 75460-6298
County: Lamar FICE Identification: 003601
Unit ID: 227401
Telephone: (903) 785-7661 Carnegie Class: Assoc/Pub-R-M
FAX Number: (903) 782-0370 Calendar System: Semester
URL: www.parisjc.edu
Established: 1924 Annual Undergrad Tuition & Fees (In-District): $1,890
Enrollment: 5,118 Coed
Affiliation or Control: State/Local IRS Status: 501(c)3
Highest Offering: Associate Degree
Program: Occupational; 2-Year Principally Bachelor's Creditable
Accreditation: **SC**, ADNUR, EMT, RAD, SURGT

01 President ... Dr. Pamela D. ANGLIN
32 Vice Pres Student Services ... Dr. Curtis HILL
103 Vice President Workforce Education ... Mr. John SPRADLING
35 Assoc VP Student Access/Success ... Mrs. Sheila REECE
05 Vice President of Academic Studies ... Mr. Ed MCCRAW
60 Dean Communications/Arts ... Dr. Ken HALEY
07 Director of Admissions ... Mrs. Amie CATO
06 Registrar ... Mrs. Rita TAPP
10 Controller ... Mrs. Keitha CARLTON
37 Director Student Financial Aid ... Mrs. Linda SLAWSON
38 Director Counseling ... Mrs. Barbara THOMAS
09 Director Institutional Research ... Mrs. Beverly MATTHEWS
30 Director Institutional Advancement ... Mr. Derald BULLS
35 Director Student Life ... Mr. Kenneth WEBB
13 Director Information Technology ... Mr. David NICHOLS

26 Chief Public Relations Officer ... Ms. Margaret RUFF
18 Manager Plant Operations ... Mr. Randall COX

Parker University (C)

2540 Walnut Hill Lane, Dallas TX 75229-5609
County: Dallas FICE Identification: 023053
Unit ID: 243823
Telephone: (972) 438-6932 Carnegie Class: Spec/Health
FAX Number: (214) 902-2496 Calendar System: Trimester
URL: www.parker.edu
Established: 1982 Annual Undergrad Tuition & Fees: $23,486
Enrollment: 977 Coed
Affiliation or Control: Independent Non-Profit IRS Status: 501(c)3
Highest Offering: Doctorate
Program: Professional
Accreditation: **SC**, CHIRO, COMTA

01 President ... Dr. Brian J. MCAULAY
05 Provost ... Dr. Gery HOCHANADEL
63 Vice Pres Col of Chiropractic ... Dr. Ashley CLEVELAND
29 Director Alumni Relations ... Ms. Donna WALD

Paul Quinn College (D)

3837 Simpson Stuart Road, Dallas TX 75241-4398
County: Dallas FICE Identification: 003602
Unit ID: 227429
Telephone: (214) 376-1000 Carnegie Class: Bac/Diverse
FAX Number: (214) 379-5559 Calendar System: Semester
URL: www.pqc.edu
Established: 1872 Annual Undergrad Tuition & Fees: $14,275
Enrollment: 273 Coed
Affiliation or Control: African Methodist Episcopal IRS Status: 501(c)3
Highest Offering: Baccalaureate
Program: Liberal Arts And General; Teacher Preparatory
Accreditation: **TRACS**

01 President ... Dr. Michael J. SORRELL
05 Vice Pres Academic Affairs ... Dr. Kizuwanda GRANT
10 Chief Financial Officer ... Mr. Bruce BRINSON
32 Dean of Student Talent ... Ms. Stacy CHERONES
06 Registrar ... Ms. Beverly TYLER
08 Librarian/Director LRC ... Ms. Clarice MEDLEY-WEEKS
13 Director of Technology ... Dr. John DEWITT
41 Dir Athletics/Intramural Sports ... Ms. Kelsel THOMPSON
37 Interim Director of Financial Aid ... Ms. Mildred MARTINEZ
35 Director Student Support Svcs ... Dr. Tiffany GURLEY-ALLOWAY
18 Interim Director of Facilities ... Mr. Ed WOODS
09 Instl Research Representative ... Dr. Chris DOWDY
30 Director of Development ... Mr. Dennis COLEMAN
23 Nurse ... Ms. Glenda DAVIS
07 Director of Recruiting ... Mrs. Jessika LARA

Pima Medical Institute-Houston (E)

10201-C Katy Freeway, Houston TX 77024
Telephone: (713) 778-0778 Identification: 770510
Accreditation: **ABHES**, #COARC, DH, PTAA, RAD

† Branch campus of Pima Medical Institute-Tucson, Tucson, AZ.

Quest College (F)

5430 Fredericksburg Rd, Ste 310, San Antonio TX 78229
County: Bexar FICE Identification: 034003
Unit ID: 439507
Telephone: (210) 366-2701 Carnegie Class: Not Classified
FAX Number: (210) 366-0738 Calendar System: Semester
URL: www.questcollege.edu
Established: 1995 Annual Undergrad Tuition & Fees: $24,113
Enrollment: 296 Coed
Affiliation or Control: Proprietary IRS Status: Proprietary
Highest Offering: Associate Degree
Program: Occupational
Accreditation: **COE**

01 Owner/Administrator ... Jeanne MARTIN

Ranger College (G)

1100 College Circle, Ranger TX 76470-3298
County: Eastland FICE Identification: 003603
Unit ID: 227687
Telephone: (254) 647-3234 Carnegie Class: Assoc/Pub-R-S
FAX Number: (254) 647-1656 Calendar System: Semester
URL: www.rangercollege.edu
Established: 1926 Annual Undergrad Tuition & Fees (In-District): $2,370
Enrollment: 2,033 Coed
Affiliation or Control: Local IRS Status: 501(c)3
Highest Offering: Associate Degree
Program: Occupational; 2-Year Principally Bachelor's Creditable; Technical Emphasis
Accreditation: **SC**

01 President ... Dr. William J. CAMPION
12 Executive VP Brownwood ... Vacant
12 Vice President Erath County ... Dr. Kerry SCHINDLER
84 Dean of Enrollment Management ... Mr. John SLAUGHTER
10 Chief Financial Officer ... Mr. Robert CULVERHOUSE
32 Dean of Students ... Mr. Manuel MCGRIFF
05 Dean of Student Learning ... Dr. Billy ADAMS
11 Dean of Administration ... Mrs. Cherie BELTRAN
06 Registrar ... Mr. John SLAUGHTER
08 Director of Learning Resources ... Mr. Joshua WALLACE
18 Director of Maintenance & Grounds ... Mr. Charles LEMASTER
37 Director of Financial Aid ... Mr. Don HILTON
41 Athletic Director ... Mr. Billy GILLISPIE
15 Director of Personnel ... Ms. DeLinda SPENCER
36 Director Student Placement ... Mr. Doug SMITH
38 Dir Academic Counseling & Testing ... Dr. Elizabeth PRICE
21 Bursar ... Ms. Evonne CHERRY
40 Director Bookstore ... Miss Cindy STRINGER
07 Admissions Assistant ... Ms. Mary LUCKY

Redeemer Theological Seminary (H)

6060 N Central Expressway, Ste. 700, Dallas TX 75206
County: Dallas Identification: 667055
Telephone: (214) 528-8600 Carnegie Class: Not Classified
FAX Number: N/A Calendar System: Semester
URL: www.redeemer.edu
Established: 1999 Annual Graduate Tuition & Fees: $14,700
Enrollment: 150 Coed
Affiliation or Control: Independent Non-Profit IRS Status: 501(c)3
Highest Offering: Master's; No Undergraduates
Program: Professional; Religious Emphasis
Accreditation: **THEOL**

01 President ... Dr. Martin BAN
05 Academic Dean ... Dr. Douglas M. GROPP
06 Registrar ... Ms. Mary-Chris SAYRE

Remington College-Dallas Campus (I)

1800 Eastgate Drive, Garland TX 75041-5513
County: Dallas FICE Identification: 030265
Unit ID: 223463
Telephone: (972) 686-7878 Carnegie Class: Assoc/PrivFP
FAX Number: (972) 686-5116 Calendar System: Quarter
URL: www.remingtoncollege.edu
Established: 1987 Annual Undergrad Tuition & Fees: $15,995
Enrollment: 822 Coed
Affiliation or Control: Independent Non-Profit IRS Status: 501(c)3
Highest Offering: Baccalaureate
Program: 2-Year Principally Bachelor's Creditable
Accreditation: **ACCSC**

01 Campus President ... Mr. Skip WALLS
05 Academic Dean ... Mr. Billy FERRELL

Remington College-Fort Worth Campus (J)

300 E Loop 820, Fort Worth TX 76112-1225
Telephone: (817) 451-0017 Identification: 666063
Accreditation: **ACCSC**

† Branch campus of Remington College-Dallas Campus, Garland, TX.

Remington College-Houston Southeast Campus (K)

20985 Interstate 45 South, Webster TX 77598
Telephone: (281) 554-1700 Identification: 770601
Accreditation: **ACCSC**

† Branch campus of Remington College-Dallas Campus, Garland, TX.

Remington College-North Houston Campus (L)

11310 Greens Crossing, Suite 300, Houston TX 77067
Telephone: (281) 885-4450 Identification: 770600
Accreditation: **ACCSC**

† Branch campus of Remington College-Dallas Campus, Garland, TX.

Rice University (M)

PO Box 1892, Houston TX 77251-1892
County: Harris FICE Identification: 003604
Unit ID: 227757
Telephone: (713) 348-0000 Carnegie Class: RU/VH
FAX Number: N/A Calendar System: Semester
URL: www.rice.edu
Established: 1891 Annual Undergrad Tuition & Fees: $42,253
Enrollment: 6,621 Coed
Affiliation or Control: Independent Non-Profit IRS Status: 501(c)3
Highest Offering: Doctorate
Program: Professional
Accreditation: **SC**, BUS, ENG, @TEAC

01 President ... Mr. David W. LEEBRON
101 Deputy Sec to Board of Trustees ... Ms. Cynthia L. WILSON
05 Provost ... Dr. Marie L. MIRANDA
11 Vice President Administration ... Dr. Kevin KIRBY
10 Vice President Finance ... Ms. Kathy COLLINS
30 Vice President Resource Development ... Mr. Darrow ZEIDENSTEIN
88 Vice Pres Investments/Treasurer ... Ms. Allison THACKER
84 Vice President for Enrollment ... Mr. Chris MUNOZ
26 Vice President for Public Affairs ... Ms. Linda THRANE
13 Vice Provost IT & CIO ... Ms. Klara JELINKOVA
46 Vice Provost Research ... Dr. Yousif SHAMOO
20 Vice Provost for Academic Affairs ... Dr. Paula SANDERS

88 Vice Prov Strategic Partnerships Dr. Daniel CARSON
08 Vice Provost/University Librarian Ms. Sara LOWMAN
88 Vice President Strategic Inits Dr. Caroline LEVANDER
88 Vice Provost Translational Biosci Dr. Cindy FARACH-CARSON
15 Associate Vice Pres Human Resources Ms. Mary A. CRONIN
91 Assoc Vice Pres for Admin Systems Mr. Randy CASTIGLIONI
43 General Counsel Mr. Richard A. ZANSITIS
06 Registrar Mr. David TENNEY
29 Asst VP for Alumni Affairs Ms. Marthe GOLDEN
37 Director Student Financial Services Ms. Anne E. WALKER
25 Director of Sponsored Research Ms. Melinda COTTEN
41 Director of Athletics Dr. Joseph KARLGAARD
85 Director Intl Students/Scholars Dr. Adria BAKER
39 Director of Housing & Dining Mr. Mark DITMAN
23 Director Student Health Services Dr. Stacy WARE
09 Director of Institutional Research Dr. Ratna SARKAR
21 University Controller Mr. Bradley FRALIC
21 Director of Internal Audit Ms. Janet COVINGTON
19 Chief of Campus Police Mr. Johnny WHITEHEAD
22 Director of Affirmative Action Mr. Russell BARNES
27 Director of News & Media Relations Mr. B.J ALMOND
21 Director Administrative Services Mr. Eugen RADULESCU
28 Director of Diversity Dr. Roland B. SMITH
36 Dir Center for Career Development Ms. Nicole VAN DEN HEUVEL
96 Director of Purchasing Mr. Brian SOIKA
40 Manager Bookstore Mr. Tim EDMOND
79 Dean of School of Humanities Dr. Nicolas SHUMWAY
58 Dean Graduate/Postdoctoral Stds Dr. Seiichi MATSUDA
97 Dean of Undergraduate Education Dr. John S. HUTCHINSON
48 Dean of Architecture Dr. Sarah M. WHITING
64 Dean of Shepherd School of Music Dr. Robert YEKOVICH
54 Dean GR Brown School Engineering Dr. Ned THOMAS
50 Dean JH Jones Graduate Sch Business Dr. William H. GLICK
83 Dean of Social Sciences Dr. Lyn RAGSDALE
81 Dean of Wiess Sch Natural Science Dr. Peter ROSSKY
51 Dean Glasscock Sch Continuing Stds Dr. Mary MCINTIRE
88 Asst Dean Stdnt Counsel/Jud Pgms Dr. Donald OSTDIEK

Rio Grande Bible Institute (A)

4300 South US Highway 281, Edinburg TX 78539-9650
County: Hidalgo Identification: 666395
Unit ID: 475185
Telephone: (956) 380-8100 Carnegie Class: Not Classified
FAX Number: (956) 380-8256 Calendar System: Semester
URL: www.riogrande.edu
Established: 1946 Annual Undergrad Tuition & Fees: $2,839
Enrollment: 136 Coed
Affiliation or Control: Independent Non-Profit IRS Status: 501(c)3
Highest Offering: Baccalaureate
Program: Professional; Religious Emphasis
Accreditation: BI

01 President Dr. Lawrence B. WINDLE
04 Administrative Assistant to Pres Mrs. Ruth WINDLE
05 Vice President of Education Mr. David LOYOLA
32 Dean of Students Mr. Daniel DE LEON
10 Director of Administration Dr. John TARWATER
21 Comptroller Mr. Jonathan WHITE
08 Chief Librarian Miss Mary CANO
06 Registrar Mr. Keith SWARTZBAUGH
15 Personnel Director Dr. John TARWATER
18 Vice President of Campus Services Mr. Gary WILLIAMS
26 Vice Pres Ministerial Advancement Dr. Robert CRANE

St. Edward's University (B)

3001 S Congress Avenue, Austin TX 78704-6489
County: Travis FICE Identification: 003621
Unit ID: 227845
Telephone: (512) 448-8400 Carnegie Class: Master's L
FAX Number: (512) 448-8492 Calendar System: Semester
URL: www.stedwards.edu
Established: 1885 Annual Undergrad Tuition & Fees: $38,720
Enrollment: 4,686 Coed
Affiliation or Control: Independent Non-Profit IRS Status: 501(c)3
Highest Offering: Master's
Program: Liberal Arts And General; Teacher Preparatory; Professional; Business Emphasis
Accreditation: SC, SW

01 President Dr. George E. MARTIN
03 Executive Vice President Sr. Donna M. JURICK
10 Vice President Financial Affairs Ms. Kimberly KVAAL
05 Vice President for Academic Affairs Dr. Mary K. BOYD
30 Interim VP for Advancement Mr. Joe DEMEDEIROS
26 Vice Pres Marketing/Enrollment Mgmt Ms. Paige BOOTH
32 Interim VP for Student Affairs Dr. Lisa L. KIRKPATRICK
13 Vice President Information Tech Mr. David E. WALDRON
42 Director of Campus Ministry Fr. Peter J. WALSH
09 Assoc VP Inst Effectiveness/Rsrch Mr. Bhuban R. PANDEY
88 Assoc VP for Global Initiatives Mr. William J. CLABBY
21 Assoc VP for Finance Vacant
20 Assoc VP for Academic Affairs Dr. Molly E. MINUS
88 Assoc VP Faculty Development Ms. Lori W. PETERSON
07 Assoc VP/Dean of Admission Ms. Tracy L. MANIER
37 Assoc VP Student Financial Services Ms. Doris F. CONSTANTINE
32 Interim Dean of Students Mr. Steven J. PINKENBURG
88 Assoc VP Stdnt Acad Support Svcs Ms. Nicole G. TREVINO
27 Assoc VP for Marketing Ms. Christie CAMPBELL
44 Director of Development Ms. Anne E. WESTDYKE
18 Assoc VP Facilities Mr. Michael W. PETERSON
109 Assoc VP for Financial Affairs Vacant
29 Director of Alumni & Parent Pgms Ms. Karin DICKS
100 Chief of Staff/Sustainability Coord Ms. Cristina L. BORDIN
04 Admin Assistant to President Ms. Lorraine M. PAGAN
83 Dean Behavioral & Social Sciences Dr. Brenda J. VALLANCE
50 Dean The Munday School of Business Dr. Nancy SCHREIBER
53 Dean School of Education Dr. Grant W. SIMPSON, JR.
79 Dean School of Humanities Dr. Sharon D. NELL
81 Dean School of Natural Sciences Dr. Gary MORRIS
55 Interim Dean of New College Dr. Ramsey FOWLER
97 Director of General Education Dr. Cory LOCK
89 Director Freshman Studies Ms. Alexandra L. BARRON
88 Director Capstone Course Dr. Todd D. ONDERDONK
92 Director Honors Program Dr. Steven M. RODENBORN
08 Director of Munday Library Mr. Pongracz SENNYEY
06 Registrar Dr. Lance R. HAYES
36 Dir Career & Prof Development Mr. Raymond C. ROGERS
108 Dir of Institutional Assessment Mr. David A. BLAIR
104 Director Ofc of International Educ Ms. Holly R. CARTER
91 Dir of Enterprise Info Systems Ms. Angela M. SVOBODA
88 Director Digital Infrastructure Mr. Benjamin R. HOCKENHULL
24 Director Info Technology Resources Mr. Mark D. JACAMAN
90 Dir Instructional & Emerging Tech Ms. Rebecca F. DAVIS
105 Midware/User Experience Architect Mr. Tim TASHJIAN
19 Chief of Police Mr. Rudolph L. RENDON
27 Director of Communications Ms. Mischelle R. DIAZ
15 Assistant VP of Human Resources Ms. Rosemary RUDNICKI
38 Director of Health & Counseling Ctr Dr. Calvin A. KELLY
102 Director Foundation Relations Ms. Allison M. RASP
41 Director of Athletics Ms. Debora W. TAYLOR
35 Director of Student Life Mr. Thomas B. SULLIVAN
39 Director Residence Life Ms. Alicia L. VELA
21 Controller Mr. Paul R. SINTEF
109 Assistant VP for Business Services Ms. Cyndy JOHNSON
40 Campus Stores Director Mr. Tim JACKSON

St. Mary's University (C)

One Camino Santa Maria, San Antonio TX 78228-8572
County: Bexar FICE Identification: 003623
Unit ID: 228149
Telephone: (210) 436-3011 Carnegie Class: Master's L
FAX Number: (210) 436-3500 Calendar System: Semester
URL: www.stmarytx.edu
Established: 1852 Annual Undergrad Tuition & Fees: $27,160
Enrollment: 2,322 Coed
Affiliation or Control: Roman Catholic IRS Status: 501(c)3
Highest Offering: Doctorate
Program: Liberal Arts And General; Teacher Preparatory; Professional
Accreditation: SC, BUS, CACREP, ENG, LAW, MFCD, MUS

01 President Mr. Thomas M. MENGLER
05 Int Provost/VP Academic Affairs Dr. Aaron TYLER
10 Vice Pres Administration & Finance Ms. Rebeckah J. DAY
84 Vice Pres Enrollment Management Ms. Suzanne M. PETRUSCH
32 Vice President Student Development Ms. Katherine SISOIAN
30 Vice Pres University Advancement Mr. Richard (Rick) KIMBROUGH, III
88 Vice President Mission & Identity Rev. Tim EDEN, SM
50 Dean/Bill Greehey Sch Business Dr. Tanuja SINGH
79 Dean Humanities & Social Science Dr. Janet B. DIZINNO
54 Dean Science/Engrng/Technology Dr. Winston EREVELLES
58 Interim Dean Graduate Studies Dr. Megan MUSTAIN
61 Dean of Law Mr. Steve M. SHEPPARD
39 Director Residence Life Mr. James VILLARREAL
100 Chief of Staff/Office of President Ms. Dianne L. PIPES
06 Registrar Ms. Christina VILLANUEVA
07 Dean of Admission Mr. Nelson DELGADO
08 Exec Director Louis J Blume Library Ms. Caroline BYRD
37 Director Financial Assistance Mr. David R. KRAUSE
38 Assoc Director Student Counseling Ms. Deidra COLEMAN
36 Director of Career Services Ms. Amy DIEPENBROCK
90 Exec Director Academic Technology Mr. Jeff SCHOMBURG
15 Director Human Resources Ms. Elsa YBANEZ
72 Vice Pres Info Tech/Library Svcs Mr. Curtis WHITE
91 Exec Dir Resource Mgmt/Planning Ms. Louisa A. MARTIN
13 Dir Network Security Administration Mr. Robert STOOKSBERRY
14 Director Systems Support Services Mr. Frank NIEWIERSKI
42 Director University Ministry Mr. Wayne ROMO
29 Executive Director Alumni Relations Mr. Peter HANSEN
21 Director of Finance Ms. Mei-Lin LEE
21 Director of Accounting Operations Ms. Sheila NIX
26 Dir Media Relations/Communications Mrs. Gina FARRELL
18 Exec Dir Facilities Administration Mr. Aaron HANNA

*San Jacinto College District (D)

4624 Fairmont Parkway, Pasadena TX 77504-3323
County: Harris FICE Identification: 029137
Unit ID: 227988
Telephone: (281) 998-6150 Carnegie Class: N/A
FAX Number: N/A
URL: www.sanjac.edu

00 Chancellor Dr. Brenda HELLYER
01 Deputy Chancellor and President Dr. Laurel WILLIAMSON
05 Provost Dr. Brenda JONES
05 Provost Dr. Van WIGGINTON
05 Provost Mr. William RAFFETTO
10 Vice Chancellor Fiscal Affairs Mr. Ken LYNN
15 Vice Chanc Human Resources Mr. Stephen TRNCAK
13 Interim CIO Mr. Rob STANICIC
26 Vice Chanc Marketing/Govt Rels Mrs. Teri CRAWFORD
45 Vice Chanc Strategic Initiatives Dr. Allatia HARRIS
84 Dean Enroll Mgmt/College Registrar Ms. Wanda MUNSON
09 Director of Research Mr. George GONZALEZ
37 Dean Financial Aid Services Mr. Robert MERINO
96 Director Contracts & Purchasing Ms. Ann KOKX-TEMPLET

*San Jacinto College Central (E)

8060 Spencer Highway, Pasadena TX 77505-5903
County: Harris FICE Identification: 003609
Unit ID: 227979
Telephone: (281) 476-1501 Carnegie Class: Assoc/Pub-S-MC
FAX Number: (281) 476-1892 Calendar System: Semester
URL: www.sanjac.edu
Established: 1960 Annual Undergrad Tuition & Fees (In-District): $704
Enrollment: 13,624 Coed
Affiliation or Control: Local IRS Status: 501(c)3
Highest Offering: Associate Degree
Program: Occupational; 2-Year Principally Bachelor's Creditable
Accreditation: &SC, ACFEI, ADNUR, COARC, DMS, EMT, MLTAD, RAD, SURGT

02 Deputy Chancellor and President Dr. Laurel WILLIAMSON
05 Provost Dr. Van WIGGINTON
32 Interim Vice Pres Student Services Ms. Joanna ZIMMERMAN
49 Dean Liberal Arts & Science Dr. Kelly SIMONS
75 Dean Business & Technology Mr. Jeffrey PARKS
76 Dean Health Sciences Mr. Michael KANE
11 Dean Administration Dr. James BRASWELL
07 Dean Enrollment Services Mr. Kevin MCKISSON
92 Director Honors Program Dr. Eddie WELLER
35 Interim Dean Student Development Ms. Shelley RINEHART
88 Director Dual Credit Ms. Nicole BARNES
62 Director Library Ms. Karen BLANKENSHIP
88 Director Campus Services Mr. Christopher CRUMLEY
41 Athletic Director Ms. Sharon NELSON
06 College Registrar Dr. Wanda MUNSON
88 Director Student Success Ms. Chisty KEITH
37 Dean Financial Aid Services Mr. Robert MERINO

† Regional accreditation is carried under the parent institution (district office) in Pasadena, TX.

*San Jacinto College North (F)

5800 Uvalde Road, Houston TX 77049-4599
County: Harris Identification: 666747
Unit ID: 227997
Telephone: (281) 458-4050 Carnegie Class: Not Classified
FAX Number: (281) 459-7125 Calendar System: Semester
URL: www.sanjac.edu
Established: 1974 Annual Undergrad Tuition & Fees (In-District): $844
Enrollment: 8,000 Coed
Affiliation or Control: Local IRS Status: 501(c)3
Highest Offering: Associate Degree
Program: Occupational; 2-Year Principally Bachelor's Creditable
Accreditation: &SC, ACFEI, CAHIIM, EMT, MAC

02 Deputy Chancellor and President Dr. Laurel WILLIAMSON
05 Provost Dr. William RAFFETTO
07 Dean Enrollment Services Vacant
11 Dean Administration Dr. Jerrel WADE
76 Dean Natural and Health Sciences Ms. Rhonda BELL
50 Dean Business and Technology Dr. Kerry MIX
32 Dean Student Development Ms. Clare IANNELLI
62 Director Library Ms. Lyn GARNER
49 Dean Liberal Arts Mr. Shawn SILMAN
06 College Registrar Dr. Wanda MUNSON
41 Athletic Director Mr. Tom ARRINGTON
92 Dean Honors Program Dr. Eddie WELLER
88 Dual Credit Director Ms. Jennifer MOWDY
55 Director Evening/Weekend Services Mr. Don SPIES
88 Director Student Success Center Ms. Erika HERNANDEZ
37 Dean Financial Aid Services Mr. Robert MERINO

† Regional accreditation is carried under the parent institution (district office) in Pasadena, TX.

*San Jacinto College South (G)

13735 Beamer Road, Houston TX 77089-6099
County: Harris Identification: 666748
Unit ID: 22797902
Telephone: (281) 484-1900 Carnegie Class: Not Classified
FAX Number: (281) 922-3401 Calendar System: Semester
URL: www.sanjac.edu
Established: 1979 Annual Undergrad Tuition & Fees (In-District): $844
Enrollment: 10,817 Coed
Affiliation or Control: Local IRS Status: 501(c)3
Highest Offering: Associate Degree
Program: Occupational; 2-Year Principally Bachelor's Creditable
Accreditation: &SC, ADNUR, PTAA

02 Deputy Chancellor and President Dr. Laurel WILLIAMSON
05 Provost Dr. Brenda JONES
50 Dean Business & Technology Mr. Kevin MORRIS
76 Dean Health and Natural Sciences Dr. Alexander OKWONNA
11 Dean Administration Mr. Joseph HEBERT
07 Interim Dean Enrollment Services Ms. Tami KELLY
92 Director Honors Program Dr. Eddie WELLER
55 Director Evening Division Mr. John BOGGS

62 Director Library .... Mr. Richard MCKAY
41 Director Athletics .... Ms. Kelly SAENZ
88 Dual Credit Director .... Ms. Kate GRAHAM
06 College Registrar .... Dr. Wanda MUNSON
32 Interim Dean Student Development .... Ms. Debbie SMITH
88 Director Student Success Center .... Ms. Diana SHOKRALLA
37 Dean Financial Aid Services .... Mr. Robert MERINO

† Regional accreditation is carried under the parent institution (district office) in Pasadena, TX.

Sanford-Brown College (A)

1250 W. Mockingbird Lane, Suite 500, Dallas TX 75247
County: Dallas FICE Identification: 026150
Unit ID: 404514
Telephone: (214) 459-8490 Carnegie Class: Assoc/PrivFP
FAX Number: (214) 638-6401 Calendar System: Other
URL: www.sanfordbrown.edu
Established: Annual Undergrad Tuition & Fees: $15,118
Enrollment: 490 Coed
Affiliation or Control: Proprietary IRS Status: Proprietary
Highest Offering: Associate Degree
Program: Occupational
Accreditation: ACICS, CVT, DH, DMS

01 Campus President .... David B. BOWMAN

† School is in teach-out plan.

Sanford Brown College (B)

4511 Horizon Hill Boulevard, San Antonio TX 78229
Telephone: (210) 530-9449 Identification: 666733
Accreditation: ACICS, CVT

† Branch campus of International Academy of Design and Technology, Tampa, FL. School is in teach out plan.

School of Automotive Machinists (C)

1911 Antoine Drive, Houston TX 77055
County: Harris FICE Identification: 030323
Unit ID: 377218
Telephone: (713) 683-3817 Carnegie Class: Not Classified
FAX Number: (713) 683-7077 Calendar System: Semester
URL: www.samracing.com
Established: 1985 Annual Undergrad Tuition & Fees: $37,550
Enrollment: 185 Coed
Affiliation or Control: Proprietary IRS Status: Proprietary
Highest Offering: Associate Degree
Program: Occupational
Accreditation: ACCSC

01 President/Dir of Education .... Judson MASSINGILL
11 CEO/Sch Exec Director/Administrator .... Linda MASSINGILL
07 Director of Admissions .... Scott MORRIS
37 Financial Aid Director .... Susie FAERMAN

Schreiner University (D)

2100 Memorial Boulevard, Kerrville TX 78028-5697
County: Kerr FICE Identification: 003610
Unit ID: 228042
Telephone: (830) 896-5411 Carnegie Class: Bac/Diverse
FAX Number: (830) 896-3232 Calendar System: Semester
URL: www.schreiner.edu
Established: 1923 Annual Undergrad Tuition & Fees: $23,386
Enrollment: 1,128 Coed
Affiliation or Control: Presbyterian Church (U.S.A.) IRS Status: 501(c)3
Highest Offering: Master's
Program: Liberal Arts And General; Teacher Preparatory; Professional
Accreditation: SC, NURSE

01 President .... Dr. Timothy SUMMERLIN
05 Provost/Vice Pres Acad Affairs .... Dr. Charlie T. MCCORMICK
10 Vice Pres Administration & Finance .... Mr. Bill MUSE
30 Vice Pres Advancement/Public Rels .... Mr. Mark TUSCHAK
84 Vice Pres Enrollment Services .... Dr. Larry CANTU
06 Assistant Provost & Registrar .... Ms. Darlene BANNISTER
20 Dean of Student Success .... Dr. Candice SCOTT
26 Vice President for Marketing .... Ms. Lane H. TAIT
21 Asst Vice Pres Finance/Controller .... Ms. Barbara SIEMERS
42 Campus Minister .... Rev. Virginia NORRIS-LANE
84 Dean of Enrollment Services .... Ms. Toni BRYANT
32 Dean of Students .... Dr. Charlie HUEBER
26 Director of Communications .... Ms. Amy ARMSTRONG
41 Athletic Director .... Mr. Ron MACOSKO
15 Director of Human Resource Services .... Ms. Wendy BLAETTNER
18 Director Facilities Services .... Mr. Dale MYERS
29 Associate Director Alumni Relations .... Mr. Paul CAMFIELD
38 Director Student Counseling .... Ms. Kimberly J. WOODS
36 Director Advising & Career Devel .... Ms. Cristina MARTINEZ
09 Director of Institutional Research .... Dr. Lucien COSTLEY
07 Assoc Dean of Enrollment Services .... Ms. Caroline RANDALL

Seminary of the Southwest (E)

Box 2247, Austin TX 78768-2247
County: Travis FICE Identification: 003566
Unit ID: 224712
Telephone: (512) 472-4133 Carnegie Class: Spec/Faith
FAX Number: (512) 472-3098 Calendar System: 4/1/4
URL: www.ssw.edu
Established: 1952 Annual Graduate Tuition & Fees: $14,255
Enrollment: 98 Coed
Affiliation or Control: Protestant Episcopal IRS Status: 501(c)3
Highest Offering: Master's; No Undergraduates
Program: Professional; Religious Emphasis
Accreditation: SC, THEOL

01 Dean & President .... V.Rev. Cynthia Briggs KITTREDGE
05 Academic Dean .... Dr. Scott BADER-SAYE
03 Executive Vice President .... Mr. Fred CLEMENT
26 VP of Communications .... Ms. Nancy SPRINGER-BALDWIN
30 Vice Pres Institutional Advancement .... Ms. Tara HOLLEY
10 Accounting Director .... Ms. Kathy LEBRUN
06 Registrar/Director of Assessment .... Ms. Madelyn SNODGRASS
08 Director of the Booher Library .... Ms. Alison POAGE
18 Director of Facilities Management .... Mr. Tigh WALTERS
13 Director Information Technology .... Mr. Erik MORROW
44 Sr Dir Annual Giving/Alumni Rels .... Mr. Andrew WEST
84 Enrollment Manager .... Ms. Beth JORDON

South Plains College (F)

1401 College Avenue, Levelland TX 79336-6595
County: Hockley FICE Identification: 003611
Unit ID: 228158
Telephone: (806) 894-9611 Carnegie Class: Assoc/Pub-R-L
FAX Number: (806) 894-5274 Calendar System: Semester
URL: www.southplainscollege.edu
Established: 1957 Annual Undergrad Tuition & Fees (In-State): $2,584
Enrollment: 9,661 Coed
Affiliation or Control: State IRS Status: 501(c)3
Highest Offering: Associate Degree
Program: Occupational; 2-Year Principally Bachelor's Creditable
Accreditation: SC, ADNUR, COARC, EMT, PTAA, SURGT

01 President .... Dr. Kelvin W. SHARP
05 Vice President Academic Affairs .... Mr. Jim WALKER
10 Vice Pres Business Affairs .... Ms. Teresa GREEN
32 Vice President of Student Affairs .... Mrs. Cathy MITCHELL
30 Vice Pres Institutional Advancement .... Mr. Stephen S. JOHN
49 Dean of Arts & Sciences .... Mr. Yancy NUNEZ
76 Dean of Health Occupations .... Ms. Sue Ann LOPEZ
75 Dean of Technical Education .... Mr. Robbie M. BLAIR
51 Dean Continuing & Distance Educ .... Mr. Ronald SPEARS
11 Dean Administrative Services .... Mr. Ronnie WATKINS
07 Dean of Admissions & Records .... Mrs. Andrea RANGEL
35 Dean of Students .... Mr. David CONNER
12 Dean of Reese Center .... Ms. Kara MARTINEZ
09 Assoc Dean of Research & Reports .... Mr. Jack WARDLOW
26 Assoc Dean of College Relations .... Mr. Dane DEWBRE
13 Assoc Dean Information Technology .... Mr. Tim WINDERS
88 Assoc Dean Dual Credit .... Mr. Ron SPEARS
103 Assoc Dean Workforce Development .... Mr. Rafael AGUILERA
20 Assoc Dean of Students .... Ms. Urisonya FLUNDER
38 Director of Counseling & Guidance .... Mrs. Christi ANDERSON
37 Director of Financial Aid .... Ms. Jim Ann BATENHORST
08 Director of Libraries .... Ms. Fran COTTON
44 Director of Development .... Ms. Julie GERSTENBERGER
15 Director of Human Resources .... Mrs. Jeri Ann DEWBRE
41 Director of Athletics .... Mr. Joe TUBB
06 Registrar .... Mr. Andrew RUIZ
18 Director of Physical Plant .... Mr. Cary MARROW
84 Director of Enrollment Management .... Ms. Kimbra QUINN
21 Controller .... Ms. Teresa GREEN
40 Bookstore Manager .... Mr. Roger SHULL
28 Diversity Coord/Career Counselor .... Ms. Maria LOPEZ-STRONG

South Texas College (G)

3201 W Pecan, McAllen TX 78501
County: Hidalgo FICE Identification: 031034
Unit ID: 409315
Telephone: (956) 872-5051 Carnegie Class: Assoc/Pub4
FAX Number: (956) 971-3739 Calendar System: Semester
URL: www.southtexascollege.edu
Established: 1993 Annual Undergrad Tuition & Fees (In-District): $3,270
Enrollment: 30,180 Coed
Affiliation or Control: State/Local IRS Status: 501(c)3
Highest Offering: Baccalaureate
Program: 2-Year Principally Bachelor's Creditable
Accreditation: SC, ACBSP, CAHIIM, COARC, EMT, OTA, PTAA

01 President .... Dr. Shirley A. REED
05 Int Vice Pres Academic Affs/CAO .... Dr. Anahid PETROSIAN
10 VP Finance/Administrative Svcs .... Ms. Maria G. ELIZONDO
32 Int VP Student Affairs/Enroll Mgmt .... Ms. Wanda GARCIA
13 Int VP Info Services/Planning .... Dr. David PLUMMER
30 Vice Pres Institutional Advancement .... Vacant
88 Exec Officer for NAAMRIE .... Ms. Wanda GARZA
83 Dean Liberal Arts/Soc Sci .... Dr. Margaretha BISCHOFF
50 Dean Business/Technology .... Mr. Mario REYNA
76 Int Dean Nursing/Allied Health .... Ms. Melba TREVINO
81 Dean Math/Science/BA Programs .... Dr. Ali ESMAEILI
88 Dean Bach Deg Prog/Univ Rels .... Dr. Ali ESMAEILI
24 Dir Instructional Technologies .... Mr. Cody GREGG
37 Assoc Dean Student Financial Svcs .... Mr. Mike CARRANZA
21 Comptroller .... Ms. Maria ELIZONDO
15 Director Human Resources .... Ms. Brenda Jo BALDERAZ
51 Dir Continuing/Prof & Workforce Ed .... Mr. Juan Carlos AGUIRRE
96 Director Purchasing .... Ms. Rebecca CAVAZOS
09 Dir Research/Analytical Svcs .... Mr. Serkan CELTEK
38 Dean Student Support Svcs .... Mr. Paul HERNANDEZ, JR.
18 Director Operations .... Mr. George MCCALEB
18 Director Facilities Plan/Construct .... Mr. Gerardo RODRIGUEZ, JR.
25 Dir Gr Dev/Accountability/Mgmt Svcs .... Vacant
12 Campus Administrator Starr Cty .... Dr. Arthuro MONTIEL
12 Campus Administrator Mid-Valley .... Mr. Daniel MONTEZ
88 Employee Relations Officer .... Vacant
106 Interim Director Distance Education .... Dr. Brett MILLAN
26 Director Public Rels/Marketing .... Mr. Daniel RAMIREZ
88 Dir Outreach/Orient/Wel Centers .... Ms. Kimberly MCKAY
84 Dean Enrollment Services/Registrar .... Mr. Matthew HEBBARD
88 Dir Profess Organizational Dev .... Ms. Lee GRIMES ETHERIDGE
20 Asst to VP Instructional Svcs .... Dr. Anahid PETROSIAN
19 Director Security .... Mr. Paul VARVILLE
62 Dean Library Services/Instr Tech .... Mr. Cody GREGG
103 Assc Dean Cmty Engage/Wkfrc Dev .... Vacant
13 Chief Information Officer .... Ms. Alicia GOMEZ
14 Director for IT Services .... Mr. Daniel DE LEON
08 Director Library Technical Services .... Mr. Jesus CAMPOS
08 Director Library Public Services .... Ms. Noemi GARZA
88 Dir Student Lrg Outcomes/Achievemnt .... Mr. Oscar HERNANDEZ
88 Int Dir Centers for Lrg Excellence .... Ms. Jennifer KNECHT
88 Administrator High School Programs .... Mr. Nicolas GONZALEZ
90 Dir Info Commons Open Labs .... Dr. Lelia SALINAS
35 Dean Student Affairs .... Mr. Pablo HERNANDEZ
88 Chief Information Security Officer .... Mr. Steve BOURDON
88 Curriculum/Accreditation Officer .... Ms. Laura TALBOT

South Texas College of Law/ Houston (H)

1303 San Jacinto Street, Houston TX 77002-7000
County: Harris FICE Identification: 004977
Unit ID: 228194
Telephone: (713) 659-8040 Carnegie Class: Spec/Law
FAX Number: (713) 646-2909 Calendar System: Semester
URL: www.stcl.edu
Established: 1923 Annual Graduate Tuition & Fees: $29,490
Enrollment: 1,088 Coed
Affiliation or Control: Independent Non-Profit IRS Status: 501(c)3
Highest Offering: First Professional Degree; No Undergraduates
Program: Professional
Accreditation: LAW

01 President & Dean .... Mr. Donald J. GUTER
03 Executive Vice President .... Ms. Helen JENKINS
101 Sr Exec Assistant to President/Dean .... Ms. Jennifer M. HUDSON
10 Vice President and CFO .... Mr. Gregory A. BROTHERS
30 Sr VP of Institutional Advancement .... Ms. Maya FREDRICKSON
09 Vice Pres Strategic Plng/Inst Rsrch .... Mr. Jeffrey L. RENSBERGER
08 Director Library Svcs .... Ms. Colleen MANNING
05 Vice President & Associate Dean .... Mr. Bruce MCGOVERN
05 Vice President & Associate Dean .... Mr. T. Gerald TREECE
05 Vice President & Associate Dean .... Ms. Catherine G. BURNETT
05 Vice President & Associate Dean .... Mr. John WORLEY
13 Vice President Technology .... Mr. Randy MARAK
15 Vice President for Human Resources .... Mr. Steve ALDERMAN
38 Asst Dean for Academic Assistance .... Ms. Gena L. SINGLETON
06 Registrar .... Ms. Mandi GIBSON
36 Director of Career Resources .... Ms. Ginna PASTRANO
07 Assistant Dean for Admissions .... Ms. Alicia CRAMER
21 Controller .... Ms. Nancy N. JOHNSON
37 Director of Financial Aid .... Ms. Pat MILLIGAN
26 Dir Marketing/Communications .... Ms. Diane SUMMERS
32 Assistant Dean .... Ms. Wanda MORROW
19 Director Security .... Mr. Kent BRAZELTON
09 Exec Dir of Institutional Research .... Dr. Ryan BEARD
24 Dir Instructional Technology Svcs .... Mr. Terry SMITH
14 Director Information Services .... Mr. George MILZ
43 General Counsel .... Mr. Steve ALDERMAN
30 Director of Advancement Services .... Ms. Roya ESFANDI
44 Director of Annual Giving .... Ms. Susan DIEDERICH
29 Director of Alumni Relations .... Ms. Megan GRAF
102 Dir of Foundation & Govt Relations .... Ms. Ashley ESTES
18 Chief Facilities/Physical Plant .... Mr. William HILL
96 Director of Purchasing .... Ms. Sandra KASPER

South University (I)

1220 W. Louis Henna Boulevard, Round Rock TX 78681
Telephone: (512) 516-8800 Identification: 770917
Accreditation: &SC, ACBSP, NURSE, PTAA

† Branch campus of South University, Savannah, GA.

Southern Methodist University (J)

6425 Boaz Lane, Dallas TX 75205-0100
County: Dallas FICE Identification: 003613
Unit ID: 228246
Telephone: (214) 768-2000 Carnegie Class: RU/H
FAX Number: (214) 768-1001 Calendar System: Semester
URL: www.smu.edu
Established: 1911 Annual Undergrad Tuition & Fees: $48,190
Enrollment: 11,272 Coed
Affiliation or Control: United Methodist IRS Status: 501(c)3
Highest Offering: Doctorate
Program: Liberal Arts And General; Professional
Accreditation: SC, ART, BUS, CLPSY, CS, DANCE, ENG, LAW, MUS, THEA, THEOL

01 President .... Dr. R. Gerald TURNER
05 Interim Provost/VP Academic Affairs .... Dr. Harold W. STANLEY

10 Vice President Business & Finance .... Ms. Chris C. REGIS
32 Interim VP for Student Affairs .... Dr. Joanne E. VOGEL
30 Vice Pres Devel & External Affairs .... Mr. Brad E. CHEVES
43 Gen Counsel/VP Leg Affs/Govt Rels .... Mr. Paul J. WARD
11 Vice President Executive Affairs .... Dr. Thomas E. BARRY
49 Dean Dedman College .... Dr. Thomas DIPIERO
35 Interim Dean of Student Life .... Dr. Stephen RANKIN
21 Assoc VP/Chief Risk Officer .... Ms. Ellen S. HOLLAND
45 Associate Vice President/Budgets .... Mr. Ernie BARRY
26 Assoc Vice President Public Affairs .... Ms. Patti LASALLE
44 Asst Vice Pres Univ Development .... Ms. Pam CONLIN
15 Assoc VP/Chief Human Res Officer .... Mr. Jeff STRESE
84 Interim Assoc VP Enroll Management .... Mr. Wes K. WAGGONER
109 Assoc VP of Campus Services .... Ms. Alison TWEEDY
88 Exec Dir of Program Services .... Ms. Dana AYRES
57 Dean Meadows Sch of the Arts .... Dr. Sam HOLLAND
61 Dean Dedman School of Law .... Ms. Jennifer M. COLLINS
54 Dean Lyle School of Engr .... Dr. Marc CHRISTENSEN
73 Dean Perkins School of Theology .... Dr. William B. LAWRENCE
50 Dean Cox School of Business .... Dr. Albert W. NIEMI, JR.
58 Director of Graduate Studies .... Ms. Phyllis PAYNE
46 Assoc VP Research/Dean Grad Studies .... Dr. James E. QUICK
53 Dean Sch of Educ/Human Devel .... Dr. David J. CHARD
08 Dean/Dir Central Univ Libraries .... Ms. Gillian M. MCCOMBS
20 Assoc Provost .... Ms. Julie FORRESTER
20 Assoc Provost .... Ms. Linda S. EADS
25 Int Director of Sponsored Projects .... Ms. Sandra A. OSWALT
41 Director of Athletics .... Mr. Richard L. HART
06 Registrar .... Mr. John A. HALL
37 Exec Director Financial Aid .... Mr. Marc PETERSON
39 Asst VP Student Aff/Dean of Housing .... Dr. Troy T. BEHRENS
13 Chief Information Officer .... Mr. Joe GARGIULO
38 Director of Counseling Services .... Dr. Cathey SOUTTER
23 Assoc Dean of Health Services .... Vacant
04 Ex Ast to Pres/Ex Dir Inst Acc/Eqt .... Ms. Samantha THOMAS
09 Director of Institutional Research .... Dr. Michael D. TUMEO
88 Treasurer/Chief Investment Officer .... Mr. Michael A. CONDON
96 Director of Procurement .... Mr. Terrence CONNOR
42 University Chaplain .... Dr. Stephen RANKIN
24 Asst Dean Central Univ Libraries .... Dr. Bill DWORACZYK
29 Exec Dir Alumni Relations .... Ms. Marianne B. PIEPENBURG
12 Executive Director SMU-in-Taos .... Mr. Michael ADLER
12 Campus Director SMU-in-Plano .... Ms. Kate LIVINGSTON
104 Director Study Abroad .... Dr. Catherine WINNIE
108 Director Assessment/Accreditation .... Dr. Patricia ALVEY
18 Assoc VP Facilities Plng/Management .... Mr. Philip JABOUR
27 Ex Director of Integrated Marketing .... Mr. Neil ROBINSON
19 Chief of Police .... Mr. Richard SHAFER
22 Dir Institutional Access and Equity .... Ms. Carolyn HERNANDEZ

Southwest Texas Junior College (A)

2401 Garner Field Road, Uvalde TX 78801-6221

County: Uvalde | FICE Identification: 003614 | Unit ID: 228316
Telephone: (830) 278-4401 | Carnegie Class: Assoc/Pub-R-M
FAX Number: (830) 591-7354 | Calendar System: Semester
URL: www.swtjc.net
Established: 1946 | Annual Undergrad Tuition & Fees (In-District): $266,2.5
Enrollment: 5,572 | Coed
Affiliation or Control: Local | IRS Status: 501(c)3
Highest Offering: Associate Degree
Program: Occupational; 2-Year Principally Bachelor's Creditable
Accreditation: SC

01 President .... Dr. Hector GONZALES
11 Vice President Administrative Svcs .... Mr. Joe BARKER
32 Vice President Student Services .... Mrs. Margo MATA
10 Vice President Finance .... Dr. Anne TARSKI
05 Vice President Academic Services .... Dr. Mark UNDERWOOD
30 AVP Institutional Advancement .... Vacant
12 Vice President Del Rio .... Mr. Derek M. SANDOVAL
12 Vice President Eagle Pass .... Mr. Gilbert S. BERMEA
88 Dean of College of Applied Science .... Mr. Juan Johnny C. GUZMAN
103 Dean of Workforce Education .... Ms. Romelia ARANDA
49 Dean of College of Liberal Arts .... Dr. Cheryl L. SANCHEZ
35 Director of Academic Advising .... Ms. Lorena LOPEZ
37 Director of Financial Aid .... Ms. Yvette HERNANDEZ
13 Director of Information Technology .... Mr. Agustin C. ALEJANDRO
18 Physical Plant Director .... Mr. Jesus J. MARTINEZ
35 Director Student Success .... Ms. Randa SCHELL
15 Human Resources Coordinator .... Mr. Oscar S. GARCIA
09 Director of Institutional Research .... Ms. Carol LARUE
06 Registrar .... Mr. Luis FERNANDEZ
08 Head Librarian .... Ms. Karen BAEN
19 Director Security/Safety .... Mr. Robert DOUCET
96 Director of Purchasing .... Ms. Maggie CAMSTRA

Southwest University at El Paso (B)

1414 Geronimo Drive, El Paso TX 79925

County: El Paso | FICE Identification: 041317 | Unit ID: 451556
Telephone: (915) 778-4001 | Carnegie Class: Assoc/PrivFP
FAX Number: (915) 778-1575 | Calendar System: Other
URL: www.southwestuniversity.edu
Established: 2001 | Annual Undergrad Tuition & Fees: N/A
Enrollment: 1,337 | Coed
Affiliation or Control: Proprietary | IRS Status: Proprietary
Highest Offering: Baccalaureate
Program: Occupational
Accreditation: ABHES, DMS, RAD

01 School Director .... Mr. Benjamin ARRIOLA

Southwestern Adventist University (C)

PO Box 567, 100 W Hillcrest St, Keene TX 76059-0567

County: Johnson | FICE Identification: 003619 | Unit ID: 228468
Telephone: (817) 645-3921 | Carnegie Class: Bac/Diverse
FAX Number: (817) 202-6744 | Calendar System: Semester
URL: www.swau.edu
Established: 1893 | Annual Undergrad Tuition & Fees: $19,916
Enrollment: 800 | Coed
Affiliation or Control: Seventh-day Adventist | IRS Status: 501(c)3
Highest Offering: Master's
Program: Liberal Arts And General; Teacher Preparatory; Professional
Accreditation: SC, IACBE, NURSE

01 President .... Dr. Ken SHAW
05 VP for Academic Administration .... Dr. Amy ROSENTHAL
10 VP for Financial Administration .... Mr. Joel WALLACE
84 VP for Enrollment .... Ms. Enga ALMEIDA
32 VP for Student Services .... Mr. James THE
42 VP for Spiritual Development .... Mr. Russ LAUGHLIN
30 Interim VP for Univ Advancement .... Mrs. Tiffany HERNANDEZ
09 Director of Institutional Research .... Dr. Thomas G. BUNCH
37 Asst VP for Student Finance .... Ms. Patricia A. NORWOOD
21 Asst VP Financial Administration .... Mr. Greg A. WICKLUND
06 Registrar .... Dr. Robert GARDNER
08 Librarian .... Ms. Cristina M. THOMSEN
34 Dean of Women .... Mrs. Janelle D. WILLIAMS
33 Dean of Men .... Mr. William IVERSON
13 Dir Information Technology Svcs .... Mr. E. Charles LEWIS
18 Plant Engineer .... Mr. Dale E. HAINEY
26 Director of Marketing .... Ms. Darcy FORCE
29 Director of Alumni Relations .... Vacant
38 Director of Counseling & Testing .... Dr. R. Mark ALDRIDGE
88 Director of Disability Services .... Mrs. Dorie CRUZ
88 Dir Ctr for Acad Success/Advising .... Dr. Andrew SMITH
07 Director of Admissions .... Ms. Rahneeka HAZELTON
15 Director of Human Resources .... Mrs. Denise RIVERA
19 Director Security/Safety .... Mr. Sean AMOS

Southwestern Assemblies of God University (D)

1200 Sycamore, Waxahachie TX 75165-2397

County: Ellis | FICE Identification: 003616 | Unit ID: 228325
Telephone: (972) 937-4010 | Carnegie Class: Master's S
FAX Number: (972) 923-0488 | Calendar System: Semester
URL: www.sagu.edu
Established: 1927 | Annual Undergrad Tuition & Fees: $20,530
Enrollment: 1,984 | Coed
Affiliation or Control: Assemblies Of God Church | IRS Status: 501(c)3
Highest Offering: Doctorate
Program: Liberal Arts And General; Teacher Preparatory; Religious Emphasis
Accreditation: SC

01 President .... Dr. Kermit S. BRIDGES
05 Vice President for Academics .... Dr. Paul BROOKS
32 Vice President for Student Services .... Rev. Terry PHIPPS
10 Vice Pres for Business & Finance .... Rev. David W. WILLEMSEN
30 Vice President for Univ Advancement .... Rev. Irby MCKNIGHT
84 Vice Pres Enrollment & Retention .... Rev. Eddie DAVIS
20 Dean of Academic Services .... Rev. Donny LUTRICK
58 Dean of Graduate Studies .... Dr. Robert HARDEN
73 Dean Col Bible & Church Ministries .... Dr. Michael CLARENSAU
50 Dean Col of Business & Education .... Dr. Larry GOODRICH
64 Dean Col of Music & Comm Arts .... Mr. Del GUYNES
09 Assoc Dean of Inst Effectiveness .... Dr. Kim BERNECKER
106 Asst Dean for Distance Education .... Rev. Joseph HARTMAN
06 Registrar .... Ms. Heather FRANCIS
35 Dean of Students .... Rev. Lance MECHE
89 Asst Dean for Student Success .... Rev. Rob BLAKNEY
88 Director of Learning Centers .... Mr. Nolan JONES
13 Sr Dir Information Technology .... Mr. James GRISSOM
29 Director of Alumni Relations .... Mr. Devin FERGUSON
08 Director of Learning Resources .... Mr. Eugene HOLDER
14 Director of Campus Software .... Mr. Mark WALKER
21 Dir of Business Services .... Mr. Landon ORRILL
88 Senior Director of Accounting .... Ms. Candee LUTRICK
37 Sr Director of Financial Aid .... Mr. Jeff FRANCIS
19 Director of Security .... Mr. Ron CRANE
07 Assistant Dean of Admissions .... Mr. Joshua MARTIN
24 Director of Media Services .... Mr. John COOKMAN
88 Director of Accounts Receivable .... Mr. Chris BACA
44 Sr Dir of Dev & Planned Giving .... Mr. Craig RINAS
36 Director of Career Services .... Ms. Beverly ROBINSON
41 Athletic Director .... Mr. Jesse GODDING
26 Director of University Marketing .... Mr. Ryan MCELHANY
15 Director of Human Resources .... Mrs. Ruth ROBERTS
88 Director of Educator Cert .... Ms. Janice WHITAKER
18 Projects Manager .... Mr. James DAVIS
38 Counselor .... Dr. Tim MYERS
88 Admissions Counselor .... Ms. Pat THOMPSON
88 Director of On Campus Admissions .... Vacant
88 Director of Online Admissions .... Mr. Jarrod PACE
04 Executive Asst to President .... Ms. Patricia BROOKS

Southwestern Baptist Theological Seminary (E)

PO Box 22607, Fort Worth TX 76122-0150

County: Tarrant | FICE Identification: 003617 | Unit ID: 228477
Telephone: (817) 923-1921 | Carnegie Class: Spec/Faith
FAX Number: (817) 921-8766 | Calendar System: Semester
URL: www.swbts.edu
Established: 1908 | Annual Undergrad Tuition & Fees: $8,340
Enrollment: 3,580 | Coed
Affiliation or Control: Southern Baptist | IRS Status: 501(c)3
Highest Offering: Doctorate
Program: Professional; Religious Emphasis
Accreditation: SC, MUS, THEOL

01 President .... Dr. Paige PATTERSON
05 Executive Vice President/Provost .... Dr. Craig A. BLAISING
10 Vice Pres Business Administration .... Mr. Kevin ENSLEY
30 Vice Pres Institutional Advancement .... Mr. Mike C. HUGHES
32 Vice Pres for Student Services/Comm .... Dr. Steven SMITH
108 Assoc VP Inst Assessment .... Dr. Mark LEEDS
45 Vice Pres of Strategic Initiatives .... Dr. Charles PATRICK
73 Dean of the School of Theology .... Dr. David ALLEN
53 Dean Sch of Church & Fam Ministries .... Dr. Waylan OWENS
64 Dean School of Church Music .... Dr. Leo DAY
12 Dean Havard Sch for Theol Studies .... Dr. Denny AUTREY
73 Dean Sch of Evangelism & Missions .... Dr. Keith EITEL
49 Dean College at Southwestern .... Dr. Mike WILKINSON
94 Dean of Women's Programs .... Dr. Terri STOVALL
56 Dean Center for Extension Education .... Dr. Deron BILES
35 Dean of Students .... Mr. Kyle WALKER

Southwestern Christian College (F)

Box 10, Terrell TX 75160-9002

County: Kaufman | FICE Identification: 003618 | Unit ID: 228486
Telephone: (972) 524-3341 | Carnegie Class: Bac/Assoc
FAX Number: (972) 563-7133 | Calendar System: Semester
URL: www.swcc.edu
Established: 1949 | Annual Undergrad Tuition & Fees: $7,764
Enrollment: 164 | Coed
Affiliation or Control: Churches Of Christ | IRS Status: 501(c)3
Highest Offering: Baccalaureate
Program: Liberal Arts And General
Accreditation: SC

01 President .... Dr. Jack EVANS, SR.
30 Vice President for Instl Expansion .... Dr. James MAXWELL
05 Vice President Academic Affairs .... Mrs. Zoa Ann TURNER
10 Vice President Fiscal Affairs .... Mr. Douglas HOWIE
32 Vice President Student Affairs .... Mr. Ben FOSTER
08 Librarian .... Mrs. Doris JOHNSON
07 Director of Admissions .... Mr. Warren ROBERTS
37 Director of Financial Aid .... Ms. Tanya DEAN
44 Director of Development .... Mr. Jack EVANS, JR.

Southwestern University (G)

1001 E University Avenue, Georgetown TX 78626-6144

County: Williamson | FICE Identification: 003620 | Unit ID: 228343
Telephone: (512) 863-6511 | Carnegie Class: Bac/A&S
FAX Number: (512) 863-5788 | Calendar System: Semester
URL: www.southwestern.edu
Established: 1840 | Annual Undergrad Tuition & Fees: $37,560
Enrollment: 1,538 | Coed
Affiliation or Control: United Methodist | IRS Status: 501(c)3
Highest Offering: Baccalaureate
Program: Liberal Arts And General; Teacher Preparatory
Accreditation: SC, MUS

01 President .... Dr. Edward B. BURGER
42 University Chaplain .... Rev. Megan DAVIDSON
04 Executive Asst to the President .... Ms. Francie SCHROEDER
05 Dean of Faculty .... Dr. Alisa GAUNDER
32 Vice President for Student Life .... Mr. Gerald D. BRODY
13 VP for Information Services and CIO .... Dr. Pam MCQUESTEN
10 VP for Finance and Administration .... Mr. Craig ERWIN
30 Vice Pres for University Relations .... Mr. Paul SECORD
20 Assoc VP Academic Administration .... Ms. Julie A. COWLEY
26 Chief Marketing Officer .... Mr. Gabe GOMEZ
18 Assoc VP for Facility/Campus Svcs .... Mr. Bob D. MATHIS
15 Assoc VP for Human Resources .... Ms. Elma F. BENAVIDES
39 Dean of Students/Dir Resident Life .... Ms. Jaime WOODY
29 Assoc VP for Alumni & Parents .... Ms. Megan FRISQUE
41 Assoc VP/Dir Intercollegiate Athl .... Dr. Glada C. MUNT
108 Assc Dean Faculty Devel/Inst Assess .... Dr. John MCCANN
21 Controller .... Ms. Brenda THOMPSON
19 Chief of Police .... Ms. Deborah BROWN
37 Director of Financial Aid .... Mr. James GAETA
36 Director Career Services .... Mr. Daniel OROZCO
20 Assoc Dir Academic Success .... Mr. David SEILER
88 Dir Paideia Program/Assoc Professor .... Dr. Sherry E. ADRIAN
85 Director Intercultural Learning .... Ms. Tisha TEMPLE
38 Director Counseling/Health Services .... Vacant
18 Director Physical Plant .... Mr. Joe LEPAGE
09 Director Institutional Research .... Mr. Trey BUCHANAN
28 Asst Dean Multicultural Affairs .... Ms. Terri JOHNSON
31 Director Civic Engagement .... Dr. Sarah BRACKMANN
07 Director of Admission .... Mr. Robert BALDWIN

Stephen F. Austin State University (A)

2008 Alumni Drive, Rusk 206,
Nacogdoches TX 75961-3940
County: Nacogdoches FICE Identification: 003624
Unit ID: 228431
Telephone: (936) 468-2011 Carnegie Class: Master's L
FAX Number: (936) 468-2202 Calendar System: Semester
URL: www.sfasu.edu
Established: 1921 Annual Undergrad Tuition & Fees (In-State): $9,312
Enrollment: 12,801 Coed
Affiliation or Control: State IRS Status: 501(c)3
Highest Offering: Doctorate
Program: Liberal Arts And General; Teacher Preparatory; Professional
Accreditation: SC, AAFCS, ART, BUS, CAATE, CACREP, CEA, CIDA, CORE, CS, DIETD, DIETI, MUS, NUR, SP, SW, TED, THEA

01 President Dr. Baker PATTILLO
05 Interim Provost/VP Academic Affairs Dr. Stephen A. BULLARD
10 Vice Pres Finance/Administration Mr. Danny R. GALLANT
32 Vice Pres for University Affairs Dr. Steve WESTBROOK
30 Vice Pres University Advancement Ms. Jill STILL
29 Exec Director Alumni Mr. Craig A. TURNAGE
20 Assoc Provost/VP Academic Affairs Dr. Mary Nelle BRUNSON
84 Exec Dir of Enrollment Management Ms. Monique COSSICH
26 Exec Dir Univ Mktg Comm Ms. Shirley A. LUNA
43 General Counsel Mr. Damon DERRICK
06 Registrar Ms. Lynda LANGHAM
09 Director Institutional Research Ms. Karyn HALL
08 Library Director Ms. Shirley DICKERSON
39 Director of Residence Life Mr. Winston BAKER
18 Director of Physical Plant Mr. Lee BRITTAIN
37 Director of Financial Aid Ms. Rachele GARRETT
22 Director Affirmative Action Ms. Glenda HERRINGTON
13 Director of ITS Mr. Paul DAVIS
15 Director of Human Resources Ms. Glenda HERRINGTON
19 Chief of University Police Mr. Marc COSSICH
23 Director Health Services Dr. Penny JEFFERY
41 Director of Intercol Athletics Mr. Robert W. HILL
35 Dean Student Affairs Dr. Adam PECK
36 Director of Counseling Ms. Jill MILEM
96 Director of Procurement Ms. Diana BOUBEL
45 Dir Research/Sponsored Programs Dr. Carrie BROWN
28 Director Multicultural Affairs Dr. Osaro AIREN
58 Dean Graduate School Dr. Richard BERRY
49 Dean College Liberal/Applied Arts Dr. Brian MURPHY
47 Dean College Forestry/Agriculture Dr. Steven BULLARD
53 Dean of College of Education Dr. Judy A. ABBOTT
57 Dean College Fine Arts Dr. A.C. (Buddy) HIMES
50 Dean College of Business Dr. Timothy BISPING
81 Dean College Sciences & Math Dr. Kimberly M. CHILDS
04 Special Asst to President Ms. Susan H. WILLLIAMS
101 Coordinator of Board Affairs Ms. Judith P. BUCKINGHAM
102 Exec Director of Development Mr. Joel L. TURNER, III
104 Director International Programs Ms. Heather CATTON
105 University Webmaster Mr. Jason L. JOHNSTONE
106 Director Instructional Technology Dr. Randy MCDONALD
108 Director Institutional Assessment Dr. Larry J. KING
38 Asst Dean Stdnt Affairs Support Dr. Michael E. WALKER
07 Associate Director of Admissions Mr. Kevin L. DAVIS

Tarrant County College District (B)

1500 Houston Street, Fort Worth TX 76102-6599
County: Tarrant FICE Identification: 003626
Unit ID: 228547
Telephone: (817) 515-5100 Carnegie Class: Assoc/Pub-U-MC
FAX Number: (817) 515-5350 Calendar System: Semester
URL: www.tccd.edu
Established: 1965 Annual Undergrad Tuition & Fees (In-District): $1,650
Enrollment: 50,595 Coed
Affiliation or Control: State/Local IRS Status: 501(c)3
Highest Offering: Associate Degree
Program: Occupational; 2-Year Principally Bachelor's Creditable
Accreditation: SC, ACFEI, ADNUR, CAHIIM, COARC, CONST, DH, DIETT, EMT, PTAA, RAD, SURGT

01 Chancellor Mrs. Erma C. JOHNSON HADLEY
11 Vice Chanc Admin and Gen Counsel Mrs. Angela ROBINSON
10 Vice Chancellor for Finance Mr. Mark MCCLENDON
13 Vice Chanc Info/Technical Services Mr. Timothy (Tim) MARSHALL
05 Vice Chanc Acad Affs/Stdnt Success Dr. L. Joy GATES BLACK
18 Vice Chanc Real Estate/Facilities Ms. Nina PETTY
26 VC Communications/External Affairs Mr. Reginald GATES
20 VP Academic Affairs SO Dr. Steven H. WILSON
20 VP Academic Affairs NE Mr. Gary SMITH
20 VP Academic Affairs NW Dr. Leann ELLIS
20 VP Academic Affairs SE Dr. Zena JACKSON
20 VP Academic Affairs TR Dr. Bryan STEWART
20 VP Academic Affairs TCC Connect Dr. Kelvin BENTLEY
32 VP Student Dev Services NE Dr. Magdalena DELA TEJA
32 VP Student Dev Services SE Dr. Lyvier LEFFLER
32 VP Student Dev Services SO Dr. Larry RIDEAUX
32 VP Student Dev Services TR Mr. Adrian RODRIGUEZ
32 VP Student Dev Services NW Dr. Joe RODE
32 VP Acad Outreach & SS TCC Connect Dr. Aubra J. GANNT
12 President South Campus Dr. Peter JORDAN
12 President Northwest Campus Dr. Elva C. LEBLANC
12 President Northeast Campus Dr. Allen GOBEN
12 President Southeast Campus Dr. William COPPOLA
12 President Trinity River Campus Dr. Tahita M. FULKERSON
12 President TCC Connect Dr. Carlos MORALES
84 Assoc Vice Chanc Enrollment Svcs Mr. David XIMENEZ
88 Assoc Vice Chanc Student Success Dr. Jade BORNE
15 Assoc Vice Chanc Human Resources Dr. Ricardo CORONADO
25 Assoc Vice Chanc Grants Dev/Compl Ms. Jackie MAKI
21 Assoc Vice Chancellor Finance Mrs. Nancy H. CHANG
20 Assoc Vice Chanc Academic Affairs Dr. Nancy CURE
103 Assoc Vice Chanc Econ/Workforce Dev Vacant
30 Executive Director of Development Dr. Joe MCINTOSH
09 Exec Dir Inst Intell Rsrch Dr. Rosemary REYNOLDS
27 Director Public Rels/Marketing Ms. Suzanne COTTRAUX
18 Assoc Vice Chan Real Estate/Facs Mr. Gary PREATHER
19 Chief of Police Mr. Shaun WILLIAMS
20 Dir Academic Support Services Suzanne CARTER
20 Dir Curriculum Dev/Intl Initiative Sheryl HARRIS
56 Director Distance Learning Vacant
08 Director Library Services NE Mr. Mark DOLIVE
08 Director Library Services SO Ms. Linda JENSON
08 Director Library Services NW Ms. Kristyn S. HELGE
08 Director Library Services SE Ms. Jotisa KLEMM
08 Director Library Services TR Ms. Suzanne BECKETT
06 Registrar South Campus Mr. Samuel (Tex) RUEGG
06 Registrar Northeast Campus Mr. Brian D. BARRETT
06 Registrar Northwest Campus Ms. Rebecca (Becki) GRIFFITH
06 Registrar Southeast Campus Mr. Juan C. TORRES
06 Registrar Trinity Campus Mr. Vikas RAJPUROHIT
38 Director of Counseling SO Dr. Jade BORNE
38 Director of Counseling NE Dr. Condoa PARRENT
38 Director of Counseling NW Dr. Charles (Ricks) EDMONDSON
38 Director of Counseling SE Dr. Michael DUPONT
38 Director of Counseling TR Dr. Louann T. SCHULZE
37 District Director Financial Aid Ms. Samantha STALNAKER
37 Director of Financial Aid SO Ms. JoLynn F. SPROLE
37 Director of Financial Aid NE Ms. Mary BLEDSOE
37 Director of Financial Aid NW Ms. Trina SMITH-PATTERSON
37 Director of Financial Aid SE Ms. Elizabeth LANDWERMEYER
37 Director of Financial Aid TR Mr. William MCMULLEN
35 Dir Student Develop Svcs NE Mr. Victor BALLESTEROS
35 Dir Student Develop Svcs SO Mr. Jared COBB
35 Dir Student Develop Svcs NW Ms. Vesta M. MARTINEZ
35 Dir Student Develop Svcs SE Mr. Douglas C. PEAK
35 Dir Student Develop Svcs TR Ms. Mayra OLIVARES-URUETA
96 Director of Business Services Mrs. Kathy CRUSTO-WAY
96 Director of Procurement Mr. Michael (Mike) HERNDON
18 Exec Dir Inst Strat Dev Ms. Margaret K. LUTTON
07 Director of Admissions & Records Ms. Nichole MANCONE

Temple College (C)

2600 S First Street, Temple TX 76504-7435
County: Bell FICE Identification: 003627
Unit ID: 228608
Telephone: (254) 298-8282 Carnegie Class: Assoc/Pub-R-M
FAX Number: (254) 298-8266 Calendar System: Semester
URL: www.templejc.edu
Established: 1926 Annual Undergrad Tuition & Fees (In-District): $2,670
Enrollment: 5,200 Coed
Affiliation or Control: Local IRS Status: 501(c)3
Highest Offering: Associate Degree
Program: Occupational; 2-Year Principally Bachelor's Creditable
Accreditation: SC, ADNUR, COARC, DH, DMS, EMT, SURGT

01 President Dr. Glenda O. BARRON
05 Vice Pres of Educational Services Dr. Mark A. SMITH
13 AVP Information Technology Services Mr. Gary JACKSON
11 Vice Pres Administrative Services Dr. Van MILLER
31 AVP Acad Outreach & Ext Programs Dr. Dan SPENCER
15 Assoc VP Resource Management Dr. Randy BACA
09 AVP Comm Init & Spec Programs Dr. Jimmy ROBERTS
106 Dir Web Applications & System Mr. Joe TEAKELL
84 Div Dir Student & Enrollment Svcs Mrs. Carey ROSE
08 Div Director of Learning Resources Mr. Kevin HENARD
102 Exec Dir Temple College Foundation Mrs. Jennifer GRAHAM
38 Director Student Advising Ms. Amy FLINN
04 Assistant to the President & Board Mrs. Judith DOHNALIK
37 Director of Financial Aid Ms. Peggy WATTS
26 Director Marketing & Media Relation Ms. Erin SPENCER
18 Dir Facilities/Physical Plant Mr. Skeet POWELL
96 Director of Purchasing Mr. Brian SUPAK
32 Chief Student Life Officer Mrs. Ruth BRIDGES
06 Registrar Mrs. Toni CUELLAR
41 Athletic Director Mr. Craig MCMURTRY
19 Chief of Police Mr. Michael MARKUM

Texarkana College (D)

2500 N Robison Road, Texarkana TX 75501-3099
County: Bowie FICE Identification: 003628
Unit ID: 228699
Telephone: (903) 823-3456 Carnegie Class: Assoc/Pub-R-M
FAX Number: (903) 823-3451 Calendar System: Semester
URL: www.texarkanacollege.edu
Established: 1927 Annual Undergrad Tuition & Fees (In-District): $2,420
Enrollment: 4,061 Coed
Affiliation or Control: Local IRS Status: 501(c)3
Highest Offering: Associate Degree
Program: Occupational; 2-Year Principally Bachelor's Creditable
Accreditation: SC, ADNUR

01 President Mr. James H. RUSSELL
05 Vice President of Instruction Mrs. Donna MCDANIEL
10 Chief Finance Officer Mrs. Kim JONES
32 Dean of Students Mr. Robert JONES
13 Chief Info Technology Officer Mr. Mike DUMDEI
30 Director Foundation/Development Mrs. Katie ANDRUS
09 Director Inst Rsrch & Effectiveness Mrs. Jamie ASHBY
18 Director Facilities Services Mr. Rick BOYETTE
26 Director Inst Adv/Public Relations Mrs. Suzy IRWIN
88 Director KTXK Radio Mr. Steve MITCHELL
15 Director Human Resources Mrs. Phyllis DEESE
103 Dean Workforce & Cont Education Mrs. Ronda DOZIER
81 Dean STEM Dr. Catherine HOWARD
76 Dean Health Sciences Mrs. Courtney SHOALMIRE
49 Dean Liberal & Performing Arts Mrs. Mary E. YOUNG
07 Director of Admissions Mr. Lee WILLIAMS
88 Director Advising & Registration Mr. Brandon HIGGINS
08 Director Library/Student Support Dr. Tonja MACKEY
06 Registrar Mrs. Kristi COBB
37 Director Student Financial Aid Mrs. Susan JOHNSTON
04 Presidential Events Coordinator Mrs. Mindy PRESTON

*The Texas A & M University System Office (E)

301 Tarrow Street, 7th Floor, College Station TX 77840
County: Brazos FICE Identification: 003629
Unit ID: 228732
Telephone: (979) 458-6000 Carnegie Class: N/A
FAX Number: (979) 458-6044
URL: www.tamus.edu

01 Chancellor Mr. John SHARP
05 Vice Chanc for Academic Affairs Dr. James HALLMARK
86 Vice Chanc for Federal & State Rels Mr. Tommy WILLIAMS
10 Exec VC & Chief Financial Officer Mr. Billy HAMILTON
26 Vice Chanc for Marketing & Comm Ms. Terry MCDEVITT
88 Chief Auditor Ms. Cathy SMOCK
43 General Counsel Mr. Ray BONILLA
46 Vice Chancellor for Research Dr. Jon MOGFORD
21 Vice Chanc for Business Affairs Mr. Phillip RAY
13 Chief Information Officer Mr. Mark STONE
21 Treasurer Ms. Maria ROBINSON
100 Exec Assistant to the Chancellor Ms. Trudy BENNETT

*Prairie View A & M University (F)

P.O. Box 519, Prairie View TX 77446-0519
County: Waller FICE Identification: 003630
Unit ID: 227526
Telephone: (936) 261-3311 Carnegie Class: Master's L
FAX Number: (936) 261-2115 Calendar System: Semester
URL: www.pvamu.edu
Established: 1876 Annual Undergrad Tuition & Fees (In-State): $8,638
Enrollment: 8,429 Coed
Affiliation or Control: State IRS Status: 501(c)3
Highest Offering: Doctorate
Program: Liberal Arts And General; Teacher Preparatory; Professional
Accreditation: SC, BUS, CS, DIETD, DIETI, ENG, ENGT, MUS, NUR, NURSE, SW, TED

02 President Dr. George C. WRIGHT
05 Provost/Sr VP Academic Affairs Dr. Felicia M. NAVE
20 Assoc Prov & Assoc VP Acad Afairs Dr. James J. WILSON, JR.
92 Director of Honors Program Dr. James J. WILSON, JR.
10 Sr Vice President Business Affairs Dr. Corey S. BRADFORD, SR.
32 VP for Student Affs/Inst Relations Dr. Lauretta F. BYARS
46 Vice President Research/Development Dr. Willie F. TROTTY
11 Vice Pres Administration/Aux Svcs Mr. Fred E. WASHINGTON
20 Vice President of Business Admin Dr. Michael L. MCFRAZIER
84 Assoc Provost Enrollment Mgmt Mr. Don BYARS
21 Asst VP for Financial Accounting Mr. Rod MIRELES
21 Asst VP for Financial Services Ms. Patricia BAUGHMAN
30 Director of Development Vacant
09 Director Institutional Research Mr. Dean WILLIAMSON
07 Int Dir of Undergraduate Admissions Ms. Lenice BROWN
18 Int Assistant VP of Physical Plant Mr. Charles MUSE
08 Director of Library Dr. Rosie L. ALBRITTON
15 Director of Human Resources Ms. Radhika AYYAR
37 Director of Financial Aid Vacant
36 Program Coord Residence Life Mr. Charles E. CROCKETT
63 Director Undergrad Med Acad Dr. Dennis E. DANIELS
41 Director of Athletics Mr. Ashley N. ROBINSON
13 Chief Information Officer Mr. Rodney MOORE
58 Dean of the Graduate School Dr. Willie F. TROTTY
50 Dean College of Business Dr. Munir QUDDUS
53 Dean College of Education Dr. Terence HICKS
54 Dean College of Engineering Dr. Kendall T. HARRIS
47 Dean Col Agriculture/Human Sci Dr. Alton B. JOHNSON
66 Dean College of Nursing Dr. Betty ADAMS
49 Dean College of Arts & Sciences Dr. Danny R. KELLEY
48 Dean School of Architecture Dr. Ikhlas SABOUNI
88 Dean Col of Juv Just/Psychology Dr. Tamara L. BROWN
21 Director of Treasury Services Ms. Equilla JACKSON
23 Director Health Center Ms. Thelma J. PIERRE
56 Administrator Coop Extension Dr. Carolyn J. WILLIAMS
19 Chief of Police Ms. Zena A. STEPHENS
109 Asst VP Auxiliary Enterprises Ms. Tressey D. WILSON
29 Alumni/Special Events Officer Ms. Carol CAMPBELL
06 Registrar/Records Ms. Deborah J. DUNGEY
12 Exec Dir University College Ms. Lettie M. RAAB
28 Director of Diversity Ms. Elma D. GONZALEZ
85 Immigration Services Coord Ms. Evelyn J. MCGINTY
96 Procurement Sup/HUB Coordinator Mr. Jim A. NELMS
88 Director Budget & Reconciliation Mrs. Diane T. EVANS

*Tarleton State University (A)

1333 W Washington, Box T-0001,
Stephenville TX 76402-0001
County: Erath FICE Identification: 003631
Unit ID: 228529
Telephone: (254) 968-9000 Carnegie Class: Master's L
FAX Number: (254) 968-9920 Calendar System: Semester
URL: www.tarleton.edu
Established: 1899 Annual Undergrad Tuition & Fees (In-State): $6,877
Enrollment: 11,681 Coed
Affiliation or Control: State IRS Status: 501(c)3
Highest Offering: Doctorate
Program: Liberal Arts And General; Teacher Preparatory
Accreditation: SC, ACBSP, DMOLS, ENG, HT, MLTAD, MT, MUS, NURSE, SW

02 President ... Dr. F. Dominic DOTTAVIO
100 Chief of Staff ... Dr. David WEISSENBURGER
05 Provost/Exec VPAA ... Dr. Karen MURRAY
30 Vice Pres Inst Advancement ... Dr. Kyle W. MCGREGOR
10 Vice Pres Finance/Administration ... Mr. Tye MINCKLER
32 VP Student Life/Dean Students ... Ms. Laura BOREN
84 Assoc VP Enrollment/Inform Mgmt ... Dr. Javier GARZA
20 Assoc VP for Academic Affairs ... Dr. Dwayne SNIDER
36 Director of Career Services ... Ms. Alana HEFNER
46 Assoc VP Academic Research/Grants ... Dr. Bert LITTLE
18 Director of Facilities ... Mr. Aaron WAND
21 Asst VP Finance/Administration ... Vacant
35 AVP Student Success/Multicul Init ... Dr. Jennifer T. EDWARDS
26 Assoc VP Marketing/Communications ... Ms. Janice HORAK
35 Asst VP Student Life Studies ... Dr. Ashley TULL
21 Director Business Svcs/Controller ... Ms. Lori BEATY
49 Dean College Science & Technology ... Dr. James PIERCE
50 Dean Col of Business Administration ... Dr. Steve STEED
47 Dean Col Agricul & Environ Sciences ... Dr. Donald L. CAWTHON
53 Dean College of Education ... Dr. Jordan BARKLEY
57 Dean College Liberal/Fine Arts ... Ms. Kelli STYRON
58 Dean College of Graduate Studies ... Dr. Barry LAMBERT
07 Director Undergraduate Admissions ... Ms. Cynthia HESS
28 Dir Student Disability Services ... Ms. Trina GEYE
08 University Librarian ... Mrs. Donna SAVAGE
31 Asst VP External Relations ... Ms. Janice HORAK
37 Director Student Financial Aid ... Ms. Kathy PURVIS
09 Director Institutional Research ... Dr. Mike HAYNES
13 CIO/Exec Dir Information Tech Svcs ... Ms. Rebecca GRAY
15 Asst VP Employee Services ... Ms. Angela C. BROWN
35 Asst VP for Student Life ... Ms. Darla DOTY
41 Athletic Director ... Mr. Lonn REISMAN
23 Director Student Health Center ... Ms. Bridgette BEDNARZ
19 University Police Chief ... Mr. Matt WELCH
88 Exec Dir of Student Engagement ... Mr. Darrell BROWN
28 Dir Ofc Diversity/Inclusion ... Dr. Lora HELVIE-MASON
24 Dir Center for Instr Innovation ... Dr. Kelli SHAFFER
44 Asst VP of Advancement ... Ms. Sabra GUERRA
104 Dir International Academic Programs ... Dr. Marilyn ROBITAILLE
06 Registrar ... Ms. Susan STOKER
96 Director of Purchasing/HUB ... Ms. Elaine CHEW
25 Contract Specialist ... Ms. Kim MEDFORD
40 Manager Campus Store ... Ms. Carrie MCCANN
105 Web Administrator ... Ms. Daphne HUNT
04 Administrative Asst to President ... Ms. Tauna BERTSCH
29 Director Alumni Relations ... Ms. Jessica EVANS

*Texas A & M International University (B)

5201 University Boulevard, Laredo TX 78041-1900
County: Webb FICE Identification: 009651
Unit ID: 226152
Telephone: (956) 326-2001 Carnegie Class: Master's L
FAX Number: (956) 326-2348 Calendar System: Semester
URL: www.tamiu.edu
Established: 1969 Annual Undergrad Tuition & Fees (In-State): $7,990
Enrollment: 7,554 Coed
Affiliation or Control: State IRS Status: 501(c)3
Highest Offering: Doctorate
Program: Liberal Arts And General; Teacher Preparatory
Accreditation: SC, BUS, NUR, SPAA

02 President ... Dr. Ray M. KECK, III
05 Provost/Vice Pres Academic Affs ... Dr. Pablo ARENAZ
10 Vice Pres Finance & Administration ... Mr. Juan J. CASTILLO, JR.
30 Vice Pres Institutional Advancement ... Ms. Rosanne PALACIOS
32 Vice Pres for Student Success ... Dr. Minita RAMIREZ
20 Assoc Vice Pres Academic Affairs ... Mrs. Mary T. TREVINO
11 Assoc Vice Pres for Administration ... Mr. Trevor C. LIDDLE
88 Assoc Vice Pres for Compliance ... Mrs. Lisa M. PAUL
13 Assoc VP Information Technology/CIO ... Dr. Leebrian E. GASKINS
88 Associate Provost ... Dr. Kevin D. LINDBERG
49 Dean College Arts & Sciences ... Dr. Thomas R. MITCHELL
50 Dean AR Sanchez Jr Sch of Business ... Dr. Steve R. SEARS
66 Dean Canseco School of Nursing ... Dr. Glenda C. WALKER
08 Dir Sue & Radcliffe Killam Library ... Mr. Douglas M. FERRIER
07 Director Admissions ... Mrs. Rosie A. DICKINSON
06 University Registrar ... Mr. Juan G. GARCIA, JR.
15 Director of Human Resources ... Ms. Martha O. GONZALEZ
26 Director Public Rels Mktg/Info Svcs ... Mr. Steve K. HARMON
37 Director Financial Aid ... Mrs. Laura M. ELIZONDO
41 Director of Athletics ... Mr. Gilbert G. ZIMMERMANN
18 Director Physical Plant ... Mr. Roberto A. GARZA
29 Director Alumni Relations ... Mrs. Yelitza M. HOWARD
36 Executive Director Career Services ... Mrs. Cassandra L. WHEELER
23 Interim Dir of SHS/CI Asst Prof ... Ms. Angelica M. MICHELANGELI
39 Director of Residence Life/Housing ... Ms. Mirasol TABAREZ
38 Dir Student Couns/Disb Svcs ... Ms. Aracely C. HERNANDEZ
96 Dir Purchasing & Support Services ... Ms. Ann E. GUTIERREZ
92 Assoc Prof Director Honors Pgm ... Dr. Deborah L. BLACKWELL
21 Comptroller ... Ms. Elena M. MARTINEZ
35 Associate VP of Student Affairs ... Mr. Gerardo ALVA
88 Dir Recruitment/School Relations ... Ms. Scheiby C. FISHER
88 Assoc Dir Student Orien Lead Engage ... Mr. Miguel A. TREVINO
09 Director of Institutional Research ... Ms. Elizabeth MARTINEZ

*Texas A & M University (C)

1246 TAMU, College Station TX 77843-1246
County: Brazos FICE Identification: 003632
Unit ID: 228723
Telephone: (979) 845-2217 Carnegie Class: RU/VH
FAX Number: (979) 845-5027 Calendar System: Semester
URL: www.tamu.edu
Established: 1876 Annual Undergrad Tuition & Fees (In-State): $9,428
Enrollment: 62,392 Coed
Affiliation or Control: State IRS Status: 501(c)3
Highest Offering: Doctorate
Program: Liberal Arts And General; Teacher Preparatory; Professional
Accreditation: SC, BUS, BUSA, CAATE, CEA, CLPSY, CONST, COPSY, CS, DENT, DH, DIETD, DIETI, ENG, ENGT, FEPAC, HSA, IPSY, LAW, LSAR, MED, NRPA, NURSE, PH, PLNG, SCPSY, SPAA, VET

02 President ... Mr. Michael K. YOUNG
05 Provost/Exec Vice President ... Dr. Karan L. WATSON
03 Interim Exec VP & CEO HSC ... Dr. Paul E. OGDEN
05 HSC VP Academic Affairs ... Dr. Vernon L. TESH
10 VP Finance & Administration (CFO) ... Dr. Jerry STRAWSER
32 VP Student Affairs ... Dr. Daniel J. PUGH, SR.
46 VP Research ... Dr. Glen A. LAINE
26 Int VP Marketing/Communications ... Mr. Shane HINCKLEY
86 VP Governmental Relations ... Mr. Michael O'QUINN
86 HSC VP Governmental Affairs ... Ms. Jenny E. JONES
88 HSC VP Public Health Prep & Resp . Dr. Gerald W. PARKER, JR.
12 VP TAMU/Pres TAMU-Galveston ... RAdm. Robert SMITH, III
28 Vice Pres/Assoc Prov Diversity ... Dr. Christine A. STANLEY
20 Vice Provost for Academic Affairs ... Dr. Michael BENEDIK
43 Deputy General Counsel ... Mr. Scott A. KELLY
47 Dean Agriculture & Life Science ... Dr. Mark A. HUSSEY
48 Dean Architecture ... Dr. Jorge VANEGAS
50 Dean Business ... Dr. Eli JONES
52 Dean Dentistry ... Dr. Lawrence E. WOLINSKY
53 Dean Education & Human Development ... Dr. Joyce M. ALEXANDER
54 Dean Engineering ... Dr. M. Katherine BANKS
65 Dean Geosciences ... Dr. Kate C. MILLER
80 Dean Govt & Public Policy ... Mr. Ryan C. CROCKER
61 Dean Law ... Dr. Andrew P. MORRISS
49 Dean Liberal Arts ... Dr. Pamela R. MATTHEWS
63 Int Dean Med/HSC VP Clinical Affs ... Dr. Paul E. OGDEN
66 Dean Nursing ... Dr. Sharon A. WILKERSON
67 Dean Pharmacy ... Dr. Indra K. REDDY
69 Dean Public Health ... Dr. Jay MADDOCK
81 Dean Science ... Dr. Meigan C. ARONSON
74 Dean Vet Med & Biomed Sciences ... Dr. Eleanor M. GREEN
08 Dean/Director Libraries ... Mr. David H. CARLSON
88 HSC Dir Inst Biosciences & Tech ... Dr. Cheryl L. WALKER
12 Dean & CEO Texas A&M at Qatar ... Dr. Mark H. WEICHOLD
20 Int Dean of Faculties/Assoc Prov ... Dr. Blanca LUPIANI
20 Assoc Prov Undergrad Studies ... Dr. Ann KENIMER
107 Assoc Prov Grad & Prof Studies ... Dr. Karen L. BUTLER-PURRY
13 Int Assoc VP & CIO ... Mr. Scott A. HONEA
07 Dir Admissions/Asst VP Acad Svcs ... Mr. Scott MCDONALD
37 Exec Dir Student Financial Aid ... Ms. Delisa F. FALKS
06 Registrar ... Ms. Venesa A. HEIDICK
36 Exec Dir Career Center ... Dr. J. Leigh TURNER
15 Exec Dir Human Resources ... Ms. Janelle R. RAMIREZ
14 Exec Dir Computing & Info Svcs ... Mr. Pete MARCHBANKS
23 Director Student Health Center ... Dr. Martha C. DANNENBAUM
38 Exec Dir Student Counseling Svcs ... Dr. Maggie GARTNER
39 Director Residence Life/Housing ... Ms. Chareny L. RYDL
92 Exec Director Honors Programs ... Dr. Sumana DATTA
104 Director Study Abroad ... Dr. Jane FLAHERTY
96 Exec Director Strategic Sourcing ... Mr. Rex JANNE
09 Exec Dir Data & Research Svcs ... Dr. David J. MARTIN
102 President Texas A&M Foundation ... Dr. Eddie J. DAVIS
29 Pres Assoc of Former Students ... Mr. Porter GARNER
100 Liaison to the President ... Ms. Jessica RUBIE
100 HSC Chief of Staff to Exec VP/CEO ... Ms. Patricia HAIGWOOD
19 Chief University Police ... Mr. J Michael E. REAGAN
41 Athletic Director ... Mr. Eric C. HYMAN

*Texas A & M University - Central Texas (D)

1001 Leadership Place, Killeen TX 76549
County: Bell Identification: 667086
Unit ID: 483036
Telephone: (245) 519-5400 Carnegie Class: Not Classified
FAX Number: (245) 519-5482 Calendar System: Semester
URL: www.tamuct.edu
Established: 1999 Annual Undergrad Tuition & Fees (In-State): $5,877
Enrollment: 2,316 Coed
Affiliation or Control: State IRS Status: 501(c)3
Highest Offering: Master's
Program: Liberal Arts And General
Accreditation: SC, ACBSP, @SW

02 President ... Dr. Marc A. NIGLIAZZO
04 Administrative Asst to President ... Ms. Donna J. DOBSON
05 Chief Academic Officer ... Dr. Peg GRAY-VICKREY
07 Director of Admissions ... Mr. Clifton JONES
08 Head Librarian ... Ms. Bridgit MCCAFFERTY
09 Director of Institutional Research ... Dr. Troy COURVILLE
10 Chief Business Officer ... Ms. Gaylene NUNN
13 Chief Info Technology Officer (CIO) ... Mr. Todd LUTZ
15 Director Personnel Services ... Mr. Charlie ROSENBLUM
18 Chief Facilities/Physical Plant ... Mr. Chadd WINTERBURG
22 Dir Affirmative Action/EEO ... Ms. Deserie RIVERA
26 Chief Public Relations/Marketing ... Mr. Randy MCCAULEY
30 Exec Dir Advancement & Alumni Svcs ... Dr. Karén CLOS
32 Chief Student Affairs/Student Life ... Mr. Brandon GRIGGS
36 Director Student Placement ... Ms. Cortina MERRITT
37 Director Student Financial Aid ... Mr. Clifton JONES
50 Dean of Business ... Dr. Larry GARNER
53 Dean of Education ... Dr. Jeff KIRK
86 Director Government Relations ... Dr. Tracy TEAFF
49 Dean of Arts & Science ... Dr. Jerry JONES
88 Director of Military Programs ... Dr. S. Stephen VITUCCI

*Texas A & M University - Commerce (E)

PO Box 3011, Commerce TX 75429-3011
County: Hunt FICE Identification: 003565
Unit ID: 224554
Telephone: (903) 886-5102 Carnegie Class: DRU
FAX Number: (903) 886-5888 Calendar System: Semester
URL: www.tamuc.edu
Established: 1889 Annual Undergrad Tuition & Fees (In-State): $6,202
Enrollment: 12,111 Coed
Affiliation or Control: State IRS Status: 501(c)3
Highest Offering: Doctorate
Program: Liberal Arts And General; Teacher Preparatory; Professional
Accreditation: SC, ART, BUS, CACREP, ENG, MUS, NURSE, SW

02 President ... Dr. Dan JONES
05 Provost/VP Academic Affairs ... Dr. Adolfo BENAVIDES
10 Vice Pres Business & Administration ... Ms. Alicia CURRIN
35 VP for Student Access & Success ... Dr. Mary HENDRIX
30 Vice Pres Institutional Advancement ... Mr. Randy VAN DEVEN
100 Chief of Staff ... Ms. Linda KING
31 Dir Media Relations & Cmty Engage ... Mr. Noah NELSON
26 Exec Director Mktg Communications ... Ms. Lisa MARTINEZ
41 Athletic Director ... Mr. Ryan IVEY
28 Chief Diversity Officer ... Dr. Edward W. ROMERO
20 Interim Assoc Provost Academic Affs ... Dr. Betty A. BLOCK
20 Interim Asst Provost Academic Affrs ... Dr. Madeline JUSTICE
20 Assoc VP Student Access & Success ... Dr. Sharon JOHNSON
09 Assoc Prov of Inst Effectiveness ... Dr. Marila PALMER
84 Dean of Enrollment & Retention ... Ms. Dina SOSA-HEGARTY
21 Assoc VP Business Admin/Comptroller ... Ms. Paula HANSON
21 Executive Dir of Budget & Fin Rep ... Ms. Tina LIVINGSTON
06 Registrar ... Ms. Paige BUSSELL
88 Dir of Acct & Financial Reporting ... Ms. Sarah BAKER
08 Library Director ... Mr. Gregory MITCHELL
13 Chief Information Officer ... Mr. Tim MURPHY
37 Director of Financial Aid ... Ms. Maria RAMOS
36 Director of Career Development ... Mrs. Tina BOITNOTT
58 Vice Prov of Research/Dean of Grad ... Dr. Arlene HORNE
53 Dean Education & Human Services ... Dr. Tim LETZRING
79 Dean of Humanities/Soc Sci & Art ... Dr. Salvatore ATTARDO
92 Dean of the Honors College ... Dr. Ray GREEN
81 Dean of Science & Engineering ... Dr. Brent DONHAM
50 Dean of Business ... Dr. Steve WILLIAMS
88 Dean of University College ... Dr. Ricky DOBBS
07 Director of Undergraduate Admiss ... Mr. Jody TODHUNTER
108 Director of Student Assessment ... Ms. Wendy GRUVER
32 Asst VP/Dean Campus Life/Stdnt Dev ... Mr. John KAULFUS
29 Director of Alumni Relations ... Mr. Derryle PEACE
19 University Police Chief ... Mrs. Donna SPINATO
12 Director Metroplex Center ... Mr. Russell BLANCHETT
12 Director Navarro Partnership ... Ms. Jeanetta GROCE
12 Rockwall Site Coordinator ... Mr. Chris WARNER
12 Exec Dir Universities Ctr at Dallas ... Dr. Berri O'NEAL
38 Director Counseling Center ... Dr. Linda T. CLINTON
39 Dir Residential Living & Learning ... Mr. Michael STARK
88 Dir of Safety & Risk Management ... Mr. Derek PREAS
21 Director of Emerging Financial Svcs ... Ms. Cheryl SCOTT
23 Director Student Health Services ... Ms. Maxine MENDOZA-WELCH
85 Dir International Student Services ... Mr. John Mark JONES
96 Director of Purchasing/HUB Coord ... Mr. Travis BALL
04 Assistant to the President ... Ms. Rhonda FERGUSON
104 Dir Global Programs/Study Abroad ... Mr. Jacques FUQUA
105 Web Application Developer ... Mr. Rick BARR
15 Chief Human Resource Officer ... Mrs. Barbara CORVEY
88 Chief Compliance Officer ... Ms. Heidi R. WRIGHT
18 Exec Dir Facilities Support Svcs ... Mr. David MCKENNA
22 Title IX Administrator ... Mrs. Michele VIEIRA
44 Assoc Dir of Annual/Special Pgms ... Mrs. Stephanie FIORISI

*Texas A & M University - Corpus Christi (F)

6300 Ocean Drive, Corpus Christi TX 78412
County: Nueces FICE Identification: 011161
Unit ID: 224147
Telephone: (361) 825-5700 Carnegie Class: DRU
FAX Number: (361) 825-5887 Calendar System: Semester

URL: www.tamucc.edu
Established: 1947 Annual Undergrad Tuition & Fees (In-State): $8,621
Enrollment: 11,234 Coed
Affiliation or Control: State IRS Status: 501(c)3
Highest Offering: Doctorate
Program: Liberal Arts And General; Teacher Preparatory; Professional
Accreditation: SC, BUS, BUSA, CAATE, CACREP, CS, ENGR, ENGT, MT, MUS, NURSE

02	President/CEO	Dr. Flavius C. KILLEBREW
05	Int Prov/VP for Acad Affairs	Dr. Kelly QUINTANILLA
10	Int Exec VP for Finance/Admin	Mr. Terry TATUM
30	Vice Pres Institutional Advancement	Dr. S. Trent HILL
32	VP Student Engagement & Success	Dr. Don ALBRECHT
46	VP Rsrch/Commercialization/Outreach	Dr. Luis CIFUENTES
20	Vice Provost Academic Affairs	Dr. Paul MEYER
100	Chief of Staff	Dr. Mary SHERWOOD
13	Int Assoc VP Info Technology/CIO	Mr. Edward EVANS
20	Assoc VP for Academic Affairs	Dr. David BILLEAUX
84	Assoc VP Enrollment Management	Ms. Margaret DECHANT
35	Assoc Vice Pres/Dean of Students	Ms. Ann DEGAISH
20	Assoc VP Academic Affairs	Ms. Christine SHUPALA
08	Director Bell Library	Dr. Catherine RUDOWSKY
09	Assoc VP Planning & Inst Research	Dr. Leona URBISH
26	Director of Marketing	Ms. Ashley LARRABEE
29	Exec Director Development	Ms. Jill JACOBS
06	Univ Registrar/Dir Veterans Affrs	Mr. Michael RENDON
07	Exec Director of Admissions	Mr. Oscar REYNA
37	Director of Financial Assistance	Ms. Jeannie GAGE
31	Int Director Community Outreach	Mr. Joseph MILLER
15	Director Human Resources	Ms. Debra CORTINAS
44	Director Annual Giving	Ms. Evon ENGLISH
36	Director Career Services	Ms. Terri HOWE
38	Dir Student Counseling/Development	Dr. Carla BERKICH
28	Dir Employee Develop/Compliance Svc	Mr. Sam RAMIREZ
11	Exec Dir Administrative Services	Ms. Judy HARRAL
96	Dir Procurement & Disbursements	Mr. Will HOBART
21	Bursar	Ms. Christina HOLZHEUSER
58	Dean College of Grad Studies	Dr. Jo Ann CANALES
49	Int Dean College of Liberal Arts	Dr. Mark HARTLAUB
50	Dean College of Business	Dr. John E. GAMBLE
53	Dean College of Education	Dr. Arthur HERNANDEZ
54	Dean College of Science & Engrng	Dr. Frank PEZOLD
66	Dean College of Nursing/Health Sci	Dr. Mary Jane HAMILTON

*Texas A & M University - Kingsville (A)

700 University Boulevard, Kingsville TX 78363-8202
County: Kleberg FICE Identification: 003639
Unit ID: 228705
Telephone: (361) 593-2111 Carnegie Class: DRU
FAX Number: (361) 593-3107 Calendar System: Semester
URL: www.tamuk.edu
Established: 1925 Annual Undergrad Tuition & Fees (In-State): $7,554
Enrollment: 8,728 Coed
Affiliation or Control: State IRS Status: 501(c)3
Highest Offering: Doctorate
Program: Liberal Arts And General; Teacher Preparatory; Fine Arts Emphasis
Accreditation: SC, CS, DIETD, DIETI, ENG, MUS, NAIT, PHAR, SP, SW

02	President	Dr. Steven H. TALLANT
100	Chief of Staff	Mr. Randy HUGHES
43	Director of Compliance	Ms. Karen B. ROYAL
05	Int Provost & Vice Pres Acad Affs	Dr. Duane GARDINER
10	Sr VP Fiscal Affairs	Dr. Terisa RILEY
88	Assistant Director of Budgets	Ms. Jennifer ALEXANDER
88	Comptroller	Ms. Lallah M. HOWARD
88	Risk Management	Dr. Shane CREEL
36	Exec Director of Career Services	Mr. Christian FERRIS
32	Vice President Student Affairs	Dr. Terisa C. RILEY
109	Director of Auxiliary Services	Mr. Crispin TREVINO
88	Dir of Campus Rec & Fitness	Mr. Charles ESPINOSA
84	VP Enrollment Management	Mr. Manuel LUJAN
13	Chief Information Officer	Mr. Robert PAULSON
14	Assoc CIO	Mr. Lonnie NAGEL
88	Dir Enterprise Applications	Mr. Lee MOORE
88	Dir IT Client Support Services	Mr. Val RAMIREZ
35	Dean of Students	Ms. Kristin COMPARY
20	Associate VP Academic Affairs	Dr. Duane GARDINER
85	Dir International Studies	Mr. Peter LI
88	Dir Center Teaching Effectiveness	Dr. Jaya GOSWAMI
58	Assoc VP Research & Grad Studies	Dr. Mohamed ABDELRAHMAN
88	Asst VP Student Access	Dr. Mary GONZALEZ
47	Dean Agriculture/Nat Res/Human Sci	Dr. George A. RASMUSSEN
49	Dean Arts & Sciences	Dr. Dolores GUERRERO
50	Dean Business Administration	Dr. Natalya DELCOURE
53	Dean Education & Human Performance	Dr. Alberto RUIZ
54	Dean Engineering	Dr. Stephan NIX
89	Assoc VP for Student Success	Dr. Nancy KING SANDERS
26	Exec Dir Markting/Communications	Ms. Cheryl CAIN
08	Librarian	Mr. Bruce R. SCHUENAMAN
108	Dir Planning & Assessment	Vacant
88	Director Citrus Center	Dr. John DA GRACA
88	Director King Ranch Institute	Dr. Clay P. MATHIS
88	Exec Director CKWRI	Dr. Fred BRYANT
88	Interim Dir Nat Toxins Res Ctr	Dr. Elda E. SANCHEZ
88	Director Inst Sust Energy & Env	Dr. Kim JONES
06	Registrar	Mr. George WEIR
07	Interim Dir of Admission	Ms. Jennifer MINKE
29	Director Development and Alumni Rel	Vacant
41	VP Intercollegiate Athletics & Camp	Mr. Scott GINES
40	Director Bookstore	Ms. Mary GUTIERREZ
106	Director Distance Learning	Ms. Michelle DURAN
44	Exec Dir Development & Alumni	Ms. Lori RUSSEK
88	Interim Dir Health and Wellness	Ms. Jo Elda CASTILLO-ALANIZ
09	Director Institutional Research	Ms. Miao ZHUANG
88	Director John E Conner Museum	Mr. Jonathan PLANT
15	Exec Dir HR & Payroll	Mr. Leon BAZAR
18	Director Physical Plant	Mr. Roberto RAMIREZ
96	Assoc VP Support Services	Mr. Ralph STEPHENS
25	Contract Administrator	Ms. Rachel L. BUENTELLO
39	Director Residence Life	Mr. Tom MARTIN
46	Exec Dir Research & Sponsored Pgms	Dr. Rebecca DAVIS
35	Interim Director Student Activities	Ms. Erin MCCLURE
19	Director of University Police	Mr. Felipe GARZA
37	Director Student Financial Aid	Ms. Jessica THOMAS
38	Director Student Counseling	Vacant
21	Supervisor Business Services	Ms. Janet L. POLLARD
88	Advisor Pre-profession Programs	Ms. Amanda MUNIZ
88	Bible Chair Baptist	Mr. Mike CERVANTES
88	Bible Chair Catholic	Mr. Victor RODRIGUEZ
04	Administrative Asst to President	Ms. Margie GALVAN
104	Director Study Abroad	Ms. Marilu SALAZAR

*Texas A & M University-San Antonio (B)

One University Way, San Antonio TX 78224
County: Bexar Identification: 666689
Unit ID: 22870501
Telephone: (210) 784-1000 Carnegie Class: Not Classified
FAX Number: (210) 784-6219 Calendar System: Semester
URL: www.tamusa.edu
Established: 2009 Annual Undergrad Tuition & Fees (In-District): $7,313
Enrollment: 4,521 Coed
Affiliation or Control: State/Local IRS Status: 501(c)3
Highest Offering: Master's
Program: Liberal Arts And General
Accreditation: SC

02	President	Dr. Cynthia TENIENTE-MATSON
05	Provost/VP Academic Affairs	Dr. Brent M. SNOW
10	Vice Pres Finance/Administration	Mr. Darrell MORRISON
32	Vice President for Student Affairs	Dr. Melissa MAHAN
26	Assc VP Univ Comm/Inst Advance	Ms. Marilu A. REYNA
09	Director of Institutional Research	Ms. Jane MIMS
50	Dean College of Business	Dr. Tracy HURLEY
49	Dean College of Arts & Sciences	Dr. Mirley BALASUBRAMANYA
53	Dean College of Education & Devel	Dr. Eric LOPEZ

*Texas A & M University - Texarkana (C)

7101 University Avenue, Texarkana TX 75503
County: Bowie FICE Identification: 031703
Unit ID: 224545
Telephone: (903) 223-3000 Carnegie Class: Master's L
FAX Number: (903) 832-8890 Calendar System: Semester
URL: www.tamut.edu
Established: 1971 Annual Undergrad Tuition & Fees (In-State): $6,734
Enrollment: 1,865 Coed
Affiliation or Control: State IRS Status: 501(c)3
Highest Offering: Doctorate
Program: Liberal Arts And General; Professional
Accreditation: SC, CACREP, NURSE

02	President	Dr. Emily FOURMY CUTRER
05	Provost/Vice Pres Academic Affairs	Dr. Rosanne STRIPLING
10	VP Finance & Administration	Mr. James SCOGIN
32	Asst Vice Pres for Student Success	Mrs. Elizabeth PATTERSON
30	Assoc VP University Advancement	Mrs. LeAnne WRIGHT
84	AVP Enrollment Management	Vacant
100	Chief of Staff President's Office	Mrs. Vicki HUCKABEE
13	Chief Information Technology	Mr. Jeff HINTON
20	Assoc Provost/SACSCOC Liaison	Dr. Nancy JORDAN
88	Interim Dean College of STEM	Dr. Donald PETERSON
53	Dean College Education/Liberal Art	Dr. Glenda BALLARD
50	Dean College of Business	Dr. Gary STADING
21	Controller	Mrs. Jackie ELDER
37	Dir Financial Aid & Veteran Svcs	Mr. Michael FULLER
15	Director Human Resources & EEO	Mr. Ricky NORTON
08	Director Library	Mrs. Teri STOVER
18	Director Physical Plant	Mr. Jeff PIERCE
18	Police Chief/Director Security	Mr. John GANN
96	Director Purchasing	Mrs. Cynthia HENDERSON
88	Director Payroll	Mrs. Ramona GREEN
35	Director Student & Career Services	Mr. Carl GREIG
84	Director Enrollment Management	Mr. Toney FAVORS
26	Director Communications	Ms. Carol LANGSTON
58	Dean of Graduate Studies & Research	Dr. William MCHENRY
41	Director of Athletics	Mr. Michael GALVAN

*West Texas A & M University (D)

2403 Russell C. Long Blvd., Canyon TX 79015
County: Randall FICE Identification: 003665
Unit ID: 229814
Telephone: (806) 651-0000 Carnegie Class: Master's L
FAX Number: (806) 651-2126 Calendar System: Semester
URL: www.wtamu.edu
Established: 1910 Annual Undergrad Tuition & Fees (In-State): $7,430
Enrollment: 8,970 Coed
Affiliation or Control: State IRS Status: 501(c)3
Highest Offering: Doctorate
Program: Liberal Arts And General; Teacher Preparatory; Professional; Business Emphasis
Accreditation: SC, BUS, CAATE, CS, ENG, MUS, NURSE, SP, SW, THEA

02	President/CEO	Dr. J. Patrick O'BRIEN
05	Provost/Vice Pres Acad Affairs	Dr. Wade SHAFFER
10	Vice Pres for Business and Finance	Mr. Randy RIKEL
32	Vice President for Student Affairs	Mr. Michael J. KNOX
30	Vice Pres Institutional Advancement	Mr. Tim BYNUM
84	Vice Pres of Enrollment Management	Mr. Dan D. GARCIA
28	Chief Diversity/Inclusion Officer	Ms. Angela ALLEN
06	Registrar	Ms. Tana J. MILLER
07	Director of Admissions	Mr. Kyle MOORE
08	Dir Information/Library Resources	Ms. Shawna J. KENNEDY-WITTHAR
36	Dir Career Planning/Placement	Ms. Denese SKINNER
37	Director Student Financial Aid	Ms. Marian K. GIESECKE
51	Dir Education on Demand	Ms. Andrea PORTER
23	Director Medical Service	Dr. Jim GIBBS
19	Police Chief	Chief Shawn G. BURNS
27	Director Communication Services	Ms. Ann UNDERWOOD
29	Director of Alumni Relations	Ms. Becky STOGNER
38	Director Counseling Services	Mr. Orvie NIX
41	Director of Athletics	Mr. Michael MCBROOM
09	Director Institutional Research	Mr. Jarvis D. HAMPTON
13	Chief Information Officer	Mr. James D. WEBB
96	Director of Purchasing	Mr. Brian GLENN
40	Manager Bookstore	Mr. Terry S. NEPPER
15	Director Personnel Services	Mr. Harvey L. HUDSPETH
47	Interim Dean Col Agr/Science/Eng	Dr. Doug BINGHAM
50	Dean College of Business	Dr. Neil W. TERRY
53	Dean Col Education & Social Science	Dr. Eddie W. HENDERSON
57	Dean College Fine Arts/Humanities	Dr. Jessica MALLARD
46	VP for Research & Compliance	Dr. Angela SPAULDING
66	Dean College of Nursing/Health Sci	Dr. Dirk NELSON
104	Director Study Abroad	Ms. Carolina GALLOWAY
04	Administrative Asst to President	Ms. Tracee POST

*Texas A & M University at Galveston (E)

PO Box 1675, Galveston TX 77553-1675
Telephone: (409) 740-4400 FICE Identification: 010298
Accreditation: &SC, ENG, ENGT

† Regional accreditation is carried under the parent institution Texas A & M University, College Station, TX.

Texas Chiropractic College (F)

5912 Spencer Highway, Pasadena TX 77505-1699
County: Harris FICE Identification: 003635
Unit ID: 228866
Telephone: (281) 487-1170 Carnegie Class: Spec/Health
FAX Number: (281) 487-2009 Calendar System: Trimester
URL: www.txchiro.edu
Established: 1908 Annual Undergrad Tuition & Fees: N/A
Enrollment: 260 Coed
Affiliation or Control: Independent Non-Profit IRS Status: 501(c)3
Highest Offering: Doctorate
Program: Professional
Accreditation: SC, CHIRO

01	President	Dr. Brad MCKECHNIE
10	Chief Financial Officer	Mr. Bill QUINN
05	VP of Academic Affairs	Dr. Steve FOSTER
20	Dean of Academic Affairs	Dr. John MROZEK
84	VP of Enrollment Management	Dr. Fred ZUKER
06	Registrar	Dr. Karlene DENBY
15	Director of Human Resources	Mrs. Sue ARNOLD
26	Director of Communications	Mr. Max ARCHER
09	Dir Inst Research & Accreditation	Dr. Lee VANDUSEN
88	Dean of Postgraduate Studies	Dr. Paul JASKOVIAK
08	Director of Library Services	Ms. Carol WEBB
37	Director Financial Aid	Mr. Arthur GOUDEAU
29	Director of Alumni Relations	Ms. Gabrielle GREENWADE
32	Director of Student Services	Ms. Kristina HANSON
07	Director of Admission	Ms. Monique LEWIS
04	Admin Asst to President	Ms. Glenda RAMIREZ
18	Physical Plant Supervisor	Mr. Perry LATIOLAIS

Texas Christian University (G)

2800 S University Drive, Fort Worth TX 76129-2800
County: Tarrant FICE Identification: 003636
Unit ID: 228875
Telephone: (817) 257-7000 Carnegie Class: DRU
FAX Number: (817) 257-7333 Calendar System: Semester
URL: www.tcu.edu
Established: 1873 Annual Undergrad Tuition & Fees: $40,720
Enrollment: 10,033 Coed
Affiliation or Control: Christian Church (Disciples Of Christ)
IRS Status: 501(c)3
Highest Offering: Doctorate
Program: Liberal Arts And General; Teacher Preparatory; Professional
Accreditation: SC, ANEST, ART, BUS, BUSA, CAATE, CIDA, CS, DANCE, DIETC, DIETD, ENG, JOUR, MUS, NURSE, SP, SW

01 Chancellor .... Dr. Victor J. BOSCHINI, JR.
05 Provost/Vice Chanc Academic Affairs ...... Dr. R. Nowell DONOVAN
10 Vice Chanc Finance & Administration .... Mr. Brian G. GUTIERREZ
30 Vice Chanc University Advancement . Mr. Donald J. WHELAN, JR.
32 Vice Chancellor Student Affairs .... Dr. Kathryn CAVINS-TULL
26 Vice Chanc Mktg & Communication ..... Ms. Tracy SYLER-JONES
15 Vice Chancellor Human Resources .... Ms. Karen M. BAKER
41 Director Athletics .... Mr. Christopher DEL CONTE
88 Chief Investment Officer .... Mr. Jim HILLE
13 Chief Technology Officer .... Mr. Bryan LUCAS
88 Chief University Compliance Officer .... Ms. Andrea NORDMANN
100 Chief of Staff .... Ms. Jean MRASEK
88 Chancellor's Intern .... Mr. Michael MARSHALL
29 Assoc Vice Chanc Alumni Relations .... Ms. Kristi M. HOBAN
88 Assoc Vice Chanc Advancement Ops .... Dr. Roby V. KEY
16 Assoc Vice Chanc Human Resources .... Ms. Faith PERKINS
35 Assoc VC/Dean Student Development ...... Dr. Barbara B. HERMAN
35 Assoc Vice Chanc/Dean Campus Life .... Dr. David COZZENS
21 Assoc Vice Chanc & Controller .... Ms. Cheryl L. WILSON
18 Assoc Vice Chanc for Facilities .... Mr. Todd S. WALDVOGEL
88 Associate VC Donor Relations .... Julie WHITT
35 Assoc VC of Student Affairs .... Mr. Darron TURNER
44 Assoc VC University Development .... Mr. David NOLAN
88 Asst VC School & College Develop .... Mr. Adam BAGGS
20 Assoc Provost Research .... Dr. Bonnie MELHART
20 Assoc Provost Academic Support .... Dr. Leo W. MUNSON
20 Asst Provost Academic Plng/Budget .... Ms. Megan M. SOYER
09 Assoc Provost Inst Effectiveness .... Dr. Catherine WEHLBURG
88 Assoc Provost Devel Academic Future .... Dr. David WHILLOCK
49 Dean Addran College of Liberal Arts .... Dr. Andrew SCHOOLMASTER
50 Dean Neeley School of Business .... Dr. Homer EREKSON
60 Dn Bob Schieffer Col Communication .... Dr. Kristie BUNTON
53 Dean College of Education .... Dr. Mary PATTON
57 Dean College of Fine Arts .... Dr. Ann HELMREICH
66 Dean Harris Col Nurs/Hlth Science .... Dr. Susan WEEKS
54 Dean Col of Science & Engineering .... Dr. Phil HARTMAN
92 Act Dn John V Roach Honors College .... Dr. Sarah ROBBINS
08 Dean of the Library .... Dr. June KOELKER
07 Dean of Admission .... Mr. Raymond A. BROWN
22 Affirmative Action Officer .... Mr. Darron TURNER
06 Registrar/Dir Enrollment Management .... Mr. Patrick MILLER
19 Chief TCU Police .... Mr. Steve G. MCGEE
42 Minister to the University .... Rev. Angela KAUFMAN
21 Asst Vice Chanc Finance .... Mr. Kenneth JANAK
106 Asst Provost of Educ Tech/Fac Dev .... Ms. Romana HUGHES
85 Director International Education .... Dr. Jane KUCKO
25 Director Contract Administration .... Mr. Matthew WALLIS
16 Director Employee Relations .... Ms. Kristen TAYLOR
51 Director Extended Education .... Mr. David A. GREBEL
88 Assoc Dean Dir Freshman Admission .... Mr. Heath EINSTEIN
88 Director Transfer Admission .... Ms. Amanda NICKERSON
23 Director Health Services .... Dr. Jane TORGERSON
09 Director Institutional Research .... Dr. Cathan COGHLAN
24 Director Instructional Services .... Mr. Larry E. KITCHENS
85 Director International Student Svcs .... Mr. John L. SINGLETON
38 Director Mental Health Services .... Dr. Linda WOLSZON
96 Warehouse/Purchasing Agent .... Mr. Roger D. FULLER
39 Director Housing & Residential Life .... Mr. Craig ALLEN
37 Dir Scholarships & Financial Aid .... Mr. Michael H. SCOTT
105 Director Website Management .... Mr. Victor NEIL
25 Director Sponsored Programs .... Ms. Linda FREED
36 Exec Director Career Services .... Dr. John THOMPSON

Texas College (A)

2404 N Grand Avenue, Tyler TX 75702-1962
County: Smith — FICE Identification: 003638
Unit ID: 228884
Telephone: (903) 593-8311 — Carnegie Class: Bac/Diverse
FAX Number: (903) 593-0588 — Calendar System: Semester
URL: www.texascollege.edu
Established: 1894 — Annual Undergrad Tuition & Fees: $10,008
Enrollment: 804 — Coed
Affiliation or Control: Christian Methodist Episcopal — IRS Status: 501(c)3
Highest Offering: Baccalaureate
Program: 2-Year Principally Bachelor's Creditable; Liberal Arts And General; Teacher Preparatory
Accreditation: SC

01 President .... Dr. Dwight FENNELL
05 Vice President Academic Affairs .... Dr. Cynthia MARSHALL-BIGGINS
10 Vice Pres Business & Finance .... Mr. James HARRIS
32 Vice Pres Student Affairs .... Mr. Edgar BERRY
30 Development Officer .... Mrs. Angelia FENNELL
07 Dean of Enrollment Services .... Mr. John ROBERTS
35 Dean of Admission .... Mr. Isaac WILLIAMS
06 Registrar .... Mr. John ROBERTS
09 Dir Inst Research/ Effectiveness .... Dr. Cynthia MARSHALL-BIGGINS
08 Director of Library Services .... Mrs. Linda SIMMONS-HENRY
13 Director of Information Technology .... Mr. Carl SCOTT
15 Director Human Resources .... Ms. Lois BOWIE
21 Comptroller .... Mr. Walter MOSLEY
36 Coord Counseling & Career Services .... Vacant
41 Athletic Director .... Ms. Elissia BURWELL
37 Director Financial Aid .... Mrs. Angela SPEECH
18 Director Physical Plant .... Mr. Forrest CURRY
26 Coordinator Public Relations .... Ms. Christie HOWARD
29 Coordinator Alumni Affairs .... Ms. Orenthia MASON
88 Asst to VP for AA/Dean Lower Col .... Dr. Robert HARPER

Texas Health and Science University (B)

4005 Manchaca Road, Austin TX 78704-6737
County: Travis — FICE Identification: 031795
Unit ID: 430704
Telephone: (512) 444-8082 — Carnegie Class: Spec/Health
FAX Number: (512) 444-6345 — Calendar System: Trimester
URL: www.thsu.edu
Established: 1990 — Annual Undergrad Tuition & Fees: $16,000
Enrollment: 94 — Coed
Affiliation or Control: Proprietary — IRS Status: Proprietary
Highest Offering: Master's; No Lower Division
Program: Professional
Accreditation: ACICS, ACUP

01 President .... Ms. Lisa LIN
05 Academic Dean/Biomed Dir/DAOM Dir .... Dr. Maoyi CAI
20 Vice Pres of Academics/Assessment .... Dr. David G. VEQUIST
10 Opers Dir Budget/Human Resources .... Mr. Paul LIN
11 Senior Administrator .... Ms. Wai Lan KUO
37 Fin Aid Ofcr/Dean of Stu/Safety Of .... Mr. Chris ATKINS
07 Admissions Coordinator .... Mr. Kai-Chang CHAN
88 Director Acupuncture Deparment .... Dr. Hai Tao CAO
88 Director of Herbal Department .... Ms. Jiahe JIN
08 Librarian/Systems Administrator .... Mr. Ryan HAECKER
46 Dir of Research/Clinic Director .... Dr. Lin-Ying TAN
06 Registrar/Administrator .... Ms. Julia DANG

† Offers a doctorate degree but ACICS's scope of recognition by USDE & CHEA does not currently include doctorate degrees.

Texas Lutheran University (C)

1000 W Court Street, Seguin TX 78155-5999
County: Guadalupe — FICE Identification: 003641
Unit ID: 228981
Telephone: (830) 372-8000 — Carnegie Class: Bac/Diverse
FAX Number: (830) 372-8096 — Calendar System: Semester
URL: www.tlu.edu
Established: 1891 — Annual Undergrad Tuition & Fees: $27,900
Enrollment: 1,320 — Coed
Affiliation or Control: Evangelical Lutheran Church In America — IRS Status: 501(c)3
Highest Offering: Master's
Program: Liberal Arts And General; Professional
Accreditation: SC, ACBSP, CAATE, MUS, TEAC

01 President .... Dr. Stuart B. DORSEY
05 Vice Pres for Academic Affairs .... Dr. Debbie COTTRELL
11 Asst to Pres Admin/Public Affairs ...... Mr. Stephen P. ANDERSON
10 Vice President Finance .... Mr. Andrew NELSON
84 Vice President Enrollment Services .... Mr. Thomas OLIVER
30 VP for Development/Alumni Relations .... Mr. Rick ROBERTS
32 VP/Dean of Student Life & Learning .... Ms. Kristi QUIROS
26 Vice President for Marketing Comm .... Ms. Sarah STORY
06 Director of Records & Registration .... Mr. Glenn YOCKEY
08 Library Director .... Ms. Martha RINN
37 Director of Financial Aid .... Vacant
42 Campus Pastor .... Rev. Kara STEWART
36 Director Career Development .... Vacant
38 Director Counseling Services .... Ms. Terry WEERS
07 Director of Admissions .... Mr. Adam NAVARRO-JUSINO
15 Director Personnel Services .... Mr. Andrew VASQUEZ
41 Director of Athletics .... Mr. Bill MILLER
09 Director of Institutional Research .... Ms. Jean CONSTABLE
04 Exec Assistant to the President .... Ms. Susan RINN
101 Secretary of the Institution/Board .... Ms. Susan RINN
102 Dir Foundation/Corporate Relations .... Mr. Sam EHRLICH
103 Interim Director Career Development .... Ms. Breane NAVARRO
104 Director Study Abroad .... Ms. Charla BAILEY
105 Director Web Services .... Ms. Jenni MORIN
108 Director Institutional Assessment .... Dr. Michael CZUCHRY
13 Chief Info Technology Officer (CIO) .... Mr. William SENTER
18 Chief Facilities/Physical Plant .... Mr. Kirk HERBOLD
19 University Police Chief .... Chief Gary HOPPER
29 Director Alumni Relations .... Ms. Taylor CARLETON
39 Director of Residence Life .... Mr. Kyle WYCH
44 Director Annual Giving .... Vacant
86 Director Government Relations .... Mr. Steve ANDERSON
22 Dir Affirm Action/EEO/Diversity .... Mr. Andy VASQUEZ
43 Dir Legal Services/General Counsel .... Mr. James FROST

Texas School of Business (D)

711 East Airtex Drive, Houston TX 77073
County: Harris — FICE Identification: 023122
Unit ID: 229036
Telephone: (281) 443-8900 — Carnegie Class: Assoc/PrivFP
FAX Number: (281) 443-0777 — Calendar System: Other
URL: www.tsb.edu
Established: 1983 — Annual Undergrad Tuition & Fees: $15,990
Enrollment: 334 — Coed
Affiliation or Control: Proprietary — IRS Status: Proprietary
Highest Offering: Associate Degree
Program: Occupational
Accreditation: ACICS, MAC

01 Campus Director .... Mr. Richard SAMBRANO

Texas School of Business-Friendswood (E)

3208 FM 528, Friendswood TX 77546
Telephone: (281) 648-0880 — Identification: 667051
Accreditation: ACICS, MAC

† Branch campus of Texas School of Business, Houston, TX.

Texas Southern University (F)

3100 Cleburne Street, Houston TX 77004-4584
County: Harris — FICE Identification: 003642
Unit ID: 229063
Telephone: (713) 313-7011 — Carnegie Class: DRU
FAX Number: (713) 313-1092 — Calendar System: Semester
URL: www.tsu.edu
Established: 1927 — Annual Undergrad Tuition & Fees (In-State): $8,726
Enrollment: 2,473 — Coed
Affiliation or Control: State — IRS Status: 170(c)1
Highest Offering: Doctorate
Program: Liberal Arts And General; Teacher Preparatory; Professional
Accreditation: SC, BUS, CAHIIM, COARC, DIETD, ENGT, LAW, MT, NAIT, PHAR, PLNG, SPAA, SW

01 President .... Dr. John M. RUDLEY
05 Provost/VP Academic Affs & Rsrch .... Dr. James W. WARD
10 Vice President for Admin & Finance .... Mr. E. Craig NESS
30 Vice Pres University Advancement .... Ms. Wendy H. ADAIR
100 Chief of Staff .... Ms. Janis J. NEWMAN
43 General Counsel .... Mr. Andrew C. HUGHEY
41 VP Intercollegiate Athletics .... Dr. Charles F. MCCLELLAND
32 VP Student Svcs/Dean of Students .... Dr. William T. SAUNDERS
09 Int Assoc Provost/Assoc VP Research ..... Dr. Adebayo O. OYEKAN
88 Dir Title III & Ofc of Sponsored Pr .... Ms. Demetria JOHNSON-WEEKS
15 Assoc VP of Human Resources .... Dr. Brian K. DICKENS
26 Assoc VP of Communications .... Ms. Eva K. PICKENS
84 Assoc VP Enrollment Management .... Mr. Hasan JAMIL
06 University Registrar .... Ms. Marilyn C. SQUARE
08 Exec Director Libraries/Museums .... Dr. Janice L. PAYTON
50 Dean School of Business .... Dr. Ronald A. JOHNSON
51 Int Dir Office of Cont Education .... Dr. Melanie LAWSON
53 Dean College of Education .... Dr. Lillian B. POATS
80 Dean School of Public Affairs .... Dr. Robert D. BULLARD
61 Dean School of Law .... Dr. Dannye HOLLEY
67 Int Dean Col Pharmacy & Health Sci .... Dr. Edward STEMLEY
72 Dean College of Science/Technology .... Dr. Lei YU
60 Dean School of Communications .... Dr. James W. WARD
19 Chief of Police .... Chief Roger D. BYARS
39 Asst VP of Student Housing .... Dr. William A. THOMAS
92 Dean Freeman Honors College .... Dr. Elizabeth A. BROWN-GUILLORY
96 Exec Dir Procurement Services .... Mr. Gregory G. WILLIAMS
18 Exec Director Facilities & Maint .... Mr. Tim RYCHLEC
13 CIO/Information Technology .... Mr. Luis VILLARREAL
20 Assoc Provost/Assoc VP Acad Affairs .... Vacant
58 Dean Graduate School .... Dr. Gregory H. MADDOX
21 Exec Dir Provost of Business Svcs .... Mr. Charles E. HENRY
21 Controller .... Ms. Christina ORDONEZ-CAMPOS
88 Dir Acad Ret Svcs Spec Asst/Provost .... Ms. Lori A. LABRIE
109 Asst VP of Student Auxiliary Svcs .... Dr. Najla F. NAJIEB
88 Exec Director Budget .... Mr. Elias HAILU
88 Assoc VP Treasurer & Budget .... Mr. Louis W. EDWARDS
108 Int Ex Dir Inst Assess Plng & Effec .... Dr. Rajanel CROCKEM
29 Exec Dir Alumni Rels/Spec Events .... Ms. Connie L. COCHRAN
88 Asst Dean of Student Support Svcs ...... Ms. Michara N. DELANEY
88 Director of Scholarships .... Ms. Cynthia LEE
88 Int Dir Teaching & Learning Center .... Dr. Bernnell PELZIER-GLAZE
88 Program Director Urban Academic Vil .... Mr. Darnell JOSEPH
88 Associate Director of QEP Office .... Dr. Arbolina L. JENNINGS
106 Dir Online Education/E-learning .... Mr. Remi ADEMOLA
37 Director Student Financial Aid .... Ms. Linda BALLARD
86 Director Government Relations .... Dr. Leonard H. SPEARMAN

*Texas State Technical College System (G)

3801 Campus Drive, Waco TX 76705-1607
County: McLennan — FICE Identification: 009642
Unit ID: 228671
Telephone: (254) 867-4891 — Carnegie Class: N/A
FAX Number: (254) 867-3973
URL: www.tstc.edu

01 Chancellor .... Mr. Michael L. REESER
86 VC & Chief Government Affairs Ofcr .... Mr. Roger MILLER
10 VC & Chief Financial Officer .... Mr. Jonathan HOEKSTRA
88 VC & Chf Business Intelligence Ofcr ...... Dr. J. Gary HENDRICKS
12 Interim President .... Dr. Stella GARCIA
45 VC & Chief Execution Officer .... Mr. Randall WOOTEN
11 VC & Chief Operations Officer .... Dr. Elton E. STUCKLY, JR.
88 VC & Chief Culture Officer .... Mrs. Gail LAWERENCE
13 VC & Chief Technology Officer .... Mr. Rick HERRERA
26 VC & Chief Marketing Officer .... Mr. Jeff KILGORE
101 Board of Regents Secretary .... Ms. Lillian MACIK
04 Exec Assistant to the Chancellor ...... Mrs. Madelynne JOHNSTON

*Texas State Technical College Harlingen (H)

1902 North Loop 499, Harlingen TX 78550-3697
County: Cameron — FICE Identification: 009225
Unit ID: 229319

Telephone: (956) 364-4000 Carnegie Class: Assoc/Pub-R-M
FAX Number: (965) 364-5100 Calendar System: Trimester
URL: www.harlingen.tstc.edu
Established: 1969 Annual Undergrad Tuition & Fees (In-State): $3,264
Enrollment: 5,225 Coed
Affiliation or Control: State IRS Status: 501(c)3
Highest Offering: Associate Degree
Program: Occupational; 2-Year Principally Bachelor's Creditable; Technical Emphasis
Accreditation: SC, CAHIIM, DH, MAC, SURGT

02 Interim President .... Dr. Stella E. GARCIA
05 Vice Pres for Student Learning .... Mrs. Rebecca SILVA
10 Vice Pres Financial/Admin Svcs .... Dr. Gisela FIGUEROA
88 Vice Pres College Readiness & Corp .... Mr. Javier DE LEON
32 Vice Pres for Student Develoment .... Mrs. Mary ADAMS
18 Vice Pres for Facilities .... Dr. Grady DEATON
09 AVP Institutional Assessment .... Ms. Celina GARZA
20 Associate VP of Academic Affairs .... Mrs. Nicki CONE
88 Assoc VP Col Readiness & Advancmnt .... Mrs. Sandra NIETO
31 Assoc VP Corp/Community Education ... Ms. Cledia HERNANDEZ
13 Chief Technology Officer .... Mr. Rick HERRERA
30 Director Institutional Advancement .... Ms. Amy LYNCH
26 Executive Director of Marketing .... Ms. Lynda LOPEZ
15 Director Human/Organizational Dev .... Mrs. Mary PREPEJCHAL
19 Chief of Public Safety .... Mr. Aurelio TORRES
18 Director of Physical Plant .... Mr. Juan LOPEZ
51 Director of Continuing Education .... Mr. Juan LEAL
38 Director Student Counseling .... Ms. Liz SILVA
37 Director of Financial Aid .... Mr. Fred PENA
35 Director of Student Success .... Ms. Norma SALAZAR
41 Supervisor of Intramurals .... Mr. Joe DOMINGUEZ
08 Director of the Library .... Ms. Nancy HENDRICKS
96 Exec Director of Procurement Mgmt .... Ms. Linda RODRIGUEZ-GUILLEN
36 Director Career Services .... Ms. Susan HOLMES
40 Supervisor Bookstore .... Mr. Luis LEAL
39 Supervisor Housing/Dormitories .... Mr. Carlos PEREZ
88 Director Staff Dev .... Mrs. Delia LEAL
106 Director Distance Education .... Dr. Gina CANO-MONREAL
27 Director College Information .... Ms. Dora COLVIN
22 Director Community Standards .... Ms. Edda URREA
88 Director Instructional Support Svcs .... Mr. Steve SZYMONIAK
88 Director of Curriculum .... Mr. Juan GARCIA

*Texas State Technical College Marshall (A)

2650 East End Boulevard S, Marshall TX 75672-7402
County: Harrison FICE Identification: 033965
Unit ID: 408394
Telephone: (903) 935-1010 Carnegie Class: Assoc/Pub-R-S
FAX Number: (903) 935-9554 Calendar System: Semester
URL: www.marshall.tstc.edu
Established: 1993 Annual Undergrad Tuition & Fees (In-District): $4,200
Enrollment: 800 Coed
Affiliation or Control: State/Local IRS Status: 501(c)3
Highest Offering: Associate Degree
Program: Occupational; 2-Year Principally Bachelor's Creditable; Technical Emphasis
Accreditation: SC

01 Provost .... Mr. Barton DAY
10 Vice Pres of Financial Services .... Mrs. Deborah L. SANDERS
20 Associate Dean Learning Community .... Mrs. Annette M. ELLIS
04 Exec Assistant to the Provost .... Ms. Tonya HOLLOWAY
06 Registrar .... Ms. Patricia A. ROBBINS
09 Dir of Inst Effect/Rsrch & Planning .... Dr. Afton BARBER
15 Human & Organizational Development .... Ms. Amanda OSWALT
36 Coordinator of Placement .... Mr. Benjamin CANTU
37 Financial Aid Specialist .... Mrs. Susan F. WINGATE
103 Director Workforce & Economic Dev .... Mr. Bryan MAERTINS
26 Chief Public Relations Officer .... Mr. Baily BRIGGS
96 Director of Purchasing .... Mrs. Eloise REED

*Texas State Technical College Waco (B)

3801 Campus Drive, Waco TX 76705-1695
County: McLennan FICE Identification: 003634
Unit ID: 228680
Telephone: (254) 799-3611 Carnegie Class: Assoc/Pub-R-M
FAX Number: (254) 867-2006 Calendar System: Semester
URL: www.tstc.edu
Established: 1965 Annual Undergrad Tuition & Fees (In-State): $5,436
Enrollment: 4,113 Coed
Affiliation or Control: State IRS Status: 501(c)3
Highest Offering: Associate Degree
Program: Occupational; 2-Year Principally Bachelor's Creditable; Technical Emphasis
Accreditation: SC, CAHIIM, DH, EMT, MAC, SURGT

00 Chancellor .... Mr. Mike REESER
02 Interim President .... Mr. Rob WOLAVER
11 VC & Chief Operations Officer .... Dr. Elton E. STUCKLY, JR.
05 AVC Student Learning .... Mr. Adam C. HUTCHISON
20 AVC Instructional Operations .... Ms. Kristi GILBEAUX
88 AVC of Innovation .... Dr. Irene CRAVEY
25 VP of Sponsored Programs .... Ms. Carliss HYDE
26 Director of Creative Services .... Ms. Jan OSBURN
10 VP Financial Services .... Mr. David KOFNOVEC
30 Sr Exec Dir Inst Advancement .... Dr. Terry CONROY
15 Executive Director Human Resources .... Ms. Kelly CONTELLA
32 VP of Student Development .... Ms. Sarah PATTERSON
109 AVC of Auxiliary Enterprises .... Mr. Kevin DORTON
37 Director of Financial Aid .... Ms. Jackie ADLER
06 Registrar/Dir of Admin & Records .... Ms. Mary DANIEL
08 Head Librarian .... Ms. Lianna DICK
18 Chief Facilities/Physical Plant Dir .... Mr. Selby HOLDER

*Texas State Technical College West Texas (C)

300 Homer K. Taylor Drive, Sweetwater TX 79556-4108
County: Nolan FICE Identification: 009932
Unit ID: 229328
Telephone: (325) 235-7300 Carnegie Class: Assoc/Pub-R-S
FAX Number: (325) 235-7309 Calendar System: Semester
URL: www.tstc.edu
Established: 1970 Annual Undergrad Tuition & Fees (In-State): $6,795
Enrollment: 1,457 Coed
Affiliation or Control: State IRS Status: 170(c)1
Highest Offering: Associate Degree
Program: Occupational; 2-Year Principally Bachelor's Creditable; Technical Emphasis
Accreditation: SC, CAHIIM, EMT

02 Interim President .... Mr. Kyle SMITH
00 Vice Chancellor/President Emerita .... Ms. Gail LAWRENCE
10 VP Financial Strategic Initiatives .... Ms. Karen WALLER
11 Assoc Vice Chancellor Facilities .... Mr. Ray FRIED
32 Associate VP Student Development .... Mr. Forrest MCMILLAN
05 Assoc Vice Pres Student Learning .... Mrs. Debbie KARL
84 Associate VP Enrollment Management .... Mrs. Sherry STRICKLAND
35 Director of Student Life .... Mrs. Crystal LATHAM-ALFORD
06 Registrar .... Mrs. Janyth USSERY
20 Dir Instructional Support Service .... Dr. Les PLAGENS
21 Assistant CFO .... Mr. Kevin SHIPP
19 Chief of Police .... Mr. Mike KELLER
15 Director Human Resources .... Ms. Hannah LOVE
37 Asst Director of Financial Aid .... Mrs. Gail JOHNSON
08 Director Library .... Mr. Steven PERRY
96 Director of Purchasing .... Ms. Jessica CHAVIRA
09 Dir Institutional Research .... Mrs. Kristen WALLACE
38 Coordinator Counseling & Testing .... Ms. Amy FREEMAN
36 Asst Dir Career Planning/Placement .... Ms. Julia HUMPHREY
26 Chief Public Relations Officer .... Ms. Maria AGUIRRE
39 Housing Supervisor .... Mr. Lupe NAVARRETTE
40 Bookstore Manager .... Ms. Kathy HICKSON
13 Director Support Operations .... Mr. Larry WILKE
103 Exec Director Workforce Training .... Mr. John DOSHER
46 Exec Director Strategic Initiatives .... Ms. Hannah LOVE
04 Executive Asst to President .... Mrs. Irene GILL
07 Coordinator of Recruiting .... Mrs. Kim PORTER
18 Chief Facilities/Physical Plant .... Mr. Ray FRIED

*The Texas State University System (D)

208 E 10th Street, Suite 600, Austin TX 78701-2407
County: Travis FICE Identification: 033442
Telephone: (512) 463-1808 Carnegie Class: N/A
FAX Number: (512) 463-1816
URL: www.tsus.edu

01 Chancellor .... Brian MCCALL
05 Vice Chanc for Academic Affairs .... Perry MOORE
43 Vice Chanc & General Counsel .... Fernando C. GOMEZ
10 Vice Chancellor for Finance .... Roland K. SMITH
86 Vice Chanc Government Relations .... Sean CUNNINGHAM
25 Vice Chanc Contract Administration .... Peter E. GRAVES
88 Associate General Counsel .... Diane CORLEY
18 Assoc Vice Chanc Facilities .... Rob Roy PARNELL
26 Assoc VC Govt Rels/Dir of Communic .... Mike WINTEMUTE
21 Director of Audits & Analysis .... Carole M. FOX
11 Director of Administration .... Carol TREADWAY

*Lamar Institute of Technology (E)

PO Box 10043, Beaumont TX 77710-0043
County: Jefferson FICE Identification: 036273
Unit ID: 441760
Telephone: (409) 880-8321 Carnegie Class: Assoc/Pub-S-SC
FAX Number: (409) 880-1711 Calendar System: Semester
URL: www.lit.edu
Established: 1995 Annual Undergrad Tuition & Fees (In-State): $4,401
Enrollment: 2,708 Coed
Affiliation or Control: State IRS Status: 501(c)3
Highest Offering: Associate Degree
Program: 2-Year Principally Bachelor's Creditable; Technical Emphasis
Accreditation: SC, CAHIIM, COARC, DH, DMS, EMT, RAD

02 President .... Dr. Paul SZUCH
05 Vice President for Academic Affairs .... Dr. Daniel WRIGHT
10 Vice President Finance & Operations .... Ms. Bonnie ALBRIGHT
32 Dean of Student Services .... Dr. Jason SMITH
15 Vice President for Human Resources .... Mrs. Catherine BLANCHARD
20 Dean of Instruction .... Ms. Melissa ARMENTOR
103 Dean Workforce Development .... Mr. Patrick CALHOUN
37 Director of Student Financial Aid .... Ms. Lisa SCHROEDER
13 Director of Technology Services .... Mrs. Susan COOK
30 Dir of Development/Alumni Relations .... Ms. Joanne BROWN
26 Director of Marketing/Public Info .... Ms. Beth MILLER
18 Facilities Coordinator .... Mr. Jack WIGGINS
36 Job Plcmnt/Student Activities Coord .... Vacant
09 Coord Inst Effectiveness and Grants .... Mr. David MOSLEY
04 Administrative Asst to President .... Mrs. Paula TANNER
06 Registrar .... Mr. David SHORT

*Lamar University (F)

PO Box 10009, Beaumont TX 77710-0009
County: Jefferson FICE Identification: 003581
Unit ID: 226091
Telephone: (409) 880-7011 Carnegie Class: DRU
FAX Number: (409) 880-8404 Calendar System: Semester
URL: www.lamar.edu
Established: 1923 Annual Undergrad Tuition & Fees (In-State): $9,721
Enrollment: 14,452 Coed
Affiliation or Control: State IRS Status: 501(c)3
Highest Offering: Doctorate
Program: Liberal Arts And General; Teacher Preparatory; Professional
Accreditation: SC, ACFEI, ADNUR, AUD, BUS, CONST, CS, DIETD, DIETI, ENG, MUS, NUR, SP, SW, TED

02 President .... Dr. Kenneth R. EVANS
05 Provost/Vice Pres Academic Affairs .... Dr. James W. MARQUART
10 Vice Pres Finance/Operations .... Dr. Cruse MELVIN
30 Vice President for Inst Advancement .... Mr. Juan ZABALA
58 Dean of Graduate Studies .... Dr. William HARN
20 Sr Assoc Provost for Academic Affs .... Dr. Kevin B. SMITH
15 Assoc Vice Pres Human Resources ... Ms. Catherine BLANCHARD
18 Assoc Vice Pres Facilities Mgmt .... Mr. Michael RULAND
21 Assoc Vice Pres Finance/Controller .... Ms. Twila BAKER
13 Assoc Vice Pres for Information Sys .... Ms. Priscilla PARSONS
84 Assoc VP Strategic Enrollment Mgmt .... Ms. Sherry BENOIT
49 Dean College Arts & Sciences .... Dr. Brenda NICHOLS
50 Dean College of Business .... Dr. Henry VENTA
53 Dean College of Education .... Dr. Robert SPINA
54 Dean College of Engineering .... Dr. Srinivas PALANKI
57 Dean Col Fine Arts & Communication .... Dr. Derina HOLTZHAUSEN
08 Director Library Services .... Mr. David J. CARROLL
06 Registrar .... Mr. David SHORT, JR.
106 Dir Division of Distance Learning .... Dr. Paula NICHOLS
32 Director of Academic Services .... Mr. James C. RUSH
44 Director of Development .... Ms. Ulana TRILOWSKY
09 Director Institutional Research .... Dr. Gregory MARSH
36 Dir Career Development/Placement .... Ms. Angela THOMAS
23 Director Health Services .... Ms. Shawn GRAY
19 Chief University Police .... Mr. Hector FLORES
26 Public Relations Director .... Mr. Brian SATTLER
29 Director Alumni Relations .... Ms. Shannon COPELAND
37 Director Student Financial Aid .... Ms. Jill ROWLEY
96 Director of Purchasing .... Mr. William GATES
07 Director of Admissions .... Ms. Melissa C. GALLIEN

*Lamar State College-Orange (G)

410 Front Street, Orange TX 77630-5802
County: Orange FICE Identification: 023582
Unit ID: 226107
Telephone: (409) 883-7750 Carnegie Class: Assoc/Pub-R-M
FAX Number: (409) 882-3374 Calendar System: Semester
URL: www.lsco.edu
Established: 1969 Annual Undergrad Tuition & Fees (In-State): $4,803
Enrollment: 2,259 Coed
Affiliation or Control: State IRS Status: 501(c)3
Highest Offering: Associate Degree
Program: Occupational; 2-Year Principally Bachelor's Creditable
Accreditation: SC

02 President .... Dr. J. Michael SHAHAN
05 Vice President Academic Affairs .... Dr. Gwen WHITEHEAD
10 Vice President Finance & Operations .... Mrs. Dana ROGERS
32 Vice Pres Student Svcs & Aux Ent .... Mr. Michael YEATER
08 Director of Library Services .... Ms. Mary MCCOY
06 Registrar .... Mrs. Becky J. MCANELLEY
37 Director Student Financial Aid .... Mr. Kerry J. OLSON
15 Human Resources Director .... Mrs. Alicia GRAY
18 Director of Physical Plant .... Mr. David GOINS
13 Coord Information Resources .... Ms. Linda G. BURNETT
09 Coordinator Institutional Research .... Mr. Bishar M. SETHNA
25 Contracts/Grants Administrator .... Mrs. Dana N. ROGERS
76 Director of Allied Health .... Ms. Gina A. SIMAR
72 Director of Business/Technology .... Ms. Jacqueline A. SPEARS
96 Director of Purchasing .... Ms. Tabitha EVANS

*Lamar State College-Port Arthur (H)

1500 Procter Street, Port Arthur TX 77640-6604
County: Jefferson FICE Identification: 023485
Unit ID: 226116
Telephone: (409) 983-4921 Carnegie Class: Assoc/Pub-R-M
FAX Number: (409) 984-6032 Calendar System: Semester
URL: www.lamarpa.edu
Established: 1909 Annual Undergrad Tuition & Fees (In-State): $5,294
Enrollment: 2,078 Coed
Affiliation or Control: State IRS Status: 501(c)3
Highest Offering: Associate Degree
Program: Occupational; 2-Year Principally Bachelor's Creditable
Accreditation: SC, SURGT

02 President Dr. Betty REYNARD
05 Vice President Academic Affairs Dr. Gary D. STRETCHER
10 Vice President for Finance Ms. Mary WICKLAND
32 Dean of Student Services Dr. Deborrah HEBERT
04 Admin Assistant to the President Mrs. Donna SCHION
08 Dean Library Services Mr. Peter B. KAATRUDE
06 Registrar Ms. Connie NICHOLAS
37 Director Financial Aid Ms. Connie RILEY
45 Director Inst Effectiveness Dr. Nancy STRETCHER
18 Director of Physical Plant Mr. Stephen ARNOLD
26 Public Information Officer Mr. Gerry DICKERT
56 Dir Inmate Instructional Program Dr. Barbara HUVAL
13 Dir Information Technology Services Mr. Samir GHORAYEB
15 Director Human Resources Ms. Tammy RILEY
07 Director of Admissions Ms. Connie NICHOLAS
09 Director of Institutional Research Mrs. Petra UZORUO
51 Dean Workforce/Continuing Educ Pgms Dr. Ben STAFFORD
72 Dean Technical Programs Ms. Shelia TRAHAN
81 Department Head Science & Math Dr. Percy JORDAN
50 Dept Head Business/CIS Technology Mrs. Sheila GUILLOT
83 Department Head Liberal Arts Dr. Barbara HUVAL
39 Director Student Housing Dr. Deborrah HEBERT
41 Athletic Director Mr. Scott STREET
96 Purchasing Manager Mrs. Allison WRIGHT

*Sam Houston State University (A)

1806 Avenue J, Suite 303, Huntsville TX 77341-0001

County: Walker FICE Identification: 003606
Unit ID: 227881
Telephone: (936) 294-1111 Carnegie Class: DRU
FAX Number: (936) 294-1465 Calendar System: Semester
URL: www.shsu.edu
Established: 1879 Annual Undergrad Tuition & Fees (In-State): $9,337
Enrollment: 19,573 Coed
Affiliation or Control: State IRS Status: 501(c)3
Highest Offering: Doctorate
Program: Liberal Arts And General; Professional
Accreditation: SC, ART, BUS, CACREP, CIDA, CLPSY, CS, DIETD, DIETI, FEPAC, MUS, NUR, NURSE, TED

02 President Dr. Dana G. HOYT
05 Provost/VP for Academic Affairs Dr. Jaimie HEBERT
10 VP for Finance & Operations Dr. Carlos HERNANDEZ
30 VP for University Advancement Mr. Frank HOLMES
84 VP for Enrollment Management Dr. Heather THIELEMANN
32 VP for Student Services Mr. Frank PARKER
13 VP for Information Technology Mr. Mark ADAMS
41 Athletic Director Mr. Bobby WILLIAMS
100 Chief of Staff Ms. Kathy GILCREASE
20 Vice Provost Dr. Richard EGLSAER
20 Assoc VP Academic Affairs Dr. Kandi TAYEBI
25 Assoc VP Research/Sponsored Program Dr. Jerry COOK
106 Assoc VP Distance Learning Dr. William ANGROVE
21 Assoc VP Financial Svcs/Controller Mr. Aaron LEMAY
18 Assoc VP Facilities Management Mr. Doug GREENING
15 Assoc VP for HR & Risk Management Mr. David HAMMONDS
26 Assoc VP Marketing & Comm Ms. Kris RUIZ
44 Assoc VP for Development Ms. Thelma MOONEY
88 Assoc VP Enrollment Management Mr. Scot MERTZ
35 Assoc VP Student Svcs/Rec Sports Dr. Keith JENKINS
14 Assoc VP Infrustructure/Support Svc Mr. Terrance HARRIS
88 Assoc VP Enterprise Services Mr. Jacob CHANDLER
09 Asst VP Institutional Effectiveness Ms. Donna ARTHO
50 Dean of Business Administration Dr. Mitchell MUEHSAM
61 Dean of Criminal Justice Dr. Phillip LYONS
53 Dean of Education Dr. Stacey EDMONSON
57 Dean of Fine Arts/Mass Comm Dr. Ronald SHIELDS
76 Dean of Health Sciences Dr. Michael LACOURSE
83 Dean of Humanities/Social Sciences Dr. Abbey ZINK
81 Dean of Sciences Dr. John PASCARELLA
08 Director Library Services Ms. Ann HOLDER
19 Director Public Safety Services Mr. Kevin MORRIS
06 Registrar Ms. Teresa RINGO
07 Director Undergraduate Admissions Mr. Trevor THORN
37 Director Financial Aid Ms. Lydia HALL
39 Director Residence Life Ms. Joellen TIPTON
38 AVP SS/Student Hlth & Couns Center Dr. Drew MILLER
29 Director Alumni Relations Mr. Charlie VIENNE
35 Dean of Students Mr. John YARABECK
108 Asst VP Planning & Assessment Dr. Somer FRANKLIN

*Sul Ross State University (B)

PO Box C-114, Alpine TX 79832-0001

County: Brewster FICE Identification: 003625
Unit ID: 228501
Telephone: (432) 837-8032 Carnegie Class: Master's L
FAX Number: (432) 837-8334 Calendar System: Semester
URL: www.sulross.edu
Established: 1917 Annual Undergrad Tuition & Fees (In-State): $6,900
Enrollment: 2,873 Coed
Affiliation or Control: State IRS Status: 501(c)3
Highest Offering: Master's
Program: Occupational; Liberal Arts And General; Teacher Preparatory; Professional
Accreditation: SC

02 President Dr. Bill KIBLER
05 Exec VP Academic/Stdnt Affs/Provost Dr. Jim CASE
10 Vice Pres for Finance & Operations Mr. Cesario E. VALENZUELA
84 Vice Pres Enrollment Management Ms. Denise GROVES
11 Assoc VP Fac/Plng/Construct/Ops Mr. Jim W. CLOUSE
30 Assoc Vice Pres University Services Mr. Leo G. DOMINGUEZ
12 Associate Provost & Dean RGC Dr. Paul SORRELS
04 Special Assistant to President Vacant
11 Exec Asst to President/Dir Admin Ms. Yvonne REALIVASQUEZ
06 Director Records & Registration Ms. Pamela S. PIPES
08 Dean Library & Info Technology Mr. Don DOWDEY
32 Dean of Students Mr. Leo DOMINGUEZ
92 Dir Honors Prog/Acad Ctr Excellence Dr. Kathy STEIN
26 Director News & Publications Mr. Stephen W. LANG
37 Dir Financial Assistance Mr. Mickey CORBETT
49 Dean Arts & Science Dr. Jay DOWNING
107 Int Dean Professional Studies Dr. Kip SULLIVAN
47 Dean Agricult/Natural Resource Sci Dr. Robert J. KINUCAN
15 Director of Human Resources Mrs. Judy A. PERRY
18 Asst Director of Physical Plant Mr. Edmundo NATERA
19 Director Dept of Public Safety Mr. Johnnie L. HOLBROOKS
21 Director of Accounting Services Ms. Lisa GEORGE
39 Director Residential Living Mr. Mark CHASZAR
41 Interim Athletic Director Mr. Bobby S. MESKER
38 Director of Counseling Ctr Vacant
13 Chief Information Officer Mr. David W. GIBSON
96 Director of Purchasing Mr. Noe HERNANDEZ
88 Dir Center for Big Bend Studies Mr. Andy CLOUD
29 Director Alumni Relations Ms. Aida LUEVANOS
66 Director of Vocational Nursing Ms. Krista L. POWELL
88 Director Museum of the Big Bend Ms. Elizabeth JACKSON
88 Director of Upward Bound Ms. Barbara VEGA
88 Director of University Archives Ms. Melleta BELL
88 Director Small Business Devel Ctr Mr. David WILSON
88 Director Law Enforcement Academy Vacant
07 Director Admissions & Records Ms. Claudia WRIGHT
88 Mail Service Supervisor Ms. Leticia GONZALES
88 Internal Auditor Mrs. Stephanie NELSON
36 Coord Career Services & Testing Ms. Jan L. RUEB
09 Dir of Institutional Effectiveness Dr. Jeanne QVARMSTROM

*Texas State University (C)

601 University Drive, San Marcos TX 78666-4615

County: Hays FICE Identification: 003615
Unit ID: 228459
Telephone: (512) 245-2111 Carnegie Class: Master's L
FAX Number: (512) 245-3040 Calendar System: Semester
URL: www.txstate.edu
Established: 1899 Annual Undergrad Tuition & Fees (In-State): $9,945
Enrollment: 36,790 Coed
Affiliation or Control: State IRS Status: 170(c)1
Highest Offering: Doctorate
Program: Liberal Arts And General; Teacher Preparatory; Professional
Accreditation: SC, BUS, BUSA, CAATE, CACREP, CAHIIM, CEA, CIDA, COARC, COARCP, CONST, CS, DIETD, DIETI, ENG, HSA, IPSY, JOUR, MT, MUS, NRPA, NURSE, PTA, RTT, SP, SPAA, SW, TEAC

02 President Dr. Denise M. TRAUTH
05 Provost/Vice Pres Academic Affairs Dr. Gene BOURGEOIS
100 Special Assistant to the President Dr. Vicki S. BRITTAIN
32 Vice President Student Affairs Dr. Joanne H. SMITH
10 Vice Pres Finance/Support Services Vacant
30 Vice President Univ Advancement Dr. Barbara BREIER
13 Vice Pres Information Technology Mr. Kenneth PIERCE
83 Dean College of Applied Arts Dr. T. Jaime CHAHIN
50 Dean McCoy Col of Business Admin Dr. Denise T. SMART
57 Dean College Fine Arts & Comm Dr. John FLEMING
53 Dean College of Education Dr. Stan CARPENTER
76 Dean College Health Professions Dr. Ruth B. WELBORN
83 Dean College Liberal Arts Dr. Michael HENNESSY
81 Interim Dean Col of Science & Eng Dr. Robert B. HABINGREITHER
58 Dean The Graduate College Dr. Andrea GOLATO
97 Dean Univ Col & Dir PACE Center Dr. Daniel BROWN
92 Dean Honors College Dr. Heather GALLOWAY
20 Assoc Vice Pres Academic Affairs Dr. Debbie M. THORNE
15 Asst VP of Human Resources Mr. John E. MCBRIDE
20 Associate Provost Dr. Cynthia L. OPHEIM
18 Associate VP of Facilities Mr. Juan M. GUERRA
86 Assoc VP Research & Dir of Fed Rels Dr. Bill C. COVINGTON
35 Assoc VP Stdnt Affs/Dean of Stdnt Dr. Margarita M. ARELLANO
20 Assoc Vice Pres for Inst Effective Dr. Beth E. WUEST
21 Assoc VP Financial Services Mr. Darryl BORGONAH
84 Assoc VP Enrollment Mgmt/Marketing Dr. Michael R. HEINTZE
08 Associate VP University Library Ms. Joan L. HEATH
20 Assistant VP for Academic Services Dr. Ronald C. BROWN
38 Director Counseling Center Dr. Kathlyn C. DAILEY
07 Asst VP Enroll Mgmt/Dir Ungrad Adm Ms. Stephanie ANDERSON
28 AVP/Dir Student Diversity/Inclusion Dr. Sherri BENN
88 Asst VP University Advancement Mr. Dan PERRY
89 Asst Dean of University College Dr. Laurie HINDSON
88 Assoc VP Finance/Support Svcs Plng Ms. Nancy NUSBAUM
14 Assoc VP for Technology Resources Mr. Mark HUGHES
90 Assoc VP Intstructional Tech Supp Dr. Carlos SOLIS
106 Interim Dir Distance/Extended Lrng Dr. Debbie M. THORNE
06 University Registrar Mr. Louis E. JIMENEZ
91 Director Enterprise Systems Mr. Martin MILLS
37 Director of Fin Aid & Scholarships Dr. Christopher MURR
36 Director Career Services Ms. Norma GUERRA GAIER
41 Director of Athletics Dr. Lawrence B. TEIS
29 Director of Alumni Affairs Ms. Kim GANNON
27 Director Univ News Services Mr. Jayme L. BLASCHKE
31 Chief Community Relations Ms. Kim PORTERFIELD
12 Asst VP Round Rock Campus Dr. Edna REHBEIN
25 Director of Sponsored Programs Mr. W. Scott ERWIN
19 Director University Police Mr. Ralph MEYER
23 Director Student Health Center Dr. Emilio CARRANCO
39 Director Housing & Residential Life Dr. Rosanne PROITE
40 Manager University Bookstore Ms. Jacqueline SLAUGHTER
24 Director Education Technology Ctr Mr. Michael W. FARRIS
09 Director of Institutional Research Mr. Joseph M. MEYER
22 Chief Divsty Offc/Dir Equity & Acce Dr. Gilda GARCIA
93 Dir Center for Multicul/Gender Stds Dr. Sandra MAYO
96 Director Purchasing Ms. Jacque ALLBRIGHT
26 Director of University Marketing Mr. Daniel W. EGGERS
88 Director of Audit & Compliance Mr. Steve R. MCGEE
88 Director Campus Recreation Dr. Glenn HANLEY
88 Director LBJ Student Center Mr. Jack RAHMANN
88 Director Retention Mgmt & Planning Dr. Jen BECK
88 Director Disability Services Mr. Clint-Michael RENEAU
20 Associate Academic Officer Dr. A. Lisa GARZA
104 Asst VP for International Affairs Dr. Ryan BUCK
44 Asst VP Univ Advancement Mr. Matt FLORES

*Texas Tech University System (D)

2500 Broadway Ave., Admin Bldg, Lubbock TX 79409-2013

County: Lubbock Identification: 667242
Telephone: (806) 742-1438 Carnegie Class: N/A
FAX Number: N/A
URL: www.texastech.edu

01 Chancellor Mr. Robert L. DUNCAN
05 Vice Chancellor Academic Affairs Dr. John OPPERMAN
10 Vice Chancellor & CFO Mr. Jim BRUNJES
30 Vice Chancellor Inst Advancement Ms. Lisa D. CALVERT
86 Vice Chanc Government Relations Ms. Martha BROWN
18 Vice Chanc Facil Plng/Construction Mr. Michael MOLINA

*Angelo State University (E)

2601 West Avenue N, San Angelo TX 76909-0001

County: Tom Green FICE Identification: 003541
Unit ID: 222831
Telephone: (325) 942-2555 Carnegie Class: Master's M
FAX Number: N/A Calendar System: Semester
URL: www.angelo.edu
Established: 1928 Annual Undergrad Tuition & Fees (In-State): $6,892
Enrollment: 6,494 Coed
Affiliation or Control: State IRS Status: 501(c)3
Highest Offering: Doctorate
Program: Liberal Arts And General; Teacher Preparatory; Professional; Fine Arts Emphasis
Accreditation: SC, ACBSP, ADNUR, MUS, NURSE, PTA, SW, TED

01 President Dr. Brian J. MAY
05 Provost/Vice Pres Academic Affairs Dr. Donald R. TOPLIFF
30 Exec Dir Development & Alumni Rels Ms. Jamie AKIN
10 VP for Finance and Administration Ms. Angelina WRIGHT
32 VP for Student Affs & Enroll Mgmt Dr. Javier FLORES
58 Dean College of Graduate Studies Dr. Susan KEITH
49 Dean of College of Arts & Sciences Dr. Paul SWETS
50 Dean College Business Dr. Clifton JONES
53 Dean College of Education Dr. John MIAZGA
66 Dean College Health & Human Service Dr. Leslie MAYRAND
06 Director of Registrar Services Ms. Cindy WEEAKS
89 Dean Freshman College Dr. John WEGNER
54 Chair of Civil Engineering Dept Dr. William A. KITCH
09 Director of Accountability Ms. Crystal BRADEN
08 Exec Director of Library Dr. Maurice G. FORTIN
36 Director Career Development Ms. Julie J. RUTHENBECK
15 Director of Human Resources Mr. Kurtis R. NEAL
37 Director of Student Financial Aid Mr. William BLOOM
26 Director of Communications & Mktg Ms. Rebekah BRACKIN
29 Director Development & Alumni Svcs Ms. Kimberly ADAMS
35 Exec Director of Student Affairs Dr. Bradley PETTY
18 Director of Facilities Management Mr. Jay HALBERT
39 Dir of Housing & Residential Pgm Ms. Tracy W. BAKER
40 Manager Bookstore Ms. Margaret BOX
41 Interim Athletic Director Mr. James REID
19 Chief of University Police Mr. James E. ADAMS
13 Assoc VP Information Technology/CIO Mr. Douglas FOX
21 Director of Business Services Ms. Jessica MANNING
96 Director Purchasing and Operations Ms. Margaret MATA
92 Director of Honors Program Dr. Shirley EOFF
04 Executive Asst to the President Ms. Adelina C. MORALES
104 Director of International Studies Ms. Meghan PACE
07 Director of Admissions Ms. Sharla ADAM
38 Director of Counseling Services Mr. Cleave POOL
84 Director Enrollment Management Mr. Jeffrey SEFCIK
43 Sr Exec Asst to Pres/Gen Counsel Mr. Joe MUNOZ

† Affiliated with Texas Tech University in Lubbock, TX

*Texas Tech University (F)

2500 Broadway Avenue, Lubbock TX 79409-2005

County: Lubbock FICE Identification: 003644
Unit ID: 229115
Telephone: (806) 742-2121 Carnegie Class: RU/H
FAX Number: (806) 742-2138 Calendar System: Semester
URL: www.ttu.edu
Established: 1923 Annual Undergrad Tuition & Fees (In-State): $7,811
Enrollment: 35,158 Coed
Affiliation or Control: State IRS Status: 170(c)1
Highest Offering: Doctorate

Program: Liberal Arts And General; Teacher Preparatory; Professional
Accreditation: SC, #ARCPA, ART, BUS, BUSA, CACREP, CIDA, CLPSY, COPSY, DANCE, DIETD, DIETI, ENG, ENGT, IPSY, LAW, LSAR, MED, MFCD, MIDWF, MUS, SPAA, SW, TED, THEA

00 Chancellor .... Mr. Robert L. DUNCAN
01 President .... Dr. M. Duane NELLIS
101 Sec Board Regents/Ex Asst to Chanc .... Mr. Ben W. LOCK
05 Provost and Senior Vice President .... Dr. Lawrence SCHOVANEC
10 Chief Operating Ofcr/SVP Admin/Fin .... Ms. Noel SLOAN
30 Vice Chanc Inst Advancement .... Ms. Lisa CALVERT
86 Vice Chancellor Govt Relations .... Ms. Martha BROWN
43 Vice Chanc & General Counsel .... Mr. John HUFFAKER
18 VC Facilities Planning Construction .... Mr. Michael MOLINA
20 Vice Provost Academic Affairs .... Dr. Peggy MILLER
100 President's Chief of Staff .... Ms. Grace HERNANDEZ
29 EVP & CEO Texas Tech Alumni Assoc .... Dr. Bill DEAN
88 Vice President for Research .... Dr. Robert DUNCAN
28 Vice Pres Institutional Diversity .... Dr. Juan S. MUNOZ
84 Sr Assoc VP Enrollment Management ... Dr. James BURKHALTER
20 Assoc Vice Provost Academic Affairs .... Dr. Gary ELBOW
20 Sr Vice Provost .... Dr. Rob STEWART
88 Director of External Relations .... Ms. Suzanne TAYLOR
21 Asst Vice Pres & Controller .... Ms. Sharon WILLIAMSON
82 Assoc Vice Prov International Affs .... Mr. Tibor P. NAGY
13 Assoc VP Information Technology .... Mr. Sam SEGRAN
08 Dean of Libraries .... Dr. Donald DYAL
60 Dean Media & Communications .... Dr. David PERLMUTTER
32 Int Dean Stdnts/Dir Campus Life .... Ms. Amy L. MURPHY
37 Managing Dir Financial Aid .... Ms. Becky WILSON
14 Chief Information Officer .... Ms. Kay RHODES
06 Registrar .... Ms. Bobbie BROWN
07 Managing Director of Admissions .... Dr. Ethan LOGAN
27 Managing Dir Comms & Marketing .... Mr. Chris COOK
104 Interim Director Study Abroad .... Ms. Elizabeth A. MCDANIEL
04 Executive Asst to President .... Ms. Jessica CARRILLO
31 Director Community Engagment .... Dr. Heather MARTINEZ
44 Senior Dir Annual Giving Programs .... Ms. Deborah FINLAYSON
23 Director Student Health Services .... Ms. Evelyn MCPHERSON
39 Managing Dir Student Housing .... Mr. Sean DUGGAN
36 Managing Director Career Center .... Mr. Jay KILLOUGH
15 Managing Director of HR Management .. Ms. Jodie BILLINGSLEY
22 Asst Vice Chanc Admin/Dir EEO .... Ms. Charlotte BINGHAM
38 Managing Dir Student Counseling .... Dr. Eileen NATHAN
41 Director of Athletics .... Mr. Kirby HOCUTT
47 Dean Agriculture Sci/Natural Res .... Dr. Michael GALYEAN
49 Dean of Arts & Sciences .... Dr. Brent LINDQUIST
48 Dean of Architecture .... Mr. Andrew VERNOOY
50 Dean Business Administration .... Dr. Lance NAIL
53 Dean of Education .... Dr. Scott RIDLEY
54 Dean of Engineering .... Dr. Albert SACCO
88 Dean of Human Sciences .... Dr. Linda HOOVER
61 Dean School of Law .... Darby DICKERSON
58 Dean of Graduate School .... Dr. Mark SHERIDAN
92 Interim Dean Honors College .... Dr. Stephen FRITZ
57 Dean Visual & Performing Arts .... Dr. Carol EDWARDS
19 Chief of Police .... Mr. Ronald SEACRIST
09 Managing Dir Institutional Research .... Ms. Vicki WEST
96 Dir Purchasing & Contracting .... Ms. Jennifer ADLING

*Texas Tech University Health Sciences Center (A)

3601 4th Street, Lubbock TX 79430-0001
County: Lubbock FICE Identification: 010674
Unit ID: 229337
Telephone: (806) 743-1000 Carnegie Class: Spec/Med
FAX Number: (806) 743-3027 Calendar System: Semester
URL: www.ttuhsc.edu
Established: 1969 Annual Undergrad Tuition & Fees (In-State): $7,896
Enrollment: 7,685 Coed
Affiliation or Control: State IRS Status: 501(c)3
Highest Offering: Doctorate
Program: Professional
Accreditation: SC, AUD, CAATE, CORE, DMOLS, MED, MT, NURSE, OT, PHAR, PTA, SP

01 President .... Dr. Tedd MITCHELL
10 Exec Vice Pres for Finance Admin .... Mr. Elmo M. CAVIN, JR.
05 Exec Vice Pres Academic Affairs .... Dr. Rial D. ROLFE
26 Exec Dir Communications & Mktg .... Ms. Mary CROYLE
17 Exec Vice Pres Rural/Community Hlth .. Dr. Billy U. PHILIPS, JR.
13 Vice Pres Info Tech/Chief Info Ofcr .... Dr. Chip SHAW
86 VP Federal and State Relations .... Mr. Ryan HENRY
100 Chief of Staff .... Ms. Didit MARTINEZ
43 Senior Assoc General Counsel .... Ms. Glenda HELFRICH
21 Assoc Vice Pres Business Affairs .... Mr. Mike CROWDER
46 Senior Vice President for Research .... Dr. Michael CONN
19 Information Security Officer .... Mr. Andrew HOWARD
15 Asst Vice Pres of Human Resources .... Dr. Gena JONES
18 Asst Vice Pres of Physical Plant .... Mr. George MORALES
63 Dean of Medical School .... Dr. Steven L. BERK
58 Dean Grad Sch Biomed Sciences .... Dr. Brandt L. SCHNEIDER
66 Dean of Nursing School .... Dr. Michael L. EVANS
76 Dean of Allied Health Sciences Sch .... Vacant
67 Dean of Pharmacy School .... Dr. Quentin R. SMITH
12 Reg Dean Medicine Amarillo Campus .... Dr. Richard JORDAN
12 Reg Dean Medicine Odessa Campus .... Dr. Gary VENTOLINI
66 Reg Dean Nursing Odessa Campus .... Dr. Sharon CANNON
76 Reg Dean Allied Health Amarillo .... Dr. Michael HOOTEN
76 Reg Dean Allied Health Odessa .... Dr. Tony DOMENECH
06 Registrar .... Ms. Tamara N. LANE
08 Exec Director of HSC Libraries .... Mr. Richard C. WOOD
21 Managing Dir Acct Services .... Ms. Melody MILLER
22 Director of Equal Employment .... Ms. Charlotte BINGHAM
25 Director of Sponsored Programs .... Ms. Victoria RIVERA
37 Director of Financial Aid .... Mr. Marcus WILSON
25 Sr Director of Contracting .... Mr. Jim LEWIS
96 Managing Director of Purchasing .... Mr. John G. HAYNES
09 Chief Analyst Inst Research .... Mr. Kevin MCINTYRE
32 AVP Student Services .... Ms. Margret DURAN
29 Director of Alumni Relations .... Ms. Danette BAKER
21 Asst Vice Pres of Budget .... Ms. Penny HARKEY
30 Asst VC Development .... Ms. Kendra BURRIS
88 Sr Director Office of Global Health .... Ms. Michelle ENSMINGER
108 Asst VP Academic Affairs .... Dr. Kari DICKSON
88 Vice President of Health Policy .... Dr. Cynthia JUMPER
28 VP of Diversity & Inclusion .... Dr. Kim PECK

*Texas Tech University Health Sciences Center at El Paso (B)

5001 El Paso Drive, El Paso TX 79905
Telephone: (915) 783-5510 Identification: 667243
Accreditation: &SC, MED, NURSE

† Branch campus of Texas Tech University Health Sciences Center, Lubbock, TX.

Texas Wesleyan University (C)

1201 Wesleyan, Fort Worth TX 76105-1536
County: Tarrant FICE Identification: 003645
Unit ID: 229160
Telephone: (817) 531-4444 Carnegie Class: Master's L
FAX Number: (817) 531-4425 Calendar System: Semester
URL: www.txwes.edu
Established: 1890 Annual Undergrad Tuition & Fees: $24,454
Enrollment: 2,606 Coed
Affiliation or Control: United Methodist IRS Status: 501(c)3
Highest Offering: Doctorate
Program: Liberal Arts And General; Teacher Preparatory; Professional
Accreditation: SC, ACBSP, ANEST, BUS, CAATE, MUS

01 President .... Mr. Frederick G. SLABACH
05 Provost .... Dr. Allen HENDERSON
10 Sr VP Finance & Administration .... Vacant
30 VP University Advancement .... Mr. Jim LEWIS
84 VP for Enrollment & Student Svcs .... Ms. Pati ALEXANDER
26 Vice Pres Marketing/Communications .... Mr. John VEILLEUX
20 Associate Provost .... Dr. Helena BUSSELL
41 Athletic Director .... Mr. Steven TRACHIER
53 Dean School of Education .... Dr. Carlos MARTINEZ
50 Dean of School of Business .... Dr. Hector QUINTANILLA
49 Dean School Arts & Letters .... Dr. Steven DANIELL
83 Dean School of Natural & Social Sci .... Vacant
32 Dean of Students .... Mr. Dennis HALL
39 Asst Dn of Students/Dir Resid Life .... Mr. Jon BARTLETT
06 Registrar .... Ms. Kay VANTOORN
08 Library Science Assoc Professor .... Vacant
21 Controller .... Ms. Caron PATTON
07 Enrollment Services Assistant VP .... Mr. Chadd BRIDWELL
37 Director Financial Aid .... Ms. Laurie ROSENKRANTZ
42 Chaplain .... Vacant
38 Director of Counseling .... Dr. Linda METCALF
29 Director Alumni Relations .... Mrs. DeAwna WOOD
15 AVP of Human Resources .... Mr. Wilton HOLLINS
96 Director of Purchasing .... Ms. Deborah CAVITT
36 Director of Career Services .... Ms. Robyn BONE
18 Exec Dir of Facil/Opers/Emr Svcs .... Mr. Brian FRANKS
25 Sr Dir of Sponsored Programs .... Mr. Shawn FARRELL
13 Associate Vice President & CIO .... Mr. Marcus KERR
04 Executive Assistant to the Pres .... Ms. Judi D. PARDUE
04 Executive Assistant to the Pres .... Ms. Krista HUGHES
09 Director Institutional Research .... Ms. Sherri CARABALLO
100 Chief of Staff and General Counsel .... Ms. Patti GEARHART TURNER
103 Director Career Services/Counselor .... Ms. Robyn BONE

Texas Woman's University (D)

Box 425589, Denton TX 76204-5587
County: Denton FICE Identification: 003646
Unit ID: 229179
Telephone: (940) 898-2000 Carnegie Class: DRU
FAX Number: (940) 898-3198 Calendar System: Semester
URL: www.twu.edu
Established: 1901 Annual Undergrad Tuition & Fees (In-State): $8,522
Enrollment: 15,071 Coed
Affiliation or Control: State IRS Status: 501(c)3
Highest Offering: Doctorate
Program: Liberal Arts And General; Teacher Preparatory; Professional
Accreditation: SC, ACBSP, CACREP, COPSY, DANCE, DH, DIETD, DIETI, HSA, IPSY, LIB, MUS, NURSE, OT, PTA, SCPSY, SP, SW

01 President/Chancellor .... Dr. Carine FEYTEN
05 Provost & VP Academic Affairs .... Dr. Robert NEELY
10 Vice Pres Finance/Administration .... Ms. BJ CRAIN
32 Vice President Student Life .... Dr. Monica MENDEZ-GRANT
13 Chief Information Officer .... Mr. Rob PLACIDO
20 Senior Associate Provost .... Dr. Jennifer MARTIN
108 Assoc Provost for Inst Improvement .... Dr. Michael STANKEY
26 Assoc Vice Pres Mktg/Communication .... Ms. Cindy POLLARD
84 Assoc Vice Pres Enrollment Services .... Mr. Gary RAY
21 Associate Vice President Finance .... Ms. Pam WILSON
18 Assoc Vice Pres Facilities .... Mr. Joe STANDRIDGE, JR.
15 Assoc Vice Pres Human Resources .... Mr. Lewis BENAVIDES
09 Asst Provost Institutional Research .... Dr. Mark HAMNER
49 Dean College Arts & Sciences .... Dr. Ann STATON
69 Int Dean College Health Sciences .... Dr. Gary JAMES
107 Int Dean College Prof Education .... Dr. Jerry WHITWORTH
58 Dean Graduate School .... Dr. Larry LEFLORE
07 Director of Admissions .... Ms. Erma M. NIETO-BRECHT
43 General Counsel .... Ms. Destinee WAITERS
08 Director of Libraries .... Ms. Sherilyn BIRD
37 Director Student Financial Aid .... Mr. Governor E. JACKSON
36 Director Career & Employment Svcs .... Ms. Deidre Lynn LESLIE
38 Director Counseling Center .... Dr. Denise LUCERO-MILLER
27 Director News & Information .... Ms. Amanda SIMPSON
19 Director of Public Safety .... Ms. Liz PAULEY
06 Registrar .... Mr. Bobby LOTHRINGER
41 Athletic Director .... Ms. Chalese CONNORS
23 Director Student Health Services .... Dr. Connie MENARD
39 Director University Housing .... Dr. Joe BERTHIAUME
29 Director Alumni Relations .... Ms. Anne SCOTT
96 Procurement Services .... Ms. Vanna PARR

Trinity University (E)

One Trinity Place, San Antonio TX 78212-7200
County: Bexar FICE Identification: 003647
Unit ID: 229267
Telephone: (210) 999-7011 Carnegie Class: Master's M
FAX Number: (210) 999-7696 Calendar System: Semester
URL: www.trinity.edu
Established: 1869 Annual Undergrad Tuition & Fees: $37,856
Enrollment: 2,490 Coed
Affiliation or Control: Independent Non-Profit IRS Status: 501(c)3
Highest Offering: Master's
Program: Liberal Arts And General; Teacher Preparatory; Professional
Accreditation: SC, BUS, ENG, HSA, OTA, TED

01 President .... Dr. Danny ANDERSON
05 VP Faculty and Student Affairs .... Dr. Michael R. FISCHER
10 VP Finance and Administration .... Mr. Gary LOGAN
30 VP Alumni Relations & Develop .... Mr. Michael BACON
26 VP Info Resources/Marketing & Comm .... Dr. Charles B. WHITE
20 Assoc VP Student Academic Issues .... Dr. Sheryl R. TYNES
20 Assoc VP Faculty Recruitment & Dev .... Dr. Duane COLTHARP
20 Assoc VP Budget & Research .... Dr. Mark BRODL
21 Assoc VP Budget/Business Ops .... Ms. Ana M. WINDHAM
07 Assoc VP Enrollment & Student Reten .... Vacant
08 University Librarian .... Ms. Diane J. GRAVES
06 Registrar .... Mr. Alfred RODRIGUEZ
37 Asst VP Student Financial Svcs .... Ms. Glendi GADDIS
38 Director Counseling/Health Svcs .... Dr. Gary W. NEAL
32 Assoc VP Stdnt Affs/Dean of Stdnt .... Mr. David M. TUTTLE
31 Dir Campus/Community Involvement .... Ms. Jamie THOMPSON
36 Director of Career Services .... Ms. Twyla HOUGH
15 Assistant VP Human Resources .... Ms. Pamela JOHNSTON
13 Dir/Chief Info Technology Officer .... Mr. Fred ZAPATA
27 Asst VP External Relations .... Ms. Sharon JONES SCHWEITZER
30 Asst VP Alumni Relations & Dev .... Vacant
44 Director of Planned Giving .... Ms. Kristine HOWLAND
29 Senior Director of Alumni Relations .... Dr. MaryKay COOPER
51 AVP Conferences/Special Pgms .... Ms. Ann G. KNOEBEL
04 Assistant to the President .... Ms. Claire SMITH
19 Asst VP Public Safety/Ent Risk Mgmt .... Mr. Paul CHAPA
18 Director Facility Services .... Mr. Mike SCHWEITZER
40 Director of Bookstore .... Vacant
42 Chaplain .... Rev. Stephen R. NICKLE
09 Assoc VP & Director Inst'l Research .... Dr. Diane G. SAPHIRE
96 Director of Purchasing .... Ms. Cynthia LARA
28 Director Diversity .... Ms. Jamie THOMPSON
41 Athletic Director .... Mr. Bob KING

Trinity Valley Community College (F)

100 Cardinal Drive, Athens TX 75751-2734
County: Henderson FICE Identification: 003572
Unit ID: 225308
Telephone: (903) 677-8822 Carnegie Class: Assoc/Pub-S-MC
FAX Number: (903) 675-6316 Calendar System: Semester
URL: www.tvcc.edu
Established: 1946 Annual Undergrad Tuition & Fees (In-District): $2,340
Enrollment: 6,752 Coed
Affiliation or Control: State/Local IRS Status: 501(c)3
Highest Offering: Associate Degree
Program: Occupational; 2-Year Principally Bachelor's Creditable
Accreditation: SC, ADNUR, EMT, SURGT

01 President .... Dr. Glendon S. FORGEY
05 Vice President for Instruction .... Dr. Jerry KING
30 VP of Institutional Advancement .... Ms. Mary NICHOLSON
32 Vice President Student Services .... Dr. Jay KINZER
13 VP of Information Technology .... Mr. Mike ABBOTT
10 Vice Pres Administrative Services .... Mrs. Jean MCSPADDEN
20 Assoc VP Instruction Academic Educ .... Dr. Wendy MAYS
103 Associate VP of Workforce Education .... Mr. David MCANALLY
91 Assoc VP of Information Technology .... Mr. Brett DANIEL
21 Associate Business Officer .... Ms. Courtney WALKER
12 Assoc VP of TDCJ Programs .... Dr. Sam HURLEY
18 Asst VP of Facilities Management .... Mr. David GRAEM
76 Provost Health Occupations .... Dr. Helen REID
12 Provost Kaufman County Campus .... Dr. Algia ALLEN
12 Provost Anderson County Campus .... Dr. Jeff WATSON
06 Registrar/Dean Enrollment Mgmt .... Dr. Colette HILLIARD

09 Dir Strategic Planning/SACS .... Ms. Tina RUMMEL
08 Director Learning Resource Center .... Ms. Karla BRYAN
36 Dir of Student Pathways/Success .... Ms. Shelia JONES
26 Public Information Officer .... Mr. Mark MEREDITH
07 Director School Relations .... Ms. Audrey HAWKINS
37 Dir Student Finan Aid/Veteran's Svc .... Ms. Julie LIVELY
41 Athletic Director .... Mr. Brad SMILEY
19 Director of Campus Police .... Mr. Stewart NEWBY
36 Placement Officer .... Vacant
40 Bookstore Manager .... Mrs. Beth Ann KIDD
35 Director Student Activities .... Mr. Harold JONES
31 Director Community Services .... Ms. Gayla ROBERTS
15 Director of Human Resources .... Ms. Jennifer ROBERTSON
96 Director of Purchasing .... Ms. Judith MCGILVRAY

Tyler Junior College (A)

PO Box 9020, Tyler TX 75711-9020

County: Smith FICE Identification: 003648
Unit ID: 229355
Telephone: (903) 510-2200 Carnegie Class: Assoc/Pub-R-L
FAX Number: (903) 510-2632 Calendar System: Semester
URL: www.tjc.edu
Established: 1926 Annual Undergrad Tuition & Fees (In-District): $2,352
Enrollment: 11,170 Coed
Affiliation or Control: State/Local IRS Status: 170(c)1
Highest Offering: Associate Degree
Program: Occupational; 2-Year Principally Bachelor's Creditable
Accreditation: SC, CAHIIM, COARC, DH, DMS, EMT, MLTAD, @PTAA, RAD, SURGT

01 President .... Dr. L. Michael METKE
10 Vice President Business Affairs .... Ms. Sarah E. VAN CLEEF
30 VP Advancement/External Affairs .... Dr. Kimberly A. RUSSELL
32 Provost/Vice Pres Acad & Stdnt Affs .... Dr. Juan E. MEJIA
79 Int Dean Humanities/Comm/Fine Arts .. Mrs. Sarah H. HARRISON
81 Dean Engineering/Math and Sciences ..... Dr. Kenneth R. MURPHY
76 Dean Nursing & Health Professions .... Mr. Paul R. MONAGAN
72 Assoc Vice Pres Instruction .... Dr. W. Clayton ALLEN
84 Dean Enrollment Management .... Mrs. Janna L. CHANCEY
09 Exec Dir Inst Effect/Plng & Rsrch .... Dr. Cheryl L. ROGERS
62 Director Library Services .... Mrs. Marian D. JACKSON
51 Dean Continuing Studies .... Dr. Aubrey D. SHARPE
21 Controller .... Ms. Carol A. HUTSON
06 Dir Academic Svcs/Registrar .... Mr. Thomas ELDER
37 Director Financial Aid .... Ms. Devon WIGGINS
26 Dir Public Affairs and Grant Dev .... Mr. Fred M. PETERS
35 Director Student Life .... Mrs. Lauren TYLER
29 Director Alumni Affairs .... Mr. Donald L. FRASER
36 Coordinator Career Services .... Mrs. Maggie RUELLE
07 Director Admissions .... Mrs. Nidia HASSAN
15 Exec Dir Human Resources .... Mr. S. Kevin FOWLER
88 Asst VP Student Engagement .... Dr. Timothy S. DRAIN
09 Dir Institutional Research .... Ms. Jacquelyn MESSINGER
18 Exec Dir Facilities & Construction .... Mr. William L. KING
96 Director Campus Services .... Mr. Michael CARUSO
35 Asst VP Student Services .... Dr. Thomas A. JOHNSON
13 Chief Information Officer .... Mr. Larry MENDEZ
109 Director Auxiliary Services .... Ms. Diana KAROL
44 Exec Dir Advance & Alum Engagement .... Mr. Mitch ANDREWS
36 Director Testing .... Mr. Roger GRIMM
88 Director Academic Advising .... Mrs. Jan ADAMS
88 Dean Student Success .... Ms. Lisa M. HARPER
88 Director SBDC .... Mr. Donald W. PROUDFOOT
04 Exec Asst to President .... Ms. Ellen MATTHEWS

University of Dallas (B)

1845 E Northgate Drive, Irving TX 75062-4736

County: Dallas FICE Identification: 003651
Unit ID: 224323
Telephone: (972) 721-5000 Carnegie Class: Master's L
FAX Number: (972) 721-5017 Calendar System: Semester
URL: www.udallas.edu
Established: 1956 Annual Undergrad Tuition & Fees: $35,800
Enrollment: 2,548 Coed
Affiliation or Control: Roman Catholic IRS Status: 501(c)3
Highest Offering: Doctorate
Program: Liberal Arts And General; Teacher Preparatory
Accreditation: SC, BUS

01 President .... Mr. Thomas W. KEEFE
04 Exec Admin Asst to the President .... Ms. Cathy MCCALEB
84 Sr VP Enroll Mgmt & Student Service .... Dr. John PLOTTS
10 VP and Chief Financial Officer .... Dr. Brian MURRAY
05 Provost and Chief Academic Officer .... Dr. Charles W. EAKER
30 VP for Advancement .... Ms. Joan CANTY
26 Executive VP for External Affairs .... Mr. Robert M. GALECKE
43 General Counsel .... Ms. Karin RILLEY
11 Assoc VP for Administration .... Mr. Patrick DALY
50 Interim Dean College of Business .... Dr. Brett LANDRY
49 Dean of Constantin College .... Dr. Jonathan J. SANFORD
58 Dean Grad School of Liberal Arts .... Dr. Joshua S. PARENS
73 Dean School of Ministry .... Dr. Ted WHAPHAM
08 Dean of Libraries and Research .... Ms. Cherie L. HOHERTZ
88 Assoc Dean for Constantin College .... Dr. Scott CRIDER
06 Registrar .... Mrs. Kathy MCGRAW
19 Campus Safety Supervisor .... Mr. Charles STEADMAN
90 Director of IT User Support Service .... Mr. Sabyasachi SANYAL
91 Director Information Technology .... Mr. Richard HAYTER
44 Director of Annual Giving .... Vacant
41 Director of Athletics .... Mr. Richard STROCKBINE

42 Director of Campus Ministry .... Mrs. Denise PHILLIPS
18 Director of Facilities .... Mr. Jerry HABA
21 Director of Finance .... Mr. Leonard A. ROBERTSON
15 Director of Human Resources .... Mrs. Janis TOWNSEND
09 Director of Institutional Research .... Mrs. Tanisha BARREN
26 Director of Marketing & Comm .... Mr. William HARTLEY
96 Director of Purchasing .... Mr. Alan STERLING
104 Director for Rome/Summer Programs .... Mrs. Becky DAVIES
23 Director of Student Health .... Dr. Laurie KUGELMANN DEKAT
36 Director of Career Services .... Ms. Julie JANIK

*University of Houston System (C)

212 Ezekiel Cullen Building, Houston TX 77204-2018

County: Harris FICE Identification: 011721
Unit ID: 229407
Telephone: (713) 743-1000 Carnegie Class: N/A
FAX Number: N/A
URL: www.uhsa.uh.edu

01 Chancellor .... Dr. Renu KHATOR
05 Sr VC for Academic Affairs/Provost .... Dr. Paula M. SHORT
43 Vice Chancellor/General Counsel .... Ms. Dona H. CORNELL
10 Interim VC Administration/Finance .... Mr. Jim MCSHAN
32 Vice Chancellor Student Affairs .... Dr. Richard WALKER
30 VC University Advancement .... Ms. Eloise D. STUHR
26 VP Univ Mktg/Communications/Media ...... Ms. Richie C. HUNTER
13 Assoc VC CIO/Information Technology .... Dr. Dennis FOUTY
21 Associate Vice Chancellor Finance .... Mr. Raymond BARTLETT
11 Assoc VC Administration .... Ms. Emily MESSA
86 Vice Chanc Govt Relations .... Mr. Jason S. SMITH
88 Asst VC for Planning & Policy .... Mr. Chris STANICH
15 Exec Director Human Resources .... Ms. Joan M. NELSON
21 Director Internal Auditing .... Mr. Don GUYTON
88 Treasurer .... Ms. Roberta (Robbi) PURYEAR

*University of Houston (D)

4800 Calhoun Road, Houston TX 77004

County: Harris FICE Identification: 003652
Unit ID: 225511
Telephone: (713) 743-1000 Carnegie Class: RU/VH
FAX Number: N/A Calendar System: Semester
URL: www.uh.edu
Established: 1927 Annual Undergrad Tuition & Fees (In-State): $10,273
Enrollment: 40,914 Coed
Affiliation or Control: State IRS Status: Exempt
Highest Offering: Doctorate
Program: Liberal Arts And General; Teacher Preparatory; Professional
Accreditation: SC, AAFCS, BUS, BUSA, CEA, CLPSY, CONST, COPSY, CS, DIETD, DIETI, ENG, ENGT, IPSY, LAW, MUS, OPT, OPTR, PHAR, SCPSY, SP, SW, TED

02 President .... Dr. Renu KHATOR
05 Sr VC/VP Academic Affs/Provost .... Dr. Paula M. SHORT
10 Int VC/VP Administration/Finance .... Mr. Jim MCSHAN
30 VC/VP University Advancement .... Ms. Eloise D. STUHR
32 VC/VP Student Affairs .... Dr. Richard WALKER
26 VP for Mtkg/Commun/Media Rels .... Ms. Richie C. HUNTER
20 Vice Provost Academic Programs .... Dr. Bruce A. JONES
86 VC/VP Govt & Community Relations .... Mr. Jason S. SMITH
43 VC/VP Legal Affairs & Gen Counsel .... Ms. Dona H. CORNELL
46 Int VC/VP Research/Tech Transfer .... Dr. Ramanan KRISHNAMOORTI
31 VP for Community Rels & Inst Access .... Dr. Elwyn C. LEE
88 Vice Provost Global Strategies .... Dr. Jaime ORTIZ
29 Assoc VP Alumni Association .... Mr. Mike PEDE
13 Assoc VP Information Tech/CIO .... Dr. Dennis FOUTY
26 Director Media Relations .... Ms. Shawn LINDSEY
20 Vice Provost & Dean UG Stdnts .... Dr. Teri E. LONGACRE
58 Vice Provost & Dean Grad School .... Mr. Dimitri LITVINOV
88 Int Assoc Provost Fac Dev/Affairs .... Dr. Mark CLARKE
21 Assoc Provost Finance & Admin .... Dr. Sabrina HASSUMANI
30 Assoc VP for Univ Development .... Mr. Cliff REDD
35 Assoc VC/VP Student Affairs .... Mr. Daniel MAXWELL
88 Assoc VP Stdnt Affs/Dean of Stdnts .... Dr. William MUNSON
91 Assoc VP Enterprise Sys Adm .... Dr. Arun JAIN
21 Associate VC/VP Finance .... Mr. Raymond BARTLETT
88 Assoc Prov Educ Innov & Tech .... Dr. Jeff MORGAN
22 Asst VC/VP Equal Opportunity .... Dr. Richard A. BAKER
45 AVC/Assoc Prov Inst Plng/Analy .... Mr. Chris M. STANICH
41 VP Intercollegiate Athletics .... Mr. Hunter YURACHEK
37 Exec Dir Scholarships & Fin Aid .... Mr. Sal LORIA
15 Exec Director Human Resources .... Ms. Joan NELSON
18 Int Dir Facilities Management .... Mr. Carlos VILLARREAL
51 Director Continuing Education ... Ms. Mercedes SURATY-CLARKE
06 University Registrar .... Ms. Debbie HENRY
07 Executive Director of Admissions .... Ms. Djuana YOUNG
19 Asst VC/VP Public Safety Secu .... Mr. Malcolm DAVIS
96 Director of Purchasing .... Mr. Jack TENNER
49 Int Dean Col Liberal Arts/Soc Sci .... Dr. Steven CRAIG
81 Dean Col Natural Sci & Math .... Dr. Dan WELLS
88 Interim Dean College of Optometry .... Dr. Roger BOLTZ
72 Dean College of Technology .... Dr. William E. FITZGIBBON, III
54 Dean Cullen College of Engineering .... Dr. Joseph W. TEDESCO
48 Dean College of Architecture .... Ms. Patricia Belton OLIVER
70 Dean Graduate Col of Social Work .... Dr. Alan DETLAFF
67 Dean College of Pharmacy .... Dr. Lamar PRITCHARD
53 Dean College of Education .... Dr. Robert MCPHERSON
50 Dean Bauer Col Business Admin .... Dr. Latha RAMCHAND
88 Dean Hilton Col Htl/Restaurant Mgt .... Dr. Dennis REYNOLDS
92 Dean Honors College .... Dr. William MONROE
61 Dean UH Law Center .... Mr. Leonard M. BAYNES

88 Assoc VC/VP Administration .... Ms. Emily MESSA
88 Chief Energy Officer .... Dr. Ramanan KRISHNAMOORTI
17 Interim Chief Health Officer .... Dr. Earl L. SMITH

*University of Houston - Clear Lake (E)

2700 Bay Area Boulevard, Houston TX 77058

County: Harris FICE Identification: 011711
Unit ID: 225414
Telephone: (281) 283-7600 Carnegie Class: Master's L
FAX Number: (281) 283-2219 Calendar System: Semester
URL: www.uhcl.edu
Established: 1971 Annual Undergrad Tuition & Fees (In-State): $7,473
Enrollment: 8,665 Coed
Affiliation or Control: State IRS Status: 501(c)3
Highest Offering: Doctorate
Program: Liberal Arts And General; Teacher Preparatory; Professional
Accreditation: SC, BUS, BUSA, CS, ENG, ENGR, MFCD, SW, TED

02 President .... Dr. William A. STAPLES
05 Sr Vice Pres for Academic Affairs .... Dr. Carl A. STOCKTON
10 Vice Pres Administration & Finance .... Ms. Michelle DOTTER
04 Executive Assoc to the President .. Ms. Mary Ann H. SHALLBERG
13 Assoc VP Information Resources .... Dr. A. Glen HOUSTON
20 Assoc Vice Pres Academic Affairs .... Dr. Mrinal Mugdh VARMA
30 Assoc VP University Advancement .... Ms. Rhonda THOMPSON
32 Assoc Vice Pres Student Services .... Dr. Darlene BIGGERS
21 Associate Vice President Finance .... Ms. Usha MATHEW
84 Assoc Vice Pres Enrollment Mgmt .... Dr. Yvette BENDECK
18 Assoc VP Facilities Mgmt/Construct .... Mr. Ward MARTAINDALE
50 Dean School Business .... Dr. Wm. Theodore CUMMINGS
81 Dean School Science/Computer Engr .... Dr. Zbigniew CZAJKIEWICZ
79 Dean Sch Human Sci/Humanities .... Dr. Rick SHORT
53 Dean School Education .... Dr. Mark D. SHERMIS
35 Interim Dean of Students .... Mr. David A. RACHITA
28 Asst Dean Student Diversity .... Ms. Linda C. BULLOCK
08 Exec Director Neumann Library .... Ms. Karen WIELHORSKI
85 Exec Dir Intl Admissions/Programs .... Dr. Sameer PANDE
45 Exec Dir Planning and Assessment .... Ms. Pat CUCHENS
15 Executive Director Human Resources .... Vacant
14 Exec Director University Computing .... Mr. Rodger CARR
21 Exec Dir of Procurement & Payables .... Ms. Debra CARPENTER
25 Exec Dir Sponsored Programs .... Mr. Paul MEYERS
37 Executive Director Financial Aid .... Mr. Billy SATTERFIELD
88 Exec Dir Environment Inst Houston .... Dr. George GUILLEN
06 Registrar/Director Academic Records .... Mr. Billy SATTERFIELD
56 Director Distance/Off-Campus Educ .... Ms. Lisa GABRIEL
26 Exec Dir University Communications ... Ms. Theresa PRESSWOOD
29 Dir Development & Alumni Relations .... Mr. Dwayne BUSBY
19 Director Police .... Mr. Paul WILLINGHAM
36 Ex Dir Counseling/Hlth/Career Svcs .... Dr. Cindy COOK
91 Assoc Dir Data Management .... Vacant
12 Dir Camp Operat/UHCL Pearland Camp .... Ms. Kathy DUPREE
23 Dir Health & Disability Services .... Ms. Regina PICKETT
07 Exec Director of Admissions .... Ms. Rauchelle JONES
40 Manager Bookstore .... Ms. Laura FORGEY

*University of Houston - Downtown (F)

One Main Street, Houston TX 77002-1014

County: Harris FICE Identification: 003612
Unit ID: 225432
Telephone: (713) 221-8001 Carnegie Class: Bac/Diverse
FAX Number: (713) 221-8075 Calendar System: Semester
URL: www.uhd.edu
Established: 1974 Annual Undergrad Tuition & Fees (In-State): $5,790
Enrollment: 14,439 Coed
Affiliation or Control: State IRS Status: Exempt
Highest Offering: Master's
Program: Liberal Arts And General
Accreditation: SC, BUS, ENGT, SW

02 President .... Dr. William V. FLORES
88 Special Asst to the President .... Dr. Gene PREUSS
05 Int Provost/Sr VP Acad & Stdnt Affs .... Mr. Edward HUGETZ
20 Assoc VP for Academic Affairs .... Dr. Faiza KHOJA
32 Assoc VP Student Affairs .... Ms. Tomikia P. LEGRANDE
50 Dean College of Business .... Dr. Michael FIELDS
79 Dean Col Humanities/Social Sci .... Dr. DoVeanna FULTON
88 Int Dean College of Public Service .... Dr. Leigh VAN HORN
81 Dean Col Sciences & Tech .... Dr. Akif UZMAN
97 Dean University College .... Dr. Chris BIRCHAK
88 Int Dir Comm Engage & Svc Learning .... Dr. Poonam GULATI
08 Executive Director WI Dykes Library .... Ms. Pat ENSOR
88 Asst Dir Library Plng & Assessment .... Ms. Lisa BERRY
106 Exec Dir Distance Education .... Mr. Louis D. EVANS, III
09 Director of Institutional Research .... Ms. Carol M. TUCKER
88 Asst VP Research & Spon Programs .... Dr. Sandra GARCIA
88 Dir Grant Writing & Assessment .... Dr. Kwame OPUNI
108 Director of Academic Assessment .... Dr. Lea CAMPBELL
88 Dir Co-Curricular & Oper Assessment .... Dr. Angela KOPONEN
88 Director Creative Services .... Mr. Joe WYNNE
88 Director O'Kane Gallery .... Mr. Mark CERVENKA
92 Exec Director of Scholars Academy .... Dr. Mary Jo PARKER
88 Dir Teaching & Learning Excel .... Dr. Gregory DEMENT
88 Exec Dir Academic Advising Center .... Dr. Wendy WILSON
88 Director Advising Center .... Ms. Jemma SYLVESTER-CAESAR
88 Director of Advising Services .... Ms. Reyna ROMERO
88 Director of Academic Support Center .... Dr. Isidro GRAU
88 Exec Dir Presidential Affairs & Ops .... Ms. Liza ALONZO
88 Exec Dir Academic Admin & Ops .... Ms. Elaine PEARSON

88 Dir Strategic Initiatives & Project .... Ms. Lucy BOWEN
11 Dir College Admin & Operation .... Ms. Paulette PURDY
72 Dir Applied Business/Technology Ctr .... Mr. G. V. KRISHNAN
88 Director English Language Institute .... Dr. Gail KELLERSBERGER
88 Director Criminal Justice Center .... Mr. Rex WHITE
51 Director Continuing Education .... Ms. Clara ROJAS ALVAREZ LOPEREN
88 Director Emergency Management .... Ms. Carol MANOUSOS
88 Dir Center for Entrepreneurship .... Mr. William DUDLEY
88 Director Insurance & Risk Mgmt Ctr .... Dr. Wendall BRANIFF
88 Dir COB Career Dev Center .... Mr. Brett HOBBY
88 Dir Assurance Learning & Asse .... Mr. Isiah BROWN
88 Dir of Retail Mgmt Center .... Mr. James DAVIS
10 VP Administration & Finance .... Mr. David M. BRADLEY
13 Assoc VP Information Technology .... Mr. Hossein SHAHROKHI
91 Director Enterprise Systems .... Mr. Kong YIN
88 Dir Technology Learning Services .... Mr. John LANE
88 Director Technical Services .... Ms. Grace DAVILA
88 Dir Comp/Telecom & Video Networks .... Mr. Miguel RUIZ
90 Dir User Support Services .... Mr. Said FATTOUH
109 Dir University Business Services .... Ms. Mary TORRES
88 Director of Budget & Procurement .... Ms. Theresa MENELEY
88 Dir IT Business Services .... Ms. Jacqueline SMITH
21 Asst VP Business Affairs .... Mr. George W. ANDERSON
88 Dir Financial Reporting .... Ms. Delethia MURRAY
25 Director Risk Mgmt & Compliance .... Ms. Mary COOK
18 Asst VP Facilities Management .... Mr. Chris MCCALL
88 Dir Maintenance & Renovations .... Mr. Abraham FLORES
88 Dir MEP .... Mr. Kris ZIMMERMAN
19 Chief of Police .... Mr. Richard BOYLE
88 Dir Student Acct & Collection .... Ms. Lauren BELLENGER
88 Dir Accounts Payable .... Ms. Cynthia CONNER
15 VP Employment Svcs & Operations ... Ms. Ivonne MONTALBANO
16 Exec Dir Employ Services & Opers .... Dr. Shawn MCCANN
88 Dir Benefits & Compensation .... Ms. Erica MORALES
88 Director Employment Operations .... Ms. April FRANK
88 Asst Dean Enrollment Management .. Mr. Christopher CHEATHAM
32 Dean of Students .... Vacant
35 Asst Dn Student Affs/Title IV Coord .... Mr. Tommy THOMASON
88 Int Dir Student Activities & Events .... Ms. Sara T. CRASS
28 Dir Ctr Stdnt Diversity Equ & Incl .... Dr. John HUDSON
07 Dir Graduate & Intl Admissions .... Ms. Ceshia LOVE
07 Director of Admissions .... Mr. Spencer LIGHTSY
37 Director of Scholarships & Fin Aid .... Ms. LaTasha GOUDEAU
41 Director Sports & Fitness .... Mr. Richard SEBASTIANI
36 Director Career Development Center .... Ms. Laura A. WESELEY
88 Director of Testing Services .... Vacant
88 Director Disability Services .... Dr. Meritza TAMEZ
88 Director Veterans Services .... Mr. Richard SELVERA
88 Director Talent Search .... Ms. Jennifer HIGHTOWER
92 Director Honors Porgram .... Dr. Mari NICHOLSON-PREUSS
88 Director Upward Bound .... Ms. Dawanna LEWIS
88 Pgm Dir Title V Stdnt Success Grant .... Ms. Katrina BORDERS
30 VP Advancement & External Rels .... Ms. Johanna WOLFE
26 Executive Dir University Relations .... Vacant
102 Director Corporate Relations .... Mr. Jacob LIPP
88 Director Individual Giving .... Ms. Jaha WILLIAMS
88 Director Media Relations .... Ms. Claire CATON

*University of Houston - Victoria (A)

3007 N Ben Wilson, Victoria TX 77901-4450

County: Victoria | FICE Identification: 013231 | Unit ID: 225502

Telephone: (361) 570-4848 | Carnegie Class: Master's L
FAX Number: (361) 580-5534 | Calendar System: Semester
URL: www.uhv.edu
Established: 1973 | Annual Undergrad Tuition & Fees (In-State): $5,761
Enrollment: 4,604 | Coed
Affiliation or Control: State | IRS Status: 501(c)3
Highest Offering: Master's
Program: Liberal Arts And General; Teacher Preparatory; Professional
Accreditation: **SC**, BUS, CACREP, NURSE, @TEAC

02 Interim President .... Dr. Raymond V. MORGAN, JR.
11 Vice Pres Administration & Finance .... Mr. Wayne B. BERAN
05 Provost/Vice Pres Acad Affairs .... Dr. Jeffrey CASS
32 Vice President Student Affairs .... Dr. Jay LAMBERT
49 Dean Arts & Sciences .... Dr. Jeffrey DILEO
50 Dean Business Administration .... Dr. Farhang NIROOMAND
53 Dean Education & Human Development .... Dr. Freddie LITTON
30 VP Advancement & External Relations .... Mr. Jesse D. PISORS
08 Senior Director of Library .... Dr. Joe F. DAHLSTROM
13 Sr Dir Academic & Student Tech Svcs .... Mr. Joseph S. FERGUSON
15 Dir Human Resource/Affirmative Act .... Ms. Laura L. SMITH
84 Assoc VP for Enrollment Mgmt .... Dr. Denee THOMAS
88 Dir Small Business Development Ctr .... Mr. Joe HUMPHREYS
06 Registrar .... Ms. Trudy WORTHAM
14 Director Administrative Technology .... Mr. Randy FAULK
37 Director Financial Aid .... Ms. Carolyn R. MALLORY
18 Director Facilities .... Mr. Kevin MYERS
10 Director Business Services .... Mr. Tim MICHALSKI
21 Comptroller .... Ms. Valerie WALDEN
41 Director Athletics .... Mr. Ashley WALYUCHOW
26 Director Marketing & Communications .... Ms. Paula COBLER
38 Director of Counseling Center .... Dr. Hege RIISE
35 Director of Student Life & Services .... Mr. Michael WILKINSON
09 Director Institutional Research .... Dr. Tong-Ai ZHANG
88 Director of Budget .... Ms. Karen SANDERS
39 Director Residence Life & Univ Comm .... Mr. Brandon w. LEE
88 Director Capital Projects .... Ms. Brenda SVETLIK
04 Executive Adm Asst to President .... Ms. Kathy WALTON

25 Dir Research Adm & Sponsored Pgms ... Ms. Angela HARTMANN
108 Dir Institutional Effectiveness .... Dr. Sharon M. BAILEY

University of the Incarnate Word (B)

4301 Broadway, San Antonio TX 78209-6397

County: Bexar | FICE Identification: 003578 | Unit ID: 225627

Telephone: (210) 829-6000 | Carnegie Class: Master's L
FAX Number: (210) 829-1220 | Calendar System: Semester
URL: www.uiw.edu
Established: 1881 | Annual Undergrad Tuition & Fees: $27,798
Enrollment: 8,745 | Coed
Affiliation or Control: Roman Catholic | IRS Status: 501(c)3
Highest Offering: Doctorate
Program: Liberal Arts And General; Teacher Preparatory; Professional
Accreditation: **SC**, ACBSP, CAATE, CIDA, DIETD, DIETI, HSA, MUS, NMT, NURSE, OPT, OPTR, PHAR, PTA, THEA

01 President .... Dr. Louis J. AGNESE, JR.
00 Chancellor .... Dr. Denise DOYLE
88 Vice President Mission and Ministry .... Sr. Walter MAHER
04 Executive Assistant to President .... Ms. Yvonne BURNS
26 Asst to the President/Communication .... Mr. Lou FOX
43 General Counsel .... Ms. Cindy ESCAMILLA
05 Provost .... Dr. Kathleen LIGHT
84 Vice Pres Enrollment Mgt/Stdnt Svcs .Dr. David M. JURENOVICH
30 Vice Pres Institutional Advancement .... Sr. Kathleen COUGHLIN
10 Vice Pres for Business & Finance .... Mr. Douglas ENDSLEY
104 Vice Pres International Programs .... Mr. Marcos FRAGOSO
56 Vice Pres of Ext Academic Programs .... Dr. Cyndi WILSON-PORTER
13 Vice Pres Information Resources/CIO .... Vacant
21 Comptroller .... Ms. Edith COGDELL
50 Dean H-E-B Sch Business & Admin .... Dr. Forrest F. AVEN
57 Dean Humanities Arts & Social Sci .... Dr. Kevin VICHCALES
66 Dean Nursing & Health Professions .... Dr. Mary HOKE
53 Dean Dreeben School of Education .... Dr. Denise STAUDT
54 Dean Math Science Engineering .... Dr. Carlos GARCIA
88 Dean Interactive Media & Design .... Dr. Sharon WELKEY
67 Dean Feik School of Pharmacy ..... Dr. Arcelia JOHNSON-FANNIN
88 Dean School of Optometry .... Dr. Timothy WINGERT
58 Dean of Grad Studies/Research .... Dr. Osman OZTURGUT
62 Dean of Library Services .... Dr. Cheryl ANDERSON
108 Assoc Provost/Dir of Assessment .... Dr. Glenn JAMES
55 Dean Sch of Extended Studies .... Mr. Vincent PORTER
88 Dean Univ Preparatory Programs .... Mr. Daniel OCHOA
88 Dean School Physical Therapy .... Dr. Caroline GOULET
29 Director of Alumni Relations .... Dr. Lisa MCNARY
26 Director of Public Relations .... Ms. Debra DEL TORO
84 Dean of Enrollment .... Ms. Andrea CYTERSKI-ACOSTA
32 Dean of Student Success .... Ms. Sandy MCMAKIN
38 Director of Counseling .... Vacant
20 Director of Academic Advising .... Ms. Sonia JASSO
88 Director Learning Assistance Center .... Ms. Cristina ARIZA
06 Registrar .... Dr. Bobbye G. FRY
37 Director of Financial Aid .... Ms. Amy CARCANAGUES
32 Dean of Campus Life .... Dr. Renee MOORE
39 Director of Residence Life .... Ms. Diane SANCHEZ
35 Dir University Events/Student Pgms .... Mr. Paul AYALA
23 Director of Health Services .... Vacant
42 Chaplain .... Fr. Tom DYMOWSKI
42 Director of Campus Ministry .... Ms. Elisabeth VILLARREAL
15 Director of Human Resources .... Ms. Annette THOMPSON
96 Director of Purchasing .... Mr. Sam WAGES
18 Director Facilities Mgmt & Services .... Mr. Steve HEYING
41 Director of Athletics .... Mr. Mark PAPICH
88 Director of Infrastructure Support .... Mr. Carl HAYWOOD
88 Director of Enterprise Applications .... Ms. Iris SOLCHER
88 Director Instructional Technology .... Ms. Ana GONZALES
72 Director of Technology Support .... Mr. Anthony RAMOS
09 Director of Institutional Research .... Ms. Robin LOGAN
07 Director of Admissions .... Mr. Javier LARA
36 Coordinator of Career Services .... Ms. Abreeta GOODE
100 Chief of Staff .... Mr. Vincent RODRIGUEZ
102 Dir Foundation/Corporate Relations .... Mr. Robert SOSA
105 Director Web Development .... Mr. Troy KINCKERBOCKER
19 Chief of Police .... Mr. Robert CHAVEZ
44 Dir of Major Gifts/Planned Giving .... Mr. Alex CASTANEDA
91 Sr Dir Digital Infra/User Resources .... Vacant

University of Mary Hardin-Baylor (C)

900 College Street, Belton TX 76513-2578

County: Bell | FICE Identification: 003588 | Unit ID: 226471

Telephone: (254) 295-8642 | Carnegie Class: Master's S
FAX Number: (254) 295-4535 | Calendar System: Semester
URL: www.umhb.edu
Established: 1845 | Annual Undergrad Tuition & Fees: $26,100
Enrollment: 3,733 | Coed
Affiliation or Control: Southern Baptist | IRS Status: 501(c)3
Highest Offering: Doctorate
Program: Liberal Arts And General; Teacher Preparatory; Professional
Accreditation: **SC**, CACREP, MUS, NURSE, @PTA, SW

01 President/CEO .... Dr. Randy G. O'REAR
03 Sr Vice Pres Admin/COO .... Dr. Steve THEODORE
05 Provost/Sr Vice Pres Academics .... Dr. Steve OLDHAM
00 President Emeritus .... Dr. Jerry G. BAWCOM
45 Vice Pres Campus Planning & Support .... Mr. Rick MARTINEZ
30 Vice Pres for Development .... Mr. Brent DAVISON

102 Vice Pres Communication/Spec Proj .... Dr. Paula TANNER
32 Vice Pres for Student Life .... Dr. Byron WEATHERSBEE
41 Vice Pres Athletics .... Mr. Randy MANN
10 Vice Pres Business/Finance/CFO .... Mrs. Jennifer RAMM
15 Vice Pres Human Resources .... Mrs. Susan OWENS
13 Vice Pres Information Tech .... Mr. Brent HARRIS
84 Vice Pres Enrollment Mgmt .... Dr. Gary LAMM
18 Assoc Vice Pres for Campus Planning .... Mr. Bob PATTEE
20 Vice Pres Innovation/Assoc Provost .... Dr. Tammi COOPER
21 Controller .... Mrs. Charla KAHLIG
79 Dean of Humanities & Sciences .... Dr. Danny MYNATT
66 Dean of Nursing .... Dr. Sharon SOUTER
53 Dean of Education .... Dr. Marlene ZIPPERLEN
58 Dean Graduate School .... Dr. Colin WILBORN
88 Dean of Christian Studies .... Dr. Tim CRAWFORD
57 Dean Visual/Performing Arts .... Mr. Ted BARNES
35 Dean of Students .... Mr. Ray MARTIN
39 Assoc Dean Students/Dir Residence .... Ms. Donna PLANK
04 Executive Assistant .... Mrs. Phyllis ROGERS
06 Registrar .... Mrs. Amy MCGILVRAY
88 Dir Grad Student Services/Engagemt .... Ms. Melissa WILLIAMS
07 Director of Admissions & Recruiting .... Dr. Brent BURKS
08 Director Learning Resources .... Ms. Denise KARIMKHANI
26 Director Marketing/Public Relations .... Mr. James STAFFORD
09 Director Institutional Research .... Ms. Jen JONES
37 Director Financial Aid .... Mr. Ron BROWN
92 Director Honors Program .... Dr. David HOLCOMB
19 Director Campus Police .... Mr. Gary SARGENT
96 Purchasing Manager .... Mrs. Jennifer WEBB
29 Assoc Vice Pres Development/Alumni ...... Ms. Rebecca O'BANION
42 University Chaplain .... Dr. George LOUTHERBACK
36 Director Career Services .... Mr. Don OWENS
38 Director Couns Testing & Health .... Mr. Nate WILLIAMS
85 Dir International Student Services .... Mrs. Elizabeth TANAKA
44 Director Planned Giving .... Mrs. Melissa BRAGG
40 Bookstore Manager .... Ms. Debbie COTTRELL

University of North Texas (D)

1155 Union Circle #311277, Denton TX 76203-5013

County: Denton | FICE Identification: 003594 | Unit ID: 227216

Telephone: (940) 565-2000 | Carnegie Class: RU/H
FAX Number: (940) 565-7600 | Calendar System: Semester
URL: www.unt.edu
Established: 1890 | Annual Undergrad Tuition & Fees (In-State): $10,090
Enrollment: 36,164 | Coed
Affiliation or Control: State | IRS Status: 501(c)3
Highest Offering: Doctorate
Program: Liberal Arts And General; Teacher Preparatory; Professional
Accreditation: **SC**, ART, AUD, BUS, BUSA, CACREP, CEA, CIDA, CLPSY, COPSY, CORE, CS, ENG, ENGT, FEPAC, JOUR, LIB, MUS, NRPA, SP, SPAA, SW, TED

01 President .... Dr. Neal SMATRESK
00 Chancellor .... Mr. Lee F. JACKSON
05 Provost/Vice Pres Academic Affairs .... Dr. Finley GRAVES
10 Vice Pres Finance/Administration .... Mr. Bob BROWN
46 VP Research/Economic Development .... Dr. Thomas J. MCCOY
32 Vice President Student Affairs .... Dr. Elizabeth WITH
43 Vice Chancellor/General Counsel .... Ms. Tina SIKES
26 Vice President University Relations ...... Ms. Deborah S. LELIAERT
30 VP for Advancement/Dir of Develop .... Ms. Eileen P. MORAN
84 VP for Enrollment .... Dr. Shannon M. GOODMAN
20 Vice Provost for Academic Affairs .... Dr. Christy CRUTSINGER
20 Vice Provost for Academic Resources .... Dr. Allen CLARK
20 Vice Provost for Faculty Success .... Dr. Angela WILSON
41 Athletic Director .... Mr. Rick VILLARREAL
35 Dean Students .... Dr. Maureen MCGUINNESS
13 Vice President for Information Tech .... Vacant
21 Assoc VP Budget & Analytics .... Ms. Beverly COTTON
28 VP Institutional Equity & Diversity .... Dr. Joanne WOODARD
88 Vice Prov for Transfer Articulation .... Dr. Celia WILLIAMSON
18 Assoc Vice President for Facilities .... Mr. David REYNOLDS
08 Dean of Libraries .... Dr. Martin HALBERT
37 Director Financial Aid .... Ms. Zelma DELEON
49 Dean College of Arts/Sciences .... Dr. David HOLDEMAN
50 Dean College Business .... Dr. Marilyn WILEY
53 Dean College of Education .... Dr. Jerry R. THOMAS
57 Dean Col Visual Arts & Design .... Dr. Eric LIGON
88 Dean Col Public Affs/Community Svc .... Dr. Thomas L. EVENSON
64 Dean College of Music .... Dr. James C. SCOTT
59 Dean Col of Merch/Hosp & Tourism .... Dr. Judith FORNEY
62 Dean College of Information .... Dr. Herman L. TOTTEN
58 Dean Toulouse Grad School .... Dr. Costas TSATSOULIS
92 Dean Honors College .... Dr. Glenisson DE OLIVEIRA
60 Dean Mayborn Sch of Journalism .... Dr. Dorothy BLAND
54 Dean College of Engineering .... Dr. Costas TSATSOULIS
90 Director Acad Computing/User Svcs .... Dr. Philip C. BACZEWSKI
09 Director Institutional Research .... Dr. Mary BARTON
108 Assoc Vice Provost IR&E .... Dr. Jason F. SIMON
88 Dir Institutional Effectiveness .... Ms. Elizabeth FISHER
07 Director of Admissions .... Dr. Rebecca LOTHRINGER
51 Dir Ctr for Achvmnt & Lifelng Lrng .... Ms. Marilyn D. WAGNER
06 Registrar .... Ms. Lynn MCCREARY
15 Assoc Vice Chancellor HR .... Mr. Luis LEWIN
36 Dir Career & Counseling Svcs .... Mr. Dan NAEGELI
38 Director of Counseling & Testing .... Vacant
19 Director/Chief of Police .... Mr. Ed REYNOLDS
39 Director Housing .... Mr. James FAIRCHILD
85 Vice Provost International Affairs .... Dr. Richard NADER
23 Dir Stdnt Health Ctr/Wellness Svcs .... Dr. Herschel VOORHEES
29 Exec Dir Alum Rels/N Texas Exes .... Mr. Robert MCINTURF

04 Administrative Asst to President ....Ms. Ruby RAINES
101 Secretary of the Institution/Board ....Dr. Rosemary R. HAGGETT
25 Asst VP Research/Sponsored Pgm .... Dr. David SCHULTZ
104 Director Study Abroad ....Ms. Amy SHENBERGER

University of North Texas at Dallas (A)

7300 University Hills Blvd, Dallas TX 75241
County: Dallas Identification: 667124
Telephone: (972) 780-3600 Carnegie Class: Not Classified
FAX Number: (972) 780-3606 Calendar System: Semester
URL: www.untdallas.edu
Established: 2000 Annual Undergrad Tuition & Fees (In-State): $7,860
Enrollment: 2,575 Coed
Affiliation or Control: State IRS Status: 501(c)3
Highest Offering: Doctorate
Program: Liberal Arts And General
Accreditation: SC

01 President ....Dr. Ronald BROWN
10 Chief Financial Officer .... Dr. Daniel EDELMAN
05 Provost ....Dr. Lois BECKER

University of North Texas Health Science Center at Fort Worth (B)

3500 Camp Bowie Boulevard, Fort Worth TX 76107-2699
County: Tarrant FICE Identification: 009768
Unit ID: 228909
Telephone: (817) 735-2000 Carnegie Class: Spec/Med
FAX Number: (817) 735-2486 Calendar System: Semester
URL: www.unthsc.edu
Established: 1966 Annual Graduate Tuition & Fees: $16,330
Enrollment: 2,242 Coed
Affiliation or Control: State IRS Status: 501(c)3
Highest Offering: Doctorate; No Undergraduates
Program: Professional
Accreditation: SC, ARCPA, FEPAC, HSA, OSTEO, PH, @PHAR, PTA

01 President ....Dr. Michael WILLIAMS
10 VP for Finance and CFO ....Mr. John A. HARMAN
86 Vice President Governmental Affairs ....Mr. Dan JENSEN
63 Dean Texas Col of Osteopathic Med ....Dr. Don PESKA
32 Vice Pres Student Affairs ....Dr. Thomas MOORMAN
15 Vice Pres Human Resource Svcs ....Vacant
45 VP Research & Innovation ....Dr. David CISTOLA
51 Assoc VP for Professional/Cont Edu .... Ms. Pam MCFADDEN
58 Dean Grad Sch Biomedical Sciences .... Dr. Meharvan SINGH
76 Dean School of Health Professions ....Dr. Claire PEEL
69 Dean of School of Public Health ....Dr. Richard KURZ
37 Director Student Financial Aid ....Mr. Joseph SANCHEZ
84 Executive Director Enrollment Svcs ....Mr. A.J RANDOLPH
19 Chief of Police ....Mr. Gary GAILLIARD
30 VP Institutional Advancement ....Mr. Doug WHITE
09 VP Strategy & Measurement ....Dr. Thomas FAIRCHILD
21 Controller & Chief Budget Officer ....Mr. Geoff SCARPELLI
07 Asst Dean of Admissions & Outreach ....Vacant
18 Vice President for Operations ....Mr. Stephen BARRETT
26 VP Marketing & Communications ....Ms. Jean TIPS
96 Dir Of Contract Administration ....Mrs. Lane NESTMAN
06 Registrar ....Mr. A.J RANDOLPH
100 Chief of Staff ....Mrs. Jennifer TREVINO

University of Phoenix Austin Campus (C)

10801-2 MoPac Expressway, Suite 300,
Austin TX 78759-5459
Telephone: (512) 344-1400 Identification: 770226
Accreditation: &NH, ACBSP

† Branch campus of University of Phoenix, Tempe, AZ.

University of Phoenix Dallas Campus (D)

12400 Coit Road, Dallas TX 75251-2004
Telephone: (972) 385-1055 Identification: 770227
Accreditation: &NH, ACBSP

† Branch campus of University of Phoenix, Tempe, AZ.

University of Phoenix El Paso Campus (E)

1340 Adabel Drive, El Paso TX 79936-5900
Telephone: (915) 599-5900 Identification: 770228
Accreditation: &NH, ACBSP

† Branch campus of University of Phoenix, Tempe, AZ.

University of Phoenix Houston Campus (F)

11451 Katy Freeway, Houston TX 77079-2004
Telephone: (713) 465-9966 Identification: 770229
Accreditation: &NH, ACBSP

† Branch campus of University of Phoenix, Tempe, AZ.

University of Phoenix McAllen Campus (G)

4201 South Shary Road, Mission TX 78572-1578
Telephone: (956) 519-5800 Identification: 770230
Accreditation: &NH, ACBSP

† No longer accepting campus-based students.

University of Phoenix San Antonio Campus (H)

8200 IH-10 West, Suite 1000, San Antonio TX 78230-3876
Telephone: (210) 524-2100 Identification: 770231
Accreditation: &NH, ACBSP

† Branch campus of University of Phoenix, Tempe, AZ.

University of St. Augustine for Health Sciences (I)

5401 La Crosse Ave, Austin TX 78739
Telephone: (512) 394-9766 Identification: 770940
Accreditation: &WC, DEAC, PTA

† Branch campus of University of St. Augustine for Health Sciences, San Marcos, CA.

University of St. Thomas (J)

3800 Montrose Boulevard, Houston TX 77006-4696
County: Harris FICE Identification: 003654
Unit ID: 227863
Telephone: (713) 522-7911 Carnegie Class: Master's L
FAX Number: (713) 525-2125 Calendar System: Semester
URL: www.stthom.edu
Established: 1947 Annual Undergrad Tuition & Fees: $30,310
Enrollment: 3,522 Coed
Affiliation or Control: Roman Catholic IRS Status: 501(c)3
Highest Offering: Doctorate
Program: Liberal Arts And General; Teacher Preparatory; Professional
Accreditation: SC, BUS, NURSE, TEAC, THEOL

01 President ....Dr. Robert IVANY
04 Special Assistant to the President ....Ms. Cindy VIAUD
04 Exec Assistant to the President ....Ms. Connie BICKHAM
10 Vice President for Finance ....Ms. Elizabeth CONDIC
05 Provost and VP Academic Affairs ....Dr. Dominic AQUILA
11 Assoc VP of Human Resources ....Mr. Randy GRAHAM
49 Dean Arts & Sciences ....Fr. Joseph PILSNER
73 Dean School of Theology ....Dr. Sandra C. MAGIE, CM
50 Dean Cameron School of Business ....Dr. Beena GEORGE
53 Dean School of Education ....Dr. Robert LEBLANC
08 Dean of Libraries ....Mr. James PICCININNI
58 Dir Center for Thomistic Studies ....Dr. Thomas OSBORNE
88 Director Center for Business Ethics ....Dr. Michele SIMMS
82 Director Center for Intl Studies ....Dr. Hans STOCKTON
88 Director Center for Irish Studies ....Ms. Lori GALLAGHER
13 Vice Pres Information Technology ....Mr. Gary MCCORMACK
30 Vice President for Inst Advancement ....Ms. Cynthia COLBERT RILEY
84 Vice Pres Marketing & Enroll Mgmt ....Ms. Vickie ALLEMAN
88 Director Center for Faith & Culture .... Fr. Donald NESTI, CSSP
06 Registrar ....Ms. Debra LOVELESS
90 Dir of Network & Campus Computing ....Mr. Tony REYNA
90 Director Technology Support Svcs .... Mr. Mark HENDERSON
91 Dir Administrative Computing Svcs ......Ms. Joanna E. PALASOTA
32 Vice Pres Student Affairs ....Ms. Patricia MCKINLEY
35 Dean of Students ....Ms. Lindsey MCPHERSON
38 Exec Dir Counseling & Disability ....Dr. Rose SIGNORELLO
35 Assistant VP of Campus Life ....Mr. Matthew PRASIFKA
42 Dir of Campus Ministry/Chaplain ....Fr. Michael BUENTELLO
39 Director Residence Life ....Mr. Marquis GATEWOOD
88 Asst Dir of Recreational Sports ....Ms. Mary Ann SHAW
18 Asst VP Facilities Operations ....Mr. Howard A. ROSE
21 Controller ....Ms. Brandy SHAW
88 Treasurer ....Ms. Susan ROSE
84 Asst VP of Enrollment Management ....Mr. Arthur ORTIZ
07 Dir of Transfer Adm & Veteran Svcs ....Mr. Phil BUTCHER
37 Dean of Scholarships/Financial Aid .... Ms. Lynda MCKENDREE
26 Asst VP Marketing Communications ....Ms. Sandra SOLIZ
88 Director of Creative Services ....Ms. Marionette MITCHELL
108 Assoc VP Institutional Assessment ....Dr. Siobhan FLEMING
19 Chief of Police ....Mr. James TATE
41 Athletic Director ....Mr. Todd SMITH

*University of Texas System Administration (K)

601 Colorado Street, Austin TX 78701-2982
County: Travis FICE Identification: 003655
Unit ID: 229090
Telephone: (512) 499-4201 Carnegie Class: N/A
FAX Number: (512) 499-4215
URL: www.utsystem.edu

01 Chancellor ....Mr. William H. MCRAVEN
05 Exec VC Academic Affairs ....Dr. Steve LESLIE
17 Exec Vice Chanc Health Affairs ....Dr. Raymond S. GREENBERG
10 Exec Vice Chanc Business Affairs ....Dr. Scott C. KELLEY
43 Vice Chanc & General Counsel ....Mr. Dan SHARPHORN
86 Vice Chanc for Govt Relations ....Mr. Barry MCBEE
26 Vice Chanc for External Relations ....Dr. Randa S. SAFADY
86 Vice Chanc Federal Relations ....Mr. William SHUTE
45 Vice Chanc Strategic Initiatives .... Dr. Stephanie A. BOND-HUIE
18 Assoc VC Facil Plng/Construction ....Mr. Michael O'DONNELL
13 Assoc VC & Chief Info Officer ....Mr. Mark MILSTEIN
21 Asst VC/Controller/Chief Budget Ofc .... Mr. Randy WALLACE
15 Asst Vice Chanc Employee Services .... Mr. Dan STEWART
27 Executive Director Public Affairs ... Ms. Jenny LACOSTE-CAPUTO
88 Executive Director Real Estate ....Mr. Kirk TAMES
30 Dir Development/Gift Planning Svcs .... Ms. Julie LYNCH
19 Director of Police .... Mr. Michael J. HEIDINGSFIELD

*The University of Texas at Arlington (L)

701 S Nedderman Drive, Arlington TX 76013
County: Tarrant FICE Identification: 003656
Unit ID: 228769
Telephone: (817) 272-2101 Carnegie Class: RU/H
FAX Number: (817) 272-5656 Calendar System: Semester
URL: www.uta.edu
Established: 1895 Annual Undergrad Tuition & Fees (In-State): $9,152
Enrollment: 39,740 Coed
Affiliation or Control: State IRS Status: 170(c)1
Highest Offering: Doctorate
Program: Liberal Arts And General; Teacher Preparatory; Business Emphasis
Accreditation: SC, ART, BUS, BUSA, CAATE, CEA, CIDA, CS, ENG, LSAR, MUS, NURSE, PLNG, SPAA, SW, TED

02 President ....Dr. Vistasp M. KARBHARI
05 Provost & Vice Pres Acad Affairs ..Dr. Ronald L. ELSENBAUMER
10 Vice Pres Business Affs/Controller ....Ms. Kelly DAVIS
32 VP Student Affairs ....Dr. Tim QUINNAN
30 VP Development and Alumni Relations ....Mr. Michael KINGAN
46 Vice President Research ....Dr. Duane DIMOS
13 Vice Pres Information Technology ....Vacant
11 Vice Pres Admin & Campus Operations ....Mr. John D. HALL
26 Vice President of Communications ....Ms. Lynne WATERS
15 Vice President for Human Resources ....Ms. Jean HOOD
84 Sr Assoc VP Student Enrollment Svcs ....Dr. Dale WASSON
45 Assoc Vice Provost Inst Eff/Report ....Dr. Loraine PHILLIPS
16 Asst Vice Pres Human Resources ....Ms. Eunice M. CURRIE
27 Asst Vice President Media Services .... Ms. Kristin SULLIVAN
18 Asst VP Campus Operation/Facilities ....Mr. Bill POOLE
88 Assoc Vice Prov/Dir Univ College .... Dr. Kimberly VAN NOORT
04 Special Assistant to the President ....Ms. Salma ADEM
58 Assoc Dean of Graduate Studies .... Mr. Raymond L. JACKSON
48 Dean of Arch & Urban & Public Affai ....Dr. Nan ELLIN
50 Dean Business Administration ....Dr. Rachel CROSON
54 Dean of Engineering .... Dr. Khosrow BEHBEHANI
49 Dean of Liberal Arts ....Dr. Paul WONG
66 Dean of Nursing ....Dr. Anne BAVIER
81 Interim Dean of Science ....Dr. James GROVER
70 Dean School of Social Work ....Dr. Scott RYAN
53 Dean College of Education .... Dr. Jeanne M. GERLACH
92 Dean Honors College ....Dr. Karl PETRUSO
08 Dean of Libraries ....Dr. Rebecca BICHEL
07 Exec Director Admissions & Records .... Dr. Hans GATTERDAM
12 Exec Dir of UTA Ft Worth Center ....Mr. Mike WEST
37 Director of Financial Aid .... Dr. Karen KRAUSE
23 Director Student Health Center ....Mr. Robert BLUM
22 Director Equal Opportunity Services ....Mr. Eddie FREEMAN
24 Director of Art Services ....Mr. Joel QUINTANS
41 Athletic Director ....Mr. Jim BAKER
19 Dir Environmental Health Safety ....Ms. Leah HOY
85 Executive Director Intl Education ....Mr. Jay HORN
88 Director Multicultural Outreach ....Mr. Casey GONZALES
88 Director Multicultural Affairs ....Ms. Leticia MARTINEZ
86 Director Government Relations ....Mr. Jeff JETER

*University of Texas at Austin (M)

Austin TX 78712-1111
County: Travis FICE Identification: 003658
Unit ID: 228778
Telephone: (512) 471-3434 Carnegie Class: RU/VH
FAX Number: (512) 471-2942 Calendar System: Semester
URL: www.utexas.edu
Established: 1883 Annual Undergrad Tuition & Fees (In-State): $9,810
Enrollment: 51,313 Coed
Affiliation or Control: State IRS Status: 170(c)1
Highest Offering: Doctorate
Program: Liberal Arts And General; Teacher Preparatory; Professional
Accreditation: SC, ART, AUD, BUS, BUSA, CAATE, CEA, CIDA, CLPSY, COPSY, CORE, DANCE, DIETC, DIETD, ENG, IPSY, JOUR, LAW, LIB, LSAR, #MED, MUS, NURSE, PHAR, PLNG, SCPSY, SP, SPAA, SW

02 President ....Dr. Gregory L. FENVES
05 Interim Executive VP & Provost .... Dr. Judith H. LANGOIS
10 Interim VP & Chief Fin Officer ....Ms. Mary E. KNIGHT
28 VP Diversity & Community Engagement .Mr. Gregory J. VINCENT
11 Vice Pres for University Operations ....Dr. Patricia L. CLUBB
46 Vice President Research ....Dr. Juan M. SANCHEZ
13 Chief Information Officer ....Mr. Bradley G. ENGLERT
27 Chief Communications Officer ....Ms. Maria M. ARRELLAGA
43 Vice President Legal Affairs ....Ms. Patricia A. OHLENDORF
26 Director University Media Relations ....Mr. Gary J. SUSSWEIN
04 Deputy to the President ....Dr. Harrison A. KELLER
100 Deputy to the Pres & Chief of Staff ....Ms. Nancy A. BRAZZIL
04 Executive Assistant to President ....Ms. Rebecca L. BAUGHMAN
88 Sr Vice Prov Resource Management ....Dr. Daniel T. SLESNICK
88 Sr Vice Provost Enroll/Grad Mgmt ....Dr. David A. LAUDE
32 Vice President Student Affairs ....Dr. Gage E. PAINE
84 Vice Provost for Enrollment Mgmt .... Mr. Ben CORPUS
20 Vice Provost for Faculty Affairs ....Dr. Janet M. DUKERICH
88 Vice Provost for Biomed Sciences ....Dr. Robert O. MESSING
46 Assoc VP Rsrch/Dir Spnsrd Projects ....Dr. Jason D. RICHER
08 Vice Provost/Director UT Libraries ....Dr. Lorraine J. HARICOMBE
06 Vice Provost & Registrar ....Mr. Vincent (Shelby) STANFIELD
104 Vice Provost International Programs ....Dr. Janet L. ELLZEY
58 Interim Dean Graduate Studies ....Dr. Marvin HACKERT
88 Vice Provost Inst Accred ....Dr. Linda N. DICKENS
88 Vice Provost for Higher Ed Policy ....Vacant

86 Assoc VP for Governmental Relations ....Mr. Carlos E. MARTINEZ
86 Assoc VP for Governmental Relations ......Ms. Gwen W. GRIGSBY
21 Associate Vice President ....Ms. Mary E. KNIGHT
21 Budget Director ....Ms. Elvia H. ROSALES
09 Director Institutional Research ....Ms. Tracy H. BROWN
88 Associate Vice Provost ....Ms. Kathy V. FOSTER
88 Associate Vice Provost ....Ms. Carolyn K. CONNERAT
88 Associate Vice Provost ....Mr. Phil LONG
88 Associate Vice President ....Ms. Renee L. WALLACE
30 Executive Director for Development ....Mr. Karl MILLER
19 Assoc VP Campus Safety/Security ...Dr. Gerald (Bob) R. HARKINS
18 Sr Assoc VP Facilities Management ....Mr. David L. REA
15 Associate Vice Pres Human Resources ....Dr. Debra G. KRESS
22 Asst VP Institutional Equity ....Dr. Sherri L. SANDERS
23 Director University Health Services ....Ms. Jamie L. SHUTTER
37 Director Student Financial Svcs ....Ms. Diane C. TODD
35 Sr Assoc Vice Pres/Dean of Students .... Dr. Soncia R. REAGINS-LILLY
39 Director Housing & Food Service ....Mr. Rene RODRIGUEZ
41 Interim Athletics Director ....Mr. Michael PERRIN
41 Women's Athletics Director ....Ms. Christine A. PLONSKY
29 CEO/Exec Director Texas Exes ....Ms. Leslie CEDAR
19 Chief University Police ....Mr. David CARTER
48 Dean of Architecture ....Dr. Frederick R. STEINER
50 Dean McCombs School of Business ....Dr. Laura STARKS
60 Dean of Communication ....Dr. Jay M. BERNHARDT
53 Dean of Education ....Dr. Manuel J. JUSTIZ
54 Interim Dean of Engineering ....Dr. Sharon L. WOOD
57 Dean of Fine Arts ....Dr. Douglas J. DEMPSTER
62 Dean School of Information ....Dr. Andrew P. DILLON
65 Dean Jackson School of Geosciences ....Dr. Sharon MOSHER
61 Dean School of Law ....Mr. Ward FARNSWORTH
49 Dean of Liberal Arts ....Dr. Randy L. DIEHL
63 Vice President for Medical Affairs .... Dr. S. Claiborne JOHNSTON
81 Dean of Natural Sciences ....Dr. Linda A. HICKE
66 Dean of Nursing .... Dr. Alexa M. STUIFBERGEN
67 Dean of Pharmacy ....Dr. M. Lynn CRISMON
80 Dean LBJ School Public Affs ....Dr. Robert H. WILSON
70 Dean Social Work ....Dr. Luis H. ZAYAS
97 Dean of Undergrad Studies ....Dr. Brent L. IVERSON
51 Int Exec Dir Ctr Teach and Learn ....Mr. Jeff D. TREICHEL
88 Director Internal Audits ....Mr. Michael W. VANDERVORT
18 Int Director Facilities Services ....Mr. Juan M. ONTIVEROS
88 Executive Director Univ Union ....Mr. Mulugeta FEREDE
27 Dir Univ of Texas Press ....Mr. David S. HAMRICK
88 Assoc Athl Dir/Dir Spec Events Ctr ....Mr. John M. GRAHAM
96 Assistant VP/Dir of Procurement ....Mr. Jerry A. FULLER
07 Director of Admissions ....Ms. Susan KEARNS

*The University of Texas at Dallas (A)

800 West Campbell Road, Richardson TX 75080
County: Collin FICE Identification: 009741
Unit ID: 228787
Telephone: (972) 883-2111 Carnegie Class: RU/H
FAX Number: (972) 883-2237 Calendar System: Semester
URL: www.utdallas.edu
Established: 1969 Annual Undergrad Tuition & Fees (In-State): $11,806
Enrollment: 23,095 Coed
Affiliation or Control: State IRS Status: 501(c)3
Highest Offering: Doctorate
Program: Liberal Arts And General; Professional
Accreditation: SC, ACAE, AUD, BUS, BUSA, CS, ENG, IPSY, SP, SPAA

02 President ....Dr. David E. DANIEL
05 Provost/Exec VP Academic Affairs ...Dr. B. Hobson WILDENTHAL
10 Vice President for Business Affairs ....Dr. Calvin D. JAMISON
32 Vice President Student Affairs ....Dr. Gene FITCH
46 VP Research/Economic Development ....Dr. Bruce GNADE
20 Vice Provost ....Dr. John WIORKOWSKI
30 Vice President for Advancement ....Ms. Susan ROGERS
27 VP/Chief Information Officer ....Mr. R. David CRAIN
28 Vice President of Diversity ....Dr. George W. FAIR
45 Assoc Dir Budget/Resource Plng ....Ms. Kimberly LAIRD
21 VP Finance & Controller ....Mr. Terry PANKRATZ
09 Exec Director Strategic Planning ....Dr. Lawrence J. REDLINGER
35 Dean of Students ....Vacant
58 Dean Graduate Studies ....Dr. Austin J. CUNNINGHAM
53 Dean Undergraduate Education ....Dr. Andrew BLANCHARD
79 Dean School Arts & Humanities ....Dr. Dennis KRATZ
50 Dean School of Management ....Dr. Hasan PIRKUL
81 Dean Sch of Natural Science/Math ....Dr. Bruce NOVAK
83 Dean School of Econ/Pol/Policy Sci ....Dr. Denis J. DEAN
76 Dean Sch Behavioral/Brain Science ....Dr. Bert S. MOORE
97 Dean School General Studies ....Dr. George W. FAIR
54 Dean EJ Sch of Engr/Computer Sci ....Dr. Mark W. SPONG
88 Dean Sch Arts/Tech & Emerg Media ....Vacant
08 Director of Libraries ....Dr. Ellen SAFLEY
06 Registrar ....Ms. Jennifer MCDOWELL
12 Exec Director of Callier Center .... Dr. Thomas F. CAMPBELL
25 Assoc VP Research Administration ....Mr. Rafael MARTIN
18 Assoc VP Facilities Management ....Mr. Richard DEMPSEY
15 Asst VP Human Resource Management ....Ms. Colleen DUTTON
96 Asst VP Procurement Management ....Mr. Peter BOND
19 Chief of Police ....Mr. Larry ZACHARIAS
36 Director Career Services ....Ms. Lisa GARZA
38 Director Student Counseling ....Mr. James P. CANNICI
88 Director of Audit and Compliance ....Ms. Toni STEPHENS
41 Athletics Director ....Mr. Bill PETITT
78 Director Co-operative Education ....Mr. Michael J. CHOATE
90 Director Tech Customer Services ....Mr. Donald L. DAVIS
29 Director of Alumni Relations ....Ms. Erin DOUGHERTY
04 Executive Associate to President ....Ms. Kimberly GOODFRIEND

105 Assistant VP Web Services ....Mr. Cary DELMARK
106 Director E-learning ....Mr. Darren CRONE
39 Asst VP Residential Life ....Mr. Ryan WHITE
104 Director Study Abroad ....Ms. Lisabeth LASSITER
37 Director Student Financial Aid ....Ms. Beth TOLAN
43 University Attorney ....Mr. Timothy SHAW
84 Asst Provost Enrollment Management ....Mr. Wray WELDON
86 VP Public Affairs ....Ms. Amanda O. ROCKOW

*University of Texas at El Paso (B)

500 W University Avenue, El Paso TX 79968-8900
County: El Paso FICE Identification: 003661
Unit ID: 228796
Telephone: (915) 747-5000 Carnegie Class: RU/H
FAX Number: (915) 747-5111 Calendar System: Semester
URL: www.utep.edu
Established: 1914 Annual Undergrad Tuition & Fees (In-State): $7,058
Enrollment: 23,079 Coed
Affiliation or Control: State IRS Status: 501(c)3
Highest Offering: Doctorate
Program: Liberal Arts And General; Teacher Preparatory; Professional
Accreditation: SC, BUS, BUSA, CORE, CS, ENG, MT, MUS, NURSE, OT, PH, PTA, SP, SPAA, SW

02 President ....Dr. Diana S. NATALICIO
05 Interim Provost/VPAA .... Dr. Howard DAUDISTEL
03 Executive Vice President ....Mr. Ricardo ADAUTO, III
04 Assistant to the President ....Ms. Estrella ESCOBAR
10 Interim VP Business Affairs ....Mr. Ricardo ADAUTO
46 Vice President for Research ....Dr. Roberto OSEGUEDA
09 Vice Pres Info Resources & Planning ....Dr. Steve RITER
58 Dean of Graduate School ....Dr. Charles AMBLER
32 Vice President Student Affairs ....Dr. Gary EDENS
50 Dean of Business Administration ....Dr. Robert NACHTMANN
53 Dean of Education ....Dr. Cynthia A. GIORGIS
54 Dean of Engineering ....Dr. Richard T. SCHOEPHOERSTER
49 Dean of Liberal Arts ....Dr. Patricia WITHERSPOON
66 Dean of Health Sciences ....Dr. Kathleen A. CURTIS
81 Dean of Science ....Dr. Robert KIRKEN
66 Dean of School of Nursing ....Dr. Elias PROVENCIO-VASQUEZ
18 Assoc VP Business Affs/Facilities ....Mr. Greg L. MCNICOL
08 Assoc Vice President Library ....Mr. Robert L. STAKES
26 Asst Vice Pres University Relations ....Mr. Beto LOPEZ
27 Assoc VP University Communications ....Ms. Robin STANTON GERROW
22 Asst Vice Pres EO/AA Dept ....Ms. Sandy VASQUEZ
29 Asst VP Development/Alumni Rels ....Dr. Richard DANIEL
46 Assoc Provost for Resource Mgmt ....Ms. Elizabeth FLORES
84 Asst VP Enrollment Services ....Ms. Amanda VASQUEZ
15 Assoc VP Human Resources Svcs ....Mr. Roger BROWN
19 Chief Campus Police ....Mr. Clifton WALSH
37 Assoc Dir of Student Financial Aid ....Mr. Ron WILLIAMS
23 Director of Student Health Center ....Ms. Louise P. CASTRO
36 Director of Career Services ....Mr. George W. BARTON
35 Associate VP/Dean of Students .... Ms. Catherine M. MCCORRY-ANDALIS
46 Assoc VP Inst Eval/Rsrch & Planning ....Dr. Roy MATHEW
39 Director of Housing Services ....Mr. Charlie E. GIBBENS
40 Director of University Bookstore ....Mr. Fernando PADULA
41 Athletics Director ....Mr. Robert W. STULL
38 Director Counseling Services ....Ms. Sherri I. TERRELL
96 Dir Purchasing/General Services ....Ms. Diane N. DEHOYOS
07 Dir Admissions/Recruitment ....Vacant
21 Assoc Vice Pres Business Affairs ....Mr. Anthony TURRIETTA
30 Assoc VP Institutional Advancement ....Mr. Robert STAKES

*University of Texas Rio Grande Valley (C)

1201 W University Drive, Edinburg TX 78539-2970
County: Hidalgo FICE Identification: 003599
Unit ID: 227368
Telephone: (956) 665-2011 Carnegie Class: Master's L
FAX Number: (956) 665-2150 Calendar System: Semester
URL: www.utpa.edu
Established: 1927 Annual Undergrad Tuition & Fees (In-State): $5,173
Enrollment: 21,015 Coed
Affiliation or Control: State IRS Status: 501(c)3
Highest Offering: Doctorate
Program: Liberal Arts And General; Teacher Preparatory; Professional
Accreditation: SC, ARCPA, BUS, CORE, CS, DIETC, ENG, MT, MUS, NURSE, OT, #SP, SW, THEA

02 Interim President ....Dr. Havidan RODRIGUEZ
100 Chief of Staff ....Ms. Lisa CARDOZA
05 Provost/VP Academic Affairs ....Dr. Havidan RODRIGUEZ
20 Associate Provost ....Dr. Kenneth BUCKMAN
88 Vice Provost for Faculty Affairs ....Dr. Ala QUBBAJ
10 Vice President for Business Affairs ....Mr. Martin BAYLOR
30 VP for University Advancement ....Ms. Veronica GONZALES
32 Vice President for Student Affairs ....Dr. Martha CANTU
13 Vice President for Info Technology ....Dr. Jeffrey GRAHAM
20 Vice Prov for Undergraduate Stds ....Dr. Kristin CROYLE
21 Assoc Vice Pres BA & Comptroller ....Mr. Esequiel GRANADO
07 Sr Assoc VP for Enrollment Services ....Dr. Maggie HINOJOSA
31 Exec Dir Ofc Ctr Oper/Community Svc ....Ms. Jessica SALINAS
08 Dean of the University Library ....Dr. Farzaneh RAZZAGHI
06 University Registrar ....Dr. Jeff RHODES
14 Executive Director for IT Services ....Mr. Frank ZECCA
15 Director of Human Resources ....Ms. Francisca RIOS
19 Interim Chief University Police ....Mr. James LOYA

26 Director University Relations ....Dr. Kimberly SELBER
36 Director Career Placement Services ...... Ms. Lourdes SERVANTES
37 Director Student Financial Services ....Mrs. Elaine RIVERA
29 Director Alumni Rels/Special Events ....Mrs. Debby GRANT
41 Director Intercollegiate Athletics ....Mr. Christopher KING
09 Exec Dir Inst Rsrch Effectiveness ....Dr. S.J SETHI
53 Interim Dean College of Education ....Dr. Laura SAENZ
35 Dean of Students ....Dr. Mari FUENTES-MARTIN
50 Dean Col Business Admin ....Dr. Teofilo OZUNA
38 Director of Couseling/Advisement ....Vacant
81 Dean College of Science and Math ....Dr. John M. TRANT
54 Dean College Engr/Computer Science ....Dr. Miguel GONZALEZ
84 Director of Recruitment ....Ms. Debbie GILCHRIST
76 Dean Col Health Sci/Human Svcs ....Dr. John RONNAU
49 Dean College Arts & Humanities ....Dr. Dahlia GUERRA
83 Dean Social/Behavioral Sciences ....Dr. Walter DIAZ
18 Dir for Facilities & Physical Plant ....Mr. Oscar VILLARREAL
96 Director Materials Management ....Mr. Alex VALDEZ
25 Supervisor for Grants & Contracts ....Mr. Donald MELE
22 Dir Office of Institutional Equity ....Ms. Alicia MORLEY

*University of Texas at San Antonio (D)

One UTSA Circle, San Antonio TX 78249-0169
County: Bexar FICE Identification: 010115
Unit ID: 229027
Telephone: (210) 458-4011 Carnegie Class: RU/H
FAX Number: (210) 458-4187 Calendar System: Semester
URL: www.utsa.edu
Established: 1969 Annual Undergrad Tuition & Fees (In-State): $8,737
Enrollment: 28,628 Coed
Affiliation or Control: State IRS Status: 501(c)3
Highest Offering: Doctorate
Program: Liberal Arts And General; Teacher Preparatory; Professional
Accreditation: SC, ART, BUS, BUSA, CACREP, CIDA, CONST, ENG, MUS, SPAA, SW

02 President ....Dr. Ricardo ROMO
05 Provost/Vice Pres Academic Affairs ....Dr. John FREDERICK
10 Vice Pres for Business Affairs ....Ms. Kathryn FUNK-BAXTER
46 Vice President for Research ....Dr. C. Mauli AGRAWAL
32 Vice President for Student Affairs ....Mr. Samuel GONZALES
31 Vice President Community Services ....Dr. Jude VALDEZ
30 Vice Pres for External Relations ....Ms. Marjorie M. FRENCH
11 Assoc Vice Pres for Administration ....Ms. Pamela BACON
20 Executive Vice Provost ....Mr. Julius M. GRIBOU
09 V Prov Acad Compliance/Inst Effect ....Dr. Sandra T. WELCH
12 Vice Provost for Downtown Campus ....Dr. Jesse T. ZAPATA
13 Vice Provost Information Officer ....Mr. Kenneth PIERCE
20 V Prov Acad Supt/Dean UGrad Studies ....Dr. Lawrence R. WILLIAMS
21 Associate VP Financial Affairs ....Ms. Lenora CHAPMAN
15 Associate VP Human Resources .. Ms. Barbara BARAN-CENTENO
08 Dean of Libraries ....Dr. Krisellen MALONEY
92 Dean of Honors College ....Dr. Richard A. DIEM
58 Interim Dean of Graduate School ....Dr. Page A. SMITH
50 Dean of College of Business ....Dr. Wm Gerard (Gerry) Y. SANDERS
57 Dean College of Liberal & Fine Arts ....Dr. Daniel J. GELO
54 Dean of College of Engineering ....Dr. Joann BROWNING
83 Dean of College of Sciences ....Dr. George PERRY
48 Dean School of Architecture ....Prof. John MURPHY
53 Dean College Educ/Human Development .....Dr. Betty MERCHANT
80 Dean of College of Public Policy ....Dr. Rogelio SAENZ
19 Chief of Police ....Mr. Steve V. BARRERA
41 Assoc VP Director Intcollegiate Ath ....Ms. Lynn HICKEY
29 Director Alumni Program Marketing ....Ms. Anne ENGLERT
43 Chief Legal Officer ....Ms. Gail JENSEN
26 Associate VP for Comm/Marketing ....Mr. Joe IZBRAND
86 Director of External Affairs ....Mr. Albert A. CARRISALEZ
04 Executive Assistant Office of Pres ....Ms. Patricia CARDENAS
06 Registrar ....Dr. Joesph R. DECRISTOFORO
07 Director of Admissions ....Ms. Beverly WOODSON DAY
100 Chief of Staff ....Ms. Sonia V. MARTINEZ
36 Director of Career Services ....Ms. Audrey J. MAGNUSON
104 Interim Dir of Educ Abroad Services ....Ms. Cristina SANCHEZ
105 Associate Director of Web/Portal ....Mr. Shashi B. PINHEIRO
106 Director of Online Learning ....Mr. Michael W. ANDERSON
108 Assistant Vice Provost Assessment ....Dr. Kimberly N. KLINE
18 Associate VP for Facilities ....Mr. David J. RIKER
22 Director Equal Opportunity Services ....Mr. Leonard FLAUM
25 Director of Grants/Contracts ....Ms. Shannyn ADKINS
28 Associate Provost ....Col. Lisa C. FIRMIN
37 Director of Student Financial Aid ....Ms. Diana S. MARTINEZ
38 Director of Counseling Services ....Mr. Thomas BAEZ
39 Director Student Housing/Residence ....Mr. Daniel L. GOCKLEY
44 Director of Fin Ops & Gift Services ...... Ms. Rebecca ANDERSON
84 Director Student Enrollment Svcs ....Ms. Erika M. COX
90 Director of Academic Computing ....Mr. John P. SOUDAH
91 Exec Director of Enterprise System ....Mr. Bryan P. WILSON
96 Director Purchasing/Dist Services ....Mr. Robert I. DICKENS

*University of Texas at Tyler (E)

3900 University Boulevard, Tyler TX 75799-6699
County: Smith FICE Identification: 011163
Unit ID: 228802
Telephone: (903) 566-7000 Carnegie Class: Master's L
FAX Number: (903) 566-7068 Calendar System: Semester
URL: www.uttyler.edu
Established: 1971 Annual Undergrad Tuition & Fees (In-State): $7,312
Enrollment: 8,036 Coed
Affiliation or Control: State IRS Status: 501(c)3
Highest Offering: Doctorate

Program: Liberal Arts And General; Teacher Preparatory; Professional
Accreditation: SC, BUS, CACREP, ENG, MUS, NAIT, NURSE, @PHAR

02 President ... Dr. Rodney H. MABRY
05 Provost/VP Academic Affairs ... Dr. Amir MIRMIRAN
30 Vice President Univ Advancement ... Mr. Wendell JEFFREYS
32 Vice Pres for Student Affairs ... Dr. Howard PATTERSON
13 Vice President & CIO IT ... Dr. Sherri WHATLEY
20 Vice Provost AA/Grad Studies ... Dr. William GEIGER
46 VP for Research & Technology Transf ... Dr. Michael ODELL
11 Interim VP for Administration ... Mr. David DABNEY
15 Director of Human Resources ... Ms. Amy CLEM
21 Assoc VP for Business Affairs ... Ms. Carrie CLAYTON
86 AVP for Legislative Relations ... Ms. Laura JACKSON
84 AVP for Enrollment Mgmt ... Ms. Sarah BOWDIN
108 Asst Vice Pres for Assessment/IE ... Dr. Lou Ann BERMAN
35 Asst VP Student Affs/Dean Students ... Ms. Ona TOLLIVER
49 Dean College of Arts & Sciences ... Dr. Martin SLANN
50 Dean College Business & Technology ... Dr. James LUMPKIN
53 Dean College Educ & Psych ... Dr. Ross SHERMAN
54 Dean College Engineering & Comp Sci ... Dr. James NELSON
66 Dean College Nursing & Health Sci ... Dr. Yong TAI WANG
08 Director of the Library ... Ms. Jeanne STANDLEY
21 Director of Financial Services ... Ms. Cindy TROYER
18 AVP for Facilities Management ... Mr. Chip CLARK
29 Director of Alumni Relations ... Ms. Brittany CHILDS
26 Director Mktg & Communication ... Ms. Beverley GOLDEN
38 Dir Stdnt Svc/Stdnt Couns/Test Ctr ... Ms. Kim HARVEY-LIVINGSTON
39 Director of Residence Life ... Dr. Jennifer WATERS
06 Registrar ... Ms. Sonja MORALE
09 Director of Institutional Analysis ... Ms. Shari KOUKL
19 Chief University Police ... Mr. Mike W. MEDDERS
04 Administrative Asst to President ... Ms. Janet ROBERTSON
07 Director of Admissions ... Ms. Angela COPELAND
37 Director of Student Financial Aid ... Ms. Marquita HACKETT
41 Athletic Director ... Dr. Howard PATTERSON
43 General Counsel ... Mr. Michael DONLEY

*The University of Texas Health Science Center at Houston (UTHealth) (A)

PO Box 20036, Houston TX 77225-0036

County: Harris   FICE Identification: 004951
Unit ID: 229300
Telephone: (713) 500-4472   Carnegie Class: Spec/Med
FAX Number: (713) 500-3026   Calendar System: Semester
URL: www.uth.edu
Established: 1972   Annual Undergrad Tuition & Fees (In-State): $14,025
Enrollment: 4,556   Coed
Affiliation or Control: State   IRS Status: 501(c)3
Highest Offering: Doctorate
Program: Professional
Accreditation: SC, ANEST, DENT, DH, DIETI, ENGR, MED, NURSE, PH

02 President ... Dr. Giuseppe N. COLASURDO
11 CFO/COO & Exec VP for Admin ... Mr. T. Kevin DILLON
63 Dean Medical School ... Dr. Giuseppe N. COLASURDO
69 Int Dean School of Public Health ... Dr. Osama I. MIKHAIL
52 Dean School of Dentistry ... Dr. John A. VALENZA
58 Dean Grad Sch Biomedical Sciences ... Dr. Michael BLACKBURN
66 Dean School of Nursing ... Dr. Lorraine FRAZIER
88 Dean Sch of Biomed Informatics ... Dr. Jiajie W. ZHANG
05 Exec VP Acad & Res Affs ... Dr. George M. STANCEL
45 Senior VP for Strategic Planning ... Dr. Osama I. MIKHAIL
10 Sr VP Finance & Business Svcs ... Mr. Michael TRAMONTE
46 Vice Dn Rsrch/Dir Molecular Med ... Dr. John HANCOCK
30 Vice Pres Development ... Mr. Kevin J. FOYLE
15 VP/Chief Human Resources Officer ... Mr. Eric FERNETTE
43 VP/Chief Legal & Compliance Officer ... Ms. Arlene D. STALLER
86 VP Govt Relations ... Mr. Scott FORBES
88 VP Research & Technology ... Dr. Bruce D. BUTLER
109 VP Auxiliary Enterprises ... Mr. Charles A. FIGARI
13 VP/Chief Information Officer ... Mr. Richard L. MILLER
18 VP Facilities Planning & Engr ... Mr. Richard L. MCDERMOTT
90 Asst VP Academic Technology ... Dr. William A. WEEMS
21 Asst VP & Chief Audit Officer ... Mr. Daniel SHERMAN
06 Registrar ... Mr. Robert JENKINS
19 Chief of Police ... Mr. William ADCOX
17 Exec Vice Dean Clinical Affairs ... Vacant
41 Director Recreation/Intramural Pgms ... Ms. Pauline M. HABETZ
85 Director International Affairs ... Ms. Rose Mary VALENCIA
39 Director University Housing ... Mr. Billy C. HINTON
26 Asst VP for Public Affairs ... Ms. Karen K. KAPLAN
88 Director of Media Relations ... Ms. Meredith RAINE
37 Director Student Financial Svcs ... Ms. Araceli ALVAREZ
25 Assoc VP Sponsored Projects Admin ... Ms. Jodi OGDEN
14 Director Data Center Operations ... Mr. Kevin B. GRANHOLD
88 Director Educational Tech Nursing ... Ms. Linda L. CRAYS
88 Director Biomedical Info Tech Med ... Dr. Stephen J. FATH
07 Vice Dean Admissions/Stdt Aff-Med ... Dr. Margaret MCNEESE
29 Assoc Dean Student & Alumni-SOD ... Dr. Hugh P. PIERPONT
32 Dir of Student Affairs-SBMI ... Ms. Jaime HARGRAVE
32 Director Student Affairs-SON ... Ms. Laurie G. RUTHERFORD
35 Assoc Dean of Student Affairs-SPH ... Dr. Mary A. SMITH
09 Director of Institutional Research ... Ms. Deanne HERNANDEZ

*University of Texas Health Science Center at San Antonio (B)

7703 Floyd Curl Drive, San Antonio TX 78229-3900

County: Bexar   FICE Identification: 003659
Unit ID: 228644
Telephone: (210) 567-7000   Carnegie Class: Spec/Med
FAX Number: (210) 567-2025   Calendar System: Other
URL: www.uthscsa.edu
Established: 1959   Annual Undergrad Tuition & Fees (In-State): $8,064
Enrollment: 3,147   Coed
Affiliation or Control: State   IRS Status: 501(c)3
Highest Offering: Doctorate
Program: Professional
Accreditation: SC, ARCPA, COARC, DENT, DH, DIETC, EMT, HT, IPSY, MED, MT, NURSE, OT, PTA, RADDOS

02 President ... Dr. William L. HENRICH
03 Sr Exec Vice President & COO ... Mr. Michael E. BLACK
11 Exec VP for Facility Planning/Admin ... Mr. James D. KAZEN
10 Vice President & CFO ... Ms. Andrea M. MARKS
05 VP Acad/Fac & Student Affairs ... Dr. Jacqueline L. MOK
13 Vice Pres & Chief Information Ofcr ... Mr. Yeman COLLIER
46 Vice President for Research ... Dr. Andrea GIUFFRIDA
86 VP for Governmental Relations ... Mr. Armando DIAZ
30 VP for Institutional Advancement ... Ms. Deborah H. MORRILL
15 Vice Pres of Human Resources ... Mr. J. Michael TESH
100 VP Communications & Chief of Staff ... Ms. Mary G. DELAY
21 Asst Vice Pres for Business Affairs ... Mr. Gerard E. LONG
09 Asst VP Research ... Dr. Mark J. NIJLAND
18 Asst VP for Strategic Initiatives ... Mr. Darrell MAATSCH
63 Dean School of Medicine ... Dr. Francisco GONZALEZ-SCARANO
52 Dean Dental School ... Dr. William W. DODGE
58 Dean Graduate Biomed Science ... Dr. David WEISS
76 Dean School Health Professions ... Dr. David C. SHELLEDY
66 Dean School of Nursing ... Dr. Eileen T. BRESLIN
32 Exec Dir for Student Services ... Vacant
06 Registrar ... Ms. Blanca GUERRA
08 Exec Director of Libraries ... Ms. Rajia C. TOBIA
19 Chief of Police ... Mr. Michael PARKS
88 Exec Dir Acad/Fac/Student Ombudspers ... Dr. Bonnie L. BLANKMEYER
37 Director of Financial Aid ... Ms. Ellen NYSTROM
38 Director of Student Counseling ... Dr. Mia VIVE
43 Asst VP/Chief Legal Officer ... Mr. Jack C. PARK
96 Sr Dir Supply Chain Mngmt/HUB Coord ... Ms. Vikki F. ROSS
07 Director of Admissions ... Ms. Belinda C. GONZALEZ
102 Dir Foundation/Corporate Relations ... Ms. Linda LOPEZ-GEORGE
26 Chief Marketing Officer ... Ms. Heather ADKINS
44 Sr Director Planned Giving ... Mr. W. Kent HAMILTON

*The University of Texas Health Science Center at Tyler (C)

11937 US Hwy 271, Tyler TX 75708-3154

County: Smith   Identification: 667206
Telephone: (903) 877-7777   Carnegie Class: Not Classified
FAX Number: N/A   Calendar System: Semester
URL: www.uthct.edu
Established: 1977   Annual Graduate Tuition & Fees: $6,642
Enrollment: 19   Coed
Affiliation or Control: State   IRS Status: 501(c)3
Highest Offering: Master's; No Undergraduates
Program: Professional; Technical Emphasis
Accreditation: @SC

02 President ... Dr. Kirk A. CALHOUN
03 Exec VP/Chief of Staff ... Joseph F. WOELKERS
05 Sr VP Clinical & Academic Affairs ... Dr. Jeffrey L. LEVIN
10 Sr VP Chief Business & Finance Ofcr ... Vernon H. MOORE
46 Sr VP Research & Graduate Studies ... Dr. Steven IDELL
23 Sr VP/CMO & Physician in Chief ... Dr. Steven W. COX
88 Sr VP/CAO/Hospital & Clinics ... Timothy G. OCHRAN
88 Sr VP Population Health ... Dr. David L. LAKEY
15 VP Human Resources ... Vacant
43 VP/Chief Legal Officer ... Terry WITTER
45 VP Planning & Public Policy ... Daniel DESLATTE
13 VP Information Technology (CIO) ... John YODER
18 Assoc VP Physical Plant ... Vacant
30 Assoc VP Institutional Advancement ... Derrith BONDURANT
20 Assoc VP Academic Affairs ... Dr. Pierre F. NEUENSCHWANDER
32 Director of Student Affairs ... Dr. Mickey SLIMP
08 Director of Library Services ... Thomas CRAIG
09 Director of Institutional Research ... Sara SHEPHERD
37 Director Student Financial Aid ... Araceli ALVAREZ
06 Registrar ... Robert JENKINS
04 Administrative Asst to President ... Carol DAVIS
19 Chief of Police ... Chief Robert CROMLEY
26 Exec Dir Public Affairs & Marketing ... Rhonda SCOBY
86 Dir University & Community Affairs ... Kimberly ASHLEY
96 Director of Purchasing ... Crystal SMITH

*The University of Texas M.D. Anderson Cancer Center (D)

1515 Holcombe Boulevard, Houston TX 77030-4000

County: Harris   FICE Identification: 025554
Unit ID: 416801
Telephone: (713) 792-6161   Carnegie Class: Spec/Health
FAX Number: N/A   Calendar System: Semester
URL: www.mdanderson.org
Established: 1941   Annual Undergrad Tuition & Fees (In-District): N/A
Enrollment: 303   Coed
Affiliation or Control: State/Local   IRS Status: 501(c)3
Highest Offering: Doctorate
Program: Professional
Accreditation: SC, CGTECH, CYTO, DENT, DMOLS, HT, MT, PAST, RAD, RADDOS, RADMAG, RTT

02 President ... Dr. Ronald DEPINHO
05 Provost/Executive Vice President ... Dr. Ethan DMITROVSKY
11 Exec Vice Pres/Chief Business Ofcr ... Dr. Leon LEACH

*The University of Texas Medical Branch (E)

301 University Boulevard, Galveston TX 77555-0100

County: Galveston   FICE Identification: 004952
Unit ID: 228653
Telephone: (409) 772-1011   Carnegie Class: Spec/Med
FAX Number: N/A   Calendar System: Semester
URL: www.utmb.edu
Established: 1891   Annual Undergrad Tuition & Fees (In-State): $7,075
Enrollment: 3,211   Coed
Affiliation or Control: State   IRS Status: 170(c)1
Highest Offering: Doctorate
Program: Professional
Accreditation: SC, ARCPA, BBT, COARC, DENT, @DIETI, MED, MT, NURSE, OT, PH, PTA

02 President ... Dr. David L. CALLENDER
04 Exec Asst to the President ... Ms. Jandee ALARID
05 Exec VP Provost/Dean Sch of Med ... Dr. Danny O. JACOBS
17 Exec VP & CEO Health System ... Ms. Donna K. SOLLENBERGER
10 Exec VP & Chief Business/Fin Ofcr ... Ms. Cheryl SADRO
86 Sr VP Health Policy & Legis Affairs ... Dr. Ben G. RAIMER
88 VP & Chief Physician Executive ... Dr. Rex M. MCCALLUM
17 Chief Medical Officer ... Dr. Selwyn O. ROGERS
20 VP Education & Dean Sch of Nursing ... Dr. Pamela G. WATSON
76 VP & Dean Sch of Health Professions ... Dr. Elizabeth J. PROTAS
58 VP & Dean Grad Sch of Biomed Sci ... Dr. David W. NIESEL
15 VP HR & Employee Services ... Dr. Ronald B. MCKINLEY
13 VP Information Services & CIO ... Mr. Todd A. LEACH
18 VP Business Oper & Facilities ... Mr. Michael B. SHRINER
21 VP Chief Oper Officer AE ... Vacant
21 VP Finance Clinical Enterprise ... Mr. David M. CONNAUGHTON
45 VP for Strategic Mgmt ... Dr. Rebecca SAAVEDRA
43 Sr VP General Counsel ... Ms. Carolee KING
26 VP Marketing & Communications ... Mr. Stephen CAMPBELL
88 Assoc Dean Grad Sch Biomed Sci ... Dr. Jose M. BARRAL
07 Assoc Dean Admissions Sch of Med ... Dr. Jeffrey RABEK
35 Assoc Dean Student Affairs Adm SON ... Ms. Dorothy PEARROW
46 Assoc VP Research Admin ... Ms. Toni J. D'AGOSTINO
08 Assoc VP Academic Res/Library ... Ms. Patricia A. CIEJKA
09 Assoc VP Inst Effectiveness ... Dr. John C. MCKEE
26 Assoc VP Public Affairs ... Ms. Mary G. HAVARD
21 Assoc VP Fin Plng & Perf Mgmt ... Mr. Matthew FURLONG
21 Assoc VP Budget & Analysis ... Ms. Celia BAILEY-OCHOA
88 Assoc VP Audit Services ... Ms. Kimberly K. HAGARA
30 Assoc VP Chief Develop Officer ... Ms. Betsy B. CLARDY
32 Assoc VP for Univ Student Svcs ... Vacant
29 Asst VP Alumni Relations ... Vacant
28 VP & Chief Compliance Officer ... Mr. Tobin R. BOENIG
06 AVP Univ Student Svcs & Registrar ... Mr. William S. BOEH
19 Chief of University Police ... Mr. Thomas ENGELLS
22 Dir of Diversity and Inclusion ... Ms. Adeola ODUWOLE
96 AVP Supply Chain Management ... Mr. Frank REIGHARD
38 Director Student Counseling ... Ms. Cynthia DESANTOS
100 Chief of Staff ... Ms. Sheila LIDSTONE
16 Assoc VP HR Talent Manager ... Mr. Ian BARRETT
105 Director Digital Communications ... Mr. Eduardo VALDES
106 Dir Online Education/E-learning ... Dr. Trish RICHARD
108 Asst Dir Institutional Effectivenes ... Mr. Jay HOWELL
11 Chief of Administrative Officer ... Mr. David O. ANDERSON
37 Director Student Financial Aid ... Ms. Carol CROMIE
39 AVP BOF Student Housing ... Mr. Carlos ESCOBAR
41 Athletic Director ... Mr. Gerald CLEVELAND
44 Director Annual or Planned Giving ... Ms. Marie MACZAK
10 VP & Chief Financial Officer ... Mr. Michael SCHEER
90 Asst Director Academic Computing ... Mr. David DEL PINO KLOQUES

*University of Texas of the Permian Basin (F)

4901 E University Boulevard, Odessa TX 79762-0001

County: Ector   FICE Identification: 009930
Unit ID: 229018
Telephone: (432) 552-2020   Carnegie Class: Master's M
FAX Number: (432) 552-2374   Calendar System: Semester
URL: www.utpb.edu
Established: 1969   Annual Undergrad Tuition & Fees (In-State): $6,457
Enrollment: 5,560   Coed
Affiliation or Control: State   IRS Status: 501(c)3
Highest Offering: Master's
Program: Liberal Arts And General; Teacher Preparatory; Professional
Accreditation: SC, ART, BUS, CAATE, ENG, MUS, SW, TED

02 President ... Dr. W. David WATTS
04 Assistant to the President ... Ms. Susan KIMBRIEL
05 Provost/Vice Pres Academic Affairs ... Dr. Dan HEIMMERMANN
10 Vice President Business Affairs ... Mr. Mark MCGURK
32 Sr AVP Academic & Student Services ... Ms. Teresa SEWELL
58 AVP Research/Dean Graduate Studies ... Dr. Juli RATHEAL
13 Chief Information Officer ... Mr. Lowell BALLARD
49 Dean College of Arts & Science ... Dr. Michael ZAVADA
50 Dean School of Business ... Dr. William PRICE

53 Dean School of Education ....Dr. Frank HERNANDEZ
30 Director Institutional Advancement ....Ms. Lee Anna GOOD
07 Director Admissions ....Mr. Scott SMILEY
06 Registrar ....Mr. Joe SANDERS
37 Director Financial Aid ....Ms. Jennifer TAVARES
08 Director of Library Services ....Mr. Howard MARKS
15 Director Human Resources ....Ms. Caron PERKINS
51 Director Continuing Education ....Mr. Rey LASCANO
26 Interim Public Information Officer ....Ms. Travis WOODWARD
41 Director Athletics ....Dr. Steve AICINENA
19 Chief of Police ....Chief Tom HAIN
18 Chief Facilities/Physical Plant ....Mr. Jay HANEY
36 Dir Student Placement/Counseling ....Mr. Tony LOVE
96 Interim Director of Purchasing ....Ms. Ynez ALDERSON
09 Director of Institutional Research ....Dr. Denise WATTS
29 Alumni Relations ....Mrs. Maribea MERRITT

*University of Texas Southwestern Medical Center (A)

5323 Harry Hines Boulevard, Dallas TX 75390-9002
County: Dallas FICE Identification: 010019
Unit ID: 228635
Telephone: (214) 648-3111 Carnegie Class: Spec/Med
FAX Number: N/A Calendar System: Other
URL: www.utsouthwestern.edu
Established: 1943 Annual Undergrad Tuition & Fees (In-State): N/A
Enrollment: 2,374 Coed
Affiliation or Control: State IRS Status: 501(c)3
Highest Offering: Doctorate
Program: Professional
Accreditation: SC, ARCPA, CLPSY, CORE, DIETC, EMT, IPSY, MED, OPE, PAST, PTA, RTT

02 President ....Dr. Daniel K. PODOLSKY
100 Vice President & Chief of Staff ....Dr. Robin M. JACOBY
05 Exec VP Acad Affs/Provost/Dean SMS ....Dr. Gregory FITZ
03 Exec VP Health System Affairs ....Dr. Bruce A. MEYER
10 Exec Vice Pres Business Affairs ....Mr. Arnim DONTES
46 Vice Provost/Dean of Basic Research ....Dr. David W. RUSSELL
23 Vice President Clinical Operations ....Dr. John D. RUTHERFORD
88 Vice President/CEO University Hosp ....Dr. John WARNER
88 Chief Quality Officer ....Dr. Gary REED
21 Vice President Financial Affairs ....Mr. Michael SERBER
86 Vice Pres Govt Affairs & Policy ....Ms. Angelica MARIN-HILL
26 Vice Pres Comm Mktg & Public Affs ....Mr. Steve MOORE
15 Vice President Human Resources ....Dr. William M. BEHRENDT
43 Vice President Legal Affairs ....Ms. Leah A. HURLEY
72 Vice Pres Technology Development ....Mr. Frank P. GRASSLER
30 Vice President Development ....Ms. Amanda BILLINGS
102 Vice Pres Community and Corp Rels ....Mr. Ruben E. ESQUIVEL
13 Vice Pres Information Resources ....Mr. Kirk A. KIRKSEY
18 Vice President Facilities Mgmt ....Mr. Kirby L. VAHLE
29 Vice Pres Stdnt/Alumni Affs/Admiss ....Mr. J. W. NORRED
09 Vice Pres Research Administration ....Ms. Angela WISHON
88 Assoc Vice Pres Ambulatory Care ....Dr. Stan TAYLOR
88 Assoc Vice Pres Chief Admin Ofcr ....Dr. Randall F. JONES
88 Chief Med Officer University Hosp ....Dr. Steven LEACH
88 Assoc Vice Pres Chief Nursing Ofcr ....Ms. Susan HERNANDEZ
96 Asst Vice Pres Materials Mgmt ....Mr. Paul D. BELEW
88 Assoc Vice Pres Parkland HHS Aff ....Dr. Christopher MADDEN
27 Asst Vice Pres Marketing ....Ms. Dorothea BONDS
88 Asst Vice President Communication ....Ms. Jeanne FORBIS
21 Asst Vice President Accounting ....Ms. Sharon LEARY
08 Asst Vice Pres Library Services ....Ms. Kelly GONZALEZ
20 Sr Assoc Dean Academic Admin ....Dr. Charles M. GINSBURG
45 Sr Assoc Dean Strategic Development ....Dr. Dwain L. THIELE
28 Assoc Dean Faculty Diversity & Dev ....Dr. Byron L. CRYER
88 Assoc Dean Global Health ....Dr. Fiemu E. NWARIAKU
51 Assoc Dean Grad Medical Education ....Dr. Bradley MARPLE
63 Assoc Dean Undergrad Medical Educ ....Dr. Steve CANNON
32 Assoc Dean Student Affairs ....Dr. Angela MIHALIC
32 Assoc Dean Student Affairs ....Dr. James M. WAGNER
93 Assoc Dean Minority Student Affairs ....Dr. Shawna NESBITT
88 Associate Dean ....Dr. Perrie M. ADAMS
58 Dean Grad School Biomedical Science ....Dr. Andrew ZINN
76 Dean School of Health Professions ....Dr. Jon WILLIAMSON
06 Registrar/Financial Aid ....Mr. Charles L. KETTLEWELL
07 Assoc Director of Admissions ....Ms. Anne P. MCLANE
11 Assoc VP/Chief Operating Officer ....Ms. Becky MCCULLEY
17 Assoc Vice Pres Health Sys Mgmt Svc ....Mr. Suresh GUNASEKARAN
88 Asst Vice Pres Administrative Sys ....Ms. Victoria STASINSKAYA
47 Vice President COO Academic Affairs ....Mr. Cameron SLOCUM

Vernon College (B)

4400 College Drive, Vernon TX 76384-4092
County: Wilbarger FICE Identification: 010060
Unit ID: 229504
Telephone: (940) 552-6291 Carnegie Class: Assoc/Pub-R-M
FAX Number: (940) 553-3902 Calendar System: Semester
URL: www.vernoncollege.edu
Established: 1970 Annual Undergrad Tuition & Fees (In-District): $2,450
Enrollment: 2,995 Coed
Affiliation or Control: State/Local IRS Status: 501(c)3
Highest Offering: Associate Degree
Program: Occupational; 2-Year Principally Bachelor's Creditable
Accreditation: SC, CAHIIM, SURGT

01 President ....Dr. Dusty R. JOHNSTON
04 Admin Secretary to the President ....Ms. Mary KING
05 Dean of Instructional Services ....Dr. Gary Don HARKEY
10 Dean of Administrative Services ....Mr. Garry DAVID
32 Dean of Student Svs/Athletic Dir ....Mr. John B. HARDIN, III
07 Dean Admiss/Registr/Financial Aid ....Mr. Joe HITE
103 Assoc Dean of Instructional Service ....Ms. Shana DRURY
30 Director of Inst Advancement ....Ms. Michelle ALEXANDER
88 Director of Quality Enhancement ....Ms. Criquett LEHMAN
09 Dir of Institutional Effectiveness ....Mrs. Betsy HARKEY
37 Director Financial Aid ....Mrs. Melissa J. ELLIOTT
08 Director of Library Services ....Ms. Marion GRONA
18 Director Physical Plant ....Mr. John MAHONEY
15 Director of Human Resources ....Mrs. Haven DAVID
39 Director of Housing ....Ms. Kelly EASON
35 Assoc Dean of Student Services ....Mrs. Kristin HARRIS
06 Director of Admissions & Records ....Mrs. Amanda RAINES
66 Dir Associate Degree in Nursing ....Ms. Cathy BOLTON
66 Dir Licensed Vocational Nursing ....Ms. Sherri DENHEM
35 Director of Student Activities ....Mr. Sjohonton FANNER
19 Director of Campus Police ....Mr. Chris BELL

Vet Tech Institute of Houston (C)

4669 Southwest Freeway, Suite 100, Houston TX 77027
County: Harris FICE Identification: 021448
Unit ID: 223472
Telephone: (713) 629-8940 Carnegie Class: Assoc/PrivFP
FAX Number: (713) 629-0059 Calendar System: Semester
URL: www.vettechinstitute.edu/houston
Established: 2007 Annual Undergrad Tuition & Fees: $14,120
Enrollment: 216 Coed
Affiliation or Control: Proprietary IRS Status: Proprietary
Highest Offering: Associate Degree
Program: Occupational
Accreditation: ACICS

01 Director/Chief Academic Officer ....Mr. Elbert HAMILTON, JR.

Victoria College (D)

2200 E Red River, Victoria TX 77901-4494
County: Victoria FICE Identification: 003662
Unit ID: 229540
Telephone: (361) 573-3291 Carnegie Class: Assoc/Pub-R-M
FAX Number: (361) 572-3850 Calendar System: Semester
URL: www.victoriacollege.edu
Established: 1925 Annual Undergrad Tuition & Fees (In-District): $2,640
Enrollment: 4,146 Coed
Affiliation or Control: Local IRS Status: 501(c)3
Highest Offering: Associate Degree
Program: Occupational; 2-Year Principally Bachelor's Creditable
Accreditation: SC, ADNUR, COARC, PTAA

01 President ....Dr. David HINDS
05 Vice President of Instruction ....Dr. Patricia A. VANDERVOORT
10 Vice Pres Administrative Svcs ....Mr. Keith BLUNDELL
32 Vice President of Student Services ....Dr. Florinda CORREA
30 VP College Advance/External Affairs ....Ms. Jennifer L. YANCEY
45 Exec Director Special Projects ....Dr. Larry GARRETT
09 Dir Inst Effect/Research/Assess ....Ms. Patricia REHAK
08 Director of Libraries ....Dr. Joe F. DAHLSTROM
06 Registrar Admissions & Records ....Ms. Missy KLIMITCHEK
18 Director Physical Plant ....Mr. Robert DUFFIE
37 Director Financial Aid ....Ms. Kim OBSTA
15 Director Human Resources ....Ms. Terri KURTZ
26 Dir Marketing & Communications ....Mr. Darin KAZMIR
38 Director Advising/Counseling ....Mr. Robert CUBRIEL, III
96 Director of Purchasing ....Ms. Lydia HUBER
21 Director of Finance ....Ms. Tracey BERGSTROM
35 Student Center/Activities Director ....Ms. Elaine EVERETT-HENSLEY
38 Director of Testing Center ....Ms. Donna RODRIGUEZ
13 Director Technology Services ....Mr. Andy FARRIOR
04 Admin Asst to President ....Ms. Debbie RAINS

Virginia College Austin (E)

14200 North Interstate 35, Austin TX 78728
Telephone: (512) 371-3500 Identification: 666074
Accreditation: ACICS, #COARC, DMS, MAAB, SURGT

† Branch campus of Virginia College, Birmingham, AL.

Vista College (F)

3440 Bell Street, Suite 100, Amarillo TX 79109
Telephone: (806) 372-3700 Identification: 770548
Accreditation: COE

† Branch campus of Vista College, El Paso, TX.

Vista College (G)

6101 Montana Avenue, El Paso TX 79925-2021
County: El Paso FICE Identification: 025720
Unit ID: 365204
Telephone: (915) 779-8031 Carnegie Class: Assoc/PrivFP
FAX Number: (915) 779-8097 Calendar System: Semester
URL: www.vistacollege.edu
Established: 1987 Annual Undergrad Tuition & Fees: $15,425
Enrollment: 2,951 Coed
Affiliation or Control: Proprietary IRS Status: Proprietary
Highest Offering: Associate Degree
Program: Occupational
Accreditation: #COE

01 Campus Director ....Mr. Antonio RICO
06 Registrar ....Ms. Valerie PARKS
07 Director of Admissions ....Mr. Andre ROYOS
36 Director Career Services ....Ms. Amanda CUSEO
37 Director Student Financial Aid ....Ms. Adrianna DURAN
63 Director Medical ....Ms. Juana CERVANTES

Vista College (H)

4620 50th Street, Lubbock TX 79414
Telephone: (806) 785-2100 Identification: 770549
Accreditation: COE

† Branch campus of Vista College, El Paso, TX.

Vista College-Online (I)

300 N. Coit Road, Suite 300, Richardson TX 75080
County: Davis FICE Identification: 025728
Unit ID: 377342
Telephone: (972) 707-8600 Carnegie Class: Assoc/PrivFP
FAX Number: (972) 707-8575 Calendar System: Other
URL: www.vistacollege.edu/online/
Established: Annual Undergrad Tuition & Fees: $35,000
Enrollment: 207 Coed
Affiliation or Control: Proprietary IRS Status: Proprietary
Highest Offering: Baccalaureate
Program: Occupational
Accreditation: ACCSC

01 Director ....Mr. Art WALLER

Wade College (J)

1950 Stemmons Fwy, Ste 4080, LB 562, Dallas TX 75207
County: Dallas FICE Identification: 010130
Unit ID: 226879
Telephone: (214) 637-3530 Carnegie Class: Assoc/PrivFP
FAX Number: (214) 637-0827 Calendar System: Trimester
URL: www.wadecollege.edu
Established: 1962 Annual Undergrad Tuition & Fees: $13,310
Enrollment: 207 Coed
Affiliation or Control: Proprietary IRS Status: Proprietary
Highest Offering: Baccalaureate
Program: Occupational; Fine Arts Emphasis
Accreditation: SC

01 President ....Dr. Harry DAVROS
03 Vice President ....Mr. John CONTE
05 Director of Academic Affairs ....Ms. Elizabeth JOHNSTON
11 Director of Institutional Support ....Ms. Kim PARKER
08 Head Librarian ....Mrs. Bobbie BAUMGARTEN
36 Director of Career Services ....Mrs. Jennifer MAGEE
07 Director of Admissions ....Mr. John FLORES
37 Director Student Financial Aid ....Ms. Lisa HOOVER

Wayland Baptist University (K)

1900 West Seventh, Plainview TX 79072-6998
County: Hale FICE Identification: 003663
Unit ID: 229780
Telephone: (806) 291-1000 Carnegie Class: Master's L
FAX Number: (806) 291-1960 Calendar System: Semester
URL: www.wbu.edu
Established: 1908 Annual Undergrad Tuition & Fees: $13,830
Enrollment: 5,536 Coed
Affiliation or Control: Southern Baptist IRS Status: 501(c)3
Highest Offering: Doctorate
Program: 2-Year Principally Bachelor's Creditable; Liberal Arts And General; Teacher Preparatory; Professional
Accreditation: SC, MUS, NUR

01 President ....Dr. Paul W. ARMES
05 Executive Vice President/Provost ....Dr. Bobby L. HALL
84 Vice Pres Enrollment Management ....Dr. D. Claude LUSK
20 Vice Pres of External Campuses ....Dr. Elane SEEBO
10 Chief Financial Officer ....Ms. Lezlie HUKILL
20 Associate Academic Vice President ....Dr. Stan DEMERRITT
12 Exec Dir/Campus Dean Albuquerque ....Dr. Steve SMITH
12 Exec Dir/Campus Dean Altus ....Dr. Tom FISHER
12 Exec Dir/Campus Dean Amarillo ....Dr. J. B BOREN
12 Exec Dir/Campus Dean Anchorage ....Dr. Eric ASH
12 Exec Dir/Campus Dean Clovis ....Dr. Gary MITCHELL
12 Exec Dir/Campus Dean Fairbanks ....Vacant
12 Exec Dir/Campus Dean Hawaii ....Vacant
12 Exec Dir/Campus Dean Lubbock ....Dr. David BISHOP
12 Exec Dir/Campus Dean Phoenix ....Dr. D. Glenn SIMMONS
12 Exec Dir/Campus Dean San Antonio ....Dr. James ANTENEN
12 Exec Dir/Campus Dean Sierra Vista ....Vacant
12 Exec Dir/Campus Dean Wichita Falls ....Dr. Dean DANIEL
83 Acad Dean School Behav & Soc Sci ....Dr. Estelle OWENS
50 Academic Dean School of Business ....Dr. Barry W. EVANS
53 Academic Dean School of Education ....Dr. Jimmie L. TODD
57 Academic Dean School of Fine Arts ....Dr. Marti R. RUNNELS
79 Academic Dean School of Lang & Lit ....Dr. Cindy M. MCCLENAGAN
81 Academic Dean School Math/Sciences ....Dr. Scott FRANKILIN
64 Academic Dean School of Music ....Dr. Ann B. STUTES
66 Academic Dean School of Nursing ....Dr. Diane FRAZOR
73 Academic Dean Religion & Philosophy ....Dr. Paul L. SADLER

06 Registrar .... Mrs. Julie BOWEN
32 Exec Dir Student Development .... Mr. Tom HALL
30 Executive Dir Univ Advancement .... Mr. Mike MELCHER
21 Controller .... Vacant
41 Athletic Director .... Mr. Rick COOPER
07 Director Admissions .... Mrs. Debbie STENNETT
29 Director Alumni Development .... Mr. Danny ANDREWS
88 Director Church Services .... Mr. Micheal SUMMERS
44 Director Annual Fund .... Mrs. Teresa YOUNG
44 Director Donor Relations .... Ms. Hope ENGLISH
37 Director Financial Aid .... Mrs. Karen LAQUEY
58 Director of Graduate Studies .... Ms. Amanda STANTON
15 Director Human Resources .... Mr. Ron APPLING
13 Director Information Technology .... Mrs. Katrina SMITH
09 Dir Inst Research/Effectiveness .... Dr. Andy PAGEL
12 Director Kenya Campus .... Dr. Richard SHAW
08 Director Library .... Dr. Polly R. LACKEY
88 Director Property Management .... Mr. Danny W. MURPHREE
26 Director Public Relations .... Mr. Jonathan PETTY
88 Director Special Projects .... Mrs. Penny POOLE
23 Director of Health Services .... Mrs. Lauren M. HALL
39 Director Student Housing .... Mrs. Nancy KEITH
38 Dir Counseling/Career/Disability .... Ms. Teresa MOORE
42 Director Student Ministries .... Mr. Donnie BROWN
40 Director University Services .... Mr. Eddie C. TURNER
106 Director Virtual Campus .... Dr. Trish TRIFILO
105 Director Web Services .... Mrs. Charlotte SCHUMACHER
88 Director External Records .... Mr. Daniel BROWN
19 Chief of Police/WBU .... Mr. Lonnie BURTON
18 Chief Facilities/Physical Plant .... Mr. David MURPHREE
04 Exec Admin Asst to President .... Mrs. Carolyn ANDREWS

Weatherford College (A)

225 College Park Drive, Weatherford TX 76086-5699

County: Parker
FICE Identification: 003664
Unit ID: 229799
Telephone: (817) 594-5471
Carnegie Class: Assoc/Pub-S-SC
FAX Number: (817) 598-6210
Calendar System: Semester
URL: www.wc.edu
Established: 1869
Annual Undergrad Tuition & Fees (In-District): $1,920
Enrollment: 5,624
Coed
Affiliation or Control: Local
IRS Status: 501(c)3
Highest Offering: Associate Degree
Program: Occupational; 2-Year Principally Bachelor's Creditable
Accreditation: SC, ADNUR, COARC, DMS, EMT, OTA, PHLEB, PTAA, RAD

01 President .... Dr. Kevin EATON
04 Exec Asst to the President .... Mrs. Theresa R. HUTCHISON
32 VP of Inst & Stdnt Services .... Dr. Richard BOWERS
10 Vice Pres Financial/Admin Affairs .... Mrs. Andra R. CANTRELL
30 Vice Pres Institutional Advancement .... Mr. Brent BAKER
76 Dean of Health & Human Sciences .... Ms. Katherine BOSWELL
05 Executive Dean of Academics .... Mr. Michael ENDY
53 Dean Educational/Instructional Sppt .... Ms. Rhonda TORRES
35 Executive Dean of Student Services .... Mrs. Kathy BASSHAM
103 Dean Workforce & Economic Devel .... Ms. Kay YOUNG
26 Dir Communications/Public Relations .... Mrs. Crystal BROWN
31 Dean of Community Programs .... Mr. Duane DURRETT
88 Director Truck Driving .... Mr. Bubba SWEARINGIN
09 Dir Institutional Research .... Mr. Dewayne BERRY
35 Exec Director Student Development .... Mr. Doug JEFFERSON
36 Dir of Career and Transfer Center .... Mr. John TURNTINE
88 Director Food Services .... Ms. Erin DAVIDSON
37 Director Student Financial Aid .... Mr. Donnie PURVIS
21 Controller .... Ms. Rebecca DEPUY
15 Director Human Resources .... Mrs. Ralinda STONE
07 Director of Admissions/Veterans .... Mr. Ralph WILLINGHAM
13 Director Technology Services .... Mr. Greg SHRADER
08 Director of Library Services .... Mrs. Valorie STARR
18 Director of Facilities .... Ms. Rhonda JOHNSON
96 Director of Purchasing .... Mrs. Jeanie HOBBS
45 Director of Resource Development .... Dr. Shirley CHENAULT
19 Chief of Campus Police .... Mr. Paul STONE
38 Student Counseling .... Ms. Phyllis TIFFIN
88 Director Upward Bound .... Mr. Jeff KHALDEN
29 Director Alumni Relations .... Mr. Brent BAKER
103 Director of Workforce Education .... Ms. Janetta KRUSE
53 Director of Teacher Education .... Dr. Joyce MELTON PAGES
06 Registrar .... Mrs. Vicki TRAWEEK
88 Exec Dir of Student Engagement .... Mr. Adam FINLEY
88 Director of Testing .... Ms. Lela MORRIS
88 Dir of Outreach/Student Success .... Ms. Kay LANDRUM
88 Director Special Populations .... Mrs. Dawn KAHLDEN
39 Director Student Housing .... Miss Faith STIFFLER
41 Athletic Director .... Mr. Bob MCKINLEY

West Coast University (B)

8435 N Stemmons Freeway, Dallas TX 75247-3900

Telephone: (214) 453-4533
Identification: 770485
Accreditation: &WC, @DIETC

† Branch campus of West Coast University, North Hollywood, CA.

Western Technical College (C)

9451 Diana Drive, El Paso TX 79924-6936

Telephone: (915) 566-9621
Identification: 666103
Accreditation: ACCSC

† Branch campus of Western Technical College, El Paso, TX.

Western Technical College (D)

9624 Plaza Circle, El Paso TX 79927-2105

County: El Paso
FICE Identification: 020983
Unit ID: 224679
Telephone: (915) 532-3737
Carnegie Class: Assoc/PrivFP
FAX Number: (915) 532-6946
Calendar System: Other
URL: www.westerntech.edu
Established: 1969
Annual Undergrad Tuition & Fees: $29,744
Enrollment: 940
Coed
Affiliation or Control: Proprietary
IRS Status: Proprietary
Highest Offering: Associate Degree
Program: Occupational; Technical Emphasis
Accreditation: ACCSC, PTAA

01 President/Director .... Mr. Allan SHARPE
88 Assistant Director .... Mr. Randy KUYKENDALL
11 Chief Administrative Officer .... Mr. Bill TERRELL
03 Executive VP/School Director .... Ms. Mary CANO
05 Academic Dean (Plaza) .... Ms. Lynda CERVANTES
05 Academic Dean (Diana) .... Ms. Marsha LAWLER
10 Accountant .... Ms. Celi AVILA
37 Financial Services Director .... Ms. Danielle PICCHI
36 Director Career Services .... Ms. Helen GARCIA
07 Director Admission .... Mr. Marco MARTINEZ
13 Director Information Technology .... Mr. Jose PEREZ

Western Texas College (E)

6200 College Avenue, Snyder TX 79549-6189

County: Scurry
FICE Identification: 009549
Unit ID: 229832
Telephone: (325) 573-8511
Carnegie Class: Assoc/Pub-R-M
FAX Number: (325) 573-9321
Calendar System: Semester
URL: www.wtc.edu
Established: 1969
Annual Undergrad Tuition & Fees (In-District): $2,054
Enrollment: 2,113
Coed
Affiliation or Control: State/Local
IRS Status: 501(c)3
Highest Offering: Associate Degree
Program: Occupational; 2-Year Principally Bachelor's Creditable
Accreditation: SC

01 President .... Dr. Barbara R. BEEBE
05 Vice President of Instruction .... Vacant
04 Assistant to the President .... Ms. Melanie SCHWERTNER
10 Chief Financial Officer .... Ms. Patricia CLAXTON
11 Chief Operation Officer .... Mr. Mike THORTON
09 Dean Inst Research & Effectiveness .... Mr. Britt CANADA
20 Dean of Instructional Affairs .... Ms. Stephanie DUCHENEAUX
32 Dean of Student Services .... Mr. Ralph RAMON
72 Dean of Technology .... Mr. Roy BARTELS
103 Dean Workforce Development .... Vacant
41 Athletic Director .... Ms. Tammy DAVIS
06 Registrar .... Ms. Ann GALYEAN
37 Director Financial Aid .... Mr. Greg TORRES
21 Controller .... Ms. Marjann MORROW
15 Director of Human Resources .... Ms. Kelly MCGINNIS
85 Dir International Student Services .... Ms. Melissa DOUCETTE
96 Director of Purchasing & Compliance .... Mr. Mitch CALHOUN

Wharton County Junior College (F)

911 Boling Highway, Wharton TX 77488-3298

County: Wharton
FICE Identification: 003668
Unit ID: 229841
Telephone: (979) 532-4560
Carnegie Class: Assoc/Pub-R-L
FAX Number: (979) 532-6545
Calendar System: Semester
URL: www.wcjc.edu
Established: 1946
Annual Undergrad Tuition & Fees (In-District): $2,222
Enrollment: 7,152
Coed
Affiliation or Control: Local
IRS Status: 501(c)3
Highest Offering: Associate Degree
Program: Occupational; 2-Year Principally Bachelor's Creditable
Accreditation: SC, CAHIIM, CSHSE, DH, EMT, PTAA, RAD, SURGT

01 President .... Ms. Betty A. MCCROHAN
05 Vice President of Instruction .... Ms. Leigh Ann COLLINS
10 Vice President Administrative Svcs .... Mr. Bryce KOCIAN
13 Vice President of Technology & IR .... Ms. Pamela YOUNGBLOOD
32 Vice President of Student Services .... Mr. David LEENHOUTS
21 Dean of Financial & Business Svcs .... Mr. Gus WESSELS
26 Director of Marketing & Comm .... Ms. Zina CARTER
06 Registrar .... Ms. Karen PREISLER
37 Director of Financial Aid .... Mr. Richard D. HYDE
08 Director Library Info/Tech Services .... Ms. Kwei HSU
18 Director of Facilities Management .... Mr. Mike FEYEN
15 Director of Human Resources .... Ms. Judy JONES
09 Director of Inst Effectiveness .... Dr. Danson JONES
96 Director of Purchasing .... Mr. Philip WUTHRICH

Wiley College (G)

711 Wiley Avenue, Marshall TX 75670-5199

County: Harrison
FICE Identification: 003669
Unit ID: 229887
Telephone: (903) 927-3300
Carnegie Class: Bac/Diverse
FAX Number: (903) 938-8100
Calendar System: Semester
URL: www.wileyc.edu
Established: 1873
Annual Undergrad Tuition & Fees: $11,482
Enrollment: 1,259
Coed
Affiliation or Control: United Methodist
IRS Status: 501(c)3
Highest Offering: Baccalaureate
Program: Liberal Arts And General; Teacher Preparatory
Accreditation: SC, ACBSP

01 President and CEO .... Dr. Haywood L. STRICKLAND
03 Executive Vice President & Provost .... Dr. Glenda F. CARTER
10 Vice Pres for Business & Finance .... Dr. James BATTEN
05 Vice President Academic Affairs .... Dr. Lee A. AGGISON
32 Vice President Student Affairs .... Dr. Joseph L. MORALE
30 Vice Pres Institutional Advancement .... Dr. Suzanne MAYO
13 Vice Pres Information Technology .... Mr. Nathaniel HEWITT
21 Controller .... Vacant
53 Dean of Education .... Dr. Calandra LOCKHART
42 College Chaplain .... Vacant
04 Assistant to the President .... Mrs. Karen HELTON
50 Dean of Business & Technology .... Dr. Abdalla F. HAGAN
49 Dean of Sciences .... Dr. Walter SHUMATE
97 Director Student Success Academy .... Vacant
79 Dean Social Sciences & Humanities .... Dr. Sherlynn H. BYRD
26 Director of Public Relations .... Ms. Tammy TAYLOR
08 Director of Library Services .... Mr. Christopher ALTNAU
06 Registrar .... Ms. Laura LANDER
07 Director of Admissions .... Ms. Jamecia MURRAY
15 Director of Human Resources .... Mrs. Krystal MOODY
18 Superintendent of Facilities .... Vacant
20 Assistant VP Academic Affairs .... Dr. Sherlynn BYRD
37 Director of Financial Aid .... Ms. Cecelia K. JONES
29 Director of Alumni Relations .... Ms. Alvena JONES
09 Director of Institutional Research .... Vacant
11 Director Administrative Svcs .... Mr. O. Ivan WHITE
23 College Nurse .... Ms. Shonte EPPERSON
36 Dir Student Placement/Counseling .... Ms. LaDonna GAUT
41 Director of Athletics .... Vacant
96 Director of Purchasing .... Mr. Darius Z. KIMBLE
35 Director of Student Development .... Ms. LaDonna GAUT
84 Director Enrollment Management .... Dr. Joseph L. MORALE
101 Secretary of the Institution/Board .... Mrs. Cassandra M. JOHNSON
106 Dir Online Education/E-learning .... Dr. Kim C. LONG
19 Director Security/Safety .... Mr. Winston ROBINSON
39 Director Student Housing .... Mr. Kerl NATHANIEL
43 Dir Legal Services/General Counsel .... Dr. Kim BEATON
44 Director Annual or Planned Giving .... Ms. Kimberly WOODWARD
90 Director Academic Computing .... Ms. Lisa TAYLOR

UTAH

Argosy University, Salt Lake City (H)

121 Election Road Suite 300, Draper UT 84020-7724

Telephone: (801) 601-5000
Identification: 666655
Accreditation: &WC, ACBSP, MFCD

† Regional accreditation is carried under the parent institution in Orange, CA.

The Art Institute of Salt Lake City (I)

121 West Election Road, Draper UT 84020

Telephone: (801) 601-4700
Identification: 666694
Accreditation: ACICS

† Branch campus of The Art Institute of Phoenix, AZ.

Brigham Young University (J)

Provo UT 84602-0002

County: Utah
FICE Identification: 003670
Unit ID: 230038
Telephone: (801) 422-4000
Carnegie Class: RU/H
FAX Number: (801) 422-0684
Calendar System: Semester
URL: www.byu.edu
Established: 1875
Annual Undergrad Tuition & Fees: $10,300
Enrollment: 30,484
Coed
Affiliation or Control: Latter-day Saints
IRS Status: 501(c)3
Highest Offering: Doctorate
Program: Liberal Arts And General; Teacher Preparatory; Professional
Accreditation: NW, ART, BUS, BUSA, CAATE, CLPSY, CONST, COPSY, CS, DANCE, DIETD, DIETI, ENG, ENGT, IPSY, JOUR, LAW, MFCD, MT, MUS, NRPA, NURSE, PH, SP, SPAA, SW, TEAC, THEA

01 President .... Dr. Kevin J. WORTHEN
05 Academic Vice President .... Dr. Brent W. WEBB
11 Administrative Vice President .... Mr. Brian K. EVANS
44 Advancement Vice President .... Dr. Matthew O. RICHARDSON
13 Vice Pres Info Tech/Chief Info Ofcr .... Dr. J. Kelly FLANAGAN
88 International Vice President .... Dr. Sandra ROGERS
32 Student Life Vice President .... Dr. Janet S. SCHARMAN
43 Asst to President/General Counsel .... Mr. Michael R. ORME
45 Asst to Pres Planning/Assessment .... Mr. James D. GORDON, III
27 Asst to Pres Univ Communications .... Mrs. Carri P. JENKINS
20 Assoc Acad Vice President Faculty .... Dr. Craig H. HART
20 Assoc Acad VP Undergraduate Stds .... Dr. Jeffrey D. KEITH
46 Assoc Acad VP Research/Grad Stds .... Dr. Alan R. HARKER
35 Assoc Student Life Vice Pres .... Dr. Ronald K. CHAPMAN
10 Chief Financial Officer .... Mr. Brian K. EVANS
18 Asst Admin VP Physical Facilities .... Mr. Ole M. SMITH
15 Asst Admin VP Human Resource Svcs .... Mr. Forrest FLAKE
35 Asst Admin VP/Stdnt Auxil Svc .... Mr. David A. HUNT
26 Assoc VP Alumni/External Relations .... Mr. John C. LEWIS
30 Managing Dir LDS Philanthropies .... Dr. Tanise CHUNG-HOON
36 Exec Dir Stdnt Acad/Advisement Svcs .... Mr. Norm FINLINSON
35 Dean Student Life .... Mr. Vernon L. HEPERI
37 Director Financial Aid/Scholarships .... Mr. Stephen E. HILL
88 Dean Undergraduate Education .... Dr. John D. BELL
08 University Librarian .... Ms. Jennifer PAUSTENBAUGH

58 Dean Graduate Studies ....Dr. Wynn C. STIRLING
51 Dean Continuing Education ....Dr. Lee GLINES
47 Dean Life Sciences ....Dr. Rodney J. BROWN
54 Dean Engineering & Technology ....Dr. Alan R. PARKINSON
83 Dean Family Home & Social Science ....Dr. Benjamin M. OGLES
57 Dean Fine Arts & Communications ....Dr. Stephen M. JONES
79 Dean Humanities ....Dr. John ROSENBERG
61 Dean Law School ....Dr. James R. RASBAND
50 Dean Marriott School Management ....Dr. Lee T. PERRY
53 Dean McKay School of Education ....Dr. Mary Ann PRATER
81 Dean Physical & Math Science ....Dr. Scott D. SOMMERFELDT
66 Dean Nursing ....Dr. Patricia RAVERT
73 Dean Religious Education ....Dr. Brent TOP
38 Director Counseling & Career Ctr ....Dr. Steve A. SMITH
09 Dir Institutional Assess/Analysis ....Dr. Danny R. OLSEN
06 Registrar ....Mr. Barry ALLRED
07 Director of Admissions ....Mr. R. Kirk STRONG
29 Managing Director Alumni Relations ....Ms. Linda PALMER
96 Director of Purchasing ....Mr. W. Timothy HILL
88 Dir University Accessibility Center ....Dr. Michael BROOKS
19 Director Security/Safety ....Mr. Larry STOTT
39 Director Student Housing ....Ms. Julie FRANKLIN
41 Athletic Director ....Mr. Tom HOLMOE

Broadview Entertainment Arts University (A)

240 East Morris Avenue, Salt Lake City UT 84115
Telephone: (801) 300-4300 Identification: 770809
Accreditation: ACICS

† Branch campus of Broadview University, West Jordan, UT.

Broadview University (B)

869 West Hill Field Road, Layton UT 84041
Telephone: (801) 660-6000 Identification: 770810
Accreditation: ACICS, MAAB

† Branch campus of Broadview University, West Jordan, UT.

Broadview University (C)

898 North 1200 West, Orem UT 84057
Telephone: (801) 822-5800 Identification: 770811
Accreditation: ACICS, MAAB

† Branch campus of Broadview University, West Jordan, UT.

Broadview University (D)

1902 W 7800 S, West Jordan UT 84088-4021
County: Salt Lake FICE Identification: 011166
Unit ID: 230056
Telephone: (801) 304-4224 Carnegie Class: Spec/Health
FAX Number: (801) 304-4229 Calendar System: Quarter
URL: www.broadviewuniversity.edu
Established: 1971 Annual Undergrad Tuition & Fees: $14,652
Enrollment: 219 Coed
Affiliation or Control: Proprietary IRS Status: Proprietary
Highest Offering: Master's
Program: Occupational; Technical Emphasis
Accreditation: ACICS, MAAB

01 President ....Mr. Terry MYHRE
05 Director ....Ms. Deeann KERR

Eagle Gate College (E)

915 North 400 West, Layton UT 84041
Telephone: (801) 546-7500 Identification: 770812
Accreditation: ACICS

† Branch campus of Eagle Gate College, Murray, UT.

Eagle Gate College (F)

5588 S Green Street, Murray UT 84123-6965
County: Salt Lake FICE Identification: 021785
Unit ID: 447625
Telephone: (801) 333-8100 Carnegie Class: Assoc/PrivFP4
FAX Number: (801) 263-6520 Calendar System: Other
URL: www.eaglegatecollege.edu
Established: 1979 Annual Undergrad Tuition & Fees: $15,513
Enrollment: 238 Coed
Affiliation or Control: Proprietary IRS Status: Proprietary
Highest Offering: Baccalaureate
Program: 2-Year Principally Bachelor's Creditable; Technical Emphasis
Accreditation: ACICS

01 President ....Mr. Chris NICKELL
03 Campus VP ....Ms. Jana COLYAR

Fortis College (G)

3949 South 700 East, Suite 150, Salt Lake City UT 84107
Telephone: (801) 713-0915 Identification: 666762
Accreditation: ACCSC, ADNUR, DH

† Tuition varies by degree program.

Independence University (H)

4021 South 700 East, Suite 400,
Salt Lake City UT 84107-2453
County: Salt Lake FICE Identification: 022061
Unit ID: 465812
Telephone: (800) 972-5149 Carnegie Class: Not Classified
FAX Number: (801) 263-0345 Calendar System: Other
URL: www.independence.edu
Established: 1978 Annual Undergrad Tuition & Fees: $16,968
Enrollment: 4,478 Coed
Affiliation or Control: Proprietary IRS Status: Proprietary
Highest Offering: Master's
Program: Professional
Accreditation: ACCSC, COARC

01 Executive Director ....Mr. Carl BARNEY

ITT Technical Institute (I)

920 West LeVoy Drive, Murray UT 84123-2500
Telephone: (801) 263-3313 FICE Identification: 023610
Accreditation: ACICS

† Branch campus of ITT Technical Institute, Indianapolis, IN.

LDS Business College (J)

95 North 300 West, Salt Lake City UT 84101-3500
County: Salt Lake FICE Identification: 003672
Unit ID: 230418
Telephone: (801) 524-8100 Carnegie Class: Assoc/PrivNFP
FAX Number: (801) 524-1900 Calendar System: Semester
URL: www.ldsbc.edu
Established: 1886 Annual Undergrad Tuition & Fees: $3,160
Enrollment: 2,036 Coed
Affiliation or Control: Latter-day Saints IRS Status: 501(c)3
Highest Offering: Associate Degree
Program: Occupational; 2-Year Principally Bachelor's Creditable; Business Emphasis
Accreditation: NW, #MAC

01 President ....Mr. Larry J. RICHARDS
04 Executive Admin Asst ....Ms. Jolynn WOLFGRAMM
05 Chief Academic Officer ....Mr. Ronald E. GUYMON
13 Chief Information Officer ....Mr. Mark AUGHENBAUGH
10 Vice President Finance/Controller ....Mr. Bob H. WISER
30 VP Advancement ....Mr. Craig V. NELSON
50 Director of Strategic Initiatives ....Mr. Robert SALMON
20 Dean of Insitutional Support ....Mr. Tyler S. MORGAN
15 Director of Human Resources ....Mr. Brady KIMBER
07 Asst Director of Admissions ....Ms. Dawn FELLOWS
06 Registrar ....Ms. Tamra TAYLOR
88 Director of Instructional Design ....Mr. Jared WRIGHT
88 Director of Business Solutions ....Mr. Glenn MCGETTIGAN
08 Dir of Library/Inform Resources ....Ms. Sarah SORENSEN
88 Accounting Program Director ....Mr. Bruce SCHREINER
50 Business Skills Program Director ....Mr. Scott NEWMAN
88 Entrepreneurship Program Director ....Mr. Brent ANDRUS
88 Professional Sales Program Director ....Ms. Jennifer WARNAS
50 Director Business Applications ....Mr. Mitch PENDLETON
23 Health Professions Program Director ....Ms. Olivia WEST
88 Paralegal Program Director ....Ms. Kimberly GARNER
97 Integrated Studies Program Director ....Mr. Paul RICHARDS
88 Interior Design Program Director ....Mr. Miles HUNSAKER
88 Business Info Systems Program Dir ....Mr. Spencer DEGRAW
73 Institute of Religion Director ....Mr. Keith BURKHART
21 Assistant Controller ....Mr. Chris REITZ
37 Manager Student Financial Services ....Ms. Melanie CONOVER
40 Bookstore Manager ....Ms. Rachel BINGHAM
32 Chief Student Services Officer ....Mr. Adrian JUCHAU
26 Public Affairs Director ....Mrs. Louise BROWN
88 Director of Learning Assistance Lab ....Mrs. Kathy SKENE
36 Director of Career Services ....Mr. Justin JONES
108 Director Institutional Assessment ....Mr. Michael R. DAVISON

Midwives College of Utah (K)

1174 E Graystone Way Suite 2,
Salt Lake City UT 84106-2671
County: Utah Identification: 666281
Unit ID: 480985
Telephone: (866) 680-2756 Carnegie Class: Not Classified
FAX Number: (866) 207-2024 Calendar System: Semester
URL: www.midwifery.edu
Established: 1980 Annual Undergrad Tuition & Fees: $6,000
Enrollment: 225 Coed
Affiliation or Control: Independent Non-Profit IRS Status: 501(c)3
Highest Offering: Master's
Program: Professional; Nursing Emphasis
Accreditation: MEAC

01 President ....Ms. Kristi RIDD-YOUNG
05 Academic Dean ....Ms. Nicole CROFT
17 Clinical Dean ....Ms. Sarah CARTER
06 Registrar ....Ms. Laura PARK
08 Head Librarian ....Ms. Kaylee RIDD
07 Admissions ....Ms. Mel SMITH-TOURVILLE
13 Chief Info Technology Officer (CIO) ....Mr. Alan BELLOWS

Neumont University (L)

143 South Main, Salt Lake City UT 84111
County: Salt Lake FICE Identification: 010098
Unit ID: 445692
Telephone: (801) 302-2800 Carnegie Class: Spec/Tech
FAX Number: (801) 302-2811 Calendar System: Quarter
URL: www.neumont.edu
Established: 2003 Annual Undergrad Tuition & Fees: $24,000
Enrollment: 431 Coed
Affiliation or Control: Proprietary IRS Status: Proprietary
Highest Offering: Master's
Program: Professional; Technical Emphasis
Accreditation: ACICS

01 President/Campus Dir Utah ....Shaun MCALMONT
05 Provost ....Vacant
32 Dean of Students ....Erin MCCORMACK
06 Registrar/Dir Academic Programs ....Larry CRANDALL
07 Director of Admissions ....Karick HEATON

New Charter University (M)

50 W. Broadway, Suite 300, Salt Lake City UT 84101
County: Salt Lake FICE Identification: 041292
Unit ID: 420361
Telephone: (801) 883-8336 Carnegie Class: Not Classified
FAX Number: (801) 855-5922 Calendar System: Trimester
URL: www.new.edu
Established: 1994 Annual Undergrad Tuition & Fees: $2,632
Enrollment: 350 Coed
Affiliation or Control: Proprietary IRS Status: Proprietary
Highest Offering: Master's
Program: Liberal Arts And General; Business Emphasis
Accreditation: DEAC

01 President ....Mr. David ROSS
05 Academic Dean ....Ms. Diane JOHNSON
10 Manager Operations/Student Affairs ....Ms. Char BOSEN
09 Sr Manager Institutional Research ....Ms. Debbie AUSTIN

Nightingale College (N)

4155 Harrison Blvd, Ste 100, Ogden UT 84403
County: Weber FICE Identification: 038383
Unit ID: 44787
Telephone: (801) 689-2160 Carnegie Class: Not Classified
FAX Number: (801) 689-3114 Calendar System: Semester
URL: www.nightingale.edu
Established: 2010 Annual Undergrad Tuition & Fees: $40,080
Enrollment: 156 Coed
Affiliation or Control: Proprietary IRS Status: Proprietary
Highest Offering: Baccalaureate
Program: Occupational; 2-Year Principally Bachelor's Creditable; Nursing Emphasis
Accreditation: ABHES, ADNUR

01 President/CEO ....Mr. Mikhail SHNEYDER

Ogden-Weber Applied Technology College (O)

200 North Washington Boulevard, Ogden UT 84404-4089
County: Weber FICE Identification: 023465
Unit ID: 230490
Telephone: (801) 627-8300 Carnegie Class: Assoc/Pub-U-MC
FAX Number: (801) 395-3727 Calendar System: Other
URL: www.owatc.edu
Established: 1971 Annual Undergrad Tuition & Fees (In-District): $3,588
Enrollment: 2,615 Coed
Affiliation or Control: State/Local IRS Status: 501(c)3
Highest Offering: Associate Degree
Program: Occupational; Technical Emphasis
Accreditation: COE, MAC, PNUR

01 President & Chief Executive Officer ....Collette MERCIER
05 VP for Instructional Services ....James R. TAGGART
32 VP for Student Services ....Rhonda LAURITZEN
10 VP for College Services/CFO ....Tyler CALL
04 Administrative Asst to President ....Tina SMITH
06 Registrar ....Kari MARLER
102 Dir Foundation/Corporate Relations ....Monica SCHWENK
15 Director Personnel Services ....Theresa WALKER
19 Director Security/Safety ....Fred FRAZIER
26 Chief Public Relations/Marketing ....Elsa ZWEIFEL
37 Director Student Financial Aid ....Jan BURTON

† Campus of Utah College of Applied Technology, Salt Lake City, UT.

Provo College (P)

1450 W 820 N, Provo UT 84601-1305
County: Utah FICE Identification: 023608
Unit ID: 380438
Telephone: (801) 818-8900 Carnegie Class: Assoc/PrivFP
FAX Number: (801) 375-9728 Calendar System: Other
URL: www.provocollege.edu
Established: 1984 Annual Undergrad Tuition & Fees: $14,882
Enrollment: 372 Coed
Affiliation or Control: Proprietary IRS Status: Proprietary
Highest Offering: Associate Degree

Program: Occupational; Nursing Emphasis
Accreditation: ACICS, ADNUR, PTAA

01 Campus President .... Mr. Todd SMITH
05 Academic Dean .... Mrs. Jana COLYAR
10 Business Manager .... Mr. Derrick BLOMQUIST
07 Director of Admissions .... Ms. Tania ROWLAND
37 Financial Services Assoc Director .... Ms. Julie TETRICK
06 Registrar .... Mrs. Camilla NASH
32 Director of Student Services .... Ms. Liz TIDWELL
36 Director of Career Services .... Mr. Fred OLENIK

Rocky Mountain University of Health Professions (A)

561 East 1860 South, Provo UT 84606-7312
County: Utah FICE Identification: 041932
Unit ID: 475495
Telephone: (801) 375-5125 Carnegie Class: Not Classified
FAX Number: (801) 375-2125 Calendar System: Trimester
URL: www.rmuohp.edu
Established: 1998 Annual Graduate Tuition & Fees: $20,000
Enrollment: 501 Coed
Affiliation or Control: Proprietary IRS Status: Proprietary
Highest Offering: Doctorate; No Undergraduates
Program: Professional
Accreditation: NW, #ARCPA, PTA

01 President .... Dr. Richard P. NIELSEN
05 Provost .... Dr. Hani GHAZI-BIRRY
11 Chief Operation Officer .... Dr. Michael SKURJA
10 Vice President Finance .... Mr. Jeff B. BATE
31 VP Inst Effect/Cmty Engagement .... Ms. Jessica D. EGBERT
84 VP Enrollment Management .... Dr. Erin NOSEL
09 Exec VP Inst Effect/Strategic Int .... Dr. Sandra PENNINGTON
46 Director of Research .... Dr. Brent ALVAR

Stevens-Henager College (B)

755 South Main Street, Logan UT 84321
Telephone: (435) 792-6970 Identification: 770603
Accreditation: ACCSC, MAC

† Branch campus of Stevens-Henager College, Ogden, UT.

Stevens-Henager College (C)

1890 South 1350 West, Ogden UT 84401
County: Weber FICE Identification: 003674
Unit ID: 230621
Telephone: (801) 622-1567 Carnegie Class: Bac/Assoc
FAX Number: (801) 621-0853 Calendar System: Quarter
URL: www.stevenshenager.edu
Established: 1891 Annual Undergrad Tuition & Fees: $16,968
Enrollment: 321 Coed
Affiliation or Control: Independent Non-Profit IRS Status: 501(c)3
Highest Offering: Baccalaureate
Program: Occupational; 2-Year Principally Bachelor's Creditable
Accreditation: ACCSC, ADNUR, MAC, SURGT

01 Pres of Ogden Campus/Regional Dir .... Ms. Vicky DEWSNUP
07 Director of Admissions .... Mr. Wynne HURTADO
32 Director of Student Services .... Mr. Doug BURCH
05 Chief Academic Officer .... Dr. Wayne HUNSAKER
10 Chief Business Officer .... Mr. Leland NEIL
35 Director Student Affairs .... Mr. Micah BERGER
36 Director Career Services .... Mr. Doug BURCH

Stevens-Henager College (D)

1476 S Sandhill Road, Orem UT 84058-7310
Telephone: (801) 418-1450 FICE Identification: 030030
Accreditation: ACCSC, #MAC

† Branch campus of Stevens-Henager College, Ogden, UT.

Stevens-Henager College (E)

720 South River Road, Suite C-130, St. George UT 84790
Telephone: (435) 628-9903 Identification: 770604
Accreditation: ACCSC

† Branch campus of Stevens-Henager College, Ogden, UT.

Stevens-Henager College (F)

383 W Vine Street, Salt Lake City UT 84123
Telephone: (801) 281-7620 Identification: 666038
Accreditation: ACCSC, #COARC

† Branch campus of Stevens-Henager College, Ogden, UT.

Uintah Basin Applied Technology College (G)

1100 East Lagoon Street, Roosevelt UT 84066
County: Duchesne FICE Identification: 011165
Unit ID: 230676
Telephone: (435) 722-6900 Carnegie Class: Assoc/Pub-R-S
FAX Number: (435) 722-6999 Calendar System: Semester
URL: www.ubatc.edu
Established: 1968 Annual Undergrad Tuition & Fees (In-State): $1,800
Enrollment: 1,389 Coed
Affiliation or Control: State IRS Status: 501(c)3
Highest Offering: Associate Degree
Program: Occupational; Technical Emphasis
Accreditation: COE, PNUR

01 Campus President .... Aaron K. WEIGHT
32 Vice Pres of Student Services .... Robert PETERSON
10 Vice President Fiscal Services .... Keith SPROUSE
05 Vice President Instruction .... Bob NAYLOR
04 Exec Assistant to the President .... Trenna BALLOU
06 Registrar .... Julene OLSEN
37 Financial Aid Coordinator .... Mark ANDERTON

† Campus of Utah College of Applied Technology, Salt Lake City, UT.

University of Phoenix Utah Campus (H)

5373 South Green Street, Salt Lake City UT 84123-4642
Telephone: (801) 263-1444 Identification: 770232
Accreditation: &NH, ACBSP, CACREP

† Branch campus of University of Phoenix, Tempe, AZ.

The Utah College of Dental Hygiene at Careers Unlimited (I)

1176 S 1480 W, Orem UT 84058-4905
County: Utah FICE Identification: 034633
Unit ID: 448239
Telephone: (801) 426-8234 Carnegie Class: Spec/Health
FAX Number: (801) 224-5437 Calendar System: Other
URL: www.ucdh.edu
Established: 2006 Annual Undergrad Tuition & Fees: $24,970
Enrollment: 120 Coed
Affiliation or Control: Proprietary IRS Status: Proprietary
Highest Offering: Baccalaureate
Program: Occupational; 2-Year Principally Bachelor's Creditable
Accreditation: ACCSC, DH

01 College President .... Mr. Brent MOLEN
05 Director of Education .... Mr. Kenneth MOLEN

*Utah System of Higher Education (J)

The Gateway, 60 S 400 W, Salt Lake City UT 84101-1284
County: Salt Lake FICE Identification: 009339
Telephone: (801) 321-7101 Carnegie Class: N/A
FAX Number: (801) 321-7199
URL: www.higheredutah.org

01 Exec Ofcr/Commissioner of Higher Ed .... Mr. David L. BUHLER
05 Assoc Commissioner Academic Affairs .... Dr. Elizabeth J. HITCH
10 Assoc Commissioner Finance/Facilit .... Dr. Gregory STAUFFER
37 Exec Director Student Financial Aid .... Mr. David A. FEITZ
88 UESP Executive Director .... Ms. Lynne WARD

*The University of Utah (K)

201 South 1460 East, Salt Lake City UT 84112-1107
County: Salt Lake FICE Identification: 003675
Unit ID: 230764
Telephone: (801) 581-7200 Carnegie Class: RU/VH
FAX Number: (801) 581-3007 Calendar System: Semester
URL: www.utah.edu
Established: 1850 Annual Undergrad Tuition & Fees (In-State): $8,197
Enrollment: 31,515 Coed
Affiliation or Control: State IRS Status: 501(c)3
Highest Offering: Doctorate
Program: Liberal Arts And General; Teacher Preparatory; Professional
Accreditation: NW, ARCPA, AUD, BUS, BUSA, CAATE, CEA, CLPSY, COPSY, CYTO, DANCE, DENT, DIETC, EMT, ENG, ENGR, HSA, IPSY, LAW, MED, MIDWF, MT, MUS, NMT, NRPA, NURSE, OT, PH, PHAR, PLNG, PTA, SCPSY, SP, SPAA, SW

02 President .... Dr. David W. PERSHING
05 Sr Vice Pres Academic Affairs .... Dr. Ruth WATKINS
17 Sr VP Hlth Sci/CEO Univ Ut Hlth Ctr .... Dr. Vivian S. LEE
43 Vice President & General Counsel .... Mr. John K. MORRIS
11 Vice Pres Administrative Services .... Mr. Arnold B. COMBE
10 Chief Business Officer .... Mr. John E. NIXON
32 Vice President Student Affairs .... Dr. Barbara H. SNYDER
30 Vice Pres Institutional Advancement .... Mr. Fred C. ESPLIN
86 Vice President Government Relations .... Mr. Jason PERRY
15 Assoc Vice Pres for Human Resources .... Ms. Joan GINES
46 Vice President Research .... Dr. Thomas N. PARKS
04 Exec Asst to the President .... Ms. Lisa BOUILLON
13 Interim Chief Information Officer .... Mr. Stephen HESS
21 Chief Strategy Officer .... Ms. Patricia A. ROSS
88 Chief Global Officer .... Dr. Michael L. HARDMAN
16 Chief Human Resources Officer .... Mr. Jeff HERRING
26 Chief Mktg & Commun Officer .... Mr. William J. WARREN
20 Assoc VP AA & Dean Undergrad Stds .... Dr. Martha S. BRADLEY
84 Sr Assoc VP for Enrollment Mgmt .... Ms. Mary G. PARKER
45 Assoc VP Acad Affs/Budget/Planning .... Ms. Cathy ANDERSON
18 Assoc VP Admin Services/Facilities .... Mr. Michael G. PEREZ
10 Assoc VP Admin/Finance & Bus Svcs .... Mr. Jeffrey J. WEST
20 Int Assoc VP Equity/Diversity .... Dr. Kathryn B. STOCKTON
88 Associate Vice President Research .... Dr. Cynthia M. FURSE
88 Assoc VP Acad Affs/Faculty .... Dr. Amy WILDERMUTH
35 Assoc VP Stdnt Affs/Bus/Auxil Svcs .... Dr. Jerry L. BASFORD
109 Assoc Vice Pres Admin Svc/Auxil Svc .... Mr. Gordon N. WILSON
58 Dean Graduate School .... Dr. David B. KIEDA
48 Dean Architecture & Planning .... Dr. Keith D. MOORE
50 Dean David Eccles Sch of Business .... Dr. Taylor RANDALL
52 Int Dean School of Dentistry .... Mr. Glen HANSON
53 Dean College of Education .... Dr. Maria FRANQUIZ
54 Dean College of Engineering .... Dr. Richard B. BROWN
57 Dean Col of Fine Arts/AVP the Arts .... Dr. Raymond TYMAS-JONES
68 Dean College of Health .... Dr. David H. PERRIN
92 Dean Honors College .... Dr. Sylvia TORTI
79 Dean College of Humanities .... Dr. Robert D. NEWMAN
61 Dean S J Quinney College of Law .... Dr. Robert ADLER
65 Dean Coll of Mines & Earth Science .... Dr. Francis H. BROWN
63 Dean School of Medicine .... Dr. Vivian S. LEE
66 Dean College of Nursing .... Dr. Patricia MORTON
67 Int Dean College of Pharmacy .... Dr. Kristen A. KEEFE
81 Dean College of Science .... Dr. Henry WHITE
83 Int Dean Col Social/Behav Science .... Dr. Cynthia BERG
70 Dean College of Social Work .... Mr. Hank LIESE
88 Dean of Students .... Ms. Lori MCDONALD
06 University Registrar .... Mr. Timothy J. EBNER
23 CEO University Hospitals & Clinics .... Mr. David E. ENTWISTLE
91 Exec Dir Proj/Apps/Univ Info Tech .... Ms. Deborah B. RAKHSHA
88 Director Institutional Review Board .... Mr. John P. STILLMAN
96 Director Purchasing .... Mr. James T. PARKER
94 Director Gender Studies .... Dr. Susie PORTER
77 Department Chair Sch of Computing .... Mr. Ross T. WHITAKER
52 Dir Dental Clinic/Gen Prac Residency .... Dr. James BEKKER
07 Director Admissions .... Mr. Matthew LOPEZ
29 Exec Director Alumni Association .... Mr. M. John ASHTON
44 Director Planned Giving .... Ms. Karin S. HARDY
37 Dir Financial Aid & Scholarships .... Mr. John CURL
08 Dean MLIB/University Librarian .... Ms. Alberta COMER
62 Dir Eccles Health Sciences Library .... Ms. Jean P. SHIPMAN
62 Dir S J Quinney Col of Law/Lib .... Ms. Melissa BERNSTEIN
36 Director of Career Services .... Mr. Stan D. INMAN
38 Director Counseling Center .... Dr. Lauren WEITZMAN
39 Director Housing & Res Education .... Ms. Barbara REMSBURG
39 Director Univ Student Apartments .... Mr. Richard L. JAMES
88 Dir Natural History Museum of Utah .... Dr. Sarah B. GEORGE
19 Chief of Police .... Mr. Dale G. BROPHY
40 Director Campus Bookstore .... Mr. Daniel L. ARCHER
85 Director International Center .... Ms. Chalimar L. SWAIN
41 Director Athletics .... Dr. Chris HILL
25 Dir Office of Sponsored Projects .... Mr. Brent K. BROWN
31 Director Univ-Neighborhood Partners .... Ms. Sarah MUNRO
09 Director Institutional Analysis .... Dr. Paul A. GORE

*Southern Utah University (L)

351 W University Blvd, Cedar City UT 84720-2470
County: Iron FICE Identification: 003678
Unit ID: 230603
Telephone: (435) 586-7700 Carnegie Class: Master's L
FAX Number: (435) 586-5475 Calendar System: Semester
URL: www.suu.edu
Established: 1897 Annual Undergrad Tuition & Fees (In-State): $6,300
Enrollment: 7,656 Coed
Affiliation or Control: State IRS Status: 501(c)3
Highest Offering: Master's
Program: Occupational; Liberal Arts And General; Teacher Preparatory
Accreditation: NW, ART, BUS, CAATE, CS, DANCE, ENG, ENGT, MUS, NURSE, SPAA, TEAC

02 President .... Mr. Scott L. WYATT
05 Provost .... Dr. Bradley COOK
10 Vice Pres of Finance & Admin .... Mr. Marvin DODGE
32 Asst VP/Dean Student Services .... Mr. Jason RAMIREZ
30 Vice Pres Advancement .... Mr. Stuart JONES
58 Assoc Provost/Dean of Graduate Stds .... Dr. James SAGE
13 Chief Information Officer .... Mr. Thomas MCFARLAND
18 Executive Director of FM .... Mr. Tiger FUNK
08 Dean/Director Library/Univ Studies .... Dr. Richard SAUNDERS
51 Dean of Continuing/Profess Studies .... Mr. Mark ATKINSON
21 Asst VP of Budget and Planning .... Mr. Mitchell BEALER
75 Director CTE .... Mr. David A. WARD
06 Registrar .... Mr. John ALLRED
15 Director Human Resources .... Mr. David T. MCGUIRE
88 Dean of University College .... Dr. Patrick CLARKE
37 Director of Financial Aid .... Ms. Jan CAREY-MCDONALD
29 Exec Director of Alumni Relations .... Ms. Mindy BENSON
41 Athletic Director .... Mr. Ken BEAZER
43 Legal Counsel .... Mr. D. Michael CARTER
79 Dean Col Humanities/Soc Sci .... Dr. James MCDONALD
50 Dean School of Business .... Dr. Carl R. TEMPLIN
53 Dean College of Education .... Dr. Deborah HILL
81 Dean College of Sci and Engineering .... Dr. Robert EVES
57 Dean College Performing/Visual Arts .... Mrs. Shauna MENDINI
96 Director of Purchasing .... Mr. Bradley BROWN
09 Director of Institutional Research .... Mr. Christian REINER
38 Director Student Counseling .... Dr. Curtis HILL

*Dixie State University (M)

225 S University Avenue, Saint George UT 84770-3876
County: Washington FICE Identification: 003671
Unit ID: 230171
Telephone: (435) 652-7500 Carnegie Class: Bac/Assoc
FAX Number: (435) 656-4001 Calendar System: Semester
URL: www.dixie.edu
Established: 1911 Annual Undergrad Tuition & Fees (In-State): $4,456
Enrollment: 8,570 Coed
Affiliation or Control: State IRS Status: 501(c)3
Highest Offering: Baccalaureate
Program: Occupational; 2-Year Principally Bachelor's Creditable; Liberal Arts And General; Teacher Preparatory; Professional

Accreditation: NW, ADNUR, COARC, DH, EMT, MT, MUS, NUR, PTAA, RAD, SURGT

02 President .... Dr. Richard B. WILLIAMS
11 Vice Pres Administrative Services .... Mr. Paul MORRIS
05 Exec Vice Pres Academic Services ..... Dr. William CHRISTENSEN
32 VP Student Services/Govt Relations .... Mr. Frank LOJKO
30 Vice Pres Advancement .... Mr. Brad LAST
49 Dean School of Humanities .... Dr. Don HINTON
66 Dean School Health Sciences .... Dr. Carole GRADY
50 Dean School Business .... Dr. Kyle WELLS
81 Dean Science & Technology .... Dr. Eric PEDERSEN
53 Dean Sch Education/Family Studies .... Dr. Brenda SABEY
51 Dean Academic & Community Outreach .... Ms. Becky SMITH
35 Dean of Students .... Mr. Del BEATTY
13 Chief Information Officer .... Mr. Gary J. KOEVEN
10 Asst VP of Business Services .... Mr. A. Scott TALBOT
15 Exec Director of Human Resources ...... Ms. Pamela MONTRALLO
18 Executive Director Campus Services .... Ms. Sherry RUESCH
08 Director Library .... Mr. Richard PAUSTENBAUGH
109 Executive Director Auxiliaries .... Mr. T. Randy JUDD
37 Exec Director Student Financial Aid .... Mr. J. D ROBERTSON
84 Exec Dir Enrollment Services .... Mr. David ROOS
06 Registrar .... Ms. Julie STENDER
07 Director of Admissions .... Mr. Brett SCHWARTS
38 Director Student Counseling .... Mr. Rick PALMER
26 Director Public Relations .... Mr. Steve JOHNSON
18 Director Facilities Operation .... Mr. Doug WHITEHEAD
19 Director Security/Safety .... Mr. Don C. REID
41 Athletic Director .... Mr. Jason BOOTHE
39 Director Resident Life .... Mr. Seth GUBLER
09 Director of Institutional Research .... Ms. Andrea BROWN
04 Exec Assistant to the President .... Mrs. Marilyn LAMOREAUX
35 Director of Student Involvement .... Mr. Jordon SHARP
96 Director of Purchasing .... Ms. Jackie FREEMAN
29 Director of Alumni Relations .... Ms. Kalynn LARSON
103 Dir Workforce/Career Development .... Mr. Steve BRINGHURST
105 Director of Network Services .... Mr. Jerry MATSON
25 Chief Contracts/Grants Admin .... Mr. Bill O'NEILL
28 Director of Diversity .... Ms. Kristine WHITTAKER
43 Dir Legal Services/General Counsel .... Mr. Michael CARTER
91 Director Administrative Computing .... Mr. James MILLER

*Utah State University (A)

Logan UT 84322-0001

County: Cache FICE Identification: 003677
Unit ID: 230728

Telephone: (435) 797-1000 Carnegie Class: RU/H
FAX Number: (435) 797-3880 Calendar System: Semester
URL: www.usu.edu
Established: 1888 Annual Undergrad Tuition & Fees (In-State): $6,664
Enrollment: 27,662 Coed
Affiliation or Control: State IRS Status: 501(c)3
Highest Offering: Doctorate
Program: Liberal Arts And General; Teacher Preparatory; Professional
Accreditation: NW, ART, AUD, BUS, BUSA, CEA, CIDA, CORE, CS, DIETC, DIETD, DIETI, ENG, ENGR, IPSY, LSAR, MFCD, MUS, PSPSY, SP, SW, TEAC

02 President .... Dr. Stan L. ALBRECHT
05 Provost .... Dr. Noelle E. COCKETT
43 General Counsel .... Mr. Craig J. SIMPER
10 Vice President Business & Finance .... Mr. Dave COWLEY
32 Vice President Student Services .... Mr. James MORALES
56 Vice Pres Extension & Agriculture .... Dr. Kenneth L. WHITE
46 VP Research/Dn Sch Graduate Stds .... Dr. Mark R. MCLELLAN
30 VP Univ Advance/Commercialization .... Mr. Robert BEHUNIN
13 CIO/Assoc VP Information Technology .... Dr. Eric HAWLEY
18 Associate VP for Facilities .... Mr. Charles DARNELL
07 Asst VP Recruitment/Enrollment Svcs .... Mr. John MORTENSEN
20 Vice Provost .... Dr. Laurens H. SMITH
51 Vice Prov Regional Camp/Dist Educ .... Mr. Travis PETERSON
08 Interim Dean Libraries .... Mr. Brad COLE
26 Exec Dir Public Relations/Marketing .... Mr. Tim VITALE
09 Dir Analysis Assess/Accreditation .... Mr. Michael TORRENS
22 Director Affirmative Action/EEO .... Ms. Stacy STURGEON
41 Athletic Director .... Mr. John HARTWELL
25 Exec Director Sponsored Programs .... Mr. Kevin PETERSON
86 Director Government Relations .... Mr. Neil N. ABERCROMBIE
15 Director of Human Resources .... Ms. BrandE FAUPELL
19 Director University Police Dept .... Mr. Steven J. MECHAM
06 Registrar .... Mr. Roland SQUIRE
36 Exec Dir Career Services/Coop Educ .... Ms. Donna E. CROW
37 Director of Financial Aid .... Ms. Patti KOHLER
38 Director Counseling Center .... Dr. David BUSH
40 Director of Campus Store .... Mr. David HANSEN
92 Director of Honors .... Ms. Kristine MILLER
96 Director of Purchasing .... Mr. Jeff CROSBIE
47 Dean of Agriculture .... Dr. Kenneth L. WHITE
57 Dean of Arts .... Dr. Craig JESSOP
50 Dean of Business .... Mr. Douglas D. ANDERSON
53 Dean of Education .... Dr. Beth FOLEY
54 Dean of Engineering .... Dr. Christine HAILEY
79 Dean Humanities/Social Science .... Dr. John C. ALLEN
65 Dean of Natural Resources .... Dr. Chris LUECKE
81 Interim Dean of Science .... Ms. Lisa BERREAU

*Utah Valley University (B)

800 W University Parkway, Orem UT 84058-5999

County: Utah FICE Identification: 004027
Unit ID: 230737

Telephone: (801) 863-8000 Carnegie Class: Bac/Diverse
FAX Number: (801) 226-5207 Calendar System: Semester
URL: www.uvu.edu
Established: 1941 Annual Undergrad Tuition & Fees (In-State): $2,693
Enrollment: 31,332 Coed
Affiliation or Control: State IRS Status: 501(c)3
Highest Offering: Master's
Program: Occupational; 2-Year Principally Bachelor's Creditable; Liberal Arts And General; Teacher Preparatory; Professional
Accreditation: NW, ADNUR, BUS, CAEP, CEA, CS, DH, EMT, IFSAC, MUS, NUR, SW, TEAC

02 President .... Dr. Matthew S. HOLLAND
05 Senior Vice Pres Academic Affairs .... Dr. Jeffery E. OLSON
11 Vice Pres Finance & Administration .... Dr. Val L. PETERSON
32 Vice President Student Affairs .... Dr. Michelle O. TAYLOR
30 Vice Pres Deveopment/Alumni .... Mr. Marc ARCHAMBAULT
26 Vice Pres University Relations .... Dr. Cameron K. MARTIN
45 VP Planning/Budgets & HR .... Ms. Linda MAKIN
10 Assoc Vice Pres Finance .... Mr. Michael R. FRANCIS
20 Assoc Vice Pres Engaged Learning .... Dr. Frederick H. WHITE
18 Assoc Vice Pres Facilities Planning .... Mr. Frank YOUNG
20 Assoc VP Programs .... Dr. Maureen ANDRADE
26 Assoc VP College Mktg/Communication .... Mr. Chris TAYLOR
20 Assoc VP Academic Affairs/Admin .... Dr. Kathren BROWN
35 Assoc VP Student Success/Retention .... Ms. Michelle KEARNS
88 Sr Dir Community College Programs .... Dr. Darrel L. HAMMON
21 Asst VP/Controller Business Svcs .... Mr. Kedric BLACK
07 Sr Director Admissions/One Stop .... Ms. Liz CHILDS
72 Dean Computing/Technology .... Dr. Michael SAVOIE
57 Dean School of the Arts .... Dr. Newell DAYLEY
81 Dean Science & Health .... Dr. Daniel FAIRBANKS
50 Dean School of Business .... Dr. Norman WRIGHT
97 Dean University College .... Dr. Forrest G. WILLIAMS
75 Dean Aviation and Public Services .... Dr. David MCENTIRE
53 Dean School of Education .... Dr. Parker C. FAWSON
15 Assoc VP Human Res/Equity Officer .... Mr. Mark WIESENBERG
37 Director Financial Aid/Scholarship .... Ms. Trish HOWARD
19 Dir Public Safety/Chief of Police .... Mr. John BREWER
44 Director of Planned Giving .... Ms. Cristina PIANEZZOLA
09 Director Institutional Research .... Mr. Robert LOVERIDGE
41 Assoc VP Athletics .... Mr. Vince OTOUPAL
24 Director Studios & Engineering .... Mr. Will MCKINNON
40 Director Bookstore .... Ms. Louise BRIDGE
06 Registrar .... Ms. LuAnn SMITH
28 Dir Multicultural Student Services .... Vacant
29 Director Alumni Relations .... Ms. Jeri L. ALLPHIN
38 Dir Career & Academic Counseling .... Mr. Adam BLACK
96 Director of Purchasing .... Mr. Ryan LINDSTROM
04 Executive Asst to President .... Ms. Candice L. GARDNER
08 Director Library .... Ms. Lesli BAKER
100 Chief of Staff .... Dr. Fidel A. MONTERO
102 Dir Foundation/Corporate Relations .... Vacant
103 Dir Workforce/Career Development .... Ms. Sherry HARWARD
104 Director Study Abroad .... Mr. Baldomero LAGO
105 Director Web Services .... Mr. Nathan GERBER
108 Institutional Review Board Chair .... Mr. Andrew CREER
13 Assoc Vice Pres CIO/IT .... Mr. Ray WALKER
90 Director Academic IT & Analytics .... Ms. Laura BUSBY

*Weber State University (C)

3850 Dixon Parkway, Ogden UT 84408-1001

County: Weber FICE Identification: 003680
Unit ID: 230782

Telephone: (801) 626-6000 Carnegie Class: Master's M
FAX Number: (801) 626-7922 Calendar System: Semester
URL: www.weber.edu
Established: 1889 Annual Undergrad Tuition & Fees (In-State): $4,456
Enrollment: 26,266 Coed
Affiliation or Control: State IRS Status: 501(c)3
Highest Offering: Master's
Program: Occupational; 2-Year Principally Bachelor's Creditable; Liberal Arts And General; Teacher Preparatory; Professional
Accreditation: NW, ADNUR, ART, BUS, BUSA, CAATE, CAHIIM, CEA, CIDA, COARC, CONST, CS, DH, EMT, ENGT, HSA, MLTAD, MT, MUS, NUR, SW, TEAC

02 President .... Dr. Charles A. WIGHT
05 Provost .... Dr. Madonne MINER
10 Vice Pres Administrative Services .... Dr. Norm TARBOX
30 Vice Pres for Univ Advancement .... Dr. Brad MORTENSEN
32 Vice President Student Affairs .... Dr. Janet WINNIFORD
13 VP for Information Technology .... Dr. Bret R. ELLIS
88 Vice Provost Innovation & Econo Dev .... Mr. Alexander LAWRENCE
51 Vice Prov & Dean Continuing Educ .... Dr. Bruce DAVIS
35 Assoc VP for Student Affairs .... Dr. Brett PEROZZI
21 Asst VP for Financial Services .... Mr. Steven E. NABOR
15 Asst Vice Pres for Human Resources .... Ms. Cherrie NELSON
11 Asst VP for Administrative Services .... Mr. Jerry G. GRAYBEAL
18 Assoc VP for Facilities Management .... Mr. Kevin HANSEN
84 Asst Prov for Enrollment Services .... Dr. Bruce BOWEN
20 Asst Prov & Dean of Undergraduates .... Dr. Ryan THOMAS
76 Dean Health Professions .... Dr. Yasmen SIMONIAN
50 Dean Business/Economics .... Dr. Jeffrey STEAGALL
53 Dean of Education .... Dr. Jack L. RASMUSSEN
83 Dean Social Behavioral Science .... Dr. Frank HARROLD
79 Interim Dean of Arts & Humanities .... Dr. Catherine ZUBLIN
81 Dean of Science .... Dr. David MATTY
72 Dean of Applied Science & Tech .... Dr. David FERRO
35 Dean of Students .... Dr. Jeffrey J. HURST
06 Registrar .... Mr. Casey D. BULLOCK
19 Director Public Safety .... Vacant
29 Exec Director Alumni Association .... Ms. Nancy COLLINWOOD
38 Dir Counseling & Psycholog Services .... Dr. Dianna K. ABEL
36 Director of Career Services .... Dr. Winn STANGER
37 Director of Financial Aid .... Mr. Jed SPENCER
27 Director of Media Relations .... Mr. John L. KOWALEWSKI
07 Director of Admissions .... Mr. Scott TEICHERT
08 University Librarian .... Ms. Joan HUBBARD
22 Dir Equal Opportunity/Affirm Action .... Dr. Barry G. GOMBERG
41 Dir of Intercollegiate Athletics .... Mr. Jerry BOVEE
40 Bookstore Director .... Mr. Tim ECK
25 Director Sponsored Projects .... Mr. James TAYLOR
85 Director Services Intl Students .... Mr. Morteza EMAMI
23 Director Student Health Center .... Ms. Juliana P. LARSEN
26 Director Public Relations .... Ms. Allison B. HESS
91 Director Administrative Computing .... Vacant
43 University Counsel .... Dr. G. Richard HILL
39 Director Housing & Residence Life .... Mr. Daniel KILCREASE
96 Director of Purchasing .... Ms. Nancy E. EMENGER
28 Chief Diversity Officer .... Dr. Adrienne G. GILLESPIE
92 Director of Honors Program .... Dr. Judy ELSLEY
88 Director Budget & Investments .... Mr. Brian L. SHUPPY
94 Coordinator of Women's Studies .... Dr. Parrilla DE KOKAL

*Snow College (D)

150 College Avenue, Ephraim UT 84627-1299

County: Sanpete FICE Identification: 003679
Unit ID: 230597

Telephone: (435) 283-7000 Carnegie Class: Assoc/Pub-R-M
FAX Number: (435) 283-6879 Calendar System: Semester
URL: www.snow.edu
Established: 1888 Annual Undergrad Tuition & Fees (In-State): $3,484
Enrollment: 4,800 Coed
Affiliation or Control: State IRS Status: 501(c)3
Highest Offering: Associate Degree
Program: Occupational; 2-Year Principally Bachelor's Creditable; Fine Arts Emphasis
Accreditation: NW, ACBSP, MUS, PNUR, THEA

02 President .... Dr. Gary L. CARLSTON
05 Vice President for Academic Affairs .... Dr. Steven HOOD
10 VP Finance/Administrative Services .... Mr. Brian FOISY
32 Vice President Student Success .... Mr. Craig MATHIE
35 Director of Student Life .... Ms. Michelle BROWN
75 Dean Business & Applied Tech .... Mr. Mike MEDLEY
36 Director of Student Success .... Ms. Susan LARSEN
08 Director Library/Information Svcs .... Mr. Jon OSTLER
09 Director Institutional Research .... Ms. Beckie HERMANSEN
15 Director Human Resource Development .... Mr. Wayne SQUIRE
18 Director Physical Plant Operations .... Ms. Leslee COOK
24 Director TTC .... Mr. Chase MITCHELL
39 Director Student Housing .... Ms. Jessica SIEGFRIED
41 Athletic Director .... Mr. Robert NIELSON
06 Registrar .... Mr. Micah STRAIT
07 Director Admissions .... Mr. Jeffrey SAVAGE
21 Budget Director .... Mr. Jacob DETTINGER
26 Director Public Relations .... Mr. John STEVENS
35 Director Student Affairs .... Mr. Mike ANDERSON
37 Director Student Financial Aid .... Mr. Jack DALENE
38 Director Student Counseling .... Mr. Allen RIGGS
96 Director of Purchasing .... Mr. Michael JORGENSEN
30 Chief Development Officer .... Ms. Rosie CONNOR
27 Director of Campus Relations .... Ms. Heidi STRINGHAM
04 Administrative Asst to President .... Ms. Marci LARSEN
13 Chief Info Technology Officer (CIO) .... Mr. Phil ALLRED

† Granted candidacy at the Baccalaureate level.

*Salt Lake Community College (E)

4600 S Redwood Road, Salt Lake City UT 84123-3197

County: Salt Lake FICE Identification: 005220
Unit ID: 230746

Telephone: (801) 957-4111 Carnegie Class: Assoc/Pub-U-MC
FAX Number: (801) 957-4444 Calendar System: Semester
URL: www.slcc.edu
Established: 1948 Annual Undergrad Tuition & Fees (In-State): $3,568
Enrollment: 24,253 Coed
Affiliation or Control: State IRS Status: 501(c)3
Highest Offering: Associate Degree
Program: Occupational; 2-Year Principally Bachelor's Creditable
Accreditation: NW, ACBSP, ACFEI, ADNUR, DH, FUSER, MAC, OTA, PTAA, RAD, SURGT

02 President .... Dr. Deneece HUFTALIN
05 Provost .... Dr. Clifton SANDERS
10 Business Services Vice Pres .... Mr. Dennis KLAUS
32 Student Services Vice President .... Dr. Charles LEPPER
30 Vice Pres Institutional Advancement .... Ms. Alison MCFARLANE
86 Govt & Community Relations VP .... Mr. Tim SHEEHAN
108 Vice Pres Inst Effectiveness .... Ms. Barbara GROVER
28 Spec Asst to President .... Dr. Roderic LAND
103 Assoc Provost/Econ Dev/Bus Ptnrshp .... Ms. Karen GUNN
20 Asst Provost Acad Support .... Dr. Nate SOUTHERLAND
21 Asst Vice Pres of Budget Services .... Mr. Darren MARSHALL
15 Asst Vice Pres of Human Resources .... Mr. Craig GARDNER
18 Assistant VP of Facilities .... Mr. Robert ASKERLUND
35 Dean of Students/Asst Vice Pres .... Dr. Marlin CLARK
45 Asst VP Student Plng/Support .... Dr. Nancy SINGER
84 Asst VP Student Enrollment Services .... Mr. Eric WEBER
26 AVP Inst Mktg/Communicatns .... Mr. Kent FROGLEY
88 Dean Arts/Comm/Digital Media .... Mr. Richard SCOTT
50 Dean School of Business .... Dr. Dennis BROMLEY
76 Dean Health Sciences .... Dr. JoAnne WRIGHT
79 Dean Humanities & Social Sciences .... Dr. John MCCORMICK
81 Dean Science/Math & Engineering .... Dr. Craig CALDWELL

75 Dean Technical Specialties .... Mr. Rick BOUILLON
41 Athletic Director .... Mr. Kevin M. DUSTIN
88 Dean SAT/Prof Development .... Mr. Kevin BROCKBANK
109 Sr Dir Student Ctr/Auxiliary Svc .... Mr. Jason BEAL
88 Director Technical Productions .... Mr. Seth MILLER
38 Director Academic Advising .... Ms. Sonia PARKER
36 Dir Career/Stdnt Employment .... Mr. Jack HESLEPH
88 Director Testing & Placement .... Ms. Diana HARVEY
06 Registrar .... Ms. MaryEtta CHASE
37 Director Financial Aid .... Ms. Cristi MILLARD
19 Director Public Safety .... Mr. Shane CRABTREE
13 Chief Information/Security Officer .... Mr. Bill ZOUMADAKIS
21 Controller/Business Manager .... Mr. Douglas HANSEN
22 EEO Director .... Ms. Mozelle ORTON
96 Director of Purchasing .... Ms. Lois WIESEMANN
25 Director Sponsored Projects .... Ms. Nicole OMER
30 Exec Director of Development .... Ms. Nancy MICHALKO
09 AVP Institutional Research .... Mr. Jeff AIRD
88 Risk Manager .... Ms. Mikel BIRCH
29 Alumni Coordinator .... Vacant
04 Admin Asst to President & Board Sec .... Ms. Janice SCHMIDT

* *Utah State University Eastern* (A)

451 E 400 N, Price UT 84501-2699

Telephone: (435) 613-5000 FICE Identification: 003676
Accreditation: &NW, ADNUR, PNUR

† Regional accreditation is carried under the parent institution in Logan, UT.

Western Governors University (B)

4001 S 700 E, Suite 700, Salt Lake City UT 84107-2533

County: Salt Lake FICE Identification: 033394
Unit ID: 433387
Telephone: (801) 274-3280 Carnegie Class: Master's L
FAX Number: (801) 274-3305 Calendar System: Other
URL: www.wgu.edu
Established: 1996 Annual Undergrad Tuition & Fees: $5,780
Enrollment: 53,800 Coed
Affiliation or Control: Independent Non-Profit IRS Status: 501(c)3
Highest Offering: Master's
Program: Teacher Preparatory; Professional
Accreditation: NW, CAHIIM, NURSE, TED

01 President .... Dr. Robert W. MENDENHALL
10 Vice Pres Finance/Administration .... David GROW
09 Vice Pres Quality/Inst Research .... Jason LEVIN
88 Vice Pres of Strategic Relations .... Ken SORBER
26 Vice President of Marketing .... Carey HILDERBRAND
15 Vice President of Human Resources .... Bonnie PATTEE
37 Vice Pres of Financial Aid .... Bob COLLINS
20 Associate Provost Student Mentoring .... Mitsu PHILLIPS
20 Associate Provost Academic Services .... Dr. Stacey LUDWIG-JOHNSON
76 Dean College of Health Professions .... Jan JONES-SCHENK
27 Vice President of Public Relations .... Joan MITCHELL
88 Chief Marketing Officer .... Patrick PARTRIDGE
05 Chief Academic Officer .... David LEASURE
86 Director Government Relations .... Chris BONNELL

Westminster College (C)

1840 S 1300 E, Salt Lake City UT 84105-3697

County: Salt Lake FICE Identification: 003681
Unit ID: 230807
Telephone: (801) 484-7651 Carnegie Class: Master's M
FAX Number: (801) 466-6916 Calendar System: Semester
URL: www.westminstercollege.edu
Established: 1875 Annual Undergrad Tuition & Fees: $31,228
Enrollment: 2,824 Coed
Affiliation or Control: Independent Non-Profit IRS Status: 501(c)3
Highest Offering: Master's
Program: Liberal Arts And General; Teacher Preparatory; Professional
Accreditation: NW, AAB, ACBSP, ANEST, MACTE, NURSE, PH, TEAC

01 President .... Mr. Stephen R. MORGAN
05 Provost .... Dr. Lisa GENTILE
30 Vice Pres Institutional Advancement .... Mrs. Staci CARSON
10 Vice Pres Finance & Administration .... Mr. Curtis W. RYAN
84 Vice President Enrollment Mgmt .... Dr. John BAWOROWSKY
26 Exec Dir Intgrated Marketing Comm .... Ms. Sheila YORKIN
49 Dean School of Arts & Sciences .... Dr. Lance NEWMAN
66 Dean School of Nursing/Hlth Science .... Dr. Sheryl STEADMAN
50 Dean School of Business .... Mrs. Melissa KOERNER
53 Dean School of Education .... Dr. Peter INGLE
32 Dean of Students .... Mr. Mark FERNE
29 Director Alumni Relations .... Ms. Michelle BARBER-LYHNAKIS
09 Director of Inst Research/Assess .... Ms. Nichole GREENWOOD
88 Assoc VP of College Relations .... Ms. Annalisa HOLCOMBE
13 Chief Information Officer .... Mr. Robert ALLRED
88 Director of Innovative Learning .... Vacant
43 General Counsel/Risk Management .... Ms. Melissa FLORES
21 Director of Accounting Services .... Ms. Jennifer MEDRANO
15 Director of Human Resources .... Ms. Julie FREESTONE
06 Registrar .... Ms. Mindy WENNERGREN
37 Director of Financial Aid .... Ms. Jenny RYAN
07 Director of Admissions .... Ms. Darlene DILLEY
18 Director Plant/Facilities .... Mr. Richard A. BROCKMYER
36 Director of Career Resource Center .... Vacant
08 Director Giovale Library .... Mr. Robert ALLRED
35 Assistant Dean of Students .... Mr. Karnell BLACK
39 Director of Student Involvement .... Mr. Ryan COOK
88 Director Start Center .... Ms. Deborah VICKERY
88 Director of Conferences .... Mr. Jeff BROWN
19 Director of Campus Safety .... Mr. Saeed REZAI
41 Director of Athletics .... Mr. Shay WYATT
42 Director of Spiritual Life .... Ms. Jan SAAED
38 Director of Campus Counseling .... Ms. Lisa JONES
92 Director of Honors Program .... Dr. Richard BADENHAUSEN
91 Database Administrator .... Mr. Kyle RIMA
04 Administrative Asst to President .... Ms. Emmalee SZWEDKO
22 Title IX Coordinator/EEO Complaince .... Mr. Jason SCHWARTZ
101 Secretary of the Institution/Board .... Ms. Melissa FLORES

VERMONT

Bennington College (D)

One College Drive, Bennington VT 05201-6003

County: Bennington FICE Identification: 003682
Unit ID: 230816
Telephone: (802) 442-5401 Carnegie Class: Bac/A&S
FAX Number: (802) 447-4269 Calendar System: Semester
URL: www.bennington.edu
Established: 1932 Annual Undergrad Tuition & Fees: $47,590
Enrollment: 755 Coed
Affiliation or Control: Independent Non-Profit IRS Status: 501(c)3
Highest Offering: Master's
Program: Liberal Arts And General
Accreditation: EH

01 President .... Dr. Mariko SILVER
05 Provost/Dean of the College .... Ms. Isabel ROCHE
10 VP for Finance & Administration .... Mr. Brian MURPHY
45 Sr VP for Strategic Initiatives .... Mr. David G. REES
30 VP for Institutional Advancement .... Ms. Paige BARTELS
27 VP for Communications .... Ms. Janet L. MARSDEN
20 Assoc Provost/Dean of Studies .... Mr. Duncan DOBBELMANN
09 Dean of Research/Plng/Assessment .... Mr. Zeke BERNSTEIN
15 Director of Human Resources .... Ms. Heather FALEY
29 Director of Alumni Relations .... Ms. Marie LEAHY
37 Director of Financial Aid .... Ms. Heather CLIFFORD

Burlington College (E)

351 North Avenue, Burlington VT 05401-8477

County: Chittenden FICE Identification: 012183
Unit ID: 230825
Telephone: (802) 862-9616 Carnegie Class: Bac/A&S
FAX Number: (802) 660-4331 Calendar System: Semester
URL: www.burlington.edu
Established: 1972 Annual Undergrad Tuition & Fees: $23,546
Enrollment: 200 Coed
Affiliation or Control: Independent Non-Profit IRS Status: 501(c)3
Highest Offering: Master's
Program: Liberal Arts And General; Fine Arts Emphasis
Accreditation: #EH

01 Interim President .... Dr. Carol A. MOORE
10 CFO .... Mr. Gibson SMITH
30 Dean Operations & Advancement .... Ms. Coralee A. HOLM
32 Dean of Student Services .... Mr. Greg LITCHFIELD
07 Director of Admissions .... Mr. Ryan LONGE
13 Director Information Technology .... Mr. Joel LENOIR
06 Registrar .... Ms. Meghan DALY
08 Dir Library/Information Services .... Ms. Jessica ALLARD
37 Director of Financial Aid .... Ms. Joanna MORSE
108 Director Institutional Assessment .... Mr. Piers KANIUKA

Champlain College (F)

163 S Willard Street, Burlington VT 05402-0670

County: Chittenden FICE Identification: 003684
Unit ID: 230852
Telephone: (802) 860-2700 Carnegie Class: Bac/Diverse
FAX Number: (802) 860-2750 Calendar System: Semester
URL: www.champlain.edu
Established: 1956 Annual Undergrad Tuition & Fees: $37,536
Enrollment: 3,636 Coed
Affiliation or Control: Independent Non-Profit IRS Status: 501(c)3
Highest Offering: Master's
Program: Liberal Arts And General; Teacher Preparatory; Professional
Accreditation: EH, ART, RAD, SW

01 President .... Mr. Donald J. LAACKMAN
05 Provost .... Dr. Laurie QUINN
10 Vice President Finances .... David J. PROVOST
84 Vice President Enrollment .... Catherine O'ROURKE
30 Vice President Advancement .... David J. PROVOST
32 Vice President Student Life .... Dr. Leslie AVERILL
13 Asst Vice Pres Information Systems .... Theodore LASKARIS
36 Assistant Vice Pres Career Services .... Pat BOERA
15 Assoc Vice Pres Human Resources .... Mary Margaret LEE
20 Senior Associate Provost .... Dr. Michelle MILLER
104 Associate Provost-Education Abroad .... Dr. James CROSS
101 VP & Secretary of Corporation .... Katie HAWLEY
53 Dean Education/Human Stds Div .... Dr. Laurel BONGIORNO
88 Dean Comm/Creative Media Div .... Dr. Paula WILLOQUET-MARICONDI
50 Dean Business Division .... Dr. Wes BALDA
77 Int Dean Information Tech/Science .... Dr. Robert MARINO
51 Vice President Continuing Profess .... Jayson BOYERS
07 Director of Admissions .... Vacant
06 Registrar .... Rebecca PETERSON
37 Director of Financial Aid .... Kristi JOVELL
38 Dir of Counseling & Accomodations .... Skip HARRIS
18 Director of Physical Plant .... Thomas BONNETTE
19 Director of Security & Safety .... Richard LONG
23 Director Health Services .... Cissy MCCLELLAN
22 Director of Affirmative Action .... Dana HUTCHINSON
39 Director of Residential Life .... Danelle BERUBE
85 Foreign Students Advisor .... Kathy LYNN
21 Treasurer .... Shelley NAVARI
26 Public Information & News Director .... Stephen MEASE
29 Director of Alumni Relations .... Erik OLIVER
08 Director Library .... Janet COTTRELL
28 Dir Student Diversity/Inclusion .... Ame LAMBERT
103 Director Workforce Development .... Melissa HERSH
102 Dir Foundation/Corporate Relations .... Sarah MCLANE
04 Executive Assistant .... Linda MURPHY
40 Bookstore Manager .... Kevin MCCANN

College of St. Joseph (G)

71 Clement Road, Rutland VT 05701-3899

County: Rutland FICE Identification: 003685
Unit ID: 231077
Telephone: (802) 773-5900 Carnegie Class: Master's S
FAX Number: (802) 776-5258 Calendar System: Semester
URL: www.csj.edu
Established: 1956 Annual Undergrad Tuition & Fees: $21,900
Enrollment: 332 Coed
Affiliation or Control: Roman Catholic IRS Status: 501(c)3
Highest Offering: Master's
Program: 2-Year Principally Bachelor's Creditable; Liberal Arts And General; Teacher Preparatory; Professional
Accreditation: EH

01 President .... Dr. Richard B. LLOYD
05 Vice Pres Academic Affs/Dean of Fac .... Dr. David BALFOUR
10 Vice President Business Affairs .... Mrs. Kristie JOHNSON
32 VP Student Affs/Dean of Students .... Ms. Melissa PARADEE
11 Associate VP of Administration .... Ms. Judy MORGAN
37 Director of Financial Aid .... Mrs. Julie ROSMUS
07 Director of Admissions .... Mr. Ken LABATE
30 Dir Development/Alumni Relations .... Mr. Bates CHILDRESS
41 Int Athletics Director .... Mr. Robert GODLEWSKI
06 Registrar .... Mr. Greg CHAMBERLAND
13 CIS Administrator .... Mr. Raymond GIBBS
35 Director of Learning Center .... Ms. Susan BOYCE
26 Director of Communications .... Mr. James LAMBERT
21 Controller .... Mrs. Karen REYNOLDS
18 Director of Maintenance .... Mr. Thomas BELAND
08 Librarian .... Ms. Doreen MCCULLOUGH
49 Chair Arts & Sciences .... Dr. Jonas PRIDA
50 Chair Business .... Dr. Robert GODDARD
53 Chair Education .... Dr. David ST. GERMAIN
15 Chair Psychology/Human Services .... Dr. Michael W. KESLER

Goddard College (H)

123 Pitkin Road, Plainfield VT 05667-9432

County: Washington FICE Identification: 003686
Unit ID: 230889
Telephone: (800) 468-4888 Carnegie Class: Master's M
FAX Number: (802) 454-1029 Calendar System: Semester
URL: www.goddard.edu
Established: 1863 Annual Undergrad Tuition & Fees: $15,476
Enrollment: 538 Coed
Affiliation or Control: Independent Non-Profit IRS Status: 501(c)3
Highest Offering: Master's
Program: Liberal Arts And General; Teacher Preparatory
Accreditation: EH

01 Interim President .... Mr. Robert KENNY
05 Interim Academic Dean .... Dr. Steven JAMES
10 Chief Financial Officer .... Vacant
100 Spec Asst to Pres/Chief of Staff .... Vacant
30 Chief Advancement Officer .... Vacant
32 Associate Dean of Community Life .... Ms. Susan A. WILSON
06 Registrar .... Mr. Josh CASTLE
15 DIrector of Human Resources .... Ms. Gloria ABBIATI
37 Director of Financial Aid .... Ms. Beverly JENE
88 Director of Campus Services .... Mr. Paul SHPER
08 Director of Information Access .... Ms. Clara BRUNS
18 Director of Facilities Operations .... Mr. Scott BLANCHARD
21 Director of Business Office .... Ms. Sherri MOLLEUR
07 Director of Admissions .... Mr. Gariot LOUIMA
88 Manager of WGDR/WGDH Radio .... Mr. Kris GRUEN

Green Mountain College (I)

1 Brennan Circle, Poultney VT 05764-1199

County: Rutland FICE Identification: 003687
Unit ID: 230898
Telephone: (802) 287-8000 Carnegie Class: Bac/A&S
FAX Number: (802) 287-8099 Calendar System: Semester
URL: www.greenmtn.edu
Established: 1834 Annual Undergrad Tuition & Fees: $35,340
Enrollment: 818 Coed
Affiliation or Control: Independent Non-Profit IRS Status: 501(c)3
Highest Offering: Master's
Program: Liberal Arts And General; Teacher Preparatory

Accreditation: EH

01 President .... Dr. Paul J. FONTEYN
03 Executive Vice President .... Mr. Chris HALNON
05 Vice President Academic Affairs .... Dr. Thomas MAUHS-PUGH
32 Vice President Student Affairs .... Dr. Joseph E. PETRICK
84 Vice Pres Enrollment Management .... Vacant
04 Executive Assistant to President .... Ms. Jeanne V. ROOT
20 Dean of Faculty .... Dr. James HARDING
07 Director of Admissions .... Mr. John CHAMPOLI
30 Director of Development .... Ms. Mary Lou WILLITS
06 Registrar .... Ms. Sharon L. HOFFMAN
18 Director of Facilities .... Mr. Glenn LAPLANTE
19 Director of Public Safety .... Mr. Steven BROWN
26 Director of Public Relations .... Mr. Kevin COBURN
41 Athletic Director .... Mr. Keith BOSLEY
08 Director Library & Information Svcs .... Mr. Paul MILLETTE
85 Director of International Pgms .... Vacant
13 Director Computing & Info Mgmt .... Mr. Jeffrey WRIGHT
42 Chaplain .... Ms. Shirley OSKAMP
29 Dir Alumni Relations/Annual Giving .... Ms. Michele ALMEIDA
36 Director of Career Counseling .... Ms. Maia HANRON-SANFORD
92 Director of College Honors Program .... Dr. Jennifer SELLERS
37 Director Student Financial Aid .... Ms. Wendy ELLIS
15 Director Human Resources .... Ms. Janie EVANS
38 Director Student Counseling .... Vacant
09 Director of Institutional Research .... Ms. Sharon L. HOFFMAN

Landmark College (A)

19 River Road South, Putney VT 05346
County: Windham FICE Identification: 025326
Unit ID: 247649
Telephone: (802) 387-4767 Carnegie Class: Assoc/PrivNFP
FAX Number: (802) 387-6868 Calendar System: Semester
URL: www.landmark.edu
Established: 1985 Annual Undergrad Tuition & Fees: $50,080
Enrollment: 518 Coed
Affiliation or Control: Independent Non-Profit IRS Status: 501(c)3
Highest Offering: Baccalaureate
Program: 2-Year Principally Bachelor's Creditable
Accreditation: EH

01 President .... Dr. Peter A. EDEN
05 Vice President Academic Affairs .... Dr. Monika BISSELL
30 Vice Pres Institutional Advancement .... Ms. Chelsea GWYTHER
10 Vice Pres Administration/Finance .... Mr. Jon A. MACCLAREN
32 Vice Pres Student Affairs .... Mr. Michael LUCIANI
84 Vice Pres Enrollment Management .... Mr. Gregory MATTHEWS
04 Assistant to the President .... Ms. Tiffany KERYLOW
20 Academic Dean .... Dr. Adrienne MAJOR
88 Dean Short-Term Pgms/Transfer Svcs .... Dr. John NISSEN
26 Director Marketing Communication .... Mr. Mark DIPIETRO
18 Director of Physical Plant .... Mr. James LOVERING
08 Head Librarian .... Ms. Jennifer LANN
13 Chief Technology Officer .... Ms. Corinne BELL
06 Registrar .... Ms. Karen DAMIAN
41 Director Athletics .... Mr. Matt VOLITIS
37 Director Student Financial Aid .... Ms. Jennifer DESMARAIS
38 Director of Counseling/Wellness .... Ms. Jacala MILLS
23 Director of Health Services .... Ms. Linda NAPIER
40 Bookstore Manager .... Ms. Kimberly JUDD

Marlboro College (B)

PO Box A, Marlboro VT 05344-9999
County: Windham FICE Identification: 003690
Unit ID: 230940
Telephone: (802) 257-4333 Carnegie Class: Bac/A&S
FAX Number: (802) 257-4154 Calendar System: Semester
URL: www.marlboro.edu
Established: 1946 Annual Undergrad Tuition & Fees: $38,110
Enrollment: 230 Coed
Affiliation or Control: Independent Non-Profit IRS Status: 501(c)3
Highest Offering: Master's
Program: Liberal Arts And General
Accreditation: EH

01 President .... Mr. Kevin F. QUIGLEY
10 Interim Chief Financial Officer .... Mr. Randy FOOSE
05 Dean of Faculty/Graduate Educ .... Mr. Richard GLEJZER
07 Dean of Admissions .... Ms. Brigid LAWLER
32 Interim Dean of Students .... Ms. Ariel BROOKS
58 Associate Dean Graduate School .... Mr. Sean CONLEY
84 Dir Enrollment Stdt Svc at Grad Ctr .... Mr. Matt LIVINGSTON
46 Chief Planning & Budget Officer .... Mr. Bryant MORGAN
08 Library Director .... Ms. Beth RUANE
06 Asst Registrar .... Ms. Diane HEILEMAN
30 Int Chief Development Officer .... Ms. Molly WILLIAMS
26 Dir of Marketing/Communications .... Mr. Matthew BARONE
44 Int Annual Giving Director .... Ms. Hillary TWINING
18 Director of Plant Operations .... Mr. Dan J. COTTER
82 World Studies Director .... Mr. Seth HARTER
40 Bookstore Manager .... Ms. Rebecca BARTLETT

Marlboro College Graduate School (C)

28 Vernon Street, Brattleboro VT 05301
Telephone: (802) 258-9200 Identification: 770120
Accreditation: &EH

† Branch campus of Marlboro College, Marlboro, VT.

Middlebury Bread Loaf School of English (D)

75 Franklin Street, Middlebury VT 05753
Telephone: (802) 443-5418 Identification: 770119
Accreditation: &EH

† Bread Loaf School of English is a summer graduate program and the enrollment figure is for the summer term.

Middlebury College (E)

Old Chapel, Middlebury VT 05753-6200
County: Addison FICE Identification: 003691
Unit ID: 230959
Telephone: (802) 443-5000 Carnegie Class: Bac/A&S
FAX Number: (802) 443-2071 Calendar System: 4/1/4
URL: www.middlebury.edu
Established: 1800 Annual Undergrad Tuition & Fees: $61,456
Enrollment: 2,533 Coed
Affiliation or Control: Independent Non-Profit IRS Status: 501(c)3
Highest Offering: Doctorate
Program: Liberal Arts And General
Accreditation: EH

01 President .... Dr. Laurie L. PATTON
05 Provost .... Dr. Susan BALDRIDGE
88 VP for Academic Development .... Dr. Tim SPEARS
10 VP for Finance/Treasurer .... Mr. Patrick J. NORTON
03 Sr Vice Pres/Philanthropic Advisor .... Mr. Michael SCHOENFELD
88 VP Lang Sch/Sch Abroad/Risk Officer .... Dr. Michael GEISLER
30 VP for Advancement .... Mr. James R. KEYES
88 VP Academic Affairs/Dean of Faculty .... Dr. Andrea LLOYD
26 VP for Communications & Marketing .... Mr. Bill BURGER
32 VP Student Affairs/Dean of College .... Dr. Katy SMITH ABBOTT
58 VP Acad Affs/Dean of the Institute .... Dr. Jeffrey DAYTON-JOHNSON
07 Dean of Admissions .... Mr. Gregory B. BUCKLES
104 Dean of International Programs .... Dr. Jeffrey CASON
101 Special Asst to Pres/Sec of Corp .... Mr. David A. DONAHUE
45 Assoc Provost for Planning .... Mr. LeRoy GRAHAM
08 Dean of the Library .... Mr. Michael D. ROY
37 Assoc VP Student Financial Services .... Ms. Kim DOWNS-BURNS
79 Dean of the Language Schools .... Dr. Stephen SNYDER
20 Dean of Curriculum .... Dr. Suzanne GURLAND
09 Dean for Faculty Dev & Research .... Dr. James RALPH
21 Asst Treasurer/Dir of Business Svcs .... Mr. Thomas CORBIN
29 Assoc VP Alumni Rels/Annual Giving .... Ms. Margaret STOREY GROVES
38 Exec Dir Health & Counseling Svcs .... Dr. Augustus JORDAN
42 Chaplain .... Ms. Laurie JORDAN
41 Director of Athletics .... Mr. Erin QUINN
35 Assoc Dn of the Col/Dir Pub Safety .... Ms. Elizabeth B. BURCHARD
06 Registrar .... Ms. Jennifer THOMPSON
15 Acting Assoc VP for HR .... Ms. Cheryl MULLINS
40 Bookstore Manager .... Ms. Erin JONES-POPPE

† Tuition figure is a comprehensive fees figure.

New England Culinary Institute (F)

56 College Street, Montpelier VT 05602-9720
County: Washington FICE Identification: 022540
Unit ID: 230977
Telephone: (802) 223-6324 Carnegie Class: Spec/Other
FAX Number: (802) 225-3280 Calendar System: Quarter
URL: www.neci.edu
Established: 1980 Annual Undergrad Tuition & Fees: $31,165
Enrollment: 422 Coed
Affiliation or Control: Proprietary IRS Status: Proprietary
Highest Offering: Baccalaureate
Program: Occupational; Technical Emphasis
Accreditation: ACCSC

01 CEO/President .... Mr. Francis VOIGT
10 Chief Financial Officer .... Mr. Phillip HARKER
05 Dean of Education/Dept Chr Cul Arts .... Mr. Lyndon VIRKLER
88 Exec Chef & VP Culinary Operations .... Chef Jean-Louis GERIN
88 Chair Baking & Pastry Programs .... Chef Kathleen KESSLER
88 Chair HRM Program .... Ms. Michelle FORD
20 Director of Compliance/Academics .... Ms. Laureen GAUTHIER
106 Chair Online Programs .... Chef Peg CHECCI
06 Registrar .... Ms. Liz FITZGERALD
07 Director of Admissions .... Mr. Dwight CROSS
08 Head Librarian .... Ms. Rachel BORNSTEIN
15 Director Human Resources .... Ms. Jennifer ZETARSKI
18 Director of Facilities .... Mr. William COLGAN
36 Manager Career Services .... Mr. Garth WALKER
20 Sr Dir Operations & Education .... Chef David MILES

Norwich University (G)

158 Harmon Drive, Northfield VT 05663-1000
County: Washington FICE Identification: 003692
Unit ID: 230995
Telephone: (802) 485-2000 Carnegie Class: Master's L
FAX Number: (802) 485-2032 Calendar System: Semester
URL: www.norwich.edu
Established: 1819 Annual Undergrad Tuition & Fees: $36,092
Enrollment: 2,306 Coed
Affiliation or Control: Independent Non-Profit IRS Status: 501(c)3
Highest Offering: Master's
Program: Liberal Arts And General; Teacher Preparatory; Professional
Accreditation: EH, ACBSP, CAATE, ENG, NURSE

01 President .... Dr. Richard W. SCHNEIDER
05 Senior VPAA & Dean of Faculty .... Dr. Guiyou HUANG
107 VP & Dean CGCS .... Dr. William CLEMENTS
84 VP Technology and Student Affairs .... Dr. Frank VANECEK
30 VP Alumni & Development Relations .... Mr. David J. WHALEY
13 VP Strategic Partnership .... Mr. Phillip SUSMANN
84 VP of Enrollment Management .... Mr. Greg MATTHEWS
107 Dean Col of Professional Schools .... Mr. Aron TEMKIN
83 Dean College of Liberal Arts .... Dr. Andrea TALENTINO
81 Dean College of Science/Mathematics .... Dr. Michael MCGINNIS
88 Dean School of National Services .... Col. Eric BRIGHAM
29 Assoc VP Alumni Relations .... Ms. Diane SCOLARO
20 Associate VP Academic Affairs .... Dr. Joseph BYRNE
04 Exec Assistant to President .... Ms. Laura AMELL
10 Chief Financial Officer .... Ms. Lauren WOBBY
11 Chief Administrative Officer .... Mr. David MAGIDA
88 Director Center for Student Success .... Ms. Shelby GILE
32 Dean of Students .... Ms. Martha MATHIS
08 Interim Head Librarian .... Mr. Greg SAUER
41 Athletic Director .... Mr. Anthony A. MARIANO
18 Director Facilities/Operations .... Mr. Bizhan YAHYAZADEH
37 Director Student Financial Aid .... Mr. Martin DANIELS
38 Director Student Counseling .... Dr. Melvin MILLER
07 Director of Admissions .... Mr. Tim REARDON
06 Registrar & Inst Research Dir .... Dr. Diane DOUGLAS
88 Asst VP Office of Communications .... Ms. Kathy MURPHY-MORIARITY
102 Dir Foundation/Corporate Relations .... Ms. Bridget WIFFIN
103 Dir Career Development .... Ms. Kathryn PROVOST
19 Director Security/Safety .... Mr. Michael ABRAHAM
15 Director of Human Resources .... Ms. Lisa YAEGER

Saint Michael's College (H)

One Winooski Park, Colchester VT 05439-0001
County: Chittenden FICE Identification: 003694
Unit ID: 231059
Telephone: (802) 654-2000 Carnegie Class: Bac/A&S
FAX Number: (802) 654-2297 Calendar System: Semester
URL: www.smcvt.edu
Established: 1904 Annual Undergrad Tuition & Fees: $15,430
Enrollment: 2,618 Coed
Affiliation or Control: Roman Catholic IRS Status: 501(c)3
Highest Offering: Master's
Program: Liberal Arts And General; Teacher Preparatory
Accreditation: EH, CEA

01 President .... Dr. John J. NEUHAUSER
04 Assistant to the President .... Ms. Tara L. ARCURY
05 Vice Pres Academic Affairs .... Dr. Karen A. TALENTINO
10 Vice President for Finance .... Mr. Neal ROBINSON
32 Vice President for Student Affairs .... Dr. Dawn M. ELLINWOOD
84 Vice President for Enrollment .... Dr. Sarah M. KELLY
15 Vice President for HR & Admin Svcs .... Mr. Michael J. NEW
30 VP for Institutional Advancement .... Mr. Patrick J. GALLIVAN
20 Dean of the College .... Dr. Jeffrey M. AYRES
42 Director Edmundite Campus Ministry .... Rev. Brian J. CUMMINGS, SSE
07 Director of Admission .... Ms. Jacqueline MURPHY
37 Director Student Financial Services .... Mr. Daniel R. COUTURE
06 Registrar .... Mr. John D. SHEEHEY
29 Director of Alumni/Parent Relations .... Ms. Angela ARMOUR
35 Director Student Activities .... Ms. Grace A. KELLY
93 Dir Multicultural Student Affairs .... Mr. Moise ST. LOUIS
39 Director of Residence Life .... Mr. Louis DIMASI
88 Associate Dean of the College .... Dr. Jonathan L. D'AMORE
104 Director of Study Abroad .... Ms. Peggy H. IMAI
92 Honors Program Faculty Coordinator .... Dr. Jim BYRNE
94 Coord of Gender/Women's Studies .... Dr. Patricia DELANEY
08 Dir Library & Information Services .... Mr. John K. PAYNE
13 Chief Information Officer .... Mr. William O. ANDERSON
19 Director of Public Safety .... Mr. Peter D. SOONS
18 Dir of Facilities/College Architect .... Mr. James P. FARRINGTON
38 Director of Personal Counseling .... Ms. Linda HOLLINGDALE
36 Director of Career Development .... Ms. Christine CLARY
23 Director of Health Services .... Ms. Mary MASSON
41 Director of Athletics .... Dr. Christopher KENNEY
44 Director of Advancement Services .... Ms. Linda V. DONAHUE
102 Director of Foundation Relations .... Ms. Angela IRVINE
96 Director of Business Services .... Mr. Robert ROBINSON
105 Dir of Web Site Development .... Mr. Brian MACDONALD
44 Director of Individual Giving .... Ms. Terri P. SELBY
88 Financial Accounting Manager .... Ms. Shirley J. GOODELL-LACKEY
40 Bookstore Manager .... Mr. Stephen MCMAHON
26 Marketing/Communications Manager .... Ms. Lindsay DAMICI

SIT (I)

Kipling Road, Brattleboro VT 05302-0676
County: Windham FICE Identification: 008860
Unit ID: 231068
Telephone: (802) 257-7751 Carnegie Class: Master's L
FAX Number: (802) 258-3248 Calendar System: Other
URL: www.sit.edu
Established: 1964 Annual Undergrad Tuition & Fees: $20,200
Enrollment: 912 Coed
Affiliation or Control: Independent Non-Profit IRS Status: 501(c)3
Highest Offering: Master's
Program: Liberal Arts And General; Teacher Preparatory; Professional
Accreditation: EH

01 President ... Mr. Don STEINBERG
05 Senior VP of Academic Affairs/CAO ... Dr. John LUCAS
10 CFO ... Mr. Kote LOMIDZE
15 VP of Human Resources ... Ms. Rachel HENRY
43 General Counsel ... Ms. Lisa RAE
58 Dean SIT Graduate Institute ... Mr. Daniel YALOWITZ
84 Dean External Rels/Strtgc Enrol Mgt ... Ms. Laurie BLACK
30 Director of Advancement ... Mr. Tom NAVIN
88 Director Language and Culture Dept ... Ms. Beatriz FANTINI
07 Director of Admissions ... Ms. Kim DEREGO
06 Registrar ... Ms. Ginny NELLIS
37 Director Financial Aid ... Ms. Cathy MULLINS
32 Director of Campus Life ... Mr. Stephen SWEET
26 Director of Marketing ... Vacant
04 Administrative Asst to President ... Ms. Kelly M. THERIEAU
08 Head Librarian ... Mr. Oscar LANZA-GALINDO
101 Board of trustess Corporate Secy ... Ms. Bethaney LACLAIR
104 Director Study Abroad ... Ms. Priscilla STONE
108 Director Institutional Assessment ... Ms. Ellen HOLMES
13 Chief Info Technology Officer (CIO) ... Mr. Tom TOLBERT
28 Director of Diversity ... Vacant
29 Director of Alumni Engagement ... Mr. Kevin BEAL
38 Director Student Counseling ... Ms. Jane BUCKINGHAM
39 Director Student Housing ... Mr. David FINCK

Southern Vermont College (A)

982 Mansion Drive, Bennington VT 05201-6002
County: Bennington FICE Identification: 003693
Unit ID: 231086
Telephone: (802) 442-5427 Carnegie Class: Bac/Diverse
FAX Number: (802) 447-4695 Calendar System: Semester
URL: www.svc.edu
Established: 1926 Annual Undergrad Tuition & Fees: $22,985
Enrollment: 457 Coed
Affiliation or Control: Independent Non-Profit IRS Status: 501(c)3
Highest Offering: Baccalaureate
Program: Occupational; Liberal Arts And General
Accreditation: EH, NUR, NURSE, RAD

01 President ... Dr. David R. EVANS
10 Chief Financial Officer/COO ... Ms. Claire WURMFELD
05 Provost ... Dr. James C. WHITE
04 Executive Assistant ... Ms. Robinette YEARWOOD
50 Chair Business ... Dr. Stacey HILLS
66 Chair Nursing ... Dr. Mary BOTTER
79 Chair of Humanities ... Dr. Jennifer BURG
81 Chair of Science and Technology ... Dr. Barry FLANARY
83 Chair of Social Sciences ... Mr. Scott STEIN
32 Dean of Students ... Ms. Anne M. HOPKINS GROSS
07 Int Dean of Admissions ... Mr. Daniel SUMMERS, II
08 Director Learning Resources ... Ms. Sarah SANFILIPPO
06 Registrar ... Mr. Eric PARSONS
36 Coordinator of Career Services ... Ms. Elizabeth DUNHAM
18 Director of Facilities ... Mr. Mark J. KLAUDER
41 Director of Athletics ... Mr. Michael MCDONOUGH
38 Director of Counseling ... Ms. Tara MCCUIN
39 Director of Residence Life ... Ms. Emily SCHIAVONI
19 Director of Campus Safety ... Mr. George MARSHALL
37 Director of Student Fin Svcs ... Ms. Susan ROCHETTE
30 Dir Development/Deputy COO ... Ms. Colleen LITTLE
15 Director of Human Resources ... Ms. Carole SHERINGHAM
09 Director Institutional Research ... Mr. Eric PARSONS
88 Coord Learning Disabilities ... Mr. David A. LINDENBERG
13 Director Information Technology ... Mr. Michael KEEN
26 Sr Adv Public Relations/Marketing ... Ms. Susan BIGGS
27 Asst Director of Communication ... Ms. Marion WHITEFORD

Sterling College (B)

PO Box 72, Craftsbury Common VT 05827-0072
County: Orleans FICE Identification: 021435
Unit ID: 231095
Telephone: (802) 586-7711 Carnegie Class: Bac/A&S
FAX Number: (802) 586-2596 Calendar System: Semester
URL: www.sterlingcollege.edu
Established: 1958 Annual Undergrad Tuition & Fees: $34,555
Enrollment: 116 Coed
Affiliation or Control: Independent Non-Profit IRS Status: 501(c)3
Highest Offering: Baccalaureate
Program: Liberal Arts And General
Accreditation: EH

01 President ... Mr. Matthew DERR
05 Dean of Academics ... Dr. Carol DICKSON
36 Dean of Work ... Ms. Molly CYR
07 Director of Admission ... Mr. Tim PATTERSON
30 Director of Advancement Services ... Ms. Michele MARTIN
10 Director of Finance/Operations ... Ms. Deborah CLARK
08 Librarian ... Ms. Petra VOGEL
18 Director of Facilities ... Mr. Kelly JONES
32 Dean of Community ... Ms. Favor ELLIS
06 Registrar ... Ms. Laura Lea BERRY
26 Director of Communications ... Ms. Christian FEUERSTEIN
29 Dir Advance/Alumni Relations ... Mr. Topher BORDEAU
37 Director of Financial Aid ... Ms. Barbara STUART

University of Vermont (C)

South Prospect Street, Burlington VT 05405-0160
County: Chittenden FICE Identification: 003696
Unit ID: 231174
Telephone: (802) 656-3131 Carnegie Class: RU/H
FAX Number: N/A Calendar System: Semester
URL: www.uvm.edu
Established: 1791 Annual Undergrad Tuition & Fees (In-State): $16,738
Enrollment: 11,822 Coed
Affiliation or Control: State IRS Status: 501(c)3
Highest Offering: Doctorate
Program: Liberal Arts And General; Teacher Preparatory; Professional
Accreditation: EH, BUS, CAATE, CACREP, CLPSY, CYTO, DENT, DIETC, DIETD, ENG, IPSY, MED, MT, NMT, NURSE, PTA, RTT, SP, SPAA, SW, TED

01 President ... Dr. E. Thomas SULLIVAN
05 Senior Vice President & Provost ... Dr. David V. ROSOWSKY
10 VP for Finance & Treasurer ... Mr. Richard H. CATE
86 VP University Relations & Admin ... Dr. Thomas J. GUSTAFSON
46 VP Research ... Dr. Richard A. GALBRAITH
30 CEO & President The UVM Foundation ... Mr. O. Richard BUNDY, III
43 VP Legal Affairs & General Counsel ... Ms. Francine T. BAZLUKE
84 VP Enrollment Management ... Ms. Stacey R. KOSTELL
20 Assoc Prov Faculty & International ... Dr. Gayle R. NUNLEY
20 Assoc Provost Teaching & Learning ... Dr. Brian V. REED
32 Vice Provost for Student Affairs ... Dr. Annie STEVENS
28 VP for Human Resources & Diversity ... Dr. Wanda R. HEADING-GRANT
100 VP for Executive Operations ... Dr. Gary L. DERR
18 Assoc VP Admin & Facility Services ... Mr. William P. BALLARD
15 Director Benefits & Employee Svcs ... Mr. Harold J. PIERCE
35 Dean of Students ... Dr. David A. NESTOR
29 Assoc VP for Alumni Relations ... Mr. Alan E. RYEA
63 Dean College of Medicine ... Dr. Frederick C. MORIN, III
66 Dean Nursing & Health Sciences ... Dr. Patricia A. PRELOCK
49 Interim Dean Arts & Sciences ... Dr. William A. FALLS
47 Dean Agriculture & Life Sciences ... Dr. Thomas C. VOGELMANN
54 Dean Engineering & Math Sciences ... Dr. Luis A. GARCIA
53 Int Dean Education & Social Svcs . Dr. Cynthia L. GERSTL-PEPIN
50 Dean Business Administration ... Dr. Sanjay SHARMA
92 Interim Dean Honors College ... Dr. Lisa J. SCHNELL
65 Dean Environment & Natural Resource ... Dr. Nancy E. MATHEWS
56 Dean Extension ... Dr. Douglas O. LANTAGNE
58 Dean Graduate College ... Dr. Cynthia J. FOREHAND
51 Dean Continuing & Distance Educ ... Ms. Cynthia L. BELLIVEAU
08 Dean Libraries & Learning Res & CIO ... Ms. Mara R. SAULE
06 Registrar ... Mr. Keith P. WILLIAMS
09 Director Institutional Research ... Dr. John F. RYAN
26 Director University Communications ... Mr. Enrique CORREDERA
13 Int Asc Chief Information Officer ... Ms. Julia H. RUSSELL
25 Assoc VP Research Admin ... Ms. Jennifer GAGNON
21 University Budget Director ... Mr. Alberto CITARELLA
19 Chief of Police Services ... Ms. Lianne M. TUOMEY
41 Director of Athletics ... Dr. Robert CORRAN
36 Director Career Services ... Ms. Pamela K. GARDNER
23 Director Ctr for Health & Wellbeing ... Dr. Jon K. PORTER
38 Counsel/Psych Services Program Dir ... Dr. Todd N. WEINMAN
39 Director Residential Life ... Ms. Stacey A. MILLER
40 Director University Bookstore ... Mr. Jay E. MENNINGER
85 Director Intl Education Services ... Ms. Kimberly A. HOWARD
102 COO & VP The UVM Foundation ... Mr. Mark W. DORGAN
44 Senior Development Coordinator ... Ms. Donna BURKE
22 Director AA & EO ... Mr. Jes S. KRAUS
07 Director Graduate Admissions ... Ms. Sydnee VIRAY
07 Director Undergraduate Admissions ... Dr. Elizabeth A. WISER
37 Director Student Financial Services ... Ms. Marie D. JOHNSON
96 Director Purchasing Services ... Ms. Natalie L. GUILLETTE
94 Director Women's Center ... Ms. Sarah G. WARRINGTON
24 Access/Media Services Librarian ... Mr. Aaron F. NICHOLS
101 Board of Trustees Coordinator ... Ms. Corinne B. THOMPSON

Vermont College of Fine Arts (D)

36 College Street, Montpelier VT 05602-3145
County: Washington FICE Identification: 003697
Unit ID: 455992
Telephone: (802) 828-8600 Carnegie Class: Assoc/PrivNFP4
FAX Number: (802) 828-8649 Calendar System: Semester
URL: www.vcfa.edu
Established: 2008 Annual Graduate Tuition & Fees: $23,368
Enrollment: 369 Coed
Affiliation or Control: Independent Non-Profit IRS Status: 501(c)3
Highest Offering: Master's; No Undergraduates
Program: Liberal Arts And General; Fine Arts Emphasis
Accreditation: EH

01 President ... Mr. Thomas Christopher GREENE
05 Academic Dean ... Mr. Matthew MONK
10 Chief Financial Ofcr/VP for Admin ... Ms. Erica HARE
04 Administrative Asst to President ... Ms. Angela PALADINO
26 Dir of Marketing & Communications ... Mr. Jay ERICSON
06 Registrar ... Ms. Jody MAUNSELL
08 Head Librarian ... Mr. Jim NOLTE
13 Chief Info Technology Officer (CIO) ... Mr. Peter TIMPONE
18 Chief Facilities/Physical Plant ... Mr. Bill CAMERON
29 Director Alumni Relations ... Ms. Sabrina FADIAL
84 Director Enrollment Management ... Mr. David MARKOW

† Carnegie Graduate Instructional Program classification is Postbac-A&S

Vermont Law School (E)

164 Chelsea Street, PO Box 96,
South Royalton VT 05068-0096
County: Windsor FICE Identification: 011934
Unit ID: 231147
Telephone: (802) 831-1000 Carnegie Class: Spec/Law
FAX Number: (802) 831-1163 Calendar System: Semester
URL: www.vermontlaw.edu
Established: 1972 Annual Graduate Tuition & Fees: $46,848
Enrollment: 642 Coed
Affiliation or Control: Independent Non-Profit IRS Status: 501(c)3
Highest Offering: First Professional Degree; No Undergraduates
Program: Professional
Accreditation: EH, LAW

01 President & Dean ... Mr. Marc MIHALY
05 Vice Dean for Faculty ... Ms. Jackie GARDINA
36 Vice Dean for Administration ... Ms. Stephanie WILLBANKS
10 Vice President for Finance & Admin ... Ms. Lorraine ATWOOD
100 Chief of Staff ... Ms. Kimberly EVANS
88 Asoc Dn Env Law Pgm/Dir Env Law Ctr ... Ms. Melissa SCANLAN
32 Assoc Dean Student Affs & Diversity ... Ms. Shirley JEFFERSON
20 Dep Vice Dean for Academic Affairs ... Mr. Mark LATHAM
106 Director of Distance Learning ... Ms. Adrienne SOLER
84 Assistant Dean of Admissions ... Mr. John MILLER
30 Assoc VP of Inst Advancement ... Ms. Mary WELZ
15 Human Resources Manager ... Ms. Chantelle BLAKE
08 Library Director ... Mr. Cynthia LEWIS
21 Comptroller ... Mr. Robert WEBBER
06 Registrar ... Ms. Maureen MORIARTY
37 Director of Financial Aid ... Ms. Sally KELLEY
18 Buildings & Grounds Facilities Mgr ... Mr. Andrew BRACKETT
26 Director of Communications ... Ms. Maryellen APELQUIST
13 Technology Operations Manager ... Mr. Sean LEE
04 Exec Asst to the President/Dean ... Ms. Stephanie CHIARELLA
40 Bookstore Manager ... Ms. Amy MCDOWELL
29 Asst Director of Alumni Affairs ... Ms. Melissa SCHLOBOHM

*Vermont State Colleges Office of the Chancellor (F)

PO Box 7, Montpelier VT 05601
County: Washington FICE Identification: 029162
Unit ID: 231156
Telephone: (802) 224-3000 Carnegie Class: N/A
FAX Number: (802) 224-3035
URL: www.vsc.edu

01 Chancellor ... Mr. Jeb SPAULDING
04 Exec Assistant to the Chancellor ... Ms. Elaine SOPCHAK
43 Vice President/General Counsel ... Mr. William REEDY
10 Vice Pres/Chief Financial Officer ... Mr. Thomas ROBBINS
05 Chief Academic/Tech Officer ... Dr. Yasmine ZIESLER
86 Dir External/Governmental Affairs ... Ms. Tricia COATES
26 Chief Information Officer ... Ms. Dianne POLLAK
18 Director of Facilities ... Mr. Richard ETHIER
91 Director Admin Information Systems ... Vacant
13 Director of System Info Tech ... Mr. Rick BLOOD
15 Director of Human Resources ... Ms. Nancy SHAW
09 Director of Institutional Research ... Ms. Hope BAKER-CARR
88 Director of Payroll/Benefits ... Ms. Tracy SWEET

*Castleton State College (G)

62 Alumni Drive, Castleton VT 05735-4454
County: Rutland FICE Identification: 003683
Unit ID: 230834
Telephone: (802) 468-5611 Carnegie Class: Bac/A&S
FAX Number: (802) 468-6470 Calendar System: Semester
URL: www.castleton.edu
Established: 1787 Annual Undergrad Tuition & Fees (In-State): $11,282
Enrollment: 2,184 Coed
Affiliation or Control: State IRS Status: 501(c)3
Highest Offering: Master's
Program: Liberal Arts And General; Teacher Preparatory
Accreditation: EH, ADNUR, CAATE, NURSE, SW

02 President ... Mr. David S. WOLK
04 Exec Assistant to the President ... Ms. Rita B. GENO
05 Academic Dean ... Dr. Tony PEFFER
11 Dean of Administration ... Mr. Scott DIKEMAN
10 Controller ... Ms. Heidi WHITNEY
32 Dean of Students ... Mr. Dennis PROULX
84 Dean of Enrollment ... Mr. Maurice OUIMET
15 Director of Human Resources ... Ms. Janet HAZELTON
35 Assistant Dean for Campus Life ... Ms. Victoria ANGIS
06 Registrar ... Ms. Lori ARNER
08 Director Calvin Coolidge Library ... Ms. Sandra DULING
37 Director Student Financial Aid ... Ms. Kathy O'MEARA
53 Director of Student Teaching ... Ms. Anne SLONAKER
18 Director of Physical Plant ... Mr. Chuck LAVOIE
27 Dir Marketing & Communication ... Mr. Jeff WELD
36 Dir of Career Planning/Placement ... Ms. Renee BEAUPREWHITE
23 Wellness Center Director ... Ms. Martha COULTER
38 Director Student Counseling ... Vacant

*Community College of Vermont (H)

PO Box 489, Montpelier VT 05601
County: Washington FICE Identification: 011167
Unit ID: 230861
Telephone: (802) 828-2800 Carnegie Class: Assoc/Pub-R-L
FAX Number: (802) 828-2805 Calendar System: Semester
URL: www.ccv.edu
Established: 1970 Annual Undergrad Tuition & Fees (In-State): $7,455
Enrollment: 6,631 Coed
Affiliation or Control: State IRS Status: 501(c)3
Highest Offering: Associate Degree
Program: Occupational; 2-Year Principally Bachelor's Creditable
Accreditation: EH, MAAB

02 President ....Ms. Joyce M. JUDY
11 Dean of Administration ....Dr. Barbara MARTIN
05 Dean of Academic Services ....Ms. Deborah STEWART
32 Dean of Student Services ....Ms. Heather WEINSTEIN
84 Dean Enrollment Services ....Ms. Pam CHISHOLM
20 Associate Academic Dean ....Ms. Darlene MURPHY
20 Associate Academic Dean ....Ms. Diane HERMANN-ARTIM
12 Exec Director of Academic Center ....Ms. Penne LYNCH
12 Exec Director of Academic Center ....Mr. Eric SAKAI
12 Exec Director of Academic Center ....Ms. Dee STEFFAN
12 Exec Director of Academic Center ....Ms. Tapp BARNHILL
24 Dean of Learning Technologies ....Mr. Eric SAKAI
15 Int Director Human Resources ....Ms. Julie HUDSON
06 Registrar ....Mr. Thomas ARNER
07 Director of Admissions ....Mr. Adam WARRINGTON
09 Dir Institutional Research/Planning ....Ms. Laura MASSELL
26 Chief Public Relations Officer ....Mr. Josh LARKIN
88 Director of Secondary Initiatives ....Ms. Natalie SEARLE
36 Director of Career Training Program ....Vacant
26 Dir of Marketing/Communications ....Ms. Janette SHAFFER

*Johnson State College (A)

337 College Hill, Johnson VT 05656-9898
County: Lamoille FICE Identification: 003688
Unit ID: 230913
Telephone: (802) 635-2356 Carnegie Class: Master's S
FAX Number: (802) 635-1230 Calendar System: Semester
URL: www.jsc.edu
Established: 1828 Annual Undergrad Tuition & Fees (In-State): $11,018
Enrollment: 1,661 Coed
Affiliation or Control: State IRS Status: 501(c)3
Highest Offering: Master's
Program: 2-Year Principally Bachelor's Creditable; Liberal Arts And General; Teacher Preparatory; Professional
Accreditation: EH

02 President ....Dr. Elaine C. COLLINS
05 Academic Dean ....Dr. Dan REGAN
11 Dean of Administration and CIO ....Ms. Sharron R. SCOTT
32 Dean of Student Life & College Rels ....Dr. David BERGH
84 Associate Dean of Enrollment ....Ms. Penny HOWRIGAN
35 Associate Dean of Students ....Ms. Michele WHITMORE
06 Registrar ....Mr. Douglas EASTMAN
51 Co-Director of External Degree Prgm ....Ms. Valerie EDWARDS
18 Director of Physical Plant ....Mr. Woody DIONNE
41 Director of Athletics & Recreation ....Mr. Jamey VENTURA
38 Director of Counseling Services ....Ms. Cynthia HENNARD
30 Director Development/Alumni Rels ....Ms. Lauren PHILIE
36 Director of Advising ....Ms. Sara KINERSON
89 Director of First-Year Experience ....Ms. Margo WARDEN
19 Director Safety & Security ....Mr. Michael PALAGONIA
26 Dir College Communications ....Ms. Deborah BOUTON
37 Director Student Financial Aid ....Ms. Lisa CUMMINGS
15 Director Human Resources ....Ms. Sharon SCOTT
07 Sr Assoc Director of Admissions ....Mr. Patrick ROGERS
08 Librarian ....Mr. Joseph FARARA
79 Chair Humanities ....Dr. Paul SILVER
53 Chair Education Dept ....Dr. Kathleen BRINEGAR
65 Chair Environ/Health Sciences ....Dr. Elizabeth DOLCI
57 Co-Chair Fine & Performing Arts ....Mr. Stephen BLAIR
57 Co-Chair Fine & Performing Arts ....Ms. Mary MARTIN
50 Chair Business/Economics ....Mr. Henrique CEZAR
60 Chair Writing/Literature ....Dr. Sharon TWIGG
81 Chair Mathematics ....Dr. Julie THEORET
83 Chair Behavioral Sciences ....Dr. Susan GREEN

*Lyndon State College (B)

1001 College Road, PO Box 919,
Lyndonville VT 05851-0919
County: Caledonia FICE Identification: 003689
Unit ID: 230931
Telephone: (802) 626-6200 Carnegie Class: Bac/Diverse
FAX Number: (802) 626-9770 Calendar System: Semester
URL: www.lyndonstate.edu
Established: 1911 Annual Undergrad Tuition & Fees (In-State): $11,018
Enrollment: 1,430 Coed
Affiliation or Control: State IRS Status: 501(c)3
Highest Offering: Master's
Program: Liberal Arts And General; Teacher Preparatory; Professional
Accreditation: EH, EXSC

02 President ....Dr. Joseph A. BERTOLINO
05 Interim Dean of Academic Affairs ....Dr. Nolan T. ATKINS
10 Dean of Administration ....Ms. Loren W. LOOMIS HUBBELL
20 Associate Dean of Faculty ....Mr. Thomas K. ANDERSON
32 Dean of Student Affairs ....Mr. Jonathan M. DAVIS
07 Director of Admissions ....Mr. Vincent U. MALONEY
09 Associate Dean Enrollment & IR ....Dr. Heather A. BOUCHEY
18 Director of Physical Plant ....Mr. Thomas R. ARCHER
91 Chief Technology Officer ....Mr. Michael A. DENTE
44 Director of Development ....Ms. Jennifer K. HARRIS
21 Associate Dean of Administration ....Ms. Sheilah M. EVANS
08 Interim Library Director ....Mr. Samuel C. BOSS
06 Registrar ....Ms. Miranda D. FOX
35 Director of Student Life ....Ms. Erin S. ROSSETTI
41 Director of Athletics ....Mr. Christopher T. UMMER
37 Director of Financial Aid ....Ms. Tanya W. BRADLEY
36 Director of Career Services ....Vacant
19 Director Public Safety ....Mr. George B. HACKING
88 Director Academic Support Services ....Vacant

88 Director of Broadcast Operations ....Ms. Darlene R. BOLDUC
88 Dir of Student Academic Development ....Ms. Debra M. BAILIN
26 Executive Director of Communication ....Ms. Sylvia PLUMB
88 Director of Advising Resources ....Ms. Kathleen E. GOLD
15 Director of Human Resources ....Ms. Sandra L. FRANZ

*Vermont Technical College (C)

PO Box 500, Randolph Center VT 05061-0500
County: Orange FICE Identification: 003698
Unit ID: 231165
Telephone: (802) 728-1000 Carnegie Class: Bac/Assoc
FAX Number: (802) 728-1508 Calendar System: Semester
URL: www.vtc.edu
Established: 1866 Annual Undergrad Tuition & Fees (In-State): $13,490
Enrollment: 1,542 Coed
Affiliation or Control: State IRS Status: 501(c)3
Highest Offering: Baccalaureate
Program: Occupational; 2-Year Principally Bachelor's Creditable; Professional; Technical Emphasis
Accreditation: EH, ADNUR, COARC, DH, ENGT, NUR, PNUR

02 President ....Mr. Daniel P. SMITH
05 Dean Academic Affairs ....Mr. Philip PETTY
32 Dean of Student Affairs ....Mr. John PATERSON
20 Dean Academic Pgm Development ....Mr. Brent SARGENT
13 Chief Technology Officer ....Mr. James SMITH
30 Assoc Dean Inst Advancement ....Vacant
11 Associate Dean of Administration ....Mr. Christopher BEATTIE
06 Registrar ....Ms. Sarah LEVIN
10 Controller ....Ms. Eileen DONOVAN
37 Director Financial Aid ....Ms. Catherine MCCULLOUGH
29 Assoc Dean Enrollment/Alumni Affs ....Mr. Dwight CROSS
19 Director Public Safety ....Mr. Emile FREDETTE
18 Director Physical Plant ....Mr. Theodore MANAZIR
36 Career Counseling/Placement ....Ms. Karry BOOSKA
66 Director Nursing Education ....Ms. Cindy MARTINDILL
15 Director of Human Resources ....Ms. Pamela ANKUDA
26 Dir Marketing/Communications ....Ms. Amanda CHAULK
40 Manager Bookstore ....Mr. Joe HIRAK
07 Director of Admissions ....Ms. Jessica VAN DEREN
08 Library Director ....Ms. Jane KEARNS

VIRGINIA

Advanced Technology Institute (D)

5700 Southern Boulevard, Virginia Beach VA 23462-2409
County: City of Virginia Beach FICE Identification: 031275
Unit ID: 231411
Telephone: (757) 490-1241 Carnegie Class: Assoc/PrivFP
FAX Number: (757) 499-5929 Calendar System: Semester
URL: www.auto.edu
Established: 1993 Annual Undergrad Tuition & Fees: $24,250
Enrollment: 550 Coed
Affiliation or Control: Proprietary IRS Status: Proprietary
Highest Offering: Associate Degree
Program: Occupational; Technical Emphasis
Accreditation: ACCSC

01 Campus President ....Mr. Dick DAIGLE
05 Chief Academic Officer ....Mr. Chenek PICKA
07 Director of Admissions ....Mr. Mike CORCORAN
32 Director of Student Services ....Mr. Kirk CLAYTON
37 Director Student Financial Aid ....Mr. Chad MARTS
06 Registrar ....Mrs. Shannon VOIGT
15 Director Personnel Services ....Mr. Rey LIZAN
36 Director Student Placement ....Mr. Kirk CLAYTON
39 Director Student Housing ....Mr. Kirk MANGHAM

American National University (E)

1813 E Main Street, Salem VA 24153-4598
County: Independent City FICE Identification: 003726
Unit ID: 232797
Telephone: (540) 986-1800 Carnegie Class: Assoc/PrivFP4
FAX Number: (540) 986-1344 Calendar System: Quarter
URL: www.an.edu
Established: 1886 Annual Undergrad Tuition & Fees: $11,550
Enrollment: 400 Coed
Affiliation or Control: Proprietary IRS Status: Proprietary
Highest Offering: Master's
Program: Business Emphasis
Accreditation: ACICS, CEA, EMT, MAC

01 President ....Mr. Frank E. LONGAKER
03 Vice President VA & WV Division ....Ms. Lenora S. DOWNING
05 Campus Director ....Mr. Ron BRADBURY
07 Regional Director of Admissions ....Mr. Larry W. STEELE

American National University (F)

3926 Seminole Trail, Charlottesville VA 22911-8397
Telephone: (434) 295-0136 Identification: 666501
Accreditation: ACICS, MAC

† Branch campus of American National University, Salem, VA.

American National University (G)

336 Old Riverside Drive, Danville VA 24541-1819
Telephone: (434) 793-6822 Identification: 666502
Accreditation: ACICS, MAC, SURGT

† Branch campus of American National University, Salem, VA.

American National University (H)

1515 Country Club Road, Harrisonburg VA 22801-9709
Telephone: (540) 432-0943 Identification: 666503
Accreditation: ACICS, MAC, SURGT

† Branch campus of American National University, Salem, VA.

American National University (I)

104 Candlewood Court, Lynchburg VA 24502-2653
Telephone: (434) 239-3500 Identification: 666504
Accreditation: ACICS, MAC

† Branch campus of American National University, Salem, VA.

American National University (J)

905 N. Memorial Boulevard, Martinsville VA 24112-2420
Telephone: (276) 632-5621 Identification: 666505
Accreditation: ACICS, MAC

† Branch campus of American National University, Salem, VA.

Appalachian College of Pharmacy (K)

1060 Dragon Road, Oakwood VA 24631
County: Buchanan FICE Identification: 041806
Unit ID: 449922
Telephone: (276) 498-4190 Carnegie Class: Spec/Health
FAX Number: (276) 498-4193 Calendar System: Semester
URL: www.acpharm.org
Established: 2003 Annual Graduate Tuition & Fees: $37,000
Enrollment: 214 Coed
Affiliation or Control: Independent Non-Profit IRS Status: 501(c)3
Highest Offering: Doctorate; No Undergraduates
Program: Professional
Accreditation: SC, PHAR

01 President ....Mr. Michael G. MCGLOTHLIN
05 Dean ....Dr. Susan L. MAYHEW
10 Chief Financial Officer ....Ms. Holli HARMAN
07 Dir of Admissions/Fin Aid/Registrar ....Ms. Vickie KEENE
103 Dir of Institutional Development ....Mr. Terry KILGORE

Appalachian School of Law (L)

1169 Riverside Drive, Grundy VA 24614-2825
County: Buchanan FICE Identification: 035593
Unit ID: 432348
Telephone: (800) 895-7411 Carnegie Class: Spec/Law
FAX Number: (276) 935-8261 Calendar System: Semester
URL: www.asl.edu
Established: 1995 Annual Undergrad Tuition & Fees: $31,525
Enrollment: 160 Coed
Affiliation or Control: Independent Non-Profit IRS Status: 501(c)3
Highest Offering: First Professional Degree
Program: Professional
Accreditation: LAW

01 Dean ....Mr. Daniel H. CALDWELL
08 Acting Director of Library ....Ms. Glenna OWENS
36 Director of Career Services ....Ms. Janie CASTLE
13 Director of Information Services ....Mr. Brian PRESLEY
31 Director of Community Services ....Ms. Jina M. SAULS
32 Director of Admissions ....Ms. Kendall SMITH
30 Director of Development ....Vacant
06 Registrar ....Mr. Eric VON KLEIST
37 Financial Aid Officer ....Mr. David BROOKSHIRE
09 Director of Institutional Research ....Vacant

Argosy University, Washington DC (M)

1550 Wilson Boulevard, Suite 600,
Arlington VA 22209-2435
Telephone: (703) 526-5800 Identification: 666788
Accreditation: &WC, ACBSP, CACREP, CLPSY

† Regional accreditation is carried under the parent institution in Orange, CA.

The Art Institute of Washington (N)

1820 North Fort Myer Drive, Arlington VA 22209-1802
Telephone: (703) 358-9550 Identification: 770945
Accreditation: &SC, ACFEI, CIDA

† Branch campus of The Art Institute of Atlanta, Atlanta, GA.

Atlantic University (O)

215 67th Street, Virginia Beach VA 23451-8101
County: Virginia Beach Identification: 666653
Unit ID: 231402
Telephone: (757) 631-8101 Carnegie Class: Not Classified
FAX Number: (757) 631-8096 Calendar System: Trimester

URL: www.atlanticuniv.edu
Established: 1930 Annual Graduate Tuition & Fees: $18,576
Enrollment: 13,000 Coed
Affiliation or Control: Independent Non-Profit IRS Status: 501(c)3
Highest Offering: Master's; No Undergraduates
Program: Professional
Accreditation: DEAC

01 CEO .... Kevin TODESCHI
05 Dir Academic & Administrative Affs .... James VAN AUKEN
06 Registrar .... Chantel KUMBA
88 Education Services Manager .... Rachel ALVIDREZ
84 Enrollment Clerk .... Megan STORY

Averett University (A)

420 W Main Street, Danville VA 24541-3692
County: Independent City FICE Identification: 003702
Unit ID: 231420
Telephone: (434) 791-5600 Carnegie Class: Bac/Diverse
FAX Number: (434) 791-5637 Calendar System: Semester
URL: www.averett.edu
Established: 1859 Annual Undergrad Tuition & Fees: $30,900
Enrollment: 1,990 Coed
Affiliation or Control: Independent Non-Profit IRS Status: 501(c)3
Highest Offering: Master's
Program: Liberal Arts And General; Teacher Preparatory
Accreditation: SC, CAATE

01 President .... Dr. Tiffany M. FRANKS
32 Executive Vice President .... Mr. Charles S. HARRIS
05 Vice Pres for Academic Affairs .... Dr. Timothy FULOP
10 Vice President Business & Finance .... Mr. Aaron HOWELL
30 Vice Pres Institutional Advancement .... Mr. Albert RAWLEY
15 Director of Human Resources .... Mrs. Kathie TUNE
84 Vice Pres Enrollment Management .... Ms. Stacy GATO
37 Director Student Financial Services .... Mr. Carl BRADSHER
21 Controller .... Ms. Lisa STEWART
08 Director of Library .... Ms. Elaine DAY
36 Director of Career Development .... Ms. Angie MCADAMS
06 Registrar .... Mrs. Janet ROBERSON
26 Dir of Marketing/Communications .... Mr. Ed JONES
29 Director Alumni Relations .... Mr. Dan HAYES
09 Dir Institutional Research/Effect .... Dr. Pam MCKIRDY
07 Director of Admissions .... Mr. Joel NESTER
18 Chief Facilities/Physical Plant .... Mr. Alonzo JONES
35 Director of Student Affairs .... Dr. Bill WOODWARD
38 Director of Student Counseling .... Mrs. Joan KAHWAJY-ANDERSON

Baptist Theological Seminary at Richmond (B)

8040 Villa Park Drive, Richmond VA 23228
County: Independent City FICE Identification: 031169
Unit ID: 366793
Telephone: (804) 355-8135 Carnegie Class: Spec/Faith
FAX Number: (804) 355-8182 Calendar System: Semester
URL: www.btsr.edu
Established: 1991 Annual Graduate Tuition & Fees: $16,500
Enrollment: 100 Coed
Affiliation or Control: Independent Non-Profit IRS Status: 501(c)3
Highest Offering: Doctorate; No Undergraduates
Program: Professional; Religious Emphasis
Accreditation: THEOL

01 President .... Dr. Ronald W. CRAWFORD
05 Dean .... Dr. Timothy GILBERT
30 VP Institutional Advancement .... Mr. Rob FOX
10 Dir Business Affairs & Facilities .... Dr. James F. PEAK, JR.
07 Director Admissions & Recruitment .... Dr. Melissa FALLEN
06 Registrar .... Rev. Susan BLANCHARD
13 Chief Info Technology Officer (CIO) .... Ms. Eryn VAN LEAR
27 Communications Manager .... Ms. Lacy KENDRICK

Bethel College (C)

1705 Todds Lane, Hampton VA 23666
County: Hampton City FICE Identification: 041538
Unit ID: 458113
Telephone: (757) 826-1883 Carnegie Class: Not Classified
FAX Number: (757) 826-5436 Calendar System: Semester
URL: www.bethel-college.com
Established: 2004 Annual Undergrad Tuition & Fees: $8,160
Enrollment: 57 Coed
Affiliation or Control: Assemblies Of God Church IRS Status: 501(c)3
Highest Offering: Baccalaureate
Program: Professional; Religious Emphasis
Accreditation: BI

01 President .... Dr. Glenn REYNOLDS
03 Executive Vice President .... Dr. Ron DE BERRY
05 Academic Dean .... Dr. Ron DEBERRY
32 Student Affairs .... Ms. Nanette BARTHOLOMEW
06 Registrar .... Mrs. Shawn LABADIE
08 Librarian .... Ms. Janell SANFORD
30 Director Institutional Advancement .... Ms. Audrey SOMERO

Bluefield College (D)

3000 College Avenue, Bluefield VA 24605-1799
County: Tazewell FICE Identification: 003703
Unit ID: 231554
Telephone: (276) 326-3682 Carnegie Class: Bac/Diverse
FAX Number: (276) 326-4288 Calendar System: Semester
URL: www.bluefield.edu
Established: 1922 Annual Undergrad Tuition & Fees: $23,296
Enrollment: 864 Coed
Affiliation or Control: Baptist IRS Status: 501(c)3
Highest Offering: Master's
Program: Liberal Arts And General; Teacher Preparatory; Professional
Accreditation: #SC, NURSE, TEAC

01 President .... Dr. David W. OLIVE
04 Assistant to the President .... Mrs. Diane T. SHOTT
05 VP for Academic Affairs .... Dr. Marshall FLOWERS
30 VP for Advancement .... Mrs. Ruth BLANKENSHIP
10 VP for Finance & Admin .... Ms. Laura WHITE
32 VP for Student Development .... Rev. David TAYLOR
84 VP for Enrollment Management .... Mr. Trent ARGO
07 Director of Adult Admissions .... Vacant
06 Registrar .... Mr. Joshua GRUBB
08 Director of Library Services .... Ms. Barbara GILLESPIE
26 Director of Public Relations .... Mr. Chris SHOEMAKER
29 Director of Alumni Relations .... Mr. Mark HIPES
09 Director of Institutional Research .... Mr. Bryan FRAZIER
37 Director of Financial Aid .... Ms. Carly KESTNER
42 Campus Minister .... Rev. David TAYLOR
41 Interim Athletic Director .... Mr. Mike WHITE
40 Campus Store Manager .... Mrs. Judy AKERS
18 Director of Maintenance .... Mr. Blair TAYLOR
19 Coordinator of Campus Safety .... Mr. Will ROBINSON
15 Human Resources Director .... Ms. Judy PEDNEAU
106 Dir of Online Programs .... Mr. Andrew LAWRENCE
13 Chief Info Technology Officer .... Mr. Steve KESSINGER
53 Dean School of Education .... Dr. Donna WATSON

Bon Secours Memorial College of Nursing (E)

8550 Magellan Parkway, Ste 1100, Richmond VA 23227
County: Henrico FICE Identification: 010043
Unit ID: 233356
Telephone: (804) 627-5300 Carnegie Class: Not Classified
FAX Number: (804) 627-5330 Calendar System: Semester
URL: www.bsmcon.edu
Established: 1961 Annual Undergrad Tuition & Fees: $4,871
Enrollment: 489 Coed
Affiliation or Control: Independent Non-Profit IRS Status: 501(c)3
Highest Offering: Baccalaureate
Program: Liberal Arts And General; Nursing Emphasis
Accreditation: ACICS, NURSE

05 Vice Pres Academic Affairs/Provost .... Dr. Melanie H. GREEN
66 Dean of Nursing .... Dr. Barbara C. SORBELLO
10 Dean of Administration and Finance .... Dr. Regina E. WELCH
32 Dean of Student Services .... Ms. Leslie WINSTON

Bridgewater College (F)

402 E College Street, Bridgewater VA 22812-1599
County: Rockingham FICE Identification: 003704
Unit ID: 231581
Telephone: (540) 828-8000 Carnegie Class: Bac/A&S
FAX Number: (540) 828-5479 Calendar System: 4/1/4
URL: www.bridgewater.edu
Established: 1880 Annual Undergrad Tuition & Fees: $31,480
Enrollment: 1,785 Coed
Affiliation or Control: Church Of The Brethren IRS Status: 501(c)3
Highest Offering: Baccalaureate
Program: Liberal Arts And General; Teacher Preparatory
Accreditation: SC, CAATE

01 President .... Dr. David W. BUSHMAN
03 Executive Vice President .... Mr. Roy W. FERGUSON, JR.
05 Vice Pres/Dean of Academic Affairs .... Dr. Carol A. SCHEPPARD
10 Vice Pres for Finance & Treasurer .... Ms. Anne B. KEELER
30 Vice Pres for Institutional Advance .... Dr. Maureen SILVA
26 Exec Dir Marketing & Communications .... Ms. Abbie PARKHURST
84 Vice President for Enrollment Mgmt .... Mr. Reggie WEBB
44 Director Institutional Advancement .... Vacant
18 Director of Sustainability .... Mr. Teshome H. MOLALENGE
40 Bookstore Manager .... Ms. Sarah LANDIS
20 Associate Dean of Academic Affairs .... Dr. Robert B. ANDERSEN
32 Dean of Students .... Dr. William D. MIRACLE
36 Director of Career Services .... Ms. Sherry TALBOTT
88 Director of Academic Support Svcs .... Dr. Raymond W. STUDWELL, II
42 Chaplain .... Rev. Robert R. MILLER
07 Director of Admissions .... Mr. Jarret L. SMITH
37 Director of Financial Aid .... Mr. Scott D. MORRISON
21 Director of Budget & Analysis .... Mr. Jeffrey FIKE
13 Director of Info Tech Center .... Ms. Kristy K. RHEA
41 Director of Athletics .... Mr. Curtis L. KENDALL
38 Director of Counseling Services .... Mr. Randall HOOK
29 Director of Alumni Relations .... Ms. Ellen B. MILLER
09 Director of Institutional Research .... Ms. Dawn S. DALBOW
15 Director of Human Resources .... Vacant
08 Library Director .... Mr. Andrew L. PEARSON
06 Registrar .... Ms. Cynthia K. HOWDYSHELL
21 Controller .... Ms. Mary S. SCHWAB
27 Editor/Dir of Media Relations .... Mr. Charles R. CULBERTSON
18 Director of Facilities .... Mr. David R. VANDEVANDER
19 Campus Police Chief .... Mr. Nicholas P. PICERNO
28 Minority Mentor .... Mr. James E. RAEFORD
23 Director of Student Health Services .... Ms. Paige FRENCH
28 Director of Multicultural Services .... Vacant
88 Director of Dining Services .... Ms. Mary SPEIR
04 Administrative Asst to President .... Mrs. Elaine C. DELLINGER
39 Director Student Housing .... Ms. Dawn OHANESSIAN
104 Director International Education .... Mrs. Anne MARSH

Bryant & Stratton College (G)

8141 Hull Street Road, North Chesterfield VA 23235-6411
Telephone: (804) 745-2444 Identification: 666496
Accreditation: &M, MAC

† Regional accreditation is carried under the parent institution (corporate office) in Buffalo, NY.

Bryant & Stratton College (H)

301 Centre Pointe Drive, Virginia Beach VA 23462-4417
Telephone: (757) 499-7900 FICE Identification: 010061
Accreditation: &M, MAC

† Regional accreditation is carried under the parent institution (corporate office) in Buffalo, NY.

California University of Management and Sciences Virginia (I)

400 North Washington Street, Falls Church VA 22046
Telephone: (703) 663-8088 Identification: 666734
Accreditation: ACICS

† Branch campus of California University of Management and Sciences, Anaheim, CA.

Career Training Solutions (J)

10304 Spotsylvania Avenue, Ste. 400, Fredericksburg VA 22408-8605
County: Stafford FICE Identification: 036543
Unit ID: 441858
Telephone: (540) 373-2200 Carnegie Class: Assoc/PrivFP
FAX Number: (540) 373-4465 Calendar System: Other
URL: www.careertrainingsolutions.com
Established: 2000 Annual Undergrad Tuition & Fees: $12,735
Enrollment: 203 Coed
Affiliation or Control: Proprietary IRS Status: Proprietary
Highest Offering: Associate Degree
Program: Occupational
Accreditation: COE

01 Chief Executive Officer/President .... Ms. A. Christine CARROLL

Catholic Distance University (K)

120 E Colonial Highway, Hamilton VA 20158-9012
County: Loudoun FICE Identification: 041242
Unit ID: 377430
Telephone: (540) 338-2700 Carnegie Class: Not Classified
FAX Number: (540) 338-4788 Calendar System: Other
URL: www.cdu.edu
Established: 1983 Annual Undergrad Tuition & Fees: $2,814
Enrollment: 330 Coed
Affiliation or Control: Independent Non-Profit IRS Status: 501(c)3
Highest Offering: Master's
Program: Religious Emphasis
Accreditation: DEAC

01 President .... Dr. Marianne E. MOUNT
05 Academic Dean .... Dr. Peter BROWN
20 Faculty Chair .... Dr. Matthew BUNSON
88 Dean of Catechetical Programs .... Sr. Mary Margaret SCHLATHER
06 Registrar .... Ms. Theresa SNIDER
06 Continuing Education Registrar .... Mrs. Kathleen WOODDELL
26 Director of Communications .... Vacant
07 Director of Admissions .... Ms. Carol CIULLO
10 Bursar .... Mrs. Amy SHOUSE
13 Director of Technology .... Mrs. Carol DALEY

Centra College of Nursing (L)

905 Lakeside Dr, Ste A, Lynchburg VA 24501
County: Independent City FICE Identification: 021758
Unit ID: 232618
Telephone: (434) 200-3070 Carnegie Class: Not Classified
FAX Number: (434) 200-5505 Calendar System: Semester
URL: www.centracon.edu
Established: 2011 Annual Undergrad Tuition & Fees: $12,034
Enrollment: 151 Coed
Affiliation or Control: Independent Non-Profit IRS Status: 501(c)3
Highest Offering: Associate Degree
Program: Occupational; 2-Year Principally Bachelor's Creditable; Nursing Emphasis
Accreditation: ABHES, ADNUR, DNUR, PNUR

01 Dean .... Dr. Melody SHARP
07 Assoc Dir ADN Pgm/Dean Admissions .... Ms. Rhonda WORMSER
07 Assoc Director PN Program .... Ms. Ronni MCCOMBIE
07 Director of Academic Progression .... Dr. Diane ELMORE
37 Financial Aid/Enrollment Manager .... Mr. Aaron ELLENBURG

Centura College (A)
932 Ventura Way, Chesapeake VA 23320
Telephone: (757) 549-2121 Identification: 770608
Accreditation: ACCSC

† Branch campus of Centura College, Virginia Beach, VA.

Centura College (B)
616 Denbigh Boulevard, Newport News VA 23608
Telephone: (757) 874-2121 Identification: 770606
Accreditation: ACCSC

† Branch campus of Centura College, Virginia Beach, VA.

Centura College (C)
7020 N Military Highway, Norfolk VA 23518-4202
Telephone: (757) 853-2121 Identification: 770605
Accreditation: ACCSC

† Branch campus of Centura College, Virginia Beach, VA.

Centura College (D)
7914 Midlothian Turnpike, North Chesterfield VA 23235
County: Chesterfield FICE Identification: 031264
Unit ID: 427982
Telephone: (804) 330-0111 Carnegie Class: Assoc/PrivFP
FAX Number: (804) 330-3809 Calendar System: Semester
URL: www.centuracollege.edu
Established: 1992 Annual Undergrad Tuition & Fees: $16,337
Enrollment: 167 Coed
Affiliation or Control: Proprietary IRS Status: Proprietary
Highest Offering: Associate Degree
Program: Occupational; Business Emphasis
Accreditation: ACCSC

01 Campus Executive Director .... Zoe THOMPSON
11 Director of Compliance and Admin .... Grace BLEVINS
05 Director of Education .... Ann TRIBBEY
07 Director of Admissions .... Paul WILLIAMS
06 Registrar .... Autre METAL
37 Financial Aid .... Korey HUGHES
10 Bursar .... Leslie CROCKER
32 Student Services .... Helena COOPER
36 Career Services .... Steven TERRY
08 Head Librarian .... Towana KELLY

Centura College (E)
2697 Dean Drive, Suite 100,
Virginia Beach VA 23452-7431
County: City of Virginia Beach FICE Identification: 023344
Unit ID: 232016
Telephone: (757) 340-2121 Carnegie Class: Assoc/PrivFP4
FAX Number: (757) 340-9704 Calendar System: Semester
URL: www.centuracollege.edu
Established: 1969 Annual Undergrad Tuition & Fees: $16,887
Enrollment: 181 Coed
Affiliation or Control: Proprietary IRS Status: Proprietary
Highest Offering: Baccalaureate
Program: Occupational; Business Emphasis
Accreditation: ACCSC

01 Campus Executive Director .... Ben CLARK
11 Assistant Campus Executive Director .... Wendy DAVIDSON
05 Director of Education .... Marcus WESSON
07 Director of Admissions .... Dustin SAUNDERS
06 Registrar .... Dennis RYAN
37 Financial Aid Officer .... Jennifer BROADWELL
10 Bursar .... Bernadene ALFRED
32 Student Services Coordinator .... Mary MORGAN
36 Career Services Coordinator .... Brenda HOUCK
36 Career Services Coordinator .... Shawn HUTCHINGS
08 Librarian .... Jeffery BARBOUR

Chamberlain College of Nursing - Arlington Campus (F)
2450 Crystal Drive, Suite 319, Arlington VA 22202
Telephone: (703) 416-7300 Identification: 770497
Accreditation: &NH, NURSE

† Branch campus of Chamberlain College of Nursing-Addison, Addison, IL.

Chester Career College (G)
751 West Hundred Road, Chester VA 23836-2516
County: Chesterfield FICE Identification: 034095
Telephone: (804) 751-9191 Carnegie Class: Not Classified
FAX Number: (804) 751-2599 Calendar System: Semester
URL: www.chestercareercollege.edu
Established: 1997 Annual Undergrad Tuition & Fees: N/A
Enrollment: N/A Coed
Affiliation or Control: Proprietary IRS Status: Proprietary
Highest Offering: Associate Degree
Program: Occupational; 2-Year Principally Bachelor's Creditable; Nursing Emphasis
Accreditation: COE

01 Campus Director .... Ms. Debbie HARRIS
05 Academic Dean .... Ms. Sandra KERRICK
06 Registrar .... Ms. Annette WHITE
08 Head Librarian .... Ms. Kathy PHILO
36 Director Student Placement .... Mrs. Tamara KNIGHT
37 Director Student Financial Aid .... Ms. Tammy RAINES

Christendom College (H)
134 Christendom Drive, Front Royal VA 22630-6534
County: Warren FICE Identification: 036653
Unit ID: 231703
Telephone: (540) 636-2900 Carnegie Class: Not Classified
FAX Number: (540) 636-1655 Calendar System: Semester
URL: www.christendom.edu
Established: 1977 Annual Undergrad Tuition & Fees: $23,200
Enrollment: 407 Coed
Affiliation or Control: Roman Catholic IRS Status: 501(c)3
Highest Offering: Master's
Program: Liberal Arts And General
Accreditation: SC

01 President .... Dr. Timothy T. O'DONNELL
10 Executive Vice President/CFO/COO .... Mr. Kenneth H. FERGUSON
05 Vice President Academic Affairs .... Dr. Steven C. SNYDER
30 Vice President for Advancement .... Mr. John F. CISKANIK
18 Vice Pres Operations/Facility Plng .... Mr. Michael S. FOECKLER
84 Vice Pres Enrollment & Marketing .... Mr. Thomas MCFADDEN
32 Dean of Student Life .... Mr. Chris VANDER WOUDE
20 Academic Dean .... Mr. Mark WUNSCH
06 Registrar .... Mr. Walter A. JANARO
07 Director of Admissions .... Mr. Sam PHILLIPS
08 Director of Christendom Library .... Mr. Andrew V. ARMSTRONG
37 Financial Aid Officer .... Mrs. Alisa L. POLK
29 Asst Dir Alumni/Donor Relations .... Mr. Vince CRISTE
13 Director of Computer Services .... Mr. Douglas S. BRIGGS
88 Registrar/Business Officer NDGS .... Miss Heidi KALIAN
41 Athletic Director .... Mr. Joshua PETERSEN
30 Dir Advancement Operations/Svcs .... Mr. Paul JALSEVAC
04 Exec Assistant to the President .... Ms. Brenda SEELBACH
58 Dean of the Graduate School .... Dr. Kristen BURNS

Christopher Newport University (I)
1 Avenue of the Arts, Newport News VA 23606-3072
County: Independent City FICE Identification: 003706
Unit ID: 231712
Telephone: (757) 594-7000 Carnegie Class: Master's S
FAX Number: N/A Calendar System: Semester
URL: www.cnu.edu
Established: 1960 Annual Undergrad Tuition & Fees (In-State): $12,526
Enrollment: 5,221 Coed
Affiliation or Control: State IRS Status: 501(c)3
Highest Offering: Master's
Program: Liberal Arts And General
Accreditation: SC, BUS, ENG, MUS, SW, THEA

01 President .... Sen. Paul S. TRIBLE, JR.
100 Chief of Staff .... Mrs. Cynthia R. PERRY
05 Provost .... Dr. David C. DOUGHTY
03 Executive Vice President .... Mr. William L. BRAUER
43 University Counsel .... Mrs. Maureen R. MATSEN
30 Vice Pres for Univ Advancement .... Mrs. Adelia P. THOMPSON
15 Director of Human Resources .... Mrs. Lorraine M. WESTPHAL
41 Director of Athletics .... Mr. Robert T. BROOKS
04 Exec Assistant to President/Board .... Mrs. Beverley D. MUELLER
10 University Comptroller .... Mrs. Diane REED
32 Dean of Students .... Dr. Kevin M. HUGHES
49 Dean College Arts & Humanities .... Dr. Lori J. UNDERWOOD
83 Dean College of Social Sciences .... Dr. Robert E. COLVIN
88 Dean College Nat/Behav Science .... Dr. Nicole R. GUAJARDO
07 Dean of Admission .... Mr. Robert J. LANGE
06 Registrar .... Mrs. Donna M. SHELTON
37 Director of Financial Aid .... Ms. Christina L. RUSSELL
36 Director Center of Career Planning .... Ms. Elizabeth K. WESTLEY
39 Assistant Director of Housing .... Mr. Andrew H. KOERNERT
09 Director of Institutional Research .... Ms. Donna A. VARNER
13 Chief Information Officer .... Mr. Stephen S. CAMPBELL
08 University Librarian .... Ms. Mary K. SELLEN
19 Chief of University Police .... Mr. Andrew H. ENGEMANN, JR.
21 Director of University Audit .... Ms. Faith D. BELOTE
18 Asst Director of Plant Operations .... Mr. Albert C. METZGAR
44 Sr Dir Advancement/Planned Giving .... Ms. Lucy L. LATCHUM
96 Director of Materiel Management .... Mr. Ryan A. FEREBEE
29 Dir Alumni Relations/Univ Events .... Mrs. Amie G. DALE
26 Director of Public Relations .... Ms. Lori A. JACOBS
28 Director of Title IX and EO .... Ms. Michelle L. MOODY
38 Exec Dir Counseling & HE Services .... Dr. William V. RITCHEY
26 Director of Communications .... Mr. Bruce S. BRONSTEIN, JR.
102 Dir Foundation & Corporate Giving .... Mr. Keith D. ROOTS
108 Director of Assessment .... Mr. Jason C. LYONS
45 Director of Planning & Budget .... Ms. Patricia L. MCDERMOTT
104 Coordinator of Study Abroad .... Ms. Amanda K. PIERCE
50 Dean Luter School of Business .... Dr. George EBBS
86 Asst Director Government Relations .... Mr. Thomas E. KRAMER

College of William & Mary (J)
PO Box 8795, Williamsburg VA 23187-8795
County: Independent City FICE Identification: 003705
Unit ID: 231624
Telephone: (757) 221-4000 Carnegie Class: RU/H
FAX Number: (757) 221-1259 Calendar System: Semester
URL: www.wm.edu
Established: 1693 Annual Undergrad Tuition & Fees (In-State): $19,372
Enrollment: 8,437 Coed
Affiliation or Control: State IRS Status: 501(c)3
Highest Offering: Doctorate
Program: Liberal Arts And General; Teacher Preparatory; Professional
Accreditation: SC, BUS, BUSA, CACREP, IPSY, LAW, TED

01 President .... Mr. W. Taylor REVELEY, III
05 Provost .... Dr. Michael HALLERAN
11 Vice President for Administration .... Mr. Samuel E. JONES
10 Vice President for Finance .... Mr. Samuel E. JONES
30 Vice President for Advancement .... Mr. Matthew T. LAMBERT
45 Vice Pres for Strategic Initiatives .... Mr. Henry R. BROADDUS
32 Vice President for Student Affairs .... Dr. Virginia M. AMBLER
41 Director of Athletics .... Mr. Edward (Terry) C. DRISCOLL
29 Assoc VP Alumni Engagement .... Ms. Marilyn W. MIDYETTE
49 Dean Faculty of Arts & Sciences .... Dr. Katharine CONLEY
50 Dean School of Business Admin .... Mr. Lawrence B. PULLEY
53 Dean School of Education .... Dr. Spencer NILES
61 Dean School of Law .... Mr. Davison M. DOUGLAS
88 Dean/Dir School of Marine Science .... Dr. John T. WELLS
08 Dean University Libraries .... Ms. Carrie COOPER
43 University Counsel .... Ms. Deborah A. LOVE
20 Vice Provost for Academic Affairs .... Ms. Susan S. GROVER
82 Vice Prov Intl Affairs/Reves Ctr .... Dr. Stephen E. HANSON
46 Vice Provost Rsch & Grad Prof Stds .... Dr. Dennis M. MANOS
13 Chief Information Officer .... Mr. Courtney CARPENTER
14 Deputy CIO .... Ms. Bernadette KENNEY
108 Assoc Prov Assessment & Accred .... Dr. Susan L. BOSWORTH
07 Dean of Admission/Assoc Prov Enroll .... Mr. Tim A. WOLFE
06 Assoc Provost & Univ Registrar .... Ms. Sara L. MARCHELLO
09 Director of Institutional Research .... Mr. Evan DAVIES
106 Assoc Provost ELearning .... Dr. Michele H. JACKSON
88 Dean for Educational Policy .... Dr. Lu Ann HOMZA
58 Dean Graduate Studies & Research .... Dr. Virginia TORCZON
92 Dean Honors/Interdisciplinary Stds .... Dr. Joel D. SCHWARTZ
88 Dean of Undergraduate Studies .... Dr. John GRIFFIN
104 Director of Global Education .... Ms. Sylvia MITTERNDORFER
86 Assoc VP Government Relations .... Ms. Frances C. BRADFORD
26 Director of University Relations .... Mr. Brian WHITSON
88 Assoc VP Advancement Campaign Dir .... Mr. Mark L. BEGLEY
44 Assoc VP Development/Fundraising .... Mr. Earl T. GRANGER
18 Assoc Vice Pres Facilities Mgmt .... Mr. Van DOBSON
35 Dean of Students .... Ms. Marjorie THOMAS
25 Director of Sponsored Programs .... Ms. Jane LOPEZ
22 Director of Equal Opportunity .... Ms. Sharron GATLING
37 Director Student Financial Aid .... Mr. Edward P. IRISH
15 Assoc VP Human Resources .... Mr. John POMA
38 Director Counseling Center .... Dr. Warrenetta C. MANN
36 Director Career Center .... Ms. Mary E. SCHILLING
19 Chief W&M Police Department .... Ms. Deborah CHEESBRO
21 Director Financial Operations .... Mr. Edmund (Bert) E. BRUMMER
23 Director Student Health Center .... Dr. Virginia D. WELLS
28 Dir of Ctr for Student Diversity .... Dr. Vernon HURTE
39 Asst VP Stdnt Affs/Dir of Res Life .... Ms. Deborah BOYKIN
96 Director of Procurement .... Mr. Gregory W. JOHNSON
40 Manager W&M Bookstore .... Ms. Cathy PACHECO
100 Asst to President/Chief of Staff .... Mr. Michael J. FOX
101 Secretary to the Board of Visitors .... Mr. Michael J. FOX
04 Executive Asst to President .... Ms. Cynthia A. BRAUER
105 Director of Creative Services .... Ms. Tina L. COLEMAN
88 Assoc VP for Health & Wellness .... Dr. Robert K. CRACE

Columbia College (K)
8300 Merrifield Avenue, Fairfax VA 22031
County: Fairfax FICE Identification: 041273
Unit ID: 455983
Telephone: (703) 206-0508 Carnegie Class: Assoc/PrivFP
FAX Number: (703) 206-0488 Calendar System: Other
URL: www.ccdc.edu
Established: 1999 Annual Undergrad Tuition & Fees: $7,700
Enrollment: 740 Coed
Affiliation or Control: Proprietary IRS Status: Proprietary
Highest Offering: Associate Degree
Program: Occupational; 2-Year Principally Bachelor's Creditable; Technical Emphasis
Accreditation: ACICS

01 President .... Dr. Richard K. KIM

Danville Regional Medical Center School of Health Professions (L)
142 South Main Street, Danville VA 24541
County: Independent City FICE Identification: 021116
Telephone: (434) 799-4510 Carnegie Class: Not Classified
FAX Number: (434) 799-3718 Calendar System: Semester
URL: www.danvilleregional.com
Established: 1898 Annual Undergrad Tuition & Fees: $4,882
Enrollment: 95 Coed
Affiliation or Control: Proprietary IRS Status: Proprietary
Highest Offering: Associate Degree
Program: Occupational
Accreditation: ABHES, DNUR, RAD

DeVry University - Arlington Campus (M)
2450 Crystal Drive, Arlington VA 22202-3843
Telephone: (703) 414-4000 Identification: 666220
Accreditation: &NH, ENGT

† Regional accreditation is carried under the parent institution in Downers Grove, IL.

Eastern Mennonite University (A)

1200 Park Road, Harrisonburg VA 22802-2462

County: Independent City — FICE Identification: 003708
Unit ID: 232043
Telephone: (540) 432-4000 — Carnegie Class: Bac/A&S
FAX Number: (540) 432-4444 — Calendar System: Semester
URL: www.emu.edu
Established: 1917 — Annual Undergrad Tuition & Fees: $32,300
Enrollment: 1,870 — Coed
Affiliation or Control: Mennonite Church — IRS Status: 501(c)3
Highest Offering: Master's
Program: Liberal Arts And General; Teacher Preparatory; Professional
Accreditation: SC, CACREP, NURSE, PAST, SW, TED, THEOL

01 President ... Dr. Loren E. SWARTZENDRUBER
05 Provost ... Dr. Fred L. KNISS
30 Vice President for Advancement ... Mr. Kirk L. SHISLER
10 Vice President for Finance ... Mr. Daryl W. BERT
84 Vice Pres Enrollment & Marketing ... Mr. Luke HARTMAN
32 Vice President for Student Life ... Dr. Kenneth L. NAFZIGER
20 Vice Pres & Undergrad Academic Dean ... Dr. Deirdre SMELTZER
73 Seminary Dean ... Dr. Michael A. KING
06 University Registrar ... Mr. David A. DETROW
26 Director of Marketing Services ... Ms. Andrea S. WENGER
07 Director Undergraduate Admissions ... Dr. Jason GOOD
08 Director of Libraries ... Dr. G. Marcille H. FREDERICK
37 Director of Financial Assistance ... Ms. Michele R. HENSLEY
36 Director Career Services/Testing ... Ms. Kimberly PHILLIPS
29 Director of Alumni/Parent Relations ... Mr. Jeffrey A. SHANK
09 Director Institutional Research ... Dr. BJ MILLER
04 Assistant to the President ... Ms. Twila K. YODER
41 Athletic Director ... Mr. David A. KING
42 Campus Pastor ... Mr. Brian M. BURKHOLDER
13 Director of Information Systems ... Mr. Benjamin S. BEACHY
18 Director of Physical Plant ... Mr. Eldon KURTZ
15 Director Human Resources ... Ms. Marcia J. ENGLE
21 Controller ... Mr. Timothy STUTZMAN
27 Chief Public Information Officer ... Mr. Michael J. ZUCCONI
35 Director Student Affairs ... Ms. Rachel R. SAWATZKY
38 Director Student Counseling ... Ms. Pamela D. COMER

Eastern Virginia Medical School (B)

Box 1980, Norfolk VA 23501-1980

County: Independent City — FICE Identification: 010338
Unit ID: 231970
Telephone: (757) 446-5600 — Carnegie Class: Spec/Med
FAX Number: (757) 446-5135 — Calendar System: Other
URL: www.evms.edu
Established: 1973 — Annual Graduate Tuition & Fees: $35,025
Enrollment: 1,204 — Coed
Affiliation or Control: Independent Non-Profit — IRS Status: 501(c)3
Highest Offering: Doctorate; No Undergraduates
Program: Professional
Accreditation: SC, ARCPA, CLPSY, IPSY, MED, PH, SURGA

01 President/Provost/Dean ... Dr. Richard V. HOMAN
04 Sr Exec Assistant to the President ... Ms. Barbara C. ALBRIGHT
88 Director Internal Audit ... Mr. Robert B. WOOD
100 Chief of Staff ... Mr. Brant M. COX
17 Vice Pres/Dean Sch of Health Prof ... Dr. Charles D. COMBS
88 Assoc Dean for Health Professions ... Mr. Jeffrey A. JOHNSON
10 Vice Pres Administration/Finance ... Mr. Mark R. BABASHANIAN
19 Chief of Police ... Mr. Andrew J. MITCHELL
18 Director Facilities/Physical Plant ... Mr. Doug MARTIN
28 Vice President for Diversity ... Mr. Mekbib L. GEMEDA
45 Vice Dean for Faculty Affairs ... Dr. Elza MYLONA
88 Vice Dean Clinical Affairs ... Dr. Alfred Z. ABUHAMAD
23 CEO EVMS Medical Group ... Mr. James F. LIND
05 Vice Dean Academic Affairs ... Dr. Ronald W. FLENNER
43 General Counsel ... Ms. Stacy R. PURCELL
58 Vice Dean Grad Medical Education ... Dr. Linda R. ARCHER
46 Vice Dean for Research ... Dr. Jerry L. NADLER
09 Sr Assoc Dean for Research ... Dr. William J. WASILENKO
88 Assoc Dean Hum Sub Protection/IRB ... Dr. Harry J. TILLMAN
50 Assoc Dean Business/Admin Affairs ... Mr. David E. HUBAND
84 Assoc Dean Admissions and Enroll ... Dr. Donald C. MEYER
32 Assoc Dean for Student Affairs ... Dr. Ann E. CAMPBELL
20 Asst Dean for Academic Affairs ... Dr. Senthil K. RAJASEKARAN
08 Assoc Dean Library/Lrng Resource ... Ms. Judith R. MERCER
35 Asst Dean Student Affairs ... Dr. Tereasa W. BABINEAU
07 Asst Dean of Admissions ... Dr. Thomas D. KIMBLE
93 Asst Dean for Diversity ... Ms. Gail C. WILLIAMS
06 Registrar ... Mr. Michael J. DONLAN
15 Director Human Resources ... Mr. Matthew R. SCHENK
21 Director of Finance ... Ms. Helen S. HESELIUS
72 Director for Technology Transfer ... Mr. Paul B. DIMARCO
37 Director Student Financial Aid ... Ms. Margaret L. MURPHY
21 Director for Business Management ... Ms. Tammy A. CHRISMAN
96 Director of Materials Management ... Mr. Steven LEE
13 Director of Information Technology ... Ms. Deborah A. TAYLOR
26 Director of Mktg & Communications ... Mr. Vincent A. RHODES
29 Director Alumni Relations ... Ms. Melissa W. LANG
30 Director of Development ... Ms. Connie L. MCKENZIE
88 Director of the Brock Institute ... Dr. Cynthia ROMERO
51 Director for Continuing Med Educ ... Ms. Drucie A. PAPAFIL
88 Director Occupational Health ... Ms. Heather SINGLETON
25 Director Sponsored Programs ... Ms. Yolanda F. DEMORY
88 Director Rad Safety Env Health ... Mr. Courtney A. KERR
88 Director Risk Management ... Ms. Donita M. LAMARAND

† Member of Virginia Consortium for Professional Psychology.

ECPI University (C)

5555 Greenwich Road, Virginia Beach VA 23462-6554

County: Independent City — FICE Identification: 010198
Unit ID: 248934
Telephone: (757) 671-7171 — Carnegie Class: Assoc/PrivFP4
FAX Number: (757) 671-8661 — Calendar System: Semester
URL: www.ecpi.edu
Established: 1966 — Annual Undergrad Tuition & Fees: $15,035
Enrollment: 9,840 — Coed
Affiliation or Control: Proprietary — IRS Status: Proprietary
Highest Offering: Master's
Program: Occupational
Accreditation: SC, ACFEI, MAAB, NUR

01 President ... Mr. Mark B. DREYFUS
12 Campus President ... Mr. Kevin PAVEGLIO
13 VP Info Systems/Financial Aid ... Mr. Jeff ARTHUR

Edward Via College of Osteopathic Medicine (D)

2265 Kraft Drive, Blacksburg VA 24060

County: Montgomery — FICE Identification: 037093
Unit ID: 442806
Telephone: (540) 231-4000 — Carnegie Class: Spec/Med
FAX Number: (540) 231-5252 — Calendar System: Semester
URL: www.vcom.vt.edu
Established: 2002 — Annual Graduate Tuition & Fees: $43,250
Enrollment: 1,444 — Coed
Affiliation or Control: Independent Non-Profit — IRS Status: 501(c)3
Highest Offering: Doctorate; No Undergraduates
Program: Professional
Accreditation: OSTEO

01 President ... Dr. Dixie TOOKE-RAWLINS
05 Provost/EVP & Founding Dean ... Dr. Dixie TOOKE-RAWLINS
10 Associate Vice Pres Finance/CFO ... Mr. Mark HAMRIC
32 Assoc Vice Pres Student Services ... Mr. William KING
46 Assoc Vice Pres Research/Grad Stds ... Dr. Hara P. MISRA
11 Assoc Vice President Operations ... Mr. Bill PRICE
12 Vice Dean Carolinas Campus ... Dr. Timothy J. KOWALSKI
12 Vice Dean Virginia Campus ... Dr. Jan M. WILLCOX
58 Vice Dean Post-Bac/Pre-med Program ... Dr. Francine ANDERSON
63 Vice Dean Post Baccalaureate Pgm ... Dr. Brian W. HILL

Emory & Henry College (E)

PO Box 947, 30461 Garnand Drive, Emory VA 24327-0947

County: Washington — FICE Identification: 003709
Unit ID: 232025
Telephone: (276) 944-4121 — Carnegie Class: Bac/A&S
FAX Number: (276) 944-6934 — Calendar System: Semester
URL: www.ehc.edu
Established: 1836 — Annual Undergrad Tuition & Fees: $30,700
Enrollment: 1,038 — Coed
Affiliation or Control: United Methodist — IRS Status: 501(c)3
Highest Offering: Doctorate
Program: Liberal Arts And General; Teacher Preparatory
Accreditation: SC, CAATE, @PTA, TEAC

01 President ... Mr. Jake B. SCHRUM
04 Executive Assistant to President ... Mr. Mark R. GRAHAM
05 VP Academic Affairs/Dean ... Dr. David P. HANEY
10 VP for Business and Finance ... Mr. Richard K. GAUMER
11 Vice Pres for Operations ... Dr. Dirk E. WILMOTH
32 VP Student Life/Dean of Students ... Ms. Pamela L. GOURLEY
30 VP for Institutional Advancement ... Mr. Joseph P. TAYLOR
84 Vice Pres for Enrollment Management ... Mr. Dave VOSKUIL
09 Dir Institutional Research/Effect ... Mr. Gregory G. STEINER
29 Director of Alumni Affairs ... Ms. Monica S. HOEL
37 Director of Financial Aid ... Ms. Scarlett BLEVINS
06 Registrar/Dir of CSA ... Ms. Lynn ELLIOTT
36 Director of Career Planning ... Ms. Amanda GARDNER
38 Director Student Counseling ... Ms. Jill M. SMELTZER
26 Director Public Relations ... Mr. Dirk S. MOORE
13 Chief Information Officer/Librarian ... Ms. Lorraine N. ABRAHAM
18 Dir of Facilities Management ... Mr. Scott E. WILLIAMS
40 Bookstore Manager ... Mr. Terry RICHARDSON
42 Chaplain ... Rev. Mary K. BRIGGS
15 Human Resources Manager ... Ms. Kim STEINER
20 Associate VP Academic Affairs ... Dr. Michael J. PUGLISI
35 Assistant Dean of Students ... Mr. Kyle CUTSHAW
21 Associate VP Business/Finance ... Ms. Benita BARE
07 Director of Admissions ... Mr. Matthew CRISMAN
39 Director of Housing ... Vacant
41 Director of Athletics ... Ms. Myra SIMS
19 Chief of Campus Police ... Mr. Scott POORE
102 Dir Foundation/Corporate Relations ... Ms. Erin HADARY
104 Director Study Abroad ... Dr. Celeste GAIA
105 Director Web Services ... Mr. Kevin CALL
44 Director Annual or Planned Giving ... Ms. Ronan KING
53 Director of Education Center ... Dr. Janet CRICKMER

Everest College (F)

825 Greenbrier Circle, Chesapeake VA 23320
Telephone: (757) 361-3900 — Identification: 770791
Accreditation: ACICS

† Branch campus of Everest College, Newport News, VA.

Everest College (G)

803 Diligence Drive, Newport News VA 23606

County: Independent City — FICE Identification: 009267
Unit ID: 232502
Telephone: (757) 873-1111 — Carnegie Class: Assoc/PrivFP
FAX Number: (757) 873-0728 — Calendar System: Other
URL: www.everest.edu
Established: 1941 — Annual Undergrad Tuition & Fees: $12,450
Enrollment: 433 — Coed
Affiliation or Control: Proprietary — IRS Status: Proprietary
Highest Offering: Associate Degree
Program: Occupational
Accreditation: ACICS

01 President ... Mr. Aaron MORRIS
05 Director of Education ... Ms. Wanda FLEMING

† Tuition varies by degree program.

Ferrum College (H)

PO Box 1000, 215 Ferrum Mtn Road, Ferrum VA 24088-9001

County: Franklin — FICE Identification: 003711
Unit ID: 232089
Telephone: (540) 365-2121 — Carnegie Class: Bac/Diverse
FAX Number: (540) 365-4269 — Calendar System: Semester
URL: www.ferrum.edu
Established: 1913 — Annual Undergrad Tuition & Fees: $30,835
Enrollment: 1,439 — Coed
Affiliation or Control: United Methodist — IRS Status: 501(c)3
Highest Offering: Baccalaureate
Program: Liberal Arts And General
Accreditation: SC, SW

01 President ... Dr. Jennifer L. BRAATEN
05 VP for Academic Affairs ... Dr. Gail SUMMER
10 VP for Business and Finance ... Mr. Chris BURNLEY
30 Vice Pres Institutional Advancement ... Mrs. Kimberly P. BLAIR
84 Vice Pres Enrollment Services ... Dr. Douglas E. CLARK
32 Vice President of Student Affairs ... Dr. Andrea P. ZUSCHIN
42 Dean of Chapel ... Dr. Jan C. NICHOLSON-ANGLE
04 Presidential Assistant ... Ms. Courtney L. BROWN
06 Registrar ... Mrs. Yvonne S. WALKER
84 Assoc VP for Enrollment Mgmt ... Mrs. Gilda Q. WOODS
09 Director of Inst Research ... Mrs. Ursa JOHNSON
08 Director Stanley Library ... Ms. Brandi PORTER
37 Director of Financial Aid ... Ms. Heather HOLLANDSWORTH
29 Director Alumni & Family Programs ... Mrs. Tracy S. HOLLEY
26 Director of Public Relations ... Vacant
41 Director of Athletics ... Mr. J. Abraham NAFF
44 Regional Gift Officer ... Mr. Gene BOURNE
18 Director of Physical Plant ... Mr. Sam E. MORAN
88 Dir Student Leadership & Engagement ... Mr. David A. NEWCOMBE
13 Dir of Network & Computer Svcs ... Mr. Daniel K. HODGES
15 Dir of Human Resources ... Mr. Chris CHANDLER
40 Bookstore Manager ... Ms. Patty SIGMON
19 Chief of Ferrum College Police Dept ... Lt. J. F. OWENS
36 Dir Career Svcs/Student Employment ... Mr. Roland WALTERS
88 Director of Academic Accessibility ... Ms. Nancy S. BEACH
91 Dir Administrative Computing ... Mr. Tim BELCHER
28 Asst Dir Stdnt Leadership/Engage ... Mr. Justin MUSE
79 Dean School Arts & Humanities ... Dr. David B. HOWELL
81 Dean School Natural Science & Math ... Dr. Jason POWELL
83 Dean School Social Sciences ... Dr. Kevin REILLY

Fortis College (I)

6300 Center Drive, Building 22, Norfolk VA 23502

County: Independent City — FICE Identification: 023427
Unit ID: 233329
Telephone: (757) 499-5447 — Carnegie Class: Assoc/PrivFP
FAX Number: N/A — Calendar System: Quarter
URL: www.fortis.edu/campuses
Established: — Annual Undergrad Tuition & Fees: $18,342
Enrollment: 315 — Coed
Affiliation or Control: Proprietary — IRS Status: Proprietary
Highest Offering: Associate Degree
Program: Occupational
Accreditation: ACICS

01 President ... Ms. Darleen CERNOCH

Fortis College (J)

2000 Westmoreland Street, Suite A, Richmond VA 23230
Telephone: (804) 323-1020 — Identification: 770815
Accreditation: ACICS, DA, SURGT

† Branch campus of Fortis College, Norfolk, VA.

George Mason University (K)

4400 University Drive - MSN 3A1, Fairfax VA 22030-4444

County: Fairfax — FICE Identification: 003749
Unit ID: 232186
Telephone: (703) 993-1000 — Carnegie Class: RU/H
FAX Number: N/A — Calendar System: Semester
URL: www.gmu.edu
Established: 1957 — Annual Undergrad Tuition & Fees (In-State): $10,952
Enrollment: 33,723 — Coed
Affiliation or Control: State — IRS Status: 501(c)3

Highest Offering: Doctorate
Program: Liberal Arts And General; Teacher Preparatory; Professional
Accreditation: SC, ART, BUS, BUSA, CAATE, CEA, CLPSY, CS, ENG, EXSC, HSA, IPSY, LAW, MUS, NRPA, NURSE, PH, SPAA, SW, TED

01 President .... Dr. Ángel CABRERA
100 Chief of Staff .... Mr. Frank NEVILLE
05 Provost & Executive Vice President .... Dr. David WU
10 Vice Pres Finance/Administration .... Ms. Jennifer (J.J.) DAVIS
07 Vice Pres Enrollment Management .... Mr. David BURGE
18 Vice President for Facilities .... Mr. Thomas G. CALHOUN
86 VP Government & Community Relations .... Mr. Paul LIBERTY
30 VP Univ Advancement & Alumni Rels .... Ms. Janet BINGHAM
13 VP Information Tech/CIO .... Ms. Marilyn SMITH
32 Vice President for University Life .... Ms. Rose PASCARELL
46 Interim VP Research/Economic Dev . Dr. Claudio CIOFFI-REVILLA
22 VP Compliance/Diversity & Ethics .... Mr. Julian WILLIAMS
15 VP for HR/Payroll & Fac/Staff Life .... Ms. Linda HARBER
43 University Counsel .... Mr. Thomas M. MONCURE
45 Chief Budget Officer .... Mr. David MOORE
21 VP & Controller Fiscal Services .... Ms. Lisa KEMP
20 Vice Provost Academic Affairs .... Dr. Michelle MARKS
20 Assoc Prov for Undergrad Education .... Dr. Janette MUIR
84 Assoc Prov for Enroll Plng & Admin .... Ms. Renate H. GUILFORD
58 Assoc Prov for Graduate Education .... Dr. Cody EDWARDS
35 Exec Dir Ofc of Student Involvement .... Ms. Lauren LONG
35 Assistant Vice Pres University Life .... Ms. Jana HURLEY
06 Registrar .... Ms. Eve DAUER
37 Director Student Financial Aid .... Vacant
36 Director University Career Services .... Ms. Christine Y. CRUZVERGARA
08 University Librarian .... Mr. John G. ZENELIS
23 Exec Director Student Health Svcs .... Dr. Wagida A. ABDALLA
29 Assoc VP Alumni Affairs .... Ms. Christine CLARK-TALLEY
41 Dir of Intercollegiate Athletics .... Mr. Brad EDWARDS
19 Dir & Chief of University Police .... Mr. Eric HEATH
49 Dean Col of Humanities/Social Sci ... Dr. Deborah BOEHM-DAVIS
61 Dean School of Law .... Dr. Henry BUTLER
80 Acting Dean School of Policy/Govt .... Dr. Mark ROZELL
50 Dean School of Business .... Dr. Sarah NUTTER
53 Dean College of Educ & Human Devel ..... Dr. Mark R. GINSBERG
54 Dean Volgenau School of Engineering .... Dr. Kenneth BALL
66 Dean College of Health/Human Svcs ... Dr. Thomas R. PROHASKA
81 Dean College of Science .... Dr. Peggy AGOURIS
88 Dean Sch Conflict/Anal & Resol .... Dr. Kevin AVRUCH
88 Dean CVPA/Exec Dir HPAC .... Dr. Rick DAVIS
38 Exec Dir Counseling Center .... Dr. Barbara MEEHAN
09 Assoc Prov Institutional Research .... Ms. Kris M. SMITH
96 Director of Purchasing and AP .... Mr. Cliff SHORE
04 Director of Presidential Admin .... Ms. Sharon CULLEN
101 Secretary pro tem Institution/Board .... Ms. Kathy CAGLE
39 Director Student Housing .... Ms. Denise TAYLOR
104 Assc Provost International Programs .... Dr. Yehuda LUKACS
108 Acting Dir Institutional Assessment .... Dr. Stephanie HAZEL
25 Asc VP Rsrch Ops Ofc Sponsored Pgms .... Mr. Mike LASKOFSKI
26 VP Communications & Marketing .... Ms. Renell WYNN
44 Director Annual Giving .... Mr. Nick HERMAN

Global Health College (A)

6101 Stevenson Avenue, Alexandria VA 22304
County: Independent City FICE Identification: 041400
Unit ID: 455390
Telephone: (703) 212-7410 Carnegie Class: Assoc/PrivFP
FAX Number: (703) 212-7414 Calendar System: Other
URL: www.global.edu
Established: 2004 Annual Undergrad Tuition & Fees: $20,338
Enrollment: 361 Coed
Affiliation or Control: Proprietary IRS Status: Proprietary
Highest Offering: Associate Degree
Program: Nursing Emphasis
Accreditation: ACICS

01 President .... Mariatu KARGBO
10 Vice Pres Administration/Fiscal Svc .... Bernard FRISBY

Hampden-Sydney College (B)

College Road, PO Box 128,
Hampden-Sydney VA 23943-0667
County: Prince Edward FICE Identification: 003713
Unit ID: 232256
Telephone: (434) 223-6000 Carnegie Class: Bac/A&S
FAX Number: (434) 223-6350 Calendar System: Semester
URL: www.hsc.edu
Established: 1775 Annual Undergrad Tuition & Fees: $39,920
Enrollment: 1,105 Male
Affiliation or Control: Presbyterian Church (U.S.A.) IRS Status: 501(c)3
Highest Offering: Baccalaureate
Program: Liberal Arts And General; Religious Emphasis
Accreditation: SC

01 President .... Dr. Christopher B. HOWARD
04 Special Asst to the President .... Mr. Warren H. BROWN
05 Provost & Dean of the Faculty .... Dr. Dennis G. STEVENS
10 VP Business Affairs & Finance .... Mr. W. Glenn CULLEY, JR.
30 VP Institutional Advancement .... Dr. H. Lee KING, JR.
11 VP Strategy/Admin & Board Affairs .... Dr. V. Dale JONES
07 Dean of Admissions .... Ms. Anita H. GARLAND
32 Dean of Students .... Dr. David A. KLEIN
20 Associate Dean Academic Success .... Ms. Lisa A. BURNS
41 Director of Athletics .... Mr. Richard P. EPPERSON, II
08 Director of the Library & Computing .... Dr. Cyrus I. DILLON, III
06 Registrar .... Ms. Dawn L. CONGLETON
37 Director of Financial Aid .... Ms. Zita M. BARREE
29 Director of Alumni Relations .... Mr. James E. BARTON
18 Director of Physical Plant .... Mr. John C. PRENGAMAN
36 Dir Career Ed/Vocational Reflection .... Ms. Ellen Lea MASTERS
23 Director of Student Health Center .... Ms. Margaret P. GRAHAM
15 Director of Human Resources .... Ms. Barbara S. ARMENTROUT
19 Dir Public Safety/Chief of Police .... Mr. Jeffrey S. BROWN
40 Bookstore Manager .... Ms. Kimberly S. MICHAUX
09 Assoc Dean Inst Effectiveness .... Dr. Christine C. ROSS
26 Director Communications & Marketing .... Mr. Thomas H. SHOMO
21 Controller .... Mr. Michael A. SMITH
35 Dir of Student Affairs Operations .... Ms. Sandy P. COOKE
39 Director of Residence Life .... Mr. John R C. RAMSAY
25 Director Grants & Special Projects .... Mrs. Eunice W. CARWILE
104 Dir Global Education & Study Abroad ...... Dr. Daniella WIDDOWS

Hampton University (C)

100 E. Queen Street, Hampton VA 23668
County: Independent City FICE Identification: 003714
Unit ID: 232265
Telephone: (757) 727-5000 Carnegie Class: Master's M
FAX Number: (757) 727-5085 Calendar System: Semester
URL: www.hamptonu.edu
Established: 1868 Annual Undergrad Tuition & Fees: $22,850
Enrollment: 4,400 Coed
Affiliation or Control: Independent Non-Profit IRS Status: 501(c)3
Highest Offering: Doctorate
Program: Liberal Arts And General; Teacher Preparatory; Professional
Accreditation: SC, AAB, CACREP, CS, ENG, IACBE, JOUR, MUS, NURSE, PHAR, PTA, SP, TED

01 President .... Dr. William R. HARVEY
05 Executive Vice President & Provost .... Dr. JoAnn W. HAYSBERT
10 Vice Pres Business Affs/Treasurer .... Mrs. Doretha J. SPELLS
11 Vice Pres for Administrative Svcs .... Dr. Barbara L. INMAN
43 Vice President/General Counsel .... Atty. Faye HARDY-LUCAS
30 Vice President for Development .... Mrs. Iris RAMEY
04 Executive Assistant to President .... Dr. Charrita D. DANLEY
31 Assoc Vice Pres External Relations .... Mrs. Joy JEFFERSON
32 Assoc Vice Pres for Student Affairs .... Vacant
21 Asst VP Business Affs/Comptroller .... Mrs. Denise NICHOLS
25 Asst Vice Pres Grants Management .... Mrs. Lillie F. GREEN
20 Asst Provost Academic Affairs .... Dr. Pollie MURPHY
13 Assistant Provost Technology .... Dr. Trina COLEMAN
26 Asst VP for Marketing .... Ms. B. DaVida PLUMMER
45 Asst Prov Research & Grantsmanship .... Dr. Michelle PENN-MARSHALL
33 Dean of Men .... Mr. Woodson H. HOPEWELL, JR.
34 Dean of Women .... Miss Jewel B. LONG
07 Dean of Admissions .... Mrs. Angela BOYD
06 Registrar .... Mrs. Jorsene COOPER
36 Dir Career Counsel/Planning Ctr .... Mrs. Vivian DAVID
38 Int Director Counseling Center ...... Dr. Linda KIRKLAND-HARRIS
08 Administrator University Libraries .... Vacant
29 Director of Alumni Affairs .... Mrs. Sharon FITZGERALD
15 Director of Human Resources .... Ms. Rikki THOMAS
14 Director Computer Center .... Mr. Ronnie JEFFERSON
37 Financial Aid Officer .... Mr. Martin MILES
26 Director of University Relations .... Mrs. Yuri Rodgers MILLIGAN
09 Director Institutional Research .... Mrs. Michelle CLAWSON
23 Director Student Health Services .... Dr. Bert HOLMES
42 University Chaplain .... Rev. Debra L. HAGGINS
18 Director Buildings & Grounds .... Mr. Randall HARDY
87 Director of Summer Sessions .... Dr. Pollie MURPHY
19 Chief of Campus Police .... Mr. David GLOVER
86 Director Government Relations .... Mr. Wilbert L. THOMAS
96 Director of Purchasing .... Vacant
40 University Bookstore Manager .... Ms. Michelle R. MILLER
53 Dean School of Liberal Arts .... Dr. Linda MALONE-COLON
66 Interim Dean School of Nursing .... Dr. Hilda WILLIAMSON
81 Assistant Dean School of Science .... Dr. Michelle CLAVILLE
51 Dean Sch Educ/Human Development ...... Dr. Cassandra HERRING
50 Dean School of Business .... Dr. Sid H. CREDLE
54 Dean Sch of Engineering/Technology .... Dr. Eric J. SHEPPARD
67 Dean School of Pharmacy .... Dr. Wayne HARRIS
58 Dean the Graduate College .... Dr. Patrena N. BENTON
60 Dean Scripps Howard Sch Journ/Comm .... Mr. Brett PULLEY
88 Dean University College .... Dr. Almarie MUNLEY

Hollins University (D)

PO Box 9688, Roanoke VA 24020-1688
County: Roanoke FICE Identification: 003715
Unit ID: 232308
Telephone: (540) 362-6000 Carnegie Class: Bac/A&S
FAX Number: (540) 362-6642 Calendar System: 4/1/4
URL: www.hollins.edu
Established: 1842 Annual Undergrad Tuition & Fees: $35,000
Enrollment: 769 Female
Affiliation or Control: Independent Non-Profit IRS Status: 501(c)3
Highest Offering: Master's
Program: Liberal Arts And General; Teacher Preparatory
Accreditation: SC

01 President .... Ms. Nancy O. GRAY
10 Vice Pres Finance/Administration .... Ms. Kerry EDMONDS
30 Vice Pres for External Relations .... Ms. Audrey STONE
84 Vice President of Enrollment .... Vacant
05 Chair of the Faculty .... Mr. Michael GETTINGS
32 Dean of Students .... Ms. Patty O'TOOLE
84 Sr Director Enrollment Management .... Ms. Nikki JOHNSON WILLIAMS
20 Dean Academic Services .... Ms. Rebecca BEACH
28 Associate Dean Intercultural Pgms .... Ms. Jeri L. SUAREZ
04 Executive Assistant to President .... Ms. Brook E. DICKSON
88 Director Alumnae & Donor Relations .... Vacant
06 Registrar .... Ms. Patricia BROKKEN
08 Director of the Library .... Mr. Luke VILELLE
15 Director of Human Resources .... Ms. Alicia GODZWA
26 Director of Public Relations .... Mr. Jeff HODGES
29 Director of Alumnae Relations .... Ms. Anna MONCURE
36 Director Career Development Center .... Ms. Ashley GLENN
37 Director Financial Aid .... Ms. Mary Jean CORRISS
41 Director of Athletics .... Ms. Teresa BOYLAN
09 Asst Dir Institutional Research .... Ms. Katie READ
18 Director Plant Operations/Services .... Ms. Mae RAMSEY
104 Director International Programs .... Ms. Kirsten MCKINNEY
13 Chief Info Technology Officer .... Ms. Carol REED
19 Director Security/Safety .... Mr. David CARLSON
39 Dir Housing & Residential Life .... Ms. Nicole SMITH

iGlobal University (E)

7700 Little River Turnpike, #600, Annandale VA 22003
County: Fairfax Identification: 667105
Telephone: (703) 941-2020 Carnegie Class: Not Classified
FAX Number: (703) 941-2025 Calendar System: Quarter
URL: www.iglobaluniversity.org
Established: 2008 Annual Undergrad Tuition & Fees: $13,820
Enrollment: 173 Coed
Affiliation or Control: Proprietary IRS Status: Proprietary
Highest Offering: Master's
Program: Business Emphasis
Accreditation: ACICS

01 President & CEO .... Dr. David Y. SOHN

Institute for the Psychological Sciences (F)

2001 Jefferson Davis Hwy, Ste 511,
Arlington VA 22202-3609
County: Arlington FICE Identification: 038724
Unit ID: 445869
Telephone: (703) 416-1441 Carnegie Class: Spec/Health
FAX Number: (703) 416-8588 Calendar System: Semester
URL: www.ipsciences.edu
Established: 1998 Annual Graduate Tuition & Fees: $31,434
Enrollment: 82 Coed
Affiliation or Control: Independent Non-Profit IRS Status: 501(c)3
Highest Offering: Doctorate; No Undergraduates
Program: Professional; Technical Emphasis
Accreditation: SC

00 President Emeritus .... Rev. John HOPKINS, LC
01 President .... Rev. Charles SIKORSKY, LC
30 VP for Advancement .... Rev. Edward MORAN
05 VP for Academic and Student Affairs .... Rev. Robert PERSUTTI
32 Associate VP for Student Affairs .... Ms. Tambi SPITZ
45 VP for Institutional Effectiveness .... Ms. Laura TUCKER
20 Academic Dean/Chair .... Dr. William NORDLING
06 Registrar .... Ms. Jennifer E. KARNS
106 Director of Distance Education .... Dr. Stephen GRUNDMAN
37 Financial Aid Officer .... Mr. Jeffrey ELLIOTT
10 Chief Business Officer .... Mrs. Marie STIEGMEIER
42 Chaplain .... Fr. John PIETROPAULI
28 Director of Diversity .... Dr. Sue HOLLOMAN
84 Director Enrollment Management .... Ms. Jenny KARNES

ITT Technical Institute (G)

14420 Albemarle Point Pl, Suite 100,
Chantilly VA 20151-1750
Telephone: (703) 263-2541 Identification: 666324
Accreditation: ACICS

† Branch campus of ITT Technical Institute, Indianapolis, IN.

ITT Technical Institute (H)

5425 Robin Hood Road, Suite 100, Norfolk VA 23513
Telephone: (757) 466-1260 Identification: 666555
Accreditation: ACICS

† Branch campus of ITT Technical Institute, Indianapolis, IN.

ITT Technical Institute (I)

300 Gateway Centre Parkway, Richmond VA 23235-5139
Telephone: (804) 330-4992 Identification: 666040
Accreditation: ACICS

† Branch campus of ITT Technical Institute, Indianapolis, IN.

ITT Technical Institute (J)

2159 Apperson Drive, Salem VA 24153
Telephone: (540) 989-2500 Identification: 770664
Accreditation: ACICS

† Branch campus of ITT Technical Institute, Indianapolis, IN.

ITT Technical Institute (A)
7300 Boston Boulevard, Springfield VA 22153-2804
Telephone: (703) 440-9535 Identification: 666321
Accreditation: ACICS

† Branch campus of ITT Technical Institute, Indianapolis, IN.

Ivy Christian College (B)
9401 Mathy Drive, Ste 200, Fairfax VA 22031
County: Fairfax Identification: 667213
Telephone: (703) 425-4143 Carnegie Class: Not Classified
FAX Number: (703) 425-4148 Calendar System: Quarter
URL: www.iccvau.org
Established: 2006 Annual Undergrad Tuition & Fees: $5,760
Enrollment: N/A Coed
Affiliation or Control: Independent Non-Profit IRS Status: 501(c)3
Highest Offering: Baccalaureate
Program: 2-Year Principally Bachelor's Creditable; Religious Emphasis
Accreditation: @TRACS

01 President .... Dr. David Y. PAK
05 Academic Dean .... Dr. Chang K. KIM

James Madison University (C)
800 S Main Street, Harrisonburg VA 22807-0001
County: Independent City FICE Identification: 003721
Unit ID: 232423
Telephone: (540) 568-6211 Carnegie Class: Master's L
FAX Number: N/A Calendar System: Semester
URL: www.jmu.edu
Established: 1908 Annual Undergrad Tuition & Fees (In-State): $10,018
Enrollment: 20,855 Coed
Affiliation or Control: State IRS Status: 501(c)3
Highest Offering: Doctorate
Program: Liberal Arts And General; Teacher Preparatory; Professional
Accreditation: SC, ARCPA, ART, AUD, BUS, BUSA, CAATE, CACREP, CS, DANCE, DIETD, ENGR, ENGT, IPSY, MUS, NURSE, OT, PSPSY, SP, SPAA, SW, TED, THEA

01 President .... Mr. Jonathan R. ALGER
05 Provost/Senior VP Academic Affairs .... Dr. Jerry BENSON
10 Sr Vice Pres Administration/Finance .... Mr. Charles W. KING
32 Sr VP Student Affairs/Univ Planning .... Dr. Mark J. WARNER
30 Vice Pres University Advancement .... Dr. Nick LANGRIDGE
84 VP Access and Enrollment Mgmt .... Ms. Donna L. HARPER
04 Exec Assistant to the President .Mrs. Maggie BURKHART-EVANS
81 Dean College Science/Math .... Dr. David F. BRAKKE
49 Dean College Arts/Letters .... Dr. David K. JEFFREY
76 Dean Col of Health & Behav Studies .... Dr. Sharon LOVELL
50 Dean College of Business .... Dr. Mary GOWAN
57 Dean College Visual Performing Arts .... Dr. George E. SPARKS
53 Dean College of Education .... Dr. Phillip M. WISHON
72 Dean College of Int Science & Engr .... Dr. Robert KOLVOORD
58 Interim Dean Graduate School .... Dr. Melissa C. ALEMAN
97 Dean University Studies .... Dr. Linda C. HALPERN
08 Dean of Libraries/Educ Technologies .... Dr. Adam A. MURRAY
43 University Counsel .... Ms. Susan L. WHEELER
45 Asst Vice Pres Budget Management .... Ms. Diane L. STAMP
07 Dean of Admissions .... Mr. Michael D. WALSH
37 Dir Financial Aid & Scholarships .... Ms. Lisa L. TUMER
15 Director Human Resources .... Ms. Diane YERIAN
09 Director Institutional Research .... Dr. Frank J. DOHERTY
41 Director of Athletics .... Mr. Jeffrey T. BOURNE
26 Acting Dir Comm & Univ Spokesperson .... Mr. Bill J. WYATT
06 University Registrar .... Ms. Michele M. WHITE
19 Chief of Police .... Mr. Lee A. SHIFFLETT
22 Dir of EEO .... Mr. James R. ROBINSON
29 Director Alumni Relations .... Ms. Ashley E. PRIVOTT
27 Senior Marketing Director .... Mr. David TAYLOR

Jefferson College of Health Sciences (D)
101 Elm Avenue S.E., Roanoke VA 24013
County: Independent City FICE Identification: 006622
Unit ID: 231837
Telephone: (540) 985-8483 Carnegie Class: Spec/Health
FAX Number: (540) 985-9773 Calendar System: Semester
URL: www.jchs.edu
Established: 1982 Annual Undergrad Tuition & Fees: $24,000
Enrollment: 1,131 Coed
Affiliation or Control: Independent Non-Profit IRS Status: 501(c)3
Highest Offering: Master's
Program: Professional; Nursing Emphasis
Accreditation: SC, ARCPA, COARC, EMT, MT, NURSE, OT, OTA, PTAA

01 President .... Dr. Nathaniel L. BISHOP
05 Dean Academic Affairs .... Dr. Lisa ALLISON-JONES
10 Dean Administrative Services .... Ms. Anna S. MILLIRONS
32 Dean Student Affairs .... Mr. Scott HILL
18 Safety/Physical Plant Officer .... Ms. Susan L. BOOTH
108 Assoc Dean for Inst Effectiveness .... Dr. Glen R. MAYHEW
84 Sr Director Enrollment Management .... Ms. Connie S. COOK
30 Director of Development .... Mr. Erik W. WILLIAMS
49 Chair Arts & Sciences .... Dr. Francis C. DANE
88 Chair Community Health Sciences .... Dr. Sharon L. HATFIELD
66 Chair Nursing .... Dr. Ava G. PORTER
88 Chair Rehab/Wellness .... Dr. Glen R. MAYHEW
88 Program Dir Physician Assistant .... Dr. Patricia J. AIREY
88 Program Dir Health & Exercise Sci .. Dr. Allison H. BOWERSOCK
88 Program Dir Emergency Services .... Mr. John C. COOK
88 Director Biomed/Science/Math .... Dr. Robin L. DAVIES
88 Program Dir Physical Therapy Asst .... Ms. Rebecca DUFF
88 Program Dir Occ Therapy Masters .... Dr. David A. HAYNES
79 Director Humanities & Soc Sciences .... Dr. Anthony L. LACK
88 Program Dir Medical Lab Science .... Ms. Laura R. LINK
88 Program Dir Occ Therapy Assistant .... Ms. Ave M. MITTA
88 Progr Dir Family Nurse Practitioner .... Dr. Rhoda R. MURRAY
88 Program Dir Healthcare Managemnt BS .. Ms. Carey H. PEERMAN
88 Program Dir Respiratory Therapy .... Dr. Chase POULSEN
88 Program Dir Surgical Technology .... Mr. John D. RATLIFF
88 Program Dir Health Psychology .... Dr. Robert C. REESE
88 Program Dir Healthcare Admn Masters .... Dr. Robert C. RIMKIS
88 Program Dir RN-to-BSN .... Dr. Milena STAYKOVA
88 Program Dir MS Nursing .... Dr. Patty M. VARI
88 Director InterProfessional Educ .... Ms. Whiter KIM
88 Program Dir Health Sciences .... Dr. Diana L. WILLEMAN-BUCKELEW
88 Program Dir Accelerated/Trad BSN .... Dr. Kimberly X. WILSON
21 Bursar .... Ms. Tonia Y. ANDREWS
40 Manager Bookstore .... Ms. Suzanne M. ANDERSON
35 Coordinator Student Affairs .... Ms. Elizabeth A. COSTA
25 Sponsored Projects Coordinator .... Ms. Amanda M. ELLINGER
04 Admin Secretary to President .... Ms. Dorothy J. HALL
37 Director of Financial Aid .... Ms. Debra J. JOHNSON
26 Coord Communications/Col Relations .... Mr. Mark A. LAMBERT
07 Director of Admissions .... Ms. Judith O. MCKEON
09 Institutional Research Director .... Dr. Timothy R. MILLARD
88 Director of Academic Advising .... Mr. Al W. OVERSTREET
39 Residence Life Coordinator .... Ms. Stephanie SIMPSON
38 Director Counseling and Wellness .... Dr. Jennifer J. SLUSHER
08 Director Library .... Ms. Ramona H. THISS
106 Dir Online & Continuing Education .... Ms. Margie B. VEST
06 Registrar .... Ms. Linda C. WILLIAMS
88 Disability Services Coordinator .... Ms. Katie WINTERS
15 HR Coordinator .... Ms. Kathy E. YORK

The John Leland Center for Theological Studies (E)
1306 N Highland Street, Arlington VA 22201
County: Arlington Identification: 666340
Telephone: (703) 812-4757 Carnegie Class: Not Classified
FAX Number: (703) 812-4764 Calendar System: Other
URL: www.leland.edu
Established: 1998 Annual Graduate Tuition & Fees: $11,620
Enrollment: 75 Coed
Affiliation or Control: Baptist IRS Status: 501(c)3
Highest Offering: Master's; No Undergraduates
Program: Religious Emphasis
Accreditation: THEOL

01 President .... Dr. Mark J. OLSON
05 Academic Dean .... Dr. John LEE
04 Exec Assistant to the President .... Ms. Lindsey PEREZ
08 Librarian .... Ms. Monica LEAK
06 Registrar .... Ms. Andrea BAKKE
07 Director Recruiting/Admissions .... Ms. Debbie WESLEY
10 Chief Business Officer .... Mr. Mel HARRIS
21 Associate Business Officer .... Mr. Jonathan RIDER
26 Chief Public Relations Officer .... Ms. Debbie WESLEY

Kings Park University (F)
4613-D Pinecrest Office Park Dr, Alexandria VA 22312
County: Fairfax Identification: 667158
Telephone: (703) 354-3533 Carnegie Class: Not Classified
FAX Number: (703) 354-3577 Calendar System: Trimester
URL: www.kpu.us
Established: 2000 Annual Graduate Tuition & Fees: $9,500
Enrollment: N/A Coed
Affiliation or Control: Independent Non-Profit IRS Status: 501(c)3
Highest Offering: Master's; No Undergraduates
Program: Professional; Technical Emphasis
Accreditation: @ACUP

01 President .... Rev. Tae JONG PARK

Liberty University (G)
1971 University Boulevard, Lynchburg VA 24515
County: Independent City FICE Identification: 020530
Unit ID: 232557
Telephone: (434) 582-2000 Carnegie Class: Master's L
FAX Number: (434) 582-2304 Calendar System: Semester
URL: www.liberty.edu
Established: 1971 Annual Undergrad Tuition & Fees: $21,300
Enrollment: 81,459 Coed
Affiliation or Control: Other IRS Status: 501(c)3
Highest Offering: Doctorate
Program: 2-Year Principally Bachelor's Creditable; Liberal Arts And General; Teacher Preparatory; Professional
Accreditation: SC, ACBSP, CAATE, CACREP, CS, ENG, EXSC, LAW, NURSE, @OSTEO, TED

01 President .... Mr. Jerry FALWELL, JR.
05 Provost .... Dr. Ronald E. HAWKINS
10 Chief Financial Officer .... Mr. Don MOON
32 Sr Vice President Student Affairs .... Dr. Mark L. HINE
15 Vice President Human Resources .... Mrs. Laura J. WALLACE
88 Vice Pres for Spiritual Development .... Mr. David NASSER
45 AVP for Institutional Effectiveness .... Dr. H. William WHEELER
13 Chief Information Officer .... Mr. Matthew J. ZEALAND
06 Registrar .... Mr. Luke GENTALA
84 Vice Pres Enrollment Management .... Mr. Chris JOHNSON
07 Director of Resident Admissions .... Mr. Terry ELAM
29 Director of Alumni Affairs .... Mr. Tyler FALWELL
08 Dean Jerry Falwell Library .... Ms. Angela RICE
42 Acting Dean of the Seminary .... Dr. David HIRSCHMAN
86 Dean Helms School of Government .... Mr. Shawn D. AKERS
37 Vice President of Financial Aid .... Dr. Robert L. RITZ
31 VP Community Relations .... Dr. Barry MOORE
88 Executive VP for Special Projects .... Mr. Chris KENNEDY
88 VP Special Proj & Bus Development .... Mr. Chris CARROLL
41 Director of Athletics .... Mr. Jeff BARBER
49 Dean College of Arts & Sciences .... Dr. Roger D. SCHULTZ
50 Dean School of Business .... Dr. Scott M. HICKS
60 Dean School of Communication .... Dr. Norm MINTLE
97 Dean Ctr Acad Support/Adv Svcs .... Dr. Brian YATES
73 Dean School of Religion .... Dr. Ed HINDSON
53 Dean School of Education .... Dr. Karen L. PARKER
35 Director of Campus Recreation .... Mr. Chris MISIANO
18 Vice Pres of Field Operations .... Mr. Scott STARNES
19 Chief of Police LUPD .... Col. Richard HINKLEY
72 Dean School of Engineering and CSCI .... Mr. David DONAHOO
28 Dir Ctr for Multicltrl Enrichment .... Ms. Melany PEARL
106 Exec Director Online Programs .... Mrs. Tamela CRICKENBERGER
88 Dean Academic Admin Graduate School ..... Dr. Kevin D. CORSINI
61 Interim Dean School of Law .... Ms. Rena LINDEVALDSEN
88 Dean School of Aeronautics .... Mr. David L. YOUNG
88 Dir Center for Teaching Excellence .... Mrs. Sharon WHEELER
97 Dean College of General Studies .... Dr. Emily HEADY
88 Dean English Language Institute .... Dr. Bill WEGERT
58 Dean Graduate School .... Dr. Doug MANN
76 Dean School of Health Sciences .... Dr. Ralph LINSTRA
63 Dean College of Osteopathic Med .... Dr. Ronnie MARTIN
64 Dean School of Music .... Dr. Vernon WHALEY
88 Admin Dean Undergraduate Programs .... Dr. Ben GUTIERREZ
35 Dean of Students .... Mr. Robert MULLEN
88 Director of Risk Management .... Mr. Robert WELLS
66 Dean School of Nursing .... Dr. Dea BRITT

Longwood University (H)
201 High Street, Farmville VA 23909-1801
County: Prince Edward FICE Identification: 003719
Unit ID: 232566
Telephone: (434) 395-2000 Carnegie Class: Master's M
FAX Number: (434) 395-2635 Calendar System: Semester
URL: www.longwood.edu
Established: 1839 Annual Undergrad Tuition & Fees (In-State): $11,910
Enrollment: 5,096 Coed
Affiliation or Control: State IRS Status: 501(c)3
Highest Offering: Master's
Program: Liberal Arts And General; Teacher Preparatory; Professional
Accreditation: SC, BUS, CAATE, EXSC, MUS, NRPA, NURSE, SP, SW, TED, THEA

01 President .... Mr. W. Taylor REVELEY, IV
05 Provost/Vice Pres Academic Affairs .... Dr. Joan NEFF
10 Vice Pres Administration & Finance .... Mr. Kenneth COPELAND
32 Vice President for Student Affairs .... Dr. Tim J. PIERSON
86 VP for Commonwealth Relations .... Ms. Courtney HODGES
45 VP for Strategic Operations .... Ms. Victoria KINDON
13 Chief Information Officer .... Ms. Victoria KINDON
84 Assoc VP Enrollment Management .... Dr. Jennifer K. GREEN
26 Assoc VP Publ/Mktg/Communications .... Ms. Sabrina BROWN
07 Dean of Admissions .... Vacant
09 Director Assessment & Inst Research .... Dr. Ling Y. WHITWORTH
06 Registrar .... Ms. Vikki LEVINE
08 Dean of Library .... Mrs. Suzy SZASZ-PALMER
29 Assistant VP for Alumni Relations .... Mr. Ryan CATHERWOOD
28 Dir Citizen Ldrshp/Soc Justice Educ .... Mr. Jonathan E. PAGE
38 Director Student Counseling .... Dr. Maureen J. WALLS-MCKAY
36 Director University Career Center .... Ms. Mary M. SAUNDERS
37 Director Student Financial Aid .... Ms. Melissa D. SHEPHERD
15 Chief Human Resources Officer .... Ms. Della H. WICKIZER
18 Dir Facilities Operations Services .... Mr. Alvin B. MYERS
96 Director of Materiel Management .... Ms. Cathryn B. MOBLEY
100 Chief of Staff .... Mr. Justin POPE
41 Athletic Director .... Mr. Troy AUSTIN

Lynchburg College (I)
1501 Lakeside Drive, Lynchburg VA 24501-3199
County: Independent City FICE Identification: 003720
Unit ID: 232609
Telephone: (434) 544-8100 Carnegie Class: Master's S
FAX Number: (434) 544-8499 Calendar System: Semester
URL: www.lynchburg.edu
Established: 1903 Annual Undergrad Tuition & Fees: $35,075
Enrollment: 2,736 Coed
Affiliation or Control: Christian Church (Disciples Of Christ)
IRS Status: 501(c)3
Highest Offering: Doctorate
Program: Liberal Arts And General; Teacher Preparatory; Professional
Accreditation: SC, ACBSP, #ARCPA, CAATE, CACREP, EXSC, MUS, NURSE, PTA

01 President .... Dr. Kenneth R. GARREN
05 Vice Pres & Dean for Academic Affs .... Dr. Julius A. SIGLER

10 Vice President Business & Finance .... Mr. Steve BRIGHT
30 Vice Pres Advancement .... Ms. Denise MCDONALD
84 Vice Pres Enrollment Management .... Mrs. Rita DETWILER
32 Vice Pres & Dean of Student Develop .... Mr. John G. ECCLES
09 Vice Pres Institutional Research .... Mrs. Debbie DRISCOLL
50 Dean School Business & Economics .... Dr. Joseph TUREK
53 Dean School Education/Human Devel .... Dr. Roger JONES
60 Dean Sch Communications & The Arts .... Dr. Oeida HATCHER
79 Dean Sch Humanities/Social Science .... Dr. Charles WATSON
81 Dean School of Sciences .... Dr. Barry LOBB
76 Dean Sch Health Science/Human Perf .... Dr. Jean ST. CLAIR
06 Registrar/Asst Dean Acad/Stndt Info .... Mr. Jay K. WEBB
08 Director of the Library .. Mr. Christopher A. MILLSON-MARTULA
37 Director of Financial Aid .... Ms. Michelle DAVIS
26 Dir of Marketing/Communications .. Ms. Deborah P. BLANCHARD
07 Director of Admissions .... Ms. Sharon WALTERS-BOWER

Mary Baldwin College (A)

318 Prospect Street, Staunton VA 24401
County: Augusta FICE Identification: 003723
Unit ID: 232672
Telephone: (540) 887-7000 Carnegie Class: Master's S
FAX Number: (540) 886-5561 Calendar System: Other
URL: www.mbc.edu
Established: 1842 Annual Undergrad Tuition & Fees: $30,331
Enrollment: 1,754 Female
Affiliation or Control: Presbyterian Church (U.S.A.) IRS Status: 501(c)3
Highest Offering: Doctorate
Program: Liberal Arts And General; Teacher Preparatory
Accreditation: SC, @PTA, SW, TEAC

01 President .... Dr. Pamela FOX
05 VP Academic Affairs/Dean .... Dr. Catharine O'CONNELL
10 Exec Vice President Finance/Admin .... Mr. David MOWEN
84 VP Enrollment Mgmt .... Ms. Lois H. WILLIAMS
30 Vice Pres Institutional Advancement .... Ms. Sherri MYLOTT
26 Vice Pres Comm/Mktg/Public Rels .... Ms. Crista CABE
76 VP of MDCHS .... Dr. Linda SEESTEDT-STANFORD
88 Assoc VP for Inclusive Excellence .... Rev. Andrea CORNELL-SCOTT
88 Commandant VWIL/Spec Asst to Pres .... BGen. Teresa A. DJURIC
88 Dir of Accred/Spec Asst to Pres .... Dr. Lewis D. ASKEGAARD
58 Dir of ADP/Assoc DOC .... Ms. Lallon POND
09 Dir of Inst Research & Assessment .... Ms. Christy COLE
13 Chief Information Officer .... Mr. Angus MCQUEEN
06 Registrar .... Ms. Kimberlely D. ROBINSON
08 Director of Library .... Ms. Carol CREAGER
53 Dean of College of Education .... Dr. Rachel POTTER
57 Director MLitt/MFA .... Dr. Paul MENZER
88 Dir Program for Exception Gifted .... Vacant
15 Director of Human Resources .... Ms. Shelly IRVINE
32 Exec Dir Student Life/Assoc DOC .... Ms. Lisa WELLS
18 Director Facilities Management .... Mr. Brent DOUGLASS
21 Dir of Budgets/Business Operation .... Mr. Rick CZERWINSKI
29 Director of Alumni Relations .... Ms. Kim M. HUTTO
36 Director Career Development Svcs .... Vacant
37 Director of Financial Aid .... Ms. Robin DIETRICH
04 Executive Presidential Assistant .... Ms. Sharon S. BOSSERMAN
41 Athletic Director .... Ms. Sharon S. SPALDING
07 Dir of Admiss for Adult & Grad Stds .... Mr. Daryl L. KINGREY
19 Director Security/Safety .... Mr. Thomas L. BYERLY

Marymount University (B)

2807 N Glebe Road, Arlington VA 22207-4299
County: Arlington FICE Identification: 003724
Unit ID: 232706
Telephone: (703) 522-5600 Carnegie Class: Master's L
FAX Number: (703) 284-1637 Calendar System: Semester
URL: www.marymount.edu
Established: 1950 Annual Undergrad Tuition & Fees: $28,310
Enrollment: 3,441 Coed
Affiliation or Control: Roman Catholic IRS Status: 501(c)3
Highest Offering: Doctorate
Program: Liberal Arts And General; Teacher Preparatory; Professional
Accreditation: SC, ACBSP, CACREP, CAEP, CIDA, HSA, NURSE, PTA, TED

01 President .... Dr. Matthew D. SHANK
05 Provost and Vice Pres Acad Affairs .... Dr. Sherri L. HUGHES
10 Vice Pres for Financial Affairs .... Mr. Alphonso V. DIAZ
30 Vice Pres University Advancement .... Mr. Joseph FOSTER
32 Vice Pres for Student Affairs .... Dr. Linda MCMURDOCK
09 Assoc Vice Pres Planning & Inst Eff .... Mr. Michael SCHUCHERT
20 Int Assoc Vice Pres Acad Affairs .... Dr. Bridget MURPHY
84 Assoc Vice Pres Enr Mgmt & Dir Grad .... Mrs. Francesca REED
21 Asst Vice Pres and Controller .... Mr. Ronald SOMERVELL
109 Asst Vice Pres Campus Plng & Mgmt .... Mr. Upendra MALANI
08 Dean Library & Learning Services .... Dr. Zary MOSTASHARI
35 Dean Student Services .... Mrs. Christina RAJMAIRA
36 Dean Career Services & Prof Dev .... Mr. David WILMES
49 Interim Dean Arts & Sciences .... Dr. Rosemary HUBBARD
50 Dean Business Administration .... Dr. James RYERSON
53 Dean Education & Human Services .... Dr. Lois STOVER
76 Dean Health Professions .... Dr. Jeanne MATTHEWS
58 Assoc Dean for Grad & Prof Studies .... Dr. Rita WONG
89 Assoc Dean First Year Experience .... Ms. Yolanda GIBSON
06 University Registrar .... Mr. Scott SPENCER
12 Executive Director Reston Center .... Mr. Lawrence HOFFMAN
13 Exec Director IT Services .... Mr. Steve MUNSON
15 Exec Dir Human Resource Svcs .... Vacant
104 Exec Dir Center for Global Studies .... Mr. Victor BETANCOURT SANTIAGO
88 Exec Dir Ctr Teaching & Learning .... Dr. Carolyn OXENFORD
07 Director of Undergrad Admissions .... Ms. Heather RENAULT
18 Director of Physical Plant .... Mr. Richard KAHLEY
19 Dir of Campus Safety/Transportation .... Mr. Eric HOLS
23 Director Student Health Center .... Mrs. Catherine BROCKER
25 Dir Office of Sponsored Research .... Mrs. Cheryl GREEN
29 Interim Director Alumni Relations .... Mr. Jerome MARKS
31 Assoc Director Community Engagement .... Ms. Margaret DALMUT
37 Director Financial Aid .... Ms. Deborah RAINES
38 Director Student Counseling .... Ms. Natalie MITCHELL
39 Director of Campus & Residence Life .... Ms. Tina SHEPPARD
41 Director Athletics .... Ms. Jamie REYNOLDS
42 Director Campus Ministry .... Fr. Brian BASHISTA
44 Director Annual Fund .... Ms. Erin SCHLESING
71 Dir Campus Pgms & Leadership Dev .... Mr. Vincent STOVALL
85 Director International Student Svcs .... Mrs. Aline ORFALI
91 Dir of Admin Information Services .... Ms. Gale KNOEDLER
92 Director Honors Program .... Dr. David GAMMACK
105 Director Integrated Tech Solutions .... Mr. Joseph LUCKETT
106 Dir Distance Ed & Instr Design .... Dr. Susan CONRAD
108 Director Institutional Assessment .... Dr. Ann BOUDINOT-AMIN
88 Director Acad Affairs Info Systems .... Mr. Louis FRISENDA
88 Director Budget & Risk Mgmt .... Mrs. Margaret AXELROD
88 Director Enrollment Mgmt Systems .... Mrs. Sara MEEHAN
88 Director Experiential Learning .... Mr. David POMEROY
88 Director Infrastructure & Security .... Mr. David LUTES
88 Director IT Support Services .... Mr. John TAMBERT
88 Director New Student Transitions .... Vacant
88 Director Non-Profit Center .... Ms. Anne VORDERBRUEGGE
88 Dir Special Events & Conferences .... Mr. Joseph ABLAO
88 Dir Stdnt Conduct & Acad Integrity ..... Mr. Christopher FIORELLO
88 Director Student Development .... Mrs. Marjory EISENMAN
88 Director Training/Org Development .... Mrs. Bernadette COSTELLO
04 Administrative Asst to President .... Mrs. Hilary PHILLIPS
96 Coordinator of Purchasing .... Mrs. Amy PAPPAS
40 Manager B&N Bookstore .... Ms. Kandice LARGE

Medical Careers Institute (C)

1001 Omni Boulevard Suite 200,
Newport News VA 23606-4388
Telephone: (757) 873-2423 FICE Identification: 022472
Accreditation: &SC, MAAB, PTAA, RAD

† Regional accreditation is carried under the parent institution, ECPI College of Technology, in Virginia Beach, VA.

Medical Careers Institute (D)

2809 Emerywood Parkway, Suite 400,
Richmond VA 23294
Telephone: (804) 521-5999 Identification: 667038
Accreditation: &SC, MAAB

† Regional accreditation is carried under the parent institution ECPI College of Technology, Virginia Beach, VA.

Medtech College (E)

6565 Arlington Boulevard, Suite 100,
Falls Church VA 22042
County: Fairfax FICE Identification: 025889
Unit ID: 131742
Telephone: (703) 237-6200 Carnegie Class: Assoc/PrivFP
FAX Number: (703) 533-3750 Calendar System: Semester
URL: www.medtech.edu
Established: 1939 Annual Undergrad Tuition & Fees: $14,450
Enrollment: 1,371 Coed
Affiliation or Control: Proprietary IRS Status: Proprietary
Highest Offering: Associate Degree
Program: Occupational
Accreditation: COE

01 Executive Director .... Janet BARONE

Miller-Motte Technical College (F)

1011 Creekside Lane, Lynchburg VA 24502-4353
County: Lynchburg FICE Identification: 004992
Unit ID: 233091
Telephone: (434) 239-5222 Carnegie Class: Assoc/PrivFP
FAX Number: (434) 239-1069 Calendar System: Quarter
URL: www.miller-motte.edu
Established: 1997 Annual Undergrad Tuition & Fees: $9,788
Enrollment: 409 Coed
Affiliation or Control: Proprietary IRS Status: Proprietary
Highest Offering: Associate Degree
Program: Occupational; Technical Emphasis
Accreditation: ACICS, MAC, SURGT

01 Director .... Ms. Susie ROWLAND

Miller-Motte Technical College (G)

4444-A Electric Road, Roanoke VA 24018
Telephone: (540) 597-1010 Identification: 770816
Accreditation: ACICS

† Branch campus of Miller-Motte Technical College, Lynchburg, VA.

Norfolk State University (H)

700 Park Avenue, Norfolk VA 23504-8000
County: Independent City FICE Identification: 003765
Unit ID: 232937
Telephone: (757) 823-8600 Carnegie Class: Master's L
FAX Number: (757) 823-2067 Calendar System: Semester
URL: www.nsu.edu
Established: 1935 Annual Undergrad Tuition & Fees (In-State): $7,552
Enrollment: 6,027 Coed
Affiliation or Control: State IRS Status: 501(c)3
Highest Offering: Doctorate
Program: Liberal Arts And General; Teacher Preparatory; Professional
Accreditation: #SC, ADNUR, BUS, CLPSY, CS, DIETD, ENG, JOUR, KIN, MT, MUS, NAIT, NUR, SW, TED

01 Interim President .... Mr. Eddie N. MOORE, JR.
05 Provost/Vice Pres Academic Affs .... Dr. Sandra J. DELOATCH
10 Vice Pres Finance and Admin .... Mr. Gerald E. HUNTER
30 Interim Vice Pres Univ Advancement .... Dr. Deborah C. FONTAINE
32 Vice President for Student Affairs .... Mr. Edward M. WILLIS
20 Vice Provost .... Dr. Mildred K. FULLER
20 Vice Provost .... Dr. Clarence D. COLEMAN
84 Asst Vice Pres Enrollment Mgmt .... Vacant
108 AVP Inst Research/Assessment/Plng .... Vacant
43 University Counsel .... Ms. Pamela F. BOSTON
07 Dir of Recruitment & Admissions .... Mrs. Lakeisha E. MAYES
19 Chief of Campus Police .... Mr. Troy COVINGTON
38 Director of Counseling .... Ms. Vanessa C. JENKINS
06 Registrar .... Mr. Michael CARPENTER
08 Dean of Library Services .... Vacant
37 Director of Financial Aid .... Mr. Kevin J. BURNS
36 Director of Career Services .... Vacant
15 Assoc VP Human Resources .... Ms. Mona ADKINS-EASLEY
13 Director Enterprise Information Sys .... Vacant
29 Dir Alumni Relations/Annual Giving .... Ms. Michelle D. HILL
49 Dean of Liberal Arts .... Dr. Belinda C. ANDERSON
50 Interim Dean of Business .... Dr. Bidhu D. MOHANTY
53 Interim Dean of Education .... Dr. Denise LITTLETON
76 Act Dean of Science/Eng/Technology .... Dr. Larry MATTIX
70 Interim Dean of Social Work .... Dr. Rowena G. WILSON
92 Dean of Honors College .... Dr. Page LAWS
58 Dean of Graduate Studies & Research . Dr. George E. MILLER, III
86 Legislative Liason .... Mr. Robert L. TURNER
26 Int Dir Communications & Marketing ..... Ms. Stevalynn R. ADAMS
09 Dir Institutional Research .... Dr. Alona SMOLOVA
39 Exec Dir Housing & Residence Life ... Mrs. Faith M. FITZGERALD
40 Bookstore Manager .... Ms. Angela HARRISON
41 Athletics Director .... Mr. Marty L. MILLER
18 Assoc Vice Pres Facilities Mgmt .... Mr. Anton KASHIRI
85 Dir International Student Services .... Mrs. Beverly HARRIS
96 Director of Procurement .... Mr. Eugene ANDERSON
21 University Controller .... Mrs. Karla J. AMAYA GORDON
35 Dean of Students .... Ms. Tracci JOHNSON
88 Assoc Vice Pres for Student Affairs .... Mrs. Julia WINGARD
108 Director of Assessment .... Ms. Katrice HAWTHORNE

† Member of Virginia Consortium for Professional Psychology.

Old Dominion University (I)

5115 Hampton Boulevard, Norfolk VA 23529-0001
County: Independent City FICE Identification: 003728
Unit ID: 232982
Telephone: (757) 683-3000 Carnegie Class: RU/H
FAX Number: (757) 683-4505 Calendar System: Semester
URL: www.odu.edu
Established: 1930 Annual Undergrad Tuition & Fees (In-State): $9,768
Enrollment: 24,932 Coed
Affiliation or Control: State IRS Status: 501(c)3
Highest Offering: Doctorate
Program: Liberal Arts And General; Teacher Preparatory; Professional
Accreditation: SC, ANEST, ART, BUS, BUSA, CAATE, CACREP, CLPSY, CYTO, DH, ENG, ENGT, EXSC, MT, MUS, NMT, NRPA, NURSE, PH, PTA, SP, SPAA, TED, THEA

01 President .... Mr. John R. BRODERICK
05 Acting Provost/VP Academic Affairs .... Dr. Chandra DESILVA
10 Vice President Admin & Finance .... Vacant
46 Vice President for Research .... Dr. Morris W. FOSTER
15 Vice Pres for Human Resources ... Ms. September C. SANDERLIN
30 Vice Pres University Advancement .... Mr. Alonzo C. BRANDON
32 VP Student Engagement & Enroll Svcs ...... Dr. Ellen J. NEUFELDT
88 Vice Provost for Faculty/Pgm Devel .... Vacant
88 Vice Prov Academic Programs .... Dr. Brian K. PAYNE
20 Assoc Vice Pres Academic Affairs .... Mr. James P. DUFFY
21 Assoc VP for Financial Services ...... Ms. Deborah L. SWIECINSKI
88 Asst VP Regional/Higher Educ Ctrs .... Ms. Renee OLANDER
56 Assoc VP Distance Learning .... Mr. Andrew R. CASIELLO
84 Assoc Vice Pres Enrollment Mgmt .... Ms. Jane H. DANE
44 Assoc Vice Pres for Advancement .... Mr. Daniel J. GENARD
88 Assoc VP Student Engagement .... Dr. Johnny YOUNG
109 Asst Vice Pres Auxiliary Services .... Mr. Todd JOHNSON
21 Asst VP Finance/Univ Controller .... Ms. Mary DENEEN
13 CIO/Assoc VP for University Svcs ..... Mr. James R. WATERFIELD
31 Asst Vice Pres Community Engagement .... Ms. Karen F. MEIER
35 Dean Students/AVP Stdnt Engagement .... Dr. Donald M. STANSBERRY
20 Asst VP Undergraduate Studies .... Ms. Judith M. BOWMAN
29 Asst Vice Pres of Alumni Relations .... Ms. Dana G. ALLEN
26 Int AVP Marketing & Communications ...... Ms. Giovanna GENARD
22 Asst VP Inst Equity & Diversity .... Ms. ReNee S. DUNMAN

58 Associate VP for Graduate Studies .... Dr. Robert WOJTOWICZ
49 Dean College Arts & Letters .... Dr. Charles E. WILSON, JR.
81 Dean College of Sciences .... Dr. Christopher PLATSOUCAS
76 Dean College of Health Sciences .... Dr. Shelley C. MISHOE
50 Dean Strome College of Business .... Dr. John F. TANNER
53 Dean Darden College of Education .... Dr. Jane S. BRAY
54 Dean Col Engineering & Tech .... Dr. Oktay BAYSAL
92 Dean Honors College .... Dr. David D. METZGER
20 Exec Dir of Academic Enhancement .... Ms. Lisa MAYES
36 Exec Dir Career Management Center .... Ms. Denise D. SMITH
93 Exec Dir of Intercultural Relations .... Ms. Lesa C. CLARK
43 Asst Atty Gen/Assoc Univ Counsel .... Mr. Richard E. NANCE
85 Exec Dir International Programs .... Dr. Marcelo E. SILES
08 Interim University Librarian .... Mr. George FOWLER
11 Chief Operating Officer .... Mr. David F. HARNAGE
06 University Registrar .... Ms. Mary K. SWARTZ
07 Exec Director of Admissions .... Dr. J. Christopher FLEMING
41 Director of Athletics .... Dr. C. Wood SELIG
37 Director Student Financial Aid .... Ms. Vera E. RIDDICK
31 Director of Community Relations .... Ms. Cecelia T. TUCKER
88 Director Military Affairs .... Vacant
38 Sr Exec Director Counseling Svcs .... Dr. Lenora H. THOMPSON
23 Director Student Health Center .... Ms. Jennifer J. FOSS
85 Director Intl Students/Scholar Svcs .... Ms. Robbin S. FULMORE
39 Exec Director of Student Housing .... Ms. April KONVALINKA
18 Director Facilities Management .... Mr. R. Dillard GEORGE
19 VP for Public Safety & Chief Police .... Ms. Rhonda L. HARRIS
28 Dir Inst Equity/Diversity/EO/AA .... Ms. Lanay NEWSOM
109 Actg Dir of Procurement Services .... Ms. Etta HENRY
94 Director Women's Studies .... Dr. Jennifer N. FISH
16 Dir of HR Employee Rels/Strat Init .... Ms. Kathleen WILLIAMSON
35 Dir Leadership/Student Involvement .... Ms. Nicole C. KIGER
40 University Bookstore Manager .... Mr. Darryl ATKINSON
04 Asst to the President/Asst to COO .... Ms. Velvet L. GRANT
86 Asst to Pres for Govt Relations .... Ms. Elizabeth A. KERSEY

† Member of Virginia Consortium for Professional Psychology.

Patrick Henry College (A)

Ten Patrick Henry Circle, Purcellville VA 20132

County: Loudoun FICE Identification: 039513
Telephone: (540) 338-1776 Carnegie Class: Bac/A&S
FAX Number: (540) 441-8709 Calendar System: Semester
URL: www.phc.edu
Established: 2000 Annual Undergrad Tuition & Fees: $27,922
Enrollment: 326 Coed
Affiliation or Control: Independent Non-Profit IRS Status: 501(c)3
Highest Offering: Baccalaureate
Program: Liberal Arts And General
Accreditation: TRACS

00 Chancellor .... Dr. Michael P. FARRIS
01 President .... Vacant
05 Provost .... Dr. Gene E. VEITH
03 Exec Vice President & Treasurer .... Mr. Carl W. SCHREIBER
30 Vice President for Advancement .... Mr. Tom ZIEMNICK
20 Dean of Academic Affairs .... Dr. Frank GULIUZZA
32 Dean of Student Affairs .... Ms. Sandra K. CORBITT
09 Asst VP for Inst Effectiveness .... Mr. Rodney J. SHOWALTER
08 Director of the Library .... Ms. Sara E. PENSGARD

Protestant Episcopal Theological Seminary in Virginia (B)

3737 Seminary Road, Alexandria VA 22304-5201

County: Independent City FICE Identification: 003731
Unit ID: 233259
Telephone: (703) 370-6600 Carnegie Class: Not Classified
FAX Number: (703) 370-6234 Calendar System: Semester
URL: www.vts.edu
Established: 1823 Annual Graduate Tuition & Fees: $13,530
Enrollment: 137 Coed
Affiliation or Control: Protestant Episcopal IRS Status: 501(c)3
Highest Offering: Doctorate; No Undergraduates
Program: Professional; Religious Emphasis
Accreditation: THEOL

01 Dean and President .... Rev. Ian S. MARKHAM
05 VP of Academic Affairs .... Rev. Melody D. KNOWLES
10 VP for Administration and Finance .... Mrs. Heather ZDANCEWICZ
30 VP of Institutional Advancement .... Rev. J. Barney HAWKINS
15 VP for HR and Inst Effectiveness .... Ms. Katie GLOVER
32 Assoc Dean of Students .... Rev. Justin LEWIS-ANTHONY
06 Registrar .... Mrs. Tamara A. SHEPHERD
08 Head Librarian .... Dr. Mitzi J. BUDDE
26 Director of Communications .... Mr. Curtis PRATHER
07 Director of Admissions .... Ms. Janice SIENKIEWICZ

Radford University (C)

810 East Main Street, Radford VA 24142

County: Radford City FICE Identification: 003732
Unit ID: 233277
Telephone: (540) 831-5000 Carnegie Class: Master's L
FAX Number: N/A Calendar System: Semester
URL: www.radford.edu
Established: 1910 Annual Undergrad Tuition & Fees (In-State): $9,809
Enrollment: 9,798 Coed
Affiliation or Control: State IRS Status: 170(c)1
Highest Offering: Doctorate
Program: Liberal Arts And General; Teacher Preparatory; Professional
Accreditation: SC, BUS, CAATE, CACREP, CIDA, COPSY, CS, DIETD, MUS, NRPA, NURSE, OT, PTA, SP, SW, TED, THEA

01 President .... Ms. Penelope W. KYLE
05 Provost/VP Academic Affairs .... Dr. Sam MINNER
10 VP Finance and Administration/CFO .... Mr. Richard ALVAREZ
13 VP Information Technology/CIO .... Mr. Danny KEMP
32 VP Student Affairs .... Dr. Mark SHANLEY
26 VP University Relations/CCO .... Mr. Larry CARPENTER
30 VP University Advancement .... Ms. Melissa WOHLSTEIN
50 Dean Business and Economics .... Dr. George LOW
53 Dean Education and Human Devel .... Dr. Kenna COLLEY
76 Dean Health and Human Services .... Dr. Kenneth COX
83 Dean Humanities and Behavioral Sci .... Dr. Katherine HAWKINS
81 Dean Science and Technology .... Dr. J. Orion ROGERS
57 Dean Visual and Performing Arts .... Ms. Margaret DEVANEY
58 Dean Graduate Studies and Research .... Dr. Dennis GRADY
07 Dean of Admissions/Enrollment Mgmt .... Mr. James PENNIX
08 Dean of the Library .... Mr. Steven HELM
06 Registrar .... Mr. Matthew BRUNNER
37 Director of Financial Aid .... Ms. Barbara PORTER
29 Executive Dir of Alumni Relations .... Ms. Laura TURK
41 Director Intercollegiate Athletics .... Mr. Robert LINEBURG
15 Exec Dir & Chief HR Officer .... Ms. Christina BROGDON
19 Asst VP for Public Safety .... Ms. Colleen ROBERTS
09 Director of Institutional Research .... Mr. Eric LOVIK
101 Secretary of the Board of Visitors .... Ms. Michele SCHUMACHER

Randolph College (D)

2500 Rivermont Avenue, Lynchburg VA 24503-1555

County: Independent City FICE Identification: 003734
Unit ID: 233301
Telephone: (434) 947-8000 Carnegie Class: Bac/A&S
FAX Number: (434) 947-8139 Calendar System: Semester
URL: www.randolphcollege.edu
Established: 1891 Annual Undergrad Tuition & Fees: $35,410
Enrollment: 693 Coed
Affiliation or Control: United Methodist IRS Status: 501(c)3
Highest Offering: Master's
Program: Liberal Arts And General; Teacher Preparatory
Accreditation: SC, TEAC

01 President .... Dr. Bradley W. BATEMAN
05 VP Academic Affs & Dean of College .... Dr. Carl A. GIRELLI
30 Vice Pres Institutional Advancement .... Mr. Skip KUHN
10 Vice Pres Finance & Administration .... Mr. James MANARO
32 VP Student Affs & Dean of Students .... Dr. Matha THORNTON
84 VP Enrollment Management .... Mr. Michael J. QUINN
100 VP & Chief of Staff .... Mr. Wesley FUGATE
20 Associate Dean of the College .... Ms. Paula J. WALLACE
29 Alumnae Director .... Ms. Heather A. GARNETT
09 Dir IR/Planning & Assessment .... Dr. John F. KEENER
15 Director Human Resources .... Ms. Sharon SAUNDERS
18 Chief Facilities/Physical Plant .... Mr. J.W WOOD
21 Director of Finance .... Mr. Jonathan TYREE
38 Director Student Counseling .... Dr. Anne HERSHBELL
08 Librarian .... Mr. Theodore J. HOSTETLER
06 Registrar .... Ms. Barbara S. THRASHER
37 Dir Student Financial Services .... Ms. Debi WOODALL-STEVENS
36 Director of Career Development .... Ms. Krista LEIGHTON
13 Director of Information Technology .... Mr. Victor GOSNELL
04 Administrative Asst to President .... Ms. Cindy LYONS
07 Director of Admissions .... Ms. Catherine SEE
19 Director Security/Safety .... Mr. Kris IRWIN
41 Athletic Director .... Ms. Tina HILL

Randolph-Macon College (E)

204 Henry Street, PO Box 5005, Ashland VA 23005-5505

County: Hanover FICE Identification: 003733
Unit ID: 233295
Telephone: (804) 752-7200 Carnegie Class: Bac/A&S
FAX Number: (804) 752-7231 Calendar System: Other
URL: www.rmc.edu
Established: 1830 Annual Undergrad Tuition & Fees: $36,600
Enrollment: 1,420 Coed
Affiliation or Control: United Methodist IRS Status: 501(c)3
Highest Offering: Baccalaureate
Program: Liberal Arts And General; Teacher Preparatory
Accreditation: SC, TEAC

01 President .... Mr. Robert R. LINDGREN
05 Provost/VP for Academic Affairs .... Dr. William T. FRANZ
10 Vice Pres of Admin & Finance .... Mr. Paul DAVIES
30 Vice Pres for College Advancement .... Ms. Diane M. LOWDER
84 Vice Pres for Enroll/Admiss/Fin Aid .... Dr. David L. LESESNE
32 Vice President for Student Affairs .... Dr. Grant L. AZDELL
04 Executive Assistant to the Pres .... Mrs. Jennifer L. THOMPSON
88 Exec Dir Ctr Personal/Career Dev .... Ms. Cindy SZADOKIERSKI
07 Director of Admissions .... Mr. Anthony F. AMBROGI
29 Exec Director Alumni Relations .... Mrs. Susan H. DONAVANT
26 Dir of Marketing & Communications .... Mrs. Anne Marie LAURANZON
37 Director of Financial Aid .... Mrs. Mary Y. NEAL
13 CIO and ITS Director .... Mr. Kirk BAUMBACH
06 Registrar .... Mrs. Alana DAVIS
36 Director of Counseling Services .... Dr. D. Craig ANDERSON
09 Director of Institutional Research .... Dr. Timothy W. MERRILL
18 Dir of Operations & Physical Plant .... Mr. Thomas P. DWYER
42 Chaplain .... Rev. Kendra SWAGER
19 Director of Campus Safety .... Mr. Maurice J. KIELY
41 Athletic Director .... Mr. Jeffrey S. BURNS

15 Director Human Resources .... Mrs. Sharon S. JACKSON
21 Controller .... Ms. Barbara A. DAUBERMAN
20 Associate Dean of the College .... Dr. Lauren C. BELL
36 Director of Professional Develop .... Ms. Catherine A. ROLLMAN
35 Asst Dean of Students .... Mr. James D. MCGHEE, JR.
40 Bookstore Manager .... Mrs. Barclay F. DUPRIEST
21 Director of Budget/Financial Analys .... Mrs. Caroline C. BUSCH

Reformed Theological Seminary (F)

1651 Old Meadow Road, Suite 300, McLean VA 22102

Telephone: (703) 448-3393 Identification: 666079
Accreditation: &SC, THEOL

† Regional accreditation is carried under the parent institution in Jackson, MS.

Regent University (G)

1000 Regent University Drive, Virginia Beach VA 23464-9800

County: Independent City FICE Identification: 030913
Unit ID: 231651
Telephone: (757) 352-4127 Carnegie Class: DRU
FAX Number: (757) 352-4381 Calendar System: Semester
URL: www.regent.edu
Established: 1977 Annual Undergrad Tuition & Fees: $16,700
Enrollment: 6,158 Coed
Affiliation or Control: Independent Non-Profit IRS Status: 501(c)3
Highest Offering: Doctorate
Program: Professional
Accreditation: SC, ACBSP, CACREP, CLPSY, LAW, TEAC, THEOL

01 Chancellor & CEO .... Dr. M.G. (Pat) ROBERTSON
05 Executive VP for Academic Affairs .... Dr. Gerson MORENO-RIANO
32 Executive VP for Student Life .... Dr. Joseph UMIDI
43 Senior VP & General Counsel .... Mr. Louis A. ISAKOFF
30 Vice President for Advancement .... Mrs. Ann LEBLANC
26 VP for Marketing & Public Relations .... Mrs. Sherri MILLER
10 Vice President for Finance .... Mr. Dean A. WOOTEN
15 VP for Human Resources & Admin .... Mrs. Martha J. SMITH
20 Associate VP for Academic Affairs .... Mr. Douglas COOK
88 Associate VP for Teaching/Learning .... Dr. Jason BAKER
61 Dean School of Law .... Mr. Michael HERNANDEZ
49 Dean College of Arts & Sciences .... Dr. Gerson MORENO-RIANO
08 Dean of University Library .... Dr. Sara BARON
50 Dean School of Business/Leadership .... Dr. Doris GOMEZ
80 Dean School of Government .... Dr. Eric PATTERSON
53 Dean School of Education .... Dr. Donald FINN
38 Dean Psychology & Counseling .... Dr. William HATHAWAY
60 Dean Communication & the Arts .... Dr. Mitch LAND
73 Interim Dean School of Divinity .... Dr. Joseph UMIDI
06 Registrar .... Ms. Erica LEMELLE
07 Exec Dir of University Admissions .... Mrs. Heidi CECE
35 Exec Director of Student Services .... Mrs. Carolyn HUGHES
106 Director of CTL .... Dr. Tonya AMANKWATIA
37 Director of Financial Aid .... Mrs. Dotti DAVIDSON
09 Director of Institutional Research .... Dr. Amanda WYNN
18 Dir of Facilities & Engineering .... Mr. Richard JEMIOLA
29 Director of Alumni Relations .... Ms. Melissa FUQUAY
42 Director of Campus Ministries .... Mr. Jason PEAKS
108 Director of Assessment .... Mr. Ryan MURNANE
88 Director of Military Affairs .... Mr. Dave BOISSELLE
39 Director of Residence Life .... Mr. Adam WILLIAMS
96 Manager of Purchasing .... Mrs. Pauline CARRAWAY
04 Admin Assistant to the President .... Mrs. Carol DIXON
101 Secretary of the Institution/Board .... Mrs. Carol DIXON

Richard Bland College (H)

8311 Halifax Road, Petersburg VA 23805-7100

County: Independent City FICE Identification: 003707
Unit ID: 233338
Telephone: (804) 862-6100 Carnegie Class: Assoc/Pub2in4
FAX Number: (804) 862-6207 Calendar System: Semester
URL: www.rbc.edu
Established: 1960 Annual Undergrad Tuition & Fees (In-State): $7,067
Enrollment: 1,600 Coed
Affiliation or Control: State IRS Status: 501(c)3
Highest Offering: Associate Degree
Program: 2-Year Principally Bachelor's Creditable
Accreditation: SC

01 President .... Dr. Debbie L. SYDOW
05 Dean of Faculty/Acad Effectiveness .... Dr. Vern L. LINDQUIST
10 Chief Operations Officer .... Mrs. Debra KAUFMAN
27 Director of Info and Communications .... Ms. Leslie WILLIAMS
19 Chief Campus Safety/Security .... Mr. Eric KONDZIELAWA
30 Director Advancement/Alumni .... Mr. Stephen WILSON
07 Dean of Enrollment Services .... Dr. James T. HART
06 Registrar .... Ms. Lois WRAY
08 Director of Library .... Vacant
13 Director of Info Tech Services .... Ms. Deborah JAMES
37 Director of Financial Aid .... Ms. Emily MARTIN
15 Director of Human Resources .... Vacant
88 Manager of Proj & Telecomm .... Mr. George JELLERSON
38 Dir of Counseling/Student Support .... Ms. Evanda WATTS-MARTINEZ
41 Director of Athletics .... Mr. Chuck MOORE
26 Director of Communications .... Ms. Joanne WILLIAMS
39 Assoc Dir of Residence Life .... Vacant
21 Interim Director Financial Opers .... Ms. Lauren SUMNER
88 Assoc Dean Academic Support .... Ms. Aimee JOYAUX

Riverside School of Health Careers (A)

316 Main Street, Newport News VA 23601
County: Independent City FICE Identification: 021400
Unit ID: 233408
Telephone: (757) 240-2200 Carnegie Class: Not Classified
FAX Number: (757) 240-2225 Calendar System: Trimester
URL: www.riverside.edu
Established: 1916 Annual Undergrad Tuition & Fees: $28,020
Enrollment: 300 Coed
Affiliation or Control: Independent Non-Profit IRS Status: 501(c)3
Highest Offering: Associate Degree
Program: Occupational; 2-Year Principally Bachelor's Creditable; Nursing Emphasis
Accreditation: ABHES, DNUR, PNUR, PTAA, RAD, SURGT, SURTEC

01 System Director of Education Robin M. NELHUEBEL

Roanoke College (B)

221 College Lane, Salem VA 24153-3747
County: Independent City FICE Identification: 003736
Unit ID: 233426
Telephone: (540) 375-2500 Carnegie Class: Bac/A&S
FAX Number: (540) 375-2205 Calendar System: Semester
URL: www.roanoke.edu
Established: 1842 Annual Undergrad Tuition & Fees: $39,666
Enrollment: 2,054 Coed
Affiliation or Control: Evangelical Lutheran Church In America
IRS Status: 501(c)3
Highest Offering: Baccalaureate
Program: Liberal Arts And General; Teacher Preparatory
Accreditation: SC, ACBSP, CAATE, TEAC

01 President Mr. Michael C. MAXEY
05 Vice President/Dean of the College Dr. Richard A. SMITH
84 VP of Enroll Svcs/Dean Adm/Fin Aid Dr. Brenda P. POGGENDORF
32 Vice President Student Affairs Mr. Aaron L. FETROW
10 Vice President Business Affairs Mr. Mark P. NOFTSINGER
30 Vice President Resource Development Ms. Connie K. CARMACK
13 Chief Information Officer Ms. Rebecca F. SANDLIN
09 Dir Institutional Research Dr. Jack K. STEEHLER
20 Assoc Dean Academic Affairs/Admin Dr. Jennifer K. BERENSON
06 Assoc Dean Acad Affairs/Registrar Ms. Leah L. RUSSELL
07 Director of Admissions Ms. Patricia N. LEDONNE
35 AVP/Dean of Students/Student Affs Dr. Brian T. CHISOM
39 Director of Residence Life/Housing Mr. Jimmy R. WHITED
88 Director of Colket Ctr/Student Act Vacant
92 Director of Honors Programs Dr. Michael A. HAKKENBERG
08 Director of the Library Vacant
36 Director of Career Services Ms. Toni D. MCLAWHORN
24 Media Technology Director Mr. David H. MULFORD
31 Dir of Community Programs Ms. Tanya RIDPATH
26 Director of Public Relations Ms. Teresa T. GEREAUX
44 Director of Gift Planning Mr. Richard J. POGGENDORF
29 Dir of Alumni/Family Relations Mr. Jonathan E. LEE
37 Director of Financial Aid Mr. Thomas S. BLAIR, JR.
21 Director of Finance & Budget Ms. Kathryn A. VANNESS
91 Database Director Ms. Mitzi B. STEELE
15 Director Human Resources Ms. Cathy S. DICKERSON
40 Bookstore Coordinator/Buyer Ms. Melissa B. RUTLEDGE
19 Director Campus Safety Mr. Thomas A. RAMBO
23 Dir Student Health/Counseling Svcs Ms. Sandra W. MCGHEE
41 Athletic Director Mr. M. Scott ALLISON
42 Chaplain/Dean of the Chapel Rev. Christopher M. BOWEN
43 General Counsel Mr. G. Michael PACE, JR.
104 Director International Education Dr. Pamela A. SEROTA COTE
28 Director of Multicultural Affairs Ms. Juliet J. LOWERY
04 Executive Assistant to President Ms. Joyce A. SINK

Saint Michael College of Allied Health (C)

8305 Richmond Hwy, Ste 10A, Alexandria VA 22309
County: Independent City Identification: 667226
Telephone: (703) 746-8708 Carnegie Class: Not Classified
FAX Number: (703) 746-8709 Calendar System: Other
URL: www.stmichaelcollegeva.us
Established: 2007 Annual Undergrad Tuition & Fees: N/A
Enrollment: N/A Coed
Affiliation or Control: Proprietary IRS Status: Proprietary
Highest Offering: Associate Degree
Program: Occupational; Nursing Emphasis
Accreditation: COE

01 Director Dr. Michael ADEDOKUN

Sentara College of Health Sciences (D)

1441 Crossways Boulevard, Ste 105, Chesapeake VA 23320
County: Chesapeake City FICE Identification: 031065
Unit ID: 232885
Telephone: (757) 388-2900 Carnegie Class: Not Classified
FAX Number: (757) 388-2905 Calendar System: Semester
URL: www.sentara.edu
Established: 1892 Annual Undergrad Tuition & Fees: $12,500
Enrollment: 367 Coed
Affiliation or Control: Independent Non-Profit IRS Status: 501(c)3
Highest Offering: Baccalaureate
Program: Professional; Nursing Emphasis
Accreditation: ACICS, CVT, NURSE, SURGT

01 Dean Sentara Col of Health Sciences Ms. Shelly COHEN
66 Dean of Nursing Dr. Angela TAYLOR
45 Asst Dean Institutional Effective Ms. Monique BAUCHAM
76 Asst Dean Dept of Allied Health Ms. Nora LEONARD
88 Asst Dean Information Technology Mr. Christopher NELSON
32 Asst Dean Dept of Student Svcs Ms. Sandy MOORE
08 Librarian Ms. Suzanne DUNCAN
37 Financial Aid Advisor Ms. Mary Ann RIVERA
07 Admissions Recruiter Mr. Jerome BROFFT
07 Admissions Recruiter Mr. Tony MARTIN

Shenandoah University (E)

1460 University Drive, Winchester VA 22601-5195
County: Independent City FICE Identification: 003737
Unit ID: 233541
Telephone: (540) 665-4500 Carnegie Class: Master's L
FAX Number: N/A Calendar System: Semester
URL: www.su.edu
Established: 1875 Annual Undergrad Tuition & Fees: $30,590
Enrollment: 3,693 Coed
Affiliation or Control: United Methodist IRS Status: 501(c)3
Highest Offering: Doctorate
Program: Liberal Arts And General; Teacher Preparatory; Professional
Accreditation: SC, ARCPA, BUS, CAATE, COARC, MIDWF, MUS, NURSE, OT, PHAR, PTA, TEAC

01 President Dr. Tracy FITZSIMMONS
05 VP for Academic Affairs Dr. Adrienne G. BLOSS
10 Vice Pres Administration/Finance Vacant
32 Vice President for Student Life Rev Dr. Rhonda VANDYKE COLBY
30 Vice Pres for Advancement & Plng Mr. Mitchell L. MOORE
84 VP for Enrol Mgmt & Student Success Dr. Clarresa MORTON
39 Dir Resident Life & Student Conduct Ms. Sue O'DRISCOLL
29 Assoc Vice Pres for Alumni Affairs Ms. Jane D. PITTMAN
26 Director of Media Relations Ms. Emily BURNER
49 Dean of College of Arts & Sciences Dr. Jeff COKER
50 Dean of Byrd School of Business Dr. Miles DAVIS
64 Dean of Shenandoah Conservatory Dr. Michael J. STEPNIAK
67 Dean of Dunn School of Pharmacy Dr. Alan B. MCKAY
07 Exec of Recruitment & Admissions Mr. Andy WOODALL
35 Dir of Student Engagement Mr. Doug STUMP
08 Director of Library Services Mr. Christopher A. BEAN
06 Registrar Ms. Elizabeth WHITE
21 Controller Ms. Courtney JARRETT
37 Director of Financial Aid Ms. Nancy S. BRAGG
36 Director of Career Services Ms. Jennifer A. SPATARO-WILSON
18 Director of Physical Plant Mr. Barry SCHNOOR
23 Director of Wellness Center Mr. Ronald G. STICKLEY
15 Director of Human Resources Ms. Marie C. LANDES
41 Athletic Director Mr. Doug ZIPP
91 Database & System Administrator Mr. David HOFFMAN
13 Director of Institutional Computing Mr. Quaiser ABSAR
66 Dean Custer School of Nursing Dr. Kathryn M. GANSKE
88 Director Div of Athletic Training Dr. Rose A. SCHMIEG
88 Dir Div of Occupational Therapy Dr. Leslie DAVIDSON
88 Interim Dir Div of Physical Therapy Dr. Sheri HALE
88 Sr Dir Advancement - Conservatory Mr. Bradley C. SNOWDEN
19 Chief of Public Safety Mr. Robin EBERSOLE
102 Director Foundation Relations Ms. Jennifer BOUSQUET
109 Director Auxiliary Services Mr. John V. STEVENS
88 Dir Div of Physician Asst Studies Dr. Rachel CARLSON
20 Director Learning Services Ms. Holli PHILLIPS
42 Dean of Spiritual Life Rev Dr. Justin ALLEN
88 Dir Division of Respiratory Care Ms. Stephanie CROSS
09 Director Institutional Research Dr. Howard BALLENTINE
40 Bookstore Manager Ms. Kimberly OTYENOH
96 Purchasing & Accts Pay Manager Ms. Amy DILL
24 Coordinator Media Services Ms. Val GANGWER
38 Director Student Counseling Ms. Nancy SCHULTE
04 Executive Asst to President Ms. Amy HAMMOND
101 Secretary of the Board of Trustees Ms. Lori JANNING
53 Director School of Education Dr. Dennis KELLISON

Skyline College (F)

5234 Airport Road, Roanoke VA 24012-1603
County: Roanoke FICE Identification: 030927
Unit ID: 261931
Telephone: (540) 563-8000 Carnegie Class: Bac/Assoc
FAX Number: (540) 362-5400 Calendar System: Semester
URL: www.skyline.edu
Established: 1966 Annual Undergrad Tuition & Fees: $14,245
Enrollment: 191 Coed
Affiliation or Control: Proprietary IRS Status: Proprietary
Highest Offering: Baccalaureate
Program: Occupational; 2-Year Principally Bachelor's Creditable; Technical Emphasis
Accreditation: ACCSC, MAAB

01 Campus President Mr. Michael TRAAS

South Baylo University (G)

7535 Little River Tnpk Unit 325-A, Annandale VA 22003
Telephone: (703) 642-7518 Identification: 770912
Accreditation: @ACUP

† Branch campus of South Baylo University, Anaheim, CA.

South University (H)

2151 Old Brick Road, Richmond VA 23060
Telephone: (804) 727-6800 Identification: 770919
Accreditation: &SC, ACBSP, CACREP, NURSE, PTAA

† Branch campus of South University, Savannah, GA.

South University (I)

301 Bendix Road, Suite 100, Virginia Beach VA 23452
Telephone: (757) 493-6900 Identification: 770920
Accreditation: &SC, ACBSP, NURSE, PTAA

† Branch campus of South University, Savannah, GA.

Southern Virginia University (J)

1 University Hill Drive, Buena Vista VA 24416-3097
County: Rockbridge FICE Identification: 003738
Unit ID: 233611
Telephone: (540) 261-8400 Carnegie Class: Bac/A&S
FAX Number: (540) 266-3859 Calendar System: Semester
URL: www.svu.edu
Established: 1867 Annual Undergrad Tuition & Fees: $22,500
Enrollment: 705 Coed
Affiliation or Control: Independent Non-Profit IRS Status: 501(c)3
Highest Offering: Baccalaureate
Program: Liberal Arts And General; Teacher Preparatory
Accreditation: SC

01 President Dr. Reed N. WILCOX
05 Provost Dr. Madison U. SOWELL
10 VP Finance Mr. Robert E. HUCH
30 VP Institutional Advancement Mr. Ron SEAMONS
44 University Ambassador Dr. Richard G. WHITEHEAD
07 VP Enrollment and Marketing Mr. Brett GARCIA
32 VP Student Life Mr. Charley BOWEN
46 VP Educational Research & Dev Dr. Karen M. WALKER
11 Exec Dir of Campus Operations Mr. Arthur FURLER
04 Administrative Asst to President Ms. Kristie GIBBONS
06 Registrar Ms. Whitney M. LARSEN
08 Director of Library Services Mrs. Stephanie K. HARDY
104 Director of Travel Study Mrs. Carrie P. BROTHERSON
20 Associate Provost Dr. Alan WHITEHURST
20 Assistant Provost Dr. Jon WALLIN
57 Division Chair Fine & Perf Arts Mrs. Launa WHITEHEAD
79 Division Chair Humanities Dr. Thomas R. PORTER
81 Div Chair Science & Mathematics Dr. Beth SCHRAMM
83 Div Chair Social & Behavioral Sci Dr. Frances MACDONNELL
53 Director of Teacher Education Mrs. Kimberly KEARNEY
09 Director of Institutional Research Dr. Alan WHITEHURST
21 Controller & Dir of Business Ops Mr. Jesse SEEGMILLER
37 Director of Financial Aid Mr. John BRANDT
15 Assoc Director Human Resources Mr. Tyson COOPER
88 Title IX Coordinator Mr. Hugh BOUCHELLE
96 Senior Accountant Mr. Trenton DESPAIN
88 Director of Institutional Advance Mr. William BRADDY
07 Director of Admissions Mr. Alan WHITEHEAD
41 Athletic Director Mr. Jason LAMB
27 Director of Communications Mr. Chris PENDLETON
88 Senior Women's Athletic Admin Mrs. Deidra DRYDEN
29 Alumni Relations Coordinator Mrs. Kristen S. JONES
35 Dean of Students Mr. Joseph BOUCHELLE, III
38 Director of Student Support Mr. Michael GIBBONS
36 Director Career Development Center Mr. Cameron T. CROWTHER
23 Director of Student Health Services Mrs. Ginger LANIER
85 Foreign Students PDSO Ms. Whitney M. LARSEN
19 Director Security/Safety Mr. Hugh BOUCHELLE
11 Director of Campus Operations Mr. Joseph WHETSTONE
39 Director of Food Services Mrs. Effie WALLACE
18 Asst Dir Facilities/Physical Plant Mr. Byron PORTER
90 IT Support Manager Ms. Stephanie GILMER

Southside Regional Medical Center Professional Schools (K)

430 Clairmont Court, Suite 200, Colonial Heights VA 23834
County: Independent City FICE Identification: 012744
Unit ID: 233082
Telephone: (804) 765-5800 Carnegie Class: Not Classified
FAX Number: (804) 765-5944 Calendar System: Semester
URL: www.srmconline.com
Established: 1895 Annual Undergrad Tuition & Fees: $5,800
Enrollment: 123 Coed
Affiliation or Control: Proprietary IRS Status: Proprietary
Highest Offering: Associate Degree
Program: Occupational
Accreditation: ABHES, ADNUR, DMS, DNUR, RAD

01 Vice Pres for Professional Schools Ms. Cynthia PARSONS

Standard Healthcare Services College of Nursing (L)

7704 Leesburg Pike, Suite 1000, Falls Church VA 22043
County: Fairfax Identification: 667129
Telephone: (703) 891-1787 Carnegie Class: Not Classified
FAX Number: (703) 891-1789 Calendar System: Semester
URL: www.standardcollege.edu
Established: 2004 Annual Undergrad Tuition & Fees: $21,654

Enrollment: 246 Coed
Affiliation or Control: Proprietary IRS Status: Proprietary
Highest Offering: Associate Degree
Program: 2-Year Principally Bachelor's Creditable; Nursing Emphasis
Accreditation: **ABHES**

01 Executive Director Ms. Isibor Joy NOSEGBE
06 Registrar Ms. Lisley ANCO

Stratford University (A)

7777 Leesburg Pike, Falls Church VA 22043
County: Fairfax FICE Identification: 025412
Unit ID: 438498
Telephone: (703) 821-8570 Carnegie Class: Master's L
FAX Number: N/A Calendar System: Quarter
URL: www.stratford.edu
Established: 1976 Annual Undergrad Tuition & Fees: $16,650
Enrollment: 2,971 Coed
Affiliation or Control: Proprietary IRS Status: Proprietary
Highest Offering: Master's
Program: Professional; Business Emphasis
Accreditation: **ACICS**, ACFEI, MAAB, NURSE

01 President Dr. Richard SHURTZ
05 Chief Academic Officer Vacant
12 Campus Director DC Metro Voytek PANAS
20 Campus Dean Dr. Richelle RESTO

Stratford University (B)

11104 West Broad Street, Glen Allen VA 23060
Telephone: (804) 290-4231 Identification: 770819
Accreditation: **ACICS**, ACFEI, MAAB

† Branch campus of Stratford University, Falls Church, VA.

Stratford University (C)

836 J. Clyde Morris Boulevard,
Newport News VA 23601-1303
Telephone: (757) 873-4235 Identification: 770818
Accreditation: **ACICS**, ACFEI

† Branch campus of Stratford University, Falls Church, VA.

Stratford University (D)

14340 Gideon Drive, Woodbridge VA 22192
Telephone: (703) 897-1982 Identification: 770817
Accreditation: **ACICS**, ACFEI

† Branch campus of Stratford University, Falls Church, VA.

Sweet Briar College (E)

134 Chapel Road, Sweet Briar VA 24595-9998
County: Amherst FICE Identification: 003742
Unit ID: 233718
Telephone: (434) 381-6100 Carnegie Class: Bac/A&S
FAX Number: (434) 381-6173 Calendar System: Semester
URL: www.sbc.edu
Established: 1901 Annual Undergrad Tuition & Fees: $34,460
Enrollment: 535 Female
Affiliation or Control: Independent Non-Profit IRS Status: 501(c)3
Highest Offering: Master's
Program: Liberal Arts And General
Accreditation: **SC**, ENG

01 President Mr. Phillip C. STONE
100 Vice Pres of Admin/General Counsel Ms. Nancyellen KEANE
04 Exec Asst Office of the President Mrs. Dawn GATEWOOD
09 Director Institutional Research Ms. Christy C. COLE
05 Dean of Academic Affairs Ms. Pamela DEWEESE
84 Dean of Enrollment Management Mr. Steven NAPE
08 Dir Integrated Information Systems Dr. John G. JAFFE
41 Director of Athletics Ms. Teresa BOYLAN
104 Director Junior Year in Spain Ms. Giulia V. WITCOMBE
32 Dean of Student Life/Academic Supp Mrs. Kelly KRAFT-MEYER
10 Vice Pres Finance and Treasurer Mr. Thomas CONNORS
21 Assoc VP Finance/Administration Ms. Gail D. PAYNE
15 Director of Human Resources Ms. Barbara DONELSON
18 Director Physical Plant Mr. Steve BAILEY
19 Director of Campus Safety Mr. Tony MUCHINE
37 Director Financial Aid Ms. Wanda SPRADLEY
40 Book Shop Manager Ms. Lynn LEWIS
96 Director Purchasing Ms. Cynthia L. PONTON
88 Coordinator Benefits Mrs. Judy SPROUSE
88 Director of Hospitality Ms. Cathy MAYS
44 Vice Pres Alumnae Relations/Develop Mr. A.P PERKINSON
38 Mental Health Counselor/Health Svcs Ms. Elizabeth S. BLEVINS
36 Director Career Services Mr. Wayne F. STARK
39 Director Residence Life & Housing Ms. Kerri BOND
26 Director of Media/Marketing & Comm Ms. Monica DEAN

Union Presbyterian Seminary (F)

3401 Brook Road, Richmond VA 23227-4597
County: Independent City FICE Identification: 003743
Unit ID: 233842
Telephone: (804) 355-0671 Carnegie Class: Spec/Faith
FAX Number: (804) 355-3919 Calendar System: Semester
URL: www.upsem.edu
Established: 1812 Annual Graduate Tuition & Fees: $13,800
Enrollment: 180 Coed
Affiliation or Control: Presbyterian Church (U.S.A.) IRS Status: 501(c)3
Highest Offering: Doctorate; No Undergraduates
Program: Professional; Religious Emphasis
Accreditation: **SC**, THEOL

01 President Dr. Brian K. BLOUNT
10 Vice Pres Finance & Administration Mr. Michael B. CASHWELL
30 Vice President Advancement Mr. Richard WONG
84 VP Student Life/Enrollment Mgmt Ms. Michelle WALKER
05 Dean Union Presby Sem (Richmond) Dr. Stanley SKRESLET
12 Dean Union Presby Sem (Charlotte) Dr. Thomas W. CURRIE
20 Associate Dean Academic Programs Dr. E. Carson BRISSON
07 Director of Admissions Ms. Mairi RENWICK
06 Registrar Mr. J. Stanley HARGRAVES
08 Librarian Dr. Milton J. COALTER
13 Director Technology Services Mr. John R. WILSON
36 Director Student Placement Dr. Susan E. FOX
37 Director of Financial Aid Ms. Michelle WALKER

University of Fairfax (G)

3361 Melrose Ave, NW, Roanoke VA 24017
County: Independent City Identification: 667094
Telephone: (888) 980-9151 Carnegie Class: Not Classified
FAX Number: N/A Calendar System: Other
URL: www.ufairfax.edu
Established: 2002 Annual Undergrad Tuition & Fees: N/A
Enrollment: 81 Coed
Affiliation or Control: Other IRS Status: Proprietary
Highest Offering: Doctorate
Program: Professional; Technical Emphasis
Accreditation: **DEAC**

01 President & Chief Academic Officer Dr. Dominic BOAMAH
88 Dean of Doctoral Research Dr. Alden BEAN

† Tuition is $895 per semester credit.

University of Management & Technology (H)

1901 Fort Myer Drive, Suite 700, Arlington VA 22209-1609
County: Arlington FICE Identification: 041103
Unit ID: 437097
Telephone: (703) 516-0035 Carnegie Class: Not Classified
FAX Number: (703) 516-0985 Calendar System: Semester
URL: www.umtweb.edu
Established: 1998 Annual Undergrad Tuition & Fees: $9,450
Enrollment: 1,020 Coed
Affiliation or Control: Proprietary IRS Status: Proprietary
Highest Offering: Doctorate
Program: Professional; Business Emphasis
Accreditation: **DEAC**

01 President Dr. Yanping CHEN
05 Academic Dean Dr. J. Davidson FRAME

University of Mary Washington (I)

1301 College Avenue, Fredericksburg VA 22401-5300
County: Independent City FICE Identification: 003746
Unit ID: 232681
Telephone: (540) 654-1000 Carnegie Class: Master's L
FAX Number: (540) 654-1073 Calendar System: Semester
URL: www.umw.edu
Established: 1908 Annual Undergrad Tuition & Fees (In-State): $11,070
Enrollment: 4,535 Coed
Affiliation or Control: State IRS Status: 501(c)3
Highest Offering: Master's
Program: Liberal Arts And General; Teacher Preparatory
Accreditation: **SC**, MUS

01 President Mr. Richard V. HURLEY
05 Provost Dr. Jonathan LEVIN
100 Chief of Staff Dr. Martin A. WILDER
10 VP for Admin & Finance Mr. Richard R. PEARCE
32 Vice President Student Affairs Mr. Douglas N. SEARCY
30 Vice Pres for Advance & Univ Rels Mr. Salvatore M. MERINGOLO
102 CEO of UMW Foundation Mr. Jeffrey W. ROUNTREE
13 Actg CIO Mr. Hall CHESHIRE
88 Exec Dir Economic Development Mr. Brian J. BAKER
15 Asst Vice Pres/Human Res/AAEEO Ms. Sabrina C. JOHNSON
105 Director of Digital Communication Ms. Shelley KEITH
21 Asst Vice Pres Business Svcs/CPO Ms. Erma A. BAKER
20 Associate Provost Dr. John T. MORELLO
18 Assoc Vice Pres Facilities Services Mr. John P. WILTENMUTH, III
09 Asst Prov Inst Analy & Effect Mr. Taiwo A. ANDE
84 Assoc Prov for Enrollment Mgmt Ms. Kimberley BUSTER-WILLIAMS
53 Dean of College of Education Dr. Mary L. GENDERNALIK-COOPER
50 Dean College of Business Dr. Lynne D. RICHARDSON
20 Dean College of Arts & Sciences Dr. Richard FINKELSTEIN
35 Dean of Student Life Mr. Cedric B. RUCKER
37 Director of Financial Aid Ms. Heidi HUNTER-GOLDSWORTHY
09 Director of Institutional Research Mr. Mathew C. WILKERSON
21 Internal Audit Director Ms. Tera D. KOVANES
39 Director of Residence Life Ms. Christine M. PORTER
06 Registrar Ms. Rita DUNSTON
41 Director of Athletics Mr. Ken D. TYLER
08 University Librarian Ms. Rosemary ARNESON
88 Director of Publications Ms. Neva S. TRENIS
24 Director of Dodd Auditorium Mr. Doug NOBLE
88 Assoc Dean of Advising Services Ms. Sallie W. BRAXTON
19 Chief of University Police Mr. Michael W. HALL
29 Exec Director Alumni Relations Mr. Mark THADEN
38 Director of Counseling/Psych Svcs Dr. Nicole A. SURETHING
88 Director of Disability Services Vacant
23 University Physician Dr. P. Thomas RILEY
88 Director of University Galleries Ms. Rosemary K. JESIONOWSKI
28 Spec Asst Diversity & Inclusion Dr. Leah COX
26 Associate VP University Rels Ms. Anna B. BILLINGSLEY
27 Director Media & Public Relations Ms. Marty G. MORRISON
27 Director of Marketing Mr. Malcolm HOLMES
88 Director of Design Services Ms. AJ NEWELL
29 Director National Alumni Engagement Vacant
44 Assoc VP Univ Advancemnt/Alumni Rel Mr. Kenneth L. STEEN

University of North America (J)

8618 Westwood Center Dr., Ste 100, Vienna VA 22182
County: Fairfax Identification: 667241
Telephone: (571) 633-9651 Carnegie Class: Not Classified
FAX Number: (703) 890-3372 Calendar System: Semester
URL: www.uona.edu
Established: Annual Graduate Tuition & Fees: $12,285
Enrollment: N/A Coed
Affiliation or Control: Independent Non-Profit IRS Status: 501(c)3
Highest Offering: Master's; No Undergraduates
Program: Business Emphasis
Accreditation: **ACICS**

00 Chancellor Marty MARTIN
01 President Jill MARTIN
05 Dean of Academics Jason KOO
10 Sr VP Finance & Administration Jacob H. DEBRUIN

University of Phoenix Richmond-Virginia Beach Campus (K)

9750 West Broad Street, Glen Allen VA 23060-4169
Telephone: (804) 281-3900 Identification: 770233
Accreditation: **&NH**, ACBSP

† No longer accepting campus-based students.

University of the Potomac (L)

2070 Chain Bridge Road Suite G100, Vienna VA 22182
Telephone: (888) 380-1192 Identification: 666178
Accreditation: **&M**

† Regional accreditation is carried under the parent institution in Washington, DC.

University of Richmond (M)

28 Westhampton Way, Richmond VA 23173-1903
County: Independent City FICE Identification: 003744
Unit ID: 233374
Telephone: (804) 289-8000 Carnegie Class: Bac/A&S
FAX Number: (804) 287-6540 Calendar System: Semester
URL: www.richmond.edu
Established: 1830 Annual Undergrad Tuition & Fees: $48,090
Enrollment: 4,180 Coordinate
Affiliation or Control: Independent Non-Profit IRS Status: 501(c)3
Highest Offering: Doctorate
Program: Liberal Arts And General; Professional
Accreditation: **SC**, BUS, BUSA, LAW, TEAC

01 President Dr. Ronald A. CRUTCHER
05 Provost & VP Academic Affairs Dr. Jacquelyn FETROW
10 Vice President Business & Finance Mr. David B. HALE
32 Vice President Student Affairs Dr. Stephen D. BISESE
30 Vice President Advancement Mr. Thomas C. GUTENBERGER
13 Vice Pres for Information Services Ms. Kathryn J. MONDAY
84 Vice Pres Enrollment Management Dr. Stephanie DUPAUL
100 Chief of Staff Dr. Lori G. SCHUYLER
101 Secretary Board of Trustees Ms. Ann Lloyd BREEDEN
04 Special Assistant to President Mrs. Carolyn R. MARTIN
88 CEO Spider Mgmt Company Mr. Steve KNEELEY
15 Assoc Vice Pres Human Resources Mr. Carl K. SORENSEN
18 Assoc Vice Pres Facilities Mr. Andrew S. MCBRIDE
29 Asst VP Alumni & Career Services Ms. Kristin J. WOODS
102 Asst VP Foundation/Corp/Govt Rels Ms. Michelle E. WAMSLEY
42 University Chaplain Rev. Craig T. KOCHER
07 Asst VP and Dean of Admissions Mr. Gil VILLANUEVA
08 University Librarian Mr. Kevin BUTTERFIELD
09 Dir Institutional Effectiveness Dr. Patricia B. MURPHY
06 University Registrar Ms. Susan D. BREEDEN
37 Director of Financial Aid Ms. Cynthia B. DEFFENBAUGH
36 Director Career Services Ms. Leslie W. STEVENSON
38 Director of CAPS Dr. Peter O. LEVINESS
96 Director Strategic Sourcing Ms. Jean C. HINES
35 Assoc VP Student Development Dr. Tinina Q. CADE
41 Director of Athletics Mr. Keith GILL
104 Director Study Abroad Ms. Michele D. COX
105 Director Web Services Mr. Eric F. PALMER
33 Dean of Richmond College Dr. Joseph R. BOEHMAN
34 Dean Westhampton College Dr. Juliette L. LANDPHAIR

49 Dean School of Arts & Sciences ......Dr. Kahtleen R. SKERRETT
50 Dean School of Business ......Dr. Nancy A. BAGRANOFF
61 Dean School of Law ......Dr. Wendy C. PERDUE
51 Dean School Continuing Studies ......Dr. Jamelle WILSON
88 Dean Jepson School Leader Stds ......Dr. Sandra J. PEART
19 Assoc VP Publc Sfty/Chief of Police ......Mr. David M. MCCOY
23 Director Health Center ......Dr. Lynne P. DEANE
26 Asst VP for Communications ......Vacant
40 Manager University Bookstore ......Mr. Roger L. BROOKS
28 Director Common Ground ......Dr. Glyn HUGHES
39 Director Student Housing ......Ms. Joan D. LACHOWSKI
43 VP & General Counsel ......Ms. Shannon E. SINCLAIR
91 Manager Admin Systems ......Mr. Lee PARKER, III

University of Virginia (A)

Charlottesville VA 22903
County: Independent City FICE Identification: 003745
Unit ID: 234076
Telephone: (434) 924-0311 Carnegie Class: RU/VH
FAX Number: (434) 924-0938 Calendar System: Semester
URL: www.virginia.edu
Established: 1819 Annual Undergrad Tuition & Fees (In-State): $14,678
Enrollment: 23,732 Coed
Affiliation or Control: State IRS Status: 501(c)3
Highest Offering: Doctorate
Program: Liberal Arts And General; Teacher Preparatory; Professional
Accreditation: SC, BUS, BUSA, CAATE, CACREP, CLPSY, CS, DENT, DIETI, ENG, IPSY, LAW, LSAR, MED, NURSE, PAST, PCSAS, PH, PLNG, PSPSY, SP, TEAC

01 President ......Dr. Teresa A. SULLIVAN
101 Secretary Board of Visitors ......Ms. Susan G. HARRIS
05 Exec Vice President & Provost ......Dr. John D. SIMON
17 Exec Vice Pres for Health Affairs ......Dr. Richard P. SHANNON
30 Sr Vice Pres for Univ Advancement ......Mr. Robert D. SWEENEY
03 Exec Vice Pres/Chief Operating Ofcr ......Mr. Patrick D. HOGAN
32 Vice Pres/Chief Student Affs Ofcr ......Ms. Patricia M. LAMPKIN
46 Vice President for Research ......Mr. Phillip A. PARRISH
28 VP/Chief Officer Diversity/Equity ......Mr. Marcus L. MARTIN
41 Dir Intercollegiate Athletic Pgms ......Mr. Craig K. LITTLEPAGE
88 Senior Vice Provost ......Mr. J. Milton ADAMS
23 CEO Medical Center ......Ms. Pamela M. SUTTON-WALLACE
15 VP/Chief Human Resource Officer ......Ms. Susan CARKEEK
10 Vice President Management/Budget ......Ms. Colette SHEEHY
21 Assoc Vice President for Finance ......Ms. Melody BIANCHETTO
13 Chief Info Officer ......Ms. Virginia EVANS
88 Health Sys CFO/Bus Dev Officer ......Mr. Charles B. FITZGERALD
100 Chief of Staff/Assoc VP for Admin ......Ms. Nancy A. RIVERS
20 Vice Prov for Academic Affairs ......Ms. Maurie D. MCINNIS
88 Vice Prov Faculty Affairs ......Ms. Kerry ABRAMS
88 Vice Provost for Global Affairs ......Mr. Jeffrey w. LEGRO
11 Vice Prov for Admin/Chief of Staff ......Ms. Anda L. WEBB
88 Vice Provost for the Arts ......Mr. Jody K. KIELBASA
88 Vice Prov for Faculty Development ......Dr. Sharon L. HOSTLER
88 Vice Prov for Academic Outreach ......Mr. Billy K. CANNADAY, JR.
88 Assoc VP Business Operations ......Mr. Richard A. KOVATCH
37 Asst Vice Pres Student Finan Svcs ......Mr. Stephen A. KIMATA
25 Asst VP Research Admin ......Mr. Gerald J. KANE, JR.
26 Chief Communications Officer ......Mr. David W. MARTEL
18 Chief Facilities Officer ......Mr. Donald E. SUNDGREN
88 Chief Investment Officer ......Mr. Lawrence E. KOCHARD
06 Registrar ......Ms. Carol A J. STANLEY
07 Dean of Admission ......Mr. Gregory W. ROBERTS
61 Dean School of Law ......Mr. Paul G. MAHONEY
49 Dean School of Arts & Sciences ......Mr. Ian BAUCOM
63 Dean School of Medicine ......Dr. Randolph J. CANTERBURY
66 Dean School of Nursing ......Ms. Dorrie K. FONTAINE
54 Dean Schl Engr/Applied Science ......Mr. Craig BENSON
48 Dean School of Architecture ......Ms. Elizabeth K. MEYER
50 Dean School of Commerce ......Mr. Carl P. ZEITHAML
80 Dean Sch Leadership/Public Policy ......Mr. Allan C. STAM
53 Dean School of Education ......Mr. Robert C. PIANTA
50 Dean Grad School Business Admin ......Mr. Scott C. BEARDSLEY
51 Dean Cont & Prof Studies ......Mr. Billy K. CANNADAY, JR.
35 Associate VP/Dean of Students ......Mr. Allen W. GROVES
23 Exec Director Student Health ......Dr. Christopher HOLSTEGE
43 Gen Counsel & Corporate Secretary ......Mr. Roscoe C. ROBERTS
22 Director Equal Opportunity Pgms ......Ms. Darlene SCOTT-SCURRY
08 University Librarian ......Ms. Martha SITES
09 Dir Institutional Assess & Studies ......Mr. George A. STOVALL
88 Exec Director The Jefferson Trust ......Mr. Wayne COZART
36 Exec Dir Univ Career Services ......Mr. Everette FORTNER
88 Dir Summer & Special Academic Pgms ......Mr. Dudley J. DOANE
104 Dir International Studies Office ......Mr. Dudley J. DOANE
19 Chief of Police ......Mr. Michael A. GIBSON
39 Exec Dir Housing & Residence Life ......Ms. Gay PEREZ
40 Executive Director of UVa Bookstore ......Mr. Jonathan A. KATES
38 Director Counseling/Psych Services ......Mr. Timothy DAVIS
93 Dean African-American Affairs ......Dr. Maurice APPREY
94 Dir Study in Women Gender Sexuality ......Ms. Charlotte PATTERSON
96 Director of Procurement Services ......Mr. Eric N. DENBY

The University of Virginia's College at Wise (B)

One College Avenue, Wise VA 24293-4412
County: Wise FICE Identification: 003747
Unit ID: 233897
Telephone: (276) 328-0100 Carnegie Class: Bac/A&S
FAX Number: (276) 376-1012 Calendar System: Semester
URL: www.uvawise.edu
Established: 1954 Annual Undergrad Tuition & Fees (In-State): $9,220
Enrollment: 2,182 Coed
Affiliation or Control: State IRS Status: 501(c)3
Highest Offering: Baccalaureate
Program: Liberal Arts And General; Teacher Preparatory
Accreditation: SC, CS, ENG, NURSE, TEAC

01 Chancellor ......Dr. Donna P. HENRY
46 Ex Asst to Chanc/Dir Strategic Plng ......Vacant
05 Provost/Vice Chan for Acad Affairs ......Dr. Sanders HUGUENIN
30 Vice Chanc Devel/College Relations ......Mr. Robert S. BRAGG
10 Vice Chanc Finance/Administration ......Mr. Sim E. EWING
84 Vice Chancellor Enrollment Mgmt ......Mr. Russell D. NECESSARY
41 Ast Vice Chanc Athletic Development ......Mr. Carroll W. DALE
20 Academic Dean ......Dr. Amelia J. HARRIS
32 Dean of Students ......Vacant
21 Comptroller ......Mrs. Kristy KISER
06 Registrar ......Ms. Narda PORTER
08 Director of the Library ......Mr. Robin P. BENKE
15 Director of Human Resources ......Ms. Stephanie D. PERRY
88 Director of College Services ......Mr. Joseph B. KISER
26 Director of News & Media Relations ......Ms. Kathy STILL
44 Director of Development ......Ms. Valerie LAWSON
29 Director of Alumni Relations ......Ms. Pamela J. COLLIE
37 Director of Financial Aid ......Ms. Rebecca HUFFMAN
35 Asst Dir of Student Activities ......Ms. Sarah SMITH
36 Director of Career Development ......Ms. Neva BRYAN
38 Personal Counselor/Health Services ......Ms. Rachel ROSE
19 Campus Police Chief ......Mr. Ronnie SHORTT
12 Site Director UVA-Wise Programs ......Ms. Courtney L. CONNER
18 Interim Dir Facility Planning/Mgmt ......Mr. David SHORT
27 Associate Vice Chancellor of Info ......Dr. P. Scott BEVINS
24 Director of Media Services ......Ms. Rosa BOTT
40 Bookstore Manager ......Mr. Scott LAWSON
39 Director of Residence Life ......Mr. Josh JUSTICE
108 Director Institutional Assessment ......Mr. David KLOCEK

Virginia Baptist College (C)

4105 Plank Road, Fredericksburg VA 22407-4803
County: Spotsylvania FICE Identification: 038626
Unit ID: 482228
Telephone: (540) 785-5440 Carnegie Class: Not Classified
FAX Number: (540) 785-5441 Calendar System: Semester
URL: www.vbc.edu
Established: 1984 Annual Undergrad Tuition & Fees: $6,540
Enrollment: 99 Coed
Affiliation or Control: Baptist IRS Status: 501(c)3
Highest Offering: Master's
Program: Religious Emphasis
Accreditation: TRACS

00 Chancellor ......Dr. Don FORRESTER
01 President ......Daniel STEVENS
05 Chief Academic Officer ......Dr. Tony RETTERER
32 Chief Student Affairs/Student Life ......Dr. Mickey CREED
37 Director Student Financial Aid ......Sherry DAVIS
39 Director Student Housing ......Adam DAVIS
108 Director Institutional Assessment ......Ann M. RILL

Virginia Beach Theological Seminary (D)

2221 Centerville Turnpike, Virginia Beach VA 23464-6847
County: Virginia Beach FICE Identification: 039663
Telephone: (757) 479-3706 Carnegie Class: Not Classified
FAX Number: (757) 479-4232 Calendar System: Semester
URL: www.vbts.edu
Established: 1995 Annual Graduate Tuition & Fees: $7,730
Enrollment: 42 Coed
Affiliation or Control: Baptist IRS Status: 501(c)3
Highest Offering: Master's; No Undergraduates
Program: Professional; Religious Emphasis
Accreditation: TRACS

01 President ......Dr. Daniel K. DAVEY
05 Chief Academic Officer ......Dr. Eric J. LEHNER
07 Director of Admissions ......Mr. Edward R. ESTES
10 Financial Officer ......Dr. Thomas A. KEISER
06 Registrar ......Dr. Kyle C. DUNHAM
09 Dir Institutional Effectiveness ......Dr. Robert J. TOMENENDAL

Virginia College (E)

7200 Midlothian Turnpike, Richmond VA 23225
Telephone: (804) 977-5100 Identification: 770837
Accreditation: ACICS, ACFEI, MAAB, OTA

† Branch campus of Virginia College, Birmingham, AL.

Virginia Commonwealth University (F)

901 W Franklin Street, Box 842527,
Richmond VA 23284-2527
County: Independent City FICE Identification: 003735
Unit ID: 234030
Telephone: (804) 828-0100 Carnegie Class: RU/VH
FAX Number: N/A Calendar System: Semester
URL: www.vcu.edu
Established: 1838 Annual Undergrad Tuition & Fees (In-State): $12,772
Enrollment: 31,163 Coed
Affiliation or Control: State IRS Status: 501(c)3
Highest Offering: Doctorate
Program: Liberal Arts And General; Teacher Preparatory; Professional
Accreditation: SC, ANEST, ART, BUS, BUSA, CACREP, CEA, CIDA, CLPSY, COPSY, CORE, CS, DANCE, DENT, DH, DIETI, EMT, ENG, FEPAC, HSA, IPSY, JOUR, MED, MT, MUS, NMT, NUR, OT, PAST, PH, PHAR, PLNG, PTA, RAD, RTT, SPAA, SW, TED, THEA

01 Pres VCU/Pres & Chair VCU Hlth Sys ......Dr. Michael RAO
05 Provost & VP for Academic Affair ......Dr. Gail HACKETT
17 Interim VCU VP & CEO Health System ......Dr. Jerome STRAUSS
10 Interim VP Finance & Administrat ......Mr. Jay BONFILI
46 Vice President for Research ......Dr. Francis L. MACRINA
30 Vice Pres Development & Alumni Rel ......Ms. Marsha HEIL
86 Interim Exec Dir for Govt Relations ......Ms. Karah L. GUNTHER
32 Interim Vice Prov Student Affairs ......Dr. Charles J. KLINK
88 Int Vice Prov for Life Sciences ......Dr. Leonard A. SMOCK
09 Vice Prov Planning & Decision Supp ......Ms. Kathleen SHAW
84 Vice Prov for Strategic Enrollment ......Mr. Luke D. SCHULTHEIS
13 Chief Information Officer Tech Svcs ......Mr. Alexander L. HENSON
18 Assoc Vice Pres Facilities Mgmt ......Mr. Harry E. WYATT
21 Assoc Vice Pres Finance & Admin ......Ms. Pamela A. CURREY
84 Asst Vice Provost Enroll Svcs ......Ms. Anjour HARRIS
15 Asst Vice Pres for Human Resource ......Ms. Cathleen C. BURKE
08 University Librarian ......Mr. John E. ULMSCHNEIDER
43 University Counsel ......Ms. Madelyn F. WESSEL
41 Director of Athletics ......Mr. Edward K. MCLAUGHLIN
88 Asst Vice Pres of Business Services ......Ms. Diane L. REYNOLDS
39 Exec Dir Resdential Life & Housing ......Mr. Curtis ERWIN
06 Univ Registrar & Dir Records/Regis ......Mr. Bernard C. HAMM
07 Asst VP Student Records & Admission ......Ms. Sybil C. HALLORAN
37 Executive Director of Financial Aid ......Mr. Marc VERNON
38 Dir of Counseling Services ......Dr. Jihad N. AZIZ
36 Dir of University Career Center ......Vacant
35 Assoc Vice Prov/Dean Student Affs ......Dr. Reuban B. RODRIGUEZ
29 Assoc VP University Alum Relations ......Mr. Gordon A. MCDOUGALL
88 Exec Dir Global Education Office ......Dr. R. McKenna BROWN
88 Dir Ctr for Environmental Studies ......Dr. Gregory C. GARMAN
25 Asst VP Research Admin ......Ms. Susan E. ROBB
19 Chief of Police ......Mr. John A. VENUTI
31 VProv/Div Community Engagement ......Dr. Catherine W. HOWARD
94 Chair Women's Studies ......Dr. Kimberly M. BROWN
92 Dean Honors College ......Dr. Barry L. FALK
67 Dean of Pharmacy ......Dr. Joseph T. DIPIRO
66 Dean of School of Nursing ......Dr. Jean GIDDENS
63 Dean of School of Medicine ......Dr. Jerome F. STRAUSS
53 Interim Dean School of Education ......Dr. Lelia CHRISTENBURY
52 Dean of Dentistry ......Dr. David C. SARRETT
50 Dean School of Business ......Mr. Ed A. GRIER
49 Dean Humanities & Sciences ......Dr. James S. COLEMAN
57 Dean School of Arts ......Mr. Joseph H. SEIPEL
70 Dean School of Social Work ......Dr. James E. HINTERLONG
76 Dean Allied Health Professions ......Dr. Cecil B. DRAIN
58 Dean Graduate School ......Dr. F. Douglas BOUDINOT
54 Dean of School of Engineering ......Dr. Barbara D. BOYAN
88 Assoc Director of GEO ......Mr. Osama ALAMI
96 Director Procurement Payment Svcs ......Ms. Brenda MOWEN
26 Vice President University Relations ......Ms. Pamela D. LEPLEY
104 Director Study Abroad ......Ms. Stephanie DAVENPORT TIGNOR
108 Dir of Assessment & Inst Effectiv ......Dr. Scott F. OATES
28 Vice Pres for Inclusive Excellence ......Dr. Wanda S. MITCHELL
100 Senior Executive Director ......Mr. Brian D. SHAW
106 Director of Online Academic Program ......Mr. Jonathan D. BECKER
90 Dir Academic Technologies ......Ms. Colleen BISHOP
91 Director of Administrative Systems ......Mr. Richard S. JOHN

*Virginia Community College System Office (G)

300 Arboretum Place, Suite 200, Richmond VA 23236
County: Independent City FICE Identification: 008904
Unit ID: 234146
Telephone: (804) 819-4901 Carnegie Class: N/A
FAX Number: (804) 819-4760
URL: www.vccs.edu

01 Chancellor ......Dr. Glenn DUBOIS
10 Vice Chanc Administrative Services ......Ms. Donna VANCLEAVE
05 Vice Chancellor Academic Services ......Dr. Sharon MORRISSEY
103 Vice Chanc Workforce Development ......Dr. Craig HERNDON
13 Vice Chanc Information Tech Svcs ......Dr. James DAVIS
30 Vice Chanc Institutional Advance ......Dr. Jennifer SAGER GENTRY
15 Assoc Vice Chanc Human Resource Svc ......Dr. Christopher LEE
18 Assoc Vice Chanc/Facility Mgmt ......Mr. Bert JONES
43 General Counsel ......Ms. Greer SAUNDERS
88 Director of Internal Audit ......Mr. Whit MADERE
21 Controller ......Mr. Dave MAIR
04 Exec Assistant to the Chancellor ......Ms. Marlene MONDZIEL

*Blue Ridge Community College (H)

PO Box 80, Weyers Cave VA 24486-0080
County: Augusta FICE Identification: 006819
Unit ID: 231536
Telephone: (540) 234-9261 Carnegie Class: Assoc/Pub-R-M
FAX Number: (540) 234-8189 Calendar System: Semester
URL: www.brcc.edu
Established: 1965 Annual Undergrad Tuition & Fees (In-State): $4,794
Enrollment: 4,388 Coed
Affiliation or Control: State IRS Status: 501(c)3
Highest Offering: Associate Degree
Program: Occupational; 2-Year Principally Bachelor's Creditable; Technical Emphasis
Accreditation: SC, ADNUR

02 President ... Dr. John A. DOWNEY
05 Vice Pres Instruction/Student Svcs ... Dr. Robert YOUNG
10 VP Finance/Administrative Svcs ... Dr. Robert BALDYGO
15 Director of Human Resources ... Mr. Tim NICELY
30 Executive Director Development ... Ms. Amy LASER KIGER
81 Int Dean Math/Physical Sci/Tech ... Dr. Marlena JARBOE
79 Dean Humanities/SoclSci/Workforce ... Dr. Kevin B. RATLIFF
76 Dean Life Sciences/Human Services ... Dr. David URSO
20 Dean Academic Support Services ... Ms. Annette WILLIAMS
08 Head Librarian ... Mr. Kyle MCCARRELL
26 Chief Public Relations Officer ... Ms. Bridget BAYLOR
06 Registrar/Admissions ... Ms. Erika MABREY
21 Financial Services Manager ... Ms. Franki HAMPTON
19 Security & Compliance Coordinator ... Mr. Wayne MARTIN
09 Coordinator Institutional Research ... Dr. Susan E. CROSBY
37 Financial Aid Coordinator ... Mr. Robert L. CLEMMER
36 Coord Career Services/ Recruitment ... Ms. Carmel MURPHY-NORRIS
84 Enrollment Services Specialist ... Ms. Amanda BLAND

*Central Virginia Community College (A)

3506 Wards Road, Lynchburg VA 24502-2498
County: Independent City FICE Identification: 004988
Unit ID: 231697
Telephone: (434) 832-7600 Carnegie Class: Assoc/Pub-R-M
FAX Number: (434) 386-4700 Calendar System: Semester
URL: www.cvcc.vccs.edu
Established: 1966 Annual Undergrad Tuition & Fees (In-State): $4,402
Enrollment: 4,521 Coed
Affiliation or Control: State IRS Status: 501(c)3
Highest Offering: Associate Degree
Program: Occupational; 2-Year Principally Bachelor's Creditable
Accreditation: SC, COARC, EMT, RAD

02 President ... Dr. John CAPPS
05 VP Academic/Student Services ... Mr. Will SANDIDGE
10 Vice Pres Finance & Admin Svcs ... Mr. John POOLE
103 VP Ctr Workforce Dev/Cont Educ ... Dr. Ruth HENDRICK
30 Vice Pres Institutional Advancement ... Mr. Michael BRADFORD
13 Vice Pres of Information Technology ... Mr. James D. LIGHTFOOT
45 Dean Instnl Effectiveness/Planning ... Ms. Kristen OGDEN
21 Chief Business Officer ... Mr. Daniel CHIPMAN
29 Director Alumni/Public Relations ... Vacant
84 Dean of Enrollment Management ... Mr. Michael FARRIS
15 Human Resource Manager ... Mr. Randall FRANKLIN
18 Capital Outlay Project Engineer ... Mr. Tom BUSHLEY
56 Distance Education Supervisor ... Mr. Ed MCGEE
08 Coordinator of Library Services ... Mr. Michael T. FEIN
78 Coord Apprenticeship/Coop Education ... Vacant
79 Dean Humanities/Social Science ... Dr. Muriel B. MICKLES
50 Dean of Business & Allied Health ... Dr. James LEMONS
81 Dean of Science/Math/Engineering ... Dr. Jeffrey W. LAUB

*Dabney S. Lancaster Community College (B)

PO Box 1000, Clifton Forge VA 24422-1000
County: Alleghany FICE Identification: 004996
Unit ID: 231873
Telephone: (540) 863-2800 Carnegie Class: Assoc/Pub-R-S
FAX Number: (540) 863-2915 Calendar System: Semester
URL: www.dslcc.edu
Established: 1967 Annual Undergrad Tuition & Fees (In-State): $5,238
Enrollment: 1,257 Coed
Affiliation or Control: State IRS Status: 501(c)3
Highest Offering: Associate Degree
Program: Occupational; 2-Year Principally Bachelor's Creditable
Accreditation: SC, ACFEI, ADNUR

02 President ... Dr. John J. RAINONE
10 Vice President Finance/Admin Svcs ... Mrs. Angela GRAHAM
51 VP Continuing Educ/Workforce Svcs ... Mr. Gary S. KEENER
49 Dean Arts & Sciences ... Ms. Lynn MCALLISTER
32 Director of Student Services ... Mr. Matthew MCGRAW
08 Director of Learning Resources ... Ms. Nova WRIGHT
06 Registrar ... Ms. Lorrie FERGUSON
21 Business Officer ... Ms. Pamela BROWN
18 Buildings & Grounds Supervisor ... Mr. Edward N. KENNY
13 Coord of Computer Info Systems ... Ms. Tamra LIPSCOMB
37 Coord of Student Financial Aid ... Mrs. Joy BROYLES
45 Planning & Funding Specialist ... Ms. Rachael G. THOMPSON
15 Director of Personnel Services ... Ms. April TOLLEY
108 Director Institutional Assessment ... Dr. Chris OREM

*Danville Community College (C)

1008 S Main Street, Danville VA 24541-4088
County: Independent City FICE Identification: 003758
Unit ID: 231882
Telephone: (434) 797-2222 Carnegie Class: Assoc/Pub-R-M
FAX Number: (434) 797-8514 Calendar System: Semester
URL: www.dcc.vccs.edu
Established: 1967 Annual Undergrad Tuition & Fees (In-State): $4,350
Enrollment: 3,982 Coed
Affiliation or Control: State IRS Status: 501(c)3
Highest Offering: Associate Degree
Program: Occupational; 2-Year Principally Bachelor's Creditable
Accreditation: SC

02 President ... Dr. Bruce R. SCISM
05 Vice Pres Academic/Student Services ... Dr. Debra HOLLEY
10 Vice Pres Financial/Admin Services ... Mr. Scott BARNES
30 Vice President of Development ... Mr. Shannon HAIR
09 Dir of Plng/Effectiveness/Research ... Mr. George STILL
26 Chief Public Relations Officer ... Ms. Andrea BURNEY

*Eastern Shore Community College (D)

29300 Lankford Highway, Melfa VA 23410-9755
County: Accomack FICE Identification: 003748
Unit ID: 232052
Telephone: (757) 789-1789 Carnegie Class: Assoc/Pub-R-S
FAX Number: (757) 789-1737 Calendar System: Semester
URL: www.es.vccs.edu
Established: 1971 Annual Undergrad Tuition & Fees (In-State): $4,275
Enrollment: 1,131 Coed
Affiliation or Control: State IRS Status: 501(c)3
Highest Offering: Associate Degree
Program: Occupational; 2-Year Principally Bachelor's Creditable
Accreditation: SC

02 President ... Dr. Linda THOMAS-GLOVER
05 VP of Academic & Student Svcs ... Dr. Kimberly BRITT
10 Vice Pres Finance & Administration ... Mrs. Annette EDWARDS
32 Coordinator of Student Services ... Mrs. Jody BAGGETT
08 Director Learning Resources ... Mrs. Janet JUSTIS
06 Registrar ... Ms. Kathy CARMODY
09 Director of Institutional Research ... Ms. Judith M. GRIER
26 Chief Public Relations Officer ... Vacant
37 Financial Aid Coordinator ... Ms. Carole READ
15 Director Personnel Services ... Ms. Diane WHEATLEY
18 Chief Facilities/Physical Plant ... Mr. Bobby MEARS
29 Director Alumni Relations/Devel ... Ms. Eve BELOTE
20 Assistant to the VP of Academics ... Mrs. Robin RICH-COATES

*Germanna Community College (E)

2130 Germanna Highway, Locust Grove VA 22508-2102
County: Orange FICE Identification: 008660
Unit ID: 232195
Telephone: (540) 423-9030 Carnegie Class: Assoc/Pub-R-M
FAX Number: (540) 727-3207 Calendar System: Semester
URL: www.germanna.edu
Established: 1970 Annual Undergrad Tuition & Fees (In-State): $3,660
Enrollment: 7,281 Coed
Affiliation or Control: State IRS Status: 501(c)3
Highest Offering: Associate Degree
Program: Occupational; 2-Year Principally Bachelor's Creditable
Accreditation: SC, ADNUR, DA, @PTAA

02 President ... Dr. David A. SAM
04 Exec Assistant to the President ... Ms. Pamela S. DUFF
05 VP Academic & Student Services ... Dr. Ann WOOLFORD
10 VP Finance & Administrative Svcs ... Mr. Richard BREHM
103 VP Workforce & Community Educ ... Dr. Jeanne WESLEY
30 VP Institutional Advancement ... Mr. Doug ELLIOTT
32 Dean of Student Services ... Ms. Pam FREDERICK
09 Exec Dir of Planning & Assessement ... Dr. Deborah BROCK
08 Head Librarian ... Ms. Tamara REMHOF
06 Registrar ... Ms. Ali HIEBER
72 Dean Professional & Technical Study ... Ms. Denise GUEST
55 Dean Distance Educ & Lrng Resources ... Dr. Yanyan YONG
66 Dean of Nursing & Health Technology ... Dr. Patti LISK
15 Exec Director of Human Resources ... Mr. Reginald RYALS
18 Building & Ground Supervisor ... Mr. Garland FENWICK
84 Dean of Enrollment Services ... Ms. Ali HEIBER
13 Manager Technology Services ... Ms. Jacque LARSEN
26 Director of Marketing ... Vacant
49 Dean of Arts & Sciences ... Dr. Shashuna GRAY
103 Dean of Workforce Prof Development ... Ms. Martha O'KEEFE
19 Chief of Police ... Mr. Craig BRANCH
37 Director Student Financial Aid ... Vacant

*J. Sargeant Reynolds Community College (F)

PO Box 85622, Richmond VA 23285-5622
County: Henrico FICE Identification: 003759
Unit ID: 232414
Telephone: (804) 371-3000 Carnegie Class: Assoc/Pub-U-MC
FAX Number: (804) 371-3650 Calendar System: Semester
URL: www.reynolds.edu
Established: 1972 Annual Undergrad Tuition & Fees (In-State): $4,691
Enrollment: 10,667 Coed
Affiliation or Control: State IRS Status: 501(c)3
Highest Offering: Associate Degree
Program: Occupational; 2-Year Principally Bachelor's Creditable
Accreditation: SC, ACFEI, ADNUR, COARC, DA, DT, EMT, MLTAD, OPD

02 President ... Dr. Gary L. RHODES
03 Executive Vice President ... Dr. Genene D. LEROSEN
05 Vice President Academic Affairs ... Dr. David R. LOOPE
30 Vice President Advancement ... Mrs. Elizabeth S. LITTLEFIELD
103 VP Comm Col Workforce Alliance ... Mr. Louis L. MCGINTY
10 VP Finance and Administration ... Ms. Amelia M. BRADSHAW
32 VP Student Affairs/Title IX Coord ... Dr. Thomas N. HOLLINS, JR.
45 Assoc VP Policy/Inst Effectiveness ... Mrs. Diane F. BRASINGTON
13 Vice President Technology ... Dr. Mark D. WEBSTER
79 Dean School of Humanities/Soc Sci ... Dr. Barbara M. GLENN
50 Dean School of Business ... Mr. David J. BARRISH
76 Dean School of Nursing/Allied Hlth ... Dr. Susan S. HUNTER
81 Dean School of Math Sci Engineering ... Mr. Raymond A. BURTON
20 Dean Educational Support Services ... Mr. Ty CORBIN
09 Director Office Inst Effectiveness ... Dr. Jackie R. BOURQUE
15 Assoc VP HR/Equal Emp Oppty Ofcr ... Ms. Corliss B. WOODSON
37 Director of Financial Aid ... Mrs. Kiesha L. POPE
07 Director of Admissions & Records ... Mrs. Karen M. PETTIS-WALDEN
88 Director Outreach and Recruitment ... Ms. Tracy S. GREEN
27 Director Communications ... Mr. Joseph SHILLING
26 Director of Marketing ... Ms. Kelly A. SMITH
08 Director of Info/Library Services ... Ms. Hong WU
88 Director of Learning Communities ... Mr. Charles PETERSON, JR.
18 Director Facilities Mgmt/Planning ... Mr. Michael VERDU
21 Director of Financial Operations ... Ms. Shirley L. HOPKINS
30 Director of Development ... Ms. Marianne S. MCGHEE
88 Director of Middle College ... Ms. Mary Jo WASHKO
84 Director of Enrollment Services ... Mr. Brian A. RICHARDSON
06 Registrar ... Ms. Denise S. TUNSTALL
96 Purchasing Manager ... Mr. Christopher L. COLE
19 Chief of Police ... Mr. Paul L. RONCA

*John Tyler Community College (G)

13101 Jefferson Davis Highway, Chester VA 23831-5316
County: Chesterfield FICE Identification: 004004
Unit ID: 232450
Telephone: (804) 796-4000 Carnegie Class: Assoc/Pub-S-MC
FAX Number: (804) 796-4163 Calendar System: Semester
URL: www.jtcc.edu
Established: 1965 Annual Undergrad Tuition & Fees (In-State): $4,345
Enrollment: 9,875 Coed
Affiliation or Control: State IRS Status: 501(c)3
Highest Offering: Associate Degree
Program: Occupational; 2-Year Principally Bachelor's Creditable
Accreditation: SC, ADNUR, #FUSER

02 President ... Dr. Edward E. RASPILLER
04 Executive Assistant to President ... Ms. Mara M. HILLIAR
05 VP Learning & Student Success ... Dr. William FIEGE
10 VP Finance & Admininstration ... Mr. William F. TAYLOR
103 Vice Pres for CC Workforce Alliance ... Mr. Mac L. MCGINTY
32 Dean of Students ... Ms. Sandra KIRKLAND
54 Interim Dean Engr/Bus/Public Svcs ... Dr. Julie RANSON
49 Dean Arts/Humanities/Soc Sciences ... Dr. Mikell BROWN
81 Dean Math/Natural & Health Sci ... Dr. Johanna WEISS
09 Dir Institutional Effectiveness ... Dr. Donna JOVANOVICH
08 Librarian Chester Campus ... Ms. Linda LUEBKE
15 AVP of Human Resources ... Ms. Susan GRINNAN
37 Director Financial Aid ... Mr. Tony JONES
19 Security Manager ... Mr. Frank MEDAGLIA
35 Coordinator Student Activities ... Vacant
36 Director Counseling Chester Campus ... Vacant
36 Dir Counseling Midlothian Campus ... Dr. Ruth VARNEY
18 Director Facilities Operations ... Mr. Greg A. DUNAWAY
08 Librarian Midlothian Campus ... Ms. Helen MCKANN
06 Registrar ... Ms. Joy L. JAMES
96 Director of Purchasing ... Ms. Nancy M. JIMISON
30 VP Institutional Advancement ... Ms. Rachel BIUNDO

*Lord Fairfax Community College (H)

173 Skirmisher Lane, Middletown VA 22645-1745
County: Frederick FICE Identification: 008659
Unit ID: 232575
Telephone: (540) 868-7000 Carnegie Class: Assoc/Pub-R-L
FAX Number: (540) 868-7100 Calendar System: Semester
URL: www.lfcc.edu
Established: 1970 Annual Undergrad Tuition & Fees (In-State): $4,395
Enrollment: 6,996 Coed
Affiliation or Control: State IRS Status: 501(c)3
Highest Offering: Associate Degree
Program: Occupational; 2-Year Principally Bachelor's Creditable; Business Emphasis
Accreditation: SC, EMT, SURGT

02 President ... Dr. Cheryl THOMPSON-STACY
05 VP of Academic and Student Affairs ... Dr. Chris COUTTS
10 VP of Financial & Admin Services ... Mr. Chris BOIES
103 VP Workforce Solutions/Cont Educ ... Ms. Jeanian CLARK
20 Assoc VP of Instruction Middletown ... Ms. Kim BLOSSER
20 Assoc VP of Instruction Fauquier ... Dr. Judy BATSON
32 Coord Student Life & Info Services ... Ms. Brandy BOIES
76 Assoc Dean Health Prof & Science ... Ms. Tammy WAGNER
50 Dean Bus/Tech/Dir HS Outreach ... Ms. Brenda K. BYARD
81 Dean Hum/Math/Social Sciences ... Dr. Richard L. ELAM
15 Human Resource Manager ... Ms. Karen N. FOREMAN
30 Director of Development ... Ms. Liv HEGGOY
12 Manager Luray-Page County Center ... Ms. Judith J. SUDDITH
08 Director Learning Resources Center ... Mr. David R. GRAY
09 Assoc Dir Planning/Inst Effective ... Ms. Nancy SMITH
13 Coordinator Network Security ... Mr. Douglas M. SHRIER
35 Dean of Students - Middletown ... Dr. Karen H. BUCHER
38 Dir Stdnt Learning Svcs/Counseling ... Ms. Amber FOLTZ
37 Director of Financial Aid ... Mr. Aaron WHITACRE
96 Procurement Officer ... Mr. Steve CORBIT
21 Budget and Finance Director ... Mr. Barry ORNDORFF
08 Librarian ... Mr. Gregory MACDONALD
88 Director of Transition Programs ... Ms. Lyda KISER
27 Public Info/Grant & Sponsored Pgm ... Mr. Darryl D. CRAWFORD
06 Assistant Registrar ... Ms. Tina Marie ANDERSON
18 Chief Facilities/Physical Plant ... Mr. David L. BUSHMAN

Code	Title	Name
19	Law Enforcement Manager	Mr. Rob MARSHALL
26	Public Relations Marketing Manager	Ms. Leslie G. KELLY
36	Counselor Middle College	Ms. Stacy DREW
88	Coord Student Learning & TRIO SS	Ms. Mia S. LEGGETT
88	Coord/Dir LF Small Bus Dev Center	Mr. William A. SIRBAUGH
88	Coord Business & Industry Trng	Mr. Bill PENCE
84	Dual Enrollment Coordinator	Ms. Heather BURTON

*Mountain Empire Community College (A)

3441 Mountain Empire Road,
Big Stone Gap VA 24219-4634

County: Wise — FICE Identification: 009629 — Unit ID: 232788

Telephone: (276) 523-2400 — Carnegie Class: Assoc/Pub-R-M
FAX Number: (276) 523-8297 — Calendar System: Semester
URL: www.mecc.edu
Established: 1972 — Annual Undergrad Tuition & Fees (In-State): $3,336
Enrollment: 2,718 — Coed
Affiliation or Control: State — IRS Status: 501(c)3
Highest Offering: Associate Degree
Program: Occupational; 2-Year Principally Bachelor's Creditable
Accreditation: SC, ADNUR, COARC

Code	Title	Name
02	President	Dr. Scott HAMILTON
05	VP Academic & Student Services	Ms. Vickie RATLIFF
10	Vice Pres Finance & Admin Services	Ms. Donna SHELTON
30	Vice Pres Institutional Advancement	Ms. Donna G. STANLEY
32	Dean of Student Services	Mr. Brandon DOTSON
07	Director of Enrollment Services	Ms. Kristy HALL
08	Director of Library Services	Mr. Michael GILLEY
51	Dir Continuing & Distance Education	Ms. Sue Ella BOATRIGHT-WELLS
37	Dir Financial Aid/Enrollment Svcs	Ms. Kristy HALL
13	Dir Ctr Computing & Info Technology	Mr. Rickie N. CAMPBELL
15	Director Personnel Services	Ms. Pam GILES
18	Chief Facilities/Physical Plant	Mr. Jim VICARS
49	Dean Arts & Sciences	Ms. Carolyn H. REYNOLDS
72	Dean of Industrial Tech/Health Sci	Mr. Tommy CLEMENTS
50	Dean of Business & Info Tech	Mr. Tommy CLEMENTS
26	Chief Public Relations Officer	Ms. Amy GREEAR
19	Chief of Police	Mr. Myron HATFIELD

*New River Community College (B)

5251 College Drive, Dublin VA 24084-1127

County: Pulaski — FICE Identification: 005223 — Unit ID: 232867

Telephone: (540) 674-3600 — Carnegie Class: Assoc/Pub-R-M
FAX Number: (540) 674-3642 — Calendar System: Semester
URL: www.nr.edu
Established: 1969 — Annual Undergrad Tuition & Fees (In-State): $4,351
Enrollment: 4,585 — Coed
Affiliation or Control: State — IRS Status: 501(c)3
Highest Offering: Associate Degree
Program: 2-Year Principally Bachelor's Creditable
Accreditation: SC

Code	Title	Name
02	President	Dr. Jack M. LEWIS
05	VP for Instruction/Student Svcs	Dr. Patricia B. HUBER
10	Vice Pres for Finance & Technology	Mr. John L. VAN HEMERT
30	VP for WD and External Relations	Dr. Mark C. ROWH
88	Coord of Emer Plng & Special Proj	Mrs. Amy J. HALL
49	Dean of Arts & Sciences	Dr. Janice SHELTON
50	Dean of Business & Technologies	Mr. Peter ANDERSON
09	Dir Inst Effectiveness/Research	Dr. Frederick M. STREFF
06	Registrar	Mrs. Tammy SMITH
15	Dir of Human Resources & Bus Oper	Ms. Melissa P. ANDERSON
102	Executive Director of Foundation	Ms. Angie E. COVEY
32	Director of Student Affairs	Mrs. Deborah KENNEDY
37	Director of Student Financial Aid	Ms. Lori A. NUNN
18	Chief Facilities/Physical Plant	Mr. Anthony J. NICOLO
96	Inventory and Purchasing Technician	Ms. Monica W. CARDEN
56	Dir Dist Educ/Offsite Campus Svcs	Mrs. Linda C. CLAUSSEN
08	Coordinator of Library Services	Mrs. Sandra B. SMITH
07	Coord Admissions/Records/Stdnt Svcs	Mrs. Tammy SMITH
88	Coordinator of WorkKeys Center	Mrs. Patricia RYAN
88	Coord Ctr for Disability Services	Ms. Lucy J. HOWLETT
84	Enrollment Manager Coordinator	Mrs. Deborah D. KENNEDY
26	Public Relations Specialist	Ms. Joyce K. TAYLOR

*Northern Virginia Community College (C)

4001 Wakefield Chapel Road, Annandale VA 22003-3796

County: Fairfax — FICE Identification: 003727 — Unit ID: 232946

Telephone: (703) 323-3000 — Carnegie Class: Assoc/Pub-S-MC
FAX Number: (703) 323-3767 — Calendar System: Semester
URL: www.nvcc.edu
Established: 1965 — Annual Undergrad Tuition & Fees (In-State): $4,110
Enrollment: 51,487 — Coed
Affiliation or Control: State — IRS Status: 501(c)3
Highest Offering: Associate Degree
Program: Occupational; 2-Year Principally Bachelor's Creditable
Accreditation: SC, ADNUR, CAHIIM, COARC, DA, DH, DMS, EMT, MLTAD, OTA, PTAA

Code	Title	Name
02	President	Dr. Scott RALLS
05	Exec VP/Chief Academic Officer	Dr. Mel D. SCHIAVELLI
10	Vice President Finance	Ms. Dimitrina DIMKOVA
11	Acting Vice Pres/Chief Admin Ofcr	Ms. Dimitrina DIMKOVA
13	Vice Pres of Information Technology	Dr. Steven G. SACHS
103	Acting VP of Workforce Development	Dr. Lorinzo FOXWORTH
09	VP Inst Research/Planning/Assess	Dr. George E. GABRIEL
20	Assoc VP Academic Services	Dr. Sharon N. ROBERTSON
104	Assoc Vice Pres Global Studies	Dr. Paul J. MCVEIGH
84	Assoc VP Stdnt Svcs & Enroll Mgmt	Dr. Elizabeth HARPER
12	Interim Provost Alexandria Campus	Dr. Ron BUCHANAN
12	Interim Provost Annandale Campus	Ms. Charlotte CALOBRISI
12	Provost Loudoun Campus	Dr. Julie LEIDIG
12	Provost Manassas Campus	Dr. Roger RAMSAMMY
12	Provost Medical Education Campus	Dr. Anne LOOCHTAN
12	Provost Woodbridge Campus	Dr. Sam HILL
102	Exec Dir NVCC Education Foundation	Mr. John J. RUFFINO
06	College Registrar	Ms. Alethea HAMILTON
22	Director of Diversity	Mr. Everett V. EBERHARDT
102	Assistant Dir NVCC Educ Foundation	Ms. Mary BRAMLEY
25	Director of Grants/Special Projects	Dr. Milan HAYWARD
15	Director of Human Resources	Ms. Julie A. GARCIA
96	Director of Purchasing	Mr. Edward J. MELLON
37	Dir Stdnt Financial Aid/Support Svc	Ms. Joan A. ZANDERS
21	Acting Associate VP	Mr. Frederick TITTMANN
18	Director of Facilities	Mr. Steven PATTERSON
26	Director of Media Relations	Ms. Kathy THOMPSON
19	Director Security/Safety	Chief Daniel DUSSEAU
86	Director Government Affs/Cmty Rels	Mr. Dana KAUFFMAN

*Patrick Henry Community College (D)

645 Patriot Avenue, Martinsville VA 24112

County: Henry — FICE Identification: 003751 — Unit ID: 233019

Telephone: (276) 638-8777 — Carnegie Class: Assoc/Pub-R-M
FAX Number: (276) 656-0320 — Calendar System: Semester
URL: www.ph.vccs.edu
Established: 1962 — Annual Undergrad Tuition & Fees (In-State): $4,360
Enrollment: 2,243 — Coed
Affiliation or Control: State — IRS Status: 501(c)3
Highest Offering: Associate Degree
Program: Occupational; 2-Year Principally Bachelor's Creditable
Accreditation: SC, ADNUR, EMT

Code	Title	Name
02	President	Dr. Angeline D. GODWIN
05	VP Academic/Student Develop Svcs	Dr. Kristin WESTOVER
10	Vice Pres Finance & Admin Services	Mr. John HANBURY
30	Vice Pres Inst Advancement	Mr. Christopher PARKER
103	Vice Pres Wrkfc/Econ/Comm Dev	Mrs. Rhonda HODGES
20	Dean Acad Succ & Col Transfer	Mr. Greg HODGES
76	Dean Prof Tech/Health Sciences	Mr. Jeff FIELDS
37	Financial Aid/Veterans Admin	Mrs. Cindy KELLER
81	Dean Science/Tech/Engineering/Math	Mr. Steve BRANCH
06	Registrar	Ms. Jessica CARTER
15	Director of Human Resources	Ms. Lori MCCARTY
18	Chief Facilities/Physical Plant	Ms. Roberta WRIGHT
26	Chief Public Relations/Dir Alumni	Mrs. Kristin LANDRUM
22	Affirmative Action Coordinator	Ms. Lori MCCARTY
96	Director of Purchasing	Ms. Lori CONNER
09	Coord Inst Research/Plng/Evaluation	Ms. Tandy GAFFNEY
07	Coord of Admissions & Records	Mr. Travis TISDALE
04	Administrative Asst to President	Ms. Jencie GIBSON
08	Head Librarian	Mr. Barry REYNOLDS
72	Dean of Technology	Mr. David DEAL
19	Director Security/Safety	Mr. Gary DOVE
25	Chief Contracts/Grants Admin	Ms. Sarah B. KEYSER
41	Athletic Director	Mr. Brian HENDERSON

*Paul D. Camp Community College (E)

100 N College Drive, Franklin VA 23851-0737

County: Independent City — FICE Identification: 009159 — Unit ID: 233037

Telephone: (757) 569-6700 — Carnegie Class: Assoc/Pub-R-S
FAX Number: (757) 569-6795 — Calendar System: Semester
URL: www.pdc.edu
Established: 1970 — Annual Undergrad Tuition & Fees (In-State): $4,340
Enrollment: 1,259 — Coed
Affiliation or Control: State — IRS Status: 501(c)3
Highest Offering: Associate Degree
Program: Occupational; 2-Year Principally Bachelor's Creditable
Accreditation: SC

Code	Title	Name
02	Interim President	Dr. William C. AIKEN
05	VP Academic/Student Development	Dr. Tara ATKINS-BRADY
10	Vice President Finance/Admin Svcs	Dr. Joe EDENFIELD
30	Int VP Institutional Advancement	Dr. Renee FELTS
32	Dean Student Services	Ms. Trina JONES
20	Dean of Suffolk Academic Programs	Dr. Justin OLIVER
20	Dean of Franklin Campus	Ms. Antoinette JOHNSON
08	Librarian	Mr. Troy HAND
12	Academic Director-Smithfield	Dr. Justin OLIVER
103	VP of Workforce Development	Mr. Randy BETZ
09	Director of Institutional Research	Ms. Damay J. BULLOCK
18	Chief Facilities/Physical Plant	Mr. James C. GORHAM
15	Human Resources Manager	Vacant
26	Public Relations Specialist	Ms. Wendy HARRISON
37	Financial Aid Coordinator	Ms. Teresa HARRISON
04	Assistant to the President	Ms. Cathy CUTCHINS

*Piedmont Virginia Community College (F)

501 College Drive, Charlottesville VA 22902-7589

County: Independent City — FICE Identification: 009928 — Unit ID: 233116

Telephone: (434) 977-3900 — Carnegie Class: Assoc/Pub-R-M
FAX Number: (434) 971-8232 — Calendar System: Semester
URL: www.pvcc.edu
Established: 1972 — Annual Undergrad Tuition & Fees (In-State): $3,388
Enrollment: 5,554 — Coed
Affiliation or Control: State — IRS Status: 501(c)3
Highest Offering: Associate Degree
Program: Occupational; 2-Year Principally Bachelor's Creditable; Liberal Arts And General
Accreditation: SC, ADNUR, DMS, EMT, RAD, SURGT

Code	Title	Name
02	President	Dr. Frank FRIEDMAN
05	VP Instruction/Student Svcs	Dr. John DONNELLY
10	Vice President Finance/Admin Svcs	Vacant
30	Vice Pres Advancement/Development	Dr. James ROSS
79	Dean Humanities/Fine Arts/Soc Sci	Dr. Clifford W. HAURY
50	Dean Business/Math/Technologies	Dr. Adam HASTINGS
17	Dean Health & Life Sciences	Dr. Kathy HUDSON
103	Dean Workforce Services	Ms. Valerie PALAMOUNTAIN
32	Director of Student Services	Ms. Mary Lee WALSH
13	Dir Information Technology/CIO	Ms. Sue HAAS
09	Dir Instl Research/Planning/Effect	Dr. Jolene HAMM
06	Registrar	Ms. Allyson REA
96	Business Manager	Ms. Tracy CERSLEY
18	Facilities Manager	Mr. Dennis WEIR
15	Human Resources Manager	Ms. Jennifer ATKINS
26	Marketing/Media Relations Director	Ms. Leigh-Anne LAWRENCE
84	Outreach Manager	Ms. Denise MCCLANAHAN
08	Coordinator Library Services	Ms. Crystal NEWELL
37	Coordinator Financial Aid	Ms. Carol LARSON
36	Coordinator Advising & Transfer	Mr. Kemper STEELE

*Rappahannock Community College (G)

12745 College Drive, Glenns VA 23149-0287

County: Gloucester — FICE Identification: 009160 — Unit ID: 233310

Telephone: (804) 758-6700 — Carnegie Class: Assoc/Pub-S-MC
FAX Number: (804) 758-3852 — Calendar System: Semester
URL: www.rappahannock.edu
Established: 1970 — Annual Undergrad Tuition & Fees (In-State): $3,401
Enrollment: 3,569 — Coed
Affiliation or Control: State — IRS Status: 501(c)3
Highest Offering: Associate Degree
Program: Occupational; 2-Year Principally Bachelor's Creditable
Accreditation: SC, ADNUR

Code	Title	Name
02	President	Dr. Elizabeth H. CROWTHER
32	VP Instruction/Student Development	Dr. A. Donna ALEXANDER
103	Vice Pres Workforce/Cmty Devel	Mr. Jason PERRY
05	Academic Dean	Ms. Martha BROOKS
35	Dean Student Development	Dr. Dave KEEL
106	Dean of Distance Learning/Tech	Ms. Virginia JONES
30	Dean of College Advancement	Ms. Cherie CARL
108	Dean Research/Effectiveness/Plng	Dr. Glenda D. HAYNIE
06	College Registrar	Ms. Felicia B. PACKETT
37	Financial Aid/Veteran Affairs Ofcr	Ms. Sherika CHARITY
15	Human Resources Manager	Mrs. Caroline W. STELTER
18	Facilities/Physical Plant Manager	Mr. Mark P. BEAVER
21	Business Manager	Ms. Susan S. BROADDUS
08	Library Coordinator	Mr. Dan REAM

*Southside Virginia Community College (H)

109 Campus Drive, Alberta VA 23821-2930

County: Brunswick — FICE Identification: 008661 — Unit ID: 233639

Telephone: (434) 949-1000 — Carnegie Class: Assoc/Pub-R-L
FAX Number: (434) 949-7863 — Calendar System: Semester
URL: www.southside.edu
Established: 1970 — Annual Undergrad Tuition & Fees (In-State): $3,480
Enrollment: 5,352 — Coed
Affiliation or Control: State — IRS Status: 501(c)3
Highest Offering: Associate Degree
Program: Occupational; 2-Year Principally Bachelor's Creditable
Accreditation: SC, EMT

Code	Title	Name
02	President	Dr. John J. CAVAN
12	Provost John H Daniel Campus	Dr. Paula M. GASTENVELD
12	Provost Christanna Campus	Dr. Al ROBERTS
05	Vice Pres Academics/Student Affs	Ms. Tara CARTER
10	Vice Pres Finance & Administration	Mr. Peter G. HUNT
25	VP Adult Education & Grants	Dr. Linda SHEFFIELD
13	Dean Information Services	Mr. Jack ANCELL
84	Dean Enrollment Management	Mrs. Shannon FEINMAN
20	Dean of Instruction Daniel Campus	Ms. Elizabeth ELAM
20	Dean of Instruction Christanna	Mr. Chad PATTON
09	Dean Institutional Effectiveness	Dr. Anne C. HAYES
66	Dean of Nursing/Health Technology	Ms. Michelle K. EDMONDS
102	Exec Director SVCC Foundation	Mrs. Mary Jane ELKINS
08	College Librarian	Ms. Marika PETERSON
26	Public Relations & Mktg Specialist	Ms. Christie C. HALES

37 Director of Financial Aid ... Ms. Sally THARRINGTON
15 Human Resources Manager ... Ms. Bethany W. HARRIS
18 Buildings/Grounds Supt Christanna ... Mr. Roger WRAY
38 Dir Student Counseling Christanna ... Ms. Bernadette BATTLE
38 Director Student Counseling Daniel ... Mrs. Dorethea SIZEMORE
21 Business Manager ... Mrs. Juanita GRIZZARD
29 Alumni Relations SVCC ... Mrs. Mary Jane ELKINS
06 Ofcr for Admiss/Registration Team ... Ms. Robin NELSON

*Southwest Virginia Community College (A)

Box SVCC, Richlands VA 24641-1101

County: Tazewell
FICE Identification: 007260
Unit ID: 233648
Telephone: (276) 964-2555
Carnegie Class: Assoc/Pub-R-M
FAX Number: (276) 964-9307
Calendar System: Semester
URL: www.sw.edu
Established: 1967
Annual Undergrad Tuition & Fees (In-State): $43487.92
Enrollment: 2,546
Coed
Affiliation or Control: State
IRS Status: 501(c)3
Highest Offering: Associate Degree
Program: Occupational; 2-Year Principally Bachelor's Creditable
Accreditation: SC, ADNUR, EMT, OTA, RAD

02 President ... Dr. J. Mark ESTEPP
05 VP Academics & Student Services ... Dr. Barbara J. FULLER
10 Int Vice Pres Finance & Admin Svcs ... Mr. Windell TURNER
04 General Admin Coordinator ... Ms. Rhonda L. VANDYKE
79 Dean Humanit/Sci/Math/Health Tech ... Ms. Cathy SMITH-COX
50 Dean Business/Engr & Indust Tech ... Mr. James DYE
103 Dean Cmty/Workforce & Econ Sol ... Vacant
32 Dean Student Success ... Ms. Mary A. RAGLAND
09 Institutional Research Officer ... Dr. Edmond C. SMITH
102 Exec Dir SWCC Educ Foundation & Dev ... Ms. Susan L. HAGY LOWE
15 Human Resources Director ... Ms. Martha L. RASNAKE
19 Campus Police Chief ... Mr. Ronnie KISER
21 Business Manager ... Mr. Michael BALES
18 Physical Plant Superintendent ... Mr. Tony MCGHEE
26 Public Relations Coordinator ... Ms. Patsy G. BUSSARD
08 Coordinator of Library Services ... Ms. Teresa A. YEAROUT
106 Director Distance Learning ... Ms. Dyan E. LESTER
25 Grants Coordinator ... Ms. Phyllis ROBERTS

*Thomas Nelson Community College (B)

99 Thomas Nelson Drive, Hampton VA 23666

County: Independent City
FICE Identification: 006871
Unit ID: 233754
Telephone: (757) 825-2700
Carnegie Class: Assoc/Pub-S-SC
FAX Number: (757) 825-2763
Calendar System: Semester
URL: www.tncc.edu
Established: 1967
Annual Undergrad Tuition & Fees (In-State): $4,416
Enrollment: 10,436
Coed
Affiliation or Control: State
IRS Status: 501(c)3
Highest Offering: Associate Degree
Program: Occupational; 2-Year Principally Bachelor's Creditable
Accreditation: SC, ADNUR, DH

02 President ... Dr. John T. DEVER
05 Vice President for Academic Affairs ... Dr. Lonnie SCHAFFER
32 Vice President for Student Affairs ... Dr. Daniel LUFKIN
11 Vice President for Admin/Finance .. Mr. Charles A. NURNBERGER
103 Vice Pres for Workforce Development ... Dr. Deborah G. WRIGHT
44 Vice Pres Institutional Advancement ... Ms. Cynthia CALLAWAY
35 Assoc VP for Student Affairs ... Dr. Vicki RICHMOND
13 Director of Information Tech ... Mr. Wayne DAVIS
106 Dir Distance/Distributive Learning ... Ms. Ruth SMITH
84 Int Dean of Enrollment Management ... Ms. Kris RARIG
10 Assoc VP for Financial Services ... Ms. Teresa BAILEY
103 Assoc VP for Workforce Training/CE ... Dr. Carmen BURROWS
60 Dean Communications/Social Sciences ... Mr. Patrick TOMKINS
81 Int Dean Science/Engr/Technology ... Dr. Michael REYNOLDS
50 Int Dean Bus/Public Ser/IT/Math ... Mr. Raymond MUZIA
76 Dean Health Professions ... Dr. Christy HAWKINS
38 Dean of Student Success ... Ms. Joyce JOHNSON
37 Dir Financial Aid/Veteran Affairs ... Ms. Kathryn ANDERSON
18 Mgr Facilities/Plan/Capital Outlay ... Mr. Mark KRAMER
26 Director Public Relations/Marketing ... Ms. Cecilia RAMIREZ
30 Director of Development ... Ms. Lara OVERY
08 Director of Learning Resources ... Mr. Richard HODGES
09 Dir Inst Research and Effectiveness ... Mr. Steven FELKER
21 Business Office Manager ... Mr. Phillip BRADSHAW
15 Director of Human Resources ... Ms. Joy COOKE

*Tidewater Community College (C)

121 College Place, Norfolk VA 23510

County: Independent City
FICE Identification: 003712
Unit ID: 233772
Telephone: (757) 822-1122
Carnegie Class: Assoc/Pub-S-SC
FAX Number: (757) 822-1060
Calendar System: Semester
URL: www.tcc.edu
Established: 1968
Annual Undergrad Tuition & Fees (In-State): $4,136
Enrollment: 27,646
Coed
Affiliation or Control: State
IRS Status: 501(c)3
Highest Offering: Associate Degree
Program: Occupational; 2-Year Principally Bachelor's Creditable
Accreditation: SC, ACFEI, ADNUR, CAHIIM, COARC, DMS, EMT, FUSER, MLTAD, OTA, PTAA, RAD

02 President ... Dr. Edna V. BAEHRE-KOLOVANI
03 Executive Vice President ... Mr. Franklin T. DUNN
05 VP Academic Affairs/Chief Acad Ofcr ... Dr. Daniel T. DEMARTE
32 Int VP for Student Affairs ... Dr. Michael D. SUMMERS
10 Vice President Finance ... Ms. Phyllis F. MILLOY
26 VP Public Affairs & Communications ... Mr. James P. TOSCANO
30 VP Inst Advancement/Exec Dir Devel ... Ms. Felecia W. BLOW
13 Vice President Information Systems ... Dr. Robin L P. YING
103 Int VP Regional Workforce Solutions ... Ms. Leslie K. BOUGHTON
12 Provost Chesapeake Campus ... Dr. Lisa B. RHINE
12 Provost Portsmouth Campus ... Dr. Michelle W. WOODHOUSE
12 Provost Norfolk Campus ... Dr. Jeffrey S. BOYD
12 Provost Virginia Beach Campus ... Dr. Michael D. SUMMERS
09 Dir Institutional Effectiveness ... Mr. Curtis K. AASEN
100 Chief of Staff ... Ms. Susan M. JAMES
20 AVP Academics ... Dr. Kellie C. SOREY
20 AVP Faculty Professional Dev ... Mr. Frederick E. STEMPLE, JR.
20 AVP Learning Tech Applications ... Mr. John MOREA
08 AVP for Libraries ... Mr. Steve E. LITHERLAND
84 AVP Recruitment/Admission/Enroll ... Dr. Karen D. CAMPBELL
106 Dean eLearning ... Ms. Virginia K. ZILLGES
25 AVP Grants/Sponsored Programs ... Ms. Valerie C. CHEESEMAN
26 AVP Interactive Com/Pub Info Office ... Ms. Marian L. ANDERFUREN
35 AVP for Student Success ... Ms. Christine DAMROSE-MAHLMANN
50 Dean Bus/Pub Svc/Tech Chesapeake ... Mr. James E. PERKINSON, JR.
81 Dean Lang/Math/Science Chesapeake ... Mr. Thomas B. STOUT
35 Dean of Student Svcs Chesapeake ... Dr. James E. EDWARDS
50 Dean Bus/SC/P Svcs/Tech Norfolk ... Ms. Johnna C. HARRELL
81 Dean Lang/Math/Science Norfolk ... Dr. Kerry S. RAGNO
35 Dean of Student Svcs Norfolk ... Mr. Emmanuel CHESTNUT
50 Dean Bus/Pub Svcs/Tech Portsmouth ... Ms. Ann P. AMBROSE
81 Dean Lang/Math/Science Portsmouth ... Ms. Jenefer D. SNYDER
35 Dean of Student Svcs Portsmouth ... Ms. Dana M. SINGLETON
66 Dean Beazley School Nurs Portsmouth ... Dr. Phyllis M. EATON
54 Dean Math Eng & Ind Tech Va Beach ... Mr. David A. EKKER
76 Dean Health Professions ... Mr. Thomas G. CALOGRIDES, JR.
50 Int Dean IT & Business Va Beach ... Mr. William CLEMENT
81 Dean Natural Sciences Va Beach ... Mr. Gregory P. FRANK
83 Dean Social Sci/Pub Svcs Va Beach ... Mr. Joseph J. FAIRCHILD
79 Dean Humanities Va Beach ... Ms. Marcanne ANDERSEN
35 Dean of Student Svcs Va Beach ... Dr. Marilyn R. HODGE
88 Dir Reg Automotive Ctr Chesapeake ... Mr. Beno RUBIN
14 Dir Programming Systems & Develop ... Mr. Ken BALLARD
14 Dir Network & Telecom Services ... Mr. Charles E. MCGEE
06 College Registrar ... Vacant
57 Director Visual Arts Center ... Ms. Christina M. RUPSCH
18 Director Facilities Management ... Mr. David R. GUGLIELMO
15 Int Director Human Resources ... Ms. Beth LUNDE
19 Director Safety & Security ... Mr. George J. OKATY
88 Director of Emergency Preparedness ... Mr. Pete F. SOMMER
88 Exec Dir Ctr Military Veterans Educ ... Dr. Bruce H. BRUNSON
88 Exec Dir Roper Performing Arts Ctr ... Mr. Paul H. LASAKOW
21 Director Fiscal Services ... Ms. Reyne D. BUCHHOLZ
96 Director Material Mgmt Procurement ... Ms. Robin S. MOORE
37 Director Central Financial Aid ... Ms. Jennifer E. HARPHAM
109 Director Auxiliary Services ... Ms. Bridgett M. PASSAUER
21 Dir Fin Info Systems & Operations ... Ms. Heather H. TAYLOR
88 Dir Gen Educ Asses Trans Partnershp ... Ms. Jennifer FERGUSON
88 Dir Std Mental Health & Behavior ... Dr. Jessica SMITH
45 Dir of Planning & Accountability ... Dr. Kimberly M. BOVEE
88 Director of Intercultural Learning ... Dr. Jeanne B. NATALI
88 Director Marketing ... Mr. Curt J. WYNN
105 Chief Web Communications Officer ... Ms. Allison H. TRELOAR

*Virginia Highlands Community College (D)

PO Box 828, Abingdon VA 24212-0828

County: Washington
FICE Identification: 007099
Unit ID: 233903
Telephone: (276) 739-2400
Carnegie Class: Assoc/Pub-R-M
FAX Number: (276) 739-2590
Calendar System: Semester
URL: www.vhcc.edu
Established: 1967
Annual Undergrad Tuition & Fees (In-State): $4,365
Enrollment: 2,518
Coed
Affiliation or Control: State
IRS Status: 501(c)3
Highest Offering: Associate Degree
Program: Occupational; 2-Year Principally Bachelor's Creditable
Accreditation: SC, ADNUR, OTA

02 President ... Dr. Gene C. COUCH, JR.
05 VP Instruction & Student Services ... Dr. Hara CHARLIER
10 VP Financial/Administrative Svcs ... Ms. Christine FIELDS
30 Vice Pres Institutional Advancement ... Mr. David N. MATLOCK
49 Business Humanities & Science Div ... Ms. Barbara MANUEL
72 Director of Institutional Advance ... Mr. Robert E. MAY
66 Dean of Nursing and Allied Health ... Ms. Kathy J. MITCHELL
103 VP Workforce Training & Cont Educ ... Ms. Melinda T. LELAND
08 Coordinator of Library Services ... Mr. Joel RUDY
37 Director of Financial Aid ... Ms. Karen T. CHEERS
07 Director Admission/Records ... Ms. Karen T. CHEERS
06 Registrar ... Ms. Charlene EASTRIDGE
15 Human Resource Manager ... Ms. Laura MCCLELLAN
32 Coord PR/Marketing & Alumni ... Ms. Anne DUNHAM
88 Coordinator Talent Search ... Mr. Justin NECESSARY
88 Director Project EXCEL ... Ms. Beth PAGE
38 Coordinator of Student Success ... Mr. Stacy THOMAS
21 Business Manager ... Ms. Mary SNEAD
96 Director of Purchasing ... Ms. Chelsa TAYLOR
88 Institutional Effectiveness ... Ms. Jennifer D. ADDISON
90 Coord Academic Computing/Technology ... Mr. Glen JOHNSON
26 Public Relations Officer ... Ms. Anne M. DUNHAM
09 Institutional Research Officer ... Mr. Jeff D. RUSSELL
18 Chief Facilities/Physical Plant ... Mr. Ernest L. NUNLEY
19 Campus Police Chief ... Mr. Blake ANDIS
36 Career Plng/Placement Specialist ... Mr. Michael MCBRIDE

*Virginia Western Community College (E)

PO Box 14007, Roanoke VA 24038-4007

County: Independent City
FICE Identification: 003760
Unit ID: 233949
Telephone: (540) 857-8922
Carnegie Class: Assoc/Pub-R-L
FAX Number: (540) 857-6526
Calendar System: Semester
URL: www.virginiawestern.edu
Established: 1966
Annual Undergrad Tuition & Fees (In-State): $4,713
Enrollment: 8,632
Coed
Affiliation or Control: State
IRS Status: 501(c)3
Highest Offering: Associate Degree
Program: Occupational; 2-Year Principally Bachelor's Creditable
Accreditation: SC, ACBSP, ACFEI, DH, RAD, RTT

02 President ... Dr. Robert H. SANDEL
10 Vice Pres of Finance/Admin Services ... Ms. Cheryl MILLER
05 Vice Pres Academic/Student Affs ... Dr. Elizabeth WILMER
30 Vice Pres Institutional Advancement ... Dr. Angela M. FALCONETTI
103 Vice Pres Workforce Development Svc ... Vacant
45 Dean Institutional Effectiveness .. Ms. Rachelle KOUDELIK-JONES
49 Dean Liberal Arts/Social Sciences ... Ms. Amy ANGUIANO
76 Dean Health Professions ... Ms. Carole GRAHAM
81 Dean Science/Tech/Engineering/Math ... Dr. John ANDERSON
50 Dean Business/Trades/Technology ... Ms. Deborah YANCEY
24 Dean Learning Resources ... Mr. Christopher PORTER
32 Dean of Student Services ... Ms. Lori BAKER
09 Director Institutional Research ... Ms. Carol ROWLETT
18 Director of Facilities Planning ... Mr. Kevin G. WITTER
26 Coord for Marketing/Strategic Comm ... Mr. Josh MEYER
06 Registrar ... Ms. Karin COLE
19 Campus Police Chief ... Mr. Craig HARRIS
37 Coord Financial Aid/Veterans Affs ... Mr. Chad SARTINI
103 Director Workforce Development ... Ms. Cassandra DOVE
13 Dir Information Educ Technology ... Mr. Shivaji SAMANTA
15 Assoc VP of Human Resources ... Ms. Jennifer PITTMAN
21 Business Manager ... Mrs. Fredona AARON
84 Coordinator for Enrollment Services ... Ms. Brooke FERGUSON
08 Coordinator of the Library ... Ms. Lynn HURT
36 Coordinator Career Services ... Ms. Rhonda PERDUE
25 Coord Grants Dev & Special Projects ... Ms. Marilyn J. HERBERT-ASHTON
29 Promotion Manager ... Ms. Carole TARRANT

*Wytheville Community College (F)

1000 E Main Street, Wytheville VA 24382-3308

County: Wythe
FICE Identification: 003761
Unit ID: 234377
Telephone: (276) 223-4700
Carnegie Class: Assoc/Pub-R-M
FAX Number: (276) 223-4778
Calendar System: Semester
URL: www.wcc.vccs.edu
Established: 1963
Annual Undergrad Tuition & Fees (In-State): $4,380
Enrollment: 3,302
Coed
Affiliation or Control: State
IRS Status: 501(c)3
Highest Offering: Associate Degree
Program: Occupational; 2-Year Principally Bachelor's Creditable
Accreditation: SC, ADNUR, DH, MLTAD, PTAA

02 President ... Dr. Dean SPRINKLE
05 Vice Pres Instruction/Student Devel ... Dr. Lorri HUFFARD
10 Vice Pres Finance & Admin Services ... Ms. Crystal Y. CREGGER
09 Director of Institutional Research ... Dr. Kent E. GLINDEMANN
30 Vice Pres of College Development ... Dr. Rhonda K. CATRON-WOOD
103 Vice Pres Workforce & Cont Ed ... Vacant
50 Dean of Transfer & Social Sciences ... Dr. Leroy HAMILTON
76 Dean of Health & Occupational Pgms ... Mr. Jamie EDWARDS
32 Dean of Student Services ... Ms. Renee THOMAS
13 Director Acad/Admin Computing ... Mr. Shawn MCREYNOLDS
06 Registrar ... Ms. Karen ALEXANDER
15 Human Resources Manager ... Ms. Malinda EVERSOLE
26 Public Relations Coordinator ... Vacant
08 Coordinator of Library Services ... Mr. George E. MATTIS, JR.
96 Procurement Officer ... Ms. Vivian FANNING
106 Dir of Distance & Distrib Learning ... Mr. Kenneth E. FAIRBANKS
37 Coordinator Financial Aid ... Ms. Mary Beth GALLAGHER
04 Administrative Asst to President ... Ms. Denita BURNETT

Virginia International University (G)

11200 Waples Mill Road, Suite 360, Fairfax VA 22030

County: Fairfax
FICE Identification: 041440
Telephone: (703) 591-7042
Carnegie Class: Not Classified
FAX Number: (703) 591-7046
Calendar System: Semester
URL: www.viu.edu
Established: 1998
Annual Undergrad Tuition & Fees: $9,840
Enrollment: 337
Coed
Affiliation or Control: Independent Non-Profit
IRS Status: 501(c)3
Highest Offering: Master's
Program: Professional; Business Emphasis

Accreditation: ACICS

01 President .... Dr. Isa SARAC
03 Vice President University Affairs .... Ms. Christine KOONTS

Virginia Military Institute (A)

319 Letcher Avenue, Lexington VA 24450-0304
County: Independent City FICE Identification: 003753
Unit ID: 234085
Telephone: (540) 464-7230 Carnegie Class: Bac/A&S
FAX Number: (540) 464-7583 Calendar System: Semester
URL: www.vmi.edu
Established: 1839 Annual Undergrad Tuition & Fees (In-State): $25,202
Enrollment: 1,700 Coed
Affiliation or Control: State IRS Status: 501(c)3
Highest Offering: Baccalaureate
Program: Liberal Arts And General
Accreditation: SC, BUS, ENG

01 Superintendent .... Gen. J. H. Binford PEAY
05 Dean of the Faculty .... BGen. Jeffrey G. SMITH
10 Deputy Superintendent Finance/Admin .... BGen. Robert L. GREEN
32 Commandant of Cadets .... Col. William J. WANOVICH
100 Chief of Staff .... Col. James P. INMAN
04 Assistant to the Superintendent .... Col. Sean P. HARRINGTON
21 Assoc Business Exec/Treasurer .... Col. Jeffrey L. LAWHORNE
07 Director of Admissions .... Col. Vernon L. BEITZEL
88 Exec Director Museum Programs .... Col. Keith E. GIBSON
37 Director of Financial Aid .... Col. Timothy P. GOLDEN
35 Deputy Commandant .... Col. L. E. HURLBUT
36 Director of Career Services .... Col. R. Samuel RATCLIFFE
41 Director Intercollegiate Athletics .... Mr. David L. DILES
26 Director Communications & Marketing .... Col. Stewart D. MACINNIS
29 Executive VP Alumni Association .... Col. Adam C. VOLANT
102 Exec VP VMI Foundation/Fund Raising ... Mr. Brian S. CROCKETT
88 Exec VP Keydet Club/Athletic Fund . Mr. Gregory M. CAVALLARO
06 Registrar .... Col. Janet M. BATTAGLIA
15 Director Human Resources .... Col. Robert B. SPORE
18 Director Physical Plant .... LtCol. James L. WILLIAMS, JR.
09 Director Institutional Research .... LtCol. Lee L. RAKES
109 Director Auxiliary Services .... Col. David P. WILLIAMS
40 Manager Bookstore .... Mr. Bradley N. MCDOUGAL
42 Institute Chaplain .... Col. James S. PARK
17 Institute Physician .... Dr. David L. COPELAND
88 Director of Athletic Communications .... Mr. Wade H. BRANNER
08 Head Librarian .... Col. Donald H. SAMDAHL, JR.
38 Director of Cadet Counseling .... LtCol. Sarah L. JONES
13 Director Information Technology .... Col. Thomas F. HOPKINS
96 Director of Purchasing .... Maj. Kathy H. TOMLIN

† Tuition includes required room and board and quartermaster charges.

Virginia Polytechnic Institute and State University (B)

Blacksburg VA 24061-0202
County: Montgomery FICE Identification: 003754
Unit ID: 233921
Telephone: (540) 231-6000 Carnegie Class: RU/VH
FAX Number: (540) 231-9263 Calendar System: Semester
URL: www.vt.edu
Established: 1872 Annual Undergrad Tuition & Fees (In-State): $12,485
Enrollment: 31,224 Coed
Affiliation or Control: State IRS Status: 501(c)3
Highest Offering: Doctorate
Program: Liberal Arts And General; Teacher Preparatory; Professional
Accreditation: SC, ART, BUS, BUSA, CACREP, CEA, CIDA, CLPSY, CONST, CS, DIETD, DIETI, ENG, IPSY, LSAR, MFCD, MUS, PCSAS, PH, PLNG, SPAA, TED, THEA, VET

01 President .... Timothy D. SANDS
05 Executive Vice President & Provost .... Thanassis RIKAKIS
11 Vice President for Administration .... Sherwood G. WILSON
13 Vice Pres for Information Tech .... Scott F. MIDKIFF
32 Vice President Student Affairs .... Patricia A. PERILLO
30 Vice Pres Advancemnt .... Charles D. PHLEGAR
29 Vice President Alumni Relations .... Thomas C. TILLAR, JR.
28 VP Diversity and Inclusion .... Vacant
46 Int VP for Research/Innovation .... Dennis R. DEAN
20 Vice Prov for Undergrad Acad Affs .... Rachel L. HOLLOWAY
58 Vice President and Dean Grad Educ .... Karen P. DEPAUW
56 VP Outreach/International Affs .... Guru GHOSH
10 Vice President for Finance and CFO .... M. Dwight SHELTON, JR.
07 Director of Undergrad Admissions .... Mildred JOHNSON
35 Dean of Students .... Thomas BROWN
15 Assoc Vice Pres for Human Resources .... Hal IRVIN
09 Asst Provost Inst Research/Effect .... Kristen BUSH
43 University Counsel .... Kay K. HEIDBREDER
84 Vice Prov for Enroll & Degree Mgmt .... Wanda H. DEAN
37 Dir of Scholarships/Financial Aid .... Elizabeth ARMSTRONG
23 Director Schiffert Health Center .... Kanitta CHAROENSIRI
18 Assoc Vice Pres/Chief Facilities .... Christopher KIWUS
39 Director of Dining Services .... Ted FAULKNER
39 Director of Housing and Res Life .... Eleanor FINGER
41 Athletic Director .... Whit BABCOCK
26 Assoc Vice Pres Univ Relations .... Larry HINCKER
38 Director Student Counseling .... Chris FLYNN
40 Executive Director Bookstore .... Donald J. WILLIAMS
62 Dean of Libraries .... Tyler WALTERS
47 Dean of Agriculture/Life Sciences .... Alan GRANT
48 Dean of Architecture/Urban Studies .... Jack DAVIS
49 Dean College of Science .... Lay N. CHANG
50 Dean of Business .... Robert T. SUMICHRAST
54 Dean of Engineering .... Richard BENSON
79 Dean Liberal Arts & Human Sciences .... Elizabeth SPILLER
74 Dean of Veterinary Medicine .... Cyril R. CLARKE
65 Dean of Natural Resources & Environ ...... Paul M. WINISTORFER
96 Director of Materials Management .... W. Thomas KALOUPEK
90 Director Educational Technology .... Vacant
91 Assoc Vice Pres for Enterprise Sys .... Deborah M. FULTON
12 VP for the National Capital Region .... Steven H. MCKNIGHT
102 CEO Virginia Tech Foundation .... John E. DOOLEY
04 Sr Executive Asst to President .... Sandy SMITH
06 Registrar .... Rick SPARKS
100 Chief of Staff .... Kim O'ROURKE
104 Director Global Education Office .... Theresa C. JOHANSSON
105 Director Web Communications .... John JACKSON
106 Exec Dir Tech Enhanced Learning .... Dale PIKE
108 Asst Provost Assess & Evaluation .... Steve CULVER
19 Chief of Police/Dir of Security .... Kevin FOUST
22 Dir Affirmative Action/EEO .... Karissa MOORE
25 Chief Contracts/Grants Admin .... Frank FITZGERALD
44 Director Annual or Planned Giving .... Randy HOLDEN
86 Exec Director Government Relations .... Chris YIANILOS

Virginia State University (C)

One Hayden Street, Petersburg VA 23806-0001
County: Chesterfield FICE Identification: 003764
Unit ID: 234155
Telephone: (804) 524-5000 Carnegie Class: Master's S
FAX Number: (804) 524-6506 Calendar System: Semester
URL: www.vsu.edu
Established: 1882 Annual Undergrad Tuition & Fees (In-State): $8,226
Enrollment: 5,025 Coed
Affiliation or Control: State IRS Status: 501(c)3
Highest Offering: Doctorate
Program: Liberal Arts And General; Teacher Preparatory
Accreditation: SC, ART, BUS, CS, DIETD, DIETI, ENG, ENGT, MUS, NAIT, SW, TED

01 Interim President .... Dr. Pamela HAMMOND
10 Vice Pres Administration & Finance .... Mr. Kevin DAVENPORT
05 Provost/VP for Academic Affairs .... Dr. W. Weldon HILL
32 Vice President for Student Affairs .... Dr. Letizia GAMBRELL-BOONE
30 VP for Institutional Advancement .... Vacant
20 Vice Provost .... Dr. James E. HUNTER
15 Assoc VP for Human Resource .... Vacant
84 Asst VP/Student Enrollment Services .... Mr. Henry DEBOSE
21 AVP Administration & Finance .... Ms. Sheila MCNAIR
50 Dean Reginald F Lewis Col Business . Dr. Emmanuel OMOJOKUN
54 Dean College of Engineering & Tech . Dr. Keith M. WILLIAMSON
79 Dean Col of Humananities & Soc Sci .... Dr. Andrew KANU
47 Dean College of Agriculture .... Vacant
58 Dean Graduate Studies .... Dr. James E. HUNTER
62 Dean Library & Library Services .. Dr. Elsie S. WEATHERINGTON
76 Dean College of Natural Health Sci .... Dr. Larry BROWN
44 Director of Development .... Vacant
06 Registrar .... Mrs. Debera BONNER
09 Director Inst Planning/Assessment .... Dr. Emmett L. RIDLEY
37 Director of Financial Aid .... Mrs. Myra PHILLIPS
19 Chief of Police and Public Safety .... Mr. Eddie L. PERRY
27 Media Specialist .... Mr. Jesse VAUGHAN
18 Director of Facilities .... Mr. Gilbert HANZLIK
07 Director Admissions & Recruitment .... Mrs. Irene F. LOGAN
26 Director Marketing & Media Relation .... Mr. Thomas REED
22 Human Resources Manager .... Ms. Gayle O'NEAL
100 Chief of Staff .... Mr. Hubert D. HARRIS
39 Director Residence Facilities .... Dr. Kelvin RACHELL
36 Director Career Services .... Vacant
40 Bookstore Manager .... Mr. Kevin POWELL
92 Director Honors Program .... Mr. Daniel M. ROBERTS
41 Athletic Director .... Mrs. Peggy DAVIS
42 Minister .... Rev. Delano DOUGLAS
29 Director of Alumni Relations .... Mrs. Pamela L. ORR
13 Deputy Chief Information Officer .... Ms. Stephanie A. HAYES
23 Acting Dir Student Health Services . Mrs. Tanya J. SATTERWHITE
25 Contract Manager .... Ms. Linda SCOTT
87 Director Summer School Session .... Dr. Vykuntapathi THOTA
96 Director of Purchasing .... Mrs. Yolanda BUCK
38 Director University Counseling .... Dr. Kendra L. PUGH

Virginia Tech Carilion School of Medicine (D)

2 Riverside Circle, Suite M140, Roanoke VA 24016
County: Independent City Identification: 667148
Telephone: (540) 526-2559 Carnegie Class: Not Classified
FAX Number: (540) 581-0741 Calendar System: Other
URL: www.vtc.vt.edu
Established: 2007 Annual Graduate Tuition & Fees: $47,973
Enrollment: 168 Coed
Affiliation or Control: Independent Non-Profit IRS Status: 501(c)3
Highest Offering: Doctorate; No Undergraduates
Program: Professional
Accreditation: SC, MED

01 President & Dean .... Dr. Cynda Ann JOHNSON

Virginia Union University (E)

1500 N Lombardy Street, Richmond VA 23220-1784
County: Independent City FICE Identification: 003766
Unit ID: 234164
Telephone: (804) 257-5600 Carnegie Class: Bac/Diverse
FAX Number: (804) 257-5818 Calendar System: Semester
URL: www.vuu.edu
Established: 1865 Annual Undergrad Tuition & Fees: $15,746
Enrollment: 1,720 Coed
Affiliation or Control: Baptist IRS Status: 501(c)3
Highest Offering: Doctorate
Program: Liberal Arts And General; Teacher Preparatory; Professional
Accreditation: SC, ACBSP, SW, TED, THEOL

01 President & CEO .... Dr. Claude G. PERKINS
05 VP Academic Affairs .... Dr. Zakir HOSSAIN
32 VP Enroll Mgmt & Student Affs .... Dr. A. Zachary FAISON
10 VP Financial Affairs .... Mr. Gregory LEWIS
30 Vice Pres Institutional Advancement .... Mr. Dennis C. WASHINGTON
09 VP Research/Planning & Spec Pgms .... Dr. Joy P. GOODRICH
26 Chief of Staff/Dir Public Relations .... Ms. Vanessa COOMBS
53 Dean Evelyn R Syphax Sch Ed/Psy .... Dr. Matthew LYNCH
81 Int Dean Math/Science & Technology .... Dr. Latrelle A. GREEN
50 Dean Sydney Lewis Sch of Business .... Dr. Brenda J. PONSFORD
79 Dean Sch of Humanities/Soc Sci .... Dr. Michael OROK
73 Dean School of Theology .... Dr. John W. KINNEY
25 Asst to President Title III Pgms .... Mr. Samuel T. RHOADES
15 Director Human Resources .... Ms. Hollace J. ENOCH
06 Registrar .... Ms. Marilyn A. BROOKS
38 Director Counseling .... Ms. Melody M. PANNELL
29 Director of Alumni Relations .... Ms. Charmica D. EPPS
08 Library Director .... Ms. Pamela B. FOREMAN
37 Director Financial Aid .... Mrs. Antionette T. HOUSE
13 Director Information Technology .... Mr. Robert R. GRAY
36 Director Career Services .... Ms. Takeish N. BROWN
84 Director of Enrollment Management .... Ms. Kristie L. WHITE
42 University Pastor .... Rev. Angelo V. CHATMON
41 Athletic Director .... Mr. Joseph TAYLOR
19 Chief University Police .... Col. Carlton G. EDWARDS
24 Audio Visual Coordinator .... Mr. JaPrince L. CARTER
21 Asst VP Finan Affairs/Comptroller .... Ms. Stephanie M. WHITE
40 Bookstore Manager .... Ms. Terri WYATT
39 Director of Residence Life .... Mr. Mandrake T. MILLER
31 Int Dir of Community & Student Rels .... Ms. Tyciee L. FAISON
18 Director Facilities .... Mr. David E. GORDON
96 Director of Purchasing .... Mr. Michael T. ADKINS
04 Administrative Asst to President .... Ms. Renee W. JOLLEY
104 Dir Ctr for International Studies .... Dr. David A. ADEWUYI
106 Dir Online Education/E-learning .... Dr. Shenita L. RAY
108 Director Institutional Assessment .... Dr. Patty R. YOUNG
22 Dir Affirmative Action/EEO .... Ms. Hollace J. ENOCH
44 Director Annual or Planned Giving .... Ms. Lisa D. WINN

Virginia University of Lynchburg (F)

2058 Garfield Avenue, Lynchburg VA 24501-6417
County: Independent City FICE Identification: 003762
Unit ID: 234137
Telephone: (434) 528-5276 Carnegie Class: Spec/Faith
FAX Number: (434) 528-4257 Calendar System: Semester
URL: www.vul.edu
Established: 1886 Annual Undergrad Tuition & Fees: $7,880
Enrollment: 324 Coed
Affiliation or Control: Independent Non-Profit IRS Status: 501(c)3
Highest Offering: Doctorate
Program: Liberal Arts And General; Business Emphasis
Accreditation: TRACS

01 President .... Dr. Ralph REAVIS
05 Provost/Executive Vice President .... Dr. Kathy C. FRANKLIN
10 Vice President of Finance .... Mr. Donald LESLIE
32 Vice Pres Div Student Affairs .... Dr. Terrie E. GRIFFIN
30 VP for Institutional Advancement .... Dr. Doris S. CRAWFORD
06 Registrar .... Mr. Layman FRANKLIN, JR.
35 Director Student Affairs .... Mr. Charles ALLEN
84 Dir Enrollment Management/Fin Aid .... Mrs. Bindiya SHAH
07 Director of Admissions/Marketing .... Gianne ESTOCADO

Virginia University of Oriental Medicine (G)

9401 Mathy Drive, Fairfax VA 22031
County: Fairfax Identification: 667208
Telephone: (703) 323-5690 Carnegie Class: Not Classified
FAX Number: (703) 323-5692 Calendar System: Quarter
URL: www.vuom.org
Established: Annual Graduate Tuition & Fees: N/A
Enrollment: N/A Coed
Affiliation or Control: Independent Non-Profit IRS Status: 501(c)3
Highest Offering: Master's; No Undergraduates
Program: Professional
Accreditation: ACUP

01 President .... John SHIN
05 Vice Pres Academic Affairs .... Tae CHEONG-CHOO

Virginia Wesleyan College (H)

1584 Wesleyan Drive, Norfolk VA 23502-5599
County: Independent City FICE Identification: 003767
Unit ID: 234173

Telephone: (757) 455-3200 Carnegie Class: Bac/A&S
FAX Number: (757) 461-4944 Calendar System: 4/1/4
URL: www.vwc.edu
Established: 1961 Annual Undergrad Tuition & Fees: $33,778
Enrollment: 1,501 Coed
Affiliation or Control: United Methodist IRS Status: 501(c)3
Highest Offering: Baccalaureate
Program: Liberal Arts And General; Teacher Preparatory
Accreditation: SC, NRPA, SW

01 President .... Dr. Scott D. MILLER
05 VP Academic Affs/Dean of College .... Dr. Timothy G. O'ROURKE
10 Vice President of Finance .... Mr. Cary A. SAWYER
32 VP Student Affs/Dean of Enrollment .. Mr. David E. BUCKINGHAM
30 VP for College Advancement .... Ms. Mita K. VAIL
11 Vice President of Operations .... Mr. Bruce F. VAUGHAN
45 Dir Strategic Plng/Spec Ast to Pres .... Ms. Laynee H. TIMLIN
45 Director Institutional Research .... Mr. Donald STAUFFER
09 Dir Instl Effective/Accreditation .... Dr. David DIRLAM
26 Director of Communications .... Ms. Leona BAKER
35 Dean of Students .... Dr. Keith E. MOORE
88 Assoc VP for College Advancement .... Ms. Suzanne SAVAGE
07 Dean of Admissions .... Mr. Nelson DAVIS
20 Assoc Dean Special Acad Projects .... Ms. Debbie L. HICKS
20 Assoc Dean of the College .... Dr. Sally SHEDD
39 Assoc Dean Students for Res Life .... Ms. McCarren CAPUTA
13 Chief Technology Officer .... Mr. Jack L. DMOCH
41 Director of Athletics .... Ms. Joanne M. RENN
55 Director of Adult Studies Program .... Mr. Thomas R. FARLEY
08 Library Director .... Mrs. Susan ERICKSON
15 Director of Human Resources .... Ms. Karla R. RASMUSSEN
06 Registrar .... Ms. Regina BYNUM
37 Director of Financial Aid .... Ms. Teresa L. RHYNE
96 Director of Purchasing .... Ms. Midge ZIMMERMAN
31 Director of Community Service .... Ms. Diane E. HOTALING
36 Director of Career Services .... Ms. Lisa I. FENTRESS
19 Director of Campus Security .... Mr. Jerry MANCE, JR.
29 Director of Alumni Relations .... Ms. Lina GREEN
18 Director of Physical Plant .... Mr. David R. HOPPER
42 Chaplain .... Rev. Greg WEST
38 Director of Counseling .... Mr. James W. BROWN
44 Director of Special Gifts .... Ms. Sherran A. DENKLER
44 Director of Annual Giving .... Ms. Kristin WILLIAMS
44 Director Leadership Giving .... Ms. Lori L. MCCAREL
92 Director Honors and Scholars .... Dr. Joyce B. EASTER
28 Director of International Programs .... Ms. Lena H. JOHNSON
88 Director of Student Activities .... Ms. Jennifer E. MITCHELL
23 Director of Health Services .... Ms. Valerie L. COVINGTON
91 Manager of Admin Computer Systems .... Mr. Greg BAPTISTE
40 Bookstore Manager .... Ms. Kim S. BROWN

Washington and Lee University (A)

204 W Washington Street, Lexington VA 24450-2116
County: Independent City FICE Identification: 003768
Unit ID: 234207
Telephone: (540) 458-8400 Carnegie Class: Bac/A&S
FAX Number: (540) 458-8945 Calendar System: Other
URL: www.wlu.edu
Established: 1749 Annual Undergrad Tuition & Fees: $46,417
Enrollment: 2,203 Coed
Affiliation or Control: Independent Non-Profit IRS Status: 501(c)3
Highest Offering: Doctorate
Program: Liberal Arts And General; Professional
Accreditation: SC, BUS, JOUR, LAW, TEAC

01 President .... Dr. Kenneth P. RUSCIO
05 Provost .... Dr. Daniel WUBAH
20 Associate Provost .... Dr. Marc CONNER
10 Vice Pres for Finance and Admin .... Mr. Steven G. MCALLISTER
30 Vice Pres University Advancement .... Mr. Dennis W. CROSS
32 VP for Stdnt Affs & Dean of Stdnts .... Ms. Sidney S. EVANS
04 Senior Asst to the President .... Dr. Elizabeth KNAPP
101 Sr Asst to Pres/Sec of University .... Mr. James D. FARRAR
43 General Counsel .... Ms. Leanne M. SHANK
22 Assoc Gen Counsel Compliance Spprt .... Ms. Jennifer E. KIRKLAND
49 Dean of the College .... Dr. Suzanne P. KEEN
50 Dean of Commerce/Economics/ Politics .... Mr. Robert D. STRAUGHAN
61 Dean of Law School .... Mr. Brant J. HELLWIG
26 Exec Dir of Comm/Public Affairs .... Mr. Brian ECKERT
35 Dean of Student Life .... Mr. David M. LEONARD
35 Assoc Dean of Students .... Ms. Tamara Y. FUTRELL
35 Assoc Dean of Students .... Ms. Tammi R. SIMPSON
30 Exec Dir of University Development .... Mr. Tres MULLIS
41 Director of Athletics .... Ms. Janine M. HATHORN
89 Asst Dean for 1st Yr Experience .... Mr. Jason L. RODOCKER
07 Dean of Admissions/Financial Aid .... M. Sally S. RICHMOND
09 Asst Provost for Inst Effectiveness .... Mr. Bryan PRICE
06 University Registrar .... Mr. Scott DITTMAN
08 University Librarian .... Mr. John TOMBARGE
85 Director International Education .... Dr. Mark E. RUSH
29 Exec Director of Alumni Affairs .... Mr. Waller T. DUDLEY
15 Exec Director of Human Resources .... Ms. Amy BARNES
37 Director of Financial Aid .... Mr. James D. KASTER
18 Exec Dir Facilities/Capital Plng .... Mr. John HOOGAKKER
21 Associate Treasurer & Controller .... Mrs. Deborah Z. CAYLOR
13 Chief Technology Officer .... Mr. David SAACKE
24 Senior Academic Technologist .... Mr. Brandon R. BUCY
36 Director Career Development .... Mr. John A. JENSEN
23 Director Student Health/Counseling .... Dr. Jane T. HORTON
96 Director of Dining Services .... Mr. Michael R. ZANIE
40 Director of Administrative Services .... Mr. K. C SCHAEFER

Washington University of Virginia (B)

4300 Evergreen Lane, Annandale VA 22003
County: Fairfax Identification: 666234
Telephone: (703) 333-5904 Carnegie Class: Not Classified
FAX Number: (703) 333-5906 Calendar System: Semester
URL: www.wuv.edu
Established: Annual Undergrad Tuition & Fees: $5,280
Enrollment: N/A Coed
Affiliation or Control: Baptist IRS Status: 501(c)3
Highest Offering: Doctorate
Program: Religious Emphasis
Accreditation: BI, @THEOL

01 President .... Dr. Peter M. CHANG
03 Executive Vice President .... Dr. Davis S. KIM
07 Admissions Advisor .... Mr. David Y. LEE

Wave Leadership College (C)

1000 North Great Neck Road, Virginia Beach VA 23454
County: Independent City Identification: 667210
Telephone: (757) 481-5005 Carnegie Class: Not Classified
FAX Number: (757) 496-6697 Calendar System: Semester
URL: www.wavecollege.com
Established: 2000 Annual Undergrad Tuition & Fees: $4,880
Enrollment: N/A Coed
Affiliation or Control: Independent Non-Profit IRS Status: 501(c)3
Highest Offering: Associate Degree
Program: Occupational; Religious Emphasis
Accreditation: @BI

01 President .... Steve KELLY
03 Executive Vice President .... Derek P. HOLSER
11 CSP Director .... James KNORR
05 Academic Dean .... Stephanie IAQUINTO
32 Dean of Students .... Dave M. HALL
06 Registrar .... Jacquie EVANS

Westwood College-Annandale (D)

7619 Little River Turnpike 5th Fl, Annandale VA 22003
Telephone: (877) 305-0049 Identification: 666599
Accreditation: ACICS

† Branch campus of Westwood College-South Bay, Torrance, CA.

Westwood College-Arlington Ballston (E)

4420 North Fairfax Drive, Arlington VA 22203
Telephone: (703) 243-3900 Identification: 666660
Accreditation: ACICS

† Branch campus of Westwood College-South Bay, Torrance, CA.

WASHINGTON

Antioch University Seattle (F)

2326 Sixth Avenue, Seattle WA 98121-1814
Telephone: (206) 441-5352 Identification: 666812
Accreditation: &NH, CACREP, MFCD

† Regional accreditation is carried under the parent institution in Yellow Springs, Ohio.

Argosy University, Seattle (G)

2601 A Elliott Avenue, Seattle WA 98121-1318
Telephone: (206) 283-4500 Identification: 666080
Accreditation: &WC, ACBSP

† Regional accreditation is carried under the parent institution in Orange, CA.

The Art Institute of Seattle (H)

2323 Elliott Avenue, Seattle WA 98121-1622
County: King FICE Identification: 022913
Unit ID: 234492
Telephone: (206) 448-0900 Carnegie Class: Spec/Arts
FAX Number: (206) 448-2501 Calendar System: Quarter
URL: www.ais.edu
Established: 1946 Annual Undergrad Tuition & Fees: $17,560
Enrollment: 1,327 Coed
Affiliation or Control: Proprietary IRS Status: Proprietary
Highest Offering: Baccalaureate
Program: Occupational
Accreditation: NW, ACFEI, CIDA

01 President .... Carol MENCK
05 Dean of Academic Affairs .... Dr. Scott CARNZ
15 Director of Human Resources .... Amber APPLETON
32 Dean of Student Affairs .... Angela HEDWALL
07 Senior Director of Admissions .... Liane SOOHOO
10 Regional Finance Director .... Greg WOODARD
36 Director Career Services .... Allison EGBERT

Bakke Graduate University (I)

1013 8th Avenue, Suite 401, Seattle WA 98104-1222
County: King FICE Identification: 031108
Unit ID: 420705
Telephone: (206) 264-9100 Carnegie Class: Not Classified
FAX Number: (206) 264-8828 Calendar System: Semester
URL: www.bgu.edu
Established: 1990 Annual Graduate Tuition & Fees: N/A
Enrollment: 186 Coed
Affiliation or Control: Independent Non-Profit IRS Status: 501(c)3
Highest Offering: Doctorate; No Undergraduates
Program: Professional; Religious Emphasis
Accreditation: TRACS

00 Chancellor .... Dr. Ray BAKKE
01 President .... Dr. Brad SMITH
05 Academic Dean .... Dr. Gwendolyn DEWEY
30 Vice President Advancement .... Mr. Robert STEINHAGEN
10 Chief Operations/Financial Ofcr .... Ms. Carolyn COCHRAN
06 Registrar .... Dr. Judi MELTON
07 Director of Admissions .... Ms. Diana BAKKE
09 Dir of Institutional Effectiveness .... Dr. Judi MELTON

Bastyr University (J)

14500 Juanita Drive NE, Kenmore WA 98028-4966
County: King FICE Identification: 022425
Unit ID: 235547
Telephone: (425) 602-3000 Carnegie Class: Spec/Health
FAX Number: (425) 823-6222 Calendar System: Quarter
URL: www.bastyr.edu
Established: 1978 Annual Undergrad Tuition & Fees: $24,423
Enrollment: 1,210 Coed
Affiliation or Control: Independent Non-Profit IRS Status: 501(c)3
Highest Offering: Doctorate
Program: Professional
Accreditation: NW, ACUP, DIETD, DIETI, MEAC, NATUR

01 President .... Dr. Mac POWELL
05 Senior Vice President/Provost .... Dr. Timothy C. CALLAHAN
10 Vice President for Finance & Admin .... Mr. Sheldon R. HABER
100 Chief of Staff .... Ms. Coquina L. DEGER
30 Chief Development Officer .... Vacant
32 Vice President of Student Affairs .... Ms. Susan WEIDER
07 Asst Vice Pres Recruitment & Retent .... Ms. Christine MASTERSON
08 Director of Library Services .... Ms. Jane SAXTON
29 Dir Career and Alumni Svcs .... Ms. Susan FARLEY
23 Chf Medical Ofcr Ctr Natural Health .... Dr. Jamey WALLACE
15 Exec Dir of Human Resources/IT .... Mr. Keith W. WOODY
13 Director of Information Technology .... Ms. Marsha MCGOUGH
09 Director of Research Development .... Dr. Mark MARTZEN
26 Assoc Dir of Media/Public Rels .... Mr. Derek WING
46 Senior Research Scientist .... Dr. Leanna STANDISH
40 Bookstore Manager .... Mr. Marty PETERSEN
07 Associate Director of Admissions .... Ms. Lauren SCHOEN
37 Director Financial Aid .... Ms. Danette CARTER
18 Director Facilities and Safety .... Mr. Daniel CLARK
21 Controller .... Mr. Joe PLOUF
38 Director Counseling .... Ms. Cheryln STOVER
06 Registrar .... Ms. Aracelly SALAZAR
101 Secretary of the Institution/Board .... Ms. Margaret BREVOORT
108 Director Institutional Assessment .... Ms. Erin ASELAS
19 Director Security/Safety .... Mr. Daniel CLARK
22 Dir Affirmative Action/EEO .... Mr. Keith W. WOODY
25 Chief Contracts/Grants Admin .... Mr. Dave HAMMOND
28 Director of Diversity .... Ms. Christy HOFSESS

Bates Technical College (K)

1101 S Yakima Avenue, Tacoma WA 98405-4895
County: Pierce FICE Identification: 005306
Unit ID: 235671
Telephone: (253) 680-7000 Carnegie Class: Assoc/Pub-U-MC
FAX Number: (253) 680-7101 Calendar System: Quarter
URL: www.bates.ctc.edu
Established: 1940 Annual Undergrad Tuition & Fees (In-State): $3,064
Enrollment: 2,907 Coed
Affiliation or Control: State IRS Status: 501(c)3
Highest Offering: Associate Degree
Program: Occupational; 2-Year Principally Bachelor's Creditable; Technical Emphasis
Accreditation: NW, ACFEI, DA, DT, OTA

01 President .... Dr. Ron LANGRELL
05 Exec VP of Instruction/Student Svcs .... Mr. Al GRISWOLD
04 Exec Asst to the President .... Ms. Becky WELCH
32 Vice President of Student Services .... Mr. Ivan GORNE
15 Director of Human Resources .... Mr. Geof KAUFMAN
11 Vice President of Admin Svcc .... Ms. Holly WOODMANSEE
30 Director of College Relations .... Ms. Kimberly PLEGER
18 Director Facilities & Operations .... Mr. Marty MATTES
06 Registrar .... Ms. Jaime SERENO
96 General Services Manager .... Mr. Alexander KENESSON
37 Financial Aid Officer .... Ms. Susan NEESE
13 Int Director Information Technology .... Mr. Bill STORMS
84 Dir of Enrollment Mgt/Admission .... Ms. Jaime SERENO
28 College Diversity Coordinator .... Ms. Kathy FLORES

Bellevue College (L)

3000 Landerholm Circle, SE, Bellevue WA 98007-6484
County: King FICE Identification: 003769
Unit ID: 234669
Telephone: (425) 564-1000 Carnegie Class: Assoc/Pub4
FAX Number: (425) 564-4065 Calendar System: Quarter
URL: www.bellevuecollege.edu

Established: 1965 Annual Undergrad Tuition & Fees (In-State): $4,497
Enrollment: 13,469 Coed
Affiliation or Control: State IRS Status: 501(c)3
Highest Offering: Baccalaureate
Program: Occupational; 2-Year Principally Bachelor's Creditable; Professional
Accreditation: NW, ADNUR, CIDA, DMS, NDT, NMT, NURSE, RADDOS, RTT

01 President .... Dr. David RULE
04 Exec Asst to the President .... Ms. Lisa CORCORAN
11 Vice Pres Administrative Services .... Mr. Ray WHITE
05 Vice President of Instruction .... Mr. Tom NIELSEN
15 Vice President of Human Resources .... Mr. Aaron HILLIARD
30 Vice Pres Institutional Advancement .... Ms. Gayle BARGE
32 Vice President of Student Affairs .... Dr. Ata KARIM
103 Vice Pres of Workforce Development .... Mr. Carl ELLIS
28 Vice President of Diversity .... Ms. Yoshiko HARDEN
13 Vice Pres of Information Resources .... Mr. Russell BEARD
09 Assoc VP Effect & Strat Planning .... Ms. Patricia JAMES
51 Dean Continuing Education .... Vacant
79 Dean of Arts and Humanities .... Ms. Margaret HARADA
76 Dean of HSEWI .... Ms. Leslie HEIZER NEWQUIST
83 Dean of Social Science .... Ms. Virginia BRIDWELL
88 Associate Dean of Student Programs .... Mr. Faisal JASWAL
35 Dean of Student Affairs .... Ms. Ana HERNANDEZ BLACKSTAD
85 Dean of Intl Educ & Global Init .... Mr. Jean D'ARC CAMPBELL
10 Exec Dir of Finance & Auxiliary Svc .... Ms. Jennifer STROTHER
08 Dean of Library Media Center .... Ms. Vivienne MCCLENDON
26 Director of Marketing .... Vacant
37 Director Financial Aid .... Ms. Melanie RUIZ
19 Director of Public Safety .... Mr. Tommy VU
13 Director Computing Services .... Mr. Jason AQUI
91 Manager Networking Svcs & Security .... Mr. Gary FARRIS
41 Director of Athletics .... Mr. Bill O'CONNOR
38 Student Counseling .... Mr. Harlan LEE
40 Director Bellevue College Bookstore .... Ms. Kristen CONNELY
96 Exec Director Physical Plant Ops .... Mr. Dexter JOHNSON

Bellingham Technical College (A)

3028 Lindebergh Avenue, Bellingham WA 98225-1599
County: Whatcom FICE Identification: 004999
Unit ID: 234696
Telephone: (360) 752-7000 Carnegie Class: Assoc/Pub-R-M
FAX Number: (360) 676-2798 Calendar System: Quarter
URL: www.btc.edu
Established: 1957 Annual Undergrad Tuition & Fees (In-District): $4,212
Enrollment: 2,842 Coed
Affiliation or Control: State/Local IRS Status: 501(c)3
Highest Offering: Associate Degree
Program: Occupational; 2-Year Principally Bachelor's Creditable; Technical Emphasis
Accreditation: NW, ACFEI, DA, DH, SURGT

01 President .... Dr. Kimberly PERRY
04 Exec Assistant to the President .... Ms. Ronda LAUGHLIN
05 Vice President of Instruction .... Dr. Frank POWERS
32 Vice President of Student Services .... Dr. Linda FOSSEN
11 VP of Administrative Services .... Ms. Chad STITELER
72 Dean of Professional Technical Educ .... Vacant
30 Exec Director College Advancement .... Mr. Dean FULTON
15 Director Human Resources .... Camille GATZA
37 Director Financial Aid .... Ms. Crystal BAGBY
06 Director Registration/Enrollment .... Ms. Joan KAMMERZELL
13 Dir Computer/Inform Support Svcs .... Mr. Curtis PERERA
08 Director Library .... Ms. Jane BLUME
18 Chief Facilities/Physical Plant .... Mr. David JUNGKUNTZ
26 Director of Communications .... Ms. Marni SALING MAYER
07 Director of Admissions .... Ms. Karen BADE
09 Dir of Inst Research & Planning .Ms. RaeLyn AXLUND MCBRIDE

Big Bend Community College (B)

7662 Chanute Street NE, Moses Lake WA 98837-3299
County: Grant FICE Identification: 003770
Unit ID: 234711
Telephone: (509) 793-2222 Carnegie Class: Assoc/Pub-R-M
FAX Number: (509) 762-6329 Calendar System: Quarter
URL: www.bigbend.edu
Established: 1962 Annual Undergrad Tuition & Fees (In-State): $4,000
Enrollment: 2,446 Coed
Affiliation or Control: State IRS Status: 501(c)3
Highest Offering: Associate Degree
Program: Occupational; 2-Year Principally Bachelor's Creditable
Accreditation: NW, ADNUR

01 President .... Dr. Terry LEAS
10 Vice Pres Administrative Services .... Ms. Linda SCHOONMAKER
05 Vice Pres Instruction/Student Svcs .... Mr. Bob MOHRBACHER
15 VP of Human Resources & Labor .... Mrs. Kim GARZA
75 Dean Prof Technical Education .... Ms. Daneen BERRY-GUERIN
49 Dean of Arts & Sciences .... Ms. Kara GARRETT
53 Dean Educ/Health/Language Skills .... Vacant
32 Assoc VP of Student Services .... Ms. Candis LACHER
35 Director of Student Programs .... Ms. Kim JACKSON
37 Director of Financial Aid .... Mr. Jeremy IVERSON
07 Director of Admissions .... Ms. Ruth COFFIN
08 Dean of Library Resources .... Mr. Tim FUHRMAN
41 Director of Athletics .... Mr. Preston WILKS
06 Registrar .... Ms. Candis LACHER
102 Dir Inst Advancement/Exec Dir Found .... Mrs. LeAnne PARTON
26 Publication & Information Director .... Mr. Doug SLY

21 Director of Business Services .... Ms. Charlene RIOS
40 Director of Bookstore .... Mrs. Caren COURTRIGHT
96 Director of Purchasing .... Ms. Kathy ARITA
39 Residence Hall Coordinator .... Mr. Hugh SCHOLTE
09 Dean of Institutional Research .... Ms. Valerie KIRKWOOD
13 Chief Info Technology Officer (CIO) .... Mr. Rick SPARKS
19 Director Security/Safety .... Mr. Kyle FOREMAN

Carrington College - Spokane (C)

10102 E Knox Ave., Suite 200, Spokane WA 99206-4187
Telephone: (509) 532-8888 Identification: 666385
Accreditation: &WJ, MAAB, RAD

† Regional accreditation is carried under the parent institution in Sacramento, CA.

Cascadia College (D)

18345 Campus Way, NE, Bothell WA 98011-8205
County: King FICE Identification: 034835
Unit ID: 439190
Telephone: (425) 352-8000 Carnegie Class: Assoc/Pub-S-SC
FAX Number: (425) 352-8313 Calendar System: Quarter
URL: www.cascadia.edu
Established: 2000 Annual Undergrad Tuition & Fees (In-District): $3,846
Enrollment: 4,705 Coed
Affiliation or Control: State/Local IRS Status: Exempt
Highest Offering: Associate Degree
Program: 2-Year Principally Bachelor's Creditable
Accreditation: NW

01 President .... Dr. Eric MURRAY
05 Vice Pres Student Learning/Success .... Dr. Rosemary SUTTON
20 Dean for Student Learning .... Dr. Erik TINGELSTAD
20 Dean for Student Learning .... Dr. Todd LUNDBERG
32 Dean for Student Services .... Ms. Erin BLAKENEY
06 Registrar .... Ms. Arlene HRUBY
09 Dir Institutional Research .... Mr. Glenn COLBY
10 Chief Business Officer .... Mr. Terrence HSIAO
15 Director Personnel Services .... Ms. Gina LORENZ
18 Chief Facilities/Physical Plant .... Vacant
26 Exec Director College Relations .... Ms. Meagan WALKER
35 Director of Student Life .... Ms. Becky RIOPEL
37 Director Student Financial Aid .... Ms. Sybil SMITH
30 Chief Development .... Vacant
38 Director Student Counseling .... Mr. Gordon DUTRISAC
84 Director Enrollment Management .... Mr. Shawn MILLER

† Granted candidacy at the Baccalaureate level.

Central Washington University (E)

400 E University Way, Ellensburg WA 98926-7501
County: Kittitas FICE Identification: 003771
Unit ID: 234827
Telephone: (509) 963-2111 Carnegie Class: Master's M
FAX Number: (509) 963-3206 Calendar System: Quarter
URL: www.cwu.edu
Established: 1890 Annual Undergrad Tuition & Fees (In-State): $9,282
Enrollment: 11,799 Coed
Affiliation or Control: State IRS Status: 501(c)3
Highest Offering: Master's
Program: Liberal Arts And General; Teacher Preparatory; Professional
Accreditation: NW, BUS, CACREP, CONST, DIETD, DIETI, EMT, ENGT, IPSY, MUS, TED

01 President .... Dr. James L. GAUDINO
05 Provost/VP Academic & Student Life .... Dr. Marilyn LEVINE
10 CFO/VP Business & Financial Affairs .... Mr. George CLARK
100 Chief of Staff .... Ms. Linda SCHACTLER
20 Assoc Provost Faculty Affairs .... Ms. Anne CUBILIE
21 Int Dir Student Financial Services .... Ms. Kelley CHRISTIANSON
84 Assoc VP Enrollment Management .... Mr. John SWINEY
32 Dean of Student Success .... Dr. Sarah L. SWAGER
35 Assoc Dean Student Development .... Mr. Keith M. CHAMPAGNE
88 Assoc Dean Student Achievement .... Mr. Jesse NELSON
18 Dir Plant Operations and Maintenenc .... Mr. Michael MOON
15 Dir Faculty and Labor Relations .... Mr. Don ANDERSON
13 Asst VP for Information Svcs/CIO .... Mr. Gene SHODA
58 Int Dean Graduate Studies/Research .... Dr. Kevin ARCHER
49 Int Dean College of Arts/Humanities .... Dr. Stacey ROBERTSON
50 Dean College of Business .... Dr. Kathryn MARTELL
53 Dean College of Educ/Prof Studies .... Dr. Paul BALLARD
83 Dean College of the Sciences .... Dr. Tim ENGLUND
08 Dean of Library Services .... Dr. Patricia CUTRIGHT
30 Vice Pres University Advancement .... Mr. Scott WADE
85 Exec Dir Intl Studies & Programs .... Dr. Ann RADWAN
06 Registrar .... Ms. Lindsey BROWN
22 Director at Large .... Ms. Staci SLEIGH-LAYMAN
41 Director Athletics .... Mr. Dennis FRANCOIS
12 Exec Director Extended Learning .... Ms. Melanie PALM
07 Director of Admissions .... Ms. Kathy GAER-CARLTON
37 Int AVP Financial Planning/Analysis .... Mr. Adrian NARANJO
39 Assoc Dean Student Living .... Mr. Richard DESHIELDS
19 Dir Police and Parking Services .... Chief Michael LUVERA
26 Exec Director Public Affairs .... Ms. Linda SCHACTLER
108 Exec Dir Organizational Effect .... Dr. James DEPAEPE
28 Director of Diversity .... Dr. Delores CLEARY
29 Sr Dir Alumni/Constituent Rels .... Mr. Bob FORD
36 Director Career Services .... Ms. Vicki SANNUTO
38 Director of Counseling .... Ms. Rhonda MCKINNEY
96 Purchasing Manager .... Mr. Stuart THOMPSON

21 Assoc VP Fin & Bus Auxiliaries .... Mr. Joel KLUCKING
14 Assoc VP Info Svcs & Security .... Mr. Andreas BOHMAN

Centralia College (F)

600 Centralia College Boulevard, Centralia WA 98531-4035
County: Lewis FICE Identification: 003772
Unit ID: 234845
Telephone: (360) 736-9391 Carnegie Class: Assoc/Pub-R-M
FAX Number: (360) 330-7108 Calendar System: Quarter
URL: www.centralia.edu
Established: 1925 Annual Undergrad Tuition & Fees (In-State): $4,000
Enrollment: 2,007 Coed
Affiliation or Control: State IRS Status: 501(c)3
Highest Offering: Baccalaureate
Program: Occupational; 2-Year Principally Bachelor's Creditable
Accreditation: NW

01 President .... Dr. Robert A. FROST
05 Vice President Instruction .... Mr. John MARTENS
32 Vice President of Students .... Mr. Robert COX
10 Vice Pres Finance/Administration .... Mr. Steve WARD
15 VP Human Resources/Legal Affairs .... Ms. Julie LEDFORD
103 Dean Workforce Education .... Ms. Durelle SULLIVAN
08 Dean of Library Services/E-Learning .... Ms. Sue KENNEDY
88 Dean of Academic Transfer Programs .... Mr. T. R. GRATZ
09 Director of Institutional Research .... Mr. Preston KIEKEL
103 Dir WorkFirst & Worker Retraining .... Vacant
84 Director of Enrollment Services .... Vacant
37 Director of Financial Aid .... Ms. Tracy DAHL
13 Director Information Technology .... Mr. Patrick ALLISON
41 Director of Sports Programs .... Mr. Bob PETERS
29 Director Alumni Relations .... Ms. Julie JOHNSON
96 Director of Purchasing .... Ms. Bonnie MYER
26 Dir College Relations & Events .... Ms. Amanda HAINES
06 Registration Specialist .... Ms. Rosanna SCHLAGEL
40 Bookstore Manager .... Ms. Tammy STRODEMIER
97 Program Coordinator .... Ms. Joanie ROGERSON

Charter College (G)

5278 Outlet Drive, Pasco WA 99301
Telephone: (509) 543-3388 Identification: 770821
Accreditation: ACICS

† Branch campus of Charter College, Anchorage, AK.

Charter College (H)

17200 SE Mill Plain Blvd, Suite 100, Vancouver WA 98683
Telephone: (360) 448-2000 Identification: 770822
Accreditation: ACICS

† Branch campus of Charter College, Anchorage, AK.

Charter College-Fife (I)

3700 Pacific Highway E, Suite 150, Fife WA 98424
Telephone: (775) 525-2117 Identification: 770623
Accreditation: ACICS

† Branch campus of Charter College, Anchorage, AK.

Charter College-Lynnwood (J)

19401 40th Avenue West, Lynnwood WA 98036
Telephone: (425) 275-4900 Identification: 770624
Accreditation: ACICS

† Branch campus of Charter College, Anchorage, AK.

City University of Seattle (K)

521 Wall Street, Suite 100, Seattle WA 98121
County: King FICE Identification: 013022
Unit ID: 234915
Telephone: (206) 239-4500 Carnegie Class: Master's L
FAX Number: N/A Calendar System: Quarter
URL: www.cityu.edu
Established: 1973 Annual Undergrad Tuition & Fees: $16,200
Enrollment: 3,936 Coed
Affiliation or Control: Independent Non-Profit IRS Status: 501(c)3
Highest Offering: Master's
Program: Teacher Preparatory; Professional; Business Emphasis
Accreditation: NW, ACBSP, CS

01 President .... Mr. Richard CARTER
101 Exec Asst Office of the President .... Ms. Ruth NICHOLS
32 Vice President Student Services .... Dr. Melissa E. MECHAM
05 Provost .... Dr. Steven OLSWANG
10 CFO/VP Finance & Administration .... Mr. Bruce K. BRYANT
88 Vice President European Operations .... Dr. Jan REBRO
84 Vice Pres Enrollment Management .... Ms. Marianne FINGADO
50 Dean School of Management .... Dr. Kurt KIRSTEIN
53 Dean School of Education .... Dr. Craig SCHIEBER
20 Dean Academic Affs-Europe .... Mr. David GRIFFIN
108 Director of Inst Effectiveness .... Dr. Susan SEYMOUR
21 Director of Finance .... Ms. Maria KREY
15 Director of Human Resources .... Mr. Timothy SPRAKE
08 Director Library Services .... Ms. Mary MARA
37 Assoc Dir Student Financial Svcs .... Ms. Linda COOKE

29 Alumni Relations Manager .... Mr. Alex WEBSTER
90 Director of Information Technology .... Mr. Kevin H. BROWN
88 Veterans Affairs Officer .... Ms. Sabrina JONES
07 Director Admissions .... Ms. Amy PORTWOOD
85 Director Intl Student Office .... Ms. Sabine SAWAY
18 Facilities Manager .... Mr. Troy CRABREE
26 Mgr Public Relations/Communications .... Ms. Tarsi HALL

† Granted candidacy at the Doctorate level.

Clark College (A)

1933 Fort Vancouver Way, Vancouver WA 98663-3598

County: Clark FICE Identification: 003773
Unit ID: 234933
Telephone: (360) 992-2000 Carnegie Class: Assoc/Pub-U-SC
FAX Number: (360) 992-2871 Calendar System: Quarter
URL: www.clark.edu
Established: 1933 Annual Undergrad Tuition & Fees (In-State): $4,163
Enrollment: 13,881 Coed
Affiliation or Control: State IRS Status: 501(c)3
Highest Offering: Associate Degree
Program: Occupational; 2-Year Principally Bachelor's Creditable; Business Emphasis
Accreditation: NW, ADNUR, DH, MAC, RAD

01 President .... Mr. Robert KNIGHT
05 Vice President of Instruction .... Dr. Tim COOK
32 Vice President of Student Affairs .... Mr. William BELDEN
11 Vice President of Admin Services .... Mr. Bob WILLIAMSON
15 Assoc Vice Pres of Human Resources .... Vacant
45 Assoc VP Planning/Instnl Effective .... Ms. Shanda DIEHL
51 Assoc VP Corp & Continuing Educ .... Mr. Kevin WITTE
84 Interim Dir of Enrollment/Registrar .... Ms. Mirranda SAARI
50 Dean Business/Technology .... Ms. Genevieve HOWARD
79 Int Dean Engl/Comm/Hum/Basic Educ .... Ms. Deena GODWIN
76 Dean Life Sci/Health & Phys Ed .... Vacant
83 Dean Social Sciences/Fine Arts .... Mr. Miles JACKSON
66 Assoc Dean of Nursing .... Ms. Cynthia MYERS
52 Director of Dental Hygiene .... Ms. Brenda WALSTEAD
04 Exec Assistant to the President .... Ms. Leigh KENT
41 Director of Athletics .... Ms. Ann WALKER
16 Associate Director Human Resources .... Ms. Sue WILLIAMS
08 Dir of Library Services .... Ms. Michelle BAGLEY
18 Director of Plant Services .... Mr. Tim PETTA
26 Chief Comm & Information Officer .... Mr. Chato HAZELBAKER
36 Director Career/Employment Services .... Ms. Edie BLAKELY
37 Director of Financial Aid .... Ms. Karen DRISCOLL
07 Assoc Dir of Entry Services .... Vacant
10 Director of Business Services .... Ms. Sabra SAND
35 Dir Stdnt Life/Multicult Stdnt Affs .... Ms. Sarah GRUHLER
38 Director Advising & Counseling .... Ms. Kelsey DUPRIE
25 Director of Grant Development .... Ms. Lori SILVERMAN
28 Director of Equity & Diversity .... Ms. Sirius BONNER
19 Director of Security & Safety .... Mr. Ken PACHECO
85 International Recruitment Manager .... Ms. Jane WALSTER
40 Bookstore Manager .... Ms. Monica KNOWLES
88 Mature Learning & Travel Stds Mgr .... Ms. Tracy REILLY-KELLY
96 Purchasing Manager .... Ms. Lisa NELSON
102 Foundation CEO .... Ms. Lisa GIBERT
105 Information Technology Specialist .... Mr. Chris CONCANNON
29 Director Alumni Relations .... Ms. Vivian MANNING

† Granted candidacy at the Baccalaureate level.

Clover Park Technical College (B)

4500 Steilacoom Boulevard, SW,
Lakewood WA 98499-4004

County: Pierce FICE Identification: 005752
Unit ID: 234951
Telephone: (253) 589-5800 Carnegie Class: Assoc/Pub-S-MC
FAX Number: (253) 589-5601 Calendar System: Quarter
URL: www.cptc.edu
Established: 1942 Annual Undergrad Tuition & Fees (In-State): $5,987
Enrollment: 4,338 Coed
Affiliation or Control: State IRS Status: 501(c)3
Highest Offering: Associate Degree
Program: Occupational; 2-Year Principally Bachelor's Creditable; Technical Emphasis
Accreditation: NW, DA, HT, MAC, MLTAD, SURGT

01 President .... Dr. Lonnie L. HOWARD
04 Executive Assistant .... Cherie STEELE
05 Vice President Student Learning .... Joyce LOVEDAY
10 Vice President Finance & Admin Svcs .... Larry CLARK
32 Vice President Student Success .... Ted BROUSSARD
20 Associate Vice Pres Instruction .... Mabel EDMONDS
15 Human Resources Director .... Shelby FRITZ
103 Dean of Workforce Development .... Vacant
13 Dir Information Technology .... Michael TAYLOR
37 Director Financial Aid .... Wendy JOSEPH
19 Director Plant Services & Security .... Vacant
12 Dir Northwest Career/Technical HS .... Loren DAVIS
84 Director of Enrollment Services .... Cynthia MOWRY
96 Purchasing Coord/Capital Projects .... Kate PURATICH
26 Marketing/Outreach Coordinator .... Janet HOLM
36 WorkFirst Special Projects Coord .... Christeen CROUCHET
09 Institutional Researcher .... Sara RABIN
40 Bookstore Coordinator .... Donna KOEHLER
18 Custodial Maintenance Coordinator .... Morris MILLER
06 Registrar .... Cynthia MOWRY
88 Int Dean Division I .... Claire KORSCHINOWSKI
88 Dean Division II .... Michelle HILLESLAND
88 Int Dean Division III .... Tanya SORENSON
30 Chief Development/Advancement .... Dr. Deborah RANNIGER

† Granted candidacy at the Baccalaureate level.

Columbia Basin College (C)

2600 N 20th Avenue, Pasco WA 99301-3397

County: Franklin FICE Identification: 003774
Unit ID: 234979
Telephone: (509) 547-0511 Carnegie Class: Assoc/Pub-R-L
FAX Number: (509) 546-0404 Calendar System: Quarter
URL: www.columbiabasin.edu
Established: 1955 Annual Undergrad Tuition & Fees (In-State): $4,738
Enrollment: 5,111 Coed
Affiliation or Control: State IRS Status: 170(c)1
Highest Offering: Baccalaureate
Program: Occupational; 2-Year Principally Bachelor's Creditable
Accreditation: NW, ADNUR, DH, EMT, MAC, SURGT

01 President .... Dr. Richard CUMMINS
05 Vice President Instruction .... Dr. Virginia TOMLINSON
10 Vice President of Administration .... Mr. Tyrone BROOKS
32 Vice President of Student Services .... Ms. Patricia CAMPBELL
15 VP Human Resources/Legal Affairs .... Ms. Camilla GLATT
21 Asst VP Fiscal Operations .... Vacant
09 Dean for Institutional Effectivenes .... Dr. Joe MONTGOMERY
49 Dean Arts & Humanities .... Mr. Bill MCKAY
62 Assoc Dean Library Services .... Ms. Melissa MCBURNEY
102 Executive Director Foundation .... Mr. Eric CLEMENTS
13 Director of Technology Services .... Mr. Brian DEXTER
40 Bookstore Director .... Ms. Debra BRUCE
18 Director of Plant Operations .... Mr. Chuck SCHMIDT
41 Athletic Director .... Mr. Scott ROGERS
26 Director of Communications .... Mr. Frank MURRAY
35 Director of Student Programs .... Ms. Alice SCHLEGEL
37 Director Student Financial Aid .... Mr. Ben BEUS
96 Director of Purchasing .... Ms. Sarah BROOKS
06 Associate Registrar .... Ms. Donna KORSTAD
04 Executive Asst to President .... Ms. Lupe PEREZ

*Community Colleges of Spokane District 17 (D)

501 N Riverpoint Boulevard, Ste 126,
Spokane WA 99217-6000

County: Spokane FICE Identification: 010784
Telephone: (509) 434-5107 Carnegie Class: N/A
FAX Number: (509) 434-5120
URL: www.ccs.spokane.edu

01 Chancellor .... Dr. Christine JOHNSON
12 Pres Spokane Community College .... Dr. Ryan CARSTENS
12 Pres Spokane Falls Comm College .... Dr. Janet GULLICKSON
05 Provost/Chief Learning Officer .... Dr. Nancy FAIR-SZOFRAN
20 Vice President of Learning SCC .... Ms. Rebecca RHODES
20 Vice President of Learning SFCC .... Dr. Jim MINKLER
32 VP of Student Services SCC .... Dr. Glen COSBY
32 VP of Student Services SFCC .... Mr. Darren PITCHER
10 Chief Financial Officer .... Ms. Lisa HJALTALIN
11 Chief Administration Officer .... Mr. Greg L. STEVENS
13 Chief Information Officer .... Mr. David O'NEILL
26 Public Information Officer .... Ms. Carolyn CASEY
41 Dist Director of Athletics PE/Rec .... Mr. Ken BURRUS
102 Executive Director CCS Foundation .... Mr. Tony D. HIGLEY
40 Director College Bookstores .... Ms. Shami R. RUGGLES
18 District Director of Facilities .... Mr. Dennis DUNHAM
103 Dist Dir Wkforce/Cont Ed/Corp Trng .... Ms. Sara SEXTON-JOHNSON
07 District Outreach Coordinator .... Vacant
96 Purchasing Manager .... Mr. Rod RAMER

*Spokane Community College (E)

North 1810 Greene Street, Spokane WA 99217-5499

County: Spokane FICE Identification: 003793
Unit ID: 236692
Telephone: (509) 533-7000 Carnegie Class: Assoc/Pub-R-L
FAX Number: (509) 533-8839 Calendar System: Quarter
URL: www.scc.spokane.edu
Established: 1963 Annual Undergrad Tuition & Fees (In-State): $4,300
Enrollment: 10,494 Coed
Affiliation or Control: State IRS Status: 501(c)3
Highest Offering: Associate Degree
Program: Occupational; 2-Year Principally Bachelor's Creditable; Technical Emphasis
Accreditation: NW, ACFEI, ADNUR, CAHIIM, COARC, CVT, DA, DMS, MAC, RAD, SURGT

00 District Chancellor .... Dr. Christine JOHNSON
02 President .... Dr. Ryan CARSTENS
05 Vice President of Instruction .... Dr. Rebecca RHODES
32 Interm VP of Student Services .... Mr. Glen COSBY
88 District Director Head Start .... Ms. Patty ALLEN
32 Dean of Student Support Services .... Mr. Michael LENKER
07 Director Admissions & Registration .... Ms. Roxanne BELOIT
35 Director Student Development .... Mr. Connan CAMPBELL
51 Dean Adult Basic Education .... Mr. Ragu HEGDE
49 Dean Arts & Sciences .... Ms. Vicki TRIER
50 Dean Business/Hospitality/Info Tech .... Mr. Jeff BROWN
88 Dean Corrections Education .... Mr. David MURLEY
56 Dean Extended Learning .... Ms. Jenni MARTIN
76 Dean Health & Environmental Science .... Dr. J.L HENRIKSEN
66 Associate Dean of Nursing .... Ms. Wendy BUENZLI
75 Dean for Technical Education .... Mr. Dave COX
41 Director Athletics/PE/Recreation .... Mr. Ken BURRUS
09 Director of Planning & Research .... Mr. Ben WOLFE
51 Asst Dean Adult Basic Education .... Mr. Brian DUDAK
88 Assistant Dean PACE Services .... Ms. Linda DEFORD
06 Registrar .... Ms. Roxanne BELOIT
37 Director Financial Aid .... Ms. Tammy ZIBELL
28 Director Multicultural & Outreach .... Ms. Lori HUNT
10 Chief Financial Officer .... Ms. Lisa HJALTALIN
40 Director of College Bookstores .... Ms. Shami RUGGLES
11 Chief Administration Officer .... Mr. Greg STEVENS
26 Chief Public Information Officer .... Ms. Carolyn CASEY
30 District Development Officer .... Mr. Tony HIGLEY
20 District Provost .... Dr. Nancy FAIR-SZOFRAN
38 Student Counseling Department Chair .... Mr. Bill RAMBO
96 Director of Purchasing .... Mr. Rodney RAMER
04 Administrative Asst to President .... Ms. Kathleen ROBERSON
13 Chief Info Technology Officer (CIO) .... Dr. David O'NEILL

*Spokane Falls Community College (F)

3410 W Fort George Wright Drive,
Spokane WA 99224-5288

County: Spokane FICE Identification: 009544
Unit ID: 236708
Telephone: (509) 533-3500 Carnegie Class: Assoc/Pub-R-L
FAX Number: (509) 533-3237 Calendar System: Quarter
URL: www.spokanefalls.edu
Established: 1967 Annual Undergrad Tuition & Fees (In-State): $4,389
Enrollment: 4,650 Coed
Affiliation or Control: State IRS Status: Exempt
Highest Offering: Associate Degree
Program: Occupational; 2-Year Principally Bachelor's Creditable
Accreditation: NW, OTA, PTAA

02 President .... Dr. Janet GULLICKSON
04 Exec Asst to the President .... Ms. Jan CARPENTER
05 Vice President of Learning .... Dr. James MINKLER
32 Vice President of Student Services .... Dr. Darren PITCHER
81 Dean Computing/Math & Science .... Mr. James BRADY
83 Dean Soc Sci/Acct/Econ/Hum Svcs .... Dr. Joseph JOZWIAK
79 Acting Dean Humanities .... Dr. Bonnie BRUNT
57 Dean Visual & Performing Arts .... Dr. Bonnie BRUNT
50 Dean Bus/Prof Stds/Workforce .... Ms. Lora SENF
88 Asst Dn Visual&Perf Arts/Humanities .... Dr. Craig RICKETT
12 Assistant Dean Pullman Campus .... Dr. Billy POTTER
06 Assoc Dean Enrollment Services .... Mr. Steven BAYS
36 Assoc Dean of Student Development .. Ms. Chrissy DAVIS JONES
07 Dir Recruit/New Stdnt Entry Center .... Ms. Chrissy DAVIS JONES
38 Co-Chair of Student Counseling .... Mr. Loren PEMBERTON
38 Co-Chair of Student Counseling .... Ms. Cynthia VIGIL
37 Director of Financial Aid .... Ms. Marjorie DAVIS
88 Assoc Dean Student Transitions .... Ms. Jennifer ALT
41 Athletic Director .... Mr. Ken BURRUS
19 Security & Safety Supervisor .... Mr. Kenneth DEMELLO
09 Dir Inst Effectiveness/Research .... Ms. Sally JACKSON
15 Chief Human Resources Officer .... Mr. Greg STEVENS
10 Chief Business Officer .... Ms. Lisa HJALTALIN
13 Chief Info Technology Officer (CIO) .... Dr. David O'NEILL
102 Exec Director CCS Foundation .... Mr. Tony HIGLEY
85 Vice Prov Strategic Partnerships .... Dr. Kevin BROCKBANK
08 District Director of Libraries .... Dr. Mary Ann GOODWIN
106 Interim District Dir e-Learning .... Dr. Kevin BROCKBANK
103 Chief Workforce Development Officer .... Mr. Mark MATTKE
26 Public Information Officer .... Ms. Carolyn CASEY
18 Director of Facilities .... Mr. Dennis DUNHAM
96 Director of Purchasing .... Mr. Rod RAMER

Cornish College of the Arts (G)

1000 Lenora Street, Seattle WA 98121-2707

County: King FICE Identification: 012315
Unit ID: 235024
Telephone: (206) 726-5151 Carnegie Class: Spec/Arts
FAX Number: (206) 720-1011 Calendar System: Semester
URL: www.cornish.edu
Established: 1914 Annual Undergrad Tuition & Fees: $36,840
Enrollment: 771 Coed
Affiliation or Control: Independent Non-Profit IRS Status: 501(c)3
Highest Offering: Baccalaureate
Program: Liberal Arts And General; Fine Arts Emphasis
Accreditation: NW, ART

01 President .... Dr. Nancy J. USCHER
05 Provost .... Ms. Moira SCOTT PAYNE
30 VP Institutional Advancement .... Ms. Sarah PERRY
10 VP of Finance and Administration .... Mr. Jeffrey R. RIDDELL
84 VP of Enrollment Management .... Mr. Jonathan LINDSAY
06 Dean of Academic Services/Registrar .Ms. Adrienne M. BOLYARD
32 Dean of Student Life .... Mr. Jerry HEKKEL
26 Director of Communications .... Ms. Rosemary JONES
15 Director of Human Resources .... Ms. Beverly PAGE
13 Director of Information Technology .... Mr. Ai NGUYEN
21 Controller .... Ms. Tina CHAMBERLAIN
08 Director of Library Services .... Ms. Hollis NEAR
07 Director of Admissions .... Ms. Sharron STARLING
18 Facilities Director .... Ms. Jenny FRAZIER
19 Dir of Campus Safety & Security .... Mr. Brandon BIRD
37 Director of Financial Aid .... Ms. Monique THERIAULT
38 Director Student Counseling .... Ms. Lori KORSHORK

DeVry University - Federal Way Campus (A)

3600 S 344th Way, Federal Way WA 98001-9558
Telephone: (253) 943-2800 Identification: 666224
Accreditation: &NH, ENGT

† Regional accreditation is carried under the parent institution in Downers Grove, IL. School is in teach out and plans to close Dec 2015.

DigiPen Institute of Technology (B)

9931 Willows Road, NE, Redmond WA 98052
County: King FICE Identification: 037243
Unit ID: 443410
Telephone: (425) 558-0299 Carnegie Class: Bac/Diverse
FAX Number: (425) 558-0378 Calendar System: Semester
URL: www.digipen.edu
Established: 1988 Annual Undergrad Tuition & Fees: $27,000
Enrollment: 1,018 Coed
Affiliation or Control: Proprietary IRS Status: Proprietary
Highest Offering: Master's
Program: Professional; Technical Emphasis
Accreditation: ACCSC

01 President .... Mr. Claude COMAIR
26 VP of External Affairs .... Ms. Angela KUGLER
32 Dean of Students .... Mr. Marshall TRAVERSE

Eastern Washington University (C)

526 5th Street, Cheney WA 99004-1619
County: Spokane FICE Identification: 003775
Unit ID: 235097
Telephone: (509) 359-6200 Carnegie Class: Master's L
FAX Number: (509) 359-6927 Calendar System: Quarter
URL: www.ewu.edu
Established: 1882 Annual Undergrad Tuition & Fees (In-State): $7,972
Enrollment: 13,453 Coed
Affiliation or Control: State IRS Status: 501(c)3
Highest Offering: Doctorate
Program: Liberal Arts And General; Teacher Preparatory; Professional
Accreditation: NW, BUS, CAATE, CACREP, CS, DH, ENG, ENGT, MUS, NRPA, OT, PLNG, PTA, SP, SPAA, SW

01 President .... Dr. Mary CULLINAN
05 Interim Prov/VP of Academic Affs .... Dr. Mary Ann KEOGH HOSS
10 Vice President for Business/Finance .... Ms. Mary VOVES
32 Vice President for Student Affairs . Ms. Stacey MORGAN FOSTER
30 Vice President of Advancement .... Mr. Michael WESTFALL
13 VP Info Technology/CIO .... Dr. Gary PRATT
20 Vice Prov Academic Admin .... Dr. Linda KIEFFER
88 Vice Prov Acad Plng/Grants & Res .... Dr. Colin ORMSBY
88 Vice Prov Undergrad & Stdnt Success .... Dr. Chuck LOPEZ
08 Dean of Libraries .... Dr. Suzanne MILTON
06 Registrar .... Ms. Erin MORGAN
41 Director Intercollegiate Athletics .... Mr. William CHAVES
21 Assoc VP Finance/Chief Fin Officer .... Ms. Toni HABEGGER
18 Assoc Vice Pres for Facilities .... Mr. Shawn KING
84 Assoc Vice Pres Enrollment Mgmt .... Dr. Neil WOOLF
04 Exec Assistant to the President/BOT .... Ms. Catherine MOSS
100 Assoc to the President .... Ms. Laurie CONNELLY
86 Director of Government Relations .... Mr. David BURI
36 Dir Career Services Center .... Ms. Virginia HINCH
92 Director of University Honors .... Dr. Dana ELDER
07 Director of Admissions .... Ms. Cathy SLEETH
37 Director of Fin Aid & Scholarships .... Mr. Bruce DEFRATES
40 Dir of Bookstore/Pence Union Bldg .... Mr. Robert ANDERSON
51 Dir of Continuing Education & RS .... Vacant
06 Director of Registration & Records .... Ms. Debra FOCKLER
58 Vice Provost/Graduate Research .... Dr. Colin ORMSBY
15 Director of Human Resources .... Ms. Jolynn ROGERS
29 Director of Alumni Advancement .... Ms. Lisa POPLAWSKI
109 Assoc VP/Business Auxil Svcs .... Ms. LeeAnn CASE
39 Sr Director Housing/Resid Life .... Mr. Josh ASHCROFT
38 Director Counseling & Psych Svcs .... Dr. Robert QUACKENBUSH
19 Director Public Safety/Chief Police .... Chief Timothy L. WALTERS
44 Assoc Director of Annual Giving .... Ms. Pat SPANJER
27 Director of Media Relations .... Mr. David MEANY
22 Dir Equal Opp/Affirm Action Coord .... Ms. Gayla THOMAS
50 Dean Business & Public Admin .... Dr. Martine DUCHATELET
49 Dean College Arts/Letters/Education .... Dr. Roy SONNEMA
83 Dean Col Social/Behav Sci/Soc Work .... Dr. Vickie SHIELDS
81 Dean Col Science Math & Technology .... Dr. Judd CASE
66 Dean Health Science & Public Health .... Dr. Laureen O'HANLON
35 Assoc VP/Dean of Student Life .... Dr. Amy JOHNSON
09 Assoc Director/Institutional Rsrch .... Ms. Bamby FIELDS
26 Chief Public Relations Officer .... Ms. Teresa CONWAY
104 Dir Office of Global Initiatives .... Ms. Catherine DIXON
106 Exec Director E-Learning .... Mr. Ben MEREDITH
25 Exec Dir Grants & Research Dev .... Ms. Ruth GALM

Edmonds Community College (D)

20000 68th Avenue W, Lynnwood WA 98036-5999
County: Snohomish FICE Identification: 005001
Unit ID: 235103
Telephone: (425) 640-1459 Carnegie Class: Assoc/Pub-S-MC
FAX Number: (425) 771-3366 Calendar System: Quarter
URL: www.edcc.edu
Established: 1967 Annual Undergrad Tuition & Fees (In-State): $4,308
Enrollment: 11,745 Coed
Affiliation or Control: State IRS Status: 501(c)3
Highest Offering: Associate Degree
Program: Occupational; 2-Year Principally Bachelor's Creditable
Accreditation: NW, CA, CONST

01 President .... Dr. Jean HERNANDEZ
05 Exec Vice President Instruction .... Dr. Charlie CRAWFORD
10 Vice Pres/Chief Financial Officer .... Mr. Kevin MCKAY
30 Vice Pres Col Relations/Advancement .... Dr. Tonya DRAKE
15 Int Exec Director Human Resources .... Ms. Suzanne MOREAU
32 Vice President Student Services .... Ms. Christina CASTORENA
103 VP Workforce Development/Training .... Dr. Terry COX
85 Vice Pres International Education .... Mr. David CORDELL
84 Dean Student Enroll/Financial Svcs .... Mr. Saovra EAR
35 Dean Student Life/Development .... Mr. Daniel JOHNSON
36 Dean Student Success/Retention .... Vacant
88 Interim Director Advising .... Ms. Heidi FARANI
04 Executive Asst to the President .... Ms. Patty MICHAJLA
102 Director College Foundation .... Mr. Brad THOMAS
25 Director Grants & Research .... Vacant
26 Director Communications/Marketing .... Ms. Marisa PIERCE
13 Director Information Technology .... Ms. Eva SMITH
18 Dir Facilites Planning & Operations .... Ms. Stephanie TEACHMAN
28 Int Director Equity & Inclusion .... Ms. Michele DOMINGO
96 Director of Purchasing .... Ms. Marian PAANANEN
27 Public Information Officer .... Mr. Nathan MACDONALD
19 Director Safety & Security .... Mr. Daniel GUERRERO
41 Athletic Director .... Mr. Jorge DE LA TORRE
85 Dir International Student Services .... Ms. Lisa THOMPSON
09 Institutional Researcher .... Ms. Pat HUFFMAN
108 Director Institutional Assessment .... Mr. James MULIK

Everest College (E)

155 Washington Ave, Ste 200, Bremerton WA 98337
County: Kitsap FICE Identification: 023001
Unit ID: 234739
Telephone: (360) 473-1120 Carnegie Class: Not Classified
FAX Number: (360) 792-2404 Calendar System: Quarter
URL: www.everest.edu
Established: 1960 Annual Undergrad Tuition & Fees: $16,900
Enrollment: 232 Coed
Affiliation or Control: Proprietary IRS Status: Proprietary
Highest Offering: Associate Degree
Program: Occupational
Accreditation: ACICS, MAC

01 President .... Mr. Tim ALLEN

Everest College (F)

906 SE Everett Mall Parkway, 6th FL, Everett WA 98208
Telephone: (425) 789-7960 Identification: 770793
Accreditation: ACICS, MAC

† Branch campus of Everest College, Bremerton, WA.

Everest College (G)

2156 Pacific Avenue, Tacoma WA 98402
Telephone: (253) 207-4000 Identification: 770794
Accreditation: ACICS, MAAB

† Branch campus of Everest College, Bremerton, WA.

Everest College (H)

120 NE 136th Avenue, Suite 130, Vancouver WA 98684
Telephone: (360) 254-3282 Identification: 666737
Accreditation: ACICS, MAC

† Branch campus of Everest College, Portland, OR. Tuition varies by degree program.

Everett Community College (I)

2000 Tower Street, Everett WA 98201-1390
County: Snohomish FICE Identification: 003776
Unit ID: 235149
Telephone: (425) 388-9100 Carnegie Class: Assoc/Pub-U-SC
FAX Number: (425) 388-9129 Calendar System: Quarter
URL: www.everettcc.edu
Established: 1941 Annual Undergrad Tuition & Fees (In-State): $4,500
Enrollment: 7,516 Coed
Affiliation or Control: State IRS Status: 501(c)3
Highest Offering: Associate Degree
Program: Occupational; 2-Year Principally Bachelor's Creditable
Accreditation: NW, ADNUR, MAC

01 President .... Dr. David BEYER
04 Executive Assistant to President .... Ms. Melissa GERAGHTY
05 Exec VP Instruction/Student Svcs .... Dr. Alison STEVENS
30 Vice Pres of College Advancement .... Dr. John OLSON
10 Vice Pres of Administrative Svcs .... Ms. Jennifer L. HOWARD
26 Vice Pres of College Services .... Mr. Patrick SISNEROS
12 Exec Dir Univ Ctr North Puget Sound .... Vacant
60 Dean Communication/Social Sciences .... Mr. Eugene MCAVOY
32 Dean of Student Development .... Mr. Anthony WILLIAMS
81 Dean of Math & Science .... Mr. Al FRIEDMAN
62 Dean of Arts & Learning Resources .... Ms. Jeanne LEADER
76 Dean Health Sciences/Public Safety .... Mr. Jason SMITH
53 Dean of Basic & Adult Education .... Ms. Katie JENSEN
28 Chief Diversity & Equity Officer .... Ms. Maria PENA
51 Director Continuing Education .... Ms. Karen LANDRY
84 Dean Enrollment/Student Finan Svcs .... Ms. Laurie FRANKLIN
50 Dean of Business & Applied Tech .... Mr. Ryan DAVIS
19 Dir of Campus Safety & Security .... Vacant
88 Vice Pres of Corporate Training .... Mr. John B. BONNER
09 Director Institutional Research .... Vacant
41 Director of Athletics .... Mr. Larry WALKER
40 Director of Bookstore .... Ms. Kerri KIRK
88 Dir Center for Disability Services .... Ms. Kathy COOK

The Evergreen State College (J)

2700 Evergreen Parkway, NW, Olympia WA 98505-0005
County: Thurston FICE Identification: 008155
Unit ID: 235167
Telephone: (360) 867-6000 Carnegie Class: Master's S
FAX Number: N/A Calendar System: Quarter
URL: www.evergreen.edu
Established: 1967 Annual Undergrad Tuition & Fees (In-State): $8,562
Enrollment: 4,219 Coed
Affiliation or Control: State IRS Status: 501(c)3
Highest Offering: Master's
Program: Liberal Arts And General
Accreditation: NW

01 President .... Dr. Thomas L. PURCE
05 Vice President/Provost .... Dr. Michael ZIMMERMAN
32 Vice President Student Affairs .... Dr. Wendy ENDRESS
10 Vice President Finance/Admin .... Dr. John HURLEY
30 Vice President College Advancement .... Ms. D. Lee HOEMANN
84 Assoc Vice Pres for Enrollmt Mgmt .... Mr. Steve HUNTER
15 Assoc Vice Pres for Human Resources ...... Ms. Laurel UZNANSKI
08 Dean of Library Services .... Mr. Greg MULLINS
35 Int Dir Student/Academic Supp Svcs .... Ms. Sara MARTIN
04 Deputy to President/Secretary BOT .... Mr. John CARMICHAEL
45 Exec Dir Operational Plng/Budget .... Mr. Steve TROTTER
22 Spec Asst to Pres/Equal Opportunity .... Mr. Paul GALLEGOS
22 Civil Rights Officer .... Ms. Nicole ACK
13 Director Computing/Communications .... Mr. Antonio ALFONSO
26 Dir Marketing/Comm/College Rels .... Mr. Todd SPRAGUE
37 Director of Financial Aid .... Ms. Tracy HALL
06 Registrar .... Ms. Elaine HAYASHI-PETERSEN
09 Director of Institutional Research .... Ms. Laura COGHLAN
18 Director of Facilities .... Ms. Jeanne RYNNE
21 Director of Business Services .... Mr. Dave KOHLER
29 Associate VP College Advancement .... Ms. Amanda WALKER
36 Director Career Development Center .... Mr. Steve LAING
38 Dir Counseling & Health Services .... Ms. Elizabeth MCHUGH
96 Purchasing and Contracts Manager .... Mr. Jay FIELD
07 Director of Admissions .... Mr. Phil BETZ
88 Director of Sustainability .... Mr. Scott MORGAN

Faith Evangelical College & Seminary (K)

3504 N Pearl Street, Tacoma WA 98407-2607
County: Pierce FICE Identification: 036894
Unit ID: 443049
Telephone: (253) 752-2020 Carnegie Class: Spec/Faith
FAX Number: (253) 759-1790 Calendar System: Quarter
URL: www.faithseminary.edu
Established: 1969 Annual Undergrad Tuition & Fees: $8,870
Enrollment: 320 Coed
Affiliation or Control: Interdenominational IRS Status: 501(c)3
Highest Offering: Doctorate
Program: Professional; Religious Emphasis
Accreditation: TRACS

01 President .... Dr. Michael J. ADAMS
05 Vice Pres Academic Affs/Provost .... Dr. H. Wayne HOUSE
11 VP Administrative Affs/Registrar .... Mr. John WHEELER
32 VP Student Affs/Dean of Students .... Dr. Mark WAGNER
07 Director of Admissions .... Mrs. Lorrie WHATELY
08 Library Director .... Dr. Timothy HYUN
88 Director of Korean Studies .... Dr. Kyu H. LEE
37 Director of Financial Aid .... Ms. Nor BOICE
10 Chief Financial Officer .... Dr. Douglas COLLIER
04 Exec Administrative Assistant .... Ms. Kimberly ADAMS

Gonzaga University (L)

502 E Boone Avenue, Spokane WA 99258-0001
County: Spokane FICE Identification: 003778
Unit ID: 235316
Telephone: (509) 313-4220 Carnegie Class: Master's L
FAX Number: (509) 313-5718 Calendar System: Semester
URL: www.gonzaga.edu
Established: 1887 Annual Undergrad Tuition & Fees: $37,480
Enrollment: 7,421 Coed
Affiliation or Control: Roman Catholic IRS Status: 501(c)3
Highest Offering: Doctorate
Program: Liberal Arts And General; Teacher Preparatory; Professional; Fine Arts Emphasis
Accreditation: NW, ANEST, BUS, BUSA, CACREP, CEA, ENG, LAW, MUS, NURSE, TED

01 President .... Dr. Thayne M. MCCULLOH
05 Academic Vice President .... Dr. Patricia OCONNELL KILLEN
03 Executive Vice President .... Vacant
10 Vice President for Finance .... Mr. Charles J. MURPHY
88 Vice President for Mission .... Rev. Frank E. CASE, SJ
32 VP for Student Development .... Dr. Judith BIGGS GARBUIO
30 VP for University Advancement .... Mr. Joe POSS

45 Interim VP for Admin & Planning .... Mr. John SKLUT
20 Assoc Academic Vice President .... Dr. Ron LARGE
28 Assoc AVP/Chief Diversity Officer .... Dr. Raymond REYES
06 Asst Academic Vice Pres/Registrar .... Ms. Jolanta A. WEBER
15 Asst Vice President Human Resources ... Mr. Kirk WOOD-GAINES
88 Assistant VP for Marketing/Comm .... Mr. Dave SONNTAG
88 Assistant VP for Mission .... Fr. Jim VOISS, SJ
36 Asst VP for Student Devel/Career .... Mr. O. Ray ANGLE
07 Dean of Admission .... Ms. Julie A. MCCULLOH
88 Dean of Student Well Being/Healthy .... Mr. Eric BALDWIN
08 Interim Dean of Library Services .... Ms. Kathleen O'CONNOR
37 Dean of Student Finance Services .... Mr. James WHITE
13 Interim Chief Information Officer .... Mr. Jim JONES
26 Director Cmty/Public Relations .... Ms. Mary Joan HAHN
29 Director Alumni .... Mr. Bob D. FINN
36 Director Career Center .... Dr. Mary HEITKEMPER
38 Dir Counseling/Career Assessment .... Dr. Fernando ORITZ
49 Dean Arts & Sciences .... Dr. Elisabeth MERMANN-JOZWIAK
50 Interim Dean School of Business .... Dr. Kenneth ANDERSON
107 Acting Dean School of Prof Studies .... Dr. Joe ALBERT
53 Dean of Education .... Dr. Vincent C. ALFONSO
54 Dean of Engineering & Applied Scien .... Dr. Steve SILLIMAN
61 Dean of Law .... Ms. Jane KORN
09 Director of Institutional Research .... Ms. Jolanta A. WEBER
41 Director of Athletics .... Mr. Michael L. ROTH
42 Director of University Ministry .... Mrs. Michelle M. WHEATLEY
43 General Counsel .... Ms. Maureen MCGUIRE
18 Director Plant Services .... Mr. Kenneth R. SAMMONS
92 Director Honors Program .... Rev. Tim R. CLANCY, SJ
96 Manager of Purchasing .... Mr. Steve M. LUNDEN
104 Director Study Abroad .... Mr. Richard O. MENARD
25 Director Sponsored Research & Pgm .... Dr. Joann WAITE
108 Faculty Director of Assessment .... Dr. Patrick T. MCCORMICK
66 Dean of Nursing & Human Physiology .... Dr. Brenda STEVENSON MARSHALL
20 Asst AVP for Global Engagement .... Dr. Joseph J. KINSELLA
108 Sr Dir Ext Relations/Assessment .... Ms. Sima THORPE
35 Dean of Student Engagement .... Mr. Matt LAMSMA
106 Dean of Virtual Campus .... Dr. Michael CAREY
71 Interim Director of Florence .... Mr. Henry BATTERMAN
100 Faculty Advisor to the President .... Dr. Ellen M. MACCARONE
21 Assoc Vice President of Finance .... Mr. Joe SMITH
88 Controller .... Ms. Deena PRESNELL
88 Director of Publications .... Mr. Dale GOODWIN
11 Chancellor .... Fr. Bernard J. COUGHLIN, SJ
19 Director Security/Safety .... Mr. Scott SNIDER
22 Dir Affirmative Action/EEO .... Ms. Chris PURVIANCE
39 Director Student Housing .... Mr. Dennis COLESTOCK
04 Administrative Asst to President .... Ms. Julia BJORDAHL

Grays Harbor College (A)

1620 Edward P. Smith Drive, Aberdeen WA 98520-7500

County: Grays Harbor — FICE Identification: 003779 — Unit ID: 235334
Telephone: (360) 532-9020 — Carnegie Class: Assoc/Pub-R-M
FAX Number: (360) 538-4299 — Calendar System: Quarter
URL: www.ghc.edu
Established: 1930 — Annual Undergrad Tuition & Fees (In-District): $3,846
Enrollment: 1,990 — Coed
Affiliation or Control: State/Local — IRS Status: 501(c)3
Highest Offering: Associate Degree
Program: Occupational; 2-Year Principally Bachelor's Creditable
Accreditation: NW, ADNUR

01 President .... Dr. Edward BREWSTER
04 Senior Admin Assistant to President .... Ms. Sandra ZELASKO
05 Vice President for Instruction .... Ms. Laurie CLARY
10 Chief Financial Officer .... Ms. Barbara MCCULLOUGH
32 Vice President for Student Services .... Mr. Jason HOSENEY
13 Chief Info Technology Officer/CIO .... Ms. Sandy LLOYD
75 Assoc Dean Vocational Instruction .... Mr. Mike KELLY
35 Assoc Dean for Student Services .... Ms. Nancy DEVERSE
08 Assoc Dean Library/Media Services .... Mr. Ahniwa FERRARI
07 Assoc Dean of Admissions .... Ms. Nancy DEVERSE
15 Chief Human Resources Officer .... Mr. Darrin JONES
37 Director Student Financial Aid .... Ms. Stacey SAVINO
18 Dir Campus Operations/Sfty/Security .... Mr. Lance JAMES
38 Director of Counseling .... Ms. Melissa BARNES
30 Chief Development Officer .... Ms. Jan JORGENSON
26 Director Public Relations .... Ms. Jane F. GOLDBERG
09 Chief Instnl Effect/Research/Plng .... Ms. Kristy ANDERSON
06 Registrar .... Ms. Nancy DEVERSE
41 Athletic Director .... Mr. Tom SUTERA
106 Dir Online Education/E-Learning .... Mr. James UMPHRES

Green River Community College (B)

12401 SE 320th Street, Auburn WA 98092-3699

County: King — FICE Identification: 003780 — Unit ID: 235343
Telephone: (253) 833-9111 — Carnegie Class: Assoc/Pub-S-MC
FAX Number: (253) 288-3470 — Calendar System: Quarter
URL: www.greenriver.edu
Established: 1965 — Annual Undergrad Tuition & Fees (In-State): $4,495
Enrollment: 7,915 — Coed
Affiliation or Control: State — IRS Status: 501(c)3
Highest Offering: Associate Degree
Program: Occupational; 2-Year Principally Bachelor's Creditable
Accreditation: NW, OTA, PTAA

01 President .... Dr. Eileen E. ELY
05 Vice President of Instruction .... Mr. Derek BRANDES
13 Exec Dir of Information Technology .... Ms. Camella MORGAN
10 Vice President Business Affairs .... Vacant
15 Vice President for Human Resources ...... Mr. Marshall SAMPSON
32 Vice President of Student Services . Dr. Deborah CASEY POWELL
56 VP Intl Programs/Extended Learning .... Mr. Ross JENNINGS
75 Dn Prof/Tech Ed/Trades & Technology .... Mr. Josh CLEARMAN
49 Dean Fine Arts/Math/Soc Sci/Library ...... Ms. Christie GILLILAND
88 Dean of Instr/Capital Project .... Mr. Sam BALL
84 Dean of Enrollment & Completion .... Mr. David LARSEN
06 Director of Enrollment Services .... Ms. Denise BENNATTS
37 Director of Financial Aid .... Ms. Mary EDINGTON
30 Exec Director of Development/Found .... Mr. George FRASIER
21 Director of Business Services .... Ms. Debbie KNIPSCHIELD
21 Controller .... Ms. Leda VOIGT
18 Director of Facilities .... Mr. Robert OLSON
27 Exec Director of College Relations .... Ms. Allison FRIEDLY
51 Exec Dir Cont Educ/Off-Campus Sites .... Ms. Leslie MOORE
09 Exec Dir Institutional Effectivenes .... Mr. Christopher JOHNSON
28 Dir Diversity/Equity & Inclusion .... Mr. Michael TUNCAP
96 Director of Purchasing .... Ms. Patty SIKORA
19 Director of Campus Safety .... Mr. Ron RILEY
41 Director Athletics .... Mr. Robert KICKNER

† Granted candidacy at the Baccalaureate level.

Heritage University (C)

3240 Fort Road, Toppenish WA 98948-9599

County: Yakima — FICE Identification: 003777 — Unit ID: 235422
Telephone: (509) 865-8500 — Carnegie Class: Master's M
FAX Number: (509) 865-4469 — Calendar System: Semester
URL: www.heritage.edu
Established: 1982 — Annual Undergrad Tuition & Fees: $19,123
Enrollment: 838 — Coed
Affiliation or Control: Independent Non-Profit — IRS Status: 501(c)3
Highest Offering: Master's
Program: 2-Year Principally Bachelor's Creditable; Liberal Arts And General; Teacher Preparatory; Professional
Accreditation: NW, #ARCPA, MT, SW

01 President .... Dr. John E. BASSETT
05 Vice President Academic Affairs .... Dr. Curtis GUAGLIANONE
32 Vice Pres Student Life .... Dr. Celestino LIMAS
100 Chief of Staff .... Ms. Veronica NARANJO
30 Vice President Advancement .... Mr. Michael P. MOORE
84 Assoc VP Enrollment Management .... Mr. Harold WINGOOD
10 Vice President & CFO .... Ms. Siri J. STROM
06 Registrar .... Mr. Luis GUTIERREZ
53 Dean of Education & Psychology .... Ms. Merrilou HARRISON
18 Director Physical Plant .... Mr. Rob CARROLL
37 Director of Financial Aid .... Mr. Oscar VERDUZCO
08 Library Director .... Mr. Bill MCCAY
13 Vice Pres for Information Services .... Mr. Jim BUSH
07 Director of Admissions .... Mrs. Olivia GUTIERREZ
26 Communications Officer .... Ms. Bonnie HUGHES
04 Manager Executive Offices .... Ms. Betty J. SAMPSON
09 Director of Institutional Research .... Ms. Nina OMAN
15 Director Personnel Services .... Ms. Veronica NARANJO
49 Dean Arts & Sciences .... Dr. Kazuhiro SONODA
35 Dean Student Affs/Career/Counseling .... Ms. Melissa HILL
36 Director Student Placement .... Ms. Irma DEPRIETO
96 Director of Purchasing .... Ms. Geneva SAPP
38 Counselor for Student Life .... Ms. Erica MACIAS
20 Associate Provost .... Dr. Laurie FATHE
21 Assoc Business Officer/Controller .... Mr. Mark MCNABB
29 Director of Alumni Relations .... Ms. Julia KROLIKOWSKI

Highline College (D)

PO Box 98000, 2400 S 240th Street, Des Moines WA 98198-9800

County: King — FICE Identification: 003781 — Unit ID: 235431
Telephone: (206) 878-3710 — Carnegie Class: Assoc/Pub-S-MC
FAX Number: (206) 870-3779 — Calendar System: Quarter
URL: www.highline.edu
Established: 1961 — Annual Undergrad Tuition & Fees (In-State): $4,000
Enrollment: 6,443 — Coed
Affiliation or Control: State — IRS Status: 501(c)3
Highest Offering: Associate Degree
Program: Occupational; 2-Year Principally Bachelor's Creditable
Accreditation: NW, ADNUR, COARC, MAC

01 President .... Dr. Jack BERMINGHAM
11 Vice Pres Administrative Services .... Mr. Michael PHAM
05 Vice Pres for Academic Affairs .... Mr. Jeff WAGNITZ
30 VP Inst Advancement/Cmty Rels .... Dr. Lisa SKARI
32 Vice Pres for Student Services .... Ms. Toni CASTRO
20 Dean of Instruction-Vocational .... Ms. Alice MADSEN
20 Dean of Instruction-Academics .... Dr. Rolita EZEONU
24 Dean Instructional Resources .... Ms. Monica LUCE
35 Assoc Dean Student Programs .... Mr. Jonathan BROWN
31 Exec Dir Community Education .... Ms. Judy PERRY
84 Assoc Dean Enrollment Services .... Ms. Lorraine ODOM
26 Director Communications & Marketing .... Mr. Tony JOHNSON
15 Exec Director of Human Resources .... Ms. Sue WILLIAMSON
10 Director Financial Services .... Ms. Shirley BEAN
13 Exec Dir Administrative Technology .... Vacant
18 Director Plant Operations .... Mr. Barry HOLLDORF
19 Dir Safety/Sec & Emergency Manager .... Mr. Jim BAYLOR
41 Director Athletics .... Mr. John DUNN
44 Director Resources & Development .... Mr. Rod STEPHENSON
09 Manager Institutional Research .... Ms. Emily COATES
38 Assoc Dean Counseling/Judicial .... Dr. Allison LAU
40 Bookstore Manager .... Ms. Laura NOLE
96 Manager of Purchasing .... Ms. Dianna THIELE
06 Registrar .... Ms. Debbie FAISON
07 Director of Admissions .... Ms. L. Michelle KUWASAKI
22 Program Asst Multicultural Affairs .... Ms. Barbara TALKINGTON
29 Coordinator Alumni Relations .... Ms. Madison GRIDLEY

† Granted candidacy at the Baccalaureate level.

Interface College (E)

178 South Stevens Street, Spokane WA 99201

County: Spokane — FICE Identification: 023265 — Unit ID: 235495
Telephone: (509) 467-1727 — Carnegie Class: Assoc/PrivFP
FAX Number: (509) 467-3804 — Calendar System: Semester
URL: www.interface.edu
Established: 1982 — Annual Undergrad Tuition & Fees: $14,710
Enrollment: 91 — Coed
Affiliation or Control: Proprietary — IRS Status: Proprietary
Highest Offering: Associate Degree
Program: Occupational
Accreditation: CNCE

01 President .... Walt LEATHERS
05 Director of Instruction .... Roy PRESCOTT
37 Vice Pres Financial Aid/Accounting .... Rick SINCLAIR
07 Asst Director of Admissions .... Kathy HAMMONDS

ITT Technical Institute (F)

1615 75th Street SW, Everett WA 98203-6261

Telephone: (425) 583-0200 — Identification: 666326
Accreditation: ACICS

† Branch campus of ITT Technical Institute, Spokane Valley, WA.

ITT Technical Institute (G)

12720 Gateway Drive, Suite 100, Seattle WA 98168-3334

Telephone: (206) 244-3300 — FICE Identification: 008443
Accreditation: ACICS

† Branch campus of ITT Technical Institute, Spokane Valley, WA.

ITT Technical Institute (H)

13518 East Indiana Avenue, Spokane Valley WA 99216-1589

County: Spokane — FICE Identification: 030718 — Unit ID: 235510
Telephone: (509) 926-2900 — Carnegie Class: Spec/Tech
FAX Number: (509) 926-2908 — Calendar System: Quarter
URL: www.itt-tech.edu
Established: 1985 — Annual Undergrad Tuition & Fees: N/A
Enrollment: 295 — Coed
Affiliation or Control: Proprietary — IRS Status: Proprietary
Highest Offering: Baccalaureate
Program: Technical Emphasis
Accreditation: ACICS

Lake Washington Institute of Technology (I)

11605 132nd Avenue NE, Kirkland WA 98034-8506

County: King — FICE Identification: 005373 — Unit ID: 235699
Telephone: (425) 739-8100 — Carnegie Class: Assoc/Pub-S-MC
FAX Number: (425) 739-8299 — Calendar System: Quarter
URL: www.lwtech.edu
Established: 1949 — Annual Undergrad Tuition & Fees (In-State): $4,761
Enrollment: 4,686 — Coed
Affiliation or Control: State — IRS Status: 170(c)1
Highest Offering: Baccalaureate
Program: Occupational; Technical Emphasis
Accreditation: NW, ACFEI, DA, DH, FUSER, MAC, #OTA, PTAA

01 President .... Dr. Amy M. MORRISON GOINGS
04 Exec Assistant to the President .... Ms. Heather DEGRAW
32 VP Student Services .... Dr. Ruby HAYDEN
05 VP of Instruction .... Dr. Elliot STERN
10 VP Administrative Services .... Mr. Bill THOMAS
86 Exec Dir Legislative & Ext Rels .... Ms. Terry BYINGTON
13 Exec Dir Information Technology .... Mr. Mike POTTER
102 Exec Director Foundation .... Ms. Elisabeth SORENSEN
15 Exec Director Human Resources .... Ms. Melissa LAMY
88 Spec Asst to Pres College Advance .... Ms. Andrea I. OLSON
53 Dean Gen Educ/Hospitality & Svcs .... Mr. Douglas J. EMORY
76 Dean Instruction Allied Health .... Ms. Jamilyn PENN
72 Dean Applied Design Programs .... Dr. Suzanne AMES
89 Principal/Dean High School Programs .... Dr. Kim INFINGER
08 Library Program Coordinator .... Ms. Cheyenne M. RODUIN
26 Director Communications/Marketing .... Ms. Leslie COHAN
76 Dir Phys Therapist Assistant Pgm .... Ms. Molly VERSCHUYL
88 Director Funeral Services .... Ms. Jamye CAMERON
66 Director of Nursing .... Ms. Antwinett LEE
85 Director International Programs .... Ms. Sarah ROSS

106 Director of eLearning .... Ms. Rhonda DEWITT
18 Director Facilities & Operations .... Mr. Tim WHEELER
37 Director Financial Aid .... Mr. Bill CHANEY
103 Director Workforce Development .... Ms. Demetra BIROS
25 Dir of Research & Grant Development .... Ms. Cathy COPELAND
07 Director Admissions & Outreach .... Ms. Christina HARTER
88 Director TRiO Student Support Svcs .... Dr. Patricia HUNTER
21 Controller .... Mr. Xieng LIM
88 Manager Food Service Operations .... Mr. Joe TREVINO
96 Purchasing Manager .... Mr. Gordy FUNAI
105 Website/Digital Content Specialist .... Ms. Alisa SHTROMBERG
88 Manager Student Programs .... Ms. Sheila WALTON
40 Manager Bookstore .... Mr. Russ MERKOW
19 Director Security/Safety .... Mr. Anthony BOWERS
54 Dean of Industrial Technology .... Dr. Sharon BUCK
84 Director Enrollment Services .... Ms. Larisa AKSELRUD
88 Director Student Development .... Ms. Andrea FECHNER
09 Director Research & Grants .... Ms. Cathy COPELAND
28 Interim Diversity Program Coord .... Ms. Neera MEHTA

Lower Columbia College (A)

PO Box 3010, Longview WA 98632-0310
County: Cowlitz FICE Identification: 003782
Unit ID: 235750
Telephone: (360) 442-2311 Carnegie Class: Assoc/Pub-R-M
FAX Number: (360) 442-2109 Calendar System: Quarter
URL: www.lowercolumbia.edu
Established: 1934 Annual Undergrad Tuition & Fees (In-State): $4,049
Enrollment: 2,998 Coed
Affiliation or Control: State IRS Status: 170(c)1
Highest Offering: Associate Degree
Program: Occupational; 2-Year Principally Bachelor's Creditable
Accreditation: NW, ADNUR, MAC

01 President .... Mr. Christopher C. BAILEY
05 Vice President of Instruction .... Mr. Brendan GLASER
11 Vice President Administrative Svcs .... Mr. Nolan WHEELER
32 Interim VP for Student Success .... Ms. Kendra SPRAGUE
103 Dean Workforce/Continuing Educ .... Ms. Darlene DE VIDA
20 Dean Instructional Programs .... Ms. Maggie STUART
20 Dean Instructional Programs .... Mr. Kyle HAMMON
76 Associate Dean Allied Health/Nurse .... Ms. Karen JOINER
09 Director Effectiveness & Marketing .... Ms. Wendy HALL
18 Director of Campus Services .... Mr. Richard HAMILTON
102 Director of Foundation .... Ms. Erin ZEIGER
41 Athletic Director .... Mr. Kirc J. ROLAND
21 Controller .... Vacant
15 Director of Personnel Services .... Ms. Kendra SPRAGUE
37 Financial Aid Officer .... Ms. Marisa GEIER
08 Director of Library Services .... Ms. Melinda WEATHERFORD
13 Director of Information Technology .... Mr. Brandon RAY
40 Director of Bookstore .... Mr. Cliff HICKS
07 Director Admissions/Registrar .... Ms. Nichole SEROSHEK
10 Chief Business Officer .... Mr. Nolan WHEELER
96 Director of Purchasing .... Ms. Sherry GOHN
04 Executive Assistant .... Ms. Linda J. CLARK
06 Registrar .... Ms. Nichole SEROSHEK
106 Dir Online Education/E-learning .... Vacant
19 Director Security/Safety .... Mr. Casey TILTON
29 Director Alumni Relations .... Ms. Sheila BURGIN

Moody Bible Institute-Spokane (B)

611 E Indiana Avenue, Spokane WA 99207
Telephone: (509) 570-5900 Identification: 770082
Accreditation: &NH

† Branch campus of Moody Bible Institute, Chicago, IL.

Northwest College of Art & Design (NCAD) (C)

16301 Creative Drive NE, Poulsbo WA 98370-8651
County: Kitsap FICE Identification: 026021
Unit ID: 377546
Telephone: (360) 779-9993 Carnegie Class: Spec/Arts
FAX Number: (360) 779-9933 Calendar System: Semester
URL: www.ncad.edu
Established: 1982 Annual Undergrad Tuition & Fees: $19,050
Enrollment: 95 Coed
Affiliation or Control: Proprietary IRS Status: Proprietary
Highest Offering: Baccalaureate
Program: Fine Arts Emphasis
Accreditation: ACCSC

01 President .... Craig FREEMAN
05 Director of Education .... Julius FINLEY
11 Director of Operations .... Kim PERIGARD
06 Registrar .... Danielle MACKELWICH
13 IT Admin .... Skye CARLSON
07 Assistant Director of Admissions .... Kyle TONAHILL
37 Financial Aid .... Mac FOX
08 Head Librarian .... Troy JOHNSON

Northwest Indian College (D)

2522 Kwina Road, Bellingham WA 98226-9278
County: Whatcom FICE Identification: 021800
Unit ID: 380377
Telephone: (360) 676-2772 Carnegie Class: Tribal
FAX Number: (360) 738-0136 Calendar System: Quarter
URL: www.nwic.edu
Established: 1978 Annual Undergrad Tuition & Fees: $4,407
Enrollment: 637 Coed
Affiliation or Control: Tribal Control IRS Status: 501(c)3
Highest Offering: Baccalaureate
Program: Occupational; 2-Year Principally Bachelor's Creditable
Accreditation: NW

01 President .... Dr. Justin GUILLORY
10 Vice Pres for Finance .... Ms. Karyl JEFFERSON
05 Vice Pres Instruction/Student Svcs .... Ms. Carole RAVE
11 Vice Pres Campus Development .... Mr. David OREIRO
45 VP for Research/Sponsored Programs .... Ms. Barbara ROBERTS
04 Exec Assistant to the President .... Ms. Corby DAVIS
106 Dean of Academic/Distant Learning .... Ms. Bernice PORTERVINT
32 Dean of Student Life .... Ms. Victoria RETASKET
20 Assoc Dean Academics/Dist Learning .... Mr. Don MCCLUSKEY
37 Asc Dn Students/Fin Aid Dir/Admiss .... Vacant
13 IT Director .... Mr. Michael JAMES
08 Library Director .... Ms. Valerie MCBETH
06 Registrar .... Ms. Patricia CUEVA

Northwest Institute of Literary Arts (E)

5611 Bayview Road, Langley WA 98260
County: Island FICE Identification: 041889
Unit ID: 460941
Telephone: (360) 331-0307 Carnegie Class: Not Classified
FAX Number: N/A Calendar System: Semester
URL: www.nila.edu
Established: 2005 Annual Graduate Tuition & Fees: $12,650
Enrollment: 51 Coed
Affiliation or Control: Independent Non-Profit IRS Status: 501(c)3
Highest Offering: Master's; No Undergraduates
Program: Professional; Fine Arts Emphasis
Accreditation: DEAC

01 Program Director/CAO .... Mr. Wayne UDE
06 Registrar .... Ms. Susan JANOW

Northwest School of Wooden Boatbuilding (F)

42 N Water Street, Port Hadlock WA 98339-8706
County: Jefferson FICE Identification: 041550
Unit ID: 458140
Telephone: (360) 385-4948 Carnegie Class: Not Classified
FAX Number: (360) 385-5089 Calendar System: Other
URL: www.nwboatschool.org
Established: 1981 Annual Undergrad Tuition & Fees: $14,550
Enrollment: 64 Coed
Affiliation or Control: Independent Non-Profit IRS Status: 501(c)3
Highest Offering: Associate Degree
Program: Occupational; Technical Emphasis
Accreditation: ACCSC

01 Executive Director .... Ms. Betsy DAVIS
05 Director of Education .... Ms. Pamela ROBERTS

Northwest University (G)

PO Box 579, Kirkland WA 98083-0579
County: King FICE Identification: 003783
Unit ID: 236133
Telephone: (425) 822-8266 Carnegie Class: Bac/Diverse
FAX Number: (425) 889-5224 Calendar System: Semester
URL: www.northwestu.edu
Established: 1934 Annual Undergrad Tuition & Fees: $28,086
Enrollment: 1,862 Coed
Affiliation or Control: Assemblies Of God Church IRS Status: 501(c)3
Highest Offering: Master's
Program: Liberal Arts And General; Religious Emphasis
Accreditation: NW, ACBSP, NURSE

01 President .... Dr. Joseph CASTLEBERRY
05 Provost .... Dr. Jim HEUGEL
10 Chief Financial Officer .... Mr. John JORDAN
30 Senior VP of Advancement .... Mr. Ken CORNELL
42 Campus Pastor .... Rev. Phil RASMUSSEN
06 Registrar .... Mrs. Sandy HENDRICKSON
07 Director of Admissions .... Mrs. Anna PFLUG
37 Director of Financial Aid .... Mr. Roger WILSON
41 Athletic Director .... Mr. Gary MCINTOSH
08 College Librarian .... Mr. Adam EPP
38 Director of Counseling Services .... Ms. Teresa REGAN
29 Dir of Alumni Svcs/Parent Rels .... Ms. Leanne KONZELMAN
15 Director Human Resources .... Ms. Victoria CLARK
36 Director Student Success .... Mrs. Amy JONES
32 Dean of Students .... Mr. Rick ENGSTROM
26 Director of Marketing .... Mr. Steve BOSTROM

† Granted candidacy at the Doctorate level.

Olympic College (H)

1600 Chester Avenue, Bremerton WA 98337-1699
County: Kitsap FICE Identification: 003784
Unit ID: 236188
Telephone: (360) 792-6050 Carnegie Class: Assoc/Pub4
FAX Number: (360) 475-7151 Calendar System: Quarter
URL: www.olympic.edu
Established: 1946 Annual Undergrad Tuition & Fees (In-State): $4,000
Enrollment: 8,218 Coed
Affiliation or Control: State IRS Status: 501(c)3
Highest Offering: Baccalaureate
Program: Occupational; 2-Year Principally Bachelor's Creditable
Accreditation: NW, ACFEI, ADNUR, MAC, NURSE, PTAA

01 President .... Dr. David C. MITCHELL
05 Vice President for Instruction .... Ms. Mary GARGUILE
10 Vice President for Administration .... Mr. Bruce RIVELAND
32 Vice President for Student Services .... Dr. Damon BELL
26 Vice President Equity & Inclusion .... Ms. Cheryl NUÑEZ
15 Exec Director Human Resource Svcs .... Mr. David SLOWN
51 Director of Continuing Education .... Vacant
04 Exec Assistant to the President .... Ms. Shawna BLISS
37 Director Student Financial Services .... Ms. Heidi TOWNSEND
27 Director of Communications .... Mr. Shawn DEVINE
84 Dean of Enrollment Services .... Ms. Jennifer GLASIER
18 Dir Facilities Svcs/Capital Project .... Mr. Robert PASQUARIELLO
21 Director of Business Services .... Ms. Janell WHITELEY
96 Procurement Officer .... Ms. Diana LAKE
36 Director Career Center .... Ms. Teresa MCDERMOTT
09 Dir Inst Planning/Assessmnt/Rsrch .... Ms. Summer KENESSON
28 Supervisor Multicltrl/Student Pgms .... Ms. Jodie COLLINS
103 Dean Workforce Development .... Ms. Amy HATFIELD
08 Dean Library/Lrng Resources/eLrng .... Ms. Erica COE
35 Dean of Student Development .... Mr. James MOHR
50 Dean Business & Technology .... Dr. Norma WHITACRE
81 Dean Math/Engineer/Sci/Health .... Dr. Mark HARRISON
79 Dean Humanities/Social Science .... Dr. Gina HUSTON
13 Director of Technical Services .... Ms. Evelyn HERNANDEZ
19 Director of Campus Safety .... Mr. Ed CALL
25 Director of Grants .... Ms. Sharon KLINE
29 Director of Alumni Association .... Mr. David EMMONS
41 Director of Athletics .... Mr. Barry JANUSCH

Pacific Lutheran University (I)

12180 Park Avenue S., Tacoma WA 98447-0003
County: Pierce FICE Identification: 003785
Unit ID: 236230
Telephone: (253) 531-6900 Carnegie Class: Master's M
FAX Number: (253) 535-8320 Calendar System: 4/1/4
URL: www.plu.edu
Established: 1890 Annual Undergrad Tuition & Fees: $37,600
Enrollment: 3,275 Coed
Affiliation or Control: Evangelical Lutheran Church In America
IRS Status: 501(c)3
Highest Offering: Master's
Program: Liberal Arts And General; Teacher Preparatory; Professional
Accreditation: NW, BUS, CS, ENG, MFCD, MUS, NURSE, SW, TED

01 President .... Dr. Thomas W. KRISE
100 Senior Advisor to the President .... Ms. Kris H. PLAEHN
04 Exec Assoc to the President .... Ms. Deidre N. HILL
101 Director of Admin & Sec to Board .... Ms. Vicky L. WINTERS
05 Provost/Senior VP Academic Affairs .. Dr. Steven P. STARKOVICH
10 Vice President Finance & Operations .... Mr. Allan BELTON
30 Vice Pres for Advancement .... Mr. Daniel J. LEE
32 Vice Pres for Student Life .... Dr. Joanna C. ROYCE-DAVIS
07 Dean for Enrollment Svcs .... Mr. David E. GUNOVICH
27 Vice Pres Marketing & Communication .... Ms. Donna L. GIBBS
20 Assoc Provost for Undergrad Program .... Dr. Jan P. LEWIS
21 Controller .... Vacant
08 Assoc Provost for Information Tech .... Dr. Frank X. MOORE
42 Interim University Pastor .... Rev. John ROSENBERG
57 Dean School of Arts & Communication .... Dr. Cameron D. BENNETT
50 Dean of School of Business .... Dr. Nancy ALBERS MILLER
53 Dean School of Educ & Kinesiology .... Dr. Frank M. KLINE
66 Dean School of Nursing .... Dr. Sheila K. SMITH
79 Dean of Humanities .... Dr. James M. ALBRECHT
88 Dean of Natural Sciences .... Dr. Matthew J. SMITH
83 Dean of Social Sciences .... Dr. David R. HUELSBECK
35 Dean of Students .... Dr. Eva R. FREY
51 Assoc Provost for Grad & Cont Ed .... Dr. Geoffrey E. FOY
88 Exec Dir Wang Ctr for Global Ed .... Dr. Tamara R. WILLIAMS
88 Director Academic Advising .... Mr. Hal R. DELAROSBY
41 Director Athletics & Recreation .... Ms. Laurie L. TURNER
06 Registrar .... Mr. Kevin A. BERG
39 Assoc VP for Campus Life .... Mr. Tom A. HUELSBECK
18 Assoc VP for Facilities Management .... Mr. Ray ORR
19 Director of Campus Safety & Info .... Mr. Greg V. PREMO
36 Director of Career Connections .. Ms. Catherine W. SWEARINGEN
23 Interim Director of Health Services .... Ms. Susana A. DOLL
15 Assoc Vice Pres Human Resources .... Ms. Teri P. PHILLIPS
90 Dir of Enterprise Systems & Comm .... Mr. David P. ALLEN
37 Director of Student Financial Aid .... Ms. Kay W. SOLTIS
40 Manager of Bookstore .... Ms. Amanda B. HAWKINS
09 Dir Assessment/Accreditation/Rsrch .... Dr. David A. VEAZEY
102 Dir Foundation/Corporate Relations .... Ms. Aileen Q. BACON
38 Director Counseling Center .... Dr. Joanne R. ITO
44 Director Annual Giving .... Ms. Alicia A. HINCKLEY

† Granted candidacy at the Doctorate level.

Pacific Northwest University of Health Sciences (J)

111 University Parkway, Suite 202, Yakima WA 98901
County: Yakima FICE Identification: 041305
Unit ID: 455406
Telephone: (509) 452-5100 Carnegie Class: Assoc/PrivNFP4
FAX Number: (509) 452-5101 Calendar System: Semester
URL: www.pnwu.edu
Established: 2005 Annual Graduate Tuition & Fees: $50,000

Enrollment: 540 Coed
Affiliation or Control: Independent Non-Profit IRS Status: 501(c)3
Highest Offering: Doctorate; No Undergraduates
Program: Professional
Accreditation: OSTEO

01 President Dr. Keith WATSON
05 Senior Advisor to the President Dr. Robert E. SUTTON
10 Chief Financial Officer Ms. Ann HITTLE
11 Chief Operations Officer Mr. Frank D. ALVAREZ
30 Chief Advancement Officer Mr. Wendell SNODGRASS
63 Dean Col of Osteopathic Medicine Dr. Thomas SCANDALIS
09 Chief Research Officer Dr. Bernadette HOWLETT
06 Registrar Ms. LeAnn HUNTER
08 Head Librarian Ms. Anita CLEARY
13 Chief Info Technology Officer (CIO) Mr. Cody DOWN
15 Director Personnel Services Ms. Stefanie DURAND
18 Chief Facilities/Physical Plant Mr. Dave WARNER
19 Director Security/Safety Mr. Ben HITTLE
26 Chief Public Relations/Marketing Mr. Ryan RODRUCK
29 Director Alumni Relations Mr. Adam STORY
37 Director Student Financial Aid Ms. Laura PENDLETON
45 Chief Institutional Planning Ms. Angie GIRARD

Peninsula College (A)

1502 East Lauridsen Boulevard,
Port Angeles WA 98362-6698
County: Clallam FICE Identification: 003786
Unit ID: 236258
Telephone: (360) 452-9277 Carnegie Class: Assoc/Pub4
FAX Number: (360) 457-8100 Calendar System: Quarter
URL: www.pencol.edu
Established: 1961 Annual Undergrad Tuition & Fees (In-District): $4,191
Enrollment: 2,342 Coed
Affiliation or Control: State/Local IRS Status: 501(c)3
Highest Offering: Baccalaureate
Program: Occupational; 2-Year Principally Bachelor's Creditable
Accreditation: NW, ADNUR

01 President Dr. Luke ROBINS
05 Vice President Instruction Vacant
11 Vice President Administrative Svcs Ms. Deborah FRAZIER
32 Vice President Student Services Mr. Jack HULS
45 VP Institutional Effectiveness Dr. Paula DOHERTY
50 Dir Cmty/Business Education Ms. Linty HOPIE
55 Dean Adult Basic Education Dr. Evelyn SHORT
35 Dean of Student Services Ms. Maria PENA
37 Assoc Dean Fin Aid/Enrollment Svcs Ms. Krista FRANCIS
41 Assoc Dean Athletics/Student Prgms Mr. Rick ROSS
13 Director Information Technology Mr. Steven BAXTER
04 Executive Asst to the President Ms. Pattie FISCHER
26 Director Public Information Ms. Phyllis L. VAN HOLLAND
15 Director Human Resources Ms. Bonnie H. CAUFFMAN
85 Dir Intl Stdnt Pgm/Stdnt Recruit Ms. Sophia ILIAKIS-DOHERTY
102 Exec Director College Foundation Ms. Mary HUNCHBERGER
09 Int Dir of Institutional Research Ms. Katie BRENKMAN
18 Director Physical Plant Mr. Rick CROOT
40 Bookstore Manager Mrs. Camilla RICO
88 Manager High School Program Ms. Cindy LAUDERBACK

Perry Technical Institute (B)

2011 W. Washington Avenue, Yakima WA 98903
County: Yakima FICE Identification: 009387
Unit ID: 236212
Telephone: (509) 453-0374 Carnegie Class: Not Classified
FAX Number: (509) 453-0375 Calendar System: Quarter
URL: www.perrytech.edu
Established: 1939 Annual Undergrad Tuition & Fees: $31,009
Enrollment: 791 Coed
Affiliation or Control: Independent Non-Profit IRS Status: 501(c)3
Highest Offering: Associate Degree
Program: Occupational
Accreditation: ACCSC

01 President Christine COTE

Pierce College District (C)

9401 Farwest Drive SW, Lakewood WA 98498-1999
County: Pierce FICE Identification: 005000
Unit ID: 235237
Telephone: (253) 964-6500 Carnegie Class: Assoc/Pub-S-MC
FAX Number: N/A Calendar System: Quarter
URL: www.pierce.ctc.edu
Established: 1967 Annual Undergrad Tuition & Fees (In-State): $3,642
Enrollment: 10,065 Coed
Affiliation or Control: State IRS Status: 501(c)3
Highest Offering: Associate Degree
Program: Occupational; 2-Year Principally Bachelor's Creditable
Accreditation: NW, ADNUR, DH

01 District Chancellor Dr. Michele JOHNSON
12 President Pierce College Puyallup Dr. Marty L. CAVALLUZZI
12 President Fort Steilacoom Ms. Denise YOCHUM
05 VP Learning/Student Success-PY Dr. Matthew CAMPBELL
05 Vice Pres Learning/Stdnt Success-FS Ms. Debra GILCHRIST
10 Vice Pres Administrative Services Mr. Choi HALLADAY
30 Vice President of Advancement Ms. Deidre SOILEAU
15 Vice President for Human Resources Ms. Holly GORSKI
13 Dean of Institutional Technology Mr. Mike STOCKE
06 Registrar/Dir Enrollment Svcs-Dist Ms. Anne WHITE
08 Dean Libraries & Learning Resources Ms. Christie FLYNN
26 Dir Marketing and Communications Mr. Brian BENEDETTI
32 Dean of Student Services Ms. Agnes STEWARD
35 Dir Student Programs-Ft Steilacoom Mr. Cameron COX
41 Director of Athletics Mr. Duncan STEVENSON
18 Director of Facilities & Const Mgt Mr. Jim TAYLOR
35 Dir of Student Life-Puyallup Mr. Sean COOKE
85 Exec Dir of International Education Ms. Myung PARK
19 District Manager Campus Safety Mr. Chris MACKERSIE
21 Director of Budget and Finance Ms. Sylvia DERRICK
37 Interim Director Financial Aid Ms. Anne WHITE
84 Director Enrollment Services-Puy Ms. Els DEMING
09 Institutional Researcher Mr. Erik GIMNESS
49 District Dean Arts & Humanities Dr. Holly SMITH
88 District Dean Transitional Educ Ms. Lori GRIFFIN
76 District Dean Tech/Allied Health Mr. Ronald MAY
81 District Dean Natural Sciences Mr. Thomas BROXSON
83 District Dean Social Sciences Ms. Sachi HORBACK
29 Alumni Relations Manager Ms. Marion SHARP
96 Procurement Officer Mr. Curtis LEE

Pima Medical Institute-Renton (D)

555 South Renton Village Place, Renton WA 98057
Telephone: (425) 228-9600 Identification: 770517
Accreditation: ABHES, COARC

† Branch campus of Pima Medical Institute-Tucson, Tucson, AZ.

Pima Medical Institute-Seattle (E)

9709 3rd Avenue NE, Suite 400, Seattle WA 98115-2052
Telephone: (206) 322-6100 Identification: 666172
Accreditation: ABHES, DH, OTA, PTAA, RAD

† Branch campus of Pima Medical Institute-Tucson, Tucson, AZ.

Pinchot University (F)

220 2nd Avenue South, Suite 400,
Seattle WA 98104-2617
County: King FICE Identification: 041612
Unit ID: 458159
Telephone: (206) 855-9559 Carnegie Class: Not Classified
FAX Number: (206) 682-0504 Calendar System: Quarter
URL: www.pinchot.edu
Established: 2002 Annual Undergrad Tuition & Fees: $27,720
Enrollment: 108 Coed
Affiliation or Control: Independent Non-Profit IRS Status: 501(c)3
Highest Offering: Master's
Program: Professional; Business Emphasis
Accreditation: ACICS

01 President Ms. Jill BAMBURG
05 Provost/Dean of Academic Affairs Dr. Mary Kay CHESS
10 CFO/Vice President of Operations Ms. Sandra POSSIN
06 Registrar Ms. Lynn BRAUN
07 Director of Admissions Ms. Becca BALYEAT
32 Director of Student/Academic Affs Ms. Bethany LINDSEY

Renton Technical College (G)

3000 NE Fourth Street, Renton WA 98056-4123
County: King FICE Identification: 010434
Unit ID: 236382
Telephone: (425) 235-2352 Carnegie Class: Assoc/Pub-S-SC
FAX Number: (425) 235-7832 Calendar System: Quarter
URL: www.rtc.edu
Established: 1942 Annual Undergrad Tuition & Fees (In-State): $4,735
Enrollment: 3,359 Coed
Affiliation or Control: State IRS Status: 501(c)3
Highest Offering: Associate Degree
Program: Occupational; Technical Emphasis
Accreditation: NW, ACFEI, DA, MAC, SURGT

01 President Dr. Kevin D. MCCARTHY
10 VP Finance/Administration Ms. Melinda M. MERRELL
05 Interim Vice President Instruction Ms. Jodi NOVOTNY
32 VP Student Services Ms. Jessica GILMORE ENGLISH
97 Interim Dean Basic Studies Ms. Jenna POLLOCK
76 Interim Dean Allied Health Mr. Jason BOATWRIGHT
103 Executive Dean Workforce/Econ Dev Ms. Heather WINFREY
50 Dean Bus/Educ/Hum Svcs/Gen Educ Vacant
72 Dean Automotive/Tech/Distance Educ Mr. Dante J. LEON
102 Foundation Executive Director Vacant
13 Chief Information Officer Mr. Paul CORRIGLIANO
07 Director Enrollment Services Mr. Patrick BROWN
46 Exec Dir Institutional Advancement Ms. Michelle CAMPBELL
08 Director Library Mr. Eric E. PALO
21 Director Financial Services Mr. Mark JOHNSON
15 Executive Director Human Resources Ms. Lesley HOGAN
37 Director Financial Aid Ms. Debbie SOLOMON
18 Director Plant Operations Mr. Barry A. BAKER
40 Bookstore Manager Mr. Jose A. PERDOMO
19 Safety & Security Manager Mr. Matthew VIELBIG
88 Dean Culinary Arts Mr. Doug MEDBURY
26 Dir College Relations/Marketing Ms. Melissa ROHLFS
38 Dean Counseling & Advising Mr. Scott LATIOLAIS
35 Director Student Programs Ms. Jessica SUPINSKI
06 Registration Coordinator Ms. Ly CHANG
88 Custodial Manager Mr. Mark DANIELS
88 Director Outreach/Entry Services Ms. Andrea LANCASTER
04 Executive Asst to President Ms. Di BEERS

† Granted candidacy at the Baccalaureate level.

Saint Martin's University (H)

5000 Abbey Way, SE, Lacey WA 98503-7500
County: Thurston FICE Identification: 003794
Unit ID: 236452
Telephone: (360) 491-4700 Carnegie Class: Master's S
FAX Number: (360) 459-4124 Calendar System: Semester
URL: www.stmartin.edu
Established: 1895 Annual Undergrad Tuition & Fees: $33,194
Enrollment: 1,801 Coed
Affiliation or Control: Roman Catholic IRS Status: 501(c)3
Highest Offering: Master's
Program: Liberal Arts And General; Teacher Preparatory; Professional
Accreditation: NW, ENG, NURSE, @SW, TEAC

00 Chancellor Abbot Neal G. ROTH, OSB
01 President Dr. Roy F. HEYNDERICKX
05 Provost & Vice President Dr. Molly E. SMITH
10 Vice President of Finance Ms. Susan D. HELTSLEY
30 Vice Pres Inst Advancement Ms. Cecelia LOVELESS
85 Vice Pres Intl Programs/Development Ms. Josephine YUNG
26 VP of Marketing/Communications Ms. Genevieve CANCEKO CHAN
13 Associate Vice President/CIO Mr. Greg DAVIS
15 Associate VP of Human Resources Ms. Cynthia JOHNSON
49 Dean Col of Arts & Sciences Dr. Eric APFELSTADT
53 Dean of Education Dr. Joyce WESTGARD
50 Dean of Business Dr. Richard BEER
54 Dean of Engineering Dr. Zella KAHN-JETTER
32 Dean Student Services Ms. Melanie RICHARDSON
84 Dean Enrollment Management Vacant
07 Dean Admission/Stdnt Financial Svcs Vacant
21 Controller Ms. Linda NEWMAN
37 Director Financial Aid Mr. Michael GROSSO
29 Director Alumni Relations Vacant
06 Assistant Registrar Ms. Ronda VANDERGIFF
18 Director Facilities Management Mr. Alan TYLER
44 Dir of Development/Planned Giving Ms. Katie WOJKE
36 Director of Career Placement Ms. Ann ADAMS
41 Athletic Director Mr. Bob GRISHAM
56 Director Extension Programs Mr. Cruz ARROYO
08 Library Director Mr. Scot HARRISON
42 Director Campus Ministry Mr. Jon DWYER
39 Director of Housing/Residence Life Mr. Tim MCCLAIN
38 Director Counseling Center Ms. Jan BERNEY
09 Director Institutional Grants/Rsrch Vacant

Sanford Brown College (I)

645 Andover Park West, Seattle WA 98188-3319
Telephone: (206) 575-1865 Identification: 666265
Accreditation: ACICS

† Branch campus of International Academy of Design and Technology, Tampa, FL. School is in teach out plan.

*Seattle Colleges (J)

1500 Harvard Avenue, Seattle WA 98122-3803
County: King FICE Identification: 010106
Unit ID: 236498
Telephone: (206) 934-4100 Carnegie Class: N/A
FAX Number: (206) 934-3883
URL: www.seattlecolleges.edu

01 Chancellor Dr. Jill WAKEFIELD
03 Interim Vice Chancellor Dr. Mary Ellen O'KEEFFE
10 Vice Chanc for Finance & Technology Dr. Kurt BUTTLEMAN
15 Chief Human Resources Officer Mr. Charles E. SIMS
26 Communications Director Dr. Earnest PHILLIPS
30 Assoc Vice Chanc for Advancement Mr. Bruce GENUNG
12 President South Seattle College Mr. Gary OERTLI
12 President North Seattle College Dr. Warren BROWN
12 Int Pres Seattle Central College Dr. Sheila EDWARDS LANGE

*North Seattle College (K)

9600 College Way N, Seattle WA 98103-3599
County: King FICE Identification: 009704
Unit ID: 236072
Telephone: (206) 934-3600 Carnegie Class: Assoc/Pub-U-MC
FAX Number: (206) 934-3606 Calendar System: Quarter
URL: www.northseattle.edu
Established: 1970 Annual Undergrad Tuition & Fees (In-State): $5,000
Enrollment: 6,140 Coed
Affiliation or Control: State IRS Status: 170(c)1
Highest Offering: Associate Degree
Program: Occupational; 2-Year Principally Bachelor's Creditable
Accreditation: NW, ADNUR, #MAC

02 President Dr. Warren J. BROWN
05 Vice President for Instruction Dr. Kristen JONES
32 Vice Pres Student Development Ms. Marci MYER
11 Vice President of Administration Dr. Monty MONTERECY
36 Exec Dean Career/Workforce Educ Mr. John LEDERER
79 Dean Art/Humanities/Social Sciences Dr. Julianne KIRGIS
81 Dean Math & Science Ms. Alissa AGNELLO

17 Dean Health & Human Services .... Dr. Steven THOMAS
50 Dean Business/Eng Info Tech .... Dr. Terry COX
08 Dean Library & Media Services .... Ms. Sharon SIMES
35 Assoc Dean Student Develop Svcs .... Ms. Alice MELLING
88 Dean Basic/Transitional Stds .... Mr. Curtis BONNEY
56 Assoc Dean e-Learning .... Dr. Tom BRAZIUNAS
30 Executive Director of Advancement .... Ms. Jennie DULAS
26 Dir Marketing & Public Relations .... Ms. Melissa MIXON
84 Dean Enrollment Svcs/Registrar .... Ms. Kathy RHODES
51 Director Continuing Education .... Ms. Christy ISAACSON
37 Director Financial Aid Services .... Ms. Brianne SANCHEZ
35 Dir Student Ldrshp/Multi Cult Pgms .... Mr. Jeffrey VASQUEZ
103 Director Workforce Education .... Ms. Dawn KINDER
09 Dir Institutional Effectiveness .... Dr. Stephanie DYKES
104 Director International Programs .... Mr. Ryan PACKARD
15 Director of Human Resources .... Mr. Martin LOGAN
18 Dir Facilities & Plant Operations .... Mr. Jason FRANCOIS
38 Lead Counselor .... Dr. Lydia MINATOYA
45 Director Strategic Initiatives .... Mr. Gary GORLAND
13 Chief Info Technology Officer .... Mr. Lucas REBER
19 Director Security/Safety .... Mr. Darryl JOHNSON
28 Director of Diversity & Inclusion .... Ms. Pam RACANSKY
07 Coordinator Admissions/Residency ...... Mr. Fleetwood L. WILSON
04 Executive Asst to President .... Ms. Toni STANKOVIC
10 Director Business Operations .... Mr. Dennis YASUKOCHI
25 Director of Grants .... Ms. Ann RICHARDSON
41 Athletic Director .... Ms. Carianya NAPOLI

† Granted candidacy at the Baccalaureate level.

*Seattle Central College (A)

1701 Broadway, Seattle WA 98122-2400
County: King FICE Identification: 003787
Unit ID: 236513
Telephone: (206) 587-3800 Carnegie Class: Assoc/Pub-U-MC
FAX Number: (206) 344-4390 Calendar System: Quarter
URL: seattlecentral.edu
Established: 1966 Annual Undergrad Tuition & Fees (In-State): $3,893
Enrollment: 6,773 Coed
Affiliation or Control: State IRS Status: 170(c)1
Highest Offering: Baccalaureate
Program: Occupational; 2-Year Principally Bachelor's Creditable
Accreditation: NW, ACFEI, ADNUR, COARC, DH, OPD, SURGT

02 President .... Dr. Paul T. KILLPATRICK
05 Interim Vice Pres of Instruction .... Dr. Wai-Fong LEE
11 Vice Pres Administrative Services .... Mr. Michael PHAM
32 Int Vice Pres Student Services .... Ms. Diane COLEMAN
103 Assoc Vice President Workforce Educ .... Mr. Al GRISWOLD
09 Exec Dir Strategic Initiatives & IR .... Dr. Cherisa YARKIN
35 Dean of Student Resources & Support .... Ms. Brigid MCDEVITT
37 Director of Financial Aid .... Ms. Noel MCBRIDE
102 Executive Director Foundation .... Mr. Adam NANCE
26 Interim Director of Communications .... Ms. Janet GRIMLEY
08 Exec Dean Instructional Resources .... Dr. Wai-Fong LEE
49 Dean Basic Studies .... Ms. Laura DIZAZZO
50 Dean Business IT & Creative Arts .... Vacant
76 Dean of Allied Health .... Mr. David GOURD
81 Dean Science & Mathematics .... Dr. Wendy ROCKHILL
83 Dean Humanities/Social Sciences .... Dr. Bradley LANE
88 Exec Dean International Education .... Dr. Andrea INSLEY
35 Dean Student Life & Engagement .... Ms. Lexie EVANS
13 Assoc Dean Information Technology .... Ms. Harriet WASSERMAN
12 Asst Dean Seattle Maritime Academy .... Dr. Matthew VON RUDEN
12 Director Seattle Culinary Academy .... Ms. Joy GULMON-HURI
51 Director Cmty Educ/Evening Pgm .... Mr. Jeff WEST
84 Dean Enrollment Services/Registrar .... Ms. Diane COLEMAN
19 Director Public Safety .... Mr. Ernan MCCLAIN
18 Dir Facilities/Plant Operations .... Mr. Chuck DAVIS

*South Seattle Community College (B)

6000 16th Avenue, SW, Seattle WA 98106-1499
County: King FICE Identification: 009706
Unit ID: 236504
Telephone: (206) 934-5300 Carnegie Class: Assoc/Pub4
FAX Number: (206) 934-5393 Calendar System: Quarter
URL: www.southseattle.edu
Established: 1969 Annual Undergrad Tuition & Fees (In-State): $3,824
Enrollment: 4,034 Coed
Affiliation or Control: State IRS Status: 501(c)3
Highest Offering: Baccalaureate
Program: Occupational; 2-Year Principally Bachelor's Creditable
Accreditation: NW

02 President .... Mr. Gary L. OERTLI
05 Vice Pres Instruction .... Mr. Pete LORTZ
11 Vice Pres Administrative Services .... Dr. Frank ASHBY
32 Vice President Student Services .... Dr. Rosie RIMANDO
30 Assoc Vice Pres College Advancement ... Dr. Elizabeth A. PLUHTA
45 Dean Instructional Resources .... Ms. Mary Jo WHITE
75 Executive Dean Technical Education .... Vacant
88 Exec Dn Apprenticeshp/Special Trng .... Ms. Holly MOORE
97 Dean Basic & Transitional Studies .... Mr. John BOWERS
20 Dean of Academic Programs .... Vacant
35 Dean Student Life .... Mr. Joe BARRIENTOS
103 Int Dean Workforce Educ/New Init .... Ms. Veronica WADE
17 Dean Hosp & Service Occupations .... Mr. Robert GLATT
88 Dean Multi-Trades/Info Technology .... Mr. Duncan BURGESS
84 Associate Dean Enrollment Services .... Mr. Greg DEMPSEY
88 Dean of Aviation .... Ms. Kim ALEXANDER
20 Assoc Dean Academic Programs .... Ms. Laura KINGSTON

06 Assistant Registrar .... Ms. Marilyn ANDERSON-BURT
51 Director Continuing Education .... Ms. Luisa MOTTEN
103 Dir Worksource Dev/Employment Svcs .... Ms. Deborah WHITE
37 Dir Student Financial Assistance .... Vacant
26 Director Communications .... Mr. Kevin MALONEY
15 Director Human Resources .... Ms. Kathryn A. VEDVICK
108 Dir of Planning/Research/Assessment .... Dr. Chad HICKOX
13 Dir Business Operation/IT .... Ms. Irina MINASOVA
18 Dir Facilities & Plant Operations .... Mr. Eric STEEN
28 Director of Diversity & Retention ...... Mr. Ricardo LEYVA-PUEBLA
19 Manager Safety/Security .... Mr. James E. LEWIS
40 Manager Bookstore .... Ms. Jen ROHLFS

Seattle Institute of Oriental Medicine (C)

444 Ravenna Boulevard, Suite 101, Seattle WA 98115
County: King FICE Identification: 032803
Unit ID: 439914
Telephone: (206) 517-4541 Carnegie Class: Spec/Health
FAX Number: N/A Calendar System: Trimester
URL: www.siom.edu
Established: 1994 Annual Undergrad Tuition & Fees: $19,365
Enrollment: 42 Coed
Affiliation or Control: Proprietary IRS Status: Proprietary
Highest Offering: Master's; No Lower Division
Program: Professional
Accreditation: ACUP

01 President .... Craig MITCHELL
05 Academic Dean .... Paul KARSTEN
06 Registrar .... Sarah LENOUE

Seattle Pacific University (D)

3307 Third Avenue W, Seattle WA 98119-1997
County: King FICE Identification: 003788
Unit ID: 236577
Telephone: (206) 281-2111 Carnegie Class: Master's L
FAX Number: (206) 281-2115 Calendar System: Quarter
URL: www.spu.edu
Established: 1891 Annual Undergrad Tuition & Fees: $36,684
Enrollment: 4,217 Coed
Affiliation or Control: Free Methodist IRS Status: 501(c)3
Highest Offering: Doctorate
Program: Liberal Arts And General; Teacher Preparatory; Professional
Accreditation: NW, BUS, CACREP, CLPSY, DIETD, ENG, MFCD, MUS, NURSE, TED, @THEOL

01 President .... Dr. Daniel J. MARTIN
05 Provost .... Dr. Jeffrey B. VAN DUZER
11 Sr VP for Planning & Administration .... Mr. Donald W. MORTENSON
32 VP for Student Life .... Dr. Jeffrey C. JORDAN
30 VP for Advancement .... Mrs. Louise S. FURROW
10 VP for Business & Finance .... Mr. Craig G. KISPERT
84 VP for Enrollment Mgmt & Mktg .... Mr. Nate MOUTTET
20 Vice Provost Academic Affairs .... Dr. Cynthia J. PRICE
13 Assoc VP Information/Data Mgmt .... Ms. Janet L. WARD
18 Asst VP Facility Management .... Mr. David B. CHURCH
43 Asst VP Risk Mgmt & Univ Counsel .... Mr. Nick GLANCY
14 Asst VP Technology Services .... Mr. David W. TINDALL
102 President of Seattle Pacific Fdn .... Mr. Thomas W. BOX
50 Dean School of Business/Govt/Econ .... Dr. Joseph WILLIAMS
53 Dean School of Education .... Dr. Rick EIGENBROOD
66 Dean School of Health Sciences .... Dr. Lorie WILD
81 Dean CAS - Sciences Divison .... Dr. Bruce D. CONGDON
49 Dean CAS - Arts & Humanities Div .... Dr. Debra-L SEQUEIRA
88 Dean School of Psych/Fam & Cmty .... Dr. Micheal D. ROE
73 Dean School of Theology .... Dr. Douglas M. STRONG
42 Int Dean of Students for Cmty Life . Mrs. Susan OKAMOTO-LANE
36 Dean Stdnt Lrng/Dir Ctr Career Coun .... Dr. Jacqui S. SMITH-BATES
08 University Librarian .... Mr. Michael PAULUS
38 Director Student Counseling Center .... Dr. Steven A. MAYBELL
07 Director Undergraduate Admissions .... Mr. Jobe S. KORB-NICE
07 Int Dir Graduate Admissions/Mktg .... Mr. Ted HIEMSTRA
06 University Registrar .... Mrs. Kenda GATLIN
26 Co-Director Univ Communications .... Mrs. Alison ESTEP
26 Co-Director Univ Communications .... Mr. Dale KEGLEY
88 Asst VP UG Enrollment Mgmt .... Mr. Jordan L. GRANT
27 News & Media Relations Manager .... Mrs. Tracy C. NORLEN
45 Assoc Director Projects & Planning .... Mr. Wayne H. ELLING
31 Director of University Services .... Ms. Alexis CRUIKSHANK
19 Director of Safety & Security .... Mr. Mark REID
44 Director of Advancement .... Ms. Maribeth MARTIN
29 Director of Alumni Relations .... Mr. Bryan H. JONES
41 Director of Athletics .... Ms. Erin E. O'CONNELL
15 Director of Human Resources .... Mr. Gary E. WOMELSDUFF
28 Director of the John Perkins Center .... Mr. Tali HAIRSTON
39 Director of Residence Life .... Mr. Gabe JACOBSEN
35 Director Student Programs .... Ms. Whitney BROETJE
88 Director of Multi-Ethnic Programs .. Mrs. Susan OKAMOTO LANE
104 Director of Study Abroad .... Ms. Gail DEBELL
04 Executive Asst to President .... Ms. Karen L. JACOBSON

The Seattle School of Theology and Psychology (E)

2501 Elliot Avenue, Seattle WA 98121-1177
County: King FICE Identification: 034664
Unit ID: 441131
Telephone: (206) 876-6100 Carnegie Class: Spec/Health
FAX Number: (206) 876-6195 Calendar System: Trimester
URL: www.theseattleschool.edu
Established: 2001 Annual Graduate Tuition & Fees: $14,385
Enrollment: 305 Coed
Affiliation or Control: Independent Non-Profit IRS Status: 501(c)3
Highest Offering: Master's; No Undergraduates
Program: Religious Emphasis
Accreditation: THEOL

01 President .... Dr. Keith R. ANDERSON
05 Sr Vice Pres Academic Affs/CAO .... Dr. J. Derek MCNEIL
10 Chief Financial Officer .... Mr. Phil BISHOP
30 Vice Pres Advancement .... Ms. Cathy LOERZEL
32 Dean of Students .... Mr. Paul STEINKE
20 Assistant Academic Dean .... Dr. Stephanie NEIL
08 Dir Library Svcs/Inst Assessment .... Ms. Cheryl GOODWIN
06 Dir Academic Services/Registrar .... Ms. Kristen HOUSTON
84 Director of Enrollment Management ...... Ms. Nicole GREENWALD
13 Director Computer & Info Services .... Mr. Jason BEST
15 Human Resources .... Ms. Kartha HEINZ

Seattle University (F)

901 12th Avenue, Seattle WA 98122-1090
County: King FICE Identification: 003790
Unit ID: 236595
Telephone: (206) 296-6000 Carnegie Class: Master's L
FAX Number: N/A Calendar System: Quarter
URL: www.seattleu.edu
Established: 1891 Annual Undergrad Tuition & Fees: $38,970
Enrollment: 7,273 Coed
Affiliation or Control: Roman Catholic IRS Status: 501(c)3
Highest Offering: Doctorate
Program: Liberal Arts And General; Teacher Preparatory; Professional
Accreditation: NW, BUS, CACREP, DMS, ENG, LAW, MFCD, MIDWF, NURSE, SPAA, SW, TED, THEOL

01 President .... Rev. Stephen V. SUNDBORG, SJ
05 Provost .... Dr. Isiaah CRAWFORD
11 Executive Vice President Admin .... Dr. Timothy LEARY
10 Chief Financial Officer .... Ms. Connie KANTER
43 Vice Pres and University Counsel .... Ms. Mary S. PETERSEN
30 Interim VP University Advancement .... Mr. Michael PODLIN
32 VP Student Development .... Dr. Michele MURRAY
88 Vice President Mission & Ministry .... Rev. Peter ELY, SJ
45 Vice President University Planning .... Dr. Robert DULLEA
84 Vice President for Enrollment Svcs .... Ms. Marilyn CRONE
26 Vice President for Communications .... Mr. Scott MCCLELLAN
15 Vice President Human Resources .... Mr. Gerald HUFFMAN
49 Dean of Arts & Sciences .... Dr. David POWERS
50 Dean of Business & Economics .... Dr. Joseph M. PHILLIPS
53 Dean of Education .... Dr. Deanna SANDS
66 Dean of Nursing .... Dr. Kristen SWANSON
54 Dean of Science & Engineering .... Dr. Michael QUINN
79 Dean of Matteo Ricci College .... Dr. Jodi OLSEN KELLY
61 Dean of Law .... Ms. Annette C. CLARK
73 Dean of Theology & Ministry .... Dr. Mark MARKULY
08 University Librarian .... Mr. John P. POPKO
20 Assoc Provost Academic Achievement ..... Dr. Charles LAWRENCE
20 Assoc Provost Global Engagement .... Dr. Russell POWELL
46 Assoc Provost Research & Grad Educ .... Dr. William EHMANN
13 Chief Information Officer .... Mr. Charles PORTER
21 Assoc VP of Finance .... Mr. Andrew O'BOYLE
18 Assoc VP Facilities Administration .... Mr. Robert SCHWARTZ
29 Asst VP Alumni Relations .... Ms. Susan VOSPER
14 Executive Director .... Mr. Dennis GENDRON
44 Sr Director of Planned Giving .... Ms. Sarah FINNEY
44 Director of Annual Giving .... Ms. Cathy REILLY
102 Dir of Foundation & Corporate Rels .... Ms. Jane SPALDING
35 Assoc Vice Pres Student Development ..... Dr. Alvin STURDIVANT
06 Associate Registrar .... Mr. Andrew ANDERSON
07 Dean of Admissions .... Ms. Melore NIELSEN
09 Director of Institutional Research .... Dr. Robert DUNIWAY
42 Director Campus Ministry .... Ms. Tammy LIDDELL
37 Director Student Financial Services .... Mr. Jeff SCOFIELD
41 Director of Athletics .... Mr. Bill HOGAN
19 Executive Director of Public Safety .... Mr. Timothy MARRON
35 Dean of Students .... Mr. Darrell GOODWIN
85 Director International Student Ctr .... Mr. Ryan GREENE
104 Director Education Abroad .... Ms. Gina LOPARDO
36 Executive Director Career Services .... Ms. Bethany KREITL
38 Director Counseling Center .... Dr. Kimberly CALUZA
28 Director of Multicultural Affairs .... Ms. Tiffany GRAY
39 Dir Housing & Resid Life .... Ms. Kathleen BAKER
25 Director Research & Sponsored Proj .... Dr. Nalini IYER
96 Director of Purchasing .... Ms. Marie PETERSON
23 Director Student Health Center .... Ms. Maura O'CONNOR
04 Executive Secretary to President .... Ms. Liz PILATI
100 Assistant to the President .... Ms. Kathy YBARRA
105 Web Communications Manager .... Mr. Jason BEARD
51 Dean New and Continuing Studies .. Dr. Richard FEHRENBACHER
22 Dir Professional Dev/EEO .... Ms. Helaina SOREY
86 Director of External Affairs .... Mr. Solynn MCCURDY
88 Associate Chief Information Officer .... Mr. Travis NATION

Shoreline Community College (G)

16101 Greenwood Avenue N, Shoreline WA 98133-5696
County: King FICE Identification: 003791
Unit ID: 236610
Telephone: (206) 546-4101 Carnegie Class: Assoc/Pub-S-SC
FAX Number: (206) 546-4630 Calendar System: Quarter
URL: www.shoreline.edu
Established: 1964 Annual Undergrad Tuition & Fees (In-State): $4,410

Enrollment: 6,827 Coed
Affiliation or Control: State IRS Status: 170(c)1
Highest Offering: Associate Degree
Program: Occupational; 2-Year Principally Bachelor's Creditable; Nursing Emphasis
Accreditation: NW, ADNUR, CAHIIM, DH, MLTAD

01 President ... Dr. Cheryl ROBERTS
05 VP Academic & Student Affairs ... Mr. Robert FRANCIS
11 Vice Pres Administrative Svcs ... Vacant
15 VP Human Resources/Legal Affairs ... Mr. Stephen SMITH
26 Spec Asst to Pres/Public Info/Mkt ... Mr. Jim HILLS
96 Exec Director Budget & Capital ... Ms. Dawn VINBERG
04 Exec Asst to the President ... Ms. Lori YONEMITSU
85 Exec Dir International Programs ... Ms. Diana SAMPSON
72 Director Technology Support Service ... Mr. Gary KALBFLEISCH
06 Registrar ... Ms. Chris MELTON
18 Dir Facilities/Capital Projects ... Mr. Bob ROEHL
19 Director Safety & Security ... Ms. Robin BLACKSMITH
66 Program Director Nursing ... Ms. Lynn VON SCHLIEDER
37 Acting Director Financial Aid ... Ms. Chris MELTON
38 Dir Counseling/High School Pgm ... Dr. Yvonne L. TERRELL-POWELL
109 Exec Dir Auxiliary/Logistical Svcs ... Ms. Mary E. KELEMEN
09 Dir Institutional Effectiveness ... Ms. Bayta MARING
08 Dean Library/Media/Tech ... Mr. Chris MATZ
32 Dean of Students ... Ms. Kim THOMPSON
103 Dean Workforce/Cont Educ/Automotive ... Mr. Dan FEY
31 Dean Capital Projects/Cmty Rels ... Vacant
79 Dean Humanities Division ... Ms. Kathy HUNT
70 Actg Dean Social Science/Honors ... Mr. Terry TAYLOR
81 Actg Dean Math/Science ... Mr. Guy HAMILTON
27 Asst Dir of Marketing/Communication ... Mr. Sean DUKE

Skagit Valley College (A)

2405 College Way, Mount Vernon WA 98273-5899
County: Skagit FICE Identification: 003792
Unit ID: 236638
Telephone: (360) 416-7600 Carnegie Class: Assoc/Pub-R-L
FAX Number: (360) 416-7890 Calendar System: Quarter
URL: www.skagit.edu
Established: 1926 Annual Undergrad Tuition & Fees (In-State): $3,086
Enrollment: 4,993 Coed
Affiliation or Control: State IRS Status: 501(c)3
Highest Offering: Associate Degree
Program: Occupational; 2-Year Principally Bachelor's Creditable
Accreditation: NW, ACFEI, ADNUR, MAC

01 President ... Dr. Thomas KEEGAN
05 Vice President Educational Services ... Dr. Kenneth LAWSON
10 Vice Pres Administrative Services ... Ms. Mary Alice GROBINS
12 Vice President of Whidbey Campus ... Dr. Laura CAILLOUX
32 Dean of Student Services ... Dr. David PAUL
13 Dean of Information Technology ... Mr. Andy HEISER
103 Dean Workforce Education ... Mr. Darren GREENO
20 Dean Academic Education ... Dr. Gabriel MAST
84 Assoc Dean Enrollment Services ... Ms. Sinead PLAGGE
37 Director of Financial Aid ... Ms. Crystal ALLISON
15 Exec Director of Human Resources ... Ms. Carolyn TUCKER
18 Director of Facilities & Operations ... Mr. Dave SCOTT
26 Director of Public Information ... Ms. Arden AINLEY
104 Director of International Programs ... Ms. Christa SCHULZ
40 Bookstore Manager ... Ms. Kim HALL
41 Athletic Director ... Mr. Steve EPPERSON
09 Director of Institutional Research ... Dr. Maureen PETTITT

† Granted candidacy at the Baccalaureate level.

South Puget Sound Community College (B)

2011 Mottman Road, SW, Olympia WA 98512-6292
County: Thurston FICE Identification: 005372
Unit ID: 236656
Telephone: (360) 754-7711 Carnegie Class: Assoc/Pub-R-L
FAX Number: (360) 664-0780 Calendar System: Quarter
URL: www.spscc.edu
Established: 1962 Annual Undergrad Tuition & Fees (In-State): $4,255
Enrollment: 6,158 Coed
Affiliation or Control: State IRS Status: 501(c)3
Highest Offering: Associate Degree
Program: Occupational; 2-Year Principally Bachelor's Creditable
Accreditation: NW, ACFEI, DA, IFSAC, MAC

01 President ... Dr. Timothy STOKES
04 Special Assistant to the President ... Ms. Diana TOLEDO
05 Vice President for Instruction ... Dr. Michelle ANDREAS
32 Vice President for Student Services ... Dr. David PELKEY
11 Vice Pres Administrative Services ... Mr. Albert BROWN
07 Dean of Enrollment Svcs/Registrar ... Mr. Steven ASHPOLE
18 Dean of Facilities Planning & Opers ... Vacant
26 Director College Relations & Events ... Ms. Kelly GREEN
35 Dean Student Engagement/Retention ... Ms. Jennifer MANLEY
37 Dean of Student Financial Services ... Ms. Johanna DWYER
15 Chief Human Resources Officer ... Mr. Kennith HARDEN
102 Exec Director College Foundation ... Ms. Tanya MOTE
28 Director of Diversity & Equity ... Ms. Eileen YOSHINA
09 Director of Institutional Research ... Ms. Jennifer TUIA
10 Chief Business Officer ... Mr. Albert BROWN
08 Dean of Academic Support Services ... Dr. Elizabeth HILL
19 Int Campus Security/Safety Sprvsr ... Mr. Robert SHAILOR

109 Director of Auxiliary Services ... Mr. Bryce WINKELMAN
13 Chief Information Officer ... Ms. Lori CASILE
72 Dean of Applied Technology ... Mr. Andrew BIRD
76 Dean of Natural & Applied Sciences ... Mr. Allen OLSON
79 Dean of Humanities/Communications ... Ms. Mary SOLTMAN
83 Dean of Social Sciences & Business ... Ms. Valerie SUNDBY-THORP
96 Procurement & Supply Specialist 4 ... Ms. Vida SHERRARD-HANNON

Tacoma Community College (C)

6501 S 19th Street, Tacoma WA 98466-6100
County: Pierce FICE Identification: 003796
Unit ID: 236753
Telephone: (253) 566-5000 Carnegie Class: Assoc/Pub-U-MC
FAX Number: (253) 566-5169 Calendar System: Quarter
URL: www.tacomacc.edu
Established: 1965 Annual Undergrad Tuition & Fees (In-State): $4,194
Enrollment: 8,124 Coed
Affiliation or Control: State IRS Status: 501(c)3
Highest Offering: Associate Degree
Program: Occupational; 2-Year Principally Bachelor's Creditable
Accreditation: NW, ADNUR, CAHIIM, COARC, DMS, EMT, RAD

01 President ... Dr. Sheila RUHLAND
05 Exec VP Academic/Student Affairs ... Dr. Tod TREAT
11 Vice Pres Administrative Services ... Ms. Silvia BARAJAS
32 Vice Pres Student Services ... Ms. Mary CHIKWINYA
88 Director K-12 Ptnshps/Stdnt Conduct ... Ms. Dolores HAUGEN
07 Dean for Entry & Enrollment Svcs ... Ms. Betsy ABTS
38 Dean for Advising and Counseling ... Ms. Shema HANEBUTTE
108 Dean Org Learning & Effectiveness ... Dr. Mecca SALAHUDDIN
18 Director Facilities/CapitalProjects ... Mr. Greg RANDALL
35 Director of Student Engagement ... Ms. Sonja MORGAN
37 Director Student Financial Aid ... Ms. Kim MATISON
04 Executive Asst to President ... Ms. Judy COLARUSSO
09 Director of Institutional Research ... Ms. Kelley SADLER
15 Director of Human Resources ... Ms. Beth BROOKS
25 Manager Grants & Sponsored Programs ... Vacant
26 Director Public Relations/Marketing ... Vacant
30 Vice Pres for College Advancement ... Mr. Bill RYBERG
41 Athletic Director ... Mr. Jason PRENEVOST
10 Director Financial Services ... Ms. Janice STROH
13 Director of IT ... Mr. Clay KRAUSS

Trinity Lutheran College (D)

2802 Wetmore Avenue, Everett WA 98201
County: Snohomish FICE Identification: 021067
Unit ID: 235769
Telephone: (425) 249-4800 Carnegie Class: Bac/Diverse
FAX Number: (425) 249-4801 Calendar System: 4/1/4
URL: www.tlc.edu
Established: 1944 Annual Undergrad Tuition & Fees: $29,000
Enrollment: 221 Coed
Affiliation or Control: Independent Non-Profit IRS Status: 501(c)3
Highest Offering: Baccalaureate
Program: Liberal Arts And General; Religious Emphasis
Accreditation: NW

01 President ... Mr. John REED
05 Academic Dean ... Dr. Michael DELASHMUTT
10 Vice President Finance ... Ms. Molly BRODIE
30 Vice President for Advancement ... Mr. Kelly MILLER
32 Dean of Students ... Ms. Andrea IDE
44 Associate Director of Development ... Mr. Lance GEORGESON
07 Interim Dean Admissions/Fin Aid ... Ms. Andrea PAULL
42 Campus Pastor ... Mr. Erik SAMUELSON
21 Accounting Manager ... Ms. Sanda TENNANT

University of Phoenix Western Washington Campus (E)

7100 Fort Dent Way, Suite 100, Tukwila WA 98188-8553
Telephone: (425) 572-1600 Identification: 770234
Accreditation: &NH, ACBSP

† Branch campus of University of Phoenix, Tempe, AZ.

University of Puget Sound (F)

1500 N Warner St., Tacoma WA 98416-0002
County: Pierce FICE Identification: 003797
Unit ID: 236328
Telephone: (253) 879-3100 Carnegie Class: Bac/A&S
FAX Number: (253) 879-3500 Calendar System: Semester
URL: www.pugetsound.edu
Established: 1888 Annual Undergrad Tuition & Fees: $44,976
Enrollment: 2,826 Coed
Affiliation or Control: Independent Non-Profit IRS Status: 501(c)3
Highest Offering: Doctorate
Program: Liberal Arts And General; Teacher Preparatory; Professional
Accreditation: NW, MUS, OT, PTA

01 President ... Dr. Ronald R. THOMAS
101 Board Secy/Dir Ofc of President ... Ms. Mary Elizabeth COLLINS
05 Academic VP/Dean of University ... Dr. Kristine M. BARTANEN
10 Vice Pres Finance & Admin ... Ms. Sherry B. MONDOU
26 Vice President University Relations ... Mr. David BEERS
84 Vice President for Enrollment ... Dr. Jenny RICKARD

32 VP Student Affairs/Dean of Students ... Mr. Mike SEGAWA
21 Assoc VP Accounting/Budget Svcs ... Ms. Janet S. HALLMAN
15 Assoc Vice Pres Human Resources ... Ms. Cindy MATERN
21 Assoc Vice Pres Business Services ... Mr. John M. HICKEY
18 Assoc Vice Pres Facilities Services ... Mr. Bob KIEF
37 Assoc VP for Student Financial Svcs ... Ms. Maggie A. MITTUCH
26 Executive Dir of Communications ... Ms. Gayle MCINTOSH
13 Chief Information Officer ... Mr. William MORSE
28 Dean Diversity and Inclusion ... Mr. Michael BENITEZ
20 Associate Academic Dean ... Dr. Martin JACKSON
20 Associate Academic Dean ... Dr. Sunil KUKREJA
20 Associate Academic Dean ... Dr. Lisa L. FERRARI
09 Dir Inst Research & Retention ... Ms. C. Ellen PETERS
06 Registrar ... Mr. Brad TOMHAVE
08 Library Director ... Ms. Jane CARLIN
41 Director of Athletics ... Ms. Amy E. HACKETT
29 Director Alumni & Parent Relations ... Ms. Allison CANNADY-SMITH
85 Director International Programs ... Mr. Roy ROBINSON
53 Dean School of Education ... Dr. John WOODWARD
50 Dir School of Business/Leadership ... Dr. Alva BUTCHER
64 Director of School of Music ... Dr. Keith C. WARD
88 Director of Occupational Therapy ... Dr. George TOMLIN
88 Director of Physical Therapy ... Dr. Jennifer D. HASTINGS

University of Washington (G)

Seattle WA 98195-0001
County: King FICE Identification: 003798
Unit ID: 236948
Telephone: (206) 543-2100 Carnegie Class: RU/VH
FAX Number: (206) 543-9285 Calendar System: Quarter
URL: www.washington.edu
Established: 1861 Annual Undergrad Tuition & Fees (In-State): $12,394
Enrollment: 44,784 Coed
Affiliation or Control: State IRS Status: 501(c)3
Highest Offering: Doctorate
Program: Liberal Arts And General; Teacher Preparatory; Professional
Accreditation: NW, ARCPA, AUD, BUS, BUSA, CAHIIM, CEA, CLPSY, CONST, DENT, DIETC, EMT, ENG, HSA, IPSY, JOUR, LAW, LIB, LSAR, MED, MIDWF, MT, NURSE, OPE, OT, PAST, PDPSY, PH, PHAR, PLNG, PTA, SCPSY, SP, SPAA, SW

01 Interim President ... Dr. Ana Mari CAUCE
12 Chancellor Bothell Campus ... Dr. Bjong W. YEIGH
12 Chancellor Tacoma Campus ... Dr. Mark PAGANO
05 Interim Provost ... Dr. Gerald J. BALDASTY
20 Vice Chanc Academic Affairs Tacoma ... Dr. James W. HARRINGTON
10 Int Vice Pres Finance/Facilities ... Ms. Elizabeth CHERRY
28 Int VP Minority Affs/Vice Prov Div ... Dr. Gabriel GALLARDO
17 Exec VP Med Affs/CEO UW Med/Dean ... Dr. Paul G. RAMSEY
30 Vice Pres for Univ Advancement ... Dr. Connie KRAVAS
15 Vice President Human Resources ... Ms. Mindy KORNBERG
13 VP & Vice Prov UW Info Tech ... Ms. Kelli TROSVIG
26 Vice President for External Affairs ... Mr. Randy HODGINS
46 Vice Provost Research ... Dr. Mary E. LIDSTROM
51 V Provost UW Prof & Cont Education ... Dr. David P. SZATMARY
45 Vice Prov Planning & Budgeting ... Mr. Paul JENNY
20 Sr V Provost Acad & Student Affs ... Dr. Gerald J. BALDASTY
20 Vice Prov/Dean Undergrad Acad Affs ... Dr. Ed TAYLOR
32 Vice Pres Student Life ... Mr. Denzil SUITE
88 V Provost for Academic Personnel ... Dr. Cheryl A. CAMERON
88 V Prov/UW Ctr for Commercialization ... Ms. Linden RHOADS
86 Director Federal Relations ... Ms. Christy D. GULLION
43 Division Chief Attorney General ... Mr. Gary L. IKEDA
06 University Registrar ... Ms. Virjean EDWARDS
29 Exec Dir & Assoc VP Alum Assoc ... Mr. Paul RUCKER
17 Exec Dir UW Medical Ctr Admin ... Mr. Stephen P. ZIENIEWICZ
17 Interim Exec Dir Harborview Med Ctr ... Ms. Johnese SPISSO
37 AVP Student Life/Dir Fin Aid ... Ms. Kay LEWIS
86 Director State Relations ... Ms. Margaret A. SHEPHERD
84 Asst VP Enrollment/Admissions ... Dr. Philip BALLINGER
09 Director Institutional Analysis ... Ms. Carol DIEM
36 Director Career Center ... Ms. Susan TERRY
13 CFO/UW Information Technology ... Mr. Bill FERRIS
18 Assoc Vice Pres Facilities Services ... Mr. Charles KENNEDY
92 Director Honors Program ... Dr. James J. CLAUSS
41 Director Athletics ... Mr. Scott WOODWARD
08 Dean Libraries ... Ms. Lizabeth A. WILSON
96 Director Procurement Services ... Mr. Mark CONLEY
58 Vice Prov/Dean Graduate School ... Dr. David L. EATON
49 Dean Arts & Sciences ... Dr. Robert STACEY
47 Dean Col of Built Environments ... Dr. John SCHAUFELBERGER
50 Dean Business School ... Dr. Jim JIAMBALVO
54 Dean Engineering ... Dr. Michael B. BRAGG
61 Dean Law School ... Dr. Kellye Y. TESTY
70 Dean Social Work ... Dr. Edwina UEHARA
52 Dean Dentistry ... Dr. Joel H. BERG
63 Dean Medicine ... Dr. Paul G. RAMSEY
66 Dean Nursing ... Dr. Azita EMAMI
67 Dean Pharmacy ... Dr. Thomas BAILLIE
69 Dean School of Public Health ... Dr. Howard FRUMKIN
53 Dean Education ... Dr. Tom STRITIKUS
80 Dean of Public Affairs ... Dr. Sandra O. ARCHIBALD
88 Dean Information School ... Dr. Harry BRUCE
88 Dean Col of the Environment ... Dr. Lisa GRAUMLICH

Walla Walla Community College (H)

500 Tausick Way, Walla Walla WA 99362-9267
County: Walla Walla FICE Identification: 005006
Unit ID: 236887
Telephone: (509) 522-2500 Carnegie Class: Assoc/Pub-R-L
FAX Number: (509) 527-4480 Calendar System: Quarter
URL: www.wwcc.edu

Established: 1967 Annual Undergrad Tuition & Fees (In-State): $4,376
Enrollment: 4,468 Coed
Affiliation or Control: State IRS Status: 170(c)1
Highest Offering: Associate Degree
Program: Occupational; 2-Year Principally Bachelor's Creditable; Professional
Accreditation: NW, ADNUR, MAC

01 President .... Dr. Steven L. VANAUSDLE
05 Vice President of Academic Educ .... Dr. Marleen RAMSEY
32 Vice Pres of Student Services .... Mrs. Wendy SAMITORE
10 Vice Pres of Financial Services .... Mrs. Davina K. FOGG
76 Dean of Health Sciences Education .... Ms. Kathleen ADAMSKI
30 Director of Resource Development .... Mr. Doug BAYNE
07 Director of Admissions/Registrar .... Mr. Carlos E. DELGADILLO
38 Dir Student Development Center .... Ms. Kristi WELLINGTON-BAKER
37 Financial Aid Director .... Ms. Danielle HODGEN
08 Director of Library Services .... Mrs. Stacy PREST
12 Director of Clarkston Campus .... Dr. Janet V. DANLEY
41 Athletic Director .... Mr. Jeffrey E. REINLAND
15 Director of Human Resources .... Mrs. Sharon M. HARTFORD
18 Director of Plant Facilities .... Mr. Shane LOPER
106 Director of eLearning .... Ms. Lisa CHAMBERLIN
88 Dean of Transitional Studies .... Ms. Darlene SNIDER
40 Bookstore Manager .... Ms. Alecia ANGELL
31 Coordinator of Community Education .... Ms. Jodi WORDEN
26 Dir Marketing & Communications .... Ms. Melissa THIESSEN
06 Registrar .... Mr. Carlos DELGADILLO
09 Director of Institutional Research .... Dr. Nicholas VELLUZZI
103 Dir Workforce/Career Development .... Mr. Angel REYNA
13 Chief Info Technology Officer .... Mr. Bill STORMS
50 Dean or Director Business .... Ms. Jessica GILMORE

Walla Walla University (A)

204 S College Avenue, College Place WA 99324-1198
County: Walla Walla FICE Identification: 003799
Unit ID: 236896
Telephone: (509) 527-2615 Carnegie Class: Master's M
FAX Number: (509) 527-2397 Calendar System: Quarter
URL: www.wallawalla.edu
Established: 1892 Annual Undergrad Tuition & Fees: $25,587
Enrollment: 1,887 Coed
Affiliation or Control: Seventh-day Adventist IRS Status: 501(c)3
Highest Offering: Master's
Program: Liberal Arts And General; Teacher Preparatory; Professional
Accreditation: NW, ACBSP, ACFEI, ENG, MUS, NUR, SW

01 President .... Dr. John MCVAY
05 Vice Pres Academic Administration .... Dr. Bob CUSHMAN
10 Vice Pres Financial Administration .... Mr. Steve ROSE
32 Vice Pres Student Life and Mission .... Dr. David RICHARDSON
84 VP University Relations and Advance .... Ms. Jodi WAGNER
28 Asst to President for Diversity .... Dr. Pedrito MAYNARD-REID
04 Executive Asst Office of President .... Ms. Deirdre BENWELL
20 Associate Vice Pres Academic Admin .... Dr. Scott LIGMAN
21 Associate Vice Pres Financial Admin .... Mr. Ken VYHMEISTER
08 Director of Libraries .... Ms. Carolyn GASKELL
06 Registrar .... Ms. Carolyn DENNEY
42 Chaplain .... Mr. Paddy MCCOY
29 Director of Alumni Relations .... Mrs. Terri DICKINSON NEIL
13 Director Information Services .... Mr. Scott MCFADDEN
37 Director Student Financial Services .... Ms. Cassie RAGENOVICH
15 Director Human Resources .... Ms. Jennifer CARPENTER
18 Director of Plant Services .... Mr. George BENNETT
26 Dir Marketing/University Relations .... Ms. Holley BRYANT
33 Dean of Men .... Vacant
34 Dean of Women .... Ms. Kristen TAYLOR
58 Dean of Graduate Programs .... Dr. Pam CRESS
66 Dean of School of Nursing .... Ms. Lucille KRULL
73 Dean of School of Theology .... Dr. David THOMAS
54 Dean of School of Engineering .... Mr. Doug LOGAN
07 Director of Admissions .... Mr. Dallas WEIS
36 Director Career Center .... Mr. David LINDSTROM
38 Director Student Counseling .... Mr. Don WALLACE
09 Director of Institutional Research .... Mr. Tyler STEFFANSON
41 Athletic Director .... Mr. Gerry LARSON
50 Dean of Business .... Mr. Josefer MONTES
53 Dean of Education .... Ms. Denise DUNZWEILER
19 Director Security/Safety .... Ms. Courtney BRYANT
44 Director Gift Planning .... Ms. Dorita TESSIER

Washington State University (B)

PO Box 645910, Pullman WA 99164-5910
County: Whitman FICE Identification: 003800
Unit ID: 236939
Telephone: (509) 335-3564 Carnegie Class: RU/VH
FAX Number: N/A Calendar System: Semester
URL: www.wsu.edu
Established: 1890 Annual Undergrad Tuition & Fees (In-District): $11,966
Enrollment: 28,686 Coed
Affiliation or Control: State/Local IRS Status: 501(c)3
Highest Offering: Doctorate
Program: Liberal Arts And General; Teacher Preparatory; Professional
Accreditation: NW, BUS, BUSA, CAATE, CEA, CIDA, CLPSY, CONST, COPSY, CS, DIETC, ENG, HSA, IPSY, LSAR, MUS, NURSE, PHAR, SP, SPAA, TED, VET

01 Interim President .... Dr. Daniel BERNARDO
05 Interim Co-Provost/Exec Vice Pres .... Dr. Ron MITTELHAMMER
05 Interim Co-Provost .... Dr. Erika AUSTIN
10 Interim VP Business/Administration .... Ms. Olivia YANG
30 Vice Pres Devel/CEO WSU Foundation .... Mr. John GARDNER
106 Vice Pres Global Campus .... Dr. David CILLAY
84 Int VP Student Affairs & Enrollment .... Dr. Melynda HUSKEY
13 VP Information Systems & CIO .... Vacant
46 Vice President Research .... Dr. Christopher KEANE
20 Vice Provost for Faculty Affairs .... Dr. Frances MCSWEENEY
12 Chancellor WSU Spokane .... Dr. Lisa BROWN
12 Chancellor WSU Tri-Cities .... Dr. Keith MOO-YOUNG
12 Chancellor WSU Vancouver .... Dr. Mel NETZHAMMER
43 Div Chief State Attorney Gen Office .... Ms. Danielle HESS
47 Int Dean Agric/Human Natl Res Sci .... Dr. Kimberlee KIDWELL
50 Dean Business & Economics .... Dr. Chip HUNTER
53 Dean College of Education .... Dr. Michael TREVISAN
54 Dean Engineering & Architecture .... Dr. Candis CLAIBORN
66 Interim Dean Nursing .... Dr. Cindy CORBETT
67 Dean Pharmacy .... Dr. Gary POLLACK
60 Dean College of Communication .... Dr. Lawrence E. PINTAK
49 Dean Arts & Sciences .... Dr. Daryll DEWALD
74 Dean Veterinary Medicine .... Dr. Bryan K. SLINKER
92 Dean Honors College .... Dr. M. Grant NORTON
45 Assoc VP & Chief Budget Office .... Ms. Joan KING
18 Assoc VP Facilities Services .... Ms. Olivia YANG
86 VP Government Relations .... Ms. Colleen KERR
71 Dean University College .... Dr. Mary F. WACK
08 Dean Libraries .... Mr. Joseph STARRATT
06 Registrar .... Ms. Julia POMERENK
07 Director Admissions .... Ms. Wendy PETERSON
09 Assoc Dir Institutional Research .... Ms. Fran HERMANSTON
37 Director Financial Aid .... Mr. Brian DIXON
41 Director Athletics .... Mr. William H. MOOS
88 Director Internal Audit .... Ms. Heather LOPEZ
26 Dir Marketing Communications .... Ms. Kathy BARNARD

Wenatchee Valley College (C)

1300 Fifth Street, Wenatchee WA 98801-1799
County: Chelan FICE Identification: 003801
Unit ID: 236975
Telephone: (509) 682-6800 Carnegie Class: Assoc/Pub-R-M
FAX Number: (509) 682-6541 Calendar System: Quarter
URL: www.wvc.edu
Established: 1939 Annual Undergrad Tuition & Fees (In-State): $3,808
Enrollment: 3,336 Coed
Affiliation or Control: State IRS Status: 501(c)3
Highest Offering: Associate Degree
Program: Occupational; 2-Year Principally Bachelor's Creditable
Accreditation: NW, ADNUR, MAC, MLTAD

01 President .... Mr. James RICHARDSON
05 Vice President of Instruction .... Dr. Carli SCHIFFNER
11 VP of Administrative Services .... Ms. Suzie BENSON
38 Vice President Student Development .... Vacant
49 Dean Lib Arts/Sciences/Basic Skills .... Vacant
12 Dean Omak Campus .... Vacant
103 Dean Workforce Education .... Ms. Anita JANIS
76 Dean Allied Health/Nursing .... Ms. Jenny CAPELO
15 Director Human Resources .... Ms. Reagan BELLAMY
45 Dir Institutional Effectiveness .... Dr. Susan MURRAY
32 Director Student Programs/Outreach .... Mr. Donte QUININE
37 Director Financial Aid .... Mr. Kevin BERG
18 Facilities & Operations Manager .... Mr. Rich PETERS
06 Registrar .... Mr. Bruce MAXWELL
08 Dn Libraries/Learning Technologies .... Mr. Andrew HERSH-TUDOR
10 Director of Fiscal Services .... Ms. Janice FREDSON
26 Communications Manager .... Ms. Libby SIEBENS
20 Coordinator of Adult Basic Skills .... Mr. Aaron PARROTT
27 Marketing/Graphic Design Specialist .... Mr. Nick WINTERS

† Granted candidacy at the Baccalaureate level.

Western Washington University (D)

516 High Street, Bellingham WA 98225-5950
County: Whatcom FICE Identification: 003802
Unit ID: 237011
Telephone: (360) 650-3000 Carnegie Class: Master's L
FAX Number: (360) 650-3022 Calendar System: Quarter
URL: www.wwu.edu
Established: 1893 Annual Undergrad Tuition & Fees (In-State): $8,611
Enrollment: 15,060 Coed
Affiliation or Control: State IRS Status: 501(c)3
Highest Offering: Beyond Master's But Less Than Doctorate
Program: Liberal Arts And General; Teacher Preparatory; Professional
Accreditation: NW, ART, BUS, CACREP, CORE, CS, ENGT, MUS, NRPA, NURSE, SP, TED

01 President .... Dr. Bruce SHEPARD
05 Vice Pres Academic Affairs/Provost .... Dr. Brent CARBAJAL
10 Vice Pres Business/Financial Affs .... Mr. Richard D. VAN DEN HUL
84 VP Enrollment/Student Services .... Dr. Eileen V. COUGHLIN
26 Vice Pres for University Relations .... Mr. Steve SWAN
30 Vice Pres University Advancement .... Ms. Stephanie BOWERS
32 Asst VP Enrollment/Student Services .... Dr. Kunle OJIKUTU
13 Vice Prov Info/Chief Info Officer .... Dr. John D. LAWSON
58 Vice Prov Rsch/Dean Grad Sch .... Dr. Kathleen KITTO
53 Vice Prov Undergraduate Education .... Dr. Steven L. VANDERSTAAY
22 Vice Prov Equal Oppty/Employmt Div .... Dr. Sue GUENTER-SCHLESINGER
51 Vice Provost Extended Education .... Dr. Earl F. GIBBONS
35 Dean of Students .... Mr. Theodore W. PRATT, JR.
15 Asst VP for Human Resources .... Ms. Chyerl WOLFE-LEE
06 Registrar .... Mr. David BRUNNEMER
07 Exec Dir Admissions/Financial Aid .... Ms. Clara CAPRON
36 Director Career Services Center .... Ms. Tina LOUDON
37 Director Financial Aid .... Ms. Clara CAPRON
29 Executive Director Alumni Relations .... Ms. Deborah DEWEES
27 Director University Communications .... Mr. Paul COCKE
44 Dir Plan Giving/Sr Advisor to Pres .... Vacant
08 Dean of Libraries .... Dr. Mark GREENBERG
39 Director University Residences .... Mr. Leonard JONES
04 Sr Executive Assistant to President .... Dr. Paul DUNN
09 Director of Institutional Research .... Dr. Ming ZHANG
18 Director of Facilities Management .... Mr. John A. FURMAN
19 Director of Public Safety .... Mr. Darin RASMUSSEN
41 Athletic Director .... Mr. Steven CARD
92 Director of Honors Program .... Dr. Scott LINNEMAN
96 Director of Business Services .... Mr. Pete HEILGEIST
79 Dean College of Humanities/Soc Sci .... Dr. LeaAnn MARTIN
72 Dean College of Science/Technology .... Dr. Catherine CLARK
50 Int Dean College Business & Econ .... Dr. Craig DUNN
65 Dean Huxley Col of the Environment .... Dr. Steven HOLLENHORST
57 Dean College of Fine & Perf .... Dr. Christopher SPICER
53 Dean Woodring College of Education .... Dr. Francisco RIOS
12 Dean Fairhaven College .... Dr. Jack HERRING
101 Secretary to the Board of Trustees .... Ms. Barbara A. SANDOVAL
104 Director Intl Programs & Exchanges .... Ms. Liz PARTOLAN-FRAY
25 Contracts Assistant .... Ms. Christine DEBONDT
38 Director Counseling Center .... Dr. Nancy CORBIN
43 AAG/Chief Legal Advisor .... Mr. Roger LEISHMAN
86 Director Government Relations .... Ms. Becca KENNA-SCHENK

Whatcom Community College (E)

237 W Kellogg Road, Bellingham WA 98226-8003
County: Whatcom FICE Identification: 010364
Unit ID: 237039
Telephone: (360) 383-3000 Carnegie Class: Assoc/Pub-R-M
FAX Number: (360) 383-4000 Calendar System: Quarter
URL: www.whatcom.ctc.edu
Established: 1970 Annual Undergrad Tuition & Fees (In-State): $4,310
Enrollment: 3,790 Coed
Affiliation or Control: State IRS Status: 501(c)3
Highest Offering: Associate Degree
Program: Occupational; 2-Year Principally Bachelor's Creditable; Technical Emphasis
Accreditation: NW, ADNUR, MAC, PTAA

01 President .... Dr. Kathi HIYANE-BROWN
05 Vice President for Instruction .... Mr. Curt FREED
11 Int VP for Administrative Services .... Mr. Nate LANGSTRAAT
32 Vice Pres for Student Services .... Dr. Luca LEWIS
20 Dean for Instruction .... Mr. Ed HARRI
08 Library Director .... Mr. Howard FULLER
10 Director for Business & Finance .... Mr. Ken BRONSTEIN
06 Registrar .... Mr. Michael SINGLETARY
07 Coordinator of Admissions Outreach .... Ms. Laine JOHNSTON
37 Director of Financial Aid .... Mr. David KLAFFKE
41 Director Student/Athletic Pgms .... Vacant
85 Director of International Programs .... Mr. Kelly KESTER
26 Exec Director for Comm/Marketing .... Ms. Mary VERMILLION
40 Bookstore Manager .... Mr. Jon SPORES
18 Senior Facilities Director .... Mr. Brian KEELEY
04 Exec Assistant to the President .... Ms. Rafeeka KLOKE
15 Director Human Resources .... Ms. Becky RAWLINGS
09 Director for Institutional Research .... Dr. Anne Marie KARLBERG
30 Executive Director for Advancement .... Ms. Anne BOWEN
27 Chief Public Information Officer .... Ms. Mary VERMILLION

Whitman College (F)

345 Boyer Avenue, Walla Walla WA 99362-2083
County: Walla Walla FICE Identification: 003803
Unit ID: 237057
Telephone: (509) 527-5411 Carnegie Class: Bac/A&S
FAX Number: (509) 527-5859 Calendar System: Semester
URL: www.whitman.edu
Established: 1882 Annual Undergrad Tuition & Fees: $59,102
Enrollment: 1,498 Coed
Affiliation or Control: Independent Non-Profit IRS Status: 501(c)3
Highest Offering: Baccalaureate
Program: Liberal Arts And General
Accreditation: NW

01 President .... Dr. Katherine MURRAY
05 Interim Provost/Dean of Faculty .... Dr. Patrick SPENCER
30 Vice President for Development .... Mr. John W. BOGLEY
10 Treasurer/Chief Financial Officer .... Mr. Peter W. HARVEY
32 Dean of Students .... Mr. Charles E. CLEVELAND
20 Associate Dean of Faculty .... Dr. Lisa R. PERFETTI
84 Dean of Admission/Financial Aid .... Mr. Tony A. CABASCO
13 Chief Technology Officer .... Mr. Dan M. TERRIO
18 Chief Facilities/Physical Plant .... Mr. Daniel L. PARK
08 Librarian .... Mrs. Dalia L. CORKRUM
91 Director of Enterprise Technology .... Mr. Michael W. QUINER
07 Director of Admissions .... Mr. Adam MILLER
09 Director of Institutional Research .... Dr. Neal J. CHRISTOPHERSON
20 Assistant Dean of Faculty .... Ms. Kendra J. GOLDEN
35 Associate Dean of Students .... Ms. Barbara A. MAXWELL
26 Chief Communications Officer .... Ms. Michelle MA
38 Director Student Counseling .... Mr. F. 'Thatcher' CARTER
39 Director Residence Life & Housing .... Ms. Nancy J. TAVELLI
29 Director Alumni Relations .... Ms. Nancy L. MITCHELL

104 Director of Off-Campus Studies .... Ms. Susan H. HOLME
15 Director Human Resources .... Mr. Dennis T. HOPWOOD
06 Registrar .... Ms. Stacey J. GIUSTI
19 Director of Security .... Mr. Mattew STROE
23 Director Health Services .... Ms. Claudia L. NESS
36 Director of Career Center .... Ms. Susan M. BUCHANAN
37 Director of Financial Aid Services .... Ms. Marilyn K. PONTI
41 Athletic Director .... Mr. Dean C. SNIDER
42 Coordinator of Spiritual Life .... Mr. Adam M. KIRTLEY
04 Executive Assistant to President .... Ms. Jennifer A. CASPER
44 Director of Annual Giving .... Mr. Brian DOHE

Whitworth University (A)

300 W Hawthorne Road, Spokane WA 99251-0001
County: Spokane FICE Identification: 003804
Unit ID: 237066
Telephone: (509) 777-1000 Carnegie Class: Master's M
FAX Number: (509) 777-4763 Calendar System: 4/1/4
URL: www.whitworth.edu
Established: 1890 Annual Undergrad Tuition & Fees: $38,914
Enrollment: 2,982 Coed
Affiliation or Control: Presbyterian IRS Status: 501(c)3
Highest Offering: Master's
Program: Liberal Arts And General; Teacher Preparatory; Professional
Accreditation: NW, CAATE, MUS, NURSE, TED

01 President .... Dr. Beck A. TAYLOR
05 Provost & Executive Vice President .... Dr. Caroline J. SIMON
100 Chief of Staff .... Ms. Rhosetta R. RHODES
10 VP Finance & Administration .... Mr. Gerald L. GEMMILL
30 VP Institutional Advancement .... Dr. Scott A. MCQUILKIN
32 VP for Student Life .... Dr. Richard G. MANDEVILLE
84 VP Admissions & Financial Aid .... Mr. Greg ORWIG
28 Asst VP Diversity/Intercultural .... Dr. Lawrence A. BURNLEY
15 Assoc VP Human Resources .... Ms. Dolores J. HUMISTON
42 Dir Office of Church Engagement .... Dr. Terry P. MCGONIGAL
88 Assoc Provost Fac Devel/Schlrshp .... Dr. Kathleen H. STORM
06 Registrar .... Ms. Beverly S. KLEEMAN
88 Assoc Dean Com Stndrds/Compliance .... Dr. Craig CHATRIAND
20 Associate Provost of Instruction .... Dr. Randall B. MICHAELIS
27 Chief Information Officer .... Mr. Kenneth BROWN
88 Dean of Instructional Resources .... Mr. Kenneth D. PECKA
21 Assoc VP Finance & Administration .... Ms. Luz I. MERKEL
29 Dir Alumni/Parent Relations .... Mr. Dale W. HAMMOND
07 Director of Admissions .... Ms. Marianne W. HANSEN
51 AVP Grad Admissions & Cont Studies .... Ms. Cheryl D. VAWTER
18 Director of Facilities Services .... Mr. Christopher EICHORST
23 Director of Health Center .... Ms. Kristiana L. HOLMES
53 Dean of School of Education .... Dr. Barbara SANDERS
41 Director of Athletics .... Mr. Timothy DEMANT
37 Acting Director of Financial Aid .... Ms. Traci L. STENSLAND
35 Assoc Dean of Students/Dir HUB .... Ms. Dayna L. COLEMAN
39 Assoc Director of Student Housing .... Mr. Alan B. JACOB
39 Director of Residence Life .... Mr. Timothy CALDWELL
40 Manager of Bookstore .... Ms. Nancy G. LOOMIS
26 Director of Communications .... Ms. Nancy G. HINES
38 Director of Counseling Services .... Ms. Monica WHITLOCK
09 Director of Institutional Research .... Ms. Wendy L. OLSON
50 Dean School of Business .... Dr. Timothy J. WILKINSON
08 Director Library .... Ms. Amanda C. CLARK
19 Supr II Security Services .... Ms. Jacquelyn CHRISTENSEN
04 Executive Asst to President .... Ms. Ruth R. PELLS
104 Dir of International Education Ctr .... Ms. Sue JACKSON

Yakima Valley Community College (B)

PO Box 22520, S 16th Ave & Nob Hill,
Yakima WA 98907-2520
County: Yakima FICE Identification: 003805
Unit ID: 237109
Telephone: (509) 574-4600 Carnegie Class: Assoc/Pub-R-M
FAX Number: (509) 574-6860 Calendar System: Quarter
URL: www.yvcc.edu
Established: 1928 Annual Undergrad Tuition & Fees (In-State): $4,319
Enrollment: 5,121 Coed
Affiliation or Control: State IRS Status: 170(c)1
Highest Offering: Associate Degree
Program: Occupational; 2-Year Principally Bachelor's Creditable
Accreditation: NW, ADNUR, DH, MAC, SURGT

01 President .... Dr. Linda KAMINSKI
05 Vice Pres Instruction/Student Svcs .... Mr. Tomas YBARRA
10 Vice Pres Administrative Services .... Ms. Teresa HOLLAND
12 Dean Basic Skills/Grandview Campus .... Dr. Bryce HUMPHREYS
13 Director Tech Services .... Mr. Scott TOWSLEY
32 Dean Student Services .... Ms. Leslie BLACKABY
49 Dean Arts & Sciences .... Ms. Kerrie CAVANESS
75 Dean Workforce Education .... Ms. Paulette LOPEZ
08 Library Director .... Vacant
37 Director Student Financial Aid .... Ms. Janet CANTELON
06 Registrar/Director of Admissions .... Mr. Quinn HALE
09 Dir Institutional Effectiveness .... Ms. Sheila DELQUADRI
29 Director Alumni Relations .... Ms. Deborah WILSON
26 Community Relations Coordinator .... Ms. Nicole HOPKINS
15 Director Human Resources .... Mr. Mark ROGSTAD
18 Director Facilities/Physical Plant .... Mr. Jeff WOOD
21 Director Accounting Services .... Ms. Clarissa WOLFE
35 Student Life Coordinator .... Ms. Caitlin GOODWILL

† Granted candidacy at the Baccalaureate level.

WEST VIRGINIA

Alderson Broaddus University (C)

101 College Hill Drive, Philippi WV 26416-4600
County: Barbour FICE Identification: 003806
Unit ID: 237118
Telephone: (304) 457-1700 Carnegie Class: Bac/Diverse
FAX Number: (304) 457-6239 Calendar System: Semester
URL: www.ab.edu
Established: 1871 Annual Undergrad Tuition & Fees: $24,140
Enrollment: 1,108 Coed
Affiliation or Control: American Baptist IRS Status: 501(c)3
Highest Offering: Master's
Program: Liberal Arts And General
Accreditation: NH, ARCPA, CAATE, NUR, TEAC

01 President .... Dr. Richard A. CREEHAN
05 Provost/Executive Vice President .... Dr. Joan L. PROPST
10 Vice Pres Administration & Finance .... Mr. Bruce A. BLANKENSHIP
30 Vice Pres Institutional Advancement .... Mr. Jay E. NUSSEL
84 Vice Pres Enrollment Management .... Mr. Andrew B. SPOHN
32 Dean of Student Affairs .... Mr. Thomas F. RADULSKI
20 Associate Provost .... Mr. Eric M. SHOR
102 Exec Dir of Inst Advancement .... Vacant
63 Dean Col of Physician Asst Studies .... Mr. Thomas F. MOORE
76 Dean College of Health Sciences .... Dr. Brenda A. MASON
53 Dean College of Education and Music .... Dr. Mary K. DEVONO
50 Dean Col of Business & Management .... Mr. Richard T. FOLEY
79 Dean Col of Humanities & Soc Sci .... Dr. Andrea J. BUCKLEW
81 Dean College of Science/Tech/Math .... Dr. Ross A. BRITTAIN
06 Registrar .... Dr. Saundra E. HOXIE
08 Director of Library Services .... Mr. David E. HOXIE
41 Athletic Director .... Mr. Dennis W. CREEHAN
42 Chaplain .... Vacant
08 Dir Academic Ctr for Educ Success .... Dr. Amy MASON
21 Director of Accounting Services .... Ms. Kim MOORE
29 Director of Alumni Relations .... Mr. Joshua D. ALLEN
44 Director of Annual Giving .... Ms. Dionne T. ANDREWS
40 Director of Campus Services .... Mr. Ed BURDA
36 Director of Career Services .... Ms. Teresa D. VAN ALSBURG
38 Director of Counseling Services .... Mr. Chad HOSTETLER
37 Director of Financial Aid .... Ms. Amy L. KING
18 Director of Facilities .... Mr. Lawrence J. TALLMAN
27 Dir of Information and Research .... Ms. Julia M. MORRIS
13 Director of Information Technology .... Ms. Carol WEAVER
26 Director of Mktg/Communications .... Ms. Ashley E. MITTELMEIER
39 Director Student Housing .... Mr. David A. FALLETA
19 Director Security/Safety .... Mr. Matthew SISK
04 Exec Asst to Pres/Sec to the Board .... Ms. Juliet A. SPRUILL
105 Web Content Editor .... Ms. Eva M. TREFETHEN
15 Director of Human Resources .... Ms. Jaunita COLEMAN

American National University (D)

110 Park Center Drive, Parkersburg WV 26101
Telephone: (304) 699-3005 Identification: 770787
Accreditation: ACICS, MAC

† Branch campus of American National University, Salem, VA.

American National University (E)

421 Hilltop Drive, Princeton WV 24740
Telephone: (304) 487-3845 Identification: 666499
Accreditation: ACICS, MAC

† Branch campus of American National University, Salem, VA.

American Public University System (F)

111 W Congress Street, Charles Town WV 25414-1621
County: Jefferson FICE Identification: 035393
Unit ID: 449339
Telephone: (304) 724-3700 Carnegie Class: Master's L
FAX Number: (304) 724-3780 Calendar System: Other
URL: www.apus.edu
Established: 1991 Annual Undergrad Tuition & Fees: $6,400
Enrollment: 57,539 Coed
Affiliation or Control: Proprietary IRS Status: Proprietary
Highest Offering: Master's
Program: 2-Year Principally Bachelor's Creditable; Liberal Arts And General; Professional
Accreditation: NH, ACBSP, NURSE

01 President/CEO .... Dr. Wallace E. BOSTON
05 Exec VP & Provost .... Dr. Karan H. POWELL
88 Exec VP & CDO .... Mr. Harry WILKINS
26 Exec VP Programs & Marketing .... Ms. Carol S. GILBERT
10 Exec VP & CFO .... Mr. Richard SUNDERLAND, JR.
11 SVP/Chief Admin Officer .... Mr. Pete W. GIBBONS
13 SVP/Chief Information Officer .... Mr. Mike MIOTTO
20 SVP/Academic Opers Officer .... Dr. Gwen HALL
88 SVP/Acad Prgm Dev & Outreach .... Mr. Michael NETZER
06 VP/Registrar .... Ms. Lyn GEER
84 VP Enrollment Mgt & Student Support .... Ms. Terry GRANT
31 VP Community Relations .... Dr. John HOUGH
46 VP Research & Development .... Dr. Phil ICE
32 VP Student Services .... Ms. Caroline SIMPSON
09 VP Institutional Research & Assess .... Dr. Jennifer HELM
08 VP Library and Educ Materials .... Mr. Hedi BENAICHA
88 VP Military/Veteran & Comm College .... Mr. Jim SWEIZER
15 VP Human Resources .... Ms. Amy PANZARELLA
37 VP Financial Aid & Compliance .... Mr. Keith WELLINGS
88 VP Ombudsman .... Ms. Lynn C. WALLACE

Appalachian Bible College (G)

161 College Drive, Mt. Hope WV 25880
County: Raleigh FICE Identification: 007544
Unit ID: 237136
Telephone: (304) 877-6428 Carnegie Class: Spec/Faith
FAX Number: (304) 877-5082 Calendar System: Semester
URL: www.abc.edu
Established: 1950 Annual Undergrad Tuition & Fees: $13,590
Enrollment: 210 Coed
Affiliation or Control: Independent Non-Profit IRS Status: 501(c)3
Highest Offering: Master's
Program: 2-Year Principally Bachelor's Creditable; Liberal Arts And General; Teacher Preparatory; Religious Emphasis
Accreditation: NH, BI

01 President .... Dr. Daniel L. ANDERSON
05 Vice President for Academics .... Mr. Daniel S. HANSHEW
10 Vice President for Business .... Mr. Kenneth E. LILLY
30 Vice President for Development .... Rev. Jonathan A. RINKER
32 Vice President for Student Services .... Rev. David E. CHILDS
42 Vice Pres for Extension Ministries .... Mr. David J. HOLLOWAY
33 Dean of Men .... Mr. Kevin GULLION
34 Dean of Women .... Mrs. Linda J. CHILDS
06 Registrar .... Dr. John RINEHART
07 Director of Admissions .... Mr. Benjamin CALE
08 Librarian .... Mr. David W. DUNKERTON
37 Director of Financial Aid .... Ms. Deana B. STEINKE
04 Admin Assistant to the President .... Mrs. Elisabeth I. GOLDEN
26 Director of Public Relations .... Miss Karisa A. CLARK

Bethany College (H)

31 E. Campus Drive, Bethany WV 26032-3002
County: Brooke FICE Identification: 003808
Unit ID: 237181
Telephone: (304) 829-7000 Carnegie Class: Bac/A&S
FAX Number: (304) 829-7700 Calendar System: 4/1/4
URL: www.bethanywv.edu
Established: 1840 Annual Undergrad Tuition & Fees: $25,736
Enrollment: 757 Coed
Affiliation or Control: Christian Church (Disciples Of Christ)
IRS Status: 501(c)3
Highest Offering: Master's
Program: Liberal Arts And General; Teacher Preparatory
Accreditation: NH, SW, TED

01 Int President of the College .... Mr. Sven M. DE JONG
05 Vice Pres for Academic Affairs .... Dr. Katrina L. D'AQUIN
10 Vice President for Finance .... Mrs. Eileen GREAF
30 AVP Advancement .... Dr. Mort GAMBLE
04 Asst to the President .... Ms. Stephanie GORDON
100 Executive Asst to the President .... Dr. Mort GAMBLE
20 Asst Vice President Academic Affs .... Vacant
32 Dean of Students .... Mr. Gerald STEBBINS
37 Director of Financial Aid .... Mr. Jason MCCLAIN
41 Director of Athletics & Recreation .... Mr. Brian ROSE
09 Dir Institutional Research/Records .... Mrs. Carolyn WALSH
88 Director of McCann Learning Center .... Dr. Christina SAMPSON
88 Dir Student Engag/Responsibility .... Ms. Malorie PORTER
89 Director of First Year Experience .... Dr. Katrina D'AQUIN
104 Director of International Programs .... Dr. Harald MENZ
36 Director of Student Placement .... Mr. John OSBORNE
23 Director of the Byrd Health Center .... Mrs. Carol TYLER
26 Director of Communications .... Ms. Rebecca ROSE
29 Director of Alumni/Parent Relations .... Ms. Ashley KANOTZ
44 Director of Advancement Services .... Ms. Shirley KEMP
88 Director of Sports Information .... Mr. Jerrod PLATE
88 Director of Church Relations .... Dr. Larry GRIMES
18 Director of Physical Plant .... Mr. Theodore D. WILLIAMS
21 Asst Vice President for Finance .... Ms. Deidra R. HALL-NUZUM
21 Director of Business Affairs .... Ms. Saralyn DAGUE
19 Director of Safety & Security .... Mr. Robert RIBAR
15 Director of Human Resources .... Mr. Douglas MCCONAHY
07 Director of Admissions .... Ms. Karina J. DAYICH-MCCABE
39 Director of Residence Life .... Mr. Andrew LEWIS
35 Director of Student Activiites .... Mr. Samuel GOODGE
42 Chaplain .... Rev. Scott THAYER
08 Director of the Libraries .... Mrs. Heather MAY-RICCIUTI
24 Dir Media Services/Classroom Tech .... Mr. Thomas V. FURBEE
88 Public Services Librarian .... Mr. Trevor ONEST
06 Registrar .... Ms. Lisa CUCARESE
84 Director of Enrollment Mgmt .... Ms. Mollie CECERE
88 General Manager Conference Center .... Ms. Donna WHITE
88 Director of Dining Services .... Mrs. Necol M. DUNSON
40 Manager of the Bookstore .... Mr. Bradly MCDOUGAL
38 College Counselor .... Ms. Renee STOCK

Davis & Elkins College (I)

100 Campus Drive, Elkins WV 26241-3996
County: Randolph FICE Identification: 003811
Unit ID: 237358
Telephone: (304) 637-1900 Carnegie Class: Bac/Diverse
FAX Number: (304) 637-1413 Calendar System: 4/1/4
URL: www.dewv.edu
Established: 1904 Annual Undergrad Tuition & Fees: $27,492

Enrollment: 846 Coed
Affiliation or Control: Presbyterian Church (U.S.A.) IRS Status: 501(c)3
Highest Offering: Baccalaureate
Program: 2-Year Principally Bachelor's Creditable; Liberal Arts And General; Teacher Preparatory; Business Emphasis
Accreditation: NH, ADNUR, IACBE, THEA

01 President .... Dr. G. T. SMITH
10 VP for Business & Finance .... Ms. Greta J. TROASTLE
05 Vice President for Academic Affairs .... Dr. Joseph M. ROIDT
32 Vice President for Student Affairs .... Mr. Scott D. GODDARD
30 Vice President for Development .... Ms. Carol M. SCHULER
15 Director Human Resources .... Ms. M. J. COREY
06 Registrar .... Dr. Stephanie C. HAYNES
18 Director of Physical Plant .... Mr. Dan JUDY
37 Director Financial Planning .... Mr. Matthew A. SUMMERS
08 Assistant Director Booth Library .... Ms. Mary Jo DEJOICE
42 Chaplain .... Rev. Kevin M. STARCHER
41 Director of Athletics .... Vacant
19 Asst Director of Security .... Mr. Jake GOODEN
04 Executive Asst to the President .... Ms. Robin PRICE
13 Director of Information Services .... Ms. Amy MATTINGLY
29 Director of Alumni Engagement .... Ms. Wendy MORGAN
07 Interim Director of Admission .... Ms. Sandy NEEL
09 Director of Institutional Research .... Mr. Willis L. MCCOLLAM
26 Dir Communications & Marketing .... Ms. Nanci BROSS-FREGONARA

Future Generations Graduate School (A)

390 Road Less Traveled, Franklin WV 26807-9201
County: Pendleton Identification: 666714
Unit ID: 481030
Telephone: (304) 358-2000 Carnegie Class: Not Classified
FAX Number: (304) 358-3008 Calendar System: Other
URL: www.future.edu
Established: 2003 Annual Graduate Tuition & Fees: $17,500
Enrollment: 29 Coed
Affiliation or Control: Independent Non-Profit IRS Status: 501(c)3
Highest Offering: Master's; No Undergraduates
Program: Liberal Arts And General; Professional
Accreditation: NH

01 Executive Director .... Dr. Daniel TAYLOR
05 Academic Director .... Dr. Stuart NOBLE-GOODMAN
11 Chief Operating Officer .... Stephanie HARTMAN
32 Chief Student Affairs/Student Life .... Christie HAND

Huntington Junior College (B)

900 Fifth Avenue, Huntington WV 25701-2004
County: Cabell FICE Identification: 009047
Unit ID: 237437
Telephone: (304) 697-7550 Carnegie Class: Assoc/PrivFP
FAX Number: (304) 697-7554 Calendar System: Quarter
URL: www.huntingtonjuniorcollege.edu
Established: 1936 Annual Undergrad Tuition & Fees: $7,800
Enrollment: 685 Coed
Affiliation or Control: Proprietary IRS Status: Proprietary
Highest Offering: Associate Degree
Program: 2-Year Principally Bachelor's Creditable; Technical Emphasis
Accreditation: NH, MAC

01 President .... Carolyn A. SMITH
03 Director .... Dr. Catherine E. SNODDY
05 Academic Affairs Director .... Linda J. WEST

ITT Technical Institute (C)

5183 US Route 60, Bldg 1, Suite 40, Huntington WV 25705
Telephone: (304) 733-8700 Identification: 666709
Accreditation: ACICS

† Branch campus of ITT Technical Institute, Indianapolis, IN.

Martinsburg College (D)

341 Aikens Center, Martinsburg WV 25404
County: Berkeley Identification: 667035
Telephone: (304) 263-6262 Carnegie Class: Not Classified
FAX Number: (866) 703-6611 Calendar System: Other
URL: www.martinsburgcollege.edu
Established: 1980 Annual Undergrad Tuition & Fees: $3,000
Enrollment: 775 Coed
Affiliation or Control: Proprietary IRS Status: Proprietary
Highest Offering: Associate Degree
Program: Occupational; 2-Year Principally Bachelor's Creditable; Technical Emphasis
Accreditation: DEAC

01 President .... Paul VIBOCH
05 Chief Academic Officer .... Stella GARLICK
07 Director of Admissions .... Laurie MAURO
06 Registrar .... Debra HAYTAS

Mountain State College (E)

1508 Spring Street, Parkersburg WV 26101
County: Wood FICE Identification: 005008
Unit ID: 237598
Telephone: (304) 485-5487 Carnegie Class: Assoc/PrivFP
FAX Number: (304) 485-3524 Calendar System: Quarter
URL: www.msc.edu
Established: 1888 Annual Undergrad Tuition & Fees: $8,100
Enrollment: 278 Coed
Affiliation or Control: Proprietary IRS Status: Proprietary
Highest Offering: Associate Degree
Program: Occupational; 2-Year Principally Bachelor's Creditable; Business Emphasis
Accreditation: ACICS

01 President .... Mrs. Judith SUTTON

Ohio Valley University (F)

1 Campus View Drive, Vienna WV 26105-8000
County: Wood FICE Identification: 003819
Unit ID: 237640
Telephone: (304) 865-6000 Carnegie Class: Bac/Diverse
FAX Number: (304) 865-6001 Calendar System: Semester
URL: www.ovu.edu
Established: 1958 Annual Undergrad Tuition & Fees: $27,060
Enrollment: 431 Coed
Affiliation or Control: Churches Of Christ IRS Status: 501(c)3
Highest Offering: Master's
Program: 2-Year Principally Bachelor's Creditable; Liberal Arts And General; Teacher Preparatory; Professional; Business Emphasis
Accreditation: NH, IACBE, @TEAC

01 President .... Dr. Harold SHANK
10 CFO .... Mr. Jeffrey A. DIMICK
00 Chancellor .... Dr. Keith STOTTS
05 VP for Academic Affairs .... Dr. Joy JONES
41 Athletic Director .... Mr. Chad PORTER
30 VP Advancement .... Vacant
04 President's Office Manager .... Mrs. Missy WAYT
18 Director of Campus Operations .... Mr. David STEWART
36 Director of Career Services .... Mrs. Kathy MULLER
32 Dean of Student Life .... Mr. Jason DOUGHERTY
08 Library Director .... Mr. Rodney WOOTEN
06 Registrar .... Mrs. Amy GHERKE
07 Director of Admissions Management .... Mrs. Kay GROSE
09 Director of OIE .... Dr. Daniel BLAIR
13 Chief Info Technology Officer .... Mr. Christopher LANG
26 Director of Marketing .... Mr. Marty DAVIS
19 Director Security/Safety .... Ms. Hope ASH

Salem International University (G)

223 W Main Street, Box 500, Salem WV 26426-0500
County: Harrison FICE Identification: 003820
Unit ID: 237783
Telephone: (304) 326-1109 Carnegie Class: Master's M
FAX Number: (304) 326-1246 Calendar System: Semester
URL: www.salemu.edu
Established: 1888 Annual Undergrad Tuition & Fees: $17,700
Enrollment: 702 Coed
Affiliation or Control: Proprietary IRS Status: Proprietary
Highest Offering: Master's
Program: Occupational; 2-Year Principally Bachelor's Creditable; Teacher Preparatory; Professional; Business Emphasis
Accreditation: NH, TED

01 President .... Mr. Dan NELANT
04 Executive Asst to President .... Mrs. Barbara L. MCCLAIN
03 Executive Vice President .... Dr. Cecil E. KIRKLAND
05 Provost .... Dr. Sally H. DIGMAN
37 VP Financial Aid & Compliance .... Mr. Marty MEHRINGER
13 Director of Information Technology .... Mr. Anthony GRANT
11 VP Operations .... Ms. Natacha CRUICKSHANK
07 Director of Admissions .... Ms. Iris ROBERTSON
10 Financial Officer .... Ms. Carey R. CSESZKO
21 Controller .... Ms. Ginger RICHARDS
85 Intl Student Dir & Business Mgr .... Mrs. Stephanie ROBERTS
06 Registrar .... Mr. Joseph E. FERLIC
50 Dean of Business .... Dr. Marc D. GETTY
53 Dean of Education .... Dr. Craig S. MCCLELLAN
66 Director of Nursing Education .... Mrs. Cheryl MICHAELS
08 Dean of Library Services .... Dr. Phyllis D. FREEDMAN
32 Dean of Student Affairs .... Dr. Dennis MCNABOE
19 Director of Campus Security .... Mr. Joseph E. SHAVER
41 Director of Athletics .... Mr. Jamie SHOEMAKER
18 Assoc Dir of Campus Operations .... Mr. Keith A. BULLION

University of Charleston (H)

2300 Maccorkle Avenue, SE, Charleston WV 25304-1099
County: Kanawha FICE Identification: 003818
Unit ID: 237312
Telephone: (304) 357-4800 Carnegie Class: Bac/Diverse
FAX Number: (304) 357-4715 Calendar System: Semester
URL: www.ucwv.edu
Established: 1888 Annual Undergrad Tuition & Fees: $25,900
Enrollment: 2,111 Coed
Affiliation or Control: Independent Non-Profit IRS Status: 501(c)3
Highest Offering: Doctorate
Program: Liberal Arts And General; Teacher Preparatory; Professional; Fine Arts Emphasis
Accreditation: NH, ACFEI, #ARCPA, CAATE, CIDA, NUR, OTA, PHAR, RAD, SW, TED

01 President .... Dr. Edwin H. WELCH
05 Exec VP/Provost/Dean of Faculty .... Dr. Letha ZOOK
10 Exec VP Administration & Finance .... Mrs. Cleta M. HARLESS
30 Vice Pres for Development .... Ms. Deborah MORRIS
07 Exec VP/Chief Admissions/Mktg Ofcr .... Ms. Joan CLARK
32 Dean of Students .... Dr. Mordecai BROWNLEE
26 Director of Marketing .... Vacant
100 Chief of Staff .... Dr. Jerry FORSTER
06 Registrar .... Ms. Carol SPRADLING
29 Director of Alumni Relations .... Ms. Catherine ECKLEY
21 Controller .... Ms. Terri UNDERHILL
13 Chief Information Officer .... Mr. Scott TERRY
08 Director of Library Services .... Mr. John ADKINS
85 Director International Student Pgms .... Ms. Elizabeth SLACK
37 Associate Director Financial Aid .... Ms. Nina MORTON
35 Assistant Dean of Students .... Ms. Virginia MOORE
35 Asst Dir Student Leadership/Engag .... Ms. Meghan SPARROW
40 Bookstore Manager .... Mr. Glenn JOHNSON
18 Director of Facilities Services .... Mr. Gary BOYD
41 Athletic Director .... Dr. Bren STEVENS
88 Director of Colleague Program .... Ms. Hallie DUNLAP
09 Director of Institutional Research .... Ms. Lisa DAWKINS
50 Dean Graduate School of Business .... Dr. Scott BELLAMY
67 Dean School of Pharmacy .... Dr. Michelle EASTON
49 Dean School of Arts & Sciences .... Dr. Barbara WRIGHT
76 Actg Dean School of Health Sciences .... Dr. Letha ZOOK

Valley College - Beckley Campus (I)

120 New River Town Center, Suite C, Beckley WV 25801
County: Raleigh FICE Identification: 030844
Unit ID: 377652
Telephone: (304) 252-9547 Carnegie Class: Assoc/PrivFP
FAX Number: (304) 252-1694 Calendar System: Other
URL: www.valley.edu
Established: 1983 Annual Undergrad Tuition & Fees: $15,209
Enrollment: 331 Coed
Affiliation or Control: Proprietary IRS Status: Proprietary
Highest Offering: Associate Degree
Program: Occupational; Business Emphasis
Accreditation: ACICS

01 President .... Mr. Tony PALMIERI
05 Vice President .... Ms. Beth GARDNER

West Virginia Business College (J)

116 Pennsylvania Avenue, Nutter Fort WV 26301-4516
Telephone: (304) 624-7695 Identification: 666507
Accreditation: ACICS

† Branch campus of West Virginia Business College, Wheeling, WV.

West Virginia Business College (K)

1052 Main Street, Wheeling WV 26003-2702
County: Ohio FICE Identification: 010861
Unit ID: 237978
Telephone: (304) 232-0361 Carnegie Class: Assoc/PrivFP
FAX Number: (304) 232-0363 Calendar System: Quarter
URL: www.wvbc.edu
Established: 1881 Annual Undergrad Tuition & Fees: $10,500
Enrollment: 130 Coed
Affiliation or Control: Proprietary IRS Status: Proprietary
Highest Offering: Associate Degree
Program: Occupational
Accreditation: ACICS

01 General Manager .... Mr. James WEIR

*West Virginia Council for Community & Technical College Education (L)

1018 Kanawha Boulevard E, Suite 700, Charleston WV 25301-2800
County: Kanawha Identification: 666993
Telephone: (304) 558-0265 Carnegie Class: N/A
FAX Number: (304) 558-1646
URL: www.wvctcs.org

01 Chancellor .... James L. SKIDMORE

*Blue Ridge Community and Technical College (M)

13650 Apple Harvest Drive, Martinsburg WV 25403
County: Berkeley FICE Identification: 039573
Unit ID: 446774
Telephone: (304) 260-4380 Carnegie Class: Assoc/Pub-R-M
FAX Number: (304) 260-4376 Calendar System: Semester
URL: www.blueridgectc.edu
Established: 1974 Annual Undergrad Tuition & Fees (In-State): $3,696
Enrollment: 5,528 Coed
Affiliation or Control: State IRS Status: 501(c)3
Highest Offering: Associate Degree
Program: Occupational; 2-Year Principally Bachelor's Creditable
Accreditation: NH, ADNUR, EMT, PTAA

02 President .... Dr. Peter G. CHECKOVICH

05 Vice President of Instruction .... Dr. George PERRY
103 VP Economic and Workforce Devel .... Dr. Ann M. SHIPWAY
84 VP of Enrollment Management .... Ms. Leslie C. SEE
10 Chief Financial Officer .... Ms. Kimberly LINEBERG
50 VP Prof Studies/Univ Transfer .... Dr. Randall C. MILLER
06 Registrar .... Dr. Angie M. KINDER
32 Associate Dean of Students .... Ms. Brenda NEAL
15 Vice President Human Resources .... Mr. Justin RUBLE
13 Vice President of IT .... Mr. Michael BYERS
37 Director of Financial Aid .... Ms. Anna CRAWFORD

*BridgeValley Community & Technical College (A)

2001 Union Carbide Drive, South Charleston WV 25303
County: Kanawha　FICE Identification: 040386
Unit ID: 445018
Telephone: (304) 205-6600　Carnegie Class: Assoc/Pub-R-S
FAX Number: N/A　Calendar System: Semester
URL: www.bridgevalley.edu
Established: 2014　Annual Undergrad Tuition & Fees (In-District): $3,850
Enrollment: 2,344　Coed
Affiliation or Control: State/Local　IRS Status: Exempt
Highest Offering: Associate Degree
Program: 2-Year Principally Bachelor's Creditable
Accreditation: NH, ADNUR, COARC, DH, ENGT, MLTAD, NMT

02 President .... Dr. Beverly Jo HARRIS
10 Senior Financial Officer .... Dr. Patricia HUNT
05 Sr Vice Pres Academic/Student Affs .... Dr. Kristin MALLORY
103 Vice Pres Workforce Economic Devel .... Mr. Jeff WYCO
06 Chief Records Officer/Registrar .... Mr. Roy SIMMONS
07 Director of Admissions .... Ms. Michelle D. WICKS
37 Associate Director of Financial Aid .... Ms. Bonnie EDWARDS
15 Chief Human Resources Officer .... Ms. Michelle BISSELL
21 Chief Financial Officer .... Ms. Cathy AQUINO
96 Chief Purchasing Officer .... Mr. John POWELL
04 Administrative Asst to President .... Ms. Alicia SYNER
08 Head Librarian .... Ms. Kathleen PHILLIPS
09 Director of Institutional Research .... Mr. James FAUVER
106 Dir Online Education/E-learning .... Ms. Connie FOX
13 Chief Information/Operations Ofcr .... Mr. Thomas MINNICH
18 Chief Facilities/Physical Plant .... Mr. Jason STARK
19 Director Security/Safety .... Mr. Bazra FAKHIR
26 Chief Public Relations/Marketing .... Mr. Brian BOLYARD
30 Chief Development/Advancement .... Mr. Jack NUCKOLS
36 Director Student Placement .... Ms. Judy WHIPKEY
38 Director Student Counseling .... Ms. Carla BLANKENBUEHLER
50 Dean of Business/Legal Studies .... Ms. Megan LORENZ
72 Dean of Technology .... Mr. Norm MORTENSEN
84 Dean Enrollment Services .... Ms. Joyce SURBAUGH

*Eastern West Virginia Community and Technical College (B)

316 Eastern Drive, Moorefield WV 26836-1155
County: Hardy　FICE Identification: 041190
Unit ID: 438708
Telephone: (304) 434-8000　Carnegie Class: Assoc/Pub-R-S
FAX Number: (304) 434-7001　Calendar System: Semester
URL: www.easternwv.edu
Established: 1999　Annual Undergrad Tuition & Fees (In-State): $3,000
Enrollment: 910　Coed
Affiliation or Control: State　IRS Status: Exempt
Highest Offering: Associate Degree
Program: Occupational; 2-Year Principally Bachelor's Creditable; Technical Emphasis
Accreditation: NH, ADNUR

02 President .... Dr. Charles TERRELL
10 Exec Dean for Financial & Operation .... Ms. Penny REARDON
05 Dean for Academic & Student Service .... Vacant
32 Assoc Dean Academic & Student Svcs .... Ms. Sherry BECKER-GORBY
103 Director of Workforce Education .... Ms. Sherry WATTS
75 Dean of Career/Technical/Workforce .... Mr. Ward MALCOLM

*Mountwest Community and Technical College (C)

1 Mountwest Way, Huntington WV 25701
County: Cabell　FICE Identification: 040414
Unit ID: 444954
Telephone: (304) 710-3141　Carnegie Class: Assoc/Pub-R-M
FAX Number: (304) 710-3187　Calendar System: Semester
URL: www.mctc.edu
Established: 1975　Annual Undergrad Tuition & Fees (In-District): $3,521
Enrollment: 2,026　Coed
Affiliation or Control: State/Local　IRS Status: 501(c)3
Highest Offering: Associate Degree
Program: Occupational; 2-Year Principally Bachelor's Creditable
Accreditation: NH, ACBSP, CAHIIM, MAC, PTAA

02 President .... Dr. Keith J. COTRONEO
05 Exec Vice Pres/Chief Academic Ofcr .... Dr. Harry R. FAULK
10 Vice Pres Finance/Business/CFO .... Mr. Daniel J. FIGLER
32 Vice President of Student Services .... Ms. Billie K. BROOKS
13 VP Operations/Info Technology .... Mrs. Terri L. TOMBLIN-BYRD
06 Registrar .... Ms. Angela ROSS

*New River Community and Technical College (D)

280 University Drive, Beaver WV 25813
County: Raleigh　FICE Identification: 039603
Unit ID: 447582
Telephone: (304) 929-6703　Carnegie Class: Assoc/Pub-R-M
FAX Number: (304) 929-6719　Calendar System: Semester
URL: www.newriver.edu
Established: 2003　Annual Undergrad Tuition & Fees (In-State): $3,564
Enrollment: 1,957　Coed
Affiliation or Control: State　IRS Status: 501(c)3
Highest Offering: Associate Degree
Program: Occupational; 2-Year Principally Bachelor's Creditable
Accreditation: NH, EMT, @PTAA

02 President .... Dr. L. Marshall WASHINGTON
04 Exec Secretary to the President .... Ms. Lori A. MIDKIFF
05 Vice Pres Academic Affairs .... Dr. Amy S. DESONIA
10 Vice Pres Financial Affairs .... Mr. Stephen M. BENSON
11 Vice Pres Administrative Services .... Ms. Leah A. TAYLOR
30 VP Inst Advancement/Col Foundation .... Ms. Karen J. HARVEY
32 Vice Pres Student Services .... Dr. Allen B. WITHERS
13 Vice Pres Technology/Library Svcs .... Dr. David J. AYERSMAN
15 Director Human Resources .... Ms. Amanda L. BAKER
27 Chief Communications Officer .... Ms. Elizabeth M. BELCHER
20 Assoc VP of Academic Affairs .... Dr. Carry DEATLEY
12 Campus Dean ATC .... Dr. Carry DEATLEY
12 Campus Dean Beckley .... Dr. Renae MCGINNIS
12 Campus Dean Greenbrier Valley .... Mr. Roger D. GRIFFITH
12 Campus Dean Mercer County .... Mr. Steve WISE
12 Campus Dean Nicholas County .... Mr. Fred B. CULLER
09 Int Dir of Institutional Research .... Mr. James M. FEDDERS
06 Registrar .... Ms. Donna M. LEWIS
08 Staff Librarian .... Mr. Robert H. COSTON
37 Director of Financial Aid .... Ms. Patricia HARMON
96 Director of Purchasing .... Ms. Twana JACKSON
21 Chief Financial Officer .... Ms. Heike I. SOEFFKER-CULICERTO
18 Director of Physical Plant .... Mr. Robert RUNION
26 Director of Public Relations .... Ms. Jenni CANTERBURY
84 Director of Enrollment Services .... Ms. Tracy L. EVANS
24 Dir Ctr for Teaching Excellence .... Mr. Ralph C. PAYNE

*Pierpont Community & Technical College (E)

1201 Locust Avenue, Fairmont WV 26554-2470
County: Marion　FICE Identification: 040385
Unit ID: 443492
Telephone: (304) 367-4692　Carnegie Class: Assoc/Pub-R-M
FAX Number: (304) 367-4881　Calendar System: Semester
URL: www.pierpont.edu
Established: 1974　Annual Undergrad Tuition & Fees (In-State): $4,440
Enrollment: 2,311　Coed
Affiliation or Control: State　IRS Status: 501(c)3
Highest Offering: Associate Degree
Program: Occupational; 2-Year Principally Bachelor's Creditable; Technical Emphasis
Accreditation: NH, ACFEI, CAHIIM, #COARC, EMT, MLTAD, NAIT, PTAA

02 President .... Vacant
10 VP for Finance and Administration .... Mr. Dale R. BRADLEY
05 Provost/VP for Academic Affairs .... Ms. Leslie LOVETT
86 VP for Organization and Development .... Mr. Stephen E. LEACH
13 VP Information Technology/CIO .... Mr. Rob LINGER
103 VP Workforce & Economic Development .... Mr. Paul SCHREFFLER
04 Exec Assistant to the President .... Ms. Cyndee SENSIBAUGH
50 Dean Sch of Business/Aviation/Tech .... Dr. Gerald BACZA
76 Dean School of Health Careers .... Dr. Rosemarie ROMESBURG
79 Dean School of Human Services .... Dr. Brian FLOYD

*Southern West Virginia Community and Technical College (F)

P. O. Box 2900, Mount Gay WV 25637-2900
County: Logan　FICE Identification: 003816
Unit ID: 237817
Telephone: (304) 792-7098　Carnegie Class: Assoc/Pub-R-M
FAX Number: (304) 792-7046　Calendar System: Semester
URL: www.southernwv.edu
Established: 1971　Annual Undergrad Tuition & Fees (In-State): $3,192
Enrollment: 1,838　Coed
Affiliation or Control: State　IRS Status: 501(c)3
Highest Offering: Associate Degree
Program: Occupational; 2-Year Principally Bachelor's Creditable; Technical Emphasis
Accreditation: NH, ADNUR, COARC, MLTAD, RAD, SURGT

02 President .... Ms. Joanne J. TOMBLIN
10 VP for Finance & Administration .... Mr. Samuel M. LITTERAL
05 VP Academic Affairs & Student Svcs .... Dr. Debra K. TEACHMAN
103 VP Economic & Workforce Development .... Mr. Allyn S. BARKER
13 Chief Information Officer .... Mr. Gary HOLEMAN
30 Vice President for Development .... Mr. Ronald E. LEMON
15 Interim Human Resources Director .... Ms. Debbie C. DINGESS
04 Exec Asst to President & BOG .... Ms. Emma L. BAISDEN
09 Dir Institutional Effectiveness .... Dr. Pamela L. ALDERMAN
12 Director Wyoming Campus Operations .... Mr. David LORD
12 Dir Williamson Campus Operations .... Ms. Rita G. ROBERSON
12 Director Logan Campus Operations .... Mr. Randy SKEENS
12 Director Boone Campus Operations .... Mr. William COOK
50 Division Head HealthCare & Business .... Mr. Steven HALL
88 Div Head Applied & Industrial Tech .... Mr. Guy LOWES, JR.
88 Div Head NonTrad & Cross Over Pgm .... Mr. Steven LACEK
88 Div Head University Transfer .... Ms. Melinda D. SAUNDERS
06 Interim Registrar .... Ms. Teri WELLS
37 Dir Student Financial Assistance .... Mr. August KAFER
08 Director of Libraries .... Ms. Kimberly L. MAYNARD
96 Director of Purchasing .... Vacant
84 Dir Enroll Mgmt/Stdnt Engagement .... Mr. Darrell TAYLOR
88 Public Relations Specialist .... Ms. Carol A. COLE
22 Dir Affirmative Action/EEO .... Ms. Debbie C. DINGESS
44 Director Annual or Planned Giving .... Mr. Ronald E. LEMON
26 Public Relations Specialist .... Ms. Carol COLE
101 Secretary of the Institution/Board .... Ms. Emma L. BAISDEN

*West Virginia Northern Community College (G)

1704 Market Street, Wheeling WV 26003-3643
County: Ohio　FICE Identification: 009054
Unit ID: 238014
Telephone: (304) 233-5900　Carnegie Class: Assoc/Pub-R-M
FAX Number: (304) 232-4651　Calendar System: Semester
URL: www.wvncc.edu
Established: 1972　Annual Undergrad Tuition & Fees (In-State): $3,360
Enrollment: 1,292　Coed
Affiliation or Control: State　IRS Status: 501(c)3
Highest Offering: Associate Degree
Program: Occupational; 2-Year Principally Bachelor's Creditable
Accreditation: NH, ACFEI, ADNUR, CAHIIM, #COARC, MAC, RAD, SURGT

02 President .... Dr. Vicki RILEY
05 Vice President Academic Affairs .... Dr. Carry DEATLEY
10 CFO & VP Administrative Services .... Mr. Stephen LIPPIELLO
32 Vice President Student Services .... Mrs. Janet FIKE
31 Dean Community Relations .... Mr. Robert DEFRANCIS
18 Director of Facilities .... Mr. Jim BALLER
15 Chief Human Resource Officer .... Mrs. Peggy CARMICHAEL
12 Dean New Martinsville & Weirton .... Mr. Larry TACKETT
35 Director Student Union Activities .... Mrs. Shannon PAYTON

*New River Technical College Greenbrier Valley Campus (H)

101 Church Street, Lewisburg WV 24901-1303
Telephone: (304) 647-6560　Identification: 770468
Accreditation: &NH

† Branch campus of New River Community and Technical College, Beaver, WV.

*New River Technical College Mercer County Campus (I)

1397 Stafford Drive, Princeton WV 24740-8230
Telephone: (304) 818-2009　Identification: 770469
Accreditation: &NH

† Branch campus of New River Community and Technical College, Beaver, WV.

*New River Technical College Nicholas County Campus (J)

6101 Webster Road, Summersville WV 26651
Telephone: (304) 872-1236　Identification: 770470
Accreditation: &NH

† Branch campus of New River Community and Technical College, Beaver, WV.

*Southern West Virginia Community and Technical College-Boone/Lincoln Campus (K)

3505 Daniel Boone Parkway, Suite A,
Foster WV 25608-8126
Telephone: (304) 369-2952　Identification: 770471
Accreditation: &NH

† Branch campus of Southern West Virginia Community and Technical College, Mount Gay, WV.

*Southern West Virginia Community and Technical College-Williamson Campus (L)

1601 Armory Drive, Williamson WV 25661
Telephone: (304) 235-6046　Identification: 770473
Accreditation: &NH

† Branch campus of Southern West Virginia Community and Technical College, Mount Gay, WV.

*Southern West Virginia Community and Technical College-Wyoming/McDowell Campus (M)

128 College Drive, Saulsville WV 25876
Telephone: (304) 294-8346　Identification: 770472
Accreditation: &NH

† Branch campus of Southern West Virginia Community and Technical College, Mount Gay, WV.

* West Virginia Northern Community College (A)

141 Main Street, New Martinsville WV 26155
Telephone: (304) 455-4684 Identification: 770474
Accreditation: &NH

† Branch campus of West Virginia Northern Community College, Wheeling, WV.

* West Virginia Northern Community College (B)

150 Park Avenue, Weirton WV 26062
Telephone: (304) 723-2210 Identification: 770475
Accreditation: &NH

---

* West Virginia Higher Education Policy Commission (C)

1018 Kanawha Boulevard E, Ste 700,
Charleston WV 25301-2887
County: Kanawha FICE Identification: 033440
Unit ID: 237941
Telephone: (304) 558-2101 Carnegie Class: N/A
FAX Number: (304) 558-5719
URL: www.hepc.wvnet.edu

01 Chancellor Dr. Paul L. HILL
05 Int Chancellor Community College Dr. Sarah TUCKER
88 Interim Program Director Dr. Jan TAYLOR
26 Senior Director of Communications Ms. Jessica TICE
20 Vice Chancellor for Academic Affs Dr. Corley DENNISON
10 Vice Chancellor for Finance Dr. Edward MAGEE
32 Vice Chancellor for Student Affairs Dr. Adam GREEN
45 Vice Chancellor Policy and Planning Dr. Neal HOLLY
15 Vice Chancellor for Human Resources Ms. Trish CLAY
43 General Counsel Mr. Bruce R. WALKER
11 Exec Vice Chancellor Administration Mr. Matt TURNER
35 Dir Student/Educational Services Mr. Daniel E. CROCKETT
37 Senior Director of Financial Aid Mr. Brian WEINGART
88 Director Administrative Services Ms. Cindy L. ANDERSON

* Bluefield State College (D)

219 Rock Street, Bluefield WV 24701-2198
County: Mercer FICE Identification: 003809
Unit ID: 237215
Telephone: (304) 327-4000 Carnegie Class: Bac/Diverse
FAX Number: (304) 325-7747 Calendar System: Semester
URL: www.bluefieldstate.edu
Established: 1895 Annual Undergrad Tuition & Fees (In-State): $6,120
Enrollment: 1,563 Coed
Affiliation or Control: State IRS Status: 501(c)3
Highest Offering: Baccalaureate
Program: Liberal Arts And General; Teacher Preparatory
Accreditation: NH, ACBSP, ADNUR, ENGT, NURSE, RAD, TED

02 President Dr. Marsha V. KROTSENG
05 Vice Pres Academic Affs/Provost Dr. Zakir HOSSAIN
10 Vice Pres Financial/Admin Affairs Ms. Shelia JOHNSON
32 Vice President Student Affairs Dr. JoAnn ROBINSON
04 Dir Inst/Media Rels/Asst to Pres Mr. James A. NELSON
88 Interim Executive Dir Title III Dr. Guy SIMS
06 Registrar Ms. Terry THOMPSON
08 Director Library Services Ms. Joanna THOMPSON
24 Interim Chief Technology Officer Mr. Tom G. COOK
13 Director of Computer Services Mr. Tom G. COOK
36 Director of Placement Mr. Thomas HARRISON
07 Director of Admissions Mr. Kenneth MANDEVILLE
37 Director of Financial Aid Mr. Thomas ILSE
15 Director of Human Resources Ms. Jonette AUGHENBAUGH
18 Admin Asst Senior of Physical Plant Ms. Diana GIBSON
19 Director Public Safety Vacant
09 Director of Institutional Research Dr. Tracey ANDERSON
38 Director of Counseling Dr. Cravor JONES
29 Director Alumni Affairs Ms. Deirdre GUYTON
40 Manager Bookstore Ms. Virginia RICHARDSON
41 Athletic Director Mr. Terry BROWN
50 Dean School of Business Dr. John SNEAD
49 Dean School of Arts and Sciences Dr. Martha EBORALL
54 Dean School of Eng Tech/Comp Sci Dr. Shannon BOWLING
53 Dean School of Education Dr. Betsy STEENKEN
66 Dean School Nursing/Allied Health Ms. Angela LAMBERT
66 ADN Program Director Ms. Sandra WYNN
66 BSN Program Director Ms. Beth PRITCHETT
88 Program Dir of Radiologic Tech Ms. Melissa HAYE
61 Program Dir Criminal Justice Vacant
28 Asst to Pres Equity/Divers/Inclusn Dr. Guy SIMS
96 Director of Purchasing Mr. Paul RUTHERFORD
30 Director of Advancement/Planning Ms. Betty CARROLL

* Concord University (E)

PO Box 1000, Athens WV 24712-1000
County: Mercer FICE Identification: 003810
Unit ID: 237330
Telephone: (304) 384-3115 Carnegie Class: Bac/Diverse
FAX Number: (304) 384-9044 Calendar System: Semester
URL: www.concord.edu
Established: 1872 Annual Undergrad Tuition & Fees (In-State): $6,744
Enrollment: 2,531 Coed
Affiliation or Control: State IRS Status: 501(c)3
Highest Offering: Master's
Program: Liberal Arts And General; Teacher Preparatory; Professional
Accreditation: NH, CAATE, SW, TED

02 President Dr. Kendra BOGGESS
05 VP & Academic Dean Dr. Peter VISCUSI
30 VP for Advancement Mrs. Alicia BESENYEI
20 Associate Dean Dr. Cheryl BARNES
32 VP Student Affairs Dr. Marjie FLANIGAN
10 VP for Business & Finance Dr. Charles P. BECKER
11 VP of Administration Mr. Rick DILLON
06 Registrar Mrs. Carolyn COX
08 Director of Libraries Mrs. Connie SHUMATE
37 Director of Student Financial Aid Mrs. Debra TURNER
29 Director of Alumni Relations Ms. Sarah TURNER
88 Director Bonner Scholars Program Mrs. Kathy BALL
13 Chief Technology Officer Mr. Charles ELLIOTT
15 Human Resources Director Mr. Daniel FITZPATRICK
18 Director Physical Plant Mr. Gerry VONVILLE
19 Director of Public Safety Chief Mark STELLA
36 Director of Career Services Vacant
38 Director of Counseling Mr. David BAILEY
40 Bookstore Manager Mr. Randy JONES
41 Athletic Director Mr. Kevin GARRETT
21 Financial Reporting Officer Ms. Elizabeth J. CAHILL
09 Director of Institutional Research Vacant
24 Ctr for Academic Technologies Mr. Steve MEADOWS
26 Public Relations/Mktg Specialist Mr. Lance MCDANIEL
25 Director of Grants and Contracts Mrs. Melanie FARMER
12 Director of the Beckley Center Dr. Susan WILLIAMS
96 Contract Specialist Mr. Gary HYLTON
88 Director of Retention Ms. Sarah BEASLEY
88 Administrative Secretary to Pres Mrs. Trena STOVALL
04 Executive Secretary to President Mrs. Lora WOOLWINE
07 Director of Admissions Vacant
102 Dir Foundation/Corporate Relations Mrs. Casie JUSTICE
39 Director Student Housing Mr. Bill FRALEY

* Fairmont State University (F)

1201 Locust Avenue, Fairmont WV 26554-2470
County: Marion FICE Identification: 003812
Unit ID: 237367
Telephone: (304) 367-4000 Carnegie Class: Master's S
FAX Number: (304) 367-4789 Calendar System: Semester
URL: www.fairmontstate.edu
Established: 1865 Annual Undergrad Tuition & Fees (In-State): $6,306
Enrollment: 4,035 Coed
Affiliation or Control: State IRS Status: 501(c)3
Highest Offering: Master's
Program: Liberal Arts And General; Teacher Preparatory; Business Emphasis
Accreditation: NH, ACBSP, ADNUR, ENGR, ENGT, NURSE, TED

02 President FSU Dr. Maria C. ROSE
05 Provost/VP Academic Affairs Dr. Christina M. LAVORATA
10 Vice Pres Admin & Fiscal Affairs Mr. Enrico A. PORTO
13 VP/Chief Information Officer Mr. John LYMPANY
32 Vice Pres Student Services Ms. Kaye WIDNEY
108 VP Inst Assessment & Effectiveness Mr. Van DEMPSEY
04 Executive Asst to the President Ms. Judith E. BIAFORE
20 Assoc Provost for Academic Affs Dr. Jack R. KIRBY
26 AVP University Communications Ms. Ann B. BOOTH
18 Asst Vice Pres for Facilities Mr. Tom T. TUCKER
15 AVP for Human Resources Mrs. Cynthia S. CURRY
06 Registrar Ms. Evie BRANTMAYER
49 Dean College of Liberal Arts Dr. Deanna J. SHIELDS
72 Int Dean College of Science/Tech Dr. Donald E. TRISEL
50 Dean School of Business Dr. Richard C. HARVEY
53 Int Dean School Educ/Hlth/Hum Perf Dr. Carolyn CRISLIP-TACY
57 Int Dean School of Fine Arts Dr. Robert E. MILD
66 Dean School of Nursing Dr. Sharon BONI
07 Director of Admissions/Recruitment Mr. Amie M. FAZALARE
29 Director Alumni Relations Ms. Emily L. SWAIN
91 Dir of Applications Develop Svcs Mr. Andy RAISOVICH
41 Director of Athletics Mr. Timothy A. MCNEELY
19 Dir of Emerg Mgmt/Chief of Police Mr. Jack A. CLAYTON
38 Dir of Counseling and Disab Srvs Ms. Andrea M. PAMMER
37 Dir Financial Aid/Scholarships Ms. Tresa WEIMER
39 Interim Director of Housing Mr. Timothy S. RICE
08 Director of Library Services Ms. Thelma J. HUTCHINS
96 Director of Procurement Ms. Monica J. COCHRAN
27 Director of Public Relations Ms. Amy E. PELLEGRIN
36 Director of Student Development Ms. Sally V. FRY
90 Director of Solutions Center Ms. Joanie RAISOVICH
23 Director of Student Health Services Ms. Trish WATSON

* Glenville State College (G)

200 High Street, Glenville WV 26351-1292
County: Gilmer FICE Identification: 003813
Unit ID: 237385
Telephone: (304) 462-7361 Carnegie Class: Bac/Diverse
FAX Number: (304) 462-7610 Calendar System: Semester
URL: www.glenville.edu
Established: 1872 Annual Undergrad Tuition & Fees (In-State): $7,032
Enrollment: 1,802 Coed
Affiliation or Control: State IRS Status: 501(c)3
Highest Offering: Baccalaureate
Program: Liberal Arts And General; Teacher Preparatory
Accreditation: NH, TED

02 President Dr. Peter B. BARR
05 Int VP Academic Affairs Dr. Milan C. VAVREK
10 Exec Vice Pres Business & Finance Mr. Robert O. HARDMAN, II
26 Sr Vice Pres for External Relations Mr. James W. SPEARS
30 VP Advancement/Exec Dir GSC Found Mr. Dennis J. POUNDS
84 Assoc Vice President of Enrollment Mr. C. Gregory KING
32 Dean of Student Life Mr. D. Duane CHAPMAN
04 Executive Assistant to President Ms. Teresa G. STERNS
53 Dean of Teacher Education Dr. Kevin G. CAIN
15 Chief Human Resources Officer Ms. Krystal D. SMITH
37 Director of Financial Aid Ms. Karen D. LAY
18 Exec Director of Physical Plant Mr. Thomas R. RATLIFF
39 Director of Residence Life Mr. Jerry L. BURKHAMMER
41 Director of Athletics Ms. Janet K. BAILEY
23 Director Campus Health Services Ms. Ronda L. WILLIAMS
08 Director of Library Ms. Gail L. WESTBROOK
21 Controller Mr. Richard D. ACCORD
96 Director of Purchasing Ms. Joyce E. RIDDLE
29 Director of Alumni Affairs Ms. Debra A. NAGY
35 Director of Student Activities Ms. Jodi WALTERS
06 Registrar Ms. Ann M. REED
13 Manager of Database Admin Mr. Neal L. BENSON
36 Career Services Counselor Ms. Joanna M. DISTEFANO
38 Professional Counselor Mr. Timothy J. UNDERWOOD
07 Director of Admissions Ms. Ashley M. WEIR
19 Associate Director of Public Safety Mr. Ronald K. TAYLOR

* Marshall University (H)

1 John Marshall Drive, Huntington WV 25755-0001
County: Cabell FICE Identification: 003815
Unit ID: 237525
Telephone: (304) 696-3170 Carnegie Class: Master's L
FAX Number: (304) 696-6565 Calendar System: Semester
URL: www.marshall.edu
Established: 1837 Annual Undergrad Tuition & Fees (In-State): $6,814
Enrollment: 13,390 Coed
Affiliation or Control: State IRS Status: 501(c)3
Highest Offering: Doctorate
Program: Occupational; 2-Year Principally Bachelor's Creditable; Liberal Arts And General; Teacher Preparatory; Professional
Accreditation: NH, ADNUR, ANEST, BUS, BUSA, CAATE, CAHIIM, CLPSY, COARC, CYTO, DIETD, DIETI, ENG, ENGR, FEPAC, JOUR, MED, MLTAD, MT, MUS, NUR, @PHAR, PTA, SP, SW, TED

02 Interim President Mr. Gary WHITE
05 Provost/Sr VP Academic Affairs Dr. Gayle L. ORMISTON
43 Sr VP/Exec Affairs & Gen Counsel Mr. F. Layton COTTRILL
10 Sr VP Finance/CFO Ms. Mary Ellen HEUTON
26 Senior VP Communication/Marketing Ms. Virginia R. PAINTER
63 Dean of Medicine Dr. Joseph I. SHAPIRO
102 CEO MU Foundation Inc Dr. Ron AREA
11 Sr VP for Administration Ms. Brandi D. JACOBS
46 VP Research Mr. John MAHER
53 Dean College of Education Dr. Teresa EAGLE
29 Executive Director Alumni Relations Mr. Matthew D. HAYES
13 VP Information Technology/CIO Dr. Jan I. FOX
44 Vice President Development Mr. Lance WEST
28 Assoc VP Intercultural Affairs Mr. Maurice R. COOLEY
14 Chief Technical Officer Mr. Allen TAYLOR
07 Dir Admission Undergrad/Grad Pgms Ms. Tammy JOHNSON
32 Interim Dean Student Affairs Ms. Carla LAPELLE
106 Asst VP for OnLine learning Lib/IT Ms. Monica BROOKS
58 Interim Dean Graduate College Dr. David PITTENGER
49 Dean College Liberal Arts Dr. Robert BOOKWALTER
50 Dean College of Business Dr. Haiyang CHEN
57 Dean College of Arts & Media Mr. Donald L. VAN HORN
67 Dean School of Pharmacy Dr. Kevin W. YINGLING
66 Dean College of Health Prof Dr. Michael PREWITT
54 Dean Col of Info Tech/Engr Dr. Wael ZATAR
81 Dean College of Science Dr. Charles SOMERVILLE
41 Director of Athletics Mr. Mike HAMRICK
06 Registrar Ms. Roberta FERGUSON
37 Director Student Financial Aid Ms. Kathy BIALK
36 Director Career Services Ms. Denise HOGSETT
15 Director Human Resource Services Mr. Bruce B. FELDER
19 Director of Public Safety Mr. James E. TERRY
96 Director of Purchasing Ms. Stephanie SMITH
18 Director of Physical Plant Mr. Mark CUTLIP
39 Director Residence Services Mr. John YAUN
09 Asst to the Pres/Dir Inst Rsch/Plng Mr. Michael J. MCGUFFEY
85 Dir Ctr for Intl Programs Dr. Michael SCHMELZLE
40 Manager of Bookstore Mr. Mike CAMPBELL
22 Director Equity Programs Ms. Debra HART
88 Director Recruitment Ms. Elizabeth WOLFE

* Shepherd University (I)

PO Box 5000, Shepherdstown WV 25443-5000
County: Jefferson FICE Identification: 003822
Unit ID: 237792
Telephone: (304) 876-5000 Carnegie Class: Master's S
FAX Number: (304) 876-3101 Calendar System: Semester
URL: www.shepherd.edu
Established: 1871 Annual Undergrad Tuition & Fees (In-State): $6,830
Enrollment: 4,041 Coed
Affiliation or Control: State IRS Status: 501(c)3
Highest Offering: Doctorate
Program: Liberal Arts And General; Teacher Preparatory
Accreditation: NH, IACBE, MUS, NRPA, NURSE, SW, TED

02 Interim President Dr. Sylvia MANNING
05 Vice President Academic Affairs Dr. Christopher AMES
10 Vice President Finance/CFO Ms. Anna BARKER

32 Vice President Student Affairs ... Dr. Thomas SEGAR
30 Vice Pres of Advancement ... Dr. Diane MELBY
84 Vice President Enrollment Mgmt ... Dr. Shari PAYNE
43 General Counsel ... Mr. K. Alan PERDUE
100 Chief of Staff ... Vacant
11 Vice President Administration ... Mr. James VIGIL
35 Asst VP Stdnt Aff/Student Success ... Vacant
81 Dean Sch of Natural Sciences/Math ... Dr. Colleen NOLAN
79 Dean School of Arts & Humanities ... Mr. Dow BENEDICT
50 Dean Sch of Bus/Social Sciences ... Dr. Ann M. LEGREID
53 Dean Sch Educ/Profess Studies ... Dr. Virginia HICKS
58 AVPAA/Dean Grad Studies/Cont Ed ... Dr. Scott BEARD
88 Dean Teaching & Learning ... Dr. Laura RENNINGER
26 Exec Director Univ Communications ... Ms. Valerie OWENS
09 Director Institutional Research ... Ms. Sara MAENE
39 Director Residence Life ... Ms. Elizabeth SECHLER
21 Director of Finance ... Ms. Rebecca STOTTLEMEYER
35 Asst VP Student Aff/Student Engage ... Ms. Holly FRYE
15 Director Human Resources ... Dr. Marie DEWALT
13 Director Info Technology Services ... Mr. Joey DAGG
06 Registrar ... Ms. Tracy SEFFERS
07 Director of Admissions ... Ms. Kristen DESANTIS
37 Director of Financial Aid ... Vacant
19 Univ Police Chief ... Mr. John MCAVOY
53 Director Teacher Education ... Dr. Douglas KENNARD
18 Assistant Director of Facilities ... Vacant
41 Athletics Director ... Mr. BJ PUMROY
96 Director of Procurement Services ... Ms. Debra LANGFORD
38 Director Student Counseling ... Ms. Shanan SPENCER
29 Director Alumni Relations ... Ms. Alexis REED
92 Director Honors Program ... Dr. Mark CANTRELL
44 Director Annual Giving ... Ms. Julia KRALL
104 Director Study Abroad ... Ms. Ann HENRIKSSON
25 Director of Grant Support ... Mr. Charles BLACHFORD

*West Liberty University (A)

208 University Drive, West Liberty WV 26074
County: Ohio FICE Identification: 003823
Unit ID: 237932
Telephone: (304) 336-5000 Carnegie Class: Bac/Diverse
FAX Number: (304) 336-8403 Calendar System: Semester
URL: www.westliberty.edu
Established: 1837 Annual Undergrad Tuition & Fees (In-State): $6,702
Enrollment: 2,694 Coed
Affiliation or Control: State IRS Status: 501(c)3
Highest Offering: Master's
Program: Liberal Arts And General; Teacher Preparatory; Professional; Business Emphasis
Accreditation: NH, ARCPA, DH, IACBE, MT, MUS, NURSE, SW, TED

02 Interim President ... Dr. John P. MCCULLOUGH
05 Vice Provost ... Vacant
43 Vice President & General Counsel ... Vacant
10 Vice President of Finance ... Ms. Stephanie L. HOOPER
32 VP of Student Services/Registrar ... Mr. Scott A. COOK
10 Executive VP & CFO ... Mr. John E. WRIGHT
11 Provost ... Dr. Brian CRAWFORD
81 Dean College of Sciences ... Dr. Robert KREISBERG
49 Interim Dean College Liberal Arts ... Dr. Tammy MCCLAIN
57 Interim Dean College Arts & Comm ... Dr. Matthew HARDER
53 Dean College of Education ... Dr. Keely O. CAMDEN
66 Dir of Nursing Programs ... Dr. Rose KUTLENIOS
50 Interim Dean College of Business ... Ms. Jean A. BAILEY
35 Assoc Dean Student Services ... Ms. Marcella SNYDER
15 Vice President of Human Resources ... Vacant
13 Chief Technology Officer ... Mr. James T. CLARK
09 Dir of Inst Research & Assessment ... Ms. Paula J. TOMASIK
41 Director of Athletics ... Dr. Aaron C. HUFFMAN
07 Exec Dir of Admissions/Recruitment ... Ms. Brenda M. KING
51 Director of Cont Educ/Special Pgm ... Vacant
08 Director of Library ... Ms. Cheryl R. HARSHMAN
29 Exec Dir of Alumni/Cmty Relations ... Vacant
37 Director Student Financial Aid ... Mrs. Katie COOPER
30 VP of Institutional Advancement ... Mr. Jason W. KOEGLER
109 Director of Auxiliary Services ... Vacant
18 Chief of Operations ... Mr. Patrick J. HENRY
38 Director of Counseling ... Ms. Bridgette DAWSON
92 Director of the Honors Program ... Dr. Shannon HALICKI
88 Director Dental Hygiene Programs ... Ms. Margaret J. SIX
88 Dir Clinical Lab Science Program ... Dr. William C. WAGENER
21 Associate Business Officer ... Ms. Cindy R. MCGEE
23 Director of Health Services ... Ms. Cheryl BENNINGTON
88 Director Physican Assistant Program ... Dr. William A. CHILDERS, JR.
85 Coord International Student Rec ... Ms. Mihaela A. SZABO
26 Executive Director of Marketing ... Ms. Tammi SECRIST
101 Secretary of the Institution/Board ... Ms. Mary A. EDWARDS
104 Director Study Abroad ... Vacant
105 Director Web Services ... Ms. Whitney INKSTER
106 Dir Online Education/E-learning ... Ms. Ann ROSE
19 Director Security/Safety ... Vacant
39 Director Student Housing ... Ms. Marcella SNYDER
96 Director of Purchasing ... Ms. Katrina HYDE

*West Virginia School of Osteopathic Medicine (B)

400 N Lee Street, Lewisburg WV 24901-1196
County: Greenbrier FICE Identification: 011245
Unit ID: 237880
Telephone: (304) 645-6270 Carnegie Class: Spec/Med
FAX Number: (304) 645-4859 Calendar System: Semester
URL: www.wvsom.edu
Established: 1972 Annual Graduate Tuition & Fees: $20,450
Enrollment: 817 Coed
Affiliation or Control: State IRS Status: 501(c)3
Highest Offering: First Professional Degree; No Undergraduates
Program: Professional
Accreditation: NH, OSTEO

02 President ... Dr. Michael D. ADELMAN
05 Vice Pres Academic Affairs & Dean ... Dr. Craig BOISVERT
10 Vice Pres Finance & Facilities ... Mr. Larry WARE
11 Vice Pres for Administration ... Dr. James W. NEMITZ
15 Associate VP of Human Resources ... Ms. Leslie BICKSLER
100 Associate VP Administrative Affairs ... Ms. Marilea BUTCHER
43 General Counsel ... Mr. Jeffrey SHAWVER
04 Administrative Assistant Senior ... Ms. Marietta CHANEY
20 Assoc Dean Osteopathic Medical Educ ... Dr. Robert W. FOSTER
20 Assoc Dean Graduate Med Education ... Dr. Victoria SHUMAN
20 Assoc Dean Preclinical Education ... Dr. John SCHRIEFER
20 Assoc Dean Predoctoral Clin Educ ... Dr. George BOXWELL
108 Assoc Dean Assessment/Educ Devel ... Dr. Machelle LINSENMEYER
20 Assoc Dean Affiliated/Spons Pgms ... Dr. Malcolm MODRZAKOWSKI
88 Medical Director ... Dr. Steve HALM
88 Exec Dir Clinical Evaluation Ctr ... Ms. Stephanie SCHULER
88 Director National Boards Office ... Dr. Robert FISK
13 Director Information Technology ... Ms. Kimberly RANSOM
32 Director of Student Affairs ... Dr. Rebecca MORROW
06 Registrar ... Ms. Jennifer SEAMS
37 Director Financial Aid ... Ms. Sharon L. HOWARD
30 Director Institutional Development ... Ms. Heather ANTOLINI
29 Director Alumni Relations ... Ms. Shannon WARREN
07 Director of Admissions ... Ms. Patricia PERKINS
08 Director of Library ... Ms. Mary ESSIG
26 Director of Marketing and PR ... Ms. Amy GOETZ
24 Director of Media Services ... Mr. Richard MCMAHAN
18 Director of Physical Plant II ... Mr. William ALDER
40 Business Manager/Bookstore ... Ms. Cindi KNIGHT

*West Virginia State University (C)

PO Box 1000, Institute WV 25112-1000
County: Kanawha FICE Identification: 003826
Unit ID: 237899
Telephone: (304) 766-3000 Carnegie Class: Bac/A&S
FAX Number: (304) 720-2075 Calendar System: Semester
URL: www.wvstateu.edu
Established: 1891 Annual Undergrad Tuition & Fees (In-State): $6,662
Enrollment: 2,847 Coed
Affiliation or Control: State IRS Status: 501(c)3
Highest Offering: Master's
Program: Liberal Arts And General; Teacher Preparatory
Accreditation: NH, ACBSP, SW, TED

02 President ... Dr. Brian O. HEMPHILL
10 VP for Business and Finance ... Dr. William H. FEATHERSTONE
05 Provost and VP for Academic Affairs ... Dr. Kumara JAYASURIYA
09 Coord Institutional Research ... Dr. Danny R. CANTRELL
32 Vice President for Student Affairs ... Ms. Katherine MCCARTHY
30 VP for University Advancement ... Ms. Patricia J. SCHUMANN
20 Assoc Provost & Assoc VP Acad Affs ... Dr. T. Ramon STUART
35 Asst Vice Pres Student Affairs ... Mr. Joseph ODEN, JR.
26 Asst VP Univ/Legislation Rels ... Mr. Thomas BENNETT, II
86 VP for Research & Public Service ... Dr. Orlando F. MCMEANS
100 Chief of Staff Spec Asst to Pres ... Ms. Ashley SCHUMAKER
79 Dean Col of Arts & Humanities ... Dr. Scott WOODARD
81 Int Dean Col of Natural Sci/Math ... Dr. Naveed ZAMAN
107 Dean Col of Prof Studies ... Dr. Paige CARNEY
50 Dean Col of Bus Admin/Soc Sci ... Dr. David BEJOU
27 Director of Public Relations ... Mr. Jack BAILEY
13 Director of Information Technology ... Mr. Alan SKIDMORE
09 Actg Dir of Inst Research/Effective ... Mr. Tom BENNETT
18 Director Physical Facilities ... Mr. Marvin SMITH
06 Director Records & Registration ... Ms. Donna L. HUNTER
19 Director of Public Safety ... Chief Joseph SAUNDERS
21 Int Asst VP for Business and Fin ... Ms. Kristi WILLIAMS
08 Director of Drain-Jordan Library ... Dr. Willette STINSON
37 Director of Student Financial Asst ... Ms. JoAnn L. ROSS
29 Director of Alumni Relations ... Ms. Belinda FULLER
15 Director of Human Resources ... Ms. Joyce CHANEY
36 Dir of Career Services & Coop Educ ... Ms. Sandhya (Sandy) G. MAHARAJ
07 Director of Admissions ... Ms. Amanda ANDERSON
88 Director of New Student Programs ... Mrs. Sharon S. BANKS
96 Director of Purchasing ... Mrs. Janis A. BENNETT
106 Dir of Center for Online Learning ... Dr. Thomas KIDDIE
41 Athletic Director ... Mr. Sean LOYD
04 Executive Asst to the President ... Ms. Crystal WALKER

*West Virginia University (D)

1500 University Avenue, Morgantown WV 26506-0002
County: Monongalia FICE Identification: 003827
Unit ID: 238032
Telephone: (304) 293-0111 Carnegie Class: RU/H
FAX Number: (304) 293-5883 Calendar System: Semester
URL: www.wvu.edu
Established: 1867 Annual Undergrad Tuition & Fees (In-State): $7,632
Enrollment: 29,175 Coed
Affiliation or Control: State IRS Status: 501(c)3
Highest Offering: Doctorate
Program: Liberal Arts And General; Teacher Preparatory; Professional
Accreditation: NH, ART, AUD, BUS, BUSA, CAATE, CACREP, CLPSY, COPSY, CORE, CS, DENT, DH, DIETD, DIETI, DMS, ENG, ENGR, FEPAC, HT, IPSY, JOUR, LAW, LSAR, MED, MT, MUS, NMT, NURSE, OT, PA, PAST, PH, PHAR, PTA, RAD, RADMAG, RTT, SP, SPAA, SW, TED, THEA

02 President ... Mr. E. Gordon GEE
05 Provost & VP Acad Affairs ... Ms. Joyce MCCONNELL
10 Vice President for Admin & Finance ... Mr. Narvel G. WEESE, JR.
26 Vice Pres for University Relations ... Ms. Sharon L. MARTIN
17 Vice Pres & Ex Dean of Hlth Sci ... Dr. Clay B. MARSH
32 Vice President Student Affairs ... Dr. William SCHAFER
46 Vice President for Research ... Mr. Fred L. KING
102 President & CEO WVU Found ... Ms. Cindi ROTH
15 Interim VP for Human Resources ... Mr. Narvel G. WEESE, JR.
58 Vice Pres Health Sci Rsrch/Grad Ed ... Dr. Glen DILLON
20 Sr Assoc Provost Academic Affairs ... Dr. Russell K. DEAN
20 Assoc Provost Academic Personnel ... Dr. Cecil B. WILSON
88 Director Research & Rural Health ... Ms. Jodie JACKSON
100 VP Fed Relations & Sr Advis to Pres ... Mr. John J. COLE
88 Exec Officer for Policy Development ... Dr. Jennifer L. FISHER
43 VP Legal Affairs/General Counsel ... Mr. Rob ALSOP
21 Assoc VP & Chief Financial Officer ... Ms. Wendy L. KING
21 Sr Assoc Vice Pres for Finance ... Mr. Daniel A. DURBIN
56 Dean & Director of Extension Svcs ... Dr. Steve C. BONANNO
20 Assoc Provost Academic Programs ... Dr. Elizabeth A. DOOLEY
13 Assoc Provost IT/CIO ... Dr. John P. CAMPBELL
18 Sr Assoc VP Facilities & Svcs ... Mr. Randy HUDAK
35 Assoc Vice Pres Student Affairs ... Mr. Michael A. ELLINGTON
88 Asst VP Hlth Sci & Tech Academy ... Ms. Ann L. CHESTER
84 Interim Assoc VP Enroll Mgmt Svcs ... Mr. Stephen LEE
45 Assoc Vice Pres Planning & Treasury ... Ms. Elizabeth P. REYNOLDS
86 Assoc VP State/Corporate Relations ... Ms. Sarah A. SMITH
25 Asst VP Office of Research Admin ... Mr. Alan B. MARTIN
09 Director of Institutional Research ... Dr. Nicolas VALCIK
39 Director Res Life/Dean of Students ... Mr. G. Corey FARRIS
41 Director Intercollegiate Athletics ... Mr. Shane LYONS
23 Director of Health Services ... Dr. Jan E. PALMER
27 Asst VP News/Information Services ... Ms. Rebecca B. LOFSTEAD
29 Exec Director Alumni Association ... Mr. Stephen L. DOUGLAS
37 Director Financial Aid ... Ms. Sandra K. OERLY-BENNETT
07 Exec Director Admissions ... Dr. Stephen E. LEE
06 University Registrar ... Dr. Steve E. ROBINSON
08 Dean of Library Services ... Jon E. CAWTHORNE
38 Asst VP Student Wellness ... Dr. Catherine A. YURA
21 Director Financial Services ... Ms. Lisa A. LIVELY
19 Chief of Police/Univ Police Dept ... Capt. Bob E. ROBERTS
96 Dir Purchasing/Cont & Pay ... Ms. Brenda K. MOWEN
88 Assoc VP Intl & Global Outreach ... Dr. David C. STEWART
50 Interim Dean Business and Economics ... Dr. Nancy MCINTYRE
49 Interim Dean of Arts & Sciences ... Dr. Maryann REED
57 Dean College Creative Arts ... Dr. Paul K. KREIDER
53 Dean Educ & Human Resources ... Dr. Gypsy DENZINE
61 Dean of Law ... Mr. Gregory W. BOWMAN
63 Dean of Medicine ... Vacant
52 Dean of Dentistry ... Dr. Tom BORGIA
54 Dean of Engr/Mineral Resources ... Dr. Eugene V. CILENTO
47 Dean of Agriculture & Forestry ... Dr. Daniel J. ROBISON
67 Dean of Pharmacy ... Dr. Patricia A. CHASE
60 Dean of Journalism ... Dr. Maryanne REED
68 Dean Physical Education ... Dr. Dana D. BROOKS
66 Dean of Nursing ... Dr. Tara HULSEY
92 Dean of Honors College ... Mr. Kenneth P. BLEMINGS
88 Assoc VP Academic Innovation ... Dr. Susan D. DAY-PERROOTS
36 Director Career Services ... Mr. David L. DURHAM
88 Assoc Provost Intl Acad Affairs ... Dr. Michael LASTINGER
88 Assoc VP Acad Strategic Plng ... Dr. Nigel N. CLARK
88 Assoc Provost Grad Acad Affairs ... Dr. Katherine A. KARRAKER
35 Dean Students & Dir Housing ... Mr. G. Corey FARRIS
28 Chief Diversity Officer ... Mr. David M. FRYSON
105 Director Web Services ... Ms. Cathy ORNDORFF
106 Dir Online Education/E-learning ... Dr. Susan D. DAY-PERROOTS

*West Virginia University at Parkersburg (E)

300 Campus Drive, Parkersburg WV 26104-8647
County: Wood FICE Identification: 003828
Unit ID: 237686
Telephone: (304) 424-8000 Carnegie Class: Bac/Assoc
FAX Number: (304) 424-8315 Calendar System: Semester
URL: www.wvup.edu
Established: 1961 Annual Undergrad Tuition & Fees (In-State): $2,214
Enrollment: 2,985 Coed
Affiliation or Control: State IRS Status: 501(c)3
Highest Offering: Baccalaureate
Program: Occupational; 2-Year Principally Bachelor's Creditable; Liberal Arts And General; Teacher Preparatory
Accreditation: NH, ACBSP, ADNUR, SURGT, TED

02 President ... Dr. Fletcher LAMKIN
04 Executive Asst to the President ... Mr. Brady WHIPKEY
05 Sr Vice Pres of Academic Affairs ... Dr. Jane MILLEY
32 Vice President for Student Services ... Mr. Anthony UNDERWOOD
20 Dean for Academic Success ... Dr. Cinthia GISSY
103 Exec Dir Workforce/Community Educ ... Ms. Michele WILSON
10 Vice Pres Finance/Administration ... Ms. Alice HARRIS
26 Director Marketing/Communications ... Mrs. Katie WOOTTON
13 Chief Information Officer ... Mr. Doug ANTHONY
22 Special Asst to President ... Mrs. Debbie RICHARDS
12 Director Jackson County Center ... Mr. John GORRELL
102 Director of Development ... Ms. Senta GOUDY
18 Director Facilities & Services ... Mr. David WHITE

15 Director Human Resources ... Mr. Scott POE
09 Dir Inst Rsrch/Outcomes Assessment ... Mr. Jeremy STARKEY
06 Registrar ... Mrs. Leslie SIMS
07 Dean of Enrollment ... Mrs. Christine POST
37 Director of Financial Aid ... Mrs. Heather SKIDMORE
21 Director of Business Services ... Ms. Jeannine RATLIFFE
35 Director Student Activities ... Mr. Tom YENCHA
08 Director of Library ... Mr. Stephen HUPP
50 Chair Business/Economics/Math Div ... Dr. Larry MULLER
53 Chair Education/Humanities Division ... Dr. David LANCASTER
76 Chair Health Sciences Division ... Dr. Rose BEEBE
83 Chair Social Science/Languages Div ... Mrs. Kim KORCMAROS
72 Chair Science/Technology Division ... Mr. Jared GUMP

* *Marshall University-South Charleston Campus* (A)

100 Angus E Peyton Drive, South Charleston WV 25303
Telephone: (304) 746-2500 Identification: 770467
Accreditation: &NH

† Branch campus of Marshall University, Huntington, WV.

* *Potomac State College of West Virginia University* (B)

101 Fort Avenue, Keyser WV 26726
Telephone: (304) 788-6800 FICE Identification: 003829
Accreditation: &NH

† Branch campus of West Virginia University, Morgantown, WV.

* *West Virginia University Institute of Technology* (C)

405 Fayette Pike, Montgomery WV 25136-2436
Telephone: (304) 442-1000 FICE Identification: 003825
Accreditation: &NH, ENG, ENGT

† Branch campus of West Virginia University, Morgantown, WV.

West Virginia Junior College (D)

1000 Virginia Street East, Charleston WV 25301-2817
County: Kanawha FICE Identification: 010573
Unit ID: 237987
Telephone: (304) 345-2820 Carnegie Class: Assoc/PrivFP
FAX Number: (304) 345-1425 Calendar System: Quarter
URL: www.wvjc.edu
Established: 1892 Annual Undergrad Tuition & Fees: $12,625
Enrollment: 162 Coed
Affiliation or Control: Proprietary IRS Status: Proprietary
Highest Offering: Associate Degree
Program: 2-Year Principally Bachelor's Creditable
Accreditation: ACICS

01 Campus President ... Mr. Chad T. CALLEN

West Virginia Junior College (E)

148 Willey Street, Morgantown WV 26505-5596
County: Monongalia FICE Identification: 005007
Unit ID: 237996
Telephone: (304) 296-8282 Carnegie Class: Assoc/PrivFP
FAX Number: (304) 581-6990 Calendar System: Quarter
URL: www.wvjc.edu
Established: 1922 Annual Undergrad Tuition & Fees: $12,650
Enrollment: 333 Coed
Affiliation or Control: Proprietary IRS Status: Proprietary
Highest Offering: Associate Degree
Program: 2-Year Principally Bachelor's Creditable; Business Emphasis
Accreditation: ACICS

01 President & CEO ... Mr. Todd MATTHEWS
05 Academic Director ... Ms. Leanne CARDOSA
36 Career Services ... Ms. Elise POGORZELSKI
37 Financial Aid Director ... Ms. Patricia CALLEN

West Virginia Junior College-Bridgeport (F)

176 Thompson Drive, Bridgeport WV 26330
Telephone: (304) 842-4007 Identification: 770823
Accreditation: ACICS

† Branch campus of West Virginia Junior College, Charleston, WV.

West Virginia Wesleyan College (G)

59 College Avenue, Buckhannon WV 26201-2699
County: Upshur FICE Identification: 003830
Unit ID: 237969
Telephone: (304) 473-8000 Carnegie Class: Bac/Diverse
FAX Number: (304) 473-8187 Calendar System: Semester
URL: www.wvwc.edu
Established: 1890 Annual Undergrad Tuition & Fees: $28,792
Enrollment: 1,511 Coed
Affiliation or Control: United Methodist IRS Status: 501(c)3
Highest Offering: Master's
Program: Liberal Arts And General; Teacher Preparatory; Professional
Accreditation: NH, CAATE, MUS, NUR, TED

01 President ... Dr. Pamela BALCH
05 VP Academic Affairs & Dean of Col ... Dr. Boyd CREASMAN
10 VP Administration & Finance ... Dr. Barry PRITTS
32 VP Student Affairs ... Ms. Julia KEEHNER
84 VP Enrollment Management ... Mr. John WALTZ
30 VP Advancement ... Mr. Robert SKINNER
42 Dean of the Chapel ... Rev. Christopher SCOTT
102 Director Foundation/Govt Relations ... Ms. Nicki BENTLEY-COLTHART
11 Director of Administrative Services ... Mr. Robert KIMBLE
37 Director Financial Aid ... Ms. Susan GEORGE
29 Assoc VP Adv & Alumni Relations ... Mr. William ARMISTEAD
08 Director of Library Services ... Ms. Paula MCGREW
06 Dir Acad & Career Svcs/Registrar ... Ms. Alice CREASMAN
39 Director Campus Life & Housing ... Ms. Alisa LIVELY
09 Director of Institutional Research ... Ms. Tammy CRITES
15 Director of Human Resources ... Ms. Vickie CROWDER
18 Director of the Physical Plant ... Mr. Kenneth ANDREW
30 Director Advancement Operations ... Ms. Rose Ellen LOUDIN
88 Director of Learning Center ... Dr. Shawn KUBA
41 Director of Athletics ... Mr. Randall TENNEY
21 Controller ... Mr. Randall CRITES
40 Retail Store Manager ... Ms. Bethaney MCKISIC
92 Director Honors Program ... Mr. Douglas VAN GUNDY
93 Director Multicultural Programs ... Mr. Robert QUARLES
44 Planned Giving Coordinator ... Rev. David PETERS
38 Director of Counseling Services ... Ms. Lori THOMPSON
31 Dir of Leadership Development ... Ms. LeeAnn BROWN
13 Director of Computing Services ... Mr. Neil ROTH
23 Director of Health Services ... Ms. Angela MAHAFFEY
04 Administrative Asst to President ... Ms. Deborah K. MULLENS
19 Director of Security ... Vacant
43 Dir Legal Services/General Counsel ... Mr. David W. MCCAULEY

Wheeling Jesuit University (H)

316 Washington Avenue, Wheeling WV 26003-6295
County: Ohio FICE Identification: 003831
Unit ID: 238078
Telephone: (304) 243-2000 Carnegie Class: Bac/Diverse
FAX Number: (304) 243-2243 Calendar System: Semester
URL: www.wju.edu
Established: 1954 Annual Undergrad Tuition & Fees: $28,030
Enrollment: 1,575 Coed
Affiliation or Control: Roman Catholic IRS Status: 501(c)3
Highest Offering: Doctorate
Program: Liberal Arts And General; Teacher Preparatory; Professional; Nursing Emphasis
Accreditation: NH, ACBSP, CAATE, COARC, NMT, NURSE, PTA, TEAC

01 President ... Rev. James FLEMING, SJ
05 Chief Academic Officer ... Dr. Robert PHILLIPS
10 Chief Financial Officer/VP Admin ... Mr. Gene P. GRILLI
88 VP for Mission & Ministry ... Rev. William RICKLE, SJ
30 VP for Institutional Advancement ... Ms. Sarah KELLY
15 Dir of HR/Assoc VP Administration ... Mr. Don KAMINSKI
32 Dean for Student Development ... Ms. Christine OHL-GIGLIOTTI
58 Dean of Graduate & Professional Stu ... Mr. Chris PETROSINO
13 Assoc VP for Info Tech Services ... Mr. Daniel T. FEELEY
37 Director Financial Aid ... Ms. Christie L. TOMCZYK
21 Controller ... Mr. Stephen CRINITI
06 Registrar ... Ms. Joy CRONIN
08 Librarian ... Ms. Kelly MUMMERT
91 Systems Administrator ... Mr. Richard M. KLEMPA
42 Director of Campus Ministry ... Mr. Jamey BROGAN
41 Interim Athletic Director ... Mr. James REGAN
18 Director of Physical Plant ... Mr. Frank P. CONNELLY
85 Intl Admissions Representative ... Ms. Sunnie ENGLISH
04 Administrative Asst to President ... Ms. Mary Jo HABURSKY
100 Chief of Staff ... Mr. Mark PHILLIPS
102 Dir Foundation/Corporate Relations ... Ms. Jasmine LO
105 Director Web Services ... Mr. Christopher KREGER
106 Dir Online Education/E-learning ... Mr. D. Jason FRITZMAN
19 Director Security/Safety ... Mr. Stephen HABURSKY
29 Director Alumni Relations ... Ms. Kelly KLUBERT
38 Director Student Counseling ... Mr. Paul BELLOTTE
39 Director Student Housing ... Mr. Justin OWENS
07 Dean of Undergraduate Admissions ... Mr. Dustin JARRETT
44 Director Annual Giving ... Mr. Noah MULL

WISCONSIN

Alverno College (I)

3400 S 43rd Street, Box 343922, Milwaukee WI 53234-3922
County: Milwaukee FICE Identification: 003832
Unit ID: 238193
Telephone: (414) 382-6000 Carnegie Class: Master's S
FAX Number: (414) 382-6066 Calendar System: Semester
URL: www.alverno.edu
Established: 1887 Annual Undergrad Tuition & Fees: $25,660
Enrollment: 2,389 Female
Affiliation or Control: Independent Non-Profit IRS Status: 501(c)3
Highest Offering: Master's
Program: Liberal Arts And General; Teacher Preparatory; Professional
Accreditation: NH, MUS, NURSE, TED

01 President ... Dr. Mary J. MEEHAN
10 Sr Vice Pres Finance & Mgmt Svcs ... Mr. James OPPERMANN
05 Sr Vice Pres Academic Affairs ... Dr. Kathleen O'BRIEN
30 Vice President College Advancement ... Ms. Julie QUINLAN BRAME
20 Exec Director Academic Services ... Sr. Marlene NEISES
84 VP for Enrollment Services ... Ms. Kate LUNDEEN
32 Assoc VP/Dean of Students ... Dr. Wendy POWERS
07 Director of Admissions ... Vacant
20 Vice President for Student Success ... Dr. Kathy LAKE
20 Associate Vice President Academic ... Dr. Jeanna ABROMEIT
06 Registrar ... Ms. Patricia HARTMANN
08 Director Library ... Mr. Larry DUERR
36 Director Career Development ... Ms. Joanna PATTERSON
13 Exec Dir Information Technology ... Ms. Anita EIKENS
37 Dir Student Financial Plng ... Ms. Amy CHRISTEN
29 Director Alumnae Relations ... Ms. Mary FRIESEKE
38 Director Advising ... Ms. Katherine BUNDALO
51 Dir Institute Educational Outreach .. Ms. Judith REISETTER-HART
15 Director Human Resources ... Ms. Sharon WILCOX
41 Director of Athletics ... Mr. Brad DUCKWORTH
42 Campus Minister ... Ms. Connie POPP
96 Purchasing Agent ... Ms. Anne MCCARRON
09 Director of Institutional Research ... Dr. Glen ROGERS
14 Chief Information Officer ... Mr. Jim HILBY
50 Dean School of Business ... Dr. Eileen SHERMAN
66 Interim Dean School of Nursing ... Ms. Margaret RAUSCHENBERGER
53 Dean of School of Education ... Dr. Nancy ATHANASIOU
49 Dean School of Arts & Sciences ... Dr. Sandra GRAHAM
50 Director Master of Business Admin ... Dr. Patricia JENSEN
79 Assoc Dean Humanities Division ... Dr. John SAVAGIAN
81 Asc Dean Natl Science/Math/Tech Div ... Dr. Angela FREY
83 Assoc Dean Behavioral Sciences Div ... Dr. Julie ULLMAN
72 Assoc Dean Comm & Tech Div ... Dr. Jennifer MIKULAY
57 Assoc Dean Arts Div ... Dr. Kat GILBERT
28 Sp Asst to VP Acad Affs/Multclt Iss ... Dr. Celia JACKSON
04 Assistant to the President ... Ms. Jill DESMOND
101 Executive Assistant ... Ms. Melinda KALLENBERGER
18 Chief Facilities/Physical Plant ... Mr. John MARKS
19 Director Security/Safety ... Lt. Michelle ENGEL

The Art Institute of Wisconsin (J)

320 East Buffalo Street, Suite 100, Milwaukee WI 53202
Telephone: (877) 285-4234 Identification: 770824
Accreditation: ACICS

† Branch campus of The Art Institute of Phoenix, Phoenix, AZ.

Bellin College, Inc. (K)

3201 Eaton Road, Green Bay WI 54311
County: Brown FICE Identification: 006639
Unit ID: 238324
Telephone: (920) 433-6699 Carnegie Class: Spec/Health
FAX Number: (920) 433-1923 Calendar System: Semester
URL: www.bellincollege.edu
Established: 1909 Annual Undergrad Tuition & Fees: $21,128
Enrollment: 351 Coed
Affiliation or Control: Independent Non-Profit IRS Status: 501(c)3
Highest Offering: Master's
Program: Professional; Nursing Emphasis
Accreditation: NH, NURSE, RAD

01 President & CEO of the College ... Dr. Connie J. BOERST
10 Vice President Business & Finance ... Mrs. Ginger B. KRUMMEN SCHRAVE
05 Dean of Academic Affairs ... Dr. Stephanie M. STEWART
32 Dean of Student Services ... Dr. Nancy M. BURRUSS
30 Vice President Development & PR ... Mr. Matt G. RENTMEESTER
13 Director of Technology ... Mr. Lucas KOENIG
06 Registrar ... Mr. Russell J. LEARY
37 Director Financial Aid ... Ms. Lena C. GOODMAN
07 Director of Admissions ... Ms. Katie KLAUS
04 Administrative Asst to President ... Mrs. Ann P. WASMUND
08 Head Librarian ... Ms. Cindy REINL

Beloit College (L)

700 College Street, Beloit WI 53511-5595
County: Rock FICE Identification: 003835
Unit ID: 238333
Telephone: (608) 363-2000 Carnegie Class: Bac/A&S
FAX Number: (608) 363-2717 Calendar System: Semester
URL: www.beloit.edu
Established: 1846 Annual Undergrad Tuition & Fees: $45,050
Enrollment: 1,225 Coed
Affiliation or Control: Independent Non-Profit IRS Status: 501(c)3
Highest Offering: Baccalaureate
Program: Liberal Arts And General; Teacher Preparatory
Accreditation: NH

01 President ... Dr. Scott BIERMAN
05 Provost ... Dr. Ann DAVIES
100 Chief of Staff ... Mr. Daniel J. SCHOOFF
45 VP Budget & Planning ... Ms. Laurie STICKELMAIER
30 VP Development & Alumni Relations ... Ms. Beth MONTEIRO
15 VP Human Resources and Operations ... Ms. Lori RHEAD
84 VP Enrollment Management ... Dr. Robert MIRABILE
32 Dean of Students ... Dr. Christina KLAWITTER
08 Chief Information Officer ... Ms. Megan E. FITCH
26 Director of Communications ... Mr. Jason HUGHES
108 Dir Strategic Research & Assessment ... Ms. Ellie O'BYRNE
09 Dir Strategic Research & Planning ... Ms. Ruth VATER

06 Registrar ... Ms. Mary BOROS-KAZAI
07 Director of Enrollment Operations ... Ms. Lindsey DUERR
18 Director of Facilities Management ... Mr. Thomas VIEL
29 Sr Dir Annual Supp & Alumni/Parent ... Mr. Mark C. WOLD
39 Director Resident Life/Conferences ... Mr. John F. WINKELMANN
36 Director of Career Development ... Ms. Jessica FOX-WILSON
38 College Counselor ... Vacant
37 Dir of Student Financial Services ... Mr. Jonathan E. URISH
41 Athletic Director ... Mr. Tim SCHMIECHEN
28 Dir Intercult Pgm/Asst Dean Stdnts ... Mr. Cecil YOUNGBLOOD
40 Bookstore Director ... Mr. Peter FRONK

Brensten Education (A)

20633 Watertown Court, Waukesha WI 53186
County: Waukensha FICE Identification: 041379
Unit ID: 455424
Telephone: (262) 901-1389 Carnegie Class: Not Classified
FAX Number: (262) 832-0283 Calendar System: Semester
URL: www.bse.edu
Established: 1994 Annual Undergrad Tuition & Fees: $13,130
Enrollment: 453 Coed
Affiliation or Control: Proprietary IRS Status: Proprietary
Highest Offering: Associate Degree
Program: Occupational
Accreditation: CNCE

01 CEO/President ... James BRENT

Bryant & Stratton College (B)

310 W Wisconsin Avenue, Suite 500 E,
Milwaukee WI 53203
Telephone: (414) 276-5200 FICE Identification: 005009
Accreditation: &M, ADNUR, MAC

† Regional accreditation is carried under the parent institution (corporate office) in Buffalo, NY.

Cardinal Stritch University (C)

6801 N Yates Road, Milwaukee WI 53217-3985
County: Milwaukee FICE Identification: 003837
Unit ID: 238430
Telephone: (414) 410-4000 Carnegie Class: DRU
FAX Number: (414) 410-4239 Calendar System: Semester
URL: www.stritch.edu
Established: 1937 Annual Undergrad Tuition & Fees: $27,540
Enrollment: 3,811 Coed
Affiliation or Control: Roman Catholic IRS Status: 501(c)3
Highest Offering: Doctorate
Program: 2-Year Principally Bachelor's Creditable; Liberal Arts And General; Teacher Preparatory; Professional
Accreditation: NH, ACBSP, ADNUR, NUR, NURSE, TED

01 President ... Dr. James P. LOFTUS
00 Chancellor ... Vacant
04 Exec Assistant to the President ... Ms. Kathryn HOWELL
30 Vice President for Univ Advancement ... Dr. Robert J. BUCKLA
10 Vice President Business & Finance ... Ms. Tammy M. HOWARD
84 Vice President Enrollment Services ... Mr. Allan M. MITCHLER
13 Vice President Info Services/CIO ... Mr. Thomas J. RAINS
05 Vice President for Academic Affairs ... Dr. Jeffrey D. SENESE
66 Dean College of Nursing ... Dr. Kelly J. DRIES
50 Int Dean College of Business & Mgmt . Dr. Phillip T. ANDERSON
53 Dean College of Education & Ldrship ... Dr. Freda R. RUSSELL
49 Dean College of Arts & Sciences ... Dr. Daniel J. SCHOLZ
41 Director of Athletics ... Dr. Tim M. VAN ALSTINE
15 Director of Human Resources/Payroll ... Vacant
06 Registrar ... Ms. Kristin A. HILDEBRANDT
21 Bursar ... Ms. Lisa M. LEWIN
37 Dir of Financial Aid ... Mr. Mark W. QUISTORF
21 Dir Treasury & Risk Management ... Mr. Scott A. HELLRUNG
20 Director of Academic Affairs ... Ms. Kristin A. HILDEBRANDT
32 Sr Director Student Success ... Ms. Tracy A. FISCHER
88 Dir of Mission Engagement ... Mr. Sean T. LANSING
35 Dir Student Experience ... Vacant
36 Career Education ... Mr. Tom E. KIPP
38 Dir for Counseling/Mental Wellness ... Ms. Laura J. HEMPE
104 Coord International Education ... Ms. Sarah R. SWEENEY
09 Dir of Institutional Effectiveness ... Mr. William A. MARCOU
91 Director of Enterprise Systems ... Ms. Susan L. INGLES
08 Director of University Library .. Mr. David W. WEINBERG-KINSEY
102 Exec Dir Corporate & Foundation Rel ... MS. Tonya M. MANTILLA
44 Director Major Gifts/Planned Giving ... Mr. Chris J. LANGE
27 Sr Dir Media Relations Adv Comm ... Ms. Mary M. REINKE
29 Dir Alumni Relations/Annual Giving ... Ms. Corrine M. ANSHUS
18 Director of Facilities ... Mr. John B. GLYNN
19 Director of Security ... Mr. Andrew DE RUBERTIS

Carroll University (D)

100 N East Avenue, Waukesha WI 53186-5593
County: Waukesha FICE Identification: 003838
Unit ID: 238458
Telephone: (262) 547-1211 Carnegie Class: Master's S
FAX Number: (262) 524-7646 Calendar System: Semester
URL: www.carrollu.edu
Established: 1846 Annual Undergrad Tuition & Fees: $29,535
Enrollment: 3,481 Coed
Affiliation or Control: Presbyterian Church (U.S.A.) IRS Status: 501(c)3
Highest Offering: Doctorate
Program: Liberal Arts And General; Teacher Preparatory; Professional
Accreditation: NH, ARCPA, CAATE, NURSE, PTA

01 President ... Dr. Doug N. HASTAD
05 Provost ... Dr. Joanne PASSARO
10 Vice President for Finance ... Mr. Ron LOSTETTER
84 Vice President for Enrollment ... Mr. James V. WISEMAN
30 Vice President for Advancement ... Mr. Stephen KUHN
32 Vice President Student Affairs ... Dr. Theresa BARRY
06 Registrar ... Ms. Ann HANDFORD
21 Controller ... Ms. Deidre ERWIN
44 Sr Advancement Ofcr for Development ... Ms. Cherie SWENSON
26 Dir of Communications/Marketing ... Ms. Jeannine SHERMAN
15 Director of Human Resources ... Ms. Lorraine FORCINITO
08 Interim Library Director ... Ms. Brittany LARSON
37 Director of Student Financial Svcs ... Ms. Dawn M. SCOTT
41 Athletic Director ... Mr. Joe BAKER
88 Assoc Director of Part-Time Studies ... Ms. Linda SKLANDER
28 Director of Cultural Diversity ... Ms. Nicole LUCKETT
29 Director Alumni Relations ... Ms. Dolores M. BROWN
96 Director of Purchasing ... Ms. Char RICHARDS
07 Director of Admissions ... Ms. Kelly J. HEIMAN
18 Chief Facilities/Physical Plant ... Mr. Alan PESCHL
38 Director Student Counseling ... Ms. Angie R. BRANNAN
04 Exec Assistant to the President ... Ms. Gina M. EHLER

Carthage College (E)

2001 Alford Park Drive, Kenosha WI 53140-1994
County: Kenosha FICE Identification: 003839
Unit ID: 238476
Telephone: (262) 551-8500 Carnegie Class: Bac/A&S
FAX Number: (262) 551-6208 Calendar System: 4/1/4
URL: www.carthage.edu
Established: 1847 Annual Undergrad Tuition & Fees: $38,375
Enrollment: 3,004 Coed
Affiliation or Control: Evangelical Lutheran Church In America
IRS Status: 501(c)3
Highest Offering: Master's
Program: Liberal Arts And General; Teacher Preparatory
Accreditation: NH, CAATE, MUS, SW

01 President ... Dr. Gregory S. WOODWARD
100 Executive Director ... Ms. Karen HOWELL
05 Provost/VP Academic Affairs ... Dr. David GARCIA
20 Senior Associate Provost ... Dr. David STEEGE
06 Registrar ... Ms. Abby HEINRICHS
92 Director of Honors Program ... Dr. Paul ULRICH
36 Director Career Center ... Ms. Jean FREDERICK
108 Director Institutional Assessment ... Dr. Dana GARRIGAN
104 Study Abroad Director ... Dr. Erik KULKE
88 Chief Investment Officer ... Mr. William R. ABT
90 VP Academic Information Services ... Mr. Todd D. KELLEY
13 Director of Computer Center ... Mrs. Carol SABBAR
105 Dir Tech Integration & Infrastructr ... Mr. David ROBINSON
105 Director Online Communications ... Mrs. Elizabeth YOUNG
24 Director Media Services ... Mr. Mike LOVE
21 Associate VP for Business ... Mr. William D. HOARE
10 Chief Financial Officer ... Mr. Scot ECKER
41 Director of Athletics ... Dr. Robert R. BONN
40 Bookstore Manager ... Mrs. Pam ROBERS
18 Physical Plant Superintendent ... Mr. Dave PERTTULA
19 Director of Campus Security ... Mr. John KLABECHEK, IV
30 VP for Institutional Advancement ... Ms. Evelyn BUCHANAN
30 Assoc VP Institutional Advancement ... Ms. Elaine L. WALTON
29 Asst Director Advancement Programs ... Mrs. Mardell FISHER
44 Asst Dir Alumni/Parent Programs ... Ms. Lauren HANSEN
26 VP for Communications ... Ms. Molly POLK
84 VP for Enrollment ... Mr. Dean CLARK
37 Director Student Financial Aid ... Mr. Vatistas VATISTAS
07 Dean of Admissions ... Mr. Nick MULVEY
32 Dean Students/Assoc VP Student Life ... Mr. Jason RAMIREZ
35 Assoc Dean of Students ... Mr. Nick WINKLER
35 Asst Dean of Students ... Ms. Nina FLEMING
35 Director Student Activities ... Ms. Becky WINDBERG
38 Director Student Counseling ... Ms. Deborah BETSWORTH
42 Campus Pastor ... Rev. Kara BAYLOR
101 Secretary to the Board ... Mr. Paul HEGLAND
100 Chief of Staff/VP Strategic Init ... Mr. Thomas KLINE

College of Menominee Nation (F)

PO Box 1179, Keshena WI 54135-1179
County: Menominee FICE Identification: 031251
Unit ID: 413617
Telephone: (800) 567-2344 Carnegie Class: Tribal
FAX Number: (715) 799-1336 Calendar System: Semester
URL: www.menominee.edu
Established: 1992 Annual Undergrad Tuition & Fees: $7,500
Enrollment: 560 Coed
Affiliation or Control: Tribal Control IRS Status: 501(c)3
Highest Offering: Baccalaureate
Program: Occupational; 2-Year Principally Bachelor's Creditable; Teacher Preparatory; Business Emphasis
Accreditation: NH, ADNUR

01 President ... Dr. Verna M. FOWLER
05 Chief Academic Officer ... Dr. Diana MORRIS
10 Chief Financial Officer ... Ms. Laurie REITER
12 Vice Pres of CMN Green Bay Campus ... Mr. Chad WAUKECHON
26 Dean External Relations ... Dr. Holly YOUNGBEAR-TIBBETS
32 Dean of Student Services ... Mr. Gary BESAW
49 Dean of Letters & Science ... Dr. Chad WAUKECHON
66 Dean of Nursing ... Ms. Karen BIALCIK
75 Int Dean of Technical Education ... Ms. Antoinette DAVIDS
51 Dean of Continuing Education ... Mr. Brian BOWALKOWSKI
04 Assistant to the President ... Ms. Melinda COOK
09 Director Institutional Research ... Mr. Ronald JURGENS
30 Advancement Director ... Ms. Irene KIEFER
25 Director of Sponsored Programs ... Mrs. Jill MARTIN
13 IT Director ... Ms. Renita WILBER
18 Director of Operations ... Mr. Richard WARRINGTON
21 Business Manager ... Mr. Victor ESCALANTE
15 Human Resources Director ... Ms. Rachel RICE-TUMA
37 Director Financial Aid ... Ms. Nicole FISH
06 Registrar ... Mrs. Juanita WAUKAU-WILBER
07 Admissions Director ... Ms. Tessa JAMES
29 Dir Alumni Relations/Development ... Ms. Susan WAUKAU
88 Voc Rehab Director ... Ms. Myrna WARRINGTON
08 Library Director ... Ms. Maria ESCALANTE
88 Campus Planner ... Mr. Joel KROENKE
40 Director of Bookstore ... Ms. Verna DELEON

College of Menominee Nation Oneida Campus (G)

2733 S Ridge Road, Green Bay WI 54304
Telephone: (920) 965-0070 Identification: 770424
Accreditation: &NH

† Branch campus of College of Menominee Nation, Keshena, WI.

Columbia College of Nursing (H)

4425 N Port Washington Rd, Milwaukee WI 53212-1099
County: Milwaukee FICE Identification: 006640
Unit ID: 238573
Telephone: (414) 326-2330 Carnegie Class: Not Classified
FAX Number: (414) 236-2331 Calendar System: Semester
URL: www.ccon.edu
Established: 1901 Annual Undergrad Tuition & Fees: $27,330
Enrollment: 151 Coed
Affiliation or Control: Independent Non-Profit IRS Status: 501(c)3
Highest Offering: Baccalaureate
Program: Professional; Nursing Emphasis
Accreditation: NH, NURSE

01 President & Dean ... Dr. Jill M. WINTERS
10 Chief Financial/Business Officer ... Ms. Christina ITALIANO
05 Associate Dean of Academic Affairs ... Ms. Heather VARTANIAN
04 Exec Assistant to the President ... Ms. Gail PETERSON
20 Associate Academic Officer ... Ms. Haley GEIGER
37 Director Student Financial Aid ... Ms. Wendy HILVO
06 Registrar ... Ms. Joua XIONG
24 Director Educational Media ... Mr. Keith JACKSON
07 Admissions Specialist ... Ms. Kelsey BENNA

Concordia University Wisconsin (I)

12800 N Lake Shore Drive, Mequon WI 53097-2402
County: Ozaukee FICE Identification: 003842
Unit ID: 238616
Telephone: (262) 243-5700 Carnegie Class: Master's L
FAX Number: (262) 243-4351 Calendar System: 4/1/4
URL: www.cuw.edu
Established: 1881 Annual Undergrad Tuition & Fees: $26,840
Enrollment: 8,161 Coed
Affiliation or Control: Lutheran Church - Missouri Synod
IRS Status: 501(c)3
Highest Offering: Doctorate
Program: Liberal Arts And General; Teacher Preparatory; Professional
Accreditation: NH, #ARCPA, CAATE, IACBE, MAC, NURSE, OT, PHAR, PTA, SW

01 President ... Rev Dr. Patrick T. FERRY
11 Executive VP & Chief Oper Ofcr ... Mr. Allen J. PROCHNOW
05 Senior Vice President of Academics ... Dr. William R. CARIO
32 Vice President of Student Life ... Mr. Steve P. TAYLOR
07 Sr Vice Pres of Enrollment Services ... Mr. Kenneth K. GASCHK
13 Vice Pres of Information Technology ... Mr. Thomas G. PHILLIP
26 Vice President of Marketing ... Ms. Anita CLARK
10 VP Finance & CFO ... Ms. Joan M. SCHOLZ
20 Assistant Vice Pres of Academics ... Rev Dr. Randy L. FERGUSON
20 Assistant Vice Pres of Academics ... Dr. Bernard D. BULL
20 Assistant Vice Pres of Academics ... Dr. Leah M. DVORAK
30 Vice Pres of Advancement ... Rev Dr. Roy PETERSON
42 Campus Pastor ... Rev. Steven N. SMITH
36 Director Counseling ... Mr. David T. ENTERS
06 Registrar ... Dr. Steven MONTREAL
50 Dean School of Business ... Dr. Dan S. SEM
66 Dean School of Nursing ... Dr. Sharon L. CHAPPY
49 Dean School Arts/Sciences ... Dr. Gaylund K. STONE
53 Dean School of Education ... Dr. Michael UDEN
35 Dean of Students ... Mr. Steve P. TAYLOR
08 Library Director ... Mr. Christian HIMSEL
09 Institutional Research ... Dr. Tamara R. FERRY
29 Director of Alumni Relations ... Ms. Michelle WAGNER
39 Director Residence Life ... Ms. Beckie KRUSE
41 Athletic Director ... Dr. Rob M. BARNHILL
88 Chair Faculty Senate ... Dr. Brad CONDIE
36 Director Career Services ... Mr. Ben ROHDE
40 Director Bookstore ... Ms. Kia LOR
19 Director Campus Safety ... Mr. Mario VALDES
18 Superintendent Buildings & Grounds ... Mr. Steve V. HIBBARD
15 Director Human Resources ... Ms. Kim MASENTHIN
24 Director Instructional Technology ... Mr. Sean B. YOUNG
88 Public Relations Officer ... Mr. Jeff J. BANDURSKI

31 VP Strategy/Culture/External Aff .... Ms. Gretchen M. JAMESON
84 Senior Director Enrollment Services .... Mr. Robert J. NOWAK

Edgewood College (A)

1000 Edgewood College Drive, Madison WI 53711-1997
County: Dane FICE Identification: 003848
Unit ID: 238661
Telephone: (608) 663-4861 Carnegie Class: DRU
FAX Number: (608) 663-3291 Calendar System: Semester
URL: www.edgewood.edu
Established: 1927 Annual Undergrad Tuition & Fees: $26,550
Enrollment: 2,980 Coed
Affiliation or Control: Roman Catholic IRS Status: 501(c)3
Highest Offering: Doctorate
Program: Liberal Arts And General; Teacher Preparatory; Professional
Accreditation: NH, ACBSP, #MFCD, NURSE, TED

01 President .... Dr. Scott FLANAGAN
05 VP Academic Affs/Academic Dean .... Dr. Dean PRIBBENOW
32 VP Student Devel/Dean of Students .... Dr. Margaret R. BALISTRERI-CLARKE
10 VP Business & Finance .... Mr. Michael GUNS
84 VP Enrollment Mgmt .... Ms. Christine BENEDICT
88 VP Dominican Life & Mission .... Sr. Maggie HOPKINS, OP
30 VP Inst Advancement .... Mr. Gary KLEIN
20 Associate Academic Dean .... Dr. Kelley GRORUD
49 Dean School of Arts & Sciences .... Dr. John FIELDS
50 Interim Dean School of Business .... Dr. Amy GANNON
53 Dean School of Education .... Dr. Timothy SLEKAR
71 Dean School of Integrative Studies .... Dr. Kristine MICKELSON
66 Dean School of Nursing .... Dr. Margaret NOREUIL
07 Director Freshman Admissions .... Mr. Derek JOHNSON
13 Director Information Technology .... Mr. Deron KLING
09 Director Inst Assessment & Research .... Dr. Edward J. KEELEY
06 Registrar .... Ms. Michelle KELLEY
106 Director Online Learning .... Ms. Karen FRANKER
08 Library Director .... Dr. Sylvia CONTRERAS
36 Director Career Education .... Ms. Shawn JOHNSON
29 Alumni Director .... Ms. Kathleen O'CONNOR
26 Director Marketing & Communication .... Mr. Edward TAYLOR
15 Interim Director Human Resources .... Ms. Pamela LAVALLIERE
18 Director Facilities & Operations .... Ms. Susan SERRAULT
38 Director Personal Counseling Svcs .... Dr. Megan COBB
21 Controller .... Ms. Jane WILHELM
28 Director Diversity & Inclusion .... Mr. Tony GARCIA
37 Director Student Financial Aid .... Ms. Kari GRIBBLE
23 Director Student Health Services .... Ms. Kimberly MORELAND
41 Director Athletics .... Mr. Al BRISACK

George Williams College of Aurora University (B)

350 Constance Boulevard, Williams Bay WI 53191
Telephone: (262) 245-5531 Identification: 770066
Accreditation: &NH

† Branch campus of Aurora University, Aurora, IL.

Globe University-Appleton (C)

5045 West Grande Market Drive, Grande Chute WI 54914
Telephone: (920) 364-1100 Identification: 770800
Accreditation: ACICS, MAAB

† Branch campus of Globe University, Woodbury, MN.

Globe University-Eau Claire (D)

4955 Bullis Farm Road, Eau Claire WI 54702
Telephone: (715) 855-6600 Identification: 770801
Accreditation: ACICS, MAAB

† Branch campus of Globe University, Woodbury, MN.

Globe University-Green Bay (E)

2620 Development Drive, Bellevue WI 54311
Telephone: (920) 264-1600 Identification: 770802
Accreditation: ACICS, MAAB

† Branch campus of Globe University, Woodbury, MN.

Globe University-La Crosse (F)

2651 Midwest Drive, Third FL, Onalaska WI 54650
Telephone: (608) 779-2600 Identification: 770803
Accreditation: ACICS, MAAB

† Branch campus of Globe University, Woodbury, MN.

Globe University-Madison East (G)

4901 Eastpark Boulevard, Madison WI 53718
Telephone: (608) 216-9400 Identification: 770804
Accreditation: ACICS, MAAB

† Branch campus of Globe University, Woodbury, MN.

Globe University-Middleton (H)

1345 Deming Way, Middleton WI 53562
Telephone: (608) 830-6900 Identification: 770805
Accreditation: ACICS, MAAB

† Branch campus of Globe University, Woodbury, MN.

Globe University-Wausau (I)

1480 County Road XX, Rothschild WI 54474
Telephone: (715) 301-1300 Identification: 770806
Accreditation: ACICS, MAAB

† Branch campus of Globe University, Woodbury, MN.

Herzing University (J)

5218 E Terrace Drive, Madison WI 53718-8340
County: Dane FICE Identification: 009621
Unit ID: 240392
Telephone: (608) 249-6611 Carnegie Class: Bac/Assoc
FAX Number: (608) 249-8593 Calendar System: Semester
URL: www.herzing.edu
Established: 1948 Annual Undergrad Tuition & Fees: $12,790
Enrollment: 2,649 Coed
Affiliation or Control: Independent Non-Profit IRS Status: 501(c)3
Highest Offering: Master's
Program: Technical Emphasis
Accreditation: NH, ADNUR, IACBE, NURSE

01 President .... Ms. Renee HERZING
12 Campus President .... Mr. William VINSON
10 CFO & Vice President of Finance .... Mr. Ryan O'DESKY
05 Academic Dean .... Mr. Mark BROWN
37 Educational Funding Manager .... Mr. Clayton GROTH
32 Director of Student Services/Regist .... Ms. Robin SCHWENN
07 Director of Admissions .... Mr. Nile MCKIBBEN
36 Director of Career Development .... Mr. Jeff WESTRA

Herzing University Brookfield Campus (K)

555 South Executive Drive, Brookfield WI 53005
Telephone: (262) 649-1710 Identification: 770429
Accreditation: &NH, NURSE, @PTAA

† Branch campus of Herzing University, Madison, WI.

Herzing University Kenosha Campus (L)

4006 Washington Road, Kenosha WI 53144
Telephone: (262) 671-0675 Identification: 770430
Accreditation: &NH, MAAB, NURSE

† Branch campus of Herzing University, Madison, WI.

Herzing University Online (M)

W140N8917 Lilly Road, Menomonee Falls WI 53051
Telephone: (866) 508-0748 Identification: 770431
Accreditation: &NH, CAHIIM, MAAB

† Branch campus of Herzing University, Madison, WI.

ITT Technical Institute (N)

470 Security Boulevard, Green Bay WI 54313-9705
Telephone: (920) 662-9000 Identification: 666317
Accreditation: ACICS

† Branch campus of ITT Technical Institute, Indianapolis, IN.

ITT Technical Institute (O)

2450 Rimrock Road, Suite 100, Madison WI 53713
Telephone: (608) 288-6301 Identification: 770666
Accreditation: ACICS

† Branch campus of ITT Technical Institute, Indianapolis, IN.

Lac Courte Oreilles Ojibwa Community College (P)

13466 W Trepania Road, Hayward WI 54843-2181
County: Sawyer FICE Identification: 025322
Unit ID: 260372
Telephone: (715) 634-4790 Carnegie Class: Tribal
FAX Number: (715) 634-5049 Calendar System: Semester
URL: www.lco.edu
Established: 1982 Annual Undergrad Tuition & Fees: $4,590
Enrollment: 352 Coed
Affiliation or Control: Tribal Control IRS Status: 501(c)3
Highest Offering: Associate Degree
Program: 2-Year Principally Bachelor's Creditable
Accreditation: #NH, MAC

01 President .... Dr. Diane VERTIN
05 Academic Dean .... Dr. Beth PAAP
32 Dean of Students .... Ms. Sarah BUTLER
10 Business Office Manager .... Mr. Eugene BAYIHA
06 Registrar .... Mrs. Annette WIGGINS
37 Financial Aid Director .... Mr. Jason PAROLIN
46 Office of Sponsored Programs .... Mr. Dan GETZ
15 Human Resource Director .... Vacant

Lakeland College (Q)

PO Box 359, Sheboygan WI 53082-0359
County: Sheboygan FICE Identification: 003854
Unit ID: 238980
Telephone: (920) 565-1000 Carnegie Class: Master's L
FAX Number: (920) 565-1060 Calendar System: Semester
URL: www.lakeland.edu
Established: 1862 Annual Undergrad Tuition & Fees: $24,090
Enrollment: 3,973 Coed
Affiliation or Control: United Church Of Christ IRS Status: 501(c)3
Highest Offering: Master's
Program: Liberal Arts And General; Professional
Accreditation: NH, TEAC

01 President .... Mr. Dan W. ECK
04 Assistant to the President .... Ms. Ann M. FLAD-JESION
05 VP Academic Affairs/Dean of College .. Dr. Margaret L. ALBRINCK
30 Interim Vice President for Advance .... Ms. Beth BORGEN
103 Director of Career Development .... Mrs. Jessica LAMBRECHT
84 Vice Pres Enrollment Management .... Mr. Zach R. VOELZ
06 Registrar .... Ms. Jacquelyn MORGAN
07 Senior Dir Recruitment/Admissions .... Ms. Kristen ENGELS
10 VP of Finance & CFO .... Mrs. Carole ROBERTSON
09 Director of Institutional Research .... Mr. Paul WHITE
08 Director of Library Services .... Ms. Ann K. PENKE
37 Director of Financial Aid .... Ms. Patty L. TAYLOR
26 Director of Communications .... Mr. David D. GALLIANETTI
21 Controller .... Ms. Sharon L. ROOB
29 Dir Alumni & Church Relations .... Ms. Linda BOSMAN
15 Director of Human Resources .... Mr. Peter G. PLATTEN
18 Dir Facilities/Mgmt & Planning .... Mr. Rich N. HAEN
38 Director of Student Counselling .... Dr. Carey A. KNIER
19 Director Security/Safety .... Mr. David SIMON
39 Director of Residence Life .... Mr. Jim BAJCZYK

Lawrence University (R)

711 E. Boldt Way, Appleton WI 54911
County: Outagamie FICE Identification: 003856
Unit ID: 239017
Telephone: (920) 832-7000 Carnegie Class: Bac/A&S
FAX Number: (920) 832-6978 Calendar System: Other
URL: www.lawrence.edu
Established: 1847 Annual Undergrad Tuition & Fees: $43,740
Enrollment: 1,519 Coed
Affiliation or Control: Independent Non-Profit IRS Status: 501(c)3
Highest Offering: Baccalaureate
Program: Liberal Arts And General
Accreditation: NH, MUS

01 President .... Mr. Mark BURSTEIN
04 Executive Asst to the President .... Ms. Alice BOECKERS
05 Provost and Dean of the Faculty .... Dr. David BURROWS
10 VP Finance & Administration .... Mr. Christopher LEE
30 VP Development/Alumni Rels .... Mr. Calvin D. HUSMANN
32 VP Student Affairs & Dean .... Ms. Nancy D. TRUESDELL
29 VP Alumni/Constituency Engagement ..... Mr. Mark D. BRESEMAN
26 Assoc Vice Pres Communications .... Mr. Craig L. GAGNON
44 Campaign Dir/Principal Gifts Ofcr ..... Ms. Kristen M. MEKEMSON
30 Assoc Vice Pres Development .... Ms. Stacy J. MARA
21 Director Financial Services .... Ms. Elizabeth MILLER
64 Dean Conservatory of Music .... Mr. Brian G. PERTL
36 Dean of Career Services .... Ms. Mary T. MEANY
35 Dean Student Academic Services .... Mr. Geoff GAJEWSKI
20 Associate Dean of the Faculty .... Ms. Ruth M. LUNT
28 Asst Dean Students Multicul Affs .... Ms. Pa Lee MOUA
09 Director of Research Administration ...... Ms. Kristin L. MCKINLEY
07 Dean of Admissions & Financial Aid .... Mr. Kenneth L. ANSELMENT
37 Director of Financial Aid .... Ms. Sara C. HOLMAN
06 Registrar .... Ms. Anne S. NORMAN
08 Librarian .... Mr. Peter J. GILBERT
41 Athletic Director .... Mr. Michael W. SZKODZINSKI
13 Director Information Tech Svcs .... Mr. Steven M. ARMSTRONG
15 Director of Human Resources .... Ms. Sandy ISSELMANN
18 Director of Facility Services .... Mr. Daniel R. MEYER
38 Assoc Dean Stdnts Health/Wellness .... Mr. Scott W. RADTKE

Madison Media Institute-College of Media Arts (S)

2702 Agriculture Drive, Madison WI 53718-6787
County: Dane FICE Identification: 010913
Unit ID: 364168
Telephone: (800) 236-4997 Carnegie Class: Assoc/PrivFP
FAX Number: (608) 442-0141 Calendar System: Semester
URL: www.mediainstitute.edu
Established: 1969 Annual Undergrad Tuition & Fees: $17,600
Enrollment: 372 Coed
Affiliation or Control: Proprietary IRS Status: Proprietary
Highest Offering: Baccalaureate
Program: 2-Year Principally Bachelor's Creditable; Technical Emphasis
Accreditation: ACCSC, ACICS

01 President .... Mr. David HEALY
10 Chief Financial/Business Officer .... Mr. Kent SHEPLER
07 Admissions Director .... Mr. David HIMM
05 Academic Dean .... Ms. Mandy JOHNSON
36 Director Student Placement .... Ms. Laura MAEL

Maranatha Baptist University (T)

745 West Main Street, Watertown WI 53094-7600
County: Jefferson FICE Identification: 023172
Unit ID: 239071
Telephone: (920) 261-9300 Carnegie Class: Bac/Diverse
FAX Number: (920) 261-9109 Calendar System: Semester
URL: www.mbu.edu
Established: 1968 Annual Undergrad Tuition & Fees: $13,940

Enrollment: 1,042 Coed
Affiliation or Control: Independent Non-Profit IRS Status: 501(c)3
Highest Offering: Doctorate
Program: 2-Year Principally Bachelor's Creditable; Liberal Arts And General; Teacher Preparatory; Professional; Religious Emphasis
Accreditation: NH, NURSE

01 President ... Dr. Martin MARRIOTT
03 Executive Vice President ... Dr. Matthew DAVIS
05 Vice President for Academic Affairs ... Dr. William LICHT
30 Vice President for Inst Advancement ... Dr. Jim H. HARRISON
10 Vice President for Business Affairs ... Dr. Mark W. STEVENS
32 Dean of Students ... Dr. John DAVIS
06 Registrar ... Mr. Steve CARLSON
07 Director of Admissions ... Dr. James H. HARRISON
30 Director of Development ... Mr. Steve BOARD
09 Director of Institutional Research ... Mr. Jonathan COLEMAN
15 Director Personnel Services ... Dr. Kevin MONTNEY
26 Chief Public Relations Officer ... Mr. Peter WRIGHT
41 Athletic Director ... Mr. Robert THOMPSON
08 Librarian ... Mr. Mark HANSON
35 Director Student Affairs ... Mr. Peter HUBER
29 Director Alumni Relations ... Dr. John DAVIS
37 Director Student Financial Aid ... Mr. Randy HIBBS
13 Chief Info Technology Officer (CIO) ... Dr. Werner LUMM
19 Director Security/Safety ... Mr. Timothy JOHNS
106 Dir Online Education/E-learning ... Dr. Jeff CRUM
108 Director Institutional Assessment ... Mr. Jonathan COLEMAN

Marian University (A)

45 S National Avenue, Fond Du Lac WI 54935-4699
County: Fond Du Lac FICE Identification: 003861
Unit ID: 239080
Telephone: (920) 923-7600 Carnegie Class: Master's L
FAX Number: (920) 923-7154 Calendar System: Semester
URL: www.marianuniversity.edu
Established: 1936 Annual Undergrad Tuition & Fees: $27,210
Enrollment: 2,130 Coed
Affiliation or Control: Roman Catholic IRS Status: 501(c)3
Highest Offering: Doctorate
Program: Liberal Arts And General; Teacher Preparatory; Professional
Accreditation: NH, IACBE, NURSE, RAD, SW, TED

01 Interim President ... Mr. Robert A. FALE
05 Interim VP Academic Affairs ... Dr. Sheryl K. AYALA
10 VP Business & Finance ... Mr. Arnold HENNING
84 VP Enrollment Management ... Ms. Stacey L. AKEY
32 VP for Student Engagement ... Ms. Kate CANDEE
30 Vice President for Advancement ... Dr. George E. KOONCE, JR.
04 Executive Assistant to President ... Ms. Carey C. GARDIN
20 Associate VP Academic Affairs ... Dr. Julie A. LUETSCHWAGER
53 Dean School of Education ... Dr. Sue A. STODDART
66 Dean Nursing/Health Prof ... Dr. Linda K. MATHESON
49 Dean Arts/Sciences ... Dr. Michelle MAJEWSKIE
50 Dean Business/Public Safety ... Dr. Jeffrey G. REED
35 Dean of Student Engagement ... Mr. Paul KRIKAU
08 Director of Libraries ... Ms. Kathryn A. JOHNSTON
44 Associate VP Advancement ... Ms. Tracy L. MILKOWSKI
18 General Manager/Facilities ... Mr. Artie L. GOLD
06 Registrar ... Ms. Cheryl A. TEICHMILLER
09 Director of Institutional Research ... Mr. Thomas P. RICHTER
37 Director of Financial Aid ... Ms. Pamela WARREN
42 Director of Campus Ministry ... Sr. Marie SCOTT, CSA
26 Director University Relations ... Ms. Lisa L. KIDD
29 Director Alumni Relations ... Ms. Mary ENDRIES
07 Dean of Admission ... Ms. Shannon S. LALUZERNE
15 Director of Human Resources ... Vacant
41 Director of Athletics ... Mr. Jason BARTELT
88 Dean Advising/Academic Services ... Ms. Cathy M. MATHWEG
23 Director of Health Services ... Ms. Jodi S. SCHRAUTH
36 Coordinator Career Services ... Ms. Mary J. HATLEN
88 Director of Campus Dining Services ... Ms. Nikki A. KRAMER
13 Director of Information Technology ... Mr. Keith L. FALK
40 Director of Bookstore ... Ms. Mary MANGAN-FLOOD
38 Director of Counseling ... Ms. Ellen MERCER
92 Director Honors Program ... Dr. Mathew P. SZROMBA
108 Director of Inst Assessment ... Dr. Moreen K. CARVAN
39 Director of Student Services ... Ms. Dee HARMSEN
104 Coordinator of Study Abroad ... Ms. Andelys BOLANOS
19 Director Security/Safety ... Mr. Matt D. ROSE

Marquette University (B)

PO Box 1881, Milwaukee WI 53201-1881
County: Milwaukee FICE Identification: 003863
Unit ID: 239105
Telephone: (414) 288-7700 Carnegie Class: DRU
FAX Number: (414) 288-3300 Calendar System: Semester
URL: www.marquette.edu
Established: 1881 Annual Undergrad Tuition & Fees: $37,170
Enrollment: 11,745 Coed
Affiliation or Control: Roman Catholic IRS Status: 501(c)3
Highest Offering: Doctorate
Program: Liberal Arts And General; Teacher Preparatory; Professional
Accreditation: NH, ARCPA, BUS, BUSA, CAATE, CACREP, CLPSY, COPSY, DENT, ENG, JOUR, LAW, MIDWF, MT, NURSE, PTA, SP, TED, THEA

01 President ... Dr. Michael R. LOVELL
05 Provost ... Dr. Daniel J. MYERS
27 Vice President Public Affairs ... Ms. Rana H. ALTENBURG
43 Vice President and General Counsel ... Ms. Cynthia M. BAUER
15 Vice President Human Resources ... Mr. Octavio CASTRO
09 Vice Pres Research and Innovation ... Dr. Jeanne M. HOSSENLOPP
10 Vice President Finance ... Mr. John C. LAMB
32 Interim Vice Pres Student Affairs ... Dr. Marya L. LEATHERWOOD
20 Vice Prov Undergrad Pgms & Teaching ... Dr. Gary MEYER
26 Vice Pres Marketing & Communication ... Mr. David MURPHY
42 Vice President Mission and Ministry ... Dr. Stephanie J. RUSSELL
41 Vice Pres and Director of Athletics ... Mr. Bill SCHOLL
30 Vice Pres University Advancement ... Mr. Michael VANDERHOEF
06 Registrar ... Ms. Georgia D. MCRAE
07 Interim Dean of Admissions ... Ms. Jean BURKE
66 Dean of Nursing ... Dr. Margaret CALLAHAN
76 Dean of Health Sciences ... Dr. William CULLINAN
107 Dean of Professional Studies ... Dr. Robert J. DEAHL
60 Interim Dean of Communication ... Dr. Ana GARNER
58 Interim Dean of Graduate School ... Dr. Kevin GIBSON
53 Dean of Education ... Dr. William A. HENK
49 Dean of Arts & Sciences ... Dr. Richard C. HOLZ
61 Dean of the Law School ... Mr. Joseph D. KEARNEY
52 Dean of Dentistry ... Dr. William K. LOBB
54 Dean of Engineering ... Dr. Kristina ROPELLA
50 Dean of Business Administration ... Dr. Brian D. TILL
08 Dean of Libraries ... Ms. Janice WELBURN
101 Assistant to Pres/Corp Secretary ... Mr. Steven W. FRIEDER
13 Chief Information Officer ... Ms. Kathy J. LANG
35 Dean of Students ... Dr. Stephanie QUADE
28 Assoc Provost Diversity & Inclusion ... Dr. William WELBURN
88 Assoc Vice Prov Acad Support Pgm ... Ms. Anne D. DEAHL
90 Assoc Vice Provost Educational Tech ... Mr. G. Jon PRAY
88 Senior Assoc Vice Pres Development ... Mr. Timothy RIPPINGER
21 Senior Assoc Vice President Finance ... Ms. Mary Lou AUSTIN
45 Assoc VP Finance/Univ Architect ... Ms. Lora STRIGENS
35 Assoc Vice Pres Student Affairs ... Dr. James MCMAHON
39 Exec Dir Housing and Residence Life ... Ms. Mary JANZ
25 Exec Director of Research Support ... Ms. Katherine DURBEN
23 Exec Dir University Medical Clinic ... Dr. Carolyn S. SMITH
36 Director Career Services Center ... Ms. Laura F. KESTNER
38 Director of Counseling Center ... Dr. Michael J. ZEBROWSKI
18 Director Facilities Services ... Mr. Gregory ADAMS
37 Director of Financial Aid ... Ms. Susan M. TEERINK
104 Dir International Education Office ... Mr. Terence MILLER
40 Director Marquette Spirit Shop ... Mr. James K. GRAEBERT
29 Engagement Director ... Mr. Daniel DEWEERDT
19 Director Public Safety ... Mr. Paul MASCARI
96 Director of Purchasing ... Ms. Jenny ALEXANDER

Medical College of Wisconsin (C)

PO Box 26509, Milwaukee WI 53226-0509
County: Milwaukee FICE Identification: 024535
Unit ID: 239169
Telephone: (414) 955-8296 Carnegie Class: Spec/Med
FAX Number: (414) 955-6560 Calendar System: Other
URL: www.mcw.edu
Established: 1893 Annual Graduate Tuition & Fees: $50,935
Enrollment: 1,209 Coed
Affiliation or Control: Independent Non-Profit IRS Status: 501(c)3
Highest Offering: Doctorate; No Undergraduates
Program: Professional
Accreditation: NH, DENT, MED, PDPSY, PH

01 President & CEO ... Dr. John R. RAYMOND, SR.
05 Dean/Executive Vice President ... Dr. Joseph E. KERSCHNER
10 Sr Vice Pres Finance/Administration ... Vacant
88 Dean Grad Sch Biomedical Science ... Dr. Ravi P. MISRA
30 Vice Pres of Development ... Ms. Alice ARCHABAL
15 Vice President Human Resources ... Ms. Sherri DUCHARME-WHITE
86 Vice Pres Government/Community Affs ... Ms. Kathryn A. KUHN
28 VP Corporate Compliance Risk Mgmt ... Mr. Daniel WICKEHAM
100 Chief of Staff ... Ms. Mara LORD
44 Assoc Vice President Development ... Vacant
26 Assoc Vice Pres Public Affairs ... Mr. Richard N. KATSCHKE
20 Sr Assoc Dean for Academic Affs ... Dr. William J. HUESTON
22 Sr Asc Dean Faculty Affs/Diversity ... Dr. Alonzo P. WALKER
32 Assoc Dean for Student Affairs ... Dr. Nancy HAVAS
63 Assoc Dean Graduate Med Educ ... Dr. Kenneth B. SIMONS
46 Co-Int Senior Assoc Dean Research ... Dr. David L. MATTSON
45 Co-Int Sr Assoc Dean Research ... Dr. Cecilia J. HILLARD
20 Associate Dean Curriculum ... Dr. Travis WEBB
45 Assoc Dean Educ Support/Evaluation ... Vacant
21 Director Budget Administration ... Mr. Ryan GOERLITZ
13 Director Application Development ... Ms. Rebecca L. MORRISON
08 Director Medical Libraries ... Ms. Mary B. BLACKWELDER
07 Director Admissions ... Ms. Jennifer L. HALUZAK
06 Registrar ... Ms. Lesley A. MACK
18 Dir Facil Engineering/Maintenance ... Mr. Jeffrey BORNEMANN
37 Director Student Financial Services ... Ms. Linda L. PASCHAL
25 Director Grants & Contracts ... Ms. April HAVERTY
29 Exec Director Alumni Relations ... Mr. William A. SCHULTZ
21 Director Business Services ... Mr. Peter THOMAS
88 Medical Dir Clinical Informatics ... Dr. Rick D. GILLIS
40 Manager of Bookstore ... Ms. Cathy GRANFIELD
19 Director Security/Safety ... Mr. David C. FELLER
43 Dir Legal Services/General Counsel ... Mr. John NEWSOME

Midwest College of Oriental Medicine (D)

6232 Bankers Road, Racine WI 53403-9747
County: Racine FICE Identification: 030612
Unit ID: 383020
Telephone: (800) 593-2320 Carnegie Class: Spec/Health
FAX Number: (262) 554-7475 Calendar System: Quarter
URL: www.acupuncture.edu
Established: 1979 Annual Undergrad Tuition & Fees: $15,660
Enrollment: 93 Coed
Affiliation or Control: Proprietary IRS Status: Proprietary
Highest Offering: Master's; No Lower Division
Program: Professional
Accreditation: ACUP

01 President ... Dr. William J. DUNBAR
05 Director of Academics ... Dr. Robert CHELNICK
20 Academic Dean/Research Director ... Dr. Alan URETZ
88 Projects Director ... Dr. Kristine L. LA POINT
37 Director of Financial Aid ... Ms. Elizabeth M. HOJAN
07 Admissions Coord/Transfer Credit ... Mr. Lawrence PILOCZEWSKI
06 Records Officer/Registrar ... Ms. Amy L. BENISH
08 Dean of Students/Librarian ... Mr. John BALLARINI
32 Dean of Students ... Ms. Olga GAJDOSIK
09 Research Director ... Mr. Jin Hua XIE
63 Dean of Biomedicine Science ... Dr. Peter NIKAS
85 Dean of Foreign Students ... Dr. Duckin SUH
17 Internship Director ... Dr. Helen WU
108 Clinic Tracking/Inst Evaluation ... Ms. Deirdre M. DUNBAR
86 Compliance Officer ... Mr. Harry S. HEIFETZ
91 Information Systems ... Mr. William H. LEHMAN
26 Marketing/Student Affairs ... Mr. Chris A. KRAJNIAK
88 Office Manager ... Ms. Stephanie M. PITTMAN

Milwaukee Career College (E)

3077 North Maryfair Road, Suite 300, Milwaukee WI 53222
County: Milwaukee FICE Identification: 041174
Unit ID: 449861
Telephone: (800) 754-1009 Carnegie Class: Not Classified
FAX Number: (414) 727-9557 Calendar System: Other
URL: www.mkecc.edu
Established: 2002 Annual Undergrad Tuition & Fees: $11,800
Enrollment: 92 Coed
Affiliation or Control: Proprietary IRS Status: Proprietary
Highest Offering: Associate Degree
Program: Occupational
Accreditation: ABHES

01 President ... Jack TAKAHASHI

Milwaukee Institute of Art & Design (F)

273 E Erie Street, Milwaukee WI 53202-6003
County: Milwaukee FICE Identification: 020771
Unit ID: 239309
Telephone: (414) 847-3200 Carnegie Class: Spec/Arts
FAX Number: (414) 291-8077 Calendar System: Semester
URL: www.miad.edu
Established: 1974 Annual Undergrad Tuition & Fees: $32,190
Enrollment: 622 Coed
Affiliation or Control: Independent Non-Profit IRS Status: 501(c)3
Highest Offering: Baccalaureate
Program: Liberal Arts And General; Fine Arts Emphasis
Accreditation: NH, ART

01 President ... Mr. Jeff MORIN
05 VP of Academic Affairs ... Mr. David MARTIN
84 VP for Enrollment Management ... Ms. Mary C. SCHOPP
04 Executive Assistant to President ... Ms. Dagmar L. CARNDUFF
09 Assoc VP Academic Plng/Assessment ... Ms. Cynthia LYNCH
10 VP for Financial Affairs ... Ms. Brenda JONES
26 VP of Development & Communications ... Ms. Vivian M. ROTHSCHILD
32 Dean of Students ... Mr. Tony J. NOWAK
37 Executive Director of Financial Aid ... Ms. Carol MASSE
07 Director of Admissions ... Mr. David SIGMAN
88 Enroll Communications Specialist ... Ms. Stacey STEINBERG
08 Director of Library Services ... Ms. Cynthia D. LYNCH
36 Director of Career Services ... Mr. Duane P. SEIDENSTICKER
51 Dir Pre-College & Adult Learning ... Ms. Jill F. KUNSMANN
19 Director Security/Safety ... Mr. Keith A. KOTOWICZ
06 Director of Registration Services ... Ms. Jean WEIMER
38 Director of College Advising ... Ms. Michelle GROSS
29 Mgr of Alumni Engagment & Develop ... Ms. Annie HYMA
15 Director of Human Resources ... Ms. April FORRAY
20 Director of Academic Operations ... Ms. Marie KAMINSKI
18 Building Maintenance Manager ... Mr. Michael A. GOETZ
13 Director of Technology ... Mr. Matt OGDEN
30 Director of Development ... Ms. Vivian ROTHSCHILD

Milwaukee School of Engineering (G)

1025 N Broadway, Milwaukee WI 53202-3109
County: Milwaukee FICE Identification: 003868
Unit ID: 239318
Telephone: (414) 277-7300 Carnegie Class: Master's S
FAX Number: (414) 277-7454 Calendar System: Quarter
URL: www.msoe.edu
Established: 1903 Annual Undergrad Tuition & Fees: $34,470
Enrollment: 2,810 Coed
Affiliation or Control: Independent Non-Profit IRS Status: 501(c)3
Highest Offering: Master's
Program: Professional; Technical Emphasis
Accreditation: NH, CONST, ENG, ENGT, NURSE, PERF

01 Interim President ... Dr. Matthew A. PANHANS
05 Vice President Academics ... Dr. Fred BERRY
10 Vice President of Finance and CFO ... Ms. Dawn THIBEDEAU
30 Interim VP of Development ... Mr. Jonathan KOWALSKI
18 VP of Operations ... Mr. Kevin MORIN
84 VP of Enroll Mgmt & Dean of Student ... Dr. Timothy VALLEY
09 Dean of Institutional Research ... Dr. Deborah JACKMAN
25 Dean Grants & Projects ... Mr. Sheku KAMARA
48 Chair Architectural Engr Dept ... Dr. Blake WENTZ
50 Chair School of Business ... Mr. Steve BIALEK
54 Chair Electrical Engr/CPU Sci Dept ... Dr. Stephen WILLIAMS
97 Chair General Studies Department ... Dr. Alicia DOMACK
81 Chair Mathematics Department ... Vacant
54 Chair Mechanical Engineering Dept ... Dr. Cynthia BARNICKI
81 Chair Physics/Chemistry Dept ... Dr. Matey KALTCHEV
66 Chair Nursing Department ... Dr. Debra JENKS
21 Controller ... Ms. Janda VAVRICKA
06 Registrar ... Ms. Mary F. NIELSEN
26 Director Marketing Public Affairs ... Ms. Sandra L. EVERTS
27 Director Public & Media Relations ... Ms. JoEllen BURDUE
15 Director of Human Resources ... Mr. Kevin A. MORIN
37 Director of Financial Aid ... Mr. Steve MIDTHUN
44 Director of Development ... Mr. Jonathan V. KOWALSKI, JR.
38 Director of Counseling ... Mr. Joseph P. MELOY
32 Director Student Activities ... Mr. Nick SEIDLER
39 Director Residence Halls ... Dr. William E. BREESE
41 Director Athletics ... Mr. Dan I. HARRIS
08 Director of Library & Info Services ... Mr. Gary S. SHIMEK
105 Director of Services/Webmaster ... Mr. Kent A. PETERSON
19 Director of Public Safety ... Mr. William P. FADROWSKI
88 Director Fluid Power Institute ... Mr. Tom S. WANKE
29 Director Alumni Affairs ... Ms. Cathy VAREBROOK
13 Dir Computer/Communications Svcs ... Vacant
07 Director of Admissions ... Ms. Seandra MITCHELL
36 Director Student Placement ... Ms. Mary SPENCER
40 Bookstore Manager ... Mr. David P. ABRAHAMSON

Mount Mary University (A)

2900 N Menomonee River Parkway,
Milwaukee WI 53222-4597

County: Milwaukee FICE Identification: 003869
Unit ID: 239390
Telephone: (414) 258-4810 Carnegie Class: Master's S
FAX Number: (414) 256-1224 Calendar System: Semester
URL: www.mtmary.edu
Established: 1913 Annual Undergrad Tuition & Fees: $26,230
Enrollment: 1,296 Female
Affiliation or Control: Roman Catholic IRS Status: 501(c)3
Highest Offering: Doctorate
Program: Liberal Arts And General; Teacher Preparatory; Professional
Accreditation: NH, CIDA, DIETC, DIETI, OT, SW

01 President ... Dr. Eileen SCHWALBACH
03 Exec VP Administrative Services ... Ms. Beth WNUK
05 VP Academic/Student Affairs ... Dr. Karen FRIEDLEN
10 Senior Vice Pres Finance ... Mr. Reyes GONZALEZ
84 Vice Pres Enrollment Services ... Mr. David WEGENER
26 VP Community Impact ... Ms. Lynn SPRANGERS
30 Vice Pres Development ... Ms. Pamela OWENS
88 Vice President Mission/Identity ... Sr. Joan PENZENSTADLER, SSND
20 Dean Academic Affairs ... Dr. Wendy WEAVER
32 Dean Student Affairs ... Ms. Sarah OLEJNICZAK
58 Dean of Graduate Education ... Vacant
66 Dean Nursing Program ... Dr. Jill WINTERS
21 Controller ... Ms. Debora OLSON
06 Registrar ... Dr. Mary KARR
44 Annual Giving Officer ... Ms. Susan NIEBERLE
27 Senior Dir of Mktg/Public Relations ... Ms. Susan SEILER
29 Director of Alumnae Relations ... Ms. Andrea MILLER
07 Director of Graduate Admission ... Mr. Kirk MESSER
07 Director of Undergraduate Admission ... Ms. Rebecca SURGES
09 Director of Inst Research ... Dr. Jill MEYER
08 Director of Library ... Mr. Eric ROBINSON
13 Director of Information Technology ... Mr. Marc BELANGER
37 Director Financial Aid ... Ms. Debra DUFF
35 Director of Student Engagement ... Ms. Kayla SELL
39 Director of Residence Life ... Mr. Erich ZEIMANTZ
36 Dir of Advising/Career Development ... Ms. Michelle PLIML
104 Director of International Studies ... Ms. Nan METZGER
15 Director of Human Resources ... Ms. Sandra SIIRA
41 Athletic Director ... Mr. Marc HEIDORF
42 Director of Campus Ministry ... Ms. Lea ROSENBERG
18 Director of Buildings & Grounds ... Ms. Rebecca JOHNSON
19 Director of Security ... Mr. Paul LESHOK
40 Mgr Barnes & Noble Bookstore ... Ms. Whitney BAUMGARTEN
105 Website and Photo Manager ... Ms. Eichelle THOMPSON
04 Executive Assistant to President ... Ms. Pamela SALOUN
38 Director Student Counseling ... Ms. Jennifer LOOYSEN

Nashotah House (B)

2777 Mission Road, Nashotah WI 53058-9793

County: Waukesha FICE Identification: 003874
Unit ID: 239424
Telephone: (262) 646-6500 Carnegie Class: Spec/Faith
FAX Number: (262) 646-6504 Calendar System: Semester
URL: www.nashotah.edu
Established: 1842 Annual Graduate Tuition & Fees: $17,750
Enrollment: 106 Coed
Affiliation or Control: Protestant Episcopal IRS Status: 501(c)3
Highest Offering: Doctorate; No Undergraduates
Program: Professional; Religious Emphasis
Accreditation: THEOL

01 Dean-President ... Rev. Steven A. PEAY
10 Associate Dean of Administration ... Rev. Philip J. CUNNINGHAM
21 Controller ... Mrs. LaRae BAUMANN
13 IT/Database Administrator ... Mr. Matt BILLS
05 Associate Dean for Academic Affairs ... Rev. Andrew GROSSO
06 Registrar ... Mrs. Alane EVANS
32 Associate Dean of Students ... Rev. Rick HARTLEY
35 Student Affairs Associate ... Mrs. Kelly MEDINA
07 Director of Student Recruitment ... Mrs. Gina BOTTOM
08 Library Director ... Dr. David G. SHERWOOD
30 Dir of Annual Giving/Advancement ... Rev. Noah S. LAWSON
26 Marketing/Comunications ... Ms. Elin WILDE
18 Chief Facilities/Physical Plant ... Mrs. Dawn BERNER
101 Secretary of the Board of Trustees ... Rev. R. Brien KOEHLER

National-Louis University Milwaukee/Beloit Campus (C)

12000 W Park Place, Suite 100,
Milwaukee WI 53224-3007

Telephone: (414) 577-2658 Identification: 770088
Accreditation: &NH

† Branch campus of National-Louis University, Chicago, IL.

Northland College (D)

1411 Ellis Avenue, Ashland WI 54806-3999

County: Ashland FICE Identification: 003875
Unit ID: 239512
Telephone: (715) 682-1699 Carnegie Class: Bac/A&S
FAX Number: (715) 682-1308 Calendar System: Other
URL: www.northland.edu
Established: 1892 Annual Undergrad Tuition & Fees: $32,754
Enrollment: 575 Coed
Affiliation or Control: United Church Of Christ IRS Status: 501(c)3
Highest Offering: Baccalaureate
Program: Liberal Arts And General; Teacher Preparatory
Accreditation: NH

01 President ... Dr. Michael MILLER
05 Interim Academic Dean ... Dr. Leslie ALLDRITT
30 VP of Institutional Advancement ... Ms. Margot ZELENZ
10 VP Finance & Administration ... Mr. Robert JACKSON
32 VP of Stdnt Affairs & Inst Sustain ... Ms. Michele MEYER
88 Exec Director Environmental Inst ... Mr. Mark PETERSON
88 Exec Director of Development ... Ms. Kristy LIPHART
20 Associate Academic Dean ... Dr. Alan BREW
07 Director of Admissions ... Mr. Teege METTILLE
06 Registrar ... Ms. Kathy TRAYNOR
08 Library Director ... Ms. Julia WAGGONER
29 Director of Alumni Relations ... Ms. Jackie MOORE
13 Information Service Manager ... Mr. Todd PYDO
41 Athletic Director ... Ms. Kim FALKENHAGEN
15 Director Human Resources ... Mr. Paul SKORACZEWSKI
37 Director of Student Financial Aid ... Ms. Heather SHELLY
21 Controller ... Mr. Matt HULMER
44 Director of Annual Giving ... Ms. Carrie SLATER-DUFFY
09 Institutional Research Specialist ... Ms. Petra HOFSTEDT
04 Exec Assistant to the President ... Ms. Dawn RIVARD
39 Director of Residential Life ... Vacant
42 Campus Minister ... Mr. David SAETRE
25 Director of Grant Dev and Admin ... Ms. Lisa WILLIAMSON
26 Exec Director of Inst Marketing ... Ms. Demeri MULLIKIN

Ottawa University Wisconsin (E)

245 South Executive Drive, Brookfield WI 53005-4204

Telephone: (262) 879-0200 Identification: 666084
Accreditation: &NH

† Regional accreditation is carried under the parent institution in Ottawa, KS.

Rasmussen College - Appleton (F)

3500 E. Destination Drive, Appleton WI 54915

Telephone: (920) 750-5900 Identification: 667059
Accreditation: &NH, MAAB

† Regional accreditation is carried under the parent institution in Saint Cloud, MN. The tuition figure is an average, actual tuition may vary.

Rasmussen College - Green Bay (G)

904 South Taylor Street, Building 1, Green Bay WI 54303

Telephone: (920) 593-8400 Identification: 667063
Accreditation: &NH, CAHIIM, MAAB, MAC, MLTAD

† Regional accreditation is carried under the parent institution in Saint Cloud, MN. The tuition figure is an average, actual tuition may vary.

Rasmussen College - Wausau (H)

1101 Westwood Drive, Wausau WI 54401

Telephone: (715) 841-8000 Identification: 667068
Accreditation: &NH, MAAB

† Regional accreditation carried under the parent institution in Saint Cloud, MN. The tuition figure is an average, actual tuition may vary.

Ripon College (I)

300 West Seward Street, PO Box 248,
Ripon WI 54971-0248

County: Fond du Lac FICE Identification: 003884
Unit ID: 239628
Telephone: (920) 748-8115 Carnegie Class: Bac/A&S
FAX Number: (920) 748-7243 Calendar System: Semester
URL: www.ripon.edu
Established: 1851 Annual Undergrad Tuition & Fees: $36,214
Enrollment: 840 Coed
Affiliation or Control: Independent Non-Profit IRS Status: 501(c)3
Highest Offering: Baccalaureate
Program: Liberal Arts And General; Teacher Preparatory
Accreditation: NH

01 President ... Zachariah P. MESSITTE
04 Admin Asst to President ... Vacant
101 Special Assistant to the President ... Margaret A. CARNE
05 VP & Dean of Faculty ... Ed WINGENBACH
30 VP for Advancement ... Vacant
10 Vice President for Finance ... Thomas M. PONTO
32 Vice President Dean of Students ... Christophor M. OGLE
84 Vice President for Enrollment ... Jennifer MACHACEK
06 Assoc Dean of Faculty/Registrar ... Michele A. WITTLER
88 Exec Dir Ctr for Social Responsib ... Lindsay A. BLUMER
07 Dean of Admissions ... Leigh D. MLODZIK
21 Controller ... Lori A. SCHULZE
08 User Services Librarian ... Andrew R. PRELLWITZ
35 Dir Student Activities/Orientation ... Melissa L. BEMUS
88 Director Student Support Svcs ... Daniel J. KRHIN
39 Director of Residence Life ... Jessica L. JOANIS
26 Dir of Creative & Social Media ... Richard T. DAMM
26 Exec Dir Marketing & Communications ... Melissa K. ANDERSON
44 Exec Director of Development ... Larry P. MALCHOW
13 Exec Dir of Information Technology ... Tara A. LACHAPELL
88 General Manager Food Service ... Allison OTTO
18 Director Physical Plant ... Brian SKAMRA
41 Director of Athletics ... Julie H. JOHNSON
102 Dir Foundation & Gov Relations ... Terri L. HOLZMAN
44 Director Annual Fund ... Nancy L. HINTZ
29 Dir Constit Engagemnt & Career Svcs ... Amy L. GERRETSEN
15 Human Resource Administrator ... Jennifer FRANZ
38 Director of Counseling Services ... Cynthia S. VIERTEL
40 Bookstore Manager ... Rose OLKIEWICZ
37 Director Financial Aid ... David B. WOODWARD

Sacred Heart Seminary and School of Theology (J)

7335 S Highway 100, P.O. Box 429,
Hales Corners WI 53130-0429

County: Milwaukee FICE Identification: 020780
Unit ID: 239637
Telephone: (414) 425-8300 Carnegie Class: Spec/Faith
FAX Number: (414) 529-6999 Calendar System: Semester
URL: www.shsst.edu
Established: 1933 Annual Graduate Tuition & Fees: $17,350
Enrollment: 123 Coed
Affiliation or Control: Roman Catholic IRS Status: 501(c)3
Highest Offering: Master's; No Undergraduates
Program: Professional; Religious Emphasis
Accreditation: NH, THEOL

01 President-Rector ... Msgr. Ross A. SHECTERLE
10 VP Finance ... Ms. Sally A. SMITS
03 Vice Rector ... Vacant
05 VP Intellectual Formation ... Dr. Patrick J. RUSSELL
42 VP Human Formation ... Rev. Robert COOK, OFM
20 VP Pastoral Formation ... Rev. Donald LOSKOT, SDS
88 VP Spiritual Formation ... Rev. Paul KELLY, SCJ
08 Director Library & Acad Tech Svcs ... Ms. Susanna PATHAK
07 VP External Affairs ... Dr. Jeremy BLACKWOOD
06 Registrar ... Ms. Julie O'CONNOR
26 Director Communications ... Mr. Jonathan DRAYNA
18 Director Plant Operations ... Mr. Michael J. ERATO
04 Executive Asst to President-Rector ... Ms. Theresa M. ILLINGWORTH
13 Information Systems Coordinator ... Ms. Mary GRIEGER

Saint Norbert College (K)

100 Grant Street, De Pere WI 54115-2099

County: Brown FICE Identification: 003892
Unit ID: 239716
Telephone: (920) 403-3181 Carnegie Class: Bac/A&S
FAX Number: (920) 403-4008 Calendar System: Semester
URL: www.snc.edu
Established: 1898 Annual Undergrad Tuition & Fees: $34,237
Enrollment: 2,112 Coed
Affiliation or Control: Roman Catholic IRS Status: 501(c)3
Highest Offering: Master's
Program: Liberal Arts And General; Teacher Preparatory; Professional
Accreditation: NH

01 President ... Mr. Thomas KUNKEL
05 Vice Pres Acad Affs/Dean of Col ... Dr. Jeffrey FRICK
10 Vice President Business & Finance ... Ms. Eileen JAHNKE
30 Vice Pres Institutional Advancement ... Mr. Phil OSWALD
32 Vice Pres Mission & Student Affairs ... Rev. Jay J. FOSTNER
84 Vice Pres Enrollment Mgmt/Comm ... Mr. Edward LAMM

44 Assoc Vice Pres Inst Advancement Ms. Lynette GREEN
09 Assoc VP Instiutional Effectiveness Dr. Ray ZURAWSKI
20 Associate Academic Dean Dr. Michael ROSEWALL
36 Director Career Services Ms. Mary Ellen OLSON
35 Associate Dean Student Life Vacant
38 Dir Counseling/Career Programs Mr. Bruce ROBERTSON
07 Actg Exec Director of Admissions Mr. Mark SELIN
29 Director Alumni & Parent Relations Mr. Todd DANEN
21 Director of Finance Mr. Curt KOWALESKI
37 Director of Financial Aid Ms. Jessica RAFELD
26 Director Communications/Marketing Mr. Drew VAN FOSSEN
08 Director of Library Dr. Kristin D. VOGEL
15 Director Human Resources Mr. Gary A. UMHOEFER
41 Director Physical Educ/Athletics Mr. Tim BALD
06 Registrar Ms. Cathy TRAVIS
13 Vice Pres & Chief Info Officer Ms. Raechelle CLEMMONS
104 Assoc Academic Dir Global Affairs Ms. Gratzia VILLARROEL
28 Dir Multicultural Student Services Ms. Bridgit MARTIN
18 Director Facilities/Physical Plant Mr. Patrick WRENN
40 Manager Bookstore Operations Ms. Monica WITTROCK
04 Administrative Asst to President Ms. Jamie MCGUIRE
102 Dir Foundation/Corporate Relations Ms. Amy KUNDINGER
100 Chief of Staff Ms. Amy SORENSON
19 Director Security/Safety Mr. Steve JAKUPS
39 Director Student Housing Mr. Michael PECKHAM

Silver Lake College of the Holy Family (A)

2406 S Alverno Road, Manitowoc WI 54220-9319
County: Manitowoc FICE Identification: 003850
Unit ID: 239743
Telephone: (920) 684-6691 Carnegie Class: Bac/Diverse
FAX Number: (920) 684-7082 Calendar System: Semester
URL: www.sl.edu
Established: 1935 Annual Undergrad Tuition & Fees: $24,000
Enrollment: 629 Coed
Affiliation or Control: Roman Catholic IRS Status: 501(c)3
Highest Offering: Master's
Program: Liberal Arts And General; Teacher Preparatory; Professional
Accreditation: NH, MUS, NURSE

01 President Dr. Chris E. DOMES
05 VP Academic Affs/Dean Faculty Ms. Vicki ANSORGE
10 VP of Finance & Business Vacant
30 VP Advancement/External Relations Mr. Marc BARBEAU
42 Director of Campus Ministry Vacant
06 Registrar/Dir Institutional Rsrch Ms. Rachel FISCHER
08 Head Librarian Ms. Natalie LONG
37 Director Student Financial Aid Ms. Erica PLOECKELMAN
29 Director Alumni/Parent Relations Ms. Cindy ST. JOHN
18 Director of Facilities Mr. Rayshaun WILLIAMS
13 Director Technology Services Mr. Jeff RAHMLOW
15 Director Human Resources Vacant
36 Dir Career Res/Experiential Lrng Ms. Jan L. ALGOZINE
21 Associate Business Officer Ms. Melissa DIENER
26 Director Marketing/Communications Mr. Ben WIDEMAN
20 Associate Dean/Academic Affairs Vacant
09 Coordinator IR/Asst Registrar Ms. Amy ECKLEY
28 Chair of Diversity Ms. Julie KAUTZER
19 Director of Campus Security Mr. Randy AMMERMAN
44 Director of Annual Fund/Major Gifts Ms. Roxanna STRAWN
07 Director of Admissions Ms. Jamie GRANT
41 Athletic Director Mr. Mike FLENTJE
32 Dir Residence/Student Life Ms. Rachel FISHER
39 Director Student Housing Mr. Toushane EVANS
84 Dir Retention/Enrollment Services Mr. Dan CONNOLLY

University of Phoenix Milwaukee Main Campus (B)

10850 West Park Place, Suite 150,
Milwaukee WI 53224-3606
Telephone: (414) 410-7900 Identification: 770235
Accreditation: &NH, ACBSP

† No longer accepting campus-based students.

*University of Wisconsin System (C)

1220 Linden Dr, 1720 Van Hise Hall,
Madison WI 53706-1559
County: Dane FICE Identification: 003894
Unit ID: 240435
Telephone: (608) 262-2321 Carnegie Class: N/A
FAX Number: (608) 262-3985
URL: www.wisconsin.edu

01 President Ray W. CROSS
05 Sr Vice Pres Academic Affairs David WARD
11 Sr VP Administration/Fiscal Affairs David MILLER
10 Vice President Finance Vacant
26 Vice Pres University Relations James C. VILLA
15 Interim AVP Human Resources Margo LESSARD
09 Int AVP Policy Analysis/Research Sue BUTH
13 Assoc VP Learning/Info Tech Sasi PILLAY
45 Assoc VP Budget & Planning Freda J. HARRIS
27 AVP Ext Rels/Strategic Comm Alex HUMMEL
43 General Counsel Tomas L. STAFFORD
100 Chief of Staff Jessica TORMEY

*University of Wisconsin-Madison (D)

500 Lincoln Drive, Madison WI 53706-1380
County: Dane FICE Identification: 003895
Unit ID: 240444
Telephone: (608) 262-1234 Carnegie Class: RU/VH
FAX Number: (608) 262-0123 Calendar System: Semester
URL: www.wisc.edu
Established: 1848 Annual Undergrad Tuition & Fees (In-State): $10,691
Enrollment: 42,598 Coed
Affiliation or Control: State IRS Status: 501(c)3
Highest Offering: Doctorate
Program: Liberal Arts And General; Teacher Preparatory; Professional
Accreditation: NH, ARCPA, ART, AUD, BUS, BUSA, CAATE, CIDA, CLPSY, COPSY, CORE, CYTO, DANCE, DIETD, DMS, ENG, IPSY, LAW, LIB, LSAR, MED, MUS, NURSE, OT, PCSAS, PH, PHAR, PLNG, PTA, RAD, SCPSY, SP, SW, THEA, VET

02 Chancellor Dr. Rebecca BLANK
05 Provost Academic Affairs Dr. Sarah MANGELSDORF
11 Vice Chancellor Administration Mr. Darrell BAZZELL
13 CIO/Vice Provost Info Technology Mr. Bruce MAAS
100 Chancellor's Chief of Staff Vacant
30 Int Vice Chanc University Relations Mr. Charles HOSLET
84 Vice Provost Enrollment Management Mr. Steven HAHN
18 Assoc Vice Chanc Facil Plng/Mgmt Mr. William ELVEY
28 Vice Provost Diversity/Climate Dr. Patrick SIMS
20 Assoc Vice Chanc Faculty/Staff Pgms Dr. Michael BERNARD-DONALS
20 Assoc Vice Chanc Teaching/Learning Dr. Steven M. CRAMER
10 Asst Vice Chanc Business Services Ms. Martha KERNER
32 Dean of Students Ms. Lori BERQUAM
58 Dean Graduate School Dr. Marsha R. MAILICK
58 Assoc Dean Graduate School Ms. Petra SCHROEDER
49 Dean College Letters & Science Dr. John K. SCHOLZ
63 Dean Medicine and Public Health Dr. Robert N. GOLDEN
53 Dean School of Education Dr. Diana HESS
50 Dean School of Business Dr. Francois ORTALO-MAGNE'
67 Dean School of Pharmacy Dr. Steven M. SWANSON
54 Dean of College of Engineering Dr. Ian ROBERTSON
47 Dean of Agricultural/Life Sciences Dr. Kathryn VANDENBOSCH
66 Dean of School of Nursing Dr. Katharyn A. MAY
59 Dean of Human Ecology Dr. Soyeon SHIM
74 Dean of Veterinary Medicine Dr. Mark D. MARKEL
61 Dean of the Law School Dr. Margaret RAYMOND
82 Dean International Studies Dr. Guido PODESTÁ
43 Director of Admin Legal Services Mr. Raymond P. TAFFORA
88 Director Environmental Studies Dr. Paul ROBBINS
41 Director Intercollegiate Athletics Mr. Barry L. ALVAREZ
88 Director of Physical Plant Mr. Robert D. LAMPPA
88 Int Director of Arboretum Dr. Donna M. PAULNOCK
88 Director State Lab of Hygiene Dr. Charles BROKOPP
88 Director of Wisconsin Union Mr. Mark C. GUTHIER
07 Director of Admissions Ms. Adele BRUMFIELD
08 Director of Libraries Mr. Edward VANGEMERT
26 Director University Communications Mr. John LUCAS
102 President UW Foundation Dr. Michael M. KNETTER
29 Director of Alumni Association Ms. Paula E. BONNER
37 Director Student Financial Services Ms. Susan FISCHER
38 Director of Counseling Services Dr. Danielle OAKLEY
15 Director Human Resources Mr. Robert LAVIGNA
39 Director of University Housing Dr. Jeffrey NOVAK
51 Dean Continuing Studies Dr. Jeffrey RUSSELL
19 Director of University Police Ms. Susan RISELING
88 Director of Archives Mr. David NULL
23 Director University Health Service Dr. Sarah A. VAN ORMAN
88 Director of Space Management Mr. Douglas N. ROSE
17 President Hospital & Clinics Ms. Donna KATEN-BAHENSKY
109 Dir Auxiliary Operations Analysis Ms. Donna HALLERAN
06 Registrar Mr. Scott OWCZAREK
88 Secretary of the Faculty Mr. Steven K. SMITH
88 Secretary of Academic Staff Ms. Heather M. DANIELS
88 Director of Recreational Sports Mr. John HORN
16 Director of Academic Personnel Mr. Stephen R. LUND
16 Director Classified Personnel Mr. Mark WALTERS
85 Dir International Student Services Ms. Laurie COX
22 Dir Office of Equity & Diversity Mr. Luis A. PINERO
96 Director of Purchasing Ms. Martha KERNER
09 Dir Instl Rsrch/Acad Plng/Analysis Dr. Jocelyn L. MILNER
88 Special Asst to Provost Dr. Eden INOWAY-RONNIE
86 Sr Special Asst to Chanc Fed Rels Mr. Ben J. MILLER

*University of Wisconsin-Eau Claire (E)

105 Garfield Avenue, PO Box 4004,
Eau Claire WI 54702-4004
County: Eau Claire FICE Identification: 003917
Unit ID: 240268
Telephone: (715) 836-2637 Carnegie Class: Master's M
FAX Number: (715) 836-2902 Calendar System: Semester
URL: www.uwec.edu
Established: 1916 Annual Undergrad Tuition & Fees (In-State): $8,822
Enrollment: 10,689 Coed
Affiliation or Control: State IRS Status: 501(c)3
Highest Offering: Doctorate
Program: Liberal Arts And General; Teacher Preparatory; Professional
Accreditation: NH, BUS, CAATE, #JOUR, MUS, NURSE, SP, SW

02 Chancellor Dr. James C. SCHMIDT
05 Prov/Vice Chanc Academic Affairs Dr. Patricia A. KLEINE
100 Special Assistant to the Chancellor Ms. Mary Jane BRUKARDT
32 Vice Chanc Student Affairs Dr. Beth A. HELLWIG
46 Asst VC Research/Sponsored Pgm Dr. Karen G. HAVHOLM
18 Asst Chanc Facilities/Univ Rels Mr. Michael J. RINDO
20 Assoc Vice Chanc Academic Affairs Dr. Michael R. WICK
88 Assoc Vice Chanc Curriculium/Intl Dr. Michael J. CARNEY
35 Associate Dean of Students Ms. Jodi M. THESING-RITTER
45 Executive Director Mktg & Planning Ms. Mary Jane BRUKARDT
22 Director of Affirmative Action Ms. Teresa E. O'HALLORAN
102 Pres UWEC Found/Dir Univ Advance Ms. Kimera K. WAY
10 Director of Budget & Resource Plan Ms. Kristen M. HENDRICKSON
32 Dean of Students Dr. Joseph J. ABHOLD
07 Director of Admissions Ms. Heather M. KRETZ
28 Asst Director of Multicultural Affs Mr. Charles C. VUE
08 Director of Libraries Mr. John H. POLLITZ
13 Chief Information Officer Mr. Chip P. ECKARDT
14 Dir Learning & Technology Services Mr. Craig A. MEY
15 Director of Human Resources Mr. David J. MILLER
37 Director of Financial Aid Ms. Kathleen A. SAHLHOFF
38 Director of Counseling Ms. Lynn Y. WILSON
06 Registrar Ms. Tessa A. PERCHINSKY
36 Assoc Director Career Services Ms. Staci L. HEIDTKE
19 Director of University Police Mr. David W. SPRICK
23 Director of Student Health Services Ms. Laura G. CHELLMAN
39 Int Director of Housing/Resid Life Mr. J. Quincy CHAPMAN
41 Director of Athletics Mr. Daniel J. SCHUMACHER
51 Director Continuing Education Mr. Durwin LONG
85 Interim Director Intl Education Ms. Colleen C. MARCHWICK
29 Director Alumni Relations Mr. John G. BACHMEIER
92 Director of Honors Program Dr. Jefford B. VAHLBUSCH
26 Chief Public Relations Officer Mr. Michael J. RINDO
27 Director of Integrated Marketing Ms. Rebecca J. DIENGER
30 Chief Development/Alumni Relations Ms. Kimera K. WAY
96 Purchasing Agent Ms. Karen E. MCINTYRE
09 Institutional Planner Mr. Andrew J. NELSON
108 Director of Assessment Dr. Jennifer J. FAGER
49 Dean College of Arts & Sciences Dr. David E. LEAMAN
66 Dean Col of Nursing/Health Sciences Dr. Linda K. YOUNG
53 Dean Col Education/Human Sciences Dr. Carmen K. MANNING
50 Dean College of Business Dr. Diane HOADLEY
04 Executive Asst to Chancellor Ms. Suzanne C. OLSON

*University of Wisconsin-Green Bay (F)

2420 Nicolet Drive, Green Bay WI 54311-7001
County: Brown FICE Identification: 003899
Unit ID: 240277
Telephone: (920) 465-2000 Carnegie Class: Master's S
FAX Number: (920) 465-2032 Calendar System: Semester
URL: www.uwgb.edu
Established: 1965 Annual Undergrad Tuition & Fees (In-State): $7,824
Enrollment: 6,700 Coed
Affiliation or Control: State IRS Status: 501(c)3
Highest Offering: Master's
Program: Liberal Arts And General; Teacher Preparatory; Professional
Accreditation: NH, ART, CAHIIM, DIETD, DIETI, MUS, NURSE, SW

02 Chancellor Dr. Gary L. MILLER
05 Interim Provost/Vice Chancellor Dr. Gregory DAVIS
10 Vice Chanc Business & Finance Mr. Kelly J. FRANZ
30 Vice Chanc University Advancement Ms. Jeanne A. STANGEL
32 Dean of Students Dr. Brenda AMENSON-HILL
13 Assoc Provost Information Services Vacant
20 Assoc Provost for Academic Affairs Vacant
107 Dean Professional Studies Dr. Sue JOSEPH MATTISON
49 Dean Liberal Arts & Sciences Dr. Scott FURLONG
51 Int Dean of Continuing Education Ms. Christina TROMBLEY
43 Legal Counsel Vacant
07 Director of Admissions Ms. Pam HARVEY-JACOBS
15 Director of Human Resources Ms. Sheryl VAN GRUENSVEN
18 Dir Facilities Management/Planning Mr. Paul PINKSTON
19 Director Public Safety Mr. Thomas KUJAWA
41 Director Athletics Ms. Mary Ellen GILLESPIE
21 Controller Ms. SuAnn DETAMPEL
09 Director Institutional Research Dr. Deborah FURLONG
84 Int Dean Enrollment & Acad Svcs Mr. Timothy SEWALL
46 Director of Institute for Research Ms. Lidia NONN
37 Director Financial Aid Mr. James P. ROHAN
39 Director of Residence Life Ms. Gail SIMS-AUBERT
40 Director Bookstore Mr. Gregory KANNENBERG
24 Director Media Svcs/Telecomm Mr. William HUBBARD
23 Director Health Services Ms. Amy HENNIGES
96 Director of Institutional Support Vacant
38 Director Counseling Services Mr. Gregory L. SMITH
100 Chief of Staff Mr. Dan SPIELMANN
26 Director University Communications Mr. Christopher SAMPSON
36 Director Career Services Ms. Linda G. PEACOCK-LANDRUM
29 Director Alumni Relations Ms. Kari MOODY
35 Director Student Life Ms. Lisa TETZLOFF
06 Registrar Ms. Amanda HRUSKA
04 Administrative Asst to President Ms. Paula MARCEC
08 Library Director Ms. Paula GANYARD
104 Director Study Abroad Mr. Brent BLAHNIK
28 Director of Diversity Dr. Justin MALLETT
44 Director of Development Ms. Kim DESOTELL

*University of Wisconsin-La Crosse (G)

1725 State Street, La Crosse WI 54601-3788
County: La Crosse FICE Identification: 003919
Unit ID: 240329
Telephone: (608) 785-8000 Carnegie Class: Master's L
FAX Number: (608) 785-8492 Calendar System: Semester
URL: www.uwlax.edu
Established: 1909 Annual Undergrad Tuition & Fees (In-State): $8,962
Enrollment: 10,555 Coed

Affiliation or Control: State IRS Status: 501(c)3
Highest Offering: Doctorate
Program: Liberal Arts And General; Teacher Preparatory; Professional
Accreditation: NH, ARCPA, BUS, CAATE, MUS, NMT, NRPA, OT, PH, PTA, RADDOS, RTT

02 Chancellor Dr. Joe GOW
05 Provost/Vice Chanc Acad Affairs Dr. Betsy MORGAN
30 Vice Chancellor Advancement Mr. Greg REICHERT
10 Vice Chancellor Admin & Finance Dr. Bob HETZEL
84 Assoc Vice Chanc Enrollment Mgmt Dr. Fred PIERCE
50 Dean of Business Administration Dr. Laura MILNER
53 Director School of Education Dr. Marcie WYCOFF-HORN
79 Dean of Liberal Studies Dr. Julia JOHNSON
76 Dean Science Health Dr. Bruce RILEY
58 Assoc V Chan Acad/Dir Univ Grad Std Dr. Robert HOAR
32 Asst Chancellor & Dean of Students Dr. Paula M. KNUDSON
13 Chief Information Officer Dr. Mohamed ELHINDI
15 Director of Human Resources Ms. Madeline HOLZEM
51 Director Continuing Educ/Exten Ms. Penny TIEDT
08 Director of Library Ms. Catherine LAVALLÉE-WELCH
85 Director International Education Mr. Fred M. PIERCE
07 Director ES/Admissions Mr. Corey SJOQUIST
06 Registrar Dr. Christine S. BAKKUM
37 Director ES/Financial Aid Ms. Louise L. JANKE
38 Director Counseling/Testing Ms. Gretchen REINDERS
36 Director of Career Services Ms. Gail BEAUSOLEIL
41 Athletic Director Ms. Kim BLUM
26 Director News and Marketing Mr. Brad R. QUARBERG
29 Director Alumni Relations Ms. Janie M. MORGAN
23 Director Student Health Center Dr. Brian K. ALLEN
09 Director Institutional Research Ms. Natalie SOLVERSON
19 Interim Chief of University Police Mr. Scott MC COLLOUGH
18 Director Physical Plant Mr. Hank M. KLOS
28 Assoc Dean Campus Climate/Diversity Ms. Barbara E. STEWART
22 Director Affirmative Action Mr. Nizam ARAIN
106 Dir Online Education/E-learning Dr. Brian UDERMANN
39 Director Student Housing Mr. Nick NICKLAUS

*University of Wisconsin-Milwaukee (A)

PO Box 413, Milwaukee WI 53201-0413
County: Milwaukee FICE Identification: 003896
Unit ID: 240453
Telephone: (414) 229-1122 Carnegie Class: RU/H
FAX Number: (414) 229-6329 Calendar System: Semester
URL: www.uwm.edu
Established: 1885 Annual Undergrad Tuition & Fees (In-State): $9,429
Enrollment: 28,042 Coed
Affiliation or Control: State IRS Status: 501(c)3
Highest Offering: Doctorate
Program: Liberal Arts And General; Teacher Preparatory; Professional; Business Emphasis
Accreditation: NH, BUS, CAATE, CEA, CLPSY, COPSY, CS, DANCE, ENG, LIB, MT, MUS, NURSE, OT, PLNG, PTA, RAD, SCPSY, SP, SW

02 Chancellor Dr. Mark MONE
05 Provost/Vice Chanc Academic Affairs Dr. Johannes BRITZ
10 Vice Chanc Finance & Admin Affs Ms. Robin L. VAN HARPEN
26 Vice Chanc Univ Rels/Communications Mr. Thomas L. LULJAK
46 Interim Vice Provost of Research Dr. Mark T. HARRIS
32 Vice Chancellor Student Affairs Dr. Michael R. LALIBERTE
30 Vice Chancellor Development Dr. Patricia A. BORGER
88 Vice Chanc Global Inclusion & Engag Dr. Joan M. PRINCE
20 Assoc Vice Chanc Academic Affairs Dr. Devarajan VENUGOPALAN
20 Assoc Vice Chanc Academic Affs Dr. Phyllis KING
28 Interim Assoc VC Diversity Dr. Cheryl S. AJIROTUTU
84 Assoc Vice Chanc Enrollment Mgmt Vacant
13 Chief Information Officer Dr. Robert J. BECK
18 Assoc VC Facilities Planning/Mgmt Mr. Geoffrey HURTADO
04 Senior Advisor to the Chancellor Mr. David H. GILBERT
76 Int Dean College Health Sciences Dr. Ronald A. CISLER
48 Dean Architecture & Urban Planning Dr. Robert C. GREENSTREET
50 Int Dean School of Business Dr. Kanti PRASAD
53 Interim Dean of School of Education Dr. Barbara J. DALEY
54 Dean Col Engr & Applied Science Dr. Brett PETERS
57 Dean Peck School of the Arts Dr. Scott EMMONS
88 Dean of Freshwater Science Dr. David GARMAN
69 Int Dean School of Public Health Dr. Ronald PEREZ
58 Dean Graduate School Dr. Marija GAJDARDZISKA-JOSIFOVSKA
49 Dean College Letters & Science Dr. Rodney SWAIN
62 Dean School Information Studies Dr. Tomas LIPINSKI
66 Dean of College of Nursing Dr. Sally LUNDEEN
70 Dean Helen Bader Sch Social Welfare Dr. Stan STOJKOVIC
51 Int Dean School of Continuing Educ Dr. Paula M. RHYNER
35 Dean of Students Dr. Timothy GORDON
22 Dir Equity/Diversity Services Ms. Jazmin TAYLOR
08 Director of the Library Ms. Ewa BARCZYK
43 Director Legal Affairs Ms. Joely B. URDAN
06 Registrar Mr. Seth J. ZLOTOCHA
15 Assoc VC Human Resources Mr. Timothy DANIELSON
19 Interim Chief University Police Mr. Gregory HABECK
25 Director Office Sponsored Research Mr. Thomas MARCUSSEN
23 Director Health Center Dr. Julia BONNER
09 Dir Assessment/Institutional Rsrch Dr. Gesele DURHAM
85 Director Center for Intl Education Dr. Patrice S. PETRO
37 Int Exec Dir Financial Aid Mr. Mark LEVINE
39 Director of Residence Life Mr. Scott S. PEAK
41 Athletic Director Ms. Amanda BRAUN
40 Director Bookstore Mr. Erik G. HEMMING
36 Int Dir Career Development Center Ms. Cindy PETRITES
27 Dir Univ Communications & Media Rel Ms. Laura GLAWE
21 Dir Business & Financial Svcs Mr. Jerry TARRER
29 Director Alumni Relations Ms. Adrienne BASS
96 Purchasing Manager Ms. Joan C. AGUADO-WARE
45 Dir Budget & Planning Ms. Cindy KLUGE
07 Director of Admissions & Recruiting Mr. Brian TROYER

*University of Wisconsin-Oshkosh (B)

800 Algoma Boulevard, Oshkosh WI 54901-3551
County: Winnebago FICE Identification: 003920
Unit ID: 240365
Telephone: (920) 424-1234 Carnegie Class: Master's L
FAX Number: (920) 424-7317 Calendar System: Semester
URL: www.uwosh.edu
Established: 1871 Annual Undergrad Tuition & Fees (In-State): $7,490
Enrollment: 14,542 Coed
Affiliation or Control: State IRS Status: 501(c)3
Highest Offering: Doctorate
Program: Liberal Arts And General; Teacher Preparatory; Professional
Accreditation: NH, BUS, CAATE, CACREP, CS, CSHSE, EXSC, IFSAC, JOUR, MUS, NURSE, SW

02 Chancellor Dr. Andrew J. LEAVITT
05 Provost & Vice Chancellor Dr. Lane R. EARNS
20 Asst Vice Chanc Curricular Affairs Dr. Carleen VANDE ZANDE
20 Asst Vice Chanc Acad Support Dr. Sylvia CAREY-BUTLER
51 Asst Vice Chanc Lifelong Learning Vacant
32 Vice Chancellor Student Affairs Dr. Petra ROTER
10 Vice Chancellor Administrative Svcs Mr. Thomas G. SONNLEITNER
21 Associate Vice Chanc Admin Svcs Ms. Lori M. WORM
06 Registrar Ms. Lisa M. DANIELSON
22 Affirmative Action Officer Ms. Ameerah MCBRIDE
09 Director of Institutional Research Mr. Michael W. WATSON
38 Director of Counseling Center Dr. Sandy COX
13 CIO Director Info Technology Ms. Ann MILKOVICH
50 Dean Business Dr. William TALLON
66 Dean Nursing Dr. Leslie NEAL BOYLAN
53 Dean Education & Human Services Dr. Frederick L. YEO
49 Dean Letters & Sciences Dr. John J. KOKER
102 Pres Univ of Wisc Oshkosh Foundatn Mr. Arthur H. RATHJEN
29 Director of Alumni Association Ms. Christine M. GANTNER
37 Director of Financial Aid Mr. Kim DONAT
26 Exec Director Integrated Marketing Ms. Jamie CEMAN
25 Director Grants/Faculty Development Mr. Robert W. ROBERTS
35 Dean of Students Dr. Sharon KIPETZ
58 Director Graduate Studies Mr. Gregory WYPISZYNSKI
07 Director of Admissions Ms. Jill M. ENDRIES
15 Director of Human Resources Ms. Laurie TEXTOR
18 Facilities/Physical Plant Director Vacant
36 Director of Career Services Ms. Jaime PAGE-STADLER
96 Purchasing/Printing Manager Mr. Barry GAUTHIER
92 Director University Honors Program Dr. Laurence CARLIN
08 Director Library Mr. Patrick J. WILKINSON
04 Administrative Asst to President Ms. Suzette THIBADEAU
104 Director Study Abroad Ms. Jenna GRAFF
28 Director of Diversity Vacant
39 Director Student Housing Mr. Tom FOJTIK
41 Athletic Director Mr. Darryl SIMS
90 Director Academic Computing Ms. Laura KNAAPEN

*University of Wisconsin-Parkside (C)

900 Wood Road, Box 2000, Kenosha WI 53141-2000
County: Kenosha FICE Identification: 005015
Unit ID: 240374
Telephone: (262) 595-2345 Carnegie Class: Bac/A&S
FAX Number: (262) 595-2202 Calendar System: Semester
URL: www.uwp.edu
Established: 1968 Annual Undergrad Tuition & Fees (In-State): $7,326
Enrollment: 4,584 Coed
Affiliation or Control: State IRS Status: 501(c)3
Highest Offering: Master's
Program: Liberal Arts And General; Teacher Preparatory; Professional
Accreditation: NH, BUS

02 Chancellor Deborah L. FORD
05 Interim Provost/Vice Chancellor Fred EBEID
10 Vice Chanc Admin/Fiscal Affairs Melvin KLINKNER
32 Dean of Students Tammy MCGUCKIN
84 Assoc Vice Chanc Enrollment Mgmt DeAnn L. POSSEHL
30 Asst Chanc Univ Rels/Advancement John JARACZEWSKI
20 Associate Provost Gary WOOD
20 Assoc VC Ofc of Academic Affairs Kimberly KELLEY
28 University Diversity & Inclusion Heather KIND-KEPPEL
50 Dean Col of Bus Econ & Comput Dirk BALDWIN
49 Dean College of Arts/Humanities Lesley WALKER
81 Dean College of Nat & Hlth Sciences Emmanual OTU
83 Int Dean Social Sci & Prof Studies Peggy JAMES
31 Exec Dir Ctr for Comty Partnerships Debra KARP
08 Interim Director of the Library Anna STADICK
13 Chief Information Officer Ilya YAKOVLEV
93 Director Minority Student Services Damian EVANS
21 Dir Business Services/Controller Scott MENKE
15 Int Director Human Resources Scott MENKE
19 Dir Campus Police/Public Safety James HELLER
37 Interim Director Financial Aid Kristina KLEMENS
29 Coord Donor Relations & Stewardship Melissa GREINER
06 Registrar Rhonda KIMMEL
36 Dir of Advising/Career Center Gwen JONES
18 Director Facilities Management Donald A. KOLBE
94 Director of Women's Studies Mary LENARD
96 Director of Purchasing James EISENHAUER
35 Assoc Dean of Students Steve WALLNER
38 Dir Health/Counseling/Disability Renee KIRBY
40 Manager Bookstore Diane SESSA
07 Director Recruit & Admissions Troy MOLDENHAUER
04 Administrative Asst to President Diane DONNELLY
104 Assoc Director Intl Education Vacant
39 Director Residence Life George HOLMAN
41 Athletic Director Tamie FALK-DAY
105 Director Web Services Elizabeth MCGEE
26 Chief Public Relations/Marketing John MIELKE

*University of Wisconsin-Platteville (D)

1 University Plaza, Platteville WI 53818-3099
County: Grant FICE Identification: 003921
Unit ID: 240462
Telephone: (608) 342-1491 Carnegie Class: Master's L
FAX Number: (608) 342-1232 Calendar System: Semester
URL: www.uwplatt.edu
Established: 1866 Annual Undergrad Tuition & Fees (In-State): $7,491
Enrollment: 8,901 Coed
Affiliation or Control: State IRS Status: 501(c)3
Highest Offering: Master's
Program: Liberal Arts And General; Teacher Preparatory; Professional
Accreditation: NH, ENG, MUS, NAIT

02 Chancellor Mr. Dennis J. SHIELDS
05 Provost & Vice Chancellor Dr. Mittie NIMOCKS DEN HERDER
100 Spec Asst to Chanc/Chief of Staff Ms. Rose M. SMYRSKI
11 Vice Chanc Administrative Services Mr. Robert G. CRAMER
32 Assoc Vice Chanc Student Affairs Dr. Laura BAYLESS
30 Asst Chanc Univ Advance/Foundation Vacant
58 Director Graduate School Dr. Dominic BARRACLOUGH
06 Registrar Mr. David S. KIECKHAFER
07 Dir Admissions and Enrollment Svcs Ms. Angela M. UDELHOFEN
37 Director of Financial Aid Ms. Tracey K. MINGO
38 Director Student Counseling Ms. Deirdre L. DALSING
26 Dir Univ Info/Comm/Public Rels Mr. Paul J. ERICKSON
41 Director Intercollegiate Athletics Mr. Mark D. MOLESWORTH
39 Director of Residence Life Mrs. Linda MULROY-BOWDEN
15 Director Human Resources Mr. John LOHMANN
19 Director Security/Safety Mr. Scott E. MARQUARDT
92 Chair History Department Dr. Nancy L. TURNER
93 Dir Multicultural Educ Resource Ctr Ms. Angela M. MILLER
96 Director of Purchasing Mr. Lewis BETTINGER
08 Director of Library Ms. Zora J. SAMPSON
18 Director of Facilities Management Mr. Pete D. DAVIS
36 Director of Career Center Ms. Diana J. TRENDT
51 Director Continuing Education Ms. Marian G. MACIEJ-HINER
29 Coordinator Alumni Relations Ms. Kimberly G. SCHMELZ
49 Dean Col Liberal Arts/Education Dr. Elizabeth A. THROOP
54 Dean Col of Engr/Math/Science Dr. Molly GRIBB
47 Dean Business Life Sci/Agric Dr. Wayne C. WEBER
28 Asst Chanc/Chief Diversity Officer Dr. Jennifer M. DECOSTE
20 Asst Vice Chanc of Academic Affairs Mrs. D. Joanne WILSON
108 Exec Dir Institutional Effectivenes Ms. Nettie DANIELS
13 Chief Info Technology Officer Ms. Suzanne A. TRAXLER
22 Dir Affirmative Action/EEO Ms. Catherine M. KUTKA

*University of Wisconsin-River Falls (E)

410 S Third Street, River Falls WI 54022-5013
County: Pierce FICE Identification: 003923
Unit ID: 240471
Telephone: (715) 425-3911 Carnegie Class: Master's M
FAX Number: (715) 425-4487 Calendar System: Semester
URL: www.uwrf.edu
Established: 1874 Annual Undergrad Tuition & Fees (In-State): $8,182
Enrollment: 6,184 Coed
Affiliation or Control: State IRS Status: 501(c)3
Highest Offering: Beyond Master's But Less Than Doctorate
Program: Liberal Arts And General; Teacher Preparatory; Professional
Accreditation: NH, BUS, MACTE, MUS, SP, SW

02 Chancellor Dr. Dean A. VAN GALEN
05 Vice Chancellor & Provost Dr. Fernando P. DELGADO
10 Assistant Chancellor Bus/Finance Ms. Elizabeth FRUEH
30 Assistant Chancellor of Advancement Mr. Chris MUELLER
85 Int Asst VC for International Pgms Ms. Katrina LARSEN
20 Int Associate VC Academic Affairs Dr. Wesley CHAPIN
32 Assoc Vice Chanc Student Affs Mr. Gregg HEINSELMAN
21 Controller Mr. Joel HEUSCHELE
47 Dean Agricult/Food/Environ Sci Dr. Dale GALLENBERG
53 Dean Education/Profess Studies Dr. Larry SOLBERG
49 Dean of Arts & Sciences Dr. Bradley J. CASKEY
50 Dean Business & Economics Dr. Michael FRONMUELLER
13 Chief Information Officer Mr. Stephen REED
15 Chief Human Resources Officer Ms. Donna ROBOLE
18 Exec Dir Facilities/Planning/Mgmt Mr. Michael J. STIFTER
22 Interim Director Affirmative Action Mrs. Donna ROBOLE
88 Director of Enrollment/Student Succ Mr. Mark R. MEYDAM
06 Registrar Mr. Daniel VANDE YACHT
07 Director of Admissions Mrs. Sarah EGERSTROM
46 Director Grants & Research Ms. Molly VAN WAGNER
08 Director of Library Ms. Valerie I. MALZACHER
35 Director of Student Life Mr. Paul SHEPHERD

41 Athletic Director ... Mr. Roger TERNES
37 Director Financial Assistance ... Ms. Barbara J. STINSON
45 Director Campus Planning ... Mr. Dale K. BRAUN
19 Director of Protective Services ... Mr. Karl FLEURY
96 Director Purchasing Services ... Ms. Gail ANDERSON
88 Dir Academic Success Center ... Ms. Chuayi YANG
35 Dir Student Services & Programs ... Mr. Gregg M. HEINSELMAN
29 Director Alumni Relations ... Mr. Daniel E. MCGINTY
09 Director of Institutional Research ... Mrs. Jennifer DREWS
92 Director Honors Program ... Ms. Kathleen HUNZER
38 Director Student Counseling ... Ms. Alice REILLY-MYKLEBUST
56 Outreach Program Manager ... Ms. Pamela BOWEN
88 McNair Scholars Director ... Dr. Natalie STROBACH
26 Director of Communications and ER ... Dr. Blake W. FRY
39 Director of Student Housing ... Ms. Karla THOENNES
40 Manager Bookstore ... Ms. Liz RUST

*University of Wisconsin-Stevens Point (A)

2100 Main Street, Stevens Point WI 54481-3871
County: Portage FICE Identification: 003924
Unit ID: 240480
Telephone: (715) 346-0123 Carnegie Class: Master's M
FAX Number: (715) 346-4841 Calendar System: Semester
URL: www.uwsp.edu
Established: 1894 Annual Undergrad Tuition & Fees (In-State): $7,684
Enrollment: 9,292 Coed
Affiliation or Control: State IRS Status: 501(c)3
Highest Offering: Doctorate
Program: Liberal Arts And General; Teacher Preparatory; Professional
Accreditation: NH, ART, AUD, CAATE, CIDA, DANCE, DIETD, ENG, MT, MUS, SP, SW, THEA

02 Chancellor ... Dr. Bernie PATTERSON
05 Provost & Vice Chancellor ... Dr. Greg SUMMERS
10 Vice Chancellor Business Affairs ... Mr. Gregory M. DIEMER
32 Vice Chancellor Student Affairs ... Dr. Al THOMPSON
20 Interim AVC for Tech/Lrng/Acad Pgms ... Dr. Todd HUSPENI
100 Chief of Staff ... Dr. Robert MANZKE
15 AVC Person/Bdgt/Grants/Summer Pgms ... Dr. Katie JORE
51 Exec Dir UWSP Continuing Ed ... Mr. Tom GOSPODARCZYK
07 Director Admissions ... Mr. Bill JORDAN
37 Director of Financial Aid ... Ms. Mandy SLOWINSKI
19 Director Safety & Loss Control ... Mr. Jeff KARCHER
30 Vice Chanc Univ Advancement ... Mr. Chris RICHARDS
29 Director of Alumni Affairs ... Ms. Laura GEHRMAN-ROTTIER
26 Interim Dir Univ Relations/Comm ... Mr. Gary WESCOTT
16 Director of Personnel ... Ms. Pam DOLLARD
38 Director Counseling Center ... Dr. Stacey GERKEN
13 Dir of Information Technology ... Mr. Jim BARRETT
22 Director Equity & Affirm Act ... Ms. Pam DOLLARD
08 Director University Library ... Dr. Kathy DAVIS
06 Interim Registrar ... Mr. Ed LEE
18 Chief Facilities/Physical Plant ... Mr. Paul HASLER
36 Director Student Placement ... Dr. Angie KELLOGG
96 Director of Purchasing ... Ms. Katie SCHROTH
57 Int Dean Col Fine Arts/Communic ... Dr. Rhonda SPRAGUE
49 Dean College of Letters & Science ... Dr. Christopher CIRMO
65 Dean Coll of Natural Resources ... Dr. Christine L. THOMAS
107 Dean Col of Professional Studies ... Dr. Marty LOY
09 Director of Institutional Research ... Vacant
28 Director of Multicultural Affairs ... Mr. Ron STREGE
35 Director Student Affairs ... Dr. Al THOMPSON
04 Administrative Asst to President ... Ms. Jean SCHERER
104 Director Study Abroad ... Dr. Eric YONKE
41 Athletic Director ... Dr. Daron MONTGOMERY
50 Dean of Business ... Dr. Gary MULLINS
84 Director Enrollment Management ... Mr. Jim BARRETT
86 Director Government Relations ... Dr. Robert MANZKE
39 Director Student Housing ... Mr. Brian FAUST

*University of Wisconsin-Stout (B)

712 South Broadway, Menomonie WI 54751-2458
County: Dunn FICE Identification: 003915
Unit ID: 240417
Telephone: (715) 232-1122 Carnegie Class: Master's L
FAX Number: (715) 232-1416 Calendar System: 4/1/4
URL: www.uwstout.edu
Established: 1891 Annual Undergrad Tuition & Fees (In-State): $9,025
Enrollment: 9,371 Coed
Affiliation or Control: State IRS Status: 501(c)3
Highest Offering: Beyond Master's But Less Than Doctorate
Program: Liberal Arts And General; Teacher Preparatory; Professional
Accreditation: NH, ACBSP, ART, CACREP, CIDA, CONST, CORE, CS, DIETD, DIETI, ENG, ENGT, MFCD, TED

02 Chancellor ... Dr. Robert MEYER
05 Provost & Vice Chancellor ... Dr. Patrick GUILFOILE
10 Vice Chanc for Admin/Student Life ... Mr. Phil LYONS
20 Associate Vice Chancellor ... Dr. Glendali RODRIQUEZ
30 Vice Chanc Univ Advance/Mktg ... Mr. Mark PARSON
32 Asst VC Student Life Svcs ... Mr. Scott GRIESBACH
28 Asst Vice Chanc for Diversity ... Vacant
45 Asst Chanc Plng/Assess/Rsrch/Qual ... Dr. Meridith DRZAKOWSKI
50 Dean College of Management ... Dr. Abel ADEKOLA
49 Dean Col Arts/Humanities/Social Sci ... Dr. Maria ALM
53 Dean Col of Ed/Hlth/Hum Sci ... Dr. Mary HOPKINS-BEST
81 Dean Col of Science/Tech/Engr/Math ... Dr. Charles BOMAR
35 Dean of Students ... Ms. Joan THOMAS
06 Registrar ... Mr. Scott CORRELL
84 Director Enrollment Management ... Dr. Pamela HOLSINGER-FUCHS
36 Interim Director Career Services ... Mr. Bryan BARTS
08 Director University Library ... Ms. Marlys BRUNSTING
04 Special Assistant to the Chancellor ... Ms. Kristi KRIMPELBEIN
37 Director Student Financial Aid ... Ms. Beth BOISEN
26 Director University Communications ... Mr. Doug MELL
21 Director Business/Financial Svcs ... Ms. Kim SCHULTE-SHOBERG
13 Chief Information Officer ... Mr. Doug J. WAHL
76 Exec Director Health & Safety ... Mr. James UHLIR
15 Interim Director Human Resources ... Ms. Kristi KRIMPELBEIN
38 Director Counseling Center ... Dr. John ACHTER
105 Director Online Services ... Mr. Doug STEVENS
23 Director Student Health Services ... Ms. Janice LAWRENCE-RAMAEKER
40 Director Bookstore ... Ms. Cathy CLOSE
44 Director of the Annual Fund ... Ms. Jennifer RUDIGER
85 Director International Education ... Vacant
18 Director Physical Plant ... Ms. Shirley KLEBESADEL
96 Director Procurement/Materials Mgmt ... Mr. Brent TILTON
39 Dir University Housing ... Ms. Sandra SCOTT DUEX
41 Director Athletics ... Mr. Duey NAATZ
29 Director Alumni Relations ... Ms. Juliet FOX
19 Dir of Safety & Risk Management ... Mr. Dean A. SANKEY
19 Coordinator University Police ... Ms. Lisa A. WALTER
106 Dir Online Education/E-learning ... Mr. Doug STEVENS

*University of Wisconsin-Superior (C)

Belknap and Catlin, PO Box 2000,
Superior WI 54880-4500
County: Douglas FICE Identification: 003925
Unit ID: 240426
Telephone: (715) 394-8101 Carnegie Class: Master's S
FAX Number: (715) 394-8454 Calendar System: Semester
URL: www.uwsuper.edu
Established: 1893 Annual Undergrad Tuition & Fees (In-State): $8,037
Enrollment: 2,600 Coed
Affiliation or Control: State IRS Status: 501(c)3
Highest Offering: Beyond Master's But Less Than Doctorate
Program: Liberal Arts And General; Teacher Preparatory; Professional
Accreditation: NH, MUS, SW

02 Chancellor ... Dr. Renee WACHTER
05 Provost/Vice Chanc Academic Affairs ... Dr. Faith HENSRUD
30 Vice Chanc University Advancement ... Ms. Jeanne E. THOMPSON
32 Dean of Students ... Mr. Harry ANDERSON
21 Controller ... Mr. Robert B. WAKSDAHL
10 Vice Chanc Administration/Finance ... Ms. Gigi KOENIG
15 Director Human Resources ... Ms. Peggy A. FECKER
18 Director Facilities Management ... Mr. Tom FENNESSEY
26 Dir Communications/Government Rels ... Mr. Daniel FANNING
06 Registrar ... Mr. Jeff KIRSHLING
08 Interim Librarian ... Ms. Laura JACOBS
07 Director of Admissions ... Ms. Tonya ROTH
41 Athletic Director ... Mr. Steve NELSON
37 Director Student Financial Aid ... Ms. Donna R. DAHLVANG
13 Director Administrative Info Svcs ... Vacant
51 Dir Center Cont Educ/Online Svcs ... Mr. Ryan MATARA
56 Int Dir Distance Learning/Cont Educ ... Ms. Christina KLINE
40 Director Bookstore ... Mr. Vaughn N. RUSSOM
29 Director Alumni Relations ... Mr. Thomas K. BERGH
38 Director Advisement ... Dr. Christopher CHERRY
28 Director of Diversity ... Mr. Alvin (Chip) BEAL
84 Director Enrollment Management ... Mr. John MUELLER

*University of Wisconsin-Whitewater (D)

800 W Main, Whitewater WI 53190-1790
County: Walworth FICE Identification: 003926
Unit ID: 240189
Telephone: (262) 472-1918 Carnegie Class: Master's L
FAX Number: (262) 472-1518 Calendar System: Semester
URL: www.uww.edu
Established: 1868 Annual Undergrad Tuition & Fees (In-State): $7,600
Enrollment: 12,159 Coed
Affiliation or Control: State IRS Status: 501(c)3
Highest Offering: Doctorate
Program: Liberal Arts And General; Teacher Preparatory; Professional
Accreditation: NH, ART, BUS, CACREP, MUS, SP, SW, TED, THEA

02 Chancellor ... Dr. Beverly A. KOPPER
05 Prov/Vice Chanc Academic Affs ... Dr. John STONE
32 Vice Chancellor Student Affairs ... Dr. Thomas R. RIOS
30 VC Univ Advance/Foundation Pres ... Mr. Jonathan ENSLIN
11 Vice Chanc Administrative Affs ... Mr. Jeff (Dean) ARNOLD
20 Assoc Vice Chanc Academic Affairs ... Dr. Greg COOK
13 Asst Vice Chanc Tech/Info Resource ... Dr. Elena POKOT
84 Asst Vice Chanc Enroll/Retention ... Mr. Matt ASCHENBRENER
09 Director of Institutional Research ... Ms. Lynsey SCHWABROW
20 AVC Multicult Affs/Stdnt Success ... Dr. Richard MCGREGORY
37 Director of Financial Aid ... Ms. Carol A. MILLER
10 Chief Business Officer ... Mr. Jeff (Dean) ARNOLD
26 Chief Public Relations Officer ... Ms. Sara KUHL
21 Director of Budget ... Ms. Aimee C. ARNOLD
07 Director of Admissions ... Dr. Jeremy REED
06 Registrar ... Ms. Jodi M. HARE-PAYNTER
36 Director of Career Services ... Mr. Ron BUCHHOLZ
15 Director Human Resources/Diversity ... Ms. Judith M. TRAMPF
85 Dir Center for Global Education ... Ms. Candace A. CHENOWETH
44 Exec Dir University Development ... Ms. Kate LOFTUS
18 Director Facility Planning/Mgmt ... Mr. Greg SWANSON
38 Exec Dir Univ Health/Counseling Svc ... Dr. Richard L. JAZDZEWSKI
96 Director of Purchasing ... Mr. Michael T. HIRSCHFIELD
28 Director of Diversity ... Dr. Elizabeth OGUNSOLA
92 Director of Honors Program ... Dr. Elizabeth KIM
88 Int Dir Acad Advising/Explor Ctr ... Ms. Pamela TANNER
35 Dean Student Life ... Ms. Mary Beth MACKIN
57 Dean Arts/Communication ... Dr. Robert MERTENS
50 Dean of Business & Economics ... Dr. John CHENOWETH
53 Dean Education/Professional Studies ... Dr. Katharina E. HEYNING
49 Dean Letters & Sciences ... Dr. David TRAVIS
58 Dean Grad Stds/Continuing Educ ... Dr. Seth MEISEL
04 Executive Asst to the Chancellor ... Mrs. Kari HEIDENREICH
41 Athletic Director ... Ms. Amy EDMONDS

*University of Wisconsin Colleges (E)

432 N. Lake Street, Room 401, Madison WI 53706
County: Dane FICE Identification: 003897
Unit ID: 240055
Telephone: (608) 262-3786 Carnegie Class: Assoc/Pub2in4
FAX Number: (608) 262-7872 Calendar System: Semester
URL: www.uwc.edu
Established: 1964 Annual Undergrad Tuition & Fees (In-State): $4,938
Enrollment: 14,182 Coed
Affiliation or Control: State IRS Status: 501(c)3
Highest Offering: Baccalaureate
Program: 2-Year Principally Bachelor's Creditable
Accreditation: NH

02 Chancellor ... Dr. Cathy SANDEEN
05 Provost/Vice Chancellor ... Dr. Gregory P. LAMPE
10 Vice Chancellor Admin & Fin Svcs ... Mr. Steve C. WILDECK
32 Assoc VC Stdt Svcs & Enroll Mgmt ... Dr. Richard BARNHOUSE
20 Associate Vice Chancellor ... Dr. Joseph FOY
13 Chief Information Officer ... Mr. Werner GADE
15 Asst Vice Chanc Human Resources ... Mr. Jason BEIER
06 Registrar ... Mr. Larry GRAVES
37 Director Student Financial Aid ... Mr. William TRIPPETT
26 Exec Director University Relations ... Vacant
28 Dir Equity/Diversity & Inclusion ... Ms. Christine CURLEY
104 Director International Programs ... Mr. Tim URBONYA
12 Dean UW Baraboo/Sauk County ... Dr. Tracy WHITE
12 Dean UW Barron County (Rice Lake) ... Dr. Dean YOHNK
12 Dean UW Fond Du Lac ... Dr. John SHORT
12 Dean UW Fox Valley (Menasha) ... Dr. Martin RUDD
12 Dean UW Manitowoc ... Dr. Charles E. CLARK
12 Dean UW Marathon County ... Dr. Keith MONTGOMERY
12 Dean UW Marinette ... Ms. Paula LANGTEAU
12 Int Dean UW Marshfield/Wood County ... Dr. Keith MONTGOMERY
12 Dean UW Richland ... Dr. Patrick HAGEN
12 Dean UW Rock County ... Dr. Carmen WILSON
12 Dean UW Sheboygan ... Dr. Jackie JOSEPH-SILVERSTEIN
12 Dean UW Washington County ... Dr. Alan Paul PRICE
12 Dean UW Waukesha ... Dr. Harry P. MUIR, JR.

*University of Wisconsin Baraboo/Sauk County (F)

1006 Connie Road, Baraboo WI 53913
Telephone: (608) 355-5200 Identification: 770450
Accreditation: &NH

† Branch campus of University of Wisconsin Colleges, Madison, WI.

*University of Wisconsin Barron County (G)

1800 College Drive, Rice Lake WI 54868
Telephone: (715) 234-8176 Identification: 770457
Accreditation: &NH

† Branch campus of University of Wisconsin Colleges, Madison, WI.

*University of Wisconsin Fond du Lac (H)

400 University Drive, Fond du Lac WI 54935
Telephone: (920) 929-1100 Identification: 770451
Accreditation: &NH

† Branch campus of University of Wisconsin Colleges, Madison, WI.

*University of Wisconsin Fox Valley (I)

1478 Midway Road, Menasha WI 54952
Telephone: (920) 832-2600 Identification: 770456
Accreditation: &NH

† Branch campus of University of Wisconsin Colleges, Madison, WI.

*University of Wisconsin Manitowoc (J)

705 Viebahn Street, Manitowoc WI 54220-6699
Telephone: (920) 683-4700 Identification: 770453
Accreditation: &NH

† Branch campus of University of Wisconsin Colleges, Madison, WI.

*University of Wisconsin-Marathon County (K)

518 South 7th Avenue, Wausau WI 54401
Telephone: (715) 261-6100 Identification: 770461
Accreditation: &NH

† Branch campus of University of Wisconsin Colleges, Madison, WI.

* University of Wisconsin Marinette (A)

750 W Bay Shore Street, Marinette WI 54143-4253
Telephone: (715) 735-4300 Identification: 770454
Accreditation: &NH

† Branch campus of University of Wisconsin Colleges, Madison, WI.

* University of Wisconsin Marshfield/Wood County (B)

2200 West 5th Street, Marshfield WI 54449
Telephone: (715) 389-6530 Identification: 770455
Accreditation: &NH

† Branch campus of University of Wisconsin Colleges, Madison, WI.

* University of Wisconsin Richland (C)

1200 Highway 14 West, Richland Center WI 53581-1316
Telephone: (608) 647-6186 Identification: 770458
Accreditation: &NH

† Branch campus of University of Wisconsin Colleges, Madison, WI.

* University of Wisconsin Rock County (D)

2909 Kellogg Avenue, Janesville WI 53546
Telephone: (608) 758-6565 Identification: 770452
Accreditation: &NH

† Branch campus of University of Wisconsin Colleges, Madison, WI.

* University of Wisconsin Sheboygan (E)

One University Drive, Sheboygan WI 53081-4760
Telephone: (920) 459-6600 Identification: 770459
Accreditation: &NH

† Branch campus of University of Wisconsin Colleges, Madison, WI.

* University of Wisconsin Washington County (F)

400 University Drive, West Bend WI 53095
Telephone: (262) 335-5200 Identification: 770462
Accreditation: &NH

† Branch campus of University of Wisconsin Colleges, Madison, WI.

* University of Wisconsin Waukesha (G)

1500 N University Drive, Waukesha WI 53188-2799
Telephone: (262) 521-5200 Identification: 770460
Accreditation: &NH

† Branch campus of University of Wisconsin Colleges, Madison, WI.

Viterbo University (H)

900 Viterbo Court, La Crosse WI 54601-8802
County: La Crosse FICE Identification: 003911
Unit ID: 240107
Telephone: (608) 796-3000 Carnegie Class: Master's L
FAX Number: (608) 796-3050 Calendar System: Semester
URL: www.viterbo.edu
Established: 1890 Annual Undergrad Tuition & Fees: $23,790
Enrollment: 2,804 Coed
Affiliation or Control: Roman Catholic IRS Status: 501(c)3
Highest Offering: Doctorate
Program: Liberal Arts And General; Teacher Preparatory; Professional
Accreditation: NH, ACBSP, CACREP, DIETC, DIETI, MUS, NURSE, SW, TED

01 President .... Dr. Richard B. ARTMAN
05 Vice President for Academic Affairs .... Dr. Glena TEMPLE
32 Vice President Student Development .... Dr. Diane L. BRIMMER
10 Vice Pres Administration/Finance .... Mr. Todd M. ERICSON
30 Vice Pres Institutional Advancement .... Mr. Wendell SNODGRASS
26 Vice Pres Communications/Marketing .... Mr. Paul WILHELMSON
21 Assistant Vice President Finance .... Mr. Eugene R. ALBERTS
07 Dean of Admission .... Mr. Robert L. FORGET
42 Chaplain .... Fr. Conrad A. TARGONSKI
66 Dean School of Nursing .... Dr. Silvana F. RICHARDSON
53 Dean School of Education .... Dr. Ted WILSON
49 Dean School Letters & Sciences .... Dr. Glena G. TEMPLE
57 Dean School of Fine Arts/Humanities .... Dr. Timothy B. SCHORR
50 Dean School of Business .... Dr. Thomas E. KNOTHE
58 Dean Graduate/Prof/Adult Education .... Vacant
88 Director of Ethics in Leadership .... Dr. Richard L. KYTE
06 Registrar .... Ms. Amy S. GLEASON
08 Director of Library .... Ms. Gretel L. STOCK-KUPPERMAN
13 Director of Computer Services .... Ms. Sarah BEARBOWER
41 Athletic Director .... Mr. Barry J. FRIED
37 Director of Financial Aid .... Ms. Terry W. NORMAN
29 Director Alumni/Parent Relations .... Ms. Kathleen A. DUERWACHTER
36 Director Career Planning/Placement .... Ms. Beth D. DOLDER-ZIEKE
15 Director of Human Resources .... Ms. Sonya GANTHER
09 Director Institutional Research .... Ms. Naomi R. STENNES-SPIDAHL
18 Director Physical Plant .... Mr. Eugene M. MCCURDY
38 Dir Counseling/Student Development .... Ms. Lesley A. STUGELMAYER
39 Director of Residence Life .... Ms. Crystal LILLGE
53 Director Grad Studies in Education .... Ms. Rhonda M. RABBITT
88 Dir Faculty Dev/Internship Coord .... Dr. Theresa MOORE
88 Director of Global Education .... Mr. Shaojie JIANG
19 Campus Safety Director .... Ms. Lisa JOSVAI
07 Associate Director of Admissions .... Mr. Eric R. SCHMIDT
04 Executive Admin Asst to President .... Ms. Sheila SEVERSON

Wisconsin Lutheran College (I)

8800 W Bluemound Road, Milwaukee WI 53226-4699
County: Milwaukee FICE Identification: 021366
Unit ID: 240338
Telephone: (414) 443-8800 Carnegie Class: Bac/A&S
FAX Number: (414) 443-8514 Calendar System: Semester
URL: www.wlc.edu
Established: 1973 Annual Undergrad Tuition & Fees: $25,960
Enrollment: 1,179 Coed
Affiliation or Control: Independent Non-Profit IRS Status: 501(c)3
Highest Offering: Master's
Program: Liberal Arts And General
Accreditation: NH, NURSE

01 President .... Dr. Daniel W. JOHNSON
05 Provost & VP of Academic Affairs .... Dr. John D. KOLANDER
32 Vice President Student Life .... Mr. Nathan STROBEL
10 Vice Pres Finance & Administration .... Mr. Gary SCHMID
26 Exec Dir Marketing & Communication .... Vacant
30 Vice Pres Development .... Mr. Richard MANNISTO
15 Vice Pres of Human Resources .... Mr. Steven SCHROEDER
21 Asst Vice Pres Finance .... Mrs. Diane HOEHNKE
07 Exec Director of Admissions .... Mr. Lucas FAUST
06 Registrar .... Mr. Brett VALERIO
08 Director of Library Services .... Mrs. Starla C. SIEGMANN
37 Director Student Financial Aid .... Mrs. Linda L. LOEFFEL
42 Campus Pastor .... Rev. Nathan STROBEL
53 Director Teacher Education .... Prof. James HOLMAN
39 Director Residential Life/Housing .... Vacant
41 Athletic Director .... Mr. William CURTIS
88 Director of Arts Programming .... Mr. Daniel SCHMAL
13 Director of Information Technology .... Mr. John MEYER
29 Director of Alumni Relations .... Mrs. Lisa LEFFEL
44 Sr Director of Planned Giving .... Mrs. Kris METZGER
09 Information Systems Analyst .... Mrs. Olya FINNEGAN
102 Director Corp/Foundation Relations .... Ms. Sharon PATTERSON
18 Chief Facilities/Physical Plant .... Mr. Gary SCHMID
24 Media Services Coordinator .... Mr. Tim SNYDER

Wisconsin School of Professional Psychology (J)

9120 W Hampton Avenue, Suite 212,
Milwaukee WI 53225-4960
County: Milwaukee FICE Identification: 022713
Unit ID: 240213
Telephone: (414) 464-9777 Carnegie Class: Spec/Health
FAX Number: (414) 358-5590 Calendar System: Semester
URL: www.wspp.edu
Established: 1979 Annual Graduate Tuition & Fees: $34,400
Enrollment: 91 Coed
Affiliation or Control: Independent Non-Profit IRS Status: 501(c)3
Highest Offering: Doctorate; No Undergraduates
Program: Professional
Accreditation: NH, CLPSY

01 President .... Dr. Kathleen M. RUSCH
05 Dean .... Dr. Dale A. BESPALEC
04 Assistant to the President .... Ms. Sheri LINDGREN
17 Director Clinical Training .... Dr. Susan DVORAK

* Wisconsin Technical College System (K)

PO Box 7874, Madison WI 53707-7874
County: Dane Identification: 666185
Telephone: (608) 266-1207 Carnegie Class: N/A
FAX Number: (608) 266-1285
URL: www.wtcsystem.edu

01 President .... Ms. Morna K. FOY
03 Executive Vice President .... Mr. James ZYLSTRA
05 Provost/Vice President .... Ms. Kathleen CULLEN
86 Dir Strategic Ptrnshp/External Rels .... Mr. Conor SMYTH

* Blackhawk Technical College (L)

PO Box 5009, Janesville WI 53547-5009
County: Rock FICE Identification: 005390
Unit ID: 238397
Telephone: (608) 758-6900 Carnegie Class: Assoc/Pub-R-M
FAX Number: (608) 757-7740 Calendar System: Semester
URL: www.blackhawk.edu
Established: 1912 Annual Undergrad Tuition & Fees (In-District): $4,180
Enrollment: 2,471 Coed
Affiliation or Control: State/Local IRS Status: 501(c)3
Highest Offering: Associate Degree
Program: Occupational; Technical Emphasis
Accreditation: NH, ACFEI, ADNUR, DA, DMS, #MAC, MLTAD, PTAA, RAD

02 President .... Dr. Thomas C. ECKERT
05 Vice President Learning .... Dr. Diane NYHAMMER
10 Vice President Finance/College Oper .... Ms. Renea L. RANGUETTE
15 Vice President Human Resources .... Mr. Brian B. GOHLKE
32 Vice President Student Services .... Mr. Edward G. ROBINSON
09 Dir Institutional Effectiveness .... Mr. G. Scott DAVIS
04 Asst to President/Board Liaison .... Ms. Jacqueline J. PINS
13 Chief Information Officer .... Ms. Mary SCHOELER
26 Marketing & Communications Mgr .... Mr. Gary KOHN
97 Dean Gen Ed/Academic Support .... Dr. Sally VOGL-BAUER
88 Assoc Dean Gen Ed/Academic Supp .... Mr. Darian SNOW
76 Dean Health Sciences .... Ms. Nancy R. LIGHTFIELD
88 Dean Public Safety .... Mr. Gary TRULSON
19 Manager of Campus Safety & Security .... Mr. Brad K. SMITH
88 EMS Fire Service & Paramedic Coord .... Mr. David F. PETERSON
66 Assoc Dean Nursing .... Dr. Doris G. ELLISON
72 Dean Advanced Mfg & Transportation .... Dr. Garry D. KRAUSE
50 Dean Business and Econ Dev .... Dr. Gina MCCONOUGHEY
12 Director of Monroe Campus .... Mr. Matthew URBAN
21 Controller .... Mr. Gerri DOWNING
25 Manager Grants Administration .... Mr. Andrew S. MCGRATH
37 Director of Financial Aid .... Ms. Deena WETTSTEIN
06 Director Student Development .... Ms. Kerry K. FROEHLICH-MUELLER
18 Facilities Director .... Mr. Daniel M. LAPAZ
96 Manager Purchasing/Fac Design .... Mr. Thomas PELLIZZI
51 Continuing Education Coord .... Vacant
08 Director of Learning Resources .... Dr. Elizabeth REZEL
30 Director of Advancement & Comm Rel .... Ms. Elizabeth HORVATH
84 Director Enrollment Management .... Mr. Barrett BELL

* Chippewa Valley Technical College (M)

620 W Clairemont Avenue, Eau Claire WI 54701-6162
County: Eau Claire FICE Identification: 005304
Unit ID: 240116
Telephone: (715) 833-6200 Carnegie Class: Assoc/Pub-R-M
FAX Number: (715) 833-6470 Calendar System: Semester
URL: www.cvtc.edu
Established: 1912 Annual Undergrad Tuition & Fees (In-District): $3,856
Enrollment: 6,074 Coed
Affiliation or Control: Local IRS Status: 501(c)3
Highest Offering: Associate Degree
Program: Occupational; 2-Year Principally Bachelor's Creditable; Technical Emphasis
Accreditation: NH, ADNUR, CAHIIM, COARC, DH, DMS, MAC, MLTAD, PNUR, PTAA, RAD, SURGT

02 President .... Bruce A. BARKER
05 Vice President Education .... Julie FURST-BOWE
11 Vice President Operations .... Tom G. HUFFCUTT
32 Vice President Student Services .... Margo A. KEYS
12 River Falls Campus Administrator .... Beth A. HEIN
12 Chippewa Falls Campus Manager .... Angela STADLER
12 Menomonie Campus Manager .... Daniel LYTLE
12 Applied Technology Center .... Roxann VANDERWYST
46 Dir of College Effectiveness .... Margaret A. DICKENS
47 Dean Industry/Agricul & Energy .... Jeff SULLIVAN
06 Registrar .... Jessica SCHWARTZ
84 Director of Enrollment Services .... Paige WEGNER
37 Financial Aid Officer .... Barbara CLOUTIER
31 Dir of Mktg & Community Relations .... Pam HALLER
10 Director of Budget & Finance .... Kirk L. MOIST
88 Director of Prof Development .... Debra WALSH
13 Director of Info Technology .... Tom J. LANGE
88 Customer Service Center Spec/Mgr .... Laura ERICSON
35 Student Life Specialist .... Alisa S. SCHLEY
96 Purchasing Agent .... Doug D. DEKAN
21 Budget Manager .... Tracy M. DRIER
19 Safety/Security and Risk Manager .... William HENNING
28 Diversity/Equal Opportunity Spec .... Michael A. OJIBWAY
35 Student Services Grants/Operations .... Natalyn M. MARLAIRE
35 Dean Academic and Develop Services .... Jennifer ANDEREGG
102 Dir of CVTC Foundation/Alumni Assoc .... Aliesha R. CROWE
25 Grants & Accreditation Manager .... Shana SCHMIDT
108 Manager of Assessment .... Philip V. PALSER
50 Interim Dean of Business .... Lynette LIVINGSTON
18 Facilities Manager .... Rod BAGLEY
15 Human Resources Director .... Tam BURGAU
21 Business Office Manager .... Sara J. NICK
76 Dean Health & Emergency Services .... Shelly Y. OLSON
97 Dean General Educ & Business .... Cherrie BERGANDI
88 Assoc Dean of Transportation .... Tim STANTON
88 Assoc Dean of Manufacturing .... Jeff SULLIVAN
88 Assoc Dean of Emergency Services .... Eric ANDERSON
88 Interim Assoc Dean Curriculum .... Jodi RUST
76 Assoc Dean of Health .... Jennifer MCSORLEY

* Fox Valley Technical College (N)

1825 N Bluemound Drive, Appleton WI 54914-1643
County: Outagamie FICE Identification: 009744
Unit ID: 238722
Telephone: (920) 735-5600 Carnegie Class: Assoc/Pub-R-L
FAX Number: (920) 735-2582 Calendar System: Semester
URL: www.fvtc.edu
Established: 1967 Annual Undergrad Tuition & Fees (In-District): $4,476
Enrollment: 10,519 Coed
Affiliation or Control: State/Local IRS Status: 501(c)3
Highest Offering: Associate Degree
Program: Occupational; 2-Year Principally Bachelor's Creditable
Accreditation: NH, ACFEI, ADNUR, DA, DH, EMT, MAC, OTA

02 President ... Dr. Susan A. MAY
05 CAO/VP Instructional Services ... Dr. Christopher MATHENY
11 VP Administrative Services ... Ms. Jill MCEWEN
32 VP Student/Community Development ... Dr. Patti JORGENSEN
72 Dean Manufacturing & Agriculture ... Mr. Steve STRAUB
10 VP Financial Services/CFO ... Ms. Amy VAN STRATEN
13 VP Information Tech/CIO ... Mr. Troy KOHL
97 Dean General Studies ... Ms. Carol MAY
102 Exec Dir FVTC Foundation/Cmty Rels ... Ms. Mary DOWNS
12 Oshkosh Campus Director ... Ms. Melissa KOHN
37 Director Student Financial Svcs ... Ms. Stacy DORAN
06 Registrar ... Mr. Brian BUSS
26 Director College Marketing ... Ms. Barb DREGER
88 Director Compensation & Benefits ... Ms. Barb KIEFFER
88 Director Venture Center ... Ms. Amy PIETSCH
15 Director Employee Rels/Staff Dev ... Ms. Deb GORMAN
46 Director College Effectiveness ... Dr. Patti FROHRIB

*Gateway Technical College (A)

3520 30th Avenue, Kenosha WI 53144-1690
County: Kenosha FICE Identification: 005389
Unit ID: 238759
Telephone: (262) 564-2200 Carnegie Class: Assoc/Pub-R-L
FAX Number: (262) 564-2201 Calendar System: Semester
URL: www.gtc.edu
Established: 1912 Annual Undergrad Tuition & Fees (In-District): $4,014
Enrollment: 7,410 Coed
Affiliation or Control: State/Local IRS Status: 501(c)3
Highest Offering: Associate Degree
Program: Occupational; 2-Year Principally Bachelor's Creditable; Technical Emphasis
Accreditation: NH, ACBSP, ADNUR, DA, PTAA, SURGT

02 President ... Dr. Bryan D. ALBRECHT
05 Exec VP/Prov/Chief Academic Officer ... Ms. Zina HAYWOOD
12 Dean Racine Campus ... Mr. Ray KOUKARI
12 Dean Elkhorn Campus ... Mr. Michael O'DONNELL
12 Dean Kenosha Campus ... Mr. Gary FLYNN
10 Vice President Finance ... Ms. Bane THOMEY
86 VP Government/Community Relations ... Ms. Stephanie SKLBA
103 VP Workforce/Economic Develop Div ... Ms. Debbie DAVIDSON
32 Asst Provost/VP IE/Student Success ... Dr. John THIBODEAU
35 Associate VP Student Success ... Ms. Stacy RILEY
88 Dean Learning Success ... Dr. Tammi SUMMERS
06 Registrar ... Ms. Chrystal MOEZ
09 Associate VP Institutional Research ... Ms. Anne WHYNOTT
15 VP Human Resources and Facilities ... Mr. William WHYTE
26 Marketing Director ... Ms. Jayne HERRING
07 Director of College Access ... Ms. Angela BECERRA-CHVILICEK
18 Chief Facilities/Physical Plant ... Mr. William WHTYE
21 Controller ... Ms. Sharon JOHNSON
37 Director Student Financial Aid ... Mr. Justin KEHRING
28 Director of Diversity ... Ms. Debbie MILLER
102 Foundation Executive Director ... Dr. Jennifer CHARPENTIER
13 Chief Info Technology Officer (CIO) ... Mr. Jeff ROBSHAW

*Lakeshore Technical College (B)

1290 North Avenue, Cleveland WI 53015-1414
County: Manitowoc FICE Identification: 009194
Unit ID: 239008
Telephone: (920) 693-1000 Carnegie Class: Assoc/Pub-R-M
FAX Number: (920) 693-8078 Calendar System: Semester
URL: www.gotoltc.edu
Established: 1913 Annual Undergrad Tuition & Fees (In-District): $4,252
Enrollment: 3,008 Coed
Affiliation or Control: State/Local IRS Status: 501(c)3
Highest Offering: Associate Degree
Program: Occupational; 2-Year Principally Bachelor's Creditable; Technical Emphasis
Accreditation: NH, ADNUR, EMT, RAD

02 President ... Dr. Michael LANSER
04 Executive Assistant ... Ms. Heidi SOODSMA
05 Vice President of Instruction ... Dr. Barbara DODGE
32 Vice President of Student Services ... Dr. Douglas GOSSEN
103 Vice President Workforce Solutions ... Mr. Peter THILLMAN
15 Chief Human Resources Officer ... Ms. Kathleen KOTAJARVI
10 Chief Financial Officer ... Ms. Cindy DROSS
09 Quality/Continuous Improvement Mgr ... Ms. Cheryl TERP
26 Dir Marketing & College Relations ... Ms. Julie MIRECKI
28 Diversity Coordinator ... Ms. Nicole YANG
88 Associate Dean Mgf & Appr ... Ms. Sheila SCHETTER
50 Dean Business & Technology ... Mr. Ed JANAIRO
97 Dean General Education/Basic Skills ... Ms. Rachelle PHAKITTHONG
47 Exec Dean Mfg Trades/Agriculture ... Mr. Richard HOERTH
35 Student Services Director ... Mr. Don GEIGER
37 Financial Aid Manager ... Ms. Jessica HEMENWAY
36 Career Services Manager ... Ms. Foua HANG
18 Physical Plant Manager ... Mr. Bryan KOESER
08 Library Services Manager ... Ms. Kelly CARPENTER
22 Affirmative Action Officer ... Ms. Kathleen KOTAJARVI
40 Bookstore Manager ... Ms. Kelly WOLFERT
13 Interim Dir Information Technology ... Ms. Wendy NASGOVITZ
30 Director of Advancement ... Ms. Karla ZAHN
30 Development Director ... Ms. Katie WILLINGER

*Madison Area Technical College (C)

1701 Wright Street, Madison WI 53704-2599
County: Dane FICE Identification: 004007
Unit ID: 238263
Telephone: (608) 246-6100 Carnegie Class: Assoc/Pub-R-L
FAX Number: (608) 246-6880 Calendar System: Semester
URL: www.madisoncollege.org
Established: 1912 Annual Undergrad Tuition & Fees (In-District): $4,209
Enrollment: 17,532 Coed
Affiliation or Control: State/Local IRS Status: 501(c)3
Highest Offering: Associate Degree
Program: Occupational; 2-Year Principally Bachelor's Creditable
Accreditation: NH, ACFEI, ADNUR, COARC, CSHSE, DH, EMT, MAC, MLTAD, OPTT, OTA, PTAA, RAD, SURGT

02 President ... Dr. Jack E. DANIELS, III
04 Admin Asst to the President ... Ms. Judith CASTRO-ROMAKER
05 Provost ... Mr. Terrance S. WEBB
32 Sr VP Student Dev & Success ... Dr. Keith T. CORNILLE
26 Int Dir Commun/Strategic Marketing ... Mr. Cary R. HEYER
15 VP Human Resources ... Mr. Charles E. MCDOWELL
45 Sr Exec/Special Asst to President ... Mr. Timothy L. CASPER
11 VP Administrative Services ... Mr. Mark THOMAS
13 Chief Information Officer ... Mr. Mirwais QADER
20 Assoc VP Learner Success ... Dr. Turina R. BAKKEN
103 Dean Workforce Education ... Ms. Schauna RASMUSSEN
88 Dean Academic Advancement ... Mr. Christopher P. VANDALL
54 Dean Applied Science Engr & Tech ... Ms. Denise REIMER
49 Dean Arts & Sciences ... Dr. Todd H. STEBBINS
50 Dean Business & Applied Arts ... Mr. Bryan M. WOODHOUSE
76 Dean Health Education ... Dr. Mark C. LAUSCH
88 Assoc Dean Academic Advancement ... Ms. Janice L. METTAUER
51 Dean Community & Corporate Learning ... Ms. Kathleen A. RADIONOFF
38 Assoc Dean Guidance & Counseling ... Dr. Geraldo G. VILACRUZ
88 Dean Human & Protective Services ... Dr. Shawna M. CARTER
35 Director Student Life ... Ms. Renee M. ALFANO
12 Dean Northern Region ... Mr. John W. ALT
12 Dean Eastern Region ... Ms. Jennifer BAKKE
88 Dean Ctr Excellence Teaching/Learn ... Ms. Sarah FRITZ
19 Director Public Safety ... Mr. James A. BOTTONI
104 Dir International Education ... Dr. Geoffrey W. BRADSHAW
88 Dir Retention & Student Svcs ... Ms. Carlotta V. CALMESE
36 Dir College & Career Transitions ... Ms. Juanita COMEAU
06 Manager Records/Admissions ... Ms. Mary SCHEY
08 Director Library Services ... Ms. Julie C. GORES
41 Athletic Director ... Mr. Stephen C. HAUSER
21 Budget Director ... Ms. Sylvia RAMIREZ
108 Director Testing and Assessment ... Mr. James A. MERRITT
10 Controller ... Mr. Brian NOWICKI
12 Interim IBPS Administrator ... Dr. Kathleen A. PARIS
25 Director Grants & Special Projects ... Ms. Emily J. SANDERS
84 Dean Enrollment Services ... Ms. Lori A. SEBRANEK
18 Director Facilities Services ... Mr. Michael M. STARK
102 Chief Exec Officer Foundation ... Ms. Tammy THAYER
09 Dir Inst Research & Effectiveness ... Mr. Ali R. ZARRINNAM
12 Regional Campus Manager South ... Ms. Valentina AHEDO
21 Assistant Controller ... Ms. Dorothy CONDUAH
40 Bookstore Manager ... Mr. Scott R. HEIMAN
37 Dean Financial Aid ... Ms. Melissa HABERMAN
28 Dir Employ/Diversity & Cmty Rels ... Vacant

*Mid-State Technical College (D)

500 32nd Street N, Wisconsin Rapids WI 54494-5599
County: Wood FICE Identification: 005380
Unit ID: 239220
Telephone: (715) 422-5300 Carnegie Class: Assoc/Pub-R-M
FAX Number: (715) 422-5345 Calendar System: Semester
URL: www.mstc.edu
Established: 1967 Annual Undergrad Tuition & Fees (In-District): $3,997
Enrollment: 2,779 Coed
Affiliation or Control: State/Local IRS Status: 501(c)3
Highest Offering: Associate Degree
Program: 2-Year Principally Bachelor's Creditable; Technical Emphasis
Accreditation: NH, ADNUR, CAHIIM, COARC, EMT, MAC, PHLEB, SURGT

02 President ... Dr. Susan BUDJAC
05 Vice President Academic Affairs ... Ms. Sandy KIDDOO
32 Vice Pres Student Affairs ... Dr. Mandy LANG
10 Vice Pres Finance & IT ... Mr. Nelson D. DAHL
15 Vice President Human Resources ... Mr. Richard O'SULLIVAN
50 Dean General Education & Business ... Vacant
75 Dean Technical/Industrial Division ... Mr. Alan JAVOROSKI
76 Dean Service & Health Div ... Ms. Barb JASCOR
12 Dean Stevens Point Campus ... Mr. Volker GAUL
12 Dean Marshfield Campus ... Ms. Brenda DILLENBURG
84 Dean of Enrollment Management ... Mr. Aamer CHAUHDRI
26 Director of Communications ... Mr. Karl EASTTORP
30 Director College Advancement ... Dr. Debra HAGEN-FOLEY
102 Director Foundation and Alumni ... Ms. Jill STECKBAUER
18 Director of Facilities/Procurement ... Vacant
35 Director Student Support ... Ms. Christina LORGE-GROVER
96 Director of Purchasing ... Vacant
06 Registrar ... Ms. Denise BORLAND
08 Librarian ... Ms. Maria HERNANDEZ
37 Financial Aid Manager ... Mrs. Mary Jo GREEN

*Milwaukee Area Technical College (E)

700 W State Street, Milwaukee WI 53233-1443
County: Milwaukee FICE Identification: 003866
Unit ID: 239248
Telephone: (414) 297-6600 Carnegie Class: Assoc/Pub-U-MC
FAX Number: (414) 297-7990 Calendar System: Semester
URL: www.matc.edu
Established: 1912 Annual Undergrad Tuition & Fees (In-District): $5,578
Enrollment: 24,738 Coed
Affiliation or Control: Local IRS Status: 501(c)3
Highest Offering: Associate Degree
Program: Occupational; 2-Year Principally Bachelor's Creditable
Accreditation: NH, ACFEI, ADNUR, COARC, CVT, DH, DIETT, #FUSER, MAC, MLTAD, OTA, PHLEB, PNUR, PTAA, RAD, SURGT

02 President ... Dr. Vicki J. MARTIN
05 Provost ... Dr. Mohammad DAKWAR
32 Vice Pres Student Services ... Dr. Trevor KUBATZKE
10 Vice President of Finance ... Mr. Al SHOREIBAH
43 Vice President & Legal Counsel ... Ms. Janice FALKENBERG
13 Assoc VP Information Technology ... Mr. Michael WALSH
23 Dean Health Occupation ... Dr. Dessie LEVY
50 Int Dean Business & Graphic Arts ... Dr. Roy VARGAS
24 General Manager Public Television ... Mr. Ellis BROMBERG
35 Director Student Life ... Mr. Archie GRAHAM
08 Director of Library ... Vacant
37 Director Admissions/Financial Aid ... Ms. Camille NICOLAI
90 Director Technical Services ... Mr. Michael GAVIN
21 Controller ... Mr. Jeffrey HOLLOW
19 Director Public Safety ... Ms. Aisha BARKOW
06 Registrar ... Ms. Sarah ADAMS
09 Director Institutional Research ... Dr. Yan WANG
84 Manager Recruitment ... Ms. Sophia WILLIAMS
29 Director Alumni Relations ... Ms. Christine MCGEE
38 Director Counseling & Advising Svcs ... Mr. Walter LANIER
26 Chief Public Relations Officer ... Ms. Kathleen HOHL
96 Procurement Manager ... Ms. Laura MOORE
41 Coordinator Athletics ... Mr. Randy CASEY

*Moraine Park Technical College (F)

235 N National Avenue, Fond Du Lac WI 54936-1940
County: Fond Du Lac FICE Identification: 009256
Unit ID: 239372
Telephone: (920) 922-8611 Carnegie Class: Assoc/Pub-R-L
FAX Number: (920) 929-2471 Calendar System: Semester
URL: www.morainepark.edu
Established: 1967 Annual Undergrad Tuition & Fees (In-District): $4,151
Enrollment: 6,280 Coed
Affiliation or Control: State/Local IRS Status: 501(c)3
Highest Offering: Associate Degree
Program: Occupational; 2-Year Principally Bachelor's Creditable; Technical Emphasis
Accreditation: NH, ADNUR, CAHIIM, COARC, EMT, MAC, MLTAD, RAD, SURGT

02 President ... Bonnie BAERWALD
05 Vice Pres Academic Affairs ... James R. EDEN
10 VP Finance/Administrative Services ... Bonnie BAERWALD
15 Vice President Human Resources ... Kathleen M. BROSKE
30 VP Marketing/College Advancement ... Sharon N. HOLMES
32 Vice President Student Affairs ... Stanley CRAM
13 CIO/Vice Pres Inform Technology ... Jim BLAKESLEE
84 Vice Pres of Enrollment Management ... Bethany M. RAFFAELLI
30 Director of College Advancement ... Dana KNEBEL
12 WB & Online Campus/Cmty Partner ... Peter J. RETTLER
12 Beaver Dam Campus/Cmty Prtnr ... Karen COLEY
20 Executive Dean of Instruction ... James V. EDEN
24 Exec Dean Instructional Support ... Gerald R. EDGREN, III
76 Exec Dean Hlth Sciences/Public Svcs ... Kathy S. VANEERDEN
88 Dean of Health Sciences/Public Svcs ... Kristin M. FINNEL
06 Registrar ... Amanda HRUSKA
26 Dir Marketing/Communications ... Melissa WORTHINGTON
07 Recruitment & Retention Associate ... Sally A. RUBACK
08 Library Services Coordinator ... Hans BAIERL
109 Auxiliary Services Associate ... Jon A. SHAPIRO
18 Facilities Associate ... Timothy J. FLOOD
22 Employment/Affirmative Action Assoc ... Beth A. MENDOZA
96 Purchasing Associate ... Charles E. BIRRINGER
37 Student Financials Partner ... Karen A. ZUEHLKE

*Nicolet Area Technical College (G)

5364 College Drive, PO Box 518, Rhinelander WI 54501-0518
County: Oneida FICE Identification: 005384
Unit ID: 239442
Telephone: (715) 365-4410 Carnegie Class: Assoc/Pub-R-S
FAX Number: (715) 365-4445 Calendar System: Semester
URL: www.nicoletcollege.edu
Established: 1967 Annual Undergrad Tuition & Fees (In-State): $3,852
Enrollment: 1,139 Coed
Affiliation or Control: State IRS Status: 501(c)3
Highest Offering: Associate Degree
Program: Occupational; 2-Year Principally Bachelor's Creditable
Accreditation: NH, ADNUR, DH, MAC

02 President ... Dr. Richard R. NELSON
10 Vice Pres Finance/Col Operations ... Ms. Roxanne M. LUTGEN
05 VP Teaching/Learning/Stdnt Success ... Vacant
88 Exec Dean Econ Dev/Security ... Mr. Ron SKALLERUD
26 Executive Director ... Ms. Sandy KINNEY
102 Executive Director Foundation ... Ms. Heather SCHALLOCK
50 Dean Business/Institutional Effect ... Mr. Chuck KOMP
76 Dean of Health Occupations ... Dr. Lenore MANGLES
32 Dean of Students ... Ms. Kathleen FERREL
88 Dean of Trade/Industry/Apprentice ... Ms. Brigitte KUMBIER
49 Dean of Univ Trans/Liberal Arts ... Dr. Emily STUCKENBRUCK
13 Chief Information Officer ... Mr. Greg MILJEVICH
21 Dir of Accounting/Business Services ... Mr. John VAN DE LOO
15 Director of Human Resources ... Dr. Dan GROLEAU
37 Director Financial Aid ... Ms. Jill PRICE

103 Director Workforce Development .... Ms. Sandy BISHOP
18 Director of Facilities .... Mr. Pete VANNEY
19 Director Protective Services .... Mr. Jason GOELDNER
08 Director Library Services .... Mr. Todd MOUNTJOY
09 Planning/Development/Evaluation Mgr ... Ms. Kelly HAVERKAMPF
06 Registrar/Dir Learner Success .... Mr. Kyle GRUENING
04 Exec Asst to President/Board .... Ms. Anne E. BONACK

*Northcentral Technical College (A)

1000 W Campus Drive, Wausau WI 54401-1880

County: Marathon FICE Identification: 005387
Unit ID: 239460
Telephone: (715) 675-3331 Carnegie Class: Assoc/Pub-R-M
FAX Number: (715) 675-9776 Calendar System: Semester
URL: www.ntc.edu
Established: 1912 Annual Undergrad Tuition & Fees (In-District): $4,230
Enrollment: 4,377 Coed
Affiliation or Control: Local IRS Status: 501(c)3
Highest Offering: Associate Degree
Program: Occupational; 2-Year Principally Bachelor's Creditable; Technical Emphasis
Accreditation: NH, ADNUR, DH, EMT, MAC, MLTAD, PHLEB, RAD, SURGT

02 President .... Dr. Lori A. WEYERS
05 Vice President for Learning .... Dr. Shelly MONDEIK
15 Vice President of HR/College Advanc ..... Dr. Jeannie M. WORDEN
32 Vice President of Student Services .... Dr. Laurie BOROWICZ
10 Vice President of Finance & CFO .... Dr. Jane KITTEL
13 Chief Information Officer .... Mr. Chet A. STREBE
18 Director of Facilities .... Mr. Rob ELLIOTT
26 Director of Marketing & PR .... Mrs. Katrina FELCH
19 Dean Public Safety .... Mr. Douglas JENNINGS
47 Dean Agricultural Sciences .... Dr. Vicky PIETZ
50 Dean Business/Cmty Svc/Intntl Ed .... Mr. Christopher SEVERSON
103 Dean Business & Industry Solutions .... Mr. Mark BOROWICZ
12 Dean Regional Campuses .... Ms. Bobbi DAMROW
76 Dean of Health Sciences .... Ms. Lorraine ZOROMSKI
22 Employment Coord/Affirm Action Ofcr .... Ms. Cindy THELEN
88 Director Quality/Continuous Improv .... Mrs. Beth ELLIE
35 Director of Student Relations .... Mr. Shawn P. SULLIVAN
19 Director of Security .... Mr. Dan JACOBSON
06 Registrar .... Mr. Nick BLANCHETTE
84 Dean of College Enrollment .... Ms. Sarah DILLON
16 Director of Human Resources .... Ms. Karen BRZEZINSKI
97 Dean ESS/Interim Dean Gen Studies .... Ms. Debra STENCIL
36 Director of Transfer & Placement .... Ms. Suzi MATHIAS
38 Dean of Student Success .... Mrs. Shannon LIVINGSTON
75 Dean of Technical & Trades .... Mr. Darren ACKLEY
51 Dean Continuing Ed/Virtual College .... Mr. Brad GAST
04 Executive Asst to President .... Mrs. PaHnia THAO
09 Director of Institutional Research .... Mrs. Angela M. SERVI
37 Director Student Financial Aid .... Mr. Jeff CICHON

*Northeast Wisconsin Technical College (B)

PO Box 19042, 2740 W Mason Street,
Green Bay WI 54307-9042

County: Brown FICE Identification: 005301
Unit ID: 239488
Telephone: (920) 498-5444 Carnegie Class: Assoc/Pub-R-L
FAX Number: (920) 498-6260 Calendar System: Semester
URL: www.nwtc.edu
Established: 1913 Annual Undergrad Tuition & Fees (In-District): $4,274
Enrollment: 10,406 Coed
Affiliation or Control: State/Local IRS Status: 501(c)3
Highest Offering: Associate Degree
Program: Occupational; 2-Year Principally Bachelor's Creditable; Technical Emphasis
Accreditation: NH, ADNUR, CAHIIM, COARC, DA, DH, DMS, EMT, ENGT, MAC, MLTAD, PTAA, RAD, SURGT

02 President .... Dr. H. Jeffrey RAFN
05 Vice President of Learning .... Ms. Lori SUDDICK
32 Vice President of Student Services .... Dr. Pamela PHILLIPS
30 Vice Pres of College Advancement .... Ms. Karen SMITS
15 Vice President of Human Resources ..... Ms. Sandy RYCZKOWSKI
13 Chief Information Officer .... Ms. Linda HARTFORD
10 VP Business & Finance .... Mr. Robert MATHEWS
12 Dean Marinette Campus .... Ms. Jan SCOVILLE
50 Dn Business/Information Technology .... Mr. Randy SMITH
76 Dean Health Science .... Ms. Kay TUPALA
72 Dean Trades & Engr Technologies .... Mr. Mark WEBER
97 Dean General Education .... Ms. Michaeline SCHMIT
20 Dean Learning Solutions .... Ms. Anne KAMPS
103 Dean Corp Training & Economic Devel .... Mr. Dean STEWART
38 Dean of Student Success .... Ms. Vickie LOCK
06 Dean Enrollment Services .... Mr. Mark FRANKS
84 Mgr Assessment/Academic Coaching .. Mr. George SKENANDORE
37 Financial Aid Director .... Ms. Emily YSEBAERT
96 Director of Purchasing .... Mr. Mark CICHON
102 Foundation Director .... Ms. Crystal HARRISON
40 Director Bookstore .... Mr. Patrick SORELLE
26 Public Relations/Comm Specialist .... Ms. Kathleen FRYDA
18 Director of Facilities .... Mr. Chet LAMERS
08 Manager Library Services .... Ms. Kim LAPLANTE
104 Manager Center for Global Cultures .... Ms. Megan POPKEY
21 Director of Financial Operations .... Mr. Clark WAGNER

*Southwest Wisconsin Technical College (C)

1800 Bronson Boulevard, Fennimore WI 53809-9778

County: Grant FICE Identification: 007669
Unit ID: 239910
Telephone: (608) 822-3262 Carnegie Class: Assoc/Pub-R-M
FAX Number: (608) 822-6019 Calendar System: Semester
URL: www.swtc.edu
Established: 1967 Annual Undergrad Tuition & Fees (In-District): $4,075
Enrollment: 3,628 Coed
Affiliation or Control: State/Local IRS Status: 501(c)3
Highest Offering: Associate Degree
Program: Occupational; 2-Year Principally Bachelor's Creditable
Accreditation: NH, ADNUR, MAC, MEAC, MLTAD, PTAA

02 President .... Dr. Jason S. WOOD
10 VP for Administrative Services .... Mr. Caleb WHITE
05 VP for Student & Academic Services .... Dr. Phil THOMAS
50 Dean Business/Mgmt/General Studies .... Dr. Richard AMMON
76 Dean Health Educ/Public Safety .... Ms. Kathleen E. GARRITY
47 Dean of Industry/Trades/Agriculture .... Dr. Derek DACHELET
32 Dean of Students .... Vacant
13 Continuous Improvement/IT Supervsr .... Ms. Lisa RILEY
15 Director of Human Resources .... Ms. Krista WEBER
30 Director Institutional Advancement .... Ms. Barbara TUCKER
37 Financial Aid Manager .... Ms. Joy A. KITE
18 Director of Facilities .... Mr. Dan IMHOFF
36 Career Services Manager .... Ms. Heather FIFRICK
19 Public Safety Supervisor .... Ms. Kris WUBBEN
04 Executive Asst to Board/President .... Ms. Karen M. CAMPBELL
88 Curriculum/Staff Development .... Ms. Julie PLUEMER
26 Marketing & Public Relations Mgr .... Ms. Sue REUKAUF
21 Controller .... Ms. Kelly KELLY
88 Business & Industry Services Mgr .... Ms. Amy CHARLES

*Waukesha County Technical College (D)

800 Main Street, Pewaukee WI 53072-4696

County: Waukesha FICE Identification: 005294
Unit ID: 240125
Telephone: (262) 691-5566 Carnegie Class: Assoc/Pub-S-MC
FAX Number: (262) 691-5593 Calendar System: Semester
URL: www.wctc.edu
Established: 1923 Annual Undergrad Tuition & Fees (In-District): $4,083
Enrollment: 8,692 Coed
Affiliation or Control: State/Local IRS Status: 501(c)3
Highest Offering: Associate Degree
Program: Occupational; 2-Year Principally Bachelor's Creditable; Technical Emphasis
Accreditation: NH, ACFEI, ADNUR, CAHIIM, DH, EMT, ENGT, MAC, SURGT

02 President .... Ms. Kaylen A. BETZIG
05 VP Learning .... Ms. Denine ROOD
32 VP Student Services .... Ms. Nicole GAHAGAN
10 VP Finance .... Ms. Cary A. TESSMANN
15 VP Human Resource Svcs .... Mr. David BROWN
11 VP Grants & IRE .... Dr. Ann KRAUSE-HANSON
13 Chief Information Officer .... Mr. Rodney NOBLES
102 Dir Foundation/Corporate Relations .... Ms. Ellen PHILLIPS
50 Dean Business Occupations .... Dr. Bradley PIAZZA
75 Dean Industrial Occupations .... Mr. Michael SHIELS
76 Dean Service Occupations .... Mr. Greg WEST
97 Dean Academic Support .... Ms. Bethany LEONARD
76 Dean Health Occupations .... Ms. Sandra STEARNS
103 Dean Center/Business Performance .... Dr. Joseph WEITZER
35 Director Student Development .... Vacant
18 Director Facilities Services .... Mr. Jeffrey LEVERENZ
06 Registrar .... Ms. Jacki VANDYKE
38 Director Counsel/Acad Sup/Spec Svcs .... Vacant
36 Mgr Career Development Services .... Ms. Debra WEBER
26 Marketing & Communications Mgr .... Ms. Susan STERN
07 Manager Admiss/Advis & Assessment .... Ms. Kathleen KAZDA
106 Director Academic Technology .... Mr. Randall COOROUGH
25 Director of Grants & Contracts .... Ms. Linda J. MILLER
09 Director Inst Rsrch & Effectiveness .... Dr. Esther KRAMER
37 Manager Financial Aid .... Mr. Timothy K. JACOBSON
35 Student Life Coordinator .... Mr. Jonathan N. PEDRAZA
07 Recruitment Supervisor .... Ms. Trisha L. HORNBURG
08 Director of Library Services .... Ms. Terry KEMPER
19 Enviro Health & Safety Supervisor .... Mr. Bruce NEUMANN
26 Specialist Public Relations .... Ms. Shelly KUHN
96 Purchasing Specialist .... Ms. Victoria NASH
28 Diversity Coordinator .... Mr. Rolando DELEON
40 Bookstore Manager .... Mr. Rick MILLER
85 International Educ Coordinator .... Mr. K.Austin BAADE
04 Administrative Asst to President .... Ms. Carolyn TINDALL

*Western Technical College (E)

400 N Seventh Street, La Crosse WI 54601-3368

County: La Crosse FICE Identification: 003840
Unit ID: 240170
Telephone: (608) 785-9200 Carnegie Class: Assoc/Pub-R-M
FAX Number: (608) 785-9205 Calendar System: Trimester
URL: www.westerntc.edu
Established: 1912 Annual Undergrad Tuition & Fees (In-District): $3,784
Enrollment: 4,648 Coed
Affiliation or Control: State/Local IRS Status: 501(c)3
Highest Offering: Associate Degree
Program: Occupational; 2-Year Principally Bachelor's Creditable; Technical Emphasis
Accreditation: NH, ADNUR, CAHIIM, COARC, DA, EMT, MAC, MLTAD, OTA, PTAA, RAD, SURGT

02 President .... Dr. J. Lee RASCH
10 Vice President Finance/Operations .... Mr. Wade HACKBARTH
05 Vice President of Academic Affairs .... Dr. Roger STANFORD
32 VP Student Development & Success .... Dr. Denise T. VUJNOVICH
45 VP Strategic Effectiveness & Engag .... Ms. Amy THORNTON
12 Director of Ops-Regional Locations .... Ms. Jennifer BRAVE
102 Executive Director Foundation .... Mr. Michael SWENSON
13 Director Computer/Telecomm Svcs .... Mr. Bruce E. MATHEW
37 Financial Aid Manager .... Ms. Jerolyn R. GRANDALL
21 Controller .... Ms. Amy SCHMIDT
56 Director Business & Industry Svcs .... Ms. Patti BALACEK
38 Director Counseling Enroll Svcs .... Ms. Ann BRANDAU-HYNEK
29 Manager Alumni Relations .... Ms. Sally EMERSON
07 Manager Admissions/Registration .... Ms. Sandy PETERSON
35 Dean of Students .... Ms. Shelley MCNEELY
08 Manager Library Services .... Mr. Ron EDWARDS
27 Assoc Director Information Services .... Ms. Joan PIERCE
40 Bookstore Manager .... Mr. David R. WIGNES
72 Dean Integrated Technology .... Mr. Josh GAMER
76 Dean Health & Public Safety .... Ms. Diane NEEFE
97 Dean General Education .... Dr. Douglas STRAUSS
50 Dean Business Education .... Mr. Gary BROWN

*Wisconsin Indianhead Technical College (F)

505 Pine Ridge Drive, Shell Lake WI 54871-9300

County: Washburn FICE Identification: 011824
Unit ID: 240198
Telephone: (715) 468-2815 Carnegie Class: Assoc/Pub-R-M
FAX Number: (715) 468-2819 Calendar System: Semester
URL: www.witc.edu
Established: 1968 Annual Undergrad Tuition & Fees (In-State): $4,252
Enrollment: 3,045 Coed
Affiliation or Control: State IRS Status: Exempt
Highest Offering: Associate Degree
Program: Occupational; 2-Year Principally Bachelor's Creditable; Technical Emphasis
Accreditation: NH, ADNUR, CAHIIM, MAC, OTA

02 President .... Mr. John WILL
10 Vice Pres Finance/Bus Svcs/CFO .... Mr. Steven DECKER
05 Vice President Academic Affairs .... Dr. Bonny COPENHAVER
32 Vice President Student Affairs .... Mr. Steve BITZER
13 Vice President Technology Services .... Mr. Joe HUFTEL
51 Vice President Cont Educ/Foundation .... Mr. Craig FOWLER
09 VP Institutional Effectiveness .... Ms. Ellen RILEY HAUSER
15 VP Human Resources/Risk Mgmt .... Ms. Cher VINK
14 Sr Director Technology Services .... Mr. James DAHLBERG
37 Director Financial Aid .... Mr. Terry KLEIN
06 Registrar .... Mr. Shane EVENSON
08 Director Learning Resources .... Mr. Scott VRIEZE
84 Director of Enrollment .... Ms. Laura SULLIVAN
26 Director Marketing & Recruitment .... Ms. Jena VOGTMAN

*Chippewa Valley Technical College-Chippewa Falls Campus (G)

770 Scheidler Road, Chippewa Falls WI 54729
Telephone: (715) 738-3841 Identification: 770419
Accreditation: &NH

† Branch campus of Chippewa Valley Technical College, Eau Claire, WI.

*Chippewa Valley Technical College-Gateway (H)

2320 Alpine Road, Eau Claire WI 54703
Telephone: (715) 874-4600 Identification: 770420
Accreditation: &NH

† Branch campus of Chippewa Valley Technical College, Eau Claire, WI.

*Chippewa Valley Technical College Menomonie Campus (I)

403 Technology Drive East, Menomonie WI 54751
Telephone: (715) 232-2685 Identification: 770422
Accreditation: &NH

† Branch campus of Chippewa Valley Technical College, Eau Claire, WI.

*Chippewa Valley Technical College River Falls Campus (J)

500 South Wasson Lane, River Falls WI 54022
Telephone: (715) 425-3301 Identification: 770423
Accreditation: &NH

† Branch campus of Chippewa Valley Technical College, Eau Claire, WI.

*Chippewa Valley Technical College-West (K)

4000 Campus Road, Eau Claire WI 54703
Telephone: (715) 852-1394 Identification: 770421
Accreditation: &NH

† Branch campus of Chippewa Valley Technical College, Eau Claire, WI.

*** Fox Valley Technical College** (A)
150 N Campbell Road, Oshkosh WI 54902
Telephone: (920) 233-9191 Identification: 770425
Accreditation: &NH

† Branch campus of Fox Valley Technical College, Appleton, WI.

*** Gateway Technical College Burlington Center** (B)
496 McCanna Parkway, Burlington WI 53105
Telephone: (262) 767-5200 Identification: 770426
Accreditation: &NH, EMT

† Branch campus of Gateway Technical College, Kenosha, WI.

*** Gateway Technical College Elkhorn Campus** (C)
400 County Road H, Elkhorn WI 53121
Telephone: (262) 741-8200 Identification: 770427
Accreditation: &NH, MAC

† Branch campus of Gateway Technical College, Kenosha, WI.

*** Gateway Technical College Racine Campus** (D)
1001 S Main Street, Racine WI 53403
Telephone: (262) 619-6200 Identification: 770428
Accreditation: &NH, CAHIIM

† Branch campus of Gateway Technical College, Kenosha, WI.

*** Madison Area Technical College Commercial Avenue Education Center** (E)
2125 Commercial Avenue, Madison WI 53704
Telephone: (608) 246-6100 Identification: 770436
Accreditation: &NH

† Branch campus of Madison Area Technical College, Madison, WI.

*** Madison Area Technical College Downtown Education Center** (F)
211 North Carroll Street, Madison WI 53703
Telephone: (608) 246-6100 Identification: 770437
Accreditation: &NH

† Branch campus of Madison Area Technical College, Madison, WI.

*** Madison Area Technical College Portage** (G)
330 West Collins Street, Portage WI 53901
Telephone: (608) 745-3100 Identification: 770438
Accreditation: &NH

† Branch campus of Madison Area Technical College, Madison, WI.

*** Madison Area Technical College Fort Atkinson** (H)
827 Banker Road, Fort Atkinson WI 53538
Telephone: (920) 568-7200 Identification: 770435
Accreditation: &NH

† Branch campus of Madison Area Technical College, Madison, WI.

*** Madison Area Technical College Reedsburg** (I)
300 Alexander Avenue, Reedsburg WI 53959
Telephone: (608) 524-7800 Identification: 770439
Accreditation: &NH

† Branch campus of Madison Area Technical College, Madison, WI.

*** Madison Area Technical College Watertown** (J)
1300 West Main Street, Watertown WI 53098
Telephone: (920) 206-8000 Identification: 770440
Accreditation: &NH

† Branch campus of Madison Area Technical College, Madison, WI.

*** Mid-State Technical College Marshfield Campus** (K)
2600 West 5th Street, Marshfield WI 54449
Telephone: (715) 387-2538 Identification: 770441
Accreditation: &NH

† Branch campus of Mid-State Technical College, Wisconsin Rapids, WI.

*** Mid-State Technical College Stevens Point Campus** (L)
1001 Centerpoint Drive, Stevens Point WI 54481
Telephone: (715) 344-3063 Identification: 770442
Accreditation: &NH

† Branch campus of Mid-State Technical College, Wisconsin Rapids, WI.

*** Milwaukee Area Technical College** (M)
5555 West Highlands Road, Mequon WI 53092
Telephone: (262) 238-2200 Identification: 770443
Accreditation: &NH

† Branch campus of Milwaukee Area Technical College, Milwaukee, WI.

*** Milwaukee Area Technical College** (N)
6665 South Howell Avenue, Oak Creek WI 53154-1107
Telephone: (414) 571-4500 Identification: 770444
Accreditation: &NH

† Branch campus of Milwaukee Area Technical College, Milwaukee, WI.

*** Milwaukee Area Technical College** (O)
1200 South 71st Street, West Allis WI 53214-3110
Telephone: (414) 456-5500 Identification: 770445
Accreditation: &NH

† Branch campus of Milwaukee Area Technical College, Milwaukee, WI.

*** Moraine Park Technical College** (P)
700 Gould Street, Beaver Dam WI 53916
Telephone: (920) 887-1428 Identification: 770446
Accreditation: &NH

† Branch campus of Moraine Park Technical College, Fond Du Lac, WI.

*** Moraine Park Technical College** (Q)
2151 North Main Street, West Bend WI 53090
Telephone: (262) 335-5713 Identification: 770447
Accreditation: &NH

† Branch campus of Moraine Park Technical College, Fond Du Lac, WI.

*** Northeast Wisconsin Technical College-Marinette Campus** (R)
1601 University Drive, Marinette WI 54143
Telephone: (715) 735-9361 Identification: 770448
Accreditation: &NH

† Branch campus of Northeast Wisconsin Technical College, Green Bay, WI.

*** Northeast Wisconsin Technical College-Sturgeon Bay Campus** (S)
229 N 14th Avenue, Sturgeon Bay WI 54235
Telephone: (920) 746-4900 Identification: 770449
Accreditation: &NH

† Branch campus of Northeast Wisconsin Technical College, Green Bay, WI.

*** Wisconsin Indianhead Technical College-Ashland Campus** (T)
2100 Beaser Avenue, Ashland WI 54806
Telephone: (715) 682-8040 Identification: 770463
Accreditation: &NH, MAC

† Branch campus of Wisconsin Indianhead Technical College, Shell Lake, WI.

*** Wisconsin Indianhead Technical College-New Richmond Campus** (U)
1019 S Knowles Avenue, New Richmond WI 54017
Telephone: (715) 246-6561 Identification: 770464
Accreditation: &NH, MAC

† Branch campus of Wisconsin Indianhead Technical College, Shell Lake, WI.

*** Wisconsin Indianhead Technical College-Rice Lake Campus** (V)
1900 College Drive, Rice Lake WI 54868
Telephone: (715) 234-7082 Identification: 770465
Accreditation: &NH, DA, EMT, MAC

† Branch campus of Wisconsin Indianhead Technical College, Shell Lake, WI.

*** Wisconsin Indianhead Technical College-Superior Campus** (W)
600 North 21st Street, Superior WI 54880
Telephone: (715) 394-6677 Identification: 770466
Accreditation: &NH

† Branch campus of Wisconsin Indianhead Technical College, Shell Lake, WI.

Wright Graduate University for the Realization of Human Potential (X)
N7698 County Highway H, Elkhorn WI 53121
County: Walworth Identification: 667224
Telephone: (262) 742-4444 Carnegie Class: Not Classified
FAX Number: (262) 721-0752 Calendar System: Quarter
URL: www.wrightgrad.edu
Established: 2006 Annual Graduate Tuition & Fees: $46,687
Enrollment: N/A Coed
Affiliation or Control: Independent Non-Profit IRS Status: 501(c)3
Highest Offering: Master's; No Undergraduates
Program: Professional
Accreditation: ACICS

01 CEO .... Dr. Bob WRIGHT
05 Dean of Faculty & Curriculum .... Dr. Judith WRIGHT

WYOMING

Carbon County Higher Education Center/ Rawlins (Y)
812 E. Murray Street, Rawlins WY 82301-4466
Telephone: (307) 328-9204 Identification: 770481
Accreditation: &NH

† Branch campus of Western Wyoming Community College, Rock Springs, WY.

Casper College (Z)
125 College Drive, Casper WY 82601-2458
County: Natrona FICE Identification: 003928
Unit ID: 240505
Telephone: (307) 268-2110 Carnegie Class: Assoc/Pub-R-M
FAX Number: (307) 268-2682 Calendar System: Semester
URL: www.caspercollege.edu
Established: 1945 Annual Undergrad Tuition & Fees (In-District): $2,640
Enrollment: 3,997 Coed
Affiliation or Control: Local IRS Status: 501(c)3
Highest Offering: Associate Degree
Program: Occupational; 2-Year Principally Bachelor's Creditable
Accreditation: NH, ACBSP, ADNUR, ART, COARC, DANCE, EMT, MLTAD, MUS, OTA, RAD, THEA

01 President .... Dr. Darren D. DIVINE
05 Vice President Academic Affairs .... Vacant
32 Vice President Student Services .... Ms. Kim BYRD
10 Vice Pres Administrative Services .... Ms. Lynnde COLLING
51 Exec Dean of Continuing Education .... Dr. Laura DRISCOLL
15 Director Human Resources .... Mr. Chauncy JOHNSON
07 Director Admissions/Student Records .... Ms. Kyla FOLTZ
26 Int Director College Relations .... Mr. Pete VAN HOUTEN
18 Director Physical Plant .... Mr. Michael SAWYER
38 Director Student Counseling .... Ms. Teresa WALLACE
08 Director of the Library .... Mr. Brad MATTHIES
13 Director Information Technology .... Mr. Kent BROOKS
36 Director Placement .... Ms. Janet DE VRIES
39 Director of Housing .... Ms. Barb MERYHEW
41 Athletic Director .... Ms. Angel SHARMAN
19 Director Campus Security .... Mr. Lance JONES
102 Exec Director Foundation .... Ms. Paulann DOANE
09 Institutional Researcher .... Ms. Lynn FLETCHER
37 Director of Student Financial Aid .... Mr. Darry VOIGT
21 Dir Financial Services/Controller .... Ms. Robyn LANDEN
84 Exec Dir of Enrollment Services .... Mr. Darry VOIGT
96 Purchasing Coordinator .... Mr. Paul CHRISTMAN
06 Registrar .... Ms. Linda NICHOLS
29 Director Alumni Relations .... Ms. Linda NIX
101 Secretary of the Institution/Board .... Ms. Janice DALGARNO

Central Wyoming College (a)
2660 Peck Avenue, Riverton WY 82501-1520
County: Fremont FICE Identification: 007289
Unit ID: 240514
Telephone: (307) 855-2000 Carnegie Class: Assoc/Pub-R-M
FAX Number: (307) 855-2095 Calendar System: Semester
URL: www.cwc.edu
Established: 1966 Annual Undergrad Tuition & Fees (In-District): $2,712
Enrollment: 2,170 Coed
Affiliation or Control: Local IRS Status: 501(c)3
Highest Offering: Associate Degree
Program: Occupational; 2-Year Principally Bachelor's Creditable
Accreditation: NH, ADNUR

01 President .... Dr. Cristobal O. VALDEZ
04 Exec Asst to the President/Board .... Ms. Linda BENDER
03 Vice Pres Academic Affairs .... Dr. Brad TYNDALL
10 Vice Pres Admin Svcs/CFO .... Mr. Ron GRANGER
13 Chief Information Officer .... Mr. John WOOD
18 Chief Facilities/Physical Plant .... Mr. Wayne ROBINSON
08 Director of Library Services .... Ms. Nicole POUGET
26 Director of Marketing .... Ms. Lori RIDGWAY
15 Exec Dir for Human Resources .... Ms. Jennifer REY
21 Finance Officer .... Ms. Lindy PASKETT
19 Director of Campus Safety/Security .... Mr. Chuck CARR
96 Director of Purchasing .... Ms. Suzie KOEHN
84 Asst Dean for Enrollment Services .... Ms. Jacquelyn BURNS

103 Dean for Workforce & Cmty Educ ... Ms. Lynne MCAULIFFE
41 Director of Athletics ... Mr. Steve BARLOW
06 Assistant Registrar ... Ms. Connie NYBERG
49 Dean for Arts/English/Math ... Dr. Mark NORDEEN
50 Dean for Commerce/Allied Health ... Ms. Charlotte DONELSON
76 Dean for Health & Sciences ... Ms. Kathy WELLS
32 Assoc VP Student Services ... Ms. Cory DALY
05 Assoc VP Academic Services ... Vacant
44 Director Annual or Planned Giving ... Ms. Becky RUTHENBECK

CollegeAmerica Cheyenne (A)

6101 Yellowstone Road, Cheyenne WY 82009
Telephone: (307) 637-2044 Identification: 770609
Accreditation: #ACCSC

† Branch campus of CollegeAmerica Denver, Denver, CO.

Eastern Wyoming College (B)

3200 W C Street, Torrington WY 82240-1699
County: Goshen FICE Identification: 003929
Unit ID: 240596
Telephone: (307) 532-8200 Carnegie Class: Assoc/Pub-R-S
FAX Number: (307) 532-8229 Calendar System: Semester
URL: ewc.wy.edu/
Established: 1948 Annual Undergrad Tuition & Fees (In-District): $2,568
Enrollment: 1,846 Coed
Affiliation or Control: State/Local IRS Status: 501(c)3
Highest Offering: Associate Degree
Program: Occupational; 2-Year Principally Bachelor's Creditable
Accreditation: NH

01 President ... Dr. Richard PATTERSON
04 Exec Asst to President/Board ... Ms. Holly L. BRANHAM
05 VP for Academic Services ... Dr. Michelle LANDA
10 VP for Admin Services ... Mr. Ron LAHER
32 VP for Student Services ... Dr. Rex COGDILL
20 Assoc VP for Outreach & Learning ... Mr. Mike DURFEE
30 Dir of Institutional Development ... Vacant
08 Director of Library Services ... Mrs. Casey DEBUS
41 Director of College Athletics ... Vacant
26 Director of College Relations ... Ms. Tami AFDAHL
09 Director of Institutional Research ... Ms. Kimberly RUSSELL
18 Director of Physical Plant ... Mr. Keith JARVIS
39 Director of Residence Life ... Ms. Kellee GOODER
37 Director of Financial Aid ... Ms. Susan STEPHENSON
38 Director Counseling & Disabilities ... Vacant
15 Director Human Resources ... Vacant
21 Business Office Director ... Ms. Karen PARRIOTT

Eastern Wyoming College-Douglas Campus (C)

203 N 6th Street, Douglas WY 82633
Telephone: (307) 358-5622 Identification: 770476
Accreditation: &NH

† Branch campus of Eastern Wyoming College, Torrington, WY.

Gillette College (D)

300 West Sinclair, Gillette WY 82718
Telephone: (888) 544-5538 Identification: 770478
Accreditation: &NH

† Branch campus of Northern Wyoming Community College District, Sheridan, WY.

Institute of Business and Medical Careers (E)

1854 Dell Range Boulevard, Cheyenne WY 82009
Telephone: (307) 433-8363 Identification: 666738
Accreditation: ACICS

† Branch campus of Institute of Business and Medical Careers, Fort Collins, CO.

Laramie County Community College (F)

1400 E College Drive, Cheyenne WY 82007-3299
County: Laramie FICE Identification: 009259
Unit ID: 240620
Telephone: (307) 778-5222 Carnegie Class: Assoc/Pub-R-M
FAX Number: (307) 778-1399 Calendar System: Semester
URL: www.lccc.wy.edu
Established: 1968 Annual Undergrad Tuition & Fees (In-District): $3,564
Enrollment: 3,800 Coed
Affiliation or Control: State/Local IRS Status: 501(c)3
Highest Offering: Associate Degree
Program: Occupational; 2-Year Principally Bachelor's Creditable
Accreditation: NH, ADNUR, DH, DMS, EMT, PTAA, RAD, SURGT

01 President ... Dr. Joe SCHAFFER
05 Interim VP of Academic Affairs ... Ms. Therese HARPER
10 Vice Pres of Administration/Finance ... Mr. Rick JOHNSON
32 Vice President of Student Services ... Ms. Judy HAY
13 Chief Technology Officer ... Mr. Chad MARLEY
15 Executive Director Human Resources ... Vacant
30 Assoc VP Inst Advancement ... Ms. Lisa MURPHY
12 Assoc VP of Albany County Campus ... Dr. James MALM
45 Assc VP Institutional Effectiveness ... Dr. Kim BENDER
08 Librarian ... Ms. Karen LANGE
37 Director of Financial Aid ... Ms. Julie WILSON
26 Director of Public Relations ... Mr. Ty STOCKTON
18 Director of Physical Plant ... Mr. Timothy MACNAMARA
21 Director of Accounting Services ... Mr. Herry ANDREWS
29 Dir Alumni Affairs/Event Planning ... Ms. Lisa TRIMBLE
44 Dir Scholarships & Annual Giving ... Ms. Brenda LAIRD
09 Manager of Institutional Research ... Ms. Ann MURRAY
07 Dir of Admissions and Welcome Ctr ... Ms. Sarah HANNES
06 Registrar ... Ms. Stacy MAESTAS
49 Dean School of Arts & Humanities ... Dr. Daniel POWELL
50 Dean Sch of Bus/Ag & Tech Studies ... Mr. Melvin O. HAWKINS, JR.
76 Int Dean Sch of Health Sci & Well ... Ms. Cindy HENNING
81 Dean School of Math & Science ... Ms. Kathleen HATHAWAY
103 Dean Sch of Outreach/Workforce Dev ... Ms. Maryellen TAST
20 Dir Instructional Technologies ... Mr. Les BALSIGER
19 Director Campus Safety & Security ... Mr. James CROSBY
41 Director of Athletics ... Mr. Scott NOBLE

Laramie County Community College Albany County Campus (G)

1125 Boulder Drive, Laramie WY 82070
Telephone: (307) 721-5138 Identification: 770477
Accreditation: &NH

† Branch campus of Laramie County Community College, Cheyenne, WY.

Northern Wyoming Community College District (H)

PO Box 1500, 3059 Coffeen Avenue, Sheridan WY 82801-1500
County: Sheridan FICE Identification: 003930
Unit ID: 240666
Telephone: (307) 674-6446 Carnegie Class: Assoc/Pub-R-M
FAX Number: (307) 674-4293 Calendar System: Semester
URL: www.sheridan.edu
Established: 1948 Annual Undergrad Tuition & Fees (In-District): $2,952
Enrollment: 4,430 Coed
Affiliation or Control: Local IRS Status: 501(c)3
Highest Offering: Associate Degree
Program: Occupational; 2-Year Principally Bachelor's Creditable
Accreditation: NH, ADNUR, DH

01 President ... Dr. Paul R. YOUNG
05 VP Academic Affairs ... Dr. Richard HALL
10 VP Admin & Finance/CFO ... Ms. Cheryl A. HEATH
12 VP Gillette College/CEO ... Dr. Mark G. ENGLERT
86 VP External Affairs ... Dr. Susan BIGELOW
06 Dean Enrollment Services ... Ms. Sharon ELWOOD
32 Dean of Students ... Ms. Carol GARCIA
49 Dean Arts/Humanies & Social Science ... Dr. Mercedes AGUIRRE BATTY
76 Dean Health Sciences ... Ms. Trudy R. MUNSICK
47 Dean Culinary/Ag & Natural Science ... Dr. Ami N. ERICKSON
75 Dean Technical Education ... Mr. Jed JENSEN
15 Director Human Resources ... Ms. Jennifer MCARTHUR
26 Dir Marketing/College Information ... Ms. Wendy M. SMITH
37 Director Financial Aid Services ... Ms. Kristen GAST
13 Dir Information Technology Services ... Mr. Brady R. FACKRELL
09 Director of Institutional Research ... Ms. Sharon ELWOOD
21 Controller ... Ms. Karen B. BURTIS
07 Executive Director of Admissions ... Mr. Joe B. MUELLER
39 Director Housing & Residential Ed ... Ms. Larissa B. BONNET
88 Director Veteran Services ... Mr. Brett K. BURTIS
18 Director Facilities/Physical Plant ... Mr. Kent A. ANDERSEN
18 Director Gillette Facilities ... Mr. Mark N. ANDERSEN
106 Dir Distance & Distributive Learn ... Mr. Stoney GADDY
103 Dir Workforce Development & CE ... Ms. Karen ST. CLAIR
08 Librarian ... Ms. Katrina M. BROWN
19 Director Security/Safety ... Mr. Jason VELA
41 Athletic Director ... Ms. Jenni WINTER
04 Administrative Asst to President ... Ms. Mary Jo JOHNSON

Northwest College (I)

231 W 6th Street, Powell WY 82435
County: Park FICE Identification: 003931
Unit ID: 240657
Telephone: (307) 754-6000 Carnegie Class: Assoc/Pub-R-S
FAX Number: (307) 754-6245 Calendar System: Semester
URL: www.nwc.edu
Established: 1946 Annual Undergrad Tuition & Fees (In-District): $2,749
Enrollment: 1,719 Coed
Affiliation or Control: State/Local IRS Status: 501(c)3
Highest Offering: Associate Degree
Program: Occupational; 2-Year Principally Bachelor's Creditable
Accreditation: NH, ADNUR, ART, MUS

01 President ... Dr. Stefani HICSWA
05 Vice Pres Academic Affairs ... Dr. Gerald GIRAUD
32 Interim Vice Pres Student Affairs ... Dr. Gerald GIRAUD
11 Vice Pres Admin Services ... Ms. Lisa WATSON
26 Vice Pres College Relations ... Mr. Mark KITCHEN
102 Executive Director NWC Foundation ... Ms. Shelby WETZEL
20 Dean Student Learning/Acad Support ... Dr. Matthew EWERS
103 Dean Extended Campus/Workforce ... Ms. Ronda PEER
08 Library Director ... Dr. Susan RICHARDS
10 Interim Finance Director ... Ms. Jo Ann HEIMER
15 Human Resources Director ... Ms. Jill ANDERSON
13 Computing Services Director ... Mr. Casey DEARCORN
18 Facilities Director ... Mr. David PLUTE
06 Registrar/Admissions Director ... Mr. Brad HAMMOND
37 Financial Aid/Scholarships Director ... Mr. Shaman QUINN
39 Residence/Campus Life Director ... Mr. Dee HAVIG
04 Exec Secretary to President & Board ... Ms. Cindy CICCI
07 Admissions Manager ... Mr. West HERNANDEZ
09 Institutional Researcher ... Ms. Lisa SMITH
105 Web Developer ... Ms. Carey MILLER
108 Assessment Coordinator ... Ms. Aura NEWLIN
19 Campus Security Coordinator ... Mr. Lee BLACKMORE
25 Grant Writer ... Ms. Megan WILSON
38 Student Success Mgr & Counselor ... Ms. Cynthia GARHART
44 Development Coordinator ... Ms. Andrea SHIPLEY

Oyster Ridge Higher Education/Kemmerer (J)

PO Box 423, Kemmerer WY 83101
Telephone: (307) 877-6958 Identification: 770479
Accreditation: &NH

† Branch campus of Western Wyoming Community College, Rock Springs, WY.

University of Wyoming (K)

1000 E University Avenue, Dept 3434, Laramie WY 82071-3434
County: Albany FICE Identification: 003932
Unit ID: 240727
Telephone: (307) 766-1121 Carnegie Class: RU/H
FAX Number: (307) 766-2271 Calendar System: Semester
URL: www.uwyo.edu
Established: 1886 Annual Undergrad Tuition & Fees (In-State): $4,646
Enrollment: 12,820 Coed
Affiliation or Control: State IRS Status: 501(c)3
Highest Offering: Doctorate
Program: Liberal Arts And General; Teacher Preparatory; Professional
Accreditation: NH, BUS, CACREP, CLPSY, CS, DIETD, ENG, LAW, MUS, NURSE, PHAR, SP, SW, TED

01 President ... Dr. Richard MCGINITY
05 Vice President Academic Affairs ... Dr. David JONES
10 Vice President Administration ... Mr. Bill MAI
86 Vice Pres Govt & Community Affairs ... Mr. Chris BOSWELL
46 Vice Pres Research & Economic Dev ... Dr. William A. GERN
32 Vice President Student Affairs ... Dr. Sara L. AXELSON
13 Vice President Information Tech ... Mr. Robert R. AYLWARD
30 Vice Pres Institutional Advancement ... Mr. W. Ben BLALOCK, III
43 Vice President & General Counsel ... Mr. Richard H. MILLER
41 Director Intercollegiate Athletics ... Mr. Tom BURMAN
20 Associate VP Academic Affairs ... Dr. Anne ALEXANDER
20 Interim Assoc VP Academic Affairs ... Dr. Tami BENHAM-DEAL
20 Interim Assoc VP Academic Affairs ... Dr. Ann HILD
11 Assoc Vice Pres Operations ... Mr. Mark A. COLLINS
21 Assoc VP Fiscal Administration ... Ms. Janet S. LOWE
21 Asst Vice Pres Budget/Inst Analysis ... Ms. Arley WILLIAMS
88 Assoc Vice President Research ... Ms. Dorothy C. YATES
35 AVP Student Affairs/Dn of Students ... Mr. Sean BLACKBURN
88 Assoc VP Institutional Advancement ... Mr. John D. STARK
26 Assoc VP Communication/Marketing ... Mr. Chad BALDWIN
47 Dean of Agriculture ... Dr. Frank D. GALEY
49 Dean of Arts & Sciences ... Dr. Paula LUTZ
50 Dean of Business ... Dr. Sanjay PUTREVU
53 Dean of Education ... Dr. Ray REUTZEL
54 Dean of Engineering ... Dr. Michael PISHKO
76 Dean of Health Sciences ... Dr. Joseph F. STEINER
61 Dean of Law ... Dr. Klint ALEXANDER
56 Dean Outreach ... Dr. Susan FRYE
12 Assoc Dean UW at Casper ... Dr. Scott SEVILLE
08 Interim Dean of Libraries ... Ms. Lori PHILLIPS
65 Director Haub Sch Env/Nat Resources ... Dr. Ingrid BURKE
07 Director of Admissions ... Ms. Shelley DODD
36 Director Advising/Career Services ... Ms. Evelyn J. CHYTKA
28 Director Affirmative Action/EEO ... Ms. Oneida BLAGG
29 Exec Director Alumni Affairs ... Mr. Keener FRYE
88 Acting Dir American Heritage Center ... Mr. Rick EWIG
88 Director School of Energy Resources ... Dr. Mark NORTHAM
88 Director Art Museum ... Ms. Susan MOLDENHAUER
88 Director Campus Recreation ... Mr. Patrick MORAN
45 Director Facilities Planning ... Mr. Larry BLAKE
109 Director Auxiliary Services ... Ms. Carolyn SMITH
15 Interim Director Human Resources ... Mr. Mark BERCHENI
18 Interim Director Physical Plant ... Mr. John DAVIS
92 Interim Director Honors Program ... Dr. Susan ARONSTEIN
86 Spec Advis to the Pres for Ext Rels ... Ms. Meredith ASAY
39 Exec Dir Res Life/Dining/Stdnt Un ... Mr. Eric WEBB
37 Director Student Financial Aid ... Ms. Kathy BOBBITT
06 Interim Registrar ... Mr. Lane BUCHANAN
23 Director Student Health Service ... Dr. Joanne E. STEANE
19 Chief University Police Dept ... Mr. Mike SAMP
38 Dir University Counseling Center ... Dr. Keith EVASHEVSKI

Western Wyoming Community College (L)

PO Box 428, Rock Springs WY 82902-0428
County: Sweetwater FICE Identification: 003933
Unit ID: 240693
Telephone: (307) 382-1600 Carnegie Class: Assoc/Pub-R-M
FAX Number: (307) 382-1636 Calendar System: Semester
URL: www.wwcc.wy.edu
Established: 1959 Annual Undergrad Tuition & Fees (In-District): $2,400
Enrollment: 3,554 Coed

Affiliation or Control: State/Local IRS Status: 501(c)3
Highest Offering: Associate Degree
Program: Occupational; 2-Year Principally Bachelor's Creditable
Accreditation: NH, ADNUR

01 President .... Dr. Karla N. LEACH
05 VP of Student Learning .... Dr. Kim FARLEY
32 VP of Student Success Services .... Dr. Jackie FREEZE
11 VP for Administrative Services .... Mr. Sheldon FLOM
88 Assoc VP for Administrative Svcs .... Ms. Carla BUDD
21 Controller .... Ms. Debbie BAKER
07 Director of Admissions .... Ms. Erin GREY
06 Registrar .... Ms. Kay LEUM
37 Director of Financial Aid .... Ms. Nicole CASTILLON
08 Director of Library Services .... Ms. Janice GROVER-ROOSA
18 Director of Physical Resources .... Mr. Paul ROSS
39 Dir Residence Halls/Student Life .... Mr. Dustin CONOVER
40 Bookstore Manager .... Ms. Natalie LANE
41 Athletic Director .... Dr. Lu SWEET
92 Director of Honors Program .... Mr. Richard KEMPA
09 Director of Planning & Improvement .... Ms. Dianna RENZ
15 Director Personnel Services .... Ms. Carla BUDD
26 Coord of Marketing/Public Info .... Mr. Christopher SHEID
30 Director Community College Relation .... Mr. David TATE
36 Dir Student Engagement & Completion .... Mr. Mark REMBACZ
10 Chief Business Officer .... Ms. Debbie BAKER
38 Dir Student Counseling/Disability .... Ms. Kim DRANE
96 Director of Purchasing .... Ms. Tammy REGISTER
04 Administrative Asst to President .... Ms. Kandy FRINK
19 Protective Services Supervisor .... Mr. Mark PADILLA

Western Wyoming Community College Outreach Afton/Star Valley (A)

247 N Washington, Box 1237, Afton WY 83110
Telephone: (307) 886-3834 Identification: 770483
Accreditation: &NH

† Branch campus of Western Wyoming Community College, Rock Springs, WY.

Western Wyoming Community College Outreach Evanston (B)

1013 Cheyenne Drive, Evanston WY 82930
Telephone: (307) 789-3988 Identification: 770482
Accreditation: &NH

† Branch campus of Western Wyoming Community College, Rock Springs, WY.

Wyoming Catholic College (C)

1400 City Park Dr, PO Box 750, Lander WY 82520
County: Fremont Identification: 667227
Telephone: (307) 332-2930 Carnegie Class: Not Classified
FAX Number: (307) 332-2918 Calendar System: Semester
URL: www.wyomingcatholiccollege.com
Established: 2005 Annual Undergrad Tuition & Fees: $20,000
Enrollment: 124 Coed
Affiliation or Control: Roman Catholic IRS Status: 501(c)3
Highest Offering: Baccalaureate
Program: Liberal Arts And General
Accreditation: @NH

01 President .... Dr. Kevin D. ROBERTS
05 Academic Dean .... Dr. John MORTENSEN
10 VP for Operations & Finance .... Mr. Richard ROLLINO
26 Vice Pres for External Affairs .... Mr. Jonathan TONKOWICH
30 Asst Vice Pres of Advancement .... Ms. Mary MURRAY
32 Dean of Students .... Mr. Kyle WASHUT

WyoTech (D)

4373 N 3rd Street, Laramie WY 82072-9519
County: Albany FICE Identification: 009157
Unit ID: 240718
Telephone: (307) 742-3776 Carnegie Class: Assoc/PrivFP
FAX Number: (307) 721-4854 Calendar System: Other
URL: www.wyotech.edu
Established: 1966 Annual Undergrad Tuition & Fees: $29,250
Enrollment: 1,085 Coed
Affiliation or Control: Proprietary IRS Status: Proprietary
Highest Offering: Associate Degree
Program: Occupational
Accreditation: ACCSC

01 President .... Mr. Wm. Guy WARPNESS
05 Director of Education .... Mr. Caleb PERRITON
11 Director of Operations .... Mr. Mario IBARRA
07 Director of Admissions .... Mr. Glenn HALSEY
37 Director of Financial Aid .... Ms. Brenda COSSITT
32 Director of Student Services .... Mr. Kyle MORRIS
36 Director of Career Services .... Mr. Martin AXLUND
06 Registrar .... Ms. Revalee WEERHEIM
07 Director of Admissions .... Mr. Greg TAYLOR
39 Housing Manager .... Mr. Gabe LUCERO
04 Admin Assistant to the President .... Ms. Courtney SCHELL

US SERVICE SCHOOLS

Air Force Institute of Technology (E)

2950 Hobson Way, Wright Patterson AFB OH 45433-7765
County: Greene FICE Identification: 003009
Unit ID: 200697
Telephone: (937) 255-2321 Carnegie Class: DRU
FAX Number: (937) 656-7600 Calendar System: Quarter
URL: www.afit.edu
Established: 1919 Annual Graduate Tuition & Fees: $16,944
Enrollment: 860 Coed
Affiliation or Control: Federal IRS Status: Exempt
Highest Offering: Doctorate; No Undergraduates
Program: Professional; Technical Emphasis
Accreditation: NH, ENG, ENGR

01 Chancellor .... Dr. Todd I. STEWART
03 Commandant .... Col. Doral E. SANDLIN
05 Provost/Vice Chancellor .... Dr. Sivaguru S. SRITHARAN
54 Dean Graduate School of Engr & Mgt .... Dr. Adedeji B. BADIRU
20 Associate Provost .... Col. Tim SANDS
46 Dean for Research .... Dr. Heidi R. RIES
10 Chief Financial Officer .... Ms. Amber L. RICHEY
09 Director Institutional Research .... Dr. Nancy J. ROSZELL
06 Director Admissions/Registrar .... Mr. Robert J. LAVERRIERE
32 Associate Dean of Students .... Col. Michael L. HASTRITER
13 Dir Communications & Information .... LtCol. Darin LADD
08 Director D'Azzo Research Library .... Dr. Laurene E. ZAPROROZHETZ
15 Director Personnel Services .... Ms. Leanne HEAGLE
18 Chief Facilities/Physical Plant .... Mr. Daniel W. ROHRBACH
29 Manager Alumni Affairs .... Ms. Kathleen E. SCOTT
35 Director Student Services .... Mr. Richard GAMMON
85 Director of Intl Student Affairs .... Ms. Annette D. ROBB
40 Bookstore Supervisor .... Mr. Joseph SCOTT

Air University (F)

55 LeMay Plaza South, Maxwell AFB AL 36112-6335
County: Montgomery FICE Identification: 001001
Telephone: (334) 953-5613 Carnegie Class: Not Classified
FAX Number: (334) 953-2749 Calendar System: Other
URL: www.au.af.mil
Established: 1946 Annual Undergrad Tuition & Fees: N/A
Enrollment: 53,102 Coed
Affiliation or Control: Federal IRS Status: Exempt
Highest Offering: Doctorate
Program: Professional
Accreditation: SC

01 Commander and President .... MajGen. Steven L. KWAST
03 Vice Commander .... Vacant
05 Vice President for Academic Affairs .... Dr. Matthew C. STAFFORD
06 Registrar .... Dr. Michael J. MASTERSON
20 Deputy Director Academic Affairs .... Mr. Jay WARWICK
20 Director Academic Affairs .... Dr. Chris CAIN

† Parent institution of Community College of the Air Force, School of Advanced Air and Space Studies, and the Air Force Institute of Technology

Community College of the Air Force (G)

100 South Turner Blvd,
Maxwell AFB, Gunter Annex AL 36114-3011
Telephone: (334) 649-5000 FICE Identification: 012308
Accreditation: &SC, PTAA

† Regional accreditation is carried under the parent institution, Air University, Maxwell AFB, AL.

Defense Language Institute (H)

1759 Lewis Road, Monterey CA 93944
County: Monterey FICE Identification: 001195
Unit ID: 428222
Telephone: (831) 242-5828 Carnegie Class: Not Classified
FAX Number: (831) 242-6495 Calendar System: Other
URL: www.dliflc.edu
Established: 1941 Annual Undergrad Tuition & Fees: N/A
Enrollment: 3,800 Coed
Affiliation or Control: Federal IRS Status: Exempt
Highest Offering: Associate Degree
Program: Occupational; 2-Year Principally Bachelor's Creditable
Accreditation: WJ

01 Commandant .... Col. Phillip DEPPERT
05 Provost .... Dr. Betty Lou LEAVER
20 Associate Provost .... Dr. Jielu ZHAO
06 Registrar .... Dr. Robert SAVUKINAS

† Associate Arts in Foreign Language authorized by US Congress in December 2001 and approved by ACCJC/WASC in June 2002.

59th Dental Training Squadron (I)

Bldg 3352, Lackland AFB TX 78236
Telephone: (210) 292-7251 Identification: 770122
Accreditation: &M

† Branch campus of Uniformed Services University of the Health Sciences, Bethesda, MD.

Joint Forces Staff College (J)

7800 Hampton Boulevard, Norfolk VA 23511-1702
Telephone: (757) 443-6000 Identification: 770121
Accreditation: &M

† Branch campus of National Defense University, Washington, DC.

The Judge Advocate General's Legal Center & School (K)

600 Massie Road, Charlottesville VA 22903-1781
County: Albermarle Identification: 666974
Telephone: (434) 971-3300 Carnegie Class: Not Classified
FAX Number: (434) 971-3338 Calendar System: Quarter
URL: www.jagcnet.army.mil/tjaglcs
Established: 1951 Annual Graduate Tuition & Fees: N/A
Enrollment: 115 Coed
Affiliation or Control: Federal IRS Status: Exempt
Highest Offering: Master's; No Undergraduates
Program: Professional
Accreditation: LAW

01 Commander/Commandant .... BGen. Charles N. PEDE
05 Dean .... Col. James F. GARRETT
20 Associate Dean of Academics .... Mr. Maurice A. LESCAULT, JR.

Marine Corps University (L)

2076 South Street, Quantico VA 22134-5068
County: Prince William Identification: 666745
Unit ID: 438513
Telephone: (703) 784-2105 Carnegie Class: Not Classified
FAX Number: (703) 784-1271 Calendar System: Semester
URL: www.mcu.usmc.mil
Established: 1989 Annual Graduate Tuition & Fees: N/A
Enrollment: 535 Coed
Affiliation or Control: Federal IRS Status: Exempt
Highest Offering: Master's; No Undergraduates
Program: Professional; Technical Emphasis
Accreditation: SC

01 President .... BGen. Helen PRATT
05 Vice President for Academic Affairs .... Dr. James ANDERSON
20 Director Academic Support Division .... Mr. Jay HATTON
09 Director Institutional Research .... Dr. Susan JOHNSTON

National Defense University (M)

Fort Lesley J. McNair, Washington DC 20319-5066
FICE Identification: 031893
Unit ID: 423494
Telephone: (202) 685-3924 Carnegie Class: Not Classified
FAX Number: (202) 685-3920 Calendar System: Semester
URL: www.ndu.edu
Established: 1976 Annual Graduate Tuition & Fees: N/A
Enrollment: 1,750 Coed
Affiliation or Control: Federal IRS Status: Exempt
Highest Offering: Master's; No Undergraduates
Program: Professional
Accreditation: M

01 President .... MajGen. Frederick M. PADILLA
03 Senior Vice President .... Amb. Wanda L. NESBITT
05 Provost/Vice Pres Academic Affairs .... Dr. John W. YAEGER
11 Chief Operating Officer .... Mr. Robert C. KANE
43 General Counsel .... Ms. Mollie MURPHY
46 Senior Director of Research .... Dr. Richard D. HOOKER, JR.
88 Chancellor .... Dr. Michael S. BELL
88 Commandant .... BG. Guy T. COSENTINO
88 Commandant .... BGen. Thomas A. GORRY
88 Chancellor .... Ms. Janice M. HAMBY
88 Commandant .... RADM. John W. SMITH, JR.
107 Senior Director CAPSTONE .... Vacant
20 Deputy Vice Pres Academic Affairs .... Dr. Tim RUSSO
32 Associate Provost Student/Acad Svcs .... Vacant
06 University Registrar .... Mr. Larry JOHNSON
42 Chaplain .... COL. Jeffery ZUST
26 Director of Strategic Communication .... Mr. Mark PHILLIPS
13 Chief Information Officer .... Ms. Diane WEBBER
105 Web/Social Media Manager .... Ms. Jennifer RUSSELL
10 Director Resource Management .... Mr. Jay HELMING
25 Director Contracting .... Ms. Jenifer CUOZZO
23 Director Health Fitness .... Mr. Tony SPINOSA
15 Director Human Resources .... Mr. Tim ROBERTSON
08 Director Libraries .... Ms. Helen (Meg) TULLOCH
85 Director International Fellows .... Dr. John GODWIN
18 Chief Facilities/Physical Plant .... Mr. Charles FANSHAW
19 Director Security .... Mr. Joe PALLANEZ
88 Events Director .... Vacant
102 President/CEO NDU Foundation .... Ms. Cathleen PEARL

National Intelligence University (N)

200 MacDill Boulevard, Washington DC 20340-5100
Identification: 666393
Unit ID: 131380
Telephone: (202) 231-3344 Carnegie Class: Not Classified
FAX Number: (202) 231-3294 Calendar System: Quarter
URL: www.ni-u.edu
Established: 1962 Annual Undergrad Tuition & Fees: N/A
Enrollment: 600 Coed

Affiliation or Control: Federal IRS Status: Exempt
Highest Offering: Master's
Program: Professional
Accreditation: M

01 President .... Dr. David R. ELLISON
100 Chief of Staff .... Col. Randall H. WILLIAMSON
04 Executive Assistant to President .... Ms. Jessica M. STEINRUCK
05 Exec VP & Provost .... Dr. Susan M. STUDDS
88 Dir Ctr for International Pgms .... Mr. Lorenzo S. HIPONIA
46 Dir Ctr for Strategic Intel Rsrch .... Dr. Cathryn Q. THURSTON
09 Dir Inst Effectiveness & Assessment .... Dr. Felicia BRADSHAW
10 VP Finance & Administration .... Mr. Paul LEGERE
11 Director of Univ Operations .... Mr. Stephen J. KERDA
18 Facilities .... Dr. Richard MESTAS
19 Security Officer .... Ms. Thelma FLAMER
06 Registrar .... Mr. Eric H. STUPAR
07 Director of Admissions .... Ms. Alteia L. ROBINSON
90 Director Eductional Technology .... Vacant
08 Director Library Services .... Ms. Denise CAMPBELL
58 Dean College Strategic Intel .... Dr. Donald HANLE
12 Director NSA Campus .... Mr. Dax NORMAN
12 Director NGA Campus .... Mr. Timothy J. CHRISTENSON
12 Director Reserve Monthly Pgm .... Cmdr. Craig O"BRIEN
12 Director European Academic Cntr .... Dr. Jimmie NEWTON
12 Director Southern Academic Cntr .... Mr. Kevin TALIAFERRO
58 Dean School of Science & Tech Intel .... Dr. Brian R. SHAW
29 Dir Outreach & Alumni Affairs .... Mr. Thomas VAN WAGNER
101 Secretary of the Institution/Board .... Mr. James HUVER

Naval Postgraduate School (A)

1 University Circle, Room M10, Monterey CA 93943-5100
County: Monterey FICE Identification: 001310
Unit ID: 119678
Telephone: (831) 656-2441 Carnegie Class: Master's L
FAX Number: (831) 656-2921 Calendar System: Quarter
URL: www.nps.edu
Established: 1909 Annual Undergrad Tuition & Fees: N/A
Enrollment: 2,901 Coed
Affiliation or Control: Federal IRS Status: Exempt
Highest Offering: Doctorate
Program: Professional
Accreditation: WC, BUS, ENG, SPAA

01 President .... VAdm. Ronald A. ROUTE, RET.
100 Chief of Staff .... Capt. Deidre MCLAY
05 Provost .... Dr. Douglas A. HENSLER
13 Director Information Technology .... Mr. Joseph LOPICCOLO
20 Vice Provost for Academic Affairs .... Dr. Orrin Douglas MOSES
46 Dean of Research .... Dr. Jeffrey D. PADUAN
54 Dean Grad Sch Engr/Applied Sci .... Dr. Phillip A. DURKEE
58 Dean Sch of Intl Graduate Studies .... Dr. James J. WIRTZ
50 Dean Grad Sch Bus/Public Policy .... Dr. William R. GATES
72 Dean Grad Sch Oper & Info Sciences ... Dr. Gordon MCCORMICK
32 Dean of Students .... Capt. Matthew R. VANDERSLUIS
10 Comptroller .... Mr. Kevin K. LITTLE
18 Director Facilities Management ...... Mr. Andrew (Pete) BOERLAGE
08 University Librarian .... Ms. Eleanor S. UHLINGER
06 Registrar .... Mr. Mike ANDERSEN
15 Director Human Resources .... Ms. Ermelinda RODRIGUEZ-HEFFNER
29 Director of Alumni Relations .... Mr. Kari L. MIGLAW
19 Sr Lecturer NPS/Chief Security Ofcr .... Capt. Robert SIMERAL, RET.
28 EEO Director .... Ms. Deborah A. BAITY
56 Director of CED3 .... Mr. Tom M. MASTRE
07 Director of Admissions .... Ms. Sue DOOLEY
88 Director of Programs .... Cmdr. James V. WALSH

Naval War College (B)

686 Cushing Road, Newport RI 02841-1207
County: Newport FICE Identification: 003413
Unit ID: 432320
Telephone: (401) 841-3089 Carnegie Class: Not Classified
FAX Number: (401) 841-1297 Calendar System: Trimester
URL: www.usnwc.edu
Established: 1884 Annual Graduate Tuition & Fees: N/A
Enrollment: N/A Coed
Affiliation or Control: Federal IRS Status: Exempt
Highest Offering: Master's; No Undergraduates
Program: Professional
Accreditation: EH

01 President .... RADM. P. Gardner HOWE, III
04 Exec Assistant to the President .... LCDR. Jay BREWER
05 Provost .... Dr. Lewis M. DUNCAN
88 Chief of Staff to the Provost .... Mr. Richard R. MENARD
20 Associate Provost .... Prof. William R. SPAIN
100 Chief of Staff .... CAPT. Francis MOLINARI
20 Dean of Academic Affairs .... Dr. John GAROFANO
09 Dean Center for Warfare Studies .... Prof. Thomas CULORA
32 Dean of Students .... CAPT. John GRIFFIN
08 Director Library Services .... Dr. Allen C. BENSON
56 Dir College of Distance Education .... Dr. Jay HICKEY
06 Registrar .... Ms. Michele BLACKBURN
46 Chairman Strategy & Policy .... Dr. Michael PAVKOVIC
88 Chairman National Security Affairs .... Dr. David COOPER
88 Chairman Joint Military Operations .... CAPT. Alan ABRAMSON
10 Chief Business Officer .... Mr. Robert SAMPSON
15 Director Military Personnel Svcs .... CDR. Melanie HA'O
15 Civilian Human Resources Officer .... Ms. Charlene HANSON
18 Chief Facilities/Physical Plant .... Ms. Beth LEINBERRY
26 Chief Public Relations Officer .... CDR. Kelly BRANNON
13 Chief Information Officer .... Mr. Joseph PANGBORN
19 Director of Security .... Mr. Paul GATELY
29 Director Alumni Affairs .... Ms. Julia GAGE
88 Director Writing Center .... Vacant
104 Director International Programs .... Prof. Thomas MANGOLD
88 Dean Col Operatnl/Strategic Ldrshp .... Prof. James KELLY
88 Director of Events .... Ms. Karen SELLERS

School of Advanced Air and Space Studies (C)

125 Chennault Circle, Maxwell AFB AL 36112-6424
Telephone: (334) 953-5155 Identification: 666746
Accreditation: &SC

† Regional accreditation is carried under the parent institution, Air University, Maxwell AFB, AL.

Uniformed Services University of the Health Sciences (D)

4301 Jones Bridge Road, Bethesda MD 20814-4799
County: Montgomery FICE Identification: 021610
Unit ID: 164137
Telephone: (301) 295-3013 Carnegie Class: Not Classified
FAX Number: (301) 295-3431 Calendar System: Quarter
URL: www.usuhs.mil
Established: 1972 Annual Graduate Tuition & Fees: N/A
Enrollment: 1,181 Coed
Affiliation or Control: Federal IRS Status: Exempt
Highest Offering: Doctorate; No Undergraduates
Program: Professional
Accreditation: M, ANEST, CLPSY, ENGR, MED, NURSE, PH

01 President .... Dr. Charles L. RICE
03 Senior Vice President .... Dr. Patrick SCULLEY
05 Sr Vice Pres University Programs .... Dr. Patrick SCULLEY
10 Vice Pres Finance & Admin .... Mr. Walter TINLING
26 Vice Pres External Affairs .... Dr. Jeffrey LONGACRE
46 Vice President for Research .... Dr. Yvonne MADDOX
04 Exec Assistant to the President .... Ms. Mary L. SCHWARTZ
100 Chief of Staff .... Mr. Robert J. THOMPSON
63 Dean School of Medicine .... Dr. Arthur KELLERMANN
63 Vice Dean School of Medicine .... Dr. John MCMANIGLE
58 Actg Assoc Dean Graduate Education .... Dr. Gregory MUELLER
07 Assoc Dean Admiss & Recruiting SOM .... LTC. Aaron SAGUIL
88 Assoc Dean Graduate Medical Educ .... CAPT. Jerri CURTIS
32 Assoc Dean Student Affairs .... COL. Lisa MOORES
88 Assistant Dean Academic Support .... Dr. William WITTMAN
88 Assistant Dean Clinical Sciences .... CAPT. Patricia MCKAY
66 Dean Graduate School of Nursing .... Dr. Ada Sue HINSHAW
20 Assoc Dean Academic Affairs GSN .... Dr. Diane SEIBERT
46 Director AFRRI .... COL. Lester HUFF
13 Chief Information Officer .... Mr. Timothy RAPP
43 General Counsel .... Mr. Jason KAAR
06 Registrar .... Ms. Gail HEWITT-CLARKE
15 Director Civilian Human Res .... Mr. Darryl BROWN
08 Acting University Librarian .... Ms. Linda SPITZER
18 Director of Facilities .... Ms. Cheryl KING
96 Director of Contracting .... Mr. Anthony REVENIS
21 Associate Business Officer .... Mr. Walter TINLING
29 Director Alumni Relations .... Ms. Sharon HOLLAND
20 Assistant Dean for Curriculum .... COL. Arnyce POCK
88 Assoc Dean for Faculty .... Dr. Brian REAMY
88 Assoc Dean for Medical Education .... Dr. William GILLILAND
52 Dean Army Postgrad Dental School .... COL. Priscilla HAMILTON
52 Dean Naval Postgrad Dental School .... CAPT. Glenn MUNRO
52 Dean Air Force Postgrad Dental Sch .... COL. Drew FALLIS

United States Air Force Academy (E)

2304 Cadet Drive, Suite 2400,
USAF Academy CO 80840-5025
County: El Paso FICE Identification: 001369
Unit ID: 128328
Telephone: (719) 333-3070 Carnegie Class: Bac/A&S
FAX Number: (719) 333-3647 Calendar System: Semester
URL: www.academyadmissions.com
Established: 1954 Annual Undergrad Tuition & Fees: N/A
Enrollment: 3,952 Coed
Affiliation or Control: Federal IRS Status: Exempt
Highest Offering: Baccalaureate
Program: Liberal Arts And General; Professional
Accreditation: NH, BUS, CS, DENT, ENG

01 Superintendent .... LtGen. Michelle D. JOHNSON

United States Army Command and General Staff College (F)

100 Stimson Avenue, Fort Leavenworth KS 66027
County: Leavenworth FICE Identification: 001947
Unit ID: 156055
Telephone: (913) 684-3097 Carnegie Class: Not Classified
FAX Number: (913) 684-2906 Calendar System: Trimester
URL: usacac.army.mil/cac2/cgsc/
Established: 1881 Annual Graduate Tuition & Fees: N/A
Enrollment: 1,002 Coed
Affiliation or Control: Federal IRS Status: Exempt
Highest Offering: Master's; No Undergraduates
Program: Professional
Accreditation: NH

01 Commandant .... LtGen. Robert B. BROWN
03 Deputy Commandant .... BGen. Christopher P. HUGHES
04 Assistant Deputy Commandant .... Vacant
05 Dean of Academics .... Dr. Wendell C. KING
100 Chief of Staff .... Col. Monty L. WILLOUGHBY
58 Director Graduate Degree Programs .... Dr. Robert BAUMANN
08 Director of Library .... Mr. Ed BURGESS
32 Director CGSS School .... Col. Drew MEYEROWICH
06 Registrar .... Vacant
26 Chief Public Relations Officer .... Mr. Harry SARLES

United States Army War College (G)

122 Forbes Avenue, Carlisle PA 17013-5050
County: Cumberland Identification: 666235
Telephone: (717) 245-4711 Carnegie Class: Not Classified
FAX Number: (717) 245-4721 Calendar System: Other
URL: www.carlisle.army.mil
Established: 1901 Annual Graduate Tuition & Fees: N/A
Enrollment: N/A Coed
Affiliation or Control: Federal IRS Status: Exempt
Highest Offering: Master's; No Undergraduates
Program: Professional
Accreditation: M

01 Commandant .... MajGen. William E. RAPP
05 Provost .... Dr. Lance BETROS

United States Coast Guard Academy (H)

15 Mohegan Avenue, New London CT 06320-8100
County: New London FICE Identification: 001415
Unit ID: 130624
Telephone: (860) 444-8444 Carnegie Class: Bac/Diverse
FAX Number: (860) 444-8288 Calendar System: Semester
URL: www.cga.edu
Established: 1876 Annual Undergrad Tuition & Fees: N/A
Enrollment: 896 Coed
Affiliation or Control: Federal IRS Status: Exempt
Highest Offering: Baccalaureate
Program: Occupational; Technical Emphasis
Accreditation: EH, BUS, ENG

01 Superintendent .... RADM. James E. RENDON
03 Assistant Superintendent .... CAPT. Anthony J. VOGT
45 Planning Officer .... CDR. Timothy T. BROWN
05 Dean of Academics .... Dr. Kurt J. COLELLA
20 Associate Dean .... CDR. Gregory HALL
45 Director of Academic Resources .... Dr. Eric PAGE
07 Director of Admissions .... CAPT. Robert E. MCKENNA
32 Commandant of Cadets .... CAPT. Melissa L. RIVERIA
06 Registrar .... Mr. Donald E. DYKES
08 Librarian .... Ms. Lucia MAZIAR
10 Comptroller .... LCDR. Francisco A. ESTEVEZ
26 Communication Director .... Mr. David M. SANTOS
09 Institutional Research .... Dr. Leonard M. GIAMBRA
13 Head of Information Services .... CDR. Robert F. TAYLOR
16 Personnel Management Specialist .... Mrs. Sunnie ROBINSON
15 Chief Personnel/Administration .... CDR. David BURNS
18 Chief Facilities Engineer .... CDR. Joshua W. FANT
19 Security Chief .... CDR. Robert F. TAYLOR
22 Civil Rights Officer .... Mr. Roy P. ZIEGENGEIST
23 Chief Health Services .... CAPT. Ernest E. SULLIVENT
38 Chief Cadet Counselor .... Dr. Robert MURRAY
40 Bookstore Manager .... Ms. Lauri KERP
41 Director of Athletics .... Mr. Timothy M. FITZPATRICK
42 Command Chaplain .... CAPT. John V. DICKENS
43 Staff Legal Officer .... CDR. Stephen J. ADLER
85 International Cadet Advisor .... Dr. Kassim M. TARHINI
28 Instructor Inclusion and Diversity .... Dr. Aram DEKOVEN

† There is a one-time entrance fee of $3,000 to cover uniform, laptop, and supplies.

United States Merchant Marine Academy (I)

300 Steamboat Road, Kings Point NY 11024-1634
County: Nassau FICE Identification: 002892
Unit ID: 197027
Telephone: (516) 773-5000 Carnegie Class: Bac/Diverse
FAX Number: (516) 773-5509 Calendar System: Trimester
URL: www.usmma.edu
Established: 1943 Annual Undergrad Tuition & Fees: $1,107
Enrollment: 961 Coed
Affiliation or Control: Federal IRS Status: Exempt
Highest Offering: Master's
Program: Liberal Arts And General; Professional; Technical Emphasis
Accreditation: M, ENG

01 Superintendent .... RADM. James HELIS
03 Deputy Superintendent .... RDML. Susan L. DUNLAP
05 Academic Dean .... Dr. Shashi KUMAR
32 Commandant Midshipmen .... Vacant
20 Assistant Academic Dean .... Ms. Dianne TAHA
18 Asst Supt for Facilities .... Capt. Theodore DOGONNIUCK
30 Director Office of External Affairs .... Mr. Ben BENSON

07 Director of Admissions .... Vacant
06 Registrar .... Ms. Lisa JERRY
08 Chief Librarian .... Vacant
13 Director Computer/Information Mgmt .... Mr. Kevin CLARKE
15 Director Human Resources .... Mr. Andrew GREEN
10 Chief Financial Officer .... Mr. Jose ESCOTO
29 Director Alumni Relations .... Mr. Jim TOBIN
35 Director Student Affairs .... Vacant
36 Dir of Prof Develop/Career Services .... Capt. Gene ALBERT
37 Director Student Financial Aid .... Mr. Joseph BECKER
96 Director of Purchasing .... Mr. Max DIAH
09 Director of Institutional Research .... Vacant
19 Director Security/Safety .... Mr. David EBERT
22 Dir Affirmative Action/EEO .... Vacant
28 Director of Diversity .... Vacant

United States Military Academy (A)

West Point NY 10996-5000
County: Orange FICE Identification: 002893
Unit ID: 197036
Telephone: (845) 938-4041 Carnegie Class: Bac/A&S
FAX Number: (845) 938-3021 Calendar System: Semester
URL: www.westpoint.edu
Established: 1802 Annual Undergrad Tuition & Fees: N/A
Enrollment: 4,414 Coed
Affiliation or Control: Federal IRS Status: Exempt
Highest Offering: Baccalaureate
Program: Liberal Arts And General
Accreditation: M, CS, ENG

01 Superintendent/President .... LTG. Robert CASLEN, JR.
05 Dean of Academic Board .... BG. Timothy TRAINOR
20 Vice Dean .... Dr. Jean BLAIR
32 Commandant of Cadets .... BG. John C. THOMSON, III
100 Chief of Staff .... COL. Wayne A. GREEN
88 Garrison Commander .... COL. Landy DUNHAM
07 Director of Admissions .... COL. Deborah MCDONALD
06 Assoc Dean Operations/Registrar .... Dr. James DALTON
45 Associate Dean for Research .... LTC. John GRAHAM
09 Institutional Research .... LTC. Holly WEST
13 Chief Information Officer .... COL. Ron DODGE
10 Director of Resource Management .... Mrs. Deborah A. POOL
26 Public Affairs Officer .... LTC. Webster WRIGHT
08 USMA Library .... Mr. Christopher BARTH
29 President Association of Graduates .... COLRet. Robert MCCLURE
38 Dir Center for Personal Development .... LTC. Brian CRANDALL
41 Director Intercollegiate Athletics .... Mr. Boo CORRIGAN
18 Chief Facilities/Physical Plant .... Mr. Matthew TALABER
15 Dir Center for Faculty Excellence .... Dr. Mark EVANS
35 Dir Ctr for Enchanced Performance .... LTC. Pete JENSEN
88 Director of Cadet Activities .... LTC. Todd MESSITT
43 Chief Legal Assistance .... Mr. Micheal BARRETT

United States Naval Academy (B)

121 Blake Road, Annapolis MD 21402-5000
County: Anne Arundel FICE Identification: 030430
Unit ID: 164155
Telephone: (410) 293-1000 Carnegie Class: Bac/A&S
FAX Number: (410) 293-3734 Calendar System: Semester
URL: www.usna.edu
Established: 1845 Annual Undergrad Tuition & Fees: N/A
Enrollment: 4,511 Coed
Affiliation or Control: Federal IRS Status: Exempt
Highest Offering: Baccalaureate
Program: Liberal Arts And General; Professional; Technical Emphasis
Accreditation: M, CS, ENG

01 Superintendent .... VADM. Walter E. CARTER, JR.
32 Commandant of Midshipmen .... COL. Stephen LISZEWSKI
05 Academic Dean & Provost .... Dr. Andrew T. PHILLIPS
20 Vice Academic Dean .... Dr. Boyd A. WAITE
07 Dean of Admissions .... Capt. Bruce J. LATTA
10 Associate Dean for Finances .... Capt. Peter A. NARDI
20 Assoc Dean for Academic Affairs .... Dr. Jennifer WATERS
08 Assoc Dean Information Svcs/Library .... Mr. James RETTIG
21 CFO/Deputy for Finance .... Mr. Joseph RUBINO
100 Chief of Staff .... Capt. Steven S. VAHSEN
11 CO Naval Support Activity Annapolis .... Capt. Thomas L. REESE
06 Registrar .... Dr. Christopher A. DAVIS
26 Public Affairs Officer .... CDR. John SCHOFIELD
29 Exec Director Alumni Association .... Mr. William OCONNER
21 Comptroller .... CDR. Todd W. HAUGE
13 Chief Information Officer .... CDR. Louis J. GIANNOTTI
88 Director Academic Center .... Dr. Bruce J. BUKOWSKI
09 Director Institutional Research .... Capt. Glenn F. GOTTSCHALK
18 Public Works Officer .... Capt. Scott BERNOTAS
41 Athletic Director .... Mr. Chet GLADCHUK
42 Command Chaplain .... Capt. Michael PARISI
30 Director Officer Development .... Capt. Mike MICHEL
15 Director Human Resources .... Mr. William COFFIN
28 Director of Diversity .... Capt. Roger ISOM

AMERICAN SAMOA

American Samoa Community College (C)

PO Box 2609, Pago Pago AS 96799-2609
County: American Samoa FICE Identification: 010010
Unit ID: 240736
Telephone: (684) 699-9155 Carnegie Class: Assoc/Pub-S-SC
FAX Number: (684) 699-6259 Calendar System: Semester
URL: www.amsamoa.edu
Established: 1970 Annual Undergrad Tuition & Fees (In-State): $3,600
Enrollment: 1,276 Coed
Affiliation or Control: State IRS Status: 501(c)3
Highest Offering: Baccalaureate
Program: Occupational; 2-Year Principally Bachelor's Creditable
Accreditation: WJ

01 President .... Dr. Seth P. GALEA'I
05 Vice Pres Academic/Student Affairs .... Dr. Rosevonne PATO
11 Vice Pres Administrative Services .... Mr. Mikaele ETUALE
25 Dir Land Grant/Cmty & Natural Res .... Dr. Daniel F. AGA
10 Chief Financial Officer .... Mrs. Emey SILAFAU-TOA
102 Director Research Foundation .... Mrs. Matesina WILLIS
45 Dir Institutional Effectiveness .... Mr. Sonny J. LEOMITI
20 Dean of Academic Affairs .... Mrs. Letupu MOANANU
53 Dean of Teacher Education .... Dr. Lina GALEA'I-SCANLAN
72 Dean Trades & Technology .... Mr. Michael LEAU
32 Dean of Student Services .... Dr. Emilia LE'I
88 Dir of Samoan Studies Inst .... Mrs. Okenaisa FAUOLO-MANILA
51 Dir of Adult Educ/Lit Ext Learning .... Mr. Tauvela FALE
08 Director of Library Services .... Mr. Elvis ZODIACAL
07 Dir of Admission/Records/Fin Aid .... Mrs. Sifagatogo TUITASI
15 Director Human Resources .... Mrs. Sereima ASIFOA
13 Chief Information Officer .... Ms. Grace TULAFONO
18 Dir Physical Facilities-Maintenance .... Mr. Loligi SEUMANUTAFA
88 Director of Small Business Develop .... Dr. Herbert THWEATT
38 Director of Student Support Svcs .... Ms. Annie PANAMA
26 Director of UCEDD .... Ms. Tafaimamao TUPUOLA

FEDERATED STATES OF MICRONESIA

College of Micronesia-FSM (D)

PO Box 159 Kolonia, Pohnpei FM 96941-0159
FICE Identification: 010343
Unit ID: 243638
Telephone: (691) 320-2480 Carnegie Class: Assoc/Pub-R-M
FAX Number: (691) 320-2479 Calendar System: Semester
URL: www.comfsm.fm
Established: 1963 Annual Undergrad Tuition & Fees (In-State): $5,780
Enrollment: 2,344 Coed
Affiliation or Control: State IRS Status: 501(c)3
Highest Offering: Associate Degree
Program: Occupational; 2-Year Principally Bachelor's Creditable
Accreditation: WJ

01 President .... Dr. Joseph M. DAISY
09 Vice President IEQA .... Ms. Frankie HARRISS
05 Interim VP Instructional Affairs .... Mrs. Karen SIMION
32 Acting VP Student Services .... Mr. Joey ODUCADO
56 VP Coop Research/Ext (Land Grant) .... Mr. Walter James CURRIE
11 Vice Pres Dept of Admin Services .... Mr. Joseph HABUCHMAI
12 Dean Chuuk Campus .... Mr. Kind KANTO
12 Dean Kosrae Campus .... Mr. Kalwin KEPHAS
12 Dean Yap Campus .... Ms. Lourdes ROBOMAN
10 Acting Comptroller .... Mr. Doman DAOAS
12 Director FSM-FMI Campus .... Mr. Matthias EWARMAI
45 Director Research & Planning .... Mr. Jimmy HICKS
15 Director Human Resources .... Ms. Rencelly NELSON
20 Acting Director Academic Programs .... Mrs. Maria DISION
08 Director Learning Resource Center .... Mrs. Jennifer HAINRICK
75 Dir Career & Technical Education .... Mr. Grilly JACK
18 Director Physical Plant/Maintenance .... Mr. Francisco MENDIOLA
06 Registrar .... Mr. Joey ODUCADO
21 Business Officer Manager .... Mr. Doman DAOAS
37 Acting Director of Financial Aid .... Mrs. Arinda SWINGLY
38 Counselor .... Ms. Penselyn ETSE
13 Director Information Technology .... Mr. Gordon SEGAL
35 Director Residential/Campus Life .... Vacant
100 Chief of Staff .... Ms. Universe YAMASE
19 Director Security/Safety .... Mr. Warren CHING

GUAM

Guam Community College (E)

PO Box 23069, Barrigada GU 96921-3069
County: Guam FICE Identification: 015361
Unit ID: 240745
Telephone: (671) 735-5531 Carnegie Class: Assoc/Pub-R-S
FAX Number: (671) 734-5238 Calendar System: Semester
URL: www.guamcc.edu
Established: 1977 Annual Undergrad Tuition & Fees (In-District): $3,414
Enrollment: 2,458 Coed
Affiliation or Control: State/Local IRS Status: 501(c)3
Highest Offering: Associate Degree
Program: Occupational; 2-Year Principally Bachelor's Creditable; Technical Emphasis
Accreditation: WJ, ACFEI, MAC

01 President .... Dr. Mary Y. OKADA
05 Vice President Academic Affairs .... Dr. R. Ray D. SOMERA
10 Vice President Finance & Admin .... Ms. Carmen K. SANTOS
21 Controller .... Mr. Edwin E. LIMTUATCO
75 Dean Trades & Professional Services .... Dr. Virginia C. TUDELA
72 Dean Technology & Student Services .... Dr. Michael L. CHAN
26 Asst Dir Communications & Promo .... Ms. Jayne T. FLORES
04 Private Secretary .... Ms. Esther A. MUNA
101 Admin Secretary II BOT-Pres Ofc .... Ms. Bertha M. GUERRERO
07 Coordinator Admissions/Registration .... Mr. Patrick L. CLYMER
45 Asst Dir Planning & Development .... Ms. Doris U. PEREZ
103 Asst Dir Cont Ed & Workforce Dev .... Ms. Rowena Ellen PEREZ
88 Assoc Dean .... Ms. Elizabeth A. DIEGO
32 Assoc Dean .... Mr. Ronald G. HARTZ
15 Administrator Human Resources .... Ms. Joann W. MUNA
18 Facilities Engineer Administrator .... Mr. Lawrence P. PEREZ
08 Librarian .... Ms. Christine B. MATSON
20 Admin Ofcr VP's Ofc-Academic Affs .... Ms. Ana Mari C. ATOIGUE
09 Asst Dir AIER .... Ms. Marlena O. MONTAGUE
88 Pgm Specialist Adult Basic Edu .... Mr. Arthur D. DE ORO
88 Pgm Specialist CACGP .... Ms. Christine B. SISON
35 Pgm Spc Ctr Student Involvement .... Ms. Barbara B. LEON GUERRERO
23 School Health Counselor .... Ms. Emma R. BATACLAN
88 Program Specialist .... Mr. Wesley T. GIMA
37 Coordinator Student Financial Aid .... Ms. Esther A. RIOS
88 Pgm Specialist TRIO Programs .... Mr. Huan F. HOSEI
29 Pgm Specialist Alumni & Fundraising .... Ms. Bonnie Mae M. DATUIN
88 Pgm Specialist POST .... Vacant
88 Pgm Specialist Alumni & Fundraising .... Mr. Danilo Philbert BILONG
96 Supply Management Administrator .... Ms. Joleen M. EVANGELISTA
13 Data Processing Administrator .... Mr. Francisco C. CAMACHO
51 Pgm Specialist Continuing Educ .... Ms. Terry L. BARNHART
51 Pgm Specialist Continuing Educ .... Mr. Philip C. GUERRERO
40 Bookstore Manager .... Mr. Daniel T. OKADA
55 Pgm Specialist Night Administrator .... Ms. Ava M. GARCIA
19 Safety Admin Envir Safety Ofc .... Mr. Gregorio T. MANGLONA
88 Pgm Specialist Accomodative Svcs .... Mr. John F. PAYNE
88 Sustainability Coord .... Mr. Francisco E. PALACIOS
88 Pgm Specialist P&D .... Ms. Priscilla C. JOHNS

Pacific Islands University (F)

172 Kinney's Road, Mangilao GU 96913
County: Guam FICE Identification: 034383
Unit ID: 439862
Telephone: (671) 734-1812 Carnegie Class: Spec/Faith
FAX Number: (671) 734-1813 Calendar System: Semester
URL: www.piu.edu
Established: 1976 Annual Undergrad Tuition & Fees: $7,630
Enrollment: 72 Coed
Affiliation or Control: Independent Non-Profit IRS Status: 501(c)3
Highest Offering: Master's
Program: Liberal Arts And General; Religious Emphasis
Accreditation: TRACS

01 President/CEO .... Dr. David L. OWEN
03 Administrative Vice President .... Mr. Nino T. PATE
05 Academic Vice President .... Vacant
20 Seminary Dean .... Mr. Malcolm James SAWYER
88 Liberal Studies Chair .... Mr. James MASON
88 Biblical Studies Chair .... Mr. Michael OWEN
32 Dean of Students .... Ms. Celeste HEIMBACH
10 Operations Director .... Ms. Celia ATOIGE
04 Exec Assistant to the President .... Ms. Samantha OWEN

University of Guam (G)

UOG Station, Mangilao GU 96923-1800
County: Guam FICE Identification: 003935
Unit ID: 240754
Telephone: (671) 735-2990 Carnegie Class: Master's S
FAX Number: (671) 734-2296 Calendar System: Semester
URL: www.uog.edu
Established: 1952 Annual Undergrad Tuition & Fees (In-State): $5,338
Enrollment: 3,958 Coed
Affiliation or Control: State IRS Status: 501(c)3
Highest Offering: Master's
Program: Occupational; Liberal Arts And General; Teacher Preparatory; Professional
Accreditation: WC, IACBE, NUR, SW, TED

01 President .... Dr. Robert A. UNDERWOOD
05 Sr VP Academic & Student Affairs .... Dr. Anita B. ENRIQUEZ
10 Vice Pres Administration & Finance .... Mr. Randall V. WIEGAND
58 AVP Graduate Studies/Research & SP .... Dr. John A. PETERSON
43 University Legal Counsel .... Ms. Victorina M Y. RENACIA
88 Institutional Compliance Officer .... Ms. Elaine FACULO-GOGUE
04 Executive Assistant to President .... Ms. Louise M. TOVES
26 Director Integrated Mktg & Comm .... Mr. Jonas D. MACAPINLAC
45 Chief Planning Officer .... Mr. David S. OKADA
29 Director Dev & Alumni Affairs .... Mr. Norman ANALISTA
102 Exec Director Endowment Foundation .... Mr. Mark B. MENDIOLA
108 Dir Academic Assess/Inst Research .... Ms. Deborah D. LEON GUERRERO
49 Dean Col of Lib Arts & Social Sci .... Dr. James D. SELLMANN
47 Dean Col of Natural & Applied Sci .... Dr. Lee S. YUDIN
50 Dean Sch Business & Pub Admin .... Dr. Annette T. SANTOS
53 Dean School of Education .... Dr. John SANCHEZ
66 Dean of Nursing & Hlth Sci .... Dr. Margaret HATTORI-UCHIMA
84 Actg Dean Enroll Mgmt & Stdnt Svcs .... Ms. Remy B. CRISTOBAL
06 Registrar .... Ms. Remy B. CRISTOBAL
37 Financial Aid Director .... Mr. Mark A. DUARTE
32 Student Life Officer .... Ms. Sallie MCDONALD
88 Director Guam CEDDERS .... Dr. Heidi E. SAN NICOLAS
08 Interim Director Learning Resources .... Dr. Monique STORIE

13 Dir Info Tech Resource/Computer Ctr ....Dr. Luan P. NGUYEN
88 Dir Micronesia Area Res Center ....Dr. Monique C. STORIE
88 Director Marine Laboratory ....Dr. Terry DONALDSON
88 Dir Watr Env Rsrch Inst Wstrn Pac ....Dr. Shahram KHOSROWPANAH
88 Dir Ctr for Island Sustainability ....Dr. John A. PETERSON
88 Actg Director Prof/Intl Program ....Mr. Carlos TAITANO
88 Director TRIO Programs ....Mr. Yoichi K. RENGIIL
15 Chief Human Resources Officer ....Mr. Larry GAMBOA
18 Chief Plant Fac Ofcr Fac & Util ....Mr. Sonny P. PEREZ
41 Actg Field House/Athletics Director ....Ms. Ann S A. LEON GUERRERO
19 Safety Administrator ....Mr. Felix MANSAPIT
40 Director Bookstore & Auxillary Svcs ....Ms. Ann S A. LEON GUERRERO
21 Comptroller ....Ms. Zeny ASUNCION-NACE

MARSHALL ISLANDS

College of the Marshall Islands (A)

PO Box 1258, Majuro MH 96960-1258
County: Marshalls FICE Identification: 030224
Unit ID: 376695
Telephone: (692) 625-3394 Carnegie Class: Assoc/Pub-R-S
FAX Number: (692) 625-7203 Calendar System: Semester
URL: www.cmi.edu
Established: 1989 Annual Undergrad Tuition & Fees (In-State): $4,945
Enrollment: 1,087 Coed
Affiliation or Control: State IRS Status: 501(c)3
Highest Offering: Associate Degree
Program: 2-Year Principally Bachelor's Creditable
Accreditation: WJ

01 President ....Dr. Theresa B. KOROIVULAONO
05 VP Academic & Student Affairs ....Mr. Donald HESS
11 Vice Pres Administration ....Mr. William REIHER
10 Chief Financial Officer ....Mr. Stevenson KOTTON
20 Dean of Academic Affairs ....Ms. Ruth ABBOTT
32 Dean of Student Services ....Ms. Rachel SALOMON
06 Registrar ....Ms. Monica GORDON
07 Director of Admissions & Records ....Ms. Jomi CAPELLE
08 Director of Library Services ....Mr. Chris SEBASTIAN
15 Human Resources Director ....Ms. Agnes KOTOISUVA
51 Director Continuing/Adult Education ....Ms. Rosana JERICHO
18 Director Physical Plant ....Mr. William REIHER
13 Director Information & Technology ....Mr. Bonifacio SANCHEZ
88 Director Nuclear Institute ....Ms. Mary L. SILK
37 Financial Aid Director ....Ms. Jacinta SAMUEL
49 Chair Liberal Arts ....Ms. Laura GIARDULLO
50 Chair Business & IT ....Ms. Meitaka KENDALL-DOMNICK
66 Chair Nursing ....Ms. Florence L. PETER
19 Director Security/Safety ....Mr. David DEBRUM
38 Dir Counseling/Career & Transfer ....Mr. Terry HAZARD
09 Dir Inst Resarch & Planning ....Ms. Cherly T. VILA
108 Dir Inst Integrity & Effectiveness ....Mr. Robert R. WILLSON

NORTHERN MARIANAS

Northern Marianas College (B)

PO Box 501250, Saipan MP 96950-1250
FICE Identification: 030330
Unit ID: 240790
Telephone: (670) 234-5498 Carnegie Class: Bac/Assoc
FAX Number: (670) 234-0759 Calendar System: Semester
URL: www.marianas.edu
Established: 1976 Annual Undergrad Tuition & Fees (In-District): $3,350
Enrollment: 1,186 Coed
Affiliation or Control: State/Local IRS Status: 501(c)3
Highest Offering: Baccalaureate
Program: 2-Year Principally Bachelor's Creditable; Liberal Arts And General; Teacher Preparatory
Accreditation: WC, WJ

01 President ....Dr. Sharon Y. HART
05 Dean of Academic Programs & Svcs ..Ms. Barbara K. MERFALEN
32 Dean of Student Services ....Mr. Leo PANGELINAN
10 Chief Financial Officer ....Ms. Tracy GUERRERO
11 Dean of Admin/Resource Development ....Mr. David ATTAO
31 Dean-Director of CREES ....Mr. Ross MANGLONA
04 Executive Secretary to President ....Ms. Becky SABLAN
13 Director of Information Technology ....Mr. Jonathan LIWAG
09 Dir Institutional Effectiveness ....Ms. Jacqueline CHE
30 Director of External Relations ....Mr. Frankie M. ELIPTICO
08 Director Library Services ....Mr. Christopher TODD
53 Director School of Education ....Ms. Charlotte R. CEPEDA
51 Director of Adult Basic Education ....Ms. Lorraine T. CABRERA
07 Director Admissions & Records ....Mr. Manny CASTRO
38 Director of Counseling Services ....Dr. Timothy BAKER
37 Director of Financial Aid ....Ms. Daisy MANGLONA-PROPST
96 Procurement Manager ....Ms. Anita C. CAMACHO
15 Director of Human Resources ....Mr. Christopher TIMMONS
21 Chief Accountant ....Ms. Solita K. BARNES
36 Career Planning/Placement Coord ....Ms. Neda C. DELEON GUERRERA
18 Facilities Manager ....Mr. John GUERRERO
29 President NMC Alumni Association ....Mr. Jack O. KIYOSHI
106 Director of Distance Learning & ALO ....Ms. Amanda ALLEN

PALAU

Palau Community College (C)

PO Box 9, Koror PW 96940-0009
County: Koror FICE Identification: 011009
Unit ID: 243647
Telephone: (680) 488-2470 Carnegie Class: Assoc/Pub-R-S
FAX Number: (680) 488-2447 Calendar System: Semester
URL: www.palau.edu
Established: 1969 Annual Undergrad Tuition & Fees: $4,517
Enrollment: 604 Coed
Affiliation or Control: Federal IRS Status: Exempt
Highest Offering: Associate Degree
Program: Occupational; 2-Year Principally Bachelor's Creditable
Accreditation: WJ

01 President ....Dr. Patrick U. TELLEI
05 Vice President Education & Training ....Vacant
11 Vice Pres Administration & Finance ....Mr. Jay OLEGERIIL
46 Vice Pres Cooperative Rsrch/Exten ....Mr. Thomas TARO
04 Exec Assistant to the President ....Mr. Todd NGIRAMENGIOR
32 Dean of Students ....Mr. Sherman DANIEL
20 Dean of Academic Affairs ....Mr. Robert RAMARUI
51 Dean of Continuing Education ....Mr. William WALLY
30 Director of Development ....Mr. Tzuchie TADAO
07 Director Admissions & Financial Aid . Mrs. Dahlia M. KATOSANG
06 Registrar ....Ms. Lesley B. ADACHI
15 Director of Human Resources ....Mr. Omdasu T. UEKI
18 Director of Physical Plant ....Mr. Clement KAZUMA
13 Director of Computer Systems ....Mr. Bruce RIMIRCH
35 Director of Student Life ....Ms. Hilda NGIRALMAU
10 Director of Finance ....Ms. Uroi N. SALII
09 Institutional Researcher ....Ms. Ligaya SARA
38 Counselor ....Ms. Maurine ALEXANDER
38 Counselor ....Mr. Winfred RECHEIUNGEL
38 Counselor ....Ms. Glendalynn NGIRMERIIL
91 System Analyst ....Ms. Grace ALEXANDER
88 Accreditation Liaison Officer ....Ms. Deikola OLIKONG
08 Director of Library Services ....Mr. James THULL

PUERTO RICO

American University of Puerto Rico (D)

Box 2037, Bayamon PR 00960-2037
County: Bayamon FICE Identification: 011941
Unit ID: 241100
Telephone: (787) 620-2040 Carnegie Class: Bac/Diverse
FAX Number: (787) 785-7377 Calendar System: Other
URL: www.aupr.edu
Established: 1963 Annual Undergrad Tuition & Fees: $5,286
Enrollment: 1,688 Coed
Affiliation or Control: Independent Non-Profit IRS Status: 501(c)3
Highest Offering: Master's
Program: Liberal Arts And General; Teacher Preparatory; Business Emphasis
Accreditation: M

01 President ....Mr. Juan C. NAZARIO-TORRES
05 Vice President Acad Student Affairs ....Dr. Jose RAMIREZ-FIGUEROA
10 Vice Pres Finance & Admin Affairs ....Mrs. Magda A. CANCEL-PEREZ
32 Dean Student Affairs ....Prof. Claribel RODRIGUEZ-VARGAS
06 Registrar ....Prof. Maria RODRIGUEZ-PAZ
07 Admissions Officer ....Ms. Keren LLANOS
08 Learning Resources Center Director ....Ms. Dirza ALMESTICA
35 Students Affairs and Retention ..Mrs. Maria Waleska HERNANDEZ
37 Director Financial Aid ....Mrs. Yahaira MELENDEZ
21 Director Accounting ....Mrs. Jeanette AVILES-FERRAN
38 Director Guidance Counseling ....Mrs. Luz S. HERNANDEZ
24 Director Educational Media ....Ms. Carol SANTIAGO
41 Athletic Director ....Mr. Manfredo VEGA
13 Director Computer Center ....Mr. Juan L. RIVERA
15 Director Personnel Services ....Mrs. Lillian BELEN-NAZARIO
12 Director Manati Campus ....Prof. Milagros RIVERA-OTERO
09 Dir Research/Institutional Planning ....Vacant
18 Chief Facilities/Physical Plant ....Mr. Efrain LUGO
36 Director of Student Placement ....Vacant
84 Director Enrollment Management ....Vacant
96 Director of Purchasing ....Mrs. Celeste TRAVERSO
92 Director of Honors Program ....Prof. Claribel RODRIGUEZ
30 Chief Development ....Mr. Jaime GONZALEZ
20 Associate Academic Officer ....Prof. Milagros RIVERA
14 Director Acad Computer Center ....Mr. Juan RIVERA
53 Dept Chair School of Education ....Dr. Jose RAMIREZ
50 Dept Chair Business Admin/Sec Sci ....Vacant
49 Department Chair Arts & Sciences ......Prof. Carmen T. LANDRON
04 Administrative Asst to President ....Ms. Teresa RODRIGUEZ
100 Chief of Staff ....Ms. Rosabel VAZQUEZ
102 Dir Foundation/Corporate Relations ....Dr. Adela VAZQUEZ

Atenas College (E)

Paseo de las Atenas #101, Manati PR 00674
FICE Identification: 035443
Unit ID: 440651
Telephone: (787) 884-3838 Carnegie Class: Assoc/PrivNFP4
FAX Number: (787) 884-6754 Calendar System: Semester
URL: www.atenascollege.edu
Established: 1996 Annual Undergrad Tuition & Fees: $6,789
Enrollment: 1,102 Coed
Affiliation or Control: Independent Non-Profit IRS Status: 501(c)3
Highest Offering: Baccalaureate
Program: 2-Year Principally Bachelor's Creditable; Nursing Emphasis
Accreditation: ACCSC

01 President ....Dra. Maria L. HERNÁNDEZ NÚÑEZ
05 Associate Dean of Academic Affairs ....Dra. Cenia K. ROMANO
05 Associate Dean Academic Affairs ....Prof. Widalys GONZÁLEZ
32 Assoc Dean Acad Affairs & Student ....Prof. Rosa M. MORALES
55 Associate Dean Night ....Mrs. Luz C. REYES
07 Recruitment and Admissions Director ....Mr. Joel FIGUEROA
08 Head Librarian ....Mrs. Annette DAVILA
36 Director Student Placement ....Mrs. Sally SANTA
11 Dean of Administrative Affairs ....Mrs. Ingrid Y. COLÓN
108 VP Innovation/Institution Quality ....Mrs. Brenda HERNÁNDEZ-AVEVEDO
45 VP Inst Planning/Devel/Assessment ....Mrs. María C. MEDINA
26 Marketing Coordinator ....Mrs. Angianette RESTO
15 Human Resources and Security Dir ....Mrs. Aurea FIGUEROA
18 Operation Manager ....Mr. Carlos R. VÁZQUEZ
10 Accounting Director ....Mrs. Zulay SOTO
37 Financial Aid Administrator ....Mr. Manuel RAMÍREZ
06 Registrar ....Mrs. Yarelis RODRÍGUEZ

Atlantic University College (F)

PO Box 3918, Guaynabo PR 00970
County: Guaynabo FICE Identification: 025054
Unit ID: 241216
Telephone: (787) 720-1022 Carnegie Class: Bac/Diverse
FAX Number: (787) 720-1092 Calendar System: Quarter
URL: www.atlanticu.edu
Established: 1983 Annual Undergrad Tuition & Fees: $7,395
Enrollment: 1,496 Coed
Affiliation or Control: Independent Non-Profit IRS Status: 501(c)3
Highest Offering: Baccalaureate
Program: 2-Year Principally Bachelor's Creditable; Liberal Arts And General; Professional
Accreditation: ACICS

01 President ....Dr. Teresa DE DIOS UNANUE
13 Exec Vice Pres/Dean Technology/ Mktg ....Prof. Heri MARTINEZ DE DIOS
05 Academic Dean ....Prof. Ivette CARBONELL
10 Dean of Administration ....Prof. Heriberto MARTINEZ-ABREU
88 Dean of Digital Arts/Sciences ....Prof. Frances GRAU
06 Registrar ....Ms. Edna I. GUTIERREZ
38 Dir Student Counseling/Placement ....Ms. Wilma MARTIN
37 Director Financial Aid ....Mrs. Janice RIVERA
08 Head Librarian ....Mrs. Tania DÍAZ
07 Officer of Admissions ....Mrs. Margarita FIGUEROA
21 Bursar's Officer ....Mrs. María del C MONTESINO
15 Officer of Human Resources ....Ms. Viviana SANTIAGO

Caribbean University (G)

Box 493, Bayamon PR 00960-0493
County: Bayamon FICE Identification: 012525
Unit ID: 241377
Telephone: (787) 780-0070 Carnegie Class: Master's M
FAX Number: (787) 785-0101 Calendar System: Semester
URL: www.caribbean.edu
Established: 1969 Annual Undergrad Tuition & Fees: $5,635
Enrollment: 1,959 Coed
Affiliation or Control: Independent Non-Profit IRS Status: 501(c)3
Highest Offering: Doctorate
Program: Liberal Arts And General; Teacher Preparatory
Accreditation: M, @TEAC

01 President/CEO ....Dr. Ana E. CUCURELLA-ADORNO
03 Executive Director ....Mr. Victor T. ADORNO
05 Vice President of Academic Affairs ....Dr. Luis J. DELGADO
45 Vice President of Planning and Info ....Mr. Jorge RIEFKOHL
11 Dean Administration Affairs ....Mr. Israel RODRIGUEZ
32 Dean of Student Affairs ....Mr. Luis J. DELGADO
13 IT Interim Director ....Mr. Luis N. PRATTS
15 Human Resources Director ....Mrs. Teresita RIVERA
37 Director Student Financial Aid ....Mr. Hector GRACIA
06 Registrar ....Mrs. Kendra M. ORTIZ
08 Librarian/Director Audio-Visual ....Mrs. Carmen L. APONTE
07 Director of Admissions ....Mrs. Rosalie MORALES
12 Director of Carolina Campus ....Prof. Jose CUETO
12 Director of Ponce Campus ....Prof. Sonia PACHECO
12 Director Vega Baja Campus ....Vacant
20 Provost ....Ms. Lillian MATOS
71 Director Special Service Program ....Mrs. Maryliz AUBRET
26 Public Relations Director ....Dr. Enrique ROSARIO
58 Assoc Dean of Graduate Programs ....Dr. Luis MEJIAS
49 Director Department Arts/Science ....Prof. William PEREZ
50 Director Dept Business Admin/Sec Sc ....Mr. Jose M. CUETO
76 Health Services ....Ms. Mara MEDINA
54 Director Department of Engineering ....Dr. Hermes CALDERON
66 Director Department of Nursing ....Dr. Mildred FLORES
53 Director Department Education ....Dr. Edgardo REYES
77 Director of Computer Science ....Dr. Augusto CARVAJAL
18 Chief Facilities/Physical Plant ....Mr. Henry SEVILLA
43 Legal Advisor ....Mr. Rafael SANTIAGO
38 Director Student Counseling ....Dr. Ida Y. ALVARADO
41 Athletic Director ....Mr. Jaime VAZQUEZ
22 Director of Compliance ....Mrs. Elena GARCIA

84 Director Enrollment Management .... Vacant
09 Director of Institutional Research .... Dr. Luz D. SERRANO
96 Director of Purchasing .... Mrs. Carmen J. ROSA

Carlos Albizu University (A)

Box 9023711, San Juan PR 00902-3711
County: San Juan　FICE Identification: 010724
Unit ID: 241331
Telephone: (787) 725-6500　Carnegie Class: Spec/Health
FAX Number: (787) 721-7187　Calendar System: Semester
URL: www.albizu.edu
Established: 1966　Annual Undergrad Tuition & Fees: $5,280
Enrollment: 1,063　Coed
Affiliation or Control: Independent Non-Profit　IRS Status: 501(c)3
Highest Offering: Doctorate
Program: Professional
Accreditation: M, CLPSY, SP

00 Chair Board of Trustees .... Mr. Jaime L. ALBORS BIGAS
01 President .... Dr. Angel COLLADO-SCHWARZ
12 Chancellor of San Juan Campus . Dr. Jose J. CABIYA-MORALES
12 Int Chancellor of Miami Campus .... Dr. Irene BRAVO
07 Vice Pres Admissions/Student Affs .... Mr. Ram LAMBA
11 Spec Asst to Chanc for Admin Affs .... Mr. Luis ECHEGARAY
05 Spec Asst to Chanc for Acad Affs .... Dr. Jaime VERAY
88 Special Assistant to Vice President .... Ms. Sylvia LOPEZ
10 Exec Director of Finance .... Mrs. Syvia LOPEZ
46 Director Research Training .... Dr. Lymaries PADILLA-COTTO
88 Director General Psychology Program .... Dr. Jaime VERAY
51 Director Continuing Education .... Ms. Isabel HERNANDEZ
88 Director Internship .... Dr. Aida GARCIA
37 Director Student Financial Aid .... Mrs. Doris QUERO-MENDEZ
08 Director Library .... Ms. Yolanda ROSARIO-ROSARIO
06 Registrar .... Ms. Fina CAMPA
88 Dir Industrial/Org Psych Program ... Dr. Miguel MARTINEZ-LUGO
13 Dir Information Technology Svcs .... Mr. Luis CAMACHO
88 Administrator Community Svcs Clinic .... Mr. Rafael ORTIZ
31 Director Community Services Clinic .... Dr. Jose RODRIGUEZ-QUINONES
88 Dir PhD Clinical Psychology Program .... Dr. Jose CABIYA
88 Dir PsyD Clinical Psychology Pgm .. Dr. Nanet LOPEZ-CORDOVA
15 Exec Director of Human Resources .... Ms. Angela RAMOS
30 Director Development .... Ms. Angeles PEREZ-TORO
88 Director Clinical Training .... Dr. Noel QUINTERO-JIMENEZ
88 Director Bachelor's Program .... Dr. Jaime VERAY
38 President Student Counseling .... Mr. Ricardo DEL RIO-MORALES
11 Director Administration .... Mr. John FERNANDEZ
26 Public Relations Officer .... Rochely ESCALANTE
29 Director Alumni Relations .... Ms. Angeles PEREZ
09 Dir Inst Research/Assessment .... Mr. Rafael MELENDEZ

Center for Advanced Studies On Puerto Rico and the Caribbean (B)

PO Box 902-3970, Old San Juan PR 00902-3970
County: San Juan　FICE Identification: 021660
Unit ID: 241793
Telephone: (787) 723-4481　Carnegie Class: Spec/Other
FAX Number: (787) 723-1023　Calendar System: Semester
URL: www.ceaprc.edu
Established: 1976　Annual Graduate Tuition & Fees: $7,130
Enrollment: 644　Coed
Affiliation or Control: Independent Non-Profit　IRS Status: 501(c)3
Highest Offering: Doctorate; No Undergraduates
Program: Liberal Arts And General; Professional; Fine Arts Emphasis
Accreditation: M

01 Chancellor .... Mr. Miguel A. RODRIGUEZ-LOPEZ
05 Academic Dean .... Dr. Jaime L. RODRIGUEZ-CANCEL
06 Registrar .... Mrs. Mayra I. RAMIREZ
08 Head Librarian .... Mr. Francis J. MOJICA
10 Administration Dean .... Mrs. Lizzette CARRILLO
04 Chancellor's Assistant .... Ms. Clarissa SANTIAGO-TORO
07 Marketing and Enrollment Director ..... Mrs. Monica D. GONZALEZ
37 Financial Aid Officer .... Mrs. Lillian M. OLIVER
101 Secretary of the Institution/Board . Ms. Clarissa SANTIAGO-TORO
32 Student Affairs Officer .... Mr. Jose F. PEREZ-RODRIGUEZ

Centro de Estudios Multidisciplinarios (C)

Calle Degetau #25, Bayamon PR 00961
Telephone: (787) 780-8900　Identification: 770590
Accreditation: ACCSC

† Branch campus of Centro de Estudios Multidisciplinarios, Rio Piedras, PR.

Centro de Estudios Multidisciplinarios (D)

Calle Dr. Vidal #8 y #53, Humacao PR 00791
Telephone: (787) 850-8333　Identification: 770589
Accreditation: ACCSC

† Branch campus of Centro de Estudios Multidisciplinarios, Rio Piedras, PR.

Centro de Estudios Multidisciplinarios (E)

Calle Cristy #56, Mayaguez PR 00681
Telephone: (787) 986-7440　Identification: 770591
Accreditation: ACCSC

† Branch campus of Centro de Estudios Multidisciplinarios, Rio Piedras, PR.

Centro de Estudios Multidisciplinarios (F)

Calle 13 #1206, Ext San Agustin, Rio Piedras PR 00926
County: San Juan　FICE Identification: 021891
Unit ID: 241517
Telephone: (787) 765-4210　Carnegie Class: Assoc/PrivNFP
FAX Number: (787) 765-4277　Calendar System: Semester
URL: www.cempr.edu
Established: 1980　Annual Undergrad Tuition & Fees: $6,416
Enrollment: 892　Coed
Affiliation or Control: Independent Non-Profit　IRS Status: 501(c)3
Highest Offering: Baccalaureate
Program: Occupational; 2-Year Principally Bachelor's Creditable; Nursing Emphasis
Accreditation: ACCSC

01 President .... Mr. Juan C. PAGANI-SOTO
05 Academic Dean .... Dr. Nereida NALES
07 Director of Admissions .... Mr. Juan RESTO TORRES
06 Registrar .... Mrs. Margarita RIVERA
10 Finance Director .... Mr. Carlos RODRIGUEZ
12 Branch Director .... Mrs. Laura M. DELGADO
15 Human Resources Director ...... Mrs. Lilliana M. LOPEZ-MEDERO

Colegio de Cinematografia, Artes y Television (G)

51 Dr. Veve St, Degetau St Corner, Bayamon PR 00960
County: Bayamon　FICE Identification: 031576
Unit ID: 430935
Telephone: (787) 779-2500　Carnegie Class: Assoc/PrivFP
FAX Number: (787) 995-2525　Calendar System: Semester
URL: www.ccatpr.com/nosotros/
Established: 1993　Annual Undergrad Tuition & Fees: $6,560
Enrollment: 900　Coed
Affiliation or Control: Proprietary　IRS Status: Proprietary
Highest Offering: Associate Degree
Program: Occupational
Accreditation: ACCSC

01 President .... Mr. Jorge GARCIA

Colegio Universitario de San Juan (H)

180 Jose R. Oliver Street, San Juan PR 00918
County: San Juan　FICE Identification: 010567
Unit ID: 241720
Telephone: (787) 480-2400　Carnegie Class: Bac/Assoc
FAX Number: (787) 250-7395　Calendar System: Semester
URL: www.cunisanjuan.edu
Established: 1972　Annual Undergrad Tuition & Fees (In-District): $2,370
Enrollment: 1,405　Coed
Affiliation or Control: Local　IRS Status: 501(c)3
Highest Offering: Baccalaureate
Program: Occupational; 2-Year Principally Bachelor's Creditable; Business Emphasis
Accreditation: M, ADNUR

01 Chancellor .... Dr. Haydee M. ZAYAS-HERNÁNDEZ
45 Dir Planning/Inst Research/Ext Rels .... Prof. Ana I. LANDRON-ARANA
05 Acting Dean Academic Affairs .... Dr. Phaedra GELPI-RODRÍGUEZ
32 Acting Dean Student Affairs .... Dr. Melvin VEGA-GONZALEZ
11 Acting Dean Administrative Affairs ...... Prof. Gilberto OLIVO-CRUZ
51 Dir Continuing Educ/Extension Pgm .... Mrs. Annelis RIVERA-MARQUEZ
37 Manager Student Financial Aid .... Mrs. Kennia I. SANTOS-PEREZ
08 Head Librarian .... Mrs. Sheila VERA-MORALES
06 Registrar .... Mrs. Evelyn GUZMAN-LOPEZ
38 Counselor .... Mrs. Mara MALAVE-LASSO
36 Placement Officer .... Prof. Waleska Y. ROSA-NUÑEZ
13 Administrator Info Systems/ Telecomm .... Mr. Zacarias POURIET-DE LA CRUZ
72 Director Science & Technology .... Prof. Marcus DROZ
76 Director Health Related Science ..... Prof. Luz D. ORTEGA-RAMOS
50 Director Business Administration .... Prof. Nilda E. RODRIGUEZ-MOLINA
97 Manager General Education .... Prof. Carmen J. RODRIGUEZ
88 Manager Behavior Related Profession .... Prof. María T. PEREZ-CASANOVA

Columbia Central University (I)

PO Box 8517, Caguas PR 00726-8517
County: Caguas　FICE Identification: 008902
Unit ID: 241304
Telephone: (787) 743-4041　Carnegie Class: Master's S
FAX Number: (787) 746-5616　Calendar System: Semester
URL: www.columbiaco.edu
Established: 1966　Annual Undergrad Tuition & Fees: $6,340
Enrollment: 2,225　Coed
Affiliation or Control: Proprietary　IRS Status: Proprietary
Highest Offering: Master's
Program: Business Emphasis
Accreditation: M

01 President .... Mrs. Daritza R. MULERO
05 VP Academic Affairs .... Mrs. Carmen J. LOPEZ
03 Senior VP of Operations .... Mrs. Carmen M. RIVERA
10 VP Finance and Administration .... Mrs. Yesenia CARRION
32 VP Student Affairs .... Mrs. Brendaliz ZAYAS
26 VP Marketing and Communication .... Mr. Angel QUIÑONES
12 Chancellor of Caguas Campus .... Dra. Gladys SERRANO
12 Chancellor of Yauco Branch .... Ms. Jannette MENDEZ
35 Executive Director Student Affairs .... Mrs. Belmarie HUERTAS
20 Dean Academic Affairs .... Mr. Luis LOPEZ
08 Institutional Librarian .... Ms. Luz NEGRON
11 Administrative Support Director .... Ms. Carmen I. ROJAS
37 Financial Aid Director .... Mrs. Gloria MIRABAL
07 Coordinator of Admissions .... Mrs. Linnette MILETTI
06 Registrar .... Ms. Wilmarie TORRES
38 Student Counselor .... Ms. Ingrid CARRION
15 Director Human Resources .... Ms. Elsie M. TORRES
36 Director Student Placement .... Ms. Iris TIZOL
18 Facilities & Development Director .... Mr. Jesus M. RIVERA

Columbia Centro Universitario (J)

Box 3062, Yauco PR 00698-3062
Telephone: (787) 856-0945　Identification: 666036
Accreditation: &M

† Regional accreditation is carried under the parent institution in Caguas, PR.

Conservatory of Music of Puerto Rico (K)

951 Ponce de Leon Ave. Miramar, Santurce PR 00907
County: San Juan　FICE Identification: 010819
Unit ID: 241766
Telephone: (787) 751-0160　Carnegie Class: Spec/Arts
FAX Number: (787) 766-1216　Calendar System: Semester
URL: www.cmpr.edu
Established: 1959　Annual Undergrad Tuition & Fees (In-State): $4,420
Enrollment: 460　Coed
Affiliation or Control: State　IRS Status: 501(c)3
Highest Offering: Master's
Program: Professional; Music Emphasis
Accreditation: M

01 Chancellor .... Dr. Carlos R. CONDE
05 Dean of Academic Affairs .... Dr. Frankie KELLY
10 Dean of Finance/Administration .... Dr. Ivan SARIEGO
32 Dean Student Affairs/Financial Aid .... Mr. Luis R. DIAZ
88 Interim Dean of Preparatory School ..... Mr. Orlando MALDONADO
07 Admission Coordinator .... Mrs. Ana M. ARRAIZA
08 Librarian .... Mrs. Damaris CORDERO
30 Development & Public Relations Dir .... Vacant
15 Human Resources Director .... Ms. Alba DAVILA
38 Counselor .... Mrs. Pilar RUIBAL
06 Registrar .... Mr. Jose A. MATOS
09 Director of Institutional Research .... Mrs. Eutimia SANTIAGO
18 Chief Facilities/Physical Plant .... Mr. Armando TOLEDO

Dewey University (L)

PO Box 19538, San Juan PR 00910-1538
County: San Juan　FICE Identification: 031121
Unit ID: 431309
Telephone: (787) 753-0039　Carnegie Class: Assoc/PrivNFP
FAX Number: (787) 764-6303　Calendar System: Trimester
URL: www.dewey.edu
Established: 1992　Annual Undergrad Tuition & Fees: $7,367
Enrollment: 1,195　Coed
Affiliation or Control: Independent Non-Profit　IRS Status: 501(c)3
Highest Offering: Baccalaureate
Program: Liberal Arts And General; Business Emphasis
Accreditation: ACICS

01 President/CEO .... Mr. Carlos A. QUINONES
10 Director of Finance .... Mr. Jaime MARTIR
88 Rector .... Mrs. Vanessa BIRD

Dewey University-Bayamon (M)

Road 2 Corujo Industrial Park, Bayamon PR 00959
Telephone: (787) 778-1200　Identification: 770777
Accreditation: ACICS

† Branch campus of Dewey University, San Juan, PR.

Dewey University-Carolina (N)

Road 3 Compound 11, Lot 7, Carolina PR 00986
Telephone: (787) 769-1515　Identification: 770776
Accreditation: ACICS

† Branch campus of Dewey University, San Juan, PR.

Dewey University-Fajardo (O)

267 General Valero Street, Fajardo PR 00738
Telephone: (787) 860-1212　Identification: 770775
Accreditation: ACICS

† Branch campus of Dewey University, San Juan, PR.

Dewey University-Juana Diaz (A)

Rd 149, KM 55.9 Lomas Industrial PK,
Juana Diaz PR 00795
Telephone: (787) 260-1023 Identification: 770774
Accreditation: ACICS

† Branch campus of Dewey University, San Juan, PR.

Dewey University-Manati (B)

Rd 604,KM 49.1,Tierra Nueva Salient, Manati PR 00674
Telephone: (789) 854-3800 Identification: 770807
Accreditation: ACICS

† Branch campus of Dewey University, San Juan, PR.

Dominican Study Center of the Caribbean (C)

PO Box 1968, Bayamon PR 00960-1968
County: Bayamon Identification: 666337
Telephone: (787) 786-4508 Carnegie Class: Not Classified
FAX Number: (787) 798-2712 Calendar System: Semester
URL: www.cedoc.edu
Established: 1980 Annual Undergrad Tuition & Fees: $5,100
Enrollment: 70 Coed
Affiliation or Control: Independent Non-Profit IRS Status: 501(c)3
Highest Offering: Master's
Program: Religious Emphasis
Accreditation: THEOL

01 Dean .... Rev Dr. Yamil A. SAMALOT-RIVERA, OP
05 Associate Dean .... Vacant

EDIC College (D)

PO Box 9120, Caguas PR 00726-9120
County: Caguas FICE Identification: 030219
Unit ID: 376321
Telephone: (787) 704-1020 Carnegie Class: Assoc/PrivFP
FAX Number: (787) 746-0048 Calendar System: Semester
URL: ediccollege.edu
Established: 1987 Annual Undergrad Tuition & Fees: $6,600
Enrollment: 1,202 Coed
Affiliation or Control: Proprietary IRS Status: Proprietary
Highest Offering: Associate Degree
Program: Occupational
Accreditation: ACICS

01 President/CEO .... Mr. Jose A. CORDOVA
11 Administrator .... Mrs. Milagros CARTAGENA
88 Licensing & Accreditation Director .... Mrs. Loida R. RAMIREZ
12 Director of Branch Campus .... Mr. Reinaldo GONZALEZ
12 Director of Branch Campus .... Mr. Ricardo FLORES
05 Chief Academic Officer .... Mrs. Betsy VIDAL
10 Comptroller .... Mr. Francis HILARIO

EDP University of Puerto Rico (E)

PO Box 192303, San Juan PR 00919-2303
County: San Juan FICE Identification: 021651
Unit ID: 243832
Telephone: (787) 765-3560 Carnegie Class: Bac/Diverse
FAX Number: (787) 777-0025 Calendar System: Semester
URL: www.edpuniversity.edu
Established: 1968 Annual Undergrad Tuition & Fees: $5,940
Enrollment: 1,568 Coed
Affiliation or Control: Independent Non-Profit IRS Status: 501(c)3
Highest Offering: Master's
Program: Occupational; 2-Year Principally Bachelor's Creditable; Professional; Business Emphasis
Accreditation: M

01 President .... Mrs. Gladys T. NIEVES
03 Executive Vice President .... Dr. Marilyn PASTRANA
05 Academic Dean .... Mrs. Enid CARTAGENA
10 Vice President Finance .... Mr. Luis RIVERA
26 VP Institutional/International Rels .... Dr. Marilyn PASTRANA
108 VP Acreditation & Inst Assessment .... Dr. Alberto LOPEZ
13 AVP Administration and Technology .... Eng. Luis FUSTER
85 AVP International Affairs .... Ms. Sandra ARROYO
21 AVP Finance .... Mrs. Marie Luz PASTRANA
14 Inst Information Systems Dean .... Dr. Ramon MALLOL
06 Registrar .... Mrs. Marian DEJESUS
08 Librarian .... Mrs. Igrí ENRIQUEZ
32 Student Services Dean .... Mr. Oscar MORALES
11 AVp Assessment .... Mrs. Nydia RIVERA
37 Director of Financial Aid .... Mrs. Maria COLON
07 Director of Admissions .... Mrs. Dendy VILA
15 Director Human Resources .... Mr. Hector VAZQUEZ

EDP University of Puerto Rico (F)

PO Box 1674, 49 Betances Street,
San Sebastian PR 00685-1674
Telephone: (787) 896-2137 Identification: 666488
Accreditation: &M

† Regional accreditation is carried under the parent institution in San Juan, PR.

Escuela de Artes Plasticas de Puerto Rico (G)

PO Box 9021112, San Juan PR 00902-1112
County: San Juan FICE Identification: 025694
Unit ID: 241951
Telephone: (787) 725-8120 Carnegie Class: Spec/Arts
FAX Number: (787) 725-8111 Calendar System: Semester
URL: www.eap.edu
Established: 1966 Annual Undergrad Tuition & Fees (In-State): $3,248
Enrollment: 555 Coed
Affiliation or Control: State IRS Status: 501(c)3
Highest Offering: Baccalaureate
Program: Liberal Arts And General; Teacher Preparatory; Fine Arts Emphasis
Accreditation: M, ART

01 Chancellor .... Arch. Ivonne M. MARCIAL VEGA
11 Int Dean of Administration .... Ms. Limaris SOLO AQUINO
05 Int Dean Academic Affairs .... Prof. Teresa LOPEZ
06 Registrar .... Ms. Ileana MALDONADO
07 Officer of Admissions .... Ms. Nitza MELENDEZ
13 Chief Information Technology .... Ms. Limaris SOTO AQUINO
37 Director Student Financial Aid .... Mr. Alfred DIAZ
20 Acting Asst Dean Academic Affairs .... Ms. Ivette MUNOZ
45 Director of Planning & Development .... Mr. Carlos E. RIVERA
09 Assistant Institutional Research .... Dr. Shirley A. TAVARES
10 Chief Financial Officer .... Ms. Mayra E. DIAZ
18 Coord Facilities/Physical Plant .... Mr. Edwin ALICEA
56 Coordinator Extension Program .... Ms. Liliam NIEVES
38 Counselor Stdnt Life/Counseling .... Dr. Yadira ORTIZ COLON
88 Coordinator Cultural Activities ... Mr. Adrian O. RIVERA NEGRON
105 Director Web Services .... Mr. Celso E. PORTELA IRIGOYEN
08 Library Director .... Ms. Milagros PIZARRO
20 Asst Dean Acad/Student Affairs ..... Dr. Marcos A. VELEZ RIVERA
15 Director Human Resources .... Mr. Julio YAMIL AVILA
28 Director of Projects .... Dr. Shirley A. TAVARES
53 Director Education .... Prof. Noemi RIVERA
97 Director General Studies .... Dr. Maria VAZQUEZ
88 Director Fashion/Apparel Design .... Prof. Ana COLORADO
88 Director Industrial/Product Design .... Prof. Vladimir GARCIA
88 Dir Design/Visual Communications .... Prof. Mayela CARDENAS
88 Director Painting .... Prof. Carlos MARCIAL
88 Director Sculpture .... Prof. Linda SÁNCHEZ PINTOR
88 Director Graphics .... Prof. Luis A. ORTIZ

Evangelical Seminary of Puerto Rico (H)

Ponce De Leon Avenue 776, San Juan PR 00925-2207
County: San Juan FICE Identification: 006823
Unit ID: 243498
Telephone: (787) 763-6700 Carnegie Class: Spec/Faith
FAX Number: (787) 751-0847 Calendar System: Semester
URL: www.se-pr.edu
Established: 1919 Annual Undergrad Tuition & Fees: $5,320
Enrollment: 231 Coed
Affiliation or Control: Interdenominational IRS Status: 501(c)3
Highest Offering: Doctorate
Program: Professional; Religious Emphasis
Accreditation: M, THEOL

01 President .... Dra. Doris GARCIA RIVERA
05 Academic Dean/Chaplain .... Dr. Francisco J. GOITIA PADILLA
10 Director Administration & Finances ..Ms. Myrna E. PEREZ-LOPEZ
06 Registrar .... Miss Marie Lillian RIVERA SEVILLA
08 Head Librarian .... Mrs. Milka VIGO VERESTÍN
30 Official of Development/Planning ..... Ms. Ruth M. DIAZ SEMPRIT
37 Student Financial Aid .... Ms. Lourdes JESUS CESAREO

Huertas College (I)

PO Box 8429, Caguas PR 00726-8429
County: Caguas FICE Identification: 022608
Unit ID: 242112
Telephone: (787) 746-1400 Carnegie Class: Assoc/PrivFP
FAX Number: (787) 747-0170 Calendar System: Semester
URL: www.huertas.edu
Established: 1945 Annual Undergrad Tuition & Fees: $6,585
Enrollment: 1,184 Coed
Affiliation or Control: Proprietary IRS Status: Proprietary
Highest Offering: Baccalaureate
Program: Occupational; 2-Year Principally Bachelor's Creditable; Technical Emphasis
Accreditation: M, CAHIIM, PTAA

01 President .... Maria del Mar LOPEZ-AVILES
03 Exec Vice President and Compliance .... Raul HERNANDEZ-RODRIGUEZ
05 Vice Pres Academic/Student Affairs ... Amarillys GARCIA-ACOSTA
30 VP Planning and Development .... Ruth BONILLA
15 VP of Human Resources .... Leslie Ann GUZMAN
32 Associate VP of Student Success .... Maribel CONTRERAS
06 Registrar .... Krishna MARQUEZ
08 Head Librarian .... Glenda PEREZ
38 Director Student Counseling .... Evelyn COTTO
21 Director of Revenue .... Hector MACHIN
22 Compliance Officer .... Vacant

Humacao Community College (J)

PO Box 9139, Humacao PR 00792-9139
County: Humacao FICE Identification: 023406
Unit ID: 242121
Telephone: (787) 852-1430 Carnegie Class: Assoc/PrivNFP
FAX Number: (787) 850-1577 Calendar System: Trimester
URL: www.hccpr.edu
Established: 1978 Annual Undergrad Tuition & Fees: $5,382
Enrollment: 639 Coed
Affiliation or Control: Independent Non-Profit IRS Status: 501(c)3
Highest Offering: Baccalaureate
Program: Occupational; 2-Year Principally Bachelor's Creditable; Business Emphasis
Accreditation: ACICS

01 President .... Lic. Jorge E. MOJICA
03 Executive Vice President .... Prof. Aida E. RODRIGUEZ
05 Exec Director/Chief Academic Ofcr .... Mrs. Gladys E. FLECHA
55 Director of Evening Session .... Prof. Ada BAEZ
88 Title V Project Director .... Mrs. Brenda L. MORALES
81 STEM Projec Director .... Mr. Jaime RIVERA
37 Director Student Financial Aid .... Mrs. Cheryle PEREZ
36 Student Placement Officer .... Mr. Luis GARCIA
07 Director Admissions .... Mrs. Loalis QUIÑONES
51 Continuing Education Officer .... Mrs. Maria M. GONZALEZ
06 Registrar .... Mrs. Nildalee MELENDEZ
08 Head Librarian .... Mrs. Lourdes ELIZA
10 Treasury Officer (Finance) .... Mrs. Diana RODRIGUEZ
38 Student Counselor .... Miss Maria RODRIGUEZ
11 Chief College Administrator .... Mrs. Marianne BERRIOS
04 Admin Asst to Pres/Dir Personnel .... Mrs. Nilda E. RODRIGUEZ

ICPR Junior College (K)

558 Munoz Rivera Avenue, Hato Rey PR 00919-0304
County: San Juan FICE Identification: 011940
Unit ID: 243841
Telephone: (787) 753-6000 Carnegie Class: Assoc/PrivFP
FAX Number: (787) 622-3416 Calendar System: Semester
URL: www.icprjc.edu
Established: 1946 Annual Undergrad Tuition & Fees: $6,634
Enrollment: 688 Coed
Affiliation or Control: Proprietary IRS Status: Proprietary
Highest Offering: Associate Degree
Program: Occupational; 2-Year Principally Bachelor's Creditable; Business Emphasis
Accreditation: M

01 President/Chief Executive Officer .... Dr. Olga RIVERA
12 Hato Rey Campus Director .... Mrs. Maria de los M. RIVERA
05 Academic Affairs Dean .... Mrs. Elsa RODRIGUEZ
07 Dir Admissions/Marketing Hato Rey .... Mrs. Beatriz FLORES
07 Director Admissions Mayaguez .... Mrs. Aracelis GASTON
07 Director Admissions Arecibo .... Ms. Meysaliz GARCIA
07 Director Admissions Manati .... Mrs. Viviana TORRES
10 Finance and Accounting Director .... Mrs. Arelis DIAZ
37 Financial Aid Director .... Ms. Jennifer HERNANDEZ
12 Mayaguez Campus Director .... Dr. Luz M. ORTIZ
12 Arecibo Campus Director .... Mrs. Ivette CHARRIEZ
12 Manati Campus Director .... Mr. Fernando GONZALEZ
06 Registrar Hato Rey .... Ms. Julie MALDONADO
06 Registrar Mayaguez .... Mrs. Olga NEGRON
06 Registrar Arecibo .... Mrs. Glenda PADIN
06 Registrar Manati .... Mrs. Vanessa TRINIDAD
06 Registrar Bayamon Extension .... Mrs. Diana FREYTES
26 Institutional Admissions/Mrktng Dir .... Mr. Isander VELAZQUEZ
13 Information Systems Director .... Mr. Nelson MEJIAS
08 Learning Res Librarian Hato Rey .... Mrs. Sulynet TORRES
08 Lrng Resources Librarian Mayaguez .... Mrs. Jessica CARO
08 Lrng Resources Librarian Arecibo .... Mrs. Irma JIMENEZ
08 Learning Resources Librarian .... Mr. Martin ROSADO
38 Professional Counselor Mayaguez .... Mrs. Barbarita CUMPIANO
38 Professional Counselor Arecibo .... Mrs. Milagros AGUILAR
38 Professional Counselor Manati .... Mrs. Lourdes RIOS
38 Professional Counselor Hato Rey .... Mrs. Yarelis COLON
15 Human Resources Director .... Mrs. Daisy CASTRO
43 Institutional Compliance Director .... Mrs. Lizzette VARGAS
56 Bayamon Extension Director .... Mr. Manuel MELO
20 Academic Coordinator Mayaguez .... Mrs. Ravel BONILLA
20 Academic Coordinator Arecibo .... Mrs. Edith RAMOS
20 Academic Coordinator Manati .... Mrs. Maribel TORRES
20 Academic Coordinator Hato Rey .... Mr. Josue CINTRON

ICPR Junior College-Arecibo Campus (L)

PO Box 146007, Arecibo PR 00614-0067
Telephone: (787) 878-6000 Identification: 770166
Accreditation: &M

† Branch campus of ICPR Junior College, Hato Rey, PR.

ICPR Junior College-Manati Branch Campus (M)

PO Box 49, Manati PR 00674-0049
Telephone: (787) 884-6000 Identification: 770168
Accreditation: &M

† Branch campus of ICPR Junior College, Hato Rey, PR.

ICPR Junior College-Mayaguez Campus (A)

PO Box 1108, Mayaguez PR 00681-9913
Telephone: (787) 832-6000 Identification: 770167
Accreditation: &M

† Branch campus of ICPR Junior College, Hato Rey, PR.

Instituto de Banca y Comercio (B)

709 Ferrocarril Street, Ponce PR 00717
Telephone: (787) 840-6119 Identification: 770773
Accreditation: ACICS

† Branch campus of Instituto de Banca y Comercio, San Juan, PR.

Instituto de Banca y Comercio (C)

61 Ponce de Leon Ave, San Juan PR 00917
Identification: 667107
Telephone: (787) 754-7120 Carnegie Class: Not Classified
FAX Number: (787) 754-7143 Calendar System: Other
URL: www.ibanca.net
Established: 1975 Annual Undergrad Tuition & Fees: $9,900
Enrollment: 1,000 Coed
Affiliation or Control: Proprietary IRS Status: Proprietary
Highest Offering: Associate Degree
Program: Occupational; Technical Emphasis
Accreditation: ACICS

01 President ... Sr. Guillermo NIGAGLIONI
05 Director ... Mr. Wilfredo HERNANDEZ

*Inter American University of Puerto Rico Central Office (D)

GPO Box 363255, San Juan PR 00936-3255
County: San Juan FICE Identification: 008242
Unit ID: 242671
Telephone: (787) 766-1912 Carnegie Class: N/A
FAX Number: (787) 751-3375
URL: www.inter.edu

01 President ... Mr. Manuel J. FERNOS
05 Vice Pres Academic & Student Affrs ... Mr. Agustin ECHEVARRIA
10 VP Financial Affairs/Services ... Mr. Luis ESQUILIN
42 Vice President Religious Affairs ... Rev. Norberto DOMINGUEZ
20 Associate VP Academic Affairs ... Dr. Rafael CABRERA
21 Assoc VP Financial Affairs/Services ... Ms. Olga LUNA
32 Associate Vice Pres Student Affairs ... Dr. Karen WOOLCOCK
04 Exec Assistant to the President ... Mr. Dominique GILORMINI-DE GRACIA
26 Dir Public Rels & Communications ... Mrs. Zaima NEGRON
30 Dir Inst Prom/Stdnt Recruit/Alumni ... Mr. Eduardo LAMADRID
09 Exec Director Inst Research ... Vacant
13 Dir Information/Telecommunications ... Mrs. Jossie SALGUERO
43 Director Legal Services ... Mrs. Lorraine JUARBE
43 Director Federal Legal Services ... Mr. Vladimir ROMAN
15 Exec Director Human Resources ... Ms. Maggie COLON

*Inter American University of Puerto Rico Aguadilla Campus (E)

Box 20000, Aguadilla PR 00605-9001
County: Aguadilla FICE Identification: 003939
Unit ID: 242626
Telephone: (787) 891-0925 Carnegie Class: Master's S
FAX Number: (787) 882-3020 Calendar System: Other
URL: www.aguadilla.inter.edu
Established: 1957 Annual Undergrad Tuition & Fees: $5,882
Enrollment: 4,668 Coed
Affiliation or Control: Independent Non-Profit IRS Status: 501(c)3
Highest Offering: Master's
Program: Occupational; Liberal Arts And General; Teacher Preparatory; Professional
Accreditation: M, NUR, TEAC

02 Chancellor ... Dr. Elie AGESILAS
05 Dean of Studies ... Mrs. Nilsa M. ROMAN
32 Dean of Student Affairs ... Mrs. Ana C. LAUSELL
13 Director Information and Technology ... Mr. Asdrubal JIMENEZ
90 Information Systems Administrator ... Mr. Jossue MORALES
10 Dean of Administrative Affairs ... Mr. Israel AYALA
20 Associate Dean of Studies ... Dr. Luis A. ACEVEDO
30 Development Director ... Miss Sacha M. RUIZ
08 Library Director ... Mrs. Monserrate YULFO
07 Admissions Director ... Mrs. Doris PEREZ
06 Registrar ... Mrs. Maria PEREZ
37 Financial Aid Director ... Mrs. Gloria CORTES
21 Bursar ... Mrs. Yanira GONZALEZ
15 Human Resources Director ... Mr. Jose R. AREIZAGA
96 Purchasing Officer ... Ms. Wanda VARGAS
35 Student Support Services Director ... Mrs. Ivonne ACEVEDO
81 Director of Science and Technology ... Prof. Jose SOLORZANO
79 Director of Education & Hum Studies ... Mrs. Ramonita ROSA
50 Director Economic Science & Admin ... Prof. Magda RUIZ
53 Dir of Social & Behavioral Sciences ... Prof. Gerardo LÓPEZ
42 Chaplain ... Dr. Pablo E. ROJAS
88 Director of Upward Bound Program ... Ms. Mayra ROZADA
88 Dir Campus Learning Center ... Ms. Yamilette PROSPER
18 Dir Building Maintenance/Univ Guard ... Mr. Jose CABAN

38 Director of Counseling Office ... Ms. Dary ACEVEDO
41 Sports Director ... Ms. Yolanda PAGAN
84 Enrollment Manager ... Prof. Myriam MARCIAL

*Inter American University of Puerto Rico Arecibo Campus (F)

PO Box 4050, Arecibo PR 00614-4050
County: Arecibo FICE Identification: 005026
Unit ID: 242635
Telephone: (787) 878-5475 Carnegie Class: Master's S
FAX Number: (787) 880-1624 Calendar System: Semester
URL: www.arecibo.inter.edu
Established: 1957 Annual Undergrad Tuition & Fees: $4,962
Enrollment: 4,713 Coed
Affiliation or Control: Independent Non-Profit IRS Status: 501(c)3
Highest Offering: Master's
Program: Occupational; Liberal Arts And General; Teacher Preparatory
Accreditation: M, ANEST, NUR, SW, TEAC

02 Chancellor ... Dr. Rafael RAMIREZ- RIVERA
05 Dean of Academic Affairs ... Dr. Annette VEGA
11 Dean of Administrative Affairs ... Ms. Wanda PEREZ
32 Dean of Student Affairs ... Mrs. Ilvis AGUIRRE
20 Assoc Dean of Academic Affairs ... Prof. Wanda BALSEIRO
08 Educational Resources Center Dir ... Mrs. Sara ABREU
10 Bursar ... Mr. Victor MALDONADO
37 Student Financial Aid Director ... Mr. Ramon DE JESUS
06 Registrar ... Mrs. Carmen RODRIGUEZ
07 Director of Admissions ... Mrs. Provi MONTALVO
04 Executive Assistant to Chancellor ... Mrs. Enid ARBELO
56 Distance Learning Director ... Prof. Ebigaly OLIVER
45 Planning Director ... Mrs. Enid ARBELO
42 Religious Life Director ... Mr. Amilcar SOTO
15 Personnel Director ... Mrs. Maritza SANTOS
41 Athletic Department ... Ms. Ileana MORALES
50 Director Econ & Adms Sciences Dept ... Prof. Elba TORO
51 Continuing Education Director ... Mrs. Mariel LLERANDI
53 Director of Education Department ... Dr. Auris MARTINEZ
66 Director of Nursing Department ... Dr. Frances CORTES
79 Dir of Humanities Department ... Prof. Maria L. DELGADO
81 Director of Sciences & Tech Dept ... Dr. Lizbeth ROMERO
83 Director of Social Sciences Dept ... Dr. Lourdes CARRION
30 Development Director ... Vacant
38 Director Student Counseling ... Ms. Abigail TORRES
13 Director of Computing Center ... Mr. Jose SEGARRA
58 Director Graduate Program in Educ ... Dra. Ramonita DIAZ
18 Chief Facilities/Physical Plant ... Mr. Jose SANCHEZ
84 Director Enrollment Management ... Mrs. Carmen MONTALVO
88 Dir Graduate Program Anesthesia ... Prof. Josue RAMOS
96 Purchasing Officer ... Mrs. Sonia VILLAIZAN
92 Coordinator Honor Program ... Ms. Vilmaris VAZQUEZ
108 Director Institutional Assessment ... Dr. Pedro RIVERA
26 Director of Marketing ... Mr. Juan RODRIGUEZ

*Inter American University of Puerto Rico Barranquitas Campus (G)

PO Box 517, Barranquitas PR 00794-0517
County: Barranquitas FICE Identification: 005027
Unit ID: 242644
Telephone: (787) 857-3600 Carnegie Class: Bac/Diverse
FAX Number: (787) 857-2244 Calendar System: Semester
URL: www.br.inter.edu
Established: 1957 Annual Undergrad Tuition & Fees: $6,952
Enrollment: 3,833 Coed
Affiliation or Control: Independent Non-Profit IRS Status: 501(c)3
Highest Offering: Master's
Program: Occupational; 2-Year Principally Bachelor's Creditable; Liberal Arts And General; Teacher Preparatory; Professional; Nursing Emphasis
Accreditation: M, TEAC

02 Chancellor ... Dr. Irene FERNANDEZ
05 Dean Academic Affairs ... Dr. Patricia ALVAREZ
09 Director of Institutional Research ... Dr. Maribel LÓPEZ
10 Bursar Director ... Mr. Antonio J. ROSARIO
06 Registrar ... Mrs. Sandra M. MORALES
32 Dean Student Affairs ... Mrs. Aramilda CARTAGENA
11 Dean Administrative Affairs ... Mr. Jose E. ORTIZ-ZAYAS
08 Librarian ... Mrs. Maria del C RIVERA
38 Director Upward Bound Program ... Mrs. Saraliz GONZALEZ
84 Director Recruitment/Promotion ... Mrs. Ana Isabel COLON
37 Financial Aid Director ... Mr. Eduardo FONTANEZ
84 Enrollment Manager ... Mrs. Lydia ARCE
07 Director of Admissions ... Mr. Edgardo CINTRON
53 Dir Education/Social Sci/Humanities ... Dr. Filomena CINTRON
81 Dir Natural Sciences/Technology ... Prof. Jose PEREZ
88 Director Admin & Economics Sciences ... Dr. Alfredo J. LEBRON KURI
76 Dir Health Department ... Dr. Omar GUERRERO
51 Director Continuing Education ... Mrs. Aixa SERRANO
29 Director Alumni Relations ... Mr. Elvin J. ORTIZ
15 Director Human Resources ... Mr. Victor SANTIAGO

*Inter American University of Puerto Rico Bayamon Campus (H)

500 Road 830, Bayamon PR 00957
County: Bayamon FICE Identification: 005028
Unit ID: 242705
Telephone: (787) 279-1912 Carnegie Class: Bac/Diverse
FAX Number: (787) 279-2205 Calendar System: Semester
URL: bayamon.inter.edu
Established: 1912 Annual Undergrad Tuition & Fees: $4,852
Enrollment: 4,826 Coed
Affiliation or Control: Independent Non-Profit IRS Status: 501(c)3
Highest Offering: Master's
Program: Technical Emphasis
Accreditation: M, AAB, ENG, OPTR

02 Chancellor ... Prof. Juan F. MARTINEZ
04 Assistant to Chancellor ... Mr. Antonio L. PANTOJA
04 Assistant to Chancellor ... Dr. Ramon E. FERNANDEZ
30 Chief Development ... Mr. Jaime COLON
05 Chief Academic Officer ... Dr. Carlos J. OLIVARES
20 Associate Academic Officer ... Dra. Irma ALVARADO
55 Assoc Dean Studies II-Evening Pgm ... Mr. Carlos N. ALICEA
88 Director Student Support Services ... Mrs. Vilma L. MALDONADO
08 Head Librarian ... Mrs. Sandra ROSA
88 Interships and Exchanges Officer ... Mrs. Maritza ZAMBRANA
88 Dean School of Aeronautics ... Prof. Jorge CALAF
54 Dean School of Engineering ... Dr. Javier QUINTANA
54 Director Electrical Engr Dept ... Prof. Ruben FLORES
54 Director Industrial Engr Dept ... Dr. Heriberto BARRIERA
54 Director Mechanical Engr Dept ... Dr. Eduardo PEREZ
81 Director Mathematics/Sciences ... Dr. Rafael CANALES
50 Dir Business Administration Dept ... Dr. Francisco MONTALVO
60 Director Communications Dept ... Prof. Ruth E. HERNANDEZ
77 Director Computer Sciences Dept ... Prof. Jose RODRIGUEZ
76 Director of Health Science ... Dra. Silvia ROSADO
79 Director Humanities/Language Dept ... Dra. Isabel GARAYTA
75 Director Tech Institute ... Mrs. Liza FREYTES
32 Chief Students Life Officer ... Mrs. Gema C. TORRES
35 Student Affairs Assistant ... Mrs. Grace GOMEZ
38 Director Student Counseling ... Mrs. Magali PALMER
35 Student Activities Director ... Mrs. Cybel BETANCOURT
41 Athletic Director ... Mr. Reynaldo ROLON
23 Infirmary ... Mrs. Maria ROSADO
10 Chief Financial/Business Officer ... Mr. Juan C. HERNANDEZ
96 Purchasing Officer ... Mrs. Gladys ARROYO
21 Associate Business Officer ... Mr. Serafin RIVERA
18 Chief Facilities/Physical Plant ... Eng. Jose A. FUENTES
15 Human Resources Director ... Mrs. Migdalia ORTIZ
46 Chief Research and Development ... Dr. Armando RODRIGUEZ
84 Director Enrollment Services ... Miss Ivette NIEVES
07 Director of Admissions ... Vacant
06 Registrar ... Mr. Eddie AYALA
13 Director Information Technology ... Mr. Edwin RIVERA
42 Director of Chaplaincy Office ... Rvda. Carmen I. PEREZ
106 Dir Online Education/E-learning ... Dr. Jose G. SANTIAGO
09 Director of Institutional Research ... Dr. Ramon E. FERNANDEZ

*Inter American University of Puerto Rico Fajardo Campus (I)

Call Box 70003, Fajardo PR 00738-7003
County: Fajardo FICE Identification: 022828
Unit ID: 242680
Telephone: (787) 863-2390 Carnegie Class: Bac/Diverse
FAX Number: (787) 860-3470 Calendar System: Semester
URL: fajardo.inter.edu
Established: 1960 Annual Undergrad Tuition & Fees: $6,300
Enrollment: 2,115 Coed
Affiliation or Control: Independent Non-Profit IRS Status: 501(c)3
Highest Offering: Master's
Program: Liberal Arts And General; Fine Arts Emphasis
Accreditation: M, SW, TEAC

02 Chancellor ... Dr. Ismael SUAREZ-HERRERO
05 Dean Academic Affairs ... Dr. Paula SAGARDIA OLIVERAS
11 Dean Administrative Affairs ... Ms. Lydia E. SANTIAGO ROSADO
32 Dean for Student Affairs ... Dr. Javier MARTINEZ
06 Registrar ... Mrs. Arlene PARRILLA
07 Director of Admissions ... Mrs. Ada CARABALLO
37 Director Student Financial Aid ... Mrs. Marilyn MARTINEZ
08 Librarian ... Ms. Angie COLON
15 Director of Personnel Office ... Mrs. Maria A. RAMOS
09 Planning Director ... Ms. Hilda L. ORTIZ
41 Athletic Director ... Mr. Jose RUIZ
18 Physical Plant Supervisor ... Mr. Angel J. RUIZ
42 Chaplain/Director Campus Ministry ... Rev. Rafael HIRALDO
50 Chairperson Business Department ... Prof. Wilfredo DEL VALLE
53 Chairperson Educ & Social Sci Dept ... Dr. Porfirio MONTES
79 Chairperson Humanities Dept .. Prof. Lourdes PEREZ DEL VALLE
81 Chairperson Math/Science Dept ... Prof. Irma MORALES
84 Director Enrollment Management ... Mrs. Glenda DIAZ

*Inter American University of Puerto Rico Guayama Campus (J)

Call Box 10004, Guayama PR 00785
County: Guayama FICE Identification: 022827
Unit ID: 242699
Telephone: (787) 864-2222 Carnegie Class: Bac/Diverse
FAX Number: (787) 866-5006 Calendar System: Semester
URL: www.guayama.inter.edu
Established: 1958 Annual Undergrad Tuition & Fees: $5,450
Enrollment: 2,151 Coed
Affiliation or Control: Independent Non-Profit IRS Status: 501(c)3
Highest Offering: Master's
Program: 2-Year Principally Bachelor's Creditable; Liberal Arts And General; Nursing Emphasis
Accreditation: M, TEAC

02 President ... Mr. Manuel J. FERNOS
00 Chancellor ... Prof. Carlos E. COLON-RAMOS
06 Registrar ... Mr. Luis A. SOTO
08 Librarian ... Mrs. Edny SANTIAGO
10 Bursar ... Ms. Teresa MANAUTOU
05 Dean of Studies ... Dr. Angela DE JESUS
11 Dean of Administration ... Mr. Nestor A. LEBRON
32 Dean of Students ... Dr. Rosa J. MARTINEZ
07 Director Admissions ... Mrs. Laura FERRER
37 Director Financial Aid ... Mr. Jose A. VECHINI
29 Director Alumni Relations ... Dr. Rosa J. MARTINEZ
51 Director Continuing Education ... Mrs. Diannie RIVERA
15 Human Resources Officer ... Mrs. Maria MARES
18 Chief Facilities/Physical Plant ... Mr. Benjamin AYALA
45 Dir Evaluation & Strategic Planning ... Mrs. Claribel RODRIGUEZ
30 Chief Devel/Dir Annual Plan Giv ... Vacant
42 Chaplain Director ... Rvdo. Arnaldo CINTRON
84 Director Enrollment Management ... Mrs. Eileen RIVERA
96 Director of Purchasing ... Mrs. Maria VAZQUEZ
31 Dir of Community & New Student Rels ... Mrs. Luz ORTIZ
23 Director Health Services ... Mrs. Arcilia RIVERA
66 Director Nursing Program ... Dr. Minerva MULERO
88 Dir Adult Higher Education Program ... Mrs. Carmen G. RIVERA
50 Dir Dept Business Admin/Econ Sci ... Dr. Rosalia MORALES
53 Dir Dept Education/Soc Sci/Hum Std ... Dr. Ray ROBLES
81 Dir Dept Natural & Applied Science ... Prof. Carmen TORRES
09 Director of Institutional Research ... Mr. Tomas JIMENEZ

*Inter American University of Puerto Rico / Metropolitan Campus (A)

PO Box 191293, San Juan PR 00919-1293

County: San Juan — FICE Identification: 003940
Unit ID: 242653
Telephone: (787) 250-1912 — Carnegie Class: DRU
FAX Number: (787) 250-0742 — Calendar System: Trimester
URL: www.metro.inter.edu
Established: 1962 — Annual Undergrad Tuition & Fees: $7,122
Enrollment: 9,649 — Coed
Affiliation or Control: Independent Non-Profit — IRS Status: 501(c)3
Highest Offering: Doctorate
Program: 2-Year Principally Bachelor's Creditable; Liberal Arts And General; Teacher Preparatory; Professional
Accreditation: M, ADNUR, MT, NUR, SW, TEAC

02 Chancellor ... Prof. Marilina L. WAYLAND
05 Dean of Studies ... Prof. Migdalia TEXIDOR
32 Dean of Students ... Dr. Carmen OQUENDO
10 Dean of Administration ... Mr. Jimmy CANCEL
11 Dean of Faculty Cs Economics & Adm ... Prof. Fredrick VEGA
53 Dean of Education & Behavioral Sci ... Dr. Carmen COLLAZO
83 Director School of Psychology ... Dr. Jaime SANTIAGO
79 Dean Faculty of Humanities ... Dr. Oscar CRUZ
66 Director of Nursing ... Dr. Ivette CORA
72 Director of Medical Technology ... Dr. Ida A. MEJIAS
81 Dean Faculty of Science & Technolog ... Vacant
06 Registrar ... Ms. Lisette RIVERA
84 Enrollment Management ... Mr. Luis E. RUIZ
20 Associate Dean of Studies ... Ms. Blanca M. GONZALEZ
08 Dir of Ctr for Access Info ... Ms. Maria de Lourdes RESTO
15 Human Resources Officer ... Mrs. Darlin TORRES
37 Director of Financial Aid ... Ms. Lillian CONCEPCION
18 Dir Conservation & General Services ... Ing. Marina O. RIVERA
38 Dir Student Placement/Guidanc/Couns ... Ms. Beatriz RIVERA
83 Director School of Social Work ... Dr. Elizabeth MIRANDA
58 Director School of Education ... Dr. Maria D. RUBERO
85 Coord International Rels Office ... Prof. Ramon AYALA
73 Dir School of Theology ... Dr. Angel VELEZ
88 Dir School of Criminal Justice ... Prof. Luis ACEVEDO
13 Director Informatic/Telecomm Center ... Mr. Eduardo ORTIZ
36 Director Student Placement ... Mrs. Adabel-Vanessa COLON
07 Director of Admissions ... Ms. Janies OLIVIERI
09 Dean Inst Research/External Rsrch ... Vacant
30 Development & Fund Raising ... Mrs. Evelyn VEGA
96 Purchasing Officer ... Mrs. Patricia GONZALEZ
92 Coordinator of Honors Program ... Prof. Mariusz JACKO
88 Bursar ... Ms. Carmen RIVERA

*Inter American University of Puerto Rico Ponce Campus (B)

104 Turpo Industrial Park Road, #1, Mercedita PR 00715-1602

County: Ponce — FICE Identification: 005029
Unit ID: 242662
Telephone: (787) 284-1912 — Carnegie Class: Bac/Diverse
FAX Number: (787) 841-0103 — Calendar System: Semester
URL: ponce.inter.edu
Established: 1962 — Annual Undergrad Tuition & Fees: $4,852
Enrollment: 5,788 — Coed
Affiliation or Control: Independent Non-Profit — IRS Status: 501(c)3
Highest Offering: Doctorate
Program: 2-Year Principally Bachelor's Creditable; Liberal Arts And General; Teacher Preparatory
Accreditation: M, OTA, PTAA, RAD, TEAC

02 Chancellor ... Dr. Vilma E. COLON
05 Dean of Studies ... Dr. Jacqueline ALVAREZ
32 Dean of Students ... Mrs. Edda COSTAS
11 Dean of Administrative Affairs ... Eng. Victor A. FELIBERTY
08 Director Education Resource Center ... Mrs. Maria SILVESTRINI
35 Director Student Services ... Mrs. Miriam MARTINEZ
10 Bursar ... Mrs. Nilda RODRIGUEZ
06 Registrar ... Mrs. Maria del C PEREZ
30 Director of Development ... Mrs. Hilda V. STELLA
07 Director of Admissions ... Mr. Franco L. DIAZ
88 Ctr Academic Retention/Integration ... Dr. Eunice CORDERO
15 Human Resource Officer ... Vacant
19 Supervisor of University Guard ... Mr. Reinaldo ROSADO
37 Director Student Financial Aid ... Mrs. Debra MARTINEZ
41 Athletic Director ... Mr. Raul HERNANDEZ
58 Director of Graduate Programs ... Vacant
50 Director Business & Administration ... Mrs. Alma SEGARRA
51 Director Continuing Education ... Mrs. Evelyn CASTILLO
79 Act Dir Humanistics/Pedagogical Std ... Mrs. Santy CORREA
81 Director Mathematics/Sciences ... Dr. Hector W. COLON
83 Dir Social/Behavioral Science ... Ms. Lidis L. JUSINO
76 Director Health Science ... Dra. Lourdes ASTACIO
38 Dir Univ Integration Services Ofc ... Mr. Hector MARTINEZ
13 Director Computer Center ... Mr. Antonio RAMOS
26 Public Relations Officer ... Vacant
04 Chief Executive Assistant ... Mrs. Yinaira SANTIAGO
88 Dir Marketing & Student Promotion ... Mrs. Vanessa PAGAN
106 Director Distance Education Program ... Dr. Omayra CARABALLO
88 Accreditation/Certification Officer ... Vacant
45 Director of Evaluation & Planning ... Vacant
18 Chief Facilities/Physical Plant ... Mr. Julio C. MUNOZ
36 Director Student Placement ... Mr. Hector MARTINEZ
84 Director Enrollment Management ... Mrs. Miriam MARTINEZ

*Inter American University of Puerto Rico San German Campus (C)

PO Box 5100, San German PR 00683-9801

County: San German — FICE Identification: 003938
Unit ID: 242617
Telephone: (787) 264-1912 — Carnegie Class: Master's M
FAX Number: (787) 892-6350 — Calendar System: Semester
URL: www.intersg.edu
Established: 1912 — Annual Undergrad Tuition & Fees: $5,920
Enrollment: 5,223 — Coed
Affiliation or Control: Independent Non-Profit — IRS Status: 501(c)3
Highest Offering: Doctorate
Program: Occupational; 2-Year Principally Bachelor's Creditable; Liberal Arts And General; Teacher Preparatory; Professional
Accreditation: M, IACBE, MT, RAD, TEAC

02 Chancellor ... Prof. Agnes MOJICA
05 Dean of Academic Affairs ... Dr. Nyvia ALVARADO
11 Dean of Administration ... Mrs. Frances CARABALLO
32 Dean of Students ... Mr. Raúl MEDINA
20 Associate Dean of Academic Affairs ... Prof. Vilma MARTÍNEZ
21 Auxiliary Dean of Administration ... Mrs. Marisol GONZÁLEZ
15 Director of Human Resources ... Mrs. Evelyn TORRES
18 Chief Facilities/Physical Plant ... Mr. José A. RIVERA
37 Director Financial Aid ... Mrs. María Inés LUGO
06 Registrar ... Mrs. Arleen SANTANA
07 Director of Admissions ... Mrs. Mildred CAMACHO
08 Director of Library ... Mrs. Doris ASENCIO
38 Director Student Counseling ... Mrs. Daisy PÉREZ
09 Dir Plng Evaluation/Inst Studies ... Miss María MORALES MARTÍNEZ
19 Director of Security ... Mr. Víctor BONILLA
13 Director of Computer Center ... Mr. Rogelio TORO-ZAPATA
41 Athletic Director ... Prof. Francisco ACEVEDO
39 Director of Men Student Housing ... Mrs. Erlinda VEGA
39 Director of Women Student Housing ... Mrs. Hilda CRUZ
42 Dir Chaplaincy/Spiritual Well-being ... Rev. Pablo CARABALLO
04 Special Assistant of the Chancellor ... Mrs. Tary GARCÍA
35 Manager of Student Services ... Mrs. María Gil MARTÍNEZ
51 Director of Continuing Education ... Vacant
58 Director Graduate Programs ... Dr. Ailín T. PADILLA
88 Manager of Food Services ... Mr. Héctor CABASSA
17 Director of Medical Services ... Vacant
109 Auxiliary Dean of Students ... Mrs. Janet RIVERA
30 Chief Development Officer ... Miss Leticia MARTÍNEZ
96 Director of Purchasing ... Mr. Israel CRUZ
10 Director Bursar's Office ... Mr. Carlos SEGARRA
53 Director of Education ... Dr. Miriam PADILLA
83 Director of Social Scieces & Libera ... Dr. Felipe MARTÍNEZ
50 Director of Entreprenurial & Mgmt ... Dr. Milsa MORALES
88 Director of Biology & Environmental ... Prof. Iris SEDA
72 Director of Technical Studies ... Prof. Mildred ORTIZ
57 Director of Fine Arts ... Prof. Samuel ROSADO
76 Director of Health Sciences ... Prof. Maritza ORTIZ
88 Director of Language & Literature ... Dr. María BODEGA
81 Director of Math & Applied Sciences ... Prof. Yvonne AVILÉS
92 Director of Honor Program ... Miss Sulmarie MORALES
26 Director of External Resources ... Prof. Mildred DE SANTIAGO
106 Dir Online Education/E-learning ... Prof. Luis ZORNOSA
108 Coordinator of Assessment ... Dr. Dalila LÓPEZ

*Inter American University of Puerto Rico School of Law (D)

PO Box 70351, San Juan PR 00936-8351

County: San Juan — Identification: 666813
Unit ID: 242723
Telephone: (787) 751-1912 — Carnegie Class: Spec/Law
FAX Number: (787) 751-2975 — Calendar System: Semester
URL: www.derecho.inter.edu
Established: 1961 — Annual Graduate Tuition & Fees: $15,386
Enrollment: 849 — Coed
Affiliation or Control: Independent Non-Profit — IRS Status: 501(c)3
Highest Offering: First Professional Degree; No Undergraduates
Program: Professional
Accreditation: M, LAW

02 President ... Mr. Manuel J. FERNÓS
61 Dean ... Dr. Julio E. FONTANET-MALDONADO
05 Dean for Academic Affairs ... Dr. Yanira REYES-GIL
32 Dean of Students ... Dr. Iris M. CAMACHO-MELÉNDEZ
11 Dean of Administration ... Mr. Heriberto SOTO-LÓPEZ
06 Acting Registrar ... Mrs. Sonia I. MONTALVO-COLÓN
08 Head Librarian ... Mr. Hector Ruben SANCHEZ
61 Director of Legal Aid Clinic ... Mr. Rafael E. RODRÍGUEZ-RIVERA
37 Director of Financial Aid ... Mr. Ricardo CRESPO
07 Director of Admissions ... Mrs. Angela TORRES
18 Chief Facilities/Physical Plant ... Mr. Jose A. RIVERA
96 Director of Purchasing ... Mrs. Yajahira VIDAL
88 Director of Bursar Office ... Mrs. Ileana PIÑERO
45 Planning/Eval & Development Ofc ... Mrs. Edith C. PABON-RODRIGUEZ
88 Academic Support Program ... Mrs. Patricia OTÓN-OLIVIERI
88 Master Program Coordinator ... Mr. Cesar A. ALVARADO-TORRES
04 Executive Asst to President ... Mr. Dominique GILORMINI
13 Chief Info Technology Officer ... Ms. Olga I. CRUZ-PABÓN
15 Director Personnel Services ... Mrs. Milagros AMALBERT
19 Director Security/Safety ... Mr. Franco QUIÑONES
30 Dir Development/Alumni Rels ... Mrs. Sheila GÓMEZ
36 Director Student Placement/Counsel ... Ms. Rosyvee GUZMÁN
35 Student Services Officer ... Ms. Rosyvee GUZMÁN-CINTRÓN

*Inter American University of Puerto Rico School of Optometry (E)

500 John Will Harris Road, Bayamon PR 00957-6257

County: San Juan — Identification: 666601
Unit ID: 404222
Telephone: (787) 765-1915 — Carnegie Class: Spec/Health
FAX Number: (787) 767-3920 — Calendar System: Semester
URL: www.optonet.inter.edu
Established: 1981 — Annual Graduate Tuition & Fees: $26,500
Enrollment: 227 — Coed
Affiliation or Control: Independent Non-Profit — IRS Status: 501(c)3
Highest Offering: First Professional Degree; No Undergraduates
Program: Professional
Accreditation: M, OPT

02 Dean ... Dr. Andres PAGAN
05 Dean for Academic Affairs ... Dr. Angel ROMERO
10 Dean of Administration ... Mr. Francisco RIVERA
32 Dean of Student Affairs ... Dra. Iris CABELLO
42 Director Religious Life ... Dra. Ileana VARGAS
30 Director Development ... Mrs. Maria J. AULET
20 Director Academic Affairs ... Vacant
17 Dean of Clinical Affairs ... Dra. Damaris PAGAN
08 Library Director ... Mrs. Wilma MARRERO
15 Director Human Resources ... Mrs. Jackeline MEJIAS
37 Financial Aid Officer ... Mrs. Sirimarie MARTINEZ
04 Executive Assistant of the Dean ... Mrs. Arleen E. CORREA
06 Registrar ... Mrs. Luz OCASIO
26 Director Marketing/Promotion ... Mrs. Jaqueline PABON

Mech-Tech College (F)

PO Box 6118, Caguas PR 00726

County: Caguas — FICE Identification: 030255
Unit ID: 414461
Telephone: (787) 744-1060 — Carnegie Class: Assoc/PrivFP
FAX Number: (787) 744-1035 — Calendar System: Quarter
URL: www.mechtech.edu
Established: 1984 — Annual Undergrad Tuition & Fees: $8,992
Enrollment: 4,221 — Coed
Affiliation or Control: Proprietary — IRS Status: Proprietary
Highest Offering: Associate Degree
Program: Occupational; 2-Year Principally Bachelor's Creditable; Technical Emphasis
Accreditation: CNCE

01 President ... Mr. Edwin J. COLON COSME

National University College (G)

MSC 452, PO Box 144035, Arecibo PR 00614

Telephone: (787) 879-5044 — Identification: 666489
Accreditation: &M

† Branch campus of National University College, Bayamon, PR.

National University College (H)

State Road#2, Km.11.2, #1660, Bayamon PR 00960-2036

County: Bayamon — FICE Identification: 022606
Unit ID: 242972
Telephone: (787) 780-5134 — Carnegie Class: Bac/Assoc
FAX Number: (787) 779-4906 — Calendar System: Trimester
URL: www.nuc.edu
Established: 1982 — Annual Undergrad Tuition & Fees: $6,495
Enrollment: 5,320 — Coed
Affiliation or Control: Proprietary — IRS Status: Proprietary
Highest Offering: Master's
Program: 2-Year Principally Bachelor's Creditable; Nursing Emphasis
Accreditation: M, @TEAC

01 President ....Dr. Gloria E. BAQUERO
88 VP of Compliance ....Mr. Desi LOPEZ
05 VP Academic Affairs ....Dr. Maria ESTRADA
32 VP of Student Affairs ....Ms. Ana M. LUCUMI
00 Chancellor ....Ms. Lydia COLLAZO
46 Director Research & Development ....Mr. Angel AVILES
37 Institutional Dir Financial Aid ....Ms. Elizabeth CRUZ
06 Registrar ....Ms. Glorimar RODRIGUEZ

National University College (A)

190 Ave Gautier Benýtez esquina Ave, Caguas PR 00725
Telephone: (787) 653-4733 Identification: 770928
Accreditation: &M

† Branch campus of National University College, Bayamon, PR.

National University College Ponce Campus (B)

SR #506 KM 1.00, Bo Coto Laurel, Ponce PR 00716
Telephone: (787) 840-4474 Identification: 770169
Accreditation: &M

† Branch campus of National University College, Bayamon, PR.

National University College Rio Grande Campus (C)

Carr.#3 Km 22.01, Bo. Cienaga Baja,
Rio Grande PR 00745
Telephone: (787) 809-5100 Identification: 770170
Accreditation: &M

† Branch campus of National University College, Bayamon, PR.

Ponce Paramedical College (D)

1213 Acacia Street Villa Flores Urb,
Ponce PR 00716-2901
County: Ponce FICE Identification: 025349
Unit ID: 243072
Telephone: (787) 848-1589 Carnegie Class: Assoc/PrivFP
FAX Number: (787) 259-0169 Calendar System: Other
URL: www.popac.edu
Established: 1983 Annual Undergrad Tuition & Fees: $14,010
Enrollment: 2,607 Coed
Affiliation or Control: Proprietary IRS Status: Proprietary
Highest Offering: Associate Degree
Program: Occupational; 2-Year Principally Bachelor's Creditable; Technical Emphasis
Accreditation: ACCSC

01 President ....Mrs. Wilda VELEZ
05 Academic Dean ....Mrs. Rosa E. CRUZ
06 Registrar ....Mrs. Ivette OLIVERAS
37 Director Student Financial Aid ....Mrs. Amarilis ROCHE

Ponce School of Medicine & Health Sciences (E)

PO Box 7004, Ponce PR 00732-7004
County: Ponce FICE Identification: 024824
Unit ID: 243081
Telephone: (787) 840-2575 Carnegie Class: Assoc/PrivNFP4
FAX Number: (787) 840-9756 Calendar System: Semester
URL: www.psm.edu
Established: 1977 Annual Graduate Tuition & Fees: $24,359
Enrollment: 701 Coed
Affiliation or Control: Independent Non-Profit IRS Status: 501(c)3
Highest Offering: Doctorate; No Undergraduates
Program: Professional; Business Emphasis
Accreditation: M, CLPSY, MED, PH

01 President/CEO ....Dr. David LENIHAN
05 Vice Pres Academic Affairs ....Dr. Jose TORRES-RUIZ
32 Vice Pres Student Affairs ....Dr. Emil RIVERA
11 Chief Operations Officer ....Ms. Ann COSS
10 Chief Financial Officer ....Mr. Carlos ROJAS

The Pontifical Catholic University of Puerto Rico (F)

2250 Las Americas Avenue, Suite 564,
Ponce PR 00717-9997
County: Ponce FICE Identification: 003936
Unit ID: 241410
Telephone: (787) 841-2000 Carnegie Class: DRU
FAX Number: (787) 651-2034 Calendar System: Semester
URL: www.pucpr.edu
Established: 1948 Annual Undergrad Tuition & Fees: $5,890
Enrollment: 10,615 Coed
Affiliation or Control: Roman Catholic IRS Status: 501(c)3
Highest Offering: Doctorate
Program: Liberal Arts And General; Teacher Preparatory; Professional
Accreditation: M, CORE, LAW, MT, NUR, SW, TEAC

00 Chancellor ....M.Rev. Felix LAZARO
01 President ....Dr. Jorge I. VELEZ AROCHO
04 Executive Assistant to President ....Lic. Liza RIESTRA
05 Vice President Academic Affairs ....Dr. Leandro COLON
10 Vice President of Finance ....Prof. Irma I. RODRIGUEZ
32 Vice President for Student Affairs ....Prof. Freddie MARTINEZ
20 Assoc Vice Pres Academic Affairs ....Prof. Maria MUNIZ
35 Asst to Vice Pres Student Affairs ....Prof. Myriam D. LOPEZ
09 Vice President Inst Rsrch/Dev Plng ....Dr. Felix CORTES
12 Rector Arecibo Branch ....Dr. Edwin HERNANDEZ
12 Rector Mayaguez Branch ....Dr. Olga HERNÁNDEZ
06 Registrar ....Prof. Ivan DAVILA
07 Director of Admissions ....Dr. Ana O. BONILLA
08 Director of the Library ....Prof. Magda VARGAS
37 Director of Student Aid ....Mrs. Maria NOLASCO
36 Director of Placement Services ....Mr. Enrique ARROYO
13 Director Computer Center ....Mr. Moises CABRERA
55 Director of Evening Studies ....Prof. Caridad ALVAREZ
24 Director Educational Technology ....Dr. Edgar RODRIGUEZ
79 Dean of Arts & Humanities ....Prof. Alfonso SANTIAGO
81 Dean of Sciences ....Dra. Alma L. SANTIAGO
61 Dean of the School of Law ....Lic. Jose A. FRONTERA
50 Dean Business Administration ....Dr. David ZAYAS
53 Dean of Education ....Dr. Myriam ZAYAS
58 Dean Institute of Graduate Studies ....Dr. Hernan VERA
48 Dean School of Architecture ....Mr. Luis V. BADILLO-LOZANO
51 Coord Continuing Education Inst ....Mrs. Karen G. MORALES
27 Communications ....Mrs. Jalibeth RODRIGUEZ
29 Alumni Relations Officer ....Mrs. Maria S. MASCARO
15 Director Human Resources ....Mr. Wilfredo CORNIER
40 Director Bookstore ....Mrs. Ashley VELEZ
41 Athletic Director ....Mr. Ramon HERNANDEZ
42 Chaplain ....Rev. Juan C. RIVERA
109 Director Auxiliary Enterprises ....Mr. Julio FELIU
26 Director Public Relations ....Mrs. Irem POVENTUD
38 Director Student Counseling ....Prof. Carmen GONZALEZ
18 Physical Plant/Safety & Security ....Mr. Julio PALMER
21 Treasurer Bursar's Office ....Mr. Juan E. ROMAN
96 Director of Purchasing ....Mrs. Zoraida VELAZQUEZ
88 Exec Dir International Relations ....Dra. Enid MIRANDA
88 Director of Biotechnology ....Dra. Cariluz SANTIAGO
88 Accreditation Liaison Officer ....Dr. Carmen J. ACOSTA-FUMERO
30 Infrastructure Director ....Ing. Armando RODRIGUEZ
84 Coord Institutional Recruitment ....Sr. Rene MARRERO
89 Director of Freshmen ....Prof. Carmen Z. TORRES
106 Dir Online Education/E-learning ....Dr. Carmen BETANCOURT
19 Director Security/Safety ....Mr. Julio PALMER
43 Dir Legal Services/General Counsel ....Lic. Carolyn COSTAS
86 Director Government Relations ....Mr. Ruben COLON
100 Chief of Staff ....Lic. Liza RIESTRA
108 Director Institutional Assessment ....Dr. Jose N. CARABALLO
25 Chief Contracts/Grants Admin ....Vacant
39 Director Student Housing ....Mr. Francisco LUGO
39 Director Student Housing ....Ms. Magda PEREZ

Pontifical Catholic University of Puerto Rico-Arecibo Campus (G)

Box 144045, Arecibo PR 00614-4045
Telephone: (787) 881-1212 Identification: 666603
Accreditation: &M

† Regional accreditation is carried under the parent institution in Ponce, PR.

Pontifical Catholic University of Puerto Rico-Mayaguez Campus (H)

Box 1326, Mayaguez PR 00681-1326
Telephone: (787) 834-5151 Identification: 666605
Accreditation: &M

† Branch campus of The Pontifical Catholic University of Puerto Rico, Ponce, PR.

San Juan Bautista School of Medicine (I)

PO Box 4968, Carretera 172, Caguas PR 00726-4968
County: San Juan FICE Identification: 031773
Unit ID: 430670
Telephone: (787) 743-3038 Carnegie Class: Spec/Med
FAX Number: (787) 743-3042 Calendar System: Semester
URL: www.sanjuanbautista.edu
Established: 1978 Annual Graduate Tuition & Fees: $28,485
Enrollment: 240 Coed
Affiliation or Control: Proprietary IRS Status: Proprietary
Highest Offering: First Professional Degree; No Undergraduates
Program: Professional
Accreditation: M, MED

01 President/Dean ....Dr. Yocasta BRUGAL-MENA
11 Dean of Administration ....Mr. Carlos F. ABREU

Seminario Teologico de Puerto Rico (J)

Calle Jose Canals #458, Oficina 301, San Juan PR 00918
Telephone: (787) 274-1142 Identification: 770142
Accreditation: &M

† Branch campus of Nyack College, Nyack, NY.

*Sistema Universitario Ana G. Mendez (K)

Apartado 21345, Rio Piedras PR 00928-1341
County: San Juan FICE Identification: 029078
Unit ID: 242060
Telephone: (787) 751-0178 Carnegie Class: N/A
FAX Number: (787) 766-1706
URL: www.suagm.edu

01 President ....Mr. Jose F. MENDEZ
03 Executive Vice President ....Mr. Jose F. MENDEZ, JR.
05 Vice President for Academic Affairs ....Mr. Jorge L. CRESPO
10 Vice Pres Financial Affairs ....Mr. Alfonso L. DAVILA
32 VP Student/Marketing Affairs ....Dr. Mayra CRUZ
45 Vice President Planning & Research ....Mr. Jorge CRESPO
11 Vice Pres Administrative Affairs ....Mr. Jesus A. DIAZ
15 Vice President Human Resources ....Dr. Victoria DE JESUS
13 Chief Information Officer ....Sr. Kenneth MALDONADO
26 Director Public Relations ....Ms. Maria MARTINEZ
04 Exec Assistant to President ....Ms. Lydia I. MASSARI
06 Registrar ....Ms. Elisa QUILES
07 Director of Admissions ....Ms. Ramonita FUENTES

*Universidad del Este (L)

PO Box 2010, Carolina PR 00984-2010
County: San Juan FICE Identification: 003941
Unit ID: 243346
Telephone: (787) 257-7373 Carnegie Class: Master's L
FAX Number: (787) 776-1220 Calendar System: Semester
URL: www.suagm.edu/une
Established: 1949 Annual Undergrad Tuition & Fees: $5,820
Enrollment: 13,331 Coed
Affiliation or Control: Independent Non-Profit IRS Status: 501(c)3
Highest Offering: Master's
Program: Occupational; 2-Year Principally Bachelor's Creditable; Liberal Arts And General; Teacher Preparatory
Accreditation: M, ACBSP, ACFEI, @SW, TEAC

02 Chancellor ....Mr. Alberto MALDONADO-RUIZ
05 Vice Chancellor Academic Affairs ....Dr. Mildred HUERTAS
11 Vice Chanc Admin Affs/Ofce of Chanc ....Mrs. Maria S. DIAZ
32 Vice Chancellor Student Affairs ....Dr. María G. VEAZ
24 Vice Chanc Information Resources ....Mrs. Carmen ORTEGA
46 Vice Chanc External Resources ....Mrs. Mayra M. FERRAN
20 Assoc VC Licensing/Accreditation ....Ms. Nilda I. ROSADO
88 Assoc Vice Chanc Admin Affairs ....Mrs. Magalie ALVARADO
35 Assoc Vice Chanc Student Affairs ....Mrs. Gisela NEGRON
84 Assoc VC Enrollment Management ....Mrs. Magda E. OSTOLAZA
23 AVC Stdnt Quality of Life/Wellness .Mrs. Carmen G. VELAZQUEZ
07 Asst Vice Chan Admiss/Financial Aid ....Vacant
09 Asst Vice Chanc Academic Effective ....Dr. Claribette RODRIGUEZ
36 Exec Director Employment Placement ....Mrs. Maria M. COLON
30 Asst VC for University Advancement ...Mrs. Maria I. DE GUZMAN
15 Asst Vice Pres Human Resources ....Mr. Jorge RODRIGUEZ
10 Assistant Vice President of Budget ....Mr. Jorge A. TORRES
45 Asst Vice President of Planning ....Mr. Alberto J. CAMACHO
88 Dean Intl Sch Hosp/Culinary Arts ....Mrs. Terestella GONZÁLEZ
107 Dean Professional Studies ....Mrs. Mildred Y. RIVERA
18 Physical Plant/Operations VC ....Mr. Edgar D. RODRIGUEZ
06 Registrar ....Mrs. Elisa QUILES
37 Director of Financial Aid ....Mrs. Eigna DE JESUS
08 Director of Library ....Mrs. Elsa MARIANI
26 Director Public Relations ....Mrs. Ivonne D. ARROYO
29 Director Alumni ....Ms. Lorna M. MORLA
13 Information/Telecommunications Dir ....Mr. Nestor MAS
41 Athletic Director ....Mr. Julio FIGUEROA
19 Director Safety & Security ....Mr. Carlos E. BERROA
53 Dean of Education ....Dr. Maria del Carmen ARRIBAS
50 Dean of Business Administration ....Dr. Maritza I. ESPINA
72 Dean of Science and Technology ....Dr. Marielis E. RIVERA
76 Dean of Health Science ....Dr. Silvio VÉLEZ
83 Dean of Social Science ....Dr. Luis MAYO
51 Executive Director of Continuing Ed ....Mrs. Litza A. RIVERA
104 Director of International Affairs ....Mrs. Laurie A. MELIN

*Universidad Del Turabo (M)

Estacion Universidad, Box 3030, Gurabo PR 00778-3030
County: Gurabo FICE Identification: 011719
Unit ID: 243601
Telephone: (787) 743-7979 Carnegie Class: DRU
FAX Number: (787) 744-5394 Calendar System: Semester
URL: www.suagm.edu
Established: 1972 Annual Undergrad Tuition & Fees: $5,820
Enrollment: 17,325 Coed
Affiliation or Control: Independent Non-Profit IRS Status: 501(c)3
Highest Offering: Doctorate
Program: Liberal Arts And General; Teacher Preparatory; Professional
Accreditation: M, BUS, #DIETC, ENG, @NATUR, NURSE, SP, SW, TEAC

02 Chancellor ....Dr. Dennis ALICEA
11 Vice Chancellor of Admin Affairs ....Dr. Gladys BETANCOURT
05 Vice Chancellor Academic Affairs ....Dr. Roberto LORAN
32 Vice Chancellor of Student Affairs ....Dra. Brunilda APONTE
08 Vice Chancellor Information Res ....Dr. Sarai LASTRA
92 Vice Chancellor Honors Program ....Ms. Maricarmen SANTOS
88 Asst Vice Chanc Eval & Development ..Dra. Maria del C. SANTOS
21 Asst Vice Chanc Admin Affairs ....Mrs. Edna ORTA
53 Dean Education ....Mr. Israel RODRÍGUEZ
50 Dean Business Administration ....Dr. Marcelino RIVERA
54 Dean Engineering ....Dr. Jack T. ALLISON
72 Dean Science & Technology ....Dr. Teresa LIPSETT
83 Dean Social Sciences & Humanities ....Dr. Felix R. HUERTAS
58 Dean of Graduate Studies ....Dr. Sharon CANTRELL
06 Registrar ....Mrs. Zoraida ORTIZ
27 Director of Marketing ....Ms. Melba G. SÁNCHEZ

37 Director Office of Financial Aid ....Mrs. Carmen J. RIVERA
26 Director Public Relations ....Ms. Iris SERRANO
18 Chief Facilities/Physical Plant ....Eng. Mayra RODRIGUEZ
29 Coordinator Alumni Relations ....Ms. René S. RONDA
30 Chief Development Officer ....Ms. Alba RIVERA
96 Director of Purchasing ....Mr. Jose BERRIOS
07 Director of Admissions ....Mrs. Virginia GONZALEZ
09 Director of Institutional Research ....Ms. Mari G. GONZALEZ
15 Director Personnel Services ....Mrs. Iris BERRIOS
36 Assoc Vice Chanc Student Placement ....Ms. Carmen PULLIZA
84 Director Enrollment Management ....Ms. Maria V. FIGUEROA
10 Chief Business Officer ....Vacant
38 Assoc Vice Chanc Student Counseling .....Ms. Samaris COLLAZO

*Universidad Metropolitana (A)

PO Box 21150, Rio Piedras PR 00928-1150

County: San Juan FICE Identification: 025875
Unit ID: 241739
Telephone: (787) 766-1717 Carnegie Class: Master's L
FAX Number: (787) 759-7663 Calendar System: Quarter
URL: www.suagm.edu/umet
Established: 1980 Annual Undergrad Tuition & Fees: $5,660
Enrollment: 13,773 Coed
Affiliation or Control: Independent Non-Profit IRS Status: 501(c)3
Highest Offering: Doctorate
Program: Liberal Arts And General; Teacher Preparatory; Professional; Business Emphasis
Accreditation: M, ACBSP, ADNUR, NUR, @TEAC

02 SUAGM President ....Dr. José F. MENDEZ
00 Chancellor ....Dr. Carlos M. PADIN
05 Int Vice Chanc Academic Affairs ....Dra. Alice J. CASANOVA
108 Int Vice Chanc Inst Assessment ....Dr. Carmen LUNA
29 Vice Chanc Alumni Relations ....Ms. Belissa AQUINO
32 Vice Chanc for Student Affairs ....Mrs. Carmen ROSADO
102 Vice Chanc of International Affairs ....Dr. Zaida VEGA
88 Vice Chanc External Resources ....Mrs. Gladys CORA
11 Assoc Vice Chanc Admin Affairs ....Mrs. Maria del Pilar CHARNECO
88 Asst Vice Chanc for Eval/Devel ....Prof. Adanid PRIETO
11 Asst Vice Chanc for Admin Affairs ....Dr. Mildred ARBONA
15 Asst Vice Pres for Human Resources ....Mrs. Marisol MUNOZ
13 Vice Pres Information Resources ....Mr. Carlos M. DELGADO
20 Assoc Vice Chanc Eval and Develop ....Mr. Eric BARRIOS
30 Assoc Vice Chanc Dev/Retention ....Mrs. Awilda PEREZ
10 Asst Vice Pres Analysis & Budget ....Mrs. Aixa ALDARONDO
45 Asst Vice President of Planning ....Mrs. Mariela COLLAZO
44 Asst Vice Chanc Retention/Develop ....Mr. Ariel MENDEZ
49 Dean of Liberal Arts/Human & Commun ....Dr. Eloisa GORDON
50 Dean of Business Administration ....Dr. Juan OTERO
53 Dean of Education ....Dr. Judith GONZALEZ
76 Dean of Health Science ....Dr. Lourdes MALDONADO
81 Dean of Science & Technology ....Dr. Karen GONZALEZ
65 Dean of Environmental Affairs ....Dr. Carlos PADIN
83 Assoc Dean of Social Sciences ....Dr. Mariveliz CABAN
107 Assoc Dean of Professional Studies ....Ms. Melissa GUILLIANI
60 Assoc Dean of Communications ....Mr. Alfredo NIEVES
79 Assoc Dean of Humanities ....Dr. Martin CRUZ
75 Assoc Dean of Technical Studies ....Prof. Felipe ROSA
51 Assoc Dean of Continuing Education ....Ms. Lorna MARTINEZ
53 Assoc Dean of Education ....Dr. Daisy RODRIGUEZ
53 Assoc Dean of Education ....Dr. Angel CANALES
08 Head Librarian ....Mrs. Maria de los A. LUGO
18 Int Chief Facilities/Physical Plant ....Mr. Egenero FRANCISCO-CABALLO
72 Director Educational Production ....Mr. Luis MARTINEZ
76 Director of Respiratory Therapy ....Mrs. Yolanda TORRES
66 Director of Nursing ....Mrs. Yolanda TORRES
26 Director Public Relations Officer ....Ms. Yvonne GUADALUPE
06 Registrar ....Mrs. Beatriz NIEVES
12 Additional Location Dir Bayamón ....Mrs. Ibis RODRÍGUEZ
12 Additional Location Dir Aguadilla ....Mr. Luis A. RUIZ
12 Additional Location Dir Jayuya ....Mrs. Irma del Pilar CRUZ
12 Additional Location Dir Comerío ....Mr. José I. CARMONA
07 Admissions Director ....Ms. Yadira RIVERA LUGO
41 Athletic Director ....Mr. Ariel ORTIZ

Trinity College of Puerto Rico (B)

PO Box 7313, Ponce PR 00732

FICE Identification: 031159
Unit ID: 431929
Telephone: (787) 848-5739 Carnegie Class: Not Classified
FAX Number: (787) 284-2537 Calendar System: Semester
URL: www.trinitypr.edu
Established: 1969 Annual Undergrad Tuition & Fees: $6,546
Enrollment: 246 Coed
Affiliation or Control: Independent Non-Profit IRS Status: 501(c)3
Highest Offering: Associate Degree
Program: Occupational; 2-Year Principally Bachelor's Creditable
Accreditation: ACICS

01 Executive Director ....Maria DEL PILAR BONNIN OROZCO
05 Academic Director ....Elizabeth PEREZ TOLEDO

Universal Technology College of Puerto Rico (C)

111 Comercio Street, Aguadilla PR 00603

County: Aguadilla FICE Identification: 030297
Unit ID: 376385
Telephone: (787) 882-2065 Carnegie Class: Assoc/PrivNFP
FAX Number: (787) 891-2370 Calendar System: Semester
URL: www.unitecpr.edu
Established: 1987 Annual Undergrad Tuition & Fees: $10,185
Enrollment: 1,565 Coed
Affiliation or Control: Independent Non-Profit IRS Status: 501(c)3
Highest Offering: Baccalaureate
Program: Occupational; 2-Year Principally Bachelor's Creditable; Technical Emphasis
Accreditation: ACICS

01 Chief Executive Officer ....Mrs. Keila LOPEZ
11 Administrative Manager ....Vacant
04 Executive Secretary ....Mrs. Marilyn GONZALEZ
05 Chief Academic Officer ....Vacant
06 Registrar ....Ms. Maria ALVAREZ
08 Director of Library ....Ms. Airlyn VAZQUEZ
10 Accountant ....Ms. Nancy MORALES
12 Director of Branch Campus ....Ms. Nelida CARDONA
13 Director Computer Center ....Mr. Zain CORDERO
15 Director Human Resources ....Ms. Daisy VEGA
18 Chief Facilities/Physical Plant ....Mr. Danily NIEVES
32 Director Student Affairs ....Vacant
36 Student Placement Officer ....Mrs. Ada MORALES
45 Director Planning & Development ....Mrs. Evelyn TORRES
37 Director Student Financial Aid ....Mr. Samuel HERNANDEZ
38 Director Student Counsel ....Mrs. Dalia SANTIAGO
96 Purchasing Officer ....Mrs. Dolores MITJANS
23 Healthcare Services ....Mr. Silverio JIMENEZ
07 Coordinator of Admissions ....Mrs. Teresita RIVERA
50 Dir General Studies/Business Admin ....Mrs. Sandra GONZALEZ
72 Director of Industrial Technology ....Mr. Eduardo FIGUEROA

Universidad Adventista de las Antillas (D)

Box 118, Mayaguez PR 00681-0118

County: Mayaguez FICE Identification: 005019
Unit ID: 241191
Telephone: (787) 834-9595 Carnegie Class: Bac/Diverse
FAX Number: (787) 834-9597 Calendar System: Semester
URL: www.uaa.edu
Established: 1961 Annual Undergrad Tuition & Fees: $6,625
Enrollment: 1,360 Coed
Affiliation or Control: Seventh-day Adventist IRS Status: 501(c)3
Highest Offering: Master's
Program: 2-Year Principally Bachelor's Creditable; Liberal Arts And General; Teacher Preparatory; Professional
Accreditation: M, NUR, @TEAC

01 President ....Dr. Obed JIMENEZ
05 Vice President for Academic Affairs ....Dr. Myrna COLON
10 Vice President Financial Affairs ....Mr. Misael JIMENEZ
32 Vice President for Students Affairs ....Mr. Jaime LOPEZ
30 VP Planning and Development ....Dr. Jose D. GOMEZ
42 Religious Affairs Director ....Mr. Abiezer RODRIGUEZ
20 Associate VP Academic Affairs ....Mrs. Yolanda PEREZ
21 Associate Financial Vice President ....Mrs. Madeline CRUZ
88 Director Student Finance Office ....Mrs. Naobelin CASIANO
66 Dean of the School of Nursing ....Dr. Alicia FRANCO
66 Director School of Nursing ....Mrs. Maria CRUZ
53 Dean of the School of Education ....Dr. Maritza LAMBOY
50 Director of Business Administration ....Dr. David L. RAMOS
81 Director Mathematics/Sciences/Comp .. Mrs. Alicia MORADILLOS
73 Director Theology Department ....Dr. Efren PAGAN
06 Registrar ....Mrs. Ana D. TORRES
07 Director of Admissions ....Mrs. Yolanda FERRER
37 Director of Student Financial Aid ....Mrs. Awilda MATOS
26 Dir Public Relations & Promotion ....Miss Lorell VARELA
108 Dir of Institutional Effectiveness ....Dr. Zilma SANTIAGO
13 Director Computing and Information ....Mr. Heber VAZQUEZ
08 Librarian ....Mrs. Aixa VEGA
38 Counselor ....Mrs. Ivelisse PEREZ
88 Environmental Services Director ....Mr. Legna VARELA
18 Chief Facilities/Physical Plant ....Mr. Abel RODRIGUEZ
34 Dean of Women ....Mrs. Felicita CRUZ
33 Dean of Men ....Mr. Angel RODRIGUEZ
09 Institutional Researcher ....Dr. Digna M. WILLIAMS

Universidad Central de Bayamon (E)

PO Box 1725, Bayamon PR 00960-1725

County: Bayamon FICE Identification: 005022
Unit ID: 241225
Telephone: (787) 786-3030 Carnegie Class: Master's M
FAX Number: (787) 740-2200 Calendar System: Semester
URL: www.ucb.edu.pr
Established: 1961 Annual Undergrad Tuition & Fees: $6,000
Enrollment: 2,360 Coed
Affiliation or Control: Roman Catholic IRS Status: 501(c)3
Highest Offering: Master's
Program: Liberal Arts And General; Teacher Preparatory; Professional
Accreditation: M, CORE, @SW, @TEAC

01 President ....Dr. Lillian NEGRON
05 Academic Dean ....Dr. Luz C. VALENTIN
11 Administrative Dean ....Mr. Noel ORTIZ
32 Dean of Students ....Mrs. Niza ZAYAS
49 Dir College Liberal Arts/Humanities ....Vacant
53 Dir Col of Education and Behavior ....Dr. Caroline GONZALEZ
50 Dir Business Development & Tech ....Dr. Nidia COLON
08 Director Learning Resources ....Mrs. Annette VALENTIN
15 Director of Human Resources ....Mrs. Elaine NUNEZ
30 Int Dir Institutional Development ....Mr. Pedro BERMUDEZ
07 Director of Admissions ....Mrs. Christine HERNANDEZ
37 Director Student Financial Aid ....Mrs. Edna ORTIZ
38 Dir Guidance/Counseling Center ....Mrs. Milagros M. RIVERA
06 Registrar ....Mr. Victor COLON
35 Dir Center Learning Stre (CFAEE) ....Mrs. Myrna PEREZ
13 Director of Information System ....Mr. Jose R. AVILES
18 Director Physical Facilities ....Mr. Eliezer GARCIA
26 Marketing Director ....Mr. Rolando RIVERA
96 Purchase Officer ....Mrs. Jessica OJEDA
09 Institutional Research Officer ....Mrs. Luz M. PALACIOS
66 Nursing Program Coordinator ....Prof. Zaida RUIZ
20 Associate Academic Dean ....Mr. Pedro BERMUDEZ
29 Alumni Relations ....Mrs. Niza ZAYAS
84 Director Enrollment Management ....Mrs. Christine HERNANDEZ
58 Graduate Studies Director ....Dr. Nitza MARQUEZ
81 Dir College Sciences/Health Profes ....Dr. Pedro ROBLES
03 Executive Vice President ....Mr. Angel VALENTIN
04 Administrative Asst to President ....Mrs. Luz N. VALLELLANES
10 Chief Business Officer ....Mr. Noel ORTIZ
101 Secretary of the Institution/Board ....Prof. Marcelina VELEZ
105 Director Web Services ....Mr. Manuel ECHEANDIA
106 Dir Online Education/E-learning ....Mr. Jorge L. DIAZ
108 Director Institutional Assessment ....Dr. Judith TORRES
41 Athletic Director ....Mr. Edwin MORALES

Universidad Central Del Caribe (F)

PO Box 60-327, Bayamon PR 00960-6032

County: Bayamon FICE Identification: 021633
Unit ID: 243568
Telephone: (787) 798-3001 Carnegie Class: Spec/Med
FAX Number: (787) 798-6836 Calendar System: Semester
URL: www.uccaribe.edu
Established: 1976 Annual Undergrad Tuition & Fees: $8,045
Enrollment: 467 Coed
Affiliation or Control: Independent Non-Profit IRS Status: 501(c)3
Highest Offering: Doctorate
Program: 2-Year Principally Bachelor's Creditable; Professional
Accreditation: M, MED

01 President ....Dr. Jose Ginel RODRIGUEZ
05 Dean for Academic Affairs ....Dr. Nereida DIAZ-RODRIGUEZ
11 Dean Administrative Affairs ....Ms. Emilia SOTO
32 Dean Student Affairs ....Dr. Omar PEREZ
17 Dean of Medicine ....Dr. Jose Ginel RODRIGUEZ
63 Associate Dean of Medicine ....Mrs. Zilka RIOS
53 Asst Dean Professional Services ....Ms. Emilia SOTO
06 Registrar ....Ms. Nilda MONTANEZ-LOPEZ
07 Director of Admissions ....Ms. Irma L. CORDERO
37 Director Student Financial Aid ....Vacant
10 Director of Finances ....Mrs. Iris J. FONT
08 Librarian ....Ms. Mildred RIVERA
51 Director of Continuing Education ....Dr. Frances GARCIA
38 Counselor ....Ms. Mariana T. HERNÁNDEZ
46 Dean of Research and Graduate Pgms ....Dr. Luis A. CUBANO
20 Dean for Clinical & Faculty Affairs ....Dr. Harry MERCADO

Universidad Pentecostal Mizpa (G)

PO Box 20966, San Juan PR 00928-0966

County: San Juan FICE Identification: 031983
Unit ID: 441690
Telephone: (787) 720-4476 Carnegie Class: Spec/Faith
FAX Number: (787) 720-2012 Calendar System: Semester
URL: www.mizpa.edu
Established: 1937 Annual Undergrad Tuition & Fees: $4,120
Enrollment: 1,231 Coed
Affiliation or Control: Pentecostal Church of God IRS Status: 501(c)3
Highest Offering: Master's
Program: Religious Emphasis
Accreditation: BI

01 President ....Mr. Luis A. HERNANDEZ
05 Dean of Academic Affairs ....Mr. Leonardo MELENDEZ
10 Dean Administration/Finance ....Mr. Elisamuel RODRIGUEZ
32 Dean of Student Affairs ....Mr. Jorge A. BURGOS
42 Coordinator Ministerial Formation ....Mr. Harry MUNOZ
06 Registrar ....Ms. Sara MARTINEZ
08 Librarian ....Mrs. Melanie RODRIGUEZ
37 Student Financial Aid Officer ....Mrs. Myriam JUARBE
26 Chief Public Relations Officer ....Mr. Rafael LABOY
04 Administrative Asst to President ....Mrs. Maria E. VARGAS

Universidad Politecnica De Puerto Rico (H)

Ponce de Leon 377, Box 192017, San Juan PR 00919

County: San Juan FICE Identification: 021000
Unit ID: 243577
Telephone: (787) 622-8000 Carnegie Class: Spec/Engg
FAX Number: (787) 754-8268 Calendar System: Trimester
URL: www.pupr.edu
Established: 1966 Annual Undergrad Tuition & Fees: $7,200
Enrollment: 4,507 Coed
Affiliation or Control: Independent Non-Profit IRS Status: 501(c)3
Highest Offering: Master's
Program: Liberal Arts And General
Accreditation: M, ENG, ENGR, IACBE, LSAR

01 President Prof. Ernesto VAZQUEZ-BARQUET
03 Executive Vice President Mr. Ernesto VAZQUEZ-MARTINEZ
84 Vice Pres Enrollment Management Mr. Carlos PEREZ
05 Chief Academic Officer Dr. Miguel A. RIESTRA
06 Registrar Mrs. Mayra I. LOPEZ
07 Director Admissions Mrs. Teresa CARDONA
08 Head Librarian Mrs. Mirta COLON
37 Director Financial Aid Mr. Sergio VILLOLDO
09 Director of Institutional Research Dr. Miguel A. RIESTRA
15 Director Personnel Services Ms. Ana CASTELLANO
18 Chief Facilities/Physical Plant Mr. Herminio ROMERO
29 Alumni Relations Ms. Lourdes ALCRUDO
32 Director Student Affairs Mr. Carlos PEREZ
36 Director Student Placement Mrs. Angie ESCALANTE
38 Director Student Counseling Ms. Claribel DIAZ-DIAZ
21 Associate Business Officer Mrs. Olga CANCEL
96 Director of Purchasing Mr. Ramon RIVERA
19 Director Security/Safety Mr. Miguel ALBARRAN
41 Athletic Director Mr. Roberto MEDINA-ORTIZ
50 Dean of Business Eng. Jose O. RIVERA
49 Dean of Arts and Science/Education Dr. Catalina VICENS
54 Dean of Engineering Dr. Carlos J. GONZALEZ
106 Dir Online Education/E-learning Mrs. Heyda DELGADO

Universidad Teologica Del Caribe (A)

PO Box 901, Saint Just PR 00978-0901
County: Trujillo Alto FICE Identification: 023355
Unit ID: 241614
Telephone: (787) 761-0640 Carnegie Class: Spec/Faith
FAX Number: (787) 748-9220 Calendar System: Semester
URL: www.utcpr.edu
Established: 1956 Annual Undergrad Tuition & Fees: $3,784
Enrollment: 250 Coed
Affiliation or Control: Church Of God IRS Status: 501(c)3
Highest Offering: Baccalaureate
Program: Religious Emphasis
Accreditation: BI

01 President Francisco ORTIZ
05 Academic Dean Carmen AYALA
06 Registrar Maria Judith CARABALLO
10 Administration Dean Frankie NEGRON
32 Dean of Students Elizabeth GONZALEZ
37 Financial Aid Director Claudia RODRIGUEZ
08 Librarian Velma Leticia SOSA

*University of Puerto Rico-Central Administration (B)

1187 Flamboyan Street, San Juan PR 00926-1117
County: San Juan FICE Identification: 003942
Unit ID: 243160
Telephone: (787) 250-0000 Carnegie Class: N/A
FAX Number: (787) 759-6917
URL: www.upr.edu

01 President Dr. Uroyoan R. WALKER-RAMOS
03 Executive Director Lic. Manuel E. CAMARA-MONTULL
05 Vice President for Academic Affairs Dra. Delia M. CAMACHO
09 Vice President for Research Dr. José A. LASALDE-DOMINICCI
32 Vice Pres for Student Affairs Dra. Margarita E. VILLAMIL-TORRES
12 Chancellor UPR-Rio Piedras Campus Dr. Carlos E. SEVERINO-VALDEZ
12 Chancellor UPR-Mayaguez Campus Dr. John FERNANDEZ
12 Chanc UPR-Medical Sciences Campus Dr. Noel J. AYMAT-SANTANA
12 Chancellor UPR-Cayey Campus Dr. Mario MEDINA-CABAN
12 Chancellor UPR-Humacao Campus Dr. Efrain VAZQUEZ-VERA
12 Chancellor UPR-Bayamon Campus Prof. Margarita FERNANDEZ-ZAVALA
12 Chancellor UPR-Ponce Campus Dr. Leonardo MORALES-TOMASSINI
12 Chancellor UPR-Carolina Campus Dr. Moises ORENGO-AVILES
12 Chancellor UPR-Utuado Campus Dra. Raquel G. VARGAS-GOMEZ
12 Chancellor UPR-Aguadilla Campus Dr. Nelson A. VERA-HERNANDEZ
12 Chancellor UPR-Arecibo Campus Dr. Otilio GONZALEZ-CORTES
30 Dir Devel & Alumni Affairs Office Sra. Gretchen KRANS
88 Dir Ctrl Designer Construction Arq. Alejandro ARGUELLES
10 Director Finance Office Lic. Angel O. VEGA-SANTIAGO
15 Director Human Resources Office Sra. Erika DIAZ-RIOS
11 Director Administrative Service Mr. Juan M. ORTIZ-VAZQUEZ
13 Director Information Systems Office Mr. Victor DIAZ-RODRIGUEZ
37 Director Student Financial Aid Vacant
43 Director Legal Affairs Office Lic. Cristina ALCARAZ-EMMANUELLI
88 Administrator Botanical Garden Sr. Juan M. ORTIZ-VAZQUEZ
27 University Press & Communications Sra. Olga L. VELEZ-ROLON
101 Exec Secretary University Board Sra. Mayra M. FLORES-SANTOS
21 Director Budget Office Mr. Basilio RIVERA-ARROYO
18 Dir Physical Dev/Infrastrcture Ofc Arq. Fernando PLA-GOMEZ

*University of Puerto Rico-Aguadilla (C)

PO Box 6150, Aguadilla PR 00604-6150
County: Aguadilla FICE Identification: 012123
Unit ID: 243106
Telephone: (787) 890-2681 Carnegie Class: Bac/Diverse
FAX Number: (787) 891-3455 Calendar System: Semester
URL: www.uprag.edu
Established: 1972 Annual Undergrad Tuition & Fees (In-State): $2,212
Enrollment: 2,927 Coed
Affiliation or Control: State IRS Status: 501(c)3
Highest Offering: Baccalaureate
Program: Occupational; 2-Year Principally Bachelor's Creditable; Liberal Arts And General
Accreditation: M, ACBSP, ENGT, TED

02 Chancellor Dr. Nelson A. VERA HERNANDEZ
05 Dean Academic Affairs Dr. Herminia ALEMANY-VALDEZ
11 Dean Administration Mr. Luis ALVAREZ-RUIZ
32 Dean Student Affairs Dr. Migdalia GONZALEZ-GUERRA
06 Registrar Mrs. Zaida SERRANO
07 Admissions Officer Mrs. Melba SERRANO
08 Head Librarian Prof. Elsa MATOS
13 Director of Computer Center Mr. Ismael VILLANUEVA
15 Director of Personnel Mrs. Nilsa MORALES TORRES
19 Director of Security/Safety Mr. Edwin VAZQUEZ MEDINA
37 Director Student Financial Aid Mrs. Yanira MATOS
51 Director Continuing Education Prof. Luis R. RIVERA
38 Director Student Counseling Dr. Gilberto HERRERA
45 Dir Planning/Inst Research Office Mr. Gerardo JAVARIZ
18 Chief Facilities/Physical Plant Mr. Luis GARCIA
29 Director Alumni Relations Mrs. Jeannette AQUINO
96 Purchasing Supervisor Mrs. Widylia MEDINA

*University of Puerto Rico at Arecibo (D)

Call Box 4010, Arecibo PR 00614-4010
County: Arecibo FICE Identification: 007228
Unit ID: 243115
Telephone: (787) 815-0000 Carnegie Class: Bac/Diverse
FAX Number: (787) 880-2245 Calendar System: Semester
URL: www.upra.edu
Established: 1967 Annual Undergrad Tuition & Fees (In-State): $1,870
Enrollment: 3,790 Coed
Affiliation or Control: State IRS Status: 501(c)3
Highest Offering: Baccalaureate
Program: Occupational; Liberal Arts And General
Accreditation: M, ACBSP, ADNUR, CS, ENGT, JOUR, NUR, TED

02 Chancellor Dr. Otilio GONZALEZ CORTES
05 Dean of Academic Affairs Dra. Ana GARCIA ADARNE
11 Dean of Administrative Affairs Prof. Rafael GARCIA TOULET
32 Dean of Student Affairs Dra. Nayla BAEZ
09 Dir Planning/Institutional Research Prof. Sylka TORRES
06 Registrar Mrs. Widilia RODRIGUEZ
07 Director of Admissions Mrs. Magaly MENDEZ
08 Head Librarian Prof. Robert ROSADO
15 Director Human Resources Mr. Luis LARACUENTE
38 Director Student Counseling Prof. Pilar CORDERO
04 Assistant to the Chancellor Prof. Juan PUIG
51 Dir Continuing Education/Prof Stds Prof. Nayla BAEZ
37 Director Student Financial Aid Ms. Daliana FRESSE
41 Athletic Director Prof. Ruth NIEVES
13 Computing & Information Management Prof. Luis COLON
20 Assoc Dean of Academic Affairs Prof. Wanda DELGADO RODRIGUEZ
29 Director Alumni Relations Mrs. Mariely ORTIZ
92 Director Honors Program Dra. Jane ALBERDESTON
96 Director of Purchasing Mrs. Rosaura QUINTANA
18 Chief Facilities/Physical Plant Mr. Edwin RAMOS

*University of Puerto Rico at Bayamon (E)

Carr. 174 #170 Industrial Minillas,
Bayamon PR 00959-1911
County: Bayamon FICE Identification: 010975
Unit ID: 243133
Telephone: (787) 993-0000 Carnegie Class: Bac/Diverse
FAX Number: (787) 993-8900 Calendar System: Semester
URL: www.uprb.edu
Established: 1971 Annual Undergrad Tuition & Fees (In-State): $2,212
Enrollment: 4,974 Coed
Affiliation or Control: State IRS Status: 501(c)3
Highest Offering: Baccalaureate
Program: Liberal Arts And General
Accreditation: M, ACBSP, CS, ENGT, TED

02 Chancellor Prof. Margarita FERNÁNDEZ-ZAVALA
05 Dean Academic Affairs Dr. Rosa RIVERA-ALAMO
32 Dean Student Affairs Dr. Elsa GELPI-BAÍZ
06 Registrar Ms. Carmen CINTRON-OTERO
07 Director Admissions Mrs. Carmen MONTES-BURGOS
08 Director Learning Resources Prof. Maria de los Angeles ZAVALA-COLÓN
11 Dean Administrative Affairs Prof. Carlos SANDOVAL-LEMUS
15 Director Human Resources Mrs. Mayra DIAZ
35 Director Student Activities Mrs. Maribelle PERGOLA-RIVERA
36 Director Student Placement Prof. Nelson VÁZQUEZ-ESPEJO
37 Director Student Financial Aid Mr. Marcos DE JESÚS
38 Director Student Counseling Ms. Guadalupe VEGA-GUTIERREZ
81 Director Biology Dr. Nilda APONTE-AVELLANET
50 Director Business Administration Prof. Anabel TORRES-ORTIZ
09 Director Planning & Inst Research Mr. Javier ZAVALA-QUIÑONES
53 Director Education Prof. María A. GONZÁLEZ DE RESENDE
54 Director Engineering Prof. Jorge VELAR-PRIETO
68 Director Physical Education Prof. Carlos MARICHAL-LUGO
79 Director Humanities Dr. Nora RODRÍGUEZ-VALLÉS
83 Director Social Sciences Dr. Elizabeth CRESPO-KEBLER
77 Director Computer Science Dr. Nelliud TORRES-BATISTA
75 Director Secretarial Sciences Prof. Nancy JIMÉNEZ-PÉREZ
72 Director Electronics Prof. Jesús ORTIZ-CINTRÓN
23 Director Health Services Dr. Adelaida L. ORTIZ-GÓMEZ
96 Director Purchasing Ms. María I. CRESPO-MARTÍNEZ
88 Director Special Services Ms. Shelciy COLLAZO-CASTRO
81 Director Physics Dr. Solange BENITEZ-RAMÍREZ
88 Director English Prof. Carmen SKERRETT-LLANOS
88 Director Spanish Dr. Amarilis TORRES-FUENTES
81 Director Mathematics Prof. Angel MORERA-GONZÁLEZ
88 Director Chemistry Dr. Solange BENÍTEZ-RAMÍREZ
18 Coord Facilities/Physical Plant Mr. Omar MUÑIZ-MUÑOZ
10 Director Finance Ms. María FIGUEROA-AGOSTO
21 Director Budget Mr. Wilfredo ORTIZ-RUÍZ
13 Director Information Systems Ms. Marcia RODRÍGUEZ-ORTIZ
105 Director Web Services Mr. Orlando ORENGO-ORTEGA
19 Director Security/Safety Ms. Yermarie COSME-FERNANDEZ
41 Athletic Director Mr. Gerardo BATISTA-SANTIAGO
43 Dir Legal Services/General Counsel Ms. Melysa RODRÍGUEZ-BONANO

*University of Puerto Rico-Carolina (F)

PO Box 4800, Carolina PR 00984-4800
County: San Juan FICE Identification: 030160
Unit ID: 243142
Telephone: (787) 257-0000 Carnegie Class: Bac/Diverse
FAX Number: (787) 750-7940 Calendar System: Quarter
URL: www.uprc.edu
Established: 1974 Annual Undergrad Tuition & Fees (In-State): $3,026
Enrollment: 3,843 Coed
Affiliation or Control: State IRS Status: 501(c)3
Highest Offering: Baccalaureate
Program:
Accreditation: M, ACBSP

02 Chancellor Dr. Moises ORENGO
05 Dean of Academic Affairs Dr. Awilda NUNEZ
11 Dean Administrative Affairs Prof. Víctor PÉREZ
32 Dean Student Affairs Dr. Jaime CABRERA
06 Registrar Mr. Abelardo MARTINEZ
15 Human Resources Director Mr. Gregory BERMUDEZ
09 Director of Planning/Inst Research Prof. Carmen L. CRUZ
08 Director Learning Resources Center Prof. Stanley PORTELA
51 Director Continuing Education Mrs. Luaida OYOLA
07 Admissions Officer Mrs. Celia MENDEZ
13 Coord/Dir Computer Sys Center Mr. Liberty ROLON
37 Financial Aid Director Mr. Rafael RUIZ
22 Affirmative Action Officer Mrs. Rosa QUINONES
88 Director Graphic Arts/Advertising Dr. Carmen ORTIZ
50 Director Banking/Finance/Insurance Prof. George OTERO
81 Director Natural Sciences Dr. Maristella RESTO
88 Director Secretarial Sciences Prof. Josefina RODRIGUEZ
83 Director Social Sciences Dr. Gerardo PERFECTO
68 Director Physical Education Prof. Walbert MARCANO
88 Director Auto Tech/Mech Engineering Prof. Narcisa MEZA
79 Director Humanities Dra. Amalia ALSINA
88 Director Spanish Dr. Mayra ENCARNACION
88 Director English Prof. Wanda RODRIGUEZ
88 Dean Hotel Administration School Dr. Paul RIVERA
23 Director Health Care Dr. Zaida DIAZ
18 Supt Operations & Maintenance Mr. Herman MUNIZ
41 Athletic Director Mr. Arcadio OCASIO
96 Director of Purchasing Vacant
10 Chief Business Officer Mrs. Sarahi GUADALUPE

*University of Puerto Rico at Cayey (G)

PO BOX 372230, Cayey PR 00737-2230
County: Cayey FICE Identification: 007206
Unit ID: 243151
Telephone: (787) 738-2161 Carnegie Class: Bac/Diverse
FAX Number: (787) 738-8039 Calendar System: Semester
URL: www.cayey.upr.edu
Established: 1967 Annual Undergrad Tuition & Fees (In-State): $4,848
Enrollment: 3,687 Coed
Affiliation or Control: State IRS Status: 501(c)3
Highest Offering: Baccalaureate
Program: Teacher Preparatory; Professional; Business Emphasis
Accreditation: M, ACBSP, TED

02 Chancellor Dr. Mario MEDINA
05 Dean of Academic Affairs Dr. Raul CASTRO
11 Dean of Administration Affairs Prof. Belma BORRAS
32 Dean of Student Affairs Dr. Rochellie MARTINEZ
08 Director Library Dr. Juan BERRIOS
06 Registrar Mrs. Daisy RAMOS
15 Director Human Resources Mrs. Gema FIGUEROA
56 Head Extension Division Mr. Jesus MARTINEZ
37 Director Student Financial Aid Mrs. Sonia PLACERES
38 Director Student Counseling Dr. Carilu PEREZ
36 Interim Director Student Placement Mrs. Rosa ORTIZ
13 Director Computer Center Mrs. Minerva DIAZ
45 Director Planning & Development Prof. Fernando VAZQUEZ-CALLE
07 Director Admissions Mr. Wilfredo LOPEZ
18 Director Facilities/Physical Plant Mr. Hector FELIX
23 Director Health Services Dr. Sandra LISBOA

19 Director Security/Safety Mr. Carlos VAZQUEZ
92 Director Honor Program Prof. Irmannette TORRES-LUGO
20 Associate Academic Officer Dr. Maria I. RODRIGUEZ
41 Director Athletic Program Prof. Efrain COLON
29 Director Alumni Relations Mrs. Leilany C. RIVERA
96 Director Purchasing Mrs. Maria CORTES
43 Director Legal Services Mr. Francisco MORENO
88 Student Ombudsman Prof. Rolando CID
53 Education Dr. Ricardo MOLINA
79 Humanities Prof. Harry HERNANDEZ
83 Social Sciences Dr. Angel RODRIGUEZ
88 Hispanic Studies Prof. Jose PEREZ
88 English Prof. David LIZARDI
81 Chemistry Vacant
65 Natural Science Dr. Glorivee ROSARIO
88 Biology Dr. Rosa del C TORRES
94 Women's Studies Dr. Sarah MALAVE
09 Director Assess & Inst Research Prof. Fernando VAZQUEZCALLE
10 Chief Business Officer Mrs. Lourdes VEGA
88 Director Budgeting Mrs. Maria SANTIAGO
81 Mathematics-Physics Vacant
50 Business Administration Vacant
72 Technology & Office Administration Prof. Awilda M. CARABALLO
68 Physical Education Prof. Efrain COLON
88 RISE Program Dr. Robert ROSS
88 Commission on Prevention of Viol Dr. Jose VARGAS
88 Iterdisciplinary Research Institute Ms. Vionex MARTI
88 Museum Dr. Humberto FIGUEROA
100 Chief of Staff Prof. Gladys RAMOS
101 Secretary of the Institution/Board Mrs. Sylvia TUBENS
104 Director Study Abroad Mr. Arturo J. COLLADO

*University of Puerto Rico-Humacao (A)

Call box 860, Humacao PR 00792

County: Humacao FICE Identification: 003943
Unit ID: 243179
Telephone: (787) 850-0000 Carnegie Class: Bac/Diverse
FAX Number: (787) 852-4638 Calendar System: Semester
URL: www.uprh.edu
Established: 1962 Annual Undergrad Tuition & Fees (In-State): $2,049
Enrollment: 3,628 Coed
Affiliation or Control: State IRS Status: 501(c)3
Highest Offering: Baccalaureate
Program: Liberal Arts And General; Teacher Preparatory
Accreditation: M, ACBSP, ADNUR, ENGT, NUR, PTAA, SW, TED

02 Chancellor Dr. Efraín VÁZQUEZ
05 Dean of Academic Affairs Dr. Carlos GALIANO
11 Dean Administrative Affairs Prof. Luis R. RODRIGUEZ
04 Assistant to the Chancellor Lic. Ricardo DIAZ
32 Dean of Student Affairs Prof. Ricardo ROHENA
20 Assistant Dean of Academic Affairs Dr. Anibal MUÑOZ
09 Dir Planning/IR and Accreditation Prof. Jose A. BALDAGUEZ
06 Registrar Mr. Jorge ACEVEDO
07 Director of Admissions Mrs. Milagros ALVAREZ
08 Director of the Library Mr. Luis RODRÍGUEZ
13 Dir Computer/Commun & Info Mgmt Eng. Luis GONZALEZ
15 Director Human Resources Mrs. Janice A. MARTINEZ
10 Director of Finance Mrs. Ines SANCHEZ
37 Asst Financial Aid Officer Mrs. Brunilda LÓPEZ
88 Director Interdis/Intreg Dev Std Dr. Castula SANTIAGO
51 Dir Continuing Education/Extension Dr. José M. ENCARNACIÓN
23 Director Health Services Vacant
18 Chief Facilities/Physical Plant Eng. Daniel ROSARIO
19 Director Security/Safety Mr. Jerry DIAZ
96 Purchase Supervisor Mr. Javier A. MUYET
88 Student Ombuds Person Prof. Elizabeth R. HODGUES
41 Athletic Activities Director Mr. Elmer WILLIAMS
21 Director of Budget Office Mrs. Iris N. CARRASQUILLO
108 Office of Institutional Assessment Mrs. Viviana CRUZ
88 Director Svcs Population Disabil Prof. Carmen SEPÚLVEDA
101 Sec of Academic Senate/Adm Board Prof. Amelia MALDONADO
29 Alumni Relations Mrs. Jose N. GONZALEZ
88 Envir Health & Occupational Safety Mrs. Angélica TORRES
27 Press Relations Mrs. Iraida CINTRON
50 Director of Business Administration Prof. Enrique SUAREZ
88 Director of Biology Dept Dr. Hector AYALA
88 Director of Chemistry Dept Dr. Rolando TREMONT
60 Director of Communication Dept Prof. Hector PIÑERO
53 Director of Education Dept Dr. Luz I. RIVERA
88 Director of English Dept Dr. Giovanna BALAGUER
79 Director of Humanities Dept Dr. Zoé JIMENEZ
81 Director of Mathematics Dept Prof. Barbara SANTIAGO
66 Director of Nursing Dept Prof. Alba PEREZ
88 Dir of Occupational Therapy Dept Prof. Mayra LEBRON
88 Director of Office System Adm Dept Prof. Ivelisse REYES
88 Director of Physical Therapy Dept Prof. Carmen E. COTTO
88 Dir of Physics & Electronics Dept Dr. Rogerio FURLAN
83 Director of Social Science Dept Dr. Alice OUSLAN
70 Director of Social Work Dept Dr. Evelyn CRUZ
88 Director of Spanish Dept Dr. Carmen ORAMA
92 Dir of Academic Honor Program Dept Dr. Maria MULERO
88 Dir of Communication Competences Prof. Margarita PARRILLA
88 Graphics Art Supervisor Mr. Carlos LAZÚ
22 Dir Affirmative Action/EEO Mrs. Mariolga ROTGER
88 Director of Cultural Activities Dr. José E. HERNÁNDEZ
88 Director of CEITICA Dr. Alex CAMACHO
46 Dir Subsidized Research & Programs Dr. Lilliam CASILLA
88 Director Day Care Center Mrs. Carmen LUNA

*University of Puerto Rico-Mayaguez Campus (B)

PO Box 9000, Mayaguez PR 00681-9000

County: Mayaguez FICE Identification: 003944
Unit ID: 243197
Telephone: (787) 832-4040 Carnegie Class: DRU
FAX Number: (787) 834-3031 Calendar System: Semester
URL: www.uprm.edu
Established: 1911 Annual Undergrad Tuition & Fees (In-State): $2,212
Enrollment: 12,130 Coed
Affiliation or Control: State IRS Status: 501(c)3
Highest Offering: Doctorate
Program: Occupational; Liberal Arts And General; Teacher Preparatory; Professional
Accreditation: M, ENG, NUR, TED

02 Chancellor Dr. John FERNANDEZ VAN CLEVE
05 Dean of Academic Affairs Dr. Jaime SEGUEL
10 Dean of Administration Prof. Lucas N. AVILÉS RODRÍGUEZ
32 Dean of Students Dr. Francisco MALDONADO FORTUNET
49 Dean of Arts & Sciences Dr. Manuel VALDÉS PIZZINI
54 Dean of Engineering Dr. Agustín RULLÁN
47 Acting Dean Agricultural Sciences Dr. Raul MACCHIAVELLI
50 Dean Business Administration Prof. Ana MARTIN
58 Acting Director of Graduate Studies Dr. Didier VALDES
13 Director of Computer Center Mr. Martin MELENDEZ
06 Registrar Mrs. Xenia RAMÍREZ
08 Director of the Library Prof. Elsie TORRES
07 Director of Admissions Sra. Maria ALEMAÑY
37 Dir Student Financial Aid Mrs. Nannette HERNÁNDEZ
36 Director Student Placement Mrs. Nancy NIEVES
26 Press Office Director Mrs. Mariam L. ROSA VELEZ
45 Director Inst Research/Planning Prof. Mercedes FERRER
29 Director Alumni Association Miss Yomarachaliff LUCIANO-FIGUEROA
15 Director Personnel Services Mrs. Lissette V. GONZÁLEZ
18 Acting Director Physical Resources Eng. Wilson ORTIZ
38 Acting Director Student Counseling Dra. Zaida CALDERON
21 Director Financial Services Mr. Angél F. PÉREZ PACHECO
51 Director Continuing Education Prof. Silvestre COLÓN
19 Acting Director Security/Safety Ms. Marisabel FERNANDEZ
23 Director Health Services Mrs. Rosie TORRES
41 Director Athletic Activities Mr. Ray QUINONES
43 Director Legal Services Lcda. Gretchen HUYKE
108 Director Institutional Assessment Prof. Betsy MORALES

*University of Puerto Rico-Medical Sciences Campus (C)

PO Box 365067, San Juan PR 00936-5067

County: San Juan FICE Identification: 024600
Unit ID: 243203
Telephone: (787) 758-2525 Carnegie Class: Spec/Med
FAX Number: (787) 758-2556 Calendar System: Other
URL: www.rcm.upr.edu
Established: 1950 Annual Undergrad Tuition & Fees (In-State): $4,369
Enrollment: 2,221 Coed
Affiliation or Control: State IRS Status: 501(c)3
Highest Offering: Doctorate
Program: Professional
Accreditation: M, ANEST, #AUD, CAHIIM, CYTO, DA, DENT, DIETI, HSA, MED, MIDWF, MT, NMT, NURSE, OT, PH, PHAR, PTA, RAD, SP

02 Chancellor Dr. Noel J. AYMAT SANTANA
05 Dean Academic Affairs Dr. Ramon GONZALEZ
32 Dean Students Affairs Dr. Nitza RIVERA
11 Dean of Administration Prof. Carlos ORTIZ
63 Dean School of Medicine Dr. Edgar COLON NEGRON
52 Dean School Dental Medicine Dr. Ana LOPEZ
69 Dean Grad School Public Health Dr. Ralph RIVERA
67 Dean School of Pharmacy Dr. Wanda MALDONADO
76 Dean School Health Prof Dr. Barbara SEGARRA
66 Dean School of Nursing Dr. Suane SANCHEZ
100 Chief of Staff Mrs. Lilia FIGUERA
20 Associate Academic Officer Dr. Jose CAPRILES
13 Director Information Technology Mr. Francisco PEREZ
43 Director Legal Services Mrs. Irene REYES
26 Chief Information Officer Mr. Angel HOYOS
06 Registrar Mr. Reinaldo POMALES
08 Library Director Dr. Irma QUINONES
09 Director Inst & Academic Research Dr. Wanda BARRETO
24 Director Educational Media Prof. Luis ESTREMERA
35 Director Student Affairs Mrs. Rosa VELEZ
07 Director of Admissions Mrs. Maribel ORTIZ
38 Director of Student Counseling Prof. Blanca AMOROS
37 Director of Student Financial Aid Mrs. Yolanda RIVERA
10 Chief Financial Officer Mrs. Yolanda QUIÑONES
15 Director Personnel Services Mrs. Maria Teresa GONZALEZ
18 Chief Facilities/Physical Plant Mr. Julio A. COLLAZO
96 Director of Purchasing Mr. Jose CARDONA
19 Director Security Office Mr. William FIGUEROA
108 Director Institutional Assessment Prof. Lillian RIOS
25 Chief Contracts/Grants Admin Dr. Marcia CRUZ

*University of Puerto Rico at Ponce (D)

PO Box 7186, Ponce PR 00732-7186

County: Ponce FICE Identification: 009652
Unit ID: 243212
Telephone: (787) 844-8181 Carnegie Class: Bac/Diverse
FAX Number: (787) 844-8679 Calendar System: Semester
URL: www.uprp.edu
Established: 1970 Annual Undergrad Tuition & Fees (In-State): $14,442
Enrollment: 3,229 Coed
Affiliation or Control: State IRS Status: 501(c)3
Highest Offering: Baccalaureate
Program: Occupational; Liberal Arts And General
Accreditation: M, ACBSP, ENGT, PTAA, TED

02 Chancellor Dr. Leonardo MORALES
04 Executive Officer III Mrs. Reina M. GONZALEZ
04 Assistant to the Chancellor Dr. Drianfel E. VAZQUEZ
05 Dean Academic Affairs Dr. Jose V. MADERA
11 Dean Administrative Affairs Prof. Enrico ENCARNACION
32 Dean Student Affairs Mrs. Acmin VELAZQUEZ
20 Associate Academic Dean Mrs. Joycette SANTOS
45 Dir Inst Research/Planning Officer Dr. Jennifer ALICEA
08 Director Library Prof. Brett DIAZ
06 Registrar Mrs. Marya Z. SANTIAGO
38 Director of Student Counseling Dr. Efrain RIOS
07 Director of Admissions Mrs. Emily MATOS
37 Director of Financial Aid Mr. Arturo ALMODOVAR
15 Director of Personnel Services Mr. Juan C. LEON
88 Director of Cultural Activities Mr. Jose L. PONS
13 Director of Computer Center Mr. Juan VEGA
18 Chief Facilities/Physical Plant Mr. Alberto GARCIA
40 Director Bookstore Vacant
41 Athletic Director Mrs. Lesbia COLON
23 Director Health Services Dr. Sandra I. TOUCET
29 Director Alumni Relations Mrs. Valerie DÍAZ
30 Chief Development Vacant
19 Director of Security/Traffic Mr. German PIMENTEL
88 Coordinator Security/Safety Mrs. Celia GONZÁLEZ
22 Coordinator Affirmative Action Mrs. Ginny VELEZ

*University of Puerto Rico-Rio Piedras Campus (E)

PO Box 23300, Rio Piedras PR 00931-3300

County: San Juan FICE Identification: 007108
Unit ID: 243221
Telephone: (787) 763-7099 Carnegie Class: RU/H
FAX Number: (787) 764-8799 Calendar System: Semester
URL: www.uprrp.edu
Established: 1903 Annual Undergrad Tuition & Fees (In-State): $2,019
Enrollment: 15,659 Coed
Affiliation or Control: State IRS Status: 501(c)3
Highest Offering: Doctorate
Program: Liberal Arts And General; Teacher Preparatory; Professional
Accreditation: M, ACBSP, BUS, CORE, CS, DIETD, JOUR, LAW, LIB, PLNG, SPAA, SW, TED

02 Chancellor Dr. Carlos E. SEVERINO VALDEZ
05 Dean Academic Affairs Dr. Palmira RIOS GONZÁLEZ
11 Dean of Administration Dr. Grisel E. MELÉNDEZ RAMOS
32 Dean of Students Dr. Gloria DÍAZ URBINA
20 Associate Dean Academic Affairs Dr. Agnes BOSCH
50 Dean Business Administration Dr. José A. GONZÁLEZ TABOADA
48 Dean of Architecture Prof. Francisco RODRIGUEZ
81 Dean of Natural Sciences Dr. Carlos GONZÁLEZ
83 Dean of Social Sciences Dr. Dagmar GUARDIOLA
61 Dean of Law Ms. Vivian NEPTUNE
97 Dean of General Studies Dr. Carlos RODRIGUEZ
79 Dean of Humanities Dr. Maria de los A CASTRO
58 Dean Graduate Studies/ Research Dr. Pedro J. RODRIGUEZ ESQUERDO
53 Dean of Education Dr. Roamé TORRES
35 Asst Dean Student Affairs Ms. Estela PEREZ RIESTRA
38 Director of Student Counseling Mrs. Maria JIMENEZ CHAFEY
30 Int Dir Devel & Alumni Relations Mrs. Elsa MARIN
06 Registrar Mr. Juan M. APONTE
08 Director of Library System Dr. Ada M. FELICIE
15 Director of Human Resources Mrs. Aida ROSARIO
07 Director of Admissions Mrs. Cruz Belinda VALENTIN
13 Director of Computer Center Mr. Alfredo FIGUEROA
62 Director Grad Sch Library/Info Sci Dr. José SÁNCHEZ
60 Director School of Communication Dr. Jimmy TORRES
58 Dir Graduate Sch of Planning Dr. Carmen CONCEPCIÓN
51 Dir Continuing Educ/Extension Dr. Carlos ROSADO
09 Director of Institutional Research Prof. Zulyn RODRIGUEZ
18 Chief Planning/Physical Devel Ofc Arq. Cesar VISSEPÓ
26 Chief Public Relations Officer Mrs. Lorna CASTRO
37 Director of Student Financial Aid Mr. Anibal ALVALLE
96 Director of Purchasing Mrs. Ivonne MATIENZO-CARRERO

*University of Puerto Rico at Utuado (F)

PO Box 2500, Utuado PR 00641-2500

County: Utuado FICE Identification: 029384
Unit ID: 243188
Telephone: (787) 894-2828 Carnegie Class: Bac/Diverse
FAX Number: (787) 894-1081 Calendar System: Semester
URL: www.uprutuado.edu
Established: 1979 Annual Undergrad Tuition & Fees (In-State): $2,212
Enrollment: 1,385 Coed
Affiliation or Control: State IRS Status: 501(c)3
Highest Offering: Baccalaureate
Program: Occupational; 2-Year Principally Bachelor's Creditable; Liberal Arts And General; Teacher Preparatory; Business Emphasis
Accreditation: M, ACBSP, TED

02 Chancellor ..... Prof. Raquel G. VARGAS GOMEZ
05 Academic Dean ..... Prof. Horacio SERRANO
10 Chief Business Officer ..... Dr. Lisette MARRERO
32 Chief Student Life Officer ..... Prof. Ana ARCE
08 Library Director ..... Prof. Yesenia HERNANDEZ
09 Director Institutional Research ..... Dr. Javier LUGO
06 Registrar ..... Mrs. Ivelisse RIVERA
07 Director of Admission ..... Mrs. María V. ROBLES
15 Int Director Human Resources ..... Ms. Luz E. MARTÍNEZ
38 Director Student Counseling ..... Mr. Amilcar GONZALEZ
37 Director Student Financial Aid ..... Mrs. Edymariel CORTES
13 Director Information Systems ..... Mr. Hector L. LOPEZ
18 Chief Facilities/Physical Plant ..... Vacant
19 Director Security/Safety ..... Mr. Miguel TORRES
41 Director of Athletics ..... Mr. Miguel RODRIGUEZ
47 Director of Agriculture ..... Prof. Eladio GONZALEZ
50 Dir Office Systems/Business Admin ..... Dr. Luis A. TAPIA
96 Director of Purchasing ..... Ms. Deborah RODRÍGUEZ
51 Director Continuing Education ..... Mr. Miguel SALVA
53 Director Education ..... Mrs. Vilmaris CESTEROS
65 Director Natural Sciences ..... Prof. Osvaldo LAMBOY
79 Director Humanities/Spanish/English ..... Prof. Hector M. REYES

University of the Sacred Heart (A)

PO Box 12383, San Juan PR 00914-8505

County: San Juan FICE Identification: 003937
Unit ID: 243443
Telephone: (787) 728-1515 Carnegie Class: Master's M
FAX Number: (787) 728-1692 Calendar System: Semester
URL: www.sagrado.edu
Established: 1935 Annual Undergrad Tuition & Fees: $5,700
Enrollment: 5,261 Coed
Affiliation or Control: Roman Catholic IRS Status: 501(c)3
Highest Offering: Master's
Program: Occupational; Liberal Arts And General; Teacher Preparatory; Professional
Accreditation: M, SW, TED

01 President ..... Dr. Gilberto MARXUACH-TORROS
84 Chief of Staff/Dir Enrollment Mgmt ..... Mrs. Lourdes BERTRAN-PASARELL
05 Dean Academic/Student Affairs ..... Dr. Lydia ESPINET
11 Dean of Administration ..... Mr. Jose L. RICCI
30 Dean of Development ..... Prof. Adlin RIOS
10 Int Chief Financial Officer ..... Mrs. Rebecca QUINTERO
20 Associate Academic Dean ..... Prof. Yezmin HERNANDEZ-SOTO
32 Associate Students Dean ..... Prof. Pedro FRAILE
09 Director of Inst Research Office ..... Dr. Maria DEL C. RODRIGUEZ
07 Director of Admissions ..... Prof. Lilia PLANELL
06 Registrar ..... Ms. Mildred PINEIRO
26 Chief Public Relations Officer .. Mrs. Maria E. MADRID-GUZMAN
21 Director of Budgeting ..... Mrs. Maribel VALENTIN
91 Director Admin Computer Center ..... Ms. Carmen CINTRON
18 Chief Facilities/Physical Plant ..... Mr. Jose L. RICCI
15 Director Human Resources ..... Ms. Sol A. GOMILA
29 Director Alumni Relations ..... Mrs. Elizabeth VARGAS
08 Head Librarian ..... Mrs. Sonia DIAZ
37 Director of Financial Aid ..... Ms. June C. ANDRADE
39 Director Student Housing ..... Ms. Livia D. PASTRANA
41 Athletic Director ..... Mr. Jose L. BURGOS
50 Director Business Administration ..... Prof. Marta ALMEYDA
53 Director Education Department ..... Dr. Migdalia OQUENDO
81 Director Natural Sciences ..... Prof. Agda CARDERO
79 Dir Fac Intdspln Human/Social Stds ..... Prof. Isabel YAMÍN
21 Internal Auditor ..... Mr. Ricardo AGUIRRE
24 Dir Center for FAC/Rchmnt/Educ Tech ..... Mrs. Sylvia ALVAREZ
51 Assoc Director Continuing Education ..... Mrs. Elvia AGOSTO
19 Director Security/Safety ..... Capt. Jose LOZADA
88 Coord Educ Tech CFRET/FAC/Rchmnt ..... Ms. Sylvia ALVAREZ

VIRGIN ISLANDS

University of the Virgin Islands (B)

#2 John Brewers Bay, Saint Thomas VI 00802-9990

FICE Identification: 003946
Unit ID: 243665
Telephone: (340) 776-9200 Carnegie Class: Bac/Diverse
FAX Number: (340) 693-1005 Calendar System: Semester
URL: www.uvi.edu
Established: 1962 Annual Undergrad Tuition & Fees (In-State): $4,794
Enrollment: 2,110 Coed
Affiliation or Control: State IRS Status: 501(c)3
Highest Offering: Doctorate
Program: 2-Year Principally Bachelor's Creditable; Liberal Arts And General; Teacher Preparatory; Professional
Accreditation: M, ADNUR, NUR

01 President ..... Dr. David HALL
88 VP/Business Development/Innovation ..... Dr. Haldane DAVIES
100 Chief of Staff ..... Vacant
04 Executive Asst to President ..... Ms. Una DYER
101 Liaison to the Board ..... Ms. Gail T. STEELE
22 Dir Affirmative Action/EEO ..... Vacant
05 Provost/Vice Pres Academic Affairs ..... Dr. Camille MCKAYLE-STOLZ
46 Interim Vice Provost/ECC/RPS ..... Dr. Frank MILLS
25 Asst Dir Spec Proj/Grants/Agreement ..... Vacant
53 Dean School of Education ..... Dr. Linda THOMAS
81 Interim Dean College of Sci & Math ..... Dr. Sandra ROMANO
50 Dean School of Business ..... Dr. Stephen REAMES
79 Interim Dean Col Lib Arts/Soc Sci ..... Dr. Marie ENGERMAN
66 Dean School of Nursing ..... Ms. Beverly A. LANSIQUOT
104 Co-Director Study Abroad/Spanish ..... Dr. Maria DELGADO
104 Co-Director Study Abroad/French ..... Mr. Robert TERRASI
84 Vice Provost Access/Enroll Services ..... Dr. Nicole L. GIBBS
07 Dir Admissions/Recruitment ..... Dr. Xuri M. ALLEN
06 Registrar ..... Ms. Monifa POTTER
37 Director of Financial Aid ..... Ms. Cheryl A. ROBERTS
41 Athletics Director ..... Mr. Curtis GILPIN
31 Dir Community/Personal Develop ..... Ms. ILene HEYWARD
32 Dean of Students-STT Campus ..... Ms. Verna J. RIVERS
36 Dir Counseling & Career Services ..... Ms. Patricia TOWAL
38 Director of Counseling Services ..... Ms. Dahlia STRIDIRON
39 Student Housing Supervisor/STT ..... Mr. Sean GEORGES
32 Dean of Students-AAS Campus ..... Mr. Stephan T. MOORE
106 Online Education/E-learning ..... Dr. Christy L. VINEYARD
30 VP Institutional Advancement ..... Mr. Mitchell NEAVES
29 Director of Alumni Affairs ..... Ms. Linda SMITH
44 Capital Campaign Manager ..... Mr. Jose Raul CARRILLO
26 Director Public Relations ..... Ms. Nanyamka FARRELLY
88 Special Events Coordinator ..... Ms. Liza MARGOLIS
102 Dir Corp/Foundation/Govt Relations ..... Mr. Richard CLEAVER
96 Purchasing Supervisor ..... Mr. Eric CHRISTIAN
105 Webmaster ..... Ms. Moneca K. PINKETT
10 VP Administration & Finance ..... Ms. Shirley LAKE-KING
21 Controller ..... Ms. Peggy SMITH
15 Director of HR/Org Development ..... Mr. Charles Ronald MEEK
16 Assoc Dir HR/Org Development ..... Vacant
40 Bookstore Manager-STT Campus ..... Mr. Mervin V. TAYLOR
40 Bookstore Manager-AAS Campus ..... Ms. Laurel A. HECKER
19 Acting Chief/Campus Police/ Security ..... Mr. Theodore E. GLASFORD
18 Director of Physical Plant ..... Mr. Charles MARTIN
13 VP/Info Technology and Assessment ..... Ms. Tina M. KOOPMANS
14 Assistant Chief Information Officer ..... Ms. Sharlene J. HARRIS
08 Director of Libraries ..... Ms. Judith ROGERS
27 Marketing Manager ..... Ms. Caroline POLYDORE-SIMON
09 Program Coordinator/Inst Research ..... Mrs. Laurence BLAKE

University of the Virgin Islands-St. Croix (C)

RR1 10,000, Kingshill VI 00850-9781

Telephone: (340) 778-1620 Identification: 770173
Accreditation: &M

† Branch campus of University of the Virgin Islands, Saint Thomas, VI.

Index of Key Administrators

A

ABSTON, Byron .... 205-391-2388.... 7 A
babston@sheltonstate.edu
ABSTON, Kara .... 501-279-4442.. 21 A
kabston@harding.edu
ABT, William, R .... 262-551-6200 535 E
wabt@carthage.edu
ABTS, Betsy .... 253-566-5326 527 C
babts@tacomacc.edu
ABU-GHAZALEH, Nabil . 619-644-7100.. 46 H
ABUHAMAD, Alfred, Z .. 757-446-7979 507 B
abuhamaz@evms.edu
ABUKHALAF, Ronnie .... 561-912-2166 102 N
rabukhalaf@evergladesuniversity.edu
ABUSHABAN, Sahar ..... 619-660-4654.. 46 G
sahar.abushaban@gcccd.edu
ABUTIN, Albert .... 714-992-7076.. 56 F
aabutin@fullcoll.edu
ABUZNEID,
Abdelshakour, A .... 203-576-4113.. 92 B
abuzneid@bridgeport.edu
ACARDO, John .... 815-825-2086 149 E
john.acardo@kishwaukeecollege.edu
ACCAPADI, Mamta .... 407-646-2185 111 H
maccapadi@rollins.edu
ACCARDI, Michael .... 978-837-5062 233 G
accardim@merrimack.edu
ACCIARDO, Linda, A ..... 401-874-2116 442 E
lindaa@advance.uri.edu
ACCOMANDO, Annette .. 504-278-6422 204 B
aaccomando@nunez.edu
ACCORD, Richard, D .... 304-462-6182 532 G
richard.accord@glenville.edu
ACEBO, Kayla 918-631-2565 403M
kayla-acebo@utulsa.edu
ACEVEDO, Beatriz .... 212-924-5900 349 D
bursar@swedishinstitute.edu
ACEVEDO, Dary .... 787-891-0925 553 E
dacevedo@aguadilla.inter.edu
ACEVEDO, Francisco ..... 787-264-1912 554 C
facevedo@intersg.edu
ACEVEDO, Gerald, C ..... 847-592-6600 156 B
gacevedo@princeinstitute.edu
ACEVEDO, Ivonne .... 787-891-0925 553 E
iaecheva@ns.inter.edu
ACEVEDO, Jorge .... 787-850-9380 558 A
jorge.acevedo4@upr.edu
ACEVEDO, Luis .... 787-250-1912 554 A
laacevedo@metro.inter.edu
ACEVEDO, Luis, A .... 787-891-0925 553 E
luacevedo@aguadilla.inter.edu
ACEVES, Salvador, D .... 303-458-4144.. 85 G
saceves@regis.edu
ACH, Richard .... 928-350-4501.. 17 K
richard.ach@prescott.edu
ACHARYA, Suresh .... 269-749-7666 249 A
sacharya@olivetcollege.edu
ACHEMIRE, Roy .... 918-293-4724 400 E
roy.achemire@okstate.edu
ACHENBACH, USMS,
Gerard .... 231-995-1203 248 C
gachenbach@nmc.edu
ACHENBACH, Laurie ..... 618-453-7984 159 H
laurie@science.siu.edu
ACHESON, Carol .... 503-253-3443 408 B
cacheson@ocom.edu
ACHING, Gerard, L .... 607-255-4625 323 C
gla23@cornell.edu
ACHS, Carol .... 480-461-7742.. 15 A
carol.achs@mesacc.edu
ACHTER, John .... 715-232-2468 541 B
achterj@uwstout.edu
ACHTERBERG,
Cheryl, L .... 614-292-2461 389 A
achterberg.1@osu.edu
ACHTERMAN, Douglas .. 408-848-4809.. 45 G
dachterman@gavilan.edu
ACIERNO, Lou .... 212-752-1530 330 C
lou.acierno@limcollege.edu
ACK, Nicole .... 360-867-5371 522 J
ackn@evergreen.edu
ACKER, Janet .... 207-985-7976 210 H
janetacker@landingschool.edu
ACKERKNECHT,
Steven, M .... 518-255-5214 346 E
ackerksm@cobleskill.edu
ACKERLEY, Roseanne ... 513-487-3234 327 C
rackerley@huc.edu
ACKERMAN, Aidan .... 617-262-5000 223 G
Aidan.Ackerman@the-bac.edu
ACKERMAN, Dean .... 812-888-4447 174 F
ackerman@vinu.edu
ACKERMAN, Debbie ...... 217-732-3155 150 H
dackerman@lincolncollege.edu
ACKERMAN, Deborah ... 503-253-3443 408 B
dackerman@ocom.edu
ACKERMAN, Denise ...... 845-758-7625 315 G
ackerman@bard.edu
ACKERMAN, Judy .... 240-567-5010 217 B
judy.ackerman@montgomerycollege.edu
ACKERMAN, Kathy .... 828-395-1522 363 D
kackerman@isothermal.edu
ACKERMAN, Tom .... 352-271-2905 112 H
thomas.ackerman@sfcollege.edu
ACKERMAN, Traci .... 954-492-5353 100 G
ackerman@citycollege.edu
ACKERMANN, Arthur, J 314-935-5582 285 E
ackermann@wustl.edu
ACKERSON, Kelly .... 858-653-3000.. 31 I
kackerson@calmu.edu
ACKLAND, Terri .... 520-494-5227.. 12 R
terri.ackland@centralaz.edu
ACKLEH, Azmy .... 337-482-6986 208 F
asa5773@louisiana.edu
ACKLEY, Brian .... 607-844-8222 350 A
ackleyb@TC3.edu
ACKLEY, Darren .... 715-675-3331 544 A
ackley@ntc.edu
ACKLEY, Lavon .... 229-430-0415 119 I
lackley@albanytech.edu
ACORACE, Joan .... 603-206-8012 297 A
jacorace@ccsnh.edu
ACOSTA, Araceli .... 210-924-4338 469 B
araceli.acosta@bua.edu
ACOSTA, Esmeralda, M 623-845-3012.. 14 N
esmeralda.acosta@gccaz.edu
ACOSTA, Lydia, M .... 954-262-4640 109 E
lacosta@nsu.nova.edu
ACOSTA, Maria .... 773-838-7984 142 C
macosta68@ccc.edu
ACOSTA, Pilar .... 407-708-2432 113 A
acostap@seminolestate.edu
ACOSTA, R. Alexander .. 305-348-1118 114 G
ACOSTA, Reynold .... 407-303-8016.. 97 J
reynold.acosta@adu.edu
ACOSTA, Vanessa .... 714-966-8500.. 75 F
vacosta@ves.edu
ACOSTA-FUMERO,
Carmen, J .... 787-841-2000 555 F
cacosta@pucpr.edu
ACQUAAH, George .... 301-860-3610 220 B
gacquaah@bowiestae.edu
ACREE, Cheryl .... 229-333-2126 134 I
cheryl.acree@wiregrass.edu
ACREE, Elizabeth, A ...... 520-621-5200.. 18 E
acree@email.arizona.edu
ACREE, Jenny .... 785-243-1435 186 A
jacree@cloud.edu
ACTON, Anne .... 617-422-7282 234 J
aacton@nesl.edu
ACTON, James .... 312-567-5000 147 E
jacton@iit.edu
ACTOR-ENGEL, Rose ..... 215-635-7300 419 D
raengel@gratz.edu
ACUESTA, Sylvia .... 718-636-3523 338 E
sacuesta@pratt.edu
ACUNA, Matt .... 714-556-3610.. 75 A
foundersclerk@vanguard.edu
ADACHI, Lesley, B .... 680-488-2471 550 C
lbadachi@gmail.com
ADACHI, Themy .... 510-430-3285.. 54 F
themy@mills.edu
ADADE, Anthony .... 508-929-8714 230 G
aadade@worcester.edu
ADADEVOH, Vidal .... 205-453-6300.. 96 H
ADAIR, Adam .... 870-512-7801.. 19 I
adam_adair@asun.edu
ADAIR, Brian .... 510-466-7269.. 59 C
badair@peralta.edu
ADAIR, Kathy .... 906-248-8404 240 J
kadair@bmcc.edu
ADAIR, Russell, K .... 203-432-4469.. 93 C
russell.adair@yale.edu
ADAIR, Wendy, H .... 713-313-7455 487 F
adairw@tsu.edu
ADAM, Baba .... 530-895-2987.. 30 B
adamba@butte.edu
ADAM, Charles, A .... 563-333-6151 182 E
AdamCharlesA@sau.edu
ADAM, Michelle .... 305-809-3279 104 A
ADAM, Nabil .... 973-353-5541 307 C
adam@adam.rutgers.edu
ADAM, Sharla .... 325-942-2041 489 E
sharla.adam@angelo.edu
ADAMES, Jose .... 214-860-2010 472 F
jose.adames@dcccd.edu
ADAMO, Clare .... 860-632-3009.. 90 H
library@holyapostles.edu
ADAMO, Paul, J .... 607-436-2535 344 B
adamopj@oneonta.edu
ADAMS, Adam .... 870-759-4142.. 25 I
aadams@wbcoll.edu
ADAMS, Amanda .... 423-354-5143 463 D
acadams@northeaststate.edu
ADAMS, Amy .... 614-236-6242 378 H
aadams@capital.edu
ADAMS, Ann .... 312-491-2869 155 D
a-adams@northwestern.edu
ADAMS, Ann .... 360-438-4382 525 H
aadams@stmartin.edu
ADAMS, Ann Clay .... 404-687-4524 123 C
adamsa@ctsnet.edu
ADAMS, Anthony, T ..... 334-229-5176.... 1 D
anthony-adams@alasu.edu
ADAMS, Barbara, B ...... 847-866-3939 145 C
barbara.adams@garrett.edu
ADAMS, Barbara, L ...... 803-536-8980 448 H
badams@scsu.edu
ADAMS, Barresa .... 478-445-7305 125 A
barresa.adams@gcsu.edu
ADAMS, Betty .... 713-797-7000 484 F
bnadams@pvamu.edu
ADAMS, Billy .... 254-647-3234 480 G
badams@rangercollege.edu
ADAMS, Blake .... 678-839-5053 133 F
badams@westga.edu
ADAMS, Brad .... 865-251-1800 460 J
badams@southcollegetn.edu
ADAMS, Brenda .... 501-450-1226.. 21 C
adams@hendrix.edu
ADAMS, Brett, C .... 443-352-4250 218 E
bcadams@stevenson.edu
ADAMS, Carey .... 314-719-3609 275 B
ADAMS, Carole .... 515-643-6601 181 B
cadams1@mercydesmoines.org
ADAMS, Catherine .... 706-396-8105 129 H
cladams@paine.edu
ADAMS, Cathryn .... 972-860-8269 472 D
cadams@dcccd.edu
ADAMS, Chadd .... 205-665-6155.... 9 C
cadams3@montevallo.edu
ADAMS, Chris .... 573-840-9666 283 D
cadams@trcc.edu
ADAMS, Christopher, J 631-451-4118 348 E
adamsc@sunysuffolk.edu
ADAMS, Corey .... 607-729-1581 324 A
cadams@davisny.edu
ADAMS, Cynthia .... 620-365-5116 184 C
adams@allencc.edu
ADAMS, Dana .... 773-508-8077 151 E
dadams2@luc.edu
ADAMS, Darly .... 620-223-2700 187 B
darlya@fortscott.edu
ADAMS, Dean .... 270-384-8036 198 C
adamsd@lindsey.edu
ADAMS, DeAnna .... 901-843-3885 460 F
registrar@rhodes.edu
ADAMS, Debbie .... 423-697-2493 462 C
debbie.adams@chattanoogastate.edu
ADAMS, Denise .... 530-895-2329.. 30 B
adamsde@butte.edu
ADAMS, Don .... 210-485-0088 466 J
dadams@alamo.edu
ADAMS, Edward .... 646-312-1190 318 C
Edward.Adams@baruch.cuny.edu
ADAMS, Elizabeth .... 912-583-3242 121 H
eadams@bpc.edu
ADAMS, Elizabeth, T .... 818-677-2969.. 34 D
elizabeth.t.adams@csun.edu
ADAMS, Ellen .... 718-631-6269 320 F
eadams@qcc.cuny.edu
ADAMS, Gary .... 218-733-2005 259 C
g.adams@lsc.edu
ADAMS, Gary .... 972-241-3371 472 A
gadams@dallas.edu
ADAMS, Grantley .... 860-738-6333.. 89 G
gadams@nwcc.commnet.edu
ADAMS, Gregory .... 414-288-1656 537 B
gregory.adams@marquette.edu
ADAMS, J. Milton .... 434-924-3728 514 A
jma@virginia.edu
ADAMS, Jacob .... 909-607-3318.. 39 E
jacob.adams@cgu.edu
ADAMS, James .... 201-200-3191 304 C
jadams@njcu.edu
ADAMS, JR., James ..... 859-257-6654 200 G
J.P.Adams@uky.edu
ADAMS, James, E .... 325-942-2071 489 E
james.adams@angelo.edu
ADAMS, Jan .... 903-510-3287 491 A
jada@tjc.edu
ADAMS, Jane, A .... 352-392-4574 115 D
jane-adams@ufl.edu
ADAMS, Janieth .... 601-979-0928 267 H
janieth.f.wilson_adams@jsums.edu
ADAMS, Jason .... 303-762-6936.. 82 C
jason.adams@denverseminary.edu
ADAMS, Jeffrey, M .... 336-841-4581 357 E
jeadams@highpoint.edu
ADAMS, Jeffrey, R .... 717-871-7462 431 E
jeffrey.adams@millersville.edu
ADAMS, Jennifer .... 925-473-7302.. 42 F
jadams@losmedanos.edu
ADAMS, Jennifer .... 334-347-2623.... 3 H
jadams@escc.edu
ADAMS, Jennifer .... 315-792-7810 348 D
jennifer.adams@sunyit.edu
ADAMS, Jennifer .... 614-236-6170 378 H
jadams@capital.edu
ADAMS, Jim, J .... 909-599-5433.. 50 H
jjadams@lifepacific.edu
ADAMS, John .... 570-662-4000 431 D
jadams@mansfield.edu
ADAMS, Joseph .... 301-985-7785 220 A
joseph.adams@umuc.edu
ADAMS, Joshua .... 707-524-1731.. 65 C
jadams2@santarosa.edu
ADAMS, Julie .... 973-655-7067 304 A
adamsju@mail.montclair.edu
ADAMS, Karen .... 785-242-5200 190 D
karen.adams@ottawa.edu
ADAMS, Karen .... 812-856-5596 167 J
kadams@iu.edu
ADAMS, Karen .... 918-495-7163 401 B
kaadams@oru.edu
ADAMS, Karen, H .... 812-856-5596 167 I
kadams@indiana.edu
ADAMS, Kelly, L .... 315-792-3047 351 G
kadams@utica.edu
ADAMS, Ken .... 412-359-1000 437 F
kadams@triangle-tech.edu
ADAMS, Ken .... 814-453-6016 437 D
ADAMS, Kent .... 620-672-5641 190 H
kenta@prattcc.edu
ADAMS, Kimberly .... 325-942-2122 489 E
kadams15@angelo.edu
ADAMS, Kimberly .... 253-752-2020 522 K
kimadams@faithseminary.edu
ADAMS, Kris .... 620-252-7137 186 C
adams.kris@coffeyville.edu
ADAMS, Linda .... 706-379-3111 134 J
leadams@yhc.edu
ADAMS, Linda .... 610-738-3892 432 B
ladams@wcupa.edu
ADAMS, Lisa .... 678-839-6428 133 F
ladams@westga.edu
ADAMS, Lita .... 413-748-3695 236 H
ladams@springfieldcollege.edu
ADAMS, Mack .... 575-527-7550 312 D
madams@nmsu.edu
ADAMS, Mark .... 208-885-4977 139 C
marka@uidaho.edu
ADAMS, Mark .... 936-294-1158 489 A
ucs_mca@shsu.edu
ADAMS, Marsha .... 256-824-6345.... 9 A
marsha.adams@uah.edu
ADAMS, Mary .... 956-364-4300 487 H
mary.adams@tstc.edu
ADAMS, Mary, A .... 303-991-1575.. 78 K
mary.adams@americansentinel.edu
ADAMS, Melvin .... 207-255-1305 212 G
melvin.adams@maine.edu
ADAMS, Michael .... 910-893-1686 355 C
adams@campbell.edu
ADAMS, Michael, J .... 888-777-7675 522 K
mjadams@faithseminary.edu
ADAMS, Michelle .... 603-641-7243 298 F
mkadams@anselm.edu
ADAMS, Molly-Dodd .... 352-588-8291 111 L
molly-dodd.adams@saintleo.edu
ADAMS, N. Scott .... 828-669-8012 359 K
nadams@montreat.edu
ADAMS, Neale, J .... 515-574-1284 179 F
adams_n@iowacentral.edu
ADAMS, Patrick .... 516-876-3194 345 E
adamsp@oldwestbury.edu
ADAMS, Paul .... 785-628-5866 187 A
padams@fhsu.edu
ADAMS, Paul, S .... 570-408-4114 440 B
paul.adams@wilkes.edu
ADAMS, Perrie, M .... 214-648-2258 496 A
perrie.adams@utsouthwestern.edu
ADAMS, Phillip, D .... 912-358-3059 131 A
adamsp@savannahstate.edu
ADAMS, Randall .... 202-885-8664.. 97 E
radams@wesleyseminary.edu
ADAMS, Rita, S .... 618-393-2982 146 F
adamsr@iecc.edu
ADAMS, Robert .... 575-492-2597 311 J
radams@nmjc.edu
ADAMS, Rodney .... 843-525-8219 449 E
radams@tcl.edu
ADAMS, Sarah .... 414-297-6595 543 E
adamss4@matc.edu
ADAMS, Shawn .... 404-627-2681 121 F
shawn.adams@beulah.org
ADAMS, Sheila, V .... 662-329-7299 269 B
svadams@muw.edu
ADAMS, Shirley, M .... 860-515-3836.. 88 B
sadams@charteroak.edu
ADAMS, Stephen .... 413-572-5394 230 F
sadams@westfield.ma.edu
ADAMS, Stevalynn, R .... 757-823-8373 510 H
ADAMS, Susanne, H ..... 910-755-7302 360 E
adamss@brunswickcc.edu
ADAMS, Tammy .... 361-354-2245 470 K
tadams@coastalbend.edu
ADAMS, Terri .... 202-806-7040.. 96 B
tadams-fuller@howard.edu
ADAMS, Tila .... 401-277-4909 442 B
madams@risd.edu

AHERN, Catherine 585-785-1273 325 E
catherine.ahern@flcc.edu
AHERN, Jack 413-545-2710 228 F
jfa@ipo.umass.edu
AHERN, Joseph, F 845-758-7178 315 G
ahern@bard.edu
AHERN, Karen 508-362-2131 231 D
kahern@capecod.edu
AHERN, Martin 617-984-1635 235 H
mahern@quincycollege.edu
AHERNE, John 845-341-4710 337 G
john.aherne@sunyorange.edu
AHERON, Michelle, L 336-322-2115 364 G
Michelle.Aheron@piedmontcc.edu
AHLBAUM, Mitch 212-772-4946 319 E
mahlbaum@hunter.cuny.edu
AHLBRAND, Eric 270-831-9848 196 C
eric.ahlbrand@kctcs.edu
AHLEMANN, Tina 843-574-6142 449 G
tina.ahlemann@tridenttech.edu
AHLQUIST, Michelle 320-762-4918 257 O
michellea@alextech.edu
AHMAD, Maria 765-455-9203 168 B
activities@iuk.edu
AHMED, Andrea 520-383-8401 18 A
aahmed@tocc.edu
AHMED, Haroon 909-962-6762 39 G
hahmed@cst.edu
AHMED, Haseeb 419-448-2284 383 C
hahmed@heidelberg.edu
AHMED, Jameel 812-877-8956 172 C
ahmed@rose-hulman.edu
AHMED, Juzar 812-465-7160 174 D
juzar@usi.edu
AHMED, M. Monir 909-537-3132 35 A
mahmed@csusb.edu
AHMED, Mirza, F 313-496-2674 252 A
fahmed1@wcccd.edu
AHMED, Mustaq 419-358-3237 377 H
ahmedm@bluffton.edu
AHMED, Shahzad 320-308-5151 261 E
shah@stcloudstate.edu
AHMED, Shariq 909-748-8352 73 K
shariq_ahmed@redlands.edu
AHMED, Zahir 573-986-6863 282 C
zahmed@semo.edu
AHN, Hee Young 323-731-2383 57 H
president@psuca.edu
AHN, Hong Jun 714-533-3946 36 D
AHN, Karen 213-385-2322 77 H
karenahn@wmu.edu
AHN, Kelly 212-229-5600 334 C
ahnk@newschool.edu
AHN, Young Jin 714-533-1495 67 A
admission@southbaylo.edu
AHO, Lynn 906-524-8313 245 B
laho@kbocc.edu
AHO, Marie 906-227-2981 248 B
mariaho@nmu.edu
AHOLA, Scott 605-642-6359 453 G
scott.ahola@bhsu.edu
AHORRIO, Beatriz 212-694-1000 316 J
bahorrio@boricuacollege.edu
AHRENHOLZ, Mark 630-752-5128 163 G
mark.ahrenholz@wheaton.edu
AHRENS, Emily 218-285-2203 261 A
emily.ahrens@rainyriver.edu
AHRENS, Rebecca 417-873-7523 274 E
bahrens@drury.edu
AHUMADA, Martin 928-724-6671 13 J
mahumada@dinecollege.edu
AICINENA, Steve 432-552-2675 495 F
aicinena_s@utpb.edu
AIKEN, Adel, G 724-847-5002 419 B
aaiken@geneva.edu
AIKEN, Donn 518-464-8765 325 B
daiken@excelsior.edu
AIKEN, Ryan 413-775-1309 231 E
aikenr@gcc.mass.edu
AIKEN, William, C 757-569-6712 516 E
baiken@pdc.edu
AIKENS, Jane 641-472-7000 181 A
jaikens@mum.edu
AILSTOCK, M. Stephen 410-777-2230 213 E
smailstock@aacc.edu
AIMONE, Chris 812-877-8498 172 C
aimone@rose-hulman.edu
AINLAY, Stephen, C 518-388-6101 350 K
ainlays@union.edu
AINLEY, Arden 360-416-7716 527 A
arden.ainley@skagit.edu
AINSLEIGH, Susan 413-565-1000 222 G
sainsleigh@baypath.edu
AINSLEY, Sharon 610-647-4400 421 B
sainsley@immaculata.edu
AINSLIE, Andrew 585-275-3316 351 D
andrew.ainslie@simon.rochester.edu
AINSLIE, Carolyn, N 609-258-1447 305 C
ainslie@princeton.edu
AINSWORTH, Emma, L 662-685-4771 266 G
eainsworth@bmc.edu
AINSWORTH, Jerald 423-425-4633 465 E
jerald-ainsworth@utc.edu
AINSWORTH, Jerry 618-634-3396 159 A
jerrya@shawneecc.edu
AINSWORTH, Patricia 978-542-6446 230 E
painsworth@salemstate.edu
AIRD, Jeff 801-957-4090 500 E
jeffrey.aird@slcc.edu
AIREN, Osaro 936-468-1073 484 A
aireno@sfasu.edu
AIREY, Linda 317-738-8225 166 B
lairey@franklincollege.edu
AIREY, Patricia, J 540-985-8376 509 D
pjairey@jchs.edu
AIROZO, Paul 508-830-5051 230 D
pairozo@maritime.edu
AISHMAN, Steve 912-525-5000 130 H
saishman@scad.edu
AISTRUP, Joe 334-844-4026 1 G
jaa0025@auburn.edu
AITCHISON, Cecile 207-780-4708 213 A
caitchison@usm.maine.edu
AITKEN, Derek 510-885-3877 33 C
derek.aitken@csueastbay.edu
AITSON-ROESSLER,
Mechelle 405-733-7308 401 L
maitson-roessler@rose.edu
AIZENSTAT, Stephen 805-969-3626 57 J
saizenstat@pacifica.edu
AJE, John 609-984-1130 308 H
jaje@tesc.edu
AJILO, Robbin 303-329-6355 81 B
robbinajilo@cstcm.edu
AJIROTUTU, Cheryl, S 414-229-3038 540 A
yinka@uwm.edu
AKAKPO, Koffi 419-755-4702 387 E
kakakpo@ncstatecollege.edu
AKANDE, Benjamin 573-592-5315 285 J
akande@westminster-mo.edu
AKANDE, Benjamin, O 314-968-5951 285 G
akandeb@webster.edu
AKBAR, Maksood 847-290-6425 155 A
AKBARI, Hamid 507-457-5014 262 D
hakbari@winona.edu
AKCHIN, Lisa, G 410-455-2889 219 F
akchin@umbc.edu
AKE, Barbara 505-566-3218 312 K
akeb@sanjuancollege.edu
AKENS, Cathy 305-919-5943 114 G
akens@fiu.edu
AKENS, Jeff 916-388-2800 36 H
jakens@carrington.edu
AKERMAN, Patricia 320-308-5966 261 F
pakerman@sctcc.edu
AKERS, Judy 276-326-4260 505 D
jvannoy@bluefield.edu
AKERS, Lex, A 309-677-2721 140 H
lakers@bradley.edu
AKERS, Mary Anne 443-885-3225 217 C
maryanne.akers@morgan.edu
AKERS, Matthew, P 330-972-7954 392 H
akers1@uakron.edu
AKERS, Shawn, D 434-592-5451 509 G
sdakers@liberty.edu
AKEY, Lynn 507-389-2419 260 A
lynn.akey@mnsu.edu
AKEY, Stacey, L 920-923-7652 537 A
sakey@marianuniversity.edu
AKHATAR, Sumaira 510-356-4760 78 G
AKHAVI, Seyed 212-594-4000 349 J
sakhavi@tricollege.edu
AKHAVI, Seyed 315-792-5469 333 D
sakhavi@mvcc.edu
AKIE, Ronald, E 617-928-4790 234 D
reakie@mountida.edu
AKIN, Daniel, L 919-761-2222 368 K
dakin@sebts.edu
AKIN, Hudson 765-285-1633 164 D
hakin@bsu.edu
AKIN, Jamie 325-942-2116 489 E
jamie.akin@angelo.edu
AKIN, Joeleen 404-471-6133 119 G
jakin@agnesscott.edu
AKIN, Renea 270-534-3461 197 E
renea.akin@kctcs.edu
AKINKUOYE, Nicholas 760-355-6215 47 G
nicholas.akinkuoye@imperial.edu
AKINLEYE, Johnson 919-530-6230 370 C
johnson.akinleye@nccu.edu
AKINS, Mike 904-596-2464 117 G
makins@tbc.edu
AKKAWI, Kayed 312-935-6025 157 A
kakkawi@robertmorris.edu
AKL, Fred, A 610-499-4036 439 G
faakl@widener.edu
AKL, Hatem 732-255-0400 304 E
hakl@ocean.edu
AKMAN, Jeffrey, S 202-741-2880 95 D
akman@gwu.edu
AKOB, Joe 570-422-3291 430 F
jakob@esu.edu
AKOJIE, Patricia, A 270-686-4200 193 G
patricia.akojie@brescia.edu
AKRIDGE, Travis 478-299-3530 132 A
takridge@southeasterntech.edu
AKSELRUD, Larisa 425-739-8515 523 I
larisa.akselrud@lwtech.edu
AKSU, Mert 313-994-6620 250 H
aksumn@udmercy.edu
AL-AMIN, John 323-953-4000 51 E
alminja@lacitycollege.edu
AL-ASSAF, Yousef 585-475-2411 339 G
ymacad@rit.edu
AL-HAZZAM DAWASARI,
Elizabeth 480-860-2700 13 Q
edawsari@taliesin.edu
ALADE, Ayodele, J 410-651-6327 219 H
ajalade@umes.edu
ALAIMO, Joseph 215-951-1974 422 F
alaimo@lasalle.edu
ALAIMO, Kathleen 773-298-3090 158 F
alaimo@sxu.edu
ALAM, Maria 901-678-2867 462 B
malam@memphis.edu
ALAM, Mohammad 212-220-1299 318 D
malam@bmcc.cuny.edu
ALAMEIDA, Marshall 415-485-9326 41 B
malameida@marin.edu
ALAMI, Osama 804-827-7474 514 F
oalami@vcu.edu
ALAMPI, Janet 860-512-2813 89 D
jalampi@manchestercc.edu
ALANDER, Link 832-813-6842 477 I
link.s.alander@lonestar.edu
ALANGAR, Sadhana 734-864-4202 241 B
sadhana@cleary.edu
ALARID, Jandee 409-772-9868 495 E
jalarid@utmb.edu
ALASIO, Claire 732-571-3463 303 G
calasio@monmouth.edu
ALAVALAPATI,
Janaki, R 334-844-1007 1 G
jra0024@auburn.edu
ALAVI, Maryam 404-894-2600 125 D
maryam.alavi@scheller.gatech.edu
ALBA, Suzanna 401-456-8086 442 A
salba@ric.edu
ALBANESE, Karli 909-599-5433 50 H
kalbanese@lifepacific.edu
ALBANESE, Linda 516-323-4025 333 E
lalbanese@molloy.edu
ALBANESE, Marc 610-282-1100 416 I
marc.albanese@desales.edu
ALBANO, John 209-386-6777 54 C
albano.j@mccd.edu
ALBANO, Ralph 202-319-5218 95 A
albano@cua.edu
ALBANO, Stephen, D 609-984-1100 308 H
salbano@tesc.edu
ALBANO, Thomas 219-785-5273 172 A
talbano@pnc.edu
ALBARRAN, Agustin 619-644-7161 46 H
agustin.albarran@gcccd.edu
ALBARRAN, Miguel 787-622-8000 556 H
malbarran@pupr.edu
ALBAWANEH,
Mahmoud 949-783-4807 75 K
mAlbawaneh@westcoastuniversity.edu
ALBAWANEH,
Mahmoud 562-985-5462 33 F
mahmoud.albawaneh@csulb.edu
ALBAYYARI, Jay 419-586-0341 396 A
jay.albayyari@wright.edu
ALBERDESTON, Jane 787-815-0000 557 D
jane.alberdeston@upr.edu
ALBERS, Jhett 605-642-6885 453 G
jhett.albers@bhsu.edu
ALBERS MILLER,
Nancy 253-535-7251 524 I
alberns-miller@plu.edu
ALBERT, Angelique 406-275-4820 288 H
angelique_albert@skc.edu
ALBERT, Barbara, J 570-326-3761 429 J
balbert@pct.edu
ALBERT, David 773-702-9800 161 D
dalbert@medicine.bsd.uchicago.edu
ALBERT, Gene 516-773-5000 548 I
albertg@usmma.edu
ALBERT, Jennifer 631-656-2128 326 B
jennifer.albert@ftc.edu
ALBERT, Joe 509-313-3564 522 L
albert@gonzaga.edu
ALBERT, Juline 712-274-6400 184 A
juline.albert@witcc.edu
ALBERT, Karen 215-951-2843 432 F
albertk@philau.edu
ALBERT, Katrice 612-624-0594 265 C
ka225@umn.edu
ALBERT, Marianne 724-222-5330 428 B
malbert@penncommercial.edu
ALBERT, OP, Peg 517-264-7000 250 B
palbert@sienaheights.edu
ALBERT, Rita 561-237-7231 108 E
ralbert@lynn.edu
ALBERT, Robert 606-783-5158 198 H
r.albert@moreheadstate.edu
ALBERT, Scott 724-738-9000 432 A
ALBERT-GREEN,
DeEadra 512-313-3000 471 H
deeadra.green@concordia.edu
ALBERT-KNOPP,
Heather 207-801-5640 210 B
halbert-Knopp@coa.edu
ALBERT LINK, Cindy 617-266-1400 223 F
ALBERTA, Vince 702-895-5165 295 G
vince.alberta@unlv.edu
ALBERTO, Paul, A 404-413-8100 126 D
palberto@gsu.edu
ALBERTS, Eugene, R 608-796-3849 542 H
eralberts@viterbo.edu
ALBERTS, Kristin, R 904-256-7180 106 Q
kalbert@ju.edu
ALBERTS, Trev 402-554-2305 294 A
talberts@unomaha.edu
ALBERTSON, Hattie 701-228-5454 374 F
hattie.c.albertson@dakotacollege.edu
ALBERTSON, Kay, H 919-735-5151 367 A
kha@waynecc.edu
ALBIERI, Guilherme 212-938-5500 347 C
galbieri@sunyopt.edu
ALBIN-HILL, Jill 708-524-6980 144 C
jalbin@dom.edu
ALBINA, Adam, R 603-641-7266 298 F
aalbina@anselm.edu
ALBINI, Marisa 401-333-7150 441 C
malbini@ccri.edu
ALBINSON, Erik 319-399-8843 176 G
ealbinso@coe.edu
ALBO-LOPEZ, Nicole 213-763-7025 52 A
albolonm@lattc.edu
ALBON, Darrell, J 740-368-3070 390 B
djalbon@owu.edu
ALBORS BIGAS,
Jaime, L 787-725-6500 551 A
jalbors@pfizer.com
ALBRECHT, Bryan, D 262-564-3000 543 A
albrechtb@gtc.edu
ALBRECHT, Catherine 419-772-2130 388 I
c-albrecht@onu.edu
ALBRECHT, Christal, M 281-756-3598 467 D
calbrecht@alvincollege.edu
ALBRECHT, Daniel 408-278-4343 77 F
dalbrecht@jessup.edu
ALBRECHT, Don 361-825-2612 485 F
don.albrecht@tamucc.edu
ALBRECHT, James, M 253-535-7698 524 I
albrecjm@plu.edu
ALBRECHT, Jana 309-438-2231 147 I
jlalbre2@ilstu.edu
ALBRECHT, John 775-673-7261 295 D
jalbrecht@tmcc.com
ALBRECHT, Kelli 501-760-4349 21 H
kalbrecht@npcc.edu
ALBRECHT, Stan, L 435-797-7172 500 A
stan.albrecht@usu.edu
ALBRIGHT, Barbara, C 757-446-5800 507 B
albrigbc@evms.edu
ALBRIGHT, Bonnie 409-880-7633 488 E
bsalbright@lit.edu
ALBRIGHT, Geri 205-929-6315 5 E
galbright@lawsonstate.edu
ALBRIGHT, Ken 530-895-2298 30 B
albrightke@butte.edu
ALBRIGHT, Mike 845-341-4728 337 G
mike.albright@sunyorange.edu
ALBRIGHT, Thomas 601-979-2580 267 H
thomas.e.albright@jsums.edu
ALBRINCK, Margaret, L 920-565-1021 536 Q
albrinckm@lakeland.edu
ALBRITTON, Kristen 678-359-5009 126 E
kristena@gordonstate.edu
ALBRITTON, Rosie, L 936-261-1510 484 F
rlalbritton@pvamu.edu
ALBRITTON, Sheila 423-697-4710 462 C
sheila.albritton@chattanoogastate.edu
ALBURCHER, Ronald 650-723-2300 68 G
ALBUS, Alana, M 484-664-3170 427 C
aalbus@muhlenberg.edu
ALCAINO, Ricardo 805-893-4504 72 D
ricardo.alcaino@oeo.ucsb.edu
ALCALA, Celena 310-287-4290 52 C
alcalac@wlac.edu
ALCALA, Emma 719-549-3327 85 A
emma.alcala@pueblocc.edu
ALCANTARA, Ryan 310-377-5501 53 E
ralcantara@marymountcalifornia.edu
ALCARAZ-EMMANUELLI,
Cristina 787-250-0000 557 B
cristina.alcaraz@upr.edu

ALKALY, Benjamin .... 310-338-7854.. 53 C
benjamin.alkaly@lmu.edu
ALKANAT, Gokhan .... 334-244-4023.... 2 A
galkanat@aum.edu
ALKIRE, Amy .... 612-330-1188 253 K
alkire@augsburg.edu
ALKIRE, Laurie .... 308-635-6036 294 C
alkirel@wncc.edu
ALKIRE, Laurie, A .... 308-635-6036 294 C
alkirel@wncc.edu
ALLADA, Venkata .... 573-341-4573 284 C
allada@mst.edu
ALLAN, Bill .... 316-295-5567 187 C
ballan@friends.edu
ALLAN, Bill .... 316-295-5891 187 C
ballan@friends.edu
ALLAN, Linda .... 412-809-5100 433 D
allan.linda@pti.edu
ALLAN, Mark .... 215-951-1395 422 F
allanm@lasalle.edu
ALLARD, Don .... 919-761-2310 368 K
dallard@sebts.edu
ALLARD, Elaine .... 603-535-2458 299 E
eallard@plymouth.edu
ALLARD, Ingrid, M .... 518-262-5919 314 I
allardi@mail.amc.edu
ALLARD, Jessica .... 802-862-9616 501 E
jallard@burlington.edu
ALLARD, Lee .... 518-782-6737 342 H
lallard@siena.edu
ALLARD, Michael .... 518-828-4181 322 E
allard@sunycgcc.edu
ALLARD, Nicholas, W ... 718-780-7902 317 A
nicholas.allard@brooklaw.edu
ALLBAUGH, Jonathan ... 714-556-3610.. 75 A
jonathan.allbaugh@vanguard.edu
ALLBEE, Bob .... 563-288-6002 178 C
ballbee@eicc.edu
ALLBRIGHT, Jacque ...... 512-245-2521 489 C
ja14@txstate.edu
ALLBRITTEN, Jeffery ..... 239-489-9211 104 G
president@fsw.edu
ALLCORN, Terry, A .... 417-268-6003 272 F
tallcorn@gobbc.edu
ALLDREDGE, Annita ...... 415-749-4560.. 62 I
aalldredge@sfai.edu
ALLDREDGE, Brian .... 415-514-0421.. 72 C
brian.alldredge@ucsf.edu
ALLDRITT, Leslie .... 715-682-1358 538 D
lalldritt@northland.edu
ALLEE, Kelly .... 217-234-5215 150 B
kallee@lakeland.cc.il.us
ALLEGRETTA, Kerri .... 516-403-5392 352 D
kallegretta@webb.edu
ALLEMAN, Vickie .... 713-942-3466 493 J
alleman@stthom.edu
ALLEMAN-BEYERS,
Natalie .... 913-468-8500 188 E
nalleman@jccc.edu
ALLEN, Al .... 386-822-8808 117 A
aallen@stetson.edu
ALLEN, Algia .... 972-563-9573 490 F
aallen@tvcc.edu
ALLEN, Amanda .... 670-234-5498 550 B
amanda.allen@marianas.edu
ALLEN, Amy .... 320-762-4591 257 O
amya@alextech.edu
ALLEN, Andrew, T .... 619-260-4553.. 74 B
provost@sandiego.edu
ALLEN, Angela .... 806-651-8482 486 D
aallen@mail.wtamu.edu
ALLEN, Anita, L .... 215-898-4032 437 I
aallen@law.upenn.edu
ALLEN, Anna, M .... 215-951-1374 422 F
aallen@lasalle.edu
ALLEN, Anthony .... 718-933-6700 333 F
aallen@monroecollege.edu
ALLEN, Anthony, W .... 573-629-3252 275 F
anthony.allen@hlg.edu
ALLEN, Bonita .... 251-405-7040.... 2 D
ballen@bishop.edu
ALLEN, Bonnie, J .... 615-898-2772 461 E
bonnie.allen@mtsu.edu
ALLEN, Brenda .... 303-315-2104.. 86 G
brenda.j.allen@ucdenver.edu
ALLEN, Brenda .... 336-750-2200 372 D
allenba@wssu.edu
ALLEN, Brian .... 815-939-5258 155 G
ballen@olivet.edu
ALLEN, Brian, K .... 608-785-8558 539 G
ballen@uwlax.edu
ALLEN, C. Leonard .... 615-966-6064 458 C
leonard.allen@lipscomb.edu
ALLEN, Calhoun .... 318-869-5120 202 D
callen@centenary.edu
ALLEN, Carol, M .... 443-412-2144 215 D
caallen@harford.edu
ALLEN, Carolyn, H .... 479-575-6702.. 23 G
challen@uark.edu
ALLEN, Charles .... 434-528-5276 518 F
callen@vul.edu
ALLEN, SJ, Charles, H . 203-254-4000.. 90 E
executive@fairfield.edu
ALLEN, Charley, B .... 270-809-3919 198 I
callen@murraystate.edu
ALLEN, Chaunda 225-578-4339 204M
call18@lsu.edu
ALLEN, Cindy .... 517-787-0800 244 H
allencynthiaa@jccmi.edu
ALLEN, Craig .... 817-257-7865 486 G
c.allen2@tcu.edu
ALLEN, Dale .... 508-854-2733 232 F
dallen@qcc.mass.edu
ALLEN, Dana, G .... 757-683-3097 510 I
dallen@odu.edu
ALLEN, Daniel .... 602-331-7500.. 12 C
dallen@aii.edu
ALLEN, Daniel, T .... 267-502-2636 413 C
daniel.allen@brynathyn.edu
ALLEN, Darren .... 205-929-6361.... 5 E
dallen@lawsonstate.edu
ALLEN, David .... 386-481-2497.. 99 F
Allend@ookman.edu
ALLEN, David .... 508-678-2811 231 B
david.allen@bristolcc.edu
ALLEN, David .... 817-923-1921 483 E
dallen@swbts.edu
ALLEN, JR., David .... 386-481-2497.. 99 F
allend@cookman.edu
ALLEN, David, D .... 662-915-7265 270 G
allen@olemiss.edu
ALLEN, David, N .... 520-621-7262.. 18 E
allendn@email.arizona.edu
ALLEN, David, P .... 253-535-7524 524 I
david.allen@plu.edu
ALLEN, David, W .... 916-339-4336.. 55 C
dallen@mticollege.edu
ALLEN, Dee Dee .... 501-450-1228.. 21 C
allendd@hendrix.edu
ALLEN, Dennis .... 541-776-9942 408 G
ALLEN, Diane, D .... 410-548-3374 220 E
ddallen@salisbury.edu
ALLEN, Donna, Y .... 870-235-4012.. 23 D
dyallen@saumag.edu
ALLEN, Douglas, W ...... 320-222-5201 261 B
douglas.allen@ridgewater.edu
ALLEN, OP,
Elizabeth Anne .... 615-297-7545 455 A
sreanne@aquinascollege.edu
ALLEN, Emily .... 302-343-4500.. 34 A
eallen3@calstatela.edu
ALLEN, Eric .... 724-589-2186 436 E
eallen@thiel.edu
ALLEN, Erika .... 208-792-2458 138 E
elallen@lcsc.edu
ALLEN, Erin .... 704-991-0261 366 D
eallen4640@stanly.edu
ALLEN, Forrest .... 432-685-4580 478 F
fallen@midland.edu
ALLEN, Gary, K .... 573-882-9200 283 G
allengk@umsystem.edu
ALLEN, Gary, K .... 573-882-9200 283 H
allengk@missouri.edu
ALLEN, George .... 517-607-2556 243 J
gallen@hillsdale.edu
ALLEN, Greg .... 402-557-7581 289 B
greg.allen@bellevue.edu
ALLEN, Gregg, N .... 207-780-5097 213 A
gregg@usm.maine.edu
ALLEN, Helen .... 205-348-7949.... 8 E
helen.allen@ua.edu
ALLEN, Hilary .... 919-760-8548 359 B
allenh@meredith.edu
ALLEN, Ivan .... 478-757-3501 122 E
iallen@centralgatech.edu
ALLEN, Ivan, H .... 478-988-6800 122 F
iallen@centralgatech.edu
ALLEN, JR., James .... 301-387-3006 215 A
james.allen@garrettcollege.edu
ALLEN, James, S .... 618-453-7653 159 H
jsallen@siu.edu
ALLEN, Janine .... 503-581-8166 405 F
jallen@corban.edu
ALLEN, Jason, K .... 816-414-3700 278 E
president@mbts.edu
ALLEN, Jay, S .... 270-707-3705 196 D
ALLEN, Jeffrey .... 814-619-3183 414 E
jallen@crbc.net
ALLEN, Jen .... 706-419-1119 123 F
jennifer.allen@covenant.edu
ALLEN, Jennie .... 909-447-2502.. 39 G
jallen@cst.edu
ALLEN, Jerry .... 510-594-3641.. 30 G
jallen@cca.edu
ALLEN, Jim .... 419-434-4207 395 H
jallen@winebrenner.edu
ALLEN, Jo .... 919-760-8511 359 B
jallen@meredith.edu
ALLEN, Jody .... 405-692-3130 398 I
jallen@macu.edu
ALLEN, John, A .... 614-885-5585 390 G
jallen@pcj.edu
ALLEN, John, C .... 435-797-1195 500 A
john.allen@usu.edu
ALLEN, John, W .... 580-327-8594 399 F
jwallen@nwosu.edu
ALLEN, Joshua, D .... 304-457-6392 529 C
allenjd@ab.edu
ALLEN, Judy .... 207-801-5680 210 B
jallen@coa.edu
ALLEN, Julia .... 704-922-6511 362 G
allen.julia@gaston.edu
ALLEN, Justin .... 540-535-3561 512 E
jallen3@su.edu
ALLEN, Kanya .... 270-707-3827 196 D
kanya.allen@kctcs.edu
ALLEN, Kate .... 913-469-8500 188 E
kallen@jccc.edu
ALLEN, Katherine .... 313-593-5300 251 D
kmaallen@umich.edu
ALLEN, Kathy .... 501-279-4263.. 21 A
kallen@harding.edu
ALLEN, Kathy .... 828-694-1773 360 D
allenkc@blueridge.edu
ALLEN, Kellie .... 606-326-2044 195 H
kellie.allen@kctcs.edu
ALLEN, Kent .... 405-425-5194 399 J
kent.allen@oc.edu
ALLEN, Kirsten .... 316-322-3192 185 F
kallen@butlercc.edu
ALLEN, Kitty .... 605-995-2612 452 C
kiallen1@dwu.edu
ALLEN, Larry, K .... 518-564-3282 346 B
lalle001@plattsburgh.edu
ALLEN, Linda .... 417-865-2815 274 L
allenl@evangel.edu
ALLEN, Linda, A .... 319-296-4201 179 B
linda.allen@hawkeyecollege.edu
ALLEN, Linda, D .... 617-373-2307 235 D
ALLEN, Lindsay .... 508-793-7666 225 B
liallen@clarku.edu
ALLEN, Lonny .... 419-448-3359 392 B
lallen@tiffin.edu
ALLEN, Lori .... 312-942-8708 158 A
lori_j_allen@rush.edu
ALLEN, Lori .... 575-527-7727 312 D
allen@nmsu.edu
ALLEN, Lynne .... 617-353-3350 224 E
cfadean@bu.edu
ALLEN, Mark .... 719-384-6830.. 84 I
mark.allen@ojc.edu
ALLEN, Mark .... 918-293-4830 400 E
mark.allen@okstate.edu
ALLEN, Mark, R .... 570-408-4103 440 B
mark.allen@wilkes.edu
ALLEN, Martha .... 218-935-0417 266 A
martha.allen@wetcc.edu
ALLEN, Mary .... 410-225-4255 216 F
mallen01@mica.edu
ALLEN, Mary Louise ..... 610-896-1183 420 J
mlallen@haverford.edu
ALLEN, Matt .... 406-683-7450 287 E
matt.allen@umwestern.edu
ALLEN, Max .... 864-656-3413 444 E
maallenn@clemson.edu
ALLEN, Melissa .... 607-431-4130 327 B
allenm2@hartwick.edu
ALLEN, Meredith .... 512-313-3000 471 H
meredith.allen@concordia.edu
ALLEN, Michael .... 406-496-4399 288 C
mallen@mtech.edu
ALLEN, Michael .... 818-364-7635.. 51 G
ALLEN, Michael .... 559-453-2038.. 45 E
michael.allen@fresno.edu
ALLEN, Michael .... 954-771-0376 107 V
mallen@knoxseminary.edu
ALLEN, Michael, K .... 818-364-7635.. 51 G
allenm@lamission.edu
ALLEN, Michael, S .... 202-319-5619.. 95 A
allen@cua.edu
ALLEN, Michele .... 816-604-4023 278 A
michele.allen@mcckc.edu
ALLEN, Myrna, L .... 386-312-4249 111 K
myrnaallen@sjrstate.edu
ALLEN, Nancy .... 303-871-2094.. 86 H
nallen@du.edu
ALLEN, Nancy .... 919-684-2965 356 E
nancy.allen@duke.edu
ALLEN, Norma, L .... 972-599-3159 471 C
nsmith@collin.edu
ALLEN, Patricia .... 503-534-7022 407 A
pallen@marylhurst.edu
ALLEN, Patrick .... 816-654-7287 276 G
pallen@kcumb.edu
ALLEN, Patty .... 509-533-4820 521 E
patty.allen@scc.spokane.edu
ALLEN, Philip, D .... 229-333-5952 133 H
pdallen@valdosta.edu
ALLEN, Preston, C .... 805-756-1226.. 32 E
pallen@calpoly.edu
ALLEN, Rachael .... 503-821-8920 408 H
rallen@pnca.edu
ALLEN, Remy, E .... 504-568-4802 205 C
rall1@lsuhsc.edu
ALLEN, Renee .... 505-346-2346 313 G
renee.allen@bie.edu
ALLEN, Robert .... 910-755-7321 360 E
allenr@brunswickcc.edu
ALLEN, Robin .... 610-796-8392 412 C
robin.allen@alvernia.edu
ALLEN, Rondall, E .... 410-651-8350 219 H
reallen@umes.edu
ALLEN, Rosemary .... 502-863-8146 195 A
rosemary_allen@georgetowncollege.edu
ALLEN, Rusty .... 620-947-3121 191 E
rustya@tabor.edu
ALLEN, Ryan .... 757-881-5100.. 96 H
ALLEN, Scott, T .... 203-596-4590.. 91 D
scallen@post.edu
ALLEN, Seth .... 909-621-8134.. 60 A
seth.allen@pomona.edu
ALLEN, Seth .... 866-931-4300 281 A
library@rockbridge.edu
ALLEN, Shannon .... 270-824-1785 196 F
shannon.allen@kctcs.edu
ALLEN, Sharlene .... 218-299-6894 259 H
sharlene.allen@minnesota.edu
ALLEN, Sharon .... 928-428-8342.. 13 L
sharon.allen@eac.edu
ALLEN, Sheila, W .... 706-542-3461 132 H
sallen01@uga.edu
ALLEN, Shelli, R .... 636-584-6565 274 J
shelli.allen@eastcentral.edu
ALLEN, Stacey .... 505-566-3515 312 K
allens@sanjuancollege.edu
ALLEN, Steve .... 606-539-4219 200 F
steve.allen@ucumberlands.edu
ALLEN, Steven, R .... 419-866-0261 391 L
srallen@stautzenberger.com
ALLEN, Susan .... 478-445-5650 125 A
susan.allen@gcsu.edu
ALLEN, Susan, K .... 603-862-3600 299 B
suzy.allen@unh.edu
ALLEN, Ted .... 503-554-2161 406 A
tallen@georgefox.edu
ALLEN, Teresa .... 912-287-5818 123 A
tallen@coastalpines.edu
ALLEN, Terry, D .... 859-257-9293 200 G
tallen@email.uky.edu
ALLEN, Thomas .... 845-437-7267 351 H
thallen@vassar.edu
ALLEN, Tim .... 360-473-1120 522 E
tiallen@cci.edu
ALLEN, Tom .... 443-334-2955 218 E
tallen@stevenson.edu
ALLEN, Tom .... 864-977-7135 448 A
tom.allen@ngu.edu
ALLEN, Tony .... 731-989-6055 456 K
tallen@fhu.edu
ALLEN, Travis, E .... 207-941-7130 210 C
allentr@husson.edu
ALLEN, Travis, J .... 714-816-0366.. 70 D
travis.allend@trident.edu
ALLEN, Valerie, M .... 812-888-4156 174 F
vallen@vinu.edu
ALLEN, W. Clayton .... 903-510-2507 491 A
call2@tjc.edu
ALLEN, Wanda .... 267-256-0200.. 96 H
ALLEN, William, R .... 530-898-5623.. 33 A
ballen@csuchico.edu
ALLEN, Xuri, M .... 340-693-1224 559 B
xallen@live.uvi.edu
ALLEN, Yvonne .... 216-373-5343 388 A
yallen@ndc.edu
ALLEN, Zachery .... 701-224-2524 374 E
zachery.allen@bismarckstate.edu
ALLEN-DIAZ,
Barbara, H .... 510-987-9359.. 70 J
barbara.allen-diaz@ucop.edu
ALLEN-KELSEY, Janice .. 386-481-2459.. 99 F
kelseyj@cookman.edu
ALLEN-SHARPE,
Regina, C .... 302-356-6790.. 94 G
regina.a.sharpe@wilmu.edu
ALLEN-STUCK,
Kimberly, M .... 610-660-1339 434 G
kallen@sju.edu
ALLENBY, Daniel .... 617-353-1068 224 E
dallenby@bu.edu
ALLER, Gary .... 202-448-6968.. 95 C
gary.aller@gallaudet.edu
ALLERY, Laisee .... 701-477-7862 375 H
lallery@tm.edu
ALLES, Patrick .... 317-788-2063 173 I
alles@uindy.edu
ALLETTO, Philip .... 912-525-5000 130 H
palletto@scad.edu
ALLEVA, Joe 225-578-3600 204M
athletics@lsu.edu
ALLEY, Brien .... 402-363-5624 294 G
balley@york.edu
ALLEY, Carolyn, W .... 828-694-1730 360 D
carolyna@blueridge.edu

ALLEY, Christy ... 620-672-5641 190 H
christya@prattcc.edu
ALLEY, Jerome ... 303-867-1155.. 87 K
Alley@TaftU.edu
ALLEY, Kathryn, E ... 605-394-6952 454 B
kate.jansak@sdsmt.edu
ALLEY, Kristen ... 660-359-3948 279 L
kalley@mail.ncmissouri.edu
ALLGOOD, John ... 225-214-6975 206 F
john.allgood@ololcollege.edu
ALLGOOD, Michael ... 918-540-6311 398 L
michael.allgood@neo.edu
ALLGRETTI, Marguerite . 312-752-2432 149 D
marguerite.allgretti@kendall.edu
ALLINA, Babette ... 401-454-6317 442 B
ballina@risd.edu
ALLING, David, C ... 860-628-4751.. 91 A
dalling@lincolncollegene.edu
ALLINSON, Roy ... 562-903-5344.. 29 F
roy.allinson@biola.edu
ALLIS, Celeste, H ... 336-342-4261 365 E
allisc@rockinghamcc.edu
ALLISON, Andrea ... 864-488-4394 447 F
aallison@limestone.edu
ALLISON, Angela ... 714-895-8156.. 40 C
aallison@gwc.cccd.edu
ALLISON, Crystal ... 360-416-7771 527 A
crystal.allison@skagit.edu
ALLISON, Dwayne ... 570-484-2022 431 C
dallison@lhup.edu
ALLISON, Harriet ... 678-717-3419 133 A
harriet.allison@ung.edu
ALLISON, Jack, T ... 787-743-7979 555 M
jaallison@suagm.edu
ALLISON, JR.,
James, M ... 410-810-7490 221 D
jallison2@washcoll.edu
ALLISON, Jennifer, R ... 864-597-4030 451 J
allisonjr@wofford.edu
ALLISON, Jim ... 502-863-7922 195 A
jim_allison@georgetowncollege.edu
ALLISON, Lorri ... 336-506-4133 359 N
lorri.allison@alamancecc.edu
ALLISON, M. Scott ... 540-375-2337 512 B
allison@roanoke.edu
ALLISON, Patrick ... 360-736-9391 520 F
pallison@centralia.edu
ALLISON, Robert ... 724-503-1001 439 B
rallison@washjeff.edu
ALLISON, Rose Mariee . 864-231-2099 443 E
rallison@andersonuniversity.edu
ALLISON, Sherry ... 505-346-2348 313 G
sherry.allison@bie.edu
ALLISON, Terry, L ... 574-520-4220 168 F
tlalliso@iusb.edu
ALLISON, William ... 914-594-4226 335 H
william_allison@nymc.edu
ALLISON-JONES, Lisa ... 540-224-6970 509 D
LAllisonjones@jchs.edu
ALLMAKER, Peter ... 413-662-5592 230 C
peter.allmaker@mcla.edu
ALLMAN, Marion, K ... 513-751-1206 376 A
aic@theartinstituteofcincinnati.com
ALLMAN, Martha, B ... 336-758-5201 372 G
allanmb@wfu.edu
ALLMON, Suzanne ... 325-674-2412 466 I
allmons@acu.edu
ALLOCCO ALLEN, Jare .. 410-617-2917 216 D
jalloccoallen@loyola.edu
ALLPHIN, Jeri, L ... 801-863-8553 500 B
jeri.allphin@uvu.edu
ALLRED, Barry ... 801-422-4530 497 J
barry_allred@byu.edu
ALLRED, J. Michael ... 530-754-9868.. 71 A
jmallred@ucdavis.edu
ALLRED, Jeremy, P ... 323-265-8802.. 51 D
allredjp@elac.edu
ALLRED, John ... 435-586-7715 499 L
johnallred1@suu.edu
ALLRED, Judy ... 970-675-3305.. 80 L
judy.allred@cncc.edu
ALLRED, Phil ... 435-283-7660 500 D
phil.allred@snow.edu
ALLRED, Robert ... 801-832-2013 501 C
rallred@westminstercollege.edu
ALLSHOUSE, Kent ... 316-284-5279 185 B
kellshouse@bethelks.edu
ALLY, Ron ... 847-925-6380 145 F
rally@harpercollege.edu
ALLYN, Julie ... 805-482-2755.. 61 F
julie@stjohnsem.edu
ALM, Deborah ... 413-748-3216 236 H
dalm@springfieldcollege.edu
ALM, Maria ... 715-232-2596 541 B
almm@uwstout.edu
ALM, Odessa ... 704-971-8500 355 J
oalm@charlottelaw.edu
ALMAGUER, Michael ... 925-969-2347.. 42 E
malmaguer@dvc.edu
ALMEDA, Delilah ... 305-237-0642 108 L
dalmeda1@mdc.edu
ALMEIDA, Craig ... 508-565-1325 237 A
calmeida@stonehill.edu
ALMEIDA, Enga ... 817-202-6494 483 C
ealmeida@swau.edu
ALMEIDA, James ... 201-692-7200 302 H
almeida@fdu.edu
ALMEIDA, Michele ... 802-287-8293 501 I
michele.almeida@greenmtn.edu
ALMENDAREZ, Elena ... 412-536-1053 422 E
elena.almendarez@laroche.edu
ALMER, Deb ... 507-537-6243 262 B
Deb.Almer@smsu.edu
ALMESTICA, Dirza ... 787-620-2040 550 D
dalmestica@aupr.edu
ALMEYDA, Marta ... 787-728-1515 559 A
malmeyda@sagrado.edu
ALMODOVAR, Arturo ... 787-844-8181 558 D
arturo.almodovar@upr.edu
ALMON, Robert, C ... 212-346-1200 337 I
ralmon@pace.edu
ALMOND, B.J ... 713-348-6770 480 M
balmond@rice.edu
ALMOND, James, S ... 765-494-9706 171 K
jsalmond@purdue.edu
ALMONTE, Loreto ... 305-821-3333 104 C
lalmonte@fnu.edu
ALMQUIST, Arne, J ... 859-572-5483 199 A
almquista@nku.edu
ALMQUIST, Brian ... 843-574-6011 449 G
brian.almquist@tridenttech.edu
ALMQUIST, Cathy ... 843-574-6750 449 G
cathy.almquist@tridenttech.edu
ALMQUIST, Jacqueline . 402-457-2745 291 E
jalmquist@mccneb.edu
ALO, Richard ... 601-979-2153 267 H
richard.a.alo@jsums.edu
ALOIA, Gregory, F ... 912-279-5705 123 B
president@ccga.edu
ALONSO, Carlos, J ... 212-854-6935 322 F
ca2201@columbia.edu
ALONSO, David ... 212-998-1077 336 C
david.alonso@nyu.edu
ALONSO, CSC, Jesus ... 574-239-8366 167 C
jalonso@hcc-nd.edu
ALONSO, John ... 860-628-4751.. 91 A
jalonso@lincolncollegene.edu
ALONZO, Erin, R ... 716-878-3640 345 B
alonzoer@buffalostate.edu
ALONZO, Jamie ... 408-288-3716.. 64 A
jamie.alonzo@sjcc.edu
ALONZO, Liza ... 713-221-8682 491 F
alonzol@uhd.edu
ALONZO, Patricia ... 989-775-4123 249 F
alonzo.patricia@sagchip.edu
ALOYO, JR., Victor ... 609-688-1940 305 B
victor.aloyo@ptsem.edu
ALP, Neslihan ... 423-425-2256 465 E
neslihan-alp@utc.edu
ALPERIN, Diane ... 561-297-3068 114 E
alperind@fau.edu
ALPERIN, Samantha ... 901-321-3116 455 I
salperin@cbu.edu
ALPERN, Robert, J ... 203-785-4672.. 93 C
robert.alpern@yale.edu
ALPHORD, Jeremy, R ... 334-727-8011.... 8 B
ALPIN, Jolie ... 760-366-3791.. 42 G
jalpin@cmccd.edu
ALSHEIMER, Michael ... 315-464-8824 344 E
alsheimm@upstate.edu
ALSINA, Amalia ... 787-257-0000 557 F
amalia.alsina@upr.edu
ALSING, Melissa ... 724-830-1850 435 E
malsing@setonhill.edu
ALSIP, David ... 270-824-1990 196 F
david.alsip@kctcs.edu
ALSIP, Morgan ... 405-692-3244 398 I
malsip@macu.edu
ALSOBROOK, Joe ... 636-949-4853 276 L
jalsobrook@lindenwood.edu
ALSOBROOKS,
David, S ... 601-403-1241 270 A
salsobrooks@prcc.edu
ALSOP, Rob ... 304-293-5772 533 D
rob.alsop@mail.wvu.edu
ALSOP, Robert ... 641-585-8130 183 I
alsopb@waldorf.edu
ALSTER, Kristine ... 617-287-5638 228 G
kristine.alster@umb.edu
ALSTON, Dawn ... 404-270-5077 132 D
dalston@spelman.edu
ALSTON, Melissa, F ... 706-771-4171 121 B
mfalston@augustatech.edu
ALSTON, Reginald ... 217-333-6394 162 A
alston@illinois.edu
ALSTON, Sharon ... 202-885-6053.. 94 H
salston@american.edu
ALSTON, Vickie ... 479-979-1000.. 25 H
ALSTON-BROWN,
Michelle ... 404-756-4442 120 H
malston@atlm.edu
ALSTON FORBES,
Lakesha ... 252-328-6804 369 E
alstonl@ecu.edu
ALSTON-PINCKNEY,
Elizabeth ... 704-216-6100 358 I
ealston-pinckney@livingstone.edu
ALSTROM, Mike ... 231-777-0307 247 G
mike.alstrom@muskegoncc.edu
ALSUP, Greer ... 931-393-1529 463 B
galsup@mscc.edu
ALT, Al ... 209-575-6867.. 78 C
alta@mjc.edu
ALT, Greg ... 309-438-2143 147 I
gaalt@ilstu.edu
ALT, Jennifer ... 509-533-3723 521 F
jennifer.alt@sfcc.spokane.edu
ALT, John, W ... 608-524-7825 543 C
jalt@madisoncollege.edu
ALTAMIRANO,
Rodolfo, R ... 215-573-6332 437 I
rudiea@pobox.upenn.edu
ALTARRIBA, Jeanette ... 518-442-3950 343 C
ugeducation@albany.edu
ALTAYLI, Z. Benek ... 719-255-3257.. 86 F
azltayli@uccs.edu
ALTEMOSE, Jane ... 610-758-4637 424 B
jca209@lehigh.edu
ALTEMOSE, Rodney, H . 215-258-7750 413 F
altemose@bucks.edu
ALTENBURG,
Deborah, E ... 202-220-1320 339 D
altend@rpi.edu
ALTENBURG, Rana, H ... 414-288-7430 537 B
rana.altenburg@marquette.edu
ALTENKIRCH, Robert, A 256-824-6340.... 9 A
robert.altenkirch@uah.edu
ALTIER, Jeffrey, P ... 386-822-8100 117 A
jaltier@stetson.edu
ALTIER, Matthew ... 504-671-5447 203 F
maltie@dcc.edu
ALTIERE, Ralph ... 303-724-2887.. 86 G
ralph.altiere@ucdenver.edu
ALTIERI, Guy ... 240-500-2000 215 C
galtieri@hagerstowncc.edu
ALTIERI, Jason, C ... 281-873-0262 471 D
j.altieri@commonwealth.edu
ALTIERI, Paul ... 570-484-2278 431 C
paltieri@lhup.edu
ALTIERO, Nicholas, J ... 504-865-5764 207 F
altiero@tulane.edu
ALTIKULAC, John ... 770-426-2644 128 C
jaltikulac@life.edu
ALTMAN, Barbara ... 570-577-1561 413 E
ALTMAN, Carolyn ... 912-486-1149 126 B
caltman@georgiasouthern.edu
ALTMAN, Don ... 660-626-2820 271 G
daltman@atsu.edu
ALTMAN, J.J ... 912-871-1648 129 E
jaltman@ogeecheetech.edu
ALTMAN, Joanne, D ... 336-841-9613 357 E
jaltman0@highpoint.edu
ALTMAN, Miranda ... 410-778-7261 221 D
maltman2@washcoll.edu
ALTNAU, Christopher ... 903-927-3274 497 G
caltnau@wileyc.edu
ALTOMARI, Helen, N ... 239-304-7819.. 98 O
helen.altomari@avemaria.edu
ALTON, Stevan ... 586-445-7374 246 A
altons@macomb.edu
ALTSCHULER, Glenn, C 607-255-7393 323 C
gca1@cornell.edu
ALTSHER, Deborah ... 508-626-4534 230 A
daltsher@framingham.edu
ALTSHULER, Gina ... 215-335-0800 424 D
galtshuler@lincolntech.edu
ALTUCHER, Kristine ... 607-844-8222 350 A
altuchk@tc3.edu
ALTUSKY,
Shlomo Avidgor ... 718-868-2300 316 B
ALTWINE, Chad ... 402-375-7274 292 D
chaltwi1@wsc.edu
ALUMBAUGH, Heather .. 718-405-3275 322 A
heather.alumbaugh@mountsaintvincent.edu
ALVA, Gerardo ... 956-326-2284 485 B
gerardo.alva@tamiu.edu
ALVA, Sylvia, A ... 909-869-4382.. 32 F
saalva@cpp.edu
ALVA, Sylvia, A ... 818-677-3001.. 34 D
sylvia.alva@csun.edu
ALVALLE, Anibal ... 787-764-0000 558 E
anibal.alvalle@upr.edu
ALVAR, Brent ... 801-375-5125 499 A
balvar@rmuohp.edu
ALVARADO, Cecilia ... 951-222-8073.. 61 B
cecilia.alvarado@rcc.edu
ALVARADO, Christian ... 949-582-4340.. 67 F
calvarado@saddleback.edu
ALVARADO, Christian ... 949-582-4860.. 67 F
calvarado@saddleback.edu
ALVARADO, Eddie, D ... 661-336-5143.. 49 D
ealvarad@kccd.edu
ALVARADO, Ida, Y ... 787-780-0070 550 G
ialvarado@caribbean.edu
ALVARADO, Irma ... 787-279-1912 553 H
ialvarado@bayamon.inter.edu
ALVARADO,
Johnathan, E ... 404-627-2681 121 F
johnathan.alvarado@beulah.org
ALVARADO, Magalie ... 787-257-7373 555 L
ue_malvarado@suagm.edu
ALVARADO, Miguel ... 617-422-7423 234 J
malvarado@nesl.edu
ALVARADO, Norman ... 718-779-1430 338 D
nalvarado@plazacollege.edu
ALVARADO, Nyvia ... 787-892-4300 554 C
nialvara@intersg.edu
ALVARADO, Phil ... 530-938-5233.. 41 E
alvarado@siskiyous.edu
ALVARADO-TORRES,
Cesar, A ... 787-751-1912 554 D
calvarado@juris.inter.edu
ALVAREZ, Abigail ... 858-505-1100.. 47 M
aalvarez@ipsb.edu
ALVAREZ, Albert ... 818-364-7600.. 51 G
LAMCFoundation@lamission.edu
ALVAREZ, Alvin ... 415-338-3326.. 36 A
aalvarez@sfsu.edu
ALVAREZ, Araceli ... 713-500-3871 495 A
Araceli.Alvarez@uth.tmc.edu
ALVAREZ, Araceli ... 903-877-7777 495 C
ALVAREZ, Armando ... 305-273-4499 100 K
armando.alvarez@cbt.edu
ALVAREZ, Barry, L ... 608-262-4312 539 D
bla@athletics.wisc.edu
ALVAREZ, Brian ... 516-364-0808 335 A
itsupport@nycollege.edu
ALVAREZ, Caridad ... 787-841-2000 555 F
caridad_alvarez@pucpr.edu
ALVAREZ, Celso ... 305-474-6868 112 B
cjalvarez@stu.edu
ALVAREZ, Celso, J ... 305-474-6868 112 B
cjalvarez@stu.edu
ALVAREZ, Frank, D ... 509-452-5100 524 J
falvarez@pnwu.edu
ALVAREZ, Ivonne ... 619-388-2689.. 62 G
ialvarez@sdccd.edu
ALVAREZ, Jackie ... 541-737-2131 408 F
jackie.alvarez@oregonstate.edu
ALVAREZ, Jacqueline ... 413-542-2354 222 A
jalvarez@amherst.edu
ALVAREZ, Jacqueline ... 787-284-1912 554 B
jalvarez@ponce.inter.edu
ALVAREZ, Leticia ... 559-638-3641.. 69 C
letty.alvarez@reedleycollege.edu
ALVAREZ, Lourdes ... 203-932-7257.. 92 G
lavarez@newhaven.edu
ALVAREZ, Maria ... 787-882-2065 556 C
registraduria@unitecpr.net
ALVAREZ, Maria, L ... 305-899-3085.. 99 B
malvarez@barry.edu
ALVAREZ, Milagros ... 787-850-9301 558 A
milagros.alvarez@upr.edu
ALVAREZ, Patricia ... 787-857-3600 553 G
palvarez@br.inter.edu
ALVAREZ, Patricia ... 559-730-3988.. 41 D
patriciaa@cos.edu
ALVAREZ, Raul ... 714-484-7128.. 56 E
ralvarez@cypresscollege.edu
ALVAREZ, Richard ... 540-831-5411 511 C
ralvarez@radford.edu
ALVAREZ, Richard, P ... 646-664-9100 318 B
ALVAREZ, Sylvia ... 787-728-1515 559 A
salvarez@sagrado.edu
ALVAREZ, Timothy ... 701-231-7701 374 C
timothy.alvarez@ndsu.edu
ALVAREZ-ROBINSON,
Sonia ... 404-385-3306 125 D
sonia@consulting.gatech.edu
ALVAREZ-RUIZ, Luis ... 787-890-2681 557 C
luis.alvarez8@upr.edu
ALVARO, Tammy ... 989-386-6622 247 B
talvaro@midmich.edu
ALVERSON, Amelia, J ... 212-851-7929 322 F
amelia.alverson@columbia.edu
ALVES, Eddie ... 541-881-4863 410 D
Eddie.J.Alves@doc.state.or.us
ALVES, Jeffrey ... 570-408-4725 440 B
jeffrey.alves@wilkes.edu
ALVES, Stephanie ... 925-969-2082.. 42 E
salves@dvc.edu
ALVEY, Patricia ... 214-768-4519 482 J
palvey@smu.edu
ALVIDREZ, Rachel ... 757-631-8101 504 O
rachel.alvidrez@atlanticuniv.edu
ALVIENE, Jason ... 561-912-1211 102 N
jalviene@evergladesuniversity.edu
ALVINO, Kathleen, M ... 401-865-2430 441 F
kalvino@providence.edu
ALVIS, Robert ... 812-357-6543 173 A
ralvis@saintmeinrad.edu

ALY, Mai ... 773-481-8061 142 D
maly@ccc.edu
ALY, Nael ... 209-667-3288.. 35 C
naly@csustan.edu
ALZAHABI, Basem ... 810-762-7893 245 A
balzahab@kettering.edu
AMACK, April ... 970-542-3187.. 84 A
april.amack@morgancc.edu
AMADI, Emmanual ... 662-254-3363 269 C
amadi@mvsu.edu
AMADO, Manuel ... 303-458-4122.. 85 G
mamado@regis.edu
AMADOR, Lui ... 657-278-8660.. 33 E
lamador@fullerton.edu
AMAKER, Corey ... 864-644-5001 449 B
camaker@swu.edu
AMALBERT, Milagros ... 787-751-1912 554 D
mamalber@juris.inter.edu
AMAN, Rick, K ... 208-535-5366 138 B
strick.aman@my.eitc.edu
AMANKWATIA, Tonya ... 757-352-4886 511 G
tamankwatia@regent.edu
AMAR, Vikram ... 217-333-0931 162 A
amar@illinois.edu
AMASON, Allen ... 912-478-2622 126 B
aamason@georgiasouthern.edu
AMASON, Amy ... 706-776-0104 130 B
aamason@piedmont.edu
AMATO, Paula ... 603-428-2461 298 B
pamato@nec.edu
AMATO, Paula, A ... 603-428-2461 298 B
pamato@nec.edu
AMATO, Roseann ... 407-708-2713 113 A
amator@seminolestate.edu
AMATOR, Shelley ... 505-566-3466 312 K
amators@sanjuancollege.edu
AMAVIZCA, Gabriela ... 520-417-4708.. 13 B
amavizcag@cochise.edu
AMAYA, Mercedes ... 305-237-2325 108 L
mamaya@mdc.edu
AMAYA GORDON,
Karla, J ... 757-823-8275 510 H
kjagordon@nsu.edu
AMBACH, Robert ... 513-556-2413 393 B
robert.ambach@uc.edu
AMBAR, Carmen, T ... 610-606-4612 415 A
president@cedarcrest.edu
AMBELANG, Charlie ... 408-551-1940.. 65 A
cambelang@scu.edu
AMBLER, Anthony, P ... 803-777-7356 450 B
ambler@cec.sc.edu
AMBLER, Charles ... 915-747-5950 494 B
cambler@utep.edu
AMBLER, Virginia, M ... 757-221-1236 506 J
vmambl@wm.edu
AMBRA, Stephen ... 603-271-6484 297 C
sambra@ccsnh.edu
AMBRIZ-GALAVIZ,
Norma ... 510-436-2501.. 59 C
nambrizgalaviz@peralta.edu
AMBROGI, Anthony, F . 804-752-7362 511 E
aambrogi@rmc.edu
AMBROISE, Danielle ... 503-493-6508 405 E
dambrose@cu-portland.edu
AMBRON, Sueann ... 303-315-8001.. 86 G
sueann.ambron@ucdenver.edu
AMBROSE, Ann, P ... 757-822-2301 517 C
aambrose@tcc.edu
AMBROSE, AnneMarie .. 315-866-0300 327 E
ambroseac@herkimer.edu
AMBROSE, Charles, M . 660-543-4112 283 F
ambrose@ucmo.edu
AMBROSE, James ... 315-786-2490 329 G
jambrose@sunyjefferson.edu
AMBROSE, Molly, B ... 617-228-2457 231 C
mambrose@bhcc.mass.edu
AMBROSE, Pam ... 312-915-7602 151 E
pambros@luc.edu
AMBROSE, Susan ... 617-373-2170 235 D
AMBROSIA, Todd ... 212-614-6110 338 C
tambrosia@chpnet.org
AMBROSON, Gene ... 712-274-5293 181 C
ambroson@morningside.edu
AMBUR, Roberta, S ... 605-677-5661 453 F
roberta.ambur@usd.edu
AMBURGEY, Jeff, S ... 859-985-3082 193 F
jeff_amburgey@berea.edu
AMBUSKE, Joseph ... 614-236-6116 378 H
jambuske@capital.edu
AMDUR, Nick ... 617-619-1900 227 G
nick.amdur@faculty.hult.edu
AMEER, Inge-Lise ... 603-643-3113 297 G
inge-lise.ameer@dartmouth.edu
AMEIGH, Michael ... 315-312-3500 346 A
michael.ameigh@oswego.edu
AMELING, Brian, F ... 864-488-8200 447 F
bameling@limestone.edu
AMELING, Jerry ... 419-372-2694 377 I
jamelin@bgsu.edu
AMELL, Laura ... 802-485-2065 502 G
lamell@norwich.edu
AMELSBERG, James ... 641-585-8164 183 I
amelsbergj@waldorf.edu
AMEN, Barbara, A ... 503-777-7259 409 E
barbara.amen@reed.edu
AMEND, John ... 402-554-2242 294 A
jamend@unomaha.edu
AMENSON-HILL,
Brenda ... 920-465-2159 539 F
hillb@uwgb.edu
AMENT, Rebecca, R ... 740-588-1322 396 E
bament@zanestate.edu
AMENTA, Paula ... 847-214-7273 144 F
pamenta@elgin.edu
AMERIN, Kylea, C ... 580-327-8601 399 F
kcamerin@nwosu.edu
AMERIO, Barbara ... 661-763-7881.. 69 E
bamerio@taftcollege.edu
AMERO, Carolina ... 678-466-4217 122 J
carolinaamero@clayton.edu
AMERSHEK, Tom ... 620-235-4775 190 G
tamershek@pittstate.edu
AMES, Christopher ... 304-876-5176 532 I
cames@shepherd.edu
AMES, Frank ... 303-373-2008.. 85 I
fames@rvu.edu
AMES, Lynda, J ... 518-564-3310 346 B
amesIj@plattsburgh.edu
AMES, Marilyn ... 914-337-9300 323 A
marilyn.ames@concordia-ny.edu
AMES, Mark ... 405-382-9950 402 C
m.ames@sscok.edu
AMES, Skip ... 334-983-6556.... 8 A
oames@troy.edu
AMES, Susan, E ... 315-445-4227 330 B
amesse@lemoyne.edu
AMES, Suzanne ... 425-739-8410 523 I
suzanne.ames@lwtech.edu
AMES, Trevor, R ... 612-624-6244 265 C
amesx001@umn.edu
AMEY, Carol, J ... 859-858-3511 193 A
camey@asbury.edu
AMEY, Tracey ... 570-327-4503 429 J
tamey@pct.edu
AMEZCUA, Jason ... 217-228-5432 156 D
amezcja@quincy.edu
AMEZCUA, Victoria ... 626-396-2278.. 28 J
victoria.amezcua@artcenter.edu
AMI, Dawn ... 505-346-2339 313 G
dawn.ami@bie.edu
AMICK, Michael ... 218-855-8268 258 C
MAmick@clcmn.edu
AMICK, Patricia, A ... 816-604-1130 277 F
patricia.amick@mcckc.edu
AMICO, David ... 315-792-5318 333 D
damico@mvcc.edu
AMIDON, Howard ... 978-921-4242 234 B
howard.amidon@montserrat.edu
AMIDON, Jacob, E ... 585-785-1418 325 E
jacob.amidon@flcc.edu
AMIDON, James, L ... 765-361-6364 175 B
amidonj@wabash.edu
AMIDON, JR.,
James, L ... 765-361-6364 175 B
amidonj@wabash.edu
AMIE, Torrion ... 952-358-8505 260 D
torrion.amie@mormandale.edu
AMINY, Marina ... 949-582-4365.. 67 F
AMIRIDIS, Michael ... 312-413-3350 161 F
chancellor@uic.edu
AMIRIDIS, Michael ... 312-413-3350 161 E
amiridis@uic.edu
AMIRTHARAJ, Merlin ... 704-991-0207 366 D
mamirtharaj5283@stanly.edu
AMIS, Eric, J ... 330-972-7500 392 H
amis@uakron.edu
AMLANER, Charles, J ... 470-578-6738 127M
camlaner@kennesaw.edu
AMLER, Robert, W ... 914-594-4531 335 H
robert_amler@nymc.edu
AMMAR, Salwa ... 718-862-7440 331 H
salwa.ammar@manhattan.edu
AMMERMAN, Randy ... 920-686-6179 539 A
Randy.Ammerman@sl.edu
AMMETER, Tony ... 662-915-7621 270 G
AMMIDOWN, Darla ... 603-577-6533 297 F
dammidown@dwc.edu
AMMIGAN, Ravi ... 302-831-2115.. 94 D
rammigan@udel.edu
AMMON, Darryl, C ... 660-263-3900 272M
darrylammon@cccb.edu
AMMON, Janice, S ... 609-497-7890 305 B
chapel@ptsem.edu
AMMON, Richard ... 608-822-2421 544 C
rammon@swtc.edu
AMMONS, Brian ... 828-298-3325 373 A
bammons@warren-wilson.edu
AMMONS, Don ... 704-922-6240 362 G
ammons.don@gaston.edu
AMMONS, Kevin ... 334-347-2623.... 3 H
kammons@escc.edu
AMMONS, Lee ... 205-391-5830.... 7 A
wammons@sheltonstate.edu
AMMONS, Sandy ... 910-630-7114 359 C
sammons@methodist.edu
AMODIO, Francis ... 845-569-3154 333 I
francis.amodio@msmc.edu
AMODIO, Greg ... 203-582-8200.. 91 E
greg.amodio@quinnipiac.edu
AMOKE, William ... 619-298-1829.. 68 C
wamoke@ssu.edu
AMON, Julie ... 856-225-6108 307 A
julie.amon@camden.rutgers.edu
AMOO, Judith, L ... 308-635-6702 294 C
amooj@wncc.edu
AMORE, Elizabeth ... 305-284-6266 118 A
eamore@miami.edu
AMOROS, Blanca ... 787-758-2525 558 C
blanca.amoros@upr.edu
AMOS, Anthea ... 850-484-4436 110 D
aamos@pensacolastate.edu
AMOS, Maureen, T ... 773-442-5000 154 H
m-amos@neiu.edu
AMOS, Sean ... 817-202-6740 483 C
samos@swau.edu
AMOS PALMER,
Susan, M ... 651-793-1823 259 E
sueamos.palmer@metrostate.edu
AMOTT, Teresa, L ... 309-341-7210 149 G
tamott@knox.edu
AMOUZEGAR, Mahyar .. 909-869-2472.. 32 F
mahyar@cpp.edu
AMPARO, Frank ... 623-935-8872.. 14 L
frank.amparo@estrellamountain.edu
AMPIL, Isaac ... 630-620-2175 154 J
iampil@seminary.edu
AMRHEIN, Rick ... 219-464-6777 174 E
rick.amrhein@valpo.edu
AMRHEIN, Rick ... 219-464-5777 174 E
rick.amrhein@valpo.edu
AMRIKHAS, Violet ... 818-947-2533.. 52 B
amrikhv@lavc.edu
AMSBERRYAUGIER,
Lora ... 504-280-5563 205 G
slamsberr@uno.edu
AMSEL, Shimshon ... 732-370-1560 300 A
AMSPAUGH,
Melissa, A ... 440-525-7357 385 C
mamspaugh@lakelandcc.edu
AMSTER, Yosef ... 516-295-5700 354 A
AMSTUTZ, Margaret ... 706-542-0383 132 H
mastutz@uga.edu
AMUNDSEN,
Minakshi, M ... 207-859-5002 210 A
mina.amundsen@colby.edu
AMUNDSEN, Scott ... 714-816-0366.. 70 D
scott.amundsen@trident.edu
AMUNDSON, Bret ... 218-625-4983 255 A
bamundson@css.edu
AMUNDSON,
Elizabeth, A ... 202-994-4900.. 95 D
amundson@gwu.edu
AMUNDSON, Jhennifer . 847-628-1019 149 A
jamundson@judsonu.edu
AMUNDSON, Shannon . 319-895-4174 177 A
samundson@cornellcollege.edu
AMYOT, Maribeth ... 513-745-3445 396 B
amyotm@xavier.edu
AMYX, Tim ... 615-230-3614 464 B
tim.amyx@volstate.edu
AN, Nana ... 202-885-2729.. 94 H
nanaan@american.edu
ANACKER, Gayne ... 951-343-4682.. 30 D
ganaker@calbaptist.edu
ANAHITA, Sine ... 907-474-6515.. 10 I
sine.anahita@alaska.edu
ANALISTA, Norman ... 671-735-2586 549 G
nanalista@uguam.uog.edu
ANANOU, Simeon ... 410-543-6112 220 E
CIO@salisbury.edu
ANASAGASTI, Rogelio .. 713-718-5001 475 C
rogelio.anasagasti@hccs.edu
ANASTASSIOU,
Pamela, L ... 928-523-2109.. 16 C
Pamela.Anastassiou@nau.edu
ANAWALT, Deborah ... 410-626-2504 218 A
debbie.anawalt@sjc.edu
ANAYA, Angela ... 505-888-8898 313 C
financialaid@acupuncturecollege.edu
ANAYA, Jose ... 310-660-6464.. 43 G
janaya@elcamino.edu
ANAYA, Nena ... 505-424-2331 310 L
nanaya@iaia.edu
ANCELL, Jack ... 434-949-1066 516 H
jack.ancell@southside.edu
ANCHOR, Rebecca, E ... 585-245-5100 345 D
anchor@geneseo.edu
ANCI, Diane ... 413-538-2515 234 C
danci@mtholyoke.edu
ANCI, Diane ... 740-427-5778 384 P
ancid@kenyon.edu
ANCO, Lisley ... 703-891-1787 512 L
ANCTIL, Robin ... 641-844-5571 179 J
robin.anctil@iavalley.edu
ANDE, Taiwo, A ... 540-654-1282 513 I
tande@umw.edu
ANDELIBI, Jila ... 714-867-5009.. 67 C
ANDELMAN, Julia ... 212-678-8893 329 H
juandelman@jtsa.edu
ANDERECK, Barbara, S . 740-368-3773 390 B
bsandere@owu.edu
ANDEREGG, Jennifer ... 715-833-6361 542M
janderegg2@cvtc.edu
ANDERFUREN,
Marian, L ... 757-822-1940 517 C
manderfuren@tcc.edu
ANDERLEY, Gerald, M .. 651-962-6061 265 F
ANDERMAN, Lynea ... 610-892-1524 429M
landerman@pit.edu
ANDERS, Lee ... 620-862-5252 184 H
andle@barclaycollege.edu
ANDERS, Peter, J ... 717-871-5972 431 E
peter.anders@millersville.edu
ANDERS, Steven ... 641-784-5178 178 G
anders@graceland.edu
ANDERSEN, Catherine .. 410-837-6205 221 B
candersen@ubalt.edu
ANDERSEN, Charles, N 208-496-1124 137 F
andersenc@byui.edu
ANDERSEN, Jim ... 209-384-6396.. 54 C
andersen.j@mccd.edu
ANDERSEN, Kathy ... 717-728-2503 415 B
kathyandersen@centralpenn.edu
ANDERSEN, Kent ... 205-226-4679.... 2 C
kanderse@bsc.edu
ANDERSEN, Kent, A ... 307-674-6446 546 H
kandersen@sheridan.edu
ANDERSEN, Leslie ... 714-816-0366.. 70 D
leslie.andersen@trident.edu
ANDERSEN, Marcanne .. 757-822-7184 517 C
mandersen@tcc.edu
ANDERSEN, Mark, N ... 307-686-0254 546 H
mandersen@sheridan.edu
ANDERSEN, Mary ... 719-775-8873.. 84 A
mary.andersen@morgancc.edu
ANDERSEN, Mike ... 831-656-1062 548 A
manderse@nps.edu
ANDERSEN, Patricia, M 605-394-1261 454 B
patricia.andersen@sdsmt.edu
ANDERSEN, Robert ... 309-298-2446 163 A
r-andersen@wiu.edu
ANDERSEN, Robert, B .. 540-828-5350 505 F
randerse@bridgewater.edu
ANDERSEN, Sherry ... 508-362-2131 231 D
sanderse@capecod.edu
ANDERSEN, Stephen ... 706-764-6936 125 F
sandersen@gntc.edu
ANDERSEN,
Thomas Ove ... 828-884-8320 355 A
ove.andersen@brevard.edu
ANDERSON, Aime ... 662-562-3305 269 E
aanderson@northwestms.edu
ANDERSON, Al ... 406-275-4833 288 H
al_anderson@skc.edu
ANDERSON, Amanda ... 304-204-4340 533 C
aanderson13@wvstateu.edu
ANDERSON, Amber ... 661-763-7870.. 69 E
aanderson@taftcollege.edu
ANDERSON, Amie ... 989-686-9472 242 I
amieanderson@delta.edu
ANDERSON, Amy ... 269-782-1367 250 D
aanderson@swmich.edu
ANDERSON, Amy ... 352-340-4801 110 B
andersa@phsc.edu
ANDERSON, Amy ... 828-898-8845 358 F
andersona@lmc.edu
ANDERSON, Amy, A ... 212-749-2802 331 I
aanderson@msmnyc.edu
ANDERSON, Andrea ... 706-432-0729 129 H
aanderson@paine.edu
ANDERSON, Andrew ... 206-296-5858 526 F
registrar@seattleu.edu
ANDERSON, Andy ... 913-469-8500 188 E
aanders@jccc.edu
ANDERSON, Angela ... 970-521-6730.. 84 H
angela.anderson@njc.edu
ANDERSON, Angela, B . 740-376-4711 386 A
angela.anderson@marietta.edu
ANDERSON, Angela, D . 301-322-0699 217 G
andersad@pgcc.edu
ANDERSON, Angela, R . 252-328-6747 369 E
andersona@ecu.edu
ANDERSON, Antje ... 402-461-7351 290 G
aanderson@hastings.edu
ANDERSON, Ashley ... 405-878-5168 402 A
ananderson@stgregorys.edu
ANDERSON, Audrey, J . 615-322-8965 465 H
audrey.j.anderson@vanderbilt.edu
ANDERSON, Barbara ... 660-248-6320 272 N
banderso@centralmethodist.edu
ANDERSON, Barbara ... 818-710-4151.. 51 H
andersbm@piercecollege.edu

ANDERSON, Rayelle ..... 208-769-5978 138 G
rayelle_anderson@nic.edu
ANDERSON, Rebecca .... 210-458-4132 494 D
REBECCA.ANDERSON@UTSA.EDU
ANDERSON, Rebecca .... 704-337-2485 368 B
andersonr@queens.edu
ANDERSON, Rhonda, C 989-837-4455 248 D
rca@northwood.edu
ANDERSON, Rick .... 252-940-6417 360 B
rick.anderson@beaufortccc.edu
ANDERSON, Rick, L ..... 785-670-1634 192 B
rick.anderson@washburn.edu
ANDERSON, Robert ...... 517-629-0446 239 A
banderson@albion.edu
ANDERSON, Robert ...... 509-359-2531 522 C
randerson@ewu.edu
ANDERSON, Robin, D .. 503-943-7224 410 H
anderson@up.edu
ANDERSON, Roger .... 908-852-1400 301 C
andersonr@centenarycollege.edu
ANDERSON, Ron .... 651-201-1498 257 N
ron.anderson@so.mnscu.edu
ANDERSON, Ronald, M 859-858-3511 193 A
ron.anderson@asbury.edu
ANDERSON, Russell ..... 601-266-4153 271 B
rusty.anderson@usm.edu
ANDERSON, Ryan .... 718-405-3403 322 A
ryan.anderson@mountsaintvincent.edu
ANDERSON, Sandy .... 907-745-3201.. 10 B
sanderson@akbible.edu
ANDERSON, Scott, R .... 815-599-3604 146 B
scott.anderson@highland.edu
ANDERSON, Sharee ...... 208-535-5333 138 B
sharee.anderson@my.eitc.edu
ANDERSON, Sharon ..... 805-756-7745.. 32 E
sander17@calpoly.edu
ANDERSON, Sharon, D 336-734-7735 362 F
sanderson@forsythtech.edu
ANDERSON, Shawn ...... 218-299-6535 259 H
shawn.anderson@minnesota.edu
ANDERSON, Shayna ..... 661-362-2203.. 53 F
sanderson@masters.edu
ANDERSON, Sherry ...... 270-534-3145 197 E
sherry.anderson@kctcs.edu
ANDERSON, Stephanie . 512-245-2803 489 C
sa35@txstate.edu
ANDERSON,
Stephen, P .... 830-372-8020 487 C
sanderson@tlu.edu
ANDERSON, Steve .... 803-372-8022 487 C
sanderson@tlu.edu
ANDERSON, Susan .... 978-656-3483 232 B
andersons@middlesex.mass.edu
ANDERSON, Susan .... 216-373-6396 388 A
andersons@ndc.edu
ANDERSON, Susan, M . 530-898-6472.. 33 A
sanderson@csuchico.edu
ANDERSON, Suzanne ... 701-777-2711 373 G
suzanne.anderson@und.edu
ANDERSON,
Suzanne, M .... 540-853-0691 509 D
srmcquire@carilionclinic.org
ANDERSON, Sylvia, C .. 919-530-6681 370 C
sander55@nccu.edu
ANDERSON, Tamara ..... 508-565-1661 237 A
tanderson@stonehill.edu
ANDERSON, Therese ..... 215-596-8813 438 E
registrar@usciences.edu
ANDERSON,
Thomas, K .... 802-626-6497 504 B
thomas.anderson@lyndonstate.edu
ANDERSON, Timothy, J 413-545-6388 228 F
tjanderson@ecs.umass.edu
ANDERSON, Tina, K ..... 229-333-2119 134 I
tina.anderson@wiregrass.edu
ANDERSON,
Tina Marie .... 540-868-7107 515 H
tanderson@lfcc.edu
ANDERSON, Todd .... 910-521-6371 371 D
todd.anderson@uncp.edu
ANDERSON, Tracey ...... 304-327-4331 532 D
tanderson@bluefieldstate.edu
ANDERSON, Vanessa .... 303-797-5930.. 79 A
vanessa.anderson@arapahoe.edu
ANDERSON, Wanda ...... 302-736-2443.. 94 E
wanda.anderson@wesley.edu
ANDERSON, Warren ...... 724-738-2003 432 A
warren.anderson@sru.edu
ANDERSON, William ..... 845-431-8961 324 D
william.anderson@sunydutchess.edu
ANDERSON, William, L 301-322-0622 217 G
anderswl@pgcc.edu
ANDERSON, William, O 610-660-1276 434 G
banderso@sju.edu
ANDERSON, William, O 802-654-2252 502 H
wanderson@smcvt.edu
ANDERSON,
Yolanda, B .... 919-530-6738 370 C
yandersn@nccu.edu
ANDERSON-BINA,
Cindy .... 218-235-2121 262 C
c.bina@vcc.edu
ANDERSON-BURT,
Marilyn .... 206-934-5144 526 B
marilyn.anderson-burt@seattlecolleges.edu
ANDERSON-REID,
Marcia .... 507-284-3627 254 G
marcis.andersonreid@mayo.edu
ANDERSON-SAPATA,
Barbara .... 847-233-7700 155 B
banderson-sapata@nc.edu
ANDERSON WIECK,
Patricia .... 503-594-6000 405 A
patricia.anderson@clackamas.edu
ANDERSON-WILLIAMS,
Sandra .... 615-327-6683 458 F
williamss@mmc.edu
ANDERTON, Mark .... 435-722-6900 499 G
marka@ubatc.edu
ANDIS, Blake .... 276-739-2582 517 D
bandis@vhcc.edu
ANDORS, Allison .... 516-686-7737 335 F
aandors@nyit.edu
ANDRACKI, Jason .... 814-332-3100 411 F
ANDRADE, Alicia .... 559-453-2220.. 45 E
alicia.andrade@fresno.edu
ANDRADE, Anne, M ..... 401-254-3207 442 C
amandrade@rwu.edu
ANDRADE, Estevan .... 208-426-1698 137 E
EstevanAndrade@boisestate.edu
ANDRADE, June, C ...... 787-728-1515 559 A
jandrade@sagrado.edu
ANDRADE, Kim .... 405-422-1267 401 H
andradek@redlandscc.edu
ANDRADE, Maureen ..... 801-863-6158 500 B
maureen.andrade@uvu.edu
ANDRADE, Raul .... 312-939-0111 144 D
raul@eastwest.edu
ANDRAOS, Amale .... 212-854-3473 322 F
aa3217@columbia.edu
ANDREA, Francine .... 201-559-6181 302 I
andreaf@felician.edu
ANDREA, JR.,
Robert, K .... 518-956-8206 343 C
randrea@albany.edu
ANDREANI, Scott .... 330-494-6170 391 J
sandreani@starkstate.edu
ANDREAS, Marc .... 616-222-3000 245 D
mandreas@kuyper.edu
ANDREAS, Michelle ...... 360-596-5209 527 B
mandreas@spscc.edu
ANDREASEN,
Michael, C .... 541-346-0869 410 F
miandrea@uoregon.edu
ANDREASEN,
Niels-Erik, A .... 269-471-3100 239 D
neaa@andrews.edu
ANDRECHAK, Michael .. 404-727-9252 124 D
michael.j.andrechak@emory.edu
ANDREINI, Janelle, S ... 402-465-2414 292 E
jsa@nebrwesleyan.edu
ANDREJCZYK, Rose, L . 413-205-3248 221 G
rose.andrejczyk@aic.edu
ANDREOLA, Michael ..... 412-536-1096 422 E
michael.andreola@laroche.edu
ANDREOTTI, Carole ...... 617-588-1369 223 D
candreotti@bfit.edu
ANDRESEN, Julie, A ..... 573-629-4001 275 F
jandresen@hlg.edu
ANDRESEN, Sharla .... 541-383-7208 404 K
sandresen@cocc.edu
ANDRESS-MARTIN,
Holly .... 583-288-6421 274 C
handress@culver.edu
ANDREU, Angel, E .... 585-292-3031 333 G
aandreu@monroecc.edu
ANDREU, Frank .... 305-821-3333 104 C
fandreu@fnu.edu
ANDREW, Aletha .... 919-735-5151 367 A
raandrew@waynecc.edu
ANDREW, Barbara .... 973-720-3657 309 I
andrewb@wpunj.edu
ANDREW, Damon, P 225-578-2043 204M
damonandrew@lsu.edu
ANDREW, Kenneth .... 304-473-8367 534 G
andrew_k@wvwc.edu
ANDREW, Martha .... 575-758-8914 311 F
marcya@midwiferycollege.edu
ANDREW, Matthew .... 320-308-4072 261 E
mjandrew@stcloudstate.edu
ANDREW, Paul .... 617-495-1000 227 D
paul_andrew@harvard.edu
ANDREWS, Aaron .... 870-759-4105.. 25 I
aandrews@wbcoll.edu
ANDREWS, Adrienne .... 530-344-5716.. 53 A
andrewa@flc.losrios.edu
ANDREWS, AnneMarie . 845-431-8980 324 D
Amandrews@sunydutchess.edu
ANDREWS, Arthur, W ... 919-866-5688 366 H
awandrews@waketech.edu
ANDREWS, Beverly .... 269-467-9945 243 A
bandrews@glenoaks.edu
ANDREWS, Bradley, J .. 620-229-6223 191 B
brad.andrews@sckans.edu
ANDREWS, Carolyn ...... 806-291-3400 496 K
andrewsc@wbu.edu
ANDREWS, Chip, L ...... 770-534-6759 121 G
candrews@brenau.edu
ANDREWS, Cyndi .... 503-594-3025 405 A
cyndia@clackamas.edu
ANDREWS, Danielle ...... 614-508-7219 383 L
dandrews@hondros.edu
ANDREWS, Danny .... 806-291-3600 496 K
andrewsd@wbu.edu
ANDREWS, David, W .... 410-516-7820 216 A
davidandrews@jhu.edu
ANDREWS, Diane, L ..... 814-865-5423 428 C
dla6@psu.edu
ANDREWS, Dianna, L ... 904-264-2172 111 G
dianna.andrews@iws.edu
ANDREWS, Dionne, T ... 304-457-6324 529 C
andrewsdt@ab.edu
ANDREWS, Donald, R .. 225-771-5640 207 A
jazandrews@yahoo.com
ANDREWS, Evelyn .... 707-654-1794.. 34 B
eandrews@csum.edu
ANDREWS, George .... 305-237-3316 108 L
gandrews@mdc.edu
ANDREWS, Herry .... 307-778-1231 546 F
handrews@lccc.wy.edu
ANDREWS, Jeannette .... 803-777-3862 450 B
jandrews@mailbox.sc.edu
ANDREWS, Jeff .... 601-318-6741 271 F
jeff.andrews@wmcarey.edu
ANDREWS, Kim .... 660-543-8059 283 F
andrews@ucmo.edu
ANDREWS, Kim .... 318-335-3944 203 C
ANDREWS, Linda .... 713-798-4620 469 C
landrews@bcm.edu
ANDREWS, Loretta .... 406-447-4508 286 D
landrews@carroll.edu
ANDREWS, Lynn .... 503-554-2112 406 A
landrews@georgefox.edu
ANDREWS, Margaret .... 810-762-3420 251 E
mmandrew@umflint.edu
ANDREWS, Margaret .... 617-619-1900 227 G
margaret.andrews@hult.edu
ANDREWS, Mark .... 770-228-7367 132 B
mandrews@sctech.edu
ANDREWS, Michael, F . 503-943-8628 410 H
andrews@up.edu
ANDREWS, Mitch .... 903-510-2034 491 A
mand@tjc.edu
ANDREWS, Nancy .... 919-684-2455 356 E
nancy.andrews@mc.duke.edu
ANDREWS, Nikki .... 508-373-9701 223 C
nikki.andrews@becker.edu
ANDREWS, Rebecca ..... 615-794-4254 460 A
randrews@omorecollege.edu
ANDREWS, Richard ...... 916-691-7423.. 52 J
andrewr@crc.losrios.edu
ANDREWS, Robert .... 386-822-7082 117 A
randrews@stetson.edu
ANDREWS, Robert .... 423-775-6596 460 B
ANDREWS, Robert .... 704-847-5600 369 A
randrews@ses.edu
ANDREWS, Rodrick ...... 904-632-5903 105 A
randrews@fscj.edu
ANDREWS, Roy .... 503-255-0332 407 D
randrews@multnomah.edu
ANDREWS, Sabrina, L .. 330-972-6959 392 H
sabrin7@uakron.edu
ANDREWS, Serena .... 979-230-3245 469 G
serena.andrews@brazosport.edu
ANDREWS, Sheila .... 317-632-5553 170 Z
sandrews@lincolntech.com
ANDREWS, Sona .... 503-725-5257 409 D
sona.andrews@pdx.edu
ANDREWS, Spring .... 831-477-5220.. 30 C
spandrew@cabrillo.edu
ANDREWS, Stacie .... 814-254-0557 415 F
standrews@pa.gov
ANDREWS, Tasha, A .... 919-516-5082 368 E
taandrews@st-aug.edu
ANDREWS, Tim .... 913-360-7363 184 K
tandrews@benedictine.edu
ANDREWS, Todd, G ...... 401-863-6331 441 A
todd_andrews@brown.edu
ANDREWS, Todd, J ...... 860-727-6937.. 90 F
tandrews@goodwin.edu
ANDREWS, Tonia, Y ..... 540-985-9784 509 D
tyandrews@jchs.edu
ANDREWS, Traci .... 954-923-4440 107 U
financialaid@keycollege.edu
ANDREWS, Trisha .... 847-543-2007 142 G
tandrews@clcillinois.edu
ANDREWS, Warren .... 914-654-5926 322 B
wandrews@cnr.edu
ANDREWS, Wayne, D ... 606-783-2022 198 H
w.andrews@moreheadstate.edu
ANDRIASSIAN, Alen ..... 323-953-4000.. 51 E
andriaar@lacitycollege.edu
ANDRIATCH, Michael ... 585-395-5809 345 A
mandriat@brockport.edu
ANDRICK, Christina ...... 310-577-3000.. 77 K
admissions@yosan.edu
ANDRICK, John .... 701-845-7302 374 D
john.andrick@vcsu.edu
ANDRIOLA, Tom .... 510-987-0405.. 70 J
tom.andriola@ucop.edu
ANDROUIN, George ..... 904-620-4222 116 A
gandroui@unf.edu
ANDRUS, Brent .... 801-524-8131 498 J
brenta51@ldsbc.edu
ANDRUS, Dionne .... 225-216-8221 202 N
andrusd@mybrcc.edu
ANDRUS, Katie .... 903-823-3125 484 D
katie.andrus@texarkanacollege.edu
ANDRUS, Steven .... 225-216-8550 202 N
andruss@mybrcc.edu
ANDRZEJEWSKI,
Margaret .... 716-827-2564 350 H
andrzejewskim@trocaire.edu
ANDRZJEWSKI,
Linda, M .... 302-356-6754.. 94 G
linda.m.andrzjewski@wilmu.edu
ANDUJAR-WENDLAND,
Sandra .... 212-686-9040 352 H
s.andujar@woodtobecoburn.edu
ANEMA, Elizabeth, A .... 413-542-2313 222 A
alumni@amherst.edu
ANEMA, Laurie .... 708-974-5343 153 D
anema@morainevalley.edu
ANG, Catharina .... 808-947-4788 137 C
cathyang2008@gmail.com
ANGE, Crystal .... 252-940-6216 360 B
crystal.ange@beaufortccc.edu
ANGEL, David, P .... 508-793-7320 225 B
dangel@clarku.edu
ANGEL, Julian .... 305-899-2908.. 99 B
jangel@barry.edu
ANGELI, Valerie, G .... 717-867-6232 423 I
angeli@lvc.edu
ANGELIS, Peter .... 310-825-4941.. 71 D
pangelis@ha.ucla.edu
ANGELL, Alecia .... 509-527-3683 527 H
alecia.angell@wwcc.edu
ANGELL, Lance .... 617-879-1209 238 C
langell@wheelock.edu
ANGELL, Mary .... 505-473-6322 313 B
mary.angell@santafeuniversity.edu
ANGELL, Townsend .... 503-777-7763 409 E
townsend.angell@reed.edu
ANGELO, Lisa .... 215-968-8306 413 F
lisa.angelo@bucks.edu
ANGELONI, Lisa .... 609-771-3080 301 E
angeloni@tcnj.edu
ANGELOTTI, Linda .... 408-855-5123.. 76 E
linda.angelotti@wvm.edu
ANGEMI, Karen .... 909-621-8384.. 46 K
kangemi@hmc.edu
ANGEMI, Karen .... 909-621-8384.. 46 K
karen_angemi@hmc.edu
ANGER, Donna .... 907-474-6131.. 10 I
dmanger@alaska.edu
ANGER, Paul .... 928-428-6260.. 13 L
paul.anger@eac.edu
ANGERMEIER, Jaclyn .... 609-894-9311 306 B
jangermeier@bcc.edu
ANGEVINE, Roger, L .... 606-878-4801 197 B
roger.angevine@kctcs.edu
ANGIS, Victoria .... 802-468-1231 503 G
victoria.angis@castleton.edu
ANGLE, J. Scott .... 706-542-3924 132 H
caesdean@uga.edu
ANGLE, O. Ray .... 509-313-4100 522 L
ANGLE, Perry .... 559-442-4600.. 69 B
perry.angle@fresnocitycollege.edu
ANGLE, Ray .... 919-962-4481 371 A
rayangle@email.unc.edu
ANGLE, Steven .... 423-425-4141 465 E
steven-angle@utc.edu
ANGLIM, Sean .... 315-568-3092 334 F
sanglim@nycc.edu
ANGLIN, AJ .... 479-968-0319.. 20 C
ajanglin@atu.edu
ANGLIN, Jennifer .... 866-251-3244.. 98 A
ANGLIN, Pamela, D ...... 903-785-7661 480 B
panglin@parisjc.edu
ANGRISANI, Vincent ..... 718-997-5600 320 E
vincent.angrisani@qc.cuny.edu
ANGROVE, William .... 936-294-2774 489 A
wla002@shsu.edu
ANGST, JR., Arthur, H . 516-876-3094 345 E
angsta@oldwestbury.edu
ANGSTADT, Peter .... 541-956-7000 409 F
pangstadt@roguecc.edu
ANGSTER, Sherrie .... 626-966-4576.. 27 I
studentservices@agu.edu

ANGUEIRA, Annette ...... 315-228-7130 321 H aangueira@colgate.edu
ANGUIANO, Amy .... 540-857-7254 517 E aanguiano@virginiawestern.edu
ANGUIANO, Maria .... 951-827-7310.. 72 A maria.anguiano@ucr.edu
ANGULO, Michael .... 609-652-4295 308 E michael.angulo@stockton.edu
ANGULO, Susan .... 305-628-6566 112 B cangulo@stu.edu
ANICH, Kenneth .... 563-876-3353 177 I kanich@dwci.edu
ANID, Nada .... 516-686-7931 335 F nanid@nyit.edu
ANKE, Robin .... 724-838-4260 435 E anke@setonhill.edu
ANKE, Sharla, M .... 724-287-8711 413 G sharla.anke@bc3.edu
ANKENY, Mark .... 503-352-2924 408 I mankeny@pacificu.edu
ANKER, Laura, M .... 516-876-3460 345 E ankerl@oldwestbury.edu
ANKER, Perryne .... 310-824-1586.. 25 K
ANKERBERG, Erik .... 512-313-3000 471 H erik.ankerberg@concordia.edu
ANKERSEN, Lynne .... 843-574-6137 449 G lynne.ankersen@tridenttech.edu
ANKSORUS, Remington 815-928-5554 155 G rjanksorus@olivet.edu
ANKUDA, Pamela .... 802-728-1530 504 C pankuda@vtc.edu
ANNA, Gary, M .... 309-677-3150 140 H gma@bradley.edu
ANNAN, Jack .... 970-521-6690.. 84 H jack.annan@njc.edu
ANNARELLI, James, J .. 727-864-8243 101 P annarejj@eckerd.edu
ANNE, Kirk .... 585-245-5577 345 D kma@geneseo.edu
ANNETT, JR., Bruce, J . 248-204-2200 245 J bannett@ltu.edu
ANNETTE, Harold .... 218-322-2353 259 B harold.annette@itascacc.edu
ANNINO, Louis .... 203-932-7153.. 92 G lannino@newhaven.edu
ANNIS, David, L .... 405-325-2300 403 I dannis@ou.edu
ANNIS, Dominique, A .. 815-740-3398 162 F dannis@stfrancis.edu
ANNUNZIATO, Frank, P .... 215-204-7366 436 C frank.annunziato@temple.edu
ANSARI, Parviz, H .... 618-650-3779 159 I pansari@siue.edu
ANSARI, Shahid .... 781-239-4277 222 E sansari@babson.edu
ANSBOURY, Pamela ..... 210-485-0307 466 J pansboury@alamo.edu
ANSEL, Stuart .... 718-252-7800 350 C sansel@touro.edu
ANSELMENT, Kenneth, L .... 920-832-6992 536 R ken.anselment@lawrence.edu
ANSELMI, Michael, A ... 410-704-4008 221 A manselmi@towson.edu
ANSERT, Janet, M .... 215-898-5777 437 I ansertjm@upenn.edu
ANSHUS, Corrine, M .... 414-410-4203 535 C cmanshus@stritch.edu
ANSON, Catherine, T .... 216-397-4520 384 F canson@jcu.edu
ANSON, Regan .... 402-872-2429 292 C ranson@peru.edu
ANSORGE, Vicki .... 920-686-6203 539 A Vicki.Ansorge@sl.edu
ANSTEY, Barbara .... 603-271-6484 297 C banstey@ccsnh.edu
ANSTOETTER, Donald ... 314-792-6120 276 H anstoetter@kenrick.edu
ANSTROM, Deborah ..... 828-298-3325 373 A danstrom@warren-wilson.edu
ANSTROM, Deborah ..... 828-298-3325 373 A purchasing@warren-wilson.edu
ANT, Susan .... 952-358-8906 260 D susan.ant@normandale.edu
ANTCZAK, Frederick ..... 616-331-2495 243 E antczakf@gvsu.edu
ANTCZAK, Laura .... 239-985-3475 104 G lantczak@fsw.edu
ANTEL, Lisa .... 203-596-4585.. 91 D lantel@post.edu
ANTELMAN, Kristin .... 626-395-6416.. 31 D kristin.antelman@caltech.edu
ANTENEN, James .... 210-826-7595 496 K antenenj@wbu.edu
ANTER, David .... 805-378-1415.. 75 C danter@vcccd.edu
ANTHONY, Cynthia .... 334-347-2623.... 3 H canthony@escc.edu
ANTHONY, David .... 315-464-8047 344 E anthonyd@upstate.edu
ANTHONY, Doug .... 304-424-8280 533 E doug.anthony@wvup.edu
ANTHONY, Kathy .... 610-526-6045 420 C kanthony@harcum.edu
ANTHONY, Linda .... 612-338-7224 265 G Linda.Anthony@laureate.net
ANTHONY, Michael ...... 847-635-1745 155 E manthony@oakton.edu
ANTHONY, Miriam .... 708-596-2000 159 D manthony@ssc.edu
ANTHONY, Pamela .... 515-294-1022 175 G panthony@iastate.edu
ANTHONY, Philadelphia .... 336-750-3301 372 D philadelphiawa@wssu.edu
ANTHONY, Sharon .... 215-572-2850 412 F anthony@arcadia.edu
ANTHONY, Yvonne, E .. 617-427-0060 233 A YAnthony@rcc.mass.edu
ANTHWAL, Sunny .... 845-398-4061 341 H sunny@stac.edu
ANTILLA, Margaret .... 503-338-2428 405 B mantilla@clatsopcc.edu
ANTILLON, Susan .... 386-506-3656 101 I antills@DaytonaState.edu
ANTKOWIAK, Alex .... 410-337-6060 215 B alex.antkowiak@goucher.edu
ANTKOWIAK, Bruce ...... 724-805-2940 435 B bruce.antkowiak@stvincent.edu
ANTMAN, Karen, H .... 617-638-5300 224 E kha4@bu.edu
ANTOBELLO, Maria, R .. 603-647-3530 297 H antobellom@franklinpierce.edu
ANTOINE, Linda, B .... 225-771-4580 207 A linda_antoine@subr.edu
ANTOKHIN, Kathleen .... 510-649-2463.. 46 E kantokhin@gtu.edu
ANTOLINI, Heather .... 304-647-6374 533 B hantolini@osteo.wvsom.edu
ANTONAKAKIS, Helen .. 856-227-7200 301 A hantonakakis@camdencc.edu
ANTONELLO, Michael ... 561-237-7960 108 E mantonello@lynn.edu
ANTONETTI, Nina .... 413-369-4044 225 E antonetti@csld.edu
ANTONIA, Keith .... 706-867-2886 133 A keith.antonia@ung.edu
ANTONIO, Edward .... 303-765-3163.. 83 C eantonio@iliff.edu
ANTONS, Christopher ... 415-482-1932.. 43 D christopher.antons@dominican.edu
ANTONUCCI, Carl .... 860-832-2099.. 88 D antonucci@ccsu.edu
ANTONUCCI, Dorothy, M .... 412-578-8770 414 I dmantonucci@carlow.edu
ANTONUCCI, Toni, C .... 734-763-5846 251 C tca@umich.edu
ANTROBUS, Barbara ..... 859-858-2285 192 O
ANTROP-GONZALEZ, Rene .... 651-999-5959 259 E rene.antropgonzalez@metrostate.edu
ANTUNES, Nancy .... 781-891-2686 223 E nantunes@bentley.edu
ANTURKAR, Anjali, N ... 734-764-5132 251 C anturkar@umich.edu
ANWAY, Amy .... 419-559-2371 392 A aanway01@terra.edu
ANYANWU, FitzPatrick . 337-421-6905 204 F fitzpatrick.anyanwu@sowela.edu
ANYANWU, Fitzpatrick, U .... 337-421-6905 204 F fitzpatrick.anyanwu@sowela.edu
ANZ, Susan .... 254-710-8641 469 D susan_anz@baylor.edu
ANZALDUA, Ricardo ..... 212-237-8316 319 F ranzaldua@jjay.cuny.edu
ANZALONE, Roseann .... 518-743-2242 347 E anzalonr@sunyacc.edu
AOUN, Joseph, E .... 617-373-2101 235 D
APANEL, Stephen, J ..... 570-577-1195 413 E stephen.apanel@bucknell.edu
APANOVICH, Val .... 570-674-6749 426 D vapanovi@misericordia.edu
APAW, David .... 410-225-2464 216 F dapaw@mica.edu
APEL, Scott .... 562-985-4031.. 33 F scott.apel@csulb.edu
APELIAN, Bill .... 864-242-5100 443 G
APELQUIST, Maryellen .. 802-831-1228 503 E mapelquist@vermontlaw.edu
APER, Jeffery, P .... 217-424-6220 153 A japer@millikin.edu
APFELSTADT, Eric .... 360-438-4564 525 H eapfelstadt@stmartin.edu
APFELTHALER, Gerhard 805-493-3352.. 31 H apfeltha@callutheran.edu
APIGIAN, Caitlin .... 719-389-6705.. 79M
APLIN, Greg .... 334-222-6591.... 5 G jgaplin@lbwcc.edu
APODACA, Phillip, C .... 719-389-6613.. 79M papodaca@coloradocollege.edu
APODACA, Rennette ...... 575-646-2916 312 A rennette@nmsu.edu
APOLLO, Richard, M .... 516-463-5405 328 A richard.apollo@hofstra.edu
APONTE, Arcelio .... 973-353-5541 307 C arcelio.aponte@rutgers.edu
APONTE, Brunilda .... 787-743-7979 555M baponte@suagm.edu
APONTE, Carmen, L ..... 787-780-0070 550 G caponte@caribbean.edu
APONTE, Juan, M .... 787-764-0000 558 E juan.aponte6@upr.edu
APONTE, Julio .... 787-274-1142 337 B japonte@stdpr.org
APONTE-AVELLANET, Nilda .... 787-993-8861 557 E nilda.aponte2@upr.edu
APPAVOO, Suresh .... 415-485-3598.. 43 D sappavoo@dominican.edu
APPEL, Marie-Noel .... 212-229-5662 334 C appelm@newschool.edu
APPELBAUM, Marla ...... 212-229-5192 334 C marla@newschool.edu
APPELGET, Kristin .... 609-258-3018 305 C appelget@princeton.edu
APPELL, Breck, H .... 515-964-0601 178 F appellb@faith.edu
APPELSMITH, Jacob, A . 530-754-6295.. 71 A jappelsmith@ucdavis.edu
APPELT, Uschi .... 812-866-7221 166 E appelt@hanover.edu
APPIAH-PADI, Stephen, K .... 570-577-3796 413 E s.appiahpadi@bucknell.edu
APPIARIUS, Donald, B . 260-399-7700 174 C dappiarius@sf.edu
APPLE, Mark .... 317-955-6775 171 A mapple@marian.edu
APPLE, Ryan .... 517-321-0242 243 H rapple@glcc.edu
APPLE VANALSTINE, Judy .... 317-788-3271 173 I japplevanal@uindy.edu
APPLEBURY, Gene .... 901-751-8453 459 C gapplebury@mabts.edu
APPLEBY, Charley .... 870-680-8717.. 19 I charley_appleby@asun.edu
APPLEGATE, J. Phillip .. 918-631-2070 403M phil-applegate@utulsa.edu
APPLEGATE, John .... 812-855-9198 167 I jsapple@iu.edu
APPLEGATE, John, S .... 812-855-9198 167 J jsapple@indiana.edu
APPLEGATE, Rachel .... 317-278-2376 168 E rapplega@iupui.edu
APPLEGRAD, Yaakov ...... 732-367-1060 300 D
APPLEMAN, Boomer .... 508-559-5208 397 K bappleman@ecok.edu
APPLETON, Amber .... 503-382-4743 519 H aappleton@aii.edu
APPLETON, Judith, A .... 607-255-9970 323 C jaa2@cornell.edu
APPLETON, Kevin .... 410-651-6230 219 H kappleton@umes.edu
APPLETON, Lea .... 909-445-2590.. 39 G lappleton@cst.edu
APPLIN, Cynthia .... 937-328-6147 379 L applinc@clarkstate.edu
APPLIN, Mary Beth .... 601-857-3253 267 D mary.applin@hindscc.edu
APPLING, Ron .... 806-291-3451 496 K applingr@wbu.edu
APPOLONIA, Terry .... 814-938-6711 431 A Terry.Appolonia@iup.edu
APPREY, Augustine .... 717-290-8747 423 E aapprey@lancasterseminary.edu
APPREY, Maurice .... 434-924-7923 514 A ma9h@virginia.edu
APSEY, Curt .... 406-447-5479 286 D capsey@carroll.edu
AQUI, Jason .... 425-564-4128 519 L jason.aqui@bellevuecollege.edu
AQUILA, Dominic .... 713-525-2164 493 J aquilad@stthom.edu
AQUILA, Jennifer, K ..... 610-799-1120 424 A jaquila@lccc.edu
AQUILA, Scott, W .... 610-799-1550 424 A saquila@lccc.edu
AQUINO, Belissa .... 787-766-1717 556 A beaquino@suagm.edu
AQUINO, Carlos .... 815-740-3398 162 F caquino@stfrancis.edu
AQUINO, Cathy .... 304-734-6611 531 A cathy.aquino@bridgevalley.edu
AQUINO, Eufemia .... 650-493-4430.. 66 H eufemia.aquino@sofia.edu
AQUINO, Jeannette .... 787-890-2681 557 C jeanette.aquino@upr.edu
ARABIA, Caprice .... 716-926-8942 327 F carabia@hilbert.edu
ARACENA, Beth .... 610-790-1981 412 C beth.aracena@alvernia.edu
ARADHYA, Jennifer, M . 781-280-3511 232 B loucksb@middlesex.mass.edu
ARAGON, Paul .... 575-769-4165 310 G paul.aragon@clovis.edu
ARAGON, Ruben .... 505-454-3330 311 H rubenaragon@nmhu.edu
ARAIMO, Angelo, G ..... 718-390-3412 352 C aaraimo@wagner.edu
ARAIN, Nizam .... 608-785-8541 539 G narain@uwlax.edu
ARAIZA, Claudia .... 619-298-1829.. 68 C caraiza@ssu.edu
ARAIZA, William .... 718-780-7955 317 A bill.araiza@brooklaw.edu
ARALDI, Mary-Jane, S . 518-471-3260 332 D maryjane.araldi@sphp.com
ARAMMASH, Fouzi, H .. 803-705-4311 443 F arammashf@benedict.edu
ARANDA, Eileen .... 909-667-4411.. 39 C president@claremontlincoln.org
ARANDA, Romelia .... 830-758-4125 483 A rdaranda@swtjc.edu
ARANEO, Mary Lou .... 631-451-4611 348 E araneom@sunysuffolk.edu
ARANT, Mark .... 918-444-2060 398M arant@nsuok.edu
ARANT, TJ .... 717-815-1231 440 H tarant@ycp.edu
ARAS, Kate .... 949-794-9090.. 68 F karas@stanbridge.edu
ARAUJO, Lisa .... 516-877-3230 314 F araujo@adelphi.edu
ARAVENA, Carmen .... 217-424-6202 153 A caravena@millikin.edu
ARBELO, Enid .... 787-878-5475 553 F earbelo@arecibo.inter.edu
ARBIDE, Donna, A .... 305-284-2873 118 A darbide@miami.edu
ARBOGAST DIMARCANTONIO, Laura .... 212-217-3762 325 C laura_arbogast@fitnyc.edu
ARBONA, Mildred .... 787-766-1717 556 A um_marbona@suagm.edu
ARBONEAUX, Annette ... 985-448-4041 208 C annette.arboneaux@nicholls.edu
ARBUCKLE, Joanne .... 212-217-4680 325 C joanne_arbuckle@fitnyc.edu
ARBUSTO, Joan .... 203-575-8091.. 89 F jarbusto@nv.edu
ARBUTHNOT, Beth .... 706-864-1441 133 A beth.arbuthnot@ung.edu
ARCADI, Margaret .... 716-270-5312 325 A arcadim@ecc.edu
ARCARESE, Chris .... 303-352-3032.. 81 J chris.arcarese@ccd.edu
ARCARIO, Paul .... 718-482-5400 320 B arcariop@lagcc.cuny.edu
ARCE, Ana .... 787-894-2828 558 F ana.arce1@upr.edu
ARCE, Elsa, M .... 412-365-1282 415 C arce@chatham.edu
ARCE, Frank .... 312-752-2478 149 D frank.arce@kendall.edu
ARCE, Joshua .... 785-749-8482 187 F jarce@haskell.edu
ARCE, Katherine .... 310-338-2881.. 53 C Katherine.Arce@lmu.edu
ARCE, Lydia .... 787-857-3600 553 G larce@br.inter.edu
ARCELUS, Victor, J .... 860-439-2834.. 90 D victor.arcelus@conncoll.edu
ARCHABAL, Alice .... 414-955-4718 537 C aarchabal@mcw.edu
ARCHAMBAULT, Marc .... 801-863-8568 500 B marc.archambault@uvu.edu
ARCHBALD, Patrick, T .. 413-545-2125 228 F archbald@umass.edu
ARCHBOLD, David, J .... 248-370-3358 248 K archbold@oakland.edu
ARCHER, Chris .... 603-623-0313 298 C chrisarcher@nhia.edu
ARCHER, Daniel, L .... 801-581-6326 499 K darcher@campusstore.utah.edu
ARCHER, Deborah .... 212-431-2138 335 G Deborah.Archer@nyls.edu
ARCHER, Elizabeth .... 619-477-6310.. 70 G earcher@usuniversity.edu
ARCHER, III, Frank .... 229-430-3686 119 H frank.archer@asurams.edu
ARCHER, Gie .... 940-668-7731 479 K marcher@nctc.edu
ARCHER, Keith .... 765-658-4165 165 G keitharcher@depauw.edu
ARCHER, Keith, A .... 309-341-7212 149 G kaarcher@knox.edu
ARCHER, Kevin .... 509-963-3101 520 E archerkc@cwu.edu

ARCHER, Len .... 407-303-5619.. 97 J
len.archer@adu.edu

ARCHER, Linda, R .... 757-446-6190 507 B
archerlr@evms.edu

ARCHER, Lynn .... 412-536-1182 422 E
lynn.archer@laroche.edu

ARCHER, Max .... 281-998-6024 486 F
marcher@txchiro.edu

ARCHER, Nicole .... 415-771-7020.. 62 I
narcher@sfai.edu

ARCHER, Rebecca .... 321-674-7571 103 R
rarcher@fit.edu

ARCHER, Ron .... 714-879-3901.. 47 D
rarcher@hiu.edu

ARCHER, Ryan .... 316-295-5410 187 C
archerr@friends.edu

ARCHER, Santee .... 229-732-5977 120 B
santeearcher@andrewcollege.edu

ARCHER, Thomas, R .... 802-626-6454 504 B
thomas.archer@lyndonstate.edu

ARCHER-RIERSON,
Abby .... 620-242-0439 189 E
archera@mcpherson.edu

ARCHEY, Larry .... 413-559-5767 227 C

ARCHIBALD, James, G . 229-333-5941 133 H
jgarchibald@valdosta.edu

ARCHIBALD, Michael .... 909-621-8152.. 65 E
michael.archibald@scrippscollege.edu

ARCHIBALD, Sandra, O 206-616-1648 527 G
sarch@uw.edu

ARCHIE, Tiffenia, D .... 215-204-9213 436 C
tiffenia.archie@temple.edu

ARCHINAL, Ginette .... 336-278-7230 356 F
garchinal@elon.edu

ARCHULETA, Irma .... 408-223-6749.. 63 P
irma.archuleta@evc.edu

ARCHULETA, Renee .... 303-914-6345.. 85 C
renee.archuleta@rrcc.edu

ARCILA, Luz .... 727-864-7748 101 P
arcilal@eckerd.edu

ARCUINO, Cathy, L .... 620-235-4680 190 G
carcuino@pittstate.edu

ARCURY, Tara, L .... 802-654-2212 502 H
tarcury@smcvt.edu

ARD, Aaron .... 803-584-3446 450 F
ajard@mailbox.sc.edu

ARDAIOLO, Frank, P .... 803-323-2251 451 I
ardaiolof@winthrop.edu

ARDALAN, Shah .... 281-290-2777 477 I
shah.ardalan@lonestar.edu

ARDEN, Warwick, A .... 919-515-2195 370 D
warwick_arden@ncsu.edu

ARDIS, Ann .... 302-831-2054.. 94 D
aardis@udel.edu

ARDREY, Melantha .... 843-953-3257 445 B
ardreym@cofc.edu

AREA, Ron .... 304-696-2826 532 H
area@marshall.edu

AREBALOS, Jason .... 760-773-2552.. 41 A
Jarebalos@collegeofthedesert.edu

AREIZAGA, Jose, R .... 787-891-0925 553 E
jareizag@aguadilla.inter.edu

ARELLANO, Jerry .... 210-486-3884 467 A
jarellano59@alamo.edu

ARELLANO,
Margarita, M .... 512-245-2124 489 C
ma33@txstate.edu

ARENA, John .... 706-771-5730 121 B
jarena@augustatech.edu

ARENA, Maryanne .... 585-345-6802 326 F
mcarena@genesee.edu

ARENA, Meaghan .... 585-245-5619 345 D
arena@geneseo.edu

ARENA, Michael .... 646-664-9100 318 B

ARENAZ, Pablo .... 956-326-2240 485 B
pablo.arenaz@tamiu.edu

AREND, Lori .... 412-536-2506 422 E
lori.arend@laroche.edu

AREND, Matthew .... 517-629-0521 239 A
marend@albion.edu

ARENDT, Ben .... 616-526-6000 240 L

ARENDT, Thomas, K .... 562-902-3355.. 67 J
tomarendt@scuhs.edu

ARENIVAS, Marisol .... 520-417-4115.. 13 B
arenivasm@cochise.edu

ARENS, Dave .... 712-279-1715 176 B
dave.arens@briarcliff.edu

ARENS, Timothy, E .... 312-329-4191 153 C
timothy.arens@moody.edu

ARES, Doreen .... 978-665-3123 229 D
dares@fitchburgstate.edu

ARESON, Ann, H .... 814-332-6556 411 F
aareson@allegheny.edu

ARETS, Wiel .... 312-567-3263 147 E
wiel.arets@iit.edu

AREY, Emily .... 704-669-4139 361 E
areye@clevelandcc.edu

AREY, George, A .... 617-552-4725 224 B
george.arey@bc.edu

AREY, Jason .... 207-216-4399 211 F
jarey@yccc.edu

AREY, Jason .... 603-206-8011 297 A
jarey@ccsnh.edu

ARFSTEN, Cheri .... 719-502-3054.. 84 J
cheri.arfsten@ppcc.edu

ARGENTIERI, Colleen .... 607-587-3932 347 D
argentch@alfredstate.edu

ARGIRI, Elizabeth .... 586-445-7306 246 A
argiril@macomb.edu

ARGO, Mike, A .... 870-235-4083.. 23 D
maargo@saumag.edu

ARGO, Scott .... 706-667-4095 121 C
sargo@gru.edu

ARGO, Trent .... 276-326-4217 505 D
targo@bluefield.edu

ARGUELLES, Adrianna .. 718-939-5100 330 E
aarguelles@libi.edu

ARGUELLES, Alejandro . 787-250-0000 557 B
alejandro.arguelles@upr.edu

ARGYRIS, Steven, G .... 510-649-2430.. 46 E
sargyris@gtu.edu

ARHIN, Afua .... 910-672-1924 370 A
aarhin@uncfsu.edu

ARHIPOV, Sergei, D .... 570-581-1818 435 A
sergei.arhipov@stots.edu

ARIANO, Pat .... 630-829-6003 140 A
pariano@ben.edu

ARIAS, Fenix .... 718-289-5210 318 E
fenix.arias@bcc.cuny.edu

ARIAS, Michael, R .... 949-824-5661.. 71 C
mrarias@uci.edu

ARICK, Bruce, E .... 317-940-9481 164 L
barick@butler.edu

ARIDA, Lisa, A .... 716-839-8218 323 F
larida@daemen.edu

ARILSON, Barbara .... 440-375-7000 385 B
barilson@lec.edu

ARIOLAN-SUKISAKI,
Kainoa .... 808-932-7777 135 I
kariolal@hawaii.edu

ARIOSTO, Robert .... 609-894-9311 306 B
rariosto@bcc.edu

ARISMENDEZ, Dee Dee 361-664-2981 470 K
deedeea@coastalbend.edu

ARISTIZABAL,
Humberto, X .... 410-543-6426 220 E
hxarisitzabal@salisbury.edu

ARITA, Kathy .... 509-793-2016 520 B
kathyar@bigbend.edu

ARIZA, Cristina .... 210-829-3870 492 B
mariza@uiwtx.edu

ARIZA, Diane, M .... 203-582-8939.. 91 E
diane.ariza@quinnipiac.edu

ARIZA, Ricardo, M .... 402-280-2469 290 B
ariza@creighton.edu

ARJUNE, Ricky, B .... 904-620-2502 116 A
rarjune@unf.edu

ARLINGTON, David, L .. 716-851-1987 325 A
arlington@ecc.edu

ARLITSCH, Kenning .... 406-994-6978 287 G
kenning.arlitsch@montana.edu

ARMAGOST, Mark, S .... 814-863-4308 428 C
msa17@psu.edu

ARMBRUSTER, Shirley .. 559-278-2795.. 33 D
shirleya@csufresno.edu

ARMENDARIZ, John .... 617-373-2133 235 D

ARMENTA, Richard, R .. 512-223-7795 468 H
rarmenta@austincc.edu

ARMENTOR, Melissa .... 409-880-8853 488 E
mfarmentor@lit.edu

ARMENTROUT,
Barbara, S .... 434-223-6220 508 B
barmentrout@hsc.edu

ARMES, Paul, W .... 806-291-3400 496 K
armesp@wbu.edu

ARMES, Traci .... 812-941-2260 169 A
trarmes@ius.edu

ARMESTO, Laura .... 859-846-5332 198 G
larmesto@midway.edu

ARMEY, Edith .... 701-662-1593 375 A
edith.armey@lrsc.edu

ARMIJO, Danny .... 575-624-8250 311 K
darmijo@nmmi.edu

ARMIJO, Lillian .... 575-835-5780 311 I
larmijo@admin.nmt.edu

ARMINANA, Ruben .... 707-664-2156.. 36 C
ruben.arminana@sonoma.edu

ARMINGTON, Thomas .. 610-526-1391 412 D
tom.armington@theamericancollege.edu

ARMINI, Michael, A .... 617-373-5718 235 D

ARMINIAK, Anthony .... 734-374-3227 252 A
aarmini1@wcccd.edu

ARMISTEAD, Lisa, P .... 404-413-2091 126 D
larmistead@gsu.edu

ARMISTEAD, William .... 304-473-8509 534 G
armistead_w@wvwc.edu

ARMITANO, Karen, A .... 970-945-8691.. 80 D

ARMOND, Pashuan .... 919-466-4400.. 96 H

ARMOR, Thomas, W .... 317-738-8045 166 B
tarmor@franklincollege.edu

ARMOUR, Angela .... 802-654-2527 502 H
aarmour@smcvt.edu

ARMOUR, Janet, Y .... 662-620-5092 267 F
jyamour@iccms.edu

ARMOUR, Lisa .... 352-381-3642 112 H
lisa.armour@sfcollege.edu

ARMOUR, Robert .... 606-546-1799 200 E
rarmour@unionky.edu

ARMOUR, Robin .... 925-473-7501.. 42 F
rarmour@losmedanos.edu

ARMOZA, Marcela .... 718-260-4999 320 D
marmoza@citytech.cuny.edu

ARMS, Gina .... 516-686-7902 335 F
garms@nyit.edu

ARMSTRONG, Albert .... 305-899-3250.. 99 B
aarmstrong@barry.edu

ARMSTRONG, Amy .... 830-792-7405 482 D
anarmstrong@schreiner.edu

ARMSTRONG,
Andrew, V .... 540-636-2900 506 H
armstrong@christendom.edu

ARMSTRONG, Booker ... 816-604-4125 278 A
booker.armstrong@mcckc.edu

ARMSTRONG, Dale .... 615-966-5148 458 C
dale.armstrong@lipscomb.edu

ARMSTRONG, David .... 706-865-2134 132 G
darmstrong@truett.edu

ARMSTRONG, David, A 859-344-3348 200 C
darmstrong@thomasmore.edu

ARMSTRONG,
David, M .... 816-501-2423 272 E
david.armstrong@avila.edu

ARMSTRONG, Donald ... 716-614-5950 336 D
hr@niagaracc.suny.edu

ARMSTRONG, Donald ... 716-614-5950 336 D
armstrong@niagaracc.suny.edu

ARMSTRONG, Elizabeth 540-231-7197 518 B
beth1@vt.edu

ARMSTRONG, Franca .... 315-334-7701 333 D
farmstrong@mvcc.edu

ARMSTRONG, Gary .... 816-415-7651 285 K
armstrongg@william.jewell.edu

ARMSTRONG, JR.,
J. David .... 954-201-7401.. 99 G
darmstro@broward.edu

ARMSTRONG,
Jeffrey, D .... 805-756-1111.. 32 E
presidentsoffice@calpoly.edu

ARMSTRONG,
Jeffrey, M .... 563-556-5110 181 F
armstroj@nicc.edu

ARMSTRONG, Keith .... 719-590-6758.. 81 H
karmstrong@coloradotech.edu

ARMSTRONG, Keith .... 877-701-3800 139 H

ARMSTRONG, Kelli, J ... 617-552-0585 224 B
kelli.armstrong@bc.edu

ARMSTRONG, Kevin .... 402-375-7534 292 D
kearmst1@wsc.edu

ARMSTRONG, Kim .... 501-337-5000.. 20 H
karmstrong@coto.edu

ARMSTRONG, Kimberly 717-291-3985 418 J
kim.armstrong@fandm.edu

ARMSTRONG, Lee, F .... 334-844-5176.... 1 G
armstlf@auburn.edu

ARMSTRONG, Lori, B ... 410-704-3570 221 A
larmstrong@towson.edu

ARMSTRONG,
Mary Beth .... 205-665-6720.... 9 C
armstrom@montevallo.edu

ARMSTRONG, Molly .... 252-246-1396 367 D
marmstrong@wilsoncc.edu

ARMSTRONG, Myeshia .. 562-908-3404.. 60 I
marmstrong@riohondo.edu

ARMSTRONG, Nancy, A 419-772-2251 388 I
n-armstrong@onu.edu

ARMSTRONG,
Patricia, J .... 615-353-3758 463 C
patricia.armstrong@nscc.edu

ARMSTRONG, Peter .... 402-465-2153 292 E
parmstro@nebrwesleyan.edu

ARMSTRONG, Scott .... 815-825-2086 149 E
scott.armstrong@kishwaukeecollege.edu

ARMSTRONG, Shelly .... 231-591-3825 242 L
ShellyArmstrong@ferris.edu

ARMSTRONG, Shirley ... 229-430-3511 119 I
sarmstrong@albanytech.edu

ARMSTRONG,
Steven, M .... 920-832-6769 536 R
steven.m.armstrong@lawrence.edu

ARMSTRONG, Susan .... 318-675-5241 205 D
sarmst@lsuhsc.edu

ARMSTRONG, Terri, A .. 530-251-8839.. 50 B
tarmstrong@lassencollege.edu

ARMSTRONG, Thomas .. 760-232-2411.. 29 C
tarmstrong1@barstow.edu

ARMSTRONG, Tonya .... 919-572-1625 354 F
tarmstrong@apexsot.edu

ARMSTRONG,
William, L .... 303-963-3350.. 79 L
warmstrong@ccu.edu

ARMUSEWICZ, Allison .. 716-614-6238 336 D
aarmusewicz@niagaracc.suny.edu

ARN, Diana .... 501-977-2001.. 25 A
arn@uaccm.edu

ARNADE, Peter .... 808-956-6460 135 J
parnade@hawaii.edu

ARNDT, Steve, A .... 919-515-8851 370 D
saarndt@ncsu.edu

ARNDT, Wayne, S .... 732-987-2237 302 J
arndt@georgian.edu

ARNENDARIC, Louis .... 323-319-9500.. 70 F

ARNER, Joseph .... 352-588-7548 111 L
joseph.arner@saintleo.edu

ARNER, Lori .... 802-468-1211 503 G
lori.arner@castleton.edu

ARNER, Lynette .... 330-263-2139 380 E
larner@wooster.edu

ARNER, Thomas .... 802-828-2800 503 H
arnert@ccv.edu

ARNESON, Rosemary .... 540-654-1000 513 I
rarneso3@umw.edu

ARNETT, Brad, K .... 770-484-1204 128 D
brad.arnett@lutherrice.edu

ARNETT, David, J .... 978-478-3400 235 E
darnett@northpoint.edu

ARNETT, Harold .... 620-441-6584 186 E
harold.arnett@cowley.edu

ARNETT, Katy .... 240-895-4451 218 B
kearnett@smcm.edu

ARNETT, Ron, W .... 606-474-3151 195 F
rarnett@kcu.edu

ARNN, Larry .... 517-607-2301 243 J
larnn@hillsdale.edu

ARNO, Marlene .... 716-851-1431 325 A
arno@ecc.edu

ARNOLD, Aimee, C .... 262-472-5955 541 D
mccanna@uww.edu

ARNOLD, Angela .... 952-358-9045 260 D
angela.arnold@normandale.edu

ARNOLD, Ashley .... 785-784-6606 184 I
arnolda@bartonccc.edu

ARNOLD, Carl .... 903-233-4320 477 G
carlarnold@letu.edu

ARNOLD, Carolyn .... 510-723-6965.. 37 N
carnold@chabotcollege.edu

ARNOLD, Christina .... 616-234-3532 243 D
carnold@grcc.edu

ARNOLD, Clinton, E .... 562-903-4816.. 29 F
clinton.arnold@biola.edu

ARNOLD, David .... 575-492-2124 314 D
darnold@usw.edu

ARNOLD, George .... 310-954-4015.. 54 I
garnold@msmu.edu

ARNOLD, Harvey, E .... 772-462-6210 106 F
harnold@irsc.edu

ARNOLD, J. David .... 309-467-6322 145 A
arnold@eureka.edu

ARNOLD, Jeanne .... 717-337-6375 419 C
jarnold@gettysburg.edu

ARNOLD, Jeff (Dean) ... 262-472-1922 541 D
arnoldd@uww.edu

ARNOLD, Joan .... 575-624-7261 310 J
joan.arnold@roswell.enmu.edu

ARNOLD, Jon .... 714-895-8183.. 40 C
jarnold@gwc.cccd.edu

ARNOLD, Jon .... 931-540-2538 462 E
jarnold15@columbiastate.edu

ARNOLD, Joshua .... 909-599-5433.. 50 H
jarnold@lifepacific.edu

ARNOLD, Julie .... 419-448-2953 383 C
jarnold3@heidelberg.edu

ARNOLD, Kathy .... 512-313-3000 471 H
kathy.arnold@concordia.edu

ARNOLD, Kelly .... 405-224-3140 403 L
karnold@usao.edu

ARNOLD, Kenneth, L .... 707-256-3331.. 55 E
karnold@napavalley.edu

ARNOLD, Lester .... 336-750-2000 372 D

ARNOLD, Lorene, R .... 260-399-7700 174 C
larnold@sf.edu

ARNOLD, Lorin .... 856-256-4290 306 D
arnold@rowan.edu

ARNOLD, Mary, M .... 651-641-8268 255 C
marnold@csp.edu

ARNOLD, Michael, A .... 302-831-1916.. 94 D
marnold@udel.edu

ARNOLD, Patrick .... 845-569-3508 333 I
patrick.arnold@msmc.edu

ARNOLD, Robert .... 815-836-5488 150 F
arnoldro@lewisu.edu

ARNOLD, Robert .... 901-321-4299 455 I
rarnold@cbu.edu

ARNOLD, Rodney .... 870-743-3000.. 22 A
rarnold@northark.edu

ARNOLD, Ronald, M .... 312-935-6646 157 A
rarnold@robertmorris.edu

ARNOLD, Sally .... 978-232-2029 226 C
sarnold@endicott.edu

ARNOLD, Shirley, E .... 828-884-8329 355 A
arnoldse@brevard.edu

ARNOLD, Stephen .... 409-984-6249 488 H
stephen.arnold@lamarpa.edu

ARNOLD, Sue .... 281-487-1170 486 F sarnold@txchiro.edu
ARNOLD, Susan .... 610-606-4609 415 A swarnold@cedarcrest.edu
ARNOLD, Tai .... 518-587-2100 348 A tai.arnold@esc.edu
ARNOLD, Virginia .... 404-872-3593 121 A varnold@johnmarshall.edu
ARNOLD, III, W. Ellis .. 501-450-1223.. 21 C arnold@hendrix.edu
ARNONE, Harriet .... 516-686-7517 335 F harnone@nyit.edu
ARNOULD, Karen, A ..... 810-762-3344 251 E karnould@umflint.edu
ARNST, Scott .... 810-762-3123 251 E sarnst@umflint.edu
ARNZEN, Diane .... 636-481-3282 276 E darnzen@jeffco.edu
AROBBA, Sarah .... 605-856-5880 453 B sarah.arobba@sintegleska.edu
AROMANDO, Drew, C .. 609-896-5178 306 A aromando@rider.edu
ARON, Deborah .... 215-635-7300 419 D daron@gratz.edu
ARONSON, Donna .... 507-457-6900 264 B daronson@smumn.edu
ARONSON, Ed .... 541-881-5875 410 D earonson@tvcc.cc
ARONSON, Linda .... 508-849-3458 222 C laronson@annamaria.edu
ARONSON, Meigan, C .. 979-845-7361 485 C
ARONSON, Roberta, C . 412-396-1818 417 I aronson@duq.edu
ARONSON, Susan .... 213-624-1200.. 44 I saronson@fidm.edu
ARONSTAM, Robert, S .. 570-389-5333 430 B aronstam@bloomu.edu
ARONSTEIN, Susan ...... 307-766-4110 546 K aronstei@uwyo.edu
ARORA, Deepa .... 478-934-6588 128 H deepa.arora@mga.edu
ARORA SINGH, Alka .... 623-845-3968.. 14 N alka.arora.singh@gccaz.edu
AROZ, Susan, D .... 480-732-7075.. 14 K Sue.Aroz@cgc.edu
ARP, Dan .... 541-737-2331 408 F dan.arp@oregonstate.edu
ARP, Robert .... 707-654-1037.. 34 B rarp@csum.edu
ARP, Virginia .... 419-448-3400 392 B arpvp@tiffin.edu
ARP, William .... 225-771-3092 207 A william_arp@subr.edu
ARPEY, Sharon, A .... 518-580-5590 342 I sarpey@skidmore.edu
ARPINO, Donald .... 617-879-7899 230 B darpino@massart.edu
ARQUETTE, Mary .... 419-824-3969 385 F marquette@lourdes.edu
ARRAIZA, Ana, M .... 787-751-0160 551 K aarraiza@cmpr.pr.gov
ARREDONDO, Arnold .... 901-572-2455 455 C arnold.arredondo@bchs.edu
ARREDONDO, Marisol .. 714-628-7339.. 38 B arredond@chapman.edu
ARREGUIN, David .... 361-698-1703 473 F darreguin@delmar.edu
ARRELLAGA, Maria, M . 512-471-6080 493 M arrellaga@utexas.edu
ARRIAZA, Cecilia .... 714-992-7087.. 56 F carriaza@fullcoll.edu
ARRIBAS, Maria del Carmen ...... 787-257-7373 555 L ue_marribas@suagm.edu
ARRINGTON, Cedric ...... 256-551-1711.... 4 J cedric.arrington@drakestate.edu
ARRINGTON, Doris, B .. 860-906-5085.. 89 A darrington@ccc.commnet.edu
ARRINGTON, Michelle .. 601-266-6698 271 B michelle.arrington@usm.edu
ARRINGTON, Pam .... 330-966-5460 391 J parrington@starkstate.edu
ARRINGTON, Pamela .... 334-241-9592.... 8 A parrington@troy.edu
ARRINGTON, Tom .... 281-459-7613 481 F tom.arrington@sjcd.edu
ARRINGTON, Trey .... 864-587-4396 449 D arringtont@smcsc.edu
ARRINGTON-JONES, Angela .... 773-291-6297 142 B aarrington@ccc.edu
ARRIOLA, Benjamin ...... 915-778-4001 483 B
ARROWOOD, Roarke .... 828-835-4305 366 F rarrowood@tricountycc.edu
ARROYO, Cheryl .... 219-989-2977 171 L cheryl.arroyo@purduecal.edu
ARROYO, Cruz .... 253-964-4688 525 H carroyo@stmartin.edu
ARROYO, Enrique .... 787-841-2000 555 F earroyo@pucpr.edu
ARROYO, Gladys .... 787-279-1912 553 H garroyo@bayamon.inter.edu
ARROYO, Ivonne, D ..... 787-257-7323 555 L iarroyo@suagm.edu
ARROYO, Patti .... 303-404-5111.. 82 J patti.arroyo@frontrange.edu
ARROYO, Sandra .... 787-765-3560 552 E sarroyo@edpuniversity.edu
ARRUDA, Yvonne, D .... 401-865-2480 441 F yarruda@providence.edu
ARSHACK, Susan .... 912-344-2596 120 D susan.arshack@armstrong.edu
ARSHADI, Nasser .... 314-516-5899 284 B arshadi@umsl.edu
ARSLANIAN, Susan ...... 978-468-7111 227 B sarslanian@gcts.edu
ARTALE, Maureen, P .... 607-436-3216 344 B artalemp@oneonta.edu
ARTEAGA, Joseph .... 805-546-3205.. 42 H joseph_arteaga@cuesta.edu
ARTEAGA-JOHNSON, Craig .... 909-607-6643.. 60 A craig.arteagajohnson@pomona.edu
ARTECONA, Sarah, N .... 305-284-5490 118 A sartecona@miami.edu
ARTENIAN, Aida .... 818-767-0888.. 77 G aida.artenian@woodbury.edu
ARTER, Neil .... 405-425-5906 399 J neil.arter@oc.edu
ARTERBERRY, Stan, R .. 707-864-7112.. 66 J stan.arterberry@solano.edu
ARTERBURN, Dave .... 256-824-6846.... 9 A david.r.arterburn@uah.edu
ARTHO, Donna .... 936-294-3101 489 A artho@shsu.edu
ARTHUR, Christon .... 269-471-3405 239 D christon@andrews.edu
ARTHUR, Dave .... 512-476-2772 468 I finaid@austingrad.edu
ARTHUR, Gwendolynne 508-793-7384 225 B garthur@clarku.edu
ARTHUR, Jeff .... 757-671-7171 507 C jarthur@ecpi.edu
ARTHUR, Mark .... 405-789-7661 402 F mark.arthur@swcu.edu
ARTHUR, Michelle .... 310-660-3504.. 43 G marthur@elcamino.edu
ARTHUR, Salinda .... 912-478-5253 126 B sarthur@georgiasouthern.edu
ARTHUR, Scott .... 303-724-8469.. 86 G scott.arthur@ucdenver.edu
ARTHUR, Virginia .... 651-793-1920 259 E ginny.arthur@metrostate.edu
ARTHURS, Margaret ..... 607-431-4061 327 B arthursm@hartwick.edu
ARTIBEE, Jessica .... 952-446-4130 255 E artibeej@crown.edu
ARTIGUES, Jay .... 985-549-2253 208 E
ARTIM, Chris .... 219-844-0100 170 X cartim@kaplan.edu
ARTIM, Michael .... 814-619-3183 414 E martim@crbc.net
ARTIS, Christine .... 718-933-6700 333 F cartis@monroecollege.edu
ARTIS, Frederick, D ...... 918-595-7898 403 A frederick.artis@tulsacc.edu
ARTIS, Lori .... 618-468-3000 150 E lartis@lc.edu
ARTMAN, Richard, B .... 608-796-3001 542 H rbartman@viterbo.edu
ARTMAN, Vickie .... 618-634-3219 159 A vickiea@shawneecc.edu
ARUNACHALAM, Vairam .... 573-882-3225 283 H arunachalam@missouri.edu
ARVELO, Wildolfo .... 603-427-7602 296 K warvelo@ccsnh.edu
ARVIN, Ann .... 650-498-6227.. 68 G aarvin@stanford.edu
ARVIN, Lorraine .... 503-517-7625 409 E arvinl@reed.edu
ARVISO, Jason .... 505-786-4193 311 G jarviso@navajotech.edu
ARVIZU, Mimi .... 408-848-4840.. 45 G marvizu@gavilan.edu
ARVIZU, Primavera .... 661-395-4863.. 49 E prarvizu@bakersfieldcollege.edu
ARZOLA, Fernando .... 646-378-6150 337 B fernando.arzola@nyack.edu
ARZROUNI-CHAHINIAN, Chaghig .... 510-987-9452.. 27 K
ASADOORIAN, III, Malcolm, O .... 781-768-7077 236 A malcolm.asadoorian@regiscollege.edu
ASAMOAH, Yaw, A .... 724-357-2280 431 A osebo@iup.edu
ASARO, Diane, C .... 773-508-2543 151 E dasaro@luc.edu
ASATO, Susan .... 760-757-2121.. 54 G sasato@miracosta.edu
ASAWA, Archibald, E .... 949-480-4006.. 66 I asawa@soka.edu
ASAY, Meredith .... 307-766-2903 546 K masay@uwyo.edu
ASBILL, Jonathan .... 918-456-5511 398 M asbill01@nsuok.edu
ASBURY, Debbie .... 410-532-5340 217 F dasbury@ndm.edu
ASBURY, Denise .... 423-652-4895 457 J dasbury@king.edu
ASBURY, Jo-Ellen .... 410-334-2181 218 E jasbury@stevenson.edu
ASBURY, Sean .... 614-287-2525 380 G sasbury@cscc.edu
ASCARELLI, Daniela ...... 215-895-6280 417 E ascareld@drexel.edu
ASCENCIO, Mario .... 626-396-2231.. 28 J mario.ascencio@artcenter.edu
ASCH, Emily .... 651-690-6650 263 V ejasch@stkate.edu
ASCHE, Hylee .... 308-398-7407 289 D hasche@cccneb.edu
ASCHENBRENER, Matt .. 262-472-1570 541 D aschenbm@uww.edu
ASCHENDRENER, Saundra .... 480-990-3773.. 14 I
ASCHER, Marie .... 914-594-4200 335 H marie_ascher@nymc.edu
ASCHIM, Joan .... 541-463-5591 406 F aschimj@lanecc.edu
ASCHLIMAN, David, A .. 260-422-5561 167 F daaschliman@indianatech.edu
ASCIONE, Lou .... 619-388-7873.. 62 H lascione@sdccd.edu
ASDURIAN, Emil .... 718-261-5800 316 K easdurianmd@bramsonort.edu
ASELAS, Erin .... 425-602-3181 519 J easelas@bastyr.edu
ASENCIO, Doris .... 787-892-5115 554 C dasencio@intersg.edu
ASENCIO-PINTO, Aida .. 708-209-3492 143 D aida.asencio-pinto@cuchicago.edu
ASH, Christine, A .... 216-368-4350 378 J caa2@case.edu
ASH, Eric .... 907-375-4515 496 K ash@wbu.edu
ASH, Hope .... 304-865-6015 530 F hope.ash@ovu.edu
ASH, Kenya, D .... 513-529-7157 386 K ashkd@miamioh.edu
ASH, Michael .... 319-208-5050 183 B mash@scciowa.edu
ASH, Steven .... 352-854-2322 100 P ashs@cf.edu
ASHANTIZA, Elizabeth .. 612-436-7538 257 K eashantiza@msbcollege.edu
ASHAOLU, John .... 724-480-3470 416 A john.ashaolu@ccbc.edu
ASHBAUGH, Jackie, E .. 330-684-8973 393 A jackie1@uakron.edu
ASHBRIDGE, Susie .... 541-956-7239 409 F sashbridge@roguecc.edu
ASHBROOK, Richard, M .... 614-236-6108 378 H rashbrook@capital.edu
ASHBURN, Beth, D .... 336-725-8344 368 A ashburnb@piedmontu.edu
ASHBURN, Elyse .... 410-455-2065 219 F eashburn@umbc.edu
ASHBURN, Gwen .... 828-251-6505 370 E gashburn@unca.edu
ASHBY, Brendan .... 651-846-1314 261 G brendan.ashby@saintpaul.edu
ASHBY, Frank .... 206-934-6417 526 B frank.ashby@seattlecolleges.edu
ASHBY, Jamie .... 903-823-3319 484 D jamie.ashby@texarkanacollege.edu
ASHBY, Patti .... 405-912-9017 398 B pashby@hc.edu
ASHBY, Rosemary .... 617-731-7101 235 F
ASHBY, Thomas .... 405-682-1611 399 K tashby@occc.edu
ASHBY, Valerie .... 919-684-4510 356 E asdean@duke.edu
ASHCRAFT, Chester ...... 870-460-1018.. 24 C ashcraft@uamont.edu
ASHCRAFT, Matthew ..... 480-461-7215.. 15 A Matthew.Aschcraft@mesacc.edu
ASHCROFT, Josh .... 509-359-6916 522 C jashcroft@ewu.edu
ASHDOWN, Jane .... 516-877-4065 314 F jashdown@adelphi.edu
ASHENMACHER, Robert, J .... 218-723-6075 255 A rashenma@css.edu
ASHER, Adam .... 708-239-4709 160 L adam.asher@trnty.edu
ASHER, Bernadette .... 404-627-2681 121 F bernadette.asher@beulah.org
ASHER, Curt .... 661-654-3042.. 32 G casher@csub.edu
ASHER, Joy .... 859-238-5284 194 E joy.asher@centre.edu
ASHER, Pamela .... 816-268-5442 279 K pjasher@nts.edu
ASHFORD, Bruce, R ...... 919-761-2435 368 K bashford@sebts.edu
ASHFORD, Rebecca, L .. 865-694-6552 463 E rlashford@pstcc.edu
ASHFORD, Scott .... 541-737-1211 408 F scott.ashford@oregonstate.edu
ASHFORD-LIGON, Latonya .... 609-586-4800 303 D ashfordl@mccc.edu
ASHLEY, Bill .... 601-276-3717 270 E bashley@smcc.edu
ASHLEY, Donna .... 646-717-9706 326 E ashley@gts.edu
ASHLEY, Garrett, P .... 562-951-4625.. 32 D gashley@calstate.edu
ASHLEY, Kimberly .... 903-877-5739 495 C kimberly.ashley@uthct.edu
ASHLEY, Kurt .... 724-589-2115 436 E kashley@thiel.edu
ASHLEY, Mark .... 909-621-8090.. 46 K mark_ashley@hmc.edu
ASHLEY, Mary Ellen ...... 937-775-4271 396 A maryellen.ashley@wright.edu
ASHLEY, Richard .... 704-272-5463 366 A rashley@spcc.edu
ASHLEY, Traci, D .... 919-209-2563 363 F tdashley@johnstoncc.edu
ASHLEY, SR., Willard W.C .... 732-247-5241 304 B washley@nbts.edu
ASHLEY-PAULEY, Jonita .... 423-798-7830 464 F jpauley@tusculum.edu
ASHMON, Rosa .... 334-872-2533.... 6 G
ASHOUR, Cheryl .... 780-744-1150.. 58 D cashour@palomar.edu
ASHPOLE, Steven .... 360-596-5240 527 B sashpole@spscc.edu
ASHRAF, Tasneem .... 520-335-1883.. 13 B ashraft@cochise.edu
ASHTON, Andrew .... 845-437-5785 351 H anashton@vassar.edu
ASHTON, Catherine .... 319-385-6227 180 A catherine.ashton@iw.edu
ASHTON, M. John .... 801-581-3055 499 K john.ashton@alumni.utah.edu
ASHTON, Nadine .... 313-664-7673 241 D nashton@collegeforcreativestudies.edu
ASHTON, Sharon .... 904-620-2115 116 A sashton@unf.edu
ASHTON-MILLER, James, A .... 734-764-7516 251 C jaam@umich.edu
ASHTON-PRITTING, Randi, L .... 860-768-4268.. 92 F pritting@hartford.edu
ASHWELL, Dru .... 417-626-1234 280 B dashwell@occ.edu
ASHWORTH, Dennis ..... 706-355-5167 120 G dashworth@athenstech.edu
ASHWORTH, Edward, N 207-581-3202 212 C edward.ashworth@maine.edu
ASHWORTH, James .... 352-638-9723.. 99 D jashworth@beaconcollege.edu
ASHWORTH, W. Brett ... 843-953-6779 444 C washwort@citadel.edu
ASIAMAH-ANDRADE, Akua .... 856-225-6322 307 A andradea@camlink.rutgers.edu
ASIFOA, Sereima .... 684-699-9155 549 C s.asifoa@amsamoa.edu
ASKA, Aaron .... 201-200-3035 304 C aaska@njcu.edu
ASKEGAARD, Lewis, D . 540-887-7071 510 A laskegaa@mbc.edu
ASKELSON, Denise .... 218-935-0417 266 A denise.askelson@wetcc.edu
ASKELSON, Mary, M ..... 503-788-6644 409 E askelsom@reed.edu
ASKERLUND, Robert ..... 801-957-4101 500 E robert.askerlund@slcc.edu
ASKEW, George, R .... 864-656-3140 444 E gaskew@clemson.edu
ASKEW, Joseph .... 731-989-6651 456 K jaskew@fhu.edu
ASKEW, Susan, S .... 931-598-1710 460 I saskew@sewanee.edu
ASKEW, Tara .... 706-649-1901 123 E taskew@columbustech.edu
ASKEW-ROBINSON, Jipaum .... 618-634-3364 159 A jipaum@shawneecc.edu
ASKINS, Rana .... 903-813-2444 468 G raskins@austincollege.edu
ASKREN, Mark .... 402-472-2311 293 H maskren1@unl.edu

ASMUS, Colleen, M ..... 850-474-2642 116 E
casmus@uwf.edu
ASONEVICH, Walter, J .. 814-262-3820 429 K
wasonevich@pennhighlands.edu
ASOODEH, Mike, M ..... 985-549-2314 208 E
asoodeh@selu.edu
ASPAN, Paul .... 610-660-1000 434 G
paspan@sju.edu
ASPELUND, Jan .... 970-945-8691.. 80 D
ASPERGER, Joseph .... 810-762-9749 245 A
jasperge@kettering.edu
ASPINALL, David .... 910-221-2224 357 A
daspinall@gcd.edu
ASPINALL, Robin, J ...... 909-621-8116.. 39 F
robin.aspinall@cmc.edu
ASPINWALL, Neil .... 337-421-6900 204 F
neil.aspinwall@sowela.edu
ASQUINO, Daniel, M .... 978-632-0001 232 C
d_asquino@mwcc.mass.edu
ASSAD, Arjang, A .... 412-648-1500 437 K
aassad@pitt.edu
ASSAEL, Leon .... 612-624-2424 265 C
assael@umn.edu
ASSAF, Michael .... 413-775-1318 231 E
assafm@gcc.mass.edu
ASSANIS, Dennis, N ..... 631-632-4360 344 C
dennis.assanis@stonybrook.edu
ASSANTE, Javonda, T ... 979-313-6211 308 C
javonda.assante@shu.edu
ASSELIN, Edward .... 518-255-5215 346 E
asselie@cobleskill.edu
ASSELIN, Edward, E ..... 518-255-5215 346 E
asselie@cobleskill.edu
ASSELIN, Martha, J ...... 581-381-1336 342 E
asselimj@sunysccc.edu
AST, Nicholas .... 405-878-5411 402 A
frnicholas@stgregorys.edu
ASTACIO, Lourdes .... 787-284-1912 554 B
lastacio@ponce.inter.edu
ASTARITA, Susan .... 973-290-4410 301 F
sastarita@cse.edu
ASTEMBORSKI-DECKER,
Cynthia .... 518-381-1353 342 E
astembc@sunysccc.edu
ASTI, Martha, S .... 704-233-8123 373 C
asti@wingate.edu
ASTI, Tony .... 602-286-8000.. 14 M
anthony.asti@gatewaycc.edu
ASTOLFI, Amy .... 978-232-2001 226 C
aastolfi@endicott.edu
ASTON, Mary Kay .... 570-941-5984 438 F
marykay.aston@scranton.edu
ASTON, Rollah .... 575-624-7281 310 J
rollah.aston@roswell.enmu.edu
ASTON, Sheree .... 909-706-3502.. 76 I
saston@westernu.edu
ASUKILE, Imani, D .... 727-816-3192 110 B
asukili@phsc.edu
ASUNCION-NACE, Zeny 671-735-2942 549 G
znace@uguam.uog.edu
ASWEGAN, Kathie .... 319-226-2003 175 D
Kathie.Aswegan@AllenCollege.edu
ATALLAH, Zahi .... 831-755-6960.. 46 J
zatallah@hartnell.edu
ATAYDE, Nancy .... 951-343-4210.. 30 D
natayde@calbaptist.edu
ATCHISON, Kathryn ...... 310-794-0212.. 71 D
katchison@resadmin.ucla.edu
ATCHLEY, Stephen .... 562-868-6488.. 49 H
ATENCIO, Elaine .... 619-260-4520.. 74 B
atencio@sandiego.edu
ATENCIO, Wilma .... 719-846-5555.. 86 A
wilma.atencio@trinidadstate.edu
ATES, Clarence .... 508-854-7515 232 F
cates@qcc.mass.edu
ATES, Kerry, A .... 410-516-8068 216 A
kates1@jhu.edu
ATEWOLOGUN,
Adenuga .... 507-433-0607 261 C
adenuga.atewologun@riverland.edu
ATHANASIOU, Nancy .... 414-382-6195 534 I
nancy.athanasiou@alverno.edu
ATHANS, Stephan .... 919-718-7287 361 C
sathans@cccc.edu
ATHERTON, Beth .... 512-313-3000 471 H
beth.atherton@concordia.edu
ATHERTON, Dennis .... 575-492-2763 311 J
datherton@nmjc.edu
ATHERTON, Joe .... 707-467-3067.. 54 A
jatherton@mendocino.edu
ATHEY, Rochelle .... 702-895-5541 295 G
rochelle.athey@unlv.edu
ATIEH, Lute .... 816-279-7000 271 H
lute@abtu.edu
ATIEH, Ramsey .... 816-279-7000 271 H
ramsey@abtu.edu
ATIEH, Sam .... 816-279-7000 271 H
president@abtu.edu
ATKIN, Michael, B .... 818-947-2600.. 52 B
atkinmb@lavc.edu
ATKINS, Angie, S .... 662-329-7126 269 B
aatkins@muw.edu
ATKINS, Chris .... 512-444-8082 487 B
faid@thsu.edu
ATKINS, Christine .... 203-401-4071.. 87 M
catkins@albertus.edu
ATKINS, Darlenna, M ... 318-797-5237 205 F
darlenna.atkins@lsus.edu
ATKINS, Deb .... 763-424-0993 260 E
datkins@nhcc.edu
ATKINS, Douglas, G ..... 603-526-3738 296 I
datkins@colby-sawyer.edu
ATKINS, Elizabeth, A .... 856-225-6161 307 A
atkins1@camden.rutgers.edu
ATKINS, Garry, L .... 205-726-2763.... 6 F
glatkins@samford.edu
ATKINS, Jennifer .... 434-961-5245 516 F
jatkins@pvcc.edu
ATKINS, Katharine, H ... 704-894-3098 356 D
kaatkins@davidson.edu
ATKINS, Kemal .... 603-358-2108 299 D
Kemal.Atkins@keene.edu
ATKINS, Marsha .... 312-850-7202 142 E
matkins15@ccc.edu
ATKINS, Nolan, T .... 802-626-6406 504 B
nolan.atkins@lyndonstate.edu
ATKINS, Norman .... 212-228-1888 339 C
ATKINS, Paula, B .... 318-795-5365 205 F
paula.atkins@lsus.edu
ATKINS, Priscilla, D ..... 616-395-7986 244 A
atkinsp@hope.edu
ATKINS, Rodney .... 903-730-4890 476 L
RAtkins@jarvis.edu
ATKINS-BRADY, Tara .... 757-569-6713 516 E
tatkins-brady@pdc.edu
ATKINSON, Barbara ...... 702-895-3524 295 G
barbara.atkinson@unlv.edu
ATKINSON, Darryl .... 757-683-3407 510 I
datkinso@odu.edu
ATKINSON, Debra, J .... 620-276-9533 187 D
debbie.atkinson@gcccks.edu
ATKINSON, Eva, G .... 270-686-4282 193 G
eva.atkinson@brescia.edu
ATKINSON, Frank .... 405-466-3370 398 E
fatkinson@langston.edu
ATKINSON, J. Scott .... 585-395-2501 345 A
satkinso@brockport.edu
ATKINSON, James .... 575-562-2467 310 I
james.atkinson@enmu.edu
ATKINSON, Jane, M ...... 503-768-7200 406 H
ATKINSON, Janet .... 208-426-1689 137 E
jatkinson@boisestate.edu
ATKINSON, Jeffrey .... 704-233-8117 373 C
atkinson@wingate.edu
ATKINSON, Joseph, C .. 202-526-3799.. 96 F
ATKINSON, Judith .... 856-415-2115 306 C
jatkinson@rcgc.edu
ATKINSON, Justin .... 559-323-2100.. 63 C
jatkinson@sjcl.edu
ATKINSON, Kacey .... 561-276-6520 131 F
katkinson@southuniversity.edu
ATKINSON, Linda .... 301-784-5000 213 C
latkinson@allegany.edu
ATKINSON, Mark .... 435-586-1966 499 L
markatkinson@suu.edu
ATKINSON, Rose .... 406-768-6317 286 H
ratkinson@fpcc.edu
ATKINSON, Sander .... 601-484-8707 268 B
satkinson@meridiancc.edu
ATKINSON, Susan, J ..... 714-449-7442.. 53 D
satkinson@ketchum.edu
ATKINSON, Thomas .... 269-782-1276 250 D
tatkinson@swmich.edu
ATKINSON, Vicki .... 847-925-6208 145 F
vatkinso@harpercollege.edu
ATKINSON-ALSTON,
Stephanie .... 310-233-4025.. 51 F
atkinssa@lahc.edu
ATKINSON-WILLOUGHBY,
Brenda .... 202-687-5677.. 95 E
ba3@georgetown.edu
ATLAS, Gordan .... 607-871-2924 314 J
atlas@alfred.edu
ATLAS, Jamie .... 615-794-4254 460 A
jatlas@omorecollege.edu
ATO, Gladys .... 408-273-2697.. 55 G
gato@nhu.edu
ATO, Gladys .... 408-273-2204.. 55 G
gato@nhu.edu
ATO, Gladys .... 408-273-2683.. 55 G
gato@nhu.edu
ATOIGE, Celia .... 671-734-1812 549 F
catoige@piu.edu
ATOIGUE, Ana Mari, C . 671-735-5527 549 E
anamari.atoigue@guamcc.edu
ATTANASIO, Ann .... 410-617-2510 216 D
aattanasio@loyola.edu
ATTAO, David .... 670-237-6801 550 B
david.attao@marianas.edu
ATTARDO, Salvatore ..... 903-886-5166 485 E
salvatore.attardo@tamuc.edu
ATTEBERY, Philip .... 903-586-2501 469 A
philip.attebery@bmats.edu
ATTERBURY,
G. Burnham 'Burnie' .. 209-932-2967.. 73 C
batterbury@pacific.edu
ATTIA, Magdy .... 704-378-1140 358 B
mattia@jcsu.edu
ATTIG, Ann, M .... 719-884-5000.. 84 G
AMAttig@nbc.edu
ATTOH, Samuel .... 312-915-7585 151 E
sattoh@luc.edu
ATTOH, Samuel, A .... 773-508-8948 151 E
sattoh@luc.edu
ATTOH, Samuel, A .... 773-508-2975 151 E
sattoh@luc.edu
ATTRIDGE, Daniel, F .... 202-319-5139.. 95 A
attridge@cua.edu
ATUAHENE, Francis ...... 610-436-3505 432 B
fatuahene@wcupa.edu
ATWATER, Ken .... 813-253-7050 106 C
katwater@hccfl.edu
ATWELL, Patrick .... 573-288-6424 274 C
patwell@culver.edu
ATWELL, Scott .... 850-644-2761 115 A
satwell@fsu.edu
ATWOOD, Julie .... 601-477-4055 268 A
julie.atwood@jcjc.edu
ATWOOD, Kim .... 502-456-6504 200 B
katwood@sullivan.edu
ATWOOD, Lorraine .... 802-831-1204 503 E
latwood@vermontlaw.edu
ATWOOD, Steve .... 573-840-9708 283 D
satwood@trcc.edu
ATWOOD, Tom .... 202-462-2101.. 96 C
atwood@iwp.edu
ATZERT, Andy .... 212-229-8947 334 C
atzerta@newschool.edu
AU, Gerard .... 909-537-5100.. 35 A
gau@csusb.edu
AU, Peggy .... 510-628-8038.. 50 I
peggyau@lincolnuca.edu
AU, Simon .... 408-435-8989.. 66 F
AU-YEUNG, Johnson .... 603-314-1494 298 H
j.au-yeung@snhu.edu
AUBEY, Hilary .... 316-295-4301 187 C
hilarya@friends.edu
AUBIN, Mary Ann .... 314-792-6302 276 H
aubin@kenrick.edu
AUBRECHT, Don .... 412-365-1231 415 C
daubrecht@chatham.edu
AUBRET, Maryliz .... 787-780-0070 550 G
maubret@caribbean.edu
AUBREY, Leonard .... 516-686-1100 335 F
laubrey@nyit.edu
AUBRY, Dawn, M .... 248-370-3364 248 K
dmaubry@oakland.edu
AUBRY, Nadine .... 617-373-2154 235 D
AUCOIN, Brent .... 765-448-1986 165 I
AUCOIN, Judi, F .... 205-726-2728.... 6 F
jfaucoin@samford.edu
AUCOIN, Martin .... 828-339-4217 366 C
m_aucoin@southwesterncc.edu
AUDAS, Jean Paul .... 405-325-1710 403 I
jaudas@ou.edu
AUDET, Suzanne .... 508-999-8076 228 H
saudet@umassd.edu
AUDETTE, Bert .... 207-509-7277 212 A
baudette@unity.edu
AUDUS, Kenneth, L ...... 785-864-3591 191 G
audus@ku.edu
AUDUSSEAU, Loïc .... 718-289-5168 318 E
loic.audusseau@bcc.cuny.edu
AUDYATIS, Todd .... 508-531-2608 229 C
taudyatis@bridgew.edu
AUER, Margaret .... 313-993-1090 250 H
auerme@udmercy.edu
AUER, Matthew, R .... 207-786-6066 209 F
mauer@bates.edu
AUERBACH, Michael ..... 843-953-5991 445 B
auerbachmh@cofc.edu
AUERBACH, Steven .... 808-845-9143 136 E
sauerbac@hawaii.edu
AUFDERHEIDE, Keith .... 404-364-8405 129 F
kaufderheide@oglethorpe.edu
AUGENSTEIN, Amee ..... 260-459-4545 169 D
aaugenstein@ibcfortwayne.edu
AUGENSTEIN, Heather .. 520-515-3649.. 13 B
augensteinh@cochise.edu
AUGHENBAUGH,
Barbara .... 410-837-5719 221 B
baughenbaugh@ubalt.edu
AUGHENBAUGH,
Jonette .... 304-327-4049 532 D
jaughenbaugh@bluefieldstate.edu
AUGHENBAUGH, Mark . 801-524-8195 498 J
Mark@ldsbc.edu
AUGOSTINI,
Christopher, L .... 202-687-7330.. 95 E
cla4@georgetown.edu
AUGSBURGER, Arol, R . 312-949-7700 146 E
aaugsburger@ico.edu
AUGSBURGER,
Carrie, A .... 515-964-0601 178 F
augsburgerc@faith.edu
AUGSBURGER,
Lance, A .... 515-964-0601 178 F
augsburgerl@faith.edu
AUGSPURGER, Bobbie .. 417-455-5750 274 B
BobbieAugspurger@Crowder.edu
AUGUISTE, Andrea .... 303-546-3594.. 84 B
aauguiste@naropa.edu
AUGUST, Bonne .... 718-260-5560 320 D
baugust@citytech.cuny.edu
AUGUST, Michele .... 620-241-0723 185 M
AUGUST-SCHWARTZ,
Suzanne .... 510-869-6511.. 61 J
saugustschwartz@samuelmerritt.edu
AUGUSTIN, Monica, L .. 408-554-6908.. 65 A
mlaugustin@scu.edu
AUGUSTINE-PLAISANCE,
LuAnn .... 718-409-7304 348 C
laugustine@sunymaritime.edu
AULD, Sandra .... 908-709-7010 309 A
auld@ucc.edu
AULET, Maria, J .... 787-765-1915 554 E
mjaulet@opto.inter.edu
AULIN, Kirsi .... 805-893-3285.. 72 D
kirsi.aulin@ucsb.edu
AULL, JR., Zeke .... 251-460-6609.... 9 F
zaull@southalabama.edu
AULT, Jill .... 530-242-7689.. 66 C
jault@shastacollege.edu
AULTMAN, Buddy .... 903-586-2518 476 K
baultman@jacksonville-college.edu
AUMAN, Timothy, L ..... 336-758-5210 372 G
aumantl@wfu.edu
AUMANN, Patricia .... 636-481-3552 276 E
paumann@jeffco.edu
AUNA, Leilani .... 808-675-3999 134 M
leilani.auna@byuh.edu
AUNE, Krystyna .... 808-956-7541 135 J
krystyna@hawaii.edu
AUNE, Mark .... 724-938-4535 430 C
aune@calu.edu
AUNGST, Donald .... 914-455-2650 332 E
daungst@mercy.edu
AURE, Aaron .... 605-688-6195 454 C
aaron.aure@sdstate.edu
AURE, Joel .... 914-251-5982 346 D
joel.aure@purchase.edu
AURICCHIO, Laura .... 212-229-5800 334 C
auricchl@newschool.edu
AURICCHIO, Michele .... 518-861-2558 331 K
mauricchiom@mariacollege.edu
AURIEMMA, Lisa .... 207-859-1233 211 I
libdir@thomas.edu
AURORA, Rosleen .... 818-785-2726.. 37 I
rosleen.aurora@casalomacollege.edu
AURYAN, Mosen .... 609-771-2143 301 E
auryanm@tcnj.edu
AUSBAND, Avrohom ..... 718-601-3523 353 O
AUSBON, Jacqueline .... 318-876-2401 203 B
AUSBORN, Dawn .... 910-630-7610 359 C
dausborn@methodist.edu
AUSBURY, Brad .... 417-862-9533 275 C
bausbury@globaluniversity.edu
AUSEL, Jill .... 412-365-1244 415 C
jausel@chatham.edu
AUSMUS, Ryan .... 620-227-9325 186 F
rausmus@dc3.edu
AUSTER, Julie .... 914-395-2365 342 C
jauster@sarahlawrence.edu
AUSTIN, Aaron, L .... 316-284-5324 185 B
aaustin@bethelks.edu
AUSTIN, Alvin .... 704-378-1110 358 B
aaustin@jcsu.edu
AUSTIN, Amy .... 678-260-3538 131 C
aaustin@shorter.edu
AUSTIN, Anne .... 870-612-2058.. 24 G
anne.austin@uaccb.edu
AUSTIN, April .... 404-270-5153 132 D
aprila@spelman.edu
AUSTIN, Brian .... 865-471-3273 455 G
baustin@cn.edu
AUSTIN, Charles .... 803-705-4967 443 F
austinc@benedict.edu
AUSTIN, Christine .... 479-880-4282.. 20 C
caustin@atu.edu
AUSTIN, Dale, F .... 616-395-7950 244 A
austin@hope.edu
AUSTIN, Debbie .... 503-207-5727 498 M
daustin@new.edu
AUSTIN, Deborah .... 717-264-4141 440 D
daustin@wilson.edu
AUSTIN, Diane .... 617-243-2124 227 K
daustin@lasell.edu
AUSTIN, Edward .... 352-588-7478 111 L
ed.austin@saintleo.edu

AUSTIN, Eric .... 612-343-4488 263 H
eaustin@northcentral.edu
AUSTIN, Erika .... 509-335-5581 528 B
eaustin@wsu.edu
AUSTIN, Jane .... 570-288-8400 418 H
janea@marcogrp.com
AUSTIN, Jim .... 541-506-6070 405 C
jaustin@cgcc.edu
AUSTIN, Joseph, M ...... 207-228-8258 213 A
austin@usm.maine.edu
AUSTIN, Kevin, P .... 626-395-8331.. 31 D
kpa@caltech.edu
AUSTIN, L. Bruce .... 847-214-7366 144 F
baustin@elgin.edu
AUSTIN, Laurie .... 718-960-8706 319 C
laurie.austin@lehman.cuny.edu
AUSTIN, Marlisa .... 502-213-5073 196 E
marlisa.austin@kctcs.edu
AUSTIN, Mary Lou .... 414-288-5163 537 B
mel.austin@marquette.edu
AUSTIN, Michael .... 316-942-4291 189 K
austinm@newmanu.edu
AUSTIN, Renee .... 615-230-3587 464 B
renee.austin@volstate.edu
AUSTIN, Robert, C .... 806-371-5024 467 E
rcaustin@actx.edu
AUSTIN, Sheila .... 334-244-3425.... 2 A
saustin1@aum.edu
AUSTIN, Suzanne, E ..... 205-934-6290.... 8 F
seaustin@uab.edu
AUSTIN, Tiffany .... 845-675-4581 337 B
tiffany.austin@nyack.edu
AUSTIN, Timothy, R ..... 412-396-6054 417 I
taustin@duq.edu
AUSTIN, Tracey, M .... 603-526-3886 296 I
taustin@colby-sawyer.edu
AUSTIN, Troy .... 434-395-2057 509 H
austints@longwood.edu
AUSTIN, William .... 908-689-7618 309 G
will@warren.edu
AUSTIN-BRUNS, Emily .. 978-665-3025 229 D
eaustinb@fitchburgstate.edu
AUTEN, Mike .... 402-844-7058 292 G
mike@northeast.edu
AUTERO, Esa .... 954-545-4500 113 B
academics@sfbc.edu
AUTIO, Wesley .... 413-545-2963 228 F
autio@umass.edu
AUTREY, Denny .... 713-634-0011 483 E
dautrey@swbts.edu
AUTRY, Dean .... 270-686-4464 197 A
dean.autry@kctcs.edu
AUTRY, Shanna .... 850-201-8918 117 B
autrys@tcc.fl.edu
AUVENSHINE, Donnie ... 325-649-8408 475 F
dauvenshine@hputx.edu
AVALLONE, Lee .... 617-912-9213 224 C
lavallone@bostonconservatory.edu
AVALONE, Valarie, L .... 585-292-3021 333 G
vavalone@monroecc.edu
AVALOS, Andrea .... 602-944-3336.. 11 D
aavalos@aicag.edu
AVALOS, Jesus .... 219-473-4623 165 A
javalos2@ccsj.edu
AVALOS, Juan .... 949-582-4566.. 67 F
javalos@saddleback.edu
AVALOS, Manuel .... 207-780-4347 213 A
manuel.avalos@maine.edu
AVALOS, Natalie .... 818-767-0888.. 77 G
Natalie.Avalos@woodbury.edu
AVALOS, Steve .... 909-794-1084.. 41 G
savalos@communitychristiancollege.com
AVALOS, Yesenia .... 708-656-8000 153 G
yesenia.avalos@morton.edu
AVALOS-THOMPSON,
Marlena .... 708-656-8000 153 G
M.Avalos-Thompson@morton.edu
AVANT, Toni, D .... 662-915-7174 270 G
tavant@olemiss.edu
AVEILLE, Candido .... 305-821-3333 104 C
caveille@fnu.edu
AVELLANEDA, Carolina . 617-236-8859 226 F
cavellaneda@fisher.edu
AVEN, Forrest, F .... 210-829-3190 492 B
aven@uiwtx.edu
AVENDANO, John .... 815-802-8110 149 B
president@kcc.edu
AVENT, Sherri, M .... 336-334-7973 370 B
avent@ncat.edu
AVERETTE, Dan .... 864-646-1341 449 F
daveret1@tctc.edu
AVERILL, Leslie .... 802-651-5907 501 F
averill@champlain.edu
AVERILL, Sue .... 330-672-2220 384 H
saveril2@kent.edu
AVERRE, Amy .... 207-941-7187 210 C
averrea@husson.edu
AVERSA, Ann .... 212-854-5561 315 J
aaversa@barnard.edu
AVERY, Barbara .... 323-259-2500.. 56 I
bavery@oxy.edu
AVERY, Brigid .... 616-632-2494 239 E
brigid.avery@aquinas.edu
AVERY, Donald .... 478-289-2015 124 B
davery@ega.edu
AVERY, Earl .... 781-891-2907 223 E
eavery@bentley.edu
AVERY, Faith .... 513-721-7944 382 K
favery@gbs.edu
AVERY, Gradin .... 607-753-2011 345 C
AVERY, James .... 731-661-5329 464 G
javery@uu.edu
AVERY, Joshua .... 513-721-7944 382 K
javery@gbs.edu
AVERY, Kathy .... 918-293-4988 400 E
kathy.avery@okstate.edu
AVERY, Kristine .... 207-893-7755 211 H
kavery@sjcme.edu
AVERY, Lisa .... 971-722-4357 409 C
lisa.avery@pcc.edu
AVERY, Margery, L .... 585-567-9350 328 C
margery.avery@houghton.edu
AVERY, Martin, D .... 315-386-7222 347 F
averym@canton.edu
AVERY, Michael, R .... 513-721-7944 382 K
president@gbs.edu
AVERY, Paula .... 310-303-7213.. 53 E
pavery@marymountcalifornia.edu
AVERY, Robert, H .... 401-254-3236 442 C
ravery@rwu.edu
AVERY, Sarah, E .... 630-637-5861 154 F
seavery@nactrl.edu
AVERYHART-FULLARD,
Vera .... 773-291-6100 142 B
vfullard@ccc.edu
AVILES, Yvonne .... 787-264-1912 554 C
yvonne_aviles_martinezr@intersg.edu
AVILES RODRIGUEZ,
Lucas, N .... 787-265-3869 558 B
decadmi@uprm.edu
AVILA, Celi .... 915-532-3737 497 D
cavila@westerntech.edu
AVILA, Glenna .... 661-255-1050.. 31 B
gavila@calarts.edu
AVILA, Lauri .... 928-428-8915.. 13 L
lauri.avila@eac.edu
AVILA, Linda, C .... 310-794-0691.. 71 D
lcavila@saa.ucla.edu
AVILA, Patricia .... 951-222-8725.. 61 B
patricia.avila@rcc.edu
AVILA, Pedro .... 559-499-6101.. 69 B
pedro.avila@scccd.edu
AVILA, Pedro .... 559-324-6474.. 68 J
pedro.avila@scccd.edu
AVILA, Susan .... 510-594-3661.. 30 G
savila@cca.edu
AVILA, Vince .... 785-864-1571 191 G
vavila1@ku.edu
AVILES, Angel .... 787-780-5134 554 H
aaviles@nuc.edu
AVILES, Gladys, M .... 248-204-4123 245 J
gaviles@ltu.edu
AVILES, John .... 859-371-9393 193 D
javiles@beckfield.edu
AVILES, Jose .... 716-645-6900 343 E
joseavil@buffalo.edu
AVILES, Jose, R .... 787-786-3030 556 E
javiles@ucb.edu.pr
AVILES-FERRAN,
Jeanette .... 787-620-2040 550 D
javiles@aupr.edu
AVILEZ, Shawnice .... 773-995-2345 141 J
savilez@csu.edu
AVISSAR, Roni .... 305-421-4000 118 A
avissar@miami.edu
AVITIA, Amber .... 559-935-3221.. 76 C
amberavitia@whccd.edu
AVRUCH, Kevin .... 703-993-1300 507 K
kavruch@gmu.edu
AW, Fanta .... 202-885-3357.. 94 H
fanta@american.edu
AWADALLAH, Baha .... 773-602-5000 142 A
AWAN, Seher .... 619-388-3428.. 62 F
sawan@sdccd.edu
AWBREY, Susan, M ...... 248-370-4955 248 K
awbrey@oakland.edu
AWE, Jacqueline .... 912-358-3114 131 A
awej@savannahstate.edu
AWE, Jennifer .... 212-799-5000 329 I
AWN, Peter .... 212-854-1932 322 F
pja3@columbia.edu
AWOLABI, Obasegun .... 718-270-4859 320 C
awolabi@mec.cuny.edu
AWOLAJU, Tafa .... 508-678-2811 231 B
tafa.awolaju@bristolcc.edu
AWONIYI, Beatrice .... 352-395-5513 112 H
bea.awoniyi@sfcollege.edu
AWUAH, Agatha .... 315-498-2500 337 F
awuaha@sunyocc.edu
AWUAH, Emmanuel ...... 630-942-2652 142 F
awuahe@cod.edu
AXELROD, Jamie .... 928-523-8773.. 16 C
Jamie.Axelrod@nau.edu
AXELROD, Larry .... 604-482-5510 139 E
laxelrod@adler.edu
AXELROD, Margaret ..... 703-284-1498 510 B
paxelrod@marymount.edu
AXELSON, Sara, L .... 307-766-5123 546 K
saxelson@uwyo.edu
AXLER, Sheldon .... 415-338-1571.. 36 A
axler@sfsu.edu
AXLUND, Martin .... 307-755-2169 547 D
maxlund@wyotechstaff.edu
AXLUND MCBRIDE,
RaeLyn .... 360-752-8344 520 A
raelyn.axlund.mcbride@btc.edu
AXTELL, Denise .... 530-242-7770.. 66 C
daxtell@shastacollege.edu
AXTELL, John .... 310-665-6957.. 57 C
AXTELL, Richard, D ...... 859-238-5342 194 E
rick.axtell@centre.edu
AXTMAN, Nichole .... 952-358-8143 260 D
nichole.axtman@normandale.edu
AXTON, Faith, M .... 660-263-3900 272 M
faithaxton@cccb.edu
AYALA, Benjamin .... 787-864-2222 553 J
benjamin.ayala@guayama.inter.edu
AYALA, Carlos .... 707-664-2132.. 36 C
dean.education@sonoma.edu
AYALA, Carmen .... 787-761-0640 557 A
decanaacademica@utcpr.edu
AYALA, Eddie .... 787-279-1912 553 H
eayala@bayamon.inter.edu
AYALA, George, M .... 956-721-5126 477 C
george.ayala@laredo.edu
AYALA, Gladys, M .... 914-594-4498 335 H
gladys_ayala@nymc.edu
AYALA, Hector .... 787-850-9187 558 A
hector.ayala5@upr.edu
AYALA, Israel .... 787-891-0925 553 E
iayala@aguadilla.inter.edu
AYALA, Mary .... 575-562-2421 310 I
mary.ayala@enmu.edu
AYALA, Oliva .... 818-364-7795.. 51 G
sancheo@lamission.edu
AYALA, Paul .... 210-805-5863 492 B
peayala@uiwtx.edu
AYALA, Ramon .... 787-250-1912 554 A
rayala@intermetro.edu
AYALA, Sheryl, K .... 920-923-7604 537 A
sayala@marianuniversity.edu
AYBAR, Jose, M .... 773-838-7511 142 C
jaybar@ccc.edu
AYCOCK, Allan .... 706-542-3196 132 H
aaycock@uga.edu
AYCOCK, Greg .... 951-739-7802.. 61 A
greg.aycock@norcocollege.edu
AYCOCK, Jim, H .... 662-246-6330 268 F
jaycock@msdelta.edu
AYCOCK, Larry, K .... 909-389-3663.. 62 B
laycock@sbccd.edu
AYDELOTT, Carla .... 541-684-7241 407 I
caydelott@nwcu.edu
AYDELOTTE, Elise .... 661-362-2267.. 53 F
eaydelotte@masters.edu
AYER, Bernice .... 270-686-4518 197 A
bernice.ayer@kctcs.edu
AYERS, Ann .... 718-390-3207 352 C
aayers@wagner.edu
AYERS, Benjamin, C ..... 706-542-8100 132 H
busdean@uga.edu
AYERS, David, J .... 724-458-2025 419 F
djayers@gcc.edu
AYERS, Donna .... 818-364-7750.. 51 G
ayersdj@lamission.edu
AYERS, Kenya .... 847-925-6404 145 F
kayers@harpercollege.edu
AYERS, Lee .... 541-552-6505 409 G
ayersl@sou.edu
AYERS, Michael, V .... 336-734-7478 362 F
mayers@forsythtech.edu
AYERS, Nancy, A .... 208-467-8542 138 H
naayers@nnu.edu
AYERS, Shari .... 419-358-3030 377 H
ayerss@bluffton.edu
AYERS, Susan .... 706-864-1998 133 A
susan.ayers@ung.edu
AYERS, Susan .... 978-232-2066 226 C
sayers@endicott.edu
AYERS, Tom .... 810-762-9787 245 A
tayers@kettering.edu
AYERS, William, J .... 302-857-1814.. 94 A
ayers@dtcc.edu
AYERSMAN, David, J .... 304-256-0281 531 D
dayersman@newriver.edu
AYKROID, David .... 847-543-2259 142 G
daykroid@clcillinois.edu
AYLESBURY, Tom .... 626-568-8850.. 49 J
AYLMER, Francoise .... 503-725-5037 409 D
francoise@pdx.edu
AYLOR, Pete .... 864-587-4229 449 D
aylorp@smcsc.edu
AYLWARD, Robert, R .... 307-766-4860 546 K
raylward@uwyo.edu
AYMAT-SANTANA,
Noel, J .... 787-758-2525 557 B
rector.rcm@upr.edu
AYMAT SANTANA,
Noel, J .... 787-758-2525 558 C
noel.aymat@upr.edu
AYON, Carlos .... 714-992-7064.. 56 F
cayon@fullcoll.edu
AYON, Maria .... 626-571-8811.. 74 E
mariaa@uwest.edu
AYON, Violet, R .... 714-808-4793.. 56 D
vayon@nocccd.edu
AYOOB, Kenneth .... 707-826-4491.. 35 D
kpa1@humboldt.edu
AYOUBI, Amjad .... 504-865-5107 207 F
aamjad@tulane.edu
AYOUCH, Karen .... 315-866-0300 327 E
ayouchka@herkimer.edu
AYRAVAINEN, Eija .... 212-772-4878 319 E
eija.ayravainen@hunter.cuny.edu
AYRE-BOGGS, Rebecca . 810-766-4044 239 H
rebecca.boggs@baker.edu
AYRES, Christina, M ..... 573-202-6959 274 J
christina.ayres@eastcentral.edu
AYRES, Dana .... 214-768-2841 482 J
dwayres@smu.edu
AYRES, Deb .... 636-949-4477 276 L
dayres@lindenwood.edu
AYRES, Jeffrey, M .... 802-654-2492 502 H
jyres@smcvt.edu
AYRES, Jessica .... 650-543-3855.. 54 B
jessica.ayres@menlo.edu
AYTCH, Keith .... 408-270-6450.. 63 P
keith.aytch@evc.edu
AYTES, Kregg .... 406-994-4423 287 G
kregg.aytes@montana.edu
AYVAZYAN, Odeta .... 866-687-2258.. 31 E
AYYAR, Radhika .... 936-261-3311 484 F
AZAIR, Cheryl .... 310-824-1586.. 25 K
cheryl@cherylazair.com
AZAR, Dimitri .... 312-996-3500 161 F
dazar@uic.edu
AZAR, Eve .... 908-835-2335 309 G
azar@warren.edu
AZAR, James, A .... 401-254-3124 442 C
jazar@rwu.edu
AZARI, Cynthia, E .... 559-489-2212.. 69 B
cynthia.azari@fresnocitycollege.edu
AZDELL, Grant, L .... 804-752-7266 511 E
gazdell@rmc.edu
AZEBEOKHAI,
Ignatius, C .... 501-569-3180.. 24 A
icazebeokhai@ualr.edu
AZEKE, Mercy .... 732-571-4409 303 G
mazeke@monmouth.edu
AZEVEDO, Hannah .... 773-244-4892 154 G
hjazevedo@northpark.edu
AZEVEDO, Mario .... 601-979-7036 267 H
mario.j.azevedo@jsums.edu
AZHAND, Hamid, U .... 909-537-5136.. 35 A
hazhand@csusb.edu
AZIZ, Jihad, N .... 804-828-6200 514 F
jnaziz@vcu.edu
AZIZ, Nadim .... 864-656-0542 444 E
aziz@clemson.edu
AZIZ, Nadim, M .... 864-656-3243 444 E
aziz@clemson.edu
AZIZAN-GARDNER,
Noor .... 573-882-6282 283 H
azizan-gardnern@missouri.edu
AZKOUL, Emilie .... 616-222-1447 241 G
emilie.azkoul@cornerstone.edu
AZLIN WRIGHT, Taisha 714-816-0366.. 70 D
taisha.wright@trident.edu
AZURE, Jackie .... 406-768-3213 286 H
jazure@fpcc.edu
AZURE, Lisa .... 701-255-3285 375 I
lazure@uttc.edu
AZURE, Melody .... 701-854-8020 375 F
melodya@sbci.edu
AZURE, Tracy .... 701-477-7862 375 H
tazure@tm.edu
A'SEE, Carlito, D .... 803-536-7485 448 H
cdasee@scsu.edu

B

BAADE, K.Austin .... 262-691-5550 544 D
kbaade@wctc.edu
BAAKKO, Lori .... 906-487-7360 242 M
lori.baakko@finlandia.edu
BAAR, Rachael .... 270-831-9803 196 C
rachael.baar@kctcs.edu
BAAR, Tricia .... 501-337-5000.. 20 H
tbaar@coto.edu
BAART, Aaron .... 712-722-6079 177 J
aaron.baart@dordt.edu
BAAS, John .... 712-722-6020 177 J
john.baas@dordt.edu

BAAS, Mark 507-332-5876 262 A mark.baas@southcentral.edu
BABALIS, Eva 718-779-1430 338 D ebabalis@mail.plazacollege.edu
BABANI, Henry 305-442-9223 108 G hbabani@mrc.edu
BABASHANIAN, Mark, R 757-446-6003 507 B babashmr@evms.edu
BABB, Brian 386-506-4457 101 I babbb@DaytonaState.edu
BABB, Brian, T 386-506-4457 101 I babbb@DaytonaState.edu
BABB, Mike 847-925-6825 145 F mbabb@harpercollege.edu
BABB, Phillip 619-702-9400.. 31 F phillip.babb@cibu.edu
BABBITT, Jeff 585-567-9211 328 C jeff.babbitt@houghton.edu
BABBITT, Steven 516-463-5019 328 A steven.babbitt@hofstra.edu
BABBITT, Terry 505-277-8392 313 H tbabbitt@unm.edu
BABBITTS, Judith 914-395-2371 342 C jbabbitts@sarahlawrence.edu
BABCOCK, Bernie 541-881-5706 410 D bbabcock@tvcc.cc
BABCOCK, Ed 309-694-5337 146 C ebabcock@icc.edu
BABCOCK, Lisa 716-614-6407 336 D lbabcock@niagaracc.suny.edu
BABCOCK, Michael 906-487-7348 242 M michael.babcock@finlandia.edu
BABCOCK, Whit 540-231-3977 518 B HokieAD@vt.edu
BABEL, Rebecca 815-753-1395 154 I rbabel@niu.edu
BABEL, Thomas 630-515-3029 144 A tbabel@devrygroup.com
BABENCHUK, Iavoslava 631-451-4409 348 E babenci@sunysuffolk.edu
BABER, Donna 636-949-4532 276 L dbaber@lindenwood.edu
BABER, James 740-264-5591 381 J jbaber@egcc.edu
BABESHOFF, Ruth 714-628-4775.. 60 H babeshoff_ruth@sccollege.edu
BABETZ, Jeffrey 843-863-7921 444 B jbabetz@csuniv.edu
BABIN, Louis 225-752-4233 202 I lbabin@iticollege.edu
BABINEAU, Tereasa, W 757-446-5116 507 B babinetw@evms.edu
BABINGTON, Cindy 765-658-4108 165 G cbabington@depauw.edu
BABINGTON, Lynn 203-254-4000.. 90 E lbabington@fairfield.edu
BABYAK, Joyce 440-775-8540 388 B joyce.babyak@oberlin.edu
BACA, Amy 575-538-6145 314 E bacaamym@wnmu.edu
BACA, Brad 970-943-2114.. 87 F bbaca@western.edu
BACA, Chris 972-825-4650 483 D cbaca@sagu.edu
BACA, Max 505-454-3117 311 H mbaca@nmhu.edu
BACA, Philip 575-624-8497 311 K baca@nmmi.edu
BACA, Randy 254-298-8582 484 C randy.baca@templejc.edu
BACA, Sylvia 505-426-2048 311 H sbaca@nmhu.edu
BACA-DOSTER, Carmen, E 303-765-3127.. 83 C cbaca@iliff.edu
BACALL, Peggy 952-358-9130 260 D peggy.bacall@normandale.edu
BACCAR, Cindy 503-725-5533 409 D baccarc@pdx.edu
BACCHETTA, Aldo 816-802-3334 276 F abacchetta@kcai.edu
BACCI, Nancy 973-748-9000 300 E nancy_bacci@bloomfield.edu
BACCUS-HAIRSTON, Nilaya 301-336-6000 217 G baccusnd@pgcc.edu
BACH, Alex 800-955-2527 187 E abach@grantham.edu
BACH, Bert, C 423-439-4219 461 D bachb@etsu.edu
BACH, Bruce 215-641-6519 426 E bbach@mc3.edu
BACH, Carol Anne 615-547-1200 456 C cbach@cumberland.edu
BACH, Larry, C 612-343-4703 263 H lcbach@northcentral.edu
BACHAND, Donald, J 989-964-4041 249 G dbachand@svsu.edu
BACHAS, Leonidas, G 305-284-4117 118 A bachas@miami.edu
BACHHER, Jagdeep, S 510-987-0260.. 70 J jagdeep.baccher@ucop.edu
BACHLE, Lori 402-552-3100 289 H
BACHMAN, Gary 517-338-3333 241 B gbachman@cleary.edu
BACHMAN, Rob 303-762-6970.. 82 C rob.bachman@denverseminary.edu
BACHMANN, Robin 714-895-8382.. 40 C rbachmann@gwc.cccd.edu
BACHMEIER, James 616-331-2188 243 E bachmeij@gvsu.edu
BACHMEIER, John, G 715-836-5189 539 E bachmejg@uwec.edu
BACHMEIER, Mark 828-262-6483 369 D bachmeiermd@appstate.edu
BACHOO, Richard, R 860-832-1776.. 88 D bachoor@ccsu.edu
BACHUS, Dan 602-639-7500.. 14 A
BACIK, Johanna 216-987-2283 381 A johanna.bacik@tri-c.edu
BACKELS, Kelsey, K 717-871-7821 431 E kelsey.backels@millersville.edu
BACKER, Carol 800-782-2422.. 32 A cbacker@mail.cnuas.edu
BACKHAUS, Kristin 845-257-2930 344 A backhauk@newpaltz.edu
BACKLIN, William 785-243-1435 186 A bbacklin@cloud.edu
BACKLUND, Lee Ann, M 931-598-1238 460 I lafton@sewanee.edu
BACKLUND, Mary, I 845-758-7472 315 G backlund@bard.edu
BACKMAN, Carey 585-389-2320 334 B cbackma2@naz.edu
BACKMAN, Danielle 800-371-6105.. 16 A danielle@nationalparalegal.edu
BACKMAN, Kelli 402-481-8698 289 C kelli.backman@bryanhealthcollege.edu
BACKMAN, Stephen, M 251-343-8200.... 6 E stephen.backman@remingtoncollege.edu
BACKOFEN, Susan 316-684-3356 191 B susan.backofen@sckans.edu
BACKOS, Dean 734-487-4428 242 J dbackos@emich.edu
BACKUS, Amy 216-368-2866 378 J amy.backus@case.edu
BACKUS, Bruce, D 314-935-9882 285 E backusb@wustl.edu
BACKUS, Robert, H 607-746-4677 347 G backusrh@delhi.edu
BACON, Aileen, Q 253-535-7385 524 I baconaq@plu.edu
BACON, Amy 417-447-2660 280 C bacona@otc.edu
BACON, Curt 541-552-6487 409 G bacon@sou.edu
BACON, Jack 610-892-1007 429 M jbacon@pit.edu
BACON, Karen 212-340-7700 353 P kbacon@yu.edu
BACON, Michael 210-999-7328 490 E
BACON, Pamela 210-458-6551 494 D pamela.bacon@utsa.edu
BACON, Robbie 717-815-6818 440 H rbacon2@ycp.edu
BACQUE, Heather 504-864-7225 206 A heather.bacque@sodexo.com
BACZA, Gerald 304-367-4632 531 E Gerald.Bacza@pierpont.edu
BACZEWSKI, Philip, C 940-565-3886 492 D baczewski@unt.edu
BADAL, Amy, A 570-577-1601 413 E amy.badal@bucknell.edu
BADAL, Ashour 209-664-6747.. 35 C abadal@csustan.edu
BADAL, Joel 317-789-8284 165 F jbadal@crossroads.edu
BADAL, Robert, S 701-252-3467 375 J badal@uj.edu
BADALYAN, Anna 213-763-7064.. 52 A badalya@lattc.edu
BADE, Karen 360-752-8324 520 A kbade@btc.edu
BADE, Michael 415-502-6460.. 72 C Michael.Bade@ucsf.edu
BADE, Robert, E 727-816-3413 110 B badeb@phsc.edu
BADE, William, D 217-786-2326 151 C bill.bade@llcc.edu
BADEAUX, Aimee 225-491-1624 206 F aimee.badeaux@ololcollege.edu
BADENHAUSEN, Richard 801-832-2460 501 C rbadenhausen@westminstercollege.edu
BADER, Greg, R 740-587-5734 381 H baderg@denison.edu
BADER, Irv 718-820-4880 350 C Irv.bader@touro.edu
BADER, Jeff 406-994-2205 287 G jeff.bader@montana.edu
BADER-SAYE, Scott 512-472-4133 482 E scott.bader-saye@ssw.edu
BADESSA, Diane 609-586-4800 303 D badessad@mccc.edu
BADGER, Nancy 423-425-4438 465 E nancy-badger@utc.edu
BADIEY, Mohsen 302-831-2841.. 94 D badiey@udel.edu
BADILLO, Toni 915-831-2164 473 J mbadill4@epcc.edu
BADILLO-LOZANO, Luis, V 787-841-2000 555 F luis_badillo@pucpr.edu
BADIRU, Adedeji, B 937-255-3025 547 E adedeji.badiru@afit.edu
BADOLATO, Michael 978-762-4000 232 D mbadolat@northshore.edu
BADOVINAC, Amanda 406-496-4828 288 C abadovinac@mtech.edu
BADOVINAC, John, C 406-496-4249 288 C jbadovinac@mtech.edu
BADOWSKA, Eva 718-817-4400 326 C
BADRY, Jay 888-442-8709.. 45 J jaybadry@ggbts.edu
BADWAL, Avi 619-260-2943.. 74 B abadwal@sandiego.edu
BAEHR, Marie 319-399-8616 176 G mbaehr@coe.edu
BAEHRE-KOLOVANI, Edna, V 757-822-1050 517 C ekolovani@tcc.edu
BAEN, Karen 830-591-7301 483 A krbaen@swtjc.edu
BAENEN, Michael 617-627-3300 237 C michael.baenen@tufts.edu
BAENNINGER, MaryAnn 973-408-3100 301 J president@drew.edu
BAER, Candace 401-454-6426 442 B cbaer@risd.edu
BAER, Catherine, E 845-437-5401 351 H cabaer@vassar.edu
BAER, Eugen 315-781-3300 327 G baer@hws.edu
BAER, Karim 415-575-6176.. 31 C kbaer@ciis.edu
BAER, Natasha 763-433-1707 257 P natasha.baer@anokaramsey.edu
BAER, Ulrich, C 212-998-8695 336 C ulrich.baer@nyu.edu
BAERWALD, Bonnie 920-929-2127 543 F bbaerwald@morainepark.edu
BAERWALD, Bonnie 920-929-2131 543 F bbaerwald@morainepark.edu
BAESLACK, III, William, A 216-368-4346 378 J william.baeslack@case.edu
BAESSLER, Laura 937-382-6661 395 F laura_baessler@wilmington.edu
BAEZ, Ada 787-285-5457 552 J abaez4@hccpr.edu
BAEZ, Juan 310-233-4427.. 51 F baejrj@lahc.edu
BAEZ, Nayla 787-878-4146 557 D nayla.baez@upr.edu
BAEZ, Nayla 787-815-0000 557 D nayla.baez@upr.edu
BAEZ, Thomas 210-458-4140 494 D THOMAS.BAEZ@UTSA.EDU
BAEZ MILAN, Tony 724-653-2183 417 D tbaez@dec.edu
BAEZA-ORTEGO, Gilda 575-538-6350 314 E ortegog@wnmu.edu
BAFFA, Joe 714-556-3610.. 75 A joe.baffa@vanguard.edu
BAGBY, Crystal 360-752-8320 520 A cbagby@btc.edu
BAGDAZIAN, Robert, A 805-525-4417.. 69 I rbagdazian@thomasaquinas.edu
BAGEL, George 770-534-6265 121 G gbagel@brenau.edu
BAGEL, Jeffrey 716-851-1991 325 A bagel@ecc.edu
BAGENTS, Bill 256-766-6610.... 4 C bbagents@hcu.edu
BAGG, Eva 562-938-4736.. 51 A ebagg@lbcc.edu
BAGG, Mary Beth 317-788-3220 173 I bagg@uindy.edu
BAGGERMAN, Thom 412-391-4100 433 F tbaggerman@pointpark.edu
BAGGETT, Cody 217-641-4360 148 J cbaggett@jwcc.edu
BAGGETT, Darla 903-233-3860 477 G darlabaggett@letu.edu
BAGGETT, Jody 757-789-1730 515 D jbaggett@es.vccs.edu
BAGGIO, Bobbe, G 215-951-1238 422 F baggio@lasalle.edu
BAGGISH, Mindy 909-593-3511.. 73 B mbaggish@laverne.edu
BAGGOT, Joseph 507-222-4075 254 D jbaggot@carleton.edu
BAGGOTT, Jacob 205-975-4041.... 8 F jbaggott@uab.edu
BAGGS, Adam 817-257-6814 486 G a.baggs@tcu.edu
BAGGS, David 843-863-7513 444 B dbaggs@csuniv.edu
BAGGSON, Gulizar 479-619-2203.. 22 B gbaggson@nwacc.edu
BAGILEO, Nick, J 202-526-3799.. 96 F
BAGIROV, Feyzi, R 617-834-6838 223 C feyzi.bagirov@becker.edu
BAGLEY, Bob 706-233-7240 131 C bbagley@shorter.edu
BAGLEY, Elizabeth 404-471-6339 119 G ebagley@agnesscott.edu
BAGLEY, Michelle 360-992-2472 521 A mbagley@clark.edu
BAGLEY, Rebecca 412-624-5530 437 K bagley@pitt.edu
BAGLEY, Rod 715-833-6480 542 M rbagley1@cvtc.edu
BAGLEY, Shawn 330-823-2280 394 A bagleysp@mountunion.edu
BAGNALL, James 928-428-8414.. 13 L jim.bagnall@eac.edu
BAGNELL, William 252-328-6858 369 E bagnellw@ecu.edu
BAGNELL FINNEGAN, Kathleen 215-951-1234 422 F finnegan@lasalle.edu
BAGNO, Sherry 847-578-3262 157 G sherry.bagno@rosalindfranklin.edu
BAGNOLI, Joseph, P 641-269-3600 178 I bagnolij@grinnell.edu
BAGRANOFF, Nancy, A 804-289-8550 513 M nbagrano@richmond.edu
BAGSBY, Tori 615-794-4254 460 A tbagsby@omorecollege.edu
BAGSTAD, Kristi 563-588-6314 176 F kristi.bagstad@clarke.edu
BAGWELL, Christopher 228-896-2500 268 G christopher.bagwell@mgccc.edu
BAGWELL, Elizabeth 828-251-6525 370 E bbagwell@unca.edu
BAGWELL, Jack 864-941-8307 448 D bagwell.j@ptc.edu
BAGWELL, Lydia 575-527-7560 312 D lbagwell@nmsu.edu
BAHAM, Anthony, L 985-380-2957 204 D anthonybaham@scl.edu
BAHAR, Sonya 314-516-7150 284 B bahars@umsl.edu
BAHARANYI, Ntam 334-727-8659.... 8 B nbaharanyi@tuskegee.edu
BAHLS, Steven, C 309-794-7208 139 K stevenbahls@augustana.edu
BAHNEY, Steve 217-245-1488 150 B steve.bahney@doc.illinois.gov
BAHNSEN, JoEllen 309-438-5667 147 I jbahnse@ilstu.edu
BAHR, Brett 218-755-2599 258 B bbahr@bemidjistate.edu
BAHR, Christine, M 618-537-6810 152 C cmbahr@mckendree.edu
BAHR, Jonathon 734-995-7311 241 F jon.bahr@cuaa.edu
BAI, Kang 573-651-2249 282 C kbai@semo.edu
BAI, Monica 928-523-6514.. 16 C Monica.Bai@nau.edu
BAI, Vinglin 516-739-1545 335 C admissions@nyctcm.edu
BAI, Yifeng 973-748-9000 300 E yifeng_bai@bloomfield.edu
BAIA, Larissa 603-524-3207 296 L lbaia@ccsnh.edu
BAIC, Beth, A 412-397-6296 434 B baic@rmu.edu
BAIDA, Ana 470-578-6555 127 M abaida@kennesaw.edu
BAIER, Henry, D 734-764-3402 251 C hbaier@umich.edu
BAIER, Valerie, A 570-326-3761 429 J vbaier@pct.edu
BAIERL, Hans 920-924-3112 543 F hbaierl@morainepark.edu
BAIERL, Kenneth, W 574-520-4560 168 F kbaierl@iusb.edu
BAIGENT, Peter, M 631-632-6700 344 C peter.baigent@stonybrook.edu
BAIK, Sang 213-763-7015.. 52 A baiks@lattc.edu
BAILARD, Rhiannon 310-506-4702.. 58 H rhiannon.bailard@pepperdine.edu
BAILES, Loretta 773-907-4418 141 O lcanett-bailes@ccc.edu

BAKER, Lori .... 540-857-6348 517 E
sdeanofstudentservices@virginiawestern.edu
BAKER, LuAnn .... 870-307-7425.. 21 G
luann.baker@lyon.edu
BAKER, Marilyn .... 816-271-4361 279 E
mbaker3@missouriwestern.edu
BAKER, Matt .... 660-562-1219 280 A
mcbaker@nwmissouri.edu
BAKER, Maureen .... 402-844-7258 292 G
maureen@northeast.edu
BAKER, Michael .... 907-564-8259.. 10 D
mbaker@alaskapacific.edu
BAKER, Michael, F .... 508-856-3040 229 B
michael.baker@umassmed.edu
BAKER, Mike .... 859-442-1153 196 A
mike.baker@kctcs.edu
BAKER, Monica .... 928-226-4262.. 13 D
monica.baker@coconino.edu
BAKER, Nancy .... 704-636-6882 357 F
nbaker@hoodseminary.edu
BAKER, Natalie .... 404-880-6879 122 I
nbaker@cau.edu
BAKER, Neal .... 765-983-1355 165 H
bakerne@earlham.edu
BAKER, Neil .... 252-823-5166 362 D
bakern@edgecombe.edu
BAKER, Nelson .... 404-894-8920 125 D
nelson.baker@pe.gatech.edu
BAKER, Nick .... 989-275-5000 245 C
nick.baker@kirtland.edu
BAKER, Nolan .... 850-718-2310 100 E
bakern@chipola.edu
BAKER, Pearl .... 606-539-4211 200 F
pearl.baker@ucumberlands.edu
BAKER, Quanda .... 919-530-5597 370 C
quanda.baker@nccu.edu
BAKER, Richard .... 601-643-8404 266 J
richard.baker@colin.edu
BAKER, Richard, A .... 713-743-8834 491 D
rabaker4@central.uh.edu
BAKER, Robert .... 617-984-5959 235 H
rbaker@quincycollege.edu
BAKER, Robert, D .... 972-238-6174 473 B
rbaker1@dcccd.edu
BAKER, Robert, T .... 336-758-5224 372 G
bakerrt@wfu.edu
BAKER, Robin, E .... 503-554-2101 406 A
rbaker@georgefox.edu
BAKER, Russell, D .... 317-921-4313 169 L
rbaker80@ivytech.edu
BAKER, Ruth, E .... 410-334-2815 221 E
rbaker@worwic.edu
BAKER, Sallie .... 828-835-4202 366 F
sbaker@tricountycc.edu
BAKER, Sandi, J .... 770-531-6408 128 A
sbaker@laniertech.edu
BAKER, Sandy .... 951-222-8408.. 61 B
sandy.baker@rcc.edu
BAKER, Sara .... 706-233-7323 131 C
sbaker@shorter.edu
BAKER, Sarah .... 910-672-1185 370 A
sdbaker@uncfsu.edu
BAKER, Sarah .... 903-886-5045 485 E
sarah.baker@tamuc.edu
BAKER, Scott .... 828-339-4249 366 C
scottb@southwesterncc.edu
BAKER, Scott, R .... 740-427-5148 384 P
bakersr@kenyon.edu
BAKER, Shawn .... 402-461-7303 290 G
sbaker@hastings.edu
BAKER, Sherry .... 731-286-3242 462 F
baker@dscc.edu
BAKER, Stephen .... 212-353-4115 323 B
baker@cooper.edu
BAKER, Stephen, N .... 401-874-2109 442 E
snbaker@uri.edu
BAKER, Steve .... 619-644-7155.. 46 H
steve.baker@gcccd.edu
BAKER, Steven .... 561-803-2223 109 G
steven_baker@pba.edu
BAKER, Susan .... 727-341-3640 112 A
baker.susan@spcollege.edu
BAKER, Susan, D .... 585-292-2124 333 G
sbaker@monroecc.edu
BAKER, Tamara .... 504-865-3860 206 A
tbaker@loyno.edu
BAKER, Tana .... 432-685-4781 478 F
tbaker@midland.edu
BAKER, Teresa .... 417-626-1234 280 B
baker.teresa@occ.edu
BAKER, Thomas, N .... 315-267-2900 346 C
bakertn@potsdam.edu
BAKER, Tiffany .... 606-218-5953 201 C
tiffanybaker@upike.edu
BAKER, Timothy .... 670-237-6777 550 B
timothy.baker@marianas.edu
BAKER, Tracy, W .... 325-942-2035 489 E
tracy.baker@angelo.edu
BAKER, Twila .... 409-880-8933 488 F
twila.baker@lamar.edu
BAKER, Valparisa .... 863-292-3602 110 E
vbaker@polk.edu
BAKER, Waylon .... 701-627-4738 373 E
wbaker@fortbertholdcc.edu
BAKER, Wayne .... 432-335-6574 479 O
wbaker@odessa.edu
BAKER, Winston .... 936-468-2601 484 A
bakerwa@sfasu.edu
BAKER-CARR, Hope .... 802-224-3000 503 F
Hope.Baker-Carr@vsc.edu
BAKER-DEMARAY,
Twila .... 701-627-4738 373 E
tbaker@fortbertholdcc.edu
BAKER-EVANS, Teresa .. 575-562-2175 310 I
teresa.baker-evans@enmu.edu
BAKER-FLOWERS, Kim . 971-722-5841 409 C
kim.bakerflowers@pcc.edu
BAKER-TATE, Ixchel .... 910-962-1112 372 A
tatei@uncw.edu
BAKER-WATSON,
Stevie .... 765-658-6075 165 G
steviebaker-watson@depauw.edu
BAKEWELL-SACHS,
Susan .... 503-494-7445 408 D
sondeansoffice@ohsu.edu
BAKHIET, Raga .... 619-482-6381.. 68 D
rbakhiet@swccd.edu
BAKHIT, Norm .... 574-535-7507 166 C
nbakhit@goshen.edu
BAKK, Kelly .... 218-749-7765 259 D
k.bakk@mesabirange.edu
BAKKE, Andrea .... 703-812-4757 509 E
abakke@leland.edu
BAKKE, Diana .... 206-264-9100 519 I
dianab@bgu.edu
BAKKE, Jennifer .... 920-568-7224 543 C
jbakke@madisoncollege.edu
BAKKE, Lisa .... 702-651-4211 295 C
lisa.bakke@csn.edu
BAKKE, Ray .... 360-927-5744 519 I
rayb@bgu.edu
BAKKEN, Jeffrey .... 309-677-3997 140 H
jbakken@bradley.edu
BAKKEN, Turina, R .... 608-246-6516 543 C
bakken@madisoncollege.edu
BAKKEN, Vickie .... 651-638-6153 254 A
vickie-bakken@bethel.edu
BAKKUM, Christine, S . 608-785-8951 539 G
cbakkum@uwlax.edu
BAKSH-JARRETT, Gail ... 718-482-5116 320 B
gailbj@lagcc.cuny.edu
BAKST, M, S .... 248-968-3360 253 D
BAKST, Y .... 248-968-3360 253 D
BAKY, John, S .... 215-951-1286 422 F
baky@lasalle.edu
BAL, Balbir .... 352-588-8599 111 L
balbir.bal@saintleo.edu
BALABAN, Michael .... 845-431-8044 324 D
michael.balaban@sunydutchess.edu
BALACEK, Patti .... 608-785-9201 544 E
balacekp@westerntc.edu
BALACHANDRAN,
Betsy .... 847-851-5309 139 H
BALAGOUR, Nina .... 215-612-6600 421 N
n_balagour@chicareers.com
BALAGUER, Giovanna ... 787-850-9337 558 A
giovanna.balaguer@upr.edu
BALAKRISHNAN, Raju .. 313-593-5248 251 D
rajub@umich.edu
BALANOFF, Janet .... 407-708-2963 113 A
balanoffj@seminolestate.edu
BALAS, E. Andrew .... 706-721-2621 121 C
andrew.balas@gru.edu
BALAS, Heather, M .... 330-569-5132 383 F
balashm@hiram.edu
BALASH, Amber, L .... 330-471-8241 385 G
abalash@malone.edu
BALASON, Severo .... 708-974-5346 153 D
balasonjrs@morainevalley.edu
BALASUBRAMANYA,
Mirley .... 210-784-2225 486 B
mbalasub@tamusa.tamus.edu
BALATBAT, Joseph .... 212-924-5900 349 D
jbalatbat@swedishinstitute.edu
BALBACH, Donna .... 812-357-6525 173 A
dbalbach@saintmeinrad.edu
BALCAZAR, Genaro .... 773-244-5705 154 G
gabalcazar@northpark.edu
BALCH, Angela .... 432-685-4508 478 F
abalch@midland.edu
BALCH, Glenna .... 512-404-4828 468 J
gbalch@austinseminary.edu
BALCH, Margaret .... 401-454-6655 442 B
mbalch@risd.edu
BALCH, Pamela .... 304-473-8181 534 G
balch@wvwc.edu
BALCH, Sue Ann .... 205-652-5456.... 9 G
sbalch@uwa.edu
BALCHAK, Sharon .... 216-373-5322 388 A
sbalchak@ndc.edu
BALD, Tim .... 920-403-3030 538 K
tim.bald@snc.edu
BALDA, Wes .... 802-865-5725 501 F
strubler@champlain.edu
BALDAGUEZ, Jose, A ... 787-850-9341 558 A
jose.baldaguez1@upr.edu
BALDASARE, Angela, Y 520-626-2885.. 18 E
baldasar@email.arizona.edu
BALDASTY, Gerald, J .... 206-685-3218 527 G
baldasty@uw.edu
BALDAUFF, John .... 708-293-4597 160 L
john.baldauff@trnty.edu
BALDEMOR, Vince .... 808-544-0209 135 C
vbaldemor@hpu.edu
BALDERAS, Maggie .... 805-585-8034.. 29 J
mbalderas@brooks.edu
BALDERAZ, Brenda Jo . 956-872-5051 482 G
BALDIN, Antoinette .... 419-995-8222 384 E
baldin.a@rhodesstate.edu
BALDINI, Fred .... 916-278-7256.. 34 E
baldinif@csus.edu
BALDONADO,
Hernando .... 713-718-5069 475 C
nandy.baldonado@hccs.edu
BALDONEDO, Claudia .. 718-482-5236 320 B
claudiab@lagcc.cuny.edu
BALDONIERI, Amy .... 412-365-1349 415 C
abaldonieri@chatham.edu
BALDREE, Megan .... 325-793-4801 478 D
baldree.megan@mcm.edu
BALDRIDGE, Amanda ... 580-387-7200 398 J
abaldridge@mscok.edu
BALDRIDGE,
Patricia, M .... 215-951-2851 432 F
baldridgep@philau.edu
BALDRIDGE, Susan .... 802-443-5518 502 E
scbaldridge@middlebury.edu
BALDUINO, Joseph, J .. 570-326-3761 429 J
jjb15@pct.edu
BALDWIN, Alphonso .... 847-543-2113 142 G
abaldwin@clcillinois.edu
BALDWIN, Anne, E .... 585-245-5547 345 D
baldwina@geneseo.edu
BALDWIN, Chad .... 307-766-2929 546 K
cbaldwin@uwyo.edu
BALDWIN, Charlene ..... 714-532-7747.. 38 B
baldwin@chapman.edu
BALDWIN, Christine, A 714-850-4800.. 87 K
Baldwin@TaftU.edu
BALDWIN, Darin .... 334-745-6437.... 7 E
dbaldwin@suscc.edu
BALDWIN, David, N ..... 508-626-4645 230 A
dbaldwin@framingham.edu
BALDWIN, Deborah, J .. 501-569-3123.. 24 A
djbaldwin@ualr.edu
BALDWIN, Dirk .... 262-595-2379 540 C
baldwin@uwp.edu
BALDWIN, Dorsey .... 912-478-5409 126 B
dbaldwin@georgiasouthern.edu
BALDWIN, Eric .... 509-313-4100 522 L
baldwine@gonzaga.edu
BALDWIN, James .... 518-464-8500 325 B
jbaldwin@excelsior.edu
BALDWIN, Joelle .... 616-632-2076 239 E
baldwjoe@aquinas.edu
BALDWIN, R. Chad .... 636-584-6609 274 J
robert.baldwin@eastcentral.edu
BALDWIN, Robert .... 512-863-1200 483 G
baldwinb@southwestern.edu
BALDWIN, Ronda .... 740-477-7713 388 F
rbaldwin@ohiochristian.edu
BALDWIN, Sarah, T .... 859-858-3511 193 A
sarah.baldwin@asbury.edu
BALDWIN, Stacy .... 601-815-3872 270 H
sbaldwin@umc.edu
BALDWIN, Stan .... 601-925-3321 268 E
sbaldwin@mc.edu
BALDWIN, Terri, M .... 740-588-1210 396 E
tbaldwin@zanestate.edu
BALDWIN, Tony .... 704-216-6272 358 I
tbaldwin@livingstone.edu
BALDWIN, Veria .... 606-589-3018 197 D
cookie.baldwin@kctcs.edu
BALDWIN-DIMEO,
Caren .... 603-526-3714 296 I
cbaldwin-dimeo@colby-sawyer.edu
BALDYGO, Robert .... 540-453-2285 514 H
baldygor@brcc.edu
BALENTINE, Jerry .... 516-686-3999 335 F
Jerry.Balentine@nyit.edu
BALENTINE, Kim .... 417-626-1234 280 B
kbalentine@occ.edu
BALES, Jennifer .... 913-621-8733 186 G
jennifer@donnelly.edu
BALES, John .... 208-885-5953 139 C
jbales@uidaho.edu
BALES, Kay .... 765-285-5344 164 D
kbales@bsu.edu
BALES, Michael .... 276-964-7323 517 A
michael.bales@sw.edu
BALES, Richard, C .... 419-772-2205 388 I
r-bales@onu.edu
BALES, Stefany .... 208-885-6567 139 C
sbales@uidaho.edu
BALES, William, J .... 615-898-5818 461 E
joe.bales@mtsu.edu
BALESTRERI, Teresa, A . 314-516-5002 284 B
tkb@umsl.edu
BALEY, Heather .... 503-244-0726 404 G
heatherbaley@achs.edu
BALFOUR, Charmaine .. 256-761-6277.... 7 H
ccbalfour@talladega.edu
BALFOUR, David .... 802-773-5900 501 G
david.balfour@csj.edu
BALGE, Daniel, N .... 507-354-8221 257 A
balgedn@mlc-wels.edu
BALI, Vinita .... 650-949-7077.. 45 A
balivinita@foothill.edu
BALINT, Bill .... 724-357-7854 431 A
wsbalint@iup.edu
BALISTRERI-CLARKE,
Margaret, R .... 608-663-2212 536 A
balistr@edgewood.edu
BALIT-MOUSSALLI,
Cinzia .... 334-833-4452.... 4 E
cinziam@huntingdon.edu
BALIUS, Cheryl .... 601-947-4201 268 G
cheryl.balius@mgccc.edu
BALL, Charles .... 574-239-8318 167 C
cball@hcc-nd.edu
BALL, Christine .... 706-771-4150 121 B
cball@augustatech.edu
BALL, Dave .... 319-296-4204 179 B
david.ball@hawkeyecollege.edu
BALL, Deborah .... 816-604-1148 277 F
deborah.ball@mcckc.edu
BALL, Deborah, L .... 734-615-4415 251 C
dball@umich.edu
BALL, Diane .... 239-513-1122 106 E
dball@hodges.edu
BALL, Don .... 330-494-6170 391 J
dball@starkstate.edu
BALL, Drexel, B .... 803-535-5263 444 D
dball@claflin.edu
BALL, Gerald, D .... 828-689-1242 359 A
gball@mhu.edu
BALL, Gregory, F .... 301-405-1691 219 D
gball@umd.edu
BALL, James, D .... 410-386-8188 214 B
jball@carrollcc.edu
BALL, Jason .... 561-297-3440 114 E
jball@fau.edu
BALL, Jennette .... 315-568-3296 334 F
jball@nycc.edu
BALL, John .... 504-568-4500 205 C
jball@lsuhsc.edu
BALL, Joshua .... 606-886-3863 195 I
jball0079@kctcs.edu
BALL, Justin .... 309-677-3850 140 H
Jball@bradley.edu
BALL, Karen .... 559-791-2420.. 49 G
kball@portervillecollege.edu
BALL, Kathy .... 304-384-6009 532 E
bonner@concord.edu
BALL, Kenneth .... 703-993-1500 507 K
kball@gmu.edu
BALL, Kevin .... 330-941-1560 396 C
keball@ysu.edu
BALL, Kim .... 704-894-2521 356 D
kiball@davidson.edu
BALL, Kimberly .... 657-278-4968.. 33 E
kball@fullerton.edu
BALL, L. Julia .... 803-641-3263 450 C
JuliaB@usca.edu
BALL, Linda .... 785-227-3380 185 A
balll@bethanylb.edu
BALL, Margaret, T .... 718-817-3010 326 C
mball@fordham.edu
BALL, Michael .... 859-246-6512 195 J
michael.ball@kctcs.edu
BALL, Sam .... 253-833-9111 523 B
sball@greenriver.edu
BALL, Scott .... 423-236-2881 460 K
sball@southern.edu
BALL, Shelley .... 865-471-3235 455 G
sball@cn.edu
BALL, Thomas, G .... 724-458-2163 419 F
tgball@gcc.edu
BALL, Travis .... 903-886-5060 485 E
travis.ball@tamuc.edu
BALL, William, S .... 513-558-0026 393 B
william.s.ball@uc.edu
BALL, Williams, S .... 513-558-7333 393 B
william.s.ball@uc.edu
BALL-WILLIAMSON,
Carrie .... 662-862-8123 267 F
cbball@iccms.edu
BALLABAN, David, C .... 610-921-7256 411 E
dballaban@albright.edu

BARABINO, Gilda 212-650-5435 318 G gbarabino@ccny.cuny.edu
BARABINO, Joseph 305-348-2494 114 G joseph.barabino@fiu.edu
BARAGONA, Fred 318-342-5141 209 A baragona@ulm.edu
BARAJAS, Daniel 928-344-7769 12 B daniel.barajas@azwestern.edu
BARAJAS, Leticia 213-763-7071 52 A barajal@lattc.edu
BARAJAS, Silvia 253-566-5050 527 C sbarajas@tacomacc.edu
BARAJAS, Sylvia 805-378-1412 75 C sbarajas@vcccd.edu
BARAKAT, Nabeel 310-233-4351 51 F barakanm@lahc.edu
BARAKAT, Nabeel, M 310-233-4351 51 F barakanm@lahc.edu
BARAKEH, Zeina 415-641-1241 62 I zbarakeh@sfai.edu
BARAN, Kelley 508-531-2492 229 C kelley.baran@bridgew.edu
BARAN-CENTENO, Barbara 210-458-4037 494 D barbara.centeno@utsa.edu
BARANICH, Debbie 614-837-4088 394 H baranichd@valorcollege.com
BARANOWSKI, Donna 941-907-2262 102 N dbaranowski@evergladesuniversity.edu
BARATO, Ruben 914-606-6777 352 G Ruben.Barato@sunywcc.edu
BARAZZONE, Esther, L 412-365-1160 415 C barazzone@chatham.edu
BARBARAK, Thomas 314-256-8886 272 B barbarak@ai.edu
BARBAREE, Joel 870-850-4821 23 C jbarbaree@seark.edu
BARBARI, Timothy 617-353-2230 224 E barbari@bu.edu
BARBATIS, Peter 561-868-3142 109 H barbatip@palmbeachstate.edu
BARBEAU, Marc 920-686-6176 539 A Marc.Barbeau@sl.edu
BARBEE, Brent 910-410-1809 365 B btbarbee@richmondcc.edu
BARBEE, Chris, W 616-331-3590 243 E barbeec@gvsu.edu
BARBER, Afton 903-923-3206 488 A afton.barber@tstc.edu
BARBER, Andrea 585-785-1216 325 E andrea.barber@flcc.edu
BARBER, Bernadette (BJ) 626-584-5238 45 F bjbarber@fuller.edu
BARBER, Billy 252-789-0303 363 H bbarber@martincc.edu
BARBER, Catherine 985-858-5746 203 G catherine.barber@fletcher.edu
BARBER, Deborah, G 803-323-2191 451 I barberdg@winthrop.edu
BARBER, Elizabeth 812-749-1242 171 I bbarber@oak.edu
BARBER, Ella 972-273-3009 473 A ebarber@dcccd.edu
BARBER, Glynis 410-951-3078 220 C gbarber@coppin.edu
BARBER, Jacques 516-877-4800 314 F jbarber@adelphi.edu
BARBER, Jeff 434-582-2100 509 G jbarber2@liberty.edu
BARBER, Jennifer 916-278-6295 34 E jbarbar@csus.edu
BARBER, Jeremiah 816-501-4587 281 B jeremiah.barber@rockhurst.edu
BARBER, Kimberly 850-644-6127 115 A kabarber@admin.fsu.edu
BARBER, Luanne 870-612-2119 24 G luanne.barber@uaccb.edu
BARBER, Marcia, A 315-470-6611 347 B mabarber@esf.edu
BARBER, Mark 828-726-2715 360 F mbarber@cccti.edu
BARBER, Michael, J 406-247-5750 287 H mbarber@msubillings.edu
BARBER, Ray, G 812-749-1213 171 I ocuexec@oak.edu
BARBER, Sharon 563-355-3500 180 F sbarber@kaplan.edu
BARBER, Susan, C 405-208-5287 400 A sbarber@okcu.edu
BARBER, Tamara 701-224-5476 374 E tamara.barber@bismarckstate.edu
BARBER, Tanyka 443-885-3559 217 C tanyka.barber@morgan.edu
BARBER, Tracy 719-255-7507 86 F tbarber@uccs.edu
BARBER, Trent, J 860-512-3353 89 D tbarber@manchestercc.edu
BARBER-LYHNAKIS, Michelle 801-832-2755 501 C mbarber@westminstercollege.edu
BARBERA, Anthony 516-876-3292 345 E barberaa@oldwestbury.edu
BARBERI, Heather 732-255-0400 304 E hbarberi@ocean.edu
BARBICH, Michelle 814-732-1457 430 G mbarbich@edinboro.edu
BARBIE, Kenneth 215-895-1335 417 E kenneth.andrew.barbee@drexel.edu
BARBIERI, Lina 610-282-1100 416 I lina.barbieri@desales.edu
BARBONI, Edward 212-772-5740 319 E edward.barboni@hunter.cuny.edu
BARBOSA, Miguel 570-422-3545 430 F mbarbosa@esu.edu
BARBOUR, A. Sandy 814-865-1086 428 C asb25@psu.edu
BARBOUR, Cheryl 303-546-3565 84 B cheryl@naropa.edu
BARBOUR, Darrell 641-585-8138 183 I darrell.barbour@waldorf.edu
BARBOUR, Jeffery 757-340-2121 506 E librariancvab@centura.edu
BARBOUR, Kathryn, A 410-827-5806 214 D kbarbour@chesapeake.edu
BARBOUR, Monica 313-993-1951 250 H barboumm@udmercy.edu
BARBOUR, Suzanne 706-542-6128 132 H sbarbour@uga.edu
BARBOUR, Wayne 301-846-2565 214 I wbarbour@frederick.edu
BARCELO, Nancy (Rusty) 505-747-2140 312 G nbarcelo@nnmc.edu
BARCHI, Robert, L 848-932-7454 306 F president@rutgers.edu
BARCKHOLTZ, Benjamin 406-657-1714 287 H benjamin.barckholtz@msubillings.edu
BARCLAY, Kent 978-232-2282 226 C kbarclay@endicott.edu
BARCLAY, Raymond 212-229-8947 334 C barclayr@newschool.edu
BARCLIFT-MCGEE, Angela 757-493-6000 96 H
BARCUS, Susan, L 706-721-0275 121 C sbarcus@gru.edu
BARCUS, Tracy 301-387-3164 215 A tracy.barcus@garrettcollege.edu
BARCZYK, Ewa 414-229-4781 540 A ewa@uwm.edu
BARD, Elizabeth 501-296-1275 24 B ebard@uams.edu
BARD, Jennifer, S 513-556-0121 393 B jennifer.bard@uc.edu
BARD, Melissa 252-328-9881 369 E bardme@ecu.edu
BARD, Sharon, K 704-463-3428 367 F sharon.bard@pfeiffer.edu
BARDEGUEZ, Lemuel 405-682-7814 399 K lbardeguez@occc.edu
BARDEGUEZ, Lemuel 405-682-7295 399 K lbardeguez@occc.edu
BARDELL, Kathleen 617-449-7070 237 E kathleen.bardell@urbancollege.edu
BARDEN, John, H 512-404-4829 468 J jbarden@austinseminary.edu
BARDILL MOSCARITOLO, Lisa 914-773-3860 337 I lbardillmoscaritolo@pace.edu
BARDO, John, W 316-978-3001 192 D john.bardo@wichita.edu
BARE, Benita 276-944-6800 507 E bbare@ehc.edu
BARE, James, S 516-739-1545 335 C admin_dean@nyctcm.edu
BAREFIELD, Frank 334-556-2235 4 A fbarefield@wallace.edu
BAREFIELD, Kevin 662-685-4771 266 G kbarefield@bmc.edu
BAREFOOT, Russell 908-526-1200 305 G Russell.Barefoot@raritanval.edu
BARELMAN, Jason 402-375-7327 292 D jabarel1@wsc.edu
BARENDS, Frans 404-894-5000 125 D frans.barends@business.gatech.edu
BARENTINE, Julie 504-816-8595 206 C housing@nobts.edu
BARES, Donna 440-375-7075 385 B dbares@lec.edu
BARFIELD, Craig 919-760-8516 359 B craigb@meredith.edu
BARFIELD, Kim 336-838-6419 367 C kim.barfield@wilkescc.edu
BARFOOT, D. Scott 214-887-5151 473 E sbarfoot@dts.edu
BARGAS, Peter 661-362-2836 53 F pbargas@masters.edu
BARGE, Gayle 425-564-2282 519 L gayle.barge@bellevuecollege.edu
BARGE, Scott 574-535-7110 166 C scottcb@goshen.edu
BARGE, Scott 574-535-7110 166 C scottb@goshen.edu
BARGE, Scott 574-535-7110 166 C scottcb@goshen.edu
BARGER, Debbie, M 515-263-6012 178 H dbarger@grandview.edu
BARGER, Debra, E 530-898-6105 33 A dbarger@csuchico.edu
BARGER, Eric, C 503-943-7337 410 H barger@up.edu
BARGER, Kyle 215-248-6325 424 G kbarger@ltsp.edu
BARGER, Peter, S 630-637-5362 154 F psbarger@noctrl.edu
BARGER, Robert, C 614-235-4136 392 D rbarger@TLSohio.edu
BARHAM, James 731-286-3371 462 F jbarham@dscc.edu
BARIL, Kathleen 419-772-2180 388 I k-baril@onu.edu
BARILAR, Stephen, J 570-577-3333 413 E steve.barilar@bucknell.edu
BARILE, Brandon 315-781-3880 327 G barile@hws.edu
BARILLO, Madeline, K 203-857-7039 89 H mbarillo@norwalk.edu
BARIOLA, Kristi 662-246-6376 268 F kbariola@msdelta.edu
BARISH, Robert, A 318-675-5240 205 D rbaris@lsuhsc.edu
BARKALOW, Susan 252-823-5166 362 D
BARKAN, Chester 516-572-7370 334 A chester.barkan@ncc.edu
BARKE, Brady, L 573-651-2322 282 C bbarke@semo.edu
BARKE, Brady, L 573-651-2229 282 C bbarke@semo.edu
BARKELOO, Mary, E 308-635-6033 294 C barkeloo@wncc.edu
BARKER, Allyn, S 304-896-7404 531 F allyn.barker@southernwv.edu
BARKER, Allyson 256-782-5820 4 L abarker@jsu.edu
BARKER, Anna 304-876-5287 532 I abarker@shepherd.edu
BARKER, Brett 843-377-2149 444 A bbarker@charlestonlaw.edu
BARKER, Brian 970-943-3038 87 F bbarker@western.edu
BARKER, Bruce, A 715-833-6221 542 M bbarker@cvtc.edu
BARKER, David, F 502-852-4676 201 A david.barker@louisville.edu
BARKER, Helen, G 301-369-2800 214 A hgbarker@captechu.edu
BARKER, Jeanette 919-530-6367 370 C jbarker@nccu.edu
BARKER, Jeffrey, H 864-596-9091 445 E jeff.barker@converse.edu
BARKER, Joe 830-591-7284 483 A jcbarker@swtjc.edu
BARKER, John 617-627-4239 237 C john.barker@tufts.edu
BARKER, John, D 864-294-2106 446 F john.barker@furman.edu
BARKER, John, F 716-286-8220 336 E jfb@niagara.edu
BARKER, Joshua 252-398-6319 356 B barkej@chowan.edu
BARKER, Lee 773-256-3000 152 D lbarker@meadville.edu
BARKER, Lisa 731-425-8835 463 A lbarker@jscc.edu
BARKER, Lorie 559-791-2370 49 G lbarker@portervillecollege.edu
BARKER, Maria, T 810-762-3322 251 E tessba@umflint.edu
BARKER, Michael 919-843-5684 371 A michael_barker@unc.edu
BARKER, Neva 909-621-8306 65 E neva.barker@scrippscollege.edu
BARKER, Randy 910-892-3178 357 D rbarker@heritagebiblecollege.edu
BARKER, Rhonda 850-872-3857 105 Q rbarker@gulfcoast.edu
BARKER, Rod 503-491-7666 407 C rod.barker@mhcc.edu
BARKLEY, Jordan 254-968-9089 485 A jbarkley@tarleton.edu
BARKLEY, Leanne 508-999-8879 228 H lbarkley@umassd.edu
BARKLEY, Robert, S 864-656-5463 444 E rbrtbkl@clemson.edu
BARKLEY, Susan, E 972-238-6943 473 B sbarkley@dcccd.edu
BARKLEY, Will 612-455-3420 254 B
BARKLEY-GIFFIN, Adrienne 618-985-3741 148 G adriennebarkley@jalc.edu
BARKMAN, Jeff 731-989-6051 456 K facilities@fhu.edu
BARKO, James, N 972-881-5721 471 C jbarko@collin.edu
BARKO, Valerie 618-985-3741 148 G valeriebarko@jalc.edu
BARKOFF, Larry 734-677-5413 251 J lbarkoff@wccnet.edu
BARKOW, Aisha 414-297-7035 543 E barkowa@matc.edu
BARKOWITZ, Daniel 386-312-4041 111 K danielbarkowitz@sjrstate.edu
BARKSCHAT, Kate 828-395-1163 363 D kbarkschat@isothermal.edu
BARKSDALE, Jeffrey 251-981-3771 3 A jeffrey.barksdale@columbiasouthern.edu
BARKSDALE, Tina, M 302-356-6940 94 G tina.m.barksdale@wilmu.edu
BARKWELL, LaRue 202-806-2500 96 B lbarkwell@howard.edu
BARKWILL, Joseph 516-463-6623 328 A joseph.barkwill@hofstra.edu
BARLAND, Karen 410-951-3704 220 C kbarland@coppin.edu
BARLETT, Paul 913-234-0632 185 N paul.barlett@cleveland.edu
BARLOK, Tracy 508-793-2011 225 C tbarlok@holycross.edu
BARLOW, Charlene 859-344-3348 200 C barlowc@thomasmore.edu
BARLOW, Christopher 405-744-7665 400 C christopher.barlow@okstate.edu
BARLOW, David 910-672-1659 370 A dbarlow@uncfsu.edu
BARLOW, Justin 678-839-5000 133 F jbarlow@westga.edu
BARLOW, Marlene, T 215-968-8000 413 F barlowm@bucks.edu
BARLOW, Michael 270-706-8614 195 K mbarlow0002@kctcs.edu
BARLOW, Steve 307-855-2029 545 a sbarlow@cwc.edu
BARLOW, William 440-775-8273 388 B bill.barlow@oberlin.edu
BARLOW-KELLEY, Jill 207-801-5633 210 B jbk@coa.edu
BARLOWE, Jamie 419-530-2413 394 E jamie.barlowe@utoledo.edu
BARNABY, Mike 218-855-8039 258 C MBarnaby@clcmn.edu
BARNARD, Cheryl, A 860-231-5267 93 A cbarnard@usj.edu
BARNARD, Cindy 865-573-4517 457 H cbarnard@johnsonU.edu
BARNARD, David 318-487-7386 202 L david.barnard@lacollege.edu
BARNARD, DeeDee 828-286-3636 363 D ddbarnard@isothermal.edu
BARNARD, Kathy 509-335-3564 528 B
BARNARD, Laura 440-525-7084 385 C lbarnard@lakelandcc.edu
BARNARD, Melinda 707-664-3236 36 C melinda.barnard@sonoma.edu
BARNARD, Mimi 615-460-8397 455 D mimi.Barnard@belmont.edu
BARNARD, Monica 806-720-7232 478 A monica.barnard@lcu.edu
BARNARD, Susan 201-447-7938 300 B sbarnard@bergen.edu
BARNARD, Tom 217-351-2582 155 I tbarnard@parkland.edu
BARNDS, W. Kent 309-794-7314 139 K wkentbarnds@augustana.edu
BARNES, Amy 540-458-8920 519 A abarnes@wlu.edu
BARNES, Andre 415-239-3151 39 A abarnes@ccsf.edu
BARNES, Andrew 718-636-3570 338 E awbarnes@pratt.edu
BARNES, Bradley 205-934-4073 8 F
BARNES, Brian, M 907-474-7649 10 I bmbarnes@alaska.edu
BARNES, Candice 252-399-6393 354 I cdbarnes@barton.edu
BARNES, Cheryl 304-384-6303 532 E cbarnes@concord.edu
BARNES, David 251-981-3771 3 A david.barnes@columbiasouthern.edu
BARNES, David, M 402-449-2809 290 F gupres@graceu.edu
BARNES, Debra 816-331-5700 280 G dbarnes@pcitraining.edu
BARNES, Elizabeth, A 248-689-8282 251 I bbarnes@walshcollege.edu
BARNES, Emanuel 601-877-6385 266 C ebarnes@alcorn.edu
BARNES, Harold, B 815-224-0450 147 J harold_barnes@ivcc.edu
BARNES, III, James, H 651-638-6230 254 A j-barnes@bethel.edu

BARNES, Jeffrey 951-552-8639 30 D jbarnes@calbaptist.edu

BARNES, Jimmy 575-624-8021 311 K jimmyb@nmmi.edu

BARNES, Joanne 765-677-2090 169 C joanne.barnes@indwes.edu

BARNES, John 831-459-2973 72 E barnes@ucsc.edu

BARNES, Juiliana 619-388-2678 62 G jbarnes@sdccd.edu

BARNES, Karen 601-925-3241 268 E misscoll@bkstr.com

BARNES, Katharine, T 401-863-1914 441 A katharine_barnes@brown.edu

BARNES, Kathleen 978-232-2292 226 C kbarnes@endicott.edu

BARNES, Keith 815-825-2086 149 E keith.barnes@kishwaukeecollege.edu

BARNES, Kelly 706-295-6842 125 F kbarnes@gntc.edu

BARNES, Kenneth, J 716-851-1157 325 A barnesk@ecc.edu

BARNES, Kiki 504-816-4752 202 F kbarnes@dillard.edu

BARNES, Kimberly 989-386-6622 247 B kbarnes@midmich.edu

BARNES, M. Craig 609-497-7800 305 B president@ptsem.edu

BARNES, Marc 504-816-4359 202 F mbarnes@dillard.edu

BARNES, Mark 217-443-8871 143 F mbarnes@dacc.edu

BARNES, Melissa 360-538-4095 523 A mbarnes@ghc.edu

BARNES, Melody, C 212-998-1212 336 C melody.barnes@nyu.edu

BARNES, Nicole 281-478-3628 481 E nicole.barnes@sjcd.edu

BARNES, Nicole 724-287-8711 413 G nicole.barnes@bc3.edu

BARNES, Peter 404-727-0419 124 D peter.barnes@emory.edu

BARNES, Randy 619-388-3523 62 F rbarnes@sdccd.edu

BARNES, Rita 931-372-3797 462 A ritabarnes@tntech.edu

BARNES, Russell 713-348-4350 480 M rcb@rice.edu

BARNES, Scott 434-797-8409 515 C sbarnes@dcc.vccs.edu

BARNES, Scott 412-648-8230 437 K sbarnes@athletics.pitt.edu

BARNES, Scott, F 724-847-6787 419 B sfbarnes@geneva.edu

BARNES, Shelly 252-527-6223 363 G swbarnes16@lenoircc.edu

BARNES, Solita, K 670-284-5698 550 B

BARNES, Ted 254-295-4678 492 C tbarnes@umhb.edu

BARNES PHARR, Cindy 480-732-7093 14 K Cindy.Barnes.Pharr@cgc.edu

BARNES-RHOADES, Dianne 252-536-7239 363 B dbarnes-rhoades128@halifaxcc.edu

BARNES-TEAMER, Toya 504-816-4916 202 F tbteamer@dillard.edu

BARNES WHYTE, Susan 503-883-2517 406 I swhyte@linfield.edu

BARNET, John 914-961-8313 341 I jbarnet@svots.edu

BARNETT, Alan 660-359-3948 279 L abarnett@mail.ncmissouri.edu

BARNETT, Alan 731-286-3259 462 F barnett@dscc.edu

BARNETT, Amy 765-998-5565 173 B ambarnett@tayloru.edu

BARNETT, Beth 201-684-7529 305 F bbarnett@ramapo.edu

BARNETT, Brooke 336-278-5659 356 F bbarnett@elon.edu

BARNETT, Bryant 828-227-7303 372 C barnett@wcu.edu

BARNETT, Charles 662-246-6304 268 F cbarnett@msdelta.edu

BARNETT, Daniel 410-617-1466 216 D djbarnett@loyola.edu

BARNETT, David 606-218-5318 201 C davidbarnett00@upike.edu

BARNETT, David, L 770-531-3172 121 G dlbarnett@brenau.edu

BARNETT, Dawn 610-902-1071 414 B dawn.barnett@cabrini.edu

BARNETT, Erin 906-487-7324 242 M erin.barnett@finlandia.edu

BARNETT, Gina 415-565-4614 71 B barnettg@uchastings.edu

BARNETT, Jacqualine 717-720-4038 430 D jbarnett@passhe.edu

BARNETT, Jahnae, H 800-995-3159 286 A jahnae.barnett@williamwoods.edu

BARNETT, James, R 850-474-2005 116 E jbarnett@uwf.edu

BARNETT, Jay 606-337-1142 194 F jbarnett@ccbbc.edu

BARNETT, Jenifer 707-664-3102 36 C jenifer.barnett@sonoma.edu

BARNETT, Kimberly 719-502-2012 84 J kimberly.barnett@ppcc.edu

BARNETT, Kristi 205-387-0511 2 B kbarnett@bscc.edu

BARNETT, Larry, E 619-260-7777 74 B larryb@sandiego.edu

BARNETT, Lee 256-924-0511 5 F

BARNETT, Lenice 954-486-7728 117 M registrar@uftl.edu

BARNETT, Lisa, P 864-597-4014 451 J barnettlp@wofford.edu

BARNETT, Michael 803-754-4100 445 D

BARNETT, Mike 785-628-4251 187 A mbarnett@fhsu.edu

BARNETT, Nicole 256-551-3114 4 J nicole.barnett@drakestate.edu

BARNETT, Pamela 202-884-9202 97 A barnettp@trinitydc.edu

BARNETT, Robert 773-602-2028 142 A rbarnett7@ccc.edu

BARNETT, Robert 810-766-6878 251 E rbarnett@umflint.edu

BARNETTE, Andrew 724-925-4047 439 F barnettea@wccc.edu

BARNETTE, Jeffrey 270-686-4359 193 G jeffrey.barnette@brescia.edu

BARNETTE, Jennifer, C 334-683-2313 5 H jbarnette@marionmilitary.edu

BARNETTE, Vivian, D 336-334-7727 370 B vdbarnet@ncat.edu

BARNETTT, Karen, L 203-576-5264 91 H Karen.Barnett@stvincentscollege.edu

BARNEY, Alfred 678-891-2362 125 G alfred.barney@gpc.edu

BARNEY, Carl 800-972-5149 498 H

BARNEY, James, N 317-916-7827 169 M jbarney6@ivytech.edu

BARNEY, Matthew, S 518-255-5628 346 E barneyms@cobleskill.edu

BARNEY, Patti 954-201-7520 99 G pbarney@broward.edu

BARNEY, Rick 502-585-9911 199 E rbarney@spalding.edu

BARNEY, Tammy 504-286-5343 207 B tbarney@suno.edu

BARNHARDT, Denise 326-249-8186 362 B dsbarnh@davidsonccc.edu

BARNHARDT, Wendy 704-216-3700 365 F wendy.barnhardt@rccc.edu

BARNHART, Amy 937-775-5721 396 A amy.barnhart@wright.edu

BARNHART, Bruce 724-938-4407 430 C barnhart@calu.edu

BARNHART, Cynthia 617-253-9742 233 C

BARNHART, Jason 419-289-5480 377 A jbarnhar@ashland.edu

BARNHART, Mitch, S 859-257-8015 200 G mbarn@email.uky.edu

BARNHART, Ross 719-549-3365 85 A ross.barnhart@pueblocc.edu

BARNHART, Terry, L 671-735-5571 549 E terry.barnhart@guamcc.edu

BARNHILL, Bridgett 573-840-9646 283 D bbarnhill@trcc.edu

BARNHILL, Carol 870-972-2028 19 F cbarnhil@astate.edu

BARNHILL, John 850-644-1224 115 A jbarnhill@admin.fsu.edu

BARNHILL, Rob, M 262-243-5700 535 I rob.barnhill@cuw.edu

BARNHILL, Tapp 802-254-6370 503 H barnhilt@ccv.edu

BARNHOUSE, Richard 608-890-2076 541 E richard.barnhouse@uwc.edu

BARNICKI, Cynthia 414-277-7287 537 G Barnicki@msoe.edu

BARNUM, Chris, C 563-333-6157 182 E BarnumChristopherC@sau.edu

BARNUM, Martin 847-566-6401 162 G mbarnum@usml.edu

BARNWELL, Jon 504-214-4098 207 F jon@tulane.edu

BARNWELL, Michael 716-286-8637 336 E barnwell@niagara.edu

BARNWELL, Vollie 828-251-6700 370 E vbarnwel@unca.edu

BARON, Bruce 909-382-4091 62 A bbaron@sbccd.cc.ca.us

BARON, Joshua, D 845-575-3000 331 L josh.baron@marist.edu

BARON, Kit 626-396-2322 28 J

BARON, Melissa, M 724-946-7927 439 D baronmm@westminster.edu

BARON, Sara 757-352-4182 511 G sbaron@regent.edu

BARON, Stuart 302-622-8000 93 D sbaron@dcad.edu

BARONE, Ann, E 401-865-2105 441 F aebarone@providence.edu

BARONE, OSF, Ann Carmen 419-824-3703 385 F acarmen@lourdes.edu

BARONE, Janet 703-237-6200 510 E

BARONE, Joseph 848-445-6814 307 B jbarone@rci.rutgers.edu

BARONE, Matthew 802-251-7644 502 B mbarone@marlboro.edu

BARONE, Michael 716-673-3323 343 F michael.barone@fredonia.edu

BARONE, Ryan 970-339-6657 78 J ryan.barone@aims.edu

BARONIO, Lisa, B 319-273-2487 176 A lisa.baronio@uni.edu

BAROODY, Fadi, N 843-349-2058 444 G fadi@coastal.edu

BAROUDI, George 516-299-3790 330 F george.baroudi@liu.edu

BARQUERO, Jason 909-607-9226 39 E jason.barquero@cgu.edu

BARQUINERO, James, M 203-365-4763 91 G barquineroj@sacredheart.edu

BARR, Carol, A 413-545-6330 228 F cbarr@provost.umass.edu

BARR, Cindy 704-645-4584 355 H clbarr14@catawba.edu

BARR, Jared, M 813-988-5131 103 L barrj@floridacollege.edu

BARR, Jason 803-536-8749 448 H jbarr2@scsu.edu

BARR, K. Jill 410-455-1337 219 F jbarr@umbc.edu

BARR, Kevin 812-237-3600 167 E kevin.barr@indstate.edu

BARR, Krispin, W 336-721-2627 368 F krispin.barr@salem.edu

BARR, Peter, B 304-462-4110 532 G peter.barr@glenville.edu

BARR, Rick 903-886-5744 485 E rick.barr@tamuc.edu

BARR, Robin 386-506-4473 101 I barrr@DaytonaState.edu

BARR, Sarah 402-465-2193 292 E sbarr@nebrwesleyan.edu

BARR, Susan 631-656-2129 326 B susan.barr@ftc.edu

BARR, Victor 865-974-2196 465 D vbarr@utk.edu

BARR-GILLESPIE, Ann 503-352-7200 408 I barr-gillespie@pacificu.edu

BARRACK, Keith 973-655-4213 304 A barrackk@mail.montclair.edu

BARRACKS, Jana, T 641-422-4269 181 E barrajan@niacc.edu

BARRACLOUGH, Diana 610-499-4153 439 G dbarraclough@widener.edu

BARRACLOUGH, Dominic 608-342-1262 540 D barracld@uwplatt.edu

BARRACLOUGH, Jessica 785-670-1723 192 B jessica.barraclough@washburn.edu

BARRAL, Jose, M 409-747-2180 495 E jmbarral@utmb.edu

BARRALE, Ralph 636-227-2100 277 A ralph.barrale@logan.edu

BARRANTES, Jane 408-554-5416 65 A jbarrantes@scu.edu

BARRAR, Elena 610-558-5516 427 D barrare@neumann.edu

BARRAS, Janet 678-359-5022 126 E janetb@gordonstate.edu

BARRAZA, Ana Lilia 562-907-4912 77 E abarraza@whittier.edu

BARREE, Zita, M 434-223-6265 508 B zbarree@hsc.edu

BARREIRO, Antonio 510-981-2881 58 J abarreiro@peralta.edu

BARREN, Tanisha 972-265-5744 491 B tbarren@udallas.edu

BARRENTINE, Debra, A 256-228-6001 6 A barrentined@nacc.edu

BARRENTINE, Jim 719-502-2148 84 J jim.barrentine@ppcc.edu

BARRENTINE, Lee 251-809-1526 5 B lee.barrentine@jdcc.edu

BARRENTINE, Roger, A 636-481-3106 276 E rbarrent@jeffco.edu

BARRERA, Adriana, D 213-891-2081 51 C barrerad@email.laccd.edu

BARRERA, Amanda 361-592-1615 470 K amanda@coastalbend.edu

BARRERA, Rosa, M 316-284-5241 185 B rbarrera@bethelks.edu

BARRERA, Steve, V 210-458-4249 494 D steve.barrera@utsa.edu

BARRESI, Lisa 859-572-5100 199 A barresi@nku.edu

BARRETO, Wanda 787-758-2480 558 C wanda.barreto@upr.edu

BARRETT, Adam 212-431-2888 335 G Adam.Barrett@nyls.edu

BARRETT, Audra 972-860-8261 472 D AudraBarrett@dcccd.edu

BARRETT, Brian, D 817-515-6960 484 B brian.barrett@tccd.edu

BARRETT, Carolyn 904-256-7090 106 Q cbarret@ju.edu

BARRETT, Christina 413-236-2112 231 A cbarrett@berkshirecc.edu

BARRETT, David 714-816-0366 70 D david.barrett@trident.edu

BARRETT, Dustin 912-650-6250 131 F dbarrett@southuniversity.edu

BARRETT, Gail 860-343-5897 89 E gbarrett@mxcc.edu

BARRETT, Ian 409-772-8692 495 E icbarret@utmb.edu

BARRETT, Jacqueline 843-349-5212 446 I jacqueline.barrett@hgtc.edu

BARRETT, Jeannie 706-754-7704 129 B jbarrett@northgatech.edu

BARRETT, Jennifer 785-827-5541 189 A jennifer.barrett@kwu.edu

BARRETT, Jim 715-346-2727 541 A jimbarrett@uwsp.edu

BARRETT, Jim 715-346-4093 541 A jbarrett@uwsp.edu

BARRETT, Joan 417-447-6914 280 C barrettj@otc.edu

BARRETT, JR., John, A 419-530-2739 394 E john.barrett@utoledo.edu

BARRETT, Karinda 850-201-6209 117 B barrettk@tcc.fl.edu

BARRETT, Kim, E 858-534-6655 72 B graduatedean@ucsd.edu

BARRETT, Kimberly 937-775-5240 396 A kimberly.barrett@wright.edu

BARRETT, Laura 845-257-3520 344 A barrettl@newpaltz.edu

BARRETT, Lawrence 386-752-1822 103 Q lawrence.barrett@fgc.edu

BARRETT, Lawrence, M 207-974-4691 211 A lbarrett@emcc.edu

BARRETT, Leah, A 585-395-2772 345 A lbarrett@brockport.edu

BARRETT, Linda 401-874-2509 442 E lindab@uri.edu

BARRETT, Liz 973-278-5400 300 C lzn@berkeleycollege.edu

BARRETT, Liz 973-278-5400 316 D lzn@berkeleycollege.edu

BARRETT, Mary, C 607-735-1790 324 J mbarrett@elmira.edu

BARRETT, Michael 616-977-0599 249 B michael.barrett@prts.edu

BARRETT, Michael 850-644-1768 115 A mgbarrett@admin.fsu.edu

BARRETT, Micheal 845-938-4041 549 A 8SJA@usma.edu

BARRETT, Monica, C 848-932-7813 306 F barrett@oldqueens.rutgers.edu

BARRETT, Pam, J 770-534-6176 121 G pbarrett@brenau.edu

BARRETT, Patrick 202-885-8600 97 E

BARRETT, Rosemary 845-341-4200 337 G rosemary.barrett@sunyorange.edu

BARRETT, Scott 765-998-4917 173 B scott_barrett@taylor.edu

BARRETT, Stephen 817-735-2261 493 B Stephen.Barrett@unthsc.edu

BARRETT, Susan 610-526-6005 420 C sbarrett@harcum.edu

BARRETT, Tim 315-445-4155 330 B barrettm@lemoyne.edu

BARRETT, William 570-740-0305 425 A wbarrett@luzerne.edu

BARRETT, Zunilka 617-287-7005 228 E zbarrett@umassp.edu

BARRETTE, Catherine 313-577-1615 252 G c.barrette@wayne.edu

BARRIENTOS, Joe 206-934-6749 526 B joe.barrientos@seattlecolleges.edu

BARRIER, Jeremy 256-766-6610 4 C jbarrier@hcu.edu

BARRIERA, Heriberto 787-279-1912 553 H hbarriera@bayamon.inter.edu

BARRINGER, Judy 212-659-7215 330 A jbarringer@tkc.edu

BARRINGER, Susan, J 336-217-7221 357 B susan.barringer@greensboro.edu

BARRINGTON, Ruth, A 401-825-2184 441 C rbarrington@ccri.edu

BARRIOS, Eric 787-766-1717 556 A ca_ebarrios@suagm.edu

BARRIOS, Eugenio .... 212-220-1266 318 D
ebarrios@bmcc.cuny.edu
BARRIOS, Francisco ..... 573-651-2154 282 C
fbarrios@semo.edu
BARRIS, Brad .... 706-236-2272 121 E
bbarris@berry.edu
BARRIS, Julie .... 814-472-3012 434 F
jbarris@francis.edu
BARRISH, David, J .... 804-523-5934 515 F
dbarrish@reynolds.edu
BARRON, Alexandra, L . 512-464-8878 481 B
alexb@stedwards.edu
BARRON, Brad, E .... 864-294-2033 446 F
brad.barron@furman.edu
BARRON, Caulyne .... 602-648-5750.. 13 K
cbarron@dunlap-stone.edu
BARRON, Dianne .... 334-670-3189.... 8 A
dlbarron@troy.edu
BARRON, Dori .... 828-448-3170 367 B
dbarron@wpcc.edu
BARRON, Eric, J .... 814-865-7611 428 C
president@psu.edu
BARRON, Glenda, O ..... 254-298-8600 484 C
glenda.barron@templejc.edu
BARRON, Jose .... 575-624-8263 311 K
Barron@nmmi.edu
BARRON, Katie .... 970-542-3108.. 84 A
katie.barron@morgancc.edu
BARRON, Kelly .... 530-895-4047.. 30 B
barronke@butte.edu
BARRON, Maria, V .... 954-308-2180.. 98 I
mbarron@aii.edu
BARRON, Matthew .... 906-786-5802 240 K
barronm@baycollege.edu
BARRON, Nicole .... 312-915-8903 151 E
nbarron@luc.edu
BARRON, Robert .... 847-970-4800 162 G
rector@usml.edu
BARRON CHUNG, Amy 415-442-6622.. 46 A
slind@ggu.edu
BARROS, Ligia .... 305-629-2929 112 D
lbarros@sanignaciocollege.edu
BARROSO, Richard .... 713-920-1120 127 E
rbarroso@ict.edu
BARROSS, Ben .... 419-530-7877 394 E
ben.barros@utoledo.edu
BARROTT, James .... 423-697-3211 462 C
jim.barrott@chattanoogastate.edu
BARROW, Carla .... 229-225-5077 132 C
cbarrow@southernregional.edu
BARROW, Christine, E . 301-322-0419 217 G
barowce@pgcc.edu
BARROW, Deborah, L .. 940-397-4212 478 G
debbie.barrow@mwsu.edu
BARROW, Linda, M ...... 770-531-6319 128 A
lbarro@laniertech.edu
BARROW, Ramona .... 270-706-8486 195 K
rbarrows0001@kctcs.edu
BARROWS, David .... 217-206-6730 161 G
barrows.david@uis.edu
BARROWS, Karen, A ..... 585-475-2396 339 G
karen.barrows@rit.edu
BARROWS, Karen, A ..... 585-475-2396 339 G
kab7050@rit.edu
BARROWS, Nancy .... 503-821-8910 408 H
nbarrows@pnca.edu
BARROWS, Robert .... 617-228-2241 231 C
rbarrows@bhcc.mass.edu
BARRY, Ann Marie .... 847-635-1699 155 E
annmarie@oakton.edu
BARRY, Barney .... 913-253-5060 190 K
bernard.barry@spst.edu
BARRY, Catherine .... 603-882-6923 297 B
cbarry@ccsnh.edu
BARRY, Donna, M .... 973-655-4361 304 A
barryd@mail.montclair.edu
BARRY, Elizabeth .... 858-566-1200.. 43 A
lbarry@disd.edu
BARRY, Ernie .... 214-768-2004 482 J
ebarry@smu.edu
BARRY, James, T .... 607-735-1770 324 J
tbarry@elmira.edu
BARRY, Jeannette .... 402-375-7466 292 D
jebarry1@wsc.edu
BARRY, Jessica .... 937-294-0592 391 B
jessica@saa.edu
BARRY, Joanne .... 607-753-2302 345 C
joanne.barry@cortland.edu
BARRY, John .... 254-710-1412 469 D
john_barry@baylor.edu
BARRY, Kevin, G .... 302-295-1170.. 94 G
kevin.g.barry@wilmu.edu
BARRY, Richard .... 610-526-6532 413 D
rbarry@brynmawr.edu
BARRY, Terry .... 570-422-3377 430 F
BARRY, Theresa .... 262-524-7334 535 D
tbarry@carrollu.edu
BARRY, Thomas, E .... 214-768-4320 482 J
tbarry@smu.edu
BARRY-ARQUIT,
Rachel, E .... 503-943-8000 410 H
BARSOM, Michelle .... 229-243-6970 121 D
michelle.barsom@bainbridge.edu
BARTA, Barbara .... 614-234-1788 386 N
bbarta@mccn.edu
BARTA, Carol .... 612-436-7576 257 K
cbarta@msbcollege.edu
BARTA, Gary .... 319-335-9435 175 H
gary-barta@uiowa.edu
BARTA, James, J .... 478-301-5397 128 G
barta_jj@mercer.edu
BARTA, Lou .... 217-641-4215 148 J
lbarta@jwcc.edu
BARTA, Sharon .... 510-485-7813.. 58 G
sbarta@patten.edu
BARTANEN, Kristine, M 253-879-3205 527 F
acadvp@pugetsound.edu
BARTEE, Robert .... 402-559-4203 293 I
bbartee@unmc.edu
BARTEL, Alexa .... 843-383-8126 445 A
abartel@coker.edu
BARTEL, Brad, N .... 615-898-2953 461 E
brad.bartel@mtsu.edu
BARTEL, Kyle, J .... 580-774-3705 402 G
kyle.bartel@swosu.edu
BARTEL, Steven, J .... 605-256-5146 453 H
steve.bartel@dsu.edu
BARTEL, Tonia .... 660-831-4105 279 D
bartelt@moval.edu
BARTELL, Sharon .... 718-270-6136 320 C
sharonb@mec.cuny.edu
BARTELL, William .... 605-331-6703 454 E
bill.bartell@usiouxfalls.edu
BARTELMAY, Ryan .... 312-752-2454 149 D
ryan.bartelmay@kendall.edu
BARTELS, Dennis .... 614-416-6200 378 B
dbartels@bradfordschoolcolumbus.edu
BARTELS, Jean .... 912-478-5258 126 B
jbartels@georgiasouthern.edu
BARTELS, Marilyn .... 800-955-2527 187 E
mbartels@grantham.edu
BARTELS, Paige .... 802-440-4336 501 D
pbartels@bennington.edu
BARTELS, Roy .... 325-574-7629 497 E
rbartels@wtc.edu
BARTELS, Suzanne, M .. 336-316-2046 357 C
bartelssm@guilford.edu
BARTELSON,
Gretchen, G .... 712-324-5061 182 A
gbartelson@nwicc.edu
BARTELT, Jason .... 920-923-8090 537 A
jbartelt@marianuniversity.edu
BARTER, John .... 251-380-4000.... 7 F
jbarter@shc.edu
BARTFIELD, Joel .... 518-262-7302 314 I
bartfi@mail.amc.edu
BARTGES, Ellyn .... 320-308-0125 261 E
elbartges@stcloudstate.edu
BARTH, Christopher ...... 845-938-3833 549 A
Christopher.Barth@usma.edu
BARTH, Cynthia .... 410-225-4223 216 F
cbarth@mica.edu
BARTH, Doug .... 785-594-4526 184 F
doug.barth@bakeru.edu
BARTH, Michael .... 406-496-4233 288 C
mbarth@mtech.edu
BARTH, Richard, P .... 410-706-7794 219 E
rbarth@ssw.umaryland.edu
BARTH, Rick .... 205-665-6239.... 9 C
rbarth@montevallo.edu
BARTHA, Jaimee .... 847-628-2514 149 A
jbartha@judsonu.edu
BARTHELL, John .... 405-974-3371 403 G
jbarthell@uco.edu
BARTHELMAS,
Frederick .... 518-587-2100 348 A
rick.barthlemas@esc.edu
BARTHOLOMEW, Craig . 480-990-3773.. 14 I
BARTHOLOMEW, Diane 660-831-4622 279 D
bartholomewd@moval.edu
BARTHOLOMEW, Lynda 256-726-7543.... 6 C
lbartholomew@oakwood.edu
BARTHOLOMEW,
Nanette .... 757-826-1883 505 C
studentaffairs@bcva.edu
BARTHOLOMEW-FEIS,
Dixee .... 712-749-2131 176 D
bartholomew@bvu.edu
BARTINE, Hunt .... 201-200-2016 304 C
hbartine@njcu.edu
BARTINI, Michael, D .... 207-725-3146 209 H
mbartini@bowdoin.edu
BARTKOWSKI, Debra .... 954-308-2434.. 98 I
dbartkowski@aii.edu
BARTL, Noelle .... 575-562-2412 310 I
noelle.bartl@enmu.edu
BARTLE, Gamin .... 973-408-3106 301 J
gbartle@drew.edu
BARTLE, John, R .... 402-554-3989 294 A
jbartle@unomaha.edu
BARTLEBAUGH,
Brenda, P .... 318-797-5009 205 F
brenda.bartlebaugh@lsus.edu
BARTLETT, Anne .... 979-230-3202 469 G
anne.bartlett@brazosport.edu
BARTLETT, Annemarie ... 610-409-3359 438 H
abartlett@ursinus.edu
BARTLETT, David, C ..... 937-766-7810 378 K
bartletd@cedarville.edu
BARTLETT, Jon .... 817-531-4870 490 C
jdbartlett@txwes.edu
BARTLETT, Julia .... 913-234-0758 185 N
julia.bartlett@cleveland.edu
BARTLETT, Noah .... 415-703-9560.. 30 G
nbartlett@cca.edu
BARTLETT, Raymond ..... 713-743-5544 491 C
rbartlett@uh.edu
BARTLETT, Raymond ..... 832-842-5544 491 D
rbartlett@uh.edu
BARTLETT, Rebecca ...... 802-258-9226 502 B
rbartlet@marlboro.edu
BARTLETT, Stacy .... 706-385-1100 130 C
stacy.bartlett@point.edu
BARTLETT, Walter, C .... 336-322-2100 364 G
Walter.Bartlett@piedmontcc.edu
BARTLEY, Jacqueline .... 973-748-9000 300 E
jackie_bartley@bloomfield.edu
BARTLEY, Kurt .... 303-964-5152.. 85 G
kbartley@regis.edu
BARTLEY, Mary, E .... 515-961-1511 182 I
mimi.bartley@simpson.edu
BARTLEY, Patricia, A .... 773-256-0717 151 H
pbartley@lstc.edu
BARTLEY, Ron .... 843-921-6901 448 B
rbartley@netc.edu
BARTLING, Jonathan .... 815-928-5405 155 G
jbartlin@olivet.edu
BARTLING, Kaitlyn .... 641-648-4611 179 K
kaitlyn.bartling@iavalley.edu
BARTLING, Kelly, H ...... 308-865-8455 293 G
bartlingkh@unk.edu
BARTLOW, Jon, A .... 620-235-4761 190 G
jbartlow@pittstate.edu
BARTO, Christopher, E . 212-752-1530 330 C
christopher.barto@limcollege.edu
BARTO, Daniel .... 727-341-3051 112 A
barto.daniel@spcollege.edu
BARTOL, Michelle, M ... 814-641-3432 421 L
bartolm@juniata.edu
BARTOLD, Melissa .... 312-225-1700 146 E
mbartold@ico.edu
BARTOLI, Andrea .... 973-313-6174 308 C
andrea.bartoli@shu.edu
BARTOLINI, Brian, J ..... 401-865-1554 441 F
bbartoli@providence.edu
BARTOLO, Tony .... 423-478-6208 462 D
tbartolo@clevelandstatecc.edu
BARTOLOTTA, Charles .. 631-451-4790 348 F
bartolc@sunysuffolk.edu
BARTOLOTTA, Charles .. 631-451-4790 348 E
bartolc@sunysuffolk.edu
BARTOLOTTA, Theresa .. 609-652-4501 308 E
theresa.bartolotta@stockton.edu
BARTON, Carolina .... 949-214-3093.. 42 B
carolina.barton@cui.edu
BARTON,
Charles (Lennie) .... 919-760-8375 359 B
bartonl@meredith.edu
BARTON, David .... 660-284-4800 275 H
BARTON, Delores .... 404-270-5376 132 D
dbarton@spelman.edu
BARTON, George, W ..... 915-747-5640 494 B
gwbarton@utep.edu
BARTON, J. Mark .... 479-394-7622.. 22 H
mbarton@rmcc.edu
BARTON, Jacqueline, K 626-395-3646.. 31 D
jkbarton@caltech.edu
BARTON, James, E .... 434-223-6148 508 B
jbarton@hsc.edu
BARTON, Jennifer, K .... 520-621-3512.. 18 E
barton@email.arizona.edu
BARTON, Judi .... 660-284-4800 275 H
registrar@heartlandcollege.org
BARTON, Kathleen .... 845-569-3355 333 I
kathleen.barton@msmc.edu
BARTON, Mary .... 940-565-2085 492 D
mary.barton@unt.edu
BARTON, Michelle .... 760-744-1150.. 58 D
mbarton@palomar.edu
BARTON, Pat .... 678-466-4185 122 J
patbarton@clayton.edu
BARTON, Patricia .... 510-136-1220.. 47 C
barton@hnu.edu
BARTON, Sara .... 310-506-4275.. 58 H
sara.barton@pepperdine.edu
BARTOW, Patricia .... 619-216-6694.. 68 D
pbartow@swccd.edu
BARTRUG, Reba .... 740-374-8716 395 D
rbartrug@wscc.edu
BARTS, Bryan .... 715-232-1469 541 B
bartsb@uwstout.edu
BARTSCH, Jonathan ...... 617-236-8800 226 F
jbartsch@fisher.edu
BARTSCHER, Patricia, B 415-338-2998.. 36 A
pattyb@sfsu.edu
BARTUNEK, Tami, A ..... 913-288-7201 188 G
tbartunek@kckcc.edu
BARTUS, Thomas, J ..... 609-258-7720 305 C
tbartus@princeton.edu
BARTUSIK, Lisa Marie .. 850-484-2014 110 D
lbartusik@pensacolastate.edu
BARWICK, Daniel, W .... 620-331-4100 188 B
dbarwick@indycc.edu
BARZACCHINI, Mike ..... 847-925-6510 145 F
mbarzacc@harpercollege.edu
BASALA, Nissim .... 732-370-1560 300 A
BASCH, Hersch .... 718-438-1002 332 F
BASCO, Chris .... 405-224-3140 403 L
cbasco@usao.edu
BASEL, Barbara .... 605-773-3455 453 E
barbara.basel@sdbor.edu
BASER, Ric .... 210-486-4908 466 J
rbaser@alamo.edu
BASER, Ric, N .... 210-486-4900 466 K
rbaser@alamo.edu
BASFORD, Jerry, L .... 801-581-7793 499 K
jbasford@sa.utah.edu
BASGEN, Brian .... 413-565-1000 222 G
bbasgen@baypath.edu
BASH, Cassaundra .... 574-936-8898 164 A
cassaundra.bash@ancilla.edu
BASHARA, Teri .... 318-678-6000 203 A
tbashara@bpcc.edu
BASHAW, Edward .... 479-968-0490.. 20 C
ebashaw@atu.edu
BASHFORD, Joanne ...... 305-237-6034 108 L
jbashfor@mdc.edu
BASHISTA, Brian .... 703-284-1607 510 B
brian.bashista@marymount.edu
BASHWINER, Bruce .... 585-273-5798 351 D
bruce.bashwiner@rochester.edu
BASIL, Meredith .... 657-278-3057.. 33 E
mbasil@fullerton.edu
BASILE, Carole, G .... 314-516-5109 284 B
basilec@umsl.edu
BASILE, Elizabeth .... 718-368-4539 320 A
ebasile@kbcc.cuny.edu
BASILEO, Paul .... 631-451-4854 348 F
basilep@sunysuffolk.edu
BASINGER, David .... 585-594-6550 339 F
basingerd@roberts.edu
BASINGER, Randall, G . 717-796-5375 426 B
rbasinge@messiah.edu
BASINSKI, Judith, B ..... 716-878-4611 345 B
basinsjb@buffalostate.edu
BASIRATMAND,
Mehran .... 561-297-0230 114 E
mehran@fau.edu
BASKER, Judith .... 541-956-7291 409 F
jbasker@roguecc.edu
BASKETTE, Shawna .... 562-860-2451.. 37 L
sbaskette@cerritos.edu
BASKIN, Richard .... 678-359-5018 126 E
rbaskin@gordonstate.edu
BASKO, Aaron, M .... 410-543-6161 220 E
ambasko@salisbury.edu
BASLER, Julie .... 303-369-5151.. 84 N
julie.basler@plattcolorado.edu
BASLER, Sandra, K .... 636-481-3298 276 E
sbasler@jeffco.edu
BASMADJIAN, Kevin ..... 203-582-3497.. 91 E
kevin.basmadjian@quinnipiac.edu
BASOA-MCMILLAN,
Ana .... 931-540-2889 462 E
abasoamcmillan@columbiastate.edu
BASOM, Richard .... 717-361-4762 418 B
basomr@etown.edu
BASRI, Gibor .... 510-642-7294.. 70 K
vcei@berkeley.edu
BASS, Adrienne .... 414-229-6410 540 A
bassa@uwm.edu
BASS, Brenda .... 319-273-2221 176 A
brenda.bass@uni.edu
BASS, Brittany .... 618-395-7777 147 A
bassb@iecc.edu
BASS, Charles .... 619-260-4819.. 74 B
charlesb@sandiego.edu
BASS, Chris .... 909-607-6999.. 39 E
chris.bass@cuc.edu
BASS, Donna .... 334-222-6591.... 5 G
dbass@lbwcc.edu
BASS, Gordon .... 904-357-8891 105 A
gbass@fscj.edu
BASS, Harry .... 252-335-3291 369 F
hsbass@ecsu.edu
BASS, Harry .... 252-335-3187 369 F
hsbass@ecsu.edu
BASS, Inga .... 601-484-8823 268 B
ibass@meridiancc.edu
BASS, Jimmy .... 910-962-4292 372 A
bassj@uncw.edu

BAUMGARDNER, Marian 918-495-7442 401 B mbaumgardner@oru.edu
BAUMGARDNER, Michael 518-244-2207 340 A baumgm@sage.edu
BAUMGARDNER, Waylon 951-343-4876 30 D wbaumgardner@calbaptist.edu
BAUMGART, Reilly 618-262-8641 147 B baumgartr@iecc.edu
BAUMGARTEN, Bobbie 214-637-3530 496 J bbaumgarten@wadecollege.edu
BAUMGARTEN, Whitney 414-256-1272 538 A MMC-Bookstore@mtmary.edu
BAUMGARTNER, Annmarie 419-772-2729 388 I a-baumgartner@onu.edu
BAUMGARTNER, Bruce 814-732-2776 430 G bbaumgartner@edinboro.edu
BAUMGARTNER, David, A 319-335-1023 175 H david-baumgartner@uiowa.edu
BAUMGARTNER, Eric, T 419-772-2372 388 I e-baumgartner@onu.edu
BAUMGARTNER, Holly, L 419-824-3756 385 F hbaumgartner@lourdes.edu
BAUMGARTNER, Renee 408-554-5344 65 A rbaumgartner@scu.edu
BAUMLER, Angela 410-532-3150 217 F abaumler@ndm.edu
BAUMLER, Kim, M 563-556-5110 181 F baumlerk@nicc.edu
BAUN, Dan 507-537-6978 262 B Dan.Baun@smsu.edu
BAUN, Jeffrey, S 610-359-5315 416 G jbaun@dccc.edu
BAUR, John 309-438-2583 147 I jebaur@ilstu.edu
BAUS, Amy 563-589-3132 183 E abaus@dbq.edu
BAUSHKE, Ken 270-745-3056 201 D ken.baushke@wku.edu
BAUSINGER, Patricia, E 570-321-4049 425 B baus@lycoming.edu
BAUSLER, Katie 907-796-6530 11 A katie.bausler@uas.alaska.edu
BAUSMAN, Marvin 319-398-5516 180 J marvin.bausman@kirkwood.edu
BAUSMITH, Shirley 843-661-1487 446 E sbausmith@fmarion.edu
BAUSS, Celia, N 864-592-4754 449 C baussc@sccsc.edu
BAUSTISTA PERTUZ, Sofia 718-817-0664 326 C spertuz@fordham.edu
BAUTISTA MOLLER, Lydia, B 954-607-4344 117 L
BAVER, Chad 406-683-7382 287 E chad.baver@umwestern.edu
BAVIER, Anne 817-272-2776 493 L bavier@uta.edu
BAVISI, Sanjay 505-922-2886 310 K
BAWA, Navraj 888-775-1514 70 H
BAWA, Opinder 415-422-2787 74 C osbawa@usfca.edu
BAWCOM, Amy 254-526-1472 470 E amy.bawcom@ctcd.edu
BAWCOM, Jerry, G 254-295-4500 492 C jbawcom@umhb.edu
BAWOROWSKY, John 801-484-7651 501 C jbaworowsky@westminstercollege.edu
BAXTER, Agnes 919-546-8212 368 G abaxter@shawu.edu
BAXTER, Aimee, F 318-257-2641 208 A abaxter@latech.edu
BAXTER, Charlene 706-880-8311 127 N cbaxter@lagrange.edu
BAXTER, Ginny 562-938-4634 51 A gbaxter@lbcc.edu
BAXTER, Jan 541-888-7259 410 A jan.baxter@socc.edu
BAXTER, Keith 580-745-2250 402 D kbaxter@se.edu
BAXTER, Pat 212-229-8947 334 C baxterp@newschool.edu
BAXTER, Randy, A 662-720-7576 269 D rabaxter@nemcc.edu
BAXTER, Steven 360-417-6300 525 A sbaxter@pencol.edu
BAYARD, Patrick 217-443-8776 143 F pbayard@dacc.edu
BAYARDELLE, Eddy 718-289-5185 318 E eddy.bayardelle@bcc.cuny.edu
BAYER, Deborah, A 248-232-4311 248 E dabayer@oaklandcc.edu
BAYER, Deborah, A 248-232-4211 248 E dabayer@oaklandcc.edu
BAYER, Richard, L 865-974-2105 465 D rbayer@utk.edu
BAYERL, Randy 763-657-2520 258 G randy.bayerl@hennepintech.edu
BAYERL, Sue 320-308-2111 261 E sjbayerl@stcloudstate.edu
BAYIHA, Eugene 715-634-4790 536 P ebayiha@lco.edu
BAYLES, Kenneth 402-559-4945 293 I kbayles@unmc.edu
BAYLESS, Debi 573-518-1330 278 F dbayless@mineralarea.edu
BAYLESS, Laura 608-342-1854 540 D baylessl@uwplatt.edu
BAYLESS, Robert 816-802-3399 276 F rbayless@kcai.edu
BAYLIS, Gordon 270-745-6733 201 D gordon.baylis@wku.edu
BAYLOR, Bridget 540-453-2358 514 H baylorb@brcc.edu
BAYLOR, Chiquita 401-341-2225 442 D chiquita.baylor@salve.edu
BAYLOR, Gail 828-298-3325 373 A gbaylor@warren-wilson.edu
BAYLOR, Jim 206-592-3443 523 D jbaylor@highline.edu
BAYLOR, Kara 262-551-5812 535 E kbaylor@carthage.edu
BAYLOR, Martin 956-665-2121 494 C baylormv@utpa.edu
BAYLOR, Monique, Y 717-736-4121 420 D mybaylor@hacc.edu
BAYNARD, Donald 617-287-7799 228 G donald.baynard@umb.edu
BAYNE, Deann 308-635-6018 292 B dbayne@csc.edu
BAYNE, Doug 509-527-4253 527 H doug.bayne@wwcc.edu
BAYNE, Sheila 617-627-2000 237 C sheila.bayne@tufts.edu
BAYNE, Suzanne 423-472-7141 462 D sbayne@clevelandstatecc.edu
BAYNES, Leonard, M 713-743-2478 491 D lbaynes@central.uh.edu
BAYOUMI, Magdy, A 337-482-6147 208 F mab@louisiana.edu
BAYS, Steven 509-533-3570 521 F steve.bays@sfcc.spokane.edu
BAYSAL, Oktay 757-683-3787 510 I obaysal@odu.edu
BAYTO, Tammy 478-274-7852 129 D tbayto@oftc.edu
BAZAN, Teresita 512-223-7950 468 H tbazan@austincc.edu
BAZAN, Yamilet 951-785-2100 49 I ybazan@lasierra.edu
BAZANT, Robert, S 724-222-5330 428 B rbazant@penncommercial.edu
BAZAR, Leon 361-593-2258 486 A kulgb000@tamuk.edu
BAZARNIC, Steve 301-784-5000 213 C sbazarnic@allegany.edu
BAZEMORE, Dennis 910-893-1540 355 C bazemored@campbell.edu
BAZEMORE, Haywood, M 803-705-4321 443 F bazemoreh@benedict.edu
BAZIJIAN, Rosann, V 336-334-3418 371 C rvbazirj@uncg.edu
BAZIL, Ted 914-961-8313 341 I ted@svots.edu
BAZILE, Samantha 845-398-4102 341 H sbazile@stac.edu
BAZLUKE, Francine, T 802-656-8585 503 C francine.bazluke@uvm.edu
BAZZELL, Darrell 608-263-2467 539 D dbazzell@vc.wisc.edu
BEA, David 520-206-4519 17 A dbea@pima.edu
BEACH, Bradley 330-244-4732 395 C bbeach@walsh.edu
BEACH, Cora 541-962-3368 405 G cbeach@eou.edu
BEACH, Gary 541-737-2815 408 F gary.beach@oregonstate.edu
BEACH, Nancy, S 540-365-4529 507 H nbeach@ferrum.edu
BEACH, Natalie 503-399-5105 404 L natalie.beach@chemeketa.edu
BEACH, Rebecca 540-362-6414 508 D rbeach@hollins.edu
BEACH, Vincent 860-628-4751 91 A vbeach@lincolncollegene.edu
BEACHAM, David, M 864-597-4206 451 J beachamdm@wofford.edu
BEACHNAU, Andrew, J 616-331-2120 243 E beachnaa@gvsu.edu
BEACHY, Benjamin, S 540-432-4478 507 A ben.beachy@emu.edu
BEACHY, Roger 530-752-7172 71 A rbeachy@ucdavis.edu
BEACON, John 812-237-3560 167 E john.beacon@indstate.edu
BEADENKOPF, Scott 610-361-5327 427 D beadenks@neumann.edu
BEADLE, Paul 724-832-1050 437 E pbeadle@triangle-tech.edu
BEAGHAN, John, W 248-370-2445 248 K beaghan@oakland.edu
BEAGLE, Donald 704-461-6740 354 J donaldbeagle@bac.edu
BEAGLE, Mike 541-552-6127 409 G beaglem@sou.edu
BEAHON, Mary Ann 573-592-1127 286 A maryann.beahon@williamwoods.edu
BEAIL, Linda 619-849-2408 59 K lindabeail@pointloma.edu
BEAL, Alvin (Chip) 715-394-8297 541 C abeal@uwsuper.edu
BEAL, Billy 601-484-8765 268 B bbeal@meridiancc.edu
BEAL, Jason 801-957-4205 500 E jason.beal@slcc.edu
BEAL, Judy 617-521-2139 236 F judy.beal@simmons.edu
BEAL, Kenton 903-813-2468 468 G bookstore@austincollege.edu
BEAL, Kevin 802-258-3158 502 I kevin.beal@worldlearning.org
BEAL, Lee 828-835-4233 366 F lbeal@tricountycc.edu
BEAL, Stephen 510-594-3630 30 G sbeal@cca.edu
BEALE, Charles, L 302-831-8107 94 D cbeale@udel.edu
BEALE, Connie, L 973-761-9401 308 C concetta.beale@shu.edu
BEALE, Leslie 210-297-7638 468 K ldbeale@baptisthealthsystem.com
BEALE, Marjorie, A 626-395-6369 31 D mbeale@caltech.edu
BEALER, Mitchell 435-586-7723 499 L bealer@suu.edu
BEALES, Sharon 610-861-5451 427 F sbeales@northampton.edu
BEALL, Brenda 818-785-2726 37 I brenda.beall@casalomacollege.edu
BEALL, David 773-508-2391 151 E dbeall@luc.edu
BEALS, Linda, M 937-327-6374 395 I lbeals@wittenberg.edu
BEALS, Michael, J 714-556-3610 75 A officeofthepresident@vanguard.edu
BEAM, Brian 309-438-8404 147 I babeam@ilstu.edu
BEAM, Carla 907-786-7711 10 G cjbeam@alaska.edu
BEAM, Gina 716-614-6220 336 D gbeam@niagaracc.suny.edu
BEAM, Jay 704-971-8500 355 J jbeam@charlottelaw.edu
BEAM, John 510-464-3474 59 B jbeam@peralta.edu
BEAM, Julie 574-807-7020 164 F julie.beam@bethelcollege.edu
BEAM, Linda 310-660-3401 43 G lbeam@elcamino.edu
BEAM, Marc 209-575-6556 78 A beamm@yosemite.edu
BEAM, Ruthanne 865-573-4517 457 H rubeam@johnsonU.edu
BEAM, Tony 864-977-2008 448 A tony.beam@ngu.edu
BEAMAN, Cynthia, A 812-888-5004 174 F cbeaman@vinu.edu
BEAMAN, Patricia, L 716-839-8538 323 F pbeaman@daemen.edu
BEAMAN, Riley 910-576-6222 364 D beamanr@montgomery.edu
BEAMAN, Warren, J 503-517-1050 411 A wbeaman@warnerpacific.edu
BEAMER, Janet 704-499-9200 96 H
BEAMER, Randy 503-222-3225 405 H randy.beamer@zenith.org
BEAMON, Stanley 312-850-7038 142 E sbeamon3@ccc.edu
BEAN, Al 207-780-5588 213 A albean@usm.maine.edu
BEAN, Alden 888-980-9151 513 G
BEAN, Athena 325-649-8810 475 F abean@hputx.edu
BEAN, Carlena 207-941-7064 210 C beanc@husson.edu
BEAN, Caronda 225-771-2191 207 A caronda_bean@subr.edu
BEAN, Christopher, A 540-665-4553 512 E cbean@su.edu
BEAN, Ethelle, S 605-256-5205 453 H ethelle.bean@dsu.edu
BEAN, James, C 617-373-2170 235 D
BEAN, Joanne 207-893-7895 211 H jbean@sjcme.edu
BEAN, Michael 603-668-6660 298 A
BEAN, Miho 603-206-8101 297 A msbean@ccsnh.edu
BEAN, Nancy 731-352-4000 455 E beann@bethelu.edu
BEAN, Paul 785-242-5200 190 D paul.bean@ottawa.edu
BEAN, Shirley 206-878-3710 523 D sbean@highline.edu
BEAN, Stacey 937-778-7844 381 K sbean@edisonohio.edu
BEAN, Steve 218-322-2351 259 B steve.bean@itascacc.edu
BEANS, Jessica 937-298-3399 385 A jessica.beans@kc.edu
BEAR, Catherine 314-529-9466 277 B cbear@maryville.edu
BEAR, Marca 813-257-3280 118 H mbear@ut.edu
BEAR, William 763-433-1132 258 A william.bear@anokaramsey.edu
BEARBOWER, Sarah 608-796-3000 542 H
BEARCE, John 702-651-7454 295 C john.bearce@csn.edu
BEARCE, Karen 609-570-3564 303 D bearcek@mccc.edu
BEARD, Aileen 218-625-4834 255 A abeard@css.edu
BEARD, Audrey, W 919-530-5327 370 C awbeard@nccu.edu
BEARD, Christopher 808-675-3368 134 M beardc@byuh.edu
BEARD, David 706-880-8175 127 N dbeard@lagrange.edu
BEARD, Jason 206-296-2499 526 F beardj@seattleu.edu
BEARD, John, P 843-349-6441 444 G johnb@coastal.edu
BEARD, Mary, A 716-851-1675 325 A beard@ecc.edu
BEARD, Richard, L 717-867-6363 423 I rbeard@lvc.edu
BEARD, Robert 918-495-6588 401 B rbeard@oru.edu
BEARD, Russell 425-564-4200 519 L russ.beard@bellevuecollege.edu
BEARD, Ryan 713-646-1811 482 H rbeard@stcl.edu
BEARD, Scott 304-876-5370 532 I sbeard@shepherd.edu
BEARD, Timothy, L 727-816-3400 110 B beardt@phsc.edu
BEARDEN, Steve 918-540-6378 398 L steve.bearden@neo.edu
BEARDMORE, Kevin 270-686-4504 197 A kevin.beardmore@kctcs.edu
BEARDMORE, Melissa, A 410-777-2532 213 E mabeardmore@aacc.edu
BEARDON, Sheiron 870-762-1020 19 C
BEARDSALL, Christopher 210-486-2312 467 B cbeardsall@alamo.edu
BEARDSLEE, Bill 603-899-4188 297 H beardsleeb@franklinpierce.edu
BEARDSLEY, Kathleen 215-572-2838 412 F beardsley@arcadia.edu
BEARDSLEY, Scott, C 434-924-7481 514 A scb4v@virginia.edu
BEARE, Paul 559-278-0210 33 D pbeare@csufresno.edu
BEARMAN, Alan 785-670-1855 192 B alan.bearman@washburn.edu
BEARROWS, Thomas, R 312-996-7762 161 F bearrows@uillinois.edu
BEARROWS, Thomas, R 312-996-7762 161 E bearrows@uillinois.edu
BEARSS, Carrie 810-989-5501 249 H cbearss@sc4.edu
BEARY, Richard 407-823-5242 115 C richard.beary@ucf.edu
BEASIMER, Linda, M 845-431-8979 324 D beasimer@sunydutchess.edu
BEASLEY, Barbara 941-907-2262 102 N bbeasley@evergladesuniversity.edu
BEASLEY, Joan 386-822-7251 117 A jlbeasle@stetson.edu
BEASLEY, Marcia 330-263-2165 380 E mbeasley@wooster.edu
BEASLEY, Norman 215-567-7080 412 G nbeasley@aii.edu
BEASLEY, Sarah 304-384-6298 532 E sbeasley@concord.edu
BEASLEY, Sharon 203-576-6262 91 H sharon.beasley@stvincentscollege.edu
BEASLEY, Teresa 903-693-2000 480 A

BEDNARZ, Bridgette ..... 254-968-9271 485 A
bednarz@tarleton.edu
BEDNEY, Elynda, A ...... 269-471-6040 239 D
bedney@andrews.edu
BEDOYA, Eduardo .... 231-777-0332 247 G
eduardo.bedoya@muskegoncc.edu
BEDOYA, Theresa .... 410-225-2434 216 F
tbedoya@mica.edu
BEDTKE, James .... 507-457-1458 264 B
jbedtke@smumn.edu
BEDWELL, Pamela .... 478-471-2730 128 H
pamela.bedwell@mga.edu
BEDWELL, Teresa, M .... 937-775-2313 396 A
teresa.bedwell@wright.edu
BEE, Richard .... 562-903-4728.. 29 F
richard.e.bee@biola.edu
BEE, Timothy, S .... 520-621-1737.. 18 E
timbee@email.arizona.edu
BEEBE, Anthony .... 619-388-3454.. 62 F
abeebe@sdccd.edu
BEEBE, Barbara, R .... 325-574-6501 497 E
bbeebe@wtc.edu
BEEBE, Gayle, D .... 805-565-6024.. 76 K
president@westmont.edu
BEEBE, Norman .... 413-775-1333 231 E
beebe@gcc.mass.edu
BEEBE, Robert, D .... 909-593-3511.. 73 B
rbeebe@laverne.edu
BEEBE, Rose .... 304-424-8286 533 E
rose.beebe@wvup.edu
BEECH, Amanda .... 661-255-1050.. 31 B
abeech@calarts.edu
BEECH, Bettina .... 601-984-1020 270 H
bbeech@umc.edu
BEECH, JR., Derrick ..... 404-756-5294 129 A
dbeech@msm.edu
BEECH, Rachel, A .... 520-621-6123.. 18 E
rabeech@email.arizona.edu
BEECHER, Brian .... 847-543-2464 142 G
bbeecher@clcillinois.edu
BEECHER, Carla, M ...... 518-564-3095 346 B
cbeec001@plattsburgh.edu
BEECHER, Shan, L .... 515-574-1985 179 F
beecher@iowacentral.edu
BEECHING, Angela .... 212-749-2802 331 I
abeeching@msmnyc.edu
BEEHLER, John, M .... 256-782-5881.... 4 L
president@jsu.edu
BEEHLER, John, M .... 412-397-5445 434 B
beehler@rmu.edu
BEEKE, Joel, R .... 616-977-0599 249 B
joel.beeke@prts.edu
BEEKE, Jonathon .... 616-977-0599 249 B
jonathon.beeke@prts.edu
BEEKE, Jonathon, D ..... 616-432-3408 249 B
jonathon.beeke@prts.edu
BEEKMAN, William, R .. 517-353-9818 246 H
beekman@msu.edu
BEELEN, Joan .... 616-957-6027 240 M
jrb44@calvinseminary.edu
BEELER, Jeremy .... 908-835-2301 309 G
jbeeler@warren.edu
BEELER, Sydney .... 913-621-8762 186 G
sbeeler@donnelly.edu
BEEMAN, Greg .... 845-675-4417 337 B
greg.beeman@nyack.edu
BEEMER, Matthew .... 904-596-2473 117 G
mbeemer@tbc.edu
BEEMER, Pamela .... 847-491-7505 155 D
p-beemer@northwestern.edu
BEEN, Sharon, A .... 501-882-8836.. 19 E
sabeen@asub.edu
BEER, Laura .... 503-699-3361 407 A
lbeer@maryhurst.edu
BEER, Patrick .... 478-387-4720 125 E
pbeer@gmc.edu
BEER, Richard .... 360-486-8784 525 H
jrbeer@stmartin.edu
BEERS, David .... 253-879-3902 527 F
dbeers@pugetsound.edu
BEERS, Di .... 425-235-2426 525 G
dbeers@rtc.edu
BEERS, Josh .... 717-560-8240 423 C
jbeers@lbc.edu
BEERS, Maggie .... 415-338-3613.. 36 A
mbeers@sfsu.edu
BEERS, Peter .... 717-560-8267 423 C
pbeers@lbc.edu
BEERS, Stephen, T .... 479-524-7252.. 21 F
sbeers@jbu.edu
BEERY, Kevin, E .... 610-917-1401 438 G
kebeery@valleyforge.edu
BEERY, Wendy .... 610-917-1429 438 G
wmbeery@valleyforge.edu
BEESLEY, Brad .... 918-781-7450 396 F
beesleyb@bacone.edu
BEESON, Duane, L .... 712-707-7116 182 C
beeson@nwciowa.edu
BEESON, Patricia, E ...... 412-624-4223 437 K
beeson@pitt.edu

BEETS, A. Ray .... 319-296-4042 179 B
ray.beets@hawkeyecollege.edu
BEETS, Shannon .... 775-831-1314 296 F
sbeets@sierranevada.edu
BEEZHOLD, Philip, D ... 616-526-6481 240 L
pdb2@calvin.edu
BEG, Christina .... 216-397-1998 384 F
cbeg@jcu.edu
BEGANY, James .... 724-357-7544 431 A
jbegany@iup.edu
BEGAY, Janice .... 785-749-8419 187 F
janice.begay@bie.edu
BEGAY, Karen, F .... 520-626-9809.. 18 E
kfbegay@email.arizona.edu
BEGG, Cori .... 412-365-1255 415 C
cbegg@chatham.edu
BEGG, Melissa, D .... 212-854-2691 322 F
mdb3@columbia.edu
BEGGS, Julie .... 303-404-5541.. 82 J
julie.beggs@frontrange.edu
BEGIAN, Jamie .... 203-837-8851.. 88 G
begianj@wcsu.edu
BEGIN, Gene .... 781-239-4512 222 E
gbegin@babson.edu
BEGLEY, John, B .... 270-384-8505 198 C
begleyj@lindsey.edu
BEGLEY, Mark, L .... 757-221-1009 506 J
mlbegly@wm.edu
BEGLEY, Mary Ann .... 415-338-3885.. 36 A
begley@sfsu.edu
BEGLEY, Thomas .... 518-276-2525 339 D
begley@rpi.edu
BEHAN, Joseph .... 718-405-3212 322 A
joseph.behan@mountsaintvincent.edu
BEHAN KRAUS,
Carolyn, A .... 203-773-8521.. 87 M
cbehan@albertus.edu
BEHAUNEK, Luke .... 515-961-1562 182 I
luke.behaunek@simpson.edu
BEHBEHANI, Khosrow .. 817-272-2571 493 L
kb@uta.edu
BEHEN, Joseph .... 312-499-4272 158 J
jbehen@saic.edu
BEHLING, David, R .... 641-585-8482 183 I
behlingd@waldorf.edu
BEHLING, Laura, L .... 309-341-7216 149 G
llbehling@knox.edu
BEHM, Bonnie Lee .... 610-519-6456 439 A
bonnie.behm@villanova.edu
BEHMAND, Mojgan .... 415-485-3276.. 43 D
mojgan.behmand@dominican.edu
BEHMER, Scott .... 440-610-2240 131 F
sbehmer@southuniversity.edu
BEHN, Julie .... 408-944-6121 182 D
julie.behn@palmer.edu
BEHNEN, Erin .... 618-650-3639 159 I
etimpe@siue.edu
BEHNKE, Laura .... 215-702-4521 414 C
lbehnke@cairn.edu
BEHR, Eileen .... 215-895-1554 417 E
eileen.w.behr@drexel.edu
BEHR, Fred, C .... 507-786-3636 264 C
behr@stolaf.edu
BEHR, John .... 914-961-8313 341 I
jbehr@svots.edu
BEHR, Kate, E .... 914-337-9300 323 A
kate.behr@concordia-ny.edu
BEHR, Michelle .... 205-226-4650.... 2 C
mbehr@bsc.edu
BEHR, Richard, A .... 239-590-7399 114 F
rbehr@fgcu.edu
BEHRE, William .... 732-987-2314 302 J
behrew@georgian.edu
BEHRENDT, William, M 214-648-6342 496 A
william.behrendt@utsouthwestern.edu
BEHRENS, Ann .... 217-228-5432 156 D
behrean@quincy.edu
BEHRENS, Kim .... 559-791-2322.. 49 G
kbehrens@portervillecollege.edu
BEHRENS, Susanne .... 713-623-2040 468 F
sbehrens@aii.edu
BEHRENS, Troy, T .... 214-768-2420 482 J
tbehrens@smu.edu
BEHRINGER, Marilyn .... 559-324-6476.. 68 J
marilyn.behringer@scccd.edu
BEHRS, David .... 814-393-2306 430 E
dbehrs@clarion.edu
BEHUNEK, Sarah .... 303-458-3535.. 85 G
sbehunek@regis.edu
BEHUNIN, Robert .... 435-797-9693 500 A
robert.behunin@usu.edu
BEIDE, Patty .... 717-262-4141 440 D
BEIDLEMAN, David, C .. 717-361-1493 418 B
beidlemand@etown.edu
BEIDLER, James .... 614-287-2646 380 G
jbeidler@cscc.edu
BEIER, Jason .... 608-890-1066 541 E
jason.beier@uwex.uwc.edu
BEIER, Nancy, A .... 410-777-2834 213 E
nabeier@aacc.edu

BEIERSCHMITT, Bill ...... 918-338-8030 401 I
bbeierschmitt@rsu.edu
BEIKIRCH, Dale .... 432-685-5539 478 F
dbeikirch@midland.edu
BEIL, Cheryl .... 202-994-6712.. 95 D
cbeil@gwu.edu
BEILOCK, Sian .... 773-834-3713 161 D
beilock@uchicago.edu
BEIMER, Connie .... 505-277-2498 313 H
cbeimer@unm.edu
BEINHOFF, Lisa .... 575-835-5615 311 I
lbeinhoff@admin.nmt.edu
BEINKE, Dayna .... 816-415-5902 285 K
beinked@william.jewell.edu
BEIRN, Jay .... 508-457-1313 234 E
BEIRNE, Chris .... 706-385-1120 130 C
chris.beirne@point.edu
BEIRNE, Jay .... 508-457-1313 234 E
BEISECKER, Mark .... 805-893-4071.. 72 D
mark.beisecker@bookstore.ucsb.edu
BEISSWENGER, Drew .... 620-331-4100 188 B
dbeisswenger@indycc.edu
BEISWANGER, Ramona . 507-389-7282 262 A
ramona.beiswanger@southcentrla.edu
BEITEL, Leland .... 443-334-2064 218 E
lbeitel@stevenson.edu
BEITEY, George .... 619-388-7860.. 62 H
gbeitey@sdccd.edu
BEITNER, Veronica .... 616-632-2458 239 E
beitnver@aquinas.edu
BEITTEL, Lisa, B .... 508-421-5913 229 B
Lisa.Beittel@umassmed.edu
BEITZEL, Vernon, L ...... 540-464-7211 518 A
beitzelvl@vmi.edu
BEITZEL, Zachery .... 301-387-3119 215 A
zachery.beitzel@garrettcollege.edu
BEJAR, Elizabeth .... 305-348-2151 114 G
elizabeth.bejar@fiu.edu
BEJNAROWICZ, Ewa ..... 312-553-3193 141 N
ebejnarowicz@ccc.edu
BEJOU, David .... 304-766-3025 533 C
dbejou@wvstateu.edu
BEJUNE, Matthew .... 508-929-8511 230 G
mbejune@worcester.edu
BEKE-HARRIGAN, Heidi 330-490-7186 395 C
hbekeharrigan@walsh.edu
BEKISZ, Pete .... 315-279-5484 329 K
pbekisz@keuka.edu
BEKKER, James .... 801-213-3505 499 K
james.bekker@hsc.utah.edu
BEKRITSKY, Brett .... 845-848-7405 324 B
brett.bekritsky@dc.edu
BELAND, Thomas .... 802-773-5900 501 G
tom.beland@csj.edu
BELANGER, OFM,
Brian, C .... 518-783-5047 342 H
bbelanger@siena.edu
BELANGER, David, J .... 413-585-2530 236 G
dbelange@smith.edu
BELANGER, Jaqueline ... 330-287-1306 389 B
belanger.24@osu.edu
BELANGER, Kenneth ..... 315-228-7220 321 H
kbelanger@colgate.edu
BELANGER, Lisa .... 860-768-4666.. 92 F
belanger@hartford.edu
BELANGER, Marc .... 414-256-1238 538 A
belangem@mtmary.edu
BELANGER-HAAS,
Aimee .... 937-328-6038 379 L
haasa@clarkstate.edu
BELAU, Don .... 402-466-4774 290 C
don.belau@doane.edu
BELCHER, Carol .... 843-574-6230 449 G
carol.belcher@tridenttech.edu
BELCHER, Chris .... 417-865-2815 274 L
belcherc@evangel.edu
BELCHER, Chris, P .... 701-483-2984 373 H
chris.belcher@dickinsonstate.edu
BELCHER, Christopher .. 701-483-2984 373 H
Christopher.Belcher@dickinsonstate.edu
BELCHER, David, O ...... 828-227-7100 372 C
dbelcher@wcu.edu
BELCHER, Elizabeth, M . 304-929-5464 531 D
ebelcher@newriver.edu
BELCHER, Jerry .... 816-654-7179 276 G
jbelcher@kcumb.edu
BELCHER, Jim .... 866-323-0233.. 60 E
president@providencecc.edu
BELCHER, Keith, E .... 912-279-5922 123 B
kbelcher@ccga.edu
BELCHER, Lawrence ...... 317-788-2397 173 I
belcherl@uindy.edu
BELCHER, Michael .... 978-934-3929 229 A
michael_belcher@uml.edu
BELCHER, Michael .... 209-946-2537.. 73 C
mbelcher@pacific.edu
BELCHER, Nicholas .... 617-850-1297 227 F
nbelcher@hchc.edu
BELCHER, Tim .... 540-365-4366 507 H
tbelcher@ferrum.edu

BELD, Jo, M .... 507-786-3632 264 C
beld@stolaf.edu
BELDEN, Eric .... 330-490-7337 395 C
ebelden@walsh.edu
BELDEN, William .... 360-992-2103 521 A
wbelden@clark.edu
BELDONA, Sam .... 415-458-3786.. 43 D
sriram.beldona@dominican.edu
BELEN-NAZARIO,
Lillian .... 787-620-2040 550 D
lbelen@aupr.edu
BELEW, Paul, D .... 214-648-6062 496 A
paul.belew@utsouthwestern.edu
BELFIELD, Kevin, D ...... 973-596-3676 304 D
kevin.d.belfield@njit.edu
BELFIELD, Sherri .... 704-378-1032 358 B
sbelfield@jcsu.edu
BELFIORE, Michael .... 718-289-5338 318 E
michael.belfiore@bcc.cuny.edu
BELFORD, Brent, A .... 763-417-8250 254 E
BELGARDE, Judy, A ..... 701-477-7978 375 H
jbelgarde@tm.edu
BELIN, Jackie .... 908-526-1200 305 G
Jacki.Belin@raritanval.edu
BELIN, Joanne .... 205-970-9215.... 7 D
jbelin@sebc.edu
BELINSKI, Victor .... 909-274-4365.. 54 J
vbelinski@mtsac.edu
BELISLE, William, R ..... 504-284-5539 207 B
wbelisle@suno.edu
BELK, Peter .... 913-469-8500 188 E
pbelk@jccc.edu
BELK, Wesley, C .... 864-429-8728 450 I
wcbelk@mailbox.sc.edu
BELKIN, Betsey .... 440-646-8184 394 G
bbelkin@ursuline.edu
BELKNAP, Cindy .... 570-577-3654 413 E
cindy.belknap@bucknell.edu
BELKNAP, Monica .... 928-776-2217.. 18 L
monica.belknap@yc.edu
BELKNAP, Peggy .... 928-536-6231.. 16 E
peggy.belknap@npc.edu
BELKO, Dawn .... 763-424-0715 260 E
dbelko@nhcc.edu
BELL, Aimee .... 440-826-2071 377 D
abell@bw.edu
BELL, Amy .... 870-743-3000.. 22 A
abell@northark.edu
BELL, Autumn .... 559-442-4600.. 69 B
autumn.bell@fresnocitycollege.edu
BELL, Barbara .... 216-987-4851 381 A
barbara.bell@tri-c.edu
BELL, Barrett .... 608-757-7670 542 L
bbell14@blackhawk.edu
BELL, Bonita .... 910-272-3331 365 D
bbell@robeson.edu
BELL, Brett .... 619-388-7810.. 62 H
bbell@sdccd.edu
BELL, Carmen .... 575-624-8080 311 K
carmen@nmmi.edu
BELL, Chris .... 940-552-6291 496 B
cbell@vernoncollege.edu
BELL, Christina .... 847-259-1840 141 L
cbell@christianlifecollege.edu
BELL, Christopher .... 207-768-9511 212 H
chris@maine.edu
BELL, Connie .... 818-243-1131.. 45 H
BELL, Corinne .... 802-387-6863 502 A
corinnebell@landmark.edu
BELL, Cynthia, M .... 330-941-3101 396 C
cmbell02@ysu.edu
BELL, Damon .... 360-475-7474 524 H
dbell@olympic.edu
BELL, Danielle .... 803-321-5128 447 L
danielle.bell@newberry.edu
BELL, David, D .... 614-823-1300 390 C
dbell@otterbein.edu
BELL, Dean .... 312-322-1791 160 E
dbell@spertus.edu
BELL, Deborah, H .... 662-915-6900 270 G
BELL, Denise .... 508-793-2397 225 C
dbell@holycross.edu
BELL, Denise .... 850-973-9481 109 C
belld@nfcc.edu
BELL, Dolores .... 678-359-5015 126 E
doloresb@gordonstate.edu
BELL, Geraldine .... 205-929-1715.... 5 I
gbell@mail.miles.edu
BELL, Gregory, J .... 570-321-4395 425 B
bell@lycoming.edu
BELL, Harold .... 404-270-5269 132 D
hbell@spelman.edu
BELL, Hershey .... 814-866-6641 423 B
hbell@lecom.edu
BELL, Jamel, S .... 309-467-6498 145 A
jbell@eureka.edu
BELL, Jennifer .... 856-256-4410 306 D
bellj@rowan.edu
BELL, Jenny .... 205-665-6565.... 9 C
jbell8@montevallo.edu

BENGFORT, Joseph ... 415-353-4273.. 72 C Joe.Bengfort@ucsf.edu

BENGINIA, Francis, A .. 610-330-5090 423 A benginif@lafayette.edu

BENGTSON, Kathy ... 612-767-7051 253 F kathy.bengtson@alfredadler.edu

BENHAM, Maenette ... 808-956-0980 135 J mbenham@hawaii.edu

BENHAM-DEAL, Tami ... 307-766-4286 546 K benham@uwyo.edu

BENINGHOVE, Linda ... 201-216-5412 308 D Linda.Beninghove@stevens.edu

BENISH, Amy, L ... 262-554-2010 537 D albenish@aol.com

BENITEZ, Hubert ... 516-918-3615 316 L hbenitez@bcl.edu

BENITEZ, Leyda, L ... 610-519-3976 439 A leyda.benitez@villanova.edu

BENITEZ, Michael ... 253-879-3929 527 F mbenitez@pugetsound.edu

BENITEZ-RAMIREZ, Solange ... 787-993-8863 557 E solange.benitez@upr.edu

BENITO, Agueda ... 312-752-2094 149 D agueda.benito@kendall.edu

BENITO, Katy ... 714-556-3610.. 75 A katy.benito@vanguard.edu

BENITZ-HODGE, Grissel ... 808-735-4852 135 A ghodge@chaminade.edu

BENJAMIN, Ashu ... 504-286-5279 207 B abenjamin@suno.edu

BENJAMIN, Bill ... 727-873-4199 116 C benjamin@mail.usf.edu

BENJAMIN, Eric, V ... 931-598-1241 460 I ebenjami@sewanee.edu

BENJAMIN, Finbar ... 256-726-7105.... 6 C fbenjamin@oakwood.edu

BENJAMIN, Gregory ... 610-399-2419 430 D gbenjamin@cheyney.edu

BENJAMIN, Guy ... 808-237-5140 135 B

BENJAMIN, Helen ... 925-229-6820.. 42 C hbenjamin@4cd.edu

BENJAMIN, Jack ... 803-641-3327 450 C

BENJAMIN, Jodi ... 402-941-6102 291 I benjamin@midlandu.edu

BENJAMIN, Mary ... 620-227-9240 186 F mbenjamin@dc3.edu

BENJAMIN, Mary, E ... 870-575-8216.. 24 D benjaminm@uapb.edu

BENJAMIN, Pamela ... 419-755-4029 387 E benjamin.155@osu.edu

BENJAMIN, Rich ... 847-628-1579 149 A rbenjamin@judsonu.edu

BENJAMIN, Robert ... 617-745-3595 225 H robert.j.benjamin@enc.edu

BENJAMIN, Robert ... 269-471-3310 239 D robertb@andrews.edu

BENJAMIN, William ... 714-432-5670.. 40 D wbenjamin1@occ.cccd.edu

BENKA, Walter ... 631-244-3083 324 C benkaw@dowling.edu

BENKE, Jack ... 573-592-5555 285 J jack.benke@westminster-mo.edu

BENKE, Robin, P ... 276-328-0151 514 B rpb@wise.edu

BENKESER, Kristina ... 724-738-2052 432 A kristina.benkeser@sru.edu

BENLOLO, Henri ... 352-854-2322 100 P benloloh@cf.edu

BENMAMOUN, Elabbas 217-333-6677 162 A benmamou@illinois.edu

BENMERGUI, Diana ... 212-960-5277 353 P benmergui@yu.edu

BENN, Sherri ... 512-245-2278 489 C sb17@txstate.edu

BENNA, Kelsey ... 414-326-1797 535 H kbenna@ccon.edu

BENNASAR, Mari Carmen ... 617-327-6777 238 D mari_bennasar@williamjames.edu

BENNATTS, Denise ... 253-833-9111 523 B dbennatts@greenriver.edu

BENNECKE, Margie ... 847-233-7700 155 B mbennecke@nc.edu

BENNEIAN, Teresa ... 717-290-8748 423 E tbenneian@lancasterseminary.edu

BENNER, Brent, W ... 813-253-6211 118 H bbenner@ut.edu

BENNER, Mary ... 405-208-5270 400 A mbenner@okcu.edu

BENNER, Tracy ... 614-823-1580 390 C tbenner@otterbein.edu

BENNETT, Amy ... 317-955-6768 171 A abennett@marian.edu

BENNETT, Bo ... 828-448-6197 358 F bennettb@lmc.edu

BENNETT, Calvin ... 601-484-8894 268 B cbennett@meridiancc.edu

BENNETT, Cameron, D . 253-535-7150 524 I bennetcd@plu.edu

BENNETT, Carolyn ... 516-876-3203 345 E bennettc@oldwestbury.edu

BENNETT, Christopher .. 440-375-7000 385 B cbennett@lec.edu

BENNETT, Daniel ... 828-669-8012 359 K dbennett@montreat.edu

BENNETT, Daniel, P ... 906-487-2216 247 A dpbennet@mtu.edu

BENNETT, David, A ... 606-474-3256 195 F dbennett@kcu.edu

BENNETT, Derwin ... 518-255-5836 346 E bennetdd@cobleskill.edu

BENNETT, Doug, L ... 740-368-3148 390 B dlbennet@owu.edu

BENNETT, Douglas ... 714-432-5126.. 40 D dbennett@occ.cccd.edu

BENNETT, Drew, A ... 417-255-7900 279 B wpchancellor@missouristate.edu

BENNETT, Drew, A ... 417-255-7900 279 A drewbennett@missouristate.edu

BENNETT, Elbert ... 870-575-8504.. 24 D bennette@uapb.edu

BENNETT, Elizabeth, C . 949-824-7982.. 71 C bennette@uci.edu

BENNETT, Elizabeth, P .. 717-290-8713 423 E ebennett@lancasterseminary.edu

BENNETT, Eric ... 212-659-7290 330 A ebennett@tkc.edu

BENNETT, Gene ... 870-780-1201.. 19 C gbennett@smail.anc.edu

BENNETT, George ... 509-527-2930 528 A george.bennett@wallawalla.edu

BENNETT, Gwendolyn, A ... 225-771-5763 207 A gwendolyn_bennett@subr.edu

BENNETT, Herman ... 212-817-7540 319 B Hbennett@gc.cuny.edu

BENNETT, Holly, L ... 561-993-1126 109 H bennetth@palmbeachstate.edu

BENNETT, James ... 913-288-7259 188 G jbennett@kckcc.edu

BENNETT, James ... 216-687-5308 380 D J.E.BENNETT90@csuohio.edu

BENNETT, Jamie ... 213-613-2200.. 67 G jamie_bennett@sciarc.edu

BENNETT, Janice, G ... 563-588-8000 178 E jbennett@emmaus.edu

BENNETT, Janis, A ... 304-766-3010 533 C bennetja@wvstateu.edu

BENNETT, Jeff ... 405-425-5903 399 J jeff.bennett@oc.edu

BENNETT, Jeffrey, L ... 570-321-4031 425 B bennett@lycoming.edu

BENNETT, Jeremy ... 580-559-5256 397 K jbennett@ecok.edu

BENNETT, Jim ... 408-551-1910.. 65 A jbbennett@scu.edu

BENNETT, Jim ... 406-265-3594 288 A james.bennett10@msun.edu

BENNETT, Joan, W ... 848-932-6223 306 F profmycogirl@yahoo.com

BENNETT, JoAnn ... 937-327-6185 395 I jbennett@wittenberg.edu

BENNETT, Joe ... 617-912-9103 224 C jbennett@bostonconservatory.edu

BENNETT, Josh ... 406-447-6932 287 F josh.bennett@umhelelna.edu

BENNETT, Kari ... 518-438-3111 331 K bennettk@mariacollege.edu

BENNETT, Kevin ... 904-256-7585 106 Q kbennet1@ju.edu

BENNETT, Kim ... 260-665-4438 173 D bennettk@trine.edu

BENNETT, Kristen ... 859-336-5082 199 B kbennett@sccky.edu

BENNETT, Laura ... 541-956-7136 409 F lbennett@roguecc.edu

BENNETT, Linda L, M .. 812-464-1756 174 D bennettl@usi.edu

BENNETT, Lisa ... 585-594-6804 337 A Bennett_Lisa@roberts.edu

BENNETT, Lori ... 805-378-1403.. 75 C lbennett@vcccd.edu

BENNETT, Marla ... 217-732-3168 150 G hr@lincolnchristian.edu

BENNETT, Matt ... 517-338-3014 241 B mbennett@cleary.edu

BENNETT, Maybelle, T .. 202-806-4771.. 96 B maybelle.bennett@howard.edu

BENNETT, Michael, J ... 727-341-3012 112 A bennett.michael@spcollege.edu

BENNETT, Mitch ... 214-333-5139 471 L mitch@dbu.edu

BENNETT, Patricia ... 850-729-4901 109 D bennettp@nwfsc.edu

BENNETT, Patrick ... 623-245-4600.. 18 C pbennett@uti.edu

BENNETT, Patrick ... 614-947-6836 382 H patrick.bennett@franklin.edu

BENNETT, Priscilla ... 617-277-3915 224 D bennettp@bgsp.edu

BENNETT, Rashad ... 954-923-4440 107 U registrar@keycollege.edu

BENNETT, Rene ... 816-604-5412 277 H rene.bennett@mcckc.edu

BENNETT, II, Richard, E ... 518-629-7205 328 D r.bennett@hvcc.edu

BENNETT, Rick ... 408-855-5232.. 76 E rick.bennett@wvm.edu

BENNETT, Robert ... 518-327-6049 338 B bbennett@paulsmiths.edu

BENNETT, Rodney ... 301-846-2501 214 I rbennett@frederick.edu

BENNETT, Rodney, D ... 601-266-5001 271 B president@usm.edu

BENNETT, Samantha ... 312-235-3511 159 B s.bennett@shimer.edu

BENNETT, Sari, M ... 603-862-4285 299 B sari.bennett@unh.edu

BENNETT, Scott ... 904-620-2002 116 A sbennett@unf.edu

BENNETT, Scott ... 281-425-6396 477 F sbennett@lee.edu

BENNETT, Sherri ... 870-838-2945.. 19 C sbennett@smail.anc.edu

BENNETT, Stephen, R ... 507-933-7526 256 A sbennett@gustavus.edu

BENNETT, Tanya Lynn .. 973-408-3718 301 J tbennett@drew.edu

BENNETT, II, Thomas ... 304-766-3032 533 C tbennett3@wvstateu.edu

BENNETT, Todd ... 404-364-8329 129 F tbennett1@oglethorpe.edu

BENNETT, Tom ... 304-766-3032 533 C tbennet3@wvstateu.edu

BENNETT, Trudy ... 979-458-6000 484 E tbennett@tamus.edu

BENNETT, Valerie ... 309-677-3961 140 H vbennett@bradley.edu

BENNETT, Vernell, A ... 502-597-6827 197 G vernell.bennett@kysu.edu

BENNETT, Wade ... 607-735-1894 324 J wbennett@elmira.edu

BENNETT-BEALER, Nichole ... 609-894-9311 306 B nbennett-bealer@bcc.edu

BENNETT-BELLAMY, Sonja, A ... 803-813-1340 448 H sbennet5@scsu.edu

BENNETT-CAMPBELL, Bonnie, L ... 815-224-0481 147 J bonnie_campbell@ivcc.edu

BENNIE, Roanna ... 925-424-1104.. 37 O rbennie@laspositascollege.edu

BENNIEFIELD, Marcus .. 619-702-9400.. 31 F

BENNIGHOFF, James ... 254-710-6500 469 D james_bennighoff@baylor.edu

BENNING, Tom ... 314-529-9304 277 B tbenning@maryville.edu

BENNINGER, Paul ... 336-917-5460 368 F paul.benninger@salem.edu

BENNINGTON, Cheryl ... 304-336-8049 533 A cbennington@westliberty.edu

BENNION, Paul ... 208-459-5841 137 J pbennion@collegeofidaho.edu

BENOIT, Andy ... 337-482-6474 208 F ajbenoit@louisiana.edu

BENOIT, Anthony ... 617-588-1324 223 D abenoit@bfit.edu

BENOIT, Debra ... 985-493-2563 208 C debi.benoit@nicholls.edu

BENOIT, Doug ... 714-992-7033.. 56 F dbenoit@fullcoll.edu

BENOIT, Kathy ... 714-992-7048.. 56 F kbenoit@fullcoll.edu

BENOIT, Michele ... 541-888-7421 410 A mbenoit@socc.edu

BENOIT, Pam ... 740-593-2600 389 H benoit@ohio.edu

BENOIT, Sherry ... 409-880-1718 488 F sherry.benoit@lamar.edu

BENOIT, Thomas ... 325-793-3869 478 D tbenoit@mcm.edu

BENOL, Christine ... 732-571-3405 303 G cbenol@monmouth.edu

BENOLIEL, Abraham ... 718-339-1090 353 J rabenoliel@mikdashmelech.org

BENOLIEL, Haim ... 718-339-1090 353 J roshyeshiva@mikdashmelech.org

BENOLKEN, Julie ... 651-450-3622 259 A jbenolk@inverhills.edu

BENRUD, Ann ... 612-874-3793 257 D abenrud@mcad.edu

BENSE, Judith, A ... 850-474-2200 116 E jbense@uwf.edu

BENSEL, Terry ... 814-332-3391 411 F tbensel@allegheny.edu

BENSEN, Steven, P ... 701-788-4761 374 A Steven.Bensen@mayvillestate.edu

BENSINK, Michael ... 508-678-2811 231 B michael.bensink@bristolcc.edu

BENSON, Allen, C ... 401-841-3397 548 B

BENSON, Ben ... 516-773-5000 548 I bensonb@usmma.edu

BENSON, Bill ... 541-962-3241 405 G wbenson@eou.edu

BENSON, Brenda ... 310-434-4433.. 65 B benson_brenda@smc.edu

BENSON, Bruce, D ... 303-860-5600.. 86 D officeofthepresident@cu.edu

BENSON, Bryan, E ... 903-233-3809 477 G bryanbenson@letu.edu

BENSON, Camesha ... 662-846-4649 267 A cbenson@deltastate.edu

BENSON, Craig ... 434-924-3593 514 A chb4x@virginia.edu

BENSON, Daniel ... 507-389-6838 260 A daniel.benson@mnsu.edu

BENSON, Dawn ... 406-275-4985 288 H dawn_benson@skc.edu

BENSON, Duane ... 712-274-5133 181 C bensond@morningside.edu

BENSON, Erin, V ... 207-768-9453 212 H erin.benson@umpi.edu

BENSON, Gus ... 859-622-3636 194 L gus.benson@eku.edu

BENSON, Jason ... 701-483-2014 373 H Jason.Bensen@sodexo.com

BENSON, Jennifer ... 706-355-5008 120 G jbenson@athenstech.edu

BENSON, Jennifer ... 706-355-5124 120 G jbenson@athenstech.edu

BENSON, Jerry ... 540-568-3429 509 C bensonaj@jmu.edu

BENSON, Jill, M ... 978-468-7111 227 B jbenson@gcts.edu

BENSON, Jocelyn ... 313-577-3933 252 G jbenson@wayne.edu

BENSON, Kristin ... 651-846-2882.. 28 G kbenson@argosy.edu

BENSON, Mark ... 518-442-2562 343 C mbenson@albany.edu

BENSON, Michael ... 859-622-2977 194 L michael.benson@eku.edu

BENSON, Mindy ... 435-586-7763 499 L benson@suu.edu

BENSON, Mitchel ... 916-568-3041.. 52 H bensonm@losrios.edu

BENSON, Neal, L ... 304-462-4117 532 G neal.benson@glenville.edu

BENSON, Patricia ... 610-526-6142 420 C pbenson@harcum.edu

BENSON, Patrick ... 312-788-1133 162 H meca@vandercook.edu

BENSON, Paul, H ... 937-229-2245 393 E pbenson1@udayton.edu

BENSON, Peter ... 203-287-3017.. 91 C paier.admin@snet.net

BENSON, Richard ... 540-231-9752 518 B deaneng@vt.edu

BENSON, Robert, M ... 865-882-4553 463 F bensonrm@roanestate.edu

BENSON, Robin ... 918-647-1344 397 C rbenson@carlalbert.edu

BENSON, Samantha ... 910-879-5567 360 C sbenson@bladencc.edu

BENSON, Stephanie, G . 706-355-5112 120 G sbenson@athenstech.edu

BENSON, Stephen ... 386-752-1822 103 Q stephen.benson@fgc.edu

BENSON, Stephen, M ... 304-929-5486 531 D sbenson@newriver.edu

BENSON, Suzie ... 509-682-6505 528 C sbenson@wvc.edu

BENSON, Todd ... 503-251-5726 410 I tbenson@uws.edu

BENSON, Vaughn ... 402-375-7245 292 D vabenso1@wsc.edu

BENSON, Wade, M ... 706-379-3111 134 J wadeb@yhc.edu

BENSON, Yolanda, C ... 502-597-5795 197 G yolanda.benson@kysu.edu

BENSON-TYUS, Hasanna ... 202-462-2101.. 96 C benson@iwp.edu

BENSTON, Kimberly ... 610-896-1021 420 J kbenston@haverford.edu

BENT, Lauren ... 978-837-5250 233 G

BENTE, James ... 630-942-2409 142 F bentej@cod.edu

BENTLEY, Candace ... 864-225-7653 446 D candacebentley@forrestcollege.edu

BENTLEY, Erik ... 952-358-8274 260 D erik.bentley@normandale.edu

BENTLEY, Jane ... 708-974-5703 153 D jane.bentley@morainevalley.edu

BENTLEY, Kelvin ... 817-515-5024 484 B kelvin.bentley@tccd.edu

BENTLEY, Marissa ... 406-496-4377 288 C mbentley@mtech.edu

BERNA, Francis, J .... 215-951-1346 422 F
berna@lasalle.edu
BERNABE, Arnaldo .... 718-518-6888 319 D
abernabe@hostos.cuny.edu
BERNAD, Manuel, A ..... 858-499-0202.. 40 G
manuelb@coleman.edu
BERNADELLE, Guary ..... 815-967-7300 157 C
bernadelle@rockfordcareercollege.edu
BERNAHL, Joni .... 217-786-9627 151 C
joni.bernahl@llcc.edu
BERNAIX, Laura .... 618-650-3969 159 I
lbernai@siue.edu
BERNAL, Deanna .... 818-785-2726.. 37 I
deanna.bernal@casalomacollege.edu
BERNAL, Elena .... 781-283-1000 237 F
ebernal@wellesley.edu
BERNAL, Erika .... 714-992-7832.. 53 D
ebernal@ketchum.edu
BERNAL, Jesse .... 616-331-3296 243 E
bernalje@gvsu.edu
BERNAL, Johnathan ...... 559-925-3253.. 76 C
johnathanbernal@whccd.edu
BERNAL-OLSON,
Patricia .... 937-229-4211 393 E
pbernalolson1@udayton.edu
BERNARD, Bill .... 212-924-5900 349 D
wbernard@swedishinstitute.edu
BERNARD, David, K ..... 314-921-9290 284 G
dbernard@ugst.edu
BERNARD, Dee .... 651-450-3522 259 A
dbernar@inverhills.edu
BERNARD, Dee .... 507-332-5890 262 A
dee.bernard@southcentral.edu
BERNARD, Donna .... 318-342-5447 209 A
bernard@ulm.edu
BERNARD, Frances .... 518-438-3111 331 K
franb@mariacollege.edu
BERNARD, Kacey .... 610-341-1389 427 I
kbernard@eastern.edu
BERNARD, Kacey .... 610-341-1481 418 A
kbernard@eastern.edu
BERNARD, Marjorie, P . 412-578-8880 414 I
mpbernard@carlow.edu
BERNARD, Nancy, M .... 334-844-4744.... 1 G
bernanm@auburn.edu
BERNARD, Nesta .... 202-238-2340.. 96 B
nbernard@howard.edu
BERNARD, Pamela .... 919-684-3955 356 E
pam.bernard@duke.edu
BERNARD, Philip .... 617-989-4162 237 G
bernardp@wit.edu
BERNARD, Renee .... 814-472-2766 434 F
rbernard@francis.edu
BERNARD, Richard .... 405-974-3493 403 G
rbernard1@uco.edu
BERNARD, Sue .... 207-768-2808 211 C
sbernard@nmcc.edu
BERNARD, Vicki .... 314-340-5112 275 G
bernardv@hssu.edu
BERNARD-DONALS,
Michael .... 608-262-5246 539 D
mfbernarddon@wisc.edu
BERNARDI, Daniel .... 415-338-1541.. 36 A
bernardi@sfsu.edu
BERNARDI, Robert .... 985-448-4794 208 C
rob.bernardi@nicholls.edu
BERNARDINO, Carole ... 937-708-5745 395 E
cbernardino@wilberforce.edu
BERNARDINO, Maria ..... 209-954-5065.. 63 D
mbernardino@deltacollege.edu
BERNARDIS, Tim .... 406-638-3113 286 I
tim@lbhc.edu
BERNARDO, Daniel .... 509-335-4200 528 B
presidentsoffice@wsu.edu
BERNARDO, Lisa, M .... 209-667-3094.. 35 C
lbernardo@csustan.edu
BERNARDO, Peter, R .... 216-397-4217 384 F
pbernardo@jcu.edu
BERNARDO-SOUSA,
Marie .... 401-598-1754 441 D
Marie.Bernardo-Sousa@jwu.edu
BERNAS, Judith, A .... 602-827-2017.. 18 E
jbernas@email.arizona.edu
BERNAUER, Edmund ..... 808-521-2288 135 E
dean@orientalmedicine.edu
BERNDT, Michael .... 651-779-3493 258 D
michael.berndt@century.edu
BERNE, Jennifer .... 847-925-6975 145 F
jbernel@harpercollege.edu
BERNE, Robert .... 212-998-2283 336 C
robert.berne@nyu.edu
BERNECKER, Kim .... 972-825-4634 483 D
kbernecker@sagu.edu
BERNEL, Liz .... 219-785-5719 172 A
ebernel@pnc.edu
BERNER, Albert, J .... 973-618-3660 300 H
aberner@caldwell.edu
BERNER, Dawn .... 262-646-6503 538 B
dberner@nashotah.edu
BERNER, JR.,
Howard, E .... 314-275-3514 156 C
howard.berner@principia.edu
BERNER, Nancy .... 931-598-1172 460 I
nberner@sewanee.edu
BERNEY, Jan .... 360-438-4513 525 H
jberney@stmartin.edu
BERNHARD, Edward, E . 574-807-7121 164 F
bernhae@bethelcollege.edu
BERNHARD, Mark, C .... 812-464-1829 174 D
mbernhard@usi.edu
BERNHARD, Robert, J .. 574-631-3902 174 A
bernhard.9@nd.edu
BERNHARDSON,
Bonnie .... 218-879-0828 258 F
bonnie@fdltcc.edu
BERNHARDSON, Mark .. 218-879-0703 258 F
mbernhar@fdltcc.edu
BERNHARDT, Jay, M 512-471-8100 493M
jay.bernhardt@austin.utexas.edu
BERNHEISEL, Susan ..... 419-251-1583 386 C
susan.bernheisel@mercycollege.edu
BERNIER, Jessica .... 845-437-5320 351 H
jebernier@vassar.edu
BERNIER, Jose .... 845-341-4689 337 G
jose.bernier@sunyorange.edu
BERNIER, Jose .... 386-822-7045 117 A
jbernier@stetson.edu
BERNIER, Julie, N .... 603-535-2230 299 E
jbernier@plymouth.edu
BERNOTAS, Scott .... 410-293-1010 549 B
scott.bernotas@navy.mil
BERNOTSKY,
R. Lorraine .... 610-436-6977 432 B
lbernotsky@wcupa.edu
BERNSTEIN, Aimee .... 718-409-5979 348 C
abernstein@sunymaritime.edu
BERNSTEIN, Alan .... 229-333-5860 133 H
abernste@valdosta.edu
BERNSTEIN, David .... 845-406-4308 353 D
BERNSTEIN, Jennifer .... 212-346-1095 337 I
jbernstein@pace.edu
BERNSTEIN, Melissa ..... 801-581-3386 499 K
melissa.bernstein@law.utah.edu
BERNSTEIN, Melvin ...... 617-373-4160 235 D
BERNSTEIN, Michael ..... 504-865-5261 207 F
mbernstein@tulane.edu
BERNSTEIN, Pamela ..... 603-880-8308 298 I
tmc@thomasmorecollege.edu
BERNSTEIN, Robin .... 402-557-7300 289 B
robin.bernstein@bellevue.edu
BERNSTEIN, Zeke .... 802-440-4594 501 D
zbernstein@bennington.edu
BERNTSON, Joan, L ..... 218-751-8670 263 J
joanberntson@oakhills.edu
BEROL, Polly .... 610-341-1386 418 A
pberol@eastern.edu
BEROWSKI, Alfred .... 315-866-0300 327 E
berowskaj@herkimer.edu
BERQUAM, Lori .... 608-263-5700 539 D
lberquam@studentlife.wisc.edu
BERQUE, David, A .... 765-658-4735 165 G
dberque@depauw.edu
BERQUIST, Gina .... 503-255-0332 407 D
ginab@multnomah.edu
BERRAHOU, Catherine .. 248-689-8282 251 I
cberraho@walshcollege.edu
BERREAU, Lisa .... 435-797-3509 500 A
lisa.berreau@usu.edu
BERRIDGE, Bob .... 773-256-0783 151 H
bberridg@lstc.edu
BERRIOS, Amy .... 610-353-7630 421 P
BERRIOS, Iris 787-743-7979 555M
ac_irberrios@suagm.edu
BERRIOS, Jose 787-751-0178 555M
ac_jberrios@suagm.edu
BERRIOS, Juan .... 787-738-2161 557 G
juan.berrios9@upr.edu
BERRIOS, Marianne .... 787-852-1430 552 J
mberrios@hccpr.edu
BERRIOS, William .... 212-592-2000 342 F
wberrios@sva.edu
BERRMAN, Terri .... 815-455-8783 152 B
tberryman@mchenry.edu
BERROA, Carlos, E .... 787-257-7373 555 L
ceberroa@suagm.edu
BERRY, Brian .... 870-777-5722.. 24 H
brian.berry@uacch.edu
BERRY, Carolynn .... 336-750-2110 372 D
berryc@wssu.edu
BERRY, Chad .... 859-985-3490 193 F
chad_berry@berea.edu
BERRY, Clay .... 870-508-6124.. 19 H
cberry@asumh.edu
BERRY, Dewayne .... 817-598-6227 497 A
dberry@wc.edu
BERRY, Donna .... 559-638-3641.. 69 C
donna.berry@reedleycollege.edu
BERRY, Edgar .... 903-593-8311 487 A
eberry@texascollege.edu
BERRY, Emily .... 513-529-9625 386 K
emily.berry@miamioh.edu
BERRY, Evan .... 772-462-7945 106 F
eberry@irsc.edu
BERRY, Fred .... 414-277-7324 537 G
berry@msoe.edu
BERRY, James .... 937-708-5701 395 E
jberry@wilberforce.edu
BERRY, Jessica .... 207-778-7295 212 E
jess.berry@maine.edu
BERRY, Joanne .... 603-427-7609 296 K
jberry@ccsnh.edu
BERRY, Joe .... 501-882-4407.. 19 E
jlberry@asub.edu
BERRY, John .... 865-981-8145 458 E
john.berry@maryvillecollege.edu
BERRY, Josh .... 785-442-6031 187 I
jberry@highlandcc.edu
BERRY, Joshua .... 203-582-8695.. 91 E
joshua.berry@quinnipiac.edu
BERRY, Keith .... 813-253-7714 106 C
kberry@hccfl.edu
BERRY, Kimberly, G ..... 518-629-8007 328 D
k.berry@hvcc.edu
BERRY, Koop .... 330-490-7058 395 C
kberry@walsh.edu
BERRY, Larry 423-614-8086 457M
lberry@leeuniversity.edu
BERRY, Laura .... 870-743-3000.. 22 A
lberry@northark.edu
BERRY, Laura Lea .... 802-586-7711 503 B
llberry@sterlingcollege.edu
BERRY, Linda, C .... 708-209-3209 143 D
linda.berry@cuchicago.edu
BERRY, Lisa .... 713-221-8468 491 F
berryl@uhd.edu
BERRY, Mario .... 281-290-3960 477 I
mario.berry@lonestar.edu
BERRY, Mark, A .... 213-621-2200.. 40 F
BERRY, Mark, E .... 843-953-7645 445 B
berrym@cofc.edu
BERRY, Mary .... 605-677-5370 453 F
mary.berry@usd.edu
BERRY, Molly .... 217-424-6335 153 A
mberry@millikin.edu
BERRY, Richard .... 936-468-2807 484 A
rberry@sfasu.edu
BERRY, Robert, L .... 904-620-2851 116 A
robert.berry@unf.edu
BERRY, Robin .... 502-410-6200 194 N
rberry@galencollege.edu
BERRY, Ronald .... 318-342-1103 209 A
rberry@ulm.edu
BERRY, Sarah .... 775-831-1314 296 F
sberry@sierranevada.edu
BERRY, Scott, D .... 864-488-4525 447 F
sberry@limestone.edu
BERRY, Steve .... 775-831-1314 296 F
sberry@sierranevada.edu
BERRY, Trey .... 870-235-4001.. 23 D
tcberry@saumag.edu
BERRY, Virginia .... 530-541-4660.. 50 A
berry@ltcc.edu
BERRY, Yvonne .... 207-893-7750 211 H
eberry@sjcme.edu
BERRY-GUERIN,
Daneen .... 509-793-2053 520 B
daneenb@bigbend.edu
BERRY-JOHNSON,
Pamela .... 478-825-6211 124 E
BERRYMAN, Daniel ...... 520-206-4740.. 17 A
dberryman@pima.edu
BERRYMAN, Davis .... 405-491-6680 402 E
dberryma@snu.edu
BERRYMAN, Jennifer .... 508-856-2900 229 B
jennifer.berryman@umassmed.edu
BERRYMAN, Joanne ..... 502-585-9911 199 E
jberryman@spalding.edu
BERRYMAN, Theresa .... 847-543-2890 142 G
tberryman@clcillinois.edu
BERSCHEIDT, Jim .... 402-280-1272 290 B
JimBerscheidt@creighton.edu
BERSHAD, Carolyn .... 607-753-4728 345 C
carolyn.bershad@cortland.edu
BERT, Daryl, W .... 540-432-4101 507 A
daryl.bert@emu.edu
BERTCH, Dennis .... 269-488-4205 244 J
dbertch@kvcc.edu
BERTEAUX, Susan .... 508-830-5035 230 D
sberteaux@maritime.edu
BERTETTO, Bill .... 217-854-3231 140 F
bill.bertetto@blackburn.edu
BERTHEL, Michael .... 516-299-2606 330 G
michael.berthel@liu.edu
BERTHELOT, Yves .... 404-385-3383 125 D
yves.berthelot@provost.gatech.edu
BERTHELSEN, Mike .... 612-624-6837 265 C
berth004@umn.edu
BERTHELSEN, Rita .... 712-325-3356 180 B
rberthelsen@iwcc.edu
BERTHIAUME, Joe .... 940-898-3676 490 D
jberthiaume@twu.edu
BERTHIAUME, Peter, L . 603-526-3675 296 I
pberthia@colby-sawyer.edu
BERTHOUMIEUX,
Rachel .... 516-686-1140 335 F
rberthou@nyit.edu
BERTI, David, M .... 617-422-7215 234 J
dberti@nesl.edu
BERTINI, Kristine .... 207-780-5180 213 A
bertini@usm.maine.edu
BERTINI, Vickie .... 847-619-8840 157 E
vbertini@roosevelt.edu
BERTOCCHI, Bonnie, M 775-445-4236 296 A
bonnie.bertocchi@wnc.edu
BERTOLI, Jim .... 812-877-8359 172 C
bertoli@rose-hulman.edu
BERTOLINI, Leonard ..... 815-836-5244 150 F
bertolle@lewisu.edu
BERTOLINO, Joseph, A 802-626-6404 504 B
joseph.bertolino@lyndonstate.edu
BERTOLUCCI, Linda ...... 619-644-7799.. 46 H
linda.bertolucci@gcccd.edu
BERTOZZI, Nicholas ..... 603-577-6640 297 F
bertozzi@dwc.edu
BERTOZZI, Stefano .... 510-642-2082.. 70 K
candido@berkeley.edu
BERTRAM, Alissa .... 617-236-8800 226 F
abertram@fisher.edu
BERTRAM, Bob .... 207-780-4546 213 A
rbertram@usm.maine.edu
BERTRAM, Brian .... 517-264-7676 250 B
bbertram@sienaheights.edu
BERTRAN-PASARELL,
Lourdes .... 787-728-1515 559 A
lbertran@sagrado.edu
BERTRAND, Andre, E .... 404-215-2717 128 L
andre.bertrand@morehouse.edu
BERTSCH, Lynda .... 701-858-3360 374 B
lynda.bertsch@minotstateu.edu
BERTSCH, Tauna .... 254-968-9921 485 A
bertsch@tarleton.edu
BERTSCHE, Allen, P ...... 309-794-8283 139 K
allenbertsche@augustana.edu
BERTSCHINGER,
Edmund .... 617-253-1000 233 C
BERTSOS, Daniel .... 937-775-4172 396 A
dan.bertsos@wright.edu
BERUBE, Danelle .... 802-860-2702 501 F
dberube@champlain.edu
BERUBE, Eric .... 661-763-7944.. 69 E
eberube@taftcollege.edu
BERUBE, Patricia .... 413-572-5415 230 F
pberube@westfield.ma.edu
BERWICK, Robert .... 386-822-7141 117 A
rberwick@stetson.edu
BERZAS, Elizabeth .... 225-768-1706 206 F
eberzas@ololcollege.edu
BESADE, Elizabeth .... 305-899-4758.. 99 B
ebesade@barry.edu
BESANA, GianMario ..... 312-362-5554 143 G
gbesana@depaul.edu
BESAW, Gary .... 800-567-2344 535 F
gbesaw@menominee.edu
BESEDA, Michael .... 503-370-6021 411 D
mbeseda@willamette.edu
BESENYEI, Alicia .... 304-384-6313 532 E
abesenyei@concord.edu
BESHARA, Alexa .... 732-255-0400 304 E
abeshara@ocean.edu
BESHARA, John .... 330-941-3527 396 C
jbeshara@ysu.edu
BESIKOF, Rudolph, J .... 818-947-2625.. 52 B
besikorj@lavc.edu
BESKID, Novella .... 803-777-0958 450 B
novella@sc.edu
BESNARD, Pamela .... 909-621-8192.. 60 A
pamela.besnard@pomona.edu
BESONG, Jeffrey, D ...... 412-392-3819 433 F
jbesong@pointpark.edu
BESPALEC, Dale, A .... 414-464-9777 542 J
dbespalec@wspp.edu
BESPALOV, Oleg .... 818-710-4292.. 51 H
bespalo@piercecollege.edu
BESS, Vivian .... 301-736-3631 216 E
vivian.bess@msbbcs.edu
BESSER, Pamela .... 502-213-2616 196 E
pam.besser@kctcs.edu
BESSESEN, Marit .... 619-594-6395.. 35 E
bessesen@mail.sdsu.edu
BESSETTE, Jeanine .... 313-577-2116 252 G
jeanine.bessette@wayne.edu
BESSETTE, Ray .... 207-941-7785 210 C
bessetter@husson.edu
BESSETTE, Roger .... 413-755-4390 233 B
rbessette@stcc.edu
BESSEY, Dean .... 207-509-7232 212 A
dbessey@unity.edu
BESSIE, Joseph .... 218-477-2415 260 B
joseph.bessie@mnstate.edu

BIERMAN, Scott ... 402-557-7245 289 B
scott.bierman@bellevue.edu
BIERMAN, Scott ... 608-363-2201 534 L
biermans@beloit.edu
BIERMANN, Mark ... 219-464-5779 174 E
mark.biermann@valpo.edu
BIERMANN, Theodore .. 734-432-5515 246 B
tbiermann@madonna.edu
BIERNBAUM, John ... 309-298-3320 163 A
j-biernbaum@wiu.edu
BIERS, Lisa, M ... 260-422-5561 167 F
lmbiers@indianatech.edu
BIES, James, B ... 605-274-4124 452 A
jim.bies@augie.edu
BIES, Susan ... 605-274-5503 452 A
susan.bies@augie.edu
BIESECKER, James ... 717-337-6700 419 C
jbieseck@gettysburg.edu
BIETELCHIES, Wade ... 517-265-5161 238 H
BIETZ, Gordon ... 423-236-2801 460 K
bietz@southern.edu
BIGARD, Heather ... 859-846-6290 198 G
hbigard@midway.edu
BIGBY, Angela, D ... 702-968-2046 296 D
abigby@roseman.edu
BIGCRANE, Michael ... 406-275-4789 288 H
michael_bigcrane@skc.edu
BIGDELI-JAHED, Fariba 502-597-6604 197 G
fariba.bigdelijahed@kysu.edu
BIGELOW, Scott ... 910-521-6351 371 D
scott.bigelow@uncp.edu
BIGELOW, Susan ... 307-674-6446 546 H
sbigelow@sheridan.edu
BIGG, Dort ... 954-763-9840.. 98 L
executivedirector@atom.edu
BIGGANE, Michael, J ... 716-851-1416 325 A
biggane@ecc.edu
BIGGER, Kimberly ... 870-248-4000.. 20 E
kim.bigger@blackrivertech.edu
BIGGER, Roberta, H ... 864-597-4040 451 J
biggerrh@wofford.edu
BIGGERS, Carla, D ... 409-944-1200 474 G
cbiggers@gc.edu
BIGGERS, Darlene ... 281-283-3000 491 E
biggers@uhcl.edu
BIGGERS, Weslynn ... 706-385-1081 130 C
weslynn.biggers@point.edu
BIGGINS, Kristin ... 401-232-6855 441 B
kbiggins@bryant.edu
BIGGIO, Nancy ... 205-726-4267.... 6 F
ncbiggio@samford.edu
BIGGS, Kristen ... 231-843-5875 252 H
kmbiggs@westshore.edu
BIGGS, Patsy ... 501-420-1201.. 19 B
patsy.biggs@arkansasbaptist.edu
BIGGS, Shirley, A ... 803-535-5268 444 D
sbiggs@claflin.edu
BIGGS, Sue, A ... 325-670-1314 474M
sbiggs@hsutx.edu
BIGGS, Susan ... 802-447-4041 503 A
sbiggs@svc.edu
BIGGS, Thomas ... 419-530-1448 394 E
thomas.biggs@utoledo.edu
BIGGS GARBUIO,
Judith ... 509-313-4100 522 L
biggsgarbuio@gonzaga.edu
BIGLIENI, Lindy ... 417-269-3083 274 A
admissions@coxcollege.edu
BIGNEY, Tracy ... 207-973-3234 212 B
bigney@maine.edu
BIGWOOD, Christine ... 401-232-6348 441 B
cbigwood@bryant.edu
BILACH, Matt ... 480-994-9244.. 17 P
mattb@swiha.edu
BILBRUCK, Tom ... 661-362-3235.. 40 H
tom.bilbruck@canyons.edu
BILCHAK, Karen ... 814-254-0471 415 F
kbilchak@pa.gov
BILDER, Kevin ... 480-517-8464.. 15 D
kevin.bilder@riosalado.edu
BILDERBACK, Rebecca . 620-365-5116 184 C
bilderback@allencc.edu
BILDERBACK, Ryan ... 620-365-5116 184 C
rbilderback@allencc.edu
BILEK, Mary Lu ... 508-985-1149 228 H
mbilek@umassd.edu
BILES, Deron ... 817-923-1921 483 E
dbiles@swbts.edu
BILGER, Cindy, L ... 570-577-1631 413 E
cbilger@bucknell.edu
BILGER, Jackie ... 570-321-4309 425 B
bilger@lycoming.edu
BILICH, Dan ... 330-867-1996 387 D
BILLARD, Trisha ... 516-876-3053 345 E
billardt@oldwestbury.edu
BILLEAUDEAU, Kim, A . 337-262-5300 208 F
kimberlyb@louisiana.edu
BILLEAUX, David ... 361-825-2393 485 F
david.billeaux@tamucc.edu
BILLECI, Celesta ... 805-893-3437.. 72 D
celesta.billeci@sa.ucsb.edu
BILLECI, Jennifer ... 925-631-4600.. 61 G
jbilleci@stmarys-ca.edu
BILLEN, Isabelle ... 405-733-7580 401 L
ibillen@rose.edu
BILLER, Gary, M ... 309-298-1814 163 A
gm-biller@wiu.edu
BILLEY, Terry, L ... 580-928-5533 402 G
terry.billey@swosu.edu
BILLHARTZ, Scott, L ... 618-537-6869 152 C
slbillhartz@mckendree.edu
BILLI, John, E ... 734-936-5214 251 C
jbilli@umich.edu
BILLICK, Tammy, N ... 971-722-7800 409 C
tbillick@pcc.edu
BILLIE, Marie, H ... 410-651-7502 219 H
mhbillie@umes.edu
BILLINGER, Kristi, M ... 785-864-7231 191 G
kristib@ku.edu
BILLINGHAM, Diana ... 352-365-3545 107 X
billingd@lssc.edu
BILLINGS, Amanda ... 214-648-2344 496 A
amanda.billings@utsouthwestern.edu
BILLINGS, Charles ... 415-485-3263.. 43 D
charles.billings@dominican.edu
BILLINGS, Christine ... 402-280-2444 290 B
ChristineBillings@creighton.edu
BILLINGS, Darron ... 731-424-3520 463 A
dbillings@jscc.edu
BILLINGS, James ... 928-541-7777.. 16 B
jbillings@ncu.edu
BILLINGSLEA, Aldo ... 408-554-5578.. 65 A
abillingslea@scu.edu
BILLINGSLEY, Anna, B . 540-654-1055 513 I
abilling@umw.edu
BILLINGSLEY, Dale, B .. 502-852-5209 201 A
dbbill01@louisville.edu
BILLINGSLEY, Jodie ... 806-742-2020 489 F
jodie.billingsley@ttu.edu
BILLINGSLEY, Linda ... 318-487-7630 202 L
linda.billingsley@lacollege.edu
BILLINGSLEY, Miron, P 919-530-6342 370 C
mpbillingsley@nccu.edu
BILLINGSLEY, Tiffany ... 870-633-4480.. 20 J
tbillingsley@eacc.edu
BILLINGTON, Suzanne .. 208-885-5867 139 C
suzib@uidaho.edu
BILLITIER, Rick ... 585-594-7777 339 F
Billitier_Rick@roberts.edu
BILLMAN, Carol ... 724-838-4204 435 E
billman@setonhill.edu
BILLMAN, Kathleen ... 773-256-0770 151 H
kbillman@lstc.edu
BILLMAN, Linda, K ... 419-289-5369 377 A
lbillman@ashland.edu
BILLMAN, Rhonda ... 330-287-1213 389 B
billman.36@osu.edu
BILLS, Andy ... 336-841-4538 357 E
abills@highpoint.edu
BILLS, Joyce ... 918-465-1777 397 L
jbills@eosc.edu
BILLS, Linda, G ... 814-332-3362 411 F
lbills@allegheny.edu
BILLS, Matt ... 262-646-6513 538 B
mbills@nashotah.edu
BILLS-WINDT, Caryn, A 312-413-8145 161 F
cabw@uic.edu
BILLUPS, Terry ... 440-646-8109 394 G
Terry.Billups@ursuline.edu
BILLUPS, Vory ... 404-225-4474 120 I
vbillups@atlantatech.edu
BILONG,
Danilo Philbert ... 671-735-5554 549 E
danilophilbert.bilong@guamcc.edu
BILOTTA, Barbara, J ... 716-880-2265 332 B
barbara.bilotta@medaille.edu
BILOTTA, Leone ... 610-917-1483 438 G
l_bilotta@valleyforge.edu
BILSKY, Edward ... 207-602-2707 213 B
ebilsky@une.edu
BILSKY, Judith ... 904-632-3105 105 A
jbilsky@fscj.edu
BIMONTE-YERGANIAN,
Maria ... 203-582-3446.. 91 E
maria.bimonte@quinnipiac.edu
BIMROSE, Irene ... 309-692-4092 152 F
ibimrose@midstate.edu
BINA, Shawn ... 218-235-2170 262 C
s.bina@vcc.edu
BINA, III, William, F ... 478-301-5570 128 G
bina_wf@mercer.edu
BINARD, Kris ... 303-404-5103.. 82 J
kris.binard@frontrange.edu
BINAU, Brad, A ... 614-235-4136 392 D
bbinau@TLSohio.edu
BINDER, Arthur ... 575-528-7070 312 D
beagle@nmsu.edu
BINDER, Holly ... 417-873-7654 274 E
hbinder@drury.edu
BINDER, Jan ... 602-285-7869.. 15 C
jan.binder@phoenixcollege.edu
BINDEWALD, Kurt ... 504-865-3226 206 A
kjbindew@loyno.edu
BINEK, Gordy ... 701-224-5697 374 E
gordon.binek@bismarckstate.edu
BINESH, Behzad ... 714-744-7099.. 38 B
binesh@chapman.edu
BING, Andrea ... 415-565-4733.. 71 B
wellesan@uchastings.edu
BING, Richard, N ... 212-998-2391 336 C
richard.bing@nyu.edu
BINGAMON, Cindy ... 314-837-6777 281 D
cbingamon@slcconline.edu
BINGEL, Laurie, A ... 618-235-2700 160 B
laurie.bingel@swic.edu
BINGER, Nancy ... 847-628-2510 149 A
nbinger@judsonu.edu
BINGHAM, Charlotte ... 806-742-3627 490 A
charlotte.bingham@ttu.edu
BINGHAM, Charlotte ... 806-742-3627 489 F
charlotte.bingham@ttu.edu
BINGHAM, Daniel, J ... 406-444-6800 287 F
daniel.bingham@umhelena.edu
BINGHAM, Doug ... 806-651-3570 486 D
dbingham@mail.wtamu.edu
BINGHAM, Janet ... 703-993-8756 507 K
bingham@gmu.edu
BINGHAM, Jeri ... 773-252-5131 156 J
jeri.bingham@resu.edu
BINGHAM, Makenzie ... 254-442-5001 470 I
makenzie.bingham@cisco.edu
BINGHAM, OP,
Mary Rose ... 615-297-7545 455 A
srmrose@aquinascollege.edu
BINGHAM, Michael ... 828-448-6020 367 B
mbingham@wpcc.edu
BINGHAM, Millard ... 601-432-6234 267 H
millard.j.bingham@jsums.edu
BINGHAM, Rachel ... 801-524-8129 498 J
rbingham@ldsbc.edu
BINGHAM, Rosie, P ... 901-678-2114 462 B
rbingham@memphis.edu
BINGHAM, Tom ... 808-956-8111 135 J
bingham@hawaii.edu
BINK, Cynthia ... 718-260-5030 320 D
cbink@citytech.cuny.edu
BINKERD, James ... 707-638-5883.. 70 B
jim.binkerd@tu.edu
BINKLEY, Kristi ... 615-514-2787 459 O
kbinkley@nossi.edu
BINKOWSKI, Marcella .. 215-637-7700 420 K
smbinkowski@holyfamily.edu
BINNEY, Craig ... 508-565-1107 237 A
cbinney@stonehill.edu
BINNEY, Diane, M ... 626-395-4638.. 31 D
dbinney@caltech.edu
BINNEY, Gayle ... 212-229-5662 334 C
binneyg@newschool.edu
BINNICKER, Paul ... 816-833-0524 178 G
binnicke@graceland.edu
BINNING, William, C ... 330-941-3436 396 C
wcbinning@ysu.edu
BINSTOCK, Jonathan ... 585-276-8903 351 D
jbinstock@mag.rochester.edu
BINSTOCK, Neal, F ... 412-397-6290 434 B
binstock@rmu.edu
BINTNER, Leslie ... 515-244-4221 175 C
bintnerl@aib.edu
BIO, Cathy ... 808-984-3515 136 H
cbio@hawaii.edu
BIONDO, Drew ... 631-451-4776 348 E
biondodr@sunysuffolk.edu
BIOTEAU, Cynthia, A ... 904-632-3222 105 A
cynthia.bioteau@fscj.edu
BIR, Chad ... 317-955-6040 171 A
cbir@marian.edu
BIRBERICK, Anne ... 815-753-0494 154 I
annie@niu.edu
BIRCH, Andrea, C ... 770-718-5325 121 G
abirch@brenau.edu
BIRCH, Barbara ... 212-960-5373 353 P
birch@yu.edu
BIRCH, Esther ... 301-736-3631 216 E
esther.birch@msbbcs.edu
BIRCH, Laura, A ... 217-420-6661 153 A
lbirch@millikin.edu
BIRCH, Mikel ... 801-957-4041 500 E
mikel.birch@slcc.edu
BIRCHAK, Chris ... 713-221-8007 491 F
birchakc@uhd.edu
BIRCHARD, Michael ... 763-424-0850 260 E
mbirchard@nhcc.edu
BIRCKBICHLER,
Carrie, J ... 724-738-2150 432 A
carrie.birckbichler@sru.edu
BIRD, Andrew ... 360-596-5219 527 B
abird@spscc.edu
BIRD, Brandon ... 206-726-5024 521 G
bbird@cornish.edu
BIRD, John ... 803-323-3374 451 I
birdj@winthrop.edu
BIRD, Keith ... 859-442-1175 196 A
keith.bird@kctcs.edu
BIRD, Lee, E ... 405-744-5328 400 C
lee.bird@okstate.edu
BIRD, Lori ... 419-267-1266 387 G
lbird@northweststate.edu
BIRD, Sheila ... 620-278-4247 191 D
sbird@sterling.edu
BIRD, Sherilyn ... 940-898-3748 490 D
sbird@twu.edu
BIRD, Su Ann ... 229-931-2110 131 E
sbird@southgatech.edu
BIRD, SuAnn ... 229-931-2110 131 E
sbird@southgatech.edu
BIRD, Vanessa ... 787-753-0039 551 L
BIRD, Veronica ... 610-917-1422 438 G
rabird@valleyforge.edu
BIRDINE, Phil ... 580-477-7700 404 D
phil.birdine@wosc.edu
BIRDSELL, David ... 646-660-6700 318 C
David.Birdsell@baruch.cuny.edu
BIRDSELL, Jo ... 858-642-8365.. 55 J
jbirdsell@nu.edu
BIRDSONG, Jeff ... 918-540-6348 398 L
jbirdsong@neo.edu
BIRDSONG, Ronnie ... 575-562-4614 310 I
ronnie.birdsong@enmu.edu
BIRDWELL, Cindy, A ... 517-264-7194 250 B
cbirdwell@sienaheights.edu
BIRDWELL, Kim ... 940-521-7101 479 K
kbirdwell@nctc.edu
BIRDWHISTELL,
Terry, L ... 859-218-1871 200 G
terry.bird@uky.edu
BIRELINE, David ... 949-214-3209.. 42 B
david.bireline@cui.edu
BIRGE, James, F ... 313-927-1208 246 D
jbirge@marygrove.edu
BIRGE, Susan, N ... 203-254-4000.. 90 E
sbirge@fairfield.edu
BIRINGER, Bobbi ... 312-261-3550 153 H
bobbi.biringer@nl.edu
BIRK, Michelle, L ... 618-235-2700 160 B
michelle.birk@swic.edu
BIRKE, Richard ... 503-370-6046 411 D
rbirke@willamette.edu
BIRKEDAHL, Patrice ... 510-659-6208.. 56 J
pbirkedahl@ohlone.edu
BIRKEDAHL, Walter ... 510-659-6216.. 56 J
wbirkedahl@ohlone.edu
BIRKENHOLTZ,
Kenneth, I ... 515-961-1512 182 I
ken.birkenholtz@simpson.edu
BIRKHEAD, Kathryn ... 479-986-4052.. 22 B
kbirkhead@nwacc.edu
BIRKHEAD, Mary ... 610-282-1100 416 I
mary.birkhead@desales.edu
BIRKHEAD, Susan ... 518-268-5130 342 B
susan.birkhead@sphp.com
BIRKHOLZ, Jane ... 419-755-4704 387 E
jbirkholz@ncstatecollege.edu
BIRKNER, Linda, M ... 501-977-2006.. 25 A
birkner@uaccm.edu
BIRKS, Robert ... 310-544-6461.. 61 I
robert.birks@usw.salvationarmy.org
BIRKS, Stacy ... 310-544-6405.. 61 I
stacy.birks@usw.salvationarmy.org
BIRKY, Ian, T ... 610-758-3880 424 B
itb0@lehigh.edu
BIRKY, Joshua ... 217-351-2376 155 I
jbirky@parkland.edu
BIRMINGHAM, Lynne ... 603-542-7744 297 D
lbirmingham@ccsnh.edu
BIRMINGHAM,
Stacy, G ... 724-458-3841 419 F
sgbirmingham@gcc.edu
BIRNBACH, David, J ... 305-284-2002 118 A
dbirnbach@miami.edu
BIRNBAUM, Ben ... 617-552-3353 224 B
ben.birnbaum@bu.edu
BIRNBAUM, Stephanie . 910-962-7187 372 A
birnbaums@uncw.edu
BIRNEY, Tyler ... 605-698-3966 453 D
tbirney@swc.tc
BIRNIE, Christine, R ... 585-385-8430 340 F
cbirnie@sjfc.edu
BIRO, Susan ... 410-386-8419 214 B
sbiro@carrollcc.edu
BIRON, Jackie ... 510-780-4500.. 50 G
jbiron@lifewest.edu
BIRON, Louise ... 518-255-5623 346 E
bironl@cobleskill.edu
BIRON, Rebecca, E ... 603-646-3113 297 G
rebecca.e.biron@dartmouth.edu
BIROS, Demetra ... 425-739-8315 523 I
demetra.biros@lwtech.edu
BIROS, Janice ... 215-895-2200 417 E
jan.biros@drexel.edu
BIRREN, Susan, J ... 781-736-3451 224 F
birren@brandeis.edu

BIRRINGER, Charles, E 920-924-3420 543 F cbirringer@morainepark.edu

BIRX, Donald, L 603-535-2210 299 E dbirx@plymouth.edu

BISBEY, CDP, Michele . 412-536-1255 422 E michele.bisbey@laroche.edu

BISCH, Debbie 620-227-9209 186 F debbieb@dc3.edu

BISCHOFF, Jeannette 916-660-7000.. 66 E jbischoff@sierracollege.edu

BISCHOFF, John 415-864-7326.. 63 A

BISCHOFF, Margaretha . 956-872-8310 482 G etybuh@southtexascollege.edu

BISCHOFF, Richard, W . 216-368-5445 378 J richard.bischoff@case.edu

BISESE, Stephen, D 804-289-8615 513 M sbisese@richmond.edu

BISH, Courtney, D 315-386-7120 347 F bish@canton.edu

BISH, Kevin 859-858-2272 192 O

BISHEL, Mary, A 219-785-5204 172 A mbishel@pnc.edu

BISHEL, Mary Ann 219-989-2510 171 L mbishel@pnc.edu

BISHOP, Brandan 616-222-1954 241 G brandan.bishop@cornerstone.edu

BISHOP, Carl 704-290-5235 366 A cbishop@spcc.edu

BISHOP, Carla 785-532-1858 188 H cbishop@ksu.edu

BISHOP, Carol 518-255-5520 346 E bishopcm@cobleskill.edu

BISHOP, Carol, M 607-746-4582 347 G bishopcm@delhi.edu

BISHOP, Carolyn 901-435-1755 457 N carolyn_bishop@loc.edu

BISHOP, Catherine, F ... 405-325-1543 403 I cbishop@ou.edu

BISHOP, Christopher .... 888-384-0849.. 26 O cjbishop@allied.edu

BISHOP, Christopher .... 970-675-3251.. 80 L christopher.bishop@cncc.edu

BISHOP, Colleen 804-828-9914 514 F cbishop4@vcu.edu

BISHOP, David 806-785-9285 496 K bishop@wbu.edu

BISHOP, Dennis 214-638-0484 476 Y dbishop@kdstudio.com

BISHOP, Donald, C 574-631-7505 174 A dbishop1@nd.edu

BISHOP, Emily, A 601-979-3975 267 H emily.a.bishop@jsums.edu

BISHOP, George 850-872-3803 105 Q gbishop@gulfcoast.edu

BISHOP, Jeffrey 314-977-6663 281 M jbisho12@slu.edu

BISHOP, Katie 518-694-7357 314 G Katie.Bishop@acphs.edu

BISHOP, Kelley 301-314-7236 219 D kbishop@umd.edu

BISHOP, Kristy 724-925-4212 439 F bishopkr@wccc.edu

BISHOP, Kristy, A 816-604-1165 277 F kristy.bishop@mcckc.edu

BISHOP, Kyle, K 240-895-4289 218 B kkbishop@smcm.edu

BISHOP, Laura 918-495-6151 401 B lbishop@oru.edu

BISHOP, Lisa, J 812-888-4274 174 F bishop@vinu.edu

BISHOP, Mike 951-552-8759.. 30 D mbishop@calbaptist.edu

BISHOP, Nancy 803-778-6638 443 I bishopnw@cctech.edu

BISHOP, Nathaniel, L ... 540-985-8484 509 D nlbishop@jchs.edu

BISHOP, Norman 606-368-6091 192 H normbishop@alc.edu

BISHOP, Pamela 614-287-2437 380 G pbishop2@cscc.edu

BISHOP, Paul 805-965-0581.. 64 N pwbishop@sbcc.edu

BISHOP, Phil 206-876-6100 526 E pbishop@theseattleschool.edu

BISHOP, Rex 770-975-4522 122 H

BISHOP, Richard 860-832-2201.. 88 D bishopr@ccsu.edu

BISHOP, Robert, H 813-974-3780 116 B robertbishop@usf.edu

BISHOP, Sandy 715-365-4564 543 G sbishop@nicoletcollege.edu

BISHOP, Selah 904-470-8952 102 A selah.bisho0911@ewc.edu

BISHOP, Shane 406-377-9421 286 F sbishop@dawson.edu

BISHOP, Steve 417-447-8152 280 C bishops@otc.edu

BISHOP, Steve 601-276-3701 270 E bishop@smcc.edu

BISHOP, Stuart 928-536-6265.. 16 E stuart.bishop@npc.edu

BISHOP, Wesley, T 504-286-5325 207 B wbishop@suno.edu

BISHOP, William 504-861-5431 206 A wgbishop@loyno.edu

BISHOP, William 916-278-7469.. 34 E william.bishop@csus.edu

BISHOP, Wilsie, S 423-439-4811 461 D bishopws@etsu.edu

BISHOP-MONROE, Robbie 404-572-3695 128 L robbie.bishopmonroe@morehouse.edu

BISIGNANO, Chris 914-251-6530 346 D chris.bisignanoi@purchase.edu

BISKUPIAK, Walter, H .. 406-447-5420 286 D bbiskupi@carroll.edu

BISMARK, Jeanie 870-235-4078.. 23 D mjbismark@saumag.edu

BISPING, Timothy 936-468-3101 484 A bispingto@sfasu.edu

BISSELL, Michelle 304-205-6640 531 A michelle.bissell@bridgevalley.edu

BISSELL, Monika 802-387-6797 502 A monikabissell@landmark.edu

BISSELL, Sandra 315-781-3312 327 G bissell@hws.edu

BISSELL PAULSON, Lisa 707-965-7362.. 57 I lpaulson@puc.edu

BISSET, Matthew, S 727-864-8482 101 P bissetms@eckerd.edu

BISSET, William, J 718-862-7200 331 H william.bisset@manhattan.edu

BISSETTE, Callie 252-399-6336 354 I cbissette@barton.edu

BISSINGER, Mary 805-482-2755.. 61 F mbissinger@stjohnsem.edu

BISSONETTE, David 218-855-8178 258 C DBissonette@clcmn.edu

BISSONETTE, Matt 507-379-3335 261 C matt.bissonette@riverland.edu

BISWAS, Harun 678-466-4240 122 J harunbiswas@clayton.edu

BITIKOFER, Scott 407-646-2121 111 H sbitikofer@rollins.edu

BITNER, Hannah 816-322-0110 272 L hannah.bitner@calvary.edu

BITNER, Scott 410-706-3822 219 E sbitner@umaryland.edu

BITNER, Teddy 816-322-0110 272 L teddy.bitner@calvary.edu

BITOK, Abe 928-724-6736.. 13 J

BITTERBAUM, Erik, J .... 607-753-2201 345 C erik.bitterbaum@cortland.edu

BITTERSFELD, Y 718-692-0208 353 H yeshivaht@gmail.com

BITTINGER, Dale 410-455-2278 219 F bittinger@umbc.edu

BITTLE, Carolyn 910-410-1751 365 B ctbittle@richmondcc.edu

BITTORF, David, C 240-500-2000 215 C dcbittorf@hagerstowncc.edu

BITZER, Michael 704-637-4466 355 H jmbitzer@catawba.edu

BITZER, Steve 715-682-4591 544 F Steve.Bitzer@witc.edu

BIUNDO, Rachel 804-594-1479 515 G rbiundo@jtcc.edu

BIVINS, Dallas 480-941-1993.. 45 J dallasbivins@ggbts.edu

BIXBY, David, E 626-815-5334.. 29 B dbixby@apu.edu

BIXBY, John, L 305-284-2211 118 A jbixby@miami.edu

BIXEL, Patricia 207-941-7144 210 C bixelp@husson.edu

BIXLER, Kirk, J 317-738-8801 166 B kbixler@franklincollege.edu

BIZON, Walter, G 248-204-3020 245 J wbizon@ltu.edu

BJARNSON, Corey 513-241-4338 376 N corey.bjarnson@antonellicollege.edu

BJELLAND, David 320-762-4407 257 O davidb@alextech.edu

BJERKE, Keith 701-231-6825 374 C keith@ndsualumni.com

BJERKLIE, Joseph, R .... 207-834-8621 212 F joseph.bjerklie@maine.edu

BJERUM, Joanna 316-284-5326 185 B jbjerum@bethelks.edu

BJOKNE, Daniel, H 515-964-0601 178 F bjokned@faith.edu

BJORDAHL, Julia 509-313-6102 522 L bjordahl@gonzaga.edu

BJORGAN, Heather 309-796-5340 140 D bjorganh@bhc.edu

BJORK, Ross 662-915-7546 270 G rbjork@olemiss.edu

BJORKLUND, Robert, B 651-638-6396 254 A robert-bjorklund@bethel.edu

BJORKMAN, David, J ... 561-297-0113 114 E dbjorkm1@fau.edu

BJORKMAN, Karen 419-530-7842 394 E karen.bjorkman@utoledo.edu

BJORN, Thorr, D 401-874-5245 442 E tbjorn@uri.edu

BJUR, Jared 909-599-5433.. 50 H jbjur@lifepacific.edu

BLACHFORD, Charles ... 304-876-5378 532 I CBLACHFO@shepherd.edu

BLACHMAN, Marvin 315-786-6542 329 G mblachman@sunyjefferson.edu

BLACK, Adam 801-863-6378 500 B blackad@uvu.edu

BLACK, Andrew 727-864-8258 101 P blackad@eckerd.edu

BLACK, Ann 505-428-1811 313 A ann.black@sfcc.edu

BLACK, Bettye, R 405-466-3294 398 E brblack@langston.edu

BLACK, Britt 630-752-5072 163 G britt.black@wheaton.edu

BLACK, Christopher, B . 260-422-5561 167 F cbblack@indianatech.edu

BLACK, Connie 208-562-3252 138 A connieblack@cwidaho.cc

BLACK, Dennis, R 716-645-2982 343 E dblack@buffalo.edu

BLACK, Diane 251-442-2209.... 9 B dblack@umobile.edu

BLACK, Ellen 843-349-5211 446 I ellen.black@hgtc.edu

BLACK, Heather 412-365-1281 415 C hblack@chatham.edu

BLACK, Jane 740-695-9500 377 F jblack@belmontcollege.edu

BLACK, Jason 205-726-3673.... 6 F jjblack@samford.edu

BLACK, Jeff 410-972-3303 218 A jeffrey.black@sjc.edu

BLACK, John Paul 252-527-6223 363 G jpblack73@lenoircc.edu

BLACK, John Paul 252-527-6223 363 G jblack@lenoircc.edu

BLACK, Joshua 864-941-8542 448 D black.j@ptc.edu

BLACK, Joshua 423-614-8370 457 M jblack@leeuniversity.edu

BLACK, Karnell 801-832-2231 501 C kblack@westminstercollege.edu

BLACK, Katherine 860-768-4103.. 92 F kablack@hartford.edu

BLACK, Kedric 801-863-8536 500 B kedric.black@uvu.edu

BLACK, Kim 970-351-1102.. 87 A kim.black@unco.edu

BLACK, Laura, L 662-329-7135 269 B llblack@muw.edu

BLACK, Laurie 802-258-3273 502 I laurie.black@worldlearning.org

BLACK, Lendley, C 218-726-7106 264 G chan@d.umn.edu

BLACK, Linda 970-351-1638.. 87 A linda.black@unco.edu

BLACK, Lynda, K 336-838-6148 367 C lynda.black@wilkescc.edu

BLACK, Mark 615-966-5709 458 C mark.black@lipscomb.edu

BLACK, Martin 724-589-2372 436 E mblack@thiel.edu

BLACK, Megan 618-544-8657 146 H blackm@iecc.edu

BLACK, Michael 404-894-2486 125 D mike.black@housing.gatech.edu

BLACK, Michael 805-922-6966.. 26 H mblack@pcpa.org

BLACK, Michael 419-267-1390 387 G mblack@northweststate.edu

BLACK, Michael, E 210-567-7103 495 B blackm@uthscsa.edu

BLACK, Michael, M 229-245-6517 133 H mmblack@valdosta.edu

BLACK, Michael, R 805-922-6966.. 26 H mblack@hancockcollege.edu

BLACK, Norman, S 808-675-3705 134 M norman.black@byuh.edu

BLACK, Rochelle, A 248-370-3682 248 K black@oakland.edu

BLACK, Sarah 318-427-4407 205 A sblack@lsua.edu

BLACK, Shaun, C 315-445-4569 330 B blacksc@lemoyne.edu

BLACK, Sul 803-705-4334 443 F blacks@benedict.edu

BLACK, Tanja 864-429-8728 450 I trblack@mailbox.sc.edu

BLACK, Thomas 650-723-1550.. 68 G thomas.black@stanford.edu

BLACK, William, N 215-204-4760 436 C william.black@temple.edu

BLACK, Willie 678-839-5344 133 F wblack@westga.edu

BLACK-GOLD, Tonia 704-637-4393 355 H tblackgo@catawba.edu

BLACKABY, Leslie 509-574-6806 529 B lblackaby@yvcc.edu

BLACKARD, Gary 417-865-2815 274 L blackardg@evangel.edu

BLACKBOURN, Richard, L 662-325-3717 269 A rlb277@msstate.edu

BLACKBURN, Amanda .. 404-233-3949 460 G ablackburn@richmont.edu

BLACKBURN, David 423-425-4495 465 E david-blackburn@utc.edu

BLACKBURN, J. Blair ... 903-923-2222 473 I bblackburn@etbu.edu

BLACKBURN, Kristi 562-860-2451.. 37 L kblackburn@cerritos.edu

BLACKBURN, Mark 605-274-4313 452 A mark.blackburn@augie.edu

BLACKBURN, Michael .. 713-500-6087 495 A Michael.R.Blackburn@uth.tmc.edu

BLACKBURN, Michele .. 401-841-6597 548 B

BLACKBURN, Sean 307-766-3296 546 K sean.blackburn@uwyo.edu

BLACKBURN, Steven 860-509-9560.. 90 G sblackburn@hartsem.edu

BLACKBURN, Terri 208-467-8673 138 H tblackburn@nnu.edu

BLACKBURN-SMITH, Jefferson 614-823-1031 390 C jblackburnsmith@otterbein.edu

BLACKFORD, Nancy 330-490-7106 395 C nblackford@walsh.edu

BLACKHURST, Anne 218-477-2243 260 B anne.blackhurst@mnstate.edu

BLACKKETTER, Donald, M 406-496-4129 288 C dblackketter@mtech.edu

BLACKLAW, Stewart 412-237-3126 415 G sblacklaw@ccc.edu

BLACKLAW, Stuart 928-717-7778.. 18 L stuart.blacklaw@yc.edu

BLACKLEY, Scott 662-407-1501 267 F jsblackley@iccms.edu

BLACKMAN, Peter 510-666-8248.. 26 C pblackman@aimc.edu

BLACKMAN, Ronda 828-277-5521 368 I rblackman@southcollegenc.edu

BLACKMON, Bruce 704-687-7010 371 B ablackm8@uncc.edu

BLACKMON, Chianti 301-447-6932 217 D blackmon@msmary.edu

BLACKMON, Luke 843-863-8004 444 B lblackmon@csuniv.edu

BLACKMON, Paul 334-420-4461.... 7 I pblackmon@trenholmstate.edu

BLACKMON, Terry, W ... 731-426-7601 457 K tblackmon@lanecollege.edu

BLACKMON, Timothy 630-752-5087 163 G chaplains.office@wheaton.edu

BLACKMORE, Lee 307-754-6067 546 I Lee.Blackmore@nwc.edu

BLACKNEY, Ken 215-895-1434 417 E Ken.Blackney@DREXEL.EDU

BLACKSHEAR, Regina, G 314-539-5123 281 H rblackshear@stlcc.edu

BLACKSMITH, Lourdes . 630-466-7900 162 K lblacksmith@waubonsee.edu

BLACKSMITH, Robin 206-546-4503 526 G rblacksmith@shoreline.edu

BLACKSTONE, Tondelaya 410-951-4265 220 C tblackstone@coppin.edu

BLACKWELDER, Mary, B 414-955-8323 537 C blackwel@mcw.edu

BLACKWELL, Amy 864-294-3496 446 F amy.blackwell@furman.edu

BLACKWELL, Ann 601-266-4568 271 B ann.blackwell@usm.edu

BLACKWELL, Bill 218-755-2590 258 B wblackwell@bemidjistate.edu

BLACKWELL, JR., Bill .. 218-335-4262 256 I bill.blackwell@lltc.edu

BLACKWELL, Billie Jo ... 908-852-1400 301 C blackwellb@centenarycollege.edu

BLACKWELL, David, W . 859-257-8939 200 G dblackwell@uky.edu

BLACKWELL, Deborah ... 704-355-5970 355 G debbie.blackwell@carolinascollege.edu

BLACKWELL, Deborah, L 956-326-2628 485 B dblackwell@tamiu.edu

BLACKWELL, Jody 405-912-9463 398 B jblackwell@hc.edu

BLACKWELL, Joe 405-789-7661 402 F joe.blackwell@swcu.edu

BLACKWELL, John 919-299-4938 369 B jblackwell@umo.edu

BLACKWELL, Kenneth ... 650-508-3502.. 56 H
safety@ndnu.edu
BLACKWELL, Mary, D ... 623-845-3305.. 14 N
m.blackwell@gccaz.edu
BLACKWELL, Samuel .... 803-780-1239 451 G
blackwell@voorhees.edu
BLACKWELL, Scott .... 601-266-4783 271 B
edward.blackwell@usm.edu
BLACKWELL, Tina .... 503-768-7680 406 H
clb@lclark.edu
BLACKWELL, Toni .... 617-266-1400 223 F
BLACKWELL-CLARK,
Edwina .... 937-376-6216 379 D
eblackwell-clark@centralstate.edu
BLACKWOOD, James .... 706-880-8050 127 N
jblackwood@lagrange.edu
BLACKWOOD, Jeremy .. 414-425-8300 538 J
jblackwood@shsst.edu
BLACKWOOD, Kathy ..... 650-358-6869.. 64 B
blackwoodk@smccd.edu
BLACKWOOD,
Rodney, B .... 806-720-7402 478 A
rod.blackwood@lcu.edu
BLADDICK, Jerry .... 618-239-6007 276 L
jbladdick@lindenwood.edu
BLADES, Dawn .... 845-257-3171 344 A
bladesd@newpaltz.edu
BLAESING, Ron .... 334-244-3758.... 2 A
rblaesin@aum.edu
BLAETTNER, Wendy ...... 830-792-7375 482 D
WLBlaettner@schreiner.edu
BLAGG, Oneida .... 307-766-3459 546 K
oblagg@uwyo.edu
BLAGG, Rosalyn .... 870-508-6128.. 19 H
rblagg@asumh.edu
BLAHNIK, Brent .... 920-465-2190 539 F
blahnikb@uwgb.edu
BLAHNIK, Jeffrey, J ...... 405-325-2252 403 I
jblahnik@ou.edu
BLAICH, Charles, F ...... 765-361-6311 175 B
blaichc@wabash.edu
BLAIFEDER, Mark .... 212-217-4020 325 C
mark_blaifeder@fitnyc.edu
BLAIN, Daniel, S .... 330-325-6261 387 F
dblain@neomed.edu
BLAIN, Judy .... 931-221-7691 461 C
blainj@apsu.edu
BLAINE, Robert .... 601-979-2127 267 H
robert.blaine@jsums.edu
BLAIR, Alan .... 413-572-5582 230 F
alan@westfield.ma.edu
BLAIR, Anthony, L .... 717-866-5775 418 E
ablair@evangelical.edu
BLAIR, Audrey, D .... 563-333-6364 182 E
BlairAudreyD@sau.edu
BLAIR, Brian .... 202-885-2842.. 94 H
bblair@american.edu
BLAIR, Brian .... 267-502-2407 413 C
brian.blair@brynathyn.edu
BLAIR, Christine .... 903-693-2075 480 A
cblair@panola.edu
BLAIR, Cinnamon .... 505-277-1806 313 H
cblair@salud.unm.edu
BLAIR, Daniel .... 304-865-6135 530 F
daniel.blair@ovu.edu
BLAIR, David, A .... 512-428-1286 481 B
davidab@stedwards.edu
BLAIR, Dena .... 734-973-3356 251 J
dlblair@wccnet.edu
BLAIR, Doug .... 574-239-8380 167 C
dblair@hcc-nd.edu
BLAIR, Eric .... 816-584-6858 280 F
eric.blair@park.edu
BLAIR, Jean .... 845-938-3615 549 A
Jean.Blair@usma.edu
BLAIR, Jeff .... 614-251-4735 388 H
blairj@ohiodominican.edu
BLAIR, John, P .... 270-745-6520 201 D
jp.blair@wku.edu
BLAIR, Kimberly, P ...... 540-365-4211 507 H
kblair@ferrum.edu
BLAIR, Linda .... 502-447-1000 199 G
lblair@spencerian.edu
BLAIR, Marilou, C .... 716-851-1832 325 A
blair@ecc.edu
BLAIR, Matthew .... 305-899-4013.. 99 B
mblair@barry.edu
BLAIR, Michael, R .... 563-387-1040 180 M
blairmic@luther.edu
BLAIR, Patricia .... 707-476-4100.. 41 C
patricia-blair@redwoods.edu
BLAIR, Paul, G .... 574-372-5100 166 D
blairp@grace.edu
BLAIR, Robbie, M .... 806-716-2336 482 F
rblair@southplainscollege.edu
BLAIR, Sara, B .... 734-764-9290 251 C
sbblair@umich.edu
BLAIR, Stephen .... 802-635-1314 504 A
stephen.blair@jsc.edu
BLAIR, Sylvia .... 410-386-8411 214 B
sblair@carrollcc.edu

BLAIR, Thomas .... 770-216-2960 127 E
tblair@ict.edu
BLAIR, JR., Thomas, S 540-375-2235 512 B
blair@roanoke.edu
BLAIR, Timothy, V .... 610-436-2739 432 B
tblair@wcupa.edu
BLAIR, Trent .... 270-745-3253 201 D
trent.blair@wku.edu
BLAIR, Wendell .... 312-553-5662 141 N
wblair@ccc.edu
BLAIR, Wray .... 301-687-4201 220 D
wnblair@frotburg.edu
BLAIS, Jessica .... 727-873-4456 116 C
blais@usfsp.edu
BLAIS, Natalie .... 413-545-2211 228 F
natalie@chancellor.umass.edu
BLAIS, Roger, N .... 918-631-2554 403 M
roger-blais@utulsa.edu
BLAISE, Butterfly, L ...... 518-564-3002 346 B
bblai001@plattsburgh.edu
BLAISING, Craig, A ...... 817-923-1921 483 E
cblaising@swbts.edu
BLAKE, Alan .... 603-271-6484 297 C
ablake@ccsnh.edu
BLAKE, Brian .... 215-895-2200 417 E
mb3545@drexel.edu
BLAKE, Chantelle .... 802-831-1308 503 E
cblake@vermontlaw.edu
BLAKE, Christopher ...... 478-471-2712 128 H
christopher.blake@mga.edu
BLAKE, Christopher, T . 631-451-4283 348 F
blakec@sunysuffolk.edu
BLAKE, Darcy .... 650-543-3901.. 54 B
dblake@menlo.edu
BLAKE, Dave .... 541-737-0546 408 F
david.blake@oregonstate.edu
BLAKE, David .... 541-737-0123 408 F
david.blake@oregonstate.edu
BLAKE, Diane, T .... 518-388-6104 350 K
blaked@union.edu
BLAKE, Erin .... 225-216-8711 202 N
blakee@mybrcc.edu
BLAKE, F. Phyllis .... 914-633-2462 328 F
pblake@iona.edu
BLAKE, Ira .... 570-389-4308 430 B
iblake@bloomu.edu
BLAKE, John .... 907-474-5188.. 10 I
jeblake@alaska.edu
BLAKE, Joi Lin .... 510-748-2273.. 59 A
jlblake@peralta.edu
BLAKE, Karen .... 203-575-8269.. 89 F
kblake@nv.edu
BLAKE, Kevin, M .... 716-888-2778 317 H
blakek@canisius.edu
BLAKE, Larry .... 859-572-1907 199 A
blakel1@nku.edu
BLAKE, Larry .... 307-766-9028 546 K
lblake3@uwyo.edu
BLAKE, Laurence .... 340-693-1017 559 B
lblake@uvi.edu
BLAKE, Lisa .... 309-341-5282 140 I
lblake@sandburg.edu
BLAKE, Lori .... 325-670-5896 474 M
lblake@hsutx.edu
BLAKE, Paul, A .... 231-591-3797 242 L
PaulBlake@ferris.edu
BLAKE, Peg .... 707-826-3361.. 35 D
plb91@humboldt.edu
BLAKE, Richard, D .... 214-887-5231 473 E
rblake@dts.edu
BLAKE, Robert, C .... 202-994-6870.. 95 D
rblake@gwu.edu
BLAKE, Scott .... 906-487-7242 242 M
scott.blake@finlandia.edu
BLAKE, Susan, N .... 470-578-3576 127 M
sblake@kennesaw.edu
BLAKE, William, J .... 330-941-2086 396 C
wjblake@ysu.edu
BLAKE-HUDSON,
Carlene .... 212-686-9040 352 H
cblakehudson@woodtobecoburn.edu
BLAKE-JUDD, Jemma ... 909-274-4750.. 54 J
jbjudd@mtsac.edu
BLAKEFIELD, Mary ...... 765-973-8522 168 A
makefi@iue.edu
BLAKELY, Craig, H .... 502-852-3297 201 A
crag.blakely@louisville.edu
BLAKELY, Dee .... 618-634-3247 159 A
deeb@shawneecc.edu
BLAKELY, Edie .... 360-992-2239 521 A
eblakely@clark.edu
BLAKELY, Robert .... 800-231-3803.. 12 G
BLAKELY, Robert .... 334-727-8011.... 8 B
BLAKELY, Zeledith .... 252-638-1587 362 A
blakelyz@cravencc.edu
BLAKEMAN, Donald, L . 502-863-8091 195 A
don_blakeman@georgetowncollege.edu
BLAKEMORE, Jerry, D .. 815-753-1000 154 I
jblakemore@niu.edu
BLAKEMORE, Patricia ... 401-739-5000 441 E
pblakemore@neit.edu

BLAKENEY, Erin .... 425-352-8307 520 D
eblakeney@cascadia.edu
BLAKESLEE, Amber .... 707-826-5702.. 35 D
amber.blakeslee@humboldt.edu
BLAKESLEE, Jim .... 920-929-2114 543 F
jblakeslee@morainepark.edu
BLAKEY, Linda .... 734-973-3536 251 J
blakey@wccnet.edu
BLAKLEY, Jackie .... 864-646-1305 449 F
jblakle1@tctc.edu
BLAKLEY, Ramon .... 478-445-1283 125 A
Ramon.Blakley@gcsu.edu
BLAKNEY, Rob .... 972-825-4643 483 D
rblakney@sagu.edu
BLALOCK, III, W. Ben .. 307-766-6300 546 K
bblalock@uwyo.edu
BLANCHARD, Andrew ... 972-883-6706 494 A
ablanch@utdallas.edu
BLANCHARD, Catherine 409-880-8375 488 F
catherine.blanchard@lamar.edu
BLANCHARD, Catherine 409-880-8355 488 E
Catherine.Blanchard@lamar.edu
BLANCHARD,
Deborah, P .... 434-544-8100 509 I
BLANCHARD, Gina, A ... 740-392-6868 387 B
gina.blanchard@mvnu.edu
BLANCHARD, Gordon ... 847-578-3232 157 G
gordon.blanchard@rosalindfranklin.edu
BLANCHARD, Jon, A .... 207-768-2795 211 C
jblanch@nmcc.edu
BLANCHARD, Joyce ...... 207-621-3403 212 D
joyceb@maine.edu
BLANCHARD, Loren, J . 562-951-4710.. 32 D
lblanchard@calstate.edu
BLANCHARD,
Marsha, L .... 573-888-0513 282 C
mblanchard@semo.edu
BLANCHARD, Myrtho ... 202-274-5946.. 97 B
mblanchard@udc.edu
BLANCHARD, Scott .... 802-322-1640 501 H
scott.blanchard@goddard.edu
BLANCHARD, Susan ...... 804-204-1218 505 B
registrar@btsr.edu
BLANCHET, Robert .... 518-255-5525 346 E
blanchrc@cobleskill.edu
BLANCHETT, Russell ..... 972-882-7520 485 E
russell.blanchett@tamuc.edu
BLANCHETT, Wanda, J . 848-932-7496 307 B
BLANCHETTE, David, M 401-456-8009 442 A
dblanchette@ric.edu
BLANCHETTE, Nick .... 715-675-3331 544 A
blanchet@ntc.edu
BLANCO, Josefina .... 818-364-7776.. 51 G
BLANCO, Mark, E .... 914-337-9300 323 A
mark.blanco@concordia-ny.edu
BLANCO, Michael .... 503-883-2616 406 I
mblanco@linfield.edu
BLAND, Amanda .... 540-234-9261 514 H
BLAND, Byron .... 650-433-3814.. 58 B
bbland@paloaltou.edu
BLAND, Constance .... 662-254-3800 269 C
cgbland@mvsu.edu
BLAND, Dorothy .... 940-367-4927 492 D
dorothy.bland@unt.edu
BLAND, Glenda .... 256-378-2004.... 2 G
gbland@cacc.edu
BLAND, James .... 937-393-3431 391 F
jbland@sscc.edu
BLAND, Janet, L .... 740-376-4741 386 A
janet.bland@marietta.edu
BLAND, John, D .... 704-687-5822 371 B
jdbland@uncc.edu
BLAND, Marissa .... 816-415-5938 285 K
blandm@william.jewell.edu
BLAND, Terry .... 662-862-8282 267 F
tgbland@iccms.edu
BLANDFORD, David, K . 989-463-7147 239 B
blandford@alma.edu
BLANDING, Bruce .... 731-424-3520 463 A
bblanding@jscc.edu
BLANEY, Diana .... 219-464-7867 174 E
diana.blaney@valpo.edu
BLANK, Dave, L .... 336-278-6705 356 F
dblank@elon.edu
BLANK, James .... 330-672-3614 384 H
jblank@kent.edu
BLANK, Michelle .... 419-783-2490 381 G
mblank@defiance.edu
BLANK, Nancy .... 303-273-3296.. 80 O
nblank@mines.edu
BLANK, Rebecca .... 608-262-9946 539 D
chancellor@news.wisc.edu
BLANKE, Raymond .... 405-733-7306 401 L
rblanke@rose.edu
BLANKENBAKER,
Zarina .... 972-238-6025 473 B
zblankenbaker@dcccd.edu
BLANKENBUEHLER,
Carla .... 304-205-6600 531 A
carla.blankenbuehler@bridgevalley.edu

BLANKENHEIM, Kim ..... 319-363-1323 181 D
kblankenheim@mtmercy.edu
BLANKENHORN, Stacie 503-359-1082 408 I
bookstore@pacificu.edu
BLANKENSHIP, Anne .... 850-644-0170 115 A
ablankenship@fsu.edu
BLANKENSHIP,
Bruce, A .... 304-457-6340 529 C
blankenshipba@ab.edu
BLANKENSHIP,
Bryan, P .... 859-858-2228 192 O
BLANKENSHIP,
Candice .... 870-762-3137.. 19 C
cblankenship@smail.anc.edu
BLANKENSHIP, Daniel .. 309-467-6301 145 A
dblankenship@eureka.edu
BLANKENSHIP, Karen ... 281-476-1850 481 E
karen.blankenship@sjcd.edu
BLANKENSHIP, Kevin ... 615-230-3428 464 B
kevin.blankenship@volstate.edu
BLANKENSHIP,
Mark, V .... 859-280-1250 198 B
mblankenship@lextheo.edu
BLANKENSHIP, Mike .... 601-605-3315 267 E
mblankenship@holmescc.edu
BLANKENSHIP, Ruth .... 276-326-4556 505 D
rblankenship@bluefield.edu
BLANKENSHIP, Tim ...... 404-471-5465 119 G
tblankenship@agnesscott.edu
BLANKENSHIP, Vince ... 903-923-2002 473 I
vblankenship@etbu.edu
BLANKINSHIP, Blair ..... 410-837-5714 221 B
bblankinship@ubalt.edu
BLANKMEYER,
Bonnie, L .... 210-567-2691 495 B
blankmeyer@uthscsa.edu
BLANKS, Janet .... 561-297-3288 114 E
blanks@fau.edu
BLANKSON, Joana .... 404-297-9522 126 A
blanksonj@gptc.edu
BLANSETT, Dewey .... 662-329-7396 269 B
dblansett@oe.muw.edu
BLANTON, Carmen .... 910-755-7332 360 E
blantonc@brunswickcc.edu
BLANTON, Jason .... 606-783-9361 198 H
j.blanton@moreheadstate.edu
BLANTON, Jay, D .... 859-257-3303 200 G
jay.blanton@uky.edu
BLANTON, Julie .... 620-665-3510 188 A
BLANTON, Ryan .... 918-463-2931 397 I
ryan.blanton@connorsstate.edu
BLANTON, Sharon .... 808-543-8000 135 C
sblanton@hpu.edu
BLANTON, Wynn .... 718-818-6470 341 G
BLAPPERT, Gerald .... 985-732-6640 203 I
BLASCHKE, Jayme, L .... 512-245-2925 489 C
jb71@txstate.edu
BLASDEL, Audra .... 317-955-6254 171 A
ablasdel@marian.edu
BLASE, Frances .... 610-896-1014 420 J
fblase@haverford.edu
BLASE, Kristen .... 603-428-2226 298 B
kblase@nec.edu
BLASIC, Michael, D ...... 607-735-1830 324 J
mblasic@elmira.edu
BLASIG, Jerry, A .... 402-557-7075 289 B
jerry.blasig@bellevue.edu
BLASINGAME, David, T 314-935-5850 285 E
david_blasingame@wustl.edu
BLASS, Tammy .... 323-226-6511.. 52 D
tblass@dhs.lacounty.gov
BLASSINGAME, Susan .. 806-720-7602 478 A
susan.blassingame@lcu.edu
BLASTING, Ralph .... 716-673-3111 343 F
ralph.blasting@fredonia.edu
BLASZAK, Julie .... 616-632-2945 239 E
jab008@aquinas.edu
BLASZKOWSKI, Remek . 561-732-4424 112 C
rblaszkowski@svdp.edu
BLATCHLEY, Richard, L 651-631-5321 265 D
rlblatchley@unwsp.edu
BLATTNER, Nancy .... 973-618-3217 300 H
nblattner@caldwell.edu
BLAU, Diane .... 248-476-1122 246 G
dblau@mispp.edu
BLAU, Kathy .... 620-276-9598 187 D
kathy.blau@gcccks.edu
BLAU, Phil .... 740-351-3137 391 C
pblau@shawnee.edu
BLAU, Thomas .... 614-251-4567 388 H
blaut@ohiodominican.edu
BLAUSTEIN, Marilyn, H 413-545-0941 228 F
blaustein@oirp.umass.edu
BLAUWKAMP, Christi ... 760-366-3791.. 42 G
cblauwkamp@cmccd.edu
BLAYLOCK, Andrew ...... 217-786-4533 151 C
andrew.blaylock@llcc.edu
BLAYLOCK, Benny .... 318-342-1603 209 A
blaylock@ulm.edu

BOCIAN, Terry, M .... 616-632-2475 239 E bociater@aquinas.edu
BOCK, Darrell, L .... 214-887-5251 473 E dbock@dts.edu
BOCK, Jim .... 610-328-8529 436 A jbock1@swarthmore.edu
BOCK, Mike .... 260-665-4878 173 D bockm@trine.edu
BOCK, Wendy .... 309-796-5180 140 D bockw@bhc.edu
BOCKSTEIN, Mindy .... 212-393-6340 319 F mbockstein@jjay.cuny.edu
BOCZER, Amy .... 203-254-4000.. 90 E aboczer@fairfield.edu
BODDIE-LAVAN, Jeanine .... 334-244-3610.... 2 A jblavan@aum.edu
BODDY, Michael .... 314-252-3132 274 K mboddy@eden.edu
BODE, Gerhard .... 314-505-7103 273 G bodeg@csl.edu
BODE, Lori .... 636-949-4925 276 L lbode@lindenwood.edu
BODEGA, María .... 787-164-1912 554 C maria_dolores_bodega_@intersg.edu
BODEN, Alison .... 609-258-6244 305 C aboden@princeton.edu
BODEN, Janet .... 773-256-0744 151 H jboden@lstc.edu
BODEN, Michael .... 845-431-8952 324 D michael.boden@sunydutchess.edu
BODIE, Cindy, H .... 336-315-8660 355 F cbodie@carolinagrad.edu
BODIE, Darryl, A .... 336-315-8660 355 F dbodie@carolinagrad.edu
BODIN, Susan .... 312-915-7454 151 E sbodin@luc.edu
BODINE, Kasey .... 706-385-1000 130 C kasey.bodine@point.edu
BODINE AL-SHARIF, Mary .... 405-682-1611 399 K mary.bodineal-sharif@occc.edu
BODMER, Brad, R .... 518-783-2315 342 H
BODNAR, Molly .... 719-389-6351.. 79 M molly.bodnar@coloradocollege.edu
BODNAR, Richard .... 718-997-5191 320 E richard.bodnar@qc.edu
BODONI, June .... 978-867-4217 227 A june.bodoni@gordon.edu
BODRATO, Kelli .... 718-405-3234 322 A kelli.bodrato@mountsaintvincent.edu
BODRATTI, Robert .... 518-828-4181 322 E bodratti@sunycgcc.edu
BODRI, Michael .... 706-864-1958 133 A michael.bodri@ung.edu
BODUR, Niyazi .... 516-686-7724 335 F nbodur@nyit.edu
BODVARSSON, Orn .... 916-278-6504.. 34 E obbodvarsson@csus.edu
BOE, Eugene .... 218-739-3375 256 K eboe@lbs.edu
BOE, Susan .... 503-255-0332 407 D sboe@multnomah.edu
BOECK, Mark .... 515-294-8959 175 G mboeck@foundation.iastate.edu
BOECKENSTEDT, Jon .... 312-362-7143 143 G jboecken@depaul.edu
BOECKERMANN, Gabriele .... 513-569-1550 379 K gabriele.boeckermann@cincinnatistate.edu
BOECKERS, Alice .... 920-832-6525 536 R alice.o.boeckers@lawrence.edu
BOECKMAN, Linda, A ... 717-262-2006 440 D linda.boeckman@wilson.edu
BOEDEKER, Katrina, P .. 260-399-7700 174 C kboedeker@sf.edu
BOEDER, John, C .... 507-354-8221 257 A boederjc@mlc-wels.edu
BOEGEL, Tom .... 415-239-3360.. 39 A tboegel@ccsf.edu
BOEH, Thomas .... 559-244-5641.. 33 D tboeh@csufresno.edu
BOEH, William, S .... 409-772-9803 495 E wsboeh@utmb.edu
BOEHLER, Susan .... 217-732-3155 150 H sboehler@lincolncollege.edu
BOEHLKE, Cassandra ... 219-785-5748 172 A cboehlke@pnc.edu
BOEHM, Beth, A .... 502-852-3975 201 A baboeh01@louisville.edu
BOEHM, Christopher .... 205-552-1222.... 3 C chris.boehm@ecacolleges.com
BOEHM, J. J .... 989-964-4055 249 G jjboehm@svsu.edu
BOEHM, Michael .... 574-284-4610 172 G mboehm@saintmarys.edu
BOEHM, Michael, J .... 614-292-5881 389 A boehm.1@osu.edu
BOEHM, Pamela .... 254-659-7501 475 A pboehm@hillcollege.edu
BOEHM-DAVIS, Deborah .... 703-993-8720 507 K dbdavis@gmu.edu
BOEHMAN, Joseph, R .. 804-289-8000 513 M jboehman@richmond.edu
BOEHME, Michael, J .... 320-234-8509 261 B mike.boehme@ridgewater.edu
BOEHMER, Ann .... 636-584-6679 274 J ann.boehmer@eastcentral.edu
BOEHMER, Brian .... 740-364-9535 378 L bboehmer@newark.ohio-state.edu
BOEHMER, Robert, G ... 478-289-2027 124 B bboehmer@ega.edu
BOEHMLER, Brook, S ... 641-422-4212 181 E boehmbro@niacc.edu
BOEHNE, Cheryl .... 618-545-3184 149 C cboehne@kaskaskia.edu
BOEHNE, Rhonda .... 618-545-3022 149 C rboehne@kaskaskia.edu
BOEHNER, Joel, D .... 574-807-7116 164 F joel.boehner@bethelcollege.edu
BOEKER, Cathy .... 979-830-4455 469 F cboeker@blinn.edu
BOELCKE, Renee, E .... 269-337-7248 244 I Renee.Boelcke@kzoo.edu
BOELE, Erin .... 599-278-2345.. 33 D eboele@csufresno.edu
BOENIG, Tobin, R .... 409-747-8702 495 E trboenig@utmb.edu
BOENINGER, Candace .. 740-593-4100 389 H boeningc@ohio.edu
BOER, Keri .... 828-669-8012 359 K kboer@montreat.edu
BOERA, Pat .... 802-865-5445 501 F boerap@champlain.edu
BOERBOOM, Chris .... 701-231-7867 374 C chris.boerboom@ndsu.edu
BOERGERMANN, Gary .. 918-343-7625 401 I gboergermann@rsu.edu
BOERLAGE, Andrew (Pete) .... 831-656-3037 548 A aboerlage@nps.edu
BOERNER, Anne .... 503-297-5544 408 A aboerner@ocac.edu
BOERNER, William .... 716-673-3358 343 F william.boerner@fredonia.edu
BOERSIG, Pam .... 612-332-3361 253 I pboersig@aii.edu
BOERSMA, Paul, H .... 616-395-7145 244 A boersma@hope.edu
BOERST, Connie, J .... 920-433-6622 534 K connie.boerst@bellincollege.edu
BOESCH, Donald .... 410-228-9250 219 G
BOESEL, Terry .... 714-997-6789.. 38 B boesel@chapman.edu
BOETTCHER, Marlene, F .... 719-384-6824.. 84 I marlene.boettcher@ojc.edu
BOEVE, Traci .... 402-461-7789 290 G tboeve@hastings.edu
BOEVINGLOH, Linda .... 636-481-3488 276 E lboeving@jeffco.edu
BOFFI, William .... 508-213-2428 235 C william.boffi@nichols.edu
BOGAGE, Alan .... 410-386-8339 214 B abogage@carrollcc.edu
BOGAN, Ivory .... 601-984-1400 270 H bogan@umc.edu
BOGAN, Jenny, G .... 864-833-8700 448 E jgbogan@presby.edu
BOGAN, Jeremy .... 518-454-5155 322 C boganj@strose.edu
BOGAN, Kim .... 619-849-2481.. 59 K kimbogan@pointloma.edu
BOGAN, Yolanda .... 850-599-3145 114 D yolanda.bogan@famu.edu
BOGARD, Karen .... 870-543-5900.. 23 C kbogard@seark.edu
BOGARD, Michele, K .... 402-280-2775 290 B bogard@creighton.edu
BOGART, Denise .... 229-333-5709 133 H dbogart@valdosta.edu
BOGART, Marti, S .... 630-637-5355 154 F msbogart@noctrl.edu
BOGART, William, T .... 865-981-8101 458 E tom.bogart@maryvillecollege.edu
BOGATSKI, Anatole .... 510-780-4500.. 50 G abogatski@lifewest.edu
BOGDALEK, Steven, J .. 248-204-3925 245 J sbogdalek@ltu.edu
BOGDAN, Sharon .... 410-532-5332 217 F sbogdan@ndm.edu
BOGDANOV, Anna .... 215-728-4177 427 H anna.bogdanov@jevs.org
BOGEN, David .... 410-669-9200 216 F
BOGEN, Janice, M .... 215-503-4335 436 F janice.bogen@jefferson.edu
BOGER, John, C .... 919-962-4417 371 A jcboger@email.unc.edu
BOGER-HAWKINS, Caitlin .... 860-738-6441.. 89 G cboger-hawkins@nwcc.commnet.edu
BOGERT, Brian .... 570-408-4015 440 B brian.bogert@wilkes.edu
BOGGAN, Jeff .... 678-717-3570 133 A jeff.boggan@ung.edu
BOGGAN, Laura, K .... 423-652-4707 457 J lkboggan@king.edu
BOGGESS, Kendra .... 304-384-5224 532 E president@concord.edu
BOGGIE, Mark .... 520-515-5451.. 13 B boggiem@cochise.edu
BOGGIO, Pamela, J .... 508-213-2483 235 C pamela.boggio@nichols.edu
BOGGS, Beverly .... 931-221-6540 461 C boggsb@apsu.edu
BOGGS, Bonnie, B .... 734-384-4268 247 C bboggs@monroeccc.edu
BOGGS, Brad .... 662-620-5302 267 F bdboggs@iccms.edu
BOGGS, Debra .... 260-481-6807 168 D debra.boggs@ipfw.edu
BOGGS, Gretchen, M ... 410-250-1088 219 H contedoc@ezy.net
BOGGS, Jill .... 260-665-4270 173 D boggsj@trine.edu
BOGGS, John .... 281-998-6150 481 G john.boggs@sjcd.edu
BOGGS, Paul, R .... 903-233-3981 477 G paulboggs@letu.edu
BOGGS, Rainie .... 859-253-3637 194 M rainie.boggs@frontier.edu
BOGH, Wayne .... 909-389-3309.. 62 B wbogh@craftonhills.edu
BOGHOSSIAN, Fikru ..... 443-885-3160 217 C fikru.boghossian@morgan.edu
BOGLE, Barry, J .... 915-831-7116 473 J bbogle@epcc.edu
BOGLE, Brittany .... 408-498-5137.. 40 E bbogle@cogswell.edu
BOGLE, Christy .... 704-991-0370 366 D cbogle9678@stanly.edu
BOGLE, Darcy .... 661-763-7889.. 69 E dbogle@taftcollege.edu
BOGLE, Yvonne .... 413-782-1594 238 A yvonne.bogle@wne.edu
BOGLEY, John, W .... 509-527-5979 528 F bogleyj@whitman.edu
BOGLIN, Amber .... 404-527-4540 122 D ahamilton@carver.edu
BOGNA, Gina .... 661-362-3376.. 40 H gina.bogna@canyons.edu
BOGNER, Drew .... 516-323-3200 333 E dbogner@molloy.edu
BOGOMILSKY, Moshe .. 718-434-0784 317 L
BOGOSINA, Deborah ..... 212-229-5600 334 C deborah.bogosian@newschool.edu
BOGUE, Michelle .... 269-782-1486 250 D mbogue@swmich.edu
BOHACH, Gregory .... 662-325-3006 269 A gbohach@dafvm.msstate.edu
BOHACZ, Candy .... 269-467-9945 243 A cbohacz@glenoaks.edu
BOHAKER, Linda, A ..... 618-374-5495 156 C linda.bohaker@principia.edu
BOHAM, Kenneth, A ..... 828-726-2211 360 F kboham@cccti.edu
BOHAM, Sandra .... 406-275-4972 288 H sandra_boham@skc.edu
BOHAN, David .... 973-378-9801 308 C david.bohan@shu.edu
BOHANNON, Betsy .... 859-622-1500 194 L betsy.bohannon@eku.edu
BOHANON, Janet .... 770-531-6315 128 A jbohanon@laniertech.edu
BOHASKA, Chris .... 410-225-2490 216 F cbohaska@mica.edu
BOHL, Kyle .... 616-538-2330 243 C kbohl@gbcol.edu
BOHLEKE, Briant .... 717-334-6286 424 F bbohleke@ltsg.edu
BOHLEN, Greg .... 303-273-3333.. 80 O gbohlen@imines.edu
BOHLENDER, Kristi .... 970-491-6533.. 81 D kristie.bohlender@colostate.edu
BOHMAN, Andreas .... 509-963-2499 520 E BohmanA@cwu.edu
BOHMAN, Bob .... 813-393-3675 131 F bbohman@southuniversity.edu
BOHMFALK, Rachel, C . 956-721-5816 477 C rbohmfalk@laredo.edu
BOHN, Bill .... 541-506-6090 405 C bbohn@cgcc.edu
BOHN, Michael .... 513-556-0626 393 B bearcAD@ucmail.uc.edu
BOHN, Nicole .... 415-405-3583.. 36 A nbohn@sfsu.edu
BOHNENBLUST, Delyna 620-421-6700 189 B delynab@labette.edu
BOHNENKAMP, John ... 502-231-5221 198 D jbohnenkamp@myLBC.us
BOHNET, Sandra .... 269-488-4409 244 J sbohnet@kvcc.edu
BOHNETT, Sally .... 419-251-8985 386 C sally.bohnett@mercycollege.edu
BOHNSACK, Jennifer .... 602-331-7500.. 12 C jbohnsack@aii.edu
BOHNY, David .... 973-618-3440 300 H dbohny@caldwell.edu
BOHREN, Karen .... 231-591-2607 242 L KarenBohren@ferris.edu
BOHRER, Joseph, S ..... 610-330-3161 423 A bohrerj@lafayette.edu
BOHRER, Robert, E ...... 717-337-6823 419 C rbohrer@gettysburg.edu
BOHRNSTEDT, Jennifer . 281-649-3321 475 B jbohrnstedt@hbu.edu
BOICE, Daniel .... 563-876-3353 177 I dboice@dwci.edu
BOICE, Nor .... 253-752-2020 522 K finaid@faithseminary.edu
BOICE-PARDEE, Heath ... 585-475-2268 339 G hbpvsa@rit.edu
BOIES, Brandy .... 540-868-7161 515 H bboies@lfcc.edu
BOIES, Chris .... 540-868-7129 515 H cboies@lfcc.edu
BOIKE, Allan .... 216-916-7468 384 H aboike1@kent.edu
BOIKE, Kristine .... 763-424-0964 260 E kboike@nhcc.edu
BOILINI, Laura, L .... 386-312-4199 111 K lauraboilini@sjrstate.edu
BOISE, Craig .... 216-687-2300 380 D c.boise@law.csuohio.edu
BOISEN, Beth .... 715-232-1695 541 B boisenb@uwstout.edu
BOISJOLY, Russell, P ... 716-673-4813 343 F russell.boisjoly@fredonia.edu
BOISSELLE, Dave .... 757-352-4757 511 G daviboi@regent.edu
BOISSELLE, Juliet .... 315-781-3952 327 G jhboiselle@hws.edu
BOISSELLE, Vincent ...... 315-781-3549 327 G boisselle@hws.edu
BOISSONEAULT, Susan 508-678-2811 231 B susan.boissoneault@bristolcc.edu
BOISVERT, Craig .... 304-647-6363 533 B cboisvert@osteo.wvsom.edu
BOISVERT, David .... 704-463-3112 367 F david.boisvert@pfeiffer.edu
BOITNOTT, Tina .... 903-886-5110 485 E tina.boitnott@tamuc.edu
BOJONCA, Victoria .... 317-299-0333 173 C
BOKOSKI, Leslie .... 610-647-4400 421 B lbokoski@immaculata.edu
BOKSAN, George .... 610-861-1421 426 H boksang@moravian.edu
BOKTOR, Monir .... 949-794-9090.. 68 F mboktor@stanbridge.edu
BOLA, William .... 207-206-2365 213 B wbola@une.edu
BOLA, William .... 207-602-2365 213 B wbola@une.edu
BOLAND, Carolyn .... 513-244-4717 387 A carolyn.boland@msj.edu
BOLAND, Kristine .... 419-783-2469 381 G kboland@defiance.edu
BOLAND, Mary, G .... 808-956-8522 135 J mgboland@hawaii.edu
BOLAND, Mary Kate ..... 610-647-4400 421 B mboland@immaculata.edu
BOLAND-CHASE, Ann ... 570-961-4728 425 D chase@marywood.edu
BOLANOS, Andelys .... 920-923-7148 537 A abolanos@marianuniversity.edu
BOLDEN, Errol .... 410-951-3542 220 C ebolden@coppin.edu
BOLDEN, Michele .... 815-825-2086 149 E michele.bolden@kishwaukeecollege.edu
BOLDMAN, Denise .... 937-484-1243 394 F dboldman@urbana.edu
BOLDREY, Penny .... 989-358-7297 239 C boldreyp@alpenacc.edu
BOLDT, Deborah .... 505-428-1704 313 A deborah.boldt@sfcc.edu
BOLDT, William .... 702-895-5895 295 G william.boldt@unlv.edu
BOLDUC, Darlene, R ..... 802-626-6490 504 B darlene.bolduc@lyndonstate.edu
BOLDUC, Michael, C .... 561-237-7180 108 E mbolduc@lynn.edu
BOLE, John .... 406-377-9416 286 F jbole@dawson.edu
BOLEK, Catherine .... 410-651-6714 219 H csbolek@umes.edu
BOLENBAUGH, Peter .... 406-657-1106 288 G peter.bolenbaugh@rocky.edu
BOLERATZ, Jonathan .... 814-332-5206 411 F jboleratz@allegheny.edu

BOOKER, Latoya 616-632-2455 239 E
latoya.booker@aquinas.edu
BOOKER, Lonnie 785-827-5541 189 A
lonnie.booker@kwu.edu
BOOKER, Marc 205-934-9847 8 F
mbooker@uab.edu
BOOKER, Mary 909-621-8205 60 A
mary.booker@pomona.edu
BOOKER, Michael 636-481-3312 276 E
mbooker@jeffco.edu
BOOKER, RhaeAnn 616-698-7111 241 I
rbooker@davenport.edu
BOOKER, Sid 814-732-2810 430 G
sbooker@edinboro.edu
BOOKER, Steve 407-646-2316 111 H
sbooker@rollins.edu
BOOKER, Steve 407-646-2395 111 H
sbooker@rollins.edu
BOOKER, Suzy 865-981-8203 458 E
suzy.booker@maryvillecollege.edu
BOOKMAN, Douglas 919-573-5350 368 H
BOOKOUT, James 334-670-3617 8 A
jbookout@troy.edu
BOOKOUT, Jeff 870-358-8614 19 I
jeff_bookout@asun.edu
BOOKSTAVER, John 636-922-8722 281 C
jbookstaver@stchas.edu
BOOKWALTER, Robert 304-696-2350 532 H
bookwalt@marshall.edu
BOOM, Philip 563-588-8000 178 E
pboom@emmaus.edu
BOOMGAARDEN,
Donald, R 570-941-7520 438 F
donald.boomgaarden@scranton.edu
BOOMS, Carole 734-432-5811 246 B
cbooms@madonna.edu
BOONE, Becky 843-349-5274 446 I
becky.boone@hgtc.edu
BOONE, Cheryl, A 513-585-0032 379 H
cheryl.boone@thechristcollege.edu
BOONE, Christopher, G 480-965-2236 11 J
christopher.g.boone@asu.edu
BOONE, Dan 615-248-1251 464 E
dboone@trevecca.edu
BOONE, Debbie 334-291-4927 2 H
debbie.boone@cv.edu
BOONE, J. Allen 901-843-3760 460 F
boone@rhodes.edu
BOONE, John, B 919-866-5923 366 H
jbboone@waketech.edu
BOONE, Kathleen, C 716-839-8301 323 F
kboone@daemen.edu
BOONE, Kyle, N 512-505-3037 475 G
knboone@htu.edu
BOONE, Loren 320-308-3151 261 E
ljboone@stcloudstate.edu
BOONE, M. Scott 404-872-3593 121 A
sboone@johnmarshall.edu
BOONE, Nick 402-941-6016 291 I
boone@midlandu.edu
BOONE, Rebecca 318-357-5621 208 D
booner@nsula.edu
BOONE, Steve, E 501-686-7348 24 B
seboone@uams.edu
BOONSTRA, Brenda 706-776-0103 130 B
bboonstra@piedmont.edu
BOOR, Kathryn, J 607-255-2241 323 C
kjb4@cornell.edu
BOOREN, Diane 303-457-2757 82 H
diane.booren@zenith.org
BOOROS, Deborah 610-282-1100 416 I
deborah.booros@desales.edu
BOOS, Jean 843-355-4167 451 H
boosj@wiltech.edu
BOOSINGER,
Timothy, R 334-844-5771 1 G
provost@auburn.edu
BOOSKA, Karry 802-728-1320 504 C
kbooska@vtc.edu
BOOSTER, Richard 541-683-5141 406 B
dbooster@gutenberg.edu
BOOTE, Marlys 319-335-2043 175 H
marlys-boote@uiowa.edu
BOOTH, Ann, B 304-367-4047 532 F
Ann.Booth@fairmontstate.edu
BOOTH, Derrick 916-484-8361 52 I
boothd@arc.losrios.edu
BOOTH, Eric, W 770-720-9198 130 E
ewb@reinhardt.edu
BOOTH, H. Austin 716-645-0983 343 E
abooth@buffalo.edu
BOOTH, Jane, E 212-854-0286 322 F
jeb@gc.columbia.edu
BOOTH, Jennifer 803-754-4100 445 D
BOOTH, Jocelyn 630-844-4647 139 L
jbooth@aurora.edu
BOOTH, LaQuita 334-229-4124 1 D
lbooth@alasu.edu
BOOTH, Molly 205-391-3978 7 A
mbooth@sheltonstate.edu
BOOTH, Paige 512-448-8429 481 B
paigeb@stedwards.edu
BOOTH, Ronnie, L 864-646-1773 449 F
rlbooth@tctc.edu
BOOTH, Scott 336-734-7317 362 F
sbooth@forsythtech.edu
BOOTH, Scott 614-947-6592 382 H
scott.booth@franklin.edu
BOOTH, Susan, A 573-629-3002 275 F
sbooth@hlg.edu
BOOTH, Susan, L 540-224-4640 509 D
slbooth1@jchs.edu
BOOTH, Terry, L 803-778-6624 443 I
boothtl@cctech.edu
BOOTH, William 410-462-8450 213 G
wbooth@bccc.edu
BOOTHBY, Mandy 712-749-2123 176 D
boothbym@bvu.edu
BOOTHBY, Rebecca 318-342-1982 209 A
ulm@campuscornerinc.com
BOOTHE, Alan 334-242-7710 8 A
aboothe@troy.edu
BOOTHE, Jason 435-652-7526 499 M
boothe@dixie.edu
BOOTHE, Shane 832-252-4646 470 L
shane.boothe@cbshouston.edu
BOOTMAN, J, L 520-626-1657 18 E
bootman@email.arizona.edu
BOOZANG, Bill 617-738-2402 235 B
bill.boozang@newbury.edu
BOOZANG, Kathleen 973-642-8750 308 C
kathleen.boozang@shu.edu
BOOZE, David 714-484-7432 56 E
dbooze@cypresscollege.edu
BOPKO, Patricia 909-652-6152 38 A
patricia.bopko@chaffey.edu
BOPP, Jodi, L 740-368-3324 390 B
jlbopp@owu.edu
BOPP, Ruthane, I 847-735-5025 149 H
bopp@lakeforest.edu
BOQUET, OSB,
Gregory, M 985-867-2232 206 J
rector@sjasc.edu
BOQUETTE, Troy 810-762-0243 247 F
troy.boquette@mcc.edu
BORAGINE, Richard 727-816-3443 110 B
boragir@phsc.edu
BORASI, Raffaella 585-275-3950 351 D
raffaella.borasi@rochester.edu
BORCHERDING, Alan 314-505-7763 273 G
borcherdinga@csl.edu
BORCHERS, Mary Ellen 614-236-6814 378 H
mborchers@capital.edu
BORCHERS, Mitch 913-469-8500 188 E
mborchers@jccc.edu
BORCHERS, Tim 402-872-2222 292 C
tborchers@peru.edu
BORCHERT, Anne, M 216-368-0242 378 J
amb14@case.edu
BORCK, Pat 478-471-2865 128 H
pat.borck@mga.edu
BORDEAU, Topher 802-586-7711 503 B
tbordeau@sterlingcollege.edu
BORDEAUX, Lionel 605-856-5880 453 B
lionel.bordeaux@sintegleska.edu
BORDEAUX, Mark 605-856-5880 453 B
mark.bordeaux@sintegleska.edu
BORDELON, Deborah 708-534-8045 145 D
dbordelon@govst.edu
BORDEN, Donald 856-227-7200 301 A
dborden@camdencc.edu
BORDEN, Jeff 352-588-8310 111 L
jeff.borden@saintleo.edu
BORDEN, M. Paige 407-823-4765 115 C
paige.borden@ucf.edu
BORDEN, Robert 216-421-7467 380 B
rborden@cia.edu
BORDEN, Sue 207-947-4591 209 G
sborden@bealcollege.edu
BORDEN, Susan 410-626-2506 218 A
susan.borden@sjc.edu
BORDER, Debra 402-481-3804 289 C
deb.border@bryanhealthcollege.edu
BORDERS, Julianna, G 419-334-8400 392 A
jborders01@terra.edu
BORDERS, Katrina 713-221-2740 491 F
bordersk@uhd.edu
BORDERS, Marianne 803-981-7320 451 K
borders@sctechsystem.edu
BORDIN, Cristina, L 512-464-8893 481 B
cristinb@stedwards.edu
BORDONARO, Vilma 914-594-4900 335 H
vilma_bordonaro@nymc.edu
BORELLI, Alysa 530-541-4660 50 A
borelli@ltcc.edu
BORELLI, Gina 714-542-8086 29 H
gborelli@bristoluniversity.edu
BORELLI, Tricia 563-588-7024 180 L
tricia.borelli@loras.edu
BOREN, David, L 405-325-3916 403 I
dboren@ou.edu
BOREN, J. B 806-352-5207 496 K
borenjb@wbu.edu
BOREN, Laura 254-968-9085 485 A
lboren@tarleton.edu
BORER,
Ralph (Sam), J 402-557-7355 289 B
sam.borer@bellevue.edu
BORES, Gerald 503-552-2007 407 F
gbores@ncnm.edu
BORFITZ, Joanne 315-228-7120 321 H
jborfitz@colgate.edu
BORGE, Keith 914-654-5552 322 B
kborge@cnr.edu
BORGEN, Beth 920-565-1023 536 Q
borgembm@lakeland.edu
BORGER, Jennika 610-861-1583 426 H
borgerj@moravian.edu
BORGER, Patricia, A 414-229-3013 540 A
pborger@uwm.edu
BORGES, Daniel 619-482-6336 68 D
dborges@swccd.edu
BORGES, Eduardo 281-649-3299 475 B
eborges@hbu.edu
BORGES, Nikki 313-993-1538 250 H
borgesnl@udmercy.edu
BORGES, Silvia 305-821-3333 104 C
sborges@fnu.edu
BORGIA, Tom 304-293-6390 533 D
aborgia@hsc.wvu.edu
BORGLUM, Karen, M 407-582-3455 118 I
kborglum@valenciacollege.edu
BORGMAN,
Cathleen, M 203-254-4081 90 E
cborgman@fairfield.edu
BORGMAN, Kenneth, L 989-463-7314 239 B
borgman@alma.edu
BORGMANN-INGWERSEN,
Marian 402-465-2415 292 E
mborgman@nebrwesleyan.edu
BORGOGNONI,
Mary, E 716-286-8352 336 E
meb@niagara.edu
BORGONAH, Darryl 512-245-2550 489 C
djb129@txstate.edu
BORGSMILLER,
Stephen 573-472-3210 282 C
sjborgsmiller@semo.edu
BORGUS, Donna 585-389-2471 334 B
dborgus8@naz.edu
BORIA, Selina, M 508-854-4203 232 F
sboria@qcc.mass.edu
BORICH, Joe 419-448-3438 392 B
borichj@tiffin.edu
BORING, David 231-348-6838 248 A
dboring@ncmich.edu
BORIS, Barbara, A 610-409-3605 438 H
bboris@ursinus.edu
BORISKIN, Ronnie 212-749-2802 331 I
rboriskin@msmnyc.edu
BORKOVICH, Bruce 231-591-5000 242 L
BruceBorkovich@ferris.edu
BORKOWSKI,
Donald, V 207-725-3947 209 H
dborkows@bowdoin.edu
BORKOWSKI, Ellen, Y 518-388-6293 350 K
borkowse@union.edu
BORLAND, Denise 715-422-5502 543 D
denise.borland@mstc.edu
BORN, Lauren 610-917-1465 438 G
leborn@valleyforge.edu
BORN, Matthew 610-436-2231 432 B
mborn@wcupa.edu
BORNE, Jade 817-515-5636 484 B
jade.borne@tccd.edu
BORNE, Jade 817-515-4742 484 B
jade.borne@tccd.edu
BORNEMANN, Jeffrey 414-955-8793 537 C
jbornema@mcw.edu
BORNHOLDT, Claudia 202-319-5115 95 A
bornholdt@cua.edu
BORNHORST, Mary 937-778-7837 381 K
mbornhorst@edisonohio.edu
BORNSTEIN, Eva 718-960-8232 319 C
eva.bornstein@lehman.cuny.edu
BORNSTEIN, Leah, L 970-339-6210 78 J
leah.bornstein@aims.edu
BORNSTEIN, Rachel 802-225-3318 502 F
rachel.bornstein@neci.edu
BORNUS, Susan 651-523-2929 256 B
sbornus@hamline.edu
BOROFSKY, David 239-513-1122 106 E
dborofsky@hodges.edu
BORONICO, Jess 516-686-7838 335 F
jboronic@nyit.edu
BORONICO, L. Christie 203-576-5238 91 H
linda.boronico@stvincentscollege.edu
BOROS, Barbara 480-461-7128 15 A
barbara.boros@mesacc.edu
BOROS-KAZAI, Mary 608-363-2640 534 L
boroskaz@beloit.edu
BOROUGHS, SJ,
Philip, L 508-793-2525 225 C
pborough@holycross.edu
BOROWICK, Matthew 973-378-9822 308 C
matthew.borowick@shu.edu
BOROWICK, Matthew 973-378-9847 308 C
matthew.borowick@shu.edu
BOROWICZ, Laurie 715-675-3331 544 A
borowiczl@ntc.edu
BOROWICZ, Mark 715-675-3331 544 A
Borowicz@ntc.edu
BORR, Mike 701-231-9535 374 C
mike.borr@ndsu.edu
BORRAS, Belma 787-738-2161 557 G
belma.borras@upr.edu
BORREGO, Paul 210-486-2194 467 B
pborrego4@alamo.edu
BORREGO, Susan, E 810-762-3322 251 E
sborrego@umflint.edu
BORREN, Tammy 931-540-2553 462 E
tborren@columbiastate.edu
BORSCH, Elva 832-813-6571 477 I
elva.borsch@lonestar.edu
BORSIG, Jim 662-329-7100 269 B
jbborsig@muw.edu
BORSKI, Brian 972-860-4116 472 C
bborski@dcccd.edu
BORST, Andrew 309-295-1414 163 A
AJ-Borst@wiu.edu
BORST, Charlotte, G 208-459-5502 137 J
cborst@collegeofidaho.edu
BORSZ, Michael 315-498-2097 337 F
m.a.borsz@sunyocc.edu
BORTH, Adam 620-417-1600 191 A
adam.borth@sccc.edu
BORTHWICK, Kristen 512-492-3011 468 A
registrar@aoma.edu
BORTMAN, Lisa 310-506-4393 58 H
lisa.bortman@pepperdine.edu
BORTMAN, Walter, J 818-364-7800 51 G
bortmawj@lamission.edu
BORTON, Jeffrey 734-462-4400 250 A
jborton@schoolcraft.edu
BORTUNK, Ayelet 305-653-8770 119 E
abortunk@lecfl.com
BORTZ, Carolyn 610-861-5434 427 F
cbortz@northampton.edu
BORUFF-JONES, Polly 765-455-9343 168 B
pboruffj@iuk.edu
BORUM, Art 618-545-3401 149 C
aborum@kaskaskia.edu
BORUSZEWSKI,
Richard 517-371-5140 252 J
boruszer@cooley.edu
BOS, James 712-722-6030 177 J
jim.bos@dordt.edu
BOS, Saskia 212-353-4203 323 B
sbos@cooper.edu
BOSACK-KOSEK,
Carol, A 570-408-5963 440 B
carol.bosack@wilkes.edu
BOSARGE, Erin 251-626-3303 8 C
ebosarge@ussa.edu
BOSCH, Agnes 787-764-0000 558 E
agnes.bosch@upr.edu
BOSCH, Debbie 405-585-4120 399 I
debbie.blue@okbu.edu
BOSCHINI, JR.,
Victor, J 817-257-7783 486 G
v.boschini@tcu.edu
BOSCHUNG, Milla 205-348-6250 8 E
mboschun@ches.ua.edu
BOSCO, Carol 518-629-7117 328 D
c.bosco@hvcc.edu
BOSCO, Mike 617-588-1364 223 D
mbosco@bfit.edu
BOSCO, Pat, J 785-532-6237 188 H
bosco@ksu.edu
BOSE, Janet 602-286-8327 14 M
janet.bose@gatewaycc.edu
BOSE, Mohua 518-608-8288 325 B
mbose@excelsior.edu
BOSE, Pradeep 859-622-1761 194 L
pradeep.bose@eku.edu
BOSEN, Char 801-883-8336 498 M
cbosen@new.edu
BOSEN, Patricia 518-580-5550 342 I
pbosen@skidmore.edu
BOSHEARS, Shannon 501-812-2221 22 F
sboshears@pulaskitech.edu
BOSIO, Katherine 810-762-9537 245 A
kbosio@kettering.edu
BOSKO, Ronna 585-245-5596 345 D
bosko@geneseo.edu
BOSLAND, Judy 575-646-1720 312 A
jbosland@nmsu.edu
BOSLEY, Amy, N 407-582-8255 118 I
abosley@valenciacollege.edu
BOSLEY, Barry 717-358-4663 418 J
barry.bosley@fandm.edu

BOWEN, Jose, A .... 410-337-6040 215 B
president@goucher.edu
BOWEN, Julie .... 806-291-3470 496 K
bowenj@wbu.edu
BOWEN, Lance .... 775-674-7552 295 F
lbowen@tmcc.edu
BOWEN, Laura .... 678-359-5011 126 E
laurab@gordonstate.edu
BOWEN, Laura .... 678-359-5585 126 E
laurab@gordonstate.edu
BOWEN, Laura .... 704-669-4106 361 E
bowen@clevelandcc.edu
BOWEN, Lauren .... 814-641-3121 421 L
bowenl@juniata.edu
BOWEN, Lucy .... 713-221-8024 491 F
bowenl@uhd.edu
BOWEN, Lynn .... 229-333-2100 134 I
lynn.bowen@wiregrass.edu
BOWEN, Marie, H .... 413-545-0360 228 F
BOWEN, Pamela .... 715-425-0633 540 E
pamela.bowen@uwrf.edu
BOWEN, Patricia, A .... 606-693-5000 197 F
pbowen@kmbc.edu
BOWEN, Rachel .... 610-526-6157 420 C
rbowen@harcum.edu
BOWEN, Randyll .... 585-292-2215 333 G
rbowen3@monroecc.edu
BOWEN, Robin, E .... 479-968-0228.. 20 C
rbowen@atu.edu
BOWEN, Roxanne .... 423-585-6806 464 C
roxanne.bowen@ws.edu
BOWEN, Sam .... 320-222-5206 261 B
sam.bowen@ridgewater.edu
BOWEN, Sharon, G .... 931-540-2548 462 E
sbowen@columbiastate.edu
BOWEN, Sherri, W .... 336-734-7200 362 F
sbowen@forsythtech.edu
BOWEN, Stephen, H .... 404-784-8300 124 D
sbowen@emory.edu
BOWEN, Susan, G .... 609-586-4800 303 D
bowens@mccc.edu
BOWEN, Terry .... 410-386-8494 214 B
tbowen@carrollcc.edu
BOWEN, Tom .... 901-678-5395 462 B
tmbowen1@memphis.edu
BOWEN, W. Ann .... 423-585-6892 464 C
ann.bowen@ws.edu
BOWENS, Laura Lee .... 201-328-5196 301 G
lbowens@ccm.edu
BOWENS, Ollie .... 662-252-8000 270 C
obowens@rustcollege.edu
BOWENS, Pacey .... 870-762-3134.. 19 C
pbowens@smail.anc.edu
BOWER, Beth, A .... 978-542-6134 230 E
bbower@salemstate.edu
BOWER, David, A .... 812-464-1918 174 D
bower@usi.edu
BOWER, Eric .... 216-791-5000 380 C
eric.bower@cim.edu
BOWER, Jami .... 678-839-6464 133 F
jbower@westga.edu
BOWER, Mike .... 567-661-7200 390 D
mike_bower@owens.edu
BOWER, Shirley .... 585-475-5034 339 G
slbwml@rit.edu
BOWER SPENCE,
Kim, D .... 570-408-4764 440 B
kimberly.bowerspence@wilkes.edu
BOWERMAN, Harley .... 907-745-3201.. 10 B
BOWERS, Angela .... 563-355-3500 180 F
abowers@kaplan.edu
BOWERS, Anthony .... 425-739-8135 523 I
anthony.bowers@lwtech.edu
BOWERS, Carol .... 803-376-5700 443 D
cbowers@allenuniversity.edu
BOWERS, David, A .... 212-938-5666 347 C
dbowers@sunyopt.edu
BOWERS, David, G .... 517-338-3021 241 B
dbowers@cleary.edu
BOWERS, J. Betsy .... 850-474-2637 116 E
bbowers@uwf.edu
BOWERS, Jan .... 607-436-3488 344 B
jan.bowers@oneonta.edu
BOWERS, Jane .... 212-237-8801 319 F
jbowers@jjay.cuny.edu
BOWERS, John .... 270-745-4278 201 D
john.bowers@wku.edu
BOWERS, John .... 206-934-6869 526 B
john.bowers@seattlecolleges.edu
BOWERS, Kathy .... 417-626-1234 280 B
kbowers@occ.edu
BOWERS, Kevin .... 618-544-8657 146 H
bowersk@iecc.edu
BOWERS, Lynn .... 773-380-6786 140 C
lbowers@bexleyseabury.edu
BOWERS, Marilyn, R .... 423-585-2633 464 C
marilyn.bowers@ws.edu
BOWERS, Marilyn, R .... 423-318-2776 464 C
marilyn.bowers@ws.edu
BOWERS, Michael, E .... 864-587-4220 449 D
bowersme@smcsc.edu
BOWERS, Richard .... 817-598-6213 497 A
rbowers@wc.edu
BOWERS, Rodney .... 321-674-8080 103 R
rbowers@fit.edu
BOWERS, Stephanie .... 360-650-2055 528 D
stephanie.bowers@wwu.edu
BOWERS, Susan .... 712-279-7969 182 F
susan.bowers@stlukescollege.edu
BOWERS, Susan .... 712-279-3149 182 F
susan.bowers@stlukescollege.edu
BOWERS, William .... 315-312-2888 346 A
william.bowers@oswego.edu
BOWERS-CAMPBELL,
Joy .... 502-863-8172 195 A
Joy_Bowers-Campbell@georgetowncollege.edu
BOWERSOCK,
Allison, H .... 540-985-9943 509 D
ahbowersock@jchs.edu
BOWERSOCK, Gary .... 303-273-3330.. 80 O
gbowerso@mines.edu
BOWERSOX, Laurie, A .... 717-270-6310 420 D
labowers@hacc.edu
BOWERSOX, Lou Ann .... 270-852-3119 198 A
lbowersox@kwc.edu
BOWES, Bill .... 501-686-6840.. 24 B
wrbowes@uams.edu
BOWES, Kristen .... 914-674-7544 332 E
kbowes@mercy.edu
BOWIE, DeWayne .... 337-482-6287 208 F
dkbowie@louisiana.edu
BOWIE, Jalonna .... 913-234-0681 185 N
jalonna.bowie@cleveland.edu
BOWIE, John .... 207-755-5432 210 L
jbowie@cmcc.edu
BOWIE, Judy .... 740-753-7032 383 G
bowiej@hocking.edu
BOWIE, Linda .... 410-951-3915 220 C
lbowie@coppin.edu
BOWIE, Lois .... 903-593-8311 487 A
lbowie@texascollege.edu
BOWIE, Michelle .... 202-884-9611.. 97 A
bowiem@trinitydc.edu
BOWIE, Staci, A .... 843-349-2227 444 G
sbowie@coastal.edu
BOWIE, Thomas .... 303-458-4040.. 85 G
tbowie@regis.edu
BOWKER, Janet, L .... 814-732-2544 430 G
bowker@edinboro.edu
BOWLAN, Ronald, E .... 215-503-7268 436 F
ron.bowlan@jefferson.edu
BOWLDS, Joy .... 270-852-8965 197 A
joy.bowlds@kctcs.edu
BOWLES, Anita, K .... 864-587-4221 449 D
bowlesa@smcsc.edu
BOWLES, Crystal .... 918-293-5274 400 E
crystal.bowles@okstate.edu
BOWLES, Deborah .... 610-399-2100 430 D
dbowles@cheyney.edu
BOWLES, Diane .... 704-378-1202 358 B
dbowles@jcsu.edu
BOWLES, Donna, J .... 812-941-2204 169 A
dbowles@ius.edu
BOWLES, James, H .... 270-824-8588 196 F
james.bowles@kctcs.edu
BOWLES, K. Johnson .... 828-298-3325 373 A
kjbowles@warren-wilson.edu
BOWLES, Ron .... 214-333-5520 471 L
ronb@dbu.edu
BOWLES, Ulisa .... 910-672-1411 370 A
ubowles@uncfsu.edu
BOWLIN, Stephanie .... 909-469-5383.. 76 I
sbowlin@westernu.edu
BOWLING, Doug .... 513-569-1752 379 K
doug.bowling@cincinnatistate.edu
BOWLING, John, C .... 815-939-5221 155 G
jbowling@olivet.edu
BOWLING, Shannon .... 304-327-4131 532 D
sbowling@bluefieldstate.edu
BOWLING, Thomas .... 301-687-4111 220 D
tbowling@frostburg.edu
BOWLUS, Robin .... 419-358-3453 377 H
bowlusr@bluffton.edu
BOWMAN, Benjamin .... 574-284-4552 172 G
bbowman@saintmarys.edu
BOWMAN, Bruce, A .... 410-777-2873 213 E
babowman2@aacc.edu
BOWMAN, Corey, L .... 660-543-4114 283 F
bowman@ucmo.edu
BOWMAN, David .... 657-278-2638.. 33 E
dbowman@fullerton.edu
BOWMAN, David, B .... 214-459-8490 482 A
BOWMAN, Denise .... 901-572-2452 455 C
denise.bowman@bchs.edu
BOWMAN, Denvy, A .... 614-236-6908 378 H
dbowman@capital.edu
BOWMAN, Donald, R .... 941-752-5301 114 B
bowmand@scf.edu
BOWMAN, Elizabeth .... 805-965-0581.. 64 N
bowmane@sbcc.edu
BOWMAN, Gail .... 859-985-3774 193 F
bowmang@berea.edu
BOWMAN, Gina .... 870-972-2250.. 19 F
gbowman@astate.edu
BOWMAN, Glen .... 252-335-3424 369 F
gcbowman@ecsu.edu
BOWMAN, Gregory, W .... 304-293-3199 533 D
gwbowman@mail.wvu.edu
BOWMAN, Helen, Y .... 215-895-2803 417 E
helen.y.bowman@drexel.edu
BOWMAN, John .... 301-687-4211 220 D
jbowman@frostburg.edu
BOWMAN, Judith, M .... 757-683-3260 510 I
jbowman@odu.edu
BOWMAN, Katie, M .... 727-816-3236 110 B
bowmank@phsc.edu
BOWMAN, Kevin .... 808-687-7032 135 C
kbowman@hpu.edu
BOWMAN, Kimberly .... 717-901-5173 420 I
kbowman@harrisburgu.edu
BOWMAN, Michael .... 510-659-6064.. 56 J
mbowman@ohlone.edu
BOWMAN, Pam .... 662-685-4771 266 G
pbowman@bmc.edu
BOWMAN, Pamela, L .... 309-298-1971 163 A
pl-bowman@wiu.edu
BOWMAN, JR.,
Ronald, L .... 330-972-2157 392 H
rbowman@uakron.edu
BOWMAN,
SallyAnn, M .... 215-746-0804 437 I
sbowman@upenn.edu
BOWMAN, Scott .... 612-874-3677 257 D
scott_bowman@mcad.edu
BOWMAN, Scott, R .... 323-343-2000.. 34 A
sbowman@calstatela.edu
BOWMAN, Stacie .... 978-837-3448 233 G
bowmans@merrimack.edu
BOWMAN, Teri, A .... 660-543-4900 283 F
tbowman@ucmo.edu
BOWMAN, Ty .... 562-860-2451.. 37 L
tbowman@cerritos.edu
BOWMANN, John .... 636-949-4678 276 L
jbowmann@lindenwood.edu
BOWNE, Kristine .... 626-396-2474.. 28 J
kristine.bowne@artcenter.edu
BOWNES, Michael, A .... 205-348-8341.... 8 D
mbownes@uasystem.ua.edu
BOWRON, Steve .... 507-433-0695 261 C
steve.bowron@riverland.edu
BOWSER, Chris .... 641-683-5155 179 C
chris.bowser@indianhills.edu
BOWSER, Steve .... 404-270-5326 132 D
sbowser@spelman.edu
BOWYER, Donald .... 870-972-3053.. 19 F
dbowyer@astate.edu
BOWYER, Karen, A .... 731-286-3301 462 F
kbowyer@dscc.edu
BOWYER, Roger .... 937-529-2201 392 G
rogerbowyer@united.edu
BOX, Jay .... 859-256-3132 195 G
jay.box@kctcs.edu
BOX, Jean, A .... 205-726-2565.... 6 F
jabox@samford.edu
BOX, Margaret .... 325-942-2335 489 E
BOX, Thomas, W .... 206-281-2108 526 D
twb@spu.edu
BOXDORFER, Bill .... 573-288-6571 274 C
bboxdorfer@culver.edu
BOXLER, Susan .... 641-673-1284 184 B
boxlers@wmpenn.edu
BOXWELL, George .... 304-647-6290 533 B
gboxwell@osteo.wvsom.edu
BOYAN, Barbara, D .... 804-828-0190 514 F
bboyan@vcu.edu
BOYCE, Eric .... 828-251-6710 370 E
eboyce@unca.edu
BOYCE, Greg .... 719-846-5530.. 86 A
greg.boyce@trinidadstate.edu
BOYCE, Lynn .... 405-224-3140 403 L
lboyce@usao.edu
BOYCE, Mary, C .... 212-854-1123 322 F
boyce@columbia.edu
BOYCE, Robert .... 301-687-4043 220 D
rjboyce@frostburg.edu
BOYCE, Susan .... 802-773-5900 501 G
susan.boyce@csj.edu
BOYD, Alan .... 440-775-5666 388 B
aboyd@oberlin.edu
BOYD, Alfredia .... 803-793-5192 445 F
boyda@denmarktech.edu
BOYD, Amanda, L .... 419-866-0261 391 L
alboyd@stautzenberger.com
BOYD, Amy .... 402-354-7073 291 P
amy.boyd@methodistcollege.edu
BOYD, Angela .... 757-727-5328 508 C
angela.boyd@hamptonu.edu
BOYD, Betsy, A .... 541-346-0946 410 F
eaboyd@uoregon.edu
BOYD, Bill .... 910-323-5614 355 E
billboyd@ccbs.edu
BOYD, Brian .... 407-823-3016 115 C
brian.boyd@ucf.edu
BOYD, Carla .... 520-515-5337.. 13 B
boydc@cochise.edu
BOYD, Carla, L .... 218-726-8795 264 G
clboyd@d.umn.edu
BOYD, Carla, M .... 217-443-8753 143 F
cboyd@dacc.edu
BOYD, Chrispher .... 336-770-3322 372 B
boydc@uncsa.edu
BOYD, Clarence .... 918-495-7767 401 B
cboyd@oru.edu
BOYD, Cristine, D .... 330-569-5288 383 F
boydcd@hiram.edu
BOYD, Cynthia .... 770-426-2756 128 C
cboyd@life.edu
BOYD, Cynthia, E .... 312-942-6915 158 A
cynthia_e_boyd@rush.edu
BOYD, Danielle .... 618-634-3298 159 A
danielleb@shawneecc.edu
BOYD, David, L .... 714-850-4800.. 69 F
boyd@taftu.edu
BOYD, Deborah .... 615-966-5708 458 C
deborah.boyd@lipscomb.edu
BOYD, Debra, C .... 803-323-2220 451 I
boydd@winthrop.edu
BOYD, Ernest .... 731-426-7531 457 K
eboyd@lanecollege.edu
BOYD, Eulas .... 718-780-7906 317 A
eulas.boyd@brooklaw.edu
BOYD, Evan .... 773-896-2400 141 K
eboyd@ctschicago.edu
BOYD, Frank, A .... 309-556-3255 148 A
fboyd@iwu.edu
BOYD, Gary .... 304-357-4704 530 H
garyboyd@ucwv.edu
BOYD, Gerald, L .... 240-629-7840 214 I
gboyd@frederick.edu
BOYD, Gwendolyn, E .... 334-229-4202.... 1 D
presgboyd@alasu.edu
BOYD, Heather .... 303-273-3221.. 80 O
hboyd@mines.edu
BOYD, JR., James, I .... 707-965-7203.. 57 I
jboyd@puc.edu
BOYD, Jean Ellen .... 618-634-3240 159 A
jeanb@shawneecc.edu
BOYD, Jeffrey, S .... 757-822-1180 517 C
jsboyd@tcc.edu
BOYD, John .... 405-682-7501 399 K
jboyd@occc.edu
BOYD, John, C .... 828-766-1270 364 A
jboyd@mayland.edu
BOYD, Karen, O .... 314-576-5923 284 B
boyd@umsl.edu
BOYD, Kathleen .... 401-341-2374 442 D
boydk@salve.edu
BOYD, Keisha .... 386-214-3653.. 99 F
boydk@cookman.edu
BOYD, Keith .... 312-942-2694 158 A
keith_boyd@rush.edu
BOYD, Ken .... 913-443-5858 131 B
kboyd@savannahtech.edu
BOYD, Ken .... 765-998-4965 173 B
knboyd@taylor.edu
BOYD, Kim .... 918-495-7108 401 B
kboyd@oru.edu
BOYD, Linda, D .... 617-732-2800 233 E
linda.boyd@mcphs.edu
BOYD, Lonnie .... 620-229-6136 191 B
lonnie.boyd@sckans.edu
BOYD, Mary, K .... 512-448-8741 481 B
mboyd@stedwards.edu
BOYD, Michael .... 706-754-7807 129 B
mboyd@northgatech.edu
BOYD, Michael .... 815-802-8360 149 B
mboyd@kcc.edu
BOYD, Monica .... 336-917-5579 368 F
monica.boyd@salem.edu
BOYD, Nick .... 530-283-0202.. 44 H
nboyd@frc.edu
BOYD, Rhonda .... 479-788-7958.. 23 H
rhonda.boyd@uafs.edu
BOYD, Robert .... 559-278-4480.. 33 D
robert_boyd@csufresno.edu
BOYD, Ruth .... 580-774-3177 402 G
ruth.boyd@swosu.edu
BOYD, Sharon, H .... 910-962-7769 372 A
boyds@uncw.edu
BOYD, Stephen .... 916-484-8406.. 52 I
boyds@arc.losrios.edu
BOYD, Steve .... 970-945-8691.. 80 D
BOYD, Susan .... 586-445-7408 246 A
boyds@macomb.edu
BOYD, Thomas .... 303-273-3247.. 80 O
tboyd@mines.edu
BOYD, Todd, T .... 580-774-3782 402 G
todd.boyd@swosu.edu
BOYD-PUGH,
Jennifer, N .... 305-899-4057.. 99 B
jboydpugh@barry.edu

BOYDSTUN, Morris 479-394-7622 22 H mboydstun@rmcc.edu

BOYE-BEAMAN, Joni, M 989-964-4062 249 G jbb@svsu.edu

BOYENS, Kathy, R 815-939-5211 155 G kboyens@olivet.edu

BOYER, Annette 724-925-4101 439 F boyera@wccc.edu

BOYER, Bruce 508-565-1380 237 A bboyer@stonehill.edu

BOYER, Bruce, E 573-875-7251 273 D beboyer@ccis.edu

BOYER, Charles 406-994-3681 287 G cboyer@montana.edu

BOYER, Debra, A 617-228-2403 231 C dboyer@bhcc.mass.edu

BOYER, John, W 773-702-8576 161 D jwboyer@uchicago.edu

BOYER, Mary 215-702-4541 414 C mboyer@cairn.edu

BOYER, Mary Jo 610-450-6524 416 G mboyer@dccc.edu

BOYER, Naomi 863-298-6854 110 E nboyer@polk.edu

BOYER, Paul, J 413-597-4181 238 E paul.j.boyer@williams.edu

BOYER, Scott 717-560-8240 423 C sboyer@lbc.edu

BOYER, Suzanne, L 410-777-2045 213 E slboyer1@aacc.edu

BOYER FERHAT, Caroline 800-995-3159 286 A caroline.boyerferhat@williamwoods.edu

BOYER-OWENS, Linda 210-485-0230 466 J lboyer-owens@alamo.edu

BOYERS, Jayson 517-586-3012 241 B jboyers@cleary.edu

BOYERS, Jayson 802-651-5824 501 F Jboyers@champlain.edu

BOYES, Jerry, S 716-878-6533 345 B boyesjs@buffalostate.edu

BOYETT, Chad 912-287-5808 123 A cboyett@coastalpines.edu

BOYETT, James, C 501-362-1125 19 E jcboyett@hebersprings.asub.edu

BOYETT, Jennifer 870-230-5401 21 B boyett@hsu.edu

BOYETT, Patricia 504-865-7880 206 A

BOYETTE, Alan, J 336-334-5494 371 C alan_boyette@uncg.edu

BOYETTE, Barbara, G 336-316-2825 357 C boyettebg@guilford.edu

BOYETTE, Don, L 252-246-1275 367 D dboyette@wilsoncc.edu

BOYETTE, Rick 903-823-3274 484 D ricky.boyette@texarkanacollege.edu

BOYKIN, Coretta 251-578-1313 6 D cboykin@rstc.edu

BOYKIN, Deborah 757-221-3178 506 J boykin@wm.edu

BOYKIN, III, George, H 919-516-4888 368 E ghboykin@st-aug.edu

BOYKIN, Karen 215-780-1420 435 D kboykin@salus.edu

BOYKIN, Lashanna 619-680-4430 30 H lashanna.boykin@cc-sd.edu

BOYKIN, Regena 601-635-2111 267 B rboykin@eccc.edu

BOYKIN, Ted 570-586-2400 435 H tboykin@summitu.edu

BOYLAN, Ellen 570-348-6203 425 D eboylan@marywood.edu

BOYLAN, Stanley, L 646-565-6000 350 C stanley.boylan@touro.edu

BOYLAN, Teresa 540-362-6435 508 D boylanta@hollins.edu

BOYLAN, Teresa 434-381-6337 513 E tboylan@sbc.edu

BOYLE, Amy 504-865-2445 206 A aboyle@loyno.edu

BOYLE, Ann 480-219-6107 271 G aboyle@atsu.edu

BOYLE, Antonio 937-708-5544 395 E aboyle@wilberforce.edu

BOYLE, Brian 251-442-2287 9 B bboyle@umobile.edu

BOYLE, Deborah 727-341-3153 112 A boyle.deborah@spcollege.edu

BOYLE, Jeanne, E 848-932-7505 307 B jeboyle@rulmail.rutgers.edu

BOYLE, Jeffery 864-592-4823 449 C boylej@sccsc.edu

BOYLE, Jerry 970-410-0456 87 L

BOYLE, Kaitlyn 215-895-2100 417 E kaitlyn.boyle@drexel.edu

BOYLE, Kevin 973-618-3372 300 H kboyle@caldwell.edu

BOYLE, Lori 619-239-0391 36 E lboyle@cwsl.edu

BOYLE, Mike, A 615-898-2177 461 E mike.boyle@mtsu.edu

BOYLE, Nuala 585-389-2670 334 B nboyle5@naz.edu

BOYLE, Patrick, M 773-508-7070 151 E pboyle@luc.edu

BOYLE, Paul 215-558-6211 426 C pboyle@phmc.org

BOYLE, Rebecca 716-827-2559 350 H boyler@trocaire.edu

BOYLE, Richard 713-221-8065 491 F boyler@uhd.edu

BOYLE, Robert, J 904-620-4663 116 A rboyle@unf.edu

BOYLE, Sharon, I 215-926-2295 436 C sharon.boyle@temple.edu

BOYLE, Susan, A 330-569-5119 383 F boylesa@hiram.edu

BOYLE, Taggart 617-984-1771 235 H tboyle@quincycollege.edu

BOYLE, Thomas, A 630-515-6166 152 H tboyle@midwestern.edu

BOYLES, Elinda 740-351-3005 391 C eboyles@shawnee.edu

BOYLES, Joel 662-562-3240 269 E jboyles@northwestms.edu

BOYLES, Robin 662-846-4804 267 A rboyles@deltastate.edu

BOYLES, Shery 919-760-8581 359 B boyless@meredith.edu

BOYLESTON, Matt 281-649-3607 475 B mboyleston@hbu.edu

BOYLL, Dave 303-937-4222 80 A dboyll@chu.edu

BOYMELGREEN, Shaya 718-434-0784 317 L

BOYNE, Andrew 985-448-7928 203 G andrew.boyne@fletcher.edu

BOYNTON, Andrew, C 617-552-4107 224 B andy.boynton@bc.edu

BOYS, Kevin, S 937-393-3431 391 F kboys@sscc.edu

BOYS, Mary 212-280-1550 351 B mboys@uts.columbia.edu

BOYSUN, Virginia 406-377-9404 286 F vboysun@dawson.edu

BOZARTH, Diane 573-288-6473 274 C dbozarth@culver.edu

BOZARTH, Peggy, I 270-707-3844 196 D peggy.bozarth@kctcs.edu

BOZEMAN-EVANS, Pamela 773-244-5662 154 G pbozeman@northpark.edu

BOZINSKI, Glenn 570-674-6434 426 D gbozinsk@misericordia.edu

BOZOVIC, Laura, B 256-765-4278 9 D lbozovic@una.edu

BOZYLINSKY, Garrett, A 401-874-4599 442 E garry@uri.edu

BOZYM, Rebecca 412-536-1158 422 E rebecca.bozym@laroche.edu

BOZZUTO, Victoria 203-285-2408 89 B vbozzuto@gwcc.commnet.edu

BRAATEN, Jennifer, L 540-365-4202 507 H jbraaten@ferrum.edu

BRAATEN, Pamela, K 701-788-4773 374 A Pamela.Braaten@mayvillestate.edu

BRAATZ, Jay 312-362-7561 143 G jbraatz@depaul.edu

BRABAZON, Jodi 215-574-9600 421 A jbrabazon@hussianart.edu

BRABHAM, Sherry, F 212-217-4020 325 C sherry_brabham@fitnyc.edu

BRABHAM, Susan, S 803-938-3795 450 H brabhams@uscsumter.edu

BRACCIANO, Susan 816-271-4214 279 E braccian@missouriwestern.edu

BRACELY, Kenesha 904-470-8445 102 A k.bracely@ewc.edu

BRACEY, Carol 951-343-4456 30 D cbracey@calbaptist.edu

BRACEY, Gerald 228-897-7101 271 F jerry.bracey@wmcarey.edu

BRACEY, Matthew 615-844-5233 466 G mbracey@welch.edu

BRACK, Jonathan, M 215-572-3878 439 E jbrack@wts.edu

BRACKEN, Damien, S 617-266-1400 223 F

BRACKEN, Gary 412-391-4100 433 F gbracken@pointpark.edu

BRACKEN, James 330-672-2962 384 H jbracke1@kent.edu

BRACKEN, Lisa 803-778-6652 443 I brackenlm@cctech.edu

BRACKETT, Andrew 802-831-1260 503 E abrackett@vermontlaw.edu

BRACKETT, Geoffrey, L 845-575-3000 331 L geoffrey.brackett@marist.edu

BRACKETT, Robert 708-563-1577 147 E rbrackett@iit.edu

BRACKETT, Stacey 828-328-7309 358 G stacey.brackett@lr.edu

BRACKIN, Chad 225-578-4736 204 L cmb@lsu.edu

BRACKIN, James 229-317-6315 123 H james.brackin@darton.edu

BRACKIN, Rebekah 325-942-2248 489 E rebekah.brackin@angelo.edu

BRACKLEY, Paul 312-329-4225 153 C paul.brackley@moody.edu

BRACKMANN, Sarah 512-863-1987 483 G brackmas@southwestern.edu

BRACKNELL, Ann 205-391-2958 7 A abracknell@sheltonstate.edu

BRACY, Judy 504-486-7411 209 E jbracy@xula.edu

BRACY, Marion 504-520-7507 209 E mbracy@xula.edu

BRACY KNIGHT, Becca 310-954-5080 29 I

BRADAC, John, P 607-274-3365 328 H jbradac@ithaca.edu

BRADACH, Carmen 218-749-7743 262 C c.bradach@mr.mnscu.edu

BRADACH, Carmen 218-749-7743 259 D c.bradach@mesabirange.edu

BRADBERRY, J. Chris 402-280-2950 290 B jcbradberry@creighton.edu

BRADBERRY, Richard 443-885-3488 217 C richard.bradberry@morgan.edu

BRADBURY, Boyd 218-477-2095 260 B bradbury@mnstate.edu

BRADBURY, Jane 309-692-4092 152 F jbradbury@midstate.edu

BRADBURY, Ron 540-986-1800 504 E rjbradbury@an.edu

BRADDER, Kelley, L 515-961-1621 182 I kelley.bradder@simpson.edu

BRADDIX, D'Andre 314-516-5205 284 B braddixd@umsl.edu

BRADDOCK, Joan 907-474-7210 10 I jfbraddock@alaska.edu

BRADDY, William 540-261-8450 512 J bill.braddy@svu.edu

BRADEEN, NJ 212-217-4370 325 C

BRADEN, Crystal 325-942-2259 489 E crystal.braden@angelo.edu

BRADEN, Jeffery, P 919-515-2468 370 D jeff_braden@ncsu.edu

BRADEN, Kale 916-484-8050 52 I bradenk@arc.losrios.edu

BRADEN, SJ, Michael, L 201-761-6014 307 K mbraden@saintpeters.edu

BRADFIELD, Anna 508-531-1201 229 C abradfield@bridgew.edu

BRADFIELD, Brett 605-331-6712 454 E brett.bradfield@usiouxfalls.edu

BRADFIELD, Carol 407-303-9585 97 J carol.bradfield@adu.edu

BRADFIELD, Jennifer, S 440-775-8400 388 B Jennifer.Bradfield@oberlin.edu

BRADFIELD, Terry 202-885-8631 97 E tbradfield@wesleyseminary.edu

BRADFORD, SR., Corey, S 936-261-2150 484 F csbradford@pvamu.edu

BRADFORD, Frances, C 757-221-7802 506 J fcbrad@wm.edu

BRADFORD, James 615-343-5705 465 H james.w.bradford@vanderbilt.edu

BRADFORD, Jerry 256-233-8278 1 F jerry.bradford@athens.edu

BRADFORD, Joy 404-880-8049 122 I jbradford@cau.edu

BRADFORD, Lawrence 323-241-5280 51 I bradfoll@lasc.edu

BRADFORD, Linda 205-247-8001 7 G lbradford@stillman.edu

BRADFORD, Michael 434-832-7293 515 A bradfordm@cvcc.vccs.edu

BRADFORD, Michele 256-439-6822 3 N mbradford@gadsdenstate.edu

BRADFORD, Peggy 914-606-6712 352 G peggy.bradford@wcc.edu

BRADFORD-PERRY, Emma 225-771-4990 207 A emma_perry@subr.edu

BRADFORD ROUSE, Teri 805-565-7255 76 K tbradfordrouse@westmont.edu

BRADIN, Bernice 617-349-8685 228 B bbradin@lesley.edu

BRADLEY, Alan 615-297-7545 455 A alanb@aquinascollege.edu

BRADLEY, Alice 704-290-5832 366 A abradley@spcc.edu

BRADLEY, Alvin 318-274-3278 207 H

BRADLEY, Angela 228-897-3886 268 G angela.bradley@mgccc.edu

BRADLEY, Brenda 712-274-6400 184 A brenda.bradley@witcc.edu

BRADLEY, Cedric 228-497-7627 268 G cedric.bradley@mgccc.edu

BRADLEY, Dale, R 304-367-4692 531 E Dale.Bradley@pierpont.edu

BRADLEY, Daniel, J 812-237-4000 167 E president@indstate.edu

BRADLEY, David, M 713-221-8610 491 F bradleyd@uhd.edu

BRADLEY, Dennis, J 814-732-1030 430 G bradley@edinboro.edu

BRADLEY, Devon 517-483-1426 245 I bradled@lcc.edu

BRADLEY, Jane 319-296-4230 179 B jane.bradley@hawkeyecollege.edu

BRADLEY, Jennifer 319-398-4913 180 J jbradley@kirkwood.edu

BRADLEY, Jennifer 334-244-3554 2 A jbradle8@aum.edu

BRADLEY, Jennifer 808-734-9890 136 C jbradley@hawaii.edu

BRADLEY, JoAnn 718-270-4418 344 D jbradley@downstate.edu

BRADLEY, Joseph 410-617-5780 216 D jbradley@loyola.edu

BRADLEY, Judy 606-218-5253 201 C judybradley@upike.edu

BRADLEY, Julie, M 972-758-3821 471 C jbradley@collin.edu

BRADLEY, Kathy 717-337-6960 419 C kbradley@gettysburg.edu

BRADLEY, Marcy, K 607-871-2350 314 J bradlemk@alfred.edu

BRADLEY, Mark 360-882-2200 45 J markbradley@ggbts.edu

BRADLEY, Martha, S 801-585-3582 499 K martha.bradley@utah.edu

BRADLEY, Miho 808-983-4163 135 D mbradley@tokai.edu

BRADLEY, Monica 318-274-6118 207 H bradleym@gram.edu

BRADLEY, Nedra 601-484-8674 268 B nbradley@meridiancc.edu

BRADLEY, Patrick, J 660-543-4515 283 F pbradley@ucmo.edu

BRADLEY, Paul, A 651-631-5592 265 D pabradley@unwsp.edu

BRADLEY, Roger 386-267-0565 101 H director@daytonacollege.edu

BRADLEY, Tanya, W 802-626-6218 504 B tanya.bradley@lyndonstate.edu

BRADLEY, Tina 870-508-6100 19 H tbradley@asumh.edu

BRADLEY, Todd 615-550-3173 466 H todd.bradley@williamsoncc.edu

BRADLEY, Tracey 865-539-7158 463 E tcbradley@pstcc.edu

BRADLEY-DOPPES, Peg 303-871-3399 86 H pbd@du.edu

BRADLEY-HASTY, Barbara 252-536-3386 363 B bhasty399@halifaxcc.edu

BRADSHAW, Amelia, M 804-523-5867 515 F abradshaw@reynolds.edu

BRADSHAW, Boyd 636-227-2100 277 A boyd.bradshaw@logan.edu

BRADSHAW, Brent 972-279-6511 467 F bbradshaw@amberton.edu

BRADSHAW, Debra 816-268-5472 279 K dlbradshaw@nts.edu

BRADSHAW, Felicia 202-231-3354 547 N felicia.bradshaw@dodiis.mil

BRADSHAW, Geoffrey, W 608-246-6165 543 C gbradshaw@madisoncollege.edu

BRADSHAW, George 909-274-4419 54 J gbradshaw@mtsac.edu

BRADSHAW, Ken 270-534-3169 197 E ken.bradshaw@kctcs.edu

BRADSHAW, Kim 704-355-5584 355 G kim.bradshaw@carolinascollege.edu

BRADSHAW, Kim 704-355-5584 355 B kim.bradshaw@carolinashealthcare.org

BRADSHAW, Marjorie 913-234-0607 185 N marjorie.bradshaw@cleveland.edu

BRADSHAW, Michael 601-477-4161 268 A michael.bradshaw@jcjc.edu

BRADSHAW, Phillip 757-825-2895 517 B bradshawp@tncc.edu

BRADSHAW, Steve 706-295-6934 125 F sbradshaw@gntc.edu

BRADSHAW, Wilson, G 239-590-1055 114 F president@fgcu.edu

BRADSHER, Carl 434-791-5646 505 A cbradshe@averett.edu

BRADSHER, Pamela, F 336-322-2102 364 G Pam.Bradsher@piedmontcc.edu

BRADT, Jeremy ... 815-599-3500 146 B
jeremy.bradt@highland.edu
BRADT, Jeremy ... 815-599-3486 146 B
jeremy.bradt@highland.edu
BRADY, Anne Marie ... 240-895-2103 218 B
ambrady@smcm.edu
BRADY, Bridget ... 805-898-4003 ... 44 J
blbrady@fielding.edu
BRADY, Christian, M ... 814-865-2631 428 C
cmb44@psu.edu
BRADY, Claire ... 352-365-3608 107 X
bradyc@lssc.edu
BRADY, David, M ... 203-576-4589 ... 92 B
dbrady@bridgeport.edu
BRADY, Emily ... 203-576-4542 ... 92 B
embrady@bridgeport.edu
BRADY, Henry, E ... 510-642-5116 ... 70 K
hbrady@econ.berkeley.edu
BRADY, James ... 509-533-3680 521 F
jim.brady@sfcc.spokane.edu
BRADY, Kathleen ... 732-987-2415 302 J
kbrady@georgian.edu
BRADY, Kathleen ... 864-503-5941 451 A
kbrady@uscupstate.edu
BRADY, Kathleen, T ... 843-792-5205 447 G
bradyk@musc.edu
BRADY, Lauren ... 480-245-7980 ... 14 D
lauren.brady@ibcs.edu
BRADY, Marilyn ... 843-574-6566 449 G
marilyn.brady@tridenttech.edu
BRADY, Michael ... 937-327-7317 395 I
bradym@wittenberg.edu
BRADY, Patricia, J ... 617-228-2000 231 C
BRADY, Thomas, F ... 219-785-5740 172 A
tfbrady@pnc.edu
BRADY, Todd ... 731-661-6566 464 G
tbrady@uu.edu
BRAENDEL, Carly ... 828-669-8012 359 K
cbraendel@montreat.edu
BRAEUTIGAM, Ronald, R ... 847-491-7040 155 D
braeutigam@northwestern.edu
BRAGA, Sophia ... 518-464-8580 325 B
SBraga@excelsior.edu
BRAGG, Chris ... 208-732-6775 137 K
cbragg@csi.edu
BRAGG, Dallas ... 704-971-8500 355 J
dbragg@charlottelaw.edu
BRAGG, Darcy ... 229-928-2378 126 C
darcy.bragg@gsw.edu
BRAGG, Elizabeth ... 503-760-3131 404 I
elizabeth@birthingway.edu
BRAGG, Melissa ... 254-295-4608 492 C
mbragg@umhb.edu
BRAGG, Michael, B ... 206-543-1829 527 G
mbragg@uw.edu
BRAGG, Nancy, S ... 540-665-4538 512 E
nbragg@su.edu
BRAGG, Robert, S ... 276-328-0129 514 B
rsb2e@uvawise.edu
BRAGIN, Marc ... 740-427-5228 384 P
braginm@kenyon.edu
BRAHA, Habtu ... 410-951-3447 220 C
hbraha@coppin.edu
BRAHA, Habtu ... 410-951-3014 220 C
hbraha@coppin.edu
BRAHAMS, Teri, T ... 865-694-6476 463 E
tbrahams@pstcc.edu
BRAHM, Gary ... 949-753-4774 ... 29 G
chancellor@brandman.edu
BRAIDES, Cheryl ... 215-612-6600 421 N
cbraides@chicareers.com
BRAILER, James ... 410-516-8070 216 A
jbraile1@jhu.edu
BRAILOW, David, G ... 317-738-8017 166 B
dbrailow@franklincollege.edu
BRAIM, Barry ... 413-775-1311 231 E
braim@gcc.mass.edu
BRAINARD, Lisa, C ... 518-292-1959 340 A
brainl@sage.edu
BRAINARD, Nancy ... 918-495-7119 401 B
nbrainard@oru.edu
BRAINER, Charles ... 765-998-5271 173 B
chbrainer@taylor.edu
BRAISHER, Lyndsey ... 405-912-9007 398 B
lbraisher@hc.edu
BRAISHER, Mark, H ... 405-912-9013 398 B
mbraisher@hc.edu
BRAKEFIELD, Jean Ann 843-349-2846 444 G
jeanann@coastal.edu
BRAKER, Regina ... 541-962-3509 405 G
rbraker@eou.edu
BRAKKE, David, F ... 540-568-3508 509 C
brakkedf@jmu.edu
BRAKKE, Karen ... 404-270-5734 132 D
kbrakke@spelman.edu
BRAKSICK, Ben ... 317-955-6319 171 A
bbraksick@marian.edu
BRALLEY, Shannon ... 254-526-1934 470 E
shannon.bralley@ctcd.edu
BRALY, JR., Cliff ... 336-272-7102 357 B
bralyc@greensboro.edu
BRAMANTE, Paula ... 617-951-2350 234 F
paula.bramante@necb.edu
BRAMBLE, Karen ... 602-944-3335 ... 11 D
kbramble@aicag.edu
BRAMBLETT, Sandra, J . 404-894-8874 125 D
sandi@gatech.edu
BRAME, David ... 407-438-6000 113 M
BRAME, Tracey ... 616-301-6800 252 J
bramet@cooley.edu
BRAMLAGE, SC, Nancy . 513-244-4844 387 A
nancy.bramlage@msj.edu
BRAMLETT, Nancy ... 913-758-4372 191 I
nancy.bramlett@stmary.edu
BRAMLETT, Rebecca ... 919-962-4388 371 A
rebecca_bramlett@unc.edu
BRAMLETTE, Jeff ... 706-291-2121 131 C
jbramlette@shorter.edu
BRAMLEY, Mary ... 703-323-3749 516 C
mbramley@nvcc.edu
BRAMMER, Erika ... 423-652-6301 457 J
ebrammer@king.edu
BRAMMER, Robyn ... 714-895-8125 ... 40 C
rbrammer@gwc.cccd.edu
BRAMUCCI, Robert, S ... 949-582-4960 ... 67 D
rbramucci@socccd.edu
BRANCA, Matthew, P ... 570-326-3761 429 J
mbranca@pct.edu
BRANCA, Mickey ... 415-241-2255 ... 39 A
mbranca@ccsf.edu
BRANCATO, Marco ... 781-239-2571 231 G
mbrancato@massbay.edu
BRANCH, Craig ... 540-891-3007 515 E
cbranch@germanna.edu
BRANCH, Deborah, G ... 252-335-3271 369 F
dgbranch@ecsu.edu
BRANCH, Gary ... 256-395-2211 ... 7 E
gbranch@suscc.edu
BRANCH, Gary, L ... 251-580-2202 ... 5 A
gary.branch@faulknerstate.edu
BRANCH, Rachel, U ... 904-819-6294 102 P
Rbranch@flagler.edu
BRANCH, Steve ... 276-656-0211 516 D
sbranch@patrickhenry.edu
BRANCH, Teresa, S ... 406-243-5225 287 D
teresa.branch@umontana.edu
BRANCHEAU, Carrie ... 303-753-6046 ... 85 H
cbrancheau@rmcad.edu
BRANCHINI, Ann, Z ... 860-215-9004 ... 90 B
abranchini@trcc.commnet.edu
BRANCIFORTE, Rosemarie ... 407-277-0311 102 N
rbranciforte@evergladesuniversity.edu
BRANCOLINI, Kristine ... 310-338-4593 ... 53 C
kbrancol@lmu.edu
BRAND, Amy ... 617-253-4078 233 C
BRAND, Amy ... 601-553-3455 268 B
abrand@meridiancc.edu
BRAND, David ... 910-678-8307 362 E
brandd@faytechcc.edu
BRAND, Frederick ... 609-984-1588 308 H
fbrand@tesc.edu
BRAND, J. Matthew ... 310-577-3000 ... 77 K
matcm@yosan.edu
BRAND, Jonathan ... 319-895-4324 177 A
jbrand@cornellcollege.edu
BRAND, Richard ... 423-968-4861 457 J
rjbrand@king.edu
BRANDAU, Janet ... 303-360-4735 ... 81 I
Janet.Brandau@CCAurora.edu
BRANDAU-HYNEK, Ann 608-785-9585 544 E
BrandauHynekA@westerntc.edu
BRANDEBERRY, Shari ... 419-434-4245 395 H
registrar@winebrenner.edu
BRANDEBURG, Rosanne ... 352-365-3515 107 X
brandebr@lssc.edu
BRANDEL, Scott ... 312-752-2104 149 D
scott.brandel@kendall.edu
BRANDEMUEHL, Kristin 734-973-3722 251 J
kbrandemuehl@wccnet.edu
BRANDEN, Karen ... 218-935-0417 266 A
karen.branden@wetcc.edu
BRANDENBURG, Aurelia ... 859-985-3173 193 F
aurelia_brandenburg@berea.edu
BRANDENBURG, Mark, C ... 843-953-5252 444 C
mark.brandenburg@citadel.edu
BRANDER, Kenneth ... 212-960-5263 353 P
brander@yu.edu
BRANDES, Derek ... 253-833-9111 523 B
dbrandes@greenriver.edu
BRANDES, Rand ... 828-328-7077 358 G
rand.brandes@lr.edu
BRANDFORD-CALVO, Dania ... 401-874-2018 442 E
brandford@uri.edu
BRANDI, Anne, E ... 516-572-7205 334 A
anne.brandi@ncc.edu
BRANDI, Erica ... 610-398-5300 424 C
ebrandi@lincolntech.edu
BRANDIMORE, Merry Jo ... 989-964-4289 249 G
mjbrand@svsu.edu
BRANDKAMP, Katelyn .. 660-263-4110 279 F
KatelynBrandkamp@macc.edu
BRANDON, Alonzo, C .. 757-683-5383 510 I
abrandon@odu.edu
BRANDON, Dave, E ... 217-424-6330 153 A
dbrandon@millikin.edu
BRANDON, Deborah, L 909-869-3427 ... 32 F
dlbrandon@cpp.edu
BRANDON, Elvis ... 615-230-3375 464 B
elvis.brandon@volstate.edu
BRANDON, Eric ... 828-328-7301 358 G
eric.brandon@lr.edu
BRANDON, Felicia ... 914-674-7718 332 E
fbrandon@mercy.edu
BRANDON, Kevin ... 708-209-3127 143 D
kevin.brandon@cuchicago.edu
BRANDON, Lisa, K ... 618-537-6865 152 C
lkbrandon@mckendree.edu
BRANDON, Mark, E ... 205-348-5117 ... 8 E
mbrandon@law.ua.edu
BRANDON, Maureen ... 970-247-7264 ... 82 I
brandon_m@fortlewis.edu
BRANDON, Michaele ... 505-566-3693 312 K
brandonm@sancollege.edu
BRANDON, Robert ... 423-478-6229 462 D
rbrandon01@clevelandstatecc.edu
BRANDON, Sonia ... 970-248-1884 ... 80 B
BRANDSEN, Cheryl ... 616-526-6102 240 L
brac@calvin.edu
BRANDSTATER, Nate ... 937-395-8618 385 A
nate.brandstater@kc.edu
BRANDT, Elaine ... 573-897-5000 282 I
BRANDT, Eric ... 218-733-7600 259 C
eric.brandt@lsc.edu
BRANDT, Jay, J ... 561-237-7947 108 E
jbrandt@lynn.edu
BRANDT, John ... 314-744-7639 278 G
brandtJ@mobap.edu
BRANDT, John ... 540-261-8467 512 J
john.brandt@svu.edu
BRANDT, Lisa ... 402-461-5177 291 C
BRANDT, Martin ... 631-420-2333 348 B
martin.brandt@farmingdale.edu
BRANDT, Mary, L ... 713-798-3380 469 C
brandt@bcm.edu
BRANDT, Scott ... 831-459-2425 ... 72 E
sbrandt@ucsc.edu
BRANDT, William ... 973-278-5400 316 D
wab@berkeleycollege.edu
BRANDT, William ... 973-278-5400 300 C
wab@berkeleycollege.edu
BRANDT-RAUF, Paul ... 312-996-5939 161 F
pwb1@uic.edu
BRANDVOLD, Kelli ... 808-734-9575 136 C
kellib@hawaii.edu
BRANGMAN, Alan ... 302-831-1110 ... 94 D
brangman@udel.edu
BRANHAM, Celeste ... 207-778-7087 212 E
cbranham@maine.edu
BRANHAM, Holly, L ... 307-532-8303 546 B
holly.branham@ewc.wy.edu
BRANHAM, Keith ... 309-672-5916 152 E
kbranham@methodistcol.edu
BRANHAM, LaTonya ... 937-376-6611 379 D
lbranham@centralstate.edu
BRANHAM, Lorraine ... 315-443-3627 349 E
lbranham@syr.edu
BRANICKY, Michael ... 785-864-3881 191 G
mbranicky@ku.edu
BRANIFF, Wendall ... 713-226-5552 491 F
braniffw@uhd.edu
BRANIGAN, Daniel, S ... 240-895-4412 218 B
dsbranigan@smcm.edu
BRANIGAN, David, E ... 814-863-9150 428 C
deb7@psu.edu
BRANKLE, Steve ... 479-524-7209 ... 21 F
SBrankle@jbu.edu
BRANN, Shawn ... 817-552-3700 477 B
shawn.brann@tku.edu
BRANNAN, Angie, R ... 262-524-7335 535 D
abrannan@carrollu.edu
BRANNAN, Cheryl ... 803-754-4100 445 D
BRANNAN, Colleen, E .. 607-436-2748 344 B
brannace@oneonta.edu
BRANNAN, Sandra ... 409-944-1387 474 G
sbrannan@gc.edu
BRANNAN, Thomas, I .. 205-935-7240 ... 8 F
tbrannan@uab.edu
BRANNER, Wade, H ... 540-464-7253 518 A
brannerwh@vmi.edu
BRANNON, Kelly ... 401-841-2220 548 B
BRANNON, Tony, L ... 270-809-3328 198 I
tbrannon@murraystate.edu
BRANSCOME, Tara ... 256-331-5299 ... 6 B
tbranscome@nwscc.edu
BRANSCUM, Cindy ... 417-455-5506 274 B
CindyBranscum@crowder.edu
BRANSFIELD, Sean ... 610-785-6205 434 E
sbransfield@scs.edu
BRANSFORD, Denise, A ... 312-341-2040 157 E
dbrandsford@roosevelt.edu
BRANSON, Angela ... 312-942-6302 158 A
Angela_Branson@rush.edu
BRANSON, Cathy ... 606-487-3550 196 B
cathy.branson@kctcs.edu
BRANSON, Diane ... 301-846-2495 214 I
dbranson@frederick.edu
BRANSON, Mark ... 312-662-4121 139 E
mbranson@adler.edu
BRANSON, Salinda Jo .. 309-649-6217 160 F
jo.branson@src.edu
BRANSON, Walter, J ... 573-341-4122 284 C
bransonwj@mst.edu
BRANSTETTER, Jeffrey, C ... 402-280-5530 290 B
jbranstetter@creighton.edu
BRANSTETTER, Kate ... 402-399-2422 289 I
kbranstetter@csm.edu
BRANSTETTER, Marie ... 913-288-7211 188 G
marie@kckcc.edu
BRANT, Christine ... 734-432-5620 246 B
cbrant@madonna.edu
BRANT, David ... 310-506-4349 ... 58 H
david.brant@pepperdine.edu
BRANT, Felicia ... 202-274-5000 ... 97 B
fbrant@udc.edu
BRANT, Kathy ... 864-646-1774 449 F
kbrand@tctc.edu
BRANT, Keith ... 831-459-0111 ... 72 E
BRANT, Todd ... 405-789-6400 402 E
tbrant@snu.edu
BRANTLEY, Brenda ... 318-678-6000 203 A
bbrantley@bpcc.edu
BRANTLEY, Kyle ... 601-925-7634 268 E
brantley@mc.edu
BRANTLEY, Linda ... 978-762-4000 232 D
lbrantley@northshore.edu
BRANTLEY, Michael ... 972-860-7640 472 E
MBrantley@dcccd.edu
BRANTMAYER, Evie ... 304-367-4141 532 F
evie.brantmayer@fairmontstate.edu
BRANTON-HOUSLEY, Mary ... 970-204-8121 ... 82 J
mary.branton-housley@frontrange.edu
BRANUM, Scott ... 409-944-1216 474 G
tbranum@gc.edu
BRAS, Duane ... 616-222-3000 245 D
dbras@kuyper.edu
BRAS, Rafael ... 404-385-5700 125 D
provost@gatech.edu
BRASE, Don ... 503-399-5184 404 L
don.brase@chemeketa.edu
BRASE, Heather ... 314-744-5342 278 G
Matlock@mobap.edu
BRASE, Ruby, F ... 217-420-6029 153 A
rbrase@millikin.edu
BRASE, Wendell, C ... 949-824-5107 ... 71 C
wcbrase@uci.edu
BRASEL, Steve ... 312-329-4194 153 C
steve.brasel@moody.edu
BRASFIELD, Julie, A ... 919-515-8008 370 D
julie_brasfield@ncsu.edu
BRASHEAR, Kurth ... 402-643-7408 289 J
Kurth.Brashear@cune.edu
BRASHEARS, Randolph . 978-934-2384 229 A
Randolph_Brashears@uml.edu
BRASHER, Christine ... 337-482-1394 208 F
cbrasher@louisiana.edu
BRASHIER, Jason ... 731-989-6571 456 K
jbrashier@fhu.edu
BRASIER, Terry ... 828-398-7146 360 A
terrygbrasier@abtech.edu
BRASINGTON, Diane, F 804-523-5130 515 F
dbrasington@reynolds.edu
BRASINGTON, Dyan, L . 410-704-3780 221 A
dbrasington@towson.edu
BRASKAMP, Larry ... 630-617-3266 144 G
president@elmhurst.edu
BRASKICH, Brian ... 651-255-6170 264 F
bbraskich@unitedseminary.edu
BRASLEY, Stephanie, L . 323-242-5512 ... 51 I
braslesl@lasc.edu
BRASSARD, Kevin, F ... 508-213-2213 235 C
kevin.brassard@nichols.edu
BRASSORD, James, D .. 413-542-2202 222 A
jdbrassord@amherst.edu
BRASTETER, Christina ... 856-256-5173 306 D
brasteter@rowan.edu
BRASWELL, Cara Mia ... 334-244-3498 ... 2 A
cbraswe2@aum.edu
BRASWELL, Frank ... 651-846-1490 261 G
frank.braswell@saintpaul.edu

BRASWELL, James .... 281-476-2771 481 E
james.braswell@sjcd.edu
BRASWELL, Kevin .... 931-372-6092 462 A
kbraswell@tntech.edu
BRATCHER, Vanetta ...... 561-803-2062 109 G
vanetta_bratcher@pba.edu
BRATCHER, Winnie .... 502-863-8024 195 A
winnie_bratcher@georgetowncollege.edu
BRATHWAITE,
Cicely Horsham .... 212-220-8141 318 D
chorshambrathwaite@bmcc.cuny.edu
BRATHWAITE, Faye ...... 256-726-7076.... 6 C
fbrathwaite@oakwood.edu
BRATHWAITE, Joy, E .... 330-471-8238 385 G
jbrathwaite@malone.edu
BRATSCH, John .... 559-730-3830.. 41 D
johnbr@cos.edu
BRATSCH-PRINCE,
Dawn .... 515-294-6410 175 G
deprince@iastate.edu
BRATT, Jonathan .... 585-594-6830 339 F
bratt_jonathan@roberts.edu
BRATTIN, Emily .... 816-584-6517 280 F
emily.brattin@park.edu
BRATTOLI, Tamara .... 815-280-2470 148 K
tbrattol@jjc.edu
BRATTON, Chris .... 617-369-3581 236 E
smfapresident@smfa.edu
BRATTON, Marissa .... 808-544-0249 135 C
mbratton@hpu.edu
BRATTON, Phyllis, K .... 701-252-3467 375 J
pbratton@uj.edu
BRATULIN, Paul .... 909-384-8978.. 62 C
BRAUCHLE, Ken .... 812-237-2334 167 E
ken.brauchle@indstate.edu
BRAUCKMULLER, Lois .. 352-854-2322 100 P
brauckml@cf.edu
BRAUER, Cynthia, A ..... 757-221-1693 506 J
cabra1@wm.edu
BRAUER, Douglas .... 217-875-7200 156 K
dbrauer@richland.edu
BRAUER, Erinn .... 308-345-8112 291 H
brauere@mpcc.edu
BRAUER, Jeanna .... 417-667-8181 273 H
jbrauer@cottey.edu
BRAUER, William, L ..... 757-594-7040 506 I
wbrauer@cnu.edu
BRAULT, Kelly, N .... 248-370-4921 248 K
brault@oakland.edu
BRAUN, Abraham .... 845-425-1370 337 E
BRAUN, Amanda .... 414-229-6599 540 A
abraun25@uwm.edu
BRAUN, Dale, K .... 715-425-3840 540 E
dale.k.braun@uwrf.edu
BRAUN, Dennis .... 508-767-7541 222 D
dbraun@assumption.edu
BRAUN, Elizabeth .... 718-818-6470 341 G
BRAUN, Eric .... 740-351-3257 391 C
ebraun@shawnee.edu
BRAUN, H. Elizabeth .... 610-328-8365 436 A
lbraun1@swarthmore.edu
BRAUN, Keith .... 518-327-6072 338 B
kbraun@paulsmiths.edu
BRAUN, Keith, V .... 727-816-3336 110 B
braunk@phsc.edu
BRAUN, Lynn .... 206-780-6221 525 F
lynn.braun@pinchot.edu
BRAUN, Mark, J .... 507-933-7541 256 A
mbraun@gustavus.edu
BRAUN, Mary .... 319-273-6144 176 A
mary.braun@uni.edu
BRAUN, Neil, S .... 212-346-1962 337 I
nbraun@pace.edu
BRAUN, Raymond .... 419-372-3411 377 I
rwbraun@bgsu.edu
BRAUN, Ronald .... 620-947-3121 191 E
ronb@tabor.edu
BRAUN, Thomas, W ...... 412-648-6801 437 K
twb3@pitt.edu
BRAUNGARD,
Elizabeth, A .... 717-361-1525 418 B
braungarde@etown.edu
BRAUNGARD, John .... 518-629-4507 328 D
j.braungard@hvcc.edu
BRAUNINGER, Mike ..... 504-280-6590 205 G
rbraunin@uno.edu
BRAVAIS-SLYMAN,
Karine .... 312-777-8674 147 C
kbravais-slyman@aii.edu
BRAVE, Jennifer .... 608-789-6248 544 E
bravej@westerntc.edu
BRAVEMAN, Daan .... 585-389-2004 334 B
dbravem7@naz.edu
BRAVER, Joel .... 845-782-1380 354 B
BRAVERMAN, Lisa .... 303-784-8225.. 83 M
lbraverman@jiu.edu
BRAVMAN, John, C .... 570-577-1511 413 E
john.bravman@bucknell.edu
BRAVO, Irene .... 305-592-1223 551 A
BRAWNER, Dan .... 615-383-4848 466 F
dbrawner@watkins.edu
BRAXTON, Joanne, E ... 631-451-4160 348 E
braxtoj@sunysuffolk.edu
BRAXTON, Pamela .... 610-519-4032 439 A
pamela.braxton@villanova.edu
BRAXTON, Phyllis .... 310-287-4333.. 52 C
braxtodl@wlac.edu
BRAXTON, Phyllis, D ... 310-233-4031.. 51 F
braxtpd@lahc.edu
BRAXTON, Sallie, W ..... 540-286-8016 513 I
sbraxton@umw.edu
BRAXTON, Weldon .... 218-322-2380 259 B
weldon.braxton@itascacc.edu
BRAY, D. John .... 716-829-7818 324 E
brayjd@dyc.edu
BRAY, Heather .... 614-222-6191 380 F
hbray@ccad.edu
BRAY, Holly .... 860-486-4241.. 92 C
holly.bray@uconn.edu
BRAY, Jane, S .... 757-683-3938 510 I
jsbray@odu.edu
BRAY, Richard .... 979-209-7285 469 F
brandon.webb@blinn.edu
BRAY, Tammy .... 541-737-3220 408 F
tammy.bray@oregonstate.edu
BRAY, Tim .... 612-624-2095 265 C
brayx010@umn.edu
BRAY MCNATT,
Rosemary .... 510-549-4724.. 68 I
rbraymcnatt@sksm.edu
BRAYSHAW, Laurie .... 505-424-2305 310 L
llogan@iaia.edu
BRAYTON, Kelley .... 310-434-3465.. 65 B
brayton_kelley@smc.edu
BRAYTON, Spencer .... 217-854-3231 140 F
spencer.brayton@blackburn.edu
BRAZ, Meredith .... 603-646-2246 297 G
meredith.braz@dartmouth.edu
BRAZA, Peter .... 719-255-4550.. 86 F
pbraza@uccs.edu
BRAZDA, Sara .... 978-837-5257 233 G
brazdas@merrimack.edu
BRAZEAU, Gayle .... 207-221-4366 213 B
gbrazeau@une.edu
BRAZELTON, Kent .... 713-646-1889 482 H
kbrazelton@stcl.edu
BRAZES, Spencer .... 503-552-2016 407 F
sbrazes@ncnm.edu
BRAZIER, Elise .... 512-313-3000 471 H
elise.brazier@concordia.edu
BRAZIUNAS, Tom .... 206-934-3619 525 K
tom.braziunas@seattlecolleges.edu
BRAZZEL, Thomas .... 979-830-4041 469 F
Thomas.Brazzel@blinn.edu
BRAZZIL, Nancy, A .... 512-471-1232 493 M
nancy@po.utexas.edu
BREANDAU, L.A .... 256-924-0511.... 5 F
BREAU, Walter, C .... 413-265-2222 225 D
breauw@elms.edu
BREAULT, Susan .... 860-932-4062.. 90 A
sbreault@qvcc.commnet.edu
BREAUX, David .... 662-846-4100 267 A
dbreaux@deltastate.edu
BREAUX, Jules .... 337-482-6471 208 F
breaux@louisiana.edu
BREAZILE, Chad .... 816-279-7000 271 H
chad@abtu.edu
BRECCIAROLI, TJ .... 256-824-6700.... 9 A
thomas.brecciaroli@uah.edu
BRECHBILL, Ryan .... 614-823-1520 390 C
rbrechbill@otterbein.edu
BRECHER, Sharon .... 305-534-7050 117 C
sbrecher@talmudicu.edu
BRECKENRIDGE, James 650-433-3826.. 58 B
jbreckenridge@paloaltou.edu
BRECKENRIDGE, Joyce . 412-237-3110 415 G
jbreckenridge@ccac.edu
BREEDEN, Amy .... 804-527-1000.. 96 H
BREEDEN, Ann Lloyd ... 804-289-8732 513 M
abreeden@richmond.edu
BREEDEN, Kathy .... 931-540-2555 462 E
mbreeden@columbiastate.edu
BREEDEN, Susan, D ..... 804-289-8400 513 M
sbreeden@richmond.edu
BREEDLOVE, Paul .... 541-880-2239 406 E
breedlove@klamathcc.edu
BREEN, Anne, L .... 603-271-6484 297 C
abreen@ccsnh.edu
BREEN, Bill .... 904-680-7674 103 K
wbreen@fcsl.edu
BREEN, Patricia, A .... 626-529-8008.. 57 F
pbreen@pacificoaks.edu
BREEN, Thomas .... 518-292-1926 340 A
breent@sage.edu
BREER, Mary .... 217-234-5401 150 B
mbreer@lakeland.cc.il.us
BREERWOOD, Adam ...... 601-403-1132 270 A
abreerwood@prcc.edu
BREES, Chris .... 641-844-5763 179 L
chris.brees@iavalley.edu
BREESE, Jeffrey .... 708-524-6813 144 C
jbreese@dom.edu
BREESE, Steven .... 203-392-5468.. 88 F
breeses1@southernct.edu
BREESE, William, E ...... 414-277-7401 537 G
breese@msoe.edu
BREFFLE, Barbara .... 714-449-7448.. 53 D
bbreffle@ketchum.edu
BREGE, Nicholas .... 989-358-7202 239 C
bregen@alpenacc.edu
BREHENY, Marie .... 413-775-1397 231 E
brehenym@gcc.mass.edu
BREHLER, Elizabeth ...... 336-506-4138 359 N
elizabeth.brehler@alamancecc.edu
BREHM, Jenna .... 701-252-3467 375 J
Jenna.Brehm@uj.edu
BREHM, Richard .... 540-423-9042 515 E
rbrehm@germanna.edu
BREIER, Barbara .... 512-245-2396 489 C
blb137@txstate.edu
BREILAND, Chris .... 918-333-6151 400 I
cbreiland@okwu.edu
BREILAND, Whitney .... 918-333-6151 400 I
wbreiland@okwu.edu
BREINER, Fred .... 865-539-7144 463 E
fjbreiner@pstcc.edu
BREINER, Ozzie .... 610-758-3500 424 B
lb05@lehigh.edu
BREITBACH, William ...... 530-242-7555.. 66 C
wbreitbach@shastacollege.edu
BREITBARTH,
Jonathan, S .... 651-641-8796 255 C
breitbarth@csp.edu
BREITENBACH, Edward . 231-777-0526 247 G
edward.breitenbach@muskegoncc.edu
BREITER, Randy .... 305-442-9223 108 G
rbreiter@mrc.edu
BREITHAUPT, Jeff .... 212-749-2802 331 I
jbreithaupt@msmnyc.edu
BREITHOLZ, Brian .... 216-523-7221 380 D
b.breittholz@csuohio.edu
BREITMEYER, Chris .... 636-922-8356 281 C
cbreitmeyer@stchas.edu
BREJA, Lisa .... 641-844-5576 179 J
lisa.breja@iavalley.edu
BREKKE, Alice .... 701-777-3511 373 G
alice.brekke@und.edu
BREKKE, Tom .... 218-723-6717 255 A
tbrekke@css.edu
BREKKEN, Kathryn, C ... 702-651-7535 295 C
kc.brekken@csn.edu
BRELAND, Byron .... 408-298-2181.. 64 A
byron.breland@sjcc.edu
BRELAND, Garry, M .... 601-318-6101 271 F
garry.breland@wmcarey.edu
BRELAND, Jason .... 601-528-8424 268 G
jason.breland@mgccc.edu
BRELAND, Roger .... 251-442-2216.... 9 B
rbreland@umobile.edu
BRELLIS, Matthew .... 631-687-4561 341 A
mbrellis@sjcny.edu
BREMER, Cris, M .... 559-489-2220.. 69 B
crism.bremer@fresnocitycollege.edu
BREMER, Melanie .... 901-321-3000 455 I
mbremer@cbu.edu
BREMMER, Zach .... 215-884-8942 440 E
zach.bremmer@woninstitute.edu
BREMS, Christiane .... 503-352-7330 408 I
cbrems@pacificu.edu
BRENEMAN, Curt .... 518-276-6305 339 D
brenec@rpi.edu
BRENER, Laura .... 503-883-2449 406 I
lbrener@linfield.edu
BRENKMAN, Katie .... 360-417-6276 525 A
kbrenkman@pencol.edu
BRENN, James, E .... 803-535-5326 444 D
jbrenn@claflin.edu
BRENNAN, Blair .... 308-432-6044 292 B
bbrennan@csc.edu
BRENNAN,
Christopher, P .... 727-864-8122 101 P
brennacp@eckerd.edu
BRENNAN, Deb .... 308-398-7305 289 D
dbrennan@cccneb.edu
BRENNAN, Jonathan, R 607-746-4670 347 G
brennajr@delhi.edu
BRENNAN, Joseph, A ... 518-956-8150 343 C
jabrennan@albany.edu
BRENNAN, Joseph, A ... 319-384-0005 175 H
joe-brennan@uiowa.edu
BRENNAN, Kara .... 914-633-2410 328 F
kbrennan@iona.edu
BRENNAN, Kelly .... 734-487-8898 242 J
kelly.brennan@emich.edu
BRENNAN, Kelly .... 212-217-3800 325 C
kelly_brennan@fitnyc.edu
BRENNAN, Kevin .... 860-486-5022.. 92 C
kevin.brennan@uconn.edu
BRENNAN, Leah .... 860-701-5061.. 91 B
brennan_l@mitchell.edu
BRENNAN, Lipa .... 718-438-2727 354 C
rlb@novominsk.com
BRENNAN, Nicole .... 617-912-9120 224 C
nbrennan@bostonconservatory.edu
BRENNAN, Rick .... 708-974-5388 153 D
brennan@morainevalley.edu
BRENNAN, Robert, J ...... 301-447-7432 217 D
brennan@msmary.edu
BRENNAN, Shannon .... 570-622-7622 425 I
shannon.brennan@mccann.edu
BRENNAN, Stephen, J .. 718-982-3214 319 A
stephen.brennan@csi.cuny.edu
BRENNAN, Susan .... 781-891-2061 223 E
sbrennan@bentley.edu
BRENNAN, Terence .... 303-373-2008.. 85 I
tbrennan@rvu.edu
BRENNAN, Terrence, P 972-881-5734 471 C
tbrennan@collin.edu
BRENNAN, Thomas .... 215-951-1516 422 F
brennan@lasalle.edu
BRENNAN, William .... 671-405-5921 235 H
wbrennan@quincycollege.edu
BRENNAN, William, J .. 207-326-2220 211 G
bill.brennan@mma.edu
BRENNEMAN, Darnell ... 740-857-1311 390 L
dbrenneman@rosedale.edu
BRENNEMAN,
James, E .... 574-535-7180 166 C
president@goshen.edu
BRENNEN, Bernadette ... 716-286-8360 336 E
bmb@niagara.edu
BRENNEN, David, A ...... 859-257-1678 200 G
david.brennen@uky.edu
BRENNER, Beth .... 909-537-7724.. 35 A
bbrenner@csusb.edu
BRENNER, Christina ...... 610-436-3511 432 B
cbrenner@wcupa.edu
BRENNER, David, A .... 858-534-1501.. 72 B
dbrenner@ucsd.edu
BRENNER, Paul .... 212-237-8968 319 F
pbrenner@jjay.cuny.edu
BRENNER, Rebecca .... 617-243-2152 227 K
rbrenner@lasell.edu
BRENNER-SCOTTI,
Laura .... 609-984-1141 308 H
lbrennerscotti@tesc.edu
BRENNIE, Matthew .... 845-688-6068 350 I
brenniem@sunyulster.edu
BRENSINGER, Terry ...... 559-453-2325.. 45 E
terry.brensinger@fresno.edu
BRENT, Daniel .... 617-327-6777 238 D
dan_brent@williamjames.edu
BRENT, James .... 262-901-1389 535 A
BRENTLINGER, Dustin .. 419-448-2062 383 C
dbrentli@heidelberg.edu
BRENZING, Pam .... 616-331-3490 243 E
brenzinp@gvsu.edu
BRESCIANI, Dean .... 701-231-7211 374 C
dean.bresciani@ndsu.edu
BRESE, James .... 808-356-5273 135 C
jbrese@hpu.edu
BRESEE, Mikel .... 313-664-1546 241 D
mbresee@collegeforcreativestudies.edu
BRESEMAN, Mark, D .... 920-832-6519 536 R
mark.d.breseman@lawrence.edu
BRESINGHAM, Ann .... 312-935-6710 157 A
abresingham@robertmorris.edu
BRESLAUER,
Kenneth, J .... 732-445-3956 306 F
kjbdna@rci.rutgers.edu
BRESLIN, Beau .... 518-580-5705 342 I
bbreslin@skidmore.edu
BRESLIN, Eileen, T .... 210-567-5800 495 B
breslin@uthscsa.edu
BRESLIN, Kathleen, A ... 610-359-5131 416 G
kbreslin@dccc.edu
BRESLIN, Lisa .... 410-857-2225 217 A
lbreslin@mcdaniel.edu
BRESNAHAN, Carol .... 407-646-2355 111 H
cbresnahan@rollins.edu
BRESSETTE, Andrew ..... 706-236-2229 121 E
abressette@berry.edu
BRESSLER, Coleen .... 402-844-7006 292 G
coleen@northeast.edu
BRESSLER, Gregory, W . 973-655-5457 304 A
bresslerg@mail.montclair.edu
BRESSLER, Rebecca, B . 662-915-7735 270 G
BRESSO, Michele .... 661-336-5041.. 49 D
mbresso@kccd.edu
BRESSO, Michelle .... 661-395-4011.. 49 E
mbresso@bakersfieldcollege.edu
BRETON, Gary .... 706-236-1756 121 E
gbreton@berry.edu
BRETSCHER, David .... 217-786-2238 151 C
david.bretscher@llcc.edu
BRETT, Jennifer .... 203-576-4122.. 92 B
acup@bridgeport.edu
BRETT, Jessie .... 541-962-3740 405 G
jbrett@eou.edu
BRETTI, Anthony .... 918-595-7833 403 A
anthony.bretti@tulsacc.edu

BRETTSCHNEIDER, Marla, B .... 603-862-4676 299 B
marla.brettschneider@unh.edu
BRETZ, Brenda, K .... 717-245-1587 417 B
bretz@dickinson.edu
BREUER, Catherine .... 952-358-8243 260 D
catherine.breuer@normandale.edu
BREVOORT, Margaret ... 425-602-3003 519 J
BREW, Alan .... 715-682-1329 538 D
abrew@northland.edu
BREWER, Athos, K .... 718-289-5869 318 E
athos.brewer@bcc.cuny.edu
BREWER, Carol, A .... 507-933-8809 256 A
cbrewer@gustavus.edu
BREWER, Chris .... 615-494-8803 461 E
chris.brewer@mtsu.edu
BREWER, Clay .... 618-985-3741 148 G
claybrewer@jalc.edu
BREWER, Craig .... 650-508-3684.. 56 H
cbrewer@ndnu.edu
BREWER, Dawn, M .... 812-888-4225 174 F
dbrewer@vinu.edu
BREWER, Deborah .... 716-614-5911 336 D
dbrewer@niagaracc.suny.edu
BREWER, Dennis .... 479-575-3301.. 23 G
dbrewer@uark.edu
BREWER, Helen .... 908-709-7142 309 A
helen.brewer@ucc.edu
BREWER, Jane, T .... 843-549-6314 450 F
jtbrewer@mailbox.sc.edu
BREWER, Janet .... 501-760-4313.. 21 H
jbrewer@npcc.edu
BREWER, Janet, L .... 765-641-4272 164 B
jlbrewer@anderson.edu
BREWER, Jay .... 401-841-7008 548 B
BREWER, Jerry, T .... 803-777-5783 450 B
jerry-brewer@sc.edu
BREWER, Jim, L .... 870-460-1274.. 24 C
brewer@uamont.edu
BREWER, John .... 801-863-8320 500 B
brewerjc@uvu.edu
BREWER, JR., John, B . 301-447-5280 217 D
brewer@msmary.edu
BREWER, Judy .... 319-656-2447 182 G
BREWER, Kristina .... 260-665-4161 173 D
brewerk@trine.edu
BREWER, Michael, H .... 484-664-3400 427 C
brewer@muhlenberg.edu
BREWER, Mondy .... 806-720-7803 478 A
mondy.brewer@lcu.edu
BREWER, Nancy .... 631-451-4469 348 F
brewern@sunysuffolk.edu
BREWER, Rick .... 916-558-2442.. 53 B
BrewerR@scc.losrios.edu
BREWER, Rick .... 318-487-7401 202 L
rick.brewer@lacollege.edu
BREWER, Robert, W ..... 336-272-7102 357 B
rbrewer@greensboro.edu
BREWER, Ryan .... 205-329-7865.... 3 C
ryan.brewer@ecacolleges.com
BREWER, Stacey .... 864-596-9050 445 E
stacey.brewer@converse.edu
BREWER, Susan .... 870-460-1050.. 24 C
brewers@uamont.edu
BREWER, Tim .... 704-878-3205 364 C
tbrewer@mitchellcc.edu
BREWINGTON, Delsey .. 910-592-8084 365 G
dbrewington@sampsoncc.edu
BREWINGTON, Donald, E .... 512-505-3054 475 G
debrewington@htu.edu
BREWINGTON, Mazie, L .... 951-222-8307.. 61 B
mazie.brewington@rcc.edu
BREWINGTON, Teare .... 803-536-7011 448 H
tbrewing@scsu.edu
BREWS, Peter, J .... 803-777-3176 450 B
peter.brews@moore.sc.edu
BREWSTER, Carrie .... 925-631-4643.. 61 G
cbrewste@stmarys-ca.edu
BREWSTER, Edward ...... 360-538-4000 523 A
brewster@ghc.edu
BREWSTER, Geoffrey ..... 918-610-8303 401 C
geoffrey.brewster@ptstulsa.edu
BREWSTER, LaRita .... 256-761-6119.... 7 H
lmbrewster@talladega.edu
BREWSTER, Shannelle .. 712-279-3149 182 F
BREWSTER, Stephen ...... 303-217-4024.. 82 M
brewsters@heritage-education.com
BREWTON, Janet, J ...... 843-953-4820 445 B
brewtonj@cofc.edu
BREY, Richard .... 208-282-2902 138 C
breyrich@isu.edu
BREZEL, Allan .... 404-872-3593 121 A
abrezel@johnmarshall.edu
BREZIL, Chris .... 212-229-5300 334 C
brezilc@newschool.edu
BREZINA, Jennifer .... 661-362-5919.. 40 H
jennifer.brezina@canyons.edu
BREZINA, Katherine ...... 508-678-2811 231 B
katherine.brezina@bristolcc.edu
BREZINSKI, Donald ...... 603-645-3109 298 H
d.brezinski@snhu.edu
BRIAN, Robert, M .... 912-583-3107 121 H
rbrian@bpc.edu
BRIAN, Thomas, J .... 918-631-2200 403 M
thomas-brian@utulsa.edu
BRIAND, Simone .... 913-234-0810 185 N
simone.briand@cleveland.edu
BRIAR, Jennifer .... 760-591-3012.. 74 A
jbriar@usa.edu
BRIAR-LAWSON, Katharine, H .... 518-442-5324 343 C
kbriarlawson@albany.edu
BRICE, Diane .... 806-371-5028 467 E
kdbrice@actx.edu
BRICE, Tanya .... 803-705-4945 443 F
bricet@benedict.edu
BRICELAND, Cynthia .... 724-503-1001 439 B
cbriceland@washjeff.edu
BRICHER, Gary .... 860-297-2331.. 92 A
gary.bricher@trincoll.edu
BRICHTA, William .... 215-780-1307 435 D
wbrichta@salus.edu
BRICK, George .... 575-624-8023 311 K
brick@nmmi.edu
BRICK, III, Harold (Ben), B .... 402-449-2893 290 F
library@graceu.edu
BRICKER, J. Douglas .... 412-396-6361 417 I
bricker@duq.edu
BRICKER, Susan .... 626-585-7614.. 58 F
BRICKETTO, Matthew, M .... 610-436-3301 432 B
mbricketto@wcupa.edu
BRICKHOUSE, Nancy ...... 314-977-2193 281 M
brickhouse@slu.edu
BRICKHOUSE, Wendy, W .... 252-335-0821 361 G
wbrickhouse@albemarle.edu
BRICKLE, Colleen .... 952-358-8158 260 D
colleen.brickle@normandale.edu
BRICKNER-WOOD, Larry .... 603-862-1165 299 B
larry.brickner-wood@unh.edu
BRIDDES, Bill .... 610-902-8526 414 B
BRIDEL, David .... 213-821-4035.. 74 D
bridel@usc.edu
BRIDGE, Louise .... 801-863-8689 500 B
bridgelo@uvu.edu
BRIDGEFORTH, Valerie . 601-318-6188 271 F
vbridgeforth@wmcarey.edu
BRIDGEMAN, Curtis ..... 503-370-6402 411 D
cbridgem@willamette.edu
BRIDGEMAN, Doris .... 601-977-7836 270 F
dbridgeman@tougaloo.edu
BRIDGEMAN, Gregory .. 270-707-3904 196 D
gbridgeman0001@kctcs.edu
BRIDGEMAN, Robert ..... 352-638-9761.. 99 D
bbridgeman@beaconcollege.edu
BRIDGEN, Erin, R .... 412-578-8725 414 I
erbridgen@carlow.edu
BRIDGENS, Marc, E ...... 570-326-3761 429 J
mbridgen@pct.edu
BRIDGER, Donald .... 303-458-4206.. 85 G
dbridger@regis.edu
BRIDGER, Seth .... 614-235-4136 392 D
sbridger@TLSohio.edu
BRIDGERS, Amy .... 252-399-6397 354 I
abbridgers@barton.edu
BRIDGES, Amanda .... 706-864-1546 133 A
amanda.bridges@ung.edu
BRIDGES, Angela .... 662-846-4380 267 A
abridges@deltastate.edu
BRIDGES, Avie .... 714-564-6910.. 60 G
bridges_avie@sac.edu
BRIDGES, Ceil, L .... 870-235-4079.. 23 D
clbridges@saumag.edu
BRIDGES, Christopher .. 570-662-4342 431 D
cbridges@mansfield.edu
BRIDGES, Clarence, F .. 312-413-5946 161 F
cbridges@uic.edu
BRIDGES, Craig .... 218-723-4822 255 A
cbridges@css.edu
BRIDGES, Daniel .... 323-343-3080.. 34 A
dbridges@cslanet.calstatela.edu
BRIDGES, Darryl .... 843-661-1295 446 E
dbridges@fmarion.edu
BRIDGES, David .... 229-391-5050 119 F
dbridges@abac.edu
BRIDGES, Harold, A ..... 310-338-2700.. 53 C
BRIDGES, Karl .... 208-282-3045 138 C
bridkarl@isu.edu
BRIDGES, Katie .... 202-462-2101.. 96 C
kbridges@iwp.edu
BRIDGES, Kermit, S .... 972-825-4652 483 D
president@sagu.edu
BRIDGES, Kristina .... 319-399-8100 176 G
kbridges@coe.edu
BRIDGES, LaDonna ...... 508-626-4906 230 A
lbridges@framingham.edu
BRIDGES, Martin .... 910-410-1818 365 B
mwbridges@richmondcc.edu
BRIDGES, Michael, W .. 412-396-6000 417 I
bridgesm@duq.edu
BRIDGES, Ruth .... 254-298-8309 484 C
ruth.bridges@templejc.edu
BRIDGES, Scott, D .... 618-453-6214 159 H
bridges@siu.edu
BRIDGES, Shelton .... 502-451-0815 200 A
sbridges@sullivan.edu
BRIDGES, Shelton .... 502-451-0815 200 B
sbridges@sullivan.edu
BRIDGES, Steven, J ...... 812-464-1849 174 D
sjbridge@usi.edu
BRIDGES, Tharsteen ..... 334-874-5700.... 3 B
tbridges@ccal.edu
BRIDGES, Vernon, D .... 818-947-2541.. 52 B
bridgevd@lavc.edu
BRIDGESMITH, Lance ... 310-506-4700.. 58 H
lance.bridgesmith@pepperdine.edu
BRIDGMAN, Christa, L . 828-298-3325 373 A
cbridgma@warren-wilson.edu
BRIDGMON, Phillip ...... 918-456-5511 398 M
bridgmon@nsuok.edu
BRIDWELL, Chadd .... 817-531-4422 490 C
cbridwell@txwes.edu
BRIDWELL, Joy .... 406-395-4875 288 I
jbridwell@stonechild.edu
BRIDWELL, Virginia ...... 425-564-2198 519 L
virginia.bridwell@bellevuecollege.edu
BRIELL, Scott .... 319-385-6231 180 A
scott.briell@iw.edu
BRIEM, Kit .... 651-255-6111 264 F
kbriem@unitedseminary.edu
BRIEN, Jane .... 845-758-4294 315 G
brien@bard.edu
BRIERE, Donna .... 603-752-1113 297 E
dbriere@ccsnh.edu
BRIETLING, Edmund ..... 202-408-2400.. 96 H
BRIGDON, Beth, P .... 706-721-9667 121 C
bbrigdon@gru.edu
BRIGGANCE, Richard .... 615-963-5171 461 F
rbriggance@tnstate.edu
BRIGGER, Clark, V .... 814-863-4774 428 C
cvb12@psu.edu
BRIGGS, Baily .... 903-923-3217 488 A
Baily.briggs@tstc.edu
BRIGGS, Catherine, R ... 609-894-9311 306 B
cbriggs@bcc.edu
BRIGGS, Charlotte .... 413-565-1000 222 G
cbriggs@baypath.edu
BRIGGS, Darcy .... 303-797-5623.. 79 A
darcy.briggs@arapahoe.edu
BRIGGS, Douglas, S ..... 540-636-2900 506 H
dougb@christendom.edu
BRIGGS, Eddie .... 864-388-8222 447 E
ebriggs@lander.edu
BRIGGS, Jeff .... 859-344-3352 200 C
briggsj@thomasmore.edu
BRIGGS, Jeff .... 785-628-4200 187 A
jbriggs@fhsu.edu
BRIGGS, Jennifer .... 812-488-2602 173 H
jb610@evansville.edu
BRIGGS, SR., Jerryl ...... 662-254-3425 269 C
jerryl.briggs@mvsu.edu
BRIGGS, Julie, A .... 585-245-5616 345 D
briggsja@geneseo.edu
BRIGGS, Karen .... 662-476-5041 267 C
kbriggs@eastms.edu
BRIGGS, Karen .... 619-260-2762.. 74 B
karenbriggs@sandiego.edu
BRIGGS, Kenneth .... 860-215-9259.. 90 B
kbriggs@trcc.commnet.edu
BRIGGS, Kennon .... 910-362-7065 360 G
kbriggs@mail.cfcc.edu
BRIGGS, LaNae, R .... 803-786-3856 445 C
lrbriggs@columbiasc.edu
BRIGGS, Larry .... 208-769-3474 138 G
ljbriggs@nic.edu
BRIGGS, Mary, K .... 276-944-6836 507 E
mkbriggs@ehc.edu
BRIGGS, Paige, D .... 505-277-5115 313 H
PDBriggs@unm.edu
BRIGGS, Pertrina .... 630-743-0695 163 D
pbriggs@westwood.edu
BRIGGS, Peter, F .... 517-353-1720 246 H
pbriggs@msu.edu
BRIGGS, Phillip .... 805-289-6000.. 75 E
pbriggs@vcccd.edu
BRIGGS, Stephen, R ..... 706-236-2281 121 E
sbriggs@berry.edu
BRIGGS, Susan .... 406-683-7031 287 E
susan.briggs@umwestern.edu
BRIGGS, Thyra .... 909-607-4408.. 46 K
thyra_briggs@hmc.edu
BRIGHAM, Bettie Ann .. 610-341-5823 418 A
bbrigham@eastern.edu
BRIGHAM, David, R ..... 215-972-2056 429 G
dbrigham@pafa.org
BRIGHAM, Eric .... 802-485-2480 502 G
ebrigham@norwich.edu
BRIGHAM, Jeffrey .... 617-964-1100 222 B
BRIGHAM, R. Scott ...... 773-907-4700 141 O
sbrigham@ccc.edu
BRIGHT, Brett .... 620-665-3579 188 A
brightb@hutchcc.edu
BRIGHT, Erin, L .... 503-943-7125 410 H
bright@up.edu
BRIGHT, Harry .... 641-472-1178 181 A
hbright@mum.edu
BRIGHT, James (Phillip) .... 731-881-7845 465 F
pbright@utm.edu
BRIGHT, Jessica .... 512-313-3000 471 H
jessica.bright@concordia.edu
BRIGHT, Marvin .... 727-712-5742 112 A
bright.marvin@spcollege.edu
BRIGHT, Richard .... 641-269-4850 178 I
bright@grinnell.edu
BRIGHT, Sarah .... 636-481-3218 276 E
sbright@jeffco.edu
BRIGHT, Steve .... 434-544-8208 509 I
bright@lynchburg.edu
BRIJBASI, Monique ...... 305-628-6648 112 B
mbrijbasi@stu.edu
BRILEY, Brantley .... 252-527-6223 363 G
bbriley@lenoircc.edu
BRILEY, Jana .... 912-478-1301 126 B
janawms@georgiasouthern.edu
BRILL, Ann .... 309-341-7130 149 G
abrill@knox.edu
BRILL, Ann, M .... 785-864-4755 191 G
abrill@ku.edu
BRILLER, Vladimir .... 718-636-4245 338 E
vbriller@pratt.edu
BRILLEY, Amy .... 217-362-6488 153 A
abrilley@millikin.edu
BRILLHART, David .... 740-366-9319 378 L
brillhart.5@osu.edu
BRIMHALL, Carrie .... 218-736-1524 259 H
carrie.brimhall@minnesota.edu
BRIMHALL, Joseph .... 503-251-5712 410 I
jebrimhall@uws.edu
BRIMHALL-VARGAS, Mark .... 617-627-3323 237 C
mark.brimhallvargas@tufts.edu
BRIMMER, Diane, L ...... 608-796-3801 542 H
dlbrimmer@viterbo.edu
BRIMMERMAN, Roger .. 847-628-2017 149 A
roger.brimmerman@judsonu.edu
BRINDLE, Denise .... 978-665-3454 229 D
dbrindl1@fitchburgstate.edu
BRINDLEY, Roger .... 813-974-1218 116 B
brindley@usf.edu
BRINEGAR, Kathleen .... 802-635-1472 504 A
kathleen.brinegar@jsc.edu
BRINER, Clare .... 708-974-5376 153 D
brinerc@morainevalley.edu
BRINEY, Colleen, M ..... 479-575-5165.. 23 G
cbriney@uark.edu
BRINGAZE, Tammy .... 413-572-5491 230 F
tbringaze@westfield.ma.edu
BRINGER, Michael .... 573-288-6300 274 C
mbringer@culver.edu
BRINGHURST, Steve ..... 435-652-7901 499 M
brings@dixie.edu
BRINGLE, Mary, L .... 828-884-8142 355 A
mbringle@brevard.edu
BRINGSJORD, Elizabeth 518-320-1251 343 B
elizabeth.bringsjord@suny.edu
BRINK, Benita .... 719-587-7426.. 78 I
babrink@adams.edu
BRINK, Laura .... 617-521-2127 236 F
laura.brink@simmons.edu
BRINK-DRESCHER, Judith .... 516-323-3925 333 E
jdrescher@molloy.edu
BRINKER, Cynthia, S .... 812-464-1774 174 D
cbrinker@usi.edu
BRINKLEY, David .... 270-745-6140 201 D
david.brinkley@wku.edu
BRINKLEY-KENNEDY, Rhonda .... 415-955-2050.. 26 I
rbrinkley-kennedy@alliant.edu
BRINKMAN, Cathy .... 818-364-7723.. 51 G
brinkmanc@lamission.edu
BRINKMAN, Kevin .... 614-251-4603 388 H
brinkmak@ohiodominican.edu
BRINKMAN, Matt .... 423-614-8395 457 M
mmbrinkman@leeuniversity.edu
BRINKOETTER, Darbe ... 217-875-7200 156 K
dbrinkoetter@richland.edu
BRINNER, Jonda .... 502-410-6200 194 N
jbrinner@galencollege.edu
BRINSON, Anne .... 317-921-4831 169 L
aebrinson@ivytech.edu
BRINSON, Bruce .... 214-379-5573 480 D
bbrinson@pqc.edu
BRINSON, Donna .... 770-781-6963 128 A
dbrinson@laniertech.edu

BRONSTEIN, Susan ...... 716-338-1035 329 E susanbronstein@mail.sunyjcc.edu
BRONSTEIN, Susan ...... 239-489-9357 104 G sbronstein@fsw.edu
BROOKBANK, Julie ...... 605-995-3026 452 H julie.brookbank@mitchelltech.edu
BROOKBANK, Maureen 202-319-5598.. 95 A brookbank@cua.edu
BROOKE, Judith .... 321-674-8053 103 R jbrooke@fit.edu
BROOKE, Patrick .... 651-638-6879 254 A pbrooke@bethel.edu
BROOKER, Paulita .... 704-463-7302 367 F paulita.brooker@pfeiffer.edu
BROOKER, Sarah .... 717-564-4112 421 M sbrooker@kaplan.edu
BROOKET, Jenn .... 517-264-7159 250 B jbrooket@sienaheights.edu
BROOKEY, Lauren, F .... 918-595-7000 403 A lauren.brookey@tulsacc.edu
BROOKING, David .... 662-329-7138 269 B dmbrooking@muw.edu
BROOKINS, Carla .... 615-966-7076 458 C carla.brookins@lipscomb.edu
BROOKINS, Laura .... 610-917-1451 438 G ljbrookins@valleyforge.edu
BROOKNER, Laurie .... 415-565-8813.. 71 B brookner@uchastings.edu
BROOKOVER, Joe .... 515-643-6611 181 B jbrookover@mercydesmoines.org
BROOKS, Ann .... 918-302-3617 397 L abrooks@eosc.edu
BROOKS, Anthony .... 919-719-1983 368 G anthony.brooks@shawu.edu
BROOKS, Ariel .... 802-451-7118 502 B abrooks@marlboro.edu
BROOKS, Audrey .... 410-532-5735 217 F abrooks@ndm.edu
BROOKS, Barbara .... 315-228-7417 321 H bbrooks@colgate.edu
BROOKS, Beth .... 253-566-5054 527 C bbrooks@tacomacc.edu
BROOKS, Beth, A .... 773-252-5311 156 J beth.brooks@resu.edu
BROOKS, Billie, K .... 304-710-3363 531 C billie.brooks@mctc.edu
BROOKS, Browning .... 850-644-8343 115 A bbrooks@fsu.edu
BROOKS, Carlton .... 719-502-2003.. 84 J carlton.brooks@ppcc.edu
BROOKS, Carolyn .... 323-856-7742.. 27 H cbrooks@afi.com
BROOKS, Carrie Allison .... 901-272-5160 459 A cbrooks@mca.edu
BROOKS, Charles, R .... 973-596-2875 304 D brooks@njit.edu
BROOKS, Christopher ... 734-207-9581 153 C chris.brooks@moody.edu
BROOKS, Cindy, L .... 610-799-1121 424 A cbrooks@lccc.edu
BROOKS, Constance ..... 702-889-8426 295 B constance_brooks@nshe.nevada.edu
BROOKS, Cynthia .... 615-963-7410 461 F cbrooks@tnstate.edu
BROOKS, Dana, D .... 304-293-8026 533 D dbrooks@mail.wvu.edu
BROOKS, Danny, K .... 336-841-9131 357 E dbrooks@highpoint.edu
BROOKS, Darlene, D .... 901-843-3901 460 F brooksd@rhodes.edu
BROOKS, DeeAnna .... 803-323-2225 451 I brooksd@winthrop.edu
BROOKS, II, Earl, D ..... 260-665-4101 173 D brookse@trine.edu
BROOKS, Elizabeth .... 215-955-0916 436 F elizabeth.brooks@jefferson.edu
BROOKS, Fred .... 252-451-8233 364 E fbrooks@nashcc.edu
BROOKS, Gene .... 402-643-7411 289 J gene.brooks@cune.edu
BROOKS, Gerald .... 504-286-5388 207 B gbrooks@suno.edu
BROOKS, Glee, R .... 530-226-4188.. 66 G gbrooks@simpsonu.edu
BROOKS, II, H. Gordon .... 337-482-6224 208 F gbrooks@louisiana.edu
BROOKS, Ian .... 510-883-2056.. 43 C ibrooks@dspt.edu
BROOKS, James, L .... 323-856-7600.. 27 H jbrooks@afi.com
BROOKS, Jane .... 219-785-5657 172 A jbrooks@pnc.edu
BROOKS, Jason .... 620-341-5481 186 H jbrooks5@emporia.edu
BROOKS, Jim .... 352-335-2332.. 97 F
BROOKS, Jim, J .... 541-346-6121 410 F brooksja@uoregon.edu
BROOKS, Joanna .... 619-594-6111.. 35 E jbrooks@mail.sdsu.edu
BROOKS, John, I .... 910-672-1060 370 A jibrooks@uncfsu.edu
BROOKS, Joseph .... 303-963-3463.. 79 L jbrooks@ccu.edu
BROOKS, Josh .... 601-974-1190 268 D Josh.Brooks@millsaps.edu
BROOKS, Juliette .... 201-692-7050 302 H juliette_brooks@fdu.edu
BROOKS, Justin, P .... 619-239-0391.. 36 E jbrooks@cwsl.edu
BROOKS, Karl .... 847-635-1739 155 E
BROOKS, Katrina .... 904-724-2229 118 F
BROOKS, Keith .... 410-706-7131 219 E kbrooks@umaryland.edu
BROOKS, Kelly .... 575-527-7650 312 D kbrooks@nmsu.edu
BROOKS, Kent .... 307-268-2703 545 Z kbrooks@caspercollege.edu
BROOKS, L. Rayburn .... 864-941-8301 448 D brooks.r@ptc.edu
BROOKS, Larry .... 701-228-5457 374 F larry.brooks@dakotacollege.edu
BROOKS, LaShon, F ..... 662-254-3425 269 C lfbrooks@mvsu.edu
BROOKS, Lisa .... 818-240-1000.. 45 I lbrooks@glendale.edu
BROOKS, Lois .... 541-737-0739 408 F lois.brooks@oregonstate.edu
BROOKS, Lyvette .... 215-751-8046 416 B lbrooks@ccp.edu
BROOKS, Marilyn, A .... 804-257-5846 518 E mabrooks2@vuu.edu
BROOKS, Mark .... 229-931-2246 131 E mbrooks@southgatech.edu
BROOKS, Mark, D .... 270-901-1117 197 C mark.brooks@kctcs.edu
BROOKS, Martha .... 804-758-6771 516 G
BROOKS, Michael .... 315-655-7141 317 J mdbrooks@cazenovia.edu
BROOKS, Michael .... 801-422-2767 497 J michael_brooks@byu.edu
BROOKS, Michelle .... 252-328-2872 369 E brooksm@ecu.edu
BROOKS, Monica .... 304-696-6474 532 H brooks@marshall.edu
BROOKS, Nancy, S .... 515-294-8757 175 G nsbrook@iastate.edu
BROOKS, Patricia .... 972-825-4652 483 D pabrooks@sagu.edu
BROOKS, Paul .... 972-825-4616 483 D pbrooks@sagu.edu
BROOKS, Paul .... 401-456-8810 442 A pbrooks@ric.edu
BROOKS, Randy, M ...... 217-424-6205 153 A rbrooks@millikin.edu
BROOKS, Rena .... 918-647-1217 397 C trbrooks@carlalbert.edu
BROOKS, Robert .... 617-928-4602 234 D rbrooks@mountida.edu
BROOKS, Robert, T ...... 757-594-7217 506 I todd.brooks@cnu.edu
BROOKS, Roger, L .... 804-289-8491 513 M rbrooks@richmond.edu
BROOKS, Ronnie .... 615-963-5671 461 F rbrooks6@tnstate.edu
BROOKS, Sarah .... 509-542-4837 521 C sbrooks@columbiabasin.edu
BROOKS, Sean .... 410-951-3455 220 C sbrooks@coppin.edu
BROOKS, Shannon .... 864-644-5072 449 B sbrooks@swu.edu
BROOKS, Sherry, L ...... 906-635-2216 245 H sbrooks1@lssu.edu
BROOKS, Teresa .... 903-693-2060 480 A trbrooks@panola.edu
BROOKS, Thom, R .... 828-339-4202 366 C tbrooks@southwesterncc.edu
BROOKS, Thomas .... 641-472-7000 181 A tbrooks@mum.edu
BROOKS, Tim .... 617-627-3986 237 C tim.brooks@tufts.edu
BROOKS, Tim .... 402-280-2564 290 B TimBrooks@creighton.edu
BROOKS, Todd .... 706-236-2260 121 E tbrooks@berry.edu
BROOKS, Tyrone .... 509-542-4408 521 C tbrooks@columbiabasin.edu
BROOKS, Tyrone, W ..... 208-885-5255 139 C tyroneb@uidaho.edu
BROOKS, Vanessa .... 734-973-3621 251 J vbrooks@wccnet.edu
BROOKS, Vera .... 410-462-8500 213 G vbrooks@bccc.edu
BROOKS, Walter, T .... 508-362-2131 231 D wbrooks@capecod.edu
BROOKS, Wendy .... 989-358-7299 239 C brooksw@alpenacc.edu
BROOKS, Wes .... 319-385-6284 180 A wesley.brooks@iw.edu
BROOKS, Will .... 678-033-1434 128 C william.brooks2@life.edu
BROOKS BLAIR, Sarah, D .... 937-529-2201 392 G sblair@united.edu
BROOKS-WALTER, Alexis .... 386-481-2668.. 99 F waltera@cookman.edu
BROOKSHIRE, David .... 800-895-7411 504 L
BROOKSHIRE, Kathy .... 601-484-8612 268 B kbrooksh@meridiancc.edu
BROOM, Cheryl .... 760-795-2121.. 54 G cbroom@miracosta.edu
BROOMALL, James, K .. 302-831-2795.. 94 D jbroom@udel.edu
BROOME, Barbara .... 330-672-8799 384 H bbroome1@kent.edu
BROOME, JR., David, E .... 704-687-5732 371 B debroome@uncc.edu
BROOME, Marion .... 919-684-3786 356 E marion.broome@duke.edu
BROOME, Melba .... 202-274-6118.. 97 B mbroome@udc.edu
BROOMHEAD, Keiko ..... 617-989-4034 237 G broomheadk@wit.edu
BROPHY, Ann .... 314-246-7422 285 G annbrophy26@webster.edu
BROPHY, Dale, G .... 801-585-2677 499 K dale.brophy@dps.utah.edu
BROPHY, Michael, S ..... 310-377-5501.. 53 E mbrophy@marymountcalifornia.edu
BROPHY, Michael, S .... 630-829-6004 140 A mbrophy@ben.edu
BROPHY, JR., William, E .... 256-824-6144.... 9 A william.brophy@uah.edu
BRORBY, Gregory .... 775-753-2260 295 D gregory.brorby@gbcnv.edu
BROSHOUS, Robert, D . 563-589-3199 183 E bbroshou@dbq.edu
BROSKE, Kathleen, M .. 920-924-2139 543 F kbroske@morainepark.edu
BROSKY, Lisa .... 502-213-2400 196 E lisa.brosky@kctcs.edu
BROSNAN, Joseph, S ... 215-489-2203 416 H Joseph.Brosnan@delval.edu
BROSNAN, Mary .... 516-323-3468 333 E mbrosnan@molloy.edu
BROSS, Scott .... 309-268-8385 145 H
BROSS-FREGONARA, Nanci .... 304-704-1162 529 I brossfregonaran@dewv.edu
BROSTROM, Nathan, E . 510-987-9029.. 70 J nathan.brostrom@ucop.edu
BROTHERS, Gregory, A 713-646-1888 482 H gbrothers@stcl.edu
BROTHERS, James, F .... 937-229-2829 393 E JBrothers1@udayton.edu
BROTHERS, Wes .... 740-477-7757 388 F wbrothers@ohiochristian.edu
BROTHERSON, Carrie, P .... 540-261-8534 512 J carrie.brotherson@svu.edu
BROTHERTON, Jeffrey ... 614-222-4014 380 F jbrotherton@ccad.edu
BROTHERTON, Thomas, S .... 712-852-5224 179 G tbrotherton@iowalakes.edu
BROUCEK, Willard .... 605-626-2401 454 A Willard.Broucek@northern.edu
BROUDE, Nancy .... 617-587-5585 234 G brouden@neco.edu
BROUGH, Aimee, B ...... 717-736-4122 420 D abbrough@hacc.edu
BROUGHTON, Nancy .... 218-879-0837 258 F sam@fdltcc.edu
BROUHARD, Nathanael, T .... 215-972-2015 429 G nbrouhard@pafa.edu
BROUILLARD-BRUCE, Torry .... 209-946-2331.. 73 C tbrouillard@pacific.edu
BROUILLET, Susan .... 603-230-3576 296 J sbrouillet@ccsnh.edu
BROUILLETTE, Domenick, R .... 816-604-1370 277 F domenick.brouillette@mcckc.edu
BROUNK, Thomas, M .. 314-935-5955 285 E tom_brounk@wustl.edu
BROUSSARD, Camille ... 212-431-2354 335 G Camille.Broussard@nyls.edu
BROUSSARD, Michael .. 337-550-1292 205 B mpbrouss@lsue.edu
BROUSSARD, Ted .... 253-589-5546 521 B ted.broussard@cptc.edu
BROUSSARD, William ... 225-771-5930 207 A will_broussard@subr.edu
BROUSSARD, Willie ...... 636-949-4705 276 L wbroussard@lindenwood.edu
BROUWER, Dustin, J .... 605-336-6588 453 C dbrouwer@sfseminary.edu
BROUWER POTTS, Natalie .... 773-442-5412 154 H n-potts@neiu.edu
BROWDER, Steven, K ... 317-738-8301 166 B sbrowder@franklincollege.edu
BROWER, Bill .... 315-445-5441 330 B browewih@lemoyne.edu
BROWER, Bob .... 619-849-2216.. 59 K bobbrower@pointloma.edu
BROWER, Jennifer .... 505-224-4669 310 F jbrower@cnm.edu
BROWER, Keith .... 718-862-7345 331 H keith.brower@manhattan.edu
BROWER, Laura .... 805-289-6460.. 75 E lbrower@vcccd.edu
BROWER, Lynn .... 818-778-5749.. 52 B browerl@lavc.edu
BROWER, Paul, O .... 508-213-2271 235 C paul.brower@nichols.edu
BROWER, Pearl, K .... 907-852-3333.. 10 F pearl.brower@ilisagvik.edu
BROWER, Roderick .... 910-678-8232 362 E browerr@faytechcc.edu
BROWN, Aaron .... 951-222-8789.. 60 J aaron.brown@rccd.edu
BROWN, Alanka .... 301-624-2826 214 I albrown@frederick.edu
BROWN, Albert .... 360-596-5268 527 B abrown@spscc.edu
BROWN, Alesia .... 864-941-8611 448 D brown.a@ptc.edu
BROWN, Alfreda .... 330-672-2442 384 H abbrown@kent.edu
BROWN, Alistair .... 630-620-2101 154 J abrown@seminary.edu
BROWN, Amon .... 202-651-5007.. 95 C amon.brown@gallaudet.edu
BROWN, Amy .... 704-463-3046 367 F amy.brown@pfeiffer.edu
BROWN, Amy, L .... 607-746-4584 347 G brownal@delhi.edu
BROWN, Andrea .... 435-652-7595 499 M abrown@dixie.edu
BROWN, Andrew .... 651-696-6069 256 L dabrown@macalester.edu
BROWN, Angela, C ...... 254-968-9128 485 A abrown@tarleton.edu
BROWN, Angela, P .... 731-425-2347 463 A abrown@jscc.edu
BROWN, Ann .... 919-516-5083 368 E abrown@st-aug.edu
BROWN, Anne .... 617-228-3267 231 C abrown@bhcc.mass.edu
BROWN, Annette .... 410-334-2900 221 E abrown@worwic.edu
BROWN, Ansel, E .... 919-530-7477 370 C browna@nccu.edu
BROWN, April .... 239-513-1122 106 E abrown@hodges.edu
BROWN, Arthur .... 870-864-7102.. 23 B abrown@southark.edu
BROWN, B, T .... 252-536-7245 363 B btbrown920@halifaxcc.edu
BROWN, Barry .... 617-928-4502 234 D barrybrown@mountida.edu
BROWN, Beverly .... 718-262-2238 321 B bbrown@york.cuny.edu
BROWN, Bill .... 919-760-2367 359 B brownw@meredith.edu
BROWN, Bill .... 913-469-8500 188 E bbrown@jccc.edu
BROWN, Bill .... 863-638-7228 118 L bill.brown@warner.edu
BROWN, Bob .... 859-233-8889 200 D robrown@transy.edu
BROWN, Bob .... 940-565-2055 492 D bob.brown@unt.edu
BROWN, Bobbie .... 806-742-3661 489 F bobbie.brown@ttu.edu
BROWN, Bonita, J .... 336-334-4244 371 C bjbrown3@uncg.edu
BROWN, Bradd .... 405-208-5001 400 A bradd.brown@okcu.edu
BROWN, Braden .... 405-382-9277 402 C b.brown@sscok.edu
BROWN, Bradley .... 435-586-7871 499 L brown@suu.edu
BROWN, Brenda, L .... 478-988-6851 122 F bbrown@centralgatech.edu
BROWN, Brent, K .... 801-581-3003 499 K brent.brown@osp.utah.edu
BROWN, Brian .... 315-364-3207 352 F bbrown@wells.edu
BROWN, JR., Buck, F .. 864-379-8805 446 B brown@erskine.edu
BROWN, Calvin .... 205-348-4767.... 8 E cbrown@alumni.ua.edu
BROWN, Calvin .... 205-348-5966.... 8 E cbrown@alumni.ua.edu
BROWN, Carl .... 614-947-6080 382 H carl.brown@franklin.edu

BROWN, Matt .... 901-381-3939 466 E
matt@visible.edu
BROWN, Max .... 603-524-3207 296 L
BROWN, Melanie, A ..... 386-312-4202 111 K
melaniebrown@sjrstate.edu
BROWN, Melissa .... 314-652-0300 281 F
mbrown@slchcmail.com
BROWN, Melissa .... 412-809-5100 433 D
brown.melissa@pti.edu
BROWN, Melissa, S ..... 909-607-7855.. 39 H
melissa_brown@kgi.edu
BROWN, Merri .... 215-248-6323 424 G
mbrown@ltsp.edu
BROWN, Merv, R .... 208-496-2010 137 F
brownme@byui.edu
BROWN, Michael .... 406-447-6947 287 F
michael.brown@umhelena.edu
BROWN, Michael .... 740-753-3591 383 G
BROWN, Michael .... 937-376-2946 390 F
mbrown@payne.edu
BROWN, II, Michael, A 336-334-7940 370 B
mabrown8@ncat.edu
BROWN, Michael, B ..... 252-985-5136 367 E
mbrown@ncwc.edu
BROWN, Michael, E ..... 202-994-6241.. 95 D
brownm@gwu.edu
BROWN, Michael, T ..... 805-893-2944.. 72 D
michael.brown@extension.ucsb.edu
BROWN, Michele .... 847-635-1724 155 E
mbrown@oakton.edu
BROWN, Michelle .... 678-717-6201 133 A
michelle.brown@ung.edu
BROWN, Michelle .... 435-283-7127 500 D
michelle.brown@snow.edu
BROWN, Mike .... 574-936-8898 164 A
mike.brown@ancilla.edu
BROWN, Mike .... 903-463-8772 474 K
mbrown@grayson.edu
BROWN, Mikell .... 804-594-1509 515 G
mbrown@jtcc.edu
BROWN, Monica, R ...... 240-567-4341 217 B
monica.brown@montgomerycollege.edu
BROWN, Naima .... 352-395-5648 112 H
naima.brown@sfcollege.edu
BROWN, Nancy, B .... 423-318-2709 464 C
nancy.brown@ws.edu
BROWN, Nicci, C .... 704-233-8126 373 C
brown@wingate.edu
BROWN, Nick .... 785-539-3571 189 D
nick.brown@mccks.edu
BROWN, Nicole .... 708-802-7750 145 B
nbrown@foxcolleg.edu
BROWN, Nicole, R .... 417-625-3137 278 I
brown-n@mssu.edu
BROWN, Pamela .... 540-863-2807 515 B
BROWN, Pamela .... 510-987-9251.. 70 J
pamela.brown@ucop.edu
BROWN, Pamela .... 718-260-5008 320 D
pbrown@citytech.cuny.edu
BROWN, Pamela .... 843-574-6246 449 G
pamela.brown@tridenttech.edu
BROWN, Pamela, S ...... 217-228-5520 140 G
pbrown@brcn.edu
BROWN, Patricia, R ...... 716-839-8484 323 F
pbrown@daemen.edu
BROWN, Patrick .... 217-245-3176 146 D
patrick.brown@mail.ic.edu
BROWN, Patrick .... 425-235-2352 525 G
pbrown@rtc.edu
BROWN, Patty .... 423-697-2437 462 C
patty.brown@chattanoogastate.edu
BROWN, Paul .... 254-659-7860 475 A
pbrown@hillcollege.edu
BROWN, Paul, R .... 732-571-3402 303 G
president@monmouth.edu
BROWN, Paula, J .... 312-942-7094 158 A
paula_j_brown@rush.edu
BROWN, Perry .... 406-243-4689 287 D
perry.brown@umontana.edu
BROWN, Peter .... 540-338-2700 505 K
pbrown@cdu.edu
BROWN, Philip, R .... 207-768-2708 211 C
pbrown@nmcc.edu
BROWN, Phillip .... 219-989-2240 171 L
brown@purduecal.edu
BROWN, Phillip, M ...... 618-650-3415 159 I
phbrown@siue.edu
BROWN, R. McKenna ... 804-828-8471 514 F
mbrown@vcu.edu
BROWN, R. Michael ..... 724-357-5924 431 A
rmbrown@iup.edu
BROWN, Rachel, A .... 202-994-6495.. 95 D
rabrown@gwu.edu
BROWN, Rachel, M ...... 615-868-6503 459 E
rachel.brown@mtsa.edu
BROWN, Ralph .... 601-366-8880 271 E
rbrown@wbs.edu
BROWN, Randy .... 408-848-4852.. 45 G
rbrown@gavilan.edu
BROWN, Rashayla .... 312-629-6869 158 J
maffai@saic.edu
BROWN, Ray .... 573-592-5238 285 J
ray.brown@westminster-mo.edu
BROWN, Raymond, A ... 610-527-0200 434 D
bbrown@rosemont.edu
BROWN, Raymond, A ... 817-257-7490 486 G
r.brown@tcu.edu
BROWN, Rebecca .... 707-826-4142.. 35 D
rebecca.brown@humboldt.edu
BROWN, Rebekkah, L ... 484-664-3247 427 C
rbrown@muhlenberg.edu
BROWN, Renee, D .... 419-559-2367 392 A
rbrown@terra.edu
BROWN, Reynolda .... 314-340-3301 275 G
brownre@hssu.edu
BROWN, Rhonda .... 773-896-2400 141 K
rhonda.brown@ctschicago.edu
BROWN, Ricardo .... 601-979-8836 267 H
ricardo.a.brown@jsums.edu
BROWN, Richard .... 856-415-2205 306 C
rbrown@rcgc.edu
BROWN, Richard .... 423-425-4393 465 E
richard-brown@utc.edu
BROWN, Richard, B ...... 801-581-6912 499 K
brown@coe.utah.edu
BROWN, Ricky .... 252-493-7259 364 H
rbrown@email.pittcc.edu
BROWN, Robert .... 410-386-8224 214 B
rbrown@carrollcc.edu
BROWN, Robert .... 502-272-8249 193 E
rbrown@bellarmine.edu
BROWN, Robert .... 478-289-2068 124 B
bbrown@ega.edu
BROWN, Robert, A .... 617-353-2200 224 E
rabrown@bu.edu
BROWN, Robert, B .... 913-684-5621 548 F
BROWN, Robert, C .... 216-368-4306 378 J
robert.c.brown@case.edu
BROWN, Robert, K .... 918-781-7218 396 F
brownr@bacone.edu
BROWN, Robert, L .... 803-981-7375 451 K
rbrown@yorktech.edu
BROWN, Robert, M ...... 251-460-6151.... 9 F
rbrown@southalabama.edu
BROWN, Robin .... 219-785-5508 172 A
rbrown@pnc.edu
BROWN, Robin, C .... 970-491-2682.. 81 D
robin.brown@colostate.edu
BROWN, Rodney, J ...... 801-422-3963 497 J
rod_brown@byu.edu
BROWN, Roger .... 901-435-1535 457 N
roger_brown@loc.edu
BROWN, Roger .... 915-747-5202 494 B
rbrown6@utep.edu
BROWN, Roger, H .... 617-266-1400 223 F
BROWN, Rolanda .... 662-621-4244 266 H
rbrown@coahomacc.edu
BROWN, Ron .... 254-295-4517 492 C
rbrown@umhb.edu
BROWN, Ronald .... 972-780-3600 493 A
BROWN, Ronald .... 334-229-7680.... 1 D
rbrown@alasu.edu
BROWN, Ronald, C .... 512-245-2205 489 C
rb04@txstate.edu
BROWN, Ronald, H .... 919-516-4859 368 E
rhbrown@st-aug.edu
BROWN, Rosann .... 814-641-3133 421 L
brownr@juniata.edu
BROWN, Roxanne .... 773-602-5016 142 A
rbrown262@ccc.edu
BROWN, Russ .... 772-462-6004 106 F
rbrown@irsc.edu
BROWN, Ryan .... 541-880-2225 406 E
brownr@klamathcc.edu
BROWN, Sabrina .... 434-395-2021 509 H
browncs2@longwood.edu
BROWN, Sandra .... 858-534-3526.. 72 B
sandrabrown@ucsd.edu
BROWN, Sandra .... 605-668-1555 452 I
sbrown@mtmc.edu
BROWN, Sara .... 501-760-4129.. 21 H
sbrown@npcc.edu
BROWN, Sean .... 405-878-5169 402 A
sdbrown@stgregorys.edu
BROWN, Shannon .... 828-726-2288 360 F
sbrown@cccti.edu
BROWN, Shannon .... 305-899-4834.. 99 B
sbrown@barry.edu
BROWN, Shannon .... 267-341-3314 420 K
sbrown10@holyfamily.edu
BROWN, Shannon .... 603-668-2211 298 H
s.brown8@snhu.edu
BROWN, Sharon .... 252-335-0821 361 G
sharon_brown@albemarle.edu
BROWN, Sheila .... 937-376-6349 379 D
sbrown@centralstate.edu
BROWN, Sheila .... 512-505-3031 475 G
stbrown@htu.edu
BROWN, Shelley .... 330-490-7134 395 C
sbrown@walsh.edu
BROWN, Simon .... 215-751-8039 416 B
sbrown@ccp.edu
BROWN, Sloane .... 918-540-6393 398 L
scbrown@neo.edu
BROWN, Stan .... 229-317-6721 123 H
stan.brown@darton.edu
BROWN, Stephan .... 352-588-8331 111 L
stephan.brown@saintleo.edu
BROWN, Stephanie .... 954-262-7456 109 E
browstep@nova.edu
BROWN, Stephanie .... 561-237-7784 108 E
scbrown@lynn.edu
BROWN, Stephanie .... 252-451-8257 364 E
sbrown@nashcc.edu
BROWN, Stephen, G .... 530-221-4275.. 66 B
sbrown@shasta.edu
BROWN, Steve .... 724-805-2534 435 B
steve.brown@email.stvincent.edu
BROWN, Steve .... 570-586-2400 435 H
sbrown@summitu.edu
BROWN, Steve, D .... 423-439-4841 461 D
browsd02@etsu.edu
BROWN, Steven .... 850-474-2222 116 E
sbrown4@uwf.edu
BROWN, Steven .... 802-287-8912 501 I
browns@greenmtn.edu
BROWN, Steven, D .... 906-227-1188 248 B
stebrown@nmu.edu
BROWN, Sue, C .... 309-655-2206 158 D
sue.c.brown@osfhealthcare.org
BROWN, Susan, M .... 859-233-8225 200 D
subrown@transy.edu
BROWN, Susie, A .... 918-595-7884 403 A
susie.brown@tulsacc.edu
BROWN, Sylvia .... 252-744-6422 369 E
brownsy@ecu.edu
BROWN, T. Rhett .... 704-233-8111 373 C
r.brown@wingate.edu
BROWN, Takeish, N ..... 804-257-5888 518 E
tnbrown@vuu.edu
BROWN, Tamara, L ...... 936-261-5205 484 F
tlbrown@pvamu.edu
BROWN, Tammie .... 406-994-2661 287 G
tdbrown@montana.edu
BROWN, Tammy .... 334-386-7264.... 3 I
tcbrown@faulkner.edu
BROWN, Tavonda .... 870-743-3000.. 22 A
tbrown@northark.edu
BROWN, Ted, R .... 931-363-9802 458 D
tbrown@martinmethodist.edu
BROWN, Teresa .... 404-225-4700 120 I
tbrown@atlantatech.edu
BROWN, Teresa, L .... 401-456-8240 442 A
tlbrown@ric.edu
BROWN, Terrence .... 901-751-8453 459 C
tbrown@mabts.edu
BROWN, Terry .... 716-673-3335 343 F
terry.brown@fredonia.edu
BROWN, Terry .... 304-327-4191 532 D
tbrown@bluefieldstate.edu
BROWN, Theresa .... 334-874-5700.... 3 B
tbrown@ccal.edu
BROWN, Therese .... 303-404-5535.. 82 J
therese.brown@frontrange.edu
BROWN, Thomas .... 205-929-1061.... 5 I
tbrown@miles.edu
BROWN, Thomas .... 540-231-3787 518 B
tbrown@vt.edu
BROWN, Thomas, W ..... 507-933-7005 256 A
brownie@gustavus.edu
BROWN, Tim .... 843-574-6424 449 G
tim.brown@tridenttech.edu
BROWN, Timothy .... 616-392-8555 253 C
tim.brown@westernsem.edu
BROWN, SJ, Timothy .... 410-617-5524 216 D
tbrown@loyola.edu
BROWN, Timothy, T ..... 860-444-8322 548 H
timothy.t.brown@uscg.mil
BROWN, Tom .... 352-638-9762.. 99 D
tbrown@beaconcollege.edu
BROWN, Tom .... 310-660-3015.. 43 G
tbrown@elcamino.edu
BROWN, Tomeka, K ...... 318-670-9319 207 C
tbrown@susla.edu
BROWN, Toneita .... 954-486-7728 117 M
universityadmission@uftl.edu
BROWN, Trachanda .... 215-242-7989 415 D
brownt@chc.edu
BROWN, Tracy, H .... 512-471-3833 493 M
tracy.brown@austin.utexas.edu
BROWN, Trevor, L .... 614-292-4533 389 A
brown.2296@osu.edu
BROWN, Trish .... 256-924-0511.... 5 F
BROWN, Venessa .... 618-650-5867 159 I
vbrown@siue.edu
BROWN, SR.,
Vernon, T .... 336-322-2215 364 G
Vernon.Brown@piedmontcc.edu
BROWN, Victor .... 937-395-5604 385 A
victor.brown@kc.edu
BROWN, JR., Walter, E 412-648-3185 437 K
walter.brown@ia.pitt.edu
BROWN, Warren .... 206-934-3601 525 J
warren.brown@seattlecolleges.edu
BROWN, Warren, H ...... 434-223-7230 508 B
hbrown@hsc.edu
BROWN, Warren, J .... 206-934-3601 525 K
warren.brown@seattlecolleges.edu
BROWN, Wayne .... 518-464-8675 325 B
wbrown@excelsior.edu
BROWN, Wes, S .... 912-260-4430 131 D
wes.brown@sgsc.edu
BROWN, Wilfred, E ...... 805-893-4155.. 72 D
wbrown@housing.ucsb.edu
BROWN, William .... 301-696-3402 215 E
brownw@hood.edu
BROWN, William .... 520-494-5340.. 12 R
william.brown@centralaz.edu
BROWN, William .... 571-334-2600.. 28 G
wbrown@argosy.edu
BROWN, William .... 973-408-3976 301 J
wbrown1@drew.edu
BROWN, William, B ..... 760-245-4271.. 75 G
bob.brown@vvc.edu
BROWN, William, H ..... 704-894-2143 356 D
wibrown@davidson.edu
BROWN, William (Bill) . 859-846-5358 198 G
bbrown@midway.edu
BROWN, William Terry . 203-332-5060.. 89 C
wbrown@housatonic.edu
BROWN, Winston, D .... 504-520-7577 209 E
wbrown@xula.edu
BROWN, Yvette .... 305-899-3600.. 99 B
ybrown@barry.edu
BROWN, Yvonne .... 843-574-6083 449 G
yvonne.brown@tridenttech.edu
BROWN, Zachary .... 607-431-4547 327 B
brownz@hartwick.edu
BROWN, Zaundra .... 404-297-9522 126 A
brownz@gptc.edu
BROWN-CORNELIUS,
Denise .... 502-272-8270 193 E
dbrowncornelius@bellarmine.edu
BROWN GIVENS,
Sonja, M .... 716-880-2242 332 B
sonja.m.browngivens@medaille.edu
BROWN GORDAN,
Loria .... 601-979-2107 267 H
loria.c.brown@jsums.edu
BROWN-GUILLORY,
Elizabeth, A .... 713-313-1983 487 F
brown-guillorye@tsu.edu
BROWN-HART, Denise .. 910-672-1856 370 A
dbrownhart@uncfsu.edu
BROWN-NEVERS,
Michelle, H .... 215-898-7233 437 I
mbnevers@upenn.edu
BROWN-SOW, Lynette .. 215-751-8859 416 B
lbrown@ccp.edu
BROWN-WELTY,
Sharon .... 909-537-8101.. 35 A
sharonb@csusb.edu
BROWN WRIGHT,
Lynda .... 404-413-2574 126 D
lwright39@gsu.edu
BROWN YOUNG,
Danita .... 612-624-3560 265 C
dbyoung@umn.edu
BROWNE, Brian .... 718-990-2762 340 G
browneb@stjohns.edu
BROWNE, Christopher .. 212-396-6533 319 E
cb1246@hunter.cuny.edu
BROWNE, Doug .... 620-417-1201 191 A
doug.browne@sccc.edu
BROWNE, Jacob .... 727-864-8846 101 P
brownejh@eckerd.edu
BROWNE, Joan, M .... 202-806-7513.. 96 B
jmbrowne@howard.edu
BROWNE, Kevin .... 312-413-3471 161 F
kbrowne@uic.edu
BROWNE, Marcus .... 718-522-9073 315 E
mbrowne@asa.edu
BROWNE, Patrick .... 503-256-3180 410 I
pbrowne@uws.edu
BROWNE, Paul .... 574-631-8696 174 A
pbrowne@nd.edu
BROWNE, Richard, M ... 305-595-9500.. 97 H
richard@amcollege.edu
BROWNE-BOATSWAIN,
Venoreen .... 763-422-6094 257 P
venoreen.browne-boatswain@
anokaramsey.edu
BROWNELL, Beverley .... 714-895-1190.. 40 C
bbrownell@gwc.cccd.edu
BROWNELL, Claire .... 303-871-4876.. 86 H
claire.brownell@du.edu
BROWNELL, Jayne, E .... 513-529-4631 386 K
browneje@miamioh.edu
BROWNELL, Jennifer .... 336-506-4140 359 N
jennifer.brownell@alamancecc.edu
BROWNELL, Scott .... 612-330-1644 253 K
brownell@augsburg.edu

BRVENIK, Andrea .... 813-882-0100.. 96 H
BRVENIK, Andrea .... 843-746-5100.. 96 H
BRY, Jay .... 978-665-3131 229 D
jbry@fitchburgstate.edu
BRYAN, Ben .... 803-754-4100 445 D
BRYAN, Brett .... 541-278-5900 404 J
bbryan@bluecc.edu
BRYAN, Derek .... 336-917-5472 368 F
derek.bryan@salem.edu
BRYAN, Doug .... 704-406-4398 356 G
dbryan@gardner-webb.edu
BRYAN, James .... 316-322-3232 185 F
jbryan8@butlercc.edu
BRYAN, Jaxie .... 919-464-2254 363 F
JLBryan1@johnstoncc.edu
BRYAN, Jessica .... 603-271-6484 297 C
jbryan@ccsnh.edu
BRYAN, John .... 413-545-2554 228 F
johnbryan@provost.umass.edu
BRYAN, Joseph .... 561-803-2127 109 G
joseph_bryan@pba.edu
BRYAN, Karla .... 903-675-6229 490 F
kbryan@tvcc.edu
BRYAN, Laura .... 859-233-8121 200 D
lbryan@transy.edu
BRYAN, Mitzi .... 718-636-3430 338 E
mbryan@pratt.edu
BRYAN, Neva .... 276-328-0126 514 B
njd8r@uvawise.edu
BRYAN, JR.,
Norman, B .... 864-833-8757 448 E
nbbryan@presby.edu
BRYAN, Paul .... 215-893-5252 416 E
paul.bryan@curtis.edu
BRYAN, Penelope .... 714-444-4141.. 77 E
pbryan@law.whittier.edu
BRYAN, Robert .... 216-987-4684 381 A
robert.bryan@tri-c.edu
BRYAN, Royce .... 620-862-5252 184 H
royce.bryan@barclaycollege.edu
BRYAN, Sandy .... 520-515-5313.. 13 B
bryans@cochise.edu
BRYAN, Sibley .... 706-453-0378 120 G
sbryan@athenstech.edu
BRYAN, Susan .... 417-865-2815 274 L
bryans@evangel.edu
BRYAN, Terry .... 832-252-4676 470 L
terry.bryan@cbshouston.edu
BRYAN, Timothy, A ...... 330-471-8539 385 G
tbryan@malone.edu
BRYAN, Wes .... 714-895-8101.. 40 C
wbryan@gwc.cccd.edu
BRYAN WILLIAMS,
Pamela .... 314-529-9614 277 B
pbryanwilliams@maryville.edu
BRYANT, America .... 650-433-3804.. 58 B
a.bryant@paloaltou.edu
BRYANT, Angela .... 336-734-7618 362 F
abryant@forsythtech.edu
BRYANT, Angela, V ...... 229-928-1378 126 C
angela.bryant@gsw.edu
BRYANT, Angie .... 615-460-6407 455 D
angie.bryant@belmont.edu
BRYANT, Bruce, K .... 206-239-4500 520 K
brucebryant@cityu.edu
BRYANT, Bryan .... 719-846-5691.. 86 A
bryant.bryant@trinidadstate.edu
BRYANT, Carlton, G ...... 800-782-2422.. 32 A
cbryant@mail.cnuas.edu
BRYANT, Charles .... 909-447-6339.. 39 G
cbryant@cst.edu
BRYANT, Cherie .... 207-741-5726 211 D
cbryant@smccme.edu
BRYANT, Clint .... 706-737-1626 121 C
cbryant1@gru.edu
BRYANT, Courtney .... 509-527-2222 528 A
courtney.bryant@wallawalla.edu
BRYANT, Daniel, C ...... 740-376-4718 386 A
dan.bryant@marietta.edu
BRYANT, David, A .... 407-303-9305.. 97 J
david.bryant@adu.edu
BRYANT, David, A .... 580-349-1302 400 B
dbryant@opsu.edu
BRYANT, Elisa .... 417-625-3039 278 I
bryant-e@mssu.edu
BRYANT, Felicia .... 856-227-7200 301 A
fbryant@camdencc.edu
BRYANT, Fred .... 361-593-3922 486 A
kffcb00@tamuk.edu
BRYANT, Gerard .... 646-781-5625 319 F
gwbryant@jjay.cuny.edu
BRYANT, Holley .... 509-527-2772 528 A
holley.bryant@wallawalla.edu
BRYANT, Jack .... 405-422-1260 401 H
jack.bryant@redlandscc.edu
BRYANT, III, James, S . 803-535-1330 448 C
bryantj@octech.edu
BRYANT, Jocelyn .... 410-951-3922 220 C
jbryant@coppin.edu
BRYANT, John .... 309-556-3449 148 A
jbryant@iwu.edu

BRYANT, Jordan .... 847-317-7074 161 B
jbryant@tiu.edu
BRYANT, Joy, L .... 864-644-5385 449 B
jbryant@swu.edu
BRYANT, Karen .... 618-842-3711 146 G
bryantk@iecc.edu
BRYANT, Kimberly .... 215-895-1121 438 E
k.bryant@usciences.edu
BRYANT, Kinney .... 405-425-5155 399 J
kinney.bryant@oc.edu
BRYANT, Mark .... 661-722-6300.. 27 P
mbryant6@avc.edu
BRYANT, Micki .... 714-564-6079.. 60 G
bryant_micki@sac.edu
BRYANT, Morgan .... 601-925-3354 268 E
mbryant@mc.edu
BRYANT, Nicole .... 305-237-5223 108 L
nbryant@mdc.edu
BRYANT, Pam .... 325-649-8401 475 F
pbryant@hputx.edu
BRYANT, Paul .... 229-430-7139 119 H
paul.bryant@asurams.edu
BRYANT, Paul .... 803-536-7000 448 H
BRYANT, Penny, J ...... 314-367-8700 281 G
penny.bryant@stlcop.edu
BRYANT, Ronnie .... 910-755-7483 360 E
bryantr@brunswickcc.edu
BRYANT, Scott .... 903-923-2173 473 I
sbryant@etbu.edu
BRYANT, Sheila, M ...... 931-221-7178 461 C
bryantsm@apsu.edu
BRYANT, Stephanie ...... 417-836-4408 279 A
stephaniebryant@missouristate.edu
BRYANT, Stephanie ...... 803-754-4100 445 D
BRYANT, Theresa .... 412-788-7360 415 G
tbryant@ccac.edu
BRYANT, Tim .... 513-244-4504 387 A
tim.bryant@msj.edu
BRYANT, Toni .... 830-792-7229 482 D
tlbyrant@schreiner.edu
BRYANT, Vickie .... 817-461-8741 468 C
vbryant@arlingtonbaptistcollege.edu
BRYANT, Wayne, H ...... 318-670-9230 207 C
wbryant@ssla.edu
BRYCE, Jeanne .... 928-428-8261.. 13 L
jeanne.bryce@eac.edu
BRYCE, Mark .... 928-428-8231.. 13 L
mark.bryce@eac.edu
BRYDE, Beverly .... 610-902-8331 414 B
beverly.reilly.bryde@cabrini.edu
BRYDEN, David, L .... 336-841-9101 357 E
dbryden@highpoint.edu
BRYDON, Lucinda, C ... 607-746-4603 347 G
brydonlm@delhi.edu
BRYENTON, John .... 270-686-4615 197 A
john.bryenton@kctcs.edu
BRYLINSKY, Jody .... 269-387-2314 252 I
jody.brylinsky@wmich.edu
BRYNTESON, Susan ...... 302-831-2231.. 94 D
susanb@udel.edu
BRYS-WILSON, Jessica . 252-985-5186 367 E
jbrys-wilson@ncwc.edu
BRYSON, Allison .... 541-880-2288 406 E
bryson@klamathcc.edu
BRYSON, Allison .... 541-880-2234 406 E
bryson@klamathcc.edu
BRYSON, Barbara .... 520-621-5511.. 18 E
bwbryson@email.arizona.edu
BRYSON, Cynthia .... 713-771-5336 127 E
cbryson@ict.edu
BRYSON, Lance .... 717-477-1451 431 F
jlbrys@ship.edu
BRYSON, Michael, A .... 480-245-7944.. 14 D
michael.bryson@ibcs.edu
BRYSON, Suzanne .... 828-251-6128 370 E
sbryson@unca.edu
BRYSON, Terri .... 256-890-4703.... 2 F
tbb@calhoun.edu
BRZENIK, Andrea .... 727-736-5082 112 I
abrzenik@schiller.edu
BRZEZINSKI, Karen ...... 715-675-3331 544 A
brzezinski@ntc.edu
BRZORAD, John .... 828-328-7606 358 G
john.brzorad@lr.edu
BRZOZOWSKI, Eileen ... 321-433-5687 101 O
brzozowskie@easternflorida.edu
BRZOZOWSKI,
Samantha .... 615-383-4848 466 F
sbrzozowski@watkins.edu
BRZYCKI, Shelly .... 847-578-8355 157 G
shelly.brzycki@rosalindfranklin.edu
BRZYTWA, MaryClare ... 415-503-6263.. 63 A
mcbrzytwa@sfcm.edu
BUBAN, Jill .... 203-591-5601.. 91 D
jbuban@post.edu
BUBAR, Nancy .... 207-941-7138 210 C
bubarn@husson.edu
BUBB, Kevin .... 517-483-9764 245 I
bubbk@lcc.edu
BUBB, Terry .... 615-230-3398 464 B
terry.bubb@volstate.edu

BUBNOVA, Elena .... 775-673-8239 295 F
ebubnova@tmcc.edu
BUCARO, S. Ted .... 937-229-4122 393 E
sbucaro1@udayton.edu
BUCCIARELLI, Roseann . 732-906-4681 303 F
rbucciarelli@middlesexcc.edu
BUCCILLI, Michael .... 203-285-2626.. 89 B
mbuccilli@gwcc.commnet.edu
BUCELL, Michael .... 814-732-2252 430 G
bucell@edinboro.edu
BUCHA, Edward, R .... 724-738-2183 432 A
ebucha@srufoundation.org
BUCHANAN, Barbara .... 775-673-7090 295 F
bbuchanan@tmcc.edu
BUCHANAN, Cindy .... 413-205-3918 221 G
cindy.buchanan@aic.edu
BUCHANAN, Evelyn ...... 262-551-6122 535 E
ebuchanan@carthage.edu
BUCHANAN, Harvey ..... 850-644-2825 115 A
buchanan@fsu.edu
BUCHANAN,
Janelle, M .... 806-720-7476 478 A
janelle.buchanan@lcu.edu
BUCHANAN, Kelly .... 619-201-8702.. 62 D
kelly.buchanan@sdcc.edu
BUCHANAN, Kyrel, L .... 256-765-4328.... 9 D
kbuchanan@una.edu
BUCHANAN, Lane .... 307-766-5272 546 K
lane@uwyo.edu
BUCHANAN, Linda, R ... 229-732-5926 120 B
lindabuchanan@andrewcollege.edu
BUCHANAN, Lori .... 931-221-6240 461 C
buchananl@apsu.edu
BUCHANAN, Martha ...... 210-486-0116 467 C
mbuchanan@alamo.edu
BUCHANAN, Merilyn .... 805-437-8579.. 32 H
merilyn.buchanan@csuci.edu
BUCHANAN, Pamela ..... 828-227-7640 372 C
pbuchanan@wcu.edu
BUCHANAN, Robin .... 828-898-8747 358 F
buchananr@lmc.edu
BUCHANAN, Ron .... 703-845-6222 516 C
rbuchanan@nvcc.edu
BUCHANAN, Russell ..... 610-292-9852 433 J
rbuchanan@reseminary.edu
BUCHANAN, Shasta ...... 971-722-6111 409 C
BUCHANAN, Stephanie . 770-426-2884 128 C
stephanie.buchanan@life.edu
BUCHANAN, Susan, M . 509-527-5183 528 F
buchansm@whitman.edu
BUCHANAN, Tony .... 330-337-6403 376 B
college@awc.edu
BUCHANAN, Trey .... 512-863-1390 483 G
buchanat@southwestern.edu
BUCHE, Nathan .... 620-665-3569 188 A
buchen@hutchcc.edu
BUCHELE, Ann .... 541-917-4211 406 J
buchela@linnbenton.edu
BUCHELI, Hernan .... 925-631-4277.. 61 G
hmb5@stmarys-ca.edu
BUCHER, Jake .... 785-594-8475 184 F
jbucher@bakeru.edu
BUCHER, Jasmine, A .... 717-867-6036 423 I
bucher@lvc.edu
BUCHER, Jennifer .... 570-372-4157 435 I
bucherjennifer@susqu.edu
BUCHER, John, E .... 440-775-6727 388 B
john.bucher@oberlin.edu
BUCHER, Karen, H .... 540-868-7132 515 H
kbucher@lfcc.edu
BUCHER, Oskar .... 541-684-7273 407 I
obucher@nwcu.edu
BUCHHOLZ, Reyne, D .. 757-822-1754 517 C
rbuchholz@tcc.edu
BUCHHOLZ, Richard ..... 405-422-6204 401 H
richard.buchholz@redlandscc.edu
BUCHHOLZ, Robert ...... 336-278-5500 356 F
rbuchholz@elon.edu
BUCHHOLZ, Ron .... 262-472-1498 541 D
buchholr@uww.edu
BUCHHOLZ, Stephen ..... 605-718-2436 454 F
stephen.buchholz@wdt.edu
BUCHMAN, Irene .... 212-217-4590 325 C
irene_buchman@fitnyc.edu
BUCHMAN, Lorne, M ... 626-396-2301.. 28 J
lorne.buchman@artcenter.edu
BUCHOLC, Stanley .... 978-665-3215 229 D
sbucholc@fitchburgstate.edu
BUCHWALD, Adam .... 503-768-7227 406 H
buchwald@lclark.edu
BUCHWALD, Carrie ...... 847-574-5164 150 A
cbuchwald@lfgsm.edu
BUCHWALD, Maurissa .. 580-581-2612 397 A
mbuchwald@cameron.edu
BUCHWALD, Rosalinda 626-914-8897.. 38 L
rbuchwald@citruscollege.edu
BUCHWALDER,
Mary, P .... 937-229-3131 393 E
mbuchwalder1@udayton.edu
BUCK, A. Scott .... 252-328-6910 369 E
bucka@ecu.edu

BUCK, Baxter .... 901-458-8232 459 B
bbuck@memphisseminary.edu
BUCK, Charles .... 208-292-1737 139 C
buck@uidaho.edu
BUCK, David .... 208-282-3111 138 C
buckdavi@isu.edu
BUCK, James, E .... 937-393-3431 391 F
jbuck@sscc.edu
BUCK, Jeff, M .... 765-641-4188 164 B
jmbuck@anderson.edu
BUCK, John .... 407-447-7300 105 E
jbuck@ftccollege.edu
BUCK, John .... 314-246-4463 285 G
buckjh@webster.edu
BUCK, Katherine .... 973-290-4204 301 F
kbuck@cse.edu
BUCK, Kavin .... 503-821-8942 408 H
kbuck@pnca.edu
BUCK, Kevan, C 918-631-3245 403M
kevan-buck@utulsa.edu
BUCK, Leah .... 207-768-2768 211 C
lbuck@nmcc.edu
BUCK, Marilyn, M .... 765-285-3716 164 D
mbuck@bsu.edu
BUCK, Mark .... 630-889-7570 144 A
mbuck@devry.edu
BUCK, Nick .... 317-931-2378 165 C
nbuck@cts.edu
BUCK, Roger .... 740-753-6095 383 G
buckr@hocking.edu
BUCK, Ryan .... 512-245-7966 489 C
r_b259@txstate.edu
BUCK, Sharon .... 425-739-8146 523 I
sharon.buck@lwtech.edu
BUCK, Sylvia, T .... 812-488-2724 173 H
sb79@evansville.edu
BUCK, Yolanda .... 804-524-5297 518 C
ybuck@vsu.edu
BUCKALEW, Danielle .... 205-652-3852.... 9 G
bdbuckalew@uwa.edu
BUCKALEW, Leslie .... 209-588-5107.. 78 B
buckalewl@yosemite.edu
BUCKALEW,
Thomas, D .... 205-652-3581.... 9 G
db@uwa.edu
BUCKELS, Carol .... 386-738-6686 117 A
cbuckels@stetson.edu
BUCKENMEYER, Janet .. 912-344-3277 120 D
janet.buckenmeyer@armstrong.edu
BUCKER, Robert .... 503-725-3340 409 D
william.robert.bucker@pdx.edu
BUCKHAULTS, Tex .... 806-874-3571 470 J
tex.buckhaults@clarendoncollege.edu
BUCKHAULTS,
Tresea, L .... 318-342-5240 209 A
buckhaults@ulm.edu
BUCKI, SJ, John, P ...... 315-445-4110 330 B
buckijp@lemoyne.edu
BUCKINGHAM,
David, E .... 757-455-3273 518 H
debuckingham@vwc.edu
BUCKINGHAM, Jane .... 802-258-3367 502 I
jane.buckingham@worldlearning.org
BUCKINGHAM, John .... 319-656-2447 182 G
BUCKINGHAM,
Judith, P .... 936-468-4048 484 A
jpbuckingham@sfasu.edu
BUCKINGHAM, Stacy .... 618-985-3741 148 G
stacybuckingham@jalc.edu
BUCKLA, Robert, J .... 414-410-4201 535 C
rbuckla@stritch.edu
BUCKLE, Eileen .... 732-255-0400 304 E
ebuckle@ocean.edu
BUCKLER, C. Adam ...... 317-896-9324 173 G
BUCKLES, Beverly, J ..... 909-558-4528.. 50 K
bbuckles@llu.edu
BUCKLES, Dale .... 270-706-8431 195 K
dale.buckles@kctcs.edu
BUCKLES, Gregory, B ... 802-443-5161 502 E
deanofadmissions@middlebury.edu
BUCKLES, Jennifer .... 423-425-4677 465 E
jennifer-buckles@utc.edu
BUCKLEW, Andrea, J .... 304-457-6438 529 C
bucklewaj@ab.edu
BUCKLEW, Kathy .... 863-297-1016 110 E
kbucklew@polk.edu
BUCKLEY, Alison .... 443-518-4133 215 F
abuckley@howardcc.edu
BUCKLEY, Anne .... 205-934-9518.... 8 F
abuckley@uab.edu
BUCKLEY, Chris .... 910-893-1208 355 C
buckley@campbell.edu
BUCKLEY, Cynthia, S ... 405-466-3204 398 E
csbuckley@langston.edu
BUCKLEY, Debi .... 479-619-4217.. 22 B
dbuckley@nwacc.edu
BUCKLEY, Emily .... 913-621-8731 186 G
ebuckley@donnelly.edu
BUCKLEY, Gerard, J ..... 585-475-6317 339 G
gbuckley@ntid.rit.edu

BUNNELL-RHYNE,
Melinda, A ... 301-369-2800 214 A
melindabunnell@captechu.edu
BUNNING, Galen ... 785-227-3380 185 A
bunningb@bethanylb.edu
BUNSON, Matthew ... 540-338-2700 505 K
mbunson@cdu.edu
BUNTEN, Tricia ... 218-726-6995 264 G
tbunten@d.umn.edu
BUNTING, Amy ... 704-463-3165 367 F
amy.bunting@pfeiffer.edu
BUNTING, Elizabeth, C . 336-334-3067 371 C
ecbuntin@uncg.edu
BUNTON, Kristie ... 817-257-6550 486 G
k.bunton@tcu.edu
BUNTON, Tim, M ... 217-443-8780 143 F
tbunton@dacc.edu
BUNYARD, Magen ... 325-649-8613 475 F
mbunyard@hputx.edu
BUNYI, Beth ... 760-630-1555.. 49 C
bbunyi@kaplan.edu
BUOL, Deborah, L ... 563-589-3223 183 E
dbuol@dbq.edu
BUONO, Lisa ... 805-493-3663.. 31 H
llbuono@callutheran.edu
BUOSCIO, Amy ... 708-237-5050 155 B
abuoscio@nc.edu
BURAK, Deborah ... 610-861-4137 427 F
dburak@northampton.edu
BURAK, Marshall, J ... 510-628-8016.. 50 I
mburak@lincolnuca.edu
BURBA, Dave ... 530-541-4660.. 50 A
burba@ltcc.edu
BURBA, Randy ... 714-997-6763.. 38 B
burba@chapman.edu
BURBAGE, Priscilla, D . 843-953-5578 445 B
burbagep@cofc.edu
BURBANK, Lynn ... 218-726-8833 264 G
lburbank@d.umn.edu
BURBANTE, Gilberto ... 985-448-4208 208 C
gilberto.burbante@nicholls.edu
BURCH, Beth ... 503-253-3443 408 B
bburch@ocom.edu
BURCH, C. Beth ... 607-777-7329 343 D
bburch@binghamton.edu
BURCH, Chuck, S ... 704-406-4342 356 G
cburch@gardner-webb.edu
BURCH, Doug ... 801-622-1573 499 C
doug.burch@stevenhenager.edu
BURCH, Doug ... 801-622-1573 499 C
doug.burch@stevenshenager.edu
BURCH, Franki ... 704-406-3522 356 G
fburch@gardner-webb.edu
BURCH, Jerome ... 808-983-4154 135 D
jburch@tokai.edu
BURCH, Jim ... 912-443-5874 131 B
jburch@savannahtech.edu
BURCH, John ... 270-789-5015 194 D
jrburch@campbellsville.edu
BURCH, Rhonda ... 812-866-7014 166 E
burch@hanover.edu
BURCH, Susan ... 406-756-3839 286 G
sburch@fvcc.edu
BURCH-SIMS,
G. Pamela ... 615-963-7043 461 F
psims@tnstate.edu
BURCHAM, Timothy ... 870-972-2085.. 19 F
tburcham@astate.edu
BURCHAM, CFRE,
Timothy, R ... 859-256-3100 195 G
tim.burcham@kctcs.edu
BURCHARD, Bob, P ... 573-875-7410 273 D
rpburchard@ccis.edu
BURCHARD,
Elizabeth, B ... 802-443-5201 502 E
eboudah@middlebury.edu
BURCHARD, Eric ... 740-593-1804 389 H
burchard@ohio.edu
BURCHARD, Faye, C ... 573-875-7400 273 D
fcburchard@ccis.edu
BURCHETT, Amy ... 432-264-5063 475 E
aburchett@howardcollege.edu
BURCHETT, Bonnie, L ... 423-439-4446 461 D
bonnie@etsu.edu
BURCHETT, Dick ... 501-812-2238.. 22 F
dburchett@pulaskitech.edu
BURCHETT, Kevin ... 734-423-2139 246 E
BURCHETT, Lance, E ... 501-686-5987.. 24 B
leburchett@uams.edu
BURCHFIELD, Doug ... 828-627-4632 363 C
ddburchfield@haywood.edu
BURCHFIELD, James ... 406-243-5521 287 D
james.burchfield@umontana.edu
BURCHFIELD, Nettie, L . 985-549-2068 208 E
nburchfield@selu.edu
BURCKHARDT, Judy ... 303-991-1575.. 78 K
judy.burckhardt@americansentinel.edu
BURD, Barbara ... 843-349-2401 444 G
bburd@coastal.edu

BURD, Gail, D ... 520-626-4099.. 18 E
gburd@email.arizona.edu
BURD, Randy, M ... 520-626-1863.. 18 E
rburd@u.arizona.edu
BURDA, Bradley ... 541-885-1180 408 E
bradley.burda@oit.edu
BURDA, Ed ... 304-457-6238 529 C
burdaep@ab.edu
BURDEN, Kathlyn ... 770-229-3328 132 B
kburden@sctech.edu
BURDEN, Matthew ... 630-637-5433 154 F
mburden@noctrl.edu
BURDEN, Regina ... 931-393-1691 463 B
rburden@mscc.edu
BURDEN, Velma ... 912-478-5421 126 B
vburden@georgiasouthern.edu
BURDETTE, David ... 270-809-6979 198 I
dburdette@murraystate.edu
BURDETTE, Ilona ... 859-336-5082 199 B
iburdette@sccky.edu
BURDETTE, Vinson ... 803-508-7244 443 C
burdettv@atc.edu
BURDI, Glenn ... 718-631-6344 320 F
gburdi@qcc.cuny.edu
BURDICK, Evelyn, P ... 708-209-3259 143 D
evelyn.burdick@cuchicago.edu
BURDICK, Jonathan ... 585-275-6805 351 D
jonathan.burdick@rochester.edu
BURDICK, Julie ... 479-788-7127.. 23 H
julie.burdick@uafs.edu
BURDICK, Mary Ellen ... 315-684-6461 347 A
burdicme@morrisville.edu
BURDICK, Phil ... 847-925-6183 145 F
pburdick@harpercollege.edu
BURDICK, Rebekah ... 863-667-5026 113 K
rburdick@seu.edu
BURDINE, Mike ... 208-459-5663 137 J
mburdine@collegeofidaho.edu
BURDOWSKI, Allen ... 718-489-5324 340 E
aburdowski@sfc.edu
BURDSALL, Dawn, M ... 610-660-1333 434 G
dburdsal@sju.edu
BURDUE, JoEllen ... 414-277-7117 537 G
burdue@msoe.edu
BURDZINSKI,
Donna, R ... 352-797-5001 110 B
burdzid@phsc.edu
BURDZINSKI,
Kenneth, R ... 727-816-3412 110 B
burdzink@phsc.edu
BURFORD, Kristina ... 501-450-1362.. 21 C
burford@hendrix.edu
BURFORD, Kyla ... 618-252-5400 159 F
kyla.burford@sic.edu
BURG, James ... 260-481-4146 168 D
burgj@ipfw.edu
BURG, Jennifer ... 802-447-6359 503 A
jburg@svc.edu
BURG, Karen, J ... 785-532-5110 188 H
kjburg@ksu.edu
BURG, Mary, G ... 785-864-3131 191 G
mburg@ku.edu
BURGARD, Bambi ... 816-802-3455 276 F
bburgard@kcai.edu
BURGAU, Tam ... 715-858-1377 542 M
tburgau@cvtc.edu
BURGAY, Stephen, P ... 617-353-1168 224 E
burgay@bu.edu
BURGE, Dale ... 785-227-3380 185 A
burgedl@bethanylb.edu
BURGE, David ... 703-993-6062 507 K
dburge@gmu.edu
BURGE, David ... 717-569-7071 423 C
dburge@lbc.edu
BURGE, Jennifer, G ... 309-677-4939 140 H
jgruening@bradley.edu
BURGE, Legand ... 334-229-4200.... 1 D
llburge@alasu.edu
BURGE, Legand, L ... 334-727-8976.... 8 B
lburge@tuskegee.edu
BURGEE, Lawrence, E .. 610-558-5596 427 D
burgeel@neumann.edu
BURGENER, Kelly, T ... 208-496-1135 137 F
burgenerk@byui.edu
BURGER, Arnold ... 615-329-8516 456 G
aburger@fisk.edu
BURGER, Avraham ... 516-295-5700 354 A
BURGER, Bill ... 802-443-5834 502 E
bburger@middlebury.edu
BURGER, Cindy, L ... 717-766-2511 426 B
cburger@messiah.edu
BURGER, Edward, B ... 512-863-1454 483 G
burger@southwestern.edu
BURGER, Lisa ... 701-777-4706 373 G
lisa.burger@und.edu
BURGER, Michael ... 334-244-3380.... 2 A
mburger1@aum.edu
BURGER, Rosemary ... 570-340-6054 425 D
burger@marywood.edu
BURGER, Shmuel ... 516-295-5700 354 A

BURGES, Jena ... 707-826-4192.. 35 D
jb139@humboldt.edu
BURGESS, Aaron ... 513-244-8112 379 I
aaron.burgess@ccuniversity.edu
BURGESS, Brenda, K ... 580-774-3015 402 G
brenda.burgess@swosu.edu
BURGESS, Charlotte, G 909-748-8281.. 73 K
char_burgess@redlands.edu
BURGESS, Colleen ... 704-403-3502 355 B
colleen.burgess@carolinashealthcare.org
BURGESS, Craig, E ... 803-533-3928 448 H
BURGESS, Douglas ... 513-556-9900 393 B
douglas.burgess@uc.edu
BURGESS, Duncan ... 206-934-6882 526 B
duncan.burgess@seattlecolleges.edu
BURGESS, Ed ... 913-758-3033 548 F
burgesse@leavenworth.army.mil
BURGESS, James ... 818-401-1030.. 41 F
jburgess@columbiacollege.edu
BURGESS, Kimberly ... 229-430-3976 119 H
kimberly.burgess@asurams.edu
BURGESS, Marcus ... 305-626-1443 104 B
Marcus.Burgess@fmuniv.edu
BURGESS, Marcus ... 803-780-1199 451 G
mburgess@voorhees.edu
BURGESS, Nancy, E ... 301-583-7011 217 G
burgesne@pgcc.edu
BURGESS, Norma ... 615-966-6146 458 C
norma.burgess@lipscomb.edu
BURGESS, Shane, C ... 520-621-7621.. 18 E
shaneburgess@email.arizona.edu
BURGESS, Sylvia ... 580-581-2284 397 A
sylviab@cameron.edu
BURGESS, Valerie ... 603-880-8308 298 I
vburgess@thomasmorecollege.edu
BURGETT, Paul, J ... 585-274-3326 351 D
pburgett@admin.rochester.edu
BURGGRAFF, Lucy ... 919-573-5350 368 H
BURGHART, Michael ... 707-826-3512.. 35 D
msb39@humboldt.edu
BURGHER, Louis, W ... 402-552-2586 289 H
burgherlouis@clarksoncollege.edu
BURGIE-BRYANT,
Willette ... 484-384-2942 418 A
wburgie@eastern.edu
BURGIE-BRYANT,
Willette, A ... 484-384-2942 427 I
wburgie@eastern.edu
BURGIN, Jeffery ... 615-460-6407 455 D
Jeffery.Burgin@belmont.edu
BURGIN, Sheila ... 360-442-2132 524 A
sburgin@lowercolumbia.edu
BURGIN, Vicki ... 251-442-2269.... 9 B
vburgin@umobile.edu
BURGIS, Laura ... 909-667-4421.. 39 C
lburgis@claremontlincoln.org
BURGMAYER, Sharon ... 610-526-5106 413 D
sburmay@brynmawr.edu
BURGMEIER, Julie ... 563-588-6374 176 F
julie.bergmeier@clarke.edu
BURGNER, Ryan, C ... 308-635-6798 294 C
burgnerr@wncc.edu
BURGOS, Jorge, A ... 787-720-4476 556 G
decanatoestudiantes@mizpa.edu
BURGOS, Jose, L ... 787-728-1515 559 A
jburgos@sagrado.edu
BURGOS, Kathy ... 562-860-2451.. 37 L
kburgos@cerritos.edu
BURGOS, Maida ... 305-821-3333 104 C
mburgos@fnu.edu
BURGOS-LOPEZ, Luz ... 410-337-6532 215 B
luz.burgoslopez@goucher.edu
BURGOYNE, Bonnie ... 870-512-7740.. 19 I
bonnie_burgoyne@asun.edu
BURI, David ... 360-359-4958 522 C
dburi@ewu.edu
BURIK, Larry ... 909-607-2226.. 59 F
larry_burik@pitzer.edu
BURISH, Thomas, G ... 574-631-6631 174 A
burish.2@nd.edu
BURK, Ann, M ... 308-432-6311 292 B
aburk@csc.edu
BURK, Kelly ... 765-983-1501 165 H
burkke@earlham.edu
BURK, Thomas ... 973-328-5037 301 G
tburk@ccm.edu
BURKARD, Donald, C .. 843-953-1432 445 B
burkardd@cofc.edu
BURKE, Barbara ... 718-260-5173 320 D
bburke@citytech.cuny.edu
BURKE, Brian, W ... 413-545-2204 228 F
bwburke@external.umass.edu
BURKE, Bridget ... 701-231-6128 374 C
bridget.burke@ndsu.edu
BURKE, Carson ... 330-923-9959 382 D
cburke@fortiscollege.edu
BURKE, Cathleen, C ... 804-828-0179 514 F
ccburke@vcu.edu
BURKE, Chelsey ... 828-251-6501 370 E
cburke@unca.edu

BURKE, Christy ... 740-376-4708 386 A
christy.burke@marietta.edu
BURKE, Clarence ... 919-572-1625 354 F
cburke@apexsot.edu
BURKE, Colleen ... 215-572-2785 412 F
burkec@arcadia.edu
BURKE, Dale ... 808-544-9394 135 C
dburke@hpu.edu
BURKE, Dana, L ... 240-895-4203 218 B
dlburke@smcm.edu
BURKE, Daniel ... 978-542-6350 230 E
daniel.burke@salemstate.edu
BURKE, David ... 626-812-3016.. 29 B
dburke@apu.edu
BURKE, Derek, A ... 252-398-6369 356 B
burked@chowan.edu
BURKE, Donald, S ... 412-624-3001 437 K
donburke@pitt.edu
BURKE, Donna ... 802-656-3402 503 C
donna.burke@uvm.edu
BURKE, Emily ... 617-746-1990 227 G
emily.burke@hult.edu
BURKE, Genevieve ... 312-752-2174 149 D
genevieve.burke@kendall.edu
BURKE, Greg ... 318-357-5251 208 D
burkeg@nsula.edu
BURKE, Ingrid ... 307-766-5080 546 K
indy.burke@uwyo.edu
BURKE, James, A ... 216-397-4484 384 F
burke@jcu.edu
BURKE, Janice, P ... 215-503-9606 436 F
janice.burke@jefferson.edu
BURKE, Jean ... 414-288-7013 537 B
jean.burke@marquette.edu
BURKE, Jeanmarie, R ... 315-568-3869 334 F
jburke@nycc.edu
BURKE, Joe ... 620-421-6700 189 B
joeburke@labette.edu
BURKE, John ... 845-848-4079 324 B
john.burke@dc.edu
BURKE, John, D ... 617-552-3387 224 B
john.burke.7@bc.edu
BURKE, Jonathan ... 949-376-6000.. 49 K
jburke@lcad.edu
BURKE, Jonathan, L ... 816-604-6620 277 G
jon.burke@mcckc.edu
BURKE, Joseph, D ... 256-228-6001.... 6 A
burkej@nacc.edu
BURKE, Joy ... 814-371-2090 437 C
jburke@triangle-tech.edu
BURKE, Judith, A ... 765-285-1847 164 D
jmoore@bsu.edu
BURKE, Kathleen, F ... 818-719-6408.. 51 H
kburke@piercecollege.edu
BURKE, Keri ... 504-394-7744 206 E
kburke@olhcc.edu
BURKE, Keri ... 503-883-2269 406 I
kburke@linfield.edu
BURKE, Kevin ... 717-291-3981 418 J
kburk2@fandm.edu
BURKE, Kimberly, G ... 601-974-1250 268 D
burkekg@millsaps.edu
BURKE, Lillian ... 410-669-9200 216 F
BURKE, Mary ... 617-984-1708 235 H
mburke@quincycollege.edu
BURKE, Matthew ... 617-928-4500 234 D
mburke@mountida.edu
BURKE, Melinda, W ... 520-621-3557.. 18 E
mwburke@email.arizona.edu
BURKE, Mia ... 808-853-1040 135 F
miaburke@pacrim.edu
BURKE, Michael, L ... 951-222-8800.. 60 J
michael.burke@rccd.edu
BURKE, Patrick ... 717-291-4270 418 J
pburke@fandm.edu
BURKE, Peggy ... 773-325-4605 143 G
pburke@depaul.edu
BURKE, Scott ... 617-928-7337 234 D
sburke@mountida.edu
BURKE, Scott, M ... 404-413-2088 126 D
sburke@gsu.edu
BURKE, Sharon ... 716-375-2102 340 C
sburke@sbu.edu
BURKE, Susan ... 781-762-1211 226 E
sburke@fmc.edu
BURKE, Ted ... 508-541-1774 225 G
tburke@dean.edu
BURKE, Thomas ... 212-343-1234 332 I
tburke@mcny.edu
BURKE, Thomas ... 601-266-5020 271 B
thomas.burke@usm.edu
BURKE, Tom, J ... 661-336-5117.. 49 D
tburke@kccd.edu
BURKE, Tracie, L ... 901-321-3357 455 I
tburke@cbu.edu
BURKE, Vic ... 912-443-5799 131 B
vburke@savannahtech.edu
BURKE, William, R ... 570-941-7887 438 F
william.burke@scranton.edu

BURKE-SULLIVAN, Eileen, C ... 402-280-3285 290 B
e_burkesullivan@creighton.edu
BURKEE, James ... 914-337-9300 323 A
james.burkee@concordia-ny.edu
BURKERT, Amy, L ... 412-268-5865 414 J
ak11@andrew.cmu.edu
BURKES, Kate ... 479-619-4299.. 22 B
kburkes@nwacc.edu
BURKET, Lisa ... 317-896-9324 173 G
BURKETT, Amy ... 704-330-5940 361 D
amy.burkett@cpcc.edu
BURKETT, Holly, L ... 865-981-5302 463 E
hlburkett@pstcc.edu
BURKETT, Kaia ... 510-587-7890.. 59 C
kburkett@peralta.edu
BURKETT, Kaia ... 510-587-7890.. 58 J
kburkett@peralta.edu
BURKETT, Kina ... 251-809-1555.... 5 B
kina.burkett@jdcc.edu
BURKETT, Nancy ... 610-328-8651 436 A
nburket1@swarthmore.edu
BURKETT, Norvel ... 865-974-3181 465 D
nburkett@utk.edu
BURKETT, Timothy ... 704-847-5600 369 A
itadmin@ses.edu
BURKEY, Daniel, E ... 402-280-2131 290 B
dburkey@creighton.edu
BURKHALTER, Carmen, L ... 256-765-4288.... 9 D
cburkhalter@una.edu
BURKHALTER, James ... 806-742-1452 489 F
j.burkhalter@ttu.edu
BURKHALTER, Shelia ... 410-837-4271 221 B
sburkhalter@ubalt.edu
BURKHAMMER, Jerry, L ... 304-462-6413 532 G
jerry.burkhammer@glenville.edu
BURKHARDT, Janet ... 303-871-4757.. 86 H
janet.burkhardt@du.edu
BURKHARDT, Lou Ann . 312-461-0600 139 G
lburkhardt@aaart.edu
BURKHARDT, Paul ... 928-350-4100.. 17 K
pburkhardt@prescott.edu
BURKHARDT, Ronald ... 856-351-2608 308 B
rburkhardt@salemcc.edu
BURKHART, Jenny ... 859-858-2318 192 O
BURKHART, Keith ... 801-524-1923 498 J
keith.burkhart@ldschurch.org
BURKHART, Patricia ... 954-492-5353 100 G
pburkhart@citycollege.edu
BURKHART, Patrick ... 480-654-7700.. 15 A
patrick.burkhart@mesacc.edu
BURKHART-EVANS, Maggie ... 540-568-5646 509 C
evansmb@jmu.edu
BURKHOLDER, Brian, M ... 540-432-4132 507 A
brian.burkholder@emu.edu
BURKHOLDER, Gary ... 408-254-6900.. 55 G
gburkholder@nhu.edu
BURKHOLDER, Mary, E 419-783-2360 381 G
mburkholder@defiance.edu
BURKHOLDER, Robert, C ... 215-503-6249 436 F
robert.burkholder@jefferson.edu
BURKINK, Timothy, J ... 308-865-8342 293 G
burkinktj@unk.edu
BURKMAN, Roger ... 502-585-9911 199 E
rburkman@spalding.edu
BURKMAN, Tom, A ... 612-343-4748 263 H
taburkma@northcentral.edu
BURKS, Barry, L ... 336-334-7995 370 B
blburks@ncat.edu
BURKS, Brent ... 254-295-4514 492 C
bburks@umhb.edu
BURKS, Bryan ... 501-279-4312.. 21 A
bburks@harding.edu
BURKS, Eric ... 785-738-9057 190 A
eburks@ncktc.edu
BURKS, Gwenevera, E .. 559-453-2010.. 45 E
gwen.burks@fresno.edu
BURKS, Laura ... 334-580-2144.... 5 A
laura.burks@faulknerstate.edu
BURKS, Scott, A ... 502-852-4661 201 A
scott.burks@louisville.edu
BURKS, Suzanne, M ... 405-744-5458 400 C
suzanne.burks@okstate.edu
BURKUM, Karen, J ... 315-268-6576 321 C
kburkum@clarkson.edu
BURLAUD, Patricia ... 516-686-7443 335 F
pburlaud@nyit.edu
BURLESON, Brooke ... 828-766-1269 364 A
bburleson@mayland.edu
BURLESON, Burt ... 254-710-3517 469 D
burt_burleson@baylor.edu
BURLESON, Susan ... 336-249-8186 362 B
sdburl@davidsonccc.edu
BURLEW, Elizabeth ... 315-655-7375 317 J
eburlew@cazenovia.edu
BURLEW, Jon ... 606-679-8501 197 B
jon.burlew@kctcs.edu
BURLEW, Lynette ... 318-473-6401 205 A
lburlew@lsua.edu
BURLINGAME, Kathy ... 502-410-6200 194 N
kburlingame@galencollege.edu
BURLISON, John ... 530-226-4140.. 66 G
jburlison@simpsonu.edu
BURMA, William, H ... 515-263-2975 178 H
bburma@grandview.edu
BURMAN, Tom ... 307-766-2292 546 K
tburman@uwyo.edu
BURMASTER, Elizabeth . 301-846-2440 214 I
eburmaster@frederick.edu
BURNAM, Paul ... 740-362-3435 386 D
pburnam@mtso.edu
BURNAM, Scott, M ... 937-778-7849 381 K
sburnam@edisonohio.edu
BURNE, Tom ... 828-898-3522 358 F
burnet@lmc.edu
BURNER, Emily ... 540-545-7334 512 E
eburner@su.edu
BURNES, Michael ... 706-236-2245 121 E
mburnes@berry.edu
BURNESS, Maria ... 410-386-8526 214 B
mburness@carrollcc.edu
BURNETT, Belinda ... 520-417-4092.. 13 B
burnettb@cochise.edu
BURNETT, Benjamin ... 601-318-6144 271 F
bburnett@wmcarey.edu
BURNETT, Bradley, T ... 405-325-5505 403 I
bburnett@ou.edu
BURNETT, Brian, D ... 573-882-3611 283 G
burnettbd@umsystem.edu
BURNETT, Catherine, G 713-646-1831 482 H
cburnett@stcl.edu
BURNETT, Daniel, C ... 606-451-6749 197 B
danielc.burnett@kctcs.edu
BURNETT, Denita ... 276-223-4769 517 F
dburnett@wcc.vccs.edu
BURNETT, Edward, T ... 508-286-8381 238 B
burnett_edward@wheatoncollege.edu
BURNETT, Elsie ... 972-860-8201 472 D
eburnett@dcccd.edu
BURNETT, Eric ... 208-882-1566 138 F
eburnett@nsa.edu
BURNETT, George, A ... 928-541-7777.. 16 B
president@ncu.edu
BURNETT, John ... 724-938-4014 430 C
burnett@calu.edu
BURNETT, Linda, G ... 409-882-3998 488 G
linda.burnett@lsco.edu
BURNETT, Lonnie ... 251-442-2319.... 9 B
lburnett@umobile.edu
BURNETT, Lori, W ... 229-430-6443 119 H
lori.burnett@asurams.edu
BURNETT, Marc ... 931-372-3411 462 A
mburnett@tntech.edu
BURNETT, Mary ... 717-477-1279 431 F
meburnett@ship.edu
BURNETT, Michael, F ... 225-578-5748 204 M
vocbur@lsu.edu
BURNETT, Myra ... 404-270-5027 132 D
mburnett@spelman.edu
BURNETT, Sharron, T ... 405-466-3579 398 E
stburnett@langston.edu
BURNETT, Sharron, T ... 405-466-3259 398 E
stburnett@langston.edu
BURNETT, Tod, A ... 949-582-4722.. 67 F
tburnett@saddleback.edu
BURNETTE, Cindy ... 270-745-2755 201 D
cindy.burnette@wku.edu
BURNETTE, Daarel ... 937-376-6201 379 D
dburnette@centralstate.edu
BURNETTE, George ... 336-770-1480 372 B
burnetteg@uncsa.edu
BURNETTE, JR., Glen, G ... 910-521-6201 371 D
glen.burnette@uncp.edu
BURNETTE, Randy ... 252-940-6426 360 B
randy.burnette@beaufortccc.edu
BURNETTE, Richard ... 850-644-1532 115 A
rburnette@admin.fsu.edu
BURNETTE, Sheryl, L ... 423-439-4230 461 D
burnetts@etsu.edu
BURNETTE, Stephanie ... 321-433-7271 101 O
burnettes@easternflorida.edu
BURNETTE, Teri ... 706-396-8132 129 H
tburnette@paine.edu
BURNEY, Andrea ... 434-797-8458 515 C
aburney@dcc.vccs.edu
BURNEY, John ... 402-826-8221 290 C
john.burney@doane.edu
BURNEY, Linda ... 910-879-5519 360 C
lburney@bladencc.edu
BURNEY, Michelle ... 662-227-2304 267 E
mburney@holmescc.edu
BURNEY, Rolanda ... 336-517-2225 354 K
rburney@bennett.edu
BURNHAM, Don ... 601-605-3301 267 E
dburnham@holmescc.edu
BURNHAM, Mark, A ... 517-353-9000 246 H
mburnham@msu.edu
BURNHAM, Willette, S . 843-792-2146 447 G
burnham@musc.edu
BURNIM, Mickey, L ... 301-860-3555 220 B
president@bowiestate.edu
BURNIP, David, W ... 330-471-8251 385 G
dburnip@malone.edu
BURNISTON, Kay ... 386-506-3658 101 I
burnisk@DaytonaState.edu
BURNLEY, Chris ... 540-365-4231 507 H
cburnley@ferrum.edu
BURNLEY, Lawrence, A 509-777-4215 529 A
lburnley@whitworth.edu
BURNLEY, Linda ... 646-888-6639 331 E
burnleyl@sloankettering.edu
BURNS, Andrew ... 970-247-7180.. 82 I
burns_a@fortlewis.edu
BURNS, Anita ... 518-464-8545 325 B
aburns@excelsior.edu
BURNS, Ann, K ... 716-673-3333 343 F
ann.burns@fredonia.edu
BURNS, Barb ... 314-392-2362 278 G
burnsba@mobap.edu
BURNS, Barbara ... 478-471-2502 128 H
barbara.burns@mga.edu
BURNS, Betty ... 812-749-1237 171 I
bburns@oak.edu
BURNS, Candace ... 973-720-2138 309 I
burnsc@wpunj.edu
BURNS, Carl, F ... 573-341-4292 284 C
carlb@mst.edu
BURNS, Cathy ... 918-343-7791 401 I
cburns@rsu.edu
BURNS, Cindy ... 910-678-8564 362 E
griffinw@faytechcc.edu
BURNS, Daniel, P ... 985-867-2225 206 J
acdean@sjasc.edu
BURNS, Dave ... 309-341-5463 140 I
dburns@sandburg.edu
BURNS, David ... 860-444-8201 548 H
David.Burns@uscg.mil
BURNS, Dianne ... 641-673-1084 184 B
burnsd@wmpenn.edu
BURNS, Elizabeth ... 315-312-4100 346 A
elizabeth.burns@oswego.edu
BURNS, Elizabeth, A ... 313-927-1207 246 D
eburns@marygrove.edu
BURNS, Erick ... 530-741-6838.. 78 F
eburns@yccd.edu
BURNS, Erin ... 510-849-8222.. 57 G
eburns@psr.edu
BURNS, Gary ... 816-501-4854 281 B
gary.burns@rockhurst.edu
BURNS, J. Joseph ... 617-552-3273 224 B
john.burns@bc.edu
BURNS, Jack ... 734-384-4249 247 C
jburns@monroeccc.edu
BURNS, Jacqueline ... 352-392-1784 115 D
jkbu@ufl.edu
BURNS, Jacquelyn ... 307-855-2150 545 a
jburns@cwc.edu
BURNS, James, R ... 617-552-1603 224 B
james.burns.3@bc.edu
BURNS, James, T ... 215-670-9235 428 A
jtburns@peirce.edu
BURNS, Janie ... 731-352-4000 455 E
burnsj@bethelu.edu
BURNS, Jeffrey, S ... 804-752-7367 511 E
jburns@rmc.edu
BURNS, Jennifer, A ... 412-365-1849 415 C
jburns@chatham.edu
BURNS, Joseph, A ... 607-255-4843 323 C
deanoffaculty-mailbox@cornell.edu
BURNS, Kathleen ... 508-678-2811 231 B
kathleen.burns@bristolcc.edu
BURNS, Kelli ... 314-539-5371 281 H
kburns@stlcc.edu
BURNS, Keri ... 678-839-6431 133 F
kburns@westga.edu
BURNS, Kevin, J ... 757-823-8879 510 H
kburns@nsu.edu
BURNS, Kimberly ... 215-567-7080 412 G
kburns@aii.edu
BURNS, Kristen ... 703-658-4304 506 H
krisburns@christendom.edu
BURNS, Laura ... 315-364-3289 352 F
lburns@wells.edu
BURNS, Lawrence, J ... 330-972-6546 392 H
lburns@uakron.edu
BURNS, Lisa, A ... 434-223-6118 508 B
lburns@hsc.edu
BURNS, Lita ... 208-769-3302 138 G
lita_burns@nic.edu
BURNS, Lucy ... 502-272-8234 193 E
lburns@bellarmine.edu
BURNS, Marie-Elaine ... 408-288-3191.. 64 A
marie-elaine.burns@sjcc.edu
BURNS, Marvin ... 405-466-6150 398 E
mburns@langston.edu
BURNS, Matthew ... 585-275-4085 351 D
matthew.burns@rochester.edu
BURNS, Max ... 678-359-5015 126 E
mburns@gordonstate.edu
BURNS, Michael ... 913-288-7670 188 G
mburns@kckcc.edu
BURNS, Michael ... 913-281-7670 188 G
mburns@kckcc.edu
BURNS, Michael ... 405-585-5253 399 I
michae.burns@okbu.edu
BURNS, Patrick ... 970-491-1833.. 81 D
patrick.burns@colostate.edu
BURNS, Patrick ... 928-776-2055.. 18 L
patrick.burns@yc.edu
BURNS, Peter ... 518-327-6017 338 B
pburns@paulsmiths.edu
BURNS, Randy ... 270-384-8170 198 C
burnsr@lindsey.edu
BURNS, Sarah, H ... 704-233-8128 373 C
shburns@wingate.edu
BURNS, Shawn, G ... 806-651-2300 486 D
sburns@mail.wtamu.edu
BURNS, Skipper ... 678-359-5739 126 E
skipperb@gordonstate.edu
BURNS, Sonya, L ... 270-824-1823 196 F
sonyal.burns@kctcs.edu
BURNS, Steven ... 845-398-4176 341 H
sburns@stac.edu
BURNS, Susan, R ... 563-588-6540 176 F
susan.burns@clarke.edu
BURNS, Thomas ... 716-286-8580 336 E
tburns@niagara.edu
BURNS, Thomas, D ... 615-460-6400 455 D
thomas.burns@belmont.edu
BURNS, Todd ... 309-268-8020 145 H
todd.burns@heartland.edu
BURNS, Wendy ... 651-523-2235 256 B
wburns@hamline.edu
BURNS, William ... 732-224-2426 300 F
wburns@brookdalecc.edu
BURNS, William ... 701-231-7671 374 C
william.burns@ndsu.edu
BURNS, Yvonne ... 210-829-3900 492 B
yburns@uiwtx.edu
BURNSIDE, Michael ... 404-225-4448 120 I
mburnside@atlantatech.edu
BURNSIDE, Virgil ... 859-985-3150 193 F
virgil_burnside@berea.edu
BURON, Otha ... 601-979-2339 267 H
otha.burton@jsums.edu
BURR, Alan ... 941-487-4245 115 B
aburr@ncf.edu
BURR, Donna ... 805-585-8058.. 29 J
dburr@brooks.edu
BURR, Jason, H ... 864-597-4381 451 J
burrjh@wofford.edu
BURR, Kim ... 828-766-1350 364 A
kburr@mayland.edu
BURR, Mei Mei ... 937-382-6661 395 F
meimei_burr@wilmington.edu
BURR, Stephen ... 313-883-8623 249 E
burr.stephen@shms.edu
BURRAGE, Sean ... 580-745-2500 402 D
sburrage@se.edu
BURRELL, Becky ... 419-995-8331 384 E
burrell.b@rhodesstate.edu
BURRELL, James ... 704-378-1081 358 B
jburrell@jcsu.edu
BURRELL, Kari ... 907-474-7907.. 10 I
kari.burrell@alaska.edu
BURRELL, Robyn ... 619-651-2482.. 70 G
rburrell@asuniversity.edu
BURRELL, Scott ... 859-371-9393 193 D
sburrell@beckfield.edu
BURRELL, Steve ... 912-478-1294 126 B
sburrell@georgiasouthern.edu
BURRELL, Todd, C ... 618-650-3705 159 I
tburrel@siue.edu
BURRESS, Diane ... 210-486-3000 467 A
BURRI, Josephine ... 215-717-6144 437 H
jburri@uarts.edu
BURRICHTER, William .. 585-567-9622 328 C
william.burrichter@houghton.edu
BURRILL, Jennifer, R ... 269-471-6601 239 D
burrillj@andrews.edu
BURRIS, David ... 530-283-0202.. 44 H
dburris@frc.edu
BURRIS, Deborah, J ... 314-516-5695 284 B
dburris@umsl.edu
BURRIS, Janssen ... 225-214-1947 206 F
janssen.burris@ololcollege.edu
BURRIS, Kendra ... 806-743-2786 490 A
kendra.burris@ttuhsc.edu
BURROUGHS, Cynthia .. 501-370-5337.. 22 E
cburroughs@philander.edu
BURROUGHS, Lisa ... 478-757-2647 128 H
lisa.burroughs@mga.edu
BURROUGHS-DAVIS, Robin ... 603-526-3752 296 I
rdavis@colby-sawyer.edu

BURROW, Susan ... 256-215-4301 ... 2 G sburrow@cacc.edu
BURROWS, Angie ... 570-372-4120 435 I burrowsa@susqu.edu
BURROWS, Carmen ... 757-825-2939 517 B burrowsc@tncc.edu
BURROWS, David ... 920-832-6528 536 R david.burrows@lawrence.edu
BURROWS, SC, Joanne, M ... 563-588-6385 176 F joanne.burrows@clarke.edu
BURROWS-SCHUMACHER, Molly ... 563-588-4981 180 L molly.burrowsschumacher@loras.edu
BURROWS-SCHUMACHER, Molly, A ... 563-588-4981 180 L molly.burrowsschumacher@loras.edu
BURRUS, Ken ... 509-533-7220 521 E ken.burrus@ccs.spokane.edu
BURRUS, Ken ... 509-533-7220 521 D kburrus@ccs.spokane.edu
BURRUS, Ken ... 509-533-3630 521 F ken.burrus@ccs.spokane.edu
BURRUS, Robert ... 910-962-3226 372 A burrusr@uncw.edu
BURRUS, Scott ... 928-541-7777 .. 16 B sburrus@ncu.edu
BURRUSS, Jennifer ... 252-789-0247 363 H jburruss@martincc.edu
BURRUSS, Nancy, M ... 920-433-6632 534 K nancy.burruss@bellincollege.edu
BURRUTO, James ... 315-781-3319 327 G burruto@hws.edu
BURSE, Raymond, M ... 502-597-6260 197 G raymond.burse@kysu.edu
BURSI, Megan, M ... 901-572-2853 455 C megan.bursi@bchs.edu
BURSON, Max ... 316-295-5521 187 C mburson@friends.edu
BURSON, Todd, E ... 740-427-5181 384 P bursont@kenyon.edu
BURSTEIN, Mark ... 920-832-6525 536 R mark.burstein@lawrence.edu
BURSTEN, Bruce ... 508-831-5222 238 G bbursten@wpi.edu
BURSTON, Gwendolyn .. 336-334-4822 363 A ggburston@gtcc.edu
BURSTYN, Yaakov ... 305-534-7050 117 C rabbiburstyn@talmudicu.edu
BURSZTYN, Jacob ... 732-367-1060 300 D jbursztyn@bmg.edu
BURT, Andrea ... 517-264-3100 238 H aburt@adrian.edu
BURT, Bobby ... 256-924-0511 ... 5 F
BURT, Bruce, E ... 937-229-2131 393 E bburt1@udayton.edu
BURT, Charles ... 617-745-3725 225 H charles.burt@enc.edu
BURT, Ernest ... 561-912-2166 102 N eburt@evergladesuniversity.edu
BURT, Mickey, G ... 563-884-5451 182 D mickey.burt@palmer.edu
BURT, Raymond ... 910-962-3346 372 A burtr@uncw.edu
BURT, Theresa, E ... 215-926-2010 436 C theresa.burt@temple.edu
BURTI, Ellen ... 718-940-5852 341 A eburti@sjcny.edu
BURTIS, Brett, K ... 307-674-6446 546 H bburtis@sheridan.edu
BURTIS, Karen, B ... 307-674-6446 546 H kburtis@sheridan.edu
BURTLEY, Harold ... 219-980-6539 168 C hburtley@iun.edu
BURTNESS, John ... 303-556-5126 .. 83 Q ua@msudenver.edu
BURTNETT, Jody ... 217-875-7211 156 K jburtnett@richland.edu
BURTON, Adam ... 951-343-4286 .. 30 D aburton@calbaptist.edu
BURTON, Adrienne ... 714-895-5103 .. 40 C aburton@gwc.cccd.edu
BURTON, Alan ... 580-745-2731 402 D aburton@se.edu
BURTON, Barbara ... 309-694-8817 146 C barbara.burton@icc.edu
BURTON, Becky ... 706-583-2818 120 G bburton@athenstech.edu
BURTON, Ben ... 317-921-4712 169 L bburton@ivytech.edu
BURTON, Carol ... 828-227-7495 372 C burton@wcu.edu
BURTON, Chet ... 775-445-4236 296 A chester.burton@wnc.edu
BURTON, Clen ... 409-933-8261 471 B clenburton@com.edu
BURTON, Courtney ... 212-799-5000 329 I
BURTON, Dan ... 513-244-8167 379 I dan.burton@ccuniversity.edu
BURTON, Derrick ... 641-585-8671 183 I derrick.burton@waldorf.edu
BURTON, Donald, N ... 602-648-5750 .. 13 K dburton@dunlap-stone.edu
BURTON, Doug ... 202-203-9883 350 J d.burton@uts.edu
BURTON, Elizabeth ... 610-399-2427 430 D eburton@cheyney.edu
BURTON, Gera, C ... 573-882-4250 283 H burtong@missouri.edu
BURTON, Gregory, A ... 973-761-9362 308 C gregory.burton@shu.edu
BURTON, Heather ... 540-868-7201 515 H hburton@lfcc.edu
BURTON, Jan ... 801-627-8309 498 O burtonj@owatc.edu
BURTON, Jennus, L ... 928-523-2708 .. 16 C Jennus.Burton@nau.edu
BURTON, Jeremy ... 918-495-6647 401 B jburton@oru.edu
BURTON, Khalilah ... 251-981-3771 ... 3 A khalilah.burton@columbiasouthern.edu
BURTON, Larry ... 336-272-7102 357 B lwburton@greensboro.edu
BURTON, Lisa, E ... 256-765-4317 ... 9 D leburton@una.edu
BURTON, Lonnie ... 806-291-3635 496 K burtonl@wbu.edu
BURTON, Marjorie ... 440-775-5782 388 B marjorie.burton@oberlin.edu
BURTON, Melody ... 503-517-1369 411 A mburton@warnerpacific.edu
BURTON, Michele ... 503-842-8222 410 C burton@tillamookbay.cc
BURTON, Patrice ... 708-596-2000 159 D pburton@ssc.edu
BURTON, Ray ... 419-995-8302 384 E burton.r@rhodesstate.edu
BURTON, Raymond, A .. 804-523-5374 515 F rburton@reynolds.edu
BURTON, Rebecca ... 972-854-5611 471 H rebecca.burton@concordia.edu
BURTON, Regina ... 334-727-8011 ... 8 B
BURTON, Robert ... 808-984-3245 136 H reburton@hawaii.edu
BURTON, Sharon ... 270-831-9646 196 C sharon.burton@kctcs.edu
BURTON, Shawntae ... 803-327-7402 444 F sburton@clintoncollege.edu
BURTON, Stacy ... 775-784-1740 295 H sburton@unr.edu
BURTON, Terrance ... 508-999-8664 228 H tburton@umassd.edu
BURTON, Timothy, P ... 516-877-3385 314 F burton@adelphi.edu
BURTON, JR., Velmer, S ... 662-915-5526 270 G vsburton@olemiss.edu
BURTON-GOSS, Sadie .. 781-239-6334 222 E sburtongoss@babson.edu
BURWELL, Elissia ... 903-593-8311 487 A eburwell@texascollege.edu
BURY, John ... 918-631-2602 403 M john-bury@utulsa.edu
BURY, Sandra ... 309-677-3100 140 H sandy@fsmail.bradley.edu
BURY, Sandra ... 309-677-2808 140 H sandy@bradley.edu
BURZACHECHI, Nancilee ... 412-237-4684 415 G nancilee@ccac.edu
BURZICHELLI, Dominick ... 856-415-2292 306 C dburzichelli@rcgc.edu
BURZINSKI, Jody ... 620-421-6700 189 B jodyb@labette.edu
BUSAM, Leah ... 513-745-4879 396 B busaml@xavier.edu
BUSBEE, Walter ... 803-508-7254 443 C busbeew@atc.edu
BUSBOOM, Margo ... 402-461-7494 290 G mbusboom@hastings.edu
BUSBY, Dwayne ... 281-283-2019 491 E busby@uhcl.edu
BUSBY, Katie ... 504-314-2898 207 F kbusby@tulane.edu
BUSBY, Laura ... 801-863-8456 500 B lbusby@uvu.edu
BUSBY, Teresa ... 601-446-1211 266 J teresa.busby@colin.edu
BUSCEMI, Vince ... 410-857-2290 217 A vbuscemi@mcdaniel.edu
BUSCH, Brian ... 252-789-0247 363 H bbusch@martincc.edu
BUSCH, Caroline, C ... 804-752-3267 511 E cbusch@rmc.edu
BUSCH, Gregory ... 419-755-4570 387 E gbusch@ncstatecollege.edu
BUSCH, Nancy ... 402-472-2526 293 H nbusch2@unl.edu
BUSCH, Nancy ... 718-817-4400 326 C busch@fordham.edu
BUSCHART, W. David ... 303-762-6907 .. 82 C david.buschart@denverseminary.edu
BUSCHMAN, John, E ... 973-761-9005 308 C john.buschman@shu.edu
BUSE, Beth, H ... 651-201-1799 257 N beth.buse@so.mnscu.edu
BUSE, Jon ... 319-398-4977 180 J jon.buse@kirkwood.edu
BUSE, Kathleen ... 973-618-3411 300 H kbuse@caldwell.edu
BUSE, William ... 212-799-5000 329 I
BUSEL, Yaakov ... 732-985-6533 305 D
BUSER, Boyd, R ... 606-218-5411 201 C boydbuser@upike.edu
BUSH, Abra ... 617-912-9124 224 C abush@bostonconservatory.edu
BUSH, Bernetta, D ... 773-995-3519 141 J bbush@csu.edu
BUSH, Catherine ... 440-525-7119 385 C cbush@lakelandcc.edu
BUSH, Cathy ... 440-525-7112 385 C cbush@lakelandcc.edu
BUSH, Darren ... 657-278-7271 .. 33 E dlbush@fullerton.edu
BUSH, David ... 435-797-1012 500 A david.bush@usu.edu
BUSH, Jim ... 509-865-8570 523 C bush_j@heritage.edu
BUSH, Katherine ... 845-437-5900 351 H kabush@vassar.edu
BUSH, Keith ... 218-751-8670 263 J it@oakhills.edu
BUSH, Kim, D ... 616-988-1000 241 E kim.b@compass.edu
BUSH, Kristen ... 540-231-1796 518 B khbush@vt.edu
BUSH, Lisa, F ... 828-398-7202 360 A lbush@abtech.edu
BUSH, Lonica ... 409-933-8413 471 B lbush@com.edu
BUSH, Michael ... 805-986-5813 .. 75 D mbush@vcccd.edu
BUSH, Mickie ... 503-494-7800 408 D regohsu@ohsu.edu
BUSH, Polly ... 585-340-9500 321 G pbush@crcds.edu
BUSH, Richard, G ... 248-204-2485 245 J rbush@ltu.edu
BUSH, TaJuan ... 215-335-0800 424 D tbush@lincolntech.edu
BUSHA, Cathy ... 503-768-7186 406 H cbusha@lclark.edu
BUSHER, Edward, J ... 937-328-6095 379 L bushere@clarkstate.edu
BUSHEY, Jane, L ... 480-245-7930 .. 14 D jane.bushey@ibcs.edu
BUSHEY, Stephanie ... 516-463-6853 328 A stephanie.bushey@hofstra.edu
BUSHLEY, Tom ... 434-832-7725 515 A bushleyt@cvcc.vccs.edu
BUSHMAN, David, L ... 540-868-7143 515 H dbushman@lfcc.edu
BUSHMAN, David, W ... 540-828-5605 505 F dbushman@bridgewater.edu
BUSHNELL, Lynn, M ... 203-582-8651 .. 91 E lynn.bushnell@quinnipiac.edu
BUSHNELL, Ryan ... 517-321-0242 243 H rbushnell@glcc.edu
BUSHONG, Sara ... 419-372-2856 377 I sbushon@bgsu.edu
BUSHWAY, Deborah ... 888-227-4149 254 C deborah.bushway@capella.edu
BUSROE, Andrew ... 606-368-6113 192 H andrewbusroe@alc.edu
BUSS, Brian ... 920-735-5792 542 N buss@fvtc.edu
BUSS, James, J ... 410-677-6556 220 E jjbuss@salisbury.edu
BUSS, Marney ... 508-213-2101 235 C marney.buss@nichols.edu
BUSSARD, Patsy, G ... 276-964-7332 517 A pat.bussard@sw.edu
BUSSE, Dan ... 850-484-1158 110 D dbusse@pensacolastate.edu
BUSSELL, Helena ... 817-531-4405 490 C hbussell@txwes.edu
BUSSELL, Paige ... 903-468-3209 485 E paige.bussell@tamuc.edu
BUSSELL, Rachelle ... 909-558-4544 .. 50 K rbussell@llu.edu
BUSSELL, Shawn ... 419-824-3785 385 F sbussell@lourdes.edu
BUSSEY, Brenda ... 508-929-8455 230 G bbussey@worcester.edu
BUSTA, Joseph, F ... 251-460-7616 ... 9 F jbusta@southalabama.edu
BUSTAMANTE, Camilla . 505-428-1388 313 A camilla.bustamante@sfcc.edu
BUSTAMANTE, Chris ... 480-517-8118 .. 15 D chris.bustamante@riosalado.edu
BUSTAMANTE, Mary ... 610-519-4300 439 A mary.bustamante@villanova.edu
BUSTARD, James ... 217-351-2211 155 I jbustard@parkland.edu
BUSTER-WILLIAMS, Kimberley ... 540-654-1618 513 I kwilli23@umw.edu
BUSTILLO, Pamela ... 408-273-2696 .. 55 G pbustillo@nhu.edu
BUSTOS, Phillip ... 505-224-4741 310 F pbustos@cnm.edu
BUTCHER, Alva ... 253-879-3394 527 F abutcher@pugetsound.edu
BUTCHER, Claudette ... 918-293-5256 400 E claudette.butcher@okstate.edu
BUTCHER, Marilea ... 304-647-6367 533 B mbutcher@osteo.wvsom.edu
BUTCHER, Michael ... 912-279-5815 123 B mbutcher@ccga.edu
BUTCHER, Phil ... 713-942-3409 493 J butchep@stthom.edu
BUTCHER, Thomas, A ... 616-331-2067 243 E butchert@gvsu.edu
BUTCHKO, Thomas ... 570-208-5928 422 D thomasbutchko@kings.edu
BUTDORFF, Carla ... 419-747-5401 387 E 196mgr@fheg.follett.com
BUTERA, Rae-Anne ... 781-292-2321 226 G rae-anne.butera@olin.edu
BUTERA, Vince ... 847-578-8374 157 G vince.butera@rosalindfranklin.edu
BUTH, Sue ... 608-262-1751 539 C sbuth@uwsa.edu
BUTIN, Dan ... 978-837-5338 233 G dan.butin@merrimack.edu
BUTKOVICH, Michelle .. 248-204-2111 245 J mbutkovic@ltu.edu
BUTKUS, Bonnie ... 585-475-5498 339 G
BUTLER, Allen, P ... 815-455-8999 152 B abutler@mchenry.edu
BUTLER, Andra ... 606-546-1224 200 E abutler@unionky.edu
BUTLER, Andrew, J ... 404-413-1082 126 D AndrewButler@gsu.edu
BUTLER, Ann ... 910-592-8081 365 G abutler@sampsoncc.edu
BUTLER, Annie ... 615-547-1247 456 C abutler@cumberland.edu
BUTLER, Beautrice ... 210-486-2300 467 B bbutler@alamo.edu
BUTLER, Brady ... 412-536-1300 422 E brady.butler@laroche.edu
BUTLER, Bruce, D ... 713-500-3369 495 A bruce.d.butler@uth.tmc.edu
BUTLER, Bryant ... 601-968-5930 266 F bbutler@belhaven.edu
BUTLER, Connie ... 402-643-7332 289 J connie.butler@cune.edu
BUTLER, Doze ... 225-771-5390 207 A doze_butler@subr.edu
BUTLER, Duan ... 540-374-4300 .. 96 H
BUTLER, Greg ... 601-477-4113 268 A greg.butler@jcjc.edu
BUTLER, Heidi ... 610-861-5453 427 F hbutler@northampton.edu
BUTLER, Henry ... 703-993-8644 507 K hnbutler@gmu.edu
BUTLER, Jack ... 931-372-3227 462 A jbutler@tntech.edu
BUTLER, James ... 301-891-4000 221 C jbutler@wau.edu
BUTLER, Janice, R ... 570-577-3973 413 E janice.butler@bucknell.edu
BUTLER, Jennifer ... 708-656-8000 153 G jennifer.butler@morton.edu
BUTLER, Jennifer ... 212-769-5055 339 E
BUTLER, Jody ... 918-463-2931 397 I jody.butler@connorsstate.edu
BUTLER, Joe, R ... 972-599-3121 471 C jrbutler@collin.edu
BUTLER, SJ, John, T ... 617-552-2257 224 B john.butler@bc.edu
BUTLER, Ken ... 484-664-3126 427 C butler@muhlenberg.edu
BUTLER, Kevin ... 702-992-2312 295 E kevin.butler@nsc.edu
BUTLER, Kim, I ... 515-263-2841 178 H maintenance@grandview.edu
BUTLER, LeRoy ... 815-836-5923 150 F butlerle@lewisu.edu
BUTLER, Linc ... 919-530-5214 370 C linc.butler@nccu.edu
BUTLER, Lisa ... 660-543-4001 283 F ljbutler@ucmo.edu
BUTLER, Lynn ... 847-543-2974 142 G lbutler@clcillinois.edu
BUTLER, Marley ... 417-626-1234 280 B recruitment@occ.edu
BUTLER, Mary Edith ... 630-466-7900 162 K mbutler@waubonsee.edu

BUTLER, Michael 909-469-5534 76 I
mbutler@westernu.edu
BUTLER, Odo 518-836-2808 342 E
butlero@sunysccc.edu
BUTLER, Patrick, B 319-335-3565 175 H
patrick-butler@uiowa.edu
BUTLER, Paul, C 856-225-6637 307 A
pbutler@camden.rutgers.edu
BUTLER, Peter, W 312-942-8801 158 A
peter_butler@rush.edu
BUTLER, Rebecca, A 419-434-5797 393 F
butlerr@findlay.edu
BUTLER, Robert 707-256-7625 55 E
rbutler@napavalley.edu
BUTLER, Sarah 715-634-4790 536 P
sbutler@lco.edu
BUTLER, Shai 518-337-2306 322 C
butlers@strose.edu
BUTLER, Sharon 517-884-0101 246 H
sbutler@msu.edu
BUTLER, Shirley 843-349-5218 446 I
shirley.butler@hgtc.edu
BUTLER, Stephen, L 251-626-3303 8 C
sbutler@ussa.edu
BUTLER, Timothy 636-627-2935 276 L
tbutler@lindenwood.edu
BUTLER, Timothy, J 215-951-2744 432 F
butlert@philau.edu
BUTLER, Vicki 870-235-4000 23 D
BUTLER, Walter 731-352-4000 455 E
butlerw@bethelu.edu
BUTLER-LUDWIG, John 773-442-4219 154 H
j-butler-ludwig1@neiu.edu
BUTLER-PURRY,
Karen, L 979-845-3628 485 C
klbutler@tamu.edu
BUTRUM, Michael 660-263-3900 272 M
michaelb@cccb.edu
BUTT, Debi, S 336-841-4524 357 E
debib@highpoint.edu
BUTT, Ryan 419-517-8929 385 F
rbutt@lourdes.edu
BUTTAFARRO, JR.,
Thomas 716-375-2155 340 C
tbuttafa@sbu.edu
BUTTENSCHON,
Marianne 315-792-5631 333 D
mbuttenschon@mvcc.edu
BUTTER, Karen 415-476-8293 72 C
Karen.Butter@ucsf.edu
BUTTERBAUGH,
Randy, R 318-797-5116 205 F
randy.butterbaugh@lsus.edu
BUTTERFIELD, Kevin 804-289-8942 513 M
kbutterf@richmond.edu
BUTTERMORE, Jim 724-964-8811 427 E
jbuttermore@ncstrades.edu
BUTTERWORTH, Betsy 708-366-2490 144 C
BUTTITTA, Deborah 818-386-5659 59 D
dbuttitta@pgi.edu
BUTTKE, Anne 320-308-2905 261 E
abuttke@stcloudstate.edu
BUTTLEMAN, Kurt 206-934-4111 525 J
kurt.buttleman@seattlecolleges.edu
BUTTRY, Tonya 573-334-6825 282 B
tbuttry@sehosp.org
BUTTS, III, Calvin, O 516-876-3160 345 E
buttsc@oldwestbury.edu
BUTTS, Dawn 803-508-7332 443 C
buttsd@atc.edu
BUTTS, Elvin 910-892-3178 357 D
ebutts@heritagebiblecollege.edu
BUTTS, Jeffrey 212-237-8486 319 F
jbutts@jjay.cuny.edu
BUTTS, Montez 970-351-3403 87 A
montez.butts@unco.edu
BUTTS, Ryan 847-566-6401 162 G
rbutts@usml.edu
BUTTS, Sue 251-981-3771 3 A
sue.butts@columbiasouthern.edu
BUTWELL, Ann 859-985-3924 193 F
butwella@berea.edu
BUTWELL, Justin 845-575-3000 331 L
justin.butwell@marist.edu
BUTWIN, Bridget, K 812-237-4141 167 E
bridget.butwin@indstate.edu
BUX, Thomas, A 610-799-1961 424 A
tbux@lccc.edu
BUXBAUM, Howard 973-748-9000 300 E
howard_buxbaum@bloomfield.edu
BUXTON, Barry, M 828-898-8785 358 F
buxtonb@lmc.edu
BUXTON, Bonnie 678-225-7465 432 E
bonnieb@pcom.edu
BUXTON, Carolyn 330-263-2631 380 E
cbuxton@wooster.edu
BUXTON, Jasmine 256-372-8094 1 A
jasmine.buxton@aamu.edu
BUXTON, Ralph, W 212-220-1432 318 D
rbuxton@bmcc.cuny.edu
BUXTON, Robert, E 423-478-7703 460 C
rbuxton@ptseminary.edu
BUYEA, James 315-786-6507 329 G
jbuyea@sunyjefferson.edu
BUZANSKI, Catherine 716-880-2179 332 B
catherine.buzanski@medaille.edu
BUZHARDT, Landee 803-321-5106 447 L
landee.buzhardt@newberry.edu
BUZZARD, Janet 575-562-2343 310 I
janet.buzzard@enmu.edu
BUZZELLI, Andrew 606-218-5511 201 C
andrewbuzzelli@upike.edu
BYAM, LaTrice 202-806-2705 96 B
latrice.byam@howard.edu
BYAM, Latrice 202-806-2763 96 B
latrice.byam@howard.edu
BYARD, Brenda, K 540-868-7208 515 H
bbyard@lfcc.edu
BYARS, Beth 251-580-2227 5 A
beth.byars@faulknerstate.edu
BYARS, Bill 706-295-6552 125 F
bbyars@gntc.edu
BYARS, Don 936-261-1057 484 F
dobyars@pvamu.edu
BYARS, Lauretta, F 936-261-2120 484 F
lfbyars@pvamu.edu
BYARS, Roger, D 713-313-1814 487 F
byarsrd@tsu.edu
BYARS, Susan 239-590-7980 114 F
sbyars@fgcu.edu
BYARS, Tracy 650-493-4430 66 H
tracy.byars@sofia.edu
BYBEE, David 808-675-4300 134 M
david.bybee@byuh.edu
BYELICH, David, S 517-355-9271 246 H
byelich@msu.edu
BYER, Shanda, R 217-786-2290 151 C
shanda.byer@llcc.edu
BYERLY, Alison, R 610-330-5200 423 A
byerlya@lafayette.edu
BYERLY, Mary Beth 770-962-7580 127 C
mbyerly@gwinnetttech.edu
BYERLY, Thomas, L 540-887-7000 510 A
tbyerly@mbc.edu
BYERS, Arthur 617-262-5000 223 G
art.byers@the-bac.edu
BYERS, Jennifer 717-334-6286 424 F
jbyers@ltsg.edu
BYERS, Merrie 970-675-3204 80 L
merrie.byers@cnc.edu
BYERS, Michael 212-817-7730 319 B
facilities@gc.cuny.edu
BYERS, Michael 304-260-4380 530 M
mbyers@blueridgectc.edu
BYERS, Michael, T 336-334-5768 371 C
mike_byers@uncg.edu
BYERS, Michelle, C 319-273-2423 176 A
michelle.byers@uni.edu
BYERS, Mike 828-227-7321 372 C
mtbyers@wcu.edu
BYERS, Randy 214-333-5691 471 L
randy@dbu.edu
BYERS, Tiffany 501-279-4531 21 A
tbyers@harding.edu
BYFORD, Tina 575-646-3616 312 A
tbyford@nmsu.edu
BYHAM, Joseph 215-503-3997 436 F
joseph.byham@jefferson.edu
BYINGTON, J. Ralph 843-349-2086 444 G
byington@coastal.edu
BYINGTON,
Kathleen, M 410-706-2802 219 E
kbyington@umaryland.edu
BYINGTON, Terry 425-739-8219 523 I
terry.byington@lwtech.edu
BYLAND, KK 800-280-0307 163 I
kk.byland@ace.edu
BYLAND, Tamara, C 816-235-1208 284 A
Bylandt@umkc.edu
BYLANDER, Joyce, A 717-245-1639 417 B
bylander@dickinson.edu
BYLSMA, Thomas, W 616-395-7781 244 A
bylsma@hope.edu
BYMAN, Gregory, P 260-422-5561 167 F
gpbyman@indianatech.edu
BYNOE, Lisa 617-369-3870 236 E
lbynoe@smfa.edu
BYNOG, Elizabeth 318-487-5443 203 D
elizabethbynog@cltc.edu
BYNUM, James 919-735-5151 367 A
jbynum@waynecc.edu
BYNUM, Jennifer 979-209-7640 469 F
jennifer.bynum@blinn.edu
BYNUM, Lou Anne 562-938-5015 51 A
lbynum@lbcc.edu
BYNUM, Lynn, M 502-272-8236 193 E
lbynum@bellarmine.edu
BYNUM, Regina 757-455-3352 518 H
rbynum@vwc.edu
BYNUM, Robin 334-983-6556 8 A
rbynum@troy.edu
BYNUM, Tim 806-651-2070 486 D
tbynum@mail.wtamu.edu
BYNUM, Torrance 415-550-4348 39 A
tbynum@ccsf.edu
BYNUM, JR., William 662-254-9041 269 C
william.bynum@mvsu.edu
BYRD, Alan 314-516-6471 284 B
byrdak@umsl.edu
BYRD, Bonita, E 410-651-6088 219 H
bebyrd@umes.edu
BYRD, Brandon 903-730-4890 476 L
bbyrd@jarvis.edu
BYRD, Cal 847-608-5457 144 F
cbyrd@elgin.edu
BYRD, Carl 334-387-3877 1 E
carlbyrd@amridgeuniversity.edu
BYRD, Carole 863-837-5925 110 E
cbyrd@polk.edu
BYRD, Caroline 210-436-3441 481 C
cbyrd@stmarytx.edu
BYRD, Christopher, D 803-777-3343 450 B
cbyrd@sc.edu
BYRD, Damon, D 404-527-4520 122 D
dbyrd@carver.edu
BYRD, David 401-874-5484 442 E
dbyrd@uri.edu
BYRD, Devin 912-650-5642 131 F
dbyrd@southuniversity.edu
BYRD, Donna 404-880-8411 122 I
dbyrd@cau.edu
BYRD, Gina 770-229-3050 132 B
gbyrd@sctech.edu
BYRD, Goldie, S 336-334-7806 370 B
gsbyrd@ncat.edu
BYRD, Herb 865-974-6621 465 C
hbyrdiii@tennessee.edu
BYRD, James 918-293-4940 400 E
james.w.byrd@okstate.edu
BYRD, Jeffrey, J 240-895-2973 218 B
jjbyrd@smcm.edu
BYRD, Joseph, K 504-520-7357 209 E
jbyrd@xula.edu
BYRD, Kim 307-268-2210 545 Z
kbyrd@caspercollege.edu
BYRD, Kimberly 803-323-2236 451 I
byrdk@winthrop.edu
BYRD, Latanya 215-728-4702 427 H
latanya.byrd@jevs.org
BYRD, Laura 704-272-5893 366 A
lbyrd@spcc.edu
BYRD, Marcia 937-529-2201 392 G
mbyrd@united.edu
BYRD, Marcus 334-229-4712 1 D
mbyrd@alasu.edu
BYRD, Mark, A 313-577-2001 252 G
mark.byrd@wayne.edu
BYRD, Michelle 704-922-6263 362 G
byrd.michelle@gaston.edu
BYRD, Nita 919-516-4241 368 E
nbyrd@st-aug.edu
BYRD, Paula 850-471-4679 110 D
pbyrd@pensacolastate.edu
BYRD, Rodney 678-839-6403 133 F
rbyrd@westga.edu
BYRD, Sherlynn 903-927-3300 497 G
sbyrd@wileyc.edu
BYRD, Sherlynn, H 903-927-3300 497 G
sbyrd@wileyc.edu
BYRD, Sherry 910-410-1772 365 B
slbyrd@richmondcc.edu
BYRD, Sherryl 931-221-7341 461 C
byrds@apsu.edu
BYRD, Sylvia 803-508-7494 443 C
byrds@atc.edu
BYRD, Theresa 619-260-7522 74 B
tsbyrd@sandiego.edu
BYRD-DANSO, Kellie 203-285-2094 89 B
kbyrd-danso@gwcc.commnet.edu
BYRD-HARRIS, Marie 559-638-3641 69 C
marie.harris@reedleycollege.edu
BYRD-LEWIS, Renee 678-407-5685 125 B
rbyrdlewis@ggc.edu
BYRDSONG, Quincy 706-721-9273 121 C
qbyrdsong@gru.edu
BYRDSONG-WOODS,
Tashaye 615-329-8894 456 G
tbyrdsong@fisk.edu
BYRN, Mary Pat 651-290-6478 266 B
marypat.byrn@wmitchell.edu
BYRNE, Barbara 712-749-2243 176 D
byrneb@bvu.edu
BYRNE, Brian, J 212-636-6265 326 C
bbyrne@fordham.edu
BYRNE, Faith 610-527-0200 434 D
fbyrne@rosemont.edu
BYRNE, Gregory, K 520-621-4622 18 E
gbyrne@email.arizona.edu
BYRNE, Jim 802-654-2390 502 H
BYRNE, Joseph 802-485-2312 502 G
byrne@norwich.edu
BYRNE, Matt 541-506-6106 405 C
mbyrne@cgcc.edu
BYRNE, Patrick 860-509-9520 90 G
pbyrne@hartsem.edu
BYRNE, Roger, A 716-673-3173 343 F
roger.byrne@fredonia.edu
BYRNE, Ryan 805-965-0581 64 N
rtbyrne@sbcc.edu
BYRNES, Josh, J 641-422-4202 181 E
byrnejos@niacc.edu
BYRNES, Julie 775-753-2271 295 D
julie.byrnes@gbcnv.edu
BYRNES, Kathleen, J 610-519-4550 439 A
kathleen.byrnes@villanova.edu
BYRNES, Mark, E 615-898-2534 461 E
mark.byrnes@mtsu.edu
BYRNS, Kristie 812-488-2478 173 H
kb241@evansville.edu
BYRON, Shelley 607-729-1581 324 A
sbyron@davisny.edu
BYSTREK, Tom 859-336-5082 199 B
tbystrek@sccky.edu
BYSTRY, Richard, L 217-245-3030 146 D
rlbystry@mail.ic.edu
BZBELL, Wally, B 518-783-2342 342 H
wbzbell@siena.edu

C

CÁRDENAS, José, A 480-965-6479 11 J
jcardenas@asu.edu
CABALLERO, Cesar 909-537-5099 35 A
ccaballe@csusb.edu
CABALLERO, Maria, C 323-226-4911 52 D
mccaballero@dhs.lacounty.gov
CABALLERO DE CORDERO,
Angela 408-864-8945 44 N
caballerodecorderoangela@deanza.edu
CABALUNA, Dawnette 801-990-1656 103 P
CABAN, Jose 352-588-8362 111 L
jose.caban@saintleo.edu
CABAN, Jose 787-891-0925 553 E
jcaban@aguadilla.inter.edu
CABAN, Mariveliz 787-766-1717 556 A
marcaban@suagm.edu
CABASA-HESS, Virginia 708-456-0300 161 C
vcabasah@triton.edu
CABASCO, Tony, A 509-527-5882 528 F
cabascja@whitman.edu
CABASSA, Héctor 787-892-1365 554 C
hector.cabassaramos@sodexo.com
CABE, Crista 540-887-7380 510 A
ccabe@mbc.edu
CABELLO, Iris 787-765-1915 554 E
icabello@opto.inter.edu
CABINTE, Ryan 415-561-6555 60 C
CABIYA, Jose 787-725-6500 551 A
jcabiya@sju.albizu.edu
CABIYA-MORALES,
Jose, J 787-725-6500 551 A
jcabiya@sju.albizu.edu
CABLE, Amy 225-216-8311 202 N
cablea@mybrcc.edu
CABLE, Christine 314-837-6777 281 D
ccable@stlchristian.edu
CABONI, Timothy 785-864-7100 191 G
caboni@ku.edu
CABOT, Jeri, O 843-953-5522 445 B
cabotj@cofc.edu
CABRAL, Jennifer, G 740-427-5171 384 P
cabral@kenyon.edu
CABRAL, Kathleen 808-455-0524 136 G
kcabral@hawaii.edu
CABRAL, Kim 805-482-2755 61 F
kcabral@stjohnsem.edu
CABRAL, Manuel, J 808-455-0215 136 G
mcabral@hawaii.edu
CABRAL-MALY,
Margarita, A 904-646-2324 105 A
mcabralm@fscj.edu
CABRALES, Joe 909-389-3368 62 B
jcabrale@craftonhills.edu
CABRALES-MEDINA,
Araceli 773-602-5365 142 A
acabreles@ccc.edu
CABRERA, Ángel 703-993-8700 507 K
president@gmu.edu
CABRERA, Isabel 212-343-1234 332 I
icabrera@mcny.edu
CABRERA, Jaime 787-257-0099 557 F
jaime.cabrera1@upr.edu
CABRERA, Lorraine, T 670-237-6708 550 B
lorraine.cabrera@marianas.edu
CABRERA, Mario 212-217-4995 325 C
mario_cabrera@fitnyc.edu
CABRERA, Moises 787-841-2000 555 F
mcabrera@pucpr.edu
CABRERA, Oscar 305-629-2929 112 D
ocabrera@sanignaciocollege.edu
CABRERA, Rafael 787-766-1912 553 D
rcabrera@inter.edu

CABRERA, Yisel .... 305-628-6562 112 B
ycabrera2@stu.edu
CABUCO, Tracy .... 818-299-5500.. 75 K
tcabuco@westcoastuniversity.edu
CABUNGCAL, Christi ..... 614-947-6542 382 H
cabungcc@franklin.edu
CABUNGCAL, Christi, L 614-947-6542 382 H
christi.cabungcal@franklin.edu
CACACE, Marie .... 301-447-5360 217 D
cacace@msmary.edu
CACCAVERI, Peter .... 513-861-6400 392 F
peter.caccaveri@myunion.edu
CACCIA, Stephen, P ...... 603-271-6484 297 C
scaccia@ccsnh.edu
CACCIATORE, Lawrence 212-353-4250 323 B
caciatl@cooper.edu
CACEDA, Luz .... 410-532-5544 217 F
lcaceda@ndm.edu
CADA, Elizabeth .... 708-534-4389 145 D
ecada@govst.edu
CADDELL, Debbie .... 870-245-5582.. 22 C
CADDY, Kurt .... 417-328-1900 282 D
kcaddy@sbuniv.edu
CADE, Eulanda .... 402-872-2230 292 C
ecade@peru.edu
CADE, Heather .... 530-541-4660.. 50 A
cade@ltcc.edu
CADE, John .... 615-963-5107 461 F
jcade@tnstate.edu
CADE, Lacrecia .... 404-681-5540 128 L
lacrecia.cade@morehouse.edu
CADE, Tinina, Q 804-289-8032 513M
tcade@richmond.edu
CADEMENOS, Anne .... 617-588-1368 223 D
CADENA, Rosa .... 978-232-2064 226 C
rcadena@endicott.edu
CADENHEAD, Robert, K 662-325-2431 269 A
rwc77@msstate.edu
CADIENTE-BROWN,
Ronalda .... 907-796-6058.. 11 A
rcadientebrown@uas.alaska.edu
CADLE, David .... 314-286-4480 280 I
dacadle@ranken.edu
CADLE, Julie .... 229-732-5927 120 B
juliecadle@andrewcollege.edu
CADLE, Shirley, A .... 719-884-5000.. 84 G
SACadle@nbc.edu
CADLE, Wendi .... 479-619-3149.. 22 B
wcadle@nwacc.edu
CADMAN, Lesley, A .... 212-517-3929 343 A
CADMUS, Ashleigh .... 410-626-2510 218 A
ashleigh.cadmus@sjc.edu
CADORETTE, Lisa .... 610-361-5484 427 D
cadoretl@neumann.edu
CADRAY, Lynell .... 404-727-2611 124 D
lynell.cadray@emory.edu
CADWALLADER,
Meghan .... 603-428-2218 298 B
mcadwallader@nec.edu
CADWALLADER, Sarah .. 620-431-2820 189 J
scadwallader@neosho.edu
CADY, Paul, S .... 208-282-3475 138 C
cady@pharmacy.isu.edu
CADY MELZER,
Deborah, M .... 315-445-4527 330 B
cadymedm@lemoyne.edu
CAFASSO, Frank .... 718-420-4220 352 C
fcafasso@wagner.edu
CAFFARELLI, Joseph ...... 973-720-2714 309 I
caffarellij@wpunj.edu
CAFFERKEY, Elizabeth ... 914-323-6800 342 C
ecafferkey@sarahlawrence.edu
CAFFERTY, Jack .... 208-459-5168 137 J
jcafferty@collegeofidaho.edu
CAFFEY, Kevin .... 903-923-2220 473 I
kcaffey@etbu.edu
CAFFEY, Walter, F .... 203-932-7205.. 92 G
wcaffey@newhaven.edu
CAFFIE, Janique .... 973-328-5149 301 G
jcaffie@ccm.edu
CAFFO, David, C .... 302-356-2474.. 94 G
david.c.caffo@wilmu.edu
CAFONCELLI, Kathy, L .. 610-921-7600 411 E
kcafoncelli@albright.edu
CAGE, Beverly .... 361-698-1279 473 F
bacage@delmar.edu
CAGE, Patrick .... 773-995-3524 141 J
pcage@csu.edu
CAGE, Stephanie .... 318-473-6424 205 A
scage@lsua.edu
CAGGIANO, Marion ...... 973-655-3417 304 A
caggianom@mail.montclair.edu
CAGIGAS, Marcia .... 323-415-5383.. 51 D
cagigamp@elac.edu
CAGLE, David .... 815-802-8128 149 B
dcagle@kcc.edu
CAGLE, David .... 251-442-2226.... 9 B
dcagle@umobile.edu
CAGLE, John 423-442-2001 456M
CAGLE, Kathy .... 703-993-8627 507 K
kcagle@gmu.edu
CAGLE, Neatha .... 903-586-2518 476 K
ncagle@jacksonville-college.edu
CAGLE, Randy, L .... 218-477-2477 260 B
caglera@mnstate.edu
CAGLE, Sheri .... 815-802-8822 149 B
scagle@kcc.edu
CAGNET, Danny .... 248-218-2190 249 D
dcagnet@rc.edu
CAHALAN, Jodi .... 515-271-1369 177 H
jodi.cahalan@dmu.edu
CAHALAN, SJ,
Patrick, J .... 310-338-5921.. 53 C
pcahalan@lmu.edu
CAHALL, Perry, J .... 614-885-5585 390 G
pcahall@pcj.edu
CAHEN, Robert .... 440-525-7097 385 C
bcahen@lakelandcc.edu
CAHILL, Bridget .... 847-925-6889 145 F
bcahilli@harpercollege.edu
CAHILL, Elizabeth, A ..... 603-526-3729 296 I
ecahill@colby-sawyer.edu
CAHILL, Elizabeth, J ..... 304-384-6003 532 E
lcahill@concord.edu
CAHILL, Holly .... 701-477-7862 375 H
hcahill@tm.edu
CAHILL, Margaret, D .... 651-962-6131 265 F
mdcahill@stthomas.edu
CAHILL, Regina .... 212-594-4000 349 J
rcahill@tcicollege.edu
CAHILL, Richard .... 859-985-3451 193 F
richard_cahill@berea.edu
CAHILL, Tina .... 617-405-5942 235 H
tcahill@quincycollege.edu
CAHOON, Amm .... 907-852-1763.. 10 F
amm.cahoon@ilisagvik.edu
CAHOON, Faye .... 252-451-8221 364 E
fcahoon@nashcc.edu
CAHOON, Kirsten .... 507-786-3268 264 C
cahoon@stolaf.edu
CAHOY, William .... 320-363-3182 264 A
bcahoy@csbsju.edu
CAI, Maoyi .... 512-444-8082 487 B
cai@thsu.edu
CAILLET, Barb .... 330-684-8935 393 A
naumoff@uakron.edu
CAILLET, Barb .... 330-684-8935 393 A
CAILLOUX, Laura .... 360-679-5333 527 A
laura.cailloux@skagit.edu
CAIMI, Steve .... 215-785-0111 429 F
CAIN, Candace .... 248-218-2040 249 D
ccain@rc.edu
CAIN, Cheryl .... 361-593-2138 486 A
cheryl.cain@tamuk.edu
CAIN, Chris .... 334-953-5159 547 F
anthony.cain@us.af.mil
CAIN, Darrell 317-917-5702 169M
dcain@ivytech.edu
CAIN, Kevin, G .... 304-462-4119 532 G
kevin.cain@glenville.edu
CAIN, Marcus .... 816-802-3468 276 F
mcain@kcai.edu
CAIN, Michael .... 716-829-2100 343 E
vphs@buffalo.edu
CAIN, Michael, E .... 716-829-3955 343 E
mcain@buffalo.edu
CAIN, R. Matthew .... 864-833-8296 448 E
mcain@presby.edu
CAIN, Ruth .... 816-235-6084 284 A
cainre@umkc.edu
CAIN, Sandra .... 508-541-1658 225 G
scain@dean.edu
CAIN, Sara Beth .... 619-388-2721.. 62 G
scain@sdccd.edu
CAIN, Stephen, D .... 240-567-1796 217 B
stephen.cain@montgomerycollege.edu
CAIN, Steven, R .... 805-525-4417.. 69 I
scain@thomasaquinas.edu
CAIN, Thomas, B .... 404-527-4522 122 D
tcain@carver.edu
CAIN, Wingate .... 820-652-0632 364 B
wingatecain@mcdowelltech.edu
CAIRES, Matthew .... 406-994-2826 287 G
mcaires@montana.edu
CAIRNS, Charles, B .... 520-626-0998.. 18 E
cairnsc@email.arizona.edu
CAIRNS, Janet 918-631-3101 403M
janet-cairns@utulsa.edu
CAIRNS, Jill .... 207-834-7602 212 F
jillb@maine.edu
CAIRNS, Linda .... 303-373-2008.. 85 I
lcairns@rvu.edu
CAIRNS, Mike .... 415-451-2817.. 63 B
mcairns@sfts.edu
CAIRO, Jim, R .... 504-568-4246 205 C
jcairo@lsuhsu.edu
CAIROL, Miguel .... 718-260-5600 320 D
mcairol@citytech.cuny.edu
CAIRY, Timothy, J .... 610-499-1193 439 G
tjcairy@widener.edu
CAISON, Anthony .... 919-866-6101 366 H
amcaison@waketech.edu
CAJAYON, Felicito .... 213-891-2056.. 51 C
cajayof@email.laccd.edu
CAKMAK, Burak .... 212-229-8966 334 C
cakmakb@newschool.edu
CAL, John .... 305-348-4001 114 G
john.cal@fiu.edu
CAL, Mark .... 575-439-3622 312 B
mcal@nmsu.edu
CALA, Catherine .... 330-941-3119 396 C
cacala@ysu.edu
CALABRESE, Nancy .... 410-626-2553 218 A
nancy.calabrese@sjc.edu
CALABRESE, Walter .... 252-444-0739 362 A
calabresew@cravencc.edu
CALABRIA, Patrick .... 631-420-2400 348 B
patrick.calabria@farmingdale.edu
CALAF, Jorge .... 787-279-1912 553 H
jcalaf@bayamon.inter.edu
CALAIS, Debra .... 337-482-6199 208 F
dcalais@louisiana.edu
CALAMAI, Anthony, G .. 828-262-3078 369 D
calamaiag@appstate.edu
CALAMAIO, Caprice .... 913-234-0733 185 N
caprice.calamaio@cleveland.edu
CALAMARE, Susan, S ... 617-422-7387 234 J
scalamare@nesl.edu
CALAME, Wanda .... 334-683-2304.... 5 H
wcalame@marionmilitary.edu
CALAMETTI, Jeffrey, D .. 251-442-2242.... 9 B
jcalametti@umobile.edu
CALAMIA, James .... 732-255-0400 304 E
jcalamia@ocean.edu
CALAMIA, John, J .... 504-865-3946 206 A
calamia@loyno.edu
CALANDRELLA, Drew .... 530-898-6131.. 33 A
dcalandrella@csuchico.edu
CALARESO, Jack, P .... 718-940-5902 341 A
jcalareso@sjcny.edu
CALARESO, Joe .... 305-595-9500.. 97 H
admissions@amcollege.edu
CALATRELLO, Stephen .. 256-306-2716.... 2 F
stc@calhoun.edu
CALCADO, Antonio .... 848-445-2474 306 F
acalcado@facilities.rutgers.edu
CALDARELLO, Beth .... 660-359-3948 279 L
bcaldarello@mail.ncmissouri.edu
CALDER, Susan .... 215-951-0981 432 F
calders@philau.edu
CALDER, Tom .... 410-516-7490 216 A
tcalder@jhu.edu
CALDERON, Ann Marie . 615-230-3401 464 B
annmarie.calderon@volstate.edu
CALDERON, Hermes ..... 787-780-0070 550 G
hcalderon@caribbean.edu
CALDERON, Janet .... 407-303-6108.. 97 J
janet.calderon@adu.edu
CALDERON, Laurena ...... 816-604-5430 277 H
laurenac.calderon@mcckc.edu
CALDERON, Nancy, T ... 408-554-4400.. 65 A
ntcalderon@scu.edu
CALDERON, Sonny .... 818-333-3558.. 56 A
CALDERON, Zaida .... 787-265-3864 558 B
zaida.calderon@upr.edu
CALDERSON, Carl .... 619-201-8780.. 62 D
Carl.Calderson@sdcc.edu
CALDWELL, Adonna ...... 901-572-2592 455 C
adonna.caldwell@bchs.edu
CALDWELL, Agnes .... 517-265-5161 238 H
acaldwell@adrian.edu
CALDWELL, Angela .... 870-248-4000.. 20 E
angelac@blackrivertech.edu
CALDWELL, Brinda, W .. 828-398-7134 360 A
bcaldwell@abtech.edu
CALDWELL, Cary .... 704-406-3939 356 G
ccaldwell@gardner-webb.edu
CALDWELL, Catherine ... 313-993-1544 250 H
caldwecr@udmercy.edu
CALDWELL, Cheryl .... 417-255-7960 279 B
cherylcaldwell@missouristate.edu
CALDWELL, Craig .... 801-957-5180 500 E
craig.caldwell@slcc.edu
CALDWELL, Dallas .... 405-974-2631 403 G
dcaldwell@uco.edu
CALDWELL, Daniel .... 601-318-6115 271 F
daniel.caldwell@wmcarey.edu
CALDWELL, Daniel, H ... 276-244-1230 504 L
dcaldwell@asl.edu
CALDWELL, David .... 615-248-1311 464 E
dcaldwell@trevecca.edu
CALDWELL, Diana .... 574-936-8898 164 A
diana.caldwell@ancilla.edu
CALDWELL, Gail .... 256-726-7024.... 6 C
gcaldwell@oakwood.edu
CALDWELL, Getchel .... 910-672-1661 370 A
gcaldwel@uncfsu.edu
CALDWELL, Helen .... 704-378-1014 358 B
hcaldwell@jcsu.edu
CALDWELL, Hollie .... 303-369-5151.. 84 N
hollie.caldwell@plattcolorado.edu
CALDWELL,
Jacqueline, H 918-631-2691 403M
jacqueline-caldwell@utulsa.edu
CALDWELL, James .... 215-780-1306 435 D
jcaldwell@salus.edu
CALDWELL, James .... 215-780-1311 435 D
jcaldwell@salus.edu
CALDWELL, Janet .... 615-327-6851 458 F
jcaldwell@mmc.edu
CALDWELL, Jeff .... 405-733-7395 401 L
jcaldwell@rose.edu
CALDWELL, Jim .... 215-780-1313 435 D
jcaldwell@salus.edu
CALDWELL, Jodi, K .... 912-478-5541 126 B
jodic@georgiasouthern.edu
CALDWELL, Katrina .... 815-753-1554 154 I
kcaldwell1@niu.edu
CALDWELL, Kisha .... 423-697-3250 462 C
kisha.caldwell@chattanoogastate.edu
CALDWELL, Larry, W .... 605-336-6588 453 C
lcaldwell@sfseminary.edu
CALDWELL, Linda .... 251-580-2247.... 5 A
linda.caldwell@faulknerstate.edu
CALDWELL, Michael ...... 559-278-3027.. 33 D
mcaldwell@csufresno.edu
CALDWELL, Nina .... 314-529-9485 277 B
ncaldwell@maryville.edu
CALDWELL, Patrice .... 575-562-2315 310 I
patrice.caldwell@enmu.edu
CALDWELL, Rachel .... 928-344-7501.. 12 B
rachel.caldwell@azwestern.edu
CALDWELL, Richard .... 402-898-1000 290 A
rich_c@creativecenter.edu
CALDWELL, Sandra .... 559-638-3641.. 69 C
sandra.caldwell@reedleycollege.edu
CALDWELL, Timothy ...... 509-777-1000 529 A
tcaldwell@whitworth.edu
CALDWELL, Trish .... 916-484-8354.. 52 I
caldwet@arc.losrios.edu
CALDWELL, Troy .... 740-695-9500 377 F
tcaldwell@belmontcollege.edu
CALDWELL, Vicki .... 704-878-3206 364 C
vcaldwell@mitchellcc.edu
CALDWELL, Ward .... 336-770-3283 372 B
caldwellw@uncsa.edu
CALDWELL, IV,
William, B .... 478-387-4774 125 E
wcaldwell@gmc.edu
CALE, Benjamin .... 304-877-6428 529 G
admissions@abc.edu
CALE, Lynn .... 252-823-5166 362 D
calel@edgecombe.edu
CALEB, Peter .... 212-749-2802 331 I
library@msmnyc.edu
CALEF, Susan, A .... 402-280-5807 290 B
scalef@creighton.edu
CALENDA, Marianne ...... 717-361-1196 418 B
calendam@etown.edu
CALERO, Teofilo .... 773-878-2998 158 C
tcalero@staugustine.edu
CALFAS, Karen, J .... 858-822-7552.. 72 B
kcalfas@ucsd.edu
CALHOON, Brian .... 617-912-9211 224 C
bcalhoon@bostonconservatory.edu
CALHOUN, Barbara, S .. 470-578-6258 127M
bcalhoun@kennesaw.edu
CALHOUN, Cheryl .... 352-395-5719 112 H
cheryl.calhoun@sfcollege.edu
CALHOUN, Deborah, C . 803-934-3216 447 K
dcalhoun@morris.edu
CALHOUN, John .... 619-849-2784.. 59 K
johncalhoun@pointloma.edu
CALHOUN, Kirk, A .... 903-877-7750 495 C
kirk.calhoun@uthct.edu
CALHOUN, Larry .... 478-289-2250 132 A
lcalhoun@southeasterntech.edu
CALHOUN, Larry, D ...... 423-439-2068 461 D
calhoun@etsu.edu
CALHOUN, Linda .... 270-686-4473 197 A
linda.calhoun@kctcs.edu
CALHOUN, Lozanne ...... 870-543-5952.. 23 C
lcalhoun@seark.edu
CALHOUN, M. Grace .... 215-898-7215 437 I
athdir@pobox.upenn.edu
CALHOUN, Matthew ...... 602-222-9300.. 11 G
mcalhoun@arizonacollege.edu
CALHOUN, Matthew ...... 601-276-3718 270 E
mattc@smcc.edu
CALHOUN, Mitch .... 325-574-7612 497 E
mcalhoun@wtc.edu
CALHOUN, Patrick .... 409-839-2014 488 E
pcalhoun@lit.edu
CALHOUN, Paul .... 518-580-5590 342 I
pcalhoun@skidmore.edu
CALHOUN, Paula, M ..... 330-471-8236 385 G
pcalhoun@malone.edu
CALHOUN, Ralph .... 901-435-1276 457 N
ralph_calhoun@loc.edu
CALHOUN, Rica .... 309-298-3070 163 A
rh-calhoun@wiu.edu

CALHOUN, Rochelle ..... 609-258-3056 305 C rochelle.calhoun@princeton.edu

CALHOUN, JR., Thomas, C ..... 256-765-4709 9 D tcalhoun@una.edu

CALHOUN, Thomas, G ..... 703-993-2541 507 K tcalhou2@gmu.edu

CALHOUN, Tony ..... 731-426-7658 457 K tcalhoun@lanecollege.edu

CALHOUN, W. Rochelle 518-580-5760 342 I rcalhoun@skidmore.edu

CALHOUN-BROWN, Allison ..... 404-413-2067 126 D acalhounbrown@gsu.edu

CALHOUN-FRENCH, Diane ..... 502-213-2120 196 E diane.calhoun-french@kctcs.edu

CALICA, Corinna ..... 925-424-1575 37 O ccalica@laspositascollege.edu

CALICO, Marla ..... 770-274-5023 125 G marla.calico@gpc.edu

CALIENDO, Evelyn ..... 847-467-3622 155 D evelyn-caliendo@northwestern.edu

CALISSI, Barbara ..... 516-323-3035 333 E bcalissi@molloy.edu

CALISTO, George, W ..... 312-553-3149 141 N gcalisto@ccc.edu

CALIXTO, Grace ..... 210-690-9000 474 L gcalixto@hallmarkuniversity.edu

CALIZ, Jason ..... 312-332-0707 160 K jason.caliz@tfa.edu

CALIZO, Lee ..... 410-455-1754 219 F calizo@umbc.edu

CALKINS, Gregory ..... 513-529-3020 386 K calkingp@miamioh.edu

CALL, Alyson ..... 620-417-1103 191 A aly.call@sccc.edu

CALL, Christopher, D ..... 805-565-6023 76 K ccall@westmont.edu

CALL, Diane ..... 718-631-6222 320 F dcall@qcc.cuny.edu

CALL, Ed ..... 360-475-7805 524 H ecall@olympic.edu

CALL, Kevin ..... 276-944-6155 507 E kcall@ehc.edu

CALL, Patrick ..... 303-871-5090 86 H Patrick.Call@du.edu

CALL, Tyler ..... 801-627-8451 498 O callt@owatc.edu

CALL, Vickie, G ..... 336-838-6146 367 C vickie.call@wilkescc.edu

CALL-BLANKINSHIP, Jamie ..... 336-770-3232 372 B callj@uncsa.edu

CALLAGHAN, Aloysius, R ..... 651-962-5777 265 F arcallaghan@stthomas.edu

CALLAGHAN, James, E ..... 740-826-8121 387 C jamesc@muskingum.edu

CALLAGHAN, Karen, A ..... 305-899-3401 99 B kcallaghan@barry.edu

CALLAGHAN, MaryEllen ..... 914-633-2512 328 F mcallaghan@iona.edu

CALLAHAN, Audra ..... 508-999-8934 228 H acallahan@umassd.edu

CALLAHAN, Brianne, S ..... 508-213-2218 235 C brianne.callahan@nichols.edu

CALLAHAN, Candice ..... 718-779-1499 338 D info@plazacollege.edu

CALLAHAN, Caroline ..... 718-779-1499 338 D cmc@plazacollege.edu

CALLAHAN, III, Charles, E ..... 718-779-1499 338 D cec3@plazacollege.edu

CALLAHAN, IV, Charles, E ..... 718-779-1499 338 D cec4@plazacollege.edu

CALLAHAN, SR., Charles, E ..... 718-779-1499 338 D cec@plazacollege.edu

CALLAHAN, Cheryl, M ..... 336-334-5099 371 C cmcallah@uncg.edu

CALLAHAN, Christopher ..... 602-496-5012 11 J christopher.callahan@asu.edu

CALLAHAN, Clara, A ..... 215-955-6983 436 F clara.callahan@jefferson.edu

CALLAHAN, Colleen ..... 843-208-8258 450 D ccallaha@uscb.edu

CALLAHAN, Elizabeth, K ..... 718-779-1499 338 D ekc@plazacollege.edu

CALLAHAN, Joy, T ..... 919-209-2027 363 F jtcallahan@johnstoncc.edu

CALLAHAN, Julie ..... 603-645-9611 298 H j.callahan@snhu.edu

CALLAHAN, Margaret ..... 414-288-7511 537 B margaret.callahan@marquette.edu

CALLAHAN, Margaret, F ..... 708-216-9222 151 E

CALLAHAN, Mary ..... 617-258-6432 233 C

CALLAHAN, Michael ..... 805-289-6344 75 E mcallahan@vcccd.edu

CALLAHAN, North ..... 914-337-9300 323 A north.callahan@concordia-ny.edu

CALLAHAN, Patricia ..... 978-762-4000 232 D tcallaha@northshore.edu

CALLAHAN, Patrick, F ..... 914-251-6435 346 D patrick.callahan@purchase.edu

CALLAHAN, Phyllis ..... 513-529-6721 386 K callahp@miamioh.edu

CALLAHAN, Robert ..... 319-363-1323 181 D rcallahan@mtmercy.edu

CALLAHAN, Timothy, C 425-602-3110 519 J tcallaha@bastyr.edu

CALLAN, Kathleen, M ..... 443-412-2129 215 D ccallan@harford.edu

CALLAN, Mike ..... 314-246-7559 285 G mikecallan@webster.edu

CALLAN, Pam ..... 325-481-8300 475 E pcallan@howardcollege.edu

CALLANAN, Cara ..... 978-921-4242 234 B cara.callanan@montserrat.edu

CALLAND, Andrea ..... 606-759-7141 196 G andrea.calland@kctcs.edu

CALLAND, Dana ..... 606-759-7141 196 G dana.calland@kctcs.edu

CALLANDRILLO, Traci ..... 202-885-3500 94 H callandr@american.edu

CALLAWAY, Cynthia ..... 757-825-2725 517 B callawayc@tncc.edu

CALLAWAY, Hannah ..... 336-721-2831 368 F hannah.callaway@salem.edu

CALLAWAY, MaryKatherine ..... 225-578-6144 204 M mkc@lsu.edu

CALLEJO PEREZ, David, M ..... 989-964-4296 249 G dmcallej@svsu.edu

CALLEN, Bruce ..... 417-873-7546 274 E bcallen@drury.edu

CALLEN, Chad, T ..... 304-345-2820 534 D ccallen@wvjc.edu

CALLEN, Edward ..... 803-641-3218 450 C edc@usca.edu

CALLEN, Patricia ..... 304-296-8282 534 E pcallen@wvjc.edu

CALLENDER, David, L ..... 409-772-1902 495 E dcallender@utmb.edu

CALLIER, Theodore ..... 504-816-4018 202 F tcallier@dillard.edu

CALLIES, Kathryn ..... 605-256-5143 453 H kathy.callies@dsu.edu

CALLINAN, Dennis ..... 845-574-4481 339 I dcallina@sunyrockland.edu

CALLIS, Keith ..... 843-863-7133 444 B kcallis@csuniv.edu

CALLOW-WRIGHT, Katie ..... 773-795-3361 161 D ccallow@uchicago.edu

CALLOWAY, Dwight ..... 707-864-7176 66 J dwight.calloway@solano.edu

CALLOWAY, Terence ..... 850-599-3256 114 D terence.calloway@famu.edu

CALLUZZO, Vincent ..... 914-633-2256 328 F vcalluzzo@iona.edu

CALLUZZO, Vincent ..... 914-633-2601 328 F vcalluzzo@iona.edu

CALLWOOD-BRATHWAITE, Denise ..... 305-623-1415 104 B denise.callwood-brathwaite@fmuniv.edu

CALMES, Daphne ..... 323-563-4816 38 C daphnecalmes@cdrewu.edu

CALMESE, Carlotta, V ..... 608-243-4270 543 C ccalmese@madisoncollege.edu

CALMET, Carlos ..... 305-223-4561 111 J

CALNAN, Kerry ..... 508-213-2207 235 C kerry.calnan@nichols.edu

CALO, Andrew ..... 617-322-3513 227 J andrew_calo@laboure.edu

CALOBRISI, Charlotte ..... 703-323-3222 516 C ccalobrisi@nvcc.edu

CALOCA, Luis ..... 208-562-3396 138 A luiscaloca@cwidaho.cc

CALOGRIDES, JR., Thomas, G ..... 757-822-7330 517 C tcalogrides@tcc.edu

CALOVINI, Susan ..... 336-721-2617 368 F susan.calovini@salem.edu

CALPIN, Fran ..... 570-945-8170 422 B fran.calpin@keystone.edu

CALTABIANO, Ronald ..... 317-940-8652 164 L rcalt@butler.edu

CALUS-MCLAIN, Martha 503-352-2764 408 I martha@pacificu.edu

CALUZA, Kimberly ..... 206-296-6090 526 F caluzak@seattleu.edu

CALVERT, Carolyn, A ..... 325-793-3808 478 D ccalvert@mcm.edu

CALVERT, Deb ..... 651-290-6310 266 B deb.calvert@wmitchell.edu

CALVERT, Lisa ..... 806-742-1780 489 F

CALVERT, Lisa, D ..... 806-742-1438 489 D

CALVERT, Maxine ..... 405-422-1466 401 H calvertm@redlandscc.edu

CALVERT, Mike ..... 620-672-2700 190 H michaelc@prattcc.edu

CALVERT, Ned ..... 903-923-2120 473 I ncalvert@etbu.edu

CALVERT, Raymond, J ..... 727-816-3418 110 B calverr@phsc.edu

CALVIN, Allen ..... 650-433-3802 58 B acalvin@paloaltou.edu

CALVIN, Brent ..... 559-730-3755 41 D brentc@cos.edu

CALVIN, Dennis, D ..... 814-865-4028 428 C ifa@psu.edu

CALVIN, Larry ..... 504-520-7537 209 E lcalvin@xula.edu

CALVO, Dean ..... 909-621-8030 39 E dean.calvo@cgu.edu

CALZADA, Maria ..... 504-865-3244 206 A calzada@loyno.edu

CALZEY, Christi ..... 503-228-6528 404 H ccalzey@aii.edu

CALZONETTI, Frank, J ..... 419-530-4749 394 E frank.calzonetti@utoledo.edu

CAMACHO, Alberto, J ..... 787-257-7373 555 L ajcamacho@suagm.edu

CAMACHO, Alex ..... 787-850-9339 558 A alex.camacho@upr.edu

CAMACHO, Anita, C ..... 670-237-6824 550 B anita.camacho@marianas.edu

CAMACHO, David, E ..... 928-523-9204 16 C David.Camacho@nau.edu

CAMACHO, Delia, M ..... 787-250-0000 557 B delia.camacho@upr.edu

CAMACHO, Francisco, C ..... 671-734-0540 549 E mis@guamcc.edu

CAMACHO, Luis ..... 787-725-6500 551 A lcamacho@sju.albizu.edu

CAMACHO, Martin ..... 940-397-4274 478 G martin.camacho@mwsu.edu

CAMACHO, Mildred ..... 787-892-3090 554 C milcama@intersg.edu

CAMACHO, Sylvia, E ..... 631-451-4049 348 F camachs@sunysuffolk.edu

CAMACHO, Sylvia, E ..... 631-451-4049 348 E camachs@sunysuffolk.edu

CAMACHO-MARÓN, Wanda ..... 617-236-8859 226 F wcamacho-maron@fisher.edu

CAMACHO-MELÉNDEZ, Iris, M ..... 787-751-1912 554 D icamacho@juris.inter.edu

CAMARA, Nivia ..... 718-933-6700 333 F ncamara@monroecollege.edu

CAMARA-MONTULL, Manuel, E ..... 787-250-0000 557 B manuel.camara@upr.edu

CAMARENA, Phame, M 989-774-3902 240 O camar1pm@cmich.edu

CAMARILLO, Jane ..... 925-631-4235 61 G jc11@stmarys-ca.edu

CAMBIA, Barbara ..... 561-237-7360 108 E bcambia@lynn.edu

CAMBONE, Joseph ..... 978-542-6266 230 E jcambone@salemstate.edu

CAMBRA, Dena ..... 570-586-2400 435 H dcambra@summitu.edu

CAMDEN, Keely, O ..... 304-336-8047 533 A kcamden@westliberty.edu

CAMELO, Kathleen, M ..... 518-564-2187 346 B camelokm@plattsburgh.edu

CAMERON, JR., A. Neill ..... 864-656-2123 444 E cameron@clemson.edu

CAMERON, Ann ..... 714-997-6611 38 B cameron@chapman.edu

CAMERON, Bill ..... 802-828-8560 503 D bill.cameron@vcfa.edu

CAMERON, Cheryl, A ..... 206-543-6616 527 G ccameron@uw.edu

CAMERON, Dwayne ..... 860-628-4751 91 A dcameron@lincolncollege.edu

CAMERON, Eleanor, W ..... 504-821-5881 202 A eleanor.cameron@cameroncollege.com

CAMERON, Helene ..... 301-934-7567 214 E hcameron@csmd.edu

CAMERON, Jamye ..... 425-739-8155 523 I jamye.cameron@lwtech.edu

CAMERON, Kenneth ..... 508-373-9452 223 C kenneth.cameron@becker.edu

CAMERON, Mark ..... 801-231-2553 144 A mcameron@devry.edu

CAMERON, Mary ..... 218-726-7912 264 G mcameron@d.umn.edu

CAMERON, Matthew, R 305-899-3875 99 B mcameron@barry.edu

CAMERON, Richard, L ..... 478-301-5500 128 G cameron_rl@mercer.edu

CAMERON, Ryan, M ..... 402-280-3434 290 B RyanCameron@creighton.edu

CAMERON, Sally, C ..... 508-678-2811 231 B sally.cameron@bristolcc.edu

CAMERON, Samantha ..... 906-248-8429 240 J scameron@bmcc.edu

CAMERON, Suzette ..... 386-506-7301 101 I cameros@DaytonaState.edu

CAMERON, Thomas ..... 630-942-2291 142 F cameron@cod.edu

CAMERON-THOMPSON, AnnMarie ..... 816-960-2008 273 B billing@cityvision.edu

CAMEY, John ..... 580-581-2267 397 A jcamey@cameron.edu

CAMFIELD, Paul ..... 830-792-7206 482 D phcamfield@schreiner.edu

CAMFIELD, Peter ..... 580-349-1514 400 B pcamfield@opsu.edu

CAMILLE, Marc ..... 410-617-2323 216 D mcamille@loyola.edu

CAMILLERI, Michael ..... 507-284-9328 254 F camilleri.michael@mayo.edu

CAMILLO, Thomas, P ..... 814-871-7413 419 A camillo001@gannon.edu

CAMMARATA, Debbie ..... 716-827-2522 350 H cammaratad@trocaire.edu

CAMMARATA, Maria ..... 510-430-3322 54 F mcammarata@mills.edu

CAMMARATA, Miki ..... 973-720-2179 309 I cammaratamj@wpunj.edu

CAMMARATA, Rita ..... 212-217-3820 325 C rita_cammarata@fitnyc.edu

CAMMISH, Peter ..... 707-864-7278 66 J peter.cammish@solano.edu

CAMOU, Fernando ..... 623-845-3677 14 N f.camou@gccaz.edu

CAMP, Aarika ..... 954-262-7052 109 E aarika@nova.edu

CAMP, Andy ..... 518-580-5745 342 I acamp@skidmore.edu

CAMP, Ann ..... 657-278-8678 33 E acamp@fullerton.edu

CAMP, Billy ..... 334-386-7255 3 I bcamp@faulkner.edu

CAMP, Carol ..... 251-442-2213 9 B ccamp@umobile.edu

CAMP, Margaret ..... 864-503-5199 451 A mcamp@uscupstate.edu

CAMP, Robert, C ..... 724-357-7889 431 A bobcamp@iup.edu

CAMP, Sue, C ..... 704-406-4378 356 G scamp@gardner-webb.edu

CAMP, Susan ..... 405-319-8570 397 A susanc@cameron.edu

CAMP, Tyler ..... 662-862-8176 267 F twcamp@iccms.edu

CAMPA, Fina ..... 787-725-6500 551 A fcampa@sju.albizu.edu

CAMPA, Jeff ..... 816-322-0110 272 L jeff.campa@calvary.edu

CAMPAGNA, Michele ..... 973-655-5369 304 A campagnam@mail.montclair.edu

CAMPANA, MaryJo ..... 570-321-4237 425 B campanam@lycoming.edu

CAMPANELLI, Kenneth ..... 718-482-5502 320 B kcampanelli@lagcc.cuny.edu

CAMPANINI, Albino, P ..... 321-674-8434 103 R bcampanini@fit.edu

CAMPBELL, Aaron ..... 661-255-1050 31 B

CAMPBELL, Abigail ..... 334-874-5700 3 B acampbell@ccal.edu

CAMPBELL, Alan ..... 563-336-3308 178 A acampbell@eicc.edu

CAMPBELL, Alton ..... 208-885-7702 139 C altonc@uidaho.edu

CAMPBELL, Amanda ..... 812-488-2241 173 H ac283@evansville.edu

CAMPBELL, Amy ..... 609-258-8896 305 C amyc@princeton.edu

CAMPBELL, Amy ..... 517-264-3910 238 H

CAMPBELL, Andrea ..... 315-279-5994 329 K

CAMPBELL, Ann, E ..... 757-446-5255 507 B campbeae@evms.edu

CAMPBELL, Anthony ..... 609-896-5101 306 A acampbel@rider.edu

CAMPBELL, Barbara ..... 606-759-7141 196 G barbara.campbell@kctcs.edu

CAMPBELL, Bill ..... 412-365-1140 415 C bcampbell@chatham.edu

CAMPBELL, Blake ..... 515-271-3077 177 K blake.campbell@drake.edu

CAMPBELL, Bonnie ..... 641-683-5108 179 C bonnie.campbell@indianhills.edu

CAMPBELL, Brett, S 918-595-7724 403 A brett.campbell@tulsacc.edu

CAMPBELL, Carol 936-261-3311 484 F

CAMPBELL, Catherine, C 252-638-7271 362 A campbelc@cravencc.edu

CAMPBELL, Celia, K 617-627-3313 237 C celia.campbell@tufts.edu

CAMPBELL, Charles 334-386-7528 3 I ccampbell@faulkner.edu

CAMPBELL, Christie 512-233-1635 481 B christie@stedwards.edu

CAMPBELL, Clark, D 562-903-4867 29 F clark.campbell@biola.edu

CAMPBELL, Connan 509-533-7081 521 E connan.campbell@scc.spokane.edu

CAMPBELL, Conway 508-767-7505 222 D ccampbel@assumption.edu

CAMPBELL, Cory 812-535-5125 172 F ccampbell2@smwc.edu

CAMPBELL, Dan 413-552-2705 231 F dcampbell@hcc.edu

CAMPBELL, Danny 432-264-3752 475 E dcampbell@howardcollege.edu

CAMPBELL, David 662-562-3231 269 E

CAMPBELL, David 601-643-8332 266 J david.campbell@colin.edu

CAMPBELL, Deanna 760-872-5301 49 F dcampbel@cerrocoso.edu

CAMPBELL, Debra 231-843-5819 252 H djcampbell@westshore.edu

CAMPBELL, Denise 202-231-3797 547 N denise.campbell@dodiis.mil

CAMPBELL, Diane 609-586-4800 303 D campbeld@mccc.edu

CAMPBELL, Diane 706-355-5048 120 G dcampbell@athenstech.edu

CAMPBELL, Donald 610-896-1100 420 J dcampbel@haverford.edu

CAMPBELL, Douglas 724-357-2141 431 A dcamp@iup.edu

CAMPBELL, Elizabeth 503-821-8881 408 H presidentsoffice@pnca.edu

CAMPBELL, Elizabeth, P 847-866-3971 145 C elizabeth.campbell@garrett.edu

CAMPBELL, Ellen 814-641-3150 421 L campbee@juniata.edu

CAMPBELL, Elreo 207-859-4814 210 A elreo.campbell@colby.edu

CAMPBELL, Elreo 617-730-7102 235 B elreo.campbell@newbury.edu

CAMPBELL, Evelyn, S 309-794-7533 139 K evelyncampbell@augustana.edu

CAMPBELL, Frances 937-766-7653 378 K campf@cedarville.edu

CAMPBELL, Gail 423-697-5718 462 C gail.campbell@chattanoogastate.edu

CAMPBELL, Garikai 404-215-2647 128 L garikai.campbell@morehouse.edu

CAMPBELL, J. David 256-228-6001 6 A campbelld@nacc.edu

CAMPBELL, Jack, M 937-327-6131 395 I jcampbell@wittenberg.edu

CAMPBELL, James, F 401-865-2343 441 F James.Campbell@providence.edu

CAMPBELL, Jamie 562-903-4555 29 F jamie.campbell@biola.edu

CAMPBELL, Jana 903-233-4186 477 G janacampbell@letu.edu

CAMPBELL, Jane, S 712-362-7947 179 G jcampbell@iowalakes.edu

CAMPBELL, Jennifer 219-989-2056 171 L Jennifer.campbell@purduecal.edu

CAMPBELL, Jennifer, D 561-868-3280 109 H campbejd@palmbeachstate.edu

CAMPBELL, Joann, N 904-620-2002 116 A jcampbel@unf.edu

CAMPBELL, Joanne 479-248-7236 20 K jcampbell@ecollege.edu

CAMPBELL, Joeseph 870-680-8725 19 I joe_campbell@asun.edu

CAMPBELL, John, B 901-722-3372 461 A jbcampbell@sco.edu

CAMPBELL, John, P 304-293-4874 533 D jpcampbe@mail.wvu.edu

CAMPBELL, Jonathan 870-230-5098 21 B campbej@hsu.edu

CAMPBELL, Karen, D 757-822-1447 517 C kcampbell@tcc.edu

CAMPBELL, Karen, M 608-822-2300 544 C kcampbell@swtc.edu

CAMPBELL, Kathy 503-399-5018 404 L kathy.campbell@chemeketa.edu

CAMPBELL, Keith, E 404-413-4465 126 D kcampbell@gsu.edu

CAMPBELL, Kelly, D 404-687-4547 123 C campbellk@ctsnet.edu

CAMPBELL, Kevin 325-674-2765 466 I kac96b@acu.edu

CAMPBELL, Kim 614-234-5144 386 N kcampbell@mccn.edu

CAMPBELL, Kimberly 913-971-3584 189 F kjcampbell@mnu.edu

CAMPBELL, Kimberly 405-491-6335 402 E kcampbell@snu.edu

CAMPBELL, Kirby, D 318-342-5147 209 A kcampbell@ulm.edu

CAMPBELL, Kristi 870-543-5959 23 C kcampbell@seark.edu

CAMPBELL, Lauren 215-637-7700 420 K lcampbell@holyfamily.edu

CAMPBELL, Lea 713-221-5548 491 F campbellc@uhd.edu

CAMPBELL, Lisa 714-992-7085 56 F lcampbell@fullcoll.edu

CAMPBELL, Lisa 775-623-4824 295 D lisa.campbell@gbcnv.edu

CAMPBELL, Lisa, M 724-287-8711 413 G lisa.campbell@bc3.edu

CAMPBELL, Lori 423-585-6933 464 C lori.campbell@ws.edu

CAMPBELL, Lucy 619-684-8783 56 B lcampbell@newschoolarch.edu

CAMPBELL, Marjorie 404-756-4025 120 H mcampbell@atlm.edu

CAMPBELL, Mark 617-266-1400 223 F

CAMPBELL, Marshall 979-230-3474 469 G

CAMPBELL, Martha 727-791-2570 112 A campbell.martha@spcollege.edu

CAMPBELL, Martin 870-230-5150 21 B campbem@hsu.edu

CAMPBELL, Mary, B 314-935-3617 285 E marycampbell@wustl.edu

CAMPBELL, Mary, B 864-488-8280 447 F mcampbell@limestone.edu

CAMPBELL, Mary, K 213-740-9464 74 D mcampbell@caps.usc.edu

CAMPBELL, Mason 870-508-6168 19 H mcampbell@asumh.edu

CAMPBELL, Matthew 253-840-8419 525 C mcampbell@pierce.ctc.edu

CAMPBELL, Michael 760-384-6159 49 F michael.campbell@cerrocoso.edu

CAMPBELL, Michael 816-279-7000 271 H michael.campbell@abtu.edu

CAMPBELL, Michael, A 423-585-2682 464 C mike.campbell@ws.edu

CAMPBELL, Michelle 425-235-2352 525 G mcampbell@rtc.edu

CAMPBELL, Mike 304-696-2456 532 H marshallbkstr@fheg.follett.com

CAMPBELL, Milt 641-673-1074 184 B campbellm@wmpenn.edu

CAMPBELL, Mitchell, L 916-558-2426 53 B campbem@scc.losrios.edu

CAMPBELL, Nicole, J 405-325-1978 403 I njudice@ou.edu

CAMPBELL, Nina 412-392-3990 433 F ncampbell@pointpark.edu

CAMPBELL, Patricia 509-542-4761 521 C pcampbell@columbiabasin.edu

CAMPBELL, Patricia 617-627-3331 237 C patricia.campbell@tufts.edu

CAMPBELL, Phyllis 731-352-4046 455 E campbellp@bethelu.edu

CAMPBELL, Randy 607-778-5196 344 F campbellrj@sunybroome.edu

CAMPBELL, Richard 832-252-4616 470 L richard.campbell@cbshouston.edu

CAMPBELL, Rickie, N 276-523-2400 516 A rcampbell@me.vccs.edu

CAMPBELL, Rina 949-214-3561 42 B rina.campbell@cui.edu

CAMPBELL, Rixon 704-378-1039 358 B rocampbell@jcsu.edu

CAMPBELL, Robert 410-704-4862 221 A rcampbell@towson.edu

CAMPBELL, Robert 631-244-5050 324 C campbelr@dowling.edu

CAMPBELL, Robert, D 212-817-7300 319 B rcampbell@gc.cuny.edu

CAMPBELL, Robin 336-517-2229 354 K rcampbell@bennett.edu

CAMPBELL, Rosana 570-484-2723 431 C rcampbel@lhup.edu

CAMPBELL, Samerah 559-244-5989 68 J samerah.campbell@scccd.edu

CAMPBELL, Sara 423-614-8525 457 M scampbell@leeuniversity.edu

CAMPBELL, Scott 773-834-3390 161 D scottcampbell@uchicago.edu

CAMPBELL, Sharon 919-760-8011 359 B sharonca@meredith.edu

CAMPBELL, Shoshanna, M 718-780-7501 317 A shoshanna.campbell@brooklaw.edu

CAMPBELL, Stanley, R 859-238-5271 194 E stan.campbell@centre.edu

CAMPBELL, Stephanie 318-357-5351 208 D campbells@nsula.edu

CAMPBELL, Stephanie 904-470-8114 102 A s.campbell@ewc.edu

CAMPBELL, Stephen 409-772-9751 495 E stepcamp@utmb.edu

CAMPBELL, Stephen 216-368-5555 378 J stephen.campbell@case.edu

CAMPBELL, Stephen, S 757-594-7663 506 I stephen.campbell@cnu.edu

CAMPBELL, Steven 423-323-0205 463 D srcampbell@northeaststate.edu

CAMPBELL, Suzanne, P 814-886-6385 427 B suzanne.campbell@mtaloy.edu

CAMPBELL, Tanna 816-415-7553 285 K campbellt@william.jewell.edu

CAMPBELL, Thomas, F 214-905-3001 494 A thomas.f.campbell@utdallas.edu

CAMPBELL, Thomas, L 610-282-1100 416 I thomas.campbell@desales.edu

CAMPBELL, Timothy, G 859-858-3511 193 A tim.campbell@asbury.edu

CAMPBELL, Timothy, M 443-334-2838 218 E tmcampbell@stevenson.edu

CAMPBELL, Tom 714-628-2516 38 B tcampbell@chapman.edu

CAMPBELL-HOOPS, Toma 406-353-2607 286 B thoops@ancollege.edu

CAMPEAU, Tony 406-994-2603 287 G tcampeau@montana.edu

CAMPER, Diane 731-286-3338 462 F camper@dscc.edu

CAMPER, Shannon 845-451-1352 323 E s_camper@culinary.edu

CAMPERI, Marcelo, F 415-422-5939 74 C camperi@usfca.edu

CAMPION, Anne 312-777-8559 147 C acampion@aii.edu

CAMPION, James, R 518-828-4181 322 E campion@sunycgcc.edu

CAMPION, William, J 254-647-3234 480 G bcampion@rangercollege.edu

CAMPLESE, Cole, W 773-702-8034 161 D kathiek@uchicago.edu

CAMPO, Carlos 419-289-5050 377 A ccampo@ashland.edu

CAMPO, Juan, E 805-893-3945 72 D jcampo@religion.ucsb.edu

CAMPO, Regina, Z 717-337-6207 419 C rcampo@gettysburg.edu

CAMPOS, Becky 714-997-6943 38 B bcampos@chapman.edu

CAMPOS, Cesar 312-939-0111 144 D cesar@eastwest.edu

CAMPOS, Connie 408-848-4802 45 G ccampos@gavilan.edu

CAMPOS, Darcie, R 708-534-5000 145 D dcampos@govst.edu

CAMPOS, Diana 575-234-9227 312 C dcampos@nmsu.edu

CAMPOS, Jesus 956-872-8330 482 G jhcampos@southtexascollege.edu

CAMPOS, Lisa 928-523-5353 16 C Lisa.Campos@nau.edu

CAMPOS, Luis 505-224-4565 310 F lcampos@cnm.edu

CAMPOS, Pete 505-454-2555 311 B pcampos@luna.edu

CAMPOS, Tom 210-486-0606 467 C tcampos1@alamo.edu

CAMPS, Manel 831-459-0111 72 E

CAMSTRA, Maggie 830-591-7342 483 A maggie.camstra@swtjc.edu

CAMUTI, Alice 931-372-6006 462 A acamuti@tntech.edu

CANADA, Allison, M 410-334-2918 221 E acanada@worwic.edu

CANADA, Britt 325-574-7671 497 E bcanada@wtc.edu

CANADA, Lisa 910-775-4201 371 D lisa.canada@uncp.edu

CANADA, Mark 765-455-9227 168 B canadam@iuk.edu

CANADA, Ruth 573-681-5975 276 K canadar@lincolnu.edu

CANADAY, Bruce 314-446-8184 281 G bruce.canaday@stlcop.edu

CANADAY, John 719-384-6819 84 I john.canaday@ojc.edu

CANADAY, Joseph 215-596-7524 438 E j.canaday@usciences.edu

CANAL, Marcie 213-738-6800 68 E administrativeservices@swlaw.edu

CANAL, Micah 937-767-1286 376 K

CANALES, Angel 787-766-1717 556 A acanales7@suagm.edu

CANALES, Carmen, I 336-758-3256 372 G ccanales@wfu.edu

CANALES, Jason, G 413-662-5413 230 C jason.canales@mcla.edu

CANALES, Jo Ann 361-825-3884 485 F joann.canales@tamucc.edu

CANALES, Luis 309-438-0287 147 I lacanal@ilstu.edu

CANALES, Rafael 787-279-1912 553 H rrcanales@bayamon.inter.edu

CANALS, Alex 718-933-6700 333 F acanals@monroecollege.edu

CANAN, Michelle 918-293-5494 400 E michelle.canan@okstate.edu

CANAS, Carlos 305-626-3698 104 B carlos.canas@fmuniv.edu

CANAVAN, Jessie 330-823-2674 394 A canavajl@mountunion.edu

CANAVAN, Linda, T 781-292-2341 226 G linda.canavan@olin.edu

CANAVAN, Terry 631-499-7100 330 E tcanavan@libi.edu

CANCEKO CHAN, Genevieve 360-491-4700 525 H gchan@stmartin.edu

CANCEL, Jimmy 787-250-1912 554 A jcancel@metro.inter.edu

CANCEL, Olga 787-754-8000 556 H ocancel@pupr.edu

CANCEL-PEREZ, Magda, A 787-620-2040 550 D mcancel@aupr.edu

CANCHOLA, Liza 210-308-8584 476 X

CANCHOLA, Rebecca 915-842-0422 475 H rebecca.canchola@ibcelpaso.edu

CANCILLA, Devon 816-235-1107 284 A cancillad@umkc.edu

CANCILLA, Mike 256-549-8311 3 N mcancilla@gadsdenstate.edu

CANDEE, Kate 920-923-8727 537 A kcandee@marianuniversity.edu

CANDELA, Natalie 810-762-9832 245 A ncandela@kettering.edu

CANDELARIA, J. Randel 336-734-7216 362 F jcandelaria@forsythtech.edu

CANDELARIA, Rene 210-733-0777 476 W rcandelaria@kaplan.edu

CANDIDO, Jacqueline, P 215-898-4970 437 I candido@upenn.edu

CANDIDO, James 512-313-3000 471 H james.candido@concordia.edu

CANDLER, George, B 212-327-7801 339 H candler@rockefeller.edu

CANDLER, Marietta 870-612-2069 24 G marietta.candler@uaccb.edu

CANDREVA, Anne, M 412-578-6043 414 I candrevaam@carlow.edu

CANEIRO-LIVINGSTON, Graciela 563-588-6406 176 F graciela.caneiro-livingston@clarke.edu

CANEPA, Janet, A 203-254-4280 90 E jcanepa@fairfield.edu

CANEPA, Thomas 513-556-2495 393 B tom.canepa@uc.edu

CANEPI, Karen 702-968-2033 296 D kcanepi@roseman.edu

CANER, Emir 706-865-2134 132 G ecaner@truett.edu

CANFIELD, Cheri 702-992-2322 295 E cheri.canfield@nsc.edu

CANFIELD, Clarke 207-741-5575 211 D ccanfield@smccme.edu

CANFIELD, Kathleen 847-925-6437 145 F kcanfiel@harpercollege.edu

CANFIELD, Kipton 309-341-5325 140 I kcanfield@sandburg.edu

CANGELLARIS, Andreas, C 217-333-2150 162 A cangella@illinois.edu

CANGEMI, Livia 212-650-3868 319 E livia.cangemi@hunter.cuny.edu

CANHAM, Drew 254-299-8645 478 C dcanham@mclennan.edu

CANHAM, Raymond, P 972-238-6248 473 B canham@dcccd.edu

CANIA, Lisa, M 315-229-5585 341 E lcania@stlawu.edu

CANICK, Simon 651-290-6301 266 B simon.canick@wmitchell.edu

CANIDA, II, Robert, L 910-522-5790 371 D canida@uncp.edu

CANIGLIA, Alan 717-291-4168 418 J alan.caniglia@fandm.edu

CANIGLIA, Alan, S 717-291-3985 418 J alan.caniglia@fandm.edu

CANIGLIA, Jason, J 303-458-4160 85 G jcaniglia@regis.edu

CANINO, Cathy 864-503-5657 451 A ccanino@uscupstate.edu

CANN, Alison 864-592-4991 449 C canna@sccsc.edu

CARDENAS, Patricia ...... 210-458-4101 494 D
PATRICIA.CARDENAS@UTSA.EDU
CARDENAS, Raul .... 303-315-2109.. 86 G
raul.cardenas@ucdenver.edu
CARDENAS, Rudolph .... 910-672-1433 370 A
rcardena@uncfsu.edu
CARDENAS, Tony .... 904-256-1231 103 K
acardenas@fcsl.edu
CARDENAS, Veronica ... 956-721-5138 477 C
veronica.cardenas@laredo.edu
CARDENAS-ADAME,
Patricia .... 623-935-8812.. 14 L
patricia.cardenas-adame@
estrellamountain.edu
CARDENAS-CLAGUE,
Adeline .... 909-593-3511.. 73 B
acardenas-clague@laverne.edu
CARDER, Rick .... 765-677-2110 169 C
rick.carder@indwes.edu
CARDERO, Agda .... 787-728-1515 559 A
acardero@sagrado.edu
CARDILLO, Rosaleen .... 845-437-5844 351 H
roecardillo@vassar.edu
CARDIN, Matt .... 585-385-8143 340 F
mcardin@sjfc.edu
CARDINAL, Jason .... 651-779-3469 258 D
jason.cardinal@century.edu
CARDINE, Darla, S .... 630-466-7900 162 K
dcardine@waubonsee.edu
CARDONA, Felix .... 718-518-6664 319 D
fcardona@hostos.cuny.edu
CARDONA, Jose .... 856-256-4236 306 D
cardona@rowan.edu
CARDONA, Jose .... 787-758-2525 558 C
jose.cardona8@upr.edu
CARDONA, Nelida .... 787-262-5786 556 C
directora_camuy@unitecpr.net
CARDONA, Teresa .... 787-754-8000 556 H
tcardona@pupr.edu
CARDONE, Stephen ...... 609-497-7730 305 B
housing@ptsem.edu
CARDOSA, Leanne .... 304-296-8282 534 E
lcardosa@wvjc.edu
CARDOZA, Carla .... 915-831-2638 473 J
ccardoza@epcc.edu
CARDOZA, Lisa .... 956-665-2100 494 C
president@utpa.edu
CARDUCCI, Jason .... 661-255-1050.. 31 B
jcarducci@calarts.edu
CARDUCCI, Vince .... 313-664-1488 241 D
vcarducci@collegeforcreativestudies.edu
CARDWELL, Cathi, A .... 740-368-3246 390 B
cacardwe@owu.edu
CARDWELL, Thomas ..... 402-228-3468 293 A
tcardwel@southeast.edu
CAREAGA, Andrew, P ... 573-341-4183 284 C
acareaga@mst.edu
CARELLA, Emily .... 704-463-3047 367 F
emily.carella@pfeiffer.edu
CARELLA, Terry .... 517-371-5140 252 J
carellat@cooley.edu
CARET, Robert, L .... 301-445-1901 219 C
rcaret@usmd.edu
CAREW, C. Racquel ...... 954-486-7728 117 M
ccarew@uftl.edu
CAREW, William .... 863-680-4305 104 F
wcarew@flsouthern.edu
CAREY, Amy .... 316-295-5888 187 C
abcarey@friends.edu
CAREY, Barbara .... 914-367-8262 341 D
bcarey@corriganlibrary.org
CAREY, Chris, J .... 858-499-0202.. 40 G
webmaster@coleman.edu
CAREY, Francis, J .... 716-839-8478 323 F
fcarey@daemen.edu
CAREY, Jason .... 718-951-5000 318 F
jcarey@brooklyn.cuny.edu
CAREY, Joe .... 317-896-9324 173 G
CAREY, Karen .... 805-437-8986.. 32 H
karen.carey@csuci.edu
CAREY, Marita .... 404-876-1227 122 A
marita.carey@bccr.edu
CAREY, Mary Beth .... 914-633-2120 328 F
mcarey@iona.edu
CAREY, Megan .... 724-266-3838 437 G
mcarey@tsm.edu
CAREY, Michael .... 718-862-8000 331 H
michael.carey@manhattan.edu
CAREY, Michael .... 509-313-3550 522 L
carey@gonzaga.edu
CAREY, Peter, M .... 716-878-6332 345 B
careypm@buffalostate.edu
CAREY, Russell, C .... 401-863-9846 441 A
russell_carey@brown.edu
CAREY, Seamus .... 859-233-8111 200 D
president@transy.edu
CAREY, Susan .... 530-895-2378.. 30 B
careysu@butte.edu
CAREY, Thomas, P .... 207-786-6254 209 F
tcarey@bates.edu
CAREY, Tim .... 607-274-3225 328 H
tcarey@ithaca.edu
CAREY, William .... 845-451-1300 323 E
w_carey@culinary.edu
CAREY-BUTLER, Sylvia .. 920-424-0348 540 B
careybus@uwosh.edu
CAREY-MCDONALD,
Jan .... 435-586-7735 499 L
careymcdonald@suu.edu
CARFAGNA, Angelo ...... 201-692-7025 302 H
angelo@fdu.edu
CARGUELLO, Brett, M ... 315-655-7150 317 J
CARHART, Tori .... 315-228-7676 321 H
tcarhart@colgate.edu
CARIAGA-LO, Liza .... 401-863-2216 441 A
liza_cariaga-lo@brown.edu
CARIDI, James, A .... 614-251-4595 388 H
caridij@ohiodominican.edu
CARIGNAN, Steven .... 413-528-7207 222 F
scarignan@simons-rock.edu
CARIKER, Heath .... 903-983-8657 477 A
hcariker@kilgore.edu
CARILLI, Vincent .... 865-974-7449 465 D
vincent.carilli@tennessee.edu
CARIN, Lawrence .... 919-681-6438 356 E
lcarin@duke.edu
CARIO, William .... 262-243-4263 241 F
william.cario@cuw.edu
CARIO, William, R .... 262-243-5700 535 I
william.cario@cuw.edu
CARISSIMI, Laura, K ..... 440-365-5222 385 E
CARITO, Phyllis .... 518-828-4181 322 E
carito@sunycgcc.edu
CARKEEK, Susan .... 434-924-4475 514 A
sc9ym@virginia.edu
CARKUM, Duane .... 504-520-7490 209 E
dcarkum@xula.edu
CARL, Ashley .... 813-253-7158 106 C
acarl@hccfl.edu
CARL, Cathy .... 845-431-8635 324 D
cathy.carl@sunydutchess.edu
CARL, Cherie .... 804-333-6705 516 G
ccarl@rappahannock.edu
CARL, David .... 505-984-6082 312 J
gi@sjc.edu
CARL, Diane .... 570-321-4101 425 B
carl@lycoming.edu
CARL, Harold, F .... 903-233-4400 477 G
haroldcarl@letu.edu
CARL, Heidi, A .... 765-361-6375 175 B
carlh@wabash.edu
CARL, James, C .... 203-396-8454.. 91 G
carlj@sacredheart.edu
CARL, Peggy .... 978-542-6517 230 E
pcarl@salemstate.edu
CARL, Steven, B .... 508-767-7267 222 D
sb.carl@assumption.edu
CARLBLOM, Shelia .... 765-677-2191 169 C
sheila.carlblom@indwes.edu
CARLETON, Dia, M .... 570-662-4052 431 D
dcarleto@mansfield.edu
CARLETON, Mary Ruth . 619-594-4562.. 35 E
mcarleto@mail.sdsu.edu
CARLETON, Taylor .... 830-372-8026 487 C
tcarleton@tlu.edu
CARLETTA, Charles, F ... 518-276-6212 339 D
carlec@rpi.edu
CARLEY, Michael .... 559-791-2275.. 49 G
mcarley@portervillecollege.edu
CARLI, Gale .... 510-742-3102.. 56 J
gcarli@ohlone.edu
CARLIN, Jane .... 253-879-3118 527 F
jcarlin@pugetsound.edu
CARLIN, Laurence .... 920-424-7364 540 B
carlin@uwosh.edu
CARLIN, Melanie .... 217-357-9117 157 A
mcarlin@robertmorris.edu
CARLIN, Michael .... 704-687-5500 371 B
Mike.Carlin@uncc.edu
CARLIN, Virginia, A .... 630-873-3485 148 H
vcarlin@ellis.edu
CARLING SMITH,
Malcolm .... 916-339-4371.. 55 C
mcarlingsmith@mticollege.edu
CARLISLE, Beth .... 602-943-2311.. 18 K
Beth.Carlisle@west.edu
CARLISLE, Brian .... 909-621-8241.. 59 F
brian_carlisle@pitzer.edu
CARLISLE, David, M ...... 323-563-4987.. 38 C
davidcarlisle@cdrewu.edu
CARLISLE, Elizabeth ...... 812-749-1241 171 I
lcarlisle@oak.edu
CARLISLE, Jerry, H .... 501-882-8835.. 19 E
jhcarlisle@asub.edu
CARLISLE, Sandra .... 320-629-5100 260 H
carlisles@pinetech.edu
CARLISLE, Siri .... 518-828-4181 322 E
carlisle@sunycgcc.edu
CARLISLE, Susan .... 502-213-5200 196 E
susan.carlisle@kctcs.edu
CARLO, Jaclyn .... 631-244-3138 324 C
carloj@dowling.edu
CARLO, Jennifer, A .... 412-578-6087 414 I
jacarlo@carlow.edu
CARLO, Luis .... 646-378-6171 337 B
luis.carlo@nyack.edu
CARLOCK, Jennifer .... 309-655-7100 158 D
jennifer.carlock@osfhealthcare.org
CARLOCK, Myra .... 731-352-4000 455 E
carlockm@bethelu.edu
CARLOCK, Ruth .... 402-363-5704 294 G
rmcarlock@york.edu
CARLSEN, Paul .... 225-308-4422 202 M
pcarlsen@lctcs.edu
CARLSON, Annie .... 828-669-8012 359 K
acarlson@montreat.edu
CARLSON, Britt .... 978-867-4221 227 A
britt.carlson@gordon.edu
CARLSON, C. Robert .... 630-682-6002 147 E
carlson@iit.edu
CARLSON, Catherina ..... 781-891-2989 223 E
ccarlson@bentley.edu
CARLSON, Cathy .... 507-222-4075 254 D
ccarlson@carleton.edu
CARLSON, Charles .... 914-637-2757 328 F
ccarlson@iona.edu
CARLSON, Chris .... 951-222-8000.. 60 J
chris.carlson@rcc.edu
CARLSON, David .... 540-362-6675 508 D
dcarlson@hollins.edu
CARLSON, David, H ...... 979-845-8160 485 C
davidcarlson@tamu.edu
CARLSON, Deborah ...... 402-354-7023 291 P
deb.carlson@methodistcollege.edu
CARLSON, Debra .... 320-308-3296 261 E
dlcarlson@stcloudstate.edu
CARLSON, Don .... 218-879-0878 258 F
dcarlson@fdltcc.edu
CARLSON, Douglas .... 415-476-4527.. 72 C
doug.carlson@ucsf.edu
CARLSON, Dusten .... 815-965-8616 157 C
CARLSON, Dylana .... 309-341-5230 140 I
dcarlson@sandburg.edu
CARLSON, Gerald, P ..... 337-482-6678 208 F
gcarlson@louisiana.edu
CARLSON, Gregory .... 701-845-7480 374 D
gregory.carlson@vcsu.edu
CARLSON, James .... 847-578-8805 157 G
James.Carlson@rosalindfrannklin.edu
CARLSON, Jeffrey .... 708-524-6814 144 C
jcarlson@dom.edu
CARLSON, Jessica .... 406-586-3585 287 B
jessica.carlson@montanabiblecollege.edu
CARLSON, Jim .... 406-586-3585 287 B
jim.carlson@montanabiblecollege.edu
CARLSON, Julie .... 402-844-7142 292 G
juliec@northeast.edu
CARLSON, Kathleen ...... 773-298-3305 158 F
carlson@sxu.edu
CARLSON, Kathleen ...... 574-284-4543 172 G
kcarlson@saintmarys.edu
CARLSON, Kenna Lee .... 402-486-2503 293 D
kecarlso@ucollege.edu
CARLSON, Kenneth .... 701-777-2127 373 G
kenneth.carlson@und.edu
CARLSON, Kevin .... 906-217-4023 240 K
kevin.carlson@baycollege.edu
CARLSON, Kurt .... 919-497-3325 358 J
kcarlson@louisburg.edu
CARLSON, Laura .... 574-631-8052 174 A
lcarlson@nd.edu
CARLSON, Libby, L .... 662-846-4268 267 A
lcarlson@deltastate.edu
CARLSON, Malinda, L .. 217-245-3011 146 D
mcarlson@mail.ic.edu
CARLSON, Mark .... 651-201-1827 257 N
mark.carlson@so.mnscu.edu
CARLSON, Mary .... 616-222-3000 245 D
mcarlson@kuyper.edu
CARLSON, Melinda .... 314-977-2824 281 M
mcarlson2@slu.edu
CARLSON, Nancy .... 303-914-6389.. 85 C
nancy.carlson@rrcc.edu
CARLSON, Neal .... 484-365-7262 424 E
ncarlson@lincoln.edu
CARLSON, Neil .... 616-526-6420 240 L
nec4@calvin.edu
CARLSON, Nicki .... 218-683-8546 260 F
nicki.carlson@northlandcollege.edu
CARLSON, Nicole .... 763-493-0597 260 E
ncarlson@nhcc.edu
CARLSON, Paul .... 815-802-8652 149 B
pcarlson@kcc.edu
CARLSON, Paula, J .... 563-387-1001 180 M
president@luther.edu
CARLSON, Rachel .... 540-545-7382 512 E
rcarlso2@su.edu
CARLSON, Ria, M .... 949-824-7911.. 71 C
ria.carlson@uci.edu
CARLSON, Rich .... 402-486-2508 293 D
ricarlso@ucollege.edu
CARLSON, Robert .... 785-227-3380 185 A
carlsonr@bethanylb.edu
CARLSON, Rosa, F .... 559-791-2316.. 49 G
rcarlson@portervillecollege.edu
CARLSON, Skye .... 360-779-9993 524 C
scarlson@ncad.edu
CARLSON, Stanley, E .... 563-884-5684 182 D
stan.carlson@palmer.edu
CARLSON, Steve .... 920-206-2342 536 T
steve.carlson@mbu.edu
CARLSON, Steven, T ..... 574-372-5100 166 D
carlsost@grace.edu
CARLSON, Susan .... 510-987-0728.. 70 J
susan.carlson@ucop.edu
CARLSON, Tammy .... 309-438-8846 147 I
tscarls@ilstu.edu
CARLSON, Tracey .... 423-614-6000 457 M
tcarlson@leeuniversity.edu
CARLSON, Wayne, E ..... 614-292-2872 389 A
carlson.8@osu.edu
CARLSON ZINK,
Deanna .... 701-777-2611 373 G
deannac@undfoundation.org
CARLSTON, Gary, L ...... 435-283-7010 500 D
gary.carlston@snow.edu
CARLSTROM, Lester, H . 773-244-5597 154 G
lcarlstrom@northpark.edu
CARLTON, Keitha .... 903-785-7661 480 B
kcarlton@parisjc.edu
CARLTON, LeAnn, K ..... 816-654-7213 276 G
lcarlton@kcumb.edu
CARLTON, William .... 912-279-5892 123 B
wcarlton@ccga.edu
CARLTON-CAREW,
Miranda .... 704-499-9200.. 96 H
CARMACK, Amy .... 781-272-0222 222 G
acarmack@baypath.edu
CARMACK, Connie, K ... 540-375-2230 512 B
carmack@roanoke.edu
CARMAN, Beth Anne ..... 614-236-6211 378 H
bcarman@capital.edu
CARMAN, Kevin .... 775-784-1740 295 H
kcarman@unr.edu
CARMEAN, John .... 352-381-3625 112 H
john.carmean@sfcollege.edu
CARMEL, Erran .... 202-885-1928.. 94 H
carmel@american.edu
CARMEL, Julie .... 508-929-8754 230 G
jcarmel@worcester.edu
CARMEN, Kim .... 318-675-5207 205 D
shvreg@lsuhsc.edu
CARMICAL, Beth .... 910-272-3343 365 D
bcarmical@robeson.edu
CARMICHAEL, Ann, C ... 803-584-3446 450 F
anncar@mailbox.sc.edu
CARMICHAEL,
Beverly, C .... 904-819-6290 102 P
bcarmichael@flagler.edu
CARMICHAEL, Brenda ... 620-343-4600 186 I
bcarmichael@fhtc.edu
CARMICHAEL, Jason ..... 970-943-2079.. 87 F
jcarmichael@western.edu
CARMICHAEL, John ...... 360-867-6100 522 J
carmichj@evergreen.edu
CARMICHAEL, Matt .... 530-752-1294.. 71 A
mecarmichael@ucdavis.edu
CARMICHAEL, Paul .... 860-343-5787.. 89 E
pcarmichael@mxcc.commnet.edu
CARMICHAEL, Peggy .... 304-214-8901 531 G
pcarmichael@wvncc.edu
CARMICHAEL, Stacey .... 770-394-8300 120 E
stacey.carmichael@cbre.com
CARMICHAEL, Stacy ..... 228-896-2503 268 G
stacy.carmichael@mgccc.edu
CARMINE, Kevin .... 718-319-7965 319 D
kcarmine@hostos.cuny.edu
CARMODY, Kathy .... 757-789-1728 515 D
kcarmody@es.vccs.edu
CARMODY, Patricia .... 507-537-6206 262 B
Patricia.Carmody@smsu.edu
CARMODY, Richard ...... 805-922-6966.. 26 H
rcarmody@hancockcollege.edu
CARMONA, José, I .... 787-875-4150 556 A
jocarmona@suagm.edu
CARNAGHI, Jan .... 317-955-6154 171 A
jcarnaghi@marian.edu
CARNAHAN, Diane .... 209-468-9155.. 69 G
dcarnahan@sjcoe.net
CARNAHAN, Scott .... 503-883-2229 406 I
scarnah@linfield.edu
CARNAROLI, Craig .... 215-898-6693 437 I
carnarol@upenn.edu
CARNDUFF, Dagmar, L . 414-847-3211 537 F
dagmarcarnduff@miad.edu
CARNE, Kim .... 906-786-5802 240 K
carnek@baycollege.edu
CARNE, Margaret, A ..... 920-748-8180 538 I
carnem@ripon.edu
CARNES, Allen .... 336-770-3320 372 B
carnesa@uncsa.edu

CARNES, Gregory, A 256-765-4245 9 D gacarnes@una.edu
CARNES, Kathy, M 252-493-7220 364 H kcarnes@email.pittcc.edu
CARNES, Peter 508-565-1206 237 A pcarnes@stonehill.edu
CARNEVALE, David 562-907-4284 77 E dcarneva@whittier.edu
CARNEY, Diane, E 412-291-6250 412 H dcarney@aii.edu
CARNEY, Edward 856-227-7200 301 A ecarney@camdencc.edu
CARNEY, Gary 610-861-1336 426 H carneyg@moravian.edu
CARNEY, OSF, Margaret 716-375-2222 340 C mcarney@sbu.edu
CARNEY, Martin 216-421-7424 380 B mcarney@cia.edu
CARNEY, Michael, J 715-836-4353 539 E carneymj@uwec.edu
CARNEY, Paige 304-766-3313 533 C carney3@wvstateu.edu
CARNEY, Paul 314-968-7086 285 G paulcarney89@webster.edu
CARNEY, Randy 618-937-2127 153 F
CARNEY, Sheila, A 412-578-6424 414 I carneysa@carlow.edu
CARNEY, Timothy 202-319-5619 95 A carneyt@cua.edu
CARNEY, Timothy, D 412-578-8712 414 I tdcarney@carlow.edu
CARNEY-DEBORD, Nan 740-587-6428 381 H carneydebord@denison.edu
CARNEY-HALL, Karla 309-556-3111 148 A dstudent@iwu.edu
CARNICOM, Scott 570-484-2204 431 C carnicom@lhup.edu
CARNIE, Andrew, H 520-621-3471 18 E carnie@email.arizona.edu
CARNLEY, Raymond 478-471-2732 128 H raymond.carnley@mga.edu
CARNS, Mary Lee 843-525-5692 449 E mcarns@tcl.edu
CARNWATH, Thomas 215-717-6640 437 H tcarnwath@uarts.edu
CARNZ, Scott 206-239-2320 519 H scarnz@aii.edu
CARO, Jessica 787-832-6000 552 K jcaro@icprjc.edu
CARO, Mary Ellen 609-984-1130 308 H mcaro@tesc.edu
CAROL, Steve 732-987-2414 302 J carols@georgian.edu
CAROLINA, Kimberly 203-575-8056 89 F kcarolina@nv.edu
CAROLLO, Chris 203-332-5078 89 C ccarollo@hcc.commnet.edu
CARON, Bob 817-552-3700 477 B bcaron@tku.edu
CARON, Rick 406-447-6937 287 F rick.caron@umhelena.edu
CAROTHERS, Amy 775-784-6620 295 H acarothers@unr.edu
CAROTHERS, Harry, G 303-963-3228 79 L hcarothers@ccu.edu
CAROTHERS, John 775-784-1394 295 H jcarothers@adv.unr.edu
CARP, Richard, M 925-631-4443 61 G rmcarp@gmail.com
CARPENTER, Andre 504-398-2110 206 E acarpenter@olhcc.edu
CARPENTER, Barbara 225-771-2613 207 A carp.subr@aol.com
CARPENTER, Brenda 405-682-1611 399 K bcarpenter@occc.edu
CARPENTER, Carol 616-977-5520 241 G carol.carpenter@cornerstone.edu
CARPENTER, Carolyn, A 573-629-3116 275 F Carolyn.Carpenter@hlg.edu
CARPENTER, Catherine 213-738-6875 68 E academicaffairs@swlaw.edu
CARPENTER, Courtney 757-221-2001 506 J cmcarp@wm.edu
CARPENTER, Dale 828-227-7311 372 C carpenter@wcu.edu
CARPENTER, Dana 225-771-2394 207 A dana_carpenter@subr.edu
CARPENTER, David 618-544-8657 146 H carpenterd@iecc.edu
CARPENTER, Debra 281-283-2150 491 E carpenter@uhcl.edu
CARPENTER, Denise 320-222-6073 261 B denise.carpenter@ridgewater.edu
CARPENTER, Dianna, M 816-604-2230 277 I dianna.carpenter@mcckc.edu
CARPENTER, Evelyn 912-583-3293 121 H ecarpenter@bpc.edu
CARPENTER, Jan 509-533-3535 521 F Jan.Carpenter@sfcc.spokane.edu
CARPENTER, Jennifer 509-527-2683 528 A jennifer.carpenter@wallawalla.edu
CARPENTER, Kae 931-372-3269 462 A kcarpenter@tntech.edu
CARPENTER, Kathryn, H 312-996-8974 161 F khc@uic.edu
CARPENTER, Kelly 920-693-1172 543 B kelly.carpenter@gotoltc.edu
CARPENTER, Kimberly 323-241-5321 51 I carpenkc@lasc.edu
CARPENTER, Larry 423-614-8440 457 M lcarpenter@leeuniversity.edu
CARPENTER, Larry 540-831-5182 511 C ljcarpenter@radford.edu
CARPENTER, Lisa 808-566-2411 135 C lcarpenter@hpu.edu
CARPENTER, Marla 336-770-3337 372 B carpem@uncsa.edu
CARPENTER, Mary 615-256-1463 454 G
CARPENTER, Michael 757-823-8104 510 H mcarpenter@nsu.edu
CARPENTER, Mike 618-262-8641 147 B carpenterm@iecc.edu
CARPENTER, Mike 402-826-6781 290 C mike.carpenter@doane.edu
CARPENTER, Monica, S 828-682-7315 364 A mscarpenter@mayland.edu
CARPENTER, Paula 217-234-5217 150 B pcarpent@lakeland.cc.il.us
CARPENTER, Robert 423-323-0259 463 D rccarpenter@northeaststate.edu
CARPENTER, Rosalie 251-380-3024 7 F rcarpenter@shc.edu
CARPENTER, Scott 541-881-5773 410 D scarpent@tvcc.cc
CARPENTER, Shelia 601-925-3200 268 E carpenter@mc.edu
CARPENTER, Stan 402-471-2505 292 A scarpenter@nscs.edu
CARPENTER, Stan 512-245-2150 489 C sc33@txstate.edu
CARPENTER, Thomas 563-333-6124 182 E CarpenterThomas@sau.edu
CARPENTER, Van 864-242-5100 443 G
CARPENTER, Virginia 954-731-8880 100 R vcarpenter@concorde.edu
CARPENTER, Wayne, D 413-782-1565 238 A wayne.carpenter@wne.edu
CARPENTER-DAVIS, Cheryl 816-604-4003 278 A cheryl.carpenter@mcckc.edu
CARPENTER-HUBIN, Julie 614-292-5915 389 A carpenter-hubin.16@osu.edu
CARPENTER LOW, Jennifer 516-299-3119 330 F jennifer.low@liu.edu
CARPENTIER, Mark 718-631-6325 320 F mcarpentier@qcc.cuny.edu
CARPENTIER, Mark 570-740-0351 425 A mcarpentier@luzerne.edu
CARPER, Kellie 815-455-8670 152 B kcarper@mchenry.edu
CARPI, Anthony 212-237-8944 319 F acarpi@jjay.cuny.edu
CARPIO, Eric 719-587-7802 78 I ecarpio@adams.edu
CARPIO, Joseph 505-346-2324 313 G joseph.carpio@bie.edu
CARPIO, Joseph 505-346-2361 313 G joseph.carpio@bie.edu
CARR, Bailey 816-501-3780 272 E bailey.carr@avila.edu
CARR, Charlene 505-428-5950 310 L ccarr@iaia.edu
CARR, Charles 940-397-4748 478 G charles.carr@mwsu.edu
CARR, Chuck 307-855-2143 545 a ccarr@cwc.edu
CARR, David 806-457-4200 474 E dcarr@fpctx.edu
CARR, Dennis 541-463-5583 406 F carrd@lanecc.edu
CARR, Ellen 617-879-7067 230 B ecarr@massart.edu
CARR, Frances 229-317-6744 123 H frances.carr@darton.edu
CARR, James, W 501-279-4406 21 A carr@harding.edu
CARR, Jeffrey 321-433-5600 101 O carrj@easternflorida.edu
CARR, Jeffrey 619-849-2415 59 K jeffreycarr@pointloma.edu
CARR, John 404-364-8439 129 F jcarr1@oglethorpe.edu
CARR, Karen 212-757-1190 315 C kcarr@funeraleducation.org
CARR, Karen, A 315-786-2404 329 G kcarr@sunyjefferson.edu
CARR, Kevin 319-208-5069 183 B kcarr@scciowa.edu
CARR, Kevin 207-780-5127 212 C kevin.carr@maine.edu
CARR, Leslie 661-362-3100 40 H leslie.carr@canyons.edu
CARR, Matthew, S 315-792-3228 351 G mcarr@utica.edu
CARR, Meagan 603-342-3086 297 E mcarr@ccsnh.edu
CARR, Michael 847-376-7046 155 E mcarr@oakton.edu
CARR, Nancy 315-498-2834 337 F carrn@sunyocc.edu
CARR, Nicole, T 251-460-6475 9 F ntcarr@southalabama.edu
CARR, Robert 601-877-6141 266 C rcarr@alcorn.edu
CARR, Rodger 281-283-2900 491 E carr@uhcl.edu
CARR, Rodney 229-243-6015 121 D rodney.carr@bainbridge.edu
CARR, Rosalie 336-315-8660 355 F rcarr@carolinagrad.edu
CARR, Sherrean 408-848-4757 45 G scarr@gavilan.edu
CARR, Steve 513-244-8473 379 I steve.carr@ccuniversity.edu
CARR, Thomas, F 607-962-9223 323 D carr_tom@corning-cc.edu
CARR ROBINETT, Angie 816-501-4541 281 B angie.carr@rockhurst.edu
CARRA, Gary 860-253-3000 88 H
CARRADINE, Tania 504-671-5155 203 F tcarra@dcc.edu
CARRAFIELLO, Susan 937-775-2660 396 A susan.carrafiello@wright.edu
CARRANCO, Emilio 512-245-2161 489 C ec05@txstate.edu
CARRANO, Julia 858-653-6740 48 Q JCarrano@JPCatholic.com
CARRANZA, Elsy 972-273-3316 473 A ecarranza@dcccd.edu
CARRANZA, James 650-574-6337 64 D carranza@smccd.edu
CARRANZA, Mike 956-872-3420 482 G mcarranz@southtexascollege.edu
CARRARO, Francine 940-397-8948 478 G francine.carraro@mwsu.edu
CARRASCO, Madeleine 619-961-4213 69 J mcarrasco@tjsl.edu
CARRASQUILLO, Iris, N 787-850-9363 558 A iris.carrasquillo@upr.edu
CARRAWAY, Jay 252-527-6223 363 G jcarraway@lenoircc.edu
CARRAWAY, Kevin 252-328-6434 369 E carrawayc@ecu.edu
CARRAWAY, Pauline 757-352-4007 511 G paulcar@regent.edu
CARRERA, Cheryl 714-564-6606 60 G carrera_cheryl@sac.edu
CARRERA, Dave 213-821-5389 74 D dcarrera@usc.edu
CARRERA, Magali 508-999-8024 228 H mcarrera@umassd.edu
CARRERE, Carol, G 919-658-7771 369 B ccarrere@umo.edu
CARRESCIA, John 718-420-4264 352 C jcarresc@wagner.edu
CARRICK, Stacy 660-562-1124 280 A carrick@nwmissouri.edu
CARRICO, John 270-534-3089 197 E john.carrico@kctcs.edu
CARRICO, Sarah 651-846-1424 261 G sarah.carrico@saintpaul.edu
CARRIER, Bryan 731-661-5090 464 G bcarrier@uu.edu
CARRIER, Laurie 603-752-1113 297 E lcarrier@ccsnh.edu
CARRIER, Shawnie 870-972-3030 19 F shawniecarrier@astate.edu
CARRIER, Steve, G 785-827-5541 189 A yotee@kwu.edu
CARRIGAN, Edward 415-338-7211 36 A edwardc@sfsu.edu
CARRIGAN, Joyce 714-484-7142 56 E jcarrigan@cypresscollege.edu
CARRIGAN, Sarah, D 336-256-0397 371 C sarah_carrigan@uncg.edu
CARRIGAN, Tena 501-812-2217 22 F tcarrigan@pulaskitech.edu
CARRILLO, Carmen 310-233-4250 51 F carrilc@lahc.edu
CARRILLO, Jessica 806-742-2121 489 F jessica.carrillo@ttu.edu
CARRILLO, Jose 760-355-6487 47 G jose.carrillo@imperial.edu
CARRILLO, Jose Raul 340-693-1043 559 B jcarril@uvi.edu
CARRILLO, Lee 505-224-3093 310 F lcarrillo@cnm.edu
CARRILLO, Lizzette 787-723-4481 551 B lcarrillo@ceaprc.edu
CARRILLO, Maria 305-220-4120 108 F mcarrillo@mattiacollege.edu
CARRINGTON, Margie 650-306-3174 64 C carringtonm@smccd.edu
CARRINO, Amy 859-442-1104 196 A amy.carrino@kctcs.edu
CARRION, Ingrid 787-743-4041 551 I icarrion@columbiacentral.edu
CARRION, Lourdes 787-878-5475 553 F lcarrion@arecibo.inter.edu
CARRION, Yesenia 787-258-1501 551 I ycarrion@columbiacentral.edu
CARRION-SILVA, Ana, M 718-518-4407 319 D amcarrion@hostos.cuny.edu
CARRISALEZ, Albert, A 210-458-5138 494 D albert.carrisalez@utsa.edu
CARRIUOLO, Nancy 401-456-8101 442 A ncarriuolo@ric.edu
CARRIZOSA, Stan, A 559-730-3731 41 D stanc@cos.edu
CARROCCI, Noreen 316-942-4291 189 K carroccin@newmanu.edu
CARROLL, A. Christine 540-373-2200 505 J christine.carroll@careertrainingsolutions.com
CARROLL, Andrew, G 419-559-2458 392 A acarroll@terra.edu
CARROLL, Barbara, L 919-515-3443 370 D barbara_carroll@ncsu.edu
CARROLL, Betty 304-327-4031 532 D bcarroll@bluefieldstate.edu
CARROLL, Brett 860-768-5708 92 F bcarroll@hartford.edu
CARROLL, Brian 863-667-5021 113 K bccarroll@seu.edu
CARROLL, Carrie 651-523-1641 256 J ccarroll002@luthersem.edu
CARROLL, Charley 575-492-2660 311 J ccarroll@nmjc.edu
CARROLL, Chris 434-592-6463 509 G cccarroll2@liberty.edu
CARROLL, Chris 570-504-9619 415 E ccarroll@tcmc.edu
CARROLL, Constance, M 619-388-6957 62 E ccarroll@sdccd.edu
CARROLL, David, J 409-880-8118 488 F david.carroll@lamar.edu
CARROLL, Denese 601-977-7720 270 F dcarroll@tougaloo.edu
CARROLL, Denise 910-521-6337 371 D denise.carroll@uncp.edu
CARROLL, Dennis, G 336-841-9229 357 E dcarroll@highpoint.edu
CARROLL, Donna, M 708-524-6817 144 C dompres@dom.edu
CARROLL, Elizabeth 845-905-4615 323 E e_carroll@culinary.edu
CARROLL, Erik, P 623-572-3326 152 H ecarro@midwestern.edu
CARROLL, Gracie 325-670-1480 474 M gcarroll@hsutx.edu
CARROLL, Gregory 386-822-7452 117 A gcarroll@stetson.edu
CARROLL, Gregory, M 315-684-6072 347 A carrolgm@morrisville.edu
CARROLL, III, James, J 734-487-3200 242 J jcarroll@emich.edu
CARROLL, Jeannie 432-264-5603 475 E jcarroll@howardcollege.edu
CARROLL, Jeffrey, G 808-956-8516 135 J jcarroll@hawaii.edu
CARROLL, Jennifer 989-686-3617 242 I jennifercarroll@delta.edu
CARROLL, Jerry 864-503-5168 451 A jcarroll@uscupstate.edu
CARROLL, Jodi 606-546-1278 200 E jcaroll@unionky.edu
CARROLL, John 718-817-4075 326 C jcarroll@fordham.edu
CARROLL, Justin, X 314-935-5050 285 E carroll@wustl.edu
CARROLL, Karen 410-225-2297 216 F kcarroll@mica.edu
CARROLL, Kathleen, A 603-526-3888 296 I kcarroll@colby-sawyer.edu
CARROLL, Kathy 402-872-2224 292 C kcarroll@peru.edu
CARROLL, Kathy 202-462-2101 96 C carroll@iwp.edu
CARROLL, Kevin 303-871-2599 86 H kevin.carroll@du.edu
CARROLL, Landera 229-430-4671 119 H LaNedra.Carroll@asurams.edu
CARROLL, Laura 325-674-2264 466 I lbc01c@acu.edu

CARROLL, Lawrence, B 630-617-3114 144 G
larryc@elmhurst.edu
CARROLL, Liz 413-775-1420 231 E
carroll@gcc.mass.edu
CARROLL, Lynn 215-489-2917 416 H
lynn.carroll@delval.edu
CARROLL, Margaret, R 248-341-2028 248 E
mrcarrol@oaklandcc.edu
CARROLL, Maria 716-270-5735 325 A
carrollm@ecc.edu
CARROLL, Mary Ellen 563-588-7575 180 L
maryellen.carroll@loras.edu
CARROLL, Matt 925-631-4378 61 G
mcarroll@stmarys-ca.edu
CARROLL, Melinda 940-668-3315 479 K
mcarroll@nctc.edu
CARROLL, Pauline 978-934-2407 229 A
Pauline_Carroll@uml.edu
CARROLL, Ramona 863-667-5041 113 K
rbcarroll@seu.edu
CARROLL, Randy 931-540-2791 462 E
rcarroll14@columbiastate.edu
CARROLL, Rebecca 912-344-2587 120 D
rebecca.carroll@armstrong.edu
CARROLL, Rob 509-865-8619 523 C
carroll_r@heritage.edu
CARROLL, Robyn 800-877-4723 225 A
robyn.carroll@cambridgecollege.edu
CARROLL, Sean, M 724-287-8711 413 G
sean.carroll@bc3.edu
CARROLL, Shannon 806-457-4200 474 E
scarroll@fpctx.edu
CARROLL, Steven 352-588-8888 111 L
steven.carroll@saintleo.edu
CARROLL, Timothy 847-578-8481 157 G
timothy.carroll@rosalindfranklin.edu
CARROLL, Timothy, D 865-882-4560 463 F
carrolltd@roanestate.edu
CARROLL, Tom 612-330-1352 253 K
carrollt@augsburg.edu
CARROLL, William 801-878-1410 296 D
wcarroll@roseman.edu
CARROLL, William 617-217-9240 223 A
wcarroll@baystate.edu
CARRON, Jennifer 254-710-3435 469 D
jennifer_carron@baylor.edu
CARRUTH, Ann 985-549-3772 208 E
acarruth@selu.edu
CARRUTHERS, Anthony 508-856-6074 229 B
anthony.carruthers@umassmed.edu
CARRUTHERS, Becky 575-769-4913 310 G
becky.carruthers@clovis.edu
CARRUTHERS, Brian, A 864-242-5100 443 G
CARRUTHERS, Garrey, E 575-646-2035 312 A
president@nmsu.edu
CARRY, Ainsley 213-740-5240 74 D
acarry@usc.edu
CARSCADDEN, Alexis 312-752-2532 149 D
alexis.carscadden@kendall.edu
CARSCALLEN, Carey 269-471-6003 239 D
ccarey@andrews.edu
CARSON, Barrett, H 404-894-1868 125 D
barrett.carson@dev.gatech.edu
CARSON, Bonnie, C 864-503-5349 451 A
BCARSON@uscupstate.edu
CARSON, Brenda, B 601-635-2111 267 B
bcarson@eccc.edu
CARSON, Carol 706-754-7703 129 B
ccarson@northgatech.edu
CARSON, Carolyn, N 865-694-6554 463 E
ccarson@pstcc.edu
CARSON, Connie, L 864-294-2202 446 F
connie.carson@furman.edu
CARSON, Cristi 225-216-8502 202 N
carsonc@mybrcc.edu
CARSON, Daniel 713-348-3347 480 M
daniel.d.carson@rice.edu
CARSON, David, L 904-819-6230 102 P
dcarson@flagler.edu
CARSON, Denise, K 785-227-3380 185 A
carsond@bethanylb.edu
CARSON, Elizabeth, M 815-395-5102 158 B
bethcarson@sacn.edu
CARSON, Geoffrey 912-478-7481 126 B
gvcarson@georgiasouthern.edu
CARSON, Jay, T 412-397-6404 434 B
carsonj@rmu.edu
CARSON, Jessica 212-237-8717 319 F
jcarson@jjay.cuny.edu
CARSON, John, J 860-768-4273 92 F
jcarson@hartford.edu
CARSON, Joyce 312-553-2500 141 M
jcarson5@ccc.edu
CARSON, Monica 800-280-0307 163 I
monica.carson@ace.edu
CARSON, Pat 740-351-3460 391 C
pcarson@shawnee.edu
CARSON, Paula 417-625-9394 278 I
carson-p@mssu.edu
CARSON, Rebecca 310-506-4558 58 H
rebecca.carson@pepperdine.edu
CARSON, Staci 801-832-2750 501 C
scarson@westminstercollege.edu
CARSON, Virginia, M 912-260-4394 131 D
virginia.carson@sgsc.edu
CARSON DALY, Anne 845-561-0800 333 I
CARSTARPHEN, Minnie 334-876-9345 4 B
mcarstarphen@wccs.edu
CARSTENS, Jeffrey 402-375-7213 292 D
jecarst1@wsc.edu
CARSTENS, Joel, B 215-898-1404 437 I
carstens@sfs.upenn.edu
CARSTENS, Lisa 503-352-2141 408 I
carstens@pacificu.edu
CARSTENS, Ryan 509-533-7042 521 D
ryan.carstens@scc.spokane.edu
CARSTENS, Ryan 509-533-7042 521 E
ryan.carstens@scc.spokane.edu
CARSTENSEN, Lundie 619-201-8705 62 D
Lundie.Carstensen@sdcc.edu
CARSWELL, Jessica 267-502-2565 413 C
jessica.carswell@anc-gc.org
CARSWELL, Linda 828-448-3110 367 B
lcarswell@wpcc.edu
CARSWELL, Pamela 386-752-1822 103 Q
pamela.carswell@fgc.edu
CARSWELL, Will 843-383-8063 445 A
wcarswell@coker.edu
CART, Robert 973-655-7028 304 A
cartr@mail.montclair.edu
CARTABUKE, Jacqueline 516-877-6004 314 F
jcartabuke@adelphi.edu
CARTAGENA, Aramilda 787-857-3600 553 G
acartagena@br.inter.edu
CARTAGENA, Carlos 520-515-5485 13 B
cartagec@cochise.edu
CARTAGENA, Enid 787-765-3560 552 E
ecartagena@edpuniversity.edu
CARTAGENA, Milagros 787-704-1020 552 D
mcartagena@ediccollege.edu
CARTE, Mandy 216-368-2595 378 J
mmc111@case.edu
CARTEE, Dawn, H 912-871-1638 129 E
dcartee@ogeecheetech.edu
CARTER, Abby 229-227-3177 132 C
acarter@southernregional.edu
CARTER, Alfonza 919-546-8527 368 G
alcarter@shawu.edu
CARTER, Allia 229-317-6728 123 H
allia.carter@darton.edu
CARTER, Allison, A 906-487-2335 247 A
allison@mtu.edu
CARTER, Amber 859-442-1712 196 A
amber.carter@kctcs.edu
CARTER, Andrew, V 580-327-8632 399 F
avcarter@nwosu.edu
CARTER, Angela, M 336-334-4822 363 A
amcarter@gtcc.edu
CARTER, Bates 302-622-8000 93 D
bcarter@dcad.edu
CARTER, Bessie 405-945-3211 400 F
cartebm@osuokc.edu
CARTER, Beth 352-588-8480 111 L
beth.carter@saintleo.edu
CARTER, Brenda, C 214-491-6271 471 C
bcarter@collin.edu
CARTER, Brett 607-778-5003 344 F
carterbd@sunybroome.edu
CARTER, Charlotte 205-366-8948 7 G
ccarter@stillman.edu
CARTER, Cindy 641-585-8130 183 I
carterc@waldorf.edu
CARTER, Clark 843-863-8008 444 B
ccarter@csuniv.edu
CARTER, Clay 252-940-6357 360 B
clay.carter@beaufortccc.edu
CARTER, Clinton, P 256-765-4233 9 D
cpcarter@una.edu
CARTER, Coletta 678-891-2455 125 G
coletta.carter@gpc.edu
CARTER, Cynthia 229-931-2057 131 E
ccarter@southgatech.edu
CARTER, Cynthia 906-786-5802 240 K
carterc@baycollege.edu
CARTER, D. Michael 435-586-7738 499 L
carter_m@suu.edu
CARTER, Danette 425-602-3083 519 J
dcarter@bastyr.edu
CARTER, Danita 314-918-2620 274 K
dcarter@eden.edu
CARTER, Darryl 716-878-6522 345 B
carterdc@buffalostate.edu
CARTER, David 512-471-4441 493 M
david.carter@austin.utexas.edu
CARTER, Deborah 517-264-7100 250 B
dcarter2@sienaheights.edu
CARTER, Derek, A 240-567-7587 217 B
derek.carter@montgomerycollege.edu
CARTER, Drake 701-224-5545 374 E
fred.carter@bismarckstate.edu
CARTER, Ed 256-331-5277 6 B
cartere@nwscc.edu
CARTER, Eloise 334-727-8953 8 B
ecarter@mytu.tuskegee.edu
CARTER, Evonne 252-335-0821 361 G
evonne_carter@albemarle.edu
CARTER, F. 'Thatcher' 509-527-5195 528 F
carterft@whitman.edu
CARTER, Fantina 615-329-8586 456 G
fcarter@fisk.edu
CARTER, Gary, L 731-661-5204 464 G
gcarter@uu.edu
CARTER, Glenda, F 903-927-3336 497 G
gcarter@wileyc.edu
CARTER, Glenn 603-577-6414 297 F
gcarter@dwc.edu
CARTER, Hasani 973-275-2385 308 C
hasani.carter@shu.edu
CARTER, Helene 706-821-8323 129 H
hcarter@paine.edu
CARTER, Holly, R 512-428-1051 481 B
hollyc@stedwards.edu
CARTER, Hugh 334-222-6591 5 G
hcarter@lbwcc.edu
CARTER, Jacque 402-826-8253 290 C
jacque.carter@doane.edu
CARTER, JaPrince, L 804-342-3895 518 E
jlcarter@vuu.edu
CARTER, Jeffrey, W 800-287-8822 164 E
president@bethanyseminary.edu
CARTER, Jennifer, L 724-847-6603 419 B
jlcarter@geneva.edu
CARTER, Jennings 618-545-3169 149 C
jcarter@kaskaskia.edu
CARTER, Jessica 276-656-0312 516 D
jcarter@patrickhenry.edu
CARTER, Joe 254-442-5106 470 I
joe.carter@cisco.edu
CARTER, John, B 413-542-2771 222 A
jbcarter@amherst.edu
CARTER, Jon 910-410-1723 365 B
jdcarter@richmondcc.edu
CARTER, Joseph 610-647-4400 421 B
jcarter@immaculata.edu
CARTER, Julien, C 617-627-3271 237 C
julien.carter@tufts.edu
CARTER, June 864-503-5881 451 A
jcarter@uscupstate.edu
CARTER, Kathryn 978-934-2741 229 A
kathryn_carter@uml.edu
CARTER, Kermit 256-306-2613 2 F
klc@calhoun.edu
CARTER, Kim, C 859-257-9420 200 G
kccarter.1@uky.edu
CARTER, Kim, C 215-895-1190 438 E
k.carter@usciences.edu
CARTER, Kyle, R 910-521-6201 371 D
chancellor@uncp.edu
CARTER, Lana 719-296-6108 85 A
lana.carter@pueblocc.edu
CARTER, Laurie 859-622-1842 194 L
laurie.carter@eku.edu
CARTER, Lawrence, E 404-215-2608 128 L
lawrence.carter@morehouse.edu
CARTER, Lawrence, L 517-321-0242 243 H
lcarter@glcc.edu
CARTER, Lennie, M 202-687-2499 95 E
carterl@georgetown.edu
CARTER, Leon 810-766-2190 239 H
leon.carter@baker.edu
CARTER, Linda 314-516-4165 284 B
cartermlin@umsl.edu
CARTER, Linda 816-604-3081 277 J
linda.carter@mcckc.edu
CARTER, Linda 606-539-4230 200 F
linda.carter@ucumberlands.edu
CARTER, Linnie, S 717-780-2321 420 D
lscarter@hacc.edu
CARTER, Luther, F 843-661-1210 446 E
lcarter@fmarion.edu
CARTER, Malika 701-777-4259 373 G
malika.carter@und.edu
CARTER, Martin 404-527-4520 122 D
mcarter@carver.edu
CARTER, Matt 505-277-3003 313 H
mdcarter@unm.edu
CARTER, Melanie 202-806-2550 96 B
melCarter@howard.edu
CARTER, Melody 478-825-6959 124 E
carterm0@fvsu.edu
CARTER, Michael 270-789-5001 194 D
mvcarter@campbellsville.edu
CARTER, Michael 661-255-1050 31 B
mcarter@calarts.edu
CARTER, Michael 435-652-7879 499 M
carter_m@dixie.edu
CARTER, Michele 254-526-1331 470 E
michele.carter@ctcd.edu
CARTER, Mike 714-879-3901 47 D
mcarter@hiu.edu
CARTER, Mike 918-495-7150 401 B
mcarter@oru.edu
CARTER, Ninette 580-581-5577 397 A
ncarter@cameron.edu
CARTER, Ninette 580-581-5577 397 A
ninettec@cameron.edu
CARTER, Phillip 615-547-1307 456 C
pcarter@cumberland.edu
CARTER, Phyllis 510-464-3232 59 B
pcarter@peralta.edu
CARTER, R. Daphne 843-661-1188 446 E
rcarter@fmarion.edu
CARTER, Regina, W 501-569-3408 24 A
rswade@ualr.edu
CARTER, Richard 309-298-2501 163 A
r-carter@wiu.edu
CARTER, Richard 309-298-1929 163 A
r-carter@wiu.edu
CARTER, Richard 206-239-4500 520 K
richardcarter@cityu.edu
CARTER, Ronald, L 909-558-7616 50 K
rcarter@llu.edu
CARTER, Ronald, L 704-378-1006 358 B
rcarter@jcsu.edu
CARTER, Sarah 801-649-5230 498 K
clinicaldean@midwifery.edu
CARTER, Saundra 202-274-6430 97 B
scarter@udc.edu
CARTER, Scott 620-278-4290 191 D
scarter@sterling.edu
CARTER, Seth, M 785-460-5400 186 D
seth.carter@colbycc.edu
CARTER, Sharon, L 714-879-3901 47 D
slcarter@hiu.edu
CARTER, Shawna, M 608-246-6249 543 C
smcarter@madisoncollege.edu
CARTER, Sheila 312-369-7994 143 C
scarter@colum.edu
CARTER, Shirley, P 336-315-8660 355 F
scarter@carolinagrad.edu
CARTER, Shree 714-556-3610 75 A
scarter@vanguard.edu
CARTER, Shree 714-556-3610 75 A
VUTrustees@vanguard.edu
CARTER, Sonja 212-875-4603 315 F
scarter@bankstreet.edu
CARTER, Spencer, D 269-471-3395 239 D
scarter@andrews.edu
CARTER, Stanley 334-514-4013 4 K
stanley.carter@istc.edu
CARTER, Steven, J 215-887-5511 439 E
scarter@wts.edu
CARTER, Suzanne 817-515-5079 484 B
suzanne.carter@tccd.edu
CARTER, Tara 434-736-2005 516 H
tara.carter@southside.edu
CARTER, Tay Sha 479-619-4396 22 B
tcarter@nwacc.edu
CARTER, Tiffany 773-291-6315 142 B
tcarter63@ccc.edu
CARTER, Todd 316-322-3201 185 F
tcarter@butlercc.edu
CARTER, Todd 620-417-1012 191 A
todd.carter@sccc.edu
CARTER, Tom 256-331-5263 6 B
tom.carter@nwscc.edu
CARTER, JR., Walter, E 410-293-1000 549 B
CARTER, William 901-448-1687 465 G
wcarte17@uthsc.edu
CARTER, William, E 713-718-8708 475 C
william.carter@hccs.edu
CARTER, William, M 412-648-1401 437 K
wmc4@pitt.edu
CARTER, Zina 979-532-6417 497 F
zinac@wcjc.edu
CARTER-CHAPMAN, Renee, M 907-786-6486 10 H
rmcarterchapman@uaa.alaska.edu
CARTER-COLEY, Stacey 252-492-2061 366 G
cartercoley@vgcc.edu
CARTER-DOVE, Bernadette 919-209-2025 363 F
bjcarterdove@johnstoncc.edu
CARTER-HARBOUR, Courtney 972-860-7335 472 E
CourtneyCarter@dcccd.edu
CARTER-STEVENS, Marilyn 718-862-7958 331 H
marilyn.carter@manhattan.edu
CARTER-TELLISON, Katrina 561-237-7210 108 E
kcarter-tellison@lynn.edu
CARTHELL, Sidney, G 270-809-6836 198 I
scarthell@murraystate.edu
CARTIER, Jennifer 207-509-7282 212 A
jcartier@unity.edu
CARTIER, Jolie, L 619-239-0391 36 E
jcartier@cwsl.edu

CASSIS, Lisa, A 859-257-5294 200 G
lcassis@uky.edu
CASTADIO, Paula 559-278-6050 33 D
pcastadio@csufresno.edu
CASTAGNERA,
James, O 609-896-5035 306 A
castagne@rider.edu
CASTALDI, Patricia 908-412-3590 309 A
castaldi@ucc.edu
CASTALDO, Annalisa 610-499-1112 439 G
acastaldo@widener.edu
CASTALDO, John 609-771-2082 301 E
castaldo@tcnj.edu
CASTANDEA, Angelia 312-935-6015 157 A
acastaneda@robertmorris.edu
CASTANEDA, Alex 210-829-6012 492 B
mcasta1@uiwtx.edu
CASTANEDA, Angelica 312-935-4556 157 A
acastaneda@robertmorris.edu
CASTANEDA, Monica 623-845-3528 14 N
monica.castaneda@gccaz.edu
CASTANEDA-CALLEROS,
Russell 562-463-7234 60 I
rcastanedacalleros@riohondo.edu
CASTANO, C. Gabriel 516-918-3705 316 L
gcastano@bcl.edu
CASTANOS, Elba 305-629-2929 112 D
ecastanos@sanignaciocollege.edu
CASTEEL, Matt 918-631-2960 403 M
matthew-casteel@utulsa.edu
CASTEEL, William 210-690-9000 474 L
wcasteel@hallmarkuniversity.edu
CASTELLANI, Patrick, E 570-348-6283 425 D
pcastellani@marywood.edu
CASTELLANO, Ana 787-622-8000 556 H
acastellano@pupr.edu
CASTELLANO, Cecilia 419-372-7803 377 I
ccast@bgsu.edu
CASTELLANO,
Deborah, A 215-871-6707 432 E
registrar@pcom.edu
CASTELLANO, Paul 407-831-9816 100 F
pcastellano@citycollege.edu
CASTELLINO, Lisa 707-826-5339 35 D
Lisa.Castellino@humboldt.edu
CASTELLO, Donald 815-836-5425 150 F
casteldo@lewisu.edu
CASTELLO, Ellen, J 575-646-2090 312 A
castello@nmsu.edu
CASTELLOE, Stephen 336-334-4822 363 A
srcastelloe@gtcc.edu
CASTENEDA, Debbie 970-542-3140 84 A
debbie.casteneda@morgancc.edu
CASTERTON, Deanna 563-387-1038 180 M
castde01@luther.edu
CASTETE, Ralynn, F 337-475-5140 208 B
rcastete@mcneese.edu
CASTIGLIA, Beth 212-986-4343 316 D
beth-castigli@berkeleycollege.edu
CASTIGLIA, Beth 973-278-5400 300 C
beth-castigli@berkeleycollege.edu
CASTIGLIA, Beth 201-559-6140 302 I
castigliab@felician.edu
CASTIGLIONE,
Joseph, R 405-325-8208 403 I
jcastiglione@ou.edu
CASTIGLIONE, Thomas 201-216-5208 308 D
Thomas.Castiglione@stevens.edu
CASTIGLIONI, Randy 713-348-5241 480 M
castigr@rice.edu
CASTILLA, Rafael 201-327-8877 302 E
rcastilla@eastwick.edu
CASTILLO, Angelina 815-455-8738 152 B
acastillo@mchenry.edu
CASTILLO, Candace 972-273-3013 473 A
ccastillo@dcccd.edu
CASTILLO, JR.,
Carmelino 956-721-5135 477 C
carmelino.castillo@laredo.edu
CASTILLO, Daniel 575-492-2135 314 D
dcastillo@usw.edu
CASTILLO, David 559-934-2166 76 A
davidcastillo2@whccd.edu
CASTILLO, Diana 254-526-1348 470 E
diana.castillo@ctcd.edu
CASTILLO, Elisa 978-542-6410 230 E
elisa.castillo@salemstate.edu
CASTILLO, Evelyn 787-284-1912 554 B
ecastillo@ponce.inter.edu
CASTILLO, Henry 718-862-7249 331 H
bookstore@manhattan.edu
CASTILLO, JR., Juan, J 956-326-2380 485 B
jjcastillo@tamiu.edu
CASTILLO, Keith 951-552-8720 30 D
kcastillo@calbaptist.edu
CASTILLO, Lida 626-873-2139 55 B
lcastillo@mtsierra.edu
CASTILLO, Maggie 623-935-8839 14 L
maggie.castillo@estrellamountain.edu
CASTILLO, Mario 832-813-6508 477 I
mario.k.castillo@lonestar.edu
CASTILLO, Mario 512-492-3005 468 A
mcastillo@aoma.edu
CASTILLO, Marvin 619-482-6330 68 D
mcastillo@swccd.edu
CASTILLO, Nicole 209-946-2496 73 C
ncastillo@pacific.edu
CASTILLO, Raul, V 818-947-2618 52 B
castilrv@lavc.edu
CASTILLO, Rosalinda 773-442-5300 154 H
r-castillo2@neiu.edu
CASTILLO, Salvador 541-737-8083 408 F
salvador.castillo@oregonstate.edu
CASTILLO, Saundra 575-527-7599 312 D
scastillo@nmsu.edu
CASTILLO, Victor 773-838-7795 142 C
vcastillo@ccc.edu
CASTILLO-ALANIZ,
Jo Elda 361-593-3991 486 A
jo.alaniz@tamuk.edu
CASTILLO CLARK,
Evette 925-631-4238 61 G
ecc4@stmarys-ca.edu
CASTILLO-FRICK, Iliana 305-237-0294 108 L
ifrick@mdc.edu
CASTILLON, Nicole 307-382-1642 546 L
ncastillon@wwcc.wy.edu
CASTILOW, Nancy 402-554-3509 294 A
ncastilow@unomaha.edu
CASTLE, Carey 218-793-8612 260 F
carey.castle@northlandcollege.edu
CASTLE, Clinton 218-683-8600 260 F
clinton.castle@northlandcollege.edu
CASTLE, Janie 276-935-4349 504 L
jcastle@asl.edu
CASTLE, Josh 802-322-1672 501 H
josh.castle@goddard.edu
CASTLE, Lyle 208-282-3218 138 C
castlyle@isu.edu
CASTLE, Lyle, W 208-282-7852 138 C
castlyle@isu.edu
CASTLE, Ruthie 662-562-3213 269 E
rcastle@northwestms.edu
CASTLE, Tom 319-363-1323 181 D
tome@mtmercy.edu
CASTLEBERRY, Joseph 425-889-4202 524 G
joseph.castleberry@northwestu.edu
CASTLEBERRY, Rita, J 580-327-8540 399 F
rjcastleberry@nwosu.edu
CASTLEBURY, Lisa 812-357-6515 173 A
lcastlebury@saintmeinrad.edu
CASTLEMAN, Janet, L 401-865-2816 441 F
jcastlem@providence.edu
CASTLEMAN, Louanna 910-678-0141 362 E
castleml@faytechcc.edu
CASTLEN, Kaye 270-686-4259 193 G
kaye.castlen@brescia.edu
CASTON, E.E 662-846-4150 267 A
ecaston@deltastate.edu
CASTON, Gay Lynn 601-857-3396 267 D
GLCaston@hindscc.edu
CASTONGUAY, Sharon 860-685-3377 93 B
scastonguay@wesleyan.edu
CASTONGUAY, Suzette 937-769-1375 376 M
scastonguay@antioch.edu
CASTONGUAY, Suzette 937-769-1375 376 L
scastonguay@antioch.edu
CASTOR, Tammy 661-362-3516 40 H
tammy.castor@canyons.edu
CASTORENA, Christina 425-640-1668 522 D
christina.castorena@edcc.edu
CASTRIOTA, Nadia 518-445-2361 314 H
ncast@albanylaw.edu
CASTRO, Adam 973-748-9000 300 E
adam_castro@bloomfield.edu
CASTRO, Bernie 856-691-8600 301 H
bcastro@cccnj.edu
CASTRO, Daisy 787-753-6335 552 K
dcastro@icprjc.edu
CASTRO, Donna 505-426-2240 311 H
dcastro@nmhu.edu
CASTRO, Evelyn 718-270-6046 320 C
ecastro@mec.cuny.edu
CASTRO, Francia, L 212-694-1000 316 J
fcastro@boricuacollege.edu
CASTRO, Ida, L 570-504-9647 415 E
icastro@tcmc.edu
CASTRO, Jill 248-476-1122 246 G
jcastro@mispp.edu
CASTRO, Joseph, I 559-278-2324 33 D
josephcastro@csufresno.edu
CASTRO, Kaye 239-687-5343 98 N
kcastro@avemarialaw.edu
CASTRO, Lori 831-459-2960 72 E
lrcastro@ucsc.edu
CASTRO, Lorna 787-764-0000 558 E
lorna.castro@upr.edu
CASTRO, Louise, P 915-747-8820 494 B
lpcastro@utep.edu
CASTRO, Madelyn 813-253-6201 118 H
macastro@ut.edu
CASTRO, Manny 670-237-6772 550 B
manny.castro@marianas.edu
CASTRO,
Maria de los A 787-767-4300 558 E
maria.castro18@upr.edu
CASTRO, Melanie 806-371-5288 467 E
m0163300@actx.edu
CASTRO, Melba 657-278-5579 33 E
melbacastro@fullerton.edu
CASTRO, Octavio 414-288-5629 537 B
octavio.castro@marquette.edu
CASTRO, Raul 787-738-2161 557 G
raul.castro@upr.edu
CASTRO, Rodrigo 305-899-4062 99 B
rcastro@barry.edu
CASTRO, Roz 630-953-3681 141 E
rcastro@chamberlain.edu
CASTRO, Toni 206-592-3351 523 D
tcastro@highline.edu
CASTRO-ROMAKER,
Judith 608-246-6678 543 C
jcastro-romaker@madisoncollege.edu
CASTRONOVO, Neil, R 508-767-7274 222 D
ncastron@assumption.edu
CASTRUITA, Javier 408-741-2042 76 D
javier_castruita@wvm.edu
CASWELL, Liz 860-723-0016 88 C
caswelle@ct.edu
CASWELL, Roger 620-341-5372 186 H
rcaswekk@emporia.edu
CATALANA, Paul 864-455-3510 450 G
pcatalana@ghs.org
CATALANA, Paul, V 864-294-2180 446 F
paul.catalana@furman.edu
CATALANO, Megan 573-288-6570 274 C
mcatalano@culver.edu
CATALANO, Mike 605-995-2669 452 C
micatala@dwu.edu
CATALANO, Steven 718-489-5309 340 E
scatalano@sfc.edu
CATALANOTTI, Robert 617-327-6777 238 D
Bob_Catalanotti@williamjames.edu
CATALDI, Jennifer 317-738-8256 166 B
jcataldi@franklincollege.edu
CATALFAMO, Kevin 856-351-2701 308 B
kcatalfamo@salemcc.edu
CATALINI, Tom 617-369-3106 236 E
tcatalini@mfa.org
CATALLOZZI, Lori, A 617-228-2048 231 C
lacatallozzi@bhcc.mass.edu
CATALON, Linda, H 225-771-2520 206 K
linda_catalon@sus.edu
CATANESE, Anthony, J 321-674-7232 103 R
catanese@fit.edu
CATANIA, Guy 412-392-3952 433 F
gcatania@pointpark.edu
CATANZARO, Sam 309-438-7018 147 I
catanzar@ilstu.edu
CATAUDELLA,
Vincent, B 203-576-5616 91 H
vincent.cataudella@stvincentscollege.edu
CATCHINGS, Robert 202-806-6700 96 B
rcatchings@howard.edu
CATE, Fred 812-855-1161 167 I
fcate@iu.edu
CATE, Jessica, M 573-288-6450 274 C
jcate@culver.edu
CATE, Richard, H 802-656-0219 503 C
richard.cate@uvm.edu
CATELLA, Rosanne 440-934-3101 388 E
rcatella@ohiobusinesscollege.edu
CATES, Damon 773-702-2151 161 D
dcates@uchicago.edu
CATES, Jared 417-255-7230 279 B
jaredcates@missouristate.edu
CATES, Tommy 731-881-7638 465 F
tcates@utm.edu
CATH, Tom 219-464-5005 174 E
tom.cath@valpo.edu
CATHCART, Scott 760-744-1150 58 D
scathcart@palomar.edu
CATHELINE, Jim 724-964-8811 427 E
jcatheline@ncstrades.edu
CATHER, Michael 410-704-4679 221 A
mcather@towson.edu
CATHERMAN, David 504-398-2279 206 E
dcatherman@olhcc.edu
CATHERWOOD, Ryan 434-395-4804 509 H
catherwoodrp@longwood.edu
CATHEY, Patrice, A 716-878-4055 345 B
catheypc@mail.buffalostate.edu
CATHEY, Ron 318-257-4336 208 A
rcathey@latech.edu
CATHIE, Julie 530-541-4660 50 A
cathie@ltcc.edu
CATIGGAY, James 415-422-6216 74 C
catiggay@usfca.edu
CATLETT, Deborrah, L 859-246-6810 195 J
deborrah.catlett@kctcs.edu
CATLETT, Jennifer 865-471-3530 455 G
jcatlett@cn.edu
CATO, Amie 903-785-7661 480 B
acato@parisjc.edu
CATO, Michael 845-437-7605 351 H
micato@vassar.edu
CATON, Brock, E 207-778-7033 212 E
brock.caton@maine.edu
CATON, Claire 713-226-5223 491 F
catonc@uhd.edu
CATON, Lisa 979-627-0286 469 F
Lisa.Caton@blinn.edu
CATON, Rhonda 479-788-7073 23 H
rhonda.caton@uafs.edu
CATOTA, Claudia 661-654-2137 32 G
ccatota@csub.edu
CATRON, Greg 904-620-2903 116 A
greg.catron@unf.edu
CATRON, Jonathan 864-644-5662 449 B
jcatron@swu.edu
CATRON, Sue 918-456-5511 398 M
catrons@nsuok.edu
CATRON-WOOD,
Rhonda, K 276-223-4772 517 F
rcatronwood@wcc.vccs.edu
CATT, Helen 229-430-3506 119 I
hcatt@albanytech.edu
CATT, Stephen, R 724-287-8711 413 G
stephen.catt@bc3.edu
CATTANACH, John, R 315-516-4100 284 B
cattanachj@umsl.edu
CATTON, Heather 936-468-5597 484 A
hcatton@sfasu.edu
CATTOOR, Chad, A 314-505-7304 273 G
cattoorc@csl.edu
CAUBERE, Monique 914-674-7510 332 E
mcaubere@mercy.edu
CAUCE, Ana Mari 206-543-5010 527 G
provost@uw.edu
CAUDA, Lisa 585-475-7721 339 G
lisa.cauda@rit.edu
CAUDILL, Helene 209-667-3407 35 C
hcaudill@csustan.edu
CAUDILL, Reggie, J 973-596-3019 304 D
reggie.j.caudil@njit.edu
CAUDLE, Mary Anne 252-789-0280 363 H
mcaudle@martincc.edu
CAUDLE, Patricia, M 909-748-8171 73 K
pat_caudle@redlands.edu
CAUFFMAN, Bonnie, H 360-417-6212 525 A
bcauffman@pencol.edu
CAUGHEY, Martha 850-484-1604 110 D
mcaughey@pensacolastate.edu
CAUGHMAN, Gretchen 706-721-4014 121 C
gcaughma@gru.edu
CAUGHMAN, S. Wright 404-778-3774 124 D
scaughm@emory.edu
CAULEY, Phil 828-227-2923 372 C
cauley@wcu.edu
CAULFIELD, Jack 508-213-2398 235 C
jack.caulfield@nichols.edu
CAULFIELD, Richard 907-796-6256 11 A
provost@uas.alaska.edu
CAULFIELD, Richard 907-796-6565 11 A
racaulfield@uas.alaska.edu
CAULFIELD,
Thomas, M 217-351-2477 155 I
tcaulfield@parkland.edu
CAULKINS, Amy 309-341-5290 140 I
acaulkins@sandburg.edu
CAUPP, Jeffrey, G 480-245-7969 14 D
jeff.caupp@ibcs.edu
CAUSBY, Cory 828-227-7218 372 C
causby@wcu.edu
CAUSEY, Bruce 256-306-2569 2 F
bcausey@calhoun.edu
CAUSEY, Jana 601-554-5506 270 A
jcausey@prcc.edu
CAUSEY, Joy 229-317-6886 123 H
joy.causey@darton.edu
CAUSEY, Katherine 901-435-1259 457 N
katherine_causey@loc.edu
CAUSEY, Mary Frances 928-350-1112 17 K
mcausey@prescott.edu
CAUSLAND, Luann 678-407-5000 125 B
lcausland@ggc.edu
CAUTIN, Robin 203-396-8020 91 G
cautinr@sacredheart.edu
CAUWELS, Beth 805-565-6101 76 K
bcauwels@westmont.edu
CAVACO, Frank 617-964-1100 222 B
fcavaco@ants.edu
CAVALIER, Amy 617-873-0106 225 A
Amy.cavalier30@go.cambridgecollege.edu
CAVALIER, Donald, R 218-281-8585 264 H
cavalier@umn.edu
CAVALIER, Philip 870-307-7202 21 G
Philip.cavalier@lyon.edu
CAVALIER, Wayne 210-341-1366 479 N
wcavalier@ost.edu

CAVALIERI, Correne ...... 718-779-1499 338 D ccavalieri@plazacollege.edu
CAVALIERI, Cristina, G . 215-503-9496 436 F cristina.cavalieri@jefferson.edu
CAVALIERI, Thomas ...... 856-566-6995 306 D cavalita@rowan.edu
CAVALLARO, Claire .... 657-278-4021.. 33 E ccavallaro@fullerton.edu
CAVALLARO, Gregory, M .... 540-464-7328 518 A gcav@vmiaa.org
CAVALLARO, Vito .... 212-938-5500 347 C vito@sunyopt.edu
CAVALLO, Julia .... 724-805-2372 435 B julia.cavallo@email.stvincent.edu
CAVALLUZZI, Marty, L .. 253-840-8421 525 C mcavalluzzi@pierce.ctc.edu
CAVALOVITCH, Renee, T .... 412-397-5262 434 B cavalovitch@rmu.edu
CAVAN, John, J .... 434-949-1003 516 H john.cavan@southside.edu
CAVANAGH, Jon .... 765-998-4161 173 B jon.cavanagh@taylor.edu
CAVANAGH, Kevin .... 914-654-5085 322 B kcavanagh@cnr.edu
CAVANAGH, Stephen .... 413-545-5093 228 F dean@nursing.umass.edu
CAVANAUGH, Amy .... 503-943-7201 410 H cavanaug@up.edu
CAVANAUGH, Brian ...... 716-829-7878 324 E cavanaub@dyc.edu
CAVANAUGH, SSJ, Cecelia .... 215-753-3623 415 D ccavanau@chc.edu
CAVANAUGH, Erica ...... 701-766-1305 373 D erica.cavanaugh@littlehoop.edu
CAVANAUGH, Kyle .... 919-684-2826 356 E kyle.cavanaugh@duke.edu
CAVANAUGH, Mary ...... 212-396-7549 319 E mary.cavanaugh@hunter.cuny.edu
CAVANAUGH, Mary Anne .... 803-641-3587 450 C maryanc@usca.edu
CAVANAUGH, Mike .... 800-670-3546 324 F
CAVANESS, Kerrie .... 509-574-4870 529 B kcavaness@yvcc.edu
CAVANUAGH, Rachel .... 910-362-7317 360 G rcavenaugh@cfcc.edu
CAVAZOS, Rebecca .... 956-664-4680 482 G beckyc@southtexascollege.edu
CAVENAUGH, Andy .... 910-296-2480 363 E acavenaugh@jamessprunt.edu
CAVENER, Douglas, R .. 814-865-9591 428 C drc9@psu.edu
CAVENY-NOECKER, Deanna, M .... 843-953-5527 445 B cavenyd@cofc.edu
CAVERLEY, Darla .... 320-629-5118 260 H calverleyd@pinetech.edu
CAVI, Sandra .... 309-438-8489 147 I skcavi@ilstu.edu
CAVICCHI, Daniel .... 401-454-6580 442 B dcavicch@risd.edu
CAVIN, JR., Elmo, M ... 806-743-3080 490 A elmo.cavin@ttuhsc.edu
CAVIN, Rita .... 541-440-4600 410 E rita.cavin@umpqua.edu
CAVIN, Wesley .... 318-255-7950 208 A wes@latechalumni.org
CAVINESS, Debbie, J .... 315-470-6632 347 B dcavines@esf.edu
CAVINESS, Howard .... 318-274-6437 207 H
CAVINS-TULL, Kathryn .. 817-257-7820 486 G k.cavins@tcu.edu
CAVIS, Mark .... 906-487-7315 242 M mark.cavis@finlandia.edu
CAVITT, Deborah .... 817-531-4298 490 C dcavitt@txwes.edu
CAWLEY, Deborah .... 610-527-0200 434 D deborah.cawley@rosemont.edu
CAWLEY, Patrick, J .... 843-792-4000 447 G cawleypj@musc.edu
CAWLEY, Steve .... 305-284-3515 118 A s.cawley@miami.edu
CAWLFIELD, Jeffrey ...... 573-341-4557 284 C jdc@mst.edu
CAWOOD, J. Scott .... 215-702-4216 414 C scawood@cairn.edu
CAWOOD, Patti .... 423-614-8316 457 M pcawood@leeuniversity.edu
CAWTHON, Donald, L .. 254-968-9227 485 A cawthon@tarleton.edu
CAWTHON, Jim .... 574-936-8898 164 A jim.cawthon@ancilla.edu
CAWTHORNE, Jon, E .... 304-293-0304 533 D jon.cawthorne@mail.wvu.edu
CAWYER, Carol, S .... 406-466-6765 398 E cscawyer@langston.edu
CAYA, Ryan .... 701-224-2412 374 E ryan.caya@bismarckstate.edu
CAYEA, Cynthia .... 516-364-0808 335 A library@nycollege.edu
CAYER, Cynthia, B .... 860-832-1741.. 88 D cayerc@ccsu.edu
CAYLOR, Deborah, Z .... 540-458-8730 519 A dcaylor@wlu.edu
CAYLOR, Mary, J .... 256-551-5219.... 4 J maryjane.caylor@drakestate.edu
CAYWOOD, Janet .... 620-278-4280 191 D jcaywood@sterling.edu
CAYWOOD, Steven .... 620-278-4240 191 D scaywood@sterling.edu
CAZALET, David .... 865-539-7350 463 E djcazalet@pstcc.edu
CAZARES, Rebecca .... 559-934-2159.. 76 A beckycazares@whccd.edu
CAZAUBON, Steven, H . 504-762-3005 203 F scazau@dcc.edu
CAZAUBON, Steven, H . 504-762-3050 203 F scazau@dcc.edu
CAZZETTA, Vinnie .... 845-341-4726 337 G vinnie.cazzetta@sunyorange.edu
CEA, Jorge .... 925-473-7430.. 42 F jcea@losmedanos.edu
CEARLEY, Anna .... 619-684-8791.. 56 B acearley@newschoolarch.edu
CEASAR, Ted .... 760-355-6312.. 47 G ted.ceasar@imperial.edu
CEBELAK, Jane, P .... 772-462-7544 106 F jcebelak@irsc.edu
CEBRICK, Daniel, T .... 570-208-5870 422 D dtcebric@kings.edu
CEBRZYNSKI, Gerard, J 847-735-5104 149 H cebrzynski@lakeforest.edu
CEBULA, Thomas .... 330-490-7051 395 C tcebula@salsh.edu
CECALA, Dianna .... 843-349-5207 446 I dianna.cecala@hgtc.edu
CECCHI, Joseph .... 505-277-5500 313 H cecchi@unm.edu
CECCHINI, Bernard .... 315-568-3127 334 F bcecchini@nycc.edu
CECCHINI, Dan .... 541-383-7700 404 K dcecchini@cocc.edu
CECE, Heidi .... 757-352-4809 511 G hcece@regent.edu
CECERE, Mollie .... 304-829-7591 529 H mcecere@bethanywv.edu
CECH, John .... 406-444-0314 287 C jcech@montana.edu
CECH, John .... 406-444-0316 287 C jcech@montana.edu
CECIL, Dale .... 270-686-4239 193 G dale.cecil@brescia.edu
CECIL, David, J .... 859-233-8239 200 D financialaid@transy.edu
CECIL, Jamie, N .... 717-867-6228 423 I cecil@lvc.edu
CECIL, Kristine .... 303-871-2412.. 86 H kristine.cecil@du.edu
CECIL, Kyle .... 309-341-5461 140 I
CECIL, Patrick, A .... 502-895-3411 198 E pcecil@lpts.edu
CECILLI, Andrea, T .... 814-886-6300 427 B
CEDAR, Leslie .... 512-471-3800 493 M cedar@alumni.utexas.edu
CEDERHOLM, Annette ... 256-840-4142.... 7 B acederholm@snead.edu
CEDILLO, Arnulfo .... 510-436-2478.. 59 C acedillo@peralta.edu
CEDRONE, David, C ...... 617-994-6904 228 D dmcedrone@bhe.mass.edu
CEGLES, Victor .... 562-985-8527.. 33 F vic.cegles@csulb.edu
CELESTIN, Irene .... 678-359-5010 126 E irenec@gordonstate.edu
CELHAY, Lilia .... 510-464-3213.. 59 B lcelhay@peralta.edu
CELL, Paul, M .... 973-655-5123 304 A cellp@mail.montclair.edu
CELLA, Barbara .... 925-473-7322.. 42 F bcella@losmedanos.edu
CELLEMME, Patricia ...... 518-292-1710 340 A cellep@sage.edu
CELLI, David, S .... 570-389-4882 430 B dcelli@bloomu.edu
CELLINI, Roger .... 909-748-8020.. 73 K roger_cellini@redlands.edu
CELLINI, Todd .... 912-201-8007 131 F tcellini@southuniversity.edu
CELTEK, Serkan .... 956-872-5577 482 G sbceltek@southtexascollege.edu
CEMAN, Jamie .... 920-424-2442 540 B cemanj@uwosh.edu
CEN, Luozhu .... 530-895-4050.. 30 B cenlu@butte.edu
CEN, Luozhu .... 530-879-4050.. 30 B cenlu@butte.edu
CENG, Kathleen .... 914-251-6507 346 D kathleen.ceng@purchase.edu
CENINA, Angela .... 714-547-9625.. 30 F acenina@calcoast.edu
CENSOR, Yerachmiel .... 845-356-7064 353 G
CENTER, Mark, R .... 210-434-6711 479 P mrcenter@lake.ollusa.edu
CENTOPANTI, Anthony (Tony) .... 203-857-7131.. 89 H acentopant@norwalk.edu
CENTOR, Josh .... 412-268-3894 414 J jcentor@andrew.cmu.edu
CEO, Nicolette .... 516-323-3282 333 E nceo@molloy.edu
CEPEDA, Adrian .... 312-935-6683 157 A acepeda@robertmorris.edu
CEPEDA, Charlotte, R ... 670-237-6751 550 B charlotte.cepeda@marianas.edu
CEPPI, Matthew .... 760-750-4040.. 35 B mceppi@csusm.edu
CEPPOS, Jerry .... 225-578-9294 204 M jceppos@lsu.edu
CEPULL, Jeff .... 215-951-2516 432 F cepullj@philau.edu
CERAVOLO, Suzanne .... 973-408-3464 301 J sceravol@drew.edu
CERCONE, Charles, P ... 260-422-5561 167 F cpcercone@indiantech.edu
CERCONE, Suzanne ...... 570-504-7954 422 G cercones@lackawanna.edu
CERES, Joanne, T .... 252-493-7208 364 H jceres@email.pittcc.edu
CERES, Sharon .... 252-493-7561 364 H sceres@email.pittcc.edu
CEREZO, Juan, E .... 718-862-7328 331 H juan.cerezo@manhattan.edu
CERILLI, Annette .... 401-232-6323 441 B acerilli@bryant.edu
CERINO, Michael, H ..... 864-488-4564 447 F mcerino@limestone.edu
CERIO, Thea .... 508-541-1565 225 G tcerio@dean.edu
CERMAK, Michael .... 630-466-7900 162 K mcermak@waubonsee.edu
CERNERO, Mark .... 215-574-9600 421 A mcernero@hussianart.edu
CERNETIC, Jeanette .... 602-243-8127.. 15 F jeanette.cernetic@southmountaincc.edu
CERNOCH, Darleen .... 757-499-5447 507 I
CERNOCH, Jeff .... 281-756-3539 467 D jcernoch@alvincollege.edu
CERNY, Glenn .... 734-462-4400 250 A gcerny@schoolcraft.edu
CERRENTANO, Cynthia . 312-553-5896 141 N ccerrentano@ccc.edu
CERSLEY, Tracy .... 434-961-5211 516 F tcersley@pvcc.edu
CERTA, Len .... 914-923-2847 337 I lcerta@pace.edu
CERULLO, Ralph .... 631-244-3101 324 C cerullor@dowling.edu
CERVANTES, Augustin ... 408-273-2751.. 55 G acervantes@nhu.edu
CERVANTES, George ..... 202-495-3828.. 96 E advance@dhs.edu
CERVANTES, Juana .... 915-779-8031 496 G jcervantes@computercareercenter.com
CERVANTES, Lynda .... 915-532-3737 497 D lcervantes@westerntech.edu
CERVANTES, Margaret ... 432-264-5009 475 E mcervantes@howardcollege.edu
CERVANTES, Mike .... 361-592-9335 486 A mike.cervantes@tamuk.edu
CERVANTES, Rafael .... 651-690-6857 263 V rcervantes@stkate.edu
CERVANTES, Richard ..... 575-835-5675 311 I rcervantes@admin.nmt.edu
CERVASIO, Nancy .... 858-513-9240.. 29 A nancy.cervasio@ashford.edu
CERVELLI, Janice, A ..... 520-621-6751.. 18 E jcervell@email.arizona.edu
CERVENKA, Mark .... 713-221-8043 491 F cervenkam@uhd.edu
CERVENY, Terri, A .... 518-388-6180 350 K cervenyt@union.edu
CERVINI, John .... 517-607-2670 243 J jcervini@hillsdale.edu
CERVONKA, Daniel .... 203-576-2400.. 92 B cervonka@bridgeport.edu
CERZA, Donna .... 570-208-5868 422 D donnacerza@kings.edu
CESAR, Aisha .... 718-261-5800 316 K acesar@bramsonort.edu
CESARANO, Betty .... 505-473-6117 313 B betty.cesarano@santafeuniversity.edu
CESAREO, Francesco, C .... 508-767-7321 222 D fcesareo@assumption.edu
CESARINI, Paola .... 617-373-2333 235 D
CESARIO, David, R .... 617-287-6200 228 G david.cesario@umb.edu
CESCA, Michele .... 657-278-4869.. 33 E mcesca@fullerton.edu
CESELSKI, Teresa .... 660-831-4139 279 D ceselskit@moval.edu
CESMEBASI, Erol .... 201-216-5576 308 D ecesmeba@stevens.edu
CESSNA, Tammy .... 859-858-2306 192 O
CESTERO, Nicolle, M .... 413-205-3800 221 G nicolle.cestero@aic.edu
CESTEROS, Vilmaris ...... 787-894-2828 558 F vilmaris.cesteros@upr.edu
CESTONE, Amy .... 302-292-6100.. 96 H
CETTIN, Matthew .... 814-732-1304 430 G mcettin@edinboro.edu
CEVALLOS, F. Javier ..... 508-626-4575 230 A jcevallos@framingham.edu
CEZAR, Henrique .... 802-635-1297 504 A henrique.cezar@jsc.edu
CHA, Jason .... 805-565-6132.. 76 K jacha@westmont.edu
CHABON, Shelly .... 503-725-3419 409 D chabonr@pdx.edu
CHABOT, Lisabeth .... 607-274-3182 328 H lchabot@ithaca.edu
CHABOT-WIEFERICH, Nicole .... 781-891-2700 223 E nchabotwieferich@bentley.edu
CHABOT-WIEFERICH, Rebecca .... 617-262-5000 223 G Rebecca.Chabot-Wieferich@the-bac.edu
CHACIN, Meredith .... 817-274-4284 469 E mchacin@bhcarroll.edu
CHACKO, Abraham .... 408-498-5123.. 40 E achacko@cogswell.edu
CHACONA, Julie, A .... 814-732-1779 430 G jchacona@edinboro.edu
CHACONIS, Alexis .... 718-260-5250 320 D achaconis@citytech.cuny.edu
CHADEN, Caryn .... 312-362-8885 143 G cchaden@depaul.edu
CHADI, Diana .... 212-960-5274 353 P diana.chadi@yu.edu
CHADWELL, Faye .... 541-737-3411 408 F faye.chadwell@oregonstate.edu
CHADWICK, Becky, J .... 313-317-1534 243 I bchadwick@hfcc.edu
CHADWICK, Cameron ... 212-349-4330 326 G coachchadwick@globe.edu
CHADWICK, Eileen, P ... 845-471-3348 314 F chadwick@adelphi.edu
CHADWICK, Gregory ..... 252-737-7030 369 E chadwickg@ecu.edu
CHADWICK, Jennifer ..... 706-867-2760 133 A jennifer.chadwick@ung.edu
CHADWICK, Scott .... 513-745-3838 396 B chadwicks@xavier.edu
CHADWICK, Susan .... 909-621-8275.. 65 E susan.chadwick@scrippscollege.edu
CHAE, Eisung .... 213-386-0080.. 54 D
CHAFEE, Julie .... 508-929-8770 230 G jchaffee1@worcester.edu
CHAFFEE, Cynthia .... 312-567-3084 147 E cchaffee@iit.edu
CHAFFEE, Reta .... 603-513-1350 299 C reta.chaffee@granite.edu
CHAFFIN, Jason .... 910-362-7275 360 G jchaffin@cfcc.edu
CHAFIN, Kris, L .... 260-359-4290 167 D kchafin@huntington.edu
CHAFIN-EVANS, Karen, S .... 606-218-5606 201 C karenevans@upike.edu
CHAGNON, William .... 203-857-7000.. 89 H
CHAGNON-BURKE, Veronique .... 212-355-1501 318 A vchagnon-burke@christies.edu
CHAHIN, T. Jaime .... 512-245-3333 489 C tc03@txstate.edu
CHAI, Lin .... 407-888-8689 103 M lchai@fcim.edu
CHAIRES-LACEY, Jackie 850-201-8510 117 B chairesj@tcc.fl.edu
CHAIREZ, Gladys .... 575-527-7664 312 D gchairez@nmsu.edu
CHAIRSELL, Christine ... 971-722-4005 409 C christine.chairsell@pcc.edu
CHAKA, Wendi .... 508-999-8711 228 H wchaka@umassd.edu
CHAKRABORTY, Dave ... 701-777-6812 373 G dave.chakraborty@und.edu
CHAKRIN, Lewis .... 201-684-7377 305 F lchakrin@ramapo.edu
CHALENBURG, Mike ...... 501-279-4041.. 21 A chalenburg@harding.edu
CHALEUNPHONH, Seuth .... 812-941-2319 169 A schaleun@ius.edu
CHALFONTE, Barb .... 413-755-4465 233 B blchalfonte@stcc.edu

CHALK, Gregg .... 508-541-1668 225 G
gchalk@dean.edu
CHALKER, Peggy .... 937-695-0751 391 F
pchalker@sscc.edu
CHALLENGER, Susan .... 781-283-2335 237 F
schallen@wellesley.edu
CHALLY, Pam .... 904-620-2810 116 A
pchally@unf.edu
CHALMERS, John .... 516-463-5791 328 A
john.chalmers@hofstra.edu
CHALMERS, Scott .... 773-256-0727 151 H
schalmer@lstc.edu
CHALMIERS, Harry .... 651-361-3441 257 B
harry.chalmiers@mcnallysmith.edu
CHALOUX, Matthew, P . 561-237-7699 108 E
mchaloux@lynn.edu
CHALOVICH, Cindy .... 561-912-1211 102 N
cchalovich@evergladesuniversity.edu
CHALTRON, Bonnie .... 231-843-5985 252 H
bchaltron@westshore.edu
CHALUPA, Leo, M .... 202-994-7315.. 95 D
lmchalupa@gwu.edu
CHALUPKA, Stephanie .. 508-929-8680 230 G
schalupka@worcester.edu
CHALYKOFF, John .... 203-396-8084.. 91 G
chalykoffj@sacredheart.edu
CHAMANDY, Susan ...... 617-730-7157 235 B
susan.chamandy@newbury.edu
CHAMBERAS, Peter .... 617-850-1237 227 F
frpac@metrocast.net
CHAMBERLAIN,
Dennis, R .... 678-359-5056 126 E
dennisc@gordonstate.edu
CHAMBERLAIN,
Enrique .... 972-273-3405 473 A
echamberlain@dcccd.edu
CHAMBERLAIN, Harvey 314-264-1000 284 J
harvey.chamberlain@vatterott.edu
CHAMBERLAIN, Katia ... 561-912-2166 102 N
kchamberlain@evergladesuniversity.edu
CHAMBERLAIN,
LaShanda .... 228-497-7630 268 G
lashanda.chamberlain@mgccc.edu
CHAMBERLAIN,
Mary Ellen, M .... 518-327-6220 338 B
mchamberlain@paulsmiths.edu
CHAMBERLAIN, Nancy . 815-921-4517 157 B
n.chamberlain@rockvalleycollege.edu
CHAMBERLAIN, Tina ..... 206-726-5197 521 G
tchamberlain@cornish.edu
CHAMBERLAND, Greg .. 802-773-5900 501 G
gregory.chamberland@csj.edu
CHAMBERLIN,
Christopher .... 212-353-4099 323 B
c.m.chamberlin@gmail.com
CHAMBERLIN, Heather . 913-253-5084 190 K
heatherc@spst.edu
CHAMBERLIN,
Jonathan .... 704-216-3765 365 F
Jonathan.Chamberlain@rccc.edu
CHAMBERLIN, Lisa .... 509-527-5145 527 H
lisa.chamberlin@wwcc.edu
CHAMBERLIN, Lyn .... 914-395-2218 342 C
lchamberlin@sarahlawrence.edu
CHAMBERLIN, Mona 918-631-2656 403M
mona-chamberlin@utulsa.edu
CHAMBERLIN, Paul, D . 603-862-2650 299 B
paul.chamberlin@unh.edu
CHAMBERS, Andy .... 314-392-2211 278 G
chambers@mobap.edu
CHAMBERS, Anthony .... 407-277-0311 102 N
achambers@evergladesuniversity.edu
CHAMBERS, Daniel, P .. 607-436-2491 344 B
daniel.cambers@oneonta.edu
CHAMBERS, Diane, M .. 330-471-8183 385 G
dchambers@malone.edu
CHAMBERS, Donna .... 405-382-9950 402 C
d.chambers@sscok.edu
CHAMBERS,
Franklin, D .... 607-436-2513 344 B
franklin.chambers@oneonta.edu
CHAMBERS, Jason .... 828-835-4297 366 F
jchambers@tricountycc.edu
CHAMBERS, Jessica, A . 240-500-2000 215 C
jachambers@hagerstowncc.edu
CHAMBERS, Kathleen ... 413-796-2080 238 A
kathleen.chambers@wne.edu
CHAMBERS, Kemba ...... 256-306-2846.... 2 F
kkc@calhoun.edu
CHAMBERS, Larry .... 518-276-6000 339 D
chamb@rpi.edu
CHAMBERS, Martha ...... 865-471-4351 455 G
mchambers@cn.edu
CHAMBERS, Melody ..... 660-785-4114 283 E
mchamber@truman.edu
CHAMBERS, Mike .... 912-478-1566 126 B
mchambers@georgiasouthern.edu
CHAMBERS, Phyllis, P . 336-272-7102 357 B
phyllis.chambers@greensboro.edu
CHAMBERS, Robert .... 617-369-3614 236 E
rchambers@smfa.edu
CHAMBERS, Steve .... 575-624-7411 310 J
steve.chambers@roswell.enmu.edu
CHAMBERS, Thomas, A 716-286-8352 336 E
chambers@niagara.edu
CHAMBLEE, Marquita ... 313-577-2003 252 G
fx1598@wayne.edu
CHAMBLEE, Tim .... 662-325-3920 269 A
t.chamblee@msstate.edu
CHAMBLIN, Cheryl, L ... 217-424-6293 153 A
cchamblin@millikin.edu
CHAMBLISS, Mary .... 256-233-8161.... 1 F
mary.chambliss@athens.edu
CHAMLEE-WRIGHT,
Emily .... 410-778-7202 221 D
echamleewright2@washcoll.edu
CHAMPA, Kristin .... 765-658-4863 165 G
kristinchampa@depauw.edu
CHAMPAGNE, Gerald .... 734-462-4400 250 A
gchampag@schoolcraft.edu
CHAMPAGNE, Keith, M 509-963-1515 520 E
champagn@cwu.edu
CHAMPAGNE, Michael .. 225-752-4233 202 I
mchampagne@iticollege.edu
CHAMPAGNE,
Ronald, O .... 607-735-1790 324 J
rchampagne@elmira.edu
CHAMPEAUX, Alison .... 218-723-7016 255 A
achampea@css.edu
CHAMPION, Jason .... 918-293-5342 400 E
jason.champion@okstate.edu
CHAMPION, John, E ..... 336-841-9196 357 E
jchampion@highpoint.edu
CHAMPION, Laura .... 616-526-6678 240 L
ldc4@calvin.edu
CHAMPION, Thomas .... 415-749-4528.. 62 I
tchampion@sfai.edu
CHAMPOLI, John .... 802-287-2150 501 I
champolij@greenmtn.edu
CHAMRA, Louay, M ..... 248-370-2217 248 K
chamra@oakland.edu
CHAN, Andy .... 336-758-4662 372 G
achan@wfu.edu
CHAN, Bill .... 614-947-6054 382 H
bill.chan@franklin.edu
CHAN, Caleb, K .... 517-750-1200 250 F
cchan@arbor.edu
CHAN, Chuen .... 510-464-3221.. 59 B
cchan@peralta.edu
CHAN, Claudia .... 718-482-5005 320 B
ClChan@lagcc.cuny.edu
CHAN, Emily .... 719-389-6679.. 79M
echan@coloradocollege.edu
CHAN, Eva .... 718-270-6487 320 C
echan@mec.cuny.edu
CHAN, Gilen .... 718-260-4981 320 D
gchan@citytech.cuny.edu
CHAN, Joe .... 312-281-3279 157 E
jchan@roosevelt.edu
CHAN, Kai-Chang .... 210-509-8080 487 B
international@thsu.edu
CHAN, Kara .... 412-521-6200 434 C
kara.chan@rosedaletech.org
CHAN, Michael, L .... 671-735-5573 549 E
michael.chan@guamcc.edu
CHAN, Paul, H .... 303-871-4646.. 86 H
phchan@du.edu
CHAN, Regina .... 212-517-0501 332 A
rchan@mmm.edu
CHANAY, Marcus .... 903-730-4890 476 L
mchanay@jarvis.edu
CHANCE, Bill .... 207-221-4373 213 B
wchance@une.edu
CHANCE, Carla .... 513-569-4755 379 K
carla.chance@cincinnatistate.edu
CHANCE, Chelsea .... 318-797-5364 205 F
chelsea.chance@lsus.edu
CHANCE, Katie .... 256-551-5214.... 4 J
katie.chance@drakestate.edu
CHANCE, Kenneth, B .... 216-368-3266 378 J
kenneth.b.chance@case.edu
CHANCE, Steve, L .... 806-371-5161 467 E
slchance@actx.edu
CHANCEY, Christine ..... 828-398-2556 368 I
cchancey@southcollegenc.edu
CHANCEY, Danny .... 251-442-2491.... 9 B
dbchancey@umobile.edu
CHANCEY, Debra, H ..... 251-442-2332.... 9 B
dchancey@umobile.edu
CHANCEY, Janna, L ...... 903-510-2298 491 A
jcha@tjc.edu
CHANDI, Balbir .... 661-362-5416.. 40 H
balbir.chandi@canyons.edu
CHANDLER, Brandon .... 856-225-6473 307 A
brandonc@rutgers.edu
CHANDLER, Chris .... 540-365-4287 507 H
cchandler@ferrum.edu
CHANDLER, Cullen, J ... 570-321-4173 425 B
chandler@lycoming.edu
CHANDLER, Derrall .... 619-388-3537.. 62 F
dchandler@sdccd.edu
CHANDLER, G. Thomas 803-777-5032 450 B
tchandler@sc.edu
CHANDLER, Jacob .... 936-294-3160 489 A
ucs_jrc@shsu.edu
CHANDLER, John, M .... 319-399-8622 176 G
jchandle@coe.edu
CHANDLER, Kim .... 651-696-6366 256 L
kchandle@macalester.edu
CHANDLER, Kirk .... 336-334-4822 363 A
kdchandler@gtcc.edu
CHANDLER, Legail, P ... 314-362-4930 285 E
legail_chandler@wustl.edu
CHANDLER, Linda .... 910-695-3961 365 H
chandlerl@sandhills.edu
CHANDLER, Luanne ...... 701-349-5793 375 G
lchandler@trinitybiblecollege.edu
CHANDLER, Maria .... 803-641-3317 450 C
mariac@usca.edu
CHANDLER, Marissa ..... 931-221-6424 461 C
chandlerm@apsu.edu
CHANDLER, Mary .... 315-445-4300 330 B
richermm@lemoyne.edu
CHANDLER, Norma .... 602-787-7073.. 15 B
norma.chandler@paradisevalley.edu
CHANDLER, Rebecca .... 310-338-2723.. 53 C
rchandler@lmu.edu
CHANDLER, Roger .... 251-575-8277.... 1 C
rchandler@ascc.edu
CHANDLER, Roger .... 303-963-3341.. 79 L
rchandler@ccu.edu
CHANDLER, Sabrina, J . 914-606-6880 352 G
sabrina.johnson.chandler@sunywcc.edu
CHANDLER, Shelly .... 352-638-9710.. 99 D
schandler@beaconcollege.edu
CHANDLER, Stephen .... 701-349-5959 375 G
schandler@trinitybiblecollege.edu
CHANDLER, Timothy ..... 410-704-2356 221 A
provost@towson.edu
CHANDO, Kristen .... 610-499-4142 439 G
kmchando@widener.edu
CHANDO, Michael .... 856-415-2282 306 C
mchando@rcgc.edu
CHANEY, Bill .... 425-739-8119 523 I
bill.chaney@lwtech.edu
CHANEY, C. Steven ...... 916-348-4689.. 43 K
stevec@chaneyassociates.com
CHANEY, Carmela .... 323-856-7698.. 27 H
cchaney@afi.com
CHANEY, Jayn .... 641-269-3200 178 I
chaneyj@grinnell.edu
CHANEY, Joyce .... 304-766-5224 533 C
jchaney@wvstateu.edu
CHANEY, Kevin .... 740-392-6868 387 B
kevin.chaney@mvnu.edu
CHANEY, Marietta .... 304-647-6400 533 B
mchaney@osteo.wvsom.edu
CHANEY, Matthew .... 231-591-2617 242 L
MatthewChaney@ferris.edu
CHANEY, Rob .... 850-201-6085 117 B
chaneyr@tcc.fl.edu
CHANEY, Steve .... 602-944-3335.. 11 D
schaney@aicag.edu
CHANEY, Steve .... 916-367-4786.. 62 D
steve.chaney@sdcc.edu
CHANG, Caroline .... 408-554-5360.. 65 A
cschang@scu.edu
CHANG, Chaw-ye .... 610-436-3043 432 B
cchang@wcupa.edu
CHANG, Christopher ..... 845-687-5096 350 I
changc@sunyulster.edu
CHANG, Cindy .... 818-719-6425.. 51 H
changck@piercecollege.edu
CHANG, Eun-Woo .... 609-586-4800 303 D
change@mccc.edu
CHANG, George .... 908-737-3600 303 C
gchang@kean.edu
CHANG, Gilbert .... 239-513-1135 119 C
gchang@wolford.edu
CHANG, Jerry .... 808-932-7339 135 I
jerry7@hawaii.edu
CHANG, Jimmy .... 727-341-4305 112 A
chang.jimmy@spcollege.edu
CHANG, Ken .... 212-226-7300 338 F
kchang@pbcny.edu
CHANG, Lay, N .... 540-231-5422 518 B
laynam@vt.edu
CHANG, Lillian .... 808-373-2849 137 C
dr.chang@wmi.edu
CHANG, Ling Ling .... 516-739-1545 335 C
library@nyctcm.edu
CHANG, Ly .... 425-235-2352 525 G
lchang@rtc.edu
CHANG, Mari .... 808-934-2526 136 D
changm@hawaii.edu
CHANG, Nancy, H .... 817-515-5222 484 B
nancy.chang@tccd.edu
CHANG, Peter, M .... 703-333-5904 519 B
CHANG, Sheng-Chung . 626-571-5110.. 50 J
shengchung@les.edu
CHANG, Shi-Kuo .... 847-679-3135 149 F
changsk@ksi.edu
CHANG, Tim .... 323-259-2531.. 56 I
tchang@oxy.edu
CHANG, Wendy .... 305-237-0244 108 L
wchang1@mdc.edu
CHANG, Young Ihl .... 770-279-0507 124 F
yichang@gcuniv.edu
CHANGNON, Susan, J .. 724-287-8711 413 G
susan.changnon@bc3.edu
CHANITZ, Shelly .... 636-227-2100 277 A
shelly.chanitz@logan.edu
CHANLER, Annette .... 318-371-3035 204 A
annettechanler@nwltc.edu
CHANNICK, Susan, A ... 619-239-0391.. 36 E
sac@cwsl.edu
CHANNING, Jill .... 815-802-8702 149 B
jchanning@kcc.edu
CHAO, Gloria .... 212-220-8304 318 D
gchao@bmcc.cuny.edu
CHAO, Xia .... 406-657-1705 287 H
xia.chao@msubillings.edu
CHAO-BUSHOVEN,
Karin .... 559-453-2058.. 45 E
karin.chao-bushoven@fresno.edu
CHAPA, Paul .... 210-999-8328 490 E
Paul.Chapa@trinity.edu
CHAPARRO, Luis .... 915-831-2132 473 J
lchapa13@epcc.edu
CHAPDELAINE,
Andrea, E .... 301-696-3855 215 E
chapdelaine@hood.edu
CHAPDELAINE, Karen ... 772-462-7465 106 F
kchapdel@irsc.edu
CHAPIN, Frank .... 513-875-3344 379 G
frank.chapin@chatfield.edu
CHAPIN, John .... 727-394-6995 112 A
chapin.john@spcollege.edu
CHAPIN, Wesley .... 715-425-0629 540 E
wes.chapin@uwrf.edu
CHAPMAN, Alisa .... 919-962-1000 369 C
chapman@northcarolina.edu
CHAPMAN, Ana .... 201-360-4244 303 A
achapman@hccc.edu
CHAPMAN, Ana .... 201-360-4242 303 A
achapman@hccc.edu
CHAPMAN, Angela .... 860-515-3880.. 88 B
achapman@charteroak.edu
CHAPMAN, Angela .... 860-515-3889.. 88 B
achapman@charteroak.edu
CHAPMAN, April .... 707-836-2904.. 65 C
achapman@santarosa.edu
CHAPMAN, Brenda, J ... 404-413-3505 126 D
bchapman@gsu.edu
CHAPMAN, Brian Keith . 678-891-3337 125 G
brian.chapman@gpc.edu
CHAPMAN, Bryce .... 314-744-7631 278 G
chapmanb@mobap.edu
CHAPMAN, D. Duane .... 304-462-6401 532 G
donald.chapman@glenville.edu
CHAPMAN, Dale, T .... 618-468-2001 150 E
dchapman@lc.edu
CHAPMAN, Dana, L .... 904-256-7682 106 Q
dchapma@ju.edu
CHAPMAN, David, W .... 205-726-2771.... 6 F
dwchapma@samford.edu
CHAPMAN, Elaine .... 626-585-7608.. 58 F
efchapman@pasadena.edu
CHAPMAN, J. Quincy .... 715-836-3630 539 E
chapmajq@uwec.edu
CHAPMAN, Katrina .... 651-638-6043 254 A
k-chapman@bethel.edu
CHAPMAN, Kendall, P .. 601-643-8364 266 J
ken.chapman@colin.edu
CHAPMAN, Lenora .... 210-458-4071 494 D
lenora.chapman@utsa.edu
CHAPMAN, Linda .... 618-468-4000 150 E
lchapman@lc.edu
CHAPMAN, Lisa 919-807-7096 359M
CHAPMAN, Matt .... 707-668-5663.. 42 K
CHAPMAN, Merv .... 816-414-3700 278 E
mchapman@mbts.edu
CHAPMAN, Michelle ...... 404-756-4054 120 H
mchapman@atlm.edu
CHAPMAN, Richard, L .. 615-898-2988 461 E
richard.chapman@mtsu.edu
CHAPMAN, Richard, N . 843-661-1281 446 E
rchapman@fmarion.edu
CHAPMAN, Robbin .... 781-283-3511 237 F
rchapman@wellesley.edu
CHAPMAN, Ronald, K ... 801-422-8157 497 J
ron_chapman@byu.edu
CHAPMAN, Sharon, H .. 803-938-3810 450 H
hamptons@uscsumter.edu
CHAPMAN, Steve, J ..... 330-569-6107 383 F
chapmansj@hiran.edu
CHAPMAN, Tasha .... 314-434-4044 273 J
tasha.chapman@covenantseminary.edu
CHAPMAN, Tim .... 785-628-5620 187 A
tdchapman@fhsu.edu

CHENEY, Richard 401-232-6707 441 B
rcheney@bryant.edu
CHENEY, Victor 904-819-6213 102 P
vcheney@flagler.edu
CHENG, Alex 662-915-7407 270 G
acheng@olemiss.edu
CHENG, Kevin 408-435-8989.. 66 F
CHENG, Rita 928-523-3232.. 16 C
Rita.Cheng@nau.edu
CHENG, Terence 718-951-5771 318 F
tcheng@brooklyn.cuny.edu
CHENG, Wayne 714-533-1495.. 67 A
waynecheng@southbaylo.edu
CHENG, Yan 954-763-9840.. 98 L
dean@atom.edu
CHENG-LEVINE, Jia-Yi .. 661-362-5806.. 40 H
jia-yi.cheng-levine@canyons.edu
CHENOWETH,
Candace, A 262-472-1592 541 D
chenowec@uww.edu
CHENOWETH, Gregg, A 574-807-7210 164 F
gregg.chenoweth@bethelcollege.edu
CHENOWETH, John 262-472-1592 541 D
chenowej@uww.edu
CHEONG-CHOO, Tae 703-323-5690 518 G
CHERAGHI, S. Hossein 413-782-1272 238 A
cheraghi@wne.edu
CHERENEGAR, Jessica .. 605-331-6671 454 E
jessica.cherenegar@usiouxfalls.edu
CHEREWICK, Daniel, P . 248-341-2011 248 E
dpcherew@oaklandcc.edu
CHERLAND, Ryan, M .... 949-824-4521.. 71 C
ryan.cherland@uci.edu
CHERMAK, Heather, A .. 208-885-2020 139 C
hchermak@uidaho.edu
CHERMONTE, Debra, J . 440-775-8411 388 B
debra.chermonte@oberlin.edu
CHERN, James 973-746-2323 304 A
chernj@mail.montclair.edu
CHERNOW, Barbara, D . 401-863-9400 441 A
barbara_chernow@brown.edu
CHERONES, Stacy 214-379-5598 480 D
scherones@pqc.edu
CHERRIN, Bruce, E 505-277-1740 313 H
cherrin@unm.edu
CHERRY, Brian 906-227-1823 248 B
bcherry@nmu.edu
CHERRY, Christopher ... 715-394-8580 541 C
rcherry@uwsuper.edu
CHERRY, Elizabeth 206-543-2100 527 G
CHERRY, Evonne 254-647-3234 480 G
echerry@rangercollege.edu
CHERRY, Jennifer 252-789-0316 363 H
jcherry@martincc.edu
CHERRY, Jewel, B 336-734-7297 362 F
jcherry@forsythtech.edu
CHERRY, Luke 661-362-2603.. 53 F
lcherry@masters.edu
CHERRY, Mark 321-433-7031 101 O
cherrym@easternflorida.edu
CHERRY, Michelle 305-809-3237 104 A
michelle.cherry@fkcc.edu
CHERRY, Norman 252-794-4861 363 H
ncherry@martincc.edu
CHERRY, Paul 501-205-8805.. 20 G
pcherry@cbc.edu
CHERRY, Shirley 870-575-8461.. 24 D
cherrys@uapb.edu
CHERRY, Stephanie 319-296-2320 179 B
stephanie.cherry@hawkeyecollege.edu
CHERRY-BECK, Kim 828-227-7170 372 C
kcherry@wcu.edu
CHERSILS, Matchez 813-889-3427 112 E
mchersils@sbtampa.com
CHERUBIN, Daniel 212-772-4161 319 E
dcherubi@hunter.cuny.edu
CHERUBINI, Angela 914-395-2567 342 C
acherubini@sarahlawrence.edu
CHERUBINO, Thomas ... 908-709-7546 309 A
cherubino@ucc.edu
CHESBRO, Steven, B 334-229-5053.... 1 D
schesbro@alasu.edu
CHESBROUGH, Ronald . 636-922-8380 281 C
rchesbrough@stchas.edu
CHESHIRE, Hall 540-654-1379 513 I
hcheshir@umw.edu
CHESLER, Barbara 973-618-3212 300 H
bchesler@caldwell.edu
CHESLEY, Laurie 616-234-3920 243 D
lchesley@grcc.edu
CHESNEY, Linda, H 718-262-5119 321 B
chesney@york.cuny.edu
CHESNEY, Scott 603-862-1870 299 B
scott.chesney@unh.edu
CHESNEY, Thom, D 972-860-4809 472 C
CHESNUT, Renae 515-271-1814 177 K
renae.chesnut@drake.edu
CHESNUT, Robert, W .... 217-581-2125 144 E
rwchesnut@eiu.edu
CHESS, Mary Kay 206-780-6213 525 F
marykay.chess@pinchot.edu

CHESSER, Ron 501-760-4230.. 21 H
rchesser@npcc.edu
CHESTER, Ann, L 304-293-1026 533 D
achester@hsc.wvu.edu
CHESTER, Brandi 870-248-4000.. 20 E
brandic@blackrivertech.edu
CHESTER, Cathie 914-251-5976 346 D
cathie.chester@purchase.edu
CHESTER, Rosalind 504-394-7744 206 E
rchester@olhcc.edu
CHESTER, Steven 860-343-5864.. 89 E
schester@mxcc.commnet.edu
CHESTER, Thomas, P ... 609-652-4384 308 E
thomas.chester@stockton.edu
CHESTER, Timothy, M .. 706-542-3145 132 H
tchester@uga.edu
CHESTNUT, SR.,
Coley, C 334-874-5700.... 3 B
cchestnut@ccal.edu
CHESTNUT, Emmanuel .. 757-822-1421 517 C
echestnut@tcc.edu
CHEU, Susan 408-864-8976.. 44 N
CHEU, Susan 408-848-4739.. 45 G
scheu@gavilan.edu
CHEUNG, Alvin 916-686-8883.. 32 B
CHEUNG, Ashley 513-305-9626 190 K
ashleyncheung@gmail.com
CHEUNG, Enos 718-939-5100 330 E
echeung@libi.edu
CHEVALIER, Jason 909-652-6904.. 38 A
CHEVALIER, JR.,
Joseph 404-756-5773 129 A
jchevalier@msm.edu
CHEVES, Brad, E 214-768-2667 482 J
bcheves@smu.edu
CHEVRETTE, II,
Joseph, M 315-733-2300 351 E
jchevrette@uscny.edu
CHEW, Elaine 254-968-9611 485 A
chew@tarleton.edu
CHEW, Kenneth 812-237-3939 167 E
kenneth.chew@indstate.edu
CHEW, Roy 937-395-8688 385 A
roy.chew@khnetwork.org
CHEW, Thomas 585-389-2884 334 B
tchew3@naz.edu
CHEZUM, Kelly, O 315-268-4483 321 C
chezumk@clarkson.edu
CHI, Selina 323-265-8154.. 51 D
chiss@elac.edu
CHI, Wenjun 610-660-1000 434 G
CHIA, Samuel 214-887-5121 473 E
schia@dts.edu
CHIACCHIERINI, Chris .. 503-253-3443 408 B
cc@ocom.edu
CHIANG, Amber 661-395-4251.. 49 E
amchiang@bakersfieldcollege.edu
CHIANG, Stacy 510-485-7836.. 58 G
schiang@patten.edu
CHIAPPETTA, Anthony .. 202-319-5623.. 95 A
chiappetta@cua.edu
CHIAPPINI, Thomas, A . 330-494-6170 391 J
tchiappini@starkstate.edu
CHIARA, Mary Jo, B .... 718-940-5574 341 A
mchiara@sjcny.edu
CHIARELLA, Stephanie .. 802-831-1237 503 E
schiarella@vermontlaw.edu
CHIAVELLI, James 978-837-5509 233 G
Chiavellij@merrimack.edu
CHICARELLI, Morgan 503-552-1602 407 F
mchicarelli@ncnm.edu
CHICHESTER, Susan, E . 585-245-5577 345 D
sue@geneseo.edu
CHICK, Brian 603-206-8158 297 A
bchick@ccsnh.edu
CHICKERING,
F. William 609-896-5111 306 A
wchickering@rider.edu
CHICO HURST, Karen ... 518-442-5540 343 C
chicohurst@albany.edu
CHICOINE, David, L 605-688-4111 454 C
david.chicoine@sdstate.edu
CHIDDICK, Troy 610-527-0200 434 D
tchiddick@rosemont.edu
CHIDIAC, George 626-585-7424.. 58 F
gchidiac@pasadena.edu
CHIELLI, Jack, A 570-408-4770 440 B
jack.chielli@wilkes.edu
CHIEN, Walter 319-363-1323 181 D
wchien@mtmercy.edu
CHIEVES, Kevin 912-443-5491 131 B
kchieves@savannahtech.edu
CHIGAWA, Steven 808-235-7457 137 A
chigawa@hawaii.edu
CHIGAZOLA, Deborah ... 707-527-4525.. 65 C
dchigazola@santarosa.edu
CHIGOS, Lisa 619-961-4326.. 69 J
lchigos@tjsl.edu
CHIH, Lo-Li 808-974-7595 135 I
loli@hawaii.edu

CHIKELEGE, Michael 870-864-7147.. 23 B
mchikelege@southark.edu
CHIKUNI, Ticha 859-336-5082 199 B
ticha.chikuni@sccky.edu
CHIKWINYA, Mary 253-566-5127 527 C
mchikwinya@tacomacc.edu
CHILCOAT, Cynthia, A .. 928-523-6120.. 16 C
Cindy.Chilcoat@nau.edu
CHILCOTE, Paul 419-289-5771 377 A
pchilcot@ashland.edu
CHILDERS, Amber 501-337-5000.. 20 H
amber@coto.edu
CHILDERS, Camille 316-978-3620 192 D
camille.childers@wichita.edu
CHILDERS, Henry, A 520-626-6779.. 18 E
hankc@email.arizona.edu
CHILDERS, Jana 415-451-2859.. 63 B
jchilders@sfts.edu
CHILDERS, Joseph 951-827-4302.. 72 A
joseph.childers@ucr.edu
CHILDERS, Karen 909-384-8987.. 62 C
kchilder@sbccd.cc.ca.us
CHILDERS, Mark 254-710-4619 469 D
Mark_Childers@baylor.edu
CHILDERS, Sharon 828-565-4094 363 C
shchilders@haywood.edu
CHILDERS, JR.,
William, A 304-336-5100 533 A
bill.childers@westliberty.edu
CHILDRES, Donna 706-236-1714 121 E
dchildres@berry.edu
CHILDRESS, Amanda 256-840-4210.... 7 B
achildress@snead.edu
CHILDRESS, Bates 802-773-5900 501 G
bates.childress@csj.edu
CHILDRESS, Jamie 919-718-7239 361 C
jchildress@cccc.edu
CHILDREY, Cynthia, A .. 928-523-6802.. 16 C
Cynthia.Childrey@nau.edu
CHILDREY, Lauren, T ... 336-272-7102 357 B
lauren.childrey@greensboro.edu
CHILDS, Brittany 903-566-7444 494 E
bchilds@uttyler.edu
CHILDS, Cindy, D 301-322-0014 217 G
childscd@pgcc.edu
CHILDS, David, E 304-877-6428 529 G
david.childs@abc.edu
CHILDS, Dee 256-824-2555.... 9 A
dee.childs@uah.edu
CHILDS, K. Paige 864-941-8688 448 D
childs.p@ptc.edu
CHILDS, Kimberly, M ... 936-468-2805 484 A
kchilds@sfasu.edu
CHILDS, Linda, J 304-877-6428 529 G
linda.childs@abc.edu
CHILDS, Liz 801-863-8460 500 B
childsli@uvu.edu
CHILDS, Nicole 919-381-6925 369 B
nchilds@umo.edu
CHILDS, Paige 864-941-8688 448 D
childs.p@ptc.edu
CHILDS, Richard, G 410-864-4274 218 C
rchilds@stmarys.edu
CHILDS, Sidney 419-372-2677 377 I
sidneyc@bgsu.edu
CHILDS, Sidney 419-372-2156 377 I
sidneyc@bgsu.edu
CHILES, Kristie 702-579-3548 294 P
kchiles@kaplan.edu
CHILES, Rebecca 503-838-8481 411 B
chilesr@wou.edu
CHILES, Thomas 617-552-6840 224 B
thomas.chiles@bc.edu
CHILICKI, Stacy 207-216-4312 211 F
schilicki@yccc.edu
CHILLO, Joseph, L 617-730-7035 235 B
joseph.chillo@newbury.edu
CHILSTRON, Brian 714-662-4402.. 57 D
bchilstron@pacific-college.edu
CHILTON, Bette 815-825-2086 149 E
bette.chilton@kishwaukeecollege.edu
CHIMENTI, Vito, R 215-670-9297 428 A
vrchimenti@peirce.edu
CHIMERA, Anthony 312-662-4031 139 E
achimera@adler.edu
CHIMIENTI, Sonia 508-856-2300 229 B
Sonia.Chimienti@Umassmemorial.org
CHIN, Deborah 203-932-7020.. 92 G
dchin@newhaven.edu
CHIN, Elaine 408-924-3601.. 36 B
elaine.chin@sjsu.edu
CHIN, Jean, E 706-542-8715 132 H
jchin@uhs.uga.edu
CHIN, Jim 559-674-4812.. 69 C
jim.chin@reedleycollege.edu
CHIN, Julie 818-299-5500.. 75 K
jChin@westcoastuniversity.edu
CHIN, Penny, J 516-876-3137 345 E
chinp@oldwestbury.edu
CHIN, Qi 219-473-4375 165 A

CHIN, Sonia 619-849-2958.. 59 K
soniachin@pointloma.edu
CHINCHILLA, Gladys .... 312-939-4975 145 G
gchinchilla@harrington.edu
CHINETTI, Peter 617-964-1100 222 B
pchinetti@ants.edu
CHING, Doris 808-689-2300 136 A
dching@hawaii.edu
CHING, Warren 691-320-2480 549 D
chiefsecurity@comfsm.fm
CHINNIAH, Nim, S 847-491-5534 155 D
nim.chinniah@northwestern.edu
CHINNICI, OFM,
Joseph 760-547-1800.. 45 B
jchinnici@fst.edu
CHINNOCK PETROSKI,
Mary, J 308-865-8655 293 G
petroskimj@unk.edu
CHINWAH, Lovette 937-376-6631 379 D
lchinwah@centralstate.edu
CHINWAH, Lovette 937-376-6210 379 D
lchinwah@centralstate.edu
CHIPMAN, Daniel 434-832-7635 515 A
chipmand@cvcc.vccs.edu
CHIPMAN, Nelson 412-392-4306 433 F
nchipman@pointpark.edu
CHIPMAN, Stephanie .... 217-245-3030 146 D
stephanie.chipman@mail.ic.edu
CHIPPS, Michael, R 402-844-7054 292 G
michaelc@northeast.edu
CHIQUITO, Yug Fon 626-529-8246.. 57 F
ychiquito@pacificoaks.edu
CHIRICO, Darlene 702-254-7577 296 B
darlene.chirico@northwestcareercollege.edu
CHIRICO, Donna 718-262-2804 321 B
dchirico@york.cuny.edu
CHISEM, Lori 205-929-3409.... 5 E
lchisem@lawsonstate.edu
CHISHOLM, Arnett 734-973-3540 251 J
achisholm@wccnet.edu
CHISHOLM, Barbara 334-727-8535.... 8 B
chisholm@mytu.tuskegee.edu
CHISHOLM,
Brendan, H 508-856-4031 229 B
brendan.chisholm@umassmed.edu
CHISHOLM, Bruce, T 336-322-2146 364 G
Bruce.Chisholm@piedmontcc.edu
CHISHOLM,
Douglas, W 937-766-7992 378 K
chisd@cedarville.edu
CHISHOLM, Pam 802-828-2800 503 H
chisholp@ccv.edu
CHISHOLM, Rex 312-503-3209 155 D
r-chisholm@northwestern.edu
CHISHOLM- BURNS,
Marie, A 901-448-6036 465 G
mchisho3@uthsc.edu
CHISLER, Christi, R 909-869-3805.. 32 F
crchisler@cpp.edu
CHISMAR, William, G ... 808-956-3400 135 J
chismar@hawaii.edu
CHISOLM, Roxanne 662-472-9079 267 E
rchisolm@holmescc.edu
CHISOM, Brian, T 540-375-2592 512 B
chisom@roanoke.edu
CHISUM, Virginia, E 432-335-6415 479 O
vchisum@odessa.edu
CHITRE, Manoj 909-607-9828.. 39 E
manoj.chitre@cgu.edu
CHITWOOD, Ashley 504-671-6603 203 F
achitw@dcc.edu
CHITWOOD, Charles 405-491-6455 402 E
cchitwood@snu.edu
CHITWOOD, James 847-969-4915.. 28 G
jchitwood@argosy.edu
CHIU, Edward 978-934-4814 229 A
Edward_Chiu@uml.edu
CHLAD, Lori 315-228-7411 321 H
lchlad@colgate.edu
CHLIWNIAK, Luba 716-614-6450 336 D
lchliwniak@niagaracc.suny.edu
CHMURA, Michael 781-239-4549 222 E
mchmura@babson.edu
CHMURA, Thomas 617-287-4087 228 E
tchmura@umassp.edu
CHO, Hyun Sung 770-279-0507 124 F
revdrcho@gmail.com
CHO, Karen 808-235-7404 137 A
kcho@hawaii.edu
CHO, Katherine H, S .... 213-413-9500.. 68 A
dean@scusoma.edu
CHO, Keum Ju 770-279-0507 124 F
keumjucho@gmail.com
CHO, Nam Hong 240-447-1664 124 F
akap1997@hotmail.com
CHOATE, Edward 417-836-6616 279 A
edchoate@missouristate.edu
CHOATE, Jim 319-398-7612 180 J
jchoate@kirkwood.edu

CHUNG, Russell ... 614-688-1698 389 A
chung.592@osu.edu
CHUNG, Silvan ... 808-845-9404 136 E
silvan@hawaii.edu
CHUNG, Tony ... 619-594-5211.. 35 E
tchung@mail.sdsu.edu
CHUNG-HOON, Tanise . 801-422-4403 497 J
tanise@byu.edu
CHUNGAG, Godwin ... 856-691-8600 301 H
gchungag@cccnj.edu
CHUNN, Patricia ... 313-831-5200 242 K
pchunn@etseminary.edu
CHUNN, Robert ... 813-253-7260 106 C
rchunn@hccfl.edu
CHUPP, Tim ... 616-222-3000 245 D
tchupp@kuyper.edu
CHURCH, Cathy ... 928-350-4100.. 17 K
cchurch@prescott.edu
CHURCH, Christine ... 517-371-5140 252 J
churchc@cooley.edu
CHURCH, David, B ... 206-281-2602 526 D
dchurch@spu.edu
CHURCH, David, M ... 719-884-5000.. 84 G
DMChurch@nbc.edu
CHURCH, Donna ... 828-726-2211 360 F
dchurch@cccti.edu
CHURCH, Jennifer, H ... 517-264-7143 250 B
jhchurch@sienaheights.edu
CHURCH, Lori ... 843-349-2751 444 G
lchurch@coastal.edu
CHURCH, Marjorie, R ... 336-841-4692 357 E
mchurch@highpoint.edu
CHURCH, Roy, A ... 440-365-5222 385 E
CHURCHILL,
Clifford, W ... 772-546-5534 106 D
cliffchurchill@hsbc.edu
CHURCHILL, David ... 405-682-1611 399 K
dchurchill@occc.edu
CHURCHILL, Mary ... 978-542-6324 230 E
mary.churchill@salemstate.edu
CHURCHILL, Robert ... 573-884-9080 283 H
churchillr@missouri.edu
CHURCHILL, Sally, J ... 734-763-5553 251 C
sjc@umich.edu
CHUSID, Eileen ... 212-410-8127 335 B
echusid@nycpm.edu
CHUSOLO, Eric, K ... 303-217-4014.. 82 M
eric@westoneducationgroup.com
CHUTE, Mary ... 609-292-6201 308 H
mchute@njstatelib.org
CHUTE, Patricia ... 516-686-3939 335 F
pchute@nyit.edu
CHYCINSKI, Jodi ... 616-331-2025 243 E
chycinsj@gvsu.edu
CHYKA, Robert, D ... 716-880-2343 332 B
robert.d.chyka@medaille.edu
CHYR, Fred, A ... 909-593-3511.. 73 B
fchyr@laverne.edu
CHYTKA, Evelyn, J ... 307-766-2398 546 K
jchytka@uwyo.edu
CIABOCCHI, Elizabeth ... 718-990-6113 340 G
ciabocce@stjohns.edu
CIACCIO, Dolores ... 631-420-2411 348 B
dolores.ciaccio@farmingdale.edu
CIANCHETTA, Susan, A 410-827-5811 214 D
scianchetta@chesapeake.edu
CIANCI, Christine ... 724-589-2195 436 E
ccianci@thiel.edu
CIANCI, Karen ... 559-453-2273.. 45 E
karen.cianci@fresno.edu
CIBUZAR, Jean ... 202-651-5282.. 95 C
jean.cibuzar@gallaudet.edu
CICALA, RSM,
Joseph, J ... 610-796-8211 412 C
joe.cicala@alvernia.edu
CICALA, Mary Ann ... 512-223-7109 468 H
mary.cicala@austincc.edu
CICCARELLI, Andrea ... 812-855-3550 167 J
aciccare@indiana.edu
CICCAZZO, Michele ... 305-348-5344 114 G
Michele.Ciccazzo@fiu.edu
CICCHELLI, Cindy ... 734-462-4400 250 A
ccicchel@schoolcraft.edu
CICCI, Cindy ... 307-754-6058 546 I
Cindy.Cicci@nwc.edu
CICCOMASCOLO, Lori ... 401-874-7074 442 E
lecicco@uri.edu
CICCONE, Joseph ... 973-290-4000 301 F
jciccone@cse.edu
CICERO, Bryan ... 303-937-4077.. 80 A
bcicero@chu.edu
CICERO, John ... 858-309-3411.. 55 J
jcicero@nu.edu
CICHOCKI, Eileen ... 707-468-3067.. 54 A
ecichock@mendocino.edu
CICHOMSKA, Grace, J .. 708-524-6288 144 C
gcichomska@dom.edu
CICHON, Jeff ... 715-675-3331 544 A
cichon@ntc.edu
CICHON, Mark ... 920-498-5759 544 B
mark.cichon@nwtc.edu

CICIRELLI, Anna ... 201-761-6036 307 K
acicirelli@saintpeters.edu
CICIRELLO, Pam ... 501-812-2774.. 22 F
pcicirello@pulaskitech.edu
CID, Carmen, R ... 860-465-5295.. 88 E
cid@easternct.edu
CID, Rolando ... 787-738-2161 557 G
rolando.cid@upr.edu
CIEJKA, Patricia, A ... 409-772-8745 495 E
pciejka@utmb.edu
CIEPLY, Kevin ... 239-687-5301.. 98 N
kcieply@avemarialaw.edu
CIFRA, Jason, S ... 808-934-2510 136 D
cifra@hawaii.edu
CIFUENTES, Geraldo ... 503-517-1017 411 A
gcifuentes@warnerpacific.edu
CIFUENTES, Luis ... 361-825-2577 485 F
luis.cifuentes@tamucc.edu
CIGANOVIC, Denny, D .. 843-953-5692 445 B
ciganovicd@cofc.edu
CIHA, Lisa ... 319-399-8669 176 G
lciha@coe.edu
CIHAK, Michael ... 320-589-6154 265 A
cihakmw@morris.umn.edu
CILENTO, Eugene, V ... 304-293-4157 533 D
gene.cilento@mail.wvu.edu
CILLAY, David ... 509-335-5454 528 B
dcillay@wsu.edu
CILLO, Robert ... 303-546-3506.. 84 B
bcillo@naropa.edu
CIMA, Cara ... 863-680-4390 104 F
ccima@flsouthern.edu
CIMA, Lauralyn ... 618-985-2828 148 G
lauralyncima@jalc.edu
CIMALORE, Ann ... 205-853-1200.... 5 C
acimalore@jeffstateonline.com
CIMBOLIC, Peter ... 614-251-4690 388 H
Peter.Cimbolic@ohiodominican.edu
CIMINELLI, Mary ... 972-273-3130 473 A
marygciminelli@dcccd.edu
CIMINELLI, Thomas, E . 716-888-2250 317 H
ciminel1@canisius.edu
CIMINERI, Christy ... 843-477-2166 446 I
christy.cimineri@hgtc.edu
CIMINO, Chris ... 865-974-9880 465 D
cimino@utk.edu
CIMITILE, Maria ... 616-331-2400 243 E
cimitilm@gvsu.edu
CIMORELLI, Abigail ... 973-290-4000 301 F
acimorelli@cse.edu
CIMORELLI, Nick ... 843-863-7581 444 B
ncimorel@csuniv.edu
CIMPL, Linda ... 605-995-2896 452 C
licimpl@dwu.edu
CINAR, Ali ... 312-567-3637 147 E
cinar@iit.edu
CINCOTTA, Josh ... 417-865-2815 274 L
cincottaj@evangel.edu
CINI, Marie ... 301-985-7174 220 A
marie.cini@umuc.edu
CINK, Janey ... 412-291-6340 412 H
jcink@aii.edu
CINNAMON, Gary ... 760-750-4675.. 35 B
cinnamon@csusm.edu
CINTORINO, Salvatore .. 860-832-1889.. 88 D
cintorino@ccsu.edu
CINTRON, Arnaldo ... 787-864-2222 553 J
arnaldo.cintron@guayama.inter.edu
CINTRON, Carmen ... 787-728-1515 559 A
crcintron@sagrado.edu
CINTRON, Edgardo ... 787-857-3600 553 G
ecintron@br.inter.edu
CINTRON, Filomena ... 787-857-3600 553 G
scintron@br.inter.edu
CINTRON, Iraida ... 787-850-9374 558 A
iraida.cintron@upr.edu
CINTRON, Josue ... 787-753-6000 552 K
jcintron@icprjc.edu
CINTRON, Nancy, A ... 718-960-8366 319 C
nancy.cintron@lehman.cuny.edu
CINTRON, Rene ... 504-762-3070 203 F
rcintr@dcc.edu
CINTRON-OTERO,
Carmen ... 787-993-8922 557 E
carmen.cintron2@upr.edu
CIOCE, Michael ... 609-894-9311 306 B
mcioce@bcc.edu
CIOFFI, Laura ... 212-752-1530 330 C
laura.cioffi@limcollege.edu
CIOFFI-REVILLA,
Claudio ... 703-993-1402 507 K
ccioffi@gmu.edu
CIOLFI, Michael, A ... 203-576-4278.. 92 B
mciolfi@bridgeport.edu
CIOPPA, Lee ... 212-799-5000 329 I
CIOSEK, Edward ... 413-748-3108 236 H
eciosek@springfieldcollege.edu
CIOTOLI, Carlo ... 212-443-1297 336 C
carlo.ciotoli@nyu.edu
CIPFL, Joseph, J ... 618-537-6462 152 C
jjcipfl@mckendree.edu

CIPOLLA, Anthony ... 845-848-7814 324 B
anthony.cipolla@dc.edu
CIPRES, Elizabeth ... 949-451-5319.. 67 E
ecipres@ivc.edu
CIPRIANI, Colleen ... 614-234-5828 386 N
ccipriani@mccn.edu
CIPRIANO, Matt, J ... 215-968-8255 413 F
cipriano@bucks.edu
CIPRIANO, Michael ... 978-934-2654 229 A
Michael_Cipriano@uml.edu
CIPRO, Cheryl ... 914-395-2535 342 C
ccipro@sarahlawrence.edu
CIPULLO, Donald, D ... 973-655-5105 304 A
cipullod@mail.montclair.edu
CIRAULO, Paul ... 212-517-0531 332 A
pciraulo@mmm.edu
CIRCE, Scott ... 305-223-4561 111 J
scirce@sjvcs.edu
CIRCLE, Kelly ... 303-914-6213.. 85 C
kelly.circle@rrcc.edu
CIRCOSTA, Amy ... 919-515-4559 370 D
accircos@ncsu.edu
CIRELLI, Rachel ... 718-862-7308 331 H
rcirelli01@manhattan.edu
CIRI, Michael ... 907-796-6452.. 11 A
michael.ciri@uas.alaska.edu
CIRI, Michael ... 907-796-6534.. 11 A
maciri@uas.alaska.edu
CIRIACO, Sandy, V ... 402-280-5560 290 B
ciriaco@creighton.edu
CIRILLO, Laureen ... 413-565-1006 222 G
lcirillo@baypath.edu
CIRILLO, Robert ... 914-606-6981 352 G
Robert.Cirillo@sunywcc.edu
CIRILLO, Susan, E ... 978-542-6232 230 E
scirillo@salemstate.edu
CIRMO, Christopher ... 715-346-4224 541 A
ccirmo@uwsp.edu
CISCO, OSB, Bede ... 812-357-6611 173 A
bcisco@saintmeinrad.edu
CISKANIK, John, F ... 800-877-5456 506 H
ciskanik@christendom.edu
CISLER, Ronald, A ... 414-229-5663 540 A
rac@uwm.edu
CISNA, Shawn ... 309-796-5000 140 D
cisnas@bhc.edu
CISNEROS, Guillermo ... 617-266-1400 223 F
CISNEROS, Maria ... 504-671-5603 203 F
mcisne@dcc.edu
CISNEROS, Teo ... 210-924-4338 469 B
teo.cisneros@bua.edu
CISSELL, Jason, A ... 502-272-8329 193 E
jcissell@bellarmine.edu
CISTOLA, David ... 817-735-2055 493 B
David.Cistola@unthsc.edu
CITARELLA, Alberto ... 802-656-3244 503 C
alberto.citarella@uvm.edu
CITRON, Chaim ... 323-937-3763.. 77 J
ccitron@yoec.edu
CITTI, Lori, A ... 410-516-6760 216 A
lcitti1@jhu.edu
CIUFFO, Patricia ... 646-565-6000 350 C
patricia.ciuffo@touro.edu
CIULLO, Carol ... 888-254-4238 505 K
cciullo@cdu.edu
CLABBY, William, J ... 512-448-8704 481 B
bclabby@stedwards.edu
CLACK, Olivia ... 870-574-4481.. 23 E
oclack@sautech.edu
CLAERBOUT, Libby ... 701-858-4155 374 B
libby.claerbout@minotstateu.edu
CLAERHOUT, Cathryn ... 231-995-1034 248 C
cclaerhout@nmc.edu
CLAFFEY, JR.,
George, F ... 860-515-3777.. 88 B
gclaffey@charteroak.edu
CLAFFEY, Marian, A ... 773-508-7473 151 E
mclaffe@luc.edu
CLAGETT, Craig, A ... 410-386-8163 214 B
cclagett@carrollcc.edu
CLAGHORN, Patricia ... 856-468-5000 306 C
pclaghorn@rcgc.edu
CLAGUE, Roger ... 707-864-7264.. 66 J
roger.clague@solano.edu
CLAIBORN, Candis ... 509-335-5593 528 B
claiborn@wsu.edu
CLAIRE, Michael ... 650-574-6222.. 64 D
clairem@smccd.edu
CLANCEY, Robert ... 863-669-2321 110 E
rclancey@polk.edu
CLANCY, Amanda ... 303-678-3736.. 82 J
amanda.clancy@frontrange.edu
CLANCY, Patricia ... 718-390-3422 352 C
patricia.clancy@wagner.edu
CLANCY, SJ, Tim, R ... 509-313-6701 522 L
clancy@gonzaga.edu
CLANTON, Ann ... 251-575-8204.... 1 C
aclanton@ascc.edu
CLANTON, Janet ... 573-897-5000 282 I
CLANTON, Karen ... 256-824-6013.... 9 A
karen.clanton@uah.edu

CLAPP, Jason ... 319-399-8526 176 G
jclapp@coe.edu
CLAPP, Kenneth, W ... 704-637-4446 355 H
kclapp@catawba.edu
CLAPPER, Mark, A ... 717-361-1499 418 B
clapperm@etown.edu
CLAPPER-DEWELL,
Theophylact ... 315-858-3914 328 B
frtheophylact@jordanville.org
CLARDY, Betsy, B ... 409-772-8789 495 E
bbclardy@utmb.edu
CLARDY, JR., Mike ... 334-844-9996.... 1 G
clardch@auburn.edu
CLARENSAU, Michael ... 972-825-4827 483 D
mclarensau@sagu.edu
CLARIDAY, Sandra ... 423-746-5249 464 D
sclariday@twcnet.edu
CLARK, Alfred ... 909-593-3511.. 73 B
aclark@laverne.edu
CLARK, Alice, M ... 662-915-7482 270 G
amclark@olemiss.edu
CLARK, Allen ... 940-565-2550 492 D
allen.clark@unt.edu
CLARK, Amanda, C ... 509-777-4482 529 A
amandaclark@whitworth.edu
CLARK, Andy, T ... 229-259-5103 133 H
atclark@valdosta.edu
CLARK, Anita ... 262-243-5700 535 I
anita.clark@cuw.edu
CLARK, Ann, B ... 860-727-6761.. 90 F
aclark@goodwin.edu
CLARK, Annette, C ... 206-398-4000 526 F
annclark@seattleu.edu
CLARK, Ben ... 757-340-2121 506 E
directorcvab@centura.edu
CLARK, Benita, I ... 919-866-7894 366 H
biclark@waketech.edu
CLARK, Bettye ... 404-880-8480 122 I
bclark@cau.edu
CLARK, Beverly ... 228-896-2512 268 G
beverly.clark@mgccc.edu
CLARK, Bill ... 252-328-6131 369 E
clarkw@ecu.edu
CLARK, Bob ... 310-506-4798.. 58 H
bob.clark@pepperdine.edu
CLARK, Bonnie, M ... 727-816-3490 110 B
clarkb@phsc.edu
CLARK, Brandi ... 520-494-5577.. 12 R
brandi.clark@centralaz.edu
CLARK, Brenda ... 803-705-4385 443 F
clarkb@benedict.edu
CLARK, Brian ... 401-427-6920 442 B
bclark@risd.edu
CLARK, Brian, J ... 207-859-4604 210 A
bjclark@colby.edu
CLARK, Brock ... 228-497-7634 268 G
brock.clark@mgccc.edu
CLARK, Bryon ... 580-745-2064 402 D
bclark@se.edu
CLARK, Carol ... 931-221-7570 461 C
clarkc@apsu.edu
CLARK, Carol, D ... 931-221-7570 461 C
clarkc@apsu.edu
CLARK, Carols ... 937-708-5738 395 E
cclark@wilberforce.edu
CLARK, Catherine ... 360-650-6400 528 D
catherine.clark@wwu.edu
CLARK, Charles ... 706-737-1738 121 C
cwclark@gru.edu
CLARK, Charles, E ... 920-683-4710 541 E
charles.clark@uwc.edu
CLARK, Charles, L ... 309-341-7399 149 G
clclark@knox.edu
CLARK, Cheryl ... 318-487-7601 202 L
cheryl.clark@lacollege.edu
CLARK, Chip ... 903-566-7431 494 E
cclark@uttyler.edu
CLARK, Chris ... 618-634-3233 159 A
chrisc@shawneecc.edu
CLARK, Craig ... 607-587-3101 347 D
clarkcr@alfredstate.edu
CLARK, Cynthia, A ... 860-628-4751.. 91 A
cclark@lincolncollegene.edu
CLARK, Dan ... 503-838-8483 411 B
clarkd@wou.edu
CLARK, Dana ... 810-766-4028 239 G
dana.clark@baker.edu
CLARK, Dana ... 810-766-4028 239 H
dana.clark@baker.edu
CLARK, Dana ... 570-740-0422 425 A
dclark@luzerne.edu
CLARK, Daniel ... 630-752-5593 163 G
daniel.clark@wheaton.edu
CLARK, Daniel ... 616-234-4354 243 D
dbclark@grcc.edu
CLARK, Daniel ... 425-602-3064 519 J
dclark@bastyr.edu
CLARK, Dave ... 701-224-5434 374 E
david.clark@bismarckstate.edu
CLARK, David ... 212-346-1590 337 I
dclark@pace.edu

CLAUSEN, Terry .... 870-543-5900.. 23 C
tclausen@seark.edu
CLAUSER, Lisa .... 573-518-2129 278 F
lisac@mineralarea.edu
CLAUSON, Kevin, L ...... 423-775-7324 455 F
kclauson4864@bryan.edu
CLAUSON BASH,
Kathleen, M .... 641-784-5064 178 G
clauson@graceland.edu
CLAUSS, James, J .... 206-221-6075 527 G
jjc@uw.edu
CLAUSS, Karl .... 610-690-5707 436 A
kclauss1@swarthmore.edu
CLAUSSEN, Ann, E .... 610-861-1492 426 H
claussena@moravian.edu
CLAUSSEN, Linda, C .... 540-674-3614 516 B
lclaussen@nr.edu
CLAVELLE, Martha .... 619-644-7000.. 46 H
martha.clavelle@gcccd.edu
CLAVERIE, Mark .... 518-587-2100 348 A
mark.claverie@esc.edu
CLAVIER, Cheri .... 423-439-7483 461 D
clavier@etsu.edu
CLAVIJO, Manuel .... 508-849-3280 222 C
mclavijo@annamaria.edu
CLAVILLE, Michelle .... 757-727-5239 508 C
michelle.claville@hamptonu.edu
CLAVIR, Kenneth, R ...... 949-214-3080.. 42 B
ken.clavir@cui.edu
CLAVIR, Pamela .... 949-214-3133.. 42 B
pam.clavir@cui.edu
CLAWSON, Dana .... 318-677-3100 208 D
roed@nsula.edu
CLAWSON, Michelle ..... 757-727-5474 508 C
michelle.clawson@hamptonu.edu
CLAXTON, Brenda .... 432-264-5160 475 E
bclaxton@howardcollege.edu
CLAXTON, Patricia .... 325-574-7607 497 E
pclaxton@wtc.edu
CLAY, Aileen .... 603-206-8175 297 A
aclay@ccsnh.edu
CLAY, Antoinette, M ..... 732-255-0400 304 E
aclay@ocean.edu
CLAY, Brian .... 501-370-5336.. 22 E
bclay@philander.edu
CLAY, Daniel .... 573-882-8524 283 H
clayda@missouri.edu
CLAY, Doreen .... 818-710-2510.. 51 H
claydj@piercecollege.edu
CLAY, George, W .... 864-656-0723 444 E
gclay@clemson.edu
CLAY, Gladys .... 904-470-8087 102 A
gladys.clay@ewc.edu
CLAY, John, L .... 256-539-0834.... 4 F
president@hbc1.edu
CLAY, Karen .... 662-329-7104 269 B
kgclay@muw.edu
CLAY, Karen .... 541-962-3792 405 G
karen.clay@eou.edu
CLAY, Lauren .... 662-476-5060 267 C
lclay@eastms.edu
CLAY, Maggie .... 310-393-0411.. 58 E
mclay@rand.org
CLAY, Makeba .... 301-934-2251 214 E
CLAY, Martyn .... 813-757-2110 106 C
mclay6@hccfl.edu
CLAY, Melanie, N .... 678-839-0627 133 F
melaniec@westga.edu
CLAY, Mercedes .... 419-783-2362 381 G
mclay@defiance.edu
CLAY, Patricia .... 610-282-1100 416 I
patricia.clay@desales.edu
CLAY, Philip, N .... 508-831-5201 238 G
pclay@wpi.edu
CLAY, Rex .... 704-922-6243 362 G
clay.rex@gaston.edu
CLAY, Rosetta, L .... 336-433-5570 370 B
rlclay@ncat.edu
CLAY, Sandra .... 903-586-2518 476 K
sclay@jacksonville-college.edu
CLAY, Sharon .... 913-758-6108 191 I
sharon.clay@stmary.edu
CLAY, Sharon .... 770-394-8300 120 E
dbclay@aii.edu
CLAY, Trish .... 304-558-2104 532 C
tclay@hepc.wvnet.edu
CLAY, Victor .... 323-259-2598.. 56 I
vclay@oxy.edu
CLAYBON, John .... 405-682-7855 399 K
jclaybon@occc.edu
CLAYBORNE, Hannah ... 502-272-8070 193 E
hclayborne@bellarmine.edu
CLAYBORNE, Hannah ... 419-289-5324 377 A
hclaybor@ashland.edu
CLAYBORNE, Staci, G ... 618-235-2700 160 B
staci.clayborne@swic.edu
CLAYBORNE-SCOTT,
Monica .... 731-426-7533 457 K
mclayborne@lanecollege.edu

CLAYBROOK,
Jennifer, D .... 706-880-8032 127 N
jclaybrook@lagrange.edu
CLAYCOMB, Donald, M 573-897-5000 282 I
CLAYCOMB, Ricka .... 502-231-5221 198 D
rclaycomb@myLBC.edu
CLAYPOOL, Joe .... 859-333-8888 200 G
joseph.claypool@uky.edu
CLAYPOOLE, Jack .... 803-777-4111 450 B
jclaypoole@mycarolina.org
CLAYTER, Seth .... 207-699-5032 210 I
sclayter@meca.edu
CLAYTON, Carrie .... 903-566-7184 494 E
cclayton@uttyler.edu
CLAYTON, Dana .... 812-488-2500 173 H
dc26@evansville.edu
CLAYTON, Ellen .... 443-334-2558 218 E
eclayton@stevenson.edu
CLAYTON, Gene, T .... 910-630-7011 359 C
gclayton@methodist.edu
CLAYTON, Jack, A .... 304-842-8269 532 F
jclayton@fairmontstate.edu
CLAYTON, Jan, L .... 918-595-7901 403 A
jan.clayton@tulsacc.edu
CLAYTON, Janet, S .... 803-934-3246 447 K
jclayton@morris.edu
CLAYTON, Jay, B .... 724-653-2202 417 D
jclayton@dec.edu
CLAYTON, Jeffrey .... 954-492-5353 100 G
jclayton@citycollege.edu
CLAYTON, John .... 417-447-2667 280 C
claytonj@otc.edu
CLAYTON, Kirk .... 757-490-1241 504 D
kclayton@auto.edu
CLAYTON, Kori .... 501-337-5000.. 20 H
kclayon@coto.edu
CLAYTON, Lisa .... 413-528-7239 222 F
lclayton@simons-rock.edu
CLAYTON, Patricia, I ..... 336-322-2105 364 G
Patti.Clayton@piedmontcc.edu
CLAYTON, Taffye, B ...... 919-962-0202 371 A
Taffye@unc.edu
CLAYTON, Tiffany .... 610-921-7795 411 E
tclayton@albright.edu
CLAYTON, Tonya, M ..... 989-386-6601 247 B
tmclayton@midmich.edu
CLAYTON, Yvette .... 256-372-5690.... 1 A
yvette.clayton@aamu.edu
CLEAR, Todd, R .... 973-353-5441 307 C
tclear@rutgers.edu
CLEARFIELD, Michael ... 707-638-5982.. 70 B
michael.clearfield@tu.edu
CLEARMAN, Josh .... 253-833-9111 523 B
jclearman@greenriver.edu
CLEARWATER, Bonnie ... 954-262-0225 109 E
bclearwater@moafl.org
CLEARY, Anita .... 509-452-5100 524 J
CLEARY, Brian .... 860-512-2613.. 89 D
bcleary@manchestercc.edu
CLEARY, Charles .... 860-773-3403.. 90 C
ccleary@txcc.commnet.edu
CLEARY, Delores .... 509-963-2152 520 E
clearyd@cwu.edu
CLEARY, Kathleen .... 937-512-3159 391 D
kathleen.cleary@sinclair.edu
CLEARY, Keelan .... 503-534-4051 407 A
kcleary@marylhurst.edu
CLEARY, Kelly .... 610-896-1181 420 J
kcleary@haverford.edu
CLEARY, Lynn .... 315-464-5387 344 E
clearyl@upstate.edu
CLEARY, Michael, J ...... 575-234-9220 312 C
mcleary@nmsu.edu
CLEARY, Paul, C .... 203-785-2867.. 93 C
paul.cleary@yale.edu
CLEARY, Sally .... 973-290-4449 301 F
scleary@cse.edu
CLEARY, Thomas .... 210-485-0500 466 J
tcleary1@alamo.edu
CLEARY, Thomas, R ...... 619-260-4297.. 74 B
tcleary@sandiego.edu
CLEARY, Valerie, A .... 503-370-6262 411 D
vcleary@willamette.edu
CLEAVER, Richard .... 340-693-1042 559 B
richard.cleaver@live.uvi.edu
CLEAVES, Laura .... 603-577-6515 297 F
lcleaves@dwc.edu
CLEAVES, Wandamae ..... 207-947-4591 209 G
bookstore@bealcollege.edu
CLEBSCH, Bill .... 650-725-0056.. 68 G
clebsch@stanford.edu
CLECKLER, Steven .... 205-970-9239.... 7 D
scleckler@sebc.edu
CLECKNER, Lisa .... 315-781-4381 327 G
cleckner@hws.edu
CLEEK, Linda, L .... 812-464-1863 174 D
lcleek@usi.edu
CLEEK, Stu .... 805-565-6029.. 76 K
scleek@westmont.edu
CLEERE, Ashley .... 706-778-8500 130 B
acleere@piedmont.edu

CLEGG, Melody .... 208-535-5403 138 B
melody.clegg@my.eitc.edu
CLEGG, Neill .... 336-272-7102 357 B
cleggn@greensboro.edu
CLEM, Amy .... 903-566-7480 494 E
aclem@uttyler.edu
CLEM, Randy .... 916-558-2424.. 53 B
clemrj@scc.losrios.edu
CLEMENS, Bonnie .... 909-607-3679.. 39 D
bonnie_clemens@cuc.claremont.edu
CLEMENS, John .... 229-317-6700 123 H
john.clemens@darton.edu
CLEMENS, Julie .... 570-849-8247.. 57 G
jclemens@psr.edu
CLEMENT, Chris, D .... 603-862-2232 299 B
christopher.clement@unh.edu
CLEMENT, Fred .... 512-472-4133 482 E
fred.clement@ssw.edu
CLEMENT, Gregory .... 978-632-6600 232 C
g_clement@mwcc.mass.edu
CLEMENT, James, A ...... 205-726-2395.... 6 F
jaclemen@samford.edu
CLEMENT, Linda, M ...... 301-314-8430 219 D
lclement@umd.edu
CLEMENT, Mercedes ...... 386-506-3440 101 I
clemenm@DaytonaState.edu
CLEMENT, Nancy .... 985-448-7915 203 G
nancy.clement@fletcher.edu
CLEMENT, Richard .... 505-277-4241 313 H
riclement@unm.edu
CLEMENT, William .... 757-822-7124 517 C
wclement@tcc.edu
CLEMENT CORNIES,
Dawn .... 901-843-3745 460 F
corniesd@rhodes.edu
CLEMENTS, Carole .... 303-546-3584.. 84 B
carole@naropa.edu
CLEMENTS, Eric .... 509-542-4688 521 C
eclements@columbiabasin.edu
CLEMENTS, Erica .... 605-256-5712 453 H
erica.clements@dsu.edu
CLEMENTS, Gary .... 252-527-6223 363 G
gclements@lenoircc.edu
CLEMENTS, Geri .... 478-553-2066 129 C
gclements@oftc.edu
CLEMENTS, James, P ... 864-656-3413 444 E
president@clemson.edu
CLEMENTS, Kieran .... 706-886-6831 132 F
clements@tfc.edu
CLEMENTS, Lee Ann, J . 904-256-7300 106 Q
lclemen@ju.edu
CLEMENTS, Mari .... 626-584-5501.. 45 F
clements@fuller.edu
CLEMENTS, Stephen, K . 859-858-3511 193 A
steve.clements@asbury.edu
CLEMENTS, Tommy ...... 276-523-7431 516 A
tclements@me.vccs.edu
CLEMENTS, Tommy ...... 276-523-7462 516 A
tclements@me.vccs.edu
CLEMENTS, Vickie .... 814-864-6666 419 E
CLEMENTS, William .... 802-485-2370 502 G
bclements@norwich.edu
CLEMETSEN, Bruce .... 541-917-4806 406 J
clemetb@linnbenton.edu
CLEMMER, Kristi .... 432-335-6865 479 O
kclemmer@odessa.edu
CLEMMER, Margaret ..... 202-885-2141.. 94 H
megc@american.edu
CLEMMER, Robert, L .... 540-453-2209 514 H
clemmerr@brcc.edu
CLEMMONS, Brian .... 828-398-7161 360 A
brianoclemmons@abtech.edu
CLEMMONS, Brian .... 732-906-2524 303 F
bclemmons@middlesexcc.edu
CLEMMONS, Raechelle . 920-403-3866 538 K
raechelle.clemmons@snc.edu
CLEMMONS, Sarah .... 850-718-2213 100 E
clemmonss@chipola.edu
CLEMO, Lorrie, A .... 315-312-2290 346 A
lorrie.clemo@oswego.edu
CLEMONS, Brian .... 816-415-7802 285 K
clemonsb@william.jewell.edu
CLEMONS, Cheryl .... 270-686-4250 193 G
cheryl.clemons@brescia.edu
CLEMONS, Chuck .... 352-395-5202 112 H
chuck.clemons@sfcollege.edu
CLEMONS, Rita .... 909-635-0250 225 A
Rita.Clemons@cambridgecollege.edu
CLENDENEN, Mike .... 252-493-7645 364 H
mclendenen@email.pittcc.edu
CLENDENIN, Larry .... 505-984-6060 312 J
admissions@sjc.edu
CLERE, Ray, R .... 859-257-2746 200 G
ray.clere@uky.edu
CLERKIN, Elizabeth ...... 440-775-8450 388 B
liz.clerkin@oberlin.edu
CLERKIN, Kris .... 603-201-0420 298 H
k.clerkin@snhu.edu
CLEROU, Diane .... 559-244-5970.. 68 J
diane.clerou@scccd.edu

CLESCERI, Michael .... 815-479-7833 152 B
mclesceri@mchenry.edu
CLEVELAND, SR.,
Alvin, A .... 334-872-2533.... 6 G
aclevesr@aol.com
CLEVELAND, Angela ...... 269-965-3931 244 L
clevelanda@kellogg.edu
CLEVELAND, Arthur .... 951-343-4215.. 30 D
acleveland@calbaptist.edu
CLEVELAND, Ashley ...... 972-438-6932 480 C
CLEVELAND, III,
Carl, S .... 913-234-0600 185 N
carl.clevelandiii@cleveland.edu
CLEVELAND, Charles, E 509-527-5158 528 F
clevelan@whitman.edu
CLEVELAND, Chris .... 978-478-3400 235 E
ccleveland@northpoint.edu
CLEVELAND, Conne .... 559-934-2383.. 76 A
conne.cleveland@whccd.edu
CLEVELAND, Gerald ...... 409-772-3689 495 E
gtclevel@utmb.edu
CLEVELAND, Melanie .... 229-243-3007 121 D
melanie.cleveland@bainbridge.edu
CLEVELAND, Tracey ...... 716-270-5735 325 A
clevelandt@ecc.edu
CLEVELAND, Vicki .... 951-552-8650.. 30 D
vdcleveland@calbaptist.edu
CLEVENGER, Brian .... 217-206-6174 161 G
clevenger.brian@uis.edu
CLEVENGER, Julie .... 217-786-2365 151 C
julie.clevenger@llcc.edu
CLEVENGER, Leah .... 704-406-4255 356 G
lclevenger@gardner-webb.edu
CLEVENGER, Tim, R ...... 541-346-2104 410 F
trc@uoregon.edu
CLEVERING, Peter .... 708-239-4770 160 L
peter.clevering@trnty.edu
CLEVINGER, Sarah .... 423-652-4715 457 J
sclevinger@king.edu
CLIATT, Cass .... 401-863-2453 441 A
cass_cliatt@brown.edu
CLICK, Sally, E .... 317-940-9854 164 L
sclick@butler.edu
CLICK, Stanley .... 606-759-7141 196 G
stanley.click@kctcs.edu
CLICK, Stanley, W .... 606-783-1538 196 G
stanley.click@kctcs.edu
CLICKNER, David .... 518-629-8068 328 D
d.clickner@hvcc.edu
CLICKNER, David, C ..... 518-629-8068 328 D
d.clickner@hvcc.edu
CLIFFORD, Alexander ... 207-454-1003 211 E
aclifford@wccc.me.edu
CLIFFORD, Christopher 205-934-8229.... 8 F
cbcliff@uab.edu
CLIFFORD, Heather .... 802-440-4325 501 D
hclifford@bennington.edu
CLIFFORD, Joan .... 518-244-2410 340 A
cliffj3@sage.edu
CLIFFORD, John, P .... 216-397-4963 384 F
jclifford@jcu.edu
CLIFFORD, Paul, J .... 541-346-6317 410 F
pjc@uoregon.edu
CLIFT, Carla .... 256-551-3120.... 4 J
carla.clift@drakestate.edu
CLIFTON, Gaye, B .... 336-342-4261 365 E
cliftong@rockinghamcc.edu
CLIFTON, SJ, James, F 402-280-2519 290 B
jclifton@creighton.edu
CLIFTON, Jamie .... 951-571-6293.. 60 K
jamie.clifton@mvc.edu
CLIFTON, Jerry .... 501-205-8789.. 20 G
jclifton@cbc.edu
CLIFTON, Lonzy .... 334-876-9251.... 4 B
lonzy.clifton@wccs.edu
CLINARD, Rhonda .... 931-363-9820 458 D
rclinard@martinmethodist.edu
CLINE, Angela .... 252-493-7679 364 H
acline@email.pittcc.edu
CLINE, Cathie .... 870-633-4480.. 20 J
ccline@eacc.edu
CLINE, Elizabeth, W ...... 330-325-6498 387 F
ecline@neomed.edu
CLINE, Gina .... 321-433-7000 101 O
clineg@easternflorida.edu
CLINE, Glen, E .... 607-587-3917 347 D
clinege@alfredstate.edu
CLINE, J. Robert .... 864-231-2077 443 E
bcline@andersonuniversity.edu
CLINE, Jack .... 240-477-9505 191 G
jackcline@ku.edu
CLINE, Joseph .... 775-784-1740 295 H
cline@unr.edu
CLINE, Kimberly, R .... 516-299-2501 330 G
president@liu.edu
CLINE, Kimberly, R .... 516-299-2501 330 F
president@liu.edu
CLINE, Laurel .... 610-796-8317 412 C
laurel.cline@alvernia.edu
CLINE, Lisa .... 913-288-7109 188 G
lcline@kckcc.edu

CODNER, Renee ... 760-630-1555.. 49 C rcodner@kaplan.edu

CODY, Doni, S ... 910-576-6222 364 D codyd@montgomery.edu

CODY, Gennie ... 662-243-1940 267 C gcody@eastms.edu

CODY, Kenneth ... 781-891-2887 223 E kcody@bentley.edu

CODY, Martha ... 805-756-6770.. 32 E mcody@calpoly.edu

CODY, Mary Ellen ... 203-285-2296.. 89 B mcody@gwcc.commnet.edu

CODY, Robert ... 508-362-2131 231 D rcody@capecod.edu

CODY, Susan ... 770-274-5402 125 G susan.cody@gpc.edu

COE, Bonnie, L ... 740-364-9509 378 L bcoe@cotc.edu

COE, Cheri ... 978-921-4242 234 B cheri.coe@montserrat.edu

COE, Douglas, A ... 406-496-4207 288 C dcoe@mtech.edu

COE, Erica ... 360-475-7263 524 H ecoe@olympic.edu

COE, Lea ... 229-931-2352 131 E lcoe@southgatech.edu

COE-SMITH, Jane ... 208-282-2794 138 C coesjane@isu.edu

COEHOORN, Joel ... 402-363-5603 294 G jcoehoorn@york.edu

COEN, Carol ... 408-274-6700.. 63 O carol.coen@sjeccd.org

COFER, Dagmar ... 909-469-5203.. 76 I dcofer@westernu.edu

COFER, Mildred ... 973-877-3468 302 F cofer@essex.edu

COFER, Stacy ... 316-323-6729 185 F scofer@butlercc.edu

COFFEE, Laura, F ... 336-342-4261 365 E coffeel@rockinghamcc.edu

COFFEY, Amanda, A ... 717-796-5300 426 B acoffey@messiah.edu

COFFEY, Paul ... 312-899-5176 158 J pcoffey@saic.edu

COFFEY, Ron, L ... 260-359-4029 167 D rcoffey@huntington.edu

COFFEY, Suzanne, R ... 413-542-2337 222 A studentaffairs@amherst.edu

COFFIN, Deborah, J ... 303-492-8447.. 86 E deb.coffin@colorado.edu

COFFIN, Gordie ... 402-465-2544 292 E gcoffin@nebrwesleyan.edu

COFFIN, Jonathan ... 765-658-4088 165 G jonathancoffin@depauw.edu

COFFIN, Lee, A ... 617-627-5275 237 C lee.coffin@tufts.edu

COFFIN, Ruth ... 509-793-2222 520 B

COFFIN, Sheila ... 312-341-3542 157 E scoffin@roosevelt.edu

COFFIN, William ... 410-293-2809 549 B coffin@usna.edu

COFFMAN, Marie, E ... 724-852-3399 439 C mcoffman@waynesburg.edu

COFFMAN, Michael ... 618-985-3741 148 G michaelcoffman@jalc.edu

COFFMAN, Renee ... 702-968-2020 296 D rcoffman@roseman.edu

COFFMAN, Robert, L ... 765-641-4063 164 B rlcoffman@anderson.edu

COFIELD, Tari, D ... 719-884-5000.. 84 G TDCofield@nbc.edu

COFONE, Albin ... 631-451-4335 348 F cofona@sunysuffolk.edu

COFRESI, Norma ... 718-960-8761 319 C norma.cofresi@lehman.cuny.edu

COGAN, Michael, F ... 651-962-6657 265 F mfcogan@stthomas.edu

COGBURN, Wendy, L ... 205-348-0537.... 8 E wcogburn@ctl.ua.edu

COGDELL, Edith ... 210-829-6037 492 B cogdell@uiwtx.edu

COGDILL, Rex ... 307-532-8257 546 B rex.cogdill@ewc.wy.edu

COGER, Robin, N ... 336-334-7589 370 B rncoger@ncat.edu

COGGIN, Rod ... 662-720-7306 269 D rcoggin@nemcc.edu

COGGINS VIENTOS, Sonja ... 615-327-6223 458 F svientos@mmc.edu

COGHLAN, Cathan ... 817-257-7793 486 G c.coghlan@tcu.edu

COGHLAN, Laura ... 360-867-6676 522 J coghlanl@evergreen.edu

COGNET, II, Guy, A ... 816-331-5700 280 G gcognet@pcitraining.edu

COGSHELL, Nickyia ... 651-779-5786 258 D nickyia.cogshell@century.edu

COGSWELL, Bob ... 910-893-1217 355 C cogswell@campbell.edu

COGSWELL, James, A ... 573-882-4701 283 H cogswellja@missouri.edu

COGSWELL, Katherine ... 315-445-6124 330 B cogswek@lemoyne.edu

COHALL, Kirkpatrick, G 212-870-1208 336 B kcohall@nyts.edu

COHAN, Leslie ... 425-739-8236 523 I leslie.cohan@lwtech.edu

COHAN, Wayne, L ... 336-322-2205 364 G Wayne.Cohan@piedmontcc.edu

COHEA, Melissa ... 707-654-1789.. 34 B mcohea@csum.edu

COHEN, Alise ... 845-848-4036 324 B alise.cohen@dc.edu

COHEN, Bernadette ... 404-270-5091 132 D bcohen@spelman.edu

COHEN, Brian ... 212-541-0365 318 B brian.cohen@cuny.edu

COHEN, Dale, S ... 916-558-2275.. 53 B cohend@scc.losrios.edu

COHEN, David ... 800-371-6105.. 16 A david@nationalparalegal.edu

COHEN, Ilene ... 732-255-0400 304 E icohen@ocean.edu

COHEN, Jason ... 413-755-4438 233 B jlcohen@stcc.edu

COHEN, Joan ... 207-741-5559 211 D jcohen@smccme.edu

COHEN, Joel, J ... 646-660-6060 318 C

COHEN, Jonah ... 203-285-2289.. 89 B jcohen@gwcc.commnet.edu

COHEN, Kathleen, L ... 607-735-1728 324 J kcohen@elmira.edu

COHEN, Laurie ... 480-423-6511.. 15 E laurie.cohen@scottsdalecc.edu

COHEN, Lisa ... 215-576-0800 433 I lcohen@rrc.edu

COHEN, Lizabeth ... 617-495-8602 227 D lizabeth_cohen@radcliffe.harvard.edu

COHEN, Mark, J ... 202-687-7610.. 95 E cohenm@georgetown.edu

COHEN, Marvin ... 312-369-7226 143 C mcohen@colum.edu

COHEN, Melissa ... 717-796-5220 426 B mcohen@messiah.edu

COHEN, Michael, E ... 772-466-4822.. 98 P m.cohen@aviator.edu

COHEN, Morris ... 513-862-2743 383 A

COHEN, Neil ... 864-578-8770 448 G ncohen@sherman.edu

COHEN, Paula ... 215-895-1821 417 E paula.marantz.cohen@drexel.edu

COHEN, Peter ... 718-368-5563 320 A pcohen@kbcc.cuny.edu

COHEN, Pinchas ... 213-740-1354.. 74 D hassy@usc.edu

COHEN, Richard ... 215-985-2500 426 C rjc@phmc.org

COHEN, Richard, L ... 847-735-5555 149 H cohen@lakeforest.edu

COHEN, Roberta ... 202-885-3415.. 94 H robertac@american.edu

COHEN, Ronald, A ... 570-372-4103 435 I cohen@susqu.edu

COHEN, Scott ... 731-425-2615 463 A scohen@jscc.edu

COHEN, Shaya ... 516-295-5700 354 A

COHEN, Shelly ... 757-388-2900 512 D sgvinson@sentara.com

COHEN, Steffaney ... 910-962-2260 372 A cohens@uncw.edu

COHEN, Susan, J ... 215-574-9600 421 A scohen@hussianart.edu

COHEN, Tamara ... 352-392-1261 115 D tamararc@dso.ufl.edu

COHEN, Veronica ... 662-254-3790 269 C veronica.cohen@mvsu.edu

COHEN, Vicki ... 201-692-2525 302 H cohen@fdu.edu

COHEN, Zoe ... 978-837-5121 233 G cohenz@merrimack.edu

COHEN-ROSE, Amy ... 617-277-3915 224 D cohenrose@bgsp.edu

COHN, Stephen, A ... 919-687-3606 356 E stevec@acpub.duke.edu

COHRS, Daniel ... 303-963-3352.. 79 L dcohrs@ccu.edu

COHUNE, Ellen ... 805-756-2527.. 32 E ecohune@calpoly.edu

COICAUD, Jean-Marc ... 973-353-3285 307 C jeanmarc.coicaud@rutgers.edu

COKER, Bryan, F ... 410-337-6150 215 B bryan.coker@goucher.edu

COKER, Dawn ... 706-880-8267 127 N dcoker@lagrange.edu

COKER, Jeff ... 540-665-4587 512 E jcoker2@su.edu

COKER, Kim ... 870-574-4533.. 23 E kcoker@sautech.edu

COKER, Melissa, A ... 843-355-4117 451 H cokerm@wiltech.edu

COKER, Scott, A ... 309-298-1834 163 A sa-coker@wiu.edu

COKER, Sherry ... 417-447-8884 280 C cokers@otc.edu

COKER, T. Kent ... 843-355-4144 451 H cokert@wiltech.edu

COKER-KOLO, Doyin ... 812-941-2333 169 A

COKKINOS, Michael ... 212-217-4476 325 C michael_cokkinos@fitnyc.edu

COLON, Ingrid, Y ... 787-884-3838 550 E administradora@atenascollege.edu

COLON, Silvestre ... 787-832-4040 558 B decep@uprm.edu

COLON, Victor ... 515-289-9200 179 E vcolon@inste.edu

COLA, Anita ... 570-504-0498 422 G colaa@lackawanna.edu

COLADARCI, Richard ... 603-230-3512 296 J rcoladarci@ccsnh.edu

COLADARCI, Ted, T ... 207-581-1415 212 C theo@maine.edu

COLAGROSS, Glenda ... 256-331-5275.... 6 B colg@nwscc.edu

COLAGROSS, Glenda ... 256-395-2211.... 7 E gcolagross@suscc.edu

COLANANNI, Terri ... 501-337-5000.. 20 H terric@coto.edu

COLANER, Kevin, T ... 909-869-3365.. 32 F ktcolaner@cpp.edu

COLANGELO, Carmon ... 314-935-9300 285 E colangelo@wustl.edu

COLANGELO, Nicholas . 319-335-5380 175 H nicholas-colangelo@uiowa.edu

COLAPIETRO, Cathy ... 816-584-6728 280 F cathy.colapietro@park.edu

COLARERI, Michael, L .. 978-468-7111 227 B mcolareri@gcts.edu

COLARIC, Susan ... 727-497-5051 112 A colaric.susan@spcollege.edu

COLARULLI, Guy, C ... 860-768-4749.. 92 F colarulli@hartford.edu

COLARUSSO, Judy ... 253-566-5136 527 C jcolarusso@tacomacc.edu

COLASURDO, Giuseppe, N ... 713-500-5700 495 A giuseppe.n.colasurdo@uth.tmc.edu

COLASURDO, Giuseppe, N ... 713-500-3000 495 A giuseppe.n.colasurdo@uth.tmc.edu

COLATCH, John, P ... 570-577-1592 413 E john.colatch@bucknell.edu

COLAW, Lee, M ... 806-371-5151 467 E lmcolaw@actx.edu

COLBAN, Tom ... 201-360-4393 303 A tcolban@follett.com

COLBECK, Ellen ... 217-875-7200 156 K ecolbeck@richland.edu

COLBERT, Carly, J ... 315-445-4312 330 B colbercj@lemoyne.edu

COLBERT, Claudia ... 718-997-3009 320 E claudia.colbert@qc.cuny.edu

COLBERT, Jeff ... 415-380-1428.. 45 J jeffcolbert@ggbts.edu

COLBERT, Mary, J ... 410-857-2214 217 A mcolbert@mcdaniel.edu

COLBERT RILEY, Cynthia ... 713-525-3119 493 J colbert@stthom.edu

COLBROOK, William ... 217-351-2884 155 I wcolbrook@parkland.edu

COLBS, Sandy ... 309-438-3655 147 I slcolbs@ilstu.edu

COLBY, Adam ... 727-864-7732 101 P colbyac@eckerd.edu

COLBY, Andrew ... 603-862-1568 299 B andy.colby@unh.edu

COLBY, Chuck ... 570-662-4952 431 D ccolby@mansfield.edu

COLBY, Glenn ... 425-352-8420 520 D gcolby@cascadia.edu

COLBY CLEMENTS, Paula ... 978-681-0800 233 D pcolby@mslaw.edu

COLCOLOUGH, Sharon . 864-646-1790 449 F scolcolo@tctc.edu

COLDREN, Brian ... 404-261-1441 129 F bcoldren@oglethorpe.edu

COLE, Amber ... 405-945-3310 400 F ambcole@osuokc.edu

COLE, Brad ... 435-797-2631 500 A brad.cole@usu.edu

COLE, Bruce ... 704-922-6309 362 G cole.bruce@gaston.edu

COLE, Carol ... 304-896-7429 531 F carol.cole@southernwv.edu

COLE, Carol, A ... 304-896-7429 531 F carol.cole@southernwv.edu

COLE, Christopher, L ... 804-523-5843 515 F ccole@reynolds.edu

COLE, Christy ... 540-887-7000 510 A

COLE, Christy, C ... 434-381-6530 513 E ccole@sbc.edu

COLE, Dan ... 402-363-5609 294 G dcole@york.edu

COLE, David ... 817-552-3700 477 B david.cole@tku.edu

COLE, David, J ... 843-792-2211 447 G coledj@musc.edu

COLE, Dayton, T ... 828-262-2751 369 D coledt@appstate.edu

COLE, Donald, R ... 662-915-7474 270 G dcole@olemiss.edu

COLE, Elyne ... 217-333-6677 162 A egcole@illinois.edu

COLE, Frank ... 505-566-3511 312 K colef@sancollege.edu

COLE, Graham ... 847-317-8086 161 B gacole@tiu.edu

COLE, Jack, T ... 717-766-2511 426 B jcole@messiah.edu

COLE, Jeffrey ... 860-439-2030.. 90 D jcole1@conncoll.edu

COLE, Jeffrey, S ... 724-847-4696 419 B jscole@geneva.edu

COLE, Jim ... 478-301-2994 128 G cole_jm@mercer.edu

COLE, Joey ... 501-812-2243.. 22 F jcole@pulaskitech.edu

COLE, John, J ... 304-293-8470 533 D jay.cole@mail.wvu.edu

COLE, Judith, M ... 617-253-8231 233 C

COLE, Karin ... 540-857-7236 517 E kcole@virginiawestern.edu

COLE, Katharine, H ... 813-253-6130 118 H kcole@ut.edu

COLE, Kathryn, B ... 601-857-3502 267 D Kathryn.Cole@hindscc.edu

COLE, Keri ... 601-857-3624 267 D KBCole@hindscc.edu

COLE, Kimberly, K ... 330-972-7608 392 H kmorgan@uakron.edu

COLE, Kristie, C ... 864-231-2067 443 E kcole@andersonuniversity.edu

COLE, Lady June ... 803-376-5701 443 D

COLE, Lance ... 318-795-2392 205 F lance.cole@lsus.edu

COLE, Lauren ... 334-670-3216.... 8 A lscole@troy.edu

COLE, Lauren, G ... 910-642-7141 366 B lauren.cole@sccnc.edu

COLE, Lisa, L ... 318-257-5222 208 A lcole@latech.edu

COLE, Lucinda ... 207-780-4093 213 A lcole@usm.maine.edu

COLE, Maria ... 816-654-7000 276 G

COLE, Mark ... 315-312-3672 346 A rmark.cole@oswego.edu

COLE, Mark ... 305-237-3242 108 L mcole@mdc.edu

COLE, Nadara, L ... 662-720-7277 269 D ncole@nemcc.edu

COLE, Nathan ... 937-381-1555 381 K ncole@edisonohio.edu

COLE, Rebecca, S ... 937-775-2350 396 A rebecca.cole@wright.edu

COLE, Richard ... 732-906-4153 303 F RCole@middlesexcc.edu

COLE, JR., Richard ... 914-633-2311 328 F rcole@iona.edu

COLE, Robert, A ... 401-254-3149 442 C rcole@rwu.edu

COLE, Ronald, B ... 814-332-3393 411 F rcole@allegheny.edu

COLE, Sherri ... 636-227-2100 277 A sherri.cole@logan.edu

COLE, Stephanie, A ... 716-286-8319 336 E scole@niagara.edu

COLE, Stephen, W ... 845-575-3000 331 L stephen.cole@marist.edu

COLE, Steve ... 870-584-4471.. 24 E scole@cccua.edu

COLE, Susan, A ... 973-655-4212 304 A coles@mail.montclair.edu

COLE, W. Scott ... 407-823-2482 115 C scott.cole@ucf.edu

COLE, Wayne ... 563-441-4011 178 D wcole@eicc.edu

COLE, Xavier, A ... 410-778-7752 221 D xcole2@washcoll.edu

COLE-VELASQUEZ, Colleen ... 575-624-8011 311 K cvelasquez@nmmi.edu

COLEAL, Sharlene ... 661-362-3405.. 40 H sharlene.coleal@canyons.edu

COLECCHIA, Carlo ... 201-355-1124 302 I colecchiac@felician.edu

COLELLA, Carlo ... 301-405-6400 219 D ccolella@umd.edu

COLELLA, Kurt, J ... 860-444-8275 548 H kurt.j.colella@uscg.mil

COLELLA, Laurie 508-831-4922 238 G lcolella@wpi.edu
COLELLO, Elizabeth 315-268-3826 321 C ecolello@clarkson.edu
COLEMAN, Alvin 870-633-4480 20 J acoleman@eacc.edu
COLEMAN, Anastasia 718-817-3112 326 C acoleman11@fordham.edu
COLEMAN, Angela 850-599-3183 114 D angela.coleman@famu.edu
COLEMAN, Anne Marie 401-874-5270 442 E amc@uri.edu
COLEMAN, Barbara 212-875-4472 315 F bcoleman@bankstreet.edu
COLEMAN, Bob, J 904-620-2700 116 A jcoleman@unf.edu
COLEMAN, Carole, T 928-344-7521 12 B carole.coleman@azwestern.edu
COLEMAN, Catherine, T 870-633-4480 20 J ccoleman@eacc.edu
COLEMAN, Chad 928-314-.953 12 B chad.coleman@azwestern.edu
COLEMAN, Chad 574-535-7292 166 C chadc@goshen.edu
COLEMAN, Clarence, D 757-823-8408 510 H cdcoleman@nsu.edu
COLEMAN, Clinton, R 443-885-3022 217 C clinton.coleman@morgan.edu
COLEMAN, Craig, S 412-397-4912 434 B colemanc@rmu.edu
COLEMAN, Daniel 410-462-8432 213 G dacoleman@bccc.edu
COLEMAN, David 859-622-1403 194 L david.coleman@eku.edu
COLEMAN, Dayna, L 509-777-4565 529 A dcoleman@whitworth.edu
COLEMAN, Deidra 210-436-3135 481 C dcoleman@stmarytx.edu
COLEMAN, Dennis 214-379-5514 480 D dcoleman@pqc.edu
COLEMAN, Diane 206-934-3842 526 A diane.coleman@seattlecolleges.edu
COLEMAN, Don 423-354-2533 463 D dscoleman@northeaststate.edu
COLEMAN, Ellen 302-736-2508 94 E ellen.coleman@wesley.edu
COLEMAN, Emily 606-539-4230 200 F emily.coleman@ucumberlands.edu
COLEMAN, F. Paul 607-431-4449 327 B colemanf@hartwick.edu
COLEMAN, Frances, N 662-325-7661 269 A fcoleman@library.msstate.edu
COLEMAN, Hardin, L 617-353-3213 224 E hardin@bu.edu
COLEMAN, James, S 804-828-1674 514 F jscoleman@vcu.edu
COLEMAN, Jaunita 304-457-6407 529 C colemanj@ab.edu
COLEMAN, Jay, T 319-352-8264 183 J todd.coleman@wartburg.edu
COLEMAN, Jessica 904-264-2172 111 G
COLEMAN, John 612-624-2535 265 C coleman@umn.edu
COLEMAN, John 903-434-8104 479 L jcoleman@ntcc.edu
COLEMAN, Jonathan 920-206-2346 536 T jonathan.coleman@mbu.edu
COLEMAN, Joyce 708-534-4124 145 D jcoleman@govst.edu
COLEMAN, Joyce 541-440-4600 410 E joyce.coleman@umpqua.edu
COLEMAN, June 620-341-5407 186 H jcoleman@emporia.edu
COLEMAN, Karen, W 773-702-7770 161 D Kwcoleman@uchicago.edu
COLEMAN, Lamar 860-465-0147 88 E colemanl@easternct.edu
COLEMAN, Larry 305-626-3713 104 B Larry.Coleman@fmuniv.edu
COLEMAN, Laura 906-786-5802 240 K colemanl@baycollege.edu
COLEMAN, Linda 610-519-4074 439 A linda.coleman@villanova.edu
COLEMAN, Lynn, C 443-518-4918 215 F lcoleman@howardcc.edu
COLEMAN, Marcus, A 225-771-3920 207 A marcus_coleman@subr.edu
COLEMAN, Marion, A 717-358-7194 418 J marion.coleman@fandm.edu
COLEMAN, Mark 270-384-8040 198 C colemanm@lindsey.edu
COLEMAN, Mark 505-538-6011 314 E colemanm1@wnmu.edu
COLEMAN, Mary 646-313-8000 321 A mary.coleman@guttman.cuny.edu
COLEMAN, Mary 617-349-8458 228 B mcolema5@lesley.edu
COLEMAN, Michael 313-664-7676 241 D mcoleman@collegeforcreativestudies.edu
COLEMAN, Mike 850-201-8427 117 B colemanm@tcc.fl.edu
COLEMAN, Mychal 301-934-7724 214 E mcoleman3@csmd.edu
COLEMAN, Rachel, C 620-417-1125 191 A rachel.coleman@sccc.edu
COLEMAN, Reggie 405-491-6366 402 E rcoleman@snu.edu
COLEMAN, Richard, A 812-888-4280 174 F rcoleman@vinu.edu
COLEMAN, Rob 562-907-4271 77 E rcoleman@whittier.edu
COLEMAN, Robert 973-275-2891 308 C robert.coleman@shu.edu
COLEMAN, Robert, M 973-275-2891 308 C robert.coleman@shu.edu
COLEMAN, Roshell 870-733-6722 19 G rfcoleman@midsouthcc.edu
COLEMAN, S. Michelle 415-575-6160 31 C mcoleman@ciis.edu
COLEMAN, Sean 412-365-1164 415 C scoleman1@chatham.edu
COLEMAN, Stephen, F 607-735-1804 324 J scoleman@elmira.edu
COLEMAN, Steve, B 864-941-8373 448 D coleman.s@ptc.edu
COLEMAN, Susan 714-432-5531 40 D scoleman@occ.cccd.edu
COLEMAN, Tammy 870-584-4471 24 E tcoleman@cccua.edu
COLEMAN, Teresa 912-538-3103 132 A tcoleman@southeasterntech.edu
COLEMAN, Tina, L 757-221-1791 506 J tina.coleman@wm.edu
COLEMAN, Tony 573-876-7299 283 A tcoleman@stephens.edu
COLEMAN, Tonya, R 678-359-5435 126 E tonya_c@gordonstate.edu
COLEMAN, Trina 757-728-6988 508 C trina.coleman@hamptonu.edu
COLEMAN, Valorie 417-690-2212 273 C vcoleman@cofo.edu
COLEMAN, Vicki 336-334-7782 370 B vcoleman@ncat.edu
COLEMAN-CARTER, Marjorie 973-655-4118 304 A carterm@mail.montclair.edu
COLES, Alvie 706-355-5175 120 G acoles@athenstech.edu
COLES, Hakien 215-785-0111 429 F
COLES, Julius 404-215-6040 128 L julius.coles@morehouse.edu
COLES, Shanna 704-687-1277 371 B shannacoles@uncc.edu
COLES, Uva, C 215-545-6400 428 A uccoles@peirce.edu
COLESTOCK, Dennis 509-313-4103 522 L colestock@gonzaga.edu
COLETTA, Gerard 617-573-8115 237 B gcoletta@suffolk.edu
COLEY, Camille 561-297-3461 114 E ccoley@fau.edu
COLEY, Karen 920-887-4426 543 F kcoley@morainepark.edu
COLEY, Kathryn, S 631-420-2719 348 B kathy.coley@farmingdale.edu
COLEY, Norman 308-635-6186 294 C coleyn@wncc.edu
COLEY, Ron, T 951-827-5135 72 A ron.coley@ucr.edu
COLEY, Soraya, M 909-869-2290 32 F president@cpp.edu
COLGAN, OSB, Tobias 812-357-6981 173 A tcolgan@saintmeinrad.edu
COLGAN, William 802-225-3342 502 F will.colgan@neci.edu
COLGATE, Beverly 805-893-2218 72 D beverly.colgate@ucsb.edu
COLGROVE, Marianne, M 503-777-7792 409 E mcolgrov@reed.edu
COLIN, Cherie 650-378-6161 64 D colinc@smccd.edu
COLIN, Cherie 650-738-4346 64 E colinc@smccd.edu
COLIP, Mark 312-949-7405 146 E mcolip@ico.edu
COLL, James, P 601-266-4491 271 B james.coll@usm.edu
COLL, Kenneth 775-682-7853 295 H kcoll@unr.edu
COLL, Stephen, W 212-854-6056 322 F steve.coll@columbia.edu
COLLADO, Arturo, J 787-728-2161 557 G arturo.collado@upr.edu
COLLADO, Shirley, M 973-353-5541 307 C shirleym.collado@rutgers.edu
COLLADO-SCHWARZ, Angel 787-725-6500 551 A acs@albizu.edu
COLLAR, Doug 419-448-2157 383 C dcollar@heidelberg.edu
COLLARD, Bruce 603-668-2211 298 H b.collard@snhu.edu
COLLAZO, Carmen 787-250-1912 554 A ccollazo@metro.inter.edu
COLLAZO, Julio, A 787-758-2525 558 C julio.collazo@upr.edu
COLLAZO, Lydia 787-780-5134 554 H lcollazo@nuc.edu
COLLAZO, Mariela 787-766-1717 556 A mcollazo@suagm.edu
COLLAZO, Samaris 787-743-7979 555 M s_collazo@suagm.edu
COLLAZO-CASTRO, Shelciy 787-993-8876 557 E shelciy.collazo@upr.edu
COLLEN, Dan 707-826-3666 35 D dgc7001@humboldt.edu
COLLEN, Jodi 612-330-1107 253 K collen@augsburg.edu
COLLER, Barry, S 212-327-7490 339 H collerb@rockefeller.edu
COLLERAN, Jeanne 216-397-4215 384 F jcolleran@jcu.edu
COLLETTI, Nikki 504-398-2130 206 E ncolletti@olhcc.edu
COLLEY, Debra, A 716-286-8560 336 E dcolley@niagara.edu
COLLEY, Karen 312-413-2548 161 F karenc@uic.edu
COLLEY, Kenna 540-831-5439 511 C kcolley@radford.edu
COLLIE, Cynthia 336-506-4410 359 N cynthia.collie@alamancecc.edu
COLLIE, Pamela, J 276-328-0128 514 B pjc9w@uvawise.edu
COLLIE, Susan, A 501-882-8967 19 E sacollie@asub.edu
COLLIER, Adrienne 585-245-5020 345 D collier@geneseo.edu
COLLIER, Barbara 323-226-6301 52 D bcollier@dhs.lacounty.gov
COLLIER, Barbara 323-226-4911 52 D bcollier@dhs.lacounty.gov
COLLIER, Barry, S 317-940-8421 164 L bcollier@butler.edu
COLLIER, Cindy 661-395-4281 49 E ccollier@bakersfieldcollege.edu
COLLIER, Diondrae 408-273-2688 55 G dcollier@nhu.edu
COLLIER, Diondrae 619-684-8803 56 B dcollier@newschoolarch.edu
COLLIER, Douglas 253-752-2020 522 K accounting@faithseminary.edu
COLLIER, Jay 402-375-7325 292 D jacolli1@wsc.edu
COLLIER, Kristen, L 937-327-7523 395 I kcollier@wittenberg.edu
COLLIER, Lauren, K 615-230-3530 464 B lauren.collier@volstate.edu
COLLIER, Li 707-524-1797 65 C lcollier@santarosa.edu
COLLIER, Lisa 217-786-2446 151 C lisa.collier@llcc.edu
COLLIER, Lula 662-254-3618 269 C lcollier@mvsu.edu
COLLIER, Richard 315-792-7100 348 D rcollier@sunycnse.com
COLLIER, Roger 918-449-6521 398 M collier@nsuok.edu
COLLIER, Sam 859-442-1146 196 A sam.collier@kctcs.edu
COLLIER, Scott 704-290-5872 366 A scollier@spcc.edu
COLLIER, Sharon 870-633-4480 20 J scollier@eacc.edu
COLLIER, Stephanie 559-730-3735 41 D stephanieco@cos.edu
COLLIER, Willyerd, R 765-361-6384 175 B collierw@wabash.edu
COLLIER, Yeman 210-567-7052 495 B colliery@uthscsa.edu
COLLIER-WHITE, Nelva, G 410-651-7700 219 H ngcollier@umes.edu
COLLING, Lynnde 307-268-2247 545 Z lcolling@caspercollege.edu
COLLINGWOOD, Tracy 716-673-3327 343 F tracy.collingwood@fredonia.edu
COLLINS, Alyssa, D 417-255-7265 279 B alyssacollins@missouristate.edu
COLLINS, Amber 606-218-5251 201 C ambercollins@upike.edu
COLLINS, Anthony, G 315-268-6444 321 C president@clarkson.edu
COLLINS, Aristide, J 202-994-6500 95 D aristide@gwu.edu
COLLINS, Ashley 703-329-9100 96 H
COLLINS, Bob 801-274-3280 501 B robert.collins@wgu.edu
COLLINS, Bruce 334-556-2447 4 A bcollins@wallace.edu
COLLINS, Bryan 516-299-2847 330 G bryan.collins@liu.edu
COLLINS, Buddy 662-862-8271 267 F bacollins@iccms.edu
COLLINS, Carri 215-871-6154 432 E carric@pcom.edu
COLLINS, Celeste 212-472-1500 336 A ccollins@nysid.edu
COLLINS, Chinneta 301-423-3600 96 H
COLLINS, Christine 337-421-6969 204 F christine.collins@sowela.edu
COLLINS, Dana 580-349-1574 400 B danac@opsu.edu
COLLINS, Darron 207-801-5601 210 B dcollins@coa.edu
COLLINS, Dave 937-512-2522 391 D dave.collins@sinclair.edu
COLLINS, David 501-279-4291 21 A dcollins@harding.edu
COLLINS, David, D 423-439-5884 461 D collinsd@etsu.edu
COLLINS, Dawn, M 773-508-3802 151 E dcollins4@luc.edu
COLLINS, Dean, C 706-385-1094 130 C dean.collins@point.edu
COLLINS, Deanne 770-531-6360 128 A dcollins@laniertech.edu
COLLINS, Deborah 870-230-5000 21 B collind@hsu.edu
COLLINS, Debra 214-333-5220 471 L debrac@dbu.edu
COLLINS, Derrick, K 773-995-3505 141 J dcollins@csu.edu
COLLINS, Dorothy 740-264-5591 381 J dcollins@egcc.edu
COLLINS, Dwight 415-561-6555 60 C
COLLINS, Elaine, C 802-635-1240 504 A jscpres@jsc.edu
COLLINS, Elizabeth 508-531-2811 229 C elizabeth.collins@bridgew.edu
COLLINS, Elizabeth 303-860-5600 86 D elizabeth.collins@cu.edu
COLLINS, Ellen 402-552-6140 289 H collins@clarksoncollege.edu
COLLINS, Ernest 215-635-7300 419 D ecollins@gratz.edu
COLLINS, Fuji 209-228-4331 71 E FCollins@UCMerced.edu
COLLINS, Gary 478-301-2970 128 G collins_g@mercer.edu
COLLINS, Gregory 530-251-8889 50 B gcollins@lassencollege.edu
COLLINS, Jacqueline, M 410-651-6407 219 H jmcollins@umes.edu
COLLINS, James 916-558-2279 53 B collins@scc.losrios.edu
COLLINS, James, E 508-793-7443 225 B jcollins@clarku.edu
COLLINS, James, E 563-588-7103 180 L jim.collins@loras.edu
COLLINS, Jennifer, M 214-768-8999 482 J jmc@smu.edu
COLLINS, Jim 256-766-6610 4 C jcollins@hcu.edu
COLLINS, Jodi 912-478-5519 126 B jcollins@georgiasouthern.edu
COLLINS, Jodie 360-475-7682 524 H jcollins@olympic.edu
COLLINS, John 707-965-6311 57 I jcollins@puc.edu
COLLINS, John 812-866-6837 166 E collins@hanover.edu
COLLINS, John 609-771-2167 301 E jcollins@tcnj.edu
COLLINS, John, D 727-816-3310 110 B collinj@phsc.edu
COLLINS, Joseph 630-942-2690 142 F collinsj@cod.edu
COLLINS, Joseph, L 630-942-2690 142 F collinsj@cod.edu
COLLINS, Justin 580-349-1522 400 B jkcollins@opsu.edu
COLLINS, Kamari 413-755-4558 233 B kacollins@stcc.edu
COLLINS, Kathy 713-348-5147 480 M kcollins@rice.edu
COLLINS, Kevin 407-366-9493 270 B kcollins@rts.edu
COLLINS, Kevin 239-590-7966 114 F kcollins@fgcu.edu
COLLINS, Kim 706-419-1439 123 F kim.collins@covenant.edu
COLLINS, Kimberley 585-292-2105 333 G kcollins@monroecc.edu
COLLINS, Kristine 208-426-2484 137 E kcollin@boisestate.edu
COLLINS, Kristy 310-506-4116 58 H kristy.collins@pepperdine.edu

COLLINS, L. Victor .... 410-704-2051 221 A
vcollins@towson.edu
COLLINS, Lance, R .... 607-255-9679 323 C
lc246@cornell.edu
COLLINS, Laverne .... 412-536-1059 422 E
laverne.collins@laroche.edu
COLLINS, Leadra .... 706-821-8233 129 H
lcollins@paine.edu
COLLINS, Leigh Ann ..... 979-532-6520 497 F
lacollins@wcjc.edu
COLLINS, Marie .... 239-489-9214 104 G
mcollins11@fsw.edu
COLLINS, Mark .... 978-837-5131 233 G
collinsma@merrimack.edu
COLLINS, Mark, A .... 307-766-4196 546 K
mcollin7@uwyo.edu
COLLINS, Mary .... 724-805-2564 435 B
mary.collins@email.stvincent.edu
COLLINS, Mary, K .... 315-445-4791 330 B
collinsm@lemoyne.edu
COLLINS,
Mary Elizabeth .... 253-879-3237 527 F
lcollins@pugetsound.edu
COLLINS, Matthew .... 502-895-3411 198 E
mcollins@lpts.edu
COLLINS, Megan .... 619-594-4562.. 35 E
mcollins@mail.sdsu.edu
COLLINS, Megan .... 619-594-5201.. 35 E
mcollins@mail.sdsu.edu
COLLINS, Michael .... 805-525-4417.. 69 I
mcollins@thomasaquinas.edu
COLLINS, Michael .... 714-564-6981.. 60 G
collins_michaelT@sac.edu
COLLINS, Michael .... 641-673-1393 184 B
collinsm@wmpenn.edu
COLLINS, Michael .... 269-488-4255 244 J
mcollins@kvcc.edu
COLLINS, Michael, F .... 508-856-8100 229 B
michael.collins@umassmed.edu
COLLINS, Michelle .... 501-205-8795.. 20 G
mcollin@cbc.edu
COLLINS, Mildred, D .... 615-327-6413 458 F
mcollins@mmc.edu
COLLINS, Miranda .... 740-376-4458 386 A
miranda.collins@marietta.edu
COLLINS, Monique .... 850-484-1630 110 D
mcollins@pensacolastate.edu
COLLINS, Nicole .... 207-509-7213 212 A
ncollins@unity.edu
COLLINS, Patti-Ann ...... 617-228-2027 231 C
pcollins@bhcc.mass.edu
COLLINS, Paul .... 312-662-4448 139 E
pcollins@adler.edu
COLLINS, Phil .... 706-864-1545 133 A
phil.collins@ung.edu
COLLINS, Ray .... 404-527-4520 122 D
rcollins@carver.edu
COLLINS, Richard .... 661-654-2221.. 32 G
rcollins6@csub.edu
COLLINS, SR.,
Ronnie, L .... 410-951-3392 220 C
rcollins@coppin.edu
COLLINS, Sarah .... 315-498-2762 337 F
collinss@sunyocc.edu
COLLINS, Scott .... 518-736-3622 326 D
scollins@fmcc.suny.edu
COLLINS, Sean .... 617-521-2296 236 F
sean.collins@simmons.edu
COLLINS, Steve .... 870-612-2026.. 24 G
steve.collins@uaccb.edu
COLLINS, Steve .... 217-732-3168 150 G
scollins@lincolnchristian.edu
COLLINS, Susan, M ...... 734-763-2258 251 C
smcol@umich.edu
COLLINS, Sylvia .... 931-393-1679 463 B
scollins@mscc.edu
COLLINS, Trudy .... 406-657-1680 287 H
tcollins@msubillings.edu
COLLINS, Valerie .... 516-323-3008 333 E
office-of-academic-affairs@molloy.edu
COLLINS, Walter .... 707-965-7500.. 57 I
wcollins@puc.edu
COLLINS, Wanda .... 919-660-1024 356 E
wanda.collins@duke.edu
COLLINS, II, William .... 716-888-8208 317 H
collinsw@canisius.edu
COLLINS, Yadigar .... 740-587-6530 381 H
collinsy@denison.edu
COLLINS-HALL, Lori ..... 937-767-1286 376 K
COLLINWOOD, Nancy ... 801-626-6569 500 C
ncollinwood@weber.edu
COLLIS, Jennifer .... 440-375-7175 385 B
jcollis@lec.edu
COLLMIER, Robert .... 973-748-9000 300 E
robert_collmier@bloomfield.edu
COLLOGAN, Jessica ...... 904-256-7269 106 Q
jcollog@ju.edu
COLLOPY, David .... 413-528-7773 222 F
dcollopy@simons-rock.edu
COLLUM, Anne .... 310-825-2827.. 71 D
acollum@asucla.ucla.edu
COLLUM, Tammy .... 770-975-4000 122 H
COLMAN, Avrohom ...... 732-367-1060 300 D
COLMAN, Glenn .... 870-743-3000.. 22 A
gcoleman@northark.edu
COLMENERO,
Jacinto (JC) .... 361-354-2559 470 K
jcolmenero@coastalbend.edu
COLMERAUER, Joanne .. 716-270-2826 325 A
colmerauer@ecc.edu
COLOM, Alberto, N .... 904-620-2881 116 A
colom@unf.edu
COLOMBAT, Andre .... 410-617-2910 216 D
acp@loyola.edu
COLOMBO, Chris .... 617-253-8566 233 C
COLOMBO, Diana .... 201-216-5213 308 D
dcolombo@stevens.edu
COLOMBO, Samuel .... 607-753-2305 345 C
samuel.colombo@cortland.edu
COLON,
Adabel-Vanessa .... 787-250-1912 554 A
avcolon@metro.inter.edu
COLON, Ana Isabel .... 787-857-3600 553 G
acolon@br.inter.edu
COLON, Angie .... 787-863-2390 553 I
angie.colon@fajardo.inter.edu
COLON, Diana, M .... 787-257-7373 555 L
dmcolon@suagm.edu
COLON, Eddie .... 816-279-7000 271 H
eddie.colon@abtu.edu
COLON, Efrain .... 787-738-2161 557 G
efrain.colon@upr.edu
COLON, Hector, W .... 787-284-1912 554 B
hwcolon@ponce.inter.edu
COLON, Jaime .... 787-279-1912 553 H
jcolon@bayamon.inter.edu
COLON, Leandro .... 787-841-2000 555 F
leandro_colon@pucpr.edu
COLON, Lesbia .... 787-844-8181 558 D
lesbia.colon@upr.edu
COLON, Luis .... 787-815-0000 557 D
luis.colon19@upr.edu
COLON, Maggie .... 787-763-1912 553 D
mcolon@inter.edu
COLON, Maria .... 787-765-3560 552 E
mscolon@edpuniversity.edu
COLON, Michelle 407-888-8689 103M
mcolon@fcim.edu
COLON, Mirta .... 787-754-8000 556 H
mcolon@pupr.edu
COLON, Myrna .... 787-834-9595 556 D
mcolon@uaa.edu
COLON, Nidia .... 787-786-3030 556 E
ncolon@ucb.edu.pr
COLON, Ruben .... 787-841-2000 555 F
ruben_colon@pucpr.edu
COLON, Victor .... 787-786-3030 556 E
vcolon@ucb.edu.pr
COLON, Vilma, E .... 787-284-1912 554 B
vcolon@ponce.inter.edu
COLON, Yarelis .... 787-753-6000 552 K
ycolon@icprjc.edu
COLON-CANALES,
Wanda .... 301-891-4000 221 C
wcolon@wau.edu
COLON COSME,
Edwin, J .... 787-744-1060 554 F
edwincolon@mechtech.edu
COLON NEGRON,
Edgar .... 787-758-2525 558 C
edgar.colon2@upr.edu
COLON-RAMOS,
Carlos, E .... 787-864-2222 553 J
carlos.colon@guayama.inter.edu
COLORADO, Ana .... 787-725-8120 552 G
acolorado0013@eap.edu
COLORETTI, Angela .... 808-735-4787 135 A
angela.coloretti@chaminade.edu
COLSON, Darrel, D .... 319-352-8450 183 J
president@wartburg.edu
COLSON, Matthew .... 631-632-4932 344 C
matthew.colson@stonybrook.edu
COLSON, Roland .... 615-320-1067 455 E
colsonr@bethelu.edu
COLTER-BRABHAM,
Constance .... 803-780-1189 451 G
cbrabham@voorhees.edu
COLTHARP, Duane .... 210-999-8201 490 E
dcolthar@trinity.edu
COLTHARP, Glenn .... 417-455-5740 274 B
GlennColtharp@crowder.edu
COLTMAN, Heather .... 561-297-3803 114 E
coltman@fau.edu
COLTRANE, Scott, L ...... 541-346-3186 410 F
provost@uoregon.edu
COLUCCI, David .... 718-779-1499 338 D
dcolluci@plazacollege.edu
COLUCCI, Rita .... 508-626-4993 230 A
rcolucci@framingham.edu
COLUMBUS, Kristi .... 319-895-4153 177 A
kcolumbus@cornellcollege.edu
COLUSSY-ESTES, Kate ... 404-471-6437 119 G
kcolussyestes@agnesscott.edu
COLVEY, Kirsten, S .... 909-389-3327.. 62 B
kcolvey@craftonhills.educa.us
COLVILLE, John .... 903-988-3747 477 A
jcolville@kilgore.edu
COLVIN, Brandon .... 701-228-5452 374 F
brandon.colvin@dakotacollege.edu
COLVIN, Christopher .... 508-213-2368 235 C
christopher.colvin@nichols.edu
COLVIN, Dora .... 956-364-4119 487 H
dora.olivares@tstc.edu
COLVIN, Robert, E .... 757-594-0723 506 I
rcolvin@cnu.edu
COLVSON, W. Mark ...... 845-257-3719 344 A
colvsonm@newpaltz.edu
COLWELL, Brad .... 419-372-7403 377 I
bcolwell@bgsu.edu
COLWELL, Ken .... 860-832-3217.. 88 D
COLWELL, Kim, H .... 217-443-8769 143 F
kcolwell@dacc.edu
COLWELL, William, B ... 618-453-2121 159 H
COLYAR, Jana .... 801-333-8100 498 F
jana.colyar@eaglegatecollege.edu
COLYAR, Jana .... 801-818-8900 498 P
jana.colyar@provocollege.edu
COMAGE, Rebecca .... 978-542-2404 230 E
rebecca.comage@salemstate.edu
COMAIR, Claude .... 425-558-0299 522 B
ccomair@digipen.edu
COMALANDER, Tammy . 251-981-3771.... 3 A
tammy.comalander@columbiasouthern.edu
COMANDA, Peter .... 815-280-6606 148 K
pcomanda@jjc.edu
COMAS, Waldemar, A ... 914-594-4567 335 H
waldemar_comas@nymc.edu
COMBE, Arnold, B .... 801-581-6404 499 K
arnie.combe@admin.utah.edu
COMBEN, Lisa .... 734-432-5601 246 B
lcomben@madonna.edu
COMBINE, Mark, S .... 724-738-2251 432 A
mark.combine@sru.edu
COMBS, Brandon .... 859-858-3511 193 A
brandon.combs@asbury.edu
COMBS, Charles, D .... 757-446-6090 507 B
combscd@evms.edu
COMBS, Delcie .... 606-487-3100 196 B
delcie.combs@kctcs.edu
COMBS, Joseph, D .... 615-322-4782 465 H
joseph.d.combs@vanderbilt.edu
COMBS, Joseph, L .... 423-585-2675 464 C
joseph.combs@ws.edu
COMBS, Kristina, A .... 415-485-9504.. 41 B
kcombs@marin.edu
COMBS, Steven .... 417-873-7204 274 E
scombs@drury.edu
COMBS, Vickie .... 606-487-3110 196 B
vickie.combs@kctcs.edu
COMEAU, Juanita .... 608-246-6596 543 C
jcomeau@madisoncollege.edu
COMEAUX, David, P ..... 337-482-0922 208 F
dcomeaux@louisiana.edu
COMEAUX, Linda .... 303-914-6403.. 85 C
linda.comeaux@rrcc.edu
COMEAUX, Mark .... 714-879-3901.. 47 D
mcomeaux@hiu.edu
COMEDY-HOLMES,
Jennifer .... 210-486-4857 466 K
jcomedy-holmes@alamo.edu
COMEGYS, Marianne .... 318-675-6065 205 D
mcomeg@lsuhsc.edu
COMER, Alberta .... 801-585-9521 499 K
alberta.comer@utah.edu
COMER, Charlotte .... 501-420-1213.. 19 B
charlotte.comer@arkansasbaptist.edu
COMER, Christopher ..... 406-243-2632 287 D
chris.comer@umontana.edu
COMER, Crystal .... 612-330-1034 253 K
comerc@augsburg.edu
COMER, Kimberly .... 229-928-1373 126 C
kim.comer@gsw.edu
COMER, Pamela, D .... 540-432-4314 507 A
pam.comer@emu.edu
COMERFORD, Ann .... 309-298-1931 163 A
at-comerford@wiu.edu
COMERFORD, John ...... 217-854-3231 140 F
john.comerford@blackburn.edu
COMERFORD,
Sandra Stefani .... 650-574-6404.. 64 D
comerford@smccd.edu
COMEY, William .... 301-934-7509 214 E
billc@csmd.edu
COMINGORE, Terry ...... 979-230-3318 469 G
terry.comingore@brazosport.edu
COMMETTE, Jeanne ...... 978-232-2344 226 C
jcommett@endicott.edu
COMMISSO, Louis .... 516-918-3609 316 L
lcommisso@bcl.edu
COMMON, Brandon, H . 309-556-3802 148 A
bcommon@iwu.edu
COMMON, Easter .... 601-977-7879 270 F
ecommon@tougaloo.edu
COMMONS, Mary .... 803-508-7413 443 C
commonsm@atc.edu
COMPAAN, Korey .... 952-446-4233 255 E
compaank@crown.edu
COMPARY, Kristin .... 361-593-3606 486 A
kristin.company@tamuk.edu
COMPHER, Jeff .... 252-737-4501 369 E
compherj@ecu.edu
COMPLIMENT, Brad ...... 562-985-4001.. 33 F
brad.compliment@csulb.edu
COMPTON, Allyssa .... 845-368-7203 342 A
allyssa.compton@use.salvationarmy.org
COMPTON, Betsy .... 205-652-3892.... 9 G
bcompton@uwa.edu
COMPTON, Duane, A .... 603-650-1200 297 G
duane.a.compton@dartmouth.edu
COMPTON, Jennifer ...... 517-264-3175 238 H
COMRIE, Andrew, C ...... 520-621-1856.. 18 E
comrie@email.arizona.edu
COMSTOCK, Alysha ...... 708-524-6296 144 C
acomstock@dom.edu
COMSTOCK, Cheryl .... 970-339-6216.. 78 J
cheryl.comstock@aims.edu
COMVALIUS-GODDARD,
Sharon .... 617-552-8259 224 B
sharon.comvalius-goddard@bc.edu
CONARD, T. Hunt .... 518-580-5940 342 I
hconard@skidmore.edu
CONASTER, Sherri .... 405-878-5416 402 A
seconaster@stgregorys.edu
CONAWAY,
Kathleen, M .... 814-332-4799 411 F
kconaway@allegheny.edu
CONBOY,
Sheila (Katie) .... 617-521-2077 236 F
katie.conboy@simmons.edu
CONCANNON, Chris ..... 360-992-2411 521 A
cconcannon@clark.edu
CONCEPCIÓN, Carmen . 787-764-0000 558 E
concepcioncm@yahoo.com
CONCEPCION, Beth .... 912-525-5000 130 H
bconcepc@scad.edu
CONCEPCION, Lillian .... 787-250-1912 554 A
lconcepcion@metro.inter.edu
CONCHA, Lee .... 847-578-8848 157 G
lee.concha@rosalindfranklin.edu
CONCILIO, Michael .... 215-335-0800 424 D
mconcilio@lincolntech.edu
CONCODORA, Jackie .... 803-323-2233 451 I
concodoraj@winthrop.edu
CONCODORA, Jackie .... 803-323-2206 451 I
concodoraj@winthrop.edu
CONDE, Carlos, R .... 787-751-0160 551 K
cconde@cmpr.pr.gov
CONDE, Jean .... 650-508-3513.. 56 H
jconde@ndnu.edu
CONDE-FRAZIER,
Elizabeth .... 215-324-0746 418 A
econdefr@eastern.edu
CONDELL, Greg .... 617-373-5144 235 D
CONDIC, Elizabeth .... 713-525-6960 493 J
condice@stthom.edu
CONDIE, Brad .... 262-243-5700 535 I
brad.condie@cuw.edu
CONDON, Jacquelyn, S 309-457-2113 153 B
jackiec@monmouthcollege.edu
CONDON, Jennifer .... 813-974-6061 116 B
jcondon@admin.usf.edu
CONDON, Jennifer, M .. 515-574-1190 179 F
condon@iowacentral.edu
CONDON, Katherine ..... 850-474-2230 116 E
kcondon@uwf.edu
CONDON, Lisa .... 860-768-4007.. 92 F
lcondon@hartford.edu
CONDON, Michael, A ... 214-768-2802 482 J
mikec@smu.edu
CONDON, Patricia .... 508-678-2811 231 B
patricia.condon@bristolcc.edu
CONDON, Sara, A .... 515-574-1005 179 F
condon_s@iowacentral.edu
CONDON, Stephen, M .. 336-887-3000 358 E
scondon@laureluniversity.edu
CONDON, Tami .... 269-471-3591 239 D
alumni@andrews.edu
CONDON, Terry .... 617-287-7800 228 G
terry.condon@umb.edu
CONDRA, Shawn, M ...... 785-539-3571 189 D
scondra@mccks.edu
CONDRON, Dan .... 707-664-2158.. 36 C
condrond@sonoma.edu
CONDRON, Leanne .... 724-480-3401 416 A
leanne.condron@ccbc.edu
CONDUAH, Dorothy ...... 608-243-4746 543 C
dconduah@madisoncollege.edu
CONE, Allen, J .... 323-265-8913.. 51 D
coneaj@elac.edu
CONE, Angela, W .... 334-420-4216.... 7 I
acone@trenholmstate.edu

CONE, Christopher .... 619-201-8970.. 67 I
christopher.cone@socalsem.edu
CONE, Diana .... 912-478-5258 126 B
dcone@georgiasouthern.edu
CONE, Janet, R .... 828-251-6922 370 E
jcone@unca.edu
CONE, Nicki .... 956-364-4602 487 H
nicki.cone@tstc.edu
CONEWAY, Raydor .... 478-275-6589 129 D
CONEWAY, Raydor .... 478-553-2065 129 C
rconeway@oftc.edu
CONEY, Lennetta .... 810-762-0269 247 F
lennetta.coney@mcc.edu
CONFER,
Christopher, L .... 765-641-4219 164 B
clconfer@anderson.edu
CONGDON, Bruce, D .... 206-281-2899 526 D
bcongdon@spu.edu
CONGER, Heather .... 609-894-9311 306 B
hconger@bcc.edu
CONGER, Lora .... 918-270-6402 401 C
lora.conger@ptstulsa.edu
CONGLETON, Dawn, L .. 434-223-6203 508 B
dcongleton@hsc.edu
CONGLETON, O. Mort .. 919-866-5926 366 H
omcongleton@waketech.edu
CONGRESSI, Karyn .... 386-752-1822 103 Q
karyn.congressi@fgc.edu
CONIGLIO, Michael ...... 706-880-8184 127 N
mconiglio@lagrange.edu
CONINE, Chris .... 423-614-8102 457 M
cconine@leeuniversity.edu
CONINE, Darren .... 978-837-5154 233 G
conined@merrimack.edu
CONINE, Frances .... 318-357-6703 208 D
coninef@nsula.edu
CONISON, Jay .... 704-971-8500 355 J
jconison@charlottelaw.edu
CONJAR, Catarin .... 610-647-4400 421 B
cconjar@immaculata.edu
CONKLIN, Barbara .... 252-399-6570 354 I
baconklin@barton.edu
CONKLIN, David .... 716-488-3026 329 D
davidconklin@jamestownbusinesscollege.edu
CONKLIN, Denise .... 405-912-9005 398 B
dconklin@hc.edu
CONKLIN, Eileen .... 915-831-4432 473 J
econklin@epcc.edu
CONKLIN, Elizabeth .... 860-486-2943.. 92 C
elizabeth.conklin@uconn.edu
CONKLIN, Kathleen ...... 517-371-5140 252 J
conklink@cooley.edu
CONKLIN, Lara, L .... 217-443-8798 143 F
lconklin@dacc.edu
CONKLIN, Margaret ...... 212-355-1501 318 A
mconklin@christies.edu
CONKLIN, Peter .... 603-513-1382 299 C
peter.conklin@granite.edu
CONKLIN, Robin .... 845-574-4484 339 I
rconklin@sunyrockland.edu
CONLEY, Aaron .... 303-492-8908.. 86 E
aaron.conley@colorado.edu
CONLEY, Bill .... 402-554-2358 294 A
bconley@unomaha.edu
CONLEY, Cary .... 270-831-9610 196 C
cary.conley@kctcs.edu
CONLEY, Dennis .... 618-395-7777 147 A
conleyd@iecc.edu
CONLEY, Heather .... 319-398-5504 180 J
heather.conley@kirkwood.edu
CONLEY, Jeremy, D ...... 515-574-1086 179 F
conley@iowacentral.edu
CONLEY, Jerome .... 513-529-2800 386 K
conleyj@miamioh.edu
CONLEY, John .... 518-562-4219 321 D
john.conley@clinton.edu
CONLEY, Johnny .... 909-384-8988.. 62 C
jconley@sbccd.cc.ca.us
CONLEY, Katharine .... 757-221-2470 506 J
kconley@wm.edu
CONLEY, Kelli .... 256-840-4101.... 7 B
kconley@snead.edu
CONLEY, Kimberley, S . 270-831-9752 196 C
kim.conley@kctcs.edu
CONLEY, Laura, H .... 330-972-5793 392 H
lhc1@uakron.edu
CONLEY, Maria .... 978-934-2383 229 A
Maria_Conley@uml.edu
CONLEY, Mark .... 206-543-4211 527 G
mconley@uw.edu
CONLEY, Marsha, A ..... 717-866-5775 418 E
mconley@evangelical.edu
CONLEY, MeShawn ...... 405-974-5944 403 G
mconley@uco.edu
CONLEY, Michael Anne 415-442-7281.. 46 A
maconley@ggu.edu
CONLEY, Sean .... 802-258-9203 502 B
sconley@marlboro.edu
CONLEY, Sonja .... 620-331-4100 188 B
sconley@indycc.edu
CONLEY, Terry .... 580-581-2308 397 A
tconley@cameron.edu
CONLEY, Tony .... 870-759-4166.. 25 I
tconley@ebcoll.edu
CONLEY, Valerie .... 719-255-4119.. 86 F
vconley@uccs.edu
CONLEY, William, J ...... 508-793-3423 225 C
wjconley@holycross.edu
CONLEY, William, T ...... 570-577-1618 413 E
bill.conley@bucknell.edu
CONLIFFE, Marcia .... 863-297-1004 110 E
mconliffe@polk.edu
CONLIN, Pam .... 214-768-3738 482 J
pconlin@smu.edu
CONLOGUE, Jon .... 413-572-5572 230 F
jconlogue@westfield.ma.edu
CONLON, Cindy, H .... 256-765-4206.... 9 D
chconlon@una.edu
CONLON, Joanne .... 610-436-3506 432 B
jconlon@wcupa.edu
CONLON, Kevin, J .... 614-222-3220 380 F
kconlon@ccad.edu
CONLON, Kevin, J .... 614-222-6171 380 F
kconlon@ccad.edu
CONN, Brian .... 423-614-8621 457 M
bconn@leeuniversity.edu
CONN, C. Paul .... 423-614-8600 457 M
pconn@leeuniversity.edu
CONN, Melinda .... 314-434-4044 273 J
melinda.conn@covenantseminary.edu
CONN, Michael .... 740-283-6319 382 G
mconn@franciscan.edu
CONN, Michael .... 806-743-3600 490 A
michael.conn@ttuhsc.edu
CONN, Robert .... 618-262-8641 147 B
connr@iecc.edu
CONN, Samuel .... 518-587-2100 348 A
samuel.conn@esc.edu
CONN-KULLING,
Nerissa .... 202-274-2303.. 97 D
admissions@potomac.edu
CONNAGHAN, Stephen . 202-319-5055.. 95 A
connaghan@cua.edu
CONNAUGHTON,
David, M .... 409-772-3446 495 E
dmconnau@utmb.edu
CONNELL, Dan, J .... 606-783-2612 198 H
d.connell@moreheadstate.edu
CONNELL, Matthew, J .. 570-688-2466 427 F
mconnell@northampton.edu
CONNELL, Rich .... 785-670-1860 192 B
rich.connell@washburn.edu
CONNELL, S. Jack .... 585-594-6200 339 F
connell_jack@roberts.edu
CONNELL,
Samuel (Jack) .... 585-594-6100 337 A
connell_jack@roberts.edu
CONNELL, Timothy .... 562-908-3413.. 60 I
tconnell@riohondo.edu
CONNELLY, Carol .... 219-785-5267 172 A
cconnelly@pnc.edu
CONNELLY, Daniel .... 503-725-4842 409 D
CONNELLY, Edward, D . 860-628-4751.. 91 A
econnelly@lincolncollegene.edu
CONNELLY, Frank, P .... 304-243-2241 534 H
fconnelly@wju.edu
CONNELLY, Krysti, H .... 618-537-6861 152 C
khconnelly@mckendree.edu
CONNELLY, Laurie .... 509-359-2371 522 C
lconnelly@ewu.edu
CONNELLY, Pamela, W . 412-624-4685 437 K
pwc4@pitt.edu
CONNELLY, Philip .... 908-737-7000 303 C
pconnell@kean.edu
CONNELLY-WEIDA,
Cecelia, A .... 610-799-1630 424 A
cconnellyweida@lccc.edu
CONNELY, Anne .... 610-398-5300 424 C
aconnely@lincolntech.edu
CONNELY, Kristen .... 425-564-2388 519 L
kristen.connely@bellevuecollege.edu
CONNER, Andrea .... 641-269-3702 178 I
conneran@grinnell.edu
CONNER, Arabie .... 785-242-5200 190 D
arabie.conner@ottawa.edu
CONNER, B. Renee .... 301-784-5206 213 C
rconner@allegany.edu
CONNER, Courtney, L .. 276-619-4317 514 B
cconner@swcenter.edu
CONNER, Cynthia .... 713-221-8614 491 F
Connerc@uhd.edu
CONNER, David .... 806-716-2380 482 F
dconner@southplainscollege.edu
CONNER, Deborah .... 843-349-2300 444 G
dconner@coastal.edu
CONNER, Jamelle .... 727-341-4656 112 A
conner.jamelle@spcollege.edu
CONNER, Lori .... 276-656-0286 516 D
lconner@patrickhenry.edu
CONNER, Marc .... 540-458-8418 519 A
connerc@wlu.edu
CONNER, Phyllis .... 402-375-7510 292 D
phconne1@wsc.edu
CONNER, Rita, D .... 828-694-1825 360 D
ritac@blueridge.edu
CONNER, Shelley .... 209-381-6585.. 54 C
shelley.conner@mccd.edu
CONNER-KERR, Teresa . 706-864-1400 133 A
teresa.conner-kerr@ung.edu
CONNERAT, Carolyn, K 512-475-9223 493 M
cconnerat@austin.utexas.edu
CONNERS, John, R .... 607-844-8222 350 A
connerj@tc3.edu
CONNERTY, Denise, A .. 215-204-0720 436 C
denise.connerty@temple.edu
CONNERY, Elizabeth, A 570-348-6200 425 D
connery@marywood.edu
CONNERY, Judith .... 401-253-1040 442 C
jconnery@rwu.edu
CONNIFF, Brian, P .... 570-941-7560 438 F
brian.conniff@scranton.edu
CONNIRY, JR.,
Charles, J .... 503-554-6152 406 A
cconniry@georgefox.edu
CONNOLLY, Adam .... 843-383-8050 445 A
aconnolly@coker.edu
CONNOLLY, Ann Marie 313-883-8500 249 E
connolly.annmarie@shms.edu
CONNOLLY, Barbara ..... 845-569-3202 333 I
barbara.connolly@msmc.edu
CONNOLLY, Dan .... 920-686-6209 539 A
Dan.Connolly@sl.edu
CONNOLLY, Derry .... 858-653-6740.. 48 Q
DConnolly@JPCatholic.com
CONNOLLY, James .... 203-332-5088.. 89 C
jconnolly@hcc.commnet.edu
CONNOLLY, James, D .. 203-332-5090.. 89 C
jconnolly@hcc.commnet.edu
CONNOLLY, Jon .... 207-453-5117 211 B
jconnolly@kvcc.me.edu
CONNOLLY, Katherine .. 781-891-2102 223 E
kconnolly@bentley.edu
CONNOLLY, Laura .... 970-351-2707.. 87 A
laura.connolly@unco.edu
CONNOLLY, Lidy .... 858-653-6740.. 48 Q
LConnolly@JPCatholic.com
CONNOLLY, Lynda .... 617-521-2164 236 F
lynda.connolly@simmons.edu
CONNOLLY, Meg .... 314-977-7121 281 M
burnsmm@slu.edu
CONNOLLY, Melissa, A 516-463-4160 328 A
melissa.a.connolly@hofstra.edu
CONNOLLY, Michael ..... 320-363-3512 264 A
mconnolly@csbsju.edu
CONNOLLY, Monika ..... 949-582-4602.. 67 F
mconnolly@saddleback.edu
CONNOLLY, Patricia, A . 412-536-1243 422 E
patricia.connolly@laroche.edu
CONNOLLY, Paula .... 978-837-5128 233 G
connollyp@merrimack.edu
CONNOLLY, Robert .... 617-287-7073 228 E
rconnolly@umassp.edu
CONNOLLY, Robert .... 404-894-2500 125 D
robert.connolly@police.gatech.edu
CONNOLLY, Tara .... 515-964-6447 177 B
tkconnolly@dmacc.edu
CONNOR, Beth .... 402-898-1000 290 A
beth_c@creativecenter.edu
CONNOR, Caroline .... 415-869-2900 227 G
caroline.connor@hult.edu
CONNOR, Cassandra .... 228-897-7137 271 F
cconnor@wmcarey.edu
CONNOR, Catherine, H 610-519-4036 439 A
catherine.connor@villanova.edu
CONNOR, Francis, P .... 260-399-7700 174 C
fconnor@sf.edu
CONNOR, Gary .... 704-216-3723 365 F
gary.connor@rccc.edu
CONNOR, Joanne .... 856-256-4102 306 D
connorj@rowan.edu
CONNOR, Pat .... 812-855-1764 167 J
connorp@indiana.edu
CONNOR, Rianne .... 707-476-4151.. 41 C
rianne-connor@redwoods.edu
CONNOR, Roger .... 203-837-9301.. 88 G
connorr@wcsu.edu
CONNOR, Rosie .... 435-283-7160 500 D
rosie.connor@snow.edu
CONNOR, Shane .... 216-687-2084 380 D
s.c.connor@csuohio.edu
CONNOR, Terrence .... 214-768-4909 482 J
connor@smu.edu
CONNOR, Terry, D .... 859-344-3308 200 C
connort@thomasmore.edu
CONNORS, Anne .... 207-453-5126 211 B
aconnors@kvcc.me.edu
CONNORS, Chalese ...... 940-898-2373 490 D
cconnors@twu.edu
CONNORS, Cheryl, C .... 401-739-5000 441 E
cconnors@neit.edu
CONNORS,
Christine, M .... 617-266-1400 223 F
CONNORS,
James (Jim) .... 251-460-6283.... 9 F
jconnors@southalabama.edu
CONNORS, John .... 215-596-8973 438 E
j.connors@usciences.edu
CONNORS, Linda .... 973-408-3322 301 J
lconnors@drew.edu
CONNORS, Michael, W 773-371-5484 141 C
mconnors@ctu.edu
CONNORS, Natalie .... 219-989-2600 171 L
Natalie.Connors@purduecal.edu
CONNORS, Natalie .... 219-785-5498 172 A
nconnors@pnc.edu
CONNORS, Thomas ...... 434-381-6300 513 E
TConnors@sbc.edu
CONNUCK, Wendy .... 215-489-2921 416 H
wendy.connuck@delval.edu
CONOLEY, Jane, C .... 562-985-4121.. 33 F
csulb-president@csulb.edu
CONOLLY, Charlene ...... 410-287-6060 214 C
cconolly@cecil.edu
CONOVER, David .... 631-632-7932 344 C
david.conover@stonybrook.edu
CONOVER, Dustin .... 307-382-1644 546 L
dconover@wwcc.wy.edu
CONOVER, Melanie .... 801-524-1927 498 J
ConoverM@ldsbc.edu
CONOVER, Randall .... 937-328-6180 379 L
conoverr@clarkstate.edu
CONOVER, Ross, P .... 240-895-4304 218 B
rpconover@smcm.edu
CONOVER, Wheeler .... 606-589-3038 197 D
wheeler.conover@kctcs.edu
CONQUE, Chasse, S ..... 501-569-3167.. 24 A
csconque@ular.edu
CONRAD, Angela .... 973-748-9000 300 E
angela_conrad@bloomfield.edu
CONRAD, Jacqueline .... 617-873-0621 225 A
Jacqueline.Conrad@cambridgecollege.edu
CONRAD, Jeffrey .... 617-236-8800 226 F
jconrad@fisher.edu
CONRAD, Jerry .... 202-319-5515.. 95 A
conradj@cua.edu
CONRAD, Jon, B .... 610-861-1526 426 H
conradj@moravian.edu
CONRAD, Kari, M .... 570-577-1217 413 E
kari.conrad@bucknell.edu
CONRAD, Rebecca .... 207-699-5017 210 I
bconrad@meca.edu
CONRAD, Rhonda .... 641-683-5115 179 C
rhonda.conrad@indianhills.edu
CONRAD, Rhonda .... 641-683-5111 179 C
rhonda.conrad@indianhills.edu
CONRAD, Robert .... 410-857-2250 217 A
rconrad@mcdaniel.edu
CONRAD, Scott .... 707-524-1553.. 65 C
sconrad@santarosa.edu
CONRAD, Susan .... 703-284-3322 510 B
susan.conrad@marymount.edu
CONRAD, Valarie .... 312-949-7304 146 E
vconrad@ico.edu
CONRADSEN, Susan ..... 706-236-5494 121 E
sconradsen@berry.edu
CONROE, Nicole .... 716-829-7645 324 E
conroen@dyc.edu
CONROY, Sarah .... 207-509-7169 212 A
sconroy@unity.edu
CONROY, Shelley, F ..... 214-820-3361 469 D
shelley_conroy@baylor.edu
CONROY, Spencer .... 219-866-6151 172 E
sconroy@saintjoe.edu
CONROY, Terry .... 254-867-3058 488 B
terry.conroy@tstc.edu
CONROY, Timothy .... 207-974-4682 211 A
tconroy@emcc.edu
CONSIDINE, Marilynn ... 503-552-1504 407 F
mconsidine@ncnm.edu
CONSIVINE-FONTES,
Lisa, M .... 401-825-2444 441 C
lfontes@ccri.edu
CONSOLVO, Camille ..... 406-771-5133 288 B
camille.consolvo@gfcmsu.edu
CONSTABLE, Jean .... 830-372-8090 487 C
jconstable@tlu.edu
CONSTABLE, Peter .... 217-333-2760 162 A
constabl@illinois.edu
CONSTANCE, Eric, F ..... 315-786-2252 329 G
econstance@sunyjefferson.edu
CONSTANINOU,
Constantia .... 631-632-7100 344 C
constantia.constantinou@stonybrook.edu
CONSTANT, Alan .... 256-824-3142.... 9 A
alan.constant@uah.edu
CONSTANT, Kathryn ...... 503-760-3131 404 I
kathryn@birthingway.edu
CONSTANTIN, Michael .. 225-216-8615 202 N
constantinm@mybrcc.edu

CONSTANTINE, Carol .... 508-678-2811 231 B
carol.constantine@bristolcc.edu
CONSTANTINE, OSB,
Cyprian, G .... 724-805-2332 435 C
cyprian.constantine@stvincent.edu
CONSTANTINE,
Doris, F .... 512-448-8525 481 B
dorisc@stedwards.edu
CONSTANTINE, Ruth, H 413-585-2200 236 G
rconstan@smith.edu
CONSTANTINO, John .... 808-245-8245 136 F
johncons@hawaii.edu
CONSTON, Marcia .... 704-330-6647 361 D
marcia.conston@cpcc.edu
CONTAG, Kimberly .... 507-389-1713 260 A
kimberly.contag@mnsu.edu
CONTARINO, Sue .... 847-925-6200 145 F
scontari@harpercollege.edu
CONTE, Daryl .... 713-623-2040 468 F
daconte@ai.edu
CONTE, Jeffrey, A .... 914-606-6795 352 G
jeffrey.conte@sunywcc.edu
CONTE, John .... 214-637-3530 496 J
jconte@wadecollege.edu
CONTE, Millie .... 718-631-6222 320 F
mconte@qcc.cuny.edu
CONTEH, Dominique .... 770-394-8300 120 E
dconteh@ai.edu
CONTELLA, Kelly .... 254-867-2368 488 B
kelly.contella@systems.tstc.edu
CONTI, Erik .... 336-506-4201 359 N
erik.conti@alamancecc.edu
CONTINO-CONNER,
Cheryl .... 828-339-4245 366 C
CONTOMANOLIS,
Emanuel .... 585-475-5464 339 G
emcoce@rit.edu
CONTOMANOLIS,
Laurel .... 585-275-3166 351 D
laurel.contomanolis@rochester.edu
CONTOS, Tanya .... 617-850-1231 227 F
tcontos@hchc.edu
CONTRERAS, Christian . 305-273-4499 100 K
christian.contreras@cbt.edu
CONTRERAS, Gilbert, J . 562-860-2451.. 37 L
gjcontreras@cerritos.edu
CONTRERAS, James ...... 202-274-6053.. 97 B
jcontreras@udc.edu
CONTRERAS, Lisa .... 312-935-6620 157 A
lcontreras@robertmorris.edu
CONTRERAS, Maribel .... 787-746-1400 552 I
mcontreras@huertas.edu
CONTRERAS, Raquel, J . 864-656-2451 444 E
rcontre@clemson.edu
CONTRERAS, JR.,
Sebastian .... 847-635-1756 155 E
scontrer@oakton.edu
CONTRERAS, Sylvia ...... 608-663-3278 536 A
scontreras@edgewood.edu
CONVER, Kathleen .... 309-677-2242 140 H
mkc@fsmail.bradley.edu
CONVERSE, Kenneth, L . 712-749-2101 176 D
conversek@bvu.edu
CONVERSE, Sharon, K .. 248-341-2154 248 E
skconver@oaklandcc.edu
CONVERSE, Wayne .... 785-784-7743 183 G
conversew@uiu.edu
CONVERTINO, Gary ...... 508-541-1681 225 G
gconvertino@dean.edu
CONWAY, Christine, G . 717-291-4083 418 J
christine.conway@fandm.edu
CONWAY, Dan .... 317-955-6280 171 A
dconway@marian.edu
CONWAY, Dennis, S ..... 518-580-5566 342 I
dconway@skidmore.edu
CONWAY, Guy .... 813-974-5400 116 B
gconway@usf.edu
CONWAY, Jean, L .... 972-860-7001 472 E
JConway@dcccd.edu
CONWAY, John .... 601-974-1138 268 D
John.conway@millsaps.edu
CONWAY, Karen .... 901-321-3536 455 I
kconway@cbu.edu
CONWAY, Katie .... 212-678-4194 349 I
conway@tc.edu
CONWAY, Linda .... 320-308-2102 261 E
lmconway@stcloudstate.edu
CONWAY, Morrie .... 402-878-3309 291 B
mconway@littlepriest.edu
CONWAY, Sharon .... 301-891-4005 221 C
sconway@wau.edu
CONWAY, Teresa .... 509-359-6489 522 C
tconway@ewu.edu
CONWAY, Thomas .... 910-672-2501 370 A
tconway@uncfsu.edu
CONWAY-TURNER,
Katherine, S .... 716-878-4101 345 B
conwayks@buffalostate.edu
CONWELL, James, C .... 812-877-8000 172 C
conwell@rose-hulman.edu

CONYERS, Calvin .... 617-879-2260 238 C
cconyers@wheelock.edu
CONYERS, Lance .... 270-831-9632 196 C
lance.conyers@kctcs.edu
CONYERS, Rhyan, M ..... 859-233-8500 200 D
rconyers@transy.edu
CONZATTI, Maria, P ..... 516-572-7600 334 A
maria.conzatti@ncc.edu
CONZEN, Christopher ... 212-752-1530 330 C
christopher.conzen@limcollege.edu
COOGAN, Janet .... 563-441-4201 178 D
jcoogan@eicc.edu
COOGAN, Jay .... 612-874-3737 257 D
president@mcad.edu
COOK, Aaron .... 303-546-5284.. 84 B
acook@naropa.edu
COOK, Allen, P .... 203-576-4206.. 92 B
acook@bridgeport.edu
COOK, Amber .... 814-871-7421 419 A
cook0692@gannon.edu
COOK, Andrea, P .... 503-517-1212 411 A
acook@warnerpacific.edu
COOK, Angela .... 207-780-5737 213 A
adcook@usm.maine.edu
COOK, Anita .... 914-606-6745 352 G
anita.cook@sunywcc.edu
COOK, Anthony .... 314-505-7774 273 G
cooka@csl.edu
COOK, Barbara Jo .... 770-467-6038 132 B
bcook@sctech.edu
COOK, Bradley .... 435-586-7704 499 L
bradcook@suu.edu
COOK, Brenda, A .... 334-683-2353.... 5 H
bcook@marionmilitary.edu
COOK, Brian .... 440-525-7720 385 C
bcook@lakelandcc.edu
COOK, Bruce .... 386-506-4417 101 I
cookb@DaytonaState.edu
COOK, Carey, W .... 208-467-8643 138 H
cwcook@nnu.edu
COOK, Charles .... 512-223-7612 468 H
charles.cook@austincc.edu
COOK, Charles, M .... 713-718-5042 475 C
charles.cook@hccs.edu
COOK, Chris .... 806-742-2136 489 F
chris.cook@ttu.edu
COOK, Cindy .... 281-283-2595 491 E
cookc@uhcl.edu
COOK, Connie, S .... 540-985-8344 509 D
cscook@jchs.edu
COOK, Corey .... 208-426-1368 137 E
coreydcook@boisestate.edu
COOK, Courtney .... 207-699-5060 210 I
ccook@meca.edu
COOK, Darrell .... 202-885-3546.. 94 H
dcook@american.edu
COOK, David .... 913-897-8400 191 G
davidcook@ku.edu
COOK, David .... 847-628-1520 149 A
dcook@judsonu.edu
COOK, David .... 309-694-8551 146 C
dcook@icc.edu
COOK, David, E .... 218-722-4000 255 F
davidc@dbumn.edu
COOK, Debra .... 918-335-6264 400 I
dcook@okwu.edu
COOK, Donelda .... 410-617-5171 216 D
dcook@loyola.edu
COOK, Donna, L .... 575-439-3699 312 B
donnac@nmsu.edu
COOK, Donna, M .... 401-341-2435 442 D
donna.cook@salve.edu
COOK, Douglas .... 757-352-4331 511 G
dougcoo@regent.edu
COOK, Edith .... 724-830-1014 435 E
ecook@setonhill.edu
COOK, Ellen, D .... 337-482-6306 208 F
edcook@louisiana.edu
COOK, Elsie .... 510-567-6174.. 69 D
drcook@sum.edu
COOK, Gary .... 214-333-5130 471 L
chancellor@dbu.edu
COOK, Gary, W .... 770-484-1204 128 D
lutherrice@lutherrice.edu
COOK, Genevieve .... 412-624-7124 437 K
gdcook@pitt.edu
COOK, Greg .... 262-472-1077 541 D
cookg@uww.edu
COOK, Howard, M .... 803-786-3343 445 C
hcook@columbiasc.edu
COOK, James .... 336-734-7311 362 F
jcook@forsythtech.edu
COOK, Jeffrey .... 657-278-4475.. 33 E
jcook@fullerton.edu
COOK, Jeffrey .... 513-569-1579 379 K
jeffrey.cook@cincinnatistate.edu
COOK, Jerry .... 918-456-5511 398 M
cookjc@nsuok.edu
COOK, Jerry .... 936-294-3620 489 A
bio_jlc@shsu.edu

COOK, Jessica .... 302-736-2435.. 94 E
jessica.cook@wesley.edu
COOK, Jim .... 573-651-2206 282 C
jcook@semo.edu
COOK, John .... 603-206-8009 297 A
jcook@ccsnh.edu
COOK, John, C .... 540-985-8317 509 D
jccook@jchs.edu
COOK, Jolane .... 870-777-5722.. 24 H
jolane.cook@uacch.edu
COOK, Judy, I .... 615-353-3236 463 C
judy.cook@nscc.edu
COOK, Karen .... 650-723-2300.. 68 G
kcook@stanford.edu
COOK, Karen .... 410-777-7370 213 E
kcook@aacc.edu
COOK, Kathy .... 425-388-9273 522 I
kcook@everettcc.edu
COOK, Kevin .... 601-984-4100 270 H
kcook@umc.edu
COOK, Larry .... 909-389-3384.. 62 B
lcook@craftonhills.edu
COOK, Les .... 906-487-1885 247 A
lpcook@mtu.edu
COOK, Les, P .... 906-487-2465 247 A
lpcook@mtu.edu
COOK, Leslee .... 435-283-7221 500 D
leslee.cook@snow.edu
COOK, Lori .... 918-495-7708 401 B
lcook@oru.edu
COOK, Mary .... 713-222-5340 491 F
cookm@uhd.edu
COOK, Melinda .... 617-670-4462 226 F
mcook1@fisher.edu
COOK, Melinda .... 800-567-2344 535 F
melcook@menominee.edu
COOK, Melissa .... 207-801-5610 210 B
mcook@coa.edu
COOK, Michelle .... 405-208-5000 400 A
michelle.cook@okcu.edu
COOK, Michelle .... 336-750-2184 372 D
cookm@wssu.edu
COOK, Michelle, G .... 706-583-8195 132 H
mgcook@uga.edu
COOK, Patrick .... 978-656-3134 232 B
COOK, Phil .... 423-614-8500 457 M
pcook@leeuniversity.edu
COOK, Randy .... 641-782-1336 183 D
rcook@swcciowa.edu
COOK, Richard, D .... 585-785-1410 325 E
richard.cook@flcc.edu
COOK, OFM, Robert ..... 414-425-8300 538 J
rcook@shsst.edu
COOK, Robert, G .... 617-627-2546 237 C
robert.cook@tufts.edu
COOK, Rosalie .... 650-493-4430.. 66 H
rosalie.cook@sofia.edu
COOK, Royrickers .... 334-844-5700.... 1 G
cookroy@auburn.edu
COOK, Ryan .... 801-832-5303 501 C
rcook@westminstercollege.edu
COOK, Sandra .... 619-594-4756.. 35 E
scook@mail.sdsu.edu
COOK, Sarah .... 404-727-6123 124 D
sccook@emory.edu
COOK, Scott .... 931-393-1844 463 B
scook@mscc.edu
COOK, Scott, A .... 304-336-8137 533 A
cookscot@westliberty.edu
COOK, Sharon, L .... 972-860-7629 472 E
SCook@dcccd.edu
COOK, Shawn .... 901-383-6750.. 96 H
COOK, Sheryl .... 319-398-5500 180 J
scook@kirkwood.edu
COOK, Stacey, A .... 408-864-8330.. 44 N
cookstacey@deanza.edu
COOK, Steve .... 502-895-3411 198 E
scook@lpts.edu
COOK, Susan .... 409-880-8195 488 E
slcook@lit.edu
COOK, Terry .... 410-455-2939 219 F
tcook@umbc.edu
COOK, Thomas .... 239-513-1135 119 C
COOK, Tim .... 360-992-2217 521 A
tcook@clark.edu
COOK, Tom, G .... 304-327-4111 532 D
tcook@bluefieldstate.edu
COOK, Toni .... 510-748-2135.. 59 A
tcook@peralta.edu
COOK, Vicki .... 231-995-1144 248 C
vcook@nmc.edu
COOK, William .... 304-307-0716 531 F
william.cook@southernwv.edu
COOK-FRANCIS,
Lynette .... 212-237-8100 319 F
lcook-francis@jjay.cuny.edu
COOK-HUFFMAN,
Daniel, J .... 814-641-3151 421 L
cookhud@juniata.edu
COOK-NOBLES, Robin .. 784-283-2839 237 F
rcooknob@wellesley.edu

COOKE, Caretta .... 504-816-4222 202 F
ccooke@dillard.edu
COOKE, Connie, F .... 716-878-4902 345 B
cookecf@buffalostate.edu
COOKE, Harry .... 704-922-6355 362 G
cooke.harry@gaston.edu
COOKE, Joy .... 757-825-2728 517 B
cookej@tncc.edu
COOKE, Linda .... 206-239-4500 520 K
lcooke@cityu.edu
COOKE, Peggy, S .... 248-370-2190 248 K
cooke@oakland.edu
COOKE, Sandy, P .... 434-223-6340 508 B
scooke@hsc.edu
COOKE, Sean .... 253-840-8472 525 C
scooke@pierce.ctc.edu
COOKE, Sunita .... 760-757-2121.. 54 G
scooke@miracosta.edu
COOKMAN, John .... 972-825-4659 483 D
jcookman@sagu.edu
COOKS, Owen, J .... 336-750-2855 372 D
cooksoj@wssu.edu
COOKSEY, Beth .... 615-230-3560 464 B
beth.cooksey@volstate.edu
COOKSEY, Gaye, M .... 972-881-5807 471 C
gcooksey@collin.edu
COOKSEY, Lynita .... 870-972-2030.. 19 F
lcooksey@astate.edu
COOKSON, Matt .... 937-769-1336 376 L
mcookson@antioch.edu
COOKSON, Nancy, B .... 402-465-2117 292 E
nbc@nebrwesleyan.edu
COOLE, Gloria, G .... 218-722-4000 255 F
finaid@dbumn.edu
COOLEY, Alvin, L .... 973-353-5882 307 C
alvin.cooley@rutgers.edu
COOLEY, Chantell .... 251-981-3771.... 3 A
chantell.cooley@columbiasouthern.edu
COOLEY, Francis .... 203-287-3029.. 91 C
paier.dean@snet.net
COOLEY, John .... 614-287-2501 380 G
jcooley3@cscc.edu
COOLEY, Lisa, K .... 336-322-2200 364 G
Lisa.Cooley@piedmontcc.edu
COOLEY, Lynn .... 203-432-2733.. 93 C
lynn.cooley@yale.edu
COOLEY, Marianne, B .. 784-283-3344 237 F
mcooley@wellesley.edu
COOLEY, Maurice, R .... 304-696-5430 532 H
cooley@marshall.edu
COOLEY, Meghan, M .... 309-794-7314 139 K
meghancooley@augustana.edu
COOLEY, Mike .... 972-860-7871 473 A
mcooley@dcccd.edu
COOLEY, Nanette .... 610-330-5114 423 A
cooleyn@lafayette.edu
COOLEY, Thomas .... 412-268-4731 414 J
tkcooley@andrew.cmu.edu
COOLEY, Tom .... 816-604-6538 277 G
thomas.cooley@mcckc.edu
COOMAR, Parmeshwar . 734-384-4209 247 C
pcoomar@monroeccc.edu
COOMBS, Gary, F .... 619-201-8989.. 67 I
gcoombs@shadowmountain.org
COOMBS, Robert .... 207-741-5569 211 D
rcoombs@smccme.edu
COOMBS, Vanessa .... 804-257-5856 518 E
vcoombs@vuu.edu
COOMER, Sue, B .... 270-384-8024 198 C
coomers@lindsey.edu
COOMES, Kerrie .... 620-431-2820 189 J
kcoomes@neosho.edu
COON, David, W .... 415-485-9502.. 41 B
dwain.coon@marin.edu
COON, Omayra .... 910-221-2224 357 A
COON, Thomas .... 405-744-2474 400 C
thomas.coon@okstate.edu
COONAN, Patrick, R ...... 516-877-4511 314 F
coonan@adelphi.edu
COONEN, Ned .... 847-214-7557 144 F
ncoonen@elgin.edu
COONER, Elizabeth .... 908-527-7213 309 A
COONEY, Anita .... 718-636-3630 338 E
acooney@pratt.edu
COONEY, Marcia, J ...... 570-577-1631 413 E
marcia.cooney@bucknell.edu
COONEY, Terry .... 410-704-2128 221 A
tcooney@towson.edu
COONEY-CONNOR,
Erica .... 315-781-3103 327 G
econnor@hws.edu
COONEY MINER,
Dianne, C .... 585-385-8472 340 F
dcooney-miner@sjfc.edu
COONING, Peggy, J ..... 615-248-1355 464 E
pcooning@trevecca.edu
COONROD, Curtis, C .... 314-516-5211 284 B
curt_coonrod@umsl.edu
COONROD, Julie .... 505-277-2711 313 H
jcoonrod@unm.edu

COONROD, Kevin .... 334-844-7170.... 1 G kcc0024@auburn.edu
COONS, Christopher, R 607-735-1806 324 J ccoons@elmira.edu
COONS, Maria .... 847-925-6143 145 F mcoons@harpercollege.edu
COONS, Patrick .... 502-272-8056 193 E pcoons@bellarmine.edu
COONS, Robert, A .... 812-877-8007 172 C robert.a.coons@rose-hulman.edu
COOPEE, Scott, J .... 413-782-1246 238 A scott.coopee@wne.edu
COOPER, Adrienne .... 386-481-2076.. 99 F coopera@cookman.edu
COOPER, Alan .... 212-678-8065 329 H alcooper@jtsa.edu
COOPER, Almeta .... 404-752-1895 129 A acooper@msm.edu
COOPER, Amy, M .... 270-384-8053 198 C coopera@lindsey.edu
COOPER, Aneita .... 870-759-4184.. 25 I acooper@wbcoll.edu
COOPER, Ann, A .... 803-778-6636 443 I cooperaa@cctech.edu
COOPER, Anne, M .... 727-341-3323 112 A cooper.anne@spcollege.edu
COOPER, Barbara, I ...... 252-222-6225 361 A cooperb@carteret.edu
COOPER, Brett .... 870-759-4107.. 25 I bcooper@wbcoll.edu
COOPER, Candace .... 704-878-3256 364 C ccooper@mitchellcc.edu
COOPER, Carrie .... 601-984-1117 270 H cecooper@umc.edu
COOPER, Carrie .... 757-221-3055 506 J clcooper@wm.edu
COOPER, Christopher ... 419-383-5320 394 E christopher.cooper@utoledo.edu
COOPER, Constance ..... 502-410-6200 194 N ccooper@galencollege.edu
COOPER, Corey .... 765-998-4694 173 B crcooper@taylor.edu
COOPER, Cynthia, L ..... 585-292-3015 333 G ccooper@monroecc.edu
COOPER, Dan .... 864-646-8361 449 F
COOPER, David .... 773-777-4220 155 B dcooper@nc.edu
COOPER, David .... 401-841-3540 548 B
COOPER, Deanna .... 660-248-6397 272 N dcooper@centralmethodist.edu
COOPER, Donna .... 423-425-4184 465 E donna-cooper@utc.edu
COOPER, Doug .... 404-653-7882 128 L douglas.cooper@morehouse.edu
COOPER, Ed .... 229-430-3577 119 I ecooper@albanytech.edu
COOPER, Emmett .... 212-875-4679 315 F ecooper@bankstreet.edu
COOPER, Erik .... 916-660-7512.. 66 E ecooper@sierracollege.edu
COOPER, Frank .... 609-771-2357 301 E fcooper@tcnj.edu
COOPER, Franklin .... 406-638-3161 286 I cooperf@lbhc.edu
COOPER, Fred .... 815-802-8752 149 B fcooper@kcc.edu
COOPER, Gail, S .... 626-585-7282.. 58 F gscooper@pasadena.edu
COOPER, Gayle .... 870-612-2004.. 24 G gayle.cooper@uaccb.edu
COOPER, Hans .... 443-885-3300 217 C hans.cooper@morgan.edu
COOPER, Helena .... 804-330-0111 506 D stuadvcrim@centura.edu
COOPER, Ingrid .... 484-654-2373 418 A icooper@eastern.edu
COOPER, James .... 773-291-6536 142 B jcooper53@ccc.edu
COOPER, James, E .... 334-727-8011.... 8 B cooper@tuskegee.edu
COOPER, James, M ...... 619-239-0391.. 36 E jcooper@cwsl.edu
COOPER, Jason .... 269-927-8165 245 E cooperj@lakemichigancollege.edu
COOPER, Jeffrey .... 215-898-1388 437 I jeffcoop@upenn.edu
COOPER, Jennifer .... 404-233-3949 460 G jcooper@richmont.edu
COOPER, Joel .... 610-328-7679 436 A jcooper2@swarthmore.edu
COOPER, John, D .... 563-333-6480 182 E CooperJohnD@sau.edu
COOPER, Jorsene .... 757-727-5323 508 C jorsene.cooper@hamptonu.edu
COOPER, Josh .... 617-327-6777 238 D josh_cooper@williamjames.edu
COOPER, Judi .... 407-708-2138 113 A cooperj@seminolestate.edu
COOPER, Karen .... 603-897-8508 298 E kcooper@rivier.edu
COOPER, Karen, S .... 650-723-0198.. 68 G karen.cooper@stanford.edu
COOPER, Karla .... 402-826-8111 290 C karla.cooper@doane.edu
COOPER, Karyn .... 850-729-6922 109 D cooperk@nwfsc.edu
COOPER, Katie .... 304-336-8131 533 A katie.mills@westliberty.edu
COOPER, Kelly .... 815-921-4092 157 B k.cooper@rockvalleycollege.edu
COOPER, Kenneth .... 505-786-4110 311 G kcooper@navajotech.edu
COOPER, Kenneth .... 845-758-7461 315 G cooper@bard.edu
COOPER, Kerrie, L .... 315-386-7616 347 F cooper@canton.edu
COOPER, Lisa, A .... 229-931-2921 126 C lcooper@gsw.edu
COOPER, Lisa, J .... 215-951-2940 432 F cooperl@philau.edu
COOPER, Marina .... 410-704-2356 221 A mcooper@towson.edu
COOPER, Mark .... 614-251-4576 388 H cooperm2@ohiodominican.edu
COOPER, Mary-Beth, A 413-748-3241 236 H mbcooper@springfieldcollege.edu
COOPER, MaryKay .... 210-999-7011 490 E marykay.cooper@trinity.edu
COOPER, Matthew .... 609-984-1140 308 H mcooper@tesc.edu
COOPER, Michael .... 908-737-4700 303 C mrcooper@kean.edu
COOPER, N. John .... 412-624-1164 437 K cooper@pitt.edu
COOPER, Nani Lou, S .. 864-488-4617 447 F ncooper@limestone.edu
COOPER, Natalie .... 215-871-6560 432 E nataliecoo@pcom.edu
COOPER, Natalie, F ...... 270-824-8599 196 F natalie.cooper@kctcs.edu
COOPER, Paul .... 631-451-4445 348 E cooperp@sunysuffolk.edu
COOPER, R. Scott .... 267-502-2681 413 C rscott.cooper@brynathyn.edu
COOPER, Rick .... 251-981-3771.... 3 A rick.cooper@columbiasouthern.edu
COOPER, Rick .... 806-291-3801 496 K rick.cooper@wbu.edu
COOPER, Ruth .... 512-313-3000 471 H ruth.cooper@concordia.edu
COOPER, Scott .... 760-776-7453.. 41 A scooper@collegeofthedesert.edu
COOPER, Stephanie ...... 973-300-2161 308 F scooper@sussex.edu
COOPER, Stewart, E ..... 219-464-5002 174 E stewart.cooper@valpo.edu
COOPER, Susan .... 657-278-1605.. 33 E scooper@fullerton.edu
COOPER, Tami, L .... 580-327-8530 399 F tlcooper@nwosu.edu
COOPER, Tammi .... 254-295-4507 492 C tcooper@umhb.edu
COOPER, Tana .... 620-792-9241 184 I coopert@bartonccc.edu
COOPER, Tara, L .... 606-546-1241 200 E tcooper@unionky.edu
COOPER, Toya .... 805-565-6832.. 76 K tcooper@westmont.edu
COOPER, Tracey, L .... 440-525-7230 385 C tcooper@lakelandcc.edu
COOPER, Tyson .... 540-261-8463 512 J tyson.cooper@svu.edu
COOPER-WHITE, Michael, L .... 717-334-6286 424 F mcooper@ltsg.edu
COOPERSMITH, Lynn .... 609-586-4800 303 D coopersl@mccc.edu
COOPWOOD, SR., Kenneth .... 417-836-3736 279 A kcoopwood@missouristate.edu
COOROUGH, Randall .... 262-691-5168 544 D rcoorough@wctc.edu
COOTE, Samra .... 404-752-1733 129 A scoote@msm.edu
COOTER, Raelynn .... 215-503-6595 436 F raelynn.cooter@jefferson.edu
COOTER, Robert, B .... 502-272-7992 193 E rcooter@bellarmine.edu
COOTS, Kevin .... 606-326-2064 195 H kevin.coots@kctcs.edu
COP, Kenneth, B .... 732-932-7211 306 F kcop@aps.rutgers.edu
COP, Kenneth, B .... 732-932-7211 307 B kcop@aps.rutgers.edu
COPAS, Tyro .... 423-354-5259 463 D tlcopas@northeaststate.edu
COPE, Glen, H .... 314-516-5373 284 B copeg@umsl.edu
COPE, Marla .... 913-234-0687 185 N marla.cope@cleveland.edu
COPE, Melody .... 631-244-3023 324 C copem@dowling.edu
COPE, Michael .... 310-506-4270.. 58 H mike.cope@pepperdine.edu
COPELAND, Angela .... 903-566-7080 494 E jcopeland@uttyler.edu
COPELAND, Brian .... 616-331-2831 243 E copelabr@gvsu.edu
COPELAND, Cathy .... 425-739-8156 523 I cathy.copeland@lwtech.edu
COPELAND, David, L .... 540-464-7218 518 A copelanddl@vmi.edu
COPELAND, Elaine, J .... 803-327-7402 444 F ecopeland@clintoncollege.edu
COPELAND, Gayle .... 530-226-4133.. 66 G gcopeland@simpsonu.edu
COPELAND, Jeff .... 813-253-7016 106 C hcopeland4@hccfl.edu
COPELAND, Jessica ...... 256-539-0834.... 4 F reg@hbc1.edu
COPELAND, Judson ...... 405-425-5129 399 J judson.copeland@oc.edu
COPELAND, Kenneth ..... 434-395-2016 509 H copelandpk@longwood.edu
COPELAND, Leigh .... 843-525-8231 449 E lcopeland@tcl.edu
COPELAND, Louise .... 651-290-6439 266 B louise.copeland@wmitchell.edu
COPELAND, Maura .... 912-478-7481 126 B mconley@georgiasouthern.edu
COPELAND, Michele ..... 612-659-6248 259 F michele.copeland@minneapolis.edu
COPELAND, Paul .... 302-736-2538.. 94 E paul.copeland@wesley.edu
COPELAND, JR., Robert, M .... 803-327-7402 444 F rcopeland@clintoncollege.edu
COPELAND, Sandra ...... 252-862-1293 365 C spcopeland7239@roanokechowan.edu
COPELAND, Sarah .... 423-473-2368 462 D SCopeland01@clevelandstatecc.edu
COPELAND, Shannon ... 409-880-8922 488 F shannon.copeland@lamar.edu
COPELAND, Wanda .... 610-796-8437 412 C wanda.copeland@alvernia.edu
COPELAND-MORGAN, Youlonda .... 310-825-2665.. 71 D ycopeland-morgan@saonet.ucla.edu
COPELY, Pat .... 937-376-2946 390 F pcopely@payne.edu
COPENHAVER, Bonny ... 715-394-6677 544 F bonny.copenhaver@witc.edu
COPENHAVER, Martin ... 617-964-1100 222 B mcopenhaver@ants.edu
COPENHAVER, Michael . 619-644-7000.. 46 H michael.coppenhaver@gcccd.edu
COPLAND, Katherine ..... 212-749-2802 331 I kcopland@msmnyc.edu
COPLIN, Kimberly, A .... 740-587-6243 381 H coplin@denison.edu
COPLIN, Louis .... 518-629-7348 328 D l.coplin@hvcc.edu
COPONITI, Laura, I .... 405-224-3140 403 L lcoponiti@usao.edu
COPONITI, Mike .... 405-224-3140 403 L mcoponiti@usao.edu
COPONITI, Mike, D ...... 405-224-3140 403 L mcoponiti@usao.edu
COPP, Crista .... 310-338-1745.. 53 C Crista.Copp@lmu.edu
COPP, Destini .... 404-432-3475 131 F acopp@southuniversity.edu
COPPEDGE, Robin .... 580-371-2371 398 J rcoppedge@mscok.edu
COPPERSMITH, Clifford 406-247-3009 287 H ccoppersmith@msubillings.edu
COPPI, Carla, E .... 618-453-7661 159 H ccoppi@siu.edu
COPPINGER, Debbie ..... 615-460-6474 455 D debbie.coppinger@belmont.edu
COPPLE, Chad .... 618-437-5321 156 I copplec@rlc.edu
COPPLE, James (Dean) 865-694-6536 463 E jdcopple@pstcc.edu
COPPOLA, David, L ...... 570-945-8500 422 B david.coppola@keystone.edu
COPPOLA, Kristin .... 503-725-8799 409 D coppola@pdx.edu
COPPOLA, Stephen, A .. 704-687-5965 371 B scoppola@uncc.edu
COPPOLA, William .... 817-515-3001 484 B william.coppola@tccd.edu
COPPRUE, Lisa .... 313-845-9610 243 I lcopprue@hfcc.edu
COQUEREL, Phoebe ...... 404-225-4529 120 I pcoquerel@atlantatech.edu
CORA, Gladys .... 787-766-1717 556 A um_gcora@suagm.edu
CORA, Ivette .... 787-250-1912 554 A icora@intermetro.com
CORAZZA, Anthony ...... 718-368-5124 320 A acorazza@kbcc.cuny.edu
CORBA, David .... 586-286-2058 246 A corbad@macomb.edu
CORBAT, Carol .... 318-473-6431 205 A ccorbat@lsua.edu
CORBETT, Ann .... 207-621-3145 212 D annie@maine.edu
CORBETT, Carrie .... 901-272-5111 459 A ccorbett@mca.edu
CORBETT, Cindy .... 509-324-7332 528 B
CORBETT, Diane .... 614-292-8595 389 A corbett.168@osu.edu
CORBETT, Faith .... 718-260-5564 320 D fcorbett@citytech.cuny.edu
CORBETT, Heather .... 860-768-2409.. 92 F hcorbett@hartford.edu
CORBETT, Keith .... 605-688-4153 454 C keith.corbett@sdstate.edu
CORBETT, Kevin, J .... 785-864-4760 191 G kcorbett@ku.edu
CORBETT, Marcus .... 803-793-5289 445 F corbettm@denmarktech.edu
CORBETT, Martin .... 315-781-3656 327 G corbett@hws.edu
CORBETT, Michele .... 619-849-2510.. 59 K michelecorbett@pointloma.edu
CORBETT, Mickey .... 432-837-8059 489 B mcorbett@sulross.edu
CORBETT, Toya .... 919-530-5547 370 C tcorbet7@nccu.edu
CORBETT, William, R .... 225-578-8324 205 E bill.corbett@law.lsu.edu
CORBIN, Amanda .... 912-583-3249 121 H acorbin@bpc.edu
CORBIN, Chuck .... 317-931-3324 165 C ccorbin@cts.edu
CORBIN, Edith .... 609-894-9311 306 B ecorbin@bcc.edu
CORBIN, Nancy .... 360-650-3000 528 D nancy.corbin@wwu.edu
CORBIN, Rebecca .... 303-753-6046.. 85 H rcorbin@rmcad.edu
CORBIN, Rebecca, A .... 609-894-9311 306 B rcorbin@bcc.edu
CORBIN, Russ .... 315-498-2831 337 F corbinr@sunyocc.edu
CORBIN, Thomas .... 802-443-5504 502 E corbin@middlebury.edu
CORBIN, Ty .... 804-523-5726 515 F tcorbin@reynolds.edu
CORBINE, Theresa, C ... 315-386-7150 347 F corbine@canton.edu
CORBIT, Steve .... 540-868-7133 515 H scorbit@lfcc.edu
CORBITT, Sandra, K ..... 540-338-1776 511 A slife@phc.edu
CORBITT, Timothy .... 315-229-5392 341 E tcorbitt@stlawu.edu
CORBITT, Zach .... 864-596-9215 445 E zach.corbitt@converse.edu
CORBOY, Lynne .... 215-780-1392 435 D lcorboy@salus.edu
CORCORAN, Heather, A 314-935-9292 285 E hcorcoran@wustl.edu
CORCORAN, Janenne .... 410-386-8444 214 B jcorcoran@carrollcc.edu
CORCORAN, Jerry, M ... 815-224-0404 147 J jerry_corcoran@ivcc.edu
CORCORAN, Kevin, J .... 248-370-2140 248 K corcoran@oakland.edu
CORCORAN, Lisa .... 425-564-2302 519 L lisa.corcoran@bellevuecollege.edu
CORCORAN, Mike .... 757-490-1241 504 D mcorcoran@auto.edu
CORCORAN, Thomas, B .... 212-678-3126 349 I corcoran@tc.columbia.edu
CORCORAN, Tim .... 619-644-7649.. 46 F tim.corcoran@gcccd.edu
CORCORAN, William ..... 201-612-5234 300 B wcorcoran@bergen.edu
CORCORAN, William, M .... 570-208-5846 422 D wmcorcor@kings.edu
CORDANO, Mark .... 978-837-5401 233 G cordanom@merrimack.edu
CORDEIRO, Wayne .... 808-853-1040 135 F
CORDEIRO, Wayne .... 541-485-1780 407 H waynecordeiro@newhope.edu
CORDEIRO, William ...... 805-437-8860.. 32 H william.cordeiro@csuci.edu
CORDELL, Barbara .... 903-694-4003 480 A bcordell@panola.edu
CORDELL, David .... 425-640-1412 522 D dcordell@edcc.edu
CORDELL, Janice, K ..... 563-387-1018 180 M cordellj@luther.edu
CORDELL, Joyce .... 915-831-6530 473 J jyamasak@epcc.edu

CORDELL, Michelle .... 479-619-4361.. 22 B
mcordell@nwacc.edu
CORDELL, Peggy .... 706-295-6959 125 F
pcordell@gntc.edu
CORDELL, Penny .... 706-272-4498 123 G
pcordell@daltonstate.edu
CORDER, Colleen .... 503-552-1702 407 F
ccorder@ncnm.edu
CORDERO, Damaris ...... 787-751-0160 551 K
dcordero@cmpr.gov.pr
CORDERO, Dona .... 847-491-3355 155 D
d-cordero@northwestern.edu
CORDERO, Edwin .... 864-578-8770 448 G
ecordero@sherman.edu
CORDERO, Eunice .... 787-284-1912 554 B
ecordero@ponce.inter.edu
CORDERO, Heather .... 847-317-7071 161 B
hcordero@tiu.edu
CORDERO, Irma, L .... 787-740-1611 556 F
irma.cordero@uccaribe.edu
CORDERO, Pilar .... 787-815-0000 557 D
pilar.cordero@upr.edu
CORDERO, Zain .... 787-882-2065 556 C
mis@unitecpr.net
CORDERY, Simon .... 706-864-1819 133 A
simon.cordery@ung.edu
CORDES, Molly .... 319-226-2091 175 D
Molly.Cordes@AllenCollege.edu
CORDIA, Judith .... 775-445-3295 296 A
judith.cordia@wnc.edu
CORDISCO, Shelli .... 607-778-5222 344 F
cordiscosl@sunybroome.edu
CORDLE, David .... 620-341-5171 186 H
dcordle@emporia.edu
CORDLE, Robbie, L ...... 301-687-4403 220 D
rcordle@frostburg.edu
CORDOVA, Damion ...... 970-339-6656.. 78 J
damion.cordova@aims.edu
CORDOVA, David .... 773-878-8756 158 C
dcordova@staugustine.edu
CORDOVA, Denise .... 775-682-6708 295 H
dcordova@unr.edu
CORDOVA, Jose, A .... 787-704-1020 552 D
jcordova@ediccollege.edu
CORDOVA, Mitchell ...... 239-590-7074 114 F
mcordova@fgcu.edu
CORDOVA, Ryan .... 505-747-2288 312 G
rcordova@nnmc.edu
CORDOVA QUERO,
Hugo .... 510-549-4705.. 68 I
hquero@sksm.edu
CORDULACK, Tricia ...... 217-875-7211 156 K
tcordulack@richland.edu
CORE, Gordon .... 724-938-5985 430 C
core@calu.edu
CORE, Jaqueline .... 724-852-3295 439 C
jcore@waynesburg.edu
CORE, Justin .... 541-881-5781 410 D
jcore@tvcc.cc
COREN, Richard, H .... 401-825-2028 441 C
rhcoren@ccri.edu
CORESSEL, James .... 419-783-2503 381 G
jcoressel@defiance.edu
COREY, Barry, H .... 562-903-4701.. 29 F
president@biola.edu
COREY, Frederick, C ..... 602-496-0624.. 11 J
frederick.corey@asu.edu
COREY, George, A .... 413-577-5211 228 F
gcorey@uhs.umass.edu
COREY, M, J .... 304-637-1344 529 I
coreym@dewv.edu
COREY, Steven .... 312-369-7844 143 C
scorey@colum.edu
COREY, Steven, M .... 269-749-7642 249 A
scorey@olivetcollege.edu
CORIA, Elizabeth .... 415-239-3382.. 39 A
ecoria@ccsf.edu
CORICH, John, S .... 480-461-7066.. 15 A
steve.corich@mesacc.edu
CORIELL, Bruce .... 719-389-6638.. 79 M
bcoriell@coloradocollege.edu
CORINO, Mark, A .... 973-618-3412 300 H
mcorino@caldwell.edu
CORKERY, John, E .... 312-987-1426 148 I
7corkery@jmls.edu
CORKILL, Jim, R .... 805-893-5882.. 72 D
jim.corkill@bfs.ucsb.edu
CORKRAN, Kenneth, F .. 508-541-1700 225 G
kcorkran@dean.edu
CORKRUM, Dalia, L ...... 509-527-5193 528 F
corkrum@whitman.edu
CORKUM, David .... 617-552-4500 224 B
david.corkum@bc.edu
CORLE, Trish .... 814-262-3841 429 K
tcorle@pennhighlands.edu
CORLEW, Amy .... 931-221-6131 461 C
corlewa@apsu.edu
CORLEY, David .... 530-257-6181.. 50 B
dcorley@lassencollege.edu
CORLEY, Diane .... 512-463-9976 488 D
diane.corley@tsus.edu

CORLEY, Raymond .... 803-327-7402 444 F
rcorley@clintoncollege.edu
CORLEY, Teresa .... 615-794-4254 460 A
tcorley@omorecollege.edu
CORLEY, Thomas .... 785-242-5200 190 D
thomas.corley@ottawa.edu
CORLISS, Bruce .... 401-874-6222 442 E
bruce.corliss@gso.uri.edu
CORLL, Thomas .... 432-685-5540 478 F
tcorll@midland.edu
CORMAN, RJ .... 828-398-7286 360 A
richardjcorman@abtech.edu
CORMIER, Cathy .... 318-473-6459 205 A
ccormier@lsua.edu
CORMIER, Garth .... 207-941-7626 210 C
cormierg@husson.edu
CORMIER, Matthew .... 508-362-2131 231 D
mcormier@capecod.edu
CORN, Melanie .... 510-594-3649.. 30 G
mcorn@cca.edu
CORNACCHIA,
Eugene, J .... 201-761-6010 307 K
ecornacchia@saintpeters.edu
CORNEAL, Maureen, K . 410-209-6045 213 G
mcorneal@bccc.edu
CORNEJO, Silvia .... 619-216-6755.. 68 D
scornejo@swccd.edu
CORNELIA, Jim .... 712-274-5234 181 C
cornelia@morningside.edu
CORNELIUS, Jerod, L ... 651-631-5320 265 D
jlcornelius@unwsp.edu
CORNELIUS, Ken .... 334-244-3000.... 2 A
kcornelius@aum.edu
CORNELIUS, Michael .... 480-423-6573.. 15 E
michael.cornelius@scottsdalecc.edu
CORNELIUS, Tim .... 479-619-3117.. 22 B
tcornelius@nwacc.edu
CORNELIUS TAYLOR,
Carmen .... 406-353-2607 286 B
ctaylor@ancollege.edu
CORNELL, Brian .... 607-735-1720 324 J
bcornell@elmira.edu
CORNELL, Craig .... 740-597-3280 389 H
cornellc@ohio.edu
CORNELL, Dennis .... 213-740-2111.. 74 D
dcornell@president.usc.edu
CORNELL, Dona, H .... 832-842-0949 491 C
dhcornell@uh.edu
CORNELL, Dona, H .... 713-743-0949 491 D
dhcornell@uh.edu
CORNELL, John .... 912-279-5703 123 B
jcornell@ccga.edu
CORNELL, Ken .... 425-889-7800 524 G
ken.cornell@northwestu.edu
CORNELL-SCOTT,
Andrea .... 540-887-7270 510 A
ascott@mbc.edu
CORNELY, Joe .... 513-244-4955 387 A
joseph.cornely@msjl.edu
CORNER, William, T ..... 616-526-6451 240 L
wtc2@calvin.edu
CORNERO, Robert .... 732-571-3424 303 G
rcornero@monmouth.edu
CORNETT, Doug .... 859-622-2301 194 L
doug.cornett@eku.edu
CORNETT, Jeff .... 317-921-4282 169 M
jcornett29@ivytech.edu
CORNETT, Megan .... 443-412-2379 215 D
mcornett@harford.edu
CORNETT, Scott .... 606-368-6120 192 H
scottcornett@alc.edu
CORNIER, Wilfredo .... 787-841-2000 555 F
wcornier@pucpr.edu
CORNILLE, Keith, T ...... 608-246-6464 543 C
kcornille@madisoncollege.edu
CORNISH, Irene, K .... 315-859-4999 327 A
icornish@hamilton.edu
CORNISH, John .... 505-224-4000 310 F
jcorn@cnm.edu
CORNISH, La Jerne ...... 410-337-6210 215 B
lcornish@goucher.edu
CORNMAN, Thomas ..... 847-317-7001 161 B
tcornman@tiu.edu
CORNNER, Ryan .... 323-265-8967.. 51 D
cornnerm@elac.edu
CORNOG, Evan, W .... 516-463-5213 328 A
evan.cornog@hofstra.edu
CORNWELL, Grant, H .... 330-263-2311 380 E
gcornwell@wooster.edu
CORNWELL, Jennifer ..... 417-667-8181 273 H
jcornwell@cottey.edu
CORNWELL, Nancy .... 406-994-6654 287 G
nancy.cornwell@montana.edu
CORNWELL, Shirley, A . 937-393-3431 391 F
scornwell@sscc.edu
COROMINAS, Mike .... 954-262-8840 109 E
coromina@nova.edu
CORONA, Lorena .... 909-652-7459.. 38 A
lorena.corona@chaffey.edu
CORONA, Nayeli .... 610-574-6909.. 57 E
ncorona@pacificcollege.edu

CORONA, Stacie .... 530-898-5103.. 33 A
scorona@csuchico.edu
CORONADO, Ricardo ..... 817-515-5234 484 B
ricardo.coronado@tccd.edu
CORONADO, Roman ..... 575-527-7694 312 D
rcorona@nmsu.edu
CORPUS, Ben .... 512-475-7326 493 M
bencorpus@utexas.edu
CORR, Daniel, P .... 480-423-6317.. 15 E
daniel.corr@scottsdalecc.edu
CORR, Marianne .... 574-631-6411 174 A
mcorr1@nd.edu
CORR, Mike, F .... 330-569-5293 383 F
corrmf@hiram.edu
CORRADETTI, Arthur ..... 718-631-6350 320 F
acorradetti@qcc.cuny.edu
CORRADO, Rebecca ...... 212-217-4202 325 C
rebecca_corrado@fitnyc.edu
CORRAL, Jeff .... 562-947-8755.. 67 J
jeffcorral@scuhs.edu
CORRAL, Nohel .... 562-938-4268.. 51 A
ncorral@lbcc.edu
CORRAL-NAVA, Nita ..... 915-831-2302 473 J
ncorraln@epcc.edu
CORRAN, Robert .... 802-656-3075 503 C
robert.corran@uvm.edu
CORREA, Arleen, E .... 787-765-1915 554 E
acorrea@opto.inter.edu
CORREA, Florinda .... 361-582-2516 496 D
florinda.correa@victoriacollege.edu
CORREA, Frank .... 714-966-8500.. 75 F
fcorrea@ves.edu
CORREA, Omar .... 402-554-2200 294 A
ogcorrea@unomaha.edu
CORREA, Peter .... 814-838-7673 418 G
pcorrea@fortisinstitute.edu
CORREA, Santy .... 787-284-1912 554 B
scorrea@ponce.inter.edu
CORREA, Sylvia .... 256-233-8116.... 1 F
sylvia.correa@athens.edu
CORREDERA, Enrique ... 802-656-2005 503 C
enrique.corredera@uvm.edu
CORREIA, Mark, E .... 724-357-2555 431 A
mark.correia@iup.edu
CORRELL, Dennis, L ..... 570-327-4761 429 J
dcorrell@pct.edu
CORRELL, Jen .... 717-728-2362 415 B
jencorrell@centralpenn.edu
CORRELL, Scott .... 715-232-2121 541 B
corrells@uwstout.edu
CORRELL-HUGHES,
Larry .... 386-822-7000 117 A
lcorrell-hughes@stetson.edu
CORRENTI, Bill .... 718-368-5066 320 A
bcorrenti@kbcc.cuny.edu
CORRIE, Rosie .... 575-769-4021 310 G
rosie.corrie@clovis.edu
CORRIGAN, Boo .... 845-938-3701 549 A
Boo.Corrigan@usma.edu
CORRIGAN,
Christopher .... 912-344-2516 120 D
christopher.corrigan@armstrong.edu
CORRIGAN, Deborah .... 518-438-3111 331 K
debc@mariacollege.edu
CORRIGAN, Kevin .... 404-727-6460 124 D
kcorrig@emory.edu
CORRIGAN, JR.,
Robert, F .... 713-798-6392 469 C
corrigan@bcm.edu
CORRIGAN, Tom .... 617-217-9205 223 A
tcorrigan@baystate.edu
CORRIGLIANO, Paul ...... 425-235-5555 525 G
pcorrigliano@rtc.edu
CORRISS, Mary Jean .... 540-362-6332 508 D
corrissmj@hollins.edu
CORRY, Alan .... 615-794-4254 460 A
acorry@omorecollege.edu
CORRY, Mac .... 706-369-5965 132 H
mcorry@uga.edu
CORSARO, Louis .... 412-392-6190 433 F
lcorsaro@pointpark.edu
CORSELLO, Christine, L 704-403-4336 355 B
christine.corsello@carolinashealthcare.org
CORSINI, Kevin, D .... 434-592-4691 509 G
kdcorsini@liberty.edu
CORSO, Melody .... 386-752-1822 103 Q
melody.corso@fgc.edu
CORSO, Michael .... 973-720-2202 309 I
corsom1@wpunj.edu
CORSO, Teri .... 973-290-4266 301 F
tcorso@cse.edu
CORSON-RIKERT,
Janet, L .... 607-255-3564 323 C
jlc18@cornell.edu
CORT, J. Thomas .... 609-497-7782 305 B
j.thomas.cort@ptsem.edu
CORTELL, Sabrina .... 619-594-0336.. 35 E
scortell@mail.sdsu.edu
CORTES, Chris .... 559-638-3641.. 69 C
chris.cortes@reedleycollege.edu

CORTES, Edymariel .... 939-292-8918 558 F
edymariel.cortes@upr.edu
CORTES, Felix .... 787-841-2000 555 F
fcortes@pucpr.edu
CORTES, Frances .... 787-878-5475 553 F
fcortes@arecibo.inter.edu
CORTES, Gloria .... 787-891-0925 553 E
gcortes@aguadilla.inter.edu
CORTES, Maria .... 787-738-2161 557 G
maria.cortes1@upr.edu
CORTES, Reinaldo .... 352-323-3691 107 X
cortesr@lssc.edu
CORTES, Tammy .... 831-813-6820 477 I
tammy.a.cortes@lonestar.edu
CORTESE, Joseph .... 570-504-9620 415 E
jcortese@tcmc.edu
CORTEZ, Allison .... 719-502-2666.. 84 J
allison.cortez@ppcc.edu
CORTEZ, Carrie .... 985-448-7936 203 G
carrie.cortez@fletcher.edu
CORTEZ, Jack .... 973-748-9000 300 E
jack_cortez@bloomfield.edu
CORTEZ, Ray .... 956-721-5303 477 C
rcortez@laredo.edu
CORTEZ, Ronald, S .... 415-338-2521.. 36 A
rscortez@sfsu.edu
CORTEZ, Sandra, L .... 956-721-5374 477 C
sandra.cortez@laredo.edu
CORTEZ-FARAH, Terre .. 619-684-8763.. 56 B
tcortez@newschoolarch.edu
CORTHELL, Ronald .... 219-989-2401 171 L
ronald.corthell@purduecal.edu
CORTI, Tom .... 631-420-2264 348 B
tom.corti@farmingdale.edu
CORTILET-ALBRECHT,
Carol .... 773-821-2215 141 J
ccortile@csu.edu
CORTINAS, Debra .... 361-825-5743 485 F
debra.cortinas@tamucc.edu
CORUM, Amanda .... 719-549-3163.. 85 A
amanda.corum@pueblocc.edu
CORVERS, Shana, L ...... 225-578-4361 205 E
shana.corvers@law.lsu.edu
CORVEY, Barbara .... 903-886-5041 485 E
barbara.corvey@tamuc.edu
CORVEY, Rebecca, J ..... 478-471-2734 128 H
rebecca.corvey@mga.edu
CORVIN, Clay, L .... 504-282-4455 206 C
claycor@wbsn.com
CORVINO, John .... 505-224-4639 310 F
jcorvino@cnm.edu
CORWIN, Courtney Lee 501-450-1352.. 21 C
corwin@hendrix.edu
CORY, Christopher .... 212-346-1117 337 I
ccory@pace.edu
CORYELL, Brett .... 815-753-2095 154 I
bcoryell@niu.edu
COSBY, Glen .... 509-533-7015 521 E
Glen.Cosby@scc.spokane.edu
COSBY, Glen .... 509-533-7015 521 D
glen.cosby@scc.spokane.edu
COSBY, Kevin, W .... 502-776-1443 199 C
srpastor1@aol.com
COSBY, Laura .... 268-488-4440 244 J
lcosby@kvcc.edu
COSBY-GAITHER,
Christine .... 502-776-1443 199 C
ccosby@simmonscollegeky.edu
COSCIA, Paul .... 336-917-5577 368 F
paul.coscia@salem.edu
COSDEN, Julie .... 239-280-2558.. 98 O
julie.cosden@avemaria.edu
COSDEN, Julie .... 239-280-2544.. 98 O
julie.cosden@avemaria.edu
COSDEN, Merith .... 805-893-2370.. 72 D
cosden@education.ucsb.edu
COSENTINO, Guy, T ...... 202-685-4342 547 M
guy.t.cosentino@ndu.edu
COSENTINO, Joseph ..... 914-323-5125 331 J
joseph.cosentino@mville.edu
COSENTINO, Lauren ...... 310-506-6202.. 58 H
lauren.cosentino@pepperdine.edu
COSENTINO, Richard, E 910-521-6209 371 D
cosentino@uncp.edu
COSENTINO, Richard, E 864-388-8300 447 E
cosentino@lander.edu
COSEY, Arnel .... 504-671-5055 203 F
acosey@dcc.edu
COSGROVE, John .... 570-662-4586 431 D
jcosgrov@mansfield.edu
COSGROVE, Mark .... 517-483-1345 245 I
cosgrom1@lcc.edu
COSIMO, Julie .... 630-829-6037 140 A
jcosimo@ben.edu
COSKY, Alicia, C .... 630-844-5116 139 L
acosky@aurora.edu
COSME-FERNANDEZ,
Yermarie .... 787-993-8898 557 E
yermarie.cosme@upr.edu
COSPER, Tracy .... 229-317-6838 123 H
tracy.cosper@darton.edu

COSS, Ann 787-840-2575 555 E
anncoss@psm.edu

COSSICH, Marc 936-468-2608 484 A
mcossich@sfasu.edu

COSSICH, Monique 936-468-2504 484 A
cossichm@sfasu.edu

COSSITT, Brenda 307-755-2244 547 D
bcossitt@wyotech.edu

COST, Timothy, P 904-256-7016 106 Q
tcost@ju.edu

COSTA, Elizabeth, A 540-985-9701 509 D
eacosta@jchs.edu

COSTA, Kathleen 925-551-1822 42 E
Kcosta@dvc.edu

COSTA, Linda, J 848-932-7743 307 B
linda.costa@rutgers.edu

COSTA, Maria, D 423-439-7737 461 D
costa@etsu.edu

COSTA, JR., Richard, F 859-371-9393 193 D
rcosta@beckfield.edu

COSTA, Tom 615-297-7545 455 A
costat@aquinascollege.edu

COSTALAS, Georgia 570-408-7854 440 B
georgia.costalas@wilkes.edu

COSTANTINI, Camilla 203-332-5222 89 C
cconstantini@housatonic.edu

COSTANTINIDIS, Teresa 415-476-9887 72 C
Teresa.Costantinidis@ucsf.edu

COSTANTINO, Andrea 716-645-2171 343 E
costanti@buffalo.edu

COSTANZA, Christine 909-621-8148 65 E
christine.costanza@scrippscollege.edu

COSTANZA, Laina 334-387-3877 1 E
lainacostanza@amridgeuniversity.edu

COSTANZA, Laina, T 334-387-3878 1 E
lainacostanza@amridgeuniversity.edu

COSTANZA, Megan 979-209-7653 469 F
megan.costanza@blinn.edu

COSTANZO, Brian 570-961-7841 422 G
costanzob@lackawanna.edu

COSTAS, Carolyn 787-841-2000 555 F
ccostas@pucpr.edu

COSTAS, Edda 787-284-1912 554 B
ecostas@ponce.inter.edu

COSTAS, Pam 312-915-6239 151 E
pcostas@luc.edu

COSTE, Mike 303-914-6636 85 C
mike.coste@rrcc.edu

COSTELLO, Bernadette 703-284-1554 510 B
bernadette.costello@marymount.edu

COSTELLO, Bernard 914-674-7569 332 E
bcostello@mercy.edu

COSTELLO, Dana 410-225-2338 216 F
dcostello@mica.edu

COSTELLO, Dennis 586-445-7318 246 A
costellod@macomb.edu

COSTELLO, Eileen 978-632-6600 232 C
e_costello@mwcc.mass.edu

COSTELLO, Georgia 618-235-2700 160 B
georgia.costello@swic.edu

COSTELLO, Gregory, W 507-344-7305 253 M
costello@blc.edu

COSTELLO, Jamie 617-879-7703 230 B
jcostello@massart.edu

COSTELLO, Janice 860-727-6919 90 F
jcostello@goodwin.edu

COSTELLO, SJ, John 312-915-6186 151 E
jcoste2@luc.edu

COSTELLO, Kathryn 270-745-6208 201 D
kathryn.costello@wku.edu

COSTELLO, Ken 602-943-2311 18 K
Ken.Costello@west.edu

COSTELLO, Kevin 617-327-6777 238 D
kevin_costello@williamjames.edu

COSTELLO, Mary Elizabeth 973-761-9175 308 C
maryelizabeth.costello@shu.edu

COSTELLO, Richard, J 219-989-2540 171 L
richard.costello@purduecal.edu

COSTELLO STANIEC, Andria 315-443-1057 349 E
costello@syr.edu

COSTELLO-SULLIVAN, Kathleen, P 315-445-4310 330 B
sullivpk@lemoyne.edu

COSTIGAN, Harry 215-567-7080 412 G
hcostigan@aii.edu

COSTIGAN, Harry 215-567-7080 412 G
hcostigan@edmc.edu

COSTLEY, Lucien 830-895-7116 482 D
lrcostley@schreiner.edu

COSTNER, Alan 937-376-2946 390 F
acostner@payne.edu

COSTNER, Carl 828-652-0614 364 B
carlc@mcdowelltech.edu

COSTON, Charlotte, M 716-851-1180 325 A
coston@ecc.edu

COSTON, D.C 701-483-2326 373 H
dc.coston@dickinsonstate.edu

COSTON, Linda 229-430-2751 119 I
lcoston@albanytech.edu

COSTON, Robert, H 304-647-6574 531 D
rcoston@newriver.edu

COSTON, Todd 661-395-4601 49 E
tcoston@bakersfieldcollege.edu

COSTON, Yvonne 919-516-4096 368 E
ycoston@st-aug.edu

COSTON-MCHUGH, Rose 856-227-7200 301 A
rcoston-mchugh@camdencc.edu

COT, Alea 504-280-6021 205 G
acot@uno.edu

COTA, Marco 909-384-8630 62 C
mcota@sbccd.cc.ca.us

COTE, Christine 509-453-0374 525 B

COTE, Deborah 413-236-1022 231 A
dcote@berkshirecc.edu

COTE, John, C 810-766-4191 239 H
john.cote@baker.edu

COTE-BONANNO, Joanne, F 973-655-6234 304 A
bonannoj@mail.montclair.edu

COTGREAVE, Bruce 806-345-5565 467 E
blcotgreave@actx.edu

COTHAM, Brian 559-278-2111 33 D
bcotham@csufresno.edu

COTHERN, John, W 615-898-2852 461 E
john.cothern@mtsu.edu

COTHERN, Susan, L 828-884-8373 355 A
strombsl@brevard.edu

COTHRAN, Rick 864-646-1701 449 F
rcothran@tctc.edu

COTLEUR, Mary Elizabeth 216-373-5316 388 A
mcotleur@ndc.edu

COTNER, Dave, R 570-326-3761 429 J
dcotner@pct.edu

COTNEY, Rachel 334-291-4979 2 H
rachel.cotney@cv.edu

COTNOIR, Jeff 212-229-5662 334 C
cotnoirj@newschool.edu

COTNOIR, Paul, D 508-373-9731 223 C
paul.cotnoir@becker.edu

COTREL, Jack, R 423-439-6900 461 D
cotrel@etsu.edu

COTRONEO, Keith, J 304-710-3355 531 C
cotroneo@mctc.edu

COTSONES, Rena 815-753-0834 154 I
rcotsones@niu.edu

COTSONIS, Joachim 617-850-1243 227 F
jcotsonis@hchc.edu

COTTAM, Michael 314-246-5972 285 G
michaelcottam@webster.edu

COTTEN, Melinda 713-348-6200 480 M
cotten@rice.edu

COTTEN-BROWN, Floya 919-572-1625 354 F
fbrown@apexsot.edu

COTTER, Bob 513-487-1144 392 F
bob.cotter@myunion.edu

COTTER, Dan, J 802-258-9297 502 B
dcotter@marlboro.edu

COTTER, Geri, E 402-465-2159 292 E
gec@nebrwesleyan.edu

COTTER, James, W 517-355-6532 246 H
cotterj@msu.edu

COTTER, Mark, S 865-539-7266 463 E
mscotter@pstcc.edu

COTTER, Michael 914-594-3675 335 H
michael_cotter@nymc.edu

COTTINGHAM, Ryan, T 517-750-1200 250 F
ryanc@arbor.edu

COTTO, Carmen, E 787-850-9390 558 A
carmen.cotto@upr.edu

COTTO, Evelyn 787-746-1400 552 I
ecoto@huertas.edu

COTTO, Marguerite, C 231-995-1775 248 C
mcotto@nmc.edu

COTTON, Beverly 940-565-4098 492 D
beverly.cotton@unt.edu

COTTON, Fran 806-894-9611 482 F
fcotton@southplainscollege.edu

COTTON, George 850-599-3491 114 D
george.cotton@famu.edu

COTTON, Sabrina 256-726-7408 6 C
cotton@oakwood.edu

COTTON, Trae 336-750-3200 372 D
cottontt@wssu.edu

COTTON KELLY, Montique 860-486-2240 92 C
montique.cotton.kelly@uconn.edu

COTTONE, John 607-753-2701 345 C
john.cottone@cortland.edu

COTTONHAM, Patricia 337-482-6266 208 F
patcottonham@louisiana.edu

COTTRAUX, Suzanne 817-515-1541 484 B
suzanne.cottraux@tccd.edu

COTTRELL, Angela 816-235-1407 284 A
cottrella@umkc.edu

COTTRELL, Debbie 830-372-8002 487 C
dcottrell@tlu.edu

COTTRELL, Debbie 254-295-5059 492 C
dcottrell@umhb.edu

COTTRELL, Janet 802-865-6492 501 F
cottrell@champlain.edu

COTTRELL, Leslie 378-839-6452 133 F
lcottrel@westga.edu

COTTRELL, Liesl 773-252-6464 156 J
liesl.cottrell@resu.edu

COTTRELL, Rick 800-962-7682 285 I
rcottrell@wma.edu

COTTRELL, Terrance, L 815-740-5041 162 F
tcottrell@stfrancis.edu

COTTRILL, Chad 503-883-2506 406 I
ccottril@linfield.edu

COTTRILL, F. Layton 304-696-6295 532 H
cottrill@marshall.edu

COTY, Mark 941-782-5980 423 B
mcoty@lecom.edu

COUCH, Alisha, M 740-368-3099 390 B
amcouch@owu.edu

COUCH, Carl 480-423-6161 15 E
carl.couch@scottsdalecc.edu

COUCH, Charlie 970-351-2231 87 A
charlie.couch@unco.edu

COUCH, JR., Gene, C 276-739-2421 517 D
gcouch@vhcc.edu

COUCH, Jennifer 208-562-3508 138 A
jennifercouch@cwidaho.cc

COUCH, Lisa 760-384-6288 49 F
lcouch@cerrocoso.edu

COUCH, Michael 513-745-1000 396 B
couch@xavier.edu

COUCH, Valerie 405-208-5440 400 A
vcouch@okcu.edu

COUCHEY, Evangeline 845-675-4733 337 B
evangeline.couchey@nyack.edu

COUCHMAN, Monte 785-309-3103 190 L
monte.couchman@salinatech.edu

COUGHENAIR, Russ 813-974-9718 116 B

COUGHENOUR, Brenda 814-262-6434 429 K
bcoughen@pennhighlands.edu

COUGHLIN, SJ, Bernard, J 509-313-5520 522 L
coughlin@gonzaga.edu

COUGHLIN, Eileen, V 360-650-3839 528 D
eileen.coughlin@wwu.edu

COUGHLIN, OFM, F. Edward 518-783-2302 342 H
ecoughlin@siena.edu

COUGHLIN, John 248-370-4618 248 K
jcoughli@oakland.edu

COUGHLIN, Kathleen 210-829-6012 492 B
coughlin@uiwtx.edu

COUGHLIN, Kevin 305-348-7347 114 G
kevin.coughlin@fiu.edu

COUGHLIN, Mary Ann 413-748-3959 236 H
mcoughlin@springfieldcollege.edu

COUGHLIN, Richard 660-785-4038 283 E
coughlin@truman.edu

COULET DUGARD, Caroline 856-351-2756 308 B
ccoulet@salemcc.edu

COULIER, Laura 616-988-1000 241 E
laura.c@compass.edu

COULLIETTE, Holly 904-808-7441 111 K
hollycoulliette@sjrstate.edu

COULOMBE, Jennifer, B 336-734-7723 362 F
jcoulombe@forsythtech.edu

COULON, Richard 949-824-6510 71 C
rcoulon@uci.edu

COULS, Lauren 803-641-2837 450 C
LaurenC@usca.edu

COULSTON, Susan 269-782-1396 250 D
scoulston@swmich.edu

COULTER, Ann 641-782-1340 183 D
coulter@swcciowa.edu

COULTER, Chris 719-389-6568 79 M
chris.coulter@coloradocollege.edu

COULTER, Cindy 828-327-7000 361 B
ccoulter@cvcc.edu

COULTER, John, P 610-758-6310 424 B
jc0i@lehigh.edu

COULTER, Kristin 512-313-3000 471 H
kristin.coulter@concordia.edu

COULTER, Laurie 903-813-2900 468 G
lcoulter@austincollege.edu

COULTER, Lisa 610-683-4072 431 B
coulter@kutztown.edu

COULTER, Martha 802-468-1314 503 G
martha.coulter@castleton.edu

COULTER, Seana 443-885-3110 217 C
seana.coulter@morgan.edu

COULTER, Tina 419-372-6894 377 I
tcoulte@bgsu.edu

COULTRY, Erin 518-956-7111 348 D
ecoultry@sunycnse.com

COUNCIL, Juanette 910-672-1208 370 A
jcouncil@uncfsu.edu

COUNIHAN, Patricia, B 207-581-1110 212 C
counihan@maine.edu

COUNSIL, Brian 620-365-5116 184 C
counsil@allencc.edu

COUNTEE, Jerome 916-484-8202 52 I
countej@arc.losrios.edu

COUNTS, LaNeta 404-471-6483 119 G
lcounts@agnesscott.edu

COURCHAINE, Jeff 714-892-7711 40 C
jcourchaine@gwc.cccd.edu

COURET, Esther 845-431-8673 324 D
esther.couret@sunydutchess.edu

COURET, Esther 845-431-8673 324 D
Esther.couret@sunydutchess.edu

COUREY, Scott 616-394-4287 241 G
scott.courey@cornerstone.edu

COURT, Kevin 516-364-0808 335 A
kcourt@nycollege.edu

COURTEMANCHE, Brian 978-927-2278 226 C
bcourtem@endicott.edu

COURTEY, Susan 818-240-1000 45 I
scourtey@glendale.edu

COURTLEY-TODD, Laura, J 305-628-6677 112 B
lcourtle@stu.edu

COURTNEY, Andalyn, M 716-888-2780 317 H
courtnea@canisius.edu

COURTNEY, Hugh 617-373-3232 235 D

COURTNEY, Justin 419-772-2145 388 I
j-courtney@onu.edu

COURTNEY, Sharon, P 504-988-3390 207 F
sharonc@tulane.edu

COURTRIGHT, Amy 209-954-5151 63 D
acourtright@deltacollege.edu

COURTRIGHT, Caren 509-793-2038 520 B
carenc@bigbend.edu

COURTWAY, Tom 501-450-5286 25 F
tcourtway@uca.edu

COURVILLE, Troy 254-519-5712 485 D
troy.courville@tamuct.edu

COURY, Michelle 913-360-7326 184 K
mcoury@benedictine.edu

COUSINS, Kathryn 212-484-1156 319 F
kcousins@jjay.cuny.edu

COUSSONS-READ, Mary 719-255-3121 86 F
mcousson@uccs.edu

COUTILISH, Theodore, G 734-487-2483 242 J
ted.coutilish@emich.edu

COUTS, Suzann 325-793-4608 478 D
couts.suzann@mcm.edu

COUTTS, Chris 540-868-7083 515 H
ccoutts@lfcc.edu

COUTURE, Daniel, R 802-654-3243 502 H
dcouture@smcvt.edu

COUTURIER, OFM, David 716-375-2000 340 C
dcouturi@sbu.edu

COVAL, Scott 610-282-1100 416 I
scott.coval@desales.edu

COVAR, Tom 864-388-8305 447 E
tcovar@lander.edu

COVAULT, Pamela 785-242-2067 189 J
pcovault@neosho.edu

COVE, Dirrane 212-217-4100 325 C
dirrane_cove@fitnyc.edu

COVE, Lorraine, D 617-573-8160 237 B
lcove@acad.suffolk.edu

COVER, Michael, S 570-577-3348 413 E
mike.cover@bucknell.edu

COVERS, Beth, A 810-762-9925 245 A
bcovers@kettering.edu

COVERSTONE, Jacob 510-780-4500 50 G
jcoverstone@lifewest.edu

COVERT, Michael 859-233-8550 200 D
mcovert@transy.edu

COVERT, Sarah 706-542-0547 132 H
covert@uga.edu

COVERT, Sheree, S 319-352-8272 183 J
sheree.covert@wartburg.edu

COVEY, Angie, E 540-674-3655 516 B
acovey@nr.edu

COVEY, Bruce 404-727-6223 124 D
bcovey@emory.edu

COVEY, Douglass, F 404-413-1500 126 D
dcovey@gsu.edu

COVINGTON, Bill, C 512-245-2314 489 C
bc18@txstate.edu

COVINGTON, Chatonda 919-530-7517 370 C
cbcovington@nccu.edu

COVINGTON, Dan 606-546-1285 200 E
dcovin@unionky.edu

COVINGTON, Dave, R 208-467-8060 138 H
dcovington@nnu.edu

COVINGTON, Dean 870-307-7206 21 G
dean.covington@lyon.edu

COVINGTON, Janet 713-348-6312 480 M
jcov@rice.edu

COVINGTON, Mary .... 919-966-9176 371 A
mary_covington@unc.edu
COVINGTON, Sim .... 315-792-7165 348 D
sim.covington@sunyit.edu
COVINGTON, Sirena ..... 312-788-1146 162 H
scovington@vandercook.edu
COVINGTON, Troy .... 757-823-9540 510 H
tjcovington@nsu.edu
COVINGTON, Valerie, L 757-455-3108 518 H
vcovington@vwc.edu
COVINO, Nicholas .... 617-327-6777 238 D
nicholas_covino@williamjames.edu
COVINO, Paul, F .... 508-767-7057 222 D
pf.covino@assumption.edu
COVINO, William, A ..... 323-343-3030.. 34 A
bill.covino@cslanet.calstatela.edu
COVITZ, Bobby .... 513-487-3259 327 C
rcovitz@huc.edu
COVONE, Michael .... 305-899-3551.. 99 B
mcovone@barry.edu
COWAN, Anthony .... 901-435-1470 457 N
anthony_cowan@loc.edu
COWAN, Carrie .... 516-367-6909 321 F
ccowan@cshl.edu
COWAN, Cindy .... 864-977-2058 448 A
cindy.cowan@ngu.edu
COWAN, David .... 507-389-2267 260 A
david.cowan@mnsu.edu
COWAN, Judith .... 803-327-7402 444 F
jcowan@clintoncollege.edu
COWAN, Kenneth, H ..... 402-559-4238 293 I
kcowan@unmc.edu
COWAN, Theresa .... 954-201-7554.. 99 G
tcowan@broward.edu
COWAN, Vickie, M .... 718-862-7398 331 H
vickie.cowan@manhattan.edu
COWARD, Darryl .... 410-617-2201 216 D
COWARD, William .... 814-536-5168 414 E
bcoward@crbc.net
COWARDIN, Anne .... 303-245-4633.. 84 B
acowardin@naropa.edu
COWART, Julian .... 406-603-7835 402 F
julian.cowart@swcu.edu
COWART, Lisa .... 803-323-2273 451 I
cowartl@winthrop.edu
COWDEN, Clint .... 559-934-2701.. 76 B
clintcowden@whccd.edu
COWDEN, Nate .... 501-450-1348.. 21 C
cowden@hendrix.edu
COWDERY, Aaron .... 740-376-4452 386 A
aaron.cowdery@marietta.edu
COWDREY, Scott .... 410-778-7894 221 D
scowdrey2@washcoll.edu
COWDREY, Scott .... 507-457-6979 264 B
rcowdrey@smumn.edu
COWELL, Elizabeth .... 831-459-2076.. 72 E
mcowell@ucsc.edu
COWELL, JR.,
James, W .... 626-395-4464.. 31 D
jcowell@caltech.edu
COWELL, Karen .... 661-722-6300.. 27 P
kcowell@avc.edu
COWELL-OATES, June ... 314-454-8694 275 D
JCowell-Oates@bjc.org
COWEN, Sonia, S .... 701-328-2965 373 F
sonia.cowen@ndus.edu
COWGER, John .... 701-594-8192 375 A
john.cowger@lrsc.edu
COWGER, Tiffany .... 618-395-7777 146 F
cowgert@iecc.edu
COWHEY, Peter, F .... 858-822-7523.. 72 B
pcowhey@uscd.edu
COWIE, Anne .... 617-369-3606 236 E
acowie@smfa.edu
COWLES, John .... 616-234-3673 243 D
jcowles@grcc.edu
COWLEY, Dave .... 435-797-1146 500 A
dave.cowley@usu.edu
COWLEY, Julie, A .... 512-863-1720 483 G
cowleyj@southwestern.edu
COWLIN, Lynn .... 815-455-8688 152 B
lcowlin@mchenry.edu
COWLING, Richard .... 630-353-8802 141 D
rcowling@chamberlain.edu
COWSER, Erin, K .... 985-549-5861 208 E
erin.moore@selu.edu
COX, Andrew .... 202-319-5305.. 95 A
coxa@cua.edu
COX, Anthony .... 706-778-3000 130 B
acox@piedmont.edu
COX, Barbara .... 850-599-3796 114 D
barbara.cox@famu.edu
COX, Barbara, J .... 619-239-0391.. 36 E
bjc@cwsl.edu
COX, Bob .... 970-339-6509.. 78 J
bob.cox@aims.edu
COX, Bobbie .... 704-406-4627 356 G
bcox@gardner-webb.edu
COX, Brandy, A .... 479-575-2801.. 23 G
brandyac@uark.edu
COX, Brant, M .... 757-446-5800 507 B
coxbm@evms.edu
COX, Cameron .... 253-964-6598 525 C
CMCox@pierce.ctc.edu
COX, Carolyn .... 304-384-5323 532 E
ccox@concord.edu
COX, Carolyn, S .... 240-500-2000 215 C
cscox@hagerstowncc.edu
COX, Cathy .... 706-379-3111 134 J
ccox@yhc.edu
COX, Charlene .... 219-464-5093 174 E
charlene.cox@valpo.edu
COX, Cheryl .... 864-592-4613 449 C
coxc@sccsc.edu
COX, Christopher .... 319-273-2737 176 A
chris.cox@uni.edu
COX, Christopher, P ..... 419-372-8932 377 I
cpcox@bgsu.edu
COX, Chuck .... 417-865-2815 274 L
coxc@evangel.edu
COX, Cleve, H .... 252-249-1851 364 F
ccox@pamlicocc.edu
COX, Colleen .... 978-656-3284 232 B
COX, Dave .... 217-234-5376 150 B
dcox5612@lakeland.cc.il.us
COX, Dave .... 509-533-7179 521 E
dave.cox@scc.spokane.edu
COX, Deborah, M .... 270-824-8609 196 F
deborah.cox@kctcs.edu
COX, Dennis .... 949-214-3182.. 42 B
dennis.cox@cui.edu
COX, Dennis .... 727-376-6911 117 H
dcox@trinitycollege.edu
COX, Donna .... 870-543-5968.. 23 C
dcox@seark.edu
COX, Ed .... 845-431-8071 324 D
ecox@sunydutchess.edu
COX, Erika, M .... 210-458-4859 494 D
ERIKA.COX@UTSA.EDU
COX, Fran .... 662-472-9035 267 E
fcox@holmescc.edu
COX, Geoffrey .... 415-955-2001.. 26 I
gcox@alliant.edu
COX, Geoffrey .... 858-635-4772.. 26 J
gcox@alliant.edu
COX, Gregg .... 561-237-7210 108 E
gcox@lynn.edu
COX, Helen .... 808-245-8210 136 F
helencox@hawaii.edu
COX, James .... 714-620-3700.. 28 G
jcox@argosy.edu
COX, Jamie, S .... 256-766-6610.... 4 C
jcox@hcu.edu
COX, Jana .... 707-524-1579.. 65 C
jcox@santarosa.edu
COX, Janet .... 513-244-4466 387 A
janet.cox@msj.edu
COX, Janet, L .... 513-529-6724 386 K
coxjl@miamioh.edu
COX, Jeff, A .... 336-838-6112 367 C
jeff.cox@wilkescc.edu
COX, Jeffrey, W .... 585-475-7433 339 G
jwccst@rit.edu
COX, Jennifer .... 503-228-6528 404 H
jcox@aii.edu
COX, Jesse .... 313-927-1404 246 D
jcox@marygrove.edu
COX, John, L .... 508-362-2131 231 D
jcox@capecod.edu
COX, Karen .... 508-854-4479 232 F
kcox@qcc.mass.edu
COX, Kelli, S .... 785-532-2118 188 H
kellicox@ksu.edu
COX, Kenneth .... 540-831-7600 511 C
kcox3@radford.edu
COX, Kevin, B .... 214-887-5233 473 E
kcox@dts.edu
COX, Kim .... 305-899-3189.. 99 B
kcox@barry.edu
COX, Lady, D .... 334-844-5672...... 1 G
ldc0006@auburn.edu
COX, Lane .... 205-348-8697..... 8 E
lcox@fa.ua.edu
COX, Larry .... 937-722-9280 394 F
larry.cox@urbana.edu
COX, Laurie .... 608-262-7890 539 D
cox@studentlife.wisc.edu
COX, Leah .... 540-654-1263 513 I
lcox@umw.edu
COX, Leana .... 970-675-3334.. 80 L
leana.cox@cncc.edu
COX, Lisa, B .... 423-869-6722 458 B
lisa.cox@lmunet.edu
COX, Lori .... 618-252-5400 159 F
lori.cox@sic.edu
COX, Lynne .... 541-917-4848 406 J
coxly@linnbenton.edu
COX, Mary .... 724-830-1027 435 E
cox@setonhill.edu
COX, Matthew .... 719-255-3375.. 86 F
mcox4@uccs.edu
COX, Megan, D .... 617-322-3568 227 J
megan_cox@laboure.edu
COX, Michele, D 804-289-8838 513M
mcox@richmond.edu
COX, Miekka, M .... 812-464-1756 174 D
mmcox1@usi.edu
COX, Monte .... 501-279-4808.. 21 A
mcox@harding.edu
COX, Nancy, M .... 859-257-4772 200 G
ncox@email.uky.edu
COX, Paul .... 305-428-5700 109 A
pmcox@aii.edu
COX, Randall .... 903-785-7661 480 B
rcox@parisjc.edu
COX, Robert .... 212-220-8041 318 D
rcox@bmcc.cuny.edu
COX, Robert .... 360-736-9391 520 F
rcox@centralia.edu
COX, Ryan .... 916-568-3101.. 52 H
coxr@losrios.edu
COX, Sam .... 405-945-6789 400 F
coxjs@osuokc.edu
COX, Sandra .... 936-633-5211 467 I
scox@angelina.edu
COX, Sandy .... 920-424-2061 540 B
coxs@uwosh.edu
COX, Steve .... 740-245-7438 394 D
scox@rio.edu
COX, Steven .... 918-595-7866 403 A
steven.cox@tulsacc.edu
COX, Steven, W .... 903-877-7456 495 C
steven.cox@uthct.edu
COX, Susan, S .... 610-606-4609 415 A
sue@cedarcrest.edu
COX, Sylvia .... 910-642-7141 366 B
scox@sccnc.edu
COX, Terry .... 425-640-1489 522 D
terry.cox@edcc.edu
COX, Terry .... 206-934-7798 525 K
terry.cox@seattlecolleges.edu
COX, Tiffa .... 615-963-7494 461 F
tcox9@tnstate.edu
COX, Traci, R .... 419-995-8040 384 E
cox.t@rhodesstate.edu
COX, Virgil .... 704-922-6295 362 G
cox.virgil@gaston.edu
COX, William .... 931-221-1400 461 C
coxw@apsu.edu
COX-KELLEY, Shannon . 903-434-8359 479 L
scoxkelley@ntcc.edu
COX-LANYON, Victoria . 508-793-7258 225 B
vcoxlanyon@clarku.edu
COX-THOMPSON,
Aleshia .... 731-410-6714 457 K
acox@lanecollege.edu
COY, Daniella .... 561-732-4424 112 C
COY, Katherine .... 847-925-6955 145 F
kcoy@harpercollege.edu
COY-OGAN, Lynne .... 207-973-1077 210 C
coyoganl@my.husson.edu
COYKENDALL, John, W 785-827-5541 189 A
john.coykendall@kwu.edu
COYLE, James .... 714-997-7074.. 38 B
coyle@chapman.edu
COYLE, Jennifer .... 503-352-2770 408 I
coylej@pacificu.edu
COYLE, John .... 814-886-6465 427 B
jcoyle@mtaloy.edu
COYLE, Judi .... 903-233-3470 477 G
judicoyle@letu.edu
COYLE, Mark .... 208-426-1826 137 E
markcoyle@boisestate.edu
COYLE, Philip .... 903-233-3200 477 G
philipcoyle@letu.edu
COYNE, Colin, M .... 205-726-4037..... 6 F
ccoyne@samford.edu
COYNE, John, B .... 330-569-5284 383 F
coyneJB@hiram.edu
COYNE, John, M .... 724-264-1328 419 F
jmcoyne@gcc.edu
COYNE, Michael .... 570-372-4128 435 I
coyne@susqu.edu
COYNE, Michael .... 928-681-0800 233 D
coyne@mslaw.edu
COZART, Melissa .... 859-858-3511 193 A
melissa.cozart@asbury.edu
COZART, Wayne .... 434-243-9041 514 A
wdc9q@virginia.edu
COZZENS, David .... 817-257-7926 486 G
d.s.cozzens@tcu.edu
COZZENS, Susan .... 404-894-5054 125 D
susan.cozzens@iac.gatech.edu
COZZOCREA, Rebecca .. 518-736-3622 326 D
rswart@fmcc.suny.edu
CRABB, Ann .... 208-467-8593 138 H
atcrabb@nnu.edu
CRABB, Jenna, S .... 505-277-2531 313 H
jennas@unm.edu
CRABBE, Kim .... 518-580-5790 342 I
kcrabbe@skidmore.edu
CRABILL, Casey .... 315-498-2211 337 F
president@sunyocc.edu
CRABREE, Troy .... 206-239-4500 520 K
troy.crabtree@cityu.edu
CRABTREE, David .... 541-683-5141 406 B
dcrabtree@gutenberg.edu
CRABTREE, Diane .... 503-883-2507 406 I
dcrabtre@linfield.edu
CRABTREE, Gina, D ...... 316-978-3672 192 D
gina.crabtree@wichita.edu
CRABTREE, JR.,
John, A .... 317-789-8288 165 F
jcrabtree@crossroads.edu
CRABTREE, Kacy .... 828-898-8739 358 F
crabtree@lmc.edu
CRABTREE, Peter .... 510-464-3218.. 59 B
pcrabtree@peralta.edu
CRABTREE, Robbin, D .. 310-338-2716.. 53 C
Robbin.Crabtree@lmu.edu
CRABTREE, Shane .... 801-957-4571 500 E
shane.crabtree@slcc.edu
CRACCO, Elizabeth .... 860-486-0744.. 92 C
elizabeth.cracco@uconn.edu
CRACCO, Elizabeth .... 860-486-4705.. 92 C
elizabeth.cracco@uconn.edu
CRACE, Robert, K .... 757-221-1236 506 J
rkcrac@wm.edu
CRACKENBERG, Peter ... 503-554-2138 406 A
pcrackenberg@georgefox.edu
CRADDOCK, Alden .... 314-529-6687 277 B
acraddock@maryville.edu
CRADDOCK,
Amanda, E .... 843-349-2979 444 G
acraddoc@coastal.edu
CRADDOCK, Chris .... 903-983-8181 477 A
ccraddock@kilgore.edu
CRADDOCK, Jackie .... 510-594-3612.. 30 G
jcraddock@cca.edu
CRADIT, J. Dennis .... 619-594-5259.. 35 E
dcradit@mail.sdsu.edu
CRADY, Thomas, M .... 507-933-7676 256 A
tcrady@gustavus.edu
CRAFT, Edwin .... 662-846-4840 267 A
ecraft@deltastate.edu
CRAFT, Linda .... 214-638-0484 476 Y
linda@kdstudio.com
CRAFT, Shonda .... 651-793-1333 259 E
shonda.craft@metrostate.edu
CRAFT, Stephen .... 205-665-6540..... 9 C
scraft@montevallo.edu
CRAFT, Terri .... 229-732-5943 120 B
terricraft@andrewcollege.edu
CRAFT, Tonya .... 601-974-1200 268 D
craftte@millsaps.edu
CRAFT, William, J .... 218-299-3000 255 B
president@cord.edu
CRAFTON, Michael .... 678-839-4875 133 F
mcrafton@westga.edu
CRAFTON, Teresa .... 478-274-7833 129 D
tcrafton@oftc.edu
CRAFTS, Deborah .... 617-236-8880 226 F
dcrafts@fisher.edu
CRAGAR, Beth .... 931-598-1312 460 I
bcragar@sewanee.edu
CRAGER, Cindy .... 609-626-3658 308 E
cindy.crager@stockton.edu
CRAGIN, Janet .... 415-575-6143.. 31 C
jcragin@ciis.edu
CRAGLE, Rachael, C ..... 865-539-7219 463 E
rccragle@pstcc.edu
CRAGO, David, C .... 419-772-2034 388 I
d-crago@onu.edu
CRAHEN, Sherri, A .... 216-397-3010 384 F
scrahen@jcu.edu
CRAIG, Barbara .... 269-695-2995 245 E
craig@lakemichigancollege.edu
CRAIG, Catharine .... 641-784-5029 178 G
ceelliot@graceland.edu
CRAIG, Christopher, J .. 417-836-5215 279 A
chriscraig@missouristate.edu
CRAIG, David .... 573-882-9570 283 H
davidcr@missouri.edu
CRAIG, David .... 406-657-2209 287 H
david.craig2@msubillings.edu
CRAIG, Dennis .... 914-251-6300 346 D
dennis.craig@purchase.edu
CRAIG, Harold .... 404-225-4488 120 I
hcraig@atlantatech.edu
CRAIG, James .... 520-206-6916.. 17 A
jcraig7@pima.edu
CRAIG, James .... 916-361-1660.. 37 A
jcraig@carrington.edu
CRAIG, Jayne .... 575-769-4031 310 G
jayne.craig@clovis.edu
CRAIG, Jennifer .... 617-964-1100 222 B
jcraig@ants.edu
CRAIG, John .... 215-953-5999.. 96 H
CRAIG, Johnny .... 773-602-5118 142 A
jcraig@ccc.edu
CRAIG, Kathleen .... 860-932-4170.. 90 A

CRAIG, Ken 828-898-8731 358 F craig@lmc.edu
CRAIG, Kenneth 910-672-1151 370 A kcraig@uncfsu.edu
CRAIG, Kim 651-603-6223 255 C craig@csp.edu
CRAIG, La Saundra 513-569-1532 379 K lasaundra.craig@cincinnatistate.edu
CRAIG, Martha, P 865-981-8167 458 E mardi.craig@maryvillecollege.edu
CRAIG, Marva 212-220-8131 318 D mcraig@bmcc.cuny.edu
CRAIG, Michael 816-501-4065 281 B michael.craig@rockhurst.edu
CRAIG, Paige 708-209-3509 143 D paige.craig@cuchicago.edu
CRAIG, Raymond 419-372-2340 377 I racraig@bgsu.edu
CRAIG, Sandy 618-262-8641 147 B craigs@iecc.edu
CRAIG, Stephanie 315-279-5609 329 K scraig@keuka.edu
CRAIG, Stephanie, A 814-371-2090 437 C scraig@triangle-tech.edu
CRAIG, Steven 713-743-3812 491 D scraig@uh.edu
CRAIG, Thomas 903-877-7442 495 C tom.craig@uthct.edu
CRAIG, Wendy 619-660-4240 46 G wendy.craig@gcccd.edu
CRAIG, William, G 732-571-3427 303 G craig@monmouth.edu
CRAIG KUNG, Pang-Jen 919-301-6500 96 H
CRAIG-MARIUS, Renee 559-442-4600 69 B renee.craig-marius@fresnocitycollege.edu
CRAIG-TAYLOR, Phyliss, V 919-530-6112 370 C pcraigtaylor@nccu.edu
CRAIGIE, Casey 541-485-1780 407 H caseycraigie@newhope.edu
CRAIGMILES, Jan 859-858-3511 193 A jan.craigmiles@asbury.edu
CRAIK, Rebecca, L 215-572-2143 412 F craikr@arcadia.edu
CRAIN, BJ 940-898-3505 490 D bcrain@twu.edu
CRAIN, John, L 985-549-2280 208 E jcrain@selu.edu
CRAIN, R. David 972-883-6900 494 A R.David.Crain@utdallas.edu
CRAIN, Terry 618-985-3741 148 G terrycrain@jalc.edu
CRAINER, Bryan, E 989-964-4091 249 G becraine@svsu.edu
CRAM, Stanley 920-924-6431 543 F scram@morainepark.edu
CRAM-RAHLF, Shelly 563-288-6011 178 C scramrahlf@eicc.edu
CRAMB, Alan 312-567-3106 147 E cramb@iit.edu
CRAMER, Alicia 713-646-1808 482 H acramer@stcl.edu
CRAMER, Gregory, D 630-889-6536 154 E gcramer@nuhs.edu
CRAMER, Janet 303-546-3588 84 B jcramer@naropa.edu
CRAMER, Joel 317-738-8197 166 B jcramer@franklincollege.edu
CRAMER, Judy 978-542-6139 230 E judy.cramer@salemstate.edu
CRAMER, Paul 717-361-1400 418 B cramerp@etown.edu
CRAMER, Rick 607-729-1581 324 A rcramer@davisny.edu
CRAMER, Robert, G 608-342-1226 540 D cramerr@uwplatt.edu
CRAMER, Steven, M 608-262-5246 539 D cramer@engr.wisc.edu
CRAMER, Walter 203-837-8547 88 G cramerw@wcsu.edu
CRAMPTON, Anne-Marie 719-336-1520 83 N anne-marie.crampton@lamarcc.edu
CRAMPTON, Roscoe 312-942-7165 158 A roscoe_crampton@rush.edu
CRAMPTON, Tom 810-762-0506 247 F thomas.crampto@mcc.edu
CRAMPTON, Troy, D 515-574-1114 179 F crampton@iowacentral.edu
CRAMSEY, Rachel 217-228-5520 140 G rcramsey@brcn.edu
CRANCE, Gina-Lyn 610-921-7611 411 E gcrance@albright.edu
CRANDALL, Brian 845-938-3327 549 A 8uscc@usma.edu
CRANDALL, Donald, W 479-524-7150 21 F dcrandal@jbu.edu
CRANDALL, James 530-242-7989 66 C jcrandall@shastacollege.edu
CRANDALL, Larry 801-302-2800 498 L larry.crandall@neumont.edu
CRANDALL, Laura 315-470-4865 347 B ldcranda@esf.edu
CRANDALL, Paige 914-395-2575 342 C pcrandall@sarahlawrence.edu
CRANDALL, Stephen, S 607-871-2184 314 J fcrandall@alfred.edu
CRANDELL, Gale, M 989-386-6664 247 B gcrandell@midmich.edu
CRANE, Amanda 817-274-4284 469 E acrane@bhcarroll.edu
CRANE, Daniel, R 651-631-5100 265 D drcrane@unwsp.edu
CRANE, David 508-531-6145 229 C dcrane@bridgew.edu
CRANE, Jeff 270-384-8150 198 C cranej@lindsey.edu
CRANE, Jennifer 203-582-5283 91 E jennifer.crane@quinnipiac.edu
CRANE, Malachi, D 517-750-1200 250 F mcrane@arbor.edu
CRANE, Peter 203-432-5109 93 C peter.crane@yale.edu
CRANE, Ramona 719-219-9636 79 K rcrane@cavt.edu
CRANE, Rob, M 913-288-7283 188 G rcrane@kckcc.edu
CRANE, Robert 956-380-8100 481 A rcrane@riogrande.edu
CRANE, Ron 972-825-4818 483 D rcrane@sagu.edu
CRANE, Sarah, R 517-750-1200 250 F scrane@arbor.edu
CRANE, Susan 914-337-9300 323 A susan.crane@concordia-ny.edu
CRANE, Susan, L 989-964-4350 249 G scrane@svsu.edu
CRANFORD, Alatorya 706-821-8248 129 H acranford@paine.edu
CRANFORD, Bill 601-925-3283 268 E cranford@mc.edu
CRANFORD, Shannon 580-628-6229 399 E shannon.cranford@noc.edu
CRANFORD, Timothy 510-869-6610 61 J tcranford@samuelmerritt.edu
CRANHAM, John, B 919-508-2336 373 B jbcranham@peace.edu
CRANK, Robert 816-322-0110 272 L bob.crank@calvary.edu
CRANMER, Wendy 585-395-2126 345 A wcranmer@brockport.edu
CRANMORE, Jill, A 217-443-8756 143 F jcranmore@dacc.edu
CRANSTON, Carey 708-444-4500 145 B
CRANSTON, Carolyn 412-924-1375 433 E ccranston@pts.edu
CRANWELL, Mary, E 732-987-2285 302 J cranwell@georgian.edu
CRAPANZANO, Vincent 845-398-4019 341 H vcrapanz@stac.edu
CRAREY, II, Patrick 301-891-4481 221 C pcrarey@wau.edu
CRARY-STACHOWIAK, Sage 413-205-3521 221 G sage.stachowiak@aic.edu
CRASS, Sara, T 713-221-8679 491 F crasss@uhd.edu
CRATER, Lucas 618-536-3331 159 G lcrater@siumed.edu
CRATSLEY, Christopher 978-665-4716 229 D ccratsley@fitchburgstate.edu
CRATTY, Frederic, W 203-837-8665 88 G crattyf@wcsu.edu
CRAVEN, Bryan, C 850-718-2375 100 E cravenb@chipola.edu
CRAVEN, Heather 973-328-5281 301 G hcraven@ccm.edu
CRAVEN, Katherine 781-239-5955 222 E kcraven@babson.edu
CRAVEN, Randy 423-236-2732 460 K rlcraven@southern.edu
CRAVENS, Michael 419-824-3620 385 F mcravens@sistersosf.org
CRAVER, Robert 303-369-5151 84 N robert.craver@plattcolorado.edu
CRAVER, III, William 678-225-7509 432 E williamcr@pcom.edu
CRAVEY, Irene 512-759-5614 488 B irene.cravey@tstc.edu
CRAVO, Ana, M 201-761-6104 307 K acravo@saintpeters.edu
CRAWFORD, Anna 304-260-4380 530 M acrawfor@blueridgectc.edu
CRAWFORD, Brian 304-336-8004 533 A brian.crawford@westliberty.edu
CRAWFORD, Brittany 334-683-2382 5 H bcrawford@marionmilitary.edu
CRAWFORD, Bruce 205-929-6312 5 E bcrawford@lawsonstate.edu
CRAWFORD, Bryan 719-562-7002 85 A bryan.crawford@pueblocc.edu
CRAWFORD, Cardon, B 843-953-6966 444 C cardon.crawford@citadel.edu
CRAWFORD, Catherine 903-923-2069 473 I ccrawford@etbu.edu
CRAWFORD, Charlie 425-640-1557 522 D charlie.crawford@edcc.edu
CRAWFORD, Chemene, L 214-860-2454 472 F chemene.crawford@dcccd.edu
CRAWFORD, Clinton 718-270-5140 320 C crawford@mec.cuny.edu
CRAWFORD, Darryl, D 540-869-0623 515 H dcrawford@lfcc.edu
CRAWFORD, David 303-797-5762 79 A david.crawford@arapahoe.edu
CRAWFORD, David 773-947-6250 152 A dcrawford@mccormick.edu
CRAWFORD, David, S 202-526-3799 96 F
CRAWFORD, Debbie 970-945-8691 80 D
CRAWFORD, Deena 601-266-4829 271 B deena.crawford@usm.edu
CRAWFORD, Diane 919-546-8309 368 G dcrawford@shawu.edu
CRAWFORD, Doris, S 434-528-5276 518 F dorisscott@vul.edu
CRAWFORD, Eboni 973-803-5000 305 A ecrawford@pillar.edu
CRAWFORD, Galen 513-562-6273 376 O gcrawford@artacademy.edu
CRAWFORD, Gregory, P 574-631-6456 174 A gregory_crawford@nd.edu
CRAWFORD, Holly 585-273-4734 351 D hcrawford@admin.rochester.edu
CRAWFORD, Isiaah 206-296-6963 526 F crawford@seattleu.edu
CRAWFORD, John 330-672-2760 384 H jcrawfor1@kent.edu
CRAWFORD, John, D 229-333-5939 133 H jdcrawford@valdosta.edu
CRAWFORD, John, P 716-880-2879 332 B jpc334@medaille.edu
CRAWFORD, Jonas 805-986-5870 75 D jcrawford@vcccd.edu
CRAWFORD, Kevin 803-641-3495 450 C KevinCr@usca.edu
CRAWFORD, Malinda 406-756-3828 286 G mcrawfor@fvcc.edu
CRAWFORD, Matthew 952-358-8454 260 D matthew.crawford@normandale.edu
CRAWFORD, Michael 773-838-7500 142 C mcrawford34@ccc.edu
CRAWFORD, Mike 863-680-6211 104 F mcrawford@flsouthern.edu
CRAWFORD, Missie 478-289-2172 124 B mcrawford@ega.edu
CRAWFORD, Patricia 765-973-8625 168 A pajames@iue.edu
CRAWFORD, R. Scott 765-361-6355 175 B crawforr@wabash.edu
CRAWFORD, Ray Scott 318-678-6000 203 A rcrawford@bpcc.edu
CRAWFORD, Rhia, M 828-448-6048 367 B rcrawford@wpcc.edu
CRAWFORD, Ronald, W 804-204-1201 505 B rcrawford@btsr.edu
CRAWFORD, Steven, R 740-587-5717 381 H crawfords@denison.edu
CRAWFORD, Teresa 863-784-7061 113 C teresa.crawford@southflorida.edu
CRAWFORD, Teri 281-998-6151 481 D teri.crawford@sjcd.edu
CRAWFORD, Tim 254-295-4180 492 C tcrawford@umhb.edu
CRAWFORD, Valerie 309-268-8150 145 H val.crawford@heartland.edu
CRAWFORD, Virginia 601-266-5390 271 B virginia.crawford@usm.edu
CRAWFORD, III, William, H 480-732-7309 14 K Bill.Crawford.III@cgc.edu
CRAWFORD, Yashica 707-864-7112 66 J yashica.crawford@solano.edu
CRAWFORD-FOWLER, Sally 620-341-5221 186 H scrowfo4@emporia.edu
CRAWLEY, Cathy 478-445-5149 125 A cathy.crawley@gcsu.edu
CRAWLEY, William 850-474-3246 116 E wcrawley@uwf.edu
CRAWMER, Martha 937-328-6031 379 L crawmerm@clarkstate.edu
CRAWSHAW, Taylor 620-331-4100 188 B tcrawshaw@indycc.edu
CRAYS, Linda, L 713-500-2080 495 A linda.l.crays@uth.tmc.edu
CRAYTON, DiOnetta 617-253-5010 233 C
CREAGER, Carol 540-887-7310 510 A ccreager@mbc.edu
CREAGH, Curtis, E 502-597-6735 197 G curtis.creagh@kysu.edu
CREAGH, CM, Kevin 716-286-8400 336 E kcreagh@niagara.edu
CREAHAN, Patricia, H 716-888-2616 317 H creahan@canisius.edu
CREAMER, Barry 214-818-1326 471 I bcreamer@criswell.edu
CREAMER, David 513-529-4225 386 K creamerd@miamioh.edu
CREAMER, Jenni 864-646-1615 449 F jevans12@tctc.edu
CREAMER, Julie 507-222-4280 254 D jcreamer@carleton.edu
CREAMER, Stephen 978-762-4000 232 D screamer@northshore.edu
CREAMER, Stephen 978-762-4000 232 D Screamer@northshore.edu
CREARY, Ferne 305-237-2222 108 L fcreary@mdc.edu
CREASMAN, Alice 304-473-8440 534 G creasman_aj@wvwc.edu
CREASMAN, Boyd 304-473-8042 534 G creasman@wvwc.edu
CREASON, Paul 562-938-4171 51 A pcreason@lbcc.edu
CREASON, Rita, A 270-789-5233 194 D racreason@campbellsville.edu
CREASY, Rick 423-472-7141 462 D RCreasy@clevelandstatecc.edu
CRECELIUS, Carolyn (Kay) 573-518-2100 278 F kayc@mineralarea.edu
CRECELIUS, Kathryn, J 443-997-2370 216 A kcrecelius@jhu.edu
CREDILLE, John 417-328-1606 282 D jcredille@sbuniv.edu
CREDLE, Sid, H 757-727-5361 508 C sid.credle@hamptonu.edu
CREE, Sara 309-344-2518 140 I scree@sandburg.edu
CREECH, Bill 918-595-7000 403 A bill.creech@tulsacc.edu
CREECH, Karlton, W 207-581-1052 212 C karlton.creech@maine.edu
CREECH, Pat 918-540-6294 398 L pcreech@neo.edu
CREECY, Scott 870-762-3159 19 C screecy@smail.anc.edu
CREED, J. Bradley 910-893-1205 355 C creed@campbell.edu
CREED, Mickey 540-785-5440 514 C mickeycreed@vbc.edu
CREED-DIKEOGU, Gloria 785-242-5200 190 D creeddikeogu@ottawa.edu
CREEDON, James 215-204-1991 436 C james.creedon@temple.edu
CREEGER, Joan 704-216-3602 365 F joan.creeger@rccc.edu
CREEHAN, Dennis, W 304-457-6404 529 C creehandw@ab.edu
CREEHAN, Richard, A 304-457-6317 529 C creehanra@ab.edu
CREEK, Frederick 541-552-7672 409 G creekf@sou.edu
CREEKMORE, Crystal 256-233-8174 1 F crystal.creekmore@athens.edu
CREEL, Angie 928-344-7776 12 B angela.creel-erb@azwestern.edu
CREEL, Ronnie 334-670-3496 8 A rcreel@troy.edu
CREEL, Shane 361-593-2237 486 A randolph.creel@tamuk.edu
CREELY, Hilliary 724-357-7730 431 A hcreely@iup.edu
CREER, Andrew 801-863-8608 500 B andrew.creer@uvu.edu
CREER, John 636-949-4777 276 L jcreer@lindenwood.edu
CREFT, Dawn, H 407-303-7894 97 J dawn.creft@adu.edu
CREGER, LeAnn 517-607-2305 243 J lcreger@hillsdale.edu
CREGGER, Crystal, Y 276-233-4762 517 F ccregger@wcc.vccs.edu
CREIGHTON, Grace 914-674-7369 332 E gcreighton@mercy.edu
CREMER, Douglas 818-767-0888 77 G douglas.cremer@woodbury.edu
CREMER, Phyllis, A 818-767-0888 77 G phyllis.cremer@woodbury.edu
CRENSHAW, Chris 601-266-4414 271 B christopher.crenshaw@usm.edu
CRENSHAW, Christine 405-744-5358 400 C christine.crenshaw@okstate.edu
CREOLA, Thomas 561-697-9200 131 F tcreola@southuniversity.edu

CRESCENZI, Nicole .... 415-351-3517.. 62 I
ncrescenzi@sfai.edu
CRESCENZO, Mario .... 212-650-5250 318 G
mcrescenzo@ccny.cuny.edu
CRESPINO, Curt, J .... 816-235-1105 284 A
crespinocj@umkc.edu
CRESPO, Jorge .... 787-751-0178 555 K
ac_jcrespo@suagm.edu
CRESPO, Jorge, L .... 787-751-0178 555 K
ac_jcrespo@suagm.edu
CRESPO, Lynn .... 864-455-7992 450 G
lcrespo@greenvillemed.sc.edu
CRESPO, Ricardo .... 787-751-1912 554 D
rcnevarez@juris.inter.edu
CRESPO-KEBLER,
Elizabeth .... 787-993-8864 557 E
elizabeth.crespo1@upr.edu
CRESPO-LOPEZ, Sylvia . 212-237-8897 319 F
sylopez@jjay.cuny.edu
CRESPO-MARTINEZ,
María, I .... 787-993-8886 557 E
maria.crespo@upr.edu
CRESPY, Charles, T ...... 989-774-2481 240 O
cresp1ct@cmich.edu
CRESS, Pam .... 509-527-2421 528 A
pam.cress@wallawalla.edu
CRESWELL, Debra .... 951-372-7016.. 61 A
debra.creswell@norcocollege.edu
CREW, Dwayne .... 478-825-6200 124 E
crewd@fvsu.edu
CREW, Rudolph, F .... 718-270-5000 320 C
rcrew@mec.cuny.edu
CREWE, Sandra .... 202-806-7300.. 96 B
screwe@howard.edu
CREWELL, Don .... 626-395-6280.. 31 D
dcrewell@caltech.edu
CREWS, Amy .... 256-765-4437.... 9 D
aecrews@una.edu
CREWS, Bradford, W .... 561-297-2190 114 E
bcrews2@fau.edu
CREWS, Chris .... 812-941-2000 169 A
cmcrews@ius.edu
CREWS, Denise .... 217-875-7200 156 K
dcrews@richland.edu
CREWS, Gordon .... 419-448-3319 392 B
crewsg@tiffin.edu
CREWS, Kimberly .... 202-274-5857.. 97 B
kcrews@udc.edu
CREWS, Lyen .... 859-336-5082 199 B
lyencrews@sccky.edu
CREWS, Micah, R .... 423-652-4773 457 J
mrcrews@king.edu
CREWS, Michele .... 617-879-2114 238 C
mcrews@wheelock.edu
CREWS, Patricia, S .... 850-484-1000 110 D
pcrews@pensacolastate.edu
CREWS, Sharon .... 205-929-6307.... 5 E
sharon.crews@lawsonstate.edu
CREWS, William, O .... 415-380-1326.. 45 J
billcrews@ggbts.edu
CREWSE, Valentina .... 602-242-6265.. 12 H
CRICK, James .... 502-451-0815 200 B
jcrick@sullivan.edu
CRICK, James .... 502-451-0815 200 A
jcrick@sullivan.edu
CRICKENBERGER,
Leslie .... 931-372-3034 462 A
lcrickenberger@tntech.edu
CRICKENBERGER,
Tamela .... 434-592-3508 509 G
tlcrickenberger@liberty.edu
CRICKMER, Janet .... 276-944-6658 507 E
jcrickme@ehc.edu
CRIDER, Scott .... 972-721-5218 491 B
crider@udallas.edu
CRIDER, Wayne .... 706-245-7226 124 C
wcrider@ec.edu
CRIGHTON, Betsy .... 909-621-8137.. 60 A
elizabeth.crighton@pomona.edu
CRILLEY, Bonnie .... 814-866-8144 423 B
bcrilley@lecom.edu
CRILLY, Sam .... 405-912-9064 398 B
scrilly@hc.edu
CRIMMIN, Nancy, P ..... 774-354-0460 223 C
nancy.crimmin@becker.edu
CRIMMINS, Cindy .... 717-815-1216 440 H
ccrimmins@ycp.edu
CRIMMINS, Kate .... 410-837-6135 221 B
kcrimmins@ubalt.edu
CRIMMINS LECHOWICZ,
Catherine .... 860-685-2841.. 93 B
ccrimmins@wesleyan.edu
CRINITI, Stephen .... 304-243-2424 534 H
scriniti@wju.edu
CRINO, Sally, E .... 563-333-6080 182 E
CrinoSallyE@sau.edu
CRIPE, Len .... 912-525-5000 130 H
lcripe@scad.edu
CRIPE, Stephen, A .... 989-837-4387 248 D
cripe@northwood.edu

CRIPPS, Kimberly .... 205-726-4180.... 6 F
kcripps@samford.edu
CRISAFULLI, Susan .... 317-738-8240 166 B
scrisafulli@franklincollege.edu
CRISER, III,
Marshall, M .... 850-245-0466 114 C
chancellor@flbog.edu
CRISLER, Pat .... 402-457-2759 291 E
pcrisler@mccneb.edu
CRISLIP, Ann .... 518-262-9550 314 I
crislipa@mail.amc.edu
CRISLIP-TACY, Carolyn . 304-367-4241 532 F
crisleptacy@fairmontstate.edu
CRISMAN, Matthew .... 276-944-6491 507 E
mcrisman@ehc.edu
CRISMAN, Steve .... 901-321-3278 455 I
scrisman@cbu.edu
CRISMON, M. Lynn 512-471-3718 493M
lynn.crismon@austin.utexas.edu
CRISP, JR., Delmas, S . 910-630-7031 359 C
dcrisp@methodist.edu
CRISP, Kathryn .... 615-904-8167 461 E
kathy.crisp@mtsu.edu
CRISP, Whitney .... 229-931-2299 131 E
wcrisp@southgatech.edu
CRISP, Winston, B .... 919-966-4045 371 A
wbcrisp@email.unc.edu
CRISPELL, Brian, L .... 813-988-5131 103 L
crispellb@floridacollege.edu
CRISS, Paul .... 901-888-3343 266 F
pcriss@belhaven.edu
CRISSINGER, Amy, S .... 605-256-5139 453 H
amy.crissinger@dsu.edu
CRIST, Diane, G .... 651-962-6765 265 F
dgcrist@stthomas.edu
CRIST, Michael, R .... 330-941-3625 396 C
mrcrist@ysu.edu
CRIST, William, J .... 337-482-2001 208 F
wjc4092@louisiana.edu
CRISTE, Vince .... 800-877-5456 506 H
alumni@christendom.edu
CRISTELLO, Justin .... 910-642-7141 366 B
justin.cristello@sccnc.edu
CRISTOBAL, Remy, B .... 671-735-2290 549 G
remybc@triton.uog.edu
CRISTOBAL, Remy, B .... 671-735-2218 549 G
remybc@triton.uog.edu
CRISTOFARO,
Theresa, R .... 856-225-6053 307 A
terri.cristofaro@rutgers.edu
CRISWELL, John .... 972-860-7786 472 B
jcriswell@dcccd.edu
CRISWELL, Pamela .... 617-369-3717 236 E
pcriswell@smfa.edu
CRITE, Ken .... 815-802-8222 149 B
kcrite@kcc.edu
CRITES, Randall .... 304-473-8030 534 G
crites@wvwc.edu
CRITES, Tammy .... 304-473-8186 534 G
crites_t@wvwc.edu
CRITTENDEN,
Barbara, J .... 641-782-1425 183 D
crittenden@swcciowa.edu
CRITTENDEN, Steve ...... 763-433-1982 257 P
steve.crittenden@anokaramsey.edu
CROCE, Edward .... 210-434-6711 479 P
ecroce@lake.ollusa.edu
CROCHET, Monique ...... 985-448-4110 208 C
monique.crochet@nicholls.edu
CROCITTO, Peter .... 954-776-4476 107 F
peterc@keiseruniversity.edu
CROCK, Veronica .... 334-347-2623.... 3 H
vcrock@escc.edu
CROCKEM, Rajanel .... 713-313-1895 487 F
CROCKER, Daniel .... 207-974-4623 211 A
dcrocker@emcc.edu
CROCKER, Heidi .... 562-947-8755.. 67 J
heidicrocker@scuhs.edu
CROCKER, Jack .... 575-538-6318 314 E
jack.crocker@wnmu.edu
CROCKER, Jane, S .... 856-415-2250 306 C
jcrocker@rcgc.edu
CROCKER, Leslie .... 804-330-0111 506 D
bursarcrim@centura.edu
CROCKER, Marjorie .... 706-419-1544 123 F
crocker@covenant.edu
CROCKER, Phyllis .... 313-596-0210 250 H
pcrocker@udmercy.edu
CROCKER, Rhonda .... 575-624-7382 310 J
rhonda.crocker@roswell.enmu.edu
CROCKER, Robert, A ...... 516-796-4800 334 F
rcrocker@nycc.edu
CROCKER, Ryan, C .... 979-862-8007 485 C
rcrocker@tamu.edu
CROCKETT, Bennie, R ... 601-318-6116 271 F
crockett@wmcarey.edu
CROCKETT, Betty, P .... 410-543-6050 220 E
bpcrockett@salisbury.edu
CROCKETT, Brian, S .... 540-464-7287 518 A
briancrockett@vmiaa.org

CROCKETT, Charles, E .. 936-261-2653 484 F
cecrockett@pvamu.edu
CROCKETT, Daniel, E .... 304-558-4618 532 C
crockett@hepc.wvnet.edu
CROCKETT, Deborah ..... 207-947-4591 209 G
dcrockett@bealcollege.edu
CROCKETT, Julie, E .... 309-794-7244 139 K
juliecrockett@augustana.edu
CROCKETT, Michael ...... 928-428-8215.. 13 L
mike.crockett@eac.edu
CROCKETT, Nathan .... 864-242-5100 443 G
CROCKETT, William, P .. 410-706-3902 219 E
bcrocket@umaryland.edu
CROCKETT-RAY, Sharon 210-486-2886 467 B
scrockett-ray@alamo.edu
CROCKETT-RAY, Sharon 210-486-2887 467 B
scrockett-ray@alamo.edu
CROCKROM, SR.,
Charles .... 205-929-1447.... 5 I
ccrockrom@miles.edu
CROCQUET, Marc .... 954-262-8842 109 E
crocquet@nsu.nova.edu
CROEKER, Jane .... 701-777-2097 373 G
jane.croeker@und.edu
CROFT, Candace .... 319-296-4432 179 B
candace.croft@hawkeyecollege.edu
CROFT, Lucy, S .... 904-620-2525 116 A
lcroft@unf.edu
CROFT, Nicole .... 866-680-2756 498 K
academicdean@midwifery.edu
CROGAN, Evelyn .... 760-795-6610.. 54 G
ecrogan@miracosta.edu
CROGHAN, David .... 301-846-2708 214 I
dcroghan@frederick.edu
CROGHAN, John .... 315-859-4129 327 A
jcroghan@hamilton.edu
CROKE, Ryan .... 217-206-7795 161 G
rcroke@uis.edu
CROLEY, Linda .... 386-752-1822 103 Q
linda.croley@fgc.edu
CROMARTIE, Anthony ... 973-877-1873 302 F
cromartie@essex.edu
CROMARTY, Geoffrey .... 215-951-2970 432 F
cromartyg@philau.edu
CROMBIE, Richard .... 651-635-8041 254 A
r-crombie@bethel.edu
CROMER, Steve .... 706-646-6234 132 B
scromer@sctech.edu
CROMIE, Carol .... 409-772-9795 495 E
cacromie@utmb.edu
CROMLEY, Brenda .... 570-389-4674 430 B
bcromley@bloomu.edu
CROMLEY, Robert .... 903-877-7455 495 C
robert.cromley@uthct.edu
CROMWELL, Dennis ...... 812-856-5594 167 J
dcromwel@iu.edu
CROMWELL, James .... 808-689-2909 136 A
cromwell@hawaii.edu
CRONAN, David .... 708-709-3585 156 A
dcronan@prairiestate.edu
CRONAUER, Alan .... 315-866-0300 327 E
cronaueab@herkimer.edu
CRONAUER, OSB,
Patrick, T .... 724-805-2324 435 C
patrick.cronauer@stvincent.edu
CRONE, Darren .... 972-883-4826 494 A
darren.crone@utdallas.edu
CRONE, Marilyn .... 206-296-5841 526 F
cronem@seattleu.edu
CRONIC, Sue .... 770-531-6332 128 A
scronic@laniertech.edu
CRONIN, Alice .... 508-565-1021 237 A
acronin@stonehill.edu
CRONIN, Barb .... 636-227-2100 277 A
barb.cronin@logan.edu
CRONIN, Charles .... 610-526-1458 412 D
tip.cronin@theamericancollege.edu
CRONIN, Deborah .... 207-509-7227 212 A
dcronin@unity.edu
CRONIN, Debra .... 312-850-7154 142 E
dcronin1@ccc.edu
CRONIN, Joy .... 304-243-2238 534 H
jcronin@wju.edu
CRONIN, Marta .... 772-462-7674 106 F
mcronin@irsc.edu
CRONIN, Mary, A 713-348-4070 480M
cronin@rice.edu
CRONIN, Shawn .... 978-762-4000 232 D
scronin@northshore.edu
CRONIN, Trish .... 508-793-7160 225 B
tcronin@clarku.edu
CRONK, Keith .... 501-279-5700.. 21 A
kcronk@harding.edu
CRONK, Nancy, L .... 765-285-1722 164 D
ncronk@bsu.edu
CRONRATH, Daniel .... 386-752-1822 103 Q
Daniel.Cronrath@fgc.edu
CRONRATH, David .... 301-405-6287 219 D
cronrath@umd.edu
CROOK, Evonne .... 423-236-2830 460 K
ercrook@southern.edu

CROOK, Linda .... 303-914-6256.. 85 C
linda.crook@rrcc.edu
CROOK, Patricia .... 615-963-5280 461 F
pcrook@tnstate.edu
CROOKENDALE,
Humphrey .... 212-343-1234 332 I
hcrookendale@mcny.edu
CROOKER, Benjamin .... 718-817-3048 326 C
crooker@fordham.edu
CROOKS, John, R .... 440-365-5222 385 E
CROOKSHANK, Gail ...... 217-420-6778 153 A
gcrookshank@millikin.edu
CROOM, Sally .... 318-675-8769 205 D
scroom@lsuhsc.edu
CROONQUIST, Matt ...... 641-673-2123 184 B
croonquistm@wmpenn.edu
CROOP, Patricia .... 518-464-8642 325 B
pcroop@excelsior.edu
CROOT, Rick .... 360-417-6553 525 A
rcroot@pencol.edu
CROPPER, USMS,
Thomas, A .... 707-654-1011.. 34 B
tacropper@csum.edu
CROPSEY, Jeffrey .... 800-955-2527 187 E
jcropsey@grantham.edu
CROSBIE, Jeff .... 435-797-1042 500 A
jeff.crosbie@usu.edu
CROSBY, Anita, L .... 334-387-3877.... 1 E
anitacrosby@amridgeuniversity.edu
CROSBY, Cherie, L .... 215-885-2360 425 C
ccrosby@manor.edu
CROSBY, Cheryl .... 352-854-2322 100 P
crosbyc@cf.edu
CROSBY, Craig .... 858-541-7780.. 55 J
ccrosby@nu.edu
CROSBY, Faye .... 831-459-3568.. 72 E
fjcrosby@ucsc.edu
CROSBY, James .... 307-778-1340 546 F
jcrosby@lccc.wy.edu
CROSBY, James, P .... 216-347-4282 384 F
jcrosby@jcu.edu
CROSBY, Jesse .... 207-947-4591 209 G
jcrosby@bealcollege.edu
CROSBY, John .... 740-284-5349 382 G
jcrosby@franciscan.edu
CROSBY, Kim .... 870-307-7275.. 21 G
kim.crosby@lyon.edu
CROSBY, Mark .... 207-859-5500 210 A
mcrosby@colby.edu
CROSBY, Pamela .... 863-667-5157 113 K
pscrosby@seu.edu
CROSBY, Susan, E .... 540-453-2363 514 H
crosbys@brcc.edu
CROSKERY, Patrick, T ... 419-772-2197 388 I
p-croskery@onu.edu
CROSLEY, Leslie, V .... 315-684-6046 347 A
croslelv@morrisville.edu
CROSLIN, Joey .... 405-208-5075 400 A
jcroslin@okcu.edu
CROSMAN, Karen .... 740-368-3104 390 B
klcrosma@owu.edu
CROSON, Rachel .... 817-272-2881 493 L
croson@uta.edu
CROSS, Berri, V .... 336-334-4822 363 A
bvcross@gtcc.edu
CROSS, Charles, E .... 415-422-6522.. 74 C
cross@usfca.edu
CROSS, Colette .... 281-649-3475 475 B
ccross@hbu.edu
CROSS, Connie .... 417-268-1000 272 D
crossc@evangel.edu
CROSS, David .... 603-862-2090 299 B
counseling.center@unh.edu
CROSS, David .... 713-718-8636 475 C
david.cross@hccs.edu
CROSS, Dean .... 916-577-2200.. 77 F
dcross@jessup.edu
CROSS, Dennis, W .... 540-458-8232 519 A
dcross@wlu.edu
CROSS, Dwight .... 802-225-6324 502 F
dwight.cross@neci.edu
CROSS, Dwight .... 802-728-1250 504 C
dcross@vtc.edu
CROSS, James .... 802-383-6633 501 F
jcross@champlain.edu
CROSS, Jeff .... 619-203-3681.. 28 G
jefcross@argosy.edu
CROSS, Jeffrey .... 248-476-1122 246 G
jcross@mispp.edu
CROSS, Jeffrey, F .... 217-581-2121 144 E
jfcross@eiu.edu
CROSS, Jesse .... 336-334-4822 363 A
jlcross@gtcc.edu
CROSS, Joe .... 858-653-6740.. 48 Q
JCross@JPCatholic.com
CROSS, Kris .... 937-393-3431 391 F
kcross@sscc.edu
CROSS, Kristen .... 870-612-2011.. 24 G
kristen.cross@uaccb.edu
CROSS, Logan .... 904-256-7137 106 Q
jcross3@ju.edu

CROSS, Mary, M .... 615-353-3301 463 C
mary.cross@nscc.edu
CROSS, Michael .... 919-209-2051 363 F
mtcross@johnstoncc.edu
CROSS, Myrna, J .... 580-477-7712 404 D
myrna.cross@wosc.edu
CROSS, Neal .... 417-328-2055 282 D
ncross@sbuniv.edu
CROSS, Penny .... 828-652-0645 364 B
penncyc@mcdowelltech.edu
CROSS, Ray, W .... 608-262-2321 539 C
rcross@uwsa.edu
CROSS, Roberta .... 724-503-1001 439 B
rcross@washjeff.edu
CROSS, Stan .... 828-298-3325 373 A
scross@warren-wilson.edu
CROSS, Stephanie .... 540-545-7245 512 E
scross92@su.edu
CROSS, Stephen .... 404-894-8885 125 D
cross@gatech.edu
CROSS, Stevan .... 530-242-7739.. 66 C
scross@shastacollege.edu
CROSS, Teresa .... 660-359-3948 279 L
tcross@mail.ncmissouri.edu
CROSS, Terry .... 423-614-8140 457 M
tcross@leeuniversity.edu
CROSS, Tim, L .... 865-974-7114 465 D
tlcross@utk.edu
CROSS, Troy .... 330-941-3035 396 C
tcross@ysu.edu
CROSSLAND, Martin ..... 913-971-3514 189 F
mcrossland@mnu.edu
CROSSLEY, John .... 315-733-2300 351 E
CROSSLEY, John, L ...... 315-733-2300 351 E
jcrossley@uscny.edu
CROSSMAN, Cynthia ...... 508-362-2131 231 D
ccrossma@capecod.edu
CROSSMAN, Herb .... 518-580-5819 342 I
hcrossma@skidmore.edu
CROSSMAN, Linda .... 727-873-4143 116 C
crossman@mail.usf.edu
CROSSMAN,
Raymond, E .... 312-662-4001 139 E
rec@adler.edu
CROSWELL, Katrina .... 510-549-4719.. 68 I
kcroswell@sksm.edu
CROTHERS, Scott .... 618-545-3176 149 C
scrothers@kaskaskia.edu
CROTTS, Glenda, S .... 704-406-4236 356 G
gcrotts@gardner-webb.edu
CROTZ, Steve .... 334-244-3541.... 2 A
scrotz@aum.edu
CROUCH, Bruce .... 714-556-3610.. 75 A
bcrouch@vanguard.edu
CROUCH, David .... 501-279-4316.. 21 A
dcrouch@harding.edu
CROUCH, Frank .... 610-861-1516 426 H
crouchf@moravian.edu
CROUCH, Julia .... 918-335-6212 400 I
jcrouch@okwu.edu
CROUCH, Michael, A .... 205-726-2820.... 6 F
mcrouch@samford.edu
CROUCH, Nancy .... 910-775-4355 371 D
nancy.crouch@uncp.edu
CROUCH, Peter, E .... 808-956-7727 135 J
pcrouch@hawaii.edu
CROUCH, Steven .... 612-624-2006 265 C
crouch@umn.edu
CROUCH, Tony .... 918-647-1320 397 C
tacrouch@carlalbert.edu
CROUCHET, Christeen ... 253-589-5895 521 B
christeen.crouchet@cptc.edu
CROUSE, Eileen .... 269-782-1369 250 D
ecrouse@swmich.edu
CROUSE, JR.,
Francis, C .... 814-886-6383 427 B
fcrouse@mtaloy.edu
CROUSE, Robert .... 573-592-5019 285 J
rob.crouse@westminster-mo.edu
CROUSE, Steve .... 864-977-7016 448 A
steve.crouse@ngu.edu
CROUTER, Ann, C .... 814-865-1420 428 C
ac1@psu.edu
CROW, Angela .... 479-968-0271.. 20 C
acrow@atu.edu
CROW, C. Robert .... 616-526-6165 240 L
rcrow@calvin.edu
CROW, Carla .... 561-803-2155 109 G
carla_crow@pba.edu
CROW, Donna, E .... 435-797-3588 500 A
donna.crow@usu.edu
CROW, Len .... 909-652-6508.. 38 A
leonard.crow@chaffey.edu
CROW, Michael, G .... 912-358-4172 131 A
crowm@savannahstate.edu
CROW, Michael, M .... 480-965-8972.. 11 J
michael.crow@asu.edu
CROW, Scott .... 916-484-8647.. 52 I
crows@arc.losrios.edu
CROW, Scott .... 419-824-3938 385 F
scrow@lourdes.edu
CROW, Steven .... 619-482-6310.. 68 D
scrow@swccd.edu
CROW, Tony, L .... 303-458-4161.. 85 G
tcrow@regis.edu
CROWDER, Annette .... 573-681-5102 276 K
crowdera@lincolnu.edu
CROWDER, Darren .... 417-328-1797 282 D
dcrowder@sbuniv.edu
CROWDER, John .... 317-789-8267 165 F
jcrowder@crossroads.edu
CROWDER, Mike .... 806-743-7865 490 A
mike.crowder@ttuhsc.edu
CROWDER, Tia .... 618-744-0426 152 C
tdcrowder@mckendree.edu
CROWDER, Vickie .... 304-473-8032 534 G
crowder_v@wvwc.edu
CROWE, Aliesha, R .... 715-833-6277 542 M
acrowe3@cvtc.edu
CROWE, Carl .... 410-778-7235 221 D
ccrowe2@washcoll.edu
CROWE, Gregg .... 503-228-6528 404 H
gcrowe@aii.edu
CROWE, Jason .... 314-454-7770 275 D
jcrowe@bjc.org
CROWE, John .... 912-525-5000 130 H
jcrowe@scad.edu
CROWE, Mary, L .... 863-680-4181 104 F
mcrowe@flsouthern.edu
CROWE, Richard .... 818-345-8414.. 41 F
rcrowe@columbiacollege.edu
CROWE, Stephanie .... 406-496-4568 288 C
scrowe@mtech.edu
CROWE, Thomas .... 847-543-2473 142 G
tcrowe@clcillinois.edu
CROWE, William, R ...... 706-542-6285 132 H
william.crowe@georgiacenter.uga.edu
CROWELL, Anthony .... 212-431-2840 335 G
Anthony.Crowell@nyls.edu
CROWELL, Heidi .... 603-577-6523 297 F
crowell@dwc.edu
CROWELL, Perry .... 850-644-4780 115 A
pcrowell@admin.fsu.edu
CROWELL, Rebecca, C . 972-516-5011 471 C
rcrowell@collin.edu
CROWELL, Scott .... 507-537-6844 262 B
Scott.Crowell@smsu.edu
CROWETIPTON,
Vaughn .... 864-294-2138 446 F
vaughn.crowetipton@furman.edu
CROWL, Rebecca, R ...... 330-363-6164 377 C
rebecca.crowl@aultman.com
CROWL, Ronald .... 330-829-2756 394 A
crowlrl@mountunion.edu
CROWLEY, Cara, J .... 806-345-5518 467 E
cjcrowley@actx.edu
CROWLEY, Kimberly, A 806-354-6087 467 E
kacrowley@actx.edu
CROWLEY, Rachel .... 605-331-6661 454 E
rachel.crowley@usiouxfalls.edu
CROWLEY, Tim .... 785-628-4236 187 A
tcrowley@fhsu.edu
CROWLEY, Timothy, D . 207-768-2811 211 C
tcrowley@nmcc.edu
CROWNE, Deborah .... 808-544-0283 135 C
dcrowne@hpu.edu
CROWNOVER, Kathleen 478-757-5224 134 E
kcrownover@wesleyancollege.edu
CROWSON, Allan .... 615-844-5221 466 G
acrowson@welch.edu
CROWSON, Dennis .... 979-830-4456 469 F
dennis.crowson@blinn.edu
CROWTHER,
Cameron, T .... 540-261-8483 512 J
cameron.crowther@svu.edu
CROWTHER, Edward ..... 719-587-7811.. 78 I
ercrowth@adams.edu
CROWTHER,
Elizabeth, H .... 804-758-6701 516 G
ecrowther@rappahannock.edu
CROWTHER, Jason .... 910-221-2224 357 A
jcrowther@gcd.edu
CROWTHER, Lori, D ..... 620-792-9216 184 I
crowtherl@bartonccc.edu
CROWTHER, Steven ...... 910-221-2224 357 A
scrowther@gcd.edu
CROX, JR., Walter, L .... 770-593-2257 127 A
wcrox@gupton-jones.edu
CROY, Jason .... 706-245-7226 124 C
jcroy@ec.edu
CROY, Lori .... 573-884-8075 283 H
croyl@missouri.edu
CROYLE, Kristin .... 956-665-7919 494 C
kcroyle@utpa.edu
CROYLE, Mary .... 806-743-2143 490 A
mary.croyle@ttuhsc.edu
CRUICKSHANK, Laura .... 860-486-2086.. 92 C
laura.cruickshank@uconn.edu
CRUICKSHANK,
Natacha .... 317-573-8942 530 G
ncruickshank@salemu.edu
CRUIKSHANK, Alexis .... 206-281-2752 526 D
acruikshank@spu.edu
CRUIKSHANK,
Nancy, L .... 724-738-4831 432 A
nancy.cruikshank@sru.edu
CRUISE, Christie .... 314-529-9684 277 B
ccruiseharper@maryville.edu
CRUISE, Deborah, J ...... 443-412-2233 215 D
dcruise@harford.edu
CRULL, Matthew .... 815-825-2086 149 E
matt.crull@kishwaukeecollege.edu
CRUM, Beth, A .... 573-629-3049 275 F
bcrum@hlg.edu
CRUM, Claude .... 606-368-6061 192 H
claudecrum@alc.edu
CRUM, Jeff .... 920-206-2323 536 T
jeff.crum@mbu.edu
CRUM, Lyndsey .... 970-351-2551.. 87 A
lyndsey.crum@unco.edu
CRUM, Michael, R .... 515-294-8105 175 G
mcrum@iastate.edu
CRUME, Gene .... 847-628-2002 149 A
gene.crume@judsonu.edu
CRUMEDY, Ron, C .... 409-944-1237 474 G
rcrumedy@gc.edu
CRUMITY, Oscar .... 850-599-3651 114 D
oscar.crumity@famu.edu
CRUMLEY, Christopher . 281-476-1810 481 E
christopher.crumley@sjcd.edu
CRUMLEY, Kristie .... 410-386-8408 214 B
kcrumley@carrollcc.edu
CRUMLEY, Linda .... 423-236-2733 460 K
lindacrumley@southern.edu
CRUMLEY, Terri .... 319-363-1323 181 D
tcrumley@mtmercy.edu
CRUMMIE, Carla, M ..... 404-527-4525 122 D
ccrummie@carver.edu
CRUMMIE, Robert, W ... 404-527-4520 122 D
rcrummie@carver.edu
CRUMP, D'adra .... 718-940-5869 341 A
dcrump@sjcny.edu
CRUMP, Laurel .... 562-907-4829.. 77 E
lcrump@whittier.edu
CRUMP, Tammy .... 704-991-0267 366 D
tcrump5648@stanly.edu
CRUMP, Virginia, S ...... 731-410-6709 457 K
vcrump@lanecollege.edu
CRUMP-PHILLIPS,
Maureen .... 773-995-3602 141 J
mcrump22@csu.edu
CRUMPACKER, Norman 919-658-7755 369 B
ncrumpacker@umo.edu
CRUMRIN, Robin .... 812-237-3700 167 E
robin.crumrin@indstate.edu
CRUSCIEL, Robert .... 814-472-3021 434 F
rcrusciel@francis.edu
CRUSE, David .... 517-265-5161 238 H
CRUSE, Kayla .... 270-686-2110 193 G
Kayla.cruse@brescia.edu
CRUSE, Susan .... 404-727-6061 124 D
scruse2@emory.edu
CRUSE, Terry .... 903-233-4310 477 G
TerryCruse@letu.edu
CRUSE, Tom .... 513-936-1538 393 C
thomas.cruse@uc.edu
CRUSOR, Grant .... 502-895-3411 198 E
gcrusor@lpts.edu
CRUSTO-WAY, Kathy ..... 817-515-5206 484 B
kathy.crustoway@tccd.edu
CRUTCHER, Caicey, L ... 620-792-9386 184 I
crutcherc@bartonccc.edu
CRUTCHER, Gary .... 816-414-3700 278 E
gcrutcher@mbts.edu
CRUTCHER, Ronald, A .. 804-289-8100 513 M
ronald.crutcher@richmond.edu
CRUTCHER, Terri .... 615-230-3343 464 B
terri.crutcher@volstate.edu
CRUTCHFIELD, Carla ..... 501-337-5000.. 20 H
ccrutchfield@coto.edu
CRUTSINGER, Christy ... 940-565-2550 492 D
christy.crutsinger@unt.edu
CRUTTENDEN, Roger .... 212-938-5945 347 C
rcruttenden@sunyopt.edu
CRUZ, Abraham .... 347-964-8600 316 J
acruz@boricuacollege.edu
CRUZ, Anthony .... 937-512-2975 391 D
anthony.cruz@sinclair.edu
CRUZ, Beatriz .... 718-429-6600 352 A
beatriz.cruz@vaughn.edu
CRUZ, Carmen, L .... 787-257-0000 557 F
carmen.cruz3@upr.edu
CRUZ, Dorie .... 817-202-6290 483 C
cruzd@swau.edu
CRUZ, Elizabeth .... 787-780-5134 554 H
ecruz@nuc.edu
CRUZ, Erin .... 559-791-2222.. 49 G
ecruz@portervillecollege.edu
CRUZ, Erin .... 559-791-2332.. 49 G
ecruz@portervillecollege.edu
CRUZ, Esteban .... 217-786-2200 151 C
esteban.cruz@llcc.edu
CRUZ, Evelyn .... 787-850-9203 558 A
evelyn.cruz1@upr.edu
CRUZ, Felicita .... 787-834-9595 556 D
fcruz@uaa.edu
CRUZ, Heather, A .... 716-851-1621 325 A
cruzh@ecc.edu
CRUZ, Hilda .... 787-164-1912 554 C
hmcruz@intersg.edu
CRUZ, Irma del Pilar .... 787-828-1319 556 A
um_idelpilar@suagm.edu
CRUZ, Israel .... 787-264-1912 554 C
icruz@intersg.edu
CRUZ, Jackie .... 831-755-6810.. 46 J
jcruz@hartnell.edu
CRUZ, Josè .... 657-278-2614.. 33 E
jcruz@fullerton.edu
CRUZ, Lambert .... 602-386-4160.. 11 F
lambert.cruz@arizonachristian.edu
CRUZ, Lourdes .... 714-542-8086.. 29 H
lcruz@bristoluniversity.edu
CRUZ, Madeline .... 787-834-9595 556 D
mcruz@uaa.edu
CRUZ, Marcia .... 787-758-2525 558 C
marcia.cruz1@upr.edu
CRUZ, Maria .... 787-834-9595 556 D
maryc@uaa.edu
CRUZ, Martin .... 787-766-1717 556 A
um_mcruzsa@suagm.edu
CRUZ, Mayra .... 787-751-0178 555 K
mcruz@suagm.edu
CRUZ, Monica .... 361-354-2258 470 K
mcruz@coastalbend.edu
CRUZ, Monica .... 361-354-2399 470 K
mcruz@coastalbend.edu
CRUZ, Nathaniel .... 718-518-4253 319 D
ncruz@hostos.cuny.edu
CRUZ, Octavio .... 408-270-6423.. 63 P
octavio.cruz@evc.edu
CRUZ, Odalis .... 352-335-2332.. 97 F
CRUZ, Oscar .... 787-250-1912 554 A
ocruz@metro.inter.edu
CRUZ, Robert .... 201-360-4051 303 A
rcruz@hccc.edu
CRUZ, Rosa, E .... 787-848-1589 555 D
rcruz@popac.edu
CRUZ, Rosalia .... 212-694-1000 316 J
rcruz@boricuacollege.edu
CRUZ, Villan .... 718-933-6700 333 F
Vcrux@monroecollege.edu
CRUZ, Viviana .... 787-850-9319 558 A
viviana.cruz1@upr.edu
CRUZ-PABÓN, Olga, I ... 787-751-1912 554 D
oicruz@juris.inter.edu
CRUZ PAUL, Theresa ... 828-227-3812 372 C
tcpaul@wcu.edu
CRUZ-URIBE, Kathyrn ... 765-973-8201 168 A
kathcruz@iue.edu
CRUZADO, Waded .... 406-994-2341 287 G
President_Cruzado@montana.edu
CRUZVERGARA,
Christine, Y .... 703-993-2370 507 K
ccruzver@gmu.edu
CRYDER, Dennis .... 660-543-4313 283 F
cryder@ucmo.edu
CRYER, Byron, L .... 214-648-2590 496 A
byron.cryer@utsouthwestern.edu
CRYLEN, Thomas .... 847-925-6169 145 F
tcrylen@harpercollege.edu
CSESZKO, Carey, R .... 317-805-1788 530 G
carey.cseszko@salemu.edu
CSOMAN, Kati, R .... 814-641-3184 421 L
csomank@juniata.edu
CUBANO, Luis, A .... 787-798-3001 556 F
luis.cubano@uccaribe.edu
CUBARRUBIA,
Archieval .... 305-237-7450 108 L
acubarru@mdc.edu
CUBBA, Stephanie .... 213-477-2766.. 54 I
scubba@msmu.edu
CUBBAGE, Alan, K .... 847-491-4886 155 D
a-cubbage@northwestern.edu
CUBBERLEY,
Frances, M .... 610-359-5141 416 G
fcubberl@dccc.edu
CUBBINS, Elaine .... 520-383-8401.. 18 A
ecubbins@tocc.edu
CUBELIC, Chuck .... 412-809-5100 433 D
cubelic.chuck@pti.edu
CUBERO, Chris .... 724-738-4267 432 A
chris.cubero@sru.edu
CUBILIE, Anne .... 509-963-1400 520 E
cubiliea@cwu.edu
CUBIT, James, R .... 847-735-5054 149 H
cubit@lakeforest.edu
CUBRIEL, III, Robert .... 361-572-6406 496 D
robert.cubriel@victoriacollege.edu
CUCARESE, Lisa .... 304-829-7831 529 H
lcucarese@bethanywv.edu
CUCCIA, Christopher .... 973-761-7554 308 C
christopher.cuccia@shu.edu

CUCHENS, Pat .... 281-283-3065 491 E
cuchens@uhcl.edu
CUCURELLA-ADORNO,
Ana, E .... 787-780-0070 550 G
acucurella@caribbean.edu
CUDD, Anne, E .... 617-353-2401 224 E
CUELLAR, Leana .... 847-635-1655 155 E
lcuellar@oakton.edu
CUELLAR, Toni .... 254-298-8333 484 C
toni.cuellar@templejc.edu
CUETO, Jose .... 787-769-0007 550 G
jcueto@caribbean.edu
CUETO, Jose, M .... 787-780-0070 550 G
jcueto@caribbean.edu
CUEVA, Patricia .... 360-676-2772 524 D
pcueva@nwic.edu
CUEVAS, Andreia .... 559-791-2457.. 49 G
andreia.cuevas@portervillecollege.edu
CUEVAS, Carmen .... 312-935-6445 157 A
ccuevas@robertmorris.edu
CUEVAS, Frank .... 865-974-2571 465 D
fcuevas@utk.edu
CUEVAS, Jessica .... 310-954-4327.. 54 I
jcuevas@msmu.edu
CUEVAS, Monica .... 559-442-4600.. 69 B
monica.cuevas@fresnocitycollege.edu
CUEVAS, Patricia .... 312-553-6029 141 N
pcuevas@ccc.edu
CUFF, Michael .... 508-830-5037 230 D
mcuff@maritime.edu
CUKANNA, Paul-James 412-396-5002 417 I
cukanna@duq.edu
CUKROWSKI, Ken, R .... 325-674-3700 466 I
cukrowskik@acu.edu
CULATTA, Victor .... 408-795-5600.. 36 B
victor.culatta@sjsu.edu
CULBERSON, Pamela .... 912-344-2518 120 D
pam.culberson@armstrong.edu
CULBERSON, Roy .... 940-498-6282 479 K
rculberson@nctc.edu
CULBERT, John .... 773-325-7954 143 G
jculbert@depaul.edu
CULBERTSON,
Charles, R .... 540-828-5720 505 F
cculbert@bridgewater.edu
CULBERTSON, Richard .. 504-568-5960 205 C
rcuble@lsuhsc.edu
CULBREATH, Jahan .... 937-376-6289 379 D
jculbreath@centralstate.edu
CULBRETH, Paul .... 717-391-1375 436 D
culbreth@stevenscollege.edu
CULHAN, Timothy, P .... 859-238-5360 194 E
tim.culhan@centre.edu
CULL, Cecelia .... 617-682-1525 226 D
ccull@eds.edu
CULLARS, Kyle .... 478-445-6804 125 A
kyle.cullars@gcsu.edu
CULLEN, Andrew .... 505-277-6465 313 H
acullen@unm.edu
CULLEN, Cathleen, R .... 508-767-7533 222 D
ccullen@assumption.edu
CULLEN, Elizabeth .... 508-373-9531 223 C
elizabeth.corcoran@becker.edu
CULLEN, Jim .... 570-961-7864 422 G
cullenj@lakcawanna.edu
CULLEN, Kathleen .... 608-266-9399 542 K
kathleen.cullen@wtcsystem.edu
CULLEN, Kevin .... 302-736-2442.. 94 E
kevin.cullen@wesley.edu
CULLEN, Laura .... 734-462-4400 250 A
lcullen@schoolcraft.edu
CULLEN, Michael .... 812-488-1178 173 H
mc42@evansville.edu
CULLEN, Sharon .... 703-993-8700 507 K
scullen1@gmu.edu
CULLENEN, Rachel .... 607-274-3306 328 H
rcullenen@ithaca.edu
CULLENS, Linda .... 831-477-3222.. 30 C
licullen@cabrillo.edu
CULLER, Angela .... 336-758-4010 372 G
culleraa@wfu.edu
CULLER, Fred, B .... 304-883-2424 531 D
fculler@newriver.edu
CULLER, Kevin, J .... 313-845-9755 243 I
kjculler@hfcc.edu
CULLER, Lori, L .... 260-359-4213 167 D
lculler@huntington.edu
CULLER, Valerie .... 734-384-4139 247 C
vculler@monroeccc.edu
CULLERTON, Laura .... 303-369-5151.. 84 N
laura.cullerton@plattcolorado.edu
CULLEY,
Christopher, M .... 614-292-0611 389 A
culley.8@osu.edu
CULLEY, JR., W. Glenn 434-223-6216 508 B
gculley@hsc.edu
CULLIGAN, Rob .... 320-363-3388 264 A
rculligan@csbsju.edu
CULLINAN, Carol .... 716-880-2211 332 B
carol.cullinan@medaille.edu
CULLINAN, Mary .... 509-359-6362 522 C
president@ewu.edu
CULLINAN, William ...... 414-288-5053 537 B
william.cullinan@marquette.edu
CULLIPHER, David .... 870-508-6100.. 19 H
CULLISON, Janet, L ...... 443-518-4904 215 F
jcullison@howardcc.edu
CULLISON, Stacy .... 415-503-6326.. 63 A
scullison@sfcm.edu
CULLITON, Pamela .... 314-529-9520 277 B
pculliton@maryville.edu
CULLITON, Richard .... 860-685-2627.. 93 B
rculliton@wesleyan.edu
CULLNANE, Chris .... 601-968-8505 266 F
ccullnane@belhaven.edu
CULLO, Len .... 814-393-2240 430 E
lcullo@clarion.edu
CULLUM, Douglas .... 585-594-6331 337 A
cullumd@nes.edu
CULLUM, John, W .... 704-687-8003 371 B
John.Cullum@uncc.edu
CULORA, Thomas .... 401-841-2200 548 B
CULP, Kristin, J .... 937-328-6087 379 L
culpk@clarkstate.edu
CULP, Mark, K .... 610-861-5301 427 F
mculp@northampton.edu
CULP, Shawn .... 412-291-6248 412 H
CULPEPPER, Anthony ... 661-395-4487.. 49 E
anthony.culpepper@bakersfieldcollege.edu
CULPEPPER, Suzann ..... 229-430-3510 119 I
sculpepper@albanytech.edu
CULSHAW, John, P .... 319-335-5867 175 H
john-culshaw@uiowa.edu
CULVAHOUSE, Dallas ... 231-439-6321 248 A
dculvahouse@ncmich.edu
CULVER, Gloria .... 585-275-2121 351 D
gloria.culver@rochester.edu
CULVER, Jay .... 863-638-2947 119 A
culverjr@webber.edu
CULVER, Joshua .... 321-674-6302 103 R
jrculver@fit.edu
CULVER, Randy .... 605-642-6245 453 G
Randy.Culver@bhsu.edu
CULVER, Richard, W ..... 410-543-6017 220 E
rwculver@salisbury.edu
CULVER, Sandi .... 907-786-1007.. 10 H
smculver@uaa.alaska.edu
CULVER, Steve .... 540-231-4581 518 B
sculver@vt.edu
CULVERHOUSE, Renee .. 256-393-2999.... 4 E
rculverhouse@huntingdon.edu
CULVERHOUSE, Robert . 254-647-3234 480 G
CUMBEE, Ann .... 903-586-2518 476 K
acumbee@jacksonville-college.edu
CUMBERLAND,
Lyndsay .... 662-329-7295 269 B
ldcumberland@muw.edu
CUMBIE, Donna, L .... 252-222-6161 361 A
cumbied@carteret.edu
CUMBIE, Michael .... 912-279-5704 123 B
mcumbie@ccga.edu
CUMBY, Rick .... 931-372-3973 462 A
rcumby@tntech.edu
CUMENS, Chris .... 270-901-1113 197 C
chris.cumens@kctcs.edu
CUMINGS, Victoria .... 503-517-1012 411 A
vcumings@warnerpacific.edu
CUMMING, Carrie .... 269-387-4300 252 I
carrie.cumming@wmich.edu
CUMMING, Tammie ...... 718-260-5007 320 D
tcumming@citytech.cuny.edu
CUMMINGS, Alison ...... 404-270-5353 132 D
acummin3@spelman.edu
CUMMINGS, Amanda .... 207-941-7875 210 C
cummingsa@husson.edu
CUMMINGS, Angela ...... 404-297-9522 126 A
cumminga@gptc.edu
CUMMINGS, SSE,
Brian, J .... 802-654-2386 502 H
bcummings@smcvt.edu
CUMMINGS, Carmen .... 850-599-3707 114 D
carmen.cummings@famu.edu
CUMMINGS,
Carmen, M .... 386-312-4152 111 K
carmencummings@sjrstate.edu
CUMMINGS, Corlis .... 678-466-4270 122 J
corliscummings@clayton.edu
CUMMINGS, Cynthia .... 508-910-6402 228 H
ccumings2@umassd.edu
CUMMINGS, Edie .... 318-869-5191 202 D
ecummings@centenary.edu
CUMMINGS,
Edmond, M .... 504-286-5258 207 B
ecumming@suno.edu
CUMMINGS, Glenn, T ... 207-780-4480 213 A
gcummings@usm.maine.edu
CUMMINGS, Jeff .... 760-366-5289.. 42 G
jcummings@cmccd.edu
CUMMINGS, Jim .... 270-745-2035 201 D
jim.cummings@wku.edu
CUMMINGS, Joseph ..... 718-489-5346 340 E
jcummings@sfc.edu
CUMMINGS, Joyce .... 954-308-2177.. 98 I
jcummings@aii.edu
CUMMINGS, Kevin, R ... 914-594-4536 335 H
webmaster@nymc.edu
CUMMINGS, Kristin ...... 651-690-6829 263 V
kacummings@stkate.edu
CUMMINGS, Lawanda ... 706-396-7597 129 H
lcummings@paine.edu
CUMMINGS, Leslie .... 205-387-0511.... 2 B
lcummings@bscc.edu
CUMMINGS, Lisa .... 802-635-1382 504 A
lisa.cummings@jsc.edu
CUMMINGS, Marge .... 606-337-1407 194 F
mcummings@ccbbc.edu
CUMMINGS, Mary .... 724-852-3271 439 C
mcumming@waynesburg.edu
CUMMINGS, JR.,
McDuffie .... 910-521-6690 371 D
mcduffie.cummings@uncp.edu
CUMMINGS, Michael, J 240-895-5000 218 B
mjcummings@smcm.edu
CUMMINGS, Monica ..... 847-578-3431 157 G
CUMMINGS, Nancy .... 785-827-5541 189 A
nancy.cummings@kwu.edu
CUMMINGS, Owen .... 503-845-3547 407 B
owen.cummings@mtangel.edu
CUMMINGS, Steve .... 503-255-0332 407 D
scummings@multnomah.edu
CUMMINGS, Victor .... 707-527-4615.. 65 C
vcummings@santarosa.edu
CUMMINGS,
Wm. Theodore .... 281-283-3100 491 E
cummings@uhcl.edu
CUMMINGS-DANSON,
Gail, L .... 518-580-5370 342 I
gcumming@skidmore.edu
CUMMINS, Cheryl .... 662-846-4405 267 A
ccummins@deltastate.edu
CUMMINS, David .... 440-365-5222 385 E
CUMMINS, F. James .... 810-766-4250 239 G
jim.cummins@baker.edu
CUMMINS, Kendra .... 918-540-6224 398 L
kendra.cummins@neo.edu
CUMMINS, Michelle ..... 812-888-4573 174 F
mcummins@vinu.edu
CUMMINS, Richard .... 509-542-4802 521 C
rcummins@columbiabasin.edu
CUMMISKEY,
Raymond, V .... 636-481-3100 276 E
rcummisk@jeffco.edu
CUMPIANO, Barbarita ... 787-832-6000 552 K
bcumpiano@icprjc.edu
CUNDALL, JR.,
Michael .... 336-285-2030 370 B
mcundall@ncat.edu
CUNDARI, Alan .... 909-469-5670.. 76 I
acundari@westernu.edu
CUNDIFF, Sarah .... 316-942-4291 189 K
cundiffs@newmanu.edu
CUNDIFF, Wendy .... 330-684-8907 393 A
wcundif@uakron.edu
CUNEAZ, Jodi .... 810-766-4015 239 H
jodi.cuneaz@baker.edu
CUNION, Jessica .... 330-823-2889 394 A
cunionjs@mountunion.edu
CUNION, William .... 216-987-2341 381 A
william.cunion@tri-c.edu
CUNNING, Charles, J ... 864-488-4540 447 F
cunning@limestone.edu
CUNNINGHAM, Al .... 912-427-5847 123 A
acunningham@coastalpines.edu
CUNNINGHAM,
Austin, J .... 972-883-2234 494 A
cunning@utdallas.edu
CUNNINGHAM, Carl, G 251-460-6895.... 9 F
ccunningham@southalabama.edu
CUNNINGHAM, Cecelia 616-632-2816 239 E
cunnicec@aquinas.edu
CUNNINGHAM, Chad ... 330-684-8910 393 A
chad6@uakron.edu
CUNNINGHAM, Damita . 918-456-5511 398 M
cunningh@nsuok.edu
CUNNINGHAM, Diane ... 270-707-3921 196 D
diane.cunningham@kctcs.edu
CUNNINGHAM, Don ..... 231-995-1705 248 C
dcunningham@nmc.edu
CUNNINGHAM, Doreen 919-546-8476 368 G
dcunningham@shawu.edu
CUNNINGHAM, Eric ..... 573-875-7649 273 D
ercunningham@ccis.edu
CUNNINGHAM, Jack, L 302-356-6921.. 94 G
john.l.cunningham@wilmu.edu
CUNNINGHAM, James .. 315-279-5228 329 K
jcunning@keuka.edu
CUNNINGHAM,
Janet, L .... 580-327-8400 399 F
jlcunningham@nwosu.edu
CUNNINGHAM, John .... 774-455-7601 228 E
jcunningham@umassonline.net
CUNNINGHAM, Joi, M . 248-370-3496 248 K
cunning3@oakland.edu
CUNNINGHAM, Julie .... 207-509-7240 212 A
jcunningham@unity.edu
CUNNINGHAM,
Karla, K .... 317-940-9570 164 L
kcunning@butler.edu
CUNNINGHAM,
Kathleen .... 610-606-4635 415 A
ksglass@cedarcrest.edu
CUNNINGHAM, Kay ...... 901-321-3430 455 I
kay.cunningham@cbu.edu
CUNNINGHAM,
Kelly, L .... 734-936-2254 251 C
kecunham@umich.edu
CUNNINGHAM,
Kevin, A .... 563-884-5898 182 D
kevin.cunningham@palmer.edu
CUNNINGHAM, Kima .... 937-376-6566 379 D
kcunningham@centralstate.edu
CUNNINGHAM,
Lawrence (Bubba), R . 919-962-8200 371 A
BubbaC@email.unc.edu
CUNNINGHAM, Marina . 973-655-7566 304 A
cunninghamm@mail.montclair.edu
CUNNINGHAM, Mark .... 404-756-4654 120 H
mcunningham@atlm.edu
CUNNINGHAM,
Michael .... 504-865-5261 207 F
mcunnin1@tulane.edu
CUNNINGHAM, II,
Michael, J .... 401-333-7121 441 C
mjcunningham2@ccri.edu
CUNNINGHAM,
Michael, M .... 570-326-3761 429 J
mike.cunningham@pct.edu
CUNNINGHAM,
Michael, R .... 858-642-8101.. 55 J
mcunningham@nu.edu
CUNNINGHAM, Nancy .. 772-462-7275 106 F
ncunning@irsc.edu
CUNNINGHAM, Pat .... 615-460-6617 455 D
Pat.Cunningham@belmont.edu
CUNNINGHAM,
Patrick, J .... 412-578-8842 414 I
pjcunningham@carlow.edu
CUNNINGHAM,
Paul R, G .... 252-744-2201 369 E
cunningham@ecu.edu
CUNNINGHAM,
Philip, J .... 262-646-6518 538 B
pcunningham@nashotah.edu
CUNNINGHAM,
R. Michael .... 217-443-8831 143 F
mcunningham@dacc.edu
CUNNINGHAM, Sean .... 512-463-4930 488 D
sean.cunningham@tsus.edu
CUNNINGHAM,
Shannon .... 405-744-2212 399 E
shannon.cunningham@noc.edu
CUNNINGHAM, Steven . 850-474-2210 116 E
scunningham1@uwf.edu
CUNNINGHAM, Tamara 201-200-3454 304 C
tcunningham@njcu.edu
CUNNINGHAM, Todd .... 724-357-7872 431 A
todd.cunningham@iup.edu
CUNNINGHAM, Tom ..... 513-861-6400 392 F
tom.cunningham@myunion.edu
CUNNINGHAM,
William, J .... 215-596-8535 438 E
w.cunningham@usciences.edu
CUNZ, Leonard .... 908-852-1400 301 C
cunzl@centenarycollege.edu
CUOMO, Robert .... 508-541-1791 225 G
rcuomo@dean.edu
CUOZZO, Frank .... 201-200-3173 304 C
fcuozzo@njcu.edu
CUOZZO, Jenifer .... 202-685-3785 547 M
cuozzoj@ndu.edu
CUP, Jo Beth .... 312-662-4101 139 E
jcup@adler.edu
CUPICH, Blase .... 847-566-6401 162 G
CUPP, Dondi, L .... 734-647-6079 251 C
dcupp@umich.edu
CUPPER, Barbara .... 415-433-6691.. 44 I
bcupper@fidm.edu
CUPRAK, Greg .... 610-436-3200 432 B
gcuprak@wcupa.edu
CURBO, Billy, D .... 254-659-7701 475 A
bdcurbo@hillcollege.edu
CURCI, Roberto .... 708-524-6826 144 C
rcurci@dom.edu
CURCITTI, Thomas .... 203-837-9090.. 88 G
crucittit@wcsu.edu
CURD, David .... 877-248-6724.. 14 C
dcurd@hmu.edu
CURD, Francis .... 941-405-1507 423 B
fcurd@lecom.edu

D

DA CRUZ, Becky .... 912-344-2613 120 D
becky.dacruz@armstrong.edu
DA GRACA, John .... 956-968-2132 486 A
j-dagraca@tamuk.edu
DAAR, Karen .... 818-947-2378.. 52 B
daarkl@lavc.edu
DAAS, Mahesh .... 785-864-3114 191 G
mahesh@ku.edu
DABIRIAN, Amir .... 657-278-5000.. 33 E
adabirian@fullerton.edu
DABNEY, David .... 903-566-7044 494 E
ddabney@uttyler.edu
DABNEY, Emily, C .... 662-846-4052 267 A
edabney@deltastate.edu
DABNEY, Jerome .... 773-602-5252 142 A
jdabney@ccc.edu
DABOVAL, Jeanne, M ... 337-475-5508 208 B
jdaboval@mcneese.edu
DABROWSKI, Jan .... 503-699-6275 407 A
jdabrowski@marylhurst.edu
DACAL, Anita, S .... 412-578-6343 414 I
dacalas@carlow.edu
DACE, Karen, L .... 317-278-3820 168 E
kdace@iupui.edu
DACEY, Susan .... 973-748-9000 300 E
susan_dacey@bloomfield.edu
DACHELET, Derek .... 608-822-2417 544 C
ddachelet@swtc.edu
DACHILLE, Nancy .... 215-248-7048 415 D
ndachill@chc.edu
DACOSTA, Herbert .... 309-694-5754 146 C
herbert.dacosta@icc.edu
DACOSTA, Tracy, M ..... 401-254-3541 442 C
tdacosta@rwu.edu
DACUS, Kent .... 951-343-4687.. 30 D
kdacus@calbaptist.edu
DADABHOY,
Khushnur, Z .... 760-252-2411.. 29 C
kdadabhoy@barstow.edu
DADABHOY, Zavareh .... 661-395-4204.. 49 E
zav.dadabhoy@bakersfieldcollege.edu
DADDONA, Sharon, N .. 860-727-6903.. 90 F
sdaddona@goodwin.edu
DADEZ, Edward .... 352-588-8206 111 L
ed.dadez@saintleo.edu
DADEZ, Teresa .... 352-588-8347 111 L
teresa.dadez@saintleo.edu
DADIAN PEREZ, Sara ... 603-623-0313 298 C
saradadian@nhia.edu
DADY, Erin .... 612-624-9022 265 C
dady@umn.edu
DAFFER, Steve .... 405-733-7424 401 L
sdaffer@rose.edu
DAFFRON, Eric .... 201-684-7532 305 F
edaffron@ramapo.edu
DAFFRON, Jeanne .... 816-271-4234 279 E
daffron@missouriwestern.edu
DAFFRON, SJ, Justin ... 312-915-7280 151 E
jdaffro@luc.edu
DAFLER, James, E .... 724-946-7317 439 D
daflerje@westminster.edu
DAGANAAR, Mark .... 913-469-8500 188 E
mdaganaar@jccc.edu
DAGG, Joey .... 304-876-5395 532 I
jdagg@shepherd.edu
DAGGETT, Michael .... 518-243-4473 316 C
daggettm@ellismedicine.org
DAGGETT, Natalie .... 575-769-4956 310 G
natalie.daggett@clovis.edu
DAGGETT, Paula .... 210-486-0224 467 C
pdaggett@alamo.edu
DAGHER, Lisa, M .... 773-947-6282 152 A
DAGUE, Saralyn .... 304-829-7835 529 H
sdague@bethanywv.edu
DAHER, Michael .... 313-845-6460 243 I
mdaher@hfcc.edu
DAHILL, Patricia .... 617-587-5632 234 G
dahillp@neco.edu
DAHILL, Rosemary .... 914-395-2202 342 C
rdahill@sarahlawrence.edu
DAHL, Barbara, A .... 219-981-4235 168 C
badahl@iun.edu
DAHL, Katie .... 303-369-5151.. 84 N
katie.dahl@plattcolorado.edu
DAHL, Mark .... 503-768-7339 406 H
dahl@lclark.edu
DAHL, Nelson, D .... 715-422-5327 543 D
nelson.dahl@mstc.edu
DAHL, Noel .... 415-703-9537.. 30 G
ndahl@cca.edu
DAHL, Tracy .... 360-736-9391 520 F
tdahl@centralia.edu
DAHLBERG, Albert, A ... 401-863-1885 441 A
albert_a_dahlberg@brown.edu
DAHLBERG, James .... 715-468-2815 544 F
jim.dahlberg@witc.edu
DAHLBERG, Steve .... 218-935-0417 266 A
sdahlberg@wetcc.edu

DAHLE, Tammi .... 205-665-6262.... 9 C
dahlet@montevallo.edu
DAHLEN, David, L .... 507-284-2749 254 F
dahlen.david@mayo.edu
DAHLEN, David, L .... 507-284-4839 254 G
dahlen.david@mayo.edu
DAHLER, Nathan .... 513-721-7944 382 K
ndahler@gbs.edu
DAHLGREN, Jerod, T .... 716-878-5569 345 B
dahlgrjt@buffalostate.edu
DAHLIN, Adrian .... 413-369-4044 225 E
dahlin@csld.edu
DAHLOR, Cara .... 816-415-5223 285 K
dahlorc@william.jewell.edu
DAHLQUIST, Kent, R .... 610-683-4027 431 B
dahlquis@kutztown.edu
DAHLQUIST, Sally .... 651-450-3567 259 A
sdahlqu@inverhills.edu
DAHLSTROM, Duane ..... 320-308-5572 261 F
ddahlstrom@sctcc.edu
DAHLSTROM, Joe, F ..... 361-570-4150 492 A
dahlstromj@uhv.edu
DAHLSTROM, Joe, F ..... 361-570-4150 496 D
joe.dahlstrom@victoriacollege.edu
DAHLSTROM, Thomas .. 610-341-5898 427 I
tdahlstro@eastern.edu
DAHLSTROM,
Thomas, A .... 610-341-5898 418 A
tdahlstr@eastern.edu
DAHLVANG, Donna, R .. 715-394-8393 541 C
ddahlva1@uwsuper.edu
DAHMES, Victoria .... 504-398-2237 206 E
vdahmes@olhcc.edu
DAHSE, Winston .... 713-718-7564 475 C
winston.dahse@hccs.edu
DAHULICH, Michael ..... 570-561-1818 435 A
bishop.michael@stots.edu
DAI, Hai-Lung .... 215-204-4775 436 C
provost@temple.edu
DAI, Hai-Lung .... 215-204-4775 436 C
hldai@temple.edu
DAIEK, Deborah .... 734-462-4400 250 A
ddaiek@schoolcraft.edu
DAIGLE, Anna .... 337-421-6954 204 F
anna.daigle@sowela.edu
DAIGLE, Claire .... 415-641-1241.. 62 I
cdaigle@sfai.edu
DAIGLE, Darren .... 251-344-1203.... 3 J
DAIGLE, David .... 207-216-4410 211 F
ddaigle@yccc.edu
DAIGLE, Dick .... 757-490-1241 504 D
ddaigle@auto.edu
DAIGLER, David .... 207-629-4000 210 K
ddaigler@mccs.me.edu
DAILEY, Bracken, J ...... 951-827-3427.. 72 A
bracken.dailey@ucr.edu
DAILEY, Brian .... 910-962-3711 372 A
daileyb@uncw.edu
DAILEY, Brooke .... 615-460-6364 455 D
brooke.dailey@belmont.edu
DAILEY, David .... 218-749-7772 259 D
d.dailey@mesabirange.edu
DAILEY, Deborah .... 215-489-2915 416 H
Deborah.Dailey@delval.edu
DAILEY, John, T .... 318-675-6468 205 D
jdaile@lsuhsc.edu
DAILEY, Kathlyn, C ...... 512-245-2208 489 C
kd01@txstate.edu
DAILEY, Ronald .... 909-558-4683.. 50 K
rdailey@llu.edu
DAILEY, Tim .... 541-888-7439 410 A
tdailey@socc.edu
DAILY, Daniel, R .... 605-677-5371 453 F
daniel.daily@usd.edu
DAILY, Hall, P .... 626-395-6256.. 31 D
hdaily@caltech.edu
DAIN, Benny .... 580-349-1560 400 B
bdain@opsu.edu
DAIN, Claudette, E .... 626-914-8886.. 38 L
cdain@citruscollege.edu
DAINES, Cameron .... 928-724-6698.. 13 J
ckdaines@dinecollege.edu
DAIS, Olga .... 646-312-3320 318 C
Olga.Dais@baruch.cuny.edu
DAISE, Abigail .... 215-887-5511 439 E
adaise@wts.edu
DAISEY, Mary Beth, B .. 856-225-2825 307 A
daisey@camden.rutgers.edu
DAISY, Joseph, M .... 691-320-2480 549 D
jdaisy@comfsm.fm
DAKWAR, Mohammad . 414-297-8087 543 E
dakwarmm@matc.edu
DALBEY, Mark .... 314-434-4044 273 J
presidentsoffice@covenantseminary.edu
DALBOW, Dawn, S .... 540-828-5310 505 F
ddalbow@bridgewater.edu
DALE, Amie, G .... 757-594-7672 506 I
amie.dale@cnu.edu
DALE, Carroll, W .... 276-376-1081 514 B
cwd7q@wise.edu

DALE, Cheryl .... 601-318-6199 271 F
cheryl.dale@wmcarey.edu
DALE, Dianna, C .... 610-361-2448 427 D
daled@neumann.edu
DALE, Elizabeth .... 215-503-5138 436 F
elizabeth.dale@jefferson.edu
DALE, Karen .... 520-452-2621.. 13 B
dalek@cochise.edu
DALE, Kim .... 970-204-8146.. 82 J
kim.dale@frontrange.edu
DALE, Kimberly .... 954-776-4476 107 F
kdale@keiseruniversity.edu
DALE, Kory, J .... 479-524-7116.. 21 F
kdale@jbu.edu
DALE, Louis .... 205-934-8762.... 8 F
ldale@uab.edu
DALE, Lynn, F .... 864-592-4833 449 C
dalel@sccsc.edu
DALE, Marc .... 630-466-7900 162 K
mdale@waubonsee.edu
DALE, Paul .... 602-787-6610.. 15 B
paul.dale@paradisevalley.edu
DALE-CARTER, April .... 909-384-8922.. 62 C
acarter@sbccd.cc.ca.us
DALEKE, David .... 812-855-6902 167 J
daleked@indiana.edu
DALENE, Jack .... 435-283-7130 500 D
jack.dalene@snow.edu
DALES, Sandra .... 910-695-3789 365 H
daless@sandhills.edu
DALEY, Barbara, J .... 414-229-4721 540 A
bdaley@uwm.edu
DALEY, Ben .... 619-398-4902.. 47 B
bdaley@hightechhigh.org
DALEY, Carol .... 540-338-2700 505 K
cdaley@cdu.edu
DALEY, David .... 530-898-5844.. 33 A
ddaley@csuchico.edu
DALEY, Elizabeth, M ..... 213-740-2804.. 74 D
edaley@cinema.usc.edu
DALEY, Karen .... 616-698-7111 241 I
kdaley@davenport.edu
DALEY, Ken .... 641-472-1163 181 A
kdaley@mum.edu
DALEY, Michael, D .... 716-673-3434 343 F
michael.daley@fredonia.edu
DALEY, Miesha, V .... 773-995-3555 141 J
mdaley@csu.edu
DALEY, Suzanne, L .... 518-564-2080 346 B
daleysl@plattsburgh.edu
DALGARNO, Janice ...... 307-268-2547 545 Z
dalgarno@caspercollege.edu
DALGLISH, Jim .... 254-659-7771 475 A
jdalglish@hillcollege.edu
DALGLISH, Lucy .... 301-405-2383 219 D
dalglish@umd.edu
DALLAM, Colleen, C .... 410-334-2864 221 E
cdallam@worwic.edu
DALLAVALLE, Nancy ..... 203-254-4000.. 90 E
DALLEY, Annique .... 510-628-8023.. 50 I
studentservices@lincolnuca.edu
DALLMAN, Bruce, D ..... 620-235-4365 190 G
bdallman@pittstate.edu
DALLMANN, Ben .... 312-329-4073 153 C
ben.dallmann@moody.edu
DALLMANN, Denise .... 503-552-1690 407 F
ddallmann@ncnm.edu
DALMUT, Margaret .... 703-284-1604 510 B
margaret.dalmut@marymount.edu
DALONZO, Beth, A .... 740-826-8041 387 C
bdalonzo@muskingum.edu
DALPE, Kyle .... 775-673-7812 295 F
kdalpe@tmcc.edu
DALRYMPLE, Jim .... 417-626-1234 280 B
dalrymple.jim@occ.edu
DALRYMPLE, Scott .... 573-875-8700 273 D
sdalrymple@ccis.edu
DALSING, Deirdre, L ... 608-342-1865 540 D
dalsingd@uwplatt.edu
DALSKE, James .... 707-654-1070.. 34 B
jdalske@csum.edu
DALTO, Joseph .... 251-344-1203.... 3 J
jdalto@fortiscollege.edu
DALTON, Amy .... 937-327-7457 395 I
daltona@wittenberg.edu
DALTON, Ben .... 740-753-6516 383 G
daltonb@hocking.edu
DALTON, Brenda .... 404-270-5245 132 D
bdalton@spelman.edu
DALTON, Brenda .... 972-860-4677 472 C
bdalton@dcccd.edu
DALTON, Brett, A .... 864-656-2444 444 E
dbrett@clemson.edu
DALTON, Brian, F .... 814-332-2102 411 F
bdalton@allegheny.edu
DALTON, Dana, L .... 336-734-7369 362 F
ddalton@forsythtech.edu
DALTON, Deborah .... 508-626-4698 230 A
ddalton@framingham.edu
DALTON, Holly .... 650-543-3910.. 54 B
holly.dalton@menlo.edu

DALTON, James .... 845-938-2050 549 A
8ord@usma.edu
DALTON, James, T ...... 734-764-7312 251 C
daltonjt@umich.edu
DALTON, Jill .... 207-699-5018 210 I
jdalton@meca.edu
DALTON, John .... 765-973-8450 168 A
jodalton@iue.edu
DALTON, Judith .... 215-572-4088 412 F
daltonj@arcadia.edu
DALTON, Karen .... 909-447-2534.. 39 G
kdalton@cst.edu
DALTON, Sue .... 937-298-3399 385 A
sue.dalton@kc.edu
DALTON, Thomas .... 518-464-8632 325 B
tdalton@excelsior.edu
DALTON, Valerie .... 404-215-2666 128 L
valerie.dalton@morehouse.edu
DALTON, Walter, H .... 828-395-1300 363 D
wdalton@isothermal.edu
DALTON-RANN,
RaVonda .... 336-750-2046 372 D
daltonrannr@wssu.edu
DALTON-RUSSELL,
Belinda .... 270-534-3081 197 E
belinda.dalton-russell@kctcs.edu
DALY, Brian .... 619-239-0391.. 36 E
bdaly@cwsl.edu
DALY, Cory .... 307-855-2186 545 a
cdaly@cwc.edu
DALY, Erin .... 952-358-8834 260 D
erin.daly@normandale.edu
DALY, Jillian .... 209-575-6149.. 78 C
DALY, Jon .... 860-628-4751.. 91 A
jdaly@lincolncollegene.edu
DALY, Jonathan, P .... 805-525-4417.. 69 I
jdaly@thomasaquinas.edu
DALY, Kathleen .... 850-644-4453 115 A
kdaly@fsu.edu
DALY, Kathleen, M .... 850-644-4453 115 A
kdaly@fsu.edu
DALY, Lois, K .... 518-783-2306 342 H
daly@siena.edu
DALY, Meghan .... 802-862-9616 501 E
mdaly@burlington.edu
DALY, Michael .... 718-429-6600 352 A
michael.daly@vaughn.edu
DALY, Patrick .... 972-721-5145 491 B
mpdaly@udallas.edu
DALY, Rebecca 906-487-7253 242M
rebecca.daly@finlandia.edu
DALY, Ross .... 914-251-6550 346 D
ross.daly@purchase.edu
DALY, Shawn, p .... 716-286-8050 336 E
sdaly@niagara.edu
DALY, Thomas .... 631-244-1372 324 C
dalyt@dowling.edu
DALY-EIMER, Anne, M . 856-691-8600 301 H
adaly@cccnj.edu
DALY-WESTON,
Marilyn .... 212-650-3995 319 E
marilyn.daley-weston@hunter.cuny.edu
DALZELL, Douglas .... 410-951-3826 220 C
ddalzell@coppin.edu
DALZIEL, Murray .... 410-837-4955 221 B
mdalziel@ubalt.edu
DAMAR, Andrea .... 212-343-1234 332 I
adamar@mcny.edu
DAMARI, David .... 231-591-3703 242 L
DavidDamari@ferris.edu
DAMAS, Tammi, L .... 202-806-4859.. 96 B
tammi.damas@howard.edu
DAMAZO, Dennis, E ..... 724-847-5678 419 B
dedamazo@geneva.edu
DAME, Robert .... 630-889-6515 154 E
rdame@nuhs.edu
DAMES, Christopher ..... 314-516-6473 284 B
cdames@umsl.edu
DAMES, Jeanine .... 203-432-0800.. 93 C
jeanine.dames@yale.edu
DAMEWOOD, Tony, M . 402-552-6109 289 H
damewood@clarksoncollege.edu
DAMHOFF, Russ, K .... 815-835-6234 158 I
russ.k.damhoff@svcc.edu
DAMIAN, Karen .... 802-387-6711 502 A
registrar@landmark.edu
DAMIANI, Glenn .... 505-224-3223 310 F
GDamiani@cnm.edu
DAMIANI, Joel, J .... 716-851-1405 325 A
damiani@ecc.edu
DAMIANI, Susan, M .... 718-990-7562 340 G
damianis@stjohns.edu
DAMIANO, Ann, E .... 717-867-6077 423 I
damiano@lvc.edu
DAMIANO, Fred .... 315-781-3955 327 G
damiano@hws.edu
DAMICI, Lindsay .... 802-654-2000 502 H
DAMICO, Debra, L .... 718-862-7213 331 H
debra.damico@manhattan.edu
DAMICO, Paul .... 252-638-0156 362 A
damicop@cravencc.edu

DARWIN, Mike .... 205-726-4241.... 6 F mdarwin@samford.edu
DAS, Dilip .... 410-951-6102 220 C ddas@coppin.edu
DAS, Pradeep, K .... 404-627-2681 121 F pradeep.das@beulah.org
DAS, Purna .... 219-785-5254 172 A pdas@pnc.edu
DASBURG, Deanne .... 828-884-8129 355 A dasburg@brevard.edu
DASENBROCK, Reed, W .... 808-956-8447 135 J rdasenbr@hawaii.edu
DASEY-MORALES, Maureen .... 316-978-3440 192 D maureen.dasey-morales@wichita.edu
DASGUPTA, Nandini ..... 510-869-8711.. 61 J ndasgupta@samuelmerritt.edu
DASHE, Alejandra .... 952-888-4777 263 I adashe@nwhealth.edu
DASHER, Leah .... 912-538-3186 132 A ldasher@southeasterntech.edu
DASHIELD, Richeleen .. 908-526-1200 305 G Richeleen.Dashield@raritanval.edu
DASHIELL, Christian ..... 620-278-4341 191 D cdashiell@sterling.edu
DASIGI, Venu .... 419-372-8719 377 I vdasigi@bgsu.edu
DASILVA, Jose .... 940-872-5211 479 K jdasilva@nctc.edu
DASILVA, Joseph .... 413-755-4889 233 B jdasilva@stcc.edu
DASINGER, Hank .... 334-285-5177.... 4 K hank.dasinger@istc.edu
DASTMOZD, Rassoul ..... 651-846-1335 261 G rassoul.dastmozd@saintpaul.edu
DATCHER, Dwight .... 617-879-2238 238 C ddatcher@wheelock.edu
DATEMA, Betsy .... 574-232-2408 172 B bdatema@rtuvt.com
DATHER, Julie .... 605-668-1525 452 I jdather@mtmc.edu
DATTA, Asoke .... 808-544-1106 135 C adatta@hpu.edu
DATTA, Rekha .... 732-571-3405 303 G rdatta@monmouth.edu
DATTA, Sumana .... 979-845-6774 485 C sumad@tamu.edu
DATTAGUPTA, Satyajit .. 410-778-7700 221 D sdattagupta2@washcoll.edu
DATUIN, Bonnie Mae, M .... 671-735-5616 549 E bonniemae.datuin@guamcc.edu
DAUBERMAN, Barbara, A .... 804-752-7300 511 E bdauberman@rmc.edu
DAUDISTEL, Howard ..... 915-747-8533 494 B hdaudistel@utep.edu
DAUER, Eve .... 703-993-2446 507 K edauer@gmu.edu
DAUGHADAY, David ..... 410-617-2349 216 D daughaday@loyola.edu
DAUGHERTY, Carolyn ... 719-549-2830.. 81 F carolyn.daugherty@csupueblo.edu
DAUGHERTY, Caron ..... 636-481-3300 276 E cdaugherty@jeffco.edu
DAUGHERTY, Craig, A .. 740-427-5430 384 P daugherty@kenyon.edu
DAUGHERTY, Debra ...... 615-230-3526 464 B debra.daugherty@volstate.edu
DAUGHERTY, Penny, J . 541-346-2971 410 F penny@uoregon.edu
DAUGHERTY, Robyn ..... 479-524-7301.. 21 F rdaugherty@jbu.edu
DAUGHERTY, Vernon, D .... 828-398-7220 360 A vdaugherty@abtech.edu
DAUGHETY, Kathy .... 252-399-6529 354 I kdaughety@barton.edu
DAUGHT, Gary .... 423-461-8799 459 I gfdaught@milligan.edu
DAUGHTREY, III, Thomas, W .... 910-630-7316 359 C tdaughtrey@methodist.edu
DAUGHTRY, Dee Dee, D .... 919-209-2066 363 F dddaughtry@johnstoncc.edu
DAULTON, Jonathan, G 864-242-5100 443 G
DAUSEY, David .... 814-824-2000 425 L
DAUSS, Jan .... 619-961-4247.. 69 J jand@tjsl.edu
DAUWALDER, David ..... 818-767-0888.. 77 G david.dauwalder@woodbury.edu
DAVALT, Greg .... 405-240-6498 402 F greg.davalt@swcu.edu
DAVAR, David .... 212-678-6161 329 H dadavar@jtsa.edu
DAVEE, Doug .... 949-376-6000.. 49 K ddavee@lcad.edu
DAVENPORT, Beverly .... 513-556-2588 393 B provost@uc.edu
DAVENPORT, Catherine, M .... 717-245-1231 417 B davenpor@dickinson.edu
DAVENPORT, Daniel, D 208-885-6312 139 C dand@uidaho.edu
DAVENPORT, Darrien .... 717-815-6663 440 H ddavenp2@ycp.edu
DAVENPORT, Derek ...... 412-924-1385 433 E ddavenport@pts.edu
DAVENPORT, Doug .... 816-271-4534 279 E ddavenport@missouriwestern.edu
DAVENPORT, Elizabeth . 773-702-8282 161 D ejld@uchicago.edu
DAVENPORT, Fiona, E .. 215-935-3868 439 E fdavenport@wts.edu
DAVENPORT, Floyd ...... 785-670-2066 192 B floyd.davenport@washburn.edu
DAVENPORT, Kevin ...... 256-306-2574.... 2 F kdavenport@calhoun.edu
DAVENPORT, Kevin ...... 804-524-5995 518 C pdjackson@vsu.edu
DAVENPORT, Lechelle .. 901-333-4195 464 A ldavenport@southwest.tn.edu
DAVENPORT, Mary .... 507-433-0530 261 C mary.davenport@riverland.edu
DAVENPORT, Mike .... 270-824-8661 196 F mike.davenport@kctcs.edu
DAVENPORT, Missy ...... 904-256-1151 103 K mdavenport@fcsl.edu
DAVENPORT, Mona ...... 217-581-6690 144 E mydavenport@eiu.edu
DAVENPORT, Nancy ..... 202-885-3200.. 94 H davenpor@american.edu
DAVENPORT, Richard ... 507-389-1111 260 A richard.davenport@mnsu.edu
DAVENPORT, Robert ..... 405-585-5301 399 I robert.davenport@okbu.edu
DAVENPORT, Robin ...... 973-618-3905 300 H rdavenport@caldwell.edu
DAVENPORT, Sara .... 503-222-3225 405 H sara.davenport@zenith.org
DAVENPORT, Shirley .... 636-481-3333 276 E sdavenp1@jeffco.edu
DAVENPORT, Susan, C 609-652-4514 308 E Susan.Davenport@stockton.edu
DAVENPORT, Tamika .... 312-850-3525 142 E Tatdavenport13@ccc.edu
DAVENPORT, Thomas ... 270-706-8699 195 K tdavenport0008@kctcs.edu
DAVENPORT, Zebulun, R .... 317-274-8990 168 E zrdavenp@iupui.edu
DAVENPORT-RAMIREZ, Keisha .... 212-229-8996 334 C davenpok@newschool.edu
DAVENPORT TIGNOR, Stephanie .... 804-828-0100 514 F davenportse@vcu.edu
DAVEY, Cathleen .... 201-684-7612 305 F cdavey@ramapo.edu
DAVEY, Daniel, K .... 757-479-3706 514 D
DAVEY, Patrick .... 202-319-6907.. 95 A daveyp@cua.edu
DAVEY, Stephen .... 919-573-5350 368 H
DAVI, Melissa .... 281-873-0262 471 D library@commonwealth.edu
DAVID, Garry .... 940-552-6291 496 B gdavid@vernoncollege.edu
DAVID, Haven .... 940-552-6291 496 B hdavid@vernoncollege.edu
DAVID, Hope .... 412-760-9967 131 F hdavid@southuniversity.edu
DAVID, Jacob .... 212-563-6647 350 J jacobdavid835@yahoo.com
DAVID, Kenneth .... 646-565-6000 350 C kenneth.david@touro.edu
DAVID, Kevin .... 918-595-7841 403 A kevin.david@tulsacc.edu
DAVID, Kimberly, C ..... 713-798-1543 469 C kcotner@bcm.edu
DAVID, Kyle .... 774-455-7560 228 E kdavid@umassp.edu
DAVID, Marcella .... 850-599-3276 114 D marcella.david@famu.edu
DAVID, Maureen .... 301-985-7047 220 A maureen.david@umuc.edu
DAVID, Paula .... 508-793-7681 225 B pdavid@clarku.edu
DAVID, Prabu .... 517-355-3410 246 H pdavid@msu.edu
DAVID, Vivian .... 757-727-5331 508 C vivian.david@hamptonu.edu
DAVIDHIZAR, Larry, J .. 312-329-4005 153 C larry.davidhizar@moody.edu
DAVIDOWITZ, Menachem .... 585-473-2810 349 F tiunyfax@gmail.com
DAVIDS, Antoinette .... 800-567-2344 535 F adavids@menominee.edu
DAVIDS, Cheryl .... 828-339-7018 366 C c_davids@southwesterncc.edu
DAVIDSEN, Susanna ..... 612-338-7224 265 G Susanna.Davidsen@waldenu.edu
DAVIDSON, Andrew, R . 212-854-6313 322 F ard2@columbia.edu
DAVIDSON, Anthony .... 914-323-5315 331 J anthony.davidson@mville.edu
DAVIDSON, Bobbie .... 928-350-1113.. 17 K bdavidson@prescott.edu
DAVIDSON, Camille ..... 704-971-8500 355 J cdavidson@charlottelaw.edu
DAVIDSON, Conrad ...... 701-858-3159 374 B conrad.davidson@minotstateu.edu
DAVIDSON, Debbie ...... 262-564-3422 543 A davidsond@gtc.edu
DAVIDSON, Don .... 719-389-6573.. 79 M ddavidson@coloradocollege.edu
DAVIDSON, Donald ...... 603-641-7287 298 F ddavidson@anselm.edu
DAVIDSON, Dotti .... 757-352-4108 511 G dorobur@regent.edu
DAVIDSON, Elizabeth ... 860-701-5155.. 91 B davidson_e@mitchell.edu
DAVIDSON, Erin .... 817-598-6285 497 A edavidson@wc.edu
DAVIDSON, Georglyn, L .... 215-968-8251 413 F davidson@bucks.edu
DAVIDSON, JaCenda .... 615-329-8712 456 G jdavidson@fisk.edu
DAVIDSON, James, A ... 410-827-5846 214 D jdavidson@chesapeake.edu
DAVIDSON, Jamie .... 702-895-3627 295 G jamie.davidson@unlv.edu
DAVIDSON, Janet .... 724-480-3395 416 A janet.davidson@ccbc.edu
DAVIDSON, John .... 870-508-6122.. 19 H jdavidson@asumh.edu
DAVIDSON, Jon .... 810-762-3300 251 E jdavidso@umflint.edu
DAVIDSON, Katrena, J . 330-941-1712 396 C katrena.davidson@ysu.edu
DAVIDSON, Keith, S ..... 410-651-6496 219 H kdavidson@umes.edu
DAVIDSON, Laura .... 919-760-8531 359 B davidsonl@meredith.edu
DAVIDSON, Leslie .... 413-528-7245 222 F leslied@simons-rock.edu
DAVIDSON, Leslie .... 540-665-5561 512 E ldavids2@su.edu
DAVIDSON, Megan .... 512-863-1056 483 G davidsom@southwestern.edu
DAVIDSON, Michael ..... 317-921-4538 169 M mdavidson40@ivytech.edu
DAVIDSON, Michael, E 404-413-3156 126 D mdavidson@gsu.edu
DAVIDSON, Mitch .... 260-481-6196 168 D davidsom@ipfw.edu
DAVIDSON, Nancy .... 605-274-5516 452 A nancy.davidson@augie.edu
DAVIDSON, Patricia ...... 410-502-2361 216 A pdavids3@jhu.edu
DAVIDSON, Richard ..... 856-351-2622 308 B rdavidson@salemcc.edu
DAVIDSON, Robert .... 636-227-2100 277 A robert.davidson@logan.edu
DAVIDSON, Shane .... 812-488-2829 173 H sd10@evansville.edu
DAVIDSON, Sharon ...... 718-262-2155 321 B sdavid@york.cuny.edu
DAVIDSON, Stephanie .. 405-692-3241 398 I sdavidson@macu.edu
DAVIDSON, Steve .... 615-966-6280 458 C steve.davidson@lipscomb.edu
DAVIDSON, Suellen ...... 870-368-2059.. 22 D sdavidson@ozarka.edu
DAVIDSON, Tracy .... 406-657-1015 288 G tracy.davidson@rocky.edu
DAVIDSON, Valerie, J .. 317-940-9281 164 L vdavidso@butler.edu
DAVIDSON, Wendy .... 757-340-2121 506 E adirectorcvab@centura.edu
DAVIE, Fred .... 212-280-1408 351 B fdavie@uts.columbia.edu
DAVIE, Karen .... 845-675-4608 337 B karen.davie@nyack.edu
DAVIE, Keith, A .... 845-675-4770 337 B keith.davie@nyack.edu
DAVIES, Ann .... 608-363-2667 534 L daviesa@beloit.edu
DAVIES, Becky .... 972-721-5206 491 B bdavies@udallas.edu
DAVIES, Bobby .... 201-327-8877 302 E bdavies@eastwick.edu
DAVIES, Evan .... 757-221-2147 506 J esdav2@wm.edu
DAVIES, Glyn .... 310-206-8041.. 71 D gdavies@ponet.ucla.edu
DAVIES, H. Dele, O ...... 402-559-5131 293 I dele.davies@unmc.edu
DAVIES, Haldane .... 340-693-1004 559 B hdavies@live.uvi.edu
DAVIES, Helen .... 603-645-9781 298 H h.davies@snhu.edu
DAVIES, Mandy .... 916-660-7302.. 66 E mdavies@sierracollege.edu
DAVIES, Marilyn, S ...... 909-593-3511.. 73 B mdavies@laverne.edu
DAVIES, Mark .... 405-208-5284 400 A mdavies@okcu.edu
DAVIES, Mark, D .... 570-577-1019 413 E mark.davies@bucknell.edu
DAVIES, Mark, Y .... 405-208-5284 400 A mdavies@okcu.edu
DAVIES, Pamela, L .... 704-337-2216 368 B daviesp@queens.edu
DAVIES, Patty .... 303-352-3037.. 81 J patty.davies@ccd.edu
DAVIES, Paul .... 804-752-7399 511 E pauldavies@rmc.edu
DAVIES, Robert, O .... 270-809-3763 198 I rdavies@murraystate.edu
DAVIES, Robin, L .... 540-224-4515 509 D RLDavies@jchs.edu
DAVIES, Sharon .... 614-688-3389 389 A davies.49@osu.edu
DAVIES, Susan .... 828-262-7244 369 D daviess@appstate.edu
DAVIES, Susan .... 810-762-9927 245 A sdavies@kettering.edu
DAVIES, William, E .... 301-447-5234 217 D davies@msmary.edu
DAVILA, Alba .... 787-751-0160 551 K adavila@cmpr.pr.gov
DAVILA, Alfonso, L ...... 787-751-0178 555 K adavila@suagm.edu
DAVILA, Annette .... 787-884-3838 550 E dircra@atenascollege.edu
DAVILA, David .... 361-698-1561 473 F ddavila23@delmar.edu
DAVILA, Grace .... 713-221-8633 491 F davilag@uhd.edu
DAVILA, Ivan .... 787-841-2000 555 F idavila@pucpr.edu
DAVIN, Donna .... 706-290-2163 121 E ddavin@berry.edu
DAVINO, Richard .... 774-354-0451 223 C rich.davino@becker.edu
DAVIS, A. Alex .... 323-953-4000.. 51 E alexanal@lacitycollege.edu
DAVIS, Adam .... 540-785-5440 514 C adamdavis@vbc.edu
DAVIS, Adrienne, D ...... 314-935-8583 285 E adriennedavis@wustl.edu
DAVIS, Alan .... 870-235-5059.. 23 D dadavis@saumag.edu
DAVIS, Alan, B .... 205-853-1200.... 5 C adavis@jeffstateonline.com
DAVIS, Alana .... 804-752-7227 511 E adavis@rmc.edu
DAVIS, Anita, A .... 901-843-3889 460 F adavis@rhodes.edu
DAVIS, Barbara .... 419-251-1704 386 C barbara.davis@mercycollege.edu
DAVIS, Barbara .... 614-222-4035 380 F bdavis@ccad.edu
DAVIS, Betsy .... 360-385-4948 524 F
DAVIS, Brad .... 405-789-7661 402 F brad.davis@swcu.edu
DAVIS, Bradley .... 408-741-2668.. 76 F bradley.davis@wvm.edu
DAVIS, Bradley, W .... 941-752-5388 114 B davisb@scf.edu
DAVIS, Bree .... 626-529-8204.. 57 F bdavis@pacificoaks.edu
DAVIS, Brenda .... 251-442-2877.... 9 B bdavis@umobile.edu
DAVIS, Brenda .... 601-928-6381 268 G brenda.davis2@mgccc.edu
DAVIS, Brent .... 559-730-3912.. 41 D brentd@cos.edu
DAVIS, Brian, E .... 330-972-6084 392 H bdavis@uakron.edu
DAVIS, Britt .... 910-893-1200 355 C davisb@campbell.edu
DAVIS, Brittany .... 850-245-0466 114 C
DAVIS, Bruce .... 801-626-6789 500 C brucedavis@weber.edu
DAVIS, Bryan .... 951-343-4721.. 30 D bdavis@calbaptist.edu
DAVIS, JR., C. Grant .... 334-844-4866.... 1 G daviscg@auburn.edu
DAVIS, C. Robert .... 405-744-3373 400 C robert.davis@okstate.edu
DAVIS, Calvin .... 305-626-3741 104 B calvin.davis@fmuniv.edu
DAVIS, Carol .... 903-877-7450 495 C carol.davis@uthct.edu

DAVIS, Carole .... 269-965-3931 244 L
davisc@kellogg.edu
DAVIS, Caroline .... 615-383-4848 466 F
cdavis@watkins.edu
DAVIS, Cassandra, E .... 973-761-7161 308 C
cassandra.davis@shu.edu
DAVIS, Catherine, C ..... 609-497-7882 305 B
student.relations@ptsem.edu
DAVIS, Cathleen, M ..... 937-775-5700 396 A
cathy.davis@wright.edu
DAVIS, Charles, N .... 706-542-1704 132 H
cndavis@uga.edu
DAVIS, Cherie .... 209-384-6000.. 54 C
cherie.davis@mccd.edu
DAVIS, Chris .... 706-385-1000 130 C
chris.davis@point.edu
DAVIS, Chris .... 501-450-3321.. 25 F
cdavis@uca.edu
DAVIS, Chris .... 910-521-6829 371 D
chris.davis@uncp.edu
DAVIS, Christine .... 479-619-3156.. 22 B
cdavis22@nwacc.edu
DAVIS, Christine .... 239-433-6950 104 G
cdavis10@fsw.edu
DAVIS, Christopher ...... 602-943-2311.. 18 K
Christopher.Davis@west.edu
DAVIS, Christopher, A .. 410-293-6381 549 B
cdavis@usna.edu
DAVIS, Chuck .... 206-934-4340 526 A
chuck.davis@seattlecolleges.edu
DAVIS, Cliff .... 417-447-2652 280 C
davisc@otc.edu
DAVIS, Colin .... 309-649-6395 160 F
colin.davis@src.edu
DAVIS, Connie .... 985-549-2094 208 E
cdavis@selu.edu
DAVIS, Corby .... 360-676-2772 524 D
cdavis@nwic.edu
DAVIS, D. Scott .... 478-301-2110 128 G
davis_ds@mercer.edu
DAVIS, Dan .... 701-228-5451 374 F
danny.davis@dakotacollege.edu
DAVIS, Daniel .... 212-854-6939 315 J
ddavis@barnard.edu
DAVIS, Daniel, P .... 817-554-5950 478 E
DAVIS, Danny .... 413-748-3532 236 H
ddavis@springfieldcollege.edu
DAVIS, Dave .... 218-855-8116 258 C
DDavis@clcmn.edu
DAVIS, David .... 601-974-1432 268 D
davisdc@millsaps.edu
DAVIS, David, H .... 828-694-1845 360 D
daviddav@blueridge.edu
DAVIS, Debra .... 419-530-8355 394 E
debra.davis@utoledo.edu
DAVIS, Debra, C .... 251-445-9404.... 9 F
ddavis@southalabama.edu
DAVIS, Deidra .... 207-326-2138 211 G
deidra.davis@mma.edu
DAVIS, Derrick .... 301-860-3427 220 B
dldavis@bowiestate.edu
DAVIS, Diana .... 513-244-4301 387 A
diana.davis@msj.edu
DAVIS, Dianne, L .... 828-398-7841 360 A
ddavis@abtech.edu
DAVIS, Dirk .... 951-343-3905.. 30 D
ddavis@calbaptist.edu
DAVIS, Don .... 626-815-3828.. 29 B
ddavis@apu.edu
DAVIS, Donald, L .... 972-883-6176 494 A
don.davis@utdallas.edu
DAVIS, Donna .... 760-757-2121.. 54 G
ddavis@miracosta.edu
DAVIS, Donna .... 636-922-8300 281 C
ddavis@stchas.edu
DAVIS, Donna, J .... 415-422-6822.. 74 C
davisdj@usfca.edu
DAVIS, Eddie .... 972-825-4686 483 D
edavis@sagu.edu
DAVIS, Eddie, J .... 979-847-8700 485 C
edavis@tamu.edu
DAVIS, Elizabeth .... 864-294-2100 446 F
elizabeth.davis@furman.edu
DAVIS, Elizabeth, B ...... 415-422-2508.. 74 C
ebdavis@usfca.edu
DAVIS, Eric .... 505-424-2351 310 L
eric.davis@iaia.edu
DAVIS, Erik .... 805-969-3626.. 57 J
edavis@pacifica.edu
DAVIS, Ernie .... 903-693-1112 480 A
edavis@panola.edu
DAVIS, Evelyn .... 423-624-0077 455 H
evelynd@chattanoogacollege.edu
DAVIS, Evett .... 706-771-4027 121 B
edavis@augustatech.edu
DAVIS, Faye .... 918-685-0724 396 F
davisf@bacone.edu
DAVIS, Fontaine .... 386-481-2005.. 99 F
davisf@cookman.edu
DAVIS, Frances .... 478-471-2472 128 H
frances.davis@mga.edu
DAVIS, G. Scott .... 608-757-7754 542 L
sdavis40@blackhawk.edu
DAVIS, Gayle, R .... 616-331-2400 243 E
davisgr@gvsu.edu
DAVIS, George .... 717-866-5775 418 E
george.davis@evangelical.edu
DAVIS, Gilda .... 504-286-5176 207 B
gdavis@suno.edu
DAVIS, Glenda .... 214-379-5526 480 D
gdavis@pqc.edu
DAVIS, Glenn .... 212-463-0400 350 C
glenn.davis2@touro.edu
DAVIS, Grant .... 610-647-4400 421 B
gdavis@immaculata.edu
DAVIS, Greg .... 360-438-8772 525 H
GDavis@stmartin.edu
DAVIS, Gregory .... 630-515-4554 144 A
gdavis@devrygroup.com
DAVIS, Gregory .... 920-465-2334 539 F
davisg@uwgb.edu
DAVIS, Guy .... 423-472-7141 462 D
GDavis08@clevelandstatecc.edu
DAVIS, Harriet, F .... 919-530-6151 370 C
hfdavis@nccu.edu
DAVIS, Hazel .... 480-517-8273.. 15 D
hazel.davis@riosalado.edu
DAVIS, Heather .... 336-750-3350 372 D
davish@wssu.edu
DAVIS, Herbert, R .... 919-572-1625 354 F
hdavis@apexsot.edu
DAVIS, Houston .... 404-962-3060 133 G
houston.davis@usg.edu
DAVIS, Howard .... 207-509-7150 212 A
hdavis@unity.edu
DAVIS, Howard .... 248-204-2316 245 J
hdavis@ltu.edu
DAVIS, Ira .... 575-624-8319 311 K
idavis@nmmi.edu
DAVIS, Jack .... 540-231-6416 518 B
davisa@vt.edu
DAVIS, James .... 410-225-4208 216 F
jdavis02@mica.edu
DAVIS, James .... 308-865-8517 293 G
DAVIS, James .... 804-819-4995 514 G
jdavis@vccs.edu
DAVIS, James .... 619-216-6759.. 68 D
jdavis@swccd.edu
DAVIS, James .... 310-206-0011.. 71 D
jdavis@conet.ucla.edu
DAVIS, James .... 972-825-4803 483 D
jdavis@sagu.edu
DAVIS, James .... 713-222-5382 491 F
davisjam@uhd.edu
DAVIS, Jamie .... 912-443-4162 131 B
jdavis@savannahtech.edu
DAVIS, Janice .... 229-931-2381 131 E
jdavis@southgatech.edu
DAVIS, Janis .... 949-794-9090.. 68 F
jdavis@stanbridge.edu
DAVIS, Jason .... 218-726-8782 264 G
jdavis@d.umn.edu
DAVIS, Jean .... 314-362-9180 275 D
Jean.Davis@bjc.org
DAVIS, Jef, C .... 330-941-2336 396 C
jcdavis05@ysu.edu
DAVIS, Jeff .... 912-871-1640 129 E
jdavis@ogeecheetech.edu
DAVIS, Jeff .... 706-802-5105 125 C
jdavis@highlands.edu
DAVIS, Jeff .... 785-539-3571 189 D
mccweb@mccks.edu
DAVIS, Jeff .... 541-757-8944 406 J
jeff.davis@linnbenton.edu
DAVIS, Jeffrey .... 662-325-3444 269 A
jdavis@alumni.msstate.edu
DAVIS, Jenna .... 719-336-1589.. 83 N
jenna.davis@lamarcc.edu
DAVIS, Jennifer .... 252-246-1228 367 D
jdavis@wilsoncc.edu
DAVIS, Jennifer, L .... 740-374-8716 395 D
jdavis@wscc.edu
DAVIS, Jennifer (J.J.) ... 703-993-8750 507 K
jjdavis@gmu.edu
DAVIS, Jerold .... 212-592-2000 342 F
jdavis@sva.edu
DAVIS, Jerome .... 212-854-5017 322 F
jd2145@columbia.edu
DAVIS, Jerome .... 205-226-4848.... 2 C
jdavis@bsc.edu
DAVIS, Jerry, C .... 417-690-2470 273 C
pres@cofo.edu
DAVIS, Jerry, W .... 260-356-6000 167 D
DAVIS, Jim, L .... 701-477-7862 375 H
jdavis@tm.edu
DAVIS, Jimmy, H .... 731-661-5461 464 G
jdavis@uu.edu
DAVIS, Joan .... 214-333-6855 471 L
joan@dbu.edu
DAVIS, Joan, Y .... 504-762-3000 203 F
jydavis@dcc.edu
DAVIS, Joanne .... 561-297-3015 114 E
joannedavis@fau.edu
DAVIS, Joe, D .... 641-422-4121 181 E
davisjoe@niacc.edu
DAVIS, Joe, M .... 765-641-4084 164 B
jmdavis@anderson.edu
DAVIS, Joel .... 973-803-5000 305 A
jdavis@pillar.edu
DAVIS, John .... 920-206-2332 536 T
john.davis@mbu.edu
DAVIS, John .... 626-873-2162.. 55 B
jdavis@mtsierra.edu
DAVIS, John .... 910-843-5304 359 L
DAVIS, John .... 920-206-2371 536 T
john.davis@mbu.edu
DAVIS, John .... 978-934-4806 229 A
John_Davis@uml.edu
DAVIS, John .... 307-766-6225 546 K
jdavis71@uwyo.edu
DAVIS, Jon .... 843-863-7218 444 B
jdavis@csuniv.edu
DAVIS, Jonathan, M ..... 802-626-6419 504 B
jonathan.davis@lyndonstate.edu
DAVIS, Julia, T .... 478-301-2644 128 G
davis_jt@mercer.edu
DAVIS, Julie .... 478-934-3518 128 H
julie.davis3@mga.edu
DAVIS, Julie .... 630-752-5079 163 G
Julie.Davis@wheaton.edu
DAVIS, Julie .... 315-268-6713 321 C
davisju@clarkson.edu
DAVIS, Julie, A .... 207-778-7264 212 E
jadavis@maine.edu
DAVIS, Julie, T .... 812-877-8988 172 C
tuttleda@rose-hulman.edu
DAVIS, June .... 910-296-2424 363 E
jdavis@jamessprunt.edu
DAVIS, Karan, P .... 850-718-2205 100 E
davisk@chipola.edu
DAVIS, Karen .... 805-493-3164.. 31 H
kdavis@callutheran.edu
DAVIS, Karen .... 401-863-3377 441 A
karen_davis@brown.edu
DAVIS, Kathleen, B .... 716-888-2500 317 H
daviskb@canisius.edu
DAVIS, Kathy .... 715-346-4193 541 A
kdavis@uwsp.edu
DAVIS, Kathy, K .... 207-768-9581 212 H
kathy.k.davis@umpi.edu
DAVIS, Katie .... 478-274-7775 129 D
kdavis@oftc.edu
DAVIS, Kelly .... 479-968-0242.. 20 C
kdavis@atu.edu
DAVIS, Kelly .... 817-272-2194 493 L
kdavis@uta.edu
DAVIS, Kelvin .... 803-376-5700 443 D
DAVIS, Ken .... 803-536-7017 448 H
ken.davis@scsu.edu
DAVIS, Ken, R .... 423-478-7898 460 C
kdavis@ptseminary.edu
DAVIS, Kenneth, L .... 212-659-9003 328 E
DAVIS, JR.,
Kenneth, M .... 919-658-2502 369 B
kdavis@umo.edu
DAVIS, Kerry .... 904-819-6200 102 P
KDavis@flagler.edu
DAVIS, Kevin, L .... 936-468-2011 484 A
DAVIS, Kim .... 843-661-1210 446 E
kdavis@fmarion.edu
DAVIS, Kimber .... 515-309-9000 183 H
kimber.davis@vatterott-college.edu
DAVIS, Kristy .... 479-968-0329.. 20 C
kdavis51@atu.edu
DAVIS, Larry, D .... 501-977-2013.. 25 A
davis@uaccm.edu
DAVIS, Larry, E .... 412-624-6304 437 K
ledavis@pitt.edu
DAVIS, Larry, J .... 314-516-5606 284 B
ldavis@umsl.edu
DAVIS, Leana .... 815-479-7661 152 B
ldavis@mchenry.edu
DAVIS, Leander .... 310-287-4314.. 52 C
davisl@wlac.edu
DAVIS, Lee .... 912-344-2535 120 D
lee.davis@armstrong.edu
DAVIS, LeeAnn .... 386-506-3404 101 I
davisl@DaytonaState.edu
DAVIS, Len, L .... 516-876-3191 345 E
davisl@oldwestbury.edu
DAVIS, Linda .... 573-592-4382 286 A
linda.davis@williamwoods.edu
DAVIS, Linda .... 617-879-2341 238 C
ldavis@wheelock.edu
DAVIS, Linda .... 810-989-5765 249 H
ldavis@sc4.edu
DAVIS, Linda, P .... 386-822-7710 117 A
ldavis@stetson.edu
DAVIS, Lois .... 503-725-2320 409 D
loisd@pdx.edu
DAVIS, Loren .... 253-589-5771 521 B
loren.davis@cptc.edu
DAVIS, Lori, A .... 502-597-6414 197 G
lori.davis@kysu.edu
DAVIS, Lorna .... 559-934-2203.. 76 B
lornadavis@whccd.edu
DAVIS, Lowell, K .... 828-227-7495 372 C
lkdavis@wcu.edu
DAVIS, LuAnn .... 402-486-2503 293 D
ludavis@ucollege.edu
DAVIS, Lynne .... 508-270-4021 231 G
ldavis@massbay.edu
DAVIS, M. Andrew .... 919-572-1625 354 F
meandavis@gmail.com
DAVIS, MacArthur .... 336-744-0900 355 D
macarthur.davis@carolina.edu
DAVIS, Maggie .... 513-244-4630 387 A
maggie.davis@msj.edu
DAVIS, Malcolm .... 832-842-4719 491 D
mdavis@uh.edu
DAVIS, Maria .... 269-749-7643 249 A
mdavis@olivetcollege.edu
DAVIS, Marie .... 229-391-4988 119 F
mdavis@abac.edu
DAVIS, Marilyn .... 404-880-8550 122 I
mdavis@cau.edu
DAVIS, Marilyn, S .... 217-424-6379 153 A
mdavis@millikin.edu
DAVIS, Marjorie .... 509-533-4152 521 F
marjorie.davis@sfcc.spokane.edu
DAVIS, Mark .... 706-880-8060 127 N
mdavis@lagrange.edu
DAVIS, Mark .... 310-506-4472.. 58 H
mark.davis@pepperdine.edu
DAVIS, Mark .... 205-652-3570.... 9 G
mdavis@uwa.edu
DAVIS, Mark, L .... 515-964-0601 178 F
davism@faith.edu
DAVIS, Marsha .... 845-758-7433 315 G
davis@bard.edu
DAVIS, Marty .... 678-839-6614 133 F
gdavis@westga.edu
DAVIS, Marty .... 304-865-6033 530 F
marty.davis@ovu.edu
DAVIS, Mary .... 212-217-4300 325 C
mary_davis@fitnyc.edu
DAVIS, Mary .... 828-298-3325 373 A
mdavis@warren-wilson.edu
DAVIS, Matthew .... 402-557-7232 289 B
matthew.davis@bellevue.edu
DAVIS, Matthew .... 920-206-2310 536 T
matthew.davis@mbu.edu
DAVIS, Matthew, D .... 812-877-8421 172 C
matthew.davis@rose-hulman.edu
DAVIS, Maureen .... 760-252-2411.. 29 C
mdavis3@barstow.edu
DAVIS, Meadow .... 207-725-3037 209 H
mdavis1@bowdoin.edu
DAVIS, Meagon .... 478-757-3803 134 E
mdavis@wesleyancollege.edu
DAVIS, Megan, W .... 603-862-2450 299 B
megan.davis@unh.edu
DAVIS, Melvin .... 601-979-1400 267 H
melvin.davis@jsums.edu
DAVIS, Melvin, D .... 256-765-4821.... 9 D
mdavis2@una.edu
DAVIS, Michael .... 770-381-7200 127 B
DAVIS, Michael .... 617-373-2121 235 D
DAVIS, Michael, G .... 985-448-4030 208 C
mike.davis@nicholls.edu
DAVIS, Michele .... 770-394-8300 120 E
mrdavis@aii.edu
DAVIS, Michelle .... 404-527-7793 127 H
lmdavis@itc.edu
DAVIS, Michelle .... 781-292-2251 226 G
michelle.davis@olin.edu
DAVIS, Michelle .... 701-228-5670 374 F
michelle.r.davis@dakotacollege.edu
DAVIS, Michelle .... 434-544-8228 509 I
davis@lynchburg.edu
DAVIS, Michelle, C ...... 336-272-7102 357 B
michelle.davis@greensboro.edu
DAVIS, Mike .... 303-360-4754.. 81 I
Mike.Davis@CCAurora.edu
DAVIS, Mike .... 386-752-1822 103 Q
mike.davis@fgc.edu
DAVIS, Miles .... 540-545-7253 512 E
mdavis3@su.edu
DAVIS, Mitch .... 970-247-7010.. 82 I
davis_m@fortlewis.edu
DAVIS, Mitch .... 251-442-2334.... 9 B
mdavis@umobile.edu
DAVIS, Mitchel, W .... 207-725-3930 209 H
mwdavis@bowdoin.edu
DAVIS, Monique, P ...... 954-308-2224.. 98 I
mpdavis@aii.edu
DAVIS, Myriah .... 740-753-7020 383 G
davism@hocking.edu
DAVIS, NaKesha .... 973-877-3306 302 F
ngreen@essex.edu
DAVIS, Nan, M .... 903-813-3000 468 G
ndavis@austincollege.edu

DAVIS, Nancy .... 619-644-7000.. 46 H
nancy.davis@gcccd.edu
DAVIS, Natalie .... 601-643-8354 266 J
natalie.davis@colin.edu
DAVIS, Nelson .... 757-455-3201 518 H
ndavis@vwc.edu
DAVIS, Pam .... 772-546-5534 106 D
admissions@hsbc.edu
DAVIS, Pamela .... 919-760-8360 359 B
davisp@meredith.edu
DAVIS, Pamela, B .... 216-368-2825 378 J
pamela.davis@case.edu
DAVIS, Patricia .... 207-780-5911 213 A
patdavis@usm.maine.edu
DAVIS, Patricia .... 972-860-8180 472 D
pdavis@dcccd.edu
DAVIS, Patricia .... 970-860-8180 472 D
pdavis@dcccd.edu
DAVIS, Patricia, A .... 251-380-3063.... 7 F
pdavis@shc.edu
DAVIS, Patti .... 410-386-8066 214 B
pdavis@carrollcc.edu
DAVIS, Paul .... 641-784-5138 178 G
padavis@graceland.edu
DAVIS, Paul .... 641-784-5422 178 G
pjdavis@graceland.edu
DAVIS, Paul .... 936-468-1111 484 A
pdavis@sfasu.edu
DAVIS, Paul, R .... 530-226-4719.. 66 G
pdavis@simpsonu.edu
DAVIS, Paula .... 609-343-5091 299 G
pdavis@atlantic.edu
DAVIS, Peggy .... 804-524-5030 518 C
pdavis@vsu.edu
DAVIS, Pete, D .... 608-342-1177 540 D
davisp@uwplatt.edu
DAVIS, Rachelle .... 301-387-3044 215 A
rachelle.davis@garrettcollege.edu
DAVIS, Raeanne .... 212-237-8604 319 F
radavis@jjay.cuny.edu
DAVIS, Ralph, U .... 843-661-1110 446 E
rdavis@fmarion.edu
DAVIS, Rance .... 315-229-5551 341 E
rdavis@stlawu.edu
DAVIS, Randy .... 502-213-2122 196 E
randall.davis@kctcs.edu
DAVIS, Randy .... 800-280-0307 163 I
randy.davis@ace.edu
DAVIS, Ray, J .... 410-651-6083 219 H
rjdavis@umes.edu
DAVIS, Rebecca .... 361-593-3344 486 A
koosr00@tamuk.edu
DAVIS, Rebecca, F .... 512-637-1949 481 B
rebeccad@stedwards.edu
DAVIS, Renee .... 334-386-7230.... 3 I
rdavis@faulkner.edu
DAVIS, Rhonda .... 817-554-5950 478 E
rdavis@messengercollege.edu
DAVIS, Richard .... 317-931-2391 165 C
ddavis@cts.edu
DAVIS, Richard .... 863-667-5310 113 K
rbdavis@seu.edu
DAVIS, Richard .... 954-262-8849 109 E
redavis@nsu.nova.edu
DAVIS, Richard, K .... 312-942-6909 158 A
Richard_K_Davis@rush.edu
DAVIS, Rick .... 850-973-9492 109 C
davisr@nfcc.edu
DAVIS, Rick .... 662-246-6441 268 F
rdavis@msdelta.edu
DAVIS, Rick .... 703-993-8624 507 K
rdavi4@gmu.edu
DAVIS, Robert, H .... 303-492-7006.. 86 E
robert.davis@colorado.edu
DAVIS, JR., Robert, W . 570-941-7500 438 F
robert.davis@scranton.edu
DAVIS, Roger .... 615-966-7161 458 C
roger.davis@lipscomb.edu
DAVIS, Ronald .... 615-353-3326 463 C
ronald.davis@nscc.edu
DAVIS, Ronnie .... 919-530-7298 370 C
rdavis82@nccu.edu
DAVIS, Ryan .... 425-388-9212 522 I
rydavis@everettcc.edu
DAVIS, Sandie .... 706-295-6339 125 C
sdavis@highlands.edu
DAVIS, Sandra, S .... 803-535-1218 448 C
davisss@octech.edu
DAVIS, Shane .... 318-487-7181 202 L
shane.davis@lacollege.edu
DAVIS, Shannon .... 901-321-3545 455 I
0478mgr@follett.com
DAVIS, Shaqualyn .... 229-732-5949 120 B
shaqualyndavis@andrewcollege.edu
DAVIS, Shara .... 440-365-5222 385 E
DAVIS, Sharon .... 513-569-1475 379 K
sharon.davis@cincinnatistate.edu
DAVIS, Sharon .... 214-860-8705 472 G
sdavis1@dcccd.edu
DAVIS, Sharon .... 254-526-1346 470 E
sharon.davis@ctcd.edu

DAVIS, Shelley .... 202-806-7141.. 96 B
shelley.davis@howard.edu
DAVIS, Shelly .... 207-893-7726 211 H
sdavis@sjcme.edu
DAVIS, Sherri .... 205-929-6357.... 5 E
sdavis@lawsonstate.edu
DAVIS, Sherri .... 828-254-1921 360 A
sherrijdavis@abtech.edu
DAVIS, Sherry .... 254-659-7602 475 A
sdavis@hillcollege.edu
DAVIS, Sherry .... 540-785-5440 514 C
sherrydavis@vbc.edu
DAVIS, Stan .... 205-726-2366.... 6 F
csdavis@samford.edu
DAVIS, Stefan, S .... 317-274-8828 168 E
ssdavis@iupui.edu
DAVIS, Stephanie .... 517-787-0800 244 H
davisstephand@jccmi.edu
DAVIS, Stephen .... 410-225-2355 216 F
sdavis@mica.edu
DAVIS, Steven .... 707-638-5270.. 70 B
steven.davis@tu.edu
DAVIS, Steven, J .... 208-496-3305 137 F
daviss@byui.edu
DAVIS, Stewart .... 256-549-8603.... 3 N
sdavis@gadsdenstate.edu
DAVIS, Sue .... 225-768-1802 206 F
sue.davis@ololcollege.edu
DAVIS, Sue, E .... 330-941-2000 396 C
sedavis@ysu.edu
DAVIS, Sue, F .... 740-587-6500 381 H
davissf@denison.edu
DAVIS, Susan, Y .... 573-875-7210 273 D
sydavis@ccis.edu
DAVIS, Suzanne .... 618-664-7004 145 E
suzanne.davis@greenville.edu
DAVIS, Suzanne, E .... 315-268-6451 321 C
daviss@clarkson.edu
DAVIS, Tamika .... 860-255-3510.. 90 C
tdavis@txcc.commnet.edu
DAVIS, Tammy .... 325-574-7695 497 E
tdavis@wtc.edu
DAVIS, Terry .... 619-482-6551.. 68 D
tdavis@swccd.edu
DAVIS, Theresa .... 657-278-7642.. 33 E
thdavis@fullerton.edu
DAVIS, Thom .... 661-654-2287.. 32 G
tdavis31@csub.edu
DAVIS, Thomas .... 803-705-4687 443 F
davist@benedict.edu
DAVIS, Tiffany .... 810-766-4277 239 G
tiffany.davis@baker.edu
DAVIS, Tim .... 606-474-3000 195 F
DAVIS, Timothy .... 434-243-5150 514 A
tld8n@virginia.edu
DAVIS, Tina .... 859-622-3876 194 L
tina.davis@eku.edu
DAVIS, Todd .... 678-359-5061 126 E
toddd@gordonstate.edu
DAVIS, Tom .... 334-670-3981.... 8 A
tomdavis@troy.edu
DAVIS, Tom .... 440-375-7170 385 B
tdavis@lec.edu
DAVIS, Tommye Lou .... 254-710-3750 469 D
tommye_lou_davis@baylor.edu
DAVIS, Traci .... 309-796-5408 140 D
davist@bhc.edu
DAVIS, Tracy .... 415-371-0002.. 57 B
DAVIS, Twyla .... 910-879-5516 360 C
tdavis@bladencc.edu
DAVIS, Tyler .... 843-574-5505 444 B
tdavis@csuniv.edu
DAVIS, Wain .... 618-393-2982 146 F
davisw@iecc.edu
DAVIS, Wayne .... 757-825-3513 517 B
davisw@tncc.edu
DAVIS, Wayne .... 865-974-5321 465 D
wtdavis@utk.edu
DAVIS, Wendy .... 520-515-3623.. 13 B
davisd@cochise.edu
DAVIS, Wendy .... 501-812-2273.. 22 F
wdavis@pulaskitech.edu
DAVIS, Wesley .... 701-477-7862 375 H
wdavis1@tm.edu
DAVIS, Wesley .... 701-477-7853 375 H
wdavis1@tm.edu
DAVIS, Whitney .... 478-757-5170 134 E
wdavis@wesleyancollege.edu
DAVIS, William .... 708-534-4105 145 D
wdavis3@govst.edu
DAVIS, William .... 610-359-6500 416 G
wdavis@dccc.edu
DAVIS, Zabe .... 662-562-3308 269 E
DAVIS-BLAKE, Alison ... 734-764-1363 251 C
alisondb@umich.edu
DAVIS-DUKES, Janet ..... 973-720-3096 309 I
davisdukesj@wpunj.edu
DAVIS-EYENE,
Mishawn .... 508-854-4576 232 F
meyene@qcc.mass.edu

DAVIS-FREEMAN,
Juana .... 803-934-3200 447 K
jdavis@morris.edu
DAVIS FREEMAN,
Louisa, M .... 413-755-4333 233 B
ldavisfreeman@stcc.edu
DAVIS-JACKSON,
Drenda .... 229-430-0664 119 I
DAVIS-JACKSON,
Latacha .... 662-254-3579 269 C
latacha.davis@mvsu.edu
DAVIS-JOHNSON, Max . 208-426-3033 137 E
maxdavisjohnson@boisestate.edu
DAVIS-JONES, Andrea .. 601-979-2245 267 H
andrea.e.davis@jsums.edu
DAVIS JONES, Chrissy . 509-533-3743 521 F
chrissy.davis@sfcc.spokane.edu
DAVIS LITTLE, Shay ...... 330-672-3000 384 H
DAVIS-SAMUELS,
Ivanetta .... 615-327-6141 458 F
isamuel@mmc.edu
DAVIS-VAN ATTA,
David .... 845-437-5276 351 H
ddavisa@vassar.edu
DAVISON, Brent .... 254-295-8642 492 C
bdavison@umhb.edu
DAVISON, Colette .... 312-893-7173 144 H
cdavison@erikson.edu
DAVISON, Don .... 513-721-7944 382 K
ddavison@gbs.edu
DAVISON, Dorothy .... 718-420-4221 352 C
ddavison@wagner.edu
DAVISON, Frieda, M .... 864-503-5610 451 A
fdavison@uscupstate.edu
DAVISON, Ian, R .... 989-774-1870 240 O
davis1ir@cmich.edu
DAVISON, Kimberly, K . 972-985-3781 471 C
kdavison@collin.edu
DAVISON, Michael, R ... 801-524-8102 498 J
mrdavison@ldsbc.edu
DAVISON, Ruth, L .... 850-474-2463 116 E
rdavison@uwf.edu
DAVISSON, Thomas, F . 502-451-0815 200 A
tdavisson@sullivan.edu
DAVISSON, Thomas, F . 502-451-0815 200 B
tdavisson@sullivan.edu
DAVITT, Jeffrey .... 904-819-6489 102 P
JDavitt@flagler.edu
DAVOLT, David .... 208-376-7731 137 D
ddavolt@boisebible.edu
DAVOUD, Mohammad .. 912-478-7412 126 B
mdavoud@georgiasouthern.edu
DAVROS, Harry .... 214-637-3530 496 J
hdavros@wadecollege.edu
DAVY, Catherine, A ...... 313-593-5030 251 D
kdavy@umich.edu
DAW, Meredith .... 773-702-7040 161 D
daw@uchicago.edu
DAW, Michael .... 415-442-6682.. 46 A
mdaw@ggu.edu
DAWE, Lloyd, A .... 803-641-3338 450 C
lloydd@usca.edu
DAWE, Richard, L .... 870-368-2006.. 22 D
rdawe@ozarka.edu
DAWES, Arlene .... 406-638-3116 286 I
dawesa@lbhc.edu
DAWES, Daniel .... 404-752-1833 129 A
ddawes@msm.edu
DAWES, Doug .... 701-845-7234 374 D
doug.dawes@vcsu.edu
DAWES, Douglas .... 209-667-3077.. 35 C
ddawes@csustan.edu
DAWES, Stephen .... 864-294-3031 446 F
steve.dawes@furman.edu
DAWKINS, E. Janyce .... 706-542-7912 132 H
edawkins@uga.edu
DAWKINS, Lisa .... 304-357-4374 530 H
lisadawkins@ucwv.edu
DAWKINS, Mark .... 904-620-2590 116 A
mark.dawkins@unf.edu
DAWKINS, Norman .... 212-431-2142 335 G
Norman.Dawkins@nyls.edu
DAWKINS, Phyllis .... 610-399-2271 430 D
pdawkins@cheyney.edu
DAWKINS, Rita .... 704-330-6862 361 D
rita.dawkins@cpcc.edu
DAWKINS, Tom .... 213-763-7361.. 52 A
dawkintl@lattc.edu
DAWKINS-FALTER,
Amelia .... 256-551-3136.... 4 J
amy.falter@drakestate.edu
DAWLEY, Anna Marie ... 315-268-6475 321 C
adawley@clarkson.edu
DAWSON, B. James ...... 423-869-6391 458 B
james.dawson@lmunet.edu
DAWSON, Brandon, T .. 607-735-1816 324 J
bdawson@elmira.edu
DAWSON, Brian .... 325-670-1253 474 M
brian.r.dawson@hsutx.edu

DAWSON, Bridgette ...... 304-336-8215 533 A
bdawson@westliberty.edu
DAWSON, Darren, M .... 785-532-5590 188 H
dmdawson@ksu.edu
DAWSON, Dave .... 479-575-5451.. 23 G
daved@uark.edu
DAWSON, David .... 401-341-2454 442 D
david.dawson@salve.edu
DAWSON, Frank .... 310-434-4585.. 65 B
dawson_frank@smc.edu
DAWSON, Imara, V ...... 765-285-5422 164 D
ivdawson@bsu.edu
DAWSON, Jim, T .... 615-353-3275 463 C
jim.dawson@nscc.edu
DAWSON, John David .. 765-983-1211 165 H
prexy@earlham.edu
DAWSON, Keith .... 574-520-4480 168 F
kdawson@iusb.edu
DAWSON, L. Wayde ...... 864-488-4522 447 F
ldawson@limestone.edu
DAWSON, Leslie .... 406-791-5294 288 J
leslie.dawson@ugf.edu
DAWSON, Randall .... 210-486-2597 467 B
rdawson@alamo.edu
DAWSON, Renita .... 919-735-5151 367 A
rddawson@waynecc.edu
DAWSON, Royal .... 312-369-7514 143 C
rdawson@colum.edu
DAWSON, Scott .... 805-756-2705.. 32 E
dcdawson@calpoly.edu
DAWSON, Theresa, R ... 308-432-6053 292 B
tdawson@csc.edu
DAWSON, JR.,
Thomas, E .... 410-951-3792 220 C
thdawson@coppin.edu
DAWSON, Timothy .... 717-901-5158 420 I
tdawson@harrisburgu.edu
DAWSON, Tony .... 630-752-5203 163 G
Tony.Dawson@wheaton.edu
DAWSON, Yolanda .... 818-401-1041.. 41 F
ydawson@columbiacollege.edu
DAWTON, Dennis .... 215-965-4073 426 G
academic@moore.edu
DAY, Barton .... 903-923-3201 488 A
bart.day@tstc.edu
DAY, Dani, R .... 972-758-3804 471 C
dday@collin.edu
DAY, Daniel, A .... 609-258-6108 305 C
dday@princeton.edu
DAY, David .... 412-536-1070 422 E
david.day@laroche.edu
DAY, Don .... 817-274-4284 469 E
dday@bhcarroll.edu
DAY, Elaine .... 434-791-5696 505 A
eday@averett.edu
DAY, Ian .... 508-999-8042 228 H
iday@umassd.edu
DAY, Jeff .... 305-222-2822 103 F
jday@careercollege.edu
DAY, John, R .... 404-413-2564 126 D
jday@gsu.edu
DAY, Lawrence .... 315-792-3099 351 G
lday@utica.edu
DAY, Leo .... 817-923-1921 483 E
lday@swbts.edu
DAY, Marc .... 212-749-2802 331 I
mday@msmnyc.edu
DAY, Mellani, J .... 303-963-3434.. 79 L
mday@ccu.edu
DAY, Michael .... 812-941-2244 169 A
micaday@ius.edu
DAY, Michelle .... 919-508-2260 373 B
michelle.day@peace.edu
DAY, Mitzi .... 231-591-3800 242 L
MitziDay@ferris.edu
DAY, Patricia .... 518-828-4181 322 E
day@sunycgcc.edu
DAY, Patrick .... 209-946-2365.. 73 C
pday@pacific.edu
DAY, Rebeckah, J .... 210-436-3727 481 C
rday@stmarytx.edu
DAY, Rondall, H .... 470-578-6074 127 M
rday9@kennesaw.edu
DAY, Thelma .... 323-953-4000.. 51 E
dayt@lacitycollege.edu
DAY, Valerie, I .... 865-471-3459 455 G
vday@cn.edu
DAY-PERROOTS,
Susan, D .... 304-293-2834 533 D
sue.day-perroots@mail.wvu.edu
DAY-PERROOTS,
Susan, D .... 304-293-3733 533 D
sue.day-perroots@mail.wvu.edu
DAYHOFF, Brenda .... 301-846-2481 214 I
bdayhoff@frederick.edu
DAYHOFF, Sharon, S ... 717-337-6276 419 C
sdayhoff@gettysburg.edu
DAYICH-MCCABE,
Karina, J .... 304-829-7000 529 H

DEBOARD, John .... 580-581-2237 397 A
jdeboard@cameron.edu
DEBOBES, Erin .... 508-531-2744 229 C
erin.debobes@bridgew.edu
DEBOCK, Devin .... 918-293-4944 400 E
devin.debock@okstate.edu
DEBOEF, Cindy, S .... 231-777-0303 247 G
cindy.deboef@muskegoncc.edu
DEBOEF, Ryan .... 417-836-8500 279 A
ryandeboef@missouristate.edu
DEBOER, Eileen .... 318-487-7222 202 L
eileen.deboer@lacollege.edu
DEBOER, Jeffrey .... 219-864-2400 171 G
jdeboer@midamerica.edu
DEBOER, Keith .... 616-222-1247 241 G
keith.deboer@cornerstone.edu
DEBOER-MORAN,
Jason .... 651-641-8766 255 C
moran@csp.edu
DEBOISE LUSTER,
Stacey .... 508-929-8022 230 G
sluster@worcester.edu
DEBOLT, Ken .... 315-781-3146 327 G
debolt@hws.edu
DEBONDT, Christine ..... 360-650-7731 528 D
christine.debondt@wwu.edu
DEBONO, Chad .... 719-336-6660.. 83 N
chad.debono@lamarcc.edu
DEBONO, Chad .... 719-336-1517.. 83 N
chad.debono@lamarcc.edu
DEBONO, Vincent .... 636-227-2100 277 A
vincent.debono@logan.edu
DEBONVILLE, Katrina .... 617-585-1157 234 H
katrina.debonville@necmusic.edu
DEBORD, Bonnie, H ..... 770-720-5502 130 E
bhd@reinhardt.edu
DEBOSE, Henry .... 804-524-5992 518 C
hdebose@vsu.edu
DEBOW, Arthur .... 503-297-5544 408 A
adebow@ocac.edu
DEBOWER, Lore .... 508-362-2131 231 D
ldebower@capecod.edu
DEBRAGA, Angie .... 775-775-2231 295 D
angie.debraga@gbcnv.edu
DEBRAGGIO,
Michael, J .... 315-859-4654 327 A
mdebragg@hamilton.edu
DEBRITO, Joannie, L .... 303-963-3378.. 79 L
jdebrito@ccu.edu
DEBRIZZI, JR.,
Thomas, A .... 203-576-4690.. 92 B
tdebriz@bridgeport.edu
DEBRUIN, Jacob, H ...... 571-633-9651 513 J
DEBRUIN, Joel .... 616-526-6127 240 L
jsd42@calvin.edu
DEBRUM, David .... 692-625-6416 550 A
ddebrum@cmi.edu
DEBURE, Olivier .... 727-864-8366 101 P
debureoc@eckerd.edu
DEBURRO, Jennifer ...... 207-602-2132 213 B
jdeburro@une.edu
DEBUS, Casey .... 307-532-8311 546 B
casey.debus@ewc.wy.edu
DEBUSK, Frankie .... 423-636-7300 464 F
fdebusk@tusculum.edu
DEC, Lynda .... 207-973-3370 212 B
lynda.dec@maine.edu
DEC, Ted .... 631-687-5155 341 A
tdec@sjcny.edu
DECAIRE, Maryann .... 847-578-3217 157 G
maryann.decaire@rosalindfranklin.edu
DECALO, Ruth .... 212-678-8915 329 H
rudecalo@jtsa.edu
DECAMILLIS, Susan ...... 231-995-1014 248 C
sdecamillis@nmc.edu
DECAMP, Alexander ...... 708-209-3505 143 D
Alexander.DeCamp@cuchicago.edu
DECANDIA, Salvatore ... 718-780-7982 317 A
salvatore.decandia@brooklaw.edu
DECAPRIO, Nicholas ..... 518-244-4551 340 A
decapn@sage.edu
DECAPUA, Lynn .... 732-987-2729 302 J
decapual@georgian.edu
DECARBO, Diane, M ..... 724-658-1938 413 G
diane.decarbo@bc3.edu
DECARIE, Linette .... 617-353-2256 224 E
decarie@bu.edu
DECARLO, Robert, L ..... 516-877-3184 314 F
decarlo@adelphi.edu
DECARO, Peter .... 212-517-0685 332 A
pdecaro@mmm.edu
DECAROLIS, Donna .... 215-895-1795 417 E
donna.marie.decarolis@drexel.edu
DECARVALHO, Fatima ... 973-655-7818 304 A
decarvalhf@mail.montclair.edu
DECASTRO-SALLIS,
Kishma .... 412-397-6238 434 B
sallis@rmu.edu
DECATUR, Jane .... 508-626-4585 230 A
jdecatur@framingham.edu
DECATUR, Sean .... 740-427-5111 384 P
decatur@kenyon.edu
DECATUR, William .... 313-577-5580 252 G
william.decatur@wayne.edu
DECAY, Jarlene .... 972-860-0800 472 D
jdecay@dcccd.edu
DECELLE, Jerry, L .... 518-564-2082 346 B
decellejl@plattsburgh.edu
DECELLES, Katherine ..... 617-558-1788 235 A
kdecelles@nesa.edu
DECENA, Peter .... 408-924-2222.. 36 B
peter.decena@sjsu.edu
DECENT,
Christopher, M .... 904-620-2131 116 A
c.decent@unf.edu
DECENZO, David, A ...... 843-349-2001 444 G
ddecenzo@coastal.edu
DECHANT, Margaret ..... 361-825-5951 485 F
margaret.dechant@tamucc.edu
DECHARINTE, Janeen ... 815-838-0500 150 F
decharja@lewisu.edu
DECHARIO, Douglas, C 785-864-9525 191 G
d325d867@ku.edu
DECHIARO, Thomas ..... 203-837-9800.. 88 G
dechiarot@wcsu.edu
DECHILLO, Neal .... 978-542-6630 230 E
ndechillo@salemstate.edu
DECICCIO, Albert .... 617-322-3507 227 J
al_deciccio@laboure.edu
DECK, Amanda .... 617-405-5967 235 H
adeck@quincycollege.edu
DECK, Joseph, G .... 210-434-6711 479 P
jgdeck@lake.ollusa.edu
DECKER, Amber .... 859-442-1147 196 A
amber.decker@kctcs.edu
DECKER, Ann .... 772-462-7240 106 F
adecker@irsc.edu
DECKER, Barbara, Q ..... 515-643-6601 181 B
bdecker@mercydesmoines.org
DECKER, Chet .... 816-268-5421 279 K
cdecker@nts.edu
DECKER, Christy .... 518-828-4181 322 E
christy.decker@sunycgcc.edu
DECKER, Craig .... 719-255-4338.. 86 F
cdecker@uccs.edu
DECKER, David, R .... 614-947-6017 382 H
DECKER, Douglas .... 724-983-0700 423 H
ddecker@laurel.edu
DECKER, Douglas, S .... 724-439-4900 423 G
ddecker@laurel.edu
DECKER, Emily .... 312-461-0600 139 G
edecker@aaart.edu
DECKER, Jennifer .... 301-696-3408 215 E
decker@hood.edu
DECKER, John .... 417-268-6002 272 F
jdecker@gobbc.edu
DECKER, Kim .... 334-244-3255.... 2 A
kdecker@aum.edu
DECKER, Nancy .... 724-983-0700 423 H
ndecker@laurel.edu
DECKER, Nancy, M .... 724-439-4900 423 G
ndecker@laurel.edu
DECKER, Pat .... 913-469-8500 188 E
pdecker5@jccc.edu
DECKER, Paul, W .... 818-767-0888.. 77 G
paul.decker@woodbury.edu
DECKER, Stephanie .... 973-684-6868 304 F
sdecker@pccc.edu
DECKER, Steven .... 715-468-2815 544 F
steven.decker@witc.edu
DECKER, Susan .... 812-535-5138 172 F
sdecker@smwc.edu
DECKER, Timothy .... 845-298-0755 324 D
tdecker@sunydutchess.edu
DECKER, William, C ..... 501-569-3302.. 24 A
wcdecker@ualr.edu
DECKERT, Glenn .... 978-867-4736 227 A
glenn.deckert@gordon.edu
DECKLER, Dan .... 330-684-8940 393 A
dcd@uakron.edu
DECKLER, Daniel, B ...... 330-684-8761 392 H
dcd@uakron.edu
DECLEENE, Catherine .... 317-738-8090 166 B
cdecleene@franklincollege.edu
DECLOUETTE, Anne .... 405-682-7546 399 K
anne.h.declouette@occc.edu
DECMAN, Mike .... 815-740-3427 162 F
mdecman@stfrancis.edu
DECOCINIS, Anthony ..... 215-972-2007 429 G
adecocinis@pafa.edu
DECOCK, Murray .... 315-228-7489 321 H
mdecock@colgate.edu
DECONCILIS,
Patricia, A .... 724-653-2213 417 D
pdeconcilis@dec.edu
DECONINCK, Lori .... 603-668-2211 298 H
l.deconinck@snhu.edu
DECONNO, David .... 518-580-5719 342 I
ddeconno@skidmore.edu
DECOOKE, Peggy .... 914-251-6485 346 D
peggy.decooke@purchase.edu
DECORDOVA, Endia ...... 860-512-2907.. 89 D
edecordova@manchestercc.edu
DECOSTA, Jean .... 805-756-5198.. 32 E
jdecosta@calpoly.edu
DECOSTA, Melvin .... 808-735-4792 135 A
security@chaminade.edu
DECOSTE, Jennifer, M .. 608-342-6152 540 D
decostej@uwplatt.edu
DECOTEAU, Katina .... 701-255-3285 375 I
kdecoteau@uttc.edu
DECOTEAU, Steve .... 701-477-7862 375 H
sdecoteau@tm.edu
DECOUDREAUX,
Alecia, A .... 510-430-2094.. 54 F
adecoudreaux@mills.edu
DECOURSEY, Paul, A .... 515-574-1055 179 F
decoursey@iowacentral.edu
DECRISTO, James .... 336-734-2862 372 B
decristoj@uncsa.edu
DECRISTOFORO,
Joesph, R .... 210-458-7070 494 D
JOE.DECRISTOFORO@UTSA.EDU
DECUIR, Anthony .... 504-865-3039 206 A
decuir@loyno.edu
DECUIR, Bobbie .... 337-482-1000 208 F
bobbie@louisiana.edu
DEDDO, Gary .... 626-650-2306.. 46 C
DEDEAUX, Vanessa ...... 601-928-6230 268 G
vanessa.dedeaux@mgccc.edu
DEDEO, Patrick .... 973-720-2224 309 I
dedeop@wpunj.edu
DEDIEMAR, Jeanette ..... 317-788-3368 173 I
DEDIOS, Paul .... 714-484-7335.. 56 E
pdedios@cypresscollege.edu
DEDONATO, Joy .... 516-572-7943 334 A
joy.dedonato@ncc.edu
DEDWYLDER, Jason ..... 601-477-4075 268 A
jason.dedwylder@jcjc.edu
DEE, Edward .... 718-779-1499 338 D
edee@plazacollege.edu
DEE, Kay, C .... 812-877-8502 172 C
dee@rose-hulman.edu
DEE, Shawn, G .... 336-334-4822 363 A
sgdee@gtcc.edu
DEE, Tina .... 231-777-0660 247 G
tina.dee@muskegoncc.edu
DEEB, Bassam, M .... 716-826-1200 350 H
deebb@trocaire.edu
DEEB, Tiffni .... 612-659-6600 259 F
tiffni.deeb@minneapolis.edu
DEEDRICK, Gary, A ...... 864-242-5100 443 G
DEEDS, Cher .... 330-684-8952 393 A
cher@uakron.edu
DEEDS, Sarene .... 417-873-7869 274 E
sdeeds@drury.edu
DEEDS, William, C .... 712-274-5103 181 C
deeds@morningside.edu
DEEG, Matthew .... 812-866-7081 166 E
deeg@hanover.edu
DEEGAN, Rosemary, L . 610-921-7202 411 E
rdeegan@albright.edu
DEEGEN, Lynn .... 601-928-6212 268 G
lynn.deegen@mgccc.edu
DEEK, Fadi, P .... 973-596-3220 304 D
fadi.deek@njit.edu
DEEL, Connie .... 785-594-8362 184 F
connie.deel@bakeru.edu
DEEL, Susan, M .... 989-463-7176 239 B
deel@alma.edu
DEEM, Marie .... 412-536-1128 422 E
marie.deem@laroche.edu
DEEN, Michael .... 903-813-2306 468 G
mdeen@austincollege.edu
DEEN, Robert .... 720-279-8990.. 82 N
bdeen@csl.org
DEEN, Stella .... 845-257-3280 344 A
provost@newpaltz.edu
DEER, Joe, W .... 308-635-6145 294 C
deerj234@wncc.edu
DEER, Susan .... 845-574-4280 339 I
sdeer@sunyrockland.edu
DEERE, Judy .... 918-270-6421 401 C
judy.deere@ptstulsa.edu
DEES, Charles .... 973-596-8293 304 D
charles.dees@njit.edu
DEES, Margaret .... 904-256-7885 106 Q
mdees@ju.edu
DEES-BURNETT,
Keichanda .... 816-235-5628 284 A
deesk@umkc.edu
DEESE, Phyllis .... 903-823-3355 484 D
phyllis.deese@texarkanacollege.edu
DEESE, Todd .... 704-403-3218 355 B
todd.deese@carolinashealthcare.org
DEESS, Eugene, P .... 973-596-3110 304 D
deess@njit.edu
DEETZ, Kristi, R .... 812-888-4358 174 F
kdeetz@vinu.edu
DEFA, Dennis .... 406-994-3651 287 G
dennis.defa@montana.edu
DEFALCO, Ron, E .... 713-718-7586 475 C
ron.defalco@hccs.edu
DEFATTA, Jerry .... 601-266-5013 271 B
jerry.defatta@usm.edu
DEFEDE, Kathryn .... 559-925-3145.. 76 A
kathryndefede@whccd.edu
DEFEIS, Evelyn .... 973-684-5900 304 F
edefeis@pccc.edu
DEFELICE, Robert .... 781-891-2256 223 E
rdefelice@bentley.edu
DEFEO, Gregory .... 412-809-5100 433 D
defeo.greg@pti.edu
DEFFENBACHER, Mark .. 559-453-2239.. 45 E
mark.deffenbacher@fresno.edu
DEFFENBAUGH,
Cynthia, B .... 804-289-8438 513 M
cdeffenb@richmond.edu
DEFOOR, Keith .... 706-379-5156 134 J
kdefoor@yhc.edu
DEFORD, J. Kevin .... 423-652-6471 457 J
DEFORD, Linda .... 509-279-6258 521 E
linda.deford@scc.spokane.edu
DEFORD, Vicki .... 651-201-1664 257 N
victoria.deford@so.mnscu.edu
DEFORE, Jody .... 678-359-5990 126 E
jody@gordonstate.edu
DEFORE, Matt .... 205-726-4021.... 6 F
mdefore@samford.edu
DEFOREST, Kristin, A ... 607-746-4590 347 G
deforeka@delhi.edu
DEFRANCIS, Robert ...... 304-214-8820 531 G
rdefrancis@wvncc.edu
DEFRANCO, Jeff .... 530-541-4660.. 50 A
defranco@ltcc.edu
DEFRATES, Bruce .... 509-359-6329 522 C
bdefrates@ewu.edu
DEFREECE, Michele, T .. 607-746-4652 347 G
defreemt@delhi.edu
DEFREITAS, Jack .... 660-263-3900 272 M
jackdefreitas@cccb.edu
DEFRIES, Robert .... 320-762-4637 257 O
bobd@alextech.edu
DEGAIN, Sabrina .... 336-506-4161 359 N
sabrina.degain@alamancecc.edu
DEGAISH, Ann .... 361-825-2612 485 F
ann.degaish@tamucc.edu
DEGARMO, David .... 417-862-9533 275 C
ddegarmo@globaluniversity.edu
DEGARMO, Kristin .... 417-862-9533 275 C
kdegarmo@globaluniversity.edu
DEGAZON, Karen .... 212-938-5654 347 C
kdegazon@sunyopt.edu
DEGEARE, Christopher . 636-481-3467 276 E
cdegear1@jeffco.edu
DEGENHARDT, Brian .... 660-626-2397 271 G
bdegenhardt@atsu.edu
DEGENHART,
Mary Louise .... 314-367-8700 281 G
mary.degenhart@stlcop.edu
DEGEORGE,
Christine, C .... 941-359-7645 111 F
ccarnegi@ringling.edu
DEGEORGE, Steven .... 812-749-1399 171 I
sdegeorge@oak.edu
DEGER, Beth .... 937-328-6023 379 L
degerb@clarkstate.edu
DEGER, Coquina, L ...... 425-602-3006 519 J
cdeger@bastyr.edu
DEGERMAN, Roger .... 336-316-2000 357 C
degerman@guildford.edu
DEGERMAN, Roger, E ... 218-299-3645 255 B
degerman@cord.edu
DEGEUS, Marilyn, J ..... 816-654-7262 276 G
mdegeus@kcumb.edu
DEGIOIA,
John (Jack), J .... 202-687-4134.. 95 E
president@georgetown.edu
DEGIOVANNI, Kim .... 301-387-3040 215 A
kim.degiovanni@garrettcollege.edu
DEGN, Jason .... 479-619-4337.. 22 B
jdegn@nwacc.edu
DEGRAAF, Donald .... 616-526-6225 240 L
ddegraaf@calvin.edu
DEGRAFFENREID,
Pamela .... 828-227-7346 372 C
degraffen@wcu.edu
DEGRANGE, Karen, A ... 812-877-8285 172 C
karen.degrange@rose-hulman.edu
DEGRAW, Heather .... 425-739-8200 523 I
heather.degraw@lwtech.edu
DEGRAW, Julie .... 419-358-3248 377 H
degrawj@bluffton.edu
DEGRAW, Spencer .... 801-524-1947 498 J
sdegraw2@ldsbc.edu
DEGROAT, Kevin .... 718-405-3400 322 A
kevin.degroat@mountsaintvincent.edu
DEGROFF, Michael .... 717-391-3510 436 D
degroft@stevenscollege.edu
DEGROOT, Bridget .... 906-786-5802 240 K
bridget.degroot@baycollege.edu

DELLICARPINI, Dominic, F ... 717-815-1303 440 H dcarpini@ycp.edu
DELLINGER, Dewey ... 704-922-6236 362 G dellinger.dewey@gaston.edu
DELLINGER, Elaine, C .. 540-828-5605 505 F edelling@bridgewater.edu
DELLINGER, Sherry, L .. 910-814-5582 355 C sdellonger@campbell.edu
DELLINGER, Tim ... 731-424-2603 463 A tdellinger1@jscc.edu
DELLINGER ACEITUNO, Leslie ... 305-284-4025 118 A leslie@miami.edu
DELLIVENERI, Richard .. 303-964-3656.. 85 G rdellive@regis.edu
DELLOLIVER, Carol ... 503-517-1119 411 A cdelloliver@warnerpacific.edu
DELLUTRI, Alexandra .... 708-237-5030 155 B adellutri@nc.edu
DELLWO, Sarah ... 406-447-6908 287 F sarah.dellwo@umhelena.edu
DELL'AQUILO, Bobbie .. 516-686-7851 335 F rdellaqu@nyit.edu
DELL'OMO, Gregory ..... 609-896-5001 306 A gdellomo@rider.edu
DELL'OMO, Gregory, G 412-397-6400 434 B president@rmu.edu
DELL'OSA, Lydia, J ... 610-359-7322 416 G ldellosa@dccc.edu
DELMAR, Cindy ... 585-345-6813 326 F cmdelmar@genesee.edu
DELMAR, Jamaica ... 763-576-4236 258 A jamaica.delmar@anokatech.edu
DELMARK, Cary ... 972-883-2590 494 A caryd@utdallas.edu
DELMORO, Leslie ... 323-463-2500.. 69 H leslied@toa.edu
DELOATCH, Eugene ... 443-885-3231 217 C eugene.deloatch@eng.morgan.edu
DELOATCH, Sandra, J .. 757-823-8408 510 H provost@nsu.edu
DELOE, Mary ... 419-473-2700 381 F mdeloe@daviscollege.edu
DELONG, Allen, W ... 207-725-3536 209 H adelong2@bowdoin.edu
DELONG, Brian, C ... 610-799-1179 424 A bdelong2@lccc.edu
DELONG, Cliff ... 605-455-6079 452 L cdelong@olc.edu
DELONG, Dianne ... 610-341-5800 418 A ddelong@eastern.edu
DELONG, Jondavid, S .. 315-386-7328 347 F delongj@canton.edu
DELONG, Laurie ... 816-936-8724 282 A ldelong@saintlukescollege.edu
DELONG, Linda ... 909-593-3511.. 73 B ledelong@laverne.edu
DELONG, Michael ... 501-812-2373.. 22 F mdelong@pulaskitech.edu
DELONG, Oscar ... 906-217-4076 240 K oscar.delong@baycollege.edu
DELONG, Stephanie ... 314-918-2628 274 K sdelong@eden.edu
DELONGORIA, Maria ... 631-451-4174 348 E delongm@sunysuffolk.edu
DELORENZO, Donna ..... 904-819-6255 102 P dDeLorenzo@flagler.edu
DELORENZO, Michael .. 217-333-1300 162 A michaeld@illinois.edu
DELORENZO, Patricia ... 410-888-9048 216 G pdelorenzo@muih.edu
DELORENZO, Patricia ... 212-443-1297 336 C patricia.delorenzo@nyu.edu
DELORT, Greg ... 785-539-3571 189 D gdelort@mccks.edu
DELOS REYES DAVIS, Mark, E ... 808-544-0803 135 C mdavis@hpu.edu
DELOZIER, Matt ... 423-323-0231 463 D jmdelozier@northeaststate.edu
DELP, Kevin ... 864-242-5100 443 G
DELP, Michael ... 850-644-1281 115 A mdelp@fsu.edu
DELPRETE, Angela ... 440-646-8371 394 G adelprete@ursuline.edu
DELQUADRI, Sheila ... 509-574-4655 529 B sdelquadri@yvcc.edu
DELROSSI, David ... 850-201-8255 117 B delrossd@tcc.fl.edu
DELUCA, Anthony, L .... 516-876-3177 345 E delucaa@oldwestbury.edu
DELUCA, Cynthia, A .... 813-974-3077 116 B deluca@usf.edu
DELUCA, Eileen ... 239-985-3498 104 G ecduluca@fsw.edu
DELUCA, Mary ... 443-840-5215 214 F mdeluca@ccbcmd.edu
DELUCA, Peter, L ... 805-525-4417.. 69 I pdeluca@thomasaquinas.edu
DELUCA, Tony ... 610-359-5110 416 G tdeluca@dccc.edu
DELUCA, Vincent, J ... 212-817-7500 319 B vdeluca@gc.cuny.edu
DELUCCHI, Jennifer ... 916-568-3039.. 52 H deluccj@losrios.edu
DELUCIA, Carla ... 617-670-4468 226 F cdelucia@fisher.edu
DELUNA, Jennifer ... 719-549-2658.. 81 F jennifer.deluna@csupueblo.edu
DELUNAS, Linda ... 219-980-6643 168 C ldelunas@iun.edu
DELVECCHIO, Edie ... 201-200-3159 304 C edelvecchio@njcu.edu
DELVENTHAL, Bruce, W ... 518-564-3140 346 B delvenbw@plattsburgh.edu
DELVISCIO, Gregory ..... 607-777-2175 343 D gregdelv@binghamton.edu
DELZEIT, Greg ... 785-442-6039 187 I gdelzeit@highlandcc.edu
DEMA, Anne, C ... 816-415-5912 285 K demaa@william.jewell.edu
DEMAIO, Dennis ... 657-278-2900.. 33 E ddemaio@fullerton.edu
DEMANT, Timothy ... 509-777-4392 529 A tdemant@whitworth.edu
DEMARCO, Deborah ... 508-856-2903 229 B deborah.demarco@umassmed.edu
DEMARESKI, Roger ... 610-330-5133 423 A demaresr@lafayette.edu
DEMAREST, David, F .... 650-724-8887.. 68 G demarest@stanford.edu
DEMAREST, Geralynn ... 518-828-4181 322 E demarest@sunycgcc.edu
DEMAREST, Terri ... 973-408-3515 301 J tdemarest@drew.edu
DEMARK, Paul ... 707-476-4358.. 41 C paul-demark@redwoods.edu
DEMARKEY, Nina ... 714-484-7188.. 56 E ndemarkey@cypresscollege.edu
DEMARS, Paula ... 406-874-6196 287 A demarsp@milescc.edu
DEMART-KRAUS, Gina .. 440-646-8334 394 G gdemart@ursuline.edu
DEMARTE, Daniel, T ..... 757-822-1061 517 C ddemarte@tcc.edu
DEMARTINO, Amanda .. 908-526-1200 305 G Amanda.DeMartino@raritanval.edu
DEMATTEO, Jeanne ... 925-631-4123.. 61 G jdematte@stmarys-ca.edu
DEMATTEO, Susan ... 908-737-3350 303 C sdematte@kean.edu
DEMBECK, Brian, B ... 443-997-3728 216 A bdembeck@jhu.edu
DEMBOSKY, Cassandra, C ... 607-255-3203 323 C ccd3@cornell.edu
DEMBOSKY, Deborah ... 910-630-7522 359 C driley@methodist.edu
DEMBY, Harold, C ... 919-516-4593 368 E hcdemby@st-aug.edu
DEMCIE, Christine ... 716-829-7688 324 E demciec@dyc.edu
DEMCZUK, Bernard ... 202-994-1000.. 95 D bdemczuk@gwu.edu
DEMEDAL, Kathryn, K .. 724-946-6338 439 D demedakk@westminster.edu
DEMEDEIROS, Joe ... 512-233-1443 481 B joed@stedwards.edu
DEMELLO, Kenneth ... 509-533-3555 521 F kennethd@sfcc.spokane.edu
DEMELO, Amy ... 417-269-3406 274 A amy.demelo@coxcollege.edu
DEMENT, Gregory ... 713-221-8280 491 F dementg@uhd.edu
DEMENT, Jennifer ... 503-491-7385 407 C jennifer.dement@mhcc.edu
DEMENT, Marilyn ... 281-756-3517 467 D mdement@alvincollege.edu
DEMENT, Marilyn ... 773-907-4755 141 O mdement@ccc.edu
DEMENT, Paul ... 732-263-5679 303 G pdement@monmouth.edu
DEMERITT, Daniel ... 207-621-3065 212 B dan.demeritt@maine.edu
DEMERRITT, Stan ... 806-291-3415 496 K demerritt@wbu.edu
DEMERS, David, M ... 716-878-3694 345 B demersdm@buffalostate.edu
DEMERS, Mary ... 207-941-7131 210 C demersm@husson.edu
DEMERS, Paul ... 603-897-8537 298 E pdemers@rivier.edu
DEMERS, Susan, S ... 727-791-2501 112 A demers.susan@spcollege.edu
DEMERS, Suzanne ... 863-784-7041 113 C suzanne.demers@southflorida.edu
DEMETRIOU, Sophia ... 212-925-6625 318 G sdemetriou@ccny.cuny.edu
DEMETROS, John ... 315-568-3213 334 F jdemetros@nycc.edu
DEMEYER, Fay ... 541-485-1780 407 H faydemeyer@newhope.edu
DEMEZZO, Robert, C .... 203-392-5886.. 88 F demezzor1@southernct.edu
DEMICHAEL, Mark ... 765-677-2317 169 C mark.demichael@indwes.edu
DEMING, Els ... 253-840-8401 525 C edeming@pierce.ctc.edu
DEMITSAS, Yiani ... 260-422-5561 167 F jdemitsas@indianatech.edu
DEMKO, Amy ... 513-244-4408 387 A amy.demko@msj.edu
DEMMINGS, Elizabeth .. 765-658-4220 165 G betsydemmings@depauw.edu
DEMMITT, Kevin ... 678-466-4802 122 J kevindemmitt@clayton.edu
DEMO, Tina ... 860-509-9549.. 90 G tdemo@hartsem.edu
DEMORY, Yolanda, F ... 757-446-8498 507 B demoryyf@evms.edu
DEMOTT, Robin ... 309-341-5221 140 I rdemott@sandburg.edu
DEMPSEY, Connie ... 570-961-4692.. 16 L connie.dempsey@pennfoster.edu
DEMPSEY, Ellen, E ... 330-569-5340 383 F dempseyee@hiram.edu
DEMPSEY, Greg ... 206-934-5378 526 B greg.dempsey@seattlecolleges.edu
DEMPSEY, Jamie ... 909-593-3511.. 73 B jdempsey@laverne.edu
DEMPSEY, John, R ... 910-695-3700 365 H dempseyj@sandhills.edu
DEMPSEY, Marianne ..... 301-447-5330 217 D dempsey@msmary.edu
DEMPSEY, Michael ... 845-848-4058 324 B michael.dempsey@dc.edu
DEMPSEY, Patricia ... 410-972-4511 218 A patricia.dempsey@sjc.edu
DEMPSEY, Richard ... 972-883-2141 494 A rmdempsey@utdallas.edu
DEMPSEY, Ron ... 816-415-5034 285 K dempseyr@william.jewell.edu
DEMPSEY, Stephanie, C ... 512-223-7736 468 H diina@austincc.edu
DEMPSEY, Van ... 304-367-4646 532 F van.dempsey@fairmontstate.edu
DEMPSEY, Van, O ... 910-962-3354 372 A dempseyv@uncw.edu
DEMPSEY, William ... 610-683-4575 431 B dempsey@kutztown.edu
DEMPSTER, Douglas, J 512-471-9601 493 M ddempster@austin.utexas.edu
DEMUTH, Paul ... 651-423-8370 258 E paul.demuth@dctc.edu
DEMYER, Craig ... 219-980-6937 168 C cdemyer@iun.edu
DEN BOER, Marten ... 312-362-8610 143 G
DENARD, Carolyn ... 478-445-2361 125 A carolyn.denard@gcsu.edu
DENARD, Jeffrey, D ... 630-637-5142 154 F jddenard@noctrl.edu
DENARD, Letitia ... 404-270-5143 132 D ldenard@spelman.edu
DENARDIS, Nick ... 313-577-4540 252 G ndenardis@wayne.edu
DENARDO, Melissa, D . 724-480-3439 416 A melissa.denardo@ccbc.edu
DENBY, Eric, N ... 434-924-4019 514 A end@virginia.edu
DENBY, Karlene ... 281-487-1170 486 F kdenby@txchiro.edu
DENEAULT, Henry ... 781-239-5700 222 E deneault@babson.edu
DENEEN, Mary ... 757-683-3211 510 I mdeneen@odu.edu
DENEEN, Tina ... 205-934-8152.... 8 F tdeneen@uab.edu
DENEUI, Dan ... 541-552-6913 409 G deneuid@sou.edu
DENG, Shery ... 718-261-5800 316 K sdeng@bramsonort.edu
DENG, Yi ... 704-687-8450 371 B Yi.Deng@uncc.edu
DENHAM, Cynthia ... 256-840-4133.... 7 B cdenham@snead.edu
DENHAM, Mark ... 313-993-3250 250 H denhamma@udmercy.edu
DENHEM, Sherri ... 940-696-8752 496 B sdenhem@vernoncollege.edu
DENHOLM, Jack ... 701-845-7160 374 D jack.denholm@vcsu.edu
DENI, Lawrence ... 716-888-8362 317 H Deni@canisius.edu
DENIO, John ... 401-232-6140 441 B jdenio@bryant.edu
DENISON, Bronda ... 334-670-5843.... 8 A bdenison@troy.edu
DENISTON, Paul ... 719-255-4665.. 86 F pdenisto@uccs.edu
DENKER, Audria ... 502-410-6200 194 N adenker@galencollege.edu
DENKER, Lee ... 402-554-2444 294 A ldenker@unomaha.edu
DENKLER, Sherran, A ... 757-455-2136 518 H sadenkler@vwc.edu
DENLEY, Tristan ... 615-366-4482 461 B tristan.denley@tbr.edu
DENLY, David ... 620-229-6104 191 B david.denly@sckans.edu
DENMAN, Bob, G ... 501-569-3194.. 24 A bgdenman@ualr.edu
DENMAN, Jillian ... 210-297-9123 468 K jldenman@baptisthealthsystem.com
DENNA, Eric ... 301-405-7700 219 D edenna@umd.edu
DENNE, Cynthia, K ... 909-593-3511.. 73 B cdenne@laverne.edu
DENNEHY, Michael ... 972-860-4607 472 C mdennehy@dcccd.edu
DENNEY, Carolyn ... 509-527-2811 528 A carolyn.denney@wallawalla.edu
DENNEY, James ... 662-329-7462 269 B jldenney@muw.edu
DENNEY, Karen ... 828-627-4546 363 C kdenney@haywood.edu
DENNEY, Martha ... 610-896-1232 420 J mdenney@haverford.edu
DENNEY, Randy ... 520-515-5455.. 13 B denneyr@cochise.edu
DENNIE, Deidra ... 912-344-2669 120 D deirdra.dennie@armstrong.edu
DENNING, CSC, John, F ... 508-565-1301 237 A jdenning@stonehill.edu
DENNING, Rusty ... 864-941-8417 448 D denning.r@ptc.edu
DENNIS, Anne ... 515-643-6640 181 B adennis@mercydesmoines.org
DENNIS, Dana ... 440-375-7000 385 B ddennis@lec.edu
DENNIS, Dave, D ... 319-363-1323 181 D ddennis@mtmercy.edu
DENNIS, Diana ... 815-753-2111 154 I ddennis@niu.edu
DENNIS, Geoff ... 502-897-4566 199 D gdennis@sbts.edu
DENNIS, James, M ... 618-537-6936 152 C jdennis@mckendree.edu
DENNIS, Jason ... 706-399-3606 129 H jdennis@paine.edu
DENNIS, Jill ... 229-226-1621 132 E jdennis@thomasu.edu
DENNIS, Larry ... 850-644-5804 115 A ldennis@cci.fsu.edu
DENNIS, Lynn, M ... 863-680-4107 104 F ldennis@flsouthern.edu
DENNIS, Marie ... 215-567-7080 412 G mdennis@edmc.edu
DENNIS, Peggy ... 419-372-8495 377 I fayed@bgsu.edu
DENNIS, Raymond ... 310-338-5994.. 53 C Raymond.Dennis@lmu.edu
DENNIS, Roger, J ... 215-571-4755 417 E rjd45@drexel.edu
DENNIS, Sara ... 575-492-2103 314 D sdennis@usw.edu
DENNIS, Suzanne ... 718-780-0314 317 A suzanne.dennis@brooklaw.edu
DENNIS, Tenique ... 614-508-7246 383 L TDennis@hondros.edu
DENNIS, Terry ... 863-680-4148 104 F vdennis@flsouthern.edu
DENNIS, Yolanda ... 508-588-9100 232 A
DENNISON, Anne ... 207-699-5054 210 I adennison@meca.edu
DENNISON, Corley ... 304-558-0261 532 C cdennison@hepc.wvnet.edu
DENNISON, Wayne ... 812-877-8858 172 C dennison@rose-hulman.edu
DENNISTON, Marsha ... 605-331-6633 454 E marsha.denniston@usiouxfalls.edu
DENNISTON, Terry ... 423-425-4203 465 E terry-denniston@utc.edu
DENNY, Christopher ..... 734-462-4400 250 A cdenny@schoolcraft.edu
DENNY, David ... 503-699-6313 407 A ddenny@marylhurst.edu
DENNY, Richard ... 501-374-6305.. 23 A
DENON, Gregory ... 978-934-2418 229 A Gregory_Denon@uml.edu
DENSBERGER, Derek ... 714-556-3610.. 75 A ddensberger@vanguard.edu
DENSBERGER, Janelle .. 314-719-8057 275 B jdensberger@fontbonne.edu
DENSE, Angela ... 417-865-2815 274 L densea@evangel.edu
DENSLOW, Kathy ... 325-793-4903 478 D kdenslow@mcm.edu

DEVER-BUMBA, Maureen .... 843-661-8141 446 C maureen.dever-bumba@fdtc.edu
DEVEREAUX, Kent .... 603-623-0313 298 C kentdevereaux@nhia.edu
DEVEREAUX, Martin, C 561-237-7151 108 E mdevereaux@lynn.edu
DEVERES, Georgette ...... 909-621-8088.. 39 F georgette.deveres@cmc.edu
DEVERICKS, Lynne Marie .... 609-894-9311 306 B ldevericks@bcc.edu
DEVERS, James .... 570-941-6267 438 F james.devers@sranton.edu
DEVERS, Margo .... 814-838-7673 418 G mdevers@fortisinstitute.edu
DEVERS, Monica .... 320-308-4894 261 E mcdevers@stcloudstate.edu
DEVERSE, Nancy .... 360-538-4030 523 A ndeverse@ghc.edu
DEVERY, Dennis .... 609-777-5693 308 H ddevery@tesc.edu
DEVEYGA, Guillermo .... 201-200-3003 304 C gdeveyga@njcu.edu
DEVIER, David .... 269-467-9945 243 A ddevier@glenoaks.edu
DEVILBISS, Mark, B ...... 937-327-7808 395 I mdevilbiss@wittenberg.edu
DEVINCENTIS, Mark ...... 585-340-9501 321 G mdevincentis@crcds.edu
DEVINE, Dennis .... 406-771-5140 288 B dennis.devine@gfcmsu.edu
DEVINE, Dick .... 513-244-8452 379 I dick.devine@ccuniversity.edu
DEVINE, Flora, B .... 470-578-3562 127 M fdevine@kennesaw.edu
DEVINE, Linda, W .... 813-253-6203 118 H ldevine@ut.edu
DEVINE, Michelle .... 989-275-5000 245 C michelle.devine@kirtland.edu
DEVINE, Scott, W .... 240-895-4295 218 B swdevine@smcm.edu
DEVINE, Shawn .... 360-475-7106 524 H sdevine@olympic.edu
DEVINNE, Christine ...... 440-646-8101 394 G cdevinne@ursuline.edu
DEVINO, SJ, Terrence, P .... 617-552-3636 224 B terrence.devino.1@bc.edu
DEVITA, Elizabeth .... 912-201-8000 131 F edevita@southuniversity.edu
DEVITO, Paul, L .... 773-298-3191 158 F pdevito@sxu.edu
DEVITO, Rose, M .... 617-984-1620 235 H rdevito@quincycollege.edu
DEVITO, Scott .... 904-680-7741 103 K sdevito@fcsl.edu
DEVITO, William, J .... 215-951-1326 422 F devito@lasalle.edu
DEVITTO, John .... 704-272-5333 366 A jdevitto@spcc.edu
DEVIVO, Sharon, B .... 718-429-6600 352 A sharon.devivo@vaughn.edu
DEVLIN, Catherine .... 413-775-1147 231 E devlinc@gcc.mass.edu
DEVLIN, George, A .... 803-705-4417 443 F devling@benedict.edu
DEVLIN, Jeffrey, P .... 412-578-8741 414 I jpdevlin@carlow.edu
DEVLIN, Thomas, C ..... 510-642-3461.. 70 K tcd@berkeley.edu
DEVOL, Purva .... 815-802-8258 149 B pdevol@kcc.edu
DEVONO, Mary, K .... 304-457-6484 529 C devonomk@ab.edu
DEVORE, Cynthia .... 651-793-1466 259 E cynthia.devore@metrostate.edu
DEVORE, Debra .... 740-392-6868 387 B debra.devore@mvnu.edu
DEVORE, Leslie .... 217-234-5211 150 B ldevore@lakeland.cc.il.us
DEVOS, Ed .... 617-327-6777 238 D Ed_DeVos@williamjames.edu
DEVOS, Edward .... 617-327-6777 238 D edward_devos@williamjames.edu
DEVRIES, Lora .... 712-722-6422 177 J lora.devries@dordt.edu
DEVRIES, Samuel .... 303-797-5073.. 79 A samuel.devries@arapahoe.edu
DEVRIES, Susann .... 734-487-2475 242 J sdevries@emich.edu
DEW, John, R .... 334-670-3201... 8 A jrdew@troy.edu
DEW, Sara .... 231-591-2115 242 L SaraDew@ferris.edu
DEW, Wendi, M .... 407-582-3841 118 I wdew@valenciacollege.edu
DEWALD, Barb .... 712-707-7192 182 C bdewald@nwciowa.edu
DEWALD, Daryll .... 509-335-5540 528 B daryll.dewald@wsu.edu
DEWALD, Howard .... 740-593-2600 389 H dewald@ohio.edu
DEWALD, Marylou .... 602-749-5108 190 D marylou.dewald@ottawa.edu
DEWALT, Carol .... 603-668-6660 298 A
DEWALT, Marie .... 304-876-5299 532 I mdewalt@shepherd.edu
DEWALT, Michael .... 410-323-6211 214 G admissions@faiththeological.org
DEWAN, Craig .... 315-792-3393 351 G cpdewan@utica.edu
DEWAN, Susan .... 518-464-8673 325 B sdewan@excelsior.edu
DEWBERRY, Angela, B . 704-894-2227 356 D andewberry@davidson.edu
DEWBERRY, Mike .... 479-986-4084.. 22 B mdewberry@nwacc.edu
DEWBERRY, Thomas .... 541-683-5141 406 B cdewberry@gutenberg.edu
DEWBRE, Dane .... 806-716-2211 482 F ddewbre@southplainscollege.edu
DEWBRE, Jeri Ann .... 806-894-9611 482 F jdewbre@southplainscollege.edu
DEWEERDT, Daniel .... 414-288-4740 537 B daniel.deweerdt@marquette.edu
DEWEERTH, Jennifer ..... 315-731-5818 333 D jdeweerth@mvcc.edu
DEWEES, Bridget .... 803-535-5793 444 D bdewees@claflin.edu
DEWEES, Deborah .... 360-560-3353 528 D deborah.dewees@wwu.edu
DEWEES, Julie .... 309-298-1800 163 A jk-dewees@wiu.edu
DEWEESE, Kass .... 580-477-7769 404 D kass.deweese@wosc.edu
DEWEESE, Pamela .... 434-381-6205 513 E deweese@sbc.edu
DEWESE, Jerima .... 718-429-6600 352 A jerima.dewese@vaughn.edu
DEWEY, Alicia, M .... 315-786-2294 329 G adewey@sunyjefferson.edu
DEWEY, Barbara, I .... 814-865-0401 428 C bid1@psu.edu
DEWEY, Greg .... 518-694-7255 314 G greg.dewey@acphs.edu
DEWEY, Gwendolyn ...... 206-264-9100 519 I gwend@bgu.edu
DEWEY, Katie .... 918-540-6211 398 L katiebs@neo.edu
DEWEY, Phyllis, K .... 716-926-8930 327 F pdewey@hilbert.edu
DEWEY, Robin .... 410-386-4699 217 A rdewey@mcdaniel.edu
DEWEY, Susan .... 607-844-8222 350 A deweys@tc3.edu
DEWEY, Tyler .... 918-540-6272 398 L deweys@neo.edu
DEWIS, Rob .... 408-855-5327.. 76 E rob.dewis@wvm.edu
DEWITT, Bob .... 937-769-1852 376 L bdewitt@antioch.edu
DEWITT, Brenda, E .... 740-368-3329 390 B bedewitt@owu.edu
DEWITT, Dan .... 502-897-4555 199 D ddewitt@sbts.edu
DEWITT, David .... 301-784-5000 213 C ddewitt@allegany.edu
DEWITT, Deborah, S ..... 937-327-7001 395 I ddewitt@wittenberg.edu
DEWITT, John .... 214-379-5542 480 D jdewitt@pqc.edu
DEWITT, Megan .... 660-359-3948 279 L mdewitt@mail.ncmissouri.edu
DEWITT, Rhonda .... 425-739-8175 523 I rhonda.dewitt@lwtech.edu
DEWITT, Siobhan, K ..... 412-578-6651 414 I skdewitt@carlow.edu
DEWOLF, Dawn .... 541-463-5315 406 F dewolfd@lanecc.edu
DEWOLF, William .... 617-824-8655 226 A william_dewolf@emerson.edu
DEWOODY, Susan .... 828-669-8012 359 K sdewoody@montreat.edu
DEWSNUP, Vicky .... 801-622-1569 499 C vicky.dewsnup@stevenshenager.edu
DEXTER, Ann .... 781-891-2640 223 E adexter@bentley.edu
DEXTER, Brian .... 509-542-4727 521 C bdexter@columbiabasin.edu
DEXTER, Kathleen, A .... 207-621-3153 212 D dexter@maine.edu
DEXTER, Kimberly .... 508-215-5859 230 A kdexter@framingham.edu
DEXTER, Lena .... 251-580-2106.... 5 A lena.dexter@faulknerstate.edu
DEXTER-WILSON, Elizabeth .... 251-380-3470.... 7 F edexterwilson@shc.edu
DEY, Anita .... 989-964-7094 249 G adey@svsu.edu
DEY, Farouk .... 650-723-1983.. 68 G fdey@stanford.edu
DEY, Kate .... 415-703-9575.. 30 G kdey@cca.edu
DEYOUNG, Jamie .... 903-233-3800 477 G jamiedeyoung@letu.edu
DEYOUNG, Michael .... 702-968-2006 296 D mdeyoung@roseman.edu
DEYOUNG, Paul, D ...... 503-777-7290 409 E paul.deyoung@reed.edu
DEYOUNG, Renee .... 231-439-6347 248 A rdeyoung@ncmich.edu
DEZEMBER, Mary .... 575-835-5172 311 I dezember@nmt.edu
DEZIEL, David .... 603-428-2417 298 B ddeziel@nec.edu
DEZIEL, Lisa .... 954-262-1387 109 E lisad@nova.edu
DEZIEL, Marissa .... 828-398-2500 368 I
DHAKAR, Vandana .... 603-206-8152 297 A vdhakar@ccsnh.edu
DHALIWAL, Jasbir .... 901-678-5402 462 B jdhaliwl@memphis.edu
DHANIE, Julianna .... 312-944-0882 150 D jdhanie@chicago.chefs.edu
DHANKHER, Veena .... 413-552-2543 231 F vdhankher@hcc.edu
DHANWADA, Kavita, R . 319-273-2518 176 A Kavita.Dhanwada@uni.edu
DHAWAN, Atam, P .... 973-596-8566 304 D atam.dhawan@njit.edu
DHILLON, Upinder, S ... 607-777-2314 343 D dhillon@binghamton.edu
DHILLON, Vineeta .... 707-654-1283.. 34 B vdhillon@csum.edu
DHIR, Krishna .... 808-932-7272 135 I kdhir@hawaii.edu
DHIR, Vijay, K .... 310-825-8507.. 71 D vdhir@seas.ucla.edu
DI DIO, Stephen .... 718-631-6044 320 F sdidio@qcc.cuny.edu
DI DONATO, Ana .... 352-588-8992 111 L ana.didonato@saintleo.edu
DI FAVA, John .... 617-252-1703 233 C
DI GUILIO, Raymond ... 916-484-8484.. 52 I diguilr@arc.losrios.edu
DI LALLA, Heather .... 610-892-1514 429 M hdilalla@pit.edu
DI LELLO, Joseph .... 914-968-6200 341 D Joseph.DiLello@archny.org
DI LULLO, Trish .... 256-233-8184.... 1 F trish.dilullo@athens.edu
DI MARE, Lesley .... 719-549-2951.. 81 F presidentsoffice@csupueblo.edu
DI MARIA, David .... 406-994-7150 287 G
DI NARDI, Jason .... 914-594-4668 335 H jason_dinardi@nymc.edu
DI NUCCI, Jo Ellen ...... 208-426-1200 137 E jedinucc@boisestate.edu
DI PASQUALE, Ray, M . 401-825-2188 441 C rmdipasquale@ccri.edu
DI SANTO, Dusty .... 630-752-5490 163 G Dusty.DiSanto@wheaton.edu
DIAB, Dorey .... 419-755-4811 387 E ddiab@ncstatecollege.edu
DIACHUN, Elizabeth ..... 661-722-6300.. 27 P ediachun@avc.edu
DIACON, Todd .... 330-672-8529 384 H tdiacon@kent.edu
DIACONT, Matthew .... 410-644-6400 218 G
DIAH, Max .... 516-773-5000 548 I diahm@usmma.edu
DIAL, Bill .... 303-914-6298.. 85 C bill.dial@rrcc.edu
DIAL, Eugene, A .... 985-448-4021 208 C eugene.dial@nicholls.edu
DIAL, Janet .... 323-343-3060.. 34 A jdial@calstatela.edu
DIAL, Miqueas .... 408-741-4619.. 76 F miqueas.dial@westvalley.edu
DIALS, Julie .... 859-572-5487 199 A dialsj1@nku.edu
DIAMANDOPOULOS, Kathy .... 610-282-1100 416 I kathy.diamandopoulos@desales.edu
DIAMOND, Christopher, R .... 860-832-1934.. 88 D diamondchr@ccsu.edu
DIAMOND, Fred .... 626-914-8691.. 38 L fdiamond@citruscollege.edu
DIAMOND, Holly .... 313-845-9887 243 I hadiamond@hfcc.edu
DIAMOND, John, N .... 207-581-1138 212 C
DIAMOND, Linda .... 336-517-2109 354 K ldiamond@bennett.edu
DIAMOND, Michael .... 706-721-6900 121 C mdiamond@gru.edu
DIAMOND, Raymond, T .... 225-578-8846 205 E ray.diamond@law.lsu.edu
DIAMOND BURROWAY, Sarah .... 606-326-2106 195 H sdiamondburrowa0001@kctc.edu
DIAMOND-ROTHSTEIN, Katherine .... 610-359-2791 416 G kdiamond@dccc.edu
DIANGELO, JR., Joseph, A .... 610-660-1645 434 G jodiange@sju.edu
DIAS, James .... 518-956-8170 343 C jdias@albany.edu
DIAS, Margaret, S .... 508-999-8791 228 H mdias@umassd.edu
DIAS, Orsete .... 212-247-3434 331 G odias@mandl.edu
DIAS, Robert .... 408-270-6400.. 63 O robert.dias@sjeccd.org
DIAZ, Alfred .... 787-725-8120 552 G adiaz@eap.edu
DIAZ, Alphonso, V .... 703-284-3847 510 B al.diaz@marymount.edu
DIAZ, Amy .... 815-921-4283 157 B a.diaz@rockvalleycollege.edu
DIAZ, Andrea .... 814-332-3100 411 F adiaz@allegheny.edu
DIAZ, Arelis .... 787-753-6335 552 K adiaz@icprjc.edu
DIAZ, Armando .... 210-567-0372 495 B diaza@uthscsa.edu
DIAZ, Brett .... 787-844-8181 558 D brett.diaz@upr.edu
DIAZ, Emiliano .... 916-278-3901.. 34 E diaze@csus.edu
DIAZ, Ester .... 219-473-4388 165 A ediaz@ccsj.edu
DIAZ, Francisco .... 973-720-3244 309 I diazf@wpunj.edu
DIAZ, Franco, L .... 787-284-1912 554 B fldiaz@ponce.inter.edu
DIAZ, Glenda .... 787-863-2390 553 I glenda.diaz@fajardo.inter.edu
DIAZ, Jackie .... 254-710-3805 469 D jackie_diaz@baylor.edu
DIAZ, Janet .... 313-883-8696 249 E diaz.janet@shms.edu
DIAZ, Jerry .... 787-850-9367 558 A jerry.diaz2@upr.edu
DIAZ, Jesus, A .... 787-751-0178 555 K ac_jdiaz@suagm.edu
DIAZ, Joel .... 805-986-5810.. 75 D jdiaz@vcccd.edu
DIAZ, Jorge, L .... 787-786-3030 556 E jdiaz@ucb.edu.pr
DIAZ, Josem .... 563-425-5231 183 G diazj93@uiu.edu
DIAZ, Leticia, M .... 321-206-5602.. 99 B ldiaz@barry.edu
DIAZ, Luis, R .... 787-751-0160 551 K lrdiaz@cmpr.pr.gov
DIAZ, Maria, S .... 787-257-7373 555 L ue_mdiaz@suagm.edu
DIAZ, Mario .... 312-850-7492 142 E mdiaz103@ccc.edu
DIAZ, Mark .... 305-284-2862 118 A markdiaz@miami.edu
DIAZ, Mauro .... 818-767-0888.. 77 G mauro.diaz@woodbury.edu
DIAZ, Mayra .... 787-993-8897 557 E mayra.diaz2@upr.edu
DIAZ, Mayra, E .... 787-725-8120 552 G mediaz@eap.edu
DIAZ, Minerva .... 787-738-2161 557 G minerva.diaz@upr.edu
DIAZ, Mischelle, R .... 512-448-8404 481 B mischeld@stedwards.edu
DIAZ, Ramonita .... 787-878-5475 553 F rdiaz@arecibo.inter.edu
DIAZ, Ricardo .... 787-850-9375 558 A ricardo.diaz6@upr.edu
DIAZ, Robert .... 212-220-8305 318 D rdiaz@bmcc.cuny.edu
DIAZ, Roberto .... 215-717-3107 416 E roberto.diaz@curtis.edu
DIAZ, Russell .... 845-848-4048 324 B russell.diaz@dc.edu
DIAZ, Sam .... 570-504-9069 415 E sdiaz@tcmc.edu
DIAZ, Sharon, C .... 510-869-6512.. 61 J sdiaz@samuelmerritt.edu
DIAZ, Sonia .... 787-728-1515 559 A sdiaz@sagrado.edu
DIAZ, Sylvia .... 631-451-4486 348 E diazs@sunysuffolk.edu
DIAZ, Veronica .... 310-434-4224.. 65 B diaz_veronica@smc.edu
DIAZ, Walter .... 860-465-5000.. 88 E diazw@easternct.edu
DIAZ, Walter .... 956-665-3551 494 C diazwr@utpa.edu
DIAZ, Zaida .... 787-257-0199 557 F zaida.diaz@upr.edu

DIAZ-ALONSO, Hernan . 213-613-2200.. 67 G
hernan@sciarc.edu
DIAZ BONACQUISTI, Judi .... 303-352-3074.. 81 J
judi.diazbonacquisti@ccd.edu
DIAZ-DIAZ, Claribel ..... 787-622-8000 556 H
dadiaz@pupr.edu
DIAZ-HERRERA, Jorge, L .... 315-279-5201 329 K
jdiazh@keuka.edu
DIAZ MORALES, Anita .. 847-578-3238 157 G
anita.diazmorales@rosalindfranklin.edu
DIAZ-RIOS, Erika .... 787-250-0000 557 B
erika.diaz1@upr.edu
DIAZ-RODRIGUEZ, Nereida .... 787-798-6732 556 F
nereida.diaz@uccaribe.edu
DIAZ-RODRIGUEZ, Victor .... 787-250-0000 557 B
victor.diaz@upr.edu
DIAZ SEMPRIT, Ruth, M .... 787-763-6700 552 H
rmdiaz@se-pr.edu
DIAZ-TORRES, Marie .... 973-353-5372 307 C
mdtorres@newark.rutgers.edu
DIBB, Andrew M, T ...... 267-502-2582 413 C
andrew.dibb@brynathyn.edu
DIBBERT, Douglas, S ... 919-962-7050 371 A
doug_dibbert@unc.edu
DIBBLE, Deborah, A ..... 716-673-3131 343 F
deborah.dibble@fredonia.edu
DIBELLA, Jeannette ...... 603-206-8006 297 A
jdibella@ccsnh.edu
DIBELLO, Nan, M .... 716-686-7800 348 A
nan.dibello@esc.edu
DIBENEDETTO, Eileen, M .... 212-854-7732 315 J
edibened@barnard.edu
DIBENEDETTO, Steve .... 847-947-5409 153 H
steve.dibenedetto@nl.edu
DIBERT, Cregg .... 814-262-3837 429 K
cdibert@pennhighlands.edu
DIBIASIO, Daniel, A ..... 419-772-2030 388 I
d-dibiasio@onu.edu
DIBISCEGLIE, Lisa .... 732-255-0400 304 E
ldibisceglie@ocean.edu
DIBLEY, Paula .... 704-216-3467 365 F
paula.dibley@rccc.edu
DIBRIGIDA, Vladimir .... 303-329-6355.. 81 B
director@cstcm.edu
DIBRITO, Kyle, J .... 717-736-4117 420 D
kjdibrit@hacc.edu
DICAPRIO, Deborah, A . 845-575-3000 331 L
deborah.dicaprio@marist.edu
DICARLO, Joseph .... 508-929-8090 230 G
jdicarlo1@worcester.edu
DICARO, David .... 585-385-8025 340 F
ddicaro@sjfc.edu
DICARO, Kim .... 313-496-2625 252 A
kdicaro1@wcccd.edu
DICE, Douglas .... 989-463-7162 239 B
dice@alma.edu
DICESARE, Deborah, A . 818-778-5522.. 52 B
dicesad@lavc.edu
DICHRISTINA, Joseph ... 860-297-2000.. 92 A
DICK, Dan .... 847-628-2086 149 A
daniel.dick@judsonu.edu
DICK, Lianna .... 254-867-2346 488 B
lianna.dick@tstc.edu
DICK, Melissa .... 724-357-2550 431 A
m.l.dick@iup.edu
DICK, Steve .... 407-869-7387 106 H
DICKENS, Brian, K .... 713-313-1379 487 F
dickensbk@tsu.edu
DICKENS, John, V .... 860-444-8480 548 H
john.v.dickens@uscg.mil
DICKENS, Linda, N .... 512-232-2646 493 M
linda.dickens@austin.utexas.edu
DICKENS, Margaret, A .. 715-833-6419 542 M
mdickens@cvtc.edu
DICKENS, Reginald ...... 704-216-6025 358 I
rdickens@livingstone.edu
DICKENS, Robert, I .... 210-458-4060 494 D
ROBERT.DICKENS@UTSA.EDU
DICKENS, Ross, N .... 731-881-7225 465 F
rdicken2@utm.edu
DICKENS, Susan .... 651-779-3298 258 D
susan.dickens@century.edu
DICKENS, Tony .... 419-720-6670 390 I
tdickens@proskills.edu
DICKER, James .... 215-204-3486 436 C
james.dicker@temple.edu
DICKERMAN, Christopher, M .... 610-359-5302 416 G
cdickerman@dccc.edu
DICKERMAN, Robert ..... 413-755-4606 233 B
dickerman@stcc.edu
DICKERSON, Aerial .... 912-279-4514 123 B
adickerson@ccga.edu
DICKERSON, Beverly .... 870-245-5299.. 22 C
DICKERSON, Cathy, S .. 540-375-2262 512 B
cdickerson@roanoke.edu
DICKERSON, Charlene .. 803-793-5134 445 F
dickersonc@denmarktech.edu
DICKERSON, Darby .... 806-742-3990 489 F
DICKERSON, Dee Ann .. 918-647-1300 397 C
ddickerson@carlalbert.edu
DICKERSON, John .... 662-325-2663 269 A
jdickerson@registrar.msstate.edu
DICKERSON, John, R ... 662-325-2663 269 A
jdickerson@registrar.msstate.edu
DICKERSON, Larry .... 816-802-3363 276 F
ldickerson@kcai.edu
DICKERSON, Leslie .... 406-496-4879 288 C
ldickerson@mtech.edu
DICKERSON, Mark .... 626-387-5763.. 29 B
mdickerson@apu.edu
DICKERSON, Mary Ann 913-469-8500 188 E
mdkerson@jccc.edu
DICKERSON, Shirley ..... 936-468-4109 484 A
sdickerson@sfasu.edu
DICKERT, Gerry .... 409-984-6342 488 H
dickertgl@lamarpa.edu
DICKES, David .... 605-668-4020 452 I
david.dickes@mtmc.edu
DICKEY, Daryl .... 678-839-6534 133 F
ddickey@westga.edu
DICKEY, Janie .... 407-277-0311 102 N
jdickey@evergladesuniversity.edu
DICKEY, M. Thaxter ...... 813-988-5131 103 L
dickeyt@floridacollege.edu
DICKEY, Marilyn .... 850-201-6652 117 B
dickeym@tcc.fl.edu
DICKEY, Matt .... 417-626-1234 280 B
dickey.matt@occ.edu
DICKEY, Todd, R .... 213-740-8184.. 74 D
svpadmin@usc.edu
DICKEY, Wanda .... 813-988-5131 103 L
library@floridacollege.edu
DICKEY, Wyman .... 904-269-7086 105 G
wdickey@fortiscollege.edu
DICKHERBER, David ..... 636-949-4907 276 L
ddickherber@lindenwood.edu
DICKINSON, Carl .... 315-279-5204 329 K
cdickinson@keuka.edu
DICKINSON, J. Barry .... 267-341-3373 420 K
bdickinson@holyfamily.edu
DICKINSON, Marjorie, M .... 530-752-2619.. 71 A
mmdickinson@ucdavis.edu
DICKINSON, Maureen ... 309-341-5327 140 I
mdickinson@sandburg.edu
DICKINSON, Michele .... 718-518-4284 319 D
mdickinson@hostos.cuny.edu
DICKINSON, Robyn, L .. 570-941-5816 438 F
robyn.dickinson@scranton.edu
DICKINSON, Rosie, A ... 956-326-2202 485 B
rosie@tamiu.edu
DICKINSON NEIL, Terri 509-527-2632 528 A
rosa.jimenez@wallawalla.edu
DICKMAN, Ellen .... 636-227-2100 277 A
ellen.dickman@logan.edu
DICKMAN, Tom .... 301-696-3494 215 E
dickman@hood.edu
DICKMEYER, Nathan ..... 718-482-6119 320 B
ndickmeyer@lagcc.cuny.edu
DICKS, Gary .... 979-230-3305 469 G
gary.dicks@brazosport.edu
DICKS, Karin .... 512-448-8405 481 B
karind@stedwards.edu
DICKSON, Betty .... 501-370-5237.. 22 E
bdickson@philander.edu
DICKSON, Brook, E ...... 540-362-6287 508 D
bdickson@hollins.edu
DICKSON, Carol .... 802-586-7711 503 B
cdickson@sterlingcollege.edu
DICKSON, Chris, M ...... 260-422-5561 167 F
cmdickson@indianatech.edu
DICKSON, John .... 727-873-4350 116 C
jdickson@mail.usf.edu
DICKSON, Kari .... 806-743-2946 490 A
kari.dickson@ttuhsc.edu
DICKSON, Kevin .... 573-651-2513 282 C
kdickson@semo.edu
DICKSON, Richard, P ... 504-865-5500 207 F
rpd@tulane.edu
DICKSON, Risa, E .... 808-956-3872 135 H
risad@hawaii.edu
DICKSON, Shannon ...... 916-691-7738.. 52 J
dicksos@crc.losrios.edu
DICOCCO, Andrea .... 617-912-9108 224 C
adicocco@bostonconservatory.edu
DICOLA, Rose Ann .... 412-237-6517 415 G
rdicola@ccac.edu
DICORLETO, Paul, E ..... 330-672-3000 384 H
DICOSTANZO, Elina ...... 910-755-8517 360 E
dicostanzoe@brunswickcc.edu
DIDIER, Kim .... 515-965-7064 177 B
kmdidier@dmacc.edu
DIDION, John .... 714-480-7489.. 60 F
didion_john@rsccd.edu
DIDION, Judy .... 419-517-8905 385 F
jdidion@lourdes.edu
DIDLAKE, Ralph, H .... 601-984-5009 270 H
rdidlake@umc.edu
DIDOMIZIO, Joseph ...... 716-896-0700 352 B
jdidomizio@villa.edu
DIDONATO, Joseph ...... 617-262-5000 223 G
Joseph.Didonato@the-bac.edu
DIEBOLD, Alain .... 315-792-7100 348 D
adiebold@sunycnse.com
DIEBOLD, Ann .... 610-519-4560 439 A
ann.diebold@villanova.edu
DIECKMAN, Stacy .... 402-844-7288 292 G
stacyd@northeast.edu
DIECKMEYER, Diane ..... 951-372-7199.. 61 A
diane.dieckmeyer@norcocollege.edu
DIEDERICH, Susan .... 713-646-1800 482 H
sdiederich@stcl.edu
DIEDRCHS, Carol, P ..... 614-292-6151 389 A
diedrichs.1@0osu.edu
DIEDRIECH, Dan .... 573-592-4220 286 A
daniel.diedriech@williamwoods.edu
DIEFENDORF, Wendy ... 518-244-2443 340 A
diefew@sage.edu
DIEGO, Elizabeth, A ..... 671-735-5506 549 E
elizabeth.diego@guamcc.edu
DIEHL, Bert .... 440-525-7140 385 C
rdiehl@lakelandcc.edu
DIEHL, Dave .... 301-696-3800 215 E
diehld@hood.edu
DIEHL, Hope, L .... 610-359-5333 416 G
hdiehl@dccc.edu
DIEHL, Joan .... 570-348-6248 425 D
1226mgr@fheg.follett.com
DIEHL, Melissa, M .... 570-577-3776 413 E
melissa.diehl@bucknell.edu
DIEHL, Michele .... 215-646-7300 420 A
diehl.m@gmercyu.edu
DIEHL, Randy, L .... 512-471-4141 493 M
diehl@austin.utexas.edu
DIEHL, Shanda .... 360-992-2421 521 A
sdiehl@clark.edu
DIEHL, Timothy .... 207-725-3716 209 H
tdiehl@bowdoin.edu
DIEKER, R. Joseph .... 319-895-4210 177 A
jdieker@cornellcollege.edu
DIEKMANN, Beth .... 507-285-7259 261 D
beth.diekmann@rctc.edu
DIEL-HUNT, Sarah .... 309-268-8593 145 H
sarah.dielhunt@heartland.edu
DIEM, Carol .... 206-543-6285 527 G
cdiem@uw.edu
DIEM, Richard, A .... 210-458-6463 494 D
richard.diem@utsa.edu
DIEMER, Gregory, M ..... 715-346-2641 541 A
gdiemer@uwsp.edu
DIEMER, Rene .... 215-248-6305 424 G
registrar@ltsp.edu
DIEMER, Robert .... 352-588-8974 111 L
robert.diemer@saintleo.edu
DIENER, Melissa .... 920-686-6146 539 A
Melissa.Diener@sl.edu
DIENGER, Rebecca, J .... 715-836-4423 539 E
diengerj@uwec.edu
DIENST, Tom .... 907-796-6497.. 11 A
tom.dienst@uas.alaska.edu
DIEPA, Evelyn .... 305-222-2812 103 F
ediepa@careercollege.edu
DIEPENBROCK, Amy ..... 210-436-3102 481 C
adiepenbrock@stmarytx.edu
DIERENFIELD, Bruce, J 716-888-2683 317 H
derenfb@canisius.edu
DIERINGER, Deanna, L . 907-474-6629.. 10 I
dldieringer@alaska.edu
DIERINGER, Dennis, D . 770-484-1204 128 D
lutherrice@lutherrice.edu
DIERINGER, Jerry, T ..... 410-704-2516 221 A
jdieringer@towson.edu
DIERKS, David, R .... 319-335-3305 175 H
david-dierks@uiowa.edu
DIERLAM, Lois .... 914-337-9300 323 A
lois.dierlam@concordia-ny.edu
DIERMEIER, Daniel .... 773-702-9623 161 D
ddiermeier@uchicago.edu
DIERS, Jane .... 217-544-6464 158 E
jane.diers@stjohnscollegespringfield.edu
DIESNER, Michael, R .... 717-867-6231 423 I
diesner@lvc.edu
DIETERICH, Scott .... 718-409-7200 348 C
DIETERLY, Catherine ..... 510-567-6174.. 69 D
cdieterly@sum.edu
DIETERLY, Don .... 510-567-6174.. 69 D
ddieterly@sum.edu
DIETRICH, David .... 330-287-1203 389 B
dietrich.114@osu.edu
DIETRICH, Julie .... 610-499-4190 439 G
jdietrich@mail.widener.edu
DIETRICH, Kim, E .... 260-399-7700 174 C
kdietrich@sf.edu
DIETRICH, Robert .... 617-373-4827 235 D
DIETRICH, Robert, C .... 570-326-3761 429 J
rdietric@pct.edu
DIETRICH, Robin .... 540-887-7025 510 A
rdietrich@mbc.edu
DIETRICH, Sandra .... 919-866-5674 366 H
sldietrich@waketech.edu
DIETZ, Carol, P .... 216-397-4314 384 F
cdietz@jcu.edu
DIETZ, Fred, K .... 270-809-2684 198 I
fdietz@murraystate.edu
DIETZ, Jonathan .... 620-792-9281 184 I
dietzj@bartonccc.edu
DIETZ, Kenneth .... 502-852-6176 201 A
kenneth.dietz@louisville.edu
DIETZ, Larry .... 309-438-5451 147 I
ldietz@ilstu.edu
DIETZ, Sally .... 607-274-3385 328 H
sdietz@ithaca.edu
DIETZ, Tim .... 309-672-4946 152 E
tdietz@methodistcol.edu
DIETZEL, Kristin, A .... 563-556-5110 181 F
dietzelk@nicc.edu
DIETZLER, Deborah .... 502-852-7155 201 A
d0diet02@louisville.edu
DIETZMAN, Cheryl, L ... 607-746-4502 347 G
dietzmcl@delhi.edu
DIETZMAN, Steve .... 520-325-0123.. 17 Q
sdietzman@suva.edu
DIEZ, Louis .... 865-981-8197 458 E
louis.diez@maryvillecollege.edu
DIEZ, Mickey .... 337-482-6287 208 F
mickey.diez@louisiana.edu
DIEZ ROUX, Ana, V .... 215-571-4013 417 E
ana.v.diezroux@drexel.edu
DIFFENDERFER, Jason .. 914-633-2373 328 F
jdiffenderfer@iona.edu
DIFFENDERFER, Pete .... 541-684-7441 407 I
pdiffenderfer@nwcu.edu
DIFFEY, Stephanie .... 662-472-9101 267 E
scdiffey@holmescc.edu
DIFFEY, Steve .... 662-472-9068 267 E
sdiffey@holmescc.edu
DIFFIE, Rita Nell .... 432-685-4503 478 F
rndiffie@midland.edu
DIFFILY, Michael, E ...... 603-577-6000 297 F
diffily@dwc.edu
DIFOLCO PARKER, Jane .... 334-844-4000.... 1 G
jdp0035@auburn.edu
DIFRANCESCO, Paul ..... 617-732-2299 233 E
paul.difrancesco@mcphs.edu
DIFRANCO, Heidi .... 803-641-3397 450 C
heidid@usca.edu
DIFRONZO-HEITZER, Nicola .... 610-647-4400 421 B
ndifronzoheitzer@immaculata.edu
DIGATE, Russell, J .... 718-990-6411 340 G
digater@stjohns.edu
DIGENNARO, John .... 440-826-2228 377 D
jdigenna@bw.edu
DIGERLANDO, Rose ...... 847-214-7635 144 F
rdigerlando@elgin.edu
DIGGS, Mawine .... 313-579-6931 252 A
mdiggs1@wcccd.edu
DIGGS, Michael .... 217-875-7200 156 K
mdiggs@richland.edu
DIGGS, Ron .... 405-878-5611 402 A
rwdiggs@stgregorys.edu
DIGIACOMO, Mary Clare .... 706-583-2760 120 G
mcdigiacomo@athenstech.edu
DIGIANFILIPPO, Denise 602-787-6693.. 15 B
denise.digianfilippo@paradisevalley.edu
DIGIOACCHINO, Dominic .... 973-803-5000 305 A
ddigioacchino@pillar.edu
DIGIRONIMO, Joseph .. 215-468-8800 421 J
director@culinaryarts.edu
DIGMAN, Jo-Ann .... 314-539-5358 281 H
jdigman1@stlcc.edu
DIGMAN, Sally, H .... 304-326-1247 530 G
sdigman@salemu.edu
DIGRANES, Jo Lynn ..... 405-208-5047 400 A
jadigranes@okcu.edu
DIGRAZIA, Lauren .... 860-486-3903.. 92 C
lauren.digrazia@uconn.edu
DIGREGORIO, Christian, M .... 570-348-6234 425 D
digregorio@marywood.edu
DIGREGORIO, Theresa . 716-614-6430 336 D
digregor@niagaracc.suny.edu
DIGREORIO, Jeffrey ...... 510-849-8283.. 46 E
jdigreorio@gtu.edu
DIGUISEPPE, Steven, A 717-871-7500 431 E
steve.diguiseppe@millersville.edu
DIJULIA, Dominick, J ... 610-660-1707 434 G
ddijulia@sju.edu
DIKEMAN, Scott .... 802-468-1214 503 G
scott.dikeman@castleton.edu

DILALLA, David ... 618-536-5535 159 H
ddilalla@siu.edu
DILANDO, Armand ... 617-254-2610 236 B
armand.dilando@sjs.edu
DILAURO, Nanette ... 212-854-2154 315 J
ndilauro@barnard.edu
DILBECK, Jack ... 270-706-8892 195 K
jdilbeck0001@kctcs.edu
DILENO, Susan, R ... 740-368-3028 390 B
srdileno@owu.edu
DILEO, Jeffrey ... 361-570-4201 492 A
dileoj@uhv.edu
DILES, David, L ... 540-464-7251 518 A
dilesdl@vmi.edu
DILGER, Patrick ... 203-392-6586.. 88 F
dilgerp1@southernct.edu
DILIBERTO, James, G ... 631-691-8733 328 G
dilibertoj@idti.edu
DILIBERTO, John, G ... 631-691-8733 328 G
johng@idti.edu
DILL, Amy ... 540-665-4513 512 E
adill@su.edu
DILL, April ... 580-477-7710 404 D
april.dill@wosc.edu
DILL, Bonnie, T ... 301-405-2095 219 D
btdill@umd.edu
DILL, Herb ... 440-375-7555 385 B
hdill@lec.edu
DILL, Jeremy ... 207-741-5821 211 D
jdill@smccme.edu
DILL, Ken ... 864-644-5431 449 B
kdill@swu.edu
DILL, Marian ... 423-614-8304 457 M
mdill@leeuniversity.edu
DILL, Randy, G ... 208-732-6600 137 K
rdill@csi.edu
DILL, Stephen ... 617-879-2355 238 C
sdill@wheelock.edu
DILL, Tracy ... 218-755-4022 258 B
tdill@bemidjistate.edu
DILLABOUGH,
Daniel, J ... 619-260-2247.. 74 B
dillaboughd@sandiego.edu
DILLANE, Robert, J ... 717-867-6060 423 I
dillane@lvc.edu
DILLARD, Abigail ... 913-288-7471 188 G
adillard@kckcc.edu
DILLARD, III, Ben, P ... 843-661-8000 446 C
ben.dillard@fdtc.edu
DILLARD, Gail ... 229-391-4782 119 F
gdillard@abac.edu
DILLARD, Glenn ... 501-279-4407.. 21 A
gdillard@harding.edu
DILLARD, Helene ... 530-752-1605.. 71 A
hrdillard@ucdavis.edu
DILLARD, Marilyn ... 601-403-1201 270 A
mdillard@prcc.edu
DILLARD, Paulette ... 919-546-8595 368 G
pdillard@shawu.edu
DILLBECK, Michael ... 641-472-1187 181 A
sdillbeck@mum.edu
DILLBECK, Susan ... 641-472-1187 181 A
sdillbeck@mum.edu
DILLE, Elizabeth, M ... 864-938-3705 448 E
emdille@presby.edu
DILLE, Wayne ... 641-628-5268 176 E
dille@central.edu
DILLENBERG, Jack ... 480-219-6081 271 G
jdillenberg@atsu.edu
DILLENBURG, Brenda ... 715-389-7011 543 D
brenda.dillenburg@mstc.edu
DILLER, Donna ... 505-224-4000 310 F
ddiller@cnm.edu
DILLER, Lisa, C ... 423-236-2417 460 K
ldiller@southern.edu
DILLER, Matthew ... 212-636-6875 326 C
DILLEY, Darlene ... 801-832-2206 501 C
ddilley@westminstercollege.edu
DILLIHAY, Adam ... 803-765-6023 443 D
adillihay@allenuniversity.edu
DILLINGHAM, Christine 620-276-9642 187 D
christine.dillingham@gcccks.edu
DILLINGHAM, Martin ... 615-383-4848 466 F
mdillingham@watkins.edu
DILLINGHAM, Sabine ... 240-895-4192 218 B
sldillingham@smcm.edu
DILLINGHAM, Tom ... 931-393-1756 463 B
tdillingham@mscc.edu
DILLION, Brennan ... 818-333-3558.. 56 A
DILLION, Diana ... 605-856-2355 453 B
diana.dillion@sintegleska.edu
DILLMAN, Joanna ... 985-732-6640 203 I
DILLMAN, Stephen ... 617-745-3558 225 H
stephen.dillman@enc.edu
DILLON, Anastacia ... 503-768-7095 406 H
adillon@lclark.edu
DILLON, Andrew, P ... 512-471-3821 493 M
adillon@ischool.utexas.edu
DILLON, Clotilde ... 212-594-4000 349 J
cdillon@tcicollege.edu

DILLON, III, Cyrus, I ... 434-223-6197 508 B
cdillon@hsc.edu
DILLON, Ellen, M ... 308-635-6787 294 C
dillone@wncc.edu
DILLON, Francis, X ... 508-565-1344 237 A
fdillon@stonehill.edu
DILLON, Glen ... 304-293-7206 533 D
ghdillon@hsc.wvu.edu
DILLON, Greg ... 765-658-4500 165 G
gdillon@depauw.edu
DILLON, James, S ... 717-720-4100 430 A
jdillon@passhe.edu
DILLON, Jennifer, A ... 216-397-1976 384 F
jdillon@jcu.edu
DILLON, John ... 610-683-4002 431 B
dillon@kutztown.edu
DILLON, Katherine, E ... 914-594-4527 335 H
katherine_dillion@nymc.edu
DILLON, Kendall ... 515-271-1661 177 H
kendall.dillon@dmu.edu
DILLON, Mary Ellen ... 704-922-6475 362 G
dillon.maryellen@gaston.edu
DILLON, Mary Jane ... 904-819-6314 102 P
dillonmj@flagler.edu
DILLON, Michael ... 423-636-7300 464 F
mdillon@tusculum.edu
DILLON, Mike ... 573-592-1632 286 A
mike.dillon@williamwoods.edu
DILLON, Patricia ... 215-951-1430 422 F
dillonp@lasalle.edu
DILLON, Paul ... 201-360-4631 303 A
pdillon@hccc.edu
DILLON, Rick ... 304-384-5231 532 E
rdillon@concord.edu
DILLON, Sarah ... 715-675-3331 544 A
Dillon@ntc.edu
DILLON, T. Kevin ... 713-500-3535 495 A
kevin.dillon@uth.tmc.edu
DILLOW, Al ... 217-245-3162 146 D
al.dillow@mail.ic.edu
DILLOW, Rhonda ... 618-634-3251 159 A
rhondad@shawneecc.edu
DILLS, Amanda ... 405-208-5584 400 A
aldills@okcu.edu
DILLSWORTH, Gary ... 716-926-8920 327 F
gdillsworth@hilbert.edu
DILMORE, Donald, H ... 814-732-2779 430 G
ddilmore@edinboro.edu
DILORENZO, Peter ... 856-227-7200 301 A
pdilorenzo@camdencc.edu
DILORENZO, Thomas ... 701-777-2167 373 G
thomas.dilorenzo@und.edu
DILORENZO, Vicki ... 518-694-7331 314 G
vicki.dilorenzo@acphs.edu
DILS, Keith ... 724-738-2292 432 A
keith.dils@sru.edu
DILUCA, Susan, A ... 502-895-3411 198 E
sdiluca@lpts.edu
DILUSTRO, John ... 252-398-6220 356 B
dilusj@chowan.edu
DIMAGGIO,
Jacqueline, R ... 864-250-8179 446 H
jacqui.dimaggio@gvltec.edu
DIMAGGIO, Mark ... 760-744-1150.. 58 D
mdimaggio@palomar.edu
DIMAGNO, Teresa ... 617-573-8483 237 B
tdimagno@suffolk.edu
DIMAIO, Amy ... 408-453-9900.. 46 L
adimaio@henley-putnam.edu
DIMAIO, Judith ... 516-686-7594 335 F
jdimaio@nyit.edu
DIMARCO, Casey ... 518-694-7278 314 G
casey.dimarco@acphs.edu
DIMARCO, Erin ... 302-356-6924.. 94 G
erin.j.dimarco@wilmu.edu
DIMARCO, Paul, B ... 757-446-5099 507 B
dimarcpb@evms.edu
DIMARCO, Scott, R ... 570-662-4689 431 D
sdimarco@mansfield.edu
DIMARIA, Karen ... 973-300-2124 308 F
kdimaria@sussex.edu
DIMARIO, Joseph, X ... 847-578-8633 157 G
joseph.dimario@rosalindfranklin.edu
DIMARZO, Dawn ... 619-388-7681.. 62 H
ddimarzo@sdccd.edu
DIMARZO, Dean ... 845-569-3219 333 I
dean.dimarzo@msmc.edu
DIMASI, Louis ... 802-654-2566 502 H
ldimasi@smcvt.edu
DIMASI, William ... 973-278-5400 300 C
wsd@berkeleycollege.edu
DIMASI, William ... 973-278-5400 316 D
wsd@berkeleycollege.edu
DIMATTIA, Andrea ... 570-504-9634 415 E
adimattia@tcmc.edu
DIMAURO, JR., Alfred ... 508-831-6678 238 G
fred@wpi.edu
DIMAURO, Giorgio, G ... 848-932-7787 307 B
gdimauro@gaiacenters.rutgers.edu
DIMAURO, Michael ... 317-813-691 327 G
dimauro@hws.edu

DIMENT, Gregory, S ... 269-337-7149 244 I
Greg.Diment@kzoo.edu
DIMICK, Jeffrey, A ... 304-865-6131 530 F
jeffrey.dimick@ovu.edu
DIMING, Mianta' ... 219-980-6620 168 C
mdiming@iun.edu
DIMINO, John, L ... 215-204-7276 436 C
john.dimino@temple.edu
DIMINO, Solweig ... 973-300-2215 308 F
sdimino@sussex.edu
DIMITROV, Danielle, E . 718-982-2250 319 A
danielle.dimitrov@csi.cuny.edu
DIMITROVA, Diana ... 604-274-3306 328 H
ddimitrova@ithaca.edu
DIMKOVA, Dimitrina ... 703-323-5053 516 C
ddimkova@nvcc.edu
DIMOLA, Anne ... 631-244-3020 324 C
dimolaa@dowling.edu
DIMOLITSAS, Spiros ... 202-687-3730.. 95 E
seniorvp@georgetown.edu
DIMON, Denise ... 619-260-6824.. 74 B
dimon@sandiego.edu
DIMOND, David ... 914-632-5400 333 F
ddimond@monroecollege.edu
DIMOS, Duane ... 817-272-1021 493 L
ddimos@uta.edu
DINALLO, JR.,
Benjamin ... 201-559-3507 302 I
dinallob@felician.edu
DINARDO, N. John ... 215-895-2510 417 E
dinardo@drexel.edu
DINDOFFER, Tamara, L 517-750-1200 250 F
tammyd@arbor.edu
DINEEN, James ... 814-838-7673 418 G
jdineen@fortisinstitute.edu
DINEGAR, Leonard ... 303-860-5600.. 86 D
leonard.dinegar@cu.edu
DINELLO, William, V ... 718-262-2350 321 B
wdinello@york.cuny.edu
DINGER, Tim ... 479-524-7234.. 21 F
tdinger@jbu.edu
DINGER-BLANTON,
Julie ... 918-463-2931 397 I
julie.dinger@connorsstate.edu
DINGESS, Debbie, C ... 304-896-7408 531 F
debbie.dingess@southernwv.edu
DINGESS, Debbie, C ... 304-896-7416 531 F
debbie.dingess@southernwv.edu
DINGFELDER, Diane ... 507-457-5138 262 D
ddingfelder@winona.edu
DINGLE, Terry ... 843-661-8321 446 C
terry.dingle@fdtc.edu
DINGLER, Mike ... 501-337-5000.. 20 H
mdingler@coto.edu
DINGMAN, Brandie ... 518-381-1280 342 E
dingmabm@sunysccc.edu
DINGMANN, Melissa ... 218-281-8576 264 H
dingmann@umn.edu
DINICE, Elizabeth, M ... 609-894-9311 306 B
edinice@bcc.edu
DINKEL, Shirley ... 785-670-1470 192 B
shirley.dinkel@washburn.edu
DINKINS, Sandy, E ... 904-264-2172 111 G
sdinkins@iws.edu
DINNAN, Matthew, A ... 203-254-4000.. 90 E
madinnan@fairfield.edu
DINNDORF,
Elizabeth, A ... 803-786-3178 445 C
bdinndorf@columbiasc.edu
DINNO, Christopher ... 707-664-2870.. 36 C
christopher.dinno@sonoma.edu
DINOVO, Carolyn ... 614-885-5585 390 G
cdinovo@pcj.edu
DINSE, Jayne ... 507-389-7269 262 A
jayne.dinse@southcentral.edu
DINWIDDIE, Ashley ... 417-328-1500 282 D
adinwiddie@sbuniv.edu
DIOGUARDI, Nicolette .. 740-753-6449 383 G
dioguardin@hocking.edu
DION, Susan ... 651-450-3568 259 A
sdion@inverhills.edu
DIONISI, Lisa ... 216-987-2340 381 A
lisa.dionisi@tri-c.edu
DIONNE, Trisha ... 603-271-6484 297 C
tdionne@ccsnh.edu
DIONNE, Woody ... 802-635-1280 504 A
woody.dionne@jsc.edu
DIORIETES, Chris ... 910-678-8443 362 E
diorietc@faytechcc.edu
DIORIO, Annette ... 610-330-5082 423 A
diorioa@lafayette.edu
DIORIO, Mary Ann ... 860-733-1404.. 90 C
mdiorio@txcc.commnet.edu
DIORIO, Nicole ... 508-767-7078 222 D
nm.diorio@assumption.edu
DIPADOVA, Audra ... 949-582-4616.. 67 F
adipadova@saddleback.edu
DIPADOVA-STOCKS,
Laurie ... 816-559-5617 280 F
laurie.dipadovastocks@park.edu

DIPALMA, Allen, A ... 412-624-7415 437 K
dipalma@pitt.edu
DIPALMA, Kristy ... 212-410-8000 335 B
kdipalma@nycpm.edu
DIPAOLA, Robert, S ... 732-235-2465 306 F
dipaolrs@cinj.rutgers.edu
DIPAOLO, Lawrence ... 610-558-5507 427 D
dipaolo@neumann.edu
DIPAOLO, Stephen, J ... 848-445-5012 306 F
sdip@uco.rutgers.edu
DIPIERO, Thomas ... 214-768-3212 482 J
tdipiero@smu.edu
DIPIERRO, John ... 269-965-3931 244 L
dipierroj@kellogg.edu
DIPIETRO, Joe ... 865-974-2241 465 C
utpresident@tennessee.edu
DIPIETRO, Mark ... 802-387-1632 502 A
markdepietro@landmark.edu
DIPIETRO, Stephen ... 215-895-4264 417 E
stephen.l.dipietro@drexel.edu
DIPIETRO-STEWART,
Suze ... 609-652-4607 308 E
suze.dipietro@stockton.edu
DIPIRO, Joseph, T ... 804-828-0100 514 F
jtdipiro@vcu.edu
DIPLOCK, Peter ... 860-486-2915.. 92 C
peter.diploc@uconn.edu
DIPLOCK, Peter ... 860-486-2915.. 92 C
peter.diplock@uconn.edu
DIPPEL, Holger ... 508-999-9181 228 H
hdippel@umassd.edu
DIPPMAN, Terry ... 419-473-2700 381 F
tdippman@daviscollege.edu
DIRADDO, Colleen ... 484-384-2943 427 I
cdiraddo@eastern.edu
DIRAIMO, Michael, J ... 814-865-6563 428 C
mjd256@psu.edu
DIRE, James ... 808-245-8229 136 F
dire@hawaii.edu
DIRIKER, Veronique, L . 410-651-8142 219 H
vdiriker@umes.edu
DIRK, Brian ... 440-375-7220 385 B
bdirk@lec.edu
DIRKS, Kathleen, M ... 815-835-6386 158 I
kathleen.m.dirks@svcc.edu
DIRKS, Nicholas, B ... 510-642-7464.. 70 K
chancellor@berkeley.edu
DIRKSCHNEIDER, Carla 402-552-6295 289 H
dirkschneider@clarksoncollege.edu
DIRKSE, John ... 661-654-6181.. 32 G
jdirkse@csub.edu
DIRKSEN, Dawn ... 866-323-0233.. 60 E
admin@providencecc.edu
DIRLAM, David ... 757-233-8893 518 H
ddirlam@vwc.edu
DIRST, Eric ... 630-515-4510 144 A
edirst@devry.edu
DISAIA, Kenneth, F ... 401-598-2346 441 D
kdisaia@jwu.edu
DISALVIO, Philip ... 617-287-7925 228 G
philip.disalvio@umb.edu
DISALVO, Anthony ... 909-652-6257.. 38 A
anthony.disalvo@chaffey.edu
DISALVO, Stephen ... 314-529-9521 277 B
sdisalvo@maryville.edu
DISALVO, Steven, R ... 603-641-7010 298 F
sdisalvo@anselm.edu
DISANO, Maria ... 401-397-7078 442 E
cdisano@mail.uri.edu
DISANTI, Francis, J ... 610-660-1506 434 G
disanti@sju.edu
DISATE, Nancy ... 303-861-1151.. 82 A
ndisate@concorde.edu
DISCALA, Anthony ... 480-517-8411.. 15 D
anthony.discale@riosalado.edu
DISCELLO, Michael ... 724-337-1000 414 G
mdiscello@careerta.edu
DISCENZA, Tobias ... 239-489-9329 104 G
tjdiscenza@fsw.edu
DISCHINO, Maureen ... 617-989-4009 237 G
dischinom@wit.edu
DISCHNER, John ... 630-942-3487 142 F
DISHMAN, Leslie, B ... 985-448-4415 208 C
leslie.dishman@nicholls.edu
DISHMAN, Marcie ... 919-718-7491 361 C
mdishman@cccc.edu
DISHNER, Annette, H ... 252-451-8236 364 E
adishner@nashcc.edu
DISION, Maria ... 691-320-2480 549 D
mdison@comfsm.fm
DISKIN, Alan ... 702-651-7924 295 C
alan.diskin@csn.edu
DISKIN, Becca, L ... 417-659-5422 278 I
diskin-b@mssu.edu
DISLER, Heather ... 727-344-8065 112 A
disler.heather@spcollege.edu
DISMUKES, David ... 225-578-4400 204 M
dismukes@lsu.edu
DISNEW, Carolyn ... 212-752-1530 330 C
carolyn.disnew@limcollege.edu

DOGAN, Can .... 832-230-5470 479 J
dogan@na.edu
DOGBEVIA, Moses .... 402-461-7466 290 G
mdogbevia@hastings.edu
DOGGETT, Jeffrey .... 978-837-5207 233 G
doggettj@merrimack.edu
DOGONNIUCK,
Theodore .... 516-773-5000 548 I
dogonniuck@usmma.edu
DOHE, Brian .... 509-527-4928 528 F
dohe@whitman.edu
DOHENY, Sarah .... 207-581-1110 212 C
sarah.doheny@maine.edu
DOHERTY, Brian .... 941-487-4300 115 B
bdoherty@ncf.edu
DOHERTY, Brian, E .... 413-265-2372 225 D
dohertyb@elms.edu
DOHERTY, Cynthia, A ... 717-736-4279 420 D
cadohert@hacc.edu
DOHERTY, Eileen .... 773-298-5060 158 F
edoherty@sxu.edu
DOHERTY, Frank, J ...... 540-568-6830 509 C
dohertfj@jmu.edu
DOHERTY, Jennifer .... 818-836-5038 150 F
dohert@lewisu.edu
DOHERTY, Kathleen, T . 717-780-2496 420 D
ktdohert@hacc.edu
DOHERTY, Kathryn .... 410-532-5316 217 F
kdoherty@ndm.edu
DOHERTY, Kenneth .... 313-577-3756 252 G
ken-doherty@wayne.edu
DOHERTY, Kevin .... 620-421-6700 189 B
kevind@labette.edu
DOHERTY, Kristal .... 864-646-1795 449 F
kdoherty@tctc.edu
DOHERTY, Leanna, J .... 620-421-6700 189 B
leannan@labette.edu
DOHERTY, Mary Jane ... 781-768-7015 236 A
mj.doherty@regiscollege.edu
DOHERTY, Paula .... 360-417-6275 525 A
pdoherty@pencol.edu
DOHERTY, Sharon .... 651-690-6783 263 V
sldoherty@stkate.edu
DOHERTY, Steve .... 269-488-4442 244 J
sdoherty@kvcc.edu
DOHERTY, Tiffany .... 603-668-6660 298 A
DOHNALIK, Judith .... 254-298-8600 484 C
j.dohnalik@templejc.edu
DOI, Tom .... 808-235-7370 137 A
tomd@hawaii.edu
DOKTOR, Caryn, G .... 212-799-5000 329 I
DOLAK, James .... 970-491-4752.. 81 D
jim.dolak@colostate.edu
DOLAK, Lisa, A .... 315-443-1860 349 E
ladolak@syr.edu
DOLAMORE, Joan .... 617-243-2485 227 K
jdolamore@lasell.edu
DOLAN, Abby .... 888-384-0849.. 26 O
adolan@allied.edu
DOLAN, Beth .... 603-513-1332 299 C
beth.dolan@granite.edu
DOLAN, Daniel .... 212-237-8900 319 F
ddolan@jjay.cuny.edu
DOLAN, Donna, M .... 617-521-2111 236 F
donna.dolan@simmons.edu
DOLAN, Gayle .... 617-277-3915 224 D
dolang@bgsp.edu
DOLAN, Jacob .... 406-994-5036 287 G
jake@montana.edu
DOLAN, James, E .... 317-381-6028 174 F
jdolan@vinu.edu
DOLAN, Jill, S .... 609-258-3040 305 C
jsdolan@princeton.edu
DOLAN, Julie, L .... 508-793-7443 225 B
jdolan@clarku.edu
DOLAN, Linda .... 320-762-4439 257 O
lindad@alextech.edu
DOLAN, Mary, K .... 315-267-4816 346 C
dolanmk@potsdam.edu
DOLAN, Stacey, L .... 312-788-1147 162 H
sdolan@vandercook.edu
DOLAN, Tim .... 303-762-6919.. 82 C
tim.dolan@denverseminary.edu
DOLAN, Tina, M .... 781-283-3501 237 F
cdolan@wellesley.edu
DOLANSKY, Brian, P .... 914-606-6284 352 G
brian.dolansky@sunywcc.edu
DOLBERRY, Carol .... 870-460-1034.. 24 C
dolberryc@uamont.edu
DOLCI, Elizabeth .... 802-635-1482 504 A
elizabeth.dolci@jsc.edu
DOLDER-ZIEKE,
Beth, D .... 608-796-3828 542 H
bdzieke@viterbo.edu
DOLDO, Frank .... 315-786-2250 329 G
fdoldo@sunyjefferson.edu
DOLHANSKY,
Barbara, A .... 215-204-7621 436 C
barbarad@temple.edu
DOLHEIMER, Mary, E ... 717-815-1274 440 H
mdolheim@ycp.edu

DOLIANITIS, Anna .... 803-508-7477 443 C
doliantisa@atc.edu
DOLINAR, Jon .... 216-987-4354 381 A
jon.dolinar@tri-c.edu
DOLIVE, Mark .... 817-515-2113 484 B
mark.dolive@tccd.edu
DOLL, Caroline .... 805-437-3232.. 32 H
caroline.doll@csuci.edu
DOLL, Cheryl, A .... 610-799-1087 424 A
cdoll@lccc.edu
DOLL, DeAnne .... 641-673-2118 184 B
dollde@wmpenn.edu
DOLL, Susana, A .... 253-535-7337 524 I
dollsa@plu.edu
DOLL, Tammy .... 620-417-1131 191 A
tammy.doll@sccc.edu
DOLLA, Marie .... 718-779-1499 338 D
mdolla@plazacollege.edu
DOLLAR, Marek .... 513-529-4036 386 K
dollarm@miamioh.edu
DOLLARD, Catherine, L 740-587-6238 381 H
dollard@denison.edu
DOLLARD, Heidi .... 413-545-6133 228 F
hdollard@oit.umass.edu
DOLLARD, Pam .... 715-346-3975 541 A
pam.dollard@uwsp.edu
DOLLING, David .... 202-994-6080.. 95 D
dolling@gwu.edu
DOLLING, Lisa .... 914-323-5262 331 J
lisa.dolling@mville.edu
DOLLING, Lisa .... 201-216-5405 308 D
ldolling@stevens.edu
DOLLY, Patricia, A .... 248-370-3500 248 K
dolly@oakland.edu
DOLLYHITE, Ronald .... 336-838-6281 367 C
ronald.dollyhite@wilkescc.edu
DOLPHIN, Jen .... 712-274-5110 181 C
dolphinj@morningside.edu
DOLS, Kenn .... 218-855-8132 258 C
KDols@clcmn.edu
DOLSEN, David, H .... 620-229-6298 191 B
david.dolsen@sckans.edu
DOMACHOWSKI,
Andrea .... 419-824-3704 385 F
adomachowski@lourdes.edu
DOMACK, Alicia .... 414-277-7351 537 G
domack@msoe.edu
DOMAN-FLYGARE,
Sarah .... 763-424-0755 260 E
SDoman-Flygare@nhcc.edu
DOMAS, Matthew, S ..... 662-562-3235 269 E
gmdomas@northwestms.edu
DOMBCHEWSKYJ, Dan . 704-290-5828 366 A
bdombchewskyj@spcc.edu
DOMBROWSKI,
Michael .... 716-614-5980 336 D
mdombrowski@niagaracc.suny.edu
DOMBROWSKI,
Teresa, A .... 630-515-6479 152 H
tdombr@midwestern.edu
DOMECK, Craig .... 561-803-2302 109 G
craig_domeck@pba.edu
DOMENECH, Manuel, A 512-394-9766.. 74 A
mdomenech@usa.edu
DOMENECH, Tony .... 432-335-5360 490 A
manuel.domenech@ttuhsc.edu
DOMENITZ, Linda .... 860-906-5153.. 89 A
ldomenitz@ccc.commnet.edu
DOMES, Chris, E .... 920-686-6138 539 A
Chris.Domes@sl.edu
DOMHOLDT, Elizabeth .. 218-723-6012 255 A
bdomhold@css.edu
DOMIANO, Sam .... 985-549-2282 208 E
sdomiano@selu.edu
DOMICK, Timothy .... 908-852-1400 301 C
library@centenarycollege.edu
DOMINE, Karen .... 541-888-7212 410 A
khelland@socc.edu
DOMINELLI, Angela .... 518-694-7333 314 G
angela.dominelli@acphs.edu
DOMINGO, Michele ...... 425-640-1562 522 D
michele.domingo@edcc.edu
DOMINGUEZ, Carmen .. 305-237-3374 108 L
cdoming3@mdc.edu
DOMINGUEZ, Carmen .. 661-362-3116.. 40 H
carmen.dominguez@canyons.edu
DOMINGUEZ, Dolores ... 859-371-9393 193 D
ddominguez@beckfield.edu
DOMINGUEZ, Israel ...... 949-582-4777.. 67 F
idominguez@saddleback.edu
DOMINGUEZ, Joe .... 956-364-4341 487 H
armando.dominguez@tstc.edu
DOMINGUEZ, Leo .... 432-837-8596 489 B
leodo@sulross.edu
DOMINGUEZ, Leo, G ..... 432-837-8033 489 B
leodo@sulross.edu
DOMINGUEZ, Mary ...... 831-755-6714.. 46 J
mdomingu@hartnell.edu
DOMINGUEZ, Niki .... 619-684-8764.. 56 B
ndominguez@newschoolarch.edu

DOMINGUEZ, Nora .... 909-593-3511.. 73 B
ndominguez@laverne.edu
DOMINGUEZ, Norberto 787-296-0453 553 D
dominguez@inter.edu
DOMINGUEZ, Randy, G 918-595-8999 403 A
randy.dominguez@tulsacc.edu
DOMINICIS, Erick .... 305-237-6151 108 L
edominic@mdc.edu
DOMINICK, Jay .... 609-258-5601 305 C
jdominick@princeton.edu
DOMINOWSKI, Jessica . 712-279-5433 176 B
jessica.dominowski@briarcliff.edu
DOMINY, Robert .... 478-757-3579 122 E
rdominy@centralgatech.edu
DOMKE-DAMONTE,
Darla, J .... 843-349-2129 444 G
ddamonte@coastal.edu
DOMMER, David .... 919-658-7854 369 B
ddommer@umo.edu
DOMNICK, Krista, R ..... 919-515-2866 370 D
krdomnic@ncsu.edu
DOMPE, Rudy .... 818-719-6440.. 51 H
domperf@piercecollege.edu
DOMPIERRE,
Michael, B .... 636-922-8355 281 C
mdompierre@stchas.edu
DOMZALSKI, Jim .... 570-740-0342 425 A
jdomzalski@luzerne.edu
DONA, David .... 541-383-7222 404 K
ddona@cocc.edu
DONAHOE, Patrick .... 406-994-4531 287 G
uccpd@montana.edu
DONAHOO, David .... 434-592-3084 509 G
ddonahoo@liberty.edu
DONAHUE, Amy .... 860-486-4037.. 92 C
amy.donahue@uconn.edu
DONAHUE, Bob .... 614-947-6010 382 H
robert.donahue@franklin.edu
DONAHUE, Colin .... 818-677-2333.. 34 D
colin.donahue@csun.edu
DONAHUE, Darrell .... 207-326-2230 211 G
darrell.donahue@mma.edu
DONAHUE, David, A .... 802-443-3060 502 E
ddonahue@middlebury.edu
DONAHUE, Eileen, B .... 203-432-5850.. 93 C
eileen.donahue@yale.edu
DONAHUE, James, A ... 925-631-4203.. 61 G
president@stmarys-ca.edu
DONAHUE, James, P ... 423-652-6002 457 J
jpd@king.edu
DONAHUE, Janice, M .. 423-585-6921 464 C
janice.donahue@ws.edu
DONAHUE, Jocelyn ...... 904-680-7734 103 K
jdonahue@fcsl.edu
DONAHUE, Joseph .... 610-526-1867 420 C
jdonahue@harcum.edu
DONAHUE, Linda, V ..... 802-654-2563 502 H
ldonahue@smcvt.edu
DONAHUE, Lorraine ...... 814-262-3822 429 K
ldonahue@pennhighlands.edu
DONAHUE, Nancy .... 865-694-6541 463 E
ndonahue@pstcc.edu
DONAHUE, Patrick .... 812-855-3207 167 J
donahued@indiana.edu
DONAHUE, Robert .... 617-353-9515 224 E
rdonahue@bu.edu
DONAHUE, Sean .... 772-462-7751 106 F
sdonahue@irsc.edu
DONALD, Christopher .. 601-974-1205 268 D
chris.donald@millsaps.edu
DONALD, Ryan, J .... 330-471-8195 385 G
rdonald@malone.edu
DONALDSON, Adam ...... 334-386-7254.... 3 I
adonaldson@faulkner.edu
DONALDSON, Anthony . 951-343-4841.. 30 D
adonaldson@calbaptist.edu
DONALDSON, Colleen .. 585-395-5118 345 A
cdonalds@brockport.edu
DONALDSON, Devlin .... 847-628-2087 149 A
devlin.donaldson@judsonu.edu
DONALDSON,
Janice, W .... 904-620-2476 116 A
jdonalds@unf.edu
DONALDSON, Jody .... 319-398-7186 180 J
jdonald@kirkwood.edu
DONALDSON, John, A . 406-265-3520 288 A
jdonaldson@msun.edu
DONALDSON, Lisa .... 719-502-3016.. 84 J
lisa.donaldson@ppcc.edu
DONALDSON, Monde ... 251-414-2291.... 7 F
mdonaldson@shc.edu
DONALDSON, Penny ...... 785-442-6054 187 I
pdonaldson@highlandcc.edu
DONALDSON, Scott ...... 510-780-4500.. 50 G
sdonaldson@lifewest.edu
DONALDSON, Stewart .. 909-607-9013.. 39 E
stewart.donaldson@cgu.edu
DONALDSON, Terry ...... 671-735-2187 549 G
terryjdonaldson@gmail.com
DONALDSON, Tracey ... 215-968-8091 413 F
donaldso@bucks.edu

DONAT, Kim .... 920-424-3377 540 B
donatk@uwosh.edu
DONATH, Ben .... 712-749-2181 176 D
donath@bvu.edu
DONATHAN, David .... 859-336-1743 195 K
david.donathan@kctcs.edu
DONATO, CSC, John, J 503-943-8532 410 H
donato@up.edu
DONATO, Michelle .... 570-674-6265 426 D
mdonato@misericordia.edu
DONAVANT, Lori, A ...... 731-881-7815 465 F
ldonavant@utm.edu
DONAVANT, Susan, H .. 804-752-7222 511 E
sdonavan@rmc.edu
DONAVON, Annette ...... 716-375-2234 340 C
amcgraw@sbu.edu
DONCEVIC, John, G ..... 724-847-6692 419 B
jgdoncev@geneva.edu
DONCITS, Diane .... 651-641-3472 256 J
ddoncits@luthersem.edu
DONCSECZ, Joseph, J .. 814-865-1355 428 C
jjd7@psu.edu
DONE, Karen .... 662-621-4153 266 H
kwdone@coahomacc.edu
DONE, Kenneth .... 662-254-3624 269 C
kennth.done@mvsu.edu
DONEGAN, Helen .... 407-317-7725 115 C
helen.donegan@ucf.edu
DONEGAN, John, P ...... 734-487-3591 242 J
jdonega1@emich.edu
DONELAN, Pam .... 605-229-8401 453 A
pam.donelan@presentation.edu
DONELSON, Barbara ..... 434-381-6708 513 E
BDonelson@SBC.EDU
DONELSON, Charlotte .. 307-855-2154 545 a
donelson@cwc.edu
DONELSON, Rollin .... 336-334-5963 371 C
rollin_donelson@uncg.edu
DONEY, Kelly, P .... 202-687-8526.. 95 E
kpdoney@georgetown.edu
DONG, Suhua .... 717-337-6487 419 C
sdong@gettysburg.edu
DONHAM, Brent .... 903-886-5390 485 E
brent.donham@tamuc.edu
DONHAM, Marilyn .... 734-973-3630 251 J
mdonham@wccnet.edu
DONHARDT, Gary, L .... 901-678-2231 462 B
donhardt@memphis.edu
DONIN, Robert, B .... 603-646-0101 297 G
robert.b.donin@dartmouth.edu
DONINI, Joseph .... 845-398-4040 341 H
jdonini@stac.edu
DONIUS, Mary Alice .... 203-365-4508.. 91 G
doniusm@sacredheart.edu
DONKERSLOOT,
Norman .... 616-392-8555 253 C
norman@westernsem.edu
DONLAN, Michael, J .... 757-446-5890 507 B
donlanmj@evms.edu
DONLEY, Bob .... 515-281-3934 175 F
bdonley@iastate.edu
DONLEY, Michael .... 903-566-7284 494 E
mdonley@uttyler.edu
DONLIN, Linda .... 701-328-2962 373 F
linda.donlin@ndus.edu
DONLIN, Mary .... 507-453-1479 259 G
mdonlin@southeastmn.edu
DONN, Denise .... 714-628-4836.. 60 H
donn_denise@sccollege.edu
DONN, Denise, C .... 209-954-5151.. 63 D
dcdonn@deltacollege.edu
DONNA, Jerry .... 863-784-7108 113 C
jerry.donna@southflorida.edu
DONNAY, Brent .... 320-308-3039 261 E
btdonnay@stcloudstate.edu
DONNELL, Kathy, S ...... 951-487-3002.. 55 A
kdonnell@msjc.edu
DONNELL, Ramsey .... 312-427-2737 148 I
rdonnell@jmls.edu
DONNELL, Richard, H .. 731-424-5883 457 K
rdonnell@lanecollege.edu
DONNELL, Robert .... 314-264-1000 284 J
robert.donnell@vatterott.edu
DONNELL, Shauna, H ... 479-968-0343.. 20 C
sdonnell@atu.edu
DONNELLA, II,
Joseph, A .... 717-337-6280 419 C
donnella@gettysburg.edu
DONNELLAN, Barbara ... 617-369-3832 236 E
bdonnellan@smfa.org
DONNELLI, Amber .... 775-753-2135 295 D
amber.donnelli@gbcnv.edu
DONNELLI-SALLEE,
Emily .... 816-584-6779 280 F
emily.donnelli@park.edu
DONNELLY, Cynthia ..... 401-341-3160 442 D
cynthia.donnelly@salve.edu
DONNELLY, Daniel .... 615-297-7545 455 A
donnellyd@aquinascollege.edu
DONNELLY, David .... 816-235-1333 284 A
donnellyd@umkc.edu

DOUCETTE, Kari .... 218-262-6735 258 H
karidoucette@hibbing.edu
DOUCETTE, Margot .... 858-566-1200.. 43 A
margot@disd.edu
DOUCETTE, Melissa ...... 325-574-7650 497 E
mdoucette@wtc.edu
DOUGAN, Thomas, R ... 401-874-2427 442 E
tdougan@uri.edu
DOUGHARTY,
W. Houston .... 516-463-6933 328 A
w.houston.doughart@hofstra.edu
DOUGHER, Mark .... 815-479-7515 152 B
mdougher@mchenry.edu
DOUGHER, Michael, J . 505-277-6128 313 H
dougher@unm.edu
DOUGHERTY,
B. Christopher .... 610-527-0200 434 D
cdougherty@rosemont.edu
DOUGHERTY,
Charles, J .... 412-396-6060 417 I
president@duq.edu
DOUGHERTY, Clint .... 760-252-2511.. 29 C
cdougherty@barstow.edu
DOUGHERTY,
Cynthia, R .... 580-774-3767 402 G
cindy.dougherty@swosu.edu
DOUGHERTY, Danny .... 740-446-4367 382 J
director@gallipoliscareercollege.edu
DOUGHERTY, Debra, K 502-852-5420 201 A
dkdough01@louisville.edu
DOUGHERTY, Dennis ... 610-647-4400 421 B
ddougherty1@immaculata.edu
DOUGHERTY,
Dennis, R .... 610-527-0200 434 D
ddougherty@rosemont.edu
DOUGHERTY, Erin .... 972-883-2586 494 A
erin.dougherty@utdallas.edu
DOUGHERTY, Gail .... 717-764-9550 416 C
gdougherty@csb.edu
DOUGHERTY, Gail, E .... 717-764-9550 416 D
gdougherty@csb.edu
DOUGHERTY, Jason ..... 304-865-6084 530 F
jason.dougherty@ovu.edu
DOUGHERTY, John .... 816-654-7303 276 G
jdougherty@kcumb.edu
DOUGHERTY, John, M . 607-871-2108 314 J
dougherty@alfred.edu
DOUGHERTY, Kathleen . 603-899-4178 297 H
doughertyk@franklinpierce.edu
DOUGHERTY, Lori .... 724-503-1001 439 B
ldougherty@washjeff.edu
DOUGHERTY, Lynne ..... 516-463-6740 328 A
lynne.dougherty@hofstra.edu
DOUGHERTY, Maureen . 856-351-2665 308 B
mdougherty@salemcc.edu
DOUGHERTY, Michael .. 303-273-3554.. 80 O
mdougher@mines.edu
DOUGHERTY,
Michele, R .... 215-955-6656 436 F
michele.dougherty@jefferson.edu
DOUGHERTY,
Shanin, L .... 570-326-3761 429 J
sdougher@pct.edu
DOUGHERTY, Sharon ... 215-248-7036 415 D
doughertys@chc.edu
DOUGHERTY, Tracy, D . 806-371-5106 467 E
tsdougherty@actx.edu
DOUGHERTY, Troy, J ... 208-496-9225 137 F
doughertyt@byui.edu
DOUGHMAN, Siham ...... 203-392-5301.. 88 F
doughmans1@southernct.edu
DOUGHTY, JR., Clyde .. 301-860-3559 220 B
cdoughty@bowiestate.edu
DOUGHTY, Corine .... 949-282-2730.. 67 E
cdoughty@ivc.edu
DOUGHTY, David, C .... 757-594-7050 506 I
doughty@cnu.edu
DOUGHTY, Karen .... 432-335-6404 479 O
kdoughty@odessa.edu
DOUGHTY, Richard ...... 503-491-7279 407 C
richard.doughty@mhcc.edu
DOUGLAS, Adrian, H .... 972-860-7603 472 E
AdrianD@dcccd.edu
DOUGLAS, Alicia, R ..... 816-501-4306 281 B
alicia.douglas@rockhurst.edu
DOUGLAS, Amy, K .... 334-844-3604.... 1 G
douglak@auburn.edu
DOUGLAS, Bernadine ... 859-985-3730 193 F
douglasb@berea.edu
DOUGLAS, Brian .... 508-286-8208 238 B
douglas_brian@wheatoncollege.edu
DOUGLAS, Brianna .... 843-383-8060 445 A
bbuncedouglas@coker.edu
DOUGLAS, Craig .... 989-964-4195 249 G
cdouglas@svsu.edu
DOUGLAS, Davison, M 757-221-3790 506 J
dmdoug@wm.edu
DOUGLAS, Delano .... 804-524-5214 518 C
ddouglas@vsu.edu
DOUGLAS, Derek .... 773-702-3627 161 D
drbdouglas@uchicago.edu
DOUGLAS, Diane .... 802-485-2035 502 G
ddouglas@norwich.edu
DOUGLAS, Jeffrey, A .... 309-341-7491 149 G
jdouglas@knox.edu
DOUGLAS, Jerome .... 610-917-3912 438 G
jndouglas@valleyforge.edu
DOUGLAS, Jim .... 508-213-2333 235 C
jim.douglas@nichols.edu
DOUGLAS,
Katherine, P .... 607-962-9232 323 D
kdouglas@corning-cc.edu
DOUGLAS, Kelly, C .... 619-260-7974.. 74 B
kdouglas@sandiego.edu
DOUGLAS, Kristen .... 678-664-0529 134 F
kristen.douglas@westgatech.edu
DOUGLAS, Kristin .... 309-794-3443 139 K
kristindouglas@augustana.edu
DOUGLAS, Laura .... 515-248-7206 177 B
lldouglas@dmacc.edu
DOUGLAS, Linda .... 919-843-9393 371 A
Linda_Douglas@unc.edu
DOUGLAS, Lindsey .... 785-864-7100 191 G
lmdouglas@ku.edu
DOUGLAS, Lisa .... 303-315-2769.. 86 G
lisa.douglas@ucdenver.edu
DOUGLAS, Malcolm, C 847-574-5166 150 A
mdouglas@lfgsm.edu
DOUGLAS, Minnie, L ... 562-408-6969.. 26 D
DOUGLAS, Shawn .... 478-471-2414 128 H
shawn.douglas@mga.edu
DOUGLAS, Sherry, L .... 308-432-6230 292 B
sdouglas@csc.edu
DOUGLAS, Stephen, L .. 304-293-4731 533 D
stephen.douglas@mail.wvu.edu
DOUGLAS CHARLES,
Rhonda .... 212-686-9040 352 H
rdouglascharles@woodtobecoburn.edu
DOUGLASS, Andraea .... 614-292-4164 389 A
douglass.101@osu.edu
DOUGLASS, Barbara ..... 860-738-6406.. 89 G
bdouglass@nwcc.commnet.edu
DOUGLASS, Brent .... 540-887-7201 510 A
bdouglass@mbc.edu
DOUGLASS, Carolinda .. 815-753-0492 154 I
cdoug@niu.edu
DOUGLASS, Claudia, B 989-774-3632 240 O
dougl1cb@cmich.edu
DOUGLASS, David, A ... 503-370-6447 411 D
ddouglas@willamette.edu
DOUGLASS, Debbie ...... 559-730-3736.. 41 D
debbied@cos.edu
DOUGLASS, James .... 507-433-0611 261 C
james.douglass@riverland.edu
DOUGLASS, Jill .... 505-428-1331 313 A
jill.douglass@sfcc.edu
DOUGLASS, Matt .... 660-263-3900 272 M
mattdouglass@cccb.edu
DOUGLASS, Scott, R .... 302-831-2200.. 94 D
douglass@udel.edu
DOUGLIS, Evan .... 518-276-6460 339 D
douglis@rpi.edu
DOUKAS, Peter, H .... 215-707-4990 436 C
peter.doukas@temple.edu
DOULIS, Peter .... 215-871-6900 432 E
peterd@pcom.edu
DOUMA, Debbie .... 850-484-1193 110 D
ddouma@pensacolastate.edu
DOURLEIN, Peter .... 520-621-9414.. 18 E
dourlein@email.arizona.edu
DOUSE, Christopher, D 260-422-5561 167 F
cddouse@indianatech.edu
DOUSTAR, Mazzie .... 718-261-5800 316 K
mdoustar@bramsonort.edu
DOUTHIT, Tricia .... 303-273-3383.. 80 O
tdouthit@mines.edu
DOVE, Bill .... 719-389-6384.. 79 M
william.dove@coloradocollege.edu
DOVE, Brooke .... 252-335-0821 361 G
brooke_dove@albemarle.edu
DOVE, Cassandra .... 540-857-6678 517 E
cdove@virginiawestern.edu
DOVE, Cathy, S .... 518-327-6223 338 B
cdove@paulsmiths.edu
DOVE, Danyele .... 610-526-6047 420 C
ddove@harcum.edu
DOVE, Gary .... 276-638-8777 516 D
gdove@patrickhenry.edu
DOVE, John .... 606-886-3863 195 I
john.dove@kctcs.edu
DOVE, Martha .... 617-322-3577 227 J
martha_dove@laboure.edu
DOVE, Robert, B .... 901-843-3800 460 F
dove@rhodes.edu
DOVE, Shirley .... 254-442-5000 470 I
DOVEY, Nicole .... 678-717-3839 133 A
nicola.dovey@ung.edu
DOVI, Sharon .... 607-844-8222 350 A
dovis@TC3.edu
DOW, Brenda .... 845-257-3231 344 A
dowb@newpaltz.edu
DOW, Evelyn .... 505-224-5217 310 F
evdow@cnm.edu
DOW, Larry .... 860-297-2157.. 92 A
larry.dow@trincoll.edu
DOW, Sarah .... 617-585-1296 234 H
sarah.dow@necmusic.edu
DOW, Steven, R .... 402-465-2255 292 E
sdow@nebrwesleyan.edu
DOW-MCDONALD,
Jennifer .... 810-762-0533 247 F
jennifer.dow@mcc.edu
DOW-ROYER, Cathy, A . 413-205-3262 221 G
cathy.dow-royer@aic.edu
DOWD, Bonnie Ann ..... 619-388-6975.. 62 E
bdowd@sdccd.edu
DOWD, Denny .... 214-333-5102 471 L
denny@dbu.edu
DOWD, Jay .... 843-953-1411 444 C
jdowd1@citadel.edu
DOWD, Julia, A .... 415-422-2531.. 74 C
dowd@usfca.edu
DOWD, Mary .... 507-389-2986 260 A
mary.dowd@mnsu.edu
DOWD, Sarah .... 864-646-1583 449 F
sdowd@tctc.edu
DOWDEN, Luke .... 337-482-6022 208 F
luke.dowden@lousiana.edu
DOWDEY, Don .... 432-837-8124 489 B
ddowdey@sulross.edu
DOWDLE, Cortney .... 229-317-6924 123 H
cortney.dowdle@darton.edu
DOWDLE, Deedie Kay .. 513-529-3637 386 K
dowdledk@miamioh.edu
DOWDY, Chris .... 214-379-5444 480 D
cdowdy@pqc.edu
DOWDY, Jacqueline ..... 904-470-8197 102 A
j.dowdy@ewc.edu
DOWDY, Kathleen, B .... 806-371-5389 467 E
kbdowdy@actx.edu
DOWDY, Michael, B ..... 410-706-3386 219 E
mdowdy@umaryland.edu
DOWDY, Ronald .... 919-546-8206 368 G
rdowdy@shawu.edu
DOWE, Peter .... 585-395-2531 345 A
pdowe@brockport.edu
DOWELL, Chanda .... 309-854-1721 140 D
dowellc@bhc.edu
DOWELL, David .... 562-985-4128.. 33 F
david.dowell@csulb.edu
DOWELL, Elise .... 212-678-8950 329 H
eldowell@jtsa.edu
DOWELL, NaTanya, F ... 404-627-2681 121 F
natanya.dowell@beulah.org
DOWEN, Chris .... 303-315-2550.. 86 G
chris.dowen@ucdenver.edu
DOWER, David .... 202-885-1000.. 94 H
dower@american.edu
DOWER, Julia .... 603-542-7744 297 D
jdower@ccsnh.edu
DOWLAND, Pam .... 812-357-6515 173 A
pdowland@saintmeinrad.edu
DOWLESS, Donald, V ... 706-233-7201 131 C
chimes@shorter.edu
DOWLING, Earl .... 630-942-3416 142 F
dowlinge@cod.edu
DOWLING, Joseph, B ... 714-895-8158.. 40 C
jdowling@gwc.cccd.edu
DOWLING, Timothy, F . 302-831-3699.. 94 D
tdowling@udel.edu
DOWLING, Victoria, A .. 618-537-2154 152 C
vadowling@mckendree.edu
DOWN, Cody .... 509-452-5100 524 J
DOWNES, Harry, W ...... 302-857-7911.. 93 E
hdownes@desu.edu
DOWNES, John .... 770-426-2646 128 C
jdownes@life.edu
DOWNES, Kelly .... 618-437-5321 156 I
downes@rlc.edu
DOWNEY, Catherine ..... 503-552-1761 407 F
cdowney@ncnm.edu
DOWNEY, Diana .... 215-248-6309 424 G
ddowney@ltsp.edu
DOWNEY, James .... 412-924-1450 433 E
jdowney@pts.edu
DOWNEY, John, A .... 540-453-2200 514 H
downeyj@brcc.edu
DOWNEY, Mechell .... 405-382-9260 402 C
m.downey@sscok.edu
DOWNEY, Nancy .... 207-859-4503 210 A
ndowney@colby.edu
DOWNEY, Nora .... 610-785-6582 434 E
ndowney@scs.edu
DOWNEY, Patricia .... 412-365-1199 415 C
downey@chatham.edu
DOWNEY, Paul .... 615-297-7545 455 A
downeyp@aquinascollege.edu
DOWNING, Amy .... 617-730-7174 235 B
amy.downing@newbury.edu
DOWNING, Arthur .... 646-312-1020 318 C
Arthur.Downing@baruch.cuny.edu
DOWNING, Beverly, L .. 502-597-6395 197 G
beverly.downing@kysu.edu
DOWNING, Gerri .... 608-757-7759 542 L
gdowning1@blackhawk.edu
DOWNING, Jay .... 432-837-8368 489 B
jdowning@sulross.edu
DOWNING, Jill .... 503-554-2121 406 A
jdowning@georgefox.edu
DOWNING, Kimberly ..... 513-556-5028 393 B
kimberly.downing@uc.edu
DOWNING, Lenora, S .. 540-986-1800 504 E
ldowning@an.edu
DOWNING, Michael .... 508-336-8700 441 D
mdowning@jwu.edu
DOWNING, Rossann ..... 816-604-4071 278 A
rossann.downing@mcckc.edu
DOWNING, Sherry .... 336-334-4822 363 A
sdowning@gtcc.edu
DOWNING, Stacy, L ..... 302-857-6300.. 93 E
sdowning@desu.edu
DOWNING, Steve .... 317-955-6351 171 A
sdowning@marian.edu
DOWNING, Tim .... 602-682-6800.. 12 A
DOWNS, Amy .... 717-815-1781 440 H
adowns@ycp.edu
DOWNS, Jesse, G .... 225-578-2162 204 M
jdowns@lsu.edu
DOWNS, Mary .... 920-735-5695 542 N
downsm@fvtc.edu
DOWNS, Sherry .... 740-593-4129 389 H
downs@ohio.edu
DOWNS, Timothy, M ..... 716-286-8342 336 E
downs@niagara.edu
DOWNS, Wil .... 812-237-4114 167 E
wil.downs@indstate.edu
DOWNS, William .... 252-328-6249 369 E
downsw14@ecu.edu
DOWNS-BURNS, Kim ... 802-443-5158 502 E
kdowns@middlebury.edu
DOXEY, Tia, M .... 919-530-7269 370 C
tdoxey@nccu.edu
DOXIE-DIXON, Eloise ... 504-520-7515 209 E
edixon@xula.edu
DOYLE, Adrian .... 310-338-1973.. 53 C
Adrian.Doyle@lmu.edu
DOYLE, Amanda .... 337-482-6730 208 F
amandad@louisiana.edu
DOYLE, Barbara .... 805-765-9300.. 64 G
DOYLE, Catherine .... 585-389-2123 334 B
cdoyle0@naz.edu
DOYLE, Cathleen, H ..... 410-777-2902 213 E
chdoyle@aacc.edu
DOYLE, Christine, M .... 610-355-7151 416 G
cdoyle@dccc.edu
DOYLE, Christy .... 208-769-3481 138 G
cadoyle@nic.edu
DOYLE, Clare .... 215-248-7071 415 D
doylec@chc.edu
DOYLE, Creig .... 610-902-8245 414 B
creig.w.doyle@cabrini.edu
DOYLE, Denise .... 210-283-6827 492 B
ddoyle@uiwtx.edu
DOYLE, Diana, M .... 303-797-5701.. 79 A
diana.doyle@arapahoe.edu
DOYLE, Eileen .... 914-633-2483 328 F
edoyle@iona.edu
DOYLE, Fiona, M .... 510-642-5472.. 70 K
graddean@berkeley.edu
DOYLE, Fred .... 518-956-7942 343 C
fdoyle@albany.edu
DOYLE, Gerald .... 312-567-5203 147 E
doyle@iit.edu
DOYLE, J. Griffin .... 706-542-8096 132 H
gdoyle@uga.edu
DOYLE, Janice, B .... 301-445-1901 219 C
jdoyle@usmd.edu
DOYLE, Jeanette, M ...... 413-748-3110 236 H
jdoyle2@springfieldcollege.edu
DOYLE, Jeff .... 254-710-1011 469 D
jeff_doyle@baylor.edu
DOYLE, Jillian .... 323-469-3300.. 26 P
DOYLE, Joy, E .... 724-847-6636 419 B
jedoyle@geneva.edu
DOYLE, Kevin .... 530-898-6222.. 33 A
kadoyle@csuchico.edu
DOYLE, Leslie .... 314-889-4503 275 B
ldoyle@fontbonne.edu
DOYLE, Lori .... 215-895-2100 417 E
lori.n.doyle@drexel.edu
DOYLE, Mary .... 831-459-4906.. 72 E
mdoyle1@ucsc.edu
DOYLE, Michael, J .... 563-588-7823 180 L
michael.doyle@loras.edu
DOYLE, Patrick .... 970-248-1847.. 80 B
pdoyle@coloradomesa.edu
DOYLE, Sheila .... 607-777-3844 343 D
sdoyle@binghamton.edu
DOYLE, Susan .... 205-726-2375.... 6 F
sdoyle@samford.edu

DOYLE, Susan, W .... 508-286-3425 238 B
doyle_susan@wheatoncollege.edu
DOYLE, Timothy .... 901-321-3548 455 I
tdoyle1@cbu.edu
DOZIER, Cheryl .... 912-358-4000 131 A
ssupresident@savannahstate.edu
DOZIER, Jack .... 417-447-7530 280 C
dozierj@otc.edu
DOZIER, Kristine, L ...... 317-788-3219 173 I
dozierk@uindy.edu
DOZIER, Luann, D .... 504-865-5794 207 F
ldozier@tulane.edu
DOZIER, Rodney .... 620-276-9603 187 D
rodney.dozier@gcccks.edu
DOZIER, Ronda .... 903-823-3088 484 D
ronda.dozier@texarkanacollege.edu
DRABIK, Joshua .... 954-545-4500 113 B
webmaster@sfbc.edu
DRABIK, Mary, A .... 954-545-4500 113 B
mdrabik@sfbc.edu
DRABIK, Tom .... 954-545-4500 113 B
registrar@sfbc.edu
DRACHMAN,
Annette, R .... 843-792-4063 447 G
drachmar@musc.edu
DRAGAN, Kimberly .... 860-738-6418.. 89 G
kdragan@nwcc.commnet.edu
DRAGOUN, Mary Beth . 805-581-1233.. 44 A
mdragoun@eternitybiblecollege.edu
DRAIN, Cecil, B .... 804-828-7247 514 F
cbdrain@vcu.edu
DRAIN, Timothy, S .... 903-510-2458 491 A
tdra@tjc.edu
DRAKE, Alison .... 708-709-3725 156 A
adrake@prairiestate.edu
DRAKE, Ann .... 315-787-4005 326 A
ann.drake@flhealth.org
DRAKE, Autumn .... 405-912-9096 398 B
adrake@hc.edu
DRAKE, Carlene .... 909-558-4581.. 50 K
cdrake@llu.edu
DRAKE, Christian .... 704-847-5600 369 A
cdrake@ses.edu
DRAKE, Edna .... 601-977-7730 270 F
edrake@tougaloo.edu
DRAKE, Eleanor .... 334-683-5100.... 5 D
DRAKE, George .... 717-871-7333 431 E
george.drake@millersville.edu
DRAKE, Jennifer, A ...... 317-791-5704 173 I
jdrake@uindy.edu
DRAKE, Kay, L .... 859-238-5467 194 E
kay.drake@centre.edu
DRAKE, Kourtney .... 816-279-7000 271 H
registrar@abtu.edu
DRAKE, Marianne .... 413-662-5224 230 C
m.drake@mcla.edu
DRAKE, Michael .... 614-292-2424 389 A
drake.379@osu.edu
DRAKE, Natricia .... 910-521-6298 371 D
natricia.drake@uncp.edu
DRAKE, Peter .... 212-966-0300 334 D
pdrake@nyaa.edu
DRAKE, Rick .... 334-229-4200.... 1 D
rdrake@alasu.edu
DRAKE, Robert .... 607-431-4000 327 B
draker@hartwick.edu
DRAKE, Roger, D .... 660-248-6221 272 N
rdrake@centralmethodist.edu
DRAKE, Sheryl .... 217-351-2280 155 I
sdrake@parkland.edu
DRAKE, Steve .... 618-283-4170 150 B
DRAKE, Susan, K .... 217-245-3041 146 D
sdrake@mail.ic.edu
DRAKE, Tom .... 575-769-4994 310 G
tom.drake@clovis.edu
DRAKE, Tonya .... 425-640-1559 522 D
tonya.drake@edcc.edu
DRAKE-DEESE, Kent ...... 603-358-2346 299 D
kdrakedeese@keene.edu
DRAKES, Gail .... 212-229-5600 334 C
drakesg@newschool.edu
DRAKSLER, Vicki .... 309-692-4092 152 F
vdraksler@midstate.edu
DRAMMEH, Lamin .... 803-793-5197 445 F
drammehl@denmarktech.edu
DRANE, Kim .... 307-382-1645 546 L
kdrane-n@wwcc.wy.edu
DRAPEAU, Guy .... 860-297-4210.. 92 A
guy.drapeau@trincoll.edu
DRAPER, Candice .... 325-481-8300 475 E
cdraper@howardcollege.edu
DRAPER, David .... 310-377-5501.. 53 E
ddraper@marymountcalifornia.edu
DRAPER, David, E .... 419-434-4202 395 H
president@winebrenner.edu
DRAPER, Dennis .... 310-338-7504.. 53 C
Dennis.Draper@lmu.edu
DRAPER, Diana, M .... 203-254-4125.. 90 E
ddraper@fairfield.edu
DRAPER, Frances .... 303-492-7531.. 86 E
frances.draper@colorado.edu
DRAPER, James .... 603-358-2492 299 D
jdraper@keene.edu
DRAPER, Jeri .... 215-751-8199 416 B
jdraper@ccp.edu
DRAPER, Mark .... 717-866-5775 418 E
mdraper@evangelical.edu
DRAPER, Nancy, J .... 405-912-9024 398 B
ndraper@hc.edu
DRASGOW, Fritz .... 217-333-1480 162 A
fdrasgow@illinois.edu
DRASS, Mike .... 302-736-2545.. 94 E
michael.drass@wesley.edu
DRAUDE, Barbara, J ...... 615-904-8189 461 E
barbara.draude@mtsu.edu
DRAUGHON, Bill .... 305-348-3961 114 G
draughon@fiu.edu
DRAUGHON,
Katherine, A .... 812-465-7107 174 D
kdraughon@usi.edu
DRAVES, Patricia, H ..... 330-823-2690 394 A
dravesph@mountunion.edu
DRAWDY, Lester, W ..... 770-720-5927 130 E
lwd@reinhardt.edu
DRAYFAHL, Perry, M ... 610-499-1291 439 G
pmdrayfahl@widener.edu
DRAYNA, Jonathan .... 414-425-8300 538 J
jdrayna@shsst.edu
DRAYTON, Paul .... 609-894-9311 306 B
DRAYTON, Ronald .... 803-738-7606 447 H
draytonr@midlandstech.edu
DREASHER, Luiza .... 651-290-6416 266 B
luiza.dreasher@wmitchell.edu
DREBIN, Diane .... 541-278-5796 404 J
ddrebin@bluecc.edu
DREES, Lynn .... 941-752-5428 114 B
dreesl@scf.edu
DREESSEN, Angela .... 309-694-5353 146 C
angela.dreessen@icc.edu
DREFFS, Daryl, A .... 603-668-2211 298 H
d.dreffs@snhu.edu
DREGER, Barb .... 920-735-4776 542 N
dreger@fvtc.edu
DREGIER, Denise, M .... 443-412-2428 215 D
ddregier@harford.edu
DREHER, H. Michael .... 914-654-5441 322 B
hdreher@cnr.edu
DREHER, Karolina .... 610-796-8218 412 C
karolina.dreher@alvernia.edu
DREIER, Alexander .... 203-432-4949.. 93 C
alexander.dreier@yale.edu
DREILING, Karolyn .... 913-758-6293 191 I
Karolyn.Dreiling@stmary.edu
DREISBACH, Joseph, H 570-941-4760 438 F
joseph.dreisbach@scranton.edu
DREISSEN, Carolyn .... 912-358-3004 131 A
DREITH, Michael .... 618-985-2637 148 G
mikedreith@jalc.edu
DRELL, Persis .... 650-723-3938.. 68 G
DRENKOW, Daniel, D ... 605-274-5251 452 A
dan.drenkow@augie.edu
DRENNEN, Rebecca, J .. 212-986-4343 316 D
rjd@berkeleycollege.edu
DRENNEN, Rebecca, J .. 973-278-5400 300 C
rjd@berkeleycollege.edu
DRESCHER, Kurt, W ...... 978-468-7111 227 B
kdrescher@gcts.edu
DRESSEN, Dan .... 507-786-3420 264 C
dressen@stolaf.edu
DRESSER, Kathy .... 914-337-9300 323 A
kathy.dresser@concordia-ny.edu
DRESSER-RECKTENWALD,
Wendy .... 607-587-4025 347 D
dressews@alfredstate.edu
DRESSLER, Chris .... 563-588-8167 176 F
chris.dressler@clarke.edu
DRESSLER, Daniel .... 405-789-7661 402 F
daniel.dressler@swcu.edu
DREVON, Charles .... 574-239-8392 167 C
cdrevon@hcc-nd.edu
DREVS, John .... 312-915-6941 151 E
jdrevs@luc.edu
DREW, Bud .... 912-260-4221 131 D
lawton.drew@sgsc.edu
DREW, Dan .... 317-278-5323 168 E
drew@iupui.edu
DREW, Daniel, J .... 716-888-2569 317 H
drewd@canisius.edu
DREW, John .... 617-827-6047 228 G
john.drew@umb.edu
DREW, Phil .... 405-425-1842 399 J
philip.drew@oc.edu
DREW, Stacy .... 540-868-7272 515 H
sdrew@lfcc.edu
DREWELOW, Lonna .... 319-363-1323 181 D
ldrewelow@mtmercy.edu
DREWENSKI, Shirley .... 708-596-2000 159 D
sdrewenski@ssc.edu
DREWS, Dani .... 518-244-2274 340 A
drewsd@sage.edu
DREWS, David .... 517-265-5161 238 H
ddrews@adrian.edu
DREWS, Jennifer .... 715-425-4481 540 E
jennifer.drews@uwrf.edu
DREXEL, Penny, M .... 814-332-4311 411 F
pdrexel@allegheny.edu
DREXLER, Brad .... 610-796-8376 412 C
bradley.drexler@alvernia.edu
DREXLER, Jim .... 706-419-1427 123 F
jim.drexler@covenant.edu
DREXLER-HINES,
Elizabeth .... 508-767-7343 222 D
ea.drexlerhines@assumption.edu
DREYER, Allen, R .... 570-586-2400 435 H
adreyer@summitu.edu
DREYER, John, M .... 260-452-3139 165 E
john.dreyer@ctsfw.edu
DREYER, Katie, E .... 513-562-8743 376 O
kdreyer@artacademy.edu
DREYER, Thomas .... 978-934-4801 229 A
Thomas_Dreyer@uml.edu
DREYFUS, Mark, B .... 757-671-7171 507 C
president@ecpi.edu
DREYFUSS, Simeon .... 503-699-3961 407 A
sdreyfuss@marylhurst.edu
DREYFUSS, Teresa .... 562-908-3403.. 60 I
tdreyfuss@riohondo.edu
DRIEDGER, Derek .... 605-995-2635 452 C
dedriedg@dwu.edu
DRIER, Tracy, M .... 715-833-6498 542 M
tdrier@cvtc.edu
DRIES, Kelly, J .... 414-410-4390 535 C
kjdries@stritch.edu
DRIESSNER, Johnnie ..... 503-493-6549 405 E
jdriessner@cu-portland.edu
DRIGGERS, Jon .... 828-898-8797 358 F
driggersj@lmc.edu
DRIGGERS, Randy .... 504-282-4455 206 C
rdriggers@nobts.edu
DRINAN, Helen, G .... 617-521-2070 236 F
helen.drinan@simmons.edu
DRINDAK, Desiree .... 518-587-2100 348 A
desiree.drindak@esc.edu
DRINKARD, Gretchen ... 314-454-7055 275 D
gdrinkard@bjc.org
DRISCOLL, Daniel, R .... 630-889-6542 154 E
ddriscoll@nuhs.edu
DRISCOLL, Debbie .... 434-544-8125 509 I
driscoll@lynchburg.edu
DRISCOLL, Diane, H ..... 603-526-3673 296 I
ddriscoll@colby-sawyer.edu
DRISCOLL,
Edward (Terry), C .... 757-221-3332 506 J
ecdris@wm.edu
DRISCOLL, Frederick .... 617-989-4135 237 G
driscollf@wit.edu
DRISCOLL, Karen .... 360-992-2260 521 A
kdriscoll@clark.edu
DRISCOLL, Kevin .... 617-873-0475 225 A
Kevin.Driscoll@cambridgecollege.edu
DRISCOLL, Laura .... 307-268-2733 545 Z
ldriscoll@caspercollege.edu
DRISCOLL, Lisa .... 508-849-3398 222 C
ldriscoll@annamaria.edu
DRISCOLL, Lori .... 850-769-1551 105 Q
ldriscoll@gulfcoast.edu
DRISCOLL, Marcy, P .... 850-644-6885 115 A
mdriscoll@fsu.edu
DRISCOLL, Marsha .... 218-755-3984 258 B
mdriscoll@bemidjistate.edu
DRISCOLL, Mary .... 803-641-3448 450 C
MaryD@usca.edu
DRISCOLL, Mary Erina . 212-650-5302 318 G
mdriscoll@ccny.cuny.edu
DRISCOLL, Michael ...... 410-837-4865 221 B
mdriscoll@ubalt.edu
DRISCOLL, Michael ...... 724-357-2200 431 A
Michael.Driscoll@iup.edu
DRISCOLL, Micheline ... 718-368-5436 320 A
mdriscoll@kbcc.cuny.edu
DRISCOLL, Michelle ...... 816-501-3608 272 E
michelle.driscoll@avila.edu
DRISCOLL, Robert, G .... 401-865-2090 441 F
rdriscol@providence.edu
DRISKELL, Chad .... 601-266-6525 271 B
chad.driskell@usm.edu
DRISKELL, Lavon .... 662-685-4771 266 G
ldriskell@bmc.edu
DRISKILL, Owen .... 865-882-4559 463 F
driskillo@roanestate.edu
DRISLANE, Kathy .... 518-743-2237 347 E
drislanek@sunyacc.edu
DRIVER, Berry .... 502-897-4807 199 D
bdriver@sbts.edu
DRIVER, Doug .... 970-943-7010.. 87 F
ddriver@western.edu
DRIVER, Louise .... 501-882-8845.. 19 E
oldriver@asub.edu
DRNEK, Jim .... 661-654-2161.. 32 G
jdrnek@csub.edu
DRODDY, Jason .... 225-578-5745 204 M
jdroddy@lsu.edu
DROEGEMEIER,
Kelvin, K .... 405-325-3806 403 I
kkd@ou.edu
DROEGEMUELLER,
Heidi .... 651-641-3528 256 J
hdroegemueller001@luthersem.edu
DROGUS, Carol .... 315-228-7216 321 H
cdrogus@colgate.edu
DROKER, Stephanie ...... 559-934-2221.. 76 B
stephaniedroker@whccd.edu
DROLL, Charlotte .... 570-389-4921 430 B
cdroll@bloomu.edu
DRONE-SILVERS, Scott . 217-234-5338 150 B
sdronesi@lakeland.cc.il.us
DRONEY, Michael .... 330-494-6170 391 J
mdroney@starkstate.edu
DRONGOWSKI, OP,
Stanley .... 616-632-8900 239 E
DROOG, Sue .... 712-722-6017 177 J
sue.droog@dordt.edu
DROPKIN, Keith .... 617-588-1363 223 D
kdropkin@bfit.edu
DROPKIN, Shelley .... 617-588-1302 223 D
sdropkin@bfit.edu
DROSS, Cindy .... 920-693-1385 543 B
cindy.dross@gotoltc.edu
DROST, Donald .... 732-906-2568 303 F
ddrost@middlesexcc.edu
DROST, Jack .... 256-824-7407.... 9 A
jack.drost@uah.edu
DROST, Jim .... 641-673-1104 184 B
drostj@wmpenn.edu
DROSTE, Pamela .... 843-574-6363 449 G
pamela.droste@tridenttech.edu
DROUGHT, Joe .... 815-921-4353 157 B
i.drought@rockvalleycollege.edu
DROUILLARD, Shelly ..... 419-530-4341 394 E
shelly.drouillard@utoledo.edu
DROUIN, Amy .... 816-501-4628 281 B
amy.drouin@rockhurst.edu
DROUIN, Jeff .... 510-723-6933.. 37 N
jdrouin@chabotcollege.edu
DROUIN, Nancy .... 207-216-4434 211 F
ndrouin@yccc.edu
DROZ, Marcus .... 787-480-2421 551 H
rrdroz@sanjuanciudadpatria.com
DRUCKER, David .... 508-541-1508 225 G
ddrucker@dean.edu
DRUCKER, Jesse .... 216-523-7440 380 D
jesse.s.drucker@csuohio.edu
DRUCKER, Monique ..... 203-582-8723.. 91 E
monique.drucker@quinnipiac.edu
DRUCKER, Sheldon ...... 201-692-7100 302 H
drucker@fdu.edu
DRUCKREY, Melissa ..... 601-979-2123 267 H
melissa.l.druckrey@jsums.edu
DRUDING, Marlene .... 856-225-6768 307 A
mdruding@camden.rutgers.edu
DRUEKE, Tim .... 803-323-4862 451 I
drueket@winthrop.edu
DRUGOVICH,
Margaret, L .... 607-431-4990 327 B
president@hartwick.edu
DRUMLUK, Sandy .... 607-844-8222 350 A
drumlus@tc3.edu
DRUMM, Kevin .... 607-778-5100 344 F
drummke@sunybroome.edu
DRUMMER, Carlee .... 860-932-4000.. 90 A
cdrummer@qvcc.commnet.edu
DRUMMER FRANCIS,
Raydora, S .... 315-470-4815 347 B
rsdrumme@esf.edu
DRUMMOND, Carl .... 260-481-6116 168 D
drummond@ipfw.edu
DRUMMOND,
Cindy-Lou .... 845-368-7208 342 A
cindy-lou.drummond@use.salvationarmy.org
DRUMMOND, Connie ... 405-682-1611 399 K
cdrummond@occc.edu
DRUMMOND, Gordon .. 480-212-1704.. 17 M
DRUMMOND, Jason, S 660-543-4157 283 F
drummond@ucmo.edu
DRUMMOND, Jerri .... 315-312-4887 346 A
jerri.drummond@oswego.edu
DRUMMOND, Qiana, J . 410-651-6283 219 H
qjdrummond@umes.edu
DRUMMOND, Sarah, B 617-964-1100 222 B
sdrummond@ants.edu
DRURY, Shana .... 940-552-6291 496 B
sdrury@vernoncollege.edu
DRY, Judy .... 314-625-0300 281 F
jdry@slchcmail.com
DRYDEN, Deidra .... 540-261-8516 512 J
deidra.dryden@svu.edu
DRYDEN, Jonathan, N .. 440-365-5222 385 E
DRYE, Theresea .... 813-974-5705 116 B
tdrye@usf.edu
DRYER, Christy .... 410-287-6060 214 C
cdryer@cecil.edu

DRYER, Michael .... 215-572-2900 412 F
dryerm@arcadia.edu
DRYER, Mike .... 215-951-2677 432 F
dryerm@philau.edu
DRYGAS, Emily .... 907-474-6631.. 10 I
emily.drygas@alaska.edu
DRZAKOWSKI,
Meridith .... 715-232-5312 541 B
drzakowskim@uwstout.edu
DU, Fang .... 330-829-8175 394 A
dufang@mountunion.edu
DU, Queenie .... 626-256-4673.. 39 B
qdu@coh.org
DUARTE, John .... 541-880-2282 406 E
registrar@klamathcc.edu
DUARTE, John .... 541-956-7176 409 F
jduarte@roguecc.edu
DUARTE, Mark, A .... 671-735-2266 549 G
mduarte@uguam.uog.edu
DUBAK, Izabela .... 630-889-6576 154 E
idubak@nuhs.edu
DUBBE, Della .... 406-447-6943 287 F
della.dubbe@umhelena.edu
DUBBERLY, Russell, G . 904-620-2769 116 A
r.dubberly@unf.edu
DUBBINI, Murad .... 909-447-6321.. 39 G
mdubbini@cst.edu
DUBE, CarolAnne .... 207-974-4817 211 A
cadube@emcc.edu
DUBEAU, Peter .... 410-225-2371 216 F
pdubeau@mica.edu
DUBEY, Steve .... 775-784-1331 295 H
sdubey@unr.edu
DUBIEL, Derek .... 575-624-7172 310 J
derek.dubiel@roswell.enmu.edu
DUBIEL, Mandy .... 517-629-0600 239 A
adubiel@albion.edu
DUBIN, Bruce, D .... 816-654-7203 276 G
bdubin@kcumb.edu
DUBINSKY, Zalman ...... 973-267-8005 305 E
zalmandubinsky@gmail.com
DUBLON, Felice .... 312-629-6800 158 J
fdublon@saic.edu
DUBOFF, Brian .... 505-428-1318 313 A
brian.duboff@sfcc.edu
DUBOIS, Andrea .... 714-449-7823.. 53 D
adubois@ketchum.edu
DUBOIS, Darcy .... 617-879-2258 238 C
ddubois@wheelock.edu
DUBOIS, Glenn .... 804-819-4903 514 G
gdubois@vccs.edu
DUBOIS, Keith .... 207-780-5250 213 A
dubois@usm.maine.edu
DUBOIS, Philip, L .... 704-687-5729 371 B
pdubois@uncc.edu
DUBOIS, Shelly .... 425-709-3968 144 A
sdubois@devry.edu
DUBOSE, Cheryl .... 843-355-4162 451 H
dubosec@wiltech.edu
DUBOSE, Lisa .... 567-661-7263 390 D
lisa_dubose@owens.edu
DUBOSE, Richard, A ..... 270-745-5405 201 D
rick.dubose@wku.edu
DUBRAY, Kirsten .... 916-484-8175.. 52 I
dubrayk@arc.losrios.edu
DUBRAY, Robert, R ...... 412-365-1641 415 C
rdubray@chatham.edu
DUBROY, Tashni-Ann .. 919-546-8300 368 G
tdubroy@shawu.edu
DUBS, Tracy .... 765-983-1582 165 H
dubstr@earlham.edu
DUBUC, Lisa .... 716-614-6798 336 D
dubuc@niagaracc.suny.edu
DUBUIS, Dina .... 734-432-5309 246 B
ddubuis@madonna.edu
DUBUQUE, Erick .... 502-585-9911 199 E
edubuque@spalding.edu
DUBUQUE, Jennifer ...... 814-886-6319 427 B
jdubuque@mtaloy.edu
DUCHARME, Gaylene .... 406-338-5441 286 C
gatk@bfcc.edu
DUCHARME, Lisa .... 413-572-8370 230 F
lducharme@westfield.ma.edu
DUCHARME-WHITE,
Sherri .... 414-955-4145 537 C
sducharm@mail.mcw.edu
DUCHATELET, Martine .. 509-828-1223 522 C
mduchatelet@ewu.edu
DUCHENEAUX,
Stephanie .... 325-574-6502 497 E
sducheneaux@wtc.edu
DUCHESNE, Kathryn ..... 603-342-3042 297 E
kduchesne@ccsnh.edu
DUCHSCHERER, Eric, D 315-267-2350 346 C
duchsced@potsdam.edu
DUCIOAME, Lynn .... 940-397-4676 478 G
lynn.ducioame@mwsu.edu
DUCK, Haley .... 601-484-8819 268 B
dhaley@meridiancc.edu
DUCKETT, Catherine ..... 732-571-3421 303 G
cduckett@monmouth.edu
DUCKETT, Dwaine, B .... 510-987-0301.. 70 J
dwaine.duckett@ucop.edu
DUCKETT, Randy .... 803-641-3480 450 C
randyd@usca.edu
DUCKHAM, James .... 765-285-1832 164 D
DUCKWORTH, Brad ...... 414-382-6323 534 I
brad.duckworth@alverno.edu
DUCKWORTH, Cory, L .. 716-338-1060 329 E
coryduckworth@mail.sunyjcc.edu
DUCKWORTH, Melinda . 301-784-5000 213 C
mduckworth@allegany.edu
DUCKWORTH, Tony ...... 918-444-3926 398 M
duckwo01@nsuok.edu
DUCLOS, Mark .... 478-445-4467 125 A
mark.duclos@gcsu.edu
DUCLOS-BARRETT,
Victoria .... 401-341-2345 442 D
duclosv@salve.edu
DUCOFFE, Robert .... 574-520-4133 168 F
ducoffe@iusb.edu
DUCRAY, Sarah .... 202-651-5000.. 95 C
sarah.ducray@gallaudet.edu
DUDA, Stephen .... 570-504-1734 422 G
dudas@lackawanna.edu
DUDA, Teri .... 201-967-9667 300 C
td@berkeleycollege.edu
DUDA, Teri .... 201-967-9667 316 D
td@berkeleycollege.edu
DUDAK, Brian .... 509-279-6066 521 E
brian.dudak@scc.spokane.edu
DUDAK, Nancy, J .... 610-519-7300 439 A
nancy.dudak@villanova.edu
DUDAS, Bertalan .... 814-866-8142 423 B
bdudas@lecom.edu
DUDAS, Jon .... 520-621-5511.. 18 E
jondudas@email.arizona.edu
DUDAS, Philip .... 651-905-3542 264 E
pdudas@browncollege.edu
DUDGEON, David .... 305-899-3727.. 99 B
ddudgeon@barry.edu
DUDLEY, Brad, D .... 310-506-4184.. 58 H
brad.dudley@pepperdine.edu
DUDLEY, Charlotte .... 404-627-2681 121 F
charlotte.dudley@beulah.org
DUDLEY,
Christopher, H .... 336-841-9127 357 E
cdudley@highpoint.edu
DUDLEY, Deborah, L .... 315-267-2113 346 C
dudleydl@potsdam.edu
DUDLEY, Erastus, C ..... 334-833-4582.... 4 E
tdudley@huntingdon.edu
DUDLEY, Erlene .... 573-592-4291 286 A
erlene.dudley@williamwoods.edu
DUDLEY, Jacklyn, K ..... 270-809-3774 198 I
jdudley@murraystate.edu
DUDLEY, Jason .... 239-489-9307 104 G
jdudley1@fsw.edu
DUDLEY, Manuel .... 336-334-4822 363 A
mcdudley@gtcc.edu
DUDLEY, Sharese .... 219-980-6791 168 C
shaadudl@iun.edu
DUDLEY, Waller, T .... 540-458-8470 519 A
wdudley@wlu.edu
DUDLEY, William .... 713-222-5368 491 F
dudleyw@uhd.edu
DUDLEY, William, C ..... 413-597-4352 238 E
william.c.dudley@williams.edu
DUDLEY-ESHBACH,
Janet, E .... 410-543-6011 220 E
jdudleyeshbach@salisbury.edu
DUDT, Susan .... 770-426-2700 128 C
sdudt@life.edu
DUELL, Charles .... 303-914-6517.. 85 C
charles.duell@rrcc.edu
DUELLO, Brenda .... 319-363-1323 181 D
bduello@mtmercy.edu
DUENAS, Felicia .... 323-241-5376.. 51 I
duenasmv@lasc.edu
DUENEZ, Nydia .... 213-738-6871.. 68 E
deanofstudents@swlaw.edu
DUERK, Jeffrey .... 216-368-3227 378 J
duerk@case.edu
DUERR, Larry .... 414-382-6173 534 I
larry.duerr@alverno.edu
DUERR, Lindsey .... 608-363-2176 534 L
duerrl@beloit.edu
DUERWACHTER,
Kathleen, A .... 608-796-3072 542 H
kaduerwachter@viterbo.edu
DUESING, Jason .... 816-414-3740 278 E
jduesing@mbts.edu
DUETT, Belinda, G .... 334-833-4519.... 4 E
bduett@huntingdon.edu
DUEWEKE, Anne, T ...... 269-337-7418 244 I
Anne.Dueweke@kzoo.edu
DUENES, Michael .... 763-424-0950 260 E
MDuenes@nhcc.edu
DUFAULT-HUNTER,
David .... 626-815-2022.. 29 B
ddhunter@apu.edu
DUFENDACH, Sarah ..... 301-985-7252 220 A
sarah.dufendach@umuc.edu
DUFF, Cathy .... 239-590-7043 114 F
cduff@fgcu.edu
DUFF, Debra .... 414-256-1258 538 A
duffd@mtmary.edu
DUFF, John .... 978-762-4000 232 D
jduff@northshore.edu
DUFF, John, A .... 727-864-8974 101 P
duffja@eckerd.edu
DUFF, Pamela, S .... 540-423-9039 515 E
pduff@germanna.edu
DUFF, Rebecca .... 540-985-8246 509 D
rduff@jchs.edu
DUFF, Sarah .... 605-995-7186 452 H
sarah.duff@mitchelltech.edu
DUFF-ANDERSON,
Rachel .... 419-824-3759 385 F
rduff-anderson@lourdes.edu
DUFFEL-JONES, Mona .. 504-816-4024 202 F
mduffeljones@dillard.edu
DUFFETT, Robert .... 610-341-5890 418 A
rduffett@eastern.edu
DUFFETT, Robert, G ...... 610-341-5890 427 I
rduffett@eastern.edu
DUFFEY, Sherry .... 850-484-1653 110 D
sduffey@pensacolastate.edu
DUFFIE, James, E .... 561-868-3077 109 H
duffiej@palmbeachstate.edu
DUFFIE, Robert .... 361-582-2469 496 D
robert.duffie@victoriacollege.edu
DUFFINS, Varo, L .... 610-328-8360 436 A
vduffin1@swarthmore.edu
DUFFOURC, Danielle .... 504-520-7563 209 E
dduffour@xula.edu
DUFFY, Brad .... 225-768-1719 206 F
brad.duffy@ololcollege.edu
DUFFY, Bre .... 212-659-3604 330 A
bduffy@tkc.edu
DUFFY, Brian .... 215-972-2030 429 G
bduffy@pafa.edu
DUFFY, Brian .... 901-381-3939 466 E
brian@visible.edu
DUFFY, Cami .... 270-809-3155 198 I
cduffy@murraystate.edu
DUFFY, Dolly .... 574-631-2788 174 A
eduffy@nd.edu
DUFFY, James, P .... 717-337-6240 419 C
jpduffy@gettysburg.edu
DUFFY, James, P .... 757-683-3808 510 I
jduffy@odu.edu
DUFFY, Joan .... 805-546-3100.. 42 H
joan_duffy@cuesta.edu
DUFFY, John .... 847-214-7374 144 F
jduffyecc@aol.com
DUFFY, Julia, A .... 203-254-4000.. 90 E
jduffy@fairfield.edu
DUFFY, Kristine .... 518-743-2237 347 E
duffyk@sunyacc.edu
DUFFY, Michael .... 517-265-5161 238 H
mduffy@adrian.edu
DUFFY, Michael .... 610-282-1100 416 I
michael.duffy@desales.edu
DUFFY, Pamela, A .... 619-239-0391.. 36 E
pduffy@cwsl.edu
DUFFY, Peter .... 508-999-9216 228 H
pduffy@umassd.edu
DUFFY, Rachelle, M ..... 517-265-5161 238 H
rduffy@adrian.edu
DUFFY, Sharon .... 617-824-8640 226 A
sharon_duffy@emerson.edu
DUFFY, Sophia .... 610-526-1255 412 D
sophia.duffy@theamericancollege.edu
DUFFY, Susan .... 781-239-6425 222 E
sduffy@babson.edu
DUFFY, II, William, R .. 563-425-5221 183 G
duffyw@uiu.edu
DUFNER, Jessie .... 406-874-6226 287 A
Dufnerj@milescc.edu
DUFORE, Timothy, R .... 330-972-7238 392 H
tdufore@uakron.edu
DUFOUR, Graciela .... 815-836-5270 150 F
dufourgr@lewisu.edu
DUFOUR, Jeff .... 518-694-7201 314 G
jeff.dufour@acphs.edu
DUFRENE, Uric .... 812-941-2208 169 A
udufrene@ius.edu
DUFRESNE-REYES,
Alice .... 408-848-4791.. 45 G
adufresnereyes@gavilan.edu
DUGAN, Brendan, J ...... 718-489-5416 340 E
bdugan@sfc.edu
DUGAN, Christine, M ... 717-245-1180 417 B
duganc@dickinson.edu
DUGAN, James, P .... 818-785-2726.. 37 I
james.dugan@casalomacollege.edu
DUGAN, Melinda, E ..... 215-887-5511 439 E
mdugan@wts.edu
DUGAN, Michael .... 410-827-5834 214 D
mdugan@chesapeake.edu
DUGAN, Robert .... 850-474-2446 116 E
rdugan@uwf.edu
DUGAN, Sharon .... 818-785-2726.. 37 I
sharon.dugan@casalomacollege.edu
DUGAN, Sharon, M ...... 818-785-2726.. 37 I
sharon.dugan@casalomacollege.edu
DUGAN, Suzanne .... 507-389-2111 260 A
suzanne.dugan@mnsu.edu
DUGAN-WOOD, Joyce .. 205-929-1458.... 5 I
jduganwood@miles.edu
DUGAS, Ross .... 952-888-4777 263 I
rdugas@nwhealth.edu
DUGATKIN, David .... 845-257-3802 344 A
dugatkind@newpaltz.edu
DUGDALE, Kathy .... 218-733-5990 259 C
k.dugdale@lsc.edu
DUGGAN, Christina ...... 781-768-7228 236 A
christina.duggan@regiscollege.edu
DUGGAN, David, B ...... 315-464-9720 344 E
duggand@upstate.edu
DUGGAN, Sean .... 806-742-2661 489 F
s.duggan@ttu.edu
DUGGAN-GOLD, Lori .... 516-877-3262 314 F
duggangold@adelphi.edu
DUGGAR, Michael .... 617-824-8268 226 A
michael_duggar@emerson.edu
DUGGER, Jim .... 901-435-1680 457 N
jim_dugger@loc.edu
DUGGER, Neil .... 214-333-5202 471 L
neil@dbu.edu
DUGUID, Stephanie ...... 601-643-8341 266 J
stephanie.duguid@colin.edu
DUHAN, Julia .... 517-371-5140 252 J
duhan@cooley.edu
DUHE, Reginald .... 650-508-3500.. 56 H
rduhe@ndnu.edu
DUHON, Gail .... 616-222-1431 241 G
gail.duhon@cornerstone.edu
DUIGNAN, Kevin .... 845-398-4017 341 H
kduignan@stac.edu
DUIN, Diane .... 406-896-5841 287 H
dduin@msubillings.edu
DUJARDIAN, Tamara ..... 407-628-5870 102 I
tamara.dujardian@zenith.org
DUKAKIS, Mary .... 603-668-2211 298 H
m.dukakis@snhu.edu
DUKE, Christopher .... 615-329-8505 456 G
cduke@fisk.edu
DUKE, Del, G .... 870-235-4171.. 23 D
dgduke@saumag.edu
DUKE, Kenneth .... 828-884-8144 355 A
dukekm@brevard.edu
DUKE, Lori .... 919-760-2291 359 B
dukel@meredith.edu
DUKE, Lynda .... 309-556-3220 148 A
lduke@iwu.edu
DUKE, Phyllis .... 908-737-5000 303 C
pduke@kean.edu
DUKE, Robert .... 626-815-5441.. 29 B
rrduke@apu.edu
DUKE, Russell .... 626-650-2308.. 46 C
DUKE, Sean .... 206-533-6659 526 G
sduke@shoreline.edu
DUKE, Shalamon .... 310-287-4423.. 52 C
dukesa@wlac.edu
DUKE, Steven .... 336-758-5938 372 G
dukest@wfu.edu
DUKE, Todd .... 765-973-8611 168 A
mtduke@iue.edu
DUKERICH, Janet, M .... 512-232-3310 493 M
janet.dukerich@austin.utexas.edu
DUKES, Charlene, M .... 301-322-0400 217 G
dukescm@pgcc.edu
DUKES, Gary .... 503-838-8221 411 B
dukesg@wou.edu
DUKES, Jimmy .... 504-816-8092 206 C
jdukes@nobts.edu
DUKES, Mona, B .... 843-355-4121 451 H
dukesm@wiltech.edu
DULABAUM, Mary .... 847-628-2089 149 A
mdulabaum@judsonu.edu
DULANEY, Jeri .... 580-477-2000 404 D
jeri.dulaney@wosc.edu
DULANY, Ann .... 740-284-5254 382 G
adulany@franciscan.edu
DULAS, Jennie .... 206-934-5661 525 K
jennie.dulas@seattlecolleges.edu
DULAY, Sarah .... 708-237-5050 155 B
sdulay@nc.edu
DULEPSKI, Deborah, L . 203-576-2388.. 92 B
ddulepsk@bridgeport.edu
DULEY, Victoria .... 518-562-4184 321 D
victoria.duley@clinton.edu
DULGAR, Laura .... 623-935-8808.. 14 L
laura.dulgar@estrellamountain.edu
DULIN, Scott .... 617-236-8800 226 F
sdulin@fisher.edu
DULING, Sandra .... 802-468-1396 503 G
sandy.duling@castleton.edu
DULL, Lindsay, N .... 607-733-7177 324 H
Ldull@ebi-college.com

DUNNAGAN, Tim .... 208-426-4116 137 E
timdunnagan@boisestate.edu

DUNNE, Jennifer .... 617-333-2271 225 F
jdunne1213@curry.edu

DUNNE, Martha, L ...... 212-998-2115 336 C
marti.dunne@nyu.edu

DUNNE, Mary, L .... 845-575-3000 331 L
Mary.Dunne@marist.edu

DUNNE, Michele, A ...... 515-263-2853 178 H
mdunne@grandview.edu

DUNNE, Nicole .... 831-646-3007.. 54 H
ndunne@mpc.edu

DUNNE, Thomas, A ...... 718-817-0180 326 C
tdunne@fordham.edu

DUNNE, Timothy .... 207-741-5506 211 D
tdunne@smccme.edu

DUNNE, Will .... 386-506-4486 101 I
dunnew@DaytonaState.edu

DUNNE-CASCIO,
Colleen .... 541-962-3476 405 G
ccascio@eou.edu

DUNNETT, Stephen, C .. 716-645-2368 343 E
dunnett@buffalo.edu

DUNNING, Arthur, N .... 229-430-4605 119 H
Art.Dunning@asurams.edu

DUNNING, Jim .... 805-756-5551.. 32 E
jdunning@calpoly.edu

DUNNING, John .... 402-375-7286 292 D
jodunni1@wsc.edu

DUNNING, Lisa .... 302-857-6050.. 93 E
ldunning@desu.edu

DUNNING, Sue .... 863-638-2937 119 A
dunnings@webber.edu

DUNNINGS, Lance .... 404-880-8051 122 I
ldunning@cau.edu

DUNNINGTON,
Sandra, F .... 301-322-0406 217 G
dunninsf@pgcc.edu

DUNNUCK, John .... 954-201-7405.. 99 G
jdunnuck@broward.edu

DUNPHE, Beth .... 212-343-1234 332 I
bdunphe@mcny.edu

DUNPHY, Michael .... 330-490-7201 395 C
mdunphy@walsh.edu

DUNSEATH, Jennifer ..... 401-454-6386 442 B
jdunseat@risd.edu

DUNSON, Kenneth .... 972-238-6171 473 B
kdunson@dcccd.edu

DUNSON, Necol, M ...... 304-829-7394 529 H
ndunson@bethanywv.edu

DUNSTON, Karen .... 503-352-2218 408 I
dunstonk@pacificu.edu

DUNSTON, Rita .... 540-654-1063 513 I
rdunston@umw.edu

DUNSWORTH,
Richard, L .... 479-979-1242.. 25 H
rdunsworth@ozarks.edu

DUNTLEY, Mark .... 503-768-7082 406 H
duntley@lclark.edu

DUNTON, Renee .... 207-947-4591 209 G
rdunton@bealcollege.edu

DUNTON, Susan .... 603-271-6484 297 C
sdunton@ccsnh.edu

DUNZWEILER, Denise ... 509-527-2615 528 A
denise.dunzweiler@wallawalla.edu

DUPAUL, Stephanie ...... 804-287-6442 513 M
sdupaul@richmond.edu

DUPEE, Daniel .... 315-786-2401 329 G
ddupee@sunyjefferson.edu

DUPELL, Linda .... 978-665-4342 229 D
ldupell@fitchburgstate.edu

DUPES, Steven .... 717-720-4100 430 A
sdupes@passhe.edu

DUPIER, Charles .... 606-539-4316 200 F
chuck.dupier@ucumberlands.edu

DUPIER, Jo .... 606-539-4208 200 F
jo.dupier@ucumberlands.edu

DUPKE, Vicki .... 567-661-7172 390 D
vicki_dupke@owens.edu

DUPLESSIS, Julie .... 319-385-6242 180 A
julie.duplessis@iw.edu

DUPONT, Joseph .... 617-552-3430 224 B
joseph.dupont@bc.edu

DUPONT, Michael .... 817-515-3584 484 B
michael.dupont@tccd.edu

DUPRA, JoAnn .... 870-543-5993.. 23 C
jdupra@seark.edu

DUPRE, Terry, G .... 985-448-4031 208 C
terry.dupre@nicholls.edu

DUPREE, Carol .... 325-794-4401 470 I
carol.dupree@cisco.edu

DUPREE, Cathy, P .... 252-823-5166 362 D
dupreec@edgecombe.edu

DUPREE, David .... 504-280-6235 205 G
ddupree@uno.edu

DUPREE, Jason, M ...... 580-774-7081 402 G
jason.dupree@swosu.edu

DUPREE, Jimmy .... 614-837-4088 394 H
dupreej@valorcollege.com

DUPREE, Kathy .... 281-212-1610 491 E
dupree@uhcl.edu

DUPREE, Paul, J .... 859-858-3511 193 A
pdupree@asbury.edu

DUPREE, Richard, K ..... 812-855-3158 167 J
rdupree@indiana.edu

DUPREY, Lorey .... 207-509-7264 212 A
lduprey@unity.edu

DUPREY, Wayne, A ...... 518-564-2033 346 B
dupreywa@plattsburgh.edu

DUPRE', Carolyn .... 601-877-4701 266 C
cdupre@alcorn.edu

DUPRIE, Kelsey .... 360-992-2505 521 A
sduprie@clark.edu

DUPRIEST, Barclay, F ... 804-752-7371 511 E
bdupries@rmc.edu

DUPUIS, Kellie, J .... 518-320-3264 343 B
kellie.dupuis@suny.edu

DURAJ, Jonathan .... 937-327-7817 395 I
jduraj@wittenberg.edu

DURAN, Adrianna .... 915-779-8031 496 G
aduran@computercareercenter.com

DURAN, Alexandra .... 408-270-6434.. 63 P
alexandra.duran@evc.edu

DURAN, Armando .... 626-585-7148.. 58 F
axduran@pasadena.edu

DURAN, Dorothy .... 507-453-2721 259 G
dduran@southeastmn.edu

DURAN, Kelly .... 716-839-8290 323 F
kduran@daemen.edu

DURAN, Margret .... 806-743-2300 490 A
margret.duran@ttuhsc.edu

DURAN, Michelle .... 361-593-5501 486 A
michelle.duran@tamuk.edu

DURAN, Veronica .... 520-494-5260.. 12 R
veronica.duran@centralaz.edu

DURAND, Bonita, R ...... 716-878-4102 345 B
durandbr@buffalostate.edu

DURAND, Stefanie .... 509-452-5100 524 J

DURAND, V. Mark .... 727-873-4324 116 C
mdurand@usfsp.edu

DURANDETTA,
Donald, W .... 302-356-6780.. 94 G
donald.w.durandetta@wilmu.edu

DURANT, Benjamin ...... 919-530-7425 370 C
benjamin.durant@nccu.edu

DURANT, Brian, M .... 315-255-1743 317 I
durantb@cayuga-cc.edu

DURANT, Joseph .... 843-661-8086 446 C
joe.durant@fdtc.edu

DURANT, Joseph, M .... 843-792-2252 447 G
durantjm@musc.edu

DURANT, Joyce, M ...... 843-661-1300 446 E
jdurant@fmarion.edu

DURANT, Leroy, A .... 803-535-5341 444 D
ldurant@claflin.edu

DURANT, Linda, S .... 610-499-4123 439 G
lsdurant@widener.edu

DURANT, Natalie .... 860-768-5565.. 92 F
ndurant@hartford.edu

DURANT, Nickeshia .... 718-357-0500 341 F
ndurant@stpaulsschoolofnursing.edu

DURANT, Zoe, W .... 580-581-2289 397 A
zoed@cameron.edu

DURANTI, Alessandro .. 310-825-4017.. 71 D
aduranti@college.ucla.edu

DURBAK, Andres .... 773-907-4708 141 O
adurbak@ccc.edu

DURBEN, Katherine .... 414-288-5470 537 B
katherine.durben@marquette.edu

DURBIN, Bryce .... 706-236-2282 121 E
bdurbin@berry.edu

DURBIN, Daniel, A .... 304-293-4008 533 D
dan.durbin@mail.wvu.edu

DURBIN, Rachel .... 503-494-7800 408 D
finaid@ohsu.edu

DURDEN, Lori .... 912-486-7607 129 E
ldurden@ogeecheetech.edu

DURDEN, Tracey .... 734-432-5673 246 B
tdurden@madonna.edu

DUREE, Christopher ...... 641-844-5720 179 J
christopher.duree@iavalley.edu

DUREE, Christopher, A . 641-844-5720 179 L
christopher.duree@iavalley.edu

DUREN, Andrew, M .... 708-974-5203 153 D
duren@morainevalley.edu

DURETTE, Kristi .... 603-645-9780 298 H
k.durette@snhu.edu

DURFEE, Carissa .... 617-989-4086 237 G
durfeec@wit.edu

DURFEE, Jeffrey, A .... 904-620-2820 116 A
jdurfee@unf.edu

DURFEE, Mike .... 307-532-8346 546 B
mike.durfee@ewc.wy.edu

DURGIN, William .... 315-792-7200 348 D
william.durgin@sunyit.edu

DURHAM, Bree .... 850-729-6458 109 D
durhamb@nwfsc.edu

DURHAM, Danielle .... 660-831-4172 279 D
durhamd@moval.edu

DURHAM, David, L ...... 304-293-8220 533 D
david.durham@mail.wvu.edu

DURHAM, Dawn, W ..... 864-833-8477 448 E
dwdurham@presby.edu

DURHAM, Ed .... 410-287-1010 214 C
edurham@cecil.edu

DURHAM, Elise .... 404-215-2680 128 L
elise.durham@morehouse.edu

DURHAM, Gesele .... 414-229-3305 540 A
gedurham@uwm.edu

DURHAM, Jerry .... 319-226-2015 175 D
Jerry.Durham@AllenCollege.edu

DURHAM, John, R .... 610-519-7164 439 A
john.durham@villanova.edu

DURHAM, Kaci .... 513-244-8100 379 I
kaci.durham@ccuniversity.edu

DURHAM, Kathy, F .... 828-448-3102 367 B
kdurham@wpcc.edu

DURHAM, Kimberly ...... 954-262-8601 109 E
durham@nova.edu

DURHAM, Lynn .... 404-894-8261 125 D
lynn.durham@carnegie.gatech.edu

DURHAM, Rhonda .... 501-882-4442.. 19 E
rsdurham@asub.edu

DURHAM, Tammara ..... 785-864-4060 191 G
tdurham@ku.edu

DURHAM, Teresa .... 269-965-3931 244 L
durhamt@kellogg.edu

DURHAM, William, H ... 704-233-8219 373 C
durham@wingate.edu

DURIAN-GAMBELL,
Angella .... 641-673-1076 184 B
gambella@wmpenn.edu

DURKEE, Gene .... 603-428-2358 298 B
edurkee@nec.edu

DURKEE, Mary Kate ..... 619-298-1829.. 68 C

DURKEE, Phillip, A .... 831-656-2517 548 A
padurkee@nps.edu

DURKEE, Robert, K .... 609-258-6428 305 C
durkee@princeton.edu

DURKIN, Karen .... 856-415-2284 306 C
kdurkin@rcgc.edu

DURKIN, Mary .... 718-429-6600 352 A
mary.durkin@vaughn.edu

DURKIN, Melissa .... 317-632-5553 170 Z
mdurkin@lincolntech.com

DURKIN, Rebecca .... 847-578-8351 157 G
rebecca.durkin@rosalindfranklin.edu

DURKLE, Robert, F .... 937-229-4411 393 E
rdurkle1@udayton.edu

DURNFORD, Ronald, R 504-520-5031 209 E
rdurnfor@xula.edu

DURNIN, Ellen .... 203-392-5356.. 88 F
durnine1@southernct.edu

DUROCHER, Becky, L ... 985-448-4510 208 C
becky.durocher@nicholls.edu

DUROJAIYE, Ande .... 561-297-3004 114 E
adurojaiye@fau.edu

DUROSS, Frank .... 315-792-5526 333 D
fduross@mvcc.edu

DURR, Elaine .... 336-278-5229 356 F
edurr@elon.edu

DURR, Jeanne .... 719-255-3969.. 86 F
jdurr@uccs.edu

DURR, Kimberly, H ...... 618-650-2477 159 I
kdurr@siue.edu

DURRETT, Duane .... 940-627-2690 497 A
ddurrett@wc.edu

DURSI, Joseph, F .... 914-594-4487 335 H
joseph_dursi@nymc.edu

DURSI, Joseph, F .... 914-594-4234 335 H
joseph_dursi@nymc.edu

DURSO, Thomas, W ..... 610-921-7526 411 E
tdurso@albright.edu

DURST, Devoiry .... 732-414-2834 309 L
yeshivatoraschaim@gmail.com

DURST, Lisa .... 440-525-7721 385 C
ldurst@lakelandcc.edu

DURST, Steve .... 231-591-2254 242 L
SteveDurst@ferris.edu

DURYEA, David .... 607-753-2211 345 C
david.duryea@cortland.edu

DUSEK, Craig .... 620-417-1204 191 A
craig.dusek@sccc.edu

DUSENBURY, Renata .... 919-546-8252 368 G
rdusenbury@shawu.edu

DUSING, Roger .... 816-584-6386 280 F
roger.dusing@park.edu

DUSSEAU, Daniel .... 703-425-5369 516 C
ddusseau@nvcc.edu

DUSSOURD, Ellen, A .... 716-645-2258 343 E
dussourd@buffalo.edu

DUSTIN, Kevin, M .... 801-957-4083 500 E
kevin.dustin@slcc.edu

DUTCH, Jennifer .... 402-363-5719 294 G
jdutch@york.edu

DUTCHER, Dave .... 315-733-2300 351 E
ddutcher@uscny.edu

DUTCHER, Debra .... 518-327-6082 338 B
ddutcher@paulsmiths.edu

DUTCHER, Donald .... 315-866-0300 327 E
dutcherdm@herkimer.edu

DUTCHER, James .... 518-255-5337 346 E
dutchejm@cobleskill.edu

DUTCHIK, Lisa .... 319-398-5431 180 J
lisa.dutchik@kirkwood.edu

DUTLER, Sue .... 312-935-2210 157 A
sdutler@robertmorris.edu

DUTREMBLE, Kathy ...... 850-484-2076 110 D
kdutremble@pensacolastate.edu

DUTRISAC, Gordon .... 425-352-8205 520 D
gdutrisac@cascadia.edu

DUTSCHKE, Jeremy, D . 870-759-4120.. 25 I
jdutschke@wbcoll.edu

DUTTA, Debasish .... 765-494-9709 171 K

DUTTA, Mitra .... 312-996-6174 161 F
dutta@uic.edu

DUTTA, Soumitra .... 607-255-6418 323 C
sd599@cornell.edu

DUTTON, Ashley .... 860-231-5245.. 93 A
adutton@usj.edu

DUTTON, Colleen .... 972-883-2221 494 A
colleen.dutton@utdallas.edu

DUTTON, Dennis .... 620-278-4364 191 D
ddutton@sterling.edu

DUTTON, Timothy .... 937-752-2189 385 A
timothy.dutton@khnetwork.org

DUTTON COX, Deborah 603-862-1627 299 B
debbie.dutton@unh.edu

DUUS, Martin .... 212-280-1426 351 B
mduus@uts.columbia.edu

DUVAL, Amanda .... 563-425-5959 183 G
duvala81@uiu.edu

DUVAL, Derethia .... 415-338-2208.. 36 A
derethia@sfsu.edu

DUVALL, C. J .... 501-370-5378.. 22 E
cjduvall@philander.edu

DUVALL, Joanna .... 740-389-4636 386 B
duvallj@mtc.edu

DUVALL, Staci .... 501-977-2087.. 25 A
duvall@uaccm.edu

DUXBURY-EDWARDS,
Chris .... 303-329-6355.. 81 B
recruiting@cstcm.edu

DVIR, Arik .... 248-370-2762 248 K
dvir@oakland.edu

DVORACSEK, Joe .... 727-341-6108 112 A
dvoracsek.joe@spcollege.edu

DVORAK, Jerome .... 570-389-4216 430 B
jdvorak@bloomufdn.org

DVORAK, Leah, M .... 262-243-5700 535 I
leah.dvorak@cuw.edu

DVORAK, Robert .... 415-380-1358.. 45 J
robertdvorak@ggbts.edu

DVORAK, Sarah .... 574-284-4587 172 G
sdvorak@saintmarys.edu

DVORAK, Susan .... 414-466-9777 542 J
sdvorak@wspp.edu

DVORKIN, Ariel .... 212-431-7959 335 G
Ariel.Dvorkin@nyls.edu

DWIGHT, Beverly, J ..... 413-796-2210 238 A
beverly.dwight@wne.edu

DWIRE, Steven, W .... 518-454-5464 322 C
dwires@strose.edu

DWORACZYK, Bill .... 214-768-3140 482 J
billd@smu.edu

DWORKIN, James, B .... 219-785-5331 172 A
jdworkin@pnc.edu

DWORSCHAK, Mark ...... 520-206-4558.. 17 A
mdworschak@pima.edu

DWYER, James, P .... 989-964-4287 249 G
jdwyer@svsu.edu

DWYER, Jim .... 970-339-6412.. 78 J
jim.dwyer@aims.edu

DWYER, Johanna .... 360-596-5235 527 B
jdwyer@spscc.edu

DWYER, Jon .... 360-412-6152 525 H
JDwyer@stmartin.edu

DWYER, Katelyn .... 617-322-3524 227 J
katelyn_dwyer@laboure.edu

DWYER, Kathleen .... 502-410-6200 194 N
kdwyer@galencollege.edu

DWYER, Ken .... 508-854-4579 232 F
krd@qcc.mass.edu

DWYER, Mary, E .... 716-878-3141 345 B
dwyerme@buffalostate.edu

DWYER, Sharon .... 805-289-8976.. 75 E
sdwyer@vcccd.edu

DWYER, Thomas .... 502-410-6200 194 N
tdwyer@galencollege.edu

DWYER, Thomas, L ...... 401-598-1000 441 D
Tom.Dwyer@jwu.edu

DWYER, Thomas, P ...... 804-752-7244 511 E
tdwyer@rmc.edu

DYAL, Donald .... 806-742-2261 489 F
donald.dyal@ttu.edu

DYBA, Christopher ...... 252-328-9565 369 E
dybac@ecu.edu

DYBICK, Thomas .... 413-205-3972 221 G
thomas.dybick@aic.edu

DYBWAD, Peter .... 510-841-9230.. 77 I
pdybwad@wi.edu

E

EASSA, Emad ... 847-214-7885 144 F
eeassa@elgin.edu

EASSON, David, D ... 508-831-4993 238 G
deasson@wpi.edu

EAST, Dwain ... 501-205-8798 .. 20 G
deast@cbc.edu

EAST, Jody, L ... 641-422-4218 181 E
eastjody@niacc.edu

EAST, Patricia, A ... 319-296-4214 179 B
patricia.east@hawkeyecollege.edu

EASTER, Joyce, B ... 757-455-2126 518 H
jeaster@vwc.edu

EASTER, Julian ... 480-677-7701 .. 12 R
julian.easter@centralaz.edu

EASTER, Lisa ... 785-227-3380 185 A
easterl@bethanylb.edu

EASTER, Michael ... 573-518-2188 278 F
mreaster@mineralarea.edu

EASTERBROOK,
Jonathan ... 860-768-4100 .. 92 F

EASTERLING, Cal ... 918-495-6538 401 B
ceasterling@oru.edu

EASTERLING, Karen ... 810-767-4000 239 H
karen.easterling@baker.edu

EASTERLING, Mayson ... 864-977-7055 448 A
mayson.easterling@ngu.edu

EASTERLING, III,
William, E ... 814-865-6546 428 C
wee2@psu.edu

EASTERWOOD, Allyson . 601-266-6986 271 B
allyson.easterwood@usm.edu

EASTHAM, Sabine ... 270-384-8236 198 C
easthams@lindsey.edu

EASTHAM, Yvette ... 270-707-3731 196 D
yvette.eastham@kctcs.edu

EASTIN, Graig, R ... 518-276-6000 339 D
easting@rpi.edu

EASTLICK, Beth ... 919-681-0405 356 E
beth.eastlick@duke.edu

EASTMAN, Callie ... 907-277-1000 .. 10 E
contact@chartercollege.edu

EASTMAN, III,
Donald, R ... 727-864-8211 101 P
deastman@eckerd.edu

EASTMAN, Douglas ... 802-635-1677 504 A
doug.eastman@jsc.edu

EASTMAN, Garrett ... 508-373-9709 223 C
garrett.eastman@becker.edu

EASTMAN, Ken ... 405-744-5064 400 C
ken.eastman@okstate.edu

EASTMAN, Lori ... 518-580-5640 342 I
leastman@skidmore.edu

EASTMAN, Mindy, R ... 641-422-4363 181 E
eastmmin@niacc.edu

EASTMAN, Nancy ... 816-802-3466 276 F
neastman@kcai.edu

EASTMAN, Nicole ... 508-756-4749 223 C
nicole.layne@becker.edu

EASTMOND, Dawn, L ... 858-784-8469 .. 66 A
eastmond@scripps.edu

EASTON, Celia, A ... 585-245-5726 345 D
easton@geneseo.edu

EASTON, Mark ... 928-226-4284 .. 13 D
mark.easton@coconino.edu

EASTON, Michelle ... 304-357-4879 530 H
michelleeaston@ucwv.edu

EASTON, Patricia ... 909-621-8965 .. 39 E
patricia.easton@cgu.edu

EASTON, Shannon ... 518-608-8234 325 B
seaston@excelsior.edu

EASTON, Tanya ... 410-532-5177 217 F
teaston@ndm.edu

EASTRIDGE, Charlene ... 276-739-2461 517 D
ceastridge@vhcc.edu

EASTTORP, Karl ... 715-422-5326 543 D
karl.easttorp@mstc.edu

EASTTY, Michelle ... 907-745-3201 .. 10 B
meastty@akbible.edu

EASTUS, Victoria ... 212-431-2870 335 G
Victoria.Eastus@nyls.edu

EASTWICK, Thomas ... 973-661-0600 302 D

EASTWICK, Thomas, M 201-327-8877 302 C
tomeastwick@aol.com

EASTWOOD, Candy ... 618-634-3231 159 A
candye@shawneecc.edu

EASTWOOD,
Gregory, L ... 315-464-5540 344 E

EATON, Arlinda ... 470-578-6117 127 M
aeaton4@kennesaw.edu

EATON, Brett ... 336-758-5237 372 G
eatonbd@wfu.edu

EATON, David, L ... 206-543-7468 527 G
deaton@uw.edu

EATON, Gary ... 713-623-2040 468 F
geaton@aii.edu

EATON, Joyce, A ... 336-316-2146 357 C
jeaton@guilford.edu

EATON, Kay ... 609-586-4800 303 D
eatonk@mccc.edu

EATON, Kent ... 713-942-9505 475 D
keaton@hgst.edu

EATON, Kevin ... 817-598-6270 497 A
keaton@wc.edu

EATON, Kristin ... 518-327-6231 338 B
keaton@paulsmiths.edu

EATON, L. David ... 845-257-3210 344 A
eatond@newpaltz.edu

EATON, Mark, A ... 636-584-6733 274 J
mark.eaton@eastcentral.edu

EATON, Michael, B ... 662-862-8001 267 F
mbeaton@iccms.edu

EATON, Patrick, D ... 662-720-7165 269 D
pdeaton@nemcc.edu

EATON, Phyllis, M ... 757-822-2308 517 C
peaton@tcc.edu

EATON, Randy ... 828-227-7338 372 C
jreaton@wcu.edu

EATON, Robert ... 401-456-8776 442 A
reaton@ric.edu

EATON, Stephanie ... 314-516-5765 284 B
stephanie@umsl.edu

EATON, Stephen, B ... 760-252-2411 .. 29 C
seaton@barstow.edu

EATON, Timothy, W ... 405-912-9456 398 B
teaton@hc.edu

EATON-CRAWFORD,
Margaret ... 617-732-2132 233 E
margaret.eaton-crawford@mcphs.edu

EATON-NEEB, Rosalyn .. 507-786-3615 264 C
eatonnee@stolaf.edu

EATON-STULL,
Yvonne, M ... 814-332-4368 411 F
yeaton@allegheny.edu

EATTIATA, Russ ... 941-355-9080 101 N
admissions@ewcollege.org

EAVES, Phil, J ... 330-569-5120 383 F
eavespj@hiram.edu

EAVES, Robert ... 803-934-3229 447 K
reaves@morris.edu

EAVES, Stephen ... 316-295-5849 187 C
stephen_eaves@friends.edu

EAVES-MCLENNAN,
Kristi ... 919-760-8455 359 B
eavesk@meredith.edu

EBARB, Lisa ... 318-675-6505 205 D
lebarb@lsuhsc.edu

EBAUGH, Carl ... 661-362-3216 .. 40 H
carl.ebaugh@canyons.edu

EBBELING, Jason ... 860-701-5197 .. 91 B
ebbeling_j@mitchell.edu

EBBERS, Daniel ... 209-946-2417 .. 73 C
debbers@pacific.edu

EBBERS, Susan ... 651-255-6143 264 F
sebbers@unitedseminary.edu

EBBERT, Deborah ... 201-761-6052 307 K
debbert@saintpeters.edu

EBBING, Jeff ... 319-208-5060 183 B
jebbing@scciowa.edu

EBBS, George ... 757-594-7184 506 I

EBEID, Fred ... 262-595-2261 540 C
ebeid@uwp.edu

EBEL, Jeffrey ... 618-545-3171 149 C
jebel@kaskaskia.edu

EBELTOFT, Gail ... 701-438-2530 373 H
gail.ebeltoft@dickinsonstate.edu

EBEN, Brian ... 712-279-1628 176 B
brian.eben@briarcliff.edu

EBENHACK-BIEBER,
Kori ... 541-956-7196 409 F
kbieber@roguecc.edu

EBERHARDT, David ... 205-226-4731 .... 2 C
deberhar@bsc.edu

EBERHARDT, Everett, V 703-323-3006 516 C
eeberhardt@nvcc.edu

EBERHART, Andy ... 563-242-4023 .. 29 A
andy.eberhart@ashford.edu

EBERHART, Becky, J ... 847-866-3938 145 C
becky.eberhart@garrett.edu

EBERHART, Cathy ... 563-884-5114 182 D
cathy.eberhart@palmer.edu

EBERHART, Joanne, L .. 330-494-6170 391 J
jeberhart@starkstate.edu

EBERHART, John ... 269-782-1207 250 D
jeberhart@swmich.edu

EBERLE, Jeanette ... 863-638-2978 119 A
eberleja@webber.edu

EBERLE, Matt ... 480-245-7969 .. 14 D
matt.eberle@tricityministries.org

EBERLE, OSB, Peter ... 503-845-3304 407 B
peter.eberle@mtangel.edu

EBERLE, Sarah ... 512-313-3000 471 H
sarah.eberle@concordia.edu

EBERLY, Jamie ... 402-872-2436 292 C
jeberly@peru.edu

EBERLY, Jeffrey, A ... 215-895-2079 417 E
jeffrey.a.eberly@drexel.edu

EBERLY, John, M ... 717-780-2648 420 D
jmeberly@hacc.edu

EBERLY, Marian ... 607-962-9231 323 D
meberly@corning-cc.edu

EBERLY, Todd, E ... 240-895-4391 218 B
teeberly@smcm.edu

EBERSOLD, E. Douglas 573-592-4339 286 A
doug.ebersold@williamwoods.edu

EBERSOLE, Bradley, J ... 740-374-8716 395 D
bebersole@wscc.edu

EBERSOLE, Erin ... 610-647-4400 421 B
eebersole@immaculata.edu

EBERSOLE, John, F ... 518-464-8500 325 B
jebersole@excelsior.edu

EBERSOLE, Mark ... 704-216-3601 365 F
mark.ebersole@rccc.edu

EBERSOLE, Robin ... 540-545-7338 512 E
rebersol@su.edu

EBERSOLE, Tim ... 717-477-1218 431 F
tmeber@ship.edu

EBERSPACHER, Brad ... 402-941-6053 291 I
eberspacherb@midlandu.edu

EBERT, David ... 516-773-5000 548 I
ebertd@usmma.edu

EBERT, Derry ... 913-971-3380 189 F
debert@mnu.edu

EBERT, Sharon ... 570-961-7860 422 G
eberts@lackawanna.edu

EBERTZ, Susan J, S ... 563-589-0265 183 K
library@wartburgseminary.edu

EBERWEIN, Howard ... 413-662-5543 230 C
h.eberwein@mcla.edu

EBERWEIN, Susan ... 785-309-3106 190 L
susan.eberwein@salinatech.edu

EBNER, Timothy, J ... 801-581-5808 499 K
tebner@sa.utah.edu

EBNER-SMITH,
Maria, E ... 248-370-4423 248 K
ebnersmi@oakland.edu

EBONG, Imeh ... 661-654-2231 .. 32 G
iebong@csub.edu

EBORALL, Martha ... 304-327-4152 532 D
meborall@bluefieldstate.edu

EBRAHAMIAN, Katrin ... 626-873-2147 .. 55 B
kebrahamian@mtsierra.edu

EBRAHIMPOUR,
Maling ... 401-874-4244 442 E

EBSTEIN, Gemma, F ... 860-685-2535 .. 93 B
gebstein@wesleyan.edu

EBY, Larry ... 302-225-6289 .. 94 B
ebylw@gbc.edu

EBY, Tim, J ... 314-516-6765 284 B
ebyt@umsl.edu

ECCLES, John, G ... 434-544-8226 509 I
eccles@lynchburg.edu

ECCLES, Tom ... 845-758-7598 315 G
ccs@bard.edu

ECHARD, B. J ... 580-559-5769 397 K
brajec@ecok.edu

ECHEANDIA, Manuel ... 787-786-3030 556 E
mecheandia@ucb.edu.pr

ECHEGARAY, Luis ... 787-725-6500 551 A
lechegaray@sju.albizu.edu

ECHEVARRI, Richard ... 215-780-1410 435 D
rech@salus.edu

ECHEVARRIA, Agustin ... 787-763-5845 553 D
aecheva@inter.edu

ECHOLS, Connie, C ... 530-226-4178 .. 66 G
cechols@simpsonu.edu

ECHOLS, Darren ... 423-614-8519 457 M
dechols@leeuniversity.edu

ECHOLS, Jacqueline ... 404-297-9522 126 A
echolsj@gptc.edu

ECHOLS, Mike ... 402-557-7851 289 B
mike.echols@bellevue.edu

ECHOLS, Steven, F ... 912-583-2241 121 H
sechols@bpc.edu

ECHOLS TOBE, Dorothy 201-684-7008 305 F
dechols@ramapo.edu

ECK, Dan, W ... 920-565-1104 536 Q
eckdw@lakeland.edu

ECK, James, C ... 919-497-3201 358 J
jeck@louisburg.edu

ECK, Kristi ... 315-312-2212 346 A
kristi.eck@oswego.edu

ECK, Stephen ... 405-425-5118 399 J
stephen.eck@oc.edu

ECK, Stephen, M ... 973-596-3306 304 D
steven.eck@njit.edu

ECK, Tim ... 801-626-6352 500 C
teck@weber.edu

ECKARDT, Chip, P ... 715-836-2381 539 E
eckardpp@uwec.edu

ECKEL, Mark ... 908-737-3150 303 C
meckel@kean.edu

ECKEL, Terri ... 928-776-2129 .. 18 L
terri.eckel@yc.edu

ECKEL, Todd ... 909-593-3511 .. 73 B
teckel@laverne.edu

ECKELS, Blaine ... 208-885-6757 139 C

ECKENRODE, Jeanine ... 315-498-2237 337 F
j.a.eckenrode@sunyocc.edu

ECKER, Brian ... 717-262-2017 440 D
brian.ecker@wilson.edu

ECKER, Scot ... 262-551-5791 535 E
secker@carthage.edu

ECKERT, Amber ... 858-513-9240 .. 29 A
Amber.Eckert@ashford.edu

ECKERT, Brian ... 540-458-8459 519 A
beckert@wlu.edu

ECKERT, Jason, C ... 937-229-2045 393 E
Jeckert1@udayton.edu

ECKERT, Steve ... 928-314-9475 .. 12 B
steve.eckert@azwestern.edu

ECKERT, Thomas, C ... 608-757-7772 542 L
tom.eckert@blackhawk.edu

ECKLES, Robert ... 212-410-8480 335 B
reckles@nycpm.edu

ECKLEY, Amy ... 920-686-6131 539 A
Amy.Eckley@sl.edu

ECKLEY, Catherine ... 304-357-4925 530 H
catherineeckley@ucwv.edu

ECKLIN, Laura ... 707-256-7105 .. 55 E
lecklin@napavalley.edu

ECKLUND, Joe ... 402-280-5531 290 B
JosephEcklund@creighton.edu

ECKLUND, Timothy ... 631-632-7320 344 C
timothy.ecklund@stonybrook.edu

ECKMAN, Charles ... 305-284-1959 118 A
ceckman@miami.edu

ECKMAN, Steven ... 386-506-3180 101 I
eckmans@DaytonaState.edu

ECKMAN, Steven, W ... 402-363-5621 294 G
seckman@york.edu

ECKRICH, Steve, E ... 541-737-4323 408 F
stevee@osubookstore.com

ECKSTEIN, Mark ... 716-829-8349 324 E
eckstein@dyc.edu

ECKSTEIN, Melanie ... 704-461-6877 354 J
MelanieEckstein@bac.edu

ECONOMOU, James, S . 310-825-7943 .. 71 D
jeconomou@conet.ucla.edu

EDBURG, Lisa ... 573-518-2294 278 F
lisae@mineralarea.edu

EDDINGER, Pam, Y ... 617-228-2400 231 C
peddinger@bhcc.mass.edu

EDDINGER, Terry, W ... 336-315-8660 355 F
teddinger@carolinagrad.edu

EDDINGTON,
Natalie, D ... 410-706-2176 219 E
neddingt@rx.umaryland.edu

EDDINS, Ledesa, J ... 240-895-4382 218 B
ljeddins@smcm.edu

EDDINS, Trevell ... 847-214-7391 144 F
teddins@elgin.edu

EDDS-ELLIS, Stacy ... 270-686-4573 197 A
stacy.edds@kctcs.edu

EDDY, Alex ... 513-244-8145 379 I
alex.eddy@ccuniversity.edu

EDDY, James, M ... 336-315-7317 371 C
jmeddy@uncg.edu

EDDY, Jean ... 401-454-6419 442 B
jeddy@risd.edu

EDDY, Laura, M ... 620-341-5465 186 H
leddy@emporia.edu

EDDY, Libby ... 907-474-7500 .. 10 I
ofeddy@alaska.edu

EDDY, Libby ... 907-450-8000 .. 10 G

EDDY, Rick ... 309-341-5234 140 I
reddy@sandburg.edu

EDDY, Shayna ... 508-626-4506 230 A
seddy@framingham.edu

EDEL, Logan ... 515-961-1579 182 I
logan.edel@simpson.edu

EDELBROCK, Craig ... 205-348-6331 .... 8 E
cedelbrock@ccs.ua.edu

EDELEN, Charles ... 812-941-2400 169 A
cedelen@ius.edu

EDELMAN, Adam ... 406-994-5091 287 G
aedelman@montana.edu

EDELMAN, Daniel ... 972-780-3600 493 A

EDELMAN, David ... 805-898-2926 .. 44 J
davidedelman@fielding.edu

EDELMAN, Peter ... 202-885-2651 .. 94 H
edelman@american.edu

EDELMAYER, Kathleen .. 734-432-5300 246 B
kodowd@madonna.edu

EDELSON, Jeffrey ... 510-642-5039 .. 70 K
swdean@berkeley.edu

EDELSON, Maurice, F ... 212-799-5000 329 I

EDELSTEIN, Ronald ... 323-563-5851 .. 38 C
ronaldedelstein@cdrewu.edu

EDELSTEIN, Ronald, A .. 323-563-4980 .. 38 C
ronaldedelstein@cdrewu.edu

EDEN, Bradford, L ... 219-464-5099 174 E
brad.eden@valpo.edu

EDEN, Gene, F ... 610-799-1146 424 A
geden@lccc.edu

EDEN, James, R ... 920-924-3317 543 F
jeden@morainepark.edu

EDEN, James, V ... 262-335-5705 543 F
jeden@morainepark.edu

EDEN, Peter, A .... 802-387-6730 502 A
petereden@landmark.edu
EDEN, SM, Tim .... 210-431-8094 481 C
teden@stmarytx.edu
EDENFIELD, Joe .... 757-569-6744 516 E
jedenfield@pdc.edu
EDENS, Barb .... 423-236-2587 460 K
barbedens@southern.edu
EDENS, Gary .... 915-747-7471 494 B
gedens@utep.edu
EDENS, Mike .... 903-693-2021 480 A
medens@panola.edu
EDENS, Mike .... 504-282-4455 206 C
medens@nobts.edu
EDENS, Ruth .... 617-964-1100 222 B
redens@ants.edu
EDENS, Whitney .... 903-693-2067 480 A
wedens@panola.edu
EDER, Robert .... 773-256-0784 151 H
reder@lstc.edu
EDGAR, Kimberly, S ..... 615-898-2622 461 E
kimberly.edgar@mtsu.edu
EDGAR, Richard, J .... 240-895-3206 218 B
rjedgar@smcm.edu
EDGAR, William, J .... 724-847-6610 419 B
wjedgar@geneva.edu
EDGE, Johnnie .... 478-553-2124 129 C
jedge@oftc.edu
EDGECOMBE, Nydia ...... 718-518-4180 319 D
nedgecombe@hostos.cuny.edu
EDGERTON, Gary .... 317-940-9825 164 L
gedgerto@butler.edu
EDGERTON, Pam .... 402-354-7000 291 P
pam.edgerton@methodistcollege.edu
EDGERTON, Teresa .... 402-486-2540 293 D
teedgert@ucollege.edu
EDGEWORTH, Lori .... 419-251-1614 386 C
lori.edgeworth@mercycollege.edu
EDGHILL-WALDEN,
Vernese .... 312-553-2500 141 M
vedghill-walden@ccc.edu
EDGINGTON, Rick .... 580-628-6220 399 E
rick.edgington@noc.edu
EDGINGTON, Steve .... 714-879-3901.. 47 D
sedgington@hiu.edu
EDGINGTON,
Thomas, J .... 574-372-5100 166 D
edging@grace.edu
EDGMON, Angie .... 615-844-5049 466 G
finaid@welch.edu
EDGREN, JR., Gerald ... 618-842-3711 146 G
edgreng@iecc.edu
EDGREN, III, Gerald, R 920-924-3184 543 F
gedgren@morainepark.edu
EDICK, Nancy .... 402-554-2719 294 A
nedick@unomaha.edu
EDINBURGH, Mary .... 518-587-2100 348 A
mary.edinburgh@esc.edu
EDINGER, Joan, B .... 318-257-3036 208 A
jedinger@latech.edu
EDINGTON, Julie .... 870-248-4000.. 20 E
julie.edington@blackrivertech.edu
EDINGTON, Mary .... 253-833-9111 523 B
medington@greenriver.edu
EDINGTON, Maurice ..... 850-412-5978 114 D
maurice.edington@famu.edu
EDINGTON, Pamela, R . 845-431-8980 324 D
Pamela.edington@sunydutchess.edu
EDISON, Monica .... 616-632-2881 239 E
edisomon@aquinas.edu
EDIZEL, Gerar .... 607-871-2412 314 J
fedizel@alfred.edu
EDLER, Casey .... 985-867-2273 206 J
cedler@sjasc.edu
EDLUND, Erin .... 651-450-3546 259 A
eedlund@inverhills.edu
EDLUND, Erin .... 651-423-8233 258 E
erin.edlund@dctc.edu
EDLUND, Matthew .... 651-361-3450 257 B
medlund@mcnallysmith.edu
EDMAN, Neal, A .... 724-946-7110 439 D
nedman@westminster.edu
EDMAN, Patricia .... 612-374-5800 255 G
pedman@dunwoody.edu
EDMAN, Sally .... 712-707-7321 182 C
sedman@nwciowa.edu
EDMINSTER, David .... 303-546-3514.. 84 B
davee@naropa.edu
EDMINSTER, Warren ..... 270-809-3166 198 I
wedminster@murraystate.edu
EDMOND, Cara .... 512-454-7001 468 A
cedmond@aoma.edu
EDMOND, Georgia .... 478-289-2112 124 B
gedmond@ega.edu
EDMOND, Steven .... 512-505-6472 475 G
ssedmond@htu.edu
EDMOND, Tim .... 713-348-4052 480 M
te6@rice.edu
EDMONDS, Amy .... 262-472-4661 541 D
edmondsa@uww.edu
EDMONDS, Charles, W 570-321-4347 425 B
edmonds@lycoming.edu
EDMONDS, Jane .... 781-239-4998 222 E
jedmonds@babson.edu
EDMONDS, Kerry .... 540-362-6630 508 D
kedmonds@hollins.edu
EDMONDS, Lawson, C . 205-652-3545.... 9 G
ledmonds@uwa.edu
EDMONDS, Lorna Jean 740-593-1889 389 H
edmonds@ohio.edu
EDMONDS, Mabel .... 253-589-4333 521 B
mabel.edmonds@cptc.edu
EDMONDS, Melody ...... 931-668-7010 463 B
medmonds@mscc.edu
EDMONDS, Michelle, K 434-949-1006 516 H
michelle.edmonds@southside.edu
EDMONDS, Mike .... 719-389-6684.. 79 M
medmonds@coloradocollege.edu
EDMONDS, William, A . 724-938-4404 430 C
edmonds@calu.edu
EDMONDSON,
Charles, M .... 607-871-2101 314 J
edmondson@alfred.edu
EDMONDSON,
Charles (Ricks) .... 817-515-7726 484 B
charles.edmondson@tccd.edu
EDMONDSON, Jackie ... 256-549-8224.... 3 N
jedmondson@gadsdenstate.edu
EDMONDSON, Lauren .. 417-873-7569 274 E
ledmondson@drury.edu
EDMONDSON,
Melanie, M .... 443-334-2272 218 E
medmondson@stevenson.edu
EDMONDSON, Michael . 309-794-7338 139 K
michaeledmondson@augustana.edu
EDMONDSON, William . 814-871-7298 419 A
edmondso002@gannon.edu
EDMONSON, Michele ... 661-362-3435.. 40 H
michele.edmonson@canyons.edu
EDMONSON, Stacey ...... 936-294-1101 489 A
edu_sle01@shsu.edu
EDMUNDSON, John ..... 928-314-9500.. 12 B
john.edmundson@azwestern.edu
EDONICK, Jessica .... 717-396-7833 429 H
jedonick@pcad.edu
EDOUARD, Randall .... 607-777-6226 343 D
redouard@binghamton.edu
EDRICH, Terri .... 972-860-4825 472 C
tedrich@dcccd.edu
EDSALL, Denese .... 954-201-7502.. 99 G
dedsall@broward.edu
EDSALL, Paul .... 724-838-4236 435 E
edsall@setonhill.edu
EDSCORN, Steven .... 918-456-5511 398 M
edscorn@nsuok.edu
EDSTROM, Julie .... 406-791-5271 288 J
jedstrom01@ugf.edu
EDUARDO, Marcelo ...... 601-925-3214 268 E
eduardo@mc.edu
EDWALDS-GILBERT,
Gretchen .... 909-607-2822.. 65 E
gretchen.edwalds-gilbert@scrippscollege.edu
EDWARD, Paul .... 978-927-2300 227 A
paul.edwards@gordon.edu
EDWARDS, Alicia .... 904-256-1184 103 K
aedwards@fcsl.edu
EDWARDS, Amy .... 217-333-3551 162 A
aledward@illinois.edu
EDWARDS, Annette .... 757-789-1768 515 D
aedwards@es.vccs.edu
EDWARDS, Bahola .... 432-685-4520 478 F
bahola@midland.edu
EDWARDS, Bambi .... 252-638-7317 362 A
edwardsb@cravencc.edu
EDWARDS, Barry .... 925-473-7391.. 42 F
bedwards@losmedanos.edu
EDWARDS, Betty .... 334-420-4321.... 7 I
bedwards@trenholmstate.edu
EDWARDS, Bonnie .... 304-205-6706 531 A
bonnie.edwards@bridgevalley.edu
EDWARDS, Brad .... 703-993-3256 507 K
bedwards@gmu.edu
EDWARDS, Bruce .... 808-356-5256 135 C
bedwards@hpu.edu
EDWARDS, Candace ..... 410-386-8505 214 B
cedwards@carrollcc.edu
EDWARDS, Carlton, G .. 804-257-5851 518 E
cgedwards@vuu.edu
EDWARDS, Carmen .... 432-685-4589 478 F
cedwards@midland.edu
EDWARDS, Carol .... 806-742-0700 489 F
carol.edwards@ttu.edu
EDWARDS, Cathy .... 214-860-8685 472 G
cedwards@dcccd.edu
EDWARDS, Chris .... 601-481-1316 268 B
cedwards@meridiancc.edu
EDWARDS,
Christopher, J .... 513-558-5233 393 B
christopher.edwards@uc.edu
EDWARDS, Cody .... 703-993-5287 507 K
cedward7@gmu.edu
EDWARDS, Cynthia ...... 404-297-9522 126 A
edwardsc@gptc.edu
EDWARDS, Danielle ...... 515-244-4221 175 C
edwardsd@aib.edu
EDWARDS, David .... 330-941-3394 396 C
dwedwards@ysu.edu
EDWARDS, David .... 732-906-2533 303 F
dedwards@middlesexcc.edu
EDWARDS, David .... 903-875-7348 479 I
david.edwards@navarrocollege.edu
EDWARDS, Donald .... 828-689-1246 359 A
dedwards@mhu.edu
EDWARDS, Doreen .... 607-871-2422 314 J
dedwards@alfred.edu
EDWARDS, Earl, W .... 858-534-8750.. 72 B
ewedwards@ucsd.edu
EDWARDS, Elizabeth .... 662-862-8265 267 F
etedwards@iccms.edu
EDWARDS, Ellen .... 207-947-4591 209 G
eedwards@bealcollege.edu
EDWARDS, Eugene .... 503-375-7010 405 F
eedwards@corban.edu
EDWARDS, Frank .... 404-880-8672 122 I
fedwards@cau.edu
EDWARDS, Gary .... 661-362-2291.. 53 F
gedwards@masters.edu
EDWARDS, Geoffrey, M 812-488-1102 173 H
ge21@evansville.edu
EDWARDS, Harry .... 562-903-4883.. 29 F
harry.edwards@biola.edu
EDWARDS, Holly .... 336-838-6175 367 C
holly.edwards@wilkescc.edu
EDWARDS, Ian, C .... 412-396-6204 417 I
edwards181@duq.edu
EDWARDS, Ishmell, H .. 662-252-8000 270 C
iedwards@rustcollege.edu
EDWARDS, Jakki .... 651-291-0177 257 B
jakki.edwards@mcnallysmith.edu
EDWARDS, James .... 252-492-2061 366 G
edwardsj@vgcc.edu
EDWARDS, James .... 202-865-6660.. 96 B
EDWARDS, James, E .... 757-822-5121 517 C
jeedwards@tcc.edu
EDWARDS, Jamie .... 276-223-4829 517 F
jedwards@wcc.vccs.edu
EDWARDS, Jan .... 719-227-8285.. 79 M
jan.edwards@coloradocollege.edu
EDWARDS, Jane .... 203-432-8680.. 93 C
jane.edwards@yale.edu
EDWARDS, Jason .... 252-985-5102 367 E
jedwards@ncwc.edu
EDWARDS, Jeff .... 337-439-5765 202 E
jeff@deltatech.edu
EDWARDS, Jennifer, T . 254-968-9480 485 A
jtedwards@tarleton.edu
EDWARDS, Jessica .... 423-746-5279 464 D
jedwards@twcnet.edu
EDWARDS, John .... 949-451-5255.. 67 E
jedwards@ivc.edu
EDWARDS, Jon .... 508-270-4102 231 G
jedwards@massbay.edu
EDWARDS,
Jonathan, P .... 843-661-1181 446 E
jedwards@fmarion.edu
EDWARDS, Joyce, P ..... 336-334-7755 370 B
edwardsj@ncat.edu
EDWARDS, Judson .... 334-670-3989.... 8 A
jcedwards@troy.edu
EDWARDS, Julie .... 417-447-8188 280 C
edwardsj@otc.edu
EDWARDS, Karen .... 251-460-7092.... 9 F
cedwards@southalabama.edu
EDWARDS, Karen .... 281-756-3639 467 D
kedwards@alvincollege.edu
EDWARDS, Karen, K ..... 641-269-3703 178 I
edwardsk@grinnell.edu
EDWARDS, Karin .... 971-722-5302 409 C
karin.edwards@pcc.edu
EDWARDS, Kelly .... 406-657-1006 288 G
kelly.edwards@rocky.edu
EDWARDS, Kelly .... 406-657-1026 288 G
kelly.edwards@rocky.edu
EDWARDS, Kendra .... 816-604-1574 277 F
kendra.edwards@mcckc.edu
EDWARDS, Kevin .... 740-477-7761 388 F
kedwards@ohiochristian.edu
EDWARDS, Lance .... 641-673-1114 184 B
edwardsl@wmpenn.edu
EDWARDS, Laurie, L .... 712-324-5061 182 A
ledwards@nwicc.edu
EDWARDS, Lisa .... 305-220-4120 108 F
ledwards@mattiacollege.edu
EDWARDS, Lisa .... 646-660-6036 318 C
Lisa.Edwards@baruch.cuny.edu
EDWARDS, Louis, W .... 713-313-6747 487 F
edwards_lw@tsu.edu
EDWARDS, Mark, H ..... 315-655-7334 317 J
medwards@cazenovia.edu
EDWARDS, Mary, A ...... 304-336-8000 533 A
edwardsm@westliberty.edu
EDWARDS, Mary Ruth .. 910-642-7141 366 B
MaryRuth.Edwards@sccnc.edu
EDWARDS, Matthew ..... 864-646-1474 449 F
medward3@tctc.edu
EDWARDS, Melinda ...... 256-352-8172.. 10 A
melinda.edwards@wallacestate.edu
EDWARDS, Michael .... 641-673-2120 184 B
edwardsml@wmpenn.edu
EDWARDS, Michael ...... 713-718-7101 475 C
michael.edwards@hccs.edu
EDWARDS, Mike .... 615-844-5246 466 G
mike.edwards@welch.edu
EDWARDS, Paul, S .... 502-597-5837 197 G
paul.edwards@kysu.edu
EDWARDS, JR.,
Quinton, T .... 662-915-3784 270 G
qtedward@olemiss.edu
EDWARDS, Randy .... 828-262-2041 369 D
edwardsrk@appstate.edu
EDWARDS, Richard .... 848-932-7821 306 F
redwards@oldqueens.rutgers.edu
EDWARDS, Richard ...... 848-932-7821 307 B
redwards@oldqueens.rutgers.edu
EDWARDS, Richard ...... 848-932-7821 306 F
redwards@oldqueens.rutgers.edu
EDWARDS, Richard ...... 518-629-7356 328 D
r.edwards@hvcc.edu
EDWARDS, Rick .... 828-395-1676 363 D
redwards@isothermal.edu
EDWARDS, Ron .... 608-785-9552 544 E
edwardsr@westerntc.edu
EDWARDS, Rosie .... 334-285-5177.... 4 K
rosie.edwards@istc.edu
EDWARDS, Shawn .... 843-953-6989 444 C
shawn.edwards@citadel.edu
EDWARDS, Stephanie ... 619-201-8713.. 62 D
stephanie.edwards@sdcc.edu
EDWARDS, TerCraig, D 336-734-7953 362 F
tedwards@forsythtech.edu
EDWARDS, Thomas ...... 207-859-1362 211 I
edwardst@thomas.edu
EDWARDS, Tim .... 205-652-3457.... 9 G
tedwards@uwa.edu
EDWARDS, Tim .... 205-652-3531.... 9 G
tedwards@uwa.edu
EDWARDS, Timothy ...... 208-882-1566 138 F
timedwards@nsa.edu
EDWARDS, Tracy .... 405-945-3376 400 F
tracyle@osuokc.edu
EDWARDS, Ulrica, S .... 318-274-6103 207 H
EDWARDS, Valerie .... 802-635-1290 504 A
valerie.edwards@jsc.edu
EDWARDS, Virjean .... 206-543-2100 527 G
vedwards@uw.edu
EDWARDS, Wanda .... 910-296-1812 363 E
wedwaeds@jamessprunt.edu
EDWARDS, Wayne .... 516-876-3175 345 E
edwardsw@oldwestbury.edu
EDWARDS- EVANS,
Nicole .... 601-979-2244 267 H
nicole.e.evans@jsums.edu
EDWARDS LANGE,
Sheila .... 206-934-4144 525 J
EERTWEGH, John .... 949-376-6000.. 49 K
jeertwegh@lcad.edu
EFF, Ryan .... 517-265-5161 238 H
reff@adrian.edu
EFFORD, Lelia, A .... 305-626-3180 104 B
laefford@fmuniv.edu
EFINGER, Cindy .... 413-528-7647 222 F
cefinger@simons-rock.edu
EFTHIMIOU, Chris .... 718-289-5169 318 E
chris.efthimiou@bcc.cuny.edu
EFTHYMIOU,
Lampeto (Betty) .... 718-631-6611 320 F
lefthymiou@qcc.cuny.edu
EFTINK, Maria .... 314-889-4533 275 B
meftink@fontbonne.edu
EFTINK, Maurice, R ...... 662-915-5974 270 G
eftink@olemiss.edu
EGAN, Brian .... 973-684-5999 304 F
began@pccc.edu
EGAN, Carolyn .... 850-644-4440 115 A
cegan@admin.fsu.edu
EGAN, Eric .... 760-921-5520.. 58 C
eegan@paloverde.edu
EGAN, Jonathon .... 315-568-3311 334 F
jegan@nycc.edu
EGAN, Maryan .... 239-590-1234 114 F
megan@fgcu.edu
EGAN, Patrick .... 312-752-2180 149 D
patrick.egan@kendall.edu
EGAN, Russi .... 760-921-5524.. 58 C
regan@paloverde.edu
EGAN, Thomas .... 215-572-2900 412 F
egant@arcadia.edu
EGAN, Todd, P .... 607-735-1888 324 J
tegan@elmira.edu

EGBE, Daniel .... 501-370-5268.. 22 E
degbe@philander.edu
EGBE, Emmanuel .... 718-270-5170 320 C
egbe@mec.cuny.edu
EGBERT, Allison .... 206-239-2302 519 H
aegbert@aii.edu
EGBERT, Jeb .... 949-783-4800.. 75 K
jegbert@westcoastuniversity.edu
EGBERT, Jessica, D .... 801-375-5125 499 A
jegbert@rmuohp.edu
EGBERT, Jessie, W .... 205-652-3535.... 9 G
jwe@uwa.edu
EGDORF, Randall .... 217-641-4973 148 J
regdorf@jwcc.edu
EGE, Daryle .... 309-467-6394 145 A
dege@eureka.edu
EGE, Sybil .... 847-214-7034 144 F
sege@elgin.edu
EGELAND, Hillary .... 845-434-5750 349 C
hegeland@sullivan.suny.edu
EGELER, William, G ...... 207-768-2792 211 C
wegeler@nmcc.edu
EGENESS, Cynthia .... 651-690-6864 263 V
cnegeness@stkate.edu
EGENREIDER, Michael .. 740-420-5926 388 F
megenreider@ohiochristian.edu
EGERER, Sarah .... 706-233-4065 121 E
segerer@berry.edu
EGERSTROM, Sarah ...... 715-425-3500 540 E
sarah.r.egerstrom@uwrf.edu
EGGEBRAATEN, Allan ... 641-585-8174 183 I
eggebraa@waldorf.edu
EGGEN, Tyler .... 907-564-8311.. 10 D
teegen@alaskapacific.edu
EGGENSPERGER,
Martin .... 870-508-6102.. 19 H
meggensperger@asumh.edu
EGGERS, Daniel, W ...... 512-245-1555 489 C
dwe16@txstate.edu
EGGERS, John, M .... 320-308-0121 261 E
jmeggers@stcloudstate.edu
EGGERS, Marilyn .... 909-558-7658.. 50 K
meggers@llu.edu
EGGERS, Troy .... 212-854-5939 322 F
te99@columbia.edu
EGGERSTEDT, Jane .... 318-675-6124 205 D
jegger@lsuhsc.edu
EGGLESTON, Chad .... 334-833-4443.... 4 E
ceggleston@huntingdon.edu
EGGLESTON, Dana, S .... 302-356-6862.. 94 G
dana.s.eggleston@wilmu.edu
EGGLESTON, Joseph ..... 562-947-8755.. 67 J
josepheggleston@scuhs.edu
EGGLESTON,
Kathryn, K .... 972-238-6364 473 B
keggleston@dcccd.edu
EGGLESTON, Latrice, E . 773-995-2548 141 J
egglest@csu.edu
EGGLESTON, Tami .... 618-537-6926 152 C
teggleston@mckendree.edu
EGGLESTON, Theresa .... 562-902-3314.. 67 J
theresaeggleston@scuhs.edu
EGGLESTON, Tryon .... 973-408-3947 301 J
tegglest@drew.edu
EGHERMAN, Mara .... 641-844-5692 179 L
mara.egherman@iavalley.edu
EGITTO, Victor, T .... 323-259-2686.. 56 I
egitto@oxy.edu
EGLE, Don .... 903-233-3290 477 G
donegle@letu.edu
EGLSAER, Richard .... 936-294-1006 489 A
eglsaer@shsu.edu
EGLY, Penny, J .... 260-422-5561 167 F
pjegly@indianatech.edu
EGRESI, Chad .... 410-888-9048 216 G
cegresi@muih.edu
EHASZ, Maribeth .... 407-823-4372 115 C
maribeth.ehasz@ucf.edu
EHENGER, Paul .... 503-375-7031 405 F
campuscare@corban.edu
EHLER, Gina, M .... 262-524-7247 535 D
gehler@carrollu.edu
EHLERS, Chris .... 918-781-7233 396 F
ehlersc@bacone.edu
EHLERS, Kathleen .... 401-739-5000 441 E
kehlers@neit.edu
EHLERS, Nancy, M .... 716-652-8900 317 M
nehlers@cks.edu
EHLERS, Pam .... 405-744-2122 400 C
pam.ehlers@okstate.edu
EHLERT, Alycia .... 615-230-3214 464 B
alycia.ehlert@volstate.edu
EHMANN, William .... 206-220-8214 526 F
ehmannw@seattleu.edu
EHMEN, Stacy, L .... 217-443-8746 143 F
stacy@dacc.edu
EHRENFELD, D .... 718-236-1171 338 K
EHRENFELD, S, B .... 718-236-1171 338 K
EHRENREICH, Yaakov ... 718-941-8000 332 H
EHRESMAN, Terry .... 620-278-4264 191 D
tehresman@sterling.edu
EHRHARDT, Tom .... 312-261-3165 153 H
tom.ehrhardt@nl.edu
EHRLICH, Anne, R .... 818-767-0888.. 77 G
anne.ehrlich@woodbury.edu
EHRLICH, Brian .... 321-674-8202 103 R
behrlich@fit.edu
EHRLICH, Jeff .... 816-584-6202 280 F
jeff.erhlich@park.edu
EHRLICH, Jonathan ...... 919-497-3428 358 J
jehrlich@louisburg.edu
EHRLICH, Margaret .... 770-274-5125 125 G
margaret.ehrlich@gpc.edu
EHRLICH, Robert .... 660-626-2297 271 G
rehrlich@atsu.edu
EHRLICH, Sam .... 830-372-8155 487 C
sehrlich@tlu.edu
EHRLICH, Steven, M .... 314-935-4320 285 E
ehrlich@wustl.edu
EHRMANTRAUT,
Dominic .... 901-321-3286 455 I
dehrmant@cbu.edu
EHST, Suzanne .... 574-535-7839 166 C
sehst@goshen.edu
EIBECK, Pamela, A .... 209-946-2223.. 73 C
president@pacific.edu
EICHELBERGER, John ... 907-474-7229.. 10 I
jceichelberger@alaska.edu
EICHELBERGER, Lisa .... 678-466-4900 122 J
lisaeichelberger@clayton.edu
EICHELROTH, Kathleen . 508-929-8098 230 G
keichelroth@worcester.edu
EICHENBERGER, Julie ... 620-223-2700 187 B
juliee@fortscott.edu
EICHENLAUB, Mark, P .. 618-235-2700 160 B
mark.eichenlaub@swic.edu
EICHENSTEIN, Joseph ... 732-985-6533 305 D
EICHER, Michael .... 614-292-9858 389 A
eicher@osu.edu
EICHFIELD, Tara .... 912-287-5809 123 A
teichfield@coastalpines.edu
EICHHORN, Edward ...... 201-559-6000 302 I
EICHHORN, Gregory, E 610-921-7260 411 E
geichhorn@albright.edu
EICHHORST, Amy .... 301-405-2102 219 D
aeich@umd.edu
EICHHORST, Carly .... 612-330-1051 253 K
eichhors@augsburg.edu
EICHLER, Barry .... 212-960-5214 353 P
eichler@yu.edu
EICHLER, Richard .... 212-854-2878 322 F
re1@columbia.edu
EICHNER, Kevin .... 785-242-5200 190 D
kevin.eichner@ottawa.edu
EICHOLTZ, Kristin .... 610-282-1100 416 I
kristin.eicholtz@desales.edu
EICHORST, Christopher 509-777-4780 529 A
ceichorst@whitworth.edu
EICHORST, Shawn .... 402-472-3011 293 H
seichorst@huskers.com
EICHTEN, Jonathan .... 320-308-5580 261 F
jeichten@sctcc.edu
EICK, Christine, L .... 334-844-4870.... 1 G
eickchr@auburn.edu
EICKHOLT, Marcia .... 419-227-3141 394 B
marcia@unoh.edu
EICKHORST, Lindsay .... 309-268-8031 145 H
lindsay.eickhorst@heartland.edu
EICKMEIER, Valerie ...... 317-920-2403 168 E
veickmei@iupui.edu
EID, Haithum .... 504-286-5010 207 B
heid@suno.edu
EIDE, Greg .... 503-375-7021 405 F
geide@corban.edu
EIDENBERG, Julia .... 503-517-1816 411 C
jeidenberg@westernseminary.edu
EIDGAHY, Saeid .... 619-388-2795.. 62 G
seidgahy@sdccd.edu
EIDSON, Kristi .... 270-686-4216 193 G
kristi.eidson@brescia.edu
EIDSON, Paul .... 714-841-6252.. 28 C
dreidson@apollosuniversity.edu
EIDSON, Rebecca, W ... 864-646-1507 449 F
reidson@tctc.edu
EIERMANN, Jason .... 985-448-4521 208 C
jason.eiermann@nicholls.edu
EIFERT, Robert .... 217-824-4004 150 B
reifert@lakeland.cc.il.us
EIGENBROOD, Rick ...... 206-281-2710 526 D
eigend@spu.edu
EIGHMY, Taylor .... 865-974-8701 465 D
vcresearch@utk.edu
EIKE, Claire .... 312-629-9379 158 J
ceike@saic.edu
EIKENBERRY, Michael .. 260-481-6461 168 D
eikenbem@ipfw.edu
EIKENS, Anita .... 414-382-6343 534 I
anita.eikens@alverno.edu
EILAND, Victoria .... 229-430-4638 119 H
victoria.eiland@asurams.edu
EILERING, Susan .... 217-479-7106 151 J
susan.eilering@mac.edu
EIMER, Greg, A .... 217-732-3155 150 H
geimer@lincolncollege.edu
EIMERS, Mardy, T .... 573-882-3412 283 H
eimersm@missouri.edu
EINFELD, Aaron .... 616-957-7035 240 M
aaron@calvinseminary.edu
EINHELLIG, Frank, E ..... 417-836-5119 279 A
frankeinhellig@missouristate.edu
EINOLF, Karl, W .... 301-447-5396 217 D
einolf@msmary.edu
EINSPAHR, Kent .... 402-643-7315 289 J
kent.einspahr@cune.edu
EINSTEIN, Heath .... 817-257-7490 486 G
h.einstein@tcu.edu
EINSTEIN, Rick .... 303-410-2440.. 85 E
reinstein@redstone.edu
EIOLA, William, T .... 419-772-2261 388 I
w-eiola@onu.edu
EIS, Linda .... 417-625-3797 278 I
eis-l@mssu.edu
EISELE, Chad .... 309-341-7280 149 G
ceisele@knox.edu
EISEN, Arnold, M .... 212-678-8072 329 H
areisen@jtsa.edu
EISEN, Jeffrey, M .... 919-658-7759 369 B
jeisen@umo.edu
EISEN, Karen .... 718-780-0343 317 A
karen.eisen@brooklaw.edu
EISENBACH, Regina ...... 760-750-4253.. 35 B
regina@csusm.edu
EISENBACH, Theresa .... 203-332-5013.. 89 C
teisenbach@hcc.commnet.edu
EISENBARTH, Jeffrey .... 407-646-2117 111 H
jeisenbarth@rollins.edu
EISENBARTH,
Kathryn, L .... 503-352-2705 408 I
eisenbak@pacificu.edu
EISENBEISER,
Colleen, K .... 410-777-1963 213 E
ckeisenbeiser@aacc.edu
EISENBERG, Eric .... 813-974-2804 116 B
eisenberg@usf.edu
EISENBERG, Jessica ..... 617-559-8775 227 E
jeisenberg@hebrewcollege.edu
EISENBERG, Larry, A .... 314-516-6469 284 B
eisenbergl@umsl.edu
EISENBERG, Martin, J .. 740-368-3112 390 B
mjeisenb@owu.edu
EISENBERGER, Israel .... 845-362-3053 316 A
EISENHARD, Craig .... 215-248-7381 424 G
ceisenhard@ltsp.edu
EISENHART, Pamela ..... 717-337-6010 419 C
peisenha@gettysburg.edu
EISENHAUER, James .... 262-595-2248 540 C
eisenhau@uwp.edu
EISENHAUER, Joseph ... 313-993-1204 250 H
eisenhjg@udmercy.edu
EISENHAUER, Walt .... 570-484-2168 431 C
weisenha@lhup.edu
EISENHUTH, Wayne ...... 507-222-4427 254 D
weisenhu@carleton.edu
EISENMAN, Ann .... 563-244-7040 178 B
aeisenman@eicc.edu
EISENMAN, Elaine .... 781-239-4355 222 E
eeisenman@babson.edu
EISENMAN, Marjory ...... 703-284-1610 510 B
marjory.eisenman@marymount.edu
EISENMANN, Linda .... 508-286-8212 238 B
eisenmann_linda@wheatoncollege.edu
EISENMENGER, Paul ..... 847-317-7087 161 B
peisenme@tiu.edu
EISENSTEIN, Laya .... 718-268-4700 339 B
EISENSTEIN, Paul .... 614-823-1609 390 C
peisenstein@otterbein.edu
EISENTRAGER, Pete ...... 816-235-2665 284 A
eisentragerp@umkc.edu
EISGRUBER,
Cristopher, L .... 609-258-3026 305 C
eisgrube@princeton.edu
EISINGER, David .... 630-844-5490 139 L
deisinger@aurora.edu
EISINGER, Robert .... 401-254-3043 442 C
reisinger@rwu.edu
EISLER, David, L .... 231-591-2500 242 L
DavidEisler@ferris.edu
EISNAUGLE, Eva .... 704-978-1344 364 C
eeisnaugle@mitchellcc.edu
EISNER, SND, Janet ...... 617-735-9825 226 B
president@emmanuel.edu
EITEL, Keith .... 817-923-1921 483 E
keitel@swbts.edu
EITEL, Norine .... 660-626-2391 271 G
neitel@atsu.edu
EJIAGA, Romanus .... 504-286-5384 207 B
rejiaga@suno.edu
EKARIUS, John .... 215-503-5017 436 F
john.ekarius@jefferson.edu
EKBOLM, Kathleen .... 508-541-1530 225 G
deanbkstr@fheg.follett.com
EKKER, David, A .... 757-822-7198 517 C
dekker@tcc.edu
EKKERS, Julie .... 651-290-6476 266 B
julie.ekkers@wmitchell.edu
EKOUE-TOTOU, Patrick . 415-883-2211.. 41 B
pekouetotou@marin.edu
EKPO, NseAbasi .... 937-376-6411 379 D
nekpo@centralstate.edu
EKSTROM, Rodney .... 603-535-2217 299 E
raekstrom@plymouth.edu
EL-AASSER,
Mohamed, S .... 610-758-2981 424 B
mse0@lehigh.edu
EL-BERMAWY,
Mohamed .... 573-288-6344 274 C
melbermawy@culver.edu
EL FATTAL, David .... 562-860-2451.. 37 L
delfattal@cerritos.edu
EL-GAYAR, Omar, F ...... 605-256-5799 453 H
omar.el-gayar@dsu.edu
EL-HAGGAN, Ahmed ..... 410-951-3850 220 C
elhaggan@coppin.edu
EL-KOURY, Rodolphe ... 305-284-9092 118 A
rxe66@miami.edu
EL-REWINI, Hesham ..... 701-777-3412 373 G
rewini@engr.und.edu
ELACHI, Charles .... 818-354-5673.. 31 D
charles.elachi@jpl.nasa.gov
ELAM, Becky .... 951-487-3011.. 55 A
belam@msjc.edu
ELAM, Demar .... 334-387-3877.... 1 E
demarelam@amridgeuniversity.edu
ELAM, Elizabeth .... 434-736-2085 516 H
elizabeth.elam@southside.edu
ELAM, Harry, J .... 650-723-2300.. 68 G
helam@stanford.edu
ELAM, Joyce .... 305-348-2779 114 G
joyce.elam@fiu.edu
ELAM, Michael, A .... 252-862-1308 365 C
elamm@roanokechowan.edu
ELAM, Richard, L .... 540-868-7042 515 H
relam@lfcc.edu
ELAM, Terry .... 434-592-3966 509 G
tlelam@liberty.edu
ELAM, Terry, D .... 706-771-4005 121 B
telam@augustatech.edu
ELANA, Baukman .... 302-736-2567.. 94 E
elana.baukman@wesley.edu
ELAND, Tom .... 612-659-6286 259 F
thomas.eland@minneapolis.edu
ELARDE, Christopher .... 212-346-1200 337 I
celarde@pace.edu
ELBE, Michael .... 217-641-4101 148 J
melbe@jwcc.edu
ELBEDOUR, Hammad ..... 703-729-8800.. 96 H
ELBOUSHI, Toni, C .... 323-563-5827.. 38 C
tonielboushi@cdrewu.edu
ELBOW, Gary .... 806-742-2184 489 F
gary.elbow@ttu.edu
ELCHANANI, Matanya ... 203-576-4322.. 92 B
matanya@btidgeport.edu
ELDAYRIE, Elias, G .... 352-273-1788 115 D
eldayrie@ufl.edu
ELDEMIRE, Flavia .... 803-376-5700 443 D
ELDER, Dana .... 509-359-6305 522 C
delder@ewu.edu
ELDER, Darla .... 814-732-2743 430 G
delder@edinboro.edu
ELDER, Jackie .... 903-223-3110 486 C
jackie.elder@tamut.edu
ELDER, Jill .... 605-718-2411 454 F
jill.elder@wdt.edu
ELDER, Laura .... 770-531-6318 128 A
lelder@laniertech.edu
ELDER, Paul .... 269-471-3284 239 D
elderp@andrews.edu
ELDER, Thomas .... 903-510-2405 491 A
teld@tjc.edu
ELDER, Vivian .... 417-447-8114 280 C
elderv@otc.edu
ELDERS, Candice .... 269-927-8198 245 E
cedlers@lakemichigancollege.edu
ELDERTON, R. Brian ..... 215-951-1540 422 F
elderton@lasalle.edu
ELDREDGE, Bradly .... 406-756-3894 286 G
beldredge@fvcc.edu
ELDRIDGE, Daryl .... 866-931-4300 281 A
daryl.eldridge@rockbridge.edu
ELDRIDGE, Jonathan ..... 415-485-9619.. 41 B
jeldridge@marin.edu
ELDRIDGE, Joseph, T ... 202-885-3336.. 94 H
eldridg@american.edu
ELDRIDGE, Karen .... 865-981-8207 458 E
karen.eldridge@maryvillecollege.edu
ELDRIDGE, Kim .... 479-524-7424.. 21 F
keldridge@adm.jbu.edu
ELDRIDGE, Linda, P ...... 859-846-5340 198 G
leldridge@midway.edu
ELDRIDGE, Marie .... 931-598-1111 460 I
police@sewanee.edu
ELDRIDGE, Maurice, G . 610-328-8312 436 A
meldrid1@swarthmore.edu

ELLISON, E. Christopher .... 614-292-2600 389 A
ellison.2@osu.edu
ELLISON, Jimmy .... 325-674-2305 466 I
jimmy.ellison@acu.edu
ELLISON, Kimberly .... 513-732-5221 393 D
kimberly.ellison@uc.edu
ELLISON, Lori .... 239-513-1135 119 C
lellison@wolford.edu
ELLISON, Maderia .... 928-532-6743.. 16 E
maderia.ellison@npc.edu
ELLISON, Marjorie .... 573-288-6541 274 C
mellison@culver.edu
ELLISON, Pamela .... 216-987-4459 381 A
pamela.ellison@tri-c.edu
ELLISON, Rich .... 859-282-8989 127 E
rellison@ict.edu
ELLISON, Ron .... 209-946-3042.. 73 C
rellison1@pacific.edu
ELLISOR, Kimberly, M .. 843-661-1190 446 E
kellisor@fmarion.edu
ELLMAN, Scott .... 858-695-8587.. 47 E
sellman@horizonuniversity.edu
ELLMORE, Philip, T ...... 609-626-3546 308 E
philip.ellmore@stockton.edu
ELLSWORTH, Tim .... 731-661-5215 464 G
tellsworth@uu.edu
ELLWANGER, Carolyn ... 712-274-6400 184 A
carolyn.ellwanger@witcc.edu
ELLZEY, Janet, L 512-471-7020 493M
jellzey@mail.utexas.edu
ELMORE, Amy .... 270-534-3118 197 E
amy.elmore@kctcs.edu
ELMORE, Cecilia .... 573-341-6798 284 C
elmorec@mst.edu
ELMORE, Chris .... 336-272-7102 357 B
chris.elmore@greensboro.edu
ELMORE, Dana .... 601-925-3371 268 E
elmore@mc.edu
ELMORE, Diane .... 434-200-3070 505 L
diane.elmore@centralhealth.com
ELMORE, Donna .... 803-535-1202 448 C
elmored@octech.edu
ELMORE, Floyd .... 704-847-5600 369 A
felmore@ses.edu
ELMORE, John .... 785-827-5541 189 A
john.elmore@kwu.edu
ELMORE, Kenneth .... 617-353-4126 224 E
kennmore@bu.edu
ELMORE, Rheena .... 251-580-2145.... 5 A
rheena.elmore@faulknerstate.edu
ELMORE, Robert .... 513-875-3344 379 G
robert.elmore@chatfield.edu
ELMORE, Ronald .... 336-841-9128 357 E
relmore@highpoint.edu
ELMORE, Troy, A .... 270-384-8144 198 C
elmoret@lindsey.edu
ELMS, Duane .... 575-624-8110 311 K
Elms@nmmi.edu
ELNASHAI, Amr, S .... 814-865-7537 428 C
ase2@psu.edu
ELNESS, Jodi, M .... 320-308-5087 261 F
jelness@sctcc.edu
ELNICK, William .... 215-572-2172 412 F
elnickb@arcadia.edu
ELOFIR, Stacey .... 410-704-4414 221 A
selofir@towson.edu
ELROD, David .... 706-272-4473 123 G
delrod@daltonstate.edu
ELROD, Eileen, R .... 408-554-4136.. 65 A
eelrod@scu.edu
ELROD, Roger .... 408-924-6112.. 36 B
roger.elrod@sjsu.edu
ELROD, Susan .... 559-278-3936.. 33 D
selrod@csufresno.edu
ELROD, Susan, L .... 530-898-6101.. 33 A
selrod@csuchico.edu
ELSASS, Susan .... 603-577-6581 297 F
elsass@dwc.edu
ELSBECK, George, J ..... 607-431-4320 327 B
elsbeckg@hartwick.edu
ELSBERRY, Erin .... 302-736-2439.. 94 E
erin.elsberry@wesley.edu
ELSBERRY, Meagan ...... 561-237-7233 108 E
melsberry@lynn.edu
ELSE, Iwalani .... 218-723-6583 255 A
ielse@css.edu
ELSE, Robert .... 805-965-0581.. 64 N
else@sbcc.edu
ELSEA, Kathy .... 660-785-4130 283 E
kelsea@truman.edu
ELSENBAUMER, Ronald, L .... 817-272-2103 493 L
elsenbaumer@uta.edu
ELSENER, Daniel, J ...... 317-955-6100 171 A
delsener@marian.edu
ELSEROAD, Arleen .... 949-451-5220.. 67 D
aelseroad@ivc.edu
ELSEROAD, Arleen .... 949-451-5416.. 67 E
alseroad@ivc.edu
ELSHAYEB, Tarek, A ..... 704-687-7781 371 B
telshaye@uncc.edu
ELSHICK, Soha .... 201-216-9901 302 A
soha.elshick@eicollege.edu
ELSLEY, Judy .... 801-626-6186 500 C
jelsley@weber.edu
ELSTER, Janette .... 315-568-3053 334 F
jelster@nycc.edu
ELSTON, Joseph, P ...... 570-340-6024 425 D
ELSTON, Timothy, G ..... 803-321-5197 447 L
timothy.elston@newberry.edu
ELSWICK, Clark .... 575-562-4352 310 I
clark.elswick@enmu.edu
ELSWICK, Clark .... 575-562-4490 310 I
clark.elswick@enmu.edu
ELTON, Nathan, J .... 704-894-2492 356 D
naelton@davidson.edu
ELVEY, William .... 608-262-3488 539 D
belvey@fpm.wisc.edu
ELVIDGE, Janet .... 207-974-4606 211 A
jelvidge@emcc.edu
ELWELL, Daniel .... 201-200-3598 304 C
delwell@njcu.edu
ELWELL, David .... 617-253-3795 233 C
ELWELL, Frank .... 918-343-7851 401 I
felwell@rsu.edu
ELWELL, Jan .... 518-255-5423 346 E
elwellja@cobleskill.edu
ELWELL, Jan, A .... 607-746-4499 347 G
elwellja@delhi.edu
ELWELL, Jeff .... 423-425-4635 465 E
jeffery-elwell@utc.edu
ELWELL, Nancy .... 402-643-7337 289 J
nancy.elwell@cune.edu
ELWOOD, Sharon .... 307-674-6446 546 H
elwood@sheridan.edu
ELWORTH, Edyce .... 336-734-7296 362 F
eelworth@forsythtech.edu
ELY, Aiden .... 916-558-2194.. 53 B
ElyA@scc.losrios.edu
ELY, Eileen, E .... 253-833-9111 523 B
eely@greenriver.edu
ELY, Janice .... 310-660-3109.. 43 G
jely@elcamino.edu
ELY, SJ, Peter .... 206-296-6158 526 F
ely@seattleu.edu
ELZARKA, Sammy .... 909-593-3511.. 73 B
selzarka@laverne.edu
EMAMI, Azita .... 206-221-2472 527 G
emamia@uw.edu
EMAMI, Morteza .... 801-626-6853 500 C
memami@weber.edu
EMANUEL, Catherine, B .... 770-720-9232 130 E
cbe@reinhardt.edu
EMBACHER, Barb .... 507-389-7493 262 A
barb.embacher@southcentral.edu
EMBERTON, Sherilyn, R .... 260-359-4050 167 D
semberton@huntington.edu
EMBRY, Greg .... 205-665-6030.... 9 C
embryg@montevallo.edu
EMBRY, Rebecka .... 501-977-2033.. 25 A
embry@uaccm.edu
EMDY, Jim .... 831-476-9424.. 44 L
librarian@fivebranches.edu
EMENGER, Nancy, E ..... 801-626-6017 500 C
nemenger@weber.edu
EMERICK, Kenneth .... 301-687-4880 220 D
kmemerick@frostburg.edu
EMERICK, Sandra, M .... 330-325-6759 387 F
semerick@neomed.edu
EMERSON, Adam .... 413-236-2131 231 A
aemerson@berkshirecc.edu
EMERSON, Brian .... 716-896-0700 352 B
bemerson@villa.edu
EMERSON, Colleen .... 401-341-2908 442 D
emersonc@salve.edu
EMERSON, Dave .... 616-222-1426 241 G
dave.emerson@cornerstone.edu
EMERSON, Karen .... 248-204-2000 245 J
kemerson@ltu.edu
EMERSON, Michael, O . 773-244-5570 154 G
moemerson@northpark.edu
EMERSON, Nate .... 507-453-2711 259 G
nemerson@southeastmn.edu
EMERSON, Sally .... 608-789-6083 544 E
emersons@westerntc.edu
EMERSON, Steve .... 951-343-4415.. 30 D
semerson@calbaptist.edu
EMERSON, Tara .... 573-592-4251 286 A
tara.emerson@williamwoods.edu
EMERSON, Tony .... 516-918-3675 316 L
temerson@bcl.edu
EMERSON, Wendy, R ... 336-734-7540 362 F
wemerson@forsythtech.edu
EMERSON, Yolanda ...... 562-908-3405.. 60 I
yemerson@riohondo.edu
EMERT, Chuck .... 619-201-8995.. 67 I
chuck.emert@socalsem.edu
EMERY, John .... 661-654-2157.. 32 G
jemery@csub.edu
EMERY, Monica .... 716-375-2400 340 C
memery@sbu.edu
EMERZIAN, Janice .... 559-442-8237.. 69 B
janice.emerzian@fresnocitycollege.edu
EMERZIAN, Janice .... 559-638-3641.. 69 C
janice.emerzian@scccd.com
EMILIO, Linda .... 909-469-8421.. 76 I
lemilio@westernu.edu
EMLET, Jerry, D .... 860-727-6906.. 90 F
jemlet@goodwin.edu
EMM, William, T .... 585-345-6811 326 F
wtemm@genesee.edu
EMMANUEL, Ted .... 315-445-4191 330 B
emmanut@lemoyne.edu
EMMANUEL, Tsegai ...... 318-274-6196 207 H
emmanuel@gram.edu
EMMANUEL-FRENEL, Rouseline .... 215-646-7300 420 A
Emmanuel.R@gmercyu.edu
EMMER, Karen .... 520-515-5417.. 13 B
emmerk@cochise.edu
EMMERICH, Linda .... 443-518-3825 215 F
lemmerich@howardcc.edu
EMMERLING, Andrew ... 717-757-1100 440 K
drew.emmerling@yti.edu
EMMERT, Heather .... 321-693-5256 103 R
hcudmore@fit.edu
EMMICK, Joseph, R ..... 630-617-6422 144 G
joseph.r.emmick@elmhurst.edu
EMMIL, Bruce .... 701-224-5758 374 E
bruce.emmil@bismarckstate.edu
EMMONS, Carol-Ann .... 312-567-3827 147 E
emmons@iit.edu
EMMONS, David .... 360-475-7120 524 H
demmons@olympic.edu
EMMONS, Don .... 315-781-3559 327 G
emmons@hws.edu
EMMONS, Ken .... 619-644-7653.. 46 H
ken.emmons@gcccd.edu
EMMONS, Luli .... 650-433-3845.. 58 B
lemmons@paloaltou.edu
EMMONS, Scott .... 414-229-4762 540 A
semm@uwm.edu
EMMONS, Todd, C .... 603-526-3076 296 I
todd.emmons@colby-sawyer.edu
EMOND, Gean Ann .... 850-484-1728 110 D
gemond@pensacolastate.edu
EMONS, Margaret, L .... 402-465-2405 292 E
memons@nebrwesleyan.edu
EMORY, Cynthia .... 301-696-3566 215 E
emory@hood.edu
EMORY, Douglas, J ...... 425-739-8311 523 I
doug.emory@lwtech.edu
EMORY, Fran .... 252-222-6144 361 A
emoryf@carteret.edu
EMORY, Julie, W .... 252-398-6252 356 B
emoryj@chowan.edu
EMORY, Kathleen .... 301-696-3215 215 E
emoryk@hood.edu
EMSLIE, A. Gordon .... 270-745-2297 201 D
gordon.emslie@wku.edu
EMSWELLER, David, W . 419-434-4578 393 F
emsweller@findlay.edu
EMSWILER, Sue .... 717-299-7730 436 D
emswiler@stevenscollege.edu
ENAMAIT, John, D .... 252-823-5166 362 D
enamaitj@edgecombe.edu
ENCARNACIÓN, José, M .... 787-850-9376 558 A
jose.encarnacion2@upr.edu
ENCARNACION, Enrico . 787-844-8991 558 D
enrico.encarnacion@upr.edu
ENCARNACION, Mayra . 787-257-0000 557 F
mayra.encarnacion@upr.edu
ENCINA, Rosalinda .... 210-486-4609 466 K
rencina@alamo.edu
ENDEAN, Kenneth, M ... 480-245-7969.. 14 D
ken.endean@ibcs.edu
ENDEAN, Robert .... 606-218-5226 201 C
robertendean@upike.edu
ENDER, Kenneth, L .... 847-925-6390 145 F
kender@harpercollege.edu
ENDER, Steven, C .... 616-234-3901 243 D
sender@grcc.edu
ENDERS, Naulayne, R ... 606-474-3276 195 F
nenders@kcu.edu
ENDERS, Thomas .... 562-985-5462.. 33 F
tom.enders@csulb.edu
ENDICOTT, Daniel, D .... 904-620-2019 116 A
dendicot@unf.edu
ENDICOTT, Jon .... 559-453-3484.. 45 E
jon.endicott@fresno.edu
ENDICOTT, Patricia .... 812-749-1435 171 I
pendicott@oak.edu
ENDRASKE, Mark .... 530-226-4108.. 66 G
mendraske@simpsonu.edu
ENDRESS, Wendy .... 360-867-6296 522 J
endressw@evergreen.edu
ENDRIES, Jill, M .... 920-424-0228 540 B
endries@uwosh.edu
ENDRIES, Mary .... 920-923-8937 537 A
mendries@marianuniversity.edu
ENDRIJONAS, Erika, A . 818-947-2600.. 52 B
ENDSLEY, Douglas .... 210-829-6004 492 B
douge@uiwtx.edu
ENDY, Michael .... 817-598-6211 497 A
mendy@wc.edu
ENG, Carla .... 605-668-1514 452 I
ceng@mtmc.edu
ENG, Dave .... 845-398-4084 341 H
deng@stac.edu
ENG, Edwin .... 559-244-5910.. 68 J
ed.eng@scccd.edu
ENGBROCK, M. Jeff ...... 409-944-1215 474 G
mengbroc@gc.edu
ENGEBRETSON, Pam .... 651-779-3994 258 D
pam.engebretson@century.edu
ENGEL, Angela .... 309-438-3305 147 I
akengel@ilstu.edu
ENGEL, Cristi, L .... 402-461-5177 291 C
ENGEL, Deidre .... 712-279-5448 176 B
deidre.engel@briarcliff.edu
ENGEL, Heather .... 585-475-2627 339 G
ncedar@rit.edu
ENGEL, Michelle .... 414-382-6037 534 I
michelle.engel@alverno.edu
ENGEL, Renata, S .... 814-863-6726 428 C
rse1@psu.edu
ENGEL, Richard, R .... 530-752-9960.. 71 A
rrengel@ucdavis.edu
ENGEL, Robert .... 718-997-4105 320 E
robert.engel@qc.cuny.edu
ENGEL, Steven .... 912-478-0357 126 B
sengel@georgiasouthern.edu
ENGELBACH, Karl, M .... 530-754-7237.. 71 A
kmengelbach@ucdavis.edu
ENGELBRECHT, Laci ..... 217-479-7043 151 J
laci.engelbrecht@mac.edu
ENGELBRECHT, Sharon . 417-626-1234 280 B
engelbrecht.sharon@occ.edu
ENGELHARDT, Kelli ...... 406-791-5237 288 J
kengelhardt01@ugf.edu
ENGELHART, Brian, W .. 260-422-5561 167 F
bwengelhart@indianatech.edu
ENGELHART, Rene .... 916-646-2774.. 61 J
rengelhart@samuelmerritt.edu
ENGELKEMIER, John ..... 312-329-2145 153 C
john.engelkemier@moody.edu
ENGELKEN, Bonnie .... 316-677-1760 192 C
bengelken@watc.edu
ENGELKING, Heather .... 407-708-2103 113 A
engelkingh@seminolestate.edu
ENGELLAND, Brian .... 202-319-5290.. 95 A
engellab@cua.edu
ENGELLANT, Roxanne ... 406-683-7305 287 E
roxanne.engellant@umwestern.edu
ENGELLS, Thomas .... 409-772-1503 495 E
tengells@utmb.edu
ENGELMEYER, Renee .... 507-285-7183 261 D
renee.engelmeyer@rctc.edu
ENGELS, Kristen .... 920-565-1102 536 Q
engelskl@lakeland.edu
ENGELSCHALL, Emily, D .... 951-827-3986.. 72 A
emily.engelschall@ucr.edu
ENGELSEN, Karen .... 805-289-6153.. 75 E
kengelsen@vcccd.edu
ENGELSMA, Chris .... 616-432-3406 249 B
chris.engelsma@prts.edu
ENGEMANN, JR., Andrew, H .... 757-594-7053 506 I
andrew.engemann@cnu.edu
ENGEN, Stuart .... 701-671-2446 375 B
stuart.engen@ndscs.edu
ENGER, Lee .... 217-228-5432 156 D
engerle@quincy.edu
ENGERMAN, Marie .... 340-693-1261 559 B
kengerm@live.uvi.edu
ENGERT, Lara .... 312-752-2130 149 D
lara.engert@kendall.edu
ENGFER, Tom .... 323-860-4349.. 55 D
tengfer@mi.edu
ENGH, SJ, Michael, E .. 408-554-4100.. 65 A
mengh@scu.edu
ENGH, Peter, M .... 508-213-2390 235 C
peter.engh@nichols.edu
ENGLAND, A, W .... 313-593-5290 251 D
england@umich.edu
ENGLAND, Amy 918-631-3288 403M
amy-england@utulsa.edu
ENGLAND, David .... 860-773-1401.. 90 C
dengland@txcc.commnet.edu
ENGLAND, David .... 615-966-6210 458 C
david.england@lipscomb.edu
ENGLAND, David, C ..... 860-255-3500.. 90 C
dengland@txcc.commnet.edu
ENGLAND, Richard .... 217-581-2017 144 E
rengland@eiu.edu

ERICKSON, Regina .... 530-226-4718.. 66 G
rerickson@simpsonu.edu
ERICKSON, Russell, E .. 651-286-7573 265 D
reerickson@unwsp.edu
ERICKSON, Scott .... 651-450-3000 259 A
serickson@inverhills.edu
ERICKSON, Scott .... 612-659-6831 259 F
scott.erickson@minneapolis.edu
ERICKSON, Siri, C .... 507-933-7446 256 A
sericks5@gustavus.edu
ERICKSON, Steve .... 218-846-3721 259 H
steve.erickson@minnesota.edu
ERICKSON, Susan .... 757-455-3220 518 H
serickson@vwc.edu
ERICKSON, Suzanne ..... 651-604-4119 257 C
ERICKSON, Suzanne ..... 770-718-5326 121 G
serickson@brenau.edu
ERICKSON, Todd .... 916-577-2200.. 77 F
terickson@jessup.edu
ERICKSON, Tony, W ..... 651-962-4340 265 F
twerickson@stthomas.edu
ERICSON, III, Ed .... 479-238-8669.. 21 F
eericson@jbu.edu
ERICSON, Jay .... 802-828-8599 503 D
jay.ericson@vcfa.edu
ERICSON, Laura .... 715-833-6232 542 M
lericson2@cvtc.edu
ERICSON, Rick, F .... 541-346-0459 410 F
rericson@uoregon.edu
ERICSON, Todd, M .... 608-796-3856 542 H
tmericson@viterbo.edu
ERIKSEN, Jennifer, A .... 207-778-7048 212 E
jennifer.eriksen@maine.edu
ERIKSEN, John .... 714-438-4680.. 40 A
jeriksen@mail.cccd.edu
ERIKSEN, John .... 401-232-6107 441 B
jeriksen@bryant.edu
ERIKSEN, Michael, P .... 404-413-1130 126 D
meriksen@gsu.edu
ERIKSMOEN, Lisa .... 701-858-3374 374 B
lisa.eriksmoen@minotstateu.edu
ERIKSON, Sherry, R ..... 828-328-7334 358 G
sherry.erikson@lr.edu
ERJAVEC, Patricia .... 719-549-3213.. 85 A
patty.erjavec@pueblocc.edu
ERKKILA, Rachel .... 515-964-6210 177 B
rrerkkila@dmacc.edu
ERLANGER, Esrael .... 718-645-0536 333 B
ERMATINGER, James .... 217-206-6512 161 G
ermatinger.james@uis.edu
ERMER, Scott .... 319-398-4944 180 J
sermer@kirkwood.edu
ERMIAS, Martha .... 323-265-8610.. 51 D
ermiasmy@elac.edu
ERMLER, Kathy .... 620-341-5403 186 H
kermler@emporia.edu
ERMOLI, Victor .... 912-525-5000 130 H
vermoli@scad.edu
ERNE, Richard .... 208-459-5334 137 J
rerne@collegeofidaho.edu
ERNEST, Ralynn .... 785-825-5422 185 D
rernest@brownmackie.edu
ERNST, Chris .... 502-456-6509 200 A
cernst@sctd.edu
ERNST, Dale, E .... 785-242-2067 189 J
dernst@neosho.edu
ERNST, John, P .... 606-783-2022 198 H
j.ernst@moreheadstate.edu
ERNST, Michelle .... 651-905-3445 264 E
mernst@browncollege.edu
ERNST, Nathan .... 630-515-6342 152 H
nernst@midwestern.edu
ERNST, Patricia .... 717-396-7833 429 H
pernst@pcad.edu
ERNST-LEONARD,
Amber .... 305-809-3531 104 A
amber.ernstleonard@fkcc.edu
ERNSTBERGER, Jon .... 706-880-8155 127 N
jernstberger@lagrange.edu
ERNSTING, Brian .... 319-352-8284 183 J
brian.ernsting@wartburg.edu
ERPELDING, Augustine . 623-845-3562.. 14 N
augustine.erpelding@gccaz.edu
ERPENBACH, Steve .... 605-697-7475 454 C
steve.erpenbach@sdsufoundation.org
ERPESTAD, Hanna .... 218-733-7600 259 C
h.erpestad@lsc.edu
ERRECA, Lori .... 619-388-3207.. 62 F
lerreca@sdccd.edu
ERRECA, Sarah .... 205-226-4905.... 2 C
serreca@bsc.edu
ERRICKSON, David, C .. 717-871-4183 431 E
david.errickson@millersville.edu
ERRIGO, Fred .... 803-321-5238 447 L
fred.errigo@newberry.edu
ERSAL, Aslam .... 973-596-5303 304 D
ersal.aslam@njit.edu
ERSKINE, Eva .... 847-476-7605 155 D
e-erskine@northwestern.edu
ERSKINE, Tina .... 207-454-1002 211 E
terskine@wccc.me.edu

ERSLAN, Bryan .... 859-622-2361 194 L
bryan.erslan@eku.edu
ERSTE, SR., Mark, A .... 740-284-5234 382 G
merste@franciscan.edu
ERSTINE, Kelley .... 501-852-0871.. 25 F
kerstine@uca.edu
ERTEL, Stefanie .... 910-221-2224 357 A
sertel@gcd.edu
ERTELT, Celeste .... 701-662-1533 375 A
celeste.m.ertelt@lrsc.edu
ERTELT, Victoria .... 503-845-3102 407 B
victoria.ertelt@mtangel.edu
ERTING, Carol, J .... 202-651-5085.. 95 C
carol.erting@gallaudet.edu
ERUZIONE, Vincent ...... 617-333-2202 225 F
veruzion@curry.edu
ERVIN, Archie .... 404-385-3686 125 D
archie.ervin@vpid.gatech.edu
ERVIN, Bob, J .... 910-678-8442 362 E
ervinb@faytechcc.edu
ERVIN, Elonda .... 812-237-2877 167 E
elonda.ervin@indstate.edu
ERVIN, Erin .... 863-680-3931 104 F
eervin@flsouthern.edu
ERVIN, Hazel .... 501-370-5276.. 22 E
hervin@philander.edu
ERVIN, Korrie .... 910-576-6222 364 D
ervink@montgomery.edu
ERVIN, Larry .... 865-981-8222 458 E
larry.ervin@maryvillecollege.edu
ERVIN, Leisa .... 662-325-7353 269 A
lbryant@audit.msstate.edu
ERVIN, Serica .... 858-279-4500.. 49 B
smartinezervin@kaplan.edu
ERWIN, Alexander .... 704-216-6899 358 I
aerwin@livingstone.edu
ERWIN, Clarissa .... 702-651-5863 295 C
clarissa.erwin@csn.edu
ERWIN, Connie, I .... 724-847-6666 419 B
cierwin@geneva.edu
ERWIN, Craig .... 512-863-1472 483 G
erwinc@southwestern.edu
ERWIN, Curtis .... 804-828-7666 514 F
cgerwin@vcu.edu
ERWIN, Deidre .... 262-524-7201 535 D
derwin@carrollu.edu
ERWIN, Gary .... 313-317-6800 243 I
gjerwin@hfcc.edu
ERWIN, John, O .... 616-885-5585 390 G
jerwin@pcj.edu
ERWIN, John, S .... 740-389-4636 386 B
erwinj@mtc.edu
ERWIN, Lisa .... 218-726-8501 264 G
laerwin@d.umn.edu
ERWIN, Pamela .... 651-638-6805 254 A
perwin@bethel.edu
ERWIN, Ryan .... 918-343-7782 401 I
rerwin@rsu.edu
ERWIN, Shari .... 918-293-4966 400 E
shari.erwin@okstate.edu
ERWIN, Steve .... 620-235-4231 190 G
serwin@pittstate.edu
ERWIN, Tom .... 316-323-6323 185 F
terwin@butlercc.edu
ERWIN, Tony .... 617-373-3190 235 D
ERWIN, W. Scott .... 512-245-2102 489 C
we10@txstate.edu
ERWIN-PLOOG, Patricia 603-513-1132 299 C
patricia.erwin-ploog@granite.edu
ERZ, Brad .... 312-629-6700 158 J
berz@saic.edu
ESBENSHADE, Melissa . 800-733-3879 144 A
mesbenshade@devrygroup.com
ESCALANTE, Angie .... 787-765-5974 556 H
aescalan@pupr.edu
ESCALANTE, Eddie .... 626-571-8811.. 74 E
eddiee@uwest.edu
ESCALANTE, Maria .... 800-567-2344 535 F
mescalante@menominee.edu
ESCALANTE, Rochely ..... 787-725-6500 551 A
rescalante@albizu.edu
ESCALANTE, Victor .... 800-567-2344 535 F
vescalante@menominee.edu
ESCAMILLA, Cindy .... 210-829-3136 492 B
cyescami@uiwtx.edu
ESCAMILLA, Mark .... 361-698-1203 473 F
mescamilla@delmar.edu
ESCH, Rod .... 970-351-3192.. 87 A
rodney.esch@unco.edu
ESCH, Terri .... 312-662-4151 139 E
tesch@adler.edu
ESCHBACH, Jeanne, M . 607-735-1825 324 J
jeschbach@elmira.edu
ESCHEN, Thomas .... 314-529-9343 277 B
teschen@maryville.edu
ESCHENBAUM, Matt ..... 303-871-4256.. 86 H
matt.eschenbaum@du.edu
ESCHENBRENNER,
Nancy .... 860-773-1304.. 90 C
neschenbrenner@txcc.commnet.edu

ESCHENBURG, Cynthia . 313-845-9820 243 I
cmeschenburg@hfcc.edu
ESCHHOLZ, Ingrid .... 303-315-2600.. 86 G
ingrid.eschholz@ucdenver.edu
ESCOBAR, Carlos .... 409-772-3569 495 E
crescoba@utmb.edu
ESCOBAR, Enrique, N ... 410-651-6206 219 H
enescobar@umes.edu
ESCOBAR, Estrella .... 915-747-5555 494 B
estrella@utep.edu
ESCOBAR, Jorge .... 408-273-2764.. 55 G
jorge.escobar@nhu.edu
ESCOBAR, Jorge .... 408-288-3723.. 64 A
jorge.escobar@sjcc.edu
ESCOBEDO, Maria .... 805-591-6220.. 42 H
maria_escobedo@cuesta.edu
ESCOLAS, Roger .... 614-222-3264 380 F
rescolas@ccad.edu
ESCOTO, Jose .... 516-773-5000 548 I
escotoj@usmma.edu
ESCRIBANO,
Dorothy, A .... 914-654-5535 322 B
describano@cnr.edu
ESFANDI, Roya .... 713-646-1796 482 H
resfandi@stcl.edu
ESHAM, Sherry, L .... 520-626-6309.. 18 E
sesham@email.arizona.edu
ESHELMAN,
Christopher .... 316-978-7007 192 D
christopher.eshelman@wichita.edu
ESHENBERG, Ardis .... 808-235-7339 137 A
ardise@hawaii.edu
ESKANDARIAN, Ali .... 202-994-8192.. 95 D
ea1102@gwu.edu
ESKER, Brian .... 312-899-5177 158 J
besker@saic.edu
ESKES, Todd .... 909-599-5433.. 50 H
teskes@lifepacific.edu
ESKEW, Ron .... 716-926-8846 327 F
reskew@hilbert.edu
ESKIN, Jim .... 210-485-0047 466 J
jeskin@alamo.edu
ESLAHI, Farokh .... 217-206-7352 161 G
eslahi.farokh@uis.edu
ESLINGER, Elise .... 507-222-5597 254 D
eeslinge@carleton.edu
ESLINGER-SCHNEIDER,
Michelle, D .... 701-777-4500 373 G
michelle.eslinger@und.edu
ESMAEILI, Ali .... 956-872-7270 482 G
esmaeili@southtexascollege.edu
ESNES, Michael .... 908-709-7046 309 A
michael.esnes@ucc.edu
ESNES-JOHNSON, Terry 631-420-2000 348 B
terry.esnes-johnson@farmingdale.edu
ESPARZA, Lou .... 214-333-5289 471 L
lou@dbu.edu
ESPER, Linda, L .... 508-373-9755 223 C
linda.esper@becker.edu
ESPESET, Rick .... 260-982-5390 170 a
rbespeset@manchester.edu
ESPEY, Shellye .... 601-481-1309 268 B
sespey@meridiancc.edu
ESPINA, Maritza, I .... 787-257-7373 555 L
mespina@suagm.edu
ESPINAL, Sonnya .... 617-873-0430 225 A
sonnya.espinal@cambridgecollege.edu
ESPINET, Lydia .... 787-727-7880 559 A
lespinet@sagrado.edu
ESPING, David .... 417-447-7552 280 C
espingd@otc.edu
ESPINOSA, Charles .... 361-593-3057 486 A
charles.espinosa@tamuk.edu
ESPINOSA, Martin .... 615-256-1463 454 G
mespinosa@abcnash.edu
ESPINOSA, Philip .... 906-635-2697 245 H
aespinosa@lssu.edu
ESPINOSA, Rene .... 210-341-1366 479 N
respinosa@ost.edu
ESPINOSA, Rosa .... 210-434-6711 479 P
raespinosar@lake.ollusa.edu
ESPINOSA-PIEB,
Christina .... 408-864-8958.. 44 N
espinosapiebchristina@deanza.edu
ESPINOSA PIEB,
Christina .... 408-864-8995.. 44 N
espinosapiebchristina@deanza.edu
ESPINOZA, Beatriz, T .... 361-354-2200 470 K
presoffice@coastalbend.edu
ESPINOZA, Christopher 210-297-9114 468 K
christopher.espinoza@baptisthealthsystem.com
ESPINOZA, Danielle ...... 210-486-3366 467 A
despinoza@alamo.edu
ESPINOZA, Dora .... 847-578-8524 157 G
dora.espinoza@rosalindfranklin.edu
ESPINOZA, Susan, B .... 210-486-0748 467 C
sespinoza@alamo.edu

ESPINOZA,
Suzanne, M .... 209-667-3177.. 35 C
sespinoza1@csustan.edu
ESPINOZA, Yolanda .... 520-206-4640.. 17 A
yespinoza5@pima.edu
ESPIRITU, Kira, A .... 619-260-8835.. 74 B
kespiritu@sandiego.edu
ESPLIN, Fred, C .... 801-581-4088 499 K
fred.esplin@utah.edu
ESPOSITO, Arthur .... 617-984-1773 235 H
aesposito@quincycollege.edu
ESPOSITO, Dominic ...... 646-312-2208 318 C
Dominic.Esposito@baruch.cuny.edu
ESPOSITO, James .... 212-678-8095 329 H
jaesposito@jtsa.edu
ESPOSITO, Richard, C .. 412-396-6607 417 I
esposito@duq.edu
ESPOSITO, Scott .... 203-254-4000.. 90 E
sesposito@fairfield.edu
ESPY, Kathlynne, D ...... 614-234-5276 386 N
kespy@mccn.edu
ESPY, Kimberly, A .... 520-621-3513.. 18 E
kespy@email.arizona.edu
ESPY, Tracy, Y .... 704-463-3440 367 F
tracy.espy@pfeiffer.edu
ESQUEDA, Angie .... 805-730-4011.. 64 N
esqueda@sbcc.edu
ESQUIBEL, Jamie .... 877-442-0505.. 87 C
jamie.esquibel@rockies.edu
ESQUILIN, Luis .... 787-758-6260 553 D
esquilin@inter.edu
ESQUITH, Stephen, L ... 517-355-0210 246 H
esquith@msu.edu
ESQUIVEL, Ruben, E ..... 214-648-0448 496 A
ruben.esquivel@utsouthwestern.edu
ESQUIVEL, Tammy .... 858-279-4500.. 49 B
tesquivel@kaplan.edu
ESQUIVEL-SWINSON,
Adela .... 510-466-7394.. 58 J
aesquivelswinson@peralta.edu
ESQUIVEL-SWINSON,
Adela .... 510-466-7374.. 59 C
aesquivelswinson@peralta.edu
ESRY, Kip .... 800-955-2527 187 E
kesry@grantham.edu
ESSAYYAD, Musa, M .... 337-475-5010 208 B
messayyad@mcneese.edu
ESSEL, Albert .... 573-681-5550 276 K
essela@lincolnu.edu
ESSENBURG, Curt .... 616-222-3000 245 D
cessenburg@kuyper.edu
ESSES, Adam .... 618-545-3146 149 C
aesses@kaskaskia.edu
ESSES, Levi .... 316-942-4291 189 K
essesl@newmanu.edu
ESSEX, Don .... 301-891-4222 221 C
dessex@wau.edu
ESSIG, Lori .... 605-995-2614 452 C
loessig@dwu.edu
ESSIG, Mary .... 304-647-6213 533 B
messig@osteo.wvsom.edu
ESTABROOK,
Madeleine, A .... 617-373-2772 235 D
ESTAPHAN, Charles, F . 508-793-2514 225 C
cestapha@holycross.edu
ESTEBAN, A. Gabriel .... 973-761-9691 308 C
gabriel.esteban@shu.edu
ESTELL, Frank, E .... 208-467-8434 138 H
festell@nnu.edu
ESTEN, Dora, E .... 818-947-2761.. 52 B
estende@lavc.edu
ESTENSON, Chad .... 701-662-1521 375 A
chad.estenson@lrsc.edu
ESTENSON, Marlene ..... 513-244-8337 379 I
marlene.estenson@ccuniversity.edu
ESTEP, Alison .... 206-378-5056 526 D
estep@spu.edu
ESTEP, Charles, R .... 864-379-8869 446 B
estep@erskine.edu
ESTEPP, J. Mark .... 276-964-7315 517 A
mark.estepp@sw.edu
ESTER, Joyce, C .... 952-358-8150 260 D
joyce.ester@normandale.edu
ESTERBERG, Kristin, G . 315-267-2100 346 C
president@potsdam.edu
ESTERLINE, David, V .... 412-924-1366 433 E
desterline@pts.edu
ESTERS, Randall .... 337-550-1308 205 B
resters@lsue.edu
ESTES, Ashley .... 713-646-1793 482 H
aestes@stcl.edu
ESTES, Edward, R .... 757-479-3706 514 D
eestes@vbts.edu
ESTES, Eric .... 440-775-8462 388 B
eric.estes@oberlin.edu
ESTES, James .... 202-885-8696.. 97 E
jestes@wesleyseminary.edu
ESTES, Lane .... 205-226-4640.... 2 C
lestes@bsc.edu

ESTES, Michael .... 601-984-1130 270 H
mestes@umc.edu
ESTES, William 423-614-8175 457M
bestes@leeuniversity.edu
ESTEVEZ, Edwin .... 618-664-7021 145 E
edwin.estevez@greenville.edu
ESTEVEZ, Francisco, A . 860-701-6728 548 H
ESTEVEZ MARTINEZ,
Jacqueline .... 212-938-5500 347 C
jmartinez@sunyopt.edu
ESTILL, Donna .... 256-306-2756.... 2 F
dre@calhoun.edu
ESTILL, Sandi, L .... 606-759-7141 196 G
sandi.estill@kctcs.edu
ESTLACK, Scarlet .... 806-874-3571 470 J
scarlet.estlack@clarendoncollege.edu
ESTLACK, Tom .... 412-809-5100 433 D
estlack.tom@pti.edu
ESTOCADO, Gianne .... 434-528-5276 518 F
gestocado@vul.edu
ESTOCK, Steven .... 575-562-2632 310 I
steven.estock@enmu.edu
ESTRADA, Donna .... 985-448-7954 203 G
donna.estrada@fletcher.edu
ESTRADA, Ella Mae ...... 212-431-2827 335 G
EllaMae.Estrada@nyls.edu
ESTRADA, George .... 203-576-4330.. 92 B
gestrada@bridgeport.edu
ESTRADA, George .... 530-242-7930.. 66 C
gestrada@shastacollege.edu
ESTRADA, Lourdes .... 520-439-6828.. 13 B
estradal@cochise.edu
ESTRADA, Maria .... 787-780-5134 554 H
mestrada@nuc.edu
ESTRADA, Rebecca .... 505-428-1604 313 A
rebecca.estrada@sfcc.edu
ESTRADA, Robert .... 925-473-7540.. 42 F
restrada@losmedanos.edu
ESTRADA-HAMBY, Lisa . 940-397-4076 478 G
lisa.hamby@mwsu.edu
ESTRELLA, JR., Joseph . 808-932-7170 135 I
josephe@hawaii.edu
ESTREMERA, Luis .... 787-758-2525 558 C
luis.estremera@upr.edu
ESTRIDGE, Gwen .... 303-477-7240.. 82M
gwene@heritage-education.com
ESTRIN, David .... 718-522-9073 315 E
david@asa.edu
ESTRIN, Elena .... 212-349-4330 326 G
eestrin@globe.edu
ESTRY, Douglas .... 517-353-5380 246 H
estry@msu.edu
ETCHEMENDY, John, W 650-724-4074.. 68 G
provost@stanford.edu
ETE, Sonia .... 310-360-8888.. 26 B
ETE, Thierry .... 310-360-8888.. 26 B
ETHIER, Richard .... 802-224-3000 503 F
richard.ethier@vsc.edu
ETHINGTON, Robert ...... 707-527-4573.. 65 C
rethington@santarosa.edu
ETINGE, Elias .... 706-821-8302 129 H
eetinge@paine.edu
ETSCHMAIER, Gale .... 619-594-1643.. 35 E
gale.etschmaier@sdsu.edu
ETSE, Penselyn .... 691-320-2480 549 D
petse@comfsm.fm
ETTARO, Barbara .... 814-863-1030 428 C
bxm7@psu.edu
ETTINGER, Sherri .... 617-521-2451 236 F
sherri.ettinger@simmons.edu
ETTLE, Violeta .... 202-885-2720.. 94 H
vi@american.edu
ETTLICH, Sherry .... 541-552-6576 409 G
ettlich@sou.edu
ETTLING, John .... 518-564-2010 346 B
president_office@plattsburgh.edu
ETTORE, JD .... 620-223-2700 187 B
jde@fortscott.edu
ETUALE, Mikaele .... 684-699-9155 549 C
m.etuale@amsamoa.edu
ETZEL, Brent .... 479-968-0417.. 20 C
betzel@atu.edu
EUBANK, Charlotte .... 573-840-9105 283 D
ceubank@trcc.edu
EUBANK, Chelsea .... 352-638-9747.. 99 D
ceubank@beaconcollege.edu
EUBANK, Gary .... 937-529-2201 392 G
geubank@united.edu
EUBANK, Jeff .... 215-702-4202 414 C
jeubank@cairn.edu
EUBANKS, Audrey, C ... 251-442-2218.... 9 B
aeubanks@umobile.edu
EUBANKS, David .... 864-294-2000 446 F
david.eubanks@furman.edu
EUBANKS, Gail .... 912-443-5443 131 B
geubanks@savannahtech.edu
EUBANKS, Jamie .... 252-399-6368 354 I
jceubanks@barton.edu
EUBANKS, Karen .... 904-259-1259 103 K
keubanks@fcsl.edu
EUBANKS, Karla .... 912-427-5899 123 A
keubanks@coastalpines.edu
EUBANKS, Kathleen, L . 508-999-8086 228 H
keubanks@umassd.edu
EUBANKS, Nekita .... 704-216-3778 365 F
nekita.eubanks@rccc.edu
EUBANKS, Philip .... 865-573-4517 457 H
peubanks@johnsonU.edu
EULAND, Linda .... 865-981-8123 458 E
linda.euland@maryvillecollege.edu
EULE, Ann .... 603-882-6923 297 B
aeule@ccsnh.edu
EUNICE, E, E .... 850-201-7000 117 B
eunicee@tcc.fl.edu
EURICH, Judy .... 252-638-7350 362 A
eurichj@cravencc.edu
EUSEBIO,
Zenda Gay, P .... 626-448-0023.. 48 C
EUSTROM, Jim .... 503-399-5144 404 L
jim.eustrom@chemeketa.edu
EVAN, Joseph .... 570-208-5895 422 D
josephevan@kings.edu
EVANCHIK, Michele ...... 609-292-2108 308 H
mevanchik@tesc.edu
EVANGELISTA,
Joleen, M .... 671-735-5540 549 E
materialsmanagement@guamcc.edu
EVANGELISTA, Nancy ... 607-871-2649 314 J
fevangel@alfred.edu
EVANOSKY, Sonya .... 630-353-8708 141 D
sevanosky@chamberlain.edu
EVANOVICH, Dolan .... 614-292-8835 389 A
evanovich.1@osu.edu
EVANS, Alana 906-487-7358 242M
alana.evans@finlandia.edu
EVANS, Alane .... 262-646-6516 538 B
aevans@nashotah.edu
EVANS, Aleia .... 216-201-9025 385 D
EVANS, Alice .... 314-434-4044 273 J
alice.evans@covenantseminary.edu
EVANS, Amy, M .... 972-599-3144 471 C
aevans@collin.edu
EVANS, Andrea .... 708-534-8396 145 D
aevans7@govst.edu
EVANS, Angela .... 269-782-1323 250 D
aevans14@swmich.edu
EVANS, Angela, J 470-578-6300 127M
aevans@kennesaw.edu
EVANS, Annette .... 706-542-7066 132 H
amevans@uga.edu
EVANS, April .... 765-998-4625 173 B
apevans@taylor.edu
EVANS, Ashley .... 478-934-3458 128 H
ashley.evans@mga.edu
EVANS, Barry, W .... 806-291-1028 496 K
evansb@wbu.edu
EVANS, Beverly, A .... 717-815-1228 440 H
behinger@ycp.edu
EVANS, Brandt .... 216-987-4294 381 A
brandt.evans@tri-c.edu
EVANS, Brenda .... 978-934-5021 229 A
Brenda_Evans@uml.edu
EVANS, Brian .... 502-863-8223 195 A
brian_evans@georgetowncollege.edu
EVANS, Brian, K .... 801-422-3760 497 J
brian_evans@byu.edu
EVANS, Carolyn, L .... 601-977-7764 270 F
cevans@tougaloo.edu
EVANS, Cheryl .... 580-628-6201 399 E
cheryl.evans@noc.edu
EVANS, Cheryl, O .... 585-385-8015 340 F
cevans@sjfc.edu
EVANS, Christina .... 314-421-0949 283 B
cevans@siba.edu
EVANS, Damian .... 262-595-2540 540 C
damian.evans@uwp.edu
EVANS, Dave .... 619-388-2737.. 62 G
devans@sdccd.edu
EVANS, David .... 229-391-2609 132 C
devans@southernregional.edu
EVANS, David .... 972-273-3561 473 A
devans@dcccd.edu
EVANS, David, R .... 802-447-6319 503 A
devans@svc.edu
EVANS, Deborah, L ...... 610-861-1340 426 H
evansd@moravian.edu
EVANS, Debra, C .... 740-376-4835 386 A
debbie.evans@marietta.edu
EVANS, Diane, T .... 936-261-2202 484 F
dtevans@pvamu.edu
EVANS, Edward .... 361-825-2693 485 F
edward.evans@tamucc.edu
EVANS, Eric, D .... 781-981-7000 233 C
EVANS, Erik .... 570-389-4047 430 B
eevans@bloomu.edu
EVANS, Frederick M, G 803-536-7133 448 H
fevans3@scsu.edu
EVANS, Gary .... 507-457-5020 262 D
gevans@winona.edu
EVANS, George .... 618-545-3030 149 C
gevans@kaskaskia.edu
EVANS, JR., Gilbert, L .. 386-312-4127 111 K
gilbertevans@sjrstate.edu
EVANS, Greg .... 847-543-2252 142 G
gevans1@clcillinois.edu
EVANS, J. David 470-578-6194 127M
devans@kennesaw.edu
EVANS, Jack .... 706-721-3964 121 C
jaevans@gru.edu
EVANS, JR., Jack .... 972-524-3341 483 F
EVANS, SR., Jack .... 972-524-3341 483 F
EVANS, Jacquie .... 757-481-5005 519 C
EVANS, Janet, D .... 412-392-3824 433 F
jevans@pointpark.edu
EVANS, Janie .... 802-287-8203 501 I
evansj@greenmtn.edu
EVANS, Jaylene .... 970-542-3168.. 84 A
jaylene.evans@morgancc.edu
EVANS, Jeannette, H .... 315-684-6067 347 A
evansjh@morrisville.edu
EVANS, Jeffrey, L .... 313-593-5110 251 D
jlevan@umich.edu
EVANS, Jennifer, M ...... 717-867-6271 423 I
jevans@lvc.edu
EVANS, Jessica .... 254-968-9682 485 A
jevans@tarleton.edu
EVANS, John .... 618-536-2384 159 H
EVANS, Joseph .... 410-706-8501 219 E
jevans@umaryland.edu
EVANS, Joy .... 231-995-1084 248 C
jevans@nmc.edu
EVANS, Julie .... 701-777-6345 373 G
julie.evans@ndus.edu
EVANS, Kaitlin .... 530-226-4166.. 66 G
1004mgr@fheg.follett.com
EVANS, Kalene .... 847-290-6425 155 A
EVANS, Karen, V .... 610-921-7630 411 E
kevans@albright.edu
EVANS, Karyn .... 937-393-3431 391 F
kevans@sscc.edu
EVANS, Katherine .... 973-761-9500 308 C
katherine.evans@shu.edu
EVANS, Kathleen .... 315-312-2240 346 A
kathleen.evans@oswego.edu
EVANS, Kenne .... 214-860-3677 472 G
klevans@dcccd.edu
EVANS, Kenneth, R .... 409-880-8405 488 F
kenneth.evans@lamar.edu
EVANS, Kevin .... 937-327-7520 395 I
kevans@wittenberg.edu
EVANS, Kimberly .... 802-831-1225 503 E
kevans@vermontlaw.edu
EVANS, Laurie .... 313-664-1501 241 D
levans@collegeforcreativestudies.edu
EVANS, Layna .... 214-333-5275 471 L
layna@dbu.edu
EVANS, Lexie .... 206-934-3890 526 A
lexie.evans@seattlecolleges.edu
EVANS, Linda .... 803-641-3342 450 C
lindae@usca.edu
EVANS, Lisa .... 513-569-1564 379 K
Lisa.evans@cincinnatistate.edu
EVANS, Lisa .... 828-398-7390 360 A
levans@abtech.edu
EVANS, Liz .... 412-392-5945 433 F
eevans@pointpark.edu
EVANS, III, Louis, D .... 713-221-2766 491 F
evansl@uhd.edu
EVANS, Marcheta .... 210-434-6711 479 P
mevans@lake.ollusa.edu
EVANS, Marisa, L .... 814-886-6336 427 B
mevans@mtaloy.edu
EVANS, Mark .... 330-672-2972 384 H
mevans@kent.edu
EVANS, Mark .... 845-938-5502 549 A
Mark.Evans@usma.edu
EVANS, Maya .... 847-635-1973 155 E
mevans@oakton.edu
EVANS, Melissa .... 315-386-7123 347 F
evansm@canton.edu
EVANS, Mercedes .... 617-879-7060 230 B
msevans@massart.edu
EVANS, Michael .... 334-420-4302.... 7 I
mevans@trenholmstate.edu
EVANS, Michael, L .... 806-743-2738 490 A
michael.evans@ttuhsc.edu
EVANS, Paul .... 317-955-6290 171 A
pevans@marian.edu
EVANS, Piper .... 212-228-1888 339 C
EVANS, R. Gregory .... 912-478-2676 126 B
rgevans@georgiasouthern.edu
EVANS, JR., R. Lee ...... 334-844-8348.... 1 G
evansrl@auburn.edu
EVANS, Rick .... 818-677-2906.. 34 D
rick.evans@csun.edu
EVANS, Robert .... 773-907-4817 141 O
REvans@ccc.edu
EVANS, Roberta .... 406-243-4911 287 D
roberta.evans@umontana.edu
EVANS, Ronda .... 719-638-6580.. 82 G
revans@cci.edu
EVANS, Sam .... 270-745-4664 201 D
sam.evans@wku.edu
EVANS, Sarah .... 317-931-2303 165 C
sevans@cts.edu
EVANS, Sarah .... 336-342-4261 365 E
evanss@rockinghamcc.edu
EVANS, Scott .... 440-375-7255 385 B
sevans@lec.edu
EVANS, Sharlotte .... 706-821-3965 225 A
Sharlotte.Evans@cambridgecollege.edu
EVANS, Sharron .... 312-341-2004 157 E
sevans12@roosevelt.edu
EVANS, Sheilah, M .... 802-626-6697 504 B
sheliah.evans@lyndonstate.edu
EVANS, Sidney .... 443-885-3144 217 C
sidney.evans@morgan.edu
EVANS, Sidney, S .... 540-458-8754 519 A
sevans@wlu.edu
EVANS, Steve .... 281-425-6887 477 F
sevans@lee.edu
EVANS, Susan .... 239-590-1057 114 F
sevans@fgcu.edu
EVANS, Tabitha .... 409-882-3319 488 G
tabitha.evans@lsco.edu
EVANS, Thomas .... 406-447-4401 286 D
tevans@carroll.edu
EVANS, Thomas, A .... 515-281-6527 175 F
taevans@iastate.edu
EVANS, Tiffany .... 270-706-8406 195 K
tevans0138@kctcs.edu
EVANS, Toushane .... 920-686-6129 539 A
Toushane.Evans@sl.edu
EVANS, Tracy, L .... 304-929-5480 531 D
tevans@newriver.edu
EVANS, Virginia .... 434-982-2249 514 A
veb5u@virginia.edu
EVANS, W. Franklin ...... 803-536-7013 448 H
wevans1@scsu.edu
EVANS, Warren .... 808-791-5200.. 28 G
waevans@argosy.edu
EVANS, Will .... 503-251-2808 410 I
wevans@uws.edu
EVANS, Zina .... 352-392-1365 115 D
zevans@ufl.edu
EVANS-COLQUITT,
Tammy .... 610-992-1700.. 96 H
EVANS-COLQUITT,
Tammy .... 610-604-7700.. 96 H
EVANS-DAME, Kimberly 315-792-5637 333 D
kevans-dame@mvcc.edu
EVANS JONES, Cheryl .. 706-396-8102 129 H
cevansjones@paine.edu
EVANS-PLANTS, Penny . 706-232-5374 121 E
peplants@berry.edu
EVANS TAYLOR,
Genevieve .... 805-437-8410.. 32 H
genevieve.evans-taylor@csuci.edu
EVASHEVSKI, Keith .... 307-766-2187 546 K
keski@uwyo.edu
EVE, Debra .... 406-353-2607 286 B
deve@ancollege.edu
EVE, Stacey .... 406-791-5306 288 J
EVELAND, Susan, M ..... 541-346-3195 410 F
seveland@uoregon.edu
EVELER, Janet .... 915-831-5202 473 J
jeveler3@epcc.edu
EVELOFF, Vivian .... 314-516-6622 284 B
eveloffv@umsl.edu
EVELYN, Alan .... 516-299-2523 330 F
alan.evelyn@liu.edu
EVEN, Brock .... 563-588-4992 180 L
brock.even@loras.edu
EVEN, Susan, E .... 573-884-9388 283 H
EvenS@health.missouri.edu
EVENBECK, Scott .... 646-313-8000 321 A
president@guttman.cuny.edu
EVENER, Julie .... 904-826-0084.. 74 A
jevener@usa.edu
EVENSON, Brad .... 620-278-4221 191 D
bevenson@sterling.edu
EVENSON, Eric .... 815-483-0062.. 28 G
eevenson@argosy.edu
EVENSON, Shane .... 715-468-2815 544 F
Shane.Evenson@witc.edu
EVENSON, Thomas, L ... 940-565-2239 492 D
evenson@unt.edu
EVENSVOLD, Marty .... 620-251-7700 186 C
martye@coffeyville.edu
EVERETT, Daniel .... 781-891-2113 223 E
deverett@bentley.edu
EVERETT, David, D .... 330-569-5353 383 F
everettdd@hiram.edu
EVERETT, Dennis, F ...... 850-718-2216 100 E
everettd@chipola.edu
EVERETT, Frankie .... 318-342-5329 209 A
everett@ulm.edu
EVERETT,
Gwendolyn, H .... 202-806-7040.. 96 B
geverett@howard.edu

EVERETT, Jamila .... 909-621-8129.. 59 F
jamila_everett@pitzer.edu
EVERETT, Joe .... 816-322-0110 272 L
joe.everett@calvary.edu
EVERETT, Julia .... 256-228-6001.... 6 A
everettj@nacc.edu
EVERETT, Kathy .... 704-669-4092 361 E
everett@clevelandcc.edu
EVERETT, Kelly .... 641-784-5144 178 G
keverett@graceland.edu
EVERETT, Lisa .... 925-424-1183.. 37 O
leverett@laspositascollege.edu
EVERETT, Marcia, K ...... 330-471-8335 385 G
meverett@malone.edu
EVERETT, Margaret .... 503-725-5258 409 D
everettm@pdx.edu
EVERETT, Montre .... 912-525-3903 121 A
meverett@savannahlawschool.org
EVERETT, Robert .... 480-732-7280.. 14 K
Robert.Everett@cgc.edu
EVERETT, Steve .... 312-996-2006 161 F
steve3@uic.edu
EVERETT, Tammy .... 641-784-5115 178 G
teverett@graceland.edu
EVERETT-HENSLEY,
Elaine .... 361-572-6440 496 D
elaine.hensley@victoriacollege.edu
EVERHART, Clinton, D .. 501-686-5113.. 24 B
CDEverhart@uams.edu
EVERHART, Deborah ..... 203-932-7330.. 92 G
deverhart@newhaven.edu
EVERINGHAM, David ..... 727-873-4995 116 C
devering@usfsp.edu
EVERITT, William .... 228-497-7789 268 G
william.everitt@mgccc.edu
EVERS, Alexander .... 773-508-2760 151 E
aevers@luc.edu
EVERS, Cynthia .... 404-756-4585 120 H
cevers@atlm.edu
EVERSLEY BRADWELL,
Nicole .... 607-274-3124 328 H
neversley@ithaca.edu
EVERSOLE, Malinda ...... 276-223-4869 517 F
meversole@wcc.vccs.edu
EVERT, Amanda .... 405-422-1445 401 H
amanda.evert@redlandscc.edu
EVERTS, Sandra, L .... 414-277-7135 537 G
everts@msoe.edu
EVERTS, Sheri, N .... 828-262-2040 369 D
evertssn@appstate.edu
EVES, Robert .... 435-586-1934 499 L
eves@suu.edu
EVETOVICH, Tammy ...... 402-375-7030 292 D
taeveto1@wsc.edu
EVINGER, Donna, J ...... 812-464-1770 174 D
devinger@usi.edu
EVITT, Regula, M .... 719-389-6706.. 79M
regula.evitt@coloradocollege.edu
EVITTS, Beth, A .... 717-339-3527 420 D
baevitts@hacc.edu
EVJEN, Art .... 831-582-3394.. 34 C
aevjen@csumb.edu
EVON, Daniel, T .... 517-355-4727 246 H
evon@cga.msu.edu
EWALD, Beth .... 810-762-9645 245 A
bewald@kettering.edu
EWALD, Paul .... 650-508-3494.. 56 H
pewald@ndnu.edu
EWALD, Stanley .... 503-251-5717 410 I
sewald@uws.edu
EWAN, Brian .... 856-691-8600 301 H
bewan@cccnj.edu
EWARMAI, Matthias ..... 691-350-5244 549 D
mewarmai@comfsm.fm
EWART, Dan .... 208-885-2271 139 C
dewart@uidaho.edu
EWART, Daniel .... 208-885-2271 139 C
dewart@uidaho.edu
EWELL, Clint .... 928-776-2166.. 18 L
clint.ewell@yc.edu
EWELL, Robbi .... 619-388-3870.. 62 F
rewell@sdccd.edu
EWEN, Bernadette .... 812-877-8697 172 C
ewen@rose-hulman.edu
EWEN, Gary .... 303-963-3166.. 79 L
gewen@ccu.edu
EWEN, Kurt, E .... 407-582-3413 118 I
kewen@valenciacollege.edu
EWEN, Lois .... 423-636-7435 464 F
lewen@tusculum.edu
EWERS, Frank, W .... 909-869-4132.. 32 F
fwewers@cpp.edu
EWERS, Matthew .... 307-754-6125 546 I
Matthew.Ewers@nwc.edu
EWERS, Terri, L .... 641-422-4106 181 E
ewerster@niacc.edu
EWIG, Rick .... 307-766-6385 546 K
rewig@uwyo.edu
EWING, April .... 706-821-8307 129 H
aewing@paine.edu
EWING, Brad .... 907-796-6457.. 11 A
brewing@uas.alaska.edu
EWING, Carol .... 847-543-2937 142 G
cewing@clcillinois.edu
EWING, Cathy .... 907-786-1558.. 10 H
clewing@uaa.alaska.edu
EWING, Douglas .... 212-817-7490 319 B
dewing@gc.cuny.edu
EWING, Eric .... 909-607-0275.. 39 E
eric.ewing@cgu.edu
EWING, James .... 954-262-8082 109 E
jewing@nova.edu
EWING, Jennifer .... 619-201-8682.. 67 I
jewing@socalsem.edu
EWING, Kamesia .... 910-672-1325 370 A
kewing@uncfsu.edu
EWING, Mike, J .... 320-363-5605 254 J
mjewing@csbsju.edu
EWING, II, Rick, M ...... 419-289-5491 377 A
pewing@ashland.edu
EWING, Sim, E .... 276-328-0133 514 B
see4r@uvawise.edu
EWING, Sunnie .... 901-722-3231 461 A
sewing@sco.edu
EWING-MORGAN,
Dawn .... 718-960-8111 319 C
dawn.ewing-morgan@lehman.cuny.edu
EXLER, Michael, J .... 215-895-6488 417 E
mexler@drexel.edu
EXLEY, Robert .... 256-840-4100.... 7 B
rexley@snead.edu
EXLINE, Teresa, D .... 812-237-7783 167 E
teresa.exline@indstate.edu
EXNER, Allen .... 301-369-2800 214 A
ahexner@captechu.edu
EXSTEEN, Shaun .... 561-237-7839 108 E
exsteen@lynn.edu
EYE, John .... 601-266-4241 271 B
john.eye@usm.edu
EYE, Kurt .... 518-244-4536 340 A
eyek@sage.edu
EYER, Paul .... 717-290-8705 423 E
peyer@lancasterseminary.edu
EYLER, Robert .... 707-664-2396.. 36 C
EYLERS, Hinrich .... 602-557-7428.. 18 H
hinrich.eylers@phoenix.edu
EYNON, Bret .... 718-482-5478 320 B
beynon@lagcc.cuny.edu
EYNON, Craig, S .... 330-325-6663 387 F
ceynon@neomed.edu
EYNON, Matthew .... 717-291-3973 418 J
matthew.eynon@fandm.edu
EYRING, Henry, J .... 208-496-1119 137 F
eyringh@byui.edu
EYSTER, Michael, E ...... 541-346-8393 410 F
meyster@uoregon.edu
EZAZ, Aron .... 334-874-5700.... 3 B
aezaz@ccal.edu
EZEIGBO, Anayo .... 704-330-1408 358 B
aezeigbo@jcsu.edu
EZELL, Cyn, D .... 813-257-3028 118 H
cezell@ut.edu
EZELL, Samantha .... 602-285-7569.. 15 C
samantha.ezell@phoenixcollege.edu
EZEONU, Rolita .... 206-878-3710 523 D
rezeonu@highline.edu
EZZEDDINE, Ahmad ...... 313-577-4450 252 G
a.m.ezzeddine@wayne.edu
EZZELL, Kevin .... 610-921-7248 411 E
kezzell@albright.edu
EZZELL, Russell .... 325-649-8040 475 F
rezzell@hputx.edu

F

FAASUA, Linda .... 805-986-5800.. 75 D
lrobison@vcccd.edu
FABBI, Jennifer .... 760-750-4330.. 35 B
jfabbi@csusm.edu
FABBRUCCI,
Stephen, W .... 978-556-3923 232 E
sfabbrucci@necc.mass.edu
FABE, Barbara, A .... 718-862-7392 331 H
barbara.fabe@manhattan.edu
FABER, Andrea .... 419-448-3375 392 B
faberad@tiffin.edu
FABER, Charles .... 208-376-7731 137 D
cfaber@boisebible.edu
FABER, Kim .... 585-245-5077 345 D
faber@geneseo.edu
FABER, Paul, W .... 785-628-4234 187 A
pfaber@fhsu.edu
FABIAN, James .... 631-632-6010 344 C
james.fabian@stonybrook.edu
FABIAN, Kim .... 708-239-4855 160 L
kim.fabian@trnty.edu
FABIANKE, Jo-Carol ..... 210-485-0169 466 J
jfabianke@alamo.edu
FABISH, David .... 562-860-2451.. 37 L
fabish@cerritos.edu
FABOS, Kristin .... 831-479-6158.. 30 C
krfabos@cabrillo.edu
FABREY, James .... 610-436-3228 432 B
jfabrey@wcupa.edu
FABRITIUS,
Stephanie, L .... 859-238-5226 194 E
stephanie.fabritius@centre.edu
FABRIZIO, Dona, M 610-892-1514 429M
dfabrizio@pit.edu
FABRIZIO, Linda .... 212-614-6113 338 C
lfabrizi@chpnet.org
FACKLER, Carol .... 207-795-2847 210 J
fackleca@cmhc.org
FACKRELL, Brady, R ..... 307-674-6446 546 H
bfackrell@sheridan.edu
FACTOR, Dan .... 405-382-9950 402 C
d.factor@sscok.edu
FACULO-GOGUE, Elaine 671-735-2244 549 G
efgogue@uguam.uog.edu
FADARIO, Adesina .... 718-270-6131 320 C
sfadairo@mec.cuny.edu
FADDEN, R. Patricia ..... 610-647-4400 421 B
pfadden@immaculata.edu
FADENRECHT, Kirby ..... 620-947-3121 191 E
kirbyf@tabor.edu
FADIAL, Sabrina .... 802-828-8544 503 D
sabrina.fadial@vcfa.edu
FADROWSKI,
William, P .... 414-277-7210 537 G
fadrowski@msoe.edu
FAEHNER, David, A ...... 269-471-3122 239 D
dfaehner@andrews.edu
FAEHNER, Frances, M .. 269-471-6686 239 D
frances@andrews.edu
FAERMAN, Larry .... 561-297-2880 114 E
FAERMAN, Sue, R .... 518-956-8240 343 C
sfaerman@albany.edu
FAERMAN, Susie .... 713-683-3817 482 C
FAGAN, Thomas, W ..... 580-774-3037 402 G
tom.fagan@swosu.edu
FAGBEYIRO, Betty, C ... 318-670-9679 207 C
bfagbeyiro@susla.edu
FAGBEYIRO, Gabriel ..... 318-670-9490 207 C
gfagbeyiro@susla.edu
FAGELLA-D'ALOSIO,
Marguerite .... 631-420-2480 348 B
marguerite.fagella@farmingdale.edu
FAGEN, Jeffrey, W .... 718-990-6068 340 G
fagenj@stjohns.edu
FAGEN, Rich, E .... 626-395-2908.. 31 D
rich@caltech.edu
FAGENSTROM, Linda .... 406-791-5223 288 J
lfagenstrom01@ugf.edu
FAGER, Jennifer, J .... 715-836-2277 539 E
fagerjj@uwec.edu
FAGLER, Mitchell .... 478-289-2272 132 A
mfagler@southeasterntech.edu
FAHEY, Jack .... 330-941-1939 396 C
jpfahey@ysu.edu
FAHEY, William, E .... 603-880-8308 298 I
wfahey@thomasmorecollege.edu
FAHNESTOCK, Bethene . 918-540-6202 398 L
bfahnestock@neo.edu
FAHNESTOCK, Brian ..... 714-808-4746.. 56 D
bfahnestock@nocccd.edu
FAHNESTOCK, Carol ..... 570-674-6216 426 D
cfahnest@misericordia.edu
FAHRENWALD, Jeffrey .. 815-394-5026 157 D
jfahrenwald@rockford.edu
FAHRENWALD, Nancy .... 605-688-5178 454 C
FAHY, Greg .... 207-621-3255 212 D
gregory.fahy@maine.edu
FAILING, Kate .... 662-246-6361 268 F
kfailing@msdelta.edu
FAILINGER, Marie .... 651-523-2941 256 B
mfailinger@hamline.edu
FAILLA, Lisa .... 785-460-5401 186 D
lisa.failla@colbycc.edu
FAIN, Carol .... 704-403-3511 355 B
carol.fain@carolinashealthcare.org
FAIN, Juanita .... 702-895-4387 295 G
juanita.fain@unlv.edu
FAIN, Starr .... 334-387-3877.... 1 E
starrfain@amridgeuniversity.edu
FAIR, George, W .... 972-883-4566 494 A
gwfair@utdallas.edu
FAIR, George, W .... 972-883-2350 494 A
gwfair@utdallas.edu
FAIR, Kathy .... 903-983-8236 477 A
kfair@kilgore.edu
FAIR, Steve .... 205-391-2384.... 7 A
sfair@sheltonstate.edu
FAIR, Terry .... 404-894-9396 125 D
terry.fair@business.gatech.edu
FAIR, Vickie .... 202-994-9633.. 95 D
vvfair14@gwu.edu
FAIR-SZOFRAN, Nancy .. 509-434-5060 521 D
nancy.szofran@ccs.spokane.edu
FAIR-SZOFRAN, Nancy . 509-434-5060 521 E
nancy.szofran@ccs.spokane.edu
FAIRBAIRN, Katie .... 707-468-3000.. 54 A
kfairbairn@mendocino.edu
FAIRBAIRN, Tina .... 650-543-3937.. 54 B
tfairbairn@menlo.edu
FAIRBANKS, Anthony ... 937-376-6373 379 D
afairbanks@centralstate.edu
FAIRBANKS, Daniel ...... 801-863-6440 500 B
daniel.fairbanks@uvu.edu
FAIRBANKS, Kathleen ... 716-926-8923 327 F
kfairbanks@hilbert.edu
FAIRBANKS,
Kenneth, E .... 276-223-4868 517 F
kfairbanks@wcc.vccs.edu
FAIRBANKS, Warren .... 508-626-4590 230 A
wfairbanks@framingham.edu
FAIRBANKS LAWSON,
Diana .... 231-995-1019 248 C
dfairbanks@nmc.edu
FAIRCHILD, Dennis ...... 315-364-3229 352 F
dfairchild@wells.edu
FAIRCHILD, Diana .... 208-426-1664 137 E
dfairchild@boisestate.edu
FAIRCHILD, James .... 940-565-2897 492 D
james.fairchild@unt.edu
FAIRCHILD, Joseph, J .. 757-822-7208 517 C
jfairchild@tcc.edu
FAIRCHILD, Thomas ..... 817-735-5497 493 B
Thomas.Fairchild@unthsc.edu
FAIRCHILDS, Angela ..... 209-588-5115.. 78 B
fairchildsa@yosemite.edu
FAIRCLOTH, Jimmy ...... 478-218-3385 122 E
jfaircloth@centralgatech.edu
FAIRFAX, Kathleen .... 605-688-4156 454 C
kathleen.fairfax@sdstate.edu
FAIRLESS, Michael, J ... 330-471-8100 385 G
mfairless@malone.edu
FAIRLEY, Danny .... 913-360-7256 184 K
dfairley@benedictine.edu
FAIRMAN, Jerilyn .... 315-786-2418 329 G
jfairman@sunyjefferson.edu
FAIROW, Greg .... 503-493-6587 405 E
gfairow@cu-portland.edu
FAISON, A. Zachary ...... 804-257-5875 518 E
azfaison@vuu.edu
FAISON, Brian .... 701-777-2234 373 G
brian.faison@und.edu
FAISON, Debbie .... 206-592-4014 523 D
dfaison@highline.edu
FAISON, Frederick .... 484-365-8075 424 E
ffaison@lincoln.edu
FAISON, Nicole .... 973-748-9000 300 E
nicole_faison@bloomfield.edu
FAISON, Tyciee, L .... 804-257-5814 518 E
tlfaison@vuu.edu
FAITH, Helen .... 541-463-5266 406 F
faithh@lanecc.edu
FAITHFUL, Mark .... 252-493-7750 364 H
mfaithful@email.pittcc.edu
FAIX, Peter, K .... 412-397-6271 434 B
faix@rmu.edu
FAJACK, Matthew, W .... 919-962-2211 371 A
FAKHIR, Bazra .... 304-205-6600 531 A
bazra.fakhir@bridgevalley.edu
FALA, Gregory .... 215-951-1907 422 F
fala@lasalle.edu
FALABELLA, Deneb .... 410-888-9048 216 G
dfalabella@muih.edu
FALARDEAU, George ..... 626-396-2201.. 28 J
george.falardeau@artcenter.edu
FALASTER, Marilyn .... 618-985-3741 148 G
marilynfalaster@jalc.edu
FALAVOLITO, Stephen .. 412-531-4433 416 F
info@deantech.edu
FALCK, Brian, G .... 717-245-1686 417 B
falckb@dickinson.edu
FALCK, Larry, B .... 843-661-1251 446 E
lfalck@fmarion.edu
FALCK-YI, Suzanne .... 641-585-8225 183 I
falckyis@waldorf.edu
FALCO, James .... 815-479-7728 152 B
jfalco@mchenry.edu
FALCO, Kathleen, P ...... 207-778-7280 212 E
kathleen.falco@maine.edu
FALCON, Kim .... 918-495-6928 401 B
kfalcon@oru.edu
FALCON, Luis .... 978-934-4000 229 A
Luis_Falcon@uml.edu
FALCON-CHANDLER,
Carole .... 406-353-2607 286 B
cfalconchan@hotmail.com
FALCONE, Alice, A .... 978-867-4208 227 A
alice.falcone@gordon.edu
FALCONER, Jameca ...... 636-227-2100 277 A
jameca.falconer@logan.edu
FALCONER, John .... 308-865-8702 293 G
falconerj@unk.edu
FALCONETTI,
Angela, M .... 540-857-6020 517 E
afalconetti@virginiawestern.edu

FALCONI, Stefano .... 617-521-2877 236 F
stefano.falconi@simmons.edu
FALDER, Mike .... 765-998-5538 173 B
mcfalder@taylor.edu
FALDUTO, Ellen .... 330-263-2230 380 E
efalduto@wooster.edu
FALE, Robert, A .... 920-923-7617 537 A
rfale@marianuniversity.edu
FALE, Tauvela .... 684-699-9155 549 C
t.fale@amsamoa.edu
FALES, Michael, F .... 269-749-7624 249 A
mfales@olivetcollege.edu
FALESE, Joseph .... 815-836-5275 150 F
falesejo@lewisu.edu
FALEY, Heather .... 802-440-4423 501 D
hfaley@bennington.edu
FALGOUT, Katherine ..... 985-380-2483 204 D
katherinefalgout@scl.edu
FALK, Adam, F .... 413-597-4233 238 E
adam.f.falk@williams.edu
FALK, Barry, L .... 804-828-1803 514 F
blfalk@vcu.edu
FALK, Dan .... 620-229-6267 191 B
dan.falk@sckans.edu
FALK, Israel .... 845-356-7065 353 G
FALK, Keith, L .... 920-923-8594 537 A
kfalk@marianuniversity.edu
FALK, Randy .... 541-917-4999 406 J
falkr@linnbenton.edu
FALK, Stephanie, A ...... 717-867-6696 423 I
falk@lvc.edu
FALK-DAY, Tamie .... 262-595-2485 540 C
falkday@uwp.edu
FALKE, Steve, J .... 814-863-0205 428 C
sjf7@psu.edu
FALKENBERG, Janice .... 414-297-8718 543 E
falkenjm@matc.edu
FALKENHAGEN,
Christopher .... 410-462-8051 213 G
cfalkenhagen@bccc.edu
FALKENHAGEN, Kim ...... 715-682-1868 538 D
kfalkenhagen@northland.edu
FALKENSTIEN,
Sarah, N .... 909-748-8044.. 73 K
sarah_falkenstien@redlands.edu
FALKIEWICZ, Linda, K .. 313-577-3550 252 G
lfalkiewicz@wayne.edu
FALKNER, Jay .... 918-647-1393 397 C
jfalkner@carlalbert.edu
FALKNER, Tina .... 612-626-0302 265 C
rovic001@umn.edu
FALKS, Delisa, F .... 979-458-5311 485 C
delisa@tamu.edu
FALKS, Jonathan .... 740-477-7789 388 F
jfalks@ohiochristian.edu
FALL, Diane .... 309-796-4840 140 D
falld@bhc.edu
FALL, Matt .... 517-483-1953 245 I
fallm@lcc.edu
FALL, Stephany .... 850-599-3203 114 D
stephany.fall@famu.edu
FALLACARO, Anthony ... 603-645-9604 298 H
a.fallacaro@snhu.edu
FALLAVOLLITA, John .... 603-623-0313 298 C
johnfallavollita@nhia.edu
FALLDINE, Cory .... 620-341-5297 186 H
cfalldin@emporia.edu
FALLEN, Melissa .... 804-204-1210 505 B
mfallen@btsr.edu
FALLERT, Danelle .... 323-265-8797.. 51 D
fallerdj@elac.edu
FALLETA, David, A .... 304-457-6213 529 C
falletada@ab.edu
FALLETTA, Eva, R .... 480-732-7231.. 14 K
Eva.Falletta@cgc.edu
FALLING, Cary .... 405-425-5290 399 J
cary.falling@oc.edu
FALLING, Sali, K .... 765-285-5162 164 D
sfalling@bsu.edu
FALLIS, Drew .... 210-292-6258 548 D
drew.fallis@us.af.mil
FALLIS, Sue .... 925-631-4856.. 61 G
sfallis@stmarys-ca.edu
FALLO, Thomas, M ...... 310-660-3111.. 43 G
tfallo@elcamino.edu
FALLON, Anne Marie .... 508-830-6485 230 D
afallon@maritime.edu
FALLON, Greg .... 973-684-5895 304 F
gfallon@pccc.edu
FALLON, III, John, A ... 765-289-1241 164 D
jafallon@bsu.edu
FALLON, Melissa, A ..... 607-436-3368 344 B
fallonma@oneonta.edu
FALLON, Thomas .... 978-556-3866 232 E
tfallon@necc.mass.edu
FALLONE, Deborah, A .. 914-323-5224 331 J
deborah.fallone@mville.edu
FALLS, Meda .... 731-925-5722 463 A
mfalls@jscc.edu
FALLS, William, A .... 802-656-3166 503 C
william.falls@uvm.edu
FALOTICO, Michael .... 312-777-7735.. 28 G
mfalotico@argosy.edu
FALTYN, Tim, W .... 918-463-2931 397 I
tfaltyn@connorsstate.edu
FALVO, Amy .... 904-819-6305 102 P
AFalvo@flagler.edu
FALWELL, JR., Jerry ..... 434-582-2957 509 G
jlfjr@liberty.edu
FALWELL, Tyler .... 434-592-3095 509 G
twfalwell2@liberty.edu
FALZERANO,
Christine, E .... 203-576-4566.. 92 B
cfalzera@bridgeport.edu
FALZONE, Kris .... 219-989-2217 171 L
Kris.falzone@purduecal.edu
FAMA, Melissa .... 978-632-6600 232 C
m_fama@mwcc.mass.edu
FAMBLE, JR., Freddie .. 325-793-4906 478 D
ffamble@mcm.edu
FAMULA, Michelle, S ... 530-752-2333.. 71 A
msfamula@ucdavis.edu
FAMULARE,
Dominick, F .... 518-388-6532 350 K
famularn@union.edu
FAMULARE, Marybeth .. 717-264-4141 440 D
marybeth.famulare@wilson.edu
FAN, C. Cindy .... 310-825-4921.. 71 D
cfan@international.ucla.edu
FAN, Lori .... 417-836-5654 279 A
lfan@missouristate.edu
FANCHER, Janet .... 620-223-2700 187 B
janetf@fortscott.edu
FANCHER, Karen .... 503-255-0332 407 D
kfancher@multnomah.edu
FANCHER, Michael .... 315-792-7100 348 D
mfancher@sunycnse.com
FANDOZZI, Melissa ...... 518-828-4181 322 E
melissa.fandozzi@sunycgcc.edu
FANDRICH, Charisse .... 701-255-3285 375 I
cfandrich@uttc.edu
FANELLI, Sean, A .... 516-463-5740 328 A
sean.fanelli@hofstra.edu
FANEUFF, Ken .... 706-379-5202 134 J
kfaneuff@yhc.edu
FANG, John .... 310-453-8300.. 43 I
john@emperors.edu
FANGMEYER, Len, J ..... 308-865-8555 293 G
fangmeyerlj@unk.edu
FANN, Erin .... 843-921-6916 448 B
efann@netc.edu
FANNAN, Lisa, L .... 816-604-2314 277 I
lisa.fannan@mcckc.edu
FANNER, Sjohonton ..... 940-552-6291 496 B
sfanner@vernoncollege.edu
FANNIN, Larry .... 801-878-1053 296 D
lfannin@roseman.edu
FANNING, Daniel .... 715-394-8213 541 C
dfanning@uwsuper.edu
FANNING, Vivian .... 276-223-4777 517 F
vfanning@wcc.vccs.edu
FANSHAW, Charles 202-685-3929 547M
fanshawc@ndu.edu
FANSLAU, Michelle .... 239-489-9478 104 G
mfanslau@fsw.edu
FANSLER, A. Gigi .... 217-732-3155 150 H
gfansler@lincolncollege.edu
FANT, JR., Gene .... 561-803-2051 109 G
gene_fant@pba.edu
FANT, Greg .... 575-646-2127 312 A
gfant@nmsu.edu
FANT, Joshua, W .... 860-701-6727 548 H
Joshua.W.Fant@uscg.mil
FANTASIA, Bethany .... 617-262-5000 223 G
Bethany.Fantasia@the-bac.edu
FANTER, Jeff .... 317-921-4502 169 L
jfanter@ivytech.edu
FANTINI, Beatriz .... 802-258-3343 502 I
beatriz.fantini@worldlearning.org
FANTINI, Maria .... 856-351-2601 308 B
mfantini@salemcc.edu
FANTOZZI, Joseph .... 212-650-7865 318 G
jfantozzi@ccny.cuny.edu
FANUTTI, Carol .... 716-827-2662 350 H
fanuttic@trocaire.edu
FANUZZI, Robert .... 718-390-4266 340 G
fanuzzir@stjohns.edu
FAONELUA, Lisa 808-675-3701 134M
lisa.faonelua@byuh.edu
FAOUR, Sheila .... 318-675-6001 205 D
sfaour@lsuhsc.edu
FAOUR, William, G ...... 423-624-0077 455 H
billf@chattanoogacollege.edu
FARACH-CARSON,
Cindy 713-348-5052 480M
farachca@rice.edu
FARAGALLA, Sameh ..... 973-661-0600 302 D
FARAHANI, Gohar .... 301-846-2451 214 I
gfarahani@frederick.edu
FARAHI, Dawood .... 908-737-7000 303 C
dfarahi@kean.edu
FARAKISH, Negar .... 908-709-7550 309 A
FARANDA, Nick .... 617-928-4648 234 D
nfaranda@mountida.edu
FARANI, Heidi .... 425-640-1049 522 D
heidi.farani@edcc.edu
FARAONE, Susan .... 312-893-7161 144 H
sfaraone@erikson.edu
FARARA, Joseph .... 802-635-1272 504 A
joe.farara@jsc.edu
FARBANIEC, David .... 845-257-3196 344 A
farbanid@newpaltz.edu
FARBER, Deborah .... 818-785-2726.. 37 I
deborah.farber@casalomacollege.edu
FARE, Bridget, M .... 412-396-6052 417 I
fareb@duq.edu
FARES, Ted .... 575-562-2511 310 I
ted.fares@enmu.edu
FARFAN, Erika, M .... 740-427-5571 384 P
farfane@kenyon.edu
FARHA, Darron .... 219-464-6702 174 E
darron.farha@valpo.edu
FARHA, Darron, C .... 219-464-6702 174 E
darron.farha@valpo.edu
FARIA, Pamela .... 617-243-2221 227 K
pfaria@lasell.edu
FARIAS, Antonio .... 860-685-3927.. 93 B
afarias@wesleyan.edu
FARIAS, Isidro .... 707-654-1127.. 34 B
ifarias@csum.edu
FARIAS, Jaime, D .... 915-831-2394 473 J
jfarias@epcc.edu
FARIAS, Richard .... 210-486-0130 467 C
rfarias14@alamo.edu
FARIDIAN, Fred .... 510-654-2934.. 44 C
ffaridian@expression.edu
FARINA, Deborah, A ..... 248-204-2308 245 J
dfarina@ltu.edu
FARINELLA, Nicole .... 312-935-6689 157 A
nfarinella@robertmorris.edu
FARINELLI, Rob .... 301-934-7539 214 E
rfarinelli@csmd.edu
FARINHOLT, Phil .... 910-362-7014 360 G
pfarinholt@cfcc.edu
FARINOS, Jose, L .... 772-462-7611 106 F
jfarinos@irsc.edu
FARISH, Donald, J .... 401-254-3201 442 C
dfarish@rwu.edu
FARISH, Guy, E .... 440-826-2478 377 D
gfarish@bw.edu
FARKAS, Abraham .... 707-524-1508.. 65 C
afarkas@santarosa.edu
FARLAND, Lisa .... 310-338-7896.. 53 C
lisa.farland@lmu.edu
FARLESS, John, A .... 812-228-5157 174 D
jafarless@usi.edu
FARLEY, Andre .... 252-335-3669 369 F
afarley@ecsu.edu
FARLEY, Barbara, A ...... 217-245-3001 146 D
barbara.farley@mail.ic.edu
FARLEY, Christy .... 602-728-9500.. 16 C
Christy.Farley@nau.edu
FARLEY, Dwayne .... 617-879-7805 230 B
dfarley@massart.edu
FARLEY, Emy .... 507-222-4289 254 D
efarley@carleton.edu
FARLEY, Erik, S .... 745-587-6605 381 H
farleye@denison.edu
FARLEY, Jeff .... 740-374-8716 395 D
jfarley1@wscc.edu
FARLEY, Jerry, B .... 785-670-1556 192 B
jerry.farley@washburn.edu
FARLEY, John .... 301-405-3205 219 D
jfarley@umd.edu
FARLEY, Karen .... 563-336-3323 178 A
kfarley@eicc.edu
FARLEY, Kay .... 785-670-1049 192 B
kay.farley@washburn.edu
FARLEY, Kim .... 307-382-1616 546 L
kfarley@wwcc.wy.edu
FARLEY, Lee .... 559-442-8231.. 69 B
lee.farley@fresnocitycollege.edu
FARLEY, Mark .... 661-255-1050.. 31 B
FARLEY, Michael .... 704-971-8500 355 J
mfarley@charlottelaw.edu
FARLEY, Patrick .... 301-891-4551 221 C
pfarley@wau.edu
FARLEY, Penelope, L .... 410-778-7224 221 D
pfarley2@washcoll.edu
FARLEY, Susan .... 425-602-3354 519 J
sfarley@bastyr.edu
FARLEY, Thomas, R ..... 757-455-3263 518 H
tfarley@vwc.edu
FARLEY, Tim .... 925-631-4830.. 61 G
tif5@stmarys-ca.edu
FARLEY, Troy .... 616-331-3311 243 E
farleytr@gvsu.edu
FARLOW, Carolyn .... 515-964-6520 177 B
cdfarlow@dmacc.edu
FARMBRY, Kyle, W .... 973-353-5834 307 C
kfarmbry@rutgers.edu
FARMER, Adam .... 765-677-2138 169 C
adam.farmer@indwes.edu
FARMER, Bradley .... 614-287-2787 380 G
bfarmer@cscc.edu
FARMER, Caleb .... 419-358-3376 377 H
Farmerc@bluffton.edu
FARMER, Carla .... 417-667-8181 273 H
cfarmer@cottey.edu
FARMER, Carter .... 717-290-8701 423 E
president@lancasterseminary.edu
FARMER, David .... 910-695-3911 365 H
farmerdj@sandhills.edu
FARMER, John .... 714-432-5017.. 40 D
jfarmer@occ.cccd.edu
FARMER, Joyce .... 610-282-1100 416 I
joyce.farmer@desales.edu
FARMER, Larry, G .... 704-637-4227 355 H
lfarmer@catawba.edu
FARMER, Lindsey .... 910-695-3726 365 H
farmerl@sandhills.edu
FARMER, Lisa, D .... 775-673-7025 295 F
ldfarmer@tmcc.edu
FARMER, Lorna .... 908-852-1400 301 C
farmer@centenarycollege.edu
FARMER, Marcella .... 513-244-8132 379 I
marcella.farmer@ccuniversity.edu
FARMER, Melanie .... 304-384-5271 532 E
mfarmer@concord.edu
FARMER, Pam .... 864-977-7009 448 A
pam.farmer@ngu.edu
FARMER, Patricia .... 603-358-2370 299 D
pfarmer@keene.edu
FARMER, Patricia J, B .. 315-229-5265 341 E
pfarmer@stlawu.edu
FARMER, Randy, L .... 901-448-7218 465 G
rfarme11@uthsc.edu
FARMER, Richard, E ..... 207-795-2846 210 J
farmerri@cmhc.org
FARMER, Ricky .... 336-322-2107 364 G
Rick.Farmer@piedmontcc.edu
FARMER, Scott .... 337-482-5393 208 F
sfarmer@louisiana.edu
FARMER, Stephen, M .... 919-966-3992 371 A
smfarmer@email.unc.edu
FARMER, Steve .... 601-968-5929 266 F
sfarmer@belhaven.edu
FARMER, Steve .... 419-227-3141 394 B
wfarmer@unoh.edu
FARMER, Will .... 928-681-5621.. 15 K
FARMER-DIXON,
Cherae .... 615-327-6207 458 F
cdixon@mmc.edu
FARMER-KAISER, Mary . 337-482-6965 208 F
kaiser@louisiana.edu
FARMER-NEAL,
Rochonda .... 254-710-1453 469 D
rochonda_farmer-neal@baylor.edu
FARMER NOONAN,
Erin .... 617-735-9991 226 B
farmer@emmanuel.edu
FARNESKI, Anna .... 201-684-6844 305 F
afarnesk@ramapo.edu
FARNEY, Kirk .... 630-752-5016 163 G
Kirk.Farney@wheaton.edu
FARNHAM, Bruce .... 619-660-4347.. 46 G
bruce.farnham@gcccd.edu
FARNHAM, Margaret, L 614-235-4136 392 D
mfarnham@TLSohio.edu
FARNHAM, Robert .... 239-304-7093.. 98 O
robert.farnham@avemaria.edu
FARNSWORTH, Scott .... 928-776-2234.. 18 L
scott.farnsworth@yc.edu
FARNSWORTH, Ward 512-232-1120 493M
wf@law.utexas.edu
FAROL, Dorothy .... 714-997-6611.. 38 B
farol@chapman.edu
FARQUHARSON,
Donald .... 816-523-9140 285 H
FARQUHARSON,
Janice, E .... 309-624-8980 158 D
janice.farquharson@osfhealthcare.org
FARR, C. Stephen .... 478-757-3700 134 E
sfarr@wesleyancollege.edu
FARR, Matthew .... 609-894-9311 306 B
mfarr@bcc.edu
FARR, Sharon .... 573-288-6633 274 C
sfarr@culver.edu
FARRAR, Gina, R .... 805-437-8503.. 32 H
gina.farrar@csuci.edu
FARRAR, James, D .... 540-458-8465 519 A
jdfarrar@wlu.edu
FARRAR, Jamiel .... 410-462-8539 213 G
jfarrar@bccc.edu
FARRAR, Jazaer .... 708-596-2000 159 D
jfouad-farrar@ssc.edu
FARRAR, Margaret .... 216-397-1886 384 F
mfarrar@jcu.edu
FARRAR, Rinalda .... 573-681-5528 276 K
farrarr@lincolnu.edu
FARRELL, Christina .... 610-558-5638 427 D
farrellc@neumann.edu

FARRELL, Courtney .... 858-513-9240.. 29 A
Courtney.Farrell@ashford.edu
FARRELL, Cynthia, H .... 724-589-2178 436 E
cfarrell@thiel.edu
FARRELL, Gene .... 714-438-4888.. 40 A
gfarrell3@cccd.edu
FARRELL, Gina .... 210-436-3517 481 C
gfarrell@stmarytx.edu
FARRELL, Gregory .... 212-220-1377 318 D
gfarrell@bmcc.cuny.edu
FARRELL, Howard, M ... 940-397-4782 478 G
howard.farrell@mwsu.edu
FARRELL, Jill .... 305-899-3649.. 99 B
jfarrell@barry.edu
FARRELL, Kathleen .... 914-251-6090 346 D
kathleen.farrell@purchase.edu
FARRELL, Lauren, M .... 724-925-4079 439 F
farrelll@wccc.edu
FARRELL, Lisa, M .... 636-584-6558 274 J
lisa.farrell@eastcentral.edu
FARRELL, Mark .... 412-392-3879 433 F
mfarrell@pointpark.edu
FARRELL, Martin, F ...... 610-660-1225 434 G
mfarrell@sju.edu
FARRELL, Mary, M .... 864-656-3026 444 E
maggie4@clemson.edu
FARRELL, Mary Ellen .... 973-275-2293 308 C
maryellen.farrell@shu.edu
FARRELL, Michael .... 716-851-1685 325 A
farrell@ecc.edu
FARRELL, Nancy .... 413-265-2389 225 D
farrelln@elms.edu
FARRELL, Pat .... 410-225-2367 216 F
pfarrell@mica.edu
FARRELL, Patrick, V ..... 610-758-3605 424 B
pvf209@lehigh.edu
FARRELL, Robert, B ...... 570-941-6213 438 F
robert.farrell@scranton.edu
FARRELL, Shawn .... 817-531-4830 490 C
sfarrell@txwes.edu
FARRELL, Suzanne .... 516-299-2916 330 F
suzanne.farrell@liu.edu
FARRELL, Terry .... 412-809-5100 433 D
farrell.terry@pti.edu
FARRELL, Thomas .... 585-275-1837 351 D
farrellt@rochester.edu
FARRELLY, Gwen .... 401-454-6725 442 B
gfarrell@risd.edu
FARRELLY, Nanyamka ... 340-693-1058 559 B
nfarrel@live.uvi.edu
FARRELLY,
Nanyamka, A .... 336-256-0863 370 B
nafarrel@ncat.edu
FARRINGTON, David .... 541-440-4600 410 E
david.farrington@umpqua.edu
FARRINGTON, Edward .. 203-837-9013.. 88 G
farringtone@wcsu.edu
FARRINGTON,
James, P .... 802-654-2000 502 H
FARRINGTON, Keisha ... 214-860-2032 472 F
kfarrington@dcccd.edu
FARRIOR, Andy .... 361-582-2547 496 D
andy.farrior@victoriacollege.edu
FARRIOR, Carolyn, P ... 321-674-7118 103 R
cfarrior@fit.edu
FARRIS, Barry .... 501-207-6201.. 19 E
bnfarris@asub.edu
FARRIS, Edward, E .... 919-735-5151 367 A
edfarris@waynecc.edu
FARRIS, G. Corey .... 304-293-4491 533 D
corey.farris@mail.wvu.edu
FARRIS, Gary .... 425-564-4077 519 L
gary.farris@bellevuecollege.edu
FARRIS, Jeffery .... 662-846-4660 267 A
jfarris@deltastate.edu
FARRIS, Joe, R .... 662-325-3221 269 A
joe.farris@pres.msstate.edu
FARRIS, Lynn, L .... 406-756-2882 286 G
lfarris@fvcc.edu
FARRIS, Michael .... 434-832-7891 515 A
farrism@cvcc.vccs.edu
FARRIS, Michael, P ...... 540-338-1776 511 A
chancellor@phc.edu
FARRIS, Michael, W ..... 512-245-2319 489 C
mf03@txstate.edu
FARRIS, Rachel .... 251-981-3771.... 3 A
rachel.farris@columbiasouthern.edu
FARRIS, Robert .... 207-255-1315 212 G
robert.farris@maine.edu
FARRIS, Thomas, N ...... 848-445-2214 307 B
tfarris@rutgers.edu
FARRIS, Tim .... 440-449-4471 394 G
tfarris@ursuline.edu
FARRIS, Victoria .... 201-761-7130 307 K
vfarris@saintpeters.edu
FARSACI, Daniel, P ...... 585-785-1286 325 E
daniel.farsaci@flcc.edu
FARSAD, Sarah .... 212-396-6863 319 E
sf957@hunter.cuny.edu
FARSON, Matthew .... 740-389-4636 386 B
farsonm@mtc.edu

FARVARDIN, Nariman ... 201-216-5213 308 D
president@stevens.edu
FARYNIAK, Karen, N .... 717-245-1323 417 B
faryniak@dickinson.edu
FASBINDER, Lori .... 714-628-5971.. 60 H
fasbinder_lori@sccollege.edu
FASLA, Cynthia, M .... 716-878-4907 345 B
faslacm@buffalostate.edu
FASS, Mark .... 507-280-5096 261 D
mark.fass@rctc.edu
FASS, Richard, A .... 909-621-8507.. 60 A
richard.fass@pomona.edu
FASSERO, Matt .... 913-360-7420 184 K
mfassero@benedictine.edu
FASSINGER,
JoAnne, M .... 315-386-7951 347 F
fassingerj@canton.edu
FASSINGER, Polly, A .... 651-696-6265 256 L
pfassing@macalester.edu
FAST, Erik .... 503-768-7922 406 H
fast@lclark.edu
FAST, Joanne, R .... 402-449-2809 290 F
jofast@graceu.edu
FAST, Linda .... 479-575-6513.. 23 G
lfast@uark.edu
FASTNOW, Chris .... 406-994-2870 287 G
cfastnow@montana.edu
FATATO, Joel, R .... 518-629-4525 328 D
j.fatato@hvcc.edu
FATH, Stephen, J .... 713-500-5202 495 A
stephen.j.fath@uth.tmc.edu
FATHE, Laurie .... 509-865-8577 523 C
fathe_l@heritage.edu
FATHERLY, Sarah .... 704-337-2568 368 B
fatherlys@queens.edu
FATICA, Jack .... 419-559-2353 392 A
jfatica@terra.edu
FATIMA, Nasrin .... 607-777-2365 343 D
nfatima@binghamton.edu
FATTIG, Teri, L .... 208-732-6501 137 K
tfattig@csi.edu
FATTOR, Stefany .... 718-817-4356 326 C
fattor@fordham.edu
FATTOUH, Said .... 713-221-8059 491 F
FattouhS@uhd.edu
FATZINGER, Jim, B .... 678-407-5866 125 B
jfatzinger@ggc.edu
FAUBERT, Bob .... 928-757-0840.. 15 K
bfaubert@mohave.edu
FAUCHET, Philippe, M . 615-322-0720 465 H
philippe.m.fauchet@vanderbilt.edu
FAUCHEUX, Brenda .... 985-448-7909 203 G
brenda.faucheux@fletcher.edu
FAUGHANAN, Timothy . 607-777-2275 343 D
tfaughn@binghamton.edu
FAUGHT, Norma .... 575-392-5018 311 J
nfaught@nmjc.edu
FAULHABER,
Gregory, M .... 716-652-8900 317 M
gfaulhaber@cks.edu
FAULHABER, Michael ... 716-652-8900 317 M
mfaulhaber@cks.edu
FAULK, Daniel .... 724-503-1001 439 B
dfaulk@washjeff.edu
FAULK, Harry, R .... 304-710-3512 531 C
faulkh@mctc.edu
FAULK, Jessica .... 617-521-1101 236 F
jess.samuels@simmons.edu
FAULK, Randy .... 361-570-4397 492 A
faulkr@uhv.edu
FAULK, Ron, H .... 405-878-5407 402 A
rhfaulk@stgregorys.edu
FAULK, Sancy .... 501-205-8799.. 20 G
sfaulk@cbc.edu
FAULKNER, J. Todd ...... 765-641-4204 164 B
jtfaulkner@anderson.edu
FAULKNER,
Jacqueline, A .... 870-512-7812.. 19 I
jacqueline.faulkner@asun.edu
FAULKNER, Jerry .... 615-230-3500 464 B
jerry.faulkner@volstate.edu
FAULKNER, Jessica .... 501-205-8800.. 20 G
jfaulkner@cbc.edu
FAULKNER, Keith .... 910-893-1380 355 C
faulknerk@campbell.edu
FAULKNER, Marquetta .. 615-327-6204 458 F
mfaulkner@mmc.edu
FAULKNER, Melissa ...... 201-559-3620 302 I
faulknerm@felician.edu
FAULKNER, Ted .... 540-231-5618 518 B
thfaulkn@vt.edu
FAULKNER, William ...... 718-281-4373 320 F
wfaulkner@qcc.cuny.edu
FAULSTICK, Donald, R . 413-542-8266 222 A
drfaulstick@amherst.edu
FAUNA, Amari .... 503-760-3131 404 I
amari@birthingway.edu
FAUNTLEROY, Carma ... 202-687-1023.. 95 E
cf274@georgetown.edu

FAUOLO-MANILA,
Okenaisa .... 684-699-9155 549 C
o.fauolo@amsamoa.edu
FAUPELL, BrandE .... 435-797-1810 500 A
brande.faupell@usu.edu
FAUROT, Sara .... 609-652-4469 308 E
sara.faurot@stockton.edu
FAUST, Brian .... 715-346-3511 541 A
brian.faust@uwsp.edu
FAUST, Deborah .... 906-635-2678 245 H
dfaust@lssu.edu
FAUST, Jeffrey .... 251-809-1581.... 5 B
jeffrey.faust@jdcc.edu
FAUST, Jennifer .... 337-482-1481 208 F
jfaust@louisiana.edu
FAUST, Kimberly, A ...... 803-323-2225 451 I
faustk@winthrop.edu
FAUST, Lucas .... 414-443-8720 542 I
lucas.faust@wlc.edu
FAUST, Margaret .... 704-637-4394 355 H
mfaust@catawba.edu
FAUST, Scott .... 218-755-2041 258 B
sfaust@bemidjistate.edu
FAUST, Teresa .... 352-854-2322 100 P
faustt@cf.edu
FAUST, William Bryant . 504-568-4829 205 C
wfaust@lsuhsc.edu
FAUSTINO, Tessie .... 808-675-3717 134 M
faustint@byuh.edu
FAUTAS, Jason .... 330-490-7437 395 C
jfautas@walsh.edu
FAUVER, James .... 304-205-6600 531 A
james.fauver@bridgevalley.edu
FAUX, Maureen .... 410-617-5817 216 D
mwfaux@loyola.edu
FAVARA, JR., Leonard .. 620-241-0723 185 M
lenny.favara@centralchristian.edu
FAVARA, Tina .... 978-556-3720 232 E
tfavara@necc.mass.edu
FAVATA, Joanne .... 845-398-4284 341 H
jfavata@stac.edu
FAVAZZA, Joseph .... 508-565-1311 237 A
jfavazza@stonehill.edu
FAVELA, Andres .... 760-750-4105.. 35 B
afavela@csusm.edu
FAVELA, Elena .... 763-576-4057 258 A
elena.favela@anokatech.edu
FAVOR, Jessica .... 803-536-8743 448 H
jfavor@scsu.edu
FAVORITO, Barbara ...... 951-785-2499.. 49 I
bfavorit@lasiera.edu
FAVORS, Toney .... 903-223-3061 486 C
toney.favors@tamut.edu
FAVRE, Cynthia, L .... 507-933-7524 256 A
cfavre@gustavus.edu
FAVRE, Martha .... 978-665-3216 229 D
mfavre@fitchburgstate.edu
FAVRE, Sherry .... 618-235-2700 160 B
sherry.favre@swic.edu
FAW, Kim, E .... 336-838-6293 367 C
kim.faw@wilkescc.edu
FAWBUSH, Jennifer, M 260-399-7700 174 C
jfawbush@sf.edu
FAWBUSH, Shanon, L .. 260-982-5029 170 a
fawbush@manchester.edu
FAWCETT, Andrew .... 631-451-4879 348 E
fawceta@sunysuffolk.edu
FAWCETT, Jeffrey, K ..... 574-372-5100 166 D
fawcettj@grace.edu
FAWCETT, Tonya, L ...... 574-372-5100 166 D
fawcettl@grace.edu
FAWKS, Melinda, D ...... 717-477-1121 431 F
mdfawk@ship.edu
FAWSON, Parker, C ...... 801-863-8006 500 B
parker.fawson@uvu.edu
FAXON, David .... 603-668-6660 298 A
FAY, III, Cornelius, R .. 301-696-3565 215 E
fay@hood.edu
FAY, Dana .... 630-515-7166 152 H
dfayxx@midwestern.edu
FAY, Derek, R .... 208-496-1450 137 F
fayd@byui.edu
FAY-REILLY, Tara .... 914-674-7762 332 E
tfreilly@mercy.edu
FAYAD, Barbara, H .... 864-938-3722 448 E
bfayad@presby.edu
FAYAD, Rosalie .... 718-368-5833 320 A
rfayad@kbcc.cuny.edu
FAYE, Janice, N .... 203-576-6355.. 91 H
jfaye@stvincentscollege.edu
FAYLOR, David, L .... 256-539-0834.... 4 F
deaninst@hbc1.edu
FAYNE, Harriet .... 718-960-8401 319 C
harriet.fayne@lehman.cuny.edu
FAYOYIN, MaryJo .... 912-358-4329 131 A
fayoyinm@savannahstate.edu
FAYTAK, Shelley .... 814-838-7673 418 G
sfaytak@fortisinstitute.edu
FAZAL, Shafeek .... 718-409-7236 348 C
sfazal@sunymaritime.edu

FAZALARE, Amie, M ..... 304-367-4867 532 F
Amie.Fazalare@fairmontstate.edu
FAZEKAS, Evelyn .... 315-792-3002 351 G
efazekas@utica.ucsu.edu
FAZIO, James, I .... 619-201-8978.. 67 I
jfazio@socalsem.edu
FAZIO, Jennifer .... 732-255-0400 304 E
jfazio@ocean.edu
FAZIO, Kari .... 610-526-5160 413 D
kfazio@brynmawr.edu
FAZIO, Patricia .... 860-486-5634.. 92 C
patricia.fazio@uconn.edu
FAZIOLI, Mark .... 860-727-6788.. 90 F
mfazioli@goodwin.edu
FAZZANO, Adriana .... 954-201-7518.. 99 G
afazzano@broward.edu
FEAGIN, Susan, K .... 212-851-7999 322 F
skf17@columbia.edu
FEAN, Judith .... 574-284-4886 172 G
jfean@saintmarys.edu
FEAR, Kevin, G .... 724-653-2222 417 D
kfear@dec.edu
FEARN, Odell .... 865-882-4679 463 F
fearnao@roanestate.edu
FEASEL, Brenda .... 740-389-4636 386 B
feaselb@mtc.edu
FEASEL, Edward, M ...... 949-480-4133.. 66 I
efeasel@soka.edu
FEASEL, Edward, M ...... 949-480-4133.. 66 I
feasel@soka.edu
FEATHERSTON, Guy ...... 903-875-7585 479 I
guy.featherston@navarrocollege.edu
FEATHERSTONE, John .. 415-476-1323.. 72 C
jdbf@ucsf.edu
FEATHERSTONE,
William, H .... 304-766-3061 533 C
wfeatherstone@wvstateu.edu
FEAVER, John, H .... 405-224-3140 403 L
jfeaver@usao.edu
FECHNER, Andrea .... 425-739-8455 523 I
andrea.fechner@lwtech.edu
FECHNER, Mary .... 575-439-3696 312 B
mfechner@nmsu.edu
FECHO, Susan .... 252-399-6480 354 I
sfecho@barton.edu
FECKER, Peggy, A .... 715-394-8365 541 C
pfecker@uwsuper.edu
FEDDEMA, Lana, L .... 320-308-1595 261 F
lfeddema@sctcc.edu
FEDDERS, James, M .... 304-929-5037 531 D
jfedders@newriver.edu
FEDELE, Dominick .... 205-329-7900.... 3 C
dominick.fedele@ecacolleges.com
FEDELE, Jennifer .... 412-392-3876 433 F
jfedele@pointpark.edu
FEDER, Mary, M .... 631-451-4256 348 E
federm@sunysuffolk.edu
FEDERER, Gina .... 972-273-3006 473 A
gfederer@dcccd.edu
FEDERLINE, Pamela ...... 252-335-0821 361 G
pamela_federline60@albemarle.edu
FEDERMAN, Robin .... 310-824-1586.. 25 K
robinfederman@hotmail.com
FEDEROFF, Howard, J .. 202-687-4600.. 95 E
hjf8@georgetown.edu
FEDEROWICZ, Jane ...... 610-527-0200 434 D
jfederowicz@rosemont.edu
FEDIN, Andrey .... 408-498-5151.. 40 E
afedin@cogswell.edu
FEDJE, Jay .... 417-873-7524 274 E
jfedje@drury.edu
FEDLER, Kyle .... 863-680-4124 104 F
kfedler@flsouthern.edu
FEDORCHAK, David .... 410-704-3974 221 A
dfedorchak@towson.edu
FEDORCHAK, Lynn .... 607-778-5319 344 F
fedorchaklm@sunybroome.edu
FEDORKO, Kathleen, C . 215-968-8220 413 F
fedorkok@bucks.edu
FEE, Glenn .... 503-253-3443 408 B
gfee@ocom.edu
FEE, Richard .... 714-484-7152.. 56 E
rfee@cypresscollege.edu
FEE, T. Joshua .... 859-858-3511 193 A
josh.fee@asbury.edu
FEEHERY, Peggy, C ...... 770-720-5548 130 E
prc@reinhardt.edu
FEELER, William .... 432-685-4626 478 F
bfeeler@midland.edu
FEELEY, Brian .... 336-278-7446 356 F
bfeeley@elon.edu
FEELEY, Daniel, T .... 304-243-2383 534 H
feeley@wju.edu
FEELEY, John .... 970-204-8131.. 82 J
john.feeley@frontrange.edu
FEELY, SND, Katherine . 216-397-1966 384 F
kfeely@jcu.edu
FEENEY, David, F .... 508-678-2811 231 B
david.feeney@bristolcc.edu
FEENEY, Gregory .... 859-246-6329 195 J
greg.feeney@kctcs.edu

FEENSTRA, Ronald, J ... 616-957-7193 240M
feenro@calvinseminary.edu
FEERER, Pam .... 620-252-7357 186 C
pamf@coffeyville.edu
FEEZELL, Travis .... 479-979-1431.. 25 H
tfeezell@ozarks.edu
FEGAN, Kevin, G .... 972-293-5449 248 D
fegan@northwood.edu
FEGELY, Neal, R .... 610-526-1501 412 D
neal.fegely@theamericancollege.edu
FEGETT, Greg .... 217-443-8888 143 F
gfegett@dacc.edu
FEGLEY, Jill .... 252-399-6345 354 I
jcfegley@barton.edu
FEGUMPS, Noel .... 386-481-2173.. 99 F
fegumpsn@cookman.edu
FEHLAU, Fred .... 626-396-2290.. 28 J
fred.fehlau@artcenter.edu
FEHLBERG, Mark .... 773-702-3321 161 D
mafehl@uchicago.edu
FEHLER, Tim, G .... 864-294-3347 446 F
tim.fehler@furman.edu
FEHN, Bruce, C .... 848-932-5661 306 F
fehn@oldqueens.rutgers.edu
FEHN, Heather .... 609-771-2101 301 E
hfehn@tcnj.edu
FEHNRICH, Jennifer ...... 567-661-7101 390 D
jennifer_fehnrich@owens.edu
FEHRENBACHER,
Richard .... 206-220-8280 526 F
fehrenbacher@seattleu.edu
FEIBEL, Ann .... 718-482-5642 320 B
afeibel@lagcc.cuny.edu
FEICHTER, Kathryn .... 330-966-5452 391 J
kfeichter@starkstate.edu
FEIER, Julie .... 970-943-2061.. 87 F
jfeier@western.edu
FEIERTAG, Jason .... 484-664-3140 427 C
feiertag@muhlenberg.edu
FEIGELSTOCK, Yitzchok 516-225-4700 338 L
rcli@mlb.edu
FEIGENBAUM, Peter ..... 718-817-1000 326 C
FEIGERT, Kendra, M ..... 717-867-6126 423 I
feigert@lvc.edu
FEIGH, Kim .... 847-735-6008 149 H
weidnerfeigh@lakeforest.edu
FEIKES, David .... 219-785-5564 172 A
dfeikes@pnc.edu
FEIL, Hallie .... 308-635-6032 294 C
feilh@wncc.edu
FEIL, Hallie, L .... 308-635-6126 294 C
feilh@wncc.edu
FEILER WHITE,
Rebecca .... 732-255-0400 304 E
rfeilerwhite@ocean.edu
FEIN, Cheri .... 212-217-4700 325 C
cheri_fein@fitnyc.edu
FEIN, Gene .... 718-817-3900 326 C
fein@fordham.edu
FEIN, Jason .... 973-408-3648 301 J
jfein@drew.edu
FEIN, Michael, T .... 434-832-7751 515 A
feinm@cvcc.vccs.edu
FEINBERG, Diane .... 405-974-2658 403 G
dfeinberg@uco.edu
FEINER, Barbara, A ...... 314-935-9842 285 E
barbara.a.feiner@wustl.edu
FEINERMAN, Frances ... 413-236-2102 231 A
ffeinerm@berkshirecc.edu
FEINGOLD, Ruth, P ...... 240-895-4922 218 B
rpfeingold@smcm.edu
FEINMAN, Shannon ...... 434-949-1012 516 H
shannon.feinman@southside.edu
FEINSTEIN, Andrew ...... 408-924-1000.. 36 B
FEINSTEIN, Bruce .... 818-767-0888.. 77 G
bruce.feinstein@woodbury.edu
FEINSTEIN, David .... 212-964-2830 332 G
FEINSTEIN, Lee .... 812-856-7900 167 J
lafeinst@indiana.edu
FEINSTEIN, Sheryl, J .... 308-865-8265 293 G
feinsteinsg@unk.edu
FEIST, K. Cameron .... 315-859-4413 327 A
cfeist@hamilton.edu
FEISTHAMEL, Kevin, P .. 330-569-5952 383 F
FEITELBERG, Daniel .... 209-228-4400.. 71 E
dfeitelberg@UCMerced.edu
FEITZ, David, A .... 801-321-7211 499 J
dfeitz@ushe.edu
FEKARIS, Cynthia .... 212-594-4000 349 J
cfekaris@tcicollege.edu
FEKE, Donald, L .... 216-368-4389 378 J
dlf4@case.edu
FEKETE, Michael .... 815-836-5549 150 F
feketemi@lewisu.edu
FEKULA, Michael .... 803-641-3340 450 C
mickf@usca.edu
FELCH, Katrina .... 715-675-3331 544 A
felch@ntc.edu
FELDBLUM, Miriam ...... 909-621-8017.. 60 A
miriam.feldblum@pomona.edu
FELDER, Bruce, B .... 304-696-3983 532 H
felder1@marshall.edu
FELDER, JR., E. Lee ..... 605-677-5671 453 F
lee.felder@usd.edu
FELDER, Luther .... 706-821-8295 129 H
lfelder@paine.edu
FELDER-DEAS,
Altoya, A .... 803-934-3167 447 K
afdeas@morris.edu
FELDHAUS, Joseph, H .. 513-745-3908 396 B
feldhausjl@xavier.edu
FELDHUES, Nicole .... 412-396-5675 417 I
feldhuesn@duq.edu
FELDHUS, Karima .... 949-451-5232.. 67 E
kfeldhus@ivc.edu
FELDMAN, Aharon .... 410-484-7200 217 E
raf@nirc.edu
FELDMAN, Andrew .... 541-917-4741 406 J
feldmana@linnbenton.edu
FELDMAN, Barbara .... 508-531-1295 229 C
barbara.feldman@bridgew.edu
FELDMAN, Dan .... 781-736-8405 224 F
feldman@brandeis.edu
FELDMAN, Harriet, R .... 212-346-1200 337 I
hfeldman@pace.edu
FELDMAN, James .... 518-225-5631 346 E
feldmajs@cobleskill.edu
FELDMAN, Leonard, C . 848-445-4524 306 F
l.c.feldman@rutgers.edu
FELDMAN, Lori .... 219-989-2388 171 L
feldman@purduecal.edu
FELDMAN, Mary Jane .. 716-614-5926 336 D
feldman@niagaracc.suny.edu
FELDMAN, Rachelle .... 510-642-7117.. 70 K
FELDMAN, Robert, S .... 413-545-2211 228 F
feldman@chancellor.umass.edu
FELDMANN, Dorothy .... 781-891-2782 223 E
dfeldmann@bentley.edu
FELDMANN, Jacob .... 718-645-0536 333 B
FELDMANN,
Raymond, C .... 410-704-4672 221 A
rfeldmann@towson.edu
FELDMEIER, Theresa ..... 614-236-6813 378 H
tfeldmei@capital.edu
FELDNER, Lisa .... 701-328-1510 373 F
lisa.feldner@ndus.edu
FELDSTEIN, Jay, S .... 215-871-6800 432 E
jfeldstein@pcom.edu
FELDT, Tina .... 318-869-5424 202 D
tfeldt@centenary.edu
FELIBERTY, Victor, A .... 787-284-1912 554 B
vfeliber@ponce.inter.edu
FELICE, Susan .... 708-656-8000 153 G
susan.felice@morton.edu
FELICIANA, Jerrye .... 301-736-3631 216 E
jerrye.feliciana@msbbcs.edu
FELICIANA, Jerrye, B .... 301-736-3631 216 E
jerrye.feliciana@msbbcs.edu
FELICIANO, Danilo .... 413-565-1000 222 G
dfeliciano@baypath.edu
FELICIANO, Idali .... 517-265-5161 238 H
ifeliciano@adrian.edu
FELICIANO, Patsy .... 813-974-3827 116 B
pfelicia@admin.usf.edu
FELICIE, Ada, M .... 787-764-0000 558 E
adamyriam15@hotmail.com
FELIO, John, R .... 518-783-2471 342 H
jfelio@siena.edu
FELIU, Julio .... 787-841-2000 555 F
jfeliu@pucpr.edu
FELIX, Hector .... 787-738-2161 557 G
hector.felix1@upr.edu
FELIX, Keny .... 404-233-3949 460 G
kfelix@richmont.edu
FELIX-MATA, Bertha ...... 559-934-2217.. 76 B
berthafelixmata@whccd.edu
FELKER, Sharon, M .... 303-963-3369.. 79 L
sfelker@ccu.edu
FELKER, Steven .... 757-825-2716 517 B
felkers@tncc.edu
FELL, Janet .... 732-923-4645 303 G
jfell@monmouth.edu
FELL, Katherine, R .... 419-434-4510 393 F
fell@findlay.edu
FELL, Stephanie 918-631-2241 403M
stephanie-fell@utulsa.edu
FELLER, David, C .... 414-955-8424 537 C
dfeller@mcw.edu
FELLER, Patricia, A .... 615-353-3572 463 C
patricia.feller@nscc.edu
FELLER, Scott .... 765-361-6224 175 B
fellers@wabash.edu
FELLINGER, Jennifer ..... 616-395-7860 244 A
fellinger@hope.edu
FELLMAN, Dorrea .... 207-621-3501 212 D
dorrea.fellman@maine.edu
FELLOWS, Dawn .... 801-524-8156 498 J
DFellows@ldsbc.edu
FELLOWS, Gail .... 610-436-3333 432 B
gfellows@wcupa.edu
FELLOWS, Maureen, O . 315-470-6621 347 B
mfellows@esf.edu
FELSER, Francis, J .... 716-250-7500 317 B
fjfelser@bryantstratton.edu
FELSKE, Eileen .... 973-618-3419 300 H
efelske@caldwell.edu
FELSKE, Julie, L .... 989-837-4436 248 D
felske@northwood.edu
FELSOVALYI, Erzsebet ... 973-748-9000 300 E
elizabeth_felsovalyi@bloomfield.edu
FELT, K.C .... 208-282-3755 138 C
feltkc@isu.edu
FELTES, Carol .... 212-327-8909 339 H
cfeltes@rockvax.rockefeller.edu
FELTHOUSEN, Mat .... 216-421-7384 380 B
mfelthousen@cia.edu
FELTHOUSEN, Robert .... 541-956-7147 409 F
rfelthousen@roguecc.edu
FELTMAN, Richard .... 718-951-5693 318 F
rfeltman@brooklyn.cuny.edu
FELTMANN, Charles ..... 636-227-2100 277 A
charles.feltmann@logan.edu
FELTNER, Michael, E .... 310-506-4280.. 58 H
michael.feltner@pepperdine.edu
FELTON, Herman .... 704-216-6044 358 I
hfelton@livingstone.edu
FELTON, III, James, A . 410-777-1472 213 E
jafelton@aacc.edu
FELTON, Jennifer .... 712-749-2120 176 D
feltonj@bvu.edu
FELTON, Karen, S .... 202-994-6040.. 95 D
kfelton@gwu.edu
FELTON, Pamela .... 312-322-1734 160 E
pfelton@spertus.edu
FELTON, Rob .... 503-554-2129 406 A
rfelton@georgefox.edu
FELTON, Shawn .... 607-255-5241 323 C
admissions@cornell.edu
FELTON, Terence .... 630-466-7900 162 K
tfelton@waubonsee.edu
FELTS, Renee .... 757-569-6760 516 E
rfelts@pdc.edu
FELTS, Ronald .... 661-726-1911.. 70 I
ron.felts@uav.edu
FELTY, Donna, H .... 423-652-4752 457 J
dhfelty@king.edu
FELVER, Eric .... 219-989-2768 171 L
eric.felver@purduecal.edu
FEMINO, Charles .... 978-232-2221 226 C
cfemino@endicott.edu
FEMINO, Donald .... 978-232-5201 226 C
dfemino@endicott.edu
FENCSIK, Alissa .... 510-204-0727.. 38 K
afencsik@cdsp.edu
FENDERS, Nancy .... 207-941-7153 210 C
fendersn@husson.edu
FENDRICH, Caleb .... 812-749-1216 171 I
cfendrich@oak.edu
FENDRICH, Chris .... 719-549-2149.. 81 F
chris.fendrich@csupueblo.edu
FENG, Tong .... 617-348-6511 237 E
tongfeng@urbancollege.edu
FENLASON, Julie .... 320-762-4531 257 O
julief@alextech.edu
FENLASON, Laurie .... 413-585-2170 236 G
lfenlaso@smith.edu
FENN, Patricia .... 732-255-0400 304 E
pfenn@ocean.edu
FENNELL, Angelia .... 903-593-8311 487 A
afennell@texascollege.edu
FENNELL, Barbara .... 432-686-4250 478 F
bfennell@midland.edu
FENNELL, Catherine ...... 610-896-1221 420 J
cfennell@haverford.edu
FENNELL, Catherine ...... 610-527-0200 434 D
fennell@roesmont.edu
FENNELL, Charles .... 901-333-4217 464 A
cfennell1@southwest.tn.edu
FENNELL, Craig .... 215-204-1492 436 C
craig.fennell@temple.edu
FENNELL, Dwight .... 903-593-8311 487 A
dfennell@texascollege.edu
FENNELL, Karla, M .... 315-267-2830 346 C
fennelkm@potsdam.edu
FENNELL, Sabrina .... 716-839-8228 323 F
sfennell@daemen.edu
FENNERN, Nicole .... 507-457-1638 264 B
nfennern@smumn.edu
FENNESSEY, Tom .... 715-394-8122 541 C
tfenness@uwsuper.edu
FENNING, Amy, E .... 731-881-7340 465 F
FENNING, Robert .... 310-243-3750.. 33 B
rfenning@csudh.edu
FENRICK, David, E .... 651-631-5229 265 D
defenrick@unwsp.edu
FENSKE, Cynthia .... 734-995-7443 241 F
cindy.fenske@cuaa.edu
FENSKE, Sue .... 719-502-2017.. 84 J
sue.fenske@ppcc.edu
FENSKE, Susanne .... 814-393-2351 430 E
sfenske@clarion.edu
FENSTAD, Terry .... 413-572-5276 230 F
tfenstad@westfield.ma.edu
FENTON, James, W ...... 419-772-2070 388 I
j-fenton.1@onu.edu
FENTON, Karl .... 515-244-4221 175 C
fentonk@aib.edu
FENTON, Patrick .... 408-741-2056.. 76 F
pat.fenton@westvalley.edu
FENTON, William, E ..... 502-272-8059 193 E
wfenton@bellarmine.edu
FENTRESS, Craig, M ..... 240-500-2000 215 C
cmfentress@hagerstowncc.edu
FENTRESS, Lisa, I .... 757-455-3337 518 H
lfentress@vwc.edu
FENTRESS, Viki, P .... 318-797-5234 205 F
viki.fentress@lsus.edu
FENVES, Gregory, L 512-471-1232 493M
president@utexas.edu
FENWICK, Garland .... 540-423-9046 515 E
gfenwick@germanna.edu
FENWICK, Jim .... 818-947-2508.. 52 B
fenwicjl@lavc.edu
FENWICK, Leslie, T ...... 202-806-7340.. 96 B
lfenwick@howard.edu
FERALDI, Corey .... 803-641-3280 450 C
coreyf@usca.edu
FERALDI, Patricia, A ..... 716-673-3553 343 F
patricia.feraldi@fredonia.edu
FERBER, Anna .... 212-431-2808 335 G
Anna.Ferber@nyls.edu
FERBER, David .... 402-399-2319 289 I
dferber@csm.edu
FERBER, Moshe .... 718-601-3523 353 O
mosheferber1@gmail.com
FERBRACHE, Jeanne ..... 402-559-3937 293 I
jferbrache@unmc.edu
FERCH, John .... 907-745-3201.. 10 B
jferch@akbible.edu
FERCH, Katie .... 907-745-3201.. 10 B
kferch@akbible.edu
FERDEN, Patricia .... 507-457-5330 262 D
pferden@winona.edu
FERDINAND, Amy .... 973-655-4367 304 A
ferdinanda@mail.montclair.edu
FERDOLAGE, Traci .... 707-826-4111.. 35 D
traci.ferdolage@humboldt.edu
FEREBEE, Cheryl .... 404-872-3593 121 A
cferebee@johnmarshall.edu
FEREBEE, Ryan, A .... 757-594-7553 506 I
ryan.ferebee@cnu.edu
FEREDE, Mulugeta 512-475-6600 493M
mferede@utexas.edu
FEREIRA, James, A .... 864-231-2075 443 E
jfereira@andersonuniversity.edu
FERGERSON, James ..... 507-222-4292 254 D
jfergers@carleton.edu
FERGERSON, Nicole ..... 775-831-1314 296 F
nfergerson@sierranevada.edu
FERGON, Elizabeth .... 661-654-3977.. 32 G
efergon@csub.edu
FERGUSON, Angela ...... 205-726-4841.... 6 F
adfergus@samford.edu
FERGUSON, Bennett ...... 678-359-5021 126 E
benf@gordonstate.edu
FERGUSON, Brandi .... 620-225-0186 186 F
bferguson@dc3.edu
FERGUSON, Brooke ...... 540-857-6323 517 E
bferguson@virginiawestern.edu
FERGUSON, Bruce .... 310-665-6979.. 57 C
FERGUSON, Charity, F . 270-384-8100 198 C
fergusonc@lindsey.edu
FERGUSON,
Christopher .... 215-571-4260 417 E
cpf42@drexel.edu
FERGUSON, Christy ...... 716-286-8345 336 E
clf@niagara.edu
FERGUSON, Cristie .... 903-693-2005 480 A
cferguson@panola.edu
FERGUSON, Daniel, W . 806-345-5582 467 E
dwferguson@actx.edu
FERGUSON, Darla .... 321-433-7080 101 O
fergusond@easternflorida.edu
FERGUSON, Devin .... 972-825-4700 483 D
dferguson@sagu.edu
FERGUSON, Donghui .... 770-279-0507 124 F
donghuijoy@gcuniv.edu
FERGUSON, Douglas, J 610-359-7399 416 G
dferguson@dccc.edu
FERGUSON, Ian .... 573-341-4778 284 C
ianf@mst.edu
FERGUSON, Jennifer ..... 757-822-1913 517 C
jferguson@tcc.edu
FERGUSON,
Jessame, E .... 410-857-2741 217 A
jferguson@mcdaniel.edu
FERGUSON, John .... 870-574-4726.. 23 E
jferguso@sautech.edu
FERGUSON, Joseph, S . 361-570-4390 492 A
fergusonj@uhv.edu
FERGUSON, Keith, D .... 615-353-3604 463 C
keith.ferguson@nscc.edu

FERGUSON, Kenneth, H .... 540-636-2900 506 H kferguson@christendom.edu
FERGUSON, Kevin .... 312-944-0882 150 D kferguson@chicago.chefs.edu
FERGUSON, Kimberly ... 404-270-5132 132 D kfergu15@spelman.edu
FERGUSON, Kyle .... 308-380-1971.. 62 D kyle.ferguson@sdcc.edu
FERGUSON, Larry .... 859-256-3100 195 G larry.ferguson@kctcs.edu
FERGUSON, Lee .... 214-333-5460 471 L lee@dbu.edu
FERGUSON, Leonard .... 605-455-6057 452 L lferguson@olc.edu
FERGUSON, Lisa, M ..... 740-283-6450 382 G lferguson@franciscan.edu
FERGUSON, Lori .... 580-349-1566 400 B lorif@opsu.edu
FERGUSON, Lorrie .... 540-863-2823 515 B lwferguson@dslcc.edu
FERGUSON, Nicole .... 775-831-1314 296 F nferguson@sierranevada.edu
FERGUSON, Noreen ...... 248-204-3106 245 J nferguson@ltu.edu
FERGUSON, Pamela ...... 973-720-2615 309 I fergusonp4@wpunj.edu
FERGUSON, Paul, W .... 765-285-5555 164 D president@bsu.edu
FERGUSON, Randy, L ... 262-243-5700 535 I randall.ferguson@cuw.edu
FERGUSON, Rhonda ..... 903-886-5014 485 E rhonda.ferguson@tamuc.edu
FERGUSON, Robert .... 212-217-4109 325 C Robert_Ferguson@fitnyc.edu
FERGUSON, Roberta ..... 304-696-6632 532 H fergusor@marshall.edu
FERGUSON, Rose, A ..... 815-599-3402 146 B rose.ferguson@highland.edu
FERGUSON, JR., Roy, W .... 540-828-5307 505 F rferguso@bridgewater.edu
FERGUSON, Sam .... 325-793-4631 478 D ferguson.sam@mcm.edu
FERGUSON, Sarah .... 972-860-4854 472 C sferguson@dcccd.edu
FERGUSON, Scott .... 419-448-3300 392 B fergusonsc@tiffin.edu
FERGUSON, Stephanie .. 417-455-5566 274 B sferguso@crowder.edu
FERGUSON, Teresa, D .. 864-587-4003 449 D fergusont@smcsc.edu
FERGUSON, Thomas ...... 614-231-3095 140 C tferguson@bexleyseabury.edu
FERGUSON, Thomas, C 614-231-3095 377 G tferguson@bexleyseabury.edu
FERGUSON, Timothy ..... 859-572-7770 199 A fergusont2@nku.edu
FERGUSON, Vicki .... 510-215-3921.. 42 D vferguson@contracosta.edu
FERGUSON, Vicki .... 405-224-3140 403 L facfergusonv@usao.edu
FERGUSON, Vincent ..... 215-248-4665 424 G vferguson@ltsp.edu
FERGUSON, William ..... 315-228-7333 321 H wferguson@colgate.edu
FERGUSON, William, L . 864-379-8881 446 B ferguson@erskine.edu
FERKINGSTAD, Suzanne .... 612-244-2800 256 E sferkingstad@ipr.edu
FERLAND, Chris .... 478-445-3350 125 A chris.ferland@gcsu.edu
FERLAND, William, R ... 401-825-1210 441 C wferland@ccri.edu
FERLEGER, Naomi, A .... 845-575-3000 331 L Naomi.Ferleger@marist.edu
FERLIC, Joseph, E .... 304-326-1304 530 G jferlic@salemu.edu
FERLO, Roger, A .... 773-380-6782 140 C rferlo@bexleyseabury.edu
FERLO, Roger, A .... 773-380-6782 377 G rferlo@bexleyseabury.edu
FERMIN, Cesar, D .... 334-727-8011.... 8 B
FERNÁNDEZ-ZAVALA, Margarita .... 787-993-8850 557 E margarita.fernandez@upr.edu
FERNÓS, Manuel, J ...... 787-766-1912 554 D mfernos@inter.edu
FERN, Kathy, T .... 314-286-4895 280 I ktfern@ranken.edu
FERNALD, Julian, L ...... 831-459-4341.. 72 E jfernald@ucsc.edu
FERNANDES, Brian .... 845-848-7807 324 B brian.fernandes@dc.edu
FERNANDES, Earl, K ..... 513-231-2223 377 B efernandes@athenaeum.edu
FERNANDES, Jamie ...... 678-891-2379 125 G jamie.fernandes@gpc.edu
FERNANDES, Jane, K ... 336-316-2146 357 C fernandesjk@guilford.edu
FERNANDES, Jill .... 724-938-4415 430 C fernandes@calu.edu
FERNANDES, Rick .... 724-805-2274 435 B rick.fernandes@stvincent.edu
FERNANDES, Sidney ..... 813-974-1780 116 B sfernand@health.usf.edu
FERNANDEZ, Diana ...... 413-549-4600 227 C
FERNANDEZ, Fabian ..... 727-736-5082 112 I ffernandez@schiller.edu
FERNANDEZ, Henry, B . 954-486-7728 117 M hfpresident@uftl.edu
FERNANDEZ, Hilda .... 305-623-2355 112 B hfernandez@stu.edu
FERNANDEZ, Irene .... 787-857-3600 553 G ifernandez@br.inter.edu
FERNANDEZ, J. Anthony .... 208-792-2216 138 E tfernandez@lcsc.edu
FERNANDEZ, Jeffrey ..... 508-289-2325 238 F jfernandez@whoi.edu
FERNANDEZ, Jim .... 225-578-6916 204 M jfernan@lsu.edu
FERNANDEZ, John .... 787-832-4040 557 B rector.uprm@upr.edu
FERNANDEZ, John .... 787-725-6500 551 A jfernandez@albizu.edu
FERNANDEZ, Jose .... 609-586-4800 303 D fernandj@mccc.edu
FERNANDEZ, Jose, B ... 407-823-2573 115 C jose.fernandez@ucf.edu
FERNANDEZ, Jose Luis 818-710-6406.. 51 H fernanjl@piercecollege.edu
FERNANDEZ, Luis .... 830-591-7276 483 A lmfernandez@swtjc.edu
FERNANDEZ, Marisabel 787-832-4040 558 B ossoa@uprm.edu
FERNANDEZ, Ramon, E 787-279-1912 553 H rfernandez@bayamon.inter.edu
FERNANDEZ, Raul .... 617-353-3635 224 E raul@bu.edu
FERNANDEZ, Ricardo, R .... 718-960-8111 319 C president.office@lehman.cuny.edu
FERNANDEZ, Rodolfo, J .... 305-284-4085 118 A rudyfernandez@miami.edu
FERNANDEZ, Vivian ...... 848-932-3020 306 F vpfsr@hr.rutgers.edu
FERNANDEZ, Wayne ..... 808-236-3597 135 C wfernandez@hpu.edu
FERNANDEZ, Yaniris .... 413-559-5781 227 C
FERNANDEZ PIZZI, Felix .... 617-912-9165 224 C ffernandez@bostonconservatory.edu
FERNANDEZ VAN CLEVE, John .... 787-265-3878 558 B rector.uprm@upr.edu
FERNANDEZ-ZAVALA, Margarita .... 787-993-0000 557 B rectoria.uprb@upr.edu
FERNANDO, Gihan .... 202-885-1804.. 94 H gihan@american.edu
FERNBERG, Jade .... 903-813-2377 468 G jfernberg@austincollege.edu
FERNE, Mark .... 801-832-2233 501 C mferne@westminstercollege.edu
FERNETTE, Eric .... 713-500-3110 495 A eric.fernette@uth.tmc.edu
FERNHALL, Bo .... 312-996-6695 161 F fernhall@uic.edu
FERNIANY, Will .... 205-975-5362.... 8 F ferniany@uab.edu
FERNOS, Manuel, J ...... 787-766-1912 553 J mfernos@inter.edu
FERNOS, Manuel, J ...... 787-763-4203 553 D mfernos@inter.edu
FERO, Laura .... 828-898-8769 358 F ferol@lmc.edu
FERRAN, Mayra, M ...... 787-257-7373 555 L mferran@suagm.edu
FERRAN, Peggy .... 315-781-3311 327 G ferran@hws.edu
FERRANTE, John .... 516-918-2787 352 D jferrante@webb.edu
FERRANTE, Regina .... 860-512-3633.. 89 D rferrante@manchestercc.edu
FERRARA, Anthony, A .. 901-448-5523 465 G aferrar1@uthsc.edu
FERRARA, Brandi .... 315-781-3517 327 G bferrara@hws.edu
FERRARA, Brendan .... 912-443-5783 131 B bferrara@savannahtech.edu
FERRARA, Hania .... 201-692-2381 302 H ferrara@fdu.edu
FERRARA, Joseph .... 202-687-4134.. 95 E jaf@georgetown.edu
FERRARA, Maria .... 201-447-7236 300 B mferrara@bergen.edu
FERRARA, Michael .... 603-862-1177 299 B mike.ferrara@unh.edu
FERRARA, Victoria .... 914-674-3094 332 E vferrara@mercy.edu
FERRARI, Ahniwa .... 360-538-4051 523 A
FERRARI, Bernard .... 410-234-9214 216 A bferrari@jhu.edu
FERRARI, Debra .... 650-685-6616.. 46 I
FERRARI, Lisa, L .... 253-879-3207 527 F lferrari@pugetsound.edu
FERRARI, Loretta .... 212-229-5860 334 C ferraril@newschool.edu
FERRARI, Susan .... 641-269-4983 178 I ferraris@grinnell.edu
FERRARO, Roger .... 860-906-5259.. 89 A rferraro@ccc.commnet.edu
FERRATO, Christy .... 505-566-3299 312 K ferratoc@sanjuancollege.edu
FERRAUILO-DAVIS, Mary-Jo .... 518-736-3622 326 D mary-jo.ferrauilo-davis@fmcc.suny.edu
FERRE, Loren .... 785-670-1794 192 B loren.ferre@washburn.edu
FERREIRA, Debora, D ... 413-545-3464 228 F ferreira@admin.umass.edu
FERREIRA, Kenneth ...... 603-899-4186 297 H ferreirak@franklinpierce.edu
FERREIRA, Lisa .... 619-961-4202.. 69 J lisaf@tjsl.edu
FERREIRA, Maritza .... 678-466-4467 122 J maritzaferreira@clayton.edu
FERREIRA, Milagros ..... 954-763-9840.. 98 L registrar@atom.edu
FERREIRA, Paul .... 207-326-2418 211 G paul.ferreira@mma.edu
FERREIRA, Robert .... 401-865-2407 441 F rferreir@providence.edu
FERREL, Kathleen .... 715-365-4685 543 G kferrel@nicoletcollege.edu
FERRELL, Amber .... 910-296-2400 363 E aferrell@jamessprunt.edu
FERRELL, Ben, B .... 512-223-7600 468 H bferrell@austincc.edu
FERRELL, Billy .... 972-686-7878 480 I
FERRELL, Jonathan .... 601-974-1060 268 D ferrej@millsaps.edu
FERRELL, Lottie .... 919-516-4351 368 E lferrell@st-aug.edu
FERRELL, Michael, T .... 318-797-5278 205 F michael.ferrell@lsus.edu
FERRENTINO, Robert, C .... 989-328-1221 247 D bobf@montcalm.edu
FERRER, Armando .... 305-237-4341 108 L aferrer@mdc.edu
FERRER, Laura .... 787-864-2222 553 J laura.ferrer@guayama.inter.edu
FERRER, Mercedes .... 787-265-3877 558 B director.oiip@upr.edu
FERRER, Yolanda .... 787-834-9595 556 D yferrer@uaa.edu
FERRER-MUNIZ, Karen . 518-629-7234 328 D k.ferrermuniz@hvcc.edu
FERRERA, Cassandra ..... 305-821-3333 104 C cferrera@fnu.edu
FERRERO, JR., Ray .... 954-262-7575 109 E ferrero@nova.edu
FERRES, Steven .... 845-574-4770 339 I sferres@sunyrockland.edu
FERRETTI, Anthony, J ... 941-756-0690 423 B aferretti@lecom.edu
FERRETTI, Bruce, S ...... 610-330-5375 423 A ferrettb@lafayette.edu
FERRETTI, John, M .... 814-866-6641 423 B hmckenzie@lecom.edu
FERRETTI, Kenneth, M .. 215-965-4007 426 G kferretti@moore.edu
FERRETTI, Silvia, M ...... 814-866-6641 423 B ckonnerth@lecom.edu
FERRETTI, Stephanie ..... 215-871-6486 432 E stephanief@pcom.edu
FERREY, Patricia, A ...... 814-332-2312 411 F pferrey@allegheny.edu
FERRIER, Douglas, M ... 956-326-2400 485 B douglas.ferrier@tamiu.edu
FERRIER, Katy .... 717-871-4625 431 E katy.ferrier@millersville.edu
FERRIER, Lawrence .... 201-684-7494 305 F lferrier@ramapo.edu
FERRILL, Mary .... 561-803-2702 109 G mary_ferrill@pba.edu
FERRIN, Susanne, E ..... 215-895-1192 438 E s.ferrin@usciences.edu
FERRIS, Adriann .... 510-780-4500.. 50 G aferris@lifewest.edu
FERRIS, Bill .... 206-543-9004 527 G bferris@uw.edu
FERRIS, Christian .... 361-593-2132 486 A christian.farris@tamuk.edu
FERRIS, Diane, L .... 727-864-7761 101 P ferrisdl@eckerd.edu
FERRIS, Jo .... 760-757-2121.. 54 G jferris@miracosta.edu
FERRIS, John .... 619-594-4967.. 35 E jferris@mail.sdsu.edu
FERRIS, Liz .... 765-973-8584 168 A liferris@iue.edu
FERRIS, Mary .... 805-893-2251.. 72 D mary.ferris@sa.ucsb.edu
FERRIS, Susan .... 518-381-1442 342 E ferrissc@sunysccc.edu
FERRITOR, Daniel, E ..... 479-575-4140.. 23 G def@uark.edu
FERRO, David .... 801-626-6303 500 C dferro@weber.edu
FERRO, Deanna .... 315-731-5797 333 D dferro@mvcc.edu
FERRO, Jennifer .... 310-450-4613.. 65 B ferro_jennifer@smc.edu
FERRO, Lynn, P .... 717-815-1558 440 H lferro@ycp.edu
FERRO, Robert .... 617-989-4557 237 G ferrob@wit.edu
FERRO, Salvatore .... 516-561-0050 317 G
FERRUCCI, Rosemary .... 516-686-1081 335 F rferrucc@nyit.edu
FERRUOLO, Stephen, C 619-260-4527.. 74 B lawdean@sandiego.edu
FERRY, Catherine, T ...... 717-291-3962 418 J cathie.ferry@fandm.edu
FERRY, Marylou .... 909-607-0283.. 60 A marylou.ferry@pomona.edu
FERRY, Michael, H .... 212-752-1530 330 C michael.ferry@limcollege.edu
FERRY, Patrick .... 734-995-7300 241 F patrick.ferry@cuw.edu
FERRY, Patrick, T .... 262-243-5700 535 I patrick.ferry@cuw.edu
FERRY, Richard, E .... 610-921-7825 411 E rferry@albright.edu
FERRY, Tamara, R .... 262-243-5700 535 I tamara.ferry@cuw.edu
FERULLO, Anthony .... 978-232-2384 226 C aferullo@endicott.edu
FERZELY, Eliza .... 402-941-6141 291 I ferzely@midlandu.edu
FESER, Edward .... 217-333-1660 162 A feser@illinois.edu
FESER, Neil .... 504-468-2900 207 E neil@southwest.edu
FESKO, John .... 760-480-8474.. 76 J jvfesko@wscal.edu
FESSENBECKER, Denise 310-377-5501.. 53 E dfessenbecker@marymountcalifornia.edu
FESSENDEN, June, S .... 623-845-3406.. 14 N june.fessenden@gccaz.edu
FESSLER, Brent .... 210-690-9000 474 L bfessler@hallmarkuniversity.edu
FESSLER, Cale .... 816-271-4226 279 E cfessler@missouriwestern.edu
FESSLER, Karen, P .... 570-326-3761 429 J kfessler@pct.edu
FESSLER, Robert .... 412-392-3479 433 F rfessler@pointpark.edu
FESTER, Rachel .... 212-986-4343 316 D rachel-fester@berkeleycollege.edu
FESTER, Rachel .... 212-986-4343 300 C rachel-fester@berkeleycollege.edu
FETICK, Fay .... 314-529-9673 277 B ffetick@maryville.edu
FETROW, Aaron, L .... 540-375-2592 512 B fetrow@roanoke.edu
FETROW, Jacquelyn ...... 804-289-8153 513 M jfetrow@richmond.edu
FETSCH, Cindy .... 701-777-3840 373 G cynthia.fetsch@und.edu
FETTER, Bridget .... 863-669-2843 110 E bfetter@polk.edu
FETTER, Wayne, R .... 337-475-5432 208 B wfetter@mcneese.edu
FETTEROLF, Bernadette, M .... 785-354-5853 184 F bfetterolf@stormontvail.org
FETTY, Gina .... 740-753-6445 383 G fettyg@hocking.edu
FEUCHT-HAVIAR, Joyce, A .... 818-677-4711.. 34 D joyce.feucht-haviar@csun.edu
FEUER, Avraham .... 732-367-1060 300 D AFeuer@bmg.edu
FEUER, Michael, J .... 202-994-6160.. 95 D mjfeuer@gwu.edu
FEUERBORN, Eric .... 405-224-3140 403 L efeuerborn@usao.edu
FEUERSTEIN, Christian . 802-586-7711 503 B cfeuerstein@sterlingcollege.edu
FEULING, Michael .... 503-838-8449 411 B feulingm@wou.edu
FEUSTLE, Judith .... 443-352-4292 218 E jfeustle@stevenson.edu
FEVIG, David .... 219-464-5304 174 E david.fevig@valpo.edu

FEVIG, Sarah .... 215-248-7182 415 D
fevigs@chc.edu
FEVOLA,
Christopher, N .... 516-299-3149 330 F
christopher.fevola@liu.edu
FEWOX, Keli .... 706-355-5081 120 G
kfewox@athenstech.edu
FEY, Charles, J .... 973-596-6476 304 D
cfey@njit.edu
FEY, Dan .... 206-546-4595 526 G
dfey@shoreline.edu
FEY, Jo .... 660-263-4110 279 F
jof@macc.edu
FEY-YENSAN, Nancy ..... 704-687-8374 371 B
nfeyyens@uncc.edu
FEYEN, Mike .... 979-532-6358 497 F
mikef@wcjc.edu
FEYERHERM, Dianne, E 254-299-8843 478 C
dfeyerherm@mclennan.edu
FEYERHERM, Sarah, R .. 410-778-7228 221 D
sfeyerherm2@washcoll.edu
FEYTEN, Carine .... 940-898-3201 490 D
cfeyten@twu.edu
FIACCO, Phil .... 518-327-6300 338 B
pfiacco@paulsmiths.edu
FIALA, Bill .... 626-815-2109.. 29 B
bfiala@apu.edu
FIALA, Kelly .... 410-543-6335 220 E
kafiala@salisbury.edu
FIANO, Jason .... 541-956-7097 409 F
jfiano@roguecc.edu
FICK, Katherine .... 507-786-3287 264 C
fick@stolaf.edu
FICK, Verlyn .... 520-515-5414.. 13 B
fickv@cochise.edu
FICKE, Joan, C .... 973-655-4368 304 A
fickej@mail.montclair.edu
FICKENSCHER, II,
Carl, C .... 260-452-2131 165 E
carl.fickenscher@ctsfw.edu
FICKLER, Debra .... 610-519-7857 439 A
debra.fickler@villanova.edu
FIDATI, Brian .... 484-664-3110 427 C
bfidati@muhlenberg.edu
FIDELI, Baycan .... 631-451-4212 348 E
fidelib@sunysuffok.edu
FIDLER, Jane, P .... 617-333-2355 225 F
jfidler0803@curry.edu
FIDLER-SHEPPARD,
Rebecca .... 856-374-4932 301 A
rsheppard@camdencc.edu
FIEBELKORN, Donna .... 906-635-2728 245 H
dfiebelkorn@lssu.edu
FIEBIG, Andrea .... 847-925-6371 145 F
afiebig@harpercollege.edu
FIEDLER, Peter .... 617-353-6500 224 E
pfiedler@bu.edu
FIEDLER, Thomas .... 617-353-3488 224 E
tfiedler@bu.edu
FIEGE, William .... 804-594-1406 515 G
bfiege@jtcc.edu
FIEGEL, Gregg .... 805-756-7029.. 32 E
gfiegel@calpoly.edu
FIELD, Darryl .... 215-591-5880 144 A
dfield@devry.edu
FIELD, Debbie .... 847-592-6600 156 B
dfield@princeinstitute.edu
FIELD, Heather, M .... 415-565-4682.. 71 B
fieldh@uchastings.edu
FIELD, Jay .... 415-239-3993.. 39 A
jfield@ccsf.edu
FIELD, Jay .... 360-867-6000 522 J
fieldj@evergreen.edu
FIELD, Sherry .... 479-968-0350.. 20 C
sfield@atu.edu
FIELD, Stephen, G .... 585-594-6150 339 F
fields@roberts.edu
FIELDER, Kala .... 931-221-1121 459 G
kala.fielder@miller-motte.com
FIELDER, Marsha .... 517-265-5161 238 H
mfielder@adrian.edu
FIELDING, Ahn .... 707-476-4140.. 41 C
ahn-fielding@redwoods.edu
FIELDING, Chad .... 870-230-5420.. 21 B
fieldic@hsu.edu
FIELDING, Ruby .... 803-376-5727 443 D
FIELDING, William .... 256-782-5773.... 4 L
fielding@jsu.edu
FIELDS, Andy .... 530-529-8980.. 66 C
afields@shastacollege.edu
FIELDS, Ann, Z .... 901-722-3230 461 A
annfields@sco.edu
FIELDS, Bamby .... 509-359-6564 522 C
bfields@ewu.edu
FIELDS, Beverly .... 806-457-4200 474 E
bfields@fpctx.edu
FIELDS, Cheryl .... 505-428-1238 313 A
cheryl.fields@sfcc.edu
FIELDS, Christine .... 276-739-2426 517 D
cfields@vhcc.edu
FIELDS, Christopher ..... 614-947-6803 382 H
christopher.fields@franklin.edu
FIELDS, Darin .... 419-434-4553 393 F
fieldsd2@findlay.edu
FIELDS, Dennis .... 717-545-4747 422 C
FIELDS, Fonda .... 931-221-6279 461 C
fieldsf@apsu.edu
FIELDS, Gene .... 337-482-9246 208 F
gene.fields@louisiana.edu
FIELDS, Jeff .... 276-656-0222 516 D
jfields@patrickhenry.edu
FIELDS, Joe .... 864-488-8347 447 F
jfields@limestone.edu
FIELDS, John .... 229-430-4711 119 H
john.fields@asurams.edu
FIELDS, John .... 608-663-3407 536 A
jfields@edgewood.edu
FIELDS, Lee, M .... 252-334-2080 359 D
lee.fields@macuniversity.edu
FIELDS, Melea .... 661-726-1911.. 70 I
melea.fields@uav.edu
FIELDS, Michael .... 707-668-5663.. 42 K
FIELDS, Michael .... 713-221-8179 491 F
fieldsm@uhd.edu
FIELDS, Mitch .... 315-312-6600 346 A
mitch.fields@oswego.edu
FIELDS, Peter .... 406-994-4221 287 G
pfields@msubobcats.com
FIELDS, Petra .... 704-991-0231 366 D
pfields7679@stanly.edu
FIELDS, Russell .... 775-784-6987 295 H
rfields@unr.edu
FIELDS, Shawn .... 860-628-4751.. 91 A
sfields@lincolncollegene.edu
FIELDS, Sheldon .... 323-568-3304.. 38 C
sheldonfields@cdrewu.edu
FIELDS, Todd, E .... 972-881-5174 471 C
tfields@collin.edu
FIELDS, Valerie .... 803-793-5108 445 F
fieldsv@denmarktech.edu
FIELDS, W. Bradley ...... 859-238-5485 194 E
brad.fields@centre.edu
FIELER, Vickie, K .... 603-594-2567 298 G
vfieler@sjhnh.org
FIENE, Jay .... 909-537-5600.. 35 A
jfiene@csusb.edu
FIENE, John, L .... 402-554-3670 294 A
jfiene@unomaha.edu
FIENSY, David, A .... 606-474-3263 195 F
dfiensy@kcu.edu
FIER, Sara .... 507-537-7150 262 B
Sara.Fier@smsu.edu
FIERBAUGH, Lee .... 423-461-8719 459 I
lfierbaugh@milligan.edu
FIERKE, Kimberly .... 607-431-4000 327 B
fierkek@hartwick.edu
FIERO, Diane .... 661-362-3424.. 40 H
diane.fiero@canyons.edu
FIERRO, Jose, L .... 562-860-2451.. 37 L
jfierro@cerritos.edu
FIESE, Richard .... 325-646-2502 475 F
rfiese@hputx.edu
FIFE, Linda, L .... 443-412-2377 215 D
lfife@harford.edu
FIFER, Susan .... 217-641-4201 148 J
sfifer@jwcc.edu
FIFER, Tom .... 660-831-4219 279 D
fifert@moval.edu
FIFRICK, Heather .... 608-822-2366 544 C
hfifrick@swtc.edu
FIGA, Jan .... 217-245-3020 146 D
jan.figa@mail.ic.edu
FIGALLO, Jessica .... 559-737-5443.. 41 D
jessicaf@cos.edu
FIGARI, Charles, A .... 713-500-8400 495 A
charles.a.figari@uth.tmc.edu
FIGGS, Joel .... 785-243-1435 186 A
jfiggs@cloud.edu
FIGHERA, Joe .... 619-482-6446.. 68 D
jfighera@swccd.edu
FIGLER, Daniel, J .... 304-710-3495 531 C
figler@mctc.edu
FIGUEIREDO, Marianne 617-521-2270 236 F
marianne.figueiredo@simmons.edu
FIGUERA, Lilia .... 787-758-2525 558 C
ayudante-rector@upr.edu
FIGUEREDO, Ann, W .... 610-896-1142 420 J
afiguere@haverford.edu
FIGUEREDO, Danilo, H . 973-748-9000 300 E
danilo_figueredo@bloomfield.edu
FIGUEREDO, Fernando . 305-348-3829 114 G
figueref@fiu.edu
FIGUEROA, Alfredo .... 787-764-0000 558 E
alfredo.figueroa@upr.edu
FIGUEROA, Aurea .... 787-884-3838 550 E
dir_rh@atenascollege.edu
FIGUEROA, Eduardo ...... 787-882-2065 556 C
technoloa_industrial@unitecpr.net
FIGUEROA, Gema .... 787-738-2161 557 G
gema.figueroa@upr.edu
FIGUEROA, Gisela .... 956-364-4400 487 H
gisela.figueroa@tstc.edu
FIGUEROA, Humberto ... 787-738-2161 557 G
humberto.figueroa@upr.edu
FIGUEROA, Jennifer, E . 570-577-1028 413 E
j.figueroa@bucknell.edu
FIGUEROA, Joel .... 787-884-3838 550 E
dir.admisiones@atenascollege.edu
FIGUEROA, Julio .... 787-257-7373 555 L
ue_jfigueroa@suagm.edu
FIGUEROA, Margarita ... 787-720-1022 550 F
admisiones@atlanticcollege.edu
FIGUEROA, Maria, V .... 787-743-7979 555 M
ut_mfigueroa@suagm.edu
FIGUEROA, Mark .... 503-768-7676 406 H
figueroa@lclark.edu
FIGUEROA, Vitaliano .... 619-594-3557.. 35 E
vfigueroa@mail.sdsu.edu
FIGUEROA, William .... 787-758-2525 558 C
william.figueroa2@upr.edu
FIGUEROA-AGOSTO,
María .... 787-993-8887 557 E
maria.figueroa7@upr.edu
FIJAL, Amanda .... 773-702-7659 161 D
afijal@uchicago.edu
FIKE, David, J .... 415-442-7059.. 46 A
dfike@ggu.edu
FIKE, Esther .... 407-831-9816 100 F
efike@citycollege.edu
FIKE, Esther .... 954-492-5353 100 G
efike@citycollege.edu
FIKE, Janet .... 304-214-8837 531 G
jfike@wvncc.edu
FIKE, Jeffrey .... 540-828-5395 505 F
jfike@bridgewater.edu
FIKE, Linda, K .... 301-387-3049 215 A
linda.fike@garrettcollege.edu
FIKES, Collette .... 334-872-2533..... 6 G
FIKES, Gloria .... 713-942-9505 475 D
gfikes@hgst.edu
FIKSE, Peggy .... 209-575-7707.. 78 C
fiksep@mjc.edu
FILAN, Sonia .... 480-461-7446.. 15 A
sonia.filan@mesacc.edu
FILARDI, Salvatore .... 203-582-8800.. 91 E
salvatore.filardi@quinnipiac.edu
FILARDO, Amy .... 410-617-5576 216 D
afilardo@loyola.edu
FILBY, Ivan .... 618-664-7000 145 E
presidentfilby@greenville.edu
FILE, Carter .... 620-665-3505 188 A
filec@hutchcc.edu
FILEMYR, Ann .... 505-467-6823 313 F
acadean@swc.edu
FILIATREAU, Amy .... 561-237-7000 108 E
afiliatreau@lynn.edu
FILIP, Janet .... 517-586-3009 241 B
jfilip@cleary.edu
FILIPP, Robert, B .... 773-442-5308 154 H
r-filipp@neiu.edu
FILIPPONE, Anne .... 610-902-8407 414 B
anne.filippone@cabrini.edu
FILIPPONE, Gregg, S .... 716-851-1073 325 A
filipponeg@ecc.edu
FILIPPONE, Robin .... 716-270-5237 325 A
filippone@ecc.edu
FILLIAN, Larry .... 212-229-5620 334 C
fillianl@newschool.edu
FILLINGER, Barbara ...... 734-973-3560 251 J
bfilling@wccnet.edu
FILLNER, Russ .... 406-447-6917 287 F
russ.fillner@umhelena.edu
FILLPOT, Jim .... 909-652-6460.. 38 A
jim.fillpot@chaffey.edu
FILORAMO, Dorothy ...... 845-848-7400 324 B
dorothy.filoramo@dc.edu
FILSON, Cori .... 518-580-5355 342 I
cfilson@skidmore.edu
FINAZZO, Susan .... 678-359-5680 126 E
sfinazzo@gordonstate.edu
FINCH, Amy .... 731-286-3347 462 F
finch@dscc.edu
FINCH, Christopher .... 201-559-6084 302 I
finchc@felician.edu
FINCH, Daniel .... 419-720-6670 390 I
dfinch@proskills.edu
FINCH, J. Howard .... 205-726-2364..... 6 F
hfinch@samford.edu
FINCH, Jack, R .... 740-377-2520 392 C
jfinch1@zoominternet.net
FINCH, Jeff .... 402-363-5651 294 G
jfinch@york.edu
FINCH, Joanna .... 636-529-0000 281 F
Jfinch@slchcmail.com
FINCH, Jonathan .... 864-646-1853 449 F
jfinch1@tctc.edu
FINCH, Judy .... 503-768-7328 406 H
finchj@lclark.edu
FINCH, Kim .... 225-222-4251 203 I
FINCH, Mary Ellen .... 314-529-9400 277 B
mfinch@maryville.edu
FINCH, Thomas .... 315-786-2235 329 G
tfinch@sunyjefferson.edu
FINCH, Tony .... 662-720-7304 269 D
tfinch@nemcc.edu
FINCH, Tracy .... 870-972-2031.. 19 F
tfinch@astate.edu
FINCHAM, Brian, S .... 515-964-0601 178 F
finchamb@faith.edu
FINCHER, David, B .... 660-263-3900 272 M
president@cccb.edu
FINCK, David .... 802-258-3365 502 I
david.finck@worldlearning.org
FINDLEY, Brenda .... 575-538-6146 314 E
Brenda.Findley@wnmu.edu
FINDLEY, Brenda .... 678-717-3614 133 A
brenda.findley@ung.edu
FINDLEY, Pamela, L ..... 256-782-5151.... 4 L
pfindley@jsu.edu
FINDT, William .... 910-879-5502 360 C
wfindt@bladencc.edu
FINE, Ricka, K .... 410-777-1868 213 E
rkfine@aacc.edu
FINE, Susan .... 575-492-2781 311 J
sfine@nmjc.edu
FINEGAN, SC,
Carol, M .... 718-405-3349 322 A
carol.finegan@mountsaintvincent.edu
FINEGAN, James, M .... 814-871-7681 419 A
finegan001@gannon.edu
FINEGAN, Kathleen .... 816-501-3621 272 E
kathleen.finegan@avila.edu
FINEGAN, Michael, J ... 570-961-4713 425 D
finegan@marywood.edu
FINEMAN, Barbara .... 401-232-6090 441 B
bfineman@bryant.edu
FINGADO, Marianne ..... 206-239-4500 520 K
mfingado@cityu.edu
FINGAR, Melissa, A ..... 585-292-2106 333 G
mfingar@monroecc.edu
FINGER, Eleanor .... 540-231-8893 518 B
efinger@vt.edu
FINGER, James .... 301-934-2251 214 E
jfinger@csmd.edu
FINGER, Mary .... 724-834-2200 435 E
mfinger@setonhill.edu
FINGERHUT, Randy ...... 215-951-1284 422 F
fingerhut@lasalle.edu
FINK, Brenda .... 626-914-8830.. 38 L
bfink@citruscollege.edu
FINK, Ernest .... 718-409-7341 348 C
efink@sunymaritime.edu
FINK, Gayle, M .... 301-860-3403 220 B
gfink@bowiestate.edu
FINK, Jonathan .... 503-725-9944 409 D
jon.fink@pdx.edu
FINK, Kathrynn .... 479-248-7236.. 20 K
kathrynn.kennedy@gmail.com
FINK, Michael .... 909-652-6453.. 38 A
michael.fink@chaffey.edu
FINK, Michael .... 912-525-5000 130 H
mfink@scad.edu
FINK, Susan .... 212-749-2802 331 I
sfink@msmnyc.edu
FINKELSTEIN, Barbara .. 207-216-4311 211 F
bfinkelstein@yccc.edu
FINKELSTEIN, Eric, M ... 718-990-2417 340 G
finkelse@stjohns.edu
FINKELSTEIN, Jerry .... 212-229-1671 334 C
finkelsj@newschool.edu
FINKELSTEIN, Monte ..... 850-201-8488 117 B
finkelsm@tcc.fl.edu
FINKELSTEIN, Richard .. 540-654-1052 513 I
rfinkels@umw.edu
FINLAY, Cheryl, S .... 412-383-4362 437 K
cfinlay@pitt.edu
FINLAYSON, Al .... 218-733-7600 259 C
a.finlayson@lsc.edu
FINLAYSON,
Alexander (Sandy) ..... 215-572-3823 439 E
sfinlayson@wts.edu
FINLAYSON, Deborah ... 806-742-0502 489 F
deborah.finlayson@ttu.edu
FINLAYSON, Jeanne ..... 508-565-1337 237 A
jfinlayson@stonehill.edu
FINLEY, Adam .... 817-598-8831 497 A
afinley@wc.edu
FINLEY, Becky .... 662-846-4051 267 A
becky@deltastate.edu
FINLEY, David .... 906-635-2426 245 H
dfinley@lssu.edu
FINLEY, Jane .... 251-442-2219.... 9 B
jfinley@umobile.edu
FINLEY, Julius .... 360-779-9993 524 C
jfinley@ncad.edu
FINLEY, Matt .... 803-321-5166 447 L
matthew.finley@newberry.edu
FINLEY, Rebecca .... 215-503-9000 436 F
rebecca.finley@jefferson.edu
FINLINSON, Norm .... 801-422-4640 497 J
norm_finlinson@byu.edu

FINN, Alan 503-725-3649 409 D alan.finn@pdx.edu
FINN, Alicia, A 603-641-7600 298 F afinn@anselm.edu
FINN, Bob, D 509-313-6100 522 L finn@gonzaga.edu
FINN, Donald 757-352-4278 511 G dfinn@regent.edu
FINN, Edward, J 563-333-6289 182 E FinnEdwardJ@sau.edu
FINN, Erin, M 215-503-1040 436 F erin.finn@jefferson.edu
FINN, Janice 267-620-4112 412 F finn@arcadia.edu
FINN, John 330-263-2373 380 E jfinn@wooster.edu
FINN, Kevin 248-204-4100 245 J kfinn@ltu.edu
FINN, Louise 410-617-5252 216 D lafinn@loyola.edu
FINN, Nathan 731-668-1818 464 G
FINN, William 708-974-5727 153 D finn@morainevalley.edu
FINN-SHERMAN, Miriam 781-768-7222 236 A miriam.sherman@regiscollege.edu
FINN-WELCH, Aliza 860-297-4054 92 A aliza.finnwelch@trincoll.edu
FINNAN, Diane, P 908-852-1400 301 C finnand@centenarycollege.edu
FINNEGAN, Barry 636-949-4455 276 L bfinnegan@lindenwood.edu
FINNEGAN, Faye, A 563-588-7155 180 L faye.finnegan@loras.edu
FINNEGAN, John 612-625-1179 265 C finne001@umn.edu
FINNEGAN, Michael, S 256-824-6480 9 A michael.finnegan@uah.edu
FINNEGAN, Olya 414-443-8867 542 I olya.finnegan@wlc.edu
FINNEGAN, Paul, J 617-495-1000 227 D
FINNEL, Kristin, M 920-922-8611 543 F kfinnel@morainepark.edu
FINNELL, John 512-454-1188 468 A jfinnell@aoma.edu
FINNELL, Karyn 928-350-3221 17 K kfinnell@prescott.edu
FINNEN, Mary 646-660-6549 318 C Mary.Finnen@baruch.cuny.edu
FINNERAN, Christina, M 207-725-3897 209 H cfinnera@bowdoin.edu
FINNERTY, Mary Beth 518-782-6818 342 H mfinnerty@siena.edu
FINNERTY, Robert 585-475-4733 339 G bob.finnerty@rit.edu
FINNEY, Andy 208-769-3266 138 G andy_finney@nic.edu
FINNEY, Howard, H 214-860-2202 472 F hfinney@dcccd.edu
FINNEY, Janice 850-644-1328 115 A jfinney@admin.fsu.edu
FINNEY, Lesley, M 717-361-1445 418 B finneylm@etown.edu
FINNEY, Marc 252-536-7237 363 B mfinney295@halifaxcc.edu
FINNEY, Sarah 206-296-6390 526 F sfinney@seattleu.edu
FINNEY, Terry 870-972-2398 19 F tfinney@astate.edu
FINNIE, David, A 937-775-2056 396 A david.finnie@wright.edu
FINNIGAN, Kristia, H 803-777-6727 450 B finnigan@sc.edu
FINNIN, Meredith 212-752-1530 330 C meredith.finnin@limcollege.edu
FINNING, Shannon 413-748-3100 236 H sfinning@springfieldcollege.edu
FINNKENNEY, Rebecca 610-796-8221 412 C rebecca.finnkenney@alvernia.edu
FINSETH, Karen 218-723-6104 255 A kfinseth@css.edu
FINSTUEN, Andrew 208-426-1205 137 E andrewfinstuen@boisestate.edu
FINTON, Steve 860-215-9003 90 B sfinton@trcc.commnet.edu
FINZEL, Bart 320-589-6015 265 A finzelbd@morris.umn.edu
FIORAVANTI, Emil 508-999-8106 228 H efioravanti@umassd.edu
FIORE, Douglas 419-289-5051 377 A dfiore2@ashland.edu
FIORE, Francesca 718-482-5332 320 B ffiore@lagcc.cuny.edu
FIORE, Laura 717-291-4278 418 J laura.fiore@fandm.edu
FIORE CONTE, Johann 607-777-2221 343 D jmfconte@binghamton.edu
FIORELLA, Cynthia 270-686-4445 197 A cindy.fiorella@kctcs.edu
FIORELLO, Christopher 703-284-1615 510 B chris.fiorello@marymount.edu
FIORENTINO, Christopher, M 610-436-2930 432 B cfiorentino@wcupa.edu
FIORENTINO, JR., Michael 570-484-2000 431 C mfiorentino@lhup.edu
FIORENZA, Anthony 305-237-2867 108 L afiorenz@mdc.edu
FIORESI, Rhonda 610-647-4400 421 B rfioresi@immaculata.edu
FIORI, Christopher 781-280-3292 232 B fioric@middlesex.mass.edu
FIORISI, Stephanie 903-468-8181 485 E stephanie.fiorisi@tamuc.edu
FIORITO, Frank 312-567-7994 147 E ffiorito@iit.edu
FIRESTONE, Bernard, J 516-463-5411 328 A bernard.j.firestone@hofstra.edu
FIRESTONE, Elizabeth, E 865-694-6457 463 E eefirestone@pstcc.edu
FIRMAN, JR., William, H 412-536-1765 422 E william.firman@laroche.edu
FIRMIN, Lisa, C 210-458-6097 494 D LISA.FIRMIN@UTSA.EDU
FIRMIN, Sally, E 254-710-3476 469 D sally_firmin@baylor.edu
FIRTH, Ann, M 574-631-9164 174 A firth.2@nd.edu
FISCH, Barry 617-587-5587 234 G fischb@neco.edu
FISCHER, Brock 815-455-8561 152 B bfischer@mchenry.edu
FISCHER, Craig 914-606-6715 352 G craig.fischer@sunywcc.edu
FISCHER, Donna 973-684-6333 304 F dfischer@pccc.edu
FISCHER, Heidi 336-841-9636 357 E hfischer@highpoint.edu
FISCHER, OSU, Helena 270-686-4248 193 G helena.fischer@brescia.edu
FISCHER, Howard 602-749-5120 190 D howard.fischer@ottawa.edu
FISCHER, Jacqueline 660-263-4110 279 F JackieFischer@macc.edu
FISCHER, John 419-372-5387 377 I jfisch@bgsu.edu
FISCHER, Kelly 712-325-3413 180 B kfischer@iwcc.edu
FISCHER, Lisa 309-467-6419 145 A lfischer@eureka.edu
FISCHER, Lynn 412-304-0712 418 F lfischer@cci.edu
FISCHER, Mark, T 585-275-3340 351 D mfische8@UR.Rochester.edu
FISCHER, Marvin, J 631-420-2702 348 B marvin.fischer@farmingdale.edu
FISCHER, Megan 605-331-6793 454 E megan.fischer@usiouxfalls.edu
FISCHER, Michael, R 210-999-8201 490 E mfischer@trinity.edu
FISCHER, Noah, M 701-788-4647 374 A noah.fischer@mayvillestate.edu
FISCHER, Paige, L 580-327-8545 399 F plfischer@nwosu.edu
FISCHER, Patricia, L 918-595-7856 403 A pat.fischer@tulsacc.edu
FISCHER, Pattie 360-417-6201 525 A pfischer@pencol.edu
FISCHER, Patty 573-875-7260 273 D pafischer@ccis.edu
FISCHER, Rachel 920-686-6231 539 A Rachel.Fischer@sl.edu
FISCHER, JR., Robert, U 615-898-2613 461 E bud.fischer@mtsu.edu
FISCHER, Stacy 973-408-3047 301 J sfischer@drew.edu
FISCHER, Susan 608-262-2087 539 D susan.fischer@finaid.wisc.edu
FISCHER, Tracy, A 414-410-4266 535 C tafischer@stritch.edu
FISCHER, William, M 937-229-3311 393 E WFischer1@udayton.edu
FISCHER-FREE, Todd 815-226-3385 157 D tfree@rockford.edu
FISCHER-FREE, Todd 815-226-3385 157 D tfischer-free@rockford.edu
FISCHER-KINNEY, Julie 419-530-7970 394 E julie.fischer@utoledo.edu
FISCHLER, Abraham 954-262-3827 109 E fischler@nova.edu
FISCHLER, Michael, L 603-535-2461 299 E mfischle@plymouth.edu
FISCUS, Ronald 702-968-5570 296 D rfiscus@roseman.edu
FISCUS, Rosemarie 856-691-8600 301 H rfiscus@cccnj.edu
FISER, Dawn, M 734-929-9086 241 B dfiser@cleary.edu
FISH, Alan 443-997-8767 216 A afish6@jhu.edu
FISH, Alicia 607-431-4021 327 B fisha@hartwick.edu
FISH, David 417-626-1234 280 B dfish@occ.edu
FISH, H. Woodrow 704-406-4254 356 G hwfish@gardner-webb.edu
FISH, Jacqueline 843-863-7504 444 B jfish@csuniv.edu
FISH, James, D 315-268-3859 321 C fishj@carkson.edu
FISH, Jennifer, N 757-683-4903 510 I jfish@odu.edu
FISH, Nicole 800-567-2344 535 F nfish@menominee.edu
FISH, Thomas, E 606-539-4214 200 F tom.fish@ucumberlands.edu
FISHBACK, Bill 325-649-8012 475 F bfishback@hputx.edu
FISHBACK, Bill 325-646-2502 475 F bfishback@hputx.edu
FISHBAUGH, Mary Susan 406-657-2285 287 H mfishbaugh@msubillings.edu
FISHBECK, Donna 701-224-5638 374 E donna.fishbeck@bismarckstate.edu
FISHBONE, Alexis 978-556-3615 232 E afishbone@necc.mass.edu
FISHEL, Teresa 651-696-6343 256 L fishel@macalester.edu
FISHER, Alec 617-746-1209 227 G alec.fisher@hult.edu
FISHER, Andrew 940-668-4234 479 K afisher@nctc.edu
FISHER, Ann 313-993-1582 250 H fisheram@udmercy.edu
FISHER, Anne, E 941-487-4254 115 B fisher@ncf.edu
FISHER, Anthony 912-525-5000 130 H afisher@scad.edu
FISHER, Barrett 651-638-6083 254 A fisbar@bethel.edu
FISHER, Bobby 610-789-6700 433 G bfisher@prismcareerinstitute.edu
FISHER, Brian 239-590-1786 114 F bfisher@fgcu.edu
FISHER, Christine 312-935-6696 157 A cfisher@robertmorris.edu
FISHER, Courtney 870-762-3191 19 C cfisher@smail.anc.edu
FISHER, Craig 325-674-2622 466 I craig.fisher@acu.edu
FISHER, David 918-540-6233 398 L dfisher@neo.edu
FISHER, David, A 864-242-5100 443 G
FISHER, Dawn 940-397-4787 478 G dawn.fisher@mwsu.edu
FISHER, Denise 412-809-5100 433 D fisher.denise@pti.edu
FISHER, Dianna, L 657-278-2586 33 E difisher@fullerton.edu
FISHER, Donna, M 620-417-1111 191 A donna.fisher@sccc.edu
FISHER, Elise 816-415-7641 285 K fishere@william.jewell.edu
FISHER, Elizabeth 940-565-2085 492 D elizabeth.fisher@unt.edu
FISHER, Elizabeth, A 205-934-2974 8 F
FISHER, Ellen 212-472-1500 336 A efisher@nysid.edu
FISHER, Farrah, E 404-872-3590 121 A ffisher@johnmarshall.edu
FISHER, Glenn, R 570-577-1921 413 E glenn.fisher@bucknell.edu
FISHER, Gloria, M 909-384-4470 62 C gfisher@sbccd.cc.ca.us
FISHER, Hilry 212-817-7523 319 B hfisher@gc.cuny.edu
FISHER, James, R 585-785-1208 325 E james.fisher@flcc.edu
FISHER, Jay 931-598-1142 460 I jafisher@sewanee.edu
FISHER, Jeffrey, A 614-222-3277 380 F jfisher@ccad.edu
FISHER, Jennifer, L 304-293-8531 533 D jennifer.fisher@mail.wvu.edu
FISHER, Jeremy, M 402-280-3819 290 B jfisher@creighton.edu
FISHER, John, S 989-774-7472 240 O john.s.fisher@cmich.edu
FISHER, Jon 334-244-3229 2 A jfisher@aum.edu
FISHER, Joseph 513-562-8754 376 O jfisher@artacademy.edu
FISHER, Joseph, B 210-690-9000 474 L jfisher@hallmarkuniversity.edu
FISHER, Joy 310-233-4033 51 F fisherjp@lahc.edu
FISHER, Judith 269-471-3470 239 D jfisher@andrews.edu
FISHER, Julie 773-896-2400 141 K julie.fisher@ctschicago.edu
FISHER, Karla 316-322-3110 185 F karla.fisher@butlercc.edu
FISHER, Katie 828-328-7247 358 G katie.fisher@lr.edu
FISHER, Kelly 978-232-2328 226 C kfisher@endicott.edu
FISHER, Kyle 412-397-5290 434 B fisherk@rmu.edu
FISHER, Laurie 406-243-6989 287 D laurie.fisher@umontana.edu
FISHER, Leona 909-652-7447 38 A leona.fisher@chaffey.edu
FISHER, Lisa 405-682-7595 399 K lisa.m.fisher@occc.edu
FISHER, Marc 805-893-3132 72 D marc.fisher@vcadmin.ucsb.edu
FISHER, Mardell 262-551-5705 535 E mfisher@carthage.edu
FISHER, Mark 417-873-7294 274 E mfisher005@drury.edu
FISHER, Michael 858-785-1458 325 E michael.fisher@flcc.edu
FISHER, Michael 541-383-7238 404 K mfisher@cocc.edu
FISHER, Michael 401-232-6000 441 B
FISHER, Myra 619-849-2388 59 K myrafisher@pointloma.edu
FISHER, Nevan 585-389-2370 334 B nfisher2@naz.edu
FISHER, Nicole 213-613-2200 67 G nicole_fisher@sciarc.edu
FISHER, P.B 843-953-7532 445 B fisherb@cofc.edu
FISHER, Patti, J 574-807-7625 164 F patti.fisher@bethelcollege.edu
FISHER, Rachel 920-686-6278 539 A Rachel.fisher@sl.edu
FISHER, Rebecca 877-248-6724 14 C rfisher@hmu.edu
FISHER, Robert 507-457-6658 264 B rfisher@smumn.edu
FISHER, Robert, C 615-460-6793 455 D bob.fisher@belmont.edu
FISHER, Robert, H 773-298-3031 158 F fisher@sxu.edu
FISHER, Scheiby, C 956-326-2780 485 B sfisher@tamiu.edu
FISHER, Thomas, R 612-624-1013 265 C fishe033@umn.edu
FISHER, Tiffany 574-936-8898 164 A tiffany.fisher@ancilla.edu
FISHER, Timothy 860-570-5127 92 C timothy.fisher@uconn.edu
FISHER, Tom 580-481-5243 496 K twfisher@wbu.edu
FISHER, William 508-793-7676 225 B wfisher@clarku.edu
FISHER, William, J 843-792-4275 447 G fisherj@musc.edu
FISHER, Witney 864-596-9139 445 E witney.fisher@converse.edu
FISHER-WILLIAMS, Nan 386-481-2098 99 F williamsnan@cookman.edu
FISHMAN, Ariel 212-960-5400 353 P afishma2@yu.edu
FISHMAN, David 845-406-4308 353 D
FISHMAN, Joan, R 212-431-2850 335 G Joan.Fishman@nyls.edu
FISHMAN, Yisroel 718-645-0536 333 B
FISHSTEIN, Janet 781-239-5840 222 E Jfishstein@babson.edu
FISK, Cheryl 952-446-4172 255 E fiskc@crown.edu
FISK, Francine, J 918-631-2495 403 M francine-fisk@utulsa.edu
FISK, Robert 304-647-6361 533 B rfisk@osteo.wvsom.edu
FISK, Tammy 864-646-1812 449 F tstout1@tctc.edu
FISKAA, Evelyn 845-848-4032 324 B evelyn.fiskaa@dc.edu
FISKE, Joshua, A 315-268-6718 321 C jfiske@clarkson.edu
FISSINGER, Matthew, X 310-338-2750 53 C mfissing@lmu.edu
FISTER, Cherie 314-529-9563 277 B cfister@maryville.edu
FISTER, K. Renee 270-809-3763 198 I kfister@murraystate.edu
FITCH, CD 620-862-5252 184 H cd.fitch@barclaycollege.edu
FITCH, Gene 972-883-6236 494 A gene.fitch@utdallas.edu
FITCH, James 940-668-4271 479 K jfitch@nctc.edu

FLEMING, Julie, C .... 770-720-5527 130 E
jcf@reinhardt.edu
FLEMING, Justin .... 507-786-3615 264 C
flemingj@stolaf.edu
FLEMING, Katherine, E . 212-998-4568 336 C
kef1@nyu.edu
FLEMING, Kevin .... 951-739-7880.. 61 A
kevin.fleming@norcocollege.edu
FLEMING, Kirsten .... 909-537-5300.. 35 A
kfleming@csusb.edu
FLEMING, Leanna .... 603-623-0313 298 C
leannafleming@nhia.edu
FLEMING, Linda .... 814-871-7549 419 A
fleming006@gannon.edu
FLEMING, Lorraine .... 202-806-6565.. 96 B
lfleming@howard.edu
FLEMING, Mark .... 973-655-5225 304 A
flemingm@mail.montclair.edu
FLEMING, Mary Kay ..... 513-244-4945 387 A
mary.kay.fleming@msj.edu
FLEMING, Michael, K ... 281-425-6231 477 F
mfleming@lee.edu
FLEMING, Mike, R .... 618-235-2700 160 B
mike.fleming@swic.edu
FLEMING, Nina .... 262-551-5800 535 E
nfleming@carthage.edu
FLEMING, Patricia, A .... 574-284-4575 172 G
pfleming@saintmarys.edu
FLEMING, Paul, C .... 504-864-7490 206 A
pcflemin@loyno.edu
FLEMING, Richard .... 443-550-6021 214 E
rfleming@csmd.edu
FLEMING, Rita .... 501-686-2920.. 23 F
rfleming@uasys.edu
FLEMING, Robert .... 617-824-8670 226 A
robert_fleming@emerson.edu
FLEMING, Saundra, K .. 773-878-4699 158 C
sfleming@staugustine.edu
FLEMING, Scott, S .... 202-687-3455.. 95 E
ssf2@georgetown.edu
FLEMING, Shezwae .... 301-624-2711 214 I
sfleming@frederick.edu
FLEMING, Siobhan .... 713-525-2112 493 J
sflemin@stthom.edu
FLEMING, Stephen .... 404-894-5217 125 D
fleming@gatech.edu
FLEMING, Tom, O .... 310-338-2714.. 53 C
tfleming@lmu.edu
FLEMING, Trish .... 215-836-2222 412 E
tfleming@antonelli.edu
FLEMING, Wanda .... 757-873-1111 507 G
wanda.fleming@zenith.org
FLEMING, William .... 919-962-4651 369 C
wafleming@northcarolina.edu
FLEMING, William, M .. 561-803-2001 109 G
william_fleming@pba.edu
FLEMING-WILLIS,
Linda .... 614-825-6255 376 C
lfleming-willis@aiam.edu
FLEMMING, Joshua ...... 518-736-3622 326 D
joshua.flemming@fmcc.suny.edu
FLEMMING, Sondra, G . 214-860-2146 472 F
sflemming@dcccd.edu
FLENIKEN, Tracey .... 940-668-4207 479 K
tfleniken@nctc.edu
FLENNER, Ronald, W ... 757-446-5829 507 B
Flennerw@evms.edu
FLENTJE, Mike .... 920-686-6137 539 A
Mike.Flentje@sl.edu
FLESCHNER, Julius .... 712-279-5451 176 B
julius.fleschner@briarcliff.edu
FLESHLER, David .... 216-368-2399 378 J
david.fleshler@case.edu
FLESHNER, Amy .... 217-351-3818 155 I
afleshner@parkland.edu
FLETCHER, Anthony, S . 972-860-7645 472 E
AnthonyFletcher@dcccd.edu
FLETCHER, Bill .... 615-898-2500 461 E
bill.fletcher@mtsu.edu
FLETCHER, Carol .... 575-562-2611 310 I
carol.fletcher@enmu.edu
FLETCHER, Courtney ..... 402-559-4333 293 I
cfletcher@unmc.edu
FLETCHER, Daryl .... 770-484-1204 128 D
library@lutherrice.edu
FLETCHER, Heidi, L ...... 410-532-5105 217 F
hfletcher@ndm.edu
FLETCHER, James, A .... 208-282-3540 138 C
fletjame@isu.edu
FLETCHER, Janice .... 617-243-2145 227 K
jfletcher@lasell.edu
FLETCHER, John .... 252-328-5817 369 E
fletcherjo@ecu.edu
FLETCHER, Kathy .... 432-685-4526 478 F
kfletcher@midland.edu
FLETCHER,
Kenneth Marty .... 808-969-8804 136 D
kmfletcher@hawaii.edu
FLETCHER, Laurонda .... 610-399-2224 430 D
lfletcher@cheyney.edu

FLETCHER, Lynn .... 307-268-2211 545 Z
lfletcher@caspercollege.edu
FLETCHER, Maria .... 208-282-5304 138 C
fletmari@isu.edu
FLETCHER, Martha .... 615-844-5048 466 G
mfletcher@welch.edu
FLETCHER, Michael .... 229-333-2100 134 I
michael.fletcher@wiregrass.edu
FLETCHER, Randy .... 217-351-2236 155 I
rfletcher@parkland.edu
FLETCHER, Richard, L ... 440-826-2323 377 D
rfletche@bw.edu
FLETCHER, Scott .... 503-768-6001 406 H
graddean@lclark.edu
FLETCHER, Stephen ...... 408-864-8642.. 44 N
fletcherstephen@deanza.edu
FLETCHER, Thomas .... 570-389-5161 430 B
tfletche@bloomu.edu
FLETCHER, Wanda .... 252-335-0821 361 G
wanda_fletcher@albemarle.edu
FLETCHER, Wesla .... 843-525-8293 449 E
wfletcher@tcl.edu
FLETCHER, William, A .. 843-953-5114 444 C
bill.fletcher@citadel.edu
FLEURISMOND, Jude .... 845-574-4224 339 I
jfleuri2@sunyrockland.edu
FLEURY, Jane .... 518-631-9851 351 A
fleuryj@uniongraduatecollege.edu
FLEURY, Karl .... 715-425-3133 540 E
karl.fleury@uwrf.edu
FLEURY, Traci .... 704-971-8500 355 J
tfleury@charlottelaw.edu
FLEWELLING, Colleen ... 570-372-4567 435 I
flewelling@susqu.edu
FLICK, Kay .... 508-849-3228 222 C
kflick@annamaria.edu
FLICK, Kenneth .... 843-525-8238 449 E
kflick@tcl.edu
FLICK, Larry .... 541-737-0123 408 F
larry.flick@oregonstate.edu
FLICK, Matt .... 937-294-0592 391 B
flick@saa.edu
FLICKER, John .... 928-350-4100.. 17 K
jflicker@prescott.edu
FLICKINGER, Catherine . 516-686-7792 335 F
cflickin@nyit.edu
FLIEGE, Cheryl .... 309-694-5599 146 C
cfliege@icc.edu
FLIER, Jeffrey, S .... 617-432-1501 227 D
FLING, Corey .... 619-849-2583.. 59 K
coreyfling@pointloma.edu
FLINN, Amy .... 254-298-8364 484 C
alflinn@templejc.edu
FLINN, Cara .... 479-979-1467.. 25 H
cflinn@ozarks.edu
FLINN, Deborah .... 860-515-3873.. 88 B
FLINN, Randal .... 219-866-6165 172 E
rflinn@saintjoe.edu
FLINT, Aaron .... 603-645-9678 298 H
a.flint@snhu.edu
FLINT, Alvin .... 504-671-5475 203 F
FLINT, Juanita .... 972-860-4694 472 C
juanitazf@dcccd.edu
FLINT, Laury .... 812-855-7621 167 J
lbarthol@indiana.edu
FLINT, Stacey .... 312-322-1707 160 E
sflint@spertus.edu
FLINT, Tora .... 310-577-3000.. 77 K
registrar@yosan.edu
FLINTOFT, Rebecca .... 303-273-3050.. 80 O
rflintof@mines.edu
FLINTON, JoElla .... 405-945-9106 400 F
fjo@osuokc.edu
FLIS, Denise .... 405-208-5848 400 A
dflis@okcu.edu
FLISS, Diana .... 507-223-1317 260 C
diana.fliss@mnwest.edu
FLLEMING, Kay .... 618-985-3741 148 G
kayfleming@jalc.edu
FLOCCHINI, Randy .... 775-674-7688 295 F
rflocchini@tmcc.edu
FLOCK, Gretchen .... 724-805-2209 435 B
gretchen.flock@email.stvincent.edu
FLOCKEN, Lise .... 760-757-2121.. 54 G
lflocken@miracosta.edu
FLOHR, Robin .... 740-264-5591 381 J
rflohr@egcc.edu
FLOM, Sheldon .... 307-382-1609 546 L
sflom@wwcc.wy.edu
FLOOD, Carolyn .... 731-352-4020 455 E
floodc@bethelu.edu
FLOOD, David .... 215-762-3699 417 E
david.flood@drexel.edu
FLOOD, Malia .... 619-216-6682.. 68 D
mflood@swccd.edu
FLOOD, Pierre .... 213-613-2200.. 67 G
pierre_flood@sciarc.edu
FLOOD, Thomas .... 718-489-5443 340 E
thomasflood@sfc.edu
FLOOD, Tim .... 619-644-7141.. 46 H
tim.flood@gcccd.edu

FLOOD, Timothy, J .... 920-929-2136 543 F
tflood@morainepark.edu
FLOOD-WEINER,
Christie .... 614-253-3502 388 H
weinerc@ohiodominican.edu
FLOOR, Gregory .... 617-850-1285 227 F
gfloor@hchc.edu
FLOR, Douglas .... 617-730-7010 235 B
doug.flor@newbury.edu
FLORA, Richard .... 727-302-6721 112 A
flora.richard@spcollege.edu
FLORCZAK, Joan, E ...... 203-576-4665.. 92 B
joan@bridgeport.edu
FLOREN, Gillian .... 503-821-8888 408 H
gfloren@pnca.edu
FLORENCE, Bob, K .... 816-604-6546 277 G
bob.florence@mcckc.edu
FLORENCE, Brad .... 563-876-3353 177 I
bflorence@dwci.edu
FLORENCE, Christopher 314-434-4044 273 J
chris.florence@covenantseminary.edu
FLORENDO, Chava .... 541-552-6128 409 G
florendch@sou.edu
FLORENTINE, Dennis .... 908-835-2326 309 G
dflorentine@warren.edu
FLORES, Abraham .... 713-221-8685 491 F
floresa@uhd.edu
FLORES, Anna .... 480-517-8171.. 15 D
anna.flores@riosalado.edu
FLORES, Baldomero ...... 510-780-4500.. 50 G
bflores@lifewest.edu
FLORES, Beatriz .... 787-753-6000 552 K
bflores@icprjc.edu
FLORES, Deanna, L ...... 407-303-1851.. 97 J
deanna.flores@adu.edu
FLORES, Eddie .... 505-538-6011 314 E
flores4@wnmu.edu
FLORES, Elizabeth .... 915-747-7872 494 B
lizaf@utep.edu
FLORES, Esmarelda ...... 210-434-6711 479 P
emflores@lake.ollusa.edu
FLORES, Fernando .... 915-831-6391 473 J
fflore63@epcc.edu
FLORES, Gustavo .... 707-664-4388.. 36 C
gustavo.flores@sonoma.edu
FLORES, Hector .... 409-880-8305 488 F
hector.flores@lamar.edu
FLORES, Hector .... 585-475-4476 339 G
hefgrad@rit.edu
FLORES, Jaime .... 860-343-5805.. 89 E
jflores@mxcc.edu
FLORES, Javier .... 325-942-2047 489 E
javier.flores@angelo.edu
FLORES, Jayne, T .... 671-735-5638 549 E
pio@guamcc.edu
FLORES, John .... 214-637-3530 496 J
jflores@wadecollege.edu
FLORES, Kathy .... 253-680-7178 519 K
kflores@bates.ctc.edu
FLORES, Laureano .... 323-265-8640.. 51 D
floresl@elac.edu
FLORES, Lucinda .... 210-297-9638 468 K
lgflores@baptisthealthsystem.com
FLORES, Marilyn .... 714-628-5030.. 60 H
marilyn_flores@sccollege.edu
FLORES, Mary .... 208-792-2325 138 E
mflores@lcsc.edu
FLORES, Matt .... 512-245-2922 489 C
mgf20@txstate.edu
FLORES, Melissa .... 801-832-2565 501 C
mflores@westminstercollege.edu
FLORES, Michael .... 305-629-2929 112 D
mflores@sanignaciocollege.edu
FLORES, Michael .... 210-486-3960 467 A
rflores@alamo.edu
FLORES, Michael .... 210-486-3963 466 J
rflores@alamo.edu
FLORES, Mildred .... 787-780-0070 550 G
mflores@caribbean.edu
FLORES, Minerva .... 707-468-3011.. 54 A
mflores@mendocino.edu
FLORES, Ricardo .... 787-701-5100 552 D
riflores@ediccollege.edu
FLORES, Robert, E .... 863-453-6661 113 C
robert.flores@southflorida.edu
FLORES, Ruben .... 787-279-1912 553 H
rflores@bayamon.inter.edu
FLORES, William, V ...... 713-221-8001 491 F
president@uhd.edu
FLORES-CHURCH,
Adriana .... 562-860-2451.. 37 L
achurch@cerritos.edu
FLORES GRIFFITH, Lisa 909-607-1887.. 39 E
lisa.griffith@cgu.edu
FLORES-LOPEZ, Brenda 423-236-2276 460 K
bfloreslopez@southern.edu
FLORES-MEDINA,
Donna .... 505-454-5328 311 B
dflores@luna.edu

FLORES-SANTOS,
Mayra, M .... 787-250-0000 557 B
mayra.flores@upr.edu
FLORESCA, Ann-Marie .. 270-745-0111 201 D
ann-marie.floresca@wku.edu
FLORIAN, Greg, E .... 217-875-7200 156 K
gflorian@richland.edu
FLORIAN, James, S ...... 520-621-3680.. 18 E
florianj@email.arizona.edu
FLORIO, Laura, L .... 712-274-5381 181 C
floriol@morningside.edu
FLOROS, John .... 785-532-6147 188 H
floros@ksu.edu
FLORY, Julie, A .... 314-935-5408 285 E
julie.flory@wustl.edu
FLOT, Rob .... 847-735-5200 149 H
flot@lakeforest.edu
FLOTTE, Terence, R ...... 508-856-8000 229 B
terry.flotte@umassmed.edu
FLOUHOUSE, Steve ...... 606-326-2055 195 H
steve.flouhouse@kctcs.edu
FLOURNOY, Jacob, W .. 501-686-2901.. 23 F
jwflournoy@uasys.edu
FLOURNOY, Sherrell ..... 706-821-8251 129 H
sflournoy@paine.edu
FLOWER KIM, Laura ..... 626-395-6330.. 31 D
laura.flowerkim@caltech.edu
FLOWERS, Carol, A ...... 404-727-0833 124 D
caflowe@emory.edu
FLOWERS, Damon .... 734-677-5322 251 J
dflowers@wccnet.edu
FLOWERS, Daniel .... 574-284-4574 172 G
dflowers@saintmarys.edu
FLOWERS, Geni .... 843-521-4122 450 D
meflower@uscb.edu
FLOWERS, George .... 334-844-4700.... 1 G
flowegt@auburn.edu
FLOWERS, Hannah .... 912-525-5000 130 H
hcrocket@scad.edu
FLOWERS, Kathleen ...... 315-781-3825 327 G
kflowers@hws.edu
FLOWERS, Ken .... 269-927-8167 245 E
flowers@lakemichigancollege.edu
FLOWERS, Laura .... 615-550-3168 466 H
laura@williamsoncc.edu
FLOWERS, Marshall .... 276-326-4202 505 D
mflowers@bluefield.edu
FLOWERS, Patricia, J .... 850-644-0415 115 A
pjflowers@fsu.edu
FLOWERS, Robert .... 315-781-3827 327 G
flowers@hws.edu
FLOWERS-HINTON,
Vonetta .... 706-821-8163 129 H
vflowers-hinton@paine.edu
FLOYD, Andrew .... 229-430-3983 119 H
andrew.floyd@asurams.edu
FLOYD, Arlene .... 330-941-2333 396 C
afloyd@ysu.edu
FLOYD, Brian .... 304-367-4298 531 E
brian.floyd@pierpont.edu
FLOYD, Brian, R .... 919-516-4093 368 E
brfloyd@st-aug.edu
FLOYD, Carey .... 580-371-2371 398 J
cfloyd@mscok.edu
FLOYD, Charlsie .... 636-949-4909 276 L
cfloyd@lindenwood.edu
FLOYD, Cindy .... 619-574-6909.. 57 E
cmfloyd@pacificcollege.edu
FLOYD, Cynthia .... 334-291-4905.... 2 H
cynthia.floyd@cv.edu
FLOYD, Daisy, H .... 478-301-2602 128 G
floyd_dh@law.mercer.edu
FLOYD, David 225-765-2437 204M
rulife1@lsu.edu
FLOYD, Deborah .... 561-297-4358 114 E
dfloyd@fau.edu
FLOYD, Donna .... 510-215-3804.. 42 D
dfloyd@contracosta.edu
FLOYD, Gregg, S .... 330-672-2422 384 H
gfloyd@kent.edu
FLOYD, James, J .... 909-621-8351.. 39 F
james.floyd@cmc.edu
FLOYD, Jennifer .... 606-539-4479 200 F
jennifer.floyd@ucumberlands.edu
FLOYD, Linda .... 706-233-7357 131 C
lfloyd@shorter.edu
FLOYD, Maurice .... 316-942-4291 189 K
floydm@newmanu.edu
FLOYD, Polly, K .... 850-263-3261.. 99 A
pkfloyd@baptistcollege.edu
FLOYD, Shawnda .... 972-273-3482 473 A
shawndafloyd@dcccd.edu
FLOYD, Steven .... 405-585-5132 399 I
steven.floyd@okbu.edu
FLOYD, Tony .... 843-383-8175 445 A
tfloyd@coker.edu
FLUEGEMAN, Tere .... 949-582-4920.. 67 D
tfluegeman@socccd.edu
FLUGSTAD, Bjorn .... 928-523-4240.. 16 C
Bjorn.Flugstad@nau.edu

FORD, Glenn ... 541-737-2447 408 F
glen.ford@oregonstate.edu
FORD, Glenn ... 870-633-4480 .. 20 J
gford@eacc.edu
FORD, Jason ... 864-592-4929 449 C
fordj@sccsc.edu
FORD, Jean ... 734-384-4274 247 C
jford@monroeccc.edu
FORD, Jeff ... 417-447-6930 280 C
fordj@otc.edu
FORD, John ... 415-476-4998 .. 72 C
jford@support.ucsf.edu
FORD, Kathy ... 909-469-5542 .. 76 I
kford@westernu.edu
FORD, Kelli ... 317-917-5731 169 M
kford50@ivytech.edu
FORD, Kim, R ... 202-274-6726 .. 97 B
kford@udc.edu
FORD, Kimberly ... 330-337-6403 376 B
college@awc.edu
FORD, Kristie, A ... 518-580-5425 342 I
kford@skidmore.edu
FORD, Lacy, K ... 803-777-2808 450 B
ford@mailbox.sc.edu
FORD, Laura, C ... 309-794-7452 139 K
lauraford@augustana.edu
FORD, Lynne, E ... 843-953-6531 445 B
fordl@cofc.edu
FORD, Madeline ... 718-518-4211 319 D
mford@hostos.cuny.edu
FORD, Mark, C ... 913-971-3614 189 F
mford@mnu.edu
FORD, Mary, J ... 603-822-5432 299 C
mary.ford@granite.edu
FORD, Mary Beth ... 412-396-6000 417 I
fordm@duq.edu
FORD, Michael ... 312-341-2098 157 E
mford@roosevelt.edu
FORD, Michael ... 312-341-2322 157 E
mford@roosevelt.edu
FORD, Michelle ... 802-764-2139 502 F
michelle.ford@neci.edu
FORD, Nadine, Y ... 919-516-4128 368 E
nford@st-aug.edu
FORD, Nancy ... 620-365-5116 184 C
ford@allencc.edu
FORD, III, Obie ... 828-298-3325 373 A
oford@warren-wilson.edu
FORD, Pamela, R ... 318-257-3031 208 A
prford@latech.edu
FORD, Patrick ... 704-461-6545 354 J
PatrickFord@bac.edu
FORD, Ralph ... 254-526-1402 470 E
ralph.ford@ctcd.edu
FORD, Ricky, G ... 662-720-7730 269 D
rgford@nemcc.edu
FORD, Robert ... 909-607-1554 .. 39 E
robert.ford@cgu.edu
FORD, Shelly ... 601-928-6222 268 G
shelly.ford@mgccc.edu
FORD, Sherry ... 970-943-7052 .. 87 F
sford@western.edu
FORD, Susan ... 618-453-5744 159 H
provost@siu.edu
FORD, Sylverna, V ... 901-678-2201 462 B
sford@memphis.edu
FORD, Wallace ... 718-270-5067 320 C
wford@mec.cuny.edu
FORD FISHER,
Margaret ... 713-718-8010 475 C
margaret.fordfisher@hccs.edu
FORD-KEE, Dianthia ... 662-254-3550 269 C
dfkee@mvsu.edu
FORDE, Althea ... 718-960-8066 319 C
althea.forde@lehman.cuny.edu
FORDE, Christopher ... 617-544-8657 146 H
fordec@iecc.edu
FORDE, Dermot, M ... 419-372-9475 377 I
dforde@bgsu.edu
FORDHAM, Traci ... 971-722-4667 409 C
traci.fordham@pcc.edu
FORDIS, JR.,
C. Michael ... 713-798-8256 469 C
fordis@bcm.edu
FORE, Janet, S ... 574-284-5281 172 G
jfore@saintmarys.edu
FORE, Marilyn ... 843-349-5208 446 I
marilyn.fore@hgtc.edu
FOREE, Amy ... 870-612-2139 .. 24 G
FOREHAND, Cynthia, J 802-656-8060 503 C
cynthia.forehand@uvm.edu
FOREMAN, Artie ... 601-635-2111 267 B
aforeman@eccc.edu
FOREMAN, David, M ... 570-577-3510 413 E
david.foreman@bucknell.edu
FOREMAN, Hank, T ... 828-262-7525 369 D
foremanht@appstate.edu
FOREMAN, Karen, N ... 540-868-7109 515 H
kforeman@lfcc.edu
FOREMAN, Kyle ... 509-793-2299 520 B
kylef@bigbend.edu

FOREMAN, Marquis, D . 312-942-7117 158 A
marquis_d_foreman@rush.edu
FOREMAN, Pamela, B .. 804-257-5821 518 E
pforeman@vuu.edu
FOREMAN, Todd, D ... 607-436-2081 344 B
foreматd@oneonta.edu
FOREST, Laura Ann ... 334-844-6444 .... 1 G
laf0009@auburn.edu
FOREST, Rebecca ... 978-632-6600 232 C
r_forest@mwcc.mass.edu
FOREST, Rebecca ... 978-630-9597 232 C
r_forest@mwcc.mass.edu
FOREST, Robert ... 610-647-4400 421 B
rforest@immaculata.edu
FORESTELL, Paul ... 315-279-5202 329 K
pforestell@keuka.edu
FORESTER, Lyn ... 402-826-8631 290 C
lyn.forester@doane.edu
FORESTER, Sherri, L ... 270-901-1115 197 C
sherri.forester@kctcs.edu
FORESYTH, Jan ... 432-264-5051 475 E
jforesyth@howardcollege.edu
FORGER, James ... 517-355-4583 246 H
forger@msu.edu
FORGET, Robert, L ... 608-796-3012 542 H
rlforget@viterbo.edu
FORGETTE,
Adrienne, M ... 712-707-7077 182 C
aforgett@nwciowa.edu
FORGETTE, Richard, G .. 662-915-7177 270 G
FORGEY, Glendon, S ... 903-675-6211 490 F
gforgey@tvcc.edu
FORGEY, Laura ... 281-283-2180 491 E
forgey@uhcl.edu
FORHAN-MULCAHY,
Katie ... 513-558-5164 393 D
foranmkn@ucmail.uc.edu
FORINA, Olga ... 718-818-6470 341 G
FORK, Patricia, A ... 614-235-4136 392 D
pfork@TLSohio.edu
FORLINES, Jon ... 615-844-5258 466 G
jforlines@welch.edu
FORLINES, Susan ... 615-844-5259 466 G
susan@welch.edu
FORMAN, David ... 502-863-8437 195 A
dforman1@georgetowncollege.edu
FORMAN, Fran ... 417-690-3223 273 C
fforman@cofo.edu
FORMAN, Gary ... 415-476-5544 .. 72 C
gary.forman@ucsf.edu
FORMAN, Kristi ... 901-321-4208 455 I
kforman@cbu.edu
FORMAN, Peter ... 201-692-9612 302 H
forman@fdu.edu
FORMAN, Robert, J ... 718-990-7552 340 G
honors@stjohns.edu
FORMAN, Robin ... 404-727-6062 124 D
robin.forman@emory.edu
FORMAN,
Scheherazade, W ... 301-322-0886 217 G
formansw@pgcc.edu
FORMAN, Tyrone, A ... 312-355-1308 161 F
tyforman@uic.edu
FORMICA, Melinda ... 203-582-3735 .. 91 E
melinda.formica@quinnipiac.edu
FORNARO, Frank ... 617-682-1520 226 D
ffornaro@eds.edu
FORNERIS, Glenda ... 815-802-8835 149 B
gforneris@kcc.edu
FORNEY, Judith ... 940-565-2436 492 D
judith.forney@unt.edu
FORNIERI, Diane, K ... 516-323-3204 333 E
dfornieri@molloy.edu
FORRAY, April ... 414-847-3233 537 F
aprilforray@miad.edu
FORREST, Adam ... 877-442-0505 .. 87 C
adam.forrest@rockies.edu
FORREST, Barbara ... 205-665-6055 .... 9 C
forrestb@montevallo.edu
FORREST, Christian ... 248-204-2204 245 J
cforrest@ltu.edu
FORREST, Christy ... 336-249-8186 362 B
clforrest@davidsonccc.edu
FORREST, Cynthia ... 207-602-2372 213 B
cforrest@une.edu
FORREST, Seth ... 410-951-6183 220 C
sforrest@coppin.edu
FORRESTER, Cynthia ... 913-758-6114 191 I
Cynthia.Forrester@stmary.edu
FORRESTER, Don ... 540-785-5440 514 C
donforrester@vbc.edu
FORRESTER, Jill, M ... 717-245-1669 417 B
forrestj@dickinson.edu
FORRESTER, Julie ... 214-768-2574 482 J
jforrest@smu.edu
FORRESTER, Liane ... 406-683-7530 287 E
liane.forrester@umwestern.edu
FORRESTER, Lyndy, D .. 806-371-5044 467 E
lforrester@actx.edu

FORRESTER,
Michael, P ... 864-592-4805 449 C
forresterm@sccsc.edu
FORRESTER, Risa ... 405-425-5954 399 J
risa.forrester@oc.edu
FORRESTER, Sallie ... 334-833-4527 .... 4 E
sforrester@huntingdon.edu
FORRIDER, Holly ... 330-337-6403 376 B
college@awc.edu
FORRIDER, Timothy ... 330-337-6403 376 B
college@awc.edu
FORRISTER, Ann ... 517-264-3999 238 H
FORRY, Jennifer ... 617-713-5901 235 B
jennifer.forry@newbury.edu
FORSBERG, Peggy ... 785-442-6013 187 I
pforsberg@highlandcc.edu
FORSDICK, Emily ... 901-321-3461 455 I
emathis@cbu.edu
FORSETH, Eric, A ... 712-722-6004 177 J
eric.forseth@dordt.edu
FORSHEE, Scott ... 406-657-2298 287 H
sforshee@msubillings.edu
FORSHEY, Jennifer ... 906-932-4231 243 B
JenniferF@gogebic.edu
FORSMAN, Carl ... 336-770-3236 372 B
forsmanc@uncsa.edu
FORSSTROM,
Janice, M ... 978-762-4000 232 D
jforsstr@northshore.edu
FORSTER, Daniel ... 617-521-2031 236 F
daniel.forster@simmons.edu
FORSTER, Jerry ... 304-929-1478 530 H
jerryforster@ucwv.edu
FORSTER, Kathy ... 716-673-3341 343 F
kathy.forster@fredonia.edu
FORSTER, Michael ... 601-266-5253 271 B
michael.forster@usm.edu
FORSTER, Patrick ... 503-821-8912 408 H
pforster@pnca.edu
FORSTER, Sarah ... 507-222-4206 254 D
sforster@carleton.edu
FORSTER, Stefanie ... 207-216-4321 211 F
sforster@yccc.edu
FORSTMAN, Valerie ... 817-257-7513 469 H
v.forstman@tcu.edu
FORSYTH, Anne, S ... 805-525-4417 .. 69 I
aforsyth@thomasaquinas.edu
FORSYTH, Nate ... 641-648-4611 179 K
nate.forsyth@iavalley.edu
FORSYTHE, Mary, E ... 910-962-3154 372 A
forsythem@uncw.edu
FORSYTHE, Robert, E ... 313-577-4501 252 G
robert.forsythe@wayne.edu
FORSYTHE, Ryan ... 508-929-8498 230 G
rforsythe@worcester.edu
FORT, Rebecca, L ... 330-471-8313 385 G
rfort@malone.edu
FORTE, Gregg ... 607-431-4026 327 B
forteg@hartwick.edu
FORTE, Paul ... 704-687-5770 371 B
pforte@uncc.edu
FORTE, Teresa (Terrie) . 413-747-0204 225 A
teresa.forte@cambridgecollege.edu
FORTE, Tyrone ... 718-368-5069 320 A
tforte@kbcc.cuny.edu
FORTE-PARNELL,
Charlotte ... 661-722-6300 .. 27 P
cforteparnell@avc.edu
FORTGANG, William ... 631-656-3189 326 B
william.fortgang@ftc.edu
FORTHMAN, Emily ... 618-634-3223 159 A
emilyf@shawneecc.edu
FORTHOFER, Scott ... 406-496-4500 288 C
sforthofer@mtech.edu
FORTI, Kevin ... 401-454-6651 442 B
kforti@risd.edu
FORTIN, Barbara ... 530-898-4113 .. 33 A
bfortin@csuchico.edu
FORTIN, Jay ... 570-504-7000 415 E
jfortin@tcmc.edu
FORTIN, Maurice, G ... 325-942-2222 489 E
maurice.fortin@angelo.edu
FORTIN, Shelley ... 843-661-8110 446 C
shelley.fortin@fdtc.edu
FORTIN-WAVRA,
Marion ... 402-554-4800 294 A
mfortin-wavra@unomaha.edu
FORTINI, Mary-Ellen ... 408-554-4806 .. 65 A
mfortini@scu.edu
FORTMAN, Brian, J ... 864-833-8258 448 E
bjfortman@presby.edu
FORTMAN, Susan ... 516-323-4311 333 E
sfortman@molloy.edu
FORTMILLER, Dan ... 503-725-4446 409 D
daniel.fortmiller@pdx.edu
FORTNER, Beverly ... 785-832-6659 187 F
beverly.fortner@bie.edu
FORTNER, Everette ... 434-924-8900 514 A
ewf5db@virginia.edu

FORTNER, James ... 404-894-7894 125 D
james.fortner@business.gatech.edu
FORTNER, Martin ... 318-670-9322 207 C
mfortner@susla.edu
FORTNER, Melissa ... 706-865-2134 132 G
mfortner@truett.edu
FORTNER, Tom ... 601-984-1100 270 H
tfortner@umc.edu
FORTNEY, Jesse ... 615-297-7545 455 A
fortneyj@aquinascollege.edu
FORTOSIS, Robert ... 727-864-8252 101 P
fortoscr@eckerd.edu
FORTSCH, Peggy ... 319-226-2031 175 D
Peggy.Fortsch@AllenCollege.edu
FORTSON, Carolyn ... 803-793-5213 445 F
fortsonc@denmarktech.edu
FORTSON, Jill ... 325-674-2653 466 I
jill.fortson@acu.edu
FORTUNATO, Frank ... 904-264-2172 111 G
Frank.Fortunato@om.org
FORTUNE, Allen ... 559-925-3326 .. 76 C
allenfortune@whccd.edu
FORTUNE, Beth ... 615-322-4234 465 H
beth.fortune@vanderbilt.edu
FORTUNE, Diana ... 518-891-2915 336 F
dfortune@nccc.edu
FOS, Peter, J ... 504-280-5536 205 G
president@uno.edu
FOSCHIA, Christine ... 724-805-2524 435 B
chris.foschia@stvincent.edu
FOSDYCK, Rick ... 641-683-5117 179 C
rick.fosdyck@indianhills.edu
FOSGARD, Steven ... 989-386-6622 247 B
sforgard@midmich.edu
FOSHEE, Brian, E ... 901-843-3870 460 F
foshee@rhodes.edu
FOSHEE, Kenneth, H ... 205-348-2857 .... 8 E
ken.foshee@ua.edu
FOSKEY, Becky ... 478-289-2104 124 B
bfoskey@ega.edu
FOSS, Anna ... 413-236-2107 231 A
afoss@berkshirecc.edu
FOSS, Ben ... 941-487-4777 115 B
bfoss@ncf.edu
FOSS, Jennifer, J ... 757-683-3132 510 I
jfoss@odu.edu
FOSS, Lisa ... 320-308-4028 261 E
lhfoss@stcloudstate.edu
FOSS, Marcia, J ... 701-845-7534 374 D
marcia.foss@vcsu.edu
FOSS, Michael, C ... 413-755-4510 233 B
mfoss@stcc.edu
FOSSEN, Linda ... 360-752-8440 520 A
lfossen@btc.edu
FOSSUM, Dallas ... 701-671-2314 375 B
dallas.fossum@ndscs.edu
FOSSUM, Scott ... 605-995-3025 452 H
scott.fossum@mitchelltech.edu
FOSSUM, Theresa, W ... 630-515-7663 152 H
tfossum@midwestern.edu
FOSTER, Adrienne ... 310-287-4589 .. 52 C
fosteraa@wlac.edu
FOSTER, Alan ... 918-781-7285 396 F
fostera@bacone.edu
FOSTER, Andrew ... 203-773-8542 .. 87 M
afoster@albertus.edu
FOSTER, Anita ... 859-336-5082 199 B
afoster@sccky.edu
FOSTER, Anne ... 513-569-1898 379 K
anne.foster@cincinnatistate.edu
FOSTER, Ben ... 972-524-3341 483 F
FOSTER, Brandi ... 406-444-0332 287 C
bfoster@montana.edu
FOSTER, Cherie, A ... 248-341-2117 248 E
cafoster@oaklandcc.edu
FOSTER, Clark, M ... 518-564-2130 346 B
fostercm@plattsburgh.edu
FOSTER, Claybourne ... 901-435-1307 457 N
claybourne_foster@loc.edu
FOSTER, Collins ... 678-891-2320 125 G
collins.foster@gpc.edu
FOSTER, Connie ... 270-745-2904 201 D
connie.foster@wku.edu
FOSTER, Delbert, T ... 803-536-8191 448 H
dfoster@scsu.edu
FOSTER, Donald, W ... 614-823-1350 390 C
dfoster@otterbein.edu
FOSTER, Donna ... 864-941-8430 448 D
foster.d@ptc.edu
FOSTER, Dyrell ... 951-571-6384 .. 60 K
dyrell.foster@mvc.edu
FOSTER, Ellen ... 251-380-3460 .... 7 F
efoster@shc.edu
FOSTER, Felecia ... 901-435-1740 457 N
felecia_foster@loc.edu
FOSTER, Gretchen, K ... 308-635-6183 294 C
fosterg2@wncc.edu
FOSTER, Isaac ... 646-378-6125 337 B
isaac.foster@nyack.edu
FOSTER, Jacqueline ... 910-362-7019 360 G
jfoster@cfcc.edu

FRALEY, Paula .... 309-694-5432 146 C
pfraley@icc.edu
FRALEY, Paula .... 309-694-5520 146 C
pfraley@icc.edu
FRALIC, Bradley .... 713-348-4927 480 M
bradley.w.fralic@rice.edu
FRALICKER, Tamara ...... 618-395-7777 147 A
fralickert@iecc.edu
FRAME, J. Davidson ..... 703-516-0035 513 H
davidson.frame@umtweb.edu
FRANCAVILLA,
Theodore .... 914-337-9300 323 A
ted.francavilla@concordia-ny.edu
FRANCE, David, A .... 601-292-9852 433 J
dfrance@reseminary.edu
FRANCE, Lucy .... 406-243-4742 287 D
lucy.france@umontana.edu
FRANCE, Melissa, H ..... 918-631-2516 403 M
melissa-france@utulsa.edu
FRANCIES, Karen .... 281-649-3450 475 B
kfrancies@hbu.edu
FRANCIOSI, Adrienne ... 617-243-2214 227 K
afranciosi@lasell.edu
FRANCIS, Amy .... 419-783-2376 381 G
afrancis@defiance.edu
FRANCIS, Charles .... 559-324-6455.. 69 A
charles.francis@scccd.edu
FRANCIS, Charles .... 559-442-4600.. 69 B
charles.francis@fresnocitycollege.edu
FRANCIS, Consuela ...... 843-953-7738 445 B
francisc@cofc.edu
FRANCIS, JR.,
D. Morgan .... 336-838-6102 367 C
morgan.francis@wilkescc.edu
FRANCIS, Diana .... 219-473-4211 165 A
dfrancis@ccsj.edu
FRANCIS, Heather .... 972-825-4627 483 D
hfrancis@sagu.edu
FRANCIS, Jason .... 601-403-1041 270 A
jfrancis@prcc.edu
FRANCIS, Jeff .... 972-825-4731 483 D
JFrancis@sagu.edu
FRANCIS, Jeffrey .... 918-631-2084 403 M
jeffrey-francis@utulsa.edu
FRANCIS, Joshua, C ..... 260-422-5561 167 F
dalatuszek@indianatech.edu
FRANCIS, Krista .... 360-417-6393 525 A
kfrancis@pencol.edu
FRANCIS, Lance .... 706-385-1062 130 C
lance.francis@point.edu
FRANCIS, Laurie, S ...... 208-496-9510 137 F
francisl@byui.edu
FRANCIS, Leon .... 610-558-5584 427 D
francisl@neumann.edu
FRANCIS, CSV, Mark, R 773-371-5420 141 C
president@ctu.edu
FRANCIS, Meg, K .... 719-884-5000.. 84 G
MKFrancis@nbc.edu
FRANCIS, Michael, R .... 801-863-8818 500 B
francimi@uvu.edu
FRANCIS, Monty, E ...... 214-860-2178 472 F
mefrancis@dcccd.edu
FRANCIS, Norman, C ... 504-520-7541 209 E
nfrancis@xula.edu
FRANCIS, Paige .... 203-254-4059.. 90 E
pfrancis@fairfield.edu
FRANCIS, Patricia .... 603-358-2111 299 D
Patricia.Francis@keene.edu
FRANCIS, Rachel .... 570-504-1588 422 G
francisr@lackawanna.edu
FRANCIS, Robert .... 206-546-4651 526 G
bfrancis@shoreline.edu
FRANCIS, Robert .... 215-895-6966 417 E
raf47@drexel.edu
FRANCIS, Sean .... 410-617-5922 216 D
sefrancis@loyola.edu
FRANCIS-CONNOLLY,
Elizabeth .... 207-221-4523 213 B
efrancisconnolly@une.edu
FRANCISCHETTI,
Jessica .... 406-657-1041 288 G
francisj@rocky.edu
FRANCISCO, Eva Lynn .. 904-819-6460 102 P
efrancisco@flagler.edu
FRANCISCO, Joseph ..... 402-472-6262 293 H
jfrancisco1@unl.edu
FRANCISCO, Renee .... 847-578-8810 157 G
Renee.Francisco@rosalindfranklin.edu
FRANCISCO-CABALLO,
Egenero .... 787-766-1717 556 A
um_efrancisco@suagm.edu
FRANCKO, David, A ..... 205-348-8280.... 8 E
dfrancko@ua.edu
FRANCO, Alicia .... 787-834-9595 556 D
afranco@uaa.edu
FRANCO, Barry .... 843-574-6796 449 G
barry.franco@tridenttech.edu
FRANCO, Darlery .... 201-360-4191 303 A
dfranco@hccc.edu
FRANCO, Juan .... 402-472-3755 293 H
jfranco2@unl.edu
FRANCO, Onorina .... 575-538-6174 314 E
francoo@wnmu.edu
FRANCO, Rita .... 209-478-0800.. 47 F
rfranco@humphreys.edu
FRANCO, Robert .... 808-734-9514 136 C
bfranco@hawaii.edu
FRANCO, Vilma .... 847-233-7700 155 B
vfranco@nc.edu
FRANCOIS, Dennis .... 509-963-1914 520 E
francoisd@cwu.edu
FRANCOIS, Jason .... 206-934-6020 525 K
jason.francois@seattlecolleges.edu
FRANCOIS-SEENY,
Denise .... 610-861-5066 427 F
dfrancois@northampton.edu
FRANCONE, Jennifer ..... 212-229-5900 334 C
franconj@newschool.edu
FRANDSEN, Michael ..... 440-775-6453 388 B
MFrandsen@oberlin.edu
FRANK, Adam .... 914-606-6709 352 G
adam.frank@sunywcc.edu
FRANK, Anthony, A ...... 970-491-6211.. 81 D
presofc@colostate.edu
FRANK, April .... 713-221-8422 491 F
FrankA@uhd.edu
FRANK, Brian .... 727-341-4143 112 A
frank.brian@spcollege.edu
FRANK, Christine, D .... 312-942-8735 158 A
christine_frank@rush.edu
FRANK, Dawn .... 605-455-6035 452 L
dfrank@olc.edu
FRANK, Gregory, P ...... 757-822-7261 517 C
gfrank@tcc.edu
FRANK, Isabel .... 718-817-4602 326 C
frank@fordham.edu
FRANK, Jonathan .... 312-793-7150 144 H
jfrank@erikson.edu
FRANK, Katherine .... 859-572-5495 199 A
frankks@nku.edu
FRANK, Larry .... 213-763-7052.. 52 A
franklb@lattc.edu
FRANK, Linda .... 415-485-9528.. 41 B
lfrank@marin.edu
FRANK, Marie .... 337-482-2148 208 F
mcf3023@louisiana.edu
FRANK, Meghan .... 707-668-5663.. 42 K
FRANK, Peter .... 704-233-8144 373 C
pfrank@wingate.edu
FRANK, Robert .... 740-593-2850 389 H
frank@ohio.edu
FRANK, Robert, G .... 505-277-2626 313 H
unmpres@unm.edu
FRANK, Sandy, K .... 812-464-1762 174 D
sfrank@usi.edu
FRANK, Shawn .... 828-328-7298 358 G
shawn.frank@lr.edu
FRANK, Tony .... 303-534-6290.. 81 C
chancellor@colostate.edu
FRANK, Vincent, P .... 717-901-5115 420 I
vfrank@harrisburgu.edu
FRANK MAYS, Karen ..... 978-665-3712 229 D
kfrankmays@fitchburgstate.edu
FRANKBERRY,
Constance .... 701-627-4738 373 E
cfrank@fortbertholdcc.edu
FRANKE, James .... 660-263-3900 272 M
jamiefranke@cccb.edu
FRANKEAS, Jacqueline . 610-225-5058 418 A
jfrankea@eastern.edu
FRANKEL, Bonnie .... 312-362-6760 143 G
bfranke2@depaul.edu
FRANKEN, Kathy .... 563-425-5868 183 G
frankenk@uiu.edu
FRANKEN, Lynn .... 724-589-2200 436 E
lfranken@thiel.edu
FRANKER, Karen .... 608-663-3408 536 A
KFranker@edgewood.edu
FRANKIEL, Tamar .... 310-824-1586.. 25 K
tamar.frankiel@ajrca.org
FRANKILIN, Scott .... 806-291-1130 496 K
franklins@wbu.edu
FRANKLAND, Phil .... 603-882-6923 297 B
pfrankland@ccsnh.edu
FRANKLIN, Audrey .... 336-517-2247 354 K
afranklin@bennett.edu
FRANKLIN, Beverly .... 202-274-6258.. 97 B
bfranklin@udc.edu
FRANKLIN, Celeste .... 505-473-6318 313 B
celeste.franklin@santafeuniversity.edu
FRANKLIN, Chris .... 205-387-0511.... 2 B
cfranklin@bscc.edu
FRANKLIN, David .... 202-274-6168.. 97 B
david.franklin@udc.edu
FRANKLIN, Janice .... 334-229-4106.... 1 D
franklin@alasu.edu
FRANKLIN, Joseph .... 575-835-5700 311 I
jfranklin@admin.nmt.edu
FRANKLIN, Julie .... 801-422-2810 497 J
julie_franklin@byu.edu
FRANKLIN, Karen .... 575-624-7138 310 J
karen.franklin@roswell.enmu.edu
FRANKLIN, Kathy, C ..... 434-528-5276 518 F
kfranklin@vul.edu
FRANKLIN, Laura .... 828-884-8112 355 A
phillil@brevard.edu
FRANKLIN, Laura .... 831-646-4816.. 54 H
lfranklin@mpc.edu
FRANKLIN, Laura, L ..... 828-883-8112 355 A
phillil@brevard.edu
FRANKLIN, Laurie .... 425-388-9035 522 I
lfranklin@everettcc.edu
FRANKLIN, JR.,
Layman .... 434-528-5276 518 F
lfranklin@vul.edu
FRANKLIN, Marshall, E 864-242-5100 443 G
FRANKLIN, Mona .... 785-749-8448 187 F
mona.franklin@bie.edu
FRANKLIN, Randall .... 434-832-7617 515 A
franklinr@cvcc.vccs.edu
FRANKLIN, Roschoune . 323-856-7621.. 27 H
rfranklin@afi.com
FRANKLIN, Shannon .... 541-278-5951 404 J
sfranklin@bluecc.edu
FRANKLIN, Somer .... 936-294-1009 489 A
somer@shsu.edu
FRANKLIN, Susan .... 402-461-7410 290 G
sfranklin@hastings.edu
FRANKLIN, Teresa .... 918-587-6789 403 F
tfranklin@twsweld.com
FRANKLIN, Timothy, V . 973-596-5515 304 D
timothy.v.franklin@njit.edu
FRANKLIN, Truitt .... 706-865-2134 132 G
tfranklin@truett.edu
FRANKLIN, William ...... 310-243-3784.. 33 B
wfranklin@csudh.edu
FRANKMAN, Tom .... 573-592-1166 286 A
tom.frankman@williamwoods.edu
FRANKOVICH, Lauren ... 212-749-2802 331 I
lfrankovich@msmnyc.edu
FRANKS, Billie .... 606-589-3029 197 D
billie.franks@kctcs.edu
FRANKS, Brian .... 817-531-4452 490 C
bfranks@txwes.edu
FRANKS, Debra, J .... 864-388-8749 447 E
jfranks@lander.edu
FRANKS, Dennis .... 336-278-5555 356 F
dfranks3@elon.edu
FRANKS, Mark .... 920-498-6269 544 B
mark.franks@nwtc.edu
FRANKS, Peter .... 215-895-0226 417 E
pjf28@drexel.edu
FRANKS, Rita .... 318-257-2577 208 A
rfranks@latech.edu
FRANKS, Tammy .... 228-497-7800 268 G
tammy.franks@mgccc.edu
FRANKS, Tiffany, M ...... 434-791-5670 505 A
tfranks@averett.edu
FRANQUIZ, Maria .... 801-581-5791 499 K
maria.franquiz@utah.edu
FRANSON, Terry .... 626-812-3061.. 29 B
tfranson@apu.edu
FRANTEL, Tracy, L .... 503-777-7508 409 E
tracy.frantel@reed.edu
FRANTZ, David .... 765-973-8337 168 A
dfrantz@iue.edu
FRANTZ, Michael .... 712-749-2140 176 D
frantzm@bvu.edu
FRANTZ, Rita, A .... 319-335-7009 175 H
rita-frantz@uiowa.edu
FRANZ, Chris .... 303-953-3415.. 79 L
cfranz@ccu.edu
FRANZ, Jennifer .... 920-748-8108 538 I
franzj@ripon.edu
FRANZ, Jonathan, R ..... 585-224-3200 348 A
jonathan.franz@esc.edu
FRANZ, Kelly, J .... 920-465-2210 539 F
franzk@uwgb.edu
FRANZ, Mark .... 314-889-1488 275 B
mfranz@fontbonne.edu
FRANZ, Matt .... 937-328-6045 379 L
franzm@clarkstate.edu
FRANZ, Sandra, L .... 802-626-4865 504 B
sandra.franz@lyndonstate.edu
FRANZ, Scott .... 620-947-3121 191 E
scottf@tabor.edu
FRANZ, William, T .... 804-752-7268 511 E
wfranz@rmc.edu
FRANZA, Thomas .... 443-412-2489 215 D
tfranza@harford.edu
FRANZBLAU, Alfred ...... 734-763-1282 251 C
afranz@umich.edu
FRANZEN, Kristine .... 563-387-1330 180 M
frankr03@luther.edu
FRAONE, Kimberly .... 908-737-4600 303 C
kfraone@kean.edu
FRASER, Donald, L .... 903-510-2371 491 A
dfra@tjc.edu
FRASER, Dori .... 919-735-5151 367 A
dori@waynecc.edu
FRASER, Greg .... 313-664-7660 241 D
gfraser@collegeforcreativestudies.edu
FRASER, Jamilah .... 718-270-6911 320 C
jfraser1@mec.cuny.edu
FRASER, Jeanmarie ...... 508-362-2131 231 D
jfraser@capecod.edu
FRASER, Julie .... 636-481-3200 276 E
jpierce@jeffco.edu
FRASER, Lynne .... 401-865-1534 441 F
lfraser1@providence.edu
FRASER, Morrison .... 217-854-3231 140 F
morrison.fraser@blackburn.edu
FRASER, Robin .... 845-368-7241 342 A
robin.fraser@use.salvationarmy.org
FRASER, Sheri .... 207-621-3136 212 D
fraser@maine.edu
FRASER, Sherry, J .... 914-337-9300 323 A
sherry.fraser@concordia-ny.edu
FRASER, Tammy .... 937-382-6661 395 F
tammy_fraser@wilmington.edu
FRASER, Wayne .... 603-366-5266 296 L
wfraser@ccsnh.edu
FRASER-MOLINA,
Maria .... 252-249-1851 364 F
mfraser-molina@pamlicocc.edu
FRASHER, Kristy .... 765-973-8275 168 A
sm628@bncollege.com
FRASIER, Darryl .... 386-481-2165.. 99 F
frazierd@cookman.edu
FRASIER, George .... 253-833-9111 523 B
gfrasier@geenriver.edu
FRASIER, Tanisha .... 602-331-7500.. 12 C
tfrasier@aii.edu
FRASSINELLI, David, W 203-254-4254.. 90 E
dfrassinelli@fairfield.edu
FRATELLA, Janet .... 541-552-6127 409 G
fratellaj@sou.edu
FRATER, Joel, L .... 585-262-1610 333 G
jfrater@monroecc.edu
FRAWLEY, Becky .... 828-669-8012 359 K
bfrawley@montreat.edu
FRAWLEY, Maria, H ...... 202-242-6817.. 95 D
mfrawley@gwu.edu
FRAZEE, David .... 216-987-5339 381 A
david.frazee@tri-c.edu
FRAZEE, Sally, M .... 215-204-8611 436 C
sally.frazee@temple.edu
FRAZER, Gael .... 850-484-1757 110 D
gfrazer@pensacolastate.edu
FRAZER, Gregory, H ..... 412-396-5303 417 I
frazer@duq.edu
FRAZER, Thomas, K ..... 352-392-9230 115 D
frazer@ufl.edu
FRAZIER, Al .... 501-279-4240.. 21 A
afrazier@harding.edu
FRAZIER, III, Arthur, E . 404-270-5436 132 D
aefrazier@spelman.edu
FRAZIER, Bryan .... 276-326-4272 505 D
bfrazier@bluefield.edu
FRAZIER, Connie .... 701-777-4251 373 G
connie.frazier@und.edu
FRAZIER, Dan .... 706-385-1017 130 C
dan.frazier@point.edu
FRAZIER, David .... 918-540-6113 398 L
david.frazier@neo.edu
FRAZIER, Deborah .... 360-417-6202 525 A
dfrazier@pencol.edu
FRAZIER, Deborah, J .... 870-612-2001.. 24 G
debbie.frazier@uaccb.edu
FRAZIER, DeWayne ...... 319-385-6205 180 A
dewayne.frazier@iw.edu
FRAZIER, Doug .... 912-344-2818 120 D
doug.frazier@armstrong.edu
FRAZIER, JR.,
Ernest, T .... 504-278-6421 204 B
cfrazier@nunez.edu
FRAZIER, Fred .... 801-627-8471 498 O
frazierf@owatc.edu
FRAZIER, Herb .... 620-862-5252 184 H
herb.frazier@barclaycollege.edu
FRAZIER, Jenny .... 206-726-5085 521 G
jfrazier@cornish.edu
FRAZIER, John .... 330-823-2243 394 A
fraziejl@mountunion.edu
FRAZIER, Julie .... 731-286-3204 462 F
frazier@dscc.edu
FRAZIER, Kimberly .... 404-225-4608 120 I
kfrazier@atlantatech.edu
FRAZIER, Larry .... 903-233-3951 477 G
larryfrazier@letu.edu
FRAZIER, Lisa .... 775-753-2147 295 D
lisa.frazier@gbcnv.edu
FRAZIER, Lorraine .... 713-500-2001 495 A
lorraine.frazier@uth.tmc.edu
FRAZIER, Renae .... 864-941-8357 448 D
frazier.r@ptc.edu
FRAZIER, Royce .... 620-862-5252 184 H
president@barclaycollege.edu
FRAZIER, Sean .... 815-753-1000 154 I
FRAZIER, Shanelle .... 662-621-4156 266 H
sfrazier@coahomacc.edu

FRAZIER, Steven, R ... 860-738-6409 .. 89 G
sfrazier@nwcc.commnet.edu
FRAZIER-HELD, Jamie .. 912-650-5672 131 F
jfrazier-held@southuniversity.edu
FRAZOR, Diane ... 210-826-7595 496 K
frazord@wbu.edu
FRAZZA, Christian ... 406-447-4344 286 D
cfrazza@carroll.edu
FREAD, Marilyn ... 630-889-6661 154 E
mfread@nuhs.edu
FREAD, Susan, J ... 610-799-1072 424 A
sfread@lccc.edu
FRECH, Leanne, C ... 717-736-4160 420 D
lcfrech@hacc.edu
FRECHETTE, Carri ... 207-699-5073 210 I
cfrechette@meca.edu
FRECHETTE, Michael ... 312-942-6256 158 A
michael_frechette@rush.edu
FRECHETTE-GUTFREUN,
Jessica ... 575-758-8914 311 F
jessicafg@midwiferycollege.edu
FRED, Leota ... 406-586-3585 287 B
leota.fred@montanabiblecollege.edu
FREDA, Kristin ... 212-875-4450 315 F
kfreda@bankstreet.edu
FREDEEN,
DonnaJean, A ... 609-896-5010 306 A
dfredeen@rider.edu
FREDERICK, Athena, D . 814-641-3171 421 L
fredera@juniata.edu
FREDERICK, Brian ... 337-482-6480 208 F
jdh7220@louisiana.edu
FREDERICK, David ... 513-721-7944 382 K
dfrederick@gbs.edu
FREDERICK, Debra ... 605-274-5514 452 A
deb.frederick@augie.edu
FREDERICK,
G. Marcille, H ... 540-432-4170 507 A
marci.frederick@emu.edu
FREDERICK, Jean ... 262-551-5959 535 E
jfrederick@carthage.edu
FREDERICK, John ... 210-458-4110 494 D
john.frederick@utsa.edu
FREDERICK, Julia ... 337-482-6700 208 F
jcg0624@louisiana.edu
FREDERICK,
Lawrence, W ... 314-516-7170 284 B
frederickl@umsl.edu
FREDERICK, Lesley, J ... 217-786-2597 151 C
lesley.frederick@llcc.edu
FREDERICK, Linda, D ... 504-286-5106 207 B
lfrederick@suno.edu
FREDERICK, Pam ... 540-423-9125 515 E
pfrederick@germanna.edu
FREDERICK, Richard ... 662-252-8000 270 C
rfrederick@rustcollege.edu
FREDERICK, Robert ... 518-381-1368 342 E
frederrg@sunysccc.edu
FREDERICK, Robert ... 256-824-7200 .... 9 A
robert.frederick@uah.edu
FREDERICK, Robert, J .. 319-273-6857 176 A
robert.frederick@uni.edu
FREDERICK, Sharon ... 254-526-1291 470 E
sharon.frederick@ctcd.edu
FREDERICK, Steven, G . 518-562-4195 321 D
steven.frederick@clinton.edu
FREDERICK, Thyssene .. 843-349-5246 446 I
thyssene.frederick@hgtc.edu
FREDERICK, Wayne ... 202-806-2500 .. 96 B
wfrederick@howard.edu
FREDERICKS, Dan ... 601-968-5977 266 F
dfredericks@belhaven.edu
FREDERICKS, Kimberly . 518-292-1782 340 A
fredek1@sage.edu
FREDERICKSON, Joel ... 651-638-6317 254 A
frejoe@bethel.edu
FREDETTE, Emile ... 802-728-1292 504 C
efredett@vtc.edu
FREDRICH, Dolores ... 516-463-1800 328 A
dolores.fredrich@hofstra.edu
FREDRICK, Kay ... 605-626-2518 454 A
Kay.Fredrick@northern.edu
FREDRICKSEN,
Donovan ... 214-333-5405 471 L
donovan@dbu.edu
FREDRICKSON, Angela . 402-375-7220 292 D
anfredr1@wsc.edu
FREDRICKSON, Kurt ... 626-584-5654 .. 45 F
kurtf@fuller.edu
FREDRICKSON, Maya ... 713-646-1801 482 H
mfredrickson@stcl.edu
FREDS, Anthony ... 989-317-4602 247 B
afreds@midmich.edu
FREDSON, Janice ... 509-682-6505 528 C
jfredson@wvc.edu
FREDSTROM, Tim ... 309-438-5386 147 I
tcfreds@ilstu.edu
FREE, Carolyn, G ... 803-536-8402 448 H
cfree@scsu.edu
FREE, Rhona, C ... 860-231-5221 .. 93 A
rfree@usj.edu
FREE, Rikky, L ... 501-882-4445 .. 19 E
rlfree@asub.edu
FREEBOURN, Randal ... 937-327-7009 395 I
freebournr@wittenberg.edu
FREED, Carol ... 507-389-7211 262 A
carol.freed@southcentral.edu
FREED, Curt ... 360-383-3230 528 E
cfreed@whatcom.ctc.edu
FREED, Linda ... 817-257-7516 486 G
linda.freed@tcu.edu
FREED, Mitchell ... 610-683-4175 431 B
freed@kutztown.edu
FREED, Suzanne, K ... 518-242-6046 343 C
sfreed@albany.edu
FREEDLAND, Gregory ... 717-871-5874 431 E
gregory.freedland@millersville.edu
FREEDMAN, Cheryl ... 215-468-8800 421 J
admissions@culinaryarts.edu
FREEDMAN, Daniel ... 845-257-3728 344 A
freedmad@newpaltz.edu
FREEDMAN, Eric ... 704-337-2384 368 B
freedmane@queens.edu
FREEDMAN, Michael ... 301-985-7200 220 A
michael.freedman@umuc.edu
FREEDMAN, Phyllis, D . 304-326-1390 530 G
pfreedman@salemu.edu
FREEDMAN, Stephen ... 718-817-3040 326 C
sfreedman@fordham.edu
FREEDMAN, Victoria ... 212-430-3179 353 P
vfreedman@aecom.yu.edu
FREEDMAN, Wendy, A . 845-437-5700 351 H
wefreedman@vassar.edu
FREEDMAN DOHERTY,
Elizabeth ... 617-287-5339 228 G
elizabeth.doherty@umb.edu
FREEH, Mary Beth ... 610-606-4605 415 A
mafreeh@cedarcrest.edu
FREEL, Lisa ... 301-846-2468 214 I
lfreel@frederick.edu
FREELAND, Kay ... 770-426-2944 128 C
freeland@life.edu
FREELAND, Megan ... 760-252-2411 .. 29 C
mfreeland@barstow.edu
FREELANDER, Chichi ... 405-491-6396 402 E
cfreelan@snu.edu
FREELS, Cindy ... 573-288-6511 274 C
cfreels@culver.edu
FREELS, Ean ... 319-208-5015 183 B
efreels@scciowa.edu
FREEMAN, Algenia ... 937-708-5704 395 E
afreeman@wilberforce.edu
FREEMAN, Alston ... 803-934-3179 447 K
afreeman@morris.edu
FREEMAN, Amy ... 325-236-8292 488 C
amy.freeman@tstc.edu
FREEMAN, Andrew ... 740-753-6079 383 G
freemana@hocking.edu
FREEMAN, Angela ... 404-752-1568 129 A
afreeman@msm.edu
FREEMAN, Bryan ... 734-677-5225 251 J
bafreeman@wccnet.edu
FREEMAN, Carol Ann ... 845-675-4794 337 B
carol_ann.freeman@nyack.edu
FREEMAN, Catharine ... 319-296-4041 179 B
catharine.freeman@hawkeyecollege.edu
FREEMAN, Chris ... 803-786-3886 445 C
bookstore@columbiasc.edu
FREEMAN, Craig ... 360-779-9993 524 C
cfreeman@ncad.edu
FREEMAN, Dave ... 530-242-2220 .. 66 C
dfreeman@shastacollege.edu
FREEMAN, Dennis ... 617-253-6056 233 C
FREEMAN, Donna, M ... 901-321-3251 455 I
dfreeman@cbu.edu
FREEMAN, Eddie ... 817-272-2106 493 L
efreeman@uta.edu
FREEMAN, Elijah, T ... 252-789-0276 363 H
efreeman@martincc.edu
FREEMAN, Everette ... 303-556-3786 .. 81 J
FREEMAN, Gary ... 402-461-7752 290 G
gfreeman@hastings.edu
FREEMAN, Ginger, C ... 615-898-2922 461 E
ginger.freeman@mtsu.edu
FREEMAN, Irving ... 724-552-2880 423 B
ifreeman@lecom.edu
FREEMAN, Jackie ... 435-652-7612 499 M
freeman@dixie.edu
FREEMAN, Jerrid ... 918-456-5511 398 M
freema22@nsuok.edu
FREEMAN, Jim ... 417-690-3248 273 C
jfreeman@cofo.edu
FREEMAN, John, E ... 937-708-5611 395 E
jfreeman@wilberforce.edu
FREEMAN, Karen, J ... 315-786-2234 329 G
kfreeman@sunyjefferson.edu
FREEMAN, Kenneth ... 314-246-5990 285 G
kennethfreeman@webster.edu
FREEMAN, Kenneth, W . 617-353-6170 224 E
kfreeman@bu.edu
FREEMAN, Kevin ... 405-974-2446 403 G
kfreeman7@uco.edu
FREEMAN, Larry ... 910-521-6601 371 D
larry.freeman@uncp.edu
FREEMAN, Lisa ... 413-572-5204 230 F
lfreeman@westfield.ma.edu
FREEMAN, Lisa ... 815-753-0493 154 I
lfreeman1@niu.edu
FREEMAN, Makiko ... 215-893-5257 416 E
makiko_freeman@curtis.edu
FREEMAN, Mark ... 215-571-3608 417 E
maf375@drexel.edu
FREEMAN, Melanie, H .. 662-329-7222 269 B
mhfreeman@muw.edu
FREEMAN, Michael ... 615-963-5644 461 F
mfreeman@tnstate.edu
FREEMAN, Renee ... 616-331-3255 243 E
freemren@gvsu.edu
FREEMAN, Roger ... 763-433-1378 257 P
roger.freeman@anokaramsey.edu
FREEMAN, Roger ... 763-576-4700 258 A
roger.freeman@anokaramsey.edu
FREEMAN, Russell ... 404-876-1227 122 A
russell.freeman@bccr.edu
FREEMAN, Russell, T ... 773-577-8100 143 E
FREEMAN, Sharon ... 662-254-3811 269 C
sharonf@mvsu.edu
FREEMAN, Sheila, D ... 662-685-4771 266 G
sfreeman@bmc.edu
FREEMAN, Stella ... 937-395-8006 385 A
stella.freeman@kc.edu
FREEMAN, Steve ... 270-534-3363 197 E
steve.freeman@kctcs.edu
FREEMAN, Susan ... 863-680-4433 104 F
sfreeman@flsouthern.edu
FREEMAN, Tierra, M ... 502-597-5932 197 G
tierra.freeman@kysu.edu
FREEMAN, Yancy ... 423-425-4662 465 E
yancy-freeman@utc.edu
FREEMAN-GALLANT,
Corey ... 518-580-5720 342 I
cfreeman@skidmore.edu
FREEMON, Yolanda ... 708-656-8000 153 G
yolanda.freemon@morton.edu
FREER, Doug ... 909-537-5130 .. 35 A
dfreer@csusb.edu
FREER, Michael ... 763-424-0955 260 E
mfreer@nhcc.edu
FREER, Steven ... 845-687-5200 350 I
freers@sunyulster.edu
FREER, Wayne ... 845-687-5053 350 I
freerw@sunyulster.edu
FREESE, Rob ... 215-340-8401 413 F
earl.freese@bucks.edu
FREESTONE, Julie ... 801-832-2573 501 C
jfreestone@westminstercollege.edu
FREEZE, Jackie ... 307-382-1639 546 L
jfreeze@wwcc.wy.edu
FREGIA, Olin ... 903-730-4890 476 L
ofregia@jarvis.edu
FREHSE, Sandra ... 518-454-5244 322 C
frehses@strose.edu
FREIBERGER, Amy, M .. 918-631-3727 403 M
amy-freiberger@utulsa.edu
FREIBURGER, Chevy ... 641-628-7637 176 E
freiburgerc@central.edu
FREIBURGER, Lisa ... 616-234-4025 243 D
lfreiburger@grcc.edu
FREIDENFELDS, Lauris . 312-947-0001 158 A
lauris_freidenfelds@rush.edu
FREIJE, Brenda ... 317-931-2301 165 C
bfreije@cts.edu
FREIJE, Margaret ... 508-793-2541 225 C
mfreije@holycross.edu
FREILER, Dan ... 717-396-7833 429 H
dfreiler@pcad.edu
FREINKEL, Lisa ... 541-346-0825 410 F
freinkel@uoregon.edu
FREIRE, Julio, A ... 731-881-7660 465 F
jfreire@utm.edu
FREISCHLAG, Julie ... 916-734-3578 .. 71 A
julie.freischlag@ucdmc.ucdavis.edu
FREITAG, Paul, A ... 612-343-4455 263 H
pafreita@northcentral.edu
FREITAS, Rockne, C ... 808-689-2770 136 A
rfreitas@hawaii.edu
FREMONT, Ronald ... 909-537-5004 .. 35 A
rfremont@csusb.edu
FRENCH, Angie ... 870-248-4000 .. 20 E
angie.french@blackrivertech.edu
FRENCH, Barbara ... 415-476-6296 .. 72 C
bfrench@ucsf.edu
FRENCH, Brian ... 406-243-2565 287 D
brian.french@umontana.edu
FRENCH, Christopher ... 860-297-5204 .. 92 A
christopher.french@trincoll.edu
FRENCH, Daniel, J ... 315-443-9732 349 E
djfrench@syr.edu
FRENCH, Daphne ... 912-260-4232 131 D
daphne.french@sgsc.edu
FRENCH, JR.,
George, T ... 205-929-1428 .... 5 I
gtfrench@aol.com
FRENCH, Joy ... 303-724-2516 .. 86 G
joy.french@ucdenver.edu
FRENCH, Kelly ... 859-344-3619 200 C
frenchk@thomasmore.edu
FRENCH, Maria ... 651-255-6107 264 F
mfrench@unitedseminary.edu
FRENCH, Marjorie, M ... 210-458-4228 494 D
marjie.french@utsa.edu
FRENCH, Mark ... 614-287-2810 380 G
mfrench1@cscc.edu
FRENCH, Paige ... 540-515-3749 505 F
pfrench@bridgewater.edu
FRENCH, CSSP,
Raymond ... 412-396-5286 417 I
french@duq.edu
FRENCH, Richard ... 774-354-0450 223 C
richard.french@becker.edu
FRENCH, Robert, C ... 315-470-6511 347 B
rcfrench@esf.edu
FRENCH, Steve ... 404-894-3380 125 D
steve.french@coa.gatech.edu
FRENCH, Sue ... 270-706-8611 195 K
sue.french@kctcs.edu
FRENCH, Vickie ... 870-248-4000 .. 20 E
vickief@blackrivertech.edu
FRENCH, William ... 609-497-7789 305 B
bill.french@ptsem.edu
FRENDEWEY, JR.,
James ... 906-487-2259 247 A
jimf@mtu.edu
FRENDIAN, Michel ... 312-893-7145 144 H
mfrendian@erikson.edu
FRENK, Julio ... 617-432-1025 227 D
jfrenk@hsph.harvard.edu
FRENK, Julio ... 305-284-5155 118 A
jfrenk@miami.edu
FRENTZOS, Karla, W ... 734-462-4400 250 A
kfrentzo@schoolcraft.edu
FRENZEL, Michelle ... 218-755-2370 258 B
mfrenzel@bemidjistate.edu
FRERE, Leslie ... 219-866-6116 172 E
lfrere@saintjoe.edu
FRERICHS, Chris ... 515-961-1711 182 I
chris.frerichs@simpson.edu
FRERIDGE, Jenifer ... 601-928-6288 268 G
jenifer.freridge@mgccc.edu
FRESA, Kerin ... 215-871-6864 432 E
kerinf@pcom.edu
FRESCH, Cathy ... 814-871-5842 419 A
fresch001@gannon.edu
FRESCHETTE, Brigitte ... 701-662-1546 375 A
brigitte.freschette@lrsc.edu
FRESE, Philip ... 814-393-2600 430 E
pfrese@clarion.edu
FRESHOUR, Brett ... 724-552-4372 435 E
b.freshour@setonhill.edu
FRESHWATER,
Laurie, A ... 252-222-6281 361 A
freshwaterl@carteret.edu
FRESHWATER,
Thomas, A ... 910-962-7673 372 A
freshwatert@uncw.edu
FRESQUEZ, Julie ... 951-343-4302 .. 30 D
jfresquez@calbaptist.edu
FRESSE, Daliana ... 787-815-0000 557 D
daliana.fresse@upr.edu
FRETWELL,
Katharine, L ... 413-542-2328 222 A
admissions@amherst.edu
FREY, Aaron ... 309-341-5301 140 I
afrey@sandburg.edu
FREY, Alicia ... 740-695-9500 377 F
afrey@belmontcollege.edu
FREY, Angela ... 414-382-6206 534 I
angela.frey@alverno.edu
FREY, Donald, R ... 402-280-2300 290 B
DonaldFrey@creighton.edu
FREY, Eva, R ... 253-535-7159 524 I
eva.frey@plu.edu
FREY, Frances ... 210-434-6711 479 P
ffrey@lake.ollusa.edu
FREY, Isabel, D ... 516-463-4779 328 A
isabel.d.frey@hofstra.edu
FREY, Joan, L ... 502-410-6200 194 N
jfrey@galencollege.edu
FREY, Len, T ... 870-972-3303 .. 19 F
lfrey@astate.edu
FREY, Lori ... 717-262-2012 440 D
lfrey@wilson.edu
FREY, Melissa ... 503-589-7652 404 L
melissa.frey@chemeketa.edu
FREY, Sandy ... 636-481-3348 276 E
sfrey@jeffco.edu
FREYBURGER, James ... 912-650-6251 131 F
jfreyburger@southuniversity.edu
FREYMAN, Debbie ... 501-337-5000 .. 20 H
dfreyman@coto.edu

FREYTAG, Peter .... 303-373-2008.. 85 I
pfreytag@rvu.edu
FREYTES, Diana .... 787-523-6000 552 K
dfreytes@icprjc.edu
FREYTES, Liza .... 787-279-1912 553 H
lfreytes@bayamon.inter.edu
FRIAS, Frank .... 626-529-8064.. 57 F
ffrias@pacificoaks.edu
FRIAS, Mary Lou .... 508-531-1252 229 C
marylou.frias@bridgew.edu
FRICK, Caroline .... 706-754-7722 129 B
cfrick@northgatech.edu
FRICK, Don .... 301-934-2251 214 E
dfrick@csmd.edu
FRICK, Jeffrey .... 920-403-3001 538 K
jeff.frick@snc.edu
FRICK, Lillian, K .... 989-386-6605 247 B
lfrick@midmich.edu
FRICK, Richard, A .... 201-692-2001 302 H
rfrick@fdu.edu
FRICK, Wanda .... 910-576-6222 364 D
frickw@montgomery.edu
FRICKE, Bob .... 419-227-3141 394 B
rlfricke@unoh.edu
FRICKE, David .... 732-906-2519 303 F
dfricke@middlesexcc.edu
FRICKE, Erik .... 805-965-0581.. 64 N
fricke@sbcc.edu
FRICKS, Brad .... 256-228-6001.... 6 A
fricksb@nacc.edu
FRICKX, Gretchen .... 312-697-8002 145 G
gfrickx@harrington.edu
FRIDAY, Brenda .... 570-422-3455 430 F
bfriday@esu.edu
FRIDAY-STROUD,
Shawnta .... 850-599-3565 114 D
shawnta.friday-stroud@famu.edu
FRIDGE, Rob .... 417-873-7527 274 E
rfridge@drury.edu
FRIEBEL, Thomas .... 718-368-6646 320 A
tfriebel@kbcc.cuny.edu
FRIED, Barry, J .... 608-796-3811 542 H
bjfried@viterbo.edu
FRIED, David .... 814-866-6641 423 B
dfried@lecom.edu
FRIED, Linda, P .... 212-305-9300 322 F
lpfried@columbia.edu
FRIED, Marc .... 785-670-1712 192 B
marc.fried@washburn.edu
FRIED, Ray .... 325-235-7302 488 C
ray.fried@tstc.edu
FRIED-GOODNIGHT,
Maud .... 856-691-8600 301 H
mgoodnight@cccnj.edu
FRIEDBERG, Connie ..... 412-809-5100 433 D
friedberg.connie@pti.edu
FRIEDEL, Kristin, M ...... 315-859-4637 327 A
kfriedel@hamilton.edu
FRIEDER, Steven, W ..... 414-288-7752 537 B
steven.frieder@marquette.edu
FRIEDHOFF, Scott .... 330-263-2118 380 E
sfriedhoff@wooster.edu
FRIEDKIN, Rebecca ...... 212-851-2273 315 J
rfriedki@barnard.edu
FRIEDLANDER, Jack ..... 805-965-0581.. 64 N
friedlan@sbcc.edu
FRIEDLEN, Karen .... 414-256-1203 538 A
friedlek@mtmary.edu
FRIEDLINE, Patrick .... 312-329-4414 153 C
patrick.friedline@moody.edu
FRIEDLY, Allison .... 253-833-9111 523 B
afriedly@greenriver.edu
FRIEDMAN, Al .... 425-388-9399 522 I
afriedman@everettcc.edu
FRIEDMAN, Avraham .... 847-982-2500 146 A
friedman@htc.edu
FRIEDMAN, Daniel, S ... 808-956-3469 135 J
friedman@hawaii.edu
FRIEDMAN, David .... 410-484-7200 217 E
dfreidman@nirc.edu
FRIEDMAN, Elizabeth .... 718-518-4314 319 D
efriedman@hostos.cuny.edu
FRIEDMAN, Eric .... 201-360-4012 303 A
efriedman@hccc.edu
FRIEDMAN, Frank .... 434-977-1620 516 F
ffriedman@pvcc.edu
FRIEDMAN, Jay, R .... 716-645-3313 343 E
jf5@buffalo.edu
FRIEDMAN, Jill, D .... 314-935-5261 285 E
jill.friedman@wustl.edu
FRIEDMAN, Joel, A ...... 401-825-2003 441 C
jafriedman@ccri.edu
FRIEDMAN, Leora .... 323-259-2500.. 56 I
lfriedman@oxy.edu
FRIEDMAN, Lori .... 617-989-4233 237 G
friedmanl@wit.edu
FRIEDMAN, Melissa ..... 212-280-6001 329 H
mefriedman@jtsa.edu
FRIEDMAN, Natalie .... 212-854-2024 315 J
nfriedma@barnard.edu
FRIEDMAN, Robert .... 212-960-5269 353 P
rfriedm2@yu.edu
FRIEDMAN, Robert, S ... 973-655-4314 304 A
FRIEDMAN, Scott .... 708-974-5359 153 D
friedmans5@morainevalley.edu
FRIEDMAN, Stephen, J . 212-346-1097 337 I
president@pace.edu
FRIEDMAN, William ...... 312-369-7623 143 C
bfriedman@colum.edu
FRIEDMAN, Yaakov ...... 847-982-2500 146 A
yfriedman@htc.edu
FRIEDMAN-LOMBARDO,
Jaclyn .... 973-655-7599 304 A
friedmanlj@mail.montclair.edu
FRIEDMANN, Mina .... 212-217-3560 325 C
mina_friedmann@fitnyc.edu
FRIEDMANN, Peggy, L . 913-288-7123 188 G
pfriedmann@kckcc.edu
FRIEDRICH, Brian, L .... 402-643-7364 289 J
brian.friedrich@cune.edu
FRIEDRICH, Dan .... 605-256-5555 453 H
dan.friedrich@dsu.edu
FRIEDRICHSEN,
Steven, W .... 909-706-3911.. 76 I
sfriedrichsen@westernu.edu
FRIEL, Lydia .... 215-780-1251 435 D
lfriel@salus.edu
FRIEL, Wm. Jake .... 724-287-8711 413 G
jake.friel@bc3.edu
FRIELER, Callie .... 570-340-6016 425 D
frieler@marywood.edu
FRIEND, Dane .... 713-798-1544 469 C
dfriend@bcm.edu
FRIEND, David .... 402-457-2770 291 E
djfriend@mccneb.edu
FRIEND, Denise .... 301-387-3125 215 A
denise.friend@garrettcollege.edu
FRIEND, Gwyn .... 312-362-6961 143 G
gfriend@depaul.edu
FRIEND, Margaret .... 918-335-6238 400 I
mfriend@okwu.edu
FRIEND, Vivian, M .... 727-816-3427 110 B
friendv@phsc.edu
FRIERMAN, Rose .... 607-777-4863 343 D
frierman@binghamton.edu
FRIERSON, Henry, T ..... 352-392-6622 115 D
hfrierson@ufl.edu
FRIERSON, Jameela ...... 714-816-0366.. 70 D
jameela.frierson@trident.edu
FRIERSON, Muriel .... 856-256-4367 306 D
frierson@rowan.edu
FRIERSON, Tobe, R ...... 864-379-6687 446 B
frierson@erskine.edu
FRIES, Jane .... 970-542-3106.. 84 A
jane.fries@morgancc.edu
FRIES, Katherine .... 203-857-7105.. 89 H
kfries@norwalk.edu
FRIESEKE, Mary .... 414-382-6098 534 I
mary.frieseke@alverno.edu
FRIESEN, Roger .... 541-245-7728 409 F
rfriesen@roguecc.edu
FRIESEN, Wilbert .... 847-628-1001 149 A
will.friesen@judsonu.edu
FRIESNER, Todd .... 989-463-7143 239 B
friesnertb@alma.edu
FRIGO, Sandy .... 213-613-2200.. 67 G
sandy_frigo@sciarc.edu
FRIGOT, Pamela, J .... 724-738-2057 432 A
pamela.frigot@sru.edu
FRINK, Dorothy .... 219-980-6994 168 C
defrink@iun.edu
FRINK, Kandy .... 307-382-1602 546 L
kfrink@wwcc.wy.edu
FRIONA, Joseph, M ...... 260-399-7700 174 C
jfriona@sf.edu
FRISBEE, Holly .... 212-966-0300 334 D
hfrisbee@nyaa.edu
FRISBEE, Stephen .... 315-792-5399 333 D
sfrisbee@mvcc.edu
FRISBIE, Kathy .... 970-542-3240.. 84 A
kathy.frisbie@morgancc.edu
FRISBY, Anthony .... 215-503-4990 436 F
anthony.frisby@jefferson.edu
FRISBY, Anthony .... 215-503-8848 436 F
anthony.frisby@jefferson.edu
FRISBY, Bernard .... 703-212-7410 508 A
FRISCH, Kim .... 303-458-4909.. 85 G
kfrisch@regis.edu
FRISCH, Randy, C .... 858-642-8105.. 55 J
rfrisch@nu.edu
FRISCH, Ronald, W ...... 412-624-8030 437 K
paurf5@pitt.edu
FRISCHMANN, John ..... 320-308-2522 261 E
jmfrischmann@stcloudstate.edu
FRISENDA, Louis .... 703-247-8341 510 B
louis.frisenda@marymount.edu
FRISHMAN, Niki .... 760-872-2000.. 42 J
nikif@deepsprings.edu
FRISINA, Warren .... 516-463-4783 328 A
warren.frisina@hofstra.edu
FRISKICS, Scott .... 406-353-2607 286 B
friskics@hotmail.com
FRISKNEY, Paul .... 513-244-8128 379 I
paul.friskney@ccuniversity.edu
FRISQUE, Megan .... 512-863-1584 483 G
frisquem@southwestern.edu
FRIST, Matthew .... 412-396-6699 417 I
FRITCH, John .... 319-273-2725 176 A
John.Fritch@uni.edu
FRITCH, Margie .... 619-388-2789.. 62 G
mfritch@sdccd.edu
FRITCHLE, Anthony .... 706-867-2712 133 A
anthony.fritchle@ung.edu
FRITSCH, Denise .... 859-442-4162 196 A
denise.fritsch@kctcs.edu
FRITSCH, Robert .... 619-388-7515.. 62 H
rfritsch@sdccd.edu
FRITSCHE, Teresa .... 570-422-3422 430 F
tfritsche@esu.edu
FRITTS, Jack .... 630-829-6060 140 A
jfritts@ben.edu
FRITTS, Mary Lou, A .... 816-235-1107 284 A
frittsml@umkc.edu
FRITZ, Greg .... 402-399-2407 289 I
gfritz@csm.edu
FRITZ, John .... 410-455-6596 219 F
fritz@umbc.edu
FRITZ, Sarah .... 608-246-6559 543 C
fritz@madisoncollege.edu
FRITZ, Shelby .... 253-589-5533 521 B
shelby.fritz@cptc.edu
FRITZ, Stephen .... 806-742-1828 489 F
steve.fritz@ttu.edu
FRITZ, Stephen, J .... 651-962-5901 265 F
sjfritz@stthomas.edu
FRITZ, Susan, M .... 402-472-5242 293 F
smfritz@nebraska.edu
FRITZ, Thomas, R .... 814-472-3006 434 F
tfritz@francis.edu
FRITZ, William, J .... 718-982-2400 319 A
president@csi.cuny.edu
FRITZE, Barbara, B .... 717-337-6582 419 C
bfritze@gettysburg.edu
FRITZE, Ronald .... 256-216-5524.... 1 F
ron.fritze@athens.edu
FRITZMAN, D. Jason .... 304-243-2043 534 H
jfritzman@wju.edu
FRIZADO, Joseph .... 419-372-7202 377 I
frizado@bgsu.edu
FRIZZELL, Christine ...... 508-999-8648 228 H
cfrizzell@umassd.edu
FRIZZELL, Douglas .... 412-396-3234 417 I
frizzelld@duq.edu
FRIZZELL, Robert .... 479-788-7205.. 23 H
robert.frizzell@uafs.edu
FROCK, Gemma .... 803-508-7277 443 C
frockg@atc.edu
FROEHLE, Mary .... 561-723-4424 112 C
mfroehle@svdp.edu
FROEHLE, Ryan .... 312-939-4975 145 G
rfroehle@harrington.edu
FROEHLICH-MUELLER,
Kerry, K .... 608-757-7654 542 L
kfroehlich-mueller@blackhawk.edu
FROGLEY, Kent .... 801-975-5094 500 E
kent.frogley@slcc.edu
FROHOFF, Katherine ..... 816-501-4151 281 B
katherine.frohoff@rockhurst.edu
FROHRIB, Patti .... 920-735-5611 542 N
frohrib@fvtc.edu
FROLE, Angelo .... 614-287-5020 380 G
afrole@cscc.edu
FROLICK, Stuart .... 661-255-1050.. 31 B
FROMBGEN, Liz .... 402-461-7321 290 G
lfrombgen@hastings.edu
FROMELL, Menachem ... 845-352-3431 353 M
shaareitorah@optonline.net
FROMENTO, Kristin ...... 740-362-3126 386 D
kfromento@mtso.edu
FROMING, William .... 650-433-3830.. 58 B
bfroming@paloaltou.edu
FROMMELT, Steve .... 309-796-5933 140 D
frommelts@bhc.edu
FRON, Ray .... 573-876-2342 283 A
rfron@stephens.edu
FRONCEK, Maureen ...... 312-341-4167 157 E
mfroncek@roosevelt.edu
FRONCZEK, Andrew, F . 216-397-4275 384 F
afronczek@jcu.edu
FRONCZEK, Walter .... 708-974-5372 153 D
fronczek@morainevalley.edu
FRONHEISER, Joey .... 405-945-3250 400 F
fronhei@osuokc.edu
FRONK, Michael, R .... 386-822-7523 117 A
mfronk@stetson.edu
FRONK, Peter .... 608-363-2375 534 L
fronkp@beloit.edu
FRONK, Suzette .... 828-898-8809 358 F
fronks@lmc.edu
FRONMUELLER,
Michael .... 715-425-3335 540 E
michael.fronmueller@uwrf.edu
FRONRATH, Scott .... 727-341-4495 112 A
fronrath.scott@spcollege.edu
FRONTERA, Jose, A ...... 787-841-2000 555 F
jose_frontera@pucpr.edu
FRONTIERA, Charlene ... 650-574-6312.. 64 D
frontierac@smccd.edu
FRONTIERA, Patrick ...... 310-338-4489.. 53 C
pfrontiera@lmu.edu
FRONZAGLIA,
Shawn, G .... 412-268-4309 414 J
sgfronza@andrew.cmu.edu
FRONZONI, Susan .... 570-674-6249 426 D
sfronzon@misericordia.edu
FROSCH, Jeff .... 512-313-3000 471 H
jeff.frosch@concordia.edu
FROSLID JONES,
Karen, L .... 202-885-6155.. 94 H
kfroslid@american.edu
FROSSARD, RET.,
Margaret O'Mara .... 312-427-2737 148 I
mfrossar@jmls.edu
FROST, Brian .... 419-473-2700 381 F
bfrost@daviscollege.edu
FROST, Catherine .... 510-215-3928.. 42 D
cfrost@contracosta.edu
FROST, Dana, L .... 864-644-5004 449 B
dfrost@swu.edu
FROST, Eric .... 315-464-4393 344 E
froste@upstate.edu
FROST, James .... 830-303-0404 487 C
frost@frostlawoffice.com
FROST, Judith .... 207-755-5265 210 L
jfrost@cmcc.edu
FROST, Julia, H .... 479-979-1401.. 25 H
jfrost@ozarks.edu
FROST, Leanne .... 406-771-4372 288 B
leanne.frost@gfcmsu.edu
FROST, Linda .... 423-425-5922 465 E
linda-frost@utc.edu
FROST, Mark .... 518-783-4100 342 H
mfrost@siena.edu
FROST, Mark .... 518-276-8246 339 D
frostm@rpi.edu
FROST, Mike .... 406-243-4711 287 D
mike.frost@umontana.edu
FROST, Richard, A .... 616-395-7800 244 A
frost@hope.edu
FROST, Robert, A .... 360-736-9391 520 F
rfrost@centralia.edu
FROST, Stacy .... 507-537-6483 262 B
Stacy.Frost@smsu.edu
FROST, Vivian .... 620-252-7199 186 C
vivianf@coffeyville.edu
FROUDE, Bill .... 859-572-5112 199 A
froudew1@nku.edu
FRUCHTHANDLER,
Abraham, H .... 718-377-0777 338 H
FRUEH, Elizabeth .... 715-425-3737 540 E
elizabeth.frueh@uwrf.edu
FRUGE, Fred .... 337-457-7311 205 B
ffruge@lsue.edu
FRUITTICHER, Lee .... 706-721-7928 121 C
lfruitticher@gru.edu
FRUM, Jennifer, L .... 706-542-6126 132 H
jfrum@uga.edu
FRUMKIN, Howard .... 206-543-2100 527 G
frumkin@uw.edu
FRUMKIN, Jeffery, R .... 734-763-4551 251 C
jfrumkin@umich.edu
FRUMKIN, Michael .... 407-823-6424 115 C
michael.frumkin@ucf.edu
FRUMKIN, Steven .... 212-217-4330 325 C
steven_frumkin@fitnyc.edu
FRUTCHEY, Shelby .... 512-516-8703 131 F
sfrutchey@southuniversity.edu
FRUZZETTI, Armida ...... 775-673-7135 295 F
afruzzetti@tmcc.edu
FRY, Angela .... 870-574-4523.. 23 E
afry@sautech.edu
FRY, Blake, W .... 715-425-3711 540 E
blake.fry@uwrf.edu
FRY, Bobbye, G .... 210-829-6006 492 B
fry@uiwtx.edu
FRY, Gary .... 615-844-5243 466 G
gfry@welch.edu
FRY, Jacy .... 605-256-5267 453 H
jacy.fry@dsu.edu
FRY, John .... 708-239-4863 160 L
john.fry@trnty.edu
FRY, John, A .... 215-895-2100 417 E
jaf@drexel.edu
FRY, Pamela .... 405-744-5627 400 C
pamela.fry@okstate.edu
FRY, Sally, V .... 304-367-4214 532 F
sally.fry@fairmontstate.edu
FRY, Scott .... 918-825-4678 400 E
scott.fry@okstate.edu

FUTRELL, Tamara, Y ..... 540-458-8766 519 A
tfutrell@wlu.edu
FUTTERER, Julie ..... 815-740-3826 162 F
jfutterer@stfrancis.edu
FUZY, Bob ..... 864-587-4295 449 D
fuzyb@smcsc.edu
FYDENKEVEZ,
Mary Ellen ..... 413-775-1469 231 E
fydenkevez@gcc.mass.edu
FYFE, Brenda, S ..... 314-968-6913 285 G
fyfebv@webster.edu
FYFE, John ..... 415-442-6540.. 46 A
jfyfe@ggu.edu
FYFFE, Richard ..... 641-269-3351 178 I
fyffe@grinnell.edu
FYFFE, Robert ..... 937-775-3336 396 A
robert.fyffe@wright.edu
FYOCK, Debra, R ..... 412-648-1458 437 K
dfyock@bc.pitt.edu

G

GÓMEZ, Sheila ..... 787-751-1912 554 D
sgomez@juris.inter.edu
GAAL, John ..... 215-276-6070 435 D
jgaal@salus.edu
GAALSWYK, Terry ..... 507-372-3491 260 C
terry.gaalswyk@mnwest.edu
GABA, Barbara ..... 908-965-6091 309 A
gaba@ucc.edu
GABBARD, Clinton ..... 269-927-8120 245 E
cgabbard@lakemichigancollege.edu
GABBARD, Elizabeth ..... 479-979-1307.. 25 H
egabbard@ozarks.edu
GABBARD, Kurt, A ..... 609-497-7705 305 B
kurt.gabbard@ptsem.edu
GABBARD, Veronica ..... 281-649-3747 475 B
vgabbard@hbu.edu
GABBERT, Jeri Pat ..... 219-981-4242 168 C
jgabbert@iun.edu
GABBERT, Paula, S ..... 864-294-2064 446 F
paula.gabbert@furman.edu
GABEHART, Alan, D ..... 318-798-4117 205 F
alan.gabehart@lsus.edu
GABEHART, Luci ..... 432-264-5074 475 E
lgabehart@howardcollege.edu
GABEL, Ann-Marie ..... 562-938-4540.. 51 A
agabel@lbcc.edu
GABEL, Barb ..... 419-448-2183 383 C
bgabel@heidelberg.edu
GABEL, Joan ..... 573-882-6688 283 H
gabelj@missouri.edu
GABEL, Joanne ..... 610-372-4721 433 H
jgabel@racc.edu
GABER, Sharon, L ..... 419-530-2211 394 E
sharon.gaber@utoledo.edu
GABERT, Glen, E ..... 201-360-4003 303 A
ggabert@hccc.edu
GABERT, Susan, S ..... 603-641-7231 298 F
sgabert@anselm.edu
GABIANELLI,
Barbara, A ..... 203-576-4134.. 92 B
bag@bridgeport.edu
GABIS, Mark, A ..... 270-926-1188 456 F
mgabis@daymargroup.com
GABLE, Carol ..... 315-229-5563 341 E
cgable@stlawu.edu
GABLE, Jeff ..... 909-599-5433.. 50 H
jgable@lifepacific.edu
GABLE, Jill ..... 828-669-8012 359 K
jgable@montreat.edu
GABLE, Jill ..... 252-335-3283 369 F
jegable@ecsu.edu
GABLE, Karla ..... 314-539-5303 281 H
kgable4@stlcc.edu
GABLE, Marsha ..... 619-660-4302.. 46 G
marsha.gable@gcccd.edu
GABLE, Nakita ..... 251-344-1203.... 3 J
GABLE, Nicole ..... 412-536-1022 422 E
nicole.gable@laroche.edu
GABOURY, John, D ..... 517-355-5767 246 H
gaboury@msu.edu
GABOURY, Mario ..... 203-932-7253.. 92 G
mgaboury@newhaven.edu
GABOVITCH, Rhonda ..... 508-678-2811 231 B
rhonda.gabovitch@bristolcc.edu
GABRIEL, George, E ..... 703-323-3129 516 C
ggabriel@nvcc.edu
GABRIEL, Lisa ..... 281-283-3032 491 E
gabriel@uhcl.edu
GABRIEL, Robert ..... 707-864-7000.. 66 J
robert.gabriel@solano.edu
GABRIELE, Gary, A ..... 610-519-5860 439 A
gary.gabriele@villanova.edu
GABRIELSE, Ken ..... 405-585-4300 399 I
ken.gabrielse@okbu.edu
GABRIELSON, Kerry ..... 719-846-5643.. 86 A
kerry.gabrielson@trinidadstate.edu
GACHETTE, Yves, M ..... 716-878-4521 345 B
gachetym@buffalostate.edu
GACKENHEIMER,
Lois, M ..... 561-683-1400.. 97 G
lgackenheimer@anho.edu
GACKLE, Joel ..... 714-556-3610.. 75 A
joel.gackle@vanguard.edu
GADBERRY, Brad ..... 770-781-6957 128 A
bgadberry@laniertech.edu
GADDE, Sandee, A ..... 989-463-7146 239 B
gadde@alma.edu
GADDIS, Glendi ..... 210-999-7011 490 E
ggaddis@trinity.edu
GADDIS, Lydia ..... 937-766-7886 378 K
lgaddis@cedarville.edu
GADDY, Stoney ..... 307-674-6446 546 H
sgaddy@sheridan.edu
GADE, Werner ..... 608-263-6012 541 E
werner.gade@uwc.edu
GADE-JONES, Tish ..... 402-465-2114 292 E
tgadejon@nebrwesleyan.edu
GADIKIAN,
Randolph Lee ..... 716-673-3181 343 F
randolph.gadikian@fredonia.edu
GADSBY, Peter ..... 845-758-7457 315 G
gadsby@bard.edu
GADSON, Mark, P ..... 610-409-3164 438 H
mgadson@ursinus.edu
GADZINSKI, James, G .. 906-227-2971 248 B
jgadzins@nmu.edu
GAER-CARLTON, Kathy . 509-963-1211 520 E
gaerk@cwu.edu
GAERTE, Phyllis ..... 585-567-9620 328 C
phyllis.gaerte@houghton.edu
GAERTNER, Michelle ..... 615-248-1463 464 E
mgaertner@trevecca.edu
GAETA, Alexa ..... 404-471-6423 119 G
agaeta@agnesscott.edu
GAETA, James ..... 512-863-1259 483 G
gaetaj@southwestern.edu
GAETA, Maria ..... 805-482-2755.. 61 F
mgaeta@stjohnsem.edu
GAETANO, Davide ..... 404-413-4469 126 D
davide@gsu.edu
GAETJENS, Stuart ..... 931-393-1663 463 B
ssgaetjens@mscc.edu
GAETZ, Ivan ..... 719-389-6070.. 79M
ivan.gaetz@coloradocollege.edu
GAFF, Crystal ..... 603-535-2338 299 E
clgaff@plymouth.edu
GAFFEY, Donna ..... 617-217-9114 223 A
dgaffey@baystate.edu
GAFFNER, Lori ..... 618-664-7120 145 E
lori.gaffner@greenville.edu
GAFFNEY, Eva ..... 508-531-1337 229 C
egaffney@bridgew.edu
GAFFNEY, FSC, James .. 815-836-5230 150 F
brjgaff@lewisu.edu
GAFFNEY, Kathryn ..... 860-701-5068.. 91 B
gaffney_K@mitchell.edu
GAFFNEY, Kevin ..... 775-445-4223 296 A
kevin.gaffney@wnc.edu
GAFFNEY, Michelle ..... 330-823-7288 394 A
gaffnemi@mountunion.edu
GAFFNEY, Michelle ..... 330-823-2496 394 A
gaffnemi@mountunion.edu
GAFFNEY, Phillip ..... 706-204-2201 125 C
pgaffney@highlands.edu
GAFFNEY, Tandy ..... 276-656-0230 516 D
tgaffney@patrickhenry.edu
GAFFNEY, Tiffany, D ..... 401-865-2191 441 F
tgaffne1@providence.edu
GAFFORD, Brian ..... 931-393-1576 463 B
bgafford@mscc.edu
GAGAN, Kelly ..... 585-389-2411 334 B
kgagan8@naz.edu
GAGE, Adrian ..... 508-929-8563 230 G
agage@worcester.edu
GAGE, Brent ..... 319-335-1548 175 H
brent-gage@uiowa.edu
GAGE, Chris ..... 812-866-7028 166 E
gage@hanover.edu
GAGE, David ..... 315-781-3734 327 G
gage@hws.edu
GAGE, J. Scott ..... 978-837-5468 233 G
j.scott.gage@merrimack.edu
GAGE, Jeannie ..... 361-825-2332 485 F
jeannie.gage@tamucc.edu
GAGE, Julia ..... 401-841-6535 548 B
julia.gage@usnwc.edu
GAGER, Sarah ..... 203-575-8034.. 89 F
sgager@nv.edu
GAGLIARDI, Cathy ..... 941-351-5100 111 F
GAGLIARDI, William ..... 989-837-4237 248 D
gagliardi@northwood.edu
GAGNE PENDLETON,
Lori ..... 860-515-3858.. 88 B
lpendleton@charteroak.edu
GAGNON, Ann, M ..... 603-899-4128 297 H
gagnonan@franklinpierce.edu
GAGNON, Craig, L ..... 920-832-6587 536 R
craig.l.gagnon@lawrence.edu
GAGNON, Grant ..... 480-423-6000.. 15 E
grant.gagnon@scottsdalecc.edu
GAGNON, Jennifer ..... 802-656-3360 503 C
jennifer.gagnon@uvm.edu
GAGNON, Karen ..... 712-274-5159 181 C
gagnon@morningside.edu
GAGNON, Paula ..... 207-216-4318 211 F
pgagnon@yccc.edu
GAGNON, Roberta ..... 269-965-3931 244 L
gagnonr@kellogg.edu
GAGNOW, Robin, W ..... 440-826-8153 377 D
rgagnow@bw.edu
GAHAGAN, Nicole ..... 262-691-5240 544 D
ngahagan@wctc.edu
GAHAGANS, Steve ..... 479-575-6626.. 23 G
steveg@uark.edu
GAHAN, Mick ..... 402-457-2402 291 E
mgahan@mccneb.edu
GAHM, Jamie, L ..... 815-224-0428 147 J
jamie_gahm@ivcc.edu
GAHMAN, Debora ..... 215-699-5700 423 F
dgahman@LSB.edu
GAIA, Celeste ..... 276-944-6917 507 E
cgaia@ehc.edu
GAIER, Mary ..... 937-512-2163 391 D
mary.gaier@sinclair.edu
GAIKO, Sylvia ..... 270-745-8985 201 D
sylvia.gaiko@wku.edu
GAIL, Jeff ..... 907-745-3201.. 10 B
jgail@akbible.edu
GAIL, Keli, A ..... 413-597-4233 238 E
kg8@williams.edu
GAILEY, Andrew ..... 706-865-2134 132 G
agailey@truett.edu
GAILEY, Kim ..... 970-943-3140.. 87 F
kgailey@western.edu
GAILLAT, Ana ..... 508-678-2811 231 B
ana.gaillat@bristolcc.edu
GAILLIARD, Gary ..... 817-735-2210 493 B
Gary.Gailliard@unthsc.edu
GAILOR, Kathleen ..... 845-451-1302 323 E
k_gailor@culinary.edu
GAINES, Adrienne, S ..... 334-833-4480.... 4 E
againes@huntingdon.edu
GAINES, Anne ..... 212-229-8933 334 C
gainesa@newschool.edu
GAINES, Chad ..... 660-248-6228 272 N
cgaines@centralmethodist.edu
GAINES, Christopher ..... 662-846-4020 267 A
cgaines@deltastate.edu
GAINES, Gina ..... 914-606-7612 352 G
gina.gaines@sunywcc.edu
GAINES, Glynnis ..... 254-299-8306 478 C
ggaines@mclennan.edu
GAINES, John ..... 615-936-2811 465 H
john.gaines@vanderbilt.edu
GAINES, Justin ..... 706-867-2781 133 A
justin.gaines@ung.edu
GAINES, Kim ..... 256-306-2592.... 2 F
kmg@calhoun.edu
GAINES, JR., Larry, R .. 856-225-6174 306 F
gaines@camden.rutgers.edu
GAINES, JR., Larry, R .. 856-225-6174 307 A
gaines@camden.rutgers.edu
GAINES, Randy ..... 208-282-2872 138 C
gainrand@isu.edu
GAINES, Shivaun, P ..... 973-655-7648 304 A
gainess@mail.montclair.edu
GAINES, Steven, D ..... 805-893-7363.. 72 D
gaines@bren.ucsb.edu
GAINEY, John ..... 601-366-8880 271 E
jgainey@wbs.edu
GAINEY, Karen, W ..... 864-488-4504 447 F
kgainey@limestone.edu
GAINOUS, Chrissy ..... 229-226-1621 132 E
cgainous@thomasu.edu
GAISER, J. Christopher 503-883-2308 406 I
cgaiser@linfield.edu
GAITAN, Deborah ..... 210-486-4454 466 K
dgaitan@alamo.edu
GAITERS-JORDAN,
Jacquelyn ..... 719-502-3078.. 84 J
jacquelyn.gaiters-jordan@ppcc.edu
GAITHER, Kimberly ..... 573-288-6340 274 C
kgaither@culver.edu
GAITHER, Sonya ..... 678-359-5078 126 E
sgaither@gordonstate.edu
GAITHER, Sophia ..... 704-216-6222 358 I
sogaither@livingstone.edu
GAJDARDZISKA-JOSIFOVSKA,
Marija ..... 414-229-5520 540 A
mgj@uwm.edu
GAJDOSIK, Olga ..... 262-554-2010 537 D
GAJEWSKI, Geoff ..... 920-832-6530 536 R
geoffrey.c.gajewski@lawrence.edu
GAJEWSKI, Jennifer ..... 410-704-2356 221 A
jgajewski@towson.edu
GAJEWSKI, Linda ..... 219-473-4217 165 A
lgajewski@ccsj.edu
GAJRIA, Meenakshi ..... 845-398-4154 341 H
mgajria@stac.edu
GALADIMA, Bulus ..... 562-903-4844.. 29 F
bulus.galadima@biola.edu
GALANES, Gloria ..... 417-836-5247 279 A
gloriagalanes@missouristate.edu
GALANSKI, Kay, A ..... 724-946-7218 439 D
galanska@westminster.edu
GALANSKY, Galia ..... 212-772-4511 319 E
galia.galansky@hunter.cuny.edu
GALARDI, Karen ..... 215-504-2000 420 K
kgalardi@holyfamily.edu
GALARRAGA,
Francesca ..... 866-621-0124.. 87 C
francesca.galarraga@rockies.edu
GALAS, James ..... 773-380-6805 163 E
jgalas@westwood.edu
GALASKA, Vickie ..... 419-448-3595 392 B
galaskavm@tiffin.edu
GALATOLO, Ron, D ..... 650-574-6550.. 64 B
galatolo@smccd.edu
GALAVIZ, Gina ..... 541-962-3496 405 G
ggalaviz@eou.edu
GALBALLY, JR.,
James, F ..... 201-559-6000 302 I
GALBAVY, Tiffany ..... 406-395-4875 288 I
tgalbavy@stonechild.edu
GALBIATI, Jacqueline ... 856-691-8600 301 H
jgalbiati@cccnj.edu
GALBIERZ, Todd ..... 636-922-8359 281 C
tgalbierz@stchas.edu
GALBRAITH, James, R .. 407-582-3420 118 I
jgalbraith1@valenciacollege.edu
GALBRAITH, Jennifer ..... 909-274-4600.. 54 J
jgalbraith@mtsac.edu
GALBRAITH, Mark ..... 619-849-2489.. 59 K
markgalbraith@pointloma.edu
GALBRAITH, OP,
Mary Sarah ..... 615-297-7545 455 A
srmsarah@aquinascollege.edu
GALBRAITH, Richard, A 802-656-2918 503 C
richard.galbraith@uvm.edu
GALBRAITH, Thomas ..... 530-226-4185.. 66 G
tgalbraith@simpsonu.edu
GALBREATH, Dodd ..... 615-966-1771 458 C
dodd.galbreath@lipscomb.edu
GALBREATH, Leslie ..... 660-562-1590 280 A
leslies@nwmissouri.edu
GALBREATH, Susan, C . 615-966-5952 458 C
susan.galbreath@lipscomb.edu
GALDIERI, Virginia ..... 908-852-1440 301 C
galdieriv@centenarycollege.edu
GALE, Andrea ..... 909-607-1236.. 39 F
andrea.gale@cmc.edu
GALE, Jennifer, D ..... 610-917-1488 438 G
jdgale@valleyforge.edu
GALE, Lewis ..... 209-946-2466.. 73 C
lgale@pacific.edu
GALE, Mary ..... 952-885-5437 263 I
mgale@nwhealth.edu
GALE, Nicole, L ..... 410-651-6458 219 H
nlgale@umes.edu
GALEA, Sandro ..... 617-638-4644 224 E
sgalea@bu.edu
GALEA'I, Seth, P ..... 684-699-9155 549 C
s.galeai@amsamoa.edu
GALEA'I-SCANLAN,
Lina ..... 684-699-9155 549 C
l.galeai-scanlan@amsamoa.edu
GALECKE, Robert, M ..... 972-721-5203 491 B
galecke@udallas.edu
GALELEI, Scott ..... 607-729-8915 324 H
sgalelei@ebi-college.com
GALEY, Frank, D ..... 307-766-4133 546 K
fgaley@uwyo.edu
GALGANO, Mark ..... 267-341-3545 420 K
mgalgano@holyfamily.edu
GALIANO, Carlos ..... 787-850-9303 558 A
carlos.galiano@upr.edu
GALICK, Robert ..... 815-825-2086 149 E
rob.galick@kishwaukeecollege.edu
GALIK, Barbara ..... 309-677-2850 140 H
barbara@bradley.edu
GALIL, Zvi ..... 404-894-8357 125 D
galil@gatech.edu
GALINDO, Emily ..... 530-752-0339.. 71 A
ecgalindo@ucdavis.edu
GALINDO, Gabriel ..... 520-287-5583.. 13 B
galindog@cochise.edu
GALINDO, Vickie ..... 575-527-7526 312 D
vigalind@nmsu.edu
GALINSKI, Bonnie ..... 978-542-2532 230 E
bgalinski@salemstate.edu
GALKIN, Daphne ..... 914-831-0413 322 D
dgalkin@cw.edu
GALL, Connie ..... 405-692-3258 398 I
cgall@macu.edu
GALL, Jen ..... 510-849-8241.. 57 G
jgall@psr.edu
GALL, Michael ..... 212-594-4000 349 J
mgall@tcicollege.edu

GALL RITCHIE, Amy, S . 800-287-8822 164 E ritcham@bethanyseminary.edu
GALLAGAN, Marilynn .. 978-656-3300 232 B gallaganm@middlesex.mass.edu
GALLAGHER, Abisola .... 201-200-3165 304 C agallagher@njcu.edu
GALLAGHER, Amber ..... 909-384-8687.. 62 C agallagher@sbccd.cc.ca.us
GALLAGHER, Amy .... 908-526-1200 305 G agallagh@raritanval.edu
GALLAGHER, Beth, E ..... 805-756-2236.. 32 E begallag@calpoly.edu
GALLAGHER, AA, Dennis, M .... 508-767-7033 222 D dgallagh@assumption.edu
GALLAGHER, Ed .... 256-766-6610.... 4 C egallagher@hcu.edu
GALLAGHER, Elizabeth . 925-631-4223.. 61 G egallagh@stmarys-ca.edu
GALLAGHER, Geraldine M, P .... 407-582-3155 118 I ggallagher@valenciacollege.edu
GALLAGHER, Helen ...... 256-215-4274.... 2 G hgallagher@cacc.edu
GALLAGHER, CSC, James, T .... 503-943-8011 410 H gallaghe@up.edu
GALLAGHER, Joan, M .. 316-295-5648 187 C gallagherj@friends.edu
GALLAGHER, Joanna .... 215-572-2187 412 F Gallagher@arcadia.edu
GALLAGHER, Jody .... 814-732-1269 430 G jgallagher@edinboro.edu
GALLAGHER, John .... 610-660-1164 434 G jgalla02@sju.edu
GALLAGHER, Karen ...... 607-753-4717 345 C karen.gallagher@cortland.edu
GALLAGHER, Karen, S .. 213-740-5756.. 74 D rsoedean@usc.edu
GALLAGHER, Kathleen .. 215-503-6959 436 F kathleen.gallagher@jefferson.edu
GALLAGHER, Leslie, D . 281-425-6301 477 F lgallagher@lee.edu
GALLAGHER, Lori .... 713-525-3592 493 J irishstudies@stthom.edu
GALLAGHER, Mary ...... 213-763-7040.. 52 A mgallagh@lattc.edu
GALLAGHER, Mary .... 213-763-7227.. 52 A gallagherm@lattc.edu
GALLAGHER, Mary Beth .... 314-719-3554 275 B mbgallagher@fontbonne.edu
GALLAGHER, Mary Beth .... 276-223-4765 517 F mgallagher@wcc.vccs.edu
GALLAGHER, Maureen .. 914-395-2385 342 C mgallagh@sarahlawrence.edu
GALLAGHER, Megan ..... 717-396-7833 429 H mgallagher@pcad.edu
GALLAGHER, Patricia .... 781-292-2416 226 G patricia.gallagher@olin.edu
GALLAGHER, Patrick ..... 412-624-4200 437 K pdg@pitt.edu
GALLAGHER, Patrick, G 978-478-3400 235 E pgallagher@northpoint.edu
GALLAGHER, Richard ... 914-968-6200 341 D richard.gallagher@archny.org
GALLAGHER, Scott .... 573-592-4337 286 A scott.gallagher@williamwoods.edu
GALLAGHER, Steve ...... 336-631-1217 372 B gallaghers@uncsa.edu
GALLAGHER, Susan, P . 518-629-8138 328 D s.gallagher@hvcc.edu
GALLAGHER, Suzanne .. 617-928-4026 234 D sgallagher@mountida.edu
GALLAGHER, Tanya, M 217-333-2131 162 A tmgallag@illinois.edu
GALLANT, Danny, R ..... 936-468-2203 484 A dgallant@sfasu.edu
GALLARDO, Gabriel ...... 206-543-2100 527 G
GALLARDO, Ignacio ...... 805-893-4412.. 72 D ignacio.gallardo@sa.ucsb.edu
GALLARDO, Mark .... 573-341-4981 284 C gallardom@mst.edu
GALLARDO, Ruben, C .. 915-831-6306 473 J rgalla16@epcc.edu
GALLART, Stephen .... 845-687-5187 350 I gallarts@sunyulster.edu
GALLATIN, Cynthia .... 203-582-8521.. 91 E cynthia.gallatin@quinnipiac.edu
GALLEGLY, Michael ...... 973-300-2306 308 F mgallegly@sussex.edu
GALLEGO, Hector, F ..... 919-516-4929 368 E hfgallego@st-aug.edu
GALLEGOS, Jeremy .... 316-295-5871 187 C jeremy_gallegos@friends.edu
GALLEGOS, Joel, A .... 704-687-7755 371 B jagalleg@uncc.edu
GALLEGOS, John .... 916-348-4689.. 43 K jgallegos@epic.edu
GALLEGOS, Jose .... 303-937-4200.. 80 A jgallegos@chu.edu
GALLEGOS, Paul .... 360-867-6368 522 J gallegos@evergreen.edu
GALLEGOS, Tommy ...... 972-860-4799 472 C tgallegos@dcccd.edu
GALLEN, Peter, C .... 864-592-4680 449 C gallenp@sccsc.edu
GALLENBERG, Dale .... 715-425-3841 540 E dale.gallenberg@uwrf.edu
GALLENTINE, Jerry, L ... 605-721-5225 452 J jgallentine@national.edu
GALLIANETTI, David, D 920-565-1119 536 Q gallianettidd@lakeland.edu
GALLIEN, Melissa, C .... 409-880-7011 488 F melissa.gallien@lamar.edu
GALLIGAN, Chad .... 623-935-8075.. 14 L chad.galligan@estrellamountain.edu
GALLIGAN, Chris .... 860-832-1764.. 88 D galliganc@ccsu.edu
GALLIGAN, Thomas, C . 603-526-3451 296 I tgalligan@colby-sawyer.edu
GALLIMORE, Anna .... 336-721-2852 368 F anna.gallimore@ssalem.edu
GALLIMORE, Sarah .... 717-815-6470 440 H sgallimo@ycp.edu
GALLINGER, Dawn .... 406-447-5179 286 D dgallinger@carroll.edu
GALLION, Melanie .... 843-525-8224 449 E mgallion@tcl.edu
GALLISATH, Glenda ...... 847-578-8787 157 G
GALLIVAN, Evan .... 617-262-5000 223 G Evan.Gallivan@the-bac.edu
GALLIVAN, Patrick, J .... 802-654-2557 502 H pgallivan@smcvt.edu
GALLIVAN, Thomas ...... 562-860-2451.. 37 L tgallivan@cerritos.edu
GALLMAN, Kathleen ..... 252-638-7233 362 A gallmank@cravencc.edu
GALLO, Eulogio .... 310-954-5080.. 29 I
GALLO, John, D .... 724-847-6796 419 B jdgallo@geneva.edu
GALLO, Kathleen .... 516-463-4074 328 A kathleen.gallo@hofstra.edu
GALLO, Kelly .... 562-902-3316.. 67 J kellygallo@scuhs.edu
GALLO, Liz .... 973-408-3097 301 J lgallo@drew.edu
GALLO, Maria .... 808-956-8234 135 J gallom@hawaii.edu
GALLON, Connie .... 931-540-2572 462 E cgallon@columbiastate.edu
GALLON, Dennis, P ...... 561-868-3500 109 H gallond@palmbeachstate.edu
GALLONIO, Anthony ..... 401-454-6636 442 B agalloni@risd.edu
GALLOUET, Catherine ... 315-781-3467 327 G gallouet@hws.edu
GALLOWAY, Alison .... 831-459-3885.. 72 E cpevc@ucsc.edu
GALLOWAY, Carolina ... 806-651-5309 486 D cgalloway@wtamu.edu
GALLOWAY, Curt .... 651-690-6980 263 V wcgalloway@stkate.edu
GALLOWAY, Cyndi .... 724-222-5330 428 B cmason@penncommercial.edu
GALLOWAY, Deborah, J .... 513-556-5054 393 B debi.galloway@uc.edu
GALLOWAY, Heather ..... 512-245-2266 489 C hg02@txstate.edu
GALLOWAY, Merrill .... 606-589-3079 197 D merrill.galloway@kctcs.edu
GALLOWAY, Peter .... 610-436-3307 432 B pgalloway@wcupa.edu
GALLOWAY, Robin .... 319-296-4292 179 B robin.galloway@hawkeyecollege.edu
GALLOWAY, Sheila .... 910-755-7312 360 E galloways@brunswickcc.edu
GALLOWAY, Tami .... 740-389-4636 386 B
GALLOWAY-PERRY, Rulisa .... 212-237-8601 319 F rgalloway@jjay.cuny.edu
GALLUCCI, Nikki .... 518-631-9836 351 A galluccn@uniongraduatecollege.edu
GALM, Molly, D .... 712-324-5061 182 A mgalm@nwicc.edu
GALM, Ruth .... 509-359-6567 522 C rgalm@ewu.edu
GALOVIC, John .... 216-373-5310 388 A jgalovic@ndc.edu
GALOYAN, Nazy .... 650-949-7772.. 45 A galoyannazy@fhda.edu
GALTNEY, Alfred .... 601-877-3965 266 C agaltney@alcorn.edu
GALUSKI, Bryan .... 336-272-7102 357 B bgaluski@greensboro.edu
GALVAN, Betty .... 210-434-6711 479 P bagalvan@lake.ollusa.edu
GALVAN, Dennis, C .... 541-346-5851 410 F dgalvan@uoregon.edu
GALVAN, Efren .... 714-432-5774.. 40 D egalvan@occ.cccd.edu
GALVAN, Joan .... 805-965-0581.. 64 N jcgalvan@sbcc.edu
GALVAN, Margie .... 361-593-3209 486 A margie.galvan@tamuk.edu
GALVAN, Michael .... 903-223-3013 486 C mgalvan@tamut.edu
GALVANONI, Mark .... 630-889-6661 154 E mgalvanoni@nuhs.edu
GALVEZ, Kathleen .... 718-982-2355 319 A kathleen.galvez@csi.cuny.edu
GALVIN, Jeanne .... 718-631-6226 320 F jgalvin@qcc.cuny.edu
GALVINHILL, Paul .... 508-793-3363 225 C pgalvin@holycross.edu
GALYEAN, Ann .... 325-574-7914 497 E agalyean@wtc.edu
GALYEAN, Michael .... 806-742-2808 489 F michael.galyean@ttu.edu
GALYEAN, Paul .... 903-586-2518 476 K pgalyean@jacksonville-college.edu
GALYON, Kim .... 800-290-4226 457 A kgalyon@hchs.edu
GAMACHE, Normand .... 401-454-6371 442 B ngamache@risd.edu
GAMBA, Raymond .... 415-239-3174.. 39 A rgamba@ccsf.edu
GAMBACINI, Michelle .. 203-591-5615.. 91 D mgambacini@post.edu
GAMBAIANA, Mark .... 660-785-4133 283 E markg@truman.edu
GAMBILL, Todd .... 765-455-9360 168 B tgambill@iuk.edu
GAMBINO, Ellen, M ..... 845-431-8954 324 D gambino@sunydutchess.edu
GAMBINO, Stephen ...... 610-436-2133 432 B sgambino@wcupa.edu
GAMBLE, Brad .... 417-328-1823 282 D bgamble@sbuniv.edu
GAMBLE, Carol .... 704-637-4411 355 H cgamble@catawba.edu
GAMBLE, Gregory .... 856-225-3999 307 A gambleg@camden.rutgers.edu
GAMBLE, Jackie .... 760-547-1800.. 45 B jgamble@fst.edu
GAMBLE, Jim .... 616-538-2330 243 C jgamble@gbcol.edu
GAMBLE, John, E .... 361-825-6045 485 F john.gamble@tamucc.edu
GAMBLE, Kay .... 334-556-2397.... 4 A kgamble@wallace.edu
GAMBLE, Melanie .... 972-860-4269 472 C mgamble@dcccd.edu
GAMBLE, Mort .... 304-829-7284 529 H mgamble@bethanywv.edu
GAMBLE, Mort .... 304-829-7111 529 H mgamble@bethanywv.edu
GAMBLE, Patrick, K .... 907-450-8000.. 10 G ua.president@alaska.edu
GAMBLE, Shawnia .... 505-786-4111 311 G sgamble@navajotech.edu
GAMBLE, Steven .... 575-562-2121 310 I steven.gamble@enmu.edu
GAMBLIN, Jeff .... 903-875-7355 479 I jeff.gamblin@navarrocollege.edu
GAMBOA, Anthony .... 773-481-8752 141 O agamboa@ccc.edu
GAMBOA, Anthony .... 773-481-8752 142 D agamboa@ccc.edu
GAMBOA, Larry .... 671-735-2359 549 G lgamboa@triton.uog.edu
GAMBOA, Noel .... 718-262-2372 321 B ngamboa@york.cuny.edu
GAMBRELL-BOONE, Letizia .... 804-524-5350 518 C lgambrell-boone@vsu.edu
GAMBRO, John, S .... 815-740-3829 162 F jgambro@stfrancis.edu
GAMELLI, Adele .... 413-572-5295 230 F agamelli@westfield.ma.edu
GAMER, Josh .... 608-785-9088 544 E gamerj@westerntc.edu
GAMER, Steve .... 858-822-0773.. 72 B sgamer@ucsd.edu
GAMMACK, David .... 703-284-1686 510 B david.gammack@marymount.edu
GAMMELL, William .... 860-723-0000.. 88 C gammellw@ct.edu
GAMMON, Marcia, L .... 480-245-7918.. 14 D marcia.gammon@ibcs.edu
GAMMON, Richard .... 937-255-6800 547 E richard.gammon@afit.edu
GAMMON, Wiley .... 478-289-2090 124 B wgammon@ega.edu
GANAHL, Gina .... 636-949-4501 276 L gganahl@lindenwood.edu
GANAS, Sean .... 617-824-8608 226 A sean_ganas@emerson.edu
GANAS, Sean .... 978-665-3599 229 D sganas@fitchburgstate.edu
GANCZ, Aharon .... 973-960-6670 305 E rgancz@aol.com
GANDHI, Ketan .... 856-351-2612 308 B kgandhi@salemcc.edu
GANDHI, Pratima, N .... 309-677-3123 140 H pratima@fsmail.bradley.edu
GANDICA, Esther .... 609-343-5688 299 G gandica@atlantic.edu
GANDRE, James .... 917-493-4477 331 I jgandre@msmnyc.edu
GANDU, Bobby .... 316-978-5675 192 D bobby.gandu@wichita.edu
GANDY, Ashley .... 404-364-8364 129 F agandy@oglethorpe.edu
GANDY, Beverly .... 310-506-4451.. 58 H beverly.gandy@pepperdine.edu
GANDY, Fredrick .... 815-836-5125 150 F gandyfr@lewisu.edu
GANDY, Rex .... 931-221-7676 461 C gandyr@apsu.edu
GANEM, Lisa .... 619-684-8794.. 56 B lganem@newschoolarch.edu
GANESAN, Arasu .... 910-672-1477 370 A aganesan@uncfsu.edu
GANESH, Jaishankar ..... 856-225-6217 307 A jganesh@camden.rutgers.edu
GANG, Martin (Marty) .. 209-575-7979.. 78 A gangm@yosemite.edu
GANGSTEAD, Sandra .... 478-445-4092 125 A sandra.gangstead@gcsu.edu
GANGWER, Val .... 540-665-4637 512 E vgangwer@su.edu
GANIO, Mary .... 619-482-6301.. 68 D mganio@swccd.edu
GANN, Alexander .... 516-367-6890 321 F ganna@cshl.edu
GANN, Brian .... 256-306-2441.... 2 F bgann@calhoun.edu
GANN, John .... 903-223-3114 486 C john.gann@tamut.edu
GANNAWAY, Anne, A ... 563-333-6283 182 E GannawayAnneM@sau.edu
GANNAWAY, Dale .... 575-492-4712 311 J dgannaway@nmjc.edu
GANNAWAY, Paula .... 806-720-7327 478 A paula.gannaway@lcu.edu
GANNETT-MALICK, Lynn .... 205-970-9218.... 7 D lynngm@sebc.edu
GANNON, Amy .... 608-663-2898 536 A agannon@edgewood.edu
GANNON, Debbie, K .... 515-263-6020 178 H dgannon@grandview.edu
GANNON, Kim .... 512-245-2371 489 C kg33@txstate.edu
GANNON, Marcy .... 301-934-7560 214 E marcyg@csmd.edu
GANNON, Susan .... 908-737-3461 303 C sgannon@kean.edu
GANNON, Violet .... 860-297-4033.. 92 A j.gannon@trincoll.edu
GANNT, Aubra, J .... 817-515-1450 484 B aubra.gantt@tccd.edu
GANO-PHILLIPS, Susasn .... 810-762-3234 251 E sganop@umflint.edu
GANONG, Rick .... 207-725-3822 209 H rganong@bowdoin.edu
GANSBERG, Alan, L ...... 818-401-1032.. 41 F agansberg@columbiacollege.edu
GANSCHOW, Darby ...... 605-677-6623 453 F darby.ganschow@usd.edu
GANSERT, Heidi .... 775-784-4778 295 H hgansert@unr.edu
GANSKE, Kathryn, M .... 540-678-4381 512 E kganske@su.edu
GANT, Jocelind, E .... 814-393-2109 430 E jgant@clarion.edu
GANT, Kim .... 828-726-2375 360 F kgant@cccti.edu
GANT, Kim .... 910-362-7003 360 G kgant@mail.cfcc.edu
GANTER, Sara .... 302-622-8000.. 93 D sganter@dcad.edu
GANTHER, Sonya .... 608-796-3930 542 H sganther@viterbo.edu
GANTMAN, Amy .... 310-665-6851.. 57 C agantman@otis.edu
GANTNER, Christine, M .... 920-424-3414 540 B gantner@uwosh.edu
GANTNER, Myrna .... 678-839-6445 133 F mgantner@westga.edu
GANTT, Bernard .... 718-289-5515 318 E bernard.gantt@bcc.cuny.edu
GANTT, Calvin .... 607-777-2791 343 D cgantt@binghamton.edu
GANTT, Kevin .... 913-758-6230 191 I ganttk@stmary.edu
GANTZ, Jennifer .... 316-942-4291 189 K gantzj@newmanu.edu

GANTZ, Katie, L ... 240-895-4491 218 B klgantz@smcm.edu
GANUES, Jeffrey ... 419-517-8894 385 F jganues@lourdes.edu
GANYARD, Paula ... 920-465-2537 539 F ganyardp@uwgb.edu
GANZEL, Toni ... 502-852-5192 201 A toni.ganzel@louisville.edu
GANZELL, Sandy ... 240-895-4371 218 B sganzell@smcm.edu
GAO, Jing ... 215-646-7300 420 A gao.j@gmercyu.edu
GAO, Lan ... 617-521-2721 236 F lan.gao@simmons.edu
GAONA, Selin ... 816-604-4190 278 A selin.gaona@mcckc.edu
GAPASIN, Nando ... 408-498-5102.. 40 E ngapasin@cogswell.edu
GAPUZ, Joanne ... 510-780-4500.. 50 G jgapuz@lifewest.edu
GARAFOLO, Rich ... 252-527-6223 363 G rmgarafolo48@lenoircc.edu
GARAJEEAGHI, Reza ... 773-477-4822.. 57 E rgarajeeaghi@pacificcollege.edu
GARANZINI, SJ, Michael, J ... 773-508-7301 151 E mgaranz@luc.edu
GARAVASO, Pieranno ... 320-589-6250 265 A garavapf@morris.umn.edu
GARAWITZ, Amy ... 212-229-5662 334 C garawita@newschool.edu
GARAY, Wendy ... 201-761-6028 307 K wgaray@saintpeters.edu
GARAYTA, Isabel ... 787-279-1912 553 H igarayta@bayamon.inter.edu
GARBADE, Henry ... 843-208-8910 450 D hgarbade@uscb.edu
GARBART, Hadley ... 410-225-2231 216 F hgarbart@mica.edu
GARBE, John ... 585-389-2038 334 B jgarbe6@naz.edu
GARBE, Theresa ... 423-461-8718 459 I tmgarbe@milligan.edu
GARBER, Alan ... 617-496-5100 227 D alan_garber@harvard.edu
GARBER, Barbara ... 415-351-3538.. 62 I bgarber@sfai.edu
GARBER, Christopher, W ... 260-982-5027 170 a cwgarber@manchester.edu
GARBER, Darrell ... 610-683-4253 431 B garber@kutztown.edu
GARBER, Gail ... 860-486-5519.. 92 C gail.garber@uconn.edu
GARBER, Kevin, S ... 913-971-3275 189 F ksgarber@mnu.edu
GARBER, Philip ... 847-214-7285 144 F pgarber@elgin.edu
GARBER BAX, Sharlene ... 660-543-4114 283 F bax@ucmo.edu
GARBINI, Dennis, J ... 973-761-9011 308 C dennis.garbini@shu.edu
GARBIOGLU, Ibrahim ... 412-237-3184 415 G igarbioglu@ccac.edu
GARBUTT, Keith ... 405-744-6799 400 C keith.garbutt@okstate.edu
GARCEAU, Hildebrand .. 805-525-4417.. 69 I hgarceau@thomasaquinas.edu
GARCES, Fred ... 619-388-7750.. 62 H fgarces@sdccd.edu
GARCIA, Abigail ... 602-331-7500.. 12 C agarcia@aii.edu
GARCIA, Adam ... 775-784-4689 295 H adam_garcia@police.unr.edu
GARCIA, Aida ... 787-725-6500 551 A agarcia@sju.albizu.edu
GARCIA, Albert ... 916-558-2337.. 53 B garciaaj@scc.losrios.edu
GARCIA, Alberto ... 787-848-0810 558 D alberto.garcia3@upr.edu
GARCIA, Alfredo ... 305-474-2445 112 B agarcia@stu.edu
GARCIA, Ana ... 408-848-4720.. 45 G
GARCIA, Andrea ... 707-638-5272.. 70 B andrea.garcia@tu.edu
GARCIA, Angelica ... 650-738-4100.. 64 E garciaa@smccd.edu
GARCIA, Ava, M ... 671-735-5558 549 E ava.garcia@guamcc.edu
GARCIA, Bo ... 517-483-9639 245 I garciab@lcc.edu
GARCIA, Bob ... 989-463-7299 239 B garciab@alma.edu
GARCIA, Bob ... 323-953-4000.. 51 E garciabj@lacitycollege.edu
GARCIA, Brenda, W ... 575-439-3697 312 B brgarcia@nmsu.edu
GARCIA, Brett ... 540-261-8401 512 J brett.garcia@svu.edu
GARCIA, Carlos ... 210-829-2717 492 B cagarci9@uiwtx.edu
GARCIA, Carol ... 718-779-1430 338 D cgarcia@plazacollege.edu
GARCIA, Carol ... 307-674-6446 546 H cgarcia@sheridan.edu
GARCIA, Caroline, M ... 520-621-3900.. 18 E cmgarcia@email.arizona.edu
GARCIA, Carrie ... 813-974-8375 116 B cagarcia@usf.edu
GARCIA, Cecilia ... 760-921-5478.. 58 C cecy.garcia@paloverde.edu
GARCIA, Christian ... 305-284-5451 118 A christian@miami.edu
GARCIA, Christina, M .. 626-914-8825.. 38 L cmgarcia@citruscollege.edu
GARCIA, Daisy ... 940-668-3330 479 K dgarcia@nctc.edu
GARCIA, Dan, D ... 806-651-2031 486 D ddgarcia@mail.wtamu.edu
GARCIA, Daniel ... 810-762-9752 245 A dgarcia@kettering.edu
GARCIA, David ... 262-551-5850 535 E dgarcia@carthage.edu
GARCIA, David ... 330-672-1001 384 H tgarcia5@kent.edu
GARCIA, Delia ... 305-348-3598 114 G garciade@fiu.edu
GARCIA, Diana ... 630-743-0680 163 D dgarcia@westwood.edu
GARCIA, Donna ... 575-461-4413 311 C donnag@mesalands.edu
GARCIA, Elena ... 787-780-0070 550 G egarcia@caribbean.edu
GARCIA, Eliezer ... 787-786-3030 556 E egarcia@ucb.edu.pr
GARCIA, Florence ... 406-247-3010 287 H florence.garcia@msubillings.edu
GARCIA, Frances ... 787-786-2412 556 F frances.garcia@uccaribe.edu
GARCIA, Gilda ... 512-245-2539 489 C gg18@txstate.edu
GARCIA, Gladys ... 661-654-3485.. 32 G ggarcia32@csub.edu
GARCIA, Heather ... 501-882-4434.. 19 E hngarcia@asub.edu
GARCIA, Helen ... 915-566-9621 497 D hgarcia@westerntech.edu
GARCIA, Herminia, C ... 561-732-4424 112 C hgarcia@svdp.edu
GARCIA, Irma ... 718-489-5490 340 E igarcia@sfc.edu
GARCIA, Isabel ... 352-723-5800 115 D agarcia2@dental.ufl.edu
GARCIA, Ivonne ... 740-427-5114 384 P garciai@kenyon.edu
GARCIA, Janet ... 605-221-3231 452 F jgarcia@kilian.edu
GARCIA, Janet, K ... 605-221-3231 452 F jgarcia@kilian.edu
GARCIA, Jessica ... 239-513-1135 119 C jgarcia@wolford.edu
GARCIA, Jessica ... 325-670-1448 474M jessica.garcia@hsutx.edu
GARCIA, Joann ... 760-252-2411.. 29 C jgarcia@barstow.edu
GARCIA, Joe ... 520-626-1197.. 18 E skipgarcia@email.arizona.edu
GARCIA, Jorge ... 787-779-2500 551 G ccat@coqui.edu
GARCIA, Joseph ... 843-953-6982 444 C jgarcia6@citadel.edu
GARCIA, Joyce ... 323-265-8732.. 51 D garciajb@elac.edu
GARCIA, Juan ... 956-364-4604 487 H juan.garcia@tstc.edu
GARCIA, Juan, B ... 575-439-3717 312 B jbgarcia@nmsu.edu
GARCIA, JR., Juan, G .. 956-326-2468 485 B jgarcia@tamiu.edu
GARCIA, Julie, A ... 703-323-2127 516 C jagarcia@nvcc.edu
GARCIA, Kellie ... 661-654-3206.. 32 G kgarcia@csub.edu
GARCIA, Kim, L ... 408-274-6700.. 63 O kim.garcia@sjeccd.org
GARCIA, Leslie ... 503-494-5657 408 D cedma@ohsu.edu
GARCIA, Luis ... 787-852-1430 552 J lgarcia@hccpr.edu
GARCIA, Luis ... 787-890-2681 557 C luis.garcia23@upr.edu
GARCIA, Luis, A ... 802-656-3390 503 C luis.garcia@uvm.edu
GARCIA, Lupe ... 805-893-4089.. 72 D lupe.garcia@sa.ucsb.edu
GARCIA, Margaret ... 323-343-3830.. 34 A mgarcia2@calstatela.edu
GARCIA, Maria ... 305-595-9500.. 97 H registrar@amcollege.edu
GARCIA, Maria ... 210-341-1366 479 N mgarcia@ost.edu
GARCIA, Melissa ... 956-721-5189 477 C melissagarcia@laredo.edu
GARCIA, Melody ... 212-659-7299 330 A mgarcia@tkc.edu
GARCIA, Meysaliz ... 787-878-6000 552 K mgarcia@icprjc.edu
GARCIA, Michael ... 973-761-9731 308 C michael.garcia@shu.edu
GARCIA, Mildred ... 657-278-3456.. 33 E presidentgarcia@fullerton.edu
GARCIA, Myra ... 909-593-3511.. 73 B mgarcia2@laverne.edu
GARCIA, Orlando ... 305-348-3357 114 G orlando.garcia@fiu.edu
GARCIA, Oscar, S ... 830-591-7330 483 A osgarcia@swtjc.edu
GARCIA, Penny, A ... 575-562-2443 310 I penny.a.garcia@enmu.edu
GARCIA, Pete ... 305-348-0504 114 G pete.garcia@fiu.edu
GARCIA, Peter ... 925-969-2001.. 42 E pgarcia@dvc.edu
GARCIA, Phil ... 916-278-8758.. 34 E garciap@csus.edu
GARCIA, Racquel ... 212-247-3434 331 G
GARCIA, Ramona ... 915-595-1935 476 R
GARCIA, Raul ... 215-717-3171 416 E raul.garcia@curtis.edu
GARCIA, Rene ... 305-237-3519 108 L rgarcia@mdc.edu
GARCIA, Rolando ... 954-201-8800.. 99 G rgarcia@broward.edu
GARCIA, Ron ... 505-454-3251 311 H garcia_rs@nmhu.edu
GARCIA, Rosella ... 212-678-3004 349 I garcia@exchange.tc.columbia.edu
GARCIA, Rudy ... 505-224-4342 310 F rudyg@cnm.edu
GARCIA, Sandra ... 713-221-8091 491 F garcias@uhd.edu
GARCIA, Sarah ... 208-769-3341 138 G sarah_garcia@nic.edu
GARCIA, Sergio, A ... 330-325-6259 387 F sgarcia@neomed.edu
GARCIA, Stella ... 956-364-4020 487 G stella.garcia@harlingen.tstc.edu
GARCIA, Stella, E ... 956-364-4020 487 H stella.garcia@tstc.edu
GARCIA, Steve ... 909-869-3020.. 32 F sngarcia@cpp.edu
GARCIA, Steve ... 760-245-4271.. 75 G steve.garcia@vvc.edu
GARCIA, Sunshine ... 805-437-3776.. 32 H sunshine.garcia@csuci.edu
GARCIA, Tania ... 805-437-8452.. 32 H tania.garcia@csuci.edu
GARCIA, Tara ... 657-278-5312.. 33 E tgarcia@fullerton.edu
GARCIA, Teresa ... 319-208-1920 183 B tgarcia@scciowa.edu
GARCIA, Tony ... 608-663-2256 536 A tgarcia@edgewood.edu
GARCIA, Valentin ... 559-791-2218.. 49 G val.garcia@portervillecollege.edu
GARCIA, Valeria ... 813-974-6987 116 B vgarcia@usf.edu
GARCIA, Veronica ... 858-642-8265.. 55 J vgarcia@nu.edu
GARCIA, Veronica ... 602-787-7668.. 15 B veronica.garcia@paradisevalley.edu
GARCIA, Viviana ... 760-750-4040.. 35 B vivigarcia@csusm.edu
GARCIA, Vladimir ... 787-725-8120 552 G vgarcia0068@eap.edu
GARCIA, Vonda ... 760-750-4852.. 35 B vgarcia@csusm.edu
GARCIA, Wanda ... 956-872-5051 482 G
GARCIA, William ... 310-660-3670.. 43 G wgarcia@elcamino.edu
GARCIA, William ... 973-596-5320 304 D william.garcia@njit.edu
GARCIA, Yolanda ... 707-527-4671.. 65 C ygarcia2@santarosa.edu
GARCIA-ACOSTA, Amarillys ... 787-746-1400 552 I agarcia@huertas.edu
GARCIA ADARNE, Ana . 787-878-9218 557 D ana.garcia6@upr.edu
GARCIA-ANOYO, Lemuel ... 512-404-4809 468 J lgarcia@austinseminary.edu
GARCIA-HANSON, Lisa . 541-552-7093 409 G garciahal@sou.edu
GARCIA-HILLS, Rosemarie ... 708-209-3257 143 D rosemarie.garcia@cuchicago.edu
GARCIA-LEON, Jose ... 212-799-5000 329 I
GARCIA-MILLER, Maria . 209-478-0800.. 47 F mgarcia@humphreys.edu
GARCIA-REYES, Ana, I .. 718-518-4313 319 D agreyes@hostos.cuny.edu
GARCIA RIVERA, Doris . 787-763-6700 552 H drdgarcia@se-pr.edu
GARCIA TOULET, Rafael ... 787-880-6577 557 D rafael.gaqrcia4@upr.edu
GARCON, Reginald ... 410-888-9048 216 G rgarcon@muih.edu
GARCIA, Tary ... 787-264-1912 554 C tdgarcia@intersg.edu
GARD, Daniel ... 708-209-3004 143 D Daniel.Gard@cuchicago.edu
GARD, Evelyn ... 203-285-2065.. 89 B egard@gwcc.commnet.edu
GARDE, Shekhar ... 518-276-6000 339 D gardes@rpi.edu
GARDEA, Oscar, M ... 415-338-2897.. 36 A omgardea@sfsu.edu
GARDELLA, Patrick ... 859-858-2130 192 O
GARDESTIG, Anders ... 785-227-3380 185 A gardestigae@bethanylb.edu
GARDI, Kerri ... 610-683-4647 431 B gardi@kutztown.edu
GARDIAL, Sarah ... 319-335-0866 175 H sarah-gardial@uiowa.edu
GARDIER PATERSON, Mary, T ... 570-340-6018 425 D paterson@marywood.edu
GARDIN, Carey, C ... 920-923-7617 537 A cgardin@marianuniversity.edu
GARDIN, Kendra ... 219-785-5519 172 A kgardin@pnc.edu
GARDINA, Jackie ... 802-831-1272 503 E jgardina@vermontlaw.edu
GARDINER, Duane ... 361-593-3098 486 A duane.gardiner@tamuk.edu
GARDINER, Duane ... 361-593-2170 486 A duane.gardiner@tamuk.edu
GARDINER, Jane, W ... 910-630-7158 359 C jgardiner@methodist.edu
GARDNER, Amanda ... 276-944-6922 507 E agardner@ehc.edu
GARDNER, Andy ... 704-669-4041 361 E gardnera@clevelandcc.edu
GARDNER, Beth ... 304-252-9547 530 I
GARDNER, Betina ... 859-622-1778 194 L betina.gardner@eku.edu
GARDNER, Bonnie, S ... 636-584-6502 274 J bonnie.gardner@eastcentral.edu
GARDNER, Brian ... 314-529-9387 277 B bgardner@maryville.edu
GARDNER, Brian ... 765-674-6901 169 C brian.gardner@indwes.edu
GARDNER, Butch ... 501-279-4454.. 21 A bgardner@harding.edu
GARDNER, Candice ... 801-863-3000 500 B candice.gardner@uvu.edu
GARDNER, Chris ... 910-410-1731 365 B csgardner@richmondcc.edu
GARDNER, Chris, L ... 864-597-4236 451 J gardnercl@wofford.edu
GARDNER, Clinton ... 202-274-2303.. 97 D president@potomac.edu
GARDNER, Craig ... 801-957-4601 500 E craig.gardner@slcc.edu
GARDNER, David ... 207-326-2485 211 G david.gardner@mma.edu
GARDNER, David, M ... 785-864-0229 191 G gardner@ku.edu
GARDNER, Denise ... 865-974-4373 465 D d.gardner@utk.edu
GARDNER, Dinelia ... 201-559-6154 302 I gardnerd@felician.edu
GARDNER, Greg ... 405-682-7534 399 K ggardner@occc.edu
GARDNER, Greg ... 405-682-7834 399 K ggardner@occc.edu
GARDNER, Henry ... 916-577-2200.. 77 F hgardner@jessup.edu
GARDNER, Iva ... 803-536-7000 448 H
GARDNER, James, A ... 716-645-2052 343 E jgard@buffalo.edu
GARDNER, Jared, L ... 208-535-5313 138 B jared.gardner@my.eitc.edu
GARDNER, Jeanne, W .. 719-549-3308.. 85 A jeanne.gardner@pueblocc.edu
GARDNER, Jeff ... 231-348-6624 248 A jgardner@ncmich.edu
GARDNER, John ... 509-335-3564 528 B gardnerj@wsu.edu
GARDNER, Judith ... 419-448-3420 392 B jgardner@tiffin.edu
GARDNER, Katherine, B ... 919-658-7746 369 B kgardner@umo.edu
GARDNER, Kelly, E ... 315-684-6363 347 A gardneke@morrisville.edu
GARDNER, Laura ... 815-802-8628 149 B lgardner@kcc.edu

GARY, Cynthia .... 405-682-1611 399 K
cynthia.d.gary@occc.edu
GARY, Kevin .... 610-527-0200 434 D
kevin.gary@rosemont.edu
GARY, Marc .... 212-678-8080 329 H
magary@jtsa.edu
GARY, William .... 216-987-3110 381 A
william.gary@tri-c.edu
GARZA, A. Lisa .... 512-245-2780 489 C
ag02@txstate.edu
GARZA, Andres .... 312-567-5755 147 E
agarza1@iit.edu
GARZA, Celina .... 956-364-4050 487 H
celina.garza@tstc.edu
GARZA, Edwardo .... 773-838-7500 142 C
egarza20@ccc.edu
GARZA, Felipe .... 361-593-2611 486 A
felipe.garza@tamuk.edu
GARZA, Fena .... 713-718-7748 475 C
fena.garza@hccs.edu
GARZA, Javier .... 254-968-9104 485 A
garza@tarleton.edu
GARZA, Kim .... 509-793-2010 520 B
kimg@bigbend.edu
GARZA, Lisa .... 972-883-4349 494 A
lisa.garza@utdallas.edu
GARZA, Noemi .... 956-872-2681 482 G
ngarza24@southtexascollege.edu
GARZA, Nora, R .... 956-721-5868 477 C
nrgarza@laredo.edu
GARZA, Rebecca, J .... 214-860-2618 472 F
rgarza@dcccd.edu
GARZA, Richie .... 806-371-5022 467 E
rrgarza@actx.edu
GARZA, Robert .... 214-860-8700 472 G
robertgarza@dcccd.edu
GARZA, Roberto .... 305-223-4561 111 J
rgarza@sjvcs.edu
GARZA, Roberto, A .... 956-326-2325 485 B
facil@tamiu.edu
GARZA, JR., Victor .... 408-274-7900.. 63 P
victor.garza@evc.edu
GARZA, Wanda .... 956-872-2770 482 G
wgarza@southtexascollege.edu
GARZA-RODERICK,
Jessie .... 209-833-7900.. 63 D
jgarza-roderick@deltacollege.edu
GARZIA, Mario, R .... 330-972-6978 392 H
mgarzia@uakron.edu
GASAWAY, Debbie .... 870-460-1622.. 24 C
gasaway@uamont.edu
GASBARRO, Dennis .... 716-614-5982 336 D
dgasbarro@niagaracc.suny.edu
GASCHK, Kenneth, K .... 262-243-5700 535 I
ken.gaschk@cuw.edu
GASCHO, Ron .... 303-762-6941.. 82 C
ron.gascho@denverseminary.edu
GASE, Chris .... 740-389-4636 386 B
gasec@mtc.edu
GASKELL, Carolyn .... 509-527-2133 528 A
carolyn.gaskell@wallawalla.edu
GASKELL, Millicent .... 610-519-6371 439 A
millicent.gaskell@villanova.edu
GASKIN, Elizabeth .... 772-462-5604 106 F
egaskin@irsc.edu
GASKIN, Keith .... 901-334-5811 459 B
kgaskin@memphisseminary.edu
GASKIN, Lori .... 805-730-4011.. 64 N
lgaskin@sbcc.edu
GASKINS, Frances .... 252-527-6223 363 G
fgaskins@lenoircc.edu
GASKINS, Laverne, L .... 229-333-5351 133 H
llgaskin@valdosta.edu
GASKINS, Leebrian, E .... 956-326-2310 485 B
lgaskins@tamiu.edu
GASOSKE, Betsy .... 314-434-4044 273 J
registrar@covenantseminary.edu
GASPAR, Leigh .... 781-891-2874 223 E
lgaspar@bentley.edu
GASPAR JARVIS,
Donna .... 207-602-2461 213 B
dgaspar@une.edu
GASPARD, Harold .... 504-671-6247 203 F
hgaspa@dcc.edu
GASPARIAN, Albert .... 714-895-8334.. 40 C
agasparian@gwc.cccd.edu
GASPARRO, Paul .... 740-699-3037 377 F
pgasparro@belmontcollege.edu
GASPER, Joseph .... 570-740-0372 425 A
jgasper@luzerne.edu
GASPER, William .... 213-763-7043.. 52 A
gasperw@lattc.edu
GASS, Melanie .... 704-403-1613 355 B
melanie.gass@carolinashealthcare.org
GASSEAU, Michelle .... 617-243-2150 227 K
mgaseau@lasell.edu
GASSIOT, Ken, W .... 706-886-6831 132 F
kgassiot@tfc.edu
GASSNER, Sheila .... 573-681-5084 276 K
gassners@lincolnu.edu

GAST, Brad .... 715-675-3331 544 A
gast@ntc.edu
GAST, Kristen .... 307-674-6446 546 H
kgast@sheridan.edu
GAST, Steve .... 712-279-1707 176 B
steve.gast@briarcliff.edu
GASTENVELD, Paula, M .... 434-736-2085 516 H
paula.gastenveld@southside.edu
GASTON, Aracelis .... 787-832-6000 552 K
agaston@icprjc.edu
GASTON, David .... 785-864-3624 191 G
adgaston@ku.edu
GASTON, Della, J .... 336-342-4261 365 E
gastond@rockinghamcc.edu
GASTON, Kenneth .... 410-651-7550 219 H
klgaston@umes.edu
GASTON, Lori .... 704-894-2208 356 D
logaston@davidson.edu
GASTON, Neely .... 704-527-9909 227 B
ngaston@gcts.edu
GASWICK, Kari .... 308-432-6487 292 B
kgaswick@csc.edu
GATCH, Denise, D .... 941-752-5325 114 B
gatchd@scf.edu
GATCHELL, Michael, D .... 864-294-2475 446 F
mike.gatchell@furman.edu
GATELY, Kevin .... 603-897-8232 298 E
kgately@rivier.edu
GATELY, Paul .... 401-841-7531 548 B
GATES, Amanda .... 617-585-1100 234 H
amanda.gates@necmusic.edu
GATES, Anne .... 216-421-7463 380 B
agates@cia.edu
GATES, Chris .... 907-745-3201.. 10 B
cgates@akbible.edu
GATES, Cynthia, K .... 405-585-5255 399 I
cynthia.gates@okbu.edu
GATES, Deb .... 315-279-5273 329 K
dgates@keuka.edu
GATES, Dennis .... 513-751-1206 376 A
dennis@aic-arts.edu
GATES, Glenn .... 973-618-3259 300 H
ggates@caldwell.edu
GATES, Jeffrey .... 315-792-3006 351 G
jtgates@utica.edu
GATES, Kathryn, F .... 662-915-7206 270 G
kfg@olemiss.edu
GATES, Kristen .... 510-780-4500.. 50 G
kgates@lifewest.edu
GATES, Leigh .... 312-697-3318 145 G
lgates@harrington.edu
GATES, Michelle .... 312-369-7215 143 C
mgates@colum.edu
GATES, Pamela, S .... 989-774-3342 240 O
gates1ps@cmich.edu
GATES, Reginald .... 817-515-5001 484 B
reginald.gates@tccd.edu
GATES, Robert .... 570-389-4015 430 B
rgates@bloomu.edu
GATES, William .... 409-880-1783 488 F
william.gates@lamar.edu
GATES, William, R .... 831-656-2754 548 A
bgates@nps.edu
GATES BLACK, L. Joy .... 817-515-5006 484 B
joy.gatesblack@tccd.edu
GATES-MILINER, Elaine .... 619-574-6909.. 57 E
egates@pacificcollege.edu
GATEWOOD, Algie, C .... 336-506-4150 359 N
algie.gatewood@alamancecc.edu
GATEWOOD, David .... 949-451-5650.. 67 E
dgatewood@ivc.edu
GATEWOOD, Dawn .... 434-381-6202 513 E
DGatewood@sbc.edu
GATEWOOD, Jessica .... 636-627-2253 276 L
jgatewood@lindenwood.edu
GATEWOOD, Marquis .... 713-525-3158 493 J
gatewom@stthom.edu
GATHERCOLE, Karen .... 321-674-7229 103 R
kgathercole@fit.edu
GATHERS, Avis .... 803-793-5241 445 F
gathersa@denmarktech.edu
GATHJE, Pete .... 901-334-5832 459 B
pgathje@memphisseminary.edu
GATHMAN, Allen .... 573-651-2682 282 C
agathman@semo.edu
GATLIN, Greg .... 617-573-8428 237 B
ggatlin@suffolk.edu
GATLIN, Kenda .... 206-281-2569 526 D
kgatlin@spu.edu
GATLING, Sharron .... 757-221-2617 506 J
sggatl@wm.edu
GATO, Stacy .... 434-791-7110 505 A
sgato@averett.edu
GATRELL, Jay, D .... 502-272-8259 193 E
jgatrell@bellarmine.edu
GATTAS, Joyce, M .... 619-594-1343.. 35 E
gattas@mail.sdsu.edu
GATTEN, Jeffrey .... 661-255-1050.. 31 B
jgatten@calarts.edu
GATTERDAM, Hans .... 817-272-3275 493 L
hgatt@uta.edu

GATTI, Robert, M .... 614-823-1250 390 C
rgatti@otterbein.edu
GATTIN, Tom .... 870-230-5135.. 21 B
gattint@hsu.edu
GATTIS, Tom .... 614-222-3237 380 F
tgattis@ccad.edu
GATTO, John .... 606-546-1728 200 E
jgatto@unionky.edu
GATTO, Joseph, C .... 716-652-8900 317 M
jgatto@cks.edu
GATTON, Pam .... 903-983-8207 477 A
pgatton@kilgore.edu
GATTON, Philip, S .... 618-453-4172 159 H
philg@pso.siu.edu
GATZA, Camille .... 360-752-8549 520 A
cgatza@btc.edu
GAUBATZ, Noreen .... 205-226-4671.... 2 C
ngaubatz@bsc.edu
GAUCHAT, Urs, P .... 973-596-3079 304 D
urs.p.gauchat@njit.edu
GAUD, Angela .... 305-443-9170 111 I
GAUDIN, Wendy .... 504-520-7469 209 E
wgaudin@xula.edu
GAUDINO, James, L .... 509-963-2111 520 E
gaudino@cwu.edu
GAUGH, Sherri .... 505-566-4007 312 K
gaughs@sanjuancollege.edu
GAUGHAN, Cheryl .... 619-849-2499.. 59 K
cherylgaughan@pointloma.edu
GAUGHF, Natalie, W .... 601-815-4236 270 H
nwgaughf1@umc.edu
GAUL, Julie, M .... 412-578-6042 414 I
gauljm@carlow.edu
GAUL, Volker .... 715-344-3063 543 D
volker.gaul@mstc.edu
GAULT, Brian, C .... 601-923-1671 270 B
bgault@rts.edu
GAULT, Carrie, J .... 724-458-2134 419 F
cjgault@gcc.edu
GAULT, Sandra .... 816-235-6234 284 A
gaults@umkc.edu
GAUMER, Richard, K .... 276-944-6966 507 E
rgaumer@ehc.edu
GAUNCE, Lori .... 606-759-7141 196 G
lori.gaunce@kctcs.edu
GAUNDER, Alisa .... 512-863-1418 483 G
gaundera@southwestern.edu
GAUNT, Victoria, F .... 410-864-4234 218 C
vgaunt@stmarys.edu
GAURMER, Terry .... 303-458-1629.. 85 G
tgaurmer@regis.edu
GAUS, Gregory, J .... 630-515-7307 152 H
ggausx@midwestern.edu
GAUSS, Nancy .... 970-943-2053.. 87 F
ngauss@western.edu
GAUSVIK, Tom .... 678-466-4000 122 J
thomasgausvik@clayton.edu
GAUT, LaDonna .... 903-923-2477 497 G
ldgaut@wileyc.edu
GAUTAM, Mridul .... 775-327-2363 295 H
mgautam@unr.edu
GAUTHIER, Ana, M .... 607-871-2082 314 J
gauthier@alfred.edu
GAUTHIER, Barry .... 920-424-1145 540 B
gauthieb@uwosh.edu
GAUTHIER, Bev .... 315-229-5011 341 E
GAUTHIER, Laureen .... 802-225-3205 502 F
laureen.gauthier@neci.edu
GAUTHIER, Theresa .... 585-785-1304 325 E
theresa.gauthier@flcc.edu
GAUTNEY, Michael, B .... 256-765-4274.... 9 D
mbgautney@una.edu
GAUVIN, Keith, R .... 203-837-9202.. 88 G
gauvink@wcsu.edu
GAVALETZ, Tami .... 618-374-5187 156 C
tami.gavaletz@principia.edu
GAVANUS, Michael .... 610-896-1249 420 J
mgavanus@haverford.edu
GAVARRA-OH,
Mary Anne .... 818-710-2234.. 51 H
gavarrm@piercecollege.edu
GAVER, Bob .... 402-363-5721 294 G
bagaver@york.edu
GAVIN, Carrie .... 850-599-3076 114 D
carrie.gavin@famu.edu
GAVIN, Jack .... 732-571-3536 303 G
gavin@monmouth.edu
GAVIN, M. F. Chip .... 207-973-3335 212 B
chip.gavin@maine.edu
GAVIN, Michael .... 414-297-6760 543 E
gavinmj@matc.edu
GAVIN, Michael, H .... 410-777-2776 213 E
mhgavin@aacc.edu
GAVIN, Mike .... 828-395-1295 363 D
mgavin@isothermal.edu
GAVIN, Todd .... 803-822-3233 447 H
gavint@midlandstech.edu
GAVLICK, Christopher .... 914-251-6916 346 D
christopher.gavlick@purchase.edu
GAVLIK, Deborah .... 937-512-3999 391 D
deborah.gavlik@sinclair.edu

GAW, Kevin, E .... 404-413-1835 126 D
kgaw@gsu.edu
GAWEL, Matthew .... 207-893-6601 211 H
mgawel@sjcme.edu
GAWELEK, Mary Ann .... 724-838-4216 435 E
gawelek@setonhill.edu
GAWENDA, Matt .... 312-922-1884 151 I
mgawenda@maccormac.edu
GAWLIK, Gail .... 815-740-5041 162 F
ggawlik@stfrancis.edu
GAWRONSKI, JR.,
Michael .... 845-341-4284 337 G
michael.gawronski@sunyorange.edu
GAWTHROP, Larry .... 810-762-0235 247 F
larry.gawthrop@mcc.edu
GAXIOLA, Thomas .... 559-443-8612.. 69 B
thom.gaxiola@fresnocitycollege.edu
GAXIOLA GAXIOLA,
Tannya, R .... 520-621-4130.. 18 E
tannya@email.arizona.edu
GAY, Bill .... 760-427-2314.. 47 G
bill.gay@imperial.edu
GAY, Cliff .... 478-289-2025 124 B
cgay@ega.edu
GAY, Gloria .... 919-536-7250 362 C
GAY, Jeff .... 315-684-6053 347 A
GAY, John .... 410-386-8434 214 B
jgay@carrollcc.edu
GAY, Judith .... 215-751-8351 416 B
jgay@ccp.edu
GAY, Michelle .... 704-403-1758 355 B
michelle.gay@carolinashealthcare.org
GAY, Shirley .... 252-862-1307 365 C
swgay6885@roanokechowan.edu
GAY, Thresa .... 404-270-5210 132 D
tgay@spelman.edu
GAY, Tim .... 510-780-4500.. 50 G
tgay@lifewest.edu
GAY, Wendy .... 413-775-1410 231 E
gay@gcc.mass.edu
GAYESKI, Diane .... 607-274-3895 328 H
gayeski@ithaca.edu
GAYLA, Shaffer .... 832-252-0750 470 L
gayla.shaffer@cbshouston.edu
GAYLARD, Cindy, M .... 850-973-1618 109 C
gaylardc@nfcc.edu
GAYLE, Robin .... 415-257-1305.. 43 D
robin.gayle@dominican.edu
GAYLE, Ruth, R .... 215-965-4002 426 G
rgayle@moore.edu
GAYLOR, IV, Charles .... 919-735-5151 367 A
cgaylor@waynecc.edu
GAYMER, Dawn, M .... 269-387-4207 252 I
dawn.gaymer@wmich.edu
GAYMON, Denise .... 256-551-1710.... 4 J
denise.gaymon@drakestate.edu
GAYMON, Joffery .... 850-474-3386 116 E
jgaymon@uwf.edu
GAYNOR, Dona, E .... 321-674-8102 103 R
dgaynor@fit.edu
GAYNOR, Julie .... 940-397-4353 478 G
julie.gaynor@mwsu.edu
GAYNOR, Michael, M .... 610-519-4000 439 A
michael.gaynor@villanova.edu
GAYNOR, Suzanne .... 607-431-4670 327 B
gaynors@hartwick.edu
GAYS, Elizabeth .... 931-372-3034 462 A
egays@tntech.edu
GAYTON, Jeffrey .... 541-552-6833 409 G
GaytonJ@sou.edu
GAZAL, Mary .... 724-805-2627 435 B
mary.gazal@stvincent.edu
GAZZALE, Bob .... 323-856-7600.. 27 H
bgazzale@afi.com
GEADELMANN,
Patricia, L .... 319-273-6144 176 A
patricia.geadelmann@uni.edu
GEAGHAN, Tom .... 216-687-4745 380 D
t.geaghan@csuohio.edu
GEALT, Adelheid .... 812-855-1039 167 J
gealta@indiana.edu
GEALT, Michael, A .... 989-774-3931 240 O
gealt1ma@cmich.edu
GEAR, Jackie .... 215-968-8416 413 F
jaclyn.gear@bucks.edu
GEAR, Lisa, L .... 213-738-6834.. 68 E
admissions@swlaw.edu
GEARAN, Mark, D .... 315-781-3309 327 G
gearan@hws.edu
GEARHART, Deb .... 740-593-2889 389 H
gearhart@ohio.edu
GEARHART, Gregory, L .... 717-691-6007 426 B
gearhart@messiah.edu
GEARHART, Rob .... 607-274-1909 328 H
rgearhart@ithaca.edu
GEARHART, Troy .... 610-917-1423 438 G
tegearhart@valleyforge.edu
GEARHART TURNER,
Patti .... 817-531-4401 490 C
pturner@txwes.edu

GEORGE, R. Dillard ...... 757-683-4156 510 I
rdgeorge@odu.edu
GEORGE, Rick .... 303-492-6591.. 86 E
rick.george@colorado.edu
GEORGE, Robert .... 941-756-0690 423 B
rgeorge@lecom.edu
GEORGE, Russell .... 970-675-3201.. 80 L
russell.george@cncc.edu
GEORGE, Sarah, B .... 801-581-6927 499 K
sgeorge@umnh.utah.edu
GEORGE, Scott .... 816-604-1087 277 F
scott.george@mcckc.edu
GEORGE, Shanika .... 713-623-2040 468 F
sgeorge@aii.edu
GEORGE, Simone, M .... 302-356-6898.. 94 G
simone.m.george@wilmu.edu
GEORGE, Stacy .... 513-529-1782 386 K
woodrus@miamioh.edu
GEORGE, Susan .... 304-473-8080 534 G
george@wvwc.edu
GEORGE, Tami, B .... 910-272-3541 365 D
tgeorge@robeson.edu
GEORGE, Terrance, C ... 270-745-3978 201 D
chris.george@wku.edu
GEORGE, Thomas, F .... 314-516-5252 284 B
tfgeorge@umsl.edu
GEORGE, Timothy, F .... 205-726-2632.... 6 F
tfgeorge@samford.edu
GEORGE, Viji, D .... 914-337-9300 323 A
viji.george@concordia-ny.edu
GEORGE, William, D .... 570-577-1228 413 E
wdgeorge@bucknell.edu
GEORGE-DYE, Amanda . 989-775-4123 249 F
george-dye.amanda@sagchip.edu
GEORGE-ROBINSON,
Avril .... 973-877-3040 302 F
agrobinson@essex.edu
GEORGE-TAYLOR,
Mosunmola .... 423-697-2552 462 C
mosunmola.georgetaylor@
chattanoogastate.edu
GEORGENES, George .... 617-850-1317 227 F
gag@hchc.edu
GEORGES, Anthony, C .. 314-516-5508 284 B
tony_georges@umsl.edu
GEORGES, John .... 212-966-0300 334 D
jgeorges@nyaa.edu
GEORGES, Sean .... 340-693-1112 559 B
sgeorge@uvi.edu
GEORGESON, Lance ..... 425-249-4752 527 D
lance.georgeson@tlc.edu
GEORGIOPOULOS,
Michael .... 407-823-5338 115 C
michaelg@ucf.edu
GEORGIOU, Tina .... 212-343-1234 332 I
tgeorgiou@mcny.edu
GEORGO, Maria .... 352-854-2322 100 P
georgom@cf.edu
GEORGOPOULOS, Terri 707-826-3739.. 35 D
tmg315@humboldt.edu
GEPHART, JR.,
George, W .... 215-299-1044 417 E
presidentsoffice@ansp.org
GERA, Holly, P .... 973-655-5234 304 A
gerah@mail.montclair.edu
GERACI, Luci .... 718-990-2023 340 G
geracil@stjohns.edu
GERAGHTY, John .... 323-563-5929.. 38 C
johngeraghty@cdrewu.edu
GERAGHTY, Melissa ..... 425-388-9572 522 I
mgeraghty@everettcc.edu
GERALD, Trudy .... 619-388-3522.. 62 F
tgerald@sdccd.edu
GERAMI, Keyvan .... 314-286-3670 280 I
kgerami@ranken.edu
GERARD, Debra .... 714-480-7450.. 60 F
gerard_debra@rsccd.edu
GERARD, Matthew, C .... 402-280-5746 290 B
mgerard@creighton.edu
GERARD, Pam .... 319-895-5267 177 A
pgerard@cornellcollege.edu
GERARD, Phil .... 864-242-5100 443 G
GERARD, Stacey .... 252-940-6241 360 B
stacey.gerard@beaufortccc.edu
GERARDO, Debbie .... 770-962-7580 127 C
dgerardo@gwinnetttech.edu
GERASSIMIDES, Gus ..... 859-985-3158 193 F
gus_gerassimides@berea.edu
GERBASI, Iris .... 714-997-6676.. 38 B
gerbasi@chapman.edu
GERBER, Andrew .... 404-894-2000 125 D
andrew.gerber@gtri.gatech.edu
GERBER, Brian .... 229-333-5353 133 H
blgerber@valdosta.edu
GERBER, Brian, L .... 229-333-5950 133 H
blgerber@valdosta.edu
GERBER, Cheryl .... 724-946-7102 439 D
gerberca@westminster.edu
GERBER, Elizabeth, L .... 815-599-3421 146 B
liz.gerber@highland.edu
GERBER, Gary .... 870-245-5129.. 22 C
gerberg@obu.edu
GERBER, Molly .... 215-955-1061 436 F
molly.gerber@jefferson.edu
GERBER, Nathan .... 801-863-7973 500 B
Nathan.Gerber@uvu.edu
GERBER, Sue .... 201-200-3042 304 C
sgerber@njcu.edu
GERBERRY, Jeffrey .... 614-947-6007 382 H
jeffrey.gerberry@franklin.edu
GERBSCH, Julie .... 912-344-2600 120 D
julie.gerbsch@armstrong.edu
GERBSCH, Reinhold ...... 912-650-5682 131 F
rgerbsch@southuniversity.edu
GERDA, Joseph .... 661-362-3452.. 40 H
joseph.gerda@canyons.edu
GERDES, Darin .... 843-574-3220 444 B
dgerdes@csuniv.edu
GERDICH, Michael .... 724-805-2895 435 B
michael.gerdich@email.stvincent.edu
GERDRUM, Kacie .... 541-684-7288 407 I
kgerdrum@nwcu.edu
GERE, Nicholas .... 207-602-2011 213 B
ngere@une.edu
GEREAUX, Teresa, T ..... 540-375-2282 512 B
gereaux@roanoke.edu
GEREMIA, Kenneth .... 413-528-7291 222 F
kgeremia@simons-rock.edu
GERENZ, Eileen .... 781-239-2522 231 G
egerenz@massbay.edu
GERETY, RSM, Jane ..... 401-341-2337 442 D
jane.gerety@salve.edu
GERGER, Rick .... 314-246-8708 285 G
rickgerger06@webster.edu
GERGES, Marilia .... 931-540-2618 462 E
mgerges@columbiastate.edu
GERHARDT, Cassie .... 701-777-4200 373 G
cassie.gerhardt@und.edu
GERHARDT, Mark .... 605-995-7174 452 H
mark.gerhardt@mitchelltech.edu
GERHARDT, Winifred .... 440-826-2222 377 D
wgerhard@bw.edu
GERHARDT,
Winifred, W .... 440-826-8002 377 D
wgerhardt@bw.edu
GERHART, Phillip, M .... 812-488-2651 173 H
pg3@evansville.edu
GERHART, Robert .... 229-391-4850 119 F
rgerhart@abac.edu
GERHOFF, Sondra .... 866-251-3244.. 98 A
GERIG, Jill .... 912-478-5367 126 B
jgerig@georgiasouthern.edu
GERIGUIS, David .... 951-785-2002.. 49 I
dgerigui@lasierra.edu
GERIK, Debbie .... 254-659-7704 475 A
debgerik@hillcollege.edu
GERIN, Jean-Louis .... 802-225-3356 502 F
jean-louis.gerin@neci.edu
GERING, Jon .... 660-785-4248 283 E
jgering@truman.edu
GERITY, Patrick, E .... 724-925-4219 439 F
gerityk@wccc.edu
GERKEN, Keith .... 907-796-6496.. 11 A
william.gerken@uas.alaska.edu
GERKEN, Stacey .... 715-346-3553 541 A
sgerken@uwsp.edu
GERKIN, Jeffrey, G .... 865-974-3131 465 D
jgerkin@utk.edu
GERKO, Danielle .... 814-262-3825 429 K
dgerko@pennhighlands.edu
GERL, Beth, R .... 410-857-2244 217 A
bgerl@mcdaniel.edu
GERLACH, Alysa .... 617-373-5144 235 D
GERLACH, David, M ...... 217-732-3155 150 H
dgerlach@lincolncollege.edu
GERLACH, Jeanne, M ... 817-272-5476 493 L
gerlach@uta.edu
GERLACH, Karen .... 202-884-9203.. 97 A
gerlachk@trinitydc.edu
GERMAN, Deborah .... 407-266-1000 115 C
deborah.german@ucf.edu
GERMAN, James, D .... 973-655-4382 304 A
GERMAN, Lisa .... 256-352-8306.. 10 A
lisa.german@wallacestate.edu
GERMANO, William .... 212-353-4274 323 B
germano@cooper.edu
GERMANY, Sylvia .... 256-726-8218..... 6 C
germany@oakwood.edu
GERMERAAD,
Stephanie .... 310-954-5080.. 29 I
GERMIC, Stephen, A ..... 406-657-1020 288 G
stephen.germic@rocky.edu
GERN, William, A .... 307-766-5353 546 K
willger@uwyo.edu
GERNERT, Maureen, C . 203-837-8266.. 88 G
gernertm@wcsu.edu
GERNES, Todd, S .... 508-565-1946 237 A
tgernes@stonehill.edu
GEROMEL, Peter .... 610-292-9852 433 J
pgeromel@reseminary.edu
GEROSIMO, Veronica ... 516-876-3079 345 E
gerosimov@oldwestbury.edu
GERRETSEN, Amy, L ..... 920-748-8353 538 I
gerretsena@ripon.edu
GERRITY, Nancy .... 405-682-7587 399 K
ngerrity@occc.edu
GERSEY, Martin, L .... 574-520-5522 168 F
mgersey@iusb.edu
GERSH, Geniene, M ..... 269-387-1880 252 I
geniene.m.gersh@wmich.edu
GERSH, Sheila .... 914-674-7339 332 E
sgersh@mercy.edu
GERSHEN, Jay, A .... 330-325-6263 387 F
president@neomed.edu
GERSHMAN, Richard .... 615-383-4848 466 F
rgershman@watkins.edu
GERSICH, Frank .... 309-457-2119 153 B
fgersich@monmouthcollege.edu
GERST, Bernard .... 410-704-2505 221 A
bgerst@towson.edu
GERSTEIN, Dean .... 909-607-9406.. 39 E
dean.gerstein@cgu.edu
GERSTEN, Karen .... 619-684-8807.. 56 B
karen.gersten@newschoolarch.edu
GERSTENBERGER, Julie 806-894-9611 482 F
jgerstenberger@southplainscollege.edu
GERSTENBERGER,
Shawn .... 702-895-1565 295 G
shawn.gerstenberger@unlv.edu
GERSTL-PEPIN,
Cynthia, L .... 802-656-3424 503 C
cynthia.gerstl-pepin@uvm.edu
GERSZEWSKI,
Raymond, H .... 701-788-4770 374 A
Ray.Gerszewski@mayvillestate.edu
GERTH, Daniel .... 314-516-7197 284 B
gerthd@umsl.edu
GERTH, Laura .... 415-422-2654.. 74 C
lgerth@usfca.edu
GERTNER, Kimberly, A . 843-953-5758 445 B
gertnerka@cofc.edu
GERTS, John .... 231-843-5850 252 H
jkgerts@westshore.edu
GERTSON, Katherine ..... 212-799-5000 329 I
GERTZ, Genie .... 202-651-5653.. 95 C
genie.gertz@gallaudet.edu
GERTZ, Tanya, M 563-387-1536 180M
gertta01@luther.edu
GERVASI, Robert .... 217-228-5432 156 D
gervasi@quincy.edu
GERZINA, Gretchen ...... 413-577-3902 228 F
dean@honors.umass.edu
GERZINA, Holly, A .... 330-325-6740 387 F
hgerzina@neomed.edu
GESO, Cristina, A .... 215-895-1674 417 E
cag58@drexel.edu
GESSLER, Klaus .... 845-431-8939 324 D
gessler@sunydutchess.edu
GESSNER, James, C ...... 570-389-4105 430 B
jgessner@bloomu.edu
GESSNER, James, R ..... 218-722-4000 255 F
jimg@dbumn.edu
GESTOSO, Llloyd .... 215-702-4275 414 C
lgestoso@cairn.edu
GESTRING, Sheila .... 605-677-5255 453 F
sheila.gestring@usd.edu
GETCHELL, JR.,
Charles, M .... 603-641-7320 298 F
cgetchell@anselm.edu
GETCHELL, Jeffrey .... 303-964-5429.. 85 G
jgetchell@regis.edu
GETCHELL,
Stephanie, L .... 919-530-7824 370 C
getchells@nccu.edu
GETKIN, Ann .... 412-924-1369 433 E
agetkin@pts.edu
GETMAN, Meghan .... 315-792-7264 348 D
meghan.getman@sunyit.edu
GETSINGER, Joseph ..... 856-415-6209 306 C
jgetsinger@rcgc.edu
GETSY, David .... 312-899-1294 158 J
dgetsy@saic.edu
GETTING, Kris, A .... 651-962-6168 265 F
kagetting@stthomas.edu
GETTING-STRAESSER,
Meghan .... 718-281-5144 320 F
mstraesser@qcc.cuny.edu
GETTINGS, Michael ...... 540-362-6432 508 D
mgettings@hollins.edu
GETTY, JacQui .... 651-523-2475 256 B
jgetty01@hamline.edu
GETTY, Larry, R .... 785-628-4513 187 A
lgetty@fhsu.edu
GETTY, Marc, D .... 304-326-1258 530 G
mgetty@salemu.edu
GETZ, Dan .... 715-634-4790 536 P
dgetz@lco.edu
GETZ, Karen .... 724-266-3838 437 G
kgetz@tsm.edu
GETZEN, Bruce .... 808-245-8355 136 F
bgetzen@hawaii.edu
GEU, Thomas .... 605-677-5443 453 F
thomas.geu@usd.edu
GEUDER, Maridith .... 662-329-7119 269 B
mgeuder@muw.edu
GEVITZ, Norman .... 660-626-2522 271 G
ngevitz@atsu.edu
GEYE, Trina .... 254-968-9400 485 A
geye@tarleton.edu
GEYER, Dennis .... 916-278-3901.. 34 E
dgeyer@csus.edu
GEYER, Enid .... 518-262-5586 314 I
geyere@mail.amc.edu
GEYER, Enid .... 518-262-6008 314 I
geyere@mail.amc.edu
GEYER, Mariann, K ...... 412-392-3805 433 F
mgeyer@pointpark.edu
GHADIALI, Khushroo .... 575-234-9414 312 C
khushroo@nmsu.edu
GHAHRAMANI, Saeed .. 413-782-1218 238 A
sghahram@wne.edu
GHAMMACHI, Gabe ...... 502-456-6504 200 B
gghammachi@sullivan.edu
GHAN, Mark .... 775-445-4468 296 A
mark.ghan@wnc.edu
GHANEM, Salma .... 312-362-8610 143 G
sghanem@depaul.edu
GHANNADIAN,
F. Frank .... 813-253-6221 118 H
fghannadian@ut.edu
GHARAKHANIAN,
Anahid .... 213-738-6786.. 68 E
academicaffairs@swlaw.edu
GHARIB, Morteza .... 626-395-6365.. 31 D
vpr@caltech.edu
GHAZARIAN, Esther, A . 781-768-7280 236 A
esther.ghazarian@regiscollege.edu
GHAZARYAN, Ashot ...... 510-987-9452.. 27 K
GHAZI-BIRRY, Hani ...... 801-375-5125 499 A
hsgbirry@rmuohp.edu
GHEE, Harry .... 910-323-5614 355 E
dean@ccbs.edu
GHERKE, Amy .... 304-865-6034 530 F
amy.gherke@ovu.edu
GHILANI, Mary .... 570-740-0456 425 A
mghilani@luzerne.edu
GHILONI, Adam .... 212-749-2802 331 I
aghiloni@msmnyc.edu
GHIO, Frederick, W ...... 401-456-8201 442 A
fghio@ric.edu
GHOLSON, Shari .... 270-534-3372 197 E
shari.gholson@kctcs.edu
GHORASHI, Bahman ..... 931-372-3224 462 A
bghorashi@tntech.edu
GHORAYEB, Samir .... 409-984-6484 488 H
samir.ghorayeb@lamarpa.edu
GHOSAL, Bobby .... 601-928-6213 268 G
bobby.ghosal@mgccc.edu
GHOSH, Avijit .... 312-355-5706 161 F
ghosha@uic.edu
GHOSH, Guru .... 540-231-3205 518 B
gghosh@vt.edu
GHOSH, Sibdas .... 914-633-2207 328 F
sghosh@iona.edu
GHOSH, Soumitra .... 217-228-5432 156 D
ghoshso@quincy.edu
GHOUS, Mostafa .... 510-981-2877.. 58 J
mghous@peralta.edu
GHYMN, Kyung-il .... 770-279-0507 124 F
Kyung.il.ghymn@gcuniv.edu
GIACCHETTI, Richard .... 408-554-4982.. 65 A
rgiacchetti@scu.edu
GIACOMINI, Michael .... 626-229-1300.. 50 E
GIACONA, Nick .... 505-984-6110 312 J
ngiacona@sjc.edu
GIAMARTINO, Gary, A .. 215-951-1040 422 F
giamartino@lasalle.edu
GIAMBRA, Leonard, M . 860-701-6679 548 H
leonard.m.giambra@uscg.mil
GIAMPAOLI,
Michael, J .... 203-576-4168.. 92 B
gmichael@bridgeport.edu
GIAMPIETRO, Michael .. 413-565-1000 222 G
mgiampietro@baypath.edu
GIANCHETTA, Larry, D .. 406-243-6195 287 D
larry.gianchetta@umontana.edu
GIANNATTASIO,
Joseph .... 305-428-5700 109 A
giannatj@aii.edu
GIANNATTASIO,
Joseph .... 215-567-7080 412 G
jgiannattasio@aii.edu
GIANNESCHI, Matt .... 970-945-8691.. 80 D
mgianneschi@coloradomtn.edu
GIANNET, Stanley, M ... 813-527-6620 110 B
giannes@phsc.edu
GIANNINI, Gaetan .... 610-606-4666 415 A
gtgianni@cedarcrest.edu

GILBERT, Peter, J ... 920-832-7353 536 R peter.j.gilbert@lawrence.edu
GILBERT, Peter, M ... 610-758-3034 424 B pmg207@lehigh.edu
GILBERT, Regina ... 615-383-4848 466 F rgilbert@watkins.edu
GILBERT, Sharon ... 603-542-7744 297 D sgilbert@ccsnh.edu
GILBERT, Susan, M ... 530-752-3136.. 71 A smvgilbert@ucdavis.edu
GILBERT, Susan, P ... 678-547-6438 128 G gilbert_sp@mercer.edu
GILBERT, Teresa ... 423-478-7702 460 C tgilbert@ptseminary.edu
GILBERT, Timothy ... 804-204-1221 505 B tgilbert@btsr.edu
GILBERT, Trent ... 309-457-2210 153 B tgilbert@monmouthcollege.edu
GILBERTSON, Rita ... 641-585-8140 183 I gilbertsr@waldorf.edu
GILBERTSON, Troy ... 218-755-2965 258 B tgilbertson@bemidjistate.edu
GILCHREST, Kendel ... 334-683-5108.... 5 D kgilchrest@judson.edu
GILCHRIST, Cheryl, B ... 502-852-8139 201 A cbgilc01@louisville.edu
GILCHRIST, Debbie ... 956-665-2140 494 C gilchrist@utpa.edu
GILCHRIST, Debra ... 253-964-6584 525 C dgilchrist@pierce.ctc.edu
GILCHRIST, Graham ... 386-481-2097.. 99 F gilchrisstg@cookman.edu
GILCHRIST, James, A ... 269-387-2382 252 I james.gilchrist@wmich.edu
GILCHRIST, Joseph ... 239-513-1122 106 E jgilchrist@hodges.edu
GILCHRIST, Lou Ann ... 660-785-4111 283 E lcg@truman.edu
GILCREASE, Kathy ... 936-294-1012 489 A gilcrease@shsu.edu
GILCREAST, Emily ... 401-598-1000 441 D EGilcreastt@jwu.edu
GILDARD, John, T ... 845-575-3000 331 L John.Gildard@marist.edu
GILDAWIE, Janice ... 413-528-7698 222 F jgildawie@simons-rock.edu
GILDEN, Bruce, F ... 858-499-0202.. 40 G bgilden@coleman.edu
GILDERSLEEVE, Elizabeth, T ... 781-283-2376 237 F egilders@wellesley.edu
GILDERSLEEVE, Susan, M ... 402-472-3886 293 H sgildersleeve1@unl.edu
GILE, Joseph ... 316-942-4291 189 K gilej@newmanu.edu
GILE, Shelby ... 802-485-2658 502 G sgile@norwich.edu
GILES, JR., Henry, C ... 864-592-4616 449 C gilesh@sccsc.edu
GILES, Marsha ... 617-537-6803 152 C magiles@mckendree.edu
GILES, Pam ... 276-523-2400 516 A pgiles@me.vccs.edu
GILES, Roger, W ... 870-235-4008.. 23 D rwgiles@saumag.edu
GILES, Timothy, W ... 904-620-4200 116 A timothy.giles@unf.edu
GILES-HISER, Gina ... 614-287-2860 380 G ggileshiser@cscc.edu
GILFERT, Christy ... 941-637-5678 104 G cgilfert@fsw.edu
GILFILLAN, Margaret ... 412-392-3994 433 F mgilfillan@pointpark.edu
GILGOUR, Joe ... 660-596-7393 282 H jgilgour@sfccmo.edu
GILKER, Bill ... 817-760-5504 475 A wmgilker@hillcollege.edu
GILKERSON, Tammeil ... 510-235-7800.. 42 D tgilkerson@contracosta.edu
GILKEY, Shane, L ... 740-593-9813 389 H gilkeys@ohio.edu
GILL, Allison ... 978-837-5174 233 G gilla@merrimack.edu
GILL, Ann, M ... 970-491-5421.. 81 D ann.gill@colostate.edu
GILL, Anne, M ... 617-989-4193 237 G gilla@wit.edu
GILL, Barbara, A ... 301-314-8350 219 D bgill@umd.edu
GILL, Barbara, A ... 301-314-8279 219 D
GILL, Barbara, J ... 850-201-6570 117 B gillb@tcc.fl.edu
GILL, Casey ... 937-327-7800 395 I gillc@wittenberg.edu
GILL, Casey ... 937-327-6231 395 I
GILL, Chris ... 515-271-3918 177 K chris.gill@drake.edu
GILL, D. Christopher ... 573-288-6322 274 C cgill@culver.edu
GILL, Dennis ... 541-881-5915 410 D dgill@tvcc.cc
GILL, Irene ... 325-235-7340 488 C irene.gill@tstc.edu
GILL, Jamie, W ... 727-864-8206 101 P gilljw@eckerd.edu
GILL, Janet ... 712-274-6400 184 A janet.gill@witcc.edu
GILL, Janet ... 303-333-4224.. 79 D
GILL, Jason ... 847-866-3987 145 C jason.gill@garrett.edu
GILL, Jeffery, A ... 574-372-5100 166 D gillja@grace.edu
GILL, Kathleen ... 914-633-2201 328 F kgill@iona.edu
GILL, Kathleen ... 516-299-4258 330 F kathleen.gill@liu.edu
GILL, Keith ... 804-289-8345 513 M kgill@richmond.edu
GILL, Lanae ... 313-993-1230 250 H gillla@udmercy.edu
GILL, Lee, A ... 330-972-7522 392 H lee16@uakron.edu
GILL, Mark ... 970-491-6211.. 81 D mark.gill@colostate.edu
GILL, Michele ... 402-844-7748 292 G micheleg@northeast.edu
GILL, Nancy ... 805-437-8456.. 32 H nancy.gill@csuci.edu
GILL, Nicholas ... 207-216-4467 211 F ngill@yccc.edu
GILL, Paula ... 615-460-6184 455 D paula.gill@belmont.edu
GILL, Rebecca ... 828-884-8233 355 A rebecca.gill@brevard.edu
GILL, Russell ... 623-261-0009 144 A rgill@devry.edu
GILL, Ruth ... 410-334-2928 221 E rgill@worwic.edu
GILL, Sandra ... 630-829-6216 140 A sgill@ben.edu
GILL, Sean ... 951-827-6063.. 72 A sean.gill@ucr.edu
GILL, Steven ... 609-258-3466 305 C sgill@princeton.edu
GILL, Tom ... 503-338-2368 405 B tgill@clatsopcc.edu
GILL-JACOBSON, Roseann ... 419-824-3829 385 F rgill-jacobson@lourdes.edu
GILLAHAN, Sheilah ... 731-286-3316 462 F gillahan@dscc.edu
GILLAM WEIR, Linda ... 501-420-1200.. 19 B linda.gillam@arkansasbaptist.edu
GILLAN, Maria ... 973-684-5904 304 F mgillan@pccc.edu
GILLARD, Natalie ... 575-461-4413 311 C natalieg@mesalands.edu
GILLARDI, Michael ... 401-598-1450 441 D mgillardi@jwu.edu
GILLASPIE, Ray ... 270-824-8592 196 F ray.gillaspie@kctcs.edu
GILLE, Chaudron ... 678-717-3835 133 A chaudron.gille@ung.edu
GILLECE, Nancy, E ... 301-696-3710 215 E gillece@hood.edu
GILLEN, Ann ... 209-946-2135.. 73 C agillen@pacific.edu
GILLEN, Dan ... 319-296-4268 179 B daniel.gillen@hawkeyecollege.edu
GILLEN, Jonathan ... 541-881-5842 410 D jgillen@tvcc.cc
GILLES, Barbara, L ... 412-578-6123 414 I gillesbl@carlow.edu
GILLESPIE, Adrienne, G 801-626-7243 500 C adrienneandrews@weber.edu
GILLESPIE, Andrew, R .. 334-844-5009.... 1 G arg0014@auburn.edu
GILLESPIE, Barbara ... 276-326-4237 505 D bgillespie@bluefield.edu
GILLESPIE, Bart ... 678-839-6582 133 F bgillesp@westga.edu
GILLESPIE, Christine ... 201-612-7488 300 B cgillespie@bergen.edu
GILLESPIE, Dave ... 402-941-6545 291 I gillespie@midlandu.edu
GILLESPIE, Greg ... 805-289-6460.. 75 E ggillespie@vcccd.edu
GILLESPIE, Heather ... 605-256-5238 453 H heather.gillespie@dsu.edu
GILLESPIE, Mary Ellen .. 920-465-2145 539 F gillespm@uwgb.edu
GILLESPIE, Melanie ... 864-644-5504 449 B mlgillespie@swu.edu
GILLESPIE, Michael ... 212-220-8323 318 D mgillespie@bmcc.cuny.edu
GILLESPIE, Michele, K .. 336-758-5000 372 G gillesmk@wfu.edu
GILLESS, J. Keith ... 510-642-7171.. 70 K gilless@berkeley.edu
GILLETT, Charisse, L ... 859-280-1230 198 B cgillett@lextheo.edu
GILLETT, William ... 603-668-2211 298 H w.gillett@snhu.edu
GILLETTE, Donna ... 207-947-4591 209 G dgillette@bealcollege.edu
GILLETTE, Jack ... 617-349-8401 228 B jgillett@lesley.edu
GILLETTE, Kimberly ... 218-282-8442 264 H gillette@umn.edu
GILLETTE, Lynn ... 985-448-4011 208 C
GILLETTE, Maureen, D .. 773-442-5500 154 H m-gillette@neiu.edu
GILLETTE, Susan ... 410-706-5353 219 E sgillett@umaryland.edu
GILLEY, Amy ... 732-255-0400 304 E agilley@ocean.edu
GILLEY, Janice ... 850-474-2218 116 E jgilley@uwf.edu
GILLEY, Michael ... 276-523-2400 516 A mgilley@me.vccs.edu
GILLIAM, Cynthia ... 832-813-6512 477 I cynthia.f.gilliam@lonestar.edu
GILLIAM, Dara ... 405-273-5331 397 N dgilliam@familyoffaithcollege.edu
GILLIAM, JR., Franklin, D ... 310-206-7568.. 71 D fgilliam@conet.ucla.edu
GILLIAM, Janice, H ... 423-323-0201 463 D jhgilliam@northeaststate.edu
GILLIAM, Kevin, E ... 616-538-2330 243 C kgilliam@gbcol.edu
GILLIAM, Nilse, F ... 662-252-8000 270 C nfurtadogilliam@rustcollege.edu
GILLIAM, Rebecca ... 318-670-9353 207 C rgilliam@susla.edu
GILLIAM, Thomas, J ... 850-484-1690 110 D tgilliam@pensacolastate.edu
GILLIAM, Tom ... 850-484-1500 110 D tgilliam@pensacolastate.edu
GILLIAM PHILLIPS, Ruth ... 919-530-7908 370 C ruth.gilliam.phillips@nccu.edu
GILLICK, Megan ... 410-617-2290 216 D mgillick@loyola.edu
GILLIESPIE, Bailey ... 951-785-2041.. 49 I bgillies@lasierra.edu
GILLIGAN, Patrick, K ... 740-427-5643 384 P gilliganp@kenyon.edu
GILLIGAN, William ... 617-824-8190 226 A william_gilligan@emerson.edu
GILLILAN, Kevin ... 256-761-0949.... 7 H kgillilan@talladega.edu
GILLILAND, Christie ... 253-833-9111 523 B cgilliland@greenriver.edu
GILLILAND, Drew ... 541-552-6319 409 G gilliland@sou.edu
GILLILAND, Jane, A ... 607-587-3979 347 D gillilja@alfredstate.edu
GILLILAND, Kimberlie .. 918-781-7226 396 F gillilandk@bacone.edu
GILLILAND, Mary, K ... 520-494-5210.. 12 R marykay.gilliland@centralaz.edu
GILLILAND, William ... 301-295-9845 548 D william.gilliland@usuhs.edu
GILLIN, Douglas, P ... 828-262-7781 369 D gillindp@appstate.edu
GILLIN, Gary ... 507-537-6221 262 B Gary.Gillin@smsu.edu
GILLIS, Chester ... 202-687-4259.. 95 E gillisc@georgetown.edu
GILLIS, Dawn ... 914-606-6844 352 G dawn.gillis@sunywcc.edu
GILLIS, Graham ... 501-450-3181.. 25 F ggillis@uca.edu
GILLIS, Ida ... 219-980-6853 168 C ilgillis@iun.edu
GILLIS, Lynette ... 512-313-3000 471 H lynette.gillis@concordia.edu
GILLIS, Rick, D ... 414-955-6333 537 C rgillis@mcw.edu
GILLIS-OLION, Marion .. 910-672-1265 370 A molion@uncfsu.edu
GILLISPIE, Billy ... 254-647-3235 480 G
GILLISS, Buster ... 701-224-5512 374 E buster.gilliss@bismarckstate.edu
GILLLILAN, Kevin, L ... 256-765-4357.... 9 D kgillilan@una.edu
GILLMAN, Howard ... 949-824-5111.. 71 C chancellor@uci.edu
GILLMAN, Rick ... 219-464-6718 174 E rick.gillman@valpo.edu
GILLMING, Kenneth, D . 617-364-3510 224 A kgillming@boston.edu
GILLOGLY, Brenda ... 870-248-4000.. 20 E brenda.gillogly@blackrivertech.edu
GILLOOLY, Jeffrey ... 508-793-7512 225 B jgillooly@clarku.edu
GILLUM, Danny ... 620-227-9359 186 F dgillum@dc3.edu
GILLUM, Deborah ... 574-807-7015 164 F gillumd@bethelcollege.edu
GILMAN, Frederick, J ... 412-268-5124 414 J gilman@andrew.cmu.edu
GILMAN, Jean ... 314-977-3415 281 M jgilman2@slu.edu
GILMAN, Josephine ... 301-387-3091 215 A josephine.gilman@garrettcollege.edu
GILMAN, Regis, M ... 217-581-6644 144 E rmgilman@eiu.edu
GILMAN, Sharon ... 520-515-5382.. 13 B gilmans@cochise.edu
GILMAN-SUR, Sarah, S 808-689-2700 136 A sgilman@hawaii.edu
GILMARTIN, Anne ... 914-674-7337 332 E agilmartin@mercy.edu
GILMARTIN, Maureen, A ... 410-827-5842 214 D mgilmartin@chesapeake.edu
GILMARTIN, Michael ... 831-646-4039.. 54 H mgilmartin@mpc.edu
GILMER, Chris ... 907-747-7704.. 11 A cgilmer2@uas.alaska.edu
GILMER, Elizabeth ... 478-289-2037 124 B egilmer@ega.edu
GILMER, Garrett ... 419-372-2081 377 I ggilmer@bgsu.edu
GILMER, Ray ... 240-567-7970 217 B ray.gilmer@montgomerycollege.edu
GILMER, Stephanie ... 540-261-8480 512 J stephanie.gilmer@svu.edu
GILMORE, Calvin, L ... 336-272-7102 357 B gilmorec@greensboro.edu
GILMORE, Chris ... 603-577-6381 297 F cgilmore@dwc.edu
GILMORE, Christopher . 518-608-8114 325 B cgilmore@excelsior.edu
GILMORE, Dan ... 856-256-4684 306 D gilmore@rowan.edu
GILMORE, David ... 401-254-3843 442 C dgilmore@rwu.edu
GILMORE, Denise ... 620-431-2820 189 J dgilmore@neosho.edu
GILMORE, Don ... 661-362-2811.. 53 F dgilmore@masters.edu
GILMORE, Grover, C ... 216-368-2270 378 J gcg@case.edu
GILMORE, Jennifer, D .. 812-888-5332 174 F jgilmore@vinu.edu
GILMORE, Jessica ... 509-527-4215 527 H jessica.gilmore@wwcc.edu
GILMORE, John, W ... 609-497-7705 305 B john.gilmore@ptsem.edu
GILMORE, Kevin, P ... 913-971-3294 189 F kgilmore@mnu.edu
GILMORE, Paul ... 848-932-2300 307 B paul.gilmore@rutgers.edu
GILMORE, Robert ... 914-323-5357 331 J robert.gilmore@mville.edu
GILMORE, Wilson ... 505-786-4114 311 G wgilmore@navajotech.edu
GILMORE ENGLISH, Jessica ... 425-235-2463 525 G jgilmoreenglishl@rtc.edu
GILMOUR, Davie, J ... 570-320-2400 428 C djg120@psu.edu
GILMOUR, Davie Jane .. 570-326-3761 429 J dgilmour@pct.edu
GILNER, David ... 513-487-3273 327 C dgilner@huc.edu
GILORMINI, Dominique 787-766-1912 554 D dgilormini@inter.edu
GILORMINI-DE GRACIA, Dominique ... 787-763-4203 553 D dgilormini@inter.edu
GILPIN, Curtis ... 340-693-1104 559 B cgilpin@live.uvi.edu
GILPIN, Sue ... 309-268-8140 145 H sue.gilpin@heartland.edu
GILPIN FAUST, Drew ... 617-495-1502 227 D president@harvard.edu
GILRAIN, Timothy ... 215-895-2159 417 E timothy.l.gilrain@drexel.edu
GILREATH, Scott ... 518-464-8550 325 B SGilreath@excelsior.edu
GILREATH, Scott, A ... 812-488-2492 173 H sg157@evansville.edu
GILROY, Janice ... 914-606-6610 352 G janice.gilroy@sunywcc.edu
GILROY, Maryellen ... 518-783-2328 342 H mgilroy@siena.edu
GILSON, David ... 216-791-5000 380 C david.gilson@cim.edu
GILSON, Jannie ... 508-588-9100 232 A
GILSON, Ken ... 562-903-4870.. 29 F ken.gilson@biola.edu
GILSTRAP, Don ... 316-978-3586 192 D don.gilstrap@wichita.edu
GILSTRAP, Linda ... 619-216-6614.. 68 D lgilstrap@swccd.edu

GLEIMER, Steven .... 212-353-4151 323 B
sgleimer@cooper.edu
GLEIXNER, Stacy .... 408-924-1177.. 36 B
stacy.gleixner@sjsu.edu
GLEJZER, Richard .... 802-258-9234 502 B
rglejzer@marlboro.edu
GLEN, Will .... 949-451-5201.. 67 E
wglen@ivc.edu
GLENDE, Leah .... 860-512-3107.. 89 D
lglende@manchestercc.edu
GLENDENING, Andrew .. 909-748-8014.. 73 K
andrew_glendening@redlands.edu
GLENMAYE, Linnea .... 316-978-5054 192 D
linnea.glenmay@wichita.edu
GLENN, Ashley .... 540-362-6609 508 D
cdc@hollins.edu
GLENN, Barbara, M ...... 804-523-5263 515 F
bglenn@reynolds.edu
GLENN, Brian .... 806-651-2105 486 D
bglenn@mail.wtamu.edu
GLENN, Brooke .... 402-465-7518 292 E
bglenn@nebrwesleyan.edu
GLENN, Chance .... 256-372-5560.... 1 A
chance.glenn@aamu.edu
GLENN, Christy .... 931-393-1682 463 B
cglenn@mscc.edu
GLENN, Crystal .... 828-327-7000 361 B
cglenn@cvcc.edu
GLENN, Darrell .... 212-217-4075 325 C
darrell_glenn@fitnyc.edu
GLENN, Daymond .... 503-517-1056 411 A
dglenn@warnerpacific.edu
GLENN, Debra .... 610-526-1399 412 D
debra.glenn@theamericancollege.edu
GLENN, Dennis, E .... 706-385-1064 130 C
dennis.glenn@point.edu
GLENN, Jenna .... 630-889-6620 154 E
jglenn@nuhs.edu
GLENN, Jonathan, A ..... 501-450-3126.. 25 F
jona@uca.edu
GLENN, Katie .... 205-226-7737.... 2 C
kglenn@bsc.edu
GLENN, Lane, A .... 978-556-3855 232 E
lglenn@necc.mass.edu
GLENN, Laverne .... 215-965-4042 426 G
lglenn@moore.edu
GLENN, Robert, K .... 256-233-8201.... 1 F
bob.glenn@athens.edu
GLENN, Susan .... 815-921-4503 157 B
s.glenn@rockvalleycollege.edu
GLENN, Thane .... 267-502-4844 413 C
thane.glenn@anc-gc.org
GLENN-SUMMITT,
Peggy .... 918-456-5511 398 M
glennsum@nsuok.edu
GLENNEN, Debrah .... 701-777-3425 373 G
debrah.glennen@und.edu
GLENNON, Jennifer ...... 410-857-2205 217 A
jglennon@mcdaniel.edu
GLETHEROW, Catherine 440-775-5547 388 B
Catherine.Gletherow@oberlin.edu
GLEW, Karen .... 207-453-5820 211 B
kglew@kvcc.me.edu
GLEZERMAN, David, R . 215-204-7269 436 C
david.glezerman@temple.edu
GLICK, Carol .... 313-593-6751 251 D
cglick@umich.edu
GLICK, Steven .... 330-263-2590 380 E
sglick@wooster.edu
GLICK, William, H .... 713-348-5928 480 M
glickb@rice.edu
GLICKMAN, Gena .... 860-512-3100.. 89 D
gglickman@manchestercc.edu
GLICKMAN, Michael ..... 516-299-3760 330 F
michael.glickman@liu.edu
GLICKSMAN, Martin ..... 321-674-7318 103 R
mglicksman@fit.edu
GLIDDEN, Laraine, M ... 240-895-4389 218 B
lmglidden@smcm.edu
GLIDDEN, Stacey, T ..... 978-468-7111 227 B
sglidden@gcts.edu
GLIDEWELL, Chris .... 618-536-3345 159 G
cglide@siu.edu
GLIDWELL, Bob .... 417-328-1550 282 D
bglidwell@sbuniv.edu
GLIEM, Valerie .... 727-864-8408 101 P
gliemvm@eckerd.edu
GLIMCHER, Laurie .... 212-746-6005 323 C
glimche@med.cornell.edu
GLINDEMANN, Kent, E . 276-223-4885 517 F
kglindemann@wcc.vccs.edu
GLINES, Carey .... 603-668-2211 298 H
c.glines@snhu.edu
GLINES, Carol, A .... 563-333-6329 182 E
GlinesCarolA@sau.edu
GLINES, Lee .... 801-422-4147 497 J
lee.glines@byu.edu
GLINES, Neil .... 707-864-7000.. 66 J
neil.glines@solano.edu
GLINIECKI, Anita, K ...... 203-576-5235.. 91 H
GLISCH, John .... 321-433-7017 101 O
glischj@easternflorida.edu
GLISSON, Altricia .... 716-270-5139 325 A
ascglissona@ecc.edu
GLISSON, Micheal .... 337-521-8954 204 E
micheal.glisson@solacc.edu
GLISSON, Tony, L .... 270-745-5360 201 D
tony.glisson@wku.edu
GLOBIS, Roxanne .... 609-633-9658 308 H
rglobis@tesc.edu
GLOCK, Jon, W .... 563-588-8000 178 E
jglock@emmaus.edu
GLOD, Carol .... 978-837-5115 233 G
glodc@merrimack.edu
GLODJO, Donna .... 618-985-2828 148 G
donnaglodjo@jalc.edu
GLOGOWSKI,
Maryruth, F .... 716-878-4716 345 B
glogowmf@buffalostate.edu
GLORE, Susan, J .... 410-871-3305 217 A
sglore@mcdaniel.edu
GLORIA, Jackie .... 858-566-1200.. 43 A
jgloria@disd.edu
GLORIA SAWYER, Rita . 323-563-4922.. 38 C
ritasawyer@cdrewu.edu
GLOSSER, Wade, W ...... 816-654-7717 276 G
bglosser@kcumb.edu
GLOSSUP, Dean .... 931-363-9800 458 D
dgloss326@martinmethodist.edu
GLOTZBACH, Philip, A . 518-580-5700 342 I
pglotzba@skidmore.edu
GLOVEN, Greta .... 303-765-3109.. 83 C
ggloven@iliff.edu
GLOVER, David .... 501-812-2318.. 22 F
dglover@pulaskitech.edu
GLOVER, David .... 757-727-5259 508 C
david.glover@hamptonu.edu
GLOVER, Devon, H .... 208-535-5394 138 B
devon.glover@my.eitc.edu
GLOVER, Glenda .... 615-963-7401 461 F
president@tnstate.edu
GLOVER, Joseph .... 352-392-2404 115 D
jglover@aa.ufl.edu
GLOVER, Joseph, M ...... 812-941-2028 169 A
joglover@ius.edu
GLOVER, Katie .... 703-370-6600 511 B
GLOVER, Kerri .... 828-254-1921 360 A
kerriaglover@abtech.edu
GLOVER, Larry .... 615-329-8826 456 G
lglover@fisk.edu
GLOVER, Laura .... 906-227-2244 248 B
lglover@nmu.edu
GLOVER, Nathaniel .... 904-470-8012 102 A
n.glover@ewc.edu
GLOVER, Paula .... 660-263-4110 279 F
paulag@macc.edu
GLOVER, Shirley .... 478-988-6890 122 F
sglover@centralgatech.edu
GLOWKA, Arthur, W ..... 770-720-5628 130 E
awg@reinhardt.edu
GLUCKOWSKY,
Moshe, M .... 718-774-3430 317 L
GLYER-CULVER, Betty ... 916-568-3068.. 52 H
glyercb@losrios.edu
GLYNN, Graham .... 785-628-4241 187 A
geglynn@fhsu.edu
GLYNN, John, B .... 414-410-4313 535 C
jbglynn@stritch.edu
GLYNN, Terry, S .... 858-499-0202.. 40 G
tglynn@coleman.edu
GMEINER, Mary, L .... 989-686-9042 242 I
marygmeiner@delta.edu
GMEINER, Rebecca .... 678-466-4145 122 J
rebeccagmeiner@clayton.edu
GNADE, Bruce .... 972-883-6636 494 A
gnade@utdallas.edu
GNADINGER, Cindy ...... 859-336-5082 199 B
cindygnadinger@sccky.edu
GNAGE, Marie, F .... 904-632-5094 105 A
marie.gnage@fscj.edu
GNAN, Peter, D .... 708-209-3192 143 D
pete.gnan@cuchicago.edu
GNASSO, Emil, A .... 610-758-3200 424 B
emg3@lehigh.edu
GNECCO, Donald .... 706-776-0117 130 B
dgnecco@piedmont.edu
GOAD, Philip .... 256-766-6610.... 4 C
pgoad@hcu.edu
GOAD, William .... 405-425-5180 399 J
bill.goad@oc.edu
GOAR, Michele .... 575-492-2161 314 D
mgoar@usw.edu
GOBBLE, Sheryl .... 619-388-7428.. 62 H
sgobble@sdccd.edu
GOBEN, Allen .... 817-515-6200 484 B
allen.goben@tccd.edu
GOBEN, Jason .... 606-693-5000 197 F
jgoben@kmbc.edu
GOBER, Chris, G .... 636-922-8211 281 C
cgober@stchas.edu
GOBER, Jerome .... 423-697-4457 462 C
jerome.gober@chattanoogastate.edu
GOBERISH, John, S ..... 724-480-3450 416 A
john.goberish@ccbc.edu
GOBLE, Allison .... 606-326-2432 195 H
allison.goble@kctcs.edu
GOBLE, Bryen .... 606-886-3863 195 I
bryen.goble@kctcs.edu
GOBLE, David, S .... 843-953-1267 444 C
dgoble@citadel.edu
GOBLET, Lois .... 518-255-5524 346 E
gobletle@cobleskill.edu
GOCHENAUR,
Heather, K .... 260-982-5873 170 a
hkgochenaur@manchester.edu
GOCHENAUR, Jack, A .. 260-982-5245 170 a
jagochenaur@manchester.edu
GOCHIS, Cheryl .... 254-710-8562 469 D
Cheryl_Gochis@baylor.edu
GOCHIS, Sue .... 530-541-4660.. 50 A
gochis@ltcc.edu
GOCHNAUER,
Richard, D .... 302-356-6795.. 94 G
richard.d.gochnauer@wilmu.edu
GOCIAL, Tammy .... 314-529-6893 277 B
tgocial@maryville.edu
GOCKLEY, Daniel, L ..... 214-458-6200 494 D
DANIEL.GOCKLEY@UTSA.EDU
GODARD, Mike .... 660-543-4811 283 F
godard@ucmo.edu
GODDARD, Courtney .... 816-584-6559 280 F
courtney.goddard@park.edu
GODDARD, Deanna ...... 507-457-2493 262 D
dgoddard@winona.edu
GODDARD, Diane, H .... 785-864-4904 191 G
dgoddard@ku.edu
GODDARD, Robert .... 802-773-5900 501 G
robert.goddard@csj.edu
GODDARD, Scott, D ..... 304-637-1352 529 I
goddards@dewv.edu
GODDARD MCGUIRK,
Lisa .... 814-871-7664 419 A
GODDARD-SOBERS,
Kelli .... 484-365-7119 424 E
kgoddard@lincoln.edu
GODDEN, Barb .... 712-325-3400 180 B
bgodden@iwcc.edu
GODDING, Jesse .... 972-825-4811 483 D
jgodding@sagu.edu
GODEK, Jim .... 949-376-6000.. 49 K
jgodek@lcad.edu
GODEL-GENGENBACH,
Kay .... 303-384-2120.. 80 O
kgengenb@mines.edu
GODENY, Elmer .... 609-343-4988 299 G
egodeny@atlantic.edu
GODENZI, Alberto, A .... 617-552-6399 224 B
alberto.godenzi@bc.edu
GODES, Iris .... 508-541-1547 225 G
igodes@dean.edu
GODFREY, Christian ..... 208-535-5387 138 B
christian.godfrey@my.eitc.edu
GODFREY, Kevin .... 805-482-2755.. 61 F
registrar-sjs@stjohnsem.edu
GODFREY, Robert .... 631-420-2700 348 B
foundation@farmingdale.edu
GODFREY, Rodney .... 662-241-7636 269 B
ragodfrey@muw.edu
GODFREY, W. Robert ... 760-480-8474.. 76 J
bvansolkema@wscal.edu
GODFREY-DAWSON,
Angela, R .... 252-335-0821 361 G
adawson@albemarle.edu
GODIN, Norm .... 951-571-6341.. 60 K
norm.godin@mvc.edu
GODIN, Patricia, A .... 919-866-5170 366 H
pagodin@waketech.edu
GODIN, Roger, A .... 717-291-3989 418 J
roger.godin@fandm.edu
GODLESKI, Mark, G ..... 315-445-4520 330 B
godlesmg@lemoyne.edu
GODLEWSKI, Robert ..... 802-773-5900 501 G
bob.godlewski@csj.edu
GODMAN, Anne .... 217-479-7141 151 J
anne.godman@mac.edu
GODO, James .... 630-637-5809 154 F
jwgodo@noctrl.edu
GODREAU, Susan, E .... 315-267-2162 346 C
godrease@potsdam.edu
GODSAVE, Sarah .... 580-699-7204 397 G
sgodsave@cnc.cc.ok.us
GODSEY, R. Kirby .... 478-330-5609 128 G
godsey_rk@mercer.edu
GODWIN, Angeline, D .. 276-656-0201 516 D
agodwin@patrickhenry.edu
GODWIN, Deena .... 360-992-2932 521 A
dgodson@clark.edu
GODWIN, Donald, R .... 619-260-4588.. 74 B
donald.godwin@sandiego.edu
GODWIN, John .... 202-685-4242 547 M
john.godwin@ndu.edu
GODWIN, King, D .... 318-274-2732 207 H
godwink@gram.edu
GODWIN, Lewis .... 678-891-3960 125 G
lewis.godwin@gpc.edu
GODWIN, Wendell .... 580-559-5274 397 K
wgodwin@ecok.edu
GODZWA, Alicia .... 540-362-6660 508 D
agodzwa@hollins.edu
GOEBEL, Jeffrey, D .... 218-477-2069 260 B
goebelj@mnstate.edu
GOEBEL, Ken .... 603-358-2378 299 D
kgoebel@keene.edu
GOEBEL, Rob .... 217-228-5432 156 D
goebero@quincy.edu
GOECKER, James, A ..... 812-877-8894 172 C
james.goecker@rose-hulman.edu
GOECKER, James, A ..... 812-877-8258 172 C
goecker@rose-hulman.edu
GOEDDE, Tony, G .... 419-434-4556 393 F
goedde@findlay.edu
GOEDERT, JoAnn .... 301-445-1921 219 C
jgoedert@usmd.edu
GOEL, Meeta .... 661-722-6300.. 27 P
mgoel@avc.edu
GOELDNER, Jason .... 715-365-4534 543 G
jgoeldner@nicoletcollege.edu
GOELLNER, Marilyn ...... 814-732-1778 430 G
mgoellner@edinboro.edu
GOELZHAUSER,
Michael, J .... 812-464-1717 174 D
mjgoelzh@usi.edu
GOEN, Jennifer .... 239-590-1020 114 F
jgoen@fgcu.edu
GOEPPINGER,
Kathleen, H .... 630-515-7300 152 H
drgoeppinger@midwestern.edu
GOERING, Doug .... 907-474-7730.. 10 I
djgoering@alaska.edu
GOERING, Wynn, M ...... 505-277-7601 313 H
wgoering@unm.edu
GOERLITZ, Ryan .... 414-955-8125 537 C
rgoerlitz@mcw.edu
GOERTEMILLER,
Paul, M .... 972-860-7091 472 E
PaulGoertemiller@dcccd.edu
GOERTZ, Christine .... 563-884-5159 182 D
christine.goertz@palmer.edu
GOERTZEN, Leroy .... 253-759-6104 405 F
lgoertzen@nbs.edu
GOERTZEN, Ryan .... 918-836-6886 402 I
rgoertzen@mail.spartan.edu
GOERZEN, Les .... 316-284-5261 185 B
lgoerzen@bethelks.edu
GOERZEN, Peter .... 316-284-5356 185 B
pgoerzen@bethelks.edu
GOETCHIUS, Stephen .... 860-215-9005.. 90 B
sgoetchius@trcc.commnet.net
GOETHE, Corey .... 989-386-6622 247 B
cgoethe@midmich.edu
GOETSCH, Lori, A .... 785-532-7402 188 H
lgoetsch@ksu.edu
GOETSCHIUS, Susan, C 607-871-2144 314 J
goetshcius@alfred.edu
GOETZ, Allison .... 215-572-4076 412 F
goetza@arcadia.edu
GOETZ, Amy .... 304-793-6845 533 B
agoetz@osteo.wvsom.edu
GOETZ, Beth .... 612-625-0775 265 C
GOETZ, Bruce, P .... 303-273-3225.. 80 O
bgoetz@mines.edu
GOETZ, Julie, K .... 260-359-4127 167 D
jgoetz@huntington.edu
GOETZ, Michael, A .... 414-847-3305 537 F
mikegoetz@miad.edu
GOETZ, Mike .... 270-686-2111 193 G
mike.goetz@brescia.edu
GOEWERT, Ed .... 618-374-5109 156 C
ed.goewert@principia.edu
GOFF, Anton .... 860-768-4989.. 92 F
hawksad@hartford.edu
GOFF, David .... 303-724-7304.. 86 G
david.goff@ucdenver.edu
GOFF, David, W .... 870-236-6901.. 20 I
dgoff@crc.edu
GOFF, Jamie .... 325-674-2751 466 I
jdb99a@acu.edu
GOFF, Jay .... 314-977-8191 281 M
goffjw@slu.edu
GOFF, Karen .... 732-987-2601 302 J
kgoff@georgian.edu
GOFF, Kim .... 916-558-2054.. 53 B
GoffK@scc.losrios.edu
GOFF, Michelle .... 478-289-2095 124 B
mgoff@ega.edu
GOFF, Mike .... 214-818-1334 471 I
mgoff@criswell.edu
GOFF, Patricia, A .... 401-865-1031 441 F
pgoff@providence.edu

GOMEZ-PALACIO, Dan .. 573-875-8700 273 D
dgomez@ccis.edu
GOMILA, Sol, A .... 787-728-1515 559 A
sgomila@sagrado.edu
GONCALVES, Andreia .... 631-370-3300 342 D
agoncalves@sbmelville.edu
GONDEK, Gretchen .... 712-274-6400 184 A
gretchen.gondek@witcc.edu
GONG, Changzhen .... 651-631-0204 253 G
tcmhealth@aol.com
GONG, Harry, S .... 716-286-8716 336 E
hgong@niagara.edu
GONG-GUY, Elizabeth ... 310-825-0768.. 71 D
egongguy@sps.ucla.edu
GONICK, Julie .... 619-684-8841.. 56 B
jgonick@newschoolarch.edu
GONSALVES-MCCABE,
Kristi .... 303-458-4153.. 85 G
kgonsalv@regis.edu
GONSER, Edward .... 716-614-6848 336 D
egonser@niagaracc.suny.edu
GONSOULIN, Sid .... 601-266-5767 271 B
sidney.gonsoulin@usm.edu
GONTHIER, Sheri .... 603-271-6484 297 C
sgonthier@ccsnh.edu
GONYEA, David .... 207-755-5251 210 L
dgonyea@cmcc.edu
GONZÁLEZ, Carlos .... 787-765-9695 558 E
carlos.gonzalez55@upr.edu
GONZÁLEZ, Celia .... 787-844-8181 558 D
celia.gonzalez@upr.edu
GONZÁLEZ, Lissette, V . 787-265-3883 558 B
lissette.gonzalez1@upr.edu
GONZÁLEZ, Marisol ...... 787-264-1912 554 C
mgonzale@intersg.edu
GONZÁLEZ, Terestella .. 787-257-7373 555 L
tergonzalez@suagm.edu
GONZÁLEZ, Widalys ..... 787-884-3838 550 E
dirdg@atenascollege.edu
GONZÁLEZ DE RESENDE,
María, A .... 787-993-8872 557 E
maria.gonzalez34@upr.edu
GONZÁLEZ TABOADA,
José, A .... 787-751-7410 558 E
jose.gonzalez63@upr.edu
GONZALES, Adrian .... 760-744-1150.. 58 D
adriangonzales@palomar.edu
GONZALES, Al .... 623-845-3035.. 14 N
al.gonzales@gccaz.edu
GONZALES, Alberto ...... 615-460-8248 455 D
alberto.gonzales@belmont.edu
GONZALES, Alfredo, M 616-395-7785 244 A
gonzales@hope.edu
GONZALES, Ana .... 210-829-3937 492 B
anagonza@uiwtx.edu
GONZALES, Benito .... 575-562-2115 310 I
benito.gonzales@enmu.edu
GONZALES, Carmen ..... 505-428-1409 313 A
carmen.gonzales1@sfcc.edu
GONZALES, Casey .... 817-272-2099 493 L
gonzales@uta.edu
GONZALES, Christina ... 303-492-8476.. 86 E
christina.gonzales@colorado.edu
GONZALES, Dianna ...... 209-954-5059.. 63 D
dgonzales@deltacollege.edu
GONZALES, Gilbert .... 505-277-8125 313 H
gonzgil@unm.edu
GONZALES, Hector .... 830-591-7281 483 A
hegonzales@swtjc.edu
GONZALES, Jenni .... 520-494-5341.. 12 R
jenni.gonzales@centralaz.edu
GONZALES, Joe .... 209-954-5139.. 63 D
jgonzales@deltacollege.edu
GONZALES, JR.,
Joseph, M .... 312-329-4202 153 C
joe.gonzales@moody.edu
GONZALES, Junius .... 919-962-4614 369 C
jjgonzales@northcarolina.edu
GONZALES, Leticia .... 432-837-8193 489 B
lgonzales@sulross.edu
GONZALES, Louis .... 432-335-6848 479 O
lgonzales@odessa.edu
GONZALES, Lucinda, A 972-860-7668 472 E
LucindaGonzales@dcccd.edu
GONZALES, Mario .... 559-638-3641.. 69 C
mario-gonzales@reedleycollege.edu
GONZALES, Mark .... 408-274-7900.. 63 P
mark.gonzales@evc.edu
GONZALES, Mary, J ..... 401-874-2101 442 E
mjgonzales@mail.uri.edu
GONZALES, Rhonda ..... 719-549-2315.. 81 F
rhonda.gonzales@csupueblo.edu
GONZALES, Richard ..... 970-947-8428.. 80 D
rgonzales4@coloradomtn.edu
GONZALES, Robert ...... 719-549-2943.. 81 F
robert.gonzales@csupueblo.edu
GONZALES, Ron .... 505-454-5305 311 B
rgonzales@luna.edu
GONZALES, Roxanne .... 814-676-6591 430 E
rgonzales@clarion.edu
GONZALES, Samuel ...... 210-458-4136 494 D
sam.gonzales@utsa.edu
GONZALES, Sandra, M . 602-944-3335.. 11 D
sgonzales@aicag.edu
GONZALES, Veronica .... 956-665-5301 494 C
gonzalesv@utpa.edu
GONZALES-MCKOSKY,
Latricia .... 505-438-8884 313 C
latricia@acupuncturecollege.edu
GONZALES-TAPIA,
Sarah .... 626-914-8556.. 38 L
sgonzales-tapia@citruscollege.edu
GONZALEZ, Alex .... 505-277-4792 313 H
agonzale@unm.edu
GONZALEZ, Alexis .... 310-377-5501.. 53 E
agonzalez@marymountcalifornia.edu
GONZALEZ, Amilcar ..... 939-292-2223 558 F
amilcar.gonzalez2@upr.edu
GONZALEZ, Anna .... 503-768-7110 406 H
annag@lclark.edu
GONZALEZ, Beatriz .... 909-593-3511.. 73 B
bgonzalez@laverne.edu
GONZALEZ, Belinda, C . 210-567-0720 495 B
chapab@uthscsa.edu
GONZALEZ, Bethaida .... 315-443-3259 349 E
bgonzale@syr.edu
GONZALEZ, Blanca, M . 787-250-1912 554 A
bmgonzalez@metro.inter.edu
GONZALEZ, Carla .... 313-664-7431 241 D
cgonzalez@collegeforcreativestudies.edu
GONZALEZ, Carlos, J ... 787-622-8000 556 H
Gonzalez@pupr.edu
GONZALEZ, Carlos, R .. 818-364-7778.. 51 G
gonzalcr@lamission.edu
GONZALEZ, Carmen ...... 787-841-2000 555 F
cgonzalez@pucpr.edu
GONZALEZ, Caroline .... 787-786-3030 556 E
cagonzalez@ucb.edu.pr
GONZALEZ, Cheryl, N .. 904-620-2507 116 A
cheryl.gonzalez@unf.edu
GONZALEZ, Diana .... 515-242-6116 175 F
gonzalez@iastate.edu
GONZALEZ, Edith .... 212-817-7520 319 B
egonzalez@gc.cuny.edu
GONZALEZ, Eladio .... 787-664-0353 558 F
eladio.gonzalez1@upr.edu
GONZALEZ, Elizabeth ... 787-761-0640 557 A
decanaestudiantes@utcpr.edu
GONZALEZ, Elma, D ..... 936-261-2124 484 F
edgonzalez@pvamu.edu
GONZALEZ, Fernando ... 787-884-6000 552 K
fgonzalez@icprjc.edu
GONZALEZ, Francisco .. 918-333-6151 400 I
francisco@gonzalezfirm.com
GONZALEZ, George ...... 281-998-6150 481 D
george.gonzalez@sjcd.edu
GONZALEZ, Gerardo ..... 812-856-8001 167 J
gonzalez@indiana.edu
GONZALEZ, Griselda ..... 212-217-3363 325 C
griselda_gonzalez@fitnyc.edu
GONZALEZ, Griselda ..... 212-217-4000 325 C
griselda_gonzalez@fitnyc.edu
GONZALEZ, Herman ...... 602-787-6601.. 15 B
herman.gonzalez@paradisevalley.edu
GONZALEZ, Jaime .... 787-620-2040 550 D
carroyo@aupr.edu
GONZALEZ, Jean .... 714-867-5009.. 67 C
GONZALEZ, Jeanette ..... 760-547-1800.. 45 B
jgonzalez@fst.edu
GONZALEZ, Jorge .... 323-259-2634.. 56 I
jorgegonzalez@oxy.edu
GONZALEZ, Jose, N ..... 787-850-9419 558 A
jose.gonzalez48@upr.edu
GONZALEZ, Juan .... 858-534-4370.. 72 B
vcsa@ucsd.edu
GONZALEZ, Judith .... 787-766-1717 556 A
jugonzalez@suagm.edu
GONZALEZ, Julio .... 516-876-5639 345 E
gonzalezj@oldwestbury.edu
GONZALEZ, Karen .... 787-766-1717 556 A
um_kgonzalez@suagm.edu
GONZALEZ, Kelly .... 214-648-3519 496 A
kelly.gonzalez@utsouthwestern.edu
GONZALEZ, Linda .... 915-831-2566 473 J
lgonz265@epcc.edu
GONZALEZ, Lizbeth ...... 603-882-6923 297 B
lgonzalez@ccsnh.edu
GONZALEZ, Luis .... 787-850-9312 558 A
luis.gonzalez35@upr.edu
GONZALEZ, Luis .... 724-357-2330 431 A
Luis.Gonzalez@iup.edu
GONZALEZ, Luz .... 559-278-3013.. 33 D
luz_gonzalez@csufresno.edu
GONZALEZ, Mari, G ...... 787-743-7979 555 M
mggonzalez@suagm.edu
GONZALEZ, Maria .... 951-372-7137.. 61 A
maria.gonzalez@norcocollege.edu
GONZALEZ, Maria, M ... 787-852-1430 552 J
mgonzalez@hccpr.edu
GONZALEZ,
Maria Teresa .... 787-758-2525 558 C
mariateresa.gonzalez@upr.edu
GONZALEZ, Marilyn ..... 787-882-2065 556 C
secretaria_ejecutiva@unitecpr.net
GONZALEZ, Martha, O . 956-326-2361 485 B
marthao.gonzalez@tamiu.edu
GONZALEZ, Mary .... 361-593-2494 486 A
kamlp00@tamuk.edu
GONZALEZ, Mauricio ... 904-620-2600 116 A
mgonzale@unf.edu
GONZALEZ, Megan .... 850-474-2658 116 E
mprawdzik@uwf.edu
GONZALEZ, Melissa ..... 281-655-3707 477 I
melissa.gonzalez@lonestar.edu
GONZALEZ, Miguel .... 956-665-3510 494 C
gonzalezma@utpa.edu
GONZALEZ, Monica, D . 787-723-4481 551 B
mgonzalez@ceaprc.edu
GONZALEZ, Nichole ..... 716-375-2572 340 C
ngonzalez@sbu.edu
GONZALEZ, Nicolas ...... 956-872-2133 482 G
ngon@southtexascollege.edu
GONZALEZ, Patricia ...... 787-250-1912 554 A
pgonzalez@metro.inter.edu
GONZALEZ, Patricia ...... 661-255-1050.. 31 B
gonzalez@calarts.edu
GONZALEZ, Ramon .... 787-758-2525 558 C
ramon.gonzalez5@upr.edu
GONZALEZ, Raul, D ..... 818-947-2606.. 52 B
gonzalrd@lavc.edu
GONZALEZ, Raymond ... 718-289-5154 318 E
raymond.gonzalez@bcc.cuny.edu
GONZALEZ, Reina, M ... 787-840-8108 558 D
reina.gonzalez@upr.edu
GONZALEZ, Reinaldo .... 787-744-8519 552 D
rgonzalez@ediccollege.edu
GONZALEZ, Reyes .... 414-256-1228 538 A
gonzaler@mtmary.edu
GONZALEZ, Roberto ...... 310-434-4912.. 65 B
gonzalez_roberto@smc.edu
GONZALEZ, Rocelia, T . 904-620-2870 116 A
rrgonz@unf.edu
GONZALEZ, Ruth .... 860-738-6315.. 89 G
rgonzalez@nwcc.commnet.edu
GONZALEZ, Sandra ...... 787-882-2065 556 C
administracion_empresas@unitecpr.net
GONZALEZ, Saraliz .... 787-857-3600 553 G
sgonzalez@br.inter.edu
GONZALEZ, Sergio, M . 305-284-4111 118 A
smgonzalez@miami.edu
GONZALEZ, Sophia ...... 210-486-2247 467 B
fklein@alamo.edu
GONZALEZ, Stacy .... 515-244-2209 340 A
gonzas@sage.edu
GONZALEZ, Steven .... 602-286-8008.. 14 M
steven.gonalez@gatewaycc.edu
GONZALEZ, Thomasa .... 609-652-4724 308 E
t.gonzalez@stockton.edu
GONZALEZ, Tina .... 212-799-5000 329 I
GONZALEZ, Virginia ..... 787-743-7979 555 M
ut_vgonzalez@suagm.edu
GONZALEZ, Yadira .... 541-278-5753 404 J
ygonzalez@bluecc.edu
GONZALEZ, Yanira .... 787-891-0925 553 E
ygonzalez@aguadilla.inter.edu
GONZALEZ-CORTES,
Otilio .... 787-815-0000 557 B
otilio.gonzalez@upr.edu
GONZALEZ CORTES,
Otilio .... 787-815-0000 557 D
otilio.gonzalez@upr.edu
GONZALEZ-DE JESUS,
Naydeen .... 201-612-5467 300 B
ngonzalezdejesus@bergen.edu
GONZALEZ-GUERRA,
Migdalia .... 787-890-2681 557 C
migdalia.gonzalez2@upr.edu
GONZALEZ-SCARANO,
Francisco .... 210-567-4432 495 B
scarano@uthscsa.edu
GOOCH, Cheryl Renee . 484-365-7664 424 E
cgooch@lincoln.edu
GOOCH, Cynthia .... 402-457-2649 291 E
cgooch@mccneb.edu
GOOCH, Ellen .... 518-327-6225 338 B
egooch@paulsmiths.edu
GOOCH, Gene .... 254-299-8649 478 C
ggooch@mclennan.edu
GOOCH, Janet .... 660-785-4383 283 E
JQuinzer@truman.edu
GOOCH, Josh .... 620-665-3594 188 A
goochj@hutchcc.edu
GOOD, Darrin .... 562-907-4204.. 77 E
dgood@whittier.edu
GOOD, Gayle, A .... 402-363-5621 294 G
gagood@york.edu
GOOD, Glenn .... 352-392-3261 115 D
ggood@coe.ufl.edu
GOOD, Jason .... 540-432-4118 507 A
jason.good@emu.edu
GOOD, Jennifer .... 251-380-2278.... 7 F
jgood@shc.edu
GOOD, Larry .... 402-363-5718 294 G
lbgood@york.edu
GOOD, Lee Anna .... 432-552-2800 495 F
good_l@utpb.edu
GOOD, Megan, R .... 334-844-4000.... 1 G
GOOD, Michael, L .... 352-273-7500 115 D
mgood@ufl.edu
GOOD, Rhonda .... 717-337-6015 419 C
rgood@gettysburg.edu
GOOD, Tina .... 518-320-1256 343 B
tina.good@suny.edu
GOOD LUCK, Aldean .... 406-638-3118 286 I
goodluckav@lbhc.edu
GOODALE, Brian .... 518-587-2100 348 A
brian.goodale@esc.edu
GOODARZI, Shirin, M .. 410-777-2148 213 E
smgoodarzi@aacc.edu
GOODBURN, Amy .... 402-472-3751 293 H
agoodburn1@unl.edu
GOODCUFF, Esther .... 516-877-3681 314 F
goodcuff@adelphi.edu
GOODE, Abreeta .... 210-829-3932 492 B
agoode@uiwtx.edu
GOODE, Debbie .... 580-581-2255 397 A
debbieg@cameron.edu
GOODE, Greg, J .... 812-237-7778 167 E
greg.goode@indstate.edu
GOODE, Gregg, R .... 785-309-3100 190 L
gregg.goode@salinatech.edu
GOODE, Mark .... 714-432-5898.. 40 D
mgoode@occ.cccd.edu
GOODE, Tammy .... 423-585-6845 464 C
tammy.goode@ws.edu
GOODE, Tyler .... 828-339-4394 366 C
t_goode@southwesterncc.edu
GOODELL-LACKEY,
Shirley, J .... 802-654-2586 502 H
sgoodell-lackey@smcvt.edu
GOODEN, Jake .... 304-704-9111 529 I
goodenj@dewv.edu
GOODER, Kellee .... 307-532-8336 546 B
kellee.gooder@ewc.wy.edu
GOODFELLOW, Sandy .. 615-844-5280 466 G
alex@welch.edu
GOODFELLOW, Tim ...... 503-554-2585 406 A
tgoodfellow@georgefox.edu
GOODFRIEND,
Kimberly .... 972-883-2201 494 A
kimberly.goodfriend@utdallas.edu
GOODGAME, Henry .... 404-215-2658 128 L
henry.goodgame@morehouse.edu
GOODGE, Samuel .... 304-829-7905 529 H
sgoodge@bethanywv.edu
GOODHEART, Marc .... 617-496-9480 227 D
marc_goodheart@harvard.edu
GOODHUE, Bill .... 607-436-2532 344 B
goodhucw@oneonta.edu
GOODHUE LYNCH,
Mary .... 508-588-9100 232 A
GOODIN, Ruth .... 925-473-7314.. 42 F
rgoodin@losmedanos.edu
GOODING, Betsy .... 903-434-8137 479 L
bgooding@ntcc.edu
GOODING, Mary, B ...... 229-333-7444 133 H
mbgooding@valdosta.edu
GOODLETT, Sean .... 978-665-3832 229 D
GOODLING, Barry, G .... 717-796-5064 426 B
bgoodlin@messiah.edu
GOODLING, Eileen, J ... 716-338-1025 329 E
eileengoodling@mail.sunyjcc.edu
GOODMAN, Brent .... 619-849-2371.. 59 K
brentgoodman@pointloma.edu
GOODMAN, Catie .... 850-201-8281 117 B
goodmanc@tcc.fl.edu
GOODMAN, Charlie ...... 606-337-1148 194 F
cgoodman@ccbbc.edu
GOODMAN, Clay .... 623-935-8456.. 14 L
clay.goodman@estrellamountain.edu
GOODMAN, Debbie .... 229-225-3978 132 C
dgoodman@southernregional.edu
GOODMAN, Grayson ...... 407-303-1631.. 97 J
grayson.goodman@adu.edu
GOODMAN, Guy .... 602-243-8000.. 15 F
guy.goodman@southmountaincc.edu
GOODMAN, J. Andy ..... 314-516-7133 284 B
goodmanjam@umsl.edu
GOODMAN, Jacque ...... 641-844-5640 179 J
Jacque.Goodman@iavalley.edu
GOODMAN, Jacque ...... 641-844-7106 179 L
jacque.goodman@iavalley.edu
GOODMAN, James .... 808-455-0664 136 G
goodmanj@hawaii.edu
GOODMAN, Jeremy ...... 781-292-2373 226 G
jeremy.goodman@olin.edu
GOODMAN, Jerry, C ..... 713-798-7234 469 C
jgoodman@bcm.edu

GOSA, Polly 520-515-8750 13 B
gosap@cochise.edu
GOSCH, Judy 865-539-7233 463 E
jagosch@pstcc.edu
GOSE, Becca 541-737-2474 408 F
GOSE, Pilar 831-582-3595 34 C
pgose@csumb.edu
GOSNELL, Victor 434-947-8138 511 D
vgosnell@randolphcollege.edu
GOSPODARCZYK, Tom 715-346-3386 541 A
Tom.Gospodarczyk@uwsp.edu
GOSS, Barbara 205-853-1200 5 C
bgoss@jeffstateonline.com
GOSS, Christopher 617-353-2288 224 E
cgoss@bu.edu
GOSS, Jonathan, D 315-268-2290 321 C
jgoss@clarkson.edu
GOSS, Leah 832-813-6636 477 I
leah.goss@lonestar.edu
GOSS, Nathan, R 770-534-6162 121 G
ngoss@brenau.edu
GOSS, Ronald 541-956-7119 409 F
rgoss@roguecc.edu
GOSSARD, Paula 215-702-4264 414 C
pgossard@cairn.edu
GOSSELIN, Grant 508-286-3780 238 B
gosselin_grant@wheatoncollege.edu
GOSSELIN, Karen 603-623-0313 298 C
karengosselin@nhia.edu
GOSSEN, Douglas 920-693-1221 543 B
doug.gossen@gotoltc.edu
GOSSEN, Ronald, H 314-516-5776 284 B
ron@umsl.edu
GOSSEN, Tim 507-457-1640 264 B
tgossen@smumn.edu
GOSSETT, Angie 303-245-4797 84 B
agossett@naropa.edu
GOSSETT, John 828-652-0676 364 B
johngossett@mcdowelltech.edu
GOSWAMI, Jaya 361-593-4411 486 A
jaya.goswami@tamuk.edu
GOSWAMI, Utpal, K 816-604-3044 277 J
utpal.goswami@mcckc.edu
GOSWICK, Barbara 501-686-2500 23 F
bgoswic@uasys.edu
GOSZ, Michael 312-567-3198 147 E
gosz@iit.edu
GOTANDA, John 610-519-7005 439 A
gotanda@law.villanova.edu
GOTCHER, Mike 931-221-7414 461 C
gotcherm@apsu.edu
GOTHAM, Kerry 585-395-2068 345 A
kgotham@brockport.edu
GOTHARD, Mathew, J 303-963-3223 79 L
mgothard@ccu.edu
GOTLIEB, Anton 941-405-1512 423 B
agotlieb@lecom.edu
GOTSCHALL, Matt, R 402-562-1211 289 D
mgotschall@cccneb.edu
GOTSHALL, Kathy 812-535-5162 172 F
kgotshal@smwc.edu
GOTT, Jared 731-989-6649 456 K
jgott@fhu.edu
GOTTARDY, John 716-645-2450 343 E
johngott@buffalo.edu
GOTTDIENER, Yitzchok 718-941-8000 332 H
GOTTFRIED, Bradley 301-934-7625 214 E
bgottfried@csmd.edu
GOTTLIEB, Jane 212-799-5000 329 I
GOTTLIEB, Rachelle 904-620-2903 116 A
r.gottlieb@unf.edu
GOTTLIEB, Tracy, T 973-761-9074 308 C
tracy.gottlieb@shu.edu
GOTTSCHALK, Glenn, F 410-293-1911 549 B
gotts@usna.edu
GOTTSCHALK,
Katherine 765-983-1267 165 H
gottska@earlham.edu
GOTTSCHALK, Sandy 785-623-6150 190 A
sgottschalk@ncktc.edu
GOTTSHALL, Lori 954-771-0376 107 V
lgottshall@knoxseminary.edu
GOTTULA, Todd 308-865-8454 293 G
gottulatm@unk.edu
GOTZON, Mary, A 610-282-1100 416 I
mary.gotzon@desales.edu
GOUBEAUX, Nolan 208-732-6225 137 K
ngoubeaux@csi.edu
GOUCH, Zanetta 615-963-7401 461 F
zgouch@tnstate.edu
GOUDEAU, Arthur 281-487-1170 486 F
agoudeau@txchiro.edu
GOUDEAU, LaTasha 713-221-8162 491 F
goudeaul@uhd.edu
GOUDY, Senta 304-424-8341 533 E
senta.goudy@wvup.edu
GOUGH, Annette 732-571-3402 303 G
gough@monmouth.edu
GOUGH, Christopher 203-332-5022 89 C
cgough@hcc.commnet.edu
GOUGH, Darby 816-501-3660 272 E
darby.gough@avila.edu
GOUGH, Richard, J 843-525-8247 449 E
rgough@tcl.edu
GOUIN, Dean 303-846-1700 87 G
GOUKER, Dan 702-651-4163 295 C
dan.gouker@csn.edu
GOUKER, Toby 301-654-7267 218 D
GOULD, Amanda 413-565-1000 222 G
agould@baypath.edu
GOULD, Brandon 478-757-5233 134 E
ltimms@wesleyancollege.edu
GOULD, Brandon 478-757-5272 134 E
bgould@wesleyancollege.edu
GOULD, Cassie 212-517-0687 332 A
cdeutsch@mmm.edu
GOULD, Holly 617-369-4041 236 E
hgould@smfa.edu
GOULD, Karen, L 718-951-5671 318 F
bcpresident@brooklyn.cuny.edu
GOULD, Mark 978-837-5072 233 G
gouldm@merrimack.edu
GOULD, Robert, J 724-503-1001 439 B
rgould@washjeff.edu
GOULD, Teresa 530-752-4557 71 A
athleticsdirector@ucdavis.edu
GOULD, Thomas 252-493-7406 364 H
tgould@email.pittcc.edu
GOULDING, Laurel 701-662-1513 375 A
laurel.goulding@lrsc.edu
GOULDING, Ruth 619-239-0391 36 E
rgoulding@cwsl.edu
GOULDSBY, Cheryl 312-341-3801 157 E
cgouldsby@roosevelt.edu
GOULET, Camille, A 213-891-2188 51 C
gouletca@laccd.edu
GOULET, Caroline 210-283-6924 492 B
goulet@uiwtx.edu
GOULET, Stephen, P 508-793-7598 225 B
sgoulet@clarku.edu
GOUNARD, Jean, F 716-878-5331 345 B
gounarjf@buffalostate.edu
GOUPIL, Sharon 951-781-2727 61 D
srgoupil@sagecollege.edu
GOURD, David 206-934-4349 526 A
david.gourd@seattlecolleges.edu
GOURDINE, Raji 334-876-9292 4 B
rgourdine@wccs.edu
GOURJI, Konstantin 650-685-6616 46 I
GOURLEY, Kristin 865-981-8194 458 E
kristin.gourley@maryvillecollege.edu
GOURLEY, Pamela, L 276-944-6122 507 E
pgourley@ehc.edu
GOURNEAU, Haven 406-768-6300 286 H
hgourneau@fpcc.edu
GOURNEAU, William 701-255-3285 375 I
wgourneau@uttc.edu
GOUSE, Richard, I 401-739-5000 441 E
rgouse@neit.edu
GOUTTIERRE,
Thomas, E 402-554-2376 294 A
teg@unomaha.edu
GOUVEIA, Jan 808-956-6405 135 H
jgouveia@hawaii.edu
GOUVIN, Eric, J 413-796-2201 238 A
eric.gouvin@law.wne.edu
GOVAN, JR., Tom 708-596-2000 159 D
tgovan@ssc.edu
GOVE, Marilyn 949-480-4131 66 I
mgove@soka.edu
GOVE, Sue 573-897-5000 282 I
GOVEA, Sam 972-860-4216 472 C
sgovea@dcccd.edu
GOVER, Bruce 606-679-8501 197 B
bruce.gover@kctcs.edu
GOVER, Kristie 904-256-7067 106 Q
kgover1@ju.edu
GOVINDAN, Indira 201-692-2060 302 H
govindan@fdu.edu
GOVINDARAJU, Venu 716-645-3321 343 E
vpr@buffalo.edu
GOVITZ, Leanne 989-686-9490 242 I
leannegovitz@delta.edu
GOVITZ, Scott 989-386-6624 247 B
sgovitz@midmich.edu
GOVONI, Mark 215-951-2700 432 F
govonim@philau.edu
GOW, Joe 608-785-8004 539 G
jgow@uwlax.edu
GOWAN, Mary 540-568-3254 509 C
gowanma@jmu.edu
GOWEN, Claire 215-885-2360 425 C
Cgowen@manor.edu
GOWENS, Krystal 714-556-3610 75 A
krystal.gowens@vanguard.edu
GOWER, John, M 848-932-4300 306 F
michael.gower@rutgers.edu
GOWER, Paula 405-585-5410 399 I
paula.gower@okbu.edu
GOYETTE, Barbara 410-295-5554 218 A
barbara.goyette@sjc.edu
GOYETTE, Syl 815-836-5974 150 F
goyettsy@lewisu.edu
GOYUNYAN, Gevorg 510-987-9452 27 K
GOZIK, Nick 617-552-3827 224 B
nick.gozik@bc.edu
GOZUM, Allan 630-829-6418 140 A
agozum@ben.edu
GRABAN, Jennifer, L 812-488-1178 173 H
jg54@evansville.edu
GRABE, David 314-977-3923 281 M
dgrabe@slu.edu
GRABE, William 928-523-4340 16 C
William.Grabe@nau.edu
GRABER, David 402-375-7257 292 D
dagrabe1@wsc.edu
GRABER, Doug 620-947-3121 191 E
dougg@tabor.edu
GRABER, Linda 866-931-4300 281 A
linda.graber@rockbridge.edu
GRABER, Thomas 570-208-5900 422 D
thomasgraber@kings.edu
GRABER, Tony 316-284-5233 185 B
tgraber@bethelks.edu
GRABOWSKA, Lynette 605-367-6122 454 D
lynette.grabowska@southeasttech.edu
GRABOWSKI, Janice, T 724-925-4123 439 F
grabowskij@wccc.edu
GRABOWSKI, John, F 410-777-2231 213 E
jfgrabowski@aacc.edu
GRABOWSKI, Lisa 303-797-5746 79 A
lisa.grabowski@arapahoe.edu
GRABOWSKI, Mark 417-328-1556 282 D
mgrabowski@sbuniv.edu
GRABOWSKI, Rod, M 513-556-6703 393 B
grabowrd@ucmail.uc.edu
GRABUS, Scott 215-572-8515 412 F
grabuss@arcadia.edu
GRACA, Michael 508-286-3503 238 B
graca_michael@wheatoncollege.edu
GRACE, Coy, F 870-633-4480 20 J
cgrace@eacc.edu
GRACE, Dennis 239-304-7093 98 O
dennis.grace@avemaria.edu
GRACE, Glenda 718-997-5559 320 E
glenda.grace@qc.cuny.edu
GRACE, John 517-264-7198 250 B
jgrace@sienaheights.edu
GRACE, Melissa, H 850-474-3423 116 E
mgrace@uwf.edu
GRACE, Michelle, M 847-543-2274 142 G
mgrace@clcillinois.edu
GRACE, Nabil, F 248-204-2500 245 J
ngrace@ltu.edu
GRACE, Selena 208-373-1874 138 C
gracsele@isu.edu
GRACE, Sherie 256-228-6001 6 A
graces@nacc.edu
GRACE, Ted, W 618-453-4485 159 H
tgrace@siu.edu
GRACIA, Hector 787-780-0070 550 G
asistenciaeconomica@caribbean.edu
GRACIA, Jessica, L 508-565-1301 237 A
jlgracia@stonehill.edu
GRACYALNY, David 410-225-2220 216 F
dgracyal@mica.edu
GRACYK, June 440-684-6083 394 G
jgracyk@ursuline.edu
GRADER, Timothy 413-205-3050 221 G
timothy.grader@aic.edu
GRADOWSKI, Charles 484-365-7404 424 E
cgradowski@lincoln.edu
GRADY, Amber 870-512-7890 19 I
amber_grady@asun.edu
GRADY, Amber, N 870-759-4188 25 I
agrady@wbcoll.edu
GRADY, Carole 453-879-4802 499 M
grady@dixie.edu
GRADY, Christine 815-753-1311 154 I
cgrady@niu.edu
GRADY, David, L 205-348-6681 8 E
david.grady@ua.edu
GRADY, Dennis 540-831-5431 511 C
dgrady4@radford.edu
GRADY, Helene 443-997-3359 216 A
hgrady1@jhu.edu
GRADY, Lynne 706-379-3111 134 J
lbgrady@yhc.edu
GRADY, Meghan 610-606-4612 415 A
megrady@cedarcrest.edu
GRADY, Sara 508-929-8130 230 G
Sara.Grady@worcester.edu
GRADY, Sarah 718-409-7262 348 C
sgrady@sunymaritime.edu
GRAEBERT, James, K 414-288-3048 537 B
james.graebert@marquette.edu
GRAEM, David 903-675-6364 490 F
dgraem@tvcc.edu
GRAETHER, Anna 816-654-7122 276 G
agraether@kcumb.edu
GRAF, Bob 651-696-6280 256 L
rgraf@macalester.edu
GRAF, Elizabeth 219-866-6195 172 E
bethg@saintjoe.edu
GRAF, Katie, M 716-839-8364 323 F
kgraf@daemen.edu
GRAF, Megan 713-646-2968 482 H
mgraf@stcl.edu
GRAFF, Eric, S 614-885-5585 390 G
egraff@pcj.edu
GRAFF, Irene 310-660-3670 43 G
igraff@elcamino.edu
GRAFF, Irene 310-660-3515 43 G
igraff@elcamino.edu
GRAFF, Jenna 920-424-0775 540 B
graff@uwosh.edu
GRAFF, Jonathan 575-624-8480 311 K
graff@nmmi.edu
GRAFF, Nadja 212-463-0400 350 C
nadja.graff@touro.edu
GRAFFICE, Anne 330-823-2030 394 A
graffiaz@mountunion.edu
GRAFFIUS, Jeff 740-753-6336 383 G
graffiusj@hocking.edu
GRAFTON, Anthony 870-307-7315 21 G
anthony.grafton@lyon.edu
GRAFTON, David 215-248-7313 424 G
dgrafton@ltsp.edu
GRAFTON, Ken 701-231-7655 374 C
k.grafton@ndsu.edu
GRAFTON, Steve, C 734-763-9730 251 C
sgrafton@umich.edu
GRAGG, Derrick 918-631-2181 403 M
derrick-gragg@utulsa.edu
GRAGG, T. Dewayne 903-875-7376 479 I
dewayne.gragg@navarrocollege.edu
GRAHAM, Amy 315-470-7858 316 I
amygraham@crouse.org
GRAHAM, Angela 540-863-2806 515 B
agraham@dslcc.edu
GRAHAM, Anthony 336-334-7757 370 B
agraham@ncat.edu
GRAHAM, April 661-362-3248 40 H
april.graham@canyons.edu
GRAHAM, Archie 414-297-6870 543 E
grahama@matc.edu
GRAHAM, Bernard 570-408-4280 440 B
bernard.graham@wilkes.edu
GRAHAM, Bobbi Jo 412-291-6286 412 H
bgraham@aii.edu
GRAHAM, Carole 540-857-6696 517 E
cgraham@virginiawestern.edu
GRAHAM, Catherine 310-338-2753 53 C
cgraham@lmu.edu
GRAHAM, Charles, W 405-325-5693 403 I
cwgraham@ou.edu
GRAHAM, Chris 858-642-8076 55 J
cgraham2@nu.edu
GRAHAM, Christy 423-869-6314 458 B
christy.graham@lmunet.edu
GRAHAM, Chuck 352-335-2332 97 F
GRAHAM, Darnell 617-989-4605 237 G
GRAHAM, Darren 641-683-4273 179 C
darren.graham@indianhills.edu
GRAHAM, Diedrick 215-596-8785 438 E
d.graham@usciences.edu
GRAHAM, Donald Kim 706-233-7469 131 C
dgraham@shorter.edu
GRAHAM, Duncan 408-298-2181 64 A
GRAHAM, Earl 203-332-5290 89 C
egraham@housatonic.edu
GRAHAM, Greg 321-674-7707 103 R
ggraham@fit.edu
GRAHAM, Gwen 219-464-5115 174 E
gwen.graham@valpo.edu
GRAHAM, James, F 660-543-4279 283 F
graham@ucmo.edu
GRAHAM, Janielle 773-995-2067 141 J
jgraham@csu.edu
GRAHAM, Jean 251-580-2293 5 A
jean.graham@faulknerstate.edu
GRAHAM, Jeanne 906-932-4231 243 B
jeanneg@gogebic.edu
GRAHAM, Jeffrey 956-665-7150 494 C
grahamja@utpa.edu
GRAHAM, Jennifer 254-298-8592 484 C
jennifer.graham@templejc.edu
GRAHAM, Joan, E 585-475-6079 339 G
jegirp@rit.edu
GRAHAM, John 845-938-5868 549 A
John.Graham@usma.edu
GRAHAM, III, John 412-346-2100 433 B
jgrahamiii@pia.edu
GRAHAM, John, D 812-855-1432 167 J
grahamjd@indiana.edu
GRAHAM, John, L 610-399-2417 430 D
jgraham@cheyney.edu
GRAHAM, John, M 512-471-4716 493 M
john.graham@athletics.utexas.edu
GRAHAM, John-Bauer 256-782-5255 4 L
jgraham@jsu.edu
GRAHAM, Kate 281-929-4653 481 G
kate.graham@sjcd.edu

GRAY, Carol .... 254-526-1668 470 E
carol.gray@ctcd.edu
GRAY, Charlotte .... 417-967-5466 283 C
GRAY, Christopher ...... 309-694-5132 146 C
christopher.gray@icc.edu
GRAY, Corey .... 402-643-3651 289 J
corey.gray@cune.edu
GRAY, Craig .... 205-665-6116.... 9 C
cgray2@montevallo.edu
GRAY, David .... 575-624-8078 311 K
david@nmmi.edu
GRAY, David, J .... 814-865-6574 428 C
djg36@psu.edu
GRAY, David, R .... 540-868-7154 515 H
dgray@lfcc.edu
GRAY, Denise .... 502-213-7202 196 E
denise.gray@kctcs.edu
GRAY, Donna, L .... 312-777-8652 147 C
dlgray@aii.edu
GRAY, Douglass, P ...... 410-827-5830 214 D
dgray@chesapeake.edu
GRAY, Gary .... 907-474-7780.. 10 I
GRAY, Gary, W .... 714-449-7481.. 53 D
ggray@ketchum.edu
GRAY, Glenn .... 319-273-2333 176 A
glenn.gray@uni.edu
GRAY, Gregory, S .... 334-727-8011.... 8 B
gsgray@tuskegee.edu
GRAY, Gregory, W .... 860-723-0011.. 88 C
grayg@ct.edu
GRAY, James .... 781-736-4520 224 F
jwgray@brandeis.edu
GRAY, Jarrod .... 217-854-3231 140 F
jarrod.gray@blackburn.edu
GRAY, Jeff .... 478-387-4781 125 E
jgray@gmc.edu
GRAY, Jeffrey .... 515-271-1506 177 H
jeffrey.gray@dmu.edu
GRAY, Jeffrey, L .... 718-817-4750 326 C
gray@fordham.edu
GRAY, Joe .... 615-547-1255 456 C
jgray@cumberland.edu
GRAY, John .... 910-755-7434 360 E
grayj@brunswickcc.edu
GRAY, John, C .... 302-295-1139.. 94 G
john.c.gray@wilmu.edu
GRAY, Karen .... 614-251-4741 388 H
Grayk4@ohiodominican.edu
GRAY, Kelly .... 419-755-4823 387 E
kgray@ncstatecollege.edu
GRAY, Kelly .... 575-769-4179 310 G
kelly.gray@clovis.edu
GRAY, Kilen .... 502-895-3411 198 E
kgray@lpts.edu
GRAY, Kristen .... 706-778-0100 130 B
kgray@piedmont.edu
GRAY, Kristen .... 616-395-7945 244 A
gray@hope.edu
GRAY, Leah .... 731-425-2606 463 A
lgray@jscc.edu
GRAY, Leslie .... 510-594-3705.. 30 G
lgray@cca.edu
GRAY, Lisa, G .... 410-546-6390 220 E
lggray@salisbury.edu
GRAY, Lydia, E .... 718-862-7231 331 H
lydia.gray@manhattan.edu
GRAY, Marisa .... 913-288-7284 188 G
mcgray@kckcc.edu
GRAY, Maryann, J .... 310-825-5573.. 71 D
mgray@conet.ucla.edu
GRAY, Megan .... 419-251-1784 386 C
megan.gray@mercycollege.edu
GRAY, Michaelle .... 580-371-2371 398 J
mgray@mscok.edu
GRAY, Nancy .... 970-339-6392.. 78 J
nancy.gray@aims.edu
GRAY, Nancy, O .... 540-362-6321 508 D
presoffc@hollins.edu
GRAY, Paul .... 314-505-7257 273 G
grayp@csl.edu
GRAY, Rebecca .... 254-968-9473 485 A
rgray@tarleton.edu
GRAY, Robert, R .... 804-257-5842 518 E
rrgray@vuu.edu
GRAY, Sandra, C .... 859-858-3511 193 A
president@asbury.edu
GRAY, Sarah .... 309-649-6265 160 F
sarah.gray@src.edu
GRAY, Seneca .... 503-768-6781 406 H
seneca@lclark.edu
GRAY, Shashuna .... 540-891-3046 515 E
dgray@germanna.edu
GRAY, Shaun .... 207-741-5580 211 D
sgray@smccme.edu
GRAY, Shawn .... 409-880-8466 488 F
shawn.gray@lamar.edu
GRAY, Sheryl .... 865-471-3240 455 G
sgray@cn.edu
GRAY, Shonda .... 443-885-3430 217 C
shonda.gray@morgan.edu
GRAY, Simon .... 716-285-1212 336 E
sgray@niagara.edu
GRAY, Susan .... 478-289-2028 124 B
sgray@ega.edu
GRAY, Tiffany .... 206-296-6070 526 F
grayt@seattleu.edu
GRAY, Tim .... 303-937-4420.. 79 E
GRAY, Tim .... 319-208-5022 183 B
tgray@scciowa.edu
GRAY, Toni .... 806-354-6083 467 E
tbgray@actx.edu
GRAY, Tracy .... 858-695-8587.. 47 E
tgray@horizonuniversity.edu
GRAY, Vance .... 404-756-4033 120 H
vgray@atlm.edu
GRAY, Velma .... 901-435-1676 457 N
velma_gray@loc.edu
GRAY, Warren .... 606-589-3070 197 D
warren.gray@kctcs.edu
GRAY, Warren, S .... 401-865-1602 441 F
wgray@providence.edu
GRAY, Wilbur, E .... 717-728-2511 415 B
billgray@centralpenn.edu
GRAY-DEVINE, Sherry .. 580-371-2371 398 J
GRAY KOGEN,
Elizabeth .... 212-472-1500 336 A
giving@nysid.edu
GRAY-LITTLE,
Bernadette .... 785-864-3131 191 G
graylittle@ku.edu
GRAY PAYTON, Pamela 619-260-4681.. 74 B
grayp@sandiego.edu
GRAY-ROBERTSON,
Beth .... 252-536-7299 363 B
bgray-robertson498@halifaxcc.edu
GRAY-SINGH, Danielle . 404-880-6161 122 I
dsingh@cau.edu
GRAY-VICKREY, Peg ..... 254-519-5447 485 D
gray-vickrey@tamuct.edu
GRAYBEAL, Clay .... 207-221-4509 213 B
cgraybeal@une.edu
GRAYBEAL, Jerry, G ..... 801-626-8114 500 C
jgraybeal@weber.edu
GRAYBEAL, Susan, E .... 423-354-2471 463 D
segraybeal@northeaststate.edu
GRAYBILL, Jody, D .... 570-577-3351 413 E
jody.graybill@bucknell.edu
GRAYBOYS, James .... 334-229-4401.... 1 D
jgrayboys@alasu.edu
GRAYLEE, Laleh .... 657-278-4228.. 33 E
lgraylee@fullerton.edu
GRAYS, Shantay .... 713-718-5053 475 C
shantay.grays@hccs.edu
GRAYSON, Chinester .... 334-874-5700.... 3 B
cgrayson@ccal.edu
GRAYSON, Denise, R ... 605-256-5152 453 H
denise.grayson@dsu.edu
GRAYSON, Lorenzo ...... 251-405-7170.... 2 D
lgrayson@bishop.edu
GRAYSON, Paul .... 212-774-0727 332 A
pgrayson@mmm.edu
GRAYSON, Shari .... 858-505-1100.. 47 M
sgrayson@ipsb.edu
GRAZIANO, Joanne ...... 516-299-2999 330 G
joanne.graziano@liu.edu
GRAZIANO, Vincent, S . 412-391-6710 413 B
vgraziano@bradfordpittsburgh.edu
GRAZZINI-OLSON,
Nancy .... 952-851-0066 253 E
GRBIC, Ana .... 313-593-5666 251 D
GREAF, Eileen .... 304-829-7633 529 H
egreaf@bethanywv.edu
GREANEY, Bryan .... 917-493-4477 331 I
bgreaney@msmnyc.edu
GREANEY, KC .... 707-778-4188.. 65 C
kgreaney@santarosa.edu
GREASON, Jessica .... 816-584-6329 280 F
jessica.greason@park.edu
GREATHOUSE, Adam .... 618-395-7777 147 A
greathousea@iecc.edu
GREATHOUSE, Jan .... 615-248-7782 464 E
jgreathouse@trevecca.edu
GREATHOUSE, Jo .... 979-230-3234 469 G
jo.greathouse@brazosport.edu
GREATHOUSE, Maren ... 973-353-3416 307 C
maren.greathouse@rutgers.edu
GREAVES, Christopher .. 718-997-3930 320 E
christopher.greaves@qc.cuny.edu
GREAVES, Matthew, C .. 202-687-3488.. 95 E
mcg3@georgetown.edu
GREB, Christine .... 215-951-2808 432 F
grebc@philau.edu
GREBEL, David, A .... 817-257-7130 486 G
d.grebel@tcu.edu
GREBERT, Robert .... 518-292-7702 340 A
greber@sage.edu
GREBIN, Kevin .... 605-331-6772 454 E
kevin.grebin@usiouxfalls.edu
GREBING, Karen .... 239-513-1122 106 E
kgrebing@hodges.edu
GREBING, Robin, E ...... 314-539-5189 281 H
rgrebing2@stlcc.edu
GRECO, Anne .... 215-751-8217 416 B
agreco@ccp.edu
GRECO, Frank, M .... 412-365-1133 415 C
greco@chatham.edu
GRECO, Juneann .... 570-340-6004 425 D
greco@marywood.edu
GRECO, Michelle .... 504-671-6001 203 F
mgreco@dcc.edu
GRECO, Peter .... 925-631-4747.. 61 G
peter.greco2@stmarys-ca.edu
GRECO, Tom .... 620-241-0723 185 M
tom.greco@centralchristian.edu
GREDER, Darcy, L .... 309-556-3541 148 A
dgreder@iwu.edu
GREEAR, Amy .... 276-523-7480 516 A
agreear@mecc.edu
GREELEY, Brian, G .... 617-333-2159 225 F
bgreeley1204@curry.edu
GREEN, Adam .... 304-558-0655 532 C
green@hepc.wvnet.edu
GREEN, Allen .... 914-395-2249 342 C
agreen@sarahlawrence.edu
GREEN, Andrew .... 516-726-6182 548 I
greena@usmma.edu
GREEN, Andy .... 256-782-5268.... 4 L
agreen@jsu.edu
GREEN, Anita .... 313-593-5190 251 D
ujima@umich.edu
GREEN, Ann, F .... 828-694-1709 360 D
anng@blueridge.edu
GREEN, Anne-Marie ..... 815-825-2086 149 E
anne-marie.green@kishwaukeecollege.edu
GREEN, Ashley .... 817-552-3700 477 B
ashley.green@tku.edu
GREEN, Audrey .... 661-362-3424.. 40 H
audrey.green@canyons.edu
GREEN, Barbara, C .... 626-395-6351.. 31 D
barbarag@caltech.edu
GREEN, Betti .... 315-781-3600 327 G
bgreen@hws.edu
GREEN, Beverly .... 909-607-7821.. 39 E
beverly.green@cgu.edu
GREEN, Bevley, W .... 251-460-6188.... 9 F
bwgreen@southalabama.edu
GREEN, Bichevia .... 803-536-0311 448 C
GREEN, Brenda .... 561-586-0121 105 R
bgreen@hci.edu
GREEN, Cheryl .... 703-526-6978 510 B
cheryl.green@marymount.edu
GREEN, Chris .... 805-546-3120.. 42 H
cgreen@cuesta.edu
GREEN, Chris .... 859-985-3727 193 F
greenchr@berea.edu
GREEN, Cindy .... 314-539-5227 281 H
cgreen2@stlcc.edu
GREEN, Clarence .... 660-562-1254 280 A
cgreen@nwmissouri.edu
GREEN, Constance, C .. 503-842-8222 410 C
green@tillamookbay.cc
GREEN, Daniel .... 518-244-2467 340 A
greend@sage.edu
GREEN, David, A .... 217-786-2406 151 C
david.green@llcc.edu
GREEN, David, M .... 818-947-2679.. 52 B
greendm@lavc.edu
GREEN, Don .... 657-278-2413.. 33 E
dgreen@fullerton.edu
GREEN, Donald .... 217-732-3168 150 G
pres@lincolnchristian.edu
GREEN, Donald, J .... 706-295-6329 125 C
dgreen@highlands.edu
GREEN, Donna .... 562-985-8416.. 33 F
donna.green@csulb.edu
GREEN, Dwayne .... 320-629-5159 260 H
greend@pinetech.edu
GREEN, Elaine .... 215-248-7063 415 D
greene@chc.edu
GREEN, Eleanor, M .... 979-845-5051 485 C
emgreen@tamu.edu
GREEN, Ellen, R .... 806-371-5131 467 E
ergreen@actx.edu
GREEN, Elna .... 408-924-2450.. 36 B
elna.green@sjsu.edu
GREEN, Gary, M .... 336-734-7200 362 F
ggreen@forsythtech.edu
GREEN, Geoff .... 805-965-0581.. 64 N
green@sbccfoundation.org
GREEN, Greg .... 512-492-3017 468 A
ggreen@aoma.edu
GREEN, Hope .... 773-380-6840 163 E
hgreen@westwood.edu
GREEN, James .... 314-340-3502 275 G
greenj@hssu.edu
GREEN, James .... 843-574-6774 449 G
james.green@tridenttech.edu
GREEN, Jean .... 217-228-5432 156 D
greenje@quincy.edu
GREEN, Jeffrey .... 312-662-4401 139 E
jgreen@adler.edu
GREEN, Jennifer .... 909-621-8000.. 46 K
jgreen@hmc.edu
GREEN, Jennifer .... 800-290-4226 457 A
jgreen@hchs.edu
GREEN, Jennifer, K .... 434-395-2944 509 H
mailto:greenjk@longwood.edu
GREEN, Jerry .... 718-817-4170 326 C
jgreen@fordham.edu
GREEN, Joel, B .... 626-584-5304.. 45 F
jbgreen@fuller.edu
GREEN, John .... 661-362-3684.. 40 H
john.green@canyons.edu
GREEN, John .... 312-369-7291 143 C
jgreen@colum.edu
GREEN, John .... 252-222-6273 361 A
greenj@carteret.edu
GREEN, John .... 610-683-4000 431 B
GREEN, John, C .... 610-683-4114 431 B
jgreen@kutztown.edu
GREEN, Jonathan, D ..... 309-556-3101 148 A
provost@iwu.edu
GREEN, Judith .... 201-684-7523 305 F
jgreen2@ramapo.edu
GREEN, Julia .... 207-941-7129 210 C
greenj@husson.edu
GREEN, Karen .... 336-517-2159 354 K
kagreen@bennett.edu
GREEN, Karen .... 484-664-3182 427 C
green@muhlenberg.edu
GREEN, Keith, A .... 717-901-5123 420 I
kgreen@harrisburgu.edu
GREEN, Kelly .... 360-596-5214 527 B
kgreen@spscc.edu
GREEN, Latrelle, A .... 804-257-5662 518 E
lagreen@vuu.edu
GREEN, Lawrence .... 610-399-2137 430 D
lgreen@cheyney.edu
GREEN, Lillie, F .... 757-727-5057 508 C
lillie.green@hamptonu.edu
GREEN, Lina .... 757-455-2115 518 H
lgreen@vwc.edu
GREEN, Lisa .... 315-792-3736 351 G
lcgreen@utica.edu
GREEN, Lois .... 310-577-3000.. 77 K
lgreen@yosan.edu
GREEN, Lorry .... 864-977-7124 448 A
lorry.green@ngu.edu
GREEN, Lynette .... 920-403-3235 538 K
lynette.green@snc.edu
GREEN, Mariah .... 970-943-7122.. 87 F
mgreen@western.edu
GREEN, Mark, A .... 618-235-2700 160 B
mark.green@swic.edu
GREEN, Mary .... 269-965-3931 244 L
greenm@kellogg.edu
GREEN, Mary Jo .... 715-422-5504 543 D
maryjo.green@mstc.edu
GREEN, Matthew .... 845-688-1568 350 I
greenm@sunyulster.edu
GREEN, Matthew .... 805-546-3924.. 42 H
mgreen@cuesta.edu
GREEN, Melanie, H .... 804-627-5300 505 E
melanie_green@bshsi.org
GREEN, Melissa .... 530-938-5374.. 41 E
mgreen8@siskiyous.edu
GREEN, Melissa .... 567-429-3535 390 D
melissa_green3@owens.edu
GREEN, III, Melvin .... 229-333-5954 133 H
GREEN, Michael, R .... 717-867-6208 423 I
mgreen@lvc.edu
GREEN, Michael, S .... 518-629-4554 328 D
m.green@hvcc.edu
GREEN, Mike .... 541-737-2092 408 F
GREEN, Mike .... 615-966-6000 458 C
mike.green@lipscomb.edu
GREEN, Moishe .... 845-352-5852 353 A
GREEN, Monica .... 951-372-7877.. 61 A
monica.green@norcocollege.edu
GREEN, Nancy .... 704-403-3599 355 B
nancy.green@carolinashealthcare.org
GREEN, Nichole .... 575-492-2122 314 D
ngreen@usw.edu
GREEN, O. Jerome .... 501-374-6305.. 23 A
GREEN, Paul .... 785-827-5541 189 A
green@kwu.edu
GREEN, Paula .... 626-914-8873.. 38 L
pgreen@citruscollege.edu
GREEN, Rachel .... 570-662-4815 431 D
rgreen@mansfield.edu
GREEN, Ragan .... 478-275-7865 129 D
rgreen@oftc.edu
GREEN, Ramona .... 903-223-3058 486 C
ramona.green@tamut.edu
GREEN, Ray .... 903-468-3005 485 E
raymond.green@tamuc.edu
GREEN, Rebecca .... 760-355-6499.. 47 G
becky.green@imperial.edu
GREEN, Renee, R .... 850-201-6564 117 B
greenr@tcc.fl.edu
GREEN, Richard .... 484-365-7400 424 E

GREEN, Robert, L .... 540-464-7321 518 A
greenrl@vmi.edu
GREEN, Ronnie .... 402-472-2871 293 F
rgreen2@unl.edu
GREEN, Ronnie, D .... 402-472-2871 293 H
rgreen2@unl.edu
GREEN, Ronnie, D .... 402-472-3751 293 H
rgreen2@unl.edu
GREEN, Rosalyn .... 405-744-9153 400 C
rosalyn.green@okstate.edu
GREEN, Ruvain .... 845-352-5852 353 A
GREEN, Ryanne .... 916-361-1660.. 37 A
rgreen@carrington.edu
GREEN, Samantha .... 973-720-2107 309 I
greens19@wpunj.edu
GREEN, Sandy, B .... 864-488-8348 447 F
sgreen@limestone.edu
GREEN, Satasha .... 773-995-3764 141 J
sgreen34@csu.edu
GREEN, Sean-Michael .. 203-932-7157.. 92 G
smgreen@newhaven.edu
GREEN, Shirley .... 602-787-6604.. 15 B
shirley.green@paradisevalley.edu
GREEN, Stacy .... 207-974-4679 211 A
sgreen@emcc.edu
GREEN, Steven, A .... 570-348-6210 425 D
sgreen@marywood.edu
GREEN, Susan .... 734-432-5595 246 B
sgreen@madonna.edu
GREEN, Susan .... 802-635-1308 504 A
susan.green@jsc.edu
GREEN, Teresa .... 806-716-2205 482 F
tgreen@southplainscollege.edu
GREEN, Teresa .... 806-894-9611 482 F
tgreen@southplainscollege.edu
GREEN, Tica, D .... 336-272-7102 357 B
tica.green@greensboro.edu
GREEN, Tiffany .... 256-539-8161.... 4 J
GREEN, Tim .... 256-549-8601.... 3 N
tgreen@gadsdenstate.edu
GREEN, Timothy, M ..... 615-248-1387 464 E
tgreen@trevecca.edu
GREEN, Tom .... 216-421-7491 380 B
tgreen@cia.edu
GREEN, Tracey .... 315-498-2532 337 F
greent@sunyocc.edu
GREEN, Tracie .... 209-384-6000.. 54 C
tracie.green@mccd.edu
GREEN, Tracy, A .... 440-365-5222 385 E
GREEN, Tracy, S .... 804-523-5789 515 F
tgreen@reynolds.edu
GREEN, Vashba .... 813-880-8013 112 E
vgreen@sbtampa.com
GREEN, Walter .... 678-359-5733 126 E
walterg@gordonstate.edu
GREEN, Wayne .... 334-974-5700.... 3 B
wgreen@ccal.edu
GREEN, Wayne, A .... 845-938-3419 549 A
8sgs@usma.edu
GREEN, William .... 423-614-8240 457 M
wgreen@leeuniversity.edu.edu
GREEN, William, S .... 305-284-2006 118 A
wgreen@miami.edu
GREEN COWLES, Maria 301-696-3811 215 E
cowles@hood.edu
GREEN-HAMANN,
Matthew .... 207-992-4951 210 C
green-hamannm@husson.edu
GREEN POWELL,
Patricia .... 850-561-2989 114 D
patricia.greenpowell@famu.edu
GREEN-YOUNG, Brian .. 405-208-5759 190 K
brian.green-young@spst.edu
GREENAN, Jennie .... 309-692-4092 152 F
jgreenan@midstate.edu
GREENBAUM,
Steven, D .... 215-885-2360 425 C
sgreenbaum@manor.edu
GREENBAUN, Yvonne ... 856-415-2138 306 C
ygreenbaun@rcgc.edu
GREENBERG, David ...... 212-854-4446 322 F
david.greenberg@columbia.edu
GREENBERG, Erika ...... 970-339-6647.. 78 J
erika.greenberg@aims.edu
GREENBERG, Mark .... 360-650-3051 528 D
mark.greenberg@wwu.edu
GREENBERG,
Penelope, S .... 610-499-4475 439 G
psgreenberg@widener.edu
GREENBERG,
Raymond, S .... 512-499-4201 493 K
GREENBERG, Roberta ... 718-933-6700 333 F
rgreenbe@monroecollege.edu
GREENBERG, Scott, B .. 508-626-4550 230 A
sgreenberg@framingham.edu
GREENBERG, Yeshaya .. 305-534-7050 117 C
GREENE, Andrew, S ..... 717-867-6200 423 I
greene@lvc.edu
GREENE, Brenda .... 718-270-4949 320 C
bgreene@mec.cuny.edu
GREENE, Carol .... 606-326-2142 195 H
Carol.Greene@kctcs.edu
GREENE, Cary .... 910-695-3781 365 H
greenec@sandhills.edu
GREENE, Christina .... 910-362-7074 360 G
cgreene@cfcc.edu
GREENE, Clark .... 401-456-8000 442 A
cgreene@ric.edu
GREENE, Dale .... 706-542-4741 132 H
wdgreene@uga.edu
GREENE, David, A .... 207-859-4604 210 A
david.greene@colby.edu
GREENE, Doug .... 641-782-1324 183 D
greene@swcciowa.edu
GREENE, Dwaine .... 502-863-8030 195 A
president@georgetowncollege.edu
GREENE, Eric .... 269-965-3931 244 L
greenee@kellogg.edu
GREENE, Gayle .... 919-866-5143 366 H
dggreene@waketech.edu
GREENE, Gloria .... 256-824-6000.... 9 A
gloria.green@uah.edu
GREENE, James .... 202-319-5247.. 95 A
greene@cua.edu
GREENE, James .... 386-506-4429 101 I
greenej@DaytonaState.edu
GREENE, Jason, T .... 618-453-7960 159 H
jgreene@cba.siu.edu
GREENE, Jeff, W .... 606-474-3298 195 F
jgreene@kcu.edu
GREENE, Jessica, A ...... 617-552-3111 224 B
jessica.greene.2@bc.edu
GREENE, Joseph, J ...... 401-598-1038 441 D
JGreene@jwu.edu
GREENE, Julia .... 860-512-3372.. 89 D
jgreene@manchestercc.edu
GREENE, Karen, L .... 614-234-5685 386 N
kgreene@mccn.edu
GREENE, Ken, S .... 252-334-2019 359 D
ken.greene@macuniversity.edu
GREENE, Kerry .... 781-762-1211 226 E
kgreene@fmc.edu
GREENE, Kimberly .... 714-556-3610.. 75 A
kimberly.greene@vanguard.edu
GREENE, Kimberly .... 417-477-8198 280 C
greenek@otc.edu
GREENE, Lori .... 317-940-6086 164 L
lgreene@butler.edu
GREENE, Michael .... 870-248-4000.. 20 E
mike.greene@blackrivertech.edu
GREENE, Mike .... 480-732-7146.. 14 K
Mike.Greene@cgc.edu
GREENE, Moshe .... 516-239-9002 342 G
GREENE, Myra .... 864-388-8351 447 E
mgreene@lander.edu
GREENE, Patricia .... 843-521-4117 450 D
pagreene@uscb.edu
GREENE, Peggy .... 503-399-6031 404 L
peggy.greene@chemeketa.edu
GREENE, Perry .... 516-877-4041 314 F
greene@adelphi.edu
GREENE, Randy .... 201-216-8761 308 D
Rgreene@stevens.edu
GREENE, Richard .... 504-278-6418 204 B
rgreene@nunez.edu
GREENE, Roger .... 212-410-8147 335 B
rgreene@nycpm.edu
GREENE, Ryan .... 206-296-6260 526 F
greener@seattleu.edu
GREENE, Sarah, E .... 717-867-6985 423 I
sgreene@lvc.edu
GREENE, Shelley, W ..... 336-633-0174 365 A
swgreene@randolph.edu
GREENE, Thomas, G .... 916-484-8211.. 52 I
greenet@arc.losrios.edu
GREENE, Thomas, G .... 503-943-7105 410 H
greene@up.edu
GREENE,
Thomas Christopher .. 802-828-8613 503 D
thomas.greene@vcfa.edu
GREENE, Timothy, J ..... 269-387-2378 252 I
tim.greene@wmich.edu
GREENE, Tom .... 718-636-3787 338 E
tgreene@pratt.edu
GREENE, Tommy .... 704-669-4084 361 E
greene@clevelandcc.edu
GREENE, Tracy .... 605-688-5248 454 C
tracy.greene@sdstate.edu
GREENE, Travis .... 661-255-1050.. 31 B
tgreene@calarts.edu
GREENE, Vanessa .... 616-395-7800 244 A
greene@hope.edu
GREENE-RAINEY, Velva 484-365-7335 424 E
vgrainey@lincoln.edu
GREENER, Kristen, A .... 610-989-1471 438 I
kgreener@vfmac.edu
GREENFELD, Shia .... 718-782-7070 351 C
swg@utsny.edu
GREENFIELD,
Brenda, T .... 315-470-6683 347 B
bgreenfield@esf.edu
GREENFIELD, Helga ...... 404-270-6425 132 D
hgreenfield@spelman.edu
GREENFIELD, Ilene .... 973-278-5400 300 C
igl@berkeleycollege.edu
GREENFIELD, Ilene .... 973-278-5400 316 D
igl@berkeleycollege.edu
GREENFIELD, Marriane . 404-527-4520 122 D
mgreenfield@carver.edu
GREENFIELD, Meg .... 504-278-6424 204 B
mgreenfield@nunez.edu
GREENFIELD,
Wendy, M .... 610-526-5221 413 D
wgreenfi@brynmawr.edu
GREENGART, Eli .... 410-484-7200 217 E
egreengart@nirc.edu
GREENHALGH, Jill .... 651-779-3338 258 D
jill.greenhalgh@century.edu
GREENHALGH, Mark ...... 714-992-7042.. 56 F
mgreenhalgh@fullcoll.edu
GREENHAW, David, M . 314-918-2620 274 K
dgreenhaw@eden.edu
GREENHAW, Eric .... 479-524-7285.. 21 F
EGreenhaw@jbu.edu
GREENHOUSE, Jeremy . 413-755-4524 233 B
jgreenhouse@stcc.edu
GREENING, Doug .... 936-294-1910 489 A
ppl_djg@shsu.edu
GREENING, Kris .... 870-743-3000.. 22 A
kgreening@northark.edu
GREENLAND, William ... 773-702-7433 161 D
greenland@uchicago.edu
GREENLAW, David, E .... 407-303-7894.. 97 J
dave.greenlaw@adu.edu
GREENLEAF, Maxine ..... 662-254-3577 269 C
max.greenleaf@mvsu.edu
GREENLEE, Carmen, M 207-725-3286 209 H
cgreenle@bowdoin.edu
GREENLEE, Lisa .... 580-477-7702 404 D
lisa.greenlee@wosc.edu
GREENO, Ben .... 847-628-2543 149 A
bgreeno@judsonu.edu
GREENO, Darren .... 360-416-7729 527 A
darren.greeno@skagit.edu
GREENO, Jimmie .... 215-972-2303 429 G
jgreeno@pafa.edu
GREENSLADE,
Ernestine .... 978-556-3862 232 E
egreenslade@necc.mass.edu
GREENSLADE-SMITH,
Toni .... 614-292-8266 389 A
greenslade-smith.1@osu.edu
GREENSTEIN, Amy .... 212-875-4402 315 F
gradcourses@bankstreet.edu
GREENSTEIN, Benjamin 319-895-4251 177 A
bgreenstein@cornellcollege.edu
GREENSTEIN, David ...... 212-353-4198 323 B
davidg@cooper.edu
GREENSTREET,
Robert, C .... 414-229-4016 540 A
bobg@uwm.edu
GREENTHAL, Joseph, T 607-587-3938 347 D
greentjt@alfredstate.edu
GREENUP, Troy .... 562-907-4287.. 77 E
greenup@whittier.edu
GREENWADE, Gabrielle 281-487-1170 486 F
ggreenwade@txchiro.edu
GREENWALD,
J. Patrick .... 716-888-8216 317 H
greenwal@canisius.edu
GREENWALD, Lorraine . 631-420-2479 348 B
lorraine.greenwald@farmingdale.edu
GREENWALD, Nicole .... 206-876-6100 526 E
ngreenwald@theseattleschool.edu
GREENWALD, Reesa ..... 973-275-2828 308 C
reesa.greenwald@shu.edu
GREENWALT, Riane, B .. 618-650-2852 159 I
rgreenw@siue.edu
GREENWAY, Adam .... 502-897-4043 199 D
agreenway@sbts.edu
GREENWAY, Janet .... 605-995-7136 452 H
janet.greenway@mitchelltech.edu
GREENWAY, Kimberly .. 256-765-4248.... 9 D
kagreenway@una.edu
GREENWAY, Lidell .... 229-468-2240 134 I
lidell.greenway@wiregrass.edu
GREENWELL, Brian .... 330-490-7282 395 C
bgreenwell@walsh.edu
GREENWELL,
Joseph, D .... 510-642-6770.. 70 K
deanofstudents@berkeley.edu
GREENWOLD, Simon .... 847-467-1829 155 D
s-greenwold@northwestern.edu
GREENWOOD, Anita ..... 978-934-4605 229 A
anita_greenwood@uml.edu
GREENWOOD, Gail .... 423-472-7141 462 D
ggreenwood@clevelandstatecc.edu
GREENWOOD, Kevin ..... 614-947-6095 382 H
kevin.greenwood@franklin.edu
GREENWOOD, Mark, D 641-422-4395 181 E
greenmar@niacc.edu
GREENWOOD, Nichole . 801-832-2027 501 C
nhg@westminstercollege.edu
GREENWOOD, Paul, G . 207-859-4776 210 A
pggreenw@colby.edu
GREENWOOD, Teresa ... 336-315-7800.. 96 H
GREENY, Erik .... 707-664-2712.. 36 C
erik.greeny@sonoma.edu
GREER, Amy .... 585-292-3010 333 G
agreer@monroecc.edu
GREER, Bobby, T .... 864-488-8251 447 F
bgreer@limestone.edu
GREER, Christine, G ..... 906-227-1700 248 B
cgreer@nmu.edu
GREER, Colleen .... 218-755-2988 258 B
cgreer@bemidjistate.edu
GREER, David .... 202-994-1000.. 95 D
dhgreer3@gwu.edu
GREER, Holly .... 337-521-8959 204 E
holly.greer@solacc.edu
GREER, James .... 325-793-4882 478 D
jgreer@mcm.edu
GREER, Jody .... 260-665-4105 173 D
greerj@trine.edu
GREER, Karla, J .... 972-860-7173 472 E
KGreer@dcccd.edu
GREER, Kevin .... 417-626-1234 280 B
greer.kevin@occ.edu
GREER, Kim .... 507-389-1333 260 A
kim.greer@mnsu.edu
GREER, M. Bradley .... 864-429-8728 450 I
greerm@mailbox.sc.edu
GREER, Rebecca .... 914-360-6220 333 H
rgreer@montefiore.org
GREER, Sherman, D ..... 901-333-4101 464 A
sdgreer@southwest.tn.edu
GREER, T. Richard .... 585-594-6160 339 F
greerR@roberts.edu
GREER, William, B .... 423-461-8710 459 I
bgreer@milligan.edu
GREESON, Tonya .... 706-419-1138 123 F
tonya.greeson@covenant.edu
GREGERSEN, Denise ...... 707-545-3647.. 29 D
denise@berginu.edu
GREGERSON,
Robert (Bob) .... 239-590-7156 114 F
rgregerson@fgcu.edu
GREGG, Chris, S .... 651-962-6390 265 F
csgregg@stthomas.edu
GREGG, Claire .... 864-455-8209 450 G
cgregg@ghs.org
GREGG, Cody .... 956-872-2528 482 G
cgregg@southtexascollege.edu
GREGG, Ellen .... 970-351-2877.. 87 A
ellen.gregg@unco.edu
GREGG, Gerald, A .... 503-943-7161 410 H
gregg@up.edu
GREGG, Karla .... 417-447-6966 280 C
greggk@otc.edu
GREGG, Kelly .... 954-262-4335 109 E
kgregg1@nova.edu
GREGG, Michael, J .... 817-552-3700 477 B
lpyun@tku.edu
GREGG, Patti .... 678-891-2571 125 G
patricia.gregg@gpc.edu
GREGG, Phyllis .... 312-362-8850 143 G
pgregg@depaul.edu
GREGG, Robert, S .... 609-652-4542 308 E
robert.gregg@stockton.edu
GREGG, Virginia .... 518-276-6524 339 D
greggv@rpi.edu
GREGGS, Rob .... 405-682-7877 399 K
rgreggs@occc.edu
GREGOIRE, David, P .... 518-564-2090 346 B
gregoidp@plattsburgh.edu
GREGOIRE, JR.,
Paul, E .... 504-282-4455 206 C
pgregoire@nobts.edu
GREGOIRE, Tom .... 614-292-9426 389 A
gregoire.5@osu.edu
GREGORI-GAHAN,
Heidi .... 812-465-1248 174 D
gahan@usi.edu
GREGOROWICZ,
Stephen .... 609-586-4800 303 D
gregoros@mccc.edu
GREGORY, Alison .... 570-321-4082 425 B
gregory@lycoming.edu
GREGORY, Anne .... 260-982-5285 170 a
GREGORY, Brent .... 662-246-6302 268 F
bgregory@msdelta.edu
GREGORY, Carolyn .... 216-368-5276 378 J
carolyn.gregory@case.edu
GREGORY, Charles .... 630-829-6009 140 A
cgregory@ben.edu
GREGORY, Christine ..... 212-774-0739 332 A
cgregory@mmm.edu
GREGORY, Christopher 508-626-4510 230 A
cgregory@framingham.edu
GREGORY, Dan .... 320-308-2192 261 E
ddgregory@stcloudstate.edu

GREGORY, Dan .... 512-313-3000 471 H
daniel.gregory@concordia.edu
GREGORY, Darlene .... 334-386-7108.... 3 I
dgregory@faulkner.edu
GREGORY, David, B ..... 615-366-4430 461 B
david.gregory@tbr.edu
GREGORY, David, D ..... 413-585-3770 236 G
dgregory@smith.edu
GREGORY, David, L ..... 606-783-5100 198 H
d.gregory@moreheadstate.edu
GREGORY, Denise .... 205-726-2725.... 6 F
djgregor@samford.edu
GREGORY, Derek .... 570-961-7839 422 G
gregoryd@lackawanna.edu
GREGORY, Ellen, D ...... 859-846-6046 198 G
egregory@midway.edu
GREGORY, Jeffery .... 570-961-7868 422 G
gregoryj@lackawanna.edu
GREGORY, Keith .... 971-722-4338 409 C
kgregory@pcc.edu
GREGORY, Lisa .... 217-875-7200 156 K
lgregory@richland.edu
GREGORY, Melissa .... 240-567-5036 217 B
melissa.gregory@montgomerycollege.edu
GREGORY, Patrick .... 334-386-7259.... 3 I
pgregory@faulkner.edu
GREGORY, Paula .... 678-225-7483 432 E
paulagr@pcom.edu
GREGORY, Rhonda .... 615-230-3668 464 B
rhonda.gregory@volstate.edu
GREGORY, Rich .... 818-909-5517.. 53 F
rgregory@tms.edu
GREGORY, Sadie, R ..... 410-951-3010 220 C
sgregory@coppin.edu
GREGORY, Steve .... 906-635-2371 245 H
sgregory@lssu.edu
GREGORY, Tiffany .... 662-915-7387 270 G
tlgregor@olemiss.edu
GREGORY, Tom, F .... 570-326-3761 429 J
tgregory@pct.edu
GREGORY, Travis .... 760-750-4954.. 35 B
tgregory@csusm.edu
GREGORY, Trisha .... 301-687-4201 220 D
tgregory@frostburg.edu
GREGORYK, Kerry .... 515-271-1665 177 H
Kerry.Gregoryk@dmu.edu
GREGORYK,
Michael, D .... 909-274-4230.. 54 J
mgregoryk@mtsac.edu
GREGSON, Donald .... 210-690-9000 474 L
dgregson@hallmarkuniversity.edu
GREGSON, Mark .... 800-422-2418.. 99 C
mgregson@baymedical.org
GREIFE, Alice, L .... 660-543-4450 283 F
greife@ucmo.edu
GREIFE, Steve, B .... 816-604-2221 277 I
steve.greife@mcckc.edu
GREIFFENDORF, OP,
Mary Agnes .... 615-256-5486 455 A
smagreiffendorf@tn-op.org
GREIG, Carl .... 903-223-3062 486 C
carl.greig@tamut.edu
GREIG, Judith, M .... 650-508-3503.. 56 H
jgreig@ndnu.edu
GREIL, Stan .... 405-733-7488 401 L
sgreil@rose.edu
GREIM, Jeffrey .... 413-565-1000 222 G
jgreim@baypath.edu
GREIMAN, Judith .... 631-632-4418 344 C
judith.greiman@stonybrook.edu
GREINER, Cathleen .... 949-451-5565.. 67 E
cgreiner@ivc.edu
GREINER, Gary .... 219-464-5130 174 E
gary.greiner@valpo.edu
GREINER, Jerry, M .... 610-499-4105 439 G
GREINER, Melissa .... 262-595-2404 540 C
greinerm@uwp.edu
GREINER, Ruta .... 440-375-7000 385 B
rgreiner@lec.edu
GREINER, Stephanie ..... 515-271-1386 177 H
stephanie.greiner@dmu.edu
GREINER, Stephen .... 606-487-3100 196 B
steve.greiner@kctcs.edu
GREINER, Susan, L .... 336-322-2245 364 G
Sue.Greiner@piedmontcc.edu
GRELLSON, Mona, S .... 651-631-5390 265 D
msgrellson@unwsp.edu
GREMILLION, Henry ..... 504-619-8500 205 C
hgremi@lsuhsc.edu
GREMMELS,
Gillian (Jill), S .... 704-894-2160 356 D
jigremmels@davidson.edu
GREMMELS, Luther .... 205-652-3768.... 9 G
gremmels@uwa.edu
GRENDER, Teresa .... 606-368-6044 192 H
teresagrender@alc.edu
GRENIER, Kyle .... 617-236-4446 226 F
kgrenier@fisher.edu
GRENIER, Tina .... 701-671-2612 375 B
tina.grenier@ndscs.edu

GRENNAN, Jon .... 845-434-5750 349 C
jgrennan@sullivan.suny.edu
GRENNAN, Jon .... 845-451-1323 323 E
j_grenna@culinary.edu
GRENON, Jamie .... 401-254-4847 442 C
jgrenon@rwu.edu
GRENOT-SCHEYER,
Marquita .... 562-985-4513.. 33 F
marquita.grenot-scheyer@csulb.edu
GRENTZ, Jennifer .... 602-243-8030.. 15 F
jennifer.grentz@southmountaincc.edu
GREPPIN-WATTS,
Monica .... 615-366-4417 461 B
monica.greppin-watts@tbr.edu
GRESH, Charles, E .... 215-951-1539 422 F
gresh@lasalle.edu
GRESHAM, John .... 314-792-6308 276 H
gresham@kenrick.edu
GRESHAM, Jonathan .... 423-636-7300 464 F
jgresham@tusculum.edu
GRESHAM, Loren, P ..... 405-491-6300 402 E
lgresham@snu.edu
GRESHAM, Susan .... 812-535-5121 172 F
sgresham@smwc.edu
GRESS, Lori .... 320-308-5937 261 F
lgress@sctcc.edu
GRESS, JR., Mark .... 215-572-2972 412 F
gressm@arcadia.edu
GRESS, Michael, E .... 812-888-4506 174 F
mgress@vinu.edu
GRESS, Vicky .... 217-333-4493 162 A
gress@illinois.edu
GRESSETT, Chris .... 305-644-1171 101 B
cgressett@dademedical.edu
GRESSLEY, Jerry, A ...... 260-359-4052 167 D
jgressley@huntington.edu
GRETCH, Jim .... 406-791-5320 288 J
jgretch@ugf.edu
GRETCH-CARTER,
Michele .... 317-274-7602 168 E
mgretch@iupui.edu
GRETZINGER, Jerry .... 315-792-7100 348 D
ggretzinger@sunycnse.com
GREUFE, Sandra .... 641-648-4611 179 K
sandra.greufe@iavalley.edu
GREVE, Debbie .... 620-235-4206 190 G
dgreve@pittstate.edu
GREVE, Jennifer .... 402-844-7062 292 G
jenniferg@northeast.edu
GREVES, Bill .... 785-827-5541 189 A
bill.greves@kwu.edu
GREVI, Laura .... 914-337-9300 323 A
laura.grevi@concordia-ny.edu
GREVING, John .... 402-465-2486 292 E
jgreving@nebrwesleyan.edu
GREWAL, Daman .... 707-654-1727.. 34 B
dgrewal@csum.edu
GREY, Erin .... 307-382-1647 546 L
egrey@wwcc.wy.edu
GREY, Kimberly .... 314-392-2241 278 G
grey@mobap.edu
GREY, Margaret .... 203-785-2393.. 93 C
margaret.grey@yale.edu
GREY, Pam .... 650-949-6193.. 44 N
greypam@fhda.edu
GREY, Thomasina .... 505-786-4186 311 G
tgrey@navajotech.edu
GREYDANUS, John .... 541-737-9099 408 F
john.greydanus@oregonstate.edu
GRIBB, Molly .... 608-342-1561 540 D
gribbm@uwplatt.edu
GRIBBEN, Les .... 212-817-7470 319 B
lgribben@gc.cuny.edu
GRIBBIN, David .... 478-289-2047 124 B
dgribbin@ega.edu
GRIBBLE, Kari .... 608-663-2305 536 A
kgribble@edgewood.edu
GRIBBLE, Scott .... 308-632-6933 293 C
GRIBBLE, Shannon, L .. 301-687-7588 220 D
slgribble@frostburg.edu
GRIBBONS, Barry .... 661-362-5500.. 40 H
barry.gribbons@canyons.edu
GRIBOU, Julius, M ...... 210-458-4110 494 D
julius.gribou@utsa.edu
GRICE, Brittany .... 805-437-3608.. 32 H
brittany.grice@csuci.edu
GRICE, Ronnie, D .... 785-532-1131 188 H
raker@ksu.edu
GRICE, Vivian, D .... 803-641-3550 450 C
viviang@usca.edu
GRIDLEY, Madison .... 206-592-3212 523 D
mgridley@highline.edu
GRIECO, Chrysanthy ..... 973-761-9022 308 C
chrysanthy.grieco@shu.edu
GRIEGER, Mary .... 414-425-8300 538 J
mgrieger@shsst.edu
GRIEGO, Brenda .... 702-968-1619 296 D
bgriego@roseman.edu
GRIEP, Mary .... 507-786-3055 264 C
griep@stolaf.edu

GRIER, Douglas, L .... 630-466-7900 162 K
dgrier@waubonsee.edu
GRIER, Ed, A .... 804-827-1062 514 F
egrier@vcu.edu
GRIER, Frank, O .... 334-833-4005.... 4 E
fgrier@huntingdon.edu
GRIER, Judith, M .... 757-789-1753 515 D
jgrier@es.vccs.edu
GRIER, Tricia, S .... 334-833-4243.... 4 E
tgrier@huntingdon.edu
GRIESBACH, Scott .... 715-232-1334 541 B
griesbachs@uwstout.edu
GRIESHEIMER, Tina ...... 303-797-5901.. 79 A
tina.griesheimer@arapahoe.edu
GRIESSE, Sarah .... 612-330-1489 253 K
griesse@augsburg.edu
GRIEVE, Cathy .... 303-871-2397.. 86 H
cgrieve@du.edu
GRIEVE, Kimberly .... 605-677-5331 453 F
kimberly.grieve@usd.edu
GRIFFEL, Michael, M ... 541-346-2667 410 F
mgriffel@uoregon.edu
GRIFFIIN-SOBEL, Joyce 315-464-3921 344 E
griffinj@upstate.edu
GRIFFIN, Adrian .... 718-260-5050 320 D
agriffin@citytech.cuny.edu
GRIFFIN, Bert .... 502-585-9911 199 E
bgriffin@spalding.edu
GRIFFIN, Bruce .... 415-351-3540.. 62 I
bgriffin@sfai.edu
GRIFFIN, Cathy .... 908-526-1200 305 G
cgriffin@raritanval.edu
GRIFFIN, Cindy .... 352-365-3521 107 X
griffinc@lssc.edu
GRIFFIN, Clifton, P ...... 410-677-0050 220 E
cpgriffin@salisbury.edu
GRIFFIN, Courtney, L ... 334-727-8011.... 8 B
GRIFFIN, Dale, M .... 405-585-5700 399 I
dale.griffin@okbu.edu
GRIFFIN, Dan .... 731-661-5120 464 G
dgriffin@uu.edu
GRIFFIN, Daniel .... 315-312-2250 346 A
daniel.griffin@oswego.edu
GRIFFIN, David .... 206-239-4500 520 K
dgriffin@cityu.edu
GRIFFIN, Deborah .... 510-659-6151.. 56 J
dgriffin@ohlone.edu
GRIFFIN, Donitha .... 334-876-9302.... 4 B
GRIFFIN, Donitha .... 334-876-9302.... 4 B
dgriffin@wccs.edu
GRIFFIN, Doris .... 559-325-5265.. 69 A
doris.griffin@scccd.edu
GRIFFIN, Elaine .... 615-966-5818 458 C
elaine.griffin@lipscomb.edu
GRIFFIN, Ellen .... 415-338-1666.. 36 A
elleng@sfsu.edu
GRIFFIN, SR., Ervin, V . 252-536-7217 363 B
egriffin518@halifaxcc.edu
GRIFFIN, Gary .... 815-939-5296 155 G
ggriffin@olivet.edu
GRIFFIN, Hayden .... 252-737-1026 369 E
griffinc@ecu.edu
GRIFFIN, Heather .... 502-895-3411 198 E
hgriffin@lpts.edu
GRIFFIN, Jacquelyn, H . 864-977-7081 448 A
jackie.griffin@ngu.edu
GRIFFIN, Janie .... 503-491-6701 407 C
janie.griffin@mhcc.edu
GRIFFIN, Jean .... 704-216-6129 358 I
jgriffin@livingstone.edu
GRIFFIN, Jeff .... 765-455-9339 168 B
griffon0@purdue.edu
GRIFFIN, Jeff, D .... 504-816-8018 206 C
jgriffin@nobts.edu
GRIFFIN, Jennifer, S .... 724-589-2069 436 E
jgriffin@thiel.edu
GRIFFIN, Joan .... 805-493-3555.. 31 H
griffin@callutheran.edu
GRIFFIN, Joel .... 864-941-8446 448 D
griffin.j@ptc.edu
GRIFFIN, John .... 401-841-6594 548 B
GRIFFIN, John .... 757-221-2498 506 J
dean-ugs@wm.edu
GRIFFIN, Jonathan .... 602-429-4912.. 16 N
GRIFFIN, Karen .... 813-253-7002 106 C
kgriffin@hccfl.edu
GRIFFIN, Karen .... 636-584-6575 274 J
karen.griffin@eastcentral.edu
GRIFFIN, Larry .... 252-399-6331 354 I
lcgriffin@barton.edu
GRIFFIN, Larry .... 901-375-4400 459 D
larrygriffin@midsouthcc.org
GRIFFIN, Leslie .... 662-846-4400 267 A
lgriffin@deltastate.edu
GRIFFIN, Lisa .... 229-217-4144 132 C
lgriffin@southernregional.edu
GRIFFIN, Lonnie .... 912-408-3024 131 B
lfgriffin@savannahtech.edu
GRIFFIN, Lori .... 253-912-3633 525 C
lgriffin@pierce.ctc.edu

GRIFFIN, Lynn .... 843-383-8071 445 A
lgriffin@coker.edu
GRIFFIN, Mark .... 973-353-1458 307 C
markg@andromeda.rutgers.edu
GRIFFIN, Michael .... 212-636-6520 326 C
mgriffinl@fordham.edu
GRIFFIN, Nancy .... 207-780-4547 213 A
ngriffin@usm.maine.edu
GRIFFIN, Neil .... 864-592-4897 449 C
griffinn@sccsc.edu
GRIFFIN, Patricia, L ..... 785-628-5377 187 A
pgriffin@fhsu.edu
GRIFFIN, Patrick .... 845-431-8924 324 D
griffin@sunydutchess.edu
GRIFFIN, CM,
Patrick, J .... 718-990-6311 340 G
griffinp@stjohns.edu
GRIFFIN, Paul, F .... 315-684-6081 347 A
griffipf@morrisville.edu
GRIFFIN, Ragan .... 814-393-2315 430 E
rwatson@clarion.edu
GRIFFIN, Randy, R .... 541-881-5595 410 D
rgriffin@tvcc.cc
GRIFFIN, Robert .... 901-375-4400 459 D
robertgriffin@midsouthcc.org
GRIFFIN, Sallie .... 601-877-6377 266 C
sgriffin@alcorn.edu
GRIFFIN, Tamara .... 870-612-2022.. 24 G
tamara.griffin@uaccb.edu
GRIFFIN, Teresa .... 330-490-7503 395 C
tgriffin@walsh.edu
GRIFFIN, Terrie, E .... 434-528-5276 518 F
tgriffin@vul.edu
GRIFFIN, Thomas, H .... 919-515-5036 370 D
thgriffi@ncsu.edu
GRIFFIN, Tim .... 602-639-7500.. 14 A
GRIFFIN, Tim .... 303-914-6516.. 85 C
tim.griffin@rrcc.edu
GRIFFIN, Timothy .... 201-216-5325 308 D
tgriffin@stevens.edu
GRIFFIN, Walt, R .... 864-488-4616 447 F
wgriffin@limestone.edu
GRIFFIN, William (Bill) 910-678-8314 362 E
griffinw@faytechcc.edu
GRIFFIN CALKINS,
Nancy .... 336-334-4822 363 A
nfgriffincalkins@gtcc.edu
GRIFFIN-DONALDSON,
Michelle .... 513-569-1515 379 K
michelle.donaldson@cincinnatistate.edu
GRIFFIS, Katie .... 270-831-9606 196 C
katie.griffis@kctcs.edu
GRIFFIS, Teresa .... 912-525-5000 130 H
tgriffis@scad.edu
GRIFFITH, Celeste .... 212-686-9040 352 H
cgriffith@woodtobecoburn.edu
GRIFFITH, Cynthia .... 281-756-3500 467 D
cgriffith@alvincollege.edu
GRIFFITH, David .... 903-813-2587 468 G
dgriffith@austincollege.edu
GRIFFITH, Denise .... 618-634-3277 159 A
deniseg@shawneecc.edu
GRIFFITH, Dennis, J ..... 330-369-3200 392 E
dgriffith@trumbull.edu
GRIFFITH, Dennis, R ..... 937-393-3431 391 F
dgriffith@soucc.sscc.edu
GRIFFITH, Jolene .... 641-782-1456 183 D
griffith@swcciowa.edu
GRIFFITH, Julie, K .... 765-494-6838 171 K
jgriff@purdue.edu
GRIFFITH, Kathy .... 740-392-6868 387 B
kathy.griffity@mvnu.edu
GRIFFITH, Larry .... 765-361-6212 175 B
griffitl@wabash.edu
GRIFFITH, Larry, K .... 724-847-6585 419 B
lkgriffith@geneva.edu
GRIFFITH, Maxine, F ..... 212-854-6524 322 F
mfg30@columbia.edu
GRIFFITH,
Rebecca (Becki) .... 817-515-7778 484 B
rebecca.griffith@tccd.edu
GRIFFITH, Roger, D ...... 304-647-6563 531 D
rgriffith@newriver.edu
GRIFFITH, Ross .... 336-414-1715 335 A
rgriffith@nycollege.edu
GRIFFITH, Ryan .... 209-946-2090.. 73 C
rgriffith@pacific.edu
GRIFFITH, Steven, J ..... 515-961-1720 182 I
steve.griffith@simpson.edu
GRIFFITH-GREEN,
Nicole .... 606-326-2000 195 H
nicole.griffithgreen@kctcs.edu
GRIFFITHS, Alison .... 646-312-3870 318 C
Alison.Griffiths@baruch.cuny.edu
GRIFFITHS, Andy .... 207-801-5605 210 B
agriffiths@coa.edu
GRIFFITHS, Geoffrey ..... 217-351-2273 155 I
GGriffiths@parkland.edu
GRIFFITHS,
José -Marie .... 605-256-5112 453 H

GRIFFUS, Randall .... 706-272-4440 123 G rgriffus@daltonstate.edu
GRIFFY, Loretta .... 931-221-7634 461 C griffyl@apsu.edu
GRIGG, Daniel, J .... 336-334-4822 363 A djgrigg@gtcc.edu
GRIGG, Eddie, G .... 704-334-6882 355 I egrigg@charlottechristian.edu
GRIGGS, Brandon .... 254-519-5748 485 D griggs@tamuct.edu
GRIGGS, Donald, R .... 843-953-5540 445 B griggsd@cofc.edu
GRIGGS, Gary, B .... 831-459-2464.. 72 E griggs@es.ucsc.edu
GRIGGS, Joyce .... 216-791-5000 380 C joyce.griggs@cim.edu
GRIGGS, LaSonya .... 607-844-8222 350 A LAG@TC3.edu
GRIGGS, Robert .... 218-333-6613 260 G robert.griggs@ntcmn.edu
GRIGGS, Robert, J .... 218-755-2097 258 B rgriggs@bemidjistate.edu
GRIGGS, Ronald, K .... 740-427-5632 384 P griggs@kenyon.edu
GRIGGS, Tanya .... 510-869-6131.. 61 J tgriggs@samuelmerritt.edu
GRIGNON, Rosemary, L .... 518-244-2311 340 A grignr@sage.edu
GRIGSBY, Beth .... 712-279-5504 176 B beth.grigsby@briarcliff.edu
GRIGSBY, Bryon, L .... 610-861-1364 426 H grigsbyb@moravian.edu
GRIGSBY, Delores .... 301-696-3440 215 E grigsby@hood.edu
GRIGSBY, Gwen, W .... 512-232-1781 493 M gwen.grigsby@austin.utexas.edu
GRIGSBY, Mark .... 918-540-6275 398 L mgrigsby@neo.edu
GRIGSBY, Rebekah .... 903-923-2217 473 I rgrigsby@etbu.edu
GRIISSER, Susan, A ...... 410-677-3160 220 E sagriisser@salisbury.edu
GRIJALVA, Norma .... 575-646-6030 312 A norma@nmsu.edu
GRIJALVA, Sara .... 575-835-5133 311 I sjgrijalva@admin.nmt.edu
GRILL, Joshua, L .... 570-577-3223 413 E josh.grill@bucknell.edu
GRILL, Stephen, A .... 574-372-5100 166 D grillsa@grace.edu
GRILLI, Gene, P .... 304-243-2389 534 H egrilli@wju.edu
GRILLO, Robert .... 305-348-2738 114 G robert.grillo@fiu.edu
GRILLOT, Suzette, R ...... 405-325-6003 403 I sgrillot@ou.edu
GRIMALDI, Dianna .... 928-523-2239.. 16 C Dianna.Grimaldi@nau.edu
GRIMALDI, Matthew ...... 570-945-8231 422 B matthew.grimaldi@keystone.edu
GRIMES, Charles, R ...... 330-471-8438 385 G cgrimes@malone.edu
GRIMES, Daniel .... 574-296-6266 163 M dgrimes@ambs.edu
GRIMES, Deborah .... 252-527-6223 363 G dgrimes@lenoircc.edu
GRIMES, Donnie .... 606-539-4197 200 F donnie.grimes@ucumberlands.edu
GRIMES, Judith .... 816-271-5991 279 E grimes@missouriwestern.edu
GRIMES, Kate .... 406-994-5326 287 G kathleen.grimes@montana.edu
GRIMES, Larry .... 304-829-7420 529 H lgrimes@bethanywv.edu
GRIMES, Marc .... 812-749-1368 171 I mgrimes@oak.edu
GRIMES, Paul .... 620-235-4598 190 G paul.grimes@pittstate.edu
GRIMES, Robert .... 212-636-6300 326 C rgrimes@fordham.edu
GRIMES, Robert (Bud), D .... 731-881-7615 465 F bgrimes@utm.edu
GRIMES, Sheila .... 530-938-5200.. 41 E grimes@siskiyous.edu
GRIMES, Steve .... 918-540-6226 398 L sgrimes@neo.edu
GRIMES, Terri, A .... 815-599-3514 146 B terri.grimes@highland.edu
GRIMES, Tresmaine .... 973-748-9000 300 E tresmaine_grimes@bloomfield.edu
GRIMES, Tresmaine .... 914-633-2206 328 F tgrimes@iona.edu
GRIMES, William, S ...... 512-505-3021 475 G wsgrimes@htu.edu
GRIMES ETHERIDGE, Lee .... 956-872-7271 482 G lgrimes@southtexascollege.edu
GRIMLEY, Janet .... 206-934-5488 526 A janet.grimley@seattlecolleges.edu
GRIMLEY, Lee Ann .... 319-895-4378 177 A lgrimley@cornellcollege.edu
GRIMM, Carol, M .... 218-477-2327 260 B grimm@mnstate.edu
GRIMM, Debra .... 740-477-7732 388 F dgrimm@ohiochristian.edu
GRIMM, Gary .... 503-370-6814 411 D ggrimm@willamette.edu
GRIMM, Keith .... 503-370-6210 411 D kgrimm@willamette.edu
GRIMM, Randy .... 816-322-0110 272 L randy.grimm@calvary.edu
GRIMM, Rich .... 847-317-7055 161 B ragrimm@tiu.edu
GRIMM, Robert, J .... 610-683-4120 431 B grimm@kutztown.edu
GRIMM, Roger .... 903-510-2389 491 A rgri2@tjc.edu
GRIMM, Tonya .... 660-626-2076 271 G tgrimm@atsu.edu
GRIMMER, Karen, D ...... 618-374-5152 156 C karen.grimmer@principia.edu
GRIMMER, Kevin, M ..... 315-792-7520 348 D grimmek@sunyit.edu
GRIMMER, Nick .... 315-792-7110 348 D nick.grimmer@sunyit.edu
GRIMMETT, Branden ...... 310-258-8779.. 53 C Branden.Grimmett@lmu.edu
GRIMSHAW-CLARK, Maria .... 315-312-4416 346 A maria.grimshaw@oswego.edu
GRIMSLEY, Deloris .... 973-877-3056 302 F dgrimsle@essex.edu
GRIMSLEY, Kim .... 719-384-6988.. 84 I kim.grimsley@ojc.edu
GRIMSLEY, Linda .... 229-430-4635 119 H linda.grimsley@asurams.edu
GRIMSON, W. Eric, L .... 617-253-5415 233 C
GRINDELL, Monique ..... 503-352-1566 408 I grindelm@pacificu.edu
GRINDLEY, Krystle .... 318-670-9472 207 C kbeauchamp@susla.edu
GRINNAGER, Donn .... 605-274-4498 452 A donn.grinnager@augie.edu
GRINNAN, Susan .... 804-706-5035 515 G sgrinnan@jtcc.edu
GRIPP, Kristine .... 216-791-5000 380 C kristine.gripp@cim.edu
GRISCOM, William, E .... 717-299-7722 436 D griscom@stevenscollege.edu
GRISHAM, Bob .... 360-438-4372 525 H bgrisham@stmartin.edu
GRISHAM, Erin .... 928-523-6990.. 16 C Erin.Grisham@nau.edu
GRISHAM, Linda .... 781-239-3147 231 G lgrisham@massbay.edu
GRISI, Mark, P .... 315-684-6465 347 A grisimp@morrisville.edu
GRISKELL, Ivory .... 601-979-4299 267 H ivory.j.griskell@jsums.edu
GRISSOM, Cytha, D ...... 717-477-1444 431 F cdgris@ship.edu
GRISSOM, James .... 972-825-4736 483 D jgrissom@sagu.edu
GRISSOM, Randy, W ...... 505-428-1201 313 A randy.grissom@sfcc.edu
GRISWOLD, Al .... 253-680-7204 519 K agriswold@bates.ctc.edu
GRISWOLD, Al .... 206-934-5482 526 A alfred.griswold@seattlecolleges.edu
GRISWOLD, Anna, M .... 814-863-0507 428 C amg5@psu.edu
GRISWOLD, Bill .... 334-290-3254.... 4 K bill.griswold@istc.edu
GRISWOLD, Emmett ...... 229-430-3396 119 I egriswold@albanytech.edu
GRISWOLD, Melissa ...... 314-529-6859 277 B mgriswold@maryville.edu
GRISWOLD, Richard, M .... 617-262-5000 223 G richard.griswold@the-bac.edu
GRITTON, Mark .... 559-934-2455.. 76 B markgritton@whccd.edu
GRIZANTI, Robert .... 716-896-0700 352 B bgrizanti@villa.edu
GRIZZARD, Juanita .... 434-949-1017 516 H juanita.grizzard@southside.edu
GRIZZELL, Kyle .... 513-562-6262 376 O kgrizzell@artacademy.edu
GRIZZLE, Debra, F .... 706-245-7226 124 C dgrizzle@ec.edu
GRIZZLE, Jeff .... 870-512-7866.. 19 I jeff_grizzle@asun.edu
GRIZZLE, Jerry, W .... 575-624-8001 311 K supt@nmmi.edu
GRMELA, Sylvia .... 716-896-0700 352 B grmela@villa.edu
GROAT, Gary .... 415-380-1330.. 45 J garygroat@ggbts.edu
GROBER, Max .... 903-813-2361 468 G mgrober@austincollege.edu
GROBINS, Mary Alice .. 360-416-7719 527 A maryalice.grobins@skagit.edu
GROBSMITH, Liz .... 928-523-8484.. 16 C Liz.Grobsmith@nau.edu
GROCE, Jeanetta .... 903-875-7619 485 E jeanetta.groce@tamuc.edu
GROCE, Robin .... 828-262-2230 369 D grocerd@appstate.edu
GRODE-HANKS, Carol .. 605-995-7103 452 H carol.grode-hanks@mitchelltech.edu
GRODSKY, Jennifer ...... 202-393-7272 224 E jgrodsky@bu.edu
GROELING, Jeff .... 765-998-5246 173 B jfgroeling@taylor.edu
GROENER, Michael .... 973-408-3501 301 J mgroener@drew.edu
GROENEVELD, Bill .... 805-565-6849.. 76 K procurement@westmont.edu
GROENHOUT, Rachel ..... 207-778-7170 212 E rachel.groenhout@maine.edu
GROENINGER, Sandra .. 847-543-2345 142 G sgroeninger@clcillinois.edu
GROENNERT, Harvey ..... 618-394-2200 150 B hgroennert@lakeland.cc.i.us
GROENWALD, Susan .... 877-751-5783 141 D sgroenwald@carrington.edu
GROESBECK, John .... 417-625-9348 278 I groesbeck-j@mssu.edu
GROFF, Keith .... 614-947-6122 382 H keith.groff@franklin.edu
GROFF, Peter .... 701-252-3467 375 J peter.groff@uj.edu
GROFF, Rodney .... 717-728-2258 415 B rodgroff@centralpenn.edu
GROFF, Susan, L .... 302-831-8063.. 94 D groff@udel.edu
GROGAN, Angela .... 573-592-5245 285 J angela.grogan@westminster-mo.edu
GROGAN, Margaret .... 714-516-5968.. 38 B grogan@chapman.edu
GROGAN, Rita .... 559-934-2180.. 76 A ritagrogan@whccd.edu
GROGAN, Rita .... 408-855-5072.. 76 E rita.grogan@wvm.edu
GROGG, Pete .... 812-855-6511 167 J pgrogg@indiana.edu
GROGG, Sam, L .... 516-877-4125 314 F sgrogg@adelphi.edu
GROGRAN, Torie .... 573-986-6191 282 C tgrogran@semo.edu
GROH, Sara .... 315-228-6134 321 H sgroh@colgate.edu
GROH BECK, Genelle .... 507-457-1421 264 B ggroh@smumn.edu
GROHMAN, Adam .... 516-299-2256 330 G adam.grohman@liu.edu
GROLEAU, Dan .... 715-365-4450 543 G dgroleau@nicoletcollege.edu
GROLEAU, Ron, W .... 815-224-0482 147 J ron_groleau@ivcc.edu
GROMAN, Elizabeth, A . 260-399-7700 174 C bgroman@sf.edu
GROMATZKY, Steven .... 913-360-7511 184 K sgromatzky@benedictine.edu
GROMIS, Jeffrey .... 610-341-1775 418 A jgromis@eastern.edu
GRONA, Marion .... 940-552-6291 496 B mgrona@vernoncollege.edu
GRONBECK-TEDESCO, Susan .... 785-864-6161 191 G slgt@ku.edu
GROND, Greta .... 712-707-7248 182 C ggrond@nwciowa.edu
GRONDAHL, Mary, M .. 518-454-5150 322 C grondahm@strose.edu
GRONER, Steve .... 618-545-3260 149 C sgroner@kaskaskia.edu
GRONEWALD, Kate .... 903-233-3291 477 G kategronewald@letu.edu
GRONNIGER, Eileen, C 785-442-6010 187 I egronniger@highlandcc.edu
GRONO, Anthony .... 718-817-4943 326 C grono@fordham.edu
GRONSKY, Jennifer, M . 215-503-8189 436 F jennifer.gronsky@jefferson.edu
GROOME, Jean, M .... 336-734-7292 362 F jgroome@forsythtech.edu
GROOMS, Craig .... 606-546-1709 200 E cgrooms@unionky.edu
GROOMS, David .... 808-984-3376 136 H grooms@hawaii.edu
GROOT, Joycelyn .... 714-241-6323.. 40 B jgroot@coastline.edu
GROOVER, John .... 912-486-7602 129 E jgroover@ogeecheetech.edu
GROPACK, Stacy .... 516-299-2900 330 G stacy.gropack@liu.edu
GROPEN, Laura .... 760-744-1150.. 58 D lgropen@palomar.edu
GROPP, Douglas, M .... 214-528-8600 480 H
GROPP, Jonathan .... 864-622-6014 443 E jgropp@andersonuniversity.edu
GROPPER, Daniel .... 561-297-3629 114 E dgropper@fau.edu
GRORUD, Kelley .... 608-663-2200 536 A KGrorud@edgewood.edu
GROS, Kathy, R .... 504-865-3237 206 A kgros@loyno.edu
GROS, Kelli .... 251-981-3771.... 3 A kelli.gros@columbiasouthern.edu
GROSBY, Karen .... 954-262-5885 109 E grosby@nsu.nova.edu
GROSE, Kay .... 304-865-6230 530 F kay.grose@ovu.edu
GROSHANS, David, E ... 308-635-6105 294 C groshans@wncc.edu
GROSLAND, David, E .... 515-574-1149 179 F grosland@iowacentral.edu
GROSOVSKY, Andrew .... 617-287-5775 228 G andrew.grosovsky@umb.edu
GROSPITCH, Eric .... 816-235-8955 284 A grospitche@umkc.edu
GROSS, Anne .... 303-871-3382.. 86 H agross@du.edu
GROSS, Bryan, J .... 413-782-1233 238 A bryan.gross@wne.edu
GROSS, Candace .... 870-512-7716.. 19 I candace_gross@asun.edu
GROSS, Carla, E .... 717-691-6027 426 B cgross@messiah.edu
GROSS, Dana .... 507-786-3624 264 C grossd@stolaf.edu
GROSS, Dolores .... 915-831-2122 473 J dgross2@epcc.edu
GROSS, Erik .... 603-862-1584 299 B erik.gross@unh.edu
GROSS, Laura .... 518-255-5626 346 E grossll@cobleskill.edu
GROSS, Linda .... 517-884-1350 246 H grossl@msu.edu
GROSS, Michael .... 732-987-2373 302 J gross@georgian.edu
GROSS, Michael .... 508-362-2131 231 D mgross@capecod.edu
GROSS, Michael, L .... 610-921-7672 411 E mgross@albright.edu
GROSS, Michelle .... 414-847-3262 537 F michellegross@miad.edu
GROSS, Michelle, R ...... 410-951-3610 220 C mgross@coppin.edu
GROSS, Monika .... 301-860-4091 220 B mgross@bowiestate.edu
GROSS, Natalie .... 914-337-0700 342 C ngross@sarahlawrence.edu
GROSS, Peter .... 503-251-5709 410 I pgross@uws.edu
GROSS, Scott .... 606-487-3528 196 B scott.gross@kctcs.edu
GROSS, Susan .... 201-692-2823 302 H swgross@fdu.edu
GROSS, Susan .... 201-216-8142 308 D Susan.Gross@stevens.edu
GROSS METHNER, Sara, E .... 651-962-5000 265 F gross6968@stthomas.edu
GROSSE, Mike .... 502-456-0004 200 A mgrosse@sullivan.edu
GROSSE, Mike .... 502-451-0815 200 B mgrosse@sullivan.edu
GROSSI, OSB, Anthony 724-537-4554 435 B anthony.grossi@email.stvincent.edu
GROSSI, Deann .... 312-777-8665 147 C dgrossi@aii.edu
GROSSINGER, Harvey ... 202-651-5000.. 95 C harvey.grossinger@gallaudet.edu
GROSSKOPF, John .... 850-973-1601 109 C grosskopfj@nfcc.edu
GROSSMAN, Claudio .... 202-274-4004.. 94 H grossman@american.edu
GROSSMAN, David .... 714-992-7046.. 56 F dgrossman@fullcoll.edu
GROSSMAN, Divina ...... 508-999-8004 228 H chancellor@umassd.edu
GROSSMAN, Joshua, M .... 240-895-4367 218 B jmgrossman@smcm.edu
GROSSMAN, LuAnn ...... 605-331-6738 454 E luann.grossman@usiouxfalls.edu
GROSSMAN, Miriam ..... 845-425-1370 337 E
GROSSMAN, Pam .... 215-898-7014 437 I grossman@gse.upenn.edu
GROSSMAN, Richard, G .... 603-535-2425 299 E rggrossman@plymouth.edu
GROSSMAN, Ruth .... 732-414-2834 309 L ytcbks@gmail.com
GROSSMAN, Susan .... 312-915-7024 151 E sgrossm@luc.edu

GROSSMANN, Jeffrey, P .... 718-990-6535 340 G grossmaj@stjohns.edu

GROSSNICKLE-BATTERTON, Jim .... 800-287-8822 164 E grossja@bethanyseminary.edu

GROSSO, Andrew .... 262-646-6510 538 B agrosso@nashotah.edu

GROSSO, Michael .... 626-571-8811.. 74 E michaelg@uwest.edu

GROSSO, Michael .... 360-486-8868 525 H michael.grosso@stmartin.edu

GROSZ, Julae .... 423-697-4721 462 C julae.grosz@chattanoogastate.edu

GROSZ, Ken .... 701-228-5403 374 F ken.grosz@dakotacollege.edu

GROSZ, Tanya, L .... 651-286-7453 265 D tlgrosz@unwsp.edu

GROTE, Lisa .... 605-626-2521 454 A Lisa.Grote@northern.edu

GROTH, Charlie .... 215-968-8285 413 F charlie.groth@bucks.edu

GROTH, Clayton .... 608-249-6611 536 J cgroth@herzing.edu

GROTH, Dennis .... 812-855-8783 167 J vpue@indiana.edu

GROTH, Katherine .... 773-380-6806 163 E kgroth@westwood.edu

GROTH, Kathy .... 219-464-5114 174 E kathy.groth@valpo.edu

GROTJAN, Gayle .... 512-313-3000 471 H gayle.grotjan@concordia.edu

GROTNESS, Ann .... 970-339-6210.. 78 J ann.grotness@aims.edu

GROTRIAN, James .... 402-457-2335 291 E jgrotrian@mccneb.edu

GROTZINGER, John, P . 626-395-6005.. 31 D grotz@gps.caltech.edu

GROUNDS, Cynthia ...... 785-749-8418 187 F cynthia.grounds@bie.edu

GROUT, David .... 574-372-5100 166 D groutd@grace.edu

GROUT, John .... 706-236-2233 121 E jgrout@berry.edu

GROVE, Amber .... 208-376-7731 137 D agrove@boisebible.edu

GROVE, Daryl .... 563-425-5311 183 G groved@uiu.edu

GROVE, Doug .... 949-214-3434.. 42 B doug.grove@cui.edu

GROVE, Kathy, M .... 641-422-4382 181 E grovekat@niacc.edu

GROVE, Laurie .... 717-396-7188 436 D grove@stevenscollege.edu

GROVE, Luke, J .... 515-574-1062 179 F grove@iowacentral.edu

GROVE, Shannon, D ..... 814-886-6391 427 B sgrove@mtaloy.edu

GROVE, Warren .... 513-244-4465 387 A warren.grove@msj.edu

GROVER, Arthur .... 215-951-1300 422 F grover77@lasalle.edu

GROVER, Barbara .... 801-957-4434 500 E barbara.grover@slcc.edu

GROVER, Carol, N .... 315-279-5252 329 K cgrover@keuka.edu

GROVER, James .... 817-272-3491 493 L grover@uta.edu

GROVER, Joni .... 602-286-8031.. 14 M joni.grover@gatewaycc.edu

GROVER, Josh .... 352-638-9773.. 99 D jgrover@beaconcollege.edu

GROVER, Rajiv .... 901-678-3633 462 B rgrover@memphis.edu

GROVER, Susan, S .... 757-221-3846 506 J ssgrov@wm.edu

GROVER-BISKER, Edna . 573-341-6170 284 C egroverb@mst.edu

GROVER-ROOSA, Janice .... 307-382-1701 546 L jgrover@wwcc.wy.edu

GROVES, Allen, W .... 434-924-7429 514 A awg8vd@virginia.edu

GROVES, Christine .... 614-251-4613 388 H grovesc@ohiodominican.edu

GROVES, Danford, F ..... 910-272-3335 365 D dgroves@robeson.edu

GROVES, Denise .... 432-837-8432 489 B dgroves@sulross.edu

GROVES, Doris .... 309-438-7304 147 I dfgrove@ilstu.edu

GROVES, Jason .... 325-674-2646 466 I jason.groves@acu.edu

GROVES, Jay .... 309-438-5631 147 I jrgrove@ilstu.edu

GROVES, Jeffrey .... 909-621-8122.. 46 K groves@hmc.edu

GROVES, Kathleen, H ... 585-395-2317 345 A kgroves@brockport.edu

GROVES, Kathy .... 573-592-1106 286 A kathy.groves@williamwoods.edu

GROVES, Robert .... 517-884-1008 246 H grovesr@msu.edu

GROVES, Robert, M ...... 202-687-6400.. 95 E provost@georgetown.edu

GROVES, William .... 937-769-1348 376 L bgroves@antioch.edu

GROVES, William .... 937-769-1348 376 M bgroves@antioch.edu

GROVES-SCOTT, Victoria .... 501-450-3175.. 25 F vickigs@uca.edu

GROW, David .... 801-274-3280 501 B dgrow@wgu.edu

GROW, Tamara, J .... 660-562-1212 280 A

GROWDEN, Melissa, A . 517-264-7614 250 B mgrowden@sienaheights.edu

GROWDON, James, F .. 610-785-6252 434 E jgrowdon@scs.edu

GROWNEY, Kathy .... 603-668-2211 298 H k.growney@snhu.edu

GROWNS, Richard, O ... 501-977-2024.. 25 A growns@uaccm.edu

GROZA, Adam .... 415-380-1448.. 45 J adamgroza@ggbts.edu

GRUBB, Dan .... 910-592-8081 365 G dgrubb@sampsoncc.edu

GRUBB, Derek .... 970-542-3158.. 84 A derek.grubb@morgancc.edu

GRUBB, Geoffrey, J ...... 419-824-3818 385 F ggrubb@lourdes.edu

GRUBB, Joshua .... 276-326-4348 505 D jgrubb@bluefield.edu

GRUBB, Lillie .... 620-223-2700 187 B lillieg@fortscott.edu

GRUBE, Dave .... 616-222-1412 241 G dave.grube@cornerstone.edu

GRUBE, M. Marshall .... 423-439-4219 461 D grube@etsu.edu

GRUBE, Sean .... 816-235-8719 284 A grubes@umkc.edu

GRUBER, Carol .... 215-646-7300 420 A gruber.c@gmercyu.edu

GRUBER, Christopher, J .... 704-894-2710 356 D chgruber@davidson.edu

GRUBER, Darlene .... 610-917-1414 438 G d_gruber@valleyforge.edu

GRUBER, Jay .... 202-687-7014.. 95 E jg1502@georgetown.edu

GRUBER, Thomas .... 504-671-6480 203 F tgrube@dcc.edu

GRUBY, Elizabeth .... 773-878-3752 158 C egruby@staugustine.edu

GRUEN, Kris .... 802-322-1721 501 H kris.gruen@goddard.edu

GRUENDLER, Donny ..... 323-860-1188.. 55 D donnyg@mi.edu

GRUENIG, Gwendolyn .. 907-450-8190.. 10 G gdgruenig@alaska.edu

GRUENING, Kyle .... 715-365-4481 543 G gruening@nicoletcollege.edu

GRUHLER, Sarah .... 360-992-2406 521 A sgruhler@clark.edu

GRUICHICH, Dawn .... 480-732-7050.. 14 K Dawn.Gruichich@cgc.edu

GRULKE, Kimmi .... 928-226-4343.. 13 D kimmi.grulke@coconino.edu

GRUNBLATT, Akiva .... 718-268-4700 339 B

GRUND, Faye .... 419-520-2602 377 A fgrund@ashland.edu

GRUNDEN, Jennifer, J .. 302-857-1040.. 94 A jgrunden@dtcc.edu

GRUNDER, Mark .... 989-358-7317 239 C grunderm@alpenacc.edu

GRUNDHAUSER, Tony .. 651-523-2219 256 B agrundhauser01@hamline.edu

GRUNDIG, John .... 863-680-6212 104 F jgrundig@flsouthern.edu

GRUNDMAN, Stephen .. 703-416-1441 508 F sgrundman@ipsciences.edu

GRUNDY, Jeffrey, W .... 973-596-2451 304 D jeffrey.w.grundy@njit.edu

GRUNDY, Marc, A .... 423-236-2875 460 K magrundy@southern.edu

GRUNER, Celeste .... 704-878-4321 364 C cgruner@mitchellcc.edu

GRUNINGER, Sandra .... 212-686-9040 352 H sgruninger@woodtobecoburn.edu

GRUNLOH, Jean Anne .. 217-234-5329 150 B jgrunloh@lakeland.cc.il.us

GRUNOW, Tamie .... 231-591-3879 242 L TamieGrunow@ferris.edu

GRUNOW, Tamie, L ...... 513-556-1015 393 B grunowtl@umail.uc.edu

GRUNTMEIR, Laura ...... 405-422-1253 401 H gruntmeirl@redlandscc.edu

GRUNWALD, Gerald ..... 215-503-8982 436 F gerald.grunwald@jefferson.edu

GRUNWALD, James, R . 507-354-8221 257 A grunwajr@mlc-wels.edu

GRUS, Shannon, M ...... 636-584-6505 274 J shannon.grus@eastcentral.edu

GRUSHINSKI, Alberta ... 570-945-8373 422 B alberta.grushinski@keystone.edu

GRUSKA, Julie .... 320-363-3395 264 A jgruska@csbsju.edu

GRUSKA, Julie, E .... 320-363-3395 254 J jgruska@csbsju.edu

GRUSKIN, Adrienne ...... 212-463-0400 350 C adrienne.gruskin@touro.edu

GRUSZKA, Bill .... 678-466-4351 122 J billgruska@clayton.edu

GRUVER, Wendy .... 903-886-5140 485 E wendy.gruver@tamuc.edu

GRZESIAK, Michael, P . 724-503-1001 439 B mgrzesiak@washjeff.edu

GRZYBOWSKI, Mark, J . 815-224-0393 147 J mark_grzybowski@ivcc.edu

GRZYWACZ, Norberto, M .... 202-687-5974.. 95 E norberto@georgetown.edu

GSCHWEND, Richard .... 217-875-7200 156 K rqschwend@richland.edu

GSTALDER, Steven .... 203-773-0129.. 87 M sgstalder@albertus.edu

GU, Sophia .... 888-488-4968.. 48 B gsophia@itu.edu

GUADAGNINO, Joseph . 954-545-4500 113 B jguadagnino@sfbc.edu

GUADALUPE, Sarahi ..... 787-276-0130 557 F sarahi.guadalupe@upr.edu

GUADALUPE, Yvonne ... 787-766-1717 556 A yguadalupe@suagm.edu

GUAGLIANONE, Curtis . 509-865-8530 523 C guaglianone_c@heritage.edu

GUAJARDO, Dan .... 918-495-7707 401 B dguajardo@oru.edu

GUAJARDO, George ...... 405-224-3140 403 L gguajardo@usao.edu

GUAJARDO, Nicole, R .. 757-594-8069 506 I nguajard@cnu.edu

GUAN, Sharon .... 773-325-7726 143 G xguan@depaul.edu

GUANCI-THERRIEN, Patricia .... 603-641-7202 298 F pguanci@anselm.edu

GUARASCI, Richard ...... 718-390-3131 352 C guarasci@wagner.edu

GUARD, Louis .... 315-781-3309 327 G guard@hws.edu

GUARDINO, Richard, V 516-463-4069 328 A richard.v.guardino@hofstra.edu

GUARDIOLA, Dagmar ... 787-767-2040 558 E dagmarguardiola2010@yahoo.com

GUARIGLIA, Carolyn, L 315-255-1743 317 I guarigliac@cayuga-cc.edu

GUARIGLIA, Daniel, M . 716-286-8431 336 E dmg@niagara.edu

GUARNIERI, Reid .... 440-375-7480 385 B rguarnieri@lec.edu

GUASCONI, Joseph ...... 973-378-2643 308 C joseph.guasconi@shu.edu

GUAY, Sheila .... 401-323-6324 441 B sguay@bryant.edu

GUBAN, Philip .... 440-943-7600 391 A pguban@dioceseofcleveland.org

GUBAN, Philip .... 440-943-7676 391 A pguban@dioceseofcleveland.org

GUBBINS, Jean, E .... 216-368-5557 378 J jeg2@case.edu

GUBLER, Seth .... 435-652-7571 499 M sgubler@dixie.edu

GUCKAVAN, Joseph ..... 215-489-2361 416 H Joseph.Guckavan@delval.edu

GUCKERT, Donald, J .... 319-335-1201 175 H don-guckert@uiowa.edu

GUDUR, Jaganmohan ... 303-458-4050.. 85 G jgudur@regis.edu

GUDVANGEN, John .... 860-685-2543.. 93 B jgudvangen@wesleyan.edu

GUDVANGEN, John, E .. 303-871-4857.. 86 H John.Gudvangen@du.edu

GUELICH, Julie .... 952-358-8156 260 D julie.guelich@normandale.edu

GUELL, Steven .... 702-567-1920 294 M sguell@cci.edu

GUENARD, Erik, M .... 906-932-4231 243 B erikg@gogebic.edu

GUENARD, Hayward ..... 985-448-4479 208 C hayward.guenard@nicholls.edu

GUENGERICH, Colleen . 575-835-5525 311 I cguengerich@admin.nmt.edu

GUENTER-SCHLESINGER, Sue .... 360-650-3307 528 D sue.guenter-schlesinger@wwu.edu

GUENTHER, Thomas ..... 847-543-2264 142 G tguenther@clcillinois.edu

GUERDAT, Kate .... 603-206-8018 297 A kguerdat@ccsnh.edu

GUERIN, David .... 318-257-4854 208 A dguerin@latech.edu

GUERIN, Donna .... 215-885-2360 425 C Dguerin@manor.edu

GUERIN, Thomas, B ..... 513-556-2389 393 B tom.guerin@uc.edu

GUERNICA, Angela .... 312-553-5901 141 N grazo@ccc.edu

GUERNSEY, Thomas, F 619-961-4272.. 69 J guernsey@tjsl.edu

GUERRA, Blanca .... 210-567-2621 495 B guerrabe@uthscsa.edu

GUERRA, Dahlia .... 956-665-2175 494 C guerrad@utpa.edu

GUERRA, Elizabeth .... 909-469-5418.. 76 I guerra@westernu.edu

GUERRA, Juan, M .... 512-245-2820 489 C jg76@txstate.edu

GUERRA, Luis .... 510-436-1516.. 47 C guerra@hnu.edu

GUERRA, Manuel .... 503-365-4684 404 L manuel.guerra@chemeketa.edu

GUERRA, Michael .... 510-628-8031.. 50 I mguerra@lincolnuca.edu

GUERRA, Nancy .... 302-831-2793.. 94 D nguerra@udel.edu

GUERRA, Olivia .... 972-860-8065 472 D oguerra@dcccd.edu

GUERRA, Sabra .... 254-968-9770 485 A sguerra@tarleton.edu

GUERRA, Yvonne .... 210-486-4339 466 K yguerra6@alamo.edu

GUERRA GAIER, Norma .... 512-245-2645 489 C ng14@txstate.edu

GUERRERO, Bertha, M . 671-735-5638 549 E boardoftrustees@guamcc.edu

GUERRERO, Daniel .... 425-640-1058 522 D daniel.guerrero@edcc.edu

GUERRERO, Daniel, G .. 310-206-6382.. 71 D dguerrero@athletics.ucla.edu

GUERRERO, Dolores ..... 361-593-2717 486 A dolores.guerrero@tamuk.edu

GUERRERO, Jennifer .... 609-984-1588 308 H jguerrero@tesc.edu

GUERRERO, John .... 670-234-5498 550 B

GUERRERO, Ken .... 909-884-8891.. 41 K

GUERRERO, Larry .... 575-492-2159 314 D lguerrero@usw.edu

GUERRERO, Omar .... 787-857-3600 553 G oguerrero@br.inter.edu

GUERRERO, Philip, C ... 671-735-5640 549 E philip.guerrero2@guamcc.edu

GUERRERO, Sherrie, L . 909-652-6131.. 38 A sherrie.guerrero@chaffey.edu

GUERRERO, Tammy .... 219-785-5249 172 A tguerrero@pnc.edu

GUERRERO, Tammy .... 219-989-2675 171 L guerrero@purduecal.edu

GUERRERO, Tim .... 303-410-2429.. 85 E tguerrero@redstone.edu

GUERRERO, Tracy .... 670-237-6714 550 B tracy.guerrero@marianas.edu

GUERRERO-LONGORIA, Marissa .... 956-721-5416 477 C marissa.longoria@laredo.edu

GUERRETTE, Leslie ...... 207-741-5715 211 D lguerrette@smccme.edu

GUERRETTE, Leslie, R .. 207-834-7550 212 F leslieg@maine.edu

GUERRIERI, Joe .... 213-763-3683.. 52 A guerrierij@lattc.edu

GUERRIERO, William .... 480-732-7012.. 14 K William.Guerriero@cgc.edu

GUERTIN, Donna .... 413-565-1000 222 G dguertin@baypath.edu

GUESS, Melissa .... 310-660-3492.. 43 G mguess@elcamino.edu

GUEST, Charles .... 251-460-6261.... 9 F cguest@southalabama.edu

GUEST, Denise .... 540-891-3040 515 E dguest@germanna.edu

GUEST, James .... 402-472-7488 293 H jguest2@unl.edu

GUEST, James, H .... 845-368-7201 342 A james.guest@use.salvationarmy.org

GUEST, Joshua .... 662-472-9023 267 E jguest@holmescc.edu

GUEST, Lois, A .... 845-368-7220 342 A lois.guest@use.salvationarmy.org

GUEST, Susan .... 870-633-4480.. 20 J sguest@eacc.edu

GUETTI, Joan .... 973-761-9018 308 C joan.guetti@shu.edu

GUEUERRA, Jonathan ... 305-809-3204 104 A jonathan.gueuerra@fkcc.edu

GUEVARA, Carla .... 631-244-3220 324 C guevara@dowling.edu

GUEVARA, Christine ..... 505-473-6652 313 B christine.guevara@santafeuniversity.edu

GUEVARA, Julia .... 616-331-2400 243 E guevaraj@gvsu.edu

GUTIERREZ, Brian, G ... 817-257-7815 486 G
brian.gutierrez@tcu.edu
GUTIERREZ, Daniel ... 505-428-1203 313 A
daniel.gutierrez@sfcc.edu
GUTIERREZ, Derrick ... 717-396-7833 429 H
dgutierrez@pcad.edu
GUTIERREZ, Diana ... 989-686-9434 242 I
dianagutierrez@delta.edu
GUTIERREZ, Dionne, K . 714-879-3901.. 47 D
dkbutler@hiu.edu
GUTIERREZ, Edna, I ... 787-720-1022 550 F
registrador@atlanticcollege.edu
GUTIERREZ, Eduardo ... 305-271-6555.. 98 C
GUTIERREZ, Javier ... 651-523-3076 256 B
jgutierrez@hamline.edu
GUTIERREZ, Juan ... 714-432-5725.. 40 D
jgutierrez@occ.cccd.edu
GUTIERREZ, Luis ... 509-865-8505 523 C
gutierrez_l@heritage.edu
GUTIERREZ, Martin ... 530-741-6939.. 78 F
mgutierr@yccd.edu
GUTIERREZ, Mary ... 650-738-4343.. 64 E
gutierrezm@smccd.edu
GUTIERREZ, Mary ... 361-593-2601 486 A
sm698@bncollege.com
GUTIERREZ, Michael, J 972-860-7196 472 E
MGutierrez@dcccd.edu
GUTIERREZ, Nancy, A .. 704-687-0081 371 B
ngutierr@uncc.edu
GUTIERREZ, Olivia ... 509-865-8508 523 C
gutierrez_o@heritage.edu
GUTIERREZ, Robert ... 212-229-8947 334 C
gutierrj@newschool.edu
GUTIERREZ, Roberto ... 541-880-2210 406 E
gutierrezr@klamathcc.edu
GUTIERREZ, Susan ... 707-664-2287.. 36 C
susan.gutierrez@sonoma.edu
GUTIERREZ, Tiffany ... 518-694-7254 314 G
tiffany.gutierrez@acphs.edu
GUTIERREZ, Tim ... 505-277-0963 313 H
tguiterr@unm.edu
GUTIERREZ KEETON,
Rebecca ... 909-869-3310.. 32 F
rgkeeton@cpp.edu
GUTIERREZ-LOPEZ,
Leticia ... 657-278-3040.. 33 E
lgutierrez-lopez@fullerton.edu
GUTIERREZ-SANDOVAL,
Yvonne ... 562-908-3411.. 60 I
ygutierrez-sandoval@riohondo.edu
GUTKIND, Susan ... 510-659-6266.. 56 J
sgutkind@ohlone.edu
GUTKNECHT, June ... 239-590-1227 114 F
jgutknec@fgcu.edu
GUTKNECHT, Leah, K ... 319-273-2846 176 A
leah.gutknecht@uni.edu
GUTMANN, Amy ... 215-898-7221 437 I
president@upenn.edu
GUTOSKEY, David, P ... 410-543-6040 220 E
dpgutoskey@salisbury.edu
GUTSTEIN, Daniel ... 410-225-4254 216 F
dgutstein@mica.edu
GUTTENTAG,
Christoph, O ... 919-684-2898 356 E
christoph.guttentag@duke.edu
GUTTERIDGE, Thomas .. 419-530-4391 394 E
thomas.gutteridge@utoledo.edu
GUTTMAN, Minerva ... 201-692-2890 302 H
minerva_guttman@fdu.edu
GUTTMAN, Stephen, J .. 610-758-4204 424 B
sjg2@lehigh.edu
GUVENDIREN, Ali ... 781-239-2557 231 G
aguvendiren@massbay.edu
GUY, Elmer ... 505-786-4112 311 G
eguy@navajotech.edu
GUY, Kristen ... 650-433-3878.. 58 B
kguy@paloaltou.edu
GUY, Shawn ... 336-517-2209 354 K
sguy@bennett.edu
GUY-SHEFTALL, Beverly 404-270-5624 132 D
bsheftall@spelman.edu
GUYDEN, Janet ... 318-247-3811 207 H
GUYER, Kim ... 402-898-1000 290 A
kim_g@creativecenter.edu
GUYETTE, Daniel ... 269-387-5810 252 I
daniel.guyette@wmich.edu
GUYETTE, Randy ... 828-835-4253 366 F
rguyette@tricountycc.edu
GUYMON, Ronald, E ... 801-524-8113 498 J
guymonre@ldsbc.edu
GUYNES, Del ... 972-923-5437 483 D
dguynes@sagu.edu
GUYOL, Kate ... 314-792-7435 276 H
guyol@kenrick.edu
GUYTON, Deirdre ... 304-327-4569 532 D
dguyton@bluefieldstate.edu
GUYTON, Don ... 713-743-8000 491 C
dguyton@uh.edu
GUYTON, Duffy ... 901-751-8453 459 C
dguyton@mabts.edu
GUYTON, Sondra ... 910-879-5634 360 C
sguyton@bladencc.edu
GUZDAR, Farida, P ... 443-518-3823 215 F
fguzdar@howardcc.edu
GUZELIMIAN, Ara ... 212-799-5000 329 I
GUZICK, David, S ... 352-733-1700 115 D
dguzick@ufl.edu
GUZMAN, Rosyvee ... 787-751-1912 554 D
roguzman@juris.inter.edu
GUZMAN-CINTRON,
Rosyvee ... 787-751-1912 554 D
roguzman@juris.inter.edu
GUZMAN, Andrew ... 213-740-7331.. 74 D
andrewgu@usc.edu
GUZMAN, Debora ... 210-434-6711 479 P
daguzman@lake.ollusa.edu
GUZMAN, Gabriel ... 708-456-0300 161 C
gguzman@triton.edu
GUZMAN, John ... 718-782-2200 316 J
jguzman@boricuacollege.edu
GUZMAN, Juan ... 308-865-8127 293 G
guzmanj@unk.edu
GUZMAN,
Juan Johnny, C ... 830-591-7264 483 A
jcguzman@swtjc.edu
GUZMAN, Leslie Ann ... 787-746-1400 552 I
lguzman@huertas.edu
GUZMAN, Margo ... 209-588-5222.. 78 B
guzmanm@yosemite.edu
GUZMAN, Ruben ... 949-451-5409.. 67 E
rguzman@ivc.edu
GUZMAN, Tobias ... 970-351-1944.. 87 A
tobias.guzman@unco.edu
GUZMAN-LOPEZ,
Evelyn ... 787-480-2455 551 H
eguzman@sanjuanciudadpatria.com
GUZOFSKY, Rosalie ... 215-635-7300 419 D
rguzofsky@gratz.edu
GUZZARDO, Joseph ... 609-777-3083 308 H
jguzzardo@tesc.edu
GUZZI, Martin ... 607-778-5245 344 F
guzzimj@sunybroome.edu
GUZZO, Linda ... 860-906-5132.. 89 A
lguzzo@ccc.commnet.edu
GWALTNEY, Darrell ... 615-460-6405 455 D
darrell.gwaltney@belmont.edu
GWARTNEY, Kurt ... 918-270-6470 401 C
kurt.gwartney@ptstulsa.edu
GWAZDA, Edward ... 609-586-4800 303 D
gwazdae@mccc.edu
GWINNER, Kevin, P ... 785-532-7227 188 H
kgwinner@ksu.edu
GWYTHER, Chelsea ... 802-387-6870 502 A
chelseagwyther@landmark.edu
GYAPONG, Samuel ... 478-825-6732 124 E
gyapongs@fvsu.edu
GYLLIN, John ... 407-708-4722 113 A
gyllinj@seminolestate.edu
GYMZIAK, Paul ... 603-623-0313 298 C
paulgymziak@nhia.edu
G'SELL, Sue ... 312-788-1154 162 H
sgsell@vandercook.edu

H

HA, Kevin ... 760-328-5554.. 53 G
HA, Viet, X ... 864-833-8193 448 E
vxha@presby.edu
HAAB, Melissa ... 251-575-8227.... 1 C
mhaab@ascc.edu
HAACK, Colleen ... 402-891-6605 290 C
colleen.haack@doane.edu
HAACK, Julie, A ... 563-333-6314 182 E
HaackJulieA@sau.edu
HAACK, Kim ... 617-912-9150 224 C
khaack@bostonconservatory.edu
HAACK, Kristen ... 617-521-2917 236 F
kristen.haack@simmons.edu
HAAG, Brandon ... 678-717-3885 133 A
brandon.haag@ung.edu
HAAGENSON, Heidi ... 763-576-4910 258 A
hhaagenson@anokatech.edu
HAAK, Robert ... 330-569-5125 383 F
haakrd@hiram.edu
HAAKE, Anne ... 585-475-4786 339 G
arhics@rit.edu
HAAKENSON,
Thomas, O ... 510-594-3655.. 30 G
thaakenson@cca.edu
HAAKONSEN, Alexis ... 203-392-5644.. 88 F
haakonsena1@southernct.edu
HAAN, Andrea ... 563-884-5447 182 D
andrea.haan@palmer.edu
HAAN, Fred ... 712-722-6050 177 J
fred.haan@dordt.edu
HAAN, Stanley, L ... 616-526-6442 240 L
haan@calvin.edu
HAAR, Jean ... 507-389-5445 260 A
jean.haar@mnsu.edu
HAAR, Scott ... 417-862-5700 272 K
shaar@bryancolleges.edu
HAARSMA, Jill ... 712-707-7100 182 C
jhaarsma@nwciowa.edu
HAAS, Bob ... 740-389-4636 386 B
HAAS, Brenda ... 740-351-3299 391 C
bhaas@shawnee.edu
HAAS, Carol, A ... 989-774-5251 240 O
haas1ca@cmich.edu
HAAS, Danielle ... 773-481-8103 142 D
dhaas3@ccc.edu
HAAS, Evelyn ... 612-767-7044 253 F
ev@alfredadler.edu
HAAS, Fritz ... 610-358-4541 427 D
haasf@neumann.edu
HAAS, Jan, M ... 215-702-4312 414 C
jhaas@cairn.edu
HAAS, Jesse ... 575-528-7548 312 D
jhaas@nmsu.edu
HAAS, Julie ... 913-469-8500 188 E
jhaas@jccc.edu
HAAS, Mark ... 517-355-5014 246 H
hass@finance.msu.edu
HAAS, Mary Ann ... 207-992-4900 210 C
haasm@husson.edu
HAAS, Mitch ... 503-251-5728 410 I
mhaas@uws.edu
HAAS, Nate ... 970-351-1763.. 87 A
nate.haas@unco.edu
HAAS, Nicole ... 718-951-5671 318 F
nicole@brooklyn.cuny.edu
HAAS, Ocki ... 417-865-2815 274 L
haaso@evangel.edu
HAAS, Patricia ... 215-503-5511 436 F
patricia.haas@jefferson.edu
HAAS, Sarah ... 573-518-2307 278 F
shaas@mineralarea.edu
HAAS, Stephen ... 800-371-6105.. 16 A
shaas@nationalparalegal.edu
HAAS, Sue ... 434-961-5229 516 F
shaas@pvcc.edu
HAAS, Thomas, J ... 616-331-2100 243 E
president@gvsu.edu
HAASE, Ryan ... 620-862-5252 184 H
rhaase@barclaycollege.edu
HAATVEDT, Chad ... 218-322-2444 259 B
chad.haatvedt@itascacc.edu
HABA, Jerry ... 972-721-5018 491 B
dhaba@udallas.edu
HABACKER, Laura ... 508-849-3447 222 C
lhabacker@annamaria.edu
HABECK, Gregory ... 414-229-4627 540 A
habeck@uwm.edu
HABECKER, Eugene, B . 765-998-5201 173 B
president@taylor.edu
HABEGER,
Christian, M ... 864-379-8813 446 B
habeger@erskine.edu
HABEGGER, Thomas ... 614-287-5422 380 G
thabegge@cscc.edu
HABEGGER, Toni ... 509-359-6373 522 C
thabegger@ewu.edu
HABEL, Heidi ... 610-902-8258 414 B
heidi.habel@cabrini.edu
HABEL, Leah ... 406-771-4327 288 B
lhabel@gfcmsu.edu
HABER, Carole ... 504-865-5225 207 F
chaber@tulane.edu
HABER, Jessica ... 914-674-7457 332 E
jhaber@mercy.edu
HABER, Melanie ... 860-512-2803.. 89 D
mhaber@manchestercc.edu
HABER, Sheldon, R ... 425-602-3040 519 J
shaber@bastyr.edu
HABERER, Ronald, J ... 716-888-8527 317 H
habererr@canisius.edu
HABERLE, Charles, J ... 401-865-1154 441 F
chaberle@providence.edu
HABERMAN, Erica ... 402-461-7487 290 G
ehaberman@hastings.edu
HABERMAN, Melissa ... 608-243-6320 543 C
mhaberman@madisoncollege.edu
HABERMAS, Mary ... 479-524-7153.. 21 F
mhaberma@jbu.edu
HABETZ, Pauline, M ... 713-500-8425 495 A
pauline.m.habetz@uth.tmc.edu
HABIB, Claudia ... 559-638-3641.. 69 C
claudia.habib@reedleycollege.edu
HABINGREITHER,
Robert, B ... 512-245-2119 489 C
rh03@txstate.edu
HABROCK, Marty ... 402-554-3408 294 A
mhabrock@unomaha.edu
HABSCHMIDT, Cathy ... 765-983-1772 165 H
habscca@earlham.edu
HABTEMARIAM,
Tsegaye ... 334-727-8174.... 8 B
thabtemariam@tuskegee.edu
HABUCHMAI, Joseph ... 691-320-2480 549 D
jhabuchmai@comfsm.fm
HABUKI, Daniel, Y ... 949-480-4005.. 66 I
habuki@soka.edu
HABURSKY, Mary Jo ... 304-243-2233 534 H
maryjoh@wju.edu
HABURSKY, Stephen ... 304-243-4453 534 H
habursky@wju.edu
HACK, Mary, C ... 609-984-1661 308 H
mhack@tesc.edu
HACKBARTH, Wade ... 608-785-9123 544 E
hackbarthw@westerntc.edu
HACKENBERG, Caitlin ... 407-646-2268 111 H
chackenberg@rollins.edu
HACKER, Carol, J ... 781-239-4220 222 E
hackerc@babson.edu
HACKER, Cheryl ... 740-351-3283 391 C
chacker@shawnee.edu
HACKERT, Marvin ... 512-232-3604 493 M
m.hackert@austin.utexas.edu
HACKET, JR.,
William, C ... 863-667-5004 113 K
wchacket@seu.edu
HACKETT, Amy, E ... 253-879-3140 527 F
ahackett@pugetsound.edu
HACKETT, Gail ... 804-828-1345 514 F
ghackett@vcu.edu
HACKETT, Georgia ... 605-856-2355 453 B
georgia.hackett@sintegleska.edu
HACKETT, Jim ... 734-764-9416 251 C
JimHackettAD@umich.edu
HACKETT, Keith ... 907-786-1250.. 10 H
khackett2@uaa.alaska.edu
HACKETT, Marquita ... 903-566-7181 494 E
mhackett@uttyler.edu
HACKETT, Mary ... 707-826-3311.. 35 D
Mary.Hackett@humboldt.edu
HACKETT, Matthew ... 859-572-5198 199 A
hackettm2@nku.edu
HACKETT, Royce ... 229-931-2074 126 C
royce.hackett@gsw.edu
HACKETT, Timothy ... 510-436-2464.. 59 C
thackett@peralta.edu
HACKETT, Tom ... 706-507-8968 123 D
hackett_tom@columbusstate.edu
HACKING, George, B ... 802-626-6200 504 B
george.hacking@lyndonstate.edu
HACKLE, Dale ... 850-973-1616 109 C
hackled@nfcc.edu
HACKLER, Gwen ... 405-789-6400 402 E
ghackler@snu.edu
HACKWORTH, Joe ... 256-331-5335.... 6 B
joehackworth@nwscc.edu
HADARY, Erin ... 276-944-6541 507 E
ehadary@ehc.edu
HADDAD, Abdallah ... 843-349-2938 444 G
abdallah@coastal.edu
HADDAD, Amy, M ... 402-280-2164 290 B
AmyHaddad@creighton.edu
HADDAD, Emily, A ... 207-581-1954 212 C
emily.haddad@maine.edu
HADDAD, Kamel ... 760-750-8034.. 35 B
khaddad@csusm.edu
HADDAWAY-WILLIAMS,
Chelsea ... 410-455-6830 219 F
chelseah@umbc.edu
HADDELAND, Patricia ... 503-883-2259 406 I
phaddel@linfield.edu
HADDOCK, Greg ... 660-562-1145 280 A
haddock@nwmissouri.edu
HADDOCK, Gregory ... 660-562-1145 280 A
haddock@nwmissouri.edu
HADDOCK, Jennifer ... 870-743-3000.. 22 A
jhaddock@northark.edu
HADDOCK, Jorge ... 617-287-7700 228 G
jorge.haddock@umb.edu
HADDON, Phoebe, A ... 856-225-6095 306 F
chancellor@camden.rutgers.edu
HADDON, Phoebe, A ... 856-225-6095 307 A
chancellor@camden.rutgers.edu
HADDOW, Deborah, E .. 607-733-2300 351 E
dhaddow@uscny.edu
HADDOW, Donna ... 719-846-5541.. 86 A
donna.haddow@trinidadstate.edu
HADEN, David, W ... 617-824-8620 226 A
david_haden@emerson.edu
HADEN, Patrick, C ... 213-740-4154.. 74 D
phaden@usc.edu
HADENFELDT, Sharon .. 402-481-8606 289 C
sharon.hadenfeldt@bryanhealthcollege.edu
HADFIELD, Christopher 218-894-5172 258 C
CHadfield@clcmn.edu
HADFIELD, Janice, M ... 402-466-4774 290 C
janice.hadfield@doane.edu
HADJEZ, Claudia ... 305-899-3970.. 99 B
chadjez@barry.edu
HADLEY, Craig ... 207-992-1953 210 C
hadleyc@husson.edu
HADLEY, H. Roger ... 909-558-4481.. 50 K
rhadley@llu.edu
HADLEY, Herbert ... 904-256-7484 106 Q
hhadley@ju.edu
HADLEY, Jeff ... 201-216-5133 308 D
Jeff.Hadley@stevens.edu

HADLEY, Jeremy ... 505-473-6411 313 B jeremy.hadley@santafeuniversity.edu
HADLEY, June, M ... 817-552-3700 477 B jhadley@tku.edu
HADLEY, Kim ... 479-524-7117.. 21 F KHadley@jbu.edu
HADLEY, Linda ... 706-568-2044 123 D hadley_linda@columbusstate.edu
HADLEY, Pamela ... 610-399-2260 430 D phadley@cheyney.edu
HADLEY, Richard ... 508-588-9100 232 A
HADLEY, Robyn, S ... 314-935-7192 285 E robyn.hadley@wustl.edu
HADLOCK, Heather ... 214-333-5340 471 L heather@dbu.edu
HADSELL, Heidi ... 860-509-9502.. 90 G hadsell@hartsem.edu
HADWIN, Denice ... 361-354-2221 470 K hadwind@coastalbend.edu
HADWIN, Julie ... 803-584-3446 450 F jhadwin@mailbox.sc.edu
HAECKER, Ryan ... 512-444-8082 487 B library@thsu.edu
HAEFNER, Jeremy, A ... 585-475-6399 339 G jahpro@rit.edu
HAEGER, Loredana, C .. 901-572-2772 455 C loredana.haeger@bchs.edu
HAELEN, Robert ... 518-320-1502 343 B bob.haelen@suny.edu
HAEN, Rich, N ... 920-565-1213 536 Q haenrn@lakeland.edu
HAERENS, Joy ... 909-652-6840.. 38 A joy.haerens@chaffey.edu
HAESLOOP, Mary ... 650-508-3651.. 56 H mhaesloop@ndnu.edu
HAFFAR, Warren ... 215-572-4094 412 F haffarw@arcadia.edu
HAFFEY, Jim ... 662-472-9013 267 E jhaffey@holmescc.edu
HAFFORD, Patrick ... 617-989-4870 237 G haffordp@wit.edu
HAFKEMEYER, Susan, P ... 563-588-7769 180 L sue.hafkemeyer@loras.edu
HAFNER, Greg ... 641-673-2168 184 B hafnerg@wmpenn.edu
HAFT, Jennifer ... 702-992-2354 295 E jennifer.haft@nsc.edu
HAFT, Tami ... 208-769-7729 138 G tami_haft@nic.edu
HAGA-DUFFY, Laura ... 541-956-7158 409 F lduffy@roguecc.edu
HAGAN, Abdalla, F ... 903-927-3343 497 G afhagan@wileyc.edu
HAGAN, Alise ... 337-482-1000 208 F alise@louisiana.edu
HAGAN, Bruce ... 949-451-5254.. 67 E bhagan@ivc.edu
HAGAN, Dara ... 763-488-2465 258 G dara.hagan@hennepintech.edu
HAGAN, Khalli ... 225-743-8500 204 C khagan@rpcc.edu
HAGAN, Lauren ... 312-915-7676 151 E lhagan@uc.edu
HAGAN, Linda ... 248-689-8282 251 I lhagan@walshcollege.edu
HAGAN, Willie, J ... 310-243-3301.. 33 B presidenthagan@csudh.edu
HAGANDER, Sonja ... 612-330-1435 253 K hagander@augsburg.edu
HAGANS, Karen ... 419-289-5067 377 A khagans@ashland.edu
HAGANS, Lori, R ... 405-878-2708 399 I lori.hagans@okbu.edu
HAGARA, Kimberly, K .. 409-747-3277 495 E kkhagara@utmb.edu
HAGE, Gloria ... 734-487-3246 242 J ghage@emich.edu
HAGEDORN, Andy ... 812-357-6520 173 A ahagedorn@saintmeinrad.edu
HAGEDORN, Christine .. 215-968-8034 413 F hagedorn@bucks.edu
HAGEDORN, Valerie, A . 412-531-4433 416 F info@deantech.edu
HAGEMAN, Kristin ... 651-773-1780 258 D kristin.hageman@century.edu
HAGEMANN, Ryan ... 503-838-8000 411 B hagemannr@wou.edu
HAGEMEYER, Gwen ... 812-535-5285 172 F ghagemeyer@smwc.edu
HAGEN, Berta ... 218-285-2207 261 A berta.hagen@rainyriver.edu
HAGEN, Cheryl, M ... 734-462-4400 250 A chagen@schoolcraft.edu
HAGEN, Gary, D ... 701-788-4754 374 A Gary.Hagen@mayvillestate.edu
HAGEN, Mike ... 641-683-5243 179 C michael.hagen@indianhills.edu
HAGEN, Patrick ... 608-647-6186 541 E patrick.hagen@uwc.edu
HAGEN, Peter ... 609-652-4504 308 E hagenp@stockton.edu
HAGEN, Stan ... 503-838-8174 411 B hagens@wou.edu
HAGEN, Susan ... 205-226-4660.... 2 C shagen@bsc.edu
HAGEN-FOLEY, Debra ... 715-422-5535 543 D debra.hagenfoley@mstc.edu
HAGEN-SWANSON, Cherish ... 218-755-4096 258 B chagenswanson@bemidjistate.edu
HAGENBAUGH, Jamie .. 610-647-4400 421 B jhagenbaugh@immaculata.edu
HAGENBAUGH, Stacie .. 413-585-2582 236 G shagenba@smith.edu
HAGER, Amy ... 660-263-4110 279 F amyh@macc.edu
HAGER, Judy ... 701-252-3467 375 J jhager@uj.edu
HAGER, Mark ... 816-322-0110 272 L mark.hager@calvary.edu
HAGER, Mary, B ... 701-355-8303 375 K mbhager@umary.edu
HAGER, Michael, A ... 319-273-2382 176 A michael.hager@uni.edu
HAGER, Tim ... 515-964-6409 177 B tjhager@dmacc.edu
HAGERMAN, Brandi, F . 336-633-0213 365 A bfhagerman@randolph.edu
HAGERMAN, Elizabeth, M ... 812-244-4100 172 C Elizabeth.Hagerman@rhventures.org
HAGERMANN, P. Donald ... 302-356-6844.. 94 G p.donald.hagermann@wilmu.edu
HAGERTY, George, J ... 352-787-7660.. 99 D ghagerty@beaconcollege.edu
HAGERTY, Michael ... 617-266-1400 223 F
HAGG, Scott ... 760-750-4826.. 35 B shagg@csusm.edu
HAGGARD, Bill ... 828-251-6474 370 E bhaggard@unca.edu
HAGGARD, David, L ... 423-775-7207 455 F david.haggard@bryan.edu
HAGGARD, Dennis ... 479-248-7236.. 20 K dennishaggard75@yahoo.com
HAGGARD, Luanne ... 816-279-7000 271 H luanne.haggard@abtu.edu
HAGGARD, Michael ... 518-355-4000 459 C mhaggard@mabtsne.edu
HAGGERTY, Angela ... 203-773-8538.. 87M ashaggerty@albertus.edu
HAGGERTY, Christina ... 815-455-8727 152 B chaggerty@mchenry.edu
HAGGERTY, Janet, A ... 918-631-2304 403M janet-haggerty@utulsa.edu
HAGGETT, Rosemary, R 214-752-5535 492 D rosemary.haggett@untsystem.edu
HAGGINS, Debra, L ... 757-727-5340 508 C debra.haggins@hamptonu.edu
HAGGINS, Isaac ... 216-201-9025 385 D
HAGGINS, Summer ... 216-201-9025 385 D
HAGGINS, Tanya ... 216-201-9025 385 D
HAGGRAY, M. Annette . 443-412-2244 215 D ahaggray@harford.edu
HAGHIGHI, Shawn ... 636-949-4726 276 L shaghighi@lindenwood.edu
HAGIN, Linwood ... 864-977-7011 448 A linwood.hagin@ngu.edu
HAGOOD, Matthew ... 305-348-2820 114 G matthew.hagood@fiu.edu
HAGOVSKY, Beth ... 610-660-1072 434 G bhagovsk@sju.edu
HAGSTROM, Fred ... 507-222-5488 254 D fhagstro@carleton.edu
HAGUE, Stephen, T ... 410-323-6211 214 G sthague@faiththeological.org
HAGY LOWE, Susan, L 276-964-7304 517 A susan.lowe@sw.edu
HAHKA, Curt ... 906-487-7380 242M curt.hahka@finlandia.edu
HAHN, Audrey ... 765-677-2408 169 C audrey.hahn@indwes.edu
HAHN, Ben ... 907-564-8289.. 10 D bhahn@alaskapacific.edu
HAHN, Ben ... 907-564-8299.. 10 D bhahn@alaskapacific.edu
HAHN, Charles ... 314-246-7457 285 G charleshahn@webster.edu
HAHN, Cynthia ... 516-562-2018 324 G chahn@nshs.edu
HAHN, Greg ... 208-426-5391 137 E greghahn@boisestate.edu
HAHN, Jack ... 760-744-1150.. 58 D jhahn@palomar.edu
HAHN, Katharine ... 216-687-2277 380 D K.HAHN@csuohio.edu
HAHN, Kelli ... 269-927-6701 245 E khahn@lakemichigancollege.edu
HAHN, Lenell ... 573-986-6012 282 C lhahn@semo.edu
HAHN, Lisa ... 516-572-7169 334 A lisa.hahn@ncc.edu
HAHN, Marc, B ... 816-654-7102 276 G mhahn@kcumb.edu
HAHN, Mary Joan ... 509-313-6095 522 L hahn@gonzaga.edu
HAHN, Richard ... 814-866-8160 423 B rhahn@lecom.edu
HAHN, Roger ... 816-268-5412 279 K rlhahn@nts.edu
HAHN, Sarah ... 530-752-0871.. 71 A shahn@shcs.ucdavis.edu
HAHN, Stephen ... 973-720-2565 309 I hahns@wpunj.edu
HAHN, Steven ... 608-262-2433 539 D smhahn@wisc.edu
HAHN, Suzan ... 907-474-7224.. 10 I uaf-library-dean@alaska.edu
HAHN, Terence ... 312-777-8705 147 C thahn@aii.edu
HAHN, Troy, J ... 631-451-4578 348 E hahnt@sunysuffolk.edu
HAHN-MURPHY, Alicia . 610-436-2122 432 B ahahn@wcupa.edu
HAHS, Sharon, K ... 773-442-5400 154 H s-hahs@neiu.edu
HAID, William, R ... 858-534-5448.. 72 B whaid@ucsd.edu
HAIDLE, Shirley, J ... 208-467-8523 138 H sjhaidle@nnu.edu
HAIGHT, Larry, L ... 530-226-4110.. 66 G lhaight@simpsonu.edu
HAIGWOOD, Patricia ... 979-436-9106 485 C haigwood@tamhsc.edu
HAIL, Amy ... 207-221-4228 213 B ahail@une.edu
HAILE, Bob, A ... 309-649-6331 160 F bob.haile@src.edu
HAILE, Christine, E ... 518-956-8080 343 C chaile@albany.edu
HAILE, Gregory, A ... 954-201-7410.. 99 G ghaile@broward.edu
HAILEY, Christine ... 435-797-2776 500 A christine.hailey@usu.edu
HAILEY, Maryann ... 903-875-7305 479 I maryann.hailey@navarrocollege.edu
HAILEY, Robert, C ... 504-862-8064 207 F rhailey@tulane.edu
HAILLE, Amy ... 207-221-4230 213 B ahaille@une.edu
HAILU, Elias ... 713-313-7879 487 F hailu_ex@tsu.edu
HAIN, C. Stuart ... 610-328-8575 436 A chain1@swarthmore.edu
HAIN, Peggy, S ... 402-465-2137 292 E phain@nebrwesleyan.edu
HAIN, Tom ... 432-552-2782 495 F hain_t@utpb.edu
HAINAJ, Rosa ... 440-365-5222 385 E
HAINES, Amanda ... 360-736-9391 520 F ahaines@centralia.edu
HAINES, Asher ... 704-357-2541 131 F ahaines@southuniversity.edu
HAINES, Christina ... 602-285-7433.. 15 C chris.haines@phoenixcollege.edu
HAINES, Chuck ... 805-893-8541.. 72 D chuck.haines@bap.ucsb.edu
HAINES, Ena ... 212-678-3486 349 I ena@tc.columbia.edu
HAINES, George ... 405-585-5504 399 I george.haines@okbu.edu
HAINES, Kairyn ... 858-566-1200.. 43 A khaines@disd.edu
HAINES, Lynne ... 912-650-5673 131 F lhaines@southuniversity.edu
HAINES, Melissa ... 610-558-5625 427 D hainesm@neumann.edu
HAINES, Paula ... 978-934-4186 229 A Paula_Haines@uml.edu
HAINES, R. Craig ... 419-434-4558 393 F haines@findlay.edu
HAINES, Rachel ... 252-335-3787 369 F rmhaines@ecsu.edu
HAINES, Rhonda ... 315-792-7100 348 D rhaines@sunycnse.com
HAINES, Terry ... 913-266-8601 190 D terry.haines@ottawa.edu
HAINEY, Dale, E ... 817-202-6519 483 C haineyd@swau.edu
HAINGRAY, Donald ... 585-567-9287 328 C donald.haingray@houghton.edu
HAINLINE, Benjamin ... 580-628-6250 399 E ben.hainline@noc.edu
HAINRICK, Jennifer ... 691-320-2480 549 D jenniferh@comfsm.fm
HAIR, Shannon ... 434-797-8495 515 C shair@dcc.vccs.edu
HAIRE, Helen, M ... 319-273-2712 176 A helen.haire@uni.edu
HAIRR, Blair ... 910-592-8084 365 G ahairr@sampsoncc.edu
HAIRSTON, Creasie ... 312-996-3219 161 F cfh@uic.edu
HAIRSTON, Gregory, G 336-750-2125 372 D hairstong@wssu.edu
HAIRSTON, Steven, E ... 919-516-4410 368 E sehairston@st-aug.edu
HAIRSTON, Tali ... 206-281-2455 526 D tali@spu.edu
HAISCH, Craig ... 503-883-2217 406 I chaisch@linfield.edu
HAISEN, Michael ... 808-735-4785 135 A mhaisen@chaminade.edu
HAISMA, Dale ... 616-632-3037 239 E haismdal@aquinas.edu
HAITCH, Russell ... 800-287-8822 164 E haitcru@bethanyseminary.edu
HAJELA, Prabhat ... 518-276-6624 339 D hajelap@rpi.edu
HAJOVSKY, Ted ... 979-209-7211 469 F thajovsky@blinn.edu
HAKA, Clifford, H ... 517-355-2341 246 H hakac@msu.edu
HAKANSON, David ... 314-977-7221 281M hakanson@slu.edu
HAKER, Catherine, A ... 518-454-5158 322 C hakerc@strose.edu
HAKES, Joseph ... 312-567-7124 147 E jhakes@iit.edu
HAKIM, George ... 810-762-3223 251 E heohak@umflint.edu
HAKIM, Iman, A ... 520-626-7083.. 18 E ihakim@email.arizona.edu
HAKKAKIAN, Eliyahu ... 410-484-7200 217 E
HAKKENBERG, Michael, A ... 540-375-2379 512 B hakkenberg@roanoke.edu
HAKL, Roberta, H ... 605-667-5651 453 F roberta.hakl@usd.edu
HAKLIN, Joseph, R ... 765-361-6233 175 B haklinj@wabash.edu
HALACO, Karen ... 518-608-8481 325 B khalaco@excelsior.edu
HALAKAN, Cathy ... 518-262-4019 314 I halakac@mail.amc.edu
HALARIS, Dimitris ... 914-633-2649 328 F dhalaris@iona.edu
HALAS, Wally ... 203-254-4000.. 90 E whalas@fairfield.edu
HALASZ, Thomas ... 803-777-3971 450 B halasztj@mailbox.sc.edu
HALBERSTADT, Joseph . 718-438-1002 332 F yhalberstadt@yeshivanet.com
HALBERSTAM, Lisa ... 646-565-6000 350 C lisa.halberstam@touro.edu
HALBERT, Jay ... 325-942-2355 489 E jay.halbert@angelo.edu
HALBERT, Martin ... 940-565-3025 492 D martin.halbert@unt.edu
HALBIG, Julie ... 765-285-1020 164 D jdhalbig@bsu.edu
HALBROOK, Anna ... 501-208-5310.. 25 A halbrook@uaccm.edu
HALBUR, Alan ... 320-762-4402 257 O alanh@alextech.edu
HALCOMB, Jonda ... 361-698-1218 473 F jhalcomb@delmar.edu
HALCROW, Katie ... 651-450-3241 259 A khalcro@inverhills.edu
HALCUMB, Cambrea ... 573-840-9658 283 D chalcumb@trcc.edu
HALDEMAN, Pam ... 310-954-4366.. 54 I phaldeman@msmu.edu
HALDER, Pradeep ... 315-792-7100 348 D phalder@sunycnse.com
HALE, Barry ... 903-923-2020 473 I bhale@etbu.edu
HALE, Brian ... 334-683-2367.... 5 H bhale@marionmilitary.edu
HALE, David, B ... 804-289-8150 513M dhale2@richmond.edu
HALE, Don ... 404-413-3025 126 D dhale@gsu.edu
HALE, Georgia ... 479-788-7030.. 23 H georgia.hale@uafs.edu
HALE, Jeffery, L ... 918-540-6201 398 L jhale@neo.edu
HALE, Jeffrey ... 605-688-5148 454 C jeffrey.hale@sdstate.edu
HALE, Jerold, L ... 843-953-0760 445 B halejl@cofc.edu
HALE, Kara, B ... 620-431-2820 189 J khale@neosho.edu
HALE, Kenneth ... 216-987-4251 381 A kenneth.hale@tri-c.edu
HALE, Lloyd ... 816-604-4062 278 A lloyd.hale@mcckc.edu
HALE, Mark ... 214-333-5503 471 L markh@dbu.edu
HALE, Nori ... 785-242-5200 190 D nori.hale@ottawa.edu

HALE, Philip, P .... 312-915-6494 151 E
phale@luc.edu
HALE, Quinn .... 509-574-4702 529 B
qhale@yvcc.edu
HALE, Richard .... 401-253-1040 442 C
rhale@rwu.edu
HALE, Sheri .... 540-545-7240 512 E
shale2@su.edu
HALE, Sheryl .... 918-293-5130 400 E
sheryl.hale@okstate.edu
HALE, Susie .... 863-784-7132 113 C
susie.hale@southflorida.edu
HALE, Ted .... 860-906-5053.. 89 A
thale@ccc.commnet.edu
HALE, Tricia, A .... 229-333-5940 133 H
tahale@valdosta.edu
HALEEM, Ali .... 312-427-2737 148 I
ahaleem@jmls.edu
HALES, Christie, C .... 434-949-1068 516 H
christie.hales@southside.edu
HALES, Erin .... 714-556-3610.. 75 A
erin.hales@vanguard.edu
HALEVY, Julia .... 617-262-5000 223 G
julia.halevy@the-bac.edu
HALEY, Donna .... 678-839-6438 133 F
dhaley@westga.edu
HALEY, John, R .... 315-445-4689 330 B
haleyjr@lemoyne.edu
HALEY, Ken .... 903-785-7661 480 B
khaley@parisjc.edu
HALEY, Lynn .... 931-372-3232 462 A
lhaley@tntech.edu
HALEY, Ted .... 508-767-7215 222 D
thaley@assumption.edu
HALEY, Terence .... 256-824-6674.... 9 A
terence.haley@uah.edu
HALEY, Thomas .... 402-280-1862 290 B
toh00008@creighton.edu
HALEY-THOMSON, Lisa 518-454-5102 322 C
thomsonl@strose.edu
HALFMANN, Tina .... 612-244-2800 256 E
thalfmann@ipr.edu
HALFORD, Sharon .... 602-285-7434.. 15 C
sharon.halford@phoenixcollege.edu
HALGERSON, Carolyn ... 605-688-4695 454 C
carolyn.halgerson@sdstate.edu
HALGREN, Cara .... 701-777-2664 373 G
cara.halgren@und.edu
HALIBURTON, Tori .... 731-426-7500 457 K
HALICKI, Shannon .... 304-336-8075 533 A
shalicki@westliberty.edu
HALIEMUN, Cynthia ..... 217-228-5432 156 D
haliecy@quincy.edu
HALL, Allyson .... 860-465-5283.. 88 E
hallall@easternct.edu
HALL, Amber, L .... 501-450-5371.. 25 F
amberh@uca.edu
HALL, Amy, J .... 540-674-3601 516 B
ahall@nr.edu
HALL, Anders, W .... 615-322-2451 465 H
anders.hall@vanderbilt.edu
HALL, Andy .... 423-585-6801 464 C
robert.hall@ws.edu
HALL, Andy .... 423-585-6801 464 C
andy.hall@ws.edu
HALL, Ann .... 989-463-7411 239 B
hall@alma.edu
HALL, Ann Lyn .... 505-224-4000 310 F
ahall@cnm.edu
HALL, Art .... 210-486-2312 467 B
ahall94@alamo.edu
HALL, Becky .... 404-364-8469 129 F
bhall1@oglethorpe.edu
HALL, Benjamin .... 740-362-3448 386 D
bhall@mtso.edu
HALL, Betty .... 864-592-4942 449 C
hallb@sccsc.edu
HALL, Bobbie .... 404-527-5264 127 H
bhall@itc.edu
HALL, Bobby, L .... 806-291-3410 496 K
hallb@wbu.edu
HALL, Bonnie .... 508-831-6645 238 G
bjhall@wpi.edu
HALL, Brad, R .... 406-338-5441 286 C
brad@bfcc.edu
HALL, C. Rick .... 706-771-4020 121 B
chall@augustatech.edu
HALL, Carol .... 734-432-5447 246 B
clhall@madonna.edu
HALL, Cassie .... 406-447-4572 286 D
chall@carroll.edu
HALL, Cathy .... 605-229-8453 453 A
cathy.hall@presentation.edu
HALL, Charles .... 252-335-3961 369 F
crhall@ecsu.edu
HALL, Charles, F .... 310-506-4532.. 58 H
charles.hall@pepperdine.edu
HALL, Cheryl .... 985-549-5312 208 E
chall@selu.edu
HALL, Chris .... 618-537-6833 152 C
chall@mckendree.edu
HALL, Chris .... 352-638-9703.. 99 D
chall@beaconcollege.edu
HALL, Cynthia .... 530-283-0202.. 44 H
chall@frc.edu
HALL, Daniel .... 502-852-6026 201 A
daniel.hall@louisville.edu
HALL, Daniel .... 763-424-0817 260 E
dhall@nhcc.edu
HALL, Dave, M .... 757-481-5005 519 C
HALL, David .... 340-693-1000 559 B
dhall@live.uvi.edu
HALL, Deborah, P .... 828-884-8262 355 A
dphall@brevard.edu
HALL, Delores .... 216-421-7423 380 B
dhall@cia.edu
HALL, Dennis .... 817-531-4872 490 C
dhall@txwes.edu
HALL, Dennis, G .... 615-322-2809 465 H
dennis.hall@vanderbilt.edu
HALL, Derek .... 906-227-2716 248 B
halld@nmu.edu
HALL, Don .... 508-854-4515 232 F
dhall@qcc.mass.edu
HALL, Donald .... 580-581-2293 397 A
dhall@cameron.edu
HALL, Donald, E .... 610-758-4570 424 B
deh211@lehigh.edu
HALL, Dorothy, J .... 540-985-8491 509 D
DJHall@jchs.edu
HALL, Elizabeth .... 856-415-2228 306 C
ehall@rcgc.edu
HALL, Ellis, F .... 317-738-8080 166 B
ehall@franklincollege.edu
HALL, Frank, L .... 603-428-2320 298 B
fhall@nec.edu
HALL, George .... 859-442-4188 196 A
george.hall@kctcs.edu
HALL, Gregory .... 860-444-8608 548 H
Gregory.Hall@uscga.edu
HALL, Gregory, V .... 863-638-7209 118 L
greg.hall@warner.edu
HALL, Gwen .... 304-724-3700 529 F
ghall@apus.edu
HALL, Heather .... 630-617-3576 144 G
heatherh@elmhurst.edu
HALL, Heather .... 616-632-2457 239 E
heather.hall@aquinas.edu
HALL, Hollie, M .... 607-587-4200 347 D
hallhm@alfredstate.edu
HALL, Jackie .... 606-487-3180 196 B
jackie.hall@kctcs.edu
HALL, James .... 520-515-5329.. 13 B
bohall@cochise.edu
HALL, James .... 251-381-3491.... 7 F
jhall@shc.edu
HALL, James .... 320-589-6378 265 A
jhall@morris.umn.edu
HALL, Jami .... 706-272-4428 123 G
jhall@daltonstate.edu
HALL, Jason .... 910-893-1291 355 C
hallj@campbell.edu
HALL, Jeffrey, B .... 706-419-1121 123 F
hall@covenant.edu
HALL, Jennifer .... 330-829-6644 394 A
halljene@mountunion.edu
HALL, Jennifer, S .... 417-268-1000 272 D
hallj@evangel.edu
HALL, Jessica .... 910-521-6571 371 D
jessica.hall@uncp.edu
HALL, Jill .... 863-297-1072 110 E
jhall@polk.edu
HALL, Jillian .... 617-730-7105 235 B
jill.hall@newbury.edu
HALL, Jim .... 631-420-2457 348 B
jim.hall@farmingdale.edu
HALL, Jim .... 479-619-4182.. 22 B
jhall@nwacc.edu
HALL, III, Jim .... 405-325-1700 403 I
tripp@ou.edu
HALL, John .... 404-880-6983 122 I
jhall@cau.edu
HALL, John, A .... 214-768-3518 482 J
jhall@smu.edu
HALL, John, D .... 817-272-2102 493 L
jhall@uta.edu
HALL, Jon Mark .... 812-464-1846 174 D
jmhall@usi.edu
HALL, Joy Lin .... 918-343-7541 401 I
jhall@rsu.edu
HALL, Juanita .... 805-493-3951.. 31 H
jahall@callutheran.edu
HALL, Julie .... 918-595-7922 403 A
julie.hall3@tulsacc.edu
HALL, Karla .... 502-213-2507 196 E
karla.hall@kctcs.edu
HALL, Karyn .... 936-468-3806 484 A
khall@sfasu.edu
HALL, Kathleen .... 252-328-9530 369 E
hallka@ecu.edu
HALL, Kathy .... 319-398-5498 180 J
khall@kirkwood.edu
HALL, Kelli .... 606-886-3863 195 I
kelli.hall@kctcs.edu
HALL, Kellie .... 701-477-7822 375 H
kmhall@tm.edu
HALL, Kelly .... 301-387-3000 215 A
kelly.hall@garrettcollege.edu
HALL, Kenneth, L .... 570-484-2598 431 C
khall@lhup.edu
HALL, Kevin .... 651-603-6165 255 C
khall@csp.edu
HALL, Kim .... 360-416-7601 527 A
kim.hall@skagit.edu
HALL, Kim, B .... 865-251-1800 460 J
khall@southcollegetn.edu
HALL, Kimberly .... 614-287-2408 380 G
khall46@cscc.edu
HALL, Kristin, E .... 845-758-7531 315 G
hall@bard.edu
HALL, Kristy .... 276-523-2400 516 A
khall@me.vccs.edu
HALL, Lanny .... 325-670-1227 474 M
lhall@hsutx.edu
HALL, Larretta .... 701-255-3285 375 I
lhall@uttc.edu
HALL, Larry .... 828-328-7112 358 G
larry.hall@lr.edu
HALL, Lataria .... 559-925-3338.. 76 C
latariahall@whccd.edu
HALL, Lauren, M .... 806-291-3763 496 K
laurie.hall@wbu.edu
HALL, Laurie .... 716-829-7640 324 E
hallla@dyc.edu
HALL, Lawrence .... 860-832-2298.. 88 D
halllaw@ccsu.edu
HALL, JR., Lawrence .... 615-327-5732 458 F
lhall@mmc.edu
HALL, Linda, M .... 585-292-2103 333 G
lhall38@monroecc.edu
HALL, Lisa .... 423-236-2900 460 K
lhwoodcock@southern.edu
HALL, Lori .... 207-741-5501 211 D
lhall@smccme.edu
HALL, Lori .... 419-448-3433 392 B
hallla@tiffin.edu
HALL, Louis, J .... 662-254-3384 269 C
ljhall@mvsu.edu
HALL, Lydia .... 936-294-3608 489 A
lth003@shsu.edu
HALL, Lynda .... 323-241-5338.. 51 I
hallj@lasc.edu
HALL, Lyndon .... 252-257-1900 366 G
halll@vgcc.edu
HALL, Lynn .... 812-866-7385 166 E
hall@hanover.edu
HALL, Mark .... 918-495-7742 401 B
mhall@oru.edu
HALL, Mark .... 919-545-8043 361 C
mhall@cccc.edu
HALL, Mark .... 734-384-4261 247 C
mhall@monroeccc.edu
HALL, Mark .... 615-297-7545 455 A
hallm@aquinascollege.edu
HALL, Marlon, R .... 530-251-8820.. 50 B
mhall@lassencollege.edu
HALL, Mary .... 828-232-5109 370 E
mhall@unca.edu
HALL, Matthew .... 502-897-4205 199 D
mhall@sbts.edu
HALL, Michael .... 302-736-2483.. 94 E
jmichael.hall@wesley.edu
HALL, Michael, R .... 336-841-9235 357 E
mhall@highpoint.edu
HALL, Michael, W .... 540-654-1025 513 I
mhall2@umw.edu
HALL, Michelle .... 985-549-2077 208 E
mhall@selu.edu
HALL, Michelle .... 404-364-8336 129 F
mhall@oglethorpe.edu
HALL, Norman, D .... 618-664-7119 145 E
norm.hall@greenville.edu
HALL, Pamela .... 313-845-6410 243 I
phall@hfcc.edu
HALL, Pat .... 620-862-5252 184 H
pat.hall@barclaycollege.edu
HALL, Patricia .... 479-394-7622.. 22 H
phall@rmcc.edu
HALL, Patty .... 402-465-2237 292 E
phall@nebrwesleyan.edu
HALL, Paulakay .... 423-775-7308 455 F
phall7036@bryan.edu
HALL, Philip, D .... 843-792-8979 447 G
hallpd@musc.edu
HALL, Ralph, G .... 972-758-3831 471 C
rhall@collin.edu
HALL, Randolph, W ...... 213-740-6709.. 74 D
rwhall@usc.edu
HALL, Raymond, D .... 810-762-3335 251 E
raydhall@umflint.edu
HALL, Renardo .... 662-254-3636 269 C
renardo.hall@mvsu.edu
HALL, Ricardo, D .... 305-284-5353 118 A
rdhall@miami.edu
HALL, Richard .... 307-674-6446 546 H
rhall@sheridan.edu
HALL, Robert .... 716-829-7657 324 E
hallrm@dyc.edu
HALL, Ron .... 865-251-1800 460 J
rhall@southcollegetn.edu
HALL, Sandy .... 325-674-2273 466 I
halls@acu.edu
HALL, Sigrid .... 336-750-3148 372 D
allensh@wssu.edu
HALL, Stacy .... 706-865-2134 132 G
shall@truett.edu
HALL, Steven .... 309-341-7823 149 G
shall@knox.edu
HALL, Steven .... 304-236-7620 531 F
steven.hall@southernwv.edu
HALL, Steven, A .... 617-358-0476 224 E
sahall@bu.edu
HALL, Susan .... 214-378-1609 472 B
shall@dcccd.edu
HALL, Susan .... 856-415-2185 306 C
shall@rcgc.edu
HALL, Tammy .... 501-279-4018.. 21 A
thall@harding.edu
HALL, Tarsi .... 206-239-4500 520 K
HALL, Teresa .... 410-704-2332 221 A
thall@towson.edu
HALL, Terry .... 415-561-1908.. 39 A
thall@ccsf.edu
HALL, Tim .... 410-455-2207 219 F
halltw@umbc.edu
HALL, Tim .... 308-535-3612 291 H
hallt@mpcc.edu
HALL, Timothy .... 914-674-7307 332 E
thall@mercy.edu
HALL, Tom .... 904-256-7715 106 Q
thall5@ju.edu
HALL, Tom .... 806-291-3750 496 K
hallt@wbu.edu
HALL, Tracy .... 845-434-5750 349 C
thall@sullivan.suny.edu
HALL, Tracy .... 360-867-6205 522 J
hallt@evergreen.edu
HALL, Tracy, A .... 336-316-2349 357 C
thall@guilford.edu
HALL, Tracy, D .... 901-333-4200 464 A
tdhall@southwest.tn.edu
HALL, Valerie .... 305-623-1409 104 B
Valerie.Hall@fmuniv.edu
HALL, Walter .... 404-364-8543 129 F
whall@oglethorpe.edu
HALL, Wayne .... 502-852-6111 201 A
whall@louisville.edu
HALL, Wendy .... 360-442-2491 524 A
whall@lowercolumbia.edu
HALL, William .... 714-997-6891.. 38 B
whall@chapman.edu
HALL, William .... 603-862-1287 299 B
bill.hall@unh.edu
HALL, JR., William .... 859-858-3511 193 A
bill.hall@asbury.edu
HALL, William, B .... 401-341-2132 442 D
hallb@salve.edu
HALL, William, C .... 617-984-1760 235 H
whall@quincycollege.edu
HALL, William, M .... 256-824-2302.... 9 A
William.Hall@uah.edu
HALL, Yvonne .... 617-322-3571 227 J
yvonne_hall@laboure.edu
HALL-JONES, Jenny ...... 740-593-2561 389 H
hallj1@ohio.edu
HALL-JONES, Jenny ...... 740-593-1800 389 H
hallj1@ohio.edu
HALL-NUZUM,
Deidra, R .... 304-829-7217 529 H
dhall-nuzum@bethanywv.edu
HALL SMITH, Willa .... 202-797-3670.... 8 B
HALL-YATES, Joyce .... 419-448-3049 392 B
hallyatesjc@tiffin.edu
HALLADAY, Choi .... 253-964-6506 525 C
challaday@pierce.ctc.edu
HALLADAY, Chris .... 610-758-3900 424 B
pch214@lehigh.edu
HALLAHAN, Kerry .... 636-227-2100 277 A
kerry.hallahan@logan.edu
HALLAHAN, Scott .... 415-581-8873.. 71 B
hallahan@uchastings.edu
HALLANGER, Nathan ..... 612-330-1674 253 K
hallange@augsburg.edu
HALLAS, Vicki .... 718-405-3332 322 A
vicki.hallas@mountsaintvincent.edu
HALLBERG, Robert .... 773-298-3109 158 F
hallberg@sxu.edu
HALLE, Kevin .... 402-375-7234 292 D
kehalle1@wsc.edu
HALLEEN, Jan .... 952-888-4777 263 I
jhalleen@nwhealth.edu
HALLER, Amy .... 815-455-8768 152 B
ahaller@mchenry.edu

HAMMAKER, Michelle .. 570-586-2400 435 H
mhammaker@summitu.edu
HAMMAN, Doug .... 541-881-5838 410 D
dhamman@tvcc.cc
HAMME, Gary .... 321-674-8832 103 R
gary@fit.edu
HAMMEKE, Curtis .... 785-628-4050 187 A
chammeke@fhsu.edu
HAMMEL, Nicole .... 484-664-3190 427 C
hammel@muhlenberg.edu
HAMMEL, Rachel .... 330-490-7452 395 C
rhammel@walsh.edu
HAMMELL, Rebecca, J . 717-245-1858 417 B
hammellr@dickinson.edu
HAMMER, Amanda .... 575-461-4413 311 C
amandah@mesalands.edu
HAMMER, Bradley, C ... 419-434-6922 393 F
hammer@findlay.edu
HAMMER,
Kimberley, A .... 412-397-6413 434 B
hammerk@rmu.edu
HAMMER, Larry .... 828-227-7232 372 C
hammer@wcu.edu
HAMMER, Lila, D .... 260-982-5234 170 a
ldhammer@manchester.edu
HAMMERMAN,
Adam, D .... 646-565-6000 350 C
adam.hammerman@touro.edu
HAMMERSCHMIDT,
David .... 734-432-5441 246 B
dhammerschmidt@madonna.edu
HAMMERSCHMIDT, Ray 517-355-2308 246 H
hammers1@msu.edu
HAMMES, Meg 563-387-1375 180M
hammma01@luther.edu
HAMMETT, Amy, S .... 216-368-4318 378 J
registrar@case.edu
HAMMETT, John .... 256-782-5445.... 4 L
jhammett@jsu.edu
HAMMETT, Maggie .... 406-994-2343 287 G
maggie.hammett@montana.edu
HAMMETT, Maria, A ..... 478-301-2670 128 G
hammett_ma@mercer.edu
HAMMILL, Graham, L .... 716-645-3786 343 E
ghammill@buffalo.edu
HAMMILL, Viv .... 406-444-0325 287 C
vhammill@montana.edu
HAMMITT, Stephanie .... 218-879-0810 258 F
shammitt@fdltcc.edu
HAMMOCK, Susan .... 478-240-5162 129 C
shammock@oftc.edu
HAMMON, Darrel, L ..... 801-863-7353 500 B
darrel.hammon@uvu.edu
HAMMON, Kyle .... 360-442-2551 524 A
khammon@lowercolumbia.edu
HAMMOND, Amy .... 540-665-4841 512 E
ahammond@su.edu
HAMMOND, Anna .... 904-470-8004 102 A
anna.hammond@ewc.edu
HAMMOND, Ben .... 781-283-2305 237 F
HAMMOND, Bill .... 402-449-2917 290 F
bhammond@graceu.edu
HAMMOND, Bill .... 913-266-8619 190 D
bill.hammond@ottawa.edu
HAMMOND, Brad .... 307-754-6400 546 I
Brad.Hammond@nwc.edu
HAMMOND, Brian .... 301-934-7853 214 E
bhammond@csmd.edu
HAMMOND, Charles ..... 646-378-6131 337 B
charles.hammond@nyack.edu
HAMMOND, Charles, A 302-225-6352.. 94 B
hammond@gbc.edu
HAMMOND,
Christine, M .... 989-386-6602 247 B
chammond@midmich.edu
HAMMOND, Dale, W ..... 509-777-3730 529 A
dhammond@whitworth.edu
HAMMOND, Dave .... 425-602-3416 519 J
dhammond@bastyr.edu
HAMMOND, Debbie ...... 843-953-5507 445 B
hammonddd@cofc.edu
HAMMOND, Denise ...... 870-584-4471.. 24 E
dhammond@cccua.edu
HAMMOND, Dianne ...... 352-245-4119 117 D
HAMMOND,
Elizabeth, D .... 478-301-2964 128 G
hammond_bd@mercer.edu
HAMMOND, Erin .... 314-256-8808 272 B
hammond@ai.edu
HAMMOND, Jamie .... 203-575-8022.. 89 F
jhammond@nv.edu
HAMMOND, Jane, F ..... 607-844-8222 350 A
hammonj@tc3.edu
HAMMOND, Jeff .... 601-266-5001 271 B
jeff.hammond@usm.edu
HAMMOND, Jerome 423-614-8310 457M
jhammond@leeuniveristy.edu
HAMMOND, Karen, S ... 240-500-2000 215 C
kshammond@hagerstowncc.edu
HAMMOND, Lesa .... 415-355-2007.. 26 I
lhammond@alliant.edu
HAMMOND, Mark .... 910-893-1211 355 C
hammond@campbell.edu
HAMMOND, Michael .... 765-998-5204 173 B
mchammond@taylor.edu
HAMMOND, Mike .... 803-535-1267 448 C
hammondm@octech.edu
HAMMOND, Pamela ..... 804-524-5000 518 C
president@vsu.edu
HAMMOND, Randy .... 717-477-1256 431 F
rphamm@ship.edu
HAMMOND, Russell ..... 845-341-4007 337 G
russell.hammond@sunyorange.edu
HAMMOND, Sue-Anne . 207-893-6633 211 H
shammond@sjcme.edu
HAMMOND, TeraKesha 773-291-6225 142 B
thammond12@ccc.edu
HAMMOND, Troy, D ..... 630-637-5454 154 F
tdhammond@noctrl.edu
HAMMOND,
Ulyssess, B .... 860-439-2046.. 90 D
ubham@conncoll.edu
HAMMOND, Vanessa 423-614-8511 457M
vhammond@leeuniversity.edu
HAMMOND NASS,
Holly .... 207-602-2306 213 B
hnass@une.edu
HAMMONDS, David ...... 936-294-2709 489 A
david.hammonds@shsu.edu
HAMMONDS, Diane, M 610-526-1407 412 D
diane.hammonds@theamericancollege.edu
HAMMONDS, Kathy ...... 509-467-1727 523 E
kathyh@interface.edu
HAMMONDS, Luke .... 601-477-4058 268 A
luke.hammonds@jcjc.edu
HAMMONDS, MarTeze . 479-880-4358.. 20 C
mhammonds2@atu.edu
HAMMONS, Chris .... 281-649-3600 475 B
chammons@hbu.edu
HAMMONS, Jamirae ..... 606-539-4201 200 F
jamirae.hammons@ucumberlands.edu
HAMMONS, Steve .... 606-679-8501 197 B
steve.hammons@kctcs.edu
HAMMONTREE, Tonya .. 501-205-8809.. 20 G
thammontree@cbc.edu
HAMNER, Elise .... 541-888-7211 410 A
elise.hamner@socc.edu
HAMNER, Mark .... 940-898-3039 490 D
mhamner@twu.edu
HAMP, Herlisa .... 408-741-4616.. 76 F
herlisa.hamp@westvalley.edu
HAMPSON, Nancy .... 970-207-4550.. 83 P
nancyh@mckinleycollege.edu
HAMPTON, Anita .... 319-385-6220 180 A
anita.hampton@iw.edu
HAMPTON, Audrey .... 661-255-1050.. 31 B
HAMPTON, Brenda .... 712-325-3402 180 B
bhampton@iwcc.edu
HAMPTON, Diane .... 870-733-6880.. 19 G
dhampton@midsouthcc.edu
HAMPTON, Franki .... 540-453-2285 514 H
hamptonf@brcc.edu
HAMPTON, Iyisha .... 334-244-3674.... 2 A
HAMPTON, Jarvis, D .... 806-651-3451 486 D
jhampton@mail.wtamu.edu
HAMPTON, Jennifer ...... 630-752-5327 163 G
jennifer.hampton@wheaton.edu
HAMPTON, Julie .... 309-649-6201 160 F
julie.hampton@src.edu
HAMPTON, Kay .... 912-279-5853 123 B
khampton@ccga.edu
HAMPTON, Lacy .... 210-486-2178 467 B
lhampton14@alamo.edu
HAMPTON, Lee .... 517-787-0800 244 H
HamptonLeeM@jccmi.edu
HAMPTON, Logan, C .... 731-426-7595 457 K
lhampton@lanecollege.edu
HAMPTON, Mark, C ..... 410-778-7264 221 D
mhampton2@washcoll.edu
HAMPTON, Michael ...... 503-883-2442 406 I
mhampton@linfield.edu
HAMPTON, Mike .... 305-919-4018 114 G
mike.hampton@fiu.edu
HAMPTON, Renee .... 417-667-8181 273 H
rhampton@cottey.edu
HAMPTON, Terri .... 626-585-7361.. 58 F
tlhampton@pasadena.edu
HAMPTON, Valerie, J ... 607-777-4775 343 D
vhampton@binghamton.edu
HAMPTON, Vickie .... 404-507-8647 128 L
vickie.hampton@morehouse.edu
HAMPTON, William .... 386-226-4811 102 B
hamptonw@erau.edu
HAMPTON, William ...... 903-730-4890 476 L
whampton@jarvis.edu
HAMRE, Lynne .... 218-723-5930 255 A
lhamre@css.edu
HAMRIC, Mark .... 540-231-1181 507 D
mhamric@vcom.vt.edu
HAMRICK, David, S 512-232-7604 493M
dhamrick@utpress.utexas.edu
HAMRICK, Howard, I ..... 281-756-3700 467 D
hhamrick@alvincollege.edu
HAMRICK, James .... 410-857-2202 217 A
jhamrick@mcdaniel.edu
HAMRICK, Jeff .... 415-422-6136.. 74 C
jhamrick@usfca.edu
HAMRICK, Mike .... 304-696-5408 532 H
hamrickm@marshall.edu
HAMRICK, Robin, G ..... 704-406-3996 356 G
rhamrick@gardner-webb.edu
HAMRICK, Sarah .... 202-651-5214.. 95 C
sarah.hamrick@gallaudet.edu
HAMSTRA, Pete .... 602-386-4114.. 11 F
pete.hamstra@arizonachristian.edu
HAMZAVI, Maria .... 858-499-0202.. 40 G
mhamzavi@coleman.edu
HAN, Joseph .... 216-687-5343 380 D
joseph.han@csuohio.edu
HAN, Ki Won .... 714-527-0691.. 44 B
HAN, Larry, L 407-888-8689 103M
lhan@fcim.edu
HAN, Peter .... 303-273-3131.. 80 O
phan@mines.edu
HAN, Sang-Ehil .... 423-478-7524 460 C
shan@ptseminary.edu
HAN, Vivian .... 847-592-6600 156 B
vhan@princeinstitute.edu
HAN, Woo Jin .... 703-244-4251.. 36 D
whan@calums.edu
HAN, Yuan-Yuan 407-888-8689 103M
y2han@fcim.edu
HANADA,
Tamone Karen .... 808-984-3527 136 H
tkhanada@hawaii.edu
HANAK, Lesley .... 912-525-5000 130 H
lhanak@scad.edu
HANBURY, II,
George, L .... 954-262-7575 109 E
hanbury@nsu.nova.edu
HANBURY, James, T .... 401-456-8684 442 A
jhanbury@ric.edu
HANBURY, John .... 276-656-0205 516 D
jhanbury@patrickhenry.edu
HANCOCK, Barry .... 618-985-3741 148 G
barryhancock@jalc.edu
HANCOCK, JR., Ben, E . 910-630-7000 359 C
bhancock@methodist.edu
HANCOCK, Blair, M ...... 336-838-6230 367 C
blair.hancock@wilkescc.edu
HANCOCK, John .... 713-500-2401 495 A
john.hancock@uth.tmc.edu
HANCOCK, John .... 503-768-7160 406 H
hancock@lclark.edu
HANCOCK, Jory, L .... 520-626-8030.. 18 E
jory@email.arizona.edu
HANCOCK, Katrina .... 620-947-3121 191 E
katrinah@tabor.edu
HANCOCK, Lori .... 810-762-0321 247 F
lori.hancock@mcc.edu
HANCOCK, Lua .... 386-822-7200 117 A
lhancock@stetson.edu
HANCOCK, Mara .... 510-594-5080.. 30 G
mhancock@cca.edu
HANCOCK, Merodie .... 518-587-2100 348 A
president@esc.edu
HANCOCK, Priscilla ...... 502-852-5667 201 A
pahanc01@louisville.edu
HANCOCK, Richard, R .. 501-450-5284.. 25 F
russh@mail.uca.edu
HANCOCK, Sean .... 760-921-5428.. 58 C
sean.hancock@paloverde.edu
HANCOCK, Wanda .... 229-225-5089 132 C
whancock@southernregional.edu
HANCOX, Robert, E 610-892-1578 429M
rhancox@pit.edu
HAND, Christie .... 304-358-2000 530 A
christie@future.edu
HAND, Jeffrey .... 856-256-5186 306 D
handj@rowan.edu
HAND, Kelli .... 704-637-4416 355 H
kmhand@catawba.edu
HAND, Natalie .... 484-664-3804 427 C
nhand@muhlenberg.edu
HAND, Theresa .... 518-244-4590 340 A
handt@sage.edu
HAND, Troy .... 757-569-6735 516 E
thand@pdc.edu
HANDCOX, Jenelle .... 910-521-6255 371 D
jenelle.handcox@uncp.edu
HANDFIELD, Sandy .... 321-433-5502 101 O
handfields@easternflorida.edu
HANDFORD, Ann .... 262-524-7211 535 D
ahandfor@carrollu.edu
HANDLER, Jan .... 319-363-1323 181 D
jhandler@mtmercy.edu
HANDLER, Jeffrey .... 201-761-7101 307 K
jhandler@saintpeters.edu
HANDLEY, Cassandra ... 912-525-5000 130 H
chandley@scad.edu
HANDLEY, Robert, L ..... 785-670-1878 192 B
bob.handley@washburn.edu
HANDLEY, Scott .... 417-626-1234 280 B
handley.scott@occ.edu
HANDOJO, Jeanne .... 626-584-5366.. 45 F
jeanne@fuller.edu
HANDS, Ashanti .... 619-388-2699.. 62 G
ahands@sdccd.edu
HANDS, Colette .... 847-635-2604 155 E
chands@oakton.edu
HANDS, Colette .... 847-635-1767 155 E
chands@oakton.edu
HANDWERK, Phil .... 336-758-5244 372 G
handwepg@wfu.edu
HANDY, Cromwell .... 334-229-4309.... 1 D
chandy@alasu.edu
HANDY, Cynthia, H ...... 404-752-1654 129 A
cynthia@msm.edu
HANDY, Linda, B .... 317-788-3349 173 I
handy@uindy.edu
HANDY, Maisha .... 404-527-7704 127 H
mhandy@itc.edu
HANDY, Ty .... 850-729-5360 109 D
handyt@nwfsc.edu
HANDZLIK, Diane, M ... 716-896-0700 352 B
dianeh@villa.edu
HANE, Jennifer .... 719-255-3180.. 86 F
jhane@uccs.edu
HANEBUTTE, Shema ..... 253-566-5352 527 C
shanebutte@tacomacc.edu
HANEFIELD, Robert ...... 580-581-2417 397 A
rhanefield@cameron.edu
HANELLY, William .... 570-484-2002 431 C
whanelly@lhup.edu
HANES, Barbara .... 484-840-4604 427 D
hanesb@neumann.edu
HANES, Billie .... 919-530-5086 370 C
bhanes@nccu.edu
HANES, Carol .... 903-875-7594 479 I
carol.hanes@navarrocollege.edu
HANES, Madlyn, L .... 814-863-0327 428 C
mqh3@psu.edu
HANES-GOODLANDER,
Lisa .... 651-846-1383 261 G
lisa.hanes@saintpaul.edu
HANEWICH, Sheila, K .. 219-866-6157 172 E
sheilah@saintjoe.edu
HANEY, Cindy, M .... 610-799-1122 424 A
chaney1@lccc.edu
HANEY, David, P .... 276-944-6168 507 E
dhaney@ehc.edu
HANEY, Frank .... 913-234-0788 185 N
frank.haney@cleveland.edu
HANEY, Jay .... 432-552-2764 495 F
haney_j@utpb.edu
HANEY, John .... 256-840-4124.... 7 B
jhaney@snead.edu
HANEY, Joyce, A .... 814-863-0274 428 C
jzh8@psu.edu
HANEY, Kent .... 661-362-2844.. 53 F
khaney@masters.edu
HANEY, Lee Anna .... 828-694-1885 360 D
leeannah@blueridge.edu
HANEY, Michele .... 303-914-6215.. 85 C
Michele.Haney@rrcc.edu
HANEY, Neil .... 512-476-2772 468 I
HANEY, Pamela .... 708-974-5204 153 D
haney@morainevalley.edu
HANEY, Regina .... 806-457-4200 474 E
rhaney@fpctx.edu
HANEY, Richard, J .... 847-543-2635 142 G
rhaney@clcillinois.edu
HANFORD, Karen .... 909-469-5243.. 76 I
khanford@westernu.edu
HANFORD, Thomas ...... 607-753-4702 345 C
thomas.hanford@cortland.edu
HANG, Foua .... 920-693-1387 543 B
foua.hang@gotoltc.edu
HANIFIN, Sheila .... 413-782-1628 238 A
shanifin@wne.edu
HANIGAN, Sherri .... 402-826-8586 290 C
sherri.hanigan@doane.edu
HANINCIK, Amanda .... 610-921-7529 411 E
ahanincik@albright.edu
HANK, Jack, L .... 210-434-6711 479 P
jlhank@lake.ollusa.edu
HANKE, Chris .... 864-503-5256 451 A
chanke@uscupstate.edu
HANKE, Robert .... 401-454-6599 442 B
rhanke@risd.edu
HANKERSON, Brian 954-486-7728 117M
bhankersoncfo@uftl.edu
HANKES, Doug .... 334-844-5123.... 1 G
hankedm@auburn.edu
HANKINS, Jeff .... 501-660-1004.. 19 D
jhankins@asusystem.edu
HANKINS, Kim .... 815-455-8778 152 B
khankins@mchenry.edu
HANKINS, Lori .... 904-826-0084.. 74 A
lhankins@usa.edu

HARDCASTLE, Bob .... 610-359-5182 416 G
bhardcastle@dccc.edu
HARDCASTLE, Louis, B . 770-484-1204 128 D
lutherrice@lutherrice.edu
HARDEE, John .... 870-230-5320.. 21 B
hardeej@hsu.edu
HARDEE, Teresa .... 302-857-6200.. 93 E
thardee@desu.edu
HARDEE, Terrence .... 609-894-9311 306 B
thardee@bcc.edu
HARDEE, Tim .... 803-778-6640 443 I
hardeebt@cctech.edu
HARDEMON, Rhonda .... 312-850-7894 142 E
rhardemon@ccc.edu
HARDEN, Daniel .... 916-348-4689.. 43 K
dharden@epic.edu
HARDEN, Derrick .... 847-543-2225 142 G
dharden@clcillinois.edu
HARDEN, Erica .... 478-553-2068 129 C
eharden@oftc.edu
HARDEN, Jim 906-487-7307 242M
jim.harden@finlandia.edu
HARDEN, Kennith .... 360-596-5360 527 B
kharden@spscc.edu
HARDEN, Mark .... 617-427-7293 227 B
mharden@gcts.edu
HARDEN, Robert .... 972-825-4814 483 D
rharden@sagu.edu
HARDEN, Ronald, W .... 916-348-4689.. 43 K
rharden@epic.edu
HARDEN, Yoshiko .... 425-564-2300 519 L
yoshiko.harden@bellevuecollege.edu
HARDEN SMITH, Lisa ... 336-770-3314 372 B
smithl@uncsa.edu
HARDER, James, M ..... 419-358-3324 377 H
harderj@bluffton.edu
HARDER, Kenette .... 816-414-3730 278 E
kharder@mbts.edu
HARDER, Larry .... 314-773-0083 272 H
HARDER, Maria, D .... 605-256-5129 453 H
maria.harder@dsu.edu
HARDER, Matthew .... 304-336-8006 533 A
mharder@westliberty.edu
HARDER, Natalie .... 337-521-8959 204 E
natalie.harder@solacc.edu
HARDERS, Michael 470-578-3007 127M
mharders@kennesaw.edu
HARDESKI, Grace, L ..... 215-955-6618 436 F
grace.hardeski@jefferson.edu
HARDESTY, Amy .... 806-720-7178 478 A
amy.hardesty@lcu.edu
HARDESTY, Jon, H .... 972-377-1725 471 C
jhardesty@collin.edu
HARDESTY, Larry, E ..... 724-458-2700 419 F
lehardesty@gcc.edu
HARDGRAVE, Bill .... 334-844-4030.... 1 G
bch0014@auburn.edu
HARDGROVE, David ..... 201-761-6454 307 K
dhardgrove@saintpeters.edu
HARDGROVE, Mark ...... 404-627-2681 121 F
mark.hardgrove@beulah.org
HARDGROVE, Mark ...... 404-627-2681 121 F
Mark.Hardgrove@beulah.org
HARDIN, Carlette .... 931-221-7511 461 C
hardinc@apsu.edu
HARDIN, Dan .... 575-492-2771 311 J
dhardin@nmjc.edu
HARDIN, David .... 910-362-7020 360 G
dhardin@cfcc.edu
HARDIN, David, M .... 910-362-7020 360 G
dhardin@cfcc.edu
HARDIN, Elizabeth, A ... 704-687-5750 371 B
eahardin@uncc.edu
HARDIN, Fred .... 864-388-8340 447 E
fhardin@lander.edu
HARDIN, III, John, B ... 940-552-6291 496 B
jhardin@vernoncollege.edu
HARDIN, Karen .... 480-461-7584.. 15 A
karen.hardin@mesacc.edu
HARDIN, Marie .... 814-863-1484 428 C
mch208@psu.edu
HARDIN, Michael .... 205-726-2718.... 6 F
mhardin@samford.edu
HARDIN, Mike, W .... 704-406-4280 356 G
mhardin@gardner-webb.edu
HARDIN, Phil .... 870-245-5400.. 22 C
hardinp@obu.edu
HARDIN, Philip, W .... 870-245-5400.. 22 C
hardinp@obu.edu
HARDIN, Richard, H ..... 636-481-3130 276 E
rhardin@jeffco.edu
HARDIN, Sally, B .... 619-260-4550.. 74 B
shardin@sandiego.edu
HARDIN, Sandy .... 575-492-4735 311 J
shardin@nmjc.edu
HARDIN, Steve, D .... 317-447-6126 166 K
Steve.Hardin@harrison.edu
HARDIN, Tammie .... 662-720-7594 269 D
twhardin@nemcc.edu
HARDIN, Walter, A .... 803-323-2261 451 I
hardinw@winthrop.edu
HARDIN, Wille .... 501-420-1252.. 19 B
willie.hardin@arkansasbaptist.edu
HARDING, Benjamin .... 215-702-4321 414 C
bharding@cairn.edu
HARDING, Hillary .... 518-608-8382 325 B
hharding@excelsior.edu
HARDING, James .... 802-287-8393 501 I
hardingj@greenmtn.edu
HARDING, Kelly 660-263-3900 272M
bookstore@cccb.edu
HARDING, Marc, L .... 412-624-7164 437 K
mharding@pitt.edu
HARDING, Mary Beth ... 615-383-4848 466 F
mharding@watkins.edu
HARDING, Millicent ...... 606-759-7141 196 G
millicent.harding@kctcs.edu
HARDING, Sally .... 212-431-2319 335 G
Sally.Harding@nyls.edu
HARDING, Sarah .... 612-874-3737 257 D
sharding@mcad.edu
HARDING, Tayloe .... 803-777-4336 450 B
tharding@mozart.sc.edu
HARDING, Teresa .... 701-766-1309 373 D
HARDING, Terry, M ...... 716-878-6112 345 B
hardintm@buffalostate.edu
HARDING, Timothy ...... 813-258-7281 118 H
tharding@ut.edu
HARDISON, Brad .... 805-965-0581.. 64 N
hardison@sbcc.edu
HARDISON, John .... 910-296-2433 363 E
jhardison@jamessprunt.edu
HARDISON, R. Karol .... 270-809-4388 198 I
rhardison@murraystate.edu
HARDISON, Roshanna .. 832-252-0728 470 L
roshanna.hardison@cbshouston.edu
HARDLEY, Michelle, M 805-565-7263.. 76 K
mhardley@westmont.edu
HARDMAN,
Alton (Tony) .... 580-349-1542 400 B
ahardman@opsu.edu
HARDMAN, John .... 870-245-5189.. 22 C
hardmanj@obu.edu
HARDMAN, Michael, L . 801-581-7200 499 K
michael.hardman@utah.edu
HARDMAN, II,
Robert, O .... 304-462-6181 532 G
robert.hardman@glenville.edu
HARDRICK, Jaffus .... 305-348-2190 114 G
jaffus.hardrick@fiu.edu
HARDT, Jim .... 412-392-6186 433 F
jhardt@pointpark.edu
HARDT, John .... 708-327-9213 151 E
jhardt@lumc.edu
HARDT, John, P .... 570-577-1232 413 E
john.hardt@bucknell.edu
HARDT, William, M .... 609-258-3379 305 C
whardt@princeton.edu
HARDWICK, James .... 813-253-6209 118 H
jhardwick@ut.edu
HARDWICK, James, D .. 406-447-4530 286 D
jhardwic@carroll.edu
HARDWICK, Monica ..... 719-549-3024.. 85 A
monica.hardwick@pueblocc.edu
HARDWRICK, Vikita, B . 870-230-5028.. 21 B
hardwrv@hsu.edu
HARDY, Anthony .... 251-809-1531.... 5 B
anthony.hardy@jdcc.edu
HARDY, Anthony .... 251-809-1531.... 5 B
HARDY, Beatriz, B .... 410-543-6130 220 E
bbhardy@salisbury.edu
HARDY, Catherine .... 203-575-8080.. 89 F
chardy@nv.edu
HARDY, Charles .... 910-962-3460 372 A
hardyc@uncw.edu
HARDY, Daniel, R .... 330-337-6403 376 B
college@awc.edu
HARDY, SR., Daniel, R . 330-337-6403 376 B
president@awc.edu
HARDY, Deborah, L ..... 440-525-7446 385 C
dhardy@lakelandcc.edu
HARDY, Deborah, L ..... 440-525-7828 385 C
dhardy@lakelandcc.edu
HARDY, Heather .... 775-784-6805 295 H
hhardy@unr.edu
HARDY, Karen .... 760-245-4271.. 75 G
karen.hardy@vvc.edu
HARDY, Karin, S .... 801-585-6220 499 K
karin.hardy@utah.edu
HARDY, Kevin .... 207-947-4591 209 G
khardy@bealcollege.edu
HARDY, Lonza .... 870-575-8471.. 24 D
hardyl@uapb.edu
HARDY, Mark, G .... 615-963-5301 461 F
mhardy@tnstate.edu
HARDY, Mia .... 773-291-6359 142 B
mhardy13@ccc.edu
HARDY, Pamela .... 619-239-0391.. 36 E
phardy@cwsl.edu
HARDY, Pollye .... 205-348-3952.... 8 E
phardy@fa.ua.edu
HARDY, Randall .... 757-727-5640 508 C
HARDY, Rebekah, L ..... 410-778-7865 221 D
rhardy2@washcoll.edu
HARDY, Richard, J .... 309-298-2228 163 A
rj-hardy@wiu.edu
HARDY, Robert, M .... 203-396-8390.. 91 G
hardyr@sacredheart.edu
HARDY, Scott, E .... 678-891-3965 125 G
scott.hardy@gpc.edu
HARDY, Stacia .... 225-216-8247 202 N
hardys@mybrcc.edu
HARDY, Stephanie, K ... 540-261-4088 512 J
stephanie.hardy@svu.edu
HARDY, Stephen, R ...... 972-985-3751 471 C
shardy@collin.edu
HARDY, Steven .... 973-684-6036 304 F
shardy@pccc.edu
HARDY, Thomas, P ...... 312-996-3772 161 E
hardyt@uillinois.edu
HARDY, Thomas, W ..... 229-333-5920 133 H
twhardy@valdosta.edu
HARDY, Tyrrell .... 505-786-4183 311 G
thardy@navajotech.edu
HARDY, Virginia .... 252-328-6541 369 E
Hardyv@ecu.edu
HARDY-LUCAS, Faye ..... 757-727-5233 508 C
faye.hardy-lucas@hamptonu.edu
HARE, Angela .... 717-766-2511 426 B
ahare@messiah.edu
HARE, Emily .... 919-718-7230 361 C
ehare@cccc.edu
HARE, Erica .... 802-828-8545 503 D
erica.hare@vcfa.edu
HARE, Michelle .... 803-323-2189 451 I
harem@winthrop.edu
HARE, Sara .... 605-256-7321 453 H
sara.hare@dsu.edu
HARE-PAYNTER,
Jodi, M .... 262-472-1570 541 D
harej@uww.edu
HARELIK, Harry .... 254-299-8606 478 C
hharelik@mclennan.edu
HAREWOOD, Anita .... 410-837-4533 221 B
aharewood@ubalt.edu
HAREWOOD, Wayne, H 718-368-5681 320 A
wharewood@kbcc.cuny.edu
HARF, James .... 314-529-6851 277 B
jharf@maryville.edu
HARFORD, Ellen .... 207-216-4435 211 F
eharford@yccc.edu
HARFST, Terry .... 618-453-3102 159 H
terriw@siu.edu
HARGER, Kathy .... 815-455-8695 152 B
kharger@mchenry.edu
HARGETT, Doug .... 256-331-5415.... 6 B
dhargett@nwscc.edu
HARGETT, Jack .... 901-321-3315 455 I
jhargett@cbu.edu
HARGIS, James .... 828-884-8282 355 A
hargisje@brevard.edu
HARGIS, Joe .... 507-222-4327 254 D
jhargis@carleton.edu
HARGIS, Michael .... 501-450-3106.. 25 F
mhargis@uca.edu
HARGIS, Randall .... 318-487-7129 202 L
randall.hargis@lacollege.edu
HARGIS, V. Burns .... 405-744-6384 400 C
osupres@okstate.edu
HARGRAVE, Alan, L ..... 765-285-8011 164 D
ahargrav@bsu.edu
HARGRAVE, Carolyn, H 225-578-6118 204 L
chargrave@lsu.edu
HARGRAVE, Gary .... 319-656-2447 182 G
HARGRAVE, Jaime .... 713-500-3476 495 A
Jaime.N.Hargrave@uth.tmc.edu
HARGRAVE, John, R ..... 580-559-5212 397 K
jhargrave@ecok.edu
HARGRAVE, Stephanie .. 336-316-2499 357 C
hargravesj@gulford.edu
HARGRAVE MEISLAHN,
Nancy .... 860-685-2269.. 93 B
nmeislahn@wesleyan.edu
HARGRAVES,
J. Stanley .... 804-278-4379 513 F
shargraves@upsem.edu
HARGROVE, Demond ... 201-200-3507 304 C
dhargrove@njcu.edu
HARGROVE, Kristi .... 615-383-4848 466 F
khargrove@watkins.edu
HARGROVE, S. Keith .... 615-963-5451 461 F
skhargrove@tnstate.edu
HARGROVE, Shannon ... 914-323-5484 331 J
shannon.hargrove@mville.edu
HARGROVE, Tony .... 870-584-4471.. 24 E
thargrove@cccua.edu
HARICHANDRAN,
Ronald .... 203-932-7167.. 92 G
rharichandran@newhaven.edu
HARICOMBE,
Lorraine, J 512-495-4350 493M
ljharic@austin.utexas.edu
HARIDAT, Anita .... 516-364-0808 335 A
aharidat@nycollege.edu
HARING, Peter .... 219-473-4323 165 A
pharing@ccsj.edu
HARING-SMITH, Tori .... 724-503-1001 439 B
tharingsmith@washjeff.edu
HARKAVY, Ira .... 215-898-5351 437 I
harkavy@upenn.edu
HARKENRIDER, Tom .... 949-480-4091.. 66 I
harkenrider@soka.edu
HARKER, Alan, R .... 801-422-5995 497 J
alan_harker@byu.edu
HARKER, David .... 719-389-7270.. 79M
david.harker@coloradocollege.edu
HARKER, Perry, L .... 252-222-6205 361 A
harkerp@carteret.edu
HARKER, Phillip .... 802-225-3201 502 F
phillip.harker@neci.edu
HARKEY, Betsy .... 940-552-6291 496 B
bharkey@vernoncollege.edu
HARKEY, Dina .... 704-216-3470 365 F
dina.harkey@rccc.edu
HARKEY, Gary Don ...... 940-552-6291 496 B
gdharkey@vernoncollege.edu
HARKEY, Penny .... 806-743-7424 490 A
penny.harkey@ttuhsc.edu
HARKINS, Dennis .... 714-432-5712.. 40 D
dharkins@occ.cccd.edu
HARKINS,
Gerald (Bob), R 512-471-5767 493M
bharkins@austin.utexas.edu
HARKINS, Vincent .... 202-885-3704.. 94 H
vharkins@american.edu
HARKLESS, Lawrence ... 909-706-3498.. 76 I
lharkless@westernu.edu
HARKNESS, Charles ..... 440-826-2426 377 D
charkness@bw.edu
HARKNESS, Kim .... 603-358-2496 299 D
kharkness@keene.edu
HARKNESS,
M. Frances .... 610-902-8546 414 B
mfrances.harkness@cabrini.edu
HARKNESS, Sarah, E .... 423-439-8304 461 D
bradfors@etsu.edu
HARKNESS, Suzan .... 573-876-7108 283 A
sharkness@stephens.edu
HARLAN, Brian .... 661-255-1050.. 31 B
bharlan@calarts.edu
HARLAN, Cathy .... 954-262-5366 109 E
charlan@nova.edu
HARLAN, Mark .... 813-974-1442 116 B
markharlan@usf.edu
HARLAND, Teresa, L .... 218-299-3733 255 B
harland@cord.edu
HARLAND-WHITE,
Faith, A .... 410-777-2961 213 E
faharlandwhite@aacc.edu
HARLANDER, Heidi .... 320-363-2724 264 A
hharlander@csbsju.edu
HARLANDER, Heidi .... 320-363-2724 254 J
hharlander@csbsju.edu
HARLESS, Cleta, M .... 304-357-4736 530 H
cletaharless@ucwv.edu
HARLESS, Debra .... 651-638-6371 254 A
d-harless@bethel.edu
HARLESS, Donna .... 704-403-1558 355 B
donna.harless@carolinashealthcare.org
HARLEY, Jay .... 214-333-6812 471 L
jay@dbu.edu
HARLEY, Joyce, W .... 973-877-4347 302 F
harley@essex.edu
HARLOW, Angie, D ...... 770-720-5603 130 E
adh@reinhardt.edu
HARLOW, Debra, B .... 336-322-2157 364 G
Debra.Harlow@piedmontcc.edu
HARLOW, Susan .... 773-380-7042 140 C
susan.harlow@seabury.edu
HARLOW, Tom .... 423-636-7300 464 F
tharlow@tusculum.edu
HARM, Joseph .... 912-650-6215 131 F
jharm@southuniversity.edu
HARMAN, Elizabeth ...... 619-260-4682.. 74 B
harman@sandiego.edu
HARMAN, Holli .... 276-498-4190 504 K
HARMAN, Jacob .... 212-960-5241 353 P
jharman@yu.edu
HARMAN, Joany .... 916-608-6500.. 53 A
harmanj@flc.losrios.edu
HARMAN, John, A .... 817-735-7600 493 B
John.Harman@unthsc.edu
HARMAN, Lisa, F .... 574-372-5100 166 D
Harmanlf@grace.edu
HARMAN, SJ, Paul, F .. 508-793-2011 225 C
pharman@holycross.edu
HARMAN, William .... 801-878-1403 296 D
wharman@roseman.edu
HARMENING, Todd .... 651-201-1856 257 N
todd.harmening@so.mnscu.edu
HARMER-BEEM, Marji .. 207-221-4314 213 B
mharmerbeem@une.edu

HARMON, Alison .... 406-994-4135 287 G
harmon@montana.edu
HARMON, Carolyn .... 252-399-6357 354 I
charmon@barton.edu
HARMON, Cindy, S ...... 573-882-2388 283 G
Harmonc@umsystem.edu
HARMON, Debbie .... 503-883-2607 406 I
dharmon@linfield.edu
HARMON, Debra, J .... 217-732-3155 150 H
dharmon@lincolncollege.edu
HARMON, Jeff .... 573-651-5910 282 C
jharmon@semo.edu
HARMON, Jeff, M .... 208-732-6210 137 K
jharmon@csi.edu
HARMON, Jeff, S .... 732-255-0400 304 E
jharmon@ocean.edu
HARMON, Justin .... 212-353-4166 323 B
jharmon@cooper.edu
HARMON, Kate .... 503-244-0726 404 G
kateharmon@achs.edu
HARMON, Kathy, M ...... 937-229-4303 393 E
KHarmon1@udayton.edu
HARMON, Kevin .... 701-858-3299 374 B
kevin.harmon@minotstateu.edu
HARMON, Ladelle .... 828-652-0626 364 B
ladelleh@mcdoweltech.edu
HARMON, LaVerne, T ... 302-356-6938.. 94 G
laverne.t.harmon@wilmu.edu
HARMON, Mark .... 706-754-7833 129 B
mharmon@northgatech.edu
HARMON, Martino .... 515-294-0754 175 G
mharmon@iastate.edu
HARMON, Martino .... 513-569-4215 379 K
martino.harmon@cincinnatistate.edu
HARMON, Mary, R .... 989-964-7117 249 G
mharmon@svsu.edu
HARMON, Melanie .... 260-982-5412 170 a
HARMON, Nathaniel, S 417-268-6007 272 F
nharmon@gobbc.edu
HARMON, Patricia .... 304-929-5460 531 D
pharmon@newriver.edu
HARMON, Steve, K .... 956-326-2180 485 B
harmon@tamiu.edu
HARMON, W. Ken 470-578-6023 127M
wharmon3@kennesaw.edu
HARMON, William .... 713-718-6041 475 C
william.harmon@hccs.edu
HARMS, Mason .... 641-585-8137 183 I
harmsm@waldorf.edu
HARMS, Steve .... 513-721-7944 382 K
sharms@gbs.edu
HARMSEN, Dee .... 920-923-8530 537 A
dharmsen@marianuniversity.edu
HARMSEN, Frederika ..... 916-278-6331.. 34 E
fraka.harmsen@csus.edu
HARMSEN, Mark .... 254-526-1365 470 E
mark.harmsen@ctcd.edu
HARN, William .... 409-880-8229 488 F
william.harn@lamar.edu
HARNAGE, David, F ...... 757-683-3159 510 I
dharnage@odu.edu
HARNDEN, Greg .... 501-279-4305.. 21 A
gharnden@harding.edu
HARNE, George, A .... 603-456-2656 298 D
administration@northeastcatholic.edu
HARNER, Holly, M .... 215-951-1865 422 F
harner@lasalle.edu
HARNER, Kristy 423-614-8110 457M
kharner@leeuniversity.edu
HARNER, Mike .... 517-607-2303 243 J
mharner@hillsdale.edu
HARNEY, Jake, P .... 770-720-9102 130 E
jph@reinhardt.edu
HARNEY, Malea .... 217-773-4441 150 B
mharney@lakeland.cc.il.us
HARNISH, Eric .... 661-259-7800.. 40 H
eric.harnish@canyons.edu
HARNUM, Donald, P ..... 609-896-5054 306 A
harnum@rider.edu
HAROLD, Martin .... 858-653-6740.. 48 Q
MHarold@JPCatholic.com
HARP, Brittaney .... 859-371-9393 193 D
bharp@beckfield.edu
HARP, Debbie .... 606-539-4259 200 F
debbie.harp@ucumberlands.edu
HARP, Jeff .... 405-974-2800 403 G
jharp@uco.edu
HARP, John, W .... 319-895-4234 177 A
jharp@cornellcollege.edu
HARP-STEPHENS,
Becky .... 859-246-6498 195 J
becky.harp@kctcs.edu
HARPE, J. Michael .... 610-399-2217 430 D
jmharpe@cheyney.edu
HARPER, Allyson, R ...... 612-874-3775 257 D
allyson_harper@mcad.edu
HARPER, Betty, J .... 814-863-8721 428 C
bjh17@psu.edu
HARPER, David .... 828-298-3325 373 A
dharper@warren-wilson.edu
HARPER, David, L .... 937-229-2973 393 E
Dharper1@udayton.edu
HARPER, Deborah .... 607-274-3136 328 H
dharper@ithaca.edu
HARPER, Donna, L .... 540-568-3705 509 C
harperdl@jmu.edu
HARPER, Doreen, C ..... 205-934-5360.... 8 F
dcharper@uab.edu
HARPER, E. Royster ..... 734-764-5132 251 C
harperer@umich.edu
HARPER, Elizabeth .... 703-323-3459 516 C
eharper@nvcc.edu
HARPER, Heather .... 615-230-3519 464 B
heather.harper@volstate.edu
HARPER, Jimmy 423-614-8420 457M
jharper@leeuniversity.edu
HARPER, Jimmy .... 912-260-4317 131 D
jimmy.harper@sgsc.edu
HARPER, Joann .... 706-245-7226 124 C
jharper@ec.edu
HARPER, Jonathan .... 617-730-7091 235 B
jonathan.harper@newbury.edu
HARPER, Josh .... 503-255-0332 407 D
jharper@multnomah.edu
HARPER, Karla .... 937-376-6444 379 D
kharper@centralstate.edu
HARPER, Kerry .... 814-641-3353 421 L
harperk@juniata.edu
HARPER, Kristin .... 205-226-4720.... 2 C
kharper@bsc.edu
HARPER, Kyle .... 405-325-4063 403 I
kyle@ou.edu
HARPER, Lisa .... 405-974-2553 403 G
lharper@uco.edu
HARPER, Lisa, D .... 859-858-3511 193 A
lisa.harper@asbury.edu
HARPER, Lisa, M .... 903-510-2147 491 A
lhar@tjc.edu
HARPER, Marilyn, A ...... 865-694-6700 463 E
maharper@pstcc.edu
HARPER, Marjoree .... 318-678-6000 203 A
mharper@bpcc.edu
HARPER, Mary, J .... 812-464-1767 174 D
mjharper@usi.edu
HARPER, Mary Ann .... 501-337-5000.. 20 H
mharper@coto.edu
HARPER, Norma .... 706-233-7268 131 C
nharper@shorter.edu
HARPER, Pam .... 270-706-8434 195 K
pamela.harper@kctcs.edu
HARPER, Patricia .... 816-654-7162 276 G
pharper@kcumb.edu
HARPER, Randy .... 870-574-4590.. 23 E
rharper@sautech.edu
HARPER, Robert .... 559-278-2482.. 33 D
roberth@csufresno.edu
HARPER, Robert .... 903-593-8311 487 A
rharper@texascollege.edu
HARPER, Rosie .... 601-977-7818 270 F
rharper@tougaloo.edu
HARPER, Sandra .... 325-793-3800 478 D
harper.sandra@mcm.edu
HARPER, Therese .... 307-778-1104 546 F
tharper@lccc.wy.edu
HARPER, Vernon .... 610-436-3416 432 B
vharper@wcupa.edu
HARPER, William .... 704-971-8500 355 J
wharper@charlottelaw.edu
HARPER, Yvonne .... 564-587-4278 449 D
harpery@smcsc.edu
HARPER HAGAN,
Mary, T .... 718-990-2505 340 G
harperm@stjohns.edu
HARPER-MARINICK,
Maria .... 480-731-8101.. 14 J
maria.harper@domail.maricopa.edu
HARPHAM, Jennifer, E . 330-972-5860 392 H
jharpham@uakron.edu
HARPHAM, Jennifer, E . 757-822-1360 517 C
jharpham@tcc.edu
HARPOLE, Jessica .... 662-329-7352 269 B
jjharpole@muw.edu
HARPOOL, David .... 928-541-7777.. 16 B
dharpool@ncu.edu
HARPS, Juanita .... 706-821-8339 129 H
jharps@paine.edu
HARPS, Trynette Lottie . 231-777-0559 247 G
trynette.lottie-harps@muskegoncc.edu
HARPST, Steve .... 845-341-4230 337 G
steve.harpst@sunyorange.edu
HARPSTER, George, F .. 717-477-1301 431 F
gfharp@ship.edu
HARR, Lois .... 718-862-7142 331 H
lois.harr@manhattan.edu
HARRA, Alice .... 503-517-7421 409 E
harraa@reed.edu
HARRAH, Scott .... 301-784-5000 213 C
sharrah@allegany.edu
HARRAL, Judy .... 361-825-2495 485 F
judy.harral@tamucc.edu
HARRAL, Kevin .... 650-949-7223.. 45 A
harralkevin@foothill.edu
HARRAL, Nicole, D .... 928-344-7600.. 12 B
nicole.harral@azwestern.edu
HARRAR, William, R ...... 570-389-4255 430 B
wharrar@bloomu.edu
HARRELD, Bruce .... 319-335-3549 175 H
HARRELL, III, Alfred, E 225-771-3911 206 K
alfred_harrell@sus.edu
HARRELL, Brian .... 478-934-3027 128 H
brian.harrell@mga.edu
HARRELL, Bryant, L ...... 860-727-6756.. 90 F
bharrell@goodwin.edu
HARRELL, Charlie, R .... 252-823-5166 362 D
harrellc@edgecombe.edu
HARRELL, David .... 972-708-7340 474 J
david_harrell@gial.edu
HARRELL,
Frank (Doug) .... 504-865-5352 207 F
fharrel@tulane.edu
HARRELL, Jerry, H 317-921-4447 169M
jeharrel@ivytech.edu
HARRELL, Jessica .... 336-506-4113 359 N
jessica.harrell@alamancecc.edu
HARRELL, Johnna, C .... 757-822-1191 517 C
jcharrell@tcc.edu
HARRELL, Kathy .... 918-775-6977 397 C
kharrell@carlalbert.edu
HARRELL, Kim .... 916-608-6500.. 53 A
harrelk@flc.losrios.edu
HARRELL, Lauren .... 229-243-6025 121 D
lauren.harrell@bainbridge.edu
HARRELL, Leslie .... 912-583-3203 121 H
lharrell@bpc.edu
HARRELL, Lou .... 704-687-1890 371 B
M.Harrell@uncc.edu
HARRELL, P. Randy ...... 252-398-6209 356 B
harrer@chowan.edu
HARRELL, Pamela, J .... 919-209-2048 363 F
pjharrell@johnstoncc.edu
HARRELL, Robin .... 404-627-2681 121 F
robin.harrell@beulah.org
HARRELL, Ronald .... 270-706-8580 195 K
ron.harrell@kctcs.edu
HARRELL, Wanda .... 423-585-6976 464 C
wanda.harrell@ws.edu
HARRELSON, Cheryl ..... 575-646-1613 312 A
cherylh@nmsu.edu
HARRELSON, Jerry, W .. 336-316-2333 357 C
jharrelson@guilford.edu
HARREYS, M. Seamus .. 617-373-4095 235 D
HARRI, Ed .... 360-383-3220 528 E
eharri@whatcom.ctc.edu
HARRI, Robert 563-387-2103 180M
harrro01@luther.edu
HARRICK, Kristie .... 205-970-9244.... 7 D
kharrick@sebc.edu
HARRIER, Briana, K ...... 515-964-0601 178 F
harrierb@faith.edu
HARRIGER, Sherill .... 863-638-7235 118 L
sherill.harriger@warner.edu
HARRILL, Thad .... 828-395-1624 363 D
tharrill@isothermal.edu
HARRILL, Thad .... 828-286-3636 363 D
HARRING, Kathleen, E . 484-664-3424 427 C
harring@muhlenberg.edu
HARRING-HENDON,
Janice, M .... 773-442-4046 154 H
j-harringhendon@neiu.edu
HARRINGTON, Angela .. 973-278-5400 316 D
angela-harringt@berkeleycollege.edu
HARRINGTON, Angela .. 973-278-5400 300 C
angela-harringt@berkeleycollege.edu
HARRINGTON, Anne, E 603-641-7465 298 F
aharrington@anselm.edu
HARRINGTON, Bonnie .. 215-751-8253 416 B
bharrington@ccp.edu
HARRINGTON, Daphne . 617-521-2754 236 F
daphne.harrington@simmons.edu
HARRINGTON, David ..... 603-641-7020 298 F
dharrington@anselm.edu
HARRINGTON, Donna ... 505-467-6831 313 F
donnaharrington@swc.edu
HARRINGTON,
James, W .... 253-692-5646 527 G
jwh@uw.edu
HARRINGTON, John ..... 603-524-3207 296 L
jharrington@ccsnh.edu
HARRINGTON, Kim .... 404-894-2499 125 D
kim.harrington@ohr.gatech.edu
HARRINGTON, Kristen .. 617-587-5624 234 G
harringtonk@neco.edu
HARRINGTON,
L. Katharine .... 213-740-7849.. 74 D
vpap@usc.edu
HARRINGTON, Lynn ..... 708-974-5704 153 D
harrington@morainevalley.edu
HARRINGTON, Maurice 541-463-5306 406 F
harringtonm@lanecc.edu
HARRINGTON, Michael 631-420-2053 348 B
michael.harrington@farmingdale.edu
HARRINGTON,
Michael, J .... 415-422-2790.. 74 C
Harrington@usfca.edu
HARRINGTON, Patricia . 570-941-7673 438 F
patricia.harrington@scranton.edu
HARRINGTON, Robert ... 417-625-3191 278 I
harrington-r@mssu.edu
HARRINGTON, Sean, P 540-464-7102 518 A
harringtonsp@vmi.edu
HARRINGTON,
Shawn, M .... 860-231-5314.. 93 A
sharrington@usj.edu
HARRINGTON,
Sherre Lee .... 706-236-2285 121 E
sharrington@berry.edu
HARRINGTON, Thomas 504-280-1154 205 G
trharrin@uno.edu
HARRINGTON-MARTIN,
Angela .... 317-543-3250 171 B
aharrington@martin.edu
HARRIOTT, Danielle ...... 815-965-8616 157 C
dharriot@rockfordcareercollege.edu
HARRIS, Alex .... 208-769-7156 138 G
afharris@nic.edu
HARRIS, Alice .... 304-424-8224 533 E
alice.harris@wvup.edu
HARRIS, Allatia .... 281-459-7140 481 D
allatia.harris@sjcd.edu
HARRIS, Alvin .... 501-370-5284.. 22 E
aharris@philander.edu
HARRIS, Amelia, J .... 276-376-4557 514 B
ajh7a@uvawise.edu
HARRIS, Andrew .... 603-358-2772 299 D
aharris5@keene.edu
HARRIS, Angela .... 478-825-6211 124 E
HARRIS, Angie .... 717-245-1556 417 B
harrisa@dickinson.edu
HARRIS, Anjour .... 804-828-2021 514 F
abharris@vcu.edu
HARRIS, Anne .... 415-338-6598.. 36 A
aharris@sfsu.edu
HARRIS, Anthony .... 610-341-5840 418 A
aharris8@eastern.edu
HARRIS, Bennie, L .... 404-752-1955 129 A
bharris@msm.edu
HARRIS, Beth .... 203-287-3023.. 91 C
paierartlibrary@snet.net
HARRIS, Bethany, W .... 434-949-1007 516 H
bethany.harris@southside.edu
HARRIS, Betsy, A .... 207-768-2791 211 C
bharris@nmcc.edu
HARRIS, Beverly .... 620-331-4100 188 B
bharris@indycc.edu
HARRIS, Beverly .... 757-823-2409 510 H
bbharris@nsu.edu
HARRIS, Beverly Jo ...... 304-205-6613 531 A
jo.harris@bridgevalley.edu
HARRIS, Brent .... 254-295-8642 492 C
bharris@umhb.edu
HARRIS, JR., Calvin ..... 410-209-6049 213 G
charris@bccc.edu
HARRIS, Camille .... 312-697-8035 145 G
charris@harrington.edu
HARRIS, Chad .... 541-383-7283 404 K
charris7@cocc.edu
HARRIS, Charles .... 334-420-4232.... 7 I
charris@trenholmstate.edu
HARRIS, Charles, S ...... 434-791-5701 505 A
csharris@averett.edu
HARRIS, Charlotte .... 937-775-2821 396 A
charlotte.harris@wright.edu
HARRIS, Chelsy .... 719-502-3034.. 84 J
chelsy.harris@ppcc.edu
HARRIS, Chris .... 949-214-3169.. 42 B
chris.harris@cui.edu
HARRIS, Chris .... 601-635-2111 267 B
charris@eccc.edu
HARRIS, Christina .... 215-568-9215 426 C
chharris@phmc.org
HARRIS, Christopher ..... 419-434-4347 393 F
harrisc1@findlay.edu
HARRIS, Clark .... 810-762-0500 247 F
clark.harris@mcc.edu
HARRIS, Clayton .... 216-987-4425 381 A
clayton.harris@tri-c.edu
HARRIS, Cliff .... 313-664-7403 241 D
charris@collegeforcreativestudies.edu
HARRIS, Connie, L .... 419-448-2000 383 C
charris@heidelberg.edu
HARRIS, Craig .... 540-857-7797 517 E
charris@virginiawestern.edu
HARRIS, Crystal .... 252-862-1246 365 C
cdharris6076@roanokechowan.edu
HARRIS, Dan, I .... 414-277-7230 537 G
harris@msoe.edu
HARRIS, Darrell, A .... 904-264-2172 111 G
dharris@iws.edu

HARRIS, David ... 805-756-1211 .. 32 E harris@calpoly.edu
HARRIS, David ... 320-308-4866 261 E djharris@stcloudstate.edu
HARRIS, David ... 718-268-4700 339 B
HARRIS, David ... 843-574-6411 449 G david.harris@tridenttech.edu
HARRIS, David, P ... 909-558-7600 .. 50 K dpharris@llu.edu
HARRIS, David, R ... 617-627-3310 237 C david.harris@tufts.edu
HARRIS, David, W ... 505-277-7520 313 H dwharris@unm.edu
HARRIS, Debbie ... 804-751-9191 506 G dharris@ccc-va.com
HARRIS, Delana ... 601-403-1197 270 A dharris@prcc.edu
HARRIS, Delphia ... 901-435-1380 457 N delphia_harris@loc.edu
HARRIS, Denise ... 716-926-8727 327 F dharris@hilbert.edu
HARRIS, Dennis ... 405-422-1283 401 H harrisd@redlandscc.edu
HARRIS, Dina ... 574-520-4131 168 F dlharris@iusb.edu
HARRIS, SR., Forrest, E ... 615-256-1463 454 G officeofthepresident@abcnash.edu
HARRIS, Fred ... 408-848-4800 .. 45 G fharris@gavilan.edu
HARRIS, Freda, J ... 608-262-6423 539 C fharris@uwsa.edu
HARRIS, G. Duncan ... 860-512-3203 .. 89 D gharris@manchestercc.edu
HARRIS, Gail ... 423-746-5208 464 D gharris@twcnet.edu
HARRIS, Gary, L ... 202-806-2550 .. 96 B gharris@howard.edu
HARRIS, Gary, L ... 202-806-6800 .. 96 B gharris@howard.edu
HARRIS, Greg ... 602-275-7133 .. 17 L greg.harris@rsiaz.edu
HARRIS, Greg ... 770-426-2836 128 C gharris@life.edu
HARRIS, Greg ... 503-584-7153 404 L greg.harris@chemeketa.edu
HARRIS, Gregory ... 336-770-3321 372 B harrisg@uncsa.edu
HARRIS, Helen ... 225-216-8287 202 N harrish@mybrcc.edu
HARRIS, Hubert, D ... 804-524-8989 518 C hharris@vsu.edu
HARRIS, James ... 903-593-8311 487 A jharris@texascollege.edu
HARRIS, James, T ... 619-260-4520 .. 74 B president@sandiego.edu
HARRIS, Janette ... 530-938-5500 .. 41 E jharris6@siskiyous.edu
HARRIS, Jay, H ... 260-481-6785 168 D harrishj@ipfw.edu
HARRIS, Jean ... 941-487-4570 115 B jharris@ncf.edu
HARRIS, Jeff ... 912-525-5000 130 H jeharris@scad.edu
HARRIS, Jeff ... 816-531-5223 273 F jharris@concorde.edu
HARRIS, Jennifer, K ... 802-626-6458 504 B jennifer.harris@lyndonstate.edu
HARRIS, Jesse ... 208-459-5222 137 J jharris@collegeofidaho.edu
HARRIS, Jewell ... 601-979-1773 267 H jewell.e.harris@jsums.edu
HARRIS, Jo-Anne ... 610-399-2247 430 D jharris@cheyney.edu
HARRIS, Joel, C ... 843-953-6841 444 C joel.harris@citadel.edu
HARRIS, John ... 601-635-2111 267 B jharris@eccc.edu
HARRIS, John ... 518-244-4582 340 A harrisj8@sage.edu
HARRIS, John ... 515-961-1626 182 I john.harris@simpson.edu
HARRIS, John ... 903-923-2181 473 I jharris@etbu.edu
HARRIS, Judy ... 760-744-1150 .. 58 D jharris@palomar.edu
HARRIS, Karen ... 828-395-1456 363 D kharris@isothermal.edu
HARRIS, Kathy ... 618-544-8657 146 H harrisk@iecc.edu
HARRIS, Kendall, T ... 936-261-9900 484 F ktharris@pvamu.edu
HARRIS, Kenneth ... 313-831-5200 242 K kharris@etseminary.edu
HARRIS, Kevin ... 573-681-5860 276 K harrisk@lincolnu.edu
HARRIS, Kim ... 662-720-7193 269 D kkharris@nemcc.edu
HARRIS, Kim ... 865-882-4695 463 F harriskb@roanestate.edu
HARRIS, Kip, B ... 208-496-9200 137 F harrisk@byui.edu
HARRIS, Kristi ... 660-359-3948 279 L kharris@mail.ncmissouri.edu
HARRIS, Kristin ... 940-855-2203 496 B kharris@vernoncollege.edu
HARRIS, Lakecia ... 334-244-3903 .... 2 A lharri18@aum.edu
HARRIS, Lamel ... 408-288-3731 .. 64 A lamel.harris@sjcc.edu
HARRIS, Lesa, C ... 270-809-3750 198 I lharris@murraystate.edu
HARRIS, Leslie ... 641-472-1126 181 A housing@mum.edu
HARRIS, Liesl, W ... 205-853-1200 .... 5 C lwharris@jeffstateonline.com
HARRIS, Lisa ... 763-433-1292 257 P lisa.harris@anokaramsey.edu
HARRIS, Lisa, B ... 208-426-1418 137 E lisaharris@boisestate.edu
HARRIS, Mark ... 336-454-1126 363 A meharris@gtcc.edu
HARRIS, Mark, D ... 856-691-8600 301 H mharris@cccnj.edu
HARRIS, Mark, T ... 414-229-8417 540 A mtharris@uwm.edu
HARRIS, Martha ... 785-594-8338 184 F martha.harris@bakeru.edu
HARRIS, Marvin ... 610-992-1700 .. 96 H
HARRIS, Mary ... 317-931-4440 165 C mharris@cts.edu
HARRIS, Mary ... 610-902-8765 414 B mary.harris@cabrini.edu
HARRIS, Mary, A ... 202-274-5498 .. 97 B mharris@udc.edu
HARRIS, Mary, E ... 512-223-7705 468 H mharris3@austincc.edu
HARRIS, Mary, R ... 575-492-2162 314 D mharris@usw.edu
HARRIS, Maurice, A ... 315-443-4734 349 E maharr17@syr.edu
HARRIS, Mel ... 703-812-4757 509 E mharris@leland.edu
HARRIS, Melissa, D ... 716-880-3368 332 B melissa.d.harris@medaille.edu
HARRIS, Melvin ... 312-942-2030 158 A melvin_harris@rush.edu
HARRIS, Melvin ... 256-726-7374 .... 6 C mharris@oakwood.edu
HARRIS, Michael, E ... 336-734-7764 362 F mharris@forsythtech.edu
HARRIS, Mitch ... 601-984-6717 270 H mharris6@umc.edu
HARRIS, Nancy ... 323-856-7600 .. 27 H nharris@afi.com
HARRIS, Ned ... 860-231-5360 .. 93 A
HARRIS, Nick, L ... 504-816-4704 202 F nharris@dillard.edu
HARRIS, Obadiah ... 323-663-2167 .. 73 E
HARRIS, Patricia ... 662-252-8000 270 C pharris@rustcollege.edu
HARRIS, Patricia, R ... 616-222-3000 245 D pharris@kuyper.edu
HARRIS, Patrick ... 406-447-4380 286 D pharris@carroll.edu
HARRIS, Patty ... 651-290-6358 266 B patty.harris@wmitchell.edu
HARRIS, Paul ... 585-475-4992 339 G pahdar@rit.edu
HARRIS, Peggy ... 850-973-1621 109 C harrisp@nfcc.edu
HARRIS, Peter ... 860-512-3213 .. 89 D pharris@manchestercc.edu
HARRIS, Peter, H ... 918-836-6886 402 I pharris@mail.spartan.edu
HARRIS, Randy ... 814-866-8416 423 B rharris@lecom.edu
HARRIS, Rhansyl ... 513-244-8668 379 I rhansyl.harris@ccuniversity.edu
HARRIS, Rhonda, L ... 757-683-4007 510 I rlharris@odu.edu
HARRIS, Richard ... 479-508-3310 .. 20 C rharris1@atu.edu
HARRIS, Richard, C ... 516-671-2215 352 D rharris@webb.edu
HARRIS, Rob ... 417-328-1827 282 D rharris@sbuniv.edu
HARRIS, Rob ... 517-787-0800 244 H HarrisRobertM@jccmi.edu
HARRIS, Robin ... 252-335-0821 361 G robin_harris@albemarle.edu
HARRIS, Rotesha ... 404-880-6917 122 I rharris@cau.edu
HARRIS, Scott ... 309-298-1949 163 A sd-harris@wiu.edu
HARRIS, Sedgwick ... 815-825-2086 149 E sedgwick.harris@kishwaukeecollege.edu
HARRIS, Sharlene, J ... 340-693-1361 559 B sharris@live.uvi.edu
HARRIS, Sheryl ... 817-515-5228 484 B sheryl.harris@tccd.edu
HARRIS, Skip ... 802-651-5961 501 F sharris@champlain.edu
HARRIS, Stephen, A ... 615-248-1245 464 E sharris@trevecca.edu
HARRIS, Susan ... 901-381-3939 466 E susan@visible.edu
HARRIS, Susan, G ... 434-924-7120 514 A sgh4c@virginia.edu
HARRIS, Suzann ... 615-248-1201 464 E sharris@trevecca.edu
HARRIS, Tamika ... 909-793-4263 .. 28 S tharris@ashdowncollege.edu
HARRIS, Tara ... 864-941-8525 448 D harris.t@ptc.edu
HARRIS, Terral ... 912-279-5726 123 B tharris@ccga.edu
HARRIS, Terrance ... 805-756-2767 .. 32 E tharris@calpoly.edu
HARRIS, Terrance ... 936-294-1325 489 A tjharris@shsu.edu
HARRIS, Terrence ... 315-786-2238 329 G tharris@sunyjefferson.edu
HARRIS, JR., Thomas .. 229-430-4650 119 H thomas.harris@asurams.edu
HARRIS, Thomas, W ... 859-257-1933 200 G tom.harris@uky.edu
HARRIS, Todd, D ... 910-630-7155 359 C toharris@methodist.edu
HARRIS, Toi, B ... 713-798-3695 469 C toih@bcm.edu
HARRIS, Tonya ... 870-838-2913 .. 19 C tharris@smail.anc.edu
HARRIS, Tosca ... 620-365-5116 184 C harris@allencc.edu
HARRIS, Tracy ... 240-725-5300 214 E tracy.harris@csmd.edu
HARRIS, Travaris ... 847-925-6673 145 F tharris@harpercollege.edu
HARRIS, Veralee ... 618-395-7777 147 A harrisv@iecc.edu
HARRIS, Wayne ... 757-727-5071 508 C wayne.harris@hamptonu.edu
HARRIS, William, L ... 859-257-9101 200 G wlharr2@email.uky.edu
HARRIS, Wilma, K ... 479-979-1215 .. 25 H wkharris@ozarks.edu
HARRIS, Yolanda ... 719-502-4689 .. 84 J yolanda.harris@ppcc.edu
HARRIS BANE, Holly ... 330-972-7508 392 H harrisb@uakron.edu
HARRIS COHEN, David . 626-264-8880 .. 73 D
HARRIS-HOOKER, Sandra ... 404-752-1725 129 A sharris-hooker@msm.edu
HARRIS-JOLLY, Stephanie ... 229-903-3609 119 H stephanie.harris-jolly@asurams.edu
HARRIS-JOLLY, Stephanie ... 229-430-4667 119 H stephanie.harris-jolly@asurams.edu
HARRIS KISUNZU, Cheryl ... 301-891-4000 221 C charris@wau.edu
HARRIS PAOLILLO, Linda ... 212-752-1530 330 C linda.harris@limcollege.edu
HARRISBANE, Holly, B . 330-972-7508 392 H harrisb@uakron.edu
HARRISON, Angela ... 757-823-2037 510 H sm505@bncollege.com
HARRISON, Antione ... 518-381-1449 342 E harrisaw@sunysccc.edu
HARRISON, B. Keith ... 251-460-6310 .... 9 F kharrison@southalabama.edu
HARRISON, B. Timothy 618-537-6962 152 C btharrison@mckendree.edu
HARRISON, Carol ... 301-934-7552 214 E carolh@csmd.edu
HARRISON, Cheryl ... 718-862-7862 331 H cheryl.harrison@manhattan.edu
HARRISON, Christopher ... 252-940-6444 360 B chris.harrison@beaufortccc.edu
HARRISON, Crystal ... 920-498-5541 544 B crystal.harrison@nwtc.edu
HARRISON, Cynthia, F . 914-968-6200 341 D
HARRISON, David ... 919-962-0330 372 B harrison@northcarolina.edu
HARRISON, David, T ... 614-287-2402 380 G dth@cscc.edu
HARRISON, Dianne, F .. 818-677-2121 .. 34 D dianne.harrison@csun.edu
HARRISON, Don ... 770-534-6136 121 G dharrison@brenau.edu
HARRISON, Elise ... 617-824-8595 226 A elise_harrison@emerson.edu
HARRISON, Fiona ... 626-395-6601 .. 31 D fiona@srl.caltech.edu
HARRISON, Fred, H ... 501-686-2515 .. 23 F fhharrison@uasys.edu
HARRISON, James, H ... 920-206-2327 536 T jim.harrison@mbu.edu
HARRISON, James, M .. 228-897-7131 271 F james.harrison@wmcarey.edu
HARRISON, Janice ... 508-565-1096 237 A jharrison@stonehill.edu
HARRISON, Jennifer ... 405-682-1611 399 K jharrison@occc.edu
HARRISON, Jim ... 478-553-2108 129 C jharrison@oftc.edu
HARRISON, Jim, H ... 920-206-2327 536 T jim.harrison@mbu.edu
HARRISON, Judy ... 870-230-5358 .. 21 B harrisj@hsu.edu
HARRISON, Justin ... 858-513-9240 .. 29 A justin.harrison@ashford.edu
HARRISON, Karen, D ... 918-465-1829 397 L kdharrison@eosc.edu
HARRISON, Kelly, G ... 904-620-1707 116 A n00874366@unf.edu
HARRISON, Kenneth ... 334-291-4963 .... 2 H kenneth.harrison@cv.edu
HARRISON, Kim, W ... 931-363-9876 458 D kharrison@martinmethodist.edu
HARRISON, Lacey ... 229-226-1621 132 E lharrison@thomasu.edu
HARRISON, Lonnie ... 575-492-2168 314 D lharrison@usw.edu
HARRISON, M. Blake ... 270-852-3460 198 A bharrison@kwc.edu
HARRISON, Malou ... 305-237-1152 108 L mharriso@mdc.edu
HARRISON, Mark ... 360-475-7700 524 H mharrison@olympic.edu
HARRISON, Merrell, J .. 606-783-2035 198 H m.harrison@moreheadstate.edu
HARRISON, Merrilou ... 509-865-8652 523 C harison_m@heritage.edu
HARRISON, Nancy ... 530-541-4660 .. 50 A harrison@ltcc.edu
HARRISON, Paul, D ... 740-245-7203 394 D harrison@rio.edu
HARRISON, Robert ... 269-927-8600 245 E harrison@lakemichigancollege.edu
HARRISON, Rodney, A . 816-414-3700 278 E rharrison@mbts.edu
HARRISON, Ryan ... 313-664-7678 241 D rharrison@collegeforcreativestudies.edu
HARRISON, Sandra ... 310-506-6500 .. 58 H sandra.k.harrison@pepperdine.edu
HARRISON, Sarah, H ... 903-510-2547 491 A shar@tjc.edu
HARRISON, Scot ... 360-438-8808 525 H sharrison@stmartin.edu
HARRISON, Scott ... 219-464-5335 174 E scott.harrison@valpo.edu
HARRISON, Shannon ... 516-877-3486 314 F sharrison@adelphi.edu
HARRISON, Sheryl, E ... 404-872-3593 121 A sharrison@johnmarshall.edu
HARRISON, Shirley, J .. 601-979-1611 267 H shirley.j.harrison@jsums.edu
HARRISON, Steve ... 843-349-6405 444 G harrison@coastal.edu
HARRISON, Suzan ... 727-864-8212 101 P harrisms@eckerd.edu
HARRISON, Tammiko ... 601-979-2345 267 H tammiko.l.harrison@jsums.edu
HARRISON, Teresa ... 757-925-6782 516 E tharrison@pdc.edu
HARRISON, Teresa, K ... 256-331-5215 .... 6 B teresah@nwscc.edu
HARRISON, Thomas ... 904-256-7347 106 Q tharris7@ju.edu
HARRISON, Thomas ... 304-327-4011 532 D tharrison@bluefieldstate.edu
HARRISON, Tim ... 805-289-6354 .. 75 E tharrison@vcccd.edu
HARRISON, Tracey ... 601-925-3239 268 E tharriso@mc.edu
HARRISON, Valerie ... 484-365-7402 424 E vharrison@lincoln.edu
HARRISON, Valerie, E .. 803-535-5225 444 D vharrison@claflin.edu
HARRISON, W. Darryl .. 706-385-1098 130 C darryl.harrison@point.edu
HARRISON, Walter ... 860-768-4417 .. 92 F horky@hartford.edu
HARRISON, Wendy ... 757-569-6792 516 E wharrison@pdc.edu
HARRISS, Frankie ... 691-320-2480 549 D frankieh@comfsm.fm
HARROD, Joseph, C ... 502-897-4215 199 D jharrod@sbts.edu
HARROLD, Cindy ... 620-429-3896 186 C cindyh@coffeyville.edu
HARROLD, Frank ... 801-626-6232 500 C frankharrold@weber.edu
HARROZ, JR., Joseph .. 405-325-4702 403 I jharroz@ou.edu

HARWARD, Brian .... 814-332-3027 411 F
bharward@allegheny.edu
HARWARD, Sherry .... 801-863-6813 500 B
sherry.harward@uvu.edu
HARWOOD, Debra .... 704-991-0206 366 D
dharwood5544@stanly.edu
HARWOOD, Gina .... 718-960-8245 319 C
gina.harwood@lehman.cuny.edu
HARWOOD, Scott .... 518-891-2915 336 F
sharwood@nccc.edu
HARYCKI, David .... 402-375-7389 292 D
daharyc1@wsc.edu
HASAN, Abul .... 918-293-4809 400 E
abul.hasan@okstate.edu
HASAN, Rashidah .... 973-877-3260 302 F
hasan@essex.edu
HASAN, Shah .... 937-484-1256 394 F
shah.hasan@urbana.edu
HASAN, Zia .... 803-535-5219 444 D
hasan@claflin.edu
HASBROUCK, Douglas .. 610-989-1451 438 I
dhasbrouck@vfmac.edu
HASELBARTH, Jared ..... 610-785-6267 434 E
jhaselbarth@scs.edu
HASELDEN,
Gregory, W .... 864-379-8812 446 B
haselden@erskine.edu
HASELOFF, Gregory, K . 859-858-3511 193 A
greg.haseloff@asbury.edu
HASH, Jennifer .... 303-722-5724.. 83 O
jhash@lincolntech.com
HASH, Joseph .... 707-476-4212.. 41 C
joe-hash@redwoods.edu
HASHEMI-BOZARTH,
Monica .... 316-295-8701 187 C
monica_hashemi@friends.edu
HASHIZUME, John .... 650-306-3325.. 64 C
hashizumej@smccd.edu
HASINGER, Guenther .... 808-956-8566 135 J
hasinger@hawaii.edu
HASKAMP, Misty .... 573-875-7582 273 D
mrhaskamp@ccis.edu
HASKETT, Tammy .... 828-227-7222 372 C
haskett@wcu.edu
HASKINS, Brenda .... 985-448-4518 208 C
brenda.haskins@nicholls.edu
HASKINS, Dana, R .... 972-860-7269 472 E
DRHaskins@dcccd.edu
HASKINS, Dennis .... 931-363-9889 458 D
dhaskins@martinmethodist.edu
HASKINS, Eileen, T ...... 401-598-1035 441 D
ehaskins@jwu.edu
HASKINS, Jamie .... 573-592-5262 285 J
jamie.haskins@westminster-mo.edu
HASKINS, Michael .... 251-460-6211.... 9 F
mhaskins@southalabama.edu
HASKINS, Rick .... 412-391-4100 433 F
rhaskins@pointpark.edu
HASLAG, Daniel .... 573-592-5282 285 J
dan.haslag@westminster-mo.edu
HASLAM, Kent .... 406-243-5348 287 D
kent.haslam@umontana.edu
HASLAM STRAUGHAN,
Hope .... 617-879-2330 238 C
hstraughan@wheelock.edu
HASLER, Paul .... 715-346-3059 541 A
phasler@uwsp.edu
HASLIM, Hue .... 602-943-2311.. 18 K
Hue.Haslim@west.edu
HASS, Marjorie .... 903-813-3001 468 G
mhass@austincollege.edu
HASS, Martha .... 518-694-7238 314 G
martha.hass@acphs.edu
HASS CORDOVA, Tracy 417-667-8181 273 H
tcordova@cottey.edu
HASSAN, Nidia .... 903-510-2883 491 A
nhas@tjc.edu
HASSANPOUR, Zinat ..... 704-403-1698 355 B
zinat.hassanpour@carolinashealthcare.org
HASSEL, George, E .... 610-499-4182 439 G
gehassel.sr@widener.edu
HASSEL, Patricia .... 513-244-4711 387 A
patricia.hassel@msj.edu
HASSELBARTH, William 518-262-6008 314 I
HASSELBLATT, Boris ..... 617-627-3419 237 C
boris.hasselblatt@tufts.edu
HASSELER, Susan, S .... 605-274-4113 452 A
susan.hasseler@augie.edu
HASSELL, Karen .... 916-686-8484.. 32 B
HASSELL, Keith .... 203-576-4466.. 92 B
khassell@bridgeport.edu
HASSELL, Rusty .... 706-385-1503 130 C
rusty.hassell@point.edu
HASSEN, Marjorie .... 207-725-3281 209 H
mhassen@bowdoin.edu
HASSENZAHL,
David, M .... 530-898-6121.. 33 A
dhassenzahl@csuchico.edu
HASSENZAHL, Roger .... 765-285-1532 164 D
rahassenzahl@bsu.edu
HASSETT, A. Tracy .... 508-831-5473 238 G
thassett@wpi.edu
HASSEVOORT, Darrin .... 423-697-3383 462 C
darrin.hassevoort@chattanoogastate.edu
HASSINGER, Steven ...... 717-728-2262 415 B
stevehassinger@centralpenn.edu
HASSLER, Ardoth .... 202-687-1780.. 95 E
hasslera@georgetown.edu
HASSLER, Gregory, L ... 252-744-2212 369 E
hasslerg@ecu.edu
HASSLER, Mary Ellen ... 856-351-2651 308 B
mhassler@salemcc.edu
HASSON, Amy, S .... 410-548-3316 220 E
ashasson@salisbury.edu
HASSUMANI, Sabrina ... 713-743-2755 491 D
shassumani@uh.edu
HASTAD, Doug, N .... 262-524-7246 535 D
dhastad@carrollu.edu
HASTED, Grigor .... 517-607-2620 243 J
ghasted@hillsdale.edu
HASTINGS, Adam .... 434-961-5348 516 F
ahastings@pvcc.edu
HASTINGS, Brian .... 402-458-1100 293 H
bhastings@nufoundation.org
HASTINGS, Dana, M ..... 785-532-6221 188 H
dhasting@ksu.edu
HASTINGS, Jan .... 818-401-1298.. 41 F
jhastings@columbiacollege.edu
HASTINGS, Jennifer, D . 253-879-2460 527 F
jhastings@pugetsound.edu
HASTINGS, Michael, M 207-581-1484 212 C
mhastings@maine.edu
HASTINGS, Nancy .... 312-329-4415 153 C
nancy.hastings@moody.edu
HASTINGS, Ron .... 909-384-8542.. 62 C
rhastings@sbccd.cc.ca.us
HASTINGS, Susan .... 651-255-6120 264 F
shastings@unitedseminary.edu
HASTRITER, Michael, L 937-255-3636 547 E
michael.hastriter@afit.edu
HASTY, Taylor .... 423-775-7568 455 F
jhasty6628@bryan.edu
HATAIER, Maria .... 212-678-3779 349 I
mrt2112@tc.columbia.edu
HATANAKA, Janice .... 562-985-7878.. 33 F
janice.hatanaka@csulb.edu
HATCH, Blaine .... 928-524-7440.. 16 E
blaine.hatch@npc.edu
HATCH, Donna, M .... 972-548-6884 471 C
dhatch@collin.edu
HATCH, SHCJ,
Jeanne Marie .... 610-527-0200 434 D
jhatch@rosemont.edu
HATCH, Jennifer .... 717-764-9550 416 D
jhatch@csb.edu
HATCH, Joy .... 785-628-4488 187 A
jhatch@fhsu.edu
HATCH, Mark .... 719-389-6805.. 79 M
mhatch@coloradocollege.edu
HATCH, Mary .... 847-214-7421 144 F
mhatch@elgin.edu
HATCH, Nathan, O .... 336-758-5211 372 G
hatch@wfu.edu
HATCHER, Betty, K .... 252-638-3745 362 A
hatcherb@cravencc.edu
HATCHER, Brian .... 410-617-5026 216 D
bhatcher@loyola.edu
HATCHER, Doreen .... 909-537-5037.. 35 A
dhatcher@csusb.edu
HATCHER, George .... 919-546-8353 368 G
ghatcher@shawu.edu
HATCHER, Kevin, L .... 909-537-5011.. 35 A
khatcher@csusb.edu
HATCHER, Oeida .... 434-544-8344 509 I
hatcher@lynchburg.edu
HATCHER, Robert .... 212-817-7020 319 B
rhatcher@gc.cuny.edu
HATCHETT, Timothy, L . 202-274-5000.. 97 B
HATFIELD, Amy .... 360-475-7555 524 H
ahatfield@olympic.edu
HATFIELD, Barbara, S .. 318-473-6446 205 A
bhatfield@lsua.edu
HATFIELD, Chad .... 914-961-8313 341 I
hatfield@svots.edu
HATFIELD, Heather .... 865-539-7331 463 E
hrhatfield@pstcc.edu
HATFIELD, Jenna .... 252-335-0821 361 G
jenna_hatfield@albemarle.edu
HATFIELD, Karen .... 352-588-8460 111 L
karen.hatfield@saintleo.edu
HATFIELD, Mark .... 662-720-7270 269 D
mahatfield@nemcc.edu
HATFIELD, Misty .... 803-938-3728 450 H
hatfielm@uscsumter.edu
HATFIELD, Myron .... 276-523-7473 516 A
mhatfield@mecc.edu
HATFIELD, Renee .... 503-222-3225 405 H
rene.hatfield@zenith.org
HATFIELD, Sharon, L ... 540-985-8263 509 D
slhatfield@jchs.edu
HATFIELD, Tish .... 419-995-8230 384 E
hatfield.t@rhodesstate.edu
HATHAWAY, Brent, A ... 702-895-3362 295 G
brent.hathaway@unlv.edu
HATHAWAY,
Charles, B .... 914-594-4480 335 H
charles_hathaway@nymc.edu
HATHAWAY,
Gretchel, L .... 518-388-8327 350 K
hathawag@union.edu
HATHAWAY, Jeffrey ...... 516-463-6750 328 A
jeffrey.hathaway@hofstra.edu
HATHAWAY, Joel .... 314-434-4044 273 J
joel.hathaway@covenantseminary.edu
HATHAWAY, Karry, L .... 443-412-2401 215 D
khathaway@harford.edu
HATHAWAY, Kathleen ... 307-778-1179 546 F
khathawa@lccc.wy.edu
HATHAWAY,
Nicholas, S .... 405-325-3916 403 I
nhathaway@ou.edu
HATHAWAY, Tom .... 513-569-1493 379 K
tom.hathaway@cincinnatistate.edu
HATHAWAY, William ...... 757-352-4294 511 G
willhat@regent.edu
HATHAWAY-CLARK,
Bill .... 303-458-4162.. 85 G
whathawa@regis.edu
HATHCOCK, Michele ..... 828-398-7203 360 A
mhathcock@abtech.edu
HATHCOTE, Jan, M ...... 706-542-6020 132 H
hathcote@uga.edu
HATHMAN, Laurie, E .... 816-501-4144 281 B
laurie.hathman@rockhurst.edu
HATHORN, Janine, M ... 540-458-8671 519 A
jhathorn@wlu.edu
HATHORN, Pamela .... 918-456-5511 398 M
hathorn@nsuok.edu
HATLEE, Mark .... 518-438-3111 331 K
mhatlee@mariacollege.edu
HATLEN, Mary, J .... 920-923-7161 537 A
mhatlen@marianuniversity.edu
HATLEY, Anita .... 501-370-5314.. 22 E
ahatley@philander.edu
HATNEY, Taura .... 706-396-7606 129 H
thatney@paine.edu
HATRAK, Gregory .... 914-961-8313 341 I
ghatrak@svots.edu
HATT, Mark .... 207-255-1221 212 G
mark.hatt@maine.edu
HATTAWAY, Trey .... 903-983-8218 477 A
thattaway@kilgore.edu
HATTEBERG,
Gregory, A .... 214-887-5101 473 E
ghatteberg@dts.edu
HATTEBERG,
Gregory, A .... 214-887-5101 473 E
alumni@dts.edu
HATTEN, Angie .... 309-692-4092 152 F
ahatten@midstate.edu
HATTENDORF, Lori .... 513-244-4230 387 A
lori.hattendorf@msj.edu
HATTERMAN, Dawn, K . 816-604-3223 277 J
dawn.hatterman@mcckc.edu
HATTMAN, Melissa .... 314-516-5708 284 B
hattmanm@umsl.edu
HATTON, Jay .... 703-784-4037 547 L
jay.hatton@usmc.mil
HATTON, John .... 314-577-8600 281 M
hattonjf@slu.edu
HATTON, Karl .... 217-479-7080 151 J
karl.hatton@mac.edu
HATTON, Martin .... 662-329-7231 269 B
mlhatton@muw.edu
HATTON, Nora .... 620-235-4276 190 G
nhatton@pittstate.edu
HATTORI-UCHIMA,
Margaret .... 671-735-2653 549 G
muchima@uguam.uog.edu
HATZENBUEHLER,
Linda .... 208-282-4899 138 C
hatzlind@isu.edu
HAUB, Elaine .... 812-941-2284 169 A
ehaub@ius.edu
HAUCK, Steven .... 605-882-5284 452 G
haucks@lakeareatech.edu
HAUCK, Tanya .... 510-885-4602.. 33 C
tanya.hauck@csueastbay.edu
HAUF, Todd .... 701-483-2570 373 H
todd.hauf@dickinsonstate.edu
HAUFF, Joel, S .... 520-621-0964.. 18 E
hauff@email.arizona.edu
HAUG, Amy .... 765-658-4181 165 G
amyhaug@depauw.edu
HAUG, Christopher ...... 503-943-7205 410 H
haug@up.edu
HAUG, Marsha, L .... 610-436-3411 432 B
mhaug@wcupa.edu
HAUGABROOK,
Adrian, K .... 617-879-2008 238 C
ahaugabrook@wheelock.edu
HAUGABROOK,
Brian, A .... 229-333-7447 133 H
bahaugab@valdosta.edu
HAUGE, Stephanie .... 973-378-9852 308 C
stephanie.hauge@shu.edu
HAUGE, Todd, W .... 410-293-1600 549 B
hauge@usna.edu
HAUGEN, Daniel .... 612-861-7554 253 F
haugen@alfredadler.edu
HAUGEN, Dolores .... 253-566-6090 527 C
dhaugen@tacomacc.edu
HAUGEN, Donna, M ...... 516-572-7809 334 A
donna.haugen@ncc.edu
HAUGEN, Doris .... 847-628-1510 149 A
dhaugen@judsonu.edu
HAUGEN, Doug .... 530-938-5295.. 41 E
haugen@siskiyous.edu
HAUGEN, Jay .... 314-977-2350 281 M
haugenjp@slu.edu
HAUGEN, Nancy .... 510-869-6511.. 61 J
nhaugen@samuelmerritt.edu
HAUGEN, Regina .... 270-384-8300 198 C
haugenr@lindsey.edu
HAUGH, Susi .... 619-702-9400.. 31 F
HAUGHT, Kenneth .... 701-483-2149 373 H
ken.haught@dickinsonstate.edu
HAUGHT, Paul .... 901-321-3230 455 I
phaught@cbu.edu
HAUK, Gary, S .... 404-727-6021 124 D
gary.hauk@emory.edu
HAUK, Matthew .... 406-791-5224 288 J
matthew.hauk@ugf.edu
HAUKE, Ray .... 785-594-8347 184 F
ray.hauke@bakeru.edu
HAUKI, Aronne .... 510-567-6174.. 69 D
ahauki@sum.edu
HAULOTTE, Erin .... 847-947-5491 153 H
erin.haulotte@nl.edu
HAUNGS, Megan .... 510-666-8248.. 26 C
mhaungs@aimc.edu
HAUPERT, Vincent, D ... 260-359-4089 167 D
vhaupert@huntington.edu
HAUPT, Benjamin .... 314-505-7040 273 G
hauptb@csl.edu
HAUPT, Diane .... 805-756-6004.. 32 E
dehaupt@calpoly.edu
HAURY, Clifford, W ...... 434-961-5380 516 F
chaury@pvcc.edu
HAUS, Teri .... 970-943-2196.. 87 F
thaus@western.edu
HAUSAMMANN,
Marilyn .... 617-495-8635 227 D
marilyn_hausammann@harvard.edu
HAUSCARRIAGUE,
Elizabeth .... 925-969-2085.. 42 E
ehauscarriague@dvc.edu
HAUSCHILD, Karen .... 843-953-5404 445 B
hauschildkb@cofc.edu
HAUSE, Jeffrey, P .... 402-280-3581 290 B
JeffreyHause@creighton.edu
HAUSER, Carrie .... 970-945-8691.. 80 D
HAUSER, Dan .... 336-841-9057 357 E
dhauser@highpoint.edu
HAUSER, John .... 336-838-6149 367 C
john.hauser@wilkescc.edu
HAUSER, Joseph, H ..... 901-722-3228 461 A
jhauser@sco.edu
HAUSER, LuAnn .... 620-431-2820 189 J
lhauser@neosho.edu
HAUSER, SJ,
Richard, J .... 402-280-3010 290 B
hausersj@creighton.edu
HAUSER, Robert .... 217-244-2807 162 A
r-hauser@illinois.edu
HAUSER, Stephen, C .... 608-246-2101 543 C
shauser@madisoncollege.edu
HAUSFELD, Mark, A ..... 417-268-1010 272 D
hausfeldm@evangel.edu
HAUSINGER, Shannon .. 281-290-2832 477 I
shannon.hausinger@lonestar.edu
HAUSKNECHT, Robert ... 708-456-0300 161 C
rhauskne@triton.edu
HAUSLER, Stephen .... 516-299-2506 330 F
stephen.hausler@liu.edu
HAUSMAN, Amy .... 973-290-4214 301 F
bookstore@cse.edu
HAUSMAN, Kristan, R .. 740-587-6271 381 H
hausmank@denison.edu
HAUSS, Kevin .... 212-237-8512 319 F
khauss@jjay.cuny.edu
HAUSSMANN, Robert ... 928-541-7777.. 16 B
rhaussmann@ncu.edu
HAUTANEN, David .... 978-837-3570 233 G
hautanend@merrimack.edu
HAUTER, Dawn .... 419-267-1339 387 G
dhauter@northweststate.edu

HAYNES, Carl, E .... 607-844-8222 350 A
haynesc@tc3.edu
HAYNES, Carolyn, A ..... 513-529-6722 386 K
haynesca@miamioh.edu
HAYNES, David, A .... 540-985-4020 509 D
DAHaynes@jchs.edu
HAYNES, Derrick .... 303-360-4721.. 81 I
Derrick.Haynes@CCAurora.edu
HAYNES, Douglas, M ... 949-824-2798.. 71 C
dhaynes@uci.edu
HAYNES, John, G .... 806-743-7387 490 A
john.g.haynes@ttuhsc.edu
HAYNES, Karen, S .... 760-750-4040.. 35 B
pres@csusm.edu
HAYNES, Leticia .... 413-597-4376 238 E
lseh1@williams.edu
HAYNES, Lisa .... 616-331-7204 243 E
haynesl@gvsu.edu
HAYNES, Martha, B ...... 906-227-2610 248 B
haynes@nmu.edu
HAYNES, Mike .... 254-968-9354 485 A
rhaynes@tarleton.edu
HAYNES, Pamela, J ...... 336-888-9055 357 E
phaynes@highpoint.edu
HAYNES, Patricia, A ..... 636-922-8427 281 C
phaynes@stchas.edu
HAYNES, Penny, A .... 518-381-1374 342 E
haynespa@sunysccc.edu
HAYNES, Ryan .... 916-577-2200.. 77 F
dgluck@jessup.edu
HAYNES, Sandra .... 303-556-2978.. 83 Q
hayness@msudenver.edu
HAYNES, Scott .... 870-245-5220.. 22 C
hayness@obu.edu
HAYNES, Sonja .... 828-339-4218 366 C
sonjah@southwesterncc.edu
HAYNES, Stephanie, C . 304-637-1335 529 I
hayness@dewv.edu
HAYNES, Tina .... 704-216-3461 365 F
tina.haynes@rccc.edu
HAYNES, Wendy .... 508-531-2809 229 C
whaynes@bridgew.edu
HAYNIE, Glenda, D ...... 804-333-6719 516 G
ghaynie@rappahannock.edu
HAYNIE, Janice .... 910-672-1211 370 A
jhaynie@uncfsu.edu
HAYNIE, Stacia 225-578-2141 204M
pohayn@lsu.edu
HAYNIE, Todd .... 928-428-8320.. 13 L
todd.haynie@eac.edu
HAYS, Antoinette, M .... 781-768-7122 236 A
antoinette.hays@regiscollege.edu
HAYS, Cheryl, M .... 412-268-6382 414 J
chays@andrew.cmu.edu
HAYS, Danny .... 870-245-5526.. 22 C
haysd@obu.edu
HAYS, Karen, L .... 410-777-2332 213 E
klhays@aacc.edu
HAYS, Kristi .... 785-825-5422 185 D
khays@brownmackie.edu
HAYS, Kristin .... 603-577-6411 297 F
khays@dwc.edu
HAYS, Kyle .... 870-307-7233.. 21 G
jason.hays@lyon.edu
HAYS, Rex .... 913-469-8500 188 E
rhays@jccc.edu
HAYS, Richard .... 919-660-3411 356 E
richard.hays@duke.edu
HAYS, Ryan .... 513-556-2201 393 B
ryan.hays@uc.edu
HAYS, Samantha .... 270-852-3130 198 A
shays@kwc.edu
HAYS, Stacie .... 712-274-5254 181 C
hays@morningside.edu
HAYS, Wm. Randy .... 859-238-5471 194 E
randy.hays@centre.edu
HAYS-MUSSOINI,
Stephanie .... 765-973-8331 168 A
shaysmus@iue.edu
HAYS-THOMAS, Helen .. 269-927-6874 245 E
hhays-thomas@lakemichigancollege.edu
HAYSBERT, JoAnn, W .. 757-727-5693 508 C
joann.haysbert@hamptonu.edu
HAYTAS, Debra .... 304-263-6262 530 D
dhaytas@martinsburginstitute.edu
HAYTER,
Christopher, A .... 614-823-1348 390 C
chayter@otterbein.edu
HAYTER, Richard .... 972-721-5227 491 B
rhayter@udallas.edu
HAYTER, Sonya .... 417-269-3469 274 A
sonya.hayter@coxcollege.edu
HAYTON, Heather .... 336-316-2397 357 C
hhayton@guilford.edu
HAYTON, James, C .... 848-932-6965 307 B
HAYWARD, Albert, G .... 803-516-4541 448 H
ahayward@scsu.edu
HAYWARD, Bill .... 847-467-5067 155 D
william.hayward@northwestern.edu
HAYWARD, Craig .... 949-451-5766.. 67 E
chayward@ivc.edu

HAYWARD, Dawn .... 215-646-7300 420 A
hayward.d@gmercyu.edu
HAYWARD, Maysa .... 732-255-0400 304 E
mhayward@ocean.edu
HAYWARD, Milan .... 703-323-3780 516 C
mhayward@nvcc.edu
HAYWOOD, Ben .... 903-233-3561 477 G
benhaywood@letu.edu
HAYWOOD, Carl .... 210-829-3935 492 B
carl@uiwtx.edu
HAYWOOD, Chanta ...... 229-430-4660 119 H
chanta.haywood@asurams.edu
HAYWOOD, Davida .... 334-229-4241.... 1 D
Dhaywood@alasu.edu
HAYWOOD, Michele ...... 910-576-6222 364 D
haywoodm@montgomery.edu
HAYWOOD, Zina .... 262-564-3104 543 A
haywoodz@gtc.edu
HAYWORTH,
Kimberly, K .... 517-750-1200 250 F
kimh@arbor.edu
HAZAM, Bruce .... 207-801-5645 210 B
bhazam@coa.edu
HAZARD, Laurie, L .... 401-232-6746 441 B
lhazard@bryant.edu
HAZARD, Terry .... 692-625-3291 550 A
thazard@cmi.edu
HAZARD, Victor, A .... 859-257-3754 200 G
vahaz@uky.edu
HAZEL, Julie .... 719-502-3005.. 84 J
julie.hazel@ppcc.edu
HAZEL, Stephanie .... 703-993-5106 507 K
shazel@gmu.edu
HAZELBAKER, Chato .... 360-992-2921 521 A
chazelbaker@clark.edu
HAZELBAKER, Nicole .... 406-683-7900 287 E
nicole.hazelbaker@umwestern.edu
HAZELETT, Margaret ..... 717-291-4000 418 J
margaret.hazelett@fandm.edu
HAZELKORN, Michael .. 912-279-5720 123 B
mhazelkorn@ccga.edu
HAZELTON, Janet .... 802-468-1208 503 G
janet.hazelton@castleton.edu
HAZELTON, Rahneeka ... 817-202-6733 483 C
rahneeka@swau.edu
HAZEN, Ian .... 315-268-6439 321 C
ihazen@clarkson.edu
HAZEN, Ron .... 615-297-7545 455 A
hazenr@aquinascollege.edu
HAZEN, Verna, J .... 585-475-5520 339 G
vjhsfa@rit.edu
HAZEN, Virginia, S .... 603-646-2451 297 G
virginia.s.hazen@dartmouth.edu
HAZLETT, Brian .... 717-871-2250 431 E
brian.hazlett@millersville.edu
HAZLETT, Laura .... 510-594-3688.. 30 G
lhazlett@cca.edu
HAZLETT, Mia .... 508-362-2131 231 D
mhazlett@capecod.edu
HAZZARD, Douglas ...... 904-256-7100 106 Q
dhazzar@ju.edu
HAZZARD, Mike .... 270-706-8686 195 K
mikew.hazzard@kctcs.edu
HAZZARD, Terry .... 251-405-7285.... 2 D
thazzard@bishop.edu
HA'O, Melanie .... 401-841-7367 548 B
HE, Phil .... 617-373-6817 235 D
HE, Yuxin .... 512-454-1188 468 A
info@aoma.edu
HEABERLIN, Robert ...... 770-254-7280 133 F
rheaber@westga.edu
HEACOCK, Maureen 937-769-1846 376M
mheacock@antioch.edu
HEACOCK, Maureen ...... 937-769-1351 376 L
mheacock@antioch.edu
HEAD, Carolyn .... 901-321-3256 455 I
chead1@cbu.edu
HEAD, Daniel .... 251-575-8259.... 1 C
dhead@ascc.edu
HEAD, John .... 678-839-6423 133 F
jhead@westg.edu
HEAD, Judith .... 214-638-0484 476 Y
jhead@kdstudio.com
HEAD, Robert, L .... 815-226-4010 157 D
rhead@rockford.edu
HEAD, Stephen .... 832-813-6515 477 I
steve.head@lonestar.edu
HEAD, Susan .... 315-792-7342 348 D
susan.head@sunyit.edu
HEADING-GRANT,
Wanda, R .... 802-656-8426 503 C
wanda.heading-grant@uvm.edu
HEADINGS, Ronald .... 419-358-3660 377 H
headingsr@bluffton.edu
HEADLEY, Julie .... 918-495-7297 401 B
jheadley@oru.edu
HEADLEY, Scot .... 503-554-2836 406 A
sheadley@georgefox.edu
HEADRICK, Dennis .... 402-323-3427 293 A
dheadric@southeast.edu

HEADRICK, Robert .... 479-248-7236.. 20 K
bheadrick@ecollege.edu
HEADY, Emily .... 434-592-3232 509 G
eheady@liberty.edu
HEAFNER, Lori .... 843-349-7871 446 I
lori.heafner@hgtc.edu
HEAGLE, Leanne .... 937-255-6565 547 E
leanne.heagle@afit.edu
HEALD, Donna .... 518-244-3190 340 A
healdd@sage.edu
HEALEY, Maureen .... 219-866-6161 172 E
maureenh@saintjoe.edu
HEALEY, Tom .... 810-762-0417 247 F
thomas.healey@mcc.edu
HEALY, Amy .... 518-255-5111 346 E
healyak@cobleskill.edu
HEALY, David .... 904-256-7024 106 Q
dhealy1@ju.edu
HEALY, David .... 608-663-2000 536 S
dhealy@mediainstitute.edu
HEALY, Diane .... 312-942-6849 158 A
diane_healy@rush.edu
HEALY, Gayle .... 518-629-7326 328 D
g.healy@hvcc.edu
HEALY, Heidi .... 847-214-7006 144 F
hhealy@elgin.edu
HEALY, Joanne .... 313-664-1474 241 D
jhealy@collegeforcreativestudies.edu
HEALY, John (Jack) ...... 218-477-2581 260 B
jack.healy@mnstate.edu
HEALY, Kevin .... 612-338-6537 253 K
healyk@augsburg.edu
HEALY, Robert .... 716-286-8341 336 E
rhealy@niagara.edu
HEALY, Rose Mary .... 973-278-5400 300 C
rmh@berkeleycollege.edu
HEALY, Rose Mary .... 973-278-5400 316 D
rmh@berkeleycollege.edu
HEALY, William, L .... 863-680-4140 104 F
whealy@flsouthern.edu
HEANEY, Nicole .... 508-678-2811 231 B
nicole.heaney@bristolcc.edu
HEANEY, Roma, E .... 313-593-5353 251 D
rheaney@umich.edu
HEAP, Jeffrey .... 815-280-2401 148 K
jheap@jjc.edu
HEARD, Anissa .... 949-451-5364.. 67 E
aheard@ivc.edu
HEARD, JR., Ernest, W 615-460-6424 455 D
ernest.heard@belmont.edu
HEARD, John .... 660-626-2397 271 G
jheard@atsu.edu
HEARD, Michael .... 229-217-4207 132 C
mheard@southernregional.edu
HEARD, Michael .... 404-756-4443 120 H
mheard@atlm.edu
HEARD, Sasha .... 888-384-0849.. 26 O
sheard@allied.edu
HEARD, Shalonda .... 229-317-6489 123 H
shalonda.heard@darton.edu
HEARIT, Keith, M .... 269-387-4360 252 I
keith.hearit@wmich.edu
HEARN, Debbie .... 620-672-2700 190 H
debbieh@prattcc.edu
HEARN, Deyna .... 310-434-4435.. 65 B
hearn_deyna@smc.edu
HEARN, Greg, K .... 706-245-7226 124 C
ghearn@lifesprings.net
HEARN, Kevin .... 716-286-8405 336 E
khearn@niagara.edu
HEARN, Maribeth .... 815-740-3384 162 F
mhearn@stfrancis.edu
HEARN, Sabrina, B .... 205-934-9176.... 8 D
shearn@uasystem.ua.edu
HEARNE, Chad .... 501-450-5015.. 25 F
HEARTLEIN, Karrie .... 309-341-7340 149 G
kheartle@knox.edu
HEASLEY, Christopher .. 215-895-6155 417 E
clh344@drexel.edu
HEASLEY, Ronald, P ..... 717-361-1558 418 B
heasleyrp@etown.edu
HEASTON, Amy .... 912-344-2505 120 D
amy.heaston@armstrong.edu
HEATER, Margaret .... 585-343-0055 326 F
meheater@genesee.edu
HEATH, Aaron .... 816-322-0110 272 L
aaron.heath@calvary.edu
HEATH, Ann .... 610-647-4400 421 B
aheath@immaculata.edu
HEATH, Bill .... 863-638-2953 119 A
heathwl@webber.edu
HEATH, Bob .... 417-626-1234 280 B
heath.bob@occ.edu
HEATH, Cassandra, A ... 530-226-4608.. 66 G
cheath@simpsonu.edu
HEATH, Cheryl, A .... 307-674-6446 546 H
cheath@sheridan.edu
HEATH, David, A .... 212-938-5650 347 C
dheath@sunyopt.edu
HEATH, Diann .... 785-825-5422 185 D
dheath@brownmackie.edu

HEATH, Eric .... 703-993-3840 507 K
eheath2@gmu.edu
HEATH, Hildy .... 415-405-4256.. 36 A
hheath@sfsu.edu
HEATH, Janie, H .... 859-257-9000 200 G
jheath@uky.edu
HEATH, Janine .... 573-840-9698 283 D
jheath@trcc.edu
HEATH, Jason .... 502-897-4106 199 D
jheath@sbts.edu
HEATH, Joan, L .... 512-245-2133 489 C
jh06@txstate.edu
HEATH, Judy .... 410-777-1177 213 E
jheath@aacc.edu
HEATH, Kathy .... 207-326-2339 211 G
kathy.heath@mma.edu
HEATH, Marie .... 904-470-8933 102 A
m.heath@ewc.edu
HEATH, Mary-Teresa .... 518-828-4181 322 E
mary-teresa.heath@sunycgcc.edu
HEATH, Richard, C .... 410-777-2204 213 E
rcheath@aacc.edu
HEATH, Robert .... 205-366-8851.... 7 G
rheath@stillman.edu
HEATHERINGTON,
Vincent, J .... 216-707-8004 384 H
vjh@kent.edu
HEATHERLY, David, L ... 910-938-6789 361 F
heatherlyd@coastalcarolina.edu
HEATON, Dennis .... 641-472-7000 181 A
dheaton@mum.edu
HEATON, Haidee .... 573-288-6434 274 C
hheaton@culver.edu
HEATON, Karick .... 801-302-2879 498 L
karick.heaton@neumont.edu
HEATON, Mandy .... 503-777-7289 409 E
heatonm@reed.edu
HEATON, Monica .... 563-425-5773 183 G
heatonm@uiu.edu
HEATON, Scott .... 209-946-2541.. 73 C
sheaton@pacific.edu
HEATON, Tim .... 605-688-5117 454 C
tim.heaton@sdstate.edu
HEATOR, Martin .... 734-462-4400 250 A
mheator@schoolcraft.edu
HEATWOLE, Deirdre ...... 617-287-5324 228 E
dheatwole@umassp.edu
HEATWOLE, Deirdre ...... 774-455-7300 228 G
DHeatwole@umassp.edu
HEAVENER, Mac .... 904-596-2400 117 G
macheavener@tbc.edu
HEAVENER, Matthew .... 904-596-2420 117 G
mheavener@tbc.org
HEAVY RUNNER, Joely 701-255-3285 375 I
jheavyrunner@uttc.edu
HEBARD, John .... 907-474-6831.. 10 I
jahebard@alaska.edu
HEBARD, Natalie, J ...... 208-535-5398 138 B
natalie.hebard@my.eitc.edu
HEBBARD, Don .... 972-279-6511 467 F
dhebbard@amberton.edu
HEBBARD, Matthew ...... 956-872-2147 482 G
mshebbar@southtexascollege.edu
HEBBE, Janet .... 505-566-3515 312 K
hebbej@sanjuancollege.edu
HEBERLE, Julia, F .... 610-921-7581 411 E
jheberle@albright.edu
HEBERT, Carolyn .... 860-515-3880.. 88 B
chebert@charteroak.edu
HEBERT, Deborrah .... 409-984-6156 488 H
hebertda@lamarpa.edu
HEBERT, Gurdeep .... 559-325-5378.. 69 A
gurdeep.hebert@scccd.edu
HEBERT, Jaimie .... 936-294-1001 489 A
hebert@shsu.edu
HEBERT, Jeanne .... 401-863-2206 441 A
jeanne_hebert@brown.edu
HEBERT, Joseph .... 281-998-6150 481 G
joseph.hebert@sjcd.edu
HEBERT, Mark .... 502-852-3133 201 A
mark.hebert@louisville.edu
HEBERT, Rudolph .... 413-572-5699 230 F
rudy@westfield.ma.edu
HECHT, Amy .... 609-771-2201 301 E
amyhecht@tcnj.edu
HECHT, Boruch .... 973-267-9404 305 E
boruch.hecht@gmail.com
HECHT, George, E .... 541-346-2290 410 F
ghecht@uoregon.edu
HECHT, Pinchas .... 718-645-0536 333 B
phecht@thejnet.com
HECK, Annie .... 541-737-0790 408 F
annie.heck@oregonstate.edu
HECK, Barbara, H .... 410-778-7805 221 D
bheck2@washcoll.edu
HECK, Catherine, J .... 740-283-6498 382 G
check@franciscan.edu
HECK, James .... 207-509-7263 212 A
jheck@unity.edu
HECK, Melissa .... 918-335-6334 400 I

HELDEROP, Sue 248-364-6135 248 K helderop@oakland.edu
HELDMAN, Lou 316-978-7114 192 D lou.heldman@wichita.edu
HELEKAR, Andrea 213-624-1200 44 I ahelekar@fidm.edu
HELEKAR, Andrea, D 213-624-1200 44 I ahelekar@fidm.edu
HELENS, Joyce, M 320-308-5017 261 F jhelens@sctcc.edu
HELFENSTEIN, Patricia 610-372-4721 433 H phelfenstein@racc.edu
HELFGOT, Steven 480-731-8098 14 J steve.helfgot@domail.maricopa.edu
HELFRICH, Glenda 806-743-2986 490 A glenda.helfrich@ttuhsc.edu
HELFRICH, Lori 314-862-3456 275 B lhelfrich@fontbonne.edu
HELGE, Kristyn, S 817-515-7463 484 B kristyn.helge@tccd.edu
HELGEN, Beth 612-330-1212 253 K helgen@augsburg.edu
HELGESEN, Paul 978-867-4730 227 A paul.helgesen@gordon.edu
HELGESEN, Pete 913-360-7476 184 K phelgesen@benedictine.edu
HELGESON, Grant 808-455-0645 136 G helgeson@hawaii.edu
HELGESON, Richard, J 731-881-7380 465 F helgeson@utm.edu
HELGESTAD, Chris 612-861-7554 253 F chris.helgestad@alfredadler.edu
HELIS, James 516-726-5815 548 I helisj@usmma.edu
HELLA, Lori, L 989-774-7194 240 O hella1ll@cmich.edu
HELLAMS, Thomas 502-897-4121 199 D thellams@sbts.edu
HELLAND, Carol 218-285-7722 261 A carol.helland@rainyriver.edu
HELLAND, Carol 218-749-7715 259 D c.helland@mesabirange.edu
HELLAND, Nathan 541-888-7316 410 A nathan.helland@socc.edu
HELLDOBLER, Richard, J 773-442-5420 154 H r-helldobler@neiu.edu
HELLENBRAND, Harry 818-677-2957 34 D harry.hellenbrand@csun.edu
HELLER, Adam 623-245-4600 18 C aheller@uti.edu
HELLER, Donald, E 517-355-1734 246 H dheller@msu.edu
HELLER, James 262-595-2455 540 C james.heller@uwp.edu
HELLER, Jennifer 913-360-7431 184 K jheller@benedictine.edu
HELLER, Joshua, J 212-752-1530 330 C joshua.heller@limcollege.edu
HELLER, Joshua, W 585-785-1335 325 E joshua.heller@flcc.edu
HELLER, Mary 406-265-4198 288 A mary.heller@msun.edu
HELLER, Matt 847-945-8800 161 B mheller@tiu.edu
HELLER, Matthew, D 607-587-3992 347 D hellermd@alfredstate.edu
HELLER, William 727-873-4979 116 C wheller@mail.usf.edu
HELLER-ROSS, Holly, B 518-564-5180 346 B hellerhb@plattsburgh.edu
HELLERMANN, David 651-290-6457 266 B david.hellermann@wmitchell.edu
HELLERSTEIN, Laurel 978-232-2153 226 C lhellers@endicott.edu
HELLERUD, Nancy 314-246-7440 285 G nancyhellerud@webster.edu
HELLIE, Thomas 503-883-2408 406 I thellie@linfield.edu
HELLIGE, Joseph, B 310-338-2733 53 C jhellige@lmu.edu
HELLING, Mary Kay 605-688-4173 454 C mary.helling@sdstate.edu
HELLING, Nathan, M 605-336-6588 453 C nhelling@sfseminary.edu
HELLMAN, Joel 202-687-0100 95 E
HELLMUND, Paul, C 413-369-4044 225 E hellmund@csld.edu
HELLRUNG, Scott, A 414-410-4697 535 C shellrung@stritch.edu
HELLUMS, Duane 502-410-6200 194 N dhellums@galencollege.edu
HELLUMS, Paula 337-421-6965 204 F
HELLWIG, Beth, A 715-836-5992 539 E hellwiba@uwec.edu
HELLWIG, Brant, J 540-458-5352 519 A hellwig@wlu.edu
HELLYER, Brenda 281-998-6100 481 D brenda.hellyer@sjcd.edu
HELM, Hunt, C 502-272-8046 193 E hhelm@bellarmine.edu
HELM, Jennifer 304-724-3700 529 F jhelm@apus.edu
HELM, Jonathan, C 254-710-8824 469 D Jonathan_Helm@baylor.edu
HELM, Lloyd 503-594-6793 405 A lloyd.helm@clackamas.edu
HELM, Matthew 309-438-8990 147 I mlhelm@ilstu.edu
HELM, Ron, C 870-368-2027 22 D rhelm@ozarka.edu
HELM, Scott 641-782-1481 183 D helm@swcciowa.edu
HELM, Steven 540-831-5471 511 C shelm@radford.edu
HELM, Thomas 603-668-2211 298 H t.helm@snhu.edu
HELMBRECHT, Alex 308-432-6212 292 B ahlembrecht@csc.edu
HELMER, Robert, C 440-826-2424 377 D rhelmer@bw.edu
HELMER, Shannon 610-799-1857 424 A shelmer@lccc.edu
HELMICH, Doris 520-494-5200 12 R doris.helmich@centralaz.edu
HELMICK, Michael 828-448-3102 367 B mhelmick@wpcc.edu
HELMICK, Tom 724-852-3210 439 C thelmick@waynesburg.edu
HELMING, Jay 202-685-3909 547 M jay.helming@ndu.edu
HELMREICH, Ann 817-257-2787 486 G
HELMS, Chris 828-766-1291 364 A chelms@mayland.edu
HELMS, James, B 256-306-2545 2 F jbh@calhoun.edu
HELMS, Lance 912-538-3207 132 A lhelms@southeasterntech.edu
HELMS, Mark 704-330-6127 361 D mark.helms@cpcc.edu
HELMS, Sherrie 478-289-2360 124 B shelms@ega.edu
HELMS, Steve 334-222-6591 5 G shelms@lbwcc.edu
HELMS, Wanda 505-224-4551 310 F whelms@cnm.edu
HELMSING, Debra, F 260-665-4240 173 D helmsingd@trine.edu
HELMSTETTER, Ashley 419-448-2231 383 C ahelmste@heidelberg.edu
HELMSTETTER, Donald, W 651-641-8227 255 C helmstetter@csp.edu
HELMUTH, Andrea, M 574-807-7351 164 F andrea.helmuth@bethelcollege.edu
HELOU, Ibrahim (Abe) 909-593-3511 73 B ihelou@laverne.edu
HELSETH, Joe 423-697-2606 462 C joe.helseth@chattanoogastate.edu
HELSPER, Nancy 320-589-6012 265 A helsper@morris.umn.edu
HELSTON, Stephanie 212-757-1190 315 C shelston@funeraleducation.org
HELTON, Karen 903-927-3369 497 G khelton@wileyc.edu
HELTON, Patti 303-871-3289 86 H phelton@du.edu
HELTON, Richard, E 812-888-4208 174 F president@vinu.edu
HELTON, Tom 706-507-8909 123 D helton_tom@columbusstate.edu
HELTSLEY, Susan, D 360-438-4534 525 H sheltsley@stmartin.edu
HELVERING, Christal, R 765-641-4205 164 B crhelvering@anderson.edu
HELVESTON, David 225-308-4420 202 M dhelveston@lctcs.edu
HELVIE-MASON, Lora 254-968-9488 485 A helviemason@tarleton.edu
HELWIG, Christine, A 518-629-7343 328 D c.helwig@hvcc.edu
HELWIG, Daniel 717-867-6220 423 I helwig@lvc.edu
HELWIG, Denice 707-826-3300 35 D dh7003@humboldt.edu
HELWIG, Susan, M 570-674-6368 426 D shelwig@misericordia.edu
HELYER, Kella 503-838-8684 411 B helyerk@wou.edu
HEMANS, Peter 828-694-1723 360 D peterh@blueridge.edu
HEMBREE, Lois, D 620-421-6700 189 B loish@labette.edu
HEMBRICK, Donna, Y 919-530-6878 370 C dhembrick@nccu.edu
HEMENWAY, David 860-629-6185 91 B hemenway_d@mitchell.edu
HEMENWAY, Jessica 920-693-1118 543 B jessica.hemenway@gotoltc.edu
HEMENWAY, Michael 303-765-3173 83 C mhemenway@iliff.edu
HEMESATH, Michael 320-363-2882 264 A sjpresident@csbsju.edu
HEMINGWAY, Wen 810-766-4036 239 H wen.hemingway@baker.edu
HEMLICK, Lisa, M 610-341-5830 418 A lhemlick@eastern.edu
HEMMASI, Harriette 401-863-2162 441 A harriette_hemmasi@brown.edu
HEMMENBACH, Jimmi 808-543-8083 135 C jhemmenbach@hpu.edu
HEMMER, Katie 212-966-0300 334 D khemmer@nyaa.edu
HEMMER, Laura 314-505-7203 273 G hemmerl@csl.edu
HEMMESCH, Michael 320-363-2595 264 A mhemmesch@csbsju.edu
HEMMILA, Deanna 906-227-2637 248 B dhemmila@nmu.edu
HEMMING, Erik, G 414-229-4201 540 A hemmingc@aux.uwm.edu
HEMMINGER, John, C 949-824-5796 71 C jchemmin@uci.edu
HEMMINGSEN, Jens 614-236-6105 378 H jhemming@capital.edu
HEMMITT, Ernita 404-880-6128 122 I ehemmitt@cau.edu
HEMPE, Laura, J 414-410-4194 535 C ljhempe@stritch.edu
HEMPEL, Lamont, C 909-748-8589 73 K monty_hempel@redlands.edu
HEMPEL-LAMER, Nele 562-985-4128 33 F nele.hempel-lamer@csulb.edu
HEMPHILL, Brian, O 304-766-3112 533 C bhemphill@wvstateu.edu
HEMPHILL, F. Bruce 337-475-5563 208 B bhemphill@mcneese.edu
HEMPHILL, Teale 719-336-1591 83 N teale.hemphill@lamarcc.edu
HEMPILL, Geoffrey 718-420-4269 352 C Geoffrey.Hempill@wagner.edu
HEMPTON, David, N 617-496-8026 227 D dhempton@hds.harvard.edu
HEMRICK, Robert, D 731-425-2636 463 A dhemrick@jscc.edu
HEMWALL, Lara 412-291-6315 412 H lhemwall@aii.edu
HEMWAY, Joseph 718-399-4293 338 E jhemway@pratt.edu
HENAHAN, David 518-587-2100 348 A david.henahan@esc.edu
HENAN, Carmen 505-424-2336 310 L chenan@iaia.edu
HENAO, Sandra 415-442-7833 46 A shenao@ggu.edu
HENARD, Kevin 254-298-8425 484 C kevin.henard@templejc.edu
HENARD, Kevin 817-760-5831 475 A khenard@hillcollege.edu
HENCHEY, Russell 740-245-7231 394 D rhenchey@rio.edu
HENCHY, Alexandra 859-858-2049 192 O
HENCHY, Dolores 201-355-1133 302 I henchyd@felician.edu
HENCK, Anita 626-815-5348 29 B ahenck@apu.edu
HENDERSHOT, Debra 256-306-2581 2 F ddg@calhoun.edu
HENDERSHOT, Jason 814-393-2111 430 E jhendershot@clarion.edu
HENDERSHOT, Stephanie, N 412-262-6251 434 B hendershot@rmu.edu
HENDERSON, Allan 314-773-0083 272 H allan.henderson@brookesbible.com
HENDERSON, Allen 817-531-4405 490 C ahenderson@txwes.edu
HENDERSON, Amanda 210-410-9159 158 H ahenderson@careered.com
HENDERSON, Andrea 309-298-1977 163 A ad-henderson@wiu.edu
HENDERSON, Angela 773-995-2411 141 J ahende22@csu.edu
HENDERSON, Brad 620-331-4100 188 B bhenderson@indycc.edu
HENDERSON, Brian 276-638-8777 516 D bhenderson@patrickhenry.edu
HENDERSON, Carl, E 443-412-2300 215 D chenderson@harford.edu
HENDERSON, Carol, E 302-831-2897 94 D ceh@udel.edu
HENDERSON, Chiquita, A 727-816-3205 110 B henderc@phsc.edu
HENDERSON, Christina 515-271-1501 177 H christina.henderson@dmu.edu
HENDERSON, Christine 773-371-5402 141 C chenderson@ctu.edu
HENDERSON, Cindy 815-753-4405 154 I chenderson@niu.edu
HENDERSON, Cynthia 903-223-3053 486 C cynthia.henderson@tamut.edu
HENDERSON, Cynthia, L 202-884-1723 96 B cynthia.henderson@howard.edu
HENDERSON, Darren 219-473-4346 165 A dhenderson@ccsj.edu
HENDERSON, Darwin, C 505-786-4300 311 G chenderson@navajotech.edu
HENDERSON, Dave 541-917-4331 406 J henderd@linnbenton.edu
HENDERSON, Dee 731-424-3520 463 A dhenderson@jscc.edu
HENDERSON, Eddie, W 806-651-2600 486 D ehenderson@mail.wtamu.edu
HENDERSON, Eric 928-524-7350 16 E eric.henderson@npc.edu
HENDERSON, Floyd 843-525-8271 449 E fhenderson@tcl.edu
HENDERSON, Gregg 626-395-4701 31 D gregg.henderson@caltech.edu
HENDERSON, Howard 580-349-1380 400 B howardh@opsu.edu
HENDERSON, Isaiah 219-785-5247 172 A ihenderson@pnc.edu
HENDERSON, Jack 847-925-6416 145 F jhenders@harpercollege.edu
HENDERSON, James 337-482-6454 208 F jim.henderson@louisiana.edu
HENDERSON, James 856-256-4175 306 D henderson@rowan.edu
HENDERSON, James, B 318-357-6441 208 D jhenderson@nsula.edu
HENDERSON, Janet 706-754-7833 129 B jhenderson@northgatech.edu
HENDERSON, Janice 850-729-5392 109 D hendersonj@nwfsc.edu
HENDERSON, John, M 601-815-4700 270 H mhenderson2@umc.edu
HENDERSON, Julie 510-987-9195 70 J julie.henderson@ucop.edu
HENDERSON, Kathy 408-855-5113 76 E kathy.henderson@missioncollege.edu
HENDERSON, Kyle, W 740-427-5729 384 P hendersonk@kenyon.edu
HENDERSON, Lennijo 972-238-6107 473 B lhenderson@dcccd.edu
HENDERSON, Lisle 718-636-3664 338 E lhenders@pratt.edu
HENDERSON, Mantra 662-254-3495 269 C mlhenderson@mvsu.edu
HENDERSON, Mark 217-244-6227 162 A
HENDERSON, Mark 713-525-3155 493 J hendermk@stthom.edu
HENDERSON, Michelle 760-252-2411 29 C mhenderson@barstow.edu
HENDERSON, Mitchell 718-482-5534 320 B mhenderson@lagcc.cuny.edu
HENDERSON, Nancy 319-296-4448 179 B nancy.henderson@hawkeyecollege.edu
HENDERSON, Necedah 256-233-8151 1 F necedah.henderson@athens.edu
HENDERSON, Pamela 251-460-6133 9 F phenderson@southalabama.edu
HENDERSON, Paul 207-602-2302 213 B phenderson@une.edu
HENDERSON, Peter 410-455-3263 219 F phenders@umbc.edu
HENDERSON, Ron, R 618-235-2700 160 B ronald.henderson@swic.edu
HENDERSON, Sandra 205-929-6333 5 E shenderson@lawsonstate.edu
HENDERSON, Sandra 845-569-3112 333 I sandra.cefaloni-henderson@msmc.edu
HENDERSON, Sean 559-265-5711 69 B sean.henderson@fresnocitycollege.edu
HENDERSON, Sharon 334-833-4482 4 E 0377mgr@fheg.follett.com
HENDERSON, Sherri 919-760-8139 359 B hendersh@meredith.edu
HENDERSON, Sue 201-200-3111 304 C shenderson@njcu.edu
HENDERSON, Susan 603-542-7744 297 D shenderson@ccsnh.edu
HENDERSON, Tammy 850-484-1766 110 D thenderson@pensacolastate.edu
HENDERSON, Thomas, W 601-974-1070 268 D hendetw@millsaps.edu
HENDERSON, Toni 910-296-2438 363 E thenderson@jamessprunt.edu
HENDERSON, Trennis 870-245-5206 22 C hendersont@obu.edu
HENDERSON, Virginia 601-968-5903 266 F vhenderson@belhaven.edu
HENDERSON-HARR, Amy 607-753-2511 345 C amy.henderson-harr@cortland.edu
HENDLER, Catherine 269-965-3931 244 L hendlerc@kellogg.edu

HENSON, Pamella, A .... 314-935-5277 285 E
hensonp@wustl.edu
HENSON, Travis .... 618-545-3177 149 C
thenson@kaskaskia.edu
HENSRUD, Faith .... 715-394-8449 541 C
fhensrud@uwsuper.edu
HENTHORN, Becky .... 580-371-2371 398 J
bhenthorn@mscok.edu
HENTHORN, Janet .... 312-235-3507 159 B
j.henthorn@shimer.edu
HENTHORNE, Michael .. 541-737-2416 408 F
michael.henthorne@oregonstate.edu
HENTON, June, M .... 334-844-4790.... 1 G
hentoju@auburn.edu
HENTSCHEL, Alain, R .... 386-312-4302 111 K
alainhentschel@sjrstate.edu
HENZEL, JR., John, R .. 706-245-7226 124 C
jhenzel@ec.edu
HEOS, Pamela .... 517-371-5140 252 J
heosp@cooley.edu
HEPBURN, Deborah, G . 814-371-2090 437 E
dhepburn@triangle-tech.edu
HEPBURN, Deborah, G . 814-371-2090 437 F
dhepburn@triangle-tech.edu
HEPERI, Vernon, L .... 801-422-7254 497 J
vernon_heperi@byu.edu
HEPLER, Lisa, L .... 814-393-2229 430 E
lhepler@clarion.edu
HEPNER, Kevin .... 617-541-5343 233 A
KHepner@rcc.mass.edu
HEPNER, Mickey .... 405-974-2809 403 G
mhepner@uco.edu
HEPPNER, Angela .... 817-554-5950 478 E
aheppner@messengercollege.edu
HEPPNER, Gloria .... 313-577-5600 252 G
heppnerg@wayne.edu
HEPPNER, Harold, H .... 406-353-2607 286 B
hheppner@ancollege.edu
HER, Chou .... 209-228-7865.. 71 E
cher@UCMerced.edu
HERALD, John .... 606-886-3863 195 I
john.herald@kctcs.edu
HERALD, Sara, B .... 305-899-3080.. 99 B
sherald@barry.edu
HERB, Amanda, K .... 740-374-8716 395 D
aherb@wscc.edu
HERB-SEPICH, Deb .... 605-331-6635 454 E
deb.sepich@usiouxfalls.edu
HERBERT, Derek .... 970-521-6714.. 84 H
derek.herbert@njc.edu
HERBERT, Eileen, C ...... 716-888-2791 317 H
herberte@canisius.edu
HERBERT, George, E .... 319-335-3179 175 H
george-herbert@uiowa.edu
HERBERT, James .... 215-895-2200 417 E
jh49@drexel.edu
HERBERT, Jane .... 212-817-7100 319 B
jherbert@gc.cuny.edu
HERBERT, Julie .... 440-375-7000 385 B
jherbert@lec.edu
HERBERT, Loren .... 215-968-8638 413 F
loren.herbert@bucks.edu
HERBERT, Mike .... 541-888-7208 410 A
mherbert@socc.edu
HERBERT, Tom .... 513-529-4029 386 K
herbertw@miamioh.edu
HERBERT-ASHTON,
Marilyn, J .... 540-857-6372 517 E
mherbert-ashton@virginiawestern.edu
HERBERT-JOHNSON,
Melissa .... 309-796-5465 140 D
herbertm@bhc.edu
HERBERTZ, Anita .... 317-955-6021 171 A
aherbertz@marian.edu
HERBOLD, Kirk .... 830-372-8150 487 C
kherbold@tlu.edu
HERBRAND, Laurie .... 209-228-2741.. 71 E
LHerbrand@UCMerced.edu
HERBST, Adam .... 320-363-3819 264 A
aherbst@csbsju.edu
HERBST, Chet .... 208-792-2240 138 E
cgherbst@lcsc.edu
HERBST, Daniel .... 480-732-7120.. 14 K
Daniel.Herbst@cgc.edu
HERBST, Joel .... 561-297-3970 114 E
jherbst1@fau.edu
HERBST, John, H .... 859-257-5781 200 G
herbst@uky.edu
HERBST, Shea, A .... 563-556-5110 181 F
herbsts@nicc.edu
HERBST, Susan .... 860-486-2337.. 92 C
president@uconn.edu
HERBSTER, David .... 605-677-5309 453 F
david.herbster@usd.edu
HERCHMER, Janice .... 716-896-0700 352 B
jherchmer@villa.edu
HERCULES, Tim .... 314-977-3434 281 M
hercultp@slu.edu
HERDLICK, Mike .... 419-448-3421 392 B
herdlickm@tiffin.edu
HEREDIA, Maria .... 619-398-4902.. 47 B
mheredia@hightechhigh.org
HEREFORD, Vicki .... 256-924-0511.... 5 F
HERENDEEN, Steve, A .. 260-422-5561 167 F
saherendeen@indianatech.edu
HERESHKO, David .... 570-784-3123 430 B
hereshko@bloomu.edu
HERGAN, Mark, J .... 443-352-4400 218 E
mhergan@stevenson.edu
HERGERT, Erin .... 719-549-3226.. 85 A
erin.hergert@pueblocc.edu
HERGERT, Travis, J ...... 641-422-4990 181 E
hergetra@niacc.edu
HERINGER, David .... 325-793-4700 478 D
heringer.david@mcm.edu
HERKELRATH, William .. 909-793-4263.. 28 S
HERKELRATH, William .. 909-793-4263.. 28 S
wherkelrath@ashdowncollege.edu
HERLETH, Sally .... 660-785-4031 283 E
sallydet@truman.edu
HERLEY, Wade .... 402-844-7299 292 G
wade@northeast.edu
HERLIHY, James .... 603-641-7107 298 F
jherlihy@anselm.edu
HERLIHY, Joseph, M .... 617-552-2855 224 B
joseph.herlihy@bc.edu
HERLOCKER, Linda, K .. 407-582-1388 118 I
lherlocker@valenciacollege.edu
HERMAN, Amber .... 336-838-6292 367 C
amber.herman@wilkescc.edu
HERMAN, Anne .... 503-352-2777 408 I
hermana@pacificu.edu
HERMAN, Barbara, B .... 817-257-7855 486 G
b.herman@tcu.edu
HERMAN, Brian .... 612-624-5054 265 C
herman@umn.edu
HERMAN, Bruce .... 410-455-2460 219 F
bherman@umbc.edu
HERMAN, David, E .... 716-673-3271 343 F
david.herman@fredonia.edu
HERMAN, Deborah .... 860-512-2872.. 89 D
dherman@manchestercc.edu
HERMAN, Harry .... 516-323-3503 333 E
hherman@molloy.edu
HERMAN, Harvey .... 605-856-5880 453 B
harvey.herman@sintegleska.edu
HERMAN, Jeanne .... 330-941-2264 396 C
jmherman@ysu.edu
HERMAN, Jeff .... 828-726-2294 360 F
jherman@cccti.edu
HERMAN, Jeffrey .... 619-849-2534.. 59 K
jeffreyherman@pointloma.edu
HERMAN, Nick .... 703-993-9515 507 K
nherman@gmu.edu
HERMAN, Terry .... 740-588-1290 396 E
therman@zanestate.edu
HERMAN, Vanessa, J ... 212-346-1025 337 I
vherman@pace.edu
HERMAN-BARLOW,
Janet .... 440-365-5222 385 E
HERMANN, David .... 815-802-8524 149 B
dhermann@kcc.edu
HERMANN, Julie, K ...... 732-445-8610 306 F
julie.hermann@rutgers.edu
HERMANN, Michael ..... 785-827-5541 189 A
mike.hermann@kwu.edu
HERMANN, Paula .... 785-827-5541 189 A
paula.hermann@kwu.edu
HERMANN-ARTIM,
Diane .... 802-388-5371 503 H
diane.hermann-artim@ccv.edu
HERMANNY,
Danielle, E .... 503-943-8715 410 H
hermannd@up.edu
HERMANO, Mara .... 401-454-6336 442 B
mhermano@risd.edu
HERMANSEN, Beckie .... 435-283-7346 500 D
beckie.hermansen@snow.edu
HERMANSTON, Fran ..... 509-335-3942 528 B
HERMES, John .... 405-425-1815 399 J
john.hermes@oc.edu
HERMES, Joseph .... 312-996-3490 161 F
jhermes@uic.edu
HERMES, Wayne, J .... 970-247-7432.. 82 I
hermes_w@fortlewis.edu
HERMON, Vada .... 620-227-9213 186 F
vhermon@dc3.edu
HERMS, Ron .... 559-453-2075.. 45 E
ron.herms@fresno.edu
HERMSEN, Cindy, L ...... 248-370-3370 248 K
hermsen@oakland.edu
HERNÁNDEZ, José, E ... 787-850-9300 558 A
jose.hernandez27@upr.edu
HERNÁNDEZ,
Mariana, T .... 787-740-1611 556 F
mariana.hernandez@uccaribe.edu
HERNÁNDEZ, Nannette . 787-265-3863 558 B
aeconomica@uprm.edu
HERNÁNDEZ, Olga .... 787-834-5151 555 F
olgan_hernandez@pucpr.edu
HERNÁNDEZ-AVEVEDO,
Brenda .... 787-884-3838 550 E
bacevedo@atenascollege.edu
HERNÁNDEZ NÚÑEZ,
Maria, L .... 787-884-3838 550 E
presidenta@atenascollege.edu
HERN, Marcia, J .... 502-852-8300 201 A
m.hern@louisville.edu
HERNANDEZ, Albert ..... 303-765-3183.. 83 C
ahernandez@iliff.edu
HERNANDEZ, Alex .... 915-831-6383 473 J
aherna78@epcc.edu
HERNANDEZ, Alfredo ... 561-732-4424 112 C
ahernandez@svdp.edu
HERNANDEZ, Ana .... 813-974-4262 116 B
ahernandez@usf.edu
HERNANDEZ, Anna .... 786-331-1000 109 B
ahernandez@maufl.edu
HERNANDEZ,
Aracely, C .... 956-326-2232 485 B
achernandez@tamiu.edu
HERNANDEZ, Arnold ..... 208-459-5868 137 J
ahernandez@collegeofidaho.edu
HERNANDEZ, Arthur ..... 361-825-2661 485 F
art.hernandez@tamucc.edu
HERNANDEZ, Axel, N .... 858-499-0202.. 40 G
ahernandez@coleman.edu
HERNANDEZ, Ayana, D 919-530-7266 370 C
ahernandez@nccu.edu
HERNANDEZ, Caridad .. 305-821-3333 104 C
csanchez@fnu.edu
HERNANDEZ, Carlos .... 936-294-2686 489 A
jch060@shsu.edu
HERNANDEZ, Carol ...... 415-485-9506.. 41 B
chernandez@marin.edu
HERNANDEZ, Carolyn .. 214-768-1979 482 J
hernandez@smu.edu
HERNANDEZ, Cathy ...... 602-286-8028.. 14 M
cathleen.hernandez@gwmail.maricopa.edu
HERNANDEZ, Christine 916-558-2438.. 53 B
hernana2@scc.losrios.edu
HERNANDEZ, Christine 787-786-3030 556 E
chernandez@ucb.edu.pr
HERNANDEZ, Cledia ..... 956-364-4530 487 H
cledia.hernandez@tstc.edu
HERNANDEZ, David ...... 805-565-6164.. 76 K
dhernand@westmont.edu
HERNANDEZ, Deanne ... 713-500-3192 495 A
Deanne.M.Hernandez@uth.tmc.edu
HERNANDEZ, Dino .... 650-508-3512.. 56 H
dhernandez@ndnu.edu
HERNANDEZ, Edwin ..... 407-303-5619.. 97 J
edwin.hernandez@adu.edu
HERNANDEZ, Edwin ..... 787-881-1212 555 F
edwin_hernandez@pucpr.edu
HERNANDEZ, Eliza .... 210-486-4913 466 K
ehernandez716@alamo.edu
HERNANDEZ, Elizabeth . 305-284-2777 108 J
elizabeth.hernandez@ncahealthcare.com
HERNANDEZ, Erika .... 281-459-7680 481 F
erika.hernandez@sjcd.edu
HERNANDEZ, Evelyn ..... 360-475-7600 524 H
ehernandez@olympic.edu
HERNANDEZ, Felix .... 805-922-6966.. 26 H
fhernandez@hancockcollege.edu
HERNANDEZ, Frank ...... 847-214-7442 144 F
fhernandez@elgin.edu
HERNANDEZ, Frank ...... 432-552-2120 495 F
hernandez_f@utpb.edu
HERNANDEZ, Grace ...... 806-742-2121 489 F
grace.hernandez@ttu.edu
HERNANDEZ, Harry ...... 787-738-2161 557 G
harry.hernandez2@upr.edu
HERNANDEZ, Isabel ..... 787-725-6500 551 A
ihernandez@sju.albizu.edu
HERNANDEZ, Jean .... 425-640-1515 522 D
jean.hernandez@edcc.edu
HERNANDEZ, Jennifer .. 787-753-6335 552 K
jhernandez@icprjc.edu
HERNANDEZ, John .... 714-628-4886.. 60 H
hernandez_john@sccollege.edu
HERNANDEZ, John, L .. 212-678-3379 349 I
hernandez@tc.columbia.edu
HERNANDEZ, Jorge ...... 808-739-4640 135 A
jhernand@chaminade.edu
HERNANDEZ, Jose .... 813-974-4373 116 B
jehernan@usf.edu
HERNANDEZ,
Josephine .... 973-341-1600 304 F
hernandez@pccc.edu
HERNANDEZ, Juan, C .. 787-279-2250 553 H
jchernandez@bayamon.inter.edu
HERNANDEZ, Justin, J . 660-944-2851 273 E
justin@conception.edu
HERNANDEZ, Kristi ...... 701-662-1692 375 A
Kristi.Hernandez@lrsc.edu
HERNANDEZ, Liliyea .... 847-290-6425 155 A
HERNANDEZ, Luis, A ... 787-720-4476 556 G
presidente@mizpa.edu
HERNANDEZ, Luz, S .... 787-620-2040 550 D
lhernandez@aupr.edu
HERNANDEZ,
Madelline .... 818-364-7618.. 51 G
hernanm@lamission.edu
HERNANDEZ, Maria ...... 715-422-5469 543 D
maria.hernandez@mstc.edu
HERNANDEZ,
Maria Waleska .... 787-620-2040 550 D
mhernandez@aupr.edu
HERNANDEZ, Michael .. 757-352-4571 511 G
michher@regent.edu
HERNANDEZ, Michelle . 212-616-7278 327 D
michelle.hernandez@heleneful d.edu
HERNANDEZ, Nina .... 908-709-7127 309 A
hernandez@ucc.edu
HERNANDEZ, Noe .... 432-837-8603 489 B
noeh@sulross.edu
HERNANDEZ, Oscar ...... 956-872-2522 482 G
oscarh@southtexascollege.edu
HERNANDEZ, Otto .... 609-343-4978 299 G
hernande@atlantic.edu
HERNANDEZ, Pablo ...... 956-872-5051 482 G
HERNANDEZ, JR., Paul 956-872-8372 482 G
phernan@southtexascollege.edu
HERNANDEZ, Rachelle . 612-625-2006 265 C
HERNANDEZ, Ramon .... 787-841-2000 555 F
ramon_hernandezcruz@pucpr.edu
HERNANDEZ, Raul .... 787-284-1912 554 B
rhernand@ponce.inter.edu
HERNANDEZ, Raymond 650-738-4221.. 64 E
hernandezr@smccd.edu
HERNANDEZ, Rebecca .. 503-554-2147 406 A
rhernandez@georgefox.edu
HERNANDEZ, Richard ... 760-252-2411.. 29 C
rhernandez@barstow.edu
HERNANDEZ, Ruth, E .... 787-279-1912 553 H
rehernandez@bayamon.inter.edu
HERNANDEZ, Samuel ... 787-882-2065 556 C
asistencia_economica@unitecpr.net
HERNANDEZ, Sheila ..... 831-582-3632.. 34 C
shernandez@csumb.edu
HERNANDEZ, Susan ..... 214-645-5485 496 A
susan.hernandez@utsouthwestern.edu
HERNANDEZ,
Thomas, J .... 585-395-2510 345 A
thernand@brockport.edu
HERNANDEZ, Tiffany .... 817-202-6628 483 C
tiffanym@swau.edu
HERNANDEZ, Todd .... 419-267-1445 387 G
thernandez@northweststate.edu
HERNANDEZ, Tracy ...... 801-878-1035 296 D
thernandez@roseman.edu
HERNANDEZ, Victoria ... 305-237-3221 108 L
vhernand@mdc.edu
HERNANDEZ, Wanda .... 646-565-6000 350 C
wandau@touro.edu
HERNANDEZ, Wendie ... 254-659-7503 475 A
whernandez@hillcollege.edu
HERNANDEZ, West .... 307-754-6103 546 I
West.Hernandez@nwc.edu
HERNANDEZ, Wilfredo . 787-754-7120 553 C
HERNANDEZ, Yesenia .. 787-894-2828 558 F
yesemoa.hernandez2@upr.edu
HERNANDEZ, Yvette ..... 830-591-7318 483 A
yvetteh@swtjc.edu
HERNANDEZ BLACKSTAD,
Ana .... 425-564-2630 519 L
ana.blackstad@bellevuecollege.edu
HERNANDEZ-HUNTER,
Anna .... 503-838-8195 411 B
hernana@wou.edu
HERNANDEZ-RODRIGUEZ,
Raul .... 787-746-1400 552 I
rahernandez@huertas.edu
HERNANDEZ-SOTO,
Yezmin .... 787-728-1515 559 A
yhernandez@sagrado.edu
HERNDON, Craig .... 804-819-4782 514 G
cherndon@vccs.edu
HERNDON, Doug .... 916-484-8101.. 52 I
herndod@arc.losrios.edu
HERNDON,
Kimmetha, D .... 205-726-2198.... 6 F
kherndon@samford.edu
HERNDON, OSB, Linda 913-360-7553 184 K
lherndon@benedictine.edu
HERNDON, Linda, M .... 229-226-1621 132 E
lherndon@thomasu.edu
HERNDON,
Michael (Mike) .... 817-515-5331 484 B
michael.herndon@tccd.edu
HERNDON, Steven, T ... 937-229-3317 393 E
SHerndon1@udayton.edu
HERNE, Jaclyn .... 716-839-8245 323 F
jherne@daemen.edu
HERNESS, Scott .... 614-292-9490 389 A
herness.1@osu.edu
HERNON, Michael .... 740-283-6447 382 G
mhernon@franciscan.edu

HEWERDINE, Kevin, L .. 812-877-8184 172 C kevin.l.hewerdine@rose-hulman.edu

HEWETSON, Hank ... 812-855-6169 167 J hhewetso@indiana.edu

HEWETT, James, E ... 712-749-2248 176 D hewettj@bvu.edu

HEWETT, Kelly ... 410-334-2908 221 E khewett@worwic.edu

HEWETT, Lamar ... 803-549-6314 450 F dlhewett@mailbox.sc.edu

HEWITT, Bradley, L ... 618-650-2871 159 I bhewitt@siue.edu

HEWITT, Chris ... 602-943-2311.. 18 K

HEWITT, Dawn ... 718-262-2060 321 B hewittd@york.cuny.edu

HEWITT, Emma ... 712-274-6400 184 A emma.hewitt@witcc.edu

HEWITT, Gordon, J ... 315-859-4084 327 A ghewitt@hamilton.edu

HEWITT, JR., Harold, W ... 714-997-6815.. 38 B hewitt@chapman.edu

HEWITT, Mark, S ... 781-736-2010 224 F mhewitt@brandeis.edu

HEWITT, Michael ... 718-951-5131 318 F mhewitt@brooklyn.cuny.edu

HEWITT, Nathaniel ... 903-923-2404 497 G nhewitt@wileyc.edu

HEWITT, Russ ... 402-826-8295 290 C russ.hewitt@doane.edu

HEWITT, Scott ... 657-278-2714.. 33 E shewitt@fullerton.edu

HEWITT, Stephany ... 843-574-6922 449 G stephany.hewitt@tridenttech.edu

HEWITT BOYD, Kimberly ... 612-624-9547 265 C boyd009@umn.edu

HEWITT-CLARKE, Gail ... 301-295-1667 548 D gail-selina.hewitt-clarke@usuhs.edu

HEWITT WATKINS, Sharon ... 718-990-3369 340 G hewittws@stjohns.edu

HEXTER, Ralph, J ... 530-752-4964.. 71 A provost@ucdavis.edu

HEY, Jeanne ... 207-602-2371 213 B Jhey@une.edu

HEYDARI, Shahryar ... 706-778-8500 130 B sheydari@piedmont.edu

HEYE, Nick ... 858-653-6740.. 48 Q NHeye@JPCatholic.com

HEYER, Cary, R ... 608-246-6443 543 C

HEYER, Doreen, E ... 213-738-6801.. 68 E academicadmin@swlaw.edu

HEYING, Lori ... 319-363-1323 181 D lheying@mtmercy.edu

HEYING, Steve ... 210-829-6023 492 B lindaw@uiwtx.edu

HEYLIGER, Wynton ... 404-527-4520 122 D wheyliger@carver.edu

HEYMAN, George ... 585-271-3657 340 B gheyman@stbernards.edu

HEYMAN, George, P ... 585-271-3657 340 B gheyman@stbernards.edu

HEYMAN, Jeffrey ... 510-466-7369.. 58 I jheyman@peralta.edu

HEYMAN, Jeffrey ... 510-466-7369.. 58 J jheyman@peralta.edu

HEYMAN, Jeffrey ... 510-466-7369.. 59 C jheyman@peralta.edu

HEYMANN, Jody ... 310-825-6381.. 71 D jheymann@ucla.edu

HEYNDERICKX, Roy, F . 360-438-4307 525 H president@stmartin.edu

HEYNING, Katharina, E 262-472-1101 541 D heyningk@uww.edu

HEYWARD, ILene ... 340-693-1101 559 B iheywar@live.uvi.edu

HEYWARD, Kerry, L ... 404-413-0500 126 D kheyward@gsu.edu

HEYWARD, Loretta ... 912-358-3049 131 A heywardl@savannahstate.edu

HEYWARD, Toyia ... 610-683-4102 431 B heyward@kutztown.edu

HIATT, Aaron ... 510-593-2923.. 65 D ahiatt@saybrook.edu

HIATT, Edwin, L ... 229-333-5886 133 H elhiatt@valdosta.edu

HIATT, Elaine ... 614-825-6255 376 C ehiatt@aiam.edu

HIATT, Jim ... 615-248-1256 464 E Jhiatt@trevecca.edu

HIATT, Jim ... 615-248-1613 464 E jhiatt@trevecca.edu

HIATT, Jon ... 605-331-6636 454 E jon.hiatt@usiouxfalls.edu

HIBBARD, J. Todd ... 313-993-1088 250 H hibbarja@udmercy.edu

HIBBARD, Steve, V ... 262-243-5700 535 I steve.hibbard@cuw.edu

HIBBARD, Susan ... 239-489-9013 104 G shibbard@fsw.edu

HIBBERD, Charles ... 402-472-2966 293 H hibberd@unl.edu

HIBBS, Randy ... 920-206-2318 536 T randy.hibbs@mbu.edu

HIBBS, Thomas, S ... 254-710-7689 469 D thomas_hibbs@baylor.edu

HIBLER, Dirk ... 904-819-6336 102 P dhibler@flagler.edu

HIBNER, Lisa ... 225-216-8244 202 N hibnerl@mybrcc.edu

HICE, Muriel ... 269-488-4410 244 J mhice@kvcc.edu

HICHWA, Richard, D ... 319-335-2106 175 H richard-hichwa@uiowa.edu

HICKE, Linda, A ... 512-471-3285 493M cnsdean@austin.utexas.edu

HICKERSON, Amanda ... 502-447-1000 199 G ahickerson@spencerian.edu

HICKERSON, Jim ... 812-866-6741 166 E hickerson@hanover.edu

HICKERSON, Keith, E ... 610-526-1000 412 D keith.hickerson@theamericancollege.edu

HICKEY, Bill ... 320-363-5480 254 J whickey@csbsju.edu

HICKEY, David ... 513-569-1448 379 K david.hickey@cincinnatistate.edu

HICKEY, Dean ... 617-243-2141 227 K dhickey@lasell.edu

HICKEY, Diane ... 678-891-2304 125 G diane.hickey@gpc.edu

HICKEY, J. Michael ... 603-641-4107 299 B mike.hickey@unh.edu

HICKEY, Jane ... 410-455-1517 219 F jchickey@umbc.edu

HICKEY, Jay ... 401-841-6515 548 B

HICKEY, John, M ... 253-879-3203 527 F hickey@pugetsound.edu

HICKEY, Lynn ... 210-458-4444 494 D lynn.hickey@utsa.edu

HICKEY, Melissa ... 845-675-4424 337 B melissa.hickey@nyack.edu

HICKEY, JR., Robert, E 937-775-3326 396 A robert.hickey@wright.edu

HICKEY, Sarah ... 614-890-3000 390 C shickey@otterbein.edu

HICKL, Frank ... 979-230-3157 469 G frank.hickl@brazosport.edu

HICKMAN, Carla ... 314-889-1416 275 B chickman@fontbonne.edu

HICKMAN, Heather ... 415-749-4540.. 62 I hhickman@sfai.edu

HICKMAN, Joseph ... 406-243-2412 287 D joseph.hickman@umontana.edu

HICKMAN, Melissa ... 706-292-3920 131 C mhickman@shorter.edu

HICKMAN, Randall ... 586-445-7866 246 A hickmanr@macomb.edu

HICKMAN, Saeedah ... 718-960-8357 319 C saeedah.hickman@lehman.cuny.edu

HICKMAN, Tanner ... 901-751-8453 459 C thickman@mabts.edu

HICKMAN, Thomas, N .. 803-323-2129 451 I hickmant@winthrop.edu

HICKMAN, Tim ... 909-558-4532.. 50 K thickman@llu.edu

HICKMAN, Tom ... 701-671-2354 375 B tom.hickman@ndscs.edu

HICKMAN, Tracy ... 386-752-1822 103 Q tracy.hickman@fgc.edu

HICKMAN, Wesley ... 803-777-7440 450 B whickman@mailbox.sc.edu

HICKMAN, Wesley, T ... 803-777-7440 450 B whickman@mailbox.sc.edu

HICKOX, Chad ... 206-934-5201 526 B chad.hickox@seattlecolleges.edu

HICKS, Barbara ... 928-541-7777.. 16 B bhicks@ncu.edu

HICKS, Brenda, D ... 620-229-6387 191 B brenda.hicks@sckans.edu

HICKS, Brian, A ... 336-734-7191 362 F bhicks@forsythtech.edu

HICKS, Bruce ... 310-287-4307.. 52 C hicksbr@wlac.edu

HICKS, Bryan ... 256-372-4014.... 1 A byran.hicks@aamu.edu

HICKS, JR., Cecil ... 402-554-2321 294 A chicks@unomaha.edu

HICKS, Cheryl ... 816-414-3700 278 E chicks@mbts.edu

HICKS, Cheryl ... 816-414-3700 278 E financialaid@mbts.edu

HICKS, Cliff ... 360-442-2441 524 A chicks@lowercolumbia.edu

HICKS, David, L ... 610-292-9852 433 J bishophicks@comcast.net

HICKS, Deanita ... 870-762-3146.. 19 C dhicks@smail.anc.edu

HICKS, Debbie, L ... 757-455-3338 518 H dlhicks@vwc.edu

HICKS, Dennis ... 765-973-8456 168 A dehicks@iue.edu

HICKS, Ed ... 334-386-7309.... 3 I ehicks@faulkner.edu

HICKS, Elena ... 410-617-2251 216 D ehicks@loyola.edu

HICKS, Elizabeth, M ... 617-253-4090 233 C

HICKS, J. David ... 423-652-4782 457 J jdhicks@king.edu

HICKS, Janet, K ... 570-586-2400 435 H jhicks@summitu.edu

HICKS, Janine, M ... 815-740-2272 162 F jhicks@stfrancis.edu

HICKS, Jim ... 423-425-4246 465 E jim-hicks@utc.edu

HICKS, Jimmy ... 691-320-2480 549 D jhicks@comfsm.fm

HICKS, Juanita ... 678-839-6424 133 F jhicks@westga.edu

HICKS, Jud ... 806-457-4200 474 E jhicks@fpctx.edu

HICKS, Julia ... 860-685-2100.. 93 B jhicks@wesleyan.edu

HICKS, Kelly ... 918-343-7573 401 I kellyhicks@rsu.edu

HICKS, Kenneth ... 215-248-7103 415 D hicksk@chc.edu

HICKS, Loretta ... 404-297-9522 126 A hicksl@gptc.edu

HICKS, Louis, E ... 240-895-4392 218 B lehicks@smcm.edu

HICKS, Marcus ... 404-297-9522 126 A hicksm@gptc.edu

HICKS, Marie ... 215-568-9215 426 C mhicks@phmc.org

HICKS, Michael ... 706-821-8350 129 H mhicks@paine.edu

HICKS, Minora ... 803-327-7402 444 F mhicks@clintoncollege.edu

HICKS, Mona, L ... 561-803-2174 109 G mona_hicks@pba.edu

HICKS, Ramona ... 314-977-5028 281M rhicks1@slu.edu

HICKS, Renee, G ... 985-493-2556 208 C renee.hicks@nicholls.edu

HICKS, Rickey, P ... 706-729-2260 121 C rhicks@gru.edu

HICKS, Scott ... 910-775-4032 371 D scott.hicks@uncp.edu

HICKS, Scott, M ... 434-592-4808 509 G smhicks@liberty.edu

HICKS, Terence ... 423-439-7616 461 D hickstl1@etsu.edu

HICKS, Terence ... 936-261-3600 484 F tlhicks@pvamu.edu

HICKS, Terri, L ... 205-226-4625.... 2 C thicks@bsc.edu

HICKS, Timothy, J ... 315-859-4790 327 A thicks@hamilton.edu

HICKS, Tom ... 319-399-8741 176 G thicks@coe.edu

HICKS, Virginia ... 304-876-5712 532 I vhicks@shepherd.edu

HICKS, Wanda ... 706-355-5160 120 G whicks@athenstech.edu

HICKS, Willie ... 501-420-1232.. 19 B willie.hicks@arkansasbaptist.edu

HICKSON, Kathy ... 325-235-7402 488 C kathy.hickson@tstc.edu

HICSWA, Stefani ... 307-754-6200 546 I Stefani.Hicswa@nwc.edu

HIDALGO, Lisa ... 985-448-7939 203 G lisa.hidalgo@fletcher.edu

HIDALGO, Rommel ... 657-278-5742.. 33 E rhidalgo@fullerton.edu

HIEBER, Ali ... 540-891-3016 515 E ahieber@germanna.edu

HIEBERT, Theodore ... 773-947-6307 152 A

HIEDEMAN, Ann ... 218-477-2066 260 B ann.hiedeman@mnstate.edu

HIEL, Edwin ... 619-388-3036.. 62 F ehiel@sdccd.edu

HIELEMA, Leslie ... 407-629-7259 103 R lhielema@fit.edu

HIEMENZ, Karen, A ... 320-308-5017 261 F khiemenz@sctcc.edu

HIEMSTRA, Ted ... 206-378-5478 526 D hiemstra@spu.edu

HIERS, Richard ... 314-434-4044 273 J richard.hiers@covenantseminary.edu

HIESIGER, Linda ... 413-585-2231 236 G lhiesige@smith.edu

HIETALA, David ... 218-855-8058 258 C DHietala@clcmn.edu

HIETALA, Robert ... 406-994-5523 287 G robert.hietala@montana.edu

HIETAPELTO, Amy ... 218-726-7281 264 G lsbe@d.umn.edu

HIETSCH, Stephen, C ... 717-245-1891 417 B hietschs@dickinson.edu

HIGA, Pat ... 949-582-4585.. 67 F phiga@saddleback.edu

HIGASHI, Guy, S ... 541-485-1780 407 H guyhigashi@newhope.edu

HIGASHI, Lori ... 541-485-1780 407 H lorihigashi@enewhope.edu

HIGBEE, Isabelle ... 601-974-1220 268 D higbeie@millsaps.edu

HIGDEM, Julie ... 763-488-2453 258 G julie.higdem@hennepintech.edu

HIGDON, Albert ... 573-629-3011 275 F Albert.Higdon@hlg.edu

HIGDON, Hal, L ... 417-447-2602 280 C higdonh@otc.edu

HIGDON, Jo Ann ... 310-660-3107.. 43 G jhigdon@elcamino.edu

HIGDON, Jo Ann ... 310-660-3670.. 43 G jhigdon@elcamino.edu

HIGGINBOTHAM, Debra ... 940-397-4120 478 G debra.higginbotham@mwsu.edu

HIGGINBOTHAM, Karen ... 212-472-1500 336 A khigginbotham@nysid.edu

HIGGINS, Brandon ... 903-823-3024 484 D brandon.higgins@texarkanacollege.edu

HIGGINS, Brenda ... 660-785-4562 283 E bhiggins@truman.edu

HIGGINS, Dalton ... 918-335-6865 400 I dhiggins@okwu.edu

HIGGINS, Dawn ... 603-271-6484 297 C dhiggins@ccsnh.edu

HIGGINS, Diana ... 309-341-5341 140 I dhiggins@sandburg.edu

HIGGINS, Elizabeth ... 207-780-4632 213 A bhiggins@maine.maine.edu

HIGGINS, Elizabeth ... 518-262-5831 314 I higgine@mail.amc.edu

HIGGINS, Kacey ... 325-670-1368 474M Kacey.Higgins@hsutx.edu

HIGGINS, Linda, A ... 803-641-3476 450 C LindaHi@usca.edu

HIGGINS, Lisa ... 716-829-7542 324 E higginsl@dyc.edu

HIGGINS, Margaret ... 828-398-7302 360 A margaretahiggins@abtech.edu

HIGGINS, Mark ... 314-977-3833 281M markhiggins@slu.edu

HIGGINS, Michael ... 314-434-4044 273 J mike.higgins@covenantseminary.edu

HIGGINS, Michael, J ... 203-371-7902.. 91 G higginsmw@sacredheart.edu

HIGGINS, TOR, Michael, J ... 760-547-1800.. 45 B mjhiggins@fst.edu

HIGGINS, Peter, J ... 678-359-5156 126 E phiggins@gordonstate.edu

HIGGINS, Richard, J ... 518-564-2040 346 B higginrj@plattsburgh.edu

HIGGINS, Ronnell, A ... 203-432-9455.. 93 C ronnell.higgins@yale.edu

HIGGINS, Sandra ... 718-260-5700 320 D shiggins@citytech.cuny.edu

HIGGINS, Sharon ... 410-617-5025 216 D sbhiggins@loyola.edu

HIGGINS, Tammy ... 620-235-4240 190 G thiggins@pittstate.edu

HIGGINS, Terri ... 641-782-1431 183 D thiggins@swcciowa.edu

HIGGINS, Thomas, J ... 518-564-3013 346 B higgintj@plattsburgh.edu

HIGGS, David ... 601-643-8376 266 J david.higgs@colin.edu

HIGGS, Jessica ... 309-677-2700 140 H jhiggs@bradley.edu

HIGGS, John ... 724-480-3558 416 A john.higgs@ccbc.edu

HIGGS, Ronnie ... 831-582-4363.. 34 C rhiggs@csumb.edu

HIGGS, Toni ... 904-256-7954 106 Q thiggs@ju.edu

HIGH, Katherine, N ... 865-974-3843 465 C khigh@tennessee.edu

HIGHAM, Pamela, S ... 814-332-3576 411 F phigham@allegheny.edu

HIGHERS, Cami ... 918-444-4200 398M highersc@nsuok.edu

HIGHERS, Michael ... 408-270-6490.. 63 P michael.highers@evc.edu

HIGHLEY, Melinda, C ... 606-783-2033 198 H m.highley@moreheadstate.edu

HIGHSMITH, Manique ... 212-247-3434 331 G rhighsmith@mandl.edu

HIGHTOWER, Damara ... 803-705-4438 443 F hightowerd@benedict.edu

HIGHTOWER, Darlene ... 405-744-3555 400 C darlene.hightower@okstate.edu

HIGHTOWER, Diane, D . 724-925-4050 439 F hightowerd@wccc.edu

HIGHTOWER, Jacqueline ... 850-599-3225 114 D jacqueline.hightower@famu.edu

HIGHTOWER, Jennifer .. 713-221-8978 491 F hightowerj@uhd.edu

HIGINBOTHAM, Lynn, E 212-998-4444 336 C lynn.higinbotham@nyu.edu

HIGLEY, Bethann 302-225-6256 94 B higleyb@gbc.edu

HIGLEY, David 203-591-5042 91 D dhigley@post.edu

HIGLEY, Tony 509-434-5123 521 E tony.higley@ccs.spokane.edu

HIGLEY, Tony 509-434-5123 521 F thigley@ccs.spokane.edu

HIGLEY, Tony, D 509-434-5123 521 D thigley@ccs.spokane.edu

HIGLEY, William, J 570-586-2400 435 H whigley@summitu.edu

HIHEGLO, Ignace 706-396-7570 129 H ihiheglo@paine.edu

HIJLEH, Mark 212-659-7200 330 A mhijleh@tkc.edu

HILARIO, Francis 787-704-1020 552 D fhilario@ediccollege.edu

HILBERT, Diane 972-238-6250 473 B dhilbert@dcccd.edu

HILBERT, Michael 814-732-2826 430 G mhilbert@edinboro.edu

HILBERT, Pamela 910-272-3230 365 D philbert@robeson.edu

HILBORN, David 216-381-1680 388 A dhilborn@ndc.edu

HILBRANDS, Steve 616-538-2330 243 C shilbrands@gbcol.edu

HILBY, Jim 414-382-6327 534 I jim.hilby@alverno.edu

HILD, Ann 307-766-4286 546 K annhild@uwyo.edu

HILD, Glenn, J 217-581-2917 144 E gjhild@eiu.edu

HILDEBRAND, Carol 415-485-9306 41 B childebrand@marin.edu

HILDEBRAND, Jane 563-387-1008 180 M hildebja@luther.edu

HILDEBRAND, Kathryn 334-670-3365 8 A khildebrand@troy.edu

HILDEBRANDT, Kristin, A 414-410-4007 535 C kahildebrandt@stritch.edu

HILDERBRAND, Carey 801-274-3280 501 B carey.hilderbrand@wgu.edu

HILDRETH, Brandon 573-681-5205 276 K hildrethb@lincolnu.edu

HILDRETH, James E.K 615-327-6904 458 F jhildreth@mmc.edu

HILEMAN, Jeffrey 814-732-1333 430 G jhileman@edinboro.edu

HILES, Jason 602-639-7500 14 A

HILES, Tom 573-882-7703 283 H hilest@missouri.edu

HILGENBRINK, Robert, J 618-235-2700 160 B robert.hilgenbrink@swic.edu

HILGERSOM, Karin, M 845-434-5750 349 C khilgersom@sunysullivan.edu

HILKE, David 412-536-1104 422 E david.hilke@laroche.edu

HILKE, Jurgen 301-846-2401 214 I jhilke@frederic.edu

HILL, Alan, P 765-361-6450 175 B hilla@wabash.edu

HILL, Amber 928-524-7484 16 E amber.hill@npc.edu

HILL, Angeline 707-476-4364 41 C angeline-hill@redwoods.edu

HILL, Art 541-278-5863 404 J ahill@bluecc.edu

HILL, Ashley 601-477-4039 268 A ashley.hill@jcjc.edu

HILL, Brandi 931-372-3317 462 A bhill@tntech.edu

HILL, Brian, W 540-231-5107 507 D bhill@vcom.vt.edu

HILL, Calvin, R 413-748-3552 236 H chill@springfieldcollege.edu

HILL, Catharine, B 845-437-7200 351 H hill@vassar.edu

HILL, Chris 801-581-5605 499 K chill@huntsman.utah.edu

HILL, Chris 619-644-7108 46 H chris.hill@gcccd.edu

HILL, Christopher, J 412-392-4707 433 F chill@pointpark.edu

HILL, Christopher, R 303-871-2539 86 H Christopher.R.Hill@du.edu

HILL, Cliff 312-752-2110 149 D clifford.hill@kendall.edu

HILL, Craig 585-389-2591 334 B chill0@naz.edu

HILL, Curtis 435-865-8621 499 L hillc@suu.edu

HILL, Curtis 903-785-7661 480 B chill@parisjc.edu

HILL, Dachea 269-387-2000 252 I dachea.hill@wmich.edu

HILL, Deana 570-484-2014 431 C dhill@lhup.edu

HILL, Deborah 435-865-8628 499 L hilld@suu.edu

HILL, Deidra, W 212-650-5310 318 G dhill@ccny.cuny.edu

HILL, Deidre, N 253-535-7101 524 I hilldn@plu.edu

HILL, Dennis 479-394-7622 22 H dhill@rmcc.edu

HILL, Diana 770-394-8300 120 E diahill@aii.edu

HILL, Diane 973-353-1630 307 C dianeh@andromeda.rutgers.edu

HILL, Doree 252-222-6282 361 A hilld@carteret.edu

HILL, Doris 763-488-0129 260 E dhill@nhcc.edu

HILL, Edward 478-825-6211 124 E

HILL, Elizabeth 360-596-5416 527 B bhill@spscc.edu

HILL, Erin 302-857-6351 93 E ehill@desu.edu

HILL, Fitz 501-420-1202 19 B fitzhill@hotmail.com

HILL, Flo 229-430-4879 119 H flo.hill@asurams.edu

HILL, G. Richard 801-626-7313 500 C grhill@weber.edu

HILL, Gladys 205-391-2457 7 A ghill@sheltonstate.edu

HILL, Henderson 931-221-6274 461 C hillh@apsu.edu

HILL, Holly, L 904-826-8636 102 P Hhill@flagler.edu

HILL, Jamie 309-796-5284 140 D hillj@bhc.edu

HILL, Janeen 714-628-7223 38 B jhill@chapman.edu

HILL, Janice 973-290-4468 301 F jhill01@cse.edu

HILL, Jean 505-454-3562 311 H jlhill@nmhu.edu

HILL, Jeff 630-434-7655 163 D jhill@westwood.edu

HILL, Jennifer 256-352-8032 10 A jennifer.hill@wallacestate.edu

HILL, John 256-726-7353 6 C jhill@oakwood.edu

HILL, Joseph 215-503-0033 436 F joseph.hill@jefferson.edu

HILL, Joslyn 405-425-5476 399 J joslyn.hill@oc.edu

HILL, Kady 336-887-3000 358 E khill@laureluniversity.edu

HILL, Kate 513-244-8181 379 I kate.hill@ccuniversity.edu

HILL, Kelli 309-268-8100 145 H kelli.hill@heartland.edu

HILL, Kelly 352-588-7560 111 L kelly.hill02@saintleo.edu

HILL, Ken 207-801-5630 210 B khill@coa.edu

HILL, Larry 773-702-2060 161 D lhill@uchicago.edu

HILL, Laura 208-769-3272 138 G ljhill2@nic.edu

HILL, Leah 252-985-5291 367 E lhill@ncwc.edu

HILL, Leon 215-641-6674 426 E hlhill@mc3.edu

HILL, Lisa 252-940-6223 360 B lisa.hill@beaufortccc.edu

HILL, Marie 617-587-5678 234 G hillm@neco.edu

HILL, Marion 214-333-5261 471 L marion@dbu.edu

HILL, Mark 651-641-8223 255 C hill@csp.edu

HILL, Mark, J 315-470-6670 347 B mjhill@esf.edu

HILL, Mary 202-806-2550 96 B marHill@howard.edu

HILL, Mary, M 989-774-3481 240 O hill1mm@cmich.edu

HILL, Mathew, B 651-631-5362 265 D mbhill@unwsp.edu

HILL, Melissa 509-865-0411 523 C hill_m@heritage.edu

HILL, Melissa, D 812-941-2359 169 A mhill02@ius.edu

HILL, Michael 610-328-8067 436 A mhill1@swarthmore.edu

HILL, Michelle 225-771-2350 206 K michelle_hill@sus.edu

HILL, Michelle, D 757-823-8135 510 H mdhill@nsu.edu

HILL, Miriam 651-638-6415 254 A m-hill@bethel.edu

HILL, Nelson, W 585-594-6944 339 F hill_nelson@roberts.edu

HILL, Paul, L 304-558-0699 532 C paul.hill@hepc.wvnet.edu

HILL, Reggie 352-588-8283 111 L reggie.hill@saintleo.edu

HILL, Reinhold 708-534-4101 145 D rhill@govst.edu

HILL, Renee 514-287-5299 380 G rhill39@cscc.edu

HILL, Rick 252-222-6153 361 A hillr@carteret.edu

HILL, Robert 701-777-2674 373 G robert.hill@und.edu

HILL, Robert, A 617-353-3560 224 E rahill@bu.edu

HILL, Robert, W 936-468-3501 484 A rhill@sfasu.edu

HILL, S. Trent 361-825-5749 485 F trent.hill@tamucc.edu

HILL, Sam 703-878-5778 516 C shill@nvcc.edu

HILL, Scott 540-985-4693 509 D bshill@jchs.edu

HILL, Sean 618-468-6000 150 E shill@lc.edu

HILL, Shannon 805-546-3279 42 H shannon_hill@cuesta.edu

HILL, Shantey 631-687-1445 341 A shill4@sjcny.edu

HILL, Sharon 781-891-2108 223 E shill@bentley.edu

HILL, Sheila, M 706-771-4840 121 B shill@augustatech.edu

HILL, Sherri 203-837-8200 88 G

HILL, Shirley 901-435-1450 457 N shirley_hill@loc.edu

HILL, Stephen, E 801-422-4104 497 J steve_hill@byu.edu

HILL, Steve 575-492-2643 311 J shill@nmjc.edu

HILL, Teresa, A 256-551-3130 4 J teresa.hill@drakestate.edu

HILL, Thomas, L 515-294-4420 175 G tomhill@iastate.edu

HILL, Tina 434-947-8537 511 D thill@randolphcollege.edu

HILL, Travis, R 315-859-4023 327 A thill@hamilton.edu

HILL, Valerie, D 512-505-3060 475 G vdhill@htu.edu

HILL, Vicki 918-647-1373 397 C vhill@carlalbert.edu

HILL, W. Timothy 801-422-7011 497 J wthill@byu.edu

HILL, W. Weldon 804-524-5997 518 C whill@vsu.edu

HILL, Walter, A 334-727-8157 8 B hillwa@mytu.tuskegee.edu

HILL, Wanda 513-921-9856 379 G wanda.hill@chatfield.edu

HILL, Wayne, R 330-972-2148 392 H whill@uakron.edu

HILL, Wes 252-246-1339 367 D whill@wilsoncc.edu

HILL, William 713-646-1764 482 H whill@kennedywilson.com

HILL, William 732-571-3580 303 G hill@monmouth.edu

HILL, II, William, L 215-965-4022 426 G whill@moore.edu

HILL, JR., Willie, L 413-545-3517 228 F drwhill@aol.com

HILL, Wynn, N 208-496-9204 137 F hillw@byui.edu

HILL-CHEATOM, Petrina 716-851-1120 325 A cheatom@ecc.edu

HILL-CLARKE, Kandi 812-237-2919 167 E kandi.hill-clarke@indstate.edu

HILL-FLANAGAN, LaVerne, M 202-274-6069 97 B lflanagan@udc.edu

HILL GETZ, Janet 309-268-8170 145 H janet.hill-getz@heartland.edu

HILLARD, Cecilia, J 414-955-8493 537 C jhillard@mcw.edu

HILLBERRY, Kai 303-477-7240 82 M kais@heritage-education.com

HILLE, Jim 817-257-7031 486 G j.hille@tcu.edu

HILLEMEIER, A. Craig 717-531-8323 428 C ach10@psu.edu

HILLENBRAND, Bruce 845-451-1286 323 E b_hillen@culinary.edu

HILLER, Jerry 315-279-5244 329 K jhiller@keuka.edu

HILLER, Renee 906-487-2281 247 A rlhiller@mtu.edu

HILLER-FREUND, Darby, L 937-327-6231 395 I hillerd@wittenberg.edu

HILLERMAN, Donnie 660-359-3948 279 L dhillerman@mail.ncmissouri.edu

HILLERY, Barbara 516-876-3915 345 E hilleryb@oldwestbury.edu

HILLES, Sharon 909-869-3261 32 F shilles@cpp.edu

HILLESLAND, Michelle 253-589-5586 521 B michelle.hillesland@cptc.edu

HILLIAR, Mara, M 804-594-1570 515 G mhilliar@jtcc.edu

HILLIARD, Aaron 425-564-2445 519 L aaron.hilliard@bellevuecollege.edu

HILLIARD, Beth 859-256-3100 195 G beth.hilliard@kctcs.edu

HILLIARD, Colette 903-675-6306 490 F chilliard@tvcc.edu

HILLIARD, Dianne 775-445-3288 296 A dianne.hilliard@wnc.edu

HILLIS, Greg 575-439-3624 312 B ghillis@nmsu.edu

HILLIS, Michael 805-493-3422 31 H mhillis@callutheran.edu

HILLMAN, Amy 480-965-3402 11 J amy.hillman@asu.edu

HILLMAN, Brenda 925-631-4457 61 G bhillman@stmarys-ca.edu

HILLMAN, Elizabeth, L 415-565-4682 71 B hillmane@uchastings.edu

HILLMAN, Gracia 202-806-2530 96 B gracia.hillman@howard.edu

HILLMAN, Jan 937-484-1297 394 F jhillman@urbana.edu

HILLMAN, Melinda 865-481-2000 463 F hillmanmk@roanestate.edu

HILLMAN, Michel 816-604-1070 277 F michel.hillman@mcckc.edu

HILLS, Amy 616-988-1000 241 E amy.h@compass.edu

HILLS, Fred 254-299-8661 478 C fhills@mclennan.edu

HILLS, Jim 206-546-4634 526 G jhills@shoreline.edu

HILLS, Michael, S 740-587-6627 381 H hills@denison.edu

HILLS, Stacey 802-447-6359 503 A shills@svc.edu

HILLS, Warren, L 269-387-3895 252 I warren.l.hills@wmich.edu

HILLSTROM, Maury 310-377-5501 53 E mhillstrom@marymountcalifornia.edu

HILLYER, Jill 336-334-4079 371 C jill_hillyer@uncg.edu

HILMEY, David 716-375-2603 340 C dhilmey@sbu.edu

HILSABECK, Alison 312-261-3149 153 H ahilsabeck@nl.edu

HILSCHER, Ted 518-828-4181 322 E ted.hilscher@sunycgcc.edu

HILT, Elizabeth 650-433-3818 58 B ehilt@paloaltou.edu

HILTERBRAN, Stephen 870-543-5907 23 C shilterbran@seark.edu

HILTON, Carol 949-582-4872 67 F chilton@saddleback.edu

HILTON, Don 254-647-3234 480 G dhilton@rangercollege.edu

HILTON, III, Earl, M 336-334-7686 370 B hiltone@ncat.edu

HILTON, Eric 215-968-8123 413 F eric.hilton@bucks.edu

HILTON, James, L 734-764-9358 251 C hilton@umich.edu

HILTON, Richard, H 315-697-2300 351 E rhilton@uscny.edu

HILTON, Stacey 928-717-7775 18 L stacey.hilton@yc.edu

HILTON, Warren 215-751-8131 416 B whilton@ccp.edu

HILTON-MORROW, Wendy, S 309-794-7282 139 K wendyhilton-morrow@augustana.edu

HILTS, Deb, B 607-431-4171 327 B hiltsd@hartwick.edu

HILVO, Wendy 414-326-2337 535 H wendy.hilvo@ccon.edu

HILYER, Billy, D 334-386-7414 3 I bhilyer@faulkner.edu

HIMBEAULT-TAYLOR, Simone 734-764-5132 251 C shtaylor@umich.edu

HIMBER, David 212-960-5330 353 P himber@yu.edu

HIMBER, Richard 985-549-2064 208 E

HIMES, A.C. (Buddy) 936-468-2801 484 A himesac@sfasu.edu

HIMES, Christine 312-567-3933 147 E chimes@iit.edu

HIMES, Shane, D .... 814-641-3141 421 L
himess@juniata.edu
HIMLEY, Margaret, R .... 315-443-1137 349 E
mrhimley@syr.edu
HIMM, David .... 608-663-2000 536 S
dhimm@mediainstitute.edu
HIMMELBERGER,
Jeffrey .... 508-793-7374 225 B
jhimmelberger@clarku.edu
HIMMELBERGER,
Stacey, J .... 315-859-4416 327 A
shimmelb@hamilton.edu
HIMMELREICH, Ellen .... 607-735-1855 324 J
ehimmelreich@elmira.edu
HIMMELSTEIN, Amos ... 323-259-1347.. 56 I
himmelstein@oxy.edu
HIMSEL, Christian .... 262-243-5700 535 I
christian.himsel@cuw.edu
HINCH, Virginia .... 509-359-2329 522 C
vhinch@ewu.edu
HINCHMAN, Mary .... 760-750-4520.. 35 B
mhinchmn@csusm.edu
HINCKER, Larry .... 540-231-5396 518 B
hincker@vt.edu
HINCKLEY, Alicia, A ..... 253-535-7447 524 I
hincklaa@plu.edu
HINCKLEY, Richard .... 702-651-7488 295 C
richard.hinckley@csn.edu
HINCKLEY, Shane .... 979-845-2217 485 C
shane.hinckley@tamu.edu
HIND, Jonathan, T .... 315-859-4116 327 A
jhind@hamilton.edu
HINDELEH, Nitsa .... 314-392-2319 278 G
hindeleh@mobap.edu
HINDERLEIDER, Maria .. 602-682-6800.. 12 A
HINDERY, Michael .... 408-554-4300.. 65 A
mhindery@scu.edu
HINDES, Victoria .... 408-741-2020.. 76 F
victoria.hindes@westvalley.edu
HINDS, David .... 301-784-5000 213 C
dhinds@allegany.edu
HINDS, David .... 361-582-2560 496 D
david.hinds@victoriacollege.edu
HINDS, M. Ray .... 813-988-5131 103 L
hindsr@floridacollege.edu
HINDS, Randy, C 470-578-6755 127M
rhinds@kennesaw.edu
HINDS, Steven .... 479-619-2220.. 22 B
schinds1@nwacc.edu
HINDSON, Ed .... 434-582-7711 509 G
ehindson@liberty.edu
HINDSON, Laurie .... 512-245-7952 489 C
lh35@txstate.edu
HINE, Christopher .... 661-336-5040.. 49 D
christopher.hine@kccd.edu
HINE, James .... 415-502-3037.. 72 C
jhine@finance.ucsf.edu
HINE, Laura .... 901-272-5115 459 A
lhine@mca.edu
HINE, Mark, L .... 434-592-3240 509 G
mhine@liberty.edu
HINE, Terry .... 203-576-5072.. 91 H
thine@stvincentscollege.edu
HINEMAN, Sheri .... 712-274-5335 181 C
hineman@morningside.edu
HINERMAN, Nate .... 415-442-6510.. 46 A
nhinerman@ggu.edu
HINES, Alexander .... 507-457-5597 262 D
ahines@winona.edu
HINES, Bonnie .... 318-473-6438 205 A
hines@lsua.edu
HINES, Clay, T .... 919-866-5699 366 H
cthines@waketech.edu
HINES, Cory .... 214-333-5628 471 L
coryh@dbu.edu
HINES, Craig .... 312-662-4111 139 E
chines@adler.edu
HINES,
Deborah Harmon .... 508-856-2444 229 B
deborah-harmon.hines@umassmed.edu
HINES, Florence, W ..... 410-857-2273 217 A
fhines@mcdaniel.edu
HINES, Jacquelyn .... 313-831-5200 242 K
jhines@etseminary.edu
HINES, Jean, C 804-289-8181 513M
jhines@richmond.edu
HINES, Joseph .... 908-497-4317 309 A
joseph.hines@ucc.edu
HINES, Joseph, D .... 724-847-6518 419 B
jdh@geneva.edu
HINES, Kenneth, D .... 919-658-7755 369 B
dhines@umo.edu
HINES, Lara .... 314-392-2242 278 G
robeyl@mobap.edu
HINES, Mark .... 978-934-4000 229 A
Mark_Hines@uml.edu
HINES, Melvin .... 334-229-4505.... 1 D
mhines@alasu.edu
HINES, Nancy, A .... 563-333-6377 182 E
HinesNancyA@sau.edu
HINES, Nancy, G .... 509-777-4638 529 A
nhines@whitworth.edu
HINES, Odessa .... 919-546-8268 368 G
ohines@shawu.edu
HINES, Patrick .... 919-536-7220 362 C
hinesp@durhamtech.edu
HINES, Patti .... 619-574-6909.. 57 E
phines@pacificcollege.edu
HINES, Resche .... 386-822-7257 117 A
rhines@stetson.edu
HINES, Ruth .... 617-427-0600 233 A
rhines@rcc.mass.edu
HINES, Scott .... 650-433-3855.. 58 B
shines@paloaltou.edu
HINES, Susan .... 208-459-5826 137 J
shines@collegeofidaho.edu
HINES, Susan .... 308-432-6494 292 B
shines@csc.edu
HINES, Wendy .... 828-565-4069 363 C
whines@haywood.edu
HINEY, Delaine, S .... 712-362-0428 179 G
dhiney@iowalakes.edu
HINGA, Beth .... 712-274-5388 181 C
hingab@morningside.edu
HINGA, Gilbert .... 308-865-8528 293 G
hingag2@unk.edu
HINGELBERG, Julie ...... 313-664-7494 241 D
julieh@collegeforcreativestudies.edu
HINGSTON, Mariko ...... 415-338-1761.. 36 A
mtodd@sfsu.edu
HINKEL, Deborah .... 610-861-1364 426 H
hinkeld@moravian.edu
HINKEN, Michele .... 415-458-3726.. 43 D
michele.hinken@dominican.edu
HINKES, Madeleine ...... 619-388-2320.. 62 G
mhinkes@sdccd.edu
HINKIN, Sue .... 303-871-2525.. 86 H
sue.hinkin@du.edu
HINKLE, Adrian .... 405-789-7661 402 F
Adrian.Hinkle@swcu.edu
HINKLE, Ana .... 907-834-1612.. 11 B
ahinkle@pwscc.edu
HINKLE, Barbara .... 724-838-4206 435 E
hinkle@setonhill.edu
HINKLE, Barbara, C ...... 724-838-4218 435 E
hinkle@setonhill.edu
HINKLE, Bernadette ...... 610-436-2961 432 B
bhinkle@wcupa.edu
HINKLE, Craig .... 214-890-3837 473 B
chinkle@dcccd.edu
HINKLE, Keith .... 310-506-4898.. 58 H
keith.hinkle@pepperdine.edu
HINKLE, Lance .... 405-744-5237 400 C
lance.hinkle@okstate.edu
HINKLE, Robin .... 502-585-9911 199 E
rhinkle@spalding.edu
HINKLE, Sandy, L .... 573-651-2250 282 C
shinkle@semo.edu
HINKLE, Sara .... 610-436-3511 432 B
shinkle@wcupa.edu
HINKLEY, Lisa .... 847-735-5235 149 H
hinkley@lakeforest.edu
HINKLEY, Richard .... 434-592-3077 509 G
rdhinkle@liberty.edu
HINKS, David .... 919-515-6500 370 D
dhinks@ncsu.edu
HINKSMAN, Paul .... 610-604-7700.. 96 H
HINKSON, Avis .... 212-854-3075 315 J
ahinkson@barnard.edu
HINNANT, Lori .... 704-233-8979 373 C
l.hinnant@wingate.edu
HINNEN, Jack .... 205-226-4761.... 2 C
jhinnen@bsc.edu
HINNEN, Marsha .... 251-981-3771.... 3 A
marsha.hinnen@columbiasouthern.edu
HINNERS, Gordon .... 828-689-1208 359 A
ghinners@mhu.edu
HINOJOSA, Felix .... 915-831-2269 473 J
fhinojo3@epcc.edu
HINOJOSA, Maggie ...... 956-665-2321 494 C
hinojosam@utpa.edu
HINOJOSA, Maria .... 210-486-2379 467 B
mhinojosa@alamo.edu
HINSHAW, Ada Sue ..... 301-295-9002 548 D
adasue.hinshaw@usuhs.edu
HINSHAW, Dana .... 620-665-3322 188 A
hinshawd@hutchcc.edu
HINSHAW, Garrett, D ... 828-327-7000 361 B
ghinshaw@cvcc.edu
HINSHAW, Jamie .... 719-549-2602.. 81 F
jamie.hinshaw@csupueblo.edu
HINSHAW, Lynn .... 828-898-3473 358 F
hinshaw@lmc.edu
HINSHAW, Stephanie ... 800-280-0307 163 I
stephanie.hinshaw@ace.edu
HINSON, Bobby .... 850-201-6071 117 B
hinsonb@tcc.fl.edu
HINSON, Brenda .... 251-460-6050.... 9 F
bhinson@southalabama.edu
HINTERLONG,
James, E .... 804-828-1036 514 F
jehinterlong@vcu.edu
HINTON, Amy, E .... 601-426-6346 270 D
ahinton@southeasternbaptist.edu
HINTON, Armenta .... 814-332-3353 411 F
ahinton@allegheny.edu
HINTON, Billy, C .... 713-500-8444 495 A
william.c.hinton@uth.tmc.edu
HINTON, Don 435-652-7651 499M
hinton@dixie.edu
HINTON, Jeff .... 903-223-3087 486 C
jhinton@tamut.edu
HINTON, John, A .... 252-398-6376 356 B
hintoj@chowan.edu
HINTON, Kisa .... 501-370-5367.. 22 E
khinton@philander.edu
HINTON, Mary .... 320-363-5505 254 J
csbpres@csbsju.edu
HINTON, Neil .... 740-753-7212 383 G
hintonn@hocking.edu
HINTON, Tim .... 205-391-2979.... 7 A
thinton@sheltonstate.edu
HINTON, Toby, R .... 770-534-6257 121 G
thinton@brenau.edu
HINTON, Wendy .... 570-955-1456 422 G
hintonw@lackawanna.edu
HINTY, Danny .... 614-222-3224 380 F
dhinty@ccad.edu
HINTZ, Carol .... 816-235-1621 284 A
hintzc@umkc.edu
HINTZ, Lynn .... 863-784-7105 113 C
lynn.hintz@southflorida.edu
HINTZ, Nancy, L .... 920-748-8346 538 I
hintzn@ripon.edu
HINTZ, Sharon .... 908-835-2356 309 G
hintz@warren.edu
HINZ, James .... 770-593-2257 127 A
jahinz@gupton-jones.edu
HINZ, Laurence, A .... 505-473-6234 313 B
president@santafeuniversity.edu
HINZMAN, Larry .... 907-474-7331.. 10 I
ldhinzman@alaska.edu
HINZMAN, Larry .... 907-474-5837.. 10 I
HIOCO, Barbara .... 559-324-6475.. 68 J
barbara.hioco@scccd.edu
HIOTT, Connie .... 912-279-5965 123 B
chiott@ccga.edu
HIPES, Mark .... 276-326-4208 505 D
mhipes@bluefield.edu
HIPOLITO, Veronica ...... 928-226-4334.. 13 D
veronica.hipolito@coconino.edu
HIPONIA, Lorenzo, S .... 202-231-8785 547 N
lorenzo.hiponia@dodiis.mil
HIPP, Joye, G .... 803-786-3178 445 C
joyehipp@columbiasc.edu
HIPP, Kathleen .... 603-577-6659 297 F
hipp@dwc.edu
HIPPEN, Kristi .... 309-457-2327 153 B
khippen@monmouthcollege.edu
HIPPLER, Stanley .... 337-475-5181 208 B
stan@mcneese.edu
HIPPOLITE WRIGHT,
Debbie 808-675-3799 134M
debbie.hippolite.wright@byuh.edu
HIPPS, OSB,
Norman, W .... 724-805-2271 435 B
norman.hipps@email.stvincent.edu
HIPPS, Suzanne .... 602-243-8153.. 15 F
suzanne.hipps@smcmail.maricopa.edu
HIRAK, Joe .... 802-728-1283 504 C
jhirak@vtc.edu
HIRALDO, Rafael .... 787-863-2390 553 I
rafael.hiraldo@fajardo.inter.edu
HIRAMOTO, Patti .... 831-582-3366.. 34 C
phiramoto@csumb.edu
HIRATA, Heather .... 808-932-7369 135 I
hiratah@hawaii.edu
HIRD, Lon .... 605-367-7284 454 D
lon.hird@southeasttech.edu
HIRDLER, Joy, L .... 707-965-6232.. 57 I
jhirdler@puc.edu
HIRE, Jack .... 740-587-5698 381 H
hire@denison.edu
HIRNEISEN, Deborah .... 610-917-2003 438 G
dghirneisen@valleyforge.edu
HIRNER, Leo, J .... 816-604-4501 277 F
leo.hirner@mcckc.edu
HIROKAWA, Randy .... 808-932-7095 135 I
randyh@hawaii.edu
HIRONAKA-JUTEAU,
Jody .... 559-278-4004.. 33 D
jhironak@csufresno.edu
HIRSCH, Andrew, H .... 570-577-3698 413 E
andy.hirsch@bucknell.edu
HIRSCH, Glenn .... 612-624-4390 265 C
ghirsch@umn.edu
HIRSCH, Linda, R .... 563-333-6296 182 E
HirschLindaR@sau.edu
HIRSCH, Michele .... 718-489-5202 340 E
mhirsch@sfc.edu
HIRSCH, Samuel .... 215-751-8160 416 B
shirsch@ccp.edu
HIRSCH, Tom .... 641-472-1170 181 A
thirsch@mum.edu
HIRSCHBECK,
Denise, R .... 314-935-5320 285 E
dhirschbeck@wustl.edu
HIRSCHFIELD,
Michael, T .... 262-472-1633 541 D
hirschfm@uww.edu
HIRSCHI, Jill .... 406-657-1005 288 G
jill.hirschi@rocky.edu
HIRSCHMAN, David ...... 434-592-4140 509 G
HIRSCHY, Margaret ...... 419-434-4260 395 H
hirschym@findlay.edu
HIRSH, Barbara .... 215-576-0800 433 I
bhirsh@rrc.edu
HIRSH, Erin .... 215-635-7300 419 D
ehirsh@gratz.edu
HIRSHMAN, Elliot .... 619-594-5201.. 35 E
presidents.office@sdsu.edu
HIRSHON, Arnold .... 216-368-5292 378 J
arnold.hirshon@case.edu
HIRST, Martha, K .... 718-817-3120 326 C
HIRST, Thomas, M .... 845-451-1204 323 E
t_hirst@culinary.edu
HIRT, E. Jill .... 610-861-5421 427 F
jhirt@northampton.edu
HIRTLE, Christopher ..... 413-572-5455 230 F
chris@westfield.ma.edu
HIS HORSE IS THUNDER,
Ron .... 402-878-2380 291 B
president@littlepriest.edu
HISAMOTO, Masashi .... 773-834-2500 160 J
hisamoto@ttic.edu
HISCANO, Lisa .... 908-965-2358 309 A
hiscano@ucc.edu
HISE, Jeremy .... 580-628-6345 399 E
jeremy.hise@noc.edu
HISE, Paul .... 806-720-7279 478 A
paul.hise@lcu.edu
HISER, Larry, R .... 740-376-4665 386 A
larry.hiser@marietta.edu
HISEY, Richard, M .... 617-266-1400 223 F
HISKES, Anne .... 616-331-8655 243 E
hiskesa@gvsu.edu
HISLE, W. Lee .... 860-439-2650.. 90 D
wlhis@conncoll.edu
HISRICH, Matt .... 765-983-1523 165 H
hisrima@earlham.edu
HISS, Nancy .... 503-699-6242 407 A
nhiss@marylhurst.edu
HISSONG, Kimberly ...... 315-229-5837 341 E
khissong@stlawu.edu
HISSONG, Wesley .... 315-786-6517 329 G
whissong@sunyjefferson.edu
HISTAND, James, L ...... 574-535-7456 166 C
jimlh@goshen.edu
HITCH, Elizabeth, J .... 801-321-7122 499 J
ehitch@ushe.edu
HITCHCOCK, Cheryl, Y . 443-885-3535 217 C
cheryl.hitchcock@morgan.edu
HITCHCOCK, Claude, E . 443-885-3938 217 C
claude.hitchcock@morgan.edu
HITCHCOCK, Eloise .... 615-547-1351 456 C
ehitchcock@cumberland.edu
HITCHCOCK,
Marjorie, C .... 607-735-1750 324 J
mhitchcock@elmira.edu
HITCHCOCK, Susan ...... 607-255-9043 323 C
sh54@cornell.edu
HITCHELL, Dan, J .... 740-368-3351 390 B
djhitche@owu.edu
HITE, Griffin .... 256-765-4400.... 9 D
una@bkstr.com
HITE, Joe .... 940-552-6291 496 B
jhite@vernoncollege.edu
HITE, Robert, D .... 415-442-7058.. 46 A
bhite@ggu.edu
HITE, Trudy, E .... 302-356-6965.. 94 G
trudy.e.hite@wilmu.edu
HITES, Michael .... 217-244-0102 161 E
hites@uillinois.edu
HITESMAN, Bill .... 402-461-2400 289 D
bhitesman@cccneb.edu
HITLIN, Amy .... 919-760-8521 359 B
hitlina@meredith.edu
HITT, Anisa .... 941-907-2262 102 N
ahitt@evergladesuniversity.edu
HITT, John, C .... 407-823-1823 115 C
john.hitt@ucf.edu
HITT, Richard, J .... 863-784-7036 113 C
richard.hitt@southflorida.edu
HITTLE, Ann .... 509-452-5100 524 J
ahittle@pnwu.edu
HITTLE, Ben .... 509-452-5100 524 J
HITZ, Randy .... 503-725-4697 409 D
hitz@pdx.edu

HIX, Ellyn ... 334-844-4512 ... 1 G hixleel@auburn.edu
HIX, Patty ... 803-754-4100 445 D
HIXENBAUGH, Steve ... 707-468-3131 .. 54 A shixenbaugh@mendocino.edu
HIXON, Sharon ... 706-272-4594 123 G shixon@daltonstate.edu
HIXSON, Carla ... 701-224-5580 374 E carla.hixson@bismarckstate.edu
HIXSON, Carol ... 561-297-3165 114 E hixson@fau.edu
HIXSON, Carol ... 727-873-4400 116 C carol.hixson@nelson.usf.edu
HIXSON, Jana ... 254-710-1421 469 D jana_hixson@baylor.edu
HIXSON, John ... 479-619-4341 .. 22 B jhixson@nwacc.edu
HIXSON-WALLACE, Julie ... 501-279-5205 .. 21 A jahixson@harding.edu
HIYANE-BROWN, Kathi . 360-383-3330 528 E khiyane-brown@whatcom.ctc.edu
HJALTALIN, Lisa ... 509-434-5275 521 D lisa.hjaltalin@ccs.spokane.edu
HJALTALIN, Lisa ... 509-434-5210 521 E lisa.hjaltalin@ccs.spokane.edu
HJALTALIN, Lisa ... 509-434-5210 521 F lisa.hjaltalin@ccs.spokane.edu
HJELLUM, Wilma ... 402-457-2723 291 E whjellum@mccneb.edu
HJERPE, Karen ... 724-938-4351 430 C hjerpe@calu.edu
HLADEK, Thomas ... 718-482-5510 320 B tomhl@lagcc.cuny.edu
HLADIK, Barbara ... 215-489-2346 416 H Barbara.Hladik@delval.edu
HLADIS, Jirka ... 303-245-4702 .. 84 B jirka@naropa.edu
HLAVENKA, Lawrence ... 201-689-7057 300 B lhlavenka@bergen.edu
HLAVIN, Karen ... 847-543-2384 142 G khlavin@clcillinois.edu
HLEBOWITSH, Peter ... 205-348-6052 ... 8 E peter.hleb@ua.edu
HLINAK, Matthew, J ... 708-524-6812 144 C mhlinak@dom.edu
HLINKA, Karen ... 270-534-3236 197 E karen.hlinka@kctcs.edu
HLUBB, Emma ... 931-424-7366 458 D ehlubb@martinmethodist.edu
HLUBB, James, R ... 931-424-7379 458 D jhlubb@martinmethodist.edu
HMIELESKI, Kristin ... 413-265-2340 225 D hmieleskik@elms.edu
HMIELEWSKI, Christopher ... 507-537-7984 262 B Christopher.Hmielewski@smsu.edu
HO, Co ... 714-992-7020 .. 56 F cho@fullcoll.edu
HO, Deanna ... 312-935-4860 157 A dho@robertmorris.edu
HO, Katy ... 808-845-9158 136 E katyho@hawaii.edu
HO, Sam ... 408-298-2181 .. 63 O sam.ho@sjeccd.org
HO, Sandra ... 603-427-7614 296 K sho@ccsnh.edu
HO, Victor ... 415-565-4624 .. 71 B hov@uchastings.edu
HOADLEY, Diane ... 715-836-2500 539 E hoadled@uwec.edu
HOAG, David ... 847-317-7128 161 B dhoag@tiu.edu
HOAG, Jamie, D ... 508-793-2011 225 C jhoag@holycross.edu
HOAG, William ... 617-541-5357 233 A whoag@rcc.mass.edu
HOANG, Minh-Ha ... 619-260-4506 .. 74 B hoangm@sandiego.edu
HOANG POE, Linh ... 808-734-9570 136 C lhoang@hawaii.edu
HOAR, Robert ... 406-657-2367 287 H rhoar@msubillings.edu
HOAR, Robert ... 608-785-8039 539 G rhoar@uwlax.edu
HOARE, William, D ... 262-551-5730 535 E whoare@carthage.edu
HOBAN, Elizabeth ... 973-328-5160 301 G ehoban@ccm.edu
HOBAN, Kristi, M ... 817-257-7803 486 G k.hoban@tcu.edu
HOBAN, Patricia, K ... 503-375-5477 411 D phoban@willamette.edu
HOBART, Will ... 361-825-2616 485 F will.hobart@tamucc.edu
HOBBIE, Lawrence ... 516-877-3165 314 F hobbie@adelphi.edu
HOBBIEBRUNKEN, Kayla ... 800-231-3803 .. 12 G
HOBBIEBRUNKEN, Kayla ... 800-354-1254 .. 16 K
HOBBS, Clinton, G ... 706-379-3111 134 J clinth@yhc.edu
HOBBS, Harriet ... 704-378-3572 358 B hhobbs@jcsu.edu
HOBBS, Jacy ... 570-558-1818 418 I jhobbs@fortisinstitute.edu
HOBBS, Jeanie ... 817-598-6267 497 A hobbs@wc.edu
HOBBS, Jeremy ... 415-351-3536 .. 62 I jhobbs@sfai.edu
HOBBS, Marcia, B ... 270-809-2193 198 I mhobbs4@murraystate.edu
HOBBS, Nancy, A ... 734-764-7270 251 C hobbsn@umich.edu
HOBBS, Nicole ... 773-291-6100 142 B nhobbs3@ccc.edu
HOBBS, Pamelia, C ... 336-322-2120 364 G Pam.Hobbs@piedmontcc.edu
HOBBS, Phillip, M ... 205-853-1200 ... 5 C mhobbs@jeffstateonline.com
HOBBS, Rick ... 408-855-5325 .. 76 E rick.hobbs@missioncollege.edu
HOBBS, Tameka ... 305-626-3955 104 B Tameka.Hobbs@fmuniv.edu
HOBBS, Teresa ... 706-379-3111 134 J teresah@yhc.edu
HOBBY, Angela ... 229-333-2100 134 I angela.hobby@wiregrass.edu
HOBBY, Brett ... 713-221-5075 491 F hobbyb@uhd.edu
HOBBY-MEARS, Michelle ... 949-480-4134 .. 66 I mhobby@soka.edu
HOBDY, Gerri ... 225-216-8401 202 N hobdyg@mybrcc.edu
HOBERMAN, Chaim ... 516-225-4700 338 L
HOBIN, Caron, T ... 413-565-1333 222 G chobin@baypath.edu
HOBIN, Gail ... 617-287-5310 228 G gail.hobin@umb.edu
HOBLER, Dean ... 419-998-3103 394 B dahobler@unoh.edu
HOBLET, Kent, H ... 662-325-1418 269 A hoblet@cvm.msstate.edu
HOBLICK, Dave ... 303-753-6046 .. 85 H dhoblick@rmcad.edu
HOBSON, Jeanne ... 503-845-3057 407 B jeanne.hobson@mtangel.edu
HOBSON, Karen ... 858-505-1100 .. 47 M khobson@ipsb.edu
HOBSON, Lynn, M ... 620-341-5267 186 H lhobson@emporia.edu
HOBSON, Paula, L ... 603-535-2212 299 E phobson@plymouth.edu
HOBSON, Sheila ... 301-860-3451 220 B shobson@bowiestate.edu
HOBSON, Tricia ... 405-422-1263 401 H hobsont@redlandscc.edu
HOBY, Lori, L ... 503-370-6546 411 D lhoby@willamette.edu
HOBYAK, Michael, S ... 215-785-0111 429 F
HOCHANADEL, Gery ... 972-438-6932 480 C ghochanadel@parkercc.edu
HOCHHALTER, Carol ... 616-222-3000 245 D chochhalter@kuyper.edu
HOCHRADEL, Ted ... 662-846-4745 267 A thochradel@deltastate.edu
HOCHSCHILD, Joshua .. 301-447-7435 217 D hochschild@msmary.edu
HOCHSTEIN, Dale ... 201-761-7827 307 K dhochstein@saintpeters.edu
HOCK, Amy ... 402-471-2505 292 A ahock@nscs.edu
HOCK, Joan ... 215-489-2975 416 H Joan.Hock@delval.edu
HOCKENBERRY, Frederick ... 301-846-2544 214 I fhockenberry@frederick.edu
HOCKENHULL, Benjamin, R ... 512-448-8688 481 B ben@stedwards.edu
HOCKENSMITH, Margaret ... 859-336-5082 199 B mhockensmith@sccky.edu
HOCKENSMITH, William ... 805-756-5301 .. 32 E whockens@calpoly.edu
HOCKETT, Anne, B ... 336-633-0218 365 A abhockett@randolph.edu
HOCKMAN, Joan ... 814-371-2090 437 C jhockman@triangle-tech.edu
HOCQUARD, Stephen, L ... 989-964-4081 249 G shoc@svsu.edu
HOCUTT, Kirby ... 806-742-3355 489 F kirby.hocutt@ttu.edu
HODA-KEARSE, Rebecca ... 315-498-2119 337 F r.a.hoda-kearse@sunyocc.edu
HODGDEN, Jessica ... 401-454-6764 442 B jhodgden@risd.edu
HODGE, Brad, K ... 215-670-9206 428 A bhodge@peirce.edu
HODGE, Charles ... 937-376-6007 379 D chodge@centralstate.edu
HODGE, David ... 513-529-2345 386 K president@miamioh.edu
HODGE, David ... 334-291-4928 ... 2 H david.hodge@cv.edu
HODGE, Dena, S ... 864-379-8833 446 B hodge@erskine.edu
HODGE, Duane ... 937-328-6063 379 L dhodge@clarkstate.edu
HODGE, Evelyn ... 334-229-4139 ... 1 D ehodge@alasu.edu
HODGE, Gary, B ... 972-881-5897 471 C ghodge@collin.edu
HODGE, Jeremy ... 334-229-4156 ... 1 D Jhodge@alasu.edu
HODGE, Jimmer ... 218-262-6705 258 H jimmerhodge@hibbing.edu
HODGE, Johnesa ... 313-496-2796 252 A jdimick1@wcccd.edu
HODGE, Margaret ... 706-385-1069 130 C margaret.hodge@point.edu
HODGE, Marilyn, R ... 757-822-7245 517 C mhodge@tcc.edu
HODGE, Michel ... 718-631-6351 320 F mhodge@qcc.cuny.edu
HODGE, Mildred ... 860-215-9252 .. 90 B mhodge@trcc.commnet.edu
HODGE, Paula ... 661-362-5108 .. 40 H paula.hodge@canyons.edu
HODGE, Rick ... 323-242-5388 .. 51 I hodgerl@lasc.edu
HODGE, Terrell, L ... 269-387-6000 252 I terrell.hodge@wmich.edu
HODGE, Tiffani ... 404-523-8520 132 D thodge3@spelman.edu
HODGEN, Danielle ... 509-527-4301 527 H danielle.hodgen@wwcc.edu
HODGES, Carolyn, R ... 865-974-3694 465 D chodges@utk.edu
HODGES, Caryl ... 650-508-3613 .. 56 H chodges@ndnu.edu
HODGES, Christopher .. 215-893-5262 416 E christopher.hodges@curtis.edu
HODGES, Courtney ... 434-395-2823 509 H hodgesmc@longwood.edu
HODGES, Dale, B ... 269-471-3321 239 D dbhodges@andrews.edu
HODGES, Daniel, K ... 540-365-4365 507 H dhodges@ferrum.edu
HODGES, Dawn ... 770-229-3293 132 B dhodges@sctech.edu
HODGES, Greg ... 276-656-0213 516 D ghodges@patrickhenry.edu
HODGES, Heath ... 918-463-2931 397 I heath.hodges@connorsstate.edu
HODGES, Jeff ... 540-362-6503 508 D jhodges@hollins.edu
HODGES, Jill ... 906-487-3310 247 A jhodges@mtu.edu
HODGES, Jimmy ... 256-352-8229 .. 10 A jimmy.hodges@wallacestate.edu
HODGES, Lorraine ... 973-803-5000 305 A lhodges@pillar.edu
HODGES, Mike ... 423-472-7141 462 D MHodges@clevelandstatecc.edu
HODGES, Omega ... 828-298-3325 373 A ohodges@warren-wilson.edu
HODGES, Rhonda ... 276-656-0256 516 D rhodges@patrickhenry.edu
HODGES, Richard ... 757-825-2868 517 B hodgesr@tncc.edu
HODGES, Ricky, C ... 336-734-7272 362 F rhodges@forsythtech.edu
HODGES, Stephen, J ... 617-746-1990 227 G stephen.hodges@hult.edu
HODGES, Tim ... 785-594-8365 184 F tim.hodges@bakeru.edu
HODGES, Tina ... 731-352-4032 455 E hodgest@bethelu.edu
HODGES, Tyler ... 601-318-6089 271 F thodges@wmcarey.edu
HODGES, YLonne ... 912-688-6922 129 E yhodges@ogeecheetech.edu
HODGES, Zachary ... 713-718-5721 475 C zachary.hodges@hccs.edu
HODGINS, Diane, W ... 850-729-6485 109 D hodginsd@nwfsc.edu
HODGINS, Ewart ... 919-573-5350 368 H
HODGINS, Randy ... 206-221-5670 527 G rhodgins@uw.edu
HODGSON, Matt ... 707-826-3321 .. 35 D matthodson@humboldt.edu
HODGSON, Robert ... 217-641-4349 148 J rhodgson@jwcc.edu
HODGUES, Elizabeth, R 787-850-9337 558 A elizabeth.hodges@upr.edu
HODNETT, James ... 478-387-4715 125 E jhodnett@gmc.edu
HODNETT, Martin ... 256-726-7052 ... 6 C mhodnett@oakwood.edu
HODOWANEC, Michael . 610-372-4721 433 H mhodowanec@racc.edu
HODOWNES, Stephen ... 603-645-9730 298 H s.hodownes@snhu.edu
HODSDON, Roger ... 626-815-5080 .. 29 B rhodsdon@apu.edu
HODSON, April ... 860-701-5027 .. 91 B hodson_a@mitchell.edu
HODSON, Brad ... 417-625-9300 278 I hodson-b@mssu.edu
HODSON, Brad ... 417-625-3072 278 I hodson-b@mssu.edu
HODSON, Luke ... 859-985-3503 193 F hodsonl@berea.edu
HODUM, Robert ... 931-372-3888 462 A rhodum@tntech.edu
HOEBEE, John ... 602-386-4810 .. 11 F john.hoebee@arizonachristian.edu
HOEBER, Mark, S ... 716-851-1413 325 A hoeber@ecc.edu
HOECK, Andreas ... 303-715-3218 .. 85 J father.hoeck@archden.org
HOEF, Ted ... 314-968-6980 285 G hoeftl@webster.edu
HOEFFNER, Denise, R .. 785-309-3110 190 L denise.hoeffner@salinatech.edu
HOEFFNER, Lori ... 516-877-3232 314 F hoeffner@adelphi.edu
HOEFLER, William ... 479-968-0353 .. 20 C whoeflerjr@atu.edu
HOEG, Portia ... 814-332-3350 411 F phoeg@allegheny.edu
HOEH, Susan ... 407-888-8689 103 M shoeh@fcim.edu
HOEHN, Alex, J ... 718-990-2998 340 G hoehna@stjohns.edu
HOEHNKE, Diane ... 414-443-8627 542 I diane.hoehnke@wlc.edu
HOEKSEMA, Jim ... 641-673-1107 184 B hoeksemaj@wmpenn.edu
HOEKSTRA, Erik ... 712-722-6002 177 J erik.hoekstra@dordt.edu
HOEKSTRA, Jack ... 803-732-6716 447 H hoekstraj@midlandstech.edu
HOEKSTRA, Jonathan ... 254-867-3929 487 G jonathan.hoekstra@systems.tstc.edu
HOEL, Aaron ... 301-687-3101 220 D ahoel@frostburg.edu
HOEL, Monica, S ... 276-944-6126 507 E mshoel@ehc.edu
HOELLEN, Kathy, L ... 803-981-7150 451 K khoellen@yorktech.edu
HOELSCHER, Ronda ... 325-793-4857 478 D hoelscher.ronda@mcm.edu
HOELTZEL, Susan ... 718-960-8731 319 C susan.hoeltzel@lehman.cuny.edu
HOEMANN, D. Lee ... 360-867-6300 522 J hoemannl@evergreen.edu
HOEPFER, Maureen, G . 717-780-1157 420 D mghoepfe@hacc.edu
HOERITZ, Kim ... 412-396-6213 417 I hoeritzk@duq.edu
HOERRNER, Keisha, L .. 470-578-3550 127 M khoerrne@kennesaw.edu
HOERSCH, Alice, L ... 215-951-1010 422 F hoersch@lasalle.edu
HOERTH, Richard ... 920-693-1237 543 B rich.hoerth@gotoltc.edu
HOESING, Paul ... 314-792-6136 276 H Hoesing@kenrick.edu
HOETING, Mark ... 678-891-2830 125 G mark.hoeting@gpc.edu
HOEWING, Rodney, E .. 217-333-2034 162 A rhoewing@illinois.edu
HOEY, John ... 508-999-8071 228 H jhoey@umassd.edu
HOFELDT, Kathryn ... 615-322-0344 465 H kathryn.hofeldt@vanderbilt.edu
HOFER, Jeanie, H ... 573-341-4208 284 C jeanie@mst.edu
HOFF, Brad ... 507-786-3310 264 C hoff@stolaf.edu
HOFF, Dianne ... 678-839-6570 133 F dhoff@westga.edu
HOFF, Kevin ... 541-956-7925 409 F khoff@roguecc.edu
HOFF, Michael, B ... 423-439-4236 461 D hoffmb@etsu.edu
HOFFHINES, Kristin ... 847-925-6522 145 F khoffhin@harpercollege.edu
HOFFLER, Undi, N ... 919-530-5140 370 C uhoffler@nccu.edu

HOFFMAN, A, P 334-556-2225 4 A ahoffman@wallace.edu
HOFFMAN, Angela 859-336-5082 199 B ahoffman@sccky.edu
HOFFMAN, Barbara 319-399-8540 176 G bhoffman@coe.edu
HOFFMAN, Bart 714-564-6800 60 G hoffman_bart@sac.edu
HOFFMAN, Beth 301-687-4101 220 D bhoffman@frostburg.edu
HOFFMAN, Carolyn, F 301-322-0561 217 G hoffmacf@pgcc.edu
HOFFMAN, Charles, E 314-516-6280 284 B hoffmance@umsl.edu
HOFFMAN, Cierra 678-331-4331 128 C cierra.hoffman@life.edu
HOFFMAN, David 540-665-5457 512 E dhoffman@su.edu
HOFFMAN, Deborah 813-935-5700 111 E deborah.hoffman@remingtoncollege.edu
HOFFMAN, Erin 847-735-5207 149 H hoffman@lakeforest.edu
HOFFMAN, H. John 203-773-6678 87 M hjhoffman@albertus.edu
HOFFMAN, Heather 770-426-2780 128 C hhoffman@life.edu
HOFFMAN, Jaime 323-259-2500 56 I jhoffman@oxy.edu
HOFFMAN, James 575-646-4083 312 A jhoffman@nmsu.edu
HOFFMAN, Jeffrey, L 315-255-1743 317 I foundation@cayuga-cc.edu
HOFFMAN, John, R 215-572-2195 412 F hoffmanj@arcadia.edu
HOFFMAN, Joseph, M 301-687-4120 220 D jhoffman@frostburg.edu
HOFFMAN, Kyle, D 209-228-4400 71 E khoffman@UCMerced.edu
HOFFMAN, Larry 914-395-2384 342 C lhoffman@sarahlawrence.edu
HOFFMAN, Laura 941-359-4237 116 D hoffman@sar.usf.edu
HOFFMAN, Lawrence 703-284-5716 510 B lhoffman@marymount.edu
HOFFMAN, LeAnn 712-274-6400 184 A leann.hoffman@witcc.edu
HOFFMAN, Lorraine, B 530-898-6231 33 A lbhoffman@csuchico.edu
HOFFMAN, Louis 410-484-7200 217 E lhoffman@nirc.edu
HOFFMAN, Marion, S 850-488-2447 115 D marionh@ufl.edu
HOFFMAN, Mark 610-341-5935 418 A hoffman@eastern.edu
HOFFMAN, SR., Martin, A 609-894-9311 306 B mhoffman@bcc.edu
HOFFMAN, Mary 719-587-7372 78 I mchoffma@adams.edu
HOFFMAN, Michael 515-965-7130 177 B mjhoffman@dmacc.edu
HOFFMAN, Michael 716-375-2530 340 C mhoffman@sbu.edu
HOFFMAN, Molly 740-362-3373 386 D mhoffman@mtso.edu
HOFFMAN, Patricia 410-706-7355 219 E phoffman@umaryland.edu
HOFFMAN, Paula 320-629-5180 260 H hoffmanp@pinetech.edu
HOFFMAN, Peter 912-877-1906 120 D peter.hoffman@armstrong.edu
HOFFMAN, Sandra 856-415-2220 306 C shoffma2@rcgc.edu
HOFFMAN, Sharon, L 802-287-8215 501 I hoffmans@greenmtn.edu
HOFFMAN, Sharon, L 802-287-8216 501 I hoffmans2@greenmtn.edu
HOFFMAN, Sonia 336-272-7102 357 B sonia.hoffman@greensboro.edu
HOFFMAN, Steven, A 859-236-6688 194 E steven.hoffman@centre.edu
HOFFMAN, Thomas 507-453-2770 259 G thoffman@southeastmn.edu
HOFFMANN, Donna 909-389-3333 62 B dhoffman@sbccd.edu
HOFFMANN, Lowell (Bud) 731-286-3307 462 F hoffmann@dscc.edu
HOFFMANN, Mark 701-777-2492 373 G mark.hoffmann@und.edu
HOFFMANN, Pauline 716-375-2578 340 C hoffmann@sbu.edu
HOFFMANN, Susie 785-670-1643 192 B susie.hoffmann@washburn.edu
HOFFMANN HARDING, Erin 574-631-7394 174 A eharding@nd.edu
HOFFMANS, Kim 805-289-6000 75 E khoffmans@vcccd.edu
HOFFMEYER, Tom 254-710-1561 469 D tom_hoffmeyer@baylor.edu
HOFFNUNG, Michele 203-582-8903 91 E michele.hoffnung@quinnipiac.edu
HOFHERR, Michael 614-292-6553 389 A hofherr3@osu.edu
HOFMANN, John 650-493-4430 66 H john.hofmann@sofia.edu
HOFMANN, John 650-508-3500 56 H jmhofmann@ndnu.edu
HOFMANN, Karen 407-823-2811 115 C karen.hofmann@ucf.edu
HOFMEISTER, David 316-295-5685 187 C david_hofmeister@friends.edu
HOFMEISTER, David 316-295-5682 187 C david_hofmeister@friends.edu
HOFMEYER, Karna 712-324-5061 182 A khofmeyer@nwicc.edu
HOFRENNING, Ilene 508-626-4900 230 A ihofrenning@framingham.edu
HOFSESS, Christy 425-602-3073 519 J chofsess@bastyr.edu
HOFSTEDT, Petra 715-682-1983 538 D phofstedt@northland.edu
HOFSTETTER, Dale 513-745-8308 393 C hofsteda@uc.edu
HOFSTETTER, Shirley, A 636-584-6704 274 J shirley.hofstetter@eastcentral.edu
HOFTIEZER, David 609-984-1164 308 H dhoftiezer@tesc.edu
HOGAN, Aaron 479-968-0376 20 C ahogan@atu.edu
HOGAN, Amy 785-242-5200 190 D amy.hogan@ottawa.edu
HOGAN, Andrea 203-582-5215 91 E andrea.hogan@quinnipiac.edu
HOGAN, Anne-Marie 502-585-9911 199 E ahogan02@spalding.edu
HOGAN, Barbara 215-248-7120 415 D hoganb@chc.edu
HOGAN, Beverly, W 601-977-7730 270 F bhogan@tougaloo.edu
HOGAN, Bill 206-296-5451 526 F hoganw@seattleu.edu
HOGAN, Brenda 478-471-6684 128 H brenda.hogan@mga.edu
HOGAN, Carrie 518-783-2554 342 H chogan@siena.edu
HOGAN, Cheryl 231-843-5864 252 H clhogan@westshore.edu
HOGAN, Christopher 617-287-6800 228 G christopher.hogan@umb.edu
HOGAN, Jennifer 810-237-6570 251 E jhogan@umflint.edu
HOGAN, Joan, P 828-448-6041 367 B jhogan@wpcc.edu
HOGAN, Joanne 508-531-1244 229 C jhogan@bridgew.edu
HOGAN, John 501-760-4200 21 H jhogan@npcc.edu
HOGAN, John 317-921-4882 169 L
HOGAN, Judith 781-280-3816 232 B hoganj@middlesex.mass.edu
HOGAN, Kay 850-973-1605 109 C hogank@nfcc.edu
HOGAN, Kimberly 860-343-5731 89 E khogan@mxcc.edu
HOGAN, Lesley 425-235-7872 525 G lhogan@rtc.edu
HOGAN, Martha, A 972-238-6210 473 B mhogan@dcccd.edu
HOGAN, Matthew 718-489-5447 340 E mhogan@sfc.edu
HOGAN, Pashia 423-354-2425 463 D phhogan@northeaststate.edu
HOGAN, Pat 910-362-7009 360 G phogan@cfcc.edu
HOGAN, Patrick, D 434-924-3252 514 A pdh9t@virginia.edu
HOGAN, Patrick, J 301-445-1927 219 C pjhogan@usmd.edu
HOGAN, Paul 603-271-6484 297 C phogan@ccsnh.edu
HOGAN, Sean 847-543-2419 142 G shogan@clcillinois.edu
HOGAN, Susan, S 413-597-4204 238 E susan.s.hogan@williams.edu
HOGAN, Terrance, E 305-474-6018 112 B thogan@stu.edu
HOGAN, Terrence 319-273-2332 176 A terry.hogan@uni.edu
HOGAN, William 907-786-4407 10 H whhogan@uaa.alaska.edu
HOGARTY, Lisa 603-646-0871 297 G lisa.hogarty@dartmouth.edu
HOGEBOOM, Cindi 510-485-7828 58 G chogeboom@patten.edu
HOGENCAMP, Kelly 909-621-8273 65 E registrar@ad.scrippscol.edu
HOGENSON, Liz 763-424-0902 260 E LHogenson@nhcc.edu
HOGGE, Jane Curley 410-617-2131 216 D jchogge@loyola.edu
HOGGLE, Layne 334-683-5110 5 D lcalhoun@judson.edu
HOGREFE, Richard 909-389-3205 62 B rhogrefe@craftonhills.edu
HOGSETT, Denise 304-696-2370 532 H hogsettd@marshall.edu
HOGUE, Belinda 334-727-8763 8 B bahoque@mytu.tuskegee.edu
HOGUE, Eileen 719-502-2419 84 J eileen.hogue@ppcc.edu
HOGUE, Eric 916-577-2200 77 F ehogue@jessup.edu
HOGUE, Gina 870-972-3057 19 F ghogue@astate.edu
HOGUE, Gina 870-972-2030 19 F ghogue@astate.edu
HOGUE, Jarrod 503-491-7019 407 C jarrod.hogue@mhcc.edu
HOGUE, Jason 620-223-2700 187 B jasonh@fortscott.edu
HOGUE, Laurel 660-543-4984 283 F lhogue@ucmo.edu
HOGUE, Matthew, L 843-349-2813 444 G dhogue@coastal.edu
HOGUE, Stacey 501-812-2299 22 F shogue@pulaskitech.edu
HOGUE, William, F 803-777-0707 450 B hogue@sc.edu
HOGYA, Tiffany 330-823-2030 394 A hogyata@mountunion.edu
HOHBERG, Tonian 213-624-1200 44 I thohberg@fidm.edu
HOHENSTEIN, Janet, M 218-477-2956 260 B hohenst@mnstate.edu
HOHERTZ, Cherie, L 972-721-5040 491 B chohertz@udallas.edu
HOHIEMER, Victoria 270-686-4512 197 A vickie.hohiemer@kctcs.edu
HOHL, David 510-780-4500 50 G dhohl@lifewest.edu
HOHL, Kathleen 414-297-6208 543 E hohlk@matc.edu
HOHMAN, Adam 260-982-5228 170 a arhohman@manchester.edu
HOI, Samuel 410-225-2237 216 F
HOIDA, Will 775-881-1314 296 F whoida@sierranevada.edu
HOIG, Todd 714-808-4849 56 D thoig@nocccd.edu
HOILMAN, Sandra, K 828-448-6020 367 B shoilman@wpcc.edu
HOISINGTON, Gloria 760-355-6244 47 G gloria.carmona@imperial.edu
HOIT, Marc, I 919-515-0141 370 D mark_hoit@ncsu.edu
HOJAN, Elizabeth, M 262-554-2010 537 D mwcfinancialaid@aol.com
HOJAN-CLARK, Jane 212-853-0469 322 F jh3574@columbia.edu
HOJSACK, Dana 619-849-2678 59 K danahojsack@pointloma.edu
HOKANSON, Sharon 928-524-7471 16 E sharon.hokanson@npc.edu
HOKE, Cynthia 229-430-4605 119 H cynthia.hoke@asurams.edu
HOKE, Mary 210-829-3982 492 B mhoke@uiwtx.edu
HOKOANA, Lui 808-984-3636 136 H lhokoana@hawaii.edu
HOLAHAN, Barbara 516-686-7533 335 F bholahan@nyit.edu
HOLAK, Susan, L 718-982-2922 319 A susan.holak@csi.cuny.edu
HOLAWAY, Rick 615-966-6133 458 C rick.holaway@lipscomb.edu
HOLBERG, Connie 315-786-2402 329 G cholberg@sunyjefferson.edu
HOLBERT, Carolyn 704-216-7223 365 F carolyn.holbert@rccc.edu
HOLBROOK, Carl 334-347-2623 3 H cholbrook@escc.edu
HOLBROOK, Catherine, B 413-662-5231 230 C catherine.holbrook@mcla.edu
HOLBROOK, Christine 413-552-2319 231 F cholbrook@hcc.edu
HOLBROOK, Eddie 704-669-4223 361 E holbrook@clevelandcc.edu
HOLBROOK, Jennifer 870-230-5275 21 B holbroj@hsu.edu
HOLBROOKS, Johnnie, L 432-837-8100 489 B johnnieh@sulross.edu
HOLCOMB, David 254-295-4184 492 C dholcomb@umhb.edu
HOLCOMB, Gay 859-858-3511 193 A gay.holcomb@asbury.edu
HOLCOMB, Glen 405-789-6400 402 E gholcomb@snu.edu
HOLCOMB, J. David 713-798-4613 469 C jholcomb@bcm.edu
HOLCOMB, Jeffrey, R 605-367-8355 454 D jeff.holcomb@southeasttech.edu
HOLCOMB, Mark 815-939-5236 155 G mholcomb@olivet.edu
HOLCOMB, Todd, R 308-635-6101 294 C holcombt@wncc.edu
HOLCOMB-MCCOY, Cheryl 410-516-8770 216 A cholcomb@jhu.edu
HOLCOMBE, Annalisa 801-832-2551 501 C asteggell@westminstercollege.edu
HOLCOMBE, Bridget 336-841-9470 357 E bholcomb@highpoint.edu
HOLCOMBE, Robert 864-429-8728 450 I reholcom@mailbox.sc.edu
HOLDA, Heather 860-509-9502 90 G hholda@hartsem.edu
HOLDA, William, M 903-983-8100 477 A bholda@kilgore.edu
HOLDEMAN, David 940-565-2497 492 D david.holdeman@unt.edu
HOLDEN, Brad 541-278-5783 404 J bholden@bluecc.edu
HOLDEN, Camille 928-757-0838 15 K cholden@mohave.edu
HOLDEN, Dave 618-664-6750 145 E dave.holden@greenville.edu
HOLDEN, Eileen 863-297-1098 110 E eholden@polk.edu
HOLDEN, Elaine, P 704-637-4402 355 H epholden@catawba.edu
HOLDEN, John 973-408-3226 301 J jholden@drew.edu
HOLDEN, Joseph, M 714-966-8500 75 F
HOLDEN, Kimberly 706-771-4019 121 B kholden@augustatech.edu
HOLDEN, Larry 615-327-6339 458 F lholden@mmc.edu
HOLDEN, Nina 313-664-7864 241 D nholden@collegeforcreativestudies.edu
HOLDEN, Randy 540-231-3171 518 B rholden@vt.edu
HOLDEN, Scott, A 212-799-5000 329 I
HOLDEN, Wesley 772-546-5534 106 D wesleyholden@hsbc.edu
HOLDEN-DUFFY, Cheryl 410-651-6460 219 H clduffy@umes.edu
HOLDER, Ann 936-294-1613 489 A lib_ahh@shsu.edu
HOLDER, Arthur 510-649-2440 46 E aholder@gtu.edu
HOLDER, Beth 336-841-9279 357 E bholder@highpoint.edu
HOLDER, Candace 336-386-3382 366 E holderc@surry.edu
HOLDER, Cheryl 618-842-3711 146 G holderc@iecc.edu
HOLDER, Dinelly 718-429-6600 352 A dinelly.holder@vaughn.edu
HOLDER, Eugene 972-825-4762 483 D eholder@sagu.edu
HOLDER, Gerald, D 412-624-9811 437 K holder@engr.pitt.edu
HOLDER, Jayne 423-425-4785 465 E jayne-holder@utc.edu
HOLDER, Jonathan 315-792-7100 348 D jholder@sunycnse.com
HOLDER, Karen, G 214-887-5221 473 E kholder@dts.edu
HOLDER, Mike 405-744-7231 400 C mike.holder@okstate.edu
HOLDER, Selby 254-867-3704 488 B selby.holder@tstc.edu
HOLDERBY, Kindle 918-781-7340 396 F holderbyk@bacone.edu
HOLDERBY, Kindle 918-781-7344 396 F holderbyk@bacone.edu
HOLDING-JORDAN, Karen, R 919-866-5838 366 H khjordan@waketech.edu
HOLDNAK, John, R 850-872-3800 105 Q jholdnak@gulfcoast.edu
HOLDSWORTH, Madeleine 312-893-7114 144 H mholdsworth@erikson.edu
HOLECHECK, Sarah 989-275-5000 245 C sarah.holecheck@kirtland.edu
HOLEMAN, Gary 304-896-7436 531 F gary.holeman@southernwv.edu
HOLESTINE, Dan 800-280-0307 163 I dan.holestine@ace.edu
HOLEY, Linka 612-728-5112 264 B lholey@smumn.edu
HOLFORD, K. Chris 219-785-5735 172 A cholford@pnc.edu
HOLGATE, Randy, L 312-893-7110 144 H rholgate@erikson.edu

HOLGER, David, K .... 515-294-7184 175 G
holger@iastate.edu
HOLGUIN, Emilsen .... 518-608-8356 325 B
eholguin@excelsior.edu
HOLGUIN, Renee .... 602-285-7433.. 15 C
renee.holguin@phoenixcollege.edu
HOLIFIELD, Brenda .... 870-780-1227.. 19 C
bholifield@smail.anc.edu
HOLL, Lynn .... 609-586-4800 303 D
holll@mccc.edu
HOLLAAR, Jean .... 218-477-2070 260 B
jean.hollaar@mnstate.edu
HOLLABAUGH, Tim ...... 559-730-3700.. 41 D
timh@cos.edu
HOLLADAY, Clare, M ... 563-333-6346 182 E
HolladayClareM@sau.edu
HOLLADAY, Kelly .... 575-492-2801 311 J
kholladay@nmjc.edu
HOLLAND, Alex .... 520-322-6330.. 14 B
alex@hanuniversity.edu
HOLLAND, Alex .... 520-322-6330.. 14 B
info@hanuniversity.edu
HOLLAND, Alice .... 610-328-8058 436 A
ahollan3@swarthmore.edu
HOLLAND, Ann, T .... 270-707-3724 196 D
ann.holland@kctcs.edu
HOLLAND, Bill .... 573-651-2332 282 C
bholland@semo.edu
HOLLAND, Christopher 904-632-3131 105 A
cholland@fscj.edu
HOLLAND, Colleen .... 417-455-5588 274 B
ColleenHolland@crowder.edu
HOLLAND, Dan .... 864-646-1552 449 F
dhollan1@tctc.edu
HOLLAND, Deana, K ..... 828-689-1275 359 A
dholland@mhu.edu
HOLLAND, Ellen, S ...... 214-768-2083 482 J
esholland@smu.edu
HOLLAND, Jann .... 417-873-7276 274 E
jholland@drury.edu
HOLLAND, Jenny .... 860-297-2139.. 92 A
jenny.holland@trincoll.edu
HOLLAND, LaTonya ...... 301-322-0007 217 G
hollanlt@pgcc.edu
HOLLAND, Leslie .... 901-722-3238 461 A
lholland@sco.edu
HOLLAND, Linda .... 501-354-7565.. 25 A
holland@uaccm.edu
HOLLAND, Lynne .... 270-745-3095 201 D
lynne.holland@wku.edu
HOLLAND, Matthew, S . 801-863-3000 500 B
president.holland@uvu.edu
HOLLAND, Melinda ...... 919-658-7702 369 B
mholland@umo.edu
HOLLAND, Melissa .... 303-546-3597.. 84 B
mholland@naropa.edu
HOLLAND, Michelle ..... 904-819-6223 102 P
Mholland@flagler.edu
HOLLAND, Nicole .... 612-338-7224 265 G
nicole.holland@waldenu.edu
HOLLAND, Rolanda, J .. 919-572-1625 354 F
rholland@apexsot.edu
HOLLAND, Sam .... 214-768-2880 482 J
sholland@smu.edu
HOLLAND, Scott .... 800-287-8822 164 E
hollasc@bethanyseminary.edu
HOLLAND, Sharon .... 301-295-3578 548 D
sharon.holland@usuhs.edu
HOLLAND, Steven, C .... 520-621-1556.. 18 E
sholland@email.arizona.edu
HOLLAND, Teresa .... 509-574-4667 529 B
tholland@yvcc.edu
HOLLAND, Tina .... 225-768-1710 206 F
tina.holland@ololcollege.edu
HOLLAND, Tony .... 334-556-2214.... 4 A
tholland@wallace.edu
HOLLANDER, Lisa .... 219-464-6882 174 E
lisa.hollander@valpo.edu
HOLLANDER, Teri .... 301-445-1909 219 C
tholland@usmd.edu
HOLLANDSWORTH,
Heather .... 540-365-4282 507 H
hhollandsworth@ferrum.edu
HOLLATZ, Gary .... 318-678-6000 203 A
ghollatz@bpcc.edu
HOLLAWAY, Jamie .... 319-352-8521 183 J
jamie.hollaway@wartburg.edu
HOLLDORF, Barry .... 206-878-3710 523 D
bholldorf@highline.edu
HOLLENBECK, Dean ...... 620-343-4600 186 I
dhollenbeck@fhtc.edu
HOLLENHORST, Steven . 360-650-3521 528 D
steve.hollenhorst@wwu.edu
HOLLER, Juanita, M ..... 413-545-1581 228 F
jholler@admin.umass.edu
HOLLER, Richard, G ..... 724-925-4129 439 F
hollerr@wccc.edu
HOLLER, Stacy .... 301-387-3045 215 A
stacy.holler@garrettcollege.edu
HOLLER, Steve .... 503-255-0332 407 D
sholler@multnomah.edu
HOLLERAN, Meghan ..... 660-263-4110 279 F
meghanh@macc.edu
HOLLERAN, Theresa ..... 614-251-4730 388 H
hollerat@ohiodominican.edu
HOLLERICH, Mary .... 612-330-1000 253 K
HOLLERN, Denny .... 740-366-9301 378 L
dhollern@cotc.edu
HOLLEY, Dannye .... 713-313-7388 487 F
dholley@tsulaw.edu
HOLLEY, Debra .... 434-797-8410 515 C
dholley@dcc.vccs.edu
HOLLEY, Earle .... 843-208-8140 450 D
eholley@uscb.edu
HOLLEY, Joey .... 334-347-2623.... 3 H
jholley@escc.edu
HOLLEY, Patricia .... 626-873-8170.. 55 B
pholley@mtsierra.edu
HOLLEY, Steven .... 325-674-6552 466 I
steven.holley@acu.edu
HOLLEY, Tara .... 512-472-4133 482 E
tara.holley@ssw.edu
HOLLEY, Tracy, S .... 540-365-4216 507 H
tholley@ferrum.edu
HOLLEY-WALKER,
Danielle, R .... 202-806-8000.. 96 B
danielle.holley-walker@howard.edu
HOLLIDAY, Chrissy ...... 719-549-2708.. 81 F
chrissy.holliday@csupueblo.edu
HOLLIDAY, Corey .... 937-328-6479 379 L
hollidayc@clarkstate.edu
HOLLIDAY, Lisa, C .... 503-370-6574 411 D
lcjones@willamette.edu
HOLLIDAY, Matthew ..... 239-489-9052 104 G
mholliday@fsw.edu
HOLLIDAY, Paul .... 213-613-2200.. 67 G
paul_holliday@sciarc.edu
HOLLIDAY, Shawn, P .... 580-327-8410 399 F
spholliday@nwosu.edu
HOLLIDAY, Theresa ...... 913-288-7110 188 G
tholliday@kckcc.edu
HOLLIER, Larry, H .... 504-568-4800 205 C
lhholl@lsuhsc.edu
HOLLIFIELD, Jim .... 901-722-3264 461 A
jhollifield@sco.edu
HOLLIMAN, Stephanie .. 641-683-5751 179 C
stephanie.holliman@indianhills.edu
HOLLIMON, Mike .... 770-531-3123 121 G
mhollimon@brenau.edu
HOLLINGDALE, Linda .... 802-654-2310 502 H
lhollingdale@smcvt.edu
HOLLINGER, Dennis ..... 978-468-7111 227 B
dhollinger@gcts.edu
HOLLINGSHEAD,
Brad, E .... 863-680-4970 104 F
bhollingshead@flsouthern.edu
HOLLINGSWORTH,
Gabe .... 704-233-8368 373 C
g.hollingsworth@wingate.edu
HOLLINGSWORTH,
Kimberly .... 312-850-7301 142 E
khollingsworth@ccc.edu
HOLLINGSWORTH,
Rusty .... 270-789-5009 194 D
rhollingsworth@campbellsville.edu
HOLLINGSWORTH,
Stacey .... 601-635-2111 267 B
sholling@eccc.edu
HOLLINS, JR.,
Thomas, N .... 804-523-5296 515 F
thollins@reynolds.edu
HOLLINS, Wilton .... 817-531-5853 490 C
wjhollins@txwes.edu
HOLLIS, Debra .... 704-378-1128 358 B
dhollis@jcsu.edu
HOLLIS, Erika, M .... 303-964-5387.. 85 G
ehollis@regis.edu
HOLLIS, Keith .... 978-837-5356 233 G
hollisk@merrimack.edu
HOLLIS, Mark .... 440-943-7600 391 A
mhollis@dioceseofcleveland.org
HOLLIS, Mark, J .... 517-432-2607 246 H
hollis@msu.edu
HOLLISTER, Jim .... 570-389-4047 430 B
jhollist@bloomu.edu
HOLLISTER, Thomas ..... 617-496-2650 227 D
thomas_hollister@harvard.edu
HOLLMAN-STANCIL,
Cynthia .... 903-730-4890 476 L
CHollman-Stancil@jarvis.edu
HOLLMANN, Joshua ..... 914-337-9300 323 A
joshua.hollmann@concordia-ny.edu
HOLLOMAN, Anthony ... 205-247-8164.... 7 G
aholloman@stillman.edu
HOLLOMAN,
Anthony, L .... 601-979-2282 267 H
anthony.l.holloman@jsums.edu
HOLLOMAN, Connie ..... 864-503-5324 451 A
cholloman@uscupstate.edu
HOLLOMAN, Darryl, B .. 404-413-1503 126 D
dholloman@gsu.edu
HOLLOMAN, Mike .... 919-497-3249 358 J
mholloman@louisburg.edu
HOLLOMAN, Sue .... 703-416-1441 508 F
sholloman@ipsciences.edu
HOLLOMAN, Suzanne ... 215-619-7397 426 E
sholloman@mc3.edu
HOLLOW, Jeffrey .... 414-297-6663 543 E
hollowj4@matc.edu
HOLLOWAY, Amy .... 478-757-3510 122 E
aholloway@centragatech.edu
HOLLOWAY, Amy, L ...... 478-988-6849 122 F
aholloway@centralgatech.edu
HOLLOWAY, Betsy, B ... 205-726-4109.... 6 F
bbhollow@samford.edu
HOLLOWAY, Brian, R ... 815-224-0491 147 J
brian_holloway@ivcc.edu
HOLLOWAY, C. Allen ... 501-977-2031.. 25 A
holloway@uaccm.edu
HOLLOWAY, David, J ... 304-877-6428 529 G
dave.holloway@abc.edu
HOLLOWAY, DeAira ...... 972-273-3163 473 A
dholloway@dcccd.edu
HOLLOWAY, Denise, W 478-757-5211 134 E
dholloway@wesleyancollege.edu
HOLLOWAY, Jackie ...... 501-337-5000.. 20 H
jholloway@coto.edu
HOLLOWAY, James, P . 734-763-0395 251 C
hagar@umich.edu
HOLLOWAY, Jerry, R 918-631-2539 403M
jerry-holloway@utulsa.edu
HOLLOWAY, Jessica ..... 479-968-0269.. 20 C
jholloway@atu.edu
HOLLOWAY, Jessica ..... 312-850-7152 142 E
jholloway@ccc.edu
HOLLOWAY, John .... 718-960-8242 319 C
john.holloway@lehman.cuny.edu
HOLLOWAY, Jonathan .. 203-432-2900.. 93 C
jonathan.holloway@yale.edu
HOLLOWAY, Leslie .... 314-340-3390 275 G
hollowal@hssu.edu
HOLLOWAY, Linda, C .. 217-581-2979 144 E
lcholloway@eiu.edu
HOLLOWAY, Lorretta ... 508-626-4926 230 A
lholloway@framingham.edu
HOLLOWAY, Michelle ... 386-752-1822 103 Q
michelle.holloway@fgc.edu
HOLLOWAY, Rachel, L . 540-231-4167 518 B
rholloway@vt.edu
HOLLOWAY, Stacy .... 618-985-3741 148 G
stacyholloway@jalc.edu
HOLLOWAY, Tonya .... 903-923-3320 488 A
Tonya.holloway@tstc.edu
HOLLOWELL, Lorna ...... 218-281-8580 264 H
lholl0we@umn.edu
HOLLOWELL,
Meghan, E .... 513-585-4841 379 H
meghan.hollowell@thechristcollege.edu
HOLLY, Gordon, K .... 330-684-8740 393 A
gholly@uakron.edu
HOLLY, Marty .... 208-459-5850 137 J
mholly@collegeofidaho.edu
HOLLY, Neal .... 304-558-1112 532 C
nholly@hepc.wvnet.edu
HOLLY, Richard .... 815-753-1138 154 I
rholly@niu.edu
HOLLY, Shelly 918-631-2550 403M
shelly-holly@utulsa.edu
HOLLY, Yvette, A .... 402-559-5678 293 I
yholly@unmc.edu
HOLLYER, William .... 480-947-6644.. 16 L
HOLM, Coralee, A .... 802-862-9616 501 E
cholm@burlington.edu
HOLM, Cyndi .... 507-537-7854 262 B
Cyndi.Holm@smsu.edu
HOLM, Janet .... 253-589-5545 521 B
janet.holm@cptc.edu
HOLMAN, Carrie .... 724-653-2190 417 D
cholman@dec.edu
HOLMAN, Dena .... 828-726-2737 360 F
dnholman@cccti.edu
HOLMAN, Fred, B .... 775-784-4853 295 H
fholman@unr.edu
HOLMAN, George .... 308-865-8208 293 G
HOLMAN, George .... 262-595-2058 540 C
Holman@uwp.edu
HOLMAN, James .... 414-443-8566 542 I
james.holman@wlc.edu
HOLMAN, Jill .... 706-867-2532 133 A
jill.holman@ung.edu
HOLMAN, John .... 606-218-5194 201 C
johnholman@upike.edu
HOLMAN, Lucy .... 606-218-5265 201 C
lucyholman@upike.edu
HOLMAN, Lucy .... 410-837-4333 221 B
lholman@ubalt.edu
HOLMAN, Mark .... 701-854-8024 375 F
markh@sbci.edu
HOLMAN, Neil .... 847-574-5230 150 A
nholman@lfgsm.edu
HOLMAN, Pat .... 505-984-6144 312 J
pat.holman@sjc.edu
HOLMAN, Sara, C .... 920-832-6583 536 R
sara.b.holman@lawrence.edu
HOLMAN, Steve, L .... 618-235-2700 160 B
steven.holman@swic.edu
HOLMAN, Steven .... 847-543-2444 142 G
sholman@clcillinois.edu
HOLMANS, Jim .... 325-674-4974 466 I
holmansj@acu.edu
HOLMBOE, Janelle .... 828-298-3325 373 A
jholmboe@warren-wilson.edu
HOLME, Susan, H .... 509-527-5790 528 F
holmesl@whitman.edu
HOLMES, Annie .... 805-756-2250.. 32 E
aholmes@calpoly.edu
HOLMES, Barbara, A .... 651-255-6106 264 F
bholmes@unitedseminary.edu
HOLMES, Barbara, J ..... 202-274-6156.. 97 B
bholmes@udc.edu
HOLMES, Bert .... 757-727-5315 508 C
bert.holmes@hamptonu.edu
HOLMES, Betsy .... 603-623-0313 298 C
betsyholmes@nhia.edu
HOLMES, Beverly .... 309-341-7755 149 G
bholmes@knox.edu
HOLMES, Carlos .... 302-857-6062.. 93 E
cholmes@desu.edu
HOLMES, Cassandra ..... 941-752-5389 114 B
holmesc@scf.edu
HOLMES, Charley .... 903-586-2501 469 A
charley.holmes@bmats.edu
HOLMES, Chris .... 617-746-1990 227 G
chris.holmes@hult.edu
HOLMES, Christine .... 508-849-3418 222 C
cholmes@annamaria.edu
HOLMES, Claire .... 510-642-6436.. 70 K
claireholmes@berkeley.edu
HOLMES, Debra .... 912-279-5787 123 B
dholmes@ccga.edu
HOLMES, Edward, J ..... 716-851-1016 325 A
holmese@ecc.edu
HOLMES, Ella .... 601-979-6858 267 H
ella.b.holmes@jsums.edu
HOLMES, Ellen .... 802-258-3139 502 I
ellen.holmes@worldlearning.org
HOLMES, Emily .... 336-272-7102 357 B
emily.holmes@greensboro.edu
HOLMES, Erica .... 520-206-4999.. 17 A
eholmes3@pima.edu
HOLMES, Erin .... 907-786-1544.. 10 H
ejholmes@uaa.alaska.edu
HOLMES, Frank .... 936-294-3625 489 A
holmes@shsu.edu
HOLMES, Gilbert .... 909-460-2000.. 73 B
gholmes@laverne.edu
HOLMES, Greg .... 541-463-5516 406 F
holmesg@lanecc.edu
HOLMES, Heather, W ... 410-677-4850 220 E
hwholmes@salisbury.edu
HOLMES, Heidi .... 314-768-7808 278 H
hholmes@missouricollege.com
HOLMES, Joan .... 813-253-7043 106 C
jholmes16@hccfl.edu
HOLMES, Johnny, B ..... 901-321-3445 455 I
jholmes@cbu.edu
HOLMES, Judy .... 785-825-5422 185 D
jholmes@brownmackie.edu
HOLMES, Kenneth .... 212-237-8211 319 F
kholmes@jjay.cuny.edu
HOLMES, Kimberly .... 912-358-4190 131 A
holmesk@savannahstate.edu
HOLMES, Kristen .... 256-352-8118.. 10 A
kristen.holmes@wallacestate.edu
HOLMES, Kristiana, L ... 509-777-4563 529 A
kholmes@whitworth.edu
HOLMES, Lloyd, A .... 585-292-2120 333 G
lholmes20@monroecc.edu
HOLMES, Lucina .... 508-362-2131 231 D
lholmes@capecod.edu
HOLMES, Malcolm .... 540-654-1617 513 I
mholmes3@umw.edu
HOLMES, Marcelena ..... 301-846-2479 214 I
mholmes@frederick.edu
HOLMES, Matthew .... 610-902-8228 414 B
matthew.holmes@cabrini.edu
HOLMES, Megan .... 314-529-9343 277 B
HOLMES, Michael, S .... 207-768-9477 212 H
michael.s.holmes@umpi.edu
HOLMES, Michelle, M .. 510-841-1905.. 27 B
mmholmes@absw.edu
HOLMES, Molly .... 651-635-8500 254 A
mp-holmes@bethel.edu
HOLMES, Myioshi, U .... 972-860-8237 472 D
muh3310@dcccd.edu
HOLMES, Owen .... 657-278-5403.. 33 E
oholmes@fullerton.edu
HOLMES, O'Neal .... 334-683-2350.... 5 H
oholmes@marionmilitary.edu
HOLMES, Phillip, M ..... 478-387-4904 125 E
mholmes@gmc.edu
HOLMES, IV, Richard ... 805-493-3586.. 31 H
holmes@callutheran.edu

HOLMES, Robert .... 602-243-8062.. 15 F
bear.holmes@southmountaincc.edu
HOLMES, Robin, H .... 541-346-1137 410 F
rhholmes@uoregon.edu
HOLMES, Rodney .... 480-461-7315.. 15 A
rodney.holmes@mesacc.edu
HOLMES, Salanna, D .... 919-866-5705 366 H
sdholmes1@waketech.edu
HOLMES, Sharon, N ..... 920-924-6326 543 F
sholmes@morainepark.edu
HOLMES, Susan .... 956-364-4107 487 H
susan.holmes@tstc.edu
HOLMES, Terrell .... 302-857-6375.. 93 E
tholmes@desu.edu
HOLMES, Tiffany .... 312-759-1671 158 J
tholmes@saic.edu
HOLMES, Tori .... 248-476-1122 246 G
tholmes@mispp.edu
HOLMES, Wanda .... 662-621-4853 266 H
wholmes@coahomacc.edu
HOLMES, Wendy .... 845-341-4662 337 G
wendy.holmes@sunyorange.edu
HOLMES, William, A .... 989-774-4308 240 O
holme1wa@cmich.edu
HOLMES BACZKOWSKI,
Helene .... 215-951-1817 422 F
holmes@lasalle.edu
HOLMES-BUTLER,
Layna .... 610-399-2461 430 D
laynaholmes@cheyney.edu
HOLMES-LEOPOLD, RJ . 319-895-4445 177 A
rholmes-leopold@cornellcollege.edu
HOLMGREN,
Richard, A .... 814-332-2898 411 F
richard.holmgren@allegheny.edu
HOLMLUND, Eric .... 518-327-6272 338 B
eholmlund@paulsmiths.edu
HOLMOE, Tom .... 801-422-7649 497 J
tom_holmoe@byu.edu
HOLMQUIST, David ...... 562-903-4886.. 29 F
dave.holmquist@biola.edu
HOLMQUIST, Eric .... 712-279-5435 176 B
eric.holmquist@briarcliff.edu
HOLMQUIST, Jake .... 718-862-7449 331 H
jake.holmquist@manhattan.edu
HOLOHAN-MOYER,
Irene .... 716-839-8214 323 F
imoyer@daemen.edu
HOLOMAN,
Christopher, L .... 716-926-8854 327 F
choloman@hilbert.edu
HOLOWICKI, Linda .... 708-209-3170 143 D
linda.holowicki@cuchicago.edu
HOLPER, Mark .... 651-779-5834 258 D
mark.holper@century.edu
HOLS, Eric .... 703-284-1601 510 B
eric.hols@marymount.edu
HOLSAPPLE, Matthew ... 301-696-3569 215 E
holsapple@hood.edu
HOLSCLAW, Sheila, K ... 859-846-5310 198 G
sholsclaw@midway.edu
HOLSENBECK, Daniel ... 407-823-2387 115 C
daniel.holsenbeck@ucf.edu
HOLSER, Derek, P .... 757-481-5005 519 C
HOLSINGER, Kent .... 860-486-2182.. 92 C
kent.holsinger@uconn.edu
HOLSINGER-FUCHS,
Pamela .... 715-232-2639 541 B
holsinger-fuchsp@uwstout.edu
HOLSOPPLE, Lee .... 202-885-3409.. 94 H
lee.holsopple@american.edu
HOLSTAD, Deb .... 320-308-3277 261 F
dholstad@sctcc.edu
HOLSTAD, Deb, A .... 320-308-3227 261 F
dholstad@sctcc.edu
HOLSTEGE, Christopher 434-924-5185 514 A
ch2fx@virginia.edu
HOLSTEIN, David .... 561-868-3004 109 H
holsteid@palmbeachstate.edu
HOLSTEIN, Michael, L .. 317-788-3214 173 I
mholstein@uindy.edu
HOLSTEN, Robert, D .... 252-246-1254 367 D
rholsten@wilsoncc.edu
HOLSTER, Melissa .... 617-228-2271 231 C
mholster@bhcc.mass.edu
HOLSTON, J.B .... 303-871-3773.. 86 H
JB.Holston@du.edu
HOLSTON, Jo-Ann, M .. 334-833-4410.... 4 E
jholston@huntingdon.edu
HOLSTON, Tavarez .... 770-531-6331 128 A
tholston@laniertech.edu
HOLSTON, William .... 336-841-9221 357 E
bookstor@highpoint.edu
HOLT, Anthony .... 313-577-2062 252 G
aa6479@wayne.edu
HOLT, Brooke .... 479-619-4298.. 22 B
bholt@nwacc.edu
HOLT, Bruce .... 865-981-8035 458 E
bruce.holt@maryvillecollege.edu

HOLT, Daniel .... 816-415-5977 285 K
holtd@william.jewell.edu
HOLT, Debbie .... 859-246-6286 195 J
debbie.holt@kctcs.edu
HOLT, Gail, W .... 413-542-2296 222 A
financialaid@amherst.edu
HOLT, Jerry .... 219-785-5200 172 A
jholt@pnc.edu
HOLT, Joseph .... 559-734-9000.. 63 E
JosephH@sjvc.edu
HOLT, Joseph, L .... 410-778-7201 221 D
jholt2@washcoll.edu
HOLT, Lynda .... 518-608-8171 325 B
lholt@excelsior.edu
HOLT, Martee .... 336-316-2198 357 C
mholt@guilford.edu
HOLT, Mary Margaret ... 405-325-4051 403 I
marymholt@ou.edu
HOLT, Raymond .... 229-931-2001 131 E
rholt@southgatech.edu
HOLT, Rosalyn, J .... 318-670-9436 207 C
rholt@susla.edu
HOLT, Russ .... 925-473-7375.. 42 F
rholt@losmedanos.edu
HOLT, Ryan, C .... 828-884-8217 355 A
holtrc@brevard.edu
HOLT, Ryan, J .... 724-847-6133 419 B
rjholt@geneva.edu
HOLT, Sam .... 580-387-7311 398 J
sholt@mscok.edu
HOLT, Shari .... 870-743-3000.. 22 A
sholt@northark.edu
HOLT, Tina .... 706-419-1275 123 F
tina.holt@covenant.edu
HOLT, Wilford .... 334-420-4400.... 7 I
wholt@trenholmstate.edu
HOLTER, Emily .... 507-288-4563 255 D
eholter@crossroadscollege.edu
HOLTER, Joan .... 218-723-6041 255 A
jholter@css.edu
HOLTGRAVE, Lorie .... 410-617-2400 216 D
LAHoltgrave@loyola.edu
HOLTGREN, Shawn, M . 574-807-7215 164 F
holtgrs@bethelcollege.edu
HOLTHAUS, Barbara ..... 217-641-4104 148 J
bholthaus@jwcc.edu
HOLTHOUSER,
David, M .... 704-894-2220 356 D
daholthouser@davidson.edu
HOLTMYER-JONES,
Larissa .... 515-294-4077 175 G
larissah@foundation.iastate.edu
HOLTON, Carol .... 910-576-6222 364 D
holtonc@montgomery.edu
HOLTON, Christa .... 708-237-5050 155 B
cholton@nc.edu
HOLTON, Kalynda .... 850-201-9856 117 B
holtonk@tcc.fl.edu
HOLTSCHNEIDER,
Dennis, H .... 312-362-8850 143 G
president@depaul.edu
HOLTZ, Daniel, F .... 320-222-5205 261 B
daniel.holtz@ridgewater.edu
HOLTZ, Eddie .... 712-325-3426 180 B
eholtz@iwcc.edu
HOLTZ, Edwin .... 712-325-3227 180 B
eholtz@iwcc.edu
HOLTZ, Ryan .... 410-706-7481 219 E
rholtz@umaryland.edu
HOLTZCLAW, Mike .... 510-659-6191.. 56 J
mholtzclaw@ohlone.edu
HOLTZCLAW, Rhonda ... 239-590-1037 114 F
rholtzcl@wgcu.edu
HOLTZEN, Wende .... 714-879-3901.. 47 D
wholtzen@hiu.edu
HOLTZHAUSEN, Derina . 409-880-8137 488 F
derina.holtzhausen@lamar.edu
HOLUBIK, Donna .... 734-487-0455 242 J
dholubik@emich.edu
HOLYFIED, Patrick .... 704-991-0235 366 D
HOLZ, Doris .... 212-220-8021 318 D
dholz@bmcc.cuny.edu
HOLZ, Richard, C .... 414-288-7230 537 B
richard.holz@marquette.edu
HOLZ-CLAUSE, Mary ..... 909-869-2200.. 32 F
msholzclause@cpp.edu
HOLZBERLEIN, Anne .... 405-974-2770 403 G
aholzberlein@uco.edu
HOLZEM, Madeline .... 608-785-8013 539 G
mholzem@uwlax.edu
HOLZEMER, William, L 732-932-1770 307 B
holzemer@andromeda.rutgers.edu
HOLZEMER, William, L 973-353-5149 307 C
holzemer@andromeda.rutgers.edu
HOLZER, Marc .... 973-353-5268 307 C
mholzer@rutgers.edu
HOLZHEUSER,
Christina .... 361-825-5975 485 F
christina.holzheuser@tamucc.edu

HOLZMAN, Terri, L ...... 920-748-8351 538 I
holzmant@ripon.edu
HOLZMER, OSF,
M. Anita .... 260-399-7700 174 C
aholzmer@sf.edu
HOM, Kevin .... 718-260-5525 320 D
khom@citytech.cuny.edu
HOMAN, David .... 847-233-7700 155 B
dhoman@nc.edu
HOMAN, Elizabeth .... 443-518-4073 215 F
ehoman@howardcc.edu
HOMAN, J. Michael ..... 507-284-9595 254 G
homan@mayo.edu
HOMAN, J. Michael ..... 507-284-9595 254 F
homan.michael@mayo.edu
HOMAN, Judi .... 901-375-4400 459 D
judiadams@midsouthcc.org
HOMAN, Patricia .... 513-875-3344 379 G
patricia.homan@chatfield.edu
HOMAN, Richard, V ..... 757-446-5800 507 B
homanrv@evms.edu
HOMANN, Gordon .... 617-912-9154 224 C
ghomann@bostonconservatory.edu
HOMARD, Jennifer .... 352-395-5493 112 H
jen.homard@sfcollege.edu
HOMBURGER, John, R . 518-564-2130 346 B
homburjr@plattsburgh.edu
HOMER, Cory .... 973-300-2116 308 F
chomer@sussex.edu
HOMESLEY, Diane .... 678-839-6582 133 F
dhomesle@westga.edu
HOMFELDT, Mike .... 541-880-2244 406 E
homfeldt@klamathcc.edu
HOMIAK, JR., Albert, J 302-831-7285.. 94 D
homiak@udel.edu
HOMICH, John .... 617-627-6333 237 C
john.homich@tufts.edu
HOMOLKA, Jessica ...... 785-242-5200 190 D
jessica.homolka@ottawa.edu
HOMOLKA, Karen, K ..... 217-245-3094 146 D
khomolk@mail.ic.edu
HOMSHER, Betsy, E ..... 810-762-9540 245 A
bhomsher@kettering.edu
HOMZA, Lu Ann .... 757-221-2469 506 J
dean-ep@wm.edu
HONAKER, Lisa .... 609-652-4505 308 E
lisa.honaker@stockton.edu
HONAN, Molly .... 617-735-9876 226 B
honanm@emmanuel.edu
HONAN, Thomas .... 716-896-0700 352 B
thonan@villa.edu
HONDA, Jacqueline ...... 808-689-2315 136 A
jn7@hawaii.edu
HONDROS, Jack .... 610-526-1445 412 D
jack.hondros@theamericancollege.edu
HONEA, Scott, A .... 979-845-2217 485 C
honea@tamu.edu
HONEGAN, Rhonda ...... 404-270-5075 132 D
rhonegan@spelman.edu
HONEGGER, Rose .... 337-482-6819 208 F
oia@louisiana.edu
HONEMAN, Donald ...... 508-793-7419 225 B
dhoneman@clarku.edu
HONEYCUTT, Tony, L .... 606-679-8501 197 B
tony.honeycutt@kctcs.edu
HONG, E-Sing .... 408-260-0208.. 44 K
chinesedoctoral@fivebranches.edu
HONG, Luoluo .... 415-338-2032.. 36 A
luoluo@sfsu.edu
HONG, Rebecca .... 562-903-6000.. 29 F
rebecca.hong@biola.edu
HONG, Steven .... 800-463-8990 315 B
shong@aada.edu
HONG, Tran .... 951-343-3907.. 30 D
thong@calbaptist.edu
HONKE, Mary, J .... 402-844-7124 292 G
maryh@northeast.edu
HONNELL, Cherie .... 503-494-7878 408 D
acad@ohsu.edu
HONTS, Arlen .... 316-295-5800 187 C
ahonts@friends.edu
HOO, Karlene .... 406-994-5555 287 G
karlene.hoo@montana.edu
HOOD, Brent .... 919-735-5151 367 A
wbhood@waynecc.edu
HOOD, Carra .... 609-652-4514 308 E
carra.hood@stockton.edu
HOOD, Donna .... 828-395-1404 363 D
dhood@isothermal.edu
HOOD, Gwendolyn, D .. 205-348-5855.... 8 E
ghood@aalan.ua.edu
HOOD, Jean .... 817-272-5554 493 L
jmhood@uta.edu
HOOD, Joshua .... 423-775-7574 455 F
jhood3724@bryan.edu
HOOD, Marcia .... 229-430-4832 119 H
marcia.hood@asurams.edu
HOOD, Michael, J .... 724-357-2397 431 A
mhood@iup.edu
HOOD, Mike .... 903-233-4115 477 G
mikehood@letu.edu

HOOD, Patricia .... 706-649-1883 123 E
phood@columbustech.edu
HOOD, Philip .... 847-735-6003 149 H
hood@lakeforest.edu
HOOD, Robin .... 931-363-9800 458 D
rhood@martinmethodist.edu
HOOD, Scott, W .... 207-725-3256 209 H
shood@bowdoin.edu
HOOD, Sonya .... 931-393-1765 463 B
shood@mscc.edu
HOOD, Steven .... 205-348-9364.... 8 E
shood1@sa.ua.edu
HOOD, Steven .... 435-283-7301 500 D
steve.hood@snow.edu
HOOD, Tim .... 815-599-3513 146 B
tim.hood@highland.edu
HOOD, W.C. (Chip) ..... 864-656-3414 444 E
chip@clemson.edu
HOOF, Tom .... 813-974-2011 116 B
HOOGAKKER, John ...... 540-458-8446 519 A
jhoogakker@wlu.edu
HOOGERHEIDE,
Katie, M .... 972-708-7379 474 J
dean-students@gial.edu
HOOK, Amy .... 617-353-2399 224 E
amyhook@bu.edu
HOOK, David .... 602-386-4131.. 11 F
david.hook@arizonachristian.edu
HOOK, Randall .... 540-828-5358 505 F
rhook@bridgewater.edu
HOOK, Rebecca .... 610-436-6973 432 B
rhook@wcupa.edu
HOOK, Samuel, S .... 864-592-4630 449 C
hooks@sccsc.edu
HOOK, Talbort .... 808-455-0611 136 G
talbort@hawaii.edu
HOOKER, Dianna .... 406-638-3142 286 I
dianna@lbhc.edu
HOOKER, George .... 814-866-8406 423 B
ghooker@lecom.edu
HOOKER, JR.,
Richard, D .... 202-685-3838 547 M
HookerR@ndu.edu
HOOKER-HARING,
Christopher .... 484-664-3245 427 C
hookerh@muhlenberg.edu
HOOKS, Alicia .... 913-288-7388 188 G
ahokks@kckcc.edu
HOOKS, Beth .... 919-735-5151 367 A
bhooks@waynecc.edu
HOOKS, Haley .... 229-317-6746 123 H
haley.hooks@darton.edu
HOOKS, Rebecca .... 704-216-3488 365 F
rebecca.hooks@rccc.edu
HOOKS, Vicky, G .... 803-778-6612 443 I
hooksvm@cctech.edu
HOOLE, Thomas .... 978-934-3509 229 A
thomas_hoole@uml.edu
HOOPER, Alice .... 864-429-8728 450 I
HOOPER, Catherine ...... 503-206-3208 410 I
chooper@uws.edu
HOOPER, Celia, R .... 336-334-5744 371 C
crhooper@uncg.edu
HOOPER, Debra, A .... 919-488-8500 358 H
dhooper@living-arts-college.edu
HOOPER, Ricardo .... 310-287-4513.. 52 C
hopperra@wlac.edu
HOOPER, Robert, D ...... 740-427-5109 384 P
hooperr@kenyon.edu
HOOPER, Stephanie, L . 304-336-8990 533 A
stephanie.hooper@westliberty.edu
HOOPER, Tia .... 603-428-2222 298 B
thooper@nec.edu
HOOPES, Robbin .... 513-569-1616 379 K
robbin.hoopes@cincinnatistate.edu
HOOPES, Tom .... 913-360-7529 184 K
thoopes@benedictine.edu
HOORNBEEK, Corbin .... 626-815-5328.. 29 B
choornbeek@apu.edu
HOOTEN, Michael .... 806-354-5589 490 A
michael.hooten@ttuhsc.edu
HOOTON, Linda, J .... 205-853-1200.... 5 C
lhooton@jeffstateonline.com
HOOTS, Cathy .... 336-750-2265 372 D
hoots@wssu.edu
HOOVER, Chris .... 620-341-5337 186 H
choover@emporia.edu
HOOVER, Douglas .... 724-938-4096 430 C
hoover@calu.edu
HOOVER, James, W ..... 214-887-5347 473 E
jhoover@dts.edu
HOOVER, Jean, B .... 717-262-2007 440 D
jhoover@wilson.edu
HOOVER, Jeffrey .... 717-560-8258 423 C
jhoover@lbc.edu
HOOVER, Jonathan .... 214-333-5821 471 L
jonh@dbu.edu
HOOVER, Kathleen .... 610-558-5560 427 D
hooverk@neumann.edu
HOOVER, Kelly .... 410-669-9200 216 F

HOOVER, Kim 601-984-6200 270 H khoover@umc.edu
HOOVER, Linda 806-742-3031 489 F linda.hoover@ttu.edu
HOOVER, Lisa 214-637-3530 496 J lhoover@wadecollege.edu
HOOVER, Lisa, D 570-577-3757 413 E lisa.hoover@bucknell.edu
HOOVER, Lorette, M 706-649-1837 123 E lhoover@columbustech.edu
HOOVER, Myrna 850-644-6089 115 A mhoover@fsu.edu
HOOVER, Nancy 503-699-6261 407 A nhoover@marylhurst.edu
HOOVER, Samantha 212-472-1500 336 A shoover@nysid.edu
HOOVER, Sara 205-226-4989 2 C shoover@bsc.edu
HOOVER, Steve 320-308-3023 261 E smhoover@stcloudstate.edu
HOOVER, Tom 423-425-5300 465 E tom-hoover@utc.edu
HOOVLER, David 216-987-4854 381 A david.hoovler@tri-c.edu
HOOYMAN, Jamie 660-359-3948 279 L jhooyman@mail.ncmissouri.edu
HOPE, Deryle 864-503-5769 451 A dhope@uscupstate.edu
HOPE, Henry 404-471-6355 119 G hhope@agnesscott.edu
HOPE, John 251-981-3771 3 A john.hope@columbiasouthern.edu
HOPE, Kelly 203-332-5085 89 C khope@hcc.commnet.edu
HOPE, Laura 909-652-6113 38 A laura.hope@chaffey.edu
HOPE, Marilyn 909-794-1084 41 G mhope@communitychristiancollege.com
HOPE, Oral 212-431-2300 335 G Oral.Hope@nyls.edu
HOPE, Thomas 407-646-1580 111 H thope@rollins.edu
HOPE, Wilbert 718-270-6961 320 C wilbert@mec.cuny.edu
HOPEWELL, JR., Woodson, H 757-727-5303 508 C woodson.hopewell@hamptonu.edu
HOPEY, Christopher, E 978-837-5110 233 G christopher.hopey@merrimack.edu
HOPIE, Linty 360-417-6504 525 A lhopie@pencol.edu
HOPKINS, Alexander, M 713-798-4262 469 C ahopkins@bcm.edu
HOPKINS, Amanda 407-646-2124 111 H ahopkins@rollins.edu
HOPKINS, Becky 323-343-3200 34 A bhopkins@cslanet.calstatela.edu
HOPKINS, Berta 864-592-4262 449 C hopkinsb@sccsc.edu
HOPKINS, Bill 650-543-3935 54 B bill.hopkins@menlo.edu
HOPKINS, Bob 601-266-4947 271 B bob.hopkins@usm.edu
HOPKINS, Boone 864-596-9183 445 E boone.hopkins@converse.edu
HOPKINS, Bruce 229-430-2837 119 I
HOPKINS, Christi 620-242-0414 189 E hopkinsc@mcpherson.edu
HOPKINS, Darlene 910-630-7150 359 C dhopkins@methodist.edu
HOPKINS, David, R 937-775-2312 396 A david.hopkins@wright.edu
HOPKINS, Denise, C 718-990-1323 340 G hopkinsd@stjohns.edu
HOPKINS, Dennis 828-726-2750 360 F dhopkins@cccti.edu
HOPKINS, Drew, W 609-984-3430 308 H dhopkins@tesc.edu
HOPKINS, Elijah 406-768-6371 286 H ehopkins@fpcc.edu
HOPKINS, Gena 260-459-4500 169 D ghopkins@ibcfortwayne.edu
HOPKINS, Hunter, H 412-338-4770 422 A hhopkins@kaplan.edu
HOPKINS, James 401-874-4977 442 E jimhopkins@uri.edu
HOPKINS, Jane, L 618-664-6600 145 E jane.hopkins@greenville.edu
HOPKINS, John 330-263-2082 380 E jhopkins@wooster.edu
HOPKINS, LC, John 703-416-1441 508 F jhopkins@ipsciences.edu
HOPKINS, Joseph 205-726-2778 6 F jhopkins@samford.edu
HOPKINS, Kathryn 870-777-5722 24 H kathryn.hopkins@uacch.edu
HOPKINS, Kent 480-965-2408 11 J kent.hopkins@asu.edu
HOPKINS, Kevin 785-594-8553 184 F kevin.hopkins@bakeru.edu
HOPKINS, Laurie, B 803-786-3669 445 C lhopkins@columbiasc.edu
HOPKINS, OP, Maggie 608-663-3388 536 A mhopkins@edgewood.edu
HOPKINS, Marilyn 707-638-5276 70 B marilyn.hopkins@tu.edu
HOPKINS, Mark 706-236-2231 121 E mhopkins@berry.edu
HOPKINS, Melissa 573-518-2177 278 F mhopkins@mineralarea.edu
HOPKINS, Nicole 509-574-6870 529 B nhopkins@yvcc.edu
HOPKINS, Paulette 619-388-7750 62 H phopkins@sdccd.edu
HOPKINS, Randy 816-501-4659 281 B randy.hopkins@rockhurst.edu
HOPKINS, Robert, P 212-353-4350 323 B bob@cooper.edu
HOPKINS, Sara 615-248-1653 464 E shopkins@trevecca.edu
HOPKINS, Shirley, L 804-523-5896 515 F shopkins@reynolds.edu
HOPKINS, Stacy 724-357-2218 431 A stacy.hopkins@iup.edu
HOPKINS, Stacy 724-357-2230 431 A stacy.hopkins@iup.edu
HOPKINS, T. Hampton 704-355-5585 355 G hampton.hopkins@carolinascollege.edu
HOPKINS, Theresa 845-451-1311 323 E t_hopkin@culinary.edu
HOPKINS, Thomas, F 540-464-7228 518 A hopkinstf@vmi.edu
HOPKINS-BEST, Mary 715-232-1168 541 B hopkinsbestm@uwstout.edu
HOPKINS GROSS, Anne, M 802-447-6323 503 A ahopkinsgross@svc.edu
HOPMANS, Jan, W 530-752-0860 71 A jwhopmans@ucdavis.edu
HOPP, Lisa 219-989-2818 171 L psgerard@purduecal.edu
HOPP, Melissa 443-840-3176 214 F mhopp@ccbcmd.edu
HOPP, Susan 503-883-2278 406 I shopp@linfield.edu
HOPPA, Anthony, T 585-245-5531 345 D thoppa@geneseo.edu
HOPPE, Elizabeth 909-706-3497 76 I shoppe@westernu.edu
HOPPE, Heather 419-251-8989 386 C heather.hoppe@mercycollege.edu
HOPPE, Jim 651-696-6220 256 L hoppe@macalester.edu
HOPPE, Ken 870-236-6901 20 I khoppe@crc.edu
HOPPER, Darla 812-535-5110 172 F dhopper@smwc.edu
HOPPER, David, R 757-455-3415 518 H dhopper@vwc.edu
HOPPER, Gary 830-372-6309 487 C ghopper@tlu.edu
HOPPER, George, M 662-325-2953 269 A ghopper@cfr.msstate.edu
HOPPER, Jeffry 501-279-4478 21 A hopper@harding.edu
HOPPER, Karen, S 870-508-6110 19 H khopper@asumh.edu
HOPPER, Lisa 501-760-4241 21 H lhopper@npcc.edu
HOPPER, Lorrie 559-325-5238 69 A lorrie.hopper@scccd.edu
HOPPER, Richard 207-453-5129 211 B president@kvcc.me.edu
HOPPER, Susan 731-661-5078 464 G shopper@uu.edu
HOPPER, William, E 305-626-3701 104 B William.Hopper@fmuniv.edu
HOPPLE, Marcella 574-936-8898 164 A marcella.hopple@ancilla.edu
HOPPLE, Stephnie 928-541-7777 16 B shopple@ncu.edu
HOPSON, April 706-649-1858 123 E
HOPSON, JR., George, A 864-977-2194 448 A george.hopson@ngu.edu
HOPSON, Pamela, F 812-465-7188 174 D pfhopson@usi.edu
HOPWOOD, Dennis, T 509-527-5172 528 F hopwoodt@whitman.edu
HORADAN, Lloyd 478-553-2060 129 C lhoradan@oftc.edu
HORADAN, Lloyd 478-553-2060 129 D lhoradan@oftc.edu
HORAK, Janice 254-968-9857 485 A jhorak@tarleton.edu
HORAK, Janice 254-968-9890 485 A jhorak@tarleton.edu
HORAK, Maureen 413-662-5205 230 C m.horak@mcla.edu
HORAK, Michael, D 972-860-8344 472 E MHorak@dcccd.edu
HORAN, Kevin 925-473-7401 42 F khoran@losmedanos.edu
HORAN, Michael, D 614-236-6813 378 H mhoran@capital.edu
HORAN, Sean 212-659-7200 330 A shoran@tkc.edu
HORAN, Thomas 909-607-3811 39 E thomas.horan@cgu.edu
HORAN, Thomas 909-607-9302 39 E thomas.horan@cgu.edu
HORBACEWICZ, Jill 212-463-0400 350 C jillh@touro.edu
HORBACK, Sachi 253-964-6531 525 C shorback@pierce.ctc.edu
HORD, Lisa 937-393-3431 391 F lhord@sscc.edu
HORGAN, Elizabeth 508-213-2289 235 C elizabeth.horgan@nichols.edu
HORGAN, Joan 518-454-5296 322 C horganj@strose.edu
HORGAN, Louise, M 732-224-2202 300 F lhorgan@brookdalecc.edu
HORGAN, Ralph, R 412-268-6156 414 J rh44@andrew.cmu.edu
HORGEN, David 808-236-5864 135 C dhorgen@hpu.edu
HORINEK, Jon 580-581-2627 397 A jhorinek@cameron.edu
HORISSIAN, Kevork, T 570-577-3623 413 E kevork.horissian@bucknell.edu
HORN, Allison 503-883-2323 406 I ahorn@linfield.edu
HORN, Brian, S 727-816-3458 110 B hornb@phsc.edu
HORN, Cindy 231-591-5309 242 L CindyHorn@ferris.edu
HORN, David, G 978-468-7111 227 B dhorn@gcts.edu
HORN, Jamie 334-386-7168 3 I jhorn@faulkner.edu
HORN, Jason 504-520-7330 209 E jhorn1@xula.edu
HORN, Jay 817-272-2355 493 L horn@uta.edu
HORN, John 608-890-0158 539 D horn1@recsports.wisc.edu
HORN, John, F 215-898-7593 437 I horn3@upenn.edu
HORN, Josh 518-828-4181 322 E josh.horn@sunycgcc.edu
HORN, Michael 704-330-5963 361 D michael.horn@cpcc.edu
HORN, Paul, M 212-998-3228 336 C paul.horn@nyu.edu
HORN, Samuel, E 864-242-5100 443 G
HORN, Vincent 215-596-7532 438 E v.horn@usciences.edu
HORN BUNK, Sheri 661-763-7936 69 E shornbunk@taftcollege.edu
HORNADAY, Kevin 910-296-2487 363 E khornaday@jamessprunt.edu
HORNBACHER, Noel 313-593-5410 251 D noelhorn@umich.edu
HORNBECK, Billi 605-455-6037 452 L bhornbeck@olc.edu
HORNBERGER, Cynthia, A 785-670-1213 192 B cynthia.hornberger@washburn.edu
HORNBERGER, Lois 503-352-2240 408 I lhornberger@pacificu.edu
HORNBERGER, Rob 417-836-6444 279 A robhornberger@missouristate.edu
HORNBOSTEL, Rachael 303-369-5151 84 N rachael.hornbostel@plattcolorado.edu
HORNBUCKLE, Jami, M 606-783-2372 198 H j.hornbuckle@moreheadstate.edu
HORNBURG, Trisha, L 262-691-5446 544 D thornburg@wctc.edu
HORNE, Arlene 903-886-5159 485 E arlene.horne@tamuc.edu
HORNE, Bart 502-863-8182 195 A bart_horne@georgetowncollege.edu
HORNE, Cathy 704-272-5337 366 A chorne@spcc.edu
HORNE, David 410-704-4236 221 A dhorne@towson.edu
HORNE, Derek 601-877-6500 266 C djhorne@alcorn.edu
HORNE, Hadie, C 252-246-1221 367 D hhorne@wilsoncc.edu
HORNE, Pamela, T 765-494-9116 171 K pamhorne@purdue.edu
HORNE, Valerie 601-403-1211 270 A vhorne@prcc.edu
HORNER, Andrew, E 937-229-3736 393 E ahorner1@udayton.edu
HORNER, Donnie 904-256-7672 106 Q dhorner3@ju.edu
HORNER, Jeff 719-502-2011 84 J jeffrey.horner@ppcc.edu
HORNER, Jeffrey, T 423-798-7952 464 C jeff.horner@ws.edu
HORNER, Jennifer 860-465-5775 88 E hornerje@easternct.edu
HORNER, Jennifer 860-768-4296 92 F horner@hartford.edu
HORNER, Jody 402-941-6000 291 I president@midlandu.edu
HORNER, Kenneth, R 931-540-2533 462 E khorner@columbiastate.edu
HORNER, Kristin 620-251-7700 186 C horner.kristin@coffeyville.edu
HORNER, Sherri 419-372-7343 377 I shorner@bgsu.edu
HORNER, Stacy 269-782-1220 250 D shorner@swmich.edu
HORNER, Taylor 617-369-3620 236 E thorner@smfa.edu
HORNER, Theresa 716-827-2485 350 H hornert@trocaire.edu
HORNICK, Robert 510-567-6174 69 D bhornick@sum.edu
HORNING, Kirsten 503-338-2341 405 B khorning@clatsopcc.edu
HORNOR, Tara, F 843-953-5336 444 C tara.mcnealy@citadel.edu
HORNS, Phyllis, N 252-744-2265 369 E hornsp@ecu.edu
HORNSBY, Jake 415-518-5396 71 B hornsbyj@uchastings.edu
HORNSBY, Sharon 225-222-4251 203 I
HOROWITZ, Avery 718-252-7800 350 C averymh@touro.edu
HOROWITZ, Boruch Avrohom 718-438-2018 338 J rcby26@aol.com
HOROWITZ, Elias 845-783-0833 351 F
HOROWITZ, Judy 716-673-3111 343 F judy.horowitz@fredonia.edu
HOROWITZ, Samuel, L 904-264-2172 111 G shorowitz@iws.edu
HOROWITZ, Sara 212-678-8838 329 H sahorowitz@jtsa.edu
HORRELL, Jeffrey, L 603-646-2235 297 G jeffrey.l.horrell@dartmouth.edu
HORSCH, Ellen, S 906-487-1737 247 A eshorsch@mtu.edu
HORSCH, Tim 515-244-4221 175 C horscht@aib.edu
HORSEY, Cheryl, L 215-641-5546 420 A horsey.c@gmercyu.edu
HORSEY, Dwight, G 717-871-5100 431 E dwight.horsey@millersville.edu
HORST, Becky 574-535-7515 166 C beckybh@goshen.edu
HORSTMEYER, Mark 708-974-5275 153 D horstmeyer@morainevalley.edu
HORTON, Becky 478-825-6226 124 E hortonb@fvsu.edu
HORTON, C, R 864-488-4586 447 F chorton@limestone.edu
HORTON, Claudia 816-833-0524 178 G horton@graceland.edu
HORTON, Connie 310-506-4210 58 H connie.horton@pepperdine.edu
HORTON, Freeman 662-621-4231 266 H fhorton@coahomacc.edu
HORTON, Gretchen 503-253-3443 408 B ghorton@ocom.edu
HORTON, Howard, E 617-951-2350 234 F howard.horton@necb.edu
HORTON, Jana 251-575-8252 1 C jhorton@ascc.edu
HORTON, Jane, T 540-458-8401 519 A jhorton@wlu.edu
HORTON, Jeff 270-707-3721 196 D jeff.horton@kctcs.edu
HORTON, Johnna 507-389-7223 262 A johnna.horton@southcentral.edu
HORTON, Joseph, M 603-641-7600 298 F jhorton@anselm.edu
HORTON, Julian, K 240-500-2000 215 C jkhorton@hagerstowncc.edu
HORTON, Kelley, R 910-775-4403 371 D kelley.horton@uncp.edu
HORTON, Kimberly 937-778-7806 381 K khorton@edisonohio.edu
HORTON, Leslie 508-854-2798 232 F lhorton@qcc.mass.edu
HORTON, Lindsey 601-979-2580 267 H lindsey.horton@jsums.edu
HORTON, Mac 251-380-2272 7 F horton@shc.edu
HORTON, Michele 850-471-4639 110 D mhorton@pensacolastate.edu
HORTON, Paul 772-462-7520 106 F phorton@irsc.edu
HORTON, Steve 318-357-5851 208 D hortons@nsula.edu
HORTON, Steve 318-357-4330 208 D hortons@nsula.edu

HORTON, Susan 845-434-5750 349 C shorton@sullivan.suny.edu
HORTON, Tracy 901-333-5760 464 A thorton@southwest.tn.edu
HORTON, JR., Walter, E 330-325-6499 387 F wehj@neomed.edu
HORTWITZ, Richard 270-926-4040 194 K rhortwitz@daymarcollege.edu
HORVATH, Elizabeth 608-757-7704 542 L ehorvath@blackhawk.edu
HORVATH, Fran 831-582-3000 34 C
HORVATH, Karl 215-646-7300 420 A horvath.k@gmercyu.edu
HORVATH, Rebecca, L 215-951-1898 422 F horvath@lasalle.edu
HORVATH, Virginia, S 716-673-3456 343 F virginia.horvath@fredonia.edu
HORVATH-PLYMAN, Melissa 201-684-7081 305 F mhorvath@ramapo.edu
HORWATH, Amy 814-536-5168 414 E ahorwath@crbc.net
HOSACK, Susan, E 314-935-5567 285 E sue.hosack@wustl.edu
HOSCH, Braden, J 631-632-6210 344 C braden.hosch@stonybrook.edu
HOSCH, Jason 504-278-6281 204 B jhosch@nunez.edu
HOSEA, Walter 865-251-1800 460 J whosea@southcollegetn.edu
HOSEI, Huan, F 671-735-5595 549 E huan.hosei@guamcc.edu
HOSELTON, Steven, A 312-341-2442 157 E shoselton@roosevelt.edu
HOSENEY, Jason 360-538-4066 523 A
HOSKEY, Lisa 607-274-3011 328 H
HOSKING, Amanda 215-567-7080 412 G ahosking@aii.edu
HOSKINS, Deb 970-641-2237 87 F dhoskins@western.edu
HOSKINS, Sheila 252-823-5166 362 D hoskinss@edgecombe.edu
HOSKINS, Steve 606-546-4151 200 E shoskins@unionky.edu
HOSKINSON, John 661-362-5900 40 H john.hoskinson@canyons.edu
HOSKOVEC, Victoria 402-399-2431 289 I vhoskovec@csm.edu
HOSKOWITZ, Joel, M 410-386-8412 214 B jhoskowitz@carrollcc.edu
HOSLET, Charles 608-265-2822 539 D choslet@wisc.edu
HOSPEDALES, Rhonda 215-572-2900 412 F
HOSS, Amy 785-227-3380 185 A hossaj@bethanylb.edu
HOSS, Cindy 620-665-3507 188 A hossc@hutchcc.edu
HOSS, Neal 760-750-4400 35 B nhoss@csusm.edu
HOSSAIN, Zakir 304-327-4161 532 D zhossain@bluefieldstate.edu
HOSSAIN, Zakir 804-257-5606 518 E zhossain@vuu.edu
HOSSENLOPP, Jeanne, M 414-288-1532 537 B jeanne.hossenlopp@marquette.edu
HOSTALKA, Amanda 443-394-9549 218 E ahostalka@stevenson.edu
HOSTELLER, Mayme 212-228-1888 339 C
HOSTER, Robert, L 570-577-3342 413 E bob.hoster@bucknell.edu
HOSTETLER, Bumper, R 812-888-4510 174 F bhostetler@vinu.edu
HOSTETLER, Chad 304-457-6320 529 C hostetlercs@ab.edu
HOSTETLER, James, D 570-577-1911 413 E jim.hostetler@bucknell.edu
HOSTETLER, Lori, J 812-888-4121 174 F lhostetler@vinu.edu
HOSTETLER, Marna, M 812-464-1834 174 D mmhostetle@usi.edu
HOSTETLER, Theodore, J 434-947-8133 511 D thostetler@randolphcollege.edu
HOSTETLER, Timothy, J 423-775-7262 455 F hostetti@bryan.edu
HOSTETTER, Julie, M 800-287-8822 164 E hosteju@bethanyseminary.edu
HOSTETTER, Larry 270-686-4236 193 G larry.hostetter@brescia.edu
HOSTETTER, Sandy 215-884-8942 440 E librarian@woninstitute.edu
HOSTETTER, Steve, J 218-751-8670 263 J stevehostetter@oakhills.edu
HOSTINA, Michael 907-450-8080 10 G mike.hostina@alaska.edu
HOSTLER, Sharon, L 434-924-9030 514 A slh2m@virginia.edu
HOTALING, Diane, E 757-455-3216 518 H dhotaling@vwc.edu
HOTALING, Marcus, S 518-388-6161 350 K hotalinm@union.edu
HOTCHKISS, Carolyn 781-239-5528 222 E hotchkiss@babson.edu
HOTCHKISS, Charles 617-989-4831 237 G hotchkissc@wit.edu
HOTEZ, Peter, J 713-798-1199 469 C hotez@bcm.edu
HOTLE, C. Patrick 573-288-6394 274 C photle@culver.edu
HOTOVY, Steve 402-471-2505 292 A shotovy@nscs.edu
HOTTA, Tomoki 808-946-3773 134 L
HOTTEL, Haven 910-893-1421 355 C hottelh@campbell.edu
HOTTEL, Timothy, L 901-448-6202 465 G thottel@uthsc.edu
HOTTENSTEIN, Kristi 517-787-0800 244 H hottenskristin@jccmi.edu
HOTZ, Lindsey 319-895-4244 177 A lhotz@cornellcollege.edu
HOTZFIELD, Brian 773-298-3096 158 F hotzfield@sxu.edu
HOTZLER, Russell, K 718-260-5400 320 D rhotzler@citytech.cuny.edu
HOU, Feng 941-752-5694 114 B houf@scf.edu
HOUBECK, JR., Robert, L 810-762-3410 251 E rhoubeck@umflint.edu
HOUCHINS, Shelia, E 270-745-4493 201 D shelia.houchins@wku.edu
HOUCK, Beth 864-977-7200 448 A beth.houck@ngu.edu
HOUCK, Brenda 757-340-2121 506 E bshouck@centura.edu
HOUCK, Clarence, M 803-934-3235 447 K chouck@morris.edu
HOUCK, James, W 814-865-4294 428 C jwh32@psu.edu
HOUCK, Jancy 803-777-8315 450 B jancyh@mailbox.sc.edu
HOUCK, Laurie 330-263-2583 380 E lhouck@wooster.edu
HOUCK, Maureen, B 516-463-6745 328 A maureen.b.houck@hofstra.edu
HOUCK, Susan 803-738-7610 447 H houcks@midlandstech.edu
HOUDE, Edward 410-228-9250 219 G
HOUDEK, Rob 605-642-6562 453 G robert.houdek@bhsu.edu
HOUDYSHELL, Michael 308-635-6123 294 C houdyshe@wncc.edu
HOUFER, Michael 651-747-4085 258 D michael.houfer@century.edu
HOUGH, Bradley 636-227-2100 277 A brad.hough@logan.edu
HOUGH, David 417-836-5254 279 A davidhough@missouristate.edu
HOUGH, John 304-724-3700 529 F jhough@apus.edu
HOUGH, Melanie 419-772-2024 388 I m-hough@onu.edu
HOUGH, Tony 803-738-7695 447 H hought@midlandstech.edu
HOUGH, Twyla 210-999-8321 490 E Twyla.Hough@trinity.edu
HOUGHTON, David, C 405-585-4400 399 I david.houghton@okbu.edu
HOUGHTON, James 212-799-5000 329 I
HOUGLAND, Dawn 312-341-3531 157 E dhougland@roosevelt.edu
HOUK, Christopher 270-686-4241 193 G chris.houk@brescia.edu
HOUK, Suzanne, N 724-458-2208 419 F snhouk@gcc.edu
HOULE, David 734-432-5380 246 B dhoule@madonna.edu
HOULE, Greg 212-938-5607 347 C ghoule@sunyopt.edu
HOULIHAN, Janet, M 714-895-8307 40 C jhoulihan@gwc.cccd.edu
HOULIHAN, Jill 501-337-5000 20 H jhoulihan@coto.edu
HOULIHAN, Robert 516-323-3457 333 E rhoulihan@molloy.edu
HOULIHAN, Timothy, J 718-489-5290 340 E thoulihan@sfc.edu
HOULT, Kevin 256-782-8122 4 L khoult@jsu.edu
HOURANY, Lance 925-631-4767 61 G lph5@stmarys-ca.edu
HOURIGAN, Christopher, P 401-456-8998 442 A chourigan@ric.edu
HOURIGAN, Gerard 216-987-4706 381 A gerard.hourigan@tri-c.edu
HOUSE, Antionette, T 804-257-5628 518 E athouse@vuu.edu
HOUSE, Brittany 574-284-4569 172 G bhouse@saintmarys.edu
HOUSE, DeAndre 601-857-3701 267 D Deandre.House@hindscc.edu
HOUSE, H. Wayne 888-777-7675 522 K hwhouse@faithseminary.edu
HOUSE, J. Daniel 815-753-6002 154 I jhouse@niu.edu
HOUSE, Jacqueline 305-628-6727 112 B jhouse@stu.edu
HOUSE, Jess 203-837-9500 88 G housej@wcsu.edu
HOUSE, Seymour 503-845-3507 407 B seymour.house@mtangel.edu
HOUSE, Stephanie 208-769-3368 138 G stephanie.house@nic.edu
HOUSE, Steven, D 336-278-6647 356 F shouse@elon.edu
HOUSE, Vicki 325-670-1276 474 M vhouse@hsutx.edu
HOUSEKNECHT, Rick 215-368-5000 412 K rhouseknecht@biblical.edu
HOUSEL, William 318-357-4592 208 D houselw@nsula.edu
HOUSENICK, Joseph 570-408-4630 440 B joseph.housenick@wilkes.edu
HOUSER, Frieda 406-444-6570 287 C fhouser@montana.edu
HOUSER, Gerald, B 503-370-6413 411 D jhouser@willamette.edu
HOUSER, Janet 303-458-4174 85 G jhouser@regis.edu
HOUSER, John 575-562-2123 310 I john.houser@enmu.edu
HOUSER, Kay 910-642-7141 366 B Kay.Houser@sccnc.edu
HOUSER, Kristin 661-362-3245 40 H kristin.houser@canyons.edu
HOUSER, Robert 970-351-1759 87 A robert.houser@ucno.edu
HOUSER, Samuel 717-291-4271 418 J sam.houser@fandm.edu
HOUSEWORTH, Julie 573-592-4260 286 A julie.houseworth@williamwoods.edu
HOUSHMAND, Ali, A 856-256-4100 306 D houshmand@rowan.edu
HOUSHOLDER, Suahil 765-641-4131 164 B srhousholder@anderson.edu
HOUSHOWER, Hans 419-358-3234 377 H houshowerh@bluffton.edu
HOUSKA, Nila 712-749-2233 176 D houskan@bvu.edu
HOUSLEY, Harold 903-875-7307 479 I harold.housley@navarrocollege.edu
HOUSLEY, Heather, L 404-413-2070 126 D heatherh@gsu.edu
HOUSLEY, La Royce 310-954-4191 54 I ldodd@msmu.edu
HOUSTON, A. Glen 281-283-3000 491 E houston@uhcl.edu
HOUSTON, Adam 760-921-5463 58 C ahouston@paloverde.edu
HOUSTON, Bernard 334-229-4200 1 D bhouston@alasu.edu
HOUSTON, Chrystal 402-363-5607 294 G chrystal.houston@york.edu
HOUSTON, Don 408-855-5428 76 E don.houston@wvm.edu
HOUSTON, Doug 636-584-6732 274 J doug.houston@eastcentral.edu
HOUSTON, Douglas, B 530-741-6971 78 D dhouston@yccd.edu
HOUSTON, Kim 731-352-6421 455 E houstonk@bethelu.edu
HOUSTON, Kristen 206-876-6100 526 E khouston@theseattleschool.edu
HOUSTON, Michael 662-621-4205 266 H mhouston@coahomacc.edu
HOUSTON, Nainsi 419-448-2108 383 C nhouston@heidelberg.edu
HOUSTON, Rachel 704-403-1228 355 B rachel.houston@carolinashealthcare.org
HOUSTON, Richard 662-846-4694 267 A rhouston@deltastate.edu
HOUSTON, Rick 978-867-4130 227 A ric.houston@gordon.edu
HOUSTON, Teresa, L 601-635-6202 267 B thouston@eccc.edu
HOUSTON, Tim 740-695-9500 377 F thouston@belmontcollege.edu
HOUSTON, Vinson 256-782-5993 4 L vhouston@jsu.edu
HOUSTON-BROWN, Clive, K 909-593-3511 73 B chouston-brown@laverne.edu
HOUSTON-PHILPOT, Kimberly, R 989-774-2085 240 O houst1kr@cmich.edu
HOUTMAN, Anne 661-654-3450 32 G ahoutman@csub.edu
HOVATTER, Angela, L 301-687-4301 220 D ahovatter@frostburg.edu
HOVEKAMP, Tina 541-383-7563 404 K thovekamp@cocc.edu
HOVEN, Les, J 405-325-5647 403 I lhoven@ou.edu
HOVERSTEN, Mark, E 208-885-5423 139 C hoverstm@uidaho.edu
HOVESTOL, Dan 406-586-3585 287 B dan.hovestol@montanabiblecollege.edu
HOVEY, Ann 503-842-8222 410 C Hovey@tillamookbay.cc
HOVEY, Jeff 314-977-8375 281 M hoveyj@slu.edu
HOVEY, Mark 860-685-2337 93 B mhover@wesleyan.edu
HOVEY, Rebecca 413-584-2700 236 G rhovey@smith.edu
HOVEY, Roger, S 308-635-6012 294 C rhovey@wncc.edu
HOW, Christine 402-557-7002 289 B christine.doocy@bellevue.edu
HOWAR, Julie 309-694-5505 146 C julie.howar@icc.edu
HOWARD, Amy 314-529-6737 277 B ahoward@maryville.edu
HOWARD, Andrew 806-743-7103 490 A andrew.howard@ttuhsc.edu
HOWARD, Angelita 404-627-2681 121 F angelita.howard@beulah.org
HOWARD, Augustus 404-527-4520 122 D ahoward@caraver.edu
HOWARD, Burgwell 847-467-0301 155 D b-howard@northwestern.edu
HOWARD, Catherine 903-823-3285 484 D catherine.howard@texarkanacollege.edu
HOWARD, Catherine, W 804-828-8790 514 F choward@vcu.edu
HOWARD, Cecil, E 717-477-1161 431 F cehoward@ship.edu
HOWARD, Chad 479-248-7236 20 K choward@ecollege.edu
HOWARD, Charles, L 215-898-8457 437 I choward@pobox.upenn.edu
HOWARD, Cheryl 617-521-2131 236 F cheryl.howard@simmons.edu
HOWARD, Christie 903-593-8311 487 A choward@texascollege.edu
HOWARD, Christopher, B 434-223-6110 508 B choward@hsc.edu
HOWARD, Cindy 800-962-7682 285 I choward@wma.edu
HOWARD, Dale, S 330-490-7303 395 C dhoward@walsh.edu
HOWARD, Dan 575-646-1727 312 A provost@nmsu.edu
HOWARD, Dana, K 318-274-3133 207 H howardd@gram.edu
HOWARD, Daniel 318-473-6444 205 A dhoward@lsua.edu
HOWARD, Doris 415-503-6214 63 A finaid@sfcm.edu
HOWARD, Douglas 603-888-1311 298 E dhoward@rivier.edu
HOWARD, JR., Eddie 330-941-2018 396 C ejhoward01@ysu.edu
HOWARD, Elizabeth 215-646-7300 420 A howard.e@gmercyu.edu
HOWARD, Ezra 662-621-4083 266 H ehoward@coahomacc.edu
HOWARD, Gail 504-865-3849 206 A ghoward@loyno.edu
HOWARD, Gary, E 859-858-3511 193 A gary.howard@asbury.edu
HOWARD, Genevieve 360-992-2936 521 A ghoward@clark.edu
HOWARD, Gerard, L 601-979-1073 267 H gerard.l.howard@jsums.edu
HOWARD, Herman 803-705-4567 443 F howardh@benedict.edu
HOWARD, James 573-681-5275 276 K jhoward@nebook.com
HOWARD, Jane 317-738-8051 166 B jhoward@franklincollege.edu
HOWARD, Jane 620-792-9208 184 I howardj@bartonccc.edu
HOWARD, Jay, R 317-940-9874 164 L jrhoward@butler.edu
HOWARD, Jeffery, S 423-439-4210 461 D howardjs@etsu.edu
HOWARD, Jennifer, L 425-388-9232 522 I jhoward@everettcc.edu
HOWARD, Jessica 971-722-6268 409 C jessica.howard@pcc.edu
HOWARD, Jonathan 202-319-5232 95 A howardjr@cua.edu
HOWARD, Keith, E 478-301-2915 128 G howard_ke@mercer.edu

HUBBARD, Janet 248-689-8282 251 I
jhubbard@walshcollege.edu

HUBBARD, Jeannette 726-946-7199 439 D
hubbarj@westminster.edu

HUBBARD, Joan 801-626-6403 500 C
jhubbard@weber.edu

HUBBARD, Laura, E 716-645-5124 343 E
laurahub@buffalo.edu

HUBBARD, Margaret 305-899-1156 99 B
mhubbard@barry.edu

HUBBARD, Michael 513-745-3741 396 B
0565mgr@fheg.follett.com

HUBBARD, Paul 617-850-1282 227 F
phubbard@hchc.edu

HUBBARD, R. Glenn 212-854-2888 322 F
rgh1@columbia.edu

HUBBARD, Robert 203-773-8563 87 M
hubbard@albertus.edu

HUBBARD, Rosemary 703-284-1560 510 B
rosemary.hubbard@marymount.edu

HUBBARD, Ruth 443-334-2203 218 E
rhubbard@stevenson.edu

HUBBARD, William 920-465-2510 539 F
hubbardw@uwgb.edu

HUBBELL, Kent, L 607-255-1115 323 C
dean_of_students@cornell.edu

HUBBELL, Lisa 510-485-7830 58 G
lhubbell@patten.edu

HUBBERT, Daron 951-552-8000 30 D
dhubbert@calbaptist.edu

HUBBS, Jocelyn 541-684-7291 407 I
jhubbs@nwcu.edu

HUBER, Amy 973-803-5000 305 A
ahuber@pillar.edu

HUBER, Bettina 818-677-3277 34 D
bettina.huber@csun.edu

HUBER, Catherine 716-829-8394 324 E
huberc@dyc.edu

HUBER, Chip 616-222-1423 241 G
chip.huber@cornerstone.edu

HUBER, Gary 239-280-2573 98 O
gary.huber@avemaria.edu

HUBER, Gary 309-796-5602 140 D
huberg@bhc.edu

HUBER, Jason 704-971-8500 355 J
jhuber@charlottelaw.edu

HUBER, Kristina 814-732-1669 430 G
khuber41@gmail.com

HUBER, Lane 701-224-5714 374 E
lane.huber@bismarckstate.edu

HUBER, Laurie, G 248-232-4513 248 E
lghuber@oaklandcc.edu

HUBER, Lydia 361-572-6461 496 D
lydia.huber@victoriacollege.edu

HUBER, Margaret 605-229-8405 453 A
margaret.huber@presentation.edu

HUBER, Mark, D 570-372-4247 435 I
huber@susqu.edu

HUBER, Michael 484-664-3150 427 C
huber@muhlenberg.edu

HUBER, Morgan 605-995-7250 452 H
morgan.huber@mitchelltech.edu

HUBER, Patricia, B 540-674-3631 516 B
phuber@nr.edu

HUBER, Peter 920-206-2347 536 T
peter.huber@mbu.edu

HUBERMAN, Jeffrey, H 309-677-2360 140 H
huberman@bradley.edu

HUBERMAN, Steven 212-463-0400 350 C
stevenh@touro.edu

HUBERS, Todd, K 616-526-6495 240 L
thubers@calvin.edu

HUBERT, Lydia 229-468-2000 134 I
lydia.hubert@wiregrass.edu

HUBINGER, Amy, M 906-227-2626 248 B
ahubinge@nmu.edu

HUBLER, Barbara 415-338-2611 36 A
bhubler@sfsu.edu

HUBREGTSE, Joyce 605-221-3113 452 F
jhubregtse@kilian.edu

HUBRIC, Kimberly, A 610-921-7629 411 E
khubric@albright.edu

HUCH, Robert, E 540-261-4098 512 J
bob.huch@svu.edu

HUCK, Alysia 701-858-3065 374 B
alysia.huck@mnotstateu.edu

HUCKABA, Sam 850-644-4404 115 A
shuckaba@fsu.edu

HUCKABAY, Sonia 559-791-2403 49 G
shuckaba@portervillecollege.edu

HUCKABEE, Vicki 903-223-3025 486 C
vhuckabee@tamut.edu

HUCKABY, Henry, M 404-962-3000 133 G
chancellor@usg.edu

HUCKESTEIN, Jim 503-594-3010 405 A
jim.huckestein@clackamas.edu

HUCKESTEIN, Julie 503-399-6591 404 L
julie.huckestein@chemeketa.edu

HUCKINS, Heather 603-535-2249 299 E
hhuckins@plymouth.edu

HUCKS, Cheri, A 864-592-4931 449 C
hucksc@sccsc.edu

HUDACK, John, J 716-827-2512 350 H
hudackj@trocaire.edu

HUDAK, Jane, E 484-664-3300 427 C
hudak@muhlenberg.edu

HUDAK, Randy 304-293-7202 533 D
randy.hudak@mail.wvu.edu

HUDAK, Sharon 570-674-6295 426 D
shudak@misericordia.edu

HUDALLA, Theo 402-935-9400 291 L
thudalla@nechristian.edu

HUDDLESTON, Gwen 805-289-6388 75 E
ghuddleston@vcccd.edu

HUDDLESTON, Mark 402-935-9400 291 L
mhuddleston@nechristian.edu

HUDDLESTON, Mark, W 603-862-2450 299 B
presidents.office@unh.edu

HUDDLESTON, Ryan 925-473-7328 42 F
rhuddleston@4cd.edu

HUDDLESTON, Scott 641-784-4744 178 G
huddlest@graceland.edu

HUDDLESTON, Sean 508-626-4515 230 A
shuddleston@framingham.edu

HUDGENS, Lisa 618-985-3741 148 G
lisahudgens@jalc.edu

HUDGIK, Mark 413-775-1810 231 E
hudgikm@gcc.mass.edu

HUDGIN, Denise 419-251-1324 386 C
denise.hudgin@mercycollege.edu

HUDGINS, Chris 702-895-0301 295 G
chris.hudgins@unlv.edu

HUDGINS, John, L 410-951-3528 220 C
jhudgins@coppin.edu

HUDGINS, V. Lavoyed 859-985-3990 193 F
hudginsv@berea.edu

HUDGINS, V. Lavoyed 859-985-3240 193 F
hudginsv@berea.edu

HUDIK, Stephen 201-684-7845 305 F
shudik@ramapo.edu

HUDLUN, Randy 417-862-9533 275 C
rhedlun@globaluniversity.edu

HUDMAN, Steve 936-639-1301 467 I
shudman@angelina.edu

HUDSON, Angela 501-686-2504 23 F
ahudson@uasys.edu

HUDSON, Bo 918-293-4912 400 E
steven.w.hudson@okstate.edu

HUDSON, Bobby 615-230-3445 464 B
bobby.hudson@volstate.edu

HUDSON, Cynthia 405-466-2915 398 E
cehudson@langston.edu

HUDSON, David, D 714-895-8907 40 C
dhudson@gwc.cccd.edu

HUDSON, Dean, P 843-349-2739 444 G
dhudson@coastal.edu

HUDSON, Donald, M 609-652-4883 308 E
donald.hudson@stockton.edu

HUDSON, Donna 888-760-2245 447 F
dhudson@limestone.edu

HUDSON, Earnest 828-227-7301 372 C
ehudson@wcu.edu

HUDSON, Elizabeth 417-334-6411 273 C
ehudson@cofo.edu

HUDSON, Elizabeth 617-373-2170 235 D

HUDSON, Garien, L 260-399-7700 174 C
ghudson@sf.edu

HUDSON, Harold 937-529-2201 392 G
hhudson@united.edu

HUDSON, Jackie 205-929-1401 5 I
jhudson@miles.edu

HUDSON, Jennifer, M 713-646-1899 482 H
jhudson@stcl.edu

HUDSON, John 713-221-8664 491 F
hudsonj@uhd.edu

HUDSON, Julie 802-828-2800 503 H
julie.hudson@ccv.edu

HUDSON, Karen 615-550-3165 466 H
karen.hudson@williamsoncc.edu

HUDSON, Kathy 434-961-5446 516 F
khudson@pvcc.edu

HUDSON, Lea Ann 404-471-6402 119 G
lhudson@agnesscott.edu

HUDSON, Lyla 843-792-8721 447 G
hudsonly@musc.edu

HUDSON, Malinda, S 270-831-9626 196 C
malinda.hudson@kctcs.edu

HUDSON, Mark, A 217-581-3923 144 E
mahudson@eiu.edu

HUDSON, Matthew 417-447-8102 280 C
hudsonm@otc.edu

HUDSON, Maureen 781-280-3506 232 B
hudsonm@middlesex.mass.edu

HUDSON, Melissa, A 530-226-4974 66 G
mhudson@simpsonu.edu

HUDSON, Michael, J 630-637-5661 154 F
mjhudson@noctrl.edu

HUDSON, Patrick 816-414-3700 278 E
phudson@mbts.edu

HUDSON, Rachel 615-297-7545 455 A
hudsonr@aquinascollege.edu

HUDSON, Richard 502-585-9911 199 E
rhudson@spalding.edu

HUDSON, Rob 812-888-2888 174 F
rhudson@vinu.edu

HUDSON, Rob 719-502-3193 84 J
rob.hudson@ppcc.edu

HUDSON, Robert 251-626-3303 8 C
rhudson@ussa.edu

HUDSON, Robert 617-353-3710 224 E
rhudson@bu.edu

HUDSON, Robert 903-233-1110 477 G
roberthudson@letu.edu

HUDSON, Rodeny, B 803-535-5470 444 D
rhudson@claflin.edu

HUDSON, Stacy 208-769-7819 138 G
stacy_hudson@nic.edu

HUDSON, Terri 601-974-5299 268 D
terri.hudson@millsaps.edu

HUDSON, Thomas 601-979-6883 267 H
thomas.k.hudson@jsums.edu

HUDSON, Tijuana, R 803-535-5197 444 D
thudson@claflin.edu

HUDSON, Tim 870-972-3030 19 F
timhudson@astate.edu

HUDSON, William 570-408-4600 440 B
william.hudson@wilkes.edu

HUDSON, JR., William 850-599-3183 114 D
william.hudson@famu.edu

HUDSPETH, Donald 585-475-7077 339 G
don.hudspeth@croatia.rit.edu

HUDSPETH, Harvey, L 806-651-2116 486 D
hhudspeth@mail.wtamu.edu

HUDY, Karen 216-421-7320 380 B
khudy@cia.edu

HUEBER, Charlie 830-792-7277 482 D
cmhueber@schreiner.edu

HUEBNER, Janet 319-352-8227 183 J
janet.huebner@wartburg.edu

HUEBNER, Joe 402-554-2322 294 A
jhuebner@unomaha.edu

HUEBNER, JR., Thomas, M 662-476-8442 267 C
thuebner@eastms.edu

HUEBOTTER, Chris 573-288-6542 274 C
chuebotter@culver.edu

HUEG, Kurt 650-949-7394 45 A
huegkurt@foothill.edu

HUEGEL, Mary 978-232-2084 226 C
mhuegel@endicott.edu

HUELSBECK, David, R 253-535-7196 524 I
huelsdr@plu.edu

HUELSBECK, Tom, A 253-535-7200 524 I
tom.huelsbeck@plu.edu

HUELSMAN, Shelly 620-227-9285 186 F
shuelsman@dc3.edu

HUENEMANN, Kurt 419-448-2351 383 C
keh@heidelberg.edu

HUERTA, David 559-278-8400 33 D
davidhu@csufresno.edu

HUERTA, Jessika 310-665-6898 57 C
otisaid@otis.edu

HUERTA, Patricia 312-362-8601 143 G
phuerta@depaul.edu

HUERTA, Paul 312-935-4569 157 A
phuerta@robertmorris.edu

HUERTA, Shanay, M 217-443-8860 143 F
shuerta@dacc.edu

HUERTAS, Belmarie 787-743-4041 551 I
bhuertas@columbiacentral.edu

HUERTAS, Carmelo, V 973-353-1670 307 C
huertacv@ca.rutgers.edu

HUERTAS, Felix, R 787-743-7979 555 M
fhuertas@suagm.edu

HUERTAS, Linda 773-481-8453 142 D
lhuertas@ccc.edu

HUERTAS, Mildred 787-257-7373 555 L
ue_mhuertas@suagm.edu

HUESER, Kyle 712-274-6400 184 A
kyle.hueser@witcc.edu

HUESING, Alan 903-923-2172 473 I
ahuesing@etbu.edu

HUESTON, William, J 414-955-8220 537 C
whueston@mcw.edu

HUET, Yvette 704-687-8696 371 B
ymhuet@uncc.edu

HUEY, Lindley 617-253-6162 233 C

HUFF, Alexandra 617-369-3659 236 E
ahuff@smfa.edu

HUFF, Cassandra 515-244-4221 175 C
huffc@aib.edu

HUFF, Eugene, C 925-229-6851 42 C
ehuff@4cd.edu

HUFF, Glenda 325-649-8014 475 F
ghuff@hputx.edu

HUFF, III, Joseph, E 409-944-1302 474 G
jhuff@gc.edu

HUFF, Kim 803-535-1210 448 C
huffk@octech.edu

HUFF, Lester 301-295-1210 548 D
lester.huff@usuhs.edu

HUFF, Liz 216-421-7957 380 B
lhuff@cia.edu

HUFF, Marie 419-372-8242 377 I
huffm@bgsu.edu

HUFF, Rick 772-546-5534 106 D
rickhuff@hsbc.edu

HUFF, Tim, T 405-744-5459 400 C
tim.huff@okstate.edu

HUFFAKER, John 806-742-2155 489 F
john.huffaker@ttu.edu

HUFFARD, Lorri 276-223-4794 517 F
lhuffard@wcc.vccs.edu

HUFFCUTT, Tom, G 715-833-6661 542 M
thuffcutt@cvtc.edu

HUFFLING, Brian 704-847-5600 369 A
bhuffling@ses.edu

HUFFMAN, Aaron, C 304-336-8200 533 A
ahuffman@westliberty.edu

HUFFMAN, Amanda 443-518-4773 215 F
ahuffman@howardcc.edu

HUFFMAN, Debbie 940-668-4475 479 K
dhuffman@nctc.edu

HUFFMAN, Don 312-662-4236 139 E
dhuffman@adler.edu

HUFFMAN, Gerald 206-296-5869 526 F
huffmanje@seattleu.edu

HUFFMAN, Jeff 865-981-8033 458 E
jeff.huffman@maryvillecollege.edu

HUFFMAN, Jeffery 419-559-2257 392 A
jhuffman01@terra.edu

HUFFMAN, Keith 740-362-3380 386 D
khuffman@mtso.edu

HUFFMAN, Lisa 580-581-2339 397 A
lhuffman@cameron.edu

HUFFMAN, Mari, L 419-866-0261 391 L
mlhuffman@stautzenberger.com

HUFFMAN, Monica, R 660-543-4106 283 F
mhuffman@ucmo.edu

HUFFMAN, Pat 425-640-1002 522 D
phuffman@edcc.edu

HUFFMAN, Rebecca 276-328-0139 514 B
reg5a@uvawise.edu

HUFFMAN, Robin 260-399-7700 174 C
rhuffman@sf.edu

HUFFMAN, Tammy, S 740-588-1212 396 E
thuffman@zanestate.edu

HUFFMAN, Virginia, A 212-327-8300 339 H
huffman@rockefeller.edu

HUFFORD, Chris 618-374-5135 156 C
chris.hufford@principia.edu

HUFFSTUTLER, Steven 618-650-5234 159 I
shuffst@siue.edu

HUFNAGEL, Michele 724-503-1001 439 B
mhufnagel@washjeff.edu

HUFSTETLER, Catrice 770-975-4000 122 H

HUFTALIN, Deneece 801-957-4226 500 E
deneece.huftalin@slcc.edu

HUFTEL, Joe 715-246-6561 544 F
joe.huftel@witc.edu

HUG, Rich 610-399-2344 430 D
rhug@cheyney.edu

HUG-ENGLISH, Cheryl 775-784-6122 295 H
cheryl h@med.unr.edu

HUGANIR, Gail 717-815-1425 440 H
ghuganir@ycp.edu

HUGER, Sophia 386-481-2951 99 F
hugers@cookman.edu

HUGETZ, Edward 713-221-8003 491 F
hugetze@uhd.edu

HUGGETT, Monica 212-799-5000 329 I

HUGGINS, Brian 314-340-3335 275 G
hugginsb@hssu.edu

HUGGINS, Derrick, E 803-777-3150 450 B
dhuggins@mailbox.sc.edu

HUGGINS, Jonathan 706-236-2217 121 E
jhuggins@berry.edu

HUGGINS, Lance 816-654-7702 276 G
lhuggins@kcumb.edu

HUGGINS, Michael 850-474-2741 116 E
mhuggins@uwf.edu

HUGGINS, Regina, M 919-866-5408 366 H
rmhuggins@waketech.edu

HUGHES, A. LeAnn 423-652-4706 457 J
lhughes@king.edu

HUGHES, Ally 912-525-5000 130 H
ahughes@scad.edu

HUGHES, Andrew 775-673-7240 295 F
ahughes@tmcc.edu

HUGHES, Angela 219-473-4227 165 A
ahughes2@ccsj.edu

HUGHES, B. Hilles 740-376-4645 386 A
hilles.hughes@marietta.edu

HUGHES, Barbara, J 814-641-3311 421 L
hughesb@juniata.edu

HUGHES, Bernice 229-391-5130 119 F
bhughes@abac.edu

HUGHES, Billy 205-665-6130 9 C
hugheswl@montevallo.edu

HUNNICUTT, Lew .... 806-648-1450 474 E
lunnicutt@fpctx.edu
HUNNICUTT, Marianne . 630-942-4306 142 F
hunnicutt@cod.edu
HUNSAKER, Deanna ..... 660-626-2356 271 G
dhunsaker@atsu.edu
HUNSAKER, Miles .... 801-524-8108 498 J
mhunsaker@ldsbc.edu
HUNSAKER, Wayne ...... 801-622-1573 499 C
wayne.hunsaker@stevenhenager.edu
HUNSBERGER, Jill .... 734-481-2324 242 J
jhunsberg1@emich.edu
HUNSICKER, Donald ..... 617-262-5000 223 G
don.hunsicker@the-bac.edu
HUNSINGER PATTEN,
Rachael .... 518-743-2243 347 E
pattenr@sunyacc.edu
HUNSINGER PATTEN,
Rachael .... 518-743-2255 347 E
pattenr@sunyacc.edu
HUNSPERGER, Susan ... 208-459-5407 137 J
shunsperger@collegeofidaho.edu
HUNSUCKER, Jeremy ... 847-467-2152 155 D
jhunsucker@northwestern.edu
HUNSUCKER, Scott, E .. 704-233-8220 373 C
scotth@wingate.edu
HUNT, Alice .... 773-896-2400 141 K
ahunt@ctschicago.edu
HUNT, Angela .... 800-955-2527 187 E
ahunt@grantham.edu
HUNT, Brittany .... 919-497-3338 358 J
bhunt@louisburg.edu
HUNT, Chris .... 610-861-1503 426 H
huntc@moravian.edu
HUNT, D. Bradford .... 312-281-3145 157 E
dbhunt@roosevelt.edu
HUNT, Daphne .... 254-968-1852 485 A
djhunt@tarleton.edu
HUNT, Darla .... 606-759-7141 196 G
darla.hunt@kctcs.edu
HUNT, David, A .... 801-422-3868 497 J
david_hunt@byu.edu
HUNT, Delores .... 704-406-4373 356 G
dhunt@gardner-webb.edu
HUNT, Denise .... 760-921-5510.. 58 C
dhunt@paloverde.edu
HUNT, Gerry .... 405-208-5582 400 A
ghunt@okcu.edu
HUNT, J. Steven .... 503-375-7591 405 F
shunt@corban.edu
HUNT, James .... 325-793-3806 478 D
hunt.james@mcm.edu
HUNT, Janet .... 501-337-5000.. 20 H
jhunt@coto.edu
HUNT, Jeff .... 864-592-4727 449 C
huntj@sccsc.edu
HUNT, Jeffrey .... 808-235-7442 137 A
jwhunt@hawaii.edu
HUNT, Jennifer .... 617-912-9130 224 C
jhunt@bostonconservatory.edu
HUNT, Jill .... 270-809-3763 198 I
thunt2@murraystate.edu
HUNT, Judith, L .... 973-655-4301 304 A
huntjl@mail.montclair.edu
HUNT, Karen .... 937-327-6377 395 I
khunt@wittenberg.edu
HUNT, Kathy .... 206-546-4741 526 G
khunt@shoreline.edu
HUNT, Larissa .... 269-927-8170 245 E
lhunt@lakemichigancollege.edu
HUNT, Lawrence .... 413-585-2260 236 G
lhunt@smith.edu
HUNT, Lisa, O .... 910-272-3501 365 D
lohunt@robeson.edu
HUNT, Lori .... 509-533-7378 521 E
lori.hunt@scc.spokane.edu
HUNT, Louis, D .... 919-515-1428 370 D
ldhunt@ncsu.edu
HUNT, Mark .... 334-386-7140.... 3 I
mhunt@faulkner.edu
HUNT, Morgan .... 910-521-6533 371 D
morgan.hunt@uncp.edu
HUNT, Patricia .... 304-205-6623 531 A
pat.hunt@bridgevalley.edu
HUNT, Patrick, G .... 240-895-4307 218 B
pghunt@smcm.edu
HUNT, Paul, M .... 517-432-4499 246 H
pmhunt@msu.edu
HUNT, Peter, G .... 434-949-1005 516 H
peter.hunt@southside.edu
HUNT, Roe, B .... 803-535-5471 444 D
rhunt@claflin.edu
HUNT, Rusty .... 336-249-8186 362 B
rthunt@davidsonccc.edu
HUNT, Sellestine .... 936-639-1301 467 I
shunt@angelina.edu
HUNT, Shane .... 870-972-3035.. 19 F
shunt@astate.edu
HUNT, Steve .... 828-327-7000 361 B
shunt@cvcc.edu

HUNT, Terry, L .... 541-346-8905 410 F
thunt@uoregon.edu
HUNT, Thomas .... 626-815-3004.. 29 B
thunt@apu.edu
HUNT, Todd, A .... 407-582-1463 118 I
thunt3@valenciacollege.edu
HUNT, Tolif, R .... 319-273-3217 176 A
tolif.hunt@uni.edu
HUNT-ALLEN, Altavese . 803-327-7402 444 F
ahunt@clintoncollege.edu
HUNT-BULL, Nicholas .. 518-327-6247 338 B
nhuntbull@paulsmiths.edu
HUNTER, Amelia .... 615-329-8537 456 G
ahunter@fisk.edu
HUNTER, Ben, D .... 317-940-9982 164 L
bdhunter@butler.edu
HUNTER, Bill .... 850-973-9448 109 C
hunterb@nfcc.edu
HUNTER, Bill .... 850-201-6556 117 B
hunterb@tcc.fl.edu
HUNTER, Bonnie, L ...... 219-464-5411 174 E
bonnie.hunter@valpo.edu
HUNTER, Brandon .... 404-756-1652 129 A
bhunter@msm.edu
HUNTER, Carolyn, A .... 513-585-2068 379 H
carolyn.hunter@thechristcollege.edu
HUNTER, Chip .... 509-335-3564 528 B
HUNTER, David .... 208-562-2089 138 A
davidshunter@cwidaho.cc
HUNTER, Donna, L .... 304-766-4146 533 C
hunterdl@wvstateu.edu
HUNTER, Gary .... 970-247-7224.. 82 I
ghunter@fortlewis.edu
HUNTER, Gayle .... 386-752-1822 103 Q
gayle.hunter@fgc.edu
HUNTER, Gerald, E .... 757-823-8011 510 H
gehunter@nsu.edu
HUNTER, JR., Jairy, C . 843-863-7500 444 B
jhunter@csuniv.edu
HUNTER, James, E .... 804-524-5997 518 C
jhunter@vsu.edu
HUNTER, Janet .... 563-387-2229 180 M
hunterja@luther.edu
HUNTER, Janice .... 760-872-2000.. 42 J
jhunter@deepsprings.edu
HUNTER, Jim .... 928-645-6681.. 13 D
Jim.Hunter@coconino.edu
HUNTER, John .... 201-216-9901 302 A
john.hunter@eicollege.edu
HUNTER, John .... 417-626-1234 280 B
library@occ.edu
HUNTER, Kim .... 513-244-4248 387 A
kim.hunter@msj.edu
HUNTER, Kymm .... 803-705-4519 443 F
hunterk@benedict.edu
HUNTER, Larry, T .... 614-236-6641 378 H
lhunter2@capital.edu
HUNTER, Laura .... 800-495-7284 222 G
lhunter@baypath.edu
HUNTER, LeAnn .... 509-452-5100 524 J
lhunter@pnwu.edu
HUNTER, Lisa .... 716-673-3717 343 F
lisa.hunter@fredonia.edu
HUNTER, Lorna .... 208-459-5319 137 J
lhunter@collegeofidaho.edu
HUNTER, Lynn .... 781-239-3120 231 G
lhunter@massbay.edu
HUNTER, Marc .... 405-382-9950 402 C
m.hunter@sscok.edu
HUNTER, Maria .... 480-994-9244.. 17 P
mariah@swiha.edu
HUNTER, Melissa .... 931-221-7315 461 C
hunterm@apsu.edu
HUNTER, Michael .... 312-850-7167 142 E
mhunter1@ccc.edu
HUNTER, Pam .... 760-773-2508.. 41 A
phunter@collegeofthedesert.edu
HUNTER, Patricia .... 425-739-8361 523 I
patricia.hunter@lwtech.edu
HUNTER, Paul .... 410-386-8429 214 B
phunter@carrollcc.edu
HUNTER, Rathenia .... 847-947-5887 153 H
rhunter@nl.edu
HUNTER, Rathenia .... 312-922-1884 151 I
rhunter@maccormac.edu
HUNTER, Rebecca .... 508-793-7561 225 B
rhunter@clarku.edu
HUNTER, Richie, C .... 713-743-0945 491 C
rchunter@uh.edu
HUNTER, Richie, C .... 713-743-0945 491 D
rchunter@uh.edu
HUNTER, Steve .... 360-867-6310 522 J
hunters@evergreen.edu
HUNTER, Susan .... 503-552-1512 407 F
shunter@ncnm.edu
HUNTER, Susan, J .... 207-581-1512 212 C
president@umaine.edu
HUNTER, Susan, S .... 804-523-5375 515 F
shunter@reynolds.edu
HUNTER, Tim, W .... 814-332-2755 411 F
thunter@allegheny.edu

HUNTER, W. Bingham .. 602-429-4431.. 16 N
bhunter@ps.edu
HUNTER-GOLDSWORTHY,
Heidi .... 540-654-2468 513 I
hhunterg@umw.edu
HUNTER-HAYES,
Tracy, J .... 410-651-6621 219 H
tjhunterhayes@umes.edu
HUNTER-RAINEY,
Sharron .... 918-877-8151 398 E
srainey@langston.edu
HUNTINGTON,
Judith, A .... 914-654-5430 322 B
president@cnr.edu
HUNTINGTON, Robert .. 419-448-2202 383 C
president@heidelberg.edu
HUNTLEY, Daniel .... 641-844-5670 179 L
daniel.huntley@iavalley.edu
HUNTLEY, Deborah, R .. 989-964-4296 249 G
huntley@svsu.edu
HUNTLEY, Julie .... 918-495-7040 401 B
jhuntley@oru.edu
HUNTLEY, Kristy .... 203-479-4559.. 92 G
khuntley@newhaven.edu
HUNTLEY, Steve, E ...... 904-264-2172 111 G
steve.huntley@iws.edu
HUNTON, Ladonna, L .. 270-745-6867 201 D
ladonna.hunton@wku.edu
HUNTOON, Ivan .... 785-594-8396 184 F
ivan.huntoon@bakeru.edu
HUNTOON,
Jacqueline, E .... 906-487-2327 247 A
jeh@mtu.edu
HUNTSINGER, Trish ...... 828-395-1297 363 D
thuntsing@isothermal.edu
HUNTSMAN,
Deborah, C .... 330-672-3237 384 H
dhuntsm1@kent.edu
HUNZER, Kathleen .... 715-425-3843 540 E
honors@uwrf.edu
HUNZIGER, Lucas .... 913-367-6204 187 I
lhunziger@highlandcc.edu
HUO,
Xiaoming (Sharon) .... 931-372-3463 462 A
xhuo@tntech.edu
HUOPPI, Jennifer .... 860-465-4357.. 88 E
huoppij@easternct.edu
HUOPPI, Margie .... 860-932-4000.. 90 A
mhuoppi@qvcc.commnet.edu
HUOT, Anne, E .... 603-358-2000 299 D
ahuot@keene.edu
HUPFER, Mary, A .... 812-464-1627 174 D
mhupfer@usi.edu
HUPKE, Doug .... 415-405-3824.. 36 A
dhupke@sfsu.edu
HUPP, Mark .... 419-755-5665 387 E
mhupp@ncstatecollege.edu
HUPP, Stephen .... 304-424-8273 533 E
stephen.hupp@wvup.edu
HUPPE, Alicia, L .... 972-377-1749 471 C
ahuppe@collin.edu
HUPPERT, Susan .... 515-271-1384 177 H
susan.huppert@dmu.edu
HURD, Cathy .... 704-378-1181 358 B
churd@jcsu.edu
HURD, James, R .... 850-474-2214 116 E
jhurd@uwf.edu
HURD, Roy .... 707-546-4000.. 43 J
rhurd@empcol.edu
HURD, Sherie .... 707-546-4000.. 43 J
shurd@empcol.edu
HURDLE, Philip, M .... 607-735-1881 324 J
phurdle@elmira.edu
HURDLE, Terri .... 513-244-4467 387 A
terri.hurdle@msj.edu
HURDLE-WINSLOW,
Lynn .... 252-335-0821 361 G
lynnhw@albermarle.edu
HURDT, Emily .... 704-669-4321 361 E
hurdte@clevelandcc.edu
HURLBURT, Linda .... 856-415-2106 306 C
lhurlbu2@rcgc.edu
HURLBUT, L, E .... 540-464-7292 518 A
hurlbutle@vmi.edu
HURLBUT, Nancy .... 909-869-2319.. 32 F
nhurlbut@cpp.edu
HURLEY, Alicia .... 212-998-6859 336 C
alicia.hurley@nyu.edu
HURLEY, Charles, T ..... 574-631-7495 174 A
hurley.32@nd.edu
HURLEY, Deanne .... 440-646-8320 394 G
dhurley@ursuline.edu
HURLEY, Deanne .... 440-646-8108 394 G
dhurley@ursuline.edu
HURLEY, Deb, B .... 336-334-5946 371 C
dbhurley@uncg.edu
HURLEY, Elizabeth .... 212-799-5000 329 I
HURLEY, Gail, A .... 814-865-5423 428 C
gah5@psu.edu

HURLEY, James .... 423-869-6254 458 B
james.hurley@lmunet.edu
HURLEY, James, B .... 601-923-1630 270 B
jhurley@rts.edu
HURLEY, James, M ...... 847-491-5114 155 D
j-hurley2@northwestern.edu
HURLEY, Jana .... 703-993-2789 507 K
jhurley4@gmu.edu
HURLEY, John .... 360-867-6500 522 J
hurleyj@evergreen.edu
HURLEY, John, J .... 716-888-2100 317 H
hurleyj@canisius.edu
HURLEY, Leah, A .... 214-648-7986 496 A
leah.hurley@utsouthwestern.edu
HURLEY, Patricia .... 818-240-1000.. 45 I
phurley@glendale.edu
HURLEY, Richard, V ..... 540-654-1301 513 I
president@umw.edu
HURLEY, Sam .... 903-928-3288 490 F
shurley@tvcc.edu
HURLEY, Tracy .... 210-784-2300 486 B
thurley@tamusa.tamus.edu
HURLEY, Travis .... 417-626-1234 280 B
hurley.travis@occ.edu
HURLEY, Wanda .... 601-635-2111 267 B
whurley@eccc.edu
HURNS, Kimberly .... 734-973-3724 251 J
khurns@wccnt.edu
HURRELL, Rockie .... 719-502-2007.. 84 J
rockie.hurrell@ppcc.edu
HURREN, Lee .... 864-503-5577 451 A
blhurren@uscupstate.edu
HURSCHMANN,
Michael .... 510-780-4500.. 50 G
mhurschmann@lifewest.edu
HURSSEY, Elizabeth ...... 662-254-3531 269 C
ejhurssey@mvsu.edu
HURST, Andrew .... 719-590-6797.. 81 H
ahurst@coloradotech.edu
HURST, Barbara .... 631-451-4829 348 F
hurstb@sunysuffolk.edu
HURST, Fred .... 928-523-6598.. 16 C
Fred.Hurst@nau.edu
HURST, Jamie .... 303-556-8452.. 83 Q
jhurst7@msudenver.edu
HURST, Jason .... 850-526-2761 100 E
hurstj@chipola.edu
HURST, Jeffrey, J .... 801-626-7256 500 C
jhurst@weber.edu
HURST, Larry .... 661-362-3875.. 40 H
larry.hurst@canyons.edu
HURST, Laura .... 610-660-1175 434 G
lannhurs@sju.edu
HURST, Mark .... 423-585-2629 464 C
mark.hurst@ws.edu
HURST, Richard, S .... 773-508-7465 151 E
rhurst@luc.edu
HURST, Susan .... 870-245-5567.. 22 C
hursts@obu.edu
HURST, Thomas, R .... 410-864-3613 218 C
thurst@stmarys.edu
HURST, Timothy .... 931-221-7671 461 C
hurstt@apsu.edu
HURT, Amelia .... 405-208-5181 400 A
aehurt@okcu.edu
HURT, Chandra .... 773-777-4220 155 B
churt@nc.edu
HURT, Lynn .... 540-857-6445 517 E
lhurt@virginiawestern.edu
HURTA, Donna .... 512-492-3014 468 A
dhurta@aoma.edu
HURTADO, Geoffrey ...... 414-229-5390 540 A
ghurtado@uwm.edu
HURTADO, Jose .... 707-256-7333.. 55 E
thurtado@napavalley.edu
HURTADO, Wynne .... 801-622-1573 499 C
wynne.hurtado@stevenshenager.edu
HURTE, Vernon .... 757-221-2300 506 J
vjhurt@wm.edu
HURTIG, Juliet, K .... 419-772-2032 388 I
j-hurtig@onu.edu
HURWITZ, T. Alan .... 202-651-5005.. 95 C
president@gallaudet.edu
HUSAK, William .... 310-338-5940.. 53 C
whusak@lmu.edu
HUSBAND-ARDOIN,
Madeline .... 337-482-6826 208 F
msh9748@louisiana.edu
HUSCHLE, Brian .... 218-793-2592 260 F
brian.huschle@northlandcollege.edu
HUSEIN, Lori .... 909-607-9192.. 39 D
Lori_Husein@cuc.claremont.edu
HUSELTON, Ken .... 412-323-4000 413 A
khuselton@mcg-btc.org
HUSHON, Kate .... 814-868-9900 418 C
kateh@erieit.edu
HUSK, Mark, A .... 317-921-4723 169 L
mhusk@ivytech.edu
HUSKEY, Jeffrey .... 605-688-6415 454 C
jeffrey.huskey@sdstate.edu

I

ICE, Phil 304-724-3700 529 F pice@apus.edu
ICE, Richard 320-363-5088 254 J rice@csbsju.edu
ICE, Richard 320-363-5503 264 A rice@csbsju.edu
ICHON, Eric 310-287-4305 52 C ichone@wlac.edu
ICHSAN, Tony 707-527-1608 65 C aichsan@santarosa.edu
ICKES, Jessica, L 717-867-6205 423 I ickes@lvc.edu
IDDINGS, R. Keith 484-384-2935 427 I semdean@eastern.edu
IDDINGS, R. Keith 610-341-4383 418 A kiddings@eastern.edu
IDE, Andrea 425-425-4723 527 D andrea.ide@tlc.edu
IDE, Melissa 570-702-8910 421 K mide@johnson.edu
IDE, Susan 248-218-2059 249 D side@rc.edu
IDELL, Steven 903-877-7674 495 C steven.idell@uthct.edu
IDETA, Lori 808-956-3290 135 J ideta@hawaii.edu
IERARDI, Kristina 508-362-2131 231 D kierardi@capecod.edu
IERIEN, Kim 503-281-4181 405 D
IGHODARO, Osaro 602-243-8036 15 F osaro.ighodaro@southmountaincc.edu
IGNAL, Howard 845-431-8937 324 D hignal@sunydutchess.edu
IGNASH, Jan 850-245-0466 114 C jan.ignash@flbog.edu
IGWEBUIKE, John 601-877-6142 266 C jigwe@alcorn.edu
IGWIKI, Richard 504-816-4830 202 F rigwiki@dillard.edu
IGYARTO, Mia 630-942-3410 142 F igyartom@cod.edu
IHDE, Rick 402-643-7422 289 J rick.ihde@cune.edu
IHRER, Kenneth 212-650-7400 318 G kihrer@ccny.cuny.edu
IHRKE, Barbara 765-677-1578 169 C barbara.ihrke@indwes.edu
IJAMES, George, R 260-399-7700 174 C gijames@sf.edu
IJIRI, Lisa 617-868-9600 228 B
IKEDA, Deborah, J 559-325-5205 69 A deborah.ikeda@scccd.edu
IKEDA, Gary, L 206-543-4150 527 G ikedagl@uw.edu
IKEDA, Kimi, M 805-756-2186 32 E kikeda@calpoly.edu
IKEM, Fidelis, M 937-376-6441 379 D fikem@centralstate.edu
IKEN, Mark 678-407-5400 125 B miken@ggc.edu
IKEN, Stacie 701-224-5491 374 E stacie.iken@bismarckstate.edu
IKENBERRY, David, L 303-492-1809 86 E david.ikenberry@colorado.edu
IKHARO, Sadiq 510-466-7336 58 J sikharo@peralta.edu
IKHARO, Sadiq 510-466-7336 59 C sikharo@peralta.edu
ILDEFONSO, Chet 630-829-6431 140 A cildefonso@ben.edu
ILER, Susan 216-791-5000 380 C susan.iler@cim.edu
ILES, Linda 530-221-4275 66 B finaid@shasta.edu
ILIAKIS-DOHERTY, Sophia 360-417-6219 525 A sdoherty@pencol.edu
ILICETO, Thomas 212-229-5101 334 C ilicetot@newschool.edu
ILLICH, Paul 402-323-3415 293 A pillich@southeast.edu
ILLIES, Diane 218-755-2448 258 B dillies@bemidjistate.edu
ILLINGWORTH, Kendra 219-866-6428 172 E kendra@saintjoe.edu
ILLINGWORTH, Theresa, M 414-425-8300 538 J tillingworth@shsst.edu
ILLUM, Brenton 417-865-2815 274 L illumb@evangel.edu
ILSE, Thomas 304-327-4022 532 D tilse@bluefieldstate.edu
ILYAS, Mohammad 561-297-3426 114 E ilyas@fau.edu
IM, Manyul 203-576-4234 92 B manyulim@bridgeport.edu
IMAI, Geri 808-235-7430 137 A gerii@hawaii.edu
IMAI, Peggy, H 802-654-2222 502 H pimai@smcvt.edu
IMASUEN, Edwin 810-762-9642 245 A eimasuen@kettering.edu
IMBIMBO, Patricia 646-312-4683 318 C Patricia.Imbimbo@baruch.cuny.edu
IMBLER, John, M 918-610-8303 401 C john.imbler@ptstulsa.edu
IMBRAGULIO, Lisa 205-726-4172 6 F lcimbrag@samford.edu
IMBRESCIA, Jeffrey, D 724-653-2200 417 D jimbrescia@dec.edu
IMBRIALE, William 212-752-1530 330 C william.imbriale@limcollege.edu
IMES, Melissa, J 717-262-2000 440 D melissa.imes@wilson.edu
IMHOF, Howard 740-366-9379 378 L himhof@cotc.edu
IMHOFF, Dan 608-822-2401 544 C dimhoff@swtc.edu
IMHOFF, Donna 412-237-2770 415 G dimhoff@ccac.edu
IMHOFF, Maren, E 212-327-8682 339 H imhoff@rockefeller.edu
IMLER, Mary Elizabeth 815-740-2274 162 F mimler@stfrancis.edu
IMLER, Sylvia, J 330-941-3370 396 C sjimler@ysu.edu
IMMERMAN, Stephen, D 978-921-4242 234 B steve.immerman@montserrat.edu
IMPELLIZZERI, Melinda, A 502-597-7010 197 G melinda.impellizzeri@kysu.edu
IMPERATO, Anthony 718-368-5902 320 A aimperato@kbcc.cuny.edu
IMWALLE, Todd, W 937-229-3299 393 E TImwalle1@udayton.edu
INABINET, Chad, E 231-843-5965 252 H ceinabinet@westshore.edu
INAFUKU, Derek 808-845-9123 136 E dinafuku@hawaii.edu
INBODY, Brian, L 620-431-2820 189 J binbody@neosho.edu
INCANDELA, Marybeth 631-420-2107 348 B marybeth.incandela@farmingdale.edu
INCH, Edward 916-278-7674 34 E edward.inch@csus.edu
INDIVERI-GANT, Jeffrey, D 973-655-6911 304 A gantj@mail.montclair.edu
INFANTI, Steven, M 717-901-5146 420 I sinfanti@harrisburgu.edu
INFINGER, Kim 425-739-8274 523 I kim.infinger@lwtech.edu
INGALLS, Keith 413-748-3946 236 H kingalls@springfieldcollege.edu
INGARGIOLA, Janet, M 217-443-8760 143 F jingarg@dacc.edu
INGBER, Marc 303-556-2870 86 G marc.ingber@ucdenver.edu
INGELSON, Jeannine 563-441-4046 178 D jingleson@eicc.edu
INGERMAN, Bret 850-201-6082 117 B ingermab@tcc.fl.edu
INGERSOLL, Christopher 419-530-5453 394 E christopher.ingersoll@utoledo.edu
INGERSOLL, Julia 610-526-6132 420 C jingersoll@harcum.edu
INGERSOLL, Pat 616-234-3869 243 D pingerso@grcc.edu
INGHAM, Joanne 212-431-2876 335 G Joanne.Ingham@nyls.edu
INGHAM, Lester, A 661-824-2977 55 I lingham@ntps.edu
INGLE, Andrea 765-285-5974 164 D akingle@bsu.edu
INGLE, Brooke 970-247-7421 82 I bookstoremgr@fortlewis.edu
INGLE, Jeffery, S 865-981-8199 458 E jeff.ingle@maryvillecollege.edu
INGLE, III, Kenneth, G 704-216-3577 365 F ken.ingle@rccc.edu
INGLE, Kent 863-667-5002 113 K kingle@seu.edu
INGLE, Peter 801-832-2474 501 C pingle@westminstercollege.edu
INGLES, Roger, D 740-368-3738 390 B rdingles@owu.edu
INGLES, Susan, L 414-410-4236 535 C slingles@stritch.edu
INGLI, Robin, C 651-523-2461 256 B robin.ingli@hamline.edu
INGLIS, Mark 216-421-7403 380 B minglis@cia.edu
INGLISH, Darla 940-397-4321 478 G darla.inglish@mwsu.edu
INGMIRE, Mac 217-732-3168 150 G mingmire@lincolnchristian.edu
INGMIRE, Randall 217-732-3168 150 G rlingmire@lincolnchristian.edu
INGOLFSLAND, Dennis 952-446-4239 255 E ingolfsland@crown.edu
INGRAHAM, Barry 207-768-2702 211 C bingraham@nmcc.edu
INGRAHAM, Timothy 978-468-7111 227 B tingraham@gcts.edu
INGRAM, Archinya 803-327-7402 444 F aingram@clintoncollege.edu
INGRAM, Beth 701-231-7131 374 C beth.ingram@ndsu.edu
INGRAM, Beverly 318-487-7694 202 L beverly.ingram@lacollege.edu
INGRAM, Brian, C 731-881-7069 465 F cingram@utm.edu
INGRAM, Charles, E 609-652-4381 308 E charles.ingram@stockton.edu
INGRAM, David 817-461-8741 468 C dingram@arlingtonbaptistcollege.edu
INGRAM, Earl 334-670-3104 8 A ingram@troy.edu
INGRAM, Geoff 951-785-2000 49 I gingram@lasierra.edu
INGRAM, Iris 310-287-4368 52 C ingramii@wlac.edu
INGRAM, J. Kevin 785-539-3571 189 D kingram@mccks.edu
INGRAM, Jim 662-862-8047 267 F jingram@iccms.edu
INGRAM, Joyce, A 850-599-3611 114 D joyce.ingram@famu.edu
INGRAM, Lashawanda, T 315-386-7128 347 F ingraml@canton.edu
INGRAM, Mark, T 205-934-0766 8 F mingram@uab.edu
INGRAM, Mike 423-746-5292 464 D mingram@twcnet.edu
INGRAM, SR., Roderick, L 330-325-6673 387 F ringram@neomed.edu
INGRAM, Trent 870-248-4000 20 E trent.ingram@blackrivertech.edu
INGRAM, Wanda Rhea 334-244-3476 2 A wingram4@aum.edu
INGRAM, William, G 919-536-7250 362 C ingramb@durhamtech.edu
INGRAM-WALLACE, Brenda, J 610-921-7585 411 E bingramwallace@albright.edu
INGS, Margaret Ann 617-824-8299 226 A margaret_ann_ings@emerson.edu
INIGUEZ, Edmond 719-549-3206 85 A edmond.iniguez@pueblocc.edu
INIGUEZ, Elizabeth 323-463-2500 69 H lizm@toa.edu
INIGUEZ-JIMENEZ, J. Alfredo 956-764-5798 477 C ainiguez@laredo.edu
INKSTER, Kathy 606-546-4151 200 E
INKSTER, Larry 606-546-1233 200 E linkster@unionky.edu
INKSTER, Whitney 304-336-8375 533 A whitney.inkster@westliberty.edu
INMAN, Ann 812-866-7013 166 E inmana@hanover.edu
INMAN, Barbara, L 757-727-5264 508 C barbara.inman@hamptonu.edu
INMAN, Dean 870-864-7142 23 B dinman@southark.edu
INMAN, Gerald 617-989-4252 237 G inmang@wit.edu
INMAN, James, P 540-464-7104 518 A inmanjp@vmi.edu
INMAN, John, G 724-458-2176 419 F jginman@gcc.edu
INMAN, Keith 502-852-6924 201 A akinma01@louisville.edu
INMAN, Leigh 619-961-4278 69 J glinman@tjsl.edu
INMAN, Linda, D 336-334-7708 370 B ldinman@ncat.edu
INMAN, Lisa 919-536-7200 362 C inmanl@durhamtech.edu
INMAN, Stan, D 801-585-5028 499 K sinman@sa.utah.edu
INNIGER, Alyssa, K 507-344-7874 253 M alyssa.inniger@blc.edu
INNISS, Courtney 973-877-4462 302 F coinniss@essex.edu
INOA, Luis 845-437-5862 351 H inoa@vassar.edu
INOUYE, Carolyn 805-986-5803 75 D cinouye@vcccd.edu
INOUYE, Susan, K 808-956-8155 135 H susani@hawaii.edu
INOWAY-RONNIE, Eden 608-265-5975 539 D etinoway@wisc.edu
INSANALLI, Dawn 914-637-2726 328 F dinsanalli@iona.edu
INSCH, Gary 419-530-5426 394 E gary.insch@utoledo.edu
INSERRA, Albert 631-244-3200 324 C inserraa@dowling.edu
INSERTO, Fathiah 714-542-8086 29 H finserto@bristoluniversity.edu
INSKO, Celeste 541-278-5780 404 J cinsko@bluecc.edu
INSKO, Thomas 541-962-3512 405 G tinsko@eou.edu
INSLER, Gayle, D 516-877-3167 314 F insler@adelphi.edu
INSLEY, Andrea 206-587-3899 526 A ainsley@sccd.ctc.edu
INSLEY, Lynn 201-216-8927 308 D linsley@stevens.edu
INSLEY, Patricia 714-547-9625 30 F pinsley@calcoast.edu
INTILLE, Amy 617-989-4885 237 G intillea@wit.edu
INTROCASO, CDP, Candace 412-536-1204 422 E cintrocaso@laroche.edu
INWOOD, Joel, D 312-939-0111 144 D joel@eastwest.edu
INZER, Monica, C 315-859-4421 327 A minzer@hamilton.edu
INZERILLA, Tina 925-424-1156 37 O tinzerilla@laspositascollege.edu
IOANNIDES, Margaret 904-256-1158 103 K mioannides@fcsl.edu
IOANNIDES, Vanessa 415-485-3235 43 D vanessa.ioannides@dominican.edu
IOANNOU, Carin 336-770-3301 372 B loannouc@uncsa.edu
IOBST, William 570-504-7000 415 E wiobst@tcmc.edu
IOCANO, Lynn 302-857-6250 93 E liocano@desu.edu
IODICE, Emilio 773-508-2760 151 E eiodice@luc.edu
IOLI, Christine 412-809-5100 433 D ioli.christine@pti.edu
IORG, Jeff 415-380-1322 45 J jeffiorg@ggbts.edu
IOSSI, Lora 402-557-7343 289 B lora.iossi@bellevue.edu
IOVANNONE, Jeffry, J 716-673-4747 343 F jeffry.iovannone@fredonia.edu
IPACH, Nichole 805-437-8893 32 H nichole.ipach@csuci.edu
IPPOLITO, Andrew 201-692-2531 302 H andrew_ippolito@fdu.edu
IPPOLITO, Elaine 860-906-5021 89 A
IRAKLIOTIS, Leonidis 508-373-9727 223 C leo.irakliotis@becker.edu
IRBY, Adam, W 336-322-2253 364 G Adam.Irby@piedmontcc.edu
IRBY, Bernice 803-934-3408 447 K birby@morris.edu
IRBY, Matthew 714-241-6104 40 B 1180mgr@follett.com
IRBY, Michele 573-651-5120 282 C mirby@semo.edu
IRBY, Sharon 770-229-3454 132 B sirby@sctech.edu
IRELAND, Alan 336-750-2935 372 D irelandag@wssu.edu
IRELAND, Asheley 270-809-5604 198 I aireland@murraystate.edu
IRELAND, Jim, D 620-792-9339 184 I irelandj@bartonccc.edu
IRELAND, Timothy 716-286-8060 336 E toi@niagara.edu
IRISH, Allyson 617-521-2324 236 F allyson.irish@simmons.edu
IRISH, Edward, P 757-221-2425 506 J epiris@wm.edu
IRISH, J. A. George 718-270-4932 320 C girish@mec.cuny.edu
IRIZARRY, Jose, R 787-296-1101 225 A Jose.Irizarry@cambridgecollege.edu
IRLA-CHESNEY, Kathy 603-862-2120 299 B kathy.irla-chesney@unh.edu
IROFF, Jayson 954-201-7423 99 G jiroff@broward.edu
IRONS, Warren 615-329-8604 456 G wirons@fisk.edu
IRUDAYAM, Irene 508-849-3410 222 C iirudayam@annamaria.edu
IRVIN, Camilla 334-833-4577 4 E cirvin@huntingdon.edu
IRVIN, Cynthia 904-680-7653 103 K cirvin@fcsl.edu
IRVIN, Dale, T 212-870-1223 336 B dirvin@nyts.edu
IRVIN, Dave 865-974-2178 465 D irvin@utk.edu
IRVIN, Hal 540-231-7784 518 B hirvin@vt.edu

J

JACKSON, Arthur, R ..... 704-687-2206 371 B
ajacks90@uncc.edu
JACKSON, Athena .... 305-626-3782 104 B
Athena.Jackson@fmuniv.edu
JACKSON, Bradley, A ... 513-585-0116 379 H
bradley.jackson@thechristcollege.edu
JACKSON, Brenda .... 251-578-1313.... 6 D
bjackson@rstc.edu
JACKSON, Brenda .... 910-695-3731 365 H
jacksonbr@sandhills.edu
JACKSON, Brenda, W ... 504-586-5274 207 B
bjackson@suno.edu
JACKSON, Brian, K .... 609-652-4521 308 E
brian.jackson@stockton.edu
JACKSON, Brooks .... 612-626-4949 265 C
jacksonb@umn.edu
JACKSON, Buddy .... 334-386-7293.... 3 I
bjackson@faulkner.edu
JACKSON, Byron, H ...... 412-924-1380 433 E
bjackson@pts.edu
JACKSON, C. C .... 803-536-7000 448 H
JACKSON, Cameron ..... 785-827-5541 189 A
cameron.jackson@kwu.edu
JACKSON, Cameron ..... 980-359-1039 373 C
c.jackson@wingate.edu
JACKSON,
Candice Love .... 601-977-7889 270 F
cljackson@tougaloo.edu
JACKSON, Carol .... 212-517-0756 332 A
cjackson@mmm.edu
JACKSON, Catrina .... 336-334-7593 370 B
sm8093@bncollege.com
JACKSON, Celia .... 414-382-6022 534 I
celia.jackson@alverno.edu
JACKSON, Charles, C ... 240-895-4413 218 B
ccjackson@smcm.edu
JACKSON, Chauncey, J 405-466-2957 398 E
cjjackson@langston.edu
JACKSON, Chris .... 719-442-0505.. 87 C
chris.jackson@rockies.edu
JACKSON, Chris .... 636-922-8271 281 C
chubbard@stchas.edu
JACKSON, Christin .... 859-371-9393 193 D
cjackson@beckfield.edu
JACKSON, Christine ...... 402-472-4455 293 H
cjackson3@unl.edu
JACKSON, Claudia .... 361-698-1247 473 F
cjackson@delmar.edu
JACKSON,
Cleveland (Tony) .... 678-422-4100.. 96 H
JACKSON, Clint .... 901-435-1233 457 N
clint_jackson@loc.edu
JACKSON, Craig .... 478-757-3508 122 E
cjackson@centralgatech.edu
JACKSON, Craig .... 478-988-6800 122 F
cjackson@centralgatech.edu
JACKSON, Craig .... 815-825-2086 149 E
craig.jackson@kishwaukeecollege.edu
JACKSON, Craig, R .... 909-558-4545.. 50 K
cjackson@llu.edu
JACKSON, Dalen, C ...... 502-863-8300 193 C
dalen.jackson@bsky.org
JACKSON, Dan .... 513-244-8437 379 I
dan.jackson@ccuniversity.edu
JACKSON, Danielle .... 406-353-2607 286 B
djackson@ancollege.edu
JACKSON, Darrick .... 773-256-3000 152 D
djackson@meadville.edu
JACKSON, Darryl .... 256-372-4854.... 1 A
darryl.jackson1@aamu.edu
JACKSON, David, H ...... 941-309-0166 111 F
djackson@ringling.edu
JACKSON, Deanne .... 573-341-4362 284 C
registrar@mst.edu
JACKSON, Debbie .... 202-319-5044.. 95 A
jacksond@cua.edu
JACKSON, Deborah .... 617-873-0172 225 A
deborah.jackson@cambridgecollege.edu
JACKSON, Debra .... 864-656-4592 444 E
dbj@clemson.edu
JACKSON, Derek, A ...... 785-532-6453 188 H
derekaj@ksu.edu
JACKSON, Dexter .... 334-874-5700.... 3 B
djackson@ccal.edu
JACKSON, Donald .... 402-461-7326 290 G
djackson@hastings.edu
JACKSON, Edison, O ..... 386-481-2001.. 99 F
jacksone@cookman.edu
JACKSON, Elizabeth ...... 432-837-8145 489 B
ejackson@sulross.edu
JACKSON, Emily, S ...... 302-225-6271.. 94 B
emily@gbc.edu
JACKSON, Equilla .... 936-261-1890 484 F
eqjackson@pvamu.edu
JACKSON, Eric .... 904-470-8216 102 A
eric.jackson@ewc.edu
JACKSON, Flossie .... 772-462-7467 106 F
fjackson@irsc.edu
JACKSON, Frances, L ... 617-333-2970 225 F
fjackson@curry.edu
JACKSON, G. Smith ...... 336-278-7220 356 F
jacksons@elon.edu
JACKSON, Gary .... 662-325-3036 269 A
gary@ext.msstate.edu
JACKSON, Gary .... 254-298-8456 484 C
gary.jackson@templejc.edu
JACKSON, Governor, E . 940-898-3050 490 D
gjackson@twu.edu
JACKSON, Grace .... 713-623-2040 468 F
dgjackson@aii.edu
JACKSON, Gregory .... 256-372-8653.... 1 A
gregory.jackson@aamu.edu
JACKSON, Harvey .... 973-328-5553 301 G
hjackson@ccm.edu
JACKSON, Heather, L ... 508-831-5211 238 G
hjackson@wpi.edu
JACKSON, Heidi .... 308-635-6395 294 C
jacksonh@wncc.edu
JACKSON, Jacob .... 559-442-4600.. 69 B
jacob.jackson@fresnocitycollege.edu
JACKSON,
Jacqueline, S .... 410-777-2830 213 E
jsjackson6@aacc.edu
JACKSON, Jae .... 305-626-3762 104 B
Jae.Jackson@fmuniv.edu
JACKSON, JR.,
James, T .... 410-777-2529 213 E
jjackson@aacc.edu
JACKSON, Jan .... 225-308-4413 202 M
jjackson@lctcs.edu
JACKSON, Jannett, N .... 925-485-5206.. 37 M
jjackson@clpccd.org
JACKSON, Jay .... 864-592-4723 449 C
jacksonj@sccsc.edu
JACKSON, Jean .... 919-760-8556 359 B
jacksonj@meredith.edu
JACKSON, Jeff .... 419-372-9487 377 I
jacksjl@bgsu.edu
JACKSON, Jerry .... 606-539-4250 200 F
jerry.jackson@ucumberlands.edu
JACKSON, Jim, C .... 580-581-2460 397 A
jjackson@cameron.edu
JACKSON, Jodie .... 304-293-6999 533 D
jjackson2@hsc.wvu.edu
JACKSON, John .... 916-577-2200.. 77 F
JACKSON, John .... 540-231-8508 518 B
johnj1@vt.edu
JACKSON, John, A .... 508-541-1814 225 G
jjackson@dean.edu
JACKSON, John, L .... 215-898-5511 437 I
jjackson@sp2.upenn.edu
JACKSON, Joseph, R .... 937-328-6003 379 L
jacksonj@clarkstate.edu
JACKSON, Judi .... 504-282-4455 206 C
jjackson@nobts.edu
JACKSON, Judy, T .... 256-765-4896.... 9 D
jtjackson@una.edu
JACKSON, Julie .... 662-846-4151 267 A
jjackson@deltastate.edu
JACKSON, Karen .... 212-787-5300 315 A
info@amda.edu
JACKSON, Karen .... 323-469-3300.. 26 P
info@amda.edu
JACKSON, Kari .... 610-861-1487 426 H
jacksonk@moravian.edu
JACKSON, Karima .... 203-932-7338.. 92 G
kjackson@newhaven.edu
JACKSON, Katherine ...... 334-244-3704.... 2 A
kjackson@outreach.aum.edu
JACKSON, Kathleen ...... 417-269-8316 274 A
kathleen.jackson@coxcollege.edu
JACKSON, Kathryn .... 773-508-7716 151 E
kjackson9@luc.edu
JACKSON, Keith .... 414-326-2335 535 H
kjackso4@ccon.edu
JACKSON, Kenneth .... 219-989-2366 171 L
kjackson@purduecal.edu
JACKSON, Kevin .... 254-710-1314 469 D
kevin_jackson@baylor.edu
JACKSON, Kim .... 509-793-2067 520 B
kimj@bigbend.edu
JACKSON, Kimberly ...... 252-940-6252 360 B
kimberly.jackson@beaufortccc.edu
JACKSON, Kristin .... 609-343-4916 299 G
kjackson@atlantic.edu
JACKSON, Laura .... 903-565-5936 494 E
laurajackson@uttyler.edu
JACKSON, Lauren .... 318-357-5961 208 D
potterl@nsula.edu
JACKSON, Lee, F .... 214-752-8585 492 D
chancellor@unt.edu
JACKSON, Linda, Y .... 512-505-3006 475 G
lyjackson@htu.edu
JACKSON, Lisa .... 225-743-8500 204 C
ljackson@rpcc.edu
JACKSON, Lisa .... 617-670-4404 226 F
ljackson@fisher.edu
JACKSON, Lisa, D .... 740-368-3002 390 B
ldjackso@owu.edu
JACKSON, Lorraine .... 516-323-3051 333 E
ljackson@molloy.edu
JACKSON, Manda .... 870-368-2045.. 22 D
manda.jackson@ozarka.edu
JACKSON, Marci .... 704-290-5833 366 A
mjackson@spcc.edu
JACKSON, Margaret, W 931-363-9836 458 D
mjackson@martinmethodist.edu
JACKSON, Marian, D .... 903-510-2759 491 A
mjac@tjc.edu
JACKSON, Marsha, D ... 716-851-1205 325 A
jacksonm@ecc.edu
JACKSON, Martin .... 253-879-3207 527 F
mjackson@pugetsound.edu
JACKSON, Mary .... 901-375-4400 459 D
maryjackson@midsouthcc.org
JACKSON, Melanie, M .. 863-784-7018 113 C
melanie.jackson@southflorida.edu
JACKSON, Melika .... 803-780-1259 451 G
mjackson@voorhees.edu
JACKSON, Michael .... 717-871-4292 431 E
michael.jackson@millersville.edu
JACKSON, Michele, H .. 757-221-2402 506 J
mhjackson@wm.edu
JACKSON, Michelle ...... 724-738-2220 432 A
michelle.jackson@sru.edu
JACKSON, Mike .... 918-463-2931 397 I
mike.jackson@connorsstate.edu
JACKSON, Miles .... 360-992-2934 521 A
mjackson@clark.edu
JACKSON, Natalie .... 567-661-2647 390 D
natalie_jackson3@owens.edu
JACKSON, Pamela .... 318-342-5230 209 A
pjackson@ulm.edu
JACKSON, Paul .... 603-880-8308 298 I
tmc@thomasmorecollege.edu
JACKSON, Paul .... 603-880-8308 298 I
pjackson@thomasmorecollege.edu
JACKSON, Paul .... 585-245-6128 345 D
jackson@geneseo.edu
JACKSON, Peggy .... 870-612-2030.. 24 G
peggy.jackson@uaccb.edu
JACKSON, Philip .... 870-972-3362.. 19 D
pjackson@asusystem.edu
JACKSON, R. Brooks .... 612-626-3700 265 C
jacksonb@umn.edu
JACKSON, Raymond, L . 817-272-3186 493 L
jackson@uta.edu
JACKSON, Richard .... 615-687-6892 454 G
rjackson@abcnash.edu
JACKSON, Rickey .... 928-289-6530.. 16 E
rickey.jackson@npc.edu
JACKSON, Robert .... 270-809-6912 198 I
rjackson@murraystate.edu
JACKSON, Robert .... 715-682-1207 538 D
rjackson@northland.edu
JACKSON, Robert, D ..... 847-578-3248 157 G
robert.jackson@rosalindfranklin.edu
JACKSON, Rodney .... 336-249-8186 362 B
rodney_jackson@davidsonccc.edu
JACKSON, Ron .... 864-592-4817 449 C
jacksonr@sccsc.edu
JACKSON, Rosemary .... 423-585-2614 464 C
rosemary.jackson@ws.edu
JACKSON, Ruth .... 207-859-4753 210 A
ruth.jackson@colby.edu
JACKSON, Ruth, R .... 405-466-3265 398 E
rrjackson@langston.edu
JACKSON, Sally .... 509-533-3123 521 F
sally.jackson@sfcc.spokane.edu
JACKSON, Sarah .... 270-686-4285 193 G
sarah.jackson@brescia.edu
JACKSON, Shanna .... 615-790-4419 462 E
sjackson@columbiatate.edu
JACKSON, Sharon, S .... 804-752-3747 511 E
sjackson@rmc.edu
JACKSON, Sherry .... 904-256-7212 106 Q
sjackso@ju.edu
JACKSON, Shirley, J ..... 202-806-7565.. 96 B
sjackson@howard.edu
JACKSON, Shirley Ann . 518-276-6211 339 D
president@rpi.edu
JACKSON, Starlene .... 919-718-7216 361 C
sjackson@cccc.edu
JACKSON, Stephanie .... 202-291-9020.. 96 G
sjackson@radianscollege.edu
JACKSON, Sue .... 509-777-4596 529 A
sjackson@whitworth.edu
JACKSON, Summer .... 606-539-4530 200 F
summer.jackson@ucumberlands.edu
JACKSON, Susan .... 406-586-3585 287 B
susan.jackson@montanabiblecollege.edu
JACKSON, Tamika .... 704-971-8500 355 J
tjackson@charlottelaw.edu
JACKSON, Tammi .... 410-337-6146 215 B
tammi.jackson@goucher.edu
JACKSON, Tekesha .... 229-732-5962 120 B
tekeshajackson@andrewcollege.edu
JACKSON, Terrence ...... 334-872-2533.... 6 G
JACKSON, Theron .... 318-670-6000 207 C
tjackson@susla.edu
JACKSON, JR.,
Thomas, H .... 706-542-8090 132 H
tjackson@uga.edu
JACKSON, Tim .... 512-448-8575 481 B
seubookstore@texasbook.com
JACKSON, Tom .... 918-456-5511 398 M
jacks009@nsuok.edu
JACKSON, JR., Tom ..... 605-642-6111 453 G
tom.jackson@bhsu.edu
JACKSON, Tondaleya .... 803-705-4479 443 F
jacksont@benedict.edu
JACKSON, Tonishea ...... 260-481-6147 168 D
jacksont@ipfw.edu
JACKSON, Twana .... 304-929-6716 531 D
tjackson@newriver.edu
JACKSON, Tyrone .... 601-857-3232 267 D
Tyrone.Jackson@hindscc.edu
JACKSON, Tyrone .... 601-857-3232 267 D
tyrone.jackson@hindscc.edu
JACKSON, Vanessa .... 312-777-8562 147 C
vjackson@aii.edu
JACKSON, Victor .... 972-708-7464 474 J
vic_jackson@gial.edu
JACKSON, Vincent .... 213-763-7035.. 52 A
vjackson@lattc.edu
JACKSON, Wayne .... 407-823-2716 115 C
wayne.jackson@ucf.edu
JACKSON, Weldon .... 301-860-3462 220 B
wjackson@bowiestate.edu
JACKSON, Wendy .... 704-216-6158 358 I
wjackso@livingstone.edu
JACKSON, William .... 301-891-4133 221 C
news@wau.edu
JACKSON, William .... 217-234-5296 150 B
wjackson60312@lakeland.cc.il.us
JACKSON, Willie .... 904-470-8277 102 A
w.b.jackson@ewc.edu
JACKSON, Wilma .... 402-826-8620 290 C
wilma.jackson@doane.edu
JACKSON, Zena .... 817-515-3010 484 B
zena.jackson@tccd.edu
JACKSON-DAVIS,
Dorothy, G .... 601-877-6460 266 C
djdavis@alcorn.edu
JACKSON-ELMOORE,
Cynthia .... 517-355-2326 246 H
jacks174@msu.edu
JACKSON-HAMMOND,
Cynthia .... 937-376-6332 379 D
chammond@centralstate.edu
JACKSON HOLLOWAY,
Melissa .... 919-530-6105 370 C
jacksonm@nccu.edu
JACKSON-LEE, Sophia .. 318-670-9355 207 C
slee@susla.edu
JACOB, Alan, B .... 509-777-3250 529 A
ajacob@whitworth.edu
JACOB, Mary, J .... 805-893-3651.. 72 D
mary.jacob@sa.ucsb.edu
JACOB, Regina .... 256-726-7146.... 6 C
rjacobs@oakwood.edu
JACOB, Shirley .... 985-549-2217 208 E
Shirley.Jacob@selu.edu
JACOB, Sinu .... 718-289-5608 318 E
sinu.jacob@bcc.cuny.edu
JACOBI, Judy, N .... 219-785-5593 172 A
jjacobi@pnc.edu
JACOBOWITZ, Chanie ... 732-367-1060 300 D
cjacobowitz@bmg.edu
JACOBOWITZ, Moses ... 845-782-1380 354 B
JACOBS, Alice, M .... 217-443-8848 143 F
amjacobs@dacc.edu
JACOBS, Alicia .... 518-464-8531 325 B
ajacobs@excelsior.edu
JACOBS, Andrew .... 334-386-7657.... 3 I
ajacobs@faulkner.edu
JACOBS, Andrew, C .... 207-834-7671 212 F
andrew.jacobs@maine.edu
JACOBS, Bernadette ...... 505-428-1778 313 A
bernadette.jacobs@sfcc.edu
JACOBS, Bonita .... 706-864-1993 133 A
president@ung.edu
JACOBS, Brandi, D .... 304-696-3328 532 H
jacobs2@marshall.edu
JACOBS, Bret .... 504-865-3979 206 A
bljacobs@loyno.edu
JACOBS, Cathleen .... 412-536-1033 422 E
cathleen.jacobs@laroche.edu
JACOBS, Craig, M .... 610-892-1509 429 M
cjacobs@pit.edu
JACOBS, Danny, O .... 409-772-4793 495 E
djacobs@utmb.edu
JACOBS, Dawn Ellen ..... 951-343-4275.. 30 D
djacobs@calbaptist.edu
JACOBS, Dennis .... 408-554-4533.. 65 A
dcjacobs@scu.edu
JACOBS, Derya .... 412-397-6363 434 B
jacobs@rmu.edu
JACOBS, Derya, A .... 412-397-6363 434 B
jacobs@rmu.edu

JAMES-MOORE, Annette .... 901-272-5153 459 A
amoore@mca.edu
JAMES PRYOR, Jennifer .... 914-323-5299 331 J
jj.pryor@mville.edu
JAMESON, Deborah .... 603-577-6161 297 F
djameson@dwc.edu
JAMESON, Dennis .... 916-577-2200.. 77 F
djameson@jessup.edu
JAMESON, Gretchen, M .... 262-243-5700 535 I
gretchen.jameson@cuw.edu
JAMESON, J, L .... 215-898-6796 437 I
ljameson@mail.med.upenn.edu
JAMESON, Kim .... 405-682-1611 399 K
kjameson@occc.edu
JAMESON, Maisha .... 510-464-3236.. 59 B
mjameson@peralta.edu
JAMESON, Sean .... 914-395-2494 342 C
sjameson@sarahlawrence.edu
JAMESON, Stacey .... 212-924-5900 349 D
sjameson@swedishinstitute.edu
JAMIESON, Michelle, E 724-287-8711 413 G
michelle.jamieson@bc3.edu
JAMIESON, Richard, J .. 216-368-3720 378 J
rjj@case.edu
JAMIESON-DRAKE, David .... 919-684-0736 356 E
david.jamieson.drake@duke.edu
JAMIL, Hasan .... 713-313-1953 487 F
jamil_hx@tsu.edu
JAMISON, Calvin, D .... 972-883-2213 494 A
cjamison@utdallas.edu
JAMISON, Charles .... 610-409-3607 438 H
cjamison@ursinus.edu
JAMISON, David, L .... 412-397-6225 434 B
jamison@rmu.edu
JAMISON, Kristin, E .... 217-245-3046 146 D
kristin.jamison@mail.ic.edu
JAMISON, Leslie .... 609-343-5004 299 G
ljamison@atlantic.edu
JAMISON, Matt .... 303-678-3845.. 82 J
matt.jamison@frontrange.edu
JAMISON, Todd, M .... 740-587-5712 381 H
jamisont@denison.edu
JAMROGOWICZ, John .. 843-574-6136 449 G
john.jamrogowicz@tridenttech.edu
JANAIRO, Ed .... 920-693-1871 543 B
ed.janairo@gotoltc.edu
JANAK, Bickram .... 443-885-3333 217 C
bickram.janak@morgan.edu
JANAK, Kenneth .... 817-257-5712 486 G
k.janak@tcu.edu
JANARO, Walter, A .... 540-636-2900 506 H
walter@christendom.edu
JANDA, Kenneth, C .... 949-824-6022.. 71 C
kcjanda@uci.edu
JANDRIS, Thomas .... 708-209-3597 143 D
thomas.jandris@cuchicago.edu
JANES, Kristin .... 828-669-8012 359 K
kjanes@montreat.edu
JANESCH, Cynthia, D ... 570-577-3763 413 E
cindy.janesch@bucknell.edu
JANG, Michelle .... 714-533-1495.. 67 A
michelle@southbaylo.edu
JANIK, Julie .... 972-721-4127 491 B
jjanik@udallas.edu
JANIK, Mary Mark .... 716-896-0700 352 B
janik@villa.edu
JANIS, Anita .... 509-682-6614 528 C
ajanis@wvc.edu
JANIS, Robert, J .... 312-362-8762 143 G
bjanis@depaul.edu
JANIS, Terry .... 218-935-0417 266 A
terry.janis@wetcc.edu
JANITZ, Suzanne .... 607-431-4244 327 B
janitzs@hartwick.edu
JANKE, Louise, L .... 608-785-8604 539 G
ljanke@uwlax.edu
JANKIEWICZ, Stacy .... 609-894-9311 306 B
sjankiewicz@bcc.edu
JANKO, Karen .... 312-777-8666 147 C
kjanko@aii.edu
JANKOVIAK, Michael, W .... 989-386-6603 247 B
mjankoviak@midmich.edu
JANKOWSKI, Cheryl .... 440-934-3101 388 E
cjankowski@ohiobusinesscollege.edu
JANKOWSKI, Mark .... 518-587-2100 348 A
mark.jankowski@esc.edu
JANKOWSKI, Phillip .... 219-989-2670 171 L
Phil.Janskowski@purduecal.edu
JANKOWSKI, Phillip, E 219-785-5404 172 A
pjankowski@pnc.edu
JANKOWSKI, Stephen, E .... 618-650-2760 159 I
sjankow@siue.edu
JANKOWSKI NIEMCZURA, Leslie .... 614-222-3225 380 F
JANNE, Rex .... 979-845-4570 485 C
r-janne@tamu.edu
JANNEY, Cindy .... 507-389-1011 260 A
cynthia.janney@mnsu.edu
JANNEY, Dell Ann .... 573-288-6388 274 C
djanney@culver.edu
JANNEY, Suzanne .... 941-487-4110 115 B
janney@ncf.edu
JANNING, Lori .... 540-678-4441 512 E
ljanning@su.edu
JANOSKY, Janine .... 313-593-5090 251 D
jjanosky@umich.edu
JANOW, Merit, E .... 212-854-4604 322 F
mj60@columbia.edu
JANOW, Susan .... 360-331-0307 524 E
registrar@nila.edu
JANOWIAK, Diane, J .... 708-709-3603 156 A
djanowiak@prairiestate.edu
JANOWSKI, Barbara .... 832-584-5122 131 F
bjanowski@southuniversity.edu
JANOWSKI, Lori .... 212-650-3133 319 E
lori.janowski@hunter.cuny.edu
JANSE, Korey .... 661-255-1050.. 31 B
JANSEN, James, S .... 402-280-1804 290 B
JimJansen@creighton.edu
JANSEN, Jennifer .... 312-499-4184 158 J
jjansen@saic.edu
JANSEN, Mark .... 815-599-3455 146 B
mark.jansen@highland.edu
JANSEN, Sandy .... 865-974-6611 465 C
sjansen@utk.edu
JANSEN, Shelley .... 970-943-2101.. 87 F
sjansen@western.edu
JANSEN, Wendy .... 605-221-3100 452 F
wjansen@kilian.edu
JANSMA, Pamela .... 303-556-2557.. 86 G
pamela.jansma@ucdenver.edu
JANSON, James .... 541-880-2242 406 E
janson@klamathcc.edu
JANSSEN, Jessica .... 402-941-6523 291 I
janssen@midlandu.edu
JANSSEN, Jill, M .... 815-599-3412 146 B
jill.janssen@highland.edu
JANSSEN, Michelle, L .. 765-361-6365 175 B
janssenm@wabash.edu
JANSSON, Jimilea .... 580-628-6771 399 E
jimilea.jansson@noc.edu
JANULIS, Jeffrey .... 773-481-8816 142 D
jjanulis@ccc.edu
JANUS, Cindy .... 808-739-4674 135 A
cindy.janus@chaminade.edu
JANUSCH, Barry .... 360-475-7458 524 H
bjanusch@olympic.edu
JANUTIS, Rachel .... 614-236-6383 378 H
rjanutis@law.capital.edu
JANZ, Curtis .... 405-425-5358 399 J
curtis.janz@oc.edu
JANZ, Kenneth .... 507-457-2299 262 D
kjanz@winona.edu
JANZ, Mary .... 414-288-7208 537 B
mary.janz@marquette.edu
JANZEN, Amy .... 405-425-5907 399 J
amy.janzen@oc.edu
JANZEN, Scott 574-296-6213 163M
registrar@ambs.edu
JANZEN, Teresa .... 616-222-3000 245 D
tjanzen@kuyper.edu
JAQUES, Kate .... 916-484-8654.. 52 I
jaquesk@arc.losrios.edu
JAQUILLARD, Jenny .... 800-869-7223 130 H
jjaquill@scad.edu
JARACZEWSKI, John .... 262-595-2591 540 C
john.jaraczewski@uwp.edu
JARAMILLO, Brooke .... 229-333-2100 134 I
brooke.jaramillo@wiregrass.edu
JARAMILLO, Fernan .... 507-222-4301 254 D
fjaramil@carleton.edu
JARAMILLO, John .... 949-582-4311.. 67 F
JARAMILLO, Justin .... 303-315-1845.. 86 G
justin.jaramillo@ucdenver.edu
JARAMILLO, Rick .... 505-454-2561 311 B
rjaramillo@luna.edu
JARAMILLO FLEMING, Melissa .... 575-835-5880 311 I
mjaramillo@admin.nmt.edu
JARBOE, Dan .... 870-245-5591.. 22 C
jarboed@obu.edu
JARBOE, Marlena .... 540-453-2260 514 H
jarboem@brcc.edu
JARDINE, Daniel, D .... 607-587-4036 347 D
JARDINE, David .... 269-471-3965 239 D
djardine@andrews.edu
JARES, Steven .... 347-886-2359 350 J
s.jares@uts.edu
JARETT, Sadie .... 334-874-5700.... 3 B
sjarret@ccal.edu
JARGO, Jeralyn .... 651-779-3235 258 D
jeralyn.jargo@century.edu
JARICH, Amy .... 510-642-3175.. 70 K
awjarich@berkeley.edu
JARLEY, Paul .... 407-823-2181 115 C
pjarley@bus.ucf.edu
JARMIN MILLER, Catherine .... 503-883-2494 406 I
cjarmin@linfield.edu
JARMUZ, Nick .... 312-935-6651 157 A
njarmuz@robertmorris.edu
JARNAGIN, Lea .... 657-278-3211.. 33 E
ljarnagin@fullerton.edu
JARNAGIN, Missy .... 805-437-3282.. 32 H
missy.jarnagin@csuci.edu
JARONSKI, Ann .... 813-974-3598 116 B
atj1@usf.edu
JAROSZ, John .... 402-354-7065 291 P
john.jarosz@methodistcollege.edu
JAROT, Lisa .... 847-628-1572 149 A
ljarot@judsonu.edu
JARR, William .... 770-426-2632 128 C
wdjarr@life.edu
JARRATT, Frances, L .... 864-503-5195 451 A
FJARRATT@uscupstate.edu
JARRELL, Bruce, E .... 410-706-2304 219 E
bjarrell@umaryland.edu
JARRELL, James .... 443-997-6393 216 A
jjarrell@jhu.edu
JARRELL, Michelle .... 205-391-2328.... 7 A
mjarrell@sheltonstate.edu
JARRELL, Sasha .... 850-729-5363 109 D
jarrells@nwfsc.edu
JARRELL, Sheila .... 928-776-2188.. 18 L
sheila.jarrell@yc.edu
JARRET, Ronald .... 508-793-2541 225 C
rjarret@holycross.edu
JARRETT, Courtney .... 540-535-3461 512 E
cjarrett1@su.edu
JARRETT, Dustin .... 304-243-2312 534 H
djarrett@wju.edu
JARRETT, James .... 863-680-4459 104 F
jjarrett@flsouthern.edu
JARRETT, Juan .... 706-542-2621 132 H
jarrettj@uga.edu
JARRETT, Katrina .... 704-216-6004 358 I
kjarrett@livingstone.edu
JARRY, Timothy .... 508-793-2515 225 C
tjarry@holycross.edu
JARSTFER, Amiel .... 423-869-6203 458 B
amiel.jarstfer@lmunet.edu
JARUSZEWICZ, Candace, L .... 843-953-5606 445 B
jaruszewiczc@cofc.edu
JARVIS, Abigail .... 617-322-3535 227 J
abigail_jarvis@laboure.edu
JARVIS, Jeffrey, A .... 419-227-3141 394 B
jjarvis@unoh.edu
JARVIS, Keith .... 307-532-8255 546 B
keith.jarvis@ewc.wy.edu
JARZABSKI, Kerri, P .... 413-782-1312 238 A
kerri.jarzabski@wne.edu
JASCOR, Barb .... 715-422-5476 543 D
barb.jascor@mstc.edu
JASEK, Michael, D .... 575-646-1722 312 A
mjasek@nmsu.edu
JASHINSKI, Michelle, L 814-371-2090 437 C
mjashinski@triangle-tech.edu
JASHO, Gay-linn .... 404-880-8892 122 I
gjasho@cau.edu
JASINSKI, John .... 660-562-1110 280 A
johnj@nwmissouri.edu
JASKEN, Julia .... 410-857-2247 217 A
jjasken@mcdaniel.edu
JASKOVIAK, Paul .... 281-487-1170 486 F
pjaskoviak@txchiro.edu
JASMAN, Troy .... 712-274-6400 184 A
troy.jasman@witcc.edu
JASMIN, Reba .... 256-372-8692.... 1 A
reba.jasmin@aamu.edu
JASON, Clayton .... 860-768-2448.. 92 F
cljason@hartford.edu
JASON, Hoerr, U .... 610-921-7221 411 E
jhoerr@albright.edu
JASON, Karen .... 508-531-2750 229 C
kjason@bridgew.edu
JASPERSON, Steve .... 909-706-8661.. 76 I
sjasperson@westernu.edu
JASS, Lori, K .... 503-517-1320 411 A
ljass@warnerpacific.edu
JASSO, Sonia .... 210-805-5814 492 B
sjasso@uiwtx.edu
JASTI, Bhaskara .... 209-946-3162.. 73 C
bjasti@pacific.edu
JASTORFF, Mark, A .... 970-247-7074.. 82 I
majastorff@fortlewis.edu
JASTORFF, Michael .... 605-642-6279 453 G
michael.jastorff@bhsu.edu
JASUR, Andela .... 631-420-2717 348 B
angela.jasur@farmingdale.edu
JASWAL, Faisal .... 425-564-6151 519 L
fjaswal@bellevuecollege.edu
JASZKA, Michael, S .... 716-286-8343 336 E
msj@niagara.edu
JATTKOWSKI-HUDSON, Anna, J .... 815-226-3392 157 D
ajattkowski-hudson@rockford.edu
JATULIS, Viltis, A .... 805-525-4417.. 69 I
vjatulis@thomasaquinas.edu
JAUNARAJS, Imants .... 740-593-2909 389 H
jaunaraj@ohio.edu
JAURON, Les .... 530-895-2266.. 30 B
jauronle@butte.edu
JAVAHERIPOUR, G. H .. 530-741-6707.. 78 F
gjavaher@yccd.edu
JAVARIZ, Gerardo .... 787-890-2681 557 C
gerardo.javariz@upr.edu
JAVDEKAR, Chitra .... 781-239-2703 231 G
cjavdekar@massbay.edu
JAVID, Sara .... 650-493-4430.. 66 H
sara.javid@sofia.edu
JAVIER, Byron, A .... 312-850-7140 142 E
bjavier@ccc.edu
JAVINAR, Jan, M .... 808-956-5283 135 H
javinar@hawaii.edu
JAVOR, Seta .... 818-767-0888.. 77 G
seta.javor@woodbury.edu
JAVOROSKI, Alan .... 715-422-5402 543 D
al.javoroski@mstc.edu
JAWAHAR, Jim .... 309-438-7018 147 I
jimoham@ilstu.edu
JAY, Ben .... 808-956-7301 135 J
athdir@hawaii.edu
JAYARAMAN, Ruki .... 312-505-0705.. 28 G
rjayaraman@argosy.edu
JAYASURIYA, Kumara ... 304-766-3146 533 C
kjayasuriya@wvstateu.edu
JAYAWICKREMA, Arosha .... 860-768-4276.. 92 F
jaya@hartford.edu
JAYE, Marilyn .... 617-559-8642 227 E
mjaye@hebrewcollege.edu
JAYNE, Bindu, K .... 828-262-2144 369 D
jaynebk@appstate.edu
JAYNE, Delaina .... 570-408-5000 440 B
JAYNE, Delaina .... 570-945-8130 422 B
delaina.jayne@keystone.edu
JAYNE, Joann .... 718-429-6600 352 A
joann.jayne@vaughn.edu
JAYNE, Lisa .... 928-524-7418.. 16 E
lisa.jayne@npc.edu
JAYNES, Jamie .... 630-353-7049 144 A
jjaynes@devry.edu
JAYNES, Kathy .... 406-265-4147 288 A
kjaynes@msun.edu
JAYNES, Lorene .... 406-771-4305 288 B
ljaynes@gfcmsu.edu
JAYNES, Tom .... 919-536-7250 362 C
jaynest@durhamtech.edu
JAZDZEWSKI, Richard, L .... 262-472-1305 541 D
jazdzewr@uww.edu
JAZWIECKI, Gabrielle, E .... 203-837-8281.. 88 G
jazwieckig@wcsu.edu
JAZZABI, Monica .... 323-343-3342.. 34 A
mjazzabi@cslanet.calstatela.edu
JBARA, Craig .... 269-353-1263 244 J
cjbara@kvcc.edu
JEAN, Libby .... 269-749-7655 249 A
ljean@olivetcollege.edu
JEAN, Martin, D .... 203-432-9681.. 93 C
martin.jean@yale.edu
JEAN, Paul .... 508-531-2660 229 C
paul.jean@bridgew.edu
JEAN-JACQUES, Alex .... 617-427-0060 233 A
ajean-jacques@rcc.mass.edu
JEAN-LOUIS, Patrick .... 617-541-5388 233 A
pjeanlouis@rcc.mass.edu
JEANCAKE, Chris .... 912-427-1958 123 A
cjeancake@coastalpines.edu
JEANFREAU, Jennifer, N .... 504-865-2282 206 A
jnjeanfr@loyno.edu
JEANOTTE, Leigh .... 701-777-4291 373 G
leigh.jeanotte@und.edu
JEBALI, Lisa .... 978-837-5109 233 G
lisa.jebali@merrimack.edu
JEBSEN, Chris .... 419-995-8020 384 E
jebsen.c@rhodesstate.edu
JECH, Sue .... 507-433-0610 261 C
sue.jech@riverland.edu
JECHURA, Kacey .... 303-300-8740.. 79 I
kacey.jechura@collegeamerica.com
JECK, Steve .... 954-771-0376 107 V
sjeck@knoxseminary.edu
JEDNAK, P. Michael .... 860-486-4741.. 92 C
michael.jednak@uconn.edu
JEELANI, Shaik .... 334-727-8970.... 8 B
jeelanis@mytu.tuskegee.edu
JEFFERS, Brenda, R .... 217-544-6464 158 E
brenda.jeffers@stjohnscollegespringfield.edu

JENSEN, Sol .... 701-777-3885 373 G
sol.jensen@und.edu
JENSEN, Stanley, C ...... 313-845-9650 243 I
sjenson@hfcc.edu
JENSEN, Steve, M .... 563-588-8000 178 E
smjensen@emmaus.edu
JENSEN, Tom, P .... 618-537-6959 152 C
tpjensen@mckendree.edu
JENSON, Linda .... 817-515-4521 484 B
linda.jenson@tccd.edu
JENT, Laura .... 931-393-1544 463 B
ljent@mscc.edu
JEONG, Peter .... 973-748-9000 300 E
peter_jeong@bloomfield.edu
JEPSON, Darla .... 815-802-8832 149 B
djepson@kcc.edu
JERALDS, Jeri Ann ...... 314-837-6777 281 D
jjeralds@stlchristian.edu
JEREBKO, Peter, J .... 716-851-1221 325 A
jerebko@ecc.edu
JEREZ, Antonio .... 201-327-8877 302 E
ajerez@eastwick.edu
JERGOVIC, Diana .... 626-395-6214.. 31 D
jergovic@caltech.edu
JERICHO, Rosana .... 692-625-4803 550 A
rjericho@cmi.edu
JERIES, John .... 651-690-6533 263 V
jjeries@stkate.edu
JERMAN, Rita, H .... 919-866-5701 366 H
whjerman@waketech.edu
JERMAN LIGUORI,
Denise .... 201-447-7480 300 B
djerman@bergen.edu
JERNBERG, Leslie .... 208-535-5353 138 B
leslie.jernberg@my.eitc.edu
JERNIEAN, Denise .... 615-361-7555 456 F
djerniean@daymarinstitute.edu
JERNIGAN, Cliff .... 516-463-4680 328 A
cliff.jernigan@hofstra.edu
JERNIGAN, Cynthia ...... 252-789-0253 363 H
cjernigan@martincc.edu
JERNIGAN, Ron .... 505-566-3035 312 K
jerniganr@sanjuancollege.edu
JERNIGAN, Tony .... 301-934-7715 214 E
tjernigan@csmd.edu
JERNIGAN, William ...... 918-495-6723 401 B
wjernigan@oru.edu
JEROME, Allison .... 808-735-4718 135 A
ajerome@chaminade.edu
JEROME, Etido, S .... 504-520-7593 209 E
ejerome@xula.edu
JEROME, Leslie .... 914-632-5400 333 F
ljerome@monroecollege.edu
JEROME, Marc, M .... 914-632-5400 333 F
mjerome@monroecollege.edu
JEROME, Priya .... 619-482-6557.. 68 D
pjerome@swccd.edu
JEROME, Stephen, J ...... 718-933-6700 333 F
sjerome@monroecollege.edu
JERRY, Lisa .... 516-726-5799 548 I
jerryl@usmma.edu
JERSKY, Brian .... 909-869-3600.. 32 F
bjersky@cpp.edu
JERZAK, Page, A .... 407-582-3865 118 I
pjerzak@valenciacollege.edu
JESIONOWSKI,
Rosemary, K .... 540-654-2037 513 I
rjesiono@umw.edu
JESKO, Rhonda .... 575-769-4043 310 G
rhonda.jesko@clovis.edu
JESME, Shannon .... 218-683-8577 260 F
shannon.jesme@northlandcollege.edu
JESPERSEN,
Christopher .... 706-864-1771 133 A
christopher.jespersen@ung.edu
JESSE, III, John, J ...... 402-280-3835 290 B
JohnJesse@creighton.edu
JESSEE, Pamela .... 815-836-5691 150 F
jesseepa@lewisu.edu
JESSELL, Kenneth .... 305-348-2101 114 G
kenneth.jessell@fiu.edu
JESSIE, Jason .... 334-222-6591.... 5 G
jjessie@lbwcc.edu
JESSOGNE, Cheryl .... 312-499-4186 158 J
cjessogne@saic.edu
JESSOP, Craig .... 435-797-3046 500 A
craig.jessop@usu.edu
JESSUP, Jim .... 916-577-2200.. 77 F
jjessup@jessup.edu
JESSUP, Len .... 702-895-3201 295 G
len.jessup@unlv.edu
JESSUP, Rhonda, E ...... 919-658-7754 369 B
rjessup@umo.edu
JESSUP, Tracy, C .... 704-406-4279 356 G
tjessup@gardner-webb.edu
JESTER, Christopher ..... 302-736-2468.. 94 E
christopher.jester@wesley.edu
JESUS CESAREO,
Lourdes .... 787-763-6700 552 H
ldjesus@se-pr.edu
JETER, Andy .... 229-732-5934 120 B
andyjeter@andrewcollege.edu
JETER, Everett .... 704-922-6226 362 G
jeter.everett@gaston.edu
JETER, Jeff .... 817-272-2101 493 L
jeter@uta.edu
JETT, Andy .... 913-344-1247 184 F
andy.jett@bakeru.edu
JETT, Melissa .... 417-255-7955 279 B
melissajett@missouristate.edu
JETT, Susan, P .... 864-429-8728 450 I
jettsp@mailbox.sc.edu
JETT, Wendy .... 541-463-5803 406 F
jettw@lanecc.edu
JETTE, Tracey .... 406-265-3708 288 A
tracey.jette@msun.edu
JETTON, Kent .... 731-286-3250 462 F
jetton@dscc.edu
JEUITT, Robert .... 601-979-2272 267 H
robert.h.jeuitt@jsums.edu
JEW, Carl .... 415-561-1875.. 39 A
cjew@ccsf.edu
JEWEL, Marion .... 210-297-9630 468 K
mtjewell@baptisthealthsystem.com
JEWELL, Christy .... 916-577-2200.. 77 F
cjewell@jessup.edu
JEWELL, Kirk .... 405-385-5100 400 C
kjewell@osugiving.com
JEWELL, Scott .... 617-349-8714 228 B
sjewell@lesley.edu
JEWELL, Shelley .... 615-460-6643 455 D
shelley.jewell@lmont.edu
JEWETT, Darla .... 207-741-5584 211 D
djewett@smccme.edu
JEWETT, Jacqueline ...... 860-701-5488.. 91 B
jewett_j@mitchell.edu
JEWETT, John .... 386-752-1822 103 Q
john.jewett@fgc.edu
JEWETT, Sherman .... 518-320-1311 343 B
sherman.jewett@suny.edu
JEWSBURY, Evan .... 417-625-9805 278 I
jewsbury-e@mssu.edu
JEZAK, Patricia .... 567-661-2650 390 D
patricia_jezak@owens.edu
JEZEK, Kenda .... 918-495-6198 401 B
kjezek@oru.edu
JEZEK-TAUSSIG,
Jennifer .... 314-968-5944 285 G
jezekjk@webster.edu
JEZIORSKI, Jennifer ..... 847-735-5242 149 H
jeziorski@lakeforest.edu
JEZUIT, Deborah .... 847-543-2339 142 G
djezuit@clcillinois.edu
JHAJ, Sukhwant, S ...... 503-725-2277 409 D
jhaj@pdx.edu
JHANJI, Andy, A .... 850-644-4747 115 A
ajhanji@foundation.fsu.edu
JHASHI, Tamara .... 914-674-7803 332 E
tjhashi@mercy.edu
JIAMBALVO, Jim .... 206-543-9132 527 G
jjiambal@uw.edu
JIANG, Jerome .... 626-289-7719.. 26 G
jjiang@amu.edu
JIANG, Shaojie .... 608-796-3172 542 H
sjiang@viterbo.edu
JIE, Yiyun .... 334-229-6859.... 1 D
yjiek@alasu.edu
JIGA, Anthony .... 212-998-2278 336 C
anthony.jiga@nyu.edu
JILES, Michael .... 678-664-0534 134 F
michael.jiles@westgatech.edu
JIMENEZ-PEREZ, Nancy 787-993-8877 557 E
nancy.jimenez1@upr.edu
JIMENEZ, Andre .... 707-654-1186.. 34 B
BookStore@csum.edu
JIMENEZ, Anna, A .... 480-732-7391.. 14 K
A.Jimenez@cgc.edu
JIMENEZ, Araceli .... 661-726-1911.. 70 I
araceli.jimenez@uav.edu
JIMENEZ, Asdrubal .... 787-891-0925 553 E
ajimenez@aguadilla.inter.edu
JIMENEZ, Audra .... 706-754-7766 129 B
ajimenez@northgatech.edu
JIMENEZ, Elena .... 773-896-2400 141 K
ejimenez@ctschicago.edu
JIMENEZ, Eva .... 530-242-7560.. 66 C
ejimenez@shastacollege.edu
JIMENEZ, Irma .... 787-878-6000 552 K
ijimenez@icprjc.edu
JIMENEZ, Julie .... 719-549-3222.. 85 A
julie.jimenez@pueblocc.edu
JIMENEZ, Louis, E .... 512-245-2158 489 C
lej27@txstate.edu
JIMENEZ, Misael .... 787-834-9595 556 D
mjimenez@uaa.edu
JIMENEZ, Obed .... 787-834-9595 556 D
ojimenez@uaa.edu
JIMENEZ, Silverio .... 787-882-2065 556 C
dispensario@unitecpr.net
JIMENEZ, Tomas .... 787-766-1912 553 J
tjimenez@inter.edu
JIMENEZ, Zoé .... 787-850-9354 558 A
zoe.jimenez@upr.edu
JIMENEZ CHAFEY,
Maria .... 787-764-0000 558 E
maria.jimenez16@upr.edu
JIMISON, Nancy, M ..... 804-706-5024 515 G
njiminson@jtcc.edu
JIMMERSON, Judy .... 229-430-3514 119 I
jjimmerson@albanytech.edu
JIN, Jiahe .... 512-444-8082 487 B
jjin@thsu.edu
JIN, Xudong .... 252-493-7354 364 H
xjin@email.pittcc.edu
JINDARYAN, Liana .... 818-767-0888.. 77 G
liana.jindaryan@woodbury.edu
JINDRA, Barbara, A ...... 972-758-3821 471 C
bjindra@collin.edu
JINKINS, Michael .... 502-895-3411 198 E
mjinkins@lpts.edu
JINRIGHT, Dwight .... 205-358-8543.... 9 C
jinrightd@montevallo.edu
JIRAK, Randy .... 785-227-3380 185 A
jirakr@bethanylb.edu
JIRON, Bill .... 541-245-7905 409 F
bjiron@roguecc.edu
JIROUSEK, Nancy .... 440-826-2298 377 D
njirouse@bw.edu
JIROVEC, Kelly .... 402-826-8265 290 C
kelly.jirovec@doane.edu
JIWANJI, Insiya .... 240-684-2124 220 A
admissions@umuc.edu
JOACHIM KITZMAN,
Patricia .... 641-628-5271 176 E
kitzmanp@central.edu
JOANIS, Jessica, L .... 920-748-8186 538 I
joanisj@ripon.edu
JOANIS, Pierre, D .... 570-577-1631 413 E
p.joanis@bucknell.edu
JOBE, Jarrett .... 405-974-2626 403 G
jjobe@uco.edu
JOBE, Steve .... 812-866-7005 166 E
jobe@hanover.edu
JOBIN, Amy .... 650-508-3761.. 56 H
ajobin@ndnu.edu
JOBSON, John, E .... 616-395-7800 244 A
jobson@hope.edu
JOBST, Ken, B .... 502-776-1443 199 C
kjobst@simmonscollegeky.edu
JOCHEMS, Jeff .... 417-447-7932 280 C
jochemsj@otc.edu
JOCHEMS, Judith .... 303-837-0825.. 79 C
jochemsj@aii.edu
JODIS, Stephen, M ...... 724-805-2358 435 B
stephen.jodis@email.stvincent.edu
JOEKEL, Brooke .... 512-313-3000 471 H
brooke.joekel@concordia.edu
JOEL, Richard, M .... 212-960-5300 353 P
president@yu.edu
JOEL PEREZ, Joel .... 562-907-4233.. 77 E
jperez@whittier.edu
JOENSEN, William .... 563-588-7104 180 L
william.joensen@loras.edu
JOERSCHKE, Bonnie, C 706-542-8208 132 H
bonniej@uga.edu
JOFEN, Avraham .... 718-382-6003 317 K
JOFEN, Mordechai .... 718-382-6003 317 K
JOHANNES, Cheri .... 406-657-2158 287 H
cjohannes@msubillings.edu
JOHANNES, Stephen .... 706-886-6831 132 F
sjohannes@tfc.edu
JOHANNESEN,
Christine .... 518-255-5522 346 E
johanncm@cobleskill.edu
JOHANNESEN, Glen ...... 410-290-7100 216 C
JOHANNSEN, Danelle .... 712-279-3149 182 F
danelle.johannsen@stlukescollege.edu
JOHANNSEN,
Danelle, D .... 712-279-3377 182 F
danelle.johannsen@stlukescollege.edu
JOHANSEN, Bob, L ...... 626-815-4603.. 29 B
bjohansen@apu.edu
JOHANSEN, Deborah .... 970-339-6459.. 78 J
deb.johansen@aims.edu
JOHANSON, Michael .... 808-675-3669 134 M
michael.johanson@byuh.edu
JOHANSON, Rod .... 503-517-1010 411 A
rjohanson@warnerpacific.edu
JOHANSON, Rosanne ... 716-664-5100 329 D
rosannejohnson@
jamestownbusinesscollege.edu
JOHANSSON,
Theresa, C .... 540-231-8205 518 B
theresaj@vt.edu
JOHN, JR., Leon, S ..... 570-422-3659 430 F
JOHN, Rebecca .... 612-330-1482 253 K
rjohn@augsburg.edu
JOHN, Richard, S .... 804-828-2111 514 F
rsjohn@vcu.edu
JOHN, Rowan .... 219-989-2654 171 L
jrowan@purduecal.edu
JOHN, Samuel .... 201-447-7868 300 B
sjohn@bergen.edu
JOHN, Stephen, S .... 806-716-2217 482 F
sjohn@southplainscollege.edu
JOHNDROW, David, A .. 570-674-6762 426 D
djohndro@misericordia.edu
JOHNOSON, April .... 301-860-3831 220 B
aljohnson@bowiestate.edu
JOHNS, David .... 606-546-4151 200 E
djohns@unionky.edu
JOHNS, Greg .... 417-865-2815 274 L
johnsg@evangel.edu
JOHNS, Marci .... 334-386-7100.... 3 I
mjohns@faulkner.edu
JOHNS, Patrick .... 218-733-7600 259 C
p.johns@lsc.edu
JOHNS, Priscilla, C ...... 671-735-5517 549 E
priscilla.johns@guamcc.edu
JOHNS, Sean .... 763-433-1124 258 A
sean.johns@anokaramsey.edu
JOHNS, Sean .... 763-433-1124 257 P
sean.johns@anokaramsey.edu
JOHNS, Sheila, R .... 308-635-6366 294 C
johnss23@wncc.edu
JOHNS, Timothy .... 920-206-2332 536 T
timothy.johns@mbu.edu
JOHNS, Xenia .... 770-228-7348 132 B
xjohns@sctech.edu
JOHNS-HINES,
Stephanie .... 316-214-1491 186 E
stephanie.johns-hines@cowley.edu
JOHNSEN, Darby .... 405-682-1611 399 K
djohnsen@occc.edu
JOHNSEN, David, C ..... 319-335-7144 175 H
david-johnsen@uiowa.edu
JOHNSEN, John, H ...... 315-792-3120 351 G
jjohnsen@utica.edu
JOHNSON, Aaron .... 303-762-6933.. 82 C
aaron.johnson@denverseminary.edu
JOHNSON, Abe .... 972-548-6677 471 C
ajohnson@collin.edu
JOHNSON, Adam .... 651-846-1782 261 G
adam.johnson@saintpaul.edu
JOHNSON, Adam .... 912-279-5739 123 B
ajohnson@ccga.edu
JOHNSON, Adam .... 405-974-2385 403 G
adjohnson@uco.edu
JOHNSON, Alan .... 662-329-7411 269 B
alan.johnson@sodexo.com
JOHNSON, JR.,
Albert, D .... 580-581-2999 397 A
aljohnson@cameron.edu
JOHNSON, Alesa .... 606-451-6693 197 B
alesa.johnson@kctcs.edu
JOHNSON, Alex .... 216-987-4853 381 A
alex.johnson@tri-c.edu
JOHNSON, Alice .... 210-486-0902 467 C
ajohnson235@alamo.edu
JOHNSON, Alisa, M ..... 207-859-4140 210 A
ajohnson@colby.edu
JOHNSON, Allen .... 951-343-4477.. 30 D
ajohnson@calbaptist.edu
JOHNSON, Allison .... 701-788-4743 374 A
allison.johnson.3@mayvillestate.edu
JOHNSON, Alton, B ...... 936-261-5125 484 F
abjohnson@pvamu.edu
JOHNSON, Amy .... 610-861-1304 426 H
johnsona@moravian.edu
JOHNSON, Amy .... 509-359-2292 522 C
amyjohns@ewu.edu
JOHNSON, Amy .... 731-286-3398 462 F
ajohnson@dscc.edu
JOHNSON, Andrea .... 870-236-6901.. 20 I
ajohnson@crc.edu
JOHNSON, Andrew .... 610-799-1155 424 A
ajohnson23@lccc.edu
JOHNSON, Andrew, W . 316-284-5230 185 B
ajohnson@bethelks.edu
JOHNSON, Angela .... 502-213-2141 196 E
angela.johnson@kctcs.edu
JOHNSON, Angela .... 216-987-4213 381 A
angela.johnson@tri-c.edu
JOHNSON, Anna .... 740-753-6553 383 G
johnson_a@hocking.edu
JOHNSON, Anne .... 651-450-3642 259 A
ajohnson@inverhills.edu
JOHNSON, Annie .... 213-624-1200.. 44 I
ajohnson@fidm.edu
JOHNSON, Anthony ...... 401-454-6638 442 B
ajohnson@risd.edu
JOHNSON, Antoinette ... 757-569-6772 516 E
ajohnson@pdc.edu
JOHNSON, Arvid, C ...... 815-740-3369 162 F
ajohnson@stfrancis.edu
JOHNSON, Ashlee .... 314-392-2305 278 G
JohnsonA@mobap.edu
JOHNSON, Ashley .... 912-844-9737 131 F
afjohnson@southuniversity.edu
JOHNSON, Barbara .... 609-777-4351 308 H
bjohnson@tesc.edu

JOHNSON, Barbara, G .. 412-578-6021 414 I
johnsonbg@carlow.edu
JOHNSON, Barbara, L .. 308-865-8205 293 G
johnsonbl@unk.edu
JOHNSON, Barry .... 704-406-4440 356 G
bjohnson@gardner-webb.edu
JOHNSON, Barry .... 408-864-5678.. 44 N
johnsonbarry@deanza.edu
JOHNSON, Bart .... 218-322-2388 259 B
bart.johnson@itascacc.edu
JOHNSON, Becky .... 903-983-8223 477 A
rjohnson@kilgore.edu
JOHNSON, Ben .... 870-235-4004.. 23 D
bfjohnson@saumag.edu
JOHNSON, Bernard, A .. 240-500-2000 215 C
bajohnson@hagerstowncc.edu
JOHNSON,
Beth Ann, H .... 203-392-5250.. 88 F
johnsonb3@southernct.edu
JOHNSON, Betsy .... 567-661-7883 390 D
betsy_johnson@owens.edu
JOHNSON, Bill .... 209-932-2824.. 73 C
bjohnson3@pacific.edu
JOHNSON, Bonnie .... 641-673-1036 184 B
johnsonb@wmpenn.edu
JOHNSON, Brad .... 859-858-3511 193 A
bjohnson@asbury.edu
JOHNSON, Brad .... 417-328-1805 282 D
bjohnson@sbuniv.edu
JOHNSON, Brad, W ...... 903-434-8102 479 L
bjohnson@ntcc.edu
JOHNSON, Brandon ...... 320-308-5166 261 E
bljohnson@stcloudstate.edu
JOHNSON, Brandon ...... 816-501-2400 272 E
brandon.johnson@avila.edu
JOHNSON, Brenda .... 773-702-8743 161 D
brendajohnson@uchicago.edu
JOHNSON, Brenda .... 510-780-4500.. 50 G
bjohnson@lifewest.edu
JOHNSON, Brenda .... 510-981-2830.. 58 J
bjohnson@peralta.edu
JOHNSON, Brian .... 504-865-5000 207 F
JOHNSON, Brian, D ...... 208-885-6246 139 C
johnsonb@uidaho.edu
JOHNSON, Brian, L ...... 334-727-8011.... 8 B
JOHNSON, Brian, T ...... 219-464-6732 174 E
brian.johnson1@valpo.edu
JOHNSON, Brooke .... 815-921-4267 157 B
b.johnson@rockvalleycollege.edu
JOHNSON, Bryan, M ..... 205-726-4036..... 6 F
bmjohnso@samford.edu
JOHNSON, C. Lynn ...... 320-222-5208 261 B
lynn.johnson@ridgewater.edu
JOHNSON, Calvin, M ..... 334-844-4546..... 1 G
johncal@auburn.edu
JOHNSON, Candace ...... 810-766-4109 239 H
candace.johnson@baker.edu
JOHNSON, Carl .... 847-317-8138 161 B
cjohnson@tiu.edu
JOHNSON, Carl .... 303-871-3111.. 86 H
cdjohnson@du.edu
JOHNSON, Carl .... 817-461-8741 468 C
cjohnson@arlingtonbaptistcollege.edu
JOHNSON, Carol .... 704-878-3225 364 C
cjohnson@mitchellcc.edu
JOHNSON, Casie .... 507-453-2663 259 G
cjohnson@southeastmn.edu
JOHNSON, Cass .... 312-362-5596 143 G
cjohn161@depaul.edu
JOHNSON, Cassandra .. 706-233-7208 131 C
cjohnson@shorter.edu
JOHNSON,
Cassandra, M .... 903-927-3336 497 G
cmjohnson@wileyc.edu
JOHNSON,
Catherine, W .... 336-506-4237 359 N
cathy.johnson@alamancecc.edu
JOHNSON, Cecelia .... 931-540-2762 462 E
cjohnson@columbiastate.edu
JOHNSON, Chacona ..... 313-577-0157 252 G
chacona.johnson@wayne.edu
JOHNSON, Chad .... 651-290-6475 266 B
chad.johnson@wmitchell.edu
JOHNSON, JR.,
Charles, R .... 812-888-4262 174 F
provost@vinu.edu
JOHNSON, Charlie .... 405-974-2315 403 G
chjohnson@uco.edu
JOHNSON, Charlotte .... 909-621-8277.. 65 E
charlotte.johnson@scrippscollege.edu
JOHNSON, Charlotte .... 870-584-4471.. 24 E
cjohnson@cccua.edu
JOHNSON, Chauncy ..... 307-268-2025 545 Z
cjohnson@caspercollege.edu
JOHNSON, Cherry .... 931-540-2582 462 E
cjohnson22@columbiastate.edu
JOHNSON, Cheryl .... 618-545-3091 149 C
cjohnson@kaskaskia.edu
JOHNSON, Cheryl, L .... 785-532-6277 188 H
cherylj2025@ksu.edu
JOHNSON, Chris .... 303-762-6924.. 82 C
chris.johnson@denverseminary.edu
JOHNSON, Chris .... 251-580-2222..... 5 A
chris.johnson@faulknerstate.edu
JOHNSON, Chris .... 434-592-3017 509 G
cjohnson@liberty.edu
JOHNSON, Christine .... 509-434-5006 521 D
cjohnson@ccs.spokane.edu
JOHNSON, Christine .... 509-434-5006 521 E
christine.johnson@ccs.spokane.edu
JOHNSON, Christine, L 859-858-2176 192 O
JOHNSON, Christol ...... 214-860-2627 472 F
christoljohnson@dcccd.edu
JOHNSON, Christopher 253-833-9111 523 B
cjohnson@greenriver.edu
JOHNSON, Cindy .... 620-235-4185 190 G
cynthia.johnson@pittstate.edu
JOHNSON, Cindy, K ..... 816-604-1011 277 F
cindy.johnson@mcckc.edu
JOHNSON, JR., Clyde .. 443-552-1659 216 F
cjohnson01@mica.edu
JOHNSON, Colleen .... 916-608-6585.. 53 A
johnsoc@flc.losrios.edu
JOHNSON, Connie .... 719-598-0200.. 81 H
cjohnson@coloradotech.edu
JOHNSON, Craig .... 870-972-2852.. 19 F
crjohnso@astate.edu
JOHNSON, Craig .... 773-244-5637 154 G
crjohnson@northpark.edu
JOHNSON, Craig .... 813-253-7051 106 C
cjohnson@hccfl.edu
JOHNSON, Croslena ..... 864-646-1568 449 F
cjohnso5@tctc.edu
JOHNSON, Curtis .... 501-420-1265.. 19 B
curtis.johnson@arkansasbaptist.edu
JOHNSON, Cuthrell ...... 336-750-2230 372 D
johnsonc@wssu.edu
JOHNSON, Cynda Ann . 540-526-2559 518 D
cajohnson@vt.edu
JOHNSON, Cyndy .... 512-448-8657 481 B
cjohns12@stedwards.edu
JOHNSON, Cynthia .... 360-486-8131 525 H
cjohnson@stmartin.edu
JOHNSON, D. Nichole .. 614-236-6945 378 H
njohnson@capital.edu
JOHNSON, Dacia .... 218-736-1512 259 H
dacia.johnson@minnesota.edu
JOHNSON, Dale .... 510-780-4500.. 50 G
djohnson@lifewest.edu
JOHNSON, Danae .... 229-226-1621 132 E
djohnson@thomasu.edu
JOHNSON, Danette ...... 604-274-1252 328 H
djohnson@ithaca.edu
JOHNSON, Daniel .... 701-662-1515 375 A
dan.johnson@lrsc.edu
JOHNSON, Daniel .... 803-584-3446 450 F
johns943@mailbox.sc.edu
JOHNSON, Daniel .... 425-640-1554 522 D
daniel.johnson@edcc.edu
JOHNSON, Daniel .... 918-456-5511 398 M
johnso89@nsuok.edu
JOHNSON, Daniel, R .... 203-582-8930.. 91 E
dan.johnson@quinnipiac.edu
JOHNSON, Daniel, W ... 414-443-8952 542 I
daniel.johnson@wlc.edu
JOHNSON, Danny .... 406-548-1986 287 B
JOHNSON, Dara .... 765-998-5113 173 B
drjohnson@taylor.edu
JOHNSON, Darren .... 518-381-1320 342 E
johnsod@sunysccc.edu
JOHNSON, Darryl .... 336-517-2358 354 K
djohnson@bennett.edu
JOHNSON, Darryl .... 206-934-3646 525 K
darryl.johnson@seattlecolleges.edu
JOHNSON, Daryl .... 651-793-1227 259 E
daryl.johnson@metrostate.edu
JOHNSON, Dave .... 909-537-5007.. 35 A
djohnson@csusb.edu
JOHNSON, David .... 256-824-6288..... 9 A
david.johnson@uah.edu
JOHNSON, David .... 606-368-6031 192 H
davidjohnson@alc.edu
JOHNSON, David .... 650-306-3336.. 64 C
johnsond@smccd.edu
JOHNSON, David .... 404-727-0640 124 D
davidjohnson@emory.edu
JOHNSON, David .... 812-855-8908 167 J
vpem@indiana.edu
JOHNSON, David .... 716-338-1002 329 E
davejohnson@mail.sunyjcc.edu
JOHNSON, David, J ...... 513-745-3202 396 B
johnsond8@xavier.edu
JOHNSON, David, N ..... 919-209-2050 363 F
dnjohnson@johnstoncc.edu
JOHNSON, Deadre .... 202-885-2721.. 94 H
deadrej@american.edu
JOHNSON, Debbie .... 218-733-6904 259 C
debra.johnson@lsc.edu
JOHNSON, Deborah ...... 419-251-1327 386 C
deborah.johnson@mercycollege.edu
JOHNSON, Deborah ..... 806-457-4200 474 E
djohnson@fpctx.edu
JOHNSON, Deborah ..... 713-798-4032 469 C
djohnson@bcm.edu
JOHNSON, Debra, J ..... 540-985-8492 509 D
djjohnson@jchs.edu
JOHNSON, Deirdra, G .. 410-334-2902 221 E
djohnson@worwic.edu
JOHNSON, Demetrius ... 504-816-4026 202 F
dpjohnson@dillard.edu
JOHNSON, Denis .... 913-971-3279 189 F
ddjohnson@mnu.edu
JOHNSON, Dennis .... 719-549-3035.. 85 A
dennis.johnson@pueblocc.edu
JOHNSON, Dennis .... 314-889-1452 275 B
djohnson@fontbonne.edu
JOHNSON, Derby .... 308-432-6224 292 B
djohnson@csc.edu
JOHNSON, Derek .... 608-663-2324 536 A
derekjohnson@edgewood.edu
JOHNSON, Derrick .... 252-335-3291 369 F
dajohnson@ecsu.edu
JOHNSON, Deshawn .... 248-204-2117 245 J
djohnson@ltu.edu
JOHNSON, DeWayne .... 213-637-1376.. 77 C
dejohnson@westwood.edu
JOHNSON, Dexter .... 425-564-4261 519 L
dexter.johnson@bellevuecollege.edu
JOHNSON, Diana .... 479-636-9222.. 22 B
JOHNSON, Diane .... 518-828-4181 322 E
diane.johnson@sunycgcc.edu
JOHNSON, Diane .... 801-883-8335 498 M
djohnson@new.edu
JOHNSON, Dianne .... 417-873-7258 274 E
djohnson021@drury.edu
JOHNSON, Donielle, R . 972-860-7014 472 E
DonielleJohnson@dcccd.edu
JOHNSON, Donna .... 845-431-8682 324 D
djohnson@sunydutchess.edu
JOHNSON, Doris .... 972-524-3341 483 F
JOHNSON, Doris, W .... 803-705-4536 443 F
johnsond@benedict.edu
JOHNSON, Doug .... 785-460-5411 186 D
doug.johnson@colbycc.edu
JOHNSON, Douglas, P . 207-581-1392 212 C
douglasj@maine.edu
JOHNSON, Duane .... 701-224-5789 374 E
duane.johnson.1@bismarckstate.edu
JOHNSON, Earl .... 918-631-3142 403 M
earl-johnson@utulsa.edu
JOHNSON, Edward .... 716-827-2456 350 H
johnsone@trocaire.edu
JOHNSON, Elise .... 586-498-4119 246 A
johnsonem@macomb.edu
JOHNSON, Elizabeth ..... 330-823-2030 394 A
johnsoec@mountunion.edu
JOHNSON, Elizabeth ..... 203-596-8598.. 91 D
ejohnson@post.edu
JOHNSON, Elizabeth ..... 813-253-7449 106 C
bjohnson@hccfl.edu
JOHNSON, Ellen .... 617-521-2515 236 F
ellen.johnson3@simmons.edu
JOHNSON, Eric .... 402-844-7236 292 G
eric@northeast.edu
JOHNSON, Eric .... 813-253-7560 106 C
ejohnson71@hccfl.edu
JOHNSON, Eric .... 219-464-5085 174 E
eric.johnson@valpo.edu
JOHNSON, Eric, C .... 617-627-5484 237 C
eric.johnson@tufts.edu
JOHNSON, Eric, P .... 218-299-3447 255 B
johnson@cord.edu
JOHNSON, Eric, S .... 207-859-4460 210 A
eric.johnson@colby.edu
JOHNSON, Eric, W .... 985-549-3860 208 E
ejohnson@selu.edu
JOHNSON, Fatima, R .... 585-245-5620 345 D
johnsonf@geneseo.edu
JOHNSON, Faye, R .... 229-226-1621 132 E
fjohnson@thomasu.edu
JOHNSON,
Fengling, M .... 651-628-3372 265 D
fmjohnson@unwsp.edu
JOHNSON, Frank .... 620-947-3121 191 E
frankj@tabor.edu
JOHNSON, Frank .... 404-756-4013 120 H
frankjohnson@atlm.edu
JOHNSON, Freddie .... 404-756-4442 120 H
fjohnson@atlm.edu
JOHNSON, Fredrick ...... 412-392-6132 433 F
fjohnson@pointpark.edu
JOHNSON, Fredrick, P . 443-412-2407 215 D
rjohnson@harford.edu
JOHNSON, G. David ..... 251-460-6261..... 9 F
djohnson@southalabama.edu
JOHNSON, Gail .... 903-730-4890 476 L
gjohnsno@jarvis.edu
JOHNSON, Gail .... 325-235-7419 488 C
gail.johnson@tstc.edu
JOHNSON, Gary .... 515-271-3133 177 K
gary.johnson@drake.edu
JOHNSON, Gary .... 573-651-2112 282 C
ggjohnson@semo.edu
JOHNSON, Gary .... 718-270-5002 320 C
gajohnson@mec.cuny.edu
JOHNSON, Gary .... 704-878-3250 364 C
gjohnson@mitchellcc.edu
JOHNSON, Gary, C ...... 402-461-7407 290 G
gcjohnson@hastings.edu
JOHNSON, George .... 256-726-8205..... 6 C
gjohnson@oakwood.edu
JOHNSON, George .... 210-486-2252 467 B
gjohnson@alamo.edu
JOHNSON, Glen .... 281-649-3801 475 B
glenjohnson@hbu.edu
JOHNSON, Glen .... 205-391-2327..... 7 A
gjohnson@sheltonstate.edu
JOHNSON, Glen .... 276-739-2467 517 D
gjohnson@vhcc.edu
JOHNSON, Glenn .... 304-929-1495 530 H
glennjohnson@ucwv.edu
JOHNSON, Gloria, C .... 615-963-7518 461 F
gjohnson@tnstate.edu
JOHNSON, Gloria, M ... 972-860-7001 472 E
GloriaJohnson@dcccd.edu
JOHNSON, Gordon, L .. 270-745-6455 201 D
gordon.johnson@wku.edu
JOHNSON, Gregory, A . 562-988-2278.. 27 L
gjohnson@auhs.edu
JOHNSON, Gregory, W 757-221-3952 506 J
gwjohnson@wm.edu
JOHNSON, H. Wayne ... 847-317-8085 161 B
wjohnson@tiu.edu
JOHNSON, H. Wilson ... 716-888-2301 317 H
johns273@canisius.edu
JOHNSON, Haley .... 615-269-8300 457 I
hjohnson@kaplan.edu
JOHNSON, Henry .... 336-517-2137 354 K
hjohnson@bennett.edu
JOHNSON, Holly .... 319-296-4283 179 B
holly.johnson@hawkeyecollege.edu
JOHNSON, J. Lee .... 517-264-7108 250 B
ljohnson@sienaheights.edu
JOHNSON, J. Theodore 704-233-8105 373 C
tjohnson@wingate.edu
JOHNSON, Jacqueline .. 320-589-6020 265 A
jrjohnso@morris.umn.edu
JOHNSON, James .... 620-235-4389 190 G
jjohnson@pittstate.edu
JOHNSON, James, F .... 215-898-2173 437 I
johnsonj@isc.upenn.edu
JOHNSON, James, K .... 651-286-7773 265 D
jkjohnson2@unwsp.edu
JOHNSON, James, M ... 630-752-5113 163 G
james.johnson@wheaton.edu
JOHNSON, James, R .... 717-477-1373 431 F
jrjohnson@ship.edu
JOHNSON, Janet, L ...... 812-464-1928 174 D
jljohnson@usi.edu
JOHNSON, Jason .... 580-628-6240 399 E
jason.johnson@noc.edu
JOHNSON, Jason, L ..... 970-491-6270.. 81 D
jason.johnson@colostate.edu
JOHNSON, Jay .... 314-889-1423 275 B
jjohnson@fontbonne.edu
JOHNSON, Jean .... 202-994-3725.. 95 D
sonjej@gwumc.edu
JOHNSON, Jean .... 785-594-8384 184 F
jean.johnson@bakeru.edu
JOHNSON, Jean .... 773-838-7544 142 C
jjohnson2@ccc.edu
JOHNSON, Jean, A .... 319-399-8561 176 G
jjohnson@coe.edu
JOHNSON, Jeff .... 318-628-4342 203 E
JOHNSON, Jeffrey .... 850-718-2237 100 E
johnsonj@chipola.edu
JOHNSON, Jeffrey, A ... 757-446-6100 507 B
johnsonja@evms.edu
JOHNSON, Jeffrey, C ... 561-237-7333 108 E
jjohnson@lynn.edu
JOHNSON, Jeffrey, W ... 515-294-6561 175 G
jjohnsn@iastate.edu
JOHNSON, Jennifer ...... 559-442-8281.. 69 B
jennifer.johnson@fresnocitycollege.edu
JOHNSON, Jennifer ...... 503-768-6626 406 H
jjj@lclark.edu
JOHNSON, Jenny .... 731-989-6378 456 K
jjohnson@fhu.edu
JOHNSON, Jerry .... 812-866-7364 166 E
johnsonj@hanover.edu
JOHNSON, Jeryl .... 843-863-8080 444 B
jjohnson@csuniv.edu
JOHNSON, Jessica ...... 918-335-6829 400 I
jjohnson@okwu.edu
JOHNSON, Jill .... 803-321-5136 447 L
jill.johnson@newberry.edu
JOHNSON, Jill .... 515-961-1595 182 I
jill.johnson@simpson.edu
JOHNSON, Jill .... 309-341-5320 140 I
jjohnson@sandburg.edu
JOHNSON, Jill, K .... 904-632-5016 105 A
jill.johnson@fscj.edu

JOHNSON, Jill, R .... 864-587-4232 449 D johnsoj@smcsc.edu
JOHNSON, Jo Ann .... 580-559-5246 397 K jajohnsn@ecok.edu
JOHNSON, JoAnna .... 254-526-1168 470 E joanna.johnson@ctcd.edu
JOHNSON, Jodi, S .... 706-272-4475 123 G jjohnson@daltonstate.edu
JOHNSON, Joel, T .... 651-631-5312 265 D jtjohnson@unwsp.edu
JOHNSON, John, J .... 361-698-1269 473 F jjohnson@delmar.edu
JOHNSON, JR., John, R .... 704-406-4303 356 G jrjohnson@gardner-webb.edu
JOHNSON, Joseph .... 484-365-7526 424 E jjohnson2@lincoln.edu
JOHNSON, JR., Joseph 619-594-1424.. 35 E jjohnson@mail.sdsu.edu
JOHNSON, Joyce .... 229-430-4792 119 H joyce.johnson@asurams.edu
JOHNSON, Joyce .... 951-639-5439.. 55 A jajohnso@msjc.edu
JOHNSON, Joyce .... 757-825-2827 517 B johnsonj@tncc.edu
JOHNSON, Joyce, B ..... 336-322-2106 364 G Joyce.Johnson@piedmontcc.edu
JOHNSON, Judy .... 309-438-7611 147 I jjohns4@ilstu.edu
JOHNSON, Julia .... 608-785-8116 539 G jjohnson2@uwlax.edu
JOHNSON, Julie .... 360-736-9391 520 F jjohnson@centralia.edu
JOHNSON, Julie .... 801-462-1056.. 28 G jljohnson@argosy.edu
JOHNSON, Julie .... 605-455-6011 452 L jjohnson@olc.edu
JOHNSON, Julie, A ...... 209-667-3351.. 35 C jjohnson34@csustan.edu
JOHNSON, Julie, A ...... 352-273-6309 115 D johnson@cop.ufl.edu
JOHNSON, Julie, H ...... 920-748-8772 538 I johnsonj@ripon.edu
JOHNSON, Karen .... 507-457-5300 262 D kjohnson@winona.edu
JOHNSON, Karen .... 402-354-7038 291 P karen.johnson@methodistcollege.edu
JOHNSON, Karen .... 918-495-7371 401 B kjohnson@oru.edu
JOHNSON, Karen, A ..... 574-284-4571 172 G kjohnson@saintmarys.edu
JOHNSON, Karen, A ..... 229-333-6024 133 H kjohnson@valdosta.edu
JOHNSON, Karen, D ..... 630-515-7268 152 H kjohns@midwestern.edu
JOHNSON, Karen, E ..... 832-826-6207 469 C karenj@bcm.edu
JOHNSON, Karen, L ..... 607-735-1827 324 J kajohnson@elmira.edu
JOHNSON, Kari .... 559-675-4835.. 69 C kari.johnson@reedleycollege.edu
JOHNSON, Katharine .. 602-787-7106.. 15 B kathaerine.johnson@paradisevalley.edu
JOHNSON, Kathleen ..... 219-785-5288 172 A kjohnson@pnc.edu
JOHNSON, Kathleen, L . 404-215-2660 128 L kathleen.johnson@morehouse.edu
JOHNSON, Kathryn, B .. 315-268-3943 321 C kjohnson@clarkson.edu
JOHNSON, Kathy .... 269-488-4223 244 J kjohnson@kvcc.edu
JOHNSON, Kathy .... 317-278-0033 168 E kjohnso@iupui.edu
JOHNSON, Kathy, J ...... 605-642-6512 453 G kathy.johnson@bhsu.edu
JOHNSON, Kaytie .... 215-965-4044 426 G kjohnson@moore.edu
JOHNSON, Keesha .... 501-337-5000.. 20 H kjohnson@coto.edu
JOHNSON, Keith .... 205-453-6300.. 96 H
JOHNSON, Keith .... 408-855-5457.. 76 E keith.johnson@wvm.edu
JOHNSON, Keith .... 270-706-8413 195 K keith.johnson@kctcs.edu
JOHNSON, Keith .... 785-242-5200 190 D keith.johnson@ottawa.edu
JOHNSON, Keith .... 701-671-2218 375 B keith.johnson@ndscs.edu
JOHNSON, Kelley .... 760-245-4271.. 75 G kelley.johnson@vvc.edu
JOHNSON, Kellye .... 405-789-7661 402 F Kellye.johnson@swcu.edu
JOHNSON, Kenneth ...... 740-593-2247 389 H Johnsok9@ohio.edu
JOHNSON, Kenneth ...... 850-644-9396 115 A ken.johnson@fsu.edu
JOHNSON, Kent, M ...... 319-273-2122 176 A kent.johnson@uni.edu
JOHNSON, Kersten .... 605-677-6713 453 F kersten.johnson@usd.edu
JOHNSON, Kevin .... 620-341-5667 186 H kjohnson@emporia.edu
JOHNSON, Kevin, R ..... 530-752-7225.. 71 A krjohnson@ucdavis.edu
JOHNSON, Kim .... 714-556-3610.. 75 A OfficeVPEM@vanguard.edu
JOHNSON, Kim, M .... 773-896-2400 141 K kjohnson@ctschicago.edu
JOHNSON, Kimberlee ... 215-769-3128 418 A kjohnso2@eastern.edu
JOHNSON, Kimberly ..... 765-361-6209 175 B johnsonk@wabash.edu
JOHNSON, Kirk .... 712-274-5116 181 C johnson@morningside.edu
JOHNSON, Kristie .... 802-773-5900 501 G kristie.johnson@csj.edu
JOHNSON, Kyle .... 808-739-8552 135 A kyle.johnson@chaminade.edu
JOHNSON, LaKenya ..... 229-931-2057 131 E ljohnson@southgatech.edu
JOHNSON, Lakeshia ..... 641-269-9801 178 I johnsola@grinnell.edu
JOHNSON, Landy, C .... 580-767-7666 222 D lajohnson@assumption.edu
JOHNSON, Landy, C .... 508-767-7666 222 D lajohnson@assumption.edu
JOHNSON, Larry .... 706-272-4571 123 G ljohnson@daltonstate.edu
JOHNSON, Larry .... 870-236-6901.. 20 I ljohnson@crc.edu
JOHNSON, Larry .... 601-977-7758 270 F ljohnson@tougaloo.edu
JOHNSON, Larry .... 202-685-2128 547 M johnsonl@ndu.edu
JOHNSON, Laura .... 870-574-4513.. 23 E ljohnson@sautech.edu
JOHNSON, Laura .... 502-863-7969 195 A Laura_Johnson@georgetowncollege.edu
JOHNSON, Laura .... 906-217-4022 240 K lauralee.johnson@baycollege.edu
JOHNSON, Laura .... 704-216-6029 358 I ljohnson@livingstone.edu
JOHNSON, Laura, T ..... 520-621-3175.. 18 E ltj@email.arizona.edu
JOHNSON, Lawrence, J 513-556-2322 393 B lawrence.johnson@uc.edu
JOHNSON, Lea .... 518-438-3111 331 K ljohnson@mariacollege.edu
JOHNSON, Leda .... 623-935-8868.. 14 L leda.johnson@estrellamountain.edu
JOHNSON, Lena, H ...... 757-455-3116 518 H ljohnson@vwc.edu
JOHNSON, Les .... 218-281-8345 264 H ljohnson@umn.edu
JOHNSON, Leslie .... 937-769-1345 376 L lbates@antioch.edu
JOHNSON, Leslie, R ..... 217-786-2848 151 C leslie.johnson@llcc.edu
JOHNSON, Levester ...... 317-940-9381 164 L ljohnson@butler.edu
JOHNSON, Lisa .... 407-646-2391 111 H adjohnson@rollins.edu
JOHNSON, Lisa .... 785-242-5200 190 D lisa.johnson@ottawa.edu
JOHNSON, Lisa .... 617-287-6020 228 G lisa.johnson@umb.edu
JOHNSON, Lisa .... 701-858-3494 373 F lisa.a.johnson@ndus.edu
JOHNSON, Lisa .... 423-636-7305 464 F ljohnson@tusculum.edu
JOHNSON, Lisa, A .... 252-335-0821 361 G lajohnson@albemarle.edu
JOHNSON, Lois, M .... 717-720-4122 430 A ljohnson@passhe.edu
JOHNSON, Louise, N ... 563-589-0201 183 K ljohnson@wartburgseminary.edu
JOHNSON, Lynda, K .... 470-578-6033 127 M ljohnson@kennesaw.edu
JOHNSON, Lynn .... 216-791-5000 380 C lynn.m.johnson@cim.edu
JOHNSON, Lynn .... 218-755-2068 258 B ljohnson@bemidjistate.edu
JOHNSON, Lynn .... 631-632-6151 344 C lynn.johnson@stonybrook.edu
JOHNSON, Lynn .... 970-491-1550.. 81 D lynn.johnson@colostate.edu
JOHNSON, Lynn .... 541-440-7690 410 E lynn.johnson@umpqua.edu
JOHNSON, Lynne .... 907-796-6416.. 11 A lynne.johnson@uas.alaska.edu
JOHNSON, Maggie, A .. 972-708-7573 474 J admissions@gial.edu
JOHNSON, Mandy .... 608-663-2000 536 S mjjohnson@mediainstitute.edu
JOHNSON, Marc .... 775-784-4805 295 H marc.johnson@unr.edu
JOHNSON, Marcia .... 803-750-2500.. 96 H
JOHNSON, Marco .... 661-726-1911.. 70 I marco.johnson@uav.edu
JOHNSON, Marcus .... 702-651-4148 295 C maracus.johnson@csn.edu
JOHNSON, Marcus .... 701-228-5674 374 F marcus.a.johnson@dakotacollege.edu
JOHNSON, Margaret ..... 208-282-3520 138 C johnmarg@isu.edu
JOHNSON, Margaret ..... 972-708-7616 474 J financial-aid@gial.edu
JOHNSON, Marguerite .. 617-732-2277 233 E peg.johnson@mcphs.edu
JOHNSON, Maria .... 909-748-8335.. 73 K maria_johnson@redlands.edu
JOHNSON, Marianne, H .... 215-699-5700 423 F mjohnson@LSB.edu
JOHNSON, Marie, D ..... 802-656-5700 503 C marie.johnson@uvm.edu
JOHNSON, Mark .... 248-218-2080 249 D mjohnson@rc.edu
JOHNSON, Mark .... 314-889-1467 275 B mjohnson@fontbonne.edu
JOHNSON, Mark .... 425-235-2352 525 G mark.johnson@rtc.edu
JOHNSON, Mark, R ..... 617-496-6847 227 D mark_johnson@harvard.edu
JOHNSON, Mark, R ...... 919-735-5151 367 A mrjohnson@waynecc.edu
JOHNSON, Martha .... 252-473-5936 361 G martha_johnson@albemarle.edu
JOHNSON, Mary .... 334-291-4973.... 2 H mary.johnson@cv.edu
JOHNSON, Mary .... 618-262-8641 147 B johnsonm@iecc.edu
JOHNSON, Mary .... 507-453-2745 259 G mjohnson@southeastmn.edu
JOHNSON, Mary .... 402-494-2311 291 M mjohnson@thenicc.edu
JOHNSON, Mary Jean .. 419-358-3272 377 H johnsonmj@bluffton.edu
JOHNSON, Mary Jo ..... 307-674-6446 546 H mjjohnson@sheridan.edu
JOHNSON, Matthew ..... 701-349-5780 375 G mjohnson@trinitybiblecollege.edu
JOHNSON, Matthew ..... 413-205-3532 221 G matthew.johnson@aic.edu
JOHNSON, McCeil .... 603-645-9664 298 H m.johnson2@snhu.edu
JOHNSON, Melissa ...... 701-671-2520 375 B melissa.j.johnson@ndscs.edu
JOHNSON, Melvina ...... 612-338-7224 265 G melvina.johnson@laureate.net
JOHNSON, Meredith, G 404-814-8813 132 H mgurley@uga.edu
JOHNSON, Merrill, L .... 503-554-2411 406 A mjohnson@georgefox.edu
JOHNSON, Michael ...... 660-562-1212 280 A mikej@nwmissouri.edu
JOHNSON, Michael ...... 615-248-7735 464 E mjohnson@trevecca.edu
JOHNSON, Michael, C . 214-860-2167 472 F mcjohnson@dcccd.edu
JOHNSON, Michael, D . 607-255-5106 323 C mdj27@cornell.edu
JOHNSON, Michael, D . 407-823-1911 115 C michael.johnson@ucf.edu
JOHNSON, Michael, L .. 270-824-8567 196 F michael.johnson@kctcs.edu
JOHNSON, Michele ...... 253-864-3100 525 C mjohnson@pierce.ctc.edu
JOHNSON, Michele ...... 973-720-2397 309 I johnsonm73j@wpunj.edu
JOHNSON, Michele ...... 567-661-7545 390 D michele_johnson@owens.edu
JOHNSON, Michelle ..... 631-420-2369 348 B michelle.johnson@farmingdale.edu
JOHNSON, Michelle ..... 626-969-3434.. 29 B mmjohnson@apu.edu
JOHNSON, Michelle, D 719-333-1818 548 E
JOHNSON, Mike .... 479-575-6601.. 23 G mrj03@uark.edu
JOHNSON, Mike .... 405-585-5130 399 I mike.johnson@okbu.edu
JOHNSON, Mildred ...... 540-231-6267 518 B mildredj@vt.edu
JOHNSON, Mimi .... 334-420-4243.... 7 I mjohnson@trenholmstate.edu
JOHNSON, Mindy .... 816-604-4339 278 A mindy.johnson@mcckc.edu
JOHNSON, Mitchell ...... 336-334-4822 363 A mjohnson@gtcc.edu
JOHNSON, Molly, B ..... 785-227-3380 185 A johnsonm@bethanylb.edu
JOHNSON, Monir .... 763-488-2415 258 G monir.johnson@hennepintech.edu
JOHNSON, Monty .... 218-631-7812 259 H monty.johnson@minnesota.edu
JOHNSON, Nadja .... 701-845-7306 374 D nadja.johnson@vcsu.edu
JOHNSON, Nancy .... 952-885-5428 263 I njohnson@nwhealth.edu
JOHNSON, Nancy .... 606-886-3863 195 I nancy.johnson@kctcs.edu
JOHNSON, Nancy, A .... 309-794-7475 139 K nancyjohnson@augustana.edu
JOHNSON, Nancy, N .... 713-646-1751 482 H njohnson@stcl.edu
JOHNSON, Nathan .... 707-664-4444.. 36 C nate.johnson@sonoma.edu
JOHNSON, Nathan .... 616-538-2330 243 C njohnson@gbcol.edu
JOHNSON, Neil .... 303-867-1155.. 87 K
JOHNSON, Nhadira ...... 714-241-6186.. 40 B
JOHNSON, Nial, L .... 309-677-2333 140 H nial@bradley.edu
JOHNSON, JR., P. Kelly .... 919-508-2329 373 B pkjohnsonjr@peace.edu
JOHNSON, Pam .... 708-524-6562 144 C pjohnson@dom.edu
JOHNSON, Pam .... 256-835-5456.... 3 N pjohnson@gadsdenstate.edu
JOHNSON, Pamela .... 903-233-3140 477 G pamjohnson@letu.edu
JOHNSON, Pamela, D .. 937-766-7765 378 K johnsonp@cedarville.edu
JOHNSON, Patricia, A .. 610-758-3178 424 B paj214@lehigh.edu
JOHNSON, Patrick .... 240-567-5288 217 B patrick.johnson@montgomerycollege.edu
JOHNSON, Patrick .... 631-244-1036 324 C jonhsonp@dowling.edu
JOHNSON, Paul .... 404-727-7727 124 D rpaul.johnson@emory.edu
JOHNSON, Paul, C ...... 303-273-3280.. 80 O presoffice@mines.edu
JOHNSON, CRM, Paula, J .... 858-534-2552.. 72 B pjjohnson@ucsd.edu
JOHNSON, Paula 'Tendai' .... 919-719-5060 368 G tejohnson@shawu.edu
JOHNSON, Paulette ...... 256-726-7250.... 6 C pjohnson@oakwood.edu
JOHNSON, Peg .... 505-428-1352 313 A peg.johnson@sfcc.edu
JOHNSON, Peter .... 415-257-1334.. 43 D peter.johnson@dominican.edu
JOHNSON, Peter, B ...... 701-777-4317 373 G peter.johnson@und.edu
JOHNSON, Phil .... 334-244-3202.... 2 A pjohns23@aum.edu
JOHNSON, Philip .... 906-487-7201 242 M philip.johnson@finlandia.edu
JOHNSON, Philip, M .... 503-255-0332 407 D pjohnson@multnomah.edu
JOHNSON, Phillip .... 205-391-2665.... 7 A pjohnson@sheltonstate.edu
JOHNSON, Phillip, A .... 574-631-8338 174 A johnson.30@nd.edu
JOHNSON, Quentin ...... 363-334-4822 363 A qrjohnson@gtcc.edu
JOHNSON, Quentin ...... 937-708-5706 395 E qjohnson@wilberforce.edu
JOHNSON, R. Stafford .. 513-745-3528 396 B johnsons@xavier.edu
JOHNSON, Rachel .... 218-751-8670 263 J
JOHNSON, Ralph .... 404-507-8697 128 L ralph.johnson@morehouse.edu
JOHNSON, Ralph .... 504-486-7411 209 E rjohns23@xula.edu
JOHNSON, Ralph .... 864-977-2077 448 A ralph.johnson@ngu.edu
JOHNSON, Ralph, F ..... 706-542-7369 132 H rfj@uga.edu
JOHNSON, Rebecca ...... 770-467-6037 132 B rajohnson@sctech.edu
JOHNSON, Rebecca ...... 541-322-3100 408 F rebecca.johnson@osucascades.edu
JOHNSON, Rebecca ...... 414-258-4810 538 A johnsonr@mtmary.edu
JOHNSON, Rebecca, D . 203-932-7176.. 92 G rjohnson@newhaven.edu
JOHNSON, Rhonda .... 817-598-6283 497 A rjohnson@wc.edu
JOHNSON, Richard .... 870-236-6901.. 20 I rjohnson@crc.edu
JOHNSON, Richard, A .. 864-597-4090 451 J johnsonra@wofford.edu
JOHNSON, Rick .... 919-684-3737 356 E
JOHNSON, Rick .... 239-590-7072 114 F rjohnson@wgcu.edu
JOHNSON, Rick .... 307-778-1281 546 F rjohnson@lccc.wy.edu
JOHNSON, Rita .... 828-328-7235 358 G rita.johnson@lr.edu
JOHNSON, Robert .... 916-691-7390.. 52 J johnsor@crc.losrios.edu
JOHNSON, Robert, E .... 913-667-5700 185 L rjohnson@cbts.edu
JOHNSON, Robert, E .... 508-373-1900 223 C robert.johnson@becker.edu
JOHNSON, Robert, E .... 704-687-8242 371 B robejohn@uncc.edu

JOINER, Karen .... 360-442-2861 524 A
kjoiner@lowercolumbia.edu
JOINER, Steve .... 615-966-7141 458 C
steve.joiner@lipscomb.edu
JOINER, Wayne .... 919-546-8251 368 G
wjoiner@shawu.edu
JOINES, Jacqueline ...... 217-234-5354 150 B
jjoines@lakeland.cc.il.us
JOKELA, Roxana .... 402-559-4385 293 I
rjokela@unmc.edu
JOKERST-HARTER, Jill .. 314-367-8700 281 G
jill.harter@stlcop.edu
JOLER-LABBE, Michelle 207-859-1240 211 I
hr@thomas.edu
JOLIE, Danielle .... 479-788-7795.. 23 H
danielle.jolie@uafs.edu
JOLINE, Mary Lou .... 717-560-8215 423 C
mjoline@lbc.edu
JOLLEY, JR.,
Edward, B .... 912-358-3000 131 A
jolleye@savannahstate.edu
JOLLEY, Kassandra .... 404-270-5323 132 D
kjolley@spelman.edu
JOLLEY, Kate .... 707-527-4413.. 65 C
kjolley@santarosa.edu
JOLLEY, Renee, W .... 804-257-5756 518 E
rwjolley@vuu.edu
JOLLEY, Rick .... 864-596-9041 445 E
rick.jolley@converse.edu
JOLLIFF, Xavier .... 702-254-7577 296 B
xavier.jolliff@northwestcareercollege.edu
JOLLIFFE, Vicki, M .... 724-439-4900 423 G
vjolliffe@laurel.edu
JOLLS, Jennifer .... 937-767-1286 376 K
JOLLY, Connie .... 843-574-6150 449 G
connie.jolly@tridenttech.edu
JOLLY, Jim .... 248-204-2400 245 J
jjolly@ltu.edu
JOLLY, Julia, A .... 916-558-2407.. 53 B
jollyj@scc.losrios.edu
JOLLY, Lawson .... 352-588-8354 111 L
lawson.jolly@saintleo.edu
JOLLY, Melody .... 714-850-4800.. 69 F
jolly@taftu.edu
JOLLY, Richard, C .... 432-685-4524 478 F
rjolly@midland.edu
JONAITIS, Aldona .... 907-474-6939.. 10 I
ajonaitis@alaska.edu
JONEN, Mike .... 520-626-5394.. 18 E
mjonen@email.arizona.edu
JONES, Aaron .... 417-873-7301 274 E
aaronjones@drury.edu
JONES, Adrianne .... 904-826-0084.. 74 A
ajones@usa.edu
JONES, Alesia, M .... 250-934-5321.... 8 F
amjones@uab.edu
JONES, Allison .... 323-953-4000.. 51 E
jonessa@lacitycollege.edu
JONES, Almarie .... 856-415-2154 306 C
ajones@rcgc.edu
JONES, Alonzo .... 434-791-4773 505 A
ajones@averett.edu
JONES, Alvena .... 903-927-3318 497 G
ajones@wileyc.edu
JONES, Amy .... 734-462-4400 250 A
ajones2@schoolcraft.edu
JONES, Amy .... 425-889-7823 524 G
amy.jones@northwestu.edu
JONES, Amy, J .... 712-749-2101 176 D
jonesa@bvu.edu
JONES, Andrea .... 404-413-1351 126 D
andreajones@gsu.edu
JONES, Andrew .... 925-229-6825.. 42 C
ajones@4cd.edu
JONES, Andrew .... 217-245-3010 146 D
andrew.jones@mail.ic.edu
JONES, Angela .... 415-817-4333.. 36 A
adjones@sfsu.edu
JONES, Angela .... 617-369-3665 236 E
ajones@smfa.edu
JONES, Angie .... 504-278-6427 204 B
ajones@nunez.edu
JONES, Annamarie .... 775-831-1314 296 F
ajones@sierranevada.edu
JONES, Anne .... 843-921-6994 448 B
ajones@netc.edu
JONES, Annie .... 603-862-2450 299 B
annie.jones@unh.edu
JONES, Anthony .... 850-201-8103 117 B
jonesa@tcc.fl.edu
JONES, Anthony, E .... 615-329-8738 456 G
ajones@fisk.edu
JONES, JR.,
Anthony, M .... 256-761-6231.... 7 H
amjones@talladega.edu
JONES, April .... 704-330-6190 361 D
april.jones@cpcc.edu
JONES, Ashley .... 678-839-6442 133 F
ashley@westga.edu
JONES, Barbara .... 870-864-7107.. 23 B
brjones@southark.edu

JONES, Barbara .... 256-372-5092.... 1 A
barbara.jones@aamu.edu
JONES, Barbara .... 617-552-2052 224 B
barbara.jones@bc.edu
JONES, Barbara .... 601-484-8804 268 B
bjones@meridiancc.edu
JONES, Barbara, E .... 607-746-4440 347 G
jonesbe@delhi.edu
JONES, Ben .... 440-775-8624 388 B
ben.jones@oberlin.edu
JONES, Benjamin, F ..... 605-256-5270 453 H
benjamin.jones@dsu.edu
JONES, Bert .... 804-819-4917 514 G
bjones@vccs.edu
JONES, Bill .... 209-543-7000.. 49 A
bjones@kaplancollege.edu
JONES, III, Bob .... 864-242-5100 443 G
JONES, Bobby, G .... 870-230-5090.. 21 B
jonesb@hsu.edu
JONES, Bonnie, J .... 941-359-4200 116 D
JONES, Bradley .... 317-738-8033 166 B
bjones@franklincollege.edu
JONES, Bradley .... 513-875-3344 379 G
brad.jones@chatfield.edu
JONES, Brenda .... 281-998-6150 481 D
brenda.jones@sjcd.edu
JONES, Brenda .... 281-922-3403 481 G
brenda.jones@sjcd.edu
JONES, Brenda .... 414-847-3231 537 F
brendajones@miad.edu
JONES, Brian .... 310-544-6442.. 61 I
brian.jones@usw.salvationarmy.org
JONES, Brian .... 704-378-1238 358 B
bjones@jcsu.edu
JONES, Brian .... 507-389-2422 260 A
brian.jones@mnsu.edu
JONES, Britt, E 325-670-1317 474M
brittj@hsutx.edu
JONES, Brontë .... 717-245-1943 417 B
jonesbro@dickinson.edu
JONES, Bruce, A .... 713-743-2490 491 D
bajones@uh.edu
JONES, Bryan, H .... 206-281-2405 526 D
bryan@spu.edu
JONES, Byron .... 602-557-9322.. 18 H
byron.jones@phoenix.edu
JONES, Candace, L .... 919-497-3237 358 J
cjones@louisburg.edu
JONES, Candice .... 404-297-9522 126 A
jonesc@gptc.edu
JONES, Carl .... 404-880-8787 122 I
cjones@cau.edu
JONES, Carl .... 318-357-4254 208 D
jonesc@nsula.edu
JONES, Carl .... 408-855-5127.. 76 E
carl.jones@missioncollege.edu
JONES, Carlee .... 405-422-1467 401 H
carlee.jones@redlandscc.edu
JONES, Carnell .... 401-874-7280 442 E
carnell@mail.uri.edu
JONES, Carol .... 706-272-4545 123 G
cjones@daltonstate.edu
JONES, Carol .... 478-218-3700 122 E
cjones@centralgatech.edu
JONES, Carol, F .... 478-988-6800 122 F
cjones@centralgatech.edu
JONES, Carolyn, J .... 412-924-1404 433 E
cjones@pts.edu
JONES, Carolyn, K .... 812-888-4182 174 F
cjones@vinu.edu
JONES, Cathy .... 704-330-1461 358 B
cjones2@jcsu.edu
JONES, Cecelia, K .... 903-927-3217 497 G
ckjones@wileyc.edu
JONES, Charles .... 478-825-6211 124 E
JONES, Chris .... 641-472-1219 181 A
cjones@mum.edu
JONES, Chris .... 641-472-7000 181 A
cjones@mum.edu
JONES, Christa, K .... 972-860-7033 472 E
christaj@dcccd.edu
JONES, Christopher ...... 978-867-4500 227 A
chris.jones@gordon.edu
JONES, Christopher ...... 309-677-2380 140 H
cmjones@fsmail.bradley.edu
JONES, Christopher ...... 313-577-2280 252 G
Christopher.Jones@wayne.edu
JONES, Cindy, M .... 417-873-7330 274 E
cjones@drury.edu
JONES, Clayton, H .... 662-915-7431 270 G
chj1@olemiss.edu
JONES, Cliff .... 870-733-6731.. 19 G
cejones@midsouthcc.edu
JONES, Clifton .... 254-519-5424 485 D
cwjones@tamuct.edu
JONES, Clifton .... 325-942-2337 489 E
clifton.jones@angelo.edu
JONES, Courtney .... 405-382-9204 402 C
c.jones@sscok.edu
JONES, Cravor .... 304-327-4016 532 D
cjones@bluefieldstate.edu

JONES, Cristen .... 410-923-4500.. 96 H
JONES, Curtis .... 912-201-6123 131 F
cejones@southuniversity.edu
JONES, Dan .... 714-546-7600.. 40 B
djones@coastline.edu
JONES, Dan .... 903-886-5011 485 E
dan.jones@tamuc.edu
JONES, Dan, L .... 828-262-3180 369 D
jonesdl@appstate.edu
JONES, Danneal .... 305-626-3711 104 B
Danneal.Jones@fmuniv.edu
JONES, Danson .... 979-532-6975 497 F
jonesd@wcjc.edu
JONES, Darci .... 814-824-2233 425 L
djones@mercyhurst.edu
JONES, Darnell .... 816-501-4117 281 B
darnell.jones@rockhurst.edu
JONES, Darren .... 501-977-2191.. 25 A
jones@uaccm.edu
JONES, Darren .... 301-736-3631 216 E
darren.jones@msbbcs.edu
JONES, Darrin .... 360-538-4234 523 A
djones@ghc.edu
JONES, Darryl .... 510-231-5000.. 48 R
JONES, Darryl .... 914-654-5522 322 B
dajones@cnr.edu
JONES, Darryll .... 407-254-3268 114 D
darryll.jones@famu.edu
JONES, David .... 931-363-9816 458 D
djones@martinmethodist.edu
JONES, David .... 573-592-5288 285 J
david.jones@westminster-mo.edu
JONES, David .... 507-389-2121 260 A
david.jones@mnsu.edu
JONES, David .... 706-542-8131 132 H
dsjones@uga.edu
JONES, David .... 251-809-1592.... 5 B
david.jones@jdcc.edu
JONES, David .... 307-766-4286 546 K
dljones@uwyo.edu
JONES, David, R .... 301-784-5000 213 C
djones@allegany.edu
JONES, Debra .... 229-430-3605 119 I
djones@albanytech.edu
JONES, Debra .... 618-374-5162 156 C
debra.jones@principia.edu
JONES, Denise .... 630-617-3012 144 G
denise.jones@elmhurst.edu
JONES, Dennis, H .... 256-766-6610.... 4 C
djones@hcu.edu
JONES, Derrick .... 303-447-3846.. 84 B
djones@naropa.edu
JONES, Diana .... 641-784-5412 178 G
dianaj@gracelend.edu
JONES, Dianna .... 781-768-7291 236 A
dianna.jones@regiscollege.edu
JONES, Dixie .... 318-675-5455 205 D
djon17@lsuhsc.edu
JONES, Don .... 617-585-1154 234 H
don.jones@necmusic.edu
JONES, Donald .... 812-488-1209 173 H
dj29@evansville.edu
JONES, Donald .... 860-768-4751.. 92 F
djones@hartford.edu
JONES, Donald, A .... 502-371-8330 193 B
djones@ata.edu
JONES, Donald, E .... 803-754-4100 445 D
JONES, Dorothy, D .... 904-743-1122 107 C
vjones@jones.edu
JONES, Doug .... 910-893-1235 355 C
jones@campbell.edu
JONES, Douglas, W .... 805-565-6048.. 76 K
vpfinance@westmont.edu
JONES, Duke .... 417-328-1714 282 D
djones@sbuniv.edu
JONES, Ed .... 434-791-5684 505 A
ejones@averett.edu
JONES, Eddie, V .... 989-964-4228 249 G
evjones@svsu.edu
JONES, JR., Edward ...... 202-274-7441.. 97 B
ejones@udc.edu
JONES, Eli .... 479-575-5949.. 23 G
ejones@walton.uark.edu
JONES, Eli .... 979-845-4712 485 C
elijones@tamu.edu
JONES, Elizabeth, R ...... 404-413-3003 126 D
bethjones@gsu.edu
JONES, Elliot .... 248-218-2036 249 D
ejones@rc.edu
JONES, Elwin .... 251-981-3771.... 3 A
elwin.jones@columbiasouthern.edu
JONES, Eric .... 641-628-5249 176 E
jonese@central.edu
JONES, Eric .... 312-915-7452 151 E
ejones6@luc.edu
JONES, Erica .... 406-683-7511 287 E
erica.jones@umwestern.edu
JONES, Ericka, D .... 512-505-3040 475 G
edjones@htu.edu
JONES, Erika .... 219-785-5200 172 A
ejones@pnc.edu

JONES, Eugene .... 352-365-3576 107 X
jonese@lssc.edu
JONES, Faye, M .... 615-353-3556 463 C
faye.jones@nscc.edu
JONES, Garry 407-679-0100 105M
gjones@fullsail.com
JONES, Garry .... 662-243-2643 267 C
gjones@eastms.edu
JONES, Gary .... 618-252-5400 159 F
gary.jones@sic.edu
JONES, Gary .... 405-425-5904 399 J
gary.jones@oc.edu
JONES, Gayle .... 352-395-5226 112 H
gayle.jones@sfcollege.edu
JONES, Gena .... 806-743-2865 490 A
gena.jones@ttuhsc.edu
JONES, Geoffrey .... 952-358-8191 260 D
geoffrey.jones@normandale.edu
JONES, George, A .... 606-759-7141 196 G
george.jones@kctcs.edu
JONES, Gerald .... 334-386-7600.... 3 I
gjones@faulkner.edu
JONES, Geraldine .... 724-938-4400 430 C
jones_gm@calu.edu
JONES, Gina, G .... 803-323-2194 451 I
jonesgg@winthrop.edu
JONES, Gladys .... 601-977-7821 270 F
gjones@tougaloo.edu
JONES, Glendell .... 870-230-5091.. 21 B
president@hsu.edu
JONES, Glenn .... 973-720-2950 309 I
jonesg13@wpunj.edu
JONES, Glenna, S .... 815-224-0230 147 J
glenna_jones@ivcc.edu
JONES, Gloria .... 803-323-3900 451 I
jonesg@winthrop.edu
JONES, Gordon .... 208-426-1000 137 E
gojones@boisestate.edu
JONES, Grady, B .... 864-833-8006 448 E
gbjones@presby.edu
JONES, Greg .... 541-552-6758 409 G
gjones@sou.edu
JONES, Gwen .... 262-595-2151 540 C
gaines@uwp.edu
JONES, Harold .... 903-675-6256 490 F
hjones@tvcc.edu
JONES, Harold, P .... 205-934-5149.... 8 F
jonesh@uab.edu
JONES, Holly .... 319-385-6246 180 A
holly.jones@iw.edu
JONES, J. Pernell .... 610-341-5948 418 A
pjones1@eastern.edu
JONES, J. Preston .... 954-262-5127 109 E
prestonj@nova.edu
JONES, Jacquelyn, K ..... 573-882-4097 283 H
jonesjk@missouri.edu
JONES, James .... 575-461-4413 311 C
jimj@mesalands.edu
JONES, James .... 903-875-7315 479 I
jim.jones@navarrocollege.edu
JONES, James, M .... 812-888-5555 174 F
jjones@vinu.edu
JONES, Jane, M .... 423-439-4211 461 D
jonesj@etsu.edu
JONES, Janet .... 256-331-5310.... 6 B
janetj@nwscc.edu
JONES, Jay .... 870-460-1020.. 24 C
jonesj@uamont.edu
JONES, Jay .... 870-460-1022.. 24 C
jonesj@uamont.edu
JONES, Jayne, W .... 479-968-0400.. 20 C
jjones@atu.edu
JONES, Jean .... 814-732-2981 430 G
jjones@edinboro.edu
JONES, Jeannine .... 541-684-7244 407 I
jjones@nwcu.edu
JONES, Jeff .... 570-422-3833 430 F
jjones@esu.edu
JONES, Jeff .... 407-823-1582 115 C
jeffrey.jones@ucf.edu
JONES, Jeffrey, A .... 724-847-6512 419 B
jajones@geneva.edu
JONES, Jen .... 254-295-8645 492 C
jen.jones@umhb.edu
JONES, Jennifer .... 815-455-8770 152 B
jjones@mchenry.edu
JONES, Jennifer .... 978-232-2042 226 C
jjones@endicott.edu
JONES, Jennifer .... 201-200-3005 304 C
jjones@njcu.edu
JONES, Jenny .... 704-687-7799 371 B
Jenny.Jones@uncc.edu
JONES, Jenny, E .... 512-452-7834 485 C
jennyjones@tamu.edu
JONES, Jeremy .... 541-962-3553 405 G
jdjones1@eou.edu
JONES, Jerry .... 254-519-5446 485 D
jerry.jones@tamuct.edu
JONES, Jessica .... 815-921-4755 157 B
j.jones@rockvalleycollege.edu

JONES, Jessica, S .... 252-246-1216 367 D jjones@wilsoncc.edu
JONES, Jessie .... 657-278-2620.. 33 E jjones@fullerton.edu
JONES, Jill .... 309-438-3135 147 I jajones2@ilstu.edu
JONES, Jill, D .... 208-467-8521 138 H jdjones@nnu.edu
JONES, Jim .... 325-670-1207 474 M jjones@hsutx.edu
JONES, Jim .... 509-313-5926 522 L jonesj@its.gonzaga.edu
JONES, John .... 904-596-2304 117 G jjones@tbc.edu
JONES, John .... 765-677-2387 169 C john.jones@indwes.edu
JONES, John .... 316-978-7751 192 D john.jones@wichita.edu
JONES, John, D .... 870-307-7326.. 21 G john.jones@lyon.edu
JONES, John, P .... 520-621-1112.. 18 E jpjones@email.arizona.edu
JONES, John, R .... 910-521-6304 371 D jrjones@uncp.edu
JONES, III, John, R ..... 205-934-4011.... 8 F
JONES, John, S .... 772-546-5534 106 D johnjones@hsbc.edu
JONES, John Mark .... 903-468-8144 485 E john.jones@tamuc.edu
JONES, Jon .... 417-268-6049 272 F jjones@gobbc.edu
JONES, Joree .... 334-291-4913.... 2 H joree.jones@cv.edu
JONES, Joshua .... 309-677-1000 140 H jejones@bradley.edu
JONES, Joy .... 304-865-6102 530 F joy.jones@ovu.edu
JONES, Joyce .... 205-391-2283.... 7 A jjones1@sheltonstate.edu
JONES, Judy .... 979-532-6561 497 F judyj@wcjc.edu
JONES, Justin .... 801-524-1922 498 J jkjones@ldsbc.edu
JONES, Karen .... 828-395-1429 363 D kjones@isothermal.edu
JONES, Karen .... 636-922-8258 281 C kjones@stchas.edu
JONES, Karen .... 803-323-3708 451 I jonesk@winthrop.edu
JONES, Karen, S .... 478-289-2012 124 B kjones@ega.edu
JONES, Katherine .... 410-334-2892 221 E kjones@worwic.edu
JONES, Katherine .... 919-735-5151 367 A kathyj@waynecc.edu
JONES, Kathleen .... 815-825-2086 149 E kathleen.jones@kishwaukeecollege.edu
JONES, Kathryn, C .... 870-972-3027.. 19 F kjones@astate.edu
JONES, Katie .... 413-565-1000 222 G kjones@baypath.edu
JONES, Katie, P .... 864-488-4597 447 F kjones@limestone.edu
JONES, Kelly .... 802-586-7711 503 B kjones@sterlingcollege.edu
JONES, Ken .... 818-767-0888.. 77 G ken.jones@woodbury.edu
JONES, Kenneth .... 501-374-6305.. 23 A
JONES, Kenneth .... 252-335-3858 369 F kljones@ecsu.edu
JONES, Kenneth, E .... 662-252-8000 270 C kjones@rustcollege.edu
JONES, Kent .... 256-228-6001.... 6 A jonesk@nacc.edu
JONES, Kevin .... 863-638-7297 118 L kevin.jones@warner.edu
JONES, Kevin .... 518-736-3622 326 D kjones@fmcc.suny.edu
JONES, Kim .... 361-593-2187 486 A krkdy00@tamuk.edu
JONES, Kim .... 903-823-3004 484 D kim.jones@texarkanacollege.edu
JONES, Kimberly .... 904-256-7048 106 Q kmarian@ju.edu
JONES, Kimberly, B ...... 334-670-3113.... 8 A kbrink@troy.edu
JONES, Kona .... 217-875-7200 156 K kona@richland.edu
JONES, Kristen .... 206-934-3701 525 K kristen.jones@seattlecolleges.edu
JONES, Kristen, S .... 540-261-8528 512 J kristen.jones@svu.edu
JONES, Lance .... 307-268-2672 545 Z ljones@caspercollege.edu
JONES, Laura, B .... 734-764-7423 251 C laurabj@umich.edu
JONES, Laurel .... 831-479-6302.. 30 C lajones@cabrillo.edu
JONES, Laurene .... 609-586-4800 303 D jonesl@mccc.edu
JONES, Laurie, S .... 706-568-2005 123 D jones_laurie@columbusstate.edu
JONES, Leonard .... 360-650-2953 528 D leonard.jones@wwu.edu
JONES, Leroy "Lee" ...... 410-516-4612 216 A
JONES, II, Leroy .... 773-995-2965 141 J ljones27@csu.edu
JONES, Leslie .... 985-448-4325 208 C leslie.jones@nicholls.edu
JONES, Linda, E .... 413-782-1247 238 A linda.jones@wne.edu
JONES, Linda, T .... 240-895-3246 218 B ltjones1@smcm.edu
JONES, Lirse .... 973-720-2101 309 I jonesl@wpunj.edu
JONES, Lisa .... 845-257-3216 344 A jonesl@newpaltz.edu
JONES, Lisa .... 801-832-2237 501 C ljones@westminstercollege.edu
JONES, Lisa .... 252-335-0821 361 G lisa_jones@albemarle.edu
JONES, Loree, D .... 856-885-6095 307 A loree.jones@rutgers.edu
JONES, Malana .... 213-252-5100.. 25 J
JONES, Marcia .... 678-466-4250 122 J marciajones@clayton.edu
JONES, Marcus .... 318-357-5701 208 D marcusj@nsula.edu
JONES, Margaret .... 914-422-4043 337 I mjones@pace.edu
JONES, Marian .... 704-378-1074 358 B myjones@jcsu.edu
JONES, Marie .... 334-876-9284.... 4 B marie.jones@wccs.edu
JONES, Marvin, L .... 410-651-6144 219 H mljones@umes.edu
JONES, Mary .... 805-289-6346.. 75 E mjones@vcccd.edu
JONES, Mary .... 913-971-3393 189 F maryjones@mnu.edu
JONES, Mary, C .... 502-213-2200 196 E maryc.jones@kctcs.edu
JONES, Mary, O .... 814-371-6920 417 F mainc@dbcollege.edu
JONES, Matteel .... 864-250-8177 446 H matteel.jones@gvltec.edu
JONES, Melanie, E .... 803-327-8012 451 K mjones@yorktech.edu
JONES, Melinda, L .... 901-678-2690 462 B mljones6@memphis.edu
JONES, Melissa .... 864-622-6011 443 E melissajones@andersonuniversity.edu
JONES, Melissa .... 217-854-5514 140 F melissa.k.jones@blackburn.edu
JONES, Melissa, A .... 910-678-8474 362 E jonesma@faytechcc.edu
JONES, Michael .... 909-607-7855.. 39 H michael_jones@kgi.edu
JONES, Michael .... 814-886-6354 427 B mjones@mtaloy.edu
JONES, Mike .... 601-925-3819 268 E jones01@mc.edu
JONES, Mike .... 325-649-8830 475 F mjones@hputx.edu
JONES, Monica .... 859-985-3795 193 F jonesmo@berea.edu
JONES, Nancy .... 714-241-6209.. 40 B njones@coastline.edu
JONES, Ned, J .... 518-783-2423 342 H jones@siena.edu
JONES, Nicholas, P ...... 814-865-2505 428 C npj1@psu.edu
JONES, Nina .... 662-915-7690 270 G nina@olemiss.edu
JONES, Nolan .... 972-825-7970 483 D nojones@sagu.edu
JONES, Norm .... 970-247-2929.. 85 A norm.jones@pueblocc.edu
JONES, Norman .... 256-372-8653.... 1 A norman.jones@aamu.edu
JONES, Olivia .... 919-530-7713 370 C ojones@nccu.edu
JONES, Para, M .... 330-494-6170 391 J pjones@starkstate.edu
JONES, Parago .... 303-329-6355.. 81 B clinicdirector@cstcm.edu
JONES, Patricia .... 301-736-3631 216 E patricia.jones@msbbcs.edu
JONES, Patricia .... 863-297-1025 110 E pjones@polk.edu
JONES, Patrick .... 904-256-7500 106 Q pjones15@ju.edu
JONES, Patrick .... 518-464-8500 325 B pjones@excelsior.edu
JONES, Paul .... 229-317-6705 123 H
JONES, Paulette .... 405-912-9020 398 B pjones@hc.edu
JONES, Peter .... 215-204-2044 436 C peter.jones@temple.edu
JONES, Phil .... 772-546-5534 106 D philjones@hsbc.edu
JONES, Philip .... 717-245-2451 417 B jonesph@dickinson.edu
JONES, JR., Philip, M .. 704-687-0514 371 B pmjones@uncc.edu
JONES, Pocahantas ...... 252-862-1222 365 C jonesp@roanokechowan.edu
JONES, R. Channing .... 910-272-3600 365 D cjones@robeson.edu
JONES, Randall, F .... 214-648-6846 496 A randall.jones@utsouthwestern.edu
JONES, Randy .... 302-857-6230.. 93 E ljones@desu.edu
JONES, Randy .... 805-565-7048.. 76 K rjones@westmont.edu
JONES, Randy .... 304-384-5385 532 E rjones@concord.edu
JONES, Rauchelle .... 281-283-2536 491 E jonesrau@uhcl.edu
JONES, Rene .... 870-733-6769.. 19 G rjones@midsouthcc.edu
JONES, Richard .... 856-256-4040 306 D jonesri@rowan.edu
JONES, Rilla, c .... 662-720-7375 269 D rcjones@nemcc.edu
JONES, Robert .... 903-823-3154 484 D robert.jones@texarkanacollege.edu
JONES, Robert .... 303-762-6913.. 82 C robert.jones@denverseminary.edu
JONES, Robert .... 239-732-3753 104 G rrjones@fsw.edu
JONES, Robert .... 401-232-6027 441 B rjones10@bryant.edu
JONES, Robert, A .... 317-788-3304 173 I rjones@uindy.edu
JONES, Robert, H .... 864-656-3940 444 E provost@clemson.edu
JONES, Robert, J .... 518-956-8010 343 C presmail@albany.edu
JONES, Robert, P .... 915-831-3112 473 J rjones35@epcc.edu
JONES, Robin .... 575-769-4921 310 G robin.jones@clovis.edu
JONES, Rockwell, F ...... 740-368-3000 390 B rfjones@owu.edu
JONES, Roger .... 434-544-8444 509 I jones@lynchburg.edu
JONES, Ronald, L .... 901-272-5100 459 A rjones@mca.edu
JONES, Rose .... 256-331-5313.... 6 B jonesr@nwscc.edu
JONES, Rosemary .... 206-726-5169 521 G
JONES, Rosetta .... 318-670-9315 207 C rjones@susla.edu
JONES, Rythee .... 301-891-4542 221 C eljones@wau.edu
JONES, Sabrina .... 206-239-4500 520 K
JONES, Sam .... 850-729-4929 109 D joness@nwfsc.edu
JONES, Sam .... 601-477-4038 268 A sam.jones@jcjc.edu
JONES, Samantha .... 417-865-2815 272 D jonessa@evangel.edu
JONES, Samuel .... 601-979-2260 267 H samuel.jones@jsums.edu
JONES, Samuel .... 731-989-6992 456 K sjones@fhu.edu
JONES, Samuel, B .... 843-953-6367 445 B jonessa@cofc.edu
JONES, Samuel, E .... 757-221-2565 506 J sejone@wm.edu
JONES, Sarah, L .... 540-464-7667 518 A jonessl10@vmi.edu
JONES, Savannah .... 714-992-7074.. 56 F sjones@fullcoll.edu
JONES, Scott .... 443-997-3715 216 A scott.jonas@jhu.edu
JONES, Scott .... 765-455-9380 168 B scotjone@iuk.edu
JONES, Serene .... 212-280-1403 351 B sjones@uts.columbia.edu
JONES, Shannon .... 843-792-8839 447 G joneshan@musc.edu
JONES, Sharon, A .... 503-943-7314 410 H joness@up.edu
JONES, Shawn .... 870-230-5072.. 21 B jonessh@hsu.edu
JONES, Sheba .... 312-662-4131 139 E sjones@adler.edu
JONES, Sheila Dove ..... 570-389-4027 430 B sjones@bloomu.edu
JONES, Shelia .... 903-675-6383 490 F sjones@tvcc.edu
JONES, Sheri .... 858-513-9240.. 29 A Sheri.Jones@ashford.edu
JONES, Sherry .... 781-762-1211 226 E sjones@fmc.edu
JONES, Sloan .... 678-717-3836 133 A sloan.jones@ung.edu
JONES, Sloan .... 678-407-5449 125 B sjones@ggc.edu
JONES, Stacey .... 479-788-7302.. 23 H stacey.jones@uafs.edu
JONES, Stacey, F .... 252-335-3228 369 F chancellor@ecsu.edu
JONES, Stanley .... 229-333-5732 133 H sjones@valdosta.edu
JONES, Stanton, L .... 630-752-5004 163 G stanton.jones@wheaton.edu
JONES, Stephen, M ...... 801-422-8271 497 J stephen_jones@byu.edu
JONES, Stephen, W ...... 330-569-5128 383 F jonessw@hiram.edu
JONES, Steve .... 704-971-8500 355 J sjones@charlottelaw.edu
JONES, Stuart .... 435-586-7775 499 L jones@suu.edu
JONES, Stuart .... 260-665-4365 173 D joness@trine.edu
JONES, Sue .... 936-633-3209 467 I sjones@angelina.edu
JONES, Susan .... 334-683-5108.... 5 D sjones@judson.edu
JONES, Susan, S .... 717-867-6184 423 I sjones@lvc.edu
JONES, Teresa, A .... 225-216-8429 202 N jonest@mybrcc.edu
JONES, Thomas, H .... 704-406-4369 356 G tjones@gardner-webb.edu
JONES, Tiffane .... 708-596-2000 159 D
JONES, Tim .... 334-493-3573.... 5 G twjones@lbwcc.edu
JONES, Tim .... 410-827-5704 214 D tjones@chesapeake.edu
JONES, Tim .... 501-812-2760.. 22 F thjones@pulaskitech.edu
JONES, Tim .... 870-230-5117.. 21 B jonest@hsu.edu
JONES, Tim .... 850-245-0466 114 C tim.jones@flbog.edu
JONES, Tim .... 412-536-1139 422 E tim.jones@laroche.edu
JONES, Timothy Paul ... 502-897-4347 199 D tjones@sbts.edu
JONES, Tina, N .... 205-652-3497.... 9 G tnj@uwa.edu
JONES, Todd .... 515-964-6242 177 B tgjones@dmacc.edu
JONES, Todd .... 706-295-6339 125 C tjones@highlands.edu
JONES, Todd .... 215-751-8167 416 B tjones@ccp.edu
JONES, Tom, O .... 870-759-4101.. 25 I tjones@wbcoll.edu
JONES, Tony .... 502-231-5221 198 D tjones@myLBC.us
JONES, Tony .... 816-472-4852 276 F tonyjones@kcai.edu
JONES, Tony .... 804-706-5235 515 G tjones@jtcc.edu
JONES, Tracie .... 810-762-9536 245 A tjones1@kettering.edu
JONES, Tracy, A .... 605-336-6588 453 C tjones@sfseminary.edu
JONES, Trevor, H .... 410-334-2828 221 E tjones@worwic.edu
JONES, Trina .... 757-569-6720 516 E tjones@pdc.edu
JONES, Tyron .... 843-661-8324 446 C tyron.jones@fdtc.edu
JONES, V. Dale .... 434-223-6116 508 B djones@hsc.edu
JONES, Valorie .... 432-335-6477 479 O vjones@odessa.edu
JONES, Verity .... 317-931-2327 165 C vjones@cts.edu
JONES, Virginia .... 804-333-6781 516 G vrjones@rappahannock.edu
JONES, Walter .... 310-287-4244.. 52 C joneswc@wlac.edu
JONES, Wayne .... 405-733-7450 401 L wzjones@rose.edu
JONES, Wendy .... 325-674-2359 466 I jonesw@acu.edu
JONES, William .... 706-880-8257 127 N wjones@lagrange.edu
JONES, William, H .... 803-754-4100 445 D
JONES, Wilma .... 718-982-4001 319 A wilma.jones@csi.cuny.edu
JONES, Winfred .... 318-274-6344 207 H jones@gram.edu
JONES, Yasemin .... 212-217-4052 325 C yasemin_jones@fitnyc.edu
JONES, Yolanda .... 622-254-3528 269 C vjones@mvsu.edu
JONES, Yvette, M .... 504-865-5259 207 F yjones@tulane.edu
JONES-DULIN, Donna .. 408-864-8209.. 44 N jonesdulindonna@fhda.edu
JONES JOHNSON, Yosette .... 212-817-7713 319 B yjonesjohnson@gc.cuny.edu

JONES-MALONE, Dionne 219-473-4305 165 A
djonesmalone@ccsj.edu
JONES-POPPE, Erin 802-443-2759 502 E
ejonespoppe@middlebury.edu
JONES ROSSI, Meredythe 651-255-6162 264 F
mrossi@unitedseminary.edu
JONES-SCHENK, Jan 801-274-3280 501 B
jjonesschenk@wgu.edu
JONES SCHWEITZER, Sharon 210-999-8406 490 E
sjones@trinity.edu
JONES-VARNELL, Karla (Page) 252-672-1751 362 A
jonesp@cravencc.edu
JONES WATKINS, Brenda 708-456-0300 161 C
bwatkins@triton.edu
JONES-WILCOX, Youlanda 731-286-3346 462 F
ywilcox@dscc.edu
JONES-WILCOX, Youlanda 731-286-3265 462 F
ywilcox@dscc.edu
JONES-WILKINS, Brenda 979-209-7264 469 F
brendawilkins@blinn.edu
JONESHILL, Nancy 870-236-6901 20 I
njoneshill@crc.edu
JONG PARK, Tae 703-354-3533 509 F
JONGSMA KNAUSS, Sonya 712-722-6024 177 J
sonya.knauss@dordt.edu
JONSE, Paula 903-813-2059 468 G
pjonse@austincollege.edu
JONTE-PACE, Diane, E 408-554-4751 65 A
djontepace@scu.edu
JOO, Kay 213-487-0150 43 E
aromc@dula.edu
JOOS DEKOVEN, Chandra 413-528-7499 222 F
cdekoven@simons-rock.edu
JOPLING, James 318-345-9266 203 H
jamesjopling@ladelta.edu
JORDAHL, Ronald, I 704-847-5600 369 A
rjordahl@ses.edu
JORDAN, A. Dane 704-233-8026 373 C
djordan@wingate.edu
JORDAN, Amber 706-295-6768 125 F
ajordan@gntc.edu
JORDAN, Andy 803-508-7241 443 C
jordana@atc.edu
JORDAN, Angela 312-935-2002 157 A
ajordan@robertmorris.edu
JORDAN, Augustus 802-443-5141 502 E
jordan@middlebury.edu
JORDAN, Austina 706-245-7226 124 C
ajordan@ec.edu
JORDAN, Belva Brown 909-447-2527 39 G
bjordan@cst.edu
JORDAN, Belva Brown 918-610-8303 401 C
belva.jordan@ptstulsa.edu
JORDAN, Ben 256-395-2211 7 E
benjordan@suscc.edu
JORDAN, Bill 715-346-2441 541 A
bjordan@uwsp.edu
JORDAN, Bradley, K 336-599-0032 364 G
Brad.Jordan@piedmontcc.edu
JORDAN, Brian 252-335-3707 369 F
bnjordan@ecsu.edu
JORDAN, Brian 718-489-5493 340 E
bjordan@sfc.edu
JORDAN, Brian, K 202-806-1100 96 B
brian.jordan@howard.edu
JORDAN, Colin 941-487-4218 115 B
cjordan@ncf.edu
JORDAN, Cordell 405-682-1611 399 K
cjordan@occc.edu
JORDAN, Corey 315-386-7319 347 F
jordanc@canton.edu
JORDAN, Dave 443-518-3801 215 F
djordan@howardcc.edu
JORDAN, Debi 281-425-6453 477 F
djordan@lee.edu
JORDAN, Diane 573-334-9181 277 C
diane@metrobusinesscollege.edu
JORDAN, Donald, K 212-650-7278 318 G
djordan@aol.com
JORDAN, Edward, K 386-312-4083 111 K
edwardjordan@sjrstate.edu
JORDAN, Elizabeth, P 302-295-1186 94 G
elizabeth.p.jordan@wilmu.edu
JORDAN, Freddie 937-708-5633 395 E
fjordan@wilberforce.edu
JORDAN, Herb 251-405-7135 2 D
hjordan@bishop.edu
JORDAN, Holly 254-526-1128 470 E
holly.jordan@ctcd.edu
JORDAN, Jeffrey, C 206-281-2123 526 D
jordaj2@spu.edu
JORDAN, Jessica 415-422-5455 74 C
jgjordan@usfca.edu
JORDAN, John 425-889-7788 524 G
john.jordan@northwestu.edu
JORDAN, Judy, G 615-547-1249 456 C
jjordan@cumberland.edu
JORDAN, Katina 877-442-0505 87 C
katina.jordan@rockies.edu
JORDAN, Kelly 574-239-8355 167 C
kjordan@hcc-nd.edu
JORDAN, Ken 217-420-6765 153 A
kjordan@millikin.edu
JORDAN, Kimberly 678-407-5000 125 B
kjordan@ggc.edu
JORDAN, L, S 678-407-5000 125 B
ljordan@ggc.edu
JORDAN, Larry, W 301-736-3631 216 E
larry.jordan@msbbcs.edu
JORDAN, Lashanda 601-979-2477 267 H
lashanda.w.jordan@jsums.edu
JORDAN, Laurie 802-443-5626 502 E
ljordan@middlebury.edu
JORDAN, Lila 919-466-4400 96 H
JORDAN, Lisa 619-239-0391 36 E
ljordan@cwsl.edu
JORDAN, Lisa 919-684-2424 356 E
Lisa.jordan@duke.edu
JORDAN, Loretta 714-628-4933 60 H
jordan_lorrie@sccollege.edu
JORDAN, Lucille, A 603-882-6923 297 B
ljordan@ccsnh.edu
JORDAN, Marilyn, L 619-239-0391 36 E
mjordan@cwsl.edu
JORDAN, Mary, V 423-439-4211 461 D
jordanm@etsu.edu
JORDAN, Megan, K 781-283-3795 237 F
mjordan@wellesley.edu
JORDAN, Michael 585-567-9228 328 C
michael.jordan@houghton.edu
JORDAN, Michael 864-977-7058 448 A
mike.jordan@ngu.edu
JORDAN, Michael, J 252-823-5166 362 D
jordanm@edgecombe.edu
JORDAN, Myron 510-748-2234 59 A
mjordan@peralta.edu
JORDAN, Nancy 603-623-0313 298 C
nancyjordan@nhia.edu
JORDAN, Nancy 903-223-3166 486 C
njordan@tamut.edu
JORDAN, Percy 409-984-6335 488 H
jordanpj@lamarpa.edu
JORDAN, Peter 817-515-4501 484 B
peter.jordan@tccd.edu
JORDAN, Richard 806-354-5401 490 A
richard.jordan@ttuhsc.edu
JORDAN, Ronald 714-997-6815 38 B
JORDAN, Sandra 803-641-3434 450 C
SandraJ@usca.edu
JORDAN, Scott 860-486-3455 92 C
scott.jordan@uconn.edu
JORDAN, Stacy 501-205-8817 20 G
sjordan@cbc.edu
JORDAN, Stephen, M 303-556-3022 83 Q
smjordan@msudenver.edu
JORDAN, Susan 870-862-8131 23 B
sjordan@southark.edu
JORDAN, Theresa 313-927-1261 246 D
tjordan@marygrove.edu
JORDAN, Tim 937-769-1304 376 L
tjordan@antioch.edu
JORDAN, Tuajuanda 240-895-4410 218 B
tcjordan@smcm.edu
JORDAN, Willis 312-980-9293 158 H
wjordan@iadtchicago.com
JORDAN-GOODEN, Joyce 601-979-1591 267 H
joyce.m.jordan-gooden@jsums.edu
JORDAN-SMITH, Barbara 518-445-3398 314 H
bjord@albanylaw.edu
JORDANO, Mark 814-871-7438 419 A
jordan001@gannon.edu
JORDAY, Kindra, K 503-370-6055 411 D
kjordan@willamette.edu
JORDE, Brad 507-288-4563 255 D
bjorde@crossroadscollege.edu
JORDEN, Rhonda 501-603-1401 24 B
JordenRhondaL@uams.edu
JORDEN, Steven 660-626-2529 271 G
sjorden@atsu.edu
JORDON, Beth 512-472-4133 482 E
bjordon@ssw.edu
JORDON, Christina 863-638-2944 119 A
cmjordon@webber.edu
JORDON, Renee 617-951-2350 234 F
renee.jordon@necb.edu
JORDRE, Todd 605-626-3005 454 A
Todd.Jordre@northern.edu
JORDT, Mary 406-756-3673 286 G
mjordt@fvcc.edu
JORE, Katie 715-346-3710 541 A
kjore@uwsp.edu
JORGENS, Amy, G 402-323-3414 293 A
ajorgens@southeast.edu
JORGENSEN, Harlan, R 712-707-7333 182 C
harlan@nwciowa.edu
JORGENSEN, Jerry 816-584-6445 280 F
jerry.jorgensen@park.edu
JORGENSEN, Jerry 605-274-4045 452 A
jerry.jorgensen@augie.edu
JORGENSEN, Laurie 630-942-2755 142 F
jorgensenl@cod.edu
JORGENSEN, Lin 727-864-8886 101 P
jorgenly@eckerd.edu
JORGENSEN, Michael 435-283-7262 500 D
michael.jorgensen@snow.edu
JORGENSEN, Oona, A 305-243-6501 118 A
a.jorgensen@med.miami.edu
JORGENSEN, Patti 920-735-5649 542 N
jorgensp@fvtc.edu
JORGENSEN, Ronald, A 712-274-5128 181 C
jorgensenr@morningside.edu
JORGENSEN, Stephen, R 573-882-6227 283 H
jorgensens@missouri.edu
JORGENSON, Evelyn, E 479-619-4191 22 B
ejorgenson@nwacc.edu
JORGENSON, Jan 360-538-4243 523 A
jjorgens@ghc.edu
JORGENSON, Jo 480-517-8538 15 D
jo.jorgenson@riosalado.edu
JORISSEN, Shari 612-338-7224 265 G
shari.jorissen@waldenu.edu
JORVIG, Erik 702-990-4433 296 D
ejorvig@roseman.edu
JOSAY ZULLO, Ashley 724-838-7832 435 E
josay@setonhill.edu
JOSCHKO, Brian 309-677-1002 140 H
bjoschko@bradley.edu
JOSE, Jorge 812-856-2408 167 J
vpr@iu.edu
JOSE, Juana Clare 520-383-8401 18 A
jjose@tocc.edu
JOSE-EGUARAS, Agnes 661-763-7945 69 E
ajeguaras@taftcollege.edu
JOSEPH, Beatriz 210-481-3936 467 A
ijospeh@alamo.edu
JOSEPH, JR., Cheney, C 225-578-8324 205 E
cheney.joseph@law.lsu.edu
JOSEPH, Cynthia 562-907-4830 77 E
cjoseph@whittier.edu
JOSEPH, Daniel, P 410-951-3549 220 C
djoseph@coppin.edu
JOSEPH, Darnell 713-313-1826 487 F
djoseph@tsu.edu
JOSEPH, Elizabeth 708-534-5000 145 D
ejoseph@govst.edu
JOSEPH, Eric 405-692-3106 398 I
ejoseph@macu.edu
JOSEPH, Gwendolyn, G 502-213-2121 196 E
gwendolyn.joseph@kctcs.edu
JOSEPH, James, E 315-445-4279 330 B
josepjae@lemoyne.edu
JOSEPH, Jann 574-520-4183 168 F
jljoseph@iusb.edu
JOSEPH, Jerry 217-206-6003 161 G
gjose1@uis.edu
JOSEPH, Joanne 315-792-7326 348 D
joanne.joseph@sunyit.edu
JOSEPH, John 810-766-4103 239 H
john.joseph@baker.edu
JOSEPH, Josh 212-960-0083 353 P
josh.joseph@yu.edu
JOSEPH, Laura 631-420-2003 348 B
laura.joseph@farmingdale.edu
JOSEPH, Laurel 281-756-3500 467 D
ljoseph@alvincollege.edu
JOSEPH, La'Vetta 510-485-7831 58 G
ljoseph@patten.edu
JOSEPH, Mark 740-284-5870 382 G
mjoseph@franciscan.edu
JOSEPH, Mary Ann 617-873-0227 225 A
maryann.joseph@cambridgecollege.edu
JOSEPH, Michael 219-464-6896 174 E
michael.joseph@valpo.edu
JOSEPH, Mitch 937-484-1262 394 F
jmjoseph@urbana.edu
JOSEPH, Noson 718-601-3523 353 O
noson.jo@juno.com
JOSEPH, Patricia, A 484-365-8152 424 E
joseph@lincoln.edu
JOSEPH, Sonya, F 407-582-7734 118 I
sjoseph@valenciacollege.edu
JOSEPH, Stephen, M 724-287-8711 413 G
steve.joseph@bc3.edu
JOSEPH, Susan 423-697-3136 462 C
susan.joseph@chattanoogastate.edu
JOSEPH, Wendy 253-589-5822 521 B
wendy.joseph@cptc.edu
JOSEPH MATTISON, Sue 920-465-2050 539 F
mattisons@uwgb.edu
JOSEPH-SILVERSTEIN, Jackie 920-459-6610 541 E
jackie.josephsilvers@uwc.edu
JOSEPHS, Nadine, W 412-291-6298 412 H
njosephs@aii.edu
JOSEPHSON, David 973-655-6956 304 A
josephsond@mail.montclair.edu
JOSEY, Peige 334-222-6591 5 G
pjosey@lbwcc.edu
JOSHEE, Jeet 562-985-4106 33 F
jeet.joshee@csulb.edu
JOSHEE, Jeet 562-985-8330 33 F
jeet.joshee@csulb.edu
JOSHI, Maulin 973-618-3519 300 H
mjoshi@caldwell.edu
JOSLIN, Dennis, A 402-354-7257 291 P
dennis.joslin@methodistcollege.edu
JOSLIN, Mike 661-362-3260 40 H
michael.joslin@canyons.edu
JOSLIN, Monica 413-662-5242 230 C
m.joslin@mcla.edu
JOSLIN, Randy 530-541-4660 50 A
joslin@ltcc.edu
JOSS, Liz 317-931-2316 165 C
ljoss@cts.edu
JOSSELL, Steven 662-621-4304 266 H
sjossell@coahomacc.edu
JOST, Bruce 502-213-7264 196 E
bruce.jost@kctcs.edu
JOST, Jenifer 402-941-6241 291 I
jostj@midlandu.edu
JOST, Steve, A 301-860-4212 220 B
sjost@bowiestate.edu
JOSVAI, Lisa 608-796-3913 542 H
lajosvai@viterbo.edu
JOTHEN, Karen, G 651-690-6666 263 V
kgjothen@stkate.edu
JOUGANATOS, Brandon 916-855-4101 55 J
bjouganatos@nu.edu
JOUGANATOS, Brandon 858-642-8066 55 J
bjouganatos@nu.edu
JOVANOVICH, Donna 804-594-1576 515 G
djovanovich@jtcc.edu
JOVELL, Kristi 802-865-5728 501 F
kjovell@champlain.edu
JOVEN, Robert 203-582-3468 91 E
robert.joven@quinnipiac.edu
JOWERS, Angel 205-652-3547 9 G
ajowers@uwa.edu
JOY, Claire 661-255-1050 31 B
cjoy@calarts.edu
JOY, Darrell 314-290-0200 273 I
JOY, John 937-393-3431 391 F
jjoy@sscc.edu
JOYAUX, Aimee 804-862-6100 511 H
ajoyaux@rbc.edu
JOYCE, David, C 828-884-8264 355 A
president@brevard.edu
JOYCE, Gerard 610-282-1100 416 I
gerard.joyce@desales.edu
JOYCE, Jane 617-349-8785 228 B
ajoyce5@lesley.edu
JOYCE, Kelly 812-866-7160 166 E
joyce@hanover.edu
JOYCE, Kevin 239-280-1695 98 O
kevin.joyce@avemaria.edu
JOYCE, Kevin 914-674-7775 332 E
kjoyce@mercy.edu
JOYCE, Mary 228-896-2517 268 G
mary.joyce@mgccc.edu
JOYCE, Paul 208-885-6338 139 C
joyce@uidaho.edu
JOYE, Teresa 510-649-2410 46 E
tjoye@gtu.edu
JOYER, Nancy 651-201-1748 257 N
nancy.joyer@so.mnscu.edu
JOYNER, Barry 912-478-5322 126 B
joyner@georgiasouthern.edu
JOYNER, Deborah 828-726-2311 360 F
djoyner@cccti.edu
JOYNER, Jill 704-847-5600 369 A
jjoyner@ses.edu
JOYNER, Kathy 415-485-9502 41 B
kathy.joyner@marin.edu
JOYNER, Laurie, M 937-327-7916 395 I
ljoyner@wittenberg.edu
JOYNER, Scott 803-321-5617 447 L
scott.joyner@newberry.edu
JOYNER, SR., Stephen 704-330-1406 358 B
sjoyner@jcsu.edu
JOYNER, Stephen, E 718-951-5114 318 F
sjoyner@brooklyn.cuny.edu

KAHWAJY-ANDERSON, Joan 434-791-5624 505 A
jkahwajy@averett.edu
KAIDEN, Drew, A 856-225-6324 307 A
drew.kaiden@rutgers.edu
KAIDER-KOROL, Michele 585-340-9669 321 G
mkaider-korol@crcds.edu
KAIL, Pam 870-933-7903 19 D
pkail@asusystem.edu
KAIN, Daniel 928-523-7122 16 C
Daniel.Kain@nau.edu
KAIN, Douglas 209-384-6344 54 C
kain.d@mccd.edu
KAIN, Gregory 708-709-3579 156 A
gkain@prairiestate.edu
KAINTH, Pritpal 516-876-3207 345 E
kainthp@oldwestbury.edu
KAINTZ, Jamie 610-807-9221 421 C
jamiekaintz@iirp.edu
KAIRO, Moses, T 410-651-6072 219 H
mkairo@umes.edu
KAISER, Joyce 716-827-2445 350 H
kaiserj@trocaire.edu
KAISER, Kathy 319-398-5625 180 J
kkaiser@kirkwood.edu
KAISER, Kenneth, H 215-204-6545 436 C
ken.kaiser@temple.edu
KAISER, Larry 215-707-8773 436 C
larry.kaiser@temple.edu
KAISER, Larry, R 215-707-8773 436 C
larry.kaiser@temple.edu
KAISER, Melissa, D 215-972-2002 429 G
mkaiser@pafa.edu
KAISER, Nancy 618-468-3315 150 E
nkaiser@lc.edu
KAISER, Sarah 805-525-4417 69 I
skaiser@thomasaquinas.edu
KAISER, Susan, B 530-752-3042 71 A
sbkaiser@ucdavis.edu
KAISRLIK, Linda 407-628-5870 102 I
linda.kaisrlik@zenith.org
KAIVOLA, Karen 612-330-1024 253 K
kaivola@augsburg.edu
KAJIC, Martin 410-532-5855 217 F
mkajic@ndm.edu
KAJIWARA, Robert 808-245-8236 136 F
kajiwara@hawaii.edu
KAJSTURA, Alex 972-775-7250 479 I
alex.kajstura@navarocollege.edu
KAKAR, Casandra 602-285-7607 15 C
casandra.kakar@phoenixcollege.edu
KAKISH, William, J 626-873-2155 55 B
bkakish@mtsierra.edu
KAKOULIDIS, Sofia 516-463-6810 328 A
sofia.kakoulidis@hofstra.edu
KAKUGAWA-LEONG, Alyson, Y 808-932-7669 135 I
alyson@hawaii.edu
KALAFATIS, Lara, A 216-368-4244 378 J
lara.kalafatis@case.edu
KALAGORGEVICH, Mark 707-546-4000 43 J
mkal@empirecollege.com
KALANTZIS, Mary 217-333-0960 162 A
kalantzi@illinois.edu
KALB, Melanie, T 740-368-3377 390 B
mtkalb@owu.edu
KALBFLEISCH, Gary 206-546-5813 526 G
garyk@shoreline.edu
KALBFLEISCH, Pamela 708-209-3255 143 D
pamela.kalbfleisch@cuchicago.edu
KALBRENER, Kristen 508-910-6503 228 H
kkalbrener@umassd.edu
KALDENBERG, Tom 319-398-5561 180 J
tom.kaldenberg@kirkwood.edu
KALDIS, Paula 978-681-0800 233 D
paulad@mslaw.edu
KALDOR, Teresa 323-259-2966 56 I
tkaldor@oxy.edu
KALE, Kathy 408-554-5021 65 A
kkale@scu.edu
KALEMBA, Lena 815-455-8581 152 B
lkalemba@mchenry.edu
KALENDAE, Jeremiah 510-549-4704 68 I
jkalendae@sksm.edu
KALER, Eric, W 612-626-1616 265 C
upres@umn.edu
KALER, Robin 217-333-5010 162 A
rkaler@illinois.edu
KALERT, David 210-341-1366 479 N
dkalert@ost.edu
KALEVELA, Sylvester 719-549-2696 81 F
sylvester.kalevela@csupueblo.edu
KALEVITCH, Maria, V 412-397-4020 434 B
kalevitch@rmu.edu
KALFAYAN, Stephanie 650-725-2788 68 G
kalfayan@stanford.edu
KALFAYAN, Terry 619-260-5998 74 B
kalfayan@sandiego.edu
KALIAN, Heidi 703-658-4304 506 H
kalian@christendom.edu
KALICKI, Scott 603-524-3207 296 L
skalicki@ccsnh.edu
KALINA, Susan 907-786-1988 10 H
smkalina@uaa.alaska.edu
KALINOWSKI, Teresa 716-270-5112 325 A
kalinowski@ecc.edu
KALIS, Michelle 860-231-5229 93 A
mkalis@usj.edu
KALISA, Marie-Chantal 402-472-3747 293 H
mkalisa2@unl.edu
KALK, Jonathan 808-245-8272 136 F
kalk@hawaii.edu
KALKBRENNER, John 641-269-4300 178 I
kalkbren@grinnell.edu
KALKBRENNER, Suzanne, K 518-629-4530 328 D
s.kalkbrenner@hvcc.edu
KALLENBERGER, Melinda 414-382-6064 534 I
melinda.kallenberger@alverno.edu
KALLIERIS, Nick, C 847-543-2476 142 G
nkallieris@clcillinois.edu
KALLIN, Robert 717-337-6301 419 C
rkallin@gettysburg.edu
KALLIO, Kenneth 585-245-5531 345 D
kallio@geneseo.edu
KALLIS, John, A 724-938-4169 430 C
kallis@calu.edu
KALM, Stephen 406-243-4970 287 D
stephen.kalm@umontana.edu
KALMANOWITZ, Osher 718-645-0536 333 B
phecht@thejnet.com
KALMANSON, Dan, P 973-378-9856 308 C
daniel.kalmanson@shu.edu
KALMEY, Jon 814-866-8147 423 B
jkalmey@lecom.edu
KALOGIANNIS, Natalie 707-664-2874 36 C
natalie.kalogiannis@sonoma.edu
KALOOSTIAN, Damita 602-243-8021 15 F
damita.kaloostian@smcmail.maricopa.edu
KALOUPEK, W. Thomas 540-231-6221 518 B
kals@vt.edu
KALOYEROS, Alain 518-956-7111 348 D
akaloyeros@sunycnse.com
KALSBEEK, David, H 312-362-8706 143 G
dkalsbee@depaul.edu
KALSCHEUR, SJ, Gregory 617-552-2393 224 B
gregory.kalscheur@bc.edu
KALTCHEV, Matey 414-277-7544 537 G
kaltchev@msoe.edu
KALTEFLEITER, Caroline 607-753-4203 345 C
caroline.kaltefleiter@cortland.edu
KALTENMARK, Michael 317-940-9672 164 L
mkaltenm@butler.edu
KALTHOFF, Theodore, J 501-882-8830 19 E
tjkalthoff@asub.edu
KALU, Mma 919-546-8350 368 G
mkalu@shawu.edu
KALUSH, Paul 213-738-6818 68 E
accounting@swlaw.edu
KALUYU, Japheth 301-548-5500 96 H
KALWEIT, Clayton 847-970-4811 162 G
ckalweit@usml.edu
KALYAYEVA, Julia 510-845-0752 77 I
jkalyayeva@wi.edu
KALYN, Andrea 440-775-8200 388 B
Andrea.Kalyn@oberlin.edu
KALYNOVSKYI, Serhii 707-965-6218 57 I
skalynovskyi@puc.edu
KAM, Jung Ae 213-381-0081 48 A
iruswkpc@gmail.com
KAM, Moshe 973-596-6506 304 D
moshe.kam@njit.edu
KAMAHELE, Ron 907-786-1419 10 H
rckamahale@uaa.alaska.edu
KAMARA, Sheku 414-277-7416 537 G
kamara@msoe.edu
KAMATH, Kiran 831-646-4034 54 H
kkamath@mpc.edu
KAMATH, Kiran 925-473-7309 42 F
kkamath@losmedanos.edu
KAMCIYAN, Jeanette 561-364-3064 99 E
KAMENETSKY, Shmuel 215-473-1212 436 B
talmudicalyeshiva@yahoo.com
KAMENETSKY, Sholom 215-477-1000 436 B
talmudicalyeshvia@yahoo.com
KAMIAB, Jane 336-770-3297 372 B
kamiabj@uncsa.edu
KAMIENIECKI, Sheldon 831-459-3212 72 E
sk1@ucsc.edu
KAMINSHINE, Steven, J 404-413-9040 126 D
skaminshine@gsu.edu
KAMINSKI, Crystal 312-752-2122 149 D
crystal.kaminski@kendall.edu
KAMINSKI, Don 304-243-8152 534 H
dkaminski@wju.edu
KAMINSKI, Janice, M 724-480-3423 416 A
jan.kaminski@ccbc.edu
KAMINSKI, Linda 509-574-4635 529 B
lkaminski@yvcc.edu
KAMINSKI, Marie 414-847-3334 537 F
mkaminski@miad.edu
KAMINSKI-LUCAS, Matthew 215-489-4851 416 H
matthew.kaminski-lucas@delval.edu
KAMINSKY, Frances, R 203-596-4580 91 D
fkaminsky@post.edu
KAMINSKY, Paul, A 615-353-3615 463 C
paul.kaminsky@nscc.edu
KAMLET, Lee 203-582-3641 91 E
lee.kamlet@quinnipiac.edu
KAMMER, Dan 573-876-7273 283 A
dkammer@stephens.edu
KAMMER, Roy 651-213-4863 256 C
rkammer@hazelden.edu
KAMMERER, Joe 417-255-7240 279 B
joekammerer@missouristate.edu
KAMMERZELL, Joan 360-752-8436 520 A
jkammerzell@btc.edu
KAMOCHE, Njambi 847-925-6764 145 F
nkamoche@harpercollege.edu
KAMP, Cyndi 317-955-6103 171 A
ckamp@marian.edu
KAMPF, Stephen 419-372-7485 377 I
skampf@bgsu.edu
KAMPHAUS, Lisa 412-536-1526 422 E
lisa.kamphaus@laroche.edu
KAMPHAUS, Randy, W 541-346-1601 410 F
randyk@uoregon.edu
KAMPS, Anne 920-498-6367 544 B
anne.kamps@nwtc.edu
KAMPS, Larissa 866-323-0233 60 E
admissions@providencecc.edu
KAMPTNER, Elaine 231-591-2504 242 L
ElaineKamptner@ferris.edu
KAMWITHI, Gina 419-755-4711 387 E
gkamwithi@ncstatecollege.edu
KANACH, Nancy, A 609-258-5524 305 C
nkanach@princeton.edu
KANANI, David 718-261-5800 316 K
dkanani@bramsonort.edu
KANAREK, Berel 914-736-1500 337 D
KANAREK, E 914-736-1500 337 D
KANDER, Ron 215-951-2106 432 F
kanderr@philau.edu
KANE, Andrew 609-258-3469 305 C
kane@princeton.edu
KANE, Barry, S 212-854-1458 322 F
barry@columbia.edu
KANE, Candice 704-233-8631 373 C
c.kane@wingate.edu
KANE, Elizabeth 201-761-6046 307 K
ekane@saintpeters.edu
KANE, JR., Gerald, J 434-924-4274 514 A
gjk5y@virginia.edu
KANE, Jeffrey 516-299-2917 330 F
jeffrey.kane@liu.edu
KANE, Katherine, J 864-938-3913 448 E
kjkane@presby.edu
KANE, Kerri 413-755-4115 233 B
kpkane@stcc.edu
KANE, Kevin, M 610-660-3020 434 G
kevin.kane@sju.edu
KANE, Luanne 763-433-1297 257 P
luanne.kane@anokaramsey.edu
KANE, Marion, J 352-323-3617 107 X
kanem@lssc.edu
KANE, Michael 859-858-3511 193 A
mike.kane@asbury.edu
KANE, Michael 281-476-1501 481 E
michael.kane@sjcd.edu
KANE, Robert, C 202-685-3927 547 M
Galen.R.Kane.mil@ndu.edu
KANE, Sara, F 863-638-7602 118 L
sara.kane@warner.edu
KANE, Scott 401-456-8061 442 A
skane@ric.edu
KANE, Terrence 607-777-5014 343 D
tkane@binghamton.edu
KANE, Terrence 607-777-2131 343 D
tkane@binghamton.edu
KANE, Thomas 401-254-3531 442 C
tkane@rwu.edu
KANE, Thomas 781-891-2340 223 E
tkane@bentley.edu
KANE, Thomas, F 570-674-6223 426 D
tkane@misericordia.edu
KANE, Victor 626-571-8811 74 E
victork@uwest.edu
KANELLIS, Jennifer 908-737-7100 303 C
jkanelli@kean.edu
KANELOS, Gwen, E 708-209-3101 143 D
gwen.kanelos@cuchicago.edu
KANELOS, Peter 219-464-5022 174 E
peter.kanelos@valpo.edu
KANEVSKAYA, Svetlana 212-752-1530 330 C
svetlana.kanevskaya@limcollege.edu
KANG, Jerry 310-825-4321 71 D
KANG, Sung Do 213-386-0080 54 D
KANG, Woo Joong 562-926-1023 60 B
wjkang@ptsa.edu
KANG, Yunn, K 215-702-4461 414 C
ykang@cairn.edu
KANGAS, Craig 906-487-7361 242 M
craig.kangas@finlandia.edu
KANGAS, Michelle 218-855-8034 258 C
MKangas@clcmn.edu
KANGAS, Richard 218-322-2319 259 B
richard.kangas@itascacc.edu
KANIA, Edward, A 704-894-2125 356 D
edkania@davidson.edu
KANIKKEBERG, Dee Dee 208-885-6571 139 C
deedeek@uidaho.edu
KANIPE, H. Dean 828-652-0634 364 B
deank@mcdowelltech.edu
KANIS, David 773-995-2497 141 J
dkanis@csu.edu
KANIUKA, Piers 802-862-9616 501 E
pkaniuka@burlington.edu
KANJA, Todd, A 808-956-2739 135 H
tkanja@hawaii.edu
KANJIRATHINKAL, Mathew 563-876-3353 177 I
mathewk@dwci.edu
KANLIOGLU, Osman 832-230-5555 479 J
osman@na.edu
KANN, Stephanie, J 847-808-8444 163 H
skann@worshamcollege.com
KANNAN, Gavindarajan 478-825-6320 124 E
kannang@fvsu.edu
KANNAN, Jack 919-735-5151 367 A
jek@waynecc.edu
KANNENBERG, Gregory 920-465-2239 539 F
kannenbg@uwgb.edu
KANNENWISCHER, Susan, E 614-236-6511 378 H
skannenwischer@capital.edu
KANONIK, Robert 815-836-5813 150 F
kanoniro@lewisu.edu
KANOTZ, Ashley 304-829-7411 529 H
akanotz@bethanywv.edu
KANT, Jack 505-566-3371 312 K
kantj@sanjuancollege.edu
KANT, Willi, E 765-641-4170 164 B
wekant@anderson.edu
KANTARDJIEFF, Katherine 760-750-7204 35 B
kkantard@csusm.edu
KANTER, Connie 206-296-6148 526 F
kanterc@seattleu.edu
KANTER, Steven 816-235-1803 284 A
kantersl@umkc.edu
KANTNER, Joanne 815-825-2086 149 E
joanne.kantner@kishwaukeecollege.edu
KANTNER, John 904-620-1360 116 A
j.kantner@unf.edu
KANTNER, John 904-620-2455 116 A
j.kantner@unf.edu
KANTNER, Michael 856-256-4566 306 D
kantner@rowan.edu
KANTO, Kind 691-330-2620 549 D
kank@comfsm.fm
KANTOR, Ali 617-521-1038 236 F
ali.kantor@simmons.edu
KANTOR, Rebecca 303-315-6343 86 G
rebecca.kantor@ucdenver.edu
KANTROWITZ, Rebecca Reed 315-443-4263 349 E
rrkantro@syr.edu
KANU, Andrew 804-524-5769 518 C
akanu@vsu.edu
KANWISCHER, Wanda, L 952-358-8123 260 D
wanda.kanwischer@normandale.edu
KAO, Chi-Chang 650-723-2300 68 G
KAO, Imin 631-632-7422 344 C
imin.kao@stonybrook.edu
KAO, Monica 628-448-0023 48 C
vp-admin@itsla.edu
KAO, Teresa 626-571-5110 50 J
teresakao@les.edu
KAOUDIS, Kathy 303-914-6341 85 C
kathy.koaudis@rrcc.edu
KAPCSOS, Kathy 610-861-5499 427 F
kkapcsos@northampton.edu
KAPITAN, George 707-476-4100 41 C
george-kapitan@redwoods.edu
KAPLA, Dale, P 906-227-2920 248 B
dkapla@nmu.edu
KAPLAN, Anne, C 815-753-9503 154 I
akaplan@niu.edu

KAUFMAN, Donald, E ... 812-888-5343 174 F dkaufman@vinu.edu

KAUFMAN, Geof .... 253-680-7180 519 K gkaufman@bates.ctc.edu

KAUFMAN, Heather ...... 808-983-4146 135 D hkaufman@tokai.edu

KAUFMAN, Helena .... 507-222-4349 254 D hkaufman@carleton.edu

KAUFMAN, Kris, A .... 716-878-3000 345 B kaufmaka@buffalostate.edu

KAUFMAN, Lon .... 212-772-4150 319 E lk506@hunter.cuny.edu

KAUFMAN, Lori .... 561-912-2166 102 N lkaufman@evergladesuniversity.edu

KAUFMAN, Michael ...... 303-384-3009.. 80 O mkaufman@mines.edu

KAUFMAN, Paulette ...... 303-751-8700.. 79 F kaufman@bel-rea.com

KAUFMAN, Steven .... 734-462-4400 250 A skaufman@schoolcraft.edu

KAUFMANN, Marta .... 215-968-8242 413 F kaufmann@bucks.edu

KAUFMANN, Sandra ..... 516-876-2715 345 E kaufmanns@oldwestbury.edu

KAUGARS, Karlis .... 607-436-3663 344 B karlis.kaugars@oneonta.edu

KAUKE, Donna .... 815-599-3688 146 B donna.kauke@highland.edu

KAUKUS, Arlene, F .... 716-645-2231 343 E arleneks@buffalo.edu

KAUL, Stephanie .... 605-995-3022 452 H stephanie.kaul@mitchelltech.edu

KAULFUS, John .... 903-886-5153 485 E john.kaulfus@tamuc.edu

KAUNITZ, Carol .... 732-255-0400 304 E ckaunitz@ocean.edu

KAUP, Joan .... 513-562-8745 376 O jkaup@artacademy.edu

KAUR, Kuldeep .... 530-741-6723.. 78 F kkaur@yccd.edu

KAUR, Kuldeep .... 530-741-6723.. 78 D kkaur@yccd.edu

KAUS, Annette .... 402-375-7230 292 D ankaus1@wsc.edu

KAUS, Cheryl .... 609-652-4512 308 E cheryl.kaus@stockton.edu

KAUSHANSKY, Kenneth 631-444-9011 344 C kenneth.kashansky@stonybrook.edu

KAUSHIK, Suresh, C ...... 334-420-4244.... 7 I skaushik@trenholmstate.edu

KAUSS, Bruce .... 541-278-5763 404 J bkauss@bluecc.edu

KAUTZ, III, John .... 561-803-2084 109 G john_kautz@pba.edu

KAUTZ, Rebecca .... 308-635-6062 294 C kautzb2@wncc.edu

KAUTZER, Julie .... 920-686-6190 539 A Julie.Kautzer@sl.edu

KAUTZMAN, Amy .... 916-278-5679.. 34 E kautzman@csus.edu

KAVAJECZ, Kenneth, A . 315-443-9494 349 E kakavaje@syr.edu

KAVALIER, Barbara .... 903-875-7306 479 I barbara.kavalier@navarrocollege.edu

KAVALIERATOS, Gerasimos (Jerry) ...... 480-860-2700.. 13 Q

KAVANAGH, Kathy, J ..... 914-594-4487 335 H kathy_johnston@nymc.edu

KAVANAGH, Kenneth .... 239-590-7007 114 F kavanagh@fgcu.edu

KAVANAUGH, Gerard .... 508-999-8002 228 H gkavanaugh@umassd.edu

KAVANAUGH, Maria, A 508-565-1331 237 A mkavanaugh@stonehill.edu

KAVANAUGH, Michael . 714-484-7108.. 56 E mkavanaugh@cypresscollege.edu

KAVANAUGH, Steven ... 610-896-1141 420 J skavanau@haverford.edu

KAVCSAK, Lynn, E .... 919-866-5696 366 H lekavcsak@waketech.edu

KAVENEY, Shannon ...... 562-860-2451.. 37 L skaveney@cerritos.edu

KAVLIE, Lucas, B .... 912-650-6233 131 F lkavlie@southuniversity.edu

KAVOURIS, John .... 312-369-8646 143 C jkavouris@colum.edu

KAVRAN, Elizabeth .... 440-646-8107 394 G ekavran@ursuline.edu

KAWAI`AE`A, Keiki .... 808-932-7360 135 I keiki@hawaii.edu

KAWAMOTO, Judy .... 401-232-6046 441 B jkawamot@bryant.edu

KAWANNA, JR., Ronald .... 708-596-2000 159 D rkawanna@ssc.edu

KAWAR, Ferris .... 310-434-3911.. 65 B kawar_ferris@smc.edu

KAWAUCHI, John .... 970-943-2206.. 87 F jkawauchi@western.edu

KAY, Carol .... 915-831-2854 473 J ckay@epcc.edu

KAY, Gilmary .... 610-785-6235 434 E gkay@scs.edu

KAY, James, F .... 609-497-7815 305 B academic.dean@ptsem.edu

KAY, Kent .... 314-539-5291 281 H kentkay@stlcc.edu

KAY, R. David .... 570-327-4770 429 J dkay@pct.edu

KAY, Sabrina .... 213-355-7777.. 45 C sabrina.kay@fremont.edu

KAY, Steve, A .... 213-740-2531.. 74 D dean@dornsife.usc.edu

KAY-WONG, Chelsea .... 808-932-7442 135 I ckwong@hawaii.edu

KAYE, Ted .... 925-424-1013.. 37 O tkaye@laspositascollege.edu

KAYLOR, Alice, J .... 724-537-4566 435 B alice.kaylor@email.stvincent.edu

KAYLOR, Christine .... 508-999-8620 228 H ckaylor@umassd.edu

KAYLOR, Debbie .... 208-426-4351 137 E debbiekaylor@boisestate.edu

KAYLOR, Sean, P .... 845-575-3000 331 L sean.kaylor@marist.edu

KAYLOR, Stacia .... 620-331-4100 188 B skaylor@indycc.edu

KAYNAMA, Shohreh, A 410-704-3342 221 A skaynama@towson.edu

KAYNARD, Meryl .... 718-997-5725 320 E meryl.kaynard@qc.cuny.edu

KAYNE, Susan .... 908-737-0580 303 C skayne@kean.edu

KAYS, Brenda .... 704-991-0220 366 D bkays2651@stanly.edu

KAYSEN-LUZBETAK, Angie .... 815-280-6679 148 K akaysen@jjc.edu

KAZAMA, Susan .... 808-734-9267 136 C smurata@hawaii.edu

KAZANECKI-KEMPTER, Diane .... 631-420-2065 348 B diane.kazanecki-kempter@farmingdale.edu

KAZARIAN, Julie .... 508-929-8077 230 G jkazarian@worcester.edu

KAZDA, Kathleen .... 262-691-5464 544 D kkazda@wctc.edu

KAZEE, Thomas, A .... 812-488-2151 173 H president@evansville.edu

KAZEN, James, D .... 210-567-0390 495 B kazen@uthscsa.edu

KAZER, Meredith, W .... 203-254-4150.. 90 E mkazer@fairfield.edu

KAZEROUNIAN, Kazem . 860-486-2221.. 92 C kazem.kazerounian@uconn.edu

KAZMAN, Nelly .... 909-593-3511.. 73 B nkazman@laverne.edu

KAZMIR, Darin .... 361-582-2417 496 D darin.kazmir@victoriacollege.edu

KAZUMA, Clement .... 680-488-2471 550 C

KAZYAKA, Carrie .... 619-961-4324.. 69 J ckazyaka@tjsl.edu

KEADY, Thomas, J .... 617-552-6795 224 B thomas.keady@bc.edu

KEAGY, Thomas, A .... 215-951-1042 422 F keagy@lasalle.edu

KEAIRNS, Kathy .... 303-871-4156.. 86 H kathy.keairns@du.edu

KEAL, Aaron, J .... 620-421-6700 189 B aaronk@labette.edu

KEALA, David .... 808-675-3572 134 M kealad@byuh.edu

KEALEY, Michelle, L ..... 814-393-2352 430 E mkealey@clarion.edu

KEAN, Linda .... 781-239-4284 222 E kean@babson.edu

KEANE, Christopher ..... 509-335-6412 528 B chris.keane@vetmed.wsu.edu

KEANE, James .... 610-896-1023 420 J jkeane@haverford.edu

KEANE, Nancyellen .... 434-381-6506 513 E NKeane@sbc.edu

KEANE, Timothy .... 303-458-1844.. 85 G keane@regis.edu

KEANE-DAWES, Jennifer, M .... 410-651-6507 219 H jmkeanedawes@umes.edu

KEARNEY, Anne, E .... 315-445-4195 330 B kearneae@lemoyne.edu

KEARNEY, Janice .... 870-575-8000.. 24 D kearneyj@uapb.edu

KEARNEY, Jeannie .... 507-433-0571 261 C jeannie.kearney@riverland.edu

KEARNEY, Joseph, D .... 414-288-1955 537 B joseph.kearney@marquette.edu

KEARNEY, Kimberly ...... 540-261-8542 512 J kim.kearney@svu.edu

KEARNEY, Margaret ...... 585-275-9093 351 D margaret.kearney@rochester.edu

KEARNEY, Matthew .... 314-889-4686 275 B mkearney@fontbonne.edu

KEARNEY, Stephen .... 617-984-1734 235 H skearney@quincycollege.edu

KEARNS, Chris .... 406-994-2828 287 G chris.kearns@montana.edu

KEARNS, Jane .... 802-728-1231 504 C jkearns@vtc.edu

KEARNS, Joanne .... 973-328-5044 301 G jkearns@ccm.edu

KEARNS, Kevin .... 716-673-3758 343 F kevin.kearns@fredonia.edu

KEARNS, Lorna, R .... 412-624-6786 437 K lrkearns@pitt.edu

KEARNS, Michael .... 928-757-0801.. 15 K mkearns@mohave.edu

KEARNS, Michelle .... 801-863-8976 500 B michelle.kearns@uvu.edu

KEARNS, Richard .... 918-631-2150 403 M richard-kearns@utulsa.edu

KEARNS, Susan .... 512-475-7326 493 M susan.kearns@austin.utexas.edu

KEARNS, Tom .... 765-983-1465 165 H kearnto@earlham.edu

KEARNS-BARRETT, Marybeth .... 508-793-2448 225 C mkearns@holycross.edu

KEAS, Lenora .... 361-698-1205 473 F lkeas@delmar.edu

KEAS, Lenora .... 361-698-1207 473 F lkeas@delmar.edu

KEASLER, Robert, L ...... 859-238-5451 194 E robert.keasler@centre.edu

KEASLING, Diane .... 423-461-8968 459 I dlkeasling@milligan.edu

KEAST, Cindy .... 620-665-3565 188 A keastc@hutchcc.edu

KEATHLEY, Gwynne ...... 410-669-9200 216 F gkeathley@mica.edu

KEATING, Brendan .... 312-915-6147 151 E bkeating@luc.edu

KEATING, Clare .... 419-559-2383 392 A ckeating01@terra.edu

KEATING, Dana .... 618-252-5400 159 F dana.keating@sic.edu

KEATING, Frederick ...... 856-415-2100 306 C fkeating@rcgc.edu

KEATING, Jeff .... 909-469-5205.. 76 I jkeating@westernu.edu

KEATING, Joseph .... 740-588-1396 396 E jkeating@zanestate.edu

KEATING, Kathy .... 616-234-4953 243 D kkeating@grcc.edu

KEATING, Lisa .... 518-454-2833 322 C keatingl@strose.edu

KEATING, MaryJo .... 860-297-5110.. 92 A maryjo.keating@trincoll.edu

KEATING, Richard, S .... 413-782-1473 238 A richard.keating@wne.edu

KEATON, Alicia .... 407-823-2827 115 C alicia.keaton@ucf.edu

KEATY, Anthony .... 781-899-5500 235 G akeaty@psjs.edu

KEBABIAN, Helen .... 315-228-7451 321 H hkebabian@colgate.edu

KEBAETSE, Masego ...... 484-384-2968 427 I mkebaets@eastern.edu

KEBISEK, Kris .... 503-297-5544 408 A kkebisek@ocac.edu

KECHICHIAN, Avedis (Avo) .... 909-593-3511.. 73 B akechichian2@laverne.edu

KECK, Jenna .... 785-539-3571 189 D jkeck@mccks.edu

KECK, Kathleen, A .... 518-327-6223 338 B kkeck@paulsmiths.edu

KECK, Kay .... 269-965-3931 244 L keckk@kellogg.edu

KECK, Michael .... 315-279-5267 329 K mkeck@keuka.edu

KECK, III, Ray, M .... 956-326-2320 485 B president@tamiu.edu

KECSKES, Gary .... 630-466-7900 162 K gkecskes@waubonsee.edu

KEDDO, Dwain .... 239-489-9205 104 G dkeddo@fsw.edu

KEDROSKI, Cristie .... 850-729-5357 109 D kedroskc@nwfsc.edu

KEDROWSKI, Jeff .... 630-617-3042 144 G jeffk@elmhurst.edu

KEDROWSKI, Karen ...... 218-744-2418 259 B kkedrowski@nhed.edu

KEDROWSKI, Karen, M 803-323-2160 451 I kedrowskik@winthrop.edu

KEDSKI, Cathy .... 508-830-5042 230 D ckedski@maritime.edu

KEE, Josh .... 870-235-4321.. 23 D jrkee@saumag.edu

KEEBLER, Dave .... 805-652-5536.. 75 B dkeebler@vcccd.edu

KEEBLER, Joel .... 503-399-6565 404 L joel.keebler@chemeketa.edu

KEECH, Brian .... 215-895-2100 417 E brian.keech@drexel.edu

KEECH, Renee .... 860-465-5348.. 88 E keechr@easternct.edu

KEEDY, Thomas, E .... 765-361-6227 175 B keedyt@wabash.edu

KEEFE, Kevin .... 973-328-5064 301 G kkeefe@ccm.edu

KEEFE, Kristen, A .... 801-585-7989 499 K k.keefe@utah.edu

KEEFE, Maureen .... 617-879-7705 230 B mkeefe@massart.edu

KEEFE, Maureen .... 415-749-4577.. 62 I mkeefe@sfai.edu

KEEFE, Phil .... 914-674-7782 332 E pkeefe@mercy.edu

KEEFE, Terri, K .... 610-799-1580 424 A tkeefe@lccc.edu

KEEFE, Thomas, W .... 972-721-5203 491 B

KEEFER, Ashley .... 575-562-2105 310 I ashley.keefer@enmu.edu

KEEFER, Elizabeth .... 216-368-4286 378 J elizabeth.keefer@case.edu

KEEFER, Maureen, H .... 412-397-6484 434 B keefer@rmu.edu

KEEFER, Michael, R ...... 814-393-1610 430 E mkeefer@cuf-inc.org

KEEFER, Sue .... 719-384-6882.. 84 I sue.keefer@ojc.edu

KEEGAN, Bridget, M ..... 402-280-4015 290 B bmkeegan@creighton.edu

KEEGAN, Joe .... 518-891-2915 336 F jkeegan@nccc.edu

KEEGAN, Kim .... 603-206-8005 297 A kkeegan@ccsnh.edu

KEEGAN, Michael .... 605-394-2336 454 B michael.keegan@sdsmt.edu

KEEGAN, Thomas .... 360-416-7997 527 A thomas.keegan@skagit.edu

KEEHLWETTER, F. Stanley .... 724-458-2142 419 F fskeehlwetter@gcc.edu

KEEHN, Jay .... 305-653-7141 392 F jay.keehn@myunion.edu

KEEHNER, Julia .... 304-473-8441 534 G keehner@wvwc.edu

KEEL, Brooks, A .... 706-721-2301 121 C president@gru.edu

KEEL, Brooks, A .... 912-478-5211 126 B bkeel@georgiasouthern.edu

KEEL, Darla, M .... 901-448-5560 465 G dkeel1@uthsc.edu

KEEL, Dave .... 804-758-6731 516 G dkeel@rappahannock.edu

KEELER, Anne, B .... 540-828-5386 505 F akeeler@bridgewater.edu

KEELER, John, T .... 412-624-7636 437 K keeler@pitt.edu

KEELER, Karen .... 603-206-8002 297 A kkeeler@ccsnh.edu

KEELER-STROM, Michela .... 402-844-7122 292 G michela@northeast.edu

KEELEY, Brian .... 360-383-3375 528 E bkeeley@whatcom.ctc.edu

KEELEY, Dan .... 845-574-4452 339 I dkeeley@sunyrockand.edu

KEELEY, Edward, J .... 608-663-2223 536 A ekeeley@edgewood.edu

KEELEY, Eileen, M .... 704-894-2422 356 D eikeeley@davidson.edu

KEELEY, Louise Carroll 508-767-7312 222 D lkeeley@assumption.edu

KEELS, Carl .... 301-736-3631 216 E genekeels@aol.com

KEEN, Cathy .... 352-395-5829 112 H cathy.keen@sfcollege.edu

KEEN, Hubert .... 631-420-2239 348 B hubert.keen@farmingdale.edu

KEEN, Larry .... 910-678-8321 362 E keenl@faytechcc.edu

KEEN, Michael .... 802-681-2848 503 A mkeen@svc.edu

KEEN, Russell .... 706-721-2301 121 C rkeen@gru.edu

KEEN, Russell .... 912-478-1583 126 B russellkeen@georgiasouthern.edu

KEEN, Suzanne, P .... 540-458-8746 519 A keens@wlu.edu

KEENAN, Claudine .... 609-652-3593 308 E claudine.keenan@stockton.edu

KEENAN, SJ, James, F . 617-552-3880 224 B james.keenan.2@bc.edu

KEENAN, Kathleen .... 617-879-7065 230 B kkeenan@massart.edu

KEENAN, Laurie .... 518-464-8575 325 B laurie@excelsior.edu

KEENAN, Mary .... 218-726-7009 264 G mkeenan@d.umn.edu

KEENAN, Maura .... 215-780-1266 435 D mkeenan@salus.edu

KELLOGG, Gary .... 530-221-4275.. 66 B gkellogg@shasta.edu
KELLOGG, John .... 612-625-3387 265 C j-kell@umn.edu
KELLOGG, Leslie .... 269-927-6188 245 E lkellogg@lakemichigancollege.edu
KELLOGG, Magdalen .... 315-568-3067 334 F mkellogg@nycc.edu
KELLOGG, Sandi .... 503-399-5041 404 L sandi.kellogg@chemeketa.edu
KELLOGG, Tonia .... 405-585-5802 399 I tonia.kellogg@okbu.edu
KELLOGG-BRADLEY, Polly .... 507-288-4563 255 D pkelloggbradley@crossroadscollege.edu
KELLY, Alan, J .... 516-463-5027 328 A alan.j.kelly@hofstra.edu
KELLY, Anita .... 484-664-3178 427 C akelly@muhlenberg.edu
KELLY, Anna .... 401-739-5000 441 E akelly@neit.edu
KELLY, Audrey .... 908-737-7000 303 C aukelly@kean.edu
KELLY, Barbara .... 334-386-7299.... 3 I bkelly@faulkner.edu
KELLY, Benji .... 270-789-5211 194 D jbkelly@campbellsville.edu
KELLY, Bonnie .... 229-468-2091 134 I bonnie.kelly@wiregrass.edu
KELLY, Brendan .... 850-474-3306 116 E bkelly@uwf.edu
KELLY, Brian .... 805-525-4417.. 69 I bkelly@thomasaquinas.edu
KELLY, Brian .... 508-541-1622 225 G bkelly@dean.edu
KELLY, Brian .... 510-780-4500.. 50 G bkelly@lifewest.edu
KELLY, Brian .... 541-463-3000 406 F kellyb@lanecc.edu
KELLY, Calvin, A .... 512-448-8538 481 B ckelly1@stedwards.edu
KELLY, Chassie .... 662-720-7239 269 D cmkelly@nemcc.edu
KELLY, Chris .... 620-235-4122 190 G ckelly@pittstate.edu
KELLY, OSB, David .... 724-805-2644 435 B david.kelly@email.stvincent.edu
KELLY, Debra .... 609-771-2161 301 E dkelly@tcnj.edu
KELLY, Dennis .... 937-382-6661 395 F dennis_kelly@wilmington.edu
KELLY, Donald .... 251-809-1521.... 5 B don.kelly@jdcc.edu
KELLY, Donald .... 203-591-7394.. 91 D dkelly@post.edu
KELLY, Drew .... 610-526-6669 420 C dkelly@harcum.edu
KELLY, Edward, J .... 423-439-8550 461 D kellye@etsu.edu
KELLY, Frances .... 541-880-2203 406 E kelly@klamathcc.edu
KELLY, Francis, E .... 845-575-3000 331 L Francis.Kelly@marist.edu
KELLY, Frankie .... 787-751-0160 551 K fkelly@cmpr.pr.gov
KELLY, George, N .... 615-327-6800 458 F gkelly@mmc.edu
KELLY, Grace, A .... 802-654-2568 502 H gkelly@smcvt.edu
KELLY, Grayson .... 864-646-8361 449 F
KELLY, Hank .... 740-420-5924 388 F hkelly@ohiochristian.edu
KELLY, Heather, A .... 302-831-2021.. 94 D hkelly@udel.edu
KELLY, Inesha .... 773-697-2093 144 B ikelly@devry.edu
KELLY, Jack .... 717-262-2013 440 D jkelly@wilson.edu
KELLY, Jack .... 617-732-2143 233 E jack.kelly@mcphs.edu
KELLY, James .... 410-617-2920 216 D jjkelly@loyola.edu
KELLY, James .... 401-841-3674 548 B
KELLY, Janet, H .... 478-988-6800 122 F jkelly@centralgatech.edu
KELLY, Jeffrey, M .... 443-352-4012 218 E jkelly@stevenson.edu
KELLY, Jennifer .... 516-686-1254 335 F jkelly16@nyit.edu
KELLY, Jennifer .... 412-338-4770 422 A jkelly@kaplan.edu
KELLY, John .... 617-735-9710 226 B kellyjo@emmanuel.edu
KELLY, John .... 561-297-3450 114 E president@fau.edu
KELLY, John, J .... 607-735-1981 324 J jkelly@elmira.edu
KELLY, Judith .... 518-454-5211 322 C kellyj@strose.edu
KELLY, Karen .... 334-291-4938.... 2 H karen.kelly@cv.edu
KELLY, Kathy .... 513-244-4418 387 A kathy.kelly@msj.edu
KELLY, Kelly .... 608-822-2305 544 C kkelly@swtc.edu
KELLY, Kevin .... 413-545-0222 228 F kk@admissions.umass.edu
KELLY, Kevin, P .... 410-269-5087 219 E kkelly@umaryland.edu
KELLY, Kevin, R .... 937-229-3557 393 E kellyker@udayton.edu
KELLY, Kirk .... 503-725-6246 409 D kkelly@pdx.edu
KELLY, Laura .... 315-312-2258 346 A laura.kelly@oswego.edu
KELLY, Lee .... 516-299-3092 330 F lee.kelly@liu.edu
KELLY, Leslie, E .... 207-834-7522 212 F lesliek@maine.edu
KELLY, Leslie, G .... 540-868-7134 515 H lkelley@lfcc.edu
KELLY, Lois, M .... 805-756-5893.. 32 E lkelly@calpoly.edu
KELLY, Lori .... 305-809-3504 104 A lori.kelly@fkcc.edu
KELLY, Lyn .... 585-475-2946 339 G lyn.kelly@rit.edu
KELLY, Lynn .... 229-226-1621 132 E lkelly@thomasu.edu
KELLY, Marcia, J .... 603-646-0445 297 G marcia.j.kelly@dartmouth.edu
KELLY, Margaret, S ...... 215-637-7700 420 K mkelly@holyfamily.edu
KELLY, Marisa .... 617-573-8120 237 B mjkelly@suffolk.edu
KELLY, Mark .... 269-927-8100 245 E kelly@lakemichigancollege.edu
KELLY, Mark .... 312-369-7650 143 C mkelly@colum.edu
KELLY, Mark, L .... 864-294-2151 446 F mark.kelly@furman.edu
KELLY, Matthew .... 908-852-1400 301 C kellym@centenarycollege.edu
KELLY, Matthew .... 740-364-9644 378 L mkelly@cotc.edu
KELLY, Maureen .... 708-235-7556 145 D mkelly7@govst.edu
KELLY, Mike .... 229-468-2034 134 I mike.kelly@wiregrass.edu
KELLY, Mike .... 360-538-4011 523 A mkelly@ghc.edu
KELLY, Paul .... 202-651-5075.. 95 C paul.kelly@gallaudet.edu
KELLY, Paul .... 760-744-1150.. 58 D pkelly@palomar.edu
KELLY, SCJ, Paul .... 414-425-8300 538 J pkelly@shsst.edu
KELLY, Renee .... 518-608-8464 325 B rkelly@excelsior.edu
KELLY, Richard .... 201-559-6000 302 I kellyr@felician.edu
KELLY, Robert .... 620-665-3417 188 A kellyr@hutchcc.edu
KELLY, Robert, D .... 518-388-6101 350 K kellyrd@union.edu
KELLY, Rosemary .... 910-678-8325 362 E kellyr@faytechcc.edu
KELLY, Roxanne .... 541-440-4662 410 E Roxanne.Kelly@umpqua.edu
KELLY, Sara .... 585-395-2122 345 A skelly@brockport.edu
KELLY, Sarah .... 304-243-8141 534 H skelly@wju.edu
KELLY, Sarah, M .... 802-654-3000 502 H skelly@smcvt.edu
KELLY, Scott .... 410-225-2256 216 F skelly@mica.edu
KELLY, Scott, A .... 979-458-6120 485 C s-kelly@tamus.edu
KELLY, Sean .... 239-590-1094 114 F skelly@fgcu.edu
KELLY, Stephanie .... 317-788-6099 173 I spkelly@uindy.edu
KELLY, Stephen .... 212-220-8261 318 D skelly@bmcc.cuny.edu
KELLY, Steve .... 757-481-5005 519 C
KELLY, Susan .... 617-287-7050 228 E skelly@umassp.edu
KELLY, T. Liisa .... 910-843-5304 359 L
KELLY, Tami .... 281-669-4708 481 G tami.kelly@sjcd.edu
KELLY, Thomas .... 607-431-4111 327 B kellyt2@hartwick.edu
KELLY, Thomas .... 601-857-3237 267 D twkelly@hindscc.edu
KELLY, Thomas, M .... 312-915-6400 151 E tkelly4@luc.edu
KELLY, Todd .... 719-549-2380.. 81 F todd.kelly@csupueblo.edu
KELLY, Tonya .... 352-854-2322 100 P kellyt@cf.edu
KELLY, Towana .... 804-330-0111 506 D
KELLY, Vieneese .... 510-567-6174.. 69 D vkelly@sum.edu
KELLY, William .... 605-642-6371 453 G William.Kelly@bhsu.edu
KELLY, Yvan, J .... 904-819-6392 102 P kellyyj@flagler.edu
KELLY-ALBERTSON, Lynn, C .... 269-387-2745 252 I lynn.kelly-albertson@wmich.edu
KELLY BATES, Martha .. 847-578-8582 157 G martha.bates@rosalindfranklin.edu
KELLY-BOWRY, Tanya .. 303-831-6192.. 86 D Tanya.KellyBowry@cu.edu
KELLY KLEESE, Christine .... 919-536-7200 362 C kleesec@durhamtech.edu
KELLY-VERGONA, Barbara .... 973-957-0188 299 F registrar@acs350.org
KELNHOFER, Jack .... 732-255-0400 304 E jkelnhofer@ocean.edu
KELPSH, Len .... 602-387-2780.. 18 H leonard.kelpsh@phoenix.edu
KELSCH, Anne .... 701-777-3325 373 G anne.kelsch@und.edu
KELSCH, Tyler .... 970-521-6615.. 84 H tyler.kelsch@njc.edu
KELSER, Sandra, B .... 334-833-4409.... 4 E skelser@huntingdon.edu
KELSEY, Craig .... 661-952-5071.. 32 G ckelsey@csub.edu
KELSEY, Jane .... 217-854-3231 140 F jane.kelsey@blackburn.edu
KELSEY, Madelaine .... 203-596-4624.. 91 D mkelsey@post.edu
KELSHEIMER, Bradley, A .... 765-658-4161 165 G bradkelsheimer@depauw.edu
KELSO, Linda, M .... 863-667-5010 113 K lmkelso@seu.edu
KELSO, William .... 912-344-2541 120 D william.kelso@armstrong.edu
KELSOE, Amanda .... 919-684-2174 356 E amanda.kelso@duke.edu
KELTER, Paul .... 701-231-8692 374 C paul.kelter@ndsu.edu
KELTING, Dan .... 518-327-6213 338 B dkelting@paulsmiths.edu
KELTNER, Tom .... 417-865-2815 274 L keltnert@evangel.edu
KELTY, Ed .... 480-731-8246.. 14 J edward.kelty@domail.maricopa.edu
KEMAH, Celestine .... 903-730-4890 476 L ckemah@jarvis.edu
KEMBLE, Karen, D .... 207-581-1226 212 C karen.kemble@maine.edu
KEMERER, John, J .... 740-593-0465 389 H kemerer@ohio.edu
KEMKER, Brett .... 504-280-6222 205 G bkemker@uno.edu
KEMMER, Corby .... 218-281-8434 264 H ckemmer@umn.edu
KEMMY, Dave .... 401-254-3428 442 C dkemmy@rwu.edu
KEMNITZ, Carl .... 661-654-3420.. 32 G ckemnitz@csub.edu
KEMP, Ann .... 501-686-2500.. 23 F pakemp@uasys.edu
KEMP, Dale, A .... 630-752-5085 163 G dale.kemp@wheaton.edu
KEMP, Danny .... 540-831-7167 511 C dmkemp@radford.edu
KEMP, Gloria .... 501-686-6728.. 24 B kempgloriad@uams.edu
KEMP, Jerylle .... 212-237-8964 319 F jkemp@jjay.cuny.edu
KEMP, John .... 864-294-3717 446 F john.kemp@furman.edu
KEMP, Josh .... 870-307-7398.. 21 G josh.kemp@lyon.edu
KEMP, Katie .... 847-317-8177 161 B katiek@tiu.edu
KEMP, Lisa .... 703-993-2483 507 K lkemp@gmu.edu
KEMP, Rick .... 480-517-8508.. 15 D rick.kemp@riosalado.edu
KEMP, Shirley .... 304-829-7485 529 H skemp@bethanywv.edu
KEMP, Stephen .... 515-292-9694 175 E stephen.kemp@antiochschool.edu
KEMP, Steve .... 760-366-5283.. 42 G skemp@cmccd.edu
KEMP, Vandy .... 865-981-8111 458 E vandy.kemp@maryvillecollege.edu
KEMPA, Richard .... 307-382-1731 546 L rkempa@wwcc.wy.edu
KEMPE, Michael, A .... 330-325-6481 387 F mkempe@neomed.edu
KEMPEL, Leo .... 517-355-5133 246 H kempel@egr.msu.edu
KEMPER, Brad .... 575-562-2425 310 I brad.kemper@enmu.edu
KEMPER, Cathy .... 281-425-6867 477 F ckemper@lee.edu
KEMPER, James .... 740-588-1209 396 E jkemper@zanestate.edu
KEMPER, Kenneth, B ... 616-538-2330 243 C preskemper@gbcol.edu
KEMPER, Terry .... 262-695-3459 544 D tkemper1@wctc.edu
KEMPF, Emily, J .... 816-501-3571 281 B emily.kempf@rockhurst.edu
KEMPF, Gary .... 620-278-4469 191 D gkempf@sterling.edu
KEMPF-LEONARD, Kimberly .... 502-852-2234 201 A asdean@louisville.edu
KEMPIAK, Robert .... 815-838-0500 150 F kempiaro@lewisu.edu
KEMPTON, Daniel .... 740-283-6228 382 G dkempton@franciscan.edu
KENAUSIS, Veronica ..... 203-837-9109.. 88 G kenausisv@wcsu.edu
KENBER, Tammy .... 707-664-3100.. 36 C kenber@sonoma.edu
KENCH, Brian .... 203-932-7115.. 92 G bkench@newhaven.edu
KENDALL, Chris .... 507-457-1640 264 B ckendall@smumn.edu
KENDALL, Christopher, W .... 734-764-0584 251 C ckndll@umich.edu
KENDALL, Curtis, L ...... 540-828-5476 505 F ckendall@bridgewater.edu
KENDALL, Deborah .... 408-554-2717.. 65 A dkendall@scu.edu
KENDALL, Donna .... 781-891-2913 223 E dkendall@bentley.edu
KENDALL, Elizabeth ...... 845-574-4269 339 I ekendall@sunyrockland.edu
KENDALL, Justin .... 620-862-5252 184 H justin.kendall@barclaycollege.edu
KENDALL, Kathy .... 970-247-7399.. 82 I kendall_k@fortlewis.edu
KENDALL, Kenny .... 315-470-7749 316 I kennethkendall@crouse.org
KENDALL, Laura .... 717-871-7026 431 E laura.kendall@millersville.edu
KENDALL, Matt .... 740-695-9500 377 F mkendall@belmontcollege.edu
KENDALL, Peter .... 828-328-7100 358 G peter.kendall@lr.edu
KENDALL, Rex .... 812-514-8446 167 E rkendall@indstatefoundation.org
KENDALL, Stephanie .... 978-837-5321 233 G kendalls@merrimack.edu
KENDALL, Susan .... 412-924-1421 433 E skendall@pts.edu
KENDALL-DOMNICK, Meitaka .... 692-625-3394 550 A mkendall@cmi.edu
KENDER, JR., Joseph, P .... 610-758-5535 424 B jkender@lehigh.edu
KENDIG, P. Tysen .... 860-486-6713.. 92 C tysen.kendig@uconn.edu
KENDJORIA, Barrett ...... 864-656-2354 444 E bkendjo@clemson.edu
KENDREX, Bradley, S ... 480-732-7379.. 14 K Bradley.Kendrex@cgc.edu
KENDRICK, Bethany ...... 620-421-6700 189 B bethanyk@labette.edu
KENDRICK, Catherine ... 978-934-2495 229 A Catherine_Kendrick@uml.edu
KENDRICK, Curtis .... 607-777-4550 343 D kendrick@binghamton.edu
KENDRICK, Dorsey, L ... 203-285-2060.. 89 B dkendrick@gwcc.commnet.edu
KENDRICK, Haley .... 704-406-3957 356 G
KENDRICK, Lacy .... 804-204-1235 505 B lkendrick@btsr.edu
KENEFICK, Timothy ...... 321-674-7259 103 R tkenefick@fit.edu
KENERSON, Laura .... 401-874-5271 442 E kenerson@uri.edu
KENERSON, Murle .... 615-963-5203 461 F mkenerson@tnstate.edu
KENESSON, Alexander . 253-680-7150 519 K akenesson@bates.ctc.edu
KENESSON, Summer .... 360-475-7108 524 H skenesson@olympic.edu
KENIMER, Ann .... 979-845-3210 485 C a-kenimer@tamu.edu
KENKEL, Kevin .... 605-995-2617 452 C kekenkel@dwu.edu
KENKEL, Mary Beth ...... 321-674-8142 103 R mkenkel@fit.edu
KENMILLE, Cleo .... 406-275-4864 288 H cleo_kenmille@skc.edu

KERSENBROCK, Angela, M .... 407-708-2483 113 A
kersenbrocka@seminolestate.edu
KERSEY, Elizabeth, A .... 757-683-3152 510 I
ekersey@odu.edu
KERSEY, Pam .... 760-366-5246.. 42 G
pkersey@cmccd.edu
KERSEY-MATUSIAK, Gloria .... 215-637-7700 420 K
gkmatusiak@holyfamily.edu
KERSH, Rogan .... 336-758-3128 372 G
kersh@wfu.edu
KERSHNER, Marcy .... 843-383-8045 445 A
mkershner@coker.edu
KERSHNER, Scott, M .... 570-372-4220 435 I
kershner@susqu.edu
KERSHNER, Ted .... 928-757-0852.. 15 K
tkershner@mohave.edu
KERSTEN, Andrew .... 208-885-7885 139 C
andrewkersten@uidaho.edu
KERSTEN, Belen .... 559-730-3794.. 41 D
belenk@cos.edu
KERSTEN, David, W ...... 773-244-6235 154 G
dwkersten@northpark.edu
KERSTEN, James, B ...... 515-574-1132 179 F
kersten@iowacentral.edu
KERSTETTER, Philip, P .. 919-658-7746 369 B
pkerstetter@umo.edu
KERSTING, Monica, R .. 218-299-4557 255 B
kersting@cord.edu
KERTULIS-TARTAR, Gina .... 706-272-4516 123 G
gkertulistartar@daltonstate.edu
KERWIN, Cornelius, M . 202-885-2121.. 94 H
president@american.edu
KERWIN, Linda .... 716-827-2454 350 H
kerwinl@trocaire.edu
KERWIN, Mark .... 617-369-3281 236 E
mkerwin@smfa.edu
KERWITZ, Ann .... 815-921-4001 157 B
a.kerwitz@rockvalleycollege.edu
KERYLOW, Tiffany .... 802-387-6725 502 A
tiffanykerylow@landmark.edu
KESARIS, Thomas, L .... 610-660-1836 434 G
tkesaris@sju.edu
KESICKI, Michael .... 814-871-5873 419 A
kesicki001@gannon.edu
KESKULA, Douglas, R .. 828-227-7271 372 C
drkeskula@wcu.edu
KESLER, Michael, W ..... 802-773-5900 501 G
michael.kesler@csj.edu
KESSEL, Joyce .... 716-896-0700 352 B
jkessel@villa.edu
KESSEL, Shelly .... 406-683-7011 287 E
shelly.kessel@umwestern.edu
KESSELMAN, Harvey ..... 609-652-4514 308 E
harvey.kesselman@stockton.edu
KESSIE, Michael .... 941-487-4212 115 B
mkessie@ncf.edu
KESSIN, Janet .... 212-799-5000 329 I
KESSINGER, Kevin, S ... 765-658-4175 165 G
kevinkessinger@depauw.edu
KESSINGER, Steve .... 276-326-4603 505 D
skessinger@bluefield.edu
KESSLER, Gene .... 219-473-4299 165 A
gkessler@ccsj.edu
KESSLER, Jeanne, D ..... 785-670-1629 192 B
jeanne.kessler@washburn.edu
KESSLER, Jeffrey, A ...... 516-877-3660 314 F
kessler@adelphi.edu
KESSLER, Jim .... 910-521-6695 371 D
KESSLER, Karen .... 850-484-1673 110 D
kkessler@pensacolastate.edu
KESSLER, Kathleen .... 802-839-8317 502 F
kathleen.kessler@neci.edu
KESSLER, Mary .... 812-488-2569 173 H
mk43@evansville.edu
KESSLER, Nevin, E .... 848-932-7890 306 F
nkessler@winants.rutgers.edu
KESSLER, Richard .... 212-580-0210 334 C
kesslerr@newschool.edu
KESSLER, Sheryl .... 215-972-7600 429 G
skessler@pafa.org
KESSLER, Susan, B .... 386-312-4021 111 K
susankessler@sjrstate.edu
KESSLER, Suzanne .... 914-251-6600 346 D
suzanne.kessler@purchase.edu
KESSLER-CLEARY, Timothy .... 973-618-3484 300 H
tcleary@caldwell.edu
KESTEN, Philip, R .... 408-554-4311.. 65 A
pkesten@scu.edu
KESTER, Karen, A .... 941-752-5329 114 B
kesterk@scf.edu
KESTER, Kelly .... 360-383-3245 528 E
kkester@whatcom.ctc.edu
KESTER, Lori .... 303-556-2906.. 81 J
lori.kester@ccd.edu
KESTERSON, Ronald, L . 865-694-6608 463 E
rkesterson@pstcc.edu
KESTNER, Carly .... 276-326-4243 505 D
ckestner@bluefield.edu
KESTNER, Jane .... 330-941-3409 396 C
jekestner@ysu.edu
KESTNER, Laura, F .... 414-288-7424 537 B
laura.kestner@marquette.edu
KETCHEN, John .... 865-573-4517 457 H
jketchen@johnsonu.edu
KETCHESON, Kathi, A ... 503-725-3425 409 D
ketchesonk@pdx.edu
KETELS, Margo .... 563-589-3131 183 E
mketels@dbq.edu
KETELSEN, Scott .... 319-273-2761 176 A
scott.ketelsen@uni.edu
KETNER, Annette .... 619-260-2925.. 74 B
aketner@sandiego.edu
KETO, Stephen, W .... 218-726-7101 264 G
vcfo@d.umn.edu
KETO, Stephen, W .... 919-515-9224 370 D
steve_keto@ncsu.edu
KETTEMAN, Paul, G ...... 615-844-5227 466 G
gketteman@welch.edu
KETTENBEIL, Kenneth ... 313-593-5140 251 D
kketten@umich.edu
KETTERER, Kathleen ...... 229-243-6960 121 D
kathleen.ketterer@bainbridge.edu
KETTERER, Patricia .... 212-237-8516 319 F
pketterer@jjay.cuny.edu
KETTERLING, Jayme ..... 208-732-6552 137 K
jketterling@csi.edu
KETTERMAN, Jesse .... 301-687-4311 220 D
jketterman@frostburg.edu
KETTING-WELLER, Ginger .... 951-785-2266.. 49 I
gketting@lasierra.edu
KETTINGER, Kirk .... 585-594-6415 339 F
Kettinger_Kirk@roberts.edu
KETTLEWELL, Charles, L .... 214-648-3606 496 A
charles.kettlewell@utsouthwestern.edu
KETTNER, Valrey, V ...... 701-231-9608 374 C
val.kettner@ndsu.edu
KETTYLE, William, M .... 617-253-1774 233 C
KEUFFEL, Elizabeth .... 603-641-7203 298 F
ekeuffel@anselm.edu
KEUP, Mike .... 309-677-2677 140 H
mkeup@bradley.edu
KEUSS, Theresa .... 314-516-4602 284 B
keusst@umsl.edu
KEVIL, Tim .... 903-875-7443 479 I
tim.kevil@navarrocollege.edu
KEVLIN, Dean .... 516-572-7771 334 A
dean.kevlin@ncc.edu
KEY, Dan .... 641-844-5741 179 L
dan.key@iavalley.edu
KEY, Dillon .... 864-977-7122 448 A
dillon.key@ngu.edu
KEY, Henry .... 908-709-7151 309 A
key@ucc.edu
KEY, Jonathan, C .... 504-282-4455 206 C
jkey@nobts.edu
KEY, Monica .... 617-989-4125 237 G
keym@wit.edu
KEY, Roby, V .... 817-257-7706 486 G
r.key@tcu.edu
KEY, Stacy .... 479-979-1360.. 25 H
skey@ozarks.edu
KEY, Stan, R .... 859-257-8907 200 G
stan.key@uky.edu
KEYES, Adam .... 508-793-7453 225 B
akeyes@clarku.edu
KEYES, Beth, H .... 937-229-3769 393 E
bkeyes@udayton.edu
KEYES, Colleen .... 510-356-4760.. 78 G
KEYES, James, R .... 802-443-5523 502 E
jkeyes@middlebury.edu
KEYES, Judy .... 617-287-6300 228 G
judy.keyes@umb.edu
KEYS, Carolyn .... 909-274-4525.. 54 J
ckeys@mtsac.edu
KEYS, James, A .... 910-843-5304 359 L
KEYS, Margo, A .... 715-858-1825 542 M
mkeys@cvtc.edu
KEYS, Marina .... 503-845-3550 407 B
marina.keys@mtangel.edu
KEYS, Terrance .... 585-292-3432 333 G
tkeys@monroecc.edu
KEYSER, Kent .... 619-388-6939.. 62 E
kkeyser@sdccd.edu
KEYSER, Sarah, B .... 276-638-8777 516 D
skeyser@patrickhenry.edu
KEZIRIAN, Wayne, M ... 401-598-1900 441 D
wkezirian@jwu.edu
KHACHATRYAN, Davit .. 949-451-5326.. 67 E
dkhachatryan@ivc.edu
KHACHIKIAN, Crist .... 818-677-2138.. 34 D
crist.khachikian@csun.edu
KHADANGA, Dave .... 334-386-7113.... 3 I
dkhadanga@faulkner.edu
KHALDEN, Jeff .... 817-598-6485 497 A
jkhalden@wc.edu
KHALEGHIRAD, Massoud .... 510-549-4706.. 68 I
mkhaleghirad@sksm.edu
KHAMSAMRAN, Anna ... 575-758-8914 311 F
annak@midwiferycollege.edu
KHAN, Adil .... 636-227-2100 277 A
adil.khan@logan.edu
KHAN, Ali .... 402-559-4950 293 I
ali.khan@unmc.edu
KHAN, Jehana .... 320-222-5986 261 B
jehana.khan@ridgewater.edu
KHAN, M. Wasiullah .... 312-939-0111 144 D
chancellor@eastwest.edu
KHAN, Raza .... 410-386-8222 214 B
rkhan@carrollcc.edu
KHAN, Rehan .... 617-373-2752 235 D
KHAN-MARCUS, Zaveeni .... 805-893-8411.. 72 D
zaveeni.khan-marcus@sa.ucsb.edu
KHANEJA, Gurvinder ..... 201-684-7766 305 F
gkhaneja@ramapo.edu
KHANI, Anthony .... 646-717-9743 326 E
khani@gts.edu
KHANNA, Pradeep .... 217-333-9525 162 A
pkhanna@illinois.edu
KHANOYAN, Gayane .... 818-988-2300.. 55 F
KHARTABIL, Basim .... 312-935-6449 157 A
bkhartabil@robertmorris.edu
KHASAWNEH, Rami ...... 815-836-5360 150 F
khasawra@lewisu.edu
KHATOR, Renu .... 713-743-8820 491 C
rkhator@uh.edu
KHATOR, Renu .... 713-743-8820 491 D
rkhator@uh.edu
KHATRI, Achal .... 617-873-0235 225 A
achal.khatri@cambridgecollege.edu
KHATTARI, Karen .... 610-606-4632 415 A
klkhatta@cedarcrest.edu
KHAYUM, Mohammed . 812-464-1718 174 D
mkhayum@usi.edu
KHEHRA, Harry .... 281-290-6576 477 I
harry.khehra@lonestar.edu
KHLEIF, Samir .... 706-721-0570 121 C
skhleif@gru.edu
KHODIER, Sayed .... 617-739-1700 234 I
skhodier@aii.edu
KHOJA, Faiza .... 713-221-8218 491 F
khojafai@uhd.edu
KHOO, Poh Lin .... 651-793-1828 259 E
pohlin.khoo@metrostate.edu
KHOSLA, Pradeep, K .... 858-534-3135.. 72 B
chancellor@ucsd.edu
KHOSRAVANI, Mariam . 714-241-6159.. 40 B
mkhosravani@coastline.edu
KHOSROWPANAH, Shahram .... 671-735-2694 549 G
khosrow@triton.uog.edu
KHOURY, Melik Peter .. 207-509-7122 212 A
mkhoury@unity.edu
KHOURY, Muna .... 313-496-2777 252 A
mkhoury1@wcccd.edu
KHOURY, Philip, S .... 617-253-0887 233 C
KHOURY, Terry .... 814-677-1322 417 F
occ@dbcollege.edu
KHOURY, Terry, L .... 814-371-6920 417 F
admissions@dbcollege.edu
KHURANA, Nikki .... 909-621-8054.. 65 E
nkhurana@scrippscollege.edu
KHURANA, Rakesh .... 617-495-4137 227 D
rkhurana@fas.harvard.edu
KIA, Norman .... 575-769-4074 310 G
norman.kia@clovis.edu
KIAMAN, Matthew .... 626-585-3200.. 58 F
mxkiaman@pasadena.edu
KIAN, David .... 561-297-3007 114 E
david.kian@fau.edu
KIANI, Tanya .... 805-756-7507.. 32 E
tkiani@calpoly.edu
KIBARDINA, Marina ..... 708-709-7921 156 A
mkibardina@prairiestate.edu
KIBLER, Bill .... 432-837-8032 489 B
president@sulross.edu
KIBLER, David .... 864-941-8475 448 D
kibler.d@ptc.edu
KIBLER, Michele .... 614-222-4009 380 F
mkibler@ccad.edu
KICKLITER, Holly .... 727-873-4455 116 C
hkicklit@mail.usf.edu
KICKNER, Robert .... 253-833-9111 523 B
rkickner@greenriver.edu
KIDD, Anessa .... 334-876-9303.... 4 B
anessa.kidd@wccs.edu
KIDD, Beth Ann .... 903-675-6223 490 F
bkidd@tvcc.edu
KIDD, Jane .... 706-369-6833 130 B
jkidd@piedmont.edu
KIDD, Kathryn .... 605-455-6055 452 L
kkidd@olc.edu
KIDD, Kevin .... 617-989-9095 237 G
kiddk@wit.edu
KIDD, Lisa, L .... 920-923-8115 537 A
llkidd@marianuniversity.edu
KIDD, Mary .... 615-514-2787 459 O
financialaid@nossi.edu
KIDD, Mike .... 828-327-7000 361 B
mkidd@cvcc.edu
KIDD, Windy .... 859-280-1237 198 B
wkidd@lextheo.edu
KIDDIE, Thomas .... 304-766-4116 533 C
tkiddie@wvstateu.edu
KIDDOO, Sandy .... 715-422-5525 543 D
sandy.kiddoo@mstc.edu
KIDESS LUCEY, Tamie .. 413-748-3161 236 H
tkidessl@springfieldcollege.edu
KIDNEY, Gary .... 203-432-6093.. 93 C
gary.kidney@yale.edu
KIDWELL, Debra .... 573-681-5418 276 K
purchasing@lincolnu.edu
KIDWELL, Eric, A .... 334-833-4420.... 4 E
ekidwell@huntingdon.edu
KIDWELL, John .... 870-460-1083.. 24 C
kidwell@uamont.edu
KIDWELL, JP .... 315-792-7225 348 D
jpkidwell@sunypoly.edu
KIDWELL, Kimberlee ..... 509-335-4561 528 B
kidwell@wsu.edu
KIDWELL, Martin .... 503-253-3443 408 B
mkidwell@ocom.edu
KIEBA-TOLKSDORF, Helen, C .... 248-689-8282 251 I
hkieba@walshcollege.edu
KIEC, Michael .... 216-373-5227 388 A
mkiec@ndc.edu
KIECKHAFER, David, S . 608-342-1321 540 D
kieckhaferd@uwplatt.edu
KIEDA, David, B .... 801-581-8796 499 K
dave.kieda@utah.edu
KIEF, Bob .... 253-879-2820 527 F
bkief@pugetsound.edu
KIEFER, Cindy .... 406-756-3843 286 G
ckiefer@fvcc.edu
KIEFER, David, E .... 626-584-5409.. 45 F
dkiefer@fuller.edu
KIEFER, Irene .... 800-567-2344 535 F
ikiefer@menominee.edu
KIEFER, William .... 412-809-5100 433 D
kiefer.william@pti.edu
KIEFFER, Barb .... 920-735-5734 542 N
kieffer@fvtc.edu
KIEFFER, Don .... 212-986-4343 300 C
dmk@berkeleycollege.edu
KIEFFER, Don .... 212-986-4343 316 D
dmk@berkeleycollege.edu
KIEFFER, Linda .... 509-359-6345 522 C
lkieffer@ewu.edu
KIEFFER, Regina .... 316-322-3104 185 F
rkieffer@butlercc.edu
KIEFFER, Shelly .... 318-473-6508 205 A
skieffer@lsua.edu
KIEFT, Thom .... 352-536-2150 107 X
kiefft@lssc.edu
KIEHL, Gregg .... 607-844-8222 350 A
kiehlg@TC3.edu
KIEHNE, Rolfe, E .... 636-327-4645 278 D
sil@midwest.edu
KIEKEL, Preston .... 360-736-9391 520 F
pkiekel@centralia.edu
KIEKLAK, Scott .... 404-526-9366 130 F
s.kieklak@sae.edu
KIEL, Cindy, M .... 530-754-1184.. 71 A
cmkiel@ucdavis.edu
KIEL, Mark .... 847-635-7122 155 E
mkiel@oakton.edu
KIEL, Micah .... 563-333-6121 182 E
KielMicahD@sau.edu
KIELBASA, Jody, K .... 434-982-5326 514 A
jkk8j@virginia.edu
KIELHOFNER, Brad, B .. 417-836-6865 279 A
bradkielhofner@missouristate.edu
KIELMEYER, David .... 419-372-8587 377 I
davidk@bgsu.edu
KIELT, Chris .... 919-962-3444 371 A
chris_kielt@unc.edu
KIELY, Maurice, J .... 804-412-2026 511 E
mkiely@rmc.edu
KIENER, Dan, W .... 412-397-5263 434 B
kiener@rmu.edu
KIENITZ, Kelli, S .... 320-222-5215 261 B
kelli.kienitz@ridgewater.edu
KIENLE-GRANZO, Elizabeth, A .... 212-998-4407 336 C
ekg241@nyu.edu
KIENOW, Sharon .... 605-626-2640 454 A
Sharon.Kienows@northern.edu
KIENTOP, Margaret .... 815-836-5230 150 F
kientoma@lewisu.edu
KIERALDO, John .... 312-553-5761 141 N
jkieraldo@ccc.edu
KIERNAN, Catherine, A 973-761-9191 308 C
catherine.kiernan@shu.edu

KINDER, Jim .... 330-287-1212 389 B
kinder.15@osu.edu
KINDER, L. Chad .... 580-774-7036 402 G
chad.kinder@swosu.edu
KINDERS, Mark .... 405-974-5560 403 G
mkinders@uco.edu
KINDL, Christine .... 724-938-5492 430 C
kindl@calu.edu
KINDLE, Derek .... 202-806-2864.. 96 B
dkindle@howard.edu
KINDLE, Jamila .... 661-252-1864.. 38 D
KINDLE, Joan .... 563-336-3488 178 A
jkindle@eicc.edu
KINDLER, Andreas .... 309-677-3107 140 H
akindler@bradley.edu
KINDON, Victoria .... 434-395-4804 509 H
kindonv@longwood.edu
KINEAVY, Jacqueline .... 973-684-6300 304 F
jkineavy@pccc.edu
KINERSON, Sara .... 802-635-1257 504 A
sara.kinerson@jsc.edu
KINES, James .... 864-231-2177 443 E
JKines@andersonuniversity.edu
KINES, Teresa .... 336-249-8186 362 B
tkines@davidsonccc.edu
KING, Adrienne .... 208-282-4407 138 C
kingadri@isu.edu
KING, Albert .... 419-289-5959 377 A
aking@ashland.edu
KING, Alissa .... 601-318-6474 271 F
aking@wmcarey.edu
KING, Amy .... 404-364-8303 129 F
aking@oglethorpe.edu
KING, Amy .... 303-871-7420.. 86 H
amking@du.edu
KING, Amy, L .... 304-457-6354 529 C
kingal@ab.edu
KING, Andrew, B .... 904-620-2602 116 A
a.king@unf.edu
KING, Angella .... 859-246-6696 195 J
angie.king@kctcs.edu
KING, Art .... 646-312-4570 318 C
Art.King@baruch.cuny.edu
KING, B, J .... 423-439-4414 461 D
kingbj@etsu.edu
KING, Barbara .... 405-682-1611 399 K
bking@occc.edu
KING, Baron .... 215-702-4224 414 C
baronking@cairn.edu
KING, Becky, L .... 254-710-4566 469 D
becky_king@baylor.edu
KING, Bob .... 210-999-7011 490 E
bob.king@trinity.edu
KING, Bobby .... 707-654-1245.. 34 B
rking@csum.edu
KING, Brenda, M .... 304-336-8076 533 A
kingbren@westliberty.edu
KING, Brian .... 916-568-3021.. 52 H
kingb@losrios.edu
KING, Brian .... 814-866-6641 423 B
bking@lecom.edu
KING, Bruce .... 510-235-7800.. 42 D
bking@contracosta.edu
KING, Bruce .... 507-786-3334 264 C
kingb@stolaf.edu
KING, C. Gregory .... 304-462-6131 532 G
greg.king@glenville.edu
KING, Carole .... 202-884-9125.. 97 A
kingc@trinitydc.edu
KING, Carolee .... 409-772-1904 495 E
caaking@utmb.edu
KING, Caroline .... 941-907-2262 102 N
caking@evergladesuniversity.edu
KING, Charles .... 409-933-8404 471 B
cking@com.edu
KING, Charles, W .... 540-568-6434 509 C
kingcw@jmu.edu
KING, Cheryl .... 301-295-3045 548 D
cheryl.king@usuhs.edu
KING, Christopher .... 956-665-2221 494 C
kingca@utpa.edu
KING, Corey .... 561-297-3988 114 E
cking14@fau.edu
KING, Craig .... 212-870-1238 336 B
cking@nyts.edu
KING, Curt .... 413-662-5062 230 C
curt.king@mcla.edu
KING, Cynthia, L .... 610-861-5510 427 F
cking@northampton.edu
KING, D. Wayne .... 859-238-5550 194 E
wayne.king@centre.edu
KING, Daniel, P .... 334-844-4810.... 1 G
dpk0002@auburn.edu
KING, David, A .... 541-737-2676 408 F
ecampus@oregonstate.edu
KING, David, A .... 540-432-4440 507 A
david.king@emu.edu
KING, David, A .... 330-471-8121 385 G
dking@malone.edu
KING, David, S .... 203-582-3213.. 91 E
david.king@quinnipiac.edu
KING, David, W .... 805-565-6036.. 76 K
dking@westmont.edu
KING, Deborah .... 870-338-6474.. 24 F
KING, Dee .... 248-204-2127 245 J
dking@ltu.edu
KING, Denise .... 423-472-7141 462 D
DKing05@clevelandstatecc.edu
KING, Dennis .... 785-628-4291 187 A
dking@fhsu.edu
KING, Dennis .... 828-398-7112 360 A
dennisfking@abtech.edu
KING, DJuana .... 314-529-9368 277 B
dking1@maryville.edu
KING, Donald .... 508-999-8575 228 H
dking@umassd.edu
KING, JR., Donald .... 765-285-1478 164 D
jking@bsu.edu
KING, Donna .... 903-463-8735 474 K
donnaking@grayson.edu
KING, Donna .... 281-290-2722 477 I
donna.l.king@lonestar.edu
KING, Dottie .... 812-535-5296 172 F
president@smwc.edu
KING, Duane .... 918-596-2710 403 M
duane-king@utulsa.edu
KING, Eddie .... 843-208-8135 450 D
eking@uscb.edu
KING, Elizabeth, H .... 316-978-3510 192 D
elizabeth.king@wichita.edu
KING, Elston, H .... 504-286-5197 207 B
eking@suno.edu
KING, Eric .... 316-978-3106 192 D
eric.king@wichita.edu
KING, Fred, L .... 304-293-3449 533 D
fred.king@mail.wvu.edu
KING, Glenda .... 662-252-8000 270 C
gking@rustcollege.edu
KING, Gordon, B .... 617-557-1520 237 B
gking@suffolk.edu
KING, Grace .... 909-537-5205.. 35 A
gking@csusb.edu
KING, Greg .... 423-236-2983 460 K
gking@southern.edu
KING, Gregory .... 330-823-2282 394 A
kinggl@mountunion.edu
KING, JR., H. Lee .... 434-223-7258 508 B
lking@hsc.edu
KING, Henry, D .... 260-422-5561 167 F
hdking@indianatech.edu
KING, Herbert .... 651-793-1508 259 E
herbert.king@metrostate.edu
KING, Irene .... 610-519-4080 439 A
irene.king@villanova.edu
KING, Jackie, E .... 585-275-1051 351 D
jking@admin.rochester.edu
KING, James .... 615-336-4470 461 B
james.king@tbr.edu
KING, Janice .... 775-753-2361 295 D
janice.king@gbcnv.edu
KING, Jean .... 508-856-4979 229 B
Jean.King@umassmed.edu
KING, Jennifer .... 413-559-5427 227 C
KING, Jerry .... 903-675-6210 490 F
jking@tvcc.edu
KING, Jim, M .... 318-257-2445 208 A
king@latech.edu
KING, Joan .... 509-335-9681 528 B
joank@wsu.edu
KING, Jodie .... 215-248-7004 415 D
kingj@chc.edu
KING, Joe, M .... 334-244-3600.... 2 A
jmking@aum.edu
KING, Joel .... 308-398-7315 289 D
joelking@cccneb.edu
KING, John .... 541-552-6261 409 G
kingjo@sou.edu
KING, John, J .... 401-254-3042 442 C
jjking@rwu.edu
KING, John, M .... 617-552-4445 224 B
john.king.2@bc.edu
KING, John, W .... 423-652-4832 457 J
jwking@king.edu
KING, Jovanna, J .... 864-656-0663 444 E
jovanna@clemson.edu
KING, Joy, S .... 512-505-3015 475 G
jsking@htu.edu
KING, Julie, A .... 803-786-3871 445 C
juking@columbiasc.edu
KING, Karen .... 505-566-3408 312 K
kingk@sanjuancollege.edu
KING, Karen, D .... 423-439-5654 461 D
kingk@etsu.edu
KING, Katherine .... 949-480-4161.. 66 I
kking@soka.edu
KING, Katie .... 405-491-6350 402 E
kking@snu.edu
KING, Kenneth .... 801-878-1419 296 D
kking@roseman.edu
KING, Kimberly .... 239-280-2500.. 98 O
kimberly.king@avemaria.edu
KING, Kristyn .... 815-394-5061 157 D
kking@rockford.edu
KING, Kwanna .... 918-463-2931 397 I
kwanna.king@connorsstate.edu
KING, L. Dianne .... 864-231-2026 443 E
ldking@andersonuniversity.edu
KING, Larry, J .... 936-468-1260 484 A
lking@sfasu.edu
KING, Laura .... 870-512-7850.. 19 I
laura_king@asun.edu
KING, Laura .... 651-846-1316 261 G
laura.king@saintpaul.edu
KING, Laura, C .... 814-393-1926 430 E
lking@clarion.edu
KING, Laura, M .... 651-201-1732 257 N
laura.king@so.mnscu.edu
KING, Lauren .... 502-447-1000 199 G
lking@spencerian.edu
KING, Leslie .... 770-426-2713 128 C
lesliek@life.edu
KING, Leslie .... 614-947-6132 382 H
leslie.king@franklin.edu
KING, Libby .... 423-869-6358 458 B
libby.king@lmunet.edu
KING, Linda .... 903-886-5013 485 E
linda.king@tamuc.edu
KING, Lonnie .... 614-688-8749 389 A
king.1518@osu.edu
KING, Lynn .... 910-879-5520 360 C
lking@bladencc.edu
KING, Lynne, O .... 518-381-1240 342 E
kinglo@sunysccc.edu
KING, Marlin .... 601-877-6471 266 C
mbking@alcorn.edu
KING, Marsha, M .... 260-399-7700 174 C
mking@sf.edu
KING, Martha .... 708-216-3354 151 E
mking17@luc.edu
KING, Mary .... 641-472-1144 181 A
registrar@mum.edu
KING, Mary .... 334-285-5177.... 4 K
mary.king@istc.edu
KING, Mary .... 940-552-6291 496 B
mking@vernoncollege.edu
KING, Mary, B .... 336-734-7901 362 F
mking@forsythtech.edu
KING, Mary Jo .... 270-706-8530 195 K
maryjo.king@kctcs.edu
KING, Maura .... 845-451-1429 323 E
m_king@culinary.edu
KING, Michael .... 706-754-7711 129 B
mking@northgatech.edu
KING, Michael, A .... 540-432-4261 507 A
michael.king@emu.edu
KING, Michelle .... 310-434-3323.. 65 B
king_michelle@smc.edu
KING, Mike .... 812-535-5273 172 F
mking2@smwc.edu
KING, Miriam, E .... 410-837-4612 221 B
mking@ubalt.edu
KING, Natalie .... 831-582-3609.. 34 C
nmking@csumb.edu
KING, Patricia, J .... 918-687-3299 396 F
kingp@bacone.edu
KING, Peggy .... 630-752-5246 163 G
peggy.king@wheaton.edu
KING, Peter .... 843-661-1362 446 E
pking@fmarion.edu
KING, Phillip .... 503-594-3430 405 A
phillipk@clackamas.edu
KING, Phyllis .... 414-229-6175 540 A
pking@wm.edu
KING, Rhonda .... 504-671-5051 203 F
rking1@dcc.edu
KING, Rhonda .... 717-766-2511 426 B
rking@messiah.edu
KING, Rochelle .... 919-546-8565 368 G
rking@shawu.edu
KING, Ronan .... 276-944-6125 507 E
rking@ehc.edu
KING, S. Bruce .... 336-758-5774 372 G
kingsb@wfu.edu
KING, Samuel .... 901-435-1509 457 N
samuel_king@loc.edu
KING, Sandra .... 507-389-1111 260 A
sandra.king@mnsu.edu
KING, Sarah .... 843-792-3621 447 G
kingsara@musc.edu
KING, Sasha .... 310-434-3404.. 65 B
king_sasha@smc.edu
KING, Shawn .... 509-359-6878 522 C
sking@ewu.edu
KING, Shelly .... 816-415-5963 285 K
kings@william.jewell.edu
KING, Stacey .... 478-289-2145 124 B
sking@ega.edu
KING, Stephanie .... 413-565-1000 222 G
sking@baypath.edu
KING, Stephanie .... 716-926-8888 327 F
sking@hilbert.edu
KING, Steven .... 413-662-5410 230 C
steven.king@mcla.edu
KING, Sue .... 816-501-3759 272 E
sue.king@avila.edu
KING, Susan, L .... 207-780-4681 213 A
susank@usm.maine.edu
KING, Susan, R .... 919-962-1204 371 A
susanking@unc.edu
KING, JR.,
Talmadge, E .... 415-476-2342.. 72 C
Talmadge.King@ucsf.edu
KING, Terry .... 765-285-1333 164 D
tsking@bsu.edu
KING, Theresa .... 201-684-7800 305 F
0396mgr@fheg.follett.com
KING, Thomas .... 610-896-1111 420 J
tking@haverford.edu
KING, Tiffany .... 708-239-4743 160 L
tiffany.king@trnty.edu
KING, Tim .... 256-782-5020.... 4 L
tbking@jsu.edu
KING, Tom .... 610-896-1111 413 D
tking01@brynmawr.edu
KING, Tom .... 216-881-1700 389 G
tking@ohiotech.edu
KING, Tommy .... 601-318-6495 271 F
pres@wmcarey.edu
KING, Venita .... 256-372-5248.... 1 A
venita.king@aamu.edu
KING, Victor, I .... 323-343-3054.. 34 A
vking@cslanet.calstatela.edu
KING, W. Cody .... 229-931-2045 126 C
cody.king@gsw.edu
KING, Wayne .... 815-280-2210 148 K
wking@jjc.edu
KING, Wendell, C .... 913-684-3280 548 F
wendell.king@leavenworth.army.mil
KING, Wendy .... 336-887-3000 358 E
KING, Wendy, L .... 304-293-7304 533 D
wking@hsc.wvu.edu
KING, William .... 540-231-5992 507 D
bking@vcom.vt.edu
KING, William, L .... 903-510-2252 491 A
bkin@tjc.edu
KING, Yolanda, M .... 617-627-3248 237 C
yolanda.king@tufts.edu
KING-JUPITER,
Kimberly .... 615-963-5446 461 F
kkingjup@tnstate.edu
KING-LEROY,
Cynthia, B .... 518-783-2420 342 H
kingleroy@siena.edu
KING SANDERS, Nancy 361-593-3290 486 A
nancy.kingsanders@tamuk.edu
KINGAN, Michael .... 817-272-2584 493 L
mkkingan@uta.edu
KINGCADE, Fawn, M .... 580-327-8533 399 F
fmkingcade@nwosu.edu
KINGHAM, Margaret, T 610-566-1776 440 C
mkingham@williamson.edu
KINGKADE, H.K .... 502-863-8209 195 A
hk_kingkade@georgetowncollege.edu
KINGREY, Daryl, L .... 540-887-7000 510 A
KINGRY, Kelly .... 912-486-7618 129 E
kkingry@ogeecheetech.edu
KINGSBURY, Judy .... 507-285-7216 261 D
judy.kingsbury@rctc.edu
KINGSFORD, Laura .... 562-985-5559.. 33 F
laura.kingsford@csulb.edu
KINGSLEY, Hal .... 716-614-6895 336 D
hkingsley@niagaracc.suny.edu
KINGSLEY, Margery .... 580-581-6900 397 A
margeryk@cameron.edu
KINGSOLVER, Robert .... 502-272-3628 193 E
kingsolver@bellarmine.edu
KINGSTON, Chris .... 419-372-7052 377 I
ckingst@bgsu.edu
KINGSTON, Jeffrey .... 925-424-1631.. 37 O
jkingston@laspositascollege.edu
KINGSTON, Jeffrey .... 925-424-1630.. 37 O
jkingston@laspositascollege.edu
KINGSTON, Laura .... 206-934-7959 526 B
laura.kingston@seattlecolleges.edu
KINGSTON, Linda .... 651-846-1411 261 G
linda.kingston@saintpaul.edu
KINGTON, Raynard, S .. 641-269-3000 178 I
kington@grinnell.edu
KINIMAKA, Malia .... 562-985-4296.. 33 F
malia.kinimaka@csulb.edu
KINKADE, Mike .... 870-584-4471.. 24 E
mkinkade@cccua.edu
KINKEL, Anthony .... 931-393-1682 463 B
tkinkel@mscc.edu
KINKELA, David .... 716-673-3529 343 F
david.kinkela@fredonia.edu
KINKELLA, John .... 775-445-3271 296 A
john.kinkella@wnc.edu
KINKELLA, John .... 775-445-3271 296 A
John.kinkella@wnc.edu
KINKEMA, Kathleen ...... 970-943-7133.. 87 F
kkinkema@western.edu

KISTLER, Kevin 209-381-6489 54 C kevin.kistler@mccd.edu
KISTLER, Ron 580-928-5533 402 G ron.kistler@swosu.edu
KISTNER, Angie 618-437-5321 156 I kistner@rlc.edu
KISTNER, Janet 850-644-7836 115 A kistner@psy.fsu.edu
KISTNER, Warren 309-556-3071 148 A wkistner@iwu.edu
KITAGAWA, Susan 831-646-4014 54 H skitagawa@mpc.edu
KITAJIMA, Naomi 650-949-7117 45 A kitajimanaomi@fhda.edu
KITCH, Rhonda 701-231-7987 374 C rhonda.k.kitch@ndsu.edu
KITCH, William, A 325-942-2483 489 E william.kitch@angelo.edu
KITCHEN, Augusta 803-780-1159 451 G akitchen@voorhees.edu
KITCHEN, Barbara 859-846-5725 198 G bkitchen@midway.edu
KITCHEN, Clifford 719-549-3121 85 A clifford.kitchen@pueblocc.edu
KITCHEN, Janie 606-326-2163 195 H janie.kitchen@kctcs.edu
KITCHEN, Mark 307-754-6405 546 I Mark.Kitchen@nwc.edu
KITCHEN, Steve 650-949-6150 44 M kitchensteve@fhda.edu
KITCHEN, Todd 479-619-4232 22 B tkitchen@nwacc.edu
KITCHENS, Elizabeth 605-999-7136 452 H elizabeth.kitchens@mitchelltech.edu
KITCHENS, Joann 701-662-1502 375 A joann.kitchens@lrsc.edu
KITCHENS, Joseph, H 770-720-5966 130 E jhk@reinhardt.edu
KITCHENS, Larry, E 817-257-7121 486 G l.kitchens@tcu.edu
KITCHENS, Penny 478-553-2060 129 C pkitchens@oftc.edu
KITCHENS, Ronnie 601-426-6346 270 D rkitchens@southeasternbaptist.edu
KITCHENS, Tempie 770-233-6170 132 B tkitchens@sctech.edu
KITCHENS, Willie 404-527-4520 122 D wkitchens@carver.edu
KITCHIN, Steven, H 401-739-5000 441 E skitchin@neit.edu
KITCHINGS, Maribeth 601-974-1002 268 D kitchme@millsaps.edu
KITE, Joy, A 608-822-2319 544 C jkite@swtc.edu
KITE, Michelle 269-782-1302 250 D mkite@swmich.edu
KITEI, Susan, C 610-758-3870 424 B sck0@lehigh.edu
KITHCART, Jane 845-687-5111 350 I kithcarj@sunyulster.edu
KITSON, Anna 502-410-6200 194 N akitson@galencollege.edu
KITTEL, Jane 715-675-3331 544 A kittelj@ntc.edu
KITTINGER, Fred 407-823-1208 115 C fred.kittinger@ucf.edu
KITTLE, Daniel 319-352-8745 183 J daniel.kittle@wartburg.edu
KITTLE, Paul 336-841-9107 357 E pkittle@highpoint.edu
KITTLE, Sandra 248-414-6900 246 F financialaid@mji.edu
KITTLESON, Mark 585-395-2350 345 A mkittleson@brockport.edu
KITTNER, Missy 254-299-8514 478 C mkittner@mclennan.edu
KITTO, Kathleen 360-650-5929 528 D kathleen.kitto@wwu.edu
KITTREDGE, Cynthia Briggs 512-472-4133 482 E cynthia.kittredge@ssw.edu
KITTRELL-MIKELL, Deborah 478-289-2161 124 B dkittrell@ega.edu
KITTS, Justin 606-546-1232 200 E jkitts@unionky.edu
KITTS, Kenneth 256-765-4211 9 D kkitts@una.edu
KITZINGER, Denis 603-880-8308 298 I dkitzinger@thomasmorecollege.edu
KITZINGER, Sara 603-880-8308 298 I skitzinger@thomasmorecollege.edu
KIVETZ, Robert 212-998-4611 336 C rsk1@nyu.edu
KIWUS, Christopher 540-231-6291 518 B chkiwus@vt.edu
KIYOSHI, Jack, O 670-234-5498 550 B
KIZINA, Terrance 412-536-1275 422 E terrance.kizina@laroche.edu
KJARTANSON, Mary 619-221-2144 62 H mkjartan@sdccd.edu
KJERULF GREER, Beau 203-396-8064 91 G greerb@sacredheart.edu
KKAYANAN, Leslie 757-382-9900 96 H
KLAAR, Desiree 619-482-6309 68 D dklaar@swccd.edu
KLAAREN, Jon 334-285-5177 4 K jon.klaaren@istc.edu
KLAAS, Carlene 312-362-8146 143 G cklaas@depaul.edu
KLAAS, Gerry 314-659-0816 276 H klaas@kenrick.edu
KLAASSEN, Sara 816-322-0110 272 L sara.klaassen@calvary.edu
KLABECHEK, IV, John 262-551-5911 535 E jklabechek@carthage.edu
KLADIVKO, Deborah 803-641-3577 450 C debk@usca.edu
KLAFFKE, David 360-383-3016 528 E dklaffke@whatcom.ctc.edu
KLAG, Michael, J 410-955-3540 216 A michaelj.klag@jhu.edu
KLAIBER, Beverly, G 530-226-4179 66 G bklaiber@simpsonu.edu
KLAIBER, James, S 440-775-5603 388 B Jim.Klaiber@oberlin.edu
KLAICH, Daniel, J 775-784-4901 295 B chancellor@nevada.edu
KLAPPER, Robert 770-729-8400 120 F
KLARE, Diane 860-685-2887 93 B dklare@wesleyan.edu
KLASEN, James 617-588-1344 223 D jklasen@bfit.edu
KLASKO, Stephen, K 215-955-6617 436 F stephen.klasko@jefferson.edu
KLASS, Stephen, P 413-597-3118 238 E stephen.p.klass@williams.edu
KLAUBER, James, S 256-306-2555 2 F jklauber@calhoun.edu
KLAUDER, Mark, J 802-447-6322 503 A mklauder@svc.edu
KLAUS, Allen, R 210-434-6711 479 P arklaus@lake.ollusa.edu
KLAUS, Carrie, F 765-658-6568 165 G cklaus@depauw.edu
KLAUS, Chad, L 609-258-5498 305 C klaus@princeton.edu
KLAUS, Dennis 801-957-4250 500 E dennis.klaus@slcc.edu
KLAUS, Eric 315-781-3304 327 G klaus@hws.edu
KLAUS, John Mark 814-472-3391 434 F jklaus@francis.edu
KLAUS, Katie 920-433-6651 534 K katie.klaus@bellincollege.edu
KLAUSMEYER, Robert 573-875-7304 273 D rklausmeyer@ccis.edu
KLAVER, Lenny 906-487-7349 242 M lenny.klaver@finlandia.edu
KLAWE, Maria, M 909-921-8120 46 K klawe@hmc.edu
KLAWITTER, Christina 608-363-2660 534 L klawitterc@beloit.edu
KLAWUNN, Margaret, M 401-863-1800 441 A margaret_klawunn@brown.edu
KLAY, Kathy, A 937-328-6085 379 L klayk@clarkstate.edu
KLEBE, Kelli 719-255-3417 86 F kklebe@uccs.edu
KLEBESADEL, Shirley 715-232-2190 541 B klebesadels@uwstout.edu
KLECKNER, Joan 610-902-8201 414 B joan.d.kleckner@cabrini.edu
KLEDZIK, Eric 321-674-8107 103 R ekledzik@fit.edu
KLEEMAN, Amy 407-582-1238 118 I akleeman@valenciacollege.edu
KLEEMAN, Beverly, S 509-777-4548 529 A bkleeman@whitworth.edu
KLEICH, Tammie 308-635-6072 294 C kleicht@wncc.edu
KLEIN, Andrew, O 508-849-3313 222 C aklein@annamaria.edu
KLEIN, Andrew, R 317-274-2581 168 E anrklein@iupui.edu
KLEIN, Barb 641-648-4611 179 K barb.klein@iavalley.edu
KLEIN, Cynthia 412-809-5100 433 D klein.cynthia@pti.edu
KLEIN, David, A 434-223-6129 508 B dklein@hsc.edu
KLEIN, Edward 518-562-4120 321 D edward.klein@clinton.edu
KLEIN, Erin 701-252-3467 375 J eklein@uj.edu
KLEIN, Gary 608-663-6713 536 A garyklein@edgewood.edu
KLEIN, Jacob 248-689-8282 251 I jklein@walshcollege.edu
KLEIN, Jacqueline 518-454-5111 322 C
KLEIN, Janie 925-631-4572 61 G mminguil@stmarys-ca.edu
KLEIN, Jeff 909-652-6317 38 A jeff.klein@chaffey.edu
KLEIN, Jim 502-456-6508 200 B jklein@sullivan.edu
KLEIN, Joanne, R 240-895-4251 218 B jrklein@smcm.edu
KLEIN, Joy 480-994-9244 17 P joyk@swiha.edu
KLEIN, Judy 267-341-3615 420 K jklein@holyfamily.edu
KLEIN, June 650-433-3849 58 B jklein@paloaltou.edu
KLEIN, Karen 580-774-3268 402 G karen.klein@swosu.edu
KLEIN, Lori 907-796-6529 11 A lori.klein@uas.alaska.edu
KLEIN, Marjorie, S 814-332-5910 411 F mklein@allegheny.edu
KLEIN, Mendel 718-384-5460 353 K
KLEIN, Michael 718-368-5087 320 A mklein@kbcc.cuny.edu
KLEIN, Michael 215-204-9570 436 C michael.klein@temple.edu
KLEIN, Michelle, W 504-866-7426 206 D finance@nds.edu
KLEIN, Paul 415-749-4589 62 I paulklein@sfai.edu
KLEIN, Ray 812-941-2457 169 A rayklein@ius.edu
KLEIN, Sandy, L 701-483-2371 373 H sandy.klein@dickinsonstate.edu
KLEIN, Sara 718-420-4518 352 C sara.klein@wagner.edu
KLEIN, Scott 812-866-7061 166 E klein@hanover.edu
KLEIN, Shalin 785-539-3571 189 D sklein@mccks.edu
KLEIN, Shelley 661-763-7711 69 E sklein@taftcollege.edu
KLEIN, Stacy 510-593-2930 65 D sklein@saybrook.edu
KLEIN, Steve 503-352-2822 408 I kleinsk@pacificu.edu
KLEIN, Steven 517-629-0321 239 A sklein@albion.edu
KLEIN, Stuart 212-431-2170 335 G Stuart.Klein@nyls.edu
KLEIN, Terry 715-468-2815 544 F Terry.Klein@witc.edu
KLEIN-WHEATON, Kristin 716-270-4432 325 A kleinwheaton@ecc.edu
KLEINDL, Brad 816-584-6308 280 F brad.kleindl@park.edu
KLEINE, Patricia, A 715-836-2320 539 E kleinepa@uwec.edu
KLEINER, Zev 347-394-1036 316 E zkleiner@ateret.net
KLEINHANS, Randy 574-372-5100 166 D kleinhrp@grace.edu
KLEINKAUFMAN, Dovid 718-327-7600 353 B yfr1@verizon.net
KLEINKOPF, Karl 208-732-6201 137 K csitrustees@csi.edu
KLEINLEIN, Tom 912-478-5047 126 B tkleinlein@georgiasouthern.edu
KLEINMAN, Gary 858-642-8357 55 J gkleinman@nu.edu
KLEINMAN, Kent 607-255-9110 323 C aapdean@cornell.edu
KLEINMAN, Naftaly 212-343-1234 332 I nkleinman@mcny.edu
KLEINMAN, Yisroel 718-853-8500 350 B
KLEINPETER, Jennifer 225-743-8500 204 C jkleinpeter@rpcc.edu
KLEINSCHMIDT, Robert 610-359-5359 416 G rkleinschmidt@dccc.edu
KLEINSORGE, Ilene, K 541-737-6024 408 F ilene.kleinsorge@bus.oregonstate.edu
KLEINWORTH, Tom 713-798-6498 469 C tklein@bcm.edu
KLEISER, Richele 559-325-3600 31 A rkleiser@chsu.org
KLEMANN, M. Adam 330-471-8308 385 G aklemann@malone.edu
KLEMENS, Kristina 262-595-2004 540 C klemens@uwp.edu
KLEMENT, Emily 940-872-4002 479 K eklement@nctc.edu
KLEMIUK, Christy 903-463-8650 474 K klemiukc@grayson.edu
KLEMM, Dave 217-732-3155 150 H dklemm@lincolncollege.edu
KLEMM, Jotisa 817-515-3083 484 B jotisa.klemm@tccd.edu
KLEMMER, John 919-658-7836 369 B jklemmer@umo.edu
KLEMPA, Richard, M 304-243-2394 534 H rklempa@wju.edu
KLEMPNER, Mark, D 508-856-8000 229 B mark.klempner@umassmed.edu
KLEN, Joseph, R 765-361-6052 175 B klenj@wabash.edu
KLENIEWSKI, Nancy 607-436-2500 344 B klenien@oneonta.edu
KLENKE, James, W 618-650-2020 159 I jklenke@siue.edu
KLEPETAR, Adam 320-308-1060 261 E ASKlepetar@stcloudstate.edu
KLEPITSCH, Heather, A 815-227-2446 158 B heatherklepitsch@sacn.edu
KLEPONIS, Stephen 610-526-6017 420 C skleponis@harcum.edu
KLESCHICK, Paul 413-205-3212 221 G paul.kleschick@aic.edu
KLESGES, Lisa, M 901-678-4637 462 B lmklsges@memphis.edu
KLESNER, Joe, L 740-427-5114 384 P klesner@kenyon.edu
KLETT, Breanna 562-903-4751 29 F breanna.klett@biola.edu
KLETZER, Lori, G 207-859-4770 210 A Lori.Kletzer@colby.edu
KLEVA, Barbara 609-984-1124 308 H bkleva@tesc.edu
KLEVENO, Robert 951-222-8000 61 B
KLEYN, Henk 616-977-0599 249 B henk.kleyn@prts.edu
KLIER, Jody 701-845-7297 374 D jody.klier@vcsu.edu
KLIEWER, Lee 570-586-2400 435 H lkliewer@summitu.edu
KLIEWONEIT, Chris 989-386-6652 247 B ckliewon@midmich.edu
KLIKA, William 201-443-8972 302 H helen_bajek@fdu.edu
KLIMA, Kris 785-670-1030 192 B kris.klima@washburn.edu
KLIMCZYK, Karen 219-464-5015 174 E karen.klimczyk@valpo.edu
KLIMITCHEK, Missy 361-572-6407 496 D missy.klimitchek@victoriacollege.edu
KLIMKOWSKI, Ann Francis 419-885-3211 385 F aklimkowski@lourdes.edu
KLIMOFF, Dodi 215-635-7300 419 D dklimoff@gratz.edu
KLIMPT, Kelly 409-944-1356 474 G kklimpt@gc.edu
KLINE, Amy 212-875-4504 315 F akline@bankstreet.edu
KLINE, Bob 251-626-3303 8 C bkline@ussa.edu
KLINE, Christina 715-394-8055 541 C ckline@uwsuper.edu
KLINE, Frank, M 253-535-7272 524 I klinefm@plu.edu
KLINE, Joseph 575-562-2733 310 I joseph.kline@enmu.edu
KLINE, Julie 651-523-2021 256 B jkline04@hamline.edu
KLINE, Julie 909-593-3511 73 B jkline@laverne.edu
KLINE, Kimberly, N 210-458-4819 494 D KIM.KLINE@UTSA.EDU
KLINE, Loni 570-321-4199 425 B klinel@lycoming.edu
KLINE, Mae 407-328-2096 113 A kline@seminolestate.edu
KLINE, Meredith 978-468-7111 227 B mmkline@gcts.edu
KLINE, Patricia 701-671-2106 375 B patty.kline@ndscs.edu
KLINE, Rebecca 573-876-7111 283 A rkline@stephens.edu
KLINE, Richard 440-375-7512 385 B rkline@lec.edu
KLINE, Ronald, J 610-861-1510 426 H kliner@moravian.edu
KLINE, Sharon 360-475-7778 524 H skline@olympic.edu
KLINE, Thomas 262-551-6036 535 E tkline@carthage.edu
KLINE, William 978-837-5134 233 G klinew@merrimack.edu
KLINE, William 812-877-8136 172 C william.kline@rose-hulman.edu
KLINE-SYMINGTON, Susan 508-362-2131 231 D sklinesy@capecod.edu
KLINESMITH, Jerry 740-264-5591 381 J jklinesmith@egcc.edu
KLING, Deron 608-663-4420 536 A dkling@edgewood.edu
KLING, Karl 517-586-3018 241 B
KLING, Lenda 850-201-8660 117 B klingl@tcc.fl.edu
KLINGBEIL, Nathan, W 937-775-5007 396 A nathan.klingbeil@wright.edu

KNOTT, William .... 616-222-1918 241 G
bill.knott@cornerstone.edu
KNOTTS, Cecil .... 318-357-5965 208 D
knottsc@nsula.edu
KNOTTS, David .... 636-798-2166 276 L
dknotts@lindenwood.edu
KNOTTS, Debby .... 505-277-5765 313 H
debby@unm.edu
KNOUSE, Christine .... 717-262-2016 440 D
cknouse@wilson.edu
KNOWLES, Harley .... 423-746-5201 464 D
hknowles@twcnet.edu
KNOWLES, Lorelette ..... 425-968-3400.. 65 D
lknowles@saybrook.edu
KNOWLES, Melody, D .. 703-370-6600 511 B
KNOWLES, Monica .... 360-992-2904 521 A
mknowles@clark.edu
KNOWLES, Susan .... 315-268-6633 321 C
sknowles@clarkson.edu
KNOWLTON, Eloise ...... 508-767-7487 222 D
eknowlton@assumption.edu
KNOX, Chrisanne .... 925-969-2048.. 42 E
cknox@dvc.edu
KNOX, Craig .... 850-201-8660 117 B
KNOX, Darby .... 585-395-5160 345 A
dknox@brockport.edu
KNOX, David, K .... 864-656-0868 444 E
knox2@clemson.edu
KNOX, George, C .... 620-421-6700 189 B
georgek@labette.edu
KNOX, Linda, B .... 219-989-3169 171 L
linda.knox@purduecal.edu
KNOX, Lindsay .... 503-554-2242 406 A
lknox@georgefox.edu
KNOX, Michael, J .... 806-651-2050 486 D
mknox@wtamu.edu
KNOX, Pamela .... 615-366-4482 461 B
pamela.knox@tbr.edu
KNOX, Ruth, A .... 478-757-5212 134 E
rknox@wesleyancollege.edu
KNOX, Teresa, L .... 918-610-0027 397 H
tknox@communitycarecollege.edu
KNOX, Tracey .... 970-521-6643.. 84 H
tracey.knox@njc.edu
KNUCKLES, Leator .... 410-238-9000.. 96 H
KNUDSEN, Alice, B ...... 510-430-2350.. 54 F
aknudsen@mills.edu
KNUDSEN, H. Peter ...... 406-496-4395 288 C
pknudsen@mtech.edu
KNUDSEN, J. Todd .... 562-902-3358.. 67 J
toddknudsen@scuhs.edu
KNUDSEN, Ross .... 208-376-7731 137 D
rknudsen@boisebible.edu
KNUDSON, Dan .... 218-299-6521 259 H
dan.knudson@minnesota.edu
KNUDSON, Edward, T .. 661-722-6300.. 27 P
eknudson@avc.edu
KNUDSON, Kari .... 701-224-5604 374 E
kari.l.knudson@bismarckstate.edu
KNUDSON, Paula, M .... 608-785-8150 539 G
pknudson@uwlax.edu
KNUDSON-CARL, Tara .. 402-399-2449 289 I
tknudsoncarl@csm.edu
KNUEPFER, Peter .... 518-320-1376 343 B
peter.knuepfer@suny.edu
KNUTEL, Phillip .... 781-239-4225 222 E
pknutel@babson.edu
KNUTH, Barbara, A ...... 607-255-5864 323 C
bak3@cornell.edu
KNUTH, Doug .... 775-784-6900 295 H
dknuth@unr.edu
KNUTSEN, Mark .... 423-697-4785 462 C
mark.knutsen@chattanoogastate.edu
KNUTSON, Craig .... 405-208-5000 400 A
crknutson@okcu.edu
KNUTSON, Jennifer .... 605-331-6611 454 E
jennifer.knutson@usiouxfalls.edu
KNUTSON, Karen .... 320-363-5922 254 J
kknutson@csbsju.edu
KNUTSON, Karen, G ..... 320-363-5922 264 A
kknutson@csbsju.edu
KNUTSON, Polly .... 208-885-6651 139 C
pknutson@uidaho.edu
KNUTSON, Sherry .... 415-749-4571.. 62 I
sknutson@sfai.edu
KNUTSON-GARCIA,
Julie .... 734-487-3152 242 J
jknutson@emich.edu
KNUTSON-KOLODZNE,
Jim .... 320-308-5447 261 E
jkolodzne@stcloudstate.edu
KNUTSON-MILLER, Kari 657-278-7511.. 33 E
kkmiller@fullerton.edu
KNUTZEN, Kathleen ...... 661-654-2210.. 32 G
kknutzen@csub.edu
KO, Jeanne .... 212-472-1500 336 A
jko@nysid.edu
KO, Shinsaeng .... 404-727-0825 124 D
shinsaeng.ko@emory.edu
KO, Vivien .... 323-343-2730.. 34 A
vko@calstatela.edu
KO, Yoo, K .... 571-730-4750 278 D
wdc@midwest.edu
KOAN, Mark .... 602-285-7855.. 15 C
mark.koan@phoenixcollege.edu
KOBACK, Beth .... 704-971-8500 355 J
bkoback@charlottelaw.edu
KOBALLA, Thomas .... 912-478-5648 126 B
tkoballa@georgiasouthern.edu
KOBAYASHI, Frank .... 916-485-6028.. 52 I
kobayaf@arc.losrios.edu
KOBERNA, Sharon .... 480-517-8220.. 15 D
sharon.koberna@riosalado.edu
KOBES, Patricia .... 845-574-4280 339 I
pkobes@sunyrockland.edu
KOBLER, Soheila .... 973-618-3724 300 H
skobler@caldwell.edu
KOBOLAKIS, Evan .... 516-876-3379 345 E
kobolakise@oldwestbury.edu
KOBRITZ, Richard .... 818-345-7921.. 41 F
rkobritz@columbiacollege.edu
KOBRYN, Danielle .... 845-398-4016 341 H
dkobryn@stac.edu
KOBUS, Gloria .... 330-941-3142 396 C
gjkobus@ysu.edu
KOBYLSKI, Janet .... 570-408-4501 440 B
janet.kobylski@wilkes.edu
KOCAR, Deb .... 617-349-8800 228 B
ugadm@lesley.edu
KOCER, Ken .... 605-668-1589 452 I
kkocer@mtmc.edu
KOCH, Bill .... 252-328-6166 369 E
kochb@ecu.edu
KOCH, Bradley .... 610-902-8571 414 B
bradley.r.koch@cabrini.edu
KOCH, Dennis .... 207-768-9560 212 H
dennis.koch@umpi.edu
KOCH, Don .... 618-634-3289 159 A
donk@shawneecc.edu
KOCH, Erec .... 646-660-6530 318 C
Erec.Koch@baruch.cuny.edu
KOCH, Greg .... 770-960-1298 127 E
gkoch@ict.edu
KOCH, Kelly .... 989-386-6639 247 B
kkoch@midmich.edu
KOCH, Kevin .... 781-762-1211 226 E
kkoch@fmc.edu
KOCH, Paul .... 831-459-5861.. 72 E
plkoch@ucolick.org
KOCH, Paul .... 563-333-6212 182 E
KochPaulC@sau.edu
KOCH, Susan .... 217-206-6634 161 E
koch@uis.edu
KOCH, Susan .... 217-206-6634 161 G
koch@uis.edu
KOCH, Thomas, L .... 520-621-2448.. 18 E
tlkoch@email.arizona.edu
KOCH, Virginia, A .... 334-844-3466.... 1 G
vak0001@auburn.edu
KOCHAN, Julie .... 518-454-5121 322 C
kochanj@strose.edu
KOCHAN, Roman .... 562-985-4047.. 33 F
roman.kochan@csulb.edu
KOCHANEK, Lea .... 210-341-1366 479 N
lkochanek@ost.edu
KOCHARD, Dale, A .... 610-758-5801 424 B
dak304@lehigh.edu
KOCHARD,
Lawrence, E .... 434-924-8976 514 A
lek8e@virginia.edu
KOCHER, Andy, M .... 317-788-3493 173 I
akocher@uindy.edu
KOCHER, Becky .... 419-372-2424 377 I
rkocher@bgsu.edu
KOCHER, Betty, A .... 269-387-2360 252 I
betty.kocher@wmich.edu
KOCHER, Craig, T 804-289-8500 513M
ckocher@richmond.edu
KOCHERA, Melissah ...... 203-596-4652.. 91 D
mkochera@post.edu
KOCHEVAR, Brenda .... 218-749-0314 259 D
b.kochevar@mesabirange.edu
KOCHEVAR, Deborah .... 508-887-4700 237 C
deborah.kochevar@tufts.edu
KOCHIEN, Kenneth, G .. 603-526-3627 296 I
kkochien@colby-sawyer.edu
KOCHIS, Stephen, J ..... 845-575-3000 331 L
stephen.kochis@marist.edu
KOCHON, Barbara .... 413-565-1000 222 G
bkochon@baypath.edu
KOCHUBA, Sara .... 724-503-1001 439 B
skochuba@washjeff.edu
KOCIAN, Bryce .... 979-532-6315 497 F
brycek@wcjc.edu
KOCIAN, Justin 402-494-2311 291M
jkocian@thenicc.edu
KOCIK, Piotr .... 718-518-6610 319 D
pkocik@hostos.cuny.edu
KOCIOLEK, Patrick .... 303-492-8464.. 86 E
patrick.kociolek@colorado.edu
KOCOUR, Bruce .... 865-471-3240 455 G
bkocour@cn.edu
KOCSIS, Katie, L .... 716-286-8669 336 E
kkocsis@niagara.edu
KOCZON, Lenore .... 701-858-3310 374 B
lenore.koczon@minotstateu.edu
KODAMA, Be-Jay .... 808-739-8526 135 A
bkodama@chaminade.edu
KODAT, Catherine .... 503-768-7100 406 H
kodat@lclark.edu
KODY, Hillary .... 617-682-1507 226 D
hkody@eds.edu
KOEBEL, Dave .... 402-457-2391 291 E
dkoebel@mccneb.edu
KOECHIG, Donna .... 541-463-5307 406 F
koechigd@lanecc.edu
KOEGLER, Jason, W ..... 304-336-8302 533 A
jkoegler@westliberty.edu
KOEHLER, Al .... 636-922-8452 281 C
alkoehler@stchas.edu
KOEHLER, David .... 308-635-6021 294 C
koehlerd@wncc.edu
KOEHLER, Donna .... 253-589-5588 521 B
donna.koehler@cptc.edu
KOEHLER, John .... 406-791-5330 288 J
jkoehler01@ugf.edu
KOEHLER, Larry .... 810-232-8153 247 F
larry.koehler@mcc.edu
KOEHLER, Martha Kaye 813-253-7007 106 C
mkoehler@hccfl.edu
KOEHLER, R. Brien .... 262-646-6545 538 B
rkoehler@nashotah.edu
KOEHLER, Randy .... 513-244-8449 379 I
randy.koehler@ccuniversity.edu
KOEHN, Effie, F .... 406-243-5580 287 D
effie.koehn@umontana.edu
KOEHN, Jack .... 224-293-5961.. 81 H
KOEHN, Michelle .... 316-226-2002 175 D
Michelle.Koehn@AllenCollege.edu
KOEHN, Suzie .... 307-855-2148 545 a
suzie@cwc.edu
KOEHNEKE, Mary, A .... 716-888-2300 317 H
mkoehneke@canisius.edu
KOEHNEMANN, Kristin . 618-664-7020 145 E
kristin.koehnemann@greenville.edu
KOEHNKE, Paul .... 704-330-6121 361 D
paul.koehnke@cpcc.edu
KOELBL, James .... 207-602-2678 213 B
jkoelbl@une.edu
KOELKER, June .... 817-257-7106 486 G
j.koelker@tcu.edu
KOELLER, Martin, E ...... 973-761-9782 308 C
martin.koeller@shu.edu
KOELTZOW, Dawn .... 309-677-2510 140 H
dkoeltzow@fsmail.bradley.edu
KOENECKE, David .... 660-626-2410 271 G
dkoenecke@atsu.edu
KOENIG, Gigi .... 715-394-8014 541 C
gkoenig1@uwsuper.edu
KOENIG, Jason, T .... 864-833-8398 448 E
jtkoenig@presby.edu
KOENIG, Jerry, L 317-921-4491 169M
jkoenig@ivytech.edu
KOENIG, Lucas .... 920-433-6621 534 K
lucas.koenig@bellincollege.edu
KOEPKE, Andrea .... 419-434-4677 393 F
koepke@findlay.edu
KOEPKE, Janelle .... 563-589-0712 183 K
jkoepke@wartburgseminary.edu
KOEPKE, Mark .... 701-252-3467 375 J
mkoepke@uj.edu
KOEPPEL, Edmund .... 516-572-7126 334 A
edmund.koeppel@ncc.edu
KOEPPEN, Bruce .... 203-528-5301.. 91 E
bruce.koeppen@quinnipiac.edu
KOERBER, Brent .... 614-236-7167 378 H
bkoerber@capital.edu
KOERNER, Mari, E .... 602-543-6352.. 11 J
mari.koerner@asu.edu
KOERNER, Melissa .... 801-832-2601 501 C
mkoerner@westminstercollege.edu
KOERNERT, Andrew, H . 757-594-8480 506 I
andrew.koernert@cnu.edu
KOERWER, V. Scott ...... 570-504-7000 415 E
vkoerwer@tcmc.edu
KOESER, Bryan .... 920-693-1731 543 B
bryan.koeser@gotoltc.edu
KOESTER, Craig .... 651-641-3471 256 J
ckoester@luthersem.edu
KOETTING, Sandy .... 573-681-5071 276 K
koettings@lincolnu.edu
KOETZNER, John .... 707-468-3000.. 54 A
jkoetzne@mendocino.edu
KOEVEN, Gary, J 435-652-7770 499M
koeven@dixie.edu
KOFFLER, Jeromy, A .... 503-943-7470 410 H
koffler@up.edu
KOFNOVEC, David .... 254-867-3791 488 B
david.kofnovec@tstc.edu
KOFRON, Cheryl, L .... 563-884-5670 182 D
cheryl.kofron@palmer.edu
KOGA, Laura, A .... 815-740-3392 162 F
lkoga@stfrancis.edu
KOGAN, Alexander .... 212-327-8001 339 H
kogana@rockefeller.edu
KOGAN, Lilly .... 212-517-3929 343 A
l.kogan@sothebysinstitute.com
KOGAN, Linda .... 719-255-3757.. 86 F
lkogan@uccs.edu
KOGUT, Leonard .... 616-632-2885 239 E
lvk001@aquinas.edu
KOHKE, Dennis .... 707-545-3647.. 29 D
dennis@berginu.edu
KOHL, Bunny .... 856-227-7200 301 A
bkohl@camdencc.edu
KOHL, James .... 978-934-2108 229 A
James_Kohl@uml.edu
KOHL, Marie .... 315-792-5340 333 D
mkohl@mvcc.edu
KOHL, Troy .... 920-735-5766 542 N
kohlt@fvtc.edu
KOHLER, Dave .... 360-867-6451 522 J
kohlerd@evergreen.edu
KOHLER, Donald .... 712-325-3262 180 B
dkohler@iwcc.edu
KOHLER, Elizabeth .... 734-462-4400 250 A
bkohler@schoolcraft.edu
KOHLER, Patti .... 435-797-0174 500 A
patti.kohler@usu.edu
KOHLER, Rebecca .... 315-866-0300 327 E
rebecca.kohler@herkimer.edu
KOHLES, Paula, S .... 402-280-2731 290 B
PaulaKohles@creighton.edu
KOHLHEPP, William, C 203-582-5226.. 91 E
william.kohlhepp@quinnipiac.edu
KOHLI, Cathy, L .... 419-995-8060 384 E
kohli.c@rhodesstate.edu
KOHLMAN, Mark .... 740-427-5000 384 P
kohlmanm@kenyon.edu
KOHLMEYER, Bill .... 503-399-6505 404 L
bill.kohlmeyer@chemeketa.edu
KOHLS, Christine .... 330-569-5134 383 F
kohlsca@hiram.edu
KOHN, David .... 845-341-4388 337 G
david.kohn@sunyorange.edu
KOHN, Gary .... 608-757-7769 542 L
gkohn@blackhawk.edu
KOHN, Lorna .... 712-279-1705 176 B
lorna.kohn@briarcliff.edu
KOHN, Melissa .... 920-236-6100 542 N
kohn@fvtc.edu
KOHN, Paul .... 404-385-3708 125 D
paul.kohn@ssc.gatech.edu
KOHN, Selina .... 706-821-8467 129 H
skohn@paine.edu
KOHN, Shayeh .... 718-327-7600 353 B
yfr1@verizon.net
KOHNEN-CAHALL, Nan . 513-569-5807 379 K
nan.cahall@cincinnatistate.edu
KOHNKE, Maria .... 805-493-3105.. 31 H
kohnke@callutheran.edu
KOHR, Lesa, J .... 585-594-6966 339 F
kohrl@roberts.edu
KOHRMAN, Robert .... 313-577-2001 252 G
dt9443@wayne.edu
KOHRMAN, Robert .... 313-577-9278 252 G
dt9443@wayne.edu
KOHRN, Lynn .... 203-932-7131.. 92 G
lkohrn@newhaven.edu
KOHRS, Becky .... 402-471-2505 292 A
bkohrs@nscs.edu
KOHSMANN, Laurie ...... 703-561-1600.. 96 H
laurie.kohsmann@strayer.edu
KOK, Cynthia .... 616-526-6125 240 L
ckok@calvin.edu
KOKAJKO, Hillary, C .... 336-841-9118 357 E
hkokajko@highpoint.edu
KOKER, John, J .... 920-424-1210 540 B
koker@uwosh.edu
KOKER, Michelle .... 612-624-2941 265 C
koker@umn.edu
KOKILEPERSAUD,
Premdat .... 443-885-3177 217 C
prem.kokilepersaud@morgan.edu
KOKINOVA,
Margarita, D .... 330-325-6333 387 F
mkokinov@neomed.edu
KOKKALA, Irene .... 706-864-1862 133 A
irene.kokkala@ung.edu
KOKOLUS, Cait .... 610-785-6280 434 E
ckokolus@scs.edu
KOKOLUS, John .... 717-361-1291 418 B
kokolusj@etown.edu
KOKONAS, Georgios .... 914-961-8313 341 I
gkokonas@svots.edu
KOKOSKA, Stephen ...... 570-389-4713 430 B
skokoska@bloomu.edu
KOKSAL, Semen .... 321-674-8887 103 R
skoksal@fit.edu
KOKX-TEMPLET, Ann .... 281-998-6103 481 D
ann.kokx-templet@sjcd.edu
KOLACINSKI, John .... 213-484-8850.. 30 A
KOLANDER, John, D .... 414-443-8816 542 I
john.kolander@wlc.edu

KOSINSKI, Mark .... 203-285-2077.. 89 B
mkosinski@gwcc.commnet.edu
KOSINSKY, James, A ... 708-209-3519 143 D
jim.kosinsky@cuchicago.edu
KOSKI, Lynne, D .... 402-844-7036 292 G
lynne@northeast.edu
KOSKY, Kristy .... 740-695-9500 377 F
kkosky@belmontcollege.edu
KOSLOSKI, James .... 516-877-3974 314 F
kosloski@adelphi.edu
KOSLOW MARTIN,
Jodi .... 773-244-5740 154 G
jkoslow@northpark.edu
KOSMICKI, Frank .... 618-453-5371 159 H
kosmicki@siu.edu
KOSMOSKI, Kathleen .... 912-486-7409 129 E
kkosmoski@ogeecheetech.edu
KOSOBUCKI, Dave .... 858-695-8587.. 47 E
dkosobucki@horizonuniversity.edu
KOSOKO-LASAKI, Sade 402-280-2332 290 B
SadeKosoko-Lasaki@creighton.edu
KOSOWSKY, Vicki .... 812-535-5216 172 F
vkosowsk@smwc.edu
KOSS, Michelle .... 586-286-2172 246 A
kossm26@macomb.edu
KOSSE, Glenn, F .... 502-272-8328 193 E
gkosse@bellarmine.edu
KOSSO, Cynthia .... 610-861-1348 426 H
kossoc@moravian.edu
KOSSUTH, Joanne .... 781-292-2431 226 G
joanne.kossuth@olin.edu
KOST, Patricia, L .... 216-368-2165 378 J
patricia.kost@case.edu
KOSTELL, Stacey, R ...... 802-656-1394 503 C
stacey.kostell@uvm.edu
KOSTELNIK, Marjorie .... 402-472-2913 293 H
mkostelnik2@unl.edu
KOSTER, Ed .... 402-761-8224 293 A
ekoster@southeast.edu
KOSTIHA, Sarah .... 440-375-7504 385 B
skostiha@lec.edu
KOSTRAB, Lynn, M ...... 330-569-5109 383 F
kostrablm@hiram.edu
KOSTRZEWA,
Waldemar .... 203-575-8297.. 89 F
wkostrzewa@nv.edu
KOSTRZEWSKI, Diana ... 303-292-0015.. 82 B
d.kostrzewski@denverschoolofnursing.edu
KOSTYUKOV, Victoria ... 718-522-9073 315 E
victoria_kostyukov@asa.edu
KOTAGAL, Nirmala .... 507-285-7143 261 D
nirmala.kotagal@rctc.edu
KOTAJARVI, Kathleen ... 920-693-1163 543 B
kathleen.kotajarvi@gotoltc.edu
KOTCAMP, Butch .... 740-351-3429 391 C
bkotcamp@shawnee.edu
KOTECKI, Kathy .... 406-657-2087 287 H
kkotecki@msubillings.edu
KOTH, Jason .... 212-592-2000 342 F
jkoth@sva.edu
KOTLER, A. Malkiel ...... 732-367-1060 300 D
KOTLER, Aaron .... 732-367-1060 300 D
akotler@bmg.edu
KOTLER, Yitzchok, S .... 732-367-1060 300 D
KOTLIKOFF, Michael, I . 607-255-2364 323 C
provost@cornell.edu
KOTLINSKI, Michael, J . 717-337-6363 419 C
mkotlinski@gettysburg.edu
KOTOISUVA, Agnes ...... 692-625-3394 550 A
KOTONIAS, Nancy .... 914-654-5914 322 B
nkotonias@cnr.edu
KOTORI, Chiaki .... 570-321-4029 425 B
kotori@lycoming.edu
KOTOWICZ, Keith, A ..... 414-847-3301 537 F
keithkotowicz@miad.edu
KOTOWSKI, Kelli .... 740-597-1819 389 H
kotowskk@ohio.edu
KOTTAS, Kathy .... 620-792-9355 184 I
kottask@bartonccc.edu
KOTTICH, Sarah .... 402-399-2427 289 I
skottich@csm.edu
KOTTON, Stevenson ..... 692-625-4931 550 A
skotton@cmi.edu
KOTTOYIL, Joseph .... 305-223-4561 111 J
josephpothen@hotmail.com
KOTULSKI, Bob, L .... 417-268-6036 272 F
bkotulski@gobbc.edu
KOTWICKI, Lee .... 941-363-7218 114 B
kotwicl@scf.edu
KOUA, Deb .... 515-965-7025 177 B
dkkoua@dmacc.edu
KOUANCHAO, Ketmani . 707-468-3013.. 54 A
kkouanchao@mendocino.edu
KOUBEK, Richard .... 225-578-1519 204 M
rkoubek@lsu.edu
KOUBEK, Richard .... 225-578-5701 204 M
rkoubek@lsu.edu
KOUCOUMARIS,
John, S .... 740-695-9500 377 F
jkoucoumaris@belmontcollege.edu

KOUDELIK-JONES,
Rachelle .... 540-857-6187 517 E
rkoudelikjones@virginiawestern.edu
KOUDOU, Nick .... 816-559-6182 280 F
nick.koudou@park.edu
KOUGH, Katherine .... 717-262-2006 440 D
kkough@wilson.edu
KOUKARI, Ray .... 262-619-6712 543 A
koukarir@gtc.edu
KOUKL, Shari .... 903-566-7214 494 E
skoukl@uttyler.edu
KOUKOLA,
Christine, H .... 573-882-4523 283 H
koukolac@missouri.edu
KOULIK, Chester .... 845-451-1347 323 E
c_koulik@culinary.edu
KOULOS, Elleni, R .... 909-593-3511.. 73 B
ekoulos@laverne.edu
KOUMARIANOS, Dee .... 603-577-6570 297 F
ykoumarianos@dwc.edu
KOUMAS, Sokratis .... 508-999-8709 228 H
skoumas@umassd.edu
KOURY, Denyel .... 716-614-6231 336 D
dkoury@niagaracc.suny.edu
KOURY, Kevin, A .... 724-938-4125 430 C
koury@calu.edu
KOUTSIDIS, Anastasia .. 646-313-8000 321 A
anastasia.koutsidis@guttman.cuny.edu
KOUTSOUTIS, Kalli .... 718-429-6600 352 A
kalli.koutsoutis@vaughn.edu
KOVAC, Matt .... 724-287-8711 413 G
matt.kovac@bc3.edu
KOVACH-ALLEN,
Katharina, E .... 585-345-6831 326 F
kekovachallen@genesee.edu
KOVACICH,
Christine, L .... 330-325-6551 387 F
ckovacich@neomed.edu
KOVACS, Anita, A .... 863-784-7123 113 C
anita.kovacs@southflorida.edu
KOVACS, Charles .... 941-359-7650 111 F
ckovacs@ringling.edu
KOVACS, Gene .... 850-245-0466 114 C
gene.kovacs@flbog.edu
KOVACS, Mark, C .... 315-792-3025 351 G
mkovacs@utica.edu
KOVAL, James .... 562-985-4691.. 33 F
james.koval@csulb.edu
KOVAL, Volga .... 707-826-4143.. 35 D
volga.koval@humboldt.edu
KOVALA, Irene, H .... 623-845-3010.. 14 N
irene.kovala@gccaz.edu
KOVALCHICK, Ann .... 209-228-4899.. 71 E
akovalchick@ucmerced.edu
KOVALCHICK, Mary ...... 610-799-1957 424 A
mkovalchick@lccc.edu
KOVALCIK, Andrew, B .. 412-648-0233 437 K
kandrew@pitt.edu
KOVALESKI, Brad .... 724-738-2727 432 A
brad.kovaleski@sru.edu
KOVANES, Tera, D .... 540-654-1042 513 I
tkovanes@umw.edu
KOVATCH, Richard, A ... 434-982-5166 514 A
rak3e@virginia.edu
KOVERMAN, Robert .... 312-369-6543 143 C
rkoverman@colum.edu
KOVEROLA, Catherine .. 617-349-8317 228 B
koverola@lesley.edu
KOVLER, Allen .... 518-828-4181 322 E
kovler@sunycgcc.edu
KOWAL, Donna, M .... 585-395-5400 345 A
dkowal@brockport.edu
KOWAL, John .... 518-438-3111 331 K
jkowal@mariacollege.edu
KOWALESKI, Curt .... 920-403-3117 538 K
curt.kowaleski@snc.edu
KOWALEWSKI, John, L 801-626-7212 500 C
jkowalewski@weber.edu
KOWALEWSKY, Lyn ...... 989-358-7280 239 C
kowalewl@alpenacc.edu
KOWALIK, Margaret ..... 315-781-3695 327 G
kowalik@hws.edu
KOWALIK, Thomas .... 607-777-2792 343 D
kowalik@binghamton.edu
KOWALSKI, Gerard, J ... 706-542-8318 132 H
kowalski@uga.edu
KOWALSKI, Jonathan ... 414-277-4510 537 G
kowalski@msoe.edu
KOWALSKI, JR.,
Jonathan, V .... 414-277-4510 537 G
kowalski@msoe.edu
KOWALSKI, Karl .... 907-450-8383.. 10 I
karl.kowalski@alaska.edu
KOWALSKI, Karl .... 907-450-8383.. 10 G
kekowalski@alaska.edu
KOWALSKI, Marion .... 212-875-4475 315 F
mkowalski@bankstreet.edu
KOWALSKI, Melanie ..... 570-504-1583 422 G
kowalskim@lackawanna.edu

KOWALSKI, Patrick, A .. 513-556-1299 393 B
patrick.kowalski@uc.edu
KOWALSKI, Sandra .... 928-523-0566.. 16 C
sandra.kowalski@nau.edu
KOWALSKI, Susan .... 717-338-3008 424 G
skowalski@ltsg.edu
KOWALSKI, Timothy, J . 864-327-9898 507 D
KOWAR, Pamela .... 860-255-3603.. 90 C
pkowar@txcc.commnet.edu
KOWCHECK, Tyler .... 724-503-1001 439 B
tkowcheck@washjeff.edu
KOWEEK, Joan .... 518-828-4181 322 E
joan.koweek@sunycgcc.edu
KOWICH, Colleen .... 816-271-5650 279 E
ckowich@missouriwestern.edu
KOWNACKI, James .... 570-484-2460 431 C
jkownack@lhup.edu
KOWTA, Mayumi .... 805-437-3107.. 32 H
mayumi.kowta@csuci.edu
KOZACHYN, Karen .... 610-359-5362 416 G
kkozachy@dccc.edu
KOZAK, Diane .... 907-786-4513.. 10 H
dhkozak@uaa.alaska.edu
KOZAK, Gregory .... 847-574-5194 150 A
gkozak@lfgsm.edu
KOZAK, Laura, A .... 410-706-8138 219 E
lkozak@umaryland.edu
KOZDEMBA, Kathy .... 412-536-1047 422 E
kozdemba@verizon.net
KOZERA, Mark .... 706-368-6945 121 E
mkozera@berry.edu
KOZERACKI, Carol .... 323-415-5374.. 51 D
kozeraca@elac.edu
KOZIATEK, Caroline ..... 203-932-7479.. 92 G
ckoziatek@newhaven.edu
KOZIEK, Timothy, J ..... 708-709-3702 156 A
tkoziek@prairiestate.edu
KOZIK, Bob .... 518-631-9881 351 A
kozikr@uniongraduatecollege.edu
KOZIKOWSKI, Mitch ..... 724-938-5706 430 C
kozikowski@calu.edu
KOZIL, Cindy, T .... 508-541-1552 225 G
ckozil@dean.edu
KOZIMOR, Renee .... 847-635-1761 155 E
rkozimor@oakton.edu
KOZIOL, Nicholas, J .... 716-880-2207 332 B
nicholas.j.koziol@medaille.edu
KOZISEK, Kelly, L .... 541-737-4261 408 F
kelly.kozisek@oregonstate.edu
KOZISEK, Sue .... 402-421-7410 291 J
KOZLOWSKI, Michael ... 860-723-0261.. 88 C
kozlowskim@ct.edu
KOZLOWSKI, Michelle .. 559-934-2240.. 76 A
michellekozlowski@whccd.edu
KOZOJED, Bob, J .... 701-788-4872 374 A
bob.kozojed@mayvillestate.edu
KOZOMAN, Robert, L ... 312-362-6695 143 G
bkozoman@depaul.edu
KOZUMA, Hikaru .... 215-898-6081 437 I
kozuma@upenn.edu
KOZY, Mallie .... 503-413-8080 406 I
mkozy@linfield.edu
KRABBENHOFT, Alan .... 765-455-9275 168 B
agkrabbe@iupui.edu
KRAEMER, David .... 212-678-8075 329 H
dakraemer@jtsa.edu
KRAEMER, Laurence ..... 516-465-8099 324 G
lkraemer@nshs.edu
KRAEMER, Ronald, D ... 574-631-9700 174 A
kraemer.5@nd.edu
KRAFT, Deborah .... 443-334-2337 218 E
dkraft@stevenson.edu
KRAFT, Deborah .... 281-756-3509 467 D
dkraft@alvincollege.edu
KRAFT, Gary, L .... 402-472-3609 293 H
gary.kraft@unl.edu
KRAFT, John .... 352-392-2398 115 D
john.kraft@warrington.ufl.edu
KRAFT, John .... 513-244-4426 387 A
john.kraft@msj.edu
KRAFT, Marian .... 816-604-1000 277 H
KRAFT, Marion .... 816-604-6550 277 G
KRAFT, Patricia .... 912-279-5858 123 B
pkraft@ccga.edu
KRAFT, Paul .... 541-881-5599 410 D
pbkraft@tvcc.cc
KRAFT, Ronald, D .... 707-256-7160.. 55 E
rkraft@napavalley.edu
KRAFT, Thomas .... 405-682-1611 399 K
tkraft@occc.edu
KRAFT, Walter .... 734-487-6895 242 J
walter.kraft@emuch.edu
KRAFT-MEYER, Kelly ..... 434-381-6425 513 E
kraft_meyer@sbc.edu
KRAGT, Donna .... 616-234-4040 243 D
dkragt@grcc.edu
KRAGULJEVIC, Nev .... 520-494-5471.. 12 R
nev.kraguljevic@centralaz.edu
KRAH, Stephanie .... 937-376-6493 379 D
skrah@centralstate.edu

KRAHE, Sharon, A .... 814-871-7670 419 A
krahe@gannon.edu
KRAHE, Stacey .... 773-697-2063 144 B
skrahe@carrington.edu
KRAHL, Tracy .... 312-362-5577 143 G
tkrahl@depaul.edu
KRAIMER, Paul .... 651-905-3509 264 E
pkraimer@browncollege.edu
KRAJEWSKI, Scott .... 612-330-1471 253 K
krajewsk@augsburg.edu
KRAJNIAK, Chris, A ..... 262-554-2010 537 D
chriskrajn@aol.com
KRAKOFF, Steve, P ...... 419-372-7127 377 I
skrakof@bgsu.edu
KRAKOW, Anne, Z .... 610-660-1905 434 G
akrakow@sju.edu
KRAL, Kathy .... 678-839-6585 133 F
kkral@westga.edu
KRAL, Martin, J .... 309-298-1838 163 A
mj-kral@wiu.edu
KRALL, Jason .... 412-578-6152 414 I
jkrall@carlow.edu
KRALL, Jim .... 479-524-7145.. 21 F
jkrall@jbu.edu
KRALL, Julia .... 304-876-5526 532 I
jkrall@shepherd.edu
KRALL, Lisi .... 607-753-4827 345 C
lisi.krall@cortland.edu
KRALLMAN, Denise, A . 513-529-7095 386 K
krallmda@miamioh.edu
KRAMER, Alan .... 229-391-4928 119 F
akramer@abac.edu
KRAMER, Alan .... 860-913-2032.. 90 F
akramer@goodwin.edu
KRAMER, Cathy .... 828-298-3325 373 A
service@warren-wilson.edu
KRAMER, Chris .... 217-234-5475 150 B
ckramer@lakeland.cc.il.us
KRAMER, Eric .... 413-528-7476 222 F
ekramer@simons-rock.edu
KRAMER, Esther .... 262-691-5040 544 D
ekramer3@wctc.edu
KRAMER, Gene .... 513-761-2020 379 J
gkramer@ccms.edu
KRAMER, Jill .... 317-921-4569 169 L
jkramer5@ivytech.edu
KRAMER, John .... 305-220-4120 108 F
acadir@mattiacollege.edu
KRAMER, Kirk, A .... 810-989-5503 249 H
kkramer@sc4.edu
KRAMER, Linda .... 507-354-8221 257 A
kramerlm@mlc-wels.edu
KRAMER, Lisa .... 415-442-7889.. 46 A
lkramer@ggu.edu
KRAMER, Mark .... 757-825-2815 517 B
kramerm@tncc.edu
KRAMER, SJ, Mark .... 314-792-6136 276 H
Kramer@kenrick.edu
KRAMER, Matt .... 617-327-6777 238 D
matt_kramer@williamjames.edu
KRAMER, Monica .... 937-484-1247 394 F
mkramer@urbana.edu
KRAMER, Monte .... 605-773-3455 453 E
monte.kramer@sdbor.edu
KRAMER, Nancy .... 319-226-2040 175 D
Nancy.Kramer@AllenCollege.edu
KRAMER, Nikki, A .... 920-923-8142 537 A
nakramer22@marianuniversity.edu
KRAMER, Pamela .... 239-687-5305.. 98 N
pkramer@avemarialaw.edu
KRAMER, Scott, E .... 270-852-3122 198 A
scottkr@kwc.edu
KRAMER, Sue .... 610-902-8781 414 B
susan.m.kramer@cabrini.edu
KRAMER, Terry .... 781-239-2431 231 G
tkramer1@massbay.edu
KRAMER, Thomas, E .... 757-594-8671 506 I
tkramer@cnu.edu
KRAMER-JEFFERSON,
Kate .... 301-846-2409 214 I
kkramerjefferson@frederick.edu
KRAMKA, James, S ...... 615-322-2591 465 H
jim.kramka@vanderbilt.edu
KRAMLICH, Carol .... 209-478-0800.. 47 F
ckramlich@humphreys.edu
KRANE, Barbara .... 954-969-9771 103 P
barbaraw@steinerleisure.com
KRANS, Gretchen .... 787-250-0000 557 B
gretchen.krans@upr.edu
KRANTZ, Margaret .... 812-866-7126 166 E
krantzm@hanover.edu
KRANTZ, Richard, N ..... 843-953-6372 445 B
krantzr@cofc.edu
KRANZ, Jason .... 858-966-3976.. 40 G
jkranz@coleman.edu
KRANZLER, Michael ...... 212-960-5277 353 P
kranzler@yu.edu
KRAPF, Audrey .... 631-420-2009 348 B
audrey.krapf@farmingdale.edu
KRAPOHL, Robert, H .... 847-317-4004 161 B
rkrapohl@tiu.edu

KROV, Matthew ... 903-813-2370 468 G mkrov@austincollege.edu
KROVI, Ravi ... 330-972-7442 392 H krovi@uakron.edu
KRSTIC, Miroslav ... 858-534-5556 72 B mkrstic@ucsd.edu
KRUCZEK, Thomas ... 216-373-5238 388 A tkruczek@ndc.edu
KRUDOP, James, D ... 334-382-2133 5 G jkrudop@lbwcc.edu
KRUEGER, Beth ... 520-515-5380 13 B kruegerbeth@cochise.edu
KRUEGER, Bryon, D ... 651-631-5392 265 D bdkrueger@unwsp.edu
KRUEGER, Cindy ... 419-267-1233 387 G ckrueger@northweststate.edu
KRUEGER, Cindy ... 419-559-2266 392 A ckrueger01@terra.edu
KRUEGER, Conrad ... 210-486-0915 467 C ckrueger@alamo.edu
KRUEGER, James, M ... 314-516-6539 284 B jimkrueger@umsl.edu
KRUEGER, Jim ... 402-399-2332 289 I jkrueger@csm.edu
KRUEGER, Joni ... 605-274-4015 452 A joni.krueger@augie.edu
KRUEGER, Justin ... 815-226-4006 157 D JKrueger@rockford.edu
KRUEGER, Karl ... 215-248-6330 424 G kkrueger@ltsp.edu
KRUEGER, Kurt, J ... 949-214-3194 42 B kurt.krueger@cui.edu
KRUEGER, Mablene ... 312-935-6645 157 A mkrueger@robertmorris.edu
KRUEGER, Mary, M ... 419-372-8034 377 I mkruege@bgsu.edu
KRUEGER, Michelle ... 941-359-4200 116 D
KRUEGER PARK, Kathleen ... 415-257-1309 43 D kathleen.kruegerpark@dominican.edu
KRUEZER, Norbert ... 612-244-2800 256 E nkreuzer@ipr.edu
KRUG, Anna ... 312-427-2737 148 I akrug@jmls.edu
KRUG, Bryce ... 314-918-2568 274 K bkrug@eden.edu
KRUG, Cherie ... 301-387-3100 215 A cherie.krug@garrettcollege.edu
KRUG, Christopher ... 858-642-8120 55 J ckrug@nu.edu
KRUG, Jeffrey ... 570-389-4745 430 B jakrug@bloomu.edu
KRUG, Sheila, R ... 620-229-6368 191 B sheila.krug@sckans.edu
KRUG, Stefan ... 617-521-3929 236 F stefan.krug@simmons.edu
KRUGER, Darrell, P ... 828-262-2070 369 D krugerdp@appstate.edu
KRUGER, Michael, J ... 704-366-5066 270 B mkruger@rts.edu
KRUHLY, Leslie, L ... 215-898-7005 437 I kruhly@upenn.edu
KRUKONES, James, H ... 216-397-4762 384 F jkrukones@jcu.edu
KRUKOWSKA, Justyna ... 510-883-2071 43 C jkrukowska@dspt.edu
KRULL, Kimberly ... 316-322-3100 185 F kim.krull@butlercc.edu
KRULL, Lucille ... 503-251-6115 528 A lucy.krull@wallawalla.edu
KRUMER, Walter ... 718-522-9073 315 E vkrumer@asa.edu
KRUMHANSL, Ezra ... 502-585-9911 199 E ekrumhansl@spalding.edu
KRUML, Susan ... 217-424-6285 153 A skruml@millikin.edu
KRUMM, Brenda, L ... 620-431-2820 189 J bkrumm@neosho.edu
KRUMM, Javier ... 951-785-2295 49 I jkrumm@lasierra.edu
KRUMMEN SCHRAVE, Ginger, B ... 920-433-6631 534 K ginger.krummen@bellincollege.edu
KRUMMRICH, Philip ... 606-783-2726 198 H p.krummrich@moreheadstate.edu
KRUMPE, Keith ... 828-250-3880 370 E kkrumpe@unca.edu
KRUPANSKY, Sharla ... 270-534-3275 197 E sharla.krupansky@kctcs.edu
KRUPICA, Suzanne ... 217-854-3231 140 F suzanne.krupica@blackburn.edu
KRUPIN, Maria ... 845-451-1385 323 E m_krupin@culinary.edu
KRUPKA, Moshe ... 646-565-6000 350 C moshe.krupka@touro.edu
KRUPNICK, Kayla ... 415-442-7228 46 A kkrupnick@ggu.edu
KRUPP, Jason ... 727-341-3339 112 A krupp.jason@spcollege.edu
KRUPP, Robert, A ... 503-517-1838 411 C rakrupp@westernseminary.edu
KRUPPS, Gina ... 309-341-5264 140 I gkrupps@sandburg.edu
KRUPPSTADT, Tom ... 877-476-8674 474 I
KRUPSKI, Eric, A ... 617-422-7232 234 J ekrupski@nesl.edu
KRUSE, Amy ... 320-629-5115 260 H krusea@pinetech.edu
KRUSE, Beckie ... 262-243-5700 535 I beckie.kruse@cuw.edu
KRUSE, Emily ... 563-588-6436 176 F emily.kruse@clarke.edu
KRUSE, Heather ... 602-285-7800 15 C heather.kruse@phoenixcollege.edu
KRUSE, Janetta ... 817-598-6391 497 A jkruse@wc.edu
KRUSE, Mary ... 517-264-7112 250 B mkruse@sienaheights.edu
KRUSE, Tracy, L ... 402-844-7056 292 G tracyk@northeast.edu
KRUSEE, Kelly ... 310-377-5501 53 E kkrusee@marymountcalifornia.edu
KRUSEMARK, Stacy, L ... 605-256-5127 453 H stacy.krusemark@dsu.edu
KRUSEMARK, Stephanie, L ... 202-884-9401 97 A krusemarks@trinitydc.edu
KRUSEN, Cynthia ... 978-840-0176 232 C c_krusen@mwcc.mass.edu
KRUSLING, James ... 415-442-7248 46 A jkrusling@ggu.edu
KRUSNIAK, Bryan ... 660-626-2364 271 G bkrusniak@atsu.edu
KRUSSEL, John ... 503-768-7563 406 H krussel@lclark.edu
KRUTKY, Judith, B ... 440-826-2257 377 D jkrutky@bw.edu
KRUTZ, Ellen ... 610-519-4237 439 A ellen.krutz@villanova.edu
KRUZANSKY, Charles ... 518-434-4157 323 C albany_office@cornell.edu
KRUZEL, Douglas ... 734-973-3497 251 J kruzel@wccnet.edu
KRYCZKA, Susan ... 518-608-8150 325 B SKryczka@excelsior.edu
KRYGOWSKI, Jean Marie ... 443-412-2102 215 D jkrygowski@harford.edu
KRYLOWICZ, Brian ... 413-748-3345 236 H bkrylowicz@springfieldcollege.edu
KRYSIAK, Richard ... 405-744-7147 400 C rick.krysiak@okstate.edu
KRZAK, Chris ... 909-593-3511 73 B ckrzak@laverne.edu
KRZANIK, Jacki ... 413-662-5421 230 C j.krzanik@mcla.edu
KRZYSTOFIAK, Susan ... 716-645-2642 343 E krzystof@buffalo.edu
KSEPKA, Matthew ... 612-330-1032 253 K ksepka@augsburg.edu
KTUL, Kathy ... 252-492-2061 366 G ktul@vgcc.edu
KUAN, Jeffrey ... 909-447-2552 39 G jkuan@cst.edu
KUBA, Jodie, M ... 808-956-3993 135 J jodiek@hawaii.edu
KUBA, Lori, P ... 602-944-3335 11 D lpryor-kuba@aicag.edu
KUBA, Shawn ... 304-473-8560 534 G kuba_s@wvwc.edu
KUBACAK, James ... 254-299-8608 478 C jkubacak@mclennan.edu
KUBAT, Robert, A ... 814-863-3681 428 C rak28@psu.edu
KUBATZKE, Trevor ... 414-297-6279 543 E kubatzkt@matc.edu
KUBB, Richard ... 314-529-9606 277 B rkubb@maryville.edu
KUBEJA, Judy ... 814-732-2729 430 G kubeja@edinboro.edu
KUBERSKI, Chris ... 815-599-3417 146 B chris.kuberski@highland.edu
KUBIK, Lesley ... 256-840-4219 7 B lkubik@snead.edu
KUBIK, Rachel ... 714-432-5834 40 D rkubik@occ.cccd.edu
KUBILUS, Norbert, J ... 858-499-0202 40 G nkubilus@coleman.edu
KUBINAK, Lois, A ... 610-921-7612 411 E lkubinak@albright.edu
KUBO, Takeo ... 408-288-3733 64 A takeo.kubo@sjcc.edu
KUBOW, Stephen ... 732-255-0356 303 C skubow@kean.edu
KUCER, Peter ... 860-632-3001 90 H pkucer@holyapostles.edu
KUCERA, Kevin ... 734-487-2390 242 J kkucera@emich.edu
KUCHARCZYK, Loretta ... 708-709-3622 156 A lkucharczyk@prairiestate.edu
KUCIA, John, F ... 513-745-3997 396 B kucia@xavier.edu
KUCIK, Maggie ... 317-955-6213 171 A mkucik@marian.edu
KUCINSKI, Nancy ... 325-670-1298 474M nkicinski@hsutx.edu
KUCKO, Jane ... 817-257-7473 486 G j.kucko@tcu.edu
KUDLAC, John ... 412-392-3920 433 F jkudlac@pointpark.edu
KUDRAVETZ, Douglas ... 202-885-3283 94 H doug@american.edu
KUE, Mailee ... 401-232-6448 441 B mkue@bryant.edu
KUEBLER, Alan, S ... 314-935-5727 285 E alan_kuebler@wustl.edu
KUECKER, Aaron ... 903-233-3309 477 G aaronkuecker@letu.edu
KUEHLER, Robert ... 303-837-2112 86 D Robert.Kuehler@cu.edu
KUEHN, Martha ... 218-855-8221 258 C MKuehn@clcmn.edu
KUEHN, Paul ... 808-455-0268 136 G pkuehn@hawaii.edu
KUEHNER, Megan, R ... 904-620-2523 116 A mkuehner@unf.edu
KUENTZEL, Jeffrey ... 313-577-2840 252 G jkuentzel@wayne.edu
KUERZI, Kenneth ... 856-256-4138 306 D kuerzi@rowan.edu
KUETER, Jeffrey, D ... 319-335-3294 175 H jeff-kueter@uiowa.edu
KUFFEL, Lorne ... 205-348-7204 8 E lkuffel@ua.edu
KUFUOR, Edward ... 718-522-9073 315 E ekufuor@asa.edu
KUGELMANN DEKAT, Laurie ... 972-721-5322 491 B ldekat@udallas.edu
KUGLER, Adriana ... 202-687-5716 95 E ak659@georgetown.edu
KUGLER, Angela ... 425-558-0299 522 B akugler@digipen.edu
KUGLER, Anne ... 216-397-4770 384 F akugler@jcu.edu
KUGLER, Sharon ... 203-432-1128 93 C sharon.kugler@yale.edu
KUHAJDA, Kimberlee, A ... 440-826-2251 377 D kkuhajda@bw.edu
KUHAR, Marilyn ... 617-228-3290 231 C mkkuhar@bhcc.mass.edu
KUHART, Mary Jeanne ... 541-463-5315 406 F kuharmj@lanecc.edu
KUHL, Colleen, M ... 563-588-7650 180 L colleen.kuhl@loras.edu
KUHL, Sara ... 262-472-1194 541 D kuhls@uww.edu
KUHLHORST, Michelle, L ... 260-399-7700 174 C mkuhlhorst@sf.edu
KUHLMAN, Ann ... 203-432-2305 93 C ann.kuhlman@yale.edu
KUHLMANN, Diana, E ... 620-341-5304 186 H dkuhlman@emporia.edu
KUHLMEIER, Sylvia ... 417-255-7949 279 B sylviakuhlmeier@missouristate.edu
KUHN, Bill ... 952-446-4227 255 E kuhnb@crown.edu
KUHN, Charles ... 301-447-5244 217 D ckuhn@msmary.edu
KUHN, Helen ... 217-245-3013 146 D registrar@mail.ic.edu
KUHN, Kathryn, A ... 414-955-8217 537 C kkuhn@mcw.edu
KUHN, Kevin ... 601-477-4108 268 A kevin.kuhn@jcjc.edu
KUHN, Paul ... 732-247-5241 304 B pkuhn@nbts.edu
KUHN, Robert ... 814-824-2104 425 L rkuhnn@mercyhurst.edu
KUHN, Sheila Jane ... 928-523-7732 16 C Jane.Kuhn@nau.edu
KUHN, Shelly ... 262-691-5450 544 D skuhn4@wctc.edu
KUHN, Skip ... 434-947-8076 511 D skughn@randolphcollege.edu
KUHN, Stephen ... 262-524-7132 535 D skuhn@carrollu.edu
KUHN-SCHNELL, Tamara ... 217-786-2353 151 C tammy.schnell@llcc.edu
KUHR, Peggy ... 406-243-2311 287 D peggy.kuhr@umontana.edu
KUIPER, Dale ... 616-222-3000 245 D dkuiper@kuyper.edu
KUIPERS, David ... 229-931-2001 131 E dkuipers@southgatech.edu
KUJAT, Marilee ... 989-386-6622 247 B mkujat@midmich.edu
KUJAWA, Lisa, R ... 248-204-2403 245 J lkujawa@ltu.edu
KUJAWA, Thomas ... 920-465-2300 539 F kujawat@uwgb.edu
KUJAWA, Tricia, A ... 217-786-2211 151 C tricia.kujawa@llcc.edu
KUJAWA-HOLBROOK, Sheryl ... 909-447-2521 39 G skujawa-holbrook@cst.edu
KUKAINIS, Maris ... 856-227-7200 301 A mkukainis@camdencc.edu
KUKAY, Mike ... 406-496-4673 288 C mkukay@mtech.edu
KUKER, Ronald ... 937-529-2201 392 G rkuker@united.edu
KUKOR, Jerome, J ... 848-932-7275 307 B kukor@aesop.rutgers.edu
KUKREJA, Anil ... 504-520-7652 209 E akukreja@xula.edu
KUKREJA, Sunil ... 253-879-3207 527 F skukreja@pugetsound.edu
KUKULIES, Emily Ann ... 808-845-9219 136 E kukulies@hawaii.edu
KULAGA, Jon, S ... 859-858-3511 193 A jon.kulaga@asbury.edu
KULBICKI, OFM CONV, Timothy, A ... 410-864-3602 218 C tkulbicki@stmarys.edu
KULECK, Gary ... 313-993-1216 250 H gary.kuleck@udmercy.edu
KULESZA, Darrell ... 508-541-1864 225 G dkulesza@dean.edu
KULESZA, Randy ... 814-866-8423 423 B rkulsza@lecom.edu
KULICH, James ... 630-617-6472 144 G jimk@elmhurst.edu
KULICK, Steven, W ... 315-445-4560 330 B kulicksw@lemoyne.edu
KULICS, Jennifer ... 330-672-9494 384 H jkulics@kent.edu
KULIK, Dmitry ... 202-462-2101 96 C kulik@iwp.edu
KULK, Allyn ... 914-964-4282 321 E
KULKARNI, Sanjeev ... 609-258-3035 305 C kulkarni@princeton.edu
KULKE, Erik ... 262-551-5916 535 E ekulke@carthage.edu
KULL, Edward, M ... 718-990-3300 340 G kulle@stjohns.edu
KULL, F. Jon ... 603-646-1552 297 G f.jon.kull@dartmouth.edu
KULL, Michael ... 219-989-2231 171 L mjkull@purduecal.edu
KULOW, Beth ... 641-782-1413 183 D kulow@swcciowa.edu
KULPA, Brian ... 734-487-2390 242 J bkulpa@emich.edu
KULWICKI, Anahid ... 617-287-7500 228 G anahid.kulwicki@umb.edu
KUMAR, Deepak ... 303-753-6046 85 H
KUMAR, Neeraj ... 312-341-3587 157 E neeraj.kumar@roosevelt.edu
KUMAR, Nikhil ... 914-323-5129 331 J nikhil.kumar@mville.edu
KUMAR, Senthil ... 617-217-9733 223 A skumar@baystate.edu
KUMAR, Shashi ... 516-726-5832 548 I kumars@usmma.edu
KUMAR, Sunil ... 773-702-1680 161 D Sunil.kumar@chicagobooth.edu
KUMAR, Thulasi ... 860-486-4240 92 C thulasi.kumar@uconn.edu
KUMARASAMY, Sundar ... 617-373-4810 235 D
KUMASHIRO, Kevin, K ... 415-422-2108 74 C kkumashiro@usfca.edu
KUMASHIRO, Kristin ... 808-956-6451 135 J kumashir@hawaii.edu
KUMBA, Chantel ... 757-631-8101 504 O chantel.kumba@atlanticuniv.edu
KUMBIER, Brigitte ... 715-365-4406 543 G bkumbier@nicoletcollege.edu
KUMLER, Kurt ... 412-268-2922 414 J kkumler@andrew.cmu.edu
KUMM, David ... 402-643-7222 289 J david.kumm@cune.edu
KUMMER, Maryann, S ... 313-927-1373 246 D mkummer@marygrove.edu
KUMMERMAN, Howard ... 562-908-3476 60 I foundation@riohondo.edu
KUMMERMAN, Howard ... 562-908-3412 60 I howard.kummerman@riohondo.edu
KUMP, Melissa ... 406-496-4108 288 C mkump@mtech.edu
KUMPF, Dan ... 805-289-6339 75 E dkumpf@vcccd.edu
KUMPF, Robert ... 732-255-0400 304 E rkumpf@ocean.edu
KUNA, Gerri ... 701-858-3497 374 B gerri.kuna@minotstateu.edu
KUNCE, Kim, M ... 708-709-3684 156 A kkunce@prairiestate.edu
KUNCL, Ralph, W ... 909-748-8390 73 K ralph_kuncl@redlands.edu

LACASCE, Cynthia .... 603-542-7744 297 D
clacasce@ccsnh.edu
LACASCHI-DECKER,
Sylvia .... 740-477-7893 388 F
slucaschi@ohiochristian.edu
LACAY, Phebe .... 973-328-5056 301 G
placay@ccm.edu
LACEK, Steven .... 304-294-2008 531 F
steven.lacek@southernwv.edu
LACEY, Aaron .... 314-264-1802 162 J
aaron.lacey@vatterott-college.edu
LACEY, Kasi .... 573-592-5269 285 J
kasi.lacey@westminster-mo.edu
LACEY, Mark .... 904-632-3381 105 A
mark.lacey@fscj.edu
LACEY, Pete .... 810-989-5561 249 H
placey@sc4.edu
LACEY, R. Alton .... 314-392-2355 278 G
president@mobap.edu
LACH, Carolyn .... 773-244-5506 154 G
clach@northpark.edu
LACHANCE, Andrea .... 607-753-5430 345 C
andrea.lachance@cortland.edu
LACHANCE, Beatrice ..... 615-547-1244 456 C
blachance@cumberland.edu
LACHANCE,
Elizabeth, A .... 585-385-8410 340 F
llachance@sjfc.edu
LACHANCE, Laurie, G ... 207-859-1201 211 I
president@thomas.edu
LACHANCE, Liz .... 585-385-8410 340 F
llachance@sjfc.edu
LACHAPELL, Tara, A ..... 920-748-8713 538 I
lachapellt@ripon.edu
LACHAPELLE, Laurie ..... 978-762-4000 232 D
llachape@northshore.edu
LACHER, Candis .... 509-793-2063 520 B
candyl@bigbend.edu
LACHER, Henry .... 615-460-6670 455 D
henry.lacher@belmont.edu
LACHICA-CHAVEZ,
Cassandra .... 575-646-7526 312 A
clachica@nmsu.edu
LACHOWSKI, Joan, D ... 804-289-8060 513 M
jlachows@richmond.edu
LACIO, Erin .... 620-672-5641 190 H
erinl@prattcc.edu
LACK, Anthony, L .... 540-985-8362 509 D
allack@jchs.edu
LACK, Paul, D .... 443-334-2205 218 E
cvanrensselaer@stevenson.edu
LACKEY, Amy .... 785-442-6023 187 I
alackey@highlandcc.edu
LACKEY, David, A .... 570-586-2400 435 H
dlackey@summitu.edu
LACKEY, Emanuel .... 662-621-4144 266 H
elackey@coahomacc.edu
LACKEY, Fred, G .... 251-442-2482.... 9 B
wbchurch@bellsouth.net
LACKEY, Mary Lou .... 209-946-2011.. 73 C
mllackey@pacific.edu
LACKEY, Miles .... 515-294-2220 175 G
mlackey@iastate.edu
LACKEY, Polly, R .... 806-291-3702 496 K
lackeyp@wbu.edu
LACKEY, Russell, L .... 515-263-6004 178 H
rlackey@grandview.edu
LACKIE, Mary .... 479-788-7021.. 23 H
mary.lackie@uafs.edu
LACKNER, Andrew .... 985-871-6201 207 F
alackner@tulane.edu
LACKNER, Elisabeth ...... 718-631-6279 320 F
elackner@qcc.cuny.edu
LACKNER, Sandra .... 252-246-1435 367 D
slackner@wilsoncc.edu
LACLAIR, Bethaney .... 802-258-3357 502 I
bethaney.laclair@worldlearning.org
LACOLA, Chris .... 803-786-3933 445 C
clacola@columbiasc.edu
LACOMBA, AJ .... 518-587-2100 348 A
aj.lacomba@esc.edu
LACOMBA, Todd .... 419-434-5184 393 F
lacomba@findlay.edu
LACOSTE-CAPUTO,
Jenny .... 512-499-4363 493 K
jcaputo@utsystem.edu
LACOUR, Joseph .... 318-670-9378 207 C
jlacour@susla.edu
LACOURSE, Michael ...... 936-294-2394 489 A
mxl035@shsu.edu
LACOURSE, Peter, W .... 231-995-1198 248 C
placourse@nmc.edu
LACOURSE, William ...... 410-455-2598 219 F
lacourse@umbc.edu
LACOVARA, Vincent, A . 202-319-6735.. 95 A
lacovara@cua.edu
LACRO, Erika .... 808-845-9225 136 E
lacro@hawaii.edu
LACROIX, Michael .... 402-554-2640 294 A
mlacroix@unomaha.edu
LACROIX, Mike .... 419-755-4048 387 E
lacroix.12@osu.edu
LACROIX, Roland, J ..... 207-581-4053 212 C
roland.j.lacroix@maine.edu
LACUEVA, Graciela .... 216-397-4625 384 F
glacueva@jcu.edu
LACY, Alan .... 309-438-8864 147 I
aclacy@ilstu.edu
LACY, Charles, F .... 702-968-2016 296 D
clacy@roseman.edu
LACY, Gary .... 914-948-6206 348 A
gary.lacy@esc.edu
LACY, Melanie .... 909-621-8129.. 59 F
melanie_lacy@pitzer.edu
LACY, Sherea .... 616-538-2330 243 C
slacy@gbcol.edu
LADAGE, Marcia .... 816-936-8716 282 A
mladage@saintlukescollege.edu
LADANY, Nicholas .... 619-260-4540.. 74 B
LADD, Cindy .... 952-358-8223 260 D
cindy.ladd@normandale.edu
LADD, Darin .... 937-255-6565 547 E
darin.ladd@afit.edu
LADD, Susan, K .... 515-271-3048 177 K
susan.ladd@drake.edu
LADE, Becky .... 515-271-1485 177 H
becky.lade@dmu.edu
LADER, Donald .... 816-279-7000 271 H
don.lader@abtu.edu
LADEWIG, Patricia, A ... 303-458-1843.. 85 G
pladewig@regis.edu
LADHA, Amin .... 734-973-3400 251 J
amin@wccnet.edu
LADITKA, Doug .... 330-263-2310 380 E
dladitka@wooster.edu
LADITKA, Robyn .... 330-263-2545 380 E
rladitka@wooster.edu
LADNER, Hilda .... 320-589-6095 265 A
hladner@morris.umn.edu
LADNER, Marilyn .... 352-854-2322 100 P
ladnerm@cf.edu
LADNER, Pam .... 228-497-7642 268 G
pamela.ladner@mgccc.edu
LADNER-MATHIS,
Jocelyn .... 216-987-4537 381 A
jocelyn.ladner-mathis@tri-c.edu
LADORE, Frank .... 203-392-5367.. 88 F
ladoref1@southernct.edu
LADUCA, Bonnie .... 651-690-8664 263 V
bsladuca@stkate.edu
LADUCER, Wanda .... 701-477-7862 375 H
wladucer@tm.edu
LADUSAW, William .... 831-459-2696.. 72 E
humdean@ucsc.edu
LADWIG, Laura .... 616-977-0599 249 B
laura.ladwig@prts.edu
LADWIG, Steven .... 707-826-4402.. 35 D
ladwig@humboldt.edu
LADY, David, E .... 970-410-0456.. 87 L
LAENEN, Carol .... 231-348-6839 248 A
claenen@ncmich.edu
LAFARGE, Vicki .... 781-891-2089 223 E
vlafarge@bentley.edu
LAFATA-JOHNSON,
Paulette .... 219-980-6769 168 C
plafataj@iun.edu
LAFAVE, Alan .... 605-626-2524 454 A
Alan.LaFave@northern.edu
LAFAY, Tressie .... 518-743-2237 347 E
lafayt@sunyacc.edu
LAFAYETTE, Jack .... 610-921-6652 411 E
jlafayette@albright.edu
LAFERLA, Chris .... 712-325-3293 180 B
claferla@iwcc.edu
LAFERLA, Frank .... 949-824-5315.. 71 C
laferla@uci.edu
LAFEVOR, Kimberly ...... 256-216-5359.... 1 F
kim.lafevor@athens.edu
LAFFERTY, T. Kevin ...... 813-258-7456 118 H
klafferty@ut.edu
LAFFERTY, William, J ... 717-337-6912 419 C
wlaffert@gettysburg.edu
LAFFEY, Brian .... 312-567-3677 147 E
blaffey1@iit.edu
LAFFITTE, Ron .... 864-587-4002 449 D
laffitter@smcsc.edu
LAFLAMME, Jacques .... 401-739-5000 441 E
jlaflamme@neit.edu
LAFLAMME, Martha ...... 603-752-1113 297 E
mlaflamme@ccsnh.edu
LAFLASH, Debra, A .... 508-854-4551 232 F
dal@qcc.mass.edu
LAFLER, Lisa .... 319-363-1323 181 D
llafler@mtmercy.edu
LAFONTAINE, Joni .... 701-477-7862 375 H
jlafontaine@tm.edu
LAFORGE, Daniel .... 207-509-7287 212 A
dlaforge@unity.edu
LAFORGE,
William (Bill) .... 662-846-4000 267 A
wlaforge@deltastate.edu
LAFORGIA, John, W ..... 507-284-2073 254 G
john.laforgia@mayo.edu
LAFRANCE, George .... 505-786-4311 311 G
glefrance@navajotech.edu
LAFRANCE, Mark .... 617-243-2178 227 K
mlafrance@lasell.edu
LAFROMEOISE, Tanya ... 605-698-3966 453 D
tlafromeoise@swc.tc
LAGARON, Elizabeth ..... 305-644-1171 101 B
LAGASSE, Ray .... 701-777-6438 373 G
raymond.lagasse@und.edu
LAGATTA, James, J ...... 518-629-4523 328 D
j.lagatta@hvcc.edu
LAGATTA, Regina .... 518-629-7736 328 D
r.lagatta@hvcc.edu
LAGEORGE, Lisa .... 661-362-2205.. 53 F
llageorge@masters.edu
LAGESON, David .... 541-962-3114 405 G
dlageson@eou.edu
LAGO, Baldomero .... 801-863-7301 500 B
lagoba@uvu.edu
LAGORIO, Grant .... 541-245-7873 409 F
glagorio@roguecc.edu
LAGRANGE, Janet .... 337-521-8900 204 E
janet.lagrange@solacc.edu
LAGRANGE, Linda .... 505-454-3578 311 H
lagrange_l@nmhu.edu
LAGRANGE, Teresa .... 216-687-4700 380 D
t.lagrange@csuohio.edu
LAGRASSA, Michael ..... 508-999-9180 228 H
mlagrassa@umassd.edu
LAGUERRE, Jowel .... 510-466-7202.. 59 C
jlaguerre@peralta.edu
LAGUERRE-BROWN,
Caroline .... 410-516-8075 216 A
clbrown@jhu.edu
LAGUNA, Robert .... 512-492-3010 468 A
rlaguna@aoma.edu
LAHAIE, Ute .... 330-490-7453 395 C
ulahaie@walsh.edu
LAHART, Edward .... 570-504-7000 415 E
elahart@tcmc.edu
LAHER, Ron .... 307-532-8218 546 B
ron.laher@ewc.wy.edu
LAHEY, John, L .... 203-582-8700.. 91 E
john.lahey@quinnipiac.edu
LAHM, Chris .... 417-626-1234 280 B
lahm.chris@occ.edu
LAHM, Terry, D .... 614-236-6800 378 H
tlahm@capital.edu
LAHODA, Anne, L .... 412-397-5235 434 B
lahoda@rmu.edu
LAHR, Sheri, K .... 580-327-8550 399 F
sklahr@nwosu.edu
LAHTI, Michele .... 209-667-3131.. 35 C
mlahti@csustan.edu
LAI, Chun .... 215-887-5511 439 E
clai@wts.edu
LAI, James .... 386-481-2306.. 99 F
laij@cookman.edu
LAI, James, S .... 408-554-5760.. 65 A
jlai@scu.edu
LAI, Mary, M .... 516-299-2502 330 F
mary.lai@liu.edu
LAI HING, Kenneth .... 256-726-7112.... 6 C
laihing@oakwood.edu
LAIBLE, Jim .... 815-967-7307 157 C
jlaible@rockfordcareercollege.edu
LAIDACKER, Crystal ...... 972-241-3371 472 A
claidacker@dallas.edu
LAINE, Glen, A .... 979-845-8585 485 C
glaine@tamu.edu
LAINE, Vance .... 309-268-4355 150 H
vlaine@lincolncollege.edu
LAING, Steve .... 360-867-6189 522 J
laings@evergreen.edu
LAINO, Nicholas .... 315-866-0300 327 E
lainonf@herkimer.edu
LAIPSON, Peter .... 413-528-7239 222 F
plaipson@simons-rock.edu
LAIR, Patrick .... 651-423-8399 258 E
patrick.lair@dctc.edu
LAIRD, Allan .... 208-459-5454 137 J
alaird@collegeofidaho.edu
LAIRD, Brenda .... 307-778-1372 546 F
blaird@lcccfoundation.edu
LAIRD, Kimberly .... 972-883-4784 494 A
kll130430@utdallas.edu
LAIRD, Richard .... 321-433-7090 101 O
lairdr@easternflorida.edu
LAIRMORE, Michael, D 530-752-1361.. 71 A
mdlairmore@ucdavis.edu
LAJEUNESSE, Deb .... 419-824-3733 385 F
dlajeunesse@lourdes.edu
LAJEUNESSE,
Mary Ellen .... 518-629-7292 328 D
m.lajeunesse@hvcc.edu
LAJINESS, Kim .... 912-583-3255 121 H
klajiness@bpc.edu
LAJINESS, Todd .... 313-883-8501 249 E
lajiness.todd@shms.edu
LAJUBUTU, Oyebanjo ... 573-341-4954 284 C
lajubutuo@mst.edu
LAKE, Diana .... 360-475-7831 524 H
dlake@olympic.edu
LAKE, Doris, J .... 270-831-9617 196 C
doris.lake@kctcs.edu
LAKE, Kathryn .... 740-427-5113 384 P
Lakek@Kenyon.edu
LAKE, Kathy .... 231-591-2113 242 L
KathyLake@ferris.edu
LAKE, Kathy .... 414-382-6084 534 I
kathy.lake@alverno.edu
LAKE, Lyndon, J .... 315-267-3274 346 C
lakelj@potsdam.edu
LAKE, Michael, P .... 850-644-2478 115 A
mlake@admin.fsu.edu
LAKE, Patti .... 406-683-7031 287 E
patricia.lake@umwestern.edu
LAKE, Rebecca .... 847-925-6633 145 F
rlake@harpercollege.edu
LAKE, Stephanie, S .... 919-866-5927 366 H
sslake@waketech.edu
LAKE, Todd .... 615-460-6628 455 D
todd.lake@belmont.edu
LAKE, Tracy .... 860-231-5447.. 93 A
tlake@usj.edu
LAKE-KING, Shirley .... 340-693-1400 559 B
sking@live.uvi.edu
LAKEN, Elizabeth, A ...... 815-740-3372 162 F
elaken@stfrancis.edu
LAKEN, Michael, J .... 630-515-6148 152 H
mlaken@midwestern.edu
LAKER, Craig .... 260-665-4862 173 D
lakerc@trine.edu
LAKES, Steven .... 859-371-9393 193 D
slakes@beckfield.edu
LAKETA, Dave .... 815-740-3464 162 F
dlaketa@stfrancis.edu
LAKEY, David, L .... 903-877-5406 495 C
david.lakey@uthct.edu
LAKHANI, Vikash .... 707-826-4402.. 35 D
vikash.lakhani@humboldt.edu
LAKIS, James .... 570-321-4141 425 B
lakis@lycoming.edu
LAKOSIL, Jennifer .... 520-515-8750.. 13 B
lakosilj@cochise.edu
LAKURIQI, Elona .... 215-951-2186 432 F
lakuriqie@philau.edu
LALANDE, Emmanuel ... 314-340-5300 275 G
lalandee@hssu.edu
LALANDE, Emmanuel ... 314-340-5112 275 G
lalandee@hssu.edu
LALANNE, Bob .... 510-643-7384.. 70 K
vcre@berkeley.edu
LALCHANDANI, Atam ..... 775-831-1314 296 F
kyoung@sierranevada.edu
LALIBERTE, Jean .... 334-670-3608.... 8 A
jlaliber@troy.edu
LALIBERTE, Michael, R . 414-229-1122 540 A
lalibert@uwm.edu
LALLA, Heather .... 603-668-6660 298 A
LALLEY, Joseph .... 740-566-7287 389 H
lalley@ohio.edu
LALLY, Jay .... 321-674-8225 103 R
jlally@fit.edu
LALLY, Kim, B .... 937-229-3902 393 E
klally1@udayton.edu
LALLY, Mary .... 617-573-8430 237 B
mlally@suffolk.edu
LALLY, Shiela .... 617-236-8800 226 F
slally@fisher.edu
LALONDE, Julie .... 209-946-2223.. 73 C
jlalonde@pacific.edu
LALOVIC-HAND, Mira .... 856-256-4146 306 D
lalovic-hand@rowan.edu
LALUZERNE, Joseph ..... 651-638-6879 254 A
j-laluzerne@bethel.edu
LALUZERNE,
Shannon, S .... 920-923-7661 537 A
slaluzerne@marianuniversity.edu
LAM, Edward .... 888-488-4968.. 48 B
edlam@itu.edu
LAM, Felix .... 212-650-8173 318 G
flam@ccny.cuny.edu
LAM, Nathan .... 310-824-1586.. 25 K
LAM, Simon, Y .... 415-338-2541.. 36 A
slam@sfsu.edu
LAM, Thien-Kieu .... 225-768-1700 206 F
LAM, Yudit .... 305-442-9223 108 G
ylam@mrc.edu
LAMADRID, Eduardo .... 787-766-1912 553 D
elamadrid@inter.edu
LAMADRID, Edward ...... 773-477-4822.. 57 E
elamadrid@pacificcollege.edu
LAMADRID, Lupe .... 225-578-1175 204 M
glamadrid@lsu.edu
LAMAGNA, Dan .... 570-961-1579 422 G
lamagnad@lackawanna.edu
LAMANA, Paul, A .... 716-851-1469 325 A
lamanna@ecc.edu

LAMANNA, Courtney .... 724-653-2221 417 D clamanna@dec.edu
LAMANNA, Richard ...... 718-289-5355 318 E richard.lamanna@bcc.cuny.edu
LAMANQUE, Andrew ..... 650-949-7179.. 45 A lamanqueandrew@foothill.edu
LAMAR, Charlene .... 912-688-6039 129 E clamar@ogeecheetech.edu
LAMAR, Melissa .... 860-773-1407.. 90 C mlamar@txcc.commnet.edu
LAMAR, Sharmaine .... 610-690-5675 436 A slamar1@swarthmore.edu
LAMARAND, Donita, M 757-446-6009 507 B lamaradm@evms.edu
LAMARCHE, Gilles .... 770-426-2674 128 C gilles.lamarche@life.edu
LAMARCHE, Paul .... 609-258-4999 305 C lamarche@princeton.edu
LAMARRE, Wayne .... 207-602-2412 213 B wlamarre@une.edu
LAMARSH, Karen .... 678-466-5115 122 J karenlamarsh@clayton.edu
LAMAS, Carmen .... 215-951-1209 422 F lamas@lasalle.edu
LAMAS, Frank .... 559-278-2541.. 33 D flamas@csufresno.edu
LAMASCUS, Scott .... 405-425-5469 399 J scott.lamascus@oc.edu
LAMASTER, Kathryn ...... 619-594-5166.. 35 E lamaster@mail.sdsu.edu
LAMB, Bill .... 319-398-5509 180 J blamb@kirkwood.edu
LAMB, Colin .... 620-276-9595 187 D colin.lamb@gcccks.edu
LAMB, Craig .... 585-345-6969 326 F crlamb@genesee.edu
LAMB, Craig .... 704-216-3500 365 F craig.lamb@rccc.edu
LAMB, Curtis, S .... 864-488-8354 447 F clamb@limestone.edu
LAMB, David .... 716-829-7652 324 E kavinokytheater@dyc.edu
LAMB, Duane .... 205-348-8092.... 8 E dlamb@fa.ua.edu
LAMB, Jason .... 540-261-8509 512 J jason.lamb@svu.edu
LAMB, John, C .... 414-288-1671 537 B john.lamb@marquette.edu
LAMB, Jon .... 734-462-4400 250 A jlamb@schoolcraft.edu
LAMB, Keith .... 940-397-4291 478 G keith.lamb@mwsu.edu
LAMB, Ken .... 513-861-6400 392 F ken.lamb@myunion.edu
LAMB, Kevin, D .... 859-238-5367 194 E kevin.lamb@centre.edu
LAMB, Krystina .... 614-251-4597 388 H lambk@ohiodominican.edu
LAMB, Linda .... 315-866-0300 327 E lamblc@herkimer.edu
LAMB, Lori .... 562-951-4455.. 32 D llamb@calstate.edu
LAMB, Margaret .... 619-388-6957.. 62 E mlamb@sdccd.edu
LAMB, Mark .... 618-664-6801 145 E mark.lamb@greenville.edu
LAMB, Mary .... 707-468-3071.. 54 A mlamb@mendocino.edu
LAMB, Marybeth .... 508-531-1353 229 C marybeth.lamb@bridgew.edu
LAMB, Rosemary .... 662-246-6256 268 F rlamb@msdelta.edu
LAMB, Susan, E .... 415-239-3303.. 39 A slamb@ccsf.edu
LAMB, Will .... 781-239-5237 222 E wlamb@babson.edu
LAMBA, Ram .... 787-725-6500 551 A rlamba@albizu.edu
LAMBDIN, Brandon .... 423-746-5337 464 D bslambdin@twcnet.edu
LAMBE, Joan .... 212-772-5462 319 E joan.lambe@hunter.cuny.edu
LAMBERT, Ame .... 802-860-2784 501 F alambert@champlain.edu
LAMBERT, Angela .... 304-327-4480 532 D alambert@bluefieldstate.edu
LAMBERT, Barry .... 254-968-9104 485 A blambert@tarleton.edu
LAMBERT, Bill .... 909-274-4215.. 54 J wlambert@mtsac.edu
LAMBERT, Chris .... 205-226-4912.... 2 C clambert@bsc.edu
LAMBERT, Cynthia, A ... 815-740-2270 162 F clambert@stfrancis.edu
LAMBERT, Dewayne ...... 985-732-6640 203 I
LAMBERT, Donovan ...... 701-255-3285 375 I dlambert@uttc.edu
LAMBERT, Edward .... 617-287-5300 228 G edward.lambert@umb.edu
LAMBERT, Elizabeth ...... 315-279-5412 329 K elambertt@keuka.edu
LAMBERT, Huntington, D .... 617-495-1000 227 D lambert@fas.harvard.edu
LAMBERT, James .... 419-372-9970 377 I jlamber@bgsu.edu
LAMBERT, James .... 802-773-5290 501 G james.lambert@csj.edu
LAMBERT, Jay .... 361-570-4290 492 A lambertj1@uhv.edu
LAMBERT, Kim, D .... 315-792-3341 351 G klambert@utica.edu
LAMBERT, III, Lake ...... 812-866-7056 166 E lambert@hanover.edu
LAMBERT, Lee, D .... 520-206-4747.. 17 A llambert@pima.edu
LAMBERT, Leo, M .... 336-278-7900 356 F lambert@elon.edu
LAMBERT, Lori, A .... 513-745-4884 396 B lambert@xavier.edu
LAMBERT, Mark, A .... 540-985-9031 509 D malambert@jchs.edu
LAMBERT, Martha .... 617-427-0060 233 A mlambert@rcc.mass.edu
LAMBERT, Matthew .... 315-786-2271 329 G mlambert@sunyjefferson.edu
LAMBERT, Matthew, T .. 757-221-1001 506 J mtlambert@wm.edu
LAMBERT, Patrick .... 845-398-4396 341 H plambert@stac.edu
LAMBERT, Peggy, E ...... 330-287-1376 389 B lambert.133@osu.edu
LAMBERT, Rebecca .... 479-524-7493.. 21 F blambert@jbu.edu
LAMBERT, Sheila .... 603-668-2211 298 H s.lambert@snhu.edu
LAMBERT, William .... 615-547-7610 456 C wlambert@cumberland.edu
LAMBERTSON, Nathaniel .... 989-775-4123 249 F lambertson.nathaniel@sagchip.edu
LAMBETH, Christopher . 513-721-7944 382 K clambeth@gbs.edu
LAMBETH, Tracie .... 407-804-1424 266 F tlambeth@belhaven.edu
LAMBIE-SIMPSON, Yasmin .... 650-543-3976.. 54 B ylambie-simpson@menlo.edu
LAMBLA, Kenneth, A .... 704-687-0090 371 B kalambla@uncc.edu
LAMBOLEY, Becky .... 701-328-4109 373 F rebecca.lamboley@ndus.edu
LAMBORGHINI, Nita ..... 978-556-3818 232 E nlamborghini@necc.mass.edu
LAMBORN, John, E ...... 765-361-6327 175 B lambornj@wabash.edu
LAMBOY, Maritza .... 787-834-9595 556 D mlamboy@uaa.edu
LAMBOY, Osvaldo .... 787-894-2828 558 F osvaldo.lamboy@upr.edu
LAMBRAKIS, Christine .. 602-286-8227.. 14 M christine.lambrakis@gwmail.maricopa.edu
LAMBRECHT, Anne, K ... 989-463-7225 239 B lambrechtak@alma.edu
LAMBRECHT, Jennifer ... 763-424-0909 260 E jsummer-lambrecht@nhcc.edu
LAMBRECHT, Jessica .... 920-565-1043 536 Q lambrechtjn@lakeland.edu
LAMBRECHT, John .... 708-456-0300 161 C jlambrec@triton.edu
LAMBRECHTSEN, Karen 916-577-2200.. 77 F klambrechtsen@jessup.edu
LAMBRIGHT, Jonathan . 912-358-3267 131 A lambrij@savannahstate.edu
LAMBRIGHT, Susie .... 214-333-6806 471 L susie@dbu.edu
LAMBSON, Leah .... 252-398-6259 356 B lambsl@chowan.edu
LAMENDOLA, Nicholas . 585-389-2072 334 B nlamend7@naz.edu
LAMERS, Chet .... 920-498-5723 544 B chet.lamers@nwtc.edu
LAMERSON, Cindy .... 581-803-2013 109 G cynthia_lamerson@pba.edu
LAMERSON, Samuel ..... 954-771-0376 107 V slamerson@knoxseminary.edu
LAMHAOUAR, Said .... 718-429-6600 352 A said.lamhaouar@vaughn.edu
LAMICA, Victoria .... 925-485-5287.. 37 N vlamica@clpccd.cc.ca.us
LAMICK, Victoria .... 708-524-6950 144 C vlamick@dom.edu
LAMIMAN, Lynne, M .... 972-708-7536 474 J
LAMKE-CALDERON, Kimberly .... 619-594-1040.. 35 E kcalderon@mail.sdsu.edu
LAMKIN, Corbet, J .... 870-574-4501.. 23 E clamkin@sautech.edu
LAMKIN, Fletcher .... 304-424-8200 533 E fletcher.lamkin@wvup.edu
LAMM, Deborah, L .... 252-823-5166 362 D lammd@edgecombe.edu
LAMM, Edward .... 920-403-3007 538 K edward.lamm@snc.edu
LAMM, Gary .... 254-295-4545 492 C glamm@umhb.edu
LAMM, Laura .... 503-251-2810 410 I lalamm@uws.edu
LAMM, Peggy .... 970-248-1020.. 80 B plamm@coloradomesa.edu
LAMMERS, Michael ...... 503-297-5544 408 A mlammers@ocac.edu
LAMMERS, Paul .... 605-668-1544 452 I plammers@mtmc.edu
LAMMONS, Anthony ..... 951-343-4217.. 30 D alammons@calbaptist.edu
LAMONACA, Stephanie . 415-451-2824.. 63 B slamonaca@sfts.edu
LAMONTAGNE, Gregory, A .... 401-825-2142 441 C glamontagne@ccri.edu
LAMONTAGNE, Ramona .... 815-836-5291 150 F lamontra@lewisu.edu
LAMONTAGNE, Susan .. 413-572-5425 230 F slamontagne@westfield.ma.edu
LAMOREAUX, Barbara .. 330-287-1214 389 B lamoreaux.1@osu.edu
LAMOREAUX, Marilyn .. 435-652-7502 499 M lamoreaux@dixie.edu
LAMORTE, Debra, A ..... 212-998-6411 336 C debra.lamorte@nyu.edu
LAMORTE, JR., Louis, A .... 215-951-1075 422 F lamorte@lasalle.edu
LAMOTHE, Stan .... 641-472-1194 181 A hrdirector@mum.edu
LAMOTHE, Vivian .... 808-934-2713 136 D vlamothe@hawaii.edu
LAMOTT, Eric, E .... 651-641-8729 255 C lamott@csp.edu
LAMOUREUX, Wayne .... 617-243-2291 227 K wlamoureux@lasell.edu
LAMPE, Gregory, P .... 608-263-1794 541 E greg.lampe@uwc.edu
LAMPE, Lawrence, P .... 513-556-2201 393 B lampelp@ucmail.uc.edu
LAMPE, Mary Beth .... 803-822-3251 447 H lampem@midlandstech.edu
LAMPE, Paul .... 636-584-6581 274 J paul.lampe@eastcentral.edu
LAMPHERE, Sue .... 740-362-3344 386 D slamphere@mtso.edu
LAMPING, Patrick .... 859-442-4175 196 A patrick.lamping@kctcs.edu
LAMPKIN, Patricia, M .. 434-924-7984 514 A pml@virginia.edu
LAMPKIN-WILLIAMS, Ann .... 313-593-5321 251 D lampkin@umich.edu
LAMPO, Jane .... 816-654-7282 276 G jlampo@kcumb.edu
LAMPPA, Robert, D ...... 608-263-3077 539 D rlamppa@fpm.wisc.edu
LAMPSHIRE, Cassie ...... 617-951-2350 234 F cassie.lampshire@necb.edu
LAMSMA, Matt .... 509-313-4100 522 L lamsma@gonzaga.edu
LAMURAGLIA, Rose ...... 619-388-3488.. 62 F rlamurag@sdccd.edu
LAMY, Melissa .... 425-739-8251 523 I melissa.lamy@lwtech.edu
LAMY, Patrick, J .... 973-748-9000 300 E patrick_lamy@bloomfield.edu
LANA, Peter .... 585-389-2344 334 B plana0@naz.edu
LANAGAN, Keni .... 865-981-8308 458 E keni.lanagan@maryvillecollege.edu
LANCASTER, Adrianna .. 580-559-5368 397 K alancaster@ecok.edu
LANCASTER, Amy, E ..... 864-597-4026 451 J lancasterae@wofford.edu
LANCASTER, Andrea ..... 425-235-2352 525 G alancaster@rtc.edu
LANCASTER, Beth .... 864-596-9704 445 E beth.lancaster@converse.edu
LANCASTER, David .... 304-424-8346 533 E david.lancaster@wvup.edu
LANCASTER, Dennis ..... 417-255-7272 279 B dennislancaster@missouristate.edu
LANCASTER, James ...... 626-852-6403.. 38 L jlancaster@citruscollege.edu
LANCASTER, Juliana .... 678-407-5834 125 B jlancaster@ggc.edu
LANCASTER, Kathy .... 864-466-1065 449 C lancasterk@sccsc.edu
LANCASTER, Loren .... 406-874-6171 287 A lancastral@milescc.edu
LANCASTER, Mark, A .... 800-287-8822 164 E lancama@bethanyseminary.edu
LANCASTER, Robin .... 501-882-4547.. 19 E rglancaster@asub.edu
LANCE, Ann, H .... 507-284-2915 254 G ann.lance@mayo.edu
LANCE, Regena .... 620-223-2700 187 B regenal@fortscott.edu
LAND, Mark .... 812-855-0850 167 I mdland@iu.edu
LAND, Matt .... 260-665-4143 173 D landm@trine.edu
LAND, Mitch .... 757-352-4916 511 G mland@regent.edu
LAND, Pammie .... 770-859-9779 128 E
LAND, Patricia .... 941-637-5656 104 G pland@fsw.edu
LAND, Richard, D .... 704-847-5600 369 A cwoodside@ses.edu
LAND, Roderic .... 801-957-4228 500 E roderic.land@slcc.edu
LAND, Sabrina .... 773-821-4976 141 J sland20@csu.edu
LANDA, Michelle .... 541-881-5583 410 D mlanda@tvcc.cc
LANDA, Michelle .... 307-532-8221 546 B michelle.landa@ewc.wy.edu
LANDAU, Lee .... 215-955-4827 436 F lee.landau@jefferson.edu
LANDEN, Jenny .... 505-428-1837 313 A jenny.landen@sfcc.edu
LANDEN, Marcia .... 601-266-4119 271 B marcia.landen@usm.edu
LANDEN, Robyn .... 307-268-2362 545 Z rlanden@caspercollege.edu
LANDER, Laura .... 903-927-3300 497 G llander@wileyc.edu
LANDER, Maria .... 704-290-5267 366 A mlander@spcc.edu
LANDER, Sharon .... 615-550-3166 466 H sharon@williamsoncc.edu
LANDERS, Joanne .... 912-344-2503 120 D joanne.landers@armstrong.edu
LANDERS, Mary, G .... 336-334-2014 371 C mglander@uncg.edu
LANDERS, Stephanie .... 313-993-1549 250 H landerss@udmercy.edu
LANDERS, Thomas, L .... 405-325-2621 403 I landers@ou.edu
LANDERS, Timothy, M . 585-343-0055 326 F tmlanders@genesee.edu
LANDES, Marie, C .... 540-665-4516 512 E mlandes@su.edu
LANDES, Mark .... 620-327-8219 187 H markl@hesston.edu
LANDETA, Christina ...... 845-431-3700 324 D christina.landeta@sunydutchess.edu
LANDEY, Sena .... 765-983-1468 165 H landse@earlham.edu
LANDGAARD, Jodi .... 507-372-3403 260 C jodi.landgaard@mnwest.edu
LANDGRAF, Tanya .... 712-749-2212 176 D landgraft@bvu.edu
LANDGREBE, Jessica .... 217-424-3965 153 A jlandgrebe@millikin.edu
LANDGREN, Peter .... 513-556-3737 393 B peter.landgren@uc.edu
LANDIS, Ann .... 229-226-1621 132 E alandis@thomasu.edu
LANDIS, Cory .... 617-730-7034 235 B cory.landis@newbury.edu
LANDIS, Jean, W .... 215-951-1000 422 F
LANDIS, Jennifer .... 620-417-1400 191 A jennifer.landis@sccc.edu
LANDIS, SCC, Marie Cecelia .... 973-957-0188 299 F spmcl@juno.com
LANDIS, Sarah .... 540-828-5334 505 F slandis@bridgewater.edu
LANDIS, Shirley, A .... 215-951-2717 432 F landiss@philau.edu
LANDPHAIR, Juliette, L 804-289-8468 513 M jlandpha@richmond.edu
LANDREBE, Robert, S .... 859-858-2192 192 O
LANDRETH, Paige .... 405-682-7503 399 K plandreth@occc.edu
LANDRITH, James, W .. 864-231-2000 443 E wlandrith@andersonuniversity.edu
LANDRON, Carmen, T .. 787-620-2040 550 D clandron@aupr.edu
LANDRON-ARANA, Ana, I .... 787-480-2450 551 H alandron@sanjuanciudadpatria.com
LANDRUM, Kay .... 817-598-6499 497 A klandrum@wc.edu
LANDRUM, Kay .... 616-222-1402 241 G kay.landrum@cornerstone.edu
LANDRUM, Kristin .... 276-656-0259 516 D klandrum@patrickhenry.edu
LANDRUM, Paul .... 575-538-6488 314 E landrump@wumu.edu
LANDRUM, Treina .... 318-342-5313 209 A landrum@ulm.edu

LANDRUM, Zalika .... 773-602-5116 142 A
zlandrum@ccc.edu

LANDRUM-SIMS, Alonzetta .... 334-347-2623.... 3 H
alandrum-sims@escc.edu

LANDRY, Abbie .... 318-357-4403 208 D
landry@nsula.edu

LANDRY, Bill .... 843-574-6745 449 G
bill.landry@tridenttech.edu

LANDRY, Brett .... 972-721-4067 491 B
rlandry@udallas.edu

LANDRY, Cara .... 225-743-8500 204 C
clandry@rpcc.edu

LANDRY, David, M .... 504-398-2109 206 E
dlandry@olhcc.edu

LANDRY, Debbie .... 918-456-5511 398 M
landry@nsuok.edu

LANDRY, Fred .... 318-869-5136 202 D
flandry@centenary.edu

LANDRY, Karen .... 425-267-0153 522 I
klandry@everettcc.edu

LANDRY, Lisa, C .... 337-482-5430 208 F
ldlandry@louisiana.edu

LANDRY, Lynette .... 808-236-5811 135 C
llandry@hpu.edu

LANDRY, Madelaine ..... 337-550-1257 205 B
mlandry@lsue.edu

LANDRY, Patrick .... 337-482-6402 208 F
pml@louisiana.edu

LANDRY, Shawntel, D .. 800-280-0307 163 I
shawntel.landry@ace.edu

LANDRY, Stephen .... 973-275-2299 308 C
stephen.landry@shu.edu

LANDSAW, Christy .... 918-456-5511 398 M
landsaw@nsuok.edu

LANDSTROM, Corey ..... 563-387-1020 180 M
clandstrom@luther.edu

LANDWER, Allan, J ...... 325-670-2222 474 M
alandwer@hsutx.edu

LANDWERMEYER, Elizabeth .... 817-515-3049 484 B
elizabeth.landwermeyer@tccd.edu

LANE, Austin .... 832-813-6522 477 I
austin.lane@lonestar.edu

LANE, Barbara .... 573-329-5160 276 K
laneb@lincolnu.edu

LANE, Bradley .... 206-934-2926 526 A
bradley.lane@seattlecolleges.edu

LANE, Carrie .... 785-628-4000 187 A
cdlane@fhsu.edu

LANE, Charles, E .... 352-392-9122 115 D
charlielane@ufl.edu

LANE, David .... 207-621-3448 212 D
dlane@maine.edu

LANE, David, J .... 585-292-3040 333 G
dlane@monroecc.edu

LANE, Deborah .... 205-348-8089.... 8 E
dlane@ur.ua.edu

LANE, Deborah .... 405-744-6384 400 C
debbie.lane@okstate.edu

LANE, Diane, C .... 410-287-1022 214 C
dlane@cecil.edu

LANE, Diane, L .... 217-362-6416 153 A
dlane@millikin.edu

LANE, Edwin, H .... 816-415-7587 285 K
lanee@william.jewell.edu

LANE, Eric .... 516-463-5854 328 A
eric.lane@hofstra.edu

LANE, Greg .... 619-574-6909.. 57 E
glane@pacificcollege.edu

LANE, Jason .... 518-320-1448 343 B
jason.lane@suny.edu

LANE, Jennifer .... 808-675-4971 134 M
jennifer.lane@byuh.edu

LANE, Jeremy .... 405-466-3428 398 E
jlane@langston.edu

LANE, Jill .... 678-466-4194 122 J
jilllane@clayton.edu

LANE, John .... 713-221-8292 491 F
lanej@uhd.edu

LANE, Jon .... 940-397-4241 478 G
jon.lane@mwsu.edu

LANE, Kim .... 909-607-3778.. 39 D
kiml@cuc.claremont.edu

LANE, Kimberly .... 216-373-5290 388 A
klane@ndc.edu

LANE, Kristi .... 218-683-8631 260 F
kristi.lane@northlandcollege.edu

LANE, Laura .... 248-476-1122 246 G
llane@mispp.edu

LANE, Marguerite .... 516-323-4014 333 E
mlane@molloy.edu

LANE, Mark .... 808-455-0213 136 G
marklane@hawaii.edu

LANE, Matt .... 717-728-2263 415 B
mattlane@centralpenn.edu

LANE, Michael .... 516-686-7723 335 F
mlane@nyit.edu

LANE, Mike .... 816-271-4476 279 E
lane@missouriwestern.edu

LANE, Natalie .... 307-382-1673 546 L
nlane@wwcc.wy.edu

LANE, Robert, J .... 515-961-1417 182 I
bob.lane@simpson.edu

LANE, Russ .... 402-557-7452 289 B
russ.lane@bellevue.edu

LANE, Shannon .... 318-487-7498 202 L
shannon.lane@lacollege.edu

LANE, Shannon .... 361-354-2271 470 K
lane@coastalbend.edu

LANE, Shelese .... 404-270-5110 132 D
sjlane@spelman.edu

LANE, Tamara, N .... 806-743-6429 490 A
tamara.lane@ttuhsc.edu

LANE, Tiletha .... 843-383-8082 445 A
tlane@coker.edu

LANE, Tracey, R .... 817-552-3700 477 B
tracey.lane@tku.edu

LANE-MARTIN, Tanya ... 585-345-6800 326 F
tmlanemartin@genesee.edu

LANE SAMPSON, Shaunda .... 610-399-2066 430 D
slsampson@cheyney.edu

LANESE, Carlos .... 213-637-1367.. 77 C
clanese@westwood.edu

LANESSKOG, Stig .... 909-621-8026.. 39 D
stig_lanesskog@cuc.claremont.edu

LANEY, Candy .... 406-874-6165 287 A
laneyc@milescc.edu

LANEY, Mary, A .... 386-312-4069 111 K
maryannelaney@sjrstate.edu

LANEY, Miriam .... 803-778-7825 443 I
laneymt@cctech.edu

LANFEAR, Jeffery .... 773-325-8308 143 G
jlanfear@depaul.edu

LANG, Anita .... 201-216-5163 308 D
alang@stevens.edu

LANG, Ashley .... 319-352-8486 183 J
ashley.lang@wartburg.edu

LANG, Christine .... 843-574-6162 449 G
chris.lang@tridenttech.edu

LANG, Christopher .... 304-865-6107 530 F
christopher.lang@ovu.edu

LANG, Cyndi .... 574-520-4490 168 F
clang@iusb.edu

LANG, Heather .... 971-722-4532 409 C
heather.lang@pcc.edu

LANG, Jean .... 808-544-0272 135 C
jlang@hpu.edu

LANG, Jennifer, R .... 718-780-0679 317 A
jennifer.lang@brooklaw.edu

LANG, Kathy, J .... 414-288-1782 537 B
kathy.lang@marquette.edu

LANG, Kenneth .... 610-917-1454 438 G
krlang@valleyforge.edu

LANG, Mandy .... 715-422-5446 543 D
mandy.lang@mstc.edu

LANG, Melissa, W .... 757-446-6054 507 B
langmw@evms.edu

LANG, Michelle .... 503-517-1190 411 A
mlang@warnerpacific.edu

LANG, Milton .... 530-752-8787.. 71 A
lmlang@ucdavis.edu

LANG, Natasha .... 925-424-1634.. 37 O
nlang@laspositascollege.edu

LANG, Stephen, W .... 432-837-8061 489 B
slang@sulross.edu

LANG, Stuart .... 612-374-5800 255 G
slang@dunwoody.edu

LANGAN, Nicole .... 570-945-8274 422 B
nicole.langan@keystone.edu

LANGAN, Rikki .... 217-479-7030 151 J
rikki.langan@mac.edu

LANGAN, Terrence, G ... 651-962-6001 265 F
tglangan@stthomas.edu

LANGDON, Deb .... 740-389-4636 386 B
langdond@mtc.edu

LANGDON, Heather, H . 828-262-2093 369 D
langdonhh@appstate.edu

LANGDON, Rita .... 516-299-2334 330 G
rita.langdon@liu.edu

LANGDON, Steven, D ... 515-643-6716 181 B
slangdon@mercydesmoines.org

LANGDON, Tennille ...... 660-831-4157 279 D
langdont@moval.edu

LANGE, Amy .... 785-243-1435 186 A
alange@cloud.edu

LANGE, Andrea, G .... 410-778-7776 221 D
alange2@washcoll.edu

LANGE, Barbara .... 352-854-2322 100 P
langeb@cf.edu

LANGE, Chris, J .... 414-410-4207 535 C
cjlange@stritch.edu

LANGE, Douglas, J .... 606-218-5988 201 C
douglaslange@upike.edu

LANGE, Janet .... 309-677-2374 140 H
lange@fsmail.bradley.edu

LANGE, Janet .... 309-677-2523 140 H
lange@bradley.edu

LANGE, Jean .... 203-582-8444.. 91 E
jean.lange@quinnipiac.edu

LANGE, OSB, Jeremiah, N .... 724-532-7961 435 C
jeremiah.lange@stvincent.edu

LANGE, Jesse .... 563-588-8000 178 E
jlange@emmaus.edu

LANGE, Karen .... 307-778-1204 546 F
klange@lccc.wy.edu

LANGE, Karen, M .... 651-962-6120 265 F
kmlange@stthomas.edu

LANGE, Mike .... 928-776-2067.. 18 L
mike.lange@yc.edu

LANGE, Robert, J .... 757-594-7036 506 I
robert.lange@cnu.edu

LANGE, Steven .... 320-629-5155 260 H
langes@pinetech.edu

LANGE, Tom, J .... 715-831-7285 542 M
tlange8@cvtc.edu

LANGE, Tyana .... 570-484-2087 431 C
tsl400@lhup.edu

LANGEN, Jill .... 810-766-4374 239 G
jill.langen@baker.edu

LANGENDORGER, Stephen, J .... 419-372-7234 377 I
slangen@bgsu.edu

LANGER, Nathan .... 218-723-6010 255 A
nlanger@css.edu

LANGER, Patricia, M ..... 651-696-6562 256 L
planger@macalester.edu

LANGER, Peter .... 617-287-5611 228 G
peter.langer@umb.edu

LANGERBEIN, Helmut ... 870-235-4200.. 23 D
helmetlangerbein@saumag.edu

LANGERUD, Steve .... 641-472-7000 181 A
slangerud@mum.edu

LANGEVIN, John .... 207-602-2549 213 B
jlangevin@une.edu

LANGFORD, Allison ...... 417-328-1601 282 D
alangford@sbuniv.edu

LANGFORD, Allison ...... 417-328-2093 282 D
alangford@sbuniv.edu

LANGFORD, David .... 201-692-9867 302 H
david_langford@fdu.edu

LANGFORD, Debra .... 304-876-5216 532 I
dlangfor@shepherd.edu

LANGFORD, Joel, C ..... 770-720-5585 130 E
jcl@reinhardt.edu

LANGFORD, Marcus ..... 516-745-5769 393 C
marcus.langford@uc.edu

LANGFORD, McKenzie .. 229-732-5956 120 B
mckenzielangford@andrewcollege.edu

LANGFORD, Pamela ..... 909-537-7454.. 35 A
plangfor@csusb.edu

LANGFORD, Russ .... 417-862-9533 275 C
rlangford@globaluniversity.edu

LANGHAM, Gay .... 601-643-8307 266 J
gay.langham@colin.edu

LANGHAM, Julie .... 706-595-0166 121 B
jlangham@augustatech.edu

LANGHAM, Lynda .... 936-468-2503 484 A
llangham@sfasu.edu

LANGHAMMER, Paul .... 401-874-9500 442 E
langhammer@uri.edu

LANGHAUSER, Derek .... 207-629-4000 210 K
dlanghauser@mccs.me.edu

LANGINESTRA, Jaime ... 212-431-2843 335 G
Jaime.Laginestra@nyls.edu

LANGIS, Gayle .... 207-893-7850 211 H
glangis@sjcme.edu

LANGKILDE, Jared .... 480-461-7396.. 15 A
jared.langkilde@mesacc.edu

LANGLAND, Meg .... 573-592-5381 285 J
meg.langland@westminster-mo.edu

LANGLEY, Amy .... 256-840-4185.... 7 B
alangley@snead.edu

LANGLEY, Angie .... 662-720-7249 269 D
alangle@nemcc.edu

LANGLEY, Goldie .... 614-947-6509 382 H
goldie.langley@franklin.edu

LANGLEY, Janet .... 623-845-3155.. 14 N
janet.langley@gccaz.edu

LANGLEY, Jesse .... 252-985-5177 367 E
jlangley@ncwc.edu

LANGLEY, Pamela .... 603-271-6484 297 C
plangley@ccsnh.edu

LANGLEY, Winston .... 617-287-5600 228 G
winston.langley@umb.edu

LANGLEY-TURNBAUGH, Samantha .... 207-780-5361 213 A
langley@usm.maine.edu

LANGLEY-TURNBAUGH, Samantha .... 859-572-7528 199 A
langleys1@nku.edu

LANGLOIS, OP, John .... 202-495-3831.. 96 E
president@dhs.edu

LANGLOIS, Mary Ann ... 716-888-2103 317 H
langloim@canisius.edu

LANGOIS, Judith, H ..... 512-232-3300 493 M
jlanglois@austin.utexas.edu

LANGRELL, Ron .... 253-680-7103 519 K
rlangrell@bates.ctc.edu

LANGRIDGE, Nick .... 540-568-3197 509 C
langrinl@jmu.edu

LANGSETH, Kay .... 319-895-4242 177 A
klangseth@cornellcollege.edu

LANGSETH, Roger .... 507-535-3309 255 D
rlangseth@crossroadscollege.edu

LANGSETH, Roger, W ... 507-288-4563 255 D
rlangseth@crossroadscollege.edu

LANGSTAFF, Kris, A ..... 606-474-3153 195 F
klangstaff@kcu.edu

LANGSTON, II, Bill, C .. 863-680-4209 104 F
blangston@flsouthern.edu

LANGSTON, Carol .... 903-334-6628 486 C
carol.langston@tamut.edu

LANGSTON, Ginna, V ... 918-631-2641 403 M
ruth-langston@utulsa.edu

LANGSTON, Randall ...... 585-395-2772 345 A
rlangsto@brockport.edu

LANGSTON, Randall ..... 585-395-2751 345 A
rlangston@brockport.edu

LANGSTRAAT, Jim .... 971-722-2913 409 C
jim.langstraat@pcc.edu

LANGSTRAAT, Jim .... 971-722-4200 409 C
jim.langstraat@pcc.edu

LANGSTRAAT, Nate .... 360-383-3350 528 E
nlangstraat@whatcom.ctc.edu

LANGTEAU, Paula .... 715-735-4339 541 E
paula.langteau@uwc.edu

LANHAM, Allen, K .... 217-581-6061 144 E
aklanham@eiu.edu

LANHAM, Heather .... 937-778-7803 381 K
hlanham@edisonohio.edu

LANHAM, Jeff .... 740-245-7485 394 D
jlanham@rio.edu

LANHAM, Terri .... 270-686-4548 197 A
terri.lanham@kctcs.edu

LANIAK, Timothy, S ..... 704-527-9909 227 B
tlaniak@gcts.edu

LANIER, Amy, S .... 803-786-3927 445 C
alanier@columbiasc.edu

LANIER, Annette .... 503-768-7685 406 H
annette@lclark.edu

LANIER, Carolyn .... 203-837-8277.. 88 G
lanierc@wcsu.edu

LANIER, David .... 478-757-3659 128 H
david.lanier@mga.edu

LANIER, Ginger .... 540-261-8469 512 J
ginger.lanier@svu.edu

LANIER, John .... 706-385-1065 130 C
john.lanier@point.edu

LANIER, Marie .... 904-743-1122 107 C
mlanier@jones.edu

LANIER, Percy .... 205-929-1663.... 5 I
plani@mail.miles.edu

LANIER, Stephen, M .... 313-577-5600 252 G
stephen.lanier@wayne.edu

LANIER, Walter .... 414-297-7710 543 E
lanierw@matc.edu

LANIER WEYERS, Anna 316-978-3001 192 D
anna.weyers@wichita.edu

LANK, Kristy .... 207-985-7976 210 H
kristy@landingschool.edu

LANKER, Jason .... 716-926-8933 327 F
jlanker@hilbert.edu

LANKES, Susan .... 716-652-8900 317 M
slankes@cks.edu

LANN, Jennifer .... 802-387-6764 502 A
jlann@landmark.edu

LANNERT, Mary .... 406-447-6944 287 F
mary.lannert@umhelena.edu

LANNING, Brek .... 828-565-4027 363 C
bwlanning@haywood.edu

LANNING, Gale .... 507-453-1443 259 G
glanning@southeastmn.edu

LANNING, Paul .... 408-924-1120.. 36 B
paul.lanning@sjsu.edu

LANNING, Stephanie .... 620-227-9370 186 F
slg@dc3.edu

LANNUTTI, Pamela .... 215-951-1935 422 F
lannuttip@lasalle.edu

LANOUE, David .... 808-544-0228 135 C
dlanoue@hpu.edu

LANOUREUX, Silvina .... 727-298-8685 117 J

LANPHER, Jim .... 803-754-4100 445 D

LANSER, Michael .... 920-693-1123 543 B
michael.lanser@gotoltc.edu

LANSING, Sean, T .... 414-410-4583 535 C
stlansing@stritch.edu

LANSIQUOT, Beverly, A 340-692-4117 559 B
beverly.lansiquot@uvi.edu

LANTAGNE, Douglas, O 802-656-2990 503 C
doug.lantagne@uvm.edu

LANTING, Mark .... 815-825-2086 149 E
mark.lanting@kishwaukeecollege.edu

LANTIS, Glenda .... 541-318-3753 404 K
glantis@cocc.edu

LANTZ, Mary Jan .... 409-944-1281 474 G
mlantz@gc.edu

LANTZ, Melody .... 423-746-5327 464 D
mlantz@twcnet.edu

LASHLEY, Jeffery .... 660-263-4110 279 F
jeffl@macc.edu
LASHLEY, Kent .... 405-733-7306 401 L
klashley@rose.edu
LASHLEY, Lynn .... 205-652-3417.... 9 G
lsl@uwa.edu
LASHLEY, Marsha .... 660-831-4115 279 D
lashleym@moval.edu
LASHLEY, Sarah, E .... 859-238-5573 194 E
sarah.lashley@centre.edu
LASHURE, Faith .... 630-466-7900 162 K
flashure@waubonsee.edu
LASICH, Deb .... 303-273-3097.. 80 O
dlasich@mines.edu
LASIEWSKI, Doreen ...... 401-739-5000 441 E
dlasiewski@neit.edu
LASITER, Paul, B .... 310-506-4497.. 58 H
paul.lasiter@pepperdine.edu
LASKA-NIXON, Diane ... 508-767-7239 222 D
dlaska@assumption.edu
LASKARIS, Maria .... 603-646-2604 297 G
maria.laskaris@dartmouth.edu
LASKARIS, Theodore .... 802-860-2757 501 F
tlaskaris@champlain.edu
LASKE, Lori, L .... 719-587-7867.. 78 I
lllaske@adams.edu
LASKER, Y. Mayer .... 718-377-0777 338 H
LASKIN, Emily .... 626-396-2200.. 28 J
emily.laskin@artcenter.edu
LASKOFSKI, Mike .... 703-993-4573 507 K
mlaskofs@gmu.edu
LASKY, Melodee, S ...... 848-932-9064 306 F
mlasky@echo.rutgers.edu
LASLEY, Steven, T .... 615-460-6404 455 D
steve.lasley@belmont.edu
LASOTA, Todd .... 773-777-4220 155 B
tlasota@nc.edu
LASSEN, Gregg .... 504-280-6207 205 G
glassen@uno.edu
LASSETTER, Jerry .... 919-761-2266 368 K
jlassetter@sebts.edu
LASSIAL, Erin .... 315-386-7608 347 F
lassiale@canton.edu
LASSITER, Carllos .... 662-252-8000 270 C
classiter@rustcollege.edu
LASSITER, Colleen .... 706-233-7337 131 C
classiter@shorter.edu
LASSITER, Donald, L .... 910-630-7081 359 C
lassiter@methodist.edu
LASSITER, Elbert, J .... 336-633-0217 365 A
ejlassiter@randolph.edu
LASSITER, Fred .... 614-251-4513 388 H
lassitef@ohiodominican.edu
LASSITER, John .... 706-295-6511 125 F
jlassiter@gntc.edu
LASSITER, Joshua .... 252-335-3665 369 F
jllassiter@ecsu.edu
LASSITER, Lisabeth .... 972-883-4715 494 A
lisabeth.lassiter@utdallas.edu
LASSNER, David, K .... 808-956-8207 135 H
david@hawaii.edu
LASSNER, Jennifer .... 319-335-2123 175 H
jennifer-lassner@uiowa.edu
LAST, Brad .... 435-652-7858 499 M
blast@dixie.edu
LASTER, Katherine .... 229-430-3848 119 H
katherine.laster@asurams.edu
LASTINGER, Michael .... 304-293-6955 533 D
michael.lastinger@mail.wvu.edu
LASTORIA, Cindy .... 585-567-9526 328 C
cindy.lastoria@houghton.edu
LASTRA, Sarai .... 787-743-7979 555 M
ut_slastra@suagm.edu
LATA, Fran .... 303-373-2008.. 85 I
flatay@rvu.edu
LATANE, Jane .... 520-383-8401.. 18 A
jlatane@tocc.edu
LATCHAW HIRSH,
Sharon .... 610-527-0200 434 D
shirsh@rosemont.edu
LATCHUM, Lucy, L .... 757-594-7702 506 I
llatchum@cnu.edu
LATCOVICH, Mark, A .... 440-943-7600 391 A
mal@dioceseofcleveland.org
LATHAM, Adrienne .... 615-329-8632 456 G
alatham@fisk.edu
LATHAM, Amy .... 662-562-3201 269 E
a_latham@northwestms.edu
LATHAM, Brenda .... 209-381-6410.. 54 C
latham.b@mccd.edu
LATHAM, Celeste .... 815-753-1000 154 I
LATHAM, Clara .... 940-397-4757 478 G
clara.latham@mwsu.edu
LATHAM, Heather .... 410-626-2511 218 A
heather.latham@sjc.edu
LATHAM, JoAnne .... 518-608-8240 325 B
jlatham@excelsior.edu
LATHAM, Linda, H .... 334-734-7582 362 F
llatham@forsythtech.edu
LATHAM, Marilae .... 618-664-7110 145 E
marilae.latham@greenville.edu
LATHAM, Mark .... 912-260-4300 131 D
mark.latham@sgsc.edu
LATHAM, Mark .... 802-831-1226 503 E
mlatham@vermontlaw.edu
LATHAM, Michael .... 641-269-3100 178 I
latham@grinnell.edu
LATHAM, Mike .... 252-443-4011 364 E
mlatham@nashcc.edu
LATHAM, Paula, J .... 606-679-8501 197 B
paula.latham@kctcs.edu
LATHAM, Sarah .... 831-459-3778.. 72 E
sclatham@ucsc.edu
LATHAM, Sheila .... 701-858-4145 374 B
sheila.latham@minotstateu.edu
LATHAM, Tricia .... 580-477-7725 404 D
tricia.latham@wosc.edu
LATHAM-ALFORD,
Crystal .... 325-235-7396 488 C
crystal.latham-alford@tstc.edu
LATHEM, Lindsay, S ..... 336-272-7102 357 B
lindsay.lathem@greensboro.edu
LATHIGARA, Rajesh ...... 650-738-7076.. 64 E
lathigarar@smccd.edu
LATHROP, Sam .... 217-228-5432 156 D
lathrsa@quincy.edu
LATIF, Niaz .... 219-989-3251 171 L
nlatif@purduecal.edu
LATIMER, Callie .... 254-526-1397 470 E
callie.latimer@ctcd.edu
LATIMER, Dewana .... 731-425-2624 463 A
dlatimer@jscc.edu
LATIMER, Maretta .... 904-470-8244 102 A
m.latimer@ewc.edu
LATIMER, Margaret .... 240-567-7711 217 B
margaret.latimer@montgomerycollege.edu
LATIMER, William .... 718-960-7306 319 C
william.latimer@lehman.cuny.edu
LATIMER-DAVIS,
Tanisha .... 803-981-7703 451 K
TLatimer-Davis@yorktech.edu
LATIMORE, Debra .... 706-821-8232 129 H
dlatimore@paine.edu
LATIMORE, Leatrice, D . 504-284-5435 207 B
llatimor@suno.edu
LATIMORE, Nancy, J .... 717-361-1407 418 B
latimonj@etown.edu
LATIN, Quinton .... 903-730-4890 476 L
quinton.latin@jarvis.edu
LATINO, Jennifer, A ...... 910-814-5577 355 C
latinoj@campbell.edu
LATINVILLE, Darlene ..... 213-624-1200.. 44 I
dlatinville@fidm.edu
LATIOLAIS, Perry .... 281-487-1170 486 F
platiolais@txchiro.edu
LATIOLAIS, Scott .... 425-235-2409 525 G
slatiolais@rtc.edu
LATORELLA, Jacqueline 813-253-6219 118 H
jlatorella@ut.edu
LATORRE, Daria .... 610-796-8481 412 C
daria.latorre@alvernia.edu
LATOUF, Christina .... 646-660-6114 318 C
Christina.Latouf@baruch.cuny.edu
LATOUR, Bill .... 217-641-4290 148 J
blatour@jwcc.edu
LATOUR, Mickey, A ...... 618-453-2469 159 H
mlatour@siu.edu
LATOUR, Terry, S .... 814-393-2343 430 E
tlatour@clarion.edu
LATSHAW, Todd, M ...... 717-867-6330 423 I
latshaw@lvc.edu
LATTA, Bruce, J .... 410-293-1801 549 B
latta@usna.edu
LATTA, Corey .... 901-381-3939 466 E
corey@visible.edu
LATTA, Mark, A .... 402-280-5061 290 B
MarkLatta@creighton.edu
LATTA, Michael .... 812-877-8975 172 C
michael.latta@rose-hulman.edu
LATTER, Deborah .... 863-784-7251 113 C
latterd@southflorida.edu
LATTER, George .... 619-849-2317.. 59 K
georgelatter@pointloma.edu
LATTIMORE, Dan, L .... 901-678-2991 462 B
dlattimr@memphis.edu
LATTIMORE, John .... 704-669-4020 361 E
lattimorej@clevelandcc.edu
LATTIMORE, Mark .... 478-825-6296 124 E
lattimorem@fvsu.edu
LATTIMORE, Vergel, L .. 704-636-6823 357 F
vlattimore@hoodseminary.edu
LATTING, John .... 404-727-6036 124 D
john.latting@emory.edu
LATVIS, Mike .... 313-436-9152 251 D
latvism@umich.edu
LATZ, Gil .... 317-278-1265 168 E
glatz@iupui.edu
LAU, Allison .... 206-878-3710 523 D
alau@highline.edu
LAU, Bradley, A .... 503-554-2312 406 A
blau@georgefox.edu
LAU, John .... 760-355-6235.. 47 G
john.lau@imperial.edu
LAU, Lawrence .... 310-577-3000.. 77 K
lau@yosan.edu
LAU, Pam .... 217-351-2542 155 I
plau@parkland.edu
LAU, Stuart .... 808-956-8010 135 J
stuartl@hawaii.edu
LAUB, Jeffrey, W .... 434-832-7707 515 A
laubj@cvcc.vccs.edu
LAUB, Joe .... 212-484-1108 319 F
jlaub@jjay.cuny.edu
LAUBAUCH, Harold ...... 954-262-1303 109 E
harold@nsu.nova.edu
LAUBE, Irene, H .... 919-536-7211 362 C
laubei@durhamtech.edu
LAUBE, Philip, E .... 740-826-8101 387 C
plaube@muskingum.edu
LAUCHNER, Kathy .... 512-313-3000 471 H
kathy.lauchner@concordia.edu
LAUDE, David, A .... 512-232-3317 493 M
dalaude@austin.utexas.edu
LAUDER, Frank .... 617-873-0137 225 A
finaid@cambridgecollege.edu
LAUDER, Sue, M .... 978-665-3313 229 D
slauder@fitchburgstate.edu
LAUDERBACK, Cindy .... 360-417-6341 525 A
clauderback@pencol.edu
LAUDERDALE, Wendy ... 985-549-5544 208 E
wlauderdale@selu.edu
LAUER, Andrew, J .... 212-960-0051 353 P
andrewlauer@yu.edu
LAUER, Bonnie .... 570-740-0734 425 A
blauer@luzerne.edu
LAUER, Brenda .... 719-502-2403.. 84 J
brenda.lauer@ppcc.edu
LAUER, John .... 719-389-6618.. 79 M
jlauer@coloradocollege.edu
LAUER, Jonathan, D ..... 717-766-2511 426 B
jlauer@messiah.edu
LAUER, Theresa .... 909-607-2760.. 46 K
theresa_lauer@hmc.edu
LAUERMAN, Meg .... 402-472-0088 293 H
mlauerman1@unl.edu
LAUFER, Marilyn .... 334-844-1486.... 1 G
laufema@auburn.edu
LAUFFENBURGER,
Linda, M .... 937-327-7811 395 I
llauffenburger@wittenberg.edu
LAUG, Adam .... 641-269-3200 178 I
laugadam@grinnell.edu
LAUGHEAD, Ross .... 210-485-0060 466 J
rlaughead@alamo.edu
LAUGHHUNN, Seirra .... 217-234-5222 150 B
slaughhunn42647@lakeland.cc.il.us
LAUGHLIN, Ed .... 978-478-3400 235 E
elaughlin@northpoint.edu
LAUGHLIN,
Frederick, L .... 231-995-1197 248 C
flaughlin@nmc.edu
LAUGHLIN, Karen, L ..... 850-644-2740 115 A
klaughlin@admin.fsu.edu
LAUGHLIN, Lynn .... 217-732-3168 150 G
llaughli@lincolnchristian.edu
LAUGHLIN, Patricia ...... 312-567-3827 147 E
plaughli@iit.edu
LAUGHLIN, Ronda .... 360-752-8334 520 A
rlaughlin@btc.ctc.edu
LAUGHLIN, Russ .... 817-202-6462 483 C
laughlinr@swau.edu
LAUGHRAN, Patrick ...... 508-626-4357 230 A
plaughran@framingham.edu
LAUGHTER, Ray .... 832-813-6621 477 I
ray.laughter@lonestar.edu
LAUGHTON, John .... 609-771-2278 301 E
jlaughto@tcnj.edu
LAUNIUS, Katy .... 918-343-7707 401 I
klaunius@rsu.edu
LAUR, Dave .... 906-786-5802 240 K
dave.laur@baycollege.edu
LAURANZON,
Anne Marie .... 804-752-7317 511 E
alauranz@rmc.edu
LAURENCE, David .... 928-776-7666.. 18 L
david.laurence@yc.edu
LAURENS, Jay .... 704-463-3026 367 F
jay.laurens@pfeiffer.edu
LAURENT, Timothy .... 406-791-5302 288 J
tlaurent01@ugf.edu
LAURENZ, Jamie .... 575-562-2312 310 I
jamie.laurenz@enmu.edu
LAURENZI, Kellie, L ...... 412-397-5201 434 B
laurenzi@rmu.edu
LAURETANO, Angela ..... 914-632-5400 333 F
alauretano@monroecollege.edu
LAURIA, James .... 412-809-5100 433 D
lauria.james@pti.edu
LAURIE, Sean .... 516-323-4820 333 E
slaurie@molloy.edu
LAURINE, Robert .... 404-962-3000 133 G
bobby.laurine@usg.edu
LAURITA, Brandi .... 419-434-4663 393 F
ankney@findlay.edu
LAURITZEN, Rhonda ..... 801-627-8388 498 O
lauritzr@owatc.edu
LAUSCH, Mark, C .... 608-243-4508 543 C
mlausch@madisoncollege.edu
LAUSELL, Ana, C .... 787-891-0925 553 E
amelon@aguadilla.inter.edu
LAUX, Carolyne .... 850-729-5360 109 D
lauxc@nwfsc.edu
LAUX, Dan .... 402-461-7301 290 G
dlaux@hastings.edu
LAUZON CLABO,
Laurie .... 313-577-4082 252 G
laurie.lauzon.clabo@wayne.edu
LAVALLÉE-WELCH,
Catherine .... 608-785-8805 539 G
clavallee-welch@uwlax.edu
LAVALLEY, Ken .... 603-862-4343 299 B
ken.lavalley@unh.edu
LAVALLIERE, Pamela .... 608-663-3317 536 A
plavalliere@edgewood.edu
LAVANIA, Ambrish .... 803-793-5263 445 F
lavaniaa@denmarktech.edu
LAVELLI, Lucinda .... 352-392-0207 115 D
llavelli@arts.ufl.edu
LAVENDER, Bernadette . 770-426-2633 128 C
bernadette.lavender@life.edu
LAVENDER, Julie .... 989-275-5000 245 C
julie.lavender@kirtland.edu
LAVENDER, Martha, G .. 256-549-8221.... 3 N
mlavender@gadsdenstate.edu
LAVENDER, Melissa ...... 850-747-3211 105 Q
mlavender@gulfcoast.edu
LAVENDER, Michael, K . 828-652-0681 364 B
michaell@mcdowelltech.edu
LAVENDER, Randall ...... 310-665-6988.. 57 C
rlavender@otis.edu
LAVERDIERE, Karen ...... 904-256-7243 106 Q
klaverd@ju.edu
LAVERGNE, Paul .... 718-429-6600 352 A
paul.lavergne@vaughn.edu
LAVERRIERE, Robert, J . 937-255-6234 547 E
robert.laverriere@afit.edu
LAVERY, Hugh, J .... 215-955-6834 436 F
hugh.lavery@jefferson.edu
LAVERY, Jim .... 740-389-4636 386 B
laveryj@mtc.edu
LAVERY, Roger .... 765-285-6000 164 D
rlavery@bsu.edu
LAVES, Beth .... 270-745-1900 201 D
beth.laves@wku.edu
LAVIAL, Pierre .... 772-466-4822.. 98 P
pierre.lavial@aviator.edu
LAVIGNA, Lisa .... 518-608-8252 325 B
llavigna@excelsior.edu
LAVIGNA, Robert .... 608-890-3888 539 D
rlavigna@ohr.wisc.edu
LAVIGNE, Robert, W ..... 508-213-2217 235 C
robert.lavigne@nichols.edu
LAVIGNE-ROHINI,
Diana .... 510-780-4500.. 50 G
dlavigne@lifewest.edu
LAVIN, Marjorie, W .... 518-587-2100 348 A
marjorie.lavin@esc.edu
LAVIN, Thomas, J .... 401-456-8094 442 A
tlavin@ric.edu
LAVINE, Danielle .... 860-509-9511.. 90 G
dlavine@hartsem.edu
LAVINE, Steven, D .... 661-255-1050.. 31 B
slavine@calarts.edu
LAVIOLETTE, Marc .... 239-590-7891 114 F
mlaviole@fgcu.edu
LAVIT, Daniel, A .... 270-809-2160 198 I
dlavit@murraystate.edu
LAVNER, Lilly .... 610-896-1228 420 J
llavner@haverford.edu
LAVOIE, Chuck .... 802-468-1250 503 G
chuck.lavoie@castleton.edu
LAVOIE, Lisa .... 860-255-3786.. 90 C
llavoie@txcc.commnet.edu
LAVOIE, Rocky .... 541-888-7425 410 A
rlavoie@socc.edu
LAVOIE, Steven .... 603-428-2386 298 B
slavoie@nec.edu
LAVORATA,
Christina, M .... 304-367-4101 532 F
Chris.Lavorata@fairmontstate.edu
LAW, Christopher, G .... 740-376-4857 386 A
christopher.law@marietta.edu
LAW, Christy .... 516-918-3650 316 L
claw@bcl.edu
LAW, John .... 413-236-3001 231 A
jlaw@berkshirecc.edu
LAW, John, W .... 630-844-5438 139 L
jlaw@aurora.edu
LAW, Kate .... 651-290-6438 266 B
kate.law@wmitchell.edu
LAW, Nancy .... 903-983-8101 477 A
nlaw@kilgore.edu

LEAHY, Mindy, S .... 563-884-5647 182 D
mindy.leahy@palmer.edu
LEAHY, Patrick, F .... 570-408-4000 440 B
patrick.leahy@wilkes.edu
LEAHY, Thomas .... 515-643-6621 181 B
tleahy@mercydesmoines.org
LEAHY, SJ, William, P . 617-552-3250 224 B
william.leahy@bc.edu
LEAK, Angela .... 336-334-4822 363 A
acleak@gtcc.edu
LEAK, Arthur, J .... 765-641-4162 164 B
ajleak@anderson.edu
LEAK, Monica .... 703-812-4757 509 E
mleak@leland.edu
LEAK, Shanna .... 269-471-6346 239 D
shannal@andrews.edu
LEAKE, Parker .... 803-777-5707 450 B
pleake@mailbox.sc.edu
LEAKS, Ileka, L .... 864-488-4557 447 F
ileaks@limestone.edu
LEAL, Delia .... 956-364-4647 487 H
delia.leal@tstc.edu
LEAL, Juan .... 956-364-4607 487 H
juan.leal@tstc.edu
LEAL, Luis .... 956-364-4443 487 H
luis.leal@tstc.edu
LEAL, Mario, A .... 512-505-3009 475 G
maleal@htu.edu
LEAL-SOTELO, Margaret 310-267-5439.. 71 D
mlealsotelo@conet.ucla.edu
LEAMAN, David, E .... 715-836-2542 539 E
leamande@uwec.edu
LEAMY, Michael, B .... 978-665-4783 229 D
mleamy1@fitchburgstate.edu
LEAO, Katie .... 775-445-3240 296 A
katie.leao@wnc.edu
LEAR, Doug .... 603-899-4123 297 H
leard@franklinpierce.edu
LEAR, Shelly .... 315-781-3388 327 G
lear@hws.edu
LEARNARD, Kim .... 678-664-0515 134 F
kim.learnard@westgatech.edu
LEARNED, Betsy, P ...... 401-254-3625 442 C
blearned@rwu.edu
LEARY, Alison, L .... 212-998-4217 336 C
alison.leary@nyu.edu
LEARY, Carol, A .... 413-565-1000 222 G
cleary@baypath.edu
LEARY, Claudine .... 740-363-1146 386 D
cleary@mtso.edu
LEARY, James .... 508-856-8200 229 B
james.leary@umassmed.edu
LEARY, Karen .... 978-665-3584 229 D
kleary10@fitchburgstate.edu
LEARY, Russell, J .... 920-433-6635 534 K
russell.leary@bellincollege.edu
LEARY, Sharon .... 214-648-0100 496 A
sharon.leary@utsouthwestern.edu
LEARY, Thomas, P .... 570-740-0388 425 A
tleary@luzerne.edu
LEARY, Timothy .... 206-296-6160 526 F
tleary@seattleu.edu
LEAS, Dawn .... 570-408-4000 440 B
dawn.leas@wilkes.edu
LEAS, Terry .... 509-793-2001 520 B
terryl@bigbend.edu
LEASE, Sharon .... 405-692-3153 398 I
slease@macu.edu
LEASE BUTTS, Jennifer . 860-486-4223.. 92 C
jennifer.lease@uconn.edu
LEASURE, David .... 801-274-3280 501 B
david.leasure@wgu.edu
LEATH, Randy .... 325-794-4407 470 I
randy.leath@cisco.edu
LEATH, Steven .... 515-294-2042 175 G
sleath@iastate.edu
LEATHERBURY, JR.,
Ernest .... 410-651-6589 219 H
eleatherbury@umes.edu
LEATHERMAN, W. Dale 870-759-4124.. 25 I
dleatherman@wbcoll.edu
LEATHERS, Barb .... 309-268-8130 145 H
barb.leathers@heartland.edu
LEATHERS, Debra, L ..... 213-738-6814.. 68 E
advancement@swlaw.edu
LEATHERS, Ed, C .... 972-881-5142 471 C
eleathers@collin.edu
LEATHERS, Mardy .... 636-584-6530 274 J
mardy.leathers@eastcentral.edu
LEATHERS, Walt .... 509-467-1727 523 E
wleather@interface.edu
LEATHERWOOD,
Cynthia .... 205-247-8038.... 7 G
cleatherwood@stillman.edu
LEATHERWOOD, Laura . 828-565-4220 363 C
lbleatherwood@haywood.edu
LEATHERWOOD,
Marya, L .... 414-288-4255 537 B
marya.leatherwood@marquette.edu
LEAU, Michael .... 684-699-9155 549 C
m.leau@amsamoa.edu

LEAVELL, Robb .... 334-683-5177.... 5 D
rleavell@judson.edu
LEAVENS, N. Dennis ..... 510-987-9452.. 27 K
LEAVER, Betty Lou .... 831-242-4404 547 H
betty.l.leaver.civ@mail.mil
LEAVER, Harold, L .... 989-964-4047 249 G
hlleaver@svsu.edu
LEAVER, Walt .... 615-966-7653 458 C
walt.leaver@lipscomb.edu
LEAVITT, Andrew, J ...... 920-424-0200 540 B
leavitt@uwosh.edu
LEAVITT, Daniel .... 312-777-8583 147 C
dleavitt@aii.edu
LEAVITT, David .... 650-433-3839.. 58 B
support@paloaltou.edu
LEAVITT, David .... 617-228-3287 231 C
djleavit@bhcc.mass.edu
LEAVITT, Gabriel .... 503-517-7696 409 E
leavittg@reed.edu
LEAVITT, Stephen, C .... 518-388-6116 350 K
leavitts@union.edu
LEBAR, Peter, M .... 814-332-5369 411 F
plebar@allegheny.edu
LEBARRON, Lynne .... 203-837-8188.. 88 G
lebarronl@wcsu.edu
LEBEAU, Bryan .... 913-758-6115 191 I
lebeau87@stmary.edu
LEBEAU, Mandie, A ...... 617-422-7499 234 J
mlebeau@nesl.edu
LEBEAU, Michael .... 205-226-4719.... 2 C
mlebeau@bsc.edu
LEBEDEFF, Alex .... 510-659-6263.. 56 J
alebedeff@ohlone.edu
LEBER, Frank, W .... 312-329-4388 153 C
frank.leber@moody.edu
LEBER, Sally, S .... 740-368-3080 390 B
ssleber@owu.edu
LEBERT, Jeff .... 918-335-6842 400 I
jlebert@okwu.edu
LEBESCH, Anna, M .... 904-276-6783 111 K
annalebesch@sjrstate.edu
LEBESCO, Kathleen .... 212-774-4861 332 A
klebesco@mmm.edu
LEBHERZ, Joe .... 301-682-8315 217 D
lebherz@msmary.edu
LEBIODA, Ed .... 805-437-8547.. 32 H
ed.lebioda@csuci.edu
LEBLANC, Ann .... 757-352-4222 511 G
aleblanc@regent.edu
LEBLANC, Elva, C .... 817-515-7750 484 B
elva.leblanc@tccd.edu
LEBLANC, Erica .... 310-434-4227.. 65 B
leblanc_erica@smc.edu
LEBLANC, Jacqueline .... 212-752-1530 330 C
jacqueline.leblanc@limcollege.edu
LEBLANC, Jerry, L .... 337-482-6235 208 F
jerrylukeleblanc@louisiana.edu
LEBLANC, Nina .... 337-439-5765 202 E
nina@deltatech.edu
LEBLANC, Paul .... 603-645-9631 298 H
p.leblanc@snhu.edu
LEBLANC, Robert .... 713-525-3540 493 J
leblancr@stthom.edu
LEBLANC, Thomas, J .... 305-284-3356 118 A
leblanc@miami.edu
LEBLANC, William .... 401-825-2225 441 C
leblanc@ccri.edu
LEBLEU BURNS,
Michele .... 408-864-8218.. 44 N
lebleuburnsmichele@deanza.edu
LEBO, Cathy, J .... 443-997-4107 216 A
lebo@jhu.edu
LEBO, Maggie .... 717-728-2406 415 B
margeretlebo@centralpenn.edu
LEBO, Russ .... 559-734-9000.. 63 E
russl@sjvc.edu
LEBRECK, Paul .... 847-925-6647 145 F
plebreck@harpercollege.edu
LEBRETON, Ryan .... 570-577-3122 413 E
ryan.lebreton@bucknell.edu
LEBRON, Mayra .... 787-850-9392 558 A
mayra.lebron@upr.edu
LEBRON, Nestor, A .... 787-864-2222 553 J
nestor.lebron@guayama.inter.edu
LEBRON KURI,
Alfredo, J .... 787-857-3600 553 G
alebron@br.inter.edu
LEBRUN, Kathy .... 512-472-4133 482 E
kathy.lebrun@ssw.edu
LEBSOCK, Gale .... 760-384-6215.. 49 F
glebsock@cerrocoso.edu
LECHE, Adriane .... 252-536-7260 363 B
aleche096@halifaxcc.edu
LECHLER, Terry .... 254-299-8652 478 C
tlechler@mclennan.edu
LECHNER, David .... 402-472-2191 293 F
dlechner@nebraska.edu
LECHTENBERG,
Melanie .... 217-641-4310 148 J
mlechtenberg@jwcc.edu

LECKONBY, Larry, W .... 704-637-4474 355 H
lleckonb14@catawba.edu
LECKRONE, Michael, J . 260-982-5004 170 a
mjleckrone@manchester.edu
LECLAIR, Mary .... 315-781-3697 327 G
leclair@hws.edu
LECLERC, Robin .... 248-204-2203 245 J
rleclerc@ltu.edu
LECOUNT, Heidi .... 919-760-8633 359 B
lecounth@meredith.edu
LECOURT, Nancy .... 707-965-6234.. 57 I
nlecourt@puc.edu
LECRONE, Jeffrey, L ..... 570-321-4112 425 B
lecrone@lycoming.edu
LEDBETTER, Beverly, E . 401-863-9900 441 A
beverly_ledbetter@brown.edu
LEDBETTER, Brad .... 828-652-0674 364 B
bradl@mcdowelltech.edu
LEDBETTER, Bronson .... 602-387-4307.. 18 H
bronson.ledbetter@phoenix.edu
LEDBETTER, Cathy .... 678-946-1103 125 C
cledbett@highlands.edu
LEDBETTER, Kim, M ...... 828-652-0602 364 B
kims@mcdowelltech.edu
LEDBETTER, Lisa .... 704-216-3620 365 F
lisa.ledbetter@rccc.edu
LEDBETTER, Mary, L ..... 828-659-6001 364 B
maryl@mcdowelltech.edu
LEDBETTER, Neal .... 251-442-2429.... 9 B
nledbetter@umobile.edu
LEDBETTER, Sislena ...... 202-274-5373.. 97 B
sledbetter@udc.edu
LEDDY, Michael .... 401-341-2195 442 D
mike.leddy@salve.edu
LEDERER, John .... 206-934-6075 525 K
john.lederer@seattlecolleges.edu
LEDERMAN, Bill .... 269-467-9945 243 A
blederman@glenoaks.edu
LEDERMANN, Sarah ...... 518-255-5516 346 E
lederms@cobleskill.edu
LEDERMANN, Stacy, A . 585-385-8142 340 F
sledermann@sjfc.edu
LEDESMA, Amadeo .... 575-527-7530 312 D
amadeol@nmsu.edu
LEDESMA, Rosalie .... 408-274-6700.. 63 O
rosalie.ledes@sjeccd.org
LEDFORD,
Catherine, M .... 858-534-3391.. 72 B
cledford@ucsd.edu
LEDFORD, Howard .... 706-335-9337 128 A
hledford@laniertech.edu
LEDFORD, Julia .... 270-686-4627 197 A
julia.ledford@kctcs.edu
LEDFORD, Julie .... 360-736-9391 520 F
jledford@centralia.edu
LEDFORD, Laura .... 217-362-6499 153 A
lledford@millikin.edu
LEDFORD, Randy .... 336-386-3279 366 E
ledfordr@surry.edu
LEDFORD, Terry .... 864-941-8568 448 D
ledford.t@ptc.edu
LEDFORD, Tommy, R ... 828-766-1190 364 A
tledford@mayland.edu
LEDLOW, Susan, E .... 407-582-3423 118 I
sledlow@valenciacollege.edu
LEDONNE, Patricia, N .. 540-375-2270 512 B
ledonne@roanoke.edu
LEDONNE, Peter .... 201-447-7159 300 B
pledonne@bergen.edu
LEDOUX, Andrew .... 518-861-2560 331 K
aledoux@mariacollege.edu
LEDOUX, Debra .... 320-762-4482 257 O
debral@alextech.edu
LEDUC, Don .... 517-371-5140 252 J
leducd@cooley.edu
LEDUC, Julaine .... 734-973-3492 251 J
jeleduc@wccnet.edu
LEDUC, Laura .... 517-371-5140 252 J
leducl@cooley.edu
LEDVINA, Anne .... 205-226-7722.... 2 C
aledvina@bsc.edu
LEDYARD,
Christopher, L .... 740-283-6437 382 G
cledyard@franciscan.edu
LEE, Abby .... 541-881-5582 410 D
alee@tvcc.cc
LEE, Allisha .... 270-707-3958 196 D
allisha.lee@kctcs.edu
LEE, Amanda .... 910-362-7555 360 G
alee@cfcc.edu
LEE, Amy .... 510-748-2288.. 59 A
ahlee@peralta.edu
LEE, Amy .... 207-741-5644 211 D
alee@smccme.edu
LEE, IHM, Andrea, J .... 651-690-6525 263 V
ajlee@stkate.edu
LEE, Angelo, C .... 717-477-1231 431 F
aclee@ship.edu
LEE, Annette .... 516-562-1108 324 G
alee@nshs.edu
LEE, Anthony .... 888-491-8686.. 76 G

LEE, Antwinett .... 425-739-8344 523 I
antwinett.lee@lwtech.edu
LEE, Asa .... 202-885-8614.. 97 E
alee@wesleyseminary.edu
LEE, Barbara, A .... 848-932-2600 306 F
blee@oldqueens.rutgers.edu
LEE, Becky .... 478-988-6852 122 F
blee@centralgatech.edu
LEE, Bob .... 907-745-3201.. 10 B
LEE, Brandon, w .... 361-485-4400 492 A
leebw@uhv.edu
LEE, Brenda .... 419-530-7730 394 E
brenda.lee@utoledo.edu
LEE, Brian, K .... 626-395-6307.. 31 D
brian.lee@caltech.edu
LEE, Bridgett, C .... 512-505-3074 475 G
bclee@htu.edu
LEE, Catherine .... 334-844-1350.... 1 G
leecath@auburn.edu
LEE, Catherine .... 910-362-7033 360 G
clee@cfcc.edu
LEE, Charley .... 714-527-0691.. 44 B
LEE, Choong .... 323-643-0301.. 27 G
LEE, Chris .... 501-882-8887.. 19 E
cllee@asub.edu
LEE, Chris .... 270-706-8622 195 K
chris.lee@kctcs.edu
LEE, Christopher .... 785-460-5509 186 D
christopher.lee@colbycc.edu
LEE, Christopher .... 804-819-4685 514 G
clee@vccs.edu
LEE, Christopher .... 920-832-7694 536 R
christopher.lee@lawrence.edu
LEE, Chul .... 812-488-2155 173 H
cl162@evansville.edu
LEE, Cindy .... 352-588-8869 111 L
cindy.lee@saintleo.edu
LEE, Crystal .... 225-743-8500 204 C
clee@rpcc.edu
LEE, Curtis .... 253-964-6595 525 C
clee@pierce.ctc.edu
LEE, Cynthia .... 713-313-7523 487 F
lee_cl@tsu.edu
LEE, D. Lynn .... 443-412-2258 215 D
llee@harford.edu
LEE, Dana .... 914-594-4567 335 H
dana_lee@nymc.edu
LEE, Daniel, J .... 253-535-7177 524 I
daniel.lee@plu.edu
LEE, David .... 213-487-0110.. 43 E
provost@dula.edu
LEE, David .... 303-273-3155.. 80 O
dlee@mines.edu
LEE, David, C .... 706-542-5969 132 H
dclee@uga.edu
LEE, David, D .... 270-745-2344 201 D
david.lee@wku.edu
LEE, David, S .... 609-258-9548 305 C
davidlee@princeton.edu
LEE, David, Y .... 703-333-5904 519 B
LEE, Deborah .... 949-854-8002.. 42 B
deborah.lee@cui.edu
LEE, Debra, A .... 330-471-8406 385 G
dlee@malone.edu
LEE, Delores .... 310-243-3189.. 33 B
dslee@csudh.edu
LEE, Dennis .... 229-227-2414 132 C
dlee@southernregional.edu
LEE, Dewain .... 907-786-1214.. 10 H
dllee@uaa.alaska.edu
LEE, Diana .... 212-349-4330 326 G
dlee@globe.edu
LEE, Diana .... 405-491-6310 402 E
dlee@snu.edu
LEE, Diane .... 212-226-7300 338 F
dlee@pbcny.edu
LEE, Diane, M .... 410-455-2859 219 F
dlee@umbc.edu
LEE, Donna .... 651-696-6220 256 L
donnalee@macalester.edu
LEE, Donna, A .... 404-471-6391 119 G
dlee@agnesscott.edu
LEE, Donny .... 501-279-4187.. 21 A
dlee@harding.edu
LEE, Donzell .... 601-877-6142 266 C
dlee@alcorn.edu
LEE, Doug .... 724-852-3212 439 C
dlee@waynesburg.edu
LEE, Douglas .... 319-335-0444 175 H
douglas-lee@uiowa.edu
LEE, Ed .... 715-346-3612 541 A
ed.lee@uwsp.edu
LEE, Eliot .... 562-926-1023.. 60 B
it@ptsa.edu
LEE, Elwyn, C .... 832-842-5090 491 D
eclee@uh.edu
LEE, Eun Moo .... 770-279-0507 124 F
academic@gcuniv.edu
LEE, Eun Moo .... 770-279-0507 124 F
emlee@gcuniv.edu

LEE, Gloria ... 203-392-5200 .. 88 F
leeg1@southernct.edu
LEE, Grayce ... 504-468-2900 207 E
drlee@southwest.edu
LEE, Harlan ... 425-564-4042 519 L
harlan.lee@bellevuecollege.edu
LEE, Hee, C ... 636-327-4645 278 D
hclee@midwest.edu
LEE, Herbert ... 831-459-2351 .. 72 E
vpaa@ucsc.edu
LEE, Ho Woo ... 770-279-0507 124 F
howard.hw.lee@gcuniv.edu
LEE, Holly ... 580-628-6274 399 E
holly.lee@noc.edu
LEE, Howoo ... 770-279-0507 124 F
howlee21@hotmail.com
LEE, Hubert ... 610-361-2499 427 D
leeh@neumann.edu
LEE, Humphrey ... 256-331-5214 .... 6 B
hlee@nwscc.edu
LEE, Jaekyung ... 716-645-6640 343 E
gscdean@buffalo.edu
LEE, James ... 617-873-0236 225 A
james.lee@cambridgecollege.edu
LEE, James, D ... 808-675-3289 134 M
james.lee@byuh.edu
LEE, James, S ... 626-448-0023 .. 48 C
president@itsla.edu
LEE, Janet ... 303-458-3552 .. 85 G
jlee@regis.edu
LEE, Jay ... 970-521-6607 .. 84 H
jay.lee@njc.edu
LEE, Jay ... 507-537-7285 262 B
Jay.Lee@smsu.edu
LEE, John ... 651-255-6156 264 F
jlee@unitedseminary.edu
LEE, John ... 707-826-3961 .. 35 D
john.lee@humboldt.edu
LEE, John ... 703-812-4757 509 E
jlee@leland.edu
LEE, Jonathan ... 310-233-4471 .. 51 F
leej@lahc.edu
LEE, Jonathan ... 508-626-4697 230 A
jlee8@framingham.edu
LEE, Jonathan, E ... 540-375-2237 512 B
jelee@roanoke.edu
LEE, Judy ... 718-818-6470 341 G
LEE, Kathleen, F ... 317-917-5935 169 M
klee@ivytech.edu
LEE, Katrina, K ... 919-658-2502 369 B
klee@umo.edu
LEE, Kenya, N ... 646-312-3322 318 C
Kenya.Lee@baruch.cuny.edu
LEE, Keum Hee ... 213-385-2322 .. 77 H
khlee@wmu.edu
LEE, Kevin ... 620-862-5252 184 H
kevin.lee@barclaycollege.edu
LEE, Kim ... 601-923-1681 270 B
klee@rts.edu
LEE, Kimberly ... 229-420-1284 119 I
klee@albanytech.edu
LEE, Kwang Hoon ... 213-381-0081 .. 48 A
khlee@irus.edu
LEE, Kyu, H ... 253-752-2020 522 K
klee@faithseminary.edu
LEE, Kyuboem ... 215-368-5000 412 K
klee@biblical.edu
LEE, Lenetta ... 484-365-7253 424 E
llee@lincoln.edu
LEE, Leon ... 212-226-7300 338 F
llee@pbcny.edu
LEE, Leslie ... 706-713-2182 132 H
lpetch@uga.edu
LEE, Linda, S ... 657-725-7789 .. 68 G
lslee@stanford.edu
LEE, Lisa ... 714-533-3946 .. 36 D
lisa@calums.edu
LEE, Lisa ... 212-410-8032 335 B
llee@nycpm.edu
LEE, Lisa ... 610-328-8402 436 A
llee2@swarthmore.edu
LEE, Marsha ... 662-246-6314 268 F
mlee@msdelta.edu
LEE, SSJ, Mary Esther .. 215-248-7062 415 D
leem@chc.edu
LEE, Mary Margaret ... 802-860-2721 501 F
mlee@champlain.edu
LEE, Mary W, L ... 630-515-7311 152 H
mleexx@midwestern.edu
LEE, Maurice, A ... 501-450-3167 .. 25 F
mauricel@uca.edu
LEE, Mei-Lin ... 210-436-3414 481 C
mlee@stmarytx.edu
LEE, Michael ... 678-225-7336 432 E
michaellee@pcom.edu
LEE, Michael, D ... 229-226-1621 132 E
mlee@thomasu.edu
LEE, Michelle ... 910-362-7733 360 G
mlee@cfcc.edu
LEE, Mike ... 386-752-1822 103 Q
mike.lee@fgc.edu
LEE, Mike, C ... 818-947-2336 .. 52 B
leemc@lavc.edu
LEE, Ming-Tung (Mike) 916-278-6312 .. 34 E
mikelee@csus.edu
LEE, Otto ... 310-233-4010 .. 51 F
leeow@lahc.edu
LEE, Pamela ... 409-944-1206 474 G
plee@gc.edu
LEE, Patricia, A ... 843-355-4127 451 H
leepa@wiltech.edu
LEE, Peter ... 651-255-6113 264 F
plee@unitedseminary.edu
LEE, Raeann ... 614-416-6239 378 B
rlee@bradfordschoolcolumbus.edu
LEE, Randall ... 601-635-6375 267 B
rlee@eccc.edu
LEE, Randolph ... 860-297-2413 .. 92 A
randolph.lee@trincoll.edu
LEE, Rebecca ... 478-757-3551 122 E
blee@centralgatech.edu
LEE, Robert, L ... 575-835-5143 311 I
lee@prrc.nmt.edu
LEE, Robert, W ... 260-399-7700 174 C
rlee@sf.edu
LEE, Roger, R ... 770-720-5537 130 E
rrl@reinhardt.edu
LEE, Samuel ... 626-914-8855 .. 38 L
slee@citruscollege.edu
LEE, Sandra ... 916-608-6500 .. 53 A
lees@flc.losrios.edu
LEE, Sandra ... 650-508-3516 .. 56 H
slee@ndnu.edu
LEE, Sang Meyng ... 562-926-1023 .. 60 B
sangmeynglee@msn.com
LEE, Sara ... 251-626-3303 .... 8 C
registrar@ussa.edu
LEE, Sean ... 802-831-1078 503 E
slee@vermontlaw.edu
LEE, Shad ... 760-921-5431 .. 58 C
shad.lee@paloverde.edu
LEE, Soo Young ... 714-527-0691 .. 44 B
LEE, Staci ... 760-921-5512 .. 58 C
staci.lee@paloverde.edu
LEE, Stephen ... 304-293-2121 533 D
stephen.lee@mail.wvu.edu
LEE, Stephen, E ... 304-293-2121 533 D
stephen.lee@mail.wvu.edu
LEE, Steven ... 757-446-5221 507 B
leect@evms.edu
LEE, Sue ... 714-533-1495 .. 67 A
LEE, Susan ... 808-956-5852 136 B
susanlee@hawaii.edu
LEE, Susan ... 765-983-1501 165 H
leesu@earlham.edu
LEE, Suzanne ... 773-298-3020 158 F
lee@sxu.edu
LEE, Tamara ... 334-229-4475 .... 1 D
Tlee@alasu.edu
LEE, Teresa ... 913-758-4359 191 I
hr@stmary.edu
LEE, Terri, S ... 919-209-2125 363 F
tslee@johnstoncc.edu
LEE, Theresa ... 865-974-4337 465 D
artscidean@utk.edu
LEE, Timothy ... 323-643-0301 .. 27 G
LEE, Timothy ... 773-995-2002 141 J
tlee27@csu.edu
LEE, Timothy ... 518-956-8219 343 C
tmlee@albany.edu
LEE, Todd, G ... 805-893-2169 .. 72 D
todd.lee@bap.ucsb.edu
LEE, Tom ... 515-433-5020 177 B
tllee@dmacc.edu
LEE, Torian ... 504-486-7411 209 E
tllee@xula.edu
LEE, Treva, A ... 504-520-7566 209 E
tlee@xula.edu
LEE, Tyjaun, A ... 301-322-0412 217 G
leeta@pgcc.edu
LEE, Vina ... 845-672-0550 325 D
LEE, Vivian, S ... 801-581-7480 499 K
vivian.lee@hsc.utah.edu
LEE, Wai-Fong ... 206-934-4062 526 A
wai-fong.lee@seattlecolleges.edu
LEE, Wai-Fong ... 206-934-5481 526 A
wai-fong.lee@seattlecolleges.edu
LEE, Wendy ... 415-257-1365 .. 43 D
wendy.lee@dominican.edu
LEE, Wendy ... 909-447-2535 .. 39 G
wlee@cst.edu
LEE, Wenshu ... 530-898-5029 .. 33 A
wslee@csuchico.edu
LEE, Wes ... 405-491-6455 402 E
wlee@snu.edu
LEE, Y. Ben ... 260-422-5561 167 F
yblee@indianatech.edu
LEE, Yi-Chia ... 408-260-8868 .. 44 K
sjclinic@fivebranches.edu
LEE, Young Gull ... 714-517-1945 .. 29 E
vicepresident@buc.edu
LEE, Yueh-TIng ... 618-453-4527 159 H
leey@siu.edu
LEE, Yuet ... 909-621-8243 .. 59 F
yuet_lee@pitzer.edu
LEE, Yung Jae ... 925-631-4610 .. 61 G
ylee@stmarys-ca.edu
LEE-BARBER, Jill ... 404-413-1640 126 D
jleebarber@gsu.edu
LEE-CLARK, Margaret ... 215-619-7413 426 E
plee@mc3.edu
LEE-COLLICK, Valescia .. 612-338-7224 265 G
valescia.lee-collick@waldenu.edu
LEE-GLAUSER, Gina ... 315-443-2492 349 E
leeglaug@syr.edu
LEE ISBARA, Jiseon ... 503-297-5544 408 A
jlee@ocac.edu
LEE-LEWIS, Sherri ... 310-434-4419 .. 65 B
lee-lewis_sherri@smc.edu
LEE-OPERARIO, Tam ... 510-436-1348 .. 47 C
lee-operario@hnu.edu
LEE-SADDUL, Claudia ... 714-895-8130 .. 40 C
clee-saddul@gwc.cccd.edu
LEE SANG, Brian ... 202-885-6108 .. 94 H
leesang@american.edu
LEEB, Fred ... 248-414-6900 246 F
fredleeb@mji.edu
LEEBRON, David, W ... 713-348-5050 480 M
president@rice.edu
LEEBRON TUTELMAN,
Elizabeth ... 215-204-7188 436 C
elizabeth.leebron@temple.edu
LEEDER, Mike ... 229-931-2222 126 C
mike.leeder@gsw.edu
LEEDS, Mark ... 817-923-1921 483 E
mleeds@swbts.edu
LEEDS, Stacy ... 479-575-4504 .. 23 G
sleeds@uark.edu
LEEDY, David ... 212-659-0741 330 A
dleedy@tkc.edu
LEEK, Linda ... 859-985-3205 193 F
leekl@berea.edu
LEEK, Marilyn, J ... 515-961-1675 182 I
marilyn.leek@simpson.edu
LEEMON, Donna ... 334-683-2362 .... 5 H
dleemon@marionmilitary.edu
LEENEY-PANAGROSSI,
Anne ... 203-773-8595 .. 87 M
panagrossi@albertus.edu
LEENHOUTS, David ... 979-532-6905 497 F
leenhoutsd@wcjc.edu
LEENHOUTS, Jim ... 828-669-8012 359 K
leenhouts-james@aramark.com
LEEPER, Greg, J ... 612-343-4457 263 H
gjleeper@northcentral.edu
LEEPER, Jeff ... 402-486-2502 293 D
jeleeper@ucollege.edu
LEEPER, Karla ... 706-721-7406 121 C
kleeper@gru.edu
LEES, David ... 610-660-1773 434 G
lees@sju.edu
LEES, Elizabeth, M ... 484-664-3116 427 C
lees@muhlenberg.edu
LEES, Melissa ... 410-532-5565 217 F
mlees@ndm.edu
LEET, Gregory, R ... 949-824-5011 .. 71 C
gregory.leet@uci.edu
LEETH, Blake ... 256-840-4170 .... 7 B
bleeth@snead.edu
LEETHAM, Lorlie ... 805-756-1131 .. 32 E
lleetham@calpoly.edu
LEFAUVE, Linda, M ... 704-894-2124 356 D
lilefauve@davidson.edu
LEFEBVRE, Carol ... 706-721-8611 121 C
clefebvr@gru.edu
LEFEBVRE, Raymond ... 508-531-2247 229 C
raymond.lefebvre@bridgew.edu
LEFELD, Amanda, L ... 740-587-6647 381 H
lefelda@denison.edu
LEFEVER-DAVIS,
Shirley ... 316-978-3301 192 D
shirley.lefever-davis@wichita.edu
LEFEVERS, William, L ... 828-448-3125 367 B
wlefevers@wpcc.edu
LEFEVRE, Lisa ... 303-360-4788 .. 81 I
Lisa.Lefevre@CCauroa.edu
LEFEVRE, Noah ... 718-862-7230 331 H
noah.lefevre@manhattan.edu
LEFF, Kelly ... 937-769-1817 376 M
kleff@antioch.edu
LEFFARD, Mary Ellen ... 770-426-2971 128 C
maryellen.leffard@life.edu
LEFFEL, Lisa ... 414-443-8796 542 I
lisa.leffel@wlc.edu
LEFFLER, Charles, D ... 919-515-2155 370 D
charles_leffler@ncsu.edu
LEFFLER, Danielle ... 812-941-2274 169 A
lefflerd@ius.edu
LEFFLER, Ernest ... 781-891-2552 223 E
eleffler@bentley.edu
LEFFLER, Lyvier ... 817-515-3015 484 B
lyvier.leffler@tccd.edu
LEFLER, Mike ... 402-826-8589 290 C
mike.lefler@doane.edu
LEFLORE, Larry ... 940-898-3415 490 D
lleflore@twu.edu
LEFOE, Grant ... 704-290-5269 366 A
glefoe@spcc.edu
LEFORT, Donna, P ... 256-765-4252 .... 9 D
dpjacobs@una.edu
LEFRANCOIS, Paul, R ... 864-488-4527 447 F
plefrancois@limestone.edu
LEFT HAND, Frederica .. 406-638-3131 286 I
lefthandfv@lbhc.edu
LEFTWICH, Shawn, B ... 630-752-5011 163 G
shawn.leftwich@wheaton.edu
LEGAKO, Jana ... 405-682-7850 399 K
jana.k.legako@occc.edu
LEGASPI, Lorenzo ... 925-485-5203 .. 37 M
llegaspi@clpccd.org
LEGENDRE, Glenda, G .. 443-352-4482 218 E
glegendre@stevenson.edu
LEGERE, Paul ... 202-231-8015 547 N
paul.legere@dodiis.mil
LEGG, David ... 865-573-4517 457 H
dlegg@johnsonU.edu
LEGG, Hal, S ... 607-436-2748 344 B
legghs@oneonta.edu
LEGG, Jamie, W ... 910-630-7028 359 C
jlegg@methodist.edu
LEGG, Margaret, A ... 423-775-7201 455 F
leggma@bryan.edu
LEGGE, Jerome, S ... 706-425-3340 132 H
jlegge@uga.edu
LEGGE, Karen ... 570-961-7886 422 G
leggek@lackawanna.edu
LEGGETT, Connie ... 229-430-1917 119 H
connie.leggett@asurams.edu
LEGGETT, Ida, F ... 615-898-5910 461 E
ida.fazillah@mtsu.edu
LEGGETT, Mia, S ... 540-868-7087 515 H
mleggett@lfcc.edu
LEGGETT, Tricia ... 740-588-1271 396 E
tleggett@zanestate.edu
LEGGETTE, Evelyn ... 601-979-2244 267 H
evelyn.j.leggette@jsums.edu
LEGGETTE, Priscilla ... 315-386-7315 347 F
leggettep@canton.edu
LEGGIO, Karyl ... 410-617-2301 216 D
kbleggio@loyola.edu
LEGGITT, Dan ... 618-544-8657 146 H
leggittd@iecc.edu
LEGLER KAPLAN,
Kristine ... 651-201-1749 257 N
kristine.kaplan@so.mnscu.edu
LEGRANDE, Tomikia, P 713-221-8100 491 F
legrandet@uhd.edu
LEGREID, Ann, M ... 304-876-5011 532 I
alegreid@shepherd.edu
LEGRO, Jeffrey, w ... 434-924-6835 514 A
legro@virginia.edu
LEGURIA, Gina ... 209-575-6507 .. 78 A
leguriag@yosemite.edu
LEHDE, Wade ... 314-454-7547 275 D
walehde@bjc.org
LEHFELDT, Elizabeth ... 216-687-3943 380 D
E.LEHFELDT@csuohio.edu
LEHMAN, Andrew ... 717-720-4030 430 A
lpandeladis@passhe.edu
LEHMAN, Ann ... 814-865-8753 428 C
axw14@psu.edu
LEHMAN, Criquett ... 940-552-6291 496 B
cslehman@vernoncollege.edu
LEHMAN, DeWayne ... 617-287-5302 228 G
deWayne.lehman@umb.edu
LEHMAN, Douglas, K ... 937-327-7016 395 I
dlehman@wittenberg.edu
LEHMAN, John, B ... 906-487-1832 247 A
jblehman@mtu.edu
LEHMAN, Joseph ... 814-472-3054 434 F
jlehman@francis.edu
LEHMAN, Mel ... 406-771-5143 288 B
melvin.lehman@gfcmsu.edu
LEHMAN, Theresa ... 317-738-8176 166 B
tlehman@franklincollege.edu
LEHMAN, Tracey, A ... 541-885-1291 408 E
tracey.lehman@oit.edu
LEHMAN, William, H ... 262-554-2010 537 D
lehmannw@yahoo.com
LEHMAN-FELTS,
Juliana ... 940-397-4193 478 G
juliana.felts@mwsu.edu
LEHMANN, Craig ... 631-444-2253 344 C
craig.lehmann@stonybrook.edu
LEHMANN, Daniel ... 617-559-8773 227 E
dlehmann@hebrewcollege.edu
LEHMPUHL, David ... 719-549-2340 .. 81 F
david.lehmpuhl@csupueblo.edu
LEHMULLER, Peter ... 401-598-4988 441 D
PLehmuller@jwu.edu
LEHN, Patty ... 217-353-2683 155 I
plehn@parkland.edu

LEHNER, Eric, J .... 757-479-3706 514 D
elehner@vbts.edu
LEHNERT, Charles .... 419-530-1447 394 E
charles.lehnert@utoledo.edu
LEHOCKY, John, F .... 847-970-4810 162 G
jlehocky@usml.edu
LEHOTAK, Ed .... 402-557-7050 289 B
ed.lehotak@bellevue.edu
LEHR, Kirk, A .... 989-317-4611 247 B
klehr@midmich.edu
LEHR, Louis .... 504-278-6474 204 B
llehr@nunez.edu
LEHR, Valerie, D .... 315-229-5993 341 E
vlehr@stlawu.edu
LEHRBERGER, Paula ..... 215-596-8891 438 E
p.lehrbe@usciences.edu
LEHRE, Elaine .... 906-248-8422 240 J
elehre@bmcc.edu
LEHRLING, Tony .... 580-745-2186 402 D
tlehrling@se.edu
LEHRMAN, III,
Kenneth, F .... 814-863-0471 428 C
kfl2@psu.edu
LEHRMAN, Sue .... 215-951-2810 432 F
Lehrmans@philau.edu
LEHRMAN, Susan .... 856-256-4000 306 D
LEHTONEN, Rona .... 856-225-2309 307 A
rlehtonen@facilities.rutgers.edu
LEHWALD, Annie .... 816-501-4276 281 B
anne.lehwald@rockhurst.edu
LEI, Joy .... 909-593-3511.. 73 B
jlei@laverne.edu
LEI, Lei .... 848-445-3600 307 B
llei@business.rutgers.edu
LEI, Lei .... 973-353-1604 307 C
llei@business.rutgers.edu
LEIBLE, Arthur .... 302-857-6060.. 93 E
aleible@desu.edu
LEIBOLD, Susanne .... 563-588-6580 176 F
susanne.leibold@clarke.edu
LEICHLITER, Kirk .... 970-351-2446.. 87 A
kirk.leichliter@unco.edu
LEICHTNAM, Marky ...... 614-885-5585 390 G
mleichtnam@pcj.edu
LEICHTY, Jeff, S .... 260-422-5561 167 F
jsleichty@indianatech.edu
LEIDERMAN, Roni .... 954-262-6930 109 E
roni@nova.edu
LEIDIG, Julie .... 703-450-2517 516 C
jleidig@nvcc.edu
LEIDIG, Mary .... 865-471-3402 455 G
mleidig@cn.edu
LEIDINGER, Angie .... 864-656-5615 444 E
angiel@clemson.edu
LEIFELD, Martin, F .... 314-516-4151 284 B
leifeldm@umsl.edu
LEIFELD, Robert, A .... 712-362-7913 179 G
rleifeld@iowalakes.edu
LEIGH, Anthony, J .... 334-833-4528.... 4 E
aleigh@huntingdon.edu
LEIGH, Bradley, K .... 419-372-2238 377 I
bleigh@bgsu.edu
LEIGH, Steven, R .... 303-492-7294.. 86 E
steven.leigh@colorado.edu
LEIGH, Thomas .... 719-590-6774.. 81 H
tleigh@coloradotech.edu
LEIGHTON, Corey .... 207-947-4591 209 G
cleighton@bealcollege.edu
LEIGHTON, Jackie .... 609-258-5006 305 C
jleighto@princeton.edu
LEIGHTON, Krista .... 434-947-8344 511 D
kleighton@randolphcollege.edu
LEIJA, Shirley .... 210-486-3608 467 A
sleija@alamo.edu
LEIKER, Jeff .... 620-252-7147 186 C
jeffl@coffeyville.edu
LEIKER, Meg .... 619-265-0107.. 59 J
mleiker@platt.edu
LEIKER, Robert, D .... 619-265-0107.. 59 J
rleiker@platt.edu
LEILER, Dina .... 773-481-8612 142 D
dleiler@ccc.edu
LEIMBACH, Bill .... 410-337-6138 215 B
bleimbach@goucher.edu
LEIMBEK, Melissa .... 763-424-0713 260 E
mleimbek@nhcc.edu
LEIMER, Christina .... 415-485-9545.. 41 B
cleimer@marin.edu
LEIMER, Jennifer .... 601-928-6211 268 G
jennifer.leimer@mgccc.edu
LEIN, Laura .... 734-764-5347 251 C
leinl@umich.edu
LEINBERRY, Beth .... 401-841-4448 548 B
LEINEN, Margaret .... 858-534-2827.. 72 B
mleinen@ucsd.edu
LEINGANG, Dan .... 701-224-5525 374 E
daniel.leingang@bismarckstate.edu
LEININGER, Earl .... 704-406-3522 356 G
eleininger@gardner-webb.edu
LEININGER, Jeffrey .... 708-209-3470 143 D
jeff.leininger@cuchicago.edu

LEINWEBER, Laura .... 619-849-2856.. 59 K
lauraleinweber@pointloma.edu
LEIPHEIMER, Jack .... 724-589-2212 436 E
jleipheimer@thiel.edu
LEIPOLD, Bil .... 973-353-5500 307 C
bil.leipold@rutgers.edu
LEISHMAN, Roger .... 360-650-2050 528 D
Roger.Leishman@wwu.edu
LEISINGER, Scott, C ..... 319-352-8495 183 J
scott.leisinger@wartburg.edu
LEIST, Terry .... 406-994-4361 287 G
tleist@montana.edu
LEITE, Randy .... 740-593-9336 389 H
leite@ohio.edu
LEITER, Dena .... 908-709-7622 309 A
leiter@ucc.edu
LEITER, Stefanie, K .... 765-641-4273 164 B
skleiter@anderson.edu
LEITHNER STAUFFER,
Andrea, C .... 570-577-1331 413 E
andrea.leithner.stauffer@bucknell.edu
LEITNER, Jennifer .... 603-882-6923 297 B
jleitner@ccsnh.edu
LEITSON, Cynthia .... 216-987-3510 381 A
cynthia.leitson@tri-c.edu
LEITZEL, Thomas, C ..... 863-784-7110 113 C
leitzelt@southflorida.edu
LEIVA, Laurie .... 504-861-5419 206 A
laleiva@loyno.edu
LEJTER, Nelly .... 603-428-2217 298 B
nlejter@nec.edu
LEKANG, Laurie .... 701-671-2871 375 B
laurie.lekang@ndscs.edu
LELAND, Chris .... 405-733-7350 401 L
cleland@rose.edu
LELAND, Dorothy .... 209-228-4417.. 71 E
Chancellor@UCMerced.edu
LELAND, John, E .... 937-229-2114 393 E
john.leland@udri.udayton.edu
LELAND, Mary .... 916-558-2198.. 53 B
lelandm@scc.losrios.edu
LELAND, Melinda, T ..... 276-739-2548 517 D
mleland@vhcc.edu
LELAND, Ted .... 209-946-2392.. 73 C
tleland@pacific.edu
LELCHOOK, Heather ...... 970-667-4611.. 78 J
heather.lelchook@aims.edu
LELE, Pradeep .... 281-618-7123 477 I
pradeep.m.lele@lonestar.edu
LELFER, John .... 704-463-3039 367 F
john.lefler@pfeiffer.edu
LELIAERT, Deborah, S .. 940-565-2108 492 D
deborah.leliaert@unt.edu
LELIK, Mary, K .... 919-515-6434 370 D
mklelik@ncsu.edu
LELONG, Kristine, D ..... 504-865-3858 206 A
klelong@loyno.edu
LELOUDIS, James, L .... 919-966-5110 371 A
leloudis@unc.edu
LEMA, Barbara .... 508-286-3542 238 B
lema_barbara@wheatoncollege.edu
LEMAHIEU, Dan .... 847-735-5083 149 H
lemahieu@lakeforest.edu
LEMAHIEU, Keith .... 219-864-2400 171 G
klemahieu@midamerica.edu
LEMAIRE, Renee .... 334-222-6591.... 5 G
rlemaire@lbwcc.edu
LEMANSKI, Kenneth ...... 413-572-5203 230 F
klemanski@westfield.ma.edu
LEMARBE, Thomas, P .. 248-370-2445 248 K
lemarbe@oakland.edu
LEMASTER, Charles ...... 254-647-3234 480 G
clemaster@rangercollege.edu
LEMASTER, J. Michael .. 937-258-8251 383 M
LEMASTERS, Michael ..... 724-357-2696 431 A
michael.lemasters@iup.edu
LEMAY, Aaron .... 936-294-3899 489 A
caaronlemay@shsu.edu
LEMAY, Eileen .... 563-589-0300 183 K
elemay@wartburgseminary.edu
LEMAY, Elaine .... 510-869-6739.. 61 J
elemay@samuelmerritt.edu
LEMAY, Jerret .... 315-312-2237 346 A
jerret.lemay@oswego.edu
LEMAY, Mitch .... 415-485-9467.. 41 B
mlemay@marin.edu
LEMBKE, Roberta .... 507-786-3097 264 C
lembke@stolaf.edu
LEMBO, Vincent, J .... 617-373-2157 235 D
LEMBURG, Mary .... 713-718-8505 475 C
mary.lemburg@hccs.edu
LEMCOE, Diane .... 908-526-1200 305 G
Diane.Lemcoe@raritanval.edu
LEMELLE, Erica .... 757-352-4778 511 G
ericlem@regent.edu
LEMERY, Cynthia .... 518-327-6399 338 B
clemery@paulsmiths.edu
LEMEUNIER, Jennifer .... 337-482-0900 208 F
jlemeunier@louisiana.edu
LEMIEN, Laura .... 603-524-3207 296 L
llemien@ccsnh.edu

LEMIRE, Mark .... 315-792-7100 348 D
mark.lemire@suny.edu
LEMISCH, Jamie .... 215-780-1391 435 D
jlemisch@salus.edu
LEMISH, Dafna, P .... 618-453-7708 159 H
dafnalemish@siu.edu
LEMKE, Chris .... 616-222-1360 241 G
chris.lemke@cornerstone.edu
LEMKE, Steve, W .... 504-282-4455 206 C
slemke@nobts.edu
LEMME, Gary, D .... 334-844-4444..... 1 G
gdl0003@aces.edu
LEMMER, Nick .... 507-457-6649 264 B
nlemmer@smumn.edu
LEMMON, Ann .... 919-962-4592 369 C
awlemmon@northcarolina.edu
LEMMON, John .... 650-508-3605.. 56 H
jlemmon@ndnu.edu
LEMOINE, Sandra, M .... 318-342-1235 209 A
slemoine@ulm.edu
LEMON, Cari .... 575-538-6675 314 E
lemonc@wnmu.edu
LEMON, Deborah, A ..... 812-855-6783 167 J
dalemon@iu.edu
LEMON, Jason .... 619-260-4585.. 74 B
jasonlemon@sandiego.edu
LEMON, Nikita .... 410-462-8056 213 G
nlemon@bccc.edu
LEMON, Ronald, E .... 304-896-7425 531 F
ronald.lemon@southernwv.edu
LEMON, William, J .... 314-516-4702 284 B
lemonj@umsl.edu
LEMONIS, Samuel .... 601-857-3204 267 D
splemonis@hindscc.edu
LEMONS, James .... 434-832-7680 515 A
lemonsj@cvcc.vccs.edu
LEMONS, L. Jay .... 570-372-4130 435 I
supres@susqu.edu
LEMUEL, Robert, L .... 989-964-4393 249 G
lemuel@svsu.edu
LEMURA, Linda, M .... 315-445-4120 330 B
president14@lemoyne.edu
LEMUS,
Maria De Jesus .... 773-371-5453 141 C
mlemus@ctu.edu
LENA, III, Hugh, F .... 401-865-2155 441 F
hlena@providence.edu
LENAHAN, Robert .... 631-632-6350 344 C
robert.lenahan@stonybrook.edu
LENARD, Mary .... 262-595-2644 540 C
mary.lenard@uwp.edu
LENCHAK, Timothy, A .. 563-876-3353 177 I
tlenchak@dwci.edu
LENCKE, Scott .... 901-381-3939 466 E
scott@visible.edu
LENCZOWSKI, John ...... 202-462-2101.. 96 C
lenczowski@iwp.edu
LENFEST, Richard .... 413-572-5405 230 F
rlenfest@westfield.ma.edu
LENGA, Kirk .... 516-299-4209 330 F
kirk.lenga@liu.edu
LENHARDT, Andrew ...... 765-973-8232 168 A
alenhard@iue.edu
LENHART, Jeff .... 704-847-5600 369 A
jlenhart@ses.edu
LENIG, Joni, L .... 931-540-2752 462 E
jlenig@columbiastate.edu
LENIHAN, Bernard .... 908-709-7605 309 A
lenihan@ucc.edu
LENIHAN, David .... 787-840-2575 555 E
dlenihan@psm.edu
LENIO, Jim .... 612-338-7224 265 G
jim.lenio@waldenu.edu
LENITNI, James, P .... 248-370-2193 248 K
jlentini@oakland.edu
LENKER, Michael .... 509-533-8280 521 E
michael.lenker@scc.spokane.edu
LENNEMAN, Marc .... 406-447-4336 286 D
mlenneman@carroll.edu
LENNERTON, Mark .... 718-289-5655 318 E
mark.lennerton@bcc.cuny.edu
LENNERTZ, Reid .... 239-590-7960 114 F
rlennert@fgcu.edu
LENNEY, Raina .... 202-885-5936.. 94 H
lenney@american.edu
LENNIE, Peter .... 585-275-5931 351 D
lennie@rochester.edu
LENNIHAN, Louise .... 212-817-7200 319 B
llennihan@gc.cuny.edu
LENNON, Craig .... 203-576-4487.. 92 B
clennon@bridgeport.edu
LENNON, John .... 845-848-4061 324 B
john.lennon@dc.edu
LENNOX, JR.,
William, J .... 352-588-8242 111 L
bill.lennox@saintleo.edu
LENO, Melissa .... 218-733-5903 259 C
m.leno@lsc.edu
LENO, Tom .... 701-224-5497 374 E
thomas.leno@bismarckstate.edu

LENOIR, Joel .... 802-862-9616 501 E
jlenoir@burlington.edu
LENOIR, Nina .... 714-997-6622.. 38 B
lenoir@chapman.edu
LENON, Fe .... 773-442-5143 154 H
f-lenon@neiu.edu
LENORE-JENKINS,
Shani .... 314-529-9350 277 B
slenore@maryville.edu
LENOSKY, Charles, A ... 402-280-2540 290 B
clenosky@creighton.edu
LENOUE, Sarah .... 206-517-4541 526 C
slenoue@siom.edu
LENOX, John, G .... 609-896-5192 306 A
jlenox@rider.edu
LENROW, Jon .... 215-670-9359 428 A
jlenrow@peirce.edu
LENSING, Peggy .... 563-387-1015 180 M
lensinpe@luther.edu
LENTING, Amy, L .... 312-788-1120 162 H
alenting@vandercook.edu
LENTINO, Nicholas .... 860-727-6765.. 90 F
nlentino@goodwin.edu
LENTNER, Nikolaus .... 914-251-6070 346 D
nikolaus.lentner@purchase.edu
LENTZ, Heather .... 605-995-7227 452 H
heather.lentz@mitchelltech.edu
LENTZ, Kristi, L .... 701-788-4772 374 A
kristi.lentz@mayvillestate.edu
LENTZ, Sherry .... 904-596-2443 117 G
slentz@tbc.edu
LENTZ, Victoria, A .... 410-543-6368 220 E
valentz@salisbury.edu
LENWAY, Stefanie, A .... 651-962-4201 265 F
lenw0002@stthomas.edu
LENZ, Christopher .... 323-343-3237.. 34 A
clenz@cslanet.calstatela.edu
LENZ, Craig, J .... 334-699-2266.... 1 B
LENZ, Joseph .... 515-271-3623 177 K
joseph.lenz@drake.edu
LENZ, Mary .... 320-762-4648 257 O
maryl@alextech.edu
LENZ, Patrick, J .... 510-987-9101.. 70 J
patrick.lenz@ucop.edu
LENZ, Suzanne .... 603-623-0313 298 C
suzannelenz@nhia.edu
LENZI, John .... 413-545-2313 228 F
jlenzi@registrar.umass.edu
LENZI, Patrick .... 610-436-1048 432 B
plenzi@wcupa.edu
LEO, Donald .... 706-542-1653 132 H
donleo@engr.uga.edu
LEO, Laurie .... 585-594-6861 337 A
Leo_Laurie@roberts.edu
LEO, Laurie .... 585-594-6861 339 F
Leo_Laurie@roberts.edu
LEO, Sydney, R .... 615-329-8663 456 G
sleo@fisk.edu
LEOMITI, Sonny, J .... 684-699-9155 549 C
s.leomiti@amsamoa.edu
LEON, Christine .... 714-564-6230.. 60 G
leon_christine@sac.edu
LEON, Christine .... 714-241-6257.. 40 B
cleon@coastline.edu
LEON, Dante, J .... 425-235-5831 525 G
dleon@rtc.edu
LEON, Gloria .... 914-606-6744 352 G
gloria.leon@sunywcc.edu
LEON, Juan, C .... 787-844-8812 558 D
juan.leon1@upr.edu
LEON, Kelly .... 513-745-3877 396 B
leon@xavier.edu
LEON, Nelson .... 212-752-1530 330 C
nelson.leon@limcollege.edu
LEON, Sam .... 909-607-4034.. 39 E
sam.leon@cgu.edu
LEON, Way .... 415-422-2868.. 74 C
leon@usfca.edu
LEON GUERRERO,
Ann S, A .... 671-735-2862 549 G
annsalg@uguam.uog.edu
LEON GUERRERO,
Ann S, A .... 671-735-2941 549 G
annsalg@uguam.uog.edu
LEON GUERRERO,
Barbara, B .... 671-735-5519 549 E
csi@guamcc.edu
LEON GUERRERO,
Deborah, D .... 671-735-2585 549 G
deborah@uguam.uog.edu
LEON-VICKS, Lilly .... 775-445-3324 296 A
lilly.leon-vicks@wnc.edu
LEONARD, Alan .... 315-228-7474 321 H
pleonard@colgate.edu
LEONARD, Bethany .... 262-695-6520 544 D
bleonard3@wctc.edu
LEONARD, Brenda .... 704-330-6626 361 D
brenda.leonard@cpcc.edu
LEONARD, Bryan .... 217-245-3048 146 D
bryan.leonard@mail.ic.edu

LEVINE, Louis, L .... 212-410-8023 335 B
llevine@nycpm.edu
LEVINE, Marilyn .... 509-963-1400 520 E
levinem@cwu.edu
LEVINE, Mark .... 414-229-6300 540 A
levinem@uwm.edu
LEVINE, Martin, L .... 213-740-2101.. 74 D
levine@usc.edu
LEVINE, Matt .... 530-251-8890.. 50 B
mlevine@lassencollege.edu
LEVINE, Michael, F ...... 716-878-4311 345 B
levinemf@buffalostate.edu
LEVINE, Shana .... 503-768-7548 406 H
slevine@lclark.edu
LEVINE, Susan .... 212-875-4657 315 F
slevine@bankstreet.edu
LEVINE, Vikki .... 434-395-2921 509 H
levinevj@longwood.edu
LEVINE, Virginia .... 607-753-2201 345 C
virginia.levine@cortland.edu
LEVINE-CLARK,
Michael .... 303-871-3176.. 86 H
miclark@du.edu
LEVINE LAUFGRABEN,
Jodi .... 215-204-7000 436 C
jodi.levine@temple.edu
LEVINESS, Peter, O .... 804-289-8119 513 M
plevines@richmond.edu
LEVINO, Evelyn .... 614-947-6765 382 H
evelyn.levino@franklin.edu
LEVINSON, David .... 203-857-7024.. 88 C
dlevinson@ncc.commnet.edu
LEVINSON, David, L ...... 203-857-7024.. 89 H
dlevinson@norwalk.edu
LEVINSON, Karen .... 215-596-8709 438 E
k.levins@usciences.edu
LEVINSTEIN, Edward ..... 585-343-0055 326 F
ejlevenstein@genesee.edu
LEVINTHAL, Keith .... 914-323-7277 331 J
keith.levinthal@mville.edu
LEVIS, Malinda .... 724-357-1358 431 A
malinda@iup.edu
LEVISEUR, Jacquelyn .... 330-941-2136 396 C
jmleviseur@ysu.edu
LEVISTER, Jason, O ...... 910-272-3533 365 D
jlevister@robeson.edu
LEVISTER, JR.,
Joseph, W .... 910-678-8327 362 E
levistej@faytechcc.edu
LEVITT, Bart .... 412-809-5100 433 D
levitt.bart@pti.edu
LEVITTE, Yael .... 607-255-6867 323 C
yael.levitte@cornell.edu
LEVITZKE, Shannon .... 334-222-6591.... 5 G
LEVY, Ben .... 201-684-7533 305 F
blevy1@ramapo.edu
LEVY, Dessie .... 414-297-6392 543 E
levyd@matc.edu
LEVY, Donald .... 773-702-1383 161 D
d-levy@uchicago.edu
LEVY, Douglas .... 586-445-7535 246 A
levyd@macomb.edu
LEVY, Gary .... 410-704-2124 221 A
glevy@towson.edu
LEVY, Kenneth, R .... 401-598-1007 441 D
klevy@jwu.edu
LEVY, Laura .... 504-988-3291 207 F
llevy@tulane.edu
LEVY, Margaree .... 651-255-6118 264 F
mlevy@unitedseminary.edu
LEVY, Mitchell .... 609-343-5087 299 G
mlevy@atlantic.edu
LEVY, Shelley .... 718-289-5119 318 E
shelley.levy@bcc.cuny.edu
LEVY CRUZ, Madeline .. 570-558-1818 418 I
LEW, Gary, B .... 716-888-2255 317 H
lew@canisius.edu
LEW, Tom .... 310-660-3316.. 43 G
tlew@elcamino.edu
LEW YAN VOON,
Lok, C .... 843-953-6682 444 C
llewyanv@citadel.edu
LEWALLEN, Willard .... 831-755-6900.. 46 J
wlewallen@hartnell.edu
LEWANDOWSKI,
Joseph, D .... 660-543-4633 283 F
lewandowski@ucmo.edu
LEWELLEN, Randy .... 903-983-8130 477 A
rlewellen@kilgore.edu
LEWICKI, Denise .... 860-628-4751.. 91 A
dlewicki@lincolncollegene.edu
LEWIN, Harris, A .... 530-754-7764.. 71 A
lewin@ucdavis.edu
LEWIN, Lisa, M .... 414-410-4230 535 C
lmlewin@stritch.edu
LEWIN, Luis .... 817-735-5097 492 D
luis.lewin@untsystem.edu
LEWIN, Ross .... 301-405-4772 219 D
rdlewin@umd.edu
LEWIS, Albert .... 708-974-5407 153 D
lewisjra@morainevalley.edu
LEWIS, Alex, O .... 405-962-1663 398 E
aolewis@langston.edu
LEWIS, Alisha .... 870-584-4471.. 24 E
alewis@cccua.edu
LEWIS, Andre .... 831-582-3044.. 34 C
alewis@csumb.edu
LEWIS, Andrew .... 304-829-7645 529 H
alewis@bethanywv.edu
LEWIS, Ann .... 208-769-7812 138 G
ann_lewis@nic.edu
LEWIS, Beth .... 409-933-8271 471 B
blewis@com.edu
LEWIS, Beverly, N .... 336-734-7512 362 F
blewis@forsythtech.edu
LEWIS, Bill .... 505-566-3339 312 K
lewisb@sanjuancollege.edu
LEWIS, Bill, E .... 314-434-2212 275 J
blewis@hickeycollege.edu
LEWIS, Blaine, D .... 330-823-7365 394 A
lewisbd@mountunion.edu
LEWIS, Brenda .... 863-680-6285 104 F
blewis@flsouthern.edu
LEWIS, Brian .... 765-677-2188 169 C
brian.lewis@indwes.edu
LEWIS, Brien .... 704-637-4414 355 H
wblewis@catawba.edu
LEWIS, Bruce .... 847-491-4933 155 D
balewis@northwestern.edu
LEWIS, Burt .... 919-658-7783 369 B
blewis@umo.edu
LEWIS, C. Jasper .... 870-235-4065.. 23 D
cjlewis@saumag.edu
LEWIS, Carolyn .... 201-559-3560 302 I
lewisc@felician.edu
LEWIS, Cassandra, B .... 601-877-3905 266 C
cblewis@alcorn.edu
LEWIS, Charles, R .... 256-782-5003.... 4 L
crlewis@jsu.edu
LEWIS, Christopher ...... 517-371-5140 252 J
lewisch@cooley.edu
LEWIS, Chuck .... 918-647-1450 397 C
cllewis@carlalbert.edu
LEWIS, Cindy .... 805-493-3199.. 31 H
clewis@callutheran.edu
LEWIS, Cindy .... 865-573-4517 457 H
clewis@johnsonU.edu
LEWIS, Crissy .... 864-578-8770 448 G
clewis@sherman.edu
LEWIS, Cyndi .... 401-232-6000 441 B
clewis@bryant.edu
LEWIS, Cynthia .... 802-831-1444 503 E
clewis@vermontlaw.edu
LEWIS, Daniel, G .... 925-631-4616.. 61 G
dlewis@stmarys-ca.edu
LEWIS, David, E .... 585-275-5240 351 D
david.lewis@rochester.edu
LEWIS, David, R .... 802-356-6824.. 94 G
david.r.lewis@wilmu.edu
LEWIS, David, W .... 317-274-0462 168 E
dlewis@iupui.edu
LEWIS, Dawanna .... 713-221-8974 491 F
lewisd@uhd.edu
LEWIS, Diane .... 530-541-4660.. 50 A
lewis@ltcc.edu
LEWIS, Don .... 763-433-1116 257 P
donald.lewis@anokaramsey.edu
LEWIS, Donald .... 763-433-1116 258 A
donald.lweis@anokaramsey.edu
LEWIS, Donna .... 601-925-3967 268 E
dlewis@mc.edu
LEWIS, Donna, M .... 304-647-6566 531 D
dlewis@newriver.edu
LEWIS, Dorothy .... 315-792-3340 351 G
dmlewis1@utica.edu
LEWIS, E. Charles .... 817-202-6720 483 C
lewisc@swau.edu
LEWIS, Edward .... 336-770-3329 372 B
lewise@uncsa.edu
LEWIS, Eleanor, M .... 717-867-6302 423 I
lewis@lvc.edu
LEWIS, Emily, G .... 860-515-3860.. 88 B
elewis1@charteroak.edu
LEWIS, Eva .... 423-697-2659 462 C
eva.lewis@chattanoogastate.edu
LEWIS, Felicia, Y .... 502-597-6286 197 G
felicia.lewis@kysu.edu
LEWIS, Fred .... 423-279-7665 463 D
fdlewis@northeaststate.edu
LEWIS, Georj .... 912-344-3562 120 D
georj.lewis@armstrong.edu
LEWIS, Gerald .... 252-328-6964 369 E
lewisge@ecu.edu
LEWIS, Gregory .... 504-816-4050 202 F
glewis@dillard.edu
LEWIS, Gregory .... 804-257-5750 518 E
gelewis@vuu.edu
LEWIS, Gregory, V .... 661-824-2977.. 55 I
glewis@ntps.edu
LEWIS, Hal, M .... 312-322-1715 160 E
LEWIS, Heather, G .... 215-573-4507 437 I
heatherl@upenn.edu
LEWIS, Jack .... 509-570-5926 153 C
jack.lewis@moody.edu
LEWIS, Jack, M .... 540-674-3601 516 B
jlewis@nr.edu
LEWIS, Jackie .... 252-985-5170 367 E
Jlewis@ncwc.edu
LEWIS, James, E .... 206-934-5157 526 B
james.lewis@seattlecolleges.edu
LEWIS, James, W .... 765-641-4525 164 B
jwlewis@anderson.edu
LEWIS, Jan .... 252-328-2267 369 E
lewisja@ecu.edu
LEWIS, Jan, P .... 253-535-7283 524 I
lewisjp@plu.edu
LEWIS, Jan Ellen .... 973-353-5213 307 C
janlewis@andromeda.rutgers.edu
LEWIS, Jane, L .... 209-946-2125.. 73 C
jlewis@pacific.edu
LEWIS, Jeanne .... 609-652-4201 308 E
jeanne.lewis@stockton.edu
LEWIS, Jeannie, M .... 559-323-2100.. 63 C
jlewis@sjcl.edu
LEWIS, Jennifer .... 619-660-4670.. 46 G
jennifer.lewis@gcccd.edu
LEWIS, Jerry .... 404-727-2793 124 D
jerrylewis@emory.edu
LEWIS, Jill .... 843-661-8003 446 C
jill.lewis@fdtc.edu
LEWIS, Jim .... 610-436-3200 432 B
jlewis@wcupa.edu
LEWIS, Jim .... 806-743-2530 490 A
jim.lewis@ttuhsc.edu
LEWIS, Jim .... 817-531-4404 490 C
jimlewis@txwes.edu
LEWIS, Jim, D .... 704-637-4720 355 H
jdlewis@catawba.edu
LEWIS, John .... 901-321-3227 455 I
john.lewis@cbu.edu
LEWIS, John, C .... 801-422-2533 497 J
john_lewis@byu.edu
LEWIS, Joseph, S .... 949-824-8792.. 71 C
jslewis@uci.edu
LEWIS, Judith .... 716-829-7776 324 E
lewisj@dyc.edu
LEWIS, Judith, H .... 914-323-5279 331 J
judith.lewis@mville.edu
LEWIS, Katherine, P ..... 570-340-6094 425 D
kplewis@marywood.edu
LEWIS, Kay .... 206-543-6107 527 G
sklewis@uw.edu
LEWIS, Keisha .... 205-929-1604.... 5 I
klewis@miles.edu
LEWIS, Kendrick, D .... 803-536-8227 448 H
klewis19@scsu.edu
LEWIS, Kenneth .... 803-536-8860 448 H
klewis31@scsu.edu
LEWIS, JR., Kenneth, A 252-492-2061 366 G
lewis@vgcc.edu
LEWIS, Kent .... 270-903-1102 198 A
klewis@kwc.edu
LEWIS, Lance .... 517-338-3431 241 B
llewis@cleary.edu
LEWIS, Larry .... 620-862-5252 184 H
larry.lewis@barclaycollege.edu
LEWIS, Laura .... 513-751-1206 376 A
laura@aic-arts.edu
LEWIS, Leslie, W .... 410-337-6044 215 B
leslie.lewis@goucher.edu
LEWIS, Lisa .... 805-898-4010.. 44 J
llewis@fielding.edu
LEWIS, Lisa .... 612-624-6142 265 C
lrlewis@umn.edu
LEWIS, Lori .... 410-857-2254 217 A
llewis@mcdaniel.edu
LEWIS, Luca .... 360-383-3076 528 E
llewis@whatcom.ctc.edu
LEWIS, Lynn .... 864-646-1437 449 F
llewis@tctc.edu
LEWIS, Lynn .... 434-381-6106 513 E
llewis@sbc.edu
LEWIS, Mark .... 952-358-8405 260 D
mark.lewis@normandale.edu
LEWIS, Mark .... 813-253-7017 106 C
mlewis73@hccfl.edu
LEWIS, Mark .... 325-674-2772 466 I
mark.lewis@acu.edu
LEWIS, Marsha, L .... 716-829-2533 343 E
UBNursingDean@buffalo.edu
LEWIS, Mary .... 772-462-7444 106 F
mlewis@irsc.edu
LEWIS, Melissa .... 505-473-6404 313 B
melissa.lewis@santafeuniversity.edu
LEWIS, Melissa .... 931-526-3660 456 H
melissa.lewis@fortisinstitute.edu
LEWIS, Michael .... 614-251-4589 388 H
lewism2@ohiodominican.edu
LEWIS, Michelle .... 314-977-6063 281 M
lewisml@slu.edu
LEWIS, Mike .... 918-463-6358 397 I
mike.lewis@connorsstate.edu
LEWIS, Mildred .... 510-464-3413.. 59 B
mildredlewis@peralta.edu
LEWIS, Mitchell, R .... 607-735-1709 324 J
mlewis@elmira.edu
LEWIS, Monique .... 281-487-1170 486 F
mlewis@txchiro.edu
LEWIS, Nora, E .... 215-746-1172 437 I
nlewis@sas.upenn.edu
LEWIS, Orlando .... 704-216-6185 358 I
olewis@livingstone.edu
LEWIS, Pat .... 704-355-2029 355 G
pat.lewis@carolinascollege.edu
LEWIS, Philip .... 701-627-4738 373 E
plewis@fortbertholdcc.edu
LEWIS, Raynold .... 508-929-8883 230 G
rlewis1@worcester.edu
LEWIS, Rebecca .... 585-245-5546 345 D
lewis@geneseo.edu
LEWIS, Rebecca, B .... 423-439-6155 461 D
bakerr@etsu.edu
LEWIS, Richard .... 928-350-1301.. 17 K
rlewis@prescott.edu
LEWIS, Richard, W .... 330-325-2511 387 F
rwl@neomed.edu
LEWIS, Rob .... 859-985-3323 193 F
lewisro@berea.edu
LEWIS, Robert, J .... 617-552-3330 224 B
robert.lewis.3@bc.edu
LEWIS, Robin .... 606-326-2423 195 H
Robin.Lewis@kctcs.edu
LEWIS, Rosalyn .... 318-247-0430 207 H
lewisros@gram.edu
LEWIS, Russ .... 951-827-3009.. 72 A
russ.lewis@ucr.edu
LEWIS, Sally .... 832-476-8211.. 44 L
clinicqualitycontrol@fivebranches.edu
LEWIS, Shaun, M .... 504-286-5292 207 B
slewis@suno.edu
LEWIS, Shirley .... 707-864-7000.. 66 J
shirley.lewis@solano.edu
LEWIS, Stephen .... 707-527-4246.. 65 C
slewis@santarosa.edu
LEWIS, Susan .... 325-674-2024 466 I
lewiss@acu.edu
LEWIS, Susan, A .... 617-262-5000 223 G
susan.lewis@the-bac.edu
LEWIS, Suzanne .... 267-341-3481 420 K
slewis10@holyfamily.edu
LEWIS, Ted, A .... 865-694-6523 463 E
talewis@pstcc.edu
LEWIS, Terry, W .... 731-881-7890 465 F
tlewis@utm.edu
LEWIS, Thomas .... 443-287-9900 216 A
tomlewis@jhu.edu
LEWIS, Thomas, C .... 404-413-1404 126 D
tomlewis@gsu.edu
LEWIS, Tiffany .... 765-677-2102 169 C
tiffany.lewis@indwes.edu
LEWIS, Tracie, O .... 888-498-6752 370 B
tolewis@ncat.edu
LEWIS, Trevor .... 305-626-3750 104 B
trevor.lewis@fmuniv.edu
LEWIS, Trey .... 502-852-6701 201 A
trey.lewis@louisville.edu
LEWIS, Urick .... 610-526-6080 420 C
ulewis@harcum.edu
LEWIS, Victoria .... 831-479-6406.. 30 C
vilewis@cabrillo.edu
LEWIS, Vivian .... 585-273-2760 351 D
vivian.lewis@rochester.edu
LEWIS, Walter .... 518-587-2100 348 A
walter.lewis@esc.edu
LEWIS, Wendy .... 330-823-6045 394 A
lewisws@mountunion.edu
LEWIS, William, A .... 601-403-1201 270 A
wlewis@prcc.edu
LEWIS-ANTHONY,
Justin .... 703-370-6600 511 B
LEWIS-BOYD, Janice .... 313-593-5200 251 D
jckboyd@umich.edu
LEWIS-JASPER, Vera ..... 409-944-1496 474 G
vlewis@gc.edu
LEWIS LOGUE, Judith .. 619-260-4720.. 74 B
jllogue@sandiego.edu
LEWIS SAULO, Mileva .. 650-292-5579.. 61 J
msaulo@samuelmerritt.edu
LEWIS-THOMAS, Janice 256-726-7840.... 6 C
jthomas@oakwood.edu
LEWIS-WHITE, Yasmin .. 202-885-8552.. 97 E
ylwhite@wesleyseminary.edu
LEWIT, Jonathan, D ...... 845-257-3130 344 A
lewit@newpaltz.edu
LEWKIEWICZ, Debra ..... 845-434-5750 349 C
dlewkiew@sullivan.suny.edu
LEWTER, Andy .... 478-445-5169 125 A
andy.lewter@gcsu.edu
LEWTHWAITE,
Barbara-Jayne .... 908-852-1400 301 C
lewthwaiteb@centenarycollege.edu

LEWY, MariLynn, J .... 941-752-5383 114 B
lewym@scf.edu
LEYBA, Johanna .... 303-871-7661.. 86 H
Johanna.Leyba@du.edu
LEYBA, Marylou .... 415-239-3291.. 39 A
mleyba@ccsf.edu
LEYDEN, John, J .... 401-865-2390 441 F
jleyden@providence.edu
LEYDON, John .... 919-962-4908 369 C
jleydon@northcarolina.edu
LEYKAM, Scott .... 503-943-7117 410 H
leykam@up.edu
LEYVA-PUEBLA,
Ricardo .... 206-934-6455 526 B
ricardo.leyva-puebla@seattlecolleges.edu
LEZAK JANOW,
Roseann .... 860-509-9501.. 90 G
rlezak@hartsem.edu
LE'I, Emilia .... 684-699-9155 549 C
e.lei@amsamoa.edu
LI, Benn .... 212-924-5900 349 D
bli@swedishinstitute.edu
LI, Dai .... 602-235-4179 190 G
dli@pittstate.edu
LI, Frank .... 916-278-6686.. 34 E
frank.li@saclink.csus.edu
LI, Haipeng .... 209-228-2579.. 71 E
hli58@UCMerced.edu
LI, Joanne .... 937-775-4859 396 A
joanne.li@wright.edu
LI, Kevin .... 773-481-8460 142 D
kli@ccc.edu
LI, Ming .... 859-336-5082 199 B
mingli@sccky.edu
LI, Ming .... 269-387-2966 252 I
ming.li@wmich.edu
LI, Peter .... 361-593-4340 486 A
peter.li@tamuk.edu
LI, Qiaoyun (Liz) .... 650-493-4430.. 66 H
liz.li@sofia.edu
LI, Rui .... 610-430-4959 432 B
rli@wcupa.edu
LI, Sharon, F .... 415-422-2790.. 74 C
lis@usfca.edu
LI, Sheng .... 714-533-1495.. 67 A
sli@southbaylo.edu
LI, Yi .... 937-775-2611 396 A
yi.li@wright.edu
LI, Yongmei .... 864-596-9752 445 E
yongmei.li@converse.edu
LI, Zhan .... 925-631-4604.. 61 G
zgl1@stmarys-ca.edu
LI-BUGG, W. Cherry ..... 714-808-4787.. 56 D
clibugg@nocccd.edu
LIANG, Bruce .... 860-679-2594.. 92 C
bliang@uchc.edu
LIANG, John Paul .... 713-780-9777 467 G
info@acaom.edu
LIANG, Mark .... 714-564-6040.. 60 G
liang_mark@sac.edu
LIANG, Sherry .... 510-628-8027.. 50 I
controller@lincolnuca.edu
LIAS CLAFFEY, Renae ... 508-929-8492 230 G
rliasclaffey@worcester.edu
LIAUTAUD, Danielle ...... 973-720-2121 309 I
liautaudd@wpunj.edu
LIBBY, Betsy .... 207-755-5250 210 L
blibby@cmcc.edu
LIBBY, Elizabeth .... 847-735-6011 149 H
libby@lakeforest.edu
LIBBY, James .... 207-859-1420 211 I
libbyj@thomas.edu
LIBBY, John .... 240-567-7951 217 B
john.libby@montgomerycollege.edu
LIBBY, Wendy, B .... 386-822-7250 117 A
wlibby@stetson.edu
LIBEN, Lucy .... 212-924-5900 349 D
lucy@swedishinstitute.edu
LIBERATI, Dennis .... 215-222-4200 434 A
dliberati@walnuthillcollege.edu
LIBERATORE,
Anthony, F .... 217-424-6338 153 A
aliberatore@millikin.edu
LIBERATORE, Debra ...... 518-454-5145 322 C
liberatd@strose.edu
LIBERATORI, Ellen, A ... 607-746-4612 347 G
liberaem@delhi.edu
LIBERATOSCIOLI,
Daniel .... 215-222-4200 434 A
president@walnuthillcollege.edu
LIBERATOSCIOLI,
Peggy .... 215-222-4200 434 A
pl@walnuthillcollege.edu
LIBERMAN, Ira .... 718-438-1002 332 F
yliberman@yeshivanet.com
LIBERTELLI, Joseph ...... 202-274-7338.. 97 B
jlibertelli@udc.edu
LIBERTO, Salvadore ...... 617-730-7135 235 B
salvadore.liberto@newbury.edu
LIBERTO, Terri .... 412-536-1813 422 E
terri.liberto@laroche.edu
LIBERTY, Bob .... 254-526-1310 470 E
bob.liberty@ctcd.edu
LIBERTY, Cindy .... 336-770-3333 372 B
libertyc@uncsa.edu
LIBERTY, Paul .... 703-993-8860 507 K
pliberty@gmu.edu
LIBERTY, Stanly, R .... 309-677-3167 140 H
sliberty@fsmail.bradley.edu
LIBET, Alice, Q .... 843-792-4930 447 G
libeta@musc.edu
LIBHART, Bonnie .... 256-652-3752 460 B
drbonnie@me.com
LIBUTTI, Dean .... 401-874-4408 442 E
dean@uri.edu
LICAR, Jason .... 918-836-6886 402 I
jlicar@mail.spartan.edu
LICARI, Frank .... 702-990-4433 296 D
flicari@roseman.edu
LICARI, Michael, J .... 812-237-2309 167 E
mike.licari@indstate.edu
LICATA, Betty Jo .... 330-941-3064 396 C
bjlicata@ysu.edu
LICATA, Christine, M .... 585-475-2953 339 G
cmlnbt@rit.edu
LICHT, Daniel .... 914-395-2301 342 C
dlicht@sarahlawrence.edu
LICHT, Jodi, N .... 212-752-1530 330 C
jodi.licht@limcollege.edu
LICHT, William .... 920-206-2320 536 T
william.licht@mbu.edu
LICHTBLAU, Jobey .... 710-231-7672 374 C
jobey.lichtblau@ndsu.edu
LICHTENBERG, Anne, V 859-257-5068 200 G
anne.lichtenberg@uky.edu
LICHTENBERGER, Lynn . 856-691-8600 301 H
llichtenberger@cccnj.edu
LICHTENFELD, Reena ..... 612-338-7224 265 G
reena.lichtenfeld@laureate.net
LICHTENSTEIN, Art .... 501-450-5202.. 25 F
artl@uca.edu
LICHTENSTEIN, Gregg ... 619-594-7351.. 35 E
lichtens@mail.sdsu.edu
LICHTENSTEIN, Mark .... 315-470-4748 347 B
malichte@esf.edu
LICHTLE, Richard .... 419-358-3314 377 H
lichtler@bluffton.edu
LICHTMAN, Louis, J ..... 607-871-2171 314 J
flich@alfred.edu
LICHTSINN, Jill .... 260-982-5015 170 a
jslichtsinn@manchester.edu
LICKISS, Steve .... 619-388-7455.. 62 H
slickiss@sdccd.edu
LICKTIEG, Elaine .... 203-285-2389.. 89 B
elicktieg@gwcc.commnet.edu
LIDDELL, Alan, C .... 908-526-1200 305 G
Alan.Liddell@raritanval.edu
LIDDELL, Peter, E .... 315-294-8861 317 I
liddell@cayuga-cc.edu
LIDDELL, Robert .... 352-588-8346 111 L
robert.liddell@saintleo.edu
LIDDELL, Tammy .... 206-296-6052 526 F
liddellt@seattleu.edu
LIDDICOAT, Al .... 805-756-2844.. 32 E
aliddico@calpoly.edu
LIDDLE, Trevor, C .... 956-326-2380 485 B
tliddle@tamiu.edu
LIDDY, Colette .... 973-618-3209 300 H
cliddy@caldwell.edu
LIDDY, Elizabeth, D ...... 315-443-2494 349 E
liddy@syr.edu
LIDERS, Gunta .... 585-275-4031 351 D
gliders@orpa.rochester.edu
LIDGUS, Jonathan, A ... 314-516-5537 284 B
lidgusj@umsl.edu
LIDH, Todd .... 828-898-8712 358 F
lidht@lmc.edu
LIDSTONE, Rhonda, W . 478-301-2005 128 G
lidstone_rw@mercer.edu
LIDSTONE, Sheila .... 409-772-9866 495 E
shlidsto@utmb.edu
LIDSTROM, Mary, E .... 206-616-0804 527 G
lidstrom@uw.edu
LIDY, Paul .... 217-362-6410 153 A
plidy@millikin.edu
LIEBAU, Linda, B .... 513-244-4593 387 A
linda.liebau@msj.edu
LIEBENGOOD, Kelly ...... 903-233-3160 477 G
kellyliebengood@letu.edu
LIEBER, Barbara .... 217-641-4535 148 J
blieber@jwcc.edu
LIEBERMAN, Abraham .. 845-782-1380 354 B
LIEBERMAN,
Devorah, A .... 909-593-3511.. 73 B
dlieberman@laverne.edu
LIEBERMAN, Ilene .... 610-499-4275 439 G
idlieberman@widener.edu
LIEBERMAN, Robert ...... 410-516-3355 216 A
rlieberman@jhu.edu
LIEBERT, Jane .... 913-758-6126 191 I
Jane.Liebert@stmary.edu
LIEBERTHAL, Susan ...... 631-451-4539 348 F
liebers@sunysuffolk.edu
LIEBESKIND, Lanny, S . 404-727-6604 124 D
chemll1@emory.edu
LIEBHABER, Karen .... 870-248-4000.. 20 E
karenl@blackrivertech.edu
LIEBOVICH, Melissa ..... 847-324-5588 141 H
mliebovich@ortchicagotech.edu
LIEBRECHT, Alan .... 310-377-5501.. 53 E
aliebrecht@marymountcalifornia.edu
LIEBROCK, Lorie .... 575-835-5481 311 I
liebrock@cs.nmt.edu
LIEBSCHER, Kim, K ...... 580-774-3776 402 G
kim.liebscher@swosu.edu
LIECHTY, Dan .... 574-535-7563 166 C
dankl@goshen.edu
LIECHTY, Jeanne, M ..... 574-535-7401 166 C
jeannem@goshen.edu
LIEDTKA, Theresa .... 423-425-4506 465 E
theresa-liedtka@utc.edu
LIEDTKE, Richard, W .... 785-670-1812 192 B
richard.liedtke@washburn.edu
LIEF, Charles, G .... 303-546-3517.. 84 B
president@naropa.edu
LIEF, Nathan, P .... 651-696-6140 256 L
nlief@macalester.edu
LIEGEL, Angela .... 312-915-6191 151 E
aliegel@luc.edu
LIEHR, Michael .... 518-956-8685 348 D
mliehr@sunycnse.com
LIEKWEG, Sarah .... 239-489-9111 104 G
sborland@fsw.edu
LIEN, Joelle .... 605-626-2558 454 A
Joelle.Lien@northern.edu
LIEN, Joelle .... 605-626-7958 454 A
Joelle.Lien@northern.edu
LIERLEY, Mark .... 480-858-9100.. 17 O
m.lierley@scnm.edu
LIERMAN, Michael .... 800-962-7682 285 I
mlierman@wma.edu
LIES, CSC, James .... 508-565-1551 237 A
jlies@stonehill.edu
LIES, CSC, William, M .. 574-631-9800 174 A
lies.7@nd.edu
LIESCH, Ed .... 717-728-2273 415 B
edliesch@centralpenn.edu
LIESE, Hank .... 801-581-6194 499 K
hank.liese@socwk.utah.edu
LIESEN, Joseph .... 573-288-6480 274 C
jliesen@culver.edu
LIESEN, Kristen .... 217-228-5432 156 D
liesekr@quincy.edu
LIESKE, Barb .... 219-464-6717 174 E
barb.lieske@valpo.edu
LIESKE, Brian .... 510-666-8248.. 26 C
blieske@aimc.edu
LIESMAN, Laura .... 732-987-2685 302 J
liesmanl@georgian.edu
LIETO, Mary .... 914-923-2690 337 I
mlieto@pace.edu
LIEU, Mark .... 510-659-6173.. 56 J
mlieu@ohlone.edu
LIEURANCE, Lorissa ..... 515-271-3781 177 K
lorissa.lieurance@drake.edu
LIEVANOS, Destry .... 760-630-1555.. 49 C
dlievanos@kaplan.edu
LIEWER, Chris .... 402-554-2200 294 A
cliewer@unomaha.edu
LIFSEY, Britt .... 678-359-5108 126 E
brittl@gordonstate.edu
LIGEIKIS, Kelli .... 607-778-5089 344 F
ligeikiskh@sunybroome.edu
LIGENZA, Jennifer .... 603-668-2211 298 H
j.ligenza@snhu.edu
LIGGETT, Shawn .... 541-888-7221 410 A
sliggett@socc.edu
LIGHT, Brad .... 336-334-4355 371 C
uncg@bkstore.com
LIGHT, Cathy .... 412-268-5345 414 J
calight@andrew.cmu.edu
LIGHT, Kathleen .... 210-829-3943 492 B
light@uiwtx.edu
LIGHT, Margaret .... 717-262-2010 440 D
margaret.light@wilson.edu
LIGHT, Michael .... 215-717-6170 437 H
mlight@uarts.edu
LIGHT, Steven .... 701-777-2167 373 G
steven.light@und.edu
LIGHTCAP, Rhonda .... 516-671-0379 352 D
rlightcap@webb.edu
LIGHTCAP, Stephen .... 215-717-6375 437 H
slightcap@uarts.edu
LIGHTFIELD, Nancy, R .. 608-757-7750 542 L
nlightfield@blackhawk.edu
LIGHTFOOD, Jennifer ..... 661-362-3482.. 40 H
jennifer.lightfoot@canyons.edu
LIGHTFOOT, Carolyn, A 281-425-6455 477 F
clightfo@lee.edu
LIGHTFOOT, Connie ..... 765-998-5105 173 B
cnlightfoot@taylor.edu
LIGHTFOOT, Douglas .... 816-604-1061 277 F
douglas.lightfoot@mcckc.edu
LIGHTFOOT, James, D .. 434-832-7643 515 A
lightfootd@cvcc.vccs.edu
LIGHTHILL, M. Joyce ... 641-784-5222 178 G
lighthil@graceland.edu
LIGHTSEY, Marissa .... 405-585-5260 399 I
marissa.lightsey@okbu.edu
LIGHTSY, Spencer .... 713-222-5391 491 F
lightsys@uhd.edu
LIGIOSO, Yulian .... 707-864-7000.. 66 J
yulian.ligioso@solano.edu
LIGMAN, Scott .... 509-527-2431 528 A
scott.ligman@wallawalla.edu
LIGNOWSKI, Beth .... 201-559-6027 302 I
0267mgr@sheg.follett.com
LIGON, Eric .... 940-565-4003 492 D
eric.ligon@unt.edu
LIGON, Theresa .... 713-780-9777 467 G
LIKENS, Erin .... 601-643-8316 266 J
erin.likens@colin.edu
LIKES, Wendy, M .... 901-448-6135 465 G
LIKNESS, Tabitha .... 605-668-1566 452 I
tabitha.likness@mtmc.edu
LILES, Jeffrey, R .... 606-783-2000 198 H
j.liles@moreheadstate.edu
LILES, Joel, O .... 740-389-4636 386 B
lilesj@mtc.edu
LILES, Kevin .... 803-641-3581 450 C
kevinl@usca.edu
LILES, Tammy .... 859-246-6449 195 J
tammy.liles@kctcs.edu
LILIENTHAL, Ronda ...... 615-248-1245 464 E
rlilienthal@trevecca.edu
LILLBACK, Peter, A .... 215-572-3811 439 E
plillback@wts.edu
LILLEBO, Troy .... 816-235-6585 284 A
lillebot@umkc.edu
LILLEHAUGEN, Sandi .... 701-662-1505 375 A
sandra.lillehaugen@lrsc.edu
LILLEMON, David .... 507-433-0543 261 C
david.lillemon@riverland.edu
LILLES, Anthony .... 805-482-2755.. 61 F
alilles@stjohnsem.edu
LILLESTON, Judith .... 914-831-0369 322 D
jlilleston@cw.edu
LILLEY, Ben .... 252-985-5113 367 E
blilley@ncwc.edu
LILLEY, Richard .... 443-840-4698 214 F
rlilley@ccbcmd.edu
LILLGE, Crystal .... 608-796-3841 542 H
clillge@viterbo.edu
LILLIBRIDGE, Fred .... 575-527-7728 312 D
flillibr@nmsu.edu
LILLIE, Deb .... 319-385-6210 180 A
deb.lillie@iw.edu
LILLIE, Sandra .... 720-890-8922.. 83 F
president@itea.edu
LILLIS, John, R .... 574-372-5100 166 D
lillisjr@grace.edu
LILLQUIST, Erik .... 973-275-4811 308 C
erik.lillquist@shu.edu
LILLQUIST, Mark .... 863-297-1083 110 E
mlilquist@polk.edu
LILLY, Claude, C .... 864-833-8222 448 E
clilly@presby.edu
LILLY, Flavius, R .... 410-706-7767 219 E
flilly@umaryland.edu
LILLY, Kenneth, E .... 304-877-6428 529 G
ken.lilly@abc.edu
LILLY, Mary .... 617-732-2144 233 E
mary.lilly@mcphs.edu
LIM, Adriene, I .... 541-346-3056 410 F
alim@uoregon.edu
LIM, Ben .... 620-229-6388 191 B
ben.lim@sckans.edu
LIM, Bob .... 785-864-4999 191 G
blim@ku.edu
LIM, Choong .... 808-735-4708 135 A
clim@chaminade.edu
LIM, Colleen .... 650-723-2300.. 68 G
LIM, Dan .... 407-303-9473.. 97 J
dan.lim@adu.edu
LIM, Gim .... 215-751-8275 416 B
glim@ccp.edu
LIM, Mercy .... 415-442-7080.. 46 A
mlim@ggu.edu
LIM, Morris .... 210-341-1366 479 N
mlim@ost.edu
LIM, Paul .... 213-385-2322.. 77 H
paul1911@wmu.edu
LIM, Sung Jin .... 213-385-2322.. 77 H
sunglim@wmu.edu
LIM, Teik, C .... 513-556-4450 393 B
teik.lim@uc.edu
LIM, Velina .... 714-533-3946.. 36 D
LIM, Xieng .... 425-739-8264 523 I
xieng.lim@lwtech.edu

LIM-THOMPSON, Soo-Yin 218-281-8248 264 H slimthom@umn.edu
LIMA, Brad 508-830-5012 230 D blima@maritime.edu
LIMA, Judy, E 205-329-7904 3 C judy.lima@ecacolleges.com
LIMAS, Celestino 509-865-8544 523 C limas_c@heritage.edu
LIMAYEM, Moez 813-974-3229 116 B mlimayem@usf.edu
LIMBAUGH, James 805-986-5808 75 D jlimbaugh@vcccd.edu
LIMBIRD, Lee 615-329-1907 456 G llimbird@fisk.edu
LIMON, Frank 773-843-7553 142 C flimon1@ccc.edu
LIMONCELLI, Jerry 516-686-7815 335 F jlimonce@nyit.edu
LIMPER, Leslie 503-352-2871 408 I limp5635@pacificu.edu
LIMTUATCO, Edwin, E 671-735-5560 549 E edwin.limtuatco@guamcc.edu
LIN, Alecia 269-927-8108 245 E lin@lakemichigancollege.edu
LIN, Alice 617-585-0100 223 G Alice.Lin@the-bac.edu
LIN, Anne 410-532-5545 217 F alin@ndm.edu
LIN, Chia-Yen 619-260-7692 74 B Linc@sandiego.edu
LIN, Ellen 408-924-5910 36 B ellen.lin@sjsu.edu
LIN, Janice 219-464-5333 174 E janice.lin@valpo.edu
LIN, Kathleen 626-571-5110 50 J kathleenlin@les.edu
LIN, Kuoliang 626-571-5110 50 J klin@les.edu
LIN, Lisa 512-444-8082 487 B lisalin@thsu.edu
LIN, Paul 512-444-8082 487 B thsu@thsu.edu
LIN, Susan, X 808-956-7161 135 H slin@hawaii.edu
LIN, Yi-Chun Tricia 203-392-6864 88 F lyny4@southernct.edu
LIN-COOK, Wendy 973-596-3309 304 D wendy.w.lin-cook@njit.edu
LINAKER, Kathleen 315-792-5376 333 D klinaker@mvcc.edu
LINAM, Alisha 251-575-8271 1 C alinam@ascc.edu
LINAM, Gail 214-333-5372 471 L gaill@dbu.edu
LINAMEN, Larry 951-552-8744 30 D llinamen@calbaptist.edu
LINBACK, John 574-936-8898 164 A john.linback@ancilla.edu
LINC, Linda 330-490-7250 395 C llinc@walsh.edu
LINCKE, James 610-353-7630 421 P jlincke@kaplan.edu
LINCOLN, Judy 314-837-6777 281 D jlincoln@stlchristian.edu
LINCOLN, Timothy 512-404-4873 468 J tlincoln@austinseminary.edu
LINCOLN-PENZEL, Brenda 314-264-1000 284 J brenda.lincoln@vatterott.edu
LIND, James, F 757-451-6200 507 B lindjf@evms.edu
LIND, Jan 812-877-8297 172 C lind@rose-hulman.edu
LIND, Kristen 218-322-2403 259 B kristen.lind@itascacc.edu
LIND, Louise 218-879-0879 258 F llind@fdltcc.edu
LIND, Steven 510-436-1131 47 C lind@hnu.edu
LIND-GONZALEZ, Patricia 631-420-2298 348 B patricia.lind-gonzalez@farmingdale.edu
LINDAHL, Roberta, D 503-943-7321 410 H lindahl@up.edu
LINDAHL, Susan 913-288-7645 188 G slindhal@kckcc.edu
LINDAHL, Susan 913-288-7645 188 G slindahl@kckcc.edu
LINDAHL, Wesley 773-244-5667 154 G wlindahl@northpark.edu
LINDBALD, Gary 562-903-4770 29 F gary.lindbald@biola.edu
LINDBERG, Brad 641-269-3250 178 I lindbergb@grinnell.edu
LINDBERG, Kevin, D 956-326-2601 485 B klindberg@tamiu.edu
LINDBERG, Maryann 603-358-2181 299 D mlindberg1@keene.edu
LINDELL, Belinda, S 218-755-2043 258 B blindell@bemidjistate.edu
LINDELL, P. Griffith 503-375-7034 405 F glindell@corban.edu
LINDEMAN, Barbara 573-882-6007 283 H lindemanb@missouri.edu
LINDEMAN, Brian 651-696-6214 256 L lindeman@macalester.edu
LINDEMAN, Craig 316-978-7282 192 D craig.lindeman@wichita.edu
LINDEMUTH, Gregory, L 610-566-1776 440 C glindemuth@williamson.edu
LINDEN, Eric 646-565-6000 350 C elinden@touro.edu
LINDEN, Erika 515-271-1526 177 H erika.linden@dmu.edu
LINDEN, James 215-489-2446 416 H James.Linden@delval.edu
LINDEN, Stephen, M 248-341-2192 248 E smlinden@oaklandcc.edu
LINDENBAUM, Sharon 816-235-2650 284 A lindenbaums@umkc.edu
LINDENBERG, David, A 802-447-6360 503 A dlindenberg@svc.edu
LINDENBERG, Joshua 701-777-5930 373 G joshea.lindenberg@und.edu
LINDENMEYER, Kriste 856-225-2809 307 A kriste.lindenmeyer@camden.rutgers.edu
LINDENMEYER, Mark, L 410-617-2576 216 D lindenmeyer@loyola.edu
LINDENMEYR, Adele 610-519-4606 439 A adele.lindenmeyr@villanova.edu
LINDER, Cynthia 912-287-4098 123 A clinder@coastalpines.edu
LINDER, Mark 256-765-4397 9 D mdlinder@una.edu
LINDEVALDSEN, Rena 434-592-5300 509 G
LINDGREN, Dianne 828-339-4268 366 C diannel@southwesterncc.edu
LINDGREN, Rita 701-224-5427 374 E rita.lindgren@bismarckstate.edu
LINDGREN, Robert, R 804-752-7211 511 E rlindgren@rmc.edu
LINDGREN, Sheri 414-464-9777 542 J sherilindgren@wspp.edu
LINDGREN, Teresa, C 606-783-2449 198 H t.lindgren@moreheadstate.edu
LINDHOLM, Denise 909-274-5431 54 J dlindholm@mtsac.edu
LINDLEY, Carolyn, V 847-491-8557 155 D c-lindley@northwestern.edu
LINDLEY, Kelli 208-467-8825 138 H klindley@nnu.edu
LINDLEY, Stu 314-744-7623 278 G lindleys@mobap.edu
LINDMAN, Barbara, A 651-631-5247 265 D balindman@unwsp.edu
LINDNER, Bill 850-644-7572 115 A blindner@fsu.edu
LINDNER, Janet, E 203-432-2188 93 C janet.lindner@yale.edu
LINDNER, JoEllen 605-626-2530 454 A JoEllen.Lindner@northern.edu
LINDNER, Roberta 937-327-6342 395 I rlindner@wittenberg.edu
LINDNER, Rosalyn, A 716-878-6939 345 B lindera@buffalostate.edu
LINDO, Patricia 860-512-3613 89 D plindo@manchestercc.edu
LINDON, Jennifer 606-487-3136 196 B jennifer.lindon@kctcs.edu
LINDOR, Keith, D 602-496-0789 11 J keith.lindor@asu.edu
LINDQUIST, Brent 806-742-2566 489 F brent.lindquist@ttu.edu
LINDQUIST, Cynthia, A 701-766-4055 373 D president@littlehoop.edu
LINDQUIST, Joyce 970-207-4500 87 D JoyceL@uscareerinstitute.edu
LINDQUIST, Joyce 970-207-4550 83 P joycel@mckinleycollege.edu
LINDQUIST, Kathy 918-335-6234 400 I klindquist@okwu.edu
LINDQUIST, Kimberly 734-384-4101 247 C klindquist@monroeccc.edu
LINDQUIST, Robert 256-824-2882 9 A robert.lindquist@uah.edu
LINDQUIST, Stefanie, A 706-542-2059 132 H slindquist@uga.edu
LINDQUIST, Vern, L 804-862-6491 511 H vllindquist@rbc.edu
LINDSAY, Barbara 303-360-4914 81 I Barbara.Lindsay@CCAurora.edu
LINDSAY, Cecile 562-985-4128 33 F cecile.lindsay@csulb.edu
LINDSAY, Charles, W 607-735-1798 324 J clindsay@elmira.edu
LINDSAY, Cheryl, A 315-255-1743 317 I cheryl.lindsay@cayuga-cc.edu
LINDSAY, Creighton 503-845-3508 407 B creighton.lindsay@mtangel.edu
LINDSAY, D. Michael 978-867-4800 227 A president@gordon.edu
LINDSAY, Dane 619-388-7823 62 H dlindsay@sdccd.edu
LINDSAY, Dawn, S 410-777-1177 213 E dslindsay@aacc.edu
LINDSAY, Dennis 541-684-7253 407 I dlindsay@nwcu.edu
LINDSAY, John 401-232-6154 441 B jlindsay@bryant.edu
LINDSAY, Jonathan 206-315-5825 521 G jlindsay@cornish.edu
LINDSAY, Kristen 419-448-2301 383 C klindsay@heidelberg.edu
LINDSAY, Nathan 406-243-4689 287 D nathan.lindsay@umontana.edu
LINDSAY, Shawn 417-626-1234 280 B lindsay.shawn@occ.edu
LINDSAY, Terry 773-244-4588 154 G tlindsay@northpark.edu
LINDSAY, Twila 410-923-4585 96 H twila.lindsay@strayer.edu
LINDSAY, Wanda 870-543-5900 23 C wlindsay@seark.edu
LINDSAY-DENNIS, LaShawnda 706-821-8726 129 H llindsaydennis@paine.edu
LINDSETH, Lori 602-787-7102 15 B lori.lindseth@paradisevalley.edu
LINDSEY, April 336-887-3000 358 E alindsey@laureluniversity.edu
LINDSEY, Bethany 206-855-9559 525 F
LINDSEY, Beverly 662-846-4648 267 A blindsey@deltastate.edu
LINDSEY, Bruce, M 314-935-6200 285 E blindsey@wustl.edu
LINDSEY, DeLois 860-768-5122 92 F lindsey@hartford.edu
LINDSEY, Earlene 205-652-3528 9 G elindsey@uwa.edu
LINDSEY, Gary 214-333-5870 471 L lindseyg@dbu.edu
LINDSEY, Heidie 337-482-6272 208 F hlindsey@louisiana.edu
LINDSEY, Johnetta 601-977-4458 270 F jlindsey@tougaloo.edu
LINDSEY, Lee 707-476-4100 41 C lee-lindsey@redwoods.edu
LINDSEY, Pamela, L 217-424-6348 153 A plindsey@millikin.edu
LINDSEY, Patrick, O 313-577-4228 252 G patrick.lindsey@wayne.edu
LINDSEY, Shannon 785-628-4462 187 A sdlindsey@fhsu.edu
LINDSEY, Shawn 713-743-5725 491 D selindsey@uh.edu
LINDSTAEDT, William 415-502-2422 72 C bill.lindstaedt@ucsf.edu
LINDSTEDT, Monique 815-394-4376 157 D mlindstedt@rockford.edu
LINDSTEN, Traci 605-331-6575 454 E traci.lindsten@usiouxfalls.edu
LINDSTROM, David 509-527-2615 528 A david.lindstrom@wallawalla.edu
LINDSTROM, Derrick 612-659-6030 259 F derrick.lindstrom@minneapolis.edu
LINDSTROM, Lynne 563-884-5313 182 D lynne.lindstrom@palmer.edu
LINDSTROM, Richard 559-442-8277 69 B richard.lindstrom@fresnocitycollege.edu
LINDSTROM, Richard, W 323-563-5832 38 C richardlindstrom@cdrewu.edu
LINDSTROM, Ryan 801-863-8303 500 B lindstry@uvu.edu
LINDTORTH, Scott, A 919-684-0539 356 E scott.lindroth@duke.edu
LINDUSKA, Kim 515-964-6628 177 B kjlinduska@dmacc.edu
LINEBAUGH, Jonathan 954-771-0376 107 V jlinebaugh@knoxseminary.edu
LINEBERG, Kimberly 304-260-4380 530 M klineberg@blueridgectc.edu
LINEBERGER, Susanne, B 386-312-4050 111 K susannelineberger@sjrstate.edu
LINEBERRY, Forrest 336-757-3396 362 F flineberry@forsythtech.edu
LINEBERRY, Gene, T 859-323-6589 200 G gt.lineberry@uky.edu
LINEBERRY, Kevin 336-249-8186 362 B kevin_lineberry@davidsonccc.edu
LINEBURG, Robert 540-831-5228 511 C rlineburg@radford.edu
LINEHAN, Rob 765-998-4905 173 B rblinehan@taylor.edu
LINEHAN, Sarah, J 518-743-2263 347 E linehans@sunyacc.edu
LINER, Andrea 979-830-4413 469 F andrea.liner@blinn.edu
LINFANTE, Patrick 973-761-9328 308 C patrick.linfante@shu.edu
LINGEFELT, Jeff 803-938-3784 450 H jdlingef@uscsumter.edu
LINGEN, Scott 701-224-5441 374 E scott.lingen@bismarckstate.edu
LINGER, Frederick, S 740-427-5250 384 P lingerf@kenyon.edu
LINGER, Rob 304-367-4692 531 E rob.linger@pierpont.edu
LINGERFELT, Harley, W 405-878-5100 402 A hwlingerfelt@stgregorys.edu
LINGLE, Richard 816-279-7000 271 H richard.lingle@abtu.edu
LINGLE, Robert 716-888-3256 317 H lingler@canisius.edu
LINGLE, Ronald, K 910-938-6211 361 F lingler@coastalcarolina.edu
LINGRELL, Scott 678-839-6423 133 F slingrel@westga.edu
LINGUA, Jan 314-256-8807 272 B lingua@ai.edu
LINGUA, Jane 310-954-4132 54 I jlingua@msmu.edu
LINHART, Lisa 303-762-6980 82 C lisa.linhart@denverseminary.edu
LINHORST, Don 314-977-2745 281 M linhorsd@slu.edu
LINIO, Richard, T 606-783-2066 198 H r.linio@moreheadstate.edu
LINK, Eric, C 260-481-5751 168 D eric.link@ipfw.edu
LINK, Harvey 701-671-2112 375 B harvey.link@ndscs.edu
LINK, Hilary, L 215-204-7000 436 C hilary.link@temple.edu
LINK, Jane, J 316-978-3186 192 D jane.link@wichita.edu
LINK, Johnson 864-656-7389 444 E jwl@clemson.edu
LINK, Laura 612-874-3700 257 D laura_link@mcad.edu
LINK, Laura, R 540-224-4668 509 D lrlink@jchs.edu
LINK, Rebecca, C 717-815-1336 440 H rlink@ycp.edu
LINK, Robert 419-434-4528 393 F link@findlay.edu
LINK, Rosemary, J 515-961-1615 182 I rosemary.link@simpson.edu
LINK, Stephen 202-687-1747 95 E spl8@georgetown.edu
LINKER, Ashley 617-588-1354 223 D alinker@bfit.edu
LINKER, Timothy, L 336-841-9313 357 E tlinker@highpoint.edu
LINKS, Jonathan 410-516-6880 216 A jlinks1@jhu.edu
LINKSZ, James 215-641-6500 426 E jlinksz@mc3.edu
LINMAN, Eric 503-255-0332 407 D elinman@multnomah.edu
LINN, Brent 901-375-4400 459 D brentlinn@midsouthcc.org
LINN, Chad 501-205-8912 20 G clinn@cbc.edu
LINN, Joseph, G 785-628-4277 187 A jlinn@fhsu.edu
LINN, Rhonda 989-386-6622 247 B rlinn@midmcih.edu
LINN, Richard, T 716-827-3451 350 H linnr@trocaire.edu
LINN, Susan 617-327-6777 238 D Susan_Linn@williamjames.edu
LINN, Susan 708-974-5335 153 D linns@morainevalley.edu
LINN, Timon 410-626-6931 218 A timon.linn@sjc.edu
LINNANE, SJ, Brian, F 410-617-2201 216 D president@loyola.edu
LINNEHAN, Francis 215-895-2122 417 E francis.linnehan@drexel.edu
LINNEHAN, JR., James, F 978-656-3151 232 B linnehanj@middlesex.mass.edu
LINNEMAN, Scott 360-650-7207 528 D scott.linneman@wwu.edu
LINNEVERS, David 831-582-3094 34 C dlinnevers@csumb.edu
LINO, Paulette 510-723-2665 37 N plino@chabotcollege.edu
LINOS, Megan, W 812-465-1061 174 D mwlinos@usi.edu
LINSALATA, Lauren 505-473-6551 313 B lauren.linsalata@santafeuniversity.edu
LINSCHEID, David 316-284-5251 185 B dlin@bethelks.edu
LINSENMEYER, Machelle 304-793-6871 533 B alinsenmeyer@osteo.wvsom.edu

LINSEY, Carolyn, R ... 203-576-2374.. 92 B clinsey@bridgeport.edu
LINSEY, Troy ... 706-265-7515 128 A tlinsey@laniertech.edu
LINSIN, James ... 618-650-2842 159 I jlinsin@siue.edu
LINSNER, Christie ... 630-620-2180 154 J
LINSON, Marci ... 417-690-2636 273 C linson@cofo.edu
LINSON, Phil ... 323-856-7792.. 27 H plinson@afi.com
LINSON, Robert ... 202-885-6013.. 94 H rlinson@american.edu
LINSTER, Michelle ... 336-517-2154 354 K mlinster@bennett.edu
LINSTRA, Ralph ... 434-582-2330 509 G rlinstra@liberty.edu
LINTHICUM, David ... 410-287-1947 214 C dlinthicum@cecil.edu
LINTHICUM, Glen ... 615-248-1243 464 E glinthicum@trevecca.edu
LINTON, Eugene ... 419-289-6995 377 A elinton@ashland.edu
LINTON, Greg ... 865-573-4517 457 H glinton@johnsonu.edu
LINTON, Leon, E ... 847-229-9595 159 C
LINTON, Pamela ... 212-752-1530 330 C pamela.linton@limcollege.edu
LINTON, Peggy ... 334-493-3573.... 5 G plinton@lbwcc.edu
LINTON, Richard, H ... 919-515-2668 370 D richard_linton@ncsu.edu
LINTS, Richard ... 978-468-7111 227 B rlints@gcts.edu
LINZER, Daniel, I ... 847-491-5117 155 D dlinzer@northwestern.edu
LINZEY, Scott ... 912-525-5000 130 H slinzey@scad.edu
LINZMEYER, Kathryn ... 510-723-6751.. 37 N klinzmeyer@chabotcollege.edu
LIOTTA, Sheila, A ... 401-865-2600 441 F sadamus@providence.edu
LIPAN, Petruta ... 314-977-3571 281M lipanp@slu.edu
LIPE, Leslie ... 503-338-2450 405 B llipe@clatsopcc.edu
LIPE, Lisa, M ... 207-834-7607 212 F lisa.lipe@maine.edu
LIPHART, Jodi ... 904-826-0084.. 74 A jliphart@usa.edu
LIPHART, Kristy ... 715-682-1496 538 D kliphart@northland.edu
LIPIEC, Susan ... 216-373-5211 388 A slipiec@ndc.edu
LIPINSKI, Tomas ... 414-229-4709 540 A tlipinski@uwm.edu
LIPKIN, Michael ... 212-463-0400 350 C michael.lipkin2@touro.edu
LIPMAN, Howard ... 305-348-6298 114 G howard.lipman@fiu.edu
LIPOLD, Tony ... 949-582-4547.. 67 F tlipold@saddleback.edu
LIPORTO, Charles ... 603-513-1354 299 C charles.liporto@granite.edu
LIPP, Evan, E ... 508-767-7285 222 D elipp@assumption.edu
LIPP, Jacob ... 713-226-5585 491 F lippp@uhd.edu
LIPPARD, Rodney ... 704-216-3686 365 F rodney.lippard@rccc.edu
LIPPE, Diane ... 954-262-4932 109 E lipped@nova.edu
LIPPE, Karen, M ... 561-868-3735 109 H lippek@palmbeachstate.edu
LIPPENS, Susan, M ... 419-866-0261 391 L smlippens@stautzenberger.com
LIPPERT, Patricia, A ... 812-488-2152 173 H pl23@evansville.edu
LIPPERT, Rebecca ... 215-702-4241 414 C blippert@cairn.edu
LIPPERT, Rebecca, M ... 215-887-5511 439 E rlippert@wts.edu
LIPPERT, Robert ... 559-453-2189.. 45 E robert.lippert@fresno.edu
LIPPIELLO, Stephen ... 304-214-8809 531 G slippiello@wvncc.edu
LIPPINCOTT, Amanda, L ... 607-274-1574 328 H alippincott@ithaca.edu
LIPPINCOTT, Doug ... 315-279-5641 329 K dlippinc@keuka.edu
LIPPINCOTT, James ... 503-375-5304 411 D jlippinc@willamette.edu
LIPPMAN, Fred ... 954-262-1508 109 E flippman@nsu.nova.edu
LIPPMAN, Stuart ... 646-565-6000 350 C stuartl@touro.edu
LIPPMANN, Frances ... 559-443-8604.. 69 B frances.lippmann@fresnocitycollege.edu
LIPSCHUTZ, Ronnie ... 831-459-3275.. 72 E rligsch@ucsc.edu
LIPSCOMB, Benjamin ... 585-567-9374 328 C benjamin.lipscomb@houghton.edu
LIPSCOMB, Jason, S ... 260-399-7700 174 C jlipscomb@sf.edu
LIPSCOMB, Kimberly ... 212-616-7283 327 D kimberly.lipscomb@helenefuld.edu
LIPSCOMB, Natasha ... 704-216-3622 365 F natasha.lipscomb@rccc.edu
LIPSCOMB, Rodney ... 940-498-6445 479 K rlipscomb@nctc.edu
LIPSCOMB, Sharyon ... 225-578-8833 204 L slipsc1@lsu.edu
LIPSCOMB, Tamra ... 540-863-2905 515 B tlipscomb@dslcc.edu
LIPSETT, Teresa ... 787-743-7979 555M ut_tlipsett@suagm.edu
LIPSHITZ, Rita ... 773-973-0241 146 A lipshitz@htc.edu
LIPSKIER, Hershel ... 973-267-9404 305 E
LIPSTREU, Tiffany ... 614-823-1414 390 C tlipstreu@otterbein.edu
LIPTON, Jeffrey ... 631-656-2122 326 B jeffrey.lipton@ftc.edu
LIPTON, Mitchell ... 212-353-4126 323 B lipton@cooper.edu
LIRLEY, Sean ... 719-336-1543.. 83 N sean.lirley@lamarcc.edu
LISBOA, Sandra ... 787-738-2161 557 G sandra.lisboa@upr.edu
LISCHIN, Renee ... 973-408-3955 301 J rlischin@drew.edu
LISCHKA, Rosemary, L . 913-288-7246 188 G rlischka@kckcc.edu
LISCHWE, Sheila, T ... 864-656-1661 444 E slischw@clemson.edu
LISCIO, Gina ... 315-792-7288 348 D gina.liscio@sunyit.edu
LISENBY, Sadie ... 901-321-3527 455 I slisenby@cbu.edu
LISENBY, Woods, B ... 334-833-4474.... 4 E chaplain@huntingdon.edu
LISI, Peter ... 860-768-2446.. 92 F lisi@hartford.edu
LISK, Patti ... 540-423-9824 515 E plisk@germanna.edu
LISKER, Donna ... 413-585-4900 236 G dlisker@smith.edu
LISLE, Cristy ... 773-602-5020 142 A clisle@ccc.edu
LISNIK, John ... 207-623-3344 212 B lisnik@maine.edu
LISS, Donna ... 660-785-4163 283 E dliss@truman.edu
LISS, Tony ... 212-650-7947 318 G tliss@ccny.cuny.edu
LISSY, Barbara, G ... 215-576-0800 433 I blissy@rrc.edu
LIST, Allison ... 631-687-5198 341 A alist@sjcny.edu
LISTER, Basil ... 816-604-6748 277 G basil.lister@mcckc.edu
LISTER, Carole, B ... 864-597-4230 451 J listercb@wofford.edu
LISTER, Charlotte, T ... 302-857-1290.. 94 A clister@dtcc.edu
LISTER, Tommy ... 626-584-5338.. 45 F tommylister@fuller.edu
LISTON, Brenda ... 614-947-6532 382 H brenda.liston@franklin.edu
LISTON, Sunny ... 503-534-4007 407 A sliston@marylhurst.edu
LISTWAK, Jeffrey, A ... 412-397-5261 434 B listwak@rmu.edu
LISZEWSKI, Stephen ... 410-293-1000 549 B
LISZKA, James ... 518-564-5402 346 B jlisz001@plattsburgh.edu
LISZKA, Justin ... 336-272-7102 357 B justin.liszka@greensboro.edu
LITCH, Mary ... 714-628-2753.. 38 B litch@chapman.edu
LITCHFIELD, Greg ... 802-862-9616 501 E glitchfield@burlington.edu
LITCHMAN, Jennifer, B . 410-706-3477 219 E jlitchman@umaryland.edu
LITHERLAND, Marisa ... 309-692-4092 152 F mlitherland@midstate.edu
LITHERLAND, Steve, E .. 757-822-1944 517 C slitherland@tcc.edu
LITKE, Russell ... 505-566-3253 312 K litker@sanjuancollege.edu
LITOLFF, Edwin ... 225-342-6950 207 G edwin.litolff@la.gov
LITT, Eleni ... 212-229-8947 334 C litte@newschool.edu
LITT, Jacquelyn, S ... 573-882-0647 283 H littj@missouri.edu
LITT, Jacquelyn, S ... 848-932-2900 307 B jacquelyn.litt@rutgers.edu
LITTERAL, Samuel, M ... 304-896-7426 531 F samuel.litteral@southernwv.edu
LITTLE, Albert ... 904-632-5167 105 A al.little@fscj.edu
LITTLE, Andrew, P ... 410-777-2227 213 E aplittle1@aacc.edu
LITTLE, Bert ... 254-968-9463 485 A little@tarleton.edu
LITTLE, Colleen ... 802-447-6319 503 A clittle@svc.edu
LITTLE, Daniel ... 313-593-5500 251 D delittle@umich.edu
LITTLE, David ... 909-793-4263.. 28 S dlittle@ashdowncollege.edu
LITTLE, Glenn, W ... 863-784-7218 113 C glenn.little@southflorida.edu
LITTLE, Jennifer ... 864-592-4808 449 C littlej@sccsc.edu
LITTLE, Jolene ... 909-793-4263.. 28 S jlittle@ashdowncollege.edu
LITTLE, Judith, W ... 510-643-6644.. 70 K jwlittle@berkeley.edu
LITTLE, Kevin, K ... 831-656-2508 548 A kllittle@nps.edu
LITTLE, Lara ... 704-463-3353 367 F lara.little@pfeiffer.edu
LITTLE, Linda ... 559-325-5205.. 69 A linda.little@scccd.edu
LITTLE, Linda ... 405-682-1611 399 K linda.k.little@occc.edu
LITTLE, Nicole ... 302-622-8000.. 93 D nlittle@dcad.edu
LITTLE, Olivia ... 850-678-5111 109 D
LITTLE, Rebecca, K ... 812-888-4220 174 F rlittle@vinu.edu
LITTLE, Scott ... 601-968-5956 266 F slittle@belhaven.edu
LITTLE, Shanon ... 415-257-1302.. 43 D shanon.little@dominican.edu
LITTLE, Sylvester ... 863-292-3762 110 E slittle@polk.edu
LITTLE, Trace ... 336-334-4104 371 C tjlittle@uncg.edu
LITTLE, Verna, S ... 334-727-8503.... 8 B little@mytu.tuskegee.edu
LITTLE, William ... 607-962-9458 323 D wlittle@corning-cc.edu
LITTLE-BERRY, Teri ... 352-854-2322 100 P berryt@cf.edu
LITTLE WHITEMAN, Iona ... 701-627-4738 373 E llittl@fortbertholdcc.edu
LITTLEBEAR, Richard ... 406-477-6215 286 E rlbear@cdkc.edu
LITTLEFIELD, Elizabeth, S ... 804-523-5181 515 F blittlefield@reynolds.edu
LITTLEFIELD, Emily ... 336-887-3000 358 E elittlefield@laureluniversity.edu
LITTLEFIELD, Julie ... 979-230-3576 469 G julie.littlefield@brazosport.edu
LITTLEJOHN, Angela, F 864-294-2171 446 F angela.littlejohn@furman.edu
LITTLEJOHN, Sylvia ... 803-738-7764 447 H littlejohns@midlandstech.edu
LITTLEPAGE, Craig, K ... 434-982-5100 514 A ckl9e@virginia.edu
LITTLES, Douglas, M ... 251-578-1313.... 6 D dlittles@rstc.edu
LITTLETON, Denise ... 757-823-8701 510 H
LITTLETON, Robert, A ... 423-652-6022 457 J ralittle@king.edu
LITTLETON-STEIB, Larissa ... 504-671-6488 203 F lsteib@dcc.edu
LITTMAN, Jared, E ... 718-990-2920 340 G littmanj@stjohns.edu
LITTON, Freddie ... 361-570-4261 492 A littonf@uhv.edu
LITTRELL, Annette ... 931-372-3979 462 A alittrell@tntech.edu
LITTRELL, Beth ... 402-461-7372 290 G blittrell@hastings.edu
LITTRELL, Johnny ... 931-540-2840 462 E jlittrell@columbiastate.edu
LITTRELL, Meghann ... 513-244-4524 387 A meghann.littrell@msj.edu
LITVINOV, Dimitri ... 713-743-4168 491 D litvinov@central.uh.edu
LITWILLER, Eric ... 316-295-5820 187 C eric_litwiller@friends.edu
LITYNSKI, Daniel, M ... 269-387-8294 252 I dan.litynski@wmich.edu
LITZ, Kerri ... 410-225-2277 216 F klitz@mica.edu
LITZIN, Louise ... 928-724-6633.. 13 J louise@dinecollege.edu
LIU, Alan ... 626-289-7719.. 26 G aliu@amu.edu
LIU, Jun ... 404-413-2536 126 D junliu@gsu.edu
LIU, Lan ... 860-343-5833.. 89 E lliu@mxcc.commnet.edu
LIU, Linyan ... 650-493-4430.. 66 H linyan.liu@itp.edu
LIU, Monika ... 415-452-5730.. 39 A mliu@ccsf.edu
LIU, Shuang ... 410-337-6062 215 B shuang.liu@goucher.edu
LIU, Victor ... 734-973-3379 251 J vliu@wccnet.edu
LIU, Ying ... 919-508-2048 373 B ying.liu@peace.edu
LIU, Ying ... 419-530-1248 394 E ying.liu3@utoledo.edu
LIU, Zhanjiang ... 334-844-4784.... 1 G liuzhan@auburn.edu
LIVELY, Alisa ... 304-473-8441 534 G lively_a@wvwc.edu
LIVELY, Julie ... 903-675-6233 490 F jlively@tvcc.edu
LIVELY, Lisa, A ... 304-293-8638 533 D lisa.lively@mail.wvu.edu
LIVELY, Robert, L ... 207-778-7277 212 E lively@maine.edu
LIVELY, Sam ... 951-343-4726.. 30 D slively@calbaptist.edu
LIVENGOOD, Lori ... 316-394-5227 185 B llivengood@bethelks.edu
LIVENGOOD, Naomi ... 269-965-3931 244 L livengoodn@kellogg.edu
LIVERMAN, Mark ... 615-333-3344 459M mliverman@national-college.edu
LIVERMORE, Jeff ... 810-762-0501 247 F jeff.livermore@mcc.edu
LIVERPOOL, Patrick, R . 410-651-6508 219 H prliverpool@umes.edu
LIVERS, John, T ... 812-888-4301 174 F jlivers@vinu.edu
LIVESAY, Stephen, D ... 423-775-7201 455 F livesast@bryan.edu
LIVESAY, Wayne ... 410-386-8249 214 B wlivesay@carrollcc.edu
LIVINGOOD, Susannah, B ... 405-325-5065 403 I slivingood@ou.edu
LIVINGSTON, Carolyn ... 507-222-4248 254 D clivingston@carleton.edu
LIVINGSTON, David, J .. 419-824-3809 385 F dlivingston@lourdes.edu
LIVINGSTON, Esther ... 859-985-3065 193 F livginstone@berea.edu
LIVINGSTON, Geraldine 803-376-5700 443 D
LIVINGSTON, Joe, A ... 407-582-8069 118 I jlivingston@valenciacollege.edu
LIVINGSTON, Kate ... 972-473-3401 482 J klivingston@smu.edu
LIVINGSTON, Kathy ... 308-865-8204 293 G livingstonke@unk.edu
LIVINGSTON, Lynette ... 715-833-1849 542M livingston3@cvtc.edu
LIVINGSTON, Matt ... 802-258-9209 502 B mlivingston@gradcenter.marlboro.edu
LIVINGSTON, Randy ... 650-724-0213.. 68 G livingston@stanford.edu
LIVINGSTON, Randy ... 321-674-8057 103 R rlivingston@fit.edu
LIVINGSTON, Sarah, M 402-399-2430 289 I slivingston@csm.edu
LIVINGSTON, Shannon . 715-675-3331 544 A livingst@ntc.edu
LIVINGSTON, Stan ... 601-477-4006 268 A stan.livingston@jcjc.edu
LIVINGSTON, Tina ... 903-886-5667 485 E tina.livingston@tamuc.edu
LIVINGSTONE, Linda, A 202-994-6380.. 95 D llivings@gwu.edu
LIVIO, Michael, D ... 609-497-7805 305 B michael.livio@ptsem.edu
LIWAG, Jonathan ... 670-237-6750 550 B jonathan.liwag@marianas.edu
LIZAN, Rey ... 757-490-1241 504 D rlizan@auto.edu
LIZARDI, David ... 787-738-2161 557 G david.lizardi@upr.edu
LIZER, Shannon, K ... 815-227-2444 158 B shannonlizer@sacn.edu
LIZOTTE, Alan, J ... 518-442-5214 343 C a.lizotte@albany.edu
LJUBICIC, Amanda ... 860-629-6115.. 91 B ljubicic_a@mitchell.edu
LJUNGDAHL, Anders ... 617-746-1990 227 G anders.ljungdahl@hult.edu
LJUTIC, Peter ... 201-200-3045 304 C pljutic@njcu.edu
LLAMAS, Elizabeth ... 760-630-1555.. 49 C ellamas@kaplan.edu
LLANA, James ... 212-237-8110 319 F jllana@jjay.cuny.edu
LLANOS, Keren ... 787-620-2040 550 D kllanos@aupr.edu
LLERANDI, Joanne, A ... 718-990-1487 340 G llerandj@stjohns.edu

LLERANDI, Mariel 787-878-5475 553 F
mllerandi@arecibo.inter.edu
LLERENA, Fernando, N 305-273-4499 100 K
fllerena@cbt.edu
LLERENA, Gladys, P 305-273-4499 100 K
gladys@cbt.edu
LLERENA, Luis, E 305-273-4499 100 K
luis@cbt.edu
LLERENA, Monica 305-273-4499 100 K
monica@cbt.edu
LLOPIZ, Maria 773-481-8323 142 D
mllopiz@ccc.edu
LLORENS, Ashley, J 410-955-5107 216 A
ashley.llorens@jhuapl.edu
LLOVIO, Kay 916-577-2200 77 F
kllovio@jessup.edu
LLOYD, Andrea 802-443-5735 502 E
lloyd@middlebury.edu
LLOYD, Celia 212-650-7859 318 G
clloyd@ccny.cuny.edu
LLOYD, Charles 603-271-6484 297 C
clloyd@ccsnh.edu
LLOYD, Chris 215-702-4339 414 C
clloyd@cairn.edu
LLOYD, Christine 239-590-1425 114 F
clloyd@fgcu.edu
LLOYD, Daniel 630-942-2865 142 F
lloydd@cod.edu
LLOYD, David 985-543-4120 203 I
LLOYD, David 765-998-4634 173 B
dvlloyd@taylor.edu
LLOYD, Don 573-897-5000 282 I
LLOYD, Giovina 607-871-2966 314 J
lloydgm@alfred.edu
LLOYD, Glen, D 507-933-6517 256 A
glloyd@gustavus.edu
LLOYD, Gweneth 845-257-2920 344 A
lloydg@newpaltz.edu
LLOYD, James, H 513-244-8138 379 I
jim.lloyd@ccuniversity.edu
LLOYD, James, W 352-392-2213 115 D
lloydjw@ufl.edu
LLOYD, Jan 407-708-2144 113 A
lloydj@seminolestate.edu
LLOYD, Jayson 208-732-6547 137 K
jlloyd@csi.edu
LLOYD, Mary, J 815-599-3418 146 B
mary.lloyd@highland.edu
LLOYD, Patrick, M 614-292-9755 389 A
lloyd.256@osu.edu
LLOYD, Rachel 918-540-6971 398 L
rlloyd@neo.edu
LLOYD, Richard, B 802-776-5236 501 G
richard.lloyd@csj.edu
LLOYD, Rodie, F 207-725-3963 209 H
rlloyd@bowdoin.edu
LLOYD, Sandy 360-538-2500 523 A
slloyd@ghc.edu
LLOYD, Sharon 678-359-5133 126 E
sharonl@gordonstate.edu
LLOYD, Willie, L 248-232-4142 248 E
wllloyd@oaklandcc.edu
LLOYD-DENNIS, Diann, L 651-631-5330 265 D
dllloyd@unwsp.edu
LLYOD, Curtis 518-320-1192 343 B
curtis.lloyd@suny.edu
LO, Angie 888-488-4968 48 B
alo@itu.edu
LO, Deborah 907-796-6123 11 A
deborah.lo@uas.alaska.edu
LO, Jasmine 304-243-8147 534 H
jlo@wju.edu
LO, Jim 765-677-1771 169 C
jim.lo@indwes.edu
LOBASSO, Lisa, M 570-941-7459 438 F
lisa.lobasso@scranton.edu
LOBASSO, Thomas 386-506-3200 101 I
lobasst@DaytonaState.edu
LOBATO, Ana 831-476-9424 44 L
studentservices@fivebranches.edu
LOBATO, Richard, L 915-831-3391 473 J
rlobato@epcc.edu
LOBB, Barry 434-544-8521 509 I
lobb@lynchburg.edu
LOBB, William, K 414-288-7485 537 B
william.lobb@marquette.edu
LOBBAN-VIRAVONG, Heather 641-269-4349 178 I
lobbanvh@grinnell.edu
LOBE, Robert 212-592-2661 342 F
rlobe@sva.edu
LOBERA, Kim 858-499-0202 40 G
klobera@coleman.edu
LOBERTINI, Jo 563-588-6432 176 F
jo.lobertini@clarke.edu
LOBIONDO, Mary 631-656-3137 326 B
mary.lobiondo@ftc.edu
LOBO, Teri, A 610-409-3000 438 H
tlobo@ursinus.edu
LOBO-TORRES, Sally 219-473-4219 165 A
slobotorres@ccs.edu
LOCANDER, William 504-864-7946 206 A
locander@loyno.edu
LOCASCIO, Patti, P 352-395-5169 112 H
patti.locascio@sfcollege.edu
LOCATELLI, Dominic 914-633-2245 328 F
dlocatelli@iona.edu
LOCH, OSB, Killian 724-805-2350 435 B
killian.loch@email.stvincent.edu
LOCH, Robert 515-643-6732 181 B
rloch@mercydesmoines.org
LOCHBAUM, Doug 770-394-8300 120 E
dlochbaum@aii.edu
LOCHE, Annette 402-494-2311 291 M
aloche@thenicc.edu
LOCHER, Linda, L 570-577-1604 413 E
linda.locher@bucknell.edu
LOCHHEAD, Michael, J 617-552-3255 224 B
michael.lochhead@bc.edu
LOCHMANN, Steve 870-575-8165 24 D
assessment@uapb.edu
LOCHMUELLER, Stephen 859-622-2120 194 L
stephen.lochmueller@eku.edu
LOCHNER, Elizabeth 215-951-5123 422 F
lochnere@lasalle.edu
LOCHNER, Mary Ann 828-227-7116 372 C
lochner@wcu.edu
LOCHSTAMPFOR, Mike 770-534-6230 121 G
mlochstampfor@brenau.edu
LOCHTE, Lynne 410-337-6572 215 B
lynne.lochte@goucher.edu
LOCICERO, Jack 336-721-2625 368 F
jack.locicero@salem.edu
LOCK, Ben, W 806-742-0012 489 F
ben.lock@ttu.edu
LOCK, Cory 512-448-8720 481 B
julial@stedwards.edu
LOCK, Vickie 920-498-5447 544 B
victoria.lock@nwtc.edu
LOCKABY, Charlotte 606-589-3020 197 D
charlotte.lockaby@kctcs.edu
LOCKE, Bruce 850-410-6161 114 D
blocke@eng.fsu.edu
LOCKE, Don 601-925-3250 268 E
locke@mc.edu
LOCKE, Dot, M 662-685-4771 266 G
dlocke@bmc.edu
LOCKE, Edward 718-631-6320 320 F
elocke@qcc.cuny.edu
LOCKE, Heidi 503-821-8976 408 H
hlocke@pnca.edu
LOCKE, Jason 607-255-2000 323 C
jcl31@cornell.edu
LOCKE, Lisa 517-629-0206 239 A
llocke@albion.edu
LOCKE, Mary, G 772-462-4702 106 F
mlocke@irsc.edu
LOCKE, Richard, M 401-863-2706 441 A
richard_locke@brown.edu
LOCKE, Samuel 860-509-9556 90 G
slocke@hartsem.edu
LOCKE, Steven, S 781-736-2000 224 F
slocke@brandeis.edu
LOCKE, Teb 717-291-4339 418 J
teb.locke@fandm.edu
LOCKETT, JR., Eugene, D 301-985-7330 220 A
cfo@umuc.edu
LOCKETT, Rose 662-621-4287 266 H
rlockett@coahomacc.edu
LOCKETT, Tom 217-224-0600 162 J
tom.lockett@vatterott-college.edu
LOCKHART, Bill 214-654-9075 218 D
LOCKHART, Calandra 903-923-2429 497 G
clockhart@wileyc.edu
LOCKHART, Earla 256-539-0834 4 F
LOCKHART, Elaine 828-726-2241 360 F
elockhart@cccti.edu
LOCKHART, Felicia 818-299-5517 75 K
Felicia@westcoastuniversity.edu
LOCKHART, Janet 310-506-4301 58 H
janet.lockhart@pepperdine.edu
LOCKHART, Janet, M 915-831-2676 473 J
jlockha2@epcc.edu
LOCKHART, Michael 212-749-2802 331 I
mlockhart@msmnyc.edu
LOCKHART, Teresa 606-218-5306 201 C
teresalockhart@upike.edu
LOCKLEAR, Amy 386-506-3079 101 I
locklea@DaytonaState.edu
LOCKLEAR, April 910-843-5304 359 L
LOCKLEAR, Chris 252-328-6105 369 E
locklearc@ecu.edu
LOCKLEAR, Marla 910-521-6201 371 D
marla.locklear@uncp.edu
LOCKLEAR, Ronnie 910-272-3347 365 D
rlocklear@robeson.edu
LOCKLEAR, William, L 910-272-3304 365 D
wlocklea@robeson.edu
LOCKLEAR, Zoe, W 910-521-6000 371 D
zoe.locklear@uncp.edu
LOCKREM, Michael 605-688-6161 454 C
michael.lockrem@sdstate.edu
LOCKWARD, Ana, C 516-323-4209 333 E
alockward@molloy.edu
LOCKWOOD, Catherine 312-935-4812 157 A
clockwood@robertmorris.edu
LOCKWOOD, Charles 813-974-0553 116 B
cjlockwood@health.usf.edu
LOCKWOOD, James, A 517-321-0242 243 H
jlockwood@glcc.edu
LOCKWOOD, Joe 405-946-7799 401 F
joel@plattcollege.org
LOCKWOOD, Lawrence, J 319-335-0217 175 H
larry-lockwood@uiowa.edu
LOCKWOOD, Matthew, T 313-577-9098 252 G
mlockwood@wayne.edu
LOCKWOOD, Sasha 517-321-0242 243 H
slockwood@glcc.edu
LOCOCO, Nina 406-447-4388 286 D
nlococo@carroll.edu
LOCURTO, Chuck 401-232-6196 441 B
clocurto@bryant.edu
LOCUST, JR., Jonathan, E 419-207-5504 377 A
jlocust@ashland.edu
LOCUST, Wayne 860-486-1463 92 C
wayne.locust@uconn.edu
LODATO, A. Michelle 864-379-6606 446 B
lodato@erskine.edu
LODEN, Kristin, B 215-893-5279 416 E
kristin.loden@curtis.edu
LODEWYCK, Becky 602-557-3170 18 H
becky.lodewyck@phoenix.edu
LODGE, Danielle 478-757-5161 134 E
dlodge@wesleyancollege.edu
LODGE, Helen 417-667-8181 273 H
hlodge@cottey.edu
LODGE, Jennifer, K 314-747-0515 285 E
lodgejk@wustl.edu
LODOVICO, John 860-733-1321 90 C
jlodovico@txcc.commnet.edu
LOE, Meika 315-228-7077 321 H
mloe@colgate.edu
LOEDEL, Peter 610-436-3515 432 B
ploedel@wcupa.edu
LOEDEL, Peter 610-738-0536 432 B
ploedel@wcupa.edu
LOEFFEL, Linda, L 414-443-8842 542 I
linda.loeffel@wlc.edu
LOEFFELHOLZ, Mary 617-373-4774 235 D
LOEFFLER, Donald 231-995-1130 248 C
dloeffler@nmc.edu
LOEFFLER, Lauren 215-968-8017 413 F
loeffler@bucks.edu
LOEHER, Larry, L 310-825-9149 71 D
lloeher@ucla.edu
LOEHFELM, Courtney 303-797-5914 79 A
courtney.loehfelm@arapahoe.edu
LOERA, Daniel, L 909-593-3511 73 B
dloera@laverne.edu
LOERZEL, Cathy 206-876-6100 526 E
LOESCH, Richard 847-578-3225 157 G
rick.loesch@rosalindfranklin.edu
LOESER, Diane 614-236-6159 378 H
dloeser@capital.edu
LOESSIN, Bruce, A 216-368-4352 378 J
bruce.loessin@case.edu
LOETHEN, Laurie 913-621-8765 186 G
lloethen@donnelly.edu
LOETTERLE, Jon 402-461-7424 290 G
jloetterle@hastings.edu
LOETZ, Devon 612-338-7224 265 G
devon.loetz@laureate.net
LOEW, Timothy 508-373-9460 223 C
timothy.loew@becker.edu
LOEWEN, Steve 620-343-4600 186 I
sloewen@fhtc.edu
LOEWY-WELLISCH, Peggy 310-233-4321 51 F
loewywp@lahc.edu
LOFALD, Dan 904-826-0084 74 A
dlofald@usa.edu
LOFFLER, Alicia 847-491-4647 155 D
a-loffler@kellogg.northwestern.edu
LOFFREDO, Joe 585-475-2829 339 G
jjlrgr@rit.edu
LOFLAND, Jessica 580-349-1362 400 B
jlofland@opsu.edu
LOFLIN, Gene 828-398-7240 360 A
williamgloflin@abtech.edu
LOFMAN, Brian 831-755-6809 46 J
blofman@hartnell.edu
LOFRANO, Bob 818-710-2823 51 H
lofranrj@piercecollege.edu
LOFSTEAD, Rebecca, B 304-293-9358 533 D
becky.lofstead@mail.wvu.edu
LOFT, Jan 507-537-6218 262 B
Jan.Loft@smsu.edu
LOFTESNES, Teresa 701-858-3000 374 B
LOFTHOUSE, David, R 951-785-2938 49 I
dlofthou@lasierra.edu
LOFTIN, Lynn 580-559-5252 397 K
lloftin@ecok.edu
LOFTIN, R. Bowen 573-882-2121 283 H
LOFTIS, Elsa 503-297-5544 408 A
eloftis@ocac.edu
LOFTON, Antwan 202-238-5960 96 B
antwan.lofton@howard.edu
LOFTUS, Edward, J 570-577-1458 413 E
edward.loftus@bucknell.edu
LOFTUS, James, K 412-624-4216 437 K
ja1216@pitt.edu
LOFTUS, James, P 414-410-4003 535 C
jploftus@stritch.edu
LOFTUS, Kate 262-472-1392 541 D
loftusk@uww.edu
LOFTUS-BERLIN, Eileen 973-278-5400 316 D
eml@berkeleyCollege.edu
LOFTUS-BERLIN, Eileen 973-278-5400 300 C
eml@berkeleycollege.edu
LOGAN, Barry 207-725-3290 209 H
blogan@bowdoin.edu
LOGAN, Bert 971-722-4490 409 C
bert.logan@pcc.edu
LOGAN, Cynthia 931-393-1588 463 B
clogan@mscc.edu
LOGAN, Debra 785-827-5541 189 A
debre.logan@kwu.edu
LOGAN, Doug 509-527-2074 528 A
doug.logan@wallawalla.edu
LOGAN, Elaine 313-593-5400 251 D
loganem@umich.edu
LOGAN, Erin 405-682-1611 399 K
elogan@occc.edu
LOGAN, Ethan 806-742-1480 489 F
ethan.logan@ttu.edu
LOGAN, F. Ward 843-953-5254 444 C
frank.logan@citadel.edu
LOGAN, Gary 210-999-7306 490 E
glogan@trinity.edu
LOGAN, Irene, F 804-524-5902 518 C
ilogan@vsu.edu
LOGAN, Jennifer 847-578-8350 157 G
Jennifer.Logan@rosalindfranklin.edu
LOGAN, Jill, B 601-643-5101 266 J
jill.logan@colin.edu
LOGAN, Linda 269-749-6669 249 A
llogan@olivetcollege.edu
LOGAN, Mark 562-860-2451 37 L
mlogan@cerritos.edu
LOGAN, Martin 206-934-7792 525 K
martin.logan@seattlecolleges.edu
LOGAN, Matt 662-621-4050 266 H
mlogan@coahomacc.edu
LOGAN, Mike 712-274-6400 184 A
mike.logan@witcc.edu
LOGAN, Penny 870-512-7827 19 I
penny_logan@asun.edu
LOGAN, Robin 210-829-3933 492 B
rlogan@uiwtx.edu
LOGAN, Ruth 585-594-6260 339 F
loganr@roberts.edu
LOGAN, Timothy, M 254-710-6665 469 D
tim_logan@baylor.edu
LOGAN, Tonya 740-264-5591 381 J
tlogan@egcc.edu
LOGAN, Traci 617-587-5711 234 G
logant@neco.edu
LOGAN-BENNETT, Lorie 410-704-2386 221 A
lloganbennett@towson.edu
LOGARAS, Stephanie, M 773-442-4670 154 H
s-logaras@neiu.edu
LOGEL, Mark, J 812-488-2941 173 H
ml44@evansville.edu
LOGGINS, Jeff 662-254-3325 269 C
jloggins@mvsu.edu
LOGHIN, Sarah 512-313-3000 471 H
sarah.loghin@concordia.edu
LOGLISCI, Marlene 856-415-2113 306 C
mloglisc@rcgc.edu
LOGSDON, Corlia, H 502-597-6863 197 G
corlia.logsdon@kysu.edu
LOGSDON, Michael 301-387-3333 215 A
michael.logsdon@garrettcollege.edu
LOGSDON, Paul 417-865-2815 274 L
logsdonp@evangel.edu
LOGUE, Mary 805-565-6251 76 K
mlogue@westmont.edu
LOGUE, Melanie 602-639-7500 14 A
LOH, Wallace, D 301-405-5803 219 D
wdloh@umd.edu
LOHAN-BREMER, Maureen 845-257-3250 344 A
sistared@newpaltz.edu
LOHDEN, Bethany, L 636-584-6503 274 J
bethany.lohden@eastcentral.edu

LOPEZ, Chas ... 503-725-4453 409 D
chlopez@pdx.edu
LOPEZ, Christine ... 847-578-8786 157 G
christine.lopez@rosalindfranklin.edu
LOPEZ, Chuck ... 509-359-2202 522 C
clopez17@ewu.edu
LOPEZ, Coral ... 775-445-4230 296 A
coral.lopez@wnc.edu
LOPEZ, Crystal ... 973-618-3472 300 H
cllopez@caldwell.edu
LOPEZ, Dana ... 310-954-4037.. 54 I
DLopez@msmu.edu
LOPEZ, JR., Daniel ... 773-442-4600 154 H
d-lopez@neiu.edu
LOPEZ, Daniel, H ... 575-835-5600 311 I
lalagarcia@admin.nmt.edu
LOPEZ, Derek ... 719-549-2535.. 81 F
derek.lopez@csupueblo.edu
LOPEZ, Desi ... 787-780-5134 554 H
dlopez@nuc.edu
LOPEZ, Don ... 559-442-4600.. 69 B
don.lopez@fresnocitycollege.edu
LOPEZ, Ed ... 337-521-8901 204 E
elopez@solacc.edu
LOPEZ, Edgar ... 949-214-3073.. 42 B
edgar.lopez@cui.edu
LOPEZ, Elias, S ... 530-752-3619.. 71 A
eslopez@ucdavis.edu
LOPEZ, Eric ... 210-784-2500 486 B
elopez@tamusa.tamus.edu
LOPEZ, Estela ... 860-723-0000.. 88 C
lopeze@ct.edu
LOPEZ, Felix, M ... 719-502-2541.. 84 J
felix.lopez@ppcc.edu
LOPEZ, Francisco ... 313-664-7428 241 D
flopez@collegeforcreativestudies.edu
LOPEZ, Frank ... 928-776-2184.. 18 L
frank.lopez@yc.edu
LOPEZ, Gersom ... 914-632-5400 333 F
glopez@monroecollege.edu
LOPEZ, Gilma ... 909-621-8055.. 46 K
gilma_lopez@hmc.edu
LOPEZ, Gloria ... 610-861-5565 427 F
glopez@northampton.edu
LOPEZ, Heather ... 509-335-2001 528 B
hlopez@wsu.edu
LOPEZ, Hector, L ... 787-894-2828 558 F
hector.lopez975@upr.edu
LOPEZ, Ignacio ... 312-261-3468 153 H
ignacio.lopez@nl.edu
LOPEZ, Jaime ... 787-834-9595 556 D
jlopez@uaa.edu
LOPEZ, Jane ... 757-221-3965 506 J
jalope@wm.edu
LOPEZ, Jarrod ... 502-863-8300 193 C
jarrod.lopez@bsky.org
LOPEZ, Jerry ... 415-439-2411.. 27 F
jlopez@act-sf.org
LOPEZ, Jilian ... 702-254-7577 296 B
jilian.lopez@northwestcareercollege.edu
LOPEZ, Jim, H ... 602-944-3335.. 11 D
jlopez@aicag.edu
LOPEZ, Jose Israel ... 347-964-8600 316 J
jilopez@boricuacollege.edu
LOPEZ, Juan ... 956-364-4206 487 H
juan.lopez@tstc.edu
LOPEZ, Keila ... 787-882-2065 556 C
presidentutc@yahoo.com
LOPEZ, Kim ... 650-306-3236.. 64 C
lopezk@smccd.edu
LOPEZ, Kimberly ... 912-525-5000 130 H
klopez@scad.edu
LOPEZ, Kristina ... 510-231-5000.. 48 R
LOPEZ, Lillian ... 712-274-5030 181 C
lopez@morningside.edu
LOPEZ, Lorena ... 818-719-6449.. 51 H
lopezl6@piercecollege.edu
LOPEZ, Lorena ... 830-591-7352 483 A
lmlopez@swtjc.edu
LOPEZ, Luis ... 787-743-4041 551 I
llopez@columbiacentral.edu
LOPEZ, Lynda ... 956-364-4114 487 H
lynda.lopez@tstc.edu
LOPEZ, Manny ... 646-313-8000 321 A
Manny.Lopez@guttman.cuny.edu
LOPEZ, Maribel ... 203-285-2029.. 89 B
mlopez@gwcc.commnet.edu
LOPEZ, Matthew ... 801-585-9453 499 K
matthew.lopez@utah.edu
LOPEZ, Mayra, I ... 787-754-8000 556 H
mlopez@pupr.edu
LOPEZ, Melissa, H ... 203-576-4712.. 92 B
melissal@bridgeport.edu
LOPEZ, Michael ... 860-215-9002.. 90 B
mlopez@trcc.commnet.edu
LOPEZ, Myriam, D ... 787-841-2000 555 F
mdlopez@pucpr.edu
LOPEZ, Oscar ... 972-860-4837 472 C
olopez@dcccd.edu
LOPEZ, Paulette ... 509-574-4901 529 B
plopez@yvcc.edu
LOPEZ, Pete ... 805-765-9300.. 64 G
LOPEZ, Priscilla ... 310-233-4605.. 51 F
lopezpa@lahc.edu
LOPEZ, Robert ... 305-821-3333 104 C
rlopez@fnu.edu
LOPEZ, Roberto ... 212-686-9244 315 B
LOPEZ, Sam, T ... 704-687-4759 371 B
slopez7@uncc.edu
LOPEZ, Santa, E ... 209-478-0800.. 47 F
selopez@humphreys.edu
LOPEZ, Sergio ... 760-355-6457.. 47 G
sergio.lopez@imperial.edu
LOPEZ, Silvia ... 305-629-2929 112 D
slopez@sanignaciocollege.edu
LOPEZ, Sonia ... 323-267-3794.. 51 D
lopezms@elac.edu
LOPEZ, Stacey, J ... 215-573-5836 437 I
staceylo@upenn.edu
LOPEZ, Sue Ann ... 806-716-2340 482 F
slopez@southplainscollege.edu
LOPEZ, Sylvia ... 787-725-6500 551 A
slopez@albizu.edu
LOPEZ, Syvia ... 787-725-6500 551 A
slopez@albizu.edu
LOPEZ, Tammy, L ... 719-587-7122.. 78 I
tllopez@adams.edu
LOPEZ, Teresa ... 787-725-8120 552 G
tlopez@eap.edu
LOPEZ, Theresa ... 562-860-2451.. 37 L
tmlopez@cerritos.edu
LOPEZ, Tom ... 818-947-2988.. 52 B
lopezt@lavc.edu
LOPEZ, Vanessa ... 718-779-1499 338 D
vlopez@plazacollege.edu
LOPEZ, Vince ... 323-343-6190.. 34 A
vlopez@cslanet.calstatela.edu
LOPEZ, Vinicio ... 714-241-6184.. 40 B
vlopez@coastline.edu
LOPEZ, Wilfredo ... 787-738-2161 557 G
wilfredo.lopez3@upr.edu
LOPEZ-AVILES,
Maria del Mar ... 787-746-1400 552 I
mlopez@huertas.edu
LOPEZ-CORDOVA,
Nanet ... 787-725-6500 551 A
nlopez@albizu.edu
LOPEZ-GEORGE, Linda . 210-567-4740 495 B
lopezgeorge@uthscsa.edu
LOPEZ-MATTHEWS,
Amy, L ... 937-229-3333 393 E
AMatthews1@udayton.edu
LOPEZ-MEDERO,
Lilliana, M ... 787-765-4210 551 F
llopez@cempr.edu
LOPEZ-PHILLIPS,
Matthew ... 707-664-2838.. 36 C
matthew.lopez-phillips@sonoma.edu
LOPEZ-ROSADO, Jorge . 239-590-1210 114 F
jlopez@fgcu.edu
LOPEZ-STRONG, Maria . 806-894-9611 482 F
mstrong@southplainscollege.edu
LOPEZ-VASQUEZ,
Alfonso ... 503-352-1437 408 I
alfonsolv@pacificu.edu
LOPEZ-WAGNER,
Muriel ... 909-537-3067.. 35 A
mclopez@csusb.edu
LOPIAN, David ... 718-339-1090 353 J
LOPIANSKY, Aaron ... 301-649-7077 221 F
alopiansky@yeshiva.edu
LOPICCOLO, Joseph ... 831-656-2994 548 A
jlopiccolo@nps.edu
LOPRESTI, James, M ... 724-458-3795 419 F
jmlopresti@gcc.edu
LOR, Kia ... 262-243-5700 535 I
kia.lor@cuw.edu
LORAINE, Donna ... 630-353-7001 144 A
dloraine@devry.edu
LORAN, James ... 406-338-5441 286 C
jloran@bfcc.edu
LORAN, Roberto ... 787-743-7979 555M
rloran@suagm.edu
LORBER, Jeffrey, D ... 217-206-7822 161 G
jlorber@uis.edu
LORCH, Teddi ... 949-582-4850.. 67 F
tlorch@socccd.org
LORD, Annette ... 702-651-5600 295 C
annette.lord@csn.edu
LORD, Ashley ... 863-680-4186 104 F
alord@flsouthern.edu
LORD, Blair, M ... 217-581-2121 144 E
blord@eiu.edu
LORD, David ... 304-294-2010 531 F
david.lord@southernwv.edu
LORD, Evelyn ... 510-464-3496.. 59 B
elord@peralta.edu
LORD, Harold, W ... 585-567-9645 328 C
harold.lord@houghton.edu
LORD, Jeanne, F ... 202-687-4056.. 95 E
lordj@georgetown.edu
LORD, Jess ... 610-896-1350 420 J
jlord@haverford.edu
LORD, Kenneth, R ... 818-677-2455.. 34 D
kenneth.lord@csun.edu
LORD, Lisa ... 337-482-6863 208 F
lisa@louisiana.edu
LORD, Mara ... 414-955-8298 537 C
mlord@mcw.edu
LORD, Marianne, E ... 617-521-2328 236 F
marianne.lord@simmons.edu
LORD, Patty, R ... 818-677-3776.. 34 D
patty.lord@csun.edu
LORD, Resa ... 334-214-4843.... 2 H
resa.lord@cv.edu
LORD, Rodney ... 251-575-8246.... 1 C
rlord@ascc.edu
LORDEN, Joan, F ... 704-687-5962 371 B
jflorden@uncc.edu
LORE, Peggy ... 303-352-3526.. 86 G
peggy.lore@ucdenver.edu
LORENSON, James, A .. 906-932-4231 243 B
LORENTZ, Gerald, F ... 518-783-6203 348 A
gerald.lorentz@esc.edu
LORENTZEN, Carol ... 707-826-5728.. 35 D
carol.lorentzen@humboldt.edu
LORENTZEN, Marcia, H 203-576-4139.. 92 B
marcia@bridgeport.edu
LORENZ, Aaron R, S ... 201-684-7624 305 F
alorenz@ramapo.edu
LORENZ, Britt ... 605-626-2371 454 A
Britt.Lorenz@northern.edu
LORENZ, Chuck ... 610-527-0200 434 D
clorenz@rosemont.edu
LORENZ, Dan, P ... 701-788-4676 374 A
daniel.lorenz@mayvillestate.edu
LORENZ, Georgia ... 310-434-4277.. 65 B
lorenz_georgia@smc.edu
LORENZ, Gina ... 425-352-8880 520 D
glorenz@cascadia.edu
LORENZ, Heather ... 603-668-2211 298 H
h.lorenz@snhu.edu
LORENZ, Megan ... 304-205-6600 531 A
megan.lorenz@bridgevalley.edu
LORENZ, Tracy ... 602-943-2311.. 18 K
Tracy.Lorenz@west.edu
LORENZA WHEELER,
Edward ... 404-527-7702 127 H
ewheeler@itc.edu
LORENZEN, Michael ... 309-298-2762 163 A
mg-lorenzen@wiu.edu
LORENZET, Steven, J ... 858-642-7281.. 55 J
slorenzet@nu.edu
LORENZO, Bernice ... 619-388-3246.. 62 F
blorenzo@sdccd.edu
LORENZO, JR., Joseph 303-797-5711.. 79 A
joe.lorenzo@arapahoe.edu
LORENZO, Lorisa ... 727-864-7810 101 P
lorenzll@eckerd.edu
LORENZO, Susan ... 650-738-4100.. 64 E
LORGAN, Jason ... 530-752-9075.. 71 A
jplorgan@ucdavis.edu
LORGE-GROVER,
Christina ... 715-422-5526 543 D
christina.lorgegrover@mstc.edu
LORIA, Sal ... 713-743-9092 491 D
sloria@uh.edu
LORIA, Tonia ... 504-278-6278 204 B
tloria@nunez.edu
LORIMER, David, W ... 606-693-5000 197 F
dlorimer@kmbc.edu
LORIMER, Stephen, A .. 606-693-5000 197 F
slorimer@kmbc.edu
LORIMER, Susan, L ... 916-568-3031.. 52 H
lorimes@losrios.edu
LORIMER, Thomas, H .. 606-693-5000 197 F
tlorimer@kmbc.edu
LORING, Christopher ... 413-585-2902 236 G
cloring@smith.edu
LORING, Trish ... 603-271-6984 297 C
tloring@ccsnh.edu
LORINO, Anthony, P ... 504-862-8698 207 F
alorino@tulane.edu
LORIUS, Billie Jo ... 701-328-4107 373 F
billiejo.lorius@ndus.edu
LORKOVICH, Malinda ... 312-996-4366 161 F
mlork@uic.edu
LORTON-ROWLAND,
Julie ... 317-921-4715 169 L
jlorton@ivytech.edu
LORTZ, Pete ... 206-934-6827 526 B
pete.lortz@seattlecolleges.edu
LOSASSO, Joseph ... 609-652-4235 308 E
joe.losasso@stockton.edu
LOSCHEIDER, Paul, H ... 630-637-5678 154 F
phloscheider@noctrl.edu
LOSCHIAVO, Linda ... 718-817-3570 326 C
loschiavo@fordham.edu
LOSE, David, J ... 215-248-6344 424 G
dlose@ltsp.edu
LOSEY, Teri ... 616-331-2100 243 E
loseyt@gvsu.edu
LOSHIN, David ... 954-262-1167 109 E
loshin@nsu.nova.edu
LOSINGER, Regina ... 607-778-5040 344 F
losingerr@sunybroome.edu
LOSKOT, SDS, Donald .. 414-425-8300 538 J
dloskot@shsst.edu
LOSS, Amy ... 618-842-3711 146 G
lossa@iecc.edu
LOSSING, David, E ... 810-766-6647 251 E
dalossin@umflint.edu
LOSTETTER, Ron ... 262-524-7200 535 D
rlosett@carrollu.edu
LOTFI, Vahid ... 810-762-3171 251 E
vahid@umflint.edu
LOTH, Karen, M ... 616-331-6000 243 E
lothk@gvsu.edu
LOTHAMER, Mary Ellen 615-383-4848 466 F
mlothamer@watkins.edu
LOTHRINGER, Bobby ... 940-898-3036 490 D
rlothringer@twu.edu
LOTHRINGER, Rebecca . 940-565-3793 492 D
rebecca.lothringer@unt.edu
LOTITO, Larry, W ... 507-354-8221 257 A
lotitolw@mlc-wels.edu
LOTITO, Tom ... 757-493-6000.. 96 H
LOTKOWICTZ, Bob ... 315-464-4448 344 E
Lotkowir@upstate.edu
LOTRIONTE, John, D ... 901-321-3550 455 I
jlotrion@cbu.edu
LOTT, Christine ... 815-967-7302 157 C
clott@rockfordcareercollege.edu
LOTT, Donalyn, L ... 504-286-5244 207 B
dlott@suno.edu
LOTT, Ilio ... 847-214-7900 144 F
ilott@elgin.edu
LOTT, Jesse ... 315-655-7161 317 J
jlott@cazenovia.edu
LOTT, Patricia, D ... 850-474-3419 116 E
plott@uwf.edu
LOTTER, Dorothea, J ... 417-268-1000 272 D
lotterd@evangel.edu
LOTTIE, Jerry, W ... 518-564-2022 346 B
lottiejw@plattsburgh.edu
LOTTO, Benjamin ... 845-437-5255 351 H
lotto@vassar.edu
LOTURCO, Jennifer ... 518-320-1805 343 B
jen.loturco@suny.edu
LOTYCZEWSKI, Halina .. 315-792-3087 351 G
halotycz@utica.edu
LOU, Kris ... 503-370-5328 411 D
klou@willamette.edu
LOUALLEN, Cheryl ... 937-382-6661 395 F
cheryl_louallen@wilmington.edu
LOUCHE, Suzee, S ... 321-674-8099 103 R
slouche@fit.edu
LOUCY, Brian, M ... 315-445-4174 330 B
loucyb@lemoyne.edu
LOUDEN, Sandy ... 731-352-4095 455 E
loudens@bethelu.edu
LOUDER, Corey ... 660-626-2203 271 G
clouder@atsu.edu
LOUDIN, Rose Ellen ... 304-473-8600 534 G
loudin_r@wvwc.edu
LOUDON, Tina ... 360-650-3240 528 D
tina.loudon@wwu.edu
LOUFER, Michelle ... 321-433-7765 101 O
louferm@easternflorida.edu
LOUGEE, Wendy, P ... 612-624-1807 265 C
wlougee@umn.edu
LOUGH, Krista, L ... 785-827-5541 189 A
krista.lough@kwu.edu
LOUGHERY, James, F .. 215-968-8041 413 F
loughery@bucks.edu
LOUGHMAN, Ann ... 518-262-5435 314 I
loughma@mail.amc.edu
LOUGHRAN, Kristine ... 513-732-5218 393 D
loughrke@ucmail.uc.edu
LOUGHRAN, Sean ... 203-837-9330.. 88 G
loughrans@wcsu.edu
LOUIE, Larry ... 415-869-2900 227 G
larry.louie@hult.edu
LOUIE-BADUA, Liane ... 650-493-4430.. 66 H
LOUIMA, Gariot ... 802-322-1676 501 H
gariot.louima@goddard.edu
LOUIS, Michael ... 314-505-7301 273 G
louism@csl.edu
LOUIS, Naomi ... 937-778-7814 381 K
nlouis@edisonohio.edu
LOUIS, Tom ... 315-792-7100 348 D
tlouis@sunycnse.com
LOUIS-NANCE, Tasha ... 803-793-5172 445 F
louis-nance@denmarktech.edu
LOUISY, Heidi ... 256-782-5007.... 4 L
hlouisy@jsu.edu
LOULA, Karianne ... 651-423-8298 258 E
karianne.loula@dctc.edu
LOURDES ELGIRUS,
Marie ... 718-289-5362 318 E
marie.elgirus@bcc.cuny.edu
LOUREIRO, Rita, D ... 561-237-7035 108 E
rloureiro@lynn.edu

LOURO, Jeffrey .... 508-999-8171 228 H
jlouro@umassd.edu
LOUTHERBACK, George 254-295-4698 492 C
gloutherback@umhb.edu
LOUTTIT, Julianne, E .... 724-287-8711 413 G
julianne.louttit@bc3.edu
LOUWAGIE, Vincent ..... 210-349-9928 479 N
vincelouwagie@ost.edu
LOVATO, Jeremy .... 505-428-1767 313 A
jeremy.lovato@sfcc.edu
LOVE, Anne .... 718-420-4212 352 C
alove@wagner.edu
LOVE, Arlyn .... 937-769-1823 376 M
alove1@antioch.edu
LOVE, Ceshia .... 713-221-8454 491 F
lovec@uhd.edu
LOVE, David .... 814-393-2334 430 E
dlove@clarion.edu
LOVE, Deborah, A .... 757-221-1306 506 J
dalove@wm.edu
LOVE, Deborah, E .... 504-862-8083 207 F
dlove1@tulane.edu
LOVE, Edna .... 972-860-4806 472 C
elove@dcccd.edu
LOVE, Eric .... 574-631-2859 174 A
elove1@nd.edu
LOVE, Hannah .... 325-236-8277 488 C
hannah.love@tstc.edu
LOVE, Jan .... 404-727-6324 124 D
jlove3@emory.edu
LOVE, Jane .... 864-294-2248 446 F
jane.love@furman.edu
LOVE, Jim .... 212-749-2802 331 I
jlove@msmnyc.edu
LOVE, Julie, B .... 800-431-8488.. 28 D
LOVE, Julie, N .... 970-247-7503.. 82 I
studenthousing@fortlewis.edu
LOVE, Kathryn .... 239-687-5430.. 98 N
klove@avemarialaw.edu
LOVE, Kathy, S .... 912-443-3024 131 B
klove@savannahtech.edu
LOVE, Kensey .... 740-753-7007 383 G
love_k@hocking.edu
LOVE, Mike .... 262-551-5900 535 E
mlove@carthage.edu
LOVE, Nikki .... 408-498-5107.. 40 E
nlove@cogswell.edu
LOVE, Patrick .... 516-686-7882 335 F
Patrick.Love@nyit.edu
LOVE, Tommy .... 503-838-8281 411 B
lovet@wou.edu
LOVE, Tony .... 432-552-2633 495 F
love_t@utpb.edu
LOVEDAY, Joyce .... 253-589-4333 521 B
joyce.loveday@cptc.edu
LOVEDER, Alan .... 212-757-1190 315 C
aloveder@funeraleducation.org
LOVEJOY, Mike .... 469-348-2500 471 G
LOVEL, Stan .... 706-754-7868 129 B
slovell@northgatech.edu
LOVELACE, Rhonda .... 501-370-5297.. 22 E
rlovelace@philander.edu
LOVELADY, III, Artis .... 832-252-4617 470 L
artis@cbshouston.edu
LOVELAND, David, A .... 607-746-4013 347 G
lovelada@delhi.edu
LOVELAND, George .... 252-399-6501 354 I
gwloveland@barton.edu
LOVELESS, Cecelia .... 360-438-4366 525 H
cloveless@stmartin.edu
LOVELESS, Debra .... 716-375-2022 340 C
dloveles@sbu.edu
LOVELESS, Debra .... 713-525-2150 493 J
registrar@stthom.edu
LOVELESS, Jill .... 928-757-0806.. 15 K
jloveless@mohave.edu
LOVELIDGE, Robert .... 979-830-4194 469 F
rlovelidge@blinn.edu
LOVELL, Cheryl .... 303-373-2008.. 85 I
president@rvu.edu
LOVELL, Ellen .... 719-336-1541.. 83 N
library@lamarcc.edu
LOVELL, JR., Ernest, L . 601-403-1183 270 A
elovell@prcc.edu
LOVELL, Kim .... 706-778-3000 130 B
klovell@piedmont.edu
LOVELL, Michael, R ...... 414-288-7223 537 B
michael.lovell@marquette.edu
LOVELL, Sharon .... 540-568-2705 509 C
lovellse@jmu.edu
LOVELL, Susan .... 706-562-1681 123 D
lovell_susan@columbusstate.edu
LOVELY, Christine, D ... 916-278-6078.. 34 E
clovely@csus.edu
LOVERIDGE, Robert ...... 801-863-8161 500 B
loveriro@uvu.edu
LOVERING, James .... 802-387-6795 502 A
jlovering@landmark.edu
LOVETT,
Christopher, M .... 814-886-6400 427 B
clovett@mtaloy.edu
LOVETT, Daniel .... 252-536-7275 363 B
dlovett037@halifaxcc.edu
LOVETT, David, L .... 717-477-1164 431 F
dllove@ship.edu
LOVETT, Leslie .... 304-367-4786 531 E
Leslie.Lovett@pierpont.edu
LOVETT, Michael .... 256-215-4247.... 2 G
mlovett@cacc.edu
LOVETT, Patricia .... 270-686-4336 193 G
patricia.lovett@brescia.edu
LOVETT, Rod, M .... 217-351-2409 155 I
rlovett@parkland.edu
LOVETT, Sandra .... 417-625-9840 278 I
lovett-s@mssu.edu
LOVICK, Reed .... 252-527-6223 363 G
rlovick@lenoircc.edu
LOVIK, Eric .... 540-831-5099 511 C
elovik@radford.edu
LOVINCE, Thomas .... 504-671-5627 203 F
tlovin@dcc.edu
LOVINGOOD,
Deborah, F .... 630-466-7900 162 K
dlovingood@waubonsee.edu
LOVINS, Greg, M .... 828-262-2030 369 D
lovinsgm@appstate.edu
LOVITT, Carl, R .... 860-832-2228.. 88 D
lovittcar@ccsu.edu
LOVSTUEN, Brenda, C .. 319-895-4292 177 A
blovstuen@cornellcollege.edu
LOVVORN, Judi .... 229-217-4198 132 C
jlovvorn@southernregional.edu
LOW,
Catherine Yu-Ling ..... 808-371-5443 135 E
cfo@orientalmedicine.edu
LOW, George .... 540-831-5187 511 C
glow@radford.edu
LOW, Kathryn, G .... 207-786-6066 209 F
klow@bates.edu
LOW, Ryan .... 207-581-1554 212 B
ryan.low@maine.edu
LOW, Ryan .... 207-581-1554 212 C
ryan.low@maine.edu
LOW, Wai Hoa .... 808-521-2288 135 E
whlow@orientalmedicine.edu
LOWBRIDGE, John, D .. 270-824-1835 196 F
john.lowbridge@kctcs.edu
LOWDEN, Paul .... 616-732-1194 241 I
plowden@davenport.edu
LOWDER, Diane, M ...... 804-752-7218 511 E
dianelowder@rmc.edu
LOWDER, Theresa .... 859-985-3313 193 F
lowdert@berea.edu
LOWDERMILK,
Robert, S .... 336-342-4261 365 E
lowdermilkb@rockinghamcc.edu
LOWE, Brenda .... 806-720-7307 478 A
brenda.lowe@lcu.edu
LOWE, Carmen .... 617-627-4239 237 C
carmen.lowe@tufts.edu
LOWE, Carrie Beth .... 865-573-4517 457 H
cblowe@johnsonU.edu
LOWE, Ellen .... 760-591-3012.. 74 A
elowe@usa.edu
LOWE, JR., Eugene, Y . 847-491-5255 155 D
eyljr@northwestern.edu
LOWE, Gee .... 626-917-9482.. 38 I
LOWE, Grant .... 706-419-1411 123 F
grant.lowe@covenant.edu
LOWE, JR., James .... 251-405-7130.... 2 D
jlowe@bishop.edu
LOWE, James, R .... 860-486-0566.. 92 C
jim.lowe@uconn.edu
LOWE, Janet, S .... 307-766-3307 546 K
jlowe@uwyo.edu
LOWE, Jeanette .... 706-771-4000 121 B
jlowe@augustatech.edu
LOWE, Jim .... 870-762-1020.. 19 C
jlowe@smail.anc.edu
LOWE, Judy .... 423-697-2686 462 C
judy.lowe@chattanoogastate.edu
LOWE, Kathy .... 606-886-3863 195 I
kathy.lowe@kctcs.edu
LOWE, Kathy .... 205-665-6100.... 9 C
lowek@montevallo.edu
LOWE, Kathy .... 707-638-5806.. 70 B
kathy.lowe@tu.edu
LOWE, Keri .... 616-988-1000 241 E
keri.l@compass.edu
LOWE, Lisa .... 404-876-1227 122 A
lisa.lowe@bccr.edu
LOWE, Mark .... 701-483-2531 373 H
mark.lowe@dickinsonstate.edu
LOWE, Melinda .... 662-241-6088 269 B
mslowe@muw.edu
LOWE, OFM, Philip, J .. 610-358-4241 427 D
lowep@neumann.edu
LOWE, Rick, D .... 910-630-7027 359 C
rlowe@methodist.edu
LOWE, Sharon .... 772-462-7476 106 F
slowe@irsc.edu
LOWE, Stephen .... 864-429-8728 450 I
lowesh@mailbox.sc.edu
LOWE, Susan, G .... 620-229-6334 191 B
susan.lowe@sckans.edu
LOWE, Tamara, A .... 330-684-8931 393 A
lowe@uakron.edu
LOWE, Tom .... 616-988-1000 241 E
tom.l@compass.edu
LOWE, Verna .... 606-539-4316 200 F
verna.lowe@ucumberlands.edu
LOWE, William, J .... 219-980-6701 168 C
wjlowe@iun.edu
LOWE-SCHNEIDER,
Katy .... 812-866-7081 166 E
lowe@hanover.edu
LOWENBERG, Ron .... 714-895-8369.. 40 C
rlowenberg@gwc.cccd.edu
LOWENSTEIN,
Daniel, H .... 415-476-4451.. 72 C
Lowenstein@ucsf.edu
LOWENSTEIN, Noah ...... 415-575-6181.. 31 C
nlowenstein@ciis.edu
LOWENTHAL, Barbara ... 212-472-1500 336 A
blowenthal@nysid.edu
LOWENTHAL, Benjamin 410-455-1720 219 F
blowenth@umbc.edu
LOWENTHAL, Tina .... 626-395-2758.. 31 D
tina.lowenthal@caltech.edu
LOWERY, Andrew .... 229-209-5239 120 B
andrewlowery@andrewcollege.edu
LOWERY, Carla .... 662-329-7197 269 B
cmlowery@muw.edu
LOWERY, Daniel .... 219-473-4333 165 A
dlowery@ccsj.edu
LOWERY, Juliet, J .... 540-375-2099 512 B
lowery@roanoke.edu
LOWERY, Kathryn .... 601-266-6775 271 B
kathryn.lowery@usm.edu
LOWERY, Kathy .... 502-213-5022 196 E
kathy.lowery@kctcs.edu
LOWERY, LaTanya .... 512-505-3035 475 G
llowery@htu.edu
LOWERY, Stan .... 615-966-6190 458 C
stan.lowery@lipscomb.edu
LOWERY, Terri .... 713-425-3100 470 N
tlowery@chcp.edu
LOWERY, Wendy .... 910-521-6252 371 D
wendy.lowery@uncp.edu
LOWERY-HART, Russell 806-371-5123 467 E
rdloweryhart@actx.edu
LOWES, JR., Guy .... 304-236-7633 531 F
guy.lowes@southernwv.edu
LOWMAN, Sara .... 713-348-2457 480 M
lowman@rice.edu
LOWMAN, Stacey, L ..... 240-500-2000 215 C
sllowman@hagerstowncc.edu
LOWMAN, Tony .... 856-256-5300 306 D
lowman@rowan.edu
LOWN, Maris .... 908-709-7006 309 A
maris.lown@ucc.edu
LOWNES-JACKSON,
Millicent .... 615-963-7142 461 F
mlownes@tnstate.edu
LOWRANCE, Jeffrey ...... 704-330-6666 361 D
jeff.lowrance@cpcc.edu
LOWREY, Brad .... 517-607-4282 243 J
blowrey@hillsdale.edu
LOWREY, Tammy .... 325-649-8043 475 F
tlowrey@hputx.edu
LOWRY, David .... 405-425-1941 399 J
david.lowry@oc.edu
LOWRY, Elisabeth .... 415-503-6258.. 63 A
elowry@sfcm.edu
LOWRY, Gail .... 317-738-8235 166 B
glowry@franklincollege.edu
LOWRY, Jenny .... 410-617-2451 216 D
jlowry@loyola.edu
LOWRY, John .... 615-966-3000 458 C
john.lowry@lipscomb.edu
LOWRY, Kimberly, M ... 972-860-7028 472 E
KimberlyMoore@dcccd.edu
LOWRY, III,
L. Randolph .... 615-966-1787 458 C
randy.lowry@lipscomb.edu
LOWRY, Meagan .... 501-205-8870.. 20 G
mlowry@cbc.edu
LOWRY, Rebekah .... 910-272-3235 365 D
relowry@robeson.edu
LOWRY, Rebekah, R ..... 910-272-3235 365 D
relowry@robeson.edu
LOWY, Laurence .... 212-410-8007 335 B
llowy@nycpm.edu
LOWY, Vivien .... 213-624-1200.. 44 I
vlowy@fidm.edu
LOX, Curt .... 618-650-3350 159 I
clox@siue.edu
LOY, Marty .... 715-346-3169 541 A
mloy@uwsp.edu
LOYA, James .... 956-665-8078 494 C
loya@utpa.edu
LOYACK, John .... 570-208-5832 422 D
johnloyack@kings.edu
LOYD, Bill .... 706-776-0104 130 B
bloyd@piedmont.edu
LOYD, James .... 706-649-1449 123 E
jloyd@columbustech.edu
LOYD, James .... 256-306-2774.... 2 F
jll@calhoun.edu
LOYD, Jo Lynn .... 972-279-6511 467 F
jloyd@amberton.edu
LOYD, Kristen, J .... 812-877-8275 172 C
loyd1@rose-hulman.edu
LOYD, Nic .... 256-824-3025.... 9 A
nicholas.loyd@uah.edu
LOYD, Nicole, L .... 610-861-1502 426 H
loydn@moravian.edu
LOYD, Sean .... 304-766-3238 533 C
loyds@wvstateu.edu
LOYD-PAIGE, Michelle . 616-526-8703 240 L
lopa@calvin.edu
LOYNAZ, Oscar .... 305-348-6796 114 G
oscar.loynaz@fiu.edu
LOYOLA, David .... 956-380-8196 481 A
dloyola@riogrande.edu
LOZA, Frank .... 325-670-1461 474 M
floza@hsutx.edu
LOZADA, Jose .... 787-727-7020 559 A
jlozada@sagrado.edu
LOZANO, Fran .... 408-848-4702.. 45 G
flozano@gavilan.edu
LOZANO, Franz .... 707-654-1032.. 34 B
flozano@csum.edu
LOZIC, Danijel .... 202-274-2303.. 97 D
marketing@potomac.edu
LOZINA, Mary .... 914-674-7651 332 E
mlozina@mercy.edu
LU, Jeffrey .... 408-433-2280.. 38 J
LU, Kuang Kai .... 323-731-2383.. 57 H
kklu@psuca.edu
LU, Wel .... 305-595-9500.. 97 H
LU, Yue .... 626-289-7719.. 26 G
ylu@amu.edu
LUALLEN, Bert .... 620-417-1563 191 A
bert.luallen@sccc.edu
LUAN, Jing .... 650-358-6880.. 64 B
luan@smccd.edu
LUBBE, Veronica, A ...... 859-344-3522 200 C
veronica.lubbe@thomas.more.edu
LUBBERDEN, Mike .... 641-628-5346 176 E
lubberdenm@central.edu
LUBBERS, Kristin .... 719-336-1518.. 83 N
kristin.lubbers@lamarcc.edu
LUBBERS, Tony .... 316-295-5200 187 C
LubbersT@friends.edu
LUBBERTS, Rhonda ...... 616-331-2525 243 E
lubbertr@gvsu.edu
LUBECK, Eileen .... 973-720-2450 309 I
lubecke@wpunj.edu
LUBECK SONENBERG,
Joyce .... 305-809-3149 104 A
joyce.lubecksonenberg@fkcc.edu
LUBECKI, Jacek .... 912-478-0332 126 B
jlubecki@georgiasouthern.edu
LUBIENECKI, Teresa ..... 716-652-8940 317 M
tlubienecki@cks.edu
LUBINSKY, Hindy .... 718-787-1602 350 C
hindy.lubinsky@touro.edu
LUBRANO, Ann .... 718-818-6470 341 G
LUCARIELLO, Joan, M .. 646-313-8000 321 A
provost@guttman.cuny.edu
LUCAS, Audrey, O .... 336-335-5090 371 C
audrey_daniel@uncg.edu
LUCAS, Bonnie .... 847-635-1711 155 E
blucas@oakton.edu
LUCAS, Bryan .... 817-257-7682 486 G
b.lucas@tcu.edu
LUCAS, Carol, A .... 516-877-3154 314 F
lucas@adelphi.edu
LUCAS, Catherine .... 303-556-5122.. 83 Q
lucascat@msudenver.edu
LUCAS, Cecilia .... 808-455-0325 136 G
cblucas@hawaii.edu
LUCAS, Dawn .... 704-463-1360 367 F
dawn.lucas@pfeiffer.edu
LUCAS, Dawn .... 704-463-3207 367 F
dawn.lucas@pfeiffer.edu
LUCAS, Dwayne .... 315-781-3304 327 G
lucas@hws.edu
LUCAS, JR., George ..... 937-772-9210 394 F
george.lucas@urbana.edu
LUCAS, Hakim, J .... 386-481-2929.. 99 F
lucash@cookman.edu
LUCAS, James .... 336-770-3317 372 B
lucasj@uncsa.edu
LUCAS, Jane, K .... 205-934-4636.... 8 F
jklucas@uab.edu
LUCAS, Jennifer, R .... 717-337-6211 419 C
jlucas@gettysburg.edu
LUCAS, Joan .... 662-325-8131 269 A
jlucas@legal.msstate.edu

LUCAS, John .... 608-262-8287 539 D
jplucas@wisc.edu

LUCAS, John .... 802-258-3266 502 I
john.lucas@sit.edu

LUCAS, Julie .... 617-253-3952 233 C

LUCAS, Karen .... 904-620-2624 116 A
karen.lucas@unf.edu

LUCAS, Kathy, A .... 765-285-5289 164 D
klucas@bsu.edu

LUCAS, LaTanya, V .... 336-744-0900 355 D
latanya@carolina.edu

LUCAS, Linda, C .... 205-934-0622.... 8 F
lucas@uab.edu

LUCAS, Mark, L .... 573-882-3621 283 H
lucasm@missouri.edu

LUCAS, Matthew .... 503-375-7019 405 F
mlucas@corban.edu

LUCAS, Megan .... 563-588-6315 176 F
megan.lucas@clarke.edu

LUCAS, Michelle .... 717-766-2511 426 B
mlucas@messiah.edu

LUCAS, Mona .... 860-486-2819.. 92 C
mona.lucas@uconn.edu

LUCAS, Pam, A .... 214-860-2097 472 F
plucas@dcccd.edu

LUCAS, Paul, M .... 724-287-8711 413 G
paul.lucas@bc3.edu

LUCAS, Phil .... 248-204-4117 245 J
plucas@ltu.edu

LUCAS, JR., Richard ..... 301-860-4303 220 B
rlucas@bowiestate.edu

LUCAS, Sandra .... 520-383-8401.. 18 A
slucas7578@aol.com

LUCAS, Sheri .... 614-222-3220 380 F
slucas@ccad.edu

LUCAS, Sophia .... 678-450-0550 127 E
slucas@ict.edu

LUCAS, Tamara, F .... 973-655-5167 304 A
lucast@mail.montclair.edu

LUCAS, Virginia, S .... 910-592-8081 365 G
vlucas@sampsoncc.edu

LUCAS-ROSS, Jennifer .. 239-687-5351.. 98 N
jlross@avemarialaw.edu

LUCAS-YOUMANS,
Tasha .... 386-481-2181.. 99 F
youmanst@cookman.edu

LUCE, Monica .... 206-878-3710 523 D
mluce@highline.edu

LUCE, Richard, E .... 405-325-2611 403 I
rluce@ou.edu

LUCERO, Cori .... 209-228-4440.. 71 E
clucero2@ucmerced.edu

LUCERO, Gabe .... 307-742-9375 547 D
glucero@wyotechstaff.edu

LUCERO, Kathy .... 909-652-6620.. 38 A
kathy.lucero@chaffey.edu

LUCERO, Louis .... 661-722-6300.. 27 P
llucero@avc.edu

LUCERO, Mark .... 714-703-1900.. 41 I

LUCERO-MILLER,
Denise .... 940-898-3801 490 D
dluceromiller@twu.edu

LUCHS, Jason .... 212-229-5626 334 C
luchsj@newschool.edu

LUCHSINGER, Andrew .. 651-638-6055 254 A
andrew-luchsinger@bethel.edu

LUCIA, Joseph .... 215-204-8231 436 C
joseph.lucia@temple.edu

LUCIANI, Michael .... 802-387-6713 502 A
mluciani@landmark.edu

LUCIANO, Jack .... 910-755-7336 360 E
lucianoj@brunswickcc.edu

LUCIANO, Jennifer, K ... 212-752-1530 330 C
jennifer.luciano@limcollege.edu

LUCIANO, Joseph .... 570-344-7101 422 G
lucianoj@lackawanna.edu

LUCIANO-FIGUEROA,
Yomarachaliff .... 787-265-3884 558 B
egresados@uprm.edu

LUCID, Robert .... 973-408-3379 301 J
rlucid@drew.edu

LUCIDO, Michael .... 314-977-8173 281 M
lucidoma@slu.edu

LUCIER, Chris .... 302-831-0746.. 94 D
clucier@udel.edu

LUCIO, Robert .... 352-588-8252 111 L
robert.lucio@saintleo.edu

LUCK, Cathy .... 616-632-2916 239 E
cathleen.luck@aquinas.edu

LUCK, Deborah, S .... 336-633-0272 365 A
dsluck@randolph.edu

LUCK, Janice, J .... 610-921-7824 411 E
jluck@albright.edu

LUCK, Renita .... 229-317-6732 123 H
renita.luck@darton.edu

LUCKADOO,
Timothy, R .... 919-515-3088 370 D
trluckad@ncsu.edu

LUCKE, Kathy, T .... 607-735-1890 324 J
klucke@elmira.edu

LUCKETT, Anita .... 718-779-1430 338 D
aluckett@plazacollege.edu

LUCKETT, Jenni .... 503-352-3006 408 I
jluckett@pacificu.edu

LUCKETT, Joseph .... 703-284-3321 510 B
joseph.luckett@marymount.edu

LUCKETT, Nicole .... 262-650-4921 535 D
nluckett@carrollu.edu

LUCKEY, Rhonda, H ..... 724-357-4040 431 A
rluckey@iup.edu

LUCKEY, JR.,
William, T .... 270-384-8001 198 C
luckeyw@lindsey.edu

LUCKIE, Sharon .... 718-289-5800 318 E
sharon.luckie@bcc.cuny.edu

LUCKING, Rachel .... 508-626-4615 230 A
rlucking@framingham.edu

LUCKY, Jana .... 318-357-4503 208 D
luckyj@nsula.edu

LUCKY, Mary .... 254-647-3234 480 G
mlucky@rangercollege.edu

LUCUMI, Ana, M .... 787-780-5134 554 H
alucumi@nuc.edu

LUCY, John .... 904-596-2507 117 G
jlucy@tbc.edu

LUDE, Judith .... 740-264-5591 381 J
jlude@egcc.edu

LUDEMAN, Angela .... 301-846-2660 214 I
aludeman@frederick.edu

LUDEMANN, Martin ..... 406-243-2277 287 D
marty.ludemann@umontana.edu

LUDLAM, Laura .... 717-477-1201 431 F
LJLudlam@ship.edu

LUDLOW, Cynthia .... 716-851-1666 325 A
ludlow@ecc.edu

LUDWIG, Amy .... 479-397-7622.. 22 H
aludwig@rmcc.edu

LUDWIG, Amy .... 479-394-7622.. 22 H
aludwig@rmcc.edu

LUDWIG, Dean .... 419-824-3686 385 F
dludwig@lourdes.edu

LUDWIG, Deborah .... 785-628-4539 187 A
dmludwig@fhsu.edu

LUDWIG, Glenn .... 717-334-6286 424 F
gludwig@ltsg.edu

LUDWIG, James .... 513-875-3344 379 G
james.ludwig@chatfield.edu

LUDWIG, James, P .... 513-875-3344 379 G
james.ludwig@chatfield.edu

LUDWIG, Nancy .... 978-837-5947 233 G
ludwign@merrimack.edu

LUDWIG, Rebecca .... 727-341-4150 112 A
ludwig.rebecca@spcollege.edu

LUDWIG, Scott .... 408-741-2031.. 76 F
scott.ludwig@westvalley.edu

LUDWIG-JOHNSON,
Stacey .... 801-274-3280 501 B
sludwig@wgu.edu

LUEBBERT, Paula, J ..... 217-782-1086 151 C
paula.luebbert@llcc.edu

LUEBKE, Linda .... 804-706-5202 515 G
lluebke@jtcc.edu

LUEBKE, Miriam .... 651-651-8825 255 C
luebke@csp.edu

LUECK, Terrie .... 507-457-6921 264 B
tlueck@smumn.edu

LUECKE, Chris .... 435-797-2452 500 A
chris.luecke@usu.edu

LUEDER, Billie .... 808-845-9187 136 E
bktakaki@hawaii.edu

LUEDERS, Carol .... 847-735-6004 149 H
lueders@lakeforest.edu

LUEKEN, Paul, A .... 724-738-2021 432 A
paul.lueken@sru.edu

LUEKENGA, Chris .... 970-943-2616.. 87 F
cluekenga@western.edu

LUESING, Anne .... 415-451-2812.. 63 B
aluesing@sfts.edu

LUESSE, Amy .... 952-446-4122 255 E
luessea@crown.edu

LUETKEHANS, Lara .... 724-357-2482 431 A
lara.luetkehans@iup.edu

LUETSCHWAGER,
Julie, A .... 920-923-8599 537 A
jaluetschwager25@marianuniversity.edu

LUETTGER, Michele .... 607-436-2514 344 B
luettgme@oneonta.edu

LUETZEN, Leigh Ann .... 617-912-9118 224 C
lluetzen@bostonconservatory.edu

LUEVANOS, Aida .... 432-837-8000 489 B
aluevanos@sulross.edu

LUFF, Debra .... 916-558-2139.. 53 B
LuffD@scc.losrios.edu

LUFF, Libby .... 615-514-2787 459 O
lfunke@nossi.edu

LUFF, Paula .... 312-362-8091 143 G
pluff@depaul.edu

LUFKIN, Daniel .... 757-825-3810 517 B
Lufkind@tncc.edu

LUFKIN, Mary Beth ..... 603-513-1328 299 C
mb.lufkin@granite.edu

LUFT, John, P .... 717-766-2511 426 B
jluft@messiah.edu

LUGEMBE, Farida .... 310-453-8300.. 43 I
farida@emperors.edu

LUGG, Thomas, W .... 610-359-5336 416 G
tlugg@dccc.edu

LUGO, Chantal .... 602-286-8330.. 14 M
chantal.lugo@gatewaycc.edu

LUGO, Daniel .... 207-859-4393 210 A
dan.lugo@colby.edu

LUGO, Efrain .... 787-620-2040 550 D
elugo@aupr.edu

LUGO, Eric .... 646-660-6095 318 C
Eric.Lugo@baruch.cuny.edu

LUGO, Francisco .... 787-841-2000 555 F
flugo@pucpr.edu

LUGO, Ivette .... 407-447-7300 105 E
ilugo@ftccollege.edu

LUGO, Javier .... 787-600-2819 558 F
javier.lugo3@upr.edu

LUGO, Maria de los, A 787-766-1717 556 A
um_mlugo@suagm.edu

LUGO, María Inés .... 787-264-1912 554 C
milugo@intersg.edu

LUGO, Udeth .... 407-646-2573 111 H
ulugo@rollins.edu

LUGO, Victoria .... 805-289-6455.. 75 E
vlugo@vcccd.edu

LUHTA, Brad .... 440-375-7585 385 B
bluhta@lec.edu

LUHTALA, Erik .... 619-684-8801.. 56 B
eluhtala@newschoolarch.edu

LUI, Kat .... 612-659-7293 259 E
kat.lui@metrostate.edu

LUIKART, Nancy .... 563-288-6073 178 C
nluikart@eicc.edu

LUIKEN, Elizabeth .... 712-325-3445 180 B
eluiken@iwcc.edu

LUINENBURG, Amber ... 507-372-3499 260 C
amber.luinenburg@mnwest.edu

LUING, Kevin, L .... 973-278-5400 316 D
kevin@berkeleycollege.edu

LUING, Kevin, L .... 973-278-5400 300 C
kevin@berkeleycollege.edu

LUJAN, Annette .... 719-846-5679.. 86 A
annette.lujan@trinidadstate.edu

LUJAN, Linda .... 480-732-7010.. 14 K
Linda.Lujan@cgc.edu

LUJAN, Manuel .... 361-593-4060 486 A
manuel.lujan@tamuk.edu

LUKAC, Dan .... 513-244-4617 387 A
dan.lukac@msj.edu

LUKACS, Yehuda .... 703-993-2156 507 K
ylukacs@gmu.edu

LUKACSKO, Debbie ...... 201-684-7535 305 F
dlukacsk@ramapo.edu

LUKAS, Veronica .... 718-631-6367 320 F
vlukas@qcc.cuny.edu

LUKASIK, Douglas, S ... 607-778-5028 344 F
lukasikds@sunybroome.edu

LUKASZEWSKI,
Patricia, L .... 919-508-2220 373 B
pllukaszewski@peace.edu

LUKE, Don, J .... 570-326-3761 429 J
dluke@pct.edu

LUKE, Gerri, F .... 570-326-3761 429 J
gluke@pct.edu

LUKE, Kristie .... 580-745-2176 402 D
kluke@se.edu

LUKE, Learie .... 803-533-3776 448 H
lluke@scsu.edu

LUKE, Learie, B .... 803-536-7180 448 H

LUKE, Sarah .... 207-801-5670 210 B
sluke@coa.edu

LUKEHART, Debra .... 515-271-2169 177 K
debra.lukehart@drake.edu

LUKEN, James, O .... 843-349-2783 444 G
joluken@coastal.edu

LUKHAUP, Walter, P .... 724-480-3376 416 A
walter.lukhaup@ccbc.edu

LUKKEN, Jeff .... 706-880-8021 127 N
jlukken@lagrange.edu

LUKKES, Nathan .... 605-773-3455 453 E
nathan.lukkes@sdbor.edu

LUKMAN, Roy .... 407-303-8520.. 97 J
roy.lukman.phd@adu.edu

LUKOSHUS, Wes, K ..... 219-989-2217 171 L
lukoshus@purduecal.edu

LUKSA, Jennifer .... 570-674-6224 426 D
jsluzele@misericordia.edu

LULJAK, Thomas, L ...... 414-229-4035 540 A
tluljak@uwm.edu

LULLI, Linda, S .... 401-232-6011 441 B
lslulli@bryant.edu

LUM-AKANA, Aileen ..... 808-455-0606 136 G
aileenla@hawaii.edu

LUMEN, Karl .... 601-366-8880 271 E
klumen@wbs.edu

LUMETTA, Joanne .... 734-432-5689 246 B
jlumetta@madonna.edu

LUMLEY, Simon, J .... 318-798-6868 201 H
simonl@bluecliffcollege.com

LUMM, Werner .... 920-206-2322 536 T
werner.lumm@mbu.edu

LUMPKIN, James .... 903-566-7346 494 E
jlumpkin@uttyler.edu

LUMPP, David, A .... 651-641-8217 255 C
lumpp@csp.edu

LUNA, Andrew, L .... 256-765-4221.... 9 D
alluna@una.edu

LUNA, Carmen .... 787-766-1717 556 A
cmluna@suagm.edu

LUNA, Carmen .... 787-850-9394 558 A
carmen.luna@upr.edu

LUNA, Edna .... 931-363-9824 458 D
eluna@martinmethodist.edu

LUNA, Leslie .... 520-383-8401.. 18 A
lluna@tocc.edu

LUNA, Mickey .... 314-977-3948 281 M
mluna@slu.edu

LUNA, Olga .... 787-766-1912 553 D
oluna@inter.edu

LUNA, Shirley, A .... 936-468-2605 484 A
sluna@sfasu.edu

LUNAN, Kathy .... 314-529-9332 277 B
klunan@maryville.edu

LUNARDI, Joseph, M ... 610-660-1221 434 G
jlunardi@sju.edu

LUNBECK, Jo .... 501-660-1030.. 19 D
jlunbeck@asusystem.edu

LUNCEFORD, Casey ...... 772-462-2505 106 F
cluncefo@irsc.edu

LUND, Bob .... 719-502-2040.. 84 J
bob.lund@ppcc.edu

LUND, Harold, E .... 530-226-4127.. 66 G
hlund@simpsonu.edu

LUND, James .... 760-480-8474.. 76 J
jlund@wscal.edu

LUND, Jon .... 563-387-1428 180 M
lundjon@luther.edu

LUND, Karla .... 406-874-6186 287 A
lundk@milescc.edu

LUND, Lisa .... 989-328-1219 247 D
lisal@montcalm.edu

LUND, Sarah .... 317-931-2311 165 C
slund@cts.edu

LUND, Stephen, R .... 608-263-5722 539 D
slund@ohr.wisc.edu

LUNDAHL, Deb .... 402-375-7209 292 D
delunda1@wsc.edu

LUNDAY, Bobbi, J .... 701-662-1501 375 A
bobbi.lunday@lrsc.edu

LUNDBERG, Cliff .... 805-565-7188.. 76 K
clundber@westmont.edu

LUNDBERG, Erik .... 734-615-4445 251 C
lerikl@umich.edu

LUNDBERG, Laura .... 407-869-7387 106 H

LUNDBERG, Njal .... 303-964-5086.. 85 G
nlundber@regis.edu

LUNDBERG, Todd .... 425-352-8168 520 D
tlundberg@cascadia.edu

LUNDBLAD, Larry, A .... 218-855-8053 258 C
LLundblad@clcmn.edu

LUNDBLAD, Tracey .... 302-736-2372.. 94 E
tracey.lundblad@wesley.edu

LUNDBURG, P. Wesley 631-451-4259 348 F
lundbuw@sunysuffolk.edu

LUNDE, Beth .... 757-822-1711 517 C
blunde@tcc.edu

LUNDEEN, Bruce .... 810-766-4018 239 G
bruce.lundeen@baker.edu

LUNDEEN, Kate .... 414-382-6103 534 I
kate.lundeen@alverno.edu

LUNDEEN, Sally .... 414-229-4189 540 A
slundeen@uwm.edu

LUNDEN, Steve, M .... 509-313-5624 522 L
slunden@plant.gonzaga.edu

LUNDERMAN, Dedria .... 850-729-5361 109 D
lundermand@nwfsc.edu

LUNDGREN, LaRae .... 951-827-2587.. 72 A
larae.lundgren@ucr.edu

LUNDGREN, LouAnne ... 505-224-4000 310 F
llundgren1@cnm.edu

LUNDQUIST, Donna ..... 337-475-5493 208 B

LUNDQUIST, Lisa, M .... 678-547-6308 128 G
lundquist_lm@mercer.edu

LUNDQUIST, Sara .... 714-564-6085.. 60 G
lundquist_sara@sac.edu

LUNDRIGAN, Kathleen .. 513-244-4330 387 A
kathleen.lundrigan@msj.edu

LUNDSTREM, Karen ...... 718-260-5140 320 D
klundstrem@citytech.cuny.edu

LUNDSTROM, Joel .... 712-792-8308 177 B
jtlundstrom@dmacc.edu

LUNDSTROM, Joel .... 785-320-4502 189 C
joellundstrom@matc.net

LUNDY, Constance, L .. 484-365-7785 424 E
lundy@lincoln.edu

LUNDY, Jennifer .... 412-365-1145 415 C
jlundy@chatham.edu

LYONS, Frankie ... 406-771-4361 288 B frankie.lyons@gfcmsu.edu
LYONS, Heather ... 910-695-3701 365 H lyonsh@sandhills.edu
LYONS, James ... 408-551-1691.. 65 A jlyons@scu.edu
LYONS, Jason, C ... 757-594-8175 506 I jason.lyons@cnu.edu
LYONS, John ... 781-280-3528 232 B
LYONS, Katherine, M ... 985-732-6640 203 I
LYONS, Kyra, A ... 202-319-5608.. 95 A lyonsk@cua.edu
LYONS, Larry ... 309-438-5626 147 I lelyons@ilstu.edu
LYONS, Lindsey ... 415-749-4512.. 62 I llyons@sfai.edu
LYONS, Marybeth ... 315-792-7505 348 D smbl@sunyit.edu
LYONS, Melinda ... 928-541-7777.. 16 B mlyons@ncu.edu
LYONS, Michael ... 781-239-2443 231 G mlyons@massbay.edu
LYONS, Nicholas, A ... 315-312-2222 346 A nicholas.lyons@oswego.edu
LYONS, Patrick, G ... 973-761-9498 308 C patrick.lyons@shu.edu
LYONS, Peter ... 404-413-2578 126 D lyonsp@gsu.edu
LYONS, Phil ... 715-232-1683 541 B lyonsp@uwstout.edu
LYONS, Phillip ... 936-294-1700 489 A icc_pml@shsu.edu
LYONS, Richard, K ... 510-643-2027.. 70 K lyons@haas.berkeley.edu
LYONS, Shane ... 304-293-5621 533 D shlyons@mail.wvu.edu
LYONS, Shawn ... 859-238-5500 194 E shawn.lyons@centre.edu
LYONS, Sheila ... 601-352-9666 266 F bookstore@belhaven.edu
LYONS, Sheri ... 601-266-5518 271 B sheri.rawls@usm.edu
LYONS, Stacy ... 404-270-5063 132 D slyons2@spelman.edu
LYONS, Steve ... 218-723-6167 255 A slyons@css.edu
LYONS, Steven, J ... 937-775-5745 396 A steven.lyons@wright.edu
LYONS, Theresa ... 907-786-1240.. 10 H tlyons@uaa.alaska.edu
LYSENG, Brenda ... 651-779-3447 258 D brenda.lyseng@century.edu
LYSIONEK, Christine ... 610-902-8416 414 B christine.lysionek@cabrini.edu
LYSLE, Jane, H ... 302-225-6274.. 94 B lyslej@gbc.edu
LYSNE, Marit ... 507-222-4080 254 D mlysne@carleton.edu
LYSSENKO, Robin ... 650-949-6233.. 44 N lyssenko@fhda.edu
LYTCH, Carol, E ... 717-290-8701 423 E president@lancasterseminary.edu
LYTLE, Anne ... 212-772-4242 319 E alytle@hunter.cuny.edu
LYTLE, Daniel ... 715-233-5358 542 M dlytle@cvtc.edu
LYTLE, David ... 210-434-6711 479 P dlytle@lake.ollusa.edu
LYTLE, James, R ... 570-586-2400 435 H jlytle@summitu.edu
LYTLE, Jesse ... 610-896-1000 420 J jlytle@haverford.edu
LYTLE, Rick, S ... 325-674-2503 466 I lytler@acu.edu
LYTLE, Rodney ... 828-298-3325 373 A rlytle@warren-wilson.edu
LYTTLE, Marsha, J ... 810-762-9660 245 A mlyttle@kettering.edu
LYTTLE, Mary Jo ... 724-357-7942 431 A mjlyttle@iup.edu
LYTTLE, Sonya ... 843-525-8248 449 E slyttle@tcl.edu
LYTTON, Billy ... 704-922-6480 362 G lytton.billy@gaston.edu
LYZUN, Nancy ... 317-940-8029 164 L nlyzun@butler.edu
L'ALLIER, Kristi ... 218-235-2171 262 C k.lallier@vcc.edu
L'ALLIER, Kristi ... 218-235-2153 262 C k.laillier@vcc.edu
L'ETOILE, Michelle ... 617-422-7210 234 J mletoile@nesl.edu
L'HEUREUX, Robert, W 712-362-0421 179 G rlheureux@iowalakes.edu

M

MA, Dongxin ... 512-454-1188 468 A info@aoma.edu
MA, Elise ... 516-739-1545 335 C financial_aid@nyctcm.edu
MA, Jennifer ... 925-473-7521.. 42 F jma@losmedanos.edu
MA, Jim ... 630-942-4034 142 F maj127@cod.edu
MA, Michelle ... 509-527-5768 528 F mamk@whitman.edu
MA, Qing ... 626-289-7719.. 26 G qma@amu.edu
MA, Qingyun ... 213-740-2083.. 74 D archdean@usc.edu
MAALOUF, Kathy ... 305-237-7440 108 L kmaalouf@mdc.edu
MAAS, Bruce ... 608-262-5381 539 D bruce.mass@cio.wisc.edu
MAAS, Paula ... 212-229-8947 334 C maasp@newschool.edu
MAASJO, Bryan ... 212-772-4582 319 E bm514@hunter.cuny.edu
MAATSCH, Darrell ... 210-567-2890 495 B maatsch@uthscsa.edu
MABE, Mark ... 816-271-4261 279 E mabe@missouriwestern.edu
MABE, Scotty ... 910-410-1684 365 B samabe@richmondcc.edu
MABERRY, Sue ... 310-665-6925.. 57 C maberry@otis.edu
MABERY, Dan ... 870-230-5101.. 21 B mayberb@hsu.edu
MABEUS, Amy ... 319-385-6478 180 A iwcbookstore@iw.edu
MABOKELA, Reitumetse ... 217-333-1828 162 A mabokela@illinois.edu
MABREY, Erika ... 540-234-9261 514 H mabreye@brcc.edu
MABRY, Aaron ... 828-627-4521 363 C acmabry@haywood.edu
MABRY, Anne ... 201-200-3001 304 C amabry@njcu.edu
MABRY, Dawn, M ... 260-399-7700 174 C dmabry@sf.edu
MABRY, Doug ... 503-517-1935 411 C dmabry@westernseminary.edu
MABRY, James, L ... 978-656-3101 232 B mabry@middlesex.mass.edu
MABRY, Rodney, H ... 903-566-7119 494 E president@uttyler.edu
MABUCHI, Julia ... 617-558-1788 235 A jmabuchi@nesa.edu
MAC PHERSON, Garry, L ... 858-822-4923.. 72 B gmacpherson@ucsd.edu
MACADAM, Martha, P .. 717-871-7520 431 E martha.macadam@millersville.edu
MACALESTER, Tom ... 704-461-6721 354 J TomMacAlester@bac.edu
MACALUSO, Anthony ... 718-990-2452 340 G macalusa@stjohns.edu
MACALUSO, Daniel ... 909-621-8335.. 46 K dmacaluso@hmc.edu
MACAN, Drew ... 386-822-7472 117 A dmacan@stetson.edu
MACAPINLAC, Jonas, D 671-735-2944 549 G jmac@triton.uog.edu
MACARI, Emir ... 504-280-7120 205 G emacari@uno.edu
MACARI, Emir ... 504-280-6836 205 G emacari@uno.edu
MACARTHUR, John ... 661-362-2220.. 53 F sstaats@masters.edu
MACARTHUR, John ... 989-463-7241 239 B macarthurjr@alma.edu
MACARTHUR, Josh ... 781-239-4528 222 E wmacarthur@babson.edu
MACAULAY, Barbara ... 508-373-5897 233 E barbara.macaulay@mcphs.edu
MACCARELLI, Lisa ... 412-586-9068 437 K lmm190@pitt.edu
MACCARONE, Ellen, M . 509-313-6136 522 L maccarone@gonzaga.edu
MACCARTHY, Stephen, J ... 215-898-8724 437 I smaccar@upenn.edu
MACCHI, Thomas, J ... 215-572-2942 412 F macchit@arcadia.edu
MACCHIARELLA, Sue, A ... 386-226-7740 102 B macchis1@erau.edu
MACCHIAVELLI, Raul ... 787-265-3850 558 B raul.macchiavelli@upr.edu
MACCLAREN, Jon, A ... 802-387-6721 502 A jonmacclaren@landmark.edu
MACCORQUODALE, Patricia ... 520-621-2848.. 18 E pmac@email.arizona.edu
MACCUISH, Spencer ... 805-581-1233.. 44 A smaccuish@eternitybiblecollege.com
MACCULLOCH, Heather . 718-409-7331 348 C hmacculloch@sunymaritime.edu
MACDONALD, Brian ... 802-654-2588 502 H bmacdonald@smcvt.edu
MACDONALD, Brian ... 610-282-1100 416 I Brian.MacDonald@desales.edu
MACDONALD, Christopher ... 912-478-5406 126 B cmacdonald@georgiasouthern.edu
MACDONALD, David ... 419-772-2200 388 I d-macdonald@onu.edu
MACDONALD, Duncan .. 607-431-4032 327 B macdonaldd@hartwick.edu
MACDONALD, Elizabeth 636-949-4396 276 L emacdonald@lindenwood.edu
MACDONALD, Gordon .. 303-762-6890.. 82 C gordon.macdonald@denverseminary.edu
MACDONALD, Gregory . 540-868-7275 515 H gmacdonald@lfcc.edu
MACDONALD, Gregory . 610-330-5069 423 A macdonag@lafayette.edu
MACDONALD, Lorri ... 313-578-0401 250 H macdonlj@udmercy.edu
MACDONALD, Lyle, W . 406-338-5441 286 C lmacdonald@bfcc.edu
MACDONALD, Mark ... 808-675-3260 134 M mark.macdonald@byuh.edu
MACDONALD, Nancy ... 518-454-2161 322 C macdonan@strose.edu
MACDONALD, Nathan ... 425-640-1423 522 D nathan.macdonald@edcc.edu
MACDONALD, Randall, M ... 863-680-4165 104 F rmacdonald1@flsouthern.edu
MACDONALD, Ronnie ... 631-656-2121 326 B ronnie.macdonald@ftc.edu
MACDONALD, William .. 218-299-4358 255 B macdonal@cord.edu
MACDONALD, William, L ... 740-366-3321 389 A macdonald.24@osu.edu
MACDONALD-DENNIS, Chris, A ... 651-696-6210 256 L cmacdona@macalester.edu
MACDONELL, Chuck, C 402-552-2693 289 H macdonell@clarksoncollege.edu
MACDONNELL, Frances 540-261-8538 512 J frances.macdonnell@svu.edu
MACDONNELL, Lisa ... 313-993-1455 250 H macdonnl@udmercy.edu
MACE, Chance ... 575-624-8214 311 K mace@nmmi.edu
MACEACHRAN, Joanne . 352-588-8462 111 L joanne.maceachran@saintleo.edu
MACEDO, Joseph ... 419-289-5090 377 A jmacedo@ashland.edu
MACELROY, Molly ... 518-388-6117 350 K macelrom@union.edu
MACEO, Brenda, K ... 213-740-5371.. 74 D maceo@usc.edu
MACEWAN, Bonnie ... 334-844-1714.... 1 G macewbj@auburn.edu
MACFARLAND, Randolph, M ... 303-762-6900.. 82 C randy.macfarland@denverseminary.edu
MACFIE, Thomas, E ... 931-598-1274 460 I tmacfie@sewanee.edu
MACGILLIVRAY, Diane, N ... 617-373-2520 235 D
MACH, Stella ... 312-935-4180 157 A smach@robertmorris.edu
MACH, Thomas ... 937-766-7936 378 K macht@cedarville.edu
MACHA, Barry ... 940-397-6225 478 G barry.macha@mwsu.edu
MACHACEK, Jennifer ... 920-748-8185 538 I machacekj@ripon.edu
MACHADO, Alyson ... 808-544-1126 135 C amachado@hpu.edu
MACHALSKI, Thomas ... 248-683-0311 250 G tmachalski@sscms.edu
MACHAMER, Claire ... 336-770-3374 372 B machamerc@uncsa.edu
MACHAN, Mark ... 937-376-6591 379 D mmachan@centralstate.edu
MACHELL, James ... 405-974-5701 403 G jmachell@uco.edu
MACHEN, Paul ... 210-486-2157 467 B pmachen@alamo.edu
MACHI, Jeffrey ... 212-650-7125 318 G jmachi@ccny.cuny.edu
MACHIA, Michael ... 580-628-6291 399 E michael.machia@noc.edu
MACHIELSON, Allen, J . 260-982-5052 170 a ajmachielson@manchester.edu
MACHIN, Hector ... 787-746-1400 552 I hmachin@huertas.edu
MACHLIS, Gedelyah ... 718-232-7800 353 F
MACHNIK, Michael, E .. 908-526-1200 305 G Mike.Machnik@raritanval.edu
MACHOVSKY, Robert ... 660-562-1248 280 A alumni@nwmissouri.edu
MACHT, Barbara, E ... 240-500-2000 215 C bemacht@hagerstowncc.edu
MACHTLEY, Ronald, K .. 401-232-6008 441 B rmac@bryant.edu
MACHUSAK, Janice, M . 313-927-1443 246 D jmachusak@marygrove.edu
MACIAG, Clark ... 704-971-8500 355 J cmaciag@charlottelaw.edu
MACIAS, Anita ... 412-563-6673 131 F amacias@southuniversity.edu
MACIAS, Benjamin ... 626-914-8611.. 38 L bmacias@citruscollege.edu
MACIAS, Erica ... 509-865-0420 523 C macias_e@heritage.edu
MACIAS, Sandy ... 650-961-9300.. 58 B smacias@paloaltou.edu
MACIAS, Tom ... 760-757-2121.. 54 G tmacias@miracosta.edu
MACIAS, Trisha ... 719-549-2951.. 81 F trisha.macias@csupueblo.edu
MACIEJ-HINER, Marian, G ... 608-342-1302 540 D maciejhm@uwplatt.edu
MACIEJEWSKI, Felice, E ... 708-524-6873 144 C fmaciejewski@dom.edu
MACIEJEWSKI, Kathryn . 906-932-4231 243 B KathrynM@gogebic.edu
MACIEL, Rene ... 210-924-4338 469 B rene.maciel@bua.edu
MACIK, Lillian ... 254-867-4893 487 G lillian.macik@systems.tstc.edu
MACINNIS, Stewart, D .. 540-464-7207 518 A macinnissd@vmi.edu
MACINTOSH, Kay, H ... 410-810-7408 221 D kmacintosh2@washcoll.edu
MACIULAITIS, Mark ... 631-632-6090 344 C mark.maciulaitis@stonybrook.edu
MACK, Arlene ... 559-453-2044.. 45 E arlene.mack@fresno.edu
MACK, Carol ... 843-525-8250 449 E cmack@tcl.edu
MACK, Cindy ... 716-614-6731 336 D cmack@niagaracc.suny.edu
MACK, Craig ... 617-732-2929 233 E craig.mack@mcphs.edu
MACK, Hailey ... 208-535-5337 138 B hailey.mack@my.eitc.edu
MACK, Jeffrey, A ... 813-974-2539 116 B jmack@admin.usf.edu
MACK, Johnny ... 503-399-6243 404 L johnny.mack@chemeketa.edu
MACK, Jon ... 610-917-1467 438 G jmack@valleyforge.edu
MACK, Joseph ... 607-431-4209 327 B mackj@hartwick.edu
MACK, Joseph, J ... 570-674-6336 426 D jmack@misericordia.edu
MACK, Kari ... 845-687-5214 350 I mackk@sunyulster.edu
MACK, Kimberly, J ... 252-536-6399 363 B kmack219@halifaxcc.edu
MACK, Lesley, A ... 414-955-8733 537 C lmack@mcw.edu
MACK, Marie ... 701-777-2746 373 G 1120mgr@follett.com
MACK, Marva ... 973-877-3346 302 F mack@essex.edu
MACK, Melvin ... 803-934-3401 447 K mmack@morris.edu
MACK, Qing, L ... 860-253-3008.. 88 H qmack@asnuntuck.edu
MACK, Sharon, K ... 207-255-1327 212 G sharon.mack@maine.edu
MACK, Teresa ... 803-793-5106 445 F mackt@denmarktech.edu
MACK, Tom ... 803-641-3479 450 C TomM@usca.edu
MACK-HISGEN, Maura .. 518-262-5033 314 I mmack@mail.amc.edu
MACKAY, Jeff ... 503-883-2436 406 I jmackay@linfield.edu
MACKE, Charles ... 931-372-3414 462 A cmacke@tntech.edu
MACKEITH, Peter ... 479-575-2702.. 23 G mackeith@uark.edu
MACKEL, Thomas, J ... 678-839-6252 133 F tmackel@westga.edu
MACKELWICH, Danielle 360-779-9993 524 C dmackelwich@ncad.edu
MACKEN, Jennifer ... 303-914-6600.. 85 C jen.macken@rrcc.edu
MACKENZIE, Lorie ... 315-229-5600 341 E lmackenzie@stlawu.edu
MACKERETH, Anne ... 952-885-5417 263 I amackereth@nwhealth.edu
MACKERSIE, Chris ... 253-912-3655 525 C cmackers@pierce.ctc.edu
MACKESY, Francis, J ... 904-620-2800 116 A f.mackesy@unf.edu

MAGHSOODI, Amin ...... 323-563-4842.. 38 C
aminmaghsoodi@cdrewu.edu
MAGHSOUD,
Amanda, F .... 803-323-4891 451 I
maghsouda@winthrop.edu
MAGID, Bruce, R .... 781-736-2256 224 F
bmagid@brandeis.edu
MAGIDA, David .... 802-485-2145 502 G
davem@norwich.edu
MAGIE, CM, Sandra, C 713-686-4345 493 J
smagie@stthom.edu
MAGIERA, Steve, L .... 239-590-1119 114 F
smagiera@fgcu.edu
MAGILL, Jim .... 828-298-3325 373 A
jmagill@warren-wilson.edu
MAGILL, M. Elizabeth ... 650-723-2300.. 68 G
MAGLIONE, Joyce .... 973-408-3631 301 J
jmaglion@drew.edu
MAGLISH, Mike .... 208-376-7731 137 D
mmaglish@boisebible.edu
MAGLIULO, Sabrina ..... 201-360-4181 303 A
smagliulo@hccc.edu
MAGNAN, Carolyn .... 860-832-3715.. 88 D
magnanc@ccsu.edu
MAGNER, Brent .... 402-363-5636 294 G
brent.magner@york.edu
MAGNER, Brent, N .... 402-363-5636 294 G
brent.magner@york.edu
MAGNER, Kevin .... 714-867-5009.. 67 C
MAGNER, Lois, B .... 620-417-1011 191 A
lois.magner@sccc.edu
MAGNER, Michael .... 978-837-5019 233 G
magnerm@merrimack.edu
MAGNER, Timothy .... 318-813-3543 205 D
tmagne@lsuhsc.edu
MAGNUS, Keith, B .... 317-940-9385 164 L
kmagnus@butler.edu
MAGNUSON, Audrey, J 210-458-6846 494 D
AUDREY.MAGNUSON@UTSA.EDU
MAGNUSON, Dave .... 803-754-4100 445 D
MAGNUSON,
Jacquelyn .... 651-641-8892 255 C
magnuson@csp.edu
MAGNUSON, Kelly, J ... 320-222-6094 261 B
kelly.magnuson@ridgewater.edu
MAGNUSON, Kendyl .... 760-744-1150.. 58 D
kmagnuson@palomar.edu
MAGNUSON, Matthew .. 559-934-2403.. 76 B
matthewmagnuson@whccd.edu
MAGNUSON, Nancy ..... 410-337-6364 215 B
nmagnuso@goucher.edu
MAGNUSON, Nancy, M 314-516-5671 284 B
magnuson@umsl.edu
MAGNUSSON, Selena ... 706-295-6866 125 F
smagnusson@gntc.edu
MAGOON, Don .... 919-735-5151 367 A
djmagoon@waynecc.edu
MAGOON, Maggie .... 989-386-6622 247 B
mmagoon@midmich.edu
MAGOULIAS, Christina . 217-424-6244 153 A
christiemagoulias@millikin.edu
MAGRETTA, Dawn .... 586-445-7302 246 A
magrettad@macomb.edu
MAGUET, Kathryn, L ..... 570-577-3700 413 E
kathryn.maguet@bucknell.edu
MAGUIRE, Eric, G .... 717-291-3953 418 J
eric.maguire@fandm.edu
MAGUIRE, Karen .... 212-355-1501 318 A
kmaguire@christies.edu
MAGUIRE, Ken .... 575-624-7160 310 J
ken.maguire@roswell.enmu.edu
MAGUIRE, Kenneth .... 575-624-7328 310 J
ken.maguire@roswell.enmu.edu
MAGUIRE, Kevin, C .... 617-627-3502 237 C
kevin.maguire@tufts.edu
MAGUIRE, Trish .... 575-562-2165 310 I
trish.maguire@enmu.edu
MAGUSIAK, Henry .... 724-738-4898 432 A
henry.magusiak@sru.edu
MAH, Al .... 323-241-5238.. 51 I
mahac@lasc.edu
MAHAFFEY, Angela .... 304-473-8100 534 G
mahaffey_a@wvwc.edu
MAHAFFEY, Danny .... 225-578-3962 204 L
dmahaf1@lsu.edu
MAHAFFEY, Dean .... 205-329-7950.... 3 C
dean.mahaffey@ecacolleges.com
MAHAFFEY, Liz .... 706-233-7974 131 C
lmahaffey@shorter.edu
MAHALINGAM,
Shankar .... 256-824-6474.... 9 A
Shankar.Mahalingam@uah.edu
MAHAN, Amy, J .... 501-882-8880.. 19 E
ajmahan@asub.edu
MAHAN, Christine, P ... 610-341-1706 418 A
cmahan@eastern.edu
MAHAN, David .... 718-862-7597 331 H
david.mahan@manhattan.edu
MAHAN, Forest .... 843-921-6919 448 B
fmahan@netc.edu
MAHAN, Karl .... 806-720-7122 478 A
karl.mahan@lcu.edu
MAHAN, Kim, B .... 806-371-5050 467 E
kbmahan@actx.edu
MAHAN, Lisa .... 317-738-8018 166 B
lmahan@franklincollege.edu
MAHAN, Marilyn .... 785-320-4501 189 C
marilynmahan@matc.net
MAHAN, Melissa .... 210-784-1350 486 B
melissa.mahan@tamusa.tamus.edu
MAHAN, Michael .... 678-359-5466 126 E
mmahan@gordonstate.edu
MAHAN, Mickie .... 417-455-5536 274 B
MickieMahan@Crowder.edu
MAHAR, Kate .... 530-242-7769.. 66 C
kmahar@shastacollege.edu
MAHARAJ, Peter .... 714-241-6297.. 40 B
pmaharaj@coastline.edu
MAHARAJ,
Sandhya (Sandy), G .. 304-766-3236 533 C
smaharaj@wvstateu.edu
MAHARAS, Marian .... 303-404-5285.. 82 J
marian.maharas@frontrange.edu
MAHDI, Johnni, F .... 315-792-3209 351 G
jmahdi@utica.edu
MAHDI, Syed .... 803-705-4576 443 F
mahdis@benedict.edu
MAHER, Brian .... 973-278-5400 300 C
bdm@berkeleycollege.edu
MAHER, Brian .... 631-420-2507 348 B
brian.maher@farmingdale.edu
MAHER, Brian .... 973-278-5400 316 D
bdm@berkeleycollege.edu
MAHER, Hannah .... 309-457-2286 153 B
hmaher@monmouthcollege.edu
MAHER, CM, James ..... 716-286-8350 336 E
jjm@niagara.edu
MAHER, James, M .... 989-964-2222 249 G
jimmaher@svsu.edu
MAHER, Jason .... 641-269-3450 178 I
maherjas@grinnell.edu
MAHER, Jeremiah, J .... 530-752-7596.. 71 A
jeremiah.maher@ucdmc.ucdavis.edu
MAHER, John .... 304-696-4748 532 H
maherj@marshall.edu
MAHER, Judith .... 724-805-2900 435 B
judith.maher@email.stvincent.edu
MAHER, Mary .... 410-837-5392 221 B
mmaher@ubalt.edu
MAHER, Peter .... 314-246-8622 285 G
maherp@webster.edu
MAHER, Stella .... 908-737-2586 303 C
smaher@kean.edu
MAHER, Susan .... 218-726-8981 264 G
smaher@d.umn.edu
MAHER, Tom .... 518-454-5216 322 C
mahert@strose.edu
MAHER, Tracy .... 701-854-8039 375 F
tracym@sbci.edu
MAHER, Walter .... 210-829-3939 492 B
maher@uiwtx.edu
MAHER, William, J .... 716-888-2970 317 H
maherw@canisius.edu
MAHFOOD, Sebastian .. 860-632-3010.. 90 H
MAHITAB, Frank .... 478-825-6211 124 E
MAHLBERG, James, A .. 712-325-3218 180 B
jmahlberg@iwcc.edu
MAHLBERG, Lynn, M ... 775-753-2282 295 D
lynn.mahlberg@gbcnv.edu
MAHLER, Craig .... 615-844-5292 466 G
cmahler@welch.edu
MAHLER, Greg .... 765-983-1318 165 H
gregm@earlham.edu
MAHLER, Stephen, J .... 337-482-6418 208 F
mahler@louisiana.edu
MAHLER, Steve .... 337-482-6780 208 F
mahler@louisiana.edu
MAHLMEISTER,
Kenneth, J .... 718-990-5883 340 G
mahlmeik@stjohns.edu
MAHON, Edward, G ..... 330-672-4704 384 H
emahon@kent.edu
MAHON, Patricia, G ..... 605-394-2416 454 B
patricia.mahon@sdsmt.edu
MAHON, Steven .... 318-342-5350 209 A
smahon@ulm.edu
MAHONE-LEIWS,
Gerald .... 254-526-1166 470 E
gerald.mahone-lewis@ctcd.edu
MAHONEY, Annie .... 215-884-8942 440 E
registrar@woninstitute.edu
MAHONEY, Deirdre, M . 231-995-1184 248 C
dmahoney@nmc.edu
MAHONEY, Erica .... 570-558-1818 418 I
emahoney@fortisinstitute.edu
MAHONEY, Jack .... 518-276-6790 339 D
mahonj@rpi.edu
MAHONEY, Janet .... 732-571-5271 303 G
jmahoney@monmouth.edu
MAHONEY, John .... 530-898-5749.. 33 A
jmahoney@csuchico.edu
MAHONEY, John .... 940-552-6291 496 B
jmahoney@vernoncollege.edu
MAHONEY, JR.,
John, L .... 617-552-3100 224 B
john.mahoney.2@bc.edu
MAHONEY, Kathleen ..... 603-899-4246 297 H
Mahonek@franklinpierce.edu
MAHONEY, Kelly .... 401-874-5053 442 E
kellymahoney@uri.edu
MAHONEY, Lynn .... 323-343-3800.. 34 A
lynn.mahoney@cslanet.calstatela.edu
MAHONEY, Michael ...... 714-816-0366.. 70 D
michael.mahoney@trident.edu
MAHONEY, Michelle, L 815-740-3372 162 F
mmahoney@stfrancis.edu
MAHONEY, Oluyemi ..... 603-656-6028 298 F
omahoney@anselm.edu
MAHONEY, Paul, G ...... 434-924-7343 514 A
pgm9h@Virginia.EDU
MAHONEY, Peter, E ..... 724-805-2241 435 B
peter.mahoney@email.stvincent.edu
MAHONEY, Sharon, A .. 508-767-7322 222 D
shmahone@assumption.edu
MAHONEY, Thomas ...... 609-771-2734 301 E
tmahoney@tcnj.edu
MAHONY, Daniel, F ..... 803-323-2225 451 I
mahonyd@winthrop.edu
MAHONY, Daniel, F ..... 330-672-2202 384 H
dmahony@kent.edu
MAHONY, James .... 517-264-3525 238 H
jmahony@adrian.edu
MAI, Bill .... 307-766-5766 546 K
william.mai@uwyo.edu
MAI, Brent .... 503-493-6560 405 E
bmai@cu-portland.edu
MAI, Uyen .... 909-274-4121.. 54 J
umai@mtsac.edu
MAIDEN, Michael .... 732-263-5285 303 G
mmaiden@monmouth.edu
MAIELLO, Gabriella ...... 800-431-8488.. 28 D
MAIENSHEIN,
Richard, W .... 215-887-5511 439 E
rmaienshein@wts.edu
MAIER, Mark .... 517-607-2445 243 J
mmaier@hillsdale.edu
MAIER, Richard, P .... 478-757-2083 134 E
rmaier@wesleyancollege.edu
MAIER-O'SHEA,
Kathryn .... 773-244-5582 154 G
kmaier@northpark.edu
MAIERHOFER, Jean ...... 763-488-2633 258 G
jean.maierhofer@hennepintech.edu
MAIETTA, Heather .... 978-837-5038 233 G
maiettah@merrimack.edu
MAIGAARD, Brenda ...... 785-864-4700 191 G
bmaigaard@ku.edu
MAILEN, Debbie .... 423-697-4487 462 C
deborah.mailen@chattanoogastate.edu
MAILHOT, John .... 413-748-3145 236 H
jmailhot@springfieldcollege.edu
MAILICK, Marsha, R ..... 608-262-1044 539 D
mmailick@wisc.edu
MAILLET, Becky .... 504-278-6477 204 B
bmaillet@nunez.edu
MAILLET, Pierrette .... 470-578-4698 127 M
pmaillet@kennesaw.edu
MAILLOUX, Colin, C .... 904-632-3232 105 A
cmaillou@fscj.edu
MAIMON, Elaine, P ...... 708-534-4130 145 D
emaimon@govst.edu
MAIMONE, Charles, A .. 336-334-5200 371 C
camaimon@uncg.edu
MAIN, Gregory .... 405-878-5422 402 A
president@stgregorys.edu
MAIN, Mary .... 207-786-6140 209 F
mmain@bates.edu
MAIN, Melissa .... 301-624-2745 214 I
mmain@frederick.edu
MAIN, Nathan .... 269-927-8169 245 E
nmain@lakemichigancollege.edu
MAIN, Sajid .... 708-534-4515 145 D
smain@govst.edu
MAINCA, Daniel .... 213-383-8999.. 26 E
MAINE, Kate .... 706-864-1950 133 A
kate.maine@ung.edu
MAINENTI, David .... 516-299-4212 330 F
David.Mainenti@liu.edu
MAIO, James .... 315-792-5401 333 D
jmaio@mvcc.edu
MAIORISI, Stephen, M . 401-863-1297 441 A
stephen_maiorisi@brown.edu
MAIR, Bernard, A .... 202-806-6700.. 96 B
bernard.mair@howard.edu
MAIR, Dave .... 804-819-4929 514 G
dmair@vccs.edu
MAIR, Rob .... 520-325-0123.. 17 Q
rmair@suva.edu
MAISEL, Jacqueline, M 410-543-6150 220 E
jmmaisel@salisbury.edu
MAISON, Amy .... 229-225-3977 132 C
amaison@southernregional.edu
MAISTO, Jeremy, A ...... 717-867-6215 423 I
maisto@lvc.edu
MAITLAND, Jason, R .... 585-785-1437 325 E
jason.maitland@flcc.edu
MAITLAND, Tina, A ...... 313-993-1005 250 H
maitlata@udmercy.edu
MAIURI, Geary .... 586-445-7579 246 A
maiurig@macomb.edu
MAIZE, Kay .... 402-481-8602 289 C
kay.maize@bryanhealthcollege.edu
MAJAK, Julieta .... 845-257-3295 344 A
majakj@newpaltz.edu
MAJEBE, Mary Cissy ..... 828-225-3993 356 C
president@daoisttraditions.edu
MAJEROWITZ,
Mordechai .... 718-851-8721 353 C
MAJERUS, Melissa .... 320-308-5922 261 F
mmajerus@sctcc.edu
MAJEWSKI, Deborah .... 508-999-9293 228 H
dmajewski@umassd.edu
MAJEWSKI, John .... 805-893-4327.. 72 D
majewski@ltsc.ucsb.edu
MAJEWSKI, Marc .... 415-338-2596.. 36 A
majewski@sfsu.edu
MAJEWSKIE, Michelle .. 920-923-8083 537 A
mmajewski@marianuniversity.edu
MAJID, Anouar .... 206-221-4447 213 B
amajid@une.edu
MAJKA, David, R .... 412-397-5443 434 B
majka@rmu.edu
MAJOR, Adrienne .... 802-387-7143 502 A
amajor@landmark.edu
MAJOR, JR.,
Anthony, W .... 505-786-4327 311 G
amajor@navajotech.edu
MAJOR, Carla .... 504-762-3003 203 F
cmajor@dcc.edu
MAJOR, Carrie .... 865-251-1800 460 J
cmajor@southcollegetn.edu
MAJOR, Lesa, H .... 812-855-8111 167 J
lhmajor@indiana.edu
MAJOR, Michael, W ..... 989-964-7130 249 G
mmajor@svsu.edu
MAJOR, Phillip .... 561-803-2034 109 G
phillip_major@pba.edu
MAJOR, Samantha .... 828-835-4203 366 F
smajor@tricountycc.edu
MAJOR, Wayne .... 785-272-0889 185 E
MAJOR-KELLY, Shanee . 703-892-5100.. 96 H
MAJORS, Jodie .... 270-852-3142 198 A
jmajors@kwc.edu
MAJZNER, Kathy .... 903-233-4381 477 G
kathymajzner@letu.edu
MAKARECHI, Pejman .... 215-503-7841 436 F
pejman.makarechi@jefferson.edu
MAKAROFF, JR.,
Christopher, A .... 513-529-4432 386 K
makaroca@miamioh.edu
MAKER, Caryn .... 412-268-1885 414 J
cmaker@andrew.cmu.edu
MAKER, Laurie .... 508-588-9100 232 A
MAKHIJA, Anil, K .... 614-292-7899 389 A
makhija.1@osu.edu
MAKI, Bill .... 218-471-0015 258 H
wmaki@nhed.edu
MAKI, David, W .... 906-227-1262 248 B
dmaki@nmu.edu
MAKI, Jackie .... 817-515-5379 484 B
jackie.maki@tccd.edu
MAKI, William .... 218-471-0015 259 D
wmaki@nhed.edu
MAKI, William, D .... 218-471-0015 259 B
wmaki@nhed.edu
MAKIN, Linda .... 801-863-8457 500 B
linda.makin@uvu.edu
MAKOFSKE, Rose .... 215-619-7383 426 E
rmakofske@mc3.edu
MAKOWSKI, Sharon ..... 203-576-5478.. 91 H
smakowski@stvincentscollege.edu
MAKREZ, Heather .... 978-934-4809 229 A
heather_makrez@uml.edu
MAKSYMICZ, Kathy, E .. 330-287-1283 389 B
maksymicz.1@osu.edu
MAKSYMIK, Michelle .... 814-262-3820 429 K
mmaksymik@pennhighlands.edu
MAKUAKANE-LUNDIN,
Gail .... 808-932-7445 135 I
gailml@hawaii.edu
MALAFA, Jeanette .... 217-652-6467 163 A
j-malafa@wiu.edu
MALANI, Upendra .... 703-284-1491 510 B
upendra.malani@marymount.edu
MALARA, Kathleen .... 718-817-4160 326 C
kmalara@fordham.edu
MALARET, Frank .... 916-558-2402.. 53 B
malarej@scc.losrios.edu
MALARTE-FELDMAN,
Claire, L .... 603-862-2398 299 B
clmf@cisunix.unh.edu

MANCOSH, Bridget .... 412-392-3992 433 F
bmancosh@pointpark.edu
MANCOSKE, Ronald ...... 504-286-5376 207 B
rmancoske@suno.edu
MANCUSO, Mary .... 607-436-3573 344 B
mary.mancuso@oneonta.edu
MANCUSO, Sandra, L ... 305-899-3072.. 99 B
smancuso@barry.edu
MANCUSO, Tracy .... 928-532-6170.. 16 E
tracy.mancuso@npc.edu
MANDAKOVIC,
Tomislav .... 305-899-3532.. 99 B
tmandakovic@barry.edu
MANDALA, Jim .... 973-408-3395 301 J
jmandala@drew.edu
MANDARINO, James .... 505-454-3199 311 H
jfmandarino@nmhu.edu
MANDAYAM,
Shreekanth .... 856-256-5150 306 D
shreek@rowan.edu
MANDEL, Carol, A .... 212-998-2444 336 C
carol.mandel@nyu.edu
MANDEL, Christine .... 315-655-7250 317 J
cmandel@cazenovia.edu
MANDEL, Christine .... 315-655-7174 317 J
cmandel@cazenovia.edu
MANDEL, Jeffrey .... 570-389-4311 430 B
jmandel@bloomu.edu
MANDEL, Larry .... 562-951-4430.. 32 D
lmandel@calstate.edu
MANDEL, Maud .... 401-863-2573 441 A
maud_mandel@brown.edu
MANDELKERN, Michael 714-432-5786.. 40 D
mmandelkern@occ.cccd.edu
MANDELL, Charlotte ..... 978-934-3954 229 A
Charlotte_Mandell@uml.edu
MANDEREN,
Michael, C .... 440-775-8413 388 B
michael.manderen@oberlin.edu
MANDERSCHEID,
David, C .... 614-292-1677 389 A
manderscheid.1@osu.edu
MANDEVILLE, Kenneth . 304-327-4067 532 D
kmandeville@bluefieldstate.edu
MANDEVILLE,
Richard, G .... 509-777-4536 529 A
rmandeville@whitworth.edu
MANDEVILLE, Steve ...... 314-529-6849 277 B
shmandeville@maryville.edu
MANDEVILLE-GAMBLE,
Steve .... 951-827-3221.. 72 A
steve.mandeville-gamble@ucr.edu
MANDL, Michael, J .... 404-778-4432 124 D
michael.mandl@emoryhealthcare.org
MANDRELL, Jon, D ...... 815-835-6344 158 I
jon.d.mandrell@svcc.edu
MANDY, Lisa .... 408-864-8403.. 44 N
mandylisa@deanza.edu
MANDYAM, Raja .... 512-454-1188 468 A
info@aoma.edu
MANER, Edward, L .... 863-667-5400 113 K
elmaner@seu.edu
MANERI, Wendy, L .... 315-568-3262 334 F
wmaneri@nycc.edu
MANESS, Terry, S .... 254-710-1211 469 D
terry_maness@baylor.edu
MANESS, Thomas .... 541-737-4279 408 F
thomas.maness@oregonstate.edu
MANEV, Ivan, M .... 207-581-1968 212 C
imanev@maine.edu
MANEY, Robert, L .... 814-863-6188 428 C
rlm1@psu.edu
MANFREDO, Francis, A 315-859-4144 327 A
fmanfred@hamilton.edu
MANGAN, Kathryn .... 510-567-6174.. 69 D
kmangan@sum.edu
MANGAN, William .... 712-279-5402 176 B
william.mangan@briarcliff.edu
MANGAN-FLOOD, Mary 920-923-7166 537 A
mmanganflood@marianuniversity.edu
MANGANARO, Marc ..... 504-865-3034 206 A
manganar@loyno.edu
MANGANARO, Robert .. 212-787-5300 315 A
MANGELS, Andrew, P ... 413-545-2141 228 F
amangels@admin.umass.edu
MANGELS, Kathy, M ..... 573-651-2570 282 C
kmangels@semo.edu
MANGELS, Susan .... 636-949-4939 276 L
smangels@lindenwood.edu
MANGELSDORF, Sarah . 608-262-1304 539 D
smangelsdorf@wisc.edu
MANGHAM, Kirk .... 757-490-1241 504 D
kmangham@auto.edu
MANGIACAPRA,
Vincent, P .... 203-932-7058.. 92 G
vmangiacapra@newhaven.edu
MANGINE, John, J .... 814-332-4356 411 F
jmangine@allegheny.edu
MANGINI, William .... 860-913-2005.. 90 F
bmangini@goodwin.edu
MANGINO, Christine .... 718-518-6611 319 D
cmangino@hostos.cuny.edu
MANGIONE, Robert, A .. 718-990-6308 340 G
mangionr@stjohns.edu
MANGIONE, Terri, L ..... 716-888-2130 317 H
mangiont@canisius.edu
MANGLES, Lenore .... 715-365-4637 543 G
lmangles@nicoletcollege.edu
MANGLITZ, Elaine .... 678-466-5433 122 J
elainemanglitz@clayton.edu
MANGLONA,
Gregorio, T .... 671-777-5591 549 E
safety@guamcc.edu
MANGLONA, Ross .... 670-237-6853 550 B
ross.manglona@marianas.edu
MANGLONA-PROPST,
Daisy .... 670-237-6792 550 B
daisy.propst@marianas.edu
MANGOLD, Thomas ..... 401-841-2074 548 B
MANGRUM, Kirk .... 615-794-4254 460 A
kmangrum@omorecollege.edu
MANGUM, Elmira .... 850-599-3000 114 D
MANGUM, Genita, D .... 717-736-4144 420 D
gdmangum@hacc.edu
MANGUM, Linda .... 336-334-7862 370 B
lmangum@ncat.edu
MANGUM, R. Todd ...... 215-368-5000 412 K
tmangum@biblical.edu
MANGUM, Steve .... 865-974-5061 465 D
smangum@utk.edu
MANGUS, Becky .... 620-229-6223 191 B
becky.mangus@sckans.edu
MANGUS, Christy .... 269-782-1473 250 D
cmangus@swmich.edu
MANHARDT, Joseph ..... 207-741-5598 211 D
jmanhardt@smccme.edu
MANIACI, Vincent, M ... 413-205-3202 221 G
vincent.maniaci@aic.edu
MANIAOL, Albert .... 909-384-8904.. 62 C
amaniaol@sbccd.cc.ca.us
MANIATIS, Marc .... 203-932-7218.. 92 G
mmaniatis@newhaven.edu
MANIER, Tracy, L .... 512-448-8602 481 B
tracym@stedwards.edu
MANIGAULT, Kimberly . 412-237-3001 415 G
kmanigault@ccac.edu
MANIGAULT, Kimberly . 937-376-6018 379 D
kmanigault@centralstate.edu
MANIGO, Venis .... 803-777-4115 450 B
venis.manigo@sc.edu
MANION, Andrew, P .... 630-844-5252 139 L
amanion@aurora.edu
MANION, Roger .... 619-260-7556.. 74 B
manion@sandiego.edu
MANION, Sheila, M ..... 314-977-2306 281 M
manionsm@slu.edu
MANIS, Christopher ..... 619-388-6546.. 62 E
cmanis@sdccd.edu
MANISCALCO,
Steven, J .... 607-436-2735 344 B
maniscsj@oneonta.edu
MANJONE, Amanda ...... 251-981-3771.... 3 A
amanda.manjone@columbiasouthern.edu
MANKEY, Gregory .... 573-876-7171 283 A
gmankey@stephens.edu
MANKEY, Richanne, C . 716-839-8519 323 F
rmankey@daemen.edu
MANKO, Tammy .... 724-357-2235 431 A
tammy.manko@iup.edu
MANKOWICH, James .... 205-929-3498.... 5 E
jmankowich@lawsonstate.edu
MANLEY, Andrew .... 785-309-3120 190 L
andrew.manley@salinatech.edu
MANLEY, Anna .... 541-956-7104 409 F
amanley@roguecc.edu
MANLEY, Colleen .... 315-229-5988 341 E
cmanley@stlawu.edu
MANLEY, Jennifer .... 360-596-5305 527 B
jmanley@spscc.edu
MANLEY, John .... 252-335-3266 369 F
jhmanley@ecsu.edu
MANLEY, Kelly .... 706-867-3230 133 A
kelly.manley@ung.edu
MANLEY, Kelly .... 706-310-6203 133 A
kelly.manley@ung.edu
MANLEY, Kyle .... 212-650-5040 318 G
kmanley@ccny.cuny.edu
MANLEY, Robert .... 631-244-3447 324 C
manleyr@dowling.edu
MANLEY, Thomas .... 603-899-1144 297 H
manleyt@franklinpierce.edu
MANLEY, Thomas .... 503-821-8881 408 H
presidentsoffice@pnca.edu
MANLEY-ROOK,
Stephanie .... 252-493-7383 364 H
sgmrook@email.pittcc.edu
MANN, April, S .... 601-984-1115 270 H
amann@umc.edu
MANN, Brian .... 813-253-7022 106 C
bmann@hccfl.edu
MANN, Charles, G .... 301-696-3611 215 E
mann@hood.edu
MANN, Christy .... 870-512-7867.. 19 I
christy_mann@asun.edu
MANN, Daniel, R .... 217-333-0100 162 A
danmann@illinois.edu
MANN, Deanna .... 620-227-9253 186 F
dmann@dc3.edu
MANN, Doug .... 434-592-6190 509 G
dmann@liberty.edu
MANN, Douglas .... 410-225-2352 216 F
dmann@mica.edu
MANN, Gwendolyn .... 334-229-4436.... 1 D
gmann@alasu.edu
MANN, Henrietta .... 580-774-7708 287 G
henriettamann@gmail.com
MANN, Henry, J .... 614-292-5711 389 A
mann.414@osu.edu
MANN, Janet .... 202-687-1307.. 95 E
mannj2@georgetown.edu
MANN, Jason .... 205-329-7875.... 3 C
jason.mann@ecacolleges.com
MANN, Jeanne, E .... 203-773-8516.. 87 M
mann@albertus.edu
MANN, Jeffery .... 610-789-6700 433 G
jmann@prismeducation.edu
MANN, Karen .... 502-585-9911 199 E
kmann@spalding.edu
MANN, Kevin, J .... 410-543-6202 220 E
kjmann@salisbury.edu
MANN, Lara, G .... 317-781-5760 173 I
mannlg@uindy.edu
MANN, Laura .... 507-457-5069 262 D
lmann@winona.edu
MANN, Lucretia .... 914-674-7492 332 E
lmann@mercy.edu
MANN, Mark .... 619-849-2359.. 59 K
markmann@pointloma.edu
MANN, Randy .... 254-295-4618 492 C
rmann@umhb.edu
MANN, Suellen .... 561-868-3450 109 H
manns@palmbeachstate.edu
MANN, Warrenetta, C ... 757-221-3620 506 J
wcmann@wm.edu
MANN, FSC, William .... 507-457-1503 264 B
wmann@smumn.edu
MANN FAULKNER,
Kenya, D .... 513-556-3483 393 B
kenya.faulkner@uc.edu
MANNELLA, Stephen .... 610-436-2242 432 B
smannella@wcupa.edu
MANNERING,
Susan, M .... 302-225-6232.. 94 B
manners@gbc.edu
MANNEY, Bill .... 218-262-6734 258 H
williammanney@hibbing.edu
MANNINEN, Kevin .... 906-487-7371 242 M
kevin.manninen@finlandia.edu
MANNING, Barbara ...... 252-823-5166 362 D
manningb@edgecombe.edu
MANNING, Beth .... 810-762-3150 251 E
bmanning@umflint.edu
MANNING, Carmen, K . 715-836-3671 539 E
manninck@uwec.edu
MANNING, Colleen ...... 713-646-1729 482 H
cmanning@stcl.edu
MANNING, Dan .... 704-878-3281 364 C
dmanning@mitchellcc.edu
MANNING, Danielle .... 617-573-8400 237 B
dmanning@suffolk.edu
MANNING, Dianne, M .. 413-662-5249 230 C
dianne.manning@mcla.edu
MANNING, Don .... 708-596-2000 159 D
dmanning@ssc.edu
MANNING, Gaye .... 870-574-4509.. 23 E
gmanning@sautech.edu
MANNING, Gerald .... 870-574-4516.. 23 E
gbmannin@sautech.edu
MANNING, Jason .... 518-458-5303 322 C
manningj@strose.edu
MANNING, Jean .... 501-374-6305.. 23 A
MANNING, Jean .... 513-569-1519 379 K
jean.manning@cincinnatistate.edu
MANNING, Jessica .... 325-942-2021 489 E
jessica.manning@angelo.edu
MANNING, Jessica .... 325-674-2751 466 I
jxm15c@acu.edu
MANNING, Joanne .... 617-682-1521 226 D
jmanning@eds.edu
MANNING, John .... 770-582-0434 121 H
johnm@lawmanning.com
MANNING, Karen .... 910-695-3995 365 H
manningk@sandhills.edu
MANNING, Kevin, J ...... 443-334-2203 218 E
rhubbard@stevenson.edu
MANNING,
Kimberly, M .... 848-932-1769 306 F
kim.manning@rutgers.edu
MANNING, Kirk .... 845-398-4066 341 H
kmanning@stac.edu
MANNING,
Lynn Etta, G .... 214-887-5366 473 E
lmanning@dts.edu
MANNING, Marcus .... 314-529-9313 277 B
mmanning@maryville.edu
MANNING, Mark .... 315-498-2268 337 F
m.r.manning@sunyocc.edu
MANNING, Noel, T .... 704-406-4631 356 G
ntmanning@gardner-webb.edu
MANNING, Patricia .... 850-201-8994 117 B
manningp@tcc.fl.edu
MANNING, Sandra, J ... 919-572-1625 354 F
smanning@apexsot.edu
MANNING, Scott .... 570-372-4256 435 I
manning@susqu.edu
MANNING, Shaun .... 218-477-2549 260 B
shaun.manning@mnstate.edu
MANNING, Sherron, K . 580-928-5533 402 G
sherron.manning@swosu.edu
MANNING, Sylvia .... 304-876-5107 532 I
smanning@shepherd.edu
MANNING, Terri .... 704-330-6592 361 D
terri.manning@cpcc.edu
MANNING, Tina .... 912-427-5814 123 A
tmanning@coastalpines.edu
MANNING, Vivian .... 360-992-2104 521 A
vmanning@clark.edu
MANNING, Wayne .... 580-349-1402 400 B
wemann@opsu.edu
MANNING-CLARK, Jean 303-273-3239.. 80 O
jeanmann@mines.edu
MANNING-MILLER,
Donald .... 662-252-8000 270 C
manningmiller@rustcollege.edu
MANNINO, Jessica, L .. 315-445-4130 330 B
hammonjl@lemoyne.edu
MANNINO, Sam .... 502-459-3535 200 B
smannino@sullivan.edu
MANNION, Joe .... 503-493-6233 405 E
jmannion@cu-portland.edu
MANNION, Tom, N .... 626-395-6174.. 31 D
mannion@caltech.edu
MANNISTO, Richard ..... 414-443-8788 542 I
rich.mannisto@wlc.edu
MANNLE, Frank .... 212-346-1743 337 I
fmannle@pace.edu
MANNO, Anthony .... 517-607-2625 243 J
amanno@hillsdale.edu
MANNO, Mariann, M ... 508-856-2323 229 B
mariann.manno@umassmed.edu
MANNO, Mechele .... 707-967-2911.. 55 E
mmanno@napavalley.edu
MANNO, Vincent, P .... 781-292-2509 226 G
vincent.manno@olin.edu
MANNOLINI, III,
Lawrence, P .... 570-321-4118 425 B
mannolin@lycoming.edu
MANNS, Derrick .... 985-448-5908 203 G
derrick.manns@fletcher.edu
MANOHAR, Aruna, S .... 410-323-6211 214 G
aruna.manohar@gmail.com
MANOHAR, John .... 410-323-6211 214 G
Jmanohar@faiththeological.org
MANOHAR, Norman, J .. 410-323-6211 214 G
nmanohar@faiththeological.org
MANOLIS, Lilly .... 617-327-6777 238 D
lilly_manolis@williamjames.edu
MANONI, Haydee .... 636-230-2100 277 A
haydee.manoni@logan.edu
MANORD, Wayne .... 256-352-8116.. 10 A
wayne.manord@wallacestate.edu
MANORY, Joseph .... 315-229-5896 341 E
jmanory@stlawu.edu
MANOS, Dennis, M ...... 757-871-9581 506 J
dmanos@wm.edu
MANOS, Steve .... 781-736-4404 224 F
ssmanos@brandeis.edu
MANOTTI, Ken .... 773-702-0686 161 D
kmanotti@uchicago.edu
MANOUSOS, Carol .... 713-221-8425 491 F
manousosc@uhd.edu
MANRIQUE, Santos ...... 620-768-2908 187 B
santosm@fortscott.edu
MANRIQUEZ, Chris ...... 310-243-3655.. 33 B
cmanriquez@csudh.edu
MANRY, J. Mark .... 248-218-2120 249 D
mmanry@rc.edu
MANSAPIT, Felix .... 671-482-8671 549 G
fmansapit@uguam.uog.edu
MANSDOERFER, Steve .. 503-517-1813 411 C
smansdoerfer@westernseminary.edu
MANSER,
Jacqueline, M .... 330-490-7117 395 C
jmanser@walsh.edu
MANSFIELD, Tim .... 315-228-7433 321 H
tmansfield@colgate.edu
MANSHEIM, Bill .... 719-587-7727.. 78 I
billmansheim@adams.edu
MANSHIP, James .... 651-690-8631 263 V
jlmanship@stkate.edu

MARINO, Robert .... 802-860-2751 501 F rmarino@champlain.edu
MARINUCCI, Dorothy .... 718-817-3000 326 C marinucci@fordham.edu
MARION, D. Keith .... 803-754-4100 445 D
MARION, Joseph .... 504-286-5389 207 B jmarion@suno.edu
MARION, Lucy, N .... 706-721-3771 121 C lumarion@gru.edu
MARION, Paul .... 978-934-3107 229 A paul_marion@uml.edu
MARION, Phyllis, C ..... 619-239-0391.. 36 E pmarion@cwsl.edu
MARISCALCO, Michele . 217-333-5465 162 A mmmaris@illinois.edu
MARISOL, Cortes .... 646-313-8000 321 A Marisol.Cortes@guttman.cuny.edu
MARIUCCI, Robert .... 805-546-3210.. 42 H rmariucc@cuesta.edu
MARIX, Amy .... 225-578-3486 204 M amarix@lsu.edu
MARK, Allan .... 704-461-6736 354 J allanmark@bac.edu
MARK, Joy .... 620-947-3121 191 E joym@tabor.edu
MARK, Marty .... 319-273-6258 176 A marty.mark@uni.edu
MARKANTONAKIS, Angelo .... 704-216-7222 365 F angelo.markantonakis@rccc.edu
MARKEL, Mark, D .... 608-263-6716 539 D markelm@svm.vetmed.wisc.edu
MARKELL, Dawn .... 517-338-3048 241 B dmarkell@cleary.edu
MARKER, John .... 831-582-4796.. 34 C jmarker@csumb.edu
MARKEY, John .... 210-341-1366 479 N jmarkey@ost.edu
MARKEY, Nanette .... 301-696-3620 215 E markey@hood.edu
MARKEY-GRABILL, Mindy .... 937-393-3431 391 F mmarkey@sscc.edu
MARKHAM, Amy, E ...... 508-286-8251 238 B markham_amy@wheatoncollege.edu
MARKHAM, Christopher .... 904-997-2900 105 A christopher.markham@fscj.edu
MARKHAM, Ian, S .... 703-370-6600 511 B
MARKHAM, Joseph ...... 770-962-7580 127 C jmarkham@gwinnetttech.edu
MARKIN, Karen .... 401-874-5971 442 E kmarkin@uri.edu
MARKIN, Rodney .... 402-559-7687 293 I rmarkin@unmc.edu
MARKLAND, Scott .... 937-512-5502 391 D scott.markland@sinclair.edu
MARKLE, Elizabeth .... 775-831-1314 296 F emarkle@sierranevada.edu
MARKLE, Suzanne .... 412-346-2100 433 B smarkle@pia.edu
MARKLE, William, J ..... 610-359-5113 416 G wmarkle@dccc.edu
MARKLEY, Bradley, A ... 717-766-2511 426 B bmarkley@messiah.edu
MARKLEY, Neil .... 707-664-4068.. 36 C neil.markley@sonoma.edu
MARKOVA, Cynthia ...... 408-273-2765.. 55 G cmarkova@nhu.edu
MARKOVA, Cynthia ...... 408-254-6900.. 55 G cmarkova@nhu.edu
MARKOVA, Cynthia ...... 408-273-2690.. 55 G cmarkova@nhu.edu
MARKOVA, Cynthia ...... 408-273-2718.. 55 G cmarkova@nhu.edu
MARKOVICH, Matt .... 415-485-9591.. 41 B mmarkovich@marin.edu
MARKOVITCH, Matthew 707-524-1849.. 65 C mmarkovitch@santarosa.edu
MARKOW, David .... 802-828-8535 503 D david.markow@vcfa.edu
MARKOW, Joanne .... 617-746-1990 227 G joanne.markow@hult.edu
MARKOWITZ, Marianne 315-448-5040 341 C
MARKOWSKI, Vincent .. 201-684-7432 305 F vmarkows@ramapo.edu
MARKS, Andrea, M ...... 210-567-7020 495 B marksa@uthscsa.edu
MARKS, Ellen .... 906-487-2500 247 A ebmarks@mtu.edu
MARKS, Erica .... 845-257-3240 344 A markse@newpaltz.edu
MARKS, Howard .... 432-552-2371 495 F marks_h@utpb.edu
MARKS, Janice, L .... 443-518-4617 215 F jmarks@howardcc.edu
MARKS, Jerome .... 703-284-3843 510 B jerome.marks@marymount.edu
MARKS, John .... 414-382-6360 534 I john.marks@alverno.edu
MARKS, Leota .... 913-288-7647 188 G lmarks@kckcc.edu
MARKS, Lilly .... 303-724-5369.. 86 G lilly.marks@ucdenver.edu
MARKS, Michelle .... 703-993-8705 507 K mmarks@gmu.edu
MARKS, Patrice .... 908-526-1200 305 G Patrice.Marks@raritanval.edu
MARKS, Ronald .... 504-865-5314 207 F rmarks@tulane.edu
MARKS, Rondah .... 601-984-1012 270 H rmarks@umc.edu
MARKS, Sandra .... 562-860-2451.. 37 L smarks@cerritos.edu
MARKS, Spider .... 602-557-9200.. 18 H spider.marks@phoenix.edu
MARKS, Steven .... 718-780-7507 317 A steven.marks@brooklaw.edu
MARKSBERRY, Annette . 513-745-4261 396 B marksberrya@xavier.edu
MARKSBURY, Rick .... 504-865-5555 207 F rmarksby@tulane.edu
MARKSON, Alison, W .. 617-333-2120 225 F amarkson1109@curry.edu
MARKULY, Mark .... 206-296-5330 526 F markulym@seattleu.edu
MARKUM, Michael .... 254-298-8291 484 C mmarkum@templejc.edu
MARKWOOD, Chris ...... 706-507-8950 123 D markwood_chris@columbusstate.edu
MARKWORD, Theresa ... 530-242-7510.. 66 C tmarkword@shastacollege.edu
MARLAIRE, Natalyn, M . 715-852-1399 542 M nmarlaire@cvtc.edu
MARLAND, Jaime .... 401-427-6954 442 B jmarland@risd.edu
MARLATT, Julie .... 630-942-2800 142 F
MARLER, Dan .... 970-542-3157.. 84 A dan.marler@morgancc.edu
MARLER, Eric .... 808-675-3708 134 M eric.marler@byuh.edu
MARLER, Janet .... 609-343-4937 299 G jmarler@atlantic.edu
MARLER, Kari .... 801-627-8392 498 O marlerk@owatc.edu
MARLETT, Keith .... 607-729-1581 324 A kmarlett@davisny.edu
MARLETTE, Marnie, S ... 336-841-4683 357 E mmarlett@highpoint.edu
MARLEY, Chad .... 307-778-1346 546 F cmarley@lccc.wy.edu
MARLEY, Robert .... 573-341-4138 284 C marleyr@mst.edu
MARLING, Garet .... 510-780-4500.. 50 G gmarling@lifewest.edu
MARLING, Janet .... 706-864-1574 133 A janet.marling@ung.edu
MARLING, Janet .... 706-864-1818 133 A janet.marling@ung.edu
MARLOW, Dan .... 816-279-7000 271 H dan@abtu.edu
MARLOW, Jean .... 859-622-1986 194 L jean.marlow@eku.edu
MARLOW, Peter .... 619-260-7460.. 74 B petermarlow@sandiego.edu
MARLOWE, Bethany ...... 803-323-4503 451 I marloweb@winthrop.edu
MARLOWE, Channing, H .... 205-391-2256.... 7 A cmarlowe@sheltonstate.edu
MARLOWE, June .... 314-991-6245 141 D jmarlowe@chamberlain.edu
MARLOWE, Monica .... 228-702-1775 271 F mmarlowe@wmcarey.edu
MARLOWE, Robert, W .. 843-953-2502 445 B marlower@cofc.edu
MARMARELLI, Beth ...... 313-593-5542 251 D bethmar@umich.edu
MARMO, Emily .... 845-569-3262 333 I emily.marmo@msmc.edu
MARMOLEJO, William .. 323-953-4000.. 51 E marmolwa@lacitycollege.edu
MARMUR, Michael .... 212-824-2215 327 C mmarmur@huc.edu
MARNEN, Ted .... 814-871-7599 419 A marnen001@gannon.edu
MARNEY, Katherine ...... 573-288-6478 274 C kmarney@culver.edu
MARNICH, Darlene .... 412-392-3474 433 F dmarnich@pointpark.edu
MAROHL, Matthew .... 507-786-3092 264 C marohl@stolaf.edu
MAROLDO, Brian .... 516-686-7449 335 F bmaroldo@nyit.edu
MARONI, Paul, L .... 860-439-2044.. 90 D plmar@conncoll.edu
MAROTTA, Marsha .... 413-572-5213 230 F mmarotta@westfield.ma.edu
MAROVICH, Diana .... 219-785-5373 172 A dmarovich@pnc.edu
MARPLE, Bradley .... 214-648-2646 496 A bradley.marple@utsouthwestern.edu
MARQUARDT, Brian ...... 231-591-3745 242 L BrianMarquardt@ferris.edu
MARQUARDT, Christopher .... 315-229-5250 341 E cmarquardt@stlawu.edu
MARQUARDT, Clifford, L .... 740-377-2520 392 C cmark@zoominternet.net
MARQUARDT, Jeanne ... 505-272-2321 313 H jmarquar@unm.edu
MARQUARDT, Richard .. 570-465-2344 422 G marquardtr@lackawanna.edu
MARQUARDT, Scott, E . 608-342-1584 540 D marquars@uwplatt.edu
MARQUARDT, Shelly .... 714-547-9625.. 30 F smarquardt@calcoast.edu
MARQUART, James, W 409-880-8398 488 F james.marquart@lamar.edu
MARQUES, Javier .... 305-348-2111 114 G javier.marques@fiu.edu
MARQUES, Jeffrey .... 413-775-1700 231 E marquesj@gcc.mass.edu
MARQUEZ, Dianne .... 575-492-2841 311 J dmarquez@nmjc.edu
MARQUEZ, JR., Felix, J .... 407-251-0007 109 F
MARQUEZ, Ivan .... 914-337-9300 323 A ivan.marquez@concordia-ny.edu
MARQUEZ, Kenneth, L . 719-587-7227.. 78 I klmarque@adams.edu
MARQUEZ, Krishna ...... 787-746-1400 552 I kmarquez@huertas.edu
MARQUEZ, Lonnie, G ... 575-835-5606 311 I lmarquez@admin.nmt.edu
MARQUEZ, Moses .... 505-454-5312 311 B mmarquez@luna.edu
MARQUEZ, Nelson .... 863-734-1509 119 A marquezNJ@webber.edu
MARQUEZ, Nitza .... 787-786-3030 556 E nimarquez@ucb.edu.pr
MARQUEZ, Nora .... 650-433-3865.. 58 B nmarquez@paloaltou.edu
MARQUEZ, Patricia ...... 619-260-7795.. 74 B pmarquez@sandiego.edu
MARQUEZ, Stephanie ... 619-961-4263.. 69 J smarquez@tjsl.edu
MARQUEZ, Walter .... 909-869-4947.. 32 F wmmarquez@cpp.edu
MARQUEZ BELL, Mary . 516-876-3082 345 E bellm@oldwestbury.edu
MARQUEZ-SCALLY, Marline .... 505-984-6075 312 J registrar@sjc.edu
MARQUIS, Jack .... 814-944-5643 440 I john.marquis@yti.edu
MARQUIS, Lauren .... 617-879-2328 238 C lmarquis@wheelock.edu
MARQUIS, Susan .... 310-393-0411.. 58 E smarquis@rand.org
MARQUSEE, Steven, J .. 315-267-2231 346 C marqussj@potsdam.edu
MARR, J, R .... 704-820-0726 354 J jrmarr@bac.edu
MARR, Jay .... 502-456-6506 200 B jmarr@sullivan.edu
MARR, Jena .... 405-422-1265 401 H jena.marr@redlandscc.edu
MARR, John .... 216-987-2296 381 A john.marr@tri-c.edu
MARR, JR., John, W .... 216-987-2296 381 A john.marr-jr@tri-c.edu
MARR, Ronda .... 209-946-2206.. 73 C rmarr@pacific.edu
MARRA, Angelina .... 718-261-5800 316 K amarra@bramsonort.edu
MARRA, Joseph .... 845-574-4156 339 I jmarra2@sunyrockland.edu
MARRABLE, Laquana ..... 678-839-6403 133 F lmarrabl@westga.edu
MARRANT, Dale .... 913-234-0612 185 N dale.marrant@cleveland.edu
MARRAPESE, Patricia .... 607-777-2510 343 D pmarra@binghamton.edu
MARRAPODI, Michael .. 617-984-1634 235 H mmarrapodi@quincycollege.edu
MARRERO, Argelio .... 860-906-5125.. 89 A amarrero@ccc.commnet.edu
MARRERO, Kyle .... 678-839-6442 133 F kmarrero@westga.edu
MARRERO, Lisette .... 787-894-2828 558 F lisette.marrero@upr.edu
MARRERO, Petrina .... 814-824-2369 425 L pwilliams@mercyhurst.edu
MARRERO, Rene .... 787-841-2000 555 F rene_marrero@pucpr.edu
MARRERO, Wilma .... 787-765-1915 554 E wmarrero@opto.inter.edu
MARRETT, Clifford .... 860-465-5577.. 88 E marrettc@easternct.edu
MARRIN, John .... 719-336-1511.. 83 N john.marrin@lamarcc.edu
MARRIOTT, Carol .... 585-343-0055 326 F cmarriott@genesee.edu
MARRIOTT, Danny .... 760-480-8474.. 76 J
MARRIOTT, Donna .... 410-386-8032 214 B dmarriott@carrollcc.edu
MARRIOTT, Jean .... 410-386-8121 214 B jmarriott@carrollcc.edu
MARRIOTT, Karin .... 951-487-3060.. 55 A kmarriott@msjc.edu
MARRIOTT, Martin .... 920-206-2310 536 T marty.marriott@mbu.edu
MARRIOTT, Russell .... 214-818-1318 471 I rmarriott@criswell.edu
MARROCCO, Susan .... 941-752-5201 114 B marrocs@scf.edu
MARROCCO, Therese .... 203-857-7311.. 89 H tmarrocco@norwalk.edu
MARROCHELLO, Drew .. 617-353-7327 224 E marroand@bu.edu
MARRON, Maria .... 402-472-3041 293 H mmarron2@unl.edu
MARRON, Timothy .... 206-296-5990 526 F marront@seattleu.edu
MARRONE, Joseph .... 203-576-5515.. 91 H jmarrone@stvincentscollege.edu
MARRONGELLE, Karen .. 503-725-5061 409 D karen.marrongelle@pdx.edu
MARROTT, Ann .... 845-687-5070 350 I marrotta@sunyulster.edu
MARROW, Cary .... 806-894-9611 482 F cmarrow@southplainscollege.edu
MARROW, Sydne, M .... 508-531-1754 229 C smarrow@bridgew.edu
MARRS, Rick .... 310-506-4261.. 58 H rick.marrs@pepperdine.edu
MARRS, Sherrie .... 606-218-5261 201 C sherriemarrs@upike.edu
MARSALEK, Lisa .... 419-783-2587 381 G lmarsalek@defiance.edu
MARSALIS, Wynton ...... 212-799-5000 329 I
MARSCH, III, Andrew, J .... 205-934-4175.... 8 F marsch@uab.edu
MARSCH, Charlotte .... 417-328-1803 282 D cmarsch@sbuniv.edu
MARSCHKE, Robyn .... 719-255-3640.. 86 F rmarschk@uccs.edu
MARSDEN, Janet, L ...... 802-440-4303 501 D jmarsden@bennington.edu
MARSDEN, John, P .... 859-846-5310 198 G jmarsden@midway.edu
MARSELIAN, Zareh .... 805-493-3119.. 31 H marselia@callutheran.edu
MARSH, Anne .... 540-828-8024 505 F atmarsh@bridgewater.edu
MARSH, Barry .... 843-349-7557 446 I barry.marsh@hgtc.edu
MARSH, Bonnie .... 724-439-4900 423 G bmarsh@laurel.edu
MARSH, Bonnie Jean ... 724-439-4900 423 G bmarsh@laurel.edu
MARSH, Brent .... 918-343-7569 401 I bmarsh@rsu.edu
MARSH, Cecilia .... 660-359-3948 279 L cmarsh@mail.ncmissouri.edu
MARSH, Clay, B .... 304-293-1024 533 D cbmarsh@hsc.wvu.edu
MARSH, David, F .... 989-837-4389 248 D dmarsh@northwood.edu
MARSH, Dawn .... 517-265-5161 238 H dmarsh@adrian.edu
MARSH, Douglas, K ...... 574-631-4200 174 A marsh.14@nd.edu
MARSH, Elinor .... 517-629-0247 239 A emarsh@albion.edu
MARSH, Geoff .... 562-903-4742.. 29 F geoff.marsh@biola.edu
MARSH, Gregory .... 409-880-2100 488 F gregory.marsh@lamar.edu
MARSH, Heather, A ...... 214-860-3611 472 G hmarsh@dcccd.edu
MARSH, James, G .... 254-710-2467 469 D jim_marsh@baylor.edu
MARSH, Janet .... 517-607-2341 243 J jmarsh@hillsdale.edu
MARSH, Jed .... 609-258-7860 305 C jmarsh@princeton.edu
MARSH, John .... 315-792-7125 348 D john.marsh@sunyit.edu
MARSH, Kathleen .... 989-358-7458 239 C marshk@alpenacc.edu
MARSH, Kent .... 970-248-1303.. 80 B kmarsh@coloradomesa.edu
MARSH, Latonia, D ...... 716-878-4618 345 B marshld@buffalostate.edu
MARSH, Mae .... 907-474-6600.. 10 I mmarsh36@alaska.edu

MARTIN, Greg .... 515-964-6368 177 B
gcmartin@dmacc.edu
MARTIN, SR.,
Harold, L .... 336-334-7940 370 B
hmartin@ncat.edu
MARTIN, Heath .... 419-559-2350 392 A
hmartin01@terra.edu
MARTIN, Irene .... 860-343-5740.. 89 E
imartin@mxcc.commnet.edu
MARTIN, Jackie, L .... 601-643-8322 266 J
jackie.martin@colin.edu
MARTIN, James .... 208-282-2341 138 C
martjame@isu.edu
MARTIN, James, J .... 501-882-8851.. 19 E
jjmartin@asub.edu
MARTIN, Jan .... 212-787-5300 315 A
MARTIN, Jana .... 918-293-5339 400 E
jana.s.martin@okstate.edu
MARTIN, Jeania .... 704-991-0114 366 D
jmartin8295@stanly.edu
MARTIN, Jeanne .... 210-366-2701 480 F
MARTIN, Jenni .... 509-279-6212 521 E
jenni.martin@scc.spokane.edu
MARTIN, Jennifer .... 940-898-3415 490 D
jmartin@twu.edu
MARTIN, Jerrold .... 312-553-2500 141 M
jmartin46@ccc.edu
MARTIN, Jerry .... 334-387-3877.... 1 E
jerrymartin@amrdigeuniversity.edu
MARTIN, Jill .... 571-633-9651 513 J
MARTIN, Jill .... 800-567-2344 535 F
jmartin@menominee.edu
MARTIN, Jim David ...... 415-575-6165.. 31 C
jmartin@ciis.edu
MARTIN, Jimmy .... 832-813-6680 477 I
james.d.martin@lonestar.edu
MARTIN, Jo Leda .... 303-963-3206.. 79 L
jomartin@ccu.edu
MARTIN, Joel .... 717-291-3986 418 J
joel.martin@fandm.edu
MARTIN, John .... 559-325-3600.. 31 A
jmartin@chsu.org
MARTIN, John .... 405-878-5293 402 A
jpmartin@stgregorys.edu
MARTIN, John, O .... 413-545-0361 228 F
jomartin@admin.umass.edu
MARTIN, John, U .... 941-487-4444 115 B
jmartin@ncf.edu
MARTIN, Joshua .... 972-825-4821 483 D
jmartin@sagu.edu
MARTIN, Joshua .... 508-854-7513 232 F
jmartin@qcc.mass.edu
MARTIN, Juanita, K ...... 330-972-7082 392 H
juanita@uakron.edu
MARTIN, Karen, O .... 912-279-5750 123 B
kmartin@ccga.edu
MARTIN, Kari .... 859-622-1260 194 L
kari.martin@eku.edu
MARTIN, Kathleen .... 413-565-1000 222 G
kmartin@baypath.edu
MARTIN, Kathy .... 208-792-2282 138 E
kmartin@lcsc.edu
MARTIN, Kathy .... 704-406-4636 356 G
kmartin@gardner-webb.edu
MARTIN, Keith .... 716-338-1261 329 E
keithmartin@mail.sunyjcc.edu
MARTIN, Keith .... 918-343-7706 401 I
kmartin@rsu.edu
MARTIN, Kelley .... 316-295-5568 187 C
kelley_martin@friends.edu
MARTIN, Kelly .... 859-572-6565 199 A
martink29@nku.edu
MARTIN, Kenneth .... 972-937-7612 479 I
kenneth.martin@navarrocollege.edu
MARTIN, Kenneth, M ... 717-815-1211 440 H
kmartin@ycp.edu
MARTIN, Kevin .... 618-650-2345 159 I
kemarti@siue.edu
MARTIN, Kevin .... 302-225-6241.. 94 B
martink@gbc.edu
MARTIN, Kevin .... 215-407-0584 429 G
kmartin@pafa.edu
MARTIN, Kim .... 949-794-9090.. 68 F
kmartin@stanbridge.edu
MARTIN, Kyle, R .... 208-496-1010 137 F
martink@byui.edu
MARTIN, Lara .... 561-237-7459 108 E
lmartin@lynn.edu
MARTIN, Larry .... 657-278-6029.. 33 E
larrymartin@fullerton.edu
MARTIN, Laura .... 404-471-6054 119 G
lmartin@agnesscott.edu
MARTIN, Laura .... 516-877-3128 314 F
lmarting@adelphi.edu
MARTIN, Laurel .... 859-246-6584 195 J
laurel.martin@kctcs.edu
MARTIN, LeaAnn .... 360-650-3763 528 D
LeaAnn.Martin@wwu.edu
MARTIN, Leandra .... 408-855-5182.. 76 E
leandra.martin@wvm.edu
MARTIN, Lee .... 419-448-2169 383 C
lmartin@heidelberg.edu
MARTIN, Lisa .... 770-962-7580 127 C
lmartin@gwinnetttech.edu
MARTIN, Lisa .... 918-343-7614 401 I
lmartin@rsu.edu
MARTIN, Lizbeth, J ...... 510-436-1040.. 47 C
martin@hnu.edu
MARTIN, Lonnie .... 717-560-8254 423 C
lmartin@lbc.edu
MARTIN, Louisa .... 603-668-2211 298 H
l.martin@snhu.edu
MARTIN, Louisa, A .... 210-431-5005 481 C
lmartin@stmarytx.edu
MARTIN, Luke .... 619-298-1829.. 68 C
lmartin@ssu.edu
MARTIN, Lynn .... 734-973-3507 251 J
lgmartin@wccnet.edu
MARTIN, Maggie .... 229-391-5135 119 F
mmartin@abac.edu
MARTIN, Marc .... 510-780-4500.. 50 G
mmartin@lifewest.edu
MARTIN, Marcus, L ...... 434-243-2079 514 A
mlm8n@Virginia.EDU
MARTIN, Margo .... 904-632-3030 105 A
margo.martin@fscj.edu
MARTIN, Maribeth .... 206-281-2448 526 D
martinm3@spu.edu
MARTIN, Marie .... 651-604-4131 257 C
mmartin@minneapolisbusinesscollege.edu
MARTIN, Marie .... 803-780-1229 451 G
martin@voorhees.edu
MARTIN, Mark, A .... 989-837-4497 248 D
martinm@northwood.edu
MARTIN, Marty .... 571-633-9651 513 J
MARTIN, Mary .... 802-635-1360 504 A
mary.martin@jsc.edu
MARTIN, Matthew, R .... 478-757-5246 134 E
mmartin@wesleyancollege.edu
MARTIN, Melissa .... 812-749-1408 171 I
mmartin@oak.edu
MARTIN, Michael .... 662-846-4638 267 A
mmartin@deltastate.edu
MARTIN, Michael .... 918-647-1360 397 C
mmartin@carlalbert.edu
MARTIN, Michele .... 802-586-7711 503 B
mmartin@sterlingcollege.edu
MARTIN, Mirta, M .... 785-628-4231 187 A
m3martin@fhsu.edu
MARTIN, Pat .... 610-328-8451 436 A
pmartin1@swarthmore.edu
MARTIN, Patrick .... 860-231-5311.. 93 A
pmartin@usj.edu
MARTIN, Paul .... 510-841-1905.. 27 B
pmartin@absw.edu
MARTIN, Paul .... 518-276-8711 339 D
martip@rpi.edu
MARTIN, Paul .... 617-730-7155 235 B
paul.martin@newbury.edu
MARTIN, Quincy .... 708-456-0300 161 C
qmartin@triton.edu
MARTIN, Rafael .... 972-883-4824 494 A
rafael.martin@utdallas.edu
MARTIN, II, Ralph, C ... 617-373-2101 235 D
MARTIN, Randy .... 870-972-2093.. 19 F
rmartin@astate.edu
MARTIN, Randy .... 724-357-2244 431 A
rmartin@iup.edu
MARTIN, Ray .... 254-295-4590 492 C
rmartin@umhb.edu
MARTIN, Richard, D ..... 706-776-0105 130 B
dmartin@piedmont.edu
MARTIN, Robert .... 202-885-8611.. 97 E
rmartin@wesleyseminary.edu
MARTIN, Robert .... 810-766-8756 239 H
robert.martin@baker.edu
MARTIN, Robert .... 505-424-2301 310 L
MARTIN, Robert, E .... 303-233-4697.. 81 A
rm@schooloftrades.edu
MARTIN, Robert, K .... 217-581-5983 144 E
rmartin@eiu.edu
MARTIN, Robyn .... 520-515-3688.. 13 B
martinrc@cochise.edu
MARTIN, Ronald, C ...... 814-732-2743 430 G
martinr@edinboro.edu
MARTIN, Roneida .... 847-543-2641 142 G
rmartin@clcillinois.edu
MARTIN, Ronnie .... 434-592-6515 509 G
rbmartin@liberty.edu
MARTIN, Rosa, L .... 706-821-8365 129 H
rmartin@paine.edu
MARTIN, Rosalee, R ..... 512-505-3098 475 G
rrmartin@htu.edu
MARTIN, Rosalynn .... 910-962-3712 372 A
martinr@uncw.edu
MARTIN, Roy, J .... 225-578-2284 204 M
rjmartin@lsu.edu
MARTIN, Russell .... 864-941-8669 448 D
martin.r@ptc.edu
MARTIN, Ruth .... 619-201-8685.. 62 D
Ruth.Martin@sdcc.edu
MARTIN, Ryan .... 201-360-4024 303 A
rmartin@hccc.edu
MARTIN, Sara .... 360-867-6034 522 J
martins@evergreen.edu
MARTIN, Sean .... 314-256-8860 272 B
martin@ai.edu
MARTIN, Sean .... 860-439-2058.. 90 D
sean.martin@conncoll.edu
MARTIN, Shane, P .... 310-338-7301.. 53 C
Shane.Martin@lmu.edu
MARTIN, Sharon, L ...... 304-293-0111 533 D
shmartin@mail.wvu.edu
MARTIN, Staci .... 903-983-8200 477 A
smartin@kilgore.edu
MARTIN, Stephanie ...... 219-464-5212 174 E
stephanie.martin1@valpo.edu
MARTIN, Steven, J .... 419-772-2277 388 I
s-martin.11@onu.edu
MARTIN, Susan .... 415-749-4533.. 62 I
smartin@sfai.edu
MARTIN, Susan, D .... 865-974-2445 465 D
sdmartin@utk.edu
MARTIN, Susan, M ...... 630-942-3324 142 F
martinsu@cod.edu
MARTIN, Susan, W ...... 408-924-1177.. 36 B
sjsupres@sjsu.edu
MARTIN, Susie .... 310-377-5501.. 53 E
smartin@marymountcalifornia.edu
MARTIN, Suzanne .... 985-448-7945 203 G
suzanne.martin@fletcher.edu
MARTIN, Terri .... 906-487-7225 242 M
terri.martin@finlandia.edu
MARTIN, Terry .... 225-743-8500 204 C
tmartin@rpcc.edu
MARTIN, Terry .... 318-487-7201 202 L
terry.martin@lacollege.edu
MARTIN, Thomas, K ..... 972-758-3817 471 C
tmartin@collin.edu
MARTIN, Timothy, J ..... 515-574-1097 179 F
martin@iowacentral.edu
MARTIN, Timothy, R .... 508-767-7373 222 D
timartin@assumption.edu
MARTIN, Tod .... 501-279-4403.. 21 A
registrar@harding.edu
MARTIN, Tom .... 361-593-3419 486 A
katdm00@tamuk.edu
MARTIN, Tony .... 757-388-2900 512 D
MARTIN, Tony, L .... 336-386-3222 366 E
martint@surry.edu
MARTIN, Traci .... 410-337-6191 215 B
tmartin@goucher.edu
MARTIN, Traycee, F ..... 229-333-5710 133 H
tmartin@valdosta.edu
MARTIN, Troy .... 716-375-2373 340 C
MARTIN, Valerie, G ...... 570-372-4288 435 I
vmartin@susqu.edu
MARTIN, Vicki, J .... 414-297-6320 543 E
martinv@matc.edu
MARTIN, Victor .... 661-654-2222.. 32 G
vmartin4@csub.edu
MARTIN, Walter .... 919-866-5385 366 H
wmartin@waketech.edu
MARTIN, Wayne .... 973-754-7192 304 F
wmartin@pccc.edu
MARTIN, Wayne .... 540-453-2347 514 H
martinw@brcc.edu
MARTIN, Willadean ...... 972-860-4817 472 C
wmartin@dcccd.edu
MARTIN, William, J ...... 614-292-8350 389 A
martin.3047@osu.edu
MARTIN, Wilma .... 787-720-1022 550 F
orientador@atlanticcollege.edu
MARTIN-BROWN,
Karen .... 352-371-2833 101 M
faa@dragonrises.edu
MARTIN-OSORIO,
Carol, J .... 615-353-3268 463 C
carol.martin-osorio@nscc.edu
MARTIN PALMER,
Barbara .... 301-447-5371 217 D
palmer@msmary.edu
MARTIN-PARISIEN,
Terri .... 701-477-7862 375 H
tmartinparisien@tm.edu
MARTIN-REND, Jill .... 814-653-8265 413 G
jill.martin-rend@bc3.edu
MARTIN-SCHRAMM,
Karen, B .... 563-387-1527 180 M
marschka@luther.edu
MARTIN TSE, Jennifer .. 315-464-4604 344 E
registrar@upstate.edu
MARTIN-VEGA,
Louis, A .... 919-515-2311 370 D
louis_martin-vega@ncsu.edu
MARTINDALE,
Jeffrey, W .... 405-466-3210 398 E
jwmartindale@langston.edu
MARTINDILL, Cindy ...... 802-728-1586 504 C
cmartindill@vtc.edu
MARTINEAU, Jim .... 503-594-3271 405 A
jmartineau@clackamas.edu
MARTINELLI, Joseph, I . 301-336-6000 217 G
jmartinelli@pgcc.edu
MARTINELLI, Joseph, L 301-322-0417 217 G
martinjl@pgcc.edu
MARTINELLI-FERNANDEZ,
Susan .... 309-298-1828 163 A
martinelli-fernandez@wiu.edu
MARTINELLO, Peter ...... 614-882-2551 382 F
MARTINEZ, Abelardo .... 787-276-8240 557 F
abelardo.martinez@upr.edu
MARTINEZ, Albert, M ... 973-596-3668 304 D
albert.martinez@njit.edu
MARTINEZ, Anthony ..... 707-527-4568.. 65 C
amartinez@santarosa.edu
MARTINEZ, Arti .... 619-477-6310.. 70 G
amartinez@usuniversity.edu
MARTINEZ, Auris .... 787-878-5475 553 F
amartinez@arecibo.inter.edu
MARTINEZ, Brenda .... 510-466-7203.. 59 C
bmartinez@peralta.edu
MARTINEZ, Carla .... 714-895-8705.. 40 C
cmartinez@gwc.cccd.edu
MARTINEZ, Carlos .... 817-531-4959 490 C
cmartinez@txwes.edu
MARTINEZ, Carlos, E ... 512-471-6519 493 M
carlos.martinez@austin.utexas.edu
MARTINEZ, Carmella ..... 505-747-2118 312 G
carmella@nnmc.edu
MARTINEZ, Carolina ..... 505-454-3269 311 H
carolina@nmhu.edu
MARTINEZ, Carriann ..... 719-549-3056.. 85 A
carriann.martinez@pueblocc.edu
MARTINEZ, Chad .... 618-650-2333 159 I
cmartaa@siue.edu
MARTINEZ, Cristina ...... 830-792-7281 482 D
cimartinez@schreiner.edu
MARTINEZ, David .... 718-960-8545 319 C
ideldavid.martinez@lehman.cuny.edu
MARTINEZ, Debra .... 787-284-1912 554 B
dmartinez@ponce.inter.edu
MARTINEZ, Diana .... 630-942-3007 142 F
martinezd59@cod.edu
MARTINEZ, Diana, S .... 210-458-7172 494 D
DIANA.MARTINEZ1@UTSA.EDU
MARTINEZ, Didit .... 806-743-2900 490 A
didit.martinez@ttuhsc.edu
MARTINEZ, Dolly .... 718-518-4300 319 D
dmartinez@hostos.cuny.edu
MARTINEZ, Elena, M .... 956-326-2433 485 B
emartinez@tamiu.edu
MARTINEZ, Elizabeth .... 956-326-2335 485 B
elizabeth@tamiu.edu
MARTINEZ, Erlinda, J ... 714-564-6975.. 60 G
martinez_erlinda@sac.edu
MARTINEZ, Everardo .... 928-314-9422.. 12 B
everardo.martinez@azwestern.edu
MARTINEZ, Freddie ...... 787-841-2000 555 F
fmartinez@pucpr.edu
MARTINEZ, Geraldine ... 575-527-7710 312 D
gerri66@nmsu.edu
MARTINEZ, German ...... 609-497-7778 305 B
facilities-security@ptsem.edu
MARTINEZ, Heather ...... 806-742-7017 489 F
heather.martinez@ttu.edu
MARTINEZ, Hector .... 787-284-1912 554 B
hmartin@ponce.inter.edu
MARTINEZ, Hector .... 787-284-1912 554 B
hemart@ponce.inter.edu
MARTINEZ, Henry .... 972-860-8142 472 D
hmartinez@dcccd.edu
MARTINEZ, Ivan .... 214-860-1416 472 F
lmartinez@dcccd.edu
MARTINEZ, Janice, A .... 787-850-9320 558 A
janice.martinez1@upr.edu
MARTINEZ, Javier .... 787-863-2390 553 I
javier.martinez@fajardo.inter.edu
MARTINEZ, Jeffrey .... 909-748-8411.. 73 K
jeffrey_martinez@redlands.edu
MARTINEZ, Jennifer ..... 619-651-2490.. 70 G
jmartinez@usuniversity.edu
MARTINEZ, Jeremy .... 432-685-5523 478 F
jmartinez@midland.edu
MARTINEZ, Jesse .... 208-885-7716 139 C
jessem@uidaho.edu
MARTINEZ, Jesus .... 787-738-2161 557 G
jesus.martinez5@upr.edu
MARTINEZ, Jesus, J ..... 830-591-7234 483 A
jjmartinez1060@swtjc.edu
MARTINEZ, Juan .... 626-584-5588.. 45 F
martinez@fuller.edu
MARTINEZ, Juan, F ...... 787-279-2220 553 H
jmartinez@bayamon.inter.edu
MARTINEZ, Kara .... 806-716-4600 482 F
kmartinez@southplainscollege.edu
MARTINEZ, Karol .... 410-225-2284 216 F
kmartinez@mica.edu
MARTINEZ, Kim .... 303-457-2757.. 82 H
kimberley.martinez@zenith.org

MASON, Tamra 505-224-4000 310 F
tmason@cnm.edu
MASON, Tisa 701-845-7102 374 D
tisa.mason@vcsu.edu
MASON, Traci 352-873-5808 100 P
masont@cf.edu
MASON, IV, W. Scott 405-325-3260 403 I
smason@ou.edu
MASON JENNINGS, Martha 269-749-7644 249 A
mjennings@olivetcollege.edu
MASON-KINSEY, Natalie, L 718-951-4128 318 F
nmasonkinsey@brooklyn.cuny.edu
MASOUM, Nazi 949-794-9090 68 F
nazim@stanbridge.edu
MASRI, Safwan, M 212-854-8716 322 F
smm1@columbia.edu
MASS, Gregory 973-596-5745 304 D
mass@njit.edu
MASSA, Gary, R 513-745-3335 396 B
massag@xavier.edu
MASSA, Laura 310-568-6130 53 C
lmassa1@lmu.edu
MASSA, Laurie, J 216-397-4661 384 F
lmassa@jcu.edu
MASSA, SJ, Mark, S 617-552-6502 224 B
mark.massa@bc.edu
MASSA, Robert 973-408-3250 301 J
rmassa@drew.edu
MASSAGUE, Joan 646-888-6639 331 E
j-massague@ski.mskcc.org
MASSANELLI, Randy 479-575-7964 23 G
jrmassan@uark.edu
MASSARI, Lydia, I 787-751-0178 555 K
ac_lmassari@suagm.edu
MASSARO, Chris, J 615-898-2450 461 E
chris.massaro@mtsu.edu
MASSARO, Patrick, W 724-287-8711 413 G
patrick.massaro@bc3.edu
MASSARO, SJ, Thomas 510-549-5040 65 A
tmassaro@jstb.edu
MASSARONI, Larry 914-606-7895 352 G
larry.massaroni@sunywcc.edu
MASSE, Carol 414-847-3270 537 F
carolmasse@miad.edu
MASSE, Michelle 225-578-3885 204 M
graddeanoffice@lsu.edu
MASSE, Raymond 207-755-5258 210 L
rmasse@cmcc.edu
MASSE, Thomas, G 386-822-8950 117 A
thomas.masse@stetson.edu
MASSELL, Laura 802-654-0532 503 H
laura.massell@mail.ccv.vsc.edu
MASSENA, James, R 269-471-3307 239 D
massenaj@andrews.edu
MASSENBURG, Gerald 973-353-5541 307 C
geraldm@andromeda.rutgers.edu
MASSET, Cara 412-624-4361 437 K
masset@pitt.edu
MASSEY, April 202-274-5194 97 B
amassey@udc.edu
MASSEY, David 503-883-2259 406 I
dmassey@linfield.edu
MASSEY, Dennis 252-493-7220 364 H
dmassey@email.pittcc.edu
MASSEY, Diane 610-647-4400 421 B
dmassey@immaculata.edu
MASSEY, Edwin, R 772-462-4701 106 F
emassey@irsc.edu
MASSEY, Gail 931-221-1139 459 G
gail.massey@miller-motte.edu
MASSEY, Jeff 318-473-6477 205 A
jmassey@lsua.edu
MASSEY, Laura 971-722-7700 409 C
laura.massey@pcc.edu
MASSEY, Margaret 251-380-3888 7 F
mmassey@shc.edu
MASSEY, Marge 972-279-6511 467 F
mmassey@amberton.edu
MASSEY, Michael 919-209-2087 363 F
mtmassey@johnstoncc.edu
MASSEY, Pamela, L 501-450-3237 25 F
pamm@uca.edu
MASSEY, Perry, A 910-672-1475 370 A
pmassey@uncfsu.edu
MASSEY, Rufus 706-368-6945 121 E
wmassey@berry.edu
MASSEY, Sandra 870-512-7851 19 I
sandra_massey@asun.edu
MASSEY, Susan, A 904-264-2172 111 G
susan.massey@iws.edu
MASSEY, Tanya 405-744-9164 400 C
tanya.massey@okstate.edu
MASSEY, Walter, E 312-899-5136 158 J
wmassey@saic.edu
MASSEY, Walter, T 404-413-3407 126 D
wmassey@gsu.edu
MASSIE, Maribeth 207-221-4519 213 B
bmassie@une.edu
MASSINGILL, Judson 713-683-3817 482 C
MASSINGILL, Linda 713-683-3817 482 C
MASSIS, Bruce 614-287-2461 380 G
bmassis@cscc.edu
MASSMAN, Joseph 816-654-7105 276 G
jmassman@kcumb.edu
MASSOELS, William 219-866-6184 172 E
billm@saintjoe.edu
MASSOGLIA, Mike 336-734-7177 362 F
mmassoglia@forsythtech.edu
MASSON, Mary 802-654-2234 502 H
mmasson@smcvt.edu
MASSOT, Devon 407-646-1943 111 H
dmassot@rollins.edu
MAST, Brian 615-966-1052 458 C
brian.mast@lipscomb.edu
MAST, Gabriel 360-416-7675 527 A
gabriel.mast@skagit.edu
MAST, Gregg, A 732-247-5241 304 B
gmast@nbts.edu
MAST, Kathryn 217-875-7211 156 K
kmast@richland.edu
MAST, Maura 617-287-6330 228 G
maura.mast@umb.edu
MAST, Maura, B 718-817-4700 326 C
MAST HEWITT, Marilyn 630-620-2136 154 J
registrar@seminary.edu
MAST HEWITT, Marilyn, R 630-620-2196 154 J
registrar@seminary.edu
MASTANDUNO, Michael 603-646-3999 297 G
michael.mastanduno@dartmouth.edu
MASTELLER, John, Q 805-525-4417 69 I
jmasteller@thomasaquinas.edu
MASTER, Jonathan, L 215-702-4358 414 C
jmaster@cairn.edu
MASTER, Sarah, L 818-364-7788 51 G
mastersl@lamission.edu
MASTERNAK, Donald 517-629-0350 239 A
dmasternak@albion.edu
MASTERS, Bradley 318-345-9239 203 H
bmasters@ladelta.edu
MASTERS, Carolynn, B 814-871-7401 419 A
masters004@gannon.edu
MASTERS, Deborah, C 415-338-1681 36 A
dmasters@sfsu.edu
MASTERS, Debra, G 405-466-2952 398 E
dgmasters@langston.edu
MASTERS, Ellen Lea 434-223-6325 508 B
emasters@hsc.edu
MASTERS, Mark 229-430-2900 119 H
mmasters@h2opolicycenter.org
MASTERS, Michael 706-272-4461 123 G
mmasters@daltonstate.edu
MASTERS, Peggy 256-824-2771 9 A
peggy.masters@uah.edu
MASTERS-DUBUCLET, Evelyn 504-286-5118 207 B
emasters@suno.edu
MASTERSON, Ana 928-692-3016 15 K
amasterson@mohave.edu
MASTERSON, Christine 425-602-3015 519 J
cmasters@bastyr.edu
MASTERSON, Dan 785-227-3380 185 A
masterson@bethanylb.edu
MASTERSON, John 864-503-5483 451 A
jmasterson@uscupstate.edu
MASTERSON, John, A 620-365-5116 184 C
masterson@allencc.edu
MASTERSON, Julie, J 417-836-5335 279 A
juliemasterson@missouristate.edu
MASTERSON, Lisanne 828-694-1806 360 D
lmasterson@blueridge.edu
MASTERSON, Michael, J 334-953-4827 547 F
michael.masterson.4@us.af.mil
MASTERSON, Robert 559-730-3862 41 D
bobm@cos.edu
MASTERSON, Tom, J 989-774-1850 240 O
maste1tj@cmich.edu
MASTERTON, Bob 603-623-0313 298 C
bobmasterton@nhia.edu
MASTRANGELO, Joseph 212-799-5000 329 I
MASTRAPA, Tania 202-462-2101 96 C
mastrapa@iwp.edu
MASTRE, Tom, M 831-656-1095 548 A
tmastre@nps.edu
MASTRIANO, Carla 518-244-6857 340 A
mastrc2@sage.edu
MASTRO, Stephen 310-243-3750 33 B
smastro@csudh.edu
MASTROIANNI, Michael 815-921-4001 157 B
m.mastroianni@rockvalleycollege.edu
MASUCCI, Michele, M 215-204-6875 436 C
michele.masucci@temple.edu
MASUDA, Andrew 805-922-6966 26 H
amasuda@hancockcollege.edu
MASUDA, Walter 530-741-6794 78 F
wmasuda@yccd.edu
MASULLO, Sharon 215-567-7080 412 G
smasullo@edmc.edu
MATA, Armanda 773-907-4350 141 O
amata@ccc.edu
MATA, Margaret 325-942-2012 489 E
margaret.mata@angelo.edu
MATA, Margo 830-591-7223 483 A
mhmata@swtjc.edu
MATACHEK, John 651-523-2252 256 B
jmatachek@hamline.edu
MATANYI, Eric 708-209-3255 143 D
eric.mantanyi@cuchicago.edu
MATARA, Ryan 715-394-8293 541 C
rmatara@uwsuper.edu
MATAREZE, Amanda 617-236-8822 226 F
amatareze@fisher.edu
MATAS, Francine 805-969-3626 57 J
fmatas@pacifica.edu
MATASAR, Richard, A 212-998-7041 336 C
richard.matasar@nyu.edu
MATASSINO, Dana 610-409-3188 438 H
dmatassino@ursinus.edu
MATCHAN, Steven 626-585-7489 58 F
sxmatchan@pasadena.edu
MATEJCIK, Mark, M 216-916-7515 384 H
mmatejci@kent.edu
MATEJKOVIC, Edward, M 610-436-3555 432 B
ematejkovic@wcupa.edu
MATEN, Lionel 662-915-7328 270 G
lmaten@olemiss.edu
MATEO, Frances 623-845-3147 14 N
frances.mateo@gccaz.edu
MATEO, Robin 407-646-2258 111 H
rmateo@rollins.edu
MATERN, Cindy 253-879-3369 527 F
cmatern@pugetsound.edu
MATES, Eileen 610-436-2128 432 B
emates@wcupa.edu
MATHAY, Patti, J 412-624-7600 437 K
mathay@pitt.edu
MATHENA, Cindy 904-826-0084 74 A
cmathena@usa.edu
MATHENEY, H. Scott 630-617-3025 144 G
hscottm@elmhurst.edu
MATHENY, Christopher 920-735-2401 542 N
matheny@fvtc.edu
MATHENY, Jacqueline 716-827-2450 350 H
mathenyj@trocaire.edu
MATHENY, Kevin 503-493-6521 405 E
kmatheny@cu-portland.edu
MATHENY, Meg 502-213-7112 196 E
meg.matheny@kctcs.edu
MATHENY, Samuel 901-448-5568 465 G
samuel.matheny@uthsc.edu
MATHENY, Stephen 828-395-1293 363 D
smatheny@isothermal.edu
MATHER, Bruce, J 630-617-3178 144 G
brucem@elmhurst.edu
MATHER, John 518-587-2100 348 A
ronnie.mather@esc.edu
MATHER, Kasey 773-602-5062 142 A
MATHER, Kim 978-867-4246 227 A
kim.mather@gordon.edu
MATHERLY, Cheryl 918-631-3225 403 M
cheryl-matherly@utulsa.edu
MATHERN, Rebecca 541-737-4331 408 F
rebecca.mathern@oregonstate.edu
MATHES, Cassie 417-625-9365 278 I
mathes-c@mssu.edu
MATHES, Dennis 717-477-1463 431 F
dhm@ship.edu
MATHES, Jonathan 606-693-5000 197 F
jmathes@kmbc.edu
MATHES, Leon 504-865-3148 206 A
mathes@loyno.edu
MATHESON, Linda, K 920-923-7668 537 A
lkmatheson85@marianuniversity.edu
MATHESON, Regina, M 563-333-5838 182 E
MathesonReginaM@sau.edu
MATHEW, Bruce, E 608-785-9214 544 E
mathewb@westerntc.edu
MATHEW, Roy 915-747-5117 494 B
rmathew@utep.edu
MATHEW, Thomson 918-495-7016 401 B
tmathew@oru.edu
MATHEW, Usha 281-283-2135 491 E
mathew@uhcl.edu
MATHEWS, Angela 507-786-3231 264 C
mathews@stolaf.edu
MATHEWS, Bruce 808-932-7036 135 I
bmathews@hawaii.edu
MATHEWS, Darren 970-247-7428 82 I
mathews_d@fortlewis.edu
MATHEWS, David 269-782-1270 250 D
president@swmich.edu
MATHEWS, Jeanne 706-236-2226 121 E
jmathews@berry.edu
MATHEWS, Jennifer 508-565-1915 237 A
jmathews@stonehill.edu
MATHEWS, John 215-968-8211 413 F
john.mathews@bucks.edu
MATHEWS, Karen 937-376-6076 379 D
kmathews@centralstate.edu
MATHEWS, Lakeisha 410-837-4030 221 B
lmathews@ubalt.edu
MATHEWS, Marc 859-233-8100 200 D
mmathews@transy.edu
MATHEWS, Marcia 405-878-5412 402 A
mamathews@stgregorys.edu
MATHEWS, Michael 918-495-6812 401 B
mmathews@oru.edu
MATHEWS, Nancy, E 802-656-4280 503 C
nancy.mathews@uvm.edu
MATHEWS, Robert 920-498-5701 544 B
robert.mathews@nwtc.edu
MATHEWS, Ruth 507-457-1481 264 B
rmathews@smumn.edu
MATHIAS, Suzi 715-675-3331 544 A
mathias@ntc.edu
MATHIASEN, Rebecca 402-354-7034 291 P
rebecca.mathiasen@methodistcollege.edu
MATHIE, Craig 435-893-2216 500 D
craig.mathie@snow.edu
MATHIESEN, Gaylan 218-739-3375 256 K
gmathiesen@lbs.edu
MATHIEU, Richard 704-337-2234 368 B
shifflerr@queens.edu
MATHIOS, Alan, D 607-255-2138 323 C
adm5@cornell.edu
MATHIS, Bob, D 512-863-1425 483 G
bmathis@southwestern.edu
MATHIS, Carolyn 626-529-8437 57 F
cmathis@pacificoaks.edu
MATHIS, Claude 915-831-2857 473 J
cmathis1@epcc.edu
MATHIS, Clay, P 361-593-5401 486 A
clay.mathis@tamuk.edu
MATHIS, Elizabeth 202-885-8601 97 E
MATHIS, Elizabeth 215-965-4017 426 G
emathis@moore.edu
MATHIS, Jennifer, M 864-388-8307 447 E
jmathis@lander.edu
MATHIS, Jon 310-506-7586 58 H
jon.mathis@pepperdine.edu
MATHIS, Larry 864-977-7160 448 A
larry.mathis@ngu.edu
MATHIS, Malissa 501-569-3110 24 A
mktrantham@ualr.edu
MATHIS, Martha 802-485-2640 502 G
martham@norwich.edu
MATHIS, Maureen 610-660-1306 434 G
mmathis@sju.edu
MATHIS, Renita 404-270-5013 132 D
rmathis@spelman.edu
MATHIS, Shawn 501-450-1333 21 C
mathis@hendrix.edu
MATHIS, Teri 229-391-5045 119 F
tmathis@abac.edu
MATHISON, Jane 440-775-8400 388 B
Jane.Mathison@oberlin.edu
MATHUES, Sabrina 732-255-0400 304 E
smathues@ocean.edu
MATHUR, Ambika 313-577-2170 252 G
ambika.mathur@wayne.edu
MATHUR, Guarav 202-651-5520 95 C
gaurav.mathur@gallaudet.edu
MATHWEG, Cathy, M 920-923-8138 537 A
cmathweg@marianuniversity.edu
MATIAS, Barbara 561-868-3110 109 H
matiasb@palmbeachstate.edu
MATIENZO-CARRERO, Ivonne 787-764-0000 558 E
ivonne.matienzo@upr.edu
MATIER, Michael 254-710-2414 469 D
michael_matier@baylor.edu
MATIJEVIC, Patricia 970-339-6374 78 J
patricia.matijevic@aims.edu
MATILDA, Mecca 831-476-9424 44 L
finaid@fivebranches.edu
MATIS, Michelle, D 407-582-3130 118 I
mmatis@valenciacollege.edu
MATISON, Kim 253-566-5194 527 C
kmatison@tacomacc.edu
MATISTA, Theresa 916-568-3058 52 H
matistt@losrios.edu
MATITIA, Abraham 440-943-5300 390 J
MATKIN, Gary, W 949-824-5525 71 C
gmatkin@uci.edu
MATKIN, H. Neil 972-758-3801 471 C
nmatkin@collin.edu
MATKIN, Neil 225-922-2373 202 M
nmatkin@lctcs.edu
MATLAK, Richard, E 508-793-2497 225 C
rmatlak@holycross.edu
MATLOCK, Bianca 214-860-3670 472 G
bmatlock@dcccd.edu
MATLOCK, David, N 276-739-2473 517 D
dmatlock@vhcc.edu

MATLOCK, Debra 312-996-7084 161 F mdebra@uic.edu
MATLOCK, Kathy 910-642-7141 366 B Kathy.Matlock@sccnc.edu
MATLOCK, Mark 814-732-1301 430 G mmatlock@edinboro.edu
MATLOCK, Maryann 973-290-4606 301 F mmatlock@cse.edu
MATNEY, Bob 419-289-5777 377 A bmatney@ashland.edu
MATOLA, Erich 719-549-2566 81 F erich.matola@csupueblo.edu
MATON, Marjane 623-845-3059 14 N marjane.maton@gccaz.edu
MATONAK, Andrew, J 518-629-4530 328 D a.matonak@hvcc.edu
MATOS, Awilda 787-834-9595 556 D amatos@uaa.edu
MATOS, Carol 212-749-2802 331 I cmatos@msmnyc.edu
MATOS, Daniel 212-650-8150 318 G dmatos@ccny.cuny.edu
MATOS, Elsa 787-890-2681 557 C elsa.matos@upr.edu
MATOS, Emily 787-844-8181 558 D emily.matos@upr.edu
MATOS, Ilia 239-939-4766 113 L imatos@southerntech.edu
MATOS, Jose, A 787-751-0160 551 K jamatos@cmpr.pr.gov
MATOS, Lillian 787-780-0070 550 G lmatos@caribbean.edu
MATOS, Lorena 718-405-3338 322 A lorena.matos@mountsaintvincent.edu
MATOS, Lynda 661-824-2977 55 I lmatos@ntps.edu
MATOS, Thomas 651-846-1362 261 G thomas.matos@saintpaul.edu
MATOS, Yanira 787-890-2681 557 C yanira.matos@upr.edu
MATOS RODRIGUEZ, Felix, V 718-997-5000 320 E qcpres@qc.cuny.edu
MATOSO, Michael 209-667-3566 35 C mmatoso@csustan.edu
MATSCHERZ, Scott 714-966-8500 75 F info@ves.edu
MATSDORF, Gary 541-485-1780 407 H garymatsdorf@newhope.edu
MATSEN, Maureen, R 757-594-7585 506 I maureen.matsen@cnu.edu
MATSON, Christine, B 671-735-0231 549 E christine.matson@guamcc.edu
MATSON, Jerry 435-652-7938 499 M matson@dixie.edu
MATSON, Pamela, A 650-723-2750 68 G pamela.matson@stanford.edu
MATSON, Ronald, R 316-978-6659 192 D ron.matson@wichita.edu
MATSON, Steven, W 919-962-3251 371 A smatson@bio.unc.edu
MATSUBARA, Melissa 808-544-0288 135 C mmatsubara@hpu.edu
MATSUDA, Matthew, K 848-932-2300 307 B matt.matsuda@rutgers.edu
MATSUDA, Seiichi 713-348-4002 480 M matsuda@rice.edu
MATSUMOTO, Mark 209-228-4021 71 E
MATSUMOTO, Rae 707-638-5926 70 B rae.matsumoto@tu.edu
MATSUO, Monica 626-396-2268 28 J monica.matsuo@artcenter.edu
MATT, Kathleen, S 302-831-8370 94 D ksmatt@udel.edu
MATTERN, Carolyn 303-914-6372 85 C carolyn.mattern@rrcc.edu
MATTES, Bill, S 717-901-5134 420 I bmattes@harrisburgu.edu
MATTES, Marty 253-680-7156 519 K mmattes@bates.ctc.edu
MATTESON, Bill 401-874-4275 442 E matteson@uri.edu
MATTESON, Christi, G 904-264-2172 111 G christi.matteson@iws.edu
MATTESON, Ryan 805-756-7676 32 E rmatteso@calpoly.edu
MATTEY, Melissa 443-518-4208 215 F mmattey@howardcc.edu
MATTHEIS, Bernd 203-575-8234 89 F bmattheis@nv.edu
MATTHES, Bruce 619-684-8871 56 B bmatthes@newschoolarch.edu
MATTHES, Mark 562-903-4875 29 F mark.matthes@biola.edu
MATTHES, Peter 319-335-3714 175 H peter-matthes@uiowa.edu
MATTHEWS, Adrienne 301-891-4177 221 C amatthew@wau.edu
MATTHEWS, Al 740-753-6590 383 G matthewsa11702@hocking.edu
MATTHEWS, Ann 573-840-9669 283 D amatthews@trcc.edu
MATTHEWS, Anne 541-888-7612 410 A amatthews@socc.edu
MATTHEWS, Beverly 903-785-7661 480 B bmatthews@parisjc.edu
MATTHEWS, Brad 845-451-1309 323 E b_matthews@culinary.edu
MATTHEWS, Bryan, L 410-778-7231 221 D bmatthews2@washcoll.edu
MATTHEWS, Caleb 585-594-6832 337 A Matthews_caleb@roberts.edu
MATTHEWS, Cassandra 205-929-6393 5 E cmatthews@lawsonstate.edu
MATTHEWS, Cissy 409-944-1203 474 G amatthew@gc.edu
MATTHEWS, Daniel 405-273-5331 397 N dmatthews@familyoffaithcollege.edu
MATTHEWS, Daniel, J 405-273-5331 397 N dmatthews@familyoffaithcollege.edu
MATTHEWS, Dennis, W 215-968-8301 413 F matthews@bucks.edu
MATTHEWS, Donnajean 714-449-7438 53 D djmatthews@ketchum.edu
MATTHEWS, Douglas, K 859-858-2206 192 O
MATTHEWS, Ellen 903-510-2380 491 A emat@tjc.edu
MATTHEWS, Elyse 212-875-4666 315 F ematthews@bankstreet.edu
MATTHEWS, Gary, C 858-534-6820 72 B gcmatthews@ucsd.edu
MATTHEWS, Grant 708-974-5566 153 D matthewsg5@morainevalley.edu
MATTHEWS, Greg 802-485-2001 502 G gmatthe2@norwich.edu
MATTHEWS, Gregory 802-387-6716 502 A gmatthews@landmark.edu
MATTHEWS, Harold, P 812-488-2051 173 H hm3@evansville.edu
MATTHEWS, Hazel 502-413-8880 200 A hmatthews@sullivan.edu
MATTHEWS, Hazel 502-413-8880 200 B hmatthews@sullivan.edu
MATTHEWS, Hewitt 678-547-6306 128 G matthews_h@mercer.edu
MATTHEWS, Janet 828-328-7254 358 G janet.matthews@lr.edu
MATTHEWS, Jeanne 703-284-1580 510 B jeanne.matthews@marymount.edu
MATTHEWS, Jennifer 202-274-5449 97 B jennifer.matthews@udc.edu
MATTHEWS, John 919-718-7405 361 C jmatthews@cccc.edu
MATTHEWS, John 201-761-7431 307 K jmatthews@saintpeters.edu
MATTHEWS, John, D 864-242-5100 443 G
MATTHEWS, Keith 937-376-6425 379 D
MATTHEWS, Kismet 252-789-0223 363 H kmatthews@martincc.edu
MATTHEWS, Leon 704-330-6524 361 D leon.matthews@cpcc.edu
MATTHEWS, Lori 502-863-8048 195 A Lori_Matthews@georgetowncollege.edu
MATTHEWS, Mary 907-474-5655 10 I mcmatthews@alaska.edu
MATTHEWS, Matt 352-854-2322 100 P matthewm@cf.edu
MATTHEWS, Michael 303-333-4224 79 D
MATTHEWS, Pamela, R 979-845-5141 485 C p-matthews@tamu.edu
MATTHEWS, Robin 252-447-3818 362 A matthewsr@cravencc.edu
MATTHEWS, Ron 704-378-1023 358 B rmatthews@jcsu.edu
MATTHEWS, Ross, D 504-864-7914 206 A rdmatthews@loyno.edu
MATTHEWS, Samuel, W 405-273-5331 397 N
MATTHEWS, Stephen, P 518-564-3824 346 B matthesp@plattsburgh.edu
MATTHEWS, Tabitha 708-293-4560 160 L tabitha.matthews@trnty.edu
MATTHEWS, Thomas 216-368-4446 378 J careers@case.edu
MATTHEWS, Todd 304-296-8282 534 E tmatthews@wvjc.edu
MATTHEWS, Valencia, E 850-599-3430 114 D valencia.matthews@famu.edu
MATTHEWS, Victor 417-836-5529 279 A victormatthews@missouristate.edu
MATTHEWS, Wesley 701-858-3352 374 B wes.matthews@minotstateu.edu
MATTHEWSON, Donald 661-255-1050 31 B dmatthewson@calarts.edu
MATTHEWSON, Mansfield 616-234-3851 243 D mmatthew@grcc.edu
MATTHIAS, Ryan 402-643-7374 289 J ryan.matthias@cune.edu
MATTHIES, Brad 307-268-2036 545 Z bmatthies@caspercollege.edu
MATTHIES, Carolyn 562-947-8755 67 J carolynmatthies@scuhs.edu
MATTIA, Antonio 305-220-4120 108 F ceo@mattiacollege.edu
MATTIA, Cynthia 732-987-2757 302 J mattiac@georgian.edu
MATTIACCI, John, A 215-629-0300 436 C john.mattiacci@temple.edu
MATTIACE, Lisa, C 419-372-6780 377 I lmattia@bgsu.edu
MATTIES, A. Joseph 518-828-4181 322 E matties@sunycgcc.edu
MATTILA, Lisa 413-236-1609 231 A lmattila@berkshirecc.edu
MATTINGLY, Amy 304-637-1273 529 I mattinglym@dewv.edu
MATTINGLY, Bruce 607-753-4312 345 C bruce.mattingly@cortland.edu
MATTINGLY, Catherine 215-572-2086 412 F mattingly@arcadia.edu
MATTINGLY, Craig 859-336-5082 199 B cmattingly@sccky.edu
MATTINGLY, Keith, E 269-471-3411 239 D matt@andrews.edu
MATTIOLI, Kathy, L 740-283-6267 382 G kmattioli@franciscan.edu
MATTIOLI, Monica 716-375-2302 340 C mmattioli@sbu.edu
MATTIS, JR., George, E 276-223-4744 517 F gmattis@wcc.vccs.edu
MATTIS, Marjorie, A 717-801-3212 420 D mamattis@hacc.edu
MATTISON, Debra 651-213-4282 256 C dmattison@hazelden.edu
MATTISON, Emily 330-823-2674 394 A mattisej@mountunion.edu
MATTISON, Gwen, M 937-775-2475 396 A gwen.mattison@wright.edu
MATTISON, Michael 605-229-8492 453 A michael.mattison@presentation.edu
MATTISON, Susie 904-470-8166 102 A smattison@ewc.edu
MATTISON, William 202-319-5683 95 A mattison@cua.edu
MATTIX, Larry 757-823-8180 510 H lmattix@nsu.edu
MATTKE, Mark 509-434-8470 521 F mark.mattke@ccs.spokane.edu
MATTOCKS, Vicki, S 417-836-5262 279 A vickimattocks@missouristate.edu
MATTOX, Bennie 229-732-5908 120 B benniemattox@andrewcollege.edu
MATTOX, Robert, J 470-578-6600 127 M bmattox@kennesaw.edu
MATTS, David 815-479-7752 152 B dmatts@mchenry.edu
MATTSON, Bob 217-443-8856 143 F bmattson@dacc.edu
MATTSON, Craig 708-239-4881 160 L craig.mattson@trnty.edu
MATTSON, David, L 414-955-8571 537 C dmattson@mcw.edu
MATTSON, Jean 308-865-8202 293 G mattsonj@unk.edu
MATTSON, Jo 314-889-4514 275 B jmattson@fontbonne.edu
MATTSON, Jo Ann 410-777-1309 213 E jmattson@aacc.edu
MATTSON, Michelle 901-843-3795 460 F mattsonm@rhodes.edu
MATTSON, Paul, R 563-387-1717 180 M paul.mattson@luther.edu
MATTY, David 801-626-6159 500 C davidmatty@weber.edu
MATTY, Joseph 815-753-8821 154 I jmatty@niu.edu
MATUCH, Kathryn 215-895-6877 417 E kathryn.matuch@drexel.edu
MATULIA, Michael, K 352-323-3643 107 X matuliam@lssc.edu
MATURANA SENDOYA, Ines 617-552-3358 224 B ines.maturana@bc.edu
MATUS, David 602-787-7872 15 B david.matus@paradisevalley.edu
MATUS, Paul 631-451-4518 348 F matusp@sunysuffolk.edu
MATUSIAK, Joseph 914-961-8313 341 I jmatusiak@svots.edu
MATUSIAK, Nina 914-961-8313 341 I nmatusiak@svots.edu
MATUSICK, Robert 386-822-7300 117 A rmatusic@stetson.edu
MATUSOW-AYRES, Helen 718-636-3639 338 E hmayres@pratt.edu
MATVEY, Jessica 218-262-7384 258 H jessicamatvey@hibbing.edu
MATWEYCHUK, Karen 610-647-4980 421 B kmatweychuk@immaculata.edu
MATYAS, Laura 480-732-7205 14 K Laura.Matyas@cgc.edu
MATYE-EDWARDS, Lisa 303-797-5601 79 A lisa.matyeedwards@arapahoe.edu
MATYSTIK, Walter, F 718-862-7268 331 H walter.matystik@manhattan.edu
MATZ, Chris 206-546-4558 526 G cmatz@shoreline.edu
MATZ, Irene 657-278-3355 33 E imatz@fullerton.edu
MATZ, Jeannine 515-643-6703 181 B jmatz@mercydesmoines.org
MATZ, Tina 517-787-0800 244 H MatzTinaM@jccmi.edu
MATZKE, Brian 616-632-2073 239 E matzkbri@aquinas.edu
MATZKE, William 989-358-7259 239 C matzkew@alpenacc.edu
MATZNER, Alan 507-537-6010 262 B Alan.Matzner@smsu.edu
MAUCH, Elizabeth 570-389-4005 430 B emauch@bloomu.edu
MAUCH, Tom 909-274-4380 54 J tmauch@mtsac.edu
MAUCH AMIR, Carol 213-740-7922 74 D cmauch@usc.edu
MAUE, Lea 618-235-2700 160 B lea.maue@swic.edu
MAUERMEYER, Henry, A 973-596-3124 304 D henry.mauermeyer@njit.edu
MAUGE, Lucille 404-880-6662 122 I lmauge@cau.edu
MAUGER, Alana 215-641-6359 426 E amauger@mc3.edu
MAUGHAN, Doug, L 208-732-6262 137 K dmaughan@csi.edu
MAUHS-PUGH, Thomas 802-287-8214 501 I mauhs-pught@greenmtn.edu
MAUK, Jean 305-296-9081 104 A wjean.mauk@fkcc.edu
MAUK, Jean 305-809-3266 104 A wjean.mauk@fkcc.edu
MAUL, Jeffrey 814-262-6431 429 K jmaul@pennhighlands.edu
MAULDIN, Angela 704-378-3578 358 B amauldin@jcsu.edu
MAULDIN, Brad 575-562-2393 310 I bradley.mauldin@enmu.edu
MAULDIN, Kim 256-765-4608 9 D komauldin@una.edu
MAULDIN, Shawn 985-448-4170 208 C shawn.mauldin@nicholls.edu
MAULDIN, Teena, P 704-463-3031 367 F teena.mauldin@pfeiffer.edu
MAULL, Perry 812-855-8961 167 J pjmaull@indiana.edu
MAULTSBY, Bill 910-642-7141 366 B Bill.Maultsby@sccnc.edu
MAUN, Duane, F 717-901-5120 420 I dmaun@harrisburgu.edu
MAUN, Robin 717-477-1302 431 F rmmaun@ship.edu
MAUNEY, Bill 910-272-3300 365 D bmauney@robeson.edu
MAUNEY, Billy, L 910-272-3330 365 D bmauney@robeson.edu
MAUNSELL, Jody 802-828-8724 503 D jody.maunsell@vcfa.edu
MAURANO, Steven, J 401-865-2775 441 F smaurano@providence.edu
MAURER, Amybeth 847-214-7423 144 F amaurer@elgin.edu
MAURER, Bobby Jo 309-341-7315 149 G bmaurer@knox.edu
MAURER, Carmen, K 402-472-3906 293 F cmaurer@nebraska.edu
MAURER, Carolyn 717-766-2511 426 B cmaurer@messiah.edu
MAURER, Charles 212-757-1190 315 C cmaurer@funeraleducation.org
MAURER, Erin, C 864-622-6074 443 E emaurer@andersonuniversity.edu
MAURER, Gaylyn 541-885-1800 408 E gaylyn.maurer@oit.edu
MAURER, Joseph 541-885-1389 408 E joseph.maurer@oit.edu
MAURER, Lynn 812-237-3087 167 E lynn.maurer@indstate.edu
MAURER, Michael, S 217-581-7568 144 E msmaurer@eiu.edu
MAURER, Paul, J 828-669-8012 359 K president@montreat.edu
MAURER, Paulette, A 708-709-3630 156 A pmaurer@prairiestate.edu

MAURER, Ryan, S .... 937-327-6114 395 I
rmaurer@wittenberg.edu
MAURER, Stacey .... 503-760-3131 404 I
stace@birthingway.edu
MAURER, William, M ... 949-824-6802.. 71 C
wmmaurer@uci.edu
MAURICE, John .... 252-334-2034 359 D
john.maurice@macuniversity.edu
MAURIELLO, Thomas ... 718-862-7241 331 H
thomas.mauriello@manhattan.edu
MAURIN, Kay .... 985-549-2118 208 E
kmaurin@selu.edu
MAURO, Laurie .... 304-263-6262 530 D
lmauro@martinsburginstitute.edu
MAURO, Steven, A .... 814-871-7618 419 A
mauro003@gannon.edu
MAUSSER, Richard, F ... 216-397-4273 384 F
rmausser@jcu.edu
MAUST, Scott .... 309-341-7892 149 G
smaust@knox.edu
MAUZ, Harry .... 281-931-7717 127 E
hmauz@ict.edu
MAUZERALL, Cynthia ... 208-459-5561 137 J
cmauzerall@collegeofidaho.edu
MAVRINAC, Mary Ann .. 585-275-4461 351 D
maryann.mavrinac@rochester.edu
MAVROGIANNIS,
Sophia .... 646-230-1360 348 A
sophia.mavrogiannis@esc.edu
MAVROS, Jeff .... 309-438-2181 147 I
MAVROUDHIS,
Athina-Eleni .... 617-850-1289 227 F
amavroudhis@hchc.edu
MAWE, Marcia .... 773-244-5750 154 G
mmawe@northpark.edu
MAX, Barbara .... 303-333-4224.. 79 D
bmax@aspen.edu
MAX, Sheryl .... 816-995-2842 280 J
sheryl.max@researchcollege.edu
MAXEINER, Amy .... 815-455-8717 152 B
amaxeiner@mchenry.edu
MAXEY, Barbara .... 270-534-3090 197 E
barbarag.maxey@kctcs.edu
MAXEY, Michael, C ...... 540-375-2200 512 B
maxey@roanoke.edu
MAXEY, Tyler .... 817-552-3700 477 B
tyler.maxey@tku.edu
MAXFIELD, Judith .... 620-225-1321 186 F
maxfield@dc3.edu
MAXFIELD, Sylvia .... 401-865-1224 441 F
maxfield@providence.edu
MAXIE-ASHFORD,
Leslie, M .... 502-272-3101 193 E
lmaxie-ashford@bellarmine.edu
MAXIN, Leslie .... 724-503-1001 439 B
lmaxin@washjeff.edu
MAXON, John .... 256-824-6108.... 9 A
john.maxon@uah.edu
MAXSON, Krista .... 405-224-3140 403 L
kmaxson@usao.edu
MAXWELL, Barbara, A .. 509-527-5208 528 F
maxwelba@whitman.edu
MAXWELL, Bruce .... 509-682-6835 528 C
bmaxwell@wvc.edu
MAXWELL, Chris .... 706-245-7226 124 C
cmaxwell@ec.edu
MAXWELL, Daniel .... 423-236-2008 460 K
dmaxwell@southern.edu
MAXWELL, Daniel .... 713-743-5390 491 D
dmmaxwell@central.uh.edu
MAXWELL, Danita .... 323-259-2613.. 56 I
dmaxwell@oxy.edu
MAXWELL, Eugene .... 706-721-8106 121 C
emaxwell@gru.edu
MAXWELL, James .... 217-479-7047 151 J
james.maxwell@mac.edu
MAXWELL, James .... 972-524-3341 483 F
MAXWELL, Jim .... 402-557-7786 289 B
jim.maxwell@bellevue.edu
MAXWELL, Kim .... 970-542-3169.. 84 A
kim.maxwell@morgancc.edu
MAXWELL, Lafayette ..... 919-572-1625 354 F
lmaxwell@nc.rr.com
MAXWELL, Laura .... 678-407-5726 125 B
lmaxwell@ggc.edu
MAXWELL, Max, A .... 502-597-5911 197 G
max.maxwell@kysu.edu
MAXWELL, Rick .... 972-860-4730 472 C
rmaxwell@dcccd.edu
MAXWELL, Sharon .... 630-844-5630 139 L
smaxwel@aurora.edu
MAXWELL, Valarie .... 940-397-4346 478 G
valarie.maxwell@mwsu.edu
MAXWELL-DOHERTY,
Melissa .... 805-493-3330.. 31 H
revmmmd@callutheran.edu
MAXWELL-DOHERTY,
Scott .... 805-493-3230.. 31 H
revsjmd@callutheran.edu

MAY, Bobbie Jo, C ...... 919-496-1567 366 G
may@vgcc.edu
MAY, Brian, J .... 325-942-2073 489 E
brian.may@angelo.edu
MAY, Bryan .... 803-778-7841 443 I
maybw@cctech.edu
MAY, Carol .... 704-463-3222 367 F
carol.may@pfeiffer.edu
MAY, Carol .... 920-735-2542 542 N
mayc@fvtc.edu
MAY, Chad, L .... 215-637-7700 420 K
cmay@holyfamily.edu
MAY, Charles, A .... 573-882-7744 283 H
mayc@missouri.edu
MAY, Christopher, V 314-977-3185 281M
cmay8@slu.edu
MAY, Daniel .... 203-932-7267.. 92 G
dmay@newhaven.edu
MAY, David, J .... 603-862-2727 299 B
david.may@unh.edu
MAY, Gary, S .... 404-894-6825 125 D
gary.may@coe.gatech.edu
MAY, Gordon, F .... 410-462-7799 213 G
MAY, Grace .... 973-275-2725 308 C
grace.may@shu.edu
MAY, Henry .... 320-308-2065 261 E
hbmay@stcloudstate.edu
MAY, Janet .... 712-279-5227 176 B
janet.may@briarcliff.edu
MAY, Janet .... 713-718-8570 475 C
may.janet@hccs.edu
MAY, Jefferson, J .... 864-388-8314 447 E
jmay@lander.edu
MAY, Jerry, A .... 734-647-6030 251 C
jamay@umich.edu
MAY, Joe, L .... 214-378-1601 472 B
jmay@dcccd.edu
MAY, PHJC, Jolise .... 574-936-8898 164 A
jolise.may@ancilla.edu
MAY, Katharyn, A .... 608-263-9725 539 D
kamay@wisc.edu
MAY, Libby .... 603-668-2211 298 H
l.may@snhu.edu
MAY, Mariani .... 310-577-3000.. 77 K
slmay@yosan.edu
MAY, Mel, A .... 216-987-2202 381 A
mel.may@tri-c.edu
MAY, Michael .... 724-738-4573 432 A
michael.may@sru.edu
MAY, Michelle .... 605-455-6064 452 L
mmay@olc.edu
MAY, Mike .... 318-678-6000 203 A
mmay@bpcc.edu
MAY, Mindy .... 937-766-7855 378 K
mkmay@cedarville.edu
MAY, Nancy, S .... 617-373-2700 235 D
MAY, Nina .... 609-586-4800 303 D
mayn@mccc.edu
MAY, Regina, A .... 573-882-4026 283 G
mayr@umsystem.edu
MAY, Robert, E .... 276-739-2436 517 D
rmay@vhcc.edu
MAY, Ron .... 423-636-7305 464 F
rmay@tusculum.edu
MAY, Ronald .... 253-964-6736 525 C
rmay@pierce.ctc.edu
MAY, Sarah, E .... 478-301-2413 128 G
may_se@mercer.edu
MAY, Susan, A .... 920-735-5731 542 N
may@fvtc.edu
MAY, Walter, P .... 770-720-5540 130 E
wpm@reinhardt.edu
MAY-RICCIUTI, Heather 304-829-7335 529 H
hricciuti@bethanywv.edu
MAYABB, Patricia .... 214-887-5022 473 E
pmayabb@dts.edu
MAYANI, Rifka 470-578-6049 127M
rmayani@kennesaw.edu
MAYATT, Darlene .... 601-484-8724 268 B
dmayatt@meridiancc.edu
MAYBANK, Denise, B ... 517-355-7535 246 H
maybank@msu.edu
MAYBELL, Steven, A ..... 206-281-2824 526 D
maybes@spu.edu
MAYBURY, Greg .... 616-395-7671 244 A
maybury@hope.edu
MAYDEN, Sharrie .... 702-895-0970 295 G
sharrie.mayden@unlv.edu
MAYE, Marilyn .... 615-871-2260.. 96 H
MAYER, Brenna, S .... 914-654-5289 322 B
bmayer@cnr.edu
MAYER, Charles .... 336-249-8186 362 B
cmayer@davidsonccc.edu
MAYER, Connie .... 518-445-2393 314 H
cmaye@albanylaw.edu
MAYER, Emily .... 215-702-4300 414 C
emayer@cairn.edu
MAYER, Russell .... 978-837-3499 233 G
mayerr@merrimack.edu
MAYERS, Darryl .... 617-287-5458 228 G
darryl.mayers@umb.edu

MAYERS, Ronnie .... 662-846-4300 267 A
rmayers@deltastate.edu
MAYERSKI, Christopher 610-558-5615 427 D
mayerskc@neumann.edu
MAYES, Brent .... 770-229-3327 132 B
bmayes@sctech.edu
MAYES, David, M .... 501-882-4420.. 19 E
dmmayes@asub.edu
MAYES, John, A .... 203-432-3503.. 93 C
john.mayes@yale.edu
MAYES, Kathleen .... 215-596-8970 438 E
president@usciences.edu
MAYES, Lakeisha, E ..... 757-823-8396 510 H
lemayes@nsu.edu
MAYES, Lisa .... 757-683-6746 510 I
lmayes@odu.edu
MAYES, Richard, A .... 336-272-7102 357 B
mayesr@greensboro.edu
MAYES, JR., Robert, G . 251-981-3771.... 3 A
robert@columbiasouthern.edu
MAYEUX, Liza .... 225-768-1737 206 F
neetu.mayeux@ololcollege.edu
MAYEUX, Teresa .... 225-752-4233 202 I
registrar@iticollege.edu
MAYEWSKI, Raymond .. 585-275-4786 351 D
Raymond_Mayewski@URMC.Rochester.
edu
MAYFIELD, Amanda, B . 860-439-2088.. 90 D
amanda.mayfield@conncoll.edu
MAYFIELD, Andrea .... 205-391-5880.... 7 A
amayfield@sheltonstate.edu
MAYFIELD, Darrell .... 808-932-7644 135 I
darrell8@hawaii.edu
MAYFIELD, Donny .... 423-746-5253 464 D
dmayfield@twcnet.edu
MAYFIELD, Mike, W ..... 828-262-7660 369 D
mayfldmw@appstate.edu
MAYFIELD, Stephen ...... 770-962-7580 127 C
smayfield@gwinnetttech.edu
MAYHER, Michael, E .... 440-525-7255 385 C
mmayher@lakelandcc.edu
MAYHEW, Glen, R .... 540-985-8539 509 D
Grmayhew@jchs.edu
MAYHEW, Kelly .... 619-388-3136.. 62 F
kmayhew@sdccd.edu
MAYHEW, Sally, A .... 618-537-6838 152 C
samayhew@mckendree.edu
MAYHEW, Sam .... 229-243-3025 121 D
sam.mayhew@bainbridge.edu
MAYHEW, Steven .... 620-231-7000 190 G
smayhew@pittstate.edu
MAYHEW, Susan, L ...... 276-498-4190 504 K
MAYHORNE, John, F .... 443-412-2382 215 D
jmayhorne@harford.edu
MAYLE, Glenn .... 928-344-7500.. 12 B
glenn.mayle@azwestern.edu
MAYLE, Teresa .... 252-536-7207 363 B
tmayle426@halifaxcc.edu
MAYLONE, Theresa, M . 718-990-2517 340 G
maylonet@stjohns.edu
MAYNARD, Francyenne 972-273-3109 473 A
fmaynard@dcccd.edu
MAYNARD, Gene .... 916-348-4689.. 43 K
gmaynard@epic.edu
MAYNARD, Jennifer 937-769-1826 376M
jmaynard@antioch.edu
MAYNARD, Kimberly, L 304-896-7345 531 F
kimberly.maynard@southernwv.edu
MAYNARD, Nelly .... 773-821-2453 141 J
nmaynard@csu.edu
MAYNARD, Pamela .... 973-877-3115 302 F
maynard@essex.edu
MAYNARD, Rebecca, A 207-768-2715 211 C
bmaynard@nmcc.edu
MAYNARD, Scott .... 662-325-3344 269 A
smaynard@career.msstate.edu
MAYNARD, Thurmond .. 301-696-3546 215 E
maynard@hood.edu
MAYNARD NELSON,
Jeanette .... 612-767-7043 253 F
jeanette@alfredadler.edu
MAYNARD-REID,
Pedrito .... 509-527-2028 528 A
pedrito.maynard-reid@wallawalla.edu
MAYNE, Deborah .... 651-779-4086 258 D
deborah.mayne@century.edu
MAYNE, Kevin .... 508-373-9400 223 C
kevin.mayne@becker.edu
MAYO, Amanda .... 712-279-5405 176 B
amanda.mayo@briarcliff.edu
MAYO, Cindy .... 870-743-3000.. 22 A
cmayo@northark.edu
MAYO, Dan .... 252-493-7304 364 H
dmayo@email.pittcc.edu
MAYO, Donna .... 706-864-1620 133 A
donna.mayo@ung.edu
MAYO, Jamaal .... 314-340-3534 275 G
mayoj@hssu.edu
MAYO, Jennifer .... 919-735-5151 367 A
jmayo@waynecc.edu

MAYO, Lindsey .... 978-556-3621 232 E
lmayo@necc.mass.edu
MAYO, Luis .... 787-257-7373 555 L
lmayo2@suagm.edu
MAYO, Michael .... 502-205-8826.. 20 G
mmayo@cbc.edu
MAYO, Michele .... 252-940-6233 360 B
michele.mayo@beaufortccc.edu
MAYO, Michelle, P .... 585-292-2370 333 G
mmayo@monroecc.edu
MAYO, Sandra .... 951-571-6160.. 60 J
sandra.mayo@mvc.edu
MAYO, Sandra .... 951-571-6160.. 60 K
sandra.mayo@mvc.edu
MAYO, Sandra .... 512-245-2361 489 C
sm37@txstate.edu
MAYO, Stephen, L .... 626-395-4951.. 31 D
steve@mayo.caltech.edu
MAYO, Suzanne .... 903-927-3386 497 G
smayo@wileyc.edu
MAYO, Tom .... 239-590-1520 114 F
tmayo@fgcu.edu
MAYRAND, Leslie .... 325-486-6247 489 E
leslie.mayrand@angelo.edu
MAYROSE, James .... 716-878-4698 345 B
mayrosj@buffalostate.edu
MAYS, Allen .... 660-562-1307 280 A
ajmays@nwmissouri.edu
MAYS, Anna .... 972-860-8261 472 D
amays@dcccd.edu
MAYS, Anna .... 972-860-2931 472 D
amays@dcccd.edu
MAYS, Beth, A .... 410-777-2480 213 E
bamays@aacc.edu
MAYS, Cathy .... 434-381-6448 513 E
CDMays@sbc.edu
MAYS, Judy .... 916-484-8376.. 52 I
maysj@arc.losrios.edu
MAYS, Marilyn .... 972-273-3501 473 A
mmays@dccd.edu
MAYS, Nathaniel .... 617-349-8539 228 B
nmays@lesley.edu
MAYS, Shirley, L .... 602-682-6870.. 12 A
smays@azsummitlaw.edu
MAYS, Susan .... 615-550-3161 466 H
susan@williamsoncc.edu
MAYS, Vida .... 662-252-8000 270 C
vmays@rustcollege.edu
MAYS, Wendy .... 903-675-6371 490 F
mays@tvcc.edu
MAYS-JACKSON, Debra 601-885-7002 267 D
Debra.Mays-Jackson@hindscc.edu
MAYSAMI, Raymin .... 601-979-2411 267 H
raymin.maysami@jsums.edu
MAYSE, Tiffany .... 859-572-5806 199 A
masyset@nku.edu
MAYSILLES, Michael, E 973-596-5642 304 D
michael.maysilles@njit.edu
MAYSON, Adrianna .... 845-434-5750 349 C
amayson@sullivan.suny.edu
MAYTON, Dana, B .... 502-852-4876 201 A
dbmayt01@louisville.edu
MAZA-DUERTO,
Aristides .... 786-331-1000 109 B
amaza@maufl.edu
MAZA-MOSS, Orianna .. 786-331-1000 109 B
omaza@maufl.edu
MAZACHEK, Juliann ..... 785-670-4483 192 B
jmazachek@wufoundation.org
MAZARIEGOS, John ..... 847-947-5086 153 H
JMazariegos@nl.edu
MAZE, Mary, C .... 248-341-2051 248 E
mcmaze@oaklandcc.edu
MAZE, Tom .... 252-399-6533 354 I
tmaze@barton.edu
MAZEL, David .... 719-587-7771.. 78 I
dbmazel@adams.edu
MAZELIN, Nikki .... 317-940-9809 164 L
nmazelin@butler.edu
MAZER, Vickie .... 301-687-4595 220 D
vmmazer@frostburg.edu
MAZEY, Mary Ellen ...... 419-372-2211 377 I
mmazey@bgsu.edu
MAZGULSKI, Judy .... 860-343-5868.. 89 E
jmazgulski@mxcc.commnet.edu
MAZIAR, Christine, M .. 574-631-2749 174 A
maziar.1@nd.edu
MAZIAR, Lucia .... 860-444-8517 548 H
Lucia.Maziar@uscga.edu
MAZICH, OSB,
Edward, M .... 724-805-2592 435 C
edward.mazich@stvincent.edu
MAZLOFF, Nina .... 508-373-9770 223 C
nina.mazloff@becker.edu
MAZUR, III, Francis, J . 352-873-5822 100 P
mazurf@cf.edu
MAZUR, JoAnne .... 440-684-6129 394 G
jmazur@ursuline.edu
MAZZA, Diane .... 203-392-5405.. 88 F
boutaughd1@southernct.edu

MCCALLUM-BEATTY, Krista ... 740-593-4330 389 H mccallum@ohio.edu
MCCAMBRIDGE, Greg ... 704-687-7683 371 B gmccambr@uncc.edu
MCCAMEY, Wade, B ... 423-585-6770 464 C wade.mccamey@ws.edu
MCCAMISH, Daniel ... 252-398-6246 356 B mccamd@chowan.edu
MCCANCE, John ... 575-492-2141 314 D jmccance@usw.edu
MCCANDLESS, Amy, T .. 843-953-1436 445 B mccandlessa@cofc.edu
MCCANDLESS, Ann ... 724-287-8711 413 G ann.mccandless@bc3.edu
MCCANDLESS, Beverly .. 270-686-4255 193 G beverly.mccandless@brescia.edu
MCCANDLESS, John ... 513-529-2223 386 K mccandjm@miamioh.edu
MCCANDLESS, Michael . 209-384-6107.. 54 C mccandless.m@mccd.edu
MCCANDLESS, N. Jane . 678-839-5170 133 F jmccandl@westga.edu
MCCANDLESS, Raymond ... 419-434-4565 393 F mccandless@findlay.edu
MCCANE, Latitia ... 251-405-7012.... 2 D lmccane@bishop.edu
MCCANN, Bonnie ... 614-947-6017 382 H bonnie.mccann@franklin.edu
MCCANN, Carrie ... 254-968-9007 485 A cmccann@tarleton.edu
MCCANN, Erin ... 607-733-7177 324 H emccann@ebi-college.com
MCCANN, Jean, A ... 636-584-6601 274 J jean.mccann@eastcentral.edu
MCCANN, John ... 512-863-1752 483 G mccannj@southwestern.edu
MCCANN, Kevin ... 802-860-2754 501 F kmccann@champlain.edu
MCCANN, Linda ... 215-968-8003 413 F mccannl@bucks.edu
MCCANN, Paul, A ... 217-581-2921 144 E pmccann@eiu.edu
MCCANN, Ralph, J ... 770-484-1204 128 D lutherrice@lutherrice.edu
MCCANN, Shawn ... 713-221-2715 491 F mccanns@uhd.edu
MCCANN, JR., Terence . 410-337-6170 215 B terence.McCann@goucher.edu
MCCANNON, Mindy ... 706-295-6846 125 F mmccannon@gntc.edu
MCCARDELL, JR., John, M ... 931-598-1101 460 I jmmccard@sewanee.edu
MCCAREL, Lori, L ... 757-455-8786 518 H lmccarel@vwc.edu
MCCARGO, Donovan ... 215-751-8876 416 B dmccargo@ccp.edu
MCCARN, Sarah ... 912-525-5000 130 H smccarn@scad.edu
MCCARRELL, Kyle ... 540-453-2269 514 H mccarrellk@brcc.edu
MCCARRICK, Richard, G ... 914-594-4503 335 H richard_mccarrick@nymc.edu
MCCARROLL, John, F ... 515-294-6137 175 G jmccarol@iastate.edu
MCCARRON, Anne ... 414-382-6068 534 I anne.mccarron@alverno.edu
MCCARRON, Tom ... 619-594-5631.. 35 E tmccarron@mail.sdsu.edu
MCCARRY, Tim ... 325-670-1434 474 M facilities@hsutx.edu
MCCART, Robert ... 517-318-3330 240 N
MCCARTER, Debbie, L .. 423-585-6844 464 C debbie.mccarter@ws.edu
MCCARTER, Rachel ... 610-902-8256 414 B rachel.mccarter@cabrini.edu
MCCARTHHY, Piper ... 775-445-3270 296 A piper.mccarthy@wnc.edu
MCCARTHY, Anne ... 651-523-2335 256 B amccarthy02@hamline.edu
MCCARTHY, Barbara ... 914-773-3741 337 I bmccarthy@pace.edu
MCCARTHY, Barbara ... 508-588-9100 232 A
MCCARTHY, Casey, J ... 218-755-3888 258 B cmccarthy@bemidjistate.edu
MCCARTHY, Colby ... 973-408-3112 301 J finaid@drew.edu
MCCARTHY, Daniel ... 985-549-2055 208 E dmccarthy@selu.edu
MCCARTHY, Dominica .. 972-860-4689 472 C dmccarthy@dcccd.edu
MCCARTHY, Douglas ... 602-285-7245.. 15 C douglas.mccarthy@phoenixcollege.edu
MCCARTHY, Elizabeth, K ... 508-678-2811 231 B elizabeth.mccarthy@bristolcc.edu
MCCARTHY, Faith ... 530-221-4275.. 66 B shastaonline@clearwire.net
MCCARTHY, Faith ... 530-221-4275.. 66 B registrar@shasta.edu
MCCARTHY, Jack, H ... 617-373-2240 235 D
MCCARTHY, James ... 610-861-5506 427 F jmccarthy@northampton.edu
MCCARTHY, Jeffrey, M . 607-255-7120 323 C jmm11@cornell.edu
MCCARTHY, John, C ... 202-319-5259.. 95 A mccartjc@cua.edu
MCCARTHY, John, J ... 413-545-5271 228 F jmccarthy@grad.umass.edu
MCCARTHY, Katherine .. 304-766-3039 533 C kmccarthy@wvstateu.edu
MCCARTHY, Kelly ... 708-235-3966 145 D kmccarthy@govst.edu
MCCARTHY, Kevin ... 315-568-3267 334 F kmccarthy@nycc.edu
MCCARTHY, Kevin ... 518-255-5217 346 E mccartk@cobleskill.edu
MCCARTHY, Kevin ... 704-330-6907 361 D kevin.mccarthy@cpcc.edu
MCCARTHY, Kevin, D ... 425-235-2235 525 G kmccarthy@rtc.edu
MCCARTHY, Margaret ... 716-888-2120 317 H mmccarth@canisius.edu
MCCARTHY, Margaret ... 716-888-2120 317 H mmccarth@canisius.edu
MCCARTHY, Margo, M . 203-576-5556.. 91 H mmccarthy@stvincentscollege.edu
MCCARTHY, Mark, D ... 216-397-4213 384 F mmccarthy@jcu.edu
MCCARTHY, Marsha ... 908-737-7100 303 C mmccarth@kean.edu
MCCARTHY, Mary ... 607-778-5210 344 F mccarthyma@sunybroome.edu
MCCARTHY, Melissa ... 401-874-2599 442 E mcmel@uri.edu
MCCARTHY, SJ, Michael ... 408-554-4715.. 65 A mcmccarthy@scu.edu
MCCARTHY, Michael, R 402-932-8600 290 B mmccarthy@mccarthycapital.com
MCCARTHY, Pamela ... 413-585-2840 236 G pmccarth@smith.edu
MCCARTHY, Patrice ... 216-373-5182 388 A mpmccarthy@ndc.edu
MCCARTHY, Rosemary .. 412-536-1173 422 E rosemary.mccarthy@laroche.edu
MCCARTHY, Sean ... 312-777-8726 147 C smccarthy@aii.edu
MCCARTHY, Sherry ... 712-279-3149 182 F sherry.mccarthy@stlukescollege.edu
MCCARTHY, Thomas ... 718-862-7977 331 H thomas.mccarthy@manhattan.edu
MCCARTNEY, Cliff ... 865-573-4517 457 H cmccartney@johnsonu.edu
MCCARTNEY, Jason ... 410-548-4085 220 E
MCCARTNEY, Jill ... 402-826-8583 290 C jill.mccartney@doane.edu
MCCARTNEY, Kathleen .. 413-585-2100 236 G kmccartney@smith.edu
MCCARTNEY, Maureen .. 413-572-8801 230 F mccartney@westfield.ma.edu
MCCARTNEY, Patrick, S 913-288-7166 188 G pmccartney@kckcc.edu
MCCARTNEY, William, G ... 765-496-2270 171 K mccart@purdue.edu
MCCARTNEY, JR., William, L ... 252-328-6050 369 E mccartneyw@ecu.edu
MCCARTY, Alison ... 617-964-1100 222 B amccarty@ants.edu
MCCARTY, II, Gerald ... 810-766-4206 239 H gerald.mccartyii@baker.edu
MCCARTY, Josh ... 870-759-4143.. 25 I jmccarty@wbcoll.edu
MCCARTY, Lori ... 276-656-0212 516 D lmccarty@patrickhenry.edu
MCCARTY, Shannon ... 480-517-8285.. 15 D shannon.mccarty@riosalado.edu
MCCARTY, Susan ... 212-772-4850 319 E susan.mccarty@hunter.cuny.edu
MCCARTY, Therese, A ... 518-388-6102 350 K mccartyt@union.edu
MCCARTY-HARRIS, Yulanda ... 216-687-2223 380 D y.mccartyharris@csuohio.edu
MCCARVEL, Thomas, J . 406-447-4409 286 D tmccarve@carroll.edu
MCCARVER, Viva ... 419-372-8421 377 I vivam@bgsu.edu
MCCARY, Jennifer, Q ... 717-337-6998 419 C jmccary@gettysburg.edu
MCCASKILL, Rock ... 912-344-2576 120 D rock.mccaskill@armstrong.edu
MCCASKILL, Sharrell ... 202-651-5642.. 95 C sharrell.mccaskill@gallaudet.edu
MCCASLAND, Shannon . 970-339-6563.. 78 J shannon.mccasland@aims.edu
MCCASLIN, James, B ... 270-901-1104 197 C james.mccaslin@kctcs.edu
MCCASLIN, John ... 931-553-0071 459 G john.mccaslin@miller-motte.com
MCCASLIN, Julie ... 423-746-5214 464 D jmccaslin@twcnet.edu
MCCASLIN, Randall ... 814-732-1346 430 G rmccaslin@edinboro.edu
MCCASLIN, Sharon ... 314-889-4567 275 B smccaslin@fontbonne.edu
MCCAULEY, David, W ... 304-473-8322 534 G mccauley@wvwc.edu
MCCAULEY, Dennis ... 215-968-8394 413 F mccauley@bucks.edu
MCCAULEY, Howard ... 816-271-4266 279 E mccaulhj@missouriwestern.edu
MCCAULEY, Laurie, K ... 734-763-3311 251 C mccauley@umich.edu
MCCAULEY, Linda ... 404-727-7976 124 D linda.mccauley@emory.edu
MCCAULEY, Randy ... 254-519-5491 485 D randymccauley@tamuct.edu
MCCAULEY, Terry, L ... 248-232-4660 248 E tlmccaul@oaklandcc.edu
MCCAULEY-JUGOVICH, Shelly ... 218-748-2416 259 D s.mccauley@mesabirange.edu
MCCAUSLAND, Bill ... 813-974-1868 116 B mccausland@usf.edu
MCCAUSLIN, Lauren ... 617-243-2139 227 K lmccauslin@lasell.edu
MCCAW, Ian, J ... 254-710-1222 469 D ian_mccaw@baylor.edu
MCCAWLEY, Loree ... 831-479-6234.. 30 C lomccawl@cabrillo.edu
MCCAY, Bill ... 509-865-8520 523 C mccay_b@heritage.edu
MCCAY, Julie ... 828-884-8264 355 A mccayjp@brevard.edu
MCCAY, Patrick ... 603-623-0313 298 C patrickmccay@nhia.edu
MCCAY, T. Dwayne ... 321-674-8889 103 R tdmccay@fit.edu
MCCHURCH, Bob ... 309-796-5000 140 D
MCCINTY, Jill ... 312-935-3033 157 A jmcginty@robertmorris.edu
MCCLAFFERTY, Joseph . 406-496-4804 288 C jmcclafferty@mtech.edu
MCCLAIN, Barbara, L ... 304-326-1234 530 G bmcclain@salemu.edu
MCCLAIN, Beth ... 309-694-5323 146 C bmcclain@icc.edu
MCCLAIN, Dale ... 847-866-3920 145 C dale.mcclain@garrett.edu
MCCLAIN, Elman ... 206-934-5437 526 A elman.mcclain@seattlecolleges.edu
MCCLAIN, Gloria ... 404-756-4098 120 H gmcclain@atlm.edu
MCCLAIN, James ... 626-914-8794.. 38 L jmcclain@citruscollege.edu
MCCLAIN, James, W ... 870-838-2910.. 19 C jmcclain@smail.anc.edu
MCCLAIN, Jason ... 304-829-7601 529 H jmcclain@bethanywv.edu
MCCLAIN, Mark ... 937-766-7933 378 K mcclain@cedarville.edu
MCCLAIN, Paula, D ... 919-681-1560 356 E pmmcclain@duke.edu
MCCLAIN, Rita ... 405-495-6300 402 E rmcclain@snu.edu
MCCLAIN, Samantha, E 515-574-1080 179 F mcclain@iowacentral.edu
MCCLAIN, Tammy ... 304-336-8023 533 A tmcclain@westliberty.edu
MCCLAIN, Tim ... 360-486-8875 525 H tmc@stmartin.edu
MCCLAIN, Tom ... 817-552-3700 477 B tom.mcclain@tku.edu
MCCLANAHAN, Ana, M 919-513-2311 366 H ammcclanahan@waketech.edu
MCCLANAHAN, Barry ... 717-477-1240 431 F bkmcca@ship.edu
MCCLANAHAN, Denise . 434-961-5275 516 F dmcclanahan@pvcc.edu
MCCLANAHAN, Keith ... 501-882-8811.. 19 E mkmcclanahan@asub.edu
MCCLANAHAN, Kimberlee, L ... 815-835-6315 158 I k.l.mcclanahan@svcc.edu
MCCLANAHAN, Thomas, H ... 559-278-0840.. 33 D thomas_mcclanahan@csufresno.edu
MCCLATCHY, Anna ... 706-886-6831 132 F amcclatchy@tfc.edu
MCCLAY, Diana, D ... 423-439-5890 461 D mcclayd@etsu.edu
MCCLAY, Kelly ... 609-343-4939 299 G mcclay@atlantic.edu
MCCLEARY, Caitlin ... 865-974-1000 465 D
MCCLEARY, Tim ... 406-638-3121 286 I baaxpaa@lbhc.edu
MCCLEERY, Steve ... 575-392-5004 311 J smccleery@nmjc.edu
MCCLELLAN, Cissy ... 802-860-2711 501 F mcclella@champlain.edu
MCCLELLAN, Craig, S ... 304-326-1465 530 G cmcclellan@salemu.edu
MCCLELLAN, Debralee .. 843-525-8210 449 E dmcclellan@tcl.edu
MCCLELLAN, Fletcher ... 717-361-1555 418 B mcclelef@etown.edu
MCCLELLAN, George, S 260-481-6844 168 D mcclellg@ipfw.edu
MCCLELLAN, Jane ... 201-200-3196 304 C jmcclellan@njcu.edu
MCCLELLAN, Laura ... 276-739-2425 517 D lMcClellan@vhcc.edu
MCCLELLAN, Mia, C ... 619-482-6369.. 68 D mmcclellan@swccd.edu
MCCLELLAN, Patricia ... 828-251-6001 370 E pmcclell@unca.edu
MCCLELLAN, Scott ... 206-220-8229 526 F mcclells@seattleu.edu
MCCLELLAN, Steve ... 662-846-4004 267 A sjmcclellan@deltastate.edu
MCCLELLAND, Charles, F ... 713-313-7216 487 F mcclellandcf@tsu.edu
MCCLELLAND, Jeremy .. 214-860-2351 472 F jmccleland@dcccd.edu
MCCLELLAND, Karin ... 925-631-4013.. 61 G klm14@stmarys-ca.edu
MCCLELLAND, Theresa . 251-580-2100..... 5 A theresa.mcclelland@faulknerstate.edu
MCCLELLAND, II, Thomas, H ... 318-257-4827 208 A tmcclelland@latech.edu
MCCLELLON, Leslie, R .. 507-285-7215 261 D leslie.mcclellon@rctc.edu
MCCLENAGAN, Cindy, M ... 806-291-1106 496 K cindym@wbu.edu
MCCLENDON, Bev ... 479-788-7082.. 23 H bev.mcclendon@uafs.edu
MCCLENDON, Jennifer .. 918-456-5511 398 M mcclendo@nsuok.edu
MCCLENDON, Karen ... 916-686-8602.. 32 B
MCCLENDON, Mark ... 817-515-5203 484 B mark.mcclendon@tccd.edu
MCCLENDON, Mark ... 940-397-4567 478 G mark.mcclendon@mwsu.edu
MCCLENDON, Vivienne . 425-564-3056 519 L vivienne.mcclendon@bellevuecollege.edu
MCCLINTOCK, Charles .. 805-765-9300.. 64 G
MCCLINTOCK, Elizabeth 724-503-1001 439 B emcclintock@washjeff.edu
MCCLINTOCK, Kate ... 707-527-4797.. 65 C kmcclintock@santarosa.edu
MCCLINTOCK, Marta ... 724-938-4251 430 C mcclintock@calu.edu
MCCLINTOCK, Melvin, A ... 240-895-4309 218 B mamcclintock@smcm.edu
MCCLINTOCK, Patty ... 812-237-2305 167 E patty.mcclintock@indstate.edu
MCCLINTOCK, Stewart .. 336-342-4261 365 E mcclintocks@rockinghamcc.edu
MCCLINTON, Ace ... 630-620-2129 154 J amcclinton@seminary.edu
MCCLINTON, JR., Flandus ... 225-771-5021 207 A flandus_mcclinton@subr.edu
MCCLINTON, Martin ... 239-489-9229 104 G mmcclinton1@fsw.edu
MCCLOSKEY, Brian ... 609-586-4800 303 D mccloskb@mccc.edu
MCCLOSKEY, Erin, E ... 814-472-3100 434 F emccloskey@francis.edu
MCCLOSKEY, James, M 302-356-6880.. 94 G james.m.mccloskey@wilmu.edu
MCCLOSKEY, JR., John, R ... 610-796-3005 412 C john.mccloskey@alvernia.edu
MCCLOUD, Alyssa ... 973-313-6146 308 C alyssa.mccloud@shu.edu
MCCLOUD, Barbara, L .. 630-515-7687 152 H bmcclo@midwestern.edu
MCCLOUD, Clarence ... 386-506-6301 101 I mcclouc@DaytonaState.edu
MCCLOUD, Elizabeth, K 717-361-1404 418 B mcclouek@etown.edu
MCCLOUD, Jennifer ... 317-822-3489 171 B jmccloud@martin.edu
MCCLOUD, Mickey ... 816-604-6621 277 G mickey.mccloud@mcckc.edu
MCCLOY, Eric ... 215-572-8521 412 F mccloy@arcadia.edu
MCCLUNEY, Alice ... 828-395-1495 363 D amccluney@isothermal.edu

MCCLUNG, Alan 423-614-8410 457 M amcclung@leeuniversity.edu
MCCLUNG, Alex 973-408-3799 301 J amcclung@drew.edu
MCCLUNG, Philip, L 336-734-7212 362 F pmcclung@forsythtech.edu
MCCLUNG, Shemeka 601-979-7030 267 H shemeka.s.mcclung@jsums.edu
MCCLURE, A. Glenn 610-917-1453 438 G agmcclure@valleyforge.edu
MCCLURE, Amber 575-461-4413 311 C amberm@mesalands.edu
MCCLURE, Amy 740-368-3562 390 B aamcclur@owu.edu
MCCLURE, Beverlee, J 719-587-7341 78 I bmcclure@adams.edu
MCCLURE, Dan 503-821-8970 408 H dmcclure@pnca.edu
MCCLURE, Erin 361-593-2795 486 A erin.mcclure@tamuk.edu
MCCLURE, Guy 256-233-8296 1 F guy.mcclure@athens.edu
MCCLURE, H. Lawrence 215-780-1331 435 D larry@salus.edu
MCCLURE, Jennifer 847-214-7319 144 F jmcclure@elgin.edu
MCCLURE, Judy 828-766-1272 364 A jmmclure@mayland.edu
MCCLURE, Ken 417-836-5233 279 A kmcclure@missuristate.edu
MCCLURE, Lawrence 215-780-1331 435 D larry@salus.edu
MCCLURE, Mike 541-956-7237 409 F mmclure@roguecc.edu
MCCLURE, Robert 845-446-1522 549 A Robert.McClure@wpaog.org
MCCLURE, Tonya 478-757-3467 122 E tmcclure@centralgatech.edu
MCCLURE, William 718-997-5790 320 E william.mcclure@qc.cuny.edu
MCCLURE, William, S 413-545-2111 228 F billmcclure@contined.umass.edu
MCCLUSKEY, Cindy 815-825-2086 149 E cindy.mccluskey@kishwaukeecollege.edu
MCCLUSKEY, Don 360-676-2772 524 D dmccluskey@nwic.edu
MCCLUSKEY, Eugene 207-768-2786 211 C emccluskey@nmcc.edu
MCCLUSKEY, Jennifer 314-529-9561 277 B jmccluskey@maryville.edu
MCCLUSKEY, Richard 978-665-3118 229 D rmccluskey@fitchburgstate.edu
MCCLUSKY, John 217-854-3231 140 F john.mcclusky@blackburn.edu
MCCLYMONT, Jay, W 717-766-2511 426 B jmcclymont@messiah.edu
MCCOEY, Margaret 215-951-1222 422 F mccoey@lasalle.edu
MCCOLGIN, Cathleen, C 315-866-0300 327 E mccolgicc@herkimer.edu
MCCOLLAM, Willis, L 304-637-1803 529 I mccollamw@dewv.edu
MCCOLLETT, Sherry 207-621-3141 212 D umafa@maine.edu
MCCOLLOCH, Mark 443-840-1021 214 F mmocolloch@ccbcmd.edu
MCCOLLOM, Keelin 909-793-4263 28 S kmccollom@ashdowncollege.edu
MCCOLLOUGH, Laura, L 907-474-1886 10 I lcmccollough@alaska.edu
MCCOLLOUGH, William, A 352-392-1202 115 D amccollough@aa.ufl.edu
MCCOLLUM, Alonzo, L 516-876-3068 345 E mccolluma@oldwestbury.edu
MCCOLLUM, Estella 785-864-2468 191 G estellam@ku.edu
MCCOLLUM, Rick, L 501-450-3132 25 F rickm@uca.edu
MCCOLLUM, Scott 937-512-3068 391 D scott.mccullum@sinclair.edu
MCCOLLUM, Susan 334-291-4953 2 H susan.mccollum@cv.edu
MCCOLSKEY, Erin, S 561-868-3139 109 H mccolske@palmbeachstate.edu
MCCOMAS, Pam 626-529-8033 57 F pmccomas@pacificoaks.edu
MCCOMAS, Richard 580-581-2524 397 A richardm@cameron.edu
MCCOMB, Brenda 541-737-4881 408 F brenda.mccomb@oregonstate.edu
MCCOMBIE, Ronni 434-200-3070 505 L ronni.mccombie@centralhealth.com
MCCOMBS, Charlie 502-213-5101 196 E charles.mccombs@kctcs.edu
MCCOMBS, Ed 928-724-6635 13 J emccombs@dinecollege.edu
MCCOMBS, Gary 864-388-8305 447 E gmccombs@lander.edu
MCCOMBS, Gillian, M 214-768-2400 482 J gmccombs@smu.edu
MCCOMBS, Laurie 216-687-3606 380 D l.mccombs11@csuohio.edu
MCCOMBS, Tyrone 856-361-2931 306 D mccombst@rowan.edu
MCCONAHAY, Mark 812-855-0121 167 J mcconaha@indiana.edu
MCCONAHY, Douglas 304-829-7131 529 H dmcconahy@bethanywv.edu
MCCONATHY, Jamie 870-864-7193 23 B jmcconathy@southark.edu
MCCONATHY, Terry, M 318-257-4262 208 A tmm@latech.edu
MCCONKEY, Dionne 410-669-9200 216 F
MCCONKEY, Susan 415-503-6285 63 A smcconkey@sfcm.edu
MCCONNAUGHEY, Scott, E 719-884-5000 84 G SEMcConnaughey@nbc.edu
MCCONNELL, Blake 618-658-8331 150 B james.mcconnell@doc.illinois.gov
MCCONNELL, Brian 607-733-7177 324 H bmcconnell@ebi-college.com
MCCONNELL, C. Douglas 626-584-5205 45 F provost@fuller.edu
MCCONNELL, Cary 617-573-8575 237 B cmcconnell@suffolk.edu
MCCONNELL, Cheryl, M 816-501-4087 281 B cheryl.mcconnell@rockhurst.edu
MCCONNELL, Frank, J 706-864-1606 133 A mac.mcconnell@ung.edu
MCCONNELL, Gaye 704-216-3600 365 F gaye.mcconnell@rccc.edu
MCCONNELL, Glenn, F 843-953-5500 445 B mcconnellgf@cofc.edu
MCCONNELL, Jason 423-869-6333 458 B jason.mcconnell@lmunet.edu
MCCONNELL, Joyce 304-293-5701 533 D joyce.mcconnell@mail.wvu.edu
MCCONNELL, Kathy 619-849-2412 59 K kathymcconnell@pointloma.edu
MCCONNELL, Penny, J 217-443-8747 143 F pmcconn@dacc.edu
MCCONNELLOGUE, Ken 303-860-5600 86 D ken.mcconnellogue@cu.edu
MCCONOUGHEY, Gina 608-757-7723 542 L gmcconoughey@blackhawk.edu
MCCOOK, Sonya 336-506-4278 359 N sonya.mccook@alamancecc.edu
MCCOOL, Bobby 606-886-3863 195 I bobby.mccool@kctcs.edu
MCCOOL, Jeff 575-492-4711 311 J jmccool@nmjc.edu
MCCOOL, Joan, L 716-878-4436 345 B mccooljl@buffalostate.edu
MCCORCLE, Michael 417-865-2815 274 L mccorclem@evangel.edu
MCCORD, Carol 812-855-8187 167 J iubdos@indiana.edu
MCCORD, Christopher 815-753-1061 154 I mccord@niu.edu
MCCORD, Elizabeth 415-451-2832 63 B emccord@sfts.edu
MCCORD, Jeff, D 423-354-5207 463 D jdmccord@northeaststate.edu
MCCORD-FITHIAN, Regina, L 812-888-5848 174 F rmccord-fithian@vinu.edu
MCCORMACK, Amy 708-524-6770 144 C amccormack@dom.edu
MCCORMACK, Bridey 806-457-4200 474 E bmccormack@fpctx.edu
MCCORMACK, Corky 417-447-8172 280 C mccormac@otc.edu
MCCORMACK, Erin 801-302-2800 498 L erin.mccormack@neumont.edu
MCCORMACK, Gary 713-942-3400 493 J mccormack@stthom.edu
MCCORMACK, Jeff 405-425-1933 399 J jeff.mccormack@oc.edu
MCCORMACK, John 708-596-2000 159 D jmccormack@ssc.edu
MCCORMACK, Laurie 816-584-6210 280 F laurie.mccormack@park.edu
MCCORMACK, Mike 205-726-2916 6 F hmmccorm@samford.edu
MCCORMICK, Adrienne 315-312-2285 346 A adrienne.mccormick@oswego.edu
MCCORMICK, Amanda 415-388-1133 45 J amanda.mccormick@lifeway.com
MCCORMICK, Brad 618-985-8340 148 G bradmccormick@jalc.edu
MCCORMICK, Brad 423-697-3264 462 C brad.mccormick@chattanoogastate.edu
MCCORMICK, Brian 319-296-4050 179 B brian.mccormick@hawkeyecollege.edu
MCCORMICK, Charlie, T 830-792-7371 482 D ctmccormick@schreiner.edu
MCCORMICK, Christine, B 413-545-2705 228 F cmccormick@educ.umass.edu
MCCORMICK, David 312-567-4972 147 E dmccormick@iitri.org
MCCORMICK, Dee 330-263-2321 380 E dmccormick@wooster.edu
MCCORMICK, Gordon 831-656-2484 548 A gmccormick@navy.edu
MCCORMICK, Heidi, A 330-263-2533 380 E hmccormick@wooster.edu
MCCORMICK, Jennifer Higgins 716-827-2455 350 H mccormickj@trocaire.edu
MCCORMICK, Jill 402-872-2257 292 C jmccormick@peru.edu
MCCORMICK, Jim, S 303-963-3363 79 L jimmccormick@ccu.edu
MCCORMICK, John 406-243-2532 287 D john.mccormick@umontana.edu
MCCORMICK, John 801-957-4024 500 E john.mccormick@slcc.edu
MCCORMICK, Joseph 303-797-4222 79 A joseph.mccormick@arapahoe.edu
MCCORMICK, Karla, S 334-844-4183 1 G ksm0010@auburn.edu
MCCORMICK, Kelly, L 303-765-3121 83 C kmccormick@iliff.edu
MCCORMICK, Kevin, M 630-515-6053 152 H kmccor@midwestern.edu
MCCORMICK, Kimberly 423-697-4792 462 C kimberly.mccormick@chattanoogastate.edu
MCCORMICK, Kirsten, M 714-879-3901 47 D kmmccormick@hiu.edu
MCCORMICK, Mark 205-247-8831 7 G mmccormick@stillman.edu
MCCORMICK, Mark 732-906-2515 303 F mmccormick@middlesexcc.edu
MCCORMICK, OSU, Mary 440-943-7600 391 A mmccormick@dioceseofcleveland.org
MCCORMICK, Megan 310-377-5501 53 E mmccormick@marymountcalifornia.edu
MCCORMICK, Michael, R 315-386-7222 347 F mccormic@canton.edu
MCCORMICK, Patrick, T 509-313-6715 522 L mccormick@calvin.gonzaga.edu
MCCORMICK, Peter 970-247-7595 82 I mccormick_p@fortrtlewis.edu
MCCORMICK, CSC, Peter, M 574-631-7800 174 A mccormick.23@nd.edu
MCCORMICK, Reenie 410-334-2939 221 E rmccormick@worwic.edu
MCCORMICK, Reid, W 714-879-3901 47 D rwmccormick@hiu.edu
MCCORMICK, Robert 312-362-6627 143 G bmccormi@depaul.edu
MCCORMICK, Robert 734-995-7391 241 F robert.mccormick@cuaa.edu
MCCORMICK, Silas 217-732-3168 150 G smccormick@lincolnchristian.edu
MCCORMICK, Stanley 229-420-7013 119 H Stanley.McCormick@asurams.edu
MCCORMICK, Susan 979-230-3423 469 G susan.mccormick@brazosport.edu
MCCORMICK, Vicky 626-396-2456 28 J vicky.mccormick@artcenter.edu
MCCORQUODALE, Duncan, L 260-422-5561 167 F dlMcCorquodale@indianatech.edu
MCCORRY, Laurie, K 617-228-2465 231 C lkmccorry@bhcc.mass.edu
MCCORRY-ANDALIS, Catherine, M 915-747-5648 494 B cmandalis@utep.edu
MCCORT, Tiffany 619-574-6909 57 E thansen@pacificcollege.edu
MCCORVEY, Angela, E 850-474-7448 116 E amccorv0@uwf.edu
MCCORY, Denise 216-987-5544 381 A denise.mccory@tri-c.edu
MCCOULLUM, Valarie, S 215-898-5337 437 I cade@upenn.edu
MCCOURT, Mary Frances 812-855-7618 167 I mmmccour@indiana.edu
MCCOURT, MaryFrances 812-855-3565 167 I mmmccour@indiana.edu
MCCOURT, MaryFrances 812-855-7114 167 J vpcfo@indiana.edu
MCCOURT, Susan 508-678-2811 231 B susan.mccourt@bristolcc.edu
MCCOWAN, Carla 217-333-3701 162 A cmccowan@illinois.edu
MCCOWN, Amber 239-489-9226 104 G amccown@fsw.edu
MCCOY, Angela, M 773-227-5193 156 J angela.mccoy@resu.edu
MCCOY, Avis, M 954-201-7401 99 G amccoy@broward.edu
MCCOY, Carole, A 315-786-2230 329 G cmccoy@sunyjefferson.edu
MCCOY, David, M 804-289-8718 513 M dmccoy2@richmond.edu
MCCOY, Holly, M 724-738-2650 432 A holly.mccoy@sru.edu
MCCOY, Janee 914-964-4282 321 E
MCCOY, John 423-236-2444 460 K jmccoy@southern.edu
MCCOY, Julie 803-938-3753 450 H jmccoy@uscsumter.edu
MCCOY, Keith 773-838-7514 142 C kmccoy@ccc.edu
MCCOY, Marilyn 847-491-4335 155 D mmccoy@northwestern.edu
MCCOY, Mark 765-658-6732 165 G markmccoy@depauw.edu
MCCOY, Mary 409-882-3080 488 G mary.mccoy@lsco.edu
MCCOY, Mary 405-682-1611 399 K mmccoy@occc.edu
MCCOY, Matthew, J 541-383-7210 404 K mmccoy@cocc.edu
MCCOY, Mike 256-216-3300 1 F mike.mccoy@athens.edu
MCCOY, Paddy 509-527-2343 528 A paddy.mccoy@wallawalla.edu
MCCOY, Patricia 800-354-1254 16 K pmccoy@brightoncollege.edu
MCCOY, Patricia 800-231-3803 12 G
MCCOY, Peggy, S 406-496-4404 288 C pmccoy@mtech.edu
MCCOY, Robert 907-474-7500 10 I rpmccoy@alaska.edu
MCCOY, Ryan 303-404-5238 82 J ryan.mccoy@frontrange.edu
MCCOY, Shauna 615-361-7555 456 F smccoy@daymarinstitute.edu
MCCOY, Shelly 931-393-1600 463 B smccoy@mscc.edu
MCCOY, Sue 916-484-8211 52 I mccoys@arc.losrios.edu
MCCOY, Sue 212-353-4167 323 B mccoy@cooper.edu
MCCOY, Thomas, J 940-369-8249 492 D thomas.mccoy@unt.edu
MCCOY, William, K 570-577-1609 413 E bill.mccoy@bucknell.edu
MCCOY GRISSOM, Shelly 419-251-1203 386 C shelly.mccoy-grissom@mercycollege.edu
MCCOY-WILSON, Sonya 404-225-4672 120 I smccoy-wilson@atlantatech.edu
MCCRACKEN, Carolyn 423-354-2509 463 D cgmccracken@northeaststate.edu
MCCRACKEN, Fawn 952-446-4325 255 E mccrackenf@crown.edu
MCCRACKEN, Jeff, B 919-966-5730 371 A jeff_mccracken@unc.edu
MCCRACKEN, Joann 610-989-1450 438 I jbmiller@vfmac.edu
MCCRACKEN, Larry 503-517-1879 411 C lmccracken@westernseminary.edu
MCCRACKEN, Mike 620-235-4624 190 G mmccracken@pittstate.edu
MCCRAE, Byron 413-559-5412 227 C bmccrae@hampshire.edu
MCCRANEY, Steven 601-925-3204 268 E smccraney@mc.edu
MCCRARY, Brian 678-839-6619 133 F bmccrary@westga.edu
MCCRARY, Cheryl 785-594-8301 184 F cheryl.mccrary@bakeru.edu
MCCRARY, Kevin 386-506-3475 101 I mccrark@DaytonaState.edu
MCCRAW, Bethany, J 254-710-1715 469 D bethany_mccraw@baylor.edu
MCCRAW, Ed 903-785-7661 480 B emccraw@parisjc.edu
MCCRAW, Liz 580-745-3212 402 D lmccraw@se.edu
MCCRAW, Patti, H 864-488-4571 447 F pmccraw@limestone.edu
MCCRAY, Carrie 573-592-4317 286 A carrie.mccray@williamwoods.edu
MCCRAY, Jacquelyn 870-575-8475 24 D mccrayj@uapb.edu
MCCRAY, JR., John, H 401-277-5489 442 E drmccray@uri.edu

MCCRAY, Suzanne .... 479-575-4883.. 23 G
smccray@uark.edu
MCCREADIE, Maureen .. 215-968-8004 413 F
mccreadi@bucks.edu
MCCREADY, Randall ..... 412-624-7180 437 K
mccready@pitt.edu
MCCREARY, Jeff .... 573-518-2308 278 F
jmccreary@mineralarea.edu
MCCREARY, Lynn .... 940-565-2378 492 D
mccreary@unt.edu
MCCREARY, William ..... 419-530-3990 394 E
william.mccreary@utoledo.edu
MCCREATH, Amy .... 617-682-1571 226 D
amccreath@eds.edu
MCCREE, Bernard, L ..... 610-683-4032 431 B
mccree@kutztown.edu
MCCREE, Robin .... 704-991-0252 366 D
MCCREE, Robin .... 704-991-0252 366 D
mmccree5540@stanly.edu
MCCREERY,
Deborah, M .... 610-921-7501 411 E
dmccreery@albright.edu
MCCREERY, Shane .... 309-438-3383 147 I
msmccre@ilstu.edu
MCCRIMMON, Samuel .. 419-530-4249 394 E
samuel.mccrimmon@utoledo.edu
MCCROHAN, Betty, A ... 979-532-6304 497 F
bettym@wcjc.edu
MCCRORY, Cynthia .... 704-922-6406 362 G
mccrory.cynthia@gaston.edu
MCCRORY, Heidi, H ...... 740-427-5154 384 P
mccroryh@kenyon.edu
MCCRORY, Robert, L .... 585-275-4973 351 D
rmcc@lle.rochester.edu
MCCROSKEY, Lorie, L ... 336-633-1118 365 A
llmccroskey@randolph.edu
MCCROW, Rich .... 661-720-2002.. 49 E
rmccrow@bakersfieldcollege.edu
MCCROY-HEINS,
Michelle .... 201-692-2190 302 H
michelle_mccroy@fdu.edu
MCCRYSTAL, Mary .... 216-373-5331 388 A
mmccrystal@ndc.edu
MCCUBBIN, Jeff .... 970-491-5841.. 81 D
jeff.mccubbin@colostate.edu
MCCUBBIN, Todd, A .... 573-882-6017 283 H
mccubbint@missouri.edu
MCCUE, Cindy .... 631-420-2319 348 B
cynthia.mccue@farmingdale.edu
MCCUE, Jennie .... 949-582-4320.. 67 F
jmccue@saddleback.edu
MCCUE, Mary, E .... 419-559-2204 392 A
mmccue@terra.edu
MCCUEN, Jan .... 714-997-6701.. 38 B
mccuen@chapman.edu
MCCUIEN-SMITH,
Cassandra .... 501-450-3173.. 25 F
cmccuien@uca.edu
MCCUIN, Tara .... 802-447-6343 503 A
tmccuin@svc.edu
MCCULLAR,
Douglas, D .... 405-878-5141 402 A
ddmccullar@stgregorys.edu
MCCULLEN, Ann, S ...... 904-620-2100 116 A
amccullen@unf.edu
MCCULLEY, Becky .... 214-645-5482 496 A
becky.mcculley@utsouthwestern.edu
MCCULLOCH, Dave .... 770-962-7580 127 C
dmcculloch@gwinnetttech.edu
MCCULLOCH, Greg .... 618-252-5400 159 F
greg.mcculloch@sic.edu
MCCULLOCH, Joseph .... 318-813-9201 205 D
jmccul@lsuhsc.edu
MCCULLOCH, Sonja ...... 912-260-4402 131 D
sonja.mcculloch@sgsc.edu
MCCULLOH, Julie, A ..... 509-313-6572 522 L
mcculloh@gu.gonzaga.edu
MCCULLOH, Thayne, M 509-313-6102 522 L
president@gonzaga.edu
MCCULLOUGH, Barbara 360-538-4034 523 A
bmccullo@ghc.edu
MCCULLOUGH, Brandi .. 252-249-1851 364 F
bmccullough@pamlicocc.edu
MCCULLOUGH, Bryan ... 336-249-4688 362 B
bryan_mccullough@davidsonccc.edu
MCCULLOUGH,
Catherine .... 802-728-1247 504 C
cmccull@vtc.edu
MCCULLOUGH,
Desiree, A .... 731-881-7014 465 F
dmccull1@utm.edu
MCCULLOUGH, Doreen . 802-773-5900 501 G
dmccullough@csj.edu
MCCULLOUGH, James .. 918-293-5068 400 E
james.mccullough@okstate.edu
MCCULLOUGH,
John, P .... 304-336-8000 533 A
mcculljp@westliberty.edu
MCCULLOUGH,
Jonathan, W .... 903-434-8115 479 L
jmccullough@ntcc.edu
MCCULLOUGH, Laura ... 912-478-5234 126 B
lmccullough@georgiasouthern.edu
MCCULLOUGH,
Laura, C .... 301-687-4068 220 D
lcmccullough@frostburg.edu
MCCULLOUGH, Laurie .. 919-508-2025 373 B
lmccullough@peace.edu
MCCULLOUGH, Lois, N 419-783-2317 381 G
lmccullough@defiance.edu
MCCULLOUGH, Randy .. 419-559-2355 392 A
rmccullough01@terra.edu
MCCULLOUGH,
Robert, R .... 216-368-5445 378 J
robert.mccullough@case.edu
MCCULLOUGH, Willie ... 606-326-2068 195 H
willie.mccullough@kctcs.edu
MCCULLUM, B. J .... 309-854-1723 140 D
mccullumb@bhc.edu
MCCULLY, Clare .... 617-730-7089 235 B
clare.mccully@newbury.edu
MCCUNE, John .... 781-239-2527 231 G
jmccune@massbay.edu
MCCUNE, Kate .... 562-947-8755.. 67 J
katmccune@scuhs.edu
MCCUNE, Mary .... 315-312-3443 346 A
mary.mccune@oswego.edu
MCCUNE, Ryan .... 620-252-7180 186 C
ryanm@coffeyville.edu
MCCURDY, Clantha .... 617-727-9420 228 D
cmccurdy@osfa.mass.edu
MCCURDY, Debra, L ..... 419-995-8200 384 E
mccurdy.d@rhodesstate.edu
MCCURDY, Eugene, M . 608-796-3921 542 H
emmccurdy@viterbo.edu
MCCURDY, Solynn .... 206-296-6116 526 F
mccurdys@seattleu.edu
MCCURLEY, Steve .... 918-540-6196 398 L
smccurley@neo.edu
MCCURREN, Cynthia ..... 616-331-3558 243 E
mccurrec@gvsu.edu
MCCURRY, David .... 864-503-5509 451 A
DMCCURRY@USCUPSTATE.EDU
MCCURRY, Faith .... 803-535-1230 448 C
mccurryf@octech.edu
MCCURRY, Faith .... 803-536-0311 448 C
MCCURRY, Ricky, N ..... 865-974-4531 465 C
rmccurry@tennessee.edu
MCCURTY, Kenyetta ...... 334-387-3877.... 1 E
kenyettamccurty@amridgeuniversity.edu
MCCUTCHAN, Molly, M 734-384-4245 247 C
mmccutchan@monroeccc.edu
MCCUTCHEN, Michael .. 731-989-6901 456 K
mmccutchen@fhu.edu
MCCUTCHEON,
Bruce, E .... 610-330-5530 423 A
mccutchb@lafayette.edu
MCCUTCHEON, John ..... 805-893-8320.. 72 D
AD@athletics.ucsb.edu
MCCUTCHEON, Ron ...... 541-885-1120 408 E
ron.mccutcheon@oit.edu
MCDADE, Kate .... 216-987-4710 381 A
kate.mcdade@tri-c.edu
MCDADE, Linda .... 570-348-6249 425 D
lmcdade@marywood.edu
MCDADE, Lucinda .... 909-625-8767.. 39 E
lucinda.mcdade@cgu.edu
MCDADE, William .... 773-834-3861 161 D
wmcdade@bsd.uchicago.edu
MCDADE-CLAY,
W. Thomas .... 585-340-9648 321 G
tmcdadeclay@crcds.edu
MCDAID, James .... 617-879-7960 230 B
jmcdaid@massart.edu
MCDANIEL, Anna, M .... 352-273-6324 115 D
annammcdaniel@ufl.edu
MCDANIEL, Chris .... 731-661-5018 464 G
cmcdaniel@uu.edu
MCDANIEL, Cliff .... 817-461-8741 468 C
cmcdaniel@arlingtonbaptistcollege.edu
MCDANIEL, Diane .... 765-677-2436 169 C
diane.mcdaniel@indwes.edu
MCDANIEL, Donna .... 903-823-3220 484 D
donna.mcdaniel@texarkanacollege.edu
MCDANIEL, Donna, N ... 402-557-7184 289 B
donna.mcdaniel@bellevue.edu
MCDANIEL,
Elizabeth, A .... 806-742-3667 489 F
elizabeth.mcdaniel@ttu.edu
MCDANIEL, Gary, R ...... 949-214-3055.. 42 B
gary.mcdaniel@cui.edu
MCDANIEL, Jervaisc ..... 619-393-2982 146 F
mcdanielj@iecc.edu
MCDANIEL, Joy .... 580-371-2371 398 J
jmcdaniel@mscok.edu
MCDANIEL, Juley .... 620-223-2700 187 B
juleym@fortscott.edu
MCDANIEL, Julie .... 937-722-9316 394 F
julie.mcdaniel@urbana.edu
MCDANIEL, Kay .... 225-359-9205 202 N
mcdanielk@mybrcc.edu
MCDANIEL, Kimberly .... 916-691-7487.. 52 J
mcdanik@crc.losrios.edu
MCDANIEL, Kristina, D . 573-840-9695 283 D
kristinamcdaniel@trcc.edu
MCDANIEL, Lance .... 304-384-5258 532 E
mcdaniell26@mycu.concord.edu
MCDANIEL, Laura .... 701-231-8330 374 C
laura.mcdaniel@ndsu.edu
MCDANIEL, Lauren .... 505-473-6440 313 B
lauren.mcdaniel@santafeuniversity.edu
MCDANIEL, Lisa .... 662-329-7377 269 B
mcmcdaniel@muw.edu
MCDANIEL, Lucinda ..... 870-933-7906.. 19 D
lmcdaniel@asusystem.edu
MCDANIEL, Mary .... 620-341-5223 186 H
mmcdanie@emporia.edu
MCDANIEL, Mary, W .... 864-388-8242 447 E
mmcdaniel@lander.edu
MCDANIEL, Mary Lee ... 601-857-3395 267 D
mlmcdaniel@hindscc.edu
MCDANIEL, Mick, R ..... 607-844-8222 350 A
mcdanim@tc3.edu
MCDANIEL, Rose .... 336-249-8186 362 B
rose_mcdaniel@davidsonccc.edu
MCDANIEL, Stephen, L . 410-651-6676 219 H
slmcdaniel@umes.edu
MCDANIEL, Wendy .... 479-394-7622.. 22 H
wmcdaniel@rmcc.edu
MCDANIELS WILSON,
Cathy .... 614-236-6114 378 H
cmcdanielswilson@capital.edu
MCDAVID, Courtney ..... 860-832-3003.. 88 D
mcdavidc@ccsu.edu
MCDAVIS, Roderick, J .. 740-593-1804 389 H
mcdavis@ohio.edu
MCDERMED,
Carolyn, G .... 541-346-4127 410 F
mcdermed@uoregon.edu
MCDERMOTT, A. Keith .. 617-541-2454 233 A
kmcderm@rcc.mass.edu
MCDERMOTT, Ann .... 401-341-2140 442 D
ann.mcdermott@salve.edu
MCDERMOTT, Ann, B ... 508-793-2443 225 C
amcdermo@holycross.edu
MCDERMOTT, Beth .... 617-552-4400 224 B
beth.mcdermott@bc.edu
MCDERMOTT, Brian .... 907-564-8248.. 10 D
bmcdermott@alaskapacific.edu
MCDERMOTT, Brian ...... 308-398-7387 289 D
bmcdermott@cccneb.edu
MCDERMOTT, Christine 315-568-3105 334 F
cmcdermott@nycc.edu
MCDERMOTT, Christine 302-736-2491.. 94 E
christine.mcdermott@wesley.edu
MCDERMOTT, Colleen .. 816-531-5223 273 F
cmcdermott@concorde.edu
MCDERMOTT, Dan .... 330-494-6170 391 J
dmcdermott@starkstate.edu
MCDERMOTT, David ...... 617-287-7128 228 E
dmcdermott@umassp.edu
MCDERMOTT, Dennis ... 718-489-5362 340 E
dmcdermott@sfc.edu
MCDERMOTT, Erin .... 773-702-7684 161 D
erinmcd@uchicago.edu
MCDERMOTT, Harry ...... 520-621-7428.. 18 E
mcdermott@email.arizona.edu
MCDERMOTT, John, R .. 563-588-7132 180 L
john.mcdermott@loras.edu
MCDERMOTT, Marty ...... 231-777-0462 247 G
marty.mcdermott@muskegoncc.edu
MCDERMOTT, Patrice .... 410-455-3150 219 F
mcdermot@umbc.edu
MCDERMOTT,
Patricia, L .... 757-594-7222 506 I
mcdermot@cnu.edu
MCDERMOTT, Patrick .... 941-377-4880 108 K
pmcdermott@meridian.edu
MCDERMOTT, Randi ...... 208-426-1493 137 E
randimcdermott@boisestate.edu
MCDERMOTT,
Richard, L .... 713-500-4963 495 A
richard.l.mcdermott@uth.tmc.edu
MCDERMOTT,
Shannon, M .... 850-245-0466 114 C
shannon.mcdermott@flbog.edu
MCDERMOTT, Teresa .... 360-475-7480 524 H
tmcdermott@olympic.edu
MCDEVITT, Brigid .... 206-934-6314 526 A
brigid.mcdevitt@seattlecolleges.edu
MCDEVITT, Jenna .... 740-587-6655 381 H
mcdevitts@denison.edu
MCDEVITT, Terry .... 979-458-6023 484 E
TMcDevitt@tamus.edu
MCDIARMID, Bill .... 919-966-1356 371 A
bmcd@email.unc.edu
MCDIARMID, Chris .... 620-331-0815 188 B
cmcdiarmid@indycc.edu
MCDILL, M. Augustus .. 843-661-1128 446 E
mmcdill@fmarion.edu
MCDILL, Sandy .... 602-787-7352.. 15 B
sandy.mcdill@paradisevalley.edu
MCDOLE, Rob .... 803-754-4100 445 D
MCDOLE, Robert .... 503-255-0332 407 D
rmcdole@multnomah.edu
MCDONAGH, David ...... 212-749-2802 331 I
dmcdonagh@msmnyc.edu
MCDONALD, Aneisa, L . 865-539-7378 463 E
almcdonald@pstcc.edu
MCDONALD, Ann, M .... 978-632-6600 232 C
a_mcdonald@mwcc.mass.edu
MCDONALD, Barbara .... 763-424-0820 260 E
BMcDonald@nhcc.edu
MCDONALD, Becky .... 937-298-3399 385 A
becky.mcdonald@kc.edu
MCDONALD, Cathy .... 701-328-4111 373 F
cathy.mcdonald@ndus.edu
MCDONALD,
Christopher .... 949-582-4820.. 67 F
cmcdonald@saddleback.edu
MCDONALD, Christy ..... 865-273-8851 458 E
christy.mcdonald@maryvillecollege.edu
MCDONALD, Clay .... 636-227-2100 277 A
Clay.McDonald@logan.edu
MCDONALD, Dalene ..... 620-229-6271 191 B
dalene.mcdonald@sckans.edu
MCDONALD, Dana .... 301-846-2458 214 I
dmcdonald@frederick.edu
MCDONALD, Danielle ... 813-974-6677 116 B
dmcdonald@usf.edu
MCDONALD, David .... 503-838-8211 411 B
mcdonald@wou.edu
MCDONALD, Debbie ..... 626-966-4576.. 27 I
info@agu.edu
MCDONALD, Deborah ... 845-938-5706 549 A
admissions@usma.edu
MCDONALD, Denise ..... 434-544-8665 509 I
mcdonald@lynchburg.edu
MCDONALD, Dennis ..... 518-454-5170 322 C
mcdonald@strose.edu
MCDONALD, Dotty .... 337-550-1357 205 B
dmcdonal@lsue.edu
MCDONALD, Eric .... 864-587-4200 449 D
mcdonalde@smcsc.edu
MCDONALD, Erin .... 312-567-5133 147 E
emcdona2@iit.edu
MCDONALD, Francis, X 508-830-5001 230 D
fmcdonald@maritime.edu
MCDONALD, Frank .... 212-346-1800 337 I
fmcdonald@pace.edu
MCDONALD, Gary .... 415-422-2699.. 74 C
mcdonald@usfca.edu
MCDONALD, Ginger ..... 978-478-3400 235 E
gmcdonald@northpoint.edu
MCDONALD, Jack .... 207-602-2562 213 B
jmcdonald10@une.edu
MCDONALD, James ...... 612-374-5800 255 G
jmcdonald@dunwoody.edu
MCDONALD, James ...... 435-586-7898 499 L
mcdonaldj@suu.edu
MCDONALD, James, L . 415-451-2810.. 63 B
jmcdonald@sfts.edu
MCDONALD, Jan .... 864-977-7151 448 A
jan.mcdonald@ngu.edu
MCDONALD, Jason, S .. 503-943-7147 410 H
mcdonaja@up.edu
MCDONALD, Jennifer ... 714-241-6163.. 40 B
jmcdonald@coastline.edu
MCDONALD, Jestinah ... 740-753-7010 383 G
mcdonaldj21@hocking.edu
MCDONALD, Joseph ..... 239-590-1102 114 F
jmcdonald@fgcu.edu
MCDONALD, Joseph ..... 256-761-6443.... 7 H
jmcdonald@talladega.edu
MCDONALD, Joseph ..... 518-631-9869 351 A
mcdonalj@uniongraduatecollege.edu
MCDONALD, Julia, J .... 270-745-4629 201 D
julia.mcdonald@wku.edu
MCDONALD, Kevin .... 585-475-6795 339 G
kgmpro@rit.edu
MCDONALD, Kimberly .. 201-219-9901 302 A
kimberly.mcdonald@eicollege.edu
MCDONALD, Kurt .... 417-690-3200 273 C
purch@cofo.edu
MCDONALD, Latrice ...... 601-928-6206 268 G
latrice.mcdonald@mgccc.edu
MCDONALD, Leander ... 701-255-3285 375 I
MCDONALD, Leann ...... 563-884-5191 182 D
leann.mcdonald@palmer.edu
MCDONALD, Loretta ..... 615-329-8503 456 G
lmcdonald@fisk.edu
MCDONALD, Lori .... 949-214-3074.. 42 B
lori.mcdonald@cui.edu
MCDONALD, Lori .... 801-581-7066 499 K
lmcdonald@sa.utah.edu
MCDONALD, Martha ..... 626-914-8602.. 38 L
mmcdonald@citruscollege.edu

MCDONALD, Matt, C .... 507-786-3255 264 C
mcdonamc@stolaf.edu
MCDONALD, Michael ... 567-661-7203 390 D
michael_mcdonald6@owens.edu
MCDONALD,
Michael, A .... 269-337-7162 244 I
Michael.McDonald@kzoo.edu
MCDONALD, Nancy, H . 662-685-4771 266 G
nmcdonald@bmc.edu
MCDONALD, Nicholas .. 978-837-3597 233 G
mcdonaldn@merrimack.edu
MCDONALD, Patrick, S 716-880-2345 332 B
patrick.s.mcdonald@medaille.edu
MCDONALD, Paul, R .... 626-966-4576.. 27 I
paulmcdonald@agu.edu
MCDONALD, Pete .... 706-295-6928 125 F
pmcdonald@gntc.edu
MCDONALD, Pete .... 706-295-6960 125 F
pmcdonald@gntc.edu
MCDONALD, Peter .... 559-278-2403.. 33 D
pmcdonald@csufresno.edu
MCDONALD, Randy ...... 936-468-1010 484 A
rmcdonald@sfasu.edu
MCDONALD, Rion .... 931-540-2523 462 E
rmcdonald11@columbiastate.edu
MCDONALD, Ryan .... 508-541-1664 225 G
rmcdonald@dean.edu
MCDONALD, Sallie .... 671-735-2233 549 G
salliemcd@uguam.uog.edu
MCDONALD, Scott .... 979-458-0996 485 C
smcdonald@tamu.edu
MCDONALD, Steven ..... 401-277-4955 442 B
smcdonal@risd.edu
MCDONALD, Tammy .... 361-698-1133 473 F
tmcdonal1@delmar.edu
MCDONALD, Thomas ... 212-752-1530 330 C
thomas.mcdonald@limcollege.edu
MCDONALD, Tim .... 770-531-6339 128 A
tmcdonal@laniertech.edu
MCDONALD, Tim .... 256-726-8399.... 6 C
tmcdonald@oakwood.edu
MCDONALD, Todd .... 217-786-2253 151 C
todd.mcdonald@llcc.edu
MCDONALD, Tracie ...... 406-275-4978 288 H
tracie_mcdonald@skc.edu
MCDONALD, William .... 315-792-5321 333 D
wmcdonald@mvcc.edu
MCDONALD,
William, A .... 973-748-9000 300 E
bill_mcdonald@bloomfield.edu
MCDONALD,
William, M .... 706-542-7774 132 H
bmcdonal@uga.edu
MCDONALD-RASH,
Jean .... 848-932-7057 306 F
jrash@rci.rutgers.edu
MCDONALD-RASH,
Jean .... 848-932-7057 307 B
jean.rash@ofa.rutgers.edu
MCDONNEL, Wendy ..... 605-221-3100 452 F
wmcdonnel@kilian.edu
MCDONNELL, Brian, A . 401-341-2185 442 D
mcdonneb@salve.edu
MCDONNELL,
Constance, F .... 570-941-7640 438 F
constance.mcdonnell@scranton.edu
MCDONNELL, John .... 773-481-8253 142 D
jmcdonnell@ccc.edu
MCDONNELL, Joseph ... 207-780-4020 213 A
jmcdonnell@usm.maine.edu
MCDONNELL, Tom .... 402-457-2716 291 E
tjmcdonnell3@mccneb.edu
MCDONOUGH, Ann ...... 702-774-4619 295 G
ann.mcdonough@unlv.edu
MCDONOUGH, David ... 207-786-6231 209 F
dmcdonou@bates.edu
MCDONOUGH, Eileen ... 305-899-3085.. 99 B
emcdonough@barry.edu
MCDONOUGH, Ellin ..... 803-323-2141 451 I
mcdonoughe@winthrop.edu
MCDONOUGH, Mary .... 973-278-5400 300 C
mmc@berkeleycollege.edu
MCDONOUGH, Mary .... 973-278-5400 316 D
mmc@berkeleycollege.edu
MCDONOUGH, Michael 908-526-1200 305 G
Michael.McDonough@raritanval.edu
MCDONOUGH, Michael 802-447-4658 503 A
mmcdonough@svc.edu
MCDONOUGH, Patrick .. 610-807-9221 421 C
mcdonough@iirp.edu
MCDONOUGH, JR.,
Peter, J .... 848-932-7741 306 F
mcdonough@oldqueens.rutgers.edu
MCDONOUGH, Shawna 630-889-6701 154 E
smcdonough@nuhs.edu
MCDORMAN, Heather ... 636-922-8277 281 C
hmcdorman@stchas.edu
MCDORMAN, Todd, F .. 765-361-6183 175 B
mcdormat@wabash.edu
MCDOUGAL,
Bradley, N .... 540-464-7637 518 A
mcdougalbn@vmi.edu
MCDOUGAL, Bradly ...... 304-829-7255 529 H
bmcdougal@bethanywv.edu
MCDOUGALL, Gerald .... 573-651-2063 282 C
gmcdougall@semo.edu
MCDOUGALL,
Gordon, A .... 804-828-8192 514 F
gamcdougall@vcu.edu
MCDOWALL, Douglass . 785-460-5484 186 D
doug.mcdowall@colbycc.edu
MCDOWALL-LONG,
Kimberly .... 701-355-8021 375 K
kmcdowalllong@umary.edu
MCDOWELL, Amy .... 802-763-7170 503 E
amcdowell@vermontlaw.edu
MCDOWELL, Chad .... 318-798-4107 205 F
chad.mcdowell@lsus.edu
MCDOWELL, Charles, E 608-243-4137 543 C
cemcdowell@madisoncollege.edu
MCDOWELL, Denise ...... 507-457-5300 262 D
dmcdowell@winona.edu
MCDOWELL, Jackie .... 706-236-2202 121 E
jmcdowell@berry.edu
MCDOWELL, James ...... 860-512-3603.. 89 D
jmcdowell@manchestercc.edu
MCDOWELL, Jennifer .... 972-883-6301 494 A
jpazik@utdallas.edu
MCDOWELL, Jill .... 203-285-2007.. 89 B
jmcdowell@gwcc.commnet.edu
MCDOWELL, Katie .... 913-360-7578 184 K
kmcdowell@benedictine.edu
MCDOWELL, N. Renee .. 724-653-2212 417 D
rmcdowell@dec.edu
MCDOWELL, Pamela ..... 507-786-3011 264 C
mcdowell@stolaf.edu
MCDOWELL, Richard, L 405-878-5350 402 A
rlmcdowell@stgregorys.edu
MCDOWELL, Scott .... 615-966-5690 458 C
scott.mcdowell@lipscomb.edu
MCDOWELL, JR., T, J .. 402-465-2149 292 E
tmcdowe2@nebrwesleyan.edu
MCDOWELL, Travis .... 864-488-4615 447 F
tmcdowell@limestone.edu
MCDOWELL, Whitney .... 601-977-7821 270 F
wmcdowell@tougaloo.edu
MCDOWN, Linda .... 405-422-1203 401 H
mcdownl@redlandscc.edu
MCDUFFIE, Georgia ...... 718-270-6222 320 C
gmcduffie@mec.cuny.edu
MCEACHARN, Lewis ..... 207-941-7020 210 C
mceacharnl@husson.edu
MCEACHERN, Daniel ..... 704-330-6395 361 D
jj.mceachern@cpcc.edu
MCELANEY-JOHNSON,
Ann .... 310-954-4011.. 54 I
amcelaney@msmu.edu
MCELHANEY, Patrick .... 706-233-7225 131 C
pmcelhaney@shorter.edu
MCELHANY, Ryan .... 972-825-4701 483 D
rmcelhany@sagu.edu
MCELHOE, Dennis .... 704-922-6266 362 G
mcelhoe.dennis@gaston.edu
MCELMURRY,
Chauvette .... 314-340-3600 275 G
mcelmurc@hssu.edu
MCELRATH, Ann .... 423-614-8105 457 M
amcelrath@leeuniversity.edu
MCELRATH, William ..... 732-571-4444 303 G
wmcelrat@monmouth.edu
MCELROY, Annie, L ...... 229-225-5200 132 C
amcelroy@southernregional.edu
MCELROY,
Catherine, C .... 215-968-8213 413 F
mcelroyc@bucks.edu
MCELROY, Clint .... 704-330-6339 361 D
clint.mcelroy@cpcc.edu
MCELROY, Coleetta .... 408-924-6086.. 36 B
coleetta.mcelroy@sjsu.edu
MCELROY, Doug .... 270-745-7009 201 D
doug.mcelroy@wku.edu
MCELROY, Edith .... 704-330-4386 361 D
edith.mcelroy@cpcc.edu
MCELROY, Emily, J ...... 402-559-7078 293 I
emily.mcelroy@unmc.edu
MCELROY, Joe .... 714-966-8500.. 75 F
info@ves.edu
MCELROY, Kevin .... 650-949-6202.. 44 M
mcelroykevin@fhda.edu
MCELROY, Neil, J .... 610-330-5150 423 A
mcelroyn@lafayette.edu
MCELROY, Tim .... 918-683-0641 398 M
mcelroyt@nsuok.edu
MCELVEEN, John .... 706-507-5341 123 D
mcelveen_john@columbusstate.edu
MCELWEE, Kay, E .... 217-581-5313 144 E
kemcelwee@eiu.edu
MCELWEE, Tim .... 260-992-5051 170 a
tamcelwee@manchester.edu
MCENEANY, Barbara ..... 845-848-4031 324 B
barbara.mceneany@dc.edu
MCENEANY, Mary .... 413-559-5528 227 C
memtr@hampshire.edu
MCENTEE, Mary .... 413-775-1203 231 E
mcenteem@gcc.mass.edu
MCENTERGART, Rory .... 302-793-1101.. 94 C
MCENTIRE, David .... 801-863-8000 500 B
MCENTIRE, Mary .... 530-221-4275.. 66 B
mmcentire09@shasta.edu
MCENTIRE, Tina, M ...... 704-687-7019 371 B
tmmcenti@uncc.edu
MCENTIRE, Tracy, D ..... 336-838-6422 367 C
tracy.mcentire@wilkescc.edu
MCEUEN, Brent .... 928-428-8201.. 13 L
brent.mceuen@eac.edu
MCEVOY, Ed, M .... 610-526-1286 412 D
ed.mcevoy@theamericancollege.edu
MCEVOY, Robert, T ...... 910-630-7182 359 C
mcevoy@methodist.edu
MCEVOY, Thomas .... 407-646-2249 111 H
tmcevoy@rollins.edu
MCEWAN, Anna, E .... 205-665-6360.... 9 C
mcewanae@montevallo.edu
MCEWEN, Beryl .... 336-334-7632 370 B
mcewenb@ncat.edu
MCEWEN, Ellen, J .... 512-505-3055 475 G
ejmcewen@htu.edu
MCEWEN, Jessie .... 312-939-4975 145 G
jmcewen@harrington.edu
MCEWEN, Jill .... 920-996-2847 542 N
mcewen@fvtc.edu
MCEWEN, Ruth .... 305-348-3264 114 G
ruthann.mcewen@fiu.edu
MCEWEN, Wendy .... 909-748-8187.. 73 K
wendy_mcewan@redlands.edu
MCFADDEN, David, F .... 260-982-5226 170 a
dfmcfadden@manchester.edu
MCFADDEN, Harry .... 914-251-6196 346 D
harry.mcfadden@purchase.edu
MCFADDEN, John .... 305-899-3208.. 99 B
jmcfadden@barry.edu
MCFADDEN, Judy .... 970-521-6660.. 84 H
judy.mcfadden@njc.edu
MCFADDEN, Mark .... 607-871-2164 314 J
mcfaddenm@alfred.edu
MCFADDEN, Mary .... 845-848-7809 324 B
mary.mcfadden@dc.edu
MCFADDEN, Mary Kay . 208-885-4200 139 C
MCFADDEN, Michael .... 202-806-1280.. 96 B
michael.mcfadden@howard.edu
MCFADDEN, Pam .... 817-735-2581 493 B
Pam.McFadden@unthsc.edu
MCFADDEN, Paul .... 870-236-6901.. 20 I
pmcfadden@crc.edu
MCFADDEN, Scott .... 509-527-2205 528 A
scott.mcfadden@wallawalla.edu
MCFADDEN, Susan .... 215-955-2867 436 F
susan.mcfadden@jefferson.edu
MCFADDEN, Tanya .... 517-483-1452 245 I
mcfaddet@lcc.edu
MCFADDEN, Thomas ..... 540-636-2900 506 H
tmcfadden@christendom.edu
MCFADDEN, Toney, C .. 423-624-0077 455 H
tonym@chattanoogacollege.edu
MCFADDIN, David .... 859-622-6220 194 L
david.mcfaddin@eku.edu
MCFALL, Jan .... 763-488-0250 260 E
jmcfall@nhcc.edu
MCFALLS-SMITH,
Tiffany .... 270-706-8419 195 K
tmcfalls0001@kctcs.edu
MCFARLAND, F. Ozzie .. 252-398-6484 356 B
mcfarf@chowan.edu
MCFARLAND, James ..... 412-731-1177 433 K
rptrustees@aol.com
MCFARLAND, Kathryn ... 813-226-4983 111 L
kathryn.mcfarland@saintleo.edu
MCFARLAND, Marielle .. 870-777-5722.. 24 H
marielle.mcfarland@uacch.edu
MCFARLAND,
Michael, S .... 570-389-4050 430 B
mcfarland@bloomu.edu
MCFARLAND, Michele .. 208-732-6304 137 K
mmcfarland@csi.edu
MCFARLAND, Mike .... 919-962-2011 371 A
Mike_McFarland@unc.edu
MCFARLAND,
Reoungeneria .... 901-435-1213 457 N
reo_mcfarland@loc.edu
MCFARLAND, Robie ...... 252-222-6021 361 A
mcfarlandr@carteret.edu
MCFARLAND, Ruth, E ... 484-384-2950 427 I
rmcfarla@eastern.edu
MCFARLAND,
Stephen, L .... 910-962-3867 372 A
mcfarlands@uncw.edu
MCFARLAND, Steven .... 630-844-5496 139 L
smcfarla@aurora.edu
MCFARLAND,
Steven, W .... 518-327-6436 338 B
smcfarland@paulsmiths.edu
MCFARLAND, Thomas .. 435-586-7785 499 L
thomasmcfarland@suu.edu
MCFARLAND, Tracy ...... 315-279-5215 329 K
tmcfarl@keuka.edu
MCFARLANE, Alison ..... 801-957-4103 500 E
alison.mcfarlane@lscc.edu
MCFARLANE, Allen, M .. 212-998-4345 336 C
allen.mcfarlane@nyu.edu
MCFARLANE, Mike .... 775-753-2266 295 D
mike.mcfarlane@gbcnv.edu
MCFARLIN, Dean, B ..... 412-396-1372 417 I
mcfarlind@duq.edu
MCFARLIN, Diane, H .... 352-392-0466 115 D
dmcfarlin@ufl.edu
MCFARLIN, Leslie .... 706-754-8128 129 B
lmcfarlin@northgatech.edu
MCFARLING,
Patricia, G .... 270-852-3257 198 A
patmc@kwc.edu
MCFATRIDGE, Michael . 310-954-4084.. 54 I
mmcfatridge@msmu.edu
MCFEE, Brenda .... 828-766-1330 364 A
bmcfee@mayland.edu
MCFETRIDGE-DURDLE,
Judith .... 850-644-3296 115 A
jdurdle@nursing.fsu.edu
MCFRAZIER,
Michael, L .... 936-261-2111 484 F
mlmcfrazier@pvamu.edu
MCFRY, Kevin .... 256-782-5002.... 4 L
kmcfry@jsu.edu
MCGAHA, SR., Gary, A 404-756-4440 120 H
gmcgaha@atlm.edu
MCGAHEY, Julia .... 303-871-4528.. 86 H
jmcgahey@du.edu
MCGALLIARD, Anna ...... 207-509-7250 212 A
amcgalliard@unity.edu
MCGANN, Robert P, H . 603-862-1360 299 B
admissions@unh.edu
MCGAREY, Tracy .... 316-942-4291 189 K
mcgareyt@newmanu.edu
MCGARITY, William, G . 706-542-9037 132 H
gmcgarity@sports.uga.edu
MCGARRITY, Maureen .. 215-637-7700 420 K
mmcgarrity@holyfamily.edu
MCGARRY, Eileen, M .... 520-621-6734.. 18 E
emcgarry@email.arizona.edu
MCGARRY, Timothy ...... 516-876-3303 345 E
mcgarryt@oldwestbury.edu
MCGARVEY, Betty, S .... 901-572-2585 455 C
bettysue.mcgarvey@bchs.edu
MCGARVEY, Scott .... 660-263-4110 279 F
scottm@macc.edu
MCGARVEY, Suzi .... 660-263-4110 279 F
suzim@macc.edu
MCGARVEY,
Vicki Lewis .... 215-204-8874 436 C
mcgarvey@temple.edu
MCGAUGH, Becky, E .... 928-523-6415.. 16 C
Becky.McGaugh@nau.edu
MCGAUGHEY, Carol ..... 281-649-3240 475 B
cmcgaughey@hbu.edu
MCGAUGHEY, Kevin, B 651-631-5318 265 D
kbmcgaughey@unwsp.edu
MCGEACHY, Neill .... 828-328-7128 358 G
neill.mcgeachy@lr.edu
MCGEE, Angel .... 337-550-1202 205 B
amcgee@lsue.edu
MCGEE, Brenda, L .... 716-375-2017 340 C
bmcgee@sbu.edu
MCGEE, Brian .... 843-953-5527 445 B
mcgeeb@cofc.edu
MCGEE, Byron .... 318-487-7259 202 L
byron.mcgee@lacollege.edu
MCGEE, Byron .... 318-487-7018 202 L
byron.mcgee@lacollege.edu
MCGEE, Charles, E .... 757-822-1947 517 C
cmcgee@tcc.edu
MCGEE, Christine .... 414-297-7997 543 E
mcgeecm@matc.edu
MCGEE, Cindy, R .... 304-336-8233 533 A
mcgeecin@westliberty.edu
MCGEE, Corlis, A .... 617-745-3702 225 H
corlis.mcgee@enc.edu
MCGEE, Deborah .... 217-875-7211 156 K
dmcgee@richland.edu
MCGEE, E. Ann .... 407-708-2009 113 A
mcgeea@seminolestate.edu
MCGEE, Ed .... 434-832-7742 515 A
mcgeee@cvcc.vccs.edu
MCGEE, Elizabeth .... 262-595-3234 540 C
mcgee@uwp.edu
MCGEE, James .... 847-214-7359 144 F
jmcgee@elgin.edu
MCGEE, James .... 708-534-4900 145 D
jmcgee@govst.edu

MCGEE, Janice 205-929-6313 5 E jmcgee@lawsonstate.edu
MCGEE, Joan 702-651-5966 295 C joan.mcgee@csn.edu
MCGEE, John 770-426-2805 128 C john.mcgee@life.edu
MCGEE, Jon 320-363-5287 264 A jmcgee@csbsju.edu
MCGEE, Jon, D 320-363-5287 254 J jmcgee@csbsju.edu
MCGEE, Laura 847-925-6686 145 F lmcgee@harpercollege.edu
MCGEE, Lynn 843-208-8240 450 D lmcgee@uscb.edu
MCGEE, Marc 707-654-1331 34 B mmcgee@csum.edu
MCGEE, Marjorie 352-854-2322 100 P mcgeem@cf.edu
MCGEE, Michael 828-328-7126 358 G michael.mcgee@lr.edu
MCGEE, Robert 910-362-7191 360 G rmcgee@cfcc.edu
MCGEE, Shawn 229-243-6030 121 D shawn.mcgee@bainbridge.edu
MCGEE, Steve, G 817-257-7930 486 G s.mcgee@tcu.edu
MCGEE, Steve, R 512-245-2533 489 C srm18@txstate.edu
MCGEE, Tammy, L 320-308-2286 261 E tlmcgee@stcloudstate.edu
MCGEE, Thomas, W 314-837-6777 281 D
MCGEE, Vincent, J 636-227-2100 277 A vince.mcgee@logan.edu
MCGEE-YUROF, Carrie 203-857-7040 89 H cmcgee-yurof@norwalk.edu
MCGEEHAN, Catherine 610-499-4396 439 G cmcgeehan@widener.edu
MCGEEHON, Carol 541-440-4600 410 E carol.mcgeehon@umpqua.edu
MCGEHEE, JR., Robert, E 501-686-5454 24 B rem@uams.edu
MCGETTIGAN, Glenn 801-524-8112 498 J Glenn@ldsbc.edu
MCGHEE, JR., James, D 804-752-3736 511 E jamesmcghee@rmc.edu
MCGHEE, Lisa 870-762-3174 19 C lmchgee@smail.anc.edu
MCGHEE, Lynold, K 717-736-4201 420 D lkmcghee@hacc.edu
MCGHEE, Marianne, S 804-523-5810 515 F mmcghee@reynolds.edu
MCGHEE, Sandra, W 540-375-2287 512 B mcghee@roanoke.edu
MCGHEE, Stephanie 417-667-8181 273 H smcghee@cottey.edu
MCGHEE, Tim 423-697-3174 462 C tim.mcghee@chattanoogastate.edu
MCGHEE, Tony 276-964-7648 517 A tony.mcghee@sw.edu
MCGHEE JOHNSON, Kassandra 773-291-6100 142 B kmcgheejohnson@ccc.edu
MCGILL, Bret 256-306-2861 2 F jbm@calhoun.edu
MCGILL, Jennifer 601-925-7782 268 E McGill@mc.edu
MCGILL, Linda 734-481-2303 242 J lmcgill@emich.edu
MCGILL, Shawna 575-769-4954 310 G shawna.mcgill@clovis.edu
MCGILL, Shelia, R 405-466-3283 398 E srmcgill@langston.edu
MCGILL, Tracy 318-678-6000 203 A tmcgill@bpcc.edu
MCGILLIS, Bill 601-266-5422 271 B bill.mcgillis@usm.edu
MCGILLOWAY, Samantha 978-762-4000 232 D smcgillo@northshore.edu
MCGILVRAY, Amy 254-295-5077 492 C amcgilvray@umhb.edu
MCGILVRAY, Judith 903-675-6240 490 F jmcgilvray@tvcc.edu
MCGILVRAY, Mary, E 918-270-6405 401 C mary.mcgilvay@ptstulsa.edu
MCGIMPSEY, Jason 406-657-2197 287 H jason.mcgimpsey@msubillings.edu
MCGINITY, Richard 307-766-4121 546 K mcginity@uwyo.edu
MCGINLEY, Anne, M 856-227-7200 301 A amcginley@camdencc.edu
MCGINLEY, Barbara 617-587-5620 234 G mcginleyb@neco.edu
MCGINLEY, Lynn, M 410-706-2889 219 E lmcginley@umaryland.edu
MCGINN, Jayne 508-929-8110 230 G jmcginn@worcester.edu

MCGINN, Joseph, P 207-778-7276 212 E joseph.mcginn@maine.edu
MCGINN, Marifrances 401-865-2774 441 F mfmcginn@providence.edu
MCGINN, III, Thomas, J 410-777-2240 213 E tjmcginn@aacc.edu
MCGINNIS, Blake 870-759-4170 25 I bmcginnis@wbcoll.edu
MCGINNIS, David 406-657-2363 287 H dmcginnis@msubillings.edu
MCGINNIS, Erik 704-463-3001 367 F erik.mcginnis@pfeiffer.edu
MCGINNIS, Grace 708-709-3519 156 A gmcginnis@prairiestate.edu
MCGINNIS, Judy 661-255-1050 31 B
MCGINNIS, Kelly 325-574-7609 497 E kmcginnis@wtc.edu
MCGINNIS, Mara 718-636-3471 338 E mmcginnis@pratt.edu
MCGINNIS, Maurice (Max) 585-594-6409 339 F mcginnis_max@roberts.edu
MCGINNIS, Michael 802-485-3338 502 G mmcginni@norwich.edu
MCGINNIS, Renae 304-256-0262 531 D rmcginnis@newriver.edu
MCGINNIS, Sharon, R 910-938-6231 361 F mcginniss@coastalcarolina.edu
MCGINNIS, William 858-822-5738 72 B areisner@ucsd.edu
MCGINNIS GONZALEZ, Sherri 312-996-2398 161 F smcginn@uic.edu
MCGINNISS, Jeremy 570-586-2400 435 H JeMcGinniss@summitu.edu
MCGINTY, Daniel, E 715-425-3505 540 E daniel.e.mcginty@uwrf.edu
MCGINTY, Evelyn, J 936-261-1725 484 F ejmcginty@pvamu.edu
MCGINTY, Felicia, E 848-932-8576 307 B felicia.mcginty@rutgers.edu
MCGINTY, Louis, L 804-523-2280 515 F mmcginty@ccwa.vccs.edu
MCGINTY, Mac, L 804-523-2280 515 G mmcginty@ccwa.vccs.edu
MCGINTY, Mary Kate 215-596-8719 438 E m.mcginty@usciences.edu
MCGIRR, Kathleen 215-641-6603 426 E kmcgirr@mc3.edu
MCGIRT, David 910-893-1265 355 C mcgirt@campbell.edu
MCGIVNEY, R, J 860-768-4401 92 F rmcgivney@hartford.edu
MCGIVNEY, Sean 719-549-2753 81 F sean.mcgivney@csupueblo.edu
MCGLADDERY, Nicole 805-581-1233 44 A nmcgladdery@eternitybiblecollege.com
MCGLADDERY, Ryan 805-581-1233 44 A rmcgladdery@eternitybiblecollege.com
MCGLADE, Charles 856-351-2649 308 B cmcglade@salemcc.edu
MCGLAMERY, Matt 970-247-7065 82 I mcglamery_m@fortlewis.edu
MCGLAMERY, Orien, S 970-247-7317 82 I mcglamery_o@fortlewis.edu
MCGLASSON, Robert 417-328-1535 282 D bmcglasson@sbuniv.edu
MCGLONE, John 606-326-2400 195 H john.mcglone@kctcs.edu
MCGLOTHIN, Kris 302-735-7696 94 E bkwesley@bncollege.edu
MCGLOTHIN-ELLER, April 847-866-3988 145 C april.mcglothin-eller@garrett.edu
MCGLOTHIN-ELLER, Vince 847-866-3907 145 C vince.mcglothin-eller@garrett.edu
MCGLOTHLIN, Michael, G 276-498-4190 504 K
MCGLOTHLIN, Sandy 559-934-2324 76 B sandymcglothlin@whccd.edu
MCGLOUGHLIN, Stephen 916-691-7589 52 J mcglous@crc.losrios.edu
MCGLYNN, Anita 845-434-5750 349 C amcglynn@sullivan.suny.edu
MCGLYNN, Ken 443-518-4802 215 F kmcglynn@howardcc.edu
MCGOFF, Michael, F 607-777-2143 343 D mmcgoff@binghamton.edu
MCGOLDRICK, John 215-951-1015 422 F mcgoldri@lasalle.edu
MCGOLDRICK, Rowena 860-515-3751 88 B rmcgoldrick@charteroak.edu
MCGOLDRICK, Sean 775-784-6514 295 H smcgoldrick@unr.edu
MCGONIGAL, Terry, P 509-777-4345 529 A tmcgonigal@whitworth.edu

MCGONIGLE, Gregory 617-627-3427 237 C gregory.mcgonigle@tufts.edu
MCGONIGLE, Mary 610-519-4070 439 A mary.mcgonigle@villanova.edu
MCGONIGLE, Robert, B 570-208-5875 422 D rbmcgoni@kings.edu
MCGONIGLE, Steve 215-951-1075 422 F mcgonigle@lasalle.edu
MCGORRY, Marian 610-359-5142 416 G mmcgorry@dccc.edu
MCGOUGH, Marsha 425-602-3036 519 J mmcgough@bastyr.edu
MCGOVERN, Bruce 713-646-2920 482 H bmcgovern@stcl.edu
MCGOVERN, Eilen 610-225-5457 418 A emcgove@eastern.edu
MCGOVERN, Lorrie 352-588-7390 111 L lorrie.mcgovern@saintleo.edu
MCGOVERN, Margaret 516-572-7124 334 A margaret.mcgovern@ncc.edu
MCGOVERN, Mark, S 401-865-2702 441 F mmcgovrn@providence.edu
MCGOVERN, Martin, P 508-565-1321 237 A mmcgovern@stonehill.edu
MCGOVERN, Terry 615-230-3352 464 B terry.mcgovern@volstate.edu
MCGOVERN, Thomas 617-236-8800 226 F tmcgovern@fisher.edu
MCGOVERN, Tina, L 570-961-4596 425 D tmcgovern@marywood.edu
MCGOWAN, Bill 828-898-8776 358 F mcgowanb@lmc.edu
MCGOWAN, Bruce, W 918-877-8116 398 E bwmcgowan@langston.edu
MCGOWAN, Charlotte 269-782-1347 250 D cmcgowan@swmich.edu
MCGOWAN, Chris 573-651-2163 282 C cwmcgowan@semo.edu
MCGOWAN, Cynthia 978-837-5139 233 G mcgowanc@merrimack.edu
MCGOWAN, Donald, A 617-627-5263 237 C donald.mcgowan@tufts.edu
MCGOWAN, James 516-877-3162 314 F mcgowan2@adelphi.edu
MCGOWAN, John 585-345-6999 326 F jmmcgowan@genesee.edu
MCGOWAN, John 205-348-5610 8 E john.mcgowan@ua.edu
MCGOWAN, Joseph, J 502-272-8234 193 E jmcgowan@bellarmine.edu
MCGOWAN, Joumana 909-274-5140 54 J jmcgowan@mtsac.edu
MCGOWAN, Katie 610-526-6062 420 C cmcgowan@harcum.edu
MCGOWAN, Kent 406-243-5373 287 D kent.mcgowan@umontana.edu
MCGOWAN, Kevin 239-687-5335 98 N kmcgowan@avemarialaw.edu
MCGOWAN, Kyle, D 615-322-6850 465 H kyle.mcgowan@vanderbilt.edu
MCGOWAN, Paul 617-552-3055 224 B paul.mcgowan.2@bc.edu
MCGOWAN, Richard 217-875-7200 156 K rmcgowan@richland.edu
MCGOWAN, Sindi 770-537-5746 134 F sindi.mcgowan@westgatech.edu
MCGOWAN, Terrance 718-933-6700 333 F tmcgowan@monroecollege.edu
MCGRADY, Patricia 973-957-0188 299 F treasurer@acs350.org
MCGRADY, Ronald, L 330-325-6799 387 F rmcgrady@neomed.edu
MCGRAIL, Annmarie 914-773-3741 337 I amcgrail@pace.edu
MCGRAIL, Frederick, J 610-758-4487 424 B fjm208@lehigh.edu
MCGRAIL, James 603-862-0927 299 A james.mcgrail@usnh.edu
MCGRAIL, III, James, J 740-264-5591 381 J jmcgrail@egcc.edu
MCGRAIL, Margaret 914-674-3031 332 E mmcgrail@mercy.edu
MCGRANAHAN, Mary, S 617-552-3300 224 B mary.mcgranahan@bc.edu
MCGRANE, Jack, V 973-748-9000 300 E jack_mcgrane@bloomfield.edu
MCGRANE, Wendy 417-625-9801 278 I mcgrane-w@mssu.edu
MCGRANN, Michael 718-940-5741 341 A mmgrann@sjcny.edu
MCGRATH, Abigail 312-567-3497 147 E amcgrat1@iit.edu
MCGRATH, Alexis 914-674-7607 332 E amcgrath3@mercy.edu
MCGRATH, Andrew, S 608-757-7764 542 L amcgrath@blackhawk.edu
MCGRATH, Brian 212-229-8955 334 C mcgrath@newschool.edu

MCGRATH, Cheryl 508-565-1111 237 A cmcgrath1@stonehill.edu
MCGRATH, Elisabeth 201-216-3389 308 D cos.mcgrath@stevens.edu
MCGRATH, Frank 239-687-5331 98 N fmcgrath@avemarialaw.edu
MCGRATH, Jamie, M 260-399-7700 174 C jmcgrath@sf.edu
MCGRATH, Jane 312-362-5765 143 G jmcgrath@depaul.edu
MCGRATH, John 212-594-4000 349 J jmcgrath@tcicollege.edu
MCGRATH, Joseph, C 800-955-2527 187 E jmcgrath@grantham.edu
MCGRATH, Karen 607-431-4130 327 B mcgrathk@hartwick.edu
MCGRATH, Laurie 503-552-1694 407 F lmcgrath@ncnm.edu
MCGRATH, Mark 215-242-1501 415 D mcgrathm@chc.edu
MCGRATH, Nicole 203-932-7077 92 G nmcgrath@newhaven.edu
MCGRATH, Patti 803-641-3569 450 C pattim@usca.edu
MCGRATH, Thomas 508-565-1086 237 A tmcgrath@stonehill.edu
MCGRATH, Tim 619-388-2600 62 G tmcgrath@sdccd.edu
MCGRATH, William 212-346-1200 337 I wmcgrath@pace.edu
MCGRAW, Darryl, D 336-256-0543 370 B ddmcgraw@ncat.edu
MCGRAW, Hesse 415-749-4580 62 I hmcgraw@sfai.edu
MCGRAW, John 904-646-2300 105 A j.mcgraw@fscj.edu
MCGRAW, Kathy 972-721-5221 491 B kmcgraw@udallas.edu
MCGRAW, Matthew 540-863-2866 515 B mmcgraw@dslcc.edu
MCGRAW, Packy 518-694-7257 314 G packy.mcgraw@acphs.edu
MCGREAL, David 706-880-8069 127 N dmcgreal@lagrange.edu
MCGREAL, Paul, E 402-280-2874 290 B PaulmcGreal@creighton.edu
MCGREEVEY, Michael 315-364-3443 352 F mmcgreevey@wells.edu
MCGREEVEY, Sean 412-365-1524 415 C
MCGREEVY, Bill 303-914-6634 85 C bill.mcgreevy@rrcc.edu
MCGREEVY, Jeanette 515-643-6717 181 B jmcgreevy@mercydesmoines.org
MCGREEVY, John, T 574-631-6642 174 A mcgreevy.5@nd.edu
MCGREGOR, Cynthia 619-427-6700 68 D cmcgregor@swccd.edu
MCGREGOR, Kyle, W 254-968-9890 485 A mcgregor@tarleton.edu
MCGREGOR, Michelle 419-755-4727 387 E mmcgregor@ncstatecollege.edu
MCGREGOR, Patricia 860-297-2120 92 A patricia.mcgregor@trincoll.edu
MCGREGOR, Tiffany 610-361-2487 427 D mcgregot@neumann.edu
MCGREGOR, Wilson, E 254-710-2663 469 D bud_mcgregor@baylor.edu
MCGREGORY, Richard 262-472-4985 541 D mcgregor@uww.edu
MCGREW, Kevin 218-723-6198 255 A kmcgrew@css.edu
MCGREW, Mackenzie 843-525-8218 449 E mmcgrew@tcl.edu
MCGREW, Martha 505-272-2165 313 H MMcGrew@salud.unm.edu
MCGREW, Paula 304-473-8461 534 G mcgrew_p@wwc.edu
MCGREW, Shea 419-372-7706 377 I smcgrew@bgsu.edu
MCGRIFF, Manuel 254-647-3234 480 G mmcgriff@rangercollege.edu
MCGRISKEN, June 718-489-5352 340 E jmcgrisken@sfc.edu
MCGRORY, Steve 615-297-7545 455 A mcgrorys@aquinascollege.edu
MCGUCKIN, Denis 516-686-7791 335 F dmcgucki@nyit.edu
MCGUCKIN, Tammy 262-595-2571 540 C mcguckin@uwp.edu
MCGUFFEY, Michael, J 304-696-3648 532 H mcguffey@marshall.edu
MCGUFFIN, Kurt 816-271-5623 279 E kmcguffin@missouriwestern.edu
MCGUINESS, Ilona 845-569-3203 333 I ilona.mcguiness@msmc.edu
MCGUINESS, Ilona 410-617-5547 216 D imcguiness@loyola.edu
MCGUINN, Ellen 215-248-7163 415 D mcguinne@chc.edu

MCGUINNESS, Maureen .... 940-565-2648 492 D
moe@unt.edu
MCGUINNESS, Paul, M 219-785-5730 172 A
mcguinpm@pnc.edu
MCGUINNESS, Scott ..... 724-503-1001 439 B
smcguinness@washjeff.edu
MCGUINNESS, Thomas, P .... 617-552-3310 224 B
thomas.mcguinness@bc.edu
MCGUIRE, Ann .... 216-421-7417 380 B
amcguire@cia.edu
MCGUIRE, Bridget .... 858-513-9240.. 29 A
bridget.mcguire@ashford.edu
MCGUIRE, Catherine ..... 559-737-5410.. 41 D
catherinemc@cos.edu
MCGUIRE, Christine ..... 617-353-4176 224 E
chmcguir@bu.edu
MCGUIRE, David, T ...... 435-586-7755 499 L
mcguire@suu.edu
MCGUIRE, Ellen .... 570-504-7000 415 E
emcguire@tcmc.edu
MCGUIRE, Jamie .... 902-403-3166 538 K
jamie.mcguire@snc.edu
MCGUIRE, Jamie .... 336-838-6482 367 C
jamie.mcguire@wilkescc.edu
MCGUIRE, Jane .... 615-230-3204 464 B
jane.mcguire@volstate.edu
MCGUIRE, Kathleen ...... 508-541-1615 225 G
kmcguire@dean.edu
MCGUIRE, Katrina .... 815-479-7510 152 B
kmcguire@mchenry.edu
MCGUIRE, Mark, T .... 740-284-5249 382 G
mmcguire@franciscan.edu
MCGUIRE, Maureen .... 509-313-6137 522 L
mcguirem@gonzaga.edu
MCGUIRE, Michael .... 303-871-3518.. 86 H
mmcguire@du.edu
MCGUIRE, Michael, J .... 785-670-1763 192 B
michael.mcguire@washburn.edu
MCGUIRE, Molly .... 205-726-4315.... 6 F
msmcguir@samford.edu
MCGUIRE, Nona, S .... 614-236-6908 378 H
nmcguire@capital.edu
MCGUIRE, Patricia, A .... 202-884-9050.. 97 A
mcguirep@trinitydc.edu
MCGUIRE, Rachel, L ...... 641-422-4104 181 E
mcguirac@niacc.edu
MCGUIRE, Ruth, A .... 651-631-5343 265 D
ramcguire@unwsp.edu
MCGUIRE, Sharon .... 208-426-4062 137 E
sharonmcguire@boisestate.edu
MCGUIRL-HADLEY, Joy 386-822-7500 117 A
jhadley@stetson.edu
MCGURE, David .... 561-697-9200 131 F
ddmcguire@southuniversity.edu
MCGURGAN, Susan ...... 513-231-2223 377 B
smcgurgan@athenaeum.edu
MCGURIMAN, Joseph ... 215-641-6605 426 E
jmcgurim@mc3.edu
MCGURIMAN, Timothy . 312-915-7802 151 E
tmcguri@luc.edu
MCGURK, Mark .... 432-552-2700 495 F
mcgurk_m@utpb.edu
MCGURN, Joseph, P .... 740-283-6278 382 G
jmcgurn@franciscan.edu
MCGURR, Paul .... 970-247-6737.. 82 I
mcgurr_p@fortlewis.edu
MCGURREN, Cynthia .... 978-542-7591 230 E
cmcgurren@salemstate.edu
MCGURTY, Thomas, S .. 617-627-3264 237 C
thomas.mcgurty@tufts.edu
MCGUTHRY, John, W ... 909-869-6442.. 32 F
jwmcguthry@cpp.edu
MCHALE, Barbara .... 215-641-5521 420 A
mchale.b@gmercyu.edu
MCHALE, JR., William .. 717-291-3870 418 J
william.mchale@fandm.edu
MCHANN, Carol .... 870-733-6740.. 19 G
clmchann@midsouthcc.edu
MCHARGUE, Jackie ...... 828-250-2370 370 E
jmchargu@unca.edu
MCHARRIS, Michael ..... 315-792-5489 333 D
mmcharris@mvcc.edu
MCHENRY, Bart .... 949-582-4907.. 67 F
bmchenry@saddleback.edu
MCHENRY, Erin .... 714-556-3610.. 75 A
erin.mchenry@vanguard.edu
MCHENRY, Lepaine ...... 405-585-4450 399 I
lepaine.mchenry@okbu.edu
MCHENRY, Stephanie .... 216-687-3673 380 D
s.y.mchenry@csuohio.edu
MCHENRY, William .... 903-223-3015 486 C
william.mchenry@tamut.edu
MCHUGH, Elizabeth ...... 360-867-6808 522 J
mchughe@evergreen.edu
MCHUGH, Evan .... 719-502-3196.. 84 J
evan.mchugh@ppcc.edu
MCHUGH, John .... 704-748-5213 362 G
mchugh.john@gaston.edu
MCHUGH, Kevin .... 207-786-6341 209 F
kmchugh@bates.edu
MCHUGH, Mary .... 978-837-5125 233 G
mary.mchugh@merrimack.edu
MCHUGH, Mary .... 845-848-7407 324 B
mary.mchugh@dc.edu
MCHUGH, Mary .... 865-251-1800 460 J
library@southcollegetn.edu
MCHUGH, Shelley .... 402-465-2123 292 E
smchugh@nebrwesleyan.edu
MCHUGH, Tracy .... 630-889-6607 154 E
tmchugh@nuhs.edu
MCILHAGGA, Doug .... 618-650-3605 159 I
dmcilha@siue.edu
MCILHENNEY, Sharon .. 717-299-7754 436 D
mcilhenney@stevenscollege.edu
MCILLECE, Michelle ...... 319-399-8844 176 G
mmcillec@coe.edu
MCILNAY, Sandy .... 816-604-4616 278 A
sandy.mcilnay@mcckc.edu
MCILROY, Julia .... 208-885-6123 139 C
juliam@uidaho.edu
MCILVANE, Amy .... 770-426-2648 128 C
mcilvane@life.edu
MCINALLY, David, W .... 319-399-8686 176 G
dmcinally@coe.edu
MCINNES, Robert .... 704-334-6882 355 I
rmcinnes@charlottechristian.edu
MCINNIS, James, P ...... 601-643-8488 266 J
jp.mcinnis@colin.edu
MCINNIS, Maurie, D .... 434-982-2334 514 A
mdm6n@virginia.edu
MCINNIS, Robert, L ...... 704-216-6400 358 I
rmcinnis@livingstone.edu
MCINNIS, W. Dale .... 910-410-1806 365 B
wdmcinnis@richmondcc.edu
MCINTEE, Justin .... 714-556-3610.. 75 A
MCINTIRE, Mary .... 713-348-2599 480 M
maryb@rice.edu
MCINTIRE, OSFS, Timothy .... 610-282-1100 416 I
Timothy.McIntire@desales.edu
MCINTOSH, Bedford ..... 909-869-4789.. 32 F
bmcintosh@cpp.edu
MCINTOSH, Cecilia, A .. 423-439-4221 461 D
mcintosc@etsu.edu
MCINTOSH, Charles ..... 352-854-2322 100 P
mcintosc@cf.edu
MCINTOSH, Craig .... 518-276-3992 339 D
mcintc@rpi.edu
MCINTOSH, Daniel .... 303-871-3712.. 86 H
daniel.mcintosh@du.edu
MCINTOSH, Gary .... 425-889-7790 524 G
gary.mcintosh@northwestu.edu
MCINTOSH, Gayle .... 253-879-3905 527 F
gmcintosh@pugetsound.edu
MCINTOSH, Glenn .... 248-370-4200 248 K
mcintosh@oakland.edu
MCINTOSH, Joe .... 817-515-5377 484 B
joe.mcintosh@tccd.edu
MCINTOSH, Joe, E .... 336-734-7297 362 F
jmcintosh@forsythtech.edu
MCINTOSH, John .... 256-331-5323.... 6 B
jmcintosh@nwscc.edu
MCINTOSH, Joshua ...... 207-786-6219 209 F
jmcintos@bates.edu
MCINTOSH, Julie .... 419-434-4062 393 F
mcintosh@findlay.edu
MCINTOSH, Keith .... 607-274-1530 328 H
kmcintosh@ithaca.edu
MCINTOSH, Tanisha ..... 734-432-5755 246 B
tmcintosh@madonna.edu
MCINTOSH, Tim .... 541-683-5141 406 B
tmcintosh@gutenberg.edu
MCINTOSH-DOTY, Mikail .... 512-313-3000 471 H
mikail.doty@concordia.edu
MCINTURF, Robert .... 940-565-4204 492 D
robert.mcinturf@unt.edu
MCINTYRE, Ashley .... 912-538-3129 132 A
amcintyre@southeasterntech.edu
MCINTYRE, Ellen, C ...... 704-687-8722 371 B
Ellen.McIntyre@uncc.edu
MCINTYRE, Faye, S ...... 678-839-6467 133 F
fmcintyr@westga.edu
MCINTYRE, Helen, M ... 205-934-8132.... 8 F
hmcintyre@uab.edu
MCINTYRE, Jacqueline . 516-364-0808 335 A
jmclntyre@nycollege.edu
MCINTYRE, Jacqueline . 516-364-0808 335 A
jmcintyre@nycollege.edu
MCINTYRE, James .... 513-244-8616 379 I
james.mcintyre@ccuniversity.edu
MCINTYRE, James, P ... 617-552-3246 224 B
james.mcintyre@bc.edu
MCINTYRE, Janet .... 503-491-7589 407 C
janet.mcintyre@mhcc.edu
MCINTYRE, Karen .... 412-392-3976 433 F
kmcintyre@pointpark.edu
MCINTYRE, Karen, E ..... 715-836-5171 539 E
mcintyke@uwec.edu
MCINTYRE, Kevin .... 217-424-6251 153 A
kmmintyre@millikin.edu
MCINTYRE, Kevin .... 806-743-7425 490 A
kevin.mcintyre@ttuhsc.edu
MCINTYRE, Leonard ..... 803-793-5101 445 F
mcintyrel@denmarktech.edu
MCINTYRE, Mary, F ...... 412-396-6668 417 I
mcintyre@duq.edu
MCINTYRE, Nancy .... 304-293-7800 533 D
nancy.mcintyre@mail.wvu.edu
MCINTYRE, Susan, H ... 252-222-6230 361 A
mcintyres@carteret.edu
MCINTYRE, William, A . 603-882-6923 297 B
bmcintyre@ccsnh.edu
MCINTYRE, Willie .... 910-672-1157 370 A
wmcintyre@uncfsu.edu
MCISAAC, Penny, J ...... 561-868-3583 109 H
mcisaacp@palmbeachstate.edu
MCIVER, John .... 208-885-6651 139 C
jmciver@uidaho.edu
MCJANNET, Cathy .... 619-216-6762.. 68 D
cmcjannet@swccd.edu
MCJUNKIN, Gayle .... 507-222-4335 254 D
gmcjunki@carleton.edu
MCKAIN, Joshua .... 617-236-8800 226 F
jmckain@fisher.edu
MCKAIN, Randy .... 218-751-8670 263 J
randymckain@oakhills.edu
MCKAMEY, Sheldon ..... 406-994-6342 287 G
smckamey@montana.edu
MCKANN, Helen .... 804-594-1523 515 G
hmckann@jtcc.edu
MCKAY, Alan, B .... 540-665-1280 512 E
amckay@su.edu
MCKAY, Ashley, M .... 812-941-2075 169 A
atronc01@ius.edu
MCKAY, Bill .... 509-542-5531 521 C
bmckay@columbiabasin.edu
MCKAY, Emily .... 701-224-2410 374 E
emily.mckay@bismarckstate.edu
MCKAY, Eugene .... 501-882-8956.. 19 E
emckay@asub.edu
MCKAY, Janet .... 203-837-8460.. 88 G
mckayj@wcsu.edu
MCKAY, Jeffrey .... 207-778-7009 212 E
jeffrey.d.mckay@maine.edu
MCKAY, Kerri .... 313-664-7441 241 D
kmckay@collegeforcreativestudies.edu
MCKAY, Kevin .... 425-640-1547 522 D
kevin.mckay@edcc.edu
MCKAY, Kimberly .... 956-872-2096 482 G
kjmckay@southtexascollege.edu
MCKAY, Kimberly .... 432-335-6683 479 O
kmckay@odessa.edu
MCKAY, Michael, E ...... 609-258-5491 305 C
mckay@princeton.edu
MCKAY, Norman .... 404-364-8322 129 F
nmckay@oglethorpe.edu
MCKAY, Patricia .... 301-295-3185 548 D
patricia.mckay@usuhs.edu
MCKAY, Richard .... 281-998-6150 481 G
richard.mckay@sjcd.edu
MCKAY, Sally .... 615-460-6456 455 D
sally.mckay@belmont.edu
MCKAY, Scott .... 870-235-4290.. 23 D
semckay@saumag.edu
MCKAY, Shaun, L .... 631-451-4736 348 E
mckays@sunysuffolk.edu
MCKAY, Tamara .... 810-762-3456 251 E
tamaramc@umflint.edu
MCKAY, Tom .... 530-741-6785.. 78 F
tmckay@yccd.edu
MCKAYLE-STOLZ, Camille .... 340-693-1201 559 B
cmckayl@uvi.edu
MCKEAN, Gerry .... 309-438-7651 147 I
gwmckea@ilstu.edu
MCKECHNIE, Brad .... 281-998-6075 486 F
bmckechnie@txchiro.edu
MCKECHNIE, Dan .... 916-484-8320.. 52 I
mckechd@arc.losrios.edu
MCKECHNIE, Janna ...... 701-858-3373 374 B
janna.mckechnie@minotstateu.edu
MCKECHNIE, Sally .... 225-578-2307 204 M
smckechnie@lsu.edu
MCKECHNIE, Susan, E . 410-706-7776 219 E
smckechnie@umaryland.edu
MCKEE, Andy .... 260-399-7700 174 C
amckee@sf.edu
MCKEE, Anne .... 865-981-8298 458 E
anne.mckee@maryvillecollege.edu
MCKEE, Bruce, G .... 641-422-4348 181 E
mckeebru@niacc.edu
MCKEE, Diann, E .... 812-237-2372 167 E
diann.mckee@indstate.edu
MCKEE, Eugenia .... 314-529-9509 277 B
gmckee@maryville.edu
MCKEE, J, P .... 803-323-2205 451 I
mckeej@winthrop.edu
MCKEE, John, C .... 409-747-9080 495 E
jcmckee@utmb.edu
MCKEE, Jonathon .... 808-984-3213 136 H
jvmckee@hawaii.edu
MCKEE, Kasey .... 636-922-8472 281 C
kmckee@stchas.edu
MCKEE, Lauren .... 408-274-7900.. 63 P
lauren.mckee@evc.edu
MCKEE, Lori .... 575-646-2172 312 A
lomckee@nmsu.edu
MCKEE, Lori .... 419-755-4828 387 E
lmckee@ncstatecollege.edu
MCKEE, Marites .... 808-687-7015 135 C
mmckee@hpu.edu
MCKEE, Michael .... 352-392-2402 115 D
mckee@ufl.edu
MCKEE, Mike .... 386-752-1822 103 Q
mike.mckee@fgc.edu
MCKEE, Richard .... 432-685-4734 478 F
rmckee@midland.edu
MCKEE, Sara .... 317-921-4607 169 M
smckee15@ivytech.edu
MCKEE, Suzanne .... 334-683-2347.... 5 H
smckee@marionmilitary.edu
MCKEE, William .... 615-547-1311 456 C
bmckee@cumberland.edu
MCKEE-LEONE, Virginia 951-222-8053.. 61 B
virginia.mckee-leone@rcc.edu
MCKEEGAN, John .... 503-883-2202 406 I
jmckeeg@linfield.edu
MCKEEN, Jerry .... 805-493-3139.. 31 H
jmckeen@callutheran.edu
MCKEEVER, Diane, M ... 312-942-6830 158 A
diane_m_mckeever@rush.edu
MCKEEVER, Kerry .... 603-899-1130 297 H
mckeeverk@franklinpierce.edu
MCKEEVER, Matt .... 303-797-5859.. 79 A
matthew.mckeever@arapahoe.edu
MCKEEVER, William, P . 716-829-7807 324 E
mckeever@dyc.edu
MCKELLIP, Mark .... 714-816-0366.. 70 D
mark.mckellip@trident.edu
MCKELLIPS, Stephen .... 901-678-5140 462 B
sjmckllp@memphis.edu
MCKELLIPS, Steve .... 901-678-5140 462 B
sjmckllp@memphis.edu
MCKELVEY, Steve .... 507-786-3421 264 C
mckelvey@stolaf.edu
MCKELVIE, OSF, Roberta .... 610-790-2876 412 C
roberta.mckelvie@alvernia.edu
MCKENDREE, Lynda ..... 713-525-2151 493 J
mckendla@stthom.edu
MCKENDRICKS, John .... 775-849-4983 407 D
jmckendricks@multnomah.edu
MCKENNA, Catherine ... 718-405-3233 322 A
catherine.mckenna@mountsaintvincent.edu
MCKENNA, Charles (Doug) .... 202-885-1052.. 94 H
dmckenna@american.edu
MCKENNA, Crichton ...... 207-453-5000 211 B
MCKENNA, David .... 903-886-5761 485 E
david.mckenna@tamuc.edu
MCKENNA, Heidi .... 510-883-7160.. 43 C
hmckenna@dspt.edu
MCKENNA, Joann .... 781-891-2455 223 E
jmckenna@bentley.edu
MCKENNA, John .... 518-587-2100 348 A
john.mckenna@esc.edu
MCKENNA, Kevin .... 914-395-2510 342 C
kmckenna@sarahlawrence.edu
MCKENNA, Kevin .... 508-793-7423 225 B
kmckenna@clarku.edu
MCKENNA, Margaret, A 617-573-8000 237 B
MCKENNA, Megan .... 440-375-7508 385 B
mmckenna@lec.edu
MCKENNA, Patrick .... 404-894-6088 125 D
pat.mckenna@carnegie.gatech.edu
MCKENNA, Rebecca ...... 970-248-1945.. 80 B
rmckenna@coloradomesa.edu
MCKENNA, Robert, E .... 860-444-8503 548 H
robert.e.mckenna@uscg.mil
MCKENNA, Sheila .... 412-392-3450 433 F
smckenna@pointpark.edu
MCKENNA, Timothy, J . 319-273-3241 176 A
Tim.McKenna@uni.edu
MCKENNA FRAZIER, Lynnette, M .... 260-399-7700 174 C
lfrazier@sf.edu
MCKENNA-JONES, Amy 573-518-2146 278 F
mjones@mineralarea.edu
MCKENNEY, William ...... 574-239-8390 167 C
wmckenney@hcc-nd.edu
MCKENZIE, Amanda ..... 478-289-2088 124 B
amckenzie@ega.edu
MCKENZIE, Andre, A .... 718-990-1892 340 G
mckenzia@stjohns.edu
MCKENZIE, Barbara, J .. 724-847-6610 419 B
bmckenzi@geneva.edu
MCKENZIE, Bruce .... 937-778-7855 381 K
bmckenzie@edisonohio.edu
MCKENZIE, Connie, L .. 757-446-6070 507 B
mckenzcl@evms.edu

MCKENZIE, Elizabeth .... 617-573-8705 237 B
emckenzi@suffolk.edu

MCKENZIE, Fred, R ...... 630-947-8930 139 L
mckenzie@aurora.edu

MCKENZIE, JoAnn .... 404-727-6052 124 D
jmckenz@emory.edu

MCKENZIE, Joy .... 615-383-4848 466 F
jmckenzie@watkins.edu

MCKENZIE, Laura .... 208-282-2661 138 C
mckelaur@isu.edu

MCKENZIE, Lester .... 931-372-3073 462 A
lmckenzie@tetech.edu

MCKENZIE, Lisa .... 518-454-5114 322 C
mckenzil@strose.edu

MCKENZIE, Natalie, E ... 530-226-4103.. 66 G
nmckenzie@simpsonu.edu

MCKENZIE, Patricia, M . 936-639-1301 467 I
mckenzie@angelina.edu

MCKENZIE, Peter, C ..... 617-552-8740 224 B
peter.mckenzie@bc.edu

MCKENZIE, Pia .... 919-807-6951 359 M
mckenziep@nccommunitycolleges.edu

MCKENZIE, Rene .... 541-956-7129 409 F
rmckenzie@roguecc.edu

MCKENZIE, Sheri .... 415-703-9535.. 30 G
smckenzie@cca.edu

MCKENZIE, Vandeen ..... 575-439-3711 312 B
vmckenzi@nmsu.edu

MCKENZIE, W. Shelby .. 225-578-4126 204 L
wmcken1@lsu.edu

MCKEON, Judith, O ...... 540-985-9083 509 D
jomckeon@jchs.edu

MCKEON, Michael .... 925-631-4552.. 61 G
mfm4@stmarys-ca.edu

MCKEOWN, Carol, M ... 585-292-2500 333 G
cmckeown2@monroecc.edu

MCKEOWN, Robert .... 716-614-6271 336 D
mckeown@niagaracc.suny.edu

MCKERNAN, Sarah .... 620-341-5551 186 H
smckerna@emporia.edu

MCKERNAN, Steve .... 505-272-2071 313 H
smckernan@salud.unm.edu

MCKESSON, Leslie .... 828-448-3156 367 B
lmckesson@wpcc.edu

MCKETHAN, Lisa, H ..... 254-710-1011 469 D
lisa_mckethan@baylor.edu

MCKIBBEN, Nile .... 608-249-6611 536 J
nmckibben@herzing.edu

MCKIBBENS, Donna ..... 617-879-2242 238 C
dmckibbens@wheelock.edu

MCKIBBIN, Barbara ...... 704-669-4116 361 E
mckibbin@clevelandcc.edu

MCKIEL, Allen .... 503-838-8886 411 B
mckiela@wou.edu

MCKIM, Dana .... 704-463-3409 367 F
dana.mckim@pfeiffer.edu

MCKINLEY, Bob .... 817-598-6256 497 A
bmckinley@wc.edu

MCKINLEY, David .... 626-448-0023.. 48 C

MCKINLEY, Elizabeth .... 816-501-3767 272 E
elizabeth.mckinley@avila.edu

MCKINLEY, Kathy .... 919-536-7244 362 C
mckinleyk@durhamtech.edu

MCKINLEY, Kristin, L ... 920-832-6532 536 R
kristin.l.mckinley@lawrence.edu

MCKINLEY, Patricia ...... 713-525-3575 493 J
mckinley@stthom.edu

MCKINLEY, Rita .... 216-987-2044 381 A
rita.mckinley@tri-c.edu

MCKINLEY, Ronald, B .. 409-772-2636 495 E
rbmckinl@utmb.edu

MCKINNEY, Andre .... 404-880-6791 122 I
amckinney@cau.edu

MCKINNEY, Bryan .... 870-245-5250.. 22 C
mckinneyb@obu.edu

MCKINNEY, Bryan .... 870-245-5513.. 22 C
mckinneyb@obu.edu

MCKINNEY, David .... 888-491-8686.. 76 G

MCKINNEY, David, C .... 828-398-7124 360 A
dmckinney@abtech.edu

MCKINNEY, Dee .... 478-289-2062 124 B
dmckinney@ega.edu

MCKINNEY, Donald, W 252-334-2084 359 D
don.mckinney@macuniversity.edu

MCKINNEY, Frances, H 410-651-6668 219 H
fhmckinney@umes.edu

MCKINNEY, Gail .... 303-797-5647.. 79 A
gail.mckinney@arapahoe.edu

MCKINNEY, Jill .... 317-940-8312 164 L
jsmckinn@butler.edu

MCKINNEY, Joan, C ..... 270-789-5214 194 D
jmckinney@campbellsville.edu

MCKINNEY, Joe .... 602-291-2237 403 F
Joe.McKinney@StrataTech.com

MCKINNEY, Kirsten .... 540-362-6307 508 D
kmckinney1@hollins.edu

MCKINNEY, Marion .... 610-436-3307 432 B
mmckinney@wcupa.edu

MCKINNEY, Michael ..... 724-589-2600 436 E
mmckinney@thiel.edu

MCKINNEY, Michele ..... 303-860-5600.. 86 D
michele.mckinney@cu.edu

MCKINNEY, Paul .... 662-325-7428 269 A
kpm137@msstate.edu

MCKINNEY, Rhonda ..... 509-963-1391 520 E
mckinner@cwu.edu

MCKINNEY, Richard, L . 785-864-3136 191 G
rlm@ku.edu

MCKINNEY, Robert .... 734-995-7328 241 F
robert.mckinney@cuaa.edu

MCKINNEY, Roger .... 612-338-7224 265 G
roger.mckinney@laureate.net

MCKINNEY, Shannon ... 813-988-5131 103 L
mckinney@floridacollege.edu

MCKINNEY, Shortie ...... 978-934-4460 229 A
Shortie_McKinney@uml.edu

MCKINNON, Brad .... 256-766-6610.... 4 C
bmckinnon@hcu.edu

MCKINNON, Keith .... 214-860-3633 472 G
kmckinnon@dcccd.edu

MCKINNON, Maureen ... 816-501-4831 281 B
maureen.mckinnon@rockhurst.edu

MCKINNON, Sarah .... 617-369-4054 236 E
smckinnon@smfa.edu

MCKINNON, Theresa .... 615-327-6185 458 F
tmckinnon@mmc.edu

MCKINNON, Will .... 801-863-8922 500 B
will.mckinnon@uvu.edu

MCKINSEY-MABRY,
Kimberly .... 585-262-1616 333 G
kmckinseymabry@monroecc.edu

MCKINTYRE, Katherine . 251-344-1203.... 3 J

MCKINZIE, Steve .... 704-637-4666 355 H
smckinzie@catawba.edu

MCKINZIE, Wes .... 405-425-5132 399 J
wes.mckinzie@oc.edu

MCKIRDY, Pam .... 434-791-5618 505 A
pmckirdy@averett.edu

MCKISIC, Bethaney .... 304-473-8017 534 G
mckisic_b@wvwc.edu

MCKISSON, Kevin .... 281-476-1501 481 E
kevin.mckisson@sjcd.edu

MCKITTRICK, Jerry .... 314-744-5345 278 G
mckittrickj@mobap.edu

MCKNIGHT, Avery .... 850-599-3591 114 D
avery.mcknight@famu.edu

MCKNIGHT, Carrie .... 650-508-3717.. 56 H
cmknight@ndnu.edu

MCKNIGHT, Cynthia ..... 440-684-6102 394 G
cmcknigh@ursuline.edu

MCKNIGHT, Frank .... 330-490-7226 395 C
fmcknight@walsh.edu

MCKNIGHT, Irby .... 972-825-4662 483 D
imcknight@sagu.edu

MCKNIGHT, Natalie .... 617-358-0180 224 E
njmck@bu.edu

MCKNIGHT, Oscar .... 419-289-5065 377 A
omcknigh@ashland.edu

MCKNIGHT, Sandra .... 216-987-4832 381 A
sandra.mcknight@tri-c.edu

MCKNIGHT, Steven, H .. 571-858-3000 518 B
shm@vt.edu

MCKONE, Kevin .... 601-643-8369 266 J
kevin.mckone@colin.edu

MCKOWN, Charles .... 620-223-2700 187 B
charlesm@fortscott.edu

MCKOWN, Johnette ...... 254-299-8601 478 C
jmckown@mclennan.edu

MCKOY, Cynthia .... 910-879-5566 360 C
cmckoy@bladencc.edu

MCKOY, Dana .... 910-362-7029 360 G
dmckoy@cfcc.edu

MCLACKEN, Susan .... 401-232-6881 441 B
smcdonal@bryant.edu

MCLAIN, Jeff, L .... 330-672-3000 384 H

MCLAIN, Katherine .... 916-691-7411.. 52 J
mclaink@crc.losrios.edu

MCLANE, Anne, P .... 214-648-5617 496 A
anne.mclane@utsouthwestern.edu

MCLANE, Sarah .... 802-860-2778 501 F
smclane@champlain.edu

MCLARAN, Diane .... 503-316-3229 404 L
diane.mclaran@chemeketa.edu

MCLAREN, Donna .... 585-594-6114 339 F
McLaren_Donna@roberts.edu

MCLAREN, Kate .... 508-531-6502 229 C
kate.mclaren@bridgew.edu

MCLAREN, Kate .... 508-830-5000 230 D

MCLARTY, Bruce, D ...... 501-279-4274.. 21 A
president@harding.edu

MCLAUGHLIN, Audrey .. 603-668-2211 298 H
a.mclaughlin1@snhu.edu

MCLAUGHLIN, Cari .... 315-470-7256 316 I
carimclaughlin@crouse.org

MCLAUGHLIN, Carrie .... 716-286-8405 336 E
cmclaughlin@niagara.edu

MCLAUGHLIN, David ..... 212-998-2415 336 C
david.mclaughlin@nyu.edu

MCLAUGHLIN,
David, B .... 419-289-5555 377 A
dmclaugh@ashland.edu

MCLAUGHLIN,
Edward, K .... 804-828-6692 514 F
athleticsdir@vcu.edu

MCLAUGHLIN,
Francis, X .... 718-817-4300 326 C
mclaughlin@fordham.edu

MCLAUGHLIN, Gerald ... 215-641-5550 420 A
mclaughlin.g@gmercyu.edu

MCLAUGHLIN, Henry, J 646-660-6000 318 C
Henry.Mclaughlin@baruch.cuny.edu

MCLAUGHLIN, James ... 518-388-6284 350 K
mclaughj@union.edu

MCLAUGHLIN, John ..... 401-456-8235 442 A
jmclaughlin@ric.edu

MCLAUGHLIN, Joyce .... 978-934-4237 229 A
Joyce_McLaughlin@uml.edu

MCLAUGHLIN, Karen .... 603-862-2140 299 B
karen.mclaughlin@unh.edu

MCLAUGHLIN, Keith ..... 708-656-8000 153 G
keith.mclaughlin@morton.edu

MCLAUGHLIN,
Kelly Anne .... 315-781-4357 327 G
mclaughlin@hws.edu

MCLAUGHLIN, Kevin .... 415-503-6253.. 63 A
kmclaughlin@sfcm.edu

MCLAUGHLIN, Kevin .... 401-863-9525 441 A
kevin_mclaughlin@brown.edu

MCLAUGHLIN, Larry ..... 661-362-3111.. 40 H
larry.mclaughlin@canyons.edu

MCLAUGHLIN, Laura .... 636-227-2100 277 A
Laura.McLaughlin@logan.edu

MCLAUGHLIN,
Laurie, L .... 612-626-1499 265 C
mclau001@umn.edu

MCLAUGHLIN, LaVerne 229-430-4799 119 H
laverne.mclaughlin@asurams.edu

MCLAUGHLIN,
Margaret .... 386-752-1822 103 Q
maggie.mclaughlin@fgc.edu

MCLAUGHLIN, Mark ..... 513-745-3409 396 B
mclaughlin@xavier.edu

MCLAUGHLIN,
Mark, W .... 860-832-0065.. 88 D
mclaughlinm@ccsu.edu

MCLAUGHLIN, Mary ..... 603-526-3755 296 I
mmclaughlin@colby-sawyer.edu

MCLAUGHLIN, Mary, R 518-454-5170 322 C
mclaughr@strose.edu

MCLAUGHLIN, Matt ...... 207-974-4869 211 A
mmclaughlin@emcc.edu

MCLAUGHLIN, Mike ...... 319-398-4947 180 J
mclaug@kirkwood.edu

MCLAUGHLIN, Nora ...... 503-777-7774 409 E
nora.mclaughlin@reed.edu

MCLAUGHLIN,
Patrick, A .... 260-481-6128 168 D
mclaughp@ipfw.edu

MCLAUGHLIN,
Robert, P .... 973-761-9545 308 C

MCLAUGHLIN, Sabrina . 850-474-2433 116 E
smclaughlin2@uwf.edu

MCLAUGHLIN, Sandee .. 805-546-3116.. 42 H
smclaugh@cuesta.edu

MCLAUGHLIN, Sean, M 614-823-1576 390 C
smclaughlin@otterbein.edu

MCLAUGHLIN, Steve ..... 612-874-3759 257 D
smclaughlin@mcad.edu

MCLAURIN, Lisa, H ...... 919-209-2178 363 F
lhmclaurin@johnstoncc.edu

MCLAWHORN, Toni, D . 540-375-2303 512 B
mclawhorn@roanoke.edu

MCLAY, Deidre .... 831-656-2511 548 A
dmclay@nps.edu

MCLEAN, Amber .... 906-635-2382 245 H
amclean@lssu.edu

MCLEAN, Anita .... 609-258-3285 305 C
amclean@princeton.edu

MCLEAN, Brandon .... 402-844-7102 292 G
brandon@northeast.edu

MCLEAN, Connie .... 309-796-5369 140 D
mcleanc@bhc.edu

MCLEAN, David .... 970-491-3366.. 81 D
david.mclean@colostate.edu

MCLEAN, Deborah .... 907-842-5109.. 10 I
dlmclean@alaska.edu

MCLEAN, Edward .... 910-672-1315 370 A
emclean@uncfsu.edu

MCLEAN, Jack .... 773-508-3912 151 E
jmclean@luc.edu

MCLEAN, Janna .... 574-807-7191 164 F
janna.mclean@bethelcollege.edu

MCLEAN, Jennifer .... 570-326-3761 429 J
jmclean@pct.edu

MCLEAN, John, A .... 734-895-3280 246 C
drjohnmclean@gmail.com

MCLEAN, Karen, P .... 515-271-1463 177 H
karen.mclean@dmu.edu

MCLEAN, Laura .... 704-378-1295 358 B
lmclean@jcsu.edu

MCLEAN, Liz .... 910-642-7141 366 B
Liz.McLean@sccnc.edu

MCLEAN, Michael, F .... 805-525-4417.. 69 I
mmclean@thomasaquinas.edu

MCLEAN, Natalie .... 336-273-4431 354 K
nmclean@bennett.edu

MCLEAN, Pat .... 417-690-3441 273 C
mclean@cofo.edu

MCLEAN, William, H .... 847-491-7050 155 D
wmclean@northwestern.edu

MCLEAN-SCANLON,
Mary .... 585-785-1778 325 E
mary.mcleanscanlon@flcc.edu

MCLEANE, David .... 870-574-4504.. 23 E
dmcleane@sautech.edu

MCLELLAN, Holly, H ..... 251-626-3303.... 8 C
hmclellan@ussa.edu

MCLELLAN, Katharyn .... 610-917-1431 438 G
kjmclellan@valleyforge.edu

MCLELLAN, Mark, R ..... 435-797-1180 500 A
mark.mclellan@usu.edu

MCLELLAND, Brandy ..... 310-243-3569.. 33 B
bmclelland@csudh.edu

MCLEMORE, Larry, A .... 620-417-1651 191 A
rry.mclemore@sccc.edu

MCLEMORE, Maria, R .... 651-201-1745 257 N
maria.mclemore@so.mnscu.edu

MCLENDON, Catrenia ... 404-297-9522 126 A
mclendon@gptc.edu

MCLENDON, Kathi .... 704-330-6976 361 D
kathi.mclendon@cpcc.edu

MCLENDON, Michael ..... 254-710-3111 469 D
Michael_McLendon@baylor.edu

MCLENDON, Sandra ...... 864-644-5354 449 B
smclendon@swu.edu

MCLENNAN, Dale .... 978-232-2101 226 C
dmclenna@endicott.edu

MCLEOD, Alisea .... 662-252-8000 270 C
amcleod@rustcollege.edu

MCLEOD, Allan .... 215-871-6826 432 E
allanm@pcom.edu

MCLEOD, Judith .... 949-794-9090.. 68 F
jmcleod@stanbridge.edu

MCLEOD, Mark .... 404-727-7457 124 D
rmcleod@emory.edu

MCLEOD, Michael .... 863-784-7441 113 C
michael.mcleod@southflorida.edu

MCLEOD, Michael, J ..... 516-877-3177 314 F
mcleod@adelphi.edu

MCLEOD, Renee .... 619-477-6310.. 70 G
rmcleod@usuniversity.edu

MCLEOD, Steve .... 706-864-1915 133 A
steve.mcleod@ung.edu

MCLESKEY, Stephanie ... 828-689-1128 359 A
smcleskey@mhu.edu

MCLLWAIN, Daryl .... 207-780-5510 213 A
darylmc@usm.maine.edu

MCLOGAN, Matthew, E . 616-331-2190 243 E
mcloganm@gvsu.edu

MCLOUGHLIN, Eileen ... 518-320-1193 343 B
eileen.mcloughlin@suny.edu

MCLOUGHLIN, II,
Paul, J .... 610-330-5082 423 A
mcloughp@lafayette.edu

MCLOUGHLIN,
Suzanne .... 516-876-3109 345 E
mcloughlins@oldwestbury.edu

MCMAHAN, Carla .... 864-977-7090 448 A
carla.mcmahan@ngu.edu

MCMAHAN,
Christopher .... 401-874-9463 442 E
cmcmahan@uri.edu

MCMAHAN, David .... 423-636-7315 464 F
dmcmahan@tusculum.edu

MCMAHAN, Kerrin .... 323-415-4135.. 51 D
mcmahakm@elac.edu

MCMAHAN, Mendi .... 214-333-5119 471 L
mendi@dbu.edu

MCMAHAN, Oliver, L .... 423-478-7037 460 C
omcmahan@ptseminary.edu

MCMAHAN, Richard .... 304-647-6410 533 B
rmcmahan@osteo.wvsom.edu

MCMAHAN, Robert, K .. 810-762-9864 245 A
mcmahan@kettering.edu

MCMAHAN, Shari .... 657-278-7000.. 33 E
smcmahan@fullerton.edu

MCMAHILL, Janet, M ... 515-271-3726 177 K
janet.mcmahill@drake.edu

MCMAHON, Beth .... 641-628-5345 176 E
mcmahone@central.edu

MCMAHON, Charles, P 504-988-8555 207 F
cpm@tulane.edu

MCMAHON, Cindy .... 212-962-0002 334 E
cmcmahon@nyci.edu

MCMAHON, David .... 413-748-3210 236 H
dmcmahon@springfieldcollege.edu

MCMAHON, Doug .... 727-864-8587 101 P
mcmahodh@eckerd.edu

MCMAHON, James .... 414-288-7206 537 B
james.mcmahon@marquette.edu

MCPHATTER, Anna .... 443-885-4325 217 C
anna.mcphatter@morgan.edu
MCPHEARSON,
Petra, R .... 731-881-7805 465 F
prencher@utm.edu
MCPHEE, Debra .... 212-636-6616 326 C
dmcphee1@fordham.edu
MCPHEE, Kelly .... 602-286-8186.. 14 M
kelly.mcphee@gwmail.maricopa.edu
MCPHEE, Scott .... 765-674-6901 169 C
scott.mcphee@indwes.edu
MCPHEE, Scott .... 912-650-5640 131 F
smcphee@southuniversity.edu
MCPHEE, Sidney, A ...... 615-898-2623 461 E
sidney.mcphee@mtsu.edu
MCPHEETERS, Andrew .. 503-768-7936 406 H
mcpheete@lclark.edu
MCPHERON, Bruce .... 614-292-6164 389 A
mcpheron.24@osu.edu
MCPHERON, Lisa .... 714-992-7014.. 56 F
mcpheron@fullcoll.edu
MCPHERREN, Ann, C ... 260-359-4225 167 D
amcpherren@huntington.edu
MCPHERSON, Brisco ..... 405-224-3140 403 L
bmcpherson@usao.edu
MCPHERSON, Evelyn .... 806-743-2860 489 F
evelyn.mcpherson@ttuhsc.edu
MCPHERSON, John .... 765-285-5600 164 D
jmcphers@bsu.edu
MCPHERSON, Lindsey .. 713-525-3639 493 J
guthmanl@stthom.edu
MCPHERSON, Mary, L .. 972-860-5097 472 F
lmcpherson@dcccd.edu
MCPHERSON, Michael .. 305-809-3280 104 A
michael.mcpherson@fkcc.edu
MCPHERSON, Mona ...... 251-981-3771.... 3 A
mona.mcpherson@columbiasouthern.edu
MCPHERSON, Penny ...... 856-256-4086 306 D
mcphersonp@rowan.edu
MCPHERSON, Robert .... 713-743-5003 491 D
bmcph@uh.edu
MCPHERSON, Terry ...... 704-378-1237 358 B
tmcpherson@jcsu.edu
MCPHERSON, Tim .... 423-266-4574 460 G
tmcpherson@richmont.edu
MCPHERSON FIELDS,
Tiffany, S .... 919-658-7714 369 B
hfields@umo.edu
MCPHILIMY, Betty, L .... 847-491-2622 155 D
b-mcphilimy@northwestern.edu
MCPIKE, Brian .... 719-255-3211.. 86 F
bmcpike@uccs.edu
MCQUADE, Robert, K .... 574-631-6161 174 A
mcquade.10@nd.edu
MCQUADE, Shauna, N . 301-784-5000 213 C
smcquade@allegany.edu
MCQUARIE, Audra .... 602-557-6151.. 18 H
audra.mcquarie@phoenix.edu
MCQUARRIE, Michael ... 410-626-2558 218 A
michael.mcquarrie@sjc.edu
MCQUAY-PENINGER,
Laurel .... 310-434-3718.. 65 B
mcquay-peninger_laurel@smc.edu
MCQUEEN, Angus .... 540-887-7012 510 A
amcqueen@mbc.edu
MCQUEEN, Lee .... 308-865-1700 293 G
mcqueenlv@unk.edu
MCQUEEN, Mary .... 361-698-1317 473 F
mmcqueen2@delmar.edu
MCQUEEN, Sylvia .... 910-642-7141 366 B
Sylvia.McQueen@sccnc.edu
MCQUEEN-BEY, Valerie 410-462-8054 213 G
vleverette-bey@bccc.edu
MCQUEENEY,
Christophe .... 315-568-3352 334 F
cmcqueeney@nycc.edu
MCQUEENY, Jane .... 785-864-3687 191 G
jane.mcqueeny@ku.edu
MCQUERRY, Marcia ...... 405-585-5101 399 I
marcia.mcquerry@okbu.edu
MCQUESTEN, Pam .... 512-863-1300 483 G
pmcquesten@southwestern.edu
MCQUILKIN, Scott, A ... 509-777-4386 529 A
smcquilkin@whitworth.edu
MCQUILLAN, Pat .... 651-423-8318 258 E
patrick.mcQuillan@dctc.edu
MCQUILLAN, Pat .... 651-450-3655 259 A
pmcquil@inverhills.edu
MCQUINN, Robert .... 847-467-2469 155 D
r-mcquinn@northwestern.edu
MCQUISTION, Chris ...... 615-383-4848 466 F
cmcquistion@watkins.edu
MCQUOWN, Daniel .... 517-629-0492 239 A
dmcquown@albion.edu
MCRAE, Alphonzo .... 910-272-3500 365 D
mcrae@robeson.edu
MCRAE, Alphonzo .... 910-272-3500 365 D
amcrae@robeson.edu
MCRAE, Georgia, D ...... 414-288-7596 537 B
georgia.mcrae@marquette.edu
MCRAE, Kevin .... 406-444-0327 287 C
kmcrae@montana.edu
MCRAE, Mary .... 215-572-2781 412 F
mcraem@arcadia.edu
MCRAE, Mary, S .... 972-881-5771 471 C
mmcrae@collin.edu
MCRAE, Maureen .... 323-259-2548.. 56 I
mmclevy@oxy.edu
MCRAE, Richard .... 502-897-4721 199 D
rmcrae@sbts.edu
MCRAE, Vanessa .... 229-430-1914 119 H
vanessa.mcrae@asurams.edu
MCRAE-BRUNSON,
Marcela, C .... 870-235-4025.. 23 D
mdbrunson@saumag.edu
MCRAVEN, William, H .. 512-499-4201 493 K
chancellor@utsystem.edu
MCRELL, Michael .... 620-341-5214 186 H
mcrellmi@emporia.edu
MCREYNOLDS, Amanda 515-271-2338 177 K
mandi.mcreynolds@drake.edu
MCREYNOLDS,
Betsy, A .... 417-667-8181 273 H
bmcreynolds@cottey.edu
MCREYNOLDS, Diane .... 805-765-9300.. 64 G
MCREYNOLDS, Karla ..... 573-288-6544 274 C
kmcreynolds@culver.edu
MCREYNOLDS, Shawn .. 276-223-4810 517 F
smcreynolds@wcc.vccs.edu
MCRIGHT, Jurgin .... 606-546-4151 200 E
mmcright@uionky.edu
MCROBBIE, Michael ..... 812-855-4613 167 J
iupres@iu.edu
MCROBBIE, Michael, A 812-855-4613 167 I
iupres@iu.edu
MCROBIE, Karen .... 415-442-6599.. 46 A
kmcrobie@ggu.edu
MCRORIE, Sally, E .... 850-644-1765 115 A
smcrorie@fsu.edu
MCSHAN, Jim .... 832-842-5550 491 C
jmcshan@uh.edu
MCSHAN, Jim .... 832-842-5530 491 D
jmcshan@central.uh.edu
MCSHANE, Bridget .... 860-439-2314.. 90 D
bamcs@conncoll.edu
MCSHANE, SJ,
Joseph, M .... 718-817-3000 326 C
MCSHAY, Kelly .... 856-351-2919 308 B
kmcshay@salemcc.edu
MCSHEA, Anitra, M ...... 570-941-7680 438 F
anitra.mcshea@scranton.edu
MCSHEEHY, Diane, M ... 303-458-4223.. 85 G
dmcsheehy@regis.edu
MCSHEFFERY, Ed .... 724-938-4299 430 C
mcsheffery@calu.edu
MCSHERRY, Bernard ..... 201-200-3321 304 C
bmcsherry@njcu.edu
MCSORLEY, Jennifer ..... 715-833-6433 542 M
jmcsorley2@cvtc.edu
MCSPADDEN, Galen, W 620-417-1550 191 A
galen.mcspadden@sccc.edu
MCSPADDEN, Jean .... 903-675-6214 490 F
jmcspadden@tvcc.edu
MCSWAIN, Garry .... 704-406-3923 356 G
gmcswain@gardner-webb.edu
MCSWAIN, Michael .... 704-669-4115 361 E
mcswainm@clevelandcc.edu
MCSWAIN, Roderick ...... 251-665-4139.... 2 D
rmcswain@bishop.edu
MCSWEENEY, Frances .. 509-335-5581 528 B
fkmcs@wsu.edu
MCSWEENEY, Jean .... 501-296-1982.. 24 B
McSweeneyJeanC@uams.edu
MCTIERNAN, Kerri-Ann 212-217-4210 325 C
kerriann_mctiernan@fitnyc.edu
MCTIERNAN, Susan ...... 401-254-3444 442 C
MCVAY, Janine .... 413-565-1000 222 G
jmcvay@baypath.edu
MCVAY, John .... 509-527-2186 528 A
john.mcvay@wallawalla.edu
MCVAY, John, R .... 575-624-8150 311 K
mcvay@nmmi.edu
MCVAY-DYCHE,
Jennifer .... 518-464-8742 325 B
JMcVay-Dyche@excelsior.edu
MCVEAN, Aaron .... 650-738-4454.. 64 E
mcveana@smccd.edu
MCVEARRY, Kenneth .... 301-447-5274 217 D
mcvearry@msmary.edu
MCVEIGH, Bob .... 303-871-4106.. 86 H
robert.mcveigh@du.edu
MCVEIGH, Paul, J .... 703-323-4224 516 C
pmcveigh@nvcc.edu
MCVETY, Paul, J .... 401-598-1775 441 D
pmcvety@jwu.edu
MCVEY, Greg .... 636-481-3386 276 E
gmcvey@jeffco.edu
MCWADE, Patricia, A .... 202-687-4547.. 95 E
mcwadep@georgetown.edu
MCWHERTER, Karen ..... 731-661-5337 464 G
kmcwhert@uu.edu
MCWHERTER, Lisa .... 864-644-5013 449 B
lmcwherter@swu.edu
MCWHORTER, Lois, A .. 606-878-4801 197 B
lois.mcwhorter@kctcs.edu
MCWHORTER,
Shirlyon, J .... 305-348-2785 114 G
shirlyon.mcwhorter@fiu.edu
MCWHORTER, Thomas . 213-740-5445.. 74 D
faodean@usc.edu
MCWILLIAMS, Mindy .... 202-687-8041.. 95 E
mcwillie@georgetown.edu
MCWILLIAMS,
Stephen, T .... 610-519-4095 439 A
stephen.mcwilliams@villanova.edu
MCWORTHY, Chance ..... 319-363-1323 181 D
cmcworthy@mtmercy.edu
MEA, William .... 212-353-4150 323 B
mea@cooper.edu
MEACHAM, Timothy, E . 843-349-2876 444 G
tmeacham@coastal.edu
MEAD, Alicia .... 303-220-1200.. 79 G
alicia.mead@cffp.edu
MEAD, JR., George, F .. 337-475-5785 208 B
mead@mcneese.edu
MEAD, K. Ann .... 270-745-2434 201 D
ann.mead@wku.edu
MEAD, Steven .... 860-733-1384.. 90 C
smead@txcc.commnet.edu
MEAD, Susan .... 845-431-8036 324 D
mead@sunydutchess.edu
MEAD-COLEGROVE,
Robert, W .... 716-878-5336 345 B
meadcorw@buffalostate.edu
MEADE, Christopher ..... 503-915-7800 406 A
cmeade@georgefox.edu
MEADE, Elizabeth .... 610-606-4637 415 A
emeade@cedarcrest.edu
MEADE, Marianne .... 610-989-1240 438 I
mmeade@vfmac.edu
MEADOR, Earl, W .... 985-448-7922 203 G
earl.meador@fletcher.edu
MEADOR, John, M .... 205-934-6360.... 8 F
jmmj@uab.edu
MEADOR, Keith, G .... 615-936-2686 465 H
keith.meador@vanderbilt.edu
MEADOR, Michele .... 775-673-7249 295 F
mmeador@tmcc.edu
MEADOR, Nancy .... 501-882-8824.. 19 E
nrmeador@asub.edu
MEADOR, Roy .... 515-643-6612 181 B
rmeador@mercydesmoines.org
MEADOR, Ruby .... 870-762-3125.. 19 C
rmeador@smail.anc.edu
MEADOR, Ryan .... 816-604-5229 277 H
ryan.meador@mcckc.edu
MEADORS, Mark .... 918-343-7860 401 I
mmeadors@rsu.edu
MEADOWS, David .... 708-534-8044 145 D
dmeadows@govst.edu
MEADOWS, David, D ..... 814-641-0714 421 L
meadowd@juniata.edu
MEADOWS, Dawn .... 863-638-7246 118 L
dawn.meadows@warner.edu
MEADOWS, Dawn .... 863-638-7654 118 L
dawn.meadows@warner.edu
MEADOWS, Dean .... 863-638-7255 118 L
dean.meadows@warner.edu
MEADOWS, Ed .... 850-484-1700 110 D
emeadows@pensacolastate.edu
MEADOWS, Mark .... 619-482-6569.. 68 D
mmeadows@swccd.edu
MEADOWS, Rebekah ..... 615-248-1436 464 E
rlmeadows@trevecca.edu
MEADOWS, Steve .... 304-384-5180 532 E
meadows@concord.edu
MEAGHER, Paula, G ..... 915-831-4530 473 J
pmeagher@epcc.edu
MEAGHER, Sharon, M .. 610-499-1260 439 G
smmeagher@widener.edu
MEALER, Angela .... 904-743-1122 107 C
amealer@jones.edu
MEALER, Donna .... 731-286-3312 462 F
mealer@dscc.edu
MEALY, Robert .... 212-799-5000 329 I
MEANA, Marta .... 702-895-2267 295 G
marta.meana@unlv.edu
MEANER,
Christopher, M .... 412-578-6069 414 I
meanercm@carlow.edu
MEANEY, Heather, L ..... 518-381-1250 342 E
meaneyhl@sunysccc.edu
MEANS, Ben .... 217-228-5432 156 D
meansbe@quincy.edu
MEANS, John .... 918-335-6892 400 I
jmeans@okwu.edu
MEANS, Laurie .... 937-328-6145 379 L
lmeans@clarkstate.edu
MEANS, Margie .... 706-776-0123 130 B
mmeans@piedmont.edu
MEANS, JR., Robert, T . 423-439-6315 461 D
deanofmedicine@etsu.edu
MEANY, Birgit .... 907-852-3333.. 10 F
birgit.meany@ilisagvik.edu
MEANY, David .... 509-359-6335 522 C
dmeany@ewu.edu
MEANY, Mary, T .... 920-832-6561 536 R
mary.t.meany@lawrence.edu
MEARA, Mark .... 609-894-9311 306 B
mmeara@bcc.edu
MEARNS, Geoffrey, S ... 859-572-5123 199 A
mearns@nku.edu
MEARNS, Raiana .... 847-543-2402 142 G
rmearns@clcillinois.edu
MEARS, Bobby .... 757-789-1747 515 D
bmears@es.vccs.edu
MEARS, Gail .... 603-535-3500 299 E
gmears@plymouth.edu
MEARS, Karen, P .... 773-244-5710 154 G
kmears@northpark.edu
MEARS, Laura .... 301-846-2429 214 I
lmears@frederick.edu
MEARS, Michael, J .... 941-752-5267 114 B
mearsm@scf.edu
MEARS, Ted .... 320-252-1489 261 E
husky@bkstr.com
MEASAMER, Ronnie ...... 919-718-7409 361 C
rmeasamer@cccc.edu
MEASE, Ervin, J .... 610-799-1112 424 A
emease@lccc.edu
MEASE, Stephen .... 802-865-6432 501 F
smease@champlain.edu
MECCA, Kim .... 570-504-0920 422 G
meccak@lackawanna.edu
MECH, Terrence, F .... 570-208-5943 422 D
tfmech@kings.edu
MECHAM, Melissa, E .... 206-239-4500 520 K
mmecham@cityu.edu
MECHAM, Steven, J ..... 435-797-1967 500 A
steve.mecham@usu.edu
MECHE, Eddie, P .... 337-475-5501 208 B
emeche@mcneese.edu
MECHE, Lance .... 972-825-4747 483 D
LMeche@sagu.edu
MECK, Bill .... 641-683-5106 179 C
bill.meck@indianhills.edu
MECKEL, David .... 415-703-9561.. 30 G
dmeckel@cca.edu
MEDA, Pat .... 626-529-8261.. 57 F
pmeda@pacificoaks.edu
MEDAGLIA, Frank .... 804-594-1414 515 G
fmedaglia@jtcc.edu
MEDAGLIA, Kimberly .... 630-752-5729 163 G
kimberly.Medaglia@wheaton.edu
MEDBURY, Doug .... 425-235-2352 525 G
dmedbury@rtc.edu
MEDCALF, Elizabeth ...... 301-687-4751 220 D
emedcalf@frostburg.edu
MEDDERS, Alan .... 706-507-8954 123 D
medders_alan@columbusstate.edu
MEDDERS, Mike, W .... 903-566-7393 494 E
mmedders@uttyler.edu
MEDDINGS, Nancy .... 805-922-6966.. 26 H
nmeddings@hancockcollege.edu
MEDEARIS, Cheryl .... 605-856-5880 453 B
cheryl.medearis@sintegleska.edu
MEDEIROS, Brad .... 508-626-4911 230 A
bmedeiros@framingham.edu
MEDEIROS, Dave .... 803-705-4586 443 F
dave@benedict.edu
MEDEIROS, Denis, M ... 816-235-1301 284 A
medeirosd@umkc.edu
MEDEL, Michael .... 805-965-0581.. 64 N
medel@sbcc.edu
MEDEMA, Pamela, S ..... 815-835-6378 158 I
pamela.s.medema@svcc.edu
MEDENBLIK, Julius, T .. 616-957-6024 240 M
jmedenblik@calvinseminary.edu
MEDFORD, Adriane .... 215-567-7080 412 G
amedford@aii.edu
MEDFORD, Kim .... 254-968-0515 485 A
medford@tarleton.edu
MEDFORD, Mike .... 404-687-4576 123 C
medfordm@ctsnet.edu
MEDINA, Cynthia .... 303-751-8700.. 79 F
medina@bel-rea.com
MEDINA, Elizabeth .... 512-313-3000 471 H
elizabeth.medina@concordia.edu
MEDINA, Gary .... 310-303-7302.. 53 E
gmedina@marymountcalifornia.edu
MEDINA, Kelly .... 262-646-6506 538 B
kmedina@nashotah.edu
MEDINA, Mara .... 787-780-0070 550 G
mmedina@caribbean.edu
MEDINA, Mario .... 787-738-4660 557 G
mario.medina@upr.edu
MEDINA, María, C .... 787-884-3838 550 E
opdai@atenascollege.edu

MEDINA, Nancy .... 773-442-5240 154 H
n-medina4@neiu.edu
MEDINA, Priscilla, G .... 956-721-5357 477 C
pmedina@laredo.edu
MEDINA, Raúl .... 787-264-0406 554 C
rimedina@intersg.edu
MEDINA, Reinalda .... 718-997-4455 320 E
reinalda.medina@qc.cuny.edu
MEDINA, Widylia .... 787-890-2681 557 C
widylia.medina@upr.edu
MEDINA-CABAN, Mario 787-738-2161 557 B
mario.medina@upr.edu
MEDINA-ORTIZ,
Roberto .... 787-622-8000 556 H
rmedina@pupr.edu
MEDLEY, Lara .... 303-273-3200.. 80 O
lmedley@mines.edu
MEDLEY, Linda, S .... 502-895-3411 198 E
lsmedley@lpts.edu
MEDLEY, Mike .... 435-896-9714 500 D
michael.medley@snow.edu
MEDLEY-WEEKS,
Clarice .... 214-379-5565 480 D
cweeks@pqc.edu
MEDLIN, Melissa, T ..... 256-765-4276.... 9 D
mtmedlin@una.edu
MEDRANO, Jennifer ..... 801-832-2126 501 C
jmedrano@westminstercollege.edu
MEDRO, Alfred .... 619-265-0107.. 59 J
amedro@platt.edu
MEDVETZ, Betsy .... 603-428-2477 298 B
bmedvetz@nec.edu
MEDWICK, Peter .... 215-972-2017 429 G
pmedwick@pafa.edu
MEE, Christine, L .... 843-349-2091 444 G
christin@coastal.edu
MEE, David .... 615-460-6785 455 D
david.mee@belmont.edu
MEEAJANE, Natasha ..... 312-922-1884 151 I
nmeeajane@maccormac.edu
MEECE, Jeffrey .... 312-369-7151 143 C
jmeece@colum.edu
MEECE, Jill, N .... 606-679-8501 197 B
jill.meece@kctcs.edu
MEEHAN, Barbara .... 703-993-2380 507 K
bmeehan@gmu.edu
MEEHAN, Barry .... 603-882-6923 297 B
bmeehan@ccsnh.edu
MEEHAN, Gabriel .... 916-558-2097.. 53 B
MeehanG@scc.losrios.edu
MEEHAN, Linda, M ...... 609-984-1105 308 H
meehan@tesc.edu
MEEHAN, Martin .... 617-287-7050 228 E
mmeehan@umassp.edu
MEEHAN, Mary, J .... 414-382-6064 534 I
mary.meehan@alverno.edu
MEEHAN, Paula, T .... 616-632-2852 239 E
meehapau@aquinas.edu
MEEHAN, Sara .... 703-284-6815 510 B
smeehan@marymount.edu
MEEK, Charles Ronald . 340-693-1421 559 B
charles.meek@uvi.edu
MEEK, Laura .... 614-251-4642 388 H
meekl@ohiodominican.edu
MEEK, Laura, E .... 740-587-6279 381 H
meekl@denison.edu
MEEK, Michelle .... 606-886-3863 195 I
michelle.meek@kctcs.edu
MEEK, Scott .... 602-787-7902.. 15 B
scott.meek@paradisevalley.edu
MEEKER, April, M .... 605-642-6092 453 G
april.meeker@bhsu.edu
MEEKER, Steve, L .... 605-642-6385 453 G
steve.meeker@bhsu.edu
MEEKMA, Glenn, A .... 269-471-3484 239 D
meekma@andrews.edu
MEEKS, Andy .... 859-572-5575 199 A
meeksa@nku.edu
MEEKS, Harry, L .... 812-888-4511 174 F
hmeeks@vinu.edu
MEEKS, J. Duane .... 561-803-2610 109 G
duane_meeks@pba.edu
MEEKS, Kimela, A .... 812-888-4377 174 F
kmeeks@vinu.edu
MEEKS, Mark .... 478-445-5851 125 A
mark.meeks@gcsu.edu
MEEKS, Matthew .... 972-241-3371 472 A
mmeeks@dallas.edu
MEEKS, Susan .... 478-387-4801 125 E
smeeks@gmc.edu
MEEKS, Tom .... 216-373-5206 388 A
tmeeks@ndc.edu
MEENTS-DECAIGNY,
Ellen .... 312-362-7298 143 G
emeentsd@depaul.edu
MEER, Jonathan, D ...... 609-896-5167 306 A
jmeer@rider.edu
MEERTS, John .... 860-685-3800.. 93 B
jmeerts@wesleyan.edu
MEES, Andrew .... 973-748-9000 300 E
andrew_mees@bloomfield.edu
MEESE, JoAnna .... 724-439-4900 423 G
jmeese@laurel.edu
MEESE, Paul .... 303-678-3707.. 82 J
paul.meese@frontrange.edu
MEESKE, Susan .... 402-461-7398 290 G
smeeske@hastings.edu
MEGAHED, Nivine .... 312-261-3232 153 H
nivine.megahed@nl.edu
MEGALE, Nicole .... 517-264-3850 238 H
MEGAW, Shelly .... 507-389-7289 262 A
shelly.megaw@southcentral.edu
MEGGERT, Shannon ..... 847-947-0575 153 H
smeggert@nl.edu
MEGORDEN,
Timothy, M .... 218-299-4161 255 B
megorden@cord.edu
MEGREDY, Jill .... 785-227-3380 185 A
megredyj@bethanylb.edu
MEHA, Arapata 808-675-3739 134M
mehaa@byuh.edu
MEHAN, Audra .... 503-552-2005 407 F
amehan@ncnm.edu
MEHAN, Uppinder .... 478-825-6211 124 E
mehanu@fvsu.edu
MEHDIZADEH, Mojdeh . 510-215-3801.. 42 D
mojdeh@contracosta.edu
MEHLER, Mark .... 609-771-2186 301 E
mehler@tcnj.edu
MEHLHOFF, Monte .... 605-626-7781 454 A
Monte.Mehlhoff@northern.edu
MEHLIG, Lisa .... 815-921-4070 157 B
l.mehlig@rockvalleycollege.edu
MEHMERT, Rebecca ...... 573-897-5000 282 I
MEHRABADI, Monte ...... 619-594-2909.. 35 E
mehrabadi@mail.sdsu.edu
MEHRHOFF, Jay .... 636-584-6585 274 J
jay.mehrhoff@eastcentral.edu
MEHRING, Tes .... 913-344-1236 184 F
tes.mehring@bakeru.edu
MEHRINGER, Marty ...... 317-805-1791 530 G
mmehringer@salemu.edu
MEHTA, Neera .... 425-739-8211 523 I
neera.mehta@lwtech.edu
MEHTA, Raj .... 513-556-6252 393 B
raj.mehta@uc.edu
MEIDLINGER, Peter, K .. 417-873-7469 274 E
pmeidlin@drury.edu
MEIER, Beth, A .... 919-760-8427 359 B
meierb@meredith.edu
MEIER, Gene .... 970-339-6662.. 78 J
gene.meier@aims.edu
MEIER, Jay .... 701-224-5666 374 E
jay.meier@bismarckstate.edu
MEIER, Karen, F .... 757-683-5026 510 I
kmeier@odu.edu
MEIER, Marina .... 208-535-5425 138 B
marina.meier@my.eitc.edu
MEIER, Neal .... 513-487-1174 392 F
neal.meier@myunion.edu
MEIER, Neal .... 916-564-1525 392 F
neal.meier@myunion.edu
MEIER WELTZIEN,
Lynn .... 406-683-7180 287 E
lynn.weltzien1@umwestern.edu
MEIERGERD, Joseph .... 314-792-6140 276 H
meiergerd@kenrick.edu
MEIGHAN, Elizabeth, A 717-334-6286 424 F
emeighan@ltsg.edu
MEIKLEJOHN, Scott, A . 207-725-3148 209 H
smeiklej@bowdoin.edu
MEIKSINS, Peter .... 216-687-5559 380 D
p.meiksins@csuohio.edu
MEILMAN, Philip, W ..... 202-687-6985.. 95 E
pwm9@georgetown.edu
MEINDL, Lidia .... 212-463-0400 350 C
lidia.meindl@touro.edu
MEINEKE, John .... 309-796-5053 140 D
meinekej@bhc.edu
MEINERT, Anita .... 641-673-1063 184 B
meinerta@wmpenn.edu
MEINERT, James .... 559-324-6481.. 68 J
jim.meinert@sccd.edu
MEINERTS, Marita, K .... 651-631-5168 265 D
mkmeinerts@unwsp.edu
MEINHARDT, Stephanie 972-881-5847 471 C
smeinhardt@collin.edu
MEINHOLD, Patricia ..... 843-383-8267 445 A
pmeinhold@coker.edu
MEINZEN, David, L ...... 260-399-7700 174 C
dmeinzen@sf.edu
MEIR, Michael .... 212-594-4000 349 J
mmeir@tcicollege.edu
MEIRICK, Craig, R .... 563-562-3263 181 F
meirickc@nicc.edu
MEIS, Aaron .... 513-745-2941 396 B
meisa@xavier.edu
MEIS, Darrell .... 719-587-7912.. 78 I
djmeis@adams.edu
MEIS, Gail, N .... 404-471-6306 119 G
gmeis@agnesscott.edu
MEISCHEID, Michelle ... 252-862-1252 365 C
mlmeischeid5257@roanokechowan.edu
MEISEL, Joseph, S .... 401-863-9499 441 A
joseph_meisel@brown.edu
MEISEL, Seth .... 262-472-1013 541 D
meisels@uww.edu
MEISELES, Gary, A .... 502-597-6438 197 G
gary.meiseles@kysu.edu
MEISENZAHL, Dan, T ... 808-956-5941 135 H
dmeisenz@hawaii.edu
MEISNER, Jane .... 515-244-4221 175 C
meisnerj@aib.edu
MEISNER, Jolene .... 570-662-4696 431 D
jmeisner@mansfield.edu
MEISSNER, Ken .... 712-749-2111 176 D
meissnerk@bvu.edu
MEISTER, Barbara .... 740-477-7858 388 F
bmeister@ohiochristian.edu
MEISTER, Bobbi .... 712-274-5606 181 C
meisterb@morningside.edu
MEISTER, Debra .... 312-915-7244 151 E
dmeiste@luc.edu
MEISTER, Tony .... 660-944-2899 273 E
tmeister@conception.edu
MEITZNER, June .... 507-285-7213 261 D
june.meitzner@rctc.edu
MEIXSEL-CORDERO,
Terri .... 623-245-4600.. 18 C
tmeixsell@uti.edu
MEJIA, Dana .... 614-837-4088 394 H
MEJIA, Gil .... 602-331-7500.. 12 C
gmejia@aii.edu
MEJIA, Juan, E .... 903-510-2261 491 A
jmej@tjc.edu
MEJIA, Laurie .... 626-966-4576.. 27 I
lauriemejia@agu.edu
MEJIA KRUG,
Miroslava .... 312-341-3583 157 E
mmkrug@roosevelt.edu
MEJIA MARTINEZ,
Marcela .... 714-997-6711.. 38 B
mamartin@chapman.edu
MEJIAS, Ida, A .... 787-250-1912 554 A
iamejias@metro.inter.edu
MEJIAS, Jackeline .... 787-765-1915 554 E
jmejias@opto.inter.edu
MEJIAS, Luis .... 787-780-0070 550 G
lmejias@caribbean.edu
MEJIAS, Nelson .... 787-753-6335 552 K
nmejias@icprjc.edu
MEJIC, Tatiana .... 718-270-6016 320 C
tmejic@mec.cuny.edu
MEKEEL, Naomi .... 518-255-5547 346 E
mekeelnf@cobleskill.edu
MEKEMSON,
Kristen, M .... 920-832-7449 536 R
kristen.mekemson@lawrence.edu
MELENDEZ RAMOS,
Grisel, E .... 787-763-6299 558 E
grisel.melendez@upr.edu
MELANSON, Chris .... 207-509-7141 212 A
cmelanson@unity.edu
MELANSON,
Leigh Anne .... 603-862-3290 299 B
leigh-anne.melanson@unh.edu
MELARAGNI, Robert ..... 617-670-4401 226 F
rmelaragni@fisher.edu
MELARAGNO, Steven .... 401-254-3667 442 C
smelaragno@rwu.edu
MELAVALIN, Robin .... 647-928-4624 234 D
rmelavalin@mountida.edu
MELBY, Darlene .... 805-378-1550.. 75 C
dmelby@vcccd.edu
MELBY, Diane .... 304-876-5378 532 I
MELBY, Laurie .... 714-241-6110.. 40 B
lmelby@coastline.edu
MELCHER, Chris .... 706-721-4018 121 C
cmelcher@gru.edu
MELCHER, Mike .... 806-291-3425 496 K
melcherp@wbu.edu
MELCHER, Rick, W .... 610-921-7748 411 E
rmelcher@albright.edu
MELCHERT, Russell, B .. 816-235-1607 284 A
melchertr@umkc.edu
MELCHIOR, Vonda .... 813-253-7107 106 C
vmelchior@hccfl.edu
MELCON, John .... 661-362-2608.. 53 F
jmelcon@masters.edu
MELDREM, Joyce, A ..... 563-588-7164 180 L
joyce.meldrem@loras.edu
MELDRUM, John .... 313-883-8512 249 E
meldrum.john@shms.edu
MELE, Donald .... 956-665-2711 494 C
meledj@utpa.edu
MELEG, Mike .... 309-796-5002 140 D
melegm@bhc.edu
MELEN, Pia .... 714-533-1495.. 67 A
pmelen@southbaylo.edu
MELENDEZ,
Georgianna .... 617-287-4818 228 G
georgianna.melendez@umb.edu
MELENDEZ, Jennifer .... 212-472-1500 336 A
jmelendez@nysid.edu
MELENDEZ, Leonardo ... 787-720-4476 556 G
decanatoacademico@mizpa.edu
MELENDEZ, Martin .... 787-834-3718 558 B
support@uprm.edu
MELENDEZ, Mercedes .. 212-343-1234 332 I
mmelendez@mcny.edu
MELENDEZ, Nildalee ..... 787-852-1430 552 J
nmelendez@hccpr.edu
MELENDEZ, Nitza .... 787-725-8120 552 G
nmelendez@eap.edu
MELENDEZ, Rafael .... 787-725-6500 551 A
rmelendez@albizu.edu
MELENDEZ, Ruben .... 908-709-7085 309 A
ruben.melendez@ucc.edu
MELENDEZ, Yahaira ...... 787-620-2040 550 D
melendezy@aupr.edu
MELENDY, Lisa, M .... 413-597-2477 238 E
lisa.m.melendy@williams.edu
MELETIES, Panayiotis ... 718-262-2780 321 B
pmeleties@york.cuny.edu
MELHART, Bonnie .... 817-257-7729 486 G
b.melhart@tcu.edu
MELIAN, Carlos .... 773-442-4400 154 H
c-melian@neiu.edu
MELIKECHI,
Noureddine .... 302-857-6656.. 93 E
nmelikechi@desu.edu
MELIKOVA, Amy .... 785-460-4608 186 D
amy.melikova@colbycc.edu
MELIN, Laurie, A .... 787-257-7373 555 L
lamelin@suagm.edu
MELINA, Livio .... 202-526-3799.. 96 F
MELINE, Douglas .... 916-568-3017.. 52 H
melined@losrios.edu
MELISI, Mary Ann .... 610-558-5611 427 D
melisim@neumann.edu
MELKONIAN,
Madeleine .... 718-405-3236 322 A
madeleine.melkonian@mountsaintvincent.edu
MELL, Doug .... 715-232-1198 541 B
melld@uwstout.edu
MELLAND, Helen .... 406-657-3784 287 G
helen.melland@montana.edu
MELLEN, Brenda .... 215-702-4843 414 C
bmellen@cairn.edu
MELLENKAMP,
Kathleen .... 606-759-7141 196 G
kathleen.mellenkamp@kctcs.edu
MELLER, Brenda .... 248-689-8282 251 I
bmeller@walshcollege.edu
MELLICHAMP,
James, F .... 706-776-0100 130 B
president@piedmont.edu
MELLING, Alice .... 206-934-3693 525 K
alice.melling@seattlecolleges.edu
MELLINGER, Laurie, A .. 717-866-7581 418 E
lmellinger@evangelical.edu
MELLO, Mary .... 559-934-2000.. 76 B
marymello@whccd.edu
MELLO, Steven .... 401-874-2698 442 E
smello@uri.edu
MELLO-GOLDNER,
Diane .... 617-731-7106 235 F
dmellogoldner@pmc.edu
MELLON, Edward, J ...... 703-323-3083 516 C
emellon@nvcc.edu
MELLON, James, P .... 808-932-7467 135 I
mellon@hawaii.edu
MELLON, Suzanne, K .... 412-578-6123 414 I
skmellon@carlow.edu
MELLONI, Suzanne .... 508-999-9299 228 H
smelloni@umassd.edu
MELLOTT, David, M ...... 717-290-8723 423 E
rgawn@lancasterseminary.edu
MELLOTT, Ramona .... 928-523-6534.. 16 C
Ramona.Mellott@nau.edu
MELLOW, Gail, O .... 718-482-5050 320 B
gmellow@lagcc.cuny.edu
MELMED, Shlomo .... 310-423-8171.. 37 K
MELNICK, Julie .... 402-844-7123 292 G
juliem@northeast.edu
MELNICK, Marie .... 215-637-7700 420 K
mmelnick@holyfamily.edu
MELNIK, JoAnn .... 724-964-8811 427 E
jmelnik@ncstrades.edu
MELNYK, Bernadette ..... 614-292-4844 389 A
melnyk.15@osu.edu
MELO, Manuel .... 787-523-6000 552 K
mmelo@icprjc.edu
MELOAN, Andrea .... 816-415-7831 285 K
meloana@william.jewell.edu
MELOAN, Ross, B .... 270-809-3735 198 I
rmeloan@murraystate.edu

MELOCHE, Catherine .... 774-354-0464 223 C
catherine.meloche@becker.edu
MELOCHE, Kyle .... 410-857-2275 217 A
kmeloche@mcdaniel.edu
MELOY, Joseph, P .... 414-277-7227 537 G
meloy@msoe.edu
MELSON, Rick .... 585-567-9340 328 C
rick.melson@houghton.edu
MELSON, Vollie, D .... 410-777-1494 213 E
vmelson@aacc.edu
MELTON, Chris .... 206-546-4613 526 G
cmelton@shoreline.edu
MELTON, David, V .... 617-364-3510 224 A
dmelton@boston.edu
MELTON, Judi .... 206-264-9100 519 I
judim@bgu.edu
MELTON, Leslie, J .... 740-368-3152 390 B
ljdelerm@owu.edu
MELTON, Mark, A .... 919-516-4029 368 E
mamelton@st-aug.edu
MELTON, Matthew .... 423-614-8115 457 M
mmelton@leeuniversity.edu
MELTON, Melissa .... 251-380-2271.... 7 F
mmelton@shc.edu
MELTON, Randall .... 269-927-8139 245 E
melton@lakemichigancollege.edu
MELTON, JR., Samuel .. 662-254-3434 269 C
smelton@mvsu.edu
MELTON, Steve .... 828-297-3811 360 F
smelton@cccti.edu
MELTON, Toni .... 901-381-3939 466 E
toni@visible.edu
MELTON PAGES, Joyce 817-598-6245 497 A
jpages@wc.edu
MELTZER, Melissa .... 970-223-2669.. 83 B
MELUSKY, Marie, B ...... 814-472-3126 434 F
mmelusky@francis.edu
MELVILLE, John .... 252-638-7260 362 A
MELVIN, Cruse .... 409-880-8395 488 F
cruse.melvin@lamar.edu
MELVIN, Cynthia .... 601-977-7716 270 F
cmelvin@tougaloo.edu
MELVIN, Dana .... 412-291-6270 412 H
dmelvin@aii.edu
MELVIN, Julie .... 216-421-7455 380 B
jrmelvin@cia.edu
MELVIN, Kari .... 301-846-2441 214 I
kmelvin@frederick.edu
MELVIN, Lee, H .... 716-645-6003 343 E
MELVIN, Marilee, A ...... 630-752-5517 163 G
marilee.melvin@wheaton.edu
MELVIN, Matt .... 785-864-4381 191 G
mattmelvin@ku.edu
MELVIN, Michael .... 770-233-6167 132 B
mmelvin@sctech.edu
MEMBRINO, Charles .... 617-585-1239 234 H
itshelp@necmusic.edu
MEMOLI, Phil .... 239-513-1122 106 E
pmemoli@hodges.edu
MEN, Su-hua .... 941-752-5250 114 B
mens@scf.edu
MENA, Clara .... 203-285-2123.. 89 B
cmena@gwcc.commnet.edu
MENA, Robert .... 213-738-6716.. 68 E
studentaffairs@swlaw.edu
MENA, Terry .... 561-297-3547 114 E
tmena@fau.edu
MENARD, Christine ...... 315-798-8144 340 D
cmenard@secon.edu
MENARD, Connie .... 940-898-3826 490 D
cmenard@twu.edu
MENARD, Ginger .... 413-662-5201 230 C
ginger.menard@mcla.edu
MENARD, Jennifer .... 508-678-2811 231 B
jennifer.menard@bristolcc.edu
MENARD, Michael .... 860-570-9208.. 92 C
michael.menard@uconn.edu
MENARD, Richard, O .... 509-313-3583 522 L
menardr@gonzaga.edu
MENARD, Richard, R .... 401-841-7004 548 B
richard.menard@usnwc.edu
MENCHION, Byron .... 850-644-1803 115 A
bmenchion@fsu.edu
MENCK, Carol .... 206-239-2315 519 H
cmenck@aii.edu
MENDEDO, Tilahun, M . 334-874-5700.... 3 B
tmendedo@ccal.edu
MENDEL, Maurice, I ..... 901-678-5877 462 B
mmendel@memphis.edu
MENDELL, Cyndi .... 513-751-1206 376 A
info@aic-arts.edu
MENDELL, Sean, M ...... 513-751-1206 376 A
sean@aic.arts.edu
MENDELSOHN, Kathy ... 831-755-6700.. 46 J
kmendelsohn@hartnell.edu
MENDELSON, Eleonor .. 831-476-9424.. 44 L
admissions@fivebranches.edu
MENDENHALL, James .. 918-463-2931 397 I
james.mendenhall@connorsstate.edu
MENDENHALL, Leslie ... 816-995-2820 280 J
leslie.mendenhall@researchcollege.edu

MENDENHALL,
Robert, W .... 801-274-3280 501 B
rwm@wgu.edu
MENDES, Godfrey .... 614-947-6027 382 H
godfrey.mendes@frankli.edu
MENDES, Susy .... 212-237-8449 319 F
smendes@jjay.cuny.edu
MENDES, Wendy .... 559-734-9000.. 63 E
wendym@sjvc.edu
MENDEZ, Ana .... 312-935-4080 157 A
amendez@robertmorris.edu
MENDEZ, Ariel .... 787-766-1717 556 A
armendez@suagm.edu
MENDEZ, Celestino ...... 605-626-2601 454 A
Tino.Mendez@northern.edu
MENDEZ, Celia .... 787-276-0130 557 F
celia.mendez@upr.edu
MENDEZ, Diana .... 760-921-5536.. 58 C
diana.mendez@paloverde.edu
MENDEZ, Jannette .... 787-856-0945 551 I
jmendez@columbiacentral.edu
MENDEZ, José, F .... 787-766-1717 556 A
ac_jmendez@suagm.edu
MENDEZ, Jose, F .... 787-751-2262 555 K
ac_jmendez@suagm.edu
MENDEZ, JR., Jose, F .. 787-751-0178 555 K
jmendez@suagm.edu
MENDEZ, Larry .... 903-510-2281 491 A
lmen@tjc.edu
MENDEZ, Magaly .... 787-815-0000 557 D
magaly.mendez@upr.edu
MENDEZ, Pedro .... 209-575-6498.. 78 C
mendezp@yosemite.cc.ca.us
MENDEZ, Raul .... 786-363-4910 101 B
rmendez@dademedical.edu
MENDEZ, Sheri .... 775-784-4176 295 H
smendez@unr.edu
MENDEZ-GRANT,
Monica .... 940-898-3601 490 D
mmendez@twu.edu
MENDICK, Kay .... 701-777-4300 373 G
kay.mendick@und.edu
MENDIETA, Juan .... 305-237-7611 108 L
jmendiet@mdc.edu
MENDIETTA, Dorianna .. 559-730-3821.. 41 D
doriannam@cos.edu
MENDINI, Shauna .... 435-865-8185 499 L
mendini_s@suu.edu
MENDIOLA, Emma .... 210-486-0373 467 C
emendiola@alamo.edu
MENDIOLA, Francisco .. 691-320-2480 549 D
mendiolaf@comfsm.fm
MENDIOLA, Mark, B ..... 671-735-2957 549 G
funduog@gmail.com
MENDOLA, Richard, A .. 404-727-6018 124 D
rich.mendola@emory.edu
MENDONEZ RUSSELL,
Bernadette .... 561-862-4400 109 H
russellb@palmbeachstate.edu
MENDOZA, Beth, A ...... 920-929-2137 543 F
bmendoza@morainepark.edu
MENDOZA, Daniel .... 845-848-7900 324 B
daniel.mendoza@dc.edu
MENDOZA, Graciano .... 831-479-6279.. 30 C
grmendoza@cabrillo.edu
MENDOZA, Pablo .... 724-357-3402 431 A
mendoza@iup.edu
MENDOZA, Sandra .... 219-980-6954 168 C
sleone@iun.edu
MENDOZA-WELCH,
Maxine .... 903-886-5851 485 E
maxine.Mmendo@tamu.edu
MENEAR, Anne .... 660-263-3900 272 M
annemenear@cccb.edu
MENEAR, Anne, P .... 660-263-3900 272 M
annemenear@cccb.edu
MENEAR, Shelley .... 301-387-3037 215 A
shelley.menear@garrettcollege.edu
MENEFEE, Jeannine ..... 303-678-3664.. 82 J
jeannine.menefee@frontrange.edu
MENELEY, Theresa .... 713-221-8612 491 F
meneleyt@uhd.edu
MENENDEZ,
Jacqueline, R .... 305-284-5505 118 A
jmenendez@miami.edu
MENENDEZ, Rasel .... 310-287-4379.. 52 C
menendrm2@wlac.edu
MENESES, Jilma .... 503-493-6411 405 E
jmeneses@cu-portland.edu
MENESES, Steven .... 541-880-2245 406 E
meneses@klamathcc.edu
MENG, Heather .... 218-683-8560 260 F
heather.meng@northlandcollege.edu
MENG, Xiao-Li .... 617-496-1464 227 D
xlmeng@fas.harvard.edu
MENGHINI, Charles, T . 312-225-6288 162 H
cmenghini@vandercook.edu
MENGINE, Tina .... 814-732-1732 430 G
tmengine@edinboro.edu

MENGLER, Thomas, M . 210-436-3722 481 C
tmengler@stmarytx.edu
MENITOFF, Michael ...... 310-824-1586.. 25 K
MENJIVAR, Claudia ...... 718-357-0500 341 F
cmenjivar@edaff.com
MENJIVAR, Claudia, I ... 650-574-6146.. 64 D
menjivarc@smccd.edu
MENJIVAR, Juan .... 562-938-4258.. 51 A
jmenjivar@lbcc.edu
MENK, David, A .... 507-933-6539 256 A
dmenk@gustavus.edu
MENKE, Brandi .... 314-768-7851 278 H
bmenke@missouricollege.com
MENKE, Lisa .... 402-363-5600 294 G
lisa.menke@york.edu
MENKE, Scott .... 262-595-2155 540 C
scott.menke@uwp.edu
MENKE-FISH, Sarah ...... 202-885-2098.. 94 H
menke@american.edu
MENKING, Cornell .... 575-646-3199 312 A
cmenking@nmsu.edu
MENN, Esther .... 773-256-0721 151 H
emenn@lstc.edu
MENNE, Renee, A .... 563-588-7130 180 L
renee.menne@loras.edu
MENNECHEY, Pamela ... 407-708-2380 113 A
mennecheyp@seminolestate.edu
MENNEKE, Beth, R .... 314-505-7761 273 G
mennekeb@csl.edu
MENNELL, Betsy .... 928-523-7128.. 16 C
Betsy.Mennell@nau.edu
MENNELLA, Hillary .... 562-860-2451.. 37 L
hmennella@cerritos.edu
MENNICKE, Sue .... 717-291-3911 418 J
susan.mennicke@fandm.edu
MENNINGER, Gaynia .... 785-242-5200 190 D
gaynia.menninger@ottawa.edu
MENNINGER, Jay, E ..... 802-656-3290 503 C
jay.menninger@uvm.edu
MENOGAN, Kelle .... 601-977-7828 270 F
kmenogan@tougaloo.edu
MENON, Ajay .... 970-491-6274.. 81 D
ajay.menon@colostate.edu
MENSAH, Michael, O .... 570-941-4049 438 F
michael.mensah@scranton.edu
MENSCHING, Ron .... 630-889-6606 154 E
rmensching@nuhs.edu
MENSHOUSE, Nancy ..... 606-326-2199 195 H
nancy.menshouse@kctcs.edu
MENTE, Patrick, J .... 607-436-2596 344 B
mentepj@oneonta.edu
MENTEL, Susan .... 718-261-5800 316 K
smentel@bramsonort.edu
MENTZER, Cathy .... 717-262-2604 440 D
cmentzer@wilson.edu
MENTZER, Stacy, L .... 515-574-1148 179 F
mentzer_s@iowacentral.edu
MENTZINGER, Bob .... 207-509-7292 212 A
bmentzinger@unity.edu
MENZ, Harald .... 304-829-7915 529 H
hmenz@bethanywv.edu
MENZ PAYTON,
Jennifer .... 918-293-5178 400 E
jennifer.menz_payton@okstate.edu
MENZEL, Carol, A .... 410-334-2946 221 E
cmenzel@worwic.edu
MENZER, Paul .... 540-887-7058 510 A
pmenzer@mbc.edu
MEONSKE, Kali, A .... 330-325-6492 387 F
kmeonske@neomed.edu
MERANDA, Seth .... 402-643-7220 289 J
seth.meranda@cune.edu
MERB, Rick .... 740-351-3610 391 C
rmerb@shawnee.edu
MERCADANTE, Richard . 727-791-2527 112 A
Mercadante.Richard@spcollege.edu
MERCADEL, Robert .... 504-520-7396 209 E
rmercade@xula.edu
MERCADO, Deborah, A . 410-777-2321 213 E
damercado@aacc.edu
MERCADO, Harry .... 787-740-3555 556 F
harry.mercado@uccaribe.edu
MERCADO,
Juan Carlos .... 212-925-6625 318 G
jmercado@ccny.cuny.edu
MERCADO, Lemuel .... 770-228-7383 132 B
lmercado@sctech.edu
MERCADO, Maritza, E ... 212-247-3434 331 G
mmercado@mandl.edu
MERCER, Brenda, D ...... 919-735-5151 367 A
bdmercer@waynecc.edu
MERCER, David, M .... 585-567-9322 328 C
david.mercer@houghton.edu
MERCER, Debbie, K ...... 785-532-5525 188 H
dmercer@ksu.edu
MERCER, Ellen .... 920-923-8112 537 A
emercer@marianuniversity.edu
MERCER, Frank .... 386-506-4461 101 I
mercerf@DaytonaState.edu
MERCER, John .... 513-745-4890 396 B
mercerjl@xavier.edu

MERCER, John, D .... 850-872-3807 105 Q
jmercer@gulfcoast.edu
MERCER, Judith, R .... 757-446-5841 507 B
mercerjr@evms.edu
MERCER, Leneil .... 313-487-7420 202 L
leneil.mercer@lacollege.edu
MERCER, Leslie, K .... 651-201-1862 257 N
leslie.mercer@so.mnscu.edu
MERCER, Molly .... 724-738-2179 432 A
molly.mercer@sru.edu
MERCER, Paul .... 207-326-2337 211 G
paul.mercer@mma.edu
MERCER, Peter, P .... 201-684-7607 305 F
pmercer@ramapo.edu
MERCER, Ralisha .... 252-335-3225 369 F
rmmercer@ecsu.edu
MERCER,
Roberta (Bobby) .... 740-377-2520 392 C
mercer.tsbc@gmail.com
MERCHANT, Betty .... 210-458-4370 494 D
betty.merchant@utsa.edu
MERCHANT, Debra, S ... 513-556-4119 393 B
debra.merchant@uc.edu
MERCHANT, Deneene ... 740-753-7080 383 G
merchantm@hocking.edu
MERCHANT, Joshua, D . 904-620-2100 116 A
joshua.merchant@unf.edu
MERCHANT, Susan .... 386-822-7120 117 A
smerchan@stetson.edu
MERCHLEWITZ, Ann, E . 507-457-1587 264 B
amerchle@smumn.edu
MERCIER, Collette .... 801-627-8304 498 O
mercierc@owatc.edu
MERCIER, Nichole, R .... 314-747-1903 285 E
nmercier@wustl.edu
MERCINCAVAGE,
Janet, E .... 570-208-5878 422 D
jemercin@kings.edu
MERCK, Dana .... 937-708-5777 395 E
dmerck@wilberforce.edu
MERCK, II, William, F .. 407-823-2351 115 C
william.merck@ucf.edu
MERCURIO, Gloria .... 201-761-6125 307 K
gmercurio@saintpeters.edu
MERCURIO, Joseph .... 617-984-1775 235 H
jmercurio@quincycollege.edu
MERCURIO, Sherry .... 614-947-6581 382 H
sherry.mercurio@franklin.edu
MEREDITH, Ben .... 509-359-6010 522 C
bmeredith@ewu.edu
MEREDITH, Brian .... 270-745-6169 201 D
brian.meredith@wku.edu
MEREDITH, Daniel .... 864-941-8442 448 D
meredith.d@ptc.edu
MEREDITH, Dave .... 252-328-4781 369 E
meredithd14@ecu.edu
MEREDITH, Derek .... 252-335-0821 361 G
derek_meredith@albemarle.edu
MEREDITH, Janette, T .. 603-899-4077 297 H
Meridethj@franklinpierce.edu
MEREDITH, Joyce .... 740-587-6515 381 H
meredithj@denison.edu
MEREDITH, Kelly .... 405-208-5088 400 A
kmeredith@okcu.edu
MEREDITH, Mark .... 903-675-6327 490 F
mark.meredith@tvcc.edu
MEREDITH, Patricia ...... 813-463-7163.. 28 G
pmeredith@argosy.edu
MEREDITH, Patrick .... 309-341-5215 140 I
pmeredith@sandburg.edu
MERESSI, Tesfay .... 508-999-8542 228 H
tmeressi@umassd.edu
MERFALEN, Barbara, K . 670-237-6706 550 B
barbara.merfalen@marianas.edu
MERGET, Kathleen .... 845-451-1776 323 E
k_merget@culinary.edu
MERGIOTTI, James, J ... 215-670-9494 428 A
president@peirce.edu
MERIAN, Dan .... 313-593-5151 251 D
dmerian@umich.edu
MERIANO, John .... 203-582-8763.. 91 E
john.meriano@quinnipiac.edu
MERIANS, Linda .... 646-313-8000 321 A
Linda.Merians@guttman.cuny.edu
MERICA, Michael .... 928-226-4212.. 13 D
Michael.Merica@coconino.edu
MERICLE, Margaret, E .. 559-442-8210.. 69 B
margaret.mericle@fresnocitycollege.edu
MERIDITH, Pamela .... 870-759-4139.. 25 I
pmeridith@wbcoll.edu
MERILLAT, Jason, C ..... 610-566-1776 440 C
jmerillat@williamson.edu
MERILLAT, Melinda .... 832-252-0745 470 L
melinda.merillat@cbshouston.edu
MERIMEE, Nancy, S ..... 913-971-3427 189 F
nsmerimee@mnu.edu
MERINAR, Whitney, A .. 570-321-4144 425 B
merinar@lycoming.edu
MERINGOLO,
Salvatore, M .... 540-654-1372 513 I
tmeringo@umw.edu

METZGER, Thomas .... 702-968-2013 296 D
tmetzger@roseman.edu

METZINGER, Michelle .. 605-229-8379 453 A
michelle.metzinger@presentation.edu

METZINGER, Ryland ..... 408-924-1800.. 36 B
ryland.metzinger@sjsu.edu

METZLER, Christopher .. 717-391-1349 436 D
metzler@stevenscollege.edu

METZLER, Christopher .. 717-299-7794 436 D
metzler@stevenscollege.edu

METZLER, Duane .... 871-568-8 .. 431 E
duane.metzler@millersville.edu

MEULEMANS, Nicole .... 651-423-8403 258 E
nicole.meulemans@dctc.edu

MEUNINGHOFF, OP,
Mary Ann .... 708-524-6521 144 C
mmeuninghoff@dom.edu

MEUSCHKE, Daylene .... 661-362-5329.. 40 H
daylene.meuschke@canyons.edu

MEUWISSEN, Daniel, J . 651-962-5100 265 F
djmeuwissen@stthomas.edu

MEY, Craig, A .... 715-836-3263 539 E
meyca@uwec.edu

MEYDAM, Mark, R .... 715-425-4095 540 E
mark.r.meydam@uwrf.edu

MEYER, Aaron, J .... 914-337-9300 323 A
aaron.meyer@concordia-ny.edu

MEYER, Adam .... 212-799-5000 329 I

MEYER, Alan, E .... 708-209-3468 143 D
alan.meyer@cuchicago.edu

MEYER, Andy .... 706-272-4420 123 G
ameyer@daltonstate.edu

MEYER, Angela .... 573-651-2292 282 C
admeyer@semo.edu

MEYER, Ann .... 312-329-4417 153 C
ann.meyer@moody.edu

MEYER, Bruce .... 419-372-6821 377 I
bameyer@bgsu.edu

MEYER, Bruce, A .... 214-648-9794 496 A
bruce.meyer@utsouthwestern.edu

MEYER, Carrie .... 260-744-8747 173 B
crmeyer@taylor.edu

MEYER, Charles .... 415-405-3835.. 36 A
cmeyer@sfsu.edu

MEYER, Chris .... 405-733-7913 401 L
cmeyer@rose.edu

MEYER, Cindy .... 660-263-3900 272 M
cindymeyer@cccb.edu

MEYER, Dale, A .... 314-505-7010 273 G
meyerd@csl.edu

MEYER, Dan .... 651-962-6151 265 F

MEYER, Daniel, R .... 920-832-6607 536 R
daniel.r.meyer@lawrence.edu

MEYER, Danielle .... 330-941-3582 396 C
dlmeyer@ysu.edu

MEYER, David .... 816-414-3700 278 E
dmeyer@mbts.edu

MEYER, David, D .... 504-865-5930 207 F
meyer@tulane.edu

MEYER, Donald, C .... 757-446-5615 507 B
meyerdc@evms.edu

MEYER, Donald, G .... 610-917-1402 438 G
president@valleyforge.edu

MEYER, Donald, J .... 319-352-8517 183 J
donald.meyer@wartburg.edu

MEYER, Doug .... 503-493-6471 405 E
dmeyer@cu-portland.edu

MEYER, Elizabeth, K ..... 434-924-7019 514 A
ekm7a@Virginia.EDU

MEYER, Ellen .... 615-383-4848 466 F
emeyer@watkins.edu

MEYER, Evie .... 610-917-1417 438 G
eemeyer@valleyforge.edu

MEYER, Gary .... 917-493-4456 331 I
gmeyer@msmnyc.edu

MEYER, Gary .... 414-288-6350 537 B
gary.meyer@marquette.edu

MEYER, Greg .... 616-632-2802 239 E
greg.meyer@aquinas.edu

MEYER, Gregg, A .... 508-531-1237 229 C
gmeyer@bridgew.edu

MEYER, Gregor .... 312-788-1132 162 H
gmeyer@vandercook.edu

MEYER, Heidi .... 217-228-5432 156 D
meyerhe@quincy.edu

MEYER, Irene .... 216-987-4469 381 A
irene.meyer@tri-c.edu

MEYER, Jan .... 325-674-2840 466 I
meyerj@acu.edu

MEYER, Jay .... 847-543-2717 142 G
jmeyer@clcillinois.edu

MEYER, Jill .... 414-258-4810 538 A
meyerj@mtmary.edu

MEYER, John .... 414-443-8910 542 I
john.meyer@wlc.edu

MEYER, John .... 239-985-3451 104 G
jmeyer9@fsw.edu

MEYER, John .... 605-626-2379 454 A
John.Meyer@northern.edu

MEYER, John, E .... 507-354-8221 257 A
meyerjd@mlc-wels.edu

MEYER, Joseph, M .... 512-245-2386 489 C
jm01@txstate.edu

MEYER, Josh .... 540-857-6311 517 E
jmeyer@virginiawestern.edu

MEYER, Kathy .... 701-483-2535 373 H
Kathleen.Meyer@dickinsonstate.edu

MEYER, Kelly .... 518-458-5402 322 C
meyerk@strose.edu

MEYER, Kevin, C .... 402-826-8258 290 C
kevin.meyer@doane.edu

MEYER, Kimberly, J ..... 574-807-7021 164 F
kimberly.meyer@bethelcollege.edu

MEYER, Kingsley .... 740-245-7365 394 D
kmeyer@rio.edu

MEYER, Kyle .... 402-559-7428 293 I
kpmeyer@unmc.edu

MEYER, Larry .... 859-572-6117 199 A
meyerl3@nku.edu

MEYER, Lisa .... 503-768-7056 406 H
lmeyer@lclark.edu

MEYER, Mary, J .... 402-844-7030 292 G
maryjm@northeast.edu

MEYER, Merry .... 845-758-7005 315 G
sm568@bncollege.com

MEYER, Michael .... 951-343-4355.. 30 D
mmeyer@calbaptist.edu

MEYER, Michael .... 808-844-2308 136 E
mmeyer@hawaii.edu

MEYER, Michele .... 407-691-1754 111 H
mmeyer@rollins.edu

MEYER, Michele .... 715-682-1674 538 D
mmeyer@northland.edu

MEYER, Michelle .... 541-885-1628 408 E
michelle.meyer@oit.edu

MEYER, Nancy, L .... 616-526-6224 240 L
meyn@calvin.edu

MEYER, Pamela .... 504-280-6159 205 G
pameyer@uno.edu

MEYER, Patricia .... 240-629-7905 214 I
pmeyer@frederick.edu

MEYER, Patricia .... 513-745-1996 396 B
meyerp@xavier.edu

MEYER, Paul .... 361-825-3996 485 F
paul.meyer@tamucc.edu

MEYER, Paul, W .... 215-247-5777 437 I
pmeyer@upenn.edu

MEYER, Peter, E .... 863-680-4264 104 F
pmeyer@flsouthern.edu

MEYER, Ralph .... 512-245-8336 489 C
rm22@txstate.edu

MEYER, Rick .... 909-599-5433.. 50 H
rmeyer@lifepacific.edu

MEYER, Robert .... 715-232-2441 541 B
meyeb@uwstout.edu

MEYER, Sabrina .... 707-468-3065.. 54 A
smeyer@mendocino.edu

MEYER, Sam .... 502-585-9911 199 E
smeyer@spalding.edu

MEYER, Shana .... 816-271-4432 279 E
slmeyer@missouriwestern.edu

MEYER, Stan .... 602-639-7500.. 14 A

MEYER, Susan .... 320-308-5512 261 F
smeyer@sctcc.edu

MEYER, Thomas .... 605-274-5330 452 A
thomas.meyer@augie.edu

MEYER, Thomas, W ..... 610-799-1517 424 A
tmeyer1@lccc.edu

MEYER, Timothy, R ...... 248-341-2116 248 E
trmeyer@oaklandcc.edu

MEYER, Tina .... 909-469-5586.. 76 I
tmeyer@westernu.edu

MEYER, Yvonne .... 816-271-4439 279 E
ymeyer@missouriwesern.edu

MEYER REIMER,
Kathryn .... 574-535-7443 166 C
kathymr@goshen.edu

MEYEROWICH, Drew ..... 913-684-7316 548 F
drew.meyerowich@leavenworth.army.mil

MEYEROWITZ, Beth, E .. 213-740-6715.. 74 D
meyerow@usc.edu

MEYERS, Aeri .... 617-732-5952 233 E
aeri.meyers@mcphs.edu

MEYERS, Andrew, W .... 901-678-2590 462 B
ameyers@memphis.edu

MEYERS, Bonnie .... 651-779-3346 258 D
bonnie.meyers@century.edu

MEYERS, Carolyn .... 601-979-2323 267 H
carolyn.meyers@jsums.edu

MEYERS, Cory, J .... 617-573-8000 237 B
cmeyers@suffolk.edu

MEYERS, Debra .... 503-699-6252 407 A
dmeyers@marylhurst.edu

MEYERS, Ernest, G .... 864-488-4367 447 F
emeyers@limestone.edu

MEYERS, Gene .... 504-865-5353 207 F
gmeyers@tulane.edu

MEYERS, Jane .... 520-795-0787.. 11 I
academicdean@asaom.edu

MEYERS, Jeffrey .... 432-335-6815 479 O
jmeyers@odessa.edu

MEYERS, Jolene .... 419-559-2147 392 A
jmeyers@terra.edu

MEYERS, Larry .... 503-768-7299 406 H
meyersl@lclark.edu

MEYERS, Michael .... 810-766-4062 239 H
michael.meyers@baker.edu

MEYERS, III, Otto .... 318-274-2245 207 H

MEYERS, Paul .... 281-283-3016 491 E
meyers@uhcl.edu

MEYERS, Ruth .... 510-204-0720.. 38 K
rmeyers@cdsp.edu

MEYERS, Sara .... 212-772-5023 319 E
sm2216@hunter.cuny.edu

MEYERS, Shelly, A .... 864-488-8207 447 F
smeyers@limestone.edu

MEYERS, Tom, J .... 574-535-7346 166 C
tomjm@goshen.edu

MEYERS, Vanessa .... 202-687-5627.. 95 E
vmm8@georgetown.edu

MEZA, Juan .... 209-228-2969.. 71 E
jmeza@ucmerced.edu

MEZA, Lorena .... 760-750-4056.. 35 B
lmeza@csusm.edu

MEZA, Narcisa .... 787-257-0000 557 F
narcisa.meza1@upr.edu

MEZIERE, Kevin .... 858-653-6740.. 48 Q
KMeziere@JPCatholic.com

MEZIK, Krista .... 315-866-1550 327 E
mezikk@herkimer.edu

MEZYNSKI, David .... 914-961-8313 341 I
dmezynski@svots.edu

MEZZACAPPA, John ..... 561-929-3405 113 B
admissions@sfbc.edu

MHLANGA, Fortune ...... 615-966-5073 458 C
fortune.mhlanga@lipscomb.edu

MI, Hanfu .... 217-206-6512 161 G
hmi2@uis.edu

MIARKA-GRZELAK,
Anna .... 518-587-2100 348 A
anna.miarka-grzelak@esc.edu

MIAZGA, John .... 325-942-2212 489 E
john.miazga@angelo.edu

MICARELLI, Stephen ..... 617-349-8705 228 B
smicarel@lesley.edu

MICCO, Melissa, A .... 412-397-5264 434 B
micco@rmu.edu

MICEK, Tyler .... 843-383-8173 445 A
tmicek@coker.edu

MICELI, Paul .... 781-899-5500 235 G
rev.miceli@psjs.edu

MICHAEL, Cheryl .... 410-334-2884 221 E
cmichael@worwic.edu

MICHAEL, Cynthia .... 937-376-6304 379 D
cmichael@centralstate.edu

MICHAEL, Donohue .... 312-777-8582 147 C
mdonohue@aii.edu

MICHAEL, Eleftherios .... 410-532-3183 217 F
emichael@ndm.edu

MICHAEL, Gage .... 719-549-3011.. 85 A
michael.gage@pueblocc.edu

MICHAEL, Jennifer .... 617-732-2871 233 E
jennifer.michael@bos.mcphs.edu

MICHAEL, Jennifer .... 315-364-3312 352 F
jmichael@wells.edu

MICHAEL, Jim .... 559-278-3923.. 33 D
jim_michael@csufresno.edu

MICHAEL, Jody .... 810-762-0048 247 F
jody.michael@mcc.edu

MICHAEL, III, Max .... 205-934-7730.... 8 F
maxm@uab.edu

MICHAEL, Renee .... 816-501-4076 281 B
renee.michael@rockhurst.edu

MICHAEL, Sandra .... 215-637-7700 420 K
smichael@holyfamily.edu

MICHAEL, Steve, O .... 323-563-5854.. 38 C
stevemichael@cdrewu.edu

MICHAEL, Thomas, R ... 217-581-2319 144 E
trmichael@eiu.edu

MICHAEL, Timothy .... 313-577-2313 252 G
tmichael@wayne.edu

MICHAEL-PICKETT,
Stephanie .... 704-922-6215 362 G
michael.stephanie@gaston.edu

MICHAELIDES, Anthony 661-362-3253.. 40 H
anthony.michaelides@canyons.edu

MICHAELIDES, Barbara . 318-342-5550 209 A
michaelides@ulm.edu

MICHAELIS, Joel .... 254-562-3848 479 I
joel.michaelis@navarrocollege.edu

MICHAELIS, Randall, B . 509-777-4303 529 A
rmichaelis@whitworth.edu

MICHAELS, Alan, C .... 614-292-2631 389 A
michaels.23@osu.edu

MICHAELS, Brent .... 910-678-8209 362 E
michaelb@faytechcc.edu

MICHAELS, Cheryl .... 304-326-1518 530 G
cmichaels@salemu.edu

MICHAELS, Craig .... 718-997-5220 320 E
craig.michaels@qc.cuny.edu

MICHAELS, Debbie .... 541-552-6590 409 G
michaeld@sou.edu

MICHAELS, Dennis .... 716-614-6744 336 D
dmichaels@niagaracc.suny.edu

MICHAELS, George, H .. 805-893-2378.. 72 D
george.michaels@id.ucsb.edu

MICHAELS, Jeff, A .... 717-477-1171 431 F
jamich@ship.edu

MICHAELS, Jon .... 605-394-1604 454 B
jon.michaels@sdsmt.edu

MICHAELS, Lynda .... 570-389-4061 430 B
lmichael@bloomu.edu

MICHAELS, Meredith .... 949-824-4923.. 71 C
m.michaels@uci.edu

MICHAELS, Sheila .... 218-935-0417 266 A
sheila.michaels@wetcc.edu

MICHAELS, Sheri .... 319-385-6229 180 A
sheri.michaels@iw.edu

MICHAELS, Sue .... 916-660-7272.. 66 E
smichaels@sierracollege.edu

MICHAELSEN, Kevin ..... 919-760-8565 359 B
michaelsen@meredith.edu

MICHAELSON, Frank ..... 805-969-3626.. 57 J
fmichaelson@pacifica.edu

MICHAELSON,
Kimberly .... 312-261-3159 153 H
Kimberly.Michaelson@nl.edu

MICHAJLA, Patty .... 425-640-1516 522 D
pmichajl@edcc.edu

MICHAL, Richard .... 317-940-9445 164 L
rmichal@butler.edu

MICHALAK, Russell ...... 302-225-6227.. 94 B
michalr@gbc.edu

MICHALAK, Sarah .... 919-962-1301 371 A
smichala@email.unc.edu

MICHALENKO, John ..... 412-397-6486 434 B
michalenko@rmu.edu

MICHALERYA,
William, D .... 610-758-5802 424 B
wdm1@lehigh.edu

MICHALKO, Nancy .... 801-957-4247 500 E
nancy.michalko@slcc.edu

MICHALSKI, Greg .... 904-632-3017 105 A
gmichals@fscj.edu

MICHALSKI, Monica ..... 718-489-5274 340 E
mmichalski@sfc.edu

MICHALSKI, Tim .... 361-570-4820 492 A
michalskit@uhv.edu

MICHAS, Harry .... 212-966-0300 334 D
harry@nyaa.edu

MICHAUD, Joanne .... 305-237-3008 108 L
jmichau1@mdc.edu

MICHAUD, Paul .... 908-526-1200 305 G
Paul.Michaud@raritanval.edu

MICHAUX, Kimberly, S 434-223-6102 508 B
kmixhaux@hsc.edu

MICHEL, Aimee .... 413-528-7293 222 F

MICHEL, Francisco .... 773-878-7950 158 C
fmichel@staugustine.edu

MICHEL, Mike .... 410-293-1901 549 B
michel@usna.edu

MICHEL, Pamela .... 315-312-2102 346 A
pamela.michel@oswego.edu

MICHEL, R. Keith .... 516-671-2277 352 D
kmichel@webb.edu

MICHELANGELI,
Angelica, M .... 956-326-2454 485 B
amichelangeli@tamiu.edu

MICHELINI, Debra .... 847-543-2383 142 G
dmichelini@clcillinois.edu

MICHELL, Peter .... 925-631-4571.. 61 G
pmichell@stmarys-ca.edu

MICHELLE, Dawn .... 915-595-1935 476 R

MICHELMAN, Jeff .... 904-620-2649 116 A
jeff.michelman@unf.edu

MICHELSON, Peggy ...... 314-529-6543 277 B
pmichelson@maryville.edu

MICHIE, Cheryl .... 641-472-7000 181 A
cmichie@mum.edu

MICHIELSSEN, Eric .... 734-647-1793 251 C
emichiel@umich.edu

MICHONG, Park .... 818-364-7868.. 51 G
ParkM@lamission.edu

MICIAK, Alan .... 216-397-1886 384 F
amiciak@jcu.edu

MICK, Kimberly, S .... 330-569-5160 383 F
mickks@hiram.edu

MICKELSEN, Scott, R .... 308-367-5253 294 B
smickelsen4@unl.edu

MICKELSON, Kristine .... 608-663-2374 536 A
kmickelson@edgewood.edu

MICKELSON, Sally .... 702-968-2004 296 D
smickelson@roseman.edu

MICKENS, Charles .... 517-371-5140 252 J
mickensc@cooley.edu

MICKENS, George .... 623-245-4600.. 18 C
gmickens@uti.edu

MICKENS, Kendrick ...... 610-359-5340 416 G
kmickens@dccc.edu

MICKEY, Marty .... 847-947-5580 153 H
mmickey@nl.edu

MICKEY, Travis .... 336-272-7102 357 B
travis.mickey@greensboro.edu

MICKEY-BOGGS, Shari 937-775-2120 396 A shari.mickey-boggs@wright.edu
MICKLER, Michael 845-752-3000 350 J mm@uts.edu
MICKLES, Muriel, B 434-832-7656 515 A micklesm@cvcc.vccs.edu
MICKOOL, Richard 937-525-3811 395 I rmickool@wittenberg.edu
MICKOOL, Richard 401-454-6390 442 B rmickool@risd.edu
MICUS, David 321-674-7400 103 R dmicus@fit.edu
MIDCAP, Richard, D 410-827-5858 214 D rmidcap@chesapeake.edu
MIDDEKER, Vicki 303-410-2438 85 E vmiddeker@westwood.edu
MIDDENDORF, Terry 651-523-2302 256 B tmiddendorf@hamline.edu
MIDDENDORF, Tom 615-248-1258 464 E tmiddendorf@trevecca.edu
MIDDLESWARTH, Jean, E 336-575-3901 362 F jmiddleswarth@forsythtech.edu
MIDDLETON, Antoinette 212-220-1267 318 D amiddleton@bmcc.cuny.edu
MIDDLETON, Dewayne 601-849-0112 266 J dewayne.middleton@colin.edu
MIDDLETON, Jacqueline 330-263-2580 380 E jkmiddleton@wooster.edu
MIDDLETON, Kenna 859-622-1721 194 L kenna.middleton@eku.edu
MIDDLETON, Lyle 501-205-8830 20 G lmiddleton@cbc.edu
MIDDLETON, Melinda, L 812-877-8259 172 C melinda.l.middleton@rose-hulman.edu
MIDDLETON, Michael 617-287-7592 228 G michael.middleton@umb.edu
MIDDLETON, Michael, A 573-882-3394 283 H middletonm@missouri.edu
MIDDLETON, Nigel, T 303-273-3327 80 O nmiddlet@mines.edu
MIDDLETON, Norma, L 336-316-2151 357 C nmiddlet@guilford.edu
MIDDLETON, Renee, A 740-593-4400 389 H middletr@ohio.edu
MIDDLETON, Rodney, C 989-328-1202 247 D rodm@montcalm.edu
MIDDLETON, Tracy 803-705-4594 443 F middletont@benedict.edu
MIDDLETON, Whittaker, V 803-535-5347 444 D wmiddleton@claflin.edu
MIDEI, Ron 954-262-5224 109 E ronmidei@nsu.nova.edu
MIDGETT, Pam 940-397-4182 478 G pam.midgett@mwsu.edu
MIDGETTE, Juanita 252-335-3586 369 F jmidgette@ecsu.edu
MIDGLEY, Michael, T 512-223-7579 468 H midgley@austincc.edu
MIDHA, Chand 330-972-7857 392 H cmidha@uakron.edu
MIDKIFF, Kittridge 270-686-4508 197 A kitt.midkiff@kctcs.edu
MIDKIFF, Lindsay 870-633-4480 20 J lindsay.midkiff@eacc.edu
MIDKIFF, Lori, A 304-929-5472 531 D lmidkiff@newriver.edu
MIDKIFF, Mike 903-923-2136 473 I mmidkiff@etbu.edu
MIDKIFF, JR., Robert, M 570-577-1547 413 E robert.midkiff@bucknell.edu
MIDKIFF, Scott, F 540-231-4227 518 B midkiff@vt.edu
MIDTHUN, Steve 414-277-7224 537 G midthun@msoe.edu
MIDURA, Matthew 310-506-4181 58 H matthew.midura@pepperdine.edu
MIDYETTE, Marilyn, W 757-221-1166 506 J mwmidyette01@wm.edu
MIEDEMA, Linda, L 321-433-7380 101 O miedemal@easternflorida.edu
MIELDEZIS, Cathie 618-937-2127 153 F
MIELISH, Julia 919-866-5649 366 H jcmielish@waketech.edu
MIELKE, Cindi 815-599-3491 146 B cindi.mielke@highland.edu
MIELKE, Dan 541-962-3833 405 G dmielke@eou.edu
MIELKE, John 262-595-3226 540 C mielke@uwp.edu
MIERA, Joseph 505-277-2511 313 H jmiera@unm.edu
MIERES, Joann, B 570-372-4049 435 I antes@susqu.edu
MIERS, Michael 508-849-3326 222 C mmiers@annamaria.edu
MIERTSCHIN, Charla 507-457-5299 262 D cmiertschin@winona.edu
MIGHTY, Hugh, E 202-806-5677 96 B hugh.mighty@howard.edu
MIGLAW, Kari, L 831-656-2077 548 A klmiglaw@nps.edu
MIGLIO, Joseph 617-873-0471 225 A joseph.miglio@cambridgecollege.edu
MIGNARDOT, Henry 505-428-1225 313 A henry.mignardot@sfcc.edu
MIGNAULT, Richard 845-451-1369 323 E r_mignau@culinary.edu
MIGNOGNA, Janice 215-780-1235 435 D janice@salus.edu
MIGUEL, George 520-383-8401 18 A gmiguel@tocc.edu
MIGYANKO, Stephanie, M 724-439-4900 423 G smigyanko@laurel.edu
MIHAL, Deborah, F 843-953-1431 445 B mihaldf@cofc.edu
MIHAL, Ruthie 704-609-1542 355 G ruthie.mihal@carolinascollege.edu
MIHALCIN, Patricia 724-287-8711 413 G patricia.mihalcin@bc3.edu
MIHALEVICH, Rick 573-897-5000 282 I
MIHALIC, Angela 214-648-2168 496 A angela.mihalic@utsouthwestern.edu
MIHALIK, Brian 803-777-1611 450 B bmahalik@hrsm.sc.edu
MIHALY, Christine 734-973-3477 251 J cmihaly@wccnet.edu
MIHALY, Marc 802-831-1237 503 E mmihaly@vermontlaw.edu
MIHALYOV, David 585-395-2577 345 A dmihalyo@brockport.edu
MIHEL, George, J 815-835-6303 158 I george.mihel@svcc.edu
MIHIR, Fnu 479-788-7456 23 H mihir@uafs.edu
MIHM-HEROLD, Wendy, A 563-562-3263 181 F mihm-heroldw@portal.nicc.edu
MIHO, Mariko 808-932-7692 135 I mariko.miho@uhfoundation.org
MIHOPULOS, Sheryl, L 516-877-3365 314 F mihopulos@adelphi.edu
MIKALSON, Joan 518-608-8144 325 B jmikalson@excelsior.edu
MIKE, James 717-477-1151 431 F jhmike@ship.edu
MIKEMAN, Cindy 405-736-0315 401 L cmikeman@rose.edu
MIKESCH, Gregory 314-792-6119 276 H mikesch@kenrick.edu
MIKESELL, Brian 413-528-7274 222 F bmikesell@simons-rock.edu
MIKESELL, Leslie 530-283-0202 44 H lmikesell@frc.edu
MIKHAIL, Michael, B 312-996-2671 161 F mmikhail@uic.edu
MIKHAIL, Mona 626-812-3013 29 B mmikhail@apu.edu
MIKHAIL, Osama, I 713-500-3047 495 A osama.i.mikhail@uth.tmc.edu
MIKKELSEN, Carmelita 251-580-2213 5 A cormelita.mikkelsen@faulknerstate.edu
MIKLOVIC, Lauren 408-498-5158 40 E lmiklovic@cogswell.edu
MIKLUSAK, Courtney 619-239-0391 36 E cmiklusak@cwsl.edu
MIKNAVICH, Marie 315-792-3111 351 G mtmiknav@utica.edu
MIKOWSKI, Thomas 616-632-2853 239 E mikowtho@aquinas.edu
MIKOYCHIK, Cindy 800-962-7682 285 I cmikoychik@wma.edu
MIKSA, Tony 815-455-8673 152 B tmiksa@mchenry.edu
MIKTARIAN, Christine 559-244-5917 68 J christine.miktarian@scccd.edu
MIKULA, Susan 630-829-6274 140 A smikula@ben.edu
MIKULAY, Jennifer 414-382-6395 534 I jennifer.mikulay@alverno.edu
MIKUS, Robert, L 717-867-6234 423 I mikus@lvc.edu
MIKUSZEWSKI, Barbara 216-987-4497 381 A barbara.mikuszewski@tri-c.edu
MILAM, B. Hofler 336-758-3121 372 G bhm@wfu.edu
MILAM, Kathy, L 937-382-6661 395 F kathy_milam@wilmington.edu
MILAM, Linda 918-781-7247 396 F milaml@bacone.edu
MILAM, Rebecca 865-694-6560 463 E bmilam@pstcc.edu
MILARDOVICH, Julia 916-278-6322 34 E juliam@csus.edu
MILAVETZ, Barry 701-777-6736 373 G barry.milavetz@research.und.edu
MILAVETZ, Barry 701-777-4278 373 G barry.milavetz@und.edu
MILBAUER, Barbara 313-993-1025 250 H barbara.milbauer@udmercy.edu
MILBERG, William 212-229-5901 334 C milbergw@newschool.edu
MILBOURNE, John, M 321-674-7160 103 R jmilbour@fit.edu
MILBURN, John 661-362-3245 40 H john.milburn@canyons.edu
MILBY, Kevin, S 859-238-5534 194 E kevin.milby@centre.edu
MILBY, Megan, H 859-238-5516 194 E megan.milby@centre.edu
MILD, Robert, E 304-367-4219 532 F robert.mild@fairmontstate.edu
MILEHAM, Mardi 503-883-2217 406 I mmileham@linfield.edu
MILEM, Jill 936-468-2401 484 A jmilem@sfasu.edu
MILES, Alicia, C 770-720-5542 130 E acm1@reinhardt.edu
MILES, Arletha 914-773-3856 337 I lmiles@pace.edu
MILES, Belinda, S 914-606-6707 352 G belinda.miles@sunywcc.edu
MILES, Cindy 619-644-7569 46 F cindy.miles@gcccd.edu
MILES, David 802-225-3240 502 F david.miles@neci.edu
MILES, David, A 201-692-2227 302 H dmiles@fdu.edu
MILES, Donald 814-472-3029 434 F dmiles@francis.edu
MILES, Donald 814-472-3360 434 F dmiles@francis.edu
MILES, Donald 803-777-2814 450 B dmiles@mailbox.sc.edu
MILES, Jennifer 662-329-7129 269 B jmmiles@muw.edu
MILES, Jennifer, P 502-597-7023 197 G jennifer.miles@kysu.edu
MILES, Keith, D 202-238-2358 96 B kmiles@howard.edu
MILES, Linda 252-398-6505 356 B milesl@chowan.edu
MILES, Lloyd 301-985-7237 220 A lloyd.miles@umuc.edu
MILES, Lora 618-650-2020 159 I lflamm@siue.edu
MILES, Mark 651-635-8065 254 A m-miles@bethel.edu
MILES, Martin 757-727-5635 508 C martin.miles@hamptonu.edu
MILES, Mary, E 502-852-6688 201 A maryelizabeth.miles@louisville.edu
MILES, Ray 337-475-5192 208 B rmiles@mcneese.edu
MILES, Richard 513-721-7944 382 K rmiles@gbs.edu
MILES, Stephannie 704-461-6873 354 J stephanniemiles@bac.edu
MILES, Stephen 941-487-4200 115 B miles@ncf.edu
MILES, Tom 478-445-4027 125 A tom.miles@gcsu.edu
MILES, Vickie 334-670-3732 8 A vmiles@troy.edu
MILES-TRIBBLE, Valerie 510-841-1905 27 B
MILETSKY, Karen 212-647-7299 338 E kmiletsk@pratt.edu
MILETTI, Linnette 787-743-4041 551 I lmiletti@columbiacentral.edu
MILETTI, Luis 404-880-8297 122 I lmiletti@cau.edu
MILEWICZ, Mark 910-521-6630 371 D mark.milewicz@uncp.edu
MILEY, Melinda 843-953-5426 445 B mileym@cofc.edu
MILEY, Tamara 812-749-1271 171 I tmiley@oak.edu
MILHAM, Donna 616-451-3511 241 I dmilham@davenport.edu
MILHAUSEN, Michael 503-399-6527 404 L michael.milhausen@chemeketa.edu
MILHOLLAND, Tom, A 325-674-2918 466 I milholland@acu.edu
MILICH, Marianne 219-980-6618 168 C mmilich@iun.edu
MILICI, Roger 212-636-6545 326 C milici@fordham.edu
MILIONI, Mark, L 417-268-6008 272 F mmilioni@gobbc.edu
MILIONIS, Daren 503-375-7012 405 F dmilionis@corban.edu
MILJEVICH, Greg 715-365-4486 543 G gmiljevidh@nicoletcollege.edu
MILKOVICH, Ann 920-424-4480 540 B milkovich@uwosh.edu
MILKOVICH, Patrice 619-575-6176 68 D pmilkovich@swccd.edu
MILKOWSKI, Rose 312-629-6182 158 J rmilkowski@saic.edu
MILKOWSKI, Tracy, L 920-923-8159 537 A tmilkowski@marianuniversity.edu
MILLA, Rosalinda 619-477-6310 70 G rmilla@usuniversity.edu
MILLAGE, Mark 605-221-3114 452 F mmillage@kilian.edu
MILLAN, Brett 956-872-7263 482 G bmillan@southtexascollege.edu
MILLANE, Maureen 716-839-8334 323 F mmillane@daemen.edu
MILLAR, Erin, O 410-576-6316 218 B
MILLAR, Janet 661-654-3366 32 G jmillar@csub.edu
MILLAR, Norman 818-767-0888 77 G norman.millar@woodbury.edu
MILLARD, Bill 765-677-2520 169 C bill.millard@indwes.edu
MILLARD, Cristi 801-957-4145 500 E cristi.millard@slcc.edu
MILLARD, James, R 252-638-7283 362 A millardj@cravencc.edu
MILLARD, Jill 704-290-5887 366 A jmillard@spcc.edu
MILLARD, Julia 702-579-3578 294 P jmillard@kaplan.edu
MILLARD, Rachel 859-233-8111 200 D rmillard@transy.edu
MILLARD, Robert, B 617-253-6700 233 C
MILLARD, Stacey 313-228-7367 321 H smillard@colgate.edu
MILLARD, Timothy, R 540-985-9781 509 D trmillard@jchs.edu
MILLAS, Nikoletta 610-896-1032 420 J nmillas@haverford.edu
MILLEA, Meghan 662-325-7476 269 A mmillea@cobilan.msstate.edu
MILLENDER, Angelia, N 773-291-6100 142 B
MILLER, Adam 509-527-5778 528 F millera@whitman.edu
MILLER, Al 251-442-2357 9 B amiller@umobile.edu
MILLER, Alex 828-669-8012 359 K amiller@montreat.edu
MILLER, Allen 803-777-2930 450 B pamiller@sc.edu
MILLER, Andrea 414-256-0170 538 A millera@mtmary.edu
MILLER, Andrea, L 225-216-8403 202 N chancellorsoffice@mybrcc.edu
MILLER, Andrew 863-667-5703 113 K aemiller@seu.edu
MILLER, Andrew, T 607-255-6384 323 C atmiller@cornell.edu
MILLER, Angela 865-981-8201 458 E angela.miller@maryvillecollege.edu
MILLER, Angela, M 608-342-1555 540 D millerang@uwplatt.edu
MILLER, Anita, L 814-871-5847 419 A miller064@gannon.edu
MILLER, Ann, S 530-226-4733 66 G amiller@simpsonu.edu
MILLER, Anna 812-888-6965 174 F amiller@vinu.edu
MILLER, Anne 212-217-4190 325 C anne_miller@fitnyc.edu
MILLER, Antoinette 216-791-5000 380 C antoinette.miller@cim.edu
MILLER, Ashley 270-384-8065 198 C millera@lindsey.edu
MILLER, Ave 770-962-7580 127 C amiller@gwinnetttech.edu
MILLER, Barbara 443-352-4369 218 E blmiller@stevenson.edu
MILLER, Barbara, R 301-447-5372 217 D brmiller@msmary.edu
MILLER, Baruch 718-382-6003 317 K
MILLER, Becky 913-360-7410 184 K beckymiller@benedictine.edu
MILLER, Ben, J 608-263-5510 539 D miller1@wisc.edu
MILLER, Beth 409-880-2292 488 E bbmiller@lit.edu
MILLER, Betsy 575-538-6118 314 E millerb@wnmu.edu
MILLER, Betty 863-680-4110 104 F bmiller@flsouthern.edu
MILLER, Bill 314-539-5220 281 H wmiller129@stlcc.edu
MILLER, Bill 830-372-8120 487 C bmiller@tlu.edu
MILLER, BJ 540-432-4304 507 A bj.miller@emu.edu
MILLER, Bo 601-968-8797 266 F bmiller@belhaven.edu
MILLER, Bob 610-526-7878 413 D rmiller03@brynmawr.edu

MILLER, Brian .... 219-785-5220 172 A
bmiller@pnc.edu
MILLER, Brian .... 501-420-1253.. 19 B
brian.miller@arkansasbaptist.edu
MILLER, Brian .... 616-451-3511 241 I
bmiller@davenport.edu
MILLER, Brian .... 616-698-7111 241 I
bmiller@davenport.edu
MILLER, Brian .... 616-451-3511 241 I
bmiller@davenport.edu
MILLER, Brian .... 252-493-7241 364 H
bmiller@email.pittcc.edu
MILLER, Bridget .... 315-655-7225 317 J
bmmiller@cazenovia.edu
MILLER, Carey .... 307-754-6114 546 I
Carey.Miller@nwc.edu
MILLER, Carla .... 231-591-3825 242 L
CarlaMiller@ferris.edu
MILLER, Carol, A .... 262-472-1130 541 D
millerc@uww.edu
MILLER, Carol, J .... 701-231-7761 374 C
carol.miller@ndsu.edu
MILLER, Carolann .... 631-656-2134 326 B
carolann.miller@ftc.edu
MILLER, Caroline, B ..... 513-556-3379 393 B
caroline.miller@uc.edu
MILLER, Carolyn .... 740-284-5822 382 G
cmiller@franciscan.edu
MILLER, Cary Beth .... 615-383-4848 466 F
cmiller@watkins.edu
MILLER, Catherine .... 203-857-3342.. 89 H
cmiller@norwalk.edu
MILLER, Catherine .... 309-438-2349 147 I
hmiller@ilstu.edu
MILLER, Chad .... 812-488-2775 173 H
cm121@evansville.edu
MILLER, Chandra .... 918-293-5266 400 E
chandra.miller@okstate.edu
MILLER, Chani .... 908-354-6057 310 A
MILLER, Cheryl .... 503-552-1510 407 F
cmiller@ncnm.edu
MILLER, Cheryl .... 540-857-7201 517 E
ccmiller@virginiawestern.edu
MILLER, Cheryl, L .... 860-439-2085.. 90 D
cheryl.miller@conncoll.edu
MILLER, Chris .... 760-744-1150.. 58 D
cmiller@palomar.edu
MILLER, Chris .... 847-317-7036 161 B
cmiller@tiu.edu
MILLER, Chris, E .... 570-326-3761 429 J
cmiller@pct.edu
MILLER, Christian .... 718-390-3153 352 C
christian.miller@wagner.edu
MILLER, Christie .... 931-540-2521 462 E
cmiller26@columbiastate.edu
MILLER, Christine .... 415-439-2350.. 27 F
MILLER, Christine, A .... 724-946-7148 439 D
millerca@westminster.edu
MILLER,
Clarence (Hank) .... 845-687-5065 350 I
millerh@sunyulster.edu
MILLER, Clinton .... 901-383-6750.. 96 H
MILLER, Colleen .... 320-589-6006 265 A
mille593@morris.umn.edu
MILLER, Craig .... 314-246-7773 285 G
craigmiller29@webster.edu
MILLER, Craig .... 484-384-2953 427 I
semregis@eastern.edu
MILLER, Curt .... 336-838-6142 367 C
curt.miller@wilkescc.edu
MILLER, Daniel, P .... 570-321-4139 425 B
millerda@lycoming.edu
MILLER, Darlene .... 973-877-3101 302 F
dmiller@essex.edu
MILLER, David .... 402-935-9400 291 L
dmiller@nechristian.edu
MILLER, David .... 563-425-5293 183 G
millerds@uiu.edu
MILLER, David .... 312-362-8720 143 G
miller@cdm.depaul.edu
MILLER, David .... 606-546-1291 200 E
dkmiller@unionky.edu
MILLER, David .... 608-262-4048 539 C
dmiller@uwsa.edu
MILLER, David, J .... 715-836-3871 539 E
milleda@uwec.edu
MILLER, David, J .... 515-294-2631 175 G
djmille@iastate.edu
MILLER, Davlon .... 662-846-4336 267 A
dmiller@deltastate.edu
MILLER, Deb .... 904-620-1416 116 A
deb.miller@unf.edu
MILLER, Debbie .... 262-564-3220 543 A
millerd@gtc.edu
MILLER, Deborah .... 714-997-6603.. 38 B
dmiller@chapman.edu
MILLER, Deborah .... 419-772-2464 388 I
d-miller@onu.edu
MILLER, Deborah, S ..... 440-826-2744 377 D
dmiller@bw.edu
MILLER, Debra .... 217-357-3129 140 I
dmiller@sandburg.edu
MILLER, Debra .... 845-687-5075 350 I
millerde@sunyulster.edu
MILLER, Debra, M .... 570-326-3761 429 J
dmiller2@pct.edu
MILLER, Dennis, R .... 570-662-4846 431 D
dmiller@mansfield.edu
MILLER, Diane .... 785-227-3380 185 A
millerde@bethanylb.edu
MILLER, Dolores, M ..... 563-562-3263 181 F
millerd@nicc.edu
MILLER, Don .... 314-514-3103 156 C
don.miller@principia.edu
MILLER, Donald .... 925-424-1383.. 37 O
dmiller@laspositascollege.edu
MILLER, Donna .... 502-213-5333 196 E
donnar.miller@kctcs.edu
MILLER, Doug .... 417-626-1234 280 B
miller.doug@occ.edu
MILLER, Draco .... 575-562-2631 310 I
draco.miller@enmu.edu
MILLER, Drew .... 936-294-1720 489 A
adm007@shsu.edu
MILLER, Drucilla, W ..... 423-798-7942 464 C
drucilla.miller@ws.edu
MILLER, Dyan .... 925-424-1275.. 37 O
dmiller@laspositascollege.edu
MILLER, E. John .... 701-231-7933 374 C
ej.miller@ndsu.edu
MILLER, Earl .... 845-675-4790 337 B
earl.miller@nyack.edu
MILLER, Edgar .... 803-777-3201 450 B
ewmiller@mailbox.sc.edu
MILLER, Elinor .... 303-964-5758.. 85 G
emiller@regis.edu
MILLER, Elizabeth .... 920-832-7164 536 R
elizabeth.miller@lawrence.edu
MILLER, Elizabeth, K .... 651-638-6215 254 A
e-miller@bethel.edu
MILLER, Ellen .... 317-791-5932 173 I
emiller@uindy.edu
MILLER, Ellen, B .... 540-828-5755 505 F
emiller@bridgewater.edu
MILLER, Enrico, A .... 315-267-2484 346 C
millerea@potsdam.edu
MILLER, Erin .... 570-321-4231 425 B
millerer@lycoming.edu
MILLER, Faith .... 706-272-4462 123 G
fmiller@daltonstate.edu
MILLER, Fayneese, S .... 651-523-2202 256 B
president@hamline.edu
MILLER, Fred .... 907-852-3333.. 10 F
fred.miller@ilisagvik.edu
MILLER, Fred .... 864-294-3800 446 F
fred.miller@furman.edu
MILLER, Galen, P .... 989-386-6644 247 B
gpmiller@midmich.edu
MILLER, Gary .... 732-987-2533 302 J
millerg@georgian.edu
MILLER, Gary .... 415-451-2806.. 63 B
maintenance@sfts.edu
MILLER, Gary .... 478-825-6228 124 E
millerg@fvsu.edu
MILLER, Gary, D .... 607-735-1777 324 J
gmiller@elmira.edu
MILLER, Gary, L .... 920-465-2207 539 F
MillerG@uwgb.edu
MILLER, Geoff .... 410-337-6385 215 B
gmiller@goucher.edu
MILLER, Geoffrey, N ..... 518-629-8172 328 D
g.miller@hvcc.edu
MILLER, III, George, E . 757-823-8015 510 H
gemiller@nsu.edu
MILLER, George, P .... 224-293-5609 139 H
MILLER, Gina .... 412-536-1085 422 E
gina.miller@laroche.edu
MILLER, Gladys .... 859-622-1571 194 L
gladys.miller@eku.edu
MILLER, Glen .... 503-399-5210 404 L
glen.miller@chemeketa.edu
MILLER, Glenn .... 800-962-7682 285 I
gmiller@wma.edu
MILLER, Glynis .... 512-223-7850 468 H
glynis.miller@austincc.edu
MILLER, Grant, T .... 208-467-8059 138 H
gtmiller@nnu.edu
MILLER, Gretchen .... 260-665-4312 173 D
millerg@trine.edu
MILLER, H. Samuel ...... 828-227-7147 372 C
sammiller@wcu.edu
MILLER, Harry, E .... 484-664-3464 427 C
hmiller@muhlenberg.edu
MILLER, Heather .... 619-201-8670.. 62 D
heather.miller@sdcc.edu
MILLER, Heather .... 972-279-6511 467 F
hmiller@amberton.edu
MILLER, Heather, C ...... 704-233-8632 373 C
h.miller@wingate.edu
MILLER, Heather, C ...... 704-233-8632 373 C
h.campbell@wingate.edu
MILLER, Henry .... 580-559-5760 397 K
bmiller@ecok.edu
MILLER, Holly, N .... 508-289-7632 238 F
hmiller@whoi.edu
MILLER, Jack .... 619-574-6909.. 57 E
jmiller@pacificcollege.edu
MILLER, Jaime, M .... 708-709-3513 156 A
jmmiller@prairiestate.edu
MILLER, James .... 630-637-5500 154 F
jlmiller@noctrl.edu
MILLER, James .... 201-447-7124 300 B
jmiller@bergen.edu
MILLER, James .... 435-652-7625 499 M
miller_j@dixie.edu
MILLER, James, A .... 256-824-2846.... 9 A
James.Miller@uah.edu
MILLER, James, G .... 585-475-6637 339 G
jgm6527@rit.edu
MILLER, James, M .... 708-209-3156 143 D
james.miller@cuchicago.edu
MILLER, James, S .... 401-863-7940 441 A
james_s_miller@brown.edu
MILLER, Jan .... 205-652-3675.... 9 G
jmiller@uwa.edu
MILLER, Janice .... 562-985-7827.. 33 F
janice.miller@csulb.edu
MILLER, Jason .... 805-447-8898.. 32 H
jason.miller@csuci.edu
MILLER, Jay .... 610-409-3790 438 H
jmiller@ursinus.edu
MILLER, Jean M, K .... 309-438-8322 147 I
jmmill5@ilstu.edu
MILLER, Jeff .... 574-296-6206 163 M
jmiller@ambs.edu
MILLER, Jeffrey .... 314-529-9350 277 B
jeffmiller@maryville.edu
MILLER, Jeffrey, A .... 412-396-5081 417 I
millerjeff@duq.edu
MILLER, Jennifer .... 805-437-8516.. 32 H
jennifer.miller@csuci.edu
MILLER, Jennifer, L ...... 330-569-5957 383 F
millerjl@hiram.edu
MILLER, Jerry .... 707-524-1506.. 65 C
jmiller@santarosa.edu
MILLER, Jessica .... 740-826-8171 387 C
jfrench@muskingum.edu
MILLER, Jim .... 724-503-1001 439 B
jbmiller@washjeff.edu
MILLER, Jim .... 603-513-1338 299 C
jim.miller@granite.edu
MILLER, Jim .... 828-227-7124 372 C
jimmiller@wcu.edu
MILLER, Jimmy .... 850-599-3413 114 D
jimmy.miller@famu.edu
MILLER, Joanne .... 508-793-7320 225 B
jmiller@clarku.edu
MILLER, Joel, C .... 319-895-4107 177 A
jmiller@cornellcollege.edu
MILLER, John .... 701-774-4231 375 C
john.s.miller@willistonstate.edu
MILLER, John .... 503-352-2215 408 I
jmiller@pacificu.edu
MILLER, John .... 256-840-4195.... 7 B
jmiller@snead.edu
MILLER, John .... 802-831-1334 503 E
jmiller@vermontlaw.edu
MILLER, John, W .... 860-832-3000.. 88 D
millerjw@ccsu.edu
MILLER, Jonathan .... 407-646-2306 111 H
jxmiller@rollins.edu
MILLER, Jonathan .... 508-854-4334 232 F
jmiller@qcc.mass.edu
MILLER, Jonathan, L .... 413-755-4230 233 B
jmiller@stcc.edu
MILLER, Joseph .... 361-825-5967 485 F
joseph.miller@tamucc.edu
MILLER, Joseph, C .... 706-880-8253 127 N
jcmiller@lagrange.edu
MILLER, Joshua .... 205-665-6245.... 9 C
millerjd@montevallo.edu
MILLER, Judith, E .... 904-620-2720 116 A
j.miller@unf.edu
MILLER, Julie, H .... 313-577-2034 252 G
julie.h.miller@wayne.edu
MILLER, Julie, L .... 317-940-9714 164 L
jlmille5@butler.edu
MILLER, K, C .... 480-994-9244.. 17 P
kc@swiha.edu
MILLER, Karen .... 507-223-7252 260 C
karen.miller@mnwest.edu
MILLER, Karen .... 216-987-3471 381 A
karen.miller@tri-c.edu
MILLER, Karl .... 512-483-1211 493 M
karl.miller@austin.utexas.edu
MILLER, Kate .... 605-995-2901 452 C
kamiller1@dwu.edu
MILLER, Kate, C .... 979-845-3651 485 C
kcmiller@tamu.edu
MILLER, Katherine .... 845-451-1261 323 E
k_miller@culinary.edu
MILLER, Katherine, A ... 407-582-6815 118 I
kmiller118@valenciacollege.edu
MILLER, Kathleen .... 239-590-7600 114 F
kmiller@fgcu.edu
MILLER, SSJ, Kathryn ... 215-248-7167 415 D
kmiller@chc.edu
MILLER, Keith .... 864-250-8175 446 H
keith.miller@gvltec.edu
MILLER, Kelly .... 425-249-4778 527 D
kelly.miller@tlc.edu
MILLER, Kelly, M .... 317-788-3437 173 I
kmiller@uindy.edu
MILLER, Ken .... 407-646-2999 111 H
kmiller@rollins.edu
MILLER, Ken .... 502-456-6506 200 B
kmiller@sullivan.edu
MILLER, Kenneth .... 740-857-1311 390 L
kmiller@rosedale.edu
MILLER, Kent .... 785-864-8989 191 G
kmiller@ku.edu
MILLER, Kent .... 573-288-6373 274 C
kmiller@culver.edu
MILLER, Kevin .... 239-489-9036 104 G
ksmiller3@fsw.edu
MILLER, Kevin, D .... 973-408-3109 301 J
theoadm@drew.edu
MILLER, Kieron .... 562-907-4236.. 77 E
kmiller@whittier.edu
MILLER, Kilohana .... 808-984-3518 136 H
kilohana@hawaii.edu
MILLER, Kim .... 336-887-3000 358 E
kmiller@laureluniversity.edu
MILLER, Kimberly, D .... 812-877-8176 172 C
kimberly.miller@rose-hulman.edu
MILLER, Kimela .... 575-835-5888 311 I
kmiller@admin.nmt.edu
MILLER, Kris .... 615-966-5722 458 C
kris.miller@lipscomb.edu
MILLER, Kristen .... 517-265-5161 238 H
kmiller5@adrian.edu
MILLER, Kristin .... 402-935-9400 291 L
kmiller@nechristian.edu
MILLER, Kristine .... 435-797-3646 500 A
kristine.miller@usu.edu
MILLER, Kyren .... 701-224-2450 374 E
kyren.miller@bismarckstate.edu
MILLER, Larry .... 228-896-2506 268 G
larry.miller@mgccc.edu
MILLER, Larry, S .... 270-686-4502 197 A
larry.miller@kctcs.edu
MILLER, Laura, M .... 717-766-2511 426 B
lmiller@messiah.edu
MILLER, Lauren .... 312-935-6026 157 A
lmiller@robertmorris.edu
MILLER, Lawrence .... 239-489-9319 104 G
lmiller17@fsw.edu
MILLER, Leilani, M .... 408-554-4439.. 65 A
lmiller@scu.edu
MILLER, Lester .... 908-526-1200 305 G
Lester.Miller@raritanval.edu
MILLER, Linda .... 618-395-1169 147 A
millerli@iecc.edu
MILLER, Linda, J .... 262-691-5526 544 D
lmiller@wctc.edu
MILLER, Lisa .... 620-672-5641 190 H
lisam@prattcc.edu
MILLER, Lisa .... 708-210-5767 159 D
lmiller@ssc.edu
MILLER, Lisa .... 563-244-7002 178 B
lmiller@eicc.edu
MILLER, Lisa .... 516-323-3046 333 E
lmiller@molloy.edu
MILLER, Lisa, R .... 318-342-5431 209 A
lmiller@ulm.edu
MILLER, Lori .... 215-702-4335 414 C
lmiller@cairn.edu
MILLER, Lucy, T .... 727-816-3448 110 B
millerl@phsc.edu
MILLER, Mandrake, T ... 804-257-5722 518 E
mtmiller@vuu.edu
MILLER, Marc .... 617-824-8953 226 A
marc_miller@emerson.edu
MILLER, Marc, L .... 520-621-1498.. 18 E
marc.miller@law.arizona.edu
MILLER, Marcia, K .... 316-284-5315 185 B
mmiller@bethelks.edu
MILLER, Margaret, C .... 847-543-2101 142 G
ecd185@clcillinois.edu
MILLER, Margaret, L .... 423-439-4300 461 D
millerml@etsu.edu
MILLER, Margaret, M ... 609-258-5813 305 C
mmmiller@princeton.edu
MILLER, Mark .... 417-447-2655 280 C
millerm@otc.edu
MILLER, Mark .... 402-472-4823 293 H
mark.miller@unl.edu
MILLER, Mark .... 318-869-5117 202 D
mmiller@centenary.edu
MILLER, Marty, L .... 757-823-9539 510 H
mlmiller@nsu.edu

MILLS, John .... 606-368-6121 192 H
johnmills@alc.edu
MILLS, Jonathan .... 415-575-6283.. 31 C
jmills@ciis.edu
MILLS, Kelly .... 863-638-7254 118 L
kelly.mills@warner.edu
MILLS, Kevin .... 209-932-3014.. 73 C
kmills@pacific.edu
MILLS, Kevin .... 828-398-7200 360 A
kevinsmills@abtech.edu
MILLS, Kimberly, A ...... 410-651-8100 219 H
kamills@umes.edu
MILLS, Laura, J .... 912-344-3073 120 D
laura.mills@armstrong.edu
MILLS, Linda .... 212-992-9712 336 C
linda.mills@nyu.edu
MILLS, Linda, G .... 212-998-9712 336 C
linda.mills@nyu.edu
MILLS, Mark .... 215-898-1453 437 I
millsme@upenn.edu
MILLS, Martin .... 512-245-2501 489 C
mm79@txstate.edu
MILLS, Marvin .... 912-478-5558 126 B
mmills@georgiasouthern.edu
MILLS, Matthew .... 912-650-6218 131 F
mmills@southuniversity.edu
MILLS, Matthew .... 210-485-0391 466 J
mmills@44@alamo.edu
MILLS, Michael .... 918-631-2510 403 M
michael-mills@utulsa.edu
MILLS, Michael, E .... 847-491-4477 155 D
michael-mills@northwestern.edu
MILLS, Nancy .... 320-308-4785 261 E
nfmills@stcloudstate.edu
MILLS, Patti .... 201-692-2132 302 H
patti_mills@fdu.edu
MILLS, Priscilla, L .... 928-523-3312.. 16 C
Priscilla.Mills@nau.edu
MILLS, R. Dean .... 573-882-6686 283 H
millsr@missouri.edu
MILLS, Randy, W .... 336-750-2706 372 D
millsrw@wssu.edu
MILLS, Richard, G .... 603-646-0459 297 G
richard.g.mills@dartmouth.edu
MILLS, Sandra, M .... 513-487-3206 327 C
smills@huc.edu
MILLS, Tegan, C .... 207-947-4591 209 G
librarian@bealcollege.edu
MILLS, Terry, L .... 216-397-4455 384 F
tmills@jcu.edu
MILLS, Tom .... 405-382-9210 402 C
t.mills@sscok.edu
MILLS, William, R .... 617-552-8661 224 B
william.mills@bc.edu
MILLS-DICK, Melissa .... 413-549-4600 227 C
MILLS-NOVOA, Avelino 612-659-6300 259 F
avelino.mills-novoa@minneapolis.edu
MILLS WOOLSEY,
Linda .... 585-567-9315 328 C
lindamills.woolsey@houghton.edu
MILLSAP, B. Burr .... 405-325-5161 403 I
bmillsap@ou.edu
MILLSAP, Pam .... 409-933-8229 471 B
pmillsap@com.edu
MILLSAP, Pam .... 409-933-8192 471 B
pmillsap@com.edu
MILLSAPPS, Michael .... 970-339-6376.. 78 J
michael.millsapps@aims.edu
MILLSAPS, Brooke .... 828-298-3325 373 A
bmillsaps@warren-wilson.edu
MILLSON-MARTULA,
Christopher, A .... 434-544-8339 509 I
millsonmartula@lynchburg.edu
MILLUSH, Mary Ann .... 630-942-2269 142 F
millush@cod.edu
MILLWOOD, Kent, A ..... 864-231-2049 443 E
kmillwood@andersonuniversity.edu
MILNE, Arryn .... 410-864-4000 218 C
amilne@stmarys.edu
MILNE, Erin, M .... 413-662-5049 230 C
erin.milne@mcla.edu
MILNE, Sheila .... 252-399-6326 354 I
smilne@barton.edu
MILNER, Devika, M ...... 305-284-6858 118 A
dmilner@miami.edu
MILNER, Eric .... 401-341-2218 442 D
eric.milner@salve.edu
MILNER, Jocelyn, L ...... 608-263-5658 539 D
jlmilner@wisc.edu
MILNER, Laura .... 608-785-8095 539 G
lmilner@uwlax.edu
MILNER, Wesley .... 812-488-2686 173 H
wm23@evansville.edu
MILON, Ronald .... 212-217-4040 325 C
Ronald_Milon@fitnyc.edu
MILONE-NUZZO,
Paula, F .... 814-863-0245 428 C
pxm36@psu.edu
MILROY, James, B .... 585-245-5601 345 D
milroy@geneseo.edu

MILSO, Lisa .... 978-762-4000 232 D
lmilso@northshore.edu
MILSOM, Penny .... 443-840-5426 214 F
mmilsom@ccbcmd.edu
MILSTEIN, Marc .... 212-960-5233 353 P
mmilstei@yu.edu
MILSTEIN, Mark .... 512-499-4246 493 K
MILSTONE, David, M .... 508-999-8640 228 H
dmilstone@umassd.edu
MILTENBERGER, Susan 410-225-2201 216 F
smiltenb@mica.edu
MILTER, Rebecca .... 404-872-3593 121 A
rmilter@johnmarshall.edu
MILTON, Alice .... 205-929-6306.... 5 E
amilton@lawsonstate.edu
MILTON, Barbara, J ...... 973-655-4349 304 A
miltonb@mail.montclair.edu
MILTON, John .... 866-323-0233.. 60 E
vpaa@providencecc.edu
MILTON, Suzanne .... 509-359-7887 522 C
smilton@ewu.edu
MILTON, Theresa .... 602-386-4159.. 11 F
theresa.milton@arizonachristian.edu
MILZ, George .... 713-646-1864 482 H
gmilz@stcl.edu
MIMMS, Jacqueline ...... 661-654-2160.. 32 G
jmimms@csub.edu
MIMMS, Lee, S .... 817-552-3700 477 B
lmimms@tku.edu
MIMS, Dana, M .... 570-577-3171 413 E
dana.mims@bucknell.edu
MIMS, Jane .... 210-784-1000 486 B
jane.mims@tamusa.tamus.edu
MIMS, Janet .... 843-863-8004 444 B
jmims@csuniv.edu
MIMS, Lloyd .... 561-803-2400 109 G
lloyd_mims@pba.edu
MIMS, Yolanda, L .... 504-286-5335 207 B
ymims@suno.edu
MIMS-DEVEZIN, Lisa .... 504-286-5064 207 B
lmims@suno.edu
MIN, John .... 949-480-4171.. 66 I
min@soka.edu
MIN, Sangki .... 913-288-7686 188 G
smin@kckcc.edu
MIN, Sarah .... 323-731-2383.. 57 H
smin@psuca.edu
MIN, William .... 714-683-1413.. 29 E
financialaid@buc.edu
MINAR, Thomas, J .... 317-738-8010 166 B
president@franklincollege.edu
MINARD, Tiffany .... 859-815-7683 196 A
tiffany.minard@kctcs.edu
MINARDI, Coco .... 717-245-1571 417 B
minardin@dickinson.edu
MINASOVA, Irina .... 206-934-6432 526 B
irina.minasova@seattlecolleges.edu
MINATOYA, Lydia .... 206-934-3712 525 K
lydia.minatoya@seattlecolleges.edu
MINCH, Kevin .... 660-785-5384 283 E
kminch@truman.edu
MINCHEFF, Chris .... 303-753-6046.. 85 H
cmincheff@rmcad.edu
MINCHELLO, Brian .... 617-879-2205 238 C
bminchello@wheelock.edu
MINCKLER, Tye .... 254-968-9877 485 A
minckler@tarleton.edu
MINCKS, Kathy .... 907-564-8272.. 10 D
kmincks.akpacprop@gci.net
MINDEMAN, Tad .... 706-419-1434 123 F
mindeman@covenant.edu
MINDEN, Courtney .... 781-239-5589 222 E
cminden@babson.edu
MINDRUM, Matthew, S 317-940-9257 164 L
mmindrum@butler.edu
MINE, Jodi .... 808-934-2742 136 D
mine@hawaii.edu
MINEHAN, Cathy .... 617-521-3806 236 F
cathy.minehan@simmons.edu
MINEHART, Heather ...... 760-252-2411.. 29 C
hminehart@barstow.edu
MINEO, Michael .... 718-817-4931 326 C
mineo@fordham.edu
MINEO, Steve .... 912-525-5000 130 H
smineo@scad.edu
MINER, Anna, G .... 603-526-3702 296 I
anna.miner@colby-sawyer.edu
MINER, Brenda .... 479-394-7622.. 22 H
bminer@rmcc.edu
MINER, Celia .... 605-668-1584 452 I
celia.miner@mtmc.edu
MINER, Judy, C .... 650-949-6100.. 44 M
minerjudy@fhda.edu
MINER, Madonne .... 801-626-6006 500 C
madonneminer@weber.edu
MINER, Marlene, R .... 513-745-5660 393 C
marlene.miner@uc.edu
MINER, R. Clinton .... 508-457-1313 234 E
cminer@ngs.edu

MINER ROMANOFF,
Karen .... 614-947-6241 382 H
karen.minerromanoff@franklin.edu
MINERVINI, Ron .... 617-730-7222 235 B
ron.minervini@newbury.edu
MINET, Jennifer, J .... 716-878-5335 345 B
siwulajj@buffalostate.edu
MINFORD, Joell .... 412-392-3422 433 F
jminford@pointpark.edu
MING, Amanda .... 248-476-1122 246 G
aming@mispp.edu
MINGEE, Sheila .... 217-709-0923 150 C
smingee@lakeviewcol.edu
MINGENBACK, Mary ...... 620-341-5413 186 H
mmingenb@emporia.edu
MINGER, David .... 541-880-2221 406 E
minger@klamathcc.edu
MINGLE, James, J .... 607-255-3903 323 C
jjm19@cornell.edu
MINGO, Dana .... 972-241-3371 472 A
dmingo@dallas.edu
MINGO, Rhonda .... 864-596-9140 445 E
rhonda.mingo@converse.edu
MINGO, Susan .... 207-454-1032 211 E
smingo@wccc.me.edu
MINGO, Tracey, K .... 608-342-1836 540 D
mingot@uwplatt.edu
MINHAS, Omer .... 419-772-2529 388 I
o-minhas@onu.edu
MINI, Susan .... 815-753-0495 154 I
smini@niu.edu
MINICK, Thomas .... 610-790-2862 412 C
thomas.minick@alvernia.edu
MINICOLA, Steven .... 215-573-0251 437 I
minicola@upenn.edu
MINICZ, Allison .... 815-479-7884 152 B
aminicz@mchenry.edu
MINIER-DELGADO,
Jesenia .... 718-289-5288 318 E
jesenia.minier-delgado@bcc.cuny.edu
MININGER, Marcus .... 219-864-2400 171 G
mmininger@midamerica.edu
MINK, Randy, L .... 412-397-4901 434 B
mink@rmu.edu
MINK, Rose .... 901-751-8453 459 C
rmink@mabts.edu
MINKE, Jennifer .... 361-593-2315 486 A
jennifer.minke@tamuk.edu
MINKLER, James .... 509-533-3764 521 F
jim.minkler@sfcc.spokane.edu
MINKLER, Jim .... 509-533-3764 521 D
jimm@spokanefalls.edu
MINKLER, Steven .... 860-343-5706.. 89 E
sminkler@mxcc.commnet.edu
MINNE, Erin .... 312-362-8663 143 G
minne@depaul.edu
MINNEMA, Emily .... 614-825-6255 376 C
eminnema@aiam.edu
MINNER, Sam .... 505-454-3269 311 H
president_office@nmhu.edu
MINNER, Sam .... 540-831-5404 511 C
sminner@radford.edu
MINNICH, Bryan, K .... 785-827-5541 189 A
bryan.minnich@kwu.edu
MINNICH, Dan .... 330-972-6476 392 H
dminnich@uakron.edu
MINNICH, Peggy .... 513-244-4531 387 A
peggy.minnich@msj.edu
MINNICH, Thomas .... 304-205-6600 531 A
thomas.minnich@bridgevalley.edu
MINNICH, William .... 650-738-4484.. 64 E
minnichw@smccd.edu
MINNICH KJESBO,
Faith .... 717-766-2511 426 B
fminnich@messiah.edu
MINNICK, Ann, M .... 651-696-6036 256 L
aminnick@macalester.edu
MINNICK, William, C ..... 712-707-7226 182 C
bminnick@nwciowa.edu
MINNIEFIELD,
Angela, L .... 323-563-4897.. 38 C
angelaminniefield@cdrewu.edu
MINNIS, Stephen, D ..... 913-360-7400 184 K
sminnis@benedictine.edu
MINNIS, Tia .... 404-880-6294 122 I
tminnis@cau.edu
MINNITI, Lea .... 513-745-3711 396 B
minnitil@xavier.edu
MINOR, Diana, Y .... 909-869-3704.. 32 F
dyminor@cpp.edu
MINOR, Diane .... 312-553-2500 141 M
dminor1@ccc.edu
MINOR, Frankie, D .... 573-882-7275 283 H
minorf@missouri.edu
MINOR, Gwen .... 817-554-5950 478 E
gminor@messengercollege.edu
MINOR, Karen .... 770-531-6347 128 A
kminor@laniertech.edu
MINOR, Leslie .... 707-864-7000.. 66 J
leslie.minor@solano.edu

MINOR, Lloyd .... 650-723-2300.. 68 G
lminor@stanford.edu
MINOR, Scott .... 916-631-8108.. 32 B
MINOR, Tamra .... 518-956-8110 343 C
tminor@albany.edu
MINOR, William .... 513-244-4261 387 A
william.minor@msj.edu
MINOW, Martha .... 617-495-4601 227 D
minow@law.harvard.edu
MINSON, Patrick .... 718-390-3304 352 C
patrick.minson@wagner.edu
MINTEN, Sam, L .... 615-868-6503 459 E
sam@mtsa.edu
MINTER, Doug, O .... 507-933-7527 256 A
dminter@gustavus.edu
MINTER, Douglas .... 309-268-8100 145 H
doug.minter@heartland.edu
MINTER, Michelle .... 609-258-6110 305 C
mminter@princeton.edu
MINTER, Penny .... 731-426-7550 457 K
pbrown@lanecollege.edu
MINTERN, Janet .... 252-493-7286 364 H
jmintern@email.pittcc.edu
MINTLE, Norm .... 434-582-2077 509 G
MINTO, Jean .... 215-702-4270 414 C
jminto@cairn.edu
MINTZ, Katrina, H .... 205-726-2896.... 6 F
kmintzi@samford.edu
MINTZ, Zev .... 732-370-1560 300 A
MINTZER, Jen .... 610-358-4547 427 D
mintzerj@neumann.edu
MINUS, Daryl .... 252-638-7200 362 A
minusd@cravencc.edu
MINUS, Molly, E .... 512-448-8581 481 B
mollym@stedwards.edu
MINUS, Monica .... 252-633-1764 362 A
minusm@cravencc.edu
MIOTTO, Mike .... 304-724-3700 529 F
mmiotto@apus.edu
MIRABAL, Gloria .... 787-743-4041 551 I
gmirabal@columbiacentral.edu
MIRABAL, Larry .... 505-424-2316 310 L
lmirabal@iaia.edu
MIRABILE, Kathleen ...... 602-212-0501.. 16 K
kmirabile@theparalegalinstitute.edu
MIRABILE, Robert .... 608-363-2380 534 L
mirabiler@beloit.edu
MIRABITO, Michael ...... 570-348-6209 425 D
mirabito@marywood.edu
MIRACKY, SJ,
James, F .... 410-617-2327 216 D
jjmiracky@loyola.edu
MIRACLE, William, D .... 540-828-5380 505 F
wmiracle@bridgewater.edu
MIRAGLIA, Gregory .... 707-256-3035.. 55 E
gmiraglia@napavalley.edu
MIRAMONTEZ, Daniel ... 619-388-7333.. 62 H
dmiramon@sdccd.edu
MIRANDA, Albert .... 714-484-7394.. 56 E
amiranda@cypresscollege.edu
MIRANDA, Alex .... 714-895-8107.. 40 C
amiranda42@gwc.cccd.edu
MIRANDA, Candida ...... 312-567-3134 147 E
miranda@iit.edu
MIRANDA, Deana .... 312-935-6657 157 A
dmiranda@robertmorris.edu
MIRANDA,
Edmund (Rick) .... 562-860-2451.. 37 L
ermiranda@cerritos.edu
MIRANDA, Elizabeth ...... 787-250-1912 554 A
emiranda@metro.inter.edu
MIRANDA, Enid .... 787-841-2000 555 F
emiranda@pucpr.edu
MIRANDA, Gloria .... 310-660-3735.. 43 G
gmiranda@elcamino.edu
MIRANDA, Luis .... 252-639-7340 369 B
lmiranda@umo.edu
MIRANDA, Marie, L ...... 734-764-2550 251 C
mlmirand@umich.edu
MIRANDA, Marie, L ...... 713-348-4026 480 M
mlm@rice.edu
MIRANDA, Mark .... 732-571-3593 303 G
mmiranda@monmouth.edu
MIRANDA, Rick .... 970-491-6614.. 81 C
rick.miranda@colostate.edu
MIRANDA, Rick .... 970-491-6614.. 81 D
rick.miranda@colostate.edu
MIRANDA, Rowan .... 773-702-4114 161 D
rmiranda@uchicago.edu
MIRCH, Mary .... 818-240-1000.. 45 I
mmirch@glendale.edu
MIRECKI, Julie .... 920-693-1193 543 B
julie.mirecki@gotoltc.edu
MIRELES, Rod .... 936-261-1905 484 F
rmireles@pvamu.edu
MIRENBERG, Mark .... 718-261-5800 316 K
mmirenberg@ortopusa.org
MIRENBERG, Mark .... 718-261-5800 316 K
mmirenberg@ortopsusa.org
MIRENDA, Rosalie, M .. 610-558-5501 427 D
rmirenda@neumann.edu

MOATS, Kyle .... 417-836-5244 279 A
kylemoats@missouristate.edu
MOATS, Scott .... 952-446-4210 255 E
moatss@crown.edu
MOBASSERI, Maria .... 217-403-4599 155 I
mmobasseri@parkland.edu
MOBERG, Bret .... 847-578-8308 157 G
bret.moberg@rosalindfranklin.edu
MOBERG, Kathleen .... 408-848-4732.. 45 G
kmoberg@gavilan.edu
MOBERLY, Jonathon ..... 402-643-7430 289 J
Jonathon.Moberly@cune.edu
MOBERLY, Tara .... 303-964-3640.. 85 G
tmoberly@regis.edu
MOBLEY, Bob .... 863-638-7213 118 L
bob.mobley@warner.edu
MOBLEY, Brandon .... 706-880-8052 127 N
mmobley@lagrange.edu
MOBLEY, Cathryn, B .... 434-395-2759 509 H
mobleycb@longwood.edu
MOBLEY, Karen .... 912-871-1638 129 E
kmobley@ogeecheetech.edu
MOBLEY, Marilyn, S ..... 216-368-8877 378 J
marilyn.mobley@case.edu
MOBLEY, Wade .... 763-544-9501 253 J
MOBLEY, Wanda .... 336-517-2267 354 K
wmobley@bennett.edu
MOBLEY-SMITH,
Miriam .... 773-821-2589 141 J
msmith56@csu.edu
MOCABEE, Norma .... 626-815-4550.. 29 B
nmocabee@apu.edu
MOCARSKI, Richard, A . 308-865-8496 293 G
mocarskira@unk.edu
MOCCIA, Mario .... 575-646-7630 312 A
moccia@nmsu.edu
MOCEK, Christian .... 812-357-6479 173 A
cmocek@saintmeinrad.edu
MOCERI, Joane, T .... 503-943-7211 410 H
moceri@up.edu
MOCK, Diana .... 559-453-5505.. 45 E
dbmock@fresno.edu
MOCK, Gerald, L .... 772-462-7315 106 F
gmock@irsc.edu
MOCK, Keith .... 334-386-7876.... 3 I
kmock@faulkner.edu
MOCK, Kelly .... 314-529-9579 277 B
kmock@maryville.edu
MOCK, Raymond, F ...... 513-529-6023 386 K
mockrf@miamioh.edu
MOCK, JR., Robert, C .. 859-257-1911 200 G
robert.mock@uky.edu
MOCNIK, Joe .... 478-445-0980 125 A
joe.mocnik@gcsu.edu
MODDER, Gail .... 916-624-3333.. 66 E
MODELANE, Dan .... 508-541-1614 225 G
dmodelane@dean.edu
MODENA, Shawn .... 478-825-6100 124 E
modenas@fvsu.edu
MODENSTEIN, Susan .... 212-592-2000 342 F
smodenstein@sva.edu
MODERSOHN, Ellen, E . 563-387-1350 180 M
ellen.modersohn@luther.edu
MODESTOU,
Jennifer, A .... 319-335-0705 175 H
jennifer-modestou@uiowa.edu
MODIC, Blaire .... 641-628-5376 176 E
modicb@central.edu
MODICA, Joseph, B ..... 610-341-5826 418 A
jmodica@eastern.edu
MODIG, James, E .... 785-864-3431 191 G
jmodig@ku.edu
MODLIN, Andy .... 336-841-9605 357 E
amodlin@highpoint.edu
MODLIN, Jason, E .... 919-497-3210 358 J
jmodlin@louisburg.edu
MODRCIN, Mary Anne . 423-869-6319 458 B
maryanne.modrcin@lmunet.edu
MODROVSKY, Amanda . 570-408-4307 440 B
amanda.modrovsky@wilkes.edu
MODRZAKOWSKI,
Malcolm .... 304-647-6302 533 B
mmodrzakowski@osteo.wvsom.edu
MOE, Karine, F .... 651-696-6160 256 L
moe@macalester.edu
MOE, Marie .... 701-483-2560 373 H
Marie.Moe@dickinsonstate.edu
MOEDER, Lawrence, E .. 785-532-6250 188 H
larrym@ksu.edu
MOEDER, Lawrence, E .. 785-532-6420 188 H
larrym@ksu.edu
MOEGENBURG, Stacey . 845-341-4286 337 G
stacey.moegenburg@sunyorange.edu
MOEGENBURGI, Stacey 845-341-4768 337 G
stacey.moegenburgi@sunyorange.edu
MOEGGENBERG, Rich ... 517-607-2348 243 J
rmoeggenberg@hillsdale.edu
MOEGLIN, Maureen ...... 402-457-2236 291 E
mmoeglin@mccneb.edu
MOEGLING, Mary Lou .. 740-374-8716 395 D
mmoegling@wscc.edu

MOELLER, Darin .... 712-274-6400 184 A
darin.moeller@witcc.edu
MOELLER, Lon .... 319-335-3565 175 H
lon-moeller@uiowa.edu
MOEN, Matthew, C .... 605-677-5221 453 F
matthew.moen@usd.edu
MOEN, Stuart .... 281-873-0262 471 D
s.moen@commonwealth.edu
MOENCH, Gerald .... 816-501-4862 281 B
gerald.moench@rockhurst.edu
MOENKHAUS, Kevin, P 515-271-3902 177 K
kevin.moenkhaus@drake.edu
MOERLAND,
Timothy, S .... 724-357-2219 431 A
tim.moerland@iup.edu
MOERMAN, LeeAnn ...... 712-722-6002 177 J
leeann.moerman@dordt.edu
MOERSCHBAECHER,
Joseph, M .... 504-568-4804 205 C
jmoers@lsuhsc.edu
MOESSNER, Phillip .... 208-282-4229 138 C
moesphil@isu.edu
MOEZ, Chrystal .... 262-619-6830 543 A
moezc@gtc.edu
MOFFAT, Barbara, A ..... 413-782-1630 238 A
barbara.moffat@wne.edu
MOFFAT, Heather .... 812-888-4120 174 F
hmoffat@vinu.edu
MOFFATT, Tammy, L .... 603-646-2811 297 G
tammy.l.moffatt@dartmouth.edu
MOFFETT, Jared, E .... 202-274-5000.. 97 B
MOFFETT, Katie .... 603-456-2656 298 D
MOFFETT, Raphael, X ... 405-466-3446 398 E
rmoffett@langston.edu
MOFFITT, Clinton .... 559-278-3902.. 33 D
clinton_moffitt@csufresno.edu
MOFFITT, Jamie, H .... 541-346-3003 410 F
jmoffitt@uoregon.edu
MOFFITT, Lisa .... 615-327-3927 457 G
moffitt@guptoncollege.edu
MOFFITT, Michael, L .... 541-346-3836 410 F
mmoffitt@uoregon.edu
MOFFITT, Thomas, J .... 610-566-1776 440 C
tmoffitt@williamson.edu
MOGCK, Steven, A .... 312-329-4131 153 C
steve.mogck@moody.edu
MOGFORD, Jon .... 979-458-0243 484 E
JMogford@tamus.edu
MOHAJIR, Terry .... 870-972-3880.. 19 F
tmohajir@astate.edu
MOHAMADIAN,
Habib, P .... 225-771-5290 207 A
mohamad@engr.subr.edu
MOHAMED, Rafik .... 909-537-5500.. 35 A
MOHAMMAD, Yatty .... 402-878-3331 291 B
ymohammad@littlepriest.edu
MOHAMMADI, Aghajan 718-262-2333 321 B
aghajan@york.cuny.edu
MOHAMMADI, Amir ..... 724-738-2002 432 A
amir.mohammadi@sru.edu
MOHAMMADI, Rameen 315-312-2232 346 A
rameen.mohammadi@oswego.edu
MOHANTY, Bidhu, D .... 757-823-8005 510 H
bbmohanty@nsu.edu
MOHAPATRA, Prasant .. 530-752-8644.. 71 A
pmohapatra@ucdavis.edu
MOHDZAIN, Zaidy .... 870-235-4057.. 23 D
azmohdzain@saumag.edu
MOHIYEDDINI, Sohila .. 714-533-1495.. 67 A
soh@southbaylo.edu
MOHLER, Nick .... 717-396-7833 429 H
nmohler@pcad.edu
MOHLER, JR.,
R. Albert .... 502-897-4121 199 D
mohler@sbts.edu
MOHNEY, David .... 908-737-4770 303 C
dmohney@kean.edu
MOHNEY, Len .... 661-362-3207.. 40 H
len.mohney@canyons.edu
MOHR, James .... 360-475-7535 524 H
jmohr@olympic.edu
MOHR, James, R .... 724-946-7115 439 D
mohrjr@westminister.edu
MOHR, Jean Marie .... 845-398-4106 341 H
jmohr@stac.edu
MOHR, Joan, I .... 203-582-8959.. 91 E
joan.isaacmohr@quinnipiac.edu
MOHR, Karl .... 530-752-2063.. 71 A
kfmohr@ucdavis.edu
MOHR, Lisa .... 507-285-7245 261 D
lisa.mohr@rctc.edu
MOHR, Marla .... 419-559-2152 392 A
mmohr@terra.edu
MOHR, Rick .... 937-529-2201 392 G
rmohr@united.edu
MOHR, Sharon .... 763-488-2525 258 G
sharon.mohr@hennepintech.edu
MOHR, Wayne, C .... 570-389-4303 430 B
wmohr@bloomu.edu

MOHRBACHER, Bob ..... 509-793-2055 520 B
Bobm@bigbend.edu
MOHRBUTTER, Trent, L 252-451-8336 364 E
tlmohrbutter@nashcc.edu
MOHRE, Trudy .... 517-264-7185 250 B
tmohre@sienaheights.edu
MOHS, Marlene .... 651-690-6932 263 V
mmohs@stkate.edu
MOHSEN, Bashir .... 201-216-9901 302 A
bashir.mohsen@eicollege.edu
MOHSINI, Virga .... 617-824-7858 226 A
virga_mohsini@emerson.edu
MOIOLA, Tena .... 858-566-1200.. 43 A
tmoiola@disd.edu
MOIR, Chris .... 216-987-3492 381 A
chris.moir@tri-c.edu
MOIST, Kirk, L .... 715-833-6224 542 M
kmoist@cvtc.edu
MOJICA, Agnes .... 787-892-4320 554 C
amojica@intersg.edu
MOJICA, Francis, J ...... 787-723-4481 551 B
fmojica@ceaprc.edu
MOJICA, Jorge, E .... 787-852-1430 552 J
jmojica@hccpr.edu
MOJOCK, Charles, R .... 352-365-3523 107 X
mojockc@lssc.edu
MOK, Jacqueline, L ...... 210-567-2004 495 B
mok@uthscsa.edu
MOKAR, Jason .... 302-622-8000.. 93 D
jmokar@dcad.edu
MOKEL, Haroon .... 703-878-2800.. 96 H
MOKREN, Jennifer .... 845-257-3860 344 A
mokrenj@newpaltz.edu
MOKU, Samuel .... 808-544-1406 135 C
smoku@hpu.edu
MOKUAU, Dawn .... 415-561-6555.. 60 C
MOKUAU, Noreen, K .... 808-956-6300 135 J
noreen@hawaii.edu
MOLALENGE,
Teshome, H .... 540-828-5750 505 F
tmolalen@bridgewater.edu
MOLCHANY, Jim .... 610-282-1100 416 I
jim.molchany@desales.edu
MOLDENHAUER, Susan 307-766-6620 546 K
amsm@uwyo.edu
MOLDENHAUER, Troy ... 262-595-2495 540 C
moldenht@uwp.edu
MOLDER, Kandi .... 918-335-6237 400 I
kmolder@okwu.edu
MOLDER, Mark .... 918-335-6843 400 I
mmolder@okwu.edu
MOLDSTAD, Donald, L . 507-344-7312 253 M
donm@blc.edu
MOLEE, Lenore .... 973-278-5400 300 C
lenore-molee@berkeleycollege.edu
MOLEE, Lenore .... 973-278-5400 316 D
lenore-molee@berkeleycollege.edu
MOLELLA, Holly .... 845-431-8953 324 D
molella@sunydutchess.edu
MOLEN, Brent .... 801-426-8234 499 I
president@ucdh.edu
MOLEN, Kenneth .... 801-426-8234 499 I
director@ucdh.edu
MOLER, Delanie, S .... 848-445-3787 306 F
delanie.moler@rutgers.edu
MOLER, Misty .... 704-216-3623 365 F
misty.moler@rccc.edu
MOLESWORTH,
Mark, D .... 608-342-1567 540 D
moleswom@uwplatt.edu
MOLEY, Linda .... 620-252-7115 186 C
lmoley@coffeyville.edu
MOLIFE, Brenda .... 508-531-2454 229 C
bmolife@bridge.edu
MOLIKEN, Laura .... 610-409-3606 438 H
lmoliken@ursinus.edu
MOLINA, Alejandra .... 315-781-3319 327 G
molina@hws.edu
MOLINA, Carlos .... 718-518-6658 319 D
cmolina@hostos.cuny.edu
MOLINA, Carlos .... 202-495-3876.. 96 E
cmolina@dhs.edu
MOLINA, Michael .... 806-742-1438 489 D
MOLINA, Michael .... 806-742-2116 489 F
michael.molina@ttu.edu
MOLINA, Ricardo .... 787-738-2161 557 G
ricardo.molina1@upr.edu
MOLINAR, Anthony .... 415-749-4524.. 62 I
amolinar@sfai.edu
MOLINARI, Francis .... 401-841-2245 548 B
MOLINARO, Brian .... 315-792-5545 333 D
bmolinaro@mvcc.edu
MOLIVER, Donald .... 732-571-3422 303 G
dmoliver@monmouth.edu
MOLL, Amy .... 208-426-5719 137 E
amoll@boisestate.edu
MOLL, John .... 602-872-7748.. 15 F
john.moll@southmountaincc.edu
MOLL, Jonathan .... 781-239-4022 222 E
jmoll@babson.edu

MOLL, Monica, M .... 419-372-2346 377 I
mmoll@bgsu.edu
MOLL, Stephen .... 305-919-5700 114 G
molls@fiu.edu
MOLLA, Mike .... 410-225-2215 216 F
mmolla@mica.edu
MOLLAHAN, David, J ... 334-683-2301.... 5 H
dmollahan@marionmilitary.edu
MOLLARD, Tikhon .... 570-561-1818 435 A
bishop.tikhon@stots.edu
MOLLEN, Elizabeth .... 607-778-5008 344 F
mollenes@sunybroome.edu
MOLLER, Amanda .... 312-752-2170 149 D
amanda.moller@kendall.edu
MOLLER, Denny .... 352-588-8250 111 L
denny.moller@saintleo.edu
MOLLER, Mark .... 740-587-6668 381 H
moller@denison.edu
MOLLER, Mary .... 503-725-9818 409 D
mollerm@pdx.edu
MOLLER, Simon .... 718-990-3917 340 G
mollers@stjohns.edu
MOLLER, Steffen .... 503-594-3390 405 A
steffenm@clackamas.edu
MOLLEUR, Sherri .... 802-322-1626 501 H
sherri.molleur@goddard.edu
MOLLFULLEDA,
Wildanette .... 312-980-9200 158 H
MOLLIS, Kristi, L .... 561-912-1211 102 N
kmollis@evergladesuniversity.edu
MOLLNER, Daniel, J ...... 507-933-7569 256 A
dmollner@gustavus.edu
MOLLOY,
Christopher, H .... 317-788-3360 173 I
cmolloy@uindy.edu
MOLLOY,
Christopher, J .... 848-932-5663 306 F
molloy@oldqueens.rutgers.edu
MOLLOY, Marcie, A ...... 410-822-5400 214 D
mamolloy@chesapeake.edu
MOLONEY, Jacqueline .. 978-934-4744 229 A
jacqueline_moloney@uml.edu
MOLTA, Phyllis .... 617-588-1347 223 D
pmolta@bfit.edu
MOLYNEUX, Annette ..... 215-895-1415 417 E
ajm26@drexel.edu
MOLZ, Chris .... 215-222-4200 434 A
cmolz@walnuthillcollege.edu
MOMAN, Frank .... 317-921-4396 169 M
fmoman@ivytech.edu
MOMAN, Orthella, P .... 601-977-7778 270 F
omoman@tougaloo.edu
MOMAN, Tim .... 602-432-8414.. 11 C
MOMANY,
Christopher, P .... 517-265-5161 238 H
cmomany@adrian.edu
MOMAYEZI, Nasser ...... 678-466-4700 122 J
nassermomayezi@clayton.edu
MOMBERG, Joel .... 813-974-1899 116 B
jmomberg@usf.edu
MOMINEY, Michael ...... 954-262-8253 109 E
mominey@nova.edu
MONACO, A.G .... 225-578-8200 204 M
amonaco@lsu.edu
MONACO, Anthony, P .. 617-627-3300 237 C
anthony.monaco@tufts.edu
MONACO, Dennis .... 978-232-2357 226 C
dmonaco@endicott.edu
MONACO, Lynn, K .... 808-956-9083 135 H
kmonaco@hawaii.edu
MONACO, Pamela .... 630-637-5384 154 F
pjmonaco@noctrl.edu
MONACO, Tana .... 510-485-7837.. 58 G
tmonaco@patten.edu
MONAGAN, Paul, R ...... 903-510-2130 491 A
pmon@tjc.edu
MONAGHAN, James ...... 858-653-6740.. 48 Q
JMonaghan@JPCatholic.com
MONAGHAN, Thomas .. 610-660-3204 434 G
tmonagha@sju.edu
MONAGHAN,
Thomas, S .... 239-280-2522.. 98 O
tmonaghan@avemaria.edu
MONAHAN, JR.,
Charles, F .... 617-732-2880 233 E
charles.monahan@mcphs.edu
MONAHAN, Joan .... 207-602-2000 213 B
jmonahan1@une.edu
MONAHAN, Kevin .... 412-268-2064 414 J
MONAHAN, Mark .... 734-487-5386 242 J
mmonahan@emich.edu
MONAHAN, Michael, D 717-245-1007 417 B
monahanm@dickinson.edu
MONAHAN, Susanne .... 503-838-8226 411 B
monahans@wou.edu
MONAN, SJ, J. Donald 617-552-2128 224 B
j.donald.monan@bc.edu
MONARCH, Laura, M ... 270-745-5334 201 D
laura.monarch@wku.edu

MONAST, Louise .... 401-341-2287 442 D
louise.monast@salve.edu
MONCK-MARCELLINO,
Caitlin .... 718-780-0322 317 A
caitlin.monck-marcellino@brooklaw.edu
MONCRIFFE, Pritchard .. 405-466-3253 398 E
pmoncriffe@langston.edu
MONCURE, Anna .... 540-362-6490 508 D
moncurea@hollins.edu
MONCURE, Betty .... 601-979-2227 267 H
betty.j.moncure@jsums.edu
MONCURE, Thomas, M 703-993-2619 507 K
tmoncure@gmu.edu
MONDAY, Eric, N .... 859-257-1841 200 G
emonday@uky.edu
MONDAY, Kathryn, J .... 804-289-8771 513 M
kmonday@richmond.edu
MONDEH, Sama .... 205-247-8070.... 7 G
smondeh@stillman.edu
MONDEIK, Shelly .... 715-675-3331 544 A
mondeik@ntc.edu
MONDELLI, Robert .... 973-684-6626 304 F
rmondelli@pccc.edu
MONDELLO-HENDREN,
Martha, C .... 216-397-4293 384 F
mhendren@jcu.edu
MONDILLO, Keith .... 215-646-7300 420 A
mondillo.k@gmercyu.edu
MONDOU, Sherry, B .... 253-879-3204 527 F
smondou@pugetsound.edu
MONDZIEL, Marlene ..... 804-819-4902 514 G
mmondziel@vccs.edu
MONE, Jennifer .... 516-463-7310 328 A
jennifer.mone@hofstra.edu
MONE, Mark .... 414-229-4331 540 A
mone@uwm.edu
MONERSON, Jodi .... 218-755-3750 258 B
jmonerson@bemidjistate.edu
MONETA, Larry .... 919-684-3737 356 E
studentaffairs@duke.edu
MONETTE, Lois, E .... 603-513-1307 299 C
lois.monette@granite.edu
MONETTE, Marliss .... 575-835-5623 311 I
mmonette@admin.nmt.edu
MONEY, Barbara .... 972-599-3151 471 C
bmoney@collin.edu
MONEY, Ken .... 601-366-8880 271 E
kmoney@wbs.edu
MONEY, Royce .... 325-674-4974 466 I
moneyr@acu.edu
MONEYHAM, Valerie, Z 850-474-2041 116 E
vmoneyha@uwf.edu
MONEYMAKER, Andrew 662-329-7127 269 B
amoneymaker@muw.edu
MONFETTE, Francine .... 401-341-2231 442 D
monfettf@salve.edu
MONG, Scott .... 740-753-7203 383 G
mongs@hocking.edu
MONGAN, Jason .... 800-444-1440 433 B
jmongan@pia.edu
MONGAN,
Jeremiah James .... 970-352-1181.. 78 H
MONGAR, Mark, J .... 402-280-2262 290 B
MarkMongar@creighton.edu
MONGELLI, Antoinette .. 310-983-3525.. 71 D
mongelli@volunteer.ucla.edu
MONGEON, Mike .... 508-373-9458 223 C
michael.mongeon@becker.edu
MONGEON-STEWART,
Karla .... 701-777-2015 373 G
karla.stewart@und.edu
MONGER, Todd .... 612-343-3513 263 H
tjmonger@northcentral.edu
MONGERSON, John ...... 815-939-5101 155 G
jmonger@olivet.edu
MONGILLO, Anne, M .... 516-463-6776 328 A
anne.mongillo@hofstra.edu
MONGO, Karen .... 214-860-2235 472 F
kmongo@dcccd.edu
MONHEIT, Yidel .... 718-853-2442 353 I
MONHOLLON, Michael . 325-670-5870 474 M
mmonholl@hsutx.edu
MONIACI, Steve, C .... 281-649-3096 475 B
smoniaci@hbu.edu
MONIODIS, Paul .... 410-837-5270 221 B
pmoniodis@ubalt.edu
MONIT, Scott .... 724-480-3356 416 A
scott.monit@ccbc.edu
MONK, David, H .... 814-865-2526 428 C
dhm6@psu.edu
MONK, Matthew .... 802-828-8556 503 D
matthew.monk@vcfa.edu
MONK, Suzanne .... 662-476-5014 267 C
smonk@eastms.edu
MONKS, Birgit .... 909-652-6876.. 38 A
birgit.monks@chaffey.edu
MONKS, Laura .... 931-438-0028 463 B
lmonks@mscc.edu
MONNAT, Angela, B ..... 585-385-8042 340 F
amonnat@sjfc.edu
MONNES, Mark, J .... 419-755-4824 387 E
mmonnes@ncstatecollege.edu
MONNIG, Amber .... 660-248-6280 272 N
armonnig@centralmethodist.edu
MONNOT, Charles .... 405-208-5295 400 A
cmonnot@okcu.edu
MONOD, Kelly .... 941-752-5491 114 B
monodk@scf.edu
MONOLO, Melissa .... 843-349-7883 446 I
melissa.monolo@hgtc.edu
MONROE, Alicia .... 713-798-2312 469 C
alicia.monroe@bcm.edu
MONROE, Dennis .... 334-420-4266.... 7 I
dmonroe@trenholmstate.edu
MONROE, Jill .... 619-849-2298.. 59 K
jillmonroe@pointloma.edu
MONROE, Joseph, W .... 859-257-5770 200 G
joe.monroe@uky.edu
MONROE, JP .... 541-346-2085 410 F
jpmonroe@uoregon.edu
MONROE, Maxine .... 845-569-3346 333 I
maxine.monroe@msmc.edu
MONROE, Randall, L .... 570-326-3761 429 J
rmonroe@pct.edu
MONROE, William .... 713-743-9007 491 D
wmonroe@uh.edu
MONROE-BAILLARGEON,
Ann .... 860-231-5322.. 93 A
annmonroe@usj.edu
MONS, Marie .... 404-894-4582 125 D
marie.mons@finaid.gatech.edu
MONSANTO, Steve .... 951-372-7140.. 61 A
steve.monsanto@norcocollege.edu
MONTAG, Jerry .... 815-753-1747 154 I
jerry.montag@niu.edu
MONTAGNE, Michael .... 617-732-2995 233 E
michael.montagne@mcphs.edu
MONTAGNINO, Chris .... 518-608-8184 325 B
cmontagnino@excelsior.edu
MONTAGUE, Evan .... 734-973-3408 251 J
elmontague@wccnet.edu
MONTAGUE, Krista .... 406-657-2061 287 H
kmontague@msubillings.edu
MONTAGUE,
Marlena, O .... 671-735-5612 549 E
marlena.montague@guamcc.edu
MONTAGUE, Orinthia .... 952-358-8283 260 D
orinthia.montague@normandale.edu
MONTALBAN, Silvia ..... 646-557-4409 319 F
smontalban@jjay.cuny.edu
MONTALBANO, Ivonne . 713-221-8060 491 F
montalbanoi@uhd.edu
MONTALVO, Carmen .... 787-878-5475 553 F
cmontalv@arecibo.inter.edu
MONTALVO, Cynthia .... 201-559-6036 302 I
montalvoc@felician.edu
MONTALVO, Francisco . 787-279-1912 553 H
fmontalvo@bayamon.inter.edu
MONTALVO, Luis .... 617-262-5000 223 G
luis.montalvo@the-bac.edu
MONTALVO, Provi .... 787-878-5475 553 F
pmontalvo@arecibo.inter.edu
MONTALVO, Veronica .... 203-596-6164.. 91 D
vmontalvo@post.edu
MONTALVO-COLON,
Sonia, I .... 787-751-1912 554 D
smontalv@juris.inter.edu
MONTANARI, James ..... 815-836-5222 150 F
montanja@lewisu.edu
MONTANEZ, John .... 212-220-8011 318 D
jmontanez@bmcc.cuny.edu
MONTANEZ, Robert ...... 916-691-7204.. 52 J
montanr@crc.losrios.edu
MONTANEZ-LOPEZ,
Nilda .... 787-740-3001 556 F
nilda.montanez@uccaribe.edu
MONTANO-CORDOVA,
Ruby, S .... 909-593-3511.. 73 B
rmontano-cordova@laverne.edu
MONTE, Renee .... 415-338-3982.. 36 A
rmonte@sfsu.edu
MONTEAGUDO, Rene .... 305-284-5511 118 A
rxm981@miami.edu
MONTEAU, Shannon .... 406-395-4875 288 I
smonteau@stonechild.edu
MONTECALVO, Frank .... 814-472-3002 434 F
fmontecalvo@francis.edu
MONTEFUSCO, Anthony 401-254-3023 442 C
amontefusco@rwu.edu
MONTEFUSCO, Luis ...... 609-343-5635 299 G
lmontefu@atlantic.edu
MONTEIRO, Beth .... 608-363-2699 534 L
monteirob@beloit.edu
MONTEIRO, Kenneth, P 415-338-1693.. 36 A
monteiro@sfsu.edu
MONTEIRO, Marconi .... 210-924-4338 469 B
marconi.monteiro@bua.edu
MONTEITH, Kellie .... 828-227-7147 372 C
monteith@wcu.edu
MONTEL, Carmen .... 954-492-5353 100 G
cmontel@citycollege.edu
MONTELEONE, Susan .... 706-233-7316 131 C
smonteleone@shorter.edu
MONTEMAYOR, Roland 408-288-3772.. 64 A
roland.montemayor@sjcc.edu
MONTEMURRO,
Kimberly .... 914-633-2246 328 F
Kmontemurro@iona.edu
MONTERECY, Monty ..... 206-934-3628 525 K
orestes.monterecy@seattlecolleges.edu
MONTERO, Fidel, A ...... 801-863-8825 500 B
fidel.montero@uvu.edu
MONTERO, Grecia .... 609-771-3132 301 E
montero@tcnj.edu
MONTERO, Ines .... 773-489-8915 142 D
imontero2@ccc.edu
MONTERO, Janina .... 310-825-1404.. 71 D
jmontero@saonet.ucla.edu
MONTES, Bruce, A .... 773-508-7601 151 E
bmontes@luc.edu
MONTES, Josefer .... 509-527-2615 528 A
josefer.montes@wallawalla.edu
MONTES, Porfirio .... 787-863-2390 553 I
porfirio.montes@fajardo.inter.edu
MONTES, Susan, R .... 305-284-6021 118 A
smontes@miami.edu
MONTES-BURGOS,
Carmen .... 787-993-8952 557 E
carmen.montes1@upr.edu
MONTES-HELU, Maria .. 520-383-8401.. 18 A
mmontes@tocc.edu
MONTES-MORALES,
Maria .... 347-964-8600 316 J
mmontes@boricuacollege.edu
MONTESINO,
María del C .... 787-720-1022 550 F
recaudaciones@atlanticcollege.edu
MONTEVIRGEN,
Alexis, S .... 219-980-6824 168 C
amontevi@iun.edu
MONTEZ, Daniel .... 956-447-6635 482 G
dmontez@southtexascollege.edu
MONTEZ, Nicholas .... 619-482-6306.. 68 D
nmontez@swccd.edu
MONTEZON, Juice .... 612-343-4188 263 H
jjmontez@northcentral.edu
MONTGOMERY,
Adrienne .... 978-837-5196 233 G
montgomerya@merrimack.edu
MONTGOMERY,
Alisa, L .... 336-322-2213 364 G
Alisa.Montgomery@piedmontcc.edu
MONTGOMERY,
Candace .... 312-553-2500 141 M
cmontgomery30@ccc.edu
MONTGOMERY, Christy 985-543-4120 203 I
MONTGOMERY, Cindy .. 229-226-1621 132 E
cmontgomery@thomasu.edu
MONTGOMERY, Clyde .. 405-466-3636 398 E
cmontgomery@langston.edu
MONTGOMERY, Dale .... 479-619-4234.. 22 B
dmontgom@nwacc.edu
MONTGOMERY, Daron .. 715-346-3688 541 A
dmontgom@uwsp.edu
MONTGOMERY, Don ...... 330-823-7803 394 A
montgojd@mountunion.edu
MONTGOMERY, Donald 337-269-0620 201 F
donaldm@bluecliffcollege.com
MONTGOMERY,
Edward, B .... 202-687-5932.. 95 E
emb48@georgetown.edu
MONTGOMERY, Eric ..... 620-331-4100 188 B
emontgomery@indycc.edu
MONTGOMERY, Francis 716-896-0700 352 B
franciscssf@villa.edu
MONTGOMERY, Grant ... 800-962-7682 285 I
gmontgomery@wma.edu
MONTGOMERY, Isalene 386-506-3961 101 I
montgoi@DaytonaState.edu
MONTGOMERY, Joe ...... 509-544-4935 521 C
jmontgomery@columbiabasin.edu
MONTGOMERY, John ..... 951-343-4963.. 30 D
jmontgomery@calbaptist.edu
MONTGOMERY, John ..... 575-562-4002 310 I
john.montgomery@enmu.edu
MONTGOMERY,
Kara, H .... 724-946-7363 439 D
montgokh@westminster.edu
MONTGOMERY, Karen .. 512-404-4816 468 J
kmontgomery@austinseminary.edu
MONTGOMERY,
Kathryn .... 864-225-7653 446 D
kathrynmontgomery@forrestcollege.edu
MONTGOMERY, Keith ... 715-261-6223 541 E
keith.montgomery@uwc.edu
MONTGOMERY, Keith ... 715-389-6538 541 E
keith.montgomery@uwc.edu
MONTGOMERY, Kit .... 214-333-5209 471 L
kit@dbu.edu
MONTGOMERY,
Laura, M .... 630-752-5227 163 G
Laura.Montgomery@wheaton.edu
MONTGOMERY, Lisa ..... 312-567-3777 147 E
montgomeryl@iit.edu
MONTGOMERY, Lisa, P 843-792-5050 447 G
montgoml@musc.edu
MONTGOMERY, Mark ... 315-733-2307 351 E
mmontgomery@uscny.edu
MONTGOMERY, Martha 254-442-5114 470 I
martha.montgomery@cisco.edu
MONTGOMERY,
Maureen .... 559-791-2209.. 49 G
maureen.montgomery@portervillecollege.edu
MONTGOMERY,
Melissa .... 517-750-6426 250 F
Melissa.Montgomery@arbor.edu
MONTGOMERY, Mike ... 937-433-3410 382 C
mmontgomery@fortiscollege.edu
MONTGOMERY, Nancy . 575-439-3798 312 B
nmontgom@nmsu.edu
MONTGOMERY, Roark .. 903-875-7487 479 I
roark.montgomery@navarrocollege.edu
MONTGOMERY, Robert . 248-232-4808 248 E
rjmontgo@oaklandcc.edu
MONTGOMERY,
Soncerey, L .... 336-750-2314 372 D
montgomerysl@wssu.edu
MONTGOMERY,
Tammy .... 916-484-8408.. 52 I
montgot2@arc.losrios.edu
MONTGOMERY,
Toni-Marie .... 847-491-7552 155 D
t-montgomery@northwestern.edu
MONTGOMERY, Tony .... 662-476-5062 267 C
tmontgomery@eastms.edu
MONTGOMERY,
Tonya, Y .... 502-597-6434 197 G
tonya.montgomery@kysu.edu
MONTGOMERY,
Walter, L .... 336-322-2211 364 G
Walter.Montgomery@piedmontcc.edu
MONTGOMERY RICE,
Valerie .... 404-752-1740 129 A
vmontgomeryrice@msm.edu
MONTI, Joseph .... 407-644-1408 111 H
jmonti@rollins.edu
MONTIEL, Arthuro .... 956-488-5808 482 G
amontiel@southtexascollege.edu
MONTIJO, Minerva .... 716-896-0700 352 B
montijom@villa.edu
MONTIJO, River .... 503-768-6030 406 H
rmontijo@lclark.edu
MONTILEAUX, Kateri .... 605-455-6051 452 L
kmontileaux@olc.edu
MONTNEY, Kevin .... 920-206-2312 536 T
kevin.montney@mbu.edu
MONTONE, Richard ...... 413-644-4776 222 F
rmontone@simons-rock.edu
MONTOYA, Adrian .... 210-486-3135 467 A
amontoya@alamo.edu
MONTOYA, Bernadette .. 575-646-2447 312 A
bermonto@nmsu.edu
MONTOYA, Denise .... 505-224-4000 310 F
montoyad@cnm.edu
MONTOYA, Jimi .... 505-747-2139 312 G
jimi.montoya@nnmc.edu
MONTOYA, Loretta .... 505-224-3457 310 F
lmontoya@cnm.edu
MONTOYA, Michael ...... 505-454-2534 311 B
mimontoya@luna.edu
MONTOYA, Michelle ..... 510-780-4500.. 50 G
mmontoya@lifewest.edu
MONTOYA, Mitzi, M ..... 480-727-1955.. 11 J
mitzi.montoya@asu.edu
MONTOYA, Rolando ..... 305-237-3872 108 L
rmontoya@mdc.edu
MONTOYA, Valerie .... 505-346-2330 313 G
valerie.montoya@bie.edu
MONTOYA, Victor .... 406-275-4974 288 H
victor_montoya@skc.edu
MONTRALLO, Pamela ... 435-652-7522 499 M
montrallo@dixie.edu
MONTREAL, Steven ...... 262-243-5700 535 I
steve.montreal@cuw.edu
MONTZ, Ruth .... 330-287-1247 389 B
montz.11@osu.edu
MOO-YOUNG, Keith ..... 509-372-7258 528 B
MOODY, Barbara .... 207-941-7000 210 C
moodyb@husson.edu
MOODY, Bill .... 678-717-3630 133 A
bill.moody@ung.edu
MOODY, Brad .... 501-760-4213.. 21 H
bmoody@npcc.edu
MOODY, Chip .... 602-429-4919.. 16 N
cmoody@ps.edu
MOODY, Chris .... 202-885-3370.. 94 H
moody@american.edu

MOODY, D. L .... 817-461-8741 468 C
dmoody@arlingtonbaptistcollege.edu
MOODY, Debra .... 334-222-6591.... 5 G
djmoody@lbwcc.edu
MOODY, Geoff .... 603-645-9611 298 H
g.moody@snhu.edu
MOODY, Jan .... 601-928-6207 268 G
janet.moody@mgccc.edu
MOODY, Jeff, T .... 219-942-1459 165 D
jmoody@ccr.edu
MOODY, Jesse .... 563-884-5306 182 D
jesse.moody@palmer.edu
MOODY, Kari .... 920-465-2226 539 F
moodyk@uwgb.edu
MOODY, Kay .... 219-942-1459 165 D
kay.moody@ccr.edu
MOODY, Krystal .... 903-927-3312 497 G
kmoody@wileyc.edu
MOODY, Linda .... 213-477-2560.. 54 I
lmoody@msmu.edu
MOODY, Lisa .... 302-857-6120.. 93 E
lmoody@desu.edu
MOODY, Marilyn .... 503-725-4616 409 D
marilynmoody@pdx.edu
MOODY, Marla .... 417-447-4842 280 C
moodym@otc.edu
MOODY, Mary .... 615-366-4437 461 B
mary.moody@tbr.edu
MOODY, Michelle, L .... 757-594-8819 506 I
mlmoody@cnu.edu
MOODY, Nancy, B .... 423-636-7301 464 F
nmoody@tusculum.edu
MOODY, Timothy .... 912-344-2518 120 D
tim.moody@armstrong.edu
MOODY, Tonia .... 601-403-1214 270 A
tmoody@prcc.edu
MOOMAW, Jillian .... 724-847-6674 419 B
jgmoomau@geneva.edu
MOON, Beverly .... 662-846-4873 267 A
bmoon@deltastate.edu
MOON, Daniel, C .... 904-620-2261 116 A
dmoon@unf.edu
MOON, David .... 719-255-3566.. 86 F
cmoon@uccs.edu
MOON, Don .... 434-592-3237 509 G
donmoon@liberty.edu
MOON, Freddie, P .... 256-766-6610.... 4 C
pmoon@hcu.edu
MOON, Greg .... 503-517-1880 411 C
gmoon@westernseminary.edu
MOON, Greta .... 760-245-4271.. 75 G
greta.moon@vvc.edu
MOON, Hope .... 440-365-5222 385 E
MOON, Hyon .... 949-480-4139.. 66 I
hmoon@soka.edu
MOON, Jennifer .... 309-794-7208 139 K
jennifermoon@augustana.edu
MOON, Jessica .... 803-508-7262 443 C
moonj@atc.edu
MOON, Joshua .... 605-626-3336 454 A
Joshua.Moon@northern.edu
MOON, Lee, L .... 904-620-2833 116 A
l.moon@unf.edu
MOON, Mary .... 212-757-1190 315 C
mmoon@funeraleducation.org
MOON, Michael .... 509-963-2213 520 E
moonm@cwu.edu
MOON, Michael, J .... 503-370-6017 411 D
mmoon@willamette.edu
MOON, Randy .... 251-460-6121.... 9 F
rmoon@southalabama.edu
MOON, Ruth .... 707-476-4264.. 41 C
ruth-moon@redwoods.edu
MOON, Sarah .... 585-785-1373 325 E
sarah.moon@flcc.edu
MOON, Sunny .... 657-278-4749.. 33 E
hmoon@fullerton.edu
MOON, Susan .... 573-288-6441 274 C
smoon@culver.edu
MOONEY, Carol Ann .... 574-284-4602 172 G
mooney@saintmarys.edu
MOONEY, Cathryn .... 631-244-3273 324 C
mooneyc@dowling.edu
MOONEY, Debra .... 513-745-3204 396 B
mooney@xavier.edu
MOONEY, Dee .... 616-222-1415 241 G
dee.mooney@cornerstone.edu
MOONEY, Denise .... 617-353-9814 224 E
dmooney@bu.edu
MOONEY, Ken .... 704-669-4030 361 E
mooneyk@clevelandcc.edu
MOONEY, Kim .... 603-899-4284 297 H
mooneyk@franklinpierce.edu
MOONEY, Laura .... 413-662-5411 230 C
laura.mooney@mcla.edu
MOONEY, Michael, C ... 585-245-5343 345 D
mooney@geneseo.edu
MOONEY, Sandra, N .... 281-649-3256 475 B
smooney@hbu.edu
MOONEY, Thelma .... 936-294-4047 489 A
tgm001@shsu.edu

MOONEY BURNS,
Mary .... 816-501-4199 281 B
mary.burns@rockhurst.edu
MOONEYHAN, Allen ..... 870-512-7864.. 19 I
allen_mooneyhan@asun.edu
MOONO, Steady .... 518-381-1200 342 E
MOORADIAN,
Ronald, G .... 562-903-4757.. 29 F
ron.mooradian@biola.edu
MOORE, Albert .... 408-741-2060.. 76 F
albert.moore@wvm.edu
MOORE, Albert .... 408-741-2060.. 76 D
albert.moore@wvm.edu
MOORE, Alicia .... 541-383-7262 404 K
amoore@cocc.edu
MOORE, Andrew .... 765-983-1672 165 H
moorean@earlham.edu
MOORE, Andrew .... 412-268-2063 414 J
awm@andrew.cmu.edu
MOORE, Anita, W .... 662-252-8000 270 C
amoore@rustcollege.edu
MOORE, Ann .... 601-403-1250 270 A
amoore@prcc.edu
MOORE, Anne .... 413-236-1641 231 A
amoore@berkshirecc.edu
MOORE, Anne, C .... 704-687-0145 371 B
amoor168@uncc.edu
MOORE, Anthony .... 270-384-8108 198 C
moorea@lindsey.edu
MOORE, A'kilah .... 925-473-7404.. 42 F
amoore@losmedanos.edu
MOORE, Barbara .... 914-251-6018 346 D
barbara.moore@purchase.edu
MOORE, Barbara .... 718-997-5421 320 E
barbara.moore@qc.cuny.edu
MOORE, Barbara .... 585-340-9593 321 G
bmoore@crcds.edu
MOORE, Barbara, C ..... 803-705-4604 443 F
mooreb@benedict.edu
MOORE, Barbara, E ...... 207-859-4250 210 A
barbara.moore@colby.edu
MOORE, Barbe .... 724-357-4077 431 A
bmoore@iup.edu
MOORE, Barry .... 434-592-3406 509 G
bnmoore@liberty.edu
MOORE, Barry, L .... 561-993-1134 109 H
mooreb@palmbeachstate.edu
MOORE, III, Berrien ..... 405-325-3095 403 I
berrien@ou.edu
MOORE, Bert, S .... 972-883-2355 494 A
bmoore@utdallas.edu
MOORE, Billy .... 662-846-4200 267 A
bmoore@deltastate.edu
MOORE, Bonnie .... 217-238-8260 150 B
bmoore71258@lakeland.cc.il.us
MOORE, Brad .... 505-224-4423 310 F
bmoore28@cnm.edu
MOORE, Brad, D .... 336-278-5490 356 F
bmoore6@elon.edu
MOORE, Brandon .... 951-639-5426.. 55 A
bmoore@msjc.edu
MOORE, Brett, C .... 607-735-1724 324 J
bmoore@elmira.edu
MOORE, Brian .... 845-569-3275 333 I
brian.moore@msmc.edu
MOORE, Brianna .... 415-703-9522.. 30 G
bmoore@cca.edu
MOORE, Bridget 325-670-1482 474M
bmoore@jsutx.edu
MOORE, Caitlan .... 970-675-3203.. 80 L
caitlan.moore@cncc.edu
MOORE, Carl .... 985-858-5956 203 G
carl.moore@fletcher.edu
MOORE, Carl, C .... 251-460-6419.... 9 F
ccmoore@southalabama.edu
MOORE, Carla .... 336-342-4261 365 E
moorec@rockinghamcc.edu
MOORE, Carla, L .... 803-786-3029 445 C
cmoore@columbiasc.edu
MOORE, Carol .... 805-922-6966.. 26 H
cvanname@hancockcollege.edu
MOORE, Carol, A .... 802-862-9616 501 E
MOORE, Caroline .... 805-756-2945.. 32 E
cmoore36@calpoly.edu
MOORE, Cathy, D .... 678-407-5000 125 B
cmoore@ggc.edu
MOORE, Charlette .... 501-882-8876.. 19 E
camoore@asub.edu
MOORE, Cherie .... 937-722-9222 394 F
cherie.moore@urbana.edu
MOORE,
Christopher, A .... 617-353-2705 224 E
mooreca@bu.edu
MOORE,
Christopher, W .... 208-496-3526 137 F
moorec@byui.edu
MOORE, Christy .... 318-678-6000 203 A
cmoore@bpcc.edu
MOORE, Chuck .... 804-862-6250 511 H
cmoore@rbc.edu

MOORE, Claire, E .... 443-352-4306 218 E
cmoore@stevenson.edu
MOORE, Cynthia .... 310-434-4305.. 65 B
moore_cynthia@smc.edu
MOORE, Dan .... 580-745-2006 402 D
dmoore@se.edu
MOORE, Dana .... 217-972-0839 429 G
dmoore@pafa.edu
MOORE, Danae .... 580-349-1356 400 B
danaem@opsu.edu
MOORE, Danny, B .... 252-398-6448 356 B
mooredd@chowan.edu
MOORE, Daryl .... 973-720-2232 309 I
moored@wpunj.edu
MOORE, David .... 714-516-4590.. 38 B
dmoore@chapman.edu
MOORE, David .... 740-593-4454 389 H
MOORE, David .... 703-993-8742 507 K
dmoorem@gmu.edu
MOORE, David, C .... 562-860-2451.. 37 L
dcmoore@cerritos.edu
MOORE, David, J .... 602-944-3335.. 11 D
dmoore@aicag.edu
MOORE, David, P .... 256-824-6285.... 9 A
david.moore@uah.edu
MOORE, Denise .... 913-469-8500 188 E
dmoore56@jccc.edu
MOORE, Dennis, T .... 585-785-1294 325 E
dennis.moore@flcc.edu
MOORE, Dirk, S .... 276-944-6810 507 E
dsmoore@ehc.edu
MOORE, Donald .... 856-256-4199 306 D
mooredo@rowan.edu
MOORE, JR., Eddie, N . 757-823-8670 510 H
president@nsu.edu
MOORE, Edwin .... 707-965-7103.. 57 I
cmoore@puc.edu
MOORE, Elinore .... 773-838-7528 142 C
emoore20@ccc.edu
MOORE, Elizabeth, M ... 336-322-2220 364 G
Libbie.McPhaul-Moore@piedmontcc.edu
MOORE, Emma .... 212-343-1234 332 I
emoore@mcny.edu
MOORE, Erin, B .... 847-866-3902 145 C
erin.moore@garrett.edu
MOORE, Faye .... 570-586-2400 435 H
fmoore@summitu.edu
MOORE, Frank, X .... 253-535-7504 524 I
moorefx@plu.edu
MOORE, Frederick, V .... 712-749-2103 176 D
mooref@bvu.edu
MOORE, Gary .... 248-364-8710 248 K
moore@oakland.edu
MOORE, Gina .... 803-705-4358 443 F
mooreg@benedict.edu
MOORE, Gregory .... 404-894-1420 125 D
gregory.moore@health.gatech.edu
MOORE, Gwendolyn ..... 912-443-5711 131 B
gmoore@savannahtech.edu
MOORE, Hallie .... 216-791-5000 380 C
hallie.moore@cim.edu
MOORE, Harry .... 215-751-8800 416 B
hmoore@ccp.edu
MOORE, Holly .... 206-934-6867 526 B
holly.moore@seattlecolleges.edu
MOORE, Hsiao-Ping, H 248-204-3500 245 J
hmoore@ltu.edu
MOORE, Jackie .... 715-682-1811 538 D
jmoore@northland.edu
MOORE, Jacques .... 207-859-4732 210 A
jrmoore@colby.edu
MOORE, James .... 520-494-5406.. 12 R
james.moore7@centralaz.edu
MOORE, James, E .... 215-951-1017 422 F
mooreje@lasalle.edu
MOORE, JR., James, H 217-333-0810 161 E
MOORE, Jan .... 912-688-6026 129 E
jmoore@ogeecheetech.edu
MOORE, Jana .... 928-317-6052.. 12 B
jana.moore@azwestern.edu
MOORE, Jason .... 205-391-5809.... 7 A
jmoore@sheltonstate.edu
MOORE, Jay .... 805-289-6340.. 75 E
jmooret@vcccd.edu
MOORE, Jennifer .... 662-329-8543 269 B
jnmoore@muw.edu
MOORE, Jeri .... 513-529-8589 386 K
moorejl@miamioh.edu
MOORE, Jim .... 417-269-8423 274 A
james.moore@coxcollege.edu
MOORE, Jim .... 831-459-0111.. 72 E
MOORE, John .... 585-475-2154 339 G
jfmfms@rit.edu
MOORE, John .... 423-869-7089 458 B
john.moore@lmunet.edu
MOORE, John, C .... 858-534-7127.. 72 B
johnmoore@ucsd.edu
MOORE, Johnny .... 903-434-8242 479 L
jmoore@ntcc.edu
MOORE, Joseph .... 630-942-2371 142 F
moorej7718@cod.edu

MOORE, Joseph, B .... 617-349-8500 228 B
jbmoore@lesley.edu
MOORE, Joshua .... 808-853-1040 135 F
joshuamoore@pacrim.edu
MOORE, Joy .... 617-552-2146 224 B
joy.moore@bc.edu
MOORE, Judy .... 219-989-2861 171 L
Judith.Moore@purduecal.edu
MOORE, Julia .... 602-787-6684.. 15 B
julia.moore@paradisevalley.edu
MOORE, Karen .... 816-604-3175 277 J
karen.moore@mcckc.edu
MOORE, Karissa .... 540-231-7518 518 B
mooreka@vt.edu
MOORE, Karla .... 386-506-3650 101 I
moorek@DaytonaState.edu
MOORE, Kathy, J .... 740-826-8114 387 C
moore@muskingum.edu
MOORE, Katie .... 417-447-8984 280 C
moorek@otc.edu
MOORE, Keith, D .... 801-581-8254 499 K
diazmoore@utah.edu
MOORE, Keith, E .... 757-455-3354 518 H
kmoore@vwc.edu
MOORE, Kelly .... 419-530-6031 394 E
kelly.moore@utoledo.edu
MOORE, Kevin .... 315-498-2220 337 F
moorek@sunyocc.edu
MOORE, Kevin .... 603-577-6529 297 F
kmoore@dwc.edu
MOORE, Kevin .... 303-273-3898.. 80 O
kmoore@mines.edu
MOORE, Kim .... 304-457-6337 529 C
moorekl@ab.edu
MOORE, Kimberly .... 850-201-8760 117 B
mooreki@tcc.fl.edu
MOORE, Kyle .... 806-651-2006 486 D
kmoore@mail.wtamu.edu
MOORE, Landa .... 218-935-0417 266 A
landa.moore@wetcc.edu
MOORE, Lara .... 541-962-3368 405 G
lmoore@eou.edu
MOORE, Lara .... 541-962-3773 405 G
lmoore@eou.edu
MOORE, Laura .... 414-297-6661 543 E
moore152@matc.edu
MOORE, Laura .... 567-661-7410 390 D
laura_moore@owens.edu
MOORE, SJ, Lawrence .. 504-861-5550 206 A
MOORE, Lee .... 361-593-2153 486 A
lee.moore@tamuk.edu
MOORE, Leeshawn .... 909-593-3511.. 73 B
lmoore@laverne.edu
MOORE, Lesa .... 251-442-2207.... 9 B
lmoore@umobile.edu
MOORE, Leslie .... 253-833-9111 523 B
lmoore@greenriver.edu
MOORE, Lew .... 501-279-4347.. 21 A
lmoore@harding.edu
MOORE, Lew Rita .... 513-861-6400 392 F
lewrita.moore@myunion.edu
MOORE, Linda .... 309-671-2734 152 E
lmoore@methodistcol.edu
MOORE, Linda, L .... 217-581-2412 144 E
llmoore@eiu.edu
MOORE, Lisa .... 925-631-4328.. 61 G
lmoore@stmarys-ca.edu
MOORE, Lisa .... 315-498-2512 337 F
l.r.moore2@sunyocc.edu
MOORE, Lisa, J .... 904-632-3326 105 A
limoore@fscj.edu
MOORE, Lisia .... 702-579-3518 294 P
lmoore@kaplan.edu
MOORE, Loretta, A .... 601-979-0552 267 H
loretta.a.moore@jsums.edu
MOORE, Lynn .... 603-752-1113 297 E
lmoore@ccsnh.edu
MOORE, Lynn .... 606-589-3001 197 D
lynn.moore@kctcs.edu
MOORE, Mable .... 912-358-4400 131 A
mooremj@savannahstate.edu
MOORE, Margie .... 405-262-2552 401 H
moorem@redlandscc.edu
MOORE, Marilyn .... 402-481-8781 289 C
marilyn.moore@bryanhealthcollege.edu
MOORE, Marilyn, A ...... 814-871-7614 419 A
moore037@gannon.edu
MOORE, Mark .... 402-363-5600 294 G
dmark.moore@gmail.com
MOORE, Mark .... 740-351-3207 391 C
mmoore@shawnee.edu
MOORE, Marlene .... 503-370-6285 411 D
moorem@willamette.edu
MOORE, Mary .... 410-287-1053 214 C
mmoore@cecil.edu
MOORE, Mary, C .... 317-788-6150 173 I
moore@uindy.edu
MOORE, Mary, E .... 617-353-3052 224 E
memoore@bu.edu
MOORE, Mary Pat .... 319-296-4255 179 B
mary.moore@hawkeyecollege.edu

MOORE, Mary Rita .... 708-456-0300 161 C
mpatrice@triton.edu
MOORE, Mary-Rita .... 708-456-0300 161 C
mmoore@triton.edu
MOORE, Matt .... 504-280-6218 205 G
msmoore2@uno.edu
MOORE, Matt .... 605-995-2187 452 C
mamoore@dwu.edu
MOORE, Matthew .... 937-512-2781 391 D
matthew.moore157@sinclair.edu
MOORE, Matthew, E ..... 718-951-5024 318 F
matthewm@brooklyn.cuny.edu
MOORE, Mazie .... 314-889-1421 275 B
mmoore@fontbonne.edu
MOORE, Michael .... 941-359-7674 111 F
mmoore@ringling.edu
MOORE, Michael .... 701-777-6772 373 G
michael.moore@research.und.edu
MOORE, Michael, A ..... 231-843-5900 252 H
mamoore@westshore.edu
MOORE, Michael, K ..... 501-686-2533.. 23 F
mmoore@uasys.edu
MOORE, Michael, P ..... 509-865-8585 523 C
moore_m@heritage.edu
MOORE, Michael, R ..... 317-274-0622 168 E
mmoore1@iupui.edu
MOORE, Mickey .... 423-614-8430 457 M
mmoore@leeuniversity.edu
MOORE, Mike .... 949-480-4155.. 66 I
mmoore@soka.edu
MOORE, Mike, K .... 701-788-4706 374 A
Mike.Moore@mayvillestate.edu
MOORE, Mitchell, L ..... 540-665-1298 512 E
mmoore7@su.edu
MOORE, Molly, E .... 605-394-2414 454 B
molly.moore@sdsmt.edu
MOORE, Nancy .... 908-526-1200 305 G
Nancy.Moore@raritanval.edu
MOORE, Natasha .... 251-380-4000.... 7 F
nmoore@shc.edu
MOORE, Paige .... 803-758-2700 443 D
pmoore@allenuniversity.edu
MOORE, Patrice .... 504-671-6535 203 F
pmoore@dcc.edu
MOORE, Perry .... 512-463-7281 488 D
perry.moore@tsus.edu
MOORE, Phil .... 860-727-6941.. 90 F
pmoore@goodwin.edu
MOORE, R. Bartley ...... 202-687-4339.. 95 E
rbm9@georgetown.edu
MOORE, Reggie .... 504-456-3141 201 G
MOORE, Regina .... 870-248-4000.. 20 E
regina.moore@blackrivertech.edu
MOORE, Renee .... 210-805-5864 492 B
reneem@uiwtx.edu
MOORE, Renee .... 865-694-6604 463 E
rmoore@pstcc.edu
MOORE, Robert .... 901-435-1627 457 N
robert_moore@loc.edu
MOORE, Robert, G .... 719-389-6693.. 79 M
robert.moore@coloradocollege.edu
MOORE, Robert, M .... 207-859-1318 211 I
moorer@thomas.edu
MOORE, Robin .... 402-323-3497 293 A
rmoore@southeast.edu
MOORE, Robin, S .... 757-822-1724 517 C
rmoore@tcc.edu
MOORE, Rod .... 316-943-2241 192 E
MOORE, Rodney .... 936-261-9311 484 F
rvmoore@pvamu.edu
MOORE, Roger .... 501-882-8906.. 19 E
rlmoore@asub.edu
MOORE, Roger .... 417-865-2815 274 L
moorer@evangel.edu
MOORE, Russell .... 303-492-2890.. 86 E
rmoore@colorado.edu
MOORE, Sandra .... 803-535-1237 448 C
mooresj@octech.edu
MOORE, Sandy .... 620-365-5116 184 C
moore@allencc.edu
MOORE, Sandy .... 620-227-9329 186 F
smoore@dc3.edu
MOORE, Sandy .... 757-388-3669 512 D
snmoore1@sentara.com
MOORE, Sara .... 212-517-3929 343 A
s.moore@sothebysinstitute.com
MOORE, Scott .... 559-278-0333.. 33 D
scottm@csufresno.edu
MOORE, Shamus .... 580-774-3001 402 G
shamus.moore@swosu.edu
MOORE, Shanee', S ...... 214-860-2138 472 F
ksmoore@dcccd.edu
MOORE, Sharon .... 860-932-4131.. 90 A
smoore@qvcc.commnet.edu
MOORE, Sharyn .... 650-543-3798.. 54 B
smoore@menlo.edu
MOORE, Shelly .... 724-480-3492 416 A
shelly.moore@ccbc.edu
MOORE, Shirley .... 937-778-7861 381 K
smoore@edisonohio.edu

MOORE, Stacey .... 330-972-5770 392 H
staceyjm@uakron.edu
MOORE, Stan .... 817-274-4284 469 E
smoore@bhcarroll.edu
MOORE, Stephan, T ..... 340-692-4188 559 B
stephan.moore@uvi.edu
MOORE, Stephany .... 575-835-5128 311 I
smoore@admin.nmt.edu
MOORE, Steve .... 781-239-3938 222 E
scmoore@babson.edu
MOORE, Steve .... 214-648-7145 496 A
steve.moore@utsouthwestern.edu
MOORE, Steven, C .... 239-590-1919 114 F
cmoore@fgcu.edu
MOORE, Stuart .... 251-380-2240.... 7 F
smoore@shc.edu
MOORE, Stuart .... 251-442-2203.... 9 B
smoore@umobile.edu
MOORE, Sue Hodges ... 859-572-5349 199 A
moores4@nku.edu
MOORE, Sylvia .... 406-683-7115 287 E
sylvia.moore@umwestern.edu
MOORE, Tammie, L ...... 985-380-2957 204 D
tammiemoore1@scl.edu
MOORE, Tammy .... 320-363-5054 254 J
tmoore@csbsju.edu
MOORE, Teresa .... 806-291-3753 496 K
teresam@wbu.edu
MOORE, Teresa, M .... 818-600-4558.. 59 D
tmoore@pgi.edu
MOORE, Tessa .... 607-735-1900 324 J
tmoore@elmira.edu
MOORE, Theresa .... 608-796-3172 542 H
trmoore@viterbo.edu
MOORE, Thomas .... 864-503-5200 451 A
tmoore@uscupstate.edu
MOORE, Thomas, F .... 304-457-6238 529 C
mooretf@ab.edu
MOORE, Thomas, J .... 989-774-3500 240 O
thomas.j.moore@cmich.edu
MOORE, Tim .... 706-379-5166 134 J
tsmoore@yhc.edu
MOORE, Timothy .... 617-353-0750 224 E
mooretj@bu.edu
MOORE, Timothy .... 847-214-7651 144 F
tmoore@elgin.edu
MOORE, Timothy .... 518-255-5323 346 E
mooretw@cobleskill.edu
MOORE, Timothy, E ...... 850-412-5102 114 D
timothy.moore@famu.edu
MOORE, Timothy, J ...... 919-530-7420 370 C
tmoore@nccu.edu
MOORE, Tina .... 217-234-5346 150 B
tmoore@lakeland.cc.il.us
MOORE, Tina .... 417-865-2815 274 L
mooret@evangel.edu
MOORE, Tonja .... 305-348-2168 114 G
tonja.moore@fiu.edu
MOORE, Tony .... 504-520-7449 209 E
tmoore15@xula.edu
MOORE, Vernon, H ...... 903-877-7750 495 C
vernon.moore@uthct.edu
MOORE, Virginia .... 304-357-4987 530 H
virginiamoore@ucwv.edu
MOORE, William (Joe) . 605-688-4692 454 C
william.moore@sdstate.edu
MOORE, Winifred, B ..... 843-953-7477 444 C
bo.moore@citadel.edu
MOORE-COOPER,
Robin .... 937-708-5488 395 E
rmoore-cooper@wilberforce.edu
MOORE-DAVIS,
Feleccia .... 850-201-8680 117 B
mooredaf@tcc.fl.edu
MOORE-GARCIA,
Beverly .... 305-237-2500 108 L
bmoorega@mdc.edu
MOORE-JONES,
Yolanda, V .... 919-536-7201 362 C
jonesym@durhamtech.edu
MOORER, Cassandra ..... 205-366-8980.... 7 G
MOORER, Cleamon .... 734-432-5366 246 B
cmoorer@madonna.edu
MOORER, Glynda, M .... 517-355-2488 246 H
moorerg@msu.edu
MOORES, Lisa .... 301-295-3185 548 D
lisa.moores@usuhs.edu
MOORHEAD, Tracey, A 219-299-3654 255 B
moorhead@cord.edu
MOORMAN, Annorrah .. 309-556-3052 148 A
amoorman@iwu.edu
MOORMAN, Cathy .... 765-998-5123 173 B
ctmoorman@taylor.edu
MOORMAN, Jack, W .... 919-515-3000 370 D
jack_moorman@ncsu.edu
MOORMAN, Nate .... 706-245-7226 124 C
nmoorman@ec.edu
MOORMAN, Thomas .... 817-735-2505 493 B
Thomas.Moorman@unthsc.edu
MOORMON, Josh .... 818-333-3558.. 56 A

MOORS, Dean .... 402-462-4000 289 D
dmoors@cccneb.edu
MOORWOOD, Woody ... 626-815-3855.. 29 B
wmoorwood@apu.edu
MOOS, Michael .... 317-917-3623 171 B
mmoos@martin.edu
MOOS, William, H .... 509-335-0200 528 B
bill.moos@wsu.edu
MOOSE, Richard, E ...... 315-267-2377 346 C
moosere@potsdam.edu
MOOSMAN, Lucas .... 916-660-8103.. 66 E
lmoosman@sierracollege.edu
MOOSMANN, Gloria ..... 216-987-4788 381 A
gloria.moosmann@tri-c.edu
MOOT, Bradley .... 212-678-8035 329 H
brmoot@jtsa.edu
MOOTHART, Kathy .... 319-385-6209 180 A
kathy.moothart@iw.edu
MOOTZ, Allison, C .... 215-885-2360 425 C
amootz@manor.edu
MOOTZ, Jay .... 916-739-7151.. 73 C
jmootz@pacific.edu
MOPPERT, Jan .... 610-499-4177 439 G
jamoppert@widener.edu
MORA, Aracely .... 714-628-4880.. 60 H
mora_aracely@sccollege.edu
MORA, Flora .... 808-984-3517 136 H
fmora@hawaii.edu
MORA, Marc .... 760-872-2000.. 42 J
mmora@deepsprings.edu
MORA, Michelle .... 818-240-1000.. 45 I
mmora@glendale.edu
MORA, Peter, L .... 609-343-4901 299 G
mora@atlantic.edu
MORA, Victoria .... 505-984-6109 312 J
vmora@sjc.edu
MORADILLOS, Alicia ..... 787-834-9595 556 D
amoradillos@uaa.edu
MORAH, Emeka .... 937-708-5685 395 E
emorah@wilberforce.edu
MORAIN, Tom .... 641-784-5053 178 G
tmorain@gracelend.edu
MORALE, Joseph, L ..... 903-927-3232 497 G
jmorale@wileyc.edu
MORALE, Sonja .... 903-566-7059 494 E
smorale@uttyler.edu
MORALES, Ada .... 787-882-2065 556 C
colocaiones@unitecpr.net
MORALES, Adelina, C ... 325-942-2073 489 E
adelina.morales@angelo.edu
MORALES, Aurea .... 718-963-4112 316 J
amorales@boricuacollege.edu
MORALES, Betsy .... 787-832-4040 558 B
MORALES, Brenda, L .... 787-852-1430 552 J
bmorales@hccpr.edu
MORALES, Carlos .... 817-515-5021 484 B
carlos.morales@tccd.edu
MORALES, Cathy, A ...... 212-870-1251 336 B
amorales@nyts.edu
MORALES, Edwin .... 787-786-3030 556 E
emorales@ucb.edu.pr
MORALES, Erica .... 713-221-8443 491 F
moralese@uhd.edu
MORALES, George .... 806-743-2952 490 A
george.morales@ttuhsc.edu
MORALES, George .... 336-917-5405 368 F
george.morales@salem.edu
MORALES, Ileana .... 787-878-5475 553 F
imorales@arecibo.inter.edu
MORALES, Irma .... 787-863-2390 553 I
irma.morales@fajardo.inter.edu
MORALES, James .... 435-797-1712 500 A
james.morales@usu.edu
MORALES, Jessica .... 575-538-6139 314 E
Jessica.Morales@wnmu.edu
MORALES, Jesus .... 408-254-6900.. 55 G
jmorales@nhu.edu
MORALES, Jossue .... 787-891-0925 553 E
jomorales@aguadilla.inter.edu
MORALES, Julie .... 575-538-6238 314 E
moralesj@wnmu.edu
MORALES, Karen, G ...... 787-841-2000 555 F
karen_morales@pucpr.edu
MORALES, Leonardo ..... 787-844-8959 558 D
leonardo.morales@upr.edu
MORALES, Lorraine ...... 520-206-6577.. 17 A
lomorales@pima.edu
MORALES, Lorraine ...... 520-206-7619.. 17 A
lomorales@pima.edu
MORALES, Marisol .... 909-593-3511.. 73 B
mmorales3@laverne.edu
MORALES, Milga .... 718-951-5352 318 F
milga@brooklyn.cuny.edu
MORALES, Milsa .... 787-264-1912 554 C
mmorale@intersg.edu
MORALES, Nancy .... 787-882-2065 556 C
controller@unitecpr.net
MORALES, Nora .... 361-354-2239 470 K
moralesn@coastlbend.edu
MORALES, Oscar .... 787-765-3560 552 E
oscarmorales@edpuniversity.edu

MORALES, Patricia .... 949-824-6701.. 71 C
patricia.morales@uci.edu
MORALES, Rachel .... 207-780-5670 213 A
rmorales@usm.maine.edu
MORALES, Robert .... 805-965-0581.. 64 N
moralesr@sbcc.edu
MORALES, Rosa, M ...... 787-884-3838 550 E
dirdt@atenascollege.edu
MORALES, Rosalia .... 787-864-2222 553 J
rosalia.morales@guayama.inter.edu
MORALES, Rosalie .... 787-780-0070 550 G
rmorales@caribbean.edu
MORALES, Sandra, M ... 787-857-3600 553 G
smmorales@br.inter.edu
MORALES, Sulmarie ..... 787-264-1912 554 C
smorales@intersg.edu
MORALES, Tomas .... 909-537-5002.. 35 A
tmorales@csusb.edu
MORALES MARTÍNEZ,
María .... 787-264-1912 554 C
marimo@intersg.edu
MORALES-TOMASSINI,
Leonardo .... 787-844-8181 557 B
leonardo.morales@upr.edu
MORALES TORRES,
Nilsa .... 787-890-2681 557 C
nilsa.morales@upr.edu
MORAMARCO, Jacques 310-453-8300.. 43 I
jacques@emperors.edu
MORAN, Al .... 850-201-6079 117 B
morana@tcc.fl.edu
MORAN, Carmella .... 630-844-5132 139 L
cmoran@aurora.edu
MORAN, Christyn .... 610-527-0200 434 D
christyn@rosemont.edu
MORAN, Edward .... 703-416-1441 508 F
emoran@ipsciences.edu
MORAN, Eileen, P .... 940-565-2010 492 D
eileen.moran@unt.edu
MORAN, James .... 314-977-3873 281 M
jemoran@slu.edu
MORAN, III, James, D . 605-677-6497 453 F
james.moran@usd.edu
MORAN, James, J .... 615-353-3249 463 C
josh.moran@nscc.edu
MORAN, Jason, R .... 570-321-4122 425 B
moran@lycoming.edu
MORAN, Jay .... 203-392-6025.. 88 F
moranj1@southernct.edu
MORAN, Joseph .... 763-424-0772 260 E
JMoran@nhcc.edu
MORAN, Karen .... 610-921-7510 411 E
kmoran@albright.edu
MORAN, Kathryn, A ..... 317-788-3367 173 I
kmoran@uindy.edu
MORAN, Kathy .... 518-464-8784 325 B
kmoran@excelsior.edu
MORAN, Ken .... 502-456-6504 200 B
kmoran@sullivan.edu
MORAN, Laura, P .... 615-353-3217 463 C
laura.moran@nscc.edu
MORAN, Maggie .... 662-562-3277 269 E
mmoran@northwestms.edu
MORAN, Matt .... 501-450-3814.. 21 C
moran@hendrix.edu
MORAN, Michael .... 413-565-1000 222 G
mmoran@baypath.edu
MORAN, Michael .... 631-656-2196 326 B
michael.moran@ftc.edu
MORAN, Patricia .... 979-830-4157 469 F
pmoran@blinn.edu
MORAN, Patrick .... 307-766-4175 546 K
pmoran5@uwyo.edu
MORAN, Paul, J .... 570-208-5948 422 D
pjmoran@kings.edu
MORAN, Rachel .... 310-825-8202.. 71 D
moran@law.ucla.edu
MORAN, Richard, A ..... 650-543-3744.. 54 B
linda.teutschel@menlo.edu
MORAN, Sam, E .... 540-365-4250 507 H
semoran@ferrum.edu
MORAN, Timothy, R ..... 610-921-7636 411 E
tmoran@albright.edu
MORAN, Virginia .... 760-245-4271.. 75 G
virginia.moran@vvc.edu
MORAN, Yvette .... 602-274-1885.. 16 M
ymoran@pihma.edu
MORANO, Lori .... 518-464-8648 325 B
lmorano@excelsior.edu
MORANSKI, Karen .... 217-206-7440 161 G
moranski.karen@uis.edu
MORANT, Blake, D .... 202-994-1000.. 95 D
morantbd@gwu.edu
MORAVEC, Todd, A ...... 518-564-2072 346 B
moraveta@plattsburgh.edu
MORAY, Yvonne .... 212-472-1500 336 A
ymoray@nysid.edu
MORAZ, Kristen, L .... 561-237-7602 108 E
kmoraz@lynn.edu
MORBER, Timothy, T ... 330-471-8279 385 G
tmorber@malone.edu

MORDACH, John .... 312-942-5600 158 A
john_mordach@rush.edu
MORE, George .... 412-304-0738 418 F
gmore@cci.edu
MOREA, John .... 757-822-1932 517 C
jmorea@tcc.edu
MOREAU, Donald .... 603-641-7350 298 F
dmoreau@anselm.edu
MOREAU, Joseph .... 650-949-6119.. 44 M
moreaujoe@fhda.edu
MOREAU, Sandra, E ..... 619-239-0391.. 36 E
sem@cwsl.edu
MOREAU, Suzanne .... 425-640-1246 522 D
suzanne.moreau@edcc.edu
MORECI, Rick .... 773-325-4283 143 G
rmoreci@depaul.edu
MOREFIELD, Bill, R ...... 423-318-2735 464 C
bill.morefield@ws.edu
MOREHEAD, Allyson .... 410-669-9200 216 F
MOREHEAD, Jere, W .... 706-542-3000 132 H
MOREHEAD, Kaleybra ... 870-543-5963.. 23 C
kmorehead@seark.edu
MOREIRA, Antonio, R ... 410-455-6576 219 F
moreira@umbc.edu
MOREL, Derek .... 504-280-6102 205 G
dmorel@uno.edu
MOREL, Luis .... 212-749-2802 331 I
lmorel@msmnyc.edu
MOREL, Nina .... 615-966-2501 458 C
nina.morel@lipscomb.edu
MORELAND, Keith .... 810-237-6503 251 E
moreland@umich.edu
MORELAND, Kimberly .. 608-663-8334 536 A
kmoreland@edgewood.edu
MORELAND, Milton .... 901-843-3795 460 F
morelandm@rhodes.edu
MORELLI, Brad .... 405-974-3573 403 G
bmorelli@uco.edu
MORELLO, Chanell .... 828-327-7000 361 B
cmorello@cvcc.edu
MORELLO, Debra .... 607-778-5199 344 F
morelloda@sunybroome.edu
MORELLO, John, T .... 540-654-1269 513 I
jmorello@umw.edu
MORELLO, Joseph .... 650-738-4271.. 64 E
morelloj@smccd.edu
MORELOCK, Luann .... 309-655-7353 158 D
luann.morelock@osfhealthcare.org
MORELOCK, Tommy ..... 352-854-2322 100 P
moreloct@cf.edu
MOREMEN, Margaret .... 207-602-2708 213 B
mmoremen@une.edu
MORENA, Pat .... 212-650-7997 318 G
MORENCY, Maurice .... 212-752-1530 330 C
maurice.morency@limcollege.edu
MORENO, Amy, R .... 717-291-3989 418 J
amy.moreno@fandm.edu
MORENO, Anthony .... 800-431-8488.. 28 D
amoreno@aptc.edu
MORENO, Ben .... 650-723-9406.. 68 G
MORENO, Francisco .... 787-738-2161 557 G
francisco.moreno@upr.edu
MORENO, Gettie .... 210-485-0374 466 J
gmoreno107@alamo.edu
MORENO, Linda .... 773-298-3379 158 F
moreno@sxu.edu
MORENO, Luis .... 309-796-5041 140 D
morenol@bhc.edu
MORENO, Marta .... 941-487-4230 115 B
mmoreno@ncf.edu
MORENO, Melissa .... 805-683-8292.. 64 N
melissa.moreno@sbcc.edu
MORENO, Patricia .... 281-873-0262 471 D
p.moreno@commonwealth.edu
MORENO-RIANO,
Gerson .... 757-352-4320 511 G
gmorenoriano@regent.edu
MORENO-WEINERT,
Inez .... 602-243-8134.. 15 F
inez.moreno-weinert@smcmail.maricopa.edu
MORENZ, Tim .... 217-854-3231 140 F
tim.morenz@blackburn.edu
MORERA-GONZÁLEZ,
Angel .... 787-993-8871 557 E
angel.morera1@upr.edu
MORESCHI, Tracy, L ..... 503-255-0332 407 D
tmoreschi@multnomah.edu
MOREST, Vanessa .... 203-857-3368.. 89 H
vmorest@norwalk.edu
MORET, Stephen .... 225-578-3811 204 M
contact@lsufoundation.org
MORETTI, James .... 610-409-3698 438 H
jcooper@ursinus.edu
MORETTI, Linda .... 716-829-7811 324 E
moretti@dyc.edu
MORETZ, Drew .... 919-962-7096 369 C
agmoretz@northcarolina.edu
MOREY, Ann, N .... 818-677-2878.. 34 D
ann.morey@csun.edu
MOREY, Megan .... 413-542-2985 222 A
mmorey@amherst.edu
MOREY, Melanie .... 650-325-5621.. 61 H
melanie.morey@stpatricksseminary.org
MOREY, Robin .... 202-687-3124.. 95 E
rm1469@georgetown.edu
MORGADO, Susan, A ... 508-286-3754 238 B
morgado_susan@wheatoncollege.edu
MORGAN, Allen .... 865-471-3372 455 G
amorgan@cn.edu
MORGAN, Amanda .... 864-388-8971 447 E
amorgan@lander.edu
MORGAN, Andrea .... 303-273-3021.. 80 O
asalazar@mines.edu
MORGAN, Andy, L .... 618-453-7524 159 H
amorgan@sdev.siu.edu
MORGAN, Anna, B .... 731-661-5410 464 G
amorgan@uu.edu
MORGAN, Annette .... 903-983-8217 477 A
amorgan@kilgore.edu
MORGAN, Barbara .... 617-879-2118 238 C
bmorgan@wheelock.edu
MORGAN, Betsy .... 608-785-8042 539 G
bmorgan@uwlax.edu
MORGAN, Betsy, S .... 269-467-9945 243 A
bmorgan@glenoaks.edu
MORGAN, Brian, J .... 858-499-0202.. 40 G
netadmin@coleman.edu
MORGAN, Bronwyn .... 870-762-3172.. 19 C
bmorgan@anc.edu
MORGAN, Bruce .... 423-775-7233 455 F
bruce.morgan@bryan.edu
MORGAN, Bryant .... 413-644-4400 222 F
MORGAN, Bryant .... 802-451-7690 502 B
bmorgan@marlboro.edu
MORGAN, Camella .... 253-833-9111 523 B
cmorgan@greenriver.edu
MORGAN, Carolyn .... 205-387-0511.... 2 B
cmorgan@bscc.edu
MORGAN, Catherine ..... 239-433-8047 104 G
cmorgan@fsw.edu
MORGAN, Chris .... 951-343-4369.. 30 D
cmorgan@calbaptist.edu
MORGAN, David .... 765-361-6382 175 B
morgand@wabash.edu
MORGAN, David .... 423-775-7597 455 F
morganda@bryan.edu
MORGAN, Deborah .... 918-540-6312 398 L
demorgan@neo.edu
MORGAN, Derek .... 303-273-3288.. 80 O
dmorgan@mines.edu
MORGAN, Dustin .... 701-349-5402 375 G
dmorgan@trinitybiblecollege.edu
MORGAN, Elizabeth .... 909-621-8101.. 39 F
elizabeth.morgan@cmc.edu
MORGAN, Emily .... 717-262-2006 440 D
emily.morgan@wilson.edu
MORGAN, Erin .... 509-359-4971 522 C
emorgan@ewu.edu
MORGAN, Gilbert .... 443-885-3125 217 C
gilbert.morgan@morgan.edu
MORGAN, Ginny .... 510-841-9230.. 77 I
vmorgan@wi.edu
MORGAN, Heath .... 660-831-4087 279 D
morganh@moval.edu
MORGAN, Helen .... 912-525-5000 130 H
hmorgan@scad.edu
MORGAN, Howard, M .. 716-286-8772 336 E
hmorgan@niagara.edu
MORGAN, J .... 859-985-3019 193 F
morganjoh@berea.edu
MORGAN, J. Reid .... 336-758-5122 372 G
jrm@wfu.edu
MORGAN, Jacquelyn .... 920-565-1041 536 Q
morganjs@lakeland.edu
MORGAN, James, F ..... 609-497-7705 305 B
james.morgan@ptsem.edu
MORGAN, Janie, M .... 608-785-8495 539 G
jspencer@uwlax.edu
MORGAN, Janifer .... 706-385-1463 130 C
janifer.morgan@point.edu
MORGAN, Jason .... 256-352-8225.. 10 A
jason.morgan@wallacestate.edu
MORGAN, Jason .... 734-477-8992 251 J
jtmorgan@wccnet.edu
MORGAN, Jeff .... 713-743-3455 491 D
jjmorgan@central.uh.edu
MORGAN, Jeffrey .... 480-219-6111 271 G
jmorgan@atsu.edu
MORGAN, Jim .... 575-461-4413 311 C
jimm@mesalands.edu
MORGAN, Joanne, L .... 919-658-8558 369 B
jmorgan@umo.edu
MORGAN, John .... 973-684-5402 304 F
jmorgan@pccc.edu
MORGAN, John .... 928-717-7721.. 18 L
john.morgan@yc.edu
MORGAN, John .... 203-582-5359.. 91 E
john.morgan@quinnipiac.edu
MORGAN, John, G .... 615-366-4403 461 B
chancellor@tbr.edu
MORGAN, Joshua .... 575-492-2769 311 J
jmorgan@nmjc.edu
MORGAN, Judy .... 802-776-5236 501 G
judy.morgan@csj.edu
MORGAN, Julie .... 585-245-5704 345 D
morgan@geneseo.edu
MORGAN, Karen .... 201-200-3003 304 C
kmorgan@njcu.edu
MORGAN, Karrie .... 605-331-6672 454 E
karrie.morgan@usiouxfalls.edu
MORGAN, Kelly .... 863-638-7244 118 L
kelly.morgan@warner.edu
MORGAN, Ken .... 478-825-6304 124 E
morgank@fvsu.edu
MORGAN, Kristy .... 903-233-4410 477 G
kristymorgan@letu.edu
MORGAN, JR., Leroy ... 706-821-8235 129 H
lmorgan@paine.edu
MORGAN, Lissa .... 901-572-2441 455 C
lissa.morgan@bchs.edu
MORGAN, Louis .... 423-614-8567 457 M
lmorgan@leeuniversity.edu
MORGAN, Lucille .... 847-947-5208 153 H
Lucille.Morgan@nl.edu
MORGAN, Luke .... 616-222-3000 245 D
lmorgan@kuyper.edu
MORGAN, Margaret ..... 706-355-5034 120 G
mmorgan@athenstech.edu
MORGAN, Mark .... 407-708-2224 113 A
morganm@seminolestate.edu
MORGAN, Mark, D .... 910-962-3719 372 A
morganm@uncw.edu
MORGAN, Marnie .... 800-962-7682 285 I
mmorgan@wma.edu
MORGAN, Mary .... 757-340-2121 506 E
stuadvcvab@centura.edu
MORGAN, Melissa .... 215-574-9600 421 A
mmorgan@hussianart.edu
MORGAN, Michael .... 901-843-3810 460 F
morganm@rhodes.edu
MORGAN, Michael, D .. 518-564-3066 346 B
morganmd@plattsburgh.edu
MORGAN, Michael, D .. 205-726-2727.... 6 F
mmorgan@samford.edu
MORGAN, Mike .... 510-666-8248.. 26 C
mmorgan@aimc.edu
MORGAN, Nancy .... 386-506-4579 101 I
morgann@DaytonaState.edu
MORGAN, Natasha .... 432-685-4534 478 F
nmorgan@midland.edu
MORGAN, Pamela .... 940-397-4785 478 G
pamela.morgan@mwsu.edu
MORGAN, Patricia .... 707-256-7305.. 55 E
pmorgan@napavalley.edu
MORGAN, Peggy .... 303-914-6337.. 85 C
peggy.morgan@rrcc.edu
MORGAN, R. Gregory ... 617-452-2082 233 C
MORGAN, Rachel, A .... 651-631-5249 265 D
ramorgan@unwsp.edu
MORGAN, Randy .... 559-791-2232.. 49 G
rmorgan@portervillecollege.edu
MORGAN, JR.,
Raymond, V .... 361-570-4332 492 A
morganrv@uhv.edu
MORGAN, Robert .... 402-228-8272 293 A
bmorgan@southeast.edu
MORGAN, Russell .... 309-298-1066 163 A
re-morgan@wiu.edu
MORGAN, Scott .... 360-867-6913 522 J
sustainabilitydirector@evergreen.edu
MORGAN, Sharon, E .... 973-596-5560 304 D
sharon.e.morgan@njit.edu
MORGAN, Sonja .... 253-566-5322 527 C
smorgan@tacomacc.edu
MORGAN, Stephen .... 626-571-8811.. 74 E
presidentoffice@uwest.edu
MORGAN, Stephen, R .. 801-832-2550 501 C
smorgan@westminstercollege.edu
MORGAN, Steve .... 602-944-3335.. 11 D
smorgan@aicag.edu
MORGAN, Steve .... 504-398-2228 206 E
smorgan@olhcc.edu
MORGAN, Steve .... 740-695-9500 377 F
smorgan@belmontcollege.edu
MORGAN, Theresa .... 845-574-4289 339 I
tmorgan5@sunyrockland.edu
MORGAN, Tyler, S .... 801-524-8161 498 J
tmorgan@ldsbc.edu
MORGAN, Warren, H .... 413-542-2267 222 A
whmorgan@amherst.edu
MORGAN, Wendy .... 304-637-1341 529 I
morganw@dewv.edu
MORGAN-CLEMENT,
Linda .... 330-263-2602 380 E
lclement@wooster.edu
MORGAN FOSTER,
Stacey .... 509-359-6015 522 C
sfoster@ewu.edu
MORGAN RIGGS, Janet 717-337-6010 419 C
jriggs@gettysburg.edu
MORGAN-RUSSELL,
Simon .... 419-372-2340 377 I
smorgan@bgsu.edu
MORGAN-ZAYACHEK,
Eileen .... 607-436-2520 344 B
eileen.morganzayachek@oneonta.edu
MORGANO, Sam, V ...... 330-569-5335 383 F
morganosv@hiram.edu
MORGANSTEIN, Penny . 212-472-1500 336 A
pmorganstein@mysid.edu
MORGENSTERN,
Patricia .... 269-467-9945 243 A
pmorgenstern@glenoaks.edu
MORGENSTERN, Teresa 239-489-9061 104 G
tmorgenstern@fsw.edu
MORGENTHALER,
Diane, S .... 203-392-6300.. 88 F
morgenthald1@southernct.edu
MORI, Darryl .... 626-396-4288.. 28 J
darryl.mori@artcenter.edu
MORIARTY, Beth .... 508-531-1277 229 C
bmoriarty@bridgew.edu
MORIARTY, Deb .... 410-704-2055 221 A
dmoriarty@towson.edu
MORIARTY, George ...... 978-659-1224 232 E
gmoriarty@necc.mass.edu
MORIARTY, Joan .... 973-618-3394 300 H
jmoriarty@caldwell.edu
MORIARTY, John .... 305-899-3957.. 99 B
jmoriarty@barry.edu
MORIARTY, Laura .... 732-571-3405 303 G
lmoriart@monmouth.edu
MORIARTY, Maureen .... 802-831-1265 503 E
mmoriarty@vermontlaw.edu
MORIARTY, Sean .... 315-312-5500 346 A
sean.moriarty@oswego.edu
MORIATY, Erin, T .... 773-508-3075 151 E
emoriar@luc.edu
MORICONI, Jill .... 814-254-0404 415 F
jmoriconi@pa.gov
MORICONI,
Kimberly, A .... 816-604-6544 277 G
kim.moriconi@mcckc.edu
MORIMOTO, Yash .... 505-428-1765 313 A
yash.morimoto@sfcc.edu
MORIN, Christine .... 207-755-5215 210 L
cmorin@cmcc.edu
MORIN, Erin .... 336-770-3296 372 B
morine@uncsa.edu
MORIN, III,
Frederick, C .... 802-656-2156 503 C
frederick.morin@uvm.edu
MORIN, Jeff .... 414-847-3210 537 F
jeffreymorin@miad.edu
MORIN, Jenni .... 830-372-8049 487 C
jmorin@tlu.edu
MORIN, Jodie .... 712-749-2097 176 D
morinj@bvu.edu
MORIN, Karen, M .... 570-577-3293 413 E
karen.morin@bucknell.edu
MORIN, Kevin .... 414-277-7129 537 G
morin@msoe.edu
MORIN, Kevin, A .... 414-277-7129 537 G
morin@msoe.edu
MORIN, Regina .... 660-785-7468 283 E
rmorin@truman.edu
MORIN, Stephen, J .... 203-932-7268.. 92 G
smorin@newhaven.edu
MORIN, Tammy .... 701-477-7862 375 H
tgmorin@tm.edu
MORINEC, Maire .... 707-864-7000.. 66 J
maire.morinec@solano.edu
MORISHITA, Leroy, M .. 510-885-3877.. 33 C
leroy.morishita@csueastbay.edu
MORISSEAU, Natalie, L 973-353-5872 307 C
natalia.morisseau@rutgers.edu
MORITZ, Thorsten .... 651-255-6126 264 F
tmoritz@unitedseminary.edu
MORLA, Lorna, M .... 787-257-7373 555 L
lmmorta@suagm.edu
MORLAN, Tom .... 503-255-0332 407 D
tmorlan@multnomah.edu
MORLEY, Alicia .... 956-665-2103 494 C
alicia@utpa.edu
MORLEY, Del .... 660-562-1363 280 A
dmorley@nwmissouri.edu
MORLEY, Elizabeth .... 607-431-4122 327 B
morleye@hartwick.edu
MORLEY, John .... 312-850-7230 142 E
jmorley@ccc.edu
MORLEY, Kathleen .... 254-710-2061 469 D
kathleen_morley@baylor.edu
MORLEY, Mary, N .... 626-395-6354.. 31 D
mmorley@caltech.edu
MORLEY, Richard, H .... 949-451-5472.. 67 E
rmorley@ivc.edu
MORLEY, Sandy .... 517-264-7193 250 B
smorley@sienaheights.edu
MORLEY, Steve .... 765-998-5344 173 B
stmorley@taylor.edu

MORLEY, Yvonne, Y ..... 859-238-5220 194 E
yvonne.morley@centre.edu
MORLEY-MOWER,
Cynthia .... 213-763-7072.. 52 A
morleycn@lattc.edu
MORLIER, Margaret, M 770-720-5579 130 E
mmm@reinhardt.edu
MORLOCK, David, R ..... 419-530-1448 394 E
david.morlock@utoledo.edu
MORNINGSTAR, Ellen ... 585-271-3657 340 B
registrar@stbernards.edu
MORNINGSTAR, Kevin .. 760-750-4775.. 35 B
kmorningstar@csusm.edu
MORNINGSTAR, Scott .. 406-586-3585 287 B
scott.morningstar@montanabiblecollege.edu
MORO, Martin .... 734-995-7589 241 F
martin.moro@cuaa.edu
MORODOMI, Joyce, K .. 559-323-2100.. 63 C
jmorodomi@sjcl.edu
MOROI, Katsumi .... 213-613-2200.. 67 G
kmoroi@sciarc.edu
MORONEY, James .... 617-254-2610 236 B
rector@sjs.edu
MORONEY, Mary, F ...... 401-232-6298 441 B
mmoroney@bryant.edu
MORONEY, Michael, R . 651-631-5482 265 D
mrmoroney@unwsp.edu
MORONG, Andrew .... 207-755-5273 210 L
amorong@cmcc.edu
MOROONEY, Kevin, M . 814-865-3540 428 C
kxm@psu.edu
MOROSKO, Linda .... 330-494-6170 391 J
lmorosko@starkstate.edu
MOROSOFF, Wendy ...... 914-251-6370 346 D
wendy.morosoff@purchase.edu
MOROTTI, Allan .... 907-474-6440.. 10 I
aamorotti@alaska.edu
MOROWSKI, James, R . 701-788-4619 374 A
james.morowski@mayvillestate.edu
MORPHEW, Vonnie .... 254-659-7502 475 A
ymorphew@hillcollege.edu
MORRAL, Melissa .... 585-340-9633 321 G
mmorral@crcds.edu
MORRELL, Chuck .... 406-496-4325 288 C
cmorrell@mtech.edu
MORRELL, Erin .... 203-773-8541.. 87 M
emorrell@albertus.edu
MORRELL, Matthew, D . 763-417-8250 254 E
MORRELL, Nancy .... 303-546-3513.. 84 B
nancym@naropa.edu
MORRELL, Richard .... 402-472-2025 293 H
richard.morrell@unl.edu
MORRELL, Sarah .... 508-678-2811 231 B
sarah.morrell@bristolcc.edu
MORRICE, Pelema, I ..... 610-526-6522 413 D
pmorrice@brynmawr.edu
MORRILL, Allen .... 724-589-2124 436 E
amorrill@thiel.edu
MORRILL, Bill .... 575-492-2791 311 J
bmorrill@nmjc.edu
MORRILL, Deborah, H .. 210-567-6395 495 B
morrill@uthscsa.edu
MORRILL, Donald, D .... 813-258-7409 118 H
dmorrill@ut.edu
MORRILL, Luke .... 904-256-8000 106 Q
lmorril1@ju.edu
MORRILL, Luke .... 904-256-7538 106 Q
lmoril1@ju.edu
MORRIS, Aaron .... 757-873-1111 507 G
aaron.morris@zenith.org
MORRIS, Adam .... 562-903-4714.. 29 F
adam.morris@biola.edu
MORRIS, Amy .... 620-431-2820 189 J
amorris@neosho.edu
MORRIS, Amy .... 702-254-7577 296 B
amy.morris@northwestcareercollege.edu
MORRIS, Ann .... 419-824-3694 385 F
amorris@lourdes.edu
MORRIS, Ann .... 704-216-3542 365 F
ann.morris@rccc.edu
MORRIS, Barbara .... 970-247-7314.. 82 I
morris_b@fortlewis.edu
MORRIS, Barbara .... 410-532-5367 217 F
bmorris@ndm.edu
MORRIS, Ben .... 252-940-6374 360 B
ben.morris@beaufortccc.edu
MORRIS, Bernadette ..... 845-257-3101 344 A
morrisb@newpaltz.edu
MORRIS, Beth .... 828-766-1257 364 A
bmorris@mayland.edu
MORRIS, Bevan, H .... 641-472-8194 181 A
president@mum.edu
MORRIS, Brenda .... 870-584-4471.. 24 E
bmorris@cccua.edu
MORRIS, Brett .... 859-622-3840 194 L
admissions@eku.edu
MORRIS, Brett .... 859-622-8835 194 L
brett.morris@eku.edu
MORRIS, Carlene .... 785-830-2702 187 F
cmorris@haskell.edu
MORRIS, Carlton, E ...... 334-724-4191.... 8 B
cmorris@mytu.tuskegee.edu
MORRIS, Charles .... 214-860-2392 472 F
cmorris@dcccd.edu
MORRIS, Clark .... 816-415-5997 285 K
morrisc@william.jewell.edu
MORRIS, Clark, W .... 816-415-5997 285 K
morrisc@william.jewell.edu
MORRIS, Claudia .... 352-365-3539 107 X
morrisc@lssc.edu
MORRIS, Connie .... 843-661-8315 446 C
connie.morris@fdtc.edu
MORRIS, Corinne .... 402-844-7361 292 G
corinne@northeast.edu
MORRIS, Craig .... 651-793-1272 259 E
craig.morris@metrostate.edu
MORRIS, Craig .... 541-552-6319 409 G
cmorris@sou.edu
MORRIS, Dan .... 702-651-5500 295 C
dan.morris@csn.edu
MORRIS, Daryl .... 334-244-3295.... 2 A
dmorris@aum.edu
MORRIS, Deborah .... 304-357-4849 530 H
deborahmorris@ucwv.edu
MORRIS, Delesa .... 561-803-2022 109 G
delesa_morris@pba.edu
MORRIS, Diana .... 800-567-2344 535 F
dmorris@menominee.edu
MORRIS, Don .... 314-968-7444 285 G
morrisdo@webster.edu
MORRIS, Dottie .... 603-358-2206 299 D
dmorris@keene.edu
MORRIS, Earl .... 808-675-3406 134 M
morrise@byuh.edu
MORRIS, Emily, F .... 716-375-2334 340 C
emorris@sbu.edu
MORRIS, Gary .... 315-312-2255 346 A
gary.morris@oswego.edu
MORRIS, Gary .... 512-448-8731 481 B
gmorris1@stedwards.edu
MORRIS, Genevieve ...... 251-380-3020.... 7 F
gmorris@shc.edu
MORRIS, Geri .... 419-998-3106 394 B
geri@unoh.edu
MORRIS, Glenn .... 352-335-2332.. 97 F
MORRIS, Henry .... 507-389-1150 260 A
henry.morris@mnsu.edu
MORRIS, Jacqueline ...... 205-366-8950.... 7 G
jmorris@stillman.edu
MORRIS, Jaime .... 661-726-1911.. 70 I
jaime.morris@uav.edu
MORRIS, Jason .... 325-674-2830 466 I
morrisj@acu.edu
MORRIS, Jeff .... 620-252-7177 186 C
jeffm@coffeyville.edu
MORRIS, Jeffery, B .... 785-532-6415 188 H
jbmorris@ksu.edu
MORRIS, Jeremy .... 731-265-1703 457 K
jkmorris@lanecollege.edu
MORRIS, John .... 928-523-6187.. 16 C
John.Morris@nau.edu
MORRIS, John .... 808-739-8555 135 A
jmorris@chaminade.edu
MORRIS, John .... 617-627-3232 237 C
john.morris@tufts.edu
MORRIS, John, K .... 801-581-4466 499 K
john.morris@legal.utah.edu
MORRIS, Joseph .... 303-797-5801.. 79 A
joseph.morris@arapahoe.edu
MORRIS, Juanita .... 601-979-2914 267 H
juanita.m.morris@jsume.edu
MORRIS, Juanita .... 731-426-7533 457 K
jmorris@lanecollege.edu
MORRIS, Julia, M .... 304-457-6205 529 C
auviljm@ab.edu
MORRIS, Karen .... 803-641-3489 450 C
karenm@usca.edu
MORRIS, Katherine, W . 937-775-2809 396 A
kathy.morris@wright.edu
MORRIS, Kathryn .... 317-940-9903 164 L
kmorris@butler.edu
MORRIS, Kay .... 229-333-2120 134 I
kay.morris@wiregrass.edu
MORRIS, Kelli .... 256-326-2602.... 2 F
kdm@calhoun.edu
MORRIS, Kelly, M .... 770-720-5897 130 E
km@reinhardt.edu
MORRIS, Ken .... 570-586-2400 435 H
kmorris@summitu.edu
MORRIS, Kevin .... 281-922-3479 481 G
kevin.morris@sjcd.edu
MORRIS, Kevin .... 936-294-1794 489 A
kmorris@shsu.edu
MORRIS, Kimberly .... 770-412-4005 132 B
kmorris@sctech.edu
MORRIS, Kizzy .... 570-422-2831 430 F
registrar@esu.edu
MORRIS, Kyle .... 307-755-2160 547 D
kmorris@wyotech.edu
MORRIS, Laura .... 832-813-6793 477 I
laura.k.morris@lonestar.edu
MORRIS, Laura, M .... 302-295-1179.. 94 G
laura.m.morris@wilmu.edu
MORRIS, Lauren, N ...... 248-204-2309 245 J
lmorris2@ltu.edu
MORRIS, Lawrence, J ... 202-319-5142.. 95 A
morrisl@cua.edu
MORRIS, Lela .... 817-598-6488 497 A
morris@wc.edu
MORRIS, Loren, L .... 620-665-3523 188 A
morrisl@hutchcc.edu
MORRIS, Malcolm, L ... 404-872-3593 121 A
mmorris@johnmarshall.edu
MORRIS, Marie, S .... 765-641-4020 164 B
msmorris@anderson.edu
MORRIS, Matt .... 661-654-6459.. 32 G
morris-matt@aramark.com
MORRIS, Melissa, M .... 334-844-7771.... 1 G
morrimm@auburn.edu
MORRIS, Nerissa, E ..... 305-284-4476 118 A
nmorris@miami.edu
MORRIS, Nora .... 763-433-1632 257 P
nora.morris@anokaramsey.edu
MORRIS, Paul .... 435-652-7504 499 M
pmorris@dixie.edu
MORRIS, Reggie .... 323-241-5200.. 51 I
morrisr@lasc.edu
MORRIS, Renea .... 740-593-2563 389 H
morrisr@ohio.edu
MORRIS, Rick .... 864-977-7777 448 A
publicsafety@ngu.edu
MORRIS, Rob .... 615-230-3312 464 B
rob.morris@volstate.edu
MORRIS, Robert .... 724-287-8711 413 G
MORRIS, Robert, D ...... 404-413-2502 126 D
robinmorris@gsu.edu
MORRIS, Robert, J .... 765-285-1300 164 D
rmorris@bsu.edu
MORRIS, Sandra, L ...... 843-792-8720 447 G
morriss@musc.edu
MORRIS, Sara, B .... 316-978-5520 192 D
sara.morris@wichita.edu
MORRIS, Scott .... 303-735-3979.. 86 E
scott.morris@Colorado.EDU
MORRIS, Scott .... 713-683-3817 482 C
MORRIS, Steve .... 270-789-5017 194 D
srmorris@campbellsville.edu
MORRIS, Steve .... 606-539-4209 200 F
steve.morris@ucumberlands.edu
MORRIS, Tama .... 704-337-2363 368 B
morrist@queens.edu
MORRIS, Tammy, H ...... 336-322-2150 364 G
Tammy.Morris@piedmontcc.edu
MORRIS, Todd .... 575-461-4413 311 C
toddm@mesalands.edu
MORRIS, Tommy .... 256-824-6576.... 9 A
tommy.morris@uah.edu
MORRIS, Tommy, A ..... 225-216-8364 202 N
morrist@mybrcc.edu
MORRIS, Tracy .... 309-694-8970 146 C
tracy.morris@icc.edu
MORRIS, Valerie, B ...... 843-953-8222 445 B
morrisv@cofc.edu
MORRIS, Wanda .... 310-660-3281.. 43 G
wmorris@elcamino.edu
MORRIS, Wendi .... 478-296-6179 129 D
wmorris@oftc.edu
MORRIS, William, G ..... 315-267-2579 346 C
morriswg@potsdam.edu
MORRIS, William, R ..... 512-492-3060 468 A
wmorris@aoma.edu
MORRIS WOOD, JR.,
Dossie .... 910-843-5304 359 L
MORRISETT, Greg .... 607-255-9188 323 C
greg.morrisett@cornell.edu
MORRISETTE, Joanna .... 919-735-5151 367 A
jmmorrisette@waynecc.edu
MORRISON, Allen .... 602-978-7203.. 11 J
allen.morrison@asu.edu
MORRISON, Angel .... 785-460-5418 186 D
angel.morrison@colbycc.edu
MORRISON, Annie .... 208-459-5016 137 J
amorrison@collegeofidaho.edu
MORRISON, Barry, F .... 401-232-6017 441 B
bmorriso@bryant.edu
MORRISON, Betty .... 630-829-6347 140 A
bmorrison@ben.edu
MORRISON, Brenda, M 443-412-2409 215 D
bmorrison@harford.edu
MORRISON,
Carberta, A .... 856-225-2949 307 A
cammor@camden.rutgers.edu
MORRISON, Carol .... 239-513-1122 106 E
cmorrison@hodges.edu
MORRISON, Cindi .... 352-854-2322 100 P
morrisoc@cf.edu
MORRISON, Darrell ...... 210-784-2000 486 B
drmorris@tamusa.tamus.edu
MORRISON, David .... 770-534-6167 121 G
dmorrison@brenau.edu
MORRISON, Don .... 641-628-5280 176 E
morrisond@central.edu
MORRISON, Edwina ..... 406-444-0326 287 C
emorrison@montana.edu
MORRISON, Gail .... 651-450-3512 259 A
gmorris@inverhills.edu
MORRISON, Jason .... 918-647-1230 397 C
jlmorrison@carlalbert.edu
MORRISON, Jean .... 617-353-2230 224 E
morrison@bu.edu
MORRISON, Jennifer .... 503-244-0726 404 G
jennifermorrison@achs.edu
MORRISON,
Jennifer, K .... 508-767-7007 222 D
jemorrison@assumption.edu
MORRISON, John .... 856-351-2628 308 B
jmorrison@salemcc.edu
MORRISON, Joseph, B . 508-767-7312 222 D
jmorrison@assumption.edu
MORRISON, Julie .... 734-973-5010 251 J
jmorriso@wccnet.edu
MORRISON, Karen .... 407-823-6479 115 C
karen.morrison@ucf.edu
MORRISON, Katrina ...... 918-270-6421 401 C
katrina.morrison@ptstulsa.edu
MORRISON, Kim .... 510-723-6762.. 37 N
kmorrison@chabotcollege.edu
MORRISON, Kirk .... 858-513-9240.. 29 A
kirk.morrison@ashford.edu
MORRISON, Laura .... 252-335-0821 361 G
laura_morrison@albemarle.edu
MORRISON, Lolita .... 404-297-9522 126 A
morrisonl@gptc.org
MORRISON, Marty, G ... 540-654-2287 513 I
mmorris3@umw.edu
MORRISON, Michael ...... 626-650-2363.. 46 C
MORRISON, Michael, L 812-888-5736 174 F
mmorrison@vinu.edu
MORRISON, Nancy, J ... 212-998-4924 336 C
nancy.morrison@nyu.edu
MORRISON, Pamela ..... 916-558-2088.. 53 B
morrisp@scc.losrios.edu
MORRISON,
Rebecca, L .... 414-955-4949 537 C
rmorriso@mcw.edu
MORRISON, Ricky .... 419-227-3141 394 B
rmorrison@unoh.edu
MORRISON, Robert ...... 312-261-3372 153 H
rob.morrison@nl.edu
MORRISON, Rodney ..... 631-632-6857 344 C
rodney.morrison@stonybrook.edu
MORRISON, Rodney ..... 419-448-2391 383 C
rmorriso@heidelberg.edu
MORRISON, Roxanne ... 619-260-4749.. 74 B
roxannemorrison@sandiego.edu
MORRISON, Scott .... 775-445-3000 296 A
scott.morrison@wnc.edu
MORRISON, Scott, D .... 540-828-5376 505 F
smorriso@bridgewater.edu
MORRISON, Sharon ..... 580-745-3172 402 D
smorrison@se.edu
MORRISON, Steven ...... 229-243-6855 121 D
steven.morrison@bainbridge.edu
MORRISON, Thomas ..... 812-855-6992 167 I
morrison@indiana.edu
MORRISON, Tom .... 812-855-6992 167 J
morrisot@indiana.edu
MORRISON, William ..... 973-684-6741 304 F
wmorrison@pccc.edu
MORRISON-BEEDY,
Dianne .... 813-974-2191 116 B
dmbeedy@health.usf.edu
MORRISON-FRONCKOWIAK,
Lisa, T .... 716-878-4500 345 B
morrislt@buffalostate.edu
MORRISON GOINGS,
Amy, M .... 425-739-8200 523 I
amy.goings@lwtech.edu
MORRISON-SHETLAR,
Alison .... 828-227-7495 372 C
aimorrison@wcu.edu
MORRISS, Andrew, P ... 817-212-4100 485 C
MORRISS-OLSON,
Melissa .... 413-565-1000 222 G
mmolson@baypath.edu
MORRISSEY, Ann, M .... 401-874-4846 442 E
morrissey@uri.edu
MORRISSEY, Jeff, P ...... 417-836-5770 279 A
jeffmorrissey@missouristate.edu
MORRISSEY, Sharon ..... 804-819-4972 514 G
smorrissey@vccs.edu
MORRISSEY, Shawn ..... 508-856-2265 229 B
shawn.morrissey@umassmed.edu
MORRO, Robert .... 610-519-4589 439 A
robert.morro@villanova.edu
MORROBEL-SOSA,
Anny .... 718-960-8111 319 C
morrobel.sosa@lehman.cuny.edu
MORRONE, Anastasia ... 317-274-3479 168 E
amorrone@iupui.edu
MORROW, Andrea .... 567-661-7104 390 D
andrea_morrow@owens.edu

MORROW, Barbara, A .. 314-340-5763 275 G morrowb@hssu.edu
MORROW, Bill, J .... 302-857-1245.. 94 A bmorrow@dtcc.edu
MORROW, Carol, K ...... 212-998-4798 336 C carol.morrow@nyu.edu
MORROW, David .... 215-222-4200 434 A dmorrow@walnuthillcollege.edu
MORROW, David, M .... 518-736-3622 326 D dmorrow@fmcc.suny.edu
MORROW, Dorothy .... 402-557-7296 289 B dorothy.morrow@bellevue.edu
MORROW, Erik .... 512-472-4133 482 E emorrow@ssw.edu
MORROW, Frances .... 330-490-7312 395 C fmorrow@walsh.edu
MORROW, Jeffrey, S .... 330-665-1084 388 G j.morrow@ocm.edu
MORROW, Jessica .... 918-335-6268 400 I jmorrow@okwu.edu
MORROW, Joyce .... 319-273-2701 176 A joyce.morrow@uni.edu
MORROW, Kieran .... 646-312-4542 318 C Kieran.Morrow@baruch.cuny.edu
MORROW, Liz .... 573-681-5011 276 K morrowl@lincolnu.edu
MORROW, Marjann ...... 325-574-7608 497 E mmorrow@wtc.edu
MORROW, Michael .... 651-523-1660 256 J mmorrow001@luthersem.edu
MORROW, Michelle .... 315-792-3111 351 G mmmorrow@utica.edu
MORROW, Rebecca ...... 304-793-6591 533 B rmorrow@osteo.wvsom.edu
MORROW, S. Rex .... 219-785-5550 172 A smorrow@pnc.edu
MORROW, Wanda .... 713-646-1825 482 H wmorrow@stcl.edu
MORROW-JENSEN, Amanda .... 408-453-9900.. 46 L amorrow-jensen@henley-putnam.edu
MORSBERGER, Michael, J .... 407-882-1250 115 C Mike.Mors@ucf.edu
MORSCHES, Michael .... 708-974-5310 153 D morschesm@morainevalley.edu
MORSE, Alicia .... 410-777-2587 213 E ammorse@aacc.edu
MORSE, Austin .... 616-988-1000 241 E austin.m@compass.edu
MORSE, Charles, C ...... 508-831-5540 238 G cmorse@wpi.edu
MORSE, Joanna .... 802-862-9616 501 E jmorse@burlington.edu
MORSE, Rachel .... 907-786-1278.. 10 H rlmorse@uaa.alaska.edu
MORSE, Susan .... 740-427-5926 384 P morses@kenyon.edu
MORSE, William .... 253-879-2808 527 F wmorse@pugetsound.edu
MORSETTE, Clarice .... 406-395-4875 288 I camorsette@yahoo.com
MORSMAN, Elaine .... 607-587-4061 347 D morsmaem@alfredstate.edu
MORSOVILLO, Michael . 708-524-6793 144 C morsomike@dom.edu
MORSS, Susan .... 520-515-3662.. 13 B morsss@cochise.edu
MORT, Dale .... 717-569-7071 423 C dmort@lbc.edu
MORTALI, Jill, M .... 603-646-3007 297 G jill.m.mortali@dartmouth.edu
MORTENSEN, Brad .... 801-626-6002 500 C bmortensen@weber.edu
MORTENSEN, Daniel, W .... 610-917-1412 438 G dwmortensen@valleyforge.edu
MORTENSEN, John .... 435-797-1110 500 A john.mortensen@usu.edu
MORTENSEN, John .... 307-332-2930 547 C jmortensen@wyomingcatholiccollege.com
MORTENSEN, Larry .... 719-587-7402.. 78 I lsmorten@adams.edu
MORTENSEN, Norm ...... 304-205-6600 531 A norm.mortensen@bridgevalley.edu
MORTENSON, Donald, W .... 206-281-2522 526 D dmort@spu.edu
MORTENSON, Gary .... 254-710-1221 469 D Gary_Mortenson@baylor.edu
MORTHLAND, Betsey .... 309-796-5049 140 D morthlandb@bhc.edu
MORTHLAND, Tim .... 618-937-2127 153 F
MORTIMER, Gayle .... 620-862-5252 184 H gayle.mortimer@barclaycollege.edu
MORTIMER, Ian .... 585-389-2525 334 B
MORTIMER, Nathan, J .. 330-972-6501 392 H njm9@uakron.edu
MORTIMER, Theresa ..... 617-287-6800 228 G theresa.mortimer@umb.edu
MORTIMEYER, Jennifer . 719-336-1572.. 83 N jennifer.mortimeyer@lamarcc.edu
MORTLAND, Stephen .... 765-998-5206 173 B stmortlan@taylor.edu
MORTON, Amy, M .... 508-831-5874 238 G ammorton@wpi.edu
MORTON, Bradley .... 732-906-2601 303 F bmorton@middlesexcc.edu
MORTON, Clarresa .... 540-665-4517 512 E cmorton@su.edu
MORTON, Jennifer .... 207-221-4273 213 B jmorton@une.edu
MORTON, John, F .... 808-956-7038 135 H jmorton@hawaii.edu
MORTON, John, F .... 808-956-7038 136 B jmorton@hawaii.edu
MORTON, Kim .... 202-884-9053.. 97 A mortonk@trinitydc.edu
MORTON, Leo, E .... 816-235-1101 284 A mortonle@umkc.edu
MORTON, Linda .... 619-239-0391.. 36 E lm@cwsl.edu
MORTON, Lisa .... 414-276-5200 165 D lisa.morton@ccr.edu
MORTON, Lynn .... 704-337-2492 368 B mortonl@queens.edu
MORTON, Marcia .... 417-667-8181 273 H mmorton@cottey.edu
MORTON, Margaret ...... 212-353-4208 323 B mortonnyc@cooper.edu
MORTON, Mary .... 518-587-2100 348 A mary.morton@esc.edu
MORTON, Matt .... 949-376-6000.. 49 K mmorton@lcad.edu
MORTON, Nina .... 304-357-4944 530 H ninamorton@ucwv.edu
MORTON, Patricia .... 801-581-8262 499 K patricia.morton@nurs.utah.edu
MORTON, Tonya, L ...... 910-938-6211 361 F mortont@coastalcarolina.edu
MORVICE, Michael .... 714-432-5741.. 40 D mmorvice@occ.cccd.edu
MORY, Scott, M .... 213-740-2383.. 74 D mory@usc.edu
MORYAN, James .... 215-489-4889 416 H james.moryan@delval.edu
MOSBURG, Calleb, N ... 580-327-8415 399 F cnmosburg@nwosu.edu
MOSBY, David, C .... 301-322-0655 217 G mosbydc@pgcc.edu
MOSBY, John .... 408-855-5195.. 76 E john.mosby@missioncollege.edu
MOSBY-WILSON, Shatiqua, A .... 504-286-5030 207 B swilson@suno.edu
MOSCA, David .... 443-367-0035 219 C dmosca@usmd.edu
MOSCA, Joseph, L .... 330-941-3321 396 C jmosca@ysu.edu
MOSCARIELLO, Dawn, M .... 610-359-5298 416 G dmoscariello@dccc.edu
MOSCATO, Robin, A ..... 609-258-3330 305 C moscato@princeton.edu
MOSCHELLA, Jayne ...... 561-912-1211 102 N jmoschella@evergladesuniversity.edu
MOSCHENROSS, Sarah . 641-269-3714 178 I moschenr@grinnell.edu
MOSELEY, David .... 479-968-0300.. 20 C dmoseley@atu.edu
MOSELEY, John .... 573-681-5333 276 K moseleyj@lincolnu.edu
MOSELEY, Lynne .... 707-638-5223.. 70 B lynne.moseley@tu.edu
MOSELEY, Pope, H .... 501-526-4533.. 24 B pmoseley@uams.edu
MOSELEY-JONES, Vickie .... 252-638-7225 362 A moseleyv@cravencc.edu
MOSELY-HAWKINS, Elizabeth .... 803-533-3681 448 H emosely@scsu.edu
MOSEMAN, Dennis .... 212-242-2692 350 G dennis.moseman@tsca.edu
MOSER, Drew .... 765-998-5384 173 B drmoser@taylor.edu
MOSER, Gary .... 707-654-1224.. 34 B gmoser@csum.edu
MOSER, Jack, T .... 662-685-4771 266 G jmoser@bmc.edu
MOSER, Jeremy .... 714-556-3610.. 75 A
MOSER, Kristin, M .... 319-273-3050 176 A kristin.moser@uni.edu
MOSER, Mike .... 808-235-7361 137 A mikem@hawaii.edu
MOSER, Patrick .... 503-838-8063 411 B moserp@wou.edu
MOSER, Shelly .... 870-612-2034.. 24 G shelly.moser@uaccb.edu
MOSER, Steven .... 601-266-4315 271 B steven.moser@usm.edu
MOSER, Tina, L .... 724-738-2000 432 A tina.moser@sru.edu
MOSER, Tracy, S .... 662-685-4771 266 G tmoser@bmc.edu
MOSES, Charles .... 404-880-8999 122 I cmoses@cau.edu
MOSES, David .... 316-978-6791 192 D david.moses@wichita.edu
MOSES, Dyann, W .... 601-877-6230 266 C dmoses@alcorn.edu
MOSES, Henry .... 615-327-6266 458 F hmoses@mmc.edu
MOSES, Lola .... 229-732-5947 120 B lolamoses@andrewcollege.edu
MOSES, Orrin Douglas . 831-656-3218 548 A dmoses@nps.edu
MOSES, Rhonda, M ...... 512-505-3075 475 G rmmoses@htu.edu
MOSES, Robert, M .... 570-422-3138 430 F bmoses@esu.edu
MOSES-HOLMES, Jeanette .... 803-934-3989 447 K jholmes@morris.edu
MOSESSO, Lynn .... 479-575-5869.. 23 G mosesso@uark.edu
MOSEY, Douglas, L ...... 860-632-3010.. 90 H rector@holyapostles.edu
MOSHER, Clifford .... 949-480-4235.. 66 I cmo@soka.edu
MOSHER, Craig .... 785-442-6019 187 I cmosher@highlandcc.edu
MOSHER, Craig .... 785-442-6017 187 I cmosher@highlandcc.edu
MOSHER, Craig, E .... 785-442-6019 187 I cmosher@highlandcc.edu
MOSHER, George .... 312-329-4268 153 C george.mosher@moody.edu
MOSHER, Michael .... 810-762-9583 245 A mmosher@kettering.edu
MOSHER, Sharon .... 512-471-6048 493 M smosher@jsg.utexas.edu
MOSHIER, Andrea .... 828-227-7212 372 C amoshier@wcu.edu
MOSHIER, Jeffrey .... 765-998-5203 173 B jfmoshier@taylor.edu
MOSIER, Greg .... 507-285-7256 261 D greg.mosier@rctc.edu
MOSIER, Gregory .... 775-784-4912 295 H greg.mosier@unr.edu
MOSIER, Julie .... 541-383-7779 404 K jmosier@cocc.edu
MOSIER, Roger .... 413-585-2400 236 G rmosier@smith.edu
MOSIER, Sarah .... 774-354-0430 223 C sarah.mosier@becker.edu
MOSKALA, Jiri .... 269-471-3648 239 D moskala@andrews.edu
MOSKOVITZ, Kristin ...... 313-664-7496 241 D kmoskovitz@collegeforcreativestudies.edu
MOSKOWITZ, Roy, P .... 212-229-5432 334 C moskowir@newschool.edu
MOSKOWITZ, Seth .... 212-960-0863 353 P seth.maskowitz@yu.edu
MOSLEY, Cal .... 320-363-3036 264 A cmosley@csbsju.edu
MOSLEY, Calvin .... 320-363-3036 254 J cmosley@csbsju.edu
MOSLEY, Carolyn .... 479-788-7856.. 23 H carolyn.mosley@uafs.edu
MOSLEY, Crystal .... 410-951-3579 220 C cmosley@coppin.edu
MOSLEY, David .... 409-880-2207 488 E dpmosley@lit.edu
MOSLEY, Eartha, J .... 803-536-7048 448 H emosely1@scsu.edu
MOSLEY, Gary .... 662-562-3216 269 E gtmosley@northwestms.edu
MOSLEY, Jenifer .... 561-237-7811 108 E jmosley@lynn.edu
MOSLEY, Juliana, M ..... 484-365-7222 424 E jmosley2@lincoln.edu
MOSLEY, Marvis .... 214-860-8758 472 G MarvisMosley@dcccd.edu
MOSLEY, Mary Lou .... 602-787-6607.. 15 B marylou.mosley@paradisevalley.edu
MOSLEY, Melissa .... 662-476-5074 267 C mmosley@eastms.edu
MOSLEY, Regina .... 734-462-4400 250 A rmosley@schoolcraft.edu
MOSLEY, Walter .... 903-593-8311 487 A wmosley@texascollege.edu
MOSLEY, Whitney .... 229-732-5950 120 B whitneymosley@andrewcollege.edu
MOSQUEDA, Leticia ...... 212-659-0736 330 A lmosqueda@tkc.edu
MOSQUEDA, Margarita . 989-686-9512 242 I momosque@delta.edu
MOSQUEDA, Rolando ... 702-651-4245 295 C rolando.mosqueda@csn.edu
MOSS, Aimi .... 810-762-3085 251 E aimi@umflint.edu
MOSS, Anne .... 828-398-2500 368 I
MOSS, Annie .... 318-670-9212 207 C amoss@susla.edu
MOSS, Ashley .... 303-333-4224.. 79 D registrar@aspen.edu
MOSS, Brendan .... 660-944-2928 273 E bmoss@conception.edu
MOSS, Catherine .... 509-359-6362 522 C cmoss4@ewu.edu
MOSS, Edwin .... 718-390-3165 352 C edwin.moss@wagner.edu
MOSS, Elizabeth, H ...... 443-518-4837 215 F emoss@howardcc.edu
MOSS, Eric, O .... 213-613-2200.. 67 G directors_office@sciarc.edu
MOSS, Michael .... 704-330-6681 361 D michael.moss@cpcc.edu
MOSS, Pamela .... 901-722-3318 461 A pmoss@sco.edu
MOSS, Renie .... 205-726-2116.... 6 F rmoss@samford.edu
MOSS, Sarah .... 712-722-6078 177 J sarah.moss@dordt.edu
MOSSER, Daniel .... 301-934-7547 214 E dmosser@csmd.edu
MOSSER, John .... 309-694-8511 146 C john.mosser@icc.edu
MOSSER, Sandra, L ...... 610-799-1172 424 A smosser@lccc.edu
MOSSEY, Christopher ... 212-799-5000 329 I
MOSTAFAVI, Moshen .... 617-495-4364 227 D moshen_mostafavi@harvard.edu
MOSTARDI, OSA, Joseph .... 610-519-4080 439 A joseph.mostardi@villanova.edu
MOSTASHARI, Zary .... 703-284-1673 510 B zary.mostashari@marymount.edu
MOSTELLER, John .... 610-896-1376 420 J jmostell@haverford.edu
MOSTILLER, Donna .... 716-286-8689 336 E dmostiller@niagara.edu
MOSTO, Pat .... 609-896-5155 306 A mosto@rider.edu
MOSTOV, Julie .... 215-895-6793 417 E julie.mostov@drexel.edu
MOTE, Jerry .... 724-266-3838 437 G jmote@tsm.edu
MOTE, Tanya .... 360-596-5204 527 B tmote@spscc.edu
MOTEN, Maria .... 847-925-6622 145 F mmoten@harpercollege.edu
MOTEN, Quevarra .... 254-526-1293 470 E quevarra.moten@ctcd.edu
MOTEN-TOLSON, Paula 919-546-8544 368 G pmotentolson@shawu.edu
MOTES, Kimberly, J ..... 651-962-6949 265 F kjmotes@stthomas.edu
MOTHERWELL, Mary ..... 734-487-2229 242 J mmotherwe@emich.edu
MOTL, Lori .... 870-245-5110.. 22 C motll@obu.edu
MOTLEY, Clay .... 239-590-7368 114 F cmotley@fgcu.edu
MOTLEY, J. Keith .... 617-287-6800 228 G keith.motley@umb.edu
MOTT, Jeanne .... 785-594-4595 184 F jeanne.mott@bakeru.edu
MOTT, Molly, A .... 315-386-7425 347 F mottma@canton.edu
MOTT, Susan .... 269-488-4217 244 J smott@kvcc.edu
MOTTE, Kristin .... 617-587-5658 234 G mottek@neco.edu
MOTTEN, Luisa .... 206-934-6782 526 B luisa.motten@seattlecolleges.edu
MOTTER, Kristi .... 256-824-4158.... 9 A kristi.motter@uah.edu
MOTTET, Timothy .... 660-562-1122 280 A tmottet@nwmissouri.edu
MOTTLEY, Darlene .... 412-365-2970 415 C dmottley@chatham.edu
MOTTLEY, Juanita, G .... 404-471-6443 119 G jgainousmottley@agnesscott.edu
MOTTOLA, Michael .... 212-217-3650 325 C Michael_Mottola@fitnyc.edu
MOTYL, Lynne, M .... 724-738-2070 432 A lynne.motyl@sru.edu
MOTZ, Arnell .... 651-582-5224 254 A a-motz@bethel.edu
MOTZER, Bill .... 402-465-2551 292 E wmotzer@nebrwesleyan.edu
MOUA, Pa Lee .... 920-832-7030 536 R palee.moua@lawrence.edu
MOUA, Phong .... 907-564-8342.. 10 D pmoua@alaskapacific.edu
MOUDGIL, Virinder, K .. 248-204-2000 245 J president@ltu.edu
MOUDIAB, Jamilah .... 973-748-9000 300 E jamilah_moudiab@bloomfield.edu

MULLEN, Steve .... 214-333-5163 471 L
stevem@dbu.edu
MULLEN, Steve, L .... 716-851-1294 325 A
mullens@ecc.edu
MULLEN, William .... 612-330-1740 253 K
mullen@augsburg.edu
MULLENIX,
Elizabeth, R .... 513-529-6010 386 K
mullener@miamioh.edu
MULLENIX, Joel .... 850-478-8496 110 C
MULLENS, Deborah, K . 304-473-8181 534 G
mullens_d@wvwc.edu
MULLENS, Liz .... 931-372-3149 462 A
lmullens@tntech.edu
MULLENS, Rob, A .... 541-346-5455 410 F
athleticdirector@uoregon.edu
MULLER, Andrew .... 843-355-4150 451 H
mullera@wiltech.edu
MULLER, Brook, W .... 541-346-3631 410 F
bmuller@uoregon.edu
MULLER, David .... 212-241-8716 328 E
MULLER, Eugene, W ...... 973-748-9000 300 E
eugene_muller@bloomfield.edu
MULLER, Glen, C .... 607-255-5070 323 C
gcm37@cornell.edu
MULLER, Joe .... 405-974-2502 403 G
jmuller2@uco.edu
MULLER, Joseph .... 860-253-3055.. 88 H
jmuller@asnuntuck.edu
MULLER, Katharine .... 310-434-3701.. 65 B
muller_katharine@smc.edu
MULLER, Kathy .... 304-865-6127 530 F
kathy.muller@ovu.edu
MULLER, Larry .... 304-424-8229 533 E
larry.muller@wvup.edu
MULLER, Nancy .... 718-818-6470 341 G
MULLER, Ralph, W .... 215-662-2203 437 I
ralph.muller@uphs.upenn.edu
MULLER, Robert .... 847-947-5065 153 H
rmuller@nl.edu
MULLER, Stephen .... 352-638-9706.. 99 D
smuller@beaconcollege.edu
MULLER, Susan .... 814-676-6591 430 E
smuller@clarion.edu
MULLERY, Colleen .... 707-826-5086.. 35 D
cbm1@humboldt.edu
MULLHOLLAND,
Angela .... 843-953-5502 445 B
mulhollandab@cofc.edu
MULLIGAN, Brendan .... 617-369-3458 236 E
bmulligan@mfa.org
MULLIGAN, Erin .... 859-572-5100 199 A
MULLIGAN, Kate, A ...... 620-417-2102 191 A
kate.mulligan@sccc.edu
MULLIGAN, Maura .... 617-989-4232 237 G
mulliganm@wit.edu
MULLIGAN, Rob .... 916-608-6736.. 53 A
mulligr@flc.losrios.edu
MULLIGAN, Susan .... 973-877-3070 302 F
mulligan@essex.edu
MULLIGAN, Zora, Z .... 573-882-2011 283 G
mulliganz@umsystem.edu
MULLIKIN, Demeri .... 715-682-1307 538 D
dmullikin@northland.edu
MULLIKIN, Jane .... 419-473-2700 381 F
jmullikin@daviscollege.edu
MULLIN, Carol .... 610-359-5318 416 G
cmullin@dccc.edu
MULLIN, OSB, Douglas 320-363-2737 264 A
dmullin@csbsju.edu
MULLIN, Joan .... 716-896-0700 352 B
mullinj@villa.edu
MULLIN, John, C .... 972-377-1575 471 C
jmullin@collin.edu
MULLIN, Joseph .... 630-942-4278 142 F
mullin@cod.edu
MULLIN, Mark, E .... 573-341-4175 284 C
memullin@mst.edu
MULLIN, II, Miles, S ... 573-629-3092 275 F
Miles.Mullin@hlg.edu
MULLINGS, Jennifer ..... 904-363-6221 112 G
MULLINS, Brian .... 859-622-2821 194 L
brian.mullins@eku.edu
MULLINS, Cathy .... 802-258-3261 502 I
cathy.mullins@sit.edu
MULLINS, Cheryl .... 802-443-5542 502 E
cmullins@middlebury.edu
MULLINS, Gary .... 715-346-3906 541 A
gmullins@uwsp.edu
MULLINS, Greg .... 360-867-6243 522 J
mullinsg@evergreen.edu
MULLINS, James, L .... 765-494-2900 171 K
jmullins@purdue.edu
MULLINS, Judy .... 660-785-4150 283 E
jmullins@truman.edu
MULLINS, Kathryn .... 616-234-4000 243 D
MULLINS, Kerry .... 908-852-1400 301 C
mullsk@centenarycollege.edu
MULLINS, Liza .... 904-256-7082 106 Q
lmullin1@ju.edu
MULLINS, Michael .... 707-546-4000.. 43 J
mmullins@empirecollege.com
MULLINS, Rachel .... 501-977-2174.. 25 A
mullins@uaccm.edu
MULLINS, Steve .... 479-968-0345.. 20 C
smullins@atu.edu
MULLINS, Steve .... 714-879-3901.. 47 D
smullins@hiu.edu
MULLINS, William, E .... 740-826-8120 387 C
wmullins@muskingum.edu
MULLION, Carrie .... 760-921-5440.. 58 C
carrie.mullion@paloverde.edu
MULLIS, Charles .... 478-934-3064 128 H
cmullis@mga.edu
MULLIS, Jay .... 478-274-7879 129 D
jmullis@oftc.edu
MULLIS, Joe, W .... 910-678-8217 362 E
mullisj@faytechcc.edu
MULLIS, Tres .... 540-458-8165 519 A
tmullis@wlu.edu
MULLISON, Mark .... 205-329-7942.... 3 C
mark.mullison@ecacolleges.com
MULLOWNEY,
William, J .... 407-582-3411 118 I
bmullowney@valenciacollege.edu
MULLOY, Josetta .... 251-380-3470.... 7 F
mulloy@shc.edu
MULRENAN, Holly .... 203-576-5518.. 91 H
hmulrenan@stvincentscollege.edu
MULROE, Michael .... 312-942-6214 158 A
mike_mulroe@rush.edu
MULROONEY, Bill .... 310-660-3418.. 43 G
bmulrooney@elcamino.edu
MULROONEY, Bill .... 310-660-3593.. 43 G
bmulrooney@elcamino.edu
MULROY, Kevin .... 909-621-8014.. 39 D
kevin_mulroy@cuc.claremont.edu
MULROY-BOWDEN,
Linda .... 608-342-1845 540 D
mulroy@uwplatt.edu
MULROY-DEGENHART,
Carmella .... 814-865-7611 428 C
qum11@psu.edu
MULRYAN, Michael .... 714-879-3901.. 47 D
mdmulryan@hiu.edu
MULSHINE, James, L ... 312-942-3589 158 A
james_l_mulshine@rush.edu
MULSO, Sara, K .... 651-641-8857 255 C
smulso@csp.edu
MULSO, William .... 507-537-6267 262 B
William.Mulso@smsu.edu
MULTARI, James .... 516-323-3060 333 E
jmultari@molloy.edu
MULTOP, Kevin .... 541-383-7578 404 K
kmultop@cocc.edu
MULVEY, Colleen .... 415-351-3508.. 62 I
cmulvey@sfai.edu
MULVEY, Julie .... 508-588-9100 232 A
MULVEY, Kristin .... 815-280-2353 148 K
kmulvey@jjc.edu
MULVEY, Nick .... 262-551-5519 535 E
nmulvey@carthage.edu
MULVILLE, Matthew, H . 716-888-2220 317 H
mulville@canisius.edu
MUMA, Richard, D .... 316-978-5761 192 D
richard.muma@wichita.edu
MUMBACH, Mary, K ..... 603-456-2656 298 D
MUMFORD, Frank .... 657-278-2423.. 33 E
fmumford@fullerton.edu
MUMFORD, Jessica .... 814-641-3331 421 L
mumforj@juniata.edu
MUMFORD, John, W .... 814-641-3452 421 L
mumford@juniata.edu
MUMM, Michele .... 320-308-4066 261 E
michelem@stcloudstate.edu
MUMM-HILL, Deb .... 503-554-2332 406 A
dmummhill@georgefox.edu
MUMMERT, Kelly .... 304-243-2226 534 H
kmummert@wju.edu
MUMMERT, Vernon .... 217-854-3231 140 F
vernon.mummert@blackburn.edu
MUMMERT, Vernon .... 480-423-6616.. 15 E
vernon.mummert@scottsdalecc.edu
MUMPER, Russ .... 706-542-0415 132 H
mumper@uga.edu
MUNA, Esther, A .... 671-735-5700 549 E
gccpresident@guamcc.edu
MUNA, Joann, W .... 671-735-5539 549 E
hr@guamcc.edu
MUNCH, Leah .... 718-405-3341 322 A
leah.munch@mountsaintvincent.edu
MUNCHEL,
Christopher, T .... 765-285-5608 164 D
cmunchel@bsu.edu
MUNCHEL, Jeff .... 410-532-5324 217 F
jmunchel@ndm.edu
MUND, Barb .... 701-671-2204 375 B
barb.mund@ndscs.edu
MUND, Catherine .... 443-518-4781 215 F
cmund@howardcc.edu
MUNDAHL, Daniel, L .... 507-344-7739 253 M
dmundahl@blc.edu
MUNDRANE, Michael ... 860-486-1777.. 92 C
michael.mundrane@uconn.edu
MUNDY, Robert .... 574-631-7305 174 A
rmundy@nd.edu
MUNDY, Susan, R .... 516-876-3033 345 E
mundys@oldwestbury.edu
MUNDY, Tiina .... 910-879-5556 360 C
tmundy@bladencc.edu
MUNFORD, Michael ...... 507-537-7858 262 B
Michael.Munford@smsu.edu
MUNGAL, Godfrey .... 408-554-2375.. 65 A
mgmungal@scu.edu
MUNGER, James .... 208-426-4010 137 E
jmunger@boisestate.edu
MUNGER, Mary Lynn ... 816-604-3155 277 J
marylynn.munger@mcckc.edu
MUNGO, T. Rein .... 843-349-2577 444 G
tmungo@coastal.edu
MUNIAK, Debby .... 330-684-8729 393 A
dmuniak@uakron.edu
MUNIER, Craig, D .... 402-472-2030 293 H
cmunier1@unl.edu
MUNIN, Art .... 309-438-2008 147 I
amunin@ilstu.edu
MUNIN, Eugene .... 312-553-2500 141 M
emunin@ccc.edu
MUNIZ, Amanda .... 361-593-3797 486 A
kaam003@tamuk.edu
MUNIZ, Herman .... 787-257-0744 557 F
herman.muniz@upr.edu
MUNIZ, Ivette .... 973-803-5000 305 A
imuniz@pillar.edu
MUNIZ, Maria .... 787-841-2000 555 F
mmuniz@pucpr.edu
MUNLEY, Almarie .... 757-727-5773 508 C
almarie.munley@hamptonu.edu
MUNLEY, Anne .... 570-348-6231 425 D
annemunley@marywood.edu
MUNN, Janet, A .... 845-368-7210 342 A
janet.munn@use.salvationarmy.org
MUNN, Kathie, A .... 906-932-4231 243 B
kathiem@gogebic.edu
MUNNELL, Barbra, M .... 724-458-3824 419 F
bmmunnell@gcc.edu
MUNNERLYN, Sam .... 334-420-4216..... 7 I
smunnerlyn@trenholmstate.edu
MUNNS, Sarah .... 573-592-6050 285 J
sarah.munns@westminster-mo.edu
MUNOZ, Candelario ...... 805-546-3147.. 42 H
cmunoz@cuesta.edu
MUNOZ, Carmen .... 818-401-1035.. 41 F
cmunoz@columbiacollege.edu
MUNOZ, Celia .... 954-763-9840.. 98 L
MUNOZ, Chris .... 713-348-6271 480 M
chris.munoz@rice.edu
MUNOZ, Harry .... 787-720-4476 556 G
serviciocristiano@mizpa.edu
MUNOZ, Ivette .... 787-725-8120 552 G
imunoz@eap.edu
MUNOZ, Joe .... 325-942-2073 489 E
joe.munoz@angelo.edu
MUNOZ, Juan, S .... 806-742-7025 489 F
juan.munoz@ttu.edu
MUNOZ, Julio, C .... 787-284-1912 554 B
jcmunoz@ponce.inter.edu
MUNOZ, Marisol .... 787-766-1717 556 A
ac_mmunoz@suagm.edu
MUNOZ, Mike .... 562-908-3467.. 60 I
mrmunoz@riohondo.edu
MUNOZ, Rene .... 717-871-4457 431 E
Rene.Munoz@millersville.edu
MUNRO, Alex .... 717-299-7776 436 D
munro@stevenscollege.edu
MUNRO, Glenn .... 301-295-0064 548 D
glenn.munro@med.navy.mil
MUNRO, Sarah .... 801-585-0970 499 K
s.munro@partners.utah.edu
MUNRO, Stuart, J .... 508-767-7041 222 D
smunro@assumption.edu
MUNROE, Amanda, L ... 972-881-5616 471 C
mmunroe@collin.edu
MUNROE, Jane Ann ...... 714-449-7446.. 53 D
jmunroe@ketchum.edu
MUNROE, Jeffrey .... 616-392-8555 253 C
jeff@westernsem.edu
MUNROE, Richard, A .... 574-807-7120 164 F
richard.munroe@bethelcollege.edu
MUNSCH, OSB, Nathan 724-805-2612 435 C
nathan.munsch@stvnicent.edu
MUNSCHY, Karl .... 706-729-2179 121 C
kmunschy@gru.edu
MUNSICK, Trudy, R ...... 307-674-6446 546 H
tmunsick@sheridan.edu
MUNSIL, Len .... 602-386-4102.. 11 F
len.munsil@arizonachristian.edu
MUNSON, David, C .... 734-647-7010 251 C
munson@umich.edu
MUNSON, Janet .... 309-649-6273 160 F
janet.munson@src.edu
MUNSON, Keith .... 612-330-1474 253 K
munsonk@augsburg.edu
MUNSON, Leo, W .... 817-257-7104 486 G
l.munson@tcu.edu
MUNSON, Robert, A ..... 312-915-8703 151 E
rmunson@luc.edu
MUNSON, Steve .... 703-284-6901 510 B
smunson@marymount.edu
MUNSON, Wanda .... 281-669-4711 481 F
wanda.munson@sjcd.edu
MUNSON, Wanda .... 281-669-4711 481 G
wanda.munson@sjcd.edu
MUNSON, Wanda .... 281-669-4711 481 E
wanda.munson@sjcd.edu
MUNSON, Wanda .... 281-998-6150 481 D
MUNSON, William .... 713-743-5470 491 D
wfmunson@central.uh.edu
MUNSON-DRYER,
Molly .... 309-556-3780 148 A
mmunsond@iwu.edu
MUNSTERMAN, Korin ... 904-680-7601 103 K
kmunsterman@fcsl.edu
MUNT, Glada, C .... 512-863-1381 483 G
muntg@southwestern.edu
MUNTER, Judith .... 415-338-2687.. 36 A
jhmunter@sfsu.edu
MUNTZ, Donna .... 740-374-8716 395 D
dmuntz@wscc.edu
MUNZER, Pat .... 785-670-2111 192 B
pat.munzer@washburn.edu
MURACA, Paul .... 713-798-6617 469 C
muraca@bcm.edu
MURAKAWA, Janelle, L 808-956-6486 135 H
jmurakaw@hawaii.edu
MURALI, Viji .... 530-752-4998.. 71 A
vpiet-sup@ucdavis.edu
MURASKO, Donna .... 215-895-1892 417 E
dm37@drexel.edu
MURASSO, Thomas ...... 914-323-5337 331 J
thomas.murasso@mville.edu
MURATORE, Lauren ...... 717-334-6286 424 F
lmuratore@ltsg.edu
MURAVCHICK, Gregg .... 859-233-8135 200 D
gmuravchick@transy.edu
MURAWSKI, Pam .... 386-752-1822 103 Q
pamela.murawski@fgc.edu
MURCH, Aimee .... 716-896-0700 352 B
murcha@villa.edu
MURCHISON, Andrea .... 310-577-3000.. 77 K
amurchison@yosan.edu
MURDAUGH, Jim .... 850-201-8660 117 B
murdaugj@tcc.fl.edu
MURDEN MCCLURE,
Tori .... 502-585-9911 199 E
tmcclure@spalding.edu
MURDEN-WALDU,
Romell .... 773-481-8451 142 D
rmurden@ccc.edu
MURDOCH, Jessica .... 978-665-3338 229 D
jmurdoch@fitchburgstate.edu
MURDOCH, William, G . 909-558-6604.. 50 K
wmurdoch@llu.edu
MURDOCK, Alan, K ...... 336-734-7757 362 F
amurdock@forsythtech.edu
MURDOCK, Rebecca ..... 402-557-7136 289 B
rebecca.murdock@bellevue.edu
MURDZAK, Karen .... 814-732-1020 430 G
kmurdzak@edinboro.edu
MURFREE, Joshua .... 478-825-6211 124 E
MURGA, Margaret .... 252-536-7242 363 B
mmurga673@halifaxcc.edu
MURGA, Mario .... 617-327-6777 238 D
mario_murga@williamjames.edu
MURGO, Joseph .... 904-470-8250 102 A
joseph.murgo@ewc.edu
MURGOLO-POORE,
Marie .... 775-337-5608 295 F
mmurgolo@tmcc.edu
MURGUIA, Stephanie ... 562-860-2451.. 37 L
smurguia@cerritos.edu
MURIANA, Joseph, P ... 718-817-3020 326 C
jmuriana@fordham.edu
MURIANKA, Luke .... 315-858-0940 328 B
lmurianka@hts.edu
MURILLO, Kindred .... 530-541-4660.. 50 A
murillo@ltcc.edu
MURKA, Adam .... 937-512-2947 391 D
adam.murka@sinclair.edu
MURLEY, David .... 509-244-6851 521 E
david.murley@scc.spokane.edu
MURNANE, Ryan .... 757-352-4891 511 G
ryanmur@regent.edu
MURO, Richae .... 708-237-5060 155 B
rmuro@nc.edu
MURPHEY, Connie .... 912-478-5413 126 B
cmurphey@georgiasouthern.edu
MURPHEY, Diane .... 580-349-1446 400 B
diane@opsu.edu
MURPHREE, Danny, W . 806-291-3635 496 K
murphree@wbu.edu

MURRY, Melanie .... 901-678-2155 462 B
mmurry@memphis.edu
MURRY, Tracy .... 941-487-4504 115 B
tmurry@ncf.edu
MURTAGH, Michael ...... 309-467-6315 145 A
mmurtagh@eureka.edu
MURTAUGH, Kelly .... 651-846-1363 261 G
kelly.murtaugh@saintpaul.edu
MURTAUGH, Peter, T ... 314-286-4813 280 I
ptmurtaugh@ranken.edu
MURTHA, Brenda .... 605-274-5217 452 A
brenda.murtha@augie.edu
MURUAKO, Dominic .... 205-366-8854.... 7 G
dmuruako@stillman.edu
MURY, Hal .... 919-209-2000 363 F
hemury@johnstoncc.edu
MUSAL, Edward .... 914-251-6923 346 D
edward.musal@purchase.edu
MUSALINI, Laneika .... 864-646-1810 449 F
lmusalin@tctc.edu
MUSANTE, Nancy, M .... 203-576-5578.. 91 H
nmusante@stvincentscollege.edu
MUSCADIN, Farah, C ... 773-995-2150 141 J
fmuscadi@csu.edu
MUSCARELLA,
Joseph, V .... 516-572-0605 334 A
joseph.muscarella@ncc.edu
MUSCARELLA, Susan .... 510-845-5373.. 31 G
MUSCENTE, Catherine ... 516-323-4710 333 E
cmuscente@molloy.edu
MUSE, Bill .... 918-463-2931 397 I
wmuse@connorsstate.edu
MUSE, Bill .... 830-792-7355 482 D
bmuse@schreiner.edu
MUSE, Charles .... 936-261-3860 484 F
cdmuse@pvamu.edu
MUSE, Clyde .... 601-857-3240 267 D
vcmuse@hindscc.edu
MUSE, Douglas .... 870-612-2167.. 24 G
douglas.muse@uaccb.edu
MUSE, Gail .... 662-472-9087 267 E
gmuse@holmescc.edu
MUSE, Justin .... 540-365-4501 507 H
jmuse@ferrum.edu
MUSEWICZ, Suellen ..... 570-961-7824 422 G
musewiczs@lackawanna.edu
MUSGROVE, Jeff .... 573-875-7663 273 D
jmusgrove@ccis.edu
MUSHRUSH-MENTZER,
Tiffany .... 440-646-8370 394 G
tmushrush@ursuline.edu
MUSIC, Amy .... 610-790-1938 412 C
amy.music@alvernia.edu
MUSICH, Michelle .... 828-766-1262 364 A
mmusich@mayland.edu
MUSICK, Kelly .... 409-933-8496 471 B
kmusick@com.edu
MUSIT, Bela .... 518-631-9890 351 A
musitsb@uniongraduatecollege.edu
MUSKAVITCH, John, W 909-389-3269.. 62 B
jmuskavitch@craftonhills.edu
MUSKETT, Milford .... 651-846-1411 261 G
milford.muskett@saintpaul.edu
MUSKRAT, Bruce .... 817-274-4284 469 E
bmuskrat@bhcarroll.edu
MUSOLF, Shelly, R .... 260-422-5561 167 F
srmusolf@indianatech.edu
MUSSA-MULDOON,
Carla, R .... 310-233-4450.. 51 F
muldoonc@lahc.edu
MUSSAT-WHITLOW,
Becky .... 336-750-2114 372 D
whitlowbm@wssu.edu
MUSSELMAN, Kathy, I .. 615-898-2929 461 E
kathy.musselman@mtsu.edu
MUSSER, Debra, S ...... 574-372-5100 166 D
musserds@grace.edu
MUSSER, Jeff .... 616-331-2207 243 E
musserj@gvsu.edu
MUSSETT, Steven, A ..... 812-488-2464 173 H
sm37@evansville.edu
MUSSO, Daniele .... 913-360-7975 184 K
dmusso@benedictine.edu
MUSTAFA, Abeer .... 336-750-3471 372 D
housing@wss.edu
MUSTAFA, Mustafa .... 201-216-9901 302 A
drmustafa@eicollege.edu
MUSTAIN, Megan .... 210-436-3176 481 C
mmustain@stmarytx.edu
MUSTARD, Barbara .... 605-394-2228 454 B
barbara.mustard@sdsmt.edu
MUSTERMAN,
Cynthia, A .... 314-421-0949 283 B
musterman@siba.edu
MUTCHLER, Jane .... 219-989-3194 171 L
Jane.Mutchler@purduecal.edu
MUTH, Richard .... 724-294-3300 431 A
Richard.Muth@iup.edu
MUTINELLI, Bobbi .... 724-589-2193 436 E
MUTONE, Paul .... 860-297-4224.. 92 A
paul.mutone@trincoll.edu
MUTTI, Anthony .... 413-782-1212 238 A
amutti@wne.edu
MUUKA, Gerry .... 270-809-4181 198 I
nmuuka@murraystate.edu
MUUS, Dan .... 701-777-2327 373 G
danm@undfoundation.org
MUYET, Javier, A .... 787-850-9318 558 A
javier.muyet@upr.edu
MUYSKENS, Judy, A ..... 402-465-2110 292 E
provost@nebrwesleyan.edu
MUZIA, Raymond .... 757-825-2900 517 B
muziar@tncc.edu
MUÑIZ-MUÑOZ, Omar . 787-993-8896 557 E
omar.muniz@upr.edu
MUÑOZ, Anibal .... 787-850-9303 558 A
anibal.munoz@upr.edu
MWANGO, Kamia .... 352-395-5018 112 H
kamia.mwango@sfcollege.edu
MWILAMBWE, Stacey ... 309-438-8611 147 I
smmwila@ilstu.edu
MYATT, Theodore, A .... 401-874-2636 442 E
tedmyatt@mail.uri.edu
MYCHASKIW, George ... 575-647-2266 310 D
MYDLOWEC, Sally, P ... 215-885-2360 425 C
smydlowec@manor.edu
MYER, Bonnie .... 360-736-9391 520 F
bmyer@centralia.edu
MYER, Marci .... 206-934-3669 525 K
marci.myer@seattlecolleges.edu
MYERS, Alvin, B .... 434-395-2740 509 H
myersab@longwood.edu
MYERS, Amy, A .... 717-291-4082 418 J
amy.myers@fandm.edu
MYERS, Andrea .... 440-375-7212 385 B
amyers@lec.edu
MYERS, Barbara, S .... 912-358-3051 131 A
myersb@savannahstate.edu
MYERS, Bianca .... 641-683-5302 179 C
bianca.myers@indianhills.edu
MYERS, Brad .... 614-292-9330 389 A
myers.7@osu.edu
MYERS, Camille .... 843-525-8359 449 E
cmyers@tcl.edu
MYERS, Charles .... 215-596-8791 438 E
c.myers@usciences.edu
MYERS, Cheryl .... 706-649-1290 123 E
cmyers@columbustech.edu
MYERS, Cheryl .... 504-571-1290 203 F
cmyers@dcc.edu
MYERS, Cynthia .... 360-992-6077 521 A
cmyers@clark.edu
MYERS, Dale .... 830-792-7235 482 D
dtmyers@schreiner.edu
MYERS, Daniel, J .... 574-631-9488 174 A
dmyers@nd.edu
MYERS, Daniel, J .... 414-288-7511 537 B
daniel.myers@marquette.edu
MYERS, Donald, C .... 901-333-5259 464 A
dmyers@southwest.tn.edu
MYERS, Donna .... 518-861-2586 331 K
dmyers@mariacollege.edu
MYERS, Eveadean .... 701-231-7703 374 C
evie.myers@ndsu.edu
MYERS, Gary .... 573-882-3246 283 H
myers@missouri.edu
MYERS, Gary .... 709-379-3111 134 J
glmyers@yhc.edu
MYERS, Gary, D .... 504-816-8003 206 C
gmeyers@nobts.edu
MYERS, James .... 650-325-9122.. 61 H
vat2ins@aol.com
MYERS, James .... 443-334-2910 218 E
jmmyers@stevenson.edu
MYERS, James .... 314-246-7080 285 G
jamesmyers79@webster.edu
MYERS, James, L .... 803-536-8480 448 H
myers@scsu.edu
MYERS, Jerry .... 404-526-7366 130 F
j.myers@sae.edu
MYERS, Joe .... 931-393-1553 463 B
jmyers@mscc.edu
MYERS, Joshua .... 734-384-4214 247 C
jmyers@monroeccc.edu
MYERS, Judi .... 570-740-0753 425 A
jmyers@luzerne.edu
MYERS, Kathryn .... 215-965-4051 426 G
kamyers@moore.edu
MYERS, Kelly .... 815-802-8260 149 B
kmyers@kcc.edu
MYERS, Ken .... 218-281-8200 264 H
kmyers@umn.edu
MYERS, Kevin .... 361-570-4840 492 A
myersk@uhv.edu
MYERS, Linda .... 937-393-3431 391 F
lmyers@sscc.edu
MYERS, Lynne, M .... 508-793-2265 225 C
lmyers@holycross.edu
MYERS, Marci .... 620-223-2700 187 B
marcim@fortscott.edu
MYERS, Mary .... 815-836-5332 150 F
myersma@lewisu.edu
MYERS, Mary .... 239-489-6768 104 G
mmyers@fsw.edu
MYERS, Mary, L .... 320-222-7534 261 B
mary.myers@ridgewater.edu
MYERS, Mary Beth .... 317-274-1505 168 E
mbmyers@iupui.edu
MYERS, Matthew, B ...... 513-529-1799 386 K
myersmb3@miamioh.edu
MYERS, Michelle .... 816-584-6727 280 F
michelle.meyers@park.edu
MYERS, Patricia .... 518-587-2100 348 A
patricia.myers@esc.edu
MYERS, Patricia, T .... 865-539-7242 463 E
pmyers@pstcc.edu
MYERS, Robert .... 310-434-4200.. 65 B
myers_robert@smc.edu
MYERS, Robert, M .... 706-886-6831 132 F
rmyers@tfc.edu
MYERS, Robin .... 870-508-6101.. 19 H
rmyers@asumh.edu
MYERS, Sara, J .... 386-312-4037 111 K
sallymyers@sjrstate.edu
MYERS, Susan .... 979-830-4273 469 F
susan.myers@blinn.edu
MYERS, Ted .... 402-844-7270 292 G
ted@northeast.edu
MYERS, Thomas .... 314-505-7329 273 G
myerst@csl.edu
MYERS, Tim .... 972-825-4723 483 D
tmyers@sagu.edu
MYERS, Tina .... 386-506-3101 101 I
myerst@DaytonaState.edu
MYETTE, Linda .... 618-664-6510 145 E
linda.myette@greenville.edu
MYHRE, Oddmund, R ... 209-667-3652.. 35 C
omyhre@csustan.edu
MYHRE, Terry .... 801-304-4224 498 D
tmyhre@globeuniversity.edu
MYKLES, Donald .... 970-491-5679.. 81 D
donald.mykles@colostate.edu
MYLETT, Brad .... 641-472-7000 181 A
bmylett@mum.edu
MYLONA, Elza .... 757-446-0340 507 B
mylonae@evms.edu
MYLOTT, Sherri .... 540-887-7386 510 A
smylott@mbc.edu
MYLREA, Brian .... 260-481-6923 168 D
mylreab@ipfw.edu
MYNATT, Danny .... 254-295-4143 492 C
dmynatt@umhb.edu
MYRICK, David .... 602-274-1885.. 16 M
dmyrick@pihma.edu
MYRICK, Justin .... 615-966-5887 458 C
justin.myrick@lipscomb.edu
MYRICK, Lynn .... 202-884-9653.. 97 A
myrickl@trinitydc.edu
MYRICK, Matt .... 218-751-8670 263 J
mmyrick@oakhills.edu
MYRON, David .... 724-838-4215 435 E
myron@setonhill.edu
MYROW, Steve .... 310-434-4871.. 65 B
myrow_steve@smc.edu
MYRTAJ, Myftar .... 617-588-1321 223 D
mmyrtaj@bfit.edu
MYRTLE, Jamie .... 913-971-3513 189 F
jmyrtle@mnu.edu
MYSCOFSKI, Carole ...... 309-556-3577 148 A
myscofsk@iwu.edu
MYSZENSKI, Rebecca ... 810-762-0317 247 F
rebecca.myszenski@mcc.edu
MYTON, David .... 906-635-2349 245 H
dmyton@lssu.edu
MYVETT, Newton .... 770-394-8300 120 E
nmyvett@aii.edu

N

NAAS, Fauzi .... 503-399-6526 404 L
fauzi.naas@chemeketa.edu
NAATZ, Duey .... 715-232-5243 541 B
naatzd@uwstout.edu
NABER, Bret .... 970-351-1887.. 87 A
bret.naber@unco.edu
NABERHAUS, Thane ..... 301-447-5617 217 D
naberhaus@msmary.edu
NABERS, JR., Drayton .. 205-726-4362..... 6 F
dnabers@samford.edu
NABI, Lynn .... 903-586-2518 476 K
lnabi@jacksonville-college.edu
NABI, Lynn .... 903-586-2518 476 K
acadean@jacksonville-college.edu
NABONNE, Michele, E . 405-325-3010 403 I
mnabonne@ou.edu
NABOR, Steven, E .... 801-626-6603 500 C
snabor@weber.edu
NABORS, Larry .... 662-246-6301 268 F
lnabors@msdelta.edu
NABORS, Marlin .... 603-668-2211 298 H
m.nabors@snhu.edu
NABORS, Melody, L ..... 901-321-3236 455 I
mnabors@cbu.edu
NABORS, Murray .... 816-271-4510 279 E
mnabors@missouriwestern.edu
NACCARATO, Shawn ...... 620-235-4128 190 G
snaccarato@pittstate.edu
NACCO, Stephen .... 908-709-7005 309 A
nacco@ucc.edu
NACE, Timothy .... 765-998-5125 173 B
tmnace@taylor.edu
NACHLAS, Rachel .... 301-846-2836 214 I
rnachlas@frederick.edu
NACHTMANN, Robert ... 915-747-5241 494 B
nachtmann@utep.edu
NACOS-BURDS,
Kathy, J .... 563-556-5110 181 F
nacos-burdsk@nicc.edu
NACSA, Beata .... 641-472-7000 181 A
bnacsa@mum.edu
NACY, Peter .... 215-596-8871 438 E
p.nacy@usciences.edu
NADARAJAN,
Gunalan, L .... 734-763-4093 251 C
guna@umich.edu
NADEAU, Evelyn .... 563-588-6557 176 F
evelyn.nadeau@clarke.edu
NADEAU, Joan, D .... 413-755-4749 233 B
jdnadeau@stcc.edu
NADEAU, Sharon, L ..... 207-778-7254 212 E
sharonn@maine.edu
NADEL, Evelyn, H .... 843-953-2211 445 B
nadele@cofc.edu
NADENICEK, Daniel, J .. 706-542-8113 132 H
dnadeni@uga.edu
NADER, John, S .... 607-746-4540 347 G
naderjs@delhi.edu
NADER, Richard .... 940-565-2197 492 D
richard.nader@unt.edu
NADERSHAHI, Nader ..... 415-929-6425.. 73 C
nnadershahi@pacific.edu
NADLER, Daniel, P .... 217-581-3221 144 E
nadler@eiu.edu
NADLER, Jerry, L .... 757-446-8920 507 B
nadlerjl@evms.edu
NADOLNY, Raymond .... 701-770-7475 375 C
raymond.nadolny@willistonstate.edu
NADOLSKI, Mike .... 269-927-8109 245 E
mnadolski@lakemichigancollege.edu
NAEGELI, Dan .... 940-565-2105 492 D
naegeli@unt.edu
NAFF, J. Abraham .... 540-365-4493 507 H
anaff@ferrum.edu
NAFFAA, Nicole .... 510-849-8231.. 57 G
nnaffaa@psr.edu
NAFFZIGER, Danielle ..... 312-935-4532 157 A
dnaffziger@robertmorris.edu
NAFIE, John .... 909-558-4562.. 50 K
jnafie@llu.edu
NAFZIGER, Kenneth, L . 540-432-4135 507 A
ken.l.nafziger@emu.edu
NAGANATHAN, Nagi ..... 419-530-8000 394 E
nagi.naganathan@utoledo.edu
NAGARKATTI, Prakash .. 803-777-5458 450 B
prakash@mailbox.sc.edu
NAGATA, Miles, K .... 808-932-7407 135 I
mnagata@hawaii.edu
NAGEL, Beverly .... 507-222-4303 254 D
bnagel@carleton.edu
NAGEL, Lonnie .... 361-593-2420 486 A
helpdesk@tamuk.edu
NAGEL, Michael .... 610-607-6294 433 H
mnagel@racc.edu
NAGEL, Michele .... 212-217-4632 325 C
michele_nagel@fitnyc.edu
NAGEL, Suzie .... 269-387-2150 252 I
suzie.nagel@wmich.edu
NAGELKERK, Jean .... 616-331-2729 243 E
nagelkej@gvsu.edu
NAGLE, Geoffrey, A ...... 312-893-7100 144 H
gnagle@erikson.edu
NAGLE, Margaret, A ..... 207-581-3743 212 C
nagle@maine.edu
NAGLE, Ryen .... 708-974-5679 153 D
nagler@morainevalley.edu
NAGLE, Stephen .... 618-453-4918 159 H
stephenn@siu.edu
NAGLE-KUCH, Abbey .... 563-884-5137 182 D
abbey.nagle-kuch@palmer.edu
NAGURA, Cynthia, K .... 619-216-6795.. 68 D
cnagura@swccd.edu
NAGY, Debra, A .... 304-462-4122 532 G
debra.nagy@glenville.edu
NAGY, Ellen .... 419-448-2063 383 C
enagy@heidelberg.edu
NAGY, Mary Anne .... 732-571-3417 303 G
mnagy@monmouth.edu
NAGY, Paul .... 813-253-7162 106 C
pnagy@hccfl.edu
NAGY, Sharon .... 864-656-1455 444 E
snagy@clemson.edu

NAYLOR MOORE, Barbara ...... 662-252-8000 270 C bmoore@rustcollege.edu
NAYOR, Greg, J ...... 716-839-8520 323 F gnayor@daemen.edu
NAZARENKO, Tatiana ... 805-565-6070.. 76 K tnazarenko@westmont.edu
NAZARIO-COLON, Ricardo ...... 606-783-9042 198 H r.nazariocolon@moreheadstate.edu
NAZARIO-TORRES, Juan, C ...... 787-620-2040 550 D jcnazario@aupr.edu
NAZE, Dave ...... 708-709-3595 156 A dnaze@prairiestate.edu
NAZZARO, Rosalyn ...... 617-369-3631 236 E rnazzaro@smfa.edu
NDIAYE, Momar ...... 860-832-2050.. 88 D mndiaye@ccsu.edu
NEAD, Margaret, A ...... 585-271-3778 321 G mnead@crcds.edu
NEAD, Margaret, A ...... 585-271-1320 321 G mnead@crcds.edu
NEAGLE, Rebecca ...... 919-866-5198 366 H
NEAL, Brenda ...... 304-260-4380 530 M bneal@blueridgectc.edu
NEAL, Brigette ...... 313-664-7470 241 D bneal@collegeforcreativestudies.edu
NEAL, Charles, V ...... 607-587-4019 347 D nealcv@alfredstate.edu
NEAL, Donna, V ...... 252-493-7309 364 H dneal@email.pittcc.edu
NEAL, Gary, W ...... 210-999-7411 490 E gneal@trinity.edu
NEAL, Jason ...... 909-593-3511.. 73 B jneal@laverne.edu
NEAL, Kathleen ...... 860-231-5271.. 93 A kneal@usj.edu
NEAL, Kurtis, R ...... 325-942-2168 489 E kurtis.neal@angelo.edu
NEAL, JR., L. Cameron 972-881-5891 471 C cneal@collin.edu
NEAL, La Vonne ...... 815-753-9055 154 I lneal1@niu.edu
NEAL, Mary, Y ...... 804-752-7259 511 E mneal@rmc.edu
NEAL, Nicole ...... 740-351-3245 391 C nneal@shawnee.edu
NEAL, Paul ...... 215-702-4307 414 C pneal@cairn.edu
NEAL, Phillip, W ...... 270-901-1111 197 C phil.neal@kctcs.edu
NEAL, Robin ...... 916-484-8172.. 52 I nealr@arc.losrios.edu
NEAL, Rodney ...... 909-558-4543.. 50 K rneal@llu.edu
NEAL, Shannon ...... 504-816-4228 202 F sneal@dillard.edu
NEAL, Susan ...... 918-631-3246 403 M susan-neal@utulsa.edu
NEAL, Thomas, J ...... 504-866-7426 206 D tneal@nds.edu
NEAL, Thomas, M ...... 714-547-9625.. 30 F tneal@calcoast.edu
NEAL, Tom ...... 503-838-8043 411 B nealt@wou.edu
NEAL, Veronica ...... 408-864-5338.. 44 N nealveronica@deanza.edu
NEAL, Willie ...... 214-860-8784 472 G wneal@dcccd.edu
NEAL, Zach ...... 501-279-4332.. 21 A zneal@harding.edu
NEAL BOYLAN, Leslie .. 920-424-3089 540 B nealboyl@uwosh.edu
NEALEIGH, Michael ...... 405-224-3140 403 L mnealeigh@usao.edu
NEALEY, Jessica ...... 859-846-5789 198 G jnealey@midway.edu
NEALON, Jackie ...... 516-299-3717 330 G jackie.nealon@liu.edu
NEALON, Michael ...... 517-483-1107 245 I nealonm@lcc.edu
NEALON-WOODS, Michele ...... 213-615-2700.. 38 G
NEAR, Hollis ...... 206-726-5040 521 G hnear@cornish.edu
NEARHOOF, Jeff ...... 312-413-4329 161 F jeff5@uic.edu
NEARY, Michele ...... 317-940-9535 164 L mneary@butler.edu
NEARY, Robert ...... 315-866-0300 327 E nearyrd@herkimer.edu
NEARY, Suzanne ...... 914-251-6000 346 D suzanne.neary@purchase.edu
NEAU, George ...... 510-567-6174.. 69 D chancellor@sum.edu
NEAULT, Lynn, C ...... 619-388-6922.. 62 E lneault@sdccd.edu
NEAVE, Jessica ...... 617-217-9448 223 A jneave@baystate.edu
NEAVES, Mitchell ...... 340-693-1040 559 B mneaves@uvi.edu
NEBEKER, Gary ...... 402-449-2915 290 F gnebeker@graceu.edu
NEBEL, Andreia ...... 402-552-6178 289 H nebel@clarksoncollege.edu
NEBEL, Andriea ...... 402-552-3373 289 H nebel@clarksoncollege.edu
NEBESKY, Michael ...... 864-656-2390 444 E mnebeske@clemson.edu
NEBLETT, Donna ...... 731-286-3327 462 F neblett@dscc.edu
NECESSARY, Justin ...... 276-739-2506 517 D jnecessary@vhcc.edu
NECESSARY, Russell, D 276-328-0322 514 B rdn2f@uvawise.edu
NECHIPURENKO, Erin ... 508-626-4951 230 A enechipurenko@framingham.edu
NECULA, Maria-Cristina ...... 718-960-2416 319 C mariacristina.necula@lehman.cuny.edu
NEDBALSKI, Coleen ...... 610-358-4587 427 D nedbalsc@neumann.edu
NEDELL, Thomas ...... 617-373-2240 235 D
NEDERHOFF, Arlan ...... 712-722-6010 177 J arlan.nederhorff@dordt.edu
NEEDHAM, Jodie ...... 312-427-2737 148 I 6needham@jmls.edu
NEEDHAM, Michele ...... 630-466-7900 162 K mneedham@waubonsee.edu
NEEDY, Bryan ...... 502-456-6504 200 B bneedy@sullivan.edu
NEEDY, Kim ...... 479-575-5900.. 23 G kneedy@uark.edu
NEEFE, Diane ...... 608-785-9539 544 E neefed@westerntc.edu
NEEL, Buster ...... 207-780-4484 213 A bneel@usm.maine.edu
NEEL, Ellen ...... 623-845-3371.. 14 N e.neel@gccaz.edu
NEEL, Joel ...... 805-756-2193.. 32 E jneel@calpoly.edu
NEEL, Linda ...... 575-624-7142 310 J linda.neel@roswell.enmu.edu
NEEL, Paul, E ...... 574-807-7035 164 F paul.neel@bethelcollege.edu
NEEL, Sandra ...... 502-852-3870 201 A sjneel01@louisville.edu
NEEL, Sandy ...... 304-650-9611 529 I neels@dewv.edu
NEELY, Jennifer ...... 615-248-1237 464 E jneely@trevecca.edu
NEELY, Renee ...... 575-562-2314 310 I renee.neely@enmu.edu
NEELY, Robert ...... 940-898-3301 490 D rneely@twu.edu
NEENAN, Benedict, T ... 660-944-2827 273 E benedict@conception.edu
NEENAN, Benedict, T ... 660-944-2859 273 E benedict@conception.edu
NEER, Stephen ...... 312-261-3031 153 H stephen.neer@nl.edu
NEESAM, Jaci, E ...... 415-422-6762.. 74 C neesam@usfca.edu
NEESE, James ...... 810-989-5585 249 H jneese@sc4.edu
NEESE, John, M ...... 325-670-1273 474 M jneese@hsutx.edu
NEESE, Susan ...... 253-680-7025 519 K sneese@bates.ctc.edu
NEESMITH, Debra ...... 704-216-3640 365 F debra.neesmith@rccc.edu
NEESON, Dave ...... 503-841-2890 408 H dneeson@pnca.edu
NEESON, Kathyrn, C ...... 716-878-4895 345 B neesonkc@buffalostate.edu
NEEVE, Tasia ...... 415-442-7820.. 46 A tneeve@ggu.edu
NEF, Dennis, L ...... 559-278-4468.. 33 D dennisn@csufresno.edu
NEFF, Charles ...... 405-208-5060 400 A cneff@okcu.edu
NEFF, Joan ...... 434-395-2256 509 H neffjl@longwood.edu
NEFF, Jon ...... 319-398-7195 180 J jneff@kirkwood.edu
NEFF, Kathryn ...... 573-518-2378 278 F kneff@mineralarea.edu
NEFF, Nancy ...... 480-423-6567.. 15 E nancy.neff@scottsdalecc.edu
NEGBENEBOR, Anthony, I ...... 704-406-2260 356 G anegbenebor@gardner-webb.edu
NEGIP, Marilyn ...... 617-243-2244 227 K mnegip@lasell.edu
NEGIP, Stephanie, E ...... 239-280-2500.. 98 O stephanie.negip@avemaria.edu
NEGLIA, Frank, A ...... 973-290-4344 301 F fneglia@cse.edu
NEGLIA, Michael, S ...... 904-620-2923 116 A mneglia@unf.edu
NEGRETE, Elizabeth ...... 818-947-2361.. 52 B negretme@lavc.edu
NEGRITTO, Leslie ...... 909-607-9060.. 39 E leslie.negritto@cgu.edu
NEGRON, Ashley ...... 417-626-1234 280 B negron.ashley@occ.edu
NEGRON, Dennis ...... 423-236-2813 460 K negron@southern.edu
NEGRON, Frankie ...... 787-761-0640 557 A decanoadministracion@utcpr.edu
NEGRON, Gisela ...... 787-257-7373 555 L gnegron@suagm.edu
NEGRON, Lillian ...... 787-786-3030 556 E lnegron@ucb.edu.pr
NEGRON, Luz ...... 787-743-4041 551 I lznegron@columbiacentral.edu
NEGRON, Olga ...... 787-832-6000 552 K mortiz@icprjc.edu
NEGRON, Zaima ...... 787-754-7597 553 D zynegron@inter.edu
NEHER, Kenneth, R ...... 618-650-2536 159 I kneher@siue.edu
NEHRA, Terese ...... 313-664-7677 241 D tnehra@collegeforcreativestudies.edu
NEHRBAS, Mark ...... 740-284-5843 382 G mnehrbas@franciscan.edu
NEHRING, Matthew, S .. 719-587-7504.. 78 I msnehrin@adams.edu
NEHRING, Wendy, M ... 423-439-7051 461 D nehringw@etsu.edu
NEIBAUER, Todd ...... 231-995-1061 248 C tneibauer@nmc.edu
NEIDECK, Robert ...... 765-998-5222 173 B rbneideck@taylor.edu
NEIDERBACH, Michael, A ...... 607-871-2329 314 J neiderbach@alfred.edu
NEIDERHISER, Jonathan ...... 605-331-6667 454 E jonathan.neiderhiser@usiouxfalls.edu
NEIDORF, David ...... 760-872-2000.. 42 J dneidorf@deepsprings.edu
NEIDY, Jon ...... 309-677-2510 140 H neidy@fsmail.bradley.edu
NEIFELD WHEELER, Wendy ...... 518-694-7319 314 G Wendy.NeifeldWheeler@acphs.edu
NEIGHBORS, Janie ...... 940-668-7333 479 K jneighbors@nctc.edu
NEIGLER, Peter ...... 212-924-5900 349 D pneigler@swedishinstitute.edu
NEIHEISEL, Steven ...... 906-227-2000 248 B sneiheis@nmu.edu
NEIHOF, Beth ...... 601-366-8880 271 E bneihof@wbs.edu
NEIHOF, JR., John, E .. 601-366-8880 271 E jneihof@wbs.edu
NEIKIRK, Mark ...... 859-572-1449 199 A neikirkm1@nku.edu
NEIL, Jon ...... 518-580-5490 342 I jneil@skidmore.edu
NEIL, Leland ...... 801-622-1573 499 C leland.neil@stevenhenager.edu
NEIL, Stephanie ...... 206-876-6100 526 E sneil@theseattleschool.edu
NEIL, Victor ...... 817-257-5218 486 G v.neil@tcu.edu
NEILL, Christine ...... 602-243-8185.. 15 F christine.neill@southmountaincc.edu
NEILL, Sarah ...... 617-521-2124 236 F sarah.neill@simmons.edu
NEILS, Kathleen, A ...... 603-862-2421 299 B kathy.neils@unh.edu
NEILSON, Eric, G ...... 312-503-0340 155 D egneilson@northwestern.edu
NEILSON, Leanne ...... 805-493-3145.. 31 H neilson@callutheran.edu
NEIMAN, Gershon ...... 845-731-3700 354 D
NEISES, Marlene ...... 414-382-6017 534 I marlene.neises@alverno.edu
NEITZ, Stephen ...... 724-805-2960 435 B stephen.neitz@stvincent.edu
NEITZEL, Alan ...... 405-736-0315 401 L aneitzel@rose.edu
NEITZKE, Eric, M ...... 641-422-4183 181 E neitzeri@niacc.edu
NEL, Stanley, D ...... 415-422-8888.. 74 C nel@usfca.edu
NELANT, Dan ...... 304-326-1234 530 G dnelant@salemu.edu
NELEN, Carla ...... 814-886-6411 427 B cnelen@mtaloy.edu
NELHUEBEL, Robin, M . 757-240-2200 512 A
NELKENBAUM, Avrohom Yaakov ...... 718-645-0536 333 B
NELL, Sharon, D ...... 512-448-8620 481 B sharonn@stedwards.edu
NELLE, Nora ...... 215-517-2659 412 F nellen@arcadia.edu
NELLER, Irene ...... 626-584-5362.. 45 F ireneneller@fuller.edu
NELLESEN, Gary ...... 909-274-4850.. 54 J gnellesen@mtsac.edu
NELLIS, Ginny ...... 802-258-3283 502 I ginny.nellis@worldlearning.org
NELLIS, M. Duane ...... 806-742-2121 489 F duane.nellis@ttu.edu
NELMS, Bruce ...... 318-797-5267 205 F bruce.nelms@lsus.edu
NELMS, Jim, A ...... 936-261-1932 484 F janelms@pvamu.edu
NELMS, Kristi ...... 217-854-3231 140 F kristi.nelms@blackburn.edu
NELSEN, Erin ...... 717-299-7772 436 D nelsen@stevenscollege.edu
NELSEN, Jeff, A ...... 515-574-1115 179 F nelsen@iowacentral.edu
NELSEN, Robert, S ...... 916-278-7737.. 34 E nelsen@csus.edu
NELSON, Andrew ...... 830-372-8011 487 C anelson@tlu.edu
NELSON, Andrew, J ...... 715-836-5368 539 E nelsonan@uwec.edu
NELSON, Anthony ...... 301-860-3590 220 B anelson@bowiestate.edu
NELSON, April ...... 580-477-7896 404 D april.nelson@wosc.edu
NELSON, Bernard ...... 504-398-2108 206 E bnelson@olhcc.edu
NELSON, Bill ...... 573-681-5555 276 K nelsonb@lincolnu.edu
NELSON, Brandi ...... 701-662-1509 375 A brandi.nelson@lrsc.edu
NELSON, Bruce, F ...... 336-278-7280 356 F bnelson@elon.edu
NELSON, Carly ...... 218-299-3020 255 B carlynelson@cord.edu
NELSON, Carol ...... 218-751-8670 263 J carolnelson@oakhills.edu
NELSON, Carolyn ...... 510-885-3942.. 33 C carolyn.nelson@csueastbay.edu
NELSON, Carolyn ...... 510-885-3711.. 33 C carolyn.nelson@csueastbay.edu
NELSON, Charles ...... 334-386-7920.... 3 I cnelson@faulkner.edu
NELSON, Cherrie ...... 801-626-7496 500 C cgnelson@weber.edu
NELSON, Christina ...... 312-944-0882 150 D CNelson@chicago.chefs.edu
NELSON, Christopher ... 757-388-2900 512 D cmnelson@sentara.com
NELSON, Christopher, B ...... 410-626-2510 218 A chris.nelson@sjc.edu
NELSON, Craig, V ...... 801-524-8103 498 J cnelson@ldsbc.edu
NELSON, Daniel ...... 651-638-6241 254 A dc-nelson@bethel.edu
NELSON, David ...... 336-770-3262 372 B nelsond@uncsa.edu
NELSON, David, A ...... 717-245-1830 417 B nelsond@dickinson.edu
NELSON, David, L ...... 313-927-1226 246 D dnelson3@marygrove.edu
NELSON, Denise ...... 603-862-2498 299 B denise.nelson@unh.edu
NELSON, Denise ...... 541-956-7001 409 F dnelson@roguecc.edu
NELSON, Denise ...... 661-255-1050.. 31 B
NELSON, Diane, L ...... 415-422-2441.. 74 C dlnelson3@usfca.edu
NELSON, Dirk ...... 806-651-2730 486 D jdnelson@mail.wtamu.edu
NELSON, Don ...... 570-740-0750 425 A dnelson@luzerne.edu
NELSON, Doug ...... 563-387-1862 180 M nelsondg@luther.edu
NELSON, Drew ...... 281-756-3718 467 D dnelson@alvincollege.edu
NELSON, Edwin, C ...... 724-925-4003 439 F nelsone@wccc.edu
NELSON, Eric ...... 805-565-6114.. 76 K enelson@westmont.edu
NELSON, Eric ...... 570-674-6725 426 D enelson@misericordia.edu
NELSON, Evelyn, C ...... 561-237-7816 108 E enelson@lynn.edu
NELSON, Fred ...... 605-642-6848 453 G fred.nelson@bhsu.edu
NELSON, Gena, C ...... 315-267-2330 346 C nelsongc@potsdam.edu
NELSON, Gersham ...... 660-543-4750 283 F ganelson@ucmo.edu
NELSON, Greg ...... 415-884-3100.. 41 B gnelson@marin.edu
NELSON, Jackie ...... 605-688-4920 454 C jacqueline.nelson@sdstate.edu
NELSON, James ...... 903-566-7002 494 E jnelson@uttyler.edu

NEUPAUER,
Nicholas, C .... 724-287-8711 413 G
nicholas.neupauer@bc3.edu
NEURAUTER, Janet .... 213-322-2450 259 B
janet.neurauter@itascacc.edu
NEUTENS, James, J ...... 865-305-9290 465 G
jneutens@mc.utmck.edu
NEUVILLE, Jeff .... 828-327-7000 361 B
jneuville@cvcc.edu
NEVAREZ, Amy .... 909-652-6020.. 38 A
amy.nevarez@chaffey.edu
NEVAREZ, Augustine .... 831-755-6825.. 46 J
anevarez@hartnell.edu
NEVAREZ, Gerard .... 575-646-3635 312 A
gerardn@nmsu.edu
NEVE, Nancy .... 906-635-2080 245 H
nneve@lssu.edu
NEVELS, Lyle .... 510-642-4096.. 70 K
lnevels@berkeley.edu
NEVELS, Tiawanna, S ... 919-516-4150 368 E
tsnevels@st-aug.edu
NEVEUX, Bettejean .... 603-206-8004 297 A
bneveux@ccsnh.edu
NEVILLE, Frank .... 703-993-8700 507 K
fnevill2@gmu.edu
NEVILLE, Nancy .... 216-421-7427 380 B
nneville@cia.edu
NEVILLS, Landee .... 417-328-1826 282 D
lnevills@sbuniv.edu
NEVIN, Amy .... 518-631-9844 351 A
nevina@uniongraduatecollege.edu
NEVINS, Daniel .... 212-678-8067 329 H
danevins@jtsa.edu
NEVOIS, Dana, A .... 636-481-3488 276 E
dnevois@jeffco.edu
NEW, Jim .... 775-856-5307 295 F
jnew@tmcc.edu
NEW, Lynn .... 903-923-2093 473 I
lnew@etbu.edu
NEW, Michael, J .... 802-654-2635 502 H
mnew@smcvt.edu
NEWALL, Edie .... 303-329-6355.. 81 B
dean@cstcm.edu
NEWALL, Edie .... 303-329-6355.. 81 B
edienewall@cstcm.edu
NEWBERG, Bella .... 760-750-4444.. 35 B
newberg@csusm.edu
NEWBERN, Judson .... 615-322-2715 465 H
judson.newbern@vanderbilt.edu
NEWBERRY, Beth .... 502-585-9911 199 E
bnewberry@spalding.edu
NEWBERRY, Byron .... 405-425-5428 399 J
byron.newberry@oc.edu
NEWBERRY, Elizabeth ... 651-450-3654 259 A
enewber@inverhills.edu
NEWBERRY, Robert .... 575-624-7180 310 J
robert.newberry@roswell.enmu.edu
NEWBOLD, Bradley, D . 573-629-3008 275 F
Brad.Newbold@hlg.edu
NEWBOLD, Ken, F .... 574-535-7550 166 C
kfnewbold@goshen.edu
NEWBOLD, Martie .... 727-864-7675 101 P
newbolhm@eckerd.edu
NEWBOLD, Pamela .... 330-823-6572 394 A
newbolph@mountunion.edu
NEWBORN, Janis .... 256-726-7460.... 6 C
jnewborn@oakwood.edu
NEWBOULD, Ian, C .... 585-385-8402 340 F
inewbould@sjfc.edu
NEWBY, Belita .... 256-726-8245.... 6 C
bfleming@oakwood.edu
NEWBY, Jennifer .... 541-383-7238 404 K
jnewby@cocc.edu
NEWBY, Stewart .... 903-675-6235 490 F
stewart.newby@tvcc.edu
NEWBY, Teresa .... 952-446-4484 255 E
newbyt@crown.edu
NEWCOMB, Bruce, C .... 208-426-1491 137 E
brucenewcomb@boisestate.edu
NEWCOMB, Ron .... 770-975-4000 122 H
NEWCOMB, Terry .... 315-364-3408 352 F
tnewcomb@wells.edu
NEWCOMBE, David, A .. 540-365-4463 507 H
dnewcombe@ferrum.edu
NEWCOMBE, Patricia .... 413-782-1201 238 A
pnewcombe@law.wne.edu
NEWCOMBE, Rodd .... 321-674-7110 103 R
newcombe@fit.edu
NEWELL, AJ .... 540-654-1934 513 I
anewell@umw.edu
NEWELL, Bridget, M ..... 570-577-1561 413 E
bridget.newell@bucknell.edu
NEWELL, Crystal .... 434-961-5339 516 F
cnewell@pvcc.edu
NEWELL, Diane .... 251-380-9090.... 3 I
dnewell@faulkner.edu
NEWELL, Glen, C .... 336-334-7731 370 B
gcnewell@ncat.edu
NEWELL, James .... 718-270-2488 344 D
james.newell@downstate.edu
NEWELL, James .... 856-256-4012 306 D
newell@rowan.edu
NEWELL, Jeffrey .... 978-921-4242 234 B
jeffrey.newell@montserrat.edu
NEWELL, Jennifer, M .... 585-343-0055 326 F
jmnewell@genesee.edu
NEWELL, Keith .... 912-260-4377 131 D
keith.newell@sgsc.edu
NEWELL, Mallory .... 408-864-8777.. 44 N
newellmallory@deanza.edu
NEWELL, Rand, E .... 207-509-7201 212 A
rnewell@unity.edu
NEWGARD, Debra .... 651-905-3400 264 E
NEWGARD, Debra .... 612-332-3361 253 I
dnewgard@aii.edu
NEWGENT, Matt .... 405-262-2552 401 H
newgentm@redlandscc.edu
NEWGENT, Matt .... 405-422-1280 401 H
matt.newgent@redlandscc.edu
NEWHALL, JR., Edward 401-454-6307 442 B
enewhall@risd.edu
NEWHOFF, Marilyn .... 619-594-6516.. 35 E
mnewhoff@mail.sdsu.edu
NEWHOUSE, Dollie .... 843-661-1362 446 E
dnewhouse@fmarion.edu
NEWHOUSE, Gary .... 847-635-1640 155 E
garyn@oakton.edu
NEWHOUSE, Greg .... 619-388-7673.. 62 H
gnewhouse@sdccd.edu
NEWHOUSE, Robin, P .. 317-274-1486 168 E
newhouse@iu.edu
NEWHOUSE, Valerie, K . 712-362-0434 179 G
vnewhouse@iowalakes.edu
NEWITZ, Laurie, H .... 718-780-7503 317 A
laurie.newitz@brooklaw.edu
NEWKIRK, Charlene ..... 412-469-6300 415 G
cnewkirk@ccac.edu
NEWKIRK, Krista, L ...... 704-687-5727 371 B
Krista.Newkirk@uncc.edu
NEWKIRK, Vann .... 252-335-3291 369 F
vrnewkirk@ecsu.edu
NEWKIRK, Vann .... 256-372-5266.... 1 A
vann.newkirk@aamu.edu
NEWKIRK, Vann .... 256-372-5104.... 1 A
vann.newkirk@aamu.edu
NEWKOFSKY, Stephen .. 315-268-6620 321 C
steve.newkofsky@clarkson.edu
NEWLAND, Carmen .... 602-285-7588.. 15 C
carmen.newland@phoenixcollege.edu
NEWLAND, Jamesetta ... 212-346-1600 337 I
jnewland@pace.edu
NEWLIN, Aura .... 307-754-6095 546 I
Aura.Newlin@nwc.edu
NEWLIN, Toni .... 765-998-5211 173 B
tnnewlin@taylor.edu
NEWLUN, Elizabeth ...... 479-248-7236.. 20 K
lnewlun@ecollege.edu
NEWMAN, Allison .... 518-276-6359 339 D
newmaa3@rpi.edu
NEWMAN, Ben .... 916-577-2200.. 77 F
bnewman@jessup.edu
NEWMAN, Benjamin ..... 618-453-3771 159 H
bnewman@siu.edu
NEWMAN, Betsy .... 617-266-1400 223 F
NEWMAN, Carolyn .... 631-656-3191 326 B
carolyn.newman@ftc.edu
NEWMAN, Carolyn .... 505-454-3146 311 H
newman_c@nmhu.edu
NEWMAN, Carrie .... 814-824-3311 425 L
cnewman@mercyhurst.edu
NEWMAN, Diane .... 212-875-4547 315 F
dnewman@bankstreet.edu
NEWMAN, Dianna .... 704-847-5600 369 A
dnewman@ses.edu
NEWMAN, Ethel .... 321-433-7060 101 O
newmane@easternflorida.edu
NEWMAN, Gail .... 925-473-7421.. 42 F
gnewman@losmedanos.edu
NEWMAN, Gilbert .... 510-841-9230.. 77 I
gnewman@wi.edu
NEWMAN, Hank .... 505-786-4188 311 G
hnewman@navajotech.edu
NEWMAN, Janice .... 916-577-2200.. 77 F
jnewman@jessup.edu
NEWMAN, Janis, J .... 713-313-1183 487 F
newmanjj@tsu.edu
NEWMAN, Jeanine .... 337-421-9615 204 F
jeanine.newman@sowela.edu
NEWMAN, Jeff .... 615-322-2476 465 H
jeffrey.k.newman@vanderbilt.edu
NEWMAN, Joan .... 865-694-6453 463 E
jnewman@pstcc.edu
NEWMAN, Katherine, S 413-545-2554 228 F
ksnewman@provost.umass.edu
NEWMAN, Kay, S .... 334-387-3877.... 1 E
kaynewman@amridgeuniversity.edu
NEWMAN, Keith .... 765-677-2105 169 C
keith.newman@indwes.edu
NEWMAN, Lance .... 801-832-2301 501 C
lnewman@westminstercollege.edu
NEWMAN, Lester, C ..... 903-730-4890 476 L
lnewman@jarvis.edu
NEWMAN, Linda .... 360-438-4584 525 H
lnewman@stmartin.edu
NEWMAN, Linda, L ...... 734-764-7403 251 C
newmanll@umich.edu
NEWMAN, Lois .... 918-495-6888 401 B
lnewman@oru.edu
NEWMAN, Louis .... 507-222-4191 254 D
lnewman@carleton.edu
NEWMAN, Michael .... 646-565-6000 350 C
michael.newman@touro.edu
NEWMAN, Nancy, J ...... 402-465-2375 292 E
njn@nebrwesleyan.edu
NEWMAN, Robert, D .... 801-581-8816 499 K
robert.newman@hum.utah.edu
NEWMAN, Rocky .... 330-337-6403 376 B
college@awc.edu
NEWMAN, Russ .... 858-635-4535.. 26 J
rnewman@alliant.edu
NEWMAN, Russ .... 858-635-4535.. 26 I
rnewman@alliant.edu
NEWMAN, Scott .... 801-524-8167 498 J
snewman@ldsbc.edu
NEWMAN, Scott .... 918-293-4666 400 E
scott.newman@okstate.edu
NEWMAN, Shannon ...... 479-248-7236.. 20 K
snewman@ecollege.edu
NEWMAN, Simon .... 301-447-5600 217 D
newman@msmary.edu
NEWMAN, William .... 615-230-3600 464 B
william.newman@volstate.edu
NEWPORT, Joseph, M .. 812-237-7829 167 E
joseph.newport@indstate.edu
NEWSCHWANDER,
Gregg .... 334-844-5662.... 1 G
gen0002@auburn.edu
NEWSOM, Andrea .... 317-791-5611 173 I
mewsoma@uindy.edu
NEWSOM, Lanay .... 757-683-3141 510 I
snewsom@odu.edu
NEWSOM, Stephanie, R 319-352-8539 183 J
stephanie.newsom@wartburg.edu
NEWSOM, Thomas, W .. 575-461-4413 311 C
thomasn@mesalands.edu
NEWSOME, Chevelle .... 916-278-6470.. 34 E
cnewsome@csus.edu
NEWSOME, Dale .... 815-939-5265 155 G
rdnewsome@olivet.edu
NEWSOME, Gary .... 815-939-5120 155 G
gnewsome@olivet.edu
NEWSOME, John .... 414-955-8203 537 C
jnewsome@mcw.edu
NEWSOME, Pam .... 612-874-3798 257 D
pam_newsome-prochniak@mcad.edu
NEWSOME, Sarah .... 850-973-9675 109 C
newsomes@nfcc.edu
NEWTON, Bryan .... 410-334-2894 221 E
bnewton@worwic.edu
NEWTON, Bryan .... 803-508-7245 443 C
newtonbd@atc.edu
NEWTON, Carolyn .... 330-263-2004 380 E
cnewton@wooster.edu
NEWTON, Christopher .. 501-370-5204.. 22 E
cnewton@philander.edu
NEWTON, Diane, D .... 501-450-3184.. 25 F
dnewton@uca.edu
NEWTON, Dusty .... 308-865-8702 293 G
newtond@unk.edu
NEWTON, Eric, D .... 864-242-5100 443 G
NEWTON, Erin .... 478-387-4731 125 E
enewton@gmc.edu
NEWTON, Franklin .... 302-831-2078.. 94 D
fanewt@udel.edu
NEWTON, Jeff .... 419-530-4484 394 E
jeff.newton2@utoledo.edu
NEWTON, Jimmie .... 202-231-3344 547 N
NEWTON, Joseph, A .... 229-333-4357 133 H
jnewton@valdosta.edu
NEWTON, Joshua .... 860-486-2709.. 92 C
jnewton@foundation.uconn.edu
NEWTON, Julianne, H .. 541-346-2167 410 F
jhnewton@uoregon.edu
NEWTON, LaCresha ...... 501-420-1203.. 19 B
lacresha.newton@arkansasbaptist.edu
NEWTON, Lynette .... 402-826-8688 290 C
lynette.newton@doane.edu
NEWTON, Martin .... 205-726-2131.... 6 F
cnewton@samford.edu
NEWTON, Michael, L ... 270-384-8099 198 C
newtonm@lindsey.edu
NEWTON, Nell, J .... 574-631-6789 174 A
nell.newton@nd.edu
NEWTON, Sandra .... 252-492-2061 366 G
newton@vgcc.edu
NEWTOWN, Michael, J . 315-386-7411 347 F
newtownm@canton.edu
NEY, Cheryl .... 323-343-4300.. 34 A
cney@cslanet.calstatela.edu
NEYENS, Richard .... 303-282-3414.. 85 J
richard.neyens@archden.org
NG, Bart .... 630-829-6187 140 A
bng@ben.edu
NG, Charles .... 800-782-2422.. 32 A
cng@mail.cnuas.edu
NG, Charles .... 760-757-2121.. 54 G
cng@miracosta.edu
NG, Michael .... 808-956-7323 135 H
ng23@hawaii.edu
NG, Peh Peh .... 320-589-6300 265 A
pehng@morris.umn.edu
NGIRALMAU, Hilda .... 680-488-3036 550 C
hildan@palau.edu
NGIRAMENGIOR, Todd . 680-488-2471 550 C
toddn@palau.edu
NGIRMERIIL,
Glendalynn .... 680-488-3036 550 C
glendalynn@palau.edu
NGO, Vincent .... 626-585-7400.. 58 F
vngo6@pasadena.edu
NGUYEN, Ai .... 206-726-5028 521 G
NGUYEN, Amanda .... 207-326-2280 211 G
amanda.nguyen@mma.edu
NGUYEN, Charles, C .... 202-319-5160.. 95 A
nguyen@cua.edu
NGUYEN, Christine .... 714-241-6144.. 40 B
cnguyen@coastline.edu
NGUYEN, Dana .... 561-912-2166 102 N
dnguyen@evergladesuniversity.edu
NGUYEN, Danny .... 408-855-5417.. 76 E
danny.nguyen@wvm.edu
NGUYEN, Dave .... 510-466-7358.. 59 C
danguyen@peralta.edu
NGUYEN, Hieu .... 951-827-1286.. 72 A
hieu.nguyen@ucr.edu
NGUYEN, Hieu .... 808-739-8577 135 A
hnguyen@chaminade.edu
NGUYEN, Hoa .... 814-824-2000 425 L
NGUYEN, Joseph .... 909-384-8677.. 62 C
jnguyen@sbccd.cc.ca.us
NGUYEN, Kay .... 714-895-8727.. 40 C
kvnguyen@gwc.cccd.edu
NGUYEN, Loan .... 510-981-2808.. 58 J
lnguyen@peralta.edu
NGUYEN, Luan, P .... 671-735-2639 549 G
nguyen@triton.uog.edu
NGUYEN, Minh .... 619-684-8778.. 56 B
mnguyen@newschoolarch.edu
NGUYEN, Nhan .... 252-985-5240 367 E
nnguyen@ncwc.edu
NGUYEN, Stacey .... 832-230-5555 479 J
snguyen@na.edu
NGUYEN, Tamie .... 323-343-5808.. 34 A
tnguyen10@cslanet.calstatela.edu
NGUYEN, Thuy, T .... 510-466-7218.. 59 B
ttnguyen@peralta.edu
NGUYEN, Thy .... 312-996-2969 161 F
thy@uic.edu
NGUYEN, Tuyen .... 714-628-4844.. 60 H
nguyen_tuyen@sccollege.edu
NGWABA, Maurice, C .. 410-651-6656 219 H
mcngwaba@umes.edu
NI, Yi .... 603-526-3648 296 I
yni@colby-sawyer.edu
NIAS, Danita .... 352-392-5401 115 D
dnias@ufalumni.ufl.edu
NICA, Claude .... 310-665-6800.. 57 C
NICASTRO, Vincent, P .. 610-519-4110 439 A
vincent.nicastro@villanova.edu
NICCHI, Frank, J .... 315-568-3100 334 F
fnicchi@nycc.edu
NICE, Steve .... 239-489-9283 104 G
snice@fsw.edu
NICELY, Nancy .... 610-328-8534 436 A
nnicely1@swarthmore.edu
NICELY, Tim .... 540-453-2371 514 H
nicelyt@brcc.edu
NICHOL, Vicki .... 303-273-3972.. 80 O
vnichol@mines.edu
NICHOLAS, Connie .... 409-984-6165 488 H
connie.nicholas@lamarpa.edu
NICHOLAS, David, R ..... 530-221-4275.. 66 B
sbcadm@shasta.edu
NICHOLAS, Donna, R ... 530-221-4275.. 66 B
donna@shasta.edu
NICHOLAS, Jim .... 661-763-7853.. 69 E
jnicholas@taftcollege.edu
NICHOLAS, Mark .... 508-626-4670 230 A
mnicholas1@framingham.edu
NICHOLAS, Mike, L .... 574-807-7875 164 F
michael.nicholas@bethelcollege.edu
NICHOLAS, Nannette .... 607-962-9229 323 D
nicholas@corning-cc.edu
NICHOLAS, Sandra .... 570-740-0730 425 A
snicholas@luzerne.edu
NICHOLES, Gary .... 559-453-7137.. 45 E
gary.nicholes@fresno.edu
NICHOLLS, Deb .... 541-888-7400 410 A
dnicholls@socc.edu
NICHOLLS, Gregory ...... 610-660-1090 434 G
gnicholl@sju.edu

NIGHSWONGER, Eve 707-527-4498 65 C enighswonger@santarosa.edu
NIGHTINGALE, Charles 443-518-4615 215 F cnightingale@howardcc.edu
NIGHTINGALE, Lisa 972-860-8051 472 D lnightingale@dcccd.edu
NIGLIAZZO, Marc, A 254-519-5720 485 D marc.nigliazzo@tamuct.edu
NIGRI, Rita 516-562-0443 324 G rnigri@nshs.edu
NIGRO, Frank 530-242-7760 66 C fnigro@shastacollege.edu
NIGRO, Nick 419-473-2700 381 F nnigro@daviscollege.edu
NIGRO, Richard, A 215-951-1360 422 F nigro@lasalle.edu
NIGRO, Sarah 402-935-9400 291 L snigro@nechristian.edu
NIGRO, Stephen, M 413-542-2101 222 A smnigro@amherst.edu
NIGUIDULA, Amanda 305-348-3532 114 G amanda.niguidula@fiu.edu
NIJLAND, Mark, J 210-567-0313 495 B nijland@uthscsa.edu
NIKAS, Peter 262-554-2010 537 D dr.peter_nikas@gmx.com
NIKIAS, C. L, M 213-740-2111 74 D president@usc.edu
NIKIRK, Sarah, F 859-218-3379 200 G s.nikirk@uky.edu
NIKOLAKIS, Michael 251-580-2121 5 A mike.nikolakis@faulknerstate.edu
NIKOPOULOS, Beth 972-273-3171 473 A bnikopoulos@dcccd.edu
NILAND, Bridget 716-839-8375 323 F bniland@daemen.edu
NILAND, Eileen, A 716-888-2620 317 H nilande@canisius.edu
NILAND, Joe 251-442-2288 9 B jniland@umobile.edu
NILES, Beau 919-546-8383 368 G bniles@shawu.edu
NILES, Maryann 781-280-3703 232 B nilesm@middlesex.mass.edu
NILES, Spencer 757-221-2315 506 J sgniles@wm.edu
NILES, Stefanie, D 717-245-1287 417 B niles@dickinson.edu
NILES-HANSEN, Diana 808-544-1102 135 C dnileshansen@hpu.edu
NILL, John (Jack) 417-862-9533 275 C info@globaluniversity.edu
NILLES, Dawnita 701-777-3239 373 G dawnita.nilles@und.edu
NILSEN, Cheryl 701-858-3150 374 B cheryl.nilsen@minotstateu.edu
NILSEN, Kenneth 201-216-5206 308 D knilsen@stevens.edu
NILSEN, Tracy 212-752-1530 330 C tracy.nilsen@limcollege.edu
NILSON, Amy 209-588-5505 78 B nilsona@yosemite.edu
NILSSON, Elizabeth 603-668-6660 298 A
NIMES, Johnny 404-527-7782 127 H jnimes@itc.edu
NIMMER, Carole 660-543-4919 283 F cnimmer@ucmo.edu
NIMMO, Pam 615-868-6503 459 E
NIMMO, Steven 706-776-0113 130 B snimmo@piedmont.edu
NIMOCKS DEN HERDER, Mittie 608-342-1261 540 D denherderm@uwplatt.edu
NIMON, Opie 312-949-7610 146 E onimon@ico.edu
NINAN, George 901-272-5125 459 A
NING, Bin 734-487-4924 242 J bning@emich.edu
NINOS, Katherine 505-467-6819 313 F katandall@aol.com
NIP, Kit 319-385-6250 180 A knip@iw.edu
NIPP, Amanda 402-844-7733 292 G amandan@northeast.edu
NIPP, Tim, J 731-881-7601 465 F timnipp@utm.edu
NIPPERT, Jennifer 740-695-9500 377 F jnippert@belmontcollege.edu
NIPPERT, Karen, F 901-333-4283 464 A knippert@southwest.tn.edu
NIRENBERG, David 773-702-8799 161 D nirenberg@uchicago.edu
NIROOMAND, Farhang 361-570-4230 492 A niroomandf@uhv.edu
NIROUMAND, Madjid 714-432-5991 40 D mniroumand@occ.cccd.edu
NISBET, Jane, A 603-862-1948 299 B jan.nisbet@unh.edu
NISBET, Kenneth, J 734-763-0614 251 C knisbet@umich.edu
NISH, Melinda 619-482-6301 68 D president@swccd.edu
NISHIGUCHI, Earl, K 808-245-8274 136 F earln@hawaii.edu
NISHIME, Jeanie 310-660-3472 43 G jnishime@elcamino.edu
NISKA, Jennifer 651-638-6891 254 A j-niska@bethel.edu
NISSEL, Chaim 646-685-0115 353 P drnissel@yu.edu
NISSEN, Jill 314-367-8700 281 G jill.nissen@stlcop.edu
NISSEN, John 802-387-7145 502 A johnnissen@landmark.edu
NISSEN, Laura 503-725-3997 409 D nissen@pdx.edu
NISSEN, Lindsey 319-296-4269 179 B lindsey.nissen@hawkeyecollege.edu
NISSEN, Sarah 701-777-3579 373 G sarah.nissen@und.edu
NISSLEY, Nick 513-569-1601 379 K nick.nissley@cincinnatistate.edu
NISUN, Michelle, L 260-399-7700 174 C mnisun@sf.edu
NISWANDER, Frederick 252-328-6975 369 E niswanderf@ecu.edu
NITECKI, Danuta 215-895-2750 417 E dan44@drexel.edu
NITSCH, Wanda 760-591-3012 74 A wnitsch@usa.edu
NITTMANN, Nydia 928-523-9488 16 C Nydia.Nittmann@nau.edu
NITZBERG, Nancy 215-635-7300 419 D nnitzberg@gratz.edu
NIVAR, Rafael 201-360-4081 303 A rnivar@hccc.edu
NIX, J. Vincent 406-377-9408 286 F jnix@dawson.edu
NIX, Julie 256-782-5815 4 L jnix@jsu.edu
NIX, Linda 307-268-2218 545 Z lnix@caspercollege.edu
NIX, Orvie 806-651-2345 486 D onix@wtamu.edu
NIX, Rachel 870-574-1521 23 E rnix@sautech.edu
NIX, Sheila 210-431-2178 481 C snix@stmarytx.edu
NIX, Stephan 361-593-2000 486 A stephan.nix@tamuk.edu
NIXON, Andrea 507-222-4043 254 D anixon@carleton.edu
NIXON, John, E 801-585-0806 499 K john.nixon@utah.edu
NIXON, Katie 731-989-6672 456 K knixon@fhu.edu
NIXON, Leah 616-234-3535 243 D commdept@grcc.edu
NIXON, LeAnne 601-477-4008 268 A leanne.nixon@jcjc.edu
NIXON, Natalie 303-991-1575 78 K natalie.nixon@americansentinel.edu
NIXON, Russell, T 215-702-4392 414 C rnixon@cairn.edu
NIXON, Susan 318-487-7401 202 L susan.nixon@lacollege.edu
NIXON, Terry 325-793-4721 478 D tnixon@mcm.edu
NIXON, Tonia 410-543-6056 220 E tcnixon@salisbury.edu
NIXON, Valerie 607-587-3985 347 D nixonvb@alfredstate.edu
NJIE, Valerie 412-402-9779 413 A vnjie@mcg-btc.org
NJOGU, Wamucii, E 773-442-5700 154 H w-njogu@neiu.edu
NNADI, Eucharia, E 702-968-2038 296 D ennadi@roseman.edu
NNOROMELE, Patrick, C 859-622-2973 194 L patrick.nnoromele@eku.edu
NNOROMELE, Salome 859-622-3855 194 L salome.nnoromele@eku.edu
NOACK, Kelly 309-794-7477 139 K kellynoack@augustana.edu
NOAH, Tara 660-359-3948 279 L tnoah@mail.ncmissouri.edu
NOAKES, John, A 215-572-2897 412 F noakesj@arcadia.edu
NOASCONO, Amanda 847-578-8489 157 G amanda.noascono@rosalindfranklin.edu
NOBEL, Michele 937-769-1802 376 M mnobel@antioch.edu
NOBILE, Bryan 601-643-8468 266 J bryan.nobile@colin.edu
NOBLE, Ann 281-649-3304 475 B aanoble@hbu.edu
NOBLE, Barbara 314-340-3621 275 G nobleb@hssu.edu
NOBLE, Darren 952-446-4352 255 E nobled@crown.edu
NOBLE, Doug 540-654-1235 513 I dnoble@umw.edu
NOBLE, Ronald 503-883-2602 406 I rnoble@linfield.edu
NOBLE, Ronald, J 209-667-3177 35 C rnoble@csustan.edu
NOBLE, Scott 307-778-4372 546 F snoble@lccc.wy.edu
NOBLE, Seth 970-542-3248 84 A seth.noble@morgancc.edu
NOBLE, Shlomo 585-473-2810 349 F
NOBLE-GOODMAN, Stuart 304-358-2000 530 A stuart.noblegoodman@future.edu
NOBLES, Daryle 910-678-8225 362 E noblesd@faytechcc.edu
NOBLES, Melissa 617-253-3450 233 C
NOBLES, Rodney 262-691-5362 544 D rnobles@wctc.edu
NOBLES, Susan, Q 252-493-7287 364 H snobles@email.pittcc.edu
NOBLEZA, Deanna 215-503-2817 436 F deanna.nobleza@jefferson.edu
NOBLITT, Jeffrey 818-677-2130 34 D jeffrey.noblitt@csun.edu
NOCE, Joe 215-780-1294 435 D pcobookstore@mattmccoy.com
NOCELLA, Frank 973-300-2115 308 F fnocella@sussex.edu
NOCHTA, Linda 724-589-2155 436 E lnochta@thiel.edu
NOCKUNAS, Michael 508-929-8045 230 G mnockunas@worcester.edu
NODES, Jennifer 239-348-4710 98 O jennifer.nodes@avemaria.edu
NODGE, Andrea 734-432-5737 246 B anodge@madonna.edu
NODINE, Barbara, F 215-572-2900 412 F nodineb@arcadia.edu
NODLAND, Rita 701-224-5692 374 E rita.nodland@bismarckstate.edu
NOE, Danielle 904-680-7659 103 K dnoe@fcsl.edu
NOE, Diane 219-464-6700 174 E diane.noe@valpo.edu
NOE, Lori 618-842-3711 146 G noel@iecc.edu
NOEL, Abraham 651-696-6000 256 L
NOEL, Amy 910-592-8081 365 G anoel@sampsoncc.edu
NOEL, Cheryl, A 724-925-4058 439 F noelc@wccc.edu
NOEL, Dan 719-638-6580 82 G dnoel@cci.edu
NOEL, Erin 559-453-5549 45 E erin.noel@fresno.edu
NOEL, JR., J. Andrew 607-255-8832 323 C jan16@cornell.edu
NOEL, John, D 563-562-3263 181 F noelj@portal.nicc.edu
NOEL, Norma 575-646-4986 312 A nnoel@nmsu.edu
NOEL, Stuart 678-891-3986 125 G stuart.noel@gpc.edu
NOEL, Terry 724-532-5095 435 B terry.noel@email.stvincent.edu
NOEL-ELKINS, Amelia 309-438-3217 147 I anoelel@ilstu.edu
NOFFSINGER, Lynda, D 336-888-6352 357 E lnoffsin@highpoint.edu
NOFFSINGER-FRAZIER, Nicole 931-598-1325 460 I nanoffsi@sewnee.edu
NOFTSINGER, Mark, P 540-375-2283 512 B noftsinger@roanoke.edu
NOGLE, Ryan 716-851-1281 325 A nogle@ecc.edu
NOHLGREN, Bethany 845-758-7099 315 G nohlgren@bard.edu
NOHNER, OSB, Sharon 320-363-5285 254 J snohner@csbsju.edu
NOHRIA, Nitin 617-495-6550 227 D nnohria@hbs.edu
NOJAN, Mehran 315-312-2345 346 A mehran.nojan@oswego.edu
NOLAN, Alanna 718-817-3080 326 C anolan@fordham.edu
NOLAN, Beth 202-994-6503 95 D bnolan@gwu.edu
NOLAN, Brian 301-447-5223 217 D nolan@msmary.edu
NOLAN, Christina 973-748-9000 300 E christina_nolan@bloomfield.edu
NOLAN, Colleen 304-876-5106 532 I cnolan@shepherd.edu
NOLAN, David 817-257-6863 486 G d.nolan@tcu.edu
NOLAN, Deborah 410-704-2452 221 A dnolan@towson.edu
NOLAN, Deborah, O 610-409-3586 438 H dnolan@ursinus.edu
NOLAN, Ernest 734-432-5313 246 B enolan@madonna.edu
NOLAN, Jamie 315-415-8514 299 B jamie.nolan@unh.edu
NOLAN, Jim 505-467-6821 313 F pres@swc.edu
NOLAN, John 216-987-4870 381 A john.nolan@tri-c.edu
NOLAN, Judy 914-251-6067 346 D judy.nolan@purchase.edu
NOLAN, Kelly 310-544-6419 61 I kelly.nolan@usw.salvationarmy.org
NOLAN, Lisa, K 515-294-9860 175 G lknolan@iastate.edu
NOLAN, Terrance 212-998-1212 336 C
NOLAN, Tiffany 217-228-5432 156 D nolanti@quincy.edu
NOLAN-WEISS, Sharon, E 716-645-2266 343 E senolan@buffalo.edu
NOLAND, Brian, E 423-439-4211 461 D president@etsu.edu
NOLAND, T. Raiford 205-652-3536 9 G trnoland@uwa.edu
NOLASCO, Maria 787-841-2000 555 F mnolasco@pucpr.edu
NOLD, Letha 816-271-4582 279 E lnold@missouriwestern.edu
NOLDER, Deborah 606-759-7141 196 G debbie.nolder@kctcs.edu
NOLDNER, Tracy 605-367-7487 454 D tracy.noldner@southeasttech.edu
NOLDON, Denise 714-808-4500 56 D dnoldon@nocccd.edu
NOLE, Laura 206-878-3710 523 D lnole@highline.edu
NOLES, Jody 334-291-4922 2 H jody.noles@cv.edu
NOLES, Kimberly 478-274-7761 129 D knoles@oftc.edu
NOLING-AUTH, Jamie 503-554-2321 406 A jnolingauth@georgefox.edu
NOLL, Cheryl 912-650-5648 131 F cnoll@southuniversity.edu
NOLL, Eric 518-388-6108 350 K nolle@union.edu
NOLL SORG, Carolyn 440-646-8114 394 G cnollsorg@ursuline.edu
NOLLAN, Damond 919-530-6399 370 C dnollan@nccu.edu
NOLLEY, Charles 708-534-5000 145 D cnolley@govst.edu
NOLSER, Michael, D 303-534-6290 81 C michael.nosler@colostate.edu
NOLT, David 406-496-4760 288 C dnolt@mtech.edu
NOLTE, Beth 573-681-5194 276 K noltem@lincolnu.edu
NOLTE, Jim 802-828-8512 503 D jim.nolte@vcfa.edu
NOLTEMEYER, J. Patrick 859-238-5218 194 E patrick.noltemeyer@centre.edu
NOMURA, Cory 909-748-8066 73 K cory_nomura@redlands.edu
NONAKA, Conrad 808-734-9539 136 C conradn@hawaii.edu
NONDORF, James 773-702-4101 161 D jnondorf@uchicago.edu
NONEMAKER, Jeffrey 909-593-3511 73 B jnonemaker@laverne.edu
NONEMAKER, Scott 315-792-3285 351 G scnonema@utica.edu
NONN, Lidia 920-465-2565 539 F nonnl@uwgb.edu
NONNAMAKER, John 504-314-2188 207 F jnonnama@tulane.edu
NOOK, Mark 406-657-2300 287 H mnook@msubillings.edu
NOOKS, Kirk, A 816-604-2044 277 I kirk.nooks@mcckc.edu
NOON, Molly 712-325-3306 180 B mnoon@iwcc.edu
NOONAN, Brigid 585-389-2396 334 B bnoonan8@naz.edu
NOONAN, Claire 708-714-9107 144 C cnoonan@dom.edu
NOONAN, Daniel 860-727-6902 90 F dnoonan@goodwin.edu
NOONAN, Ellen, R 413-205-3530 221 G ellen.noonan@aic.edu
NOONAN, John 919-660-4252 356 E john.noonan@duke.edu
NOONAN, Paul 617-730-7018 235 B paul.noonan@newbury.edu
NOONE, Anne 570-208-5899 422 D aenoone@kings.edu
NOONE, Kate 714-620-3700 28 G knoone@argosy.edu
NOONE, Pamela, K 570-577-7136 413 E noone@bucknell.edu

NOVICKI, Elizabeth 336-917-5421 368 F elizabeth.novicki@salem.edu
NOVIELLO, Sheri, R 229-333-5959 133 H srnoviello@valdosta.edu
NOVO, Frank 617-964-1111 222 B fnovo@ants.edu
NOVO, Lizza 503-223-2245 406 G lnovo@portland.chefs.edu
NOVOTNY, April 614-236-6565 378 H anovotny@capital.edu
NOVOTNY, Dorene 650-949-6210.. 44 M novotnydorene@fhda.edu
NOVOTNY, Frank, J 719-587-7622.. 78 I fjnovotn@adams.edu
NOVOTNY, Jodi 425-235-2369 525 G jnovotny@rtc.edu
NOVOTNY, Richard, J 440-525-7358 385 C rnovotny@lakelandcc.edu
NOWACZYK, Ronald 814-393-2223 430 E rnowaczyk@clarion.edu
NOWAK, Bill 502-213-2104 196 E bill.nowak@kctcs.edu
NOWAK, Jack 541-880-2224 406 E nowak@klamathcc.edu
NOWAK, Janice 904-470-8192 102 A janice.nowak@ewc.edu
NOWAK, Meg 607-431-4501 327 B nowakm@hartwick.edu
NOWAK, Patricia 219-980-6501 168 C nowakpat@iun.edu
NOWAK, Robert 847-635-1876 155 E rnowak@oakton.edu
NOWAK, Robert, J 262-243-5700 535 I robert.nowak@cuw.edu
NOWAK, Thomas, S 845-848-4000 324 B thomas.nowak@dc.edu
NOWAK, Tom 574-936-8898 164 A tom.nowak@ancilla.edu
NOWAK, Tony, J 414-847-3240 537 F tonynowak@miad.edu
NOWAR, Mariam 215-248-7311 424 G mnowar@ltsp.edu
NOWEL, OP, Mark, D 401-865-2649 441 F mnowel@providence.edu
NOWELL, Cheryl 305-348-2434 114 G nowell@fiu.edu
NOWICKI, Brian 608-258-2401 543 C bnowicki@madisoncollege.edu
NOWICKI, Laura 740-593-1969 389 H nowicki@ohio.edu
NOWICKI, Stacy, A 269-337-5750 244 I Stacy.Nowicki@kzoo.edu
NOWICKI, Stephen 919-668-3420 356 E snowicki@duke.edu
NOWICKI, Sue, A 989-837-4203 248 D nowicki@northwood.edu
NOWIK, Christine, M 717-736-4142 420 D cmnowik@hacc.edu
NOWLAN, Marilyn, L 860-727-6782.. 90 F mnowlan@goodwin.edu
NOWLIN, Brian 562-985-5537.. 33 F brian.nowlin@csulb.edu
NOWLIN, Steve 626-396-2397.. 28 J stephen.nowlin@artcenter.edu
NOWOGORSKI, Barbara 570-961-7835 422 G nowogorskib@lackawanna.edu
NOYES, Cynthia 269-749-7144 249 A cnoyes@olivetcollege.edu
NOYES, Michelle 252-451-8258 364 E
NRI, Monique, N 212-229-5592 334 C nrim@newschool.edu
NTOKO, Alfred 518-587-2100 348 A alfred.ntoko@esc.edu
NUBEL, Anna 402-280-2222 290 B AnnaNubel@creighton.edu
NUBILE, Anthony 701-349-5771 375 G tnubile@trinitybiblecollege.edu
NUCCI, John, A 617-973-1103 237 B jnucci@suffolk.edu
NUCCIARONE, Mary, B 574-631-6436 174 A Nucciarone.2@nd.edu
NUCKOLS, Jack 304-205-6600 531 A jack.nuckols@bridgevalley.edu
NUCKOLS, Melanie, L 336-734-7332 362 F mnuckols@forsythtech.edu
NUDELMAN, Felice 937-769-1351 376 L fnudelman@antioch.edu
NUESELL, Lisa, M 919-381-6912 369 B lnuesell@umo.edu
NUFER, Ken 719-549-3474.. 85 A ken.nufer@pueblocc.edu
NUGEN, Deb 402-399-2442 289 I dnugen@csm.edu
NUGENT, Barli 212-799-5000 329 I
NUGENT, Joe 831-479-6140.. 30 C jonugent@cabrillo.edu
NUGENT, John, D 860-439-5266.. 90 D john.nugent@conncoll.edu
NUGENT, Kari 815-802-8256 149 B knugent@kcc.edu
NUGENT, Katherine 601-266-5445 271 B katherine.nugent@usm.edu
NUGENT, Megan 503-251-2836 410 I mnugent@uws.edu
NUGENT, Richard 574-284-4542 172 G rnugent@saintmarys.edu
NULL, David 608-265-1988 539 D dnull@library.wisc.edu
NULL, Wesley 254-710-6120 469 D wesley_null@baylor.edu
NUMRICH, Camille 401-825-2237 441 C cnumrich@ccri.edu
NUNALEE, Carmen 252-823-5166 362 D nunaleec@edgecombe.edu
NUNAMAKER, Gail 989-386-6692 247 B gnunamaker@midmich.edu
NUNES, Grafton, J 216-421-7410 380 B gnunes@cia.edu
NUNES, Victoria 650-306-3274.. 64 C nunes@smccd.edu
NUNEZ, Anilsa, R 718-390-4006 340 G nuneza@stjohns.edu
NUNEZ, Awilda 787-769-2043 557 F awilda.nunez@upr.edu
NUNEZ, Elaine 787-786-3030 556 E enunez@ucb.edu.pr
NUNEZ, Elsa 860-465-5222.. 88 C nuneze@easternct.edu
NUNEZ, Elsa, M 860-465-5222.. 88 E nunez@easternct.edu
NUNEZ, Ivon 973-596-3478 304 D nunez@njit.edu
NUNEZ, Jose 650-358-6836.. 64 B nunezj@smccd.edu
NUNEZ, Jose Ramon 714-992-7030.. 56 F Jnunez@fullcoll.edu
NUNEZ, Steve, C 815-835-6263 158 I steve.c.nunez@svcc.edu
NUNEZ, William 402-472-2116 293 H wnunez2@unl.edu
NUNEZ, William, J 402-472-2097 293 H wnunez2@unl.edu
NUNEZ, III, William, J 337-550-1201 205 B wnunez@lsue.edu
NUNEZ, Yancy 806-716-2338 482 F ynunez@southplainscollege.edu
NUNLEY, Beth 815-802-8142 149 B bnunley@kcc.edu
NUNLEY, Ernest, L 276-739-2510 517 D enunley@vhcc.edu
NUNLEY, Gayle, R 802-656-8513 503 C gayle.nunley@uvm.edu
NUNN, Dana 970-248-1868.. 80 B dnunn@coloradomesa.edu
NUNN, Gaylene 254-519-5458 485 D nunn@tamuct.edu
NUNN, Lori, A 540-674-3615 516 B lnunn@nr.edu
NUNNA, Ramakrishna 559-278-2500.. 33 D rnunna@csufresno.edu
NUNNALLY, Delecia 209-954-5151.. 63 D dnunnally@deltacollege.edu
NUNO, Karina 707-546-4000.. 43 J knuno@empirecollege.com
NURNBERGER, Charles, A 757-825-2717 517 B nurnbergerc@tncc.edu
NUSBAUM, Nancy 512-245-2244 489 C nn01@txstate.edu
NUSENBAUM, Tatiana 212-349-4330 326 G tnusenbaum@globe.edu
NUSSBAUM, Daniel 860-231-5770.. 93 A dnussbaum@usj.edu
NUSSBAUM, Irwin 860-768-7904.. 92 F nussbaum@hartford.edu
NUSSBAUM, Renee 419-755-4772 387 E rnussbau@ncstatecollege.edu
NUSSEL, Jay, E 304-457-6581 529 C nusselje@ab.edu
NUSSEN, Jack 757-771-9978 111 L jack.nussen@saintleo.edu
NUSSER, Sarah, M 515-294-6344 175 G nusser@iastate.edu
NUSUM-SMITH, Michelle 301-846-2851 214 I mnusumsmith@frederick.edu
NUTEFALL, Jennifer 408-554-6829.. 65 A jnutefall@scu.edu
NUTER, Julie, L 515-294-6458 175 G jnuter@iastate.edu
NUTI, Larry 925-631-4901.. 61 G lnuti@stmarys-ca.edu
NUTT, Jill 616-395-7765 244 A nutt@hope.edu
NUTT, Lee Ann 281-351-3644 477 I leeann.nutt@lonestar.edu
NUTTALL, Neil 660-359-3948 279 L nnuttall@mail.ncmissouri.edu
NUTTER, April, H 606-783-9351 198 H a.nutter@moreheadstate.edu
NUTTER, Cheryl 419-251-1519 386 C cheryl.nutter@mercycollege.edu
NUTTER, Doug 301-860-3402 220 B dnutter@bowiestate.edu
NUTTER, Jeff 740-389-4636 386 B nutterj@mtc.edu
NUTTER, Mark 740-374-8716 395 D mnutter@wscc.edu
NUTTER, Sarah 703-993-1807 507 K snutter@gmu.edu
NUTTER, Susan, K 919-515-7188 370 D susan_nutter@ncsu.edu
NUTTLE, Louise, C 423-439-6052 461 D nuttle@etsu.edu
NUTTY, David 207-780-4276 213 A dnutty@usm.maine.edu
NUZZO, Jane 212-592-2000 342 F jnuzzo@sva.edu
NUÑEZ, Cheryl 360-475-7740 524 H cnunez@olympic.edu
NWAKEZE, Peter 718-933-6700 333 F pnwakeze@monroecollege.edu
NWANGWU, Winfred 401-874-1000 442 E winny@mail.uri.edu
NWANKWO, Charles 480-732-7020.. 14 K Charles.Nwankwo@cgc.edu
NWANNE, Andrew, I 575-234-9215 312 C anwanne@nmsu.edu
NWARIAKU, Fiemu, E 214-648-9968 496 A fiemu.nwariku@utsouthwestern.edu
NWOKEAFOR, Cosmos 301-860-3232 220 B cnwokeafor@bowiestate.edu
NWOSU, Peter 657-278-3602.. 33 E pnwosu@fullerton.edu
NYBERG, Christopher, L 315-684-6083 347 A nybergcl@morrisville.edu
NYBERG, Connie 307-855-2207 545 a cnyberg@cwc.edu
NYE, Jamey 916-563-3207.. 52 H nyej@crc.losrios.edu
NYE, Judith 732-571-3637 303 G nye@monmouth.edu
NYE, Robert, K 717-299-7793 436 D nye@stevenscollege.edu
NYGAARD, Steven 310-258-5522.. 53 C steven.nygaard@lmu.edu
NYGARD, Bonnie, K 907-786-6494.. 10 H bknygard@uaa.alaska.edu
NYGREEN, Ted 914-606-6789 352 G ted.nygreen@sunywcc.edu
NYHAMMER, Diane 608-757-7737 542 L dnyhammer@blackhawk.edu
NYHAN, Jeff 602-206-8220 297 A jnyhan@ccsnh.edu
NYIRENDA, Stanley, M 410-651-6672 219 H smnyirenda@umes.edu
NYLAND, Gerald 231-777-0315 247 G gerald.nyland@muskegoncc.edu
NYLEN, John 847-578-3252 157 G
NYPAVER, David 330-972-6876 392 H nypaver@uakron.edu
NYQUIST, J. Paul 312-329-4112 153 C paul.nyquist@moody.edu
NYRE, Joseph, E 914-633-2203 328 F jnyre@iona.edu
NYSTROM, Ellen 210-567-2640 495 B nystrom@uthscsa.edu
NYUL, Renata 617-373-7666 235 D
NZAMUTUNA, Issmael 951-785-2006.. 49 I inzamutu@lasierra.edu
NZEH, Okoroafor 706-821-8331 129 H onzeh@paine.edu
NZEOGWU, Okeleke 702-968-1659 296 D onzeogwu@roseman.edu

O

O"BRIEN, Craig 202-231-4133 547 N craig.o'brien@dodiis.mil
OAKES, Barbee 336-758-3106 372 G oaks@wfu.edu
OAKES, Mary 312-369-6802 143 C moakes@colum.edu
OAKLEY, Christina 561-912-1211 102 N coakley@evergladesuniversity.edu
OAKLEY, Danielle 608-262-8350 539 D droakley@uhs.wisc.edu
OAKLEY, Eloy 562-938-4122.. 51 A eoakley@lbcc.edu
OAKMAN, Tommy 828-694-1725 360 D t_oakman@blueridge.edu
OAKS, Beth 605-642-6411 453 G beth.oaks@bhsu.edu
OAKS, Diane, G 949-451-5277.. 67 E doaks@ivc.edu
OAKS, Geneva 951-343-4702.. 30 D gcooperoaks@calbaptist.edu
OAKS, Nick 605-642-6545 453 G nicholas.oaks@bhsu.edu
OAKS SMITH, Tonya 870-230-5348.. 21 B smithto@hsu.edu
OANES, Laura 507-457-6909 264 B loanes@smumn.edu
OARD, Tasha 406-586-3585 287 B tasha.oard@montanabiblecollege.edu
OATES, Bruce 847-635-1705 155 E boates@oakton.edu
OATES, Bruce 847-635-1753 155 E boates@oakton.edu
OATES, Justin 201-216-3495 308 D Justin.Oates@stevens.edu
OATES, Richard 706-864-1840 133 A richard.oates@ung.edu
OATES, Richard 706-864-1602 133 A richard.oates@ung.edu
OATES, Scott, F 804-828-9124 514 F sfoates@vcu.edu
OATEY, J. Sue 218-299-3455 255 B joatey@cord.edu
OBA, Saichi 907-450-8000.. 10 G soba@alaska.edu
OBBINK, Kim 406-994-6550 287 G kobbink@montana.edu
OBELOVA, Olga 718-522-9073 315 E obelova@asa.edu
OBER, Jay 305-442-9223 108 G jober@mrc.edu
OBERDIEK, John, F 856-225-6513 307 A oberdiek@camlaw.rutgers.edu
OBEREM, Graham 760-750-4050.. 35 B oberem@csusm.edu
OBERFELDT, Kathleen 718-390-3435 352 C koberfel@wagner.edu
OBERG, Beth 217-479-7130 151 J beth.oberg@mac.edu
OBERGFELL, Ann 260-481-6100 168 D obergfea@ipfw.edu
OBERHELMAN, Don 805-756-1407.. 32 E obe@calpoly.edu
OBERHOLTZER, Brent 717-867-6111 423 I oberholt@lvc.edu
OBERLANDER, Cyril 707-826-3441.. 35 D Cyril.Oberlander@humboldt.edu
OBERLANDER, Janell 970-824-1102.. 80 L janell.oberlander@cncc.edu
OBERMAN, Anne 320-363-5999 254 J aoberman@csbsju.edu
OBERMEISTER, Tuvia, M 718-377-0777 338 H
OBERMEYER, Carole 316-295-5779 187 C obermeyer@friends.edu
OBERMEYER, Carole 316-295-5628 187 C obermeyer@friends.edu
OBERQUELL, Christian 406-265-3761 288 A coberquell@msun.edu
OBERSTEIN, Leonard 410-484-7200 217 E loberstein@nirc.edu
OBERT, Brian 308-345-8109 291 H obertb@mpcc.edu
OBI, Stacey 717-728-2248 415 B staceyobi@centralpenn.edu
OBIELODAN, James, B 502-597-4723 197 G james.obielodan@kysu.edu
OBILADE, Sandra, O 270-686-4209 193 G sandra.obilade@brescia.edu
OBIN, Jason 773-508-8643 151 E jobin@luc.edu
OBISESAN, Thomas, O 202-806-2550.. 96 B tobisesan@howard.edu
OBLANDER, Douglas 843-208-8256 450 D Oblander@uscb.edu
OBLANDER, Frances, W 912-650-5684 131 F foblander@southuniversity.edu
OBLEY, Debora 510-987-9112.. 70 J debora.obley@ucop.edu
OBLOY, Leonard 248-683-0446 250 G lobloy@sscms.edu
OBRENTZ, Barbara 678-891-2685 125 G barbara.obrentz@gpc.edu
OBRESLEY, Amber 406-791-5248 288 J aobresley01@ugf.edu
OBSNIUK, Karen 734-432-5648 246 B kobsniuk@madonna.edu
OBST, Cheryl 619-201-8951.. 67 I registrar@socalsem.edu
OBSTA, Kim 361-572-6410 496 D kim.obsta@victoriacollege.edu
OBURN, Martha 713-718-8670 475 C martha.oburn@hccs.edu
OCAMPO, Arturo 760-750-4309.. 35 B aocampo@csusm.edu
OCAMPO, Carlotta 202-884-9209.. 97 A ocampoc@trinitydc.edu
OCASIO, Arcadio 787-257-0000 557 F arcadio.ocasio@upr.edu
OCASIO, Joseph 610-917-1430 438 G jaocasio@valleyforge.edu
OCASIO, Luz 787-765-1915 554 E locasio@opto.inter.edu

OLDHAM, Deborah .... 601-484-8636 268 B
doldham@meridiancc.edu
OLDHAM, Philip, B ...... 931-372-3241 462 A
poldham@tntech.edu
OLDHAM, Robin .... 502-863-8031 195 A
Robin_Oldham@georgetowncollege.edu
OLDHAM, Steve .... 254-295-4505 492 C
soldham@umhb.edu
OLDHAM, Todd, M .... 585-292-3057 333 G
toldham@monroecc.edu
OLDS, Carole .... 719-502-3249.. 84 J
carole.olds@ppcc.edu
OLDS, Scott .... 559-244-5957.. 68 J
scott.olds@scccd.edu
OLEGERIIL, Jay .... 680-488-2471 550 C
jayo@palau.edu
OLEJNICZAK, Sarah ...... 414-256-1211 538 A
olejnics@mtmary.edu
OLEJNICZAK-CAUSHAJ,
Joanna .... 248-683-0310 250 G
jolejniczak@sscms.edu
OLEN, Lynda .... 251-380-4195.... 7 F
lolen@shc.edu
OLEN, Simcha .... 718-252-6333 353 N
OLENDER, Ursula, J ..... 413-542-8203 222 A
uolender@amherst.edu
OLENIK, Fred .... 801-818-8900 498 P
fred.olenik@provocollege.edu
OLENIK-DORMAN, Lisa 334-833-4465.... 4 E
ldorman@huntingdon.edu
OLENYK, Mary Ellen ...... 413-662-5599 230 C
m.olenyk@mcla.edu
OLESIUK, Sue .... 828-398-7176 360 A
sueholesiuk@abtech.edu
OLESKA, Carla .... 413-594-2761 225 D
oleskac@elms.edu
OLESON, Misty .... 918-781-7225 396 F
olesonm@bacone.edu
OLGUIN, Javier, E .... 972-860-5306 472 E
JavierEOlguin@dcccd.edu
OLGUIN-RYAN,
Elizabeth .... 915-831-6325 473 J
eolguin@epcc.edu
OLIAN, Judy, D .... 310-825-7982.. 71 D
judy.olian@anderson.ucla.edu
OLIKONG, Deikola .... 680-488-2471 550 C
olikongd@gmail.com
OLIN, Jessica .... 302-736-2455.. 94 E
jessica.olin@wesley.edu
OLIN, Joanna .... 413-559-5521 227 C
OLIN, Robert, F .... 205-348-5972.... 8 E
olin@as.ua.edu
OLINER, Alex .... 212-349-4330 326 G
aoliner@globe.edu
OLINER, Martin .... 212-349-4330 326 G
moliner@globe.edu
OLING-SISAY, Mary ...... 415-955-2100.. 26 I
moling-sisay@alliant.edu
OLINGER, CSC,
Gerard, J .... 503-943-8532 410 H
olinger@up.edu
OLINGER, Richard, P ... 814-868-7767 423 B
rpolinger@mch1.org
OLINGER, Ronald, J ..... 913-360-7413 184 K
rolinger@benedictine.edu
OLIVA, Giacomo .... 212-217-4040 325 C
giacomo_oliva@fitnyc.edu
OLIVA, Joseph, E .... 718-990-6421 340 G
olivaj@stjohns.edu
OLIVA, Julia .... 718-289-5100 318 E
julia.oliva@bcc.cuny.edu
OLIVARES, Carlos, J ..... 787-279-1912 553 H
colivares@bayamon.inter.edu
OLIVARES-URUETA,
Mayra .... 817-515-1197 484 B
mayra.olivaresurueta@tccd.edu
OLIVAREZ, Juan .... 616-632-2880 239 E
edisomon@aquinas.edu
OLIVE, David, W .... 276-326-4466 505 D
dolive@bluefield.edu
OLIVE-TAYLOR, Becky .. 336-278-6500 356 F
oliveb@elon.edu
OLIVEIRA, Judy .... 808-689-2689 136 A
joliveira@hawaii.edu
OLIVEIRA, Sandra, J .... 401-865-2602 441 F
solivei6@providence.edu
OLIVER, Debra .... 937-708-5748 395 E
doliver@wilberforce.edu
OLIVER, Denita .... 256-215-4290.... 2 G
doliver@cacc.edu
OLIVER, Diane .... 585-389-2641 334 B
OLIVER, Dominick .... 412-365-1262 415 C
doliver@chatham.edu
OLIVER, Ebigaly .... 787-878-5475 553 F
eoliver@arecibo.inter.edu
OLIVER, Elizabeth .... 618-393-3491 146 F
olivere@iecc.edu
OLIVER, Erik .... 802-383-6662 501 F
eoliver@champlain.edu
OLIVER, Helen .... 662-252-8000 270 C
holiver@rustcollege.edu
OLIVER, Jeanne .... 503-352-2740 408 I
jeanne1@pacificu.edu
OLIVER, Justin .... 757-925-6342 516 E
joliver@pdc.edu
OLIVER, Justin .... 757-925-6302 516 E
joliver@pdc.edu
OLIVER, Kenneth, R ...... 660-248-6225 272 N
koliver@centralmethodist.edu
OLIVER, Lillian, M .... 787-723-4481 551 B
loliver@ceaprc.edu
OLIVER, Melvin, L .... 805-893-8354.. 72 D
moliver@ltsc.ucsb.edu
OLIVER, Michael .... 734-462-4400 250 A
moliver@schoolcraft.edu
OLIVER, Nancy .... 704-461-6257 354 J
NancyOliver@bac.edu
OLIVER, Parker .... 931-598-1586 460 I
pwoliver@sewanee.edu
OLIVER, Patricia Belton 713-743-2400 491 D
poliver@central.uh.edu
OLIVER, Ralph .... 785-864-5900 191 G
roliver@ku.edu
OLIVER, Rebecca .... 870-972-2308.. 19 F
rsoliver@astate.edu
OLIVER, Richard, E .... 573-884-6705 283 H
oliverr@missouri.edu
OLIVER, Robert, C .... 605-274-4111 452 A
rob.oliver@augie.edu
OLIVER, Robin, C .... 828-227-7337 372 C
rcoliver@wcu.edu
OLIVER, Ruben, D .... 405-466-2996 398 E
rdoliver@langston.edu
OLIVER,
Samuel (Dub), W .... 731-661-5180 464 G
doliver@uu.edu
OLIVER, Sandi .... 803-738-7699 447 H
olivers@midlandstech.edu
OLIVER, Sharon, J .... 919-530-5313 370 C
soliver@nccu.edu
OLIVER, Sharon, M ...... 207-581-1110 212 C
smoliver@maine.edu
OLIVER, Shawn .... 609-497-7818 305 B
shawn.oliver@ptsem.edu
OLIVER, Thomas .... 830-372-8050 487 C
toliver@tlu.edu
OLIVER, Tricia, M .... 508-849-3344 222 C
toliver@annamaria.edu
OLIVERA, Tammie .... 305-428-5674 109 A
tolivera@aii.edu
OLIVERAS, Ivette .... 787-848-1589 555 D
ioliveras@popac.edu
OLIVERIA, Steve .... 707-468-3081.. 54 A
soliveria@mendocino.edu
OLIVERIO, Robert .... 602-386-4110.. 11 F
robert.oliverio@arizonachristian.edu
OLIVEROS, Claire .... 503-399-5076 404 L
claire.oliveros@chemeketa.edu
OLIVEROS, Jon .... 847-397-0300 139 F
OLIVETTE, Michael .... 914-606-6912 352 G
michael.olivette@sunywcc.edu
OLIVIERE, Tod .... 617-266-1400 223 F
OLIVIERI, Janies .... 787-250-1912 554 A
jolivieri@metro.inter.edu
OLIVIERI-LENAHAN,
Elizabeth .... 914-633-2547 328 F
eolivieri@iona.edu
OLIVO, Michael .... 516-323-4840 333 E
molivo@molloy.edu
OLIVO-CRUZ, Gilberto .. 787-480-2387 551 H
golivo@sanjuanciudadpatria.com
OLKHOVSKAYA, Elena .. 510-436-1037.. 47 C
olkhovskaya@hnu.edu
OLKIEWICZ, Rose .... 920-748-8137 538 I
0342mgr@follett.com
OLLA, Phillip .... 734-432-5363 246 B
polla@madonna.edu
OLLER, Elizabeth .... 312-935-4245 148 B
eoller@icsw.edu
OLLEY EUSTICE,
Lorraine .... 847-566-6401 162 G
lolley@usml.edu
OLLIFF, Thomas .... 954-201-7693.. 99 G
toliff@broward.edu
OLLINGER, Nancy .... 610-902-8276 414 B
nancy.ollinger@cabrini.edu
OLLSON, Joanne .... 413-782-1343 238 A
joanne.ollson@wne.edu
OLMOS, Mary .... 626-568-8850.. 49 J
OLMSTEAD, Audrey .... 248-689-8282 251 I
aolmstea@walshcollege.edu
OLMSTEAD, Karen, L .... 410-543-6489 220 E
klolmstead@salisbury.edu
OLMSTEAD, Steve .... 918-293-4744 400 E
steve.olmstead@okstate.edu
OLNEY, Douglas, P ...... 218-755-2764 258 B
dolney@bemidjistate.edu
OLOGUNJA, Folake .... 212-966-0300 334 D
fologunja@nyaa.edu
OLON, John .... 724-852-3241 439 C
jolon@waynesburg.edu
OLOVSON, Matthew ...... 231-591-2152 242 L
MatthewOlovson@ferris.edu
OLSCHWANG, Alana ..... 909-607-8135.. 39 E
alana.olschwang@cgu.edu
OLSEN, Anika .... 928-523-1428.. 16 C
Anika.Olsen@nau.edu
OLSEN, Ann, E .... 502-272-8133 193 E
aolsen@bellarmine.edu
OLSEN, Danny, R .... 801-422-5648 497 J
danny_olsen@byu.edu
OLSEN, David .... 785-227-3380 185 A
olsends@bethanylb.edu
OLSEN, Gary, R .... 570-941-7723 438 F
gary.olsen@scranton.edu
OLSEN, Jamie .... 785-670-3100 192 B
jamie.colsen@washburn.edu
OLSEN, Jane .... 320-308-4958 261 E
jolsen@stcloudstate.edu
OLSEN, Jo .... 218-723-7040 255 A
jolsen@css.edu
OLSEN, Julene .... 435-722-6900 499 G
julene@ubatc.edu
OLSEN, Karin .... 406-447-4495 286 D
kjolsen@carroll.edu
OLSEN, Kris .... 714-628-7303.. 38 B
kolsen@chapman.edu
OLSEN, Matthew .... 918-495-7707 401 B
maolsen@oru.edu
OLSEN, Michelle, D ...... 417-836-5274 279 A
MOlsen@MissouriState.edu
OLSEN, Morgan, R .... 480-727-9920.. 11 J
morgan.r.olsen@asu.edu
OLSEN, Pete .... 831-645-1362.. 54 H
polsen@mpc.edu
OLSEN, Renee .... 208-792-2151 138 E
rmolsen@lcsc.edu
OLSEN, Steve .... 310-825-4321.. 71 D
OLSEN, Steven, A .... 310-825-3444.. 71 D
solsen@conet.ucla.edu
OLSEN, Steven, M .... 716-878-4113 345 B
olsensw@buffalostate.edu
OLSEN KELLY, Jodi ...... 206-296-5405 526 F
jkelly@seattleu.edu
OLSEN KRENGEL,
Jennifer .... 651-641-3516 256 J
jolsenkrengel001@luthersem.edu
OLSON, Adam, J .... 813-988-5131 103 L
olsona@floridacollege.edu
OLSON, Allen .... 360-596-5283 527 B
aolson@spscc.edu
OLSON, Alma, E .... 330-972-6577 392 H
aolson@uakron.edu
OLSON, Andrea, I .... 425-739-8127 523 I
andrea.olson@lwtech.edu
OLSON, Becky .... 907-745-3201.. 10 B
info@akbible.edu
OLSON, Ben .... 907-745-3201.. 10 B
registrar@akbible.edu
OLSON, Cari .... 701-858-3323 374 B
cari.olson@minotstateu.edu
OLSON, Carolyn .... 320-308-5156 261 F
colson@sctcc.edu
OLSON, Cathy .... 413-755-4419 233 B
colson@stcc.edu
OLSON, Christa .... 515-271-2084 177 K
christa.olson@drake.edu
OLSON, Dawn .... 701-483-2027 373 H
Dawn.M.Olson.1@dickinsonstate.edu
OLSON, Debora .... 414-256-1202 538 A
olsond@mtmary.edu
OLSON, Deborah .... 863-784-7275 113 C
deborah.olson@southflorida.edu
OLSON, Don .... 218-723-6471 255 A
dolson@css.edu
OLSON, Douglas .... 708-456-0300 161 C
dolson@triton.edu
OLSON, Dustin .... 805-893-4151.. 72 D
dustin.olson@police.ucsb.edu
OLSON, Eric .... 610-902-8275 414 B
eric.j.olson@cabrini.edu
OLSON, Gary, A .... 716-839-8210 323 F
golson@daemen.edu
OLSON, Hadley .... 701-627-4738 373 E
holson@fortbertholdcc.edu
OLSON, Heidi, L .... 320-222-5209 261 B
heidi.olson@ridgewater.edu
OLSON, Ian .... 907-474-5317.. 10 I
inolson@alaska.edu
OLSON, Jeffery, D .... 651-638-6241 254 A
jeff-olson@bethel.edu
OLSON, Jeffery, E .... 801-863-8951 500 B
JOlson@uvu.edu
OLSON, John .... 425-388-9407 522 I
jolson@everettcc.edu
OLSON, Judith .... 760-591-3012.. 74 A
jolson@usa.edu
OLSON, Kerry, J .... 409-882-3362 488 G
kerry.olson@lsco.edu
OLSON, Kristin .... 215-641-5571 420 A
olson.k@gmercyu.edu
OLSON, Ksenia .... 218-723-6139 255 A
solson19@css.edu
OLSON, Linda .... 303-871-6801.. 86 H
lolson@du.edu
OLSON, Lynette .... 620-235-4113 190 G
lolson@pittstate.edu
OLSON, Marjean .... 212-749-2802 331 I
molson@msmnyc.edu
OLSON, Mark .... 763-544-9501 253 J
OLSON, Mark, J .... 703-812-4757 509 E
molson@leland.edu
OLSON, Mary Ellen ...... 920-403-3181 538 K
maryellen.olson@snc.edu
OLSON, Matthew .... 781-280-3802 232 B
olsonm@middlesex.mass.edu
OLSON, Megan .... 907-786-1764.. 10 H
msolson5@uaa.alaska.edu
OLSON, Michael .... 202-250-2652.. 95 C
michael.olson@gallaudet.edu
OLSON, Nancy .... 641-585-8147 183 I
olsonn@waldorf.edu
OLSON, Nancy .... 217-732-3168 150 G
nolson@lincolnchristian.edu
OLSON, Neil .... 573-882-3768 283 H
olsonne@missouri.edu
OLSON, Paul .... 701-252-3467 375 J
paul.olson@uj.edu
OLSON, Peter .... 231-348-6660 248 A
polson@ncmich.edu
OLSON, Ray, A .... 614-235-4136 392 D
rolson@TLSohio.edu
OLSON, Robert .... 253-833-9111 523 B
rolson@greenriver.edu
OLSON, Sandra .... 508-929-8025 230 G
solson@worcester.edu
OLSON, Sara, M .... 402-465-2185 292 E
solson@nebrwesleyan.edu
OLSON, Scott .... 906-635-2828 245 H
solson@lssu.edu
OLSON, Scott, R .... 507-457-5003 262 D
solson@winona.edu
OLSON, Shari, L .... 602-243-8035.. 15 F
shari.olson@southmountaincc.edu
OLSON, Sharon .... 562-985-5585.. 33 F
sharon.olson@csulb.edu
OLSON, Shelly, Y .... 715-833-6675 542 M
solson@cvtc.edu
OLSON, Sheryl .... 763-424-0882 260 E
solson@nhcc.edu
OLSON, Sonja .... 605-668-1619 452 I
sonja.olson@mtmc.edu
OLSON, Stephen .... 765-998-5119 173 B
stolson@taylor.edu
OLSON, Suzanne, C ..... 715-836-2327 539 E
olsonsc@uwec.edu
OLSON, Todd .... 202-687-4056.. 95 E
tao4@georgetown.edu
OLSON, Warren .... 785-227-3380 185 A
olsonw@bethanylb.edu
OLSON, Wendy, L .... 509-777-4313 529 A
wolson@whitworth.edu
OLSON-LOY, Sandra ..... 320-589-6013 265 A
olsonloy@morris.umn.edu
OLSSON, Jackie .... 763-424-0731 260 E
jolsson@nhcc.edu
OLSSON, Roy .... 616-331-3358 243 E
olssonr@gvsu.edu
OLSTEIN, Binyamin .... 847-982-2500 146 A
olstein@htc.edu
OLSWANG, Steven .... 206-239-4500 520 K
solswang@cityu.edu
OLSZEWSKI, Gabriel, G 203-432-2330.. 93 C
gabriel.olszewski@yale.edu
OLTMAN, Eva .... 502-213-4245 196 E
eva.oltman@kctcs.edu
OLTROGGE, Michael ..... 402-494-2311 291 M
moltrogge@thenicc.edu
OLUIC, Steven .... 440-525-7079 385 C
soluic@lakelandcc.edu
OLZINSKI, Len .... 570-740-0370 425 A
lolzinski@luzerne.edu
OMACHONU, John .... 470-578-6406 127 M
jomachon@kennesaw.edu
OMACHONU, John, O .. 615-898-2329 461 E
john.omachonu@mtsu.edu
OMAN, Nina .... 509-865-8500 523 C
oman_n@heritage.edu
OMANN, Bernie .... 320-308-1600 261 E
BOmann@stcloudstate.edu
OMAR, Richard .... 646-216-2863 335 D
romar@sft.edu
OMARI, Safiya .... 601-979-6851 267 H
safiya.r.omari@jsums.edu
OMER, Nicole .... 801-957-4209 500 E
nicole.omer@slcc.edu
OMINSKY, Paul .... 609-258-3000 305 C
pominsky@princeton.edu

ORTIZ, Hilda, L ... 787-863-2390 553 I
hilda.ortiz@fajardo.inter.edu
ORTIZ, Isaac ... 210-924-4338 469 B
registrar@bua.edu
ORTIZ, Jaime ... 713-743-7310 491 D
jortiz22@uh.edu
ORTIZ, Jennifer ... 210-486-4208 466 K
jortiz157@alamo.edu
ORTIZ, Johnathan ... 505-454-2596 311 B
jortiz@luna.edu
ORTIZ, Jose, M ... 510-466-7202.. 58 I
jortiz@peralta.edu
ORTIZ, Juanita ... 405-733-7413 401 L
jrortiz@rose.edu
ORTIZ, Judy ... 714-449-7470.. 53 D
jortiz@ketchum.edu
ORTIZ, Kendra, M ... 787-780-0070 550 G
kortiz@caribbean.edu
ORTIZ, Kristina ... 212-752-1530 330 C
kristina.ortiz@limcollege.edu
ORTIZ, Laura ... 630-466-7900 162 K
lortiz@waubonsee.edu
ORTIZ, Lillian, M ... 508-854-4232 232 F
lmortiz@qcc.mass.edu
ORTIZ, Luis, A ... 787-725-8120 552 G
ORTIZ, Luz ... 787-864-2222 553 J
luz.ortiz@guayama.inter.edu
ORTIZ, Luz, M ... 787-832-6000 552 K
mortiz@icprjc.edu
ORTIZ, Maribel ... 787-758-2525 558 C
maribel.ortiz5@upr.edu
ORTIZ, Mariely ... 787-815-0000 557 D
mariely.ortiz@upr.edu
ORTIZ, Mario ... 574-520-5511 168 F
ortizmr@iusb.edu
ORTIZ, Maritza ... 787-264-1912 554 C
maritza_ortiz_figueroa@intersg.edu
ORTIZ, Mary Lou ... 848-932-1990 307 B
marylou.ortiz@oldqueens.rutgers.edu
ORTIZ, Mati ... 716-286-8504 336 E
mortiz@niagara.edu
ORTIZ, Migdalia ... 787-279-1912 553 H
morti@bayamon.inter.edu
ORTIZ, Mildred ... 787-264-1940 554 C
milortiz@intersg.edu
ORTIZ, Nancy ... 210-297-9198 468 K
nortiz@baptisthealthsystem.com
ORTIZ, Noel ... 787-786-3030 556 E
nortiz@ucb.edu.pr
ORTIZ, Nuria ... 650-289-3336.. 61 H
nuria.ortiz@stpatricksseminary.org
ORTIZ, Rafael ... 787-725-6500 551 A
rortiz@albizu.edu
ORTIZ, Rafael ... 212-280-1342 351 B
rortiz@uts.columbia.edu
ORTIZ, Ralph ... 559-734-9000.. 63 E
ralpho@sjvc.edu
ORTIZ, Rosa ... 787-738-2161 557 G
rosa.ortiz1@upr.edu
ORTIZ, Vivian ... 781-239-3101 231 G
vortiz@massbay.edu
ORTIZ, Wilson ... 787-265-5413 558 B
wilson.ortiz3@uprm.edu
ORTIZ, Zoraida ... 787-743-7979 555M
zortiz@suagm.edu
ORTIZ-CINTRÓN, Jesús 787-993-8878 557 E
jesus.ortiz3@upr.edu
ORTIZ COLON, Yadira .. 787-725-8120 552 G
yortiz@eap.edu
ORTIZ-GÓMEZ,
Adelaida, L ... 787-993-8965 557 E
adelaida.ortiz1@upr.edu
ORTIZ HENDRICKS,
Carmen ... 212-960-0820 353 P
cortiz@yu.edu
ORTIZ-MORETTA, Amy .. 937-298-3399 385 A
amy.ortiz-moretta@kc.edu
ORTIZ-RUIZ, Wilfredo ... 787-993-8855 557 E
wilfredo.ortiz5@upr.edu
ORTIZ-VAZQUEZ,
Juan, M ... 787-250-0000 557 B
juanm.ortiz@upr.edu
ORTIZ-WALTERS,
Rowena ... 518-564-3190 346 B
rorti002@plattsburgh.edu
ORTIZ-ZAYAS, Jose, E .. 787-857-3600 553 G
jeortiz@br.inter.edu
ORTMAN, William ... 973-278-5400 300 C
william-ortman@berkeleycollege.edu
ORTMAN, William ... 973-278-5400 316 D
william-ortman@berkeleycollege.edu
ORTMEIER, Shane ... 605-882-5284 452 G
ortmeiers@lakeareatech.edu
ORTMEYER, Rose Ann .. 573-681-5044 276 K
ortmeyr@lincolnu.edu
ORTNER, Richard ... 617-912-9134 224 C
rortner@bostonconservatory.edu
ORTO, Christianne ... 212-749-2802 331 I
corto@msmnyc.edu
ORTON, Donna, J ... 641-422-4216 181 E
ortondon@niacc.edu
ORTON, Mozelle ... 801-957-4561 500 E
mozelle.orton@slcc.edu
ORTON, Vince ... 562-860-2451.. 37 L
vorton@cerritos.edu
ORTQUIST-AHRENS,
Leslie ... 859-985-3670 193 F
ortquistahrensl@berea.edu
ORVIS, Arleen ... 563-387-1005 180M
orvisarl@luther.edu
ORWIG, Greg ... 509-777-4580 529 A
gorwig@whitworth.edu
ORZE, Carole ... 312-567-3636 147 E
orze@iit.edu
ORZECH, Mary Jo ... 585-395-2141 345 A
morzech@brockport.edu
ORZECHOWSKI, Laurie . 419-824-3959 385 F
lorzechowski@lourdes.edu
ORZECHOWSKI,
Michael ... 212-280-1301 351 B
morzechowski@uts.columbia.edu
ORZOLEK, Mariah ... 419-783-2358 381 G
morzolek@defiance.edu
OSADJAN, Justin ... 312-341-2128 157 E
josadjan@roosevelt.edu
OSAE-KWAPONG, John 419-434-5877 393 F
osae-kwapong@findlay.edu
OSAGIE, Linda ... 972-860-8016 472 D
losagie@dcccd.edu
OSAKWE, Nneka-Nora .. 229-430-1043 119 H
nora.osakwe@asurams.edu
OSANTOWSKI,
Kimberly ... 248-204-3940 245 J
kosantows@ltu.edu
OSBAHR, Diane ... 712-325-3235 180 B
dosbahr@iwcc.edu
OSBON, Cindy ... 301-846-2593 214 I
cosbon@frederick.edu
OSBORN, Charles ... 913-360-7601 184 K
chucko@benedictine.edu
OSBORN, Chastity ... 217-709-0945 150 C
cosborn@lakeviewcol.edu
OSBORN, Edward, H ... 860-465-5303.. 88 E
osborne@easternct.edu
OSBORN, Fred ... 541-684-4644 409 A
fosborn@pioneerpacific.edu
OSBORN, Jeffrey ... 609-771-2724 301 E
josborn@tcnj.edu
OSBORN, Kevin ... 626-584-5200.. 45 F
osborn@fuller.edu
OSBORN, Richard, E ... 423-439-8300 461 D
osbornr@etsu.edu
OSBORN, Terry ... 941-359-4200 116 D
OSBORN, William ... 928-428-8286.. 13 L
bill.osborn@eac.edu
OSBORNE, Curtis ... 510-649-2477.. 46 E
cosborne@gtu.edu
OSBORNE, Dawn ... 918-781-7281 396 F
osborned@bacone.edu
OSBORNE, Jeanne ... 330-287-1211 389 B
osborne.2@osu.edu
OSBORNE, John ... 405-425-5463 399 J
john.osborne@oc.edu
OSBORNE, John ... 305-428-5700 109 A
josborne@aii.edu
OSBORNE, John ... 304-829-7395 529 H
josborne@bethanywv.edu
OSBORNE, Kevin ... 336-342-4261 365 E
osbornek@rockinghamcc.edu
OSBORNE, Mark ... 513-244-4892 387 A
mark.osborne@msj.edu
OSBORNE, Maurice ... 501-370-5211.. 22 E
mosborne@philander.edu
OSBORNE, Michelle ... 518-454-5141 322 C
osbornem@strose.edu
OSBORNE, Shelley ... 704-991-0203 366 D
sosborne7501@stanly.edu
OSBORNE, Steven, C ... 843-953-5574 445 B
osbornes@cofc.edu
OSBORNE, Thomas ... 713-942-3483 493 J
osborntm@stthom.edu
OSBOURNE, Jesse ... 859-336-5082 199 B
jesseosbourne@sccky.edu
OSBURN, Jan ... 254-867-3014 488 B
jan.osburn@tstc.edu
OSBURN, Monica ... 919-515-2423 370 D
monica_osburn@ncsu.edu
OSBURN, Wade ... 731-989-6067 456 K
wosburn@fhu.edu
OSBY, Rachel, V ... 256-824-6549.... 9 A
Rachel.Osby@uah.edu
OSEBY, Todd ... 651-779-3276 258 D
todd.oseby@century.edu
OSEGUEDA, Roberto ... 915-747-5680 494 B
osegueda@utep.edu
OSEGUERA, Tonantzin .. 657-278-3211.. 33 E
toseguera@fullerton.edu
OSENGA, Annette ... 510-780-4500.. 50 G
aosenga@lifewest.edu
OSGOOD, Jeffery ... 610-436-0045 432 B
josgood@wcupa.edu
OSGOOD, Ken ... 303-273-3596.. 80 O
kosgood@mines.edu
OSGOOD, Patricia ... 617-989-4025 237 G
teresiak@wit.edu
OSGUTHORPE, Richard . 208-426-1611 137 E
RichardOsguthorpe@boisestate.edu
OSHIRO, Cathie, R ... 620-792-9234 184 I
oshiroc@bartonccc.edu
OSHIRO, James ... 503-554-2235 406 A
joshiro@georgefox.edu
OSHIRO, Robyn ... 808-689-2900 136 A
robyno@hawaii.edu
OSHIRO, Wayde ... 808-455-0378 136 G
waydeo@hawaii.edu
OSINGA, Mark, L ... 864-833-8310 448 E
mlosinga@presby.edu
OSIRIM, Mary, J ... 610-526-5167 413 D
mosirim@brynmawr.edu
OSISEK, Vincent ... 803-750-2510.. 96 H
OSKAMP, Shirley ... 802-287-8388 501 I
oskamps@greenmtn.edu
OSMANSON, Deb ... 402-449-2820 290 F
dosmanson@graceu.edu
OSMANSON, Deb ... 402-449-2844 290 F
dosmanson@graceu.edu
OSPITALE, Michael ... 631-632-9085 344 C
michael.ospitale@stonybrook.edu
OSSEIRAN-HANNA,
Khatmeh ... 718-982-2365 319 A
khatmeh.osseiran-hanna@csi.cuny.edu
OSTASH, Heather ... 760-384-6249.. 49 F
hostash@cerrocoso.edu
OSTDIEK, Donald ... 713-348-4786 480M
dho@rice.edu
OSTENDARP, Timothy ... 443-352-4348 218 E
tostendarp@stevenson.edu
OSTENDORF, Trevor ... 530-541-4660.. 50 A
sm420@bncollege.com
OSTENDORFF, Stephen . 212-343-1234 332 I
sostendorff@mcny.edu
OSTER, Ben Zion ... 323-937-3763.. 77 J
boster@yoec.edu
OSTER, Cynthia ... 856-691-8600 301 H
coster@cccnj.edu
OSTER, Joseph, J ... 410-704-2151 221 A
joster@towson.edu
OSTER-AALAND, Laura . 701-231-7052 374 C
laura.oster-aaland@ndsu.edu
OSTERBIND, Kelly ... 251-460-6251.... 9 F
osterbind@southalabama.edu
OSTERGREN, Warren ... 575-835-5227 311 I
vpaa@admin.nmt.edu
OSTERHOUDT, Lori, B .. 607-746-4692 347 G
osterhlb@delhi.edu
OSTERTHUN, Stu ... 402-323-3401 293 A
sosterthun@southeast.edu
OSTGAARD, Kolleen ... 916-484-8569.. 52 I
ostgaak@arc.losrios.edu
OSTLER, Jon ... 435-283-7361 500 D
jon.ostler@snow.edu
OSTLUND, Kara ... 704-637-4410 355 H
kostlund@catawba.edu
OSTOLAZA, Magda, E ... 787-257-7373 555 L
ue_mostolaza@suagm.edu
OSTRANDER, David ... 503-883-2217 406 I
dostrand@linfield.edu
OSTRANDER, Gary, K ... 850-644-3347 115 A
gary@fsu.edu
OSTRANDER, Tammy ... 218-723-6173 255 A
tostrand@css.edu
OSTROSKE, Georgette ... 516-918-3607 316 L
gostroske@bcl.edu
OSTROW, James ... 617-243-2111 227 K
jostrow@lasell.edu
OSTROWICKI,
Jacqueline ... 402-472-7130 293 F
jostrowicki@nebraska.edu
OSTRYE, Mary, E ... 317-921-4313 169 L
mostrye@ivytech.edu
OSTWINKLE, Chris ... 815-280-6635 148 K
costwink@jjc.edu
OSUNDE, Samuel ... 662-254-9041 269 C
sosunde@mvsu.edu
OSVAI, Nanci ... 704-290-5251 366 A
nosvai@spcc.edu
OSWALD, Mike, R ... 208-356-1320 137 F
oswaldrm@byui.edu
OSWALD, P.J ... 503-517-1800 411 C
pjoswald@westernseminary.edu
OSWALD, Peter ... 217-854-3231 140 F
peter.oswald@blackburn.edu
OSWALD, Phil ... 920-403-3016 538 K
phil.oswald@snc.edu
OSWALD, Sharon ... 662-325-2580 269 A
soswald@cobilan.msstate.edu
OSWALT, Amanda ... 903-923-3221 488 A
Amanda.oswalt@tstc.edu
OSWALT, Natalie ... 936-591-9075 480 A
noswalt@panola.edu
OSWALT, Sandra, A ... 214-768-4306 482 J
soswalt@smu.edu
OSWELL, Michelle ... 215-893-5265 416 E
michelle.oswell@curtis.edu
OSZUST, Renee ... 248-341-2153 248 E
raoszust@oaklandcc.edu
OTON-OLIVIERI,
Patricia ... 787-751-1912 554 D
poton@juris.inter.edu
OTERO, George ... 787-257-0000 557 F
george.otero@upr.edu
OTERO, Juan ... 787-766-1717 556 A
juotero@suagm.edu
OTERO, Neyda ... 305-237-0608 108 L
notero@mdc.edu
OTEY, Rex ... 704-637-4394 355 H
rexotey@catawba.edu
OTHMAN, Saib ... 630-844-4229 139 L
sothman@aurora.edu
OTIS, Brian ... 860-486-5960.. 92 C
botis@foundation.uconn.edu
OTIS, Linda ... 228-497-7649 268 G
linda.otis@mgccc.edu
OTO, Rod, M ... 507-222-4190 254 D
roto@carleton.edu
OTOUPAL, Vince ... 801-863-8998 500 B
vince.otoupal@uvu.edu
OTT, Alexander ... 718-289-5939 318 E
alexander.ott@bcc.cuny.edu
OTT, Amy ... 803-536-0311 448 C
OTT, Deanna ... 501-205-8838.. 20 G
dott@cbc.edu
OTT, Emlyn, A ... 614-235-4136 392 D
eott@TLSohio.edu
OTT, Luisa ... 520-494-5283.. 12 R
luisa.ott@centralaz.edu
OTT, Randall ... 202-319-5188.. 95 A
ott@cua.edu
OTT, Steven, H ... 704-687-7630 371 B
SHott@uncc.edu
OTT-HANSEN, Sarah ... 216-421-8016 380 B
saott-hansen@cia.edu
OTT ROWLANDS, Sue .. 859-572-5788 199 A
sottrowlands@nku.edu
OTTAVIANI-JONES,
Barbara ... 904-819-6603 102 P
OttovianiJB@flagler.edu
OTTAWAY, Thomas ... 208-282-3585 138 C
ottathom@isu.edu
OTTE, Bobbi ... 406-657-1086 288 G
otteb@rocky.edu
OTTEMAN, Marcie, M ... 989-774-1042 240 O
ottem1mm@cmich.edu
OTTEN, Daren ... 530-741-6853.. 78 F
dotten@yccd.edu
OTTEN, Laura ... 215-951-1118 422 F
otten@lasalle.edu
OTTEN, Valerie, A ... 626-395-6832.. 31 D
votten@caltech.edu
OTTENHOFF, John ... 208-459-5334 137 J
jottenhoff@collegeofidaho.edu
OTTER, Kelly ... 202-687-8700.. 95 E
otter@georgetown.edu
OTTERNESS, Naomi ... 828-771-3057 373 A
nottern@warren-wilson.edu
OTTERSON, Robert ... 605-688-4111 454 C
robert.otterson@sdstate.edu
OTTESON, Julie Ann ... 213-624-1200.. 44 I
jotteson@fidm.edu
OTTEY, Jacqueline ... 201-447-7204 300 B
jottey@bergen.edu
OTTINGER, Denise ... 785-670-2100 192 B
denise.ottinger@washburn.edu
OTTINGER, Marie ... 334-386-7512.... 3 I
mottinger@faulkner.edu
OTTINGER, Mary Beth .. 847-925-6341 145 F
mottinge@harpercollege.edu
OTTINO, Julio, M ... 847-491-5220 155 D
jm-ottino@northwestern.edu
OTTLEY, Alford, H ... 973-803-5000 305 A
aottley@pillar.edu
OTTMAN, Ray ... 479-788-7110.. 23 H
ray.ottman@uafs.edu
OTTO, Allison ... 920-748-8169 538 I
ottoa@ripon.edu
OTTO, Richard, H ... 312-461-0600 139 G
ifitzgerald@aaart.edu
OTTO, Rick ... 479-979-1000.. 25 H
OTTO, Sheryl ... 874-925-6342 145 F
sotto@harpercollege.edu
OTTO, Tyson ... 660-359-3948 279 L
totto@mail.ncmissouri.edu
OTTOBONI, John ... 408-554-5355.. 65 A
jottoboni@scu.edu
OTTOSSON, John ... 641-673-1076 184 B
ottossonj@wmpenn.edu
OTU, Emmanual ... 262-598-2973 540 C
otu@uwp.edu
OTUONYE, Francis, O ... 931-372-3374 462 A
fotuonye@tntech.edu

O'BRIEN, Ian ... 701-349-5405 375 G
ianobrien@trinitybiblecollege.edu

O'BRIEN, Irene ... 973-353-5541 307 C
jobrien@andromeda.rutgers.edu

O'BRIEN, J. Patrick ... 806-651-2100 486 D
pobrien@mail.wtamu.edu

O'BRIEN, J. Randall ... 865-471-3200 455 G
robrien@cn.edu

O'BRIEN, Jane ... 207-221-4102 213 B
jobrien@une.edu

O'BRIEN, Janet, L ... 912-478-5371 126 B
jlobrien@georgiasouthern.edu

O'BRIEN, Jim ... 480-965-9118.. 11 J
james.obrien@asu.edu

O'BRIEN, John, F ... 617-422-7221 234 J
jobrien@nesl.edu

O'BRIEN, Kathleen ... 414-382-6084 534 I
kathleen.obrien@alverno.edu

O'BRIEN, Katie ... 315-655-7348 317 J
kobrien@cazenovia.edu

O'BRIEN, Kelly ... 860-297-2046.. 92 A
kelly.obrien@trincoll.edu

O'BRIEN, Kevin ... 865-573-4517 457 H
kobrien@johnsonU.edu

O'BRIEN, SJ, Kevin ... 202-687-1395.. 95 E
obrienkf@georgetown.edu

O'BRIEN, Martha ... 814-472-3217 434 F
mobrien@francis.edu

O'BRIEN, Mary ... 707-546-4000.. 43 J
mobrien@empirecollege.com

O'BRIEN, Mary Eileen .. 845-848-7801 324 B
mary.eileen.obrien@dc.edu

O'BRIEN, Maryellen ... 910-272-3324 365 D
mo'brien@robeson.edu

O'BRIEN, Maureen ... 724-830-1075 435 E
obrien@setonhill.edu

O'BRIEN, Michael, E ... 419-530-4987 394 E
michael.obrien6@utoledo.edu

O'BRIEN, Michael, J ... 573-882-4421 283 H
obrienm@missouri.edu

O'BRIEN, Paul, R ... 772-462-7376 106 F
pobrien@irsc.edu

O'BRIEN, Peg ... 708-209-3528 143 D
Margaret.OBrien@cuchicago.edu

O'BRIEN, Rachel ... 214-887-5368 473 E
robrien@dts.edu

O'BRIEN, Ron ... 563-884-5856 182 D
ron.obrien@palmer.edu

O'BRIEN, Shannon ... 406-243-7852 287 D
shannon.obrien@umontana.edu

O'BRIEN, Sharon, J ... 717-245-1497 417 B
obrien@dickinson.edu

O'BRIEN, Terry ... 860-465-5395.. 88 E
obrienth@easternct.edu

O'BRIEN, Theresa ... 415-514-1455.. 72 C
Theresa.OBrien@ucsf.edu

O'BRIEN, Thomas ... 610-647-4400 421 B
tobrien@immaculata.edu

O'BRIEN, William, T ... 724-287-8711 413 G
william.obrien@bc3.edu

O'BRIEN-FOELSCH, Molly, E ... 570-577-3624 413 E
molly.obrien@bucknell.edu

O'BRIEN FRIEDERICHS, Jane ... 781-239-2461 231 G
jobrienfriederichs@massbay.edu

O'BRIEN-KNOTTS, Jennifer, E ... 610-758-4679 424 B
jeo211@lehigh.edu

O'BRIEN PEDERSEN, Julianne ... 508-541-1608 225 G
jobrienpedersen@dean.edu

O'BRYAN, Dan ... 775-831-1314 296 F
dobryan@sierranevada.edu

O'BRYANT, Theresa, M 413-662-5231 230 C
theresa.obryant@mcla.edu

O'BYRNE, Ellie ... 608-363-2014 534 L
obyrneek@beloit.edu

O'CAIN, Woody ... 386-822-7481 117 A
wocain@stetson.edu

O'CALLAGHAN, Cindy .. 617-735-9779 226 B
ocallac@emmanuel.edu

O'CALLAGHAN, Karen .. 516-463-6605 328 A
karen.ocallaghan@hofstra.edu

O'CAMPO, Kathy ... 928-314-9559.. 12 B
katheline.ocampo@azwestern.edu

O'CARROLL, Theresa ... 708-974-5248 153 D
ocarroll@morainevalley.edu

O'CINNSEALAIGH, Benedict ... 513-231-2223 377 B
bocinnsealaigh@athenaeum.edu

O'CONNELL, Catharine . 540-887-7030 510 A
coconnell@mbc.edu

O'CONNELL, Colleen ... 215-884-8942 440 E
planning@woninstitute.edu

O'CONNELL, Daniel ... 978-867-4246 227 A
daniel.oconnell@gordon.edu

O'CONNELL, Danny, J .. 330-941-3549 396 C
djoconnell@ysu.edu

O'CONNELL, Erin, E ... 206-281-2175 526 D
ocone@spu.edu

O'CONNELL, Heather, A ... 302-356-6814.. 94 G
heather.a.oconnell@wilmu.edu

O'CONNELL, John ... 260-481-6977 168 D
oconnelj@ipfw.edu

O'CONNELL, Lil ... 815-455-8676 152 B
loconnell@mchenry.edu

O'CONNELL, Mark ... 269-965-3931 244 L
oconnellm@kellogg.edu

O'CONNELL, Melissa, E ... 386-312-4232 111 K
melissaoconnell@sjrstate.edu

O'CONNELL, Robert, G . 617-333-2050 225 F
boconnell@curry.edu

O'CONNELL, Sean ... 203-773-8068.. 87 M
soconnell@albertus.edu

O'CONNER, Terrence, L ... 305-628-6516 112 B
toconner@stu.edu

O'CONNOR, Angela ... 773-481-8644 142 D
aoconnor5@ccc.edu

O'CONNOR, Angela, M 813-253-6230 118 H
aoconnor@ut.edu

O'CONNOR, Barbara ... 860-486-4806.. 92 C
barbara.o'connor@uconn.edu

O'CONNOR, OSFS, Bernard, F ... 610-282-1100 416 I
boconnor@desales.edu

O'CONNOR, Bill ... 425-564-2454 519 L
bill.oconnor@bellevuecollege.edu

O'CONNOR, Brian ... 406-994-3211 287 G
boconnor@montana.edu

O'CONNOR, Charles, D 402-472-9339 293 H
charles.oconnor@unl.edu

O'CONNOR, Christi ... 323-953-4000.. 51 E
oconnoca@lacitycollege.edu

O'CONNOR, Christopher, K ... 617-254-2610 236 B
rev.christopher.o'connor@sjs.edu

O'CONNOR, Deirdre, M ... 570-577-3141 413 E
deirdre.oconnor@bucknell.edu

O'CONNOR, Diane ... 215-641-6416 426 E
doconnor@mc3.edu

O'CONNOR, Edward, R 402-280-4076 290 B
EdwardOConnor@creighton.edu

O'CONNOR, Ellen ... 617-287-5100 228 G
ellen.oconnor@umb.edu

O'CONNOR, Ellen, M ... 215-955-6835 436 F
ellen.oconnor@jefferson.edu

O'CONNOR, J. Daniel ... 907-834-1610.. 11 B
jdoconnor@pwscc.edu

O'CONNOR, James ... 563-884-5294 182 D
james.oconnor@palmer.edu

O'CONNOR, James ... 404-894-9044 125 D
james.oconnor@oit.gatech.edu

O'CONNOR, Jasi ... 218-299-3549 255 B
oconnor@cord.edu

O'CONNOR, Jeremiah .. 508-793-2564 225 C
joconnor@holycross.edu

O'CONNOR, Jim ... 707-638-5997.. 70 B
jim.oconnor@tu.edu

O'CONNOR, Jody ... 415-575-6153.. 31 C
joconnor@ciis.edu

O'CONNOR, Joseph ... 607-778-5379 344 F
oconnorjt@sunybroome.edu

O'CONNOR, Julie ... 414-425-8300 538 J
joconnor@shsst.edu

O'CONNOR, Kathleen ... 617-243-2225 227 K
koconnor@lasell.edu

O'CONNOR, Kathleen ... 816-271-5827 279 E
koconnor5@missouriwestern.edu

O'CONNOR, Kathleen ... 608-663-6715 536 A
koconnor@edgewood.edu

O'CONNOR, Kathleen ... 509-313-6545 522 L
oconnor@gonzaga.edu

O'CONNOR, Kevin ... 949-582-4788.. 67 F
koconnor@saddleback.edu

O'CONNOR, Marcia ... 423-473-2390 462 D
moconnor@clevelandstatecc.edu

O'CONNOR, Maria, A ... 330-569-5272 383 F
occonorma@hiram.edu

O'CONNOR, Mary ... 480-731-8403.. 14 J
mary.oconnor@domail.maricopa.edu

O'CONNOR, Matthew, L ... 203-582-8297.. 91 E
matthew.oconnor@quinnipiac.edu

O'CONNOR, Maura ... 206-296-6300 526 F
oconnorm@seattleu.edu

O'CONNOR, Michael ... 410-778-7268 221 D
moconnor2@washcoll.edu

O'CONNOR, Michael ... 815-802-8908 149 B
moconnor@kcc.edu

O'CONNOR, Mike, J ... 828-262-3190 369 D
oconnormj@appstate.edu

O'CONNOR, Patrick ... 708-974-5555 153 D
oconnorp@morainevalley.edu

O'CONNOR, Patrick ... 617-879-7878 230 B
poconnor@massart.edu

O'CONNOR, Phyllis, G . 330-972-6057 392 H
oconnor@uakron.edu

O'CONNOR, Rob ... 501-450-1426.. 21 C
o'connor@hendrix.edu

O'CONNOR, Robert ... 315-781-3535 327 G
oconnor@hws.edu

O'CONNOR, Sheila ... 402-457-2733 291 E
soconnor7@mccneb.edu

O'CONNOR, Timothy ... 212-327-8080 339 H
toconnor@rockefeller.edu

O'CONNOR-BENSON, Pat ... 239-597-7101 114 F
poconnor@fgcu.edu

O'CONNOR-GOMEZ, Doreen ... 562-907-4352.. 77 E
doconnor@whittier.edu

O'DAIR, Katherine, G ... 617-552-3482 224 B
katherine.odair@bc.edu

O'DANIEL, Carolyn ... 502-213-2212 196 E
carolyn.o'daniel@kctcs.edu

O'DAY, Gail, R ... 336-758-4315 372 G
odaygr@wfu.edu

O'DAY, Patricia, G ... 607-778-5100 344 F
odaypg@sunybroome.edu

O'DAY, Steven, P ... 717-867-6407 423 I
oday@lvc.edu

O'DELL, Cynthia ... 219-980-6509 168 C
codell@iun.edu

O'DELL, James ... 617-536-6340 224 C
jodell@bostonconservatory.edu

O'DELL MAINOUS, Rosalie ... 937-775-3133 396 A
rosalie.mainous@wright.edu

O'DESKY, Ryan ... 608-249-6611 536 J
rodesky@herzing.edu

O'DONNELL, Alicia ... 402-461-7784 290 G
aodonnell@hastings.edu

O'DONNELL, Bill, J ... 574-520-4218 168 F
odonnell@iusb.edu

O'DONNELL, Brennan ... 718-862-7301 331 H
brennan.odonnell@manhattan.edu

O'DONNELL, Eileen ... 617-327-6777 238 D
eileen_odonnell@williamjames.edu

O'DONNELL, Elizabeth .. 212-353-4100 323 B

O'DONNELL, James ... 660-785-7777 283 E
jodonnell@truman.edu

O'DONNELL, James ... 716-645-2823 343 E
jod@buffalo.edu

O'DONNELL, James ... 480-965-3956.. 11 J
jjodonn2@mainex1.asu.edu

O'DONNELL, John ... 781-239-3101 231 G
jodonnell@massbay.edu

O'DONNELL, Karen ... 813-286-8087 153 H
kodonnell@nl.edu

O'DONNELL, Kitti ... 913-758-6415 191 I
odonnell61@stmary.edu

O'DONNELL, Michael ... 262-741-8538 543 A
odonnellm@gtc.edu

O'DONNELL, Michael ... 512-499-4601 493 K
modonnell@utsystem.edu

O'DONNELL, SSJ, Patricia ... 215-248-7125 415 D
podonnel@chc.edu

O'DONNELL, Patrick ... 562-860-2451.. 37 L
podonnell@cerritos.edu

O'DONNELL, Tim ... 479-575-5828.. 23 G
odonnell@uark.edu

O'DONNELL, Timothy, T ... 540-636-2900 506 H
president@christendom.edu

O'DONOVAN, Stephen . 254-526-1114 470 E
admissions.registrar@ctcd.edu

O'DRISCOLL, Brian ... 503-352-2917 408 I
odriscob@pacificu.edu

O'DRISCOLL, Daniel ... 508-541-1641 225 G
dodriscoll@dean.edu

O'DRISCOLL, Sue ... 540-545-7399 512 E
sodrisco09@su.edu

O'DWYER, Anne ... 413-528-7240 222 F
aodwyer@simons-rock.edu

O'DWYER, Timothy ... 503-768-7860 406 H
odwyer@lclark.edu

O'FARRELL, Kevin, F ... 727-816-3213 110 B
ofarrek@phsc.edu

O'FARRELL, Mark, T ... 727-376-6911 117 H
mofarrell@trinitycollege.edu

O'FLAHERTY, Kevin ... 215-646-7300 420 A
oflaherty.k@gmercyu.edu

O'FLANNERY ANDERSON, Jennifer ... 954-262-2114 109 E
joa@nova.edu

O'GEARY, Amy ... 252-492-2061 366 G
ogearya@vgcc.edu

O'GORMAN, Deb ... 775-824-3811 295 F
dogorman@tmcc.edu

O'GORMAN, Jane ... 706-864-2814 133 A
janeogorman@ung.edu

O'GORMAN, Ryan ... 845-848-7600 324 B
ryan.ogorman@dc.edu

O'GRADY, Elaine ... 845-569-3255 333 I
elaine.ogrady@msmc.edu

O'GRADY EISENMANN, Sharon ... 610-660-1290 434 G
seisenma@sju.edu

O'GWYNN, Marty ... 405-208-5120 400 A
mlogwynn@okcu.edu

O'HAGAN, Donald ... 973-618-3759 300 H
dohagan@caldwell.edu

O'HAGAN, Patricia ... 808-734-9569 136 C
ohaganp@hawaii.edu

O'HAILEY, Tina ... 912-525-5000 130 H
tohailey@scad.edu

O'HAIR, H. Dan ... 859-218-0290 200 G
ohair@uky.edu

O'HAIR, Mary John ... 859-257-2813 200 G
mjohair@uky.edu

O'HALLORAN, Teresa, E ... 715-836-2387 539 E
ohallote@uwec.edu

O'HANLON, Laureen ... 509-828-1459 522 C
lohanlon@ewu.edu

O'HARA, Christine, S ... 716-286-8792 336 E
cohara@niagara.edu

O'HARA, James, P ... 609-896-5367 306 A
johara@rider.edu

O'HARA, Kate ... 617-217-9225 223 A
kohara@baystate.edu

O'HARA, Sabine ... 202-274-7174.. 97 B
sabine.ohara@udc.edu

O'HARA, Sandra ... 631-451-4736 348 E
oharas@sunysuffolk.edu

O'HARA, William, T ... 401-232-6477 441 B
wohara@bryant.edu

O'HARE, Katie ... 617-323-6662 238 D
katie_ohare@williamjames.edu

O'HARE, Lauren ... 201-761-6272 307 K
lohare@saintpeters.edu

O'HARE, Lyn ... 828-771-3780 373 A
lohare@warren-wilson.edu

O'HARE, Sharon ... 406-243-5672 287 D
sharon1.ohare@umontana.edu

O'HARE, Susan ... 610-861-1588 426 H
ohares@moravian.edu

O'HERN, Susan ... 518-464-8822 325 B
sohern@excelsior.edu

O'HERRON, Mick ... 815-965-8616 157 C
moherron@rockfordcareercollege.edu

O'KANE, Gail ... 612-659-6299 259 F
gail.okane@minneapolis.edu

O'KARMA, Theodore ... 818-345-8414.. 41 F
tokarma@columbiacollege.edu

O'KEEFE, Barbara, J ... 847-491-7023 155 D
b-okeefe@northwestern.edu

O'KEEFE, Claire ... 239-687-5423.. 98 N
cokeefe@avemarialaw.edu

O'KEEFE, James ... 718-390-4190 340 G
okeefej@stjohns.edu

O'KEEFE, John, L ... 610-330-5803 423 A
okeefej@lafayette.edu

O'KEEFE, Louise ... 256-824-2445.... 9 A
Louise.OKeefe@uah.edu

O'KEEFE, Martha ... 540-891-3094 515 E
mokeefe@germanna.edu

O'KEEFE, Matt ... 573-341-4132 284 C
mjokeefe@mst.edu

O'KEEFE, Michael ... 845-569-3597 333 I
michael.okeefe@msmc.edu

O'KEEFE, Mildred ... 516-876-3247 345 E
okeefem@oldwestbury.edu

O'KEEFE, Patrick ... 716-829-7753 324 E
okeefep@dyc.edu

O'KEEFE, Paul ... 508-830-5063 230 D
pokeefe@maritime.edu

O'KEEFE, Steve ... 618-985-3741 148 G
steveokeefe@jalc.edu

O'KEEFE, Timothy ... 850-474-2349 116 E
tokeefe@uwf.edu

O'KEEFFE, Mary Ellen .. 206-934-4101 525 J
maryellen.okeeffe@seattlecolleges.edu

O'KELLEY, Carolyn ... 417-328-1512 282 D
cokelley@sbuniv.edu

O'KIEF, Mary ... 541-245-7596 409 F
mokief@roguecc.edu

O'LAUGHLIN, Jeanne ... 305-899-3010.. 99 B
jolaughlin@barry.edu

O'LEARY, Brendan ... 508-856-6510 229 B
brendan.o'leary@umassmed.edu

O'LEARY, David ... 610-361-2330 427 D
olearyd@neumann.edu

O'LEARY, Eileen, K ... 508-565-1347 237 A
eoleary@stonehill.edu

O'LEARY, Erin ... 912-525-5000 130 H
eoleary@scad.edu

O'LEARY, George ... 407-823-2261 115 C
mdennis@athletics.ucf.edu

O'LEARY, Kara ... 574-284-4578 172 G
koleary@saintmarys.edu

O'LEARY, Lindsay, M ... 412-578-8861 414 I
lmoleary@carlow.edu
O'LEARY, Michael .... 734-995-7314 241 F
michael.oleary@cuaa.edu
O'LEARY, Mick .... 301-846-2585 214 I
moleary@frederick.edu
O'LEARY, Patrick .... 570-849-8274.. 57 G
poleary@psr.edu
O'LEARY, Paula .... 502-447-1000 199 G
poleary@spencerian.edu
O'LEARY, Rita .... 610-647-4400 421 B
roleary@immaculata.edu
O'LEARY, Sarah .... 860-768-5101.. 92 F
saoleary@hartford.edu
O'LINGER, Jennifer ...... 256-551-3125.... 4 J
jennifer.o'linger@drakestate.edu
O'MAHONEY, Megan .... 650-433-3806.. 58 B
megano@paloaltou.edu
O'MALEY-LAMSON,
Patty .... 765-983-1424 165 H
pattyo@earlham.edu
O'MALLEY, Barbara ..... 314-246-7825 285 G
barbaraomalley25@webster.edu
O'MALLEY, Deborah, A 617-879-5097 233 E
deborah.omalley@mcphs.edu
O'MALLEY, Marjorie ..... 617-879-7045 230 B
momalley@massart.edu
O'MALLEY, Richard ...... 979-830-4054 469 F
richard.omalley@blinn.edu
O'MALLEY, Timothy, L . 619-260-4770.. 74 B
tomalley@sandiego.edu
O'MARA, Charles .... 601-984-1010 270 H
comara@umc.edu
O'MEARA, Ann .... 816-501-2422 272 E
ann.omeara@avila.edu
O'MEARA, Kathy .... 802-468-1292 503 G
kathy.omeara@castleton.edu
O'MEARA, Kyle .... 312-332-0707 160 K
O'MEARA, Patrick, D ... 701-355-8048 375 K
pdomeara@umary.edu
O'MEARA, Ron .... 229-333-2111 134 I
ron.omeara@wiregrass.edu
O'MEARA-MCKINNEY,
Colette .... 402-280-3474 290 B
ColetteOmeara@creighton.edu
O'MEARA-MCKINNEY,
Colette .... 402-280-2006 290 B
ColetteOMeara@creighton.edu
O'NEAL, Alan .... 773-821-2897 141 J
aoneal@csu.edu
O'NEAL, Andy .... 419-227-2048 394 B
aoneal@unoh.edu
O'NEAL, Berri .... 214-915-1900 485 E
berrio@ucddowntown.org
O'NEAL, Christian .... 501-683-7208.. 24 A
cxoneal@ualr.edu
O'NEAL, Dennis .... 254-710-3871 469 D
dennis_oneal@baylor.edu
O'NEAL, Gayle .... 804-524-5087 518 C
goneal@vsu.edu
O'NEAL, Ginger, H .... 252-335-0821 361 G
goneal@albemarle.edu
O'NEAL, Justin .... 660-596-7282 282 H
joneal@sfccmo.edu
O'NEAL, Kaye .... 912-344-3266 120 D
kaye.oneal@armstrong.edu
O'NEAL, Rene, S .... 202-994-9013.. 95 D
rstewartoneal@gwu.edu
O'NEAL, Sharon .... 478-553-2056 129 C
soneal@oftc.edu
O'NEAL, Tom .... 407-882-1120 115 C
oneal@ucf.edu
O'NEIL, Burton .... 864-656-4337 444 E
boneil@clemson.edu
O'NEIL, Christine .... 906-487-7328 242 M
christine.oneil@finlandia.edu
O'NEIL, Laura, L .... 607-777-2131 343 D
loneil@binghamton.edu
O'NEIL, Sally, C .... 402-280-1830 290 B
SallyONeill@creighton.edu
O'NEIL, Tabitha .... 773-602-5125 142 A
toneil@ccc.edu
O'NEIL, Tom .... 661-722-6300.. 27 P
loneil@avc.edu
O'NEIL KNIGHT,
Alicia, M .... 202-994-2371.. 95 D
aoknight@gwu.edu
O'NEILL, Amy, A .... 610-330-5000 423 A
oneilla@lafayette.edu
O'NEILL, Bettyann .... 706-236-2261 121 E
boneill@berry.edu
O'NEILL, Bill .... 435-879-4367 499 M
oneillb@dixie.edu
O'NEILL, Charles .... 724-830-1144 435 E
oneill@setonhill.edu
O'NEILL, Colin .... 612-874-3858 257 D
co5000@gmail.com
O'NEILL, Dale, A .... 919-209-2106 363 F
daoneill@johnstoncc.edu
O'NEILL, Daniel .... 978-762-4000 232 D
Daoneill@northshore.edu
O'NEILL, David .... 509-434-5425 521 D
david.o'neill@ccs.spokane.edu
O'NEILL, David .... 509-434-5425 521 F
david.oneill@ccs.spokane.edu
O'NEILL, David .... 509-434-5427 521 E
david.oneill@ccs.spokane.edu
O'NEILL, Denise .... 609-652-4332 308 E
denise.oneill@stockton.edu
O'NEILL, Dianne, M ...... 301-369-2800 214 A
dmoneill@captechu.edu
O'NEILL, Ellizabeth .... 401-232-6000 441 B
O'NEILL, F. Shawn .... 201-684-7550 305 F
soneill@ramapo.edu
O'NEILL, Gerry, J .... 252-246-1337 367 D
goneill@wilsoncc.edu
O'NEILL, Jennifer .... 603-577-6000 297 F
joneill@dwc.edu
O'NEILL, Jerry, F .... 412-731-6000 433 K
joneill@rpts.edu
O'NEILL, Joan, E .... 203-432-5461.. 93 C
joan.oneill@yale.edu
O'NEILL, Keith .... 847-925-6225 145 F
koneill@harpercollege.edu
O'NEILL, Meggan .... 201-355-1421 302 I
oneillm@feliciabn.edu
O'NEILL, Michael .... 610-519-7926 439 A
mike.oneill@villanova.edu
O'NEILL, Patrick .... 303-404-5400.. 82 J
patrick.o'neill@frontrange.edu
O'NEILL, Shannon .... 518-782-5830 342 H
soneill@siena.edu
O'NEILL, Stephen .... 507-786-3062 264 C
oneill@stolaf.edu
O'NEILL, Tess .... 504-398-2744 206 E
toneill@olhcc.edu
O'NEILL, Thomas .... 315-228-7418 321 H
toneill@colgate.edu
O'NEILL, Walter .... 616-554-5827 241 I
woneill1@davenport.edu
O'NEILL, William .... 402-559-1952 293 I
woneill@unmc.edu
O'NEILL, JR.,
William, J .... 617-573-8300 237 B
woneill@suffolk.edu
O'NIELL, Claudia .... 720-890-8922.. 83 F
registrar@itea.edu
O'QUINN, Doretha .... 714-556-3610.. 75 A
officeoftheprovost@vanguard.edu
O'QUINN, Michael .... 979-845-2217 485 C
irishmike@tamu.edu
O'QUINN, Monica .... 912-427-5840 123 A
moquinn@coastalpines.edu
O'QUINN, Robin .... 918-463-2931 397 I
robin.oquinn@connorsstate.edu
O'REAR, Matthew .... 215-248-6304 424 G
morear@ltsp.edu
O'REAR, Randy, G .... 254-295-4500 492 C
rorear@umhb.edu
O'REGAN, Danny .... 808-440-4226 135 A
daniel.oregan@chaminade.edu
O'REGGIO, Elizabeth .... 352-395-5486 112 H
elizabeth.oreggio@sfcollege.edu
O'REILLY, Jane .... 617-369-3477 236 E
joreilly@mfa.org
O'REILLY, Kevin, P .... 914-968-6200 341 D
O'REILLY, Maureen, A .. 603-641-7084 298 F
moreilly@anselm.edu
O'REILLY, Paul, J .... 805-525-4417.. 69 I
poreilly@thomasaquinas.edu
O'REILLY, Sharon .... 239-280-1654.. 98 O
sharon.oreilly@avemaria.edu
O'REILLY, Tricia .... 510-841-9230.. 77 I
toreilly@wi.edu
O'RILEY, Jane .... 318-670-9401 207 C
joriley@susla.edu
O'RILEY, Shawn .... 516-877-3404 314 F
oriley@adelphi.edu
O'RIORDAN, Steven ..... 978-934-3463 229 A
Steven_Oriordan@uml.edu
O'RORKE, Kevin .... 530-242-7629.. 66 C
kororke@shastacollege.edu
O'ROURKE, Bernard, C 973-618-3409 300 H
borourke@caldwell.edu
O'ROURKE, Brian .... 908-526-1200 305 G
Brian.O'Rourke@raritanval.edu
O'ROURKE, Brian .... 510-430-2133.. 54 F
borourke@mills.edu
O'ROURKE, Brian, J ..... 864-656-4248 444 E
orourke@clemson.edu
O'ROURKE, Catherine .. 802-651-5911 501 F
corourke@champlain.edu
O'ROURKE, John .... 413-552-2056 231 F
jorourke@hcc.edu
O'ROURKE, Kevin .... 718-489-5496 340 E
korourke@sfc.edu
O'ROURKE, Kim .... 540-231-6232 518 B
orourkek@vt.edu
O'ROURKE, Krysti .... 631-656-2163 326 B
krysti.orourke@ftc.edu
O'ROURKE,
Maureen, A .... 617-353-3112 224 E
morourke@bu.edu
O'ROURKE, Pat .... 303-860-5600.. 86 D
patrick.orourke@cu.edu
O'ROURKE, Sheila, N ... 973-618-3341 300 H
sorourke@caldwell.edu
O'ROURKE, Timothy, G 757-455-3210 518 H
torourke@vwc.edu
O'SABEN, Carol .... 928-523-2261.. 16 C
Carol.OSaben@nau.edu
O'SHAUGHNESSY,
Brian, J .... 413-205-3247 221 G
brian.oshaughnessy@aic.edu
O'SHEA, David .... 480-517-8689.. 15 D
david.oshea@riosalado.edu
O'SHEA, Dennis .... 443-287-9908 216 A
doshea@jhu.edu
O'SHEA, Donal, E .... 941-487-4100 115 B
doshea@ncf.edu
O'SHEA, Gregory, M .... 856-225-6475 307 A
osheag@camden.rutgers.edu
O'SHEA, Maureen .... 508-362-2131 231 D
moshea@capecod.edu
O'SHEA, Patrick, G .... 301-405-6499 219 D
poshea@umd.edu
O'SHEA, William .... 503-352-1419 408 I
osheawa@pacificu.edu
O'SHIELDS, Shannon ... 714-879-3901.. 47 D
soshields@hiu.edu
O'SULLIVAN, Eileen ...... 508-531-2921 229 C
eosullivan@bridgew.edu
O'SULLIVAN, Elaine ...... 617-879-7906 230 B
eo'sullivan@massart.edu
O'SULLIVAN, Gerard, P 201-761-6020 307 K
gosullivan@saintpeters.edu
O'SULLIVAN, Joseph .... 314-516-6800 284 B
osullivanj@umsl.edu
O'SULLIVAN, Leighton . 404-880-8067 122 I
losullivan@cau.edu
O'SULLIVAN,
Michael, J .... 310-338-3015.. 53 C
michael.osullivan@lmu.edu
O'SULLIVAN, Patrick .... 805-756-7244.. 32 E
posulliv@calpoly.edu
O'SULLIVAN, Patrick .... 516-876-3135 345 E
osullivanp@oldwestbury.edu
O'SULLIVAN, Richard ... 715-422-5325 543 D
richard.osullivan@mstc.edu
O'SULLIVAN, Trecia ...... 646-717-9742 326 E
osullivan@gts.edu
O'TOOLE, Beth .... 605-331-6797 454 E
elisabeth.otoole@usiouxfalls.edu
O'TOOLE, Diana .... 605-394-1288 454 B
diana.otoole@sdsmt.edu
O'TOOLE, Jason .... 620-441-5353 186 E
jason.otoole@cowley.edu
O'TOOLE, Laura, L .... 401-341-3183 442 D
laura.otoole@salve.edu
O'TOOLE, Lynne, B ...... 978-232-2030 226 C
lynne@endicott.edu
O'TOOLE, Patty .... 540-362-6588 508 D
potoole@hollins.edu
O'CARROLL, Dottie .... 480-860-2700.. 13 Q
docarroll@taliesin.edu

P

PÉREZ, Daisy .... 787-892-6442 554 C
dnperez@intersg.edu
PÉREZ, Víctor .... 787-769-9965 557 F
victor.perez4@upr.edu
PÉREZ PACHECO,
Angél, F .... 787-265-3767 558 B
finanzaz@uprm.edu
PAANANEN, Marian ...... 425-640-1680 522 D
mpaananen@edcc.edu
PAAP, Beth .... 715-634-4790 536 P
bpaap@lco.edu
PAAVOLA, Cindy, L ...... 906-227-2720 248 B
cipaavol@nmu.edu
PABARCUS, Michael ..... 314-837-6777 281 D
mpabarcus@stlchristian.edu
PABON, Jaqueline .... 787-765-1915 554 E
jpabon@opto.inter.edu
PABON-RODRIGUEZ,
Edith, C .... 787-751-1912 554 D
epabon@juris.inter.edu
PACACHA, Edith .... 772-462-7340 106 F
epacacha@irsc.edu
PACCHIANA, Patricia .... 845-398-4044 341 H
ppacchia@stac.edu
PACE, Christy .... 870-460-1121.. 24 C
pacec@uamont.edu
PACE, Danielle .... 843-921-6900 448 B
PACE, Derek .... 601-635-2111 267 B
dpace@eccc.edu
PACE, Donald, G .... 803-535-5679 444 D
dpace@claflin.edu
PACE, Duane .... 423-614-8104 457 M
dpace@leeuniversity.edu
PACE, JR., G. Michael . 540-375-2047 512 B
gpace@roanoke.edu
PACE, Gay .... 870-460-1140.. 24 C
pace@uamont.edu
PACE, Harold .... 336-758-5206 372 G
hpace@wfu.edu
PACE, Jarrod .... 972-825-5469 483 D
Japace@sagu.edu
PACE, Jessica .... 903-693-2044 480 A
jpace@panola.edu
PACE, Kris .... 816-501-4865 281 B
kristine.pace@rockhurst.edu
PACE, Lisa, L .... 843-953-4823 444 C
lisa.pace@citadel.edu
PACE, Meghan .... 325-942-2083 489 E
meghan.pace@angelo.edu
PACE, Steven .... 928-350-2243.. 17 K
space@prescott.edu
PACELLI, Kimberly, A ... 207-725-3490 209 H
kpacelli@bowdoin.edu
PACENTI, Elena .... 619-684-8802.. 56 B
epacenti@newschoolarch.edu
PACHECO, Andrea .... 505-467-6809 313 F
registrar@swc.edu
PACHECO, Anthony, R .. 718-990-2663 340 G
pachecoa@stjohns.edu
PACHECO, Caryn, L ...... 405-325-9627 403 I
cpacheco@ou.edu
PACHECO, Cathy .... 757-253-4900 506 J
cpacheco@wm.edu
PACHECO, Diane .... 816-604-1341 277 F
diane.pacheco@mcckc.edu
PACHECO, Edwin, R ..... 401-456-8000 442 A
epacheco@ric.edu
PACHECO, Jacob .... 505-747-2122 312 G
jpacheco@nnmc.edu
PACHECO, Jennifer ...... 508-531-1221 229 C
jennifer.pacheco@bridgew.edu
PACHECO, Ken .... 360-992-2413 521 A
kpacheco@clark.edu
PACHECO, Michael .... 606-218-5216 201 C
michaelpacheco@upike.edu
PACHECO, Philicia .... 508-678-2811 231 B
philicia.pacheco@bristolcc.edu
PACHECO, Randy .... 505-327-5705 312 K
pachecor@sanjuancollege.edu
PACHECO, Robert .... 760-797-2121.. 54 G
rpacheco@miracosta.edu
PACHECO, Sonia .... 787-840-2955 550 G
spacheco@ponce.caribbean.edu
PACHECO DUNN,
Tanhena .... 845-257-3172 344 A
pachecot@newpaltz.edu
PACHIS, Dimitrios, C .... 860-465-4414.. 88 E
pachis@easternct.edu
PACHUAU,
Lalsangkima .... 859-858-3581 192 O
PACIEJ-WOODRUFF,
Amy .... 570-340-6016 425 D
apaciej@marywood.edu
PACINI, Christine .... 313-993-1208 250 H
pacinicm@udmercy.edu
PACK, Della .... 606-886-3863 195 I
della.pack@kctcs.edu
PACK, Thomas, J .... 513-562-8779 376 O
tpack@artacademy.edu
PACK, W. Gary .... 513-585-1414 379 H
william.pack@thechristcollege.edu
PACKARD, James .... 573-341-4252 284 C
jpackard@mst.edu
PACKARD, Ryan .... 206-934-7804 525 K
ryan.packard@seattlecolleges.edu
PACKER, Benjamin .... 716-851-1102 325 A
packer@ecc.edu
PACKER, Mike .... 626-568-8850.. 49 J
PACKER-MUTI, Barbara . 954-262-5398 109 E
packerb@nova.edu
PACKER-WILLIAMS,
Catherine .... 251-809-1500.... 5 B
catherine.williams@jdcc.edu
PACKETT, Felicia, B ..... 804-758-6742 516 G
fpackett@rappahannock.edu
PACKEY, Matthew .... 704-337-2375 368 B
packeym@queens.edu
PACKHAM, Larry .... 310-287-4424.. 52 C
packhald@wlac.edu
PACTOL, Monica .... 916-608-6503.. 53 A
pactolm@flc.losrios.edu
PADASH, Ali .... 916-608-6648.. 53 A
padasha@flc.losrios.edu
PADDEN, Carol, A .... 858-534-6073.. 72 B
deansocsci@ucsd.edu
PADDOCK, Christopher 508-286-3506 238 B
paddock_christopher@wheatoncollege.edu
PADDOCK, Ericka .... 909-389-3457.. 62 B
epaddock@craftonhills.edu
PADDOCK, Jean .... 330-363-5205 377 C
jean.paddock@aultman.com
PADDOCK, John .... 315-498-2299 337 F
paddockj@sunyocc.edu

PADDOCK, Susan .... 815-729-9020 148 K
PADDOCK, Suzanne ...... 315-866-0300 327 E
paddocksm@herkimer.edu
PADDOCK, Will .... 267-620-4834 412 F
paddockw@arcadia.edu
PADDOCK-O'REILLY,
Kimberly .... 636-227-2100 277 A
kimberly.oreilly@logan.edu
PADEN, Katie .... 404-261-1441 129 F
PADEN, Orlando .... 662-621-4674 266 H
opaden@coahomacc.edu
PADEN, Russ .... 602-557-1723.. 18 H
russ.paden@phoenix.edu
PADGETT, Laura .... 828-898-3485 358 F
padgettl@lmc.edu
PADGETT, Mary Jean ... 601-925-3278 268 E
padgett@mc.edu
PADGETT, Mila .... 803-641-3230 450 C
milap@usca.edu
PADILLA, Ailín, T .... 787-264-1912 554 C
ailin_padilla@intersg.edu
PADILLA, Bernie .... 505-747-2160 312 G
bernie.padilla@nnmc.edu
PADILLA, Christina .... 405-692-3182 398 I
cpadilla@macu.edu
PADILLA, Eugene .... 505-224-4721 310 F
epadilla@cnm.edu
PADILLA, Frederick, M . 202-685-3924 547M
frederick.m.padilla.mil@ndu.edu
PADILLA, Jackie .... 850-484-1721 110 D
jpadilla@pensacolastate.edu
PADILLA, Jose .... 562-907-4211.. 77 E
jpadilla@whittier.edu
PADILLA, Jose, D .... 312-362-8590 143 G
jpadill7@depaul.edu
PADILLA, Mark .... 307-382-1690 546 L
mpadilla@wwcc.wy.edu
PADILLA, Melissa .... 215-780-1382 435 D
melissa@salus.edu
PADILLA, Miriam .... 787-264-1912 554 C
miriam_padilla_camacho@intersg.edu
PADILLA, Ramon .... 651-201-1800 257 N
ramon.padilla@so.mnscu.edu
PADILLA, Rene .... 402-280-4745 290 B
RenePadilla@creighton.edu
PADILLA, Sherrie .... 808-932-7451 135 I
sherriep@hawaii.edu
PADILLA-COTTO,
Lymaries .... 787-725-6500 551 A
lpadilla@sju.albizu.edu
PADIN, Carlos .... 787-766-1717 556 A
um_cpadin@suagm.edu
PADIN, Carlos, M .... 787-766-1717 556 A
um_cpadin@suagm.edu
PADIN, Glenda .... 787-878-6000 552 K
onegron@icprjc.edu
PADMANABHAM,
Ananth .... 619-594-4276.. 35 E
apadmanabham@mail.sdsu.edu
PADMANABHAN,
Anand .... 212-229-5300 334 C
anand@newschool.edu
PADOVANI, John, J ...... 607-746-4632 347 G
padovajj@delhi.edu
PADOW, Fran, A .... 816-604-1081 277 F
fran.padow@mcckc.edu
PADRON, Eduardo, J ... 305-237-3316 108 L
epadron@mdc.edu
PADRON, Margie .... 562-938-4947.. 51 A
mpadron@lbcc.edu
PADUAN, Jeffrey, D ...... 831-656-3241 548 A
jdpaduan@nps.edu
PADULA, Fernando .... 915-747-5594 494 B
lfpadula@utep.edu
PAEPLOW, Randall, K ... 863-784-7083 113 C
randall.paeplow@southflorida.edu
PAESE, Paul .... 765-455-9441 168 B
jpcpaese@iuk.edu
PAEZ-FIGUEROA, Jose . 908-709-7084 309 A
paez@ucc.edu
PAFFENDORF, Nancy .... 908-852-1400 301 C
paffendorfn@centenarycollege.edu
PAFFENROTH, Kim .... 914-633-2697 328 F
kpaffenroth@iona.edu
PAGAN, Alba .... 617-850-1261 227 F
apagan@hchc.edu
PAGAN, Andres .... 787-765-1915 554 E
apagan@opto.inter.edu
PAGAN, Damaris .... 787-765-1915 554 E
dpagan@opto.inter.edu
PAGAN, Efren .... 787-834-9595 556 D
epagan@uaa.edu
PAGAN, Linda .... 732-987-2255 302 J
paganl@georgian.edu
PAGAN, Lorraine, M .... 512-448-8411 481 B
lorraine@stedwards.edu
PAGAN, Vanessa .... 787-284-1912 554 B
vpagan@ponce.inter.edu
PAGAN, Yolanda .... 787-891-0925 553 E
ypagan@ns.inter.edu
PAGANELLI, John .... 508-531-1328 229 C
jpaganelli@bridgew.edu
PAGANI-SOTO, Juan, C 787-765-4210 551 F
jpagani@cempr.edu
PAGANO, Amy, E .... 724-458-3850 419 F
aepagano@gcc.edu
PAGANO, Jan .... 772-462-7635 106 F
jpagano@irsc.edu
PAGANO, Jeffrey, M ..... 716-839-8254 323 F
jpagano@daemen.edu
PAGANO, Mark .... 206-543-2100 527 G
PAGANO, Michael, A ... 312-413-3375 161 F
mapagano@uic.edu
PAGE, Beth .... 276-739-2561 517 D
bpage@vhcc.edu
PAGE, Beverly .... 206-726-5004 521 G
bpage@cornish.edu
PAGE, Cheryl .... 417-268-6412 272 F
cpage@gobbc.edu
PAGE, Eric .... 860-701-6117 548 H
Eric.J.Page@uscg.mil
PAGE, Heather .... 256-306-2461.... 2 F
hpage@calhoun.edu
PAGE, Hugh, R .... 574-631-7242 174 A
page.6@nd.edu
PAGE, JR., Hugh, R ..... 574-631-7147 174 A
hpage@nd.edu
PAGE, James, H .... 207-973-3220 212 B
jpage@maine.edu
PAGE, Jonathan, E .... 434-395-4808 509 H
pageje@longwood.edu
PAGE, Kelli .... 209-946-2987.. 73 C
kpage@pacific.edu
PAGE, Kim .... 207-255-1220 212 G
kpage@maine.edu
PAGE, Kimberly, D .... 207-581-1110 212 C
kimberly.page@maine.edu
PAGE, LeAnne .... 910-892-3178 357 D
lpage@heritagebiblecollege.edu
PAGE, Martin 918-631-2698 403M
martin-page@utulsa.edu
PAGE, Michael .... 781-891-2921 223 E
mpage@bentley.edu
PAGE, Pamela .... 254-442-5121 470 I
pam.page@cisco.edu
PAGE, Phillip .... 617-873-0256 225 A
Phillip.Page@cambridgecollege.edu
PAGE, Ray .... 856-415-6202 306 C
rpage@rcgc.edu
PAGE, Richard, K .... 208-496-1121 137 F
pager@byui.edu
PAGE, Robert .... 912-260-4201 131 D
robert.page@sgsc.edu
PAGE, Scott .... 503-494-8050 408 D
faclog@ohsu.edu
PAGE, Susan .... 708-456-0300 161 C
spage@triton.edu
PAGE, Yolanda .... 504-816-4368 202 F
ypage@dillard.edu
PAGE-SMITH, Julie .... 231-843-5949 252 H
jsmith@westshore.edu
PAGE-STADLER, Jaime .. 920-424-2027 540 B
pagestad@uwosh.edu
PAGEL, Andy .... 806-291-3406 496 K
andy.pagel@wbu.edu
PAGEL, Richard .... 714-432-5024.. 40 D
rpagel@occ.cccd.edu
PAGENKEMPER, Karl .... 402-449-2851 290 F
kpagenkemper@graceu.edu
PAGGI, Paula .... 818-710-2843.. 51 H
paggipm@piercecollege.edu
PAGLIARO, Joel .... 717-262-2003 440 D
conferences@wilson.edu
PAGLIARO, Phil .... 610-399-2418 430 D
ppagliaro@cheyney.edu
PAGNAM, Charles .... 617-287-4085 228 E
cpagnam@umassp.edu
PAGOR, Katherine .... 603-456-2656 298 D
PAGOTTO, Louise .... 808-734-9519 136 C
pagotto@hawaii.edu
PAGUIO, Arnold .... 510-723-6608.. 37 N
apaguio@chabotcollege.edu
PAHCODDY, JR., Lee .... 785-749-8467 187 F
lpahcoddy@haskell.edu
PAHL, Caleb .... 515-289-9200 179 E
PAHL, Jennifer, K .... 989-964-4011 249 G
jkpahl@svsu.edu
PAI, Edward .... 310-233-4044.. 51 F
paie@lahc.edu
PAIER, Daniel, L .... 203-287-3022.. 91 C
PAIER, Jonathan, E .... 203-287-3180.. 91 C
paier.jep@snet.net
PAIER, Maureen, E .... 203-287-3035.. 91 C
paier.fin@snet.net
PAIGE, Andrew .... 617-928-4519 234 D
apaige@mountida.edu
PAIGE, Brian .... 616-526-6758 240 L
bp28@calvin.edu
PAIGE, Ellen, M .... 904-256-7024 106 Q
epaige@ju.edu
PAIGE, CSC, John, R .... 574-239-8375 167 C
jpaige@hcc-nd.edu
PAIGE, Joseph, P .... 860-832-2225.. 88 D
paigejop@ccsu.edu
PAIGE, Joy .... 704-378-1024 358 B
jpaige@jcsu.edu
PAIGE, Leslie .... 785-628-4000 187 A
lpagie@fhsu.edu
PAIGE, Michael .... 978-232-2259 226 C
mpaige@endicott.edu
PAIGE, Tim .... 352-638-9737.. 99 D
tpaige@beaconcollege.edu
PAIKOWSKI, Gary .... 903-463-8707 474 K
paikowski@grayson.edu
PAINE, Brenda .... 248-689-8282 251 I
bpaine@walshcollege.edu
PAINE, Clarke, C .... 717-291-3991 418 J
clarke.paine@fandm.edu
PAINE, Dorie .... 573-341-4218 284 C
pained@mst.edu
PAINE, Gage, E 512-471-1133 493M
gage.paine@austin.utexas.edu
PAINO, Troy, D .... 660-785-4100 283 E
tpaino@truman.edu
PAINTER, Donald .... 863-669-2929 110 E
dpainter@polk.edu
PAINTER, Sherry .... 901-435-1383 457 N
sherry_painter@loc.edu
PAINTER, Virginia, R .... 304-696-4621 532 H
painterv@marshall.edu
PAIR-CUNNINGHAM,
Stephanie, S .... 301-322-0649 217 G
pairss@pgcc.edu
PAISANT, Julie .... 408-924-2250.. 36 B
julie.paisant@sjsu.edu
PAIVA, Ann .... 718-940-5902 341 A
apaiva@sjcny.edu
PAJE-MANALO, Leila, L 603-862-3491 299 B
leila.paje-manalo@unh.edu
PAJIC, Natasa .... 859-233-8213 200 D
npajic@transy.edu
PAK, David, Y .... 703-425-4143 509 B
PAK, Scott .... 714-816-0366.. 70 D
scott.pak@trident.edu
PAKALA, James, C .... 314-434-4044 273 J
jim.pakala@covenantseminary.edu
PAKIESER, Erik .... 763-424-0806 260 E
epakieser@nhcc.edu
PAKOWSKI, Lawrence .. 863-297-5282 110 E
lpakowski@polk.edu
PAKSTIS, John .... 978-934-4331 229 A
john_pakstis@uml.edu
PAKSTIS, Tracey .... 774-354-0459 223 C
tracey.claiborne@becker.edu
PALACIO, Michelle .... 305-348-1757 114 G
michelle.palacio@fiu.edu
PALACIOS, Barbara .... 406-791-5300 288 J
bpalacios01@ugf.edu
PALACIOS, Elizabeth ..... 254-710-3653 469 D
liz_palacios@baylor.edu
PALACIOS,
Francisco, E .... 671-735-5501 549 E
francisco.palacios1@guamcc.edu
PALACIOS, Luz, M .... 787-786-3030 556 E
lpalacios@ucb.edu.pr
PALACIOS, Rosanne ..... 956-326-2178 485 B
rosanne.palacios@tamiu.edu
PALACIOS, Sarah .... 505-984-6103 312 J
alumni@sjc.edu
PALADINO, Angela .... 802-828-8613 503 D
angela.paladino@vcfa.edu
PALAGANO, Nicole .... 973-748-9000 300 E
nicole_palagano@bloomfield.edu
PALAGONIA, Michael ... 802-635-1205 504 A
michael.palagonia@jsc.edu
PALAKAL, Mathew, J .... 317-278-7689 168 E
mpalakal@iupui.edu
PALAMOUNTAIN,
Valerie .... 434-961-5333 516 F
vpalamountain@pvcc.edu
PALAN, Kay .... 269-387-5069 252 I
kay.palan@wmich.edu
PALANGI, Anthony .... 518-743-2246 347 E
palangia@sunyacc.edu
PALANKI, Srinivas .... 409-880-8741 488 F
srinivas.palanki@lamar.edu
PALANTZAS, Nicholas .. 781-821-2222 232 A
PALARDY, William, B ... 781-899-5500 235 G
rev.palardy@psjs.edu
PALASOTA, Joanna, E .. 713-525-3151 493 J
palasota@stthom.edu
PALATELLA,
Anna Marie .... 724-925-4091 439 F
palatellaa@wccc.edu
PALAZOLA, Cecelia .... 901-272-5142 459 A
cpalazola@mca.edu
PALAZZI, Bea .... 910-755-7301 360 E
palazzib@brunswickcc.edu
PALAZZO, Robert .... 205-934-5643.... 8 F
rpalazzo@uab.edu
PALCZEWSKI,
Christine, E .... 716-896-0700 352 B
cepalcz@villa.edu
PALDER, Amy .... 404-364-8462 129 F
apalder@oglethorpe.edu
PALEL, Dipte .... 310-660-3444.. 43 G
dpatel@elcamino.edu
PALELLA, Rocco .... 412-237-4416 415 G
rpalella@ccac.edu
PALEN, Lisa .... 203-575-8100.. 89 F
lpalen@nv.edu
PALERMO, Lisa .... 651-730-5100 255 J
lpalermo@globeuniversity.edu
PALERMO, Pam .... 231-995-1533 248 C
ppalermo@nmc.edu
PALERMO, Pamela .... 440-375-7000 385 B
ppalermo@lec.edu
PALEY, Laura .... 847-574-5188 150 A
lbarnespaley@lfgsm.edu
PALEY, Noelle .... 607-753-2336 345 C
noelle.paley@cortland.edu
PALIAN, Paul .... 847-635-1600 155 E
PALINKAS, Robert, D ... 217-333-2711 162 A
palinkas@illinois.edu
PALINSKY, David, W ..... 661-336-5147.. 49 D
dpalinsk@kccd.edu
PALIS, Michael .... 856-225-6095 307 A
palis@camden.rutgers.edu
PALIWAL, Rupendra ...... 203-371-7851.. 91 G
paliwalr@sacredheart.edu
PALLADINO, Mark .... 215-951-2700 432 F
palladinom@philau.edu
PALLADINO, Michael ..... 732-571-3405 303 G
mpalladi@monmouth.edu
PALLADINO, Richard ..... 914-633-2351 328 F
rpalladino@iona.edu
PALLADINO, Robert ...... 740-283-6405 382 G
rpalladino@franciscan.edu
PALLANEZ, Joe 202-685-3835 547M
pallenzaj@ndu.edu
PALLAVICINI, Maria, G . 209-946-2551.. 73 C
mpallavicini@pacific.edu
PALLEMONI, Sushil .... 361-698-1207 473 F
spallemoni@delmar.edu
PALLER, Alan .... 301-654-7267 218 D
PALLONE, Donna, L ...... 724-287-8711 413 G
donna.pallone@bc3.edu
PALLOTO, Mike .... 805-289-6486.. 75 E
mpalloto@vcccd.edu
PALM, Don .... 530-747-5220.. 53 B
palmd@scc.losrios.edu
PALM, Elizabeth, A .... 847-735-5107 149 H
palm@lakeforest.edu
PALM, Matt .... 419-448-2020 383 C
mpalm@heidelberg.edu
PALM, Melanie .... 509-963-1407 520 E
palmn@cwu.edu
PALM, Risa, I .... 404-413-2574 126 D
risapalm@gsu.edu
PALMA, Eugene .... 516-877-3505 314 F
palma@adelphi.edu
PALMA, Yazmin .... 305-273-4499 100 K
yazmin@cbt.edu
PALMER, Allesandra, C 617-585-1295 234 H
allesandra.cionco@necmusic.edu
PALMER, Betty, G .... 404-627-2681 121 F
betty.palmer@beulah.org
PALMER, Brian .... 904-256-7374 106 Q
bpalmer@ju.edu
PALMER, Charles .... 813-545-4527 446 D
charlespalmer@forrrestcollege.edu
PALMER, Dale, J .... 404-413-3434 126 D
dpalmer@gsu.edu
PALMER, Daniel .... 919-761-2352 368 K
dpalmer@sebts.edu
PALMER, Daniel .... 605-773-3455 453 E
daniel.palmer2@sdbor.edu
PALMER, David .... 901-321-4321 455 I
David.Palmer@cbu.edu
PALMER, David .... 315-655-7777 317 J
dwpalmer@cazenovia.edu
PALMER, David .... 212-812-4040 335 D
dpalmer@sft.edu
PALMER, Donald, F ...... 330-672-2312 384 H
dpalmer@kent.edu
PALMER, Douglas .... 330-490-7043 395 C
dpalmer@walsh.edu
PALMER, Elizabeth .... 763-576-4700 258 A
PALMER, Elyn .... 575-492-2189 314 D
epalmer@usw.edu
PALMER, Eric .... 810-766-4237 239 G
ericpalmer@baker.edu
PALMER, Eric, F 804-287-6591 513M
epalmer@richmond.edu
PALMER, Gail .... 785-670-1151 192 B
gail.palmer@washburn.edu
PALMER, Gregory .... 914-323-5194 331 J
greg.palmer@mville.edu
PALMER, Harvey, J .... 585-475-2146 339 G
hjpeen@rit.edu

PARHAM, Sandra .... 615-966-5837 458 C
sandra.parham@lipscomb.edu
PARHAM, Thomas, A ... 949-824-4804.. 71 C
taparham@uci.edu
PARHAM, Tyrone, A ..... 814-863-2521 428 C
tap3@psu.edu
PARHAM, Walter, H ...... 803-777-7854 450 B
terry@mailbox.sc.edu
PARIANTE, Jody .... 212-431-2137 335 G
Jody.Pariante@nyls.edu
PARIGIAN, Debbie .... 503-244-0726 404 G
debbieparigian@achs.edu
PARINI, Shelly .... 503-594-3015 405 A
shellyp@clackamas.edu
PARIS, Chris .... 314-921-9290 284 G
dean@ugst.edu
PARIS, Kathleen, A .... 608-246-6498 543 C
kparis@madisoncollege.edu
PARIS, Lisa .... 215-670-9127 428 A
lparis@peirce.edu
PARIS, Mark, S .... 302-356-6829.. 94 G
mark.s.paris@wilmu.edu
PARIS, III, Oren .... 479-248-7236.. 20 K
oparis3@ecollege.edu
PARIS, Robin .... 615-383-4848 466 F
rparis@watkins.edu
PARIS, Susan .... 617-989-4589 237 G
pariss@wit.edu
PARISEAU, Anita .... 719-389-6772.. 79M
anita.pariseau@ColoradoCollege.edu
PARISH, David .... 636-227-2100 277 A
david.parish@logan.edu
PARISH, Michael, C ...... 906-248-8400 240 J
mparish@bmcc.edu
PARISHER, Deborah ...... 252-823-5166 362 D
parisherd@edgecombe.edu
PARISI, Dawn .... 352-588-8251 111 L
dawn.parisi@saintleo.edu
PARISI, Joe .... 636-949-4812 276 L
jparisi@lindenwood.edu
PARISI, Michael .... 410-293-1104 549 B
parisi@usna.edu
PARISI, Rob .... 805-922-6966.. 26 H
rparisi@hancockcollege.edu
PARISI, Robert .... 805-922-6966.. 26 H
rparisi@hancockcollege.edu
PARISIEN, Ray .... 701-477-7862 375 H
PARK, Chan, J .... 561-237-7186 108 E
cpark@lynn.edu
PARK, Choong Gi .... 562-926-1023.. 60 B
choong.park@gmail.com
PARK, Christina .... 714-533-1495.. 67 A
christina@southbaylo.edu
PARK, Daniel, L .... 509-527-5999 528 F
park@whitman.edu
PARK, Daniel, W .... 858-822-1236.. 72 B
dwpark@ucsd.edu
PARK, David .... 714-533-3946.. 36 D
dpark@calums.edu
PARK, Doug, Y .... 541-346-3082 410 F
dougpark@uoregon.edu
PARK, George .... 310-453-8300.. 43 I
george@emperors.edu
PARK, Heerei .... 408-260-0208.. 44 K
korean@fivebranches.edu
PARK, Helen .... 702-968-5248 296 D
hpark1@roseman.edu
PARK, Hojin .... 215-884-8942 440 E
hojin.park@woninstitute.edu
PARK, Hun Sung .... 213-381-0081.. 48 A
hspark@laopendoor.org
PARK, Hyung .... 213-252-5100.. 25 J
hpark@alu.edu
PARK, Jack, C .... 210-567-2020 495 B
parkjc@uthscsa.edu
PARK, James, S .... 540-464-7390 518 A
parkjs@vmi.edu
PARK, Jessica .... 213-252-5100.. 25 J
jpark@alu.edu
PARK, Jessica .... 925-631-4030.. 61 G
jep6@stmarys-ca.edu
PARK, Jinsoo .... 973-877-3588 302 F
jpark@essex.edu
PARK, Joshua .... 770-232-2717 130 D
PARK, Julia .... 213-487-0110.. 43 E
financialaid@dula.edu
PARK, Kathryn .... 409-933-8201 471 B
kpark@com.edu
PARK, Kevin .... 404-687-4533 123 C
parkk@ctsnet.edu
PARK, Laura .... 801-649-5230 498 K
office@midwifery.edu
PARK, Linda .... 315-279-5208 329 K
lpark@keuka.edu
PARK, Matthew .... 940-397-4501 478 G
matthew.park@mwsu.edu
PARK, Mi .... 562-926-1023.. 60 B
mhpark@ptsa.edu
PARK, Mimi .... 714-533-1495.. 67 A
mimi@southbaylo.edu
PARK, Min .... 213-487-0110.. 43 E
officemanager@dula.edu
PARK, Myung .... 253-964-7327 525 C
mpark@pierce.ctc.edu
PARK, No Hee .... 310-206-6063.. 71 D
npark@dent.ucla.edu
PARK, Scott .... 309-341-7459 149 G
sapark@knox.edu
PARK, Steve .... 972-860-7771 472 B
spark@dcccd.edu
PARK, Sung Uk .... 213-413-9500.. 68 A
registrar@scusoma.edu
PARK, Sung Uk .... 213-413-9500.. 68 A
sungukpark@scusoma.edu
PARK, Sunny .... 806-720-7507 478 A
sunny.park@lcu.edu
PARK, Susan .... 714-556-3610.. 75 A
susan.park@vanguard.edu
PARK, Yong Hee .... 714-533-1495.. 67 A
yhpark@southbaylo.edu
PARK, Young, S .... 636-327-4645 278 D
dl@midwest.edu
PARK, Yung Won .... 610-917-1457 438 G
ywpark@valleyforge.edu
PARK ZERBEL, Jennifer 310-360-8888.. 26 B
PARKE, Lydia .... 215-780-1417 435 D
lparke@salus.edu
PARKER, Aaron .... 212-824-2219 327 C
aparker@huc.edu
PARKER, Aaron, L .... 601-426-6346 270 D
aparker@southeasternbaptist.edu
PARKER, Andrew .... 765-677-2201 169 C
andrew.parker@indwes.edu
PARKER, Annette .... 507-389-7211 262 A
annette.parker@southcentral.edu
PARKER, Anthony, O .... 229-430-3502 119 I
aparker@albanytech.edu
PARKER, Audrey .... 252-492-2061 366 G
parkera@vgcc.edu
PARKER, Barbara .... 828-627-4515 363 C
bmparker@haywood.edu
PARKER, Beverly, J ...... 318-670-9571 207 C
bparker@susla.edu
PARKER, Brian .... 617-745-3864 225 H
brian.parker@enc.edu
PARKER, Bruce .... 406-657-1124 288 G
bruce.parker@rocky.edu
PARKER, Carol .... 505-277-2611 313 H
cparker@unm.edu
PARKER, Carol .... 617-824-8912 226 A
carol_parker@emerson.edu
PARKER, Carol, A .... 864-231-2120 443 E
cparker@andersonuniversity.edu
PARKER, Cassandra ..... 202-274-5323.. 97 B
cparker@udc.edu
PARKER, Cathy .... 601-484-8799 268 B
cparker@meridiancc.edu
PARKER, Charles, R ..... 850-263-3261.. 99 A
crparker@baptistcollege.edu
PARKER, Charlie .... 912-433-7174 131 F
ceparker@southuniversity.edu
PARKER, Christopher ... 276-656-0281 516 D
cparker@patrickhenry.edu
PARKER, Collier, B .... 570-340-6000 425 D
cbparker@marywood.edu
PARKER, Corey .... 404-297-9522 126 A
parkerc@gptc.edu
PARKER, Craig .... 502-897-4142 199 D
cparker@sbts.edu
PARKER, Cynthia, L ..... 401-598-1345 441 D
cparker@jwu.edu
PARKER, Cynthia Ann .. 609-652-4378 308 E
cynthia.parker@stockton.edu
PARKER, Dana .... 513-558-9964 393 D
dana.parker@uc.edu
PARKER, Dana, C .... 610-436-2627 432 B
dparker@wcupa.edu
PARKER, Danny, M .... 864-231-2000 443 E
dparker@andersonuniversity.edu
PARKER, Darrell .... 828-227-7401 372 C
dfparker@wcu.edu
PARKER, David .... 336-506-4301 359 N
dave.parker@alamancecc.edu
PARKER, Deborah .... 870-762-3113.. 19 C
dparker@smail.anc.edu
PARKER, Debra .... 419-434-5478 393 F
parker@findlay.edu
PARKER, Debra, O .... 919-530-5269 370 C
dparker@nccu.edu
PARKER, Diane .... 617-243-2137 227 K
dparker@lasell.edu
PARKER, Donna .... 610-399-2308 430 D
dparker@cheyney.edu
PARKER, Doug .... 859-344-3321 200 C
parkerd@thomasmore.edu
PARKER, Frank .... 936-294-1786 489 A
fparker@shsu.edu
PARKER, Gail, C .... 318-342-1961 209 A
gparker@ulm.edu
PARKER, JR.,
Gerald, W .... 979-436-0670 485 C
GParker@tamhsc.edu
PARKER, Gilbert, A .... 607-729-1581 324 A
gparker@davisny.edu
PARKER, Heidi .... 641-673-1031 184 B
parkerh@wmpenn.edu
PARKER, Jack .... 321-433-7380 101 O
parkerj@easternflorida.edu
PARKER, James, T .... 801-581-6857 499 K
jparker@purchasing.utah.edu
PARKER, Janet .... 312-355-4565 161 F
japarker@uic.edu
PARKER, Janice, C .... 312-658-5100 160 H
janice.parker@tbiil.edu
PARKER, Jeffrey .... 303-315-2750.. 86 G
jeff.parker@ucdenver.edu
PARKER, Jerome, S ...... 610-359-5100 416 G
jparker@dccc.edu
PARKER, Jill .... 530-752-2599.. 71 A
jblack@ucdavis.edu
PARKER, Jim, O .... 504-816-8592 206 C
jparker@nobts.edu
PARKER, Joe .... 970-491-3350.. 81 D
joe.parker@colostate.edu
PARKER, Joyce, E .... 310-233-4551.. 51 F
parkerje@lahc.edu
PARKER, Juli .... 508-910-4582 228 H
jparker@umassd.edu
PARKER, Julia .... 601-643-8308 266 J
julia.parker@colin.edu
PARKER, Karen, L .... 434-582-2445 509 G
kparker@liberty.edu
PARKER, Kathleen .... 320-363-5195 254 J
kparker@csbsju.edu
PARKER, Kathleen .... 320-363-2121 264 A
kparker@csbsju.edu
PARKER, Keith .... 561-732-4424 112 C
kparker@svdp.edu
PARKER, Keith, S .... 310-794-6811.. 71 D
kparker@support.ucla.edu
PARKER, Kevin .... 845-758-7511 315 G
parker@bard.edu
PARKER, Kim .... 214-637-3530 496 J
kparker@wadecollege.edu
PARKER, III, Lee 804-289-8405 513M
lparker@richmond.edu
PARKER, Linda .... 336-517-2331 354 K
lparker@bennett.edu
PARKER, Linda .... 641-673-1327 184 B
parkerl@wmpenn.edu
PARKER, Linda, M .... 518-388-6123 350 K
parkerl@union.edu
PARKER, Lionel .... 336-322-2154 364 G
Lionell.Parker@piedmontcc.edu
PARKER, Marcia .... 909-607-7855.. 39 H
PARKER, Maria .... 870-584-4471.. 24 E
mparker@cccua.edu
PARKER, Mark .... 405-208-5315 400 A
mparker@okcu.edu
PARKER, Mary .... 310-393-0411.. 58 E
mfparker@rand.org
PARKER, Mary, G .... 801-581-3490 499 K
mgparker@sa.utah.edu
PARKER, Mary Jo .... 713-221-8471 491 F
parkerm@uhd.edu
PARKER, Melanie, L ..... 617-715-5329 233 C
PARKER, Micah .... 951-343-4381.. 30 D
miparker@calbaptist.edu
PARKER, Michael .... 210-341-1366 479 N
mparker@ost.edu
PARKER, Patsy .... 580-774-3284 402 G
patsy.parker@swosu.edu
PARKER, Pennie .... 407-646-2636 111 H
pparker@rollins.edu
PARKER, Philip, L .... 812-464-1865 174 D
plparker@usi.edu
PARKER, Pippin .... 212-229-5859 334 C
parkerp@newschool.edu
PARKER, Randy .... 336-334-4822 363 A
PARKER, Robin, L .... 513-529-6734 386 K
parkerrl@miamioh.edu
PARKER, Rodney .... 410-617-2310 216 D
rparker1@loyola.edu
PARKER, Ron .... 979-230-3480 469 G
ron.parker@brazosport.edu
PARKER, Sandra .... 513-745-5736 393 C
sandra.parker@uc.edu
PARKER, Sonia .... 801-957-4446 500 E
sonia.parker@slcc.edu
PARKER, Tammie .... 541-278-5850 404 J
tparker@bluecc.edu
PARKER, Teresa .... 740-389-4636 386 B
parkert@mtc.edu
PARKER, Terry .... 303-273-3399.. 80 O
tparker@mines.edu
PARKER, Tim .... 205-879-5588.... 3 I
tparker@faulkner.edu
PARKER, Zoann, J .... 443-412-2170 215 D
zparker@harford.edu
PARKER AMES, Gwen ... 845-675-4446 337 B
gwen.ames@nyack.edu
PARKER-AYERS,
Jennifer .... 256-372-5601.... 1 A
martin.sherrill@aamu.edu
PARKER-BELL, Bernice . 904-470-8261 102 A
bparkerbell@ewc.edu
PARKER-DER BOGHOSSIAN,
John .... 651-846-1757 261 G
john.parker@saintpaul.edu
PARKER-JEANNETTE,
Cyrus .... 562-985-4376.. 33 F
cyrus.parker-jeannette@csulb.edu
PARKER-KELLY,
Darlene .... 323-563-9340.. 38 C
darleneparkerkelly@cdrewu.edu
PARKER-WOLERY,
Amanda .... 513-562-6267 376 O
aparker@artacademy.edu
PARKES, Martin, J .... 717-867-6038 423 I
parkes@ivc.edu
PARKEVICH, Michelle ... 319-385-8021 180 A
michelle.parkevich@iw.edu
PARKHILL, Molly .... 828-694-1706 360 D
mollyp@blueridge.edu
PARKHURST, Abbie ...... 540-828-5782 505 F
aparkhur@bridgewater.edu
PARKIN, Jan .... 312-341-4327 157 E
jparkin01@roosevelt.edu
PARKIN, Janice .... 312-341-4327 157 E
jparkin01@roosevelt.edu
PARKINSON, Alan, R .... 801-422-4327 497 J
alan_parkinson@byu.edu
PARKINSON, Curt .... 559-278-4062.. 33 D
cparkinson@csufresno.edu
PARKINSON, III,
Henry, C .... 978-665-3160 229 D
hparkinson@fitchburgstate.edu
PARKINSON, Michael ... 314-529-9553 277 B
mparkinson@maryville.edu
PARKINSON, Richard ... 815-772-7218 153 E
rcpark@morrisontech.edu
PARKINSON, Tracy .... 843-383-8012 445 A
tparkinson@coker.edu
PARKMAN, Julie .... 315-386-7119 347 F
parkman@canton.edu
PARKS, Amy .... 216-987-6130 381 A
amy.parks@tri-c.edu
PARKS, Ann .... 660-263-4110 279 F
annp@macc.edu
PARKS, Brenda .... 309-298-1944 163 A
bs-parks@wiu.edu
PARKS, Charlotte, P ..... 404-413-7064 126 D
cparks@gsu.edu
PARKS, Cherri, S .... 303-963-3357.. 79 L
cparks@ccu.edu
PARKS, Cynthia .... 478-825-6605 124 E
parksc@fvsu.edu
PARKS, Cynthia .... 706-737-1431 121 C
cparks1@gru.edu
PARKS, Donald, K .... 850-201-8071 102 P
Dparks@flagler.edu
PARKS, Earl .... 202-651-5494.. 95 C
earl.parks@gallaudet.edu
PARKS, Erik .... 312-332-0707 160 K
PARKS, Jason .... 318-484-2184 208 D
parksj@nsula.edu
PARKS, Jeffrey .... 281-476-1501 481 E
jeffrey.parks@sjcd.edu
PARKS, Julie .... 616-234-3714 243 D
jparks@grcc.edu
PARKS, Marshall .... 970-351-1814.. 87 A
marshall.parks@unco.edu
PARKS, Maureen .... 217-333-2590 161 E
mparks@uillinois.edu
PARKS, Michael .... 210-567-2791 495 B
parksm@uthscsa.edu
PARKS, Patricia .... 714-816-0366.. 70 D
patricia.parks@trident.edu
PARKS, Rodney .... 336-278-6677 356 F
rparks4@elon.edu
PARKS, Susan .... 714-556-3610.. 75 A
PARKS, Tammy .... 212-517-3929 343 A
t.parks@sothebysinstitute.com
PARKS, Thomas, N .... 801-581-7236 499 K
tom.parks@utah.edu
PARKS, Tom .... 617-262-5000 223 G
thomas.parks@the-bac.edu
PARKS, Valerie .... 915-779-8031 496 G
vparks@computercareercenter.com
PARKS,
Vanasia Conley .... 423-425-4467 465 E
vanasia-parks@utc.edu
PARKTON, Deanna .... 215-489-4728 416 H
deanna.parkton@delval.edu
PARKYN, David, L .... 773-244-5710 154 G
dparkyn@northpark.edu
PARLE, Joseph, D .... 713-785-5995 470 L
joe.parle@cbshouston.edu

PARLER, Branson 616-222-3000 245 D bparler@kuyper.edu
PARLETT, Lynda, W 828-339-4265 366 C l_parlett@southwesterncc.edu
PARLETT, Ray, M 585-567-9333 328 C ray.parlett@houghton.edu
PARLETT-SWEENEY, Mary, W 518-782-6988 342 H mparlett-sweeney@siena.edu
PARLETTE, Jared 800-955-2527 187 E jparlette@grantham.edu
PARLIER, Heather 828-250-3835 370 E hparlier@unca.edu
PARMAN, Traci 302-622-8000 93 D tparman@dcad.edu
PARMANN, Maureen 810-767-4000 239 H maureen.parmann@baker.edu
PARMER, David 409-212-5724 468 L
PARMER, Marsha 503-223-2245 406 G mparmer@portland.chefs.edu
PARMETER, Kim 218-733-7607 259 C k.parmeter@lsc.edu
PARNELL, John 910-521-6465 371 D john.parnell@uncp.edu
PARNELL, Kathleen 410-617-2354 216 D kmparnell@loyola.edu
PARNELL, Lauren 912-583-3211 121 H lparnell@bpc.edu
PARNELL, Paul 951-372-7015 60 J paul.parnell@nc.edu
PARNELL, Paul 951-372-7015 61 A paul.parnell@norcocollege.edu
PARNELL, Philip 701-671-2669 375 B philip.parnell@ndscs.edu
PARNELL, Rob Roy 512-463-2237 488 D robroy.parnell@tsus.edu
PARNUM CADBURY, Sarah 218-951-5144 422 F cadbury@lasalle.edu
PAROLIN, Jason 715-634-4790 536 P jparolin@lco.edu
PAROLINI, Roger, K 630-844-5489 139 L rparolin@aurora.edu
PARPART, Amanda, L 605-256-5244 453 H amanda.parpart@dsu.edu
PARR, Josephine 212-229-5667 334 C parrj@newschool.edu
PARR, Ronald, G 901-333-4737 464 A rgparr@southwest.tn.edu
PARR, Vanna 940-898-3525 490 D vparr@twu.edu
PARR WALKER, Diane 574-631-7790 174 A Diane.Parr.Walker@nd.edu
PARRA, Alicia, F 954-322-4460 107 D aliciafernandaparra@jmvu.edu
PARRAMORE, Cheri 402-375-7241 292 D chparra1@wsc.edu
PARRENT, Condoa 817-515-6532 484 B condoa.parrent@tccd.edu
PARRENT, Jay, V 270-824-8571 196 F jay.parrent@kctcs.edu
PARRENT, Rick 615-230-3321 464 B rick.parrent@volstate.edu
PARRENT, Robert 314-246-7910 285 G robertparrent@webster.edu
PARRETT, Brenda, J 601-643-8301 266 J brenda.parrett@colin.edu
PARRILL, Jacqueline 740-366-9407 378 L parrill.9@osu.edu
PARRILLA, Arlene 787-863-2390 553 I arlene.parrilla@fajardo.inter.edu
PARRILLA, Margarita 787-850-9463 558 A margarita.parrilla@upr.edu
PARRIOTT, Karen 307-532-8264 546 B karen.parriott@ewc.wy.edu
PARRISH, Austen, L 812-855-8885 167 J austparr@indiana.edu
PARRISH, Cheney 800-962-7682 285 I cparrish@wma.edu
PARRISH, Clyde 513-487-3202 327 C cparrish@huc.edu
PARRISH, Dave 770-531-6420 128 A dparrish@laniertech.edu
PARRISH, David, K 308-632-6933 293 C
PARRISH, Debra, J 906-524-8414 245 B dparrish@kbocc.edu
PARRISH, Gretchen 336-342-4261 365 E parrishg@rockinghamcc.edu
PARRISH, J. Michael 408-924-4800 36 B mparrish@science.sjsu.edu
PARRISH, John 336-342-4261 365 E parrishj@rockinghamcc.edu
PARRISH, Patricia 352-588-8417 111 L trish.parrish@saintleo.edu
PARRISH, Phillip, A 434-243-4023 514 A pap4n@virginia.edu
PARRISH, Rebecca 859-985-3524 193 F parrishr@berea.edu
PARRISH, Sid 800-845-4955 447 L
PARROTT, Aaron 509-682-6795 528 C aparrott@wvc.edu
PARROTT, Mike 843-208-8040 450 D rparrot@uscb.edu
PARROTT, Rebecca 606-242-0256 197 D rebecca.parrott@kctcs.edu
PARROTT, Roger 601-968-5919 266 F president@belhaven.edu
PARRY, John 970-491-3939 81 D john.parry@colostate.edu
PARRY, John 216-687-4808 380 D john.parry@csuohio.edu
PARRY, Laura, S 518-783-8282 342 H lparry@siena.edu
PARRY, Susan 845-341-4251 337 G susan.parry@sunyorange.edu
PARSELL RUMSEY, Leah 317-738-8141 166 B lparsellrumsey@franklincollege.edu
PARSHALL, William 215-204-1421 436 C william.parshall@temple.edu
PARSLEY, Ashton 614-837-4088 394 H parsleya@valorcollege.com
PARSLEY, Nancy, L 847-578-8401 157 G nancy.parsley@rosalindfranklin.edu
PARSNIK, Pamela 570-674-6310 426 D pparsnik@misericordia.edu
PARSON, Mark 715-232-1151 541 B parsonm@uwstout.edu
PARSON, Reginald 415-338-3068 36 A regg@sfsu.edu
PARSON, Tara 417-328-1511 282 D tparson@sbuniv.edu
PARSONS, Brian 405-208-5121 400 A pdparsons@okcu.edu
PARSONS, Bruce 606-218-5273 201 C bruceparsons@upike.edu
PARSONS, Cynthia 804-765-5800 512 K cynthia-parsons@chs.net
PARSONS, Edy 319-363-1323 181 D eparsons@mtmercy.edu
PARSONS, Eric 802-447-2878 503 A eparsons@svc.edu
PARSONS, JR., Frank, R 334-833-4294 4 E fparsons@huntingdon.edu
PARSONS, Gayle 623-245-4600 18 C gparsons@uti.edu
PARSONS, Geoffrey, J 843-349-2054 444 G parsons@coastal.edu
PARSONS, James 207-859-1250 211 I maintenance@thomas.edu
PARSONS, John 325-942-2800 475 E jparsons@howardcollege.edu
PARSONS, Kevin 910-410-1918 365 B ksparsons@richmondcc.edu
PARSONS, Leland 231-348-6615 248 A lparsons@ncmich.edu
PARSONS, Marty 207-762-0146 212 H marty.parsons@umpi.edu
PARSONS, Nancy, P 309-298-1066 163 A np-parsons@wiu.edu
PARSONS, Paul, F 336-278-5724 356 F pparsons@elon.edu
PARSONS, Priscilla 409-880-8489 488 F priscilla.parsons@lamar.edu
PARSONS, Ray, B 302-857-1050 94 A rparsons3@dtcc.edu
PARSONS, Sue 562-860-2451 37 L parsons@cerritos.edu
PARSONS, Teena 910-410-1810 365 B tlparsons@richmondcc.edu
PARSONS, Timothy 570-558-1818 418 I tparsons@fortisinstitute.edu
PARSONS-WELLS, Rachel, E 864-833-7000 448 E reparsons@presby.edu
PARTAIN, Julie 229-931-2249 131 E jpartain@southgatech.edu
PARTAIN, Pam 706-272-2985 123 G ppartain@daltonstate.edu
PARTAIN, Sandra 318-678-6000 203 A spartain@bpcc.edu
PARTCH, Nancy 815-825-2086 149 E nancy.partch@kishwaukeecollege.edu
PARTEE, Ben 805-965-0581 64 N partee@sbcc.edu
PARTELOW, Kevin 815-967-7322 157 C kpartelow@rockfordcareercollege.edu
PARTEN, Janice 559-278-2364 33 D jparten@csufresno.edu
PARTIN, Sherry 606-546-1625 200 E spartin2@unionky.edu
PARTOLAN-FRAY, Liz 360-650-7970 528 D liz.partolan-fray@wwu.edu
PARTON, Becky 217-786-2351 151 C becky.parton@llcc.edu
PARTON, LeAnne 509-793-2004 520 B leannep@bigbend.edu
PARTRIDGE, Kristen, N 405-325-3163 403 I kpartridge@ou.edu
PARTRIDGE, Patrick 801-274-3280 501 B ppartridge@wgu.edu
PARTRIDGE, Richard 803-327-8031 451 K rpartridge@yorktech.edu
PARTS, Nellis 415-955-2100 26 I nparts@alliant.edu
PARVIZI, Nasrin 607-753-5582 345 C nasrin.parvizi@cortland.edu
PARZIALE, Anthony 561-868-3239 109 H parziala@palmbeachstate.edu
PARZY, Robert 847-925-6649 145 F rparzy@harpercollege.edu
PASCAL, Sandra, E 617-989-4478 237 G pascals@wit.edu
PASCALE, Lynn 203-287-3031 91 C paier.admission@snet.net
PASCARELL, Rose 703-993-8760 507 K rpascare@gmu.edu
PASCARELLA, John 936-294-1458 489 A jbp014@shsu.edu
PASCARIELLO, Jacqueline 631-632-6840 344 C jacqueline.pascariello@stonybrook.edu
PASCHAL, Linda, L 414-955-8208 537 C lpaschal@mcw.edu
PASCHAL, Trisa Long 404-880-6186 122 I tpaschal@cau.edu
PASCHALL, Bill 720-855-6014 82 M billp@heritage-education.com
PASCHALL, Danny 562-903-4874 29 F danny.paschall@biola.edu
PASCHALL, Kimberly, S 270-809-3809 198 I kpaschall@murraystate.edu
PASCHOLD, Erika 402-465-7574 292 E epaschol@nebrwesleyan.edu
PASCO, Leslie 315-228-7481 321 H lpasco@colgate.edu
PASCOE, Frank, H 815-740-3216 162 F fpascoe@stfrancis.edu
PASCOE, Tammie 903-983-8105 477 A tpascoe@kilgore.edu
PASCOE AGUILAR, Daniel 541-346-6009 410 F dpascoe@uoregon.edu
PASCUA, Vance 916-577-2200 77 F vpascua@jessup.edu
PASCUA DEA, Tracy 925-631-4165 61 G tjp2@stmarys-ca.edu
PASCUCCI, Richard, A 215-871-6690 432 E richardp@pcom.edu
PASEK, Heidi 406-771-4397 288 B hpasek@gfcmsu.edu
PASENELLI, Rose 619-594-1630 35 E rpasenel@mail.sdsu.edu
PASHA, Stephanie 508-831-6655 238 G spasha@wpi.edu
PASIC, Amir 317-278-5652 168 E
PASKER, Mark 563-876-3353 177 I mpasker@dwci.edu
PASKETT, Lindy 307-855-2120 545 a lpaskett@cwc.edu
PASKEY, Louise 712-279-5494 176 B louise.paskey@briarcliff.edu
PASKOFF, Beth, M 225-578-1480 204 M bpaskoff@lsu.edu
PASKVAN, Brian 567-661-7742 390 D brian_paskvan@owens.edu
PASKVAN, Kevin, F 740-368-3052 390 B kfpaskva@owu.edu
PASQUARIELLO, Gino 619-200-8965 67 I gpasquariello@socalsem.edu
PASQUARIELLO, Robert 360-475-7835 524 H rpasquariello@olympic.edu
PASQUERELLA, Lynn 413-538-2500 234 C commish@mtholyoke.edu
PASS-STERN, Bernice 212-614-6176 338 C bstern@chpnet.org
PASSAFIUME, Marisa 718-862-7796 331 H marisa.passafiume@manhattan.edumanhattan.edu
PASSARO, Joanne 262-524-7364 535 D jpassaro@carrollu.edu
PASSAUER, Bridgett, M 757-822-1536 517 C bpassauer@tcc.edu
PASSE, Jeffrey 609-771-2100 301 E passej@tcnj.edu
PASSER, Christine 269-782-1316 250 D cpasser@swmich.edu
PASSERINI, Katia 973-642-7664 304 D katia.passerini@njit.edu
PASTERIS, Marc 309-467-6305 145 A mpasteris@eureka.edu
PASTERNAK, Reuven 631-444-2701 344 C reuven.pasternak@stonybrookmedicine.edu
PASTERNIAK, Sarah 870-862-8131 23 B spasterniak@southark.edu
PASTIDES, Harris 803-777-2001 450 B pastides@sc.edu
PASTIN, John, R 856-256-4550 306 D pastin@rowan.edu
PASTOOR, Robert, A 219-866-6157 172 E rpastoor@saintjoe.edu
PASTOR, Richard 386-506-4414 101 I pastorr@DaytonaState.edu
PASTORE, Michael, A 315-255-1743 317 I michael.pastore@cayuga-cc.edu
PASTORELLA, Mark, J 585-262-1509 333 G mpastorella@monroecc.edu
PASTORIZA, Nelida 718-518-4412 319 D npastoriza@hostos.cuny.edu
PASTORRES-PALFFY, Elizabeth 916-485-3276 392 F beth.pastorres-palffy@myunion.edu
PASTRANA, Livia, D 787-728-1515 559 A lpastrana@sagrado.edu
PASTRANA, Marie Luz 787-765-3560 552 E lpastrana@edpuniversity.edu
PASTRANA, Marilyn 787-765-3560 552 E mpastrana@edpuniversity.edu
PASTRANO, Ginna 713-646-1867 482 H gpastrano@stcl.edu
PASTVA, Kimberlee, M 848-932-1245 306 F pastva@oldqueens.rutgers.edu
PASZKIEWICZ, Wendy 312-662-4211 139 E paszk@adler.edu
PASZTOR, Jim 303-220-1200 79 G jim.pasztor@cffp.edu
PATALANO, Carla 617-951-2350 234 F carla.patalano@necb.edu
PATAWARAN, Arrileen 773-995-2063 141 J apatawar@csu.edu
PATCHETT, Heather 423-636-7303 464 F hpatchett@tusculum.edu
PATCHETT, Margaret, B 704-403-3077 355 B meg.patchett@carolinashealthcare.org
PATCHIN, Steve 906-487-2313 247 A shpatchi@mtu.edu
PATCHNER, Michael 317-274-8362 168 E patchner@iupui.edu
PATE, Carol 215-248-7127 415 D cmpate@chc.edu
PATE, Doug 919-209-2007 363 F mdpate@johnstoncc.edu
PATE, Herman 404-527-4520 122 D hpate@carver.edu
PATE, Juston 606-759-7141 196 G juston.pate@kctcs.edu
PATE, Kim 217-206-7592 161 G kpate80@uis.edu
PATE, Nino, T 671-734-1812 549 F npate@piu.edu
PATEE, Carla 620-227-9378 186 F cpatee@dc3.edu
PATEE, Greg 620-227-9355 186 F gpatee@dc3.edu
PATEGAS, Dianna 203-582-8797 91 E dianna.pategas@quinnipiac.edu
PATEL, Maqbool 410-951-3780 220 C mpatel@coppin.edu
PATEL, Narendra, H 404-880-8064 122 I npatel@cau.edu
PATEL, Prita 202-885-2177 94 H ppatel@american.edu
PATEL, Tarun 518-694-7337 314 G tarun.patel@acphs.edu
PATENAUDE, Craig 301-934-7643 214 E cpatenaude@csmd.edu
PATERSON, Brent 309-438-5451 147 I bgpater@ilstu.edu
PATERSON, John 802-728-1434 504 C jpaterson@vtc.edu
PATERSON, Valerie 617-682-1593 226 D vpaterson@eds.edu
PATERSON, Wendy, A 716-878-4214 345 B paterswa@buffalostate.edu
PATES, Nancy 952-358-8200 260 D nancy.pates@normandale.edu
PATH, Bill 918-293-5256 400 E bpath@okstate.edu
PATHAK, Dushyant 530-752-7309 71 A dpathak@ucdavis.edu
PATHAK, Susanna 414-425-8300 538 J spathak@shsst.edu
PATILLA, Shane 770-394-8300 120 E spatilla@aii.edu
PATINO, Beatriz 508-767-7100 222 D bpatino@assumption.edu
PATLOLLA, Babu, P 601-877-6120 266 C bpatlolla@alcorn.edu
PATNAUDE, Valerie 603-897-8533 298 E vpatnaude@rivier.edu
PATO, Rosevonne 684-699-9155 549 C r.pato@amsamoa.edu
PATON, Jeff 336-322-2237 364 G Jeff.Paton@piedmontcc.edu
PATON, Nancy, E 716-645-6969 343 E nepaton@buffalo.edu
PATOUT, Gerald 337-550-1380 205 B gpatout@lsue.edu
PATRAGNONI-SAUTER, Kirstin 215-951-2700 432 F patragnonik@philau.edu

PATRIA, Patty, L ... 508-373-1981 223 C ppatria@becker.edu

PATRIARCA, Linda ... 252-328-1000 369 E patriarcal@ecu.edu

PATRICK, Beth, G ... 606-783-2053 198 H b.patrick@moreheadstate.edu

PATRICK, Brian ... 913-288-7362 188 G bpatrick@kckcc.edu

PATRICK, Charles ... 817-923-1921 483 E cpatrick@swbts.edu

PATRICK, Craig ... 914-632-6700 333 F cpatrick@monroecollege.edu

PATRICK, Diane ... 616-234-4105 243 D dpatrick@grcc.edu

PATRICK, Diane, D ... 616-234-4101 243 D dpatrick@grcc.edu

PATRICK, Edward ... 803-536-7000 448 H

PATRICK, Garry ... 707-476-4385.. 41 C garry-patrick@redwoods.edu

PATRICK, Jamie ... 919-497-3245 358 J jpatrick@louisburg.edu

PATRICK, Juletta ... 815-455-8613 152 B jpatrick@mchenry.edu

PATRICK, Keeley ... 860-768-2441.. 92 F kpatrick@hartford.edu

PATRICK, Kim ... 616-331-2280 243 E patricki@gvsu.edu

PATRICK, Laura ... 949-376-6000.. 49 K lpatrick@lcad.edu

PATRICK, Maggie ... 507-222-5568 254 D mpatrick@carleton.edu

PATRICK, Melissa ... 502-231-5221 198 D mpatrick@myLBC.us

PATRICK, Michelle ... 610-436-2930 432 B mpatrick@wcupa.edu

PATRICK, Nicole ... 662-329-7114 269 B jnpatrick@muw.edu

PATRICK, Paul, D ... 843-953-0879 445 B patrickpd@cofc.edu

PATRICK, Paul, G ... 864-379-6675 446 B ppatrick@erskine.edu

PATRICK, Ron ... 800-422-2418.. 99 C rpatrick@baymedical.org

PATRICK, Roxann ... 937-294-0592 391 B roxann@saa.edu

PATRICK, Stan ... 601-643-8302 266 J stan.patrick@colin.edu

PATRICK-TURNER, Ronne ... 617-373-5416 235 D

PATRIDGE, Emily ... 704-403-1798 355 B emily.patridge@carolinashealthcare.org

PATRIE, Shannon ... 315-498-2802 337 F patries@sunyocc.edu

PATSALIDES, Eugene ... 270-831-9688 196 C eugenios.patsalides@kctcs.edu

PATSCHECK, Valerie ... 805-437-8878.. 32 H valerie.patscheck@csuci.edu

PATTEE, Bob ... 254-295-4524 492 C rpattee@umhb.edu

PATTEE, Bonnie ... 801-274-3280 501 B bonnie.pattee@wgu.edu

PATTEN, David, B ... 401-825-2194 441 C dpatten@ccri.edu

PATTEN, Diana, R ... 319-399-8844 176 G dpatten@coe.edu

PATTEN-LEMONS, Rebecca ... 317-921-4667 169M rpatten@ivytech.edu

PATTEN-WALLACE, Kaye ... 419-530-7963 394 E kaye.pattenwallace@utoledo.edu

PATTENAUDE, Richard .. 858-513-9240.. 29 A richard.pattenaude@ashford.edu

PATTERSON, Anthony ... 410-822-5400 214 D apatterson@chesapeake.edu

PATTERSON, Anthony ... 919-572-1625 354 F apatterson@apexsot.edu

PATTERSON, Barbara, A ... 580-774-3261 402 G barbara.patterson@swosu.edu

PATTERSON, Bart ... 702-992-2350 295 E bart.patterson@nsc.edu

PATTERSON, Becky ... 502-852-3385 201 A becky.patterson@louisville.edu

PATTERSON, Ben ... 805-565-6210.. 76 K bpatters@westmont.edu

PATTERSON, Bernie ... 715-346-2123 541 A

PATTERSON, Charles ... 912-478-2647 126 B cpatterson@georgiasouthern.edu

PATTERSON, Charles ... 912-478-5465 126 B cpatterson@georgiasouthern.edu

PATTERSON, Charles, E 229-928-1360 126 C charles.patterson@gsw.edu

PATTERSON, Charlotte .. 434-982-2961 514 A cjp@virginia.edu

PATTERSON, Christina .. 863-638-2914 119 A pattersonCM@webber.edu

PATTERSON, Corey ... 325-674-6566 466 I pattersonc@acu.edu

PATTERSON, Cynthia, A ... 252-638-7304 362 A pattersc@cravencc.edu

PATTERSON, Dale ... 918-540-6319 398 L dale.patterson@neo.edu

PATTERSON, Daniel ... 606-679-8501 197 B daniel.patterson@kctcs.edu

PATTERSON, Darrin ... 330-337-6403 376 B college@awc.edu

PATTERSON, Donald, A 716-878-3447 345 B patterda@buffalostate.edu

PATTERSON, Donald, W ... 570-484-2255 431 C dpatters@lhup.edu

PATTERSON, Dorothy ... 803-780-1192 451 G pattersn@voorhees.edu

PATTERSON, Dorsey ... 901-435-1286 457 N dorsey_patterson@loc.edu

PATTERSON, Eddie ... 803-780-1249 451 G epatterson@voorhees.edu

PATTERSON, Elice ... 202-651-5309.. 95 C elice.patterson@gallaudet.edu

PATTERSON, Elizabeth .. 903-223-6722 486 C epatterson@tamut.edu

PATTERSON, Eric ... 757-352-4616 511 G epatterson@regent.edu

PATTERSON, Felicia, L . 410-777-2718 213 E flpatterson@aacc.edu

PATTERSON, Frank ... 850-644-0453 115 A fpatterson@fsu.edu

PATTERSON, Franklin ... 386-481-2020.. 99 F pattersonf@cookman.edu

PATTERSON, Gary ... 727-873-4005 116 C gpatterson@usf.edu

PATTERSON, Howard ... 903-566-7350 494 E hpatterson@uttyler.edu

PATTERSON, James ... 860-738-6482.. 89 G jpatterson@nwcc.commnet.edu

PATTERSON, James ... 908-852-1400 301 C pattersonj@centenarycollege.edu

PATTERSON, Jana Lynn, F ... 336-278-7200 356 F patters@elon.edu

PATTERSON, Jennifer ... 614-236-6502 378 H jpatterson@capital.edu

PATTERSON, Joanna ... 414-382-6009 534 I joanna.patterson@alverno.edu

PATTERSON, John, A ... 478-301-5537 128 G patterson_ja@mercer.edu

PATTERSON, John, D ... 620-235-4108 190 G jdpatterson@pittstate.edu

PATTERSON, Johnny ... 318-274-6568 207 H pattersonj@gram.edu

PATTERSON, Jolene, M 334-844-4650.... 1 G pattejo@auburn.edu

PATTERSON, Joyce, D .. 337-475-5232 208 B alumni@mcneese.edu

PATTERSON, Kristi ... 815-479-7677 152 B kpatterson@mchenry.edu

PATTERSON, Laura, M .. 734-763-7109 251 C lmpatter@umich.edu

PATTERSON, Lauren ... 503-228-6528 404 H lpatterson@aii.edu

PATTERSON, Leni, N ... 864-833-8284 448 E lpatters@presby.edu

PATTERSON, Lisa ... 614-823-1589 390 C lphillips@otterbein.edu

PATTERSON, Liz ... 313-993-1254 250 H patterew@udmercy.edu

PATTERSON, Michael ... 843-958-5813 449 G michael.patterso12568@tridenttech.edu

PATTERSON, Michael ... 410-225-2422 216 F mpatters@mica.edu

PATTERSON, Michael ... 415-503-6237.. 63 A mpatterson@sfcm.edu

PATTERSON, Michael, J ... 570-577-1911 413 E mike.patterson@bucknell.edu

PATTERSON, Myrna ... 808-845-9115 136 E mpatters@hawaii.edu

PATTERSON, Nancy ... 423-697-2630 462 C nancy.patterson@chattanoogastate.edu

PATTERSON, Paige ... 817-923-1921 483 E presidentsoffice@swbts.edu

PATTERSON, Paul, M ... 334-844-3209.... 1 G pmp0003@auburn.edu

PATTERSON, Rae Lynn . 208-535-5361 138 B raelynn.patterson@my.eitc.edu

PATTERSON, Ralph ... 864-388-8350 447 E rpatterson@lander.edu

PATTERSON, Randall ... 847-628-2011 149 A randall.patterson@judsonu.edu

PATTERSON, Randall, B 501-569-3328.. 24 A rbpatterson@ualr.edu

PATTERSON, Richard ... 307-532-8202 546 B richard.patterson@ewc.wy.edu

PATTERSON, Ron, K ... 740-376-4600 386 A ron.patterson@marietta.edu

PATTERSON, Sarah ... 254-867-2005 488 B sarah.patterson@tstc.edu

PATTERSON, Shannon .. 706-771-4013 121 B sbentley@augustatech.edu

PATTERSON, Sharon ... 414-443-8556 542 I sharon.patterson@wlc.edu

PATTERSON, Steven ... 703-323-3554 516 C spatterson@nvcc.edu

PATTERSON, Susan ... 518-458-5358 322 C patterss@strose.edu

PATTERSON, Teresa ... 909-274-5512.. 54 J tpatterson@mtsac.edu

PATTERSON, Terry, L ... 208-732-6402 137 K tpatterson@csi.edu

PATTERSON, Thomas ... 334-387-3877.... 1 E thomaspatterson@amridgeuniversity.edu

PATTERSON, Tim ... 802-586-7711 503 B tpatterson@sterlingcollege.edu

PATTERSON, III, U, L ... 704-669-4025 361 E patterson@clevelandcc.edu

PATTERSON, Vicki ... 832-252-4624 470 L vicki@cbhouston.edu

PATTERSON, Yvonne ... 773-995-2386 141 J ypatte20@csu.edu

PATTI, Christopher, M . 510-642-7122.. 70 K cpatti@berkeley.edu

PATTI, James ... 401-232-6088 441 B jpatti@bryant.edu

PATTILLO, Andre ... 404-215-2752 128 L andre.pattillo@morehouse.edu

PATTILLO, Baker ... 936-468-2201 484 A bpattillo@sfasu.edu

PATTISALL, Jeremy ... 336-725-8344 368 A pattisallj@piedmontu.edu

PATTISON, Peggy ... 313-593-5131 251 D ppatt@umich.edu

PATTON, Barbara, L ... 615-898-2185 461 E barbara.patton@mtsu.edu

PATTON, Caron ... 817-531-6571 490 C cpatton@txwes.edu

PATTON, Chad ... 434-949-1045 516 H chad.patton@southside.edu

PATTON, Danny ... 662-329-7436 269 B dcpatton@muw.edu

PATTON, Jack ... 260-481-6710 168 D Jack.Patton@ipfw.edu

PATTON, Jeremy ... 575-439-3703 312 B patton@nmsu.edu

PATTON, John ... 314-434-4044 273 J john.patton@covenantseminary.edu

PATTON, Josh ... 607-729-8915 324 H Jpatton@ebi-college.com

PATTON, Kerry ... 203-582-3087.. 91 E kerry.patton2@quinnipiac.edu

PATTON, Laurie, L ... 802-443-5400 502 E president@middlebury.edu

PATTON, Lori ... 732-906-2574 303 F lpatton@middlesexcc.edu

PATTON, Mary ... 817-257-7660 486 G m.patton@tcu.edu

PATTON, Paul, E ... 606-218-5261 201 C pep@upike.edu

PATTON, Philip, L ... 319-273-2241 176 A philip.patton@uni.edu

PATTON, Terry ... 940-397-4088 478 G terry.patton@mwsu.edu

PATTY, Jeff ... 706-295-6775 125 C jpatty@highlands.edu

PATTY, Kevin ... 706-419-1209 123 F kevin.patty@covenant.edu

PATTY, Stacy ... 806-720-7652 478 A stacy.patty@lcu.edu

PATWARY, Mohsin ... 718-270-6217 320 C mohsin@mec.cuny.edu

PATZ, Thomas ... 317-738-8183 166 B tpatz@franklincollege.edu

PATZ, Thomas ... 317-738-8025 166 B tpatz@franklincollege.edu

PAUGH, Jerry ... 714-449-7487.. 53 D jpaugh@ketchum.edu

PAUGH, Mark ... 352-854-2322 100 P paughm@cf.edu

PAUKEN, Patrick ... 419-372-2226 377 I paukenp@bgsu.edu

PAUL, Alyson ... 706-864-1900 133 A alyson.paul@ung.edu

PAUL, Beth ... 386-822-7010 117 A bpaul@stetson.edu

PAUL, David ... 606-693-5000 197 F dpaul@kmbc.edu

PAUL, David ... 360-416-7738 527 A dave.paul@skagit.edu

PAUL, Ivan ... 217-641-4553 148 J ipaul@jwcc.edu

PAUL, Jeremy ... 617-373-5149 235 D

PAUL, Jina ... 402-552-3100 289 H

PAUL, Joseph ... 972-860-8054 472 D jpaul@dcccd.edu

PAUL, Joy ... 606-693-5000 197 F jpaul@kmbc.edu

PAUL, Kelley ... 903-923-2229 473 I kpaul@etbu.edu

PAUL, Kiesha ... 561-912-1211 102 N kpaul@evergladesuniversity.edu

PAUL, Leslie ... 603-206-8176 297 A lpaul@ccsnh.edu

PAUL, Lisa, M ... 956-326-2856 485 B lisa.paul@tamiu.edu

PAUL, Mary ... 619-849-2215.. 59 K marypaul@pointloma.edu

PAUL, Michelle ... 417-455-5675 274 B MichellePaul@crowder.edu

PAUL, Parrish ... 256-824-6203.... 9 A parrish.paul@uah.edu

PAUL, Prem, S ... 402-472-3123 293 H ppaul2@unl.edu

PAUL, Robert ... 630-515-4566 144 A rpaul@devrygroup.com

PAUL, Robert, H ... 314-516-8403 284 B paulro@umsl.edu

PAUL, Sheilah ... 718-270-4936 320 C spaul@mec.cuny.edu

PAUL, Susan ... 440-365-5222 385 E

PAUL, Tina ... 870-612-2017.. 24 G tina.paul@uaccb.edu

PAUL, Tonya ... 419-772-3106 388 I t-paul@onu.edu

PAULE, Romeo ... 415-949-7308.. 45 A pauleromeo@fhda.edu

PAULETTI, Daniel ... 610-436-2552 432 B dpauletti@wcupa.edu

PAULEY, Ann ... 202-884-9725.. 97 A pauleya@trinitydc.edu

PAULEY, II, John ... 610-341-5892 418 A casdean@eastern.edu

PAULEY, Liz ... 940-898-2911 490 D epauley@twu.edu

PAULIEN, Jon ... 909-558-4536.. 50 K jpaulien@llu.edu

PAULIN, Christopher ... 860-512-2753.. 89 D cpaulin@manchestercc.edu

PAULINE, Rose Lee ... 215-951-1014 422 F pauline@lasalle.edu

PAULISON, Wayne ... 918-631-2616 403M wayne-paulison@utulsa.edu

PAULL, Andrea ... 425-249-4777 527 D andrea.paull@tlc.edu

PAULMAN, John ... 575-527-7500 312 D jpaulma@nmsu.edu

PAULNACK, Karl ... 607-274-3343 328 H kpaulnack@ithaca.edu

PAULNOCK, Donna, M . 608-262-2748 539 D paulnock@wisc.edu

PAULO, Joseph ... 803-754-4100 445 D

PAULOS, Christine ... 651-748-2619 258 D christine.paulos@century.edu

PAULOSKI, SP, Pam ... 773-371-5420 141 C presoffice@ctu.edu

PAULSEN, Christi ... 785-227-3380 185 A paulsenc@bethanylb.edu

PAULSON, Cheri ... 781-239-3845 222 E cpaulson@babson.edu

PAULSON, Chuck ... 612-659-6102 259 F chuck.paulson@minneapolis.edu

PAULSON, Dennis, J ... 630-515-7352 152 H dpauls@midwestern.edu

PAULSON, Don ... 208-282-2130 138 C pauldona@isu.edu

PAULSON, Janet ... 503-594-3162 405 A jpaulson@clackamas.edu

PAULSON, Ken, A ... 615-898-2813 461 E ken.paulson@mtsu.edu

PAULSON, Nancy ... 218-855-8054 258 C NPaulson@clcmn.edu

PAULSON, Robert ... 361-593-5002 486 A robert.paulson@tamuk.edu

PAULSON, Susan ... 757-373-7370 111 L susan.paulson@saintleo.edu

PAULSON, Veronica ... 605-626-2537 454 A Veronica.Paulson@northern.edu

PAULUS, Jim ... 620-947-3121 191 E jimp@tabor.edu

PAULUS, Michael ... 206-281-2414 526 D paulusm@spu.edu

PAULUS, Michael, L ... 419-372-2891 377 I mpaulus@bgsu.edu

PAUSTENBAUGH, Jennifer ... 801-422-4301 497 J jennifer_paustenbaugh@byu.edu

PAUSTENBAUGH, Richard ... 435-652-7711 499M paustenbaugh@dixie.edu

PAUSTIAN, Kevin ... 563-884-5721 182 D kevin.paustian@palmer.edu

PAUSTIAN, Tony ... 515-633-2439 177 B adpaustian@dmacc.edu

PAVA, Moses ... 212-960-0845 353 P mpava@yu.edu

PAVAN, Ron ... 615-547-1348 456 C rpavan@cumberland.edu

PAVAN, Tammi ... 615-547-1228 456 C tpavan@cumberland.edu

PECSOK, Michael .... 808-455-0453 136 G
mpecsok@hawaii.edu
PECTOL, James, B .... 423-585-6823 464 C
james.pectol@ws.edu
PEDE, Charles, N .... 434-971-3301 547 K
charles.n.pede@mail.mil
PEDE, Michael .... 315-792-5411 333 D
mpede@mvcc.edu
PEDE, Mike .... 713-743-9551 491 D
mlpede@uh.edu
PEDEN, Gary, S .... 315-470-6588 347 B
gspeden@esf.edu
PEDERSEN, Daniel, T .... 320-308-2166 261 E
dtpedersen@stcloudstate.edu
PEDERSEN, Eric .... 907-474-7500.. 10 I
PEDERSEN, Eric .... 435-652-7977 499 M
pedersen@dixie.edu
PEDERSEN, Eric, R .... 907-786-1266.. 10 H
erpedersen@uaa.alaska.edu
PEDERSEN, Jeffrey, M .. 631-451-4425 348 E
pedersj@sunysuffolk.edu
PEDERSEN, Jennifer, L . 308-635-6078 294 C
pedersen@wncc.edu
PEDERSEN, Joel, D .... 402-472-1201 293 F
jdpedersen@nebraska.edu
PEDERSEN, Mary, E ...... 805-756-2246.. 32 E
mdederse@calpoly.edu
PEDERSEN, Patricia, E .. 203-436-8518.. 93 C
patty.pedersen@yale.edu
PEDERSEN, Phyllis .... 225-214-6979 206 F
phyllis.pedersen@ololcollege.edu
PEDERSON, Barb .... 701-231-7211 374 C
barbara.pederson@ndsu.edu
PEDERSON, Mark .... 765-677-2117 169 C
mark.pederson@indwes.edu
PEDERSON, Robert, A .. 207-778-7036 212 E
pederson@maine.edu
PEDESCLEAUX, Desiree 404-270-5696 132 D
dpedescl@spelman.edu
PEDIGO, Sue, H .... 615-230-3551 464 B
sue.pedigo@volstate.edu
PEDNEAU, Judy .... 276-326-4461 505 D
jpedneau@bluefield.edu
PEDRAZA, Jonathan, N 262-691-5308 544 D
jpedraza2@wctc.edu
PEDREGON, Sam .... 719-596-7400.. 83 A
spedregon@intellitecmedical.edu
PEDRICK, Andrea .... 315-786-2236 329 G
apedrick@sunyjefferson.edu
PEDRICK, Jim .... 319-385-6218 180 A
jim.pedrick@iw.edu
PEDRONE, Dino, J .... 607-729-1581 324 A
dpedrone@davisny.edu
PEDROTTY, Kate .... 318-869-5715 202 D
kpedrotty@centenary.edu
PEDUTO, Michelle, A ... 412-578-6157 414 I
mapeduto@carlow.edu
PEE, Charles, M .... 803-934-3294 447 K
cpee@morris.edu
PEEBLES, Carolyn .... 919-572-1625 354 F
cpeebles@apexsot.edu
PEEBLES, Ethel .... 704-216-6111 358 I
epeebles@livingstone.edu
PEEBLES, Henry .... 321-674-7715 103 R
peebles@fit.edu
PEEBLES, Lee .... 401-739-5000 441 E
lpeebles@neit.edu
PEEDIN, Pamela, L .... 603-646-2445 297 G
pamela.l.peedin@dartmouth.edu
PEEK, Brian .... 706-245-7226 124 C
bpeek@ec.edu
PEEK, Katherine .... 909-652-6333.. 38 A
kay.peek@chaffey.edu
PEEL, Bill .... 214-932-1112 477 G
billpeel@letu.edu
PEEL, Claire .... 817-735-2762 493 B
Claire.Peel@unthsc.edu
PEEL, Henry .... 239-489-9011 104 G
hpeel@fsw.edu
PEEL, Michael, A .... 203-432-8362.. 93 C
mike.peel@yale.edu
PEELER, Chris Goff .... 704-461-6663 354 J
chrisgoff@bac.edu
PEELER, Mark, L .... 864-379-8745 446 B
mlp@erskine.edu
PEELING, Rebecca .... 561-803-2024 109 G
becky_peeling@pba.edu
PEEPLES, Junelyn .... 909-607-3884.. 65 E
junelyn.peeples@scrippscollege.edu
PEEPLES, Terry, G .... 870-245-5169.. 22 C
peeplest@obu.edu
PEEPLES, Tim .... 336-278-5613 356 F
peeples@elon.edu
PEER, Ronda .... 307-754-6123 546 I
Ronda.Peer@nwc.edu
PEERMAN, Carey, H ..... 540-224-6973 509 D
chpeerman@jchs.edu
PEEVEY, Robin .... 617-873-0274 225 A
Robin.peevey@cambridgecollege.edu
PEFFALL, Marianne .... 610-436-2705 432 B
mpeffall@wcupa.edu
PEFFER, Deb .... 313-593-5100 251 D
dkpeffer@umich.edu
PEFFER, Tony .... 802-468-1203 503 G
tony.peffer@castleton.edu
PEFFERS, Keith .... 219-785-5720 172 A
kpeffers@pnc.edu
PEGAH, Mahmoud .... 941-359-7633 111 F
mpegah@ringling.edu
PEGG, Steven, M .... 410-777-2651 213 E
smpegg@aacc.edu
PEGGY, Allen .... 850-644-1841 115 A
mrallen@fsu.edu
PEGRAM, Mike .... 402-761-8270 293 A
mpegram@southeast.edu
PEGUES, Charlotte Fant 662-915-7792 270 G
cfant@olemiss.edu
PEGUES, John, R .... 504-568-5135 205 C
jpegue@lsuhsc.edu
PEGUES, Patricia .... 662-252-2491 270 C
ppegues@rustcollege.edu
PEGUES, Patricia .... 662-252-8000 270 C
ppegues@rustcollege.edu
PEHLMAN, Patricia, A .. 717-245-1545 417 B
pehlman@dickinson.edu
PEHRSSON,
Dale-Elizabeth .... 989-774-6995 240 O
pehrs1d@cmich.edu
PEI, Alissa .... 573-876-7212 283 A
apei@stephens.edu
PEIFER, Bruce .... 301-891-4000 221 C
bpeifer@wau.edu
PEIFER, Michelle .... 704-991-0393 366 D
mpeifer7924@stanly.edu
PEIFFER, Cyndi .... 641-673-1040 184 B
peifferc@wmpenn.edu
PEIFFER, Mark, J .... 515-271-1475 177 H
mark.peiffer@dmu.edu
PEIRCE, Nathaniel .... 603-899-4320 297 H
peircen@franklinpierce.edu
PEKRUL, William, A ...... 507-354-8221 257 A
pekrulwa@mlc-wels.edu
PELAEZ, Michelle .... 813-253-6251 118 H
mpelaez@ut.edu
PELAK, Anne, C .... 914-654-5225 322 B
apelak@cnr.edu
PELAZZA, Todd, A .... 203-254-4090.. 90 E
tapelazza@fairfield.edu
PELC, Sharon .... 308-865-8523 293 G
pelcs@unk.edu
PELISSERO, John, P ..... 312-915-6400 151 E
jpeliss@luc.edu
PELKEY, David .... 360-596-5231 527 B
dpelkey@spscc.edu
PELLEGRIN, Amy, E ...... 304-367-4135 532 F
Amy.Pellegrin@fairmontstate.edu
PELLEGRIN, Nathan ...... 510-466-7210.. 59 C
npellegrin@peralta.edu
PELLEGRINI, Larry .... 570-674-6307 426 D
lpellegr@misericordia.edu
PELLEGRINO, Debra, A . 570-941-6305 438 F
debra.pellegrino@scranton.edu
PELLEGRINO, Diane ...... 973-655-5460 304 A
pellegrinod@mail.montclair.edu
PELLEGRINO, Eric .... 856-351-2770 308 B
epellegrino@salemcc.edu
PELLEGRINO, Karen, A . 203-254-4100.. 90 E
kpellegrino@fairfield.edu
PELLEGRINO,
Thomas, C .... 203-254-4000.. 90 E
tpellegrino@fairfield.edu
PELLETIER, Corey .... 207-859-1106 211 I
pelletierc@thomas.edu
PELLETIER, Jo-Ann, M . 508-678-2811 231 B
jo-ann.pelletier@bristolcc.edu
PELLETIER, Kristan, M .. 518-629-7328 328 D
k.pelletier@hvcc.edu
PELLETT, Tracy .... 912-279-5960 123 B
tpellett@ccga.edu
PELLICANE, Patrick .... 657-278-2407.. 33 E
ppellicane@fullerton.edu
PELLICCIA, Michael, C . 516-572-7538 334 A
michael.pelliccia@ncc.edu
PELLICCIOTTI, M. Beth . 219-989-2239 171 L
pellicmb@purduecal.edu
PELLICO, Gary .... 317-921-4882 169 M
gpellico@ivytech.edu
PELLISH, Catherine .... 303-404-5022.. 82 J
catherine.pellish@frontrange.edu
PELLIZZI, Thomas .... 608-757-6328 542 L
tpellizzi@blackhawk.edu
PELLOT, Robert .... 212-938-5720 347 C
rpellot@sunyopt.edu
PELLS, Ruth, R .... 509-777-4665 529 A
rpells@whitworth.edu
PELLY, Michael .... 714-997-6982.. 38 B
pelly@chapman.edu
PELOQUIN, Andy .... 503-517-1815 411 C
apeloquin@westernseminary.edu
PELOQUIN-DODD,
Mary, T .... 919-515-2143 370 D
mary_peloquin-dodd@ncsu.edu
PELOSO, Elizabeth, D ... 215-746-0234 437 I
epeloso@upenn.edu
PELPHREY, Barry .... 606-546-1299 200 E
bpelphrey@unionky.edu
PELRINE, JR., John, P . 773-298-3121 158 F
pelrine@sxu.edu
PELTIER, Beverly .... 706-771-4023 121 B
bpeltier@augustatech.edu
PELTIER, Eileen .... 860-253-3032.. 88 H
epeltier@asnuntuck.edu
PELTIER, John .... 401-874-4530 442 E
jpeltier@uri.edu
PELTIER, Linda, M .... 937-778-7802 381 K
lpeltier@edisonohio.edu
PELTIER, Matthew, S .... 423-652-4740 457 J
mspeltie@king.edu
PELTO, William, L .... 828-262-3021 369 D
peltowl@appstate.edu
PELTON, Jack .... 208-426-4203 137 E
jpelton@boisestate.edu
PELTON, M. Lee .... 617-824-8525 226 A
lee_pelton@emerson.edu
PELTON, Mark .... 478-445-2753 125 A
mark.pelton@gcsu.edu
PELTON, Vanessa .... 805-965-0581.. 64 N
pelton@sbcc.edu
PELTON, Woody .... 336-278-6700 356 F
wpelton@elon.edu
PELTZ, Mark .... 641-269-4940 178 I
peltzm@grinnell.edu
PELUSI, Mario, J .... 309-556-3061 148 A
mpelusi@iwu.edu
PELUSO, Constance ...... 718-631-6297 320 F
cpeluso@qcc.cuny.edu
PELUSO, Eileen .... 570-321-4135 425 B
pelusoem@lycoming.edu
PELUSO-VERDEND,
Gary .... 918-270-6405 401 C
gary.peluso@ptstulsa.edu
PELY, Laszlo .... 410-617-2421 216 D
lpely@loyola.edu
PELZIER-GLAZE,
Bernnell .... 713-313-7496 487 F
glazedm@tsu.edu
PEMBERTON, Barbara ... 870-245-5541.. 22 C
pembertonb@obu.edu
PEMBERTON, Cynthia ... 701-483-2330 373 H
cynthia.pemberton@dickinsonstate.edu
PEMBERTON,
Cynthia, L .... 816-235-1107 284 A
pembertonc@umkc.edu
PEMBERTON, Loren ...... 509-533-3503 521 F
loren.pemberton@sfcc.spokane.edu
PEMBERTON, Richard ... 573-897-5000 282 I
PEMBERTON, Shelly ...... 218-335-4202 256 I
shelly.pemberton@lltc.edu
PEMBROOK,
Randall, G .... 785-670-1649 192 B
randy.pembrook@washburn.edu
PEMSTEIN, Debra .... 845-758-7405 315 G
pemstein@bard.edu
PENA, Andrew, M .... 575-646-1694 312 A
ampena@nmsu.edu
PENA, Denise .... 714-556-3610.. 75 A
denise.pena@vanguard.edu
PENA, Fred .... 956-364-4337 487 H
fred.pena@tstc.edu
PENA, Jesus .... 610-683-4700 431 B
pena@kutztown.edu
PENA, Maria .... 360-417-6340 525 A
mpena@pencol.edu
PENA, Maria .... 425-388-9979 522 I
mpena@everettcc.edu
PENA, Phil .... 636-584-6701 274 J
philip.pena@eastcentral.edu
PENA, Raquel, A .... 956-794-4988 477 C
rapena@laredo.edu
PENA, Stan .... 575-538-6470 314 E
stan.pena@wnmu.edu
PENA, Stephen, M .... 480-245-7971.. 14 D
stephen.pena@ibcs.edu
PENALOZA, Carlos .... 518-381-1381 342 E
PENCE, Bill .... 540-868-7061 515 H
bpence@lfcc.edu
PENCE, Heather .... 404-297-9522 126 A
penceh@gptc.edu
PENCE, Nadine, S .... 765-361-6434 175 B
pencen@wabash.edu
PENCIU, Cristian .... 561-912-2166 102 N
cpenciu@evergladesuniversity.edu
PENDAKUR,
Sumun (Sumi) .... 909-607-3470.. 46 K
spendakur@hmc.edu
PENDAKUR, Vijay .... 657-278-4688.. 33 E
vpendakur@fullerton.edu
PENDELTON, Alicia .... 313-577-2017 252 G
alicia.pendelton@wayne.edu
PENDERGAST,
Katherine, N .... 617-373-2230 235 D
PENDERGAST, Linda ..... 617-984-1695 235 H
lpendergast@quincycollege.edu
PENDERGRASS, Martha 919-843-5048 371 A
mjpender@email.unc.edu
PENDERGRASS, Toni .... 505-566-3209 312 K
pendergrasst@sanjuancollege.edu
PENDERGRAST, Runan . 859-246-6305 195 J
runan.pendergrast@kctcs.edu
PENDERS, Brooke .... 860-528-4111.. 90 F
bpenders@goodwin.edu
PENDHARKAR, Daya ..... 813-253-7091 106 C
dpendharkar@hccfl.edu
PENDLETON, Chris .... 540-261-8441 512 J
chris.pendleton@svu.edu
PENDLETON, Gail .... 510-981-2804.. 58 J
gpendleton@peralta.edu
PENDLETON, Janis, S ... 803-327-7402 444 F
jpendleton@clintoncollege.edu
PENDLETON, Laura .... 509-452-5100 524 J
PENDLETON, Laurence . 615-963-7923 461 F
laurence.pendleton@tnstate.edu
PENDLETON, Mitch .... 801-524-1948 498 J
mpendleton@ldsbc.edu
PENDLETON, Patrick ..... 928-541-7777.. 16 B
ppendleton@ncu.edu
PENDLETON, Penny ...... 479-788-7121.. 23 H
penny.pendleton@uafs.edu
PENDLETON, Sally .... 502-895-3411 198 E
spendleton@lpts.edu
PENDSE, Ravindra .... 401-863-7250 441 A
ravi_pendse@brown.edu
PENGRA, Matt .... 407-679-0100 105 M
mpengra@fullsail.com
PENISTEN, Douglas .... 918-456-5511 398 M
penisten@nsuok.edu
PENKALA, Robert .... 586-445-7636 246 A
penkalar@macomb.edu
PENKE, Ann, K .... 920-565-1038 536 Q
penkea@lakeland.edu
PENLAND, Joni, M .... 502-410-6200 194 N
jpenland@galencollege.edu
PENLAND, Nathan .... 417-328-1828 282 D
npenland@sbuniv.edu
PENLEY, Julie .... 915-831-7001 473 J
jpenley@epcc.edu
PENN, Brad .... 859-336-5082 199 B
bradpenn@sccky.edu
PENN, David .... 407-447-7300 105 E
dpenn@ftccollege.edu
PENN, Deborah .... 620-947-3121 191 E
deborahp@tabor.edu
PENN, Jamie .... 570-484-2322 431 C
jks109@lhup.edu
PENN, Jamilyn .... 425-739-8255 523 I
jamilyn.penn@lwtech.edu
PENN, Mark, A .... 702-802-2837 296 D
mpenn@roseman.edu
PENN-HARGROVE,
Valencia .... 773-256-3000 152 D
vpennhargrove@meadville.edu
PENN-MARSHALL,
Michelle .... 757-727-5267 508 C
michelle.penn-marshall@hamptonu.edu
PENNA, Anthony .... 617-552-3475 224 B
anthony.penna@bc.edu
PENNACHIO, Michael ... 617-521-2190 236 F
michael.pennachio@simmons.edu
PENNARTZ-BROWNING,
Kathy .... 940-397-4214 478 G
kathy.pennartz@mwsu.edu
PENNER, Julie .... 815-836-5667 150 F
pennerju@lewisu.edu
PENNER, Menachem .... 212-568-7300 338 G
PENNETTI, Dianna .... 212-854-3362 315 J
dpennetti@barnard.edu
PENNEY, Bill .... 352-395-5160 112 H
bill.penney@sfcollege.edu
PENNIECOOK, Tricia ..... 256-726-7007.... 6 C
tpenniecook@oakwood.edu
PENNIMAN, Sarah .... 717-361-1428 418 B
pennimans@etown.edu
PENNINGS, Rhonda, R . 712-324-5061 182 A
rpennings@nwicc.edu
PENNINGTON,
Josianne, E .... 410-704-3255 221 A
jpennington@towson.edu
PENNINGTON, Karen, L 973-655-4311 304 A
penningtonk@mail.montclair.edu
PENNINGTON, Kevin .... 252-399-6467 354 I
knpennington@barton.edu
PENNINGTON,
Kimberly .... 828-328-7473 358 G
kimberly.pennington@lr.edu
PENNINGTON, Laurie ... 928-428-8231.. 13 L
laurie.pennington@eac.edu
PENNINGTON, Michael 910-521-6637 371 D
michael.pennington@uncp.edu
PENNINGTON, Nicole ... 740-533-4610 389 H
penningj@ohio.edu

PERKINS, Myrna, L ...... 620-792-9270 184 I
perkinsm@bartonccc.edu
PERKINS, Patricia .... 304-645-6336 533 B
pperkins@osteo.wvsom.edu
PERKINS, Peter .... 607-753-2518 345 C
peter.perkins@cortland.edu
PERKINS, Priscilla, L .... 413-782-1531 238 A
priscilla.perkins@wne.edu
PERKINS, Russell .... 913-758-6182 191 I
registrar@stmary.edu
PERKINS, Sarah, F .... 650-738-4321.. 64 E
perkinss@smccd.edu
PERKINS, Susan, K ...... 732-906-2505 303 F
sperkins@middlesexcc.edu
PERKINS, Suzetta, M .... 910-672-1143 370 A
sperkins@uncfsu.edu
PERKINS, Will .... 503-352-2120 408 I
wperkins@pacificu.edu
PERKINS BROWN,
Jayne .... 912-478-5218 126 B
jperkins@georgiasouthern.edu
PERKINSON, A.P .... 434-381-6272 513 E
APerkinson@sbc.edu
PERKINSON, Ewa .... 330-867-1996 387 D
PERKINSON, JR.,
James, E .... 757-822-5159 517 C
jperkinson@tcc.edu
PERKINSON, Stephen ... 330-867-1996 387 D
PERKNER, Stanislav ...... 209-478-0800.. 47 F
sperkner@humphreys.edu
PERKO, Janet, A .... 330-471-8340 385 G
jperko@malone.edu
PERKOWSKI, C, L .... 718-259-2525 316 G
PERKOWSKI, Henry ...... 212-678-3016 349 I
hp2125@tc.columbia.edu
PERL, Emily .... 410-337-6122 215 B
eperl@goucher.edu
PERLAS, Char .... 510-748-2318.. 59 A
cperlas@peralta.edu
PERLICK, Nick .... 859-622-1583 194 L
nick.perlick@eku.edu
PERLIN, Jeremy .... 513-487-3215 327 C
jperlin@huc.edu
PERLMAN, Andrew .... 617-573-8157 237 B
aperlman@suffolk.edu
PERLMAN, Harvey .... 402-472-2116 293 H
hperlman1@unl.edu
PERLMAN, Lynn .... 617-277-3915 224 D
perlmanl@bgsp.edu
PERLMUTTER, David ..... 806-742-3385 489 F
david.perlmutter@ttu.edu
PERLOFF, Carey .... 415-439-2422.. 27 F
cep@act-sf.org
PERLOW, Yaakov .... 718-438-2727 354 C
PERLSTROM,
Christine, L .... 847-574-5208 150 A
cperlstrom@lfgsm.edu
PERMAN, Jay, A .... 410-706-7002 219 E
jperman@umaryland.edu
PERME, Connie .... 513-745-3992 396 B
perme@xavier.edu
PERMENTER,
Andrew, H .... 863-667-5078 113 K
ahpermenter@seu.edu
PERNA, Michael .... 201-200-3542 304 C
mperna@njcu.edu
PERNICIARO, Richard ... 609-343-5670 299 G
rpernici@atlantic.edu
PERNICK HUBER,
Maureen .... 716-827-2444 350 H
huberm@trocaire.edu
PERNOT, Laurent .... 312-553-2500 141 M
lpernot@ccc.edu
PEROLIO, Jessica .... 314-977-2154 281 M
jperolio@slu.edu
PERONE, Julie .... 610-436-2301 432 B
jperone@wcupa.edu
PERONI-CALLAHAN,
Kathy .... 617-521-2150 236 F
kathleen.peroni-callahan@simmons.edu
PEROO, Rama .... 620-441-5587 186 E
rama.peroo@cowley.edu
PEROW, Lauren, A .... 814-641-3302 421 L
perowl@juniata.edu
PEROZZI, Brett .... 801-626-6361 500 C
brettperozzi@weber.edu
PERR, Yechiel, I .... 718-327-7600 353 B
yfr1@verizon.net
PERREAULT,
Melanie, L .... 716-878-5550 345 B
perreaml@buffalostate.edu
PERREIRA, Mary .... 808-956-4650 136 B
maryperr@hawaii.edu
PERRELLI, John .... 410-337-6527 215 B
john.perrelli@goucher.edu
PERREN, Ray .... 770-533-7030 128 A
rperren@laniertech.edu
PERRENOD, William, L . 914-337-9300 323 A
william.perrenod@concordia-ny.edu
PERRES, Irving .... 718-232-7800 353 F

PERRET, Geraldine .... 973-618-3536 300 H
gperret@caldwell.edu
PERRI, Christine .... 619-216-6668.. 68 D
cperri@swccd.edu
PERRI, Geraldine, M .... 626-914-8821.. 38 L
gperri@citruscollege.edu
PERRI, Mary Lynn .... 440-646-8329 394 G
mperri@ursuline.edu
PERRI, Michael .... 352-273-6214 115 D
mperri@php.ufl.edu
PERRIEN, Shane .... 402-941-6171 291 I
perrien@midlandu.edu
PERRIER, Rochelle .... 504-398-2744 206 E
rperrier@olhcc.edu
PERRIN, Amy .... 847-214-7217 144 F
aperrin@elgin.edu
PERRIN, David, H .... 801-581-8537 499 K
david.perrin@health.utah.edu
PERRIN, L. Timothy ..... 806-720-7125 478 A
tim.perrin@lcu.edu
PERRIN, Michael .... 512-471-7575 493 M
mwp@athletics.utexas.edu
PERRIN, Nicholas .... 630-752-5227 163 G
nicholas.perrin@wheaton.edu
PERRIN, Ralph .... 530-242-7730.. 66 C
rperrin@shastacollege.edu
PERRINE, Mary, A .... 315-786-2485 329 G
mperrine@sunyjefferson.edu
PERRINE, Paul .... 828-298-3325 373 A
pperrine@warren-wilson.edu
PERRINE, Richard .... 603-897-8206 298 E
rperrine@rivier.edu
PERRITON, Caleb .... 307-755-2114 547 D
cperriton@wyotechstaff.edu
PERRON, Evelyn, R ...... 603-206-8121 297 A
eperron@ccsnh.edu
PERRON, Michael .... 508-373-9409 223 C
michael.perron@becker.edu
PERRONE, Brenda .... 815-226-4010 157 D
bperrone@rockford.edu
PERROTT, Emma .... 716-888-3145 317 H
perrotte@canisius.edu
PERROTTA, Steve .... 603-513-1341 299 C
steve.perrotta@granite.edu
PERRUCI,
Gamaliel (Gama) .... 740-376-4760 386 A
gama.perruci@marietta.edu
PERRY, Andy .... 217-443-8777 143 F
aperry@dacc.edu
PERRY, Candace .... 404-756-4004 120 H
cperry@atlm.edu
PERRY, Carolyn, J .... 573-592-5212 285 J
carolyn.perry@westminster-mo.edu
PERRY, Chris .... 877-701-3800 139 H
PERRY, Christine, M .... 617-573-8470 237 B
cperry@suffolk.edu
PERRY, Cynthia, R .... 757-594-7571 506 I
cperry@cnu.edu
PERRY, Dan .... 512-245-4440 489 C
d_p93@txstate.edu
PERRY, Darlene .... 252-538-4326 363 B
dperry934@halifaxcc.edu
PERRY, David, L .... 850-644-1240 115 A
dlperry@admin.fsu.edu
PERRY, Denah .... 812-888-4277 174 F
dperry@vinu.edu
PERRY, Derrick .... 702-579-3530 294 P
dperry@kaplan.edu
PERRY, Don .... 214-378-1732 472 B
don.perry@dcccd.edu
PERRY, Douglas, E .... 815-939-5240 155 G
dperry@olivet.edu
PERRY, Eddie, L .... 804-524-5598 518 C
eperry@vsu.edu
PERRY, Erma .... 334-687-3543.... 4 A
eperry@wallace.edu
PERRY, Foster .... 256-824-6880.... 9 A
Foster.Perry@uah.edu
PERRY, Frank, E .... 412-397-6233 434 B
perry@rmu.edu
PERRY, Gary, W .... 561-297-3062 114 E
provost@fau.edu
PERRY, George .... 210-458-4450 494 D
george.perry@utsa.edu
PERRY, George .... 304-260-4380 530 M
gperry@blueridgectc.edu
PERRY, Gretchen .... 845-758-7454 315 G
gperry@bard.edu
PERRY, James .... 903-813-2277 468 G
jperry@austincollege.edu
PERRY, Janet .... 970-207-4550.. 83 P
janetp@mckinleycollege.edu
PERRY, Janet .... 970-207-4500.. 87 D
JanetP@uscareerinstitute.edu
PERRY, Janet .... 405-682-1611 399 K
jcperry@occc.edu
PERRY, Jason .... 804-758-6751 516 G
jperry@rappahannock.edu
PERRY, Jason .... 801-581-8514 499 K
jason.perry@utah.edu

PERRY, Jay .... 605-773-3455 453 E
jay.perry@sdbor.edu
PERRY, Johanna, L ...... 914-337-9300 323 A
johanna.perry@concordia-ny.edu
PERRY, John .... 708-534-4518 145 D
jperry@govst.edu
PERRY, John, F .... 864-503-5242 451 A
jperry@uscupstate.edu
PERRY, Jonathan, C ..... 479-575-5276.. 23 G
jperry@uark.edu
PERRY, Judy .... 206-592-3349 523 D
jperry@highline.edu
PERRY, Judy, A .... 432-837-8058 489 B
jperry@sulross.edu
PERRY, Keith .... 404-297-9522 126 A
perryk@gptc.edu
PERRY, Kimberly .... 360-752-8333 520 A
kperry@btc.edu
PERRY, Laura .... 315-268-6760 321 C
lperry@clarkson.edu
PERRY, Lee, T .... 801-422-4122 497 J
lee_perry@byu.edu
PERRY, Mark .... 417-862-9533 275 C
mperry@globaluniversity.edu
PERRY, Mark .... 559-734-9000.. 63 E
president@sjvc.edu
PERRY, Marva .... 781-239-3151 231 G
mperry@massbay.edu
PERRY, Mary Elaine ..... 610-660-1045 434 G
mperry01@sju.edu
PERRY, Maryann, B ...... 508-565-1105 237 A
mperry@stonehill.edu
PERRY, Melissa .... 386-312-4058 111 K
melissaperry@sjrstate.edu
PERRY, Meredith .... 423-425-4431 465 E
meredith-perry@utc.edu
PERRY, Michael .... 559-734-9000.. 63 E
mikep@sjvc.edu
PERRY, Michael .... 321-674-7127 103 R
perrymj@fit.edu
PERRY, Michael, J .... 315-386-7623 347 F
perrymj@canton.edu
PERRY, Missy .... 864-941-8666 448 D
perry.m@ptc.edu
PERRY, Monique .... 803-981-7391 451 K
mperry@yorktech.edu
PERRY, Nancy .... 410-386-8231 214 B
nperry@carrollcc.edu
PERRY, Nauleen, A .... 302-857-1080.. 94 A
nperry@dtcc.edu
PERRY, Paul .... 231-995-1114 248 C
pperry@nmc.edu
PERRY, Rhonda .... 217-206-7796 161 G
rrperry@uillinois.edu
PERRY, Robert .... 617-879-7269 230 B
rperry@massart.edu
PERRY, Roberta .... 610-527-0200 434 D
rperry@rosemont.edu
PERRY, Robin .... 704-637-4384 355 H
raperry@catawba.edu
PERRY, Rodger .... 704-669-4032 361 E
perryr@clevelandcc.edu
PERRY, Roslyn .... 606-783-2571 198 H
ro.perry@moreheadstate.edu
PERRY, Sam, J .... 773-508-8781 151 E
sperry@luc.edu
PERRY, Sarah .... 206-726-5052 521 G
PERRY, Stacey .... 870-245-5220.. 22 C
perrys@obu.edu
PERRY, Stephanie, D .... 276-328-0240 514 B
sdh9y@uvawise.edu
PERRY, Steve .... 864-294-2458 446 F
steve.perry@furman.edu
PERRY, Steven .... 201-684-7363 305 F
sperry@ramapo.edu
PERRY, Steven .... 325-738-3341 488 C
steven.perry@tstc.edu
PERRY, Stuart .... 320-363-5047 264 A
sperry@csbsju.edu
PERRY, Stuart .... 320-363-5047 254 J
sperry@csbsju.edu
PERRY, Sue, A .... 856-691-8600 301 H
sperry@cccnj.edu
PERRY, Thomas, D .... 740-376-4408 386 A
tom.perry@marietta.edu
PERRY, Tom .... 479-524-7122.. 21 F
tperry@jbu.edu
PERRY, Walter .... 215-596-8890 438 E
w.perry@usciences.edu
PERRY-JOHNSON,
Arlethia .... 470-578-6350 127 M
aperryjo@kennesaw.edu
PERRY KEITH, Colleen . 704-463-3030 367 F
colleen.keith@pfeiffer.edu
PERRY-NAUSE, Sharon . 419-448-3504 392 B
perrynauses@tiffin.edu
PERRY-SPEARS, Megan 218-723-6029 255 A
mperryspears@css.edu
PERRYMAN,
Emily Burns .... 716-827-4347 350 H
perrymane@trocaire.edu

PERRYMAN, Nancy, S .. 309-655-4119 158 D
nancy.s.perryman@osfhealthcare.org
PERRYMAN, Patricia ..... 469-941-8300 473 D
PERSAUD, Damindra .... 718-261-5800 316 K
dpersaud@bramsonort.edu
PERSAVICH, Jon .... 626-873-2136.. 55 B
jpersavich@mtsierra.edu
PERSHING, David, W ... 801-581-5701 499 K
david.pershing@utah.edu
PERSICO, Frank, G .... 202-319-5100.. 95 A
persico@cua.edu
PERSICO, Patrice .... 570-208-5972 422 D
patricepersico@kings.edu
PERSICO, Sebastian, T . 212-817-7600 319 B
spersico@gc.cuny.edu
PERSINGER, Angela ...... 812-288-8878 171 F
apersinger@mid-america.edu
PERSINGER, Bill .... 931-221-6309 461 C
persingerb@apsu.edu
PERSKY, Ira .... 718-982-2240 319 A
ira.persky@csi.cuny.edu
PERSON, Andy .... 914-330-1450 332 E
aperson@mercy.edu
PERSON, Gretchen .... 615-322-2457 465 H
religiouslife@vanderbilt.edu
PERSON, Mark .... 601-979-2021 267 H
mark.s.person@jsums.edu
PERSON, Walter .... 202-274-2303.. 97 D
walter.person@potomac.edu
PERSON, William .... 334-229-4276.... 1 D
wperson@alasu.edu
PERSSON, Katherine ..... 281-312-1640 477 I
katherine.persson@lonestar.edu
PERSUTTI, Robert .... 703-416-1441 508 F
rpersutti@ipsciences.edu
PERTL, Brian, G .... 920-832-6614 536 R
brian.g.pertl@lawrence.edu
PERTTULA, Dave .... 262-551-5925 535 E
dperttula@carthage.edu
PERTUZ, Sofia, B .... 516-463-6716 328 A
sofia.b.pertuz@hofstra.edu
PERUMAL, Santhi .... 415-561-6555.. 60 C
PERUSKI, David .... 989-686-9291 242 I
davidperuski@delta.edu
PERUSSE, Charles, E .... 919-962-1000 369 C
ceperusse@northcarolina.edu
PERVIER, Curt .... 432-685-4677 478 F
cpervier@midland.edu
PERVINE, Robert .... 270-809-3744 198 I
rpervine@murraystate.edu
PERYGA, Erica .... 203-596-8527.. 91 D
eperyga@post.edu
PERZEKI, Donna, M ..... 216-916-7506 384 H
dmp@kent.edu
PERZYNA, Ashley, M ... 717-245-1792 417 B
perzynaa@dickinson.edu
PESARCHICK, Robert, A 610-785-6204 434 E
rpesarchick@scs.edu
PESCARMONA, Denee ... 661-362-5042.. 40 H
denee.pescarmona@canyons.edu
PESCHL, Alan .... 262-524-7343 535 D
apeschl@carrollu.edu
PESCI, Christy .... 309-341-5236 140 I
cpecsi@sandburg.edu
PESCINSKI, Robert .... 908-526-1200 305 G
Robert.Pescinski@raritanval.edu
PESHECK, Philip .... 605-642-6297 453 G
philip.pesheck@bhsu.edu
PESKA, Don .... 817-735-2149 493 B
Don.Peska@unthsc.edu
PESKA, Scott .... 630-466-7900 162 K
speska@waubonsee.edu
PESKIN, Josh .... 215-576-0800 433 I
jpeskin@rrc.edu
PESSIER, Julian .... 631-632-6720 344 C
julian.pessier@stonybrook.edu
PESTA, Donna .... 518-255-5624 346 E
Pestadh@cobleskill.edu
PESTANA, John .... 508-565-1315 237 A
jpestana@stonehill.edu
PESTELLO, Fred, P .... 314-977-7777 281 M
president@slu.edu
PETAK, Katty .... 402-399-2411 289 I
vpetak@csm.edu
PETCHER, Douglas .... 312-362-7595 143 G
dpetcher@depaul.edu
PETE, Mary, C .... 907-543-4502.. 10 I
mpete@alaska.edu
PETEET, Allison .... 903-923-2072 473 I
apeteet@etbu.edu
PETER, Beth, C .... 651-641-8795 255 C
peter@csp.edu
PETER, David, M .... 812-888-4166 174 F
dpeter@vinu.edu
PETER, Evon .... 907-474-1865.. 10 I
evon.peter@alaska.edu
PETER, Florence, L .... 692-625-0635 550 A
fpeter@cmi.edu
PETER, Lori .... 660-263-3900 272 M
loripeter@cccb.edu

PETER, Zomar ... 252-638-4597 362 A
peterz@cravencc.edu
PETERKA, Cynthia, J ... 443-518-4809 215 F
cpeterka@howardcc.edu
PETERKIN, Leron ... 843-355-4170 451 H
peterkinl@wiltech.edu
PETERMAN, Christina ... 301-624-2713 214 I
cpeterman@frederick.edu
PETERMAN, Terry ... 903-875-7419 479 I
terry.peterman@navarrocollege.edu
PETERS, Angela, W ... 803-535-5404 444 D
angela.peters@claflin.edu
PETERS, Anna ... 212-659-7281 330 A
apeters@tkc.edu
PETERS, Bob ... 360-736-9391 520 F
bpeters@centralia.edu
PETERS, Brett ... 414-229-4126 540 A
petersba@uwm.edu
PETERS, Brian, S ... 847-491-8420 155 D
b-peters2@northwestern.edu
PETERS, C. Ellen ... 253-879-3104 527 F
epeters@pugetsound.edu
PETERS, Chad ... 864-644-5325 449 B
cpeters@swu.edu
PETERS, Cherise ... 205-929-1851 ... 5 I
cpeters@miles.edu
PETERS, Craig ... 605-367-5462 454 D
craig.peters@southeasttech.edu
PETERS, Dan ... 402-461-7700 290 G
dpeters@hastings.edu
PETERS, David ... 304-473-8540 534 G
peters_d@wvwc.edu
PETERS, Denise ... 785-362-6000 187 I
dpeters@highlandcc.edu
PETERS, Doug, D ... 218-477-2306 260 B
petersd@mnstate.edu
PETERS, Earic ... 818-710-2911 .. 51 H
peterseb@piercecollege.edu
PETERS, Eva ... 909-621-8471 .. 59 F
eva_peters@pitzer.edu
PETERS, Fred, M ... 903-510-2627 491 A
fpet@tjc.edu
PETERS, Hermina, P ... 202-274-6256 .. 97 B
hpeters@udc.edu
PETERS, J. Lee ... 860-768-4165 .. 92 F
lpeters@hartford.edu
PETERS, James ... 616-538-2330 243 C
jpeters@gbcol.edu
PETERS, Jerry ... 760-252-2411 .. 29 C
jpeters@barstow.edu
PETERS, Joseph ... 478-445-4546 125 A
joseph.peters@gcsu.edu
PETERS, Joseph, R ... 502-410-6200 194 N
jpeters@galencollege.edu
PETERS, Joyce ... 662-685-4771 266 G
jpeters@bmc.edu
PETERS, Kirk ... 860-733-1482 .. 90 C
kpeters@txcc.commnet.edu
PETERS, Lee ... 617-262-5000 223 G
lee.peters@the-bac.edu
PETERS, Leonard ... 203-432-3262 .. 93 C
leonard.peters@yale.edu
PETERS, Libby ... 606-487-3087 196 B
libby.peters@kctcs.edu
PETERS, Margaret ... 505-428-1372 313 A
margaret.peters@sfcc.edu
PETERS, Mary Ann ... 404-727-3130 124 D
mary.ann.peters@emory.edu
PETERS, Matthew ... 570-961-7830 422 G
petersm@lackawanna.edu
PETERS, Melissa ... 386-822-7022 117 A
mpeters@stetson.edu
PETERS, Michael, P ... 505-984-6098 312 J
president@sjc.edu
PETERS, Michele ... 716-827-4333 350 H
petersm@trocaire.edu
PETERS, Monica ... 936-633-5250 467 I
mpeters@angelina.edu
PETERS, Nichole ... 620-365-5116 184 C
PETERS, Pamela, J ... 607-746-4635 347 G
peterspj@delhi.edu
PETERS, Rachael ... 318-869-5360 202 D
rpeters@centenary.edu
PETERS, Randall ... 770-228-7365 132 B
rpeters@sctech.edu
PETERS, Raul ... 706-821-8203 129 H
rpeters@paine.edu
PETERS, Rich ... 509-682-6465 528 C
rpeters@wvc.edu
PETERS, Sarah ... 707-668-5663 .. 42 K
PETERS, Scott ... 573-897-5000 282 I
PETERS, Shane ... 765-983-1131 165 H
petersh@earlham.edu
PETERS, Sheila ... 615-329-8575 456 G
speters@fisk.edu
PETERS, Steph ... 712-274-5261 181 C
peters@morningside.edu
PETERS, Steven ... 205-665-6663 .... 9 C
speters3@montevallo.edu
PETERS, Suzanne ... 413-545-0356 228 F
sepeters@finaid.umass.edu
PETERS, Tara ... 732-263-5690 303 G
tpeters@monmouth.edu
PETERS, Teresa, A ... 570-348-6230 425 D
peters@marywood.edu
PETERS, Thomas, A ... 417-836-4525 279 A
tpeters@missouristate.edu
PETERS, Timothy, C ... 949-214-3363 .. 42 B
tim.peters@cui.edu
PETERS, Tom, D ... 308-398-7365 289 D
tpeters@cccneb.edu
PETERS, Vincent ... 651-638-6124 254 A
v-peters@bethel.edu
PETERS-NGUYEN,
Diane ... 808-735-4772 135 A
dpeters@chaminade.edu
PETERSDORFF, Joe ... 478-988-6800 122 F
jpetersdorff@centralgatech.edu
PETERSEN, Aaron ... 517-607-2330 243 J
apetersen@hillsdale.edu
PETERSEN, Calvin ... 402-280-2796 290 B
creighton@bkstr.com
PETERSEN, Carol ... 309-341-5416 140 I
cpetersen@sandburg.edu
PETERSEN, Dana ... 207-216-4454 211 F
dpetersen@yccc.edu
PETERSEN, Donna ... 813-974-6603 116 B
dpeters@hsc.usf.edu
PETERSEN, Dorene ... 503-244-0726 404 G
dorenepetersen@achs.edu
PETERSEN, Joshua ... 540-636-2900 506 H
jpetersen@christendom.edu
PETERSEN, Karl ... 314-768-7800 278 H
kpetersen@missouricollege.com
PETERSEN, Kenneth, J .. 208-426-1135 137 E
KenPetersen@boisestate.edu
PETERSEN, Kevin ... 410-704-2487 221 A
kpetersen@towson.edu
PETERSEN, Kristin ... 402-471-2505 292 A
kpetersen@nscs.edu
PETERSEN, Linda ... 785-243-1435 186 A
lpetersen@cloud.edu
PETERSEN, Mark, A ... 336-758-6053 372 G
map@wfu.edu
PETERSEN, Marty ... 425-602-3027 519 J
mpetersen@bastyr.edu
PETERSEN, Mary, S ... 206-296-2043 526 F
marypete@seattleu.edu
PETERSEN, Melissa ... 617-217-9036 223 A
mpetersen@baystate.edu
PETERSEN, Molly ... 619-849-2463 .. 59 K
mollypetersen@pointloma.edu
PETERSEN, Page ... 507-433-0650 261 C
ppeterse@riverland.edu
PETERSEN, Steve ... 847-925-6255 145 F
speterse@harpercollege.edu
PETERSEN, Ted ... 815-802-8602 149 B
tpetersen@kcc.edu
PETERSEN, Tina ... 916-577-2200 .. 77 F
tpetersen@jessup.edu
PETERSON, Al, L ... 661-824-2977 .. 55 I
apeterson@ntps.edu
PETERSON, Andrew ... 215-596-8877 438 E
a.peterson@usciences.edu
PETERSON, Andrew, J .. 704-366-4853 270 B
apeterson@rts.edu
PETERSON, Andrew, T .. 864-833-8486 448 E
atpeterso@presby.edu
PETERSON, Andy ... 503-517-1800 411 C
apeterson@westernseminary.edu
PETERSON, Ben ... 617-262-5000 223 G
Benjamin.Peterson@the-bac.edu
PETERSON, Bill ... 413-585-3000 236 G
bpeterso@smith.edu
PETERSON, Candace ... 503-280-8500 405 E
cpeterson@cu-portland.edu
PETERSON, Carolyn ... 919-546-3750 368 G
cpeterson@shawu.edu
PETERSON, JR.,
Charles ... 804-523-5821 515 F
cpeterson@reynolds.edu
PETERSON, Charles, D . 701-231-7456 374 C
charles.peterson@ndsu.edu
PETERSON, Charles, I ... 773-244-5570 154 G
cpeterson@northpark.edu
PETERSON, Chris ... 405-491-6333 402 E
cpeterso@snu.edu
PETERSON, Christine ... 443-423-1467 216 F
cpetersn@mica.edu
PETERSON, Cindy ... 913-971-3533 189 F
cpeterso@mnu.edu
PETERSON, Cynthia ... 225-578-4202 204M
cbpeterson@lsu.edu
PETERSON, Cynthia ... 903-923-2257 473 I
cpeterson@etbu.edu
PETERSON, Cynthia, L .. 706-778-8500 130 B
cpeterson@piedmont.edu
PETERSON, Daniel ... 603-456-2656 298 D
dpeterson@northeastcatholic.edu
PETERSON, Daniel, C ... 217-244-1206 162 A
dcpeters@illinois.edu
PETERSON, David ... 260-481-6130 168 D
petersod@ipfw.edu
PETERSON, David, F ... 608-743-4525 542 L
dpeterson38@blackhawk.edu
PETERSON, Debra ... 218-755-4121 258 B
dpeterson@bemidjistate.edu
PETERSON, Derek ... 605-688-4163 454 C
derek.peterson@sdstate.edu
PETERSON, Dick ... 651-638-6805 254 A
petric@bethel.edu
PETERSON, Dolores ... 610-372-4721 433 H
dpeterson@racc.edu
PETERSON, Donald ... 903-334-6650 486 C
donald.peterson@tamut.edu
PETERSON, Donn ... 707-826-5555 .. 35 D
donn.peterson@humboldt.edu
PETERSON, Doug ... 312-322-1733 160 E
dpeterson@spertus.edu
PETERSON, Ellen ... 808-984-3582 136 H
epeterso@hawaii.edu
PETERSON, Ericka, K ... 218-299-3250 255 B
ekpeters@cord.edu
PETERSON, G. P. (Bud) 404-894-5051 125 D
president@gatech.edu
PETERSON, Gail ... 414-326-2303 535 H
gpeterso@ccon.edu
PETERSON, Graham ... 870-862-8131 .. 23 B
gpeterson@southark.edu
PETERSON, Greg ... 562-938-4140 .. 51 A
gpeterson@lbcc.edu
PETERSON, Heather ... 609-343-5008 299 G
hpeterso@atlantic.edu
PETERSON,
Jacqueline, D ... 508-793-2414 225 C
jpeterso@holycross.edu
PETERSON, James ... 510-540-7747 .. 50 I
jamespeterson@lincolnuca.edu
PETERSON, Jill ... 916-278-6940 .. 34 E
jill.peteson@csus.edu
PETERSON, Jocelyn ... 404-225-4683 120 I
jpeterson@atlantatech.edu
PETERSON, John, A ... 671-735-6912 549 G
jpeterson@uguam.uog.edu
PETERSON, Joyce, C ... 218-722-4000 255 F
joycep@dbumn.edu
PETERSON, Kate, M ... 541-737-0759 408 F
kate.peterson@oregonstate.edu
PETERSON, Kathleen ... 973-300-2235 308 F
kpeterson@sussex.edu
PETERSON, Keith ... 479-936-5145 .. 22 B
kpeterson2@nwacc.edu
PETERSON, Kellie ... 406-994-4570 287 G
kellie.peterson@montana.edu
PETERSON, Kent, A ... 414-277-7176 537 G
peterson@msoe.edu
PETERSON, Kevin ... 435-797-1223 500 A
kevin.peterson@usu.edu
PETERSON, Klay ... 864-503-5254 451 A
kpeterson@uscupstate.edu
PETERSON, Kristi ... 406-265-3536 288 A
kristi.peterson1@msun.edu
PETERSON, Larry ... 701-231-8824 374 C
larry.r.peterson@ndsu.edu
PETERSON, Laura ... 940-397-4919 478 G
laura.peterson@mwsu.edu
PETERSON, Linda, M ... 563-556-5110 181 F
petersol@nicc.edu
PETERSON, Lori ... 406-447-5432 286 D
lpeterson@carroll.edu
PETERSON, Lori, W ... 512-448-8519 481 B
lorip@stedwards.edu
PETERSON, Maggie ... 406-496-4316 288 C
mpeterson@mtech.edu
PETERSON, Marc ... 214-768-3417 482 J
mpeterso@smu.edu
PETERSON, Margrette ... 510-869-6512 .. 61 J
mpeterson@samuelmerritt.edu
PETERSON, Marie ... 206-296-6241 526 F
mpeters@seattleu.edu
PETERSON, Marika ... 434-949-1064 516 H
marika.peterson@southside.edu
PETERSON, Mark ... 651-450-3373 259 A
mpeters@inverhills.edu
PETERSON, Mark ... 715-682-1332 538 D
mpeterson@northland.edu
PETERSON, Matthew ... 303-546-3549 .. 84 B
mpeterson@naropa.edu
PETERSON, Megan ... 717-728-2398 415 B
meganpeterson@centralpenn.edu
PETERSON, Michael, W 512-448-8788 481 B
michaelp@stedwards.edu
PETERSON, Michele ... 970-247-7435 .. 82 I
peterson_m@fortlewis.edu
PETERSON, Michele ... 505-566-3363 312 K
petersonm@sanjuancollege.edu
PETERSON, Nedra ... 818-767-0888 .. 77 G
nedra.peterson@woodbury.edu
PETERSON, Nell ... 813-974-6884 116 B
ncpeterson@usf.edu
PETERSON, Nels ... 404-962-3263 133 G
nels.peterson@usg.edu
PETERSON, Nichole ... 860-768-5365 .. 92 F
npetersen@hartford.edu
PETERSON, Nicole ... 931-221-7979 461 C
petersonn@apsu.edu
PETERSON, Pamela ... 561-912-2166 102 N
ppeterson@evergladesuniversity.edu
PETERSON, Pamela ... 831-459-5380 .. 72 E
pgpeters@ucsc.edu
PETERSON,
Penelope, L ... 847-467-1190 155 D
p-peterson@northwestern.edu
PETERSON, Phyllis, M .. 815-740-3848 162 F
ppeterson@stfrancis.edu
PETERSON, Polly, J ... 701-252-3467 375 J
ppeterso@uj.edu
PETERSON, Randall ... 386-312-4022 111 K
randypeterson@sjrstate.edu
PETERSON, Randy ... 270-852-3329 198 A
rpeterson@kwc.edu
PETERSON, Rebecca ... 802-865-6425 501 F
peterson@champlain.edu
PETERSON, Robert ... 435-722-6900 499 G
bobp@ubatc.edu
PETERSON, Robert ... 216-987-2836 381 A
robert.peterson@tri-c.edu
PETERSON, Roy ... 262-243-5700 535 I
roy.peterson@cuw.edu
PETERSON, Samantha ... 918-335-6223 400 I
speterson@okwu.edu
PETERSON, Samuel ... 305-809-3179 104 A
samuel.peterson@fkcc.edu
PETERSON, Sandy ... 608-785-9207 544 E
petersons@westerntc.edu
PETERSON, Scott ... 740-392-6868 387 B
scott.peterson@mvnu.edu
PETERSON, Scott ... 864-225-7653 446 D
scottpeterson@forrestcollege.edu
PETERSON, Stella ... 770-426-2930 128 C
peterson@life.edu
PETERSON, Susan, K ... 785-532-6221 188 H
skp@ksu.edu
PETERSON, Terry ... 312-942-7020 158 A
terry_peterson@rush.edu
PETERSON, Thomas ... 732-906-2512 303 F
TPeterson@middlesexcc.edu
PETERSON, Tom ... 209-228-4439 .. 71 E
twpeterson@ucmerced.edu
PETERSON, Travis ... 435-797-2836 500 A
travis.peterson@usu.edu
PETERSON, Val, L ... 801-863-8424 500 B
petersva@uvu.edu
PETERSON, Vance ... 775-831-1314 296 F
vpeterson@sierranevada.edu
PETERSON, Wendy ... 509-335-5586 528 B
wendyp@wsu.edu
PETERSON, Yvonne ... 503-228-6528 404 H
ypeterson@aii.edu
PETERSON-SENIUK,
Peggy ... 419-473-2700 381 F
pseniuk@daviscollege.edu
PETERSON-VEATCH,
Ross ... 574-535-7503 166 C
rosspv@goshen.edu
PETERSSON, Arlette ... 561-912-1211 102 N
apetersson@evergladesuniversity.edu
PETHE-COOK, Marlyn ... 813-253-6231 118 H
mpethe@ut.edu
PETHICK, Michael ... 231-591-3900 242 L
MichaelPethick@ferris.edu
PETILLO, John, J ... 203-371-7900 .. 91 G
petilloj@sacredheart.edu
PETIPRIN, Gary ... 502-272-8480 193 E
gpetiprin@bellarmine.edu
PETIT-FRERE, Yaruby ... 908-737-0350 303 C
ypetitfr@kean.edu
PETITFILS, Brad ... 504-865-3080 206 A
bpetit@loyno.edu
PETITT, Becky, R ... 858-822-4783 .. 72 B
bpetitt@ucsd.edu
PETITT, Bill ... 972-883-6166 494 A
bpetitt@utdallas.edu
PETITT, Charles, W ... 336-725-8344 368 A
petittc@piedmontu.edu
PETITTI, Mario ... 440-525-7328 385 C
mpetitti@lakelandcc.edu
PETKASH, John ... 607-778-5011 344 F
petkashjc@sunybroome.edu
PETKO, Karen ... 859-846-5390 198 G
kpetko@midway.edu
PETLEY, Kathleen ... 518-629-4574 328 D
k.petley@hvcc.edu
PETOSKEY, Indira ... 860-465-5066 .. 88 E
petoskeyi@easternct.edu
PETR, Carrie ... 402-826-8271 290 C
carrie.petr@doane.edu
PETRAS, Donna ... 586-263-6266 246 A
petrasd@macomb.edu
PETREE, Daniel ... 585-395-2623 345 A
dpetree@brockport.edu
PETREN, Kenneth ... 513-556-5858 393 B
ken.petren@uc.edu

PETRESCU, Claudia, A .. 248-370-2100 248 K
PETRI, Elizabeth .... 413-662-5219 230 C
e.petri@mcla.edu
PETRI, OP, Thomas ...... 202-495-3832.. 96 E
dean@dhs.edu
PETRICCA, Joe .... 323-856-7721.. 27 H
jpetricca@afi.com
PETRICHENKO,
Kathleen, J .... 410-822-5400 214 D
kpetrichenko@chesapeake.edu
PETRICK, Joseph, E ...... 802-287-8377 501 I
petrickj@greenmtn.edu
PETRIDIS, Heather .... 626-815-4570.. 29 B
hpetridis@apu.edu
PETRIE, Mark .... 315-279-5254 329 K
mpetrie@keuka.edu
PETRIE, Susan .... 518-608-8156 325 B
spetrie@excelsior.edu
PETRIKAT, Douglas .... 714-547-9625.. 30 F
dpetrikat@calcoast.edu
PETRILLO, Emilia, K ..... 410-328-8404 219 E
epetr001@umaryland.edu
PETRILLOSE, Michael ... 401-598-4621 441 D
mpetrillose@jwu.edu
PETRITES, Cindy .... 414-229-4519 540 A
petrites@uwm.edu
PETRITIS, Paul .... 603-427-7630 296 K
ppetritis@ccsnh.edu
PETRIZZO, Louis, S ...... 631-451-4235 348 E
petrizl@sunysuffolk.edu
PETRO, Patrice, S .... 414-229-4523 540 A
ppetro@uwm.edu
PETROFF, Les .... 317-738-8108 166 B
lpetroff@franklincollege.edu
PETROKA, Louise, A ..... 203-285-2393.. 89 B
lpetroka@gwcc.commnet.edu
PETRONE, Eileen .... 412-536-1115 422 E
eileen.petrone@laroche.edu
PETROSIAN, Anahid ...... 956-872-8339 482 G
anahid@southtexascollege.edu
PETROSIAN, Anahid ...... 956-872-6790 482 G
anahid@southtexascollege.edu
PETROSINO, Chris .... 304-243-2165 534 H
cpetrosino@wju.edu
PETROSINO, Linda .... 607-274-3265 328 H
lpetrosino@ithaca.edu
PETROSKY, Joseph .... 586-498-4181 246 A
petroskyj@macomb.edu
PETROV, John .... 301-985-7980 220 A
john.petrov@umuc.edu
PETROVAY, George .... 740-753-6072 383 G
petrovayg@hocking.edu
PETROVICH, Tamberly .. 831-582-4137.. 34 C
tpetrovich@csumb.edu
PETRUCCI, Michele .... 724-357-2295 431 A
michelep@iup.edu
PETRUCELLI, Amanda ... 574-936-8898 164 A
amanda.petrucelli@ancilla.edu
PETRUS, Robin .... 607-778-5201 344 F
petrusre@sunybroome.edu
PETRUSCH,
Suzanne, M .... 210-436-3995 481 C
spetrusch@stmarytx.edu
PETRUSO, Karl .... 817-272-7215 493 L
petruso@uta.edu
PETRUZZELLI,
Barbara, W .... 845-569-3601 333 I
barbara.petruzzelli@msmc.edu
PETRY, Ric .... 614-222-3227 380 F
rpetry@ccad.edu
PETRYSHAK, Bruce .... 615-898-5570 461 E
bruce.petryshak@mtsu.edu
PETRYSHYN, Laryssa .... 716-829-8119 324 E
petryshl@dyc.edu
PETSCHE, Carolyn .... 815-599-3577 146 B
carolyn.petsche@highland.edu
PETSCHE, Daniel .... 660-944-2875 273 E
daniel@conception.edu
PETSCHENKO, Lisa .... 630-953-3694 141 E
lpetschenko@chamberlain.edu
PETTA, Tim .... 360-992-2408 521 A
tpetta@clark.edu
PETTAZZONI, Jodi, E .... 336-334-5531 371 C
jepettaz@uncg.edu
PETTEGREW, Larry .... 919-573-5350 368 H
PETTENGER, Wade .... 417-862-9533 275 C
wpettenger@globaluniversity.edu
PETTERELLI, Mark, J ..... 315-445-4444 330 B
pettermj@lemoyne.edu
PETTERSON, Jennifer .... 573-592-4280 286 A
jennie.petterson@williamwoods.edu
PETTEWAY, Venetia .... 810-762-7899 245 A
vpettewa@kettering.edu
PETTIBONE, John, C .... 770-720-5939 130 E
jcp@reinhardt.edu
PETTIGREW, Jason .... 605-229-8350 453 A
jason.pettigrew@presentation.edu
PETTINGER, Connie ...... 708-209-3045 143 D
constance.pettinger@cuchicago.edu
PETTINGILL, Sara, Y ..... 502-272-8401 193 E
spettingill@bellarmine.edu
PETTINICO, JR.,
Nicholas .... 860-832-1766.. 88 D
pettinico@ccsu.edu
PETTIS, Curtis .... 937-376-6207 379 D
cpettis@centralstate.edu
PETTIS, Deloris .... 617-373-2226 235 D
PETTIS, Stephanie .... 850-729-5362 109 D
pettiss@nwfsc.edu
PETTIS-WALDEN,
Karen, M .... 804-523-5029 515 F
kpettis-walden@reynolds.edu
PETTIT, Cyndi .... 214-333-5235 471 L
cyndi@dbu.edu
PETTIT, Emily .... 706-778-8500 130 B
epettit@piedmont.edu
PETTIT, Frederick .... 570-208-5881 422 D
frederickpettit@kings.edu
PETTIT, Jeanne .... 859-572-7544 199 A
pettitje@nku.edu
PETTIT, Joel .... 781-899-5500 235 G
jpettit@psjs.edu
PETTIT, Kathy .... 303-963-3327.. 79 L
kpettit@ccu.edu
PETTIT, Linda .... 517-264-7661 250 B
lpettit@sienaheights.edu
PETTIT, Martin, A .... 607-746-4702 347 G
pettitma@delhi.edu
PETTIT, Paul, E .... 214-887-5102 473 E
ppettit@dts.edu
PETTIT, Stephen, D .... 864-242-5100 443 G
PETTITT, Maureen .... 360-416-7919 527 A
maureen.pettitt@skagit.edu
PETTY, Bradley .... 325-942-2191 489 E
bradley.petty@angelo.edu
PETTY, Daniel, W .... 813-988-5131 103 L
vpres@floridacollege.edu
PETTY, JoBeth .... 601-968-8901 266 F
JBpetty@belhaven.edu
PETTY, Jonathan .... 806-291-3588 496 K
pettyj@wbu.edu
PETTY, Leslie .... 734-462-4400 250 A
lpetty@schoolcraft.edu
PETTY, Leslie .... 708-802-6213 158 F
petty@sxu.edu
PETTY, Marcia, L .... 504-865-3030 206 A
mlpetty@loyno.edu
PETTY, Mark .... 605-677-5434 453 F
mark.petty@usd.edu
PETTY, Mikel, D .... 256-824-4368.... 9 A
mikel.petty@uah.edu
PETTY, Nina .... 817-515-5433 484 B
nina.petty@tccd.edu
PETTY, Philip .... 802-728-1533 504 C
ppetty@vtc.edu
PETTY, Rachel .... 202-274-5072.. 97 B
rpetty@udc.edu
PETTY, Tanjula .... 334-420-4479.... 7 I
tpetty@trenholmstate.edu
PETTY, Yolanda .... 478-471-5364 128 H
yolanda.petty@mga.edu
PETTYJOHN, Susan, H . 828-262-2090 369 D
pettyjohnsh@appstate.edu
PETULA, Eileen, E .... 610-328-8399 436 A
epetula1@swarthmore.edu
PETZ, Dan .... 620-672-5641 190 H
danp@prattcc.edu
PETZ, Thomas .... 248-689-8282 251 I
tpetz@walshcollege.edu
PETZKE, Greg .... 704-378-1190 358 B
gpetzke@jcsu.edu
PETZNICK, Michelle, L . 641-422-4205 181 E
petznmic@niacc.edu
PEUGH-WADE,
Martha, A .... 415-422-2444.. 74 C
peugh@usfca.edu
PEWE, Rich .... 517-607-2518 243 J
rpewe@hillsdale.edu
PEYSER, Roma .... 503-297-5544 408 A
rpeyser@ocac.edu
PEYTON, Elizabeth .... 949-794-9090.. 68 F
epeyton@stanbridge.edu
PEYTON, Janice .... 936-270-7392 477 I
janice.peyton@lonestar.edu
PEYTON, Marcia .... 706-754-7789 129 B
mpeyton@northgatech.edu
PEZOLD, Frank .... 361-825-2349 485 F
frank.pezold@tamucc.edu
PEZZAROSSI, Alba .... 773-481-8059 142 D
apezzarossi@ccc.edu
PEZZELLE, Patrick .... 406-293-2721 286 G
ppezzell@fvcc.edu
PEZZI, Eileen .... 315-464-7853 344 E
pezzie@upstate.edu
PEZZOLI, Jean .... 808-984-3234 136 H
pezzoli@hawaii.edu
PEZZUTO, John .... 808-933-2909 135 I
pezzuto@hawaii.edu
PEÑA, Damien .... 805-437-3218.. 32 H
damien.pena@csuci.edu
PEÑA, Milagros .... 951-827-2762.. 72 A
milagros.pena@ucr.edu
PEÑALVER, Eduardo, M 607-255-3527 323 C
eduardo.penalver@cornell.edu
PFANNESTIEL, Todd ..... 814-393-2225 430 E
tpfannestiel@clarion.edu
PFEFER, Mark, T .... 913-234-0796 185 N
mark.pfefer@cleveland.edu
PFEFFER, Carole .... 502-272-8184 193 E
cpfeffer@bellarmine.edu
PFEFFER, Lawrence, M . 901-448-7125 465 G
lpfeffer@uthsc.edu
PFEIFER, Alan, A .... 815-835-6218 158 I
alan.pfeifer@svcc.edu
PFEIFER, Gene, R .... 507-344-7315 253 M
gpfeifer@blc.edu
PFEIFER, Glenn .... 678-891-2528 125 G
glenn.pfeifer@gpc.edu
PFEIFER, Glenn, A .... 678-407-5000 125 B
gpfeifer@ggc.edu
PFEIFER, Jane .... 419-473-2700 381 F
jpfeifer@daviscollege.edu
PFEIFER, Joseph .... 503-251-5775 410 I
jpfeifer@uws.edu
PFEIFER, Justin .... 316-677-1020 192 C
jpfeifer@watc.edu
PFEIFER, Laura .... 701-228-5432 374 F
laura.pfeifer@dakotacollege.edu
PFEIFER, Tad .... 308-535-3684 291 H
pfeifert@mpcc.edu
PFEIFFER, Francine .... 202-220-1336 306 F
francine@rutgers.edu
PFEIFFER, Glenn .... 714-997-6814.. 38 B
PFEIFFER, Kelley .... 636-922-8544 281 C
kpfeiffer@stchas.edu
PFEIFFER, Pattie .... 919-735-5151 367 A
ppfeiffer@waynecc.edu
PFLANZ, Mary .... 913-621-8764 186 G
mpflanz@donnelly.edu
PFLEIGER, Kelly .... 215-368-5000 412 K
kpfleiger@biblical.edu
PFLUG, Anna .... 425-889-5212 524 G
anna.pflug@northwestu.edu
PFURSICH, Fred .... 562-907-4236.. 77 E
fpfursich@whittier.edu
PFUTZENREUTER,
Richard, H .... 612-625-4517 265 C
pfutz001@umn.edu
PHAIAH, Peter .... 218-281-8505 264 H
phaiah@umn.edu
PHAKITTHONG,
Rachelle .... 920-693-1282 543 B
rachelle.phakitthoong@gotoltc.edu
PHAM, Hue .... 714-432-5764.. 40 D
hpham@occ.cccd.edu
PHAM, Michael .... 206-934-4193 526 A
michael.pham@seattlecolleges.edu
PHAM, Michael .... 206-878-3701 523 D
mpham@highline.edu
PHAM, Tom, C .... 617-984-1699 235 H
tpham@quincycollege.edu
PHAM, Trinh .... 323-343-5969.. 34 A
tpham4@calstatela.edu
PHAN, Nga .... 619-477-6310.. 70 G
nphan@usuniversity.edu
PHAN, Nga .... 619-684-8815.. 56 B
nphan@newschoolarch.edu
PHANNENSTIEL, Matt .... 785-227-3380 185 A
pfannenstielmm@bethanylb.edu
PHARIS, Lily .... 318-357-5960 208 D
pharrisl@nsula.edu
PHARO, SCN, Diane ...... 812-357-6598 173 A
dpharo@saintmeinrad.edu
PHARR, Dianne .... 254-442-5151 470 I
dianne.pharr@cisco.edu
PHARR, Julie .... 336-386-3452 366 E
pharrj@surry.edu
PHARR, Kathy, R .... 706-542-0054 132 H
pharr@uga.edu
PHARR, Zach .... 479-619-2664.. 22 B
zpharr@nwacc.edu
PHARRIS, Heather .... 863-680-4754 104 F
hpharis@flsouthern.edu
PHARRIS, William, A ..... 863-680-4192 104 F
wpharris@flsouthern.edu
PHEASANT, Joel, C .... 814-641-5334 421 L
pheasaj@juniata.edu
PHELAN, Carol .... 617-585-1139 234 H
carol.phelan@necmusic.edu
PHELAN, Daniel, J .... 517-787-0800 244 H
phelandanielj@jccmi.edu
PHELAN JOHNSON,
Marcia .... 860-297-2041.. 92 A
marcia.johnson@trincoll.edu
PHELON, Elmer .... 212-237-8541 319 F
ephelon@jjay.cuny.edu
PHELPS, Bill .... 870-245-5567.. 22 C
phelpswr@obu.edu
PHELPS, Celeste .... 714-484-7107.. 56 E
cphelps@cypresscollege.edu
PHELPS, Craig .... 660-626-2391 271 G
cphelps@atsu.edu
PHELPS, Debbie .... 620-331-4100 188 B
dphelps@indycc.edu
PHELPS, Dennis, L .... 504-282-4455 206 C
dphelps@nobts.edu
PHELPS, Esther .... 330-337-6403 376 B
depemp@raex.com
PHELPS, Gary, L .... 330-471-8127 385 G
gphelps@malone.edu
PHELPS, Greg .... 636-627-2938 276 L
gphelps@lindenwood.edu
PHELPS, Hilary .... 860-343-5856.. 89 E
hphelps@mxcc.commnet.edu
PHELPS, Jean .... 718-262-2285 321 B
phelps@york.cuny.edu
PHELPS, Joel .... 518-828-4181 322 E
joel.phelps@sunycgcc.edu
PHELPS, Julie .... 410-951-3000 220 C
PHELPS, Kathy .... 239-280-2500.. 98 O
kathy.phelps@avemaria.edu
PHELPS, Lena .... 863-784-7303 113 C
lena.phelps@southflorida.edu
PHELPS, Martha .... 270-824-8591 196 F
martha.phelps@kctcs.edu
PHELPS, Sherri .... 870-245-5410.. 22 C
phelpss@obu.edu
PHENICIE,
Christopher, N .... 864-488-4549 447 F
cphenicie@limestone.edu
PHENIX, Amy .... 612-626-1616 265 C
pheni001@umn.edu
PHERNETTON, Michelle 218-733-5976 259 C
michelle.phernetton@lsc.edu
PHIFER-MCGHEE,
Kimberly, C .... 919-530-7593 370 C
kpmcghee@nccu.edu
PHILBECK, Daniel, L .... 864-587-4223 449 D
philbed@smcsc.edu
PHILBERT, Martin, A .... 734-763-5454 251 C
philbert@umich.edu
PHILBIN, Catherine ...... 617-322-3505 227 J
catherine_philbin@laboure.edu
PHILEMON,
Suzanne, B .... 704-233-8303 373 C
ksbostic@wingate.edu
PHILIE, Lauren .... 802-635-1657 504 A
lauren.philie@jsc.edu
PHILION, Thomas .... 312-853-4780 157 E
tphilion@roosevelt.edu
PHILIPKOSKY,
Thomas, G .... 843-953-5092 444 C
tom.philipkosky@citadel.edu
PHILIPP, Diane .... 517-607-2333 243 J
dphilipp@hillsdale.edu
PHILIPP, Shirin .... 617-349-9600 228 B
philipp@lesley.edu
PHILIPPON, Roger .... 207-755-5357 210 L
rphilippon@cmcc.edu
PHILIPS, JR., Billy, U ... 806-743-1388 490 A
billy.philips@ttuhsc.edu
PHILLEY, Tim .... 918-495-6970 401 B
tphilley@oru.edu
PHILLIP, Thomas, G ..... 262-243-5700 535 I
thomas.phillip@cuw.edu
PHILLIPS, Alan .... 815-753-3400 154 I
aphillips9@niu.edu
PHILLIPS, Allison .... 336-838-6491 367 C
allison.phillips@wilkescc.edu
PHILLIPS, Amanda .... 724-653-2195 417 D
aphillips@dec.edu
PHILLIPS, Andrew, T .... 410-293-1583 549 B
aphillip@usna.edu
PHILLIPS, Angela .... 614-234-5717 386 N
aphillips-lowe@mccn.edu
PHILLIPS, Anita .... 501-370-8525.. 22 E
aphillips@philander.edu
PHILLIPS, Antoinette ..... 985-549-2258 208 E
Antoinette.Phillips@selu.edu
PHILLIPS, Benet .... 603-641-7402 298 F
bphillips@anselm.edu
PHILLIPS, Bob .... 415-380-1678.. 45 J
bobphillips@ggbts.edu
PHILLIPS, Brad, C .... 607-733-7177 324 H
bphillips@ebi-college.com
PHILLIPS, Brian .... 562-903-4897.. 29 F
brian.phillips@biola.edu
PHILLIPS, Calvin .... 734-487-0035 242 J
cphill34@emich.edu
PHILLIPS, Carme .... 205-970-9205.... 7 D
cphillips@sebc.edu
PHILLIPS, Carol .... 910-938-6343 361 F
phillipsc@coastalcarolina.edu
PHILLIPS, Chelsea .... 405-224-3140 403 L
cphillips@usao.edu
PHILLIPS, Christina ...... 601-974-1200 268 D
phillcl@millsaps.edu
PHILLIPS,
Christopher, G .... 410-706-2261 219 E
cphillip@umaryland.edu
PHILLIPS, Clarenda, M . 606-783-2434 198 H
c.phillips@moreheadstate.edu

PIEPER, John, A .... 314-367-8700 281 G
john.pieper@stlcop.edu
PIEPER, Michael .... 507-457-5039 262 D
mpieper@winona.edu
PIEPER, Sandi, J .... 515-574-1139 179 F
pieper@iowacentral.edu
PIER, David .... 916-608-6809.. 53 A
pierd@flc.losrios.edu
PIER, Julie, H .... 605-677-5446 453 F
julie.pier@usd.edu
PIERCE, Amanda, K ...... 757-594-8851 506 I
amanda.pierce@cnu.edu
PIERCE, Barb .... 800-962-7682 285 I
bpierce@wma.edu
PIERCE, Bill .... 479-788-7188.. 23 H
bill.pierce@uafs.edu
PIERCE, Bill .... 502-852-8372 201 A
wmpier01@louisville.edu
PIERCE, Bob .... 601-266-6796 271 B
bob.pierce@usm.edu
PIERCE, Brandon .... 316-295-5658 187 C
piercb@friends.edu
PIERCE, Brandon .... 334-347-2623.... 3 H
bpierce@escc.edu
PIERCE, Brynn .... 541-383-7402 404 K
bpierce@cocc.edu
PIERCE, Carl, G .... 610-499-4555 439 G
cgpierce@widener.edu
PIERCE, Carolyn .... 954-308-2101.. 98 I
cjpierce@aii.edu
PIERCE, Cleon .... 919-546-8244 368 G
cpierce@shawu.edu
PIERCE, Dee .... 630-752-5048 163 G
dee.pierce@wheaton.edu
PIERCE, Donald, E .... 864-294-2024 446 F
don.pierce@furman.edu
PIERCE, Donna, L .... 931-598-1880 460 I
dopierce@sewanee.edu
PIERCE, JR., Earl, E ..... 607-871-2406 314 J
pierce@alfred.edu
PIERCE, JR., Earl, E ..... 607-871-2159 314 J
pierce@alfred.edu
PIERCE, Evan, F .... 716-286-8769 336 E
epierce@niagara.edu
PIERCE, Fred .... 608-785-8376 539 G
fpierce@uwlax.edu
PIERCE, Fred, M .... 608-785-8017 539 G
fpierce@uwlax.edu
PIERCE, Frederic .... 607-753-2518 345 C
fred.pierce@cortland.edu
PIERCE, Greg .... 601-266-5006 271 B
greg.pierce@usm.edu
PIERCE, Harold, J .... 802-656-4490 503 C
harold.pierce@uvm.edu
PIERCE, Heather .... 773-252-5308 156 J
heather.pierce@resu.edu
PIERCE, James .... 254-968-9781 485 A
jrpierce@tarleton.edu
PIERCE, Jason, A .... 828-689-1237 359 A
jpierce@mhu.edu
PIERCE, Jason, L .... 937-229-2601 393 E
jpierce2@udayton.edu
PIERCE, Jeff .... 903-223-3049 486 C
jeff.pierce@tamut.edu
PIERCE, Jennifer .... 856-351-2642 308 B
jpierce@salemcc.edu
PIERCE, Jerry, D .... 318-357-6588 208 D
pierce@nsula.edu
PIERCE, Joan .... 608-785-9915 544 E
piercej@westerntc.edu
PIERCE, John .... 828-251-6742 370 E
jpierce@unca.edu
PIERCE, IV, John, Q ...... 202-687-4020.. 95 E
piercej@georgetown.edu
PIERCE, Jonathan .... 503-883-2490 406 I
jdpierce@linfield.edu
PIERCE, Joshua .... 573-629-3014 275 F
Joshua.Pierce@hlg.edu
PIERCE, Kathy .... 870-541-7850.. 21 E
PIERCE, Keith .... 803-641-3513 450 C
keithp@usca.edu
PIERCE, Kenetta .... 803-786-3848 445 C
kpierce@columbiasc.edu
PIERCE, Kenneth .... 512-245-9650 489 C
PIERCE, Kenneth .... 210-458-4555 494 D
kenneth.pierce@utsa.edu
PIERCE, Kristen .... 505-565-1075 237 A
kpierce1@stonehill.edu
PIERCE, Leighton .... 661-255-1050.. 31 B
lpierce@calarts.edu
PIERCE, Leslie .... 478-445-5596 125 A
leslie.pierce@gcsu.edu
PIERCE, Lois .... 314-516-6384 284 B
piercel@umsl.edu
PIERCE, Lori, J .... 734-764-0151 251 C
ljpierce@umich.edu
PIERCE, Malisa .... 918-270-6409 401 C
malisa.pierce@ptstulsa.edu
PIERCE, Marianne .... 864-294-2269 446 F
marianne.pierce@furman.edu
PIERCE, Marisa .... 425-640-1697 522 D
marisa.pierce@edcc.edu
PIERCE, Mark .... 518-736-3622 326 D
mpierce@fmcc.suny.edu
PIERCE, Mark .... 865-573-4517 457 H
mpierce@johnsonU.edu
PIERCE, Melody, C .... 336-334-7696 370 B
mcpierce@ncat.edu
PIERCE, Michael .... 562-903-4777.. 29 F
michael.pierce@biola.edu
PIERCE, Misti .... 970-521-6619.. 84 H
misti.pierce@njc.edu
PIERCE, Peg .... 248-204-3143 245 J
mpierce@ltu.edu
PIERCE, Sharon, J .... 443-518-4807 215 F
spierce@howardcc.edu
PIERCE, Susan .... 972-860-8058 472 D
spierce@dcccd.edu
PIERCE, Tom .... 815-479-7588 152 B
tpierce@mchenry.edu
PIERCE, Vicki, G .... 256-765-4311.... 9 D
vgpierce@una.edu
PIERCE BURNETTE,
Colette .... 512-505-3001 475 G
cburnette@htu.edu
PIERCY, Brad .... 573-840-9106 283 D
bpiercy@trcc.edu
PIERCY, Mitchell .... 417-626-1234 280 B
mpiercy@occ.edu
PIERI, Sean .... 719-389-6741.. 79 M
sean.pieri@coloradocollege.edu
PIERICK, Michael, J ..... 773-442-5100 154 H
m-pierick@neiu.edu
PIERNER, Tracy .... 313-845-9607 243 I
tpierner@hfcc.edu
PIERONI, Barbara .... 812-488-1085 173 H
bp66@evansville.edu
PIEROTTI, Laura .... 201-559-3504 302 I
PIERPOINT, Paul, E ...... 610-861-5580 427 F
ppierpoint@northampton.edu
PIERPONT, Hugh, P ..... 713-486-4151 495 A
hugh.p.pierpont@uth.tmc.edu
PIERRE, Christophe ...... 217-333-3077 161 E
chpierre@uillinois.edu
PIERRE, John, K .... 225-771-2552 207 D
PIERRE, Thelma, J .... 926-261-1401 484 F
tjpierre@pvamu.edu
PIERRE, Vivica, D .... 617-228-2366 231 C
vdpierre@bhcc.mass.edu
PIERSOL, Amy .... 785-594-7866 184 F
amy.piersol@bakeru.edu
PIERSOL, John .... 386-752-1822 103 Q
john.piersol@fgc.edu
PIERSON, Cathy .... 541-245-7912 409 F
cpierson@roguecc.edu
PIERSON, Connie .... 410-455-3055 219 F
krach@umbc.edu
PIERSON, Donald .... 978-934-2635 229 A
Donald_Pierson@uml.edu
PIERSON, Donald, E ..... 978-934-4000 229 A
PIERSON, Gary .... 970-943-2049.. 87 F
gpierson@western.edu
PIERSON, Karen .... 530-283-0202.. 44 H
KPierson@frc.edu
PIERSON, Katricia .... 580-559-5204 397 K
kpierson@ecok.edu
PIERSON, Kenn .... 562-463-3100.. 60 I
kpierson@riohondo.edu
PIERSON, Tim, J .... 434-395-2039 509 H
piersontj@longwood.edu
PIESIK, Deanette .... 701-774-4246 375 C
deanette.piesik@willistonstate.edu
PIETKIEWICZ, Michael .. 716-270-4670 325 A
pietkiewicz@ecc.edu
PIETROPAULI, John ...... 703-416-1441 508 F
jpietropauli@ipsciences.edu
PIETROWSKI, Michael .. 505-565-1082 237 A
mpietrowski@stonehill.edu
PIETRUSZKIEWICZ,
Christopher .... 727-562-7809 117 A
cmp@law.stetson.edu
PIETRYKOWSKI, Chet ... 406-791-5283 288 J
cpietrykowski@ugf.edu
PIETRYKOWSKI,
Robert, J .... 954-262-7893 109 E
rpietrykowski@nova.edu
PIETRZAK, Ted .... 716-926-8790 327 F
tedpietrzak@hilbert.edu
PIETSCH, Amy .... 920-735-2594 542 N
pietsch@fvtc.edu
PIETZ, Vicky .... 715-675-3331 544 A
pietz@ntc.edu
PIFER, Kenneth .... 503-370-6104 411 D
kpifer@willamette.edu
PIGA, John .... 781-891-2148 223 E
jpiga@bentley.edu
PIGATTI, Kimberly .... 708-596-2000 159 D
kpigatti@ssc.edu
PIGGOTT, Patrick, L ..... 209-478-0800.. 47 F
ppiggott@humphreys.edu
PIGNATELLO, Robert ..... 212-237-8500 319 F
rpignatello@jjay.cuny.edu
PIGNATO, David .... 617-254-2610 236 B
rev.david.pignato@sjs.edu
PIGORS, Aaron .... 219-980-7203 168 C
apigors@iu.edu
PIGOTT, Kelly .... 325-671-2179 474 M
kpigott@hsutx.edu
PIGOTT, Teri .... 312-915-6800 151 E
tpigott@luc.edu
PIGZA, Jennifer .... 925-631-4755.. 61 G
jpigza@stmarys-ca.edu
PIIRAINEN, Jack .... 775-445-4282 296 A
jack.piirainen@wnc.edu
PIKE, Alan .... 336-334-4822 363 A
adpike@gtcc.edu
PIKE, Dale .... 208-426-3289 137 E
dalepike@boisestate.edu
PIKE, Dale .... 540-231-7108 518 B
dalepike@vt.edu
PIKE, David .... 202-885-2996.. 94 H
dpike@american.edu
PIKE, Gary .... 317-278-2282 168 E
pikeg@iupui.edu
PIKE, Patricia .... 562-903-4713.. 29 F
patricia.pike@biola.edu
PIKKA, Joshua .... 313-831-5200 242 K
jpikka@etseminary.edu
PIKOR, Susan .... 413-542-8099 222 A
spikor@amherst.edu
PIKOWSKY, Reta .... 404-894-4181 125 D
reta.pikowsky@registrar.gatech.edu
PILACHOWSKI,
David, M .... 413-597-2502 238 E
david.m.pilachowski@williams.edu
PILATI, Liz .... 206-296-1891 526 F
pilatil@seattleu.edu
PILCHER, Benjamin, J .. 412-578-6557 414 I
bjpilcher@carlow.edu
PILCHICK, Tovia .... 718-232-7800 353 F
PILCHICK, Yochanan .... 718-232-7800 353 F
PILEWSKI, Tim, W .... 814-732-5555 430 G
pilewski@edinboro.edu
PILGRIM, Andrea .... 864-644-5000 449 B
apilgrim@swu.edu
PILGRIM, David .... 231-591-3946 242 L
DavidPilgrim@ferris.edu
PILGRIM, Jacqueline .... 617-422-7401 234 J
jpilgrim@nesl.edu
PILGRIM, Mark .... 717-477-1154 431 F
mepilg@ship.edu
PILIECI, Kim .... 616-538-2330 243 C
kpilieci@gbcol.edu
PILIPZECK, Beth .... 215-596-8970 438 E
b.pilipz@usciences.edu
PILLAI, Bindu .... 631-370-3300 342 D
BPillai@sbmelville.edu
PILLANS, Elizabeth .... 903-875-7370 479 I
elizabeth.pillans@navarrocollege.edu
PILLAR, James .... 732-571-3465 303 G
jpillar@monmouth.edu
PILLARELLI, Tina .... 734-384-4229 247 C
tpillarelli@monroeccc.edu
PILLARI, Vimala .... 404-880-8549 122 I
vpillari@cau.edu
PILLAY, Gautam .... 610-436-3592 432 B
gpillay@wcupa.edu
PILLAY, Sasi .... 608-265-4622 539 C
spillay@uwsa.edu
PILLING, Peter, E .... 212-854-4774 322 F
pp2542@columbia.edu
PILLON, Greg, S .... 615-460-6645 455 D
greg.pillon@belmont.edu
PILLOW, Kirk .... 718-636-3744 338 E
kpillow@pratt.edu
PILLOW, Peggy .... 501-205-8834.. 20 G
ppillow@cbc.edu
PILOCZEWSKI,
Lawrence .... 262-554-2010 537 D
mcomadmissions@aol.com
PILON, Maryann .... 845-569-3332 333 I
maryannpilon@msmc.edu
PILSNER, Joseph .... 713-942-5049 493 J
pilsnerj@stthom.edu
PIMBER, Lisa .... 800-371-6105.. 16 A
lisa@nationalparalegal.edu
PIMENTEL, Art .... 916-375-5513.. 53 B
pimenta@scc.losrios.edu
PIMENTEL, George .... 615-230-3557 464 B
george.pimentel@volstate.edu
PIMENTEL, German .... 787-840-8894 558 D
german.pimentel@upr.edu
PIMENTEL, Kristin .... 805-546-3182.. 42 H
kpimente@cuesta.edu
PIMENTEL, Robert .... 559-934-2793.. 76 B
robertpimentel@whccd.edu
PINA, Bernard .... 575-527-7610 312 D
bepina@nmsu.edu
PINA, Christine, M .... 860-768-2403.. 92 F
cpina@hartford.edu
PINA, Jason .... 508-531-1276 229 C
jason.pina@bridgew.edu
PINA, Tony .... 818-883-9002.. 74 F
PINAR, Kemale .... 507-457-2394 262 D
kpinar@winona.edu
PINCEK, Debra .... 724-738-2470 432 A
debra.pincek@sru.edu
PINCHBACK, G. Keith ... 870-338-6474.. 24 F
PINCHBACK, Keith .... 501-882-8855.. 19 E
gkpinchback@asub.edu
PINCHBACK, Rebekah ... 248-218-2096 249 D
rpinchback@rc.edu
PINCKNEY, Jloundia ..... 843-574-6120 449 G
jloundia.pinckney@tridenttech.edu
PINDER, Elaine .... 202-462-2101.. 96 C
pinder@iwp.edu
PINDER, Kymberly .... 505-277-2112 313 H
kpinder@unm.edu
PINE, Gary .... 626-815-5081.. 29 B
gpine@apu.edu
PINE, Nathan .... 508-793-2582 225 C
npine@holycross.edu
PINEDA, Carmen .... 617-449-7380 237 E
carmen.pineda@urbancollege.edu
PINEDA, Gladys .... 212-423-2768 327 D
gladys.pineda@helenefuld.edu
PINEDA, Marika .... 541-463-5824 406 F
pinedam@lanecc.edu
PINEIRO, Mildred .... 787-728-1515 559 A
mpineiro@sagrado.edu
PINEIRO, Pedro .... 718-997-4446 320 E
pedro.pineiro@qc.cuny.edu
PINEO, Sara .... 814-332-4392 411 F
spineo@allegheny.edu
PINERES, Sheila, A .... 903-813-2226 468 G
spineres@austincollege.edu
PINERO, Luis, A .... 608-263-2378 539 D
lapinero@vc.wisc.edu
PINERO, Ramon .... 507-389-1794 260 A
ramon.pinero@mnsu.edu
PINES, Darryll, J .... 301-405-3869 219 D
pines@umd.edu
PINESCHI, David .... 916-348-4689.. 43 K
dpineschi@epic.edu
PINET, Celine .... 831-755-6764.. 46 J
cpinet@hartnell.edu
PINHEIRO, Shashi, B ... 210-458-6466 494 D
SHASHI.PINHEIRO@UTSA.EDU
PINION, Laura .... 251-344-1203.... 3 J
PINK, Kathleen .... 641-844-5739 179 J
Kathy.Pink@iavalley.edu
PINK, Kathy .... 641-844-5539 179 L
kathy.pink@iavalley.edu
PINK, Kevin .... 641-683-5105 179 C
kevin.pink@indianhills.edu
PINK, Larry .... 619-388-7665.. 62 H
lpink@sdccd.edu
PINK, Thomas, A .... 906-635-2315 245 H
tpink@lssu.edu
PINKALL, Rita .... 620-672-5641 190 H
ritap@prattcc.edu
PINKARD, Elfred, A ...... 704-378-1000 358 B
epinkard@jcsu.edu
PINKELTON, Lawrence .. 773-995-2042 141 J
lpinkelt@csu.edu
PINKENBURG,
Steven, J .... 512-448-8408 481 B
stevep@stedwards.edu
PINKERT, Carl .... 205-348-4566.... 8 E
cap@ua.edu
PINKERTON, Nick .... 860-768-4482.. 92 F
pinkerton@hartford.edu
PINKETT, Moneca, K .... 340-693-1495 559 B
mpinket@uvi.edu
PINKHAM, JoEllen .... 585-389-2060 334 B
jpinkha0@naz.edu
PINKHAM, Wesley .... 319-656-2447 182 G
PINKNEY, Dwayne .... 919-962-1091 371 A
dpinkney@email.unc.edu
PINKNEY-PASTRANA,
Jill .... 218-726-6537 264 G
cehsp@d.umn.edu
PINKOWSKI, JR.,
Richard, J .... 716-926-8820 327 F
rickp@hilbert.edu
PINKSTON, Paul .... 920-465-2373 539 F
pinkstop@uwgb.edu
PINKSTON, Scott .... 870-368-2016.. 22 D
spinkston@ozarka.edu
PINKSTON, Terri, B ...... 405-325-3021 403 I
terri@ou.edu
PINKSTON-MCKEE, Ria . 773-291-6251 142 B
rmckee@ccc.edu
PINNELL, Julie .... 402-826-8565 290 C
julie.pinnell@doane.edu
PINNER, Ray .... 256-824-6350.... 9 A
ray.pinner@uah.edu
PINNEY, Marjorie .... 860-231-5291.. 93 A
mpinney@usj.edu
PINNEY, Pete .... 907-474-5860.. 10 I
pppinney@alaska.edu

PLEASANT, Lori .... 850-973-9469 109 C
pleasantl@nfcc.edu
PLEASANT-DOINE,
Sheia, I .... 904-819-6435 102 P
SPleasant@flagler.edu
PLEASANTS, Jane .... 919-668-2565 356 E
jane.pleasants@duke.edu
PLEGER, Kimberly .... 253-680-7102 519 K
kpleger@bates.ctc.edu
PLEGER, Thomas, C ..... 906-635-2202 245 H
tpleger@lssu.edu
PLEMMONS, Donna ...... 501-450-1351.. 21 C
plemmons@hendrix.edu
PLEMMONS, Kim .... 704-403-1751 355 B
kim.plemmons@carolinashealthcare.org
PLETCHER, Ann .... 864-596-9086 445 E
ann.pletcher@converse.edu
PLETCHER, James, R .... 740-587-6469 381 H
pletcher@denison.edu
PLETCHER, Jill, M .... 316-978-3435 192 D
jill.pletcher@wichita.edu
PLETSCHER,
Anthony, W .... 215-368-5000 412 K
tpletscher@biblical.edu
PLEUSS, Carol, J .... 330-684-8928 393 A
cjpleus@uakron.edu
PLEVER, Steve .... 828-251-6526 370 E
splever@unca.edu
PLEVIN, Cynthia .... 415-749-4523.. 62 I
ashulock@sfai.edu
PLIML, Michelle .... 414-258-4810 538 A
plimlm@mtmary.edu
PLINER, Lauren .... 215-953-5999.. 96 H
PLINER, Susan .... 315-781-3354 327 G
pliner@hws.edu
PLINSKE, Kathleen, A ... 407-582-4975 118 I
kplinske@valenciacollege.edu
PLINSKE, Paul, M .... 308-865-8332 293 G
plinskep@unk.edu
PLINSKI, Christie .... 503-491-7295 407 C
christie.plinski@mhcc.edu
PLLOG, William .... 603-641-7174 298 F
wploog@anselm.edu
PLOECKELMAN, Erica ... 920-686-6127 539 A
erica.ploeckelman@sl.edu
PLOEGER, SM, Bernard 808-735-4741 135 A
bploeger@chaminade.edu
PLONSKY, Christine, A . 512-471-4780 493M
cp@utexas.edu
PLOTKIN, David .... 503-594-3020 405 A
david.plotkin@clackamas.edu
PLOTKIN, Helen .... 501-450-1225.. 21 C
plotkin@hendrix.edu
PLOTKOWSKI, Paul ...... 616-331-6260 243 E
plotkowp@gvsu.edu
PLOTNER, Amy .... 315-312-3702 346 A
amy.plotner@oswego.edu
PLOTNICK, Tamra .... 212-346-1244 337 I
tplotnick@pace.edu
PLOTTS, Debra .... 334-214-4866.... 2 H
debra.plotts@cv.edu
PLOTTS, Douglas, J ...... 610-861-1560 426 H
plottsd@moravian.edu
PLOTTS, John .... 972-721-5266 491 B
jplotts@udallas.edu
PLOUF, Joe .... 425-602-3043 519 J
jplouf@bastyr.edu
PLOUFFE, Audrey .... 406-275-4969 288 H
audrey_plouffe@skc.edu
PLOUFFE, Jeffrey .... 401-874-4198 442 E
jeff@uri.edu
PLOURDE, Philip, D ...... 319-273-2853 176 A
Philip.Plourde@uni.edu
PLOWFIELD, Lisa .... 410-704-2132 221 A
lplowfield@towson.edu
PLOWMAN, Donde .... 402-472-9500 293 H
dplowman2@unl.edu
PLUCHUTA, Alexander .. 610-359-5057 416 G
apluchut@dccc.edu
PLUDE, Katie .... 985-867-2248 206 J
kplude@sjasc.edu
PLUDOW, Julie .... 619-388-3195.. 62 F
jpludow@sdccd.edu
PLUEMER, Julie .... 608-822-2369 544 C
jpluemer@swtc.edu
PLUHTA, Elizabeth, A ... 206-934-5141 526 B
elizabeth.pluhta@seattlecolleges.edu
PLUMB, Anne, M .... 901-572-2842 455 C
anne.plumb@bchs.edu
PLUMB, Richard, G .... 651-962-6720 265 F
rgplumb@stthomas.edu
PLUMB, Sylvia .... 802-626-6459 504 B
sylvia.plumb@lyndonstate.edu
PLUMLEE, Darrel .... 614-251-4548 388 H
plumleed@ohiodominican.edu
PLUMLEY, Kelly .... 828-327-7000 361 B
kplumley@cvcc.edu
PLUMLY, Wayne, L .... 229-245-3825 133 H
lwplumly@valdosta.edu
PLUMMER, B. DaVida .. 757-727-6698 508 C
davida.plummer@hamptonu.edu

PLUMMER, Dale, H ...... 610-566-1776 440 C
dplummer@williamson.edu
PLUMMER, David .... 956-872-5051 482 G
PLUMMER, Deborah, L . 508-856-2179 229 B
deborah.plummer@umassmed.edu
PLUMMER, Dianne .... 617-989-4036 237 G
plummerd@wit.edu
PLUMMER, Donna, M .. 859-238-5308 194 E
donna.plummer@centre.edu
PLUMMER, Eric .... 701-777-3391 373 G
eric.plummer@und.edu
PLUMMER, Lisa .... 610-902-8549 414 B
lisa.m.plummer@cabrini.edu
PLUMMER, Meredith .... 760-366-5284.. 42 G
mplummer@cmccd.edu
PLUMMER, Robert, M .. 423-439-4218 461 D
plummerb@etsu.edu
PLUMMER, Troy, A .... 515-263-6050 178 H
tplummer@grandview.edu
PLUMMER, Vince .... 701-671-2319 375 B
vince.plummer@ndscs.edu
PLUNK, Kelly .... 870-584-4471.. 24 E
kplunk@cccua.edu
PLUNKET, Chris .... 319-385-6206 180 A
chris.plunkett@iw.edu
PLUNKETT, James, C ... 215-951-1500 422 F
plunkett@lasalle.edu
PLUTCHAK, Scott .... 205-934-5460.... 8 F
tscott@uab.edu
PLUTCHOK, Yisroel ...... 718-438-5476 352 I
PLUTE, David .... 307-754-6025 546 I
David.Plute@nwc.edu
PLYLER, Chris, P .... 803-777-7695 450 B
chrisp@mailbox.sc.edu
PLYLER, Jeffrey, B .... 704-463-3042 367 F
jeff.plyler@pfeiffer.edu
PLYMALE, Chad .... 585-567-9480 328 C
chad.plymale@houghton.edu
PLYMESSER, Jillian .... 402-354-7137 291 P
jillian.plymesser@methodistcollege.edu
POAGE, Alison .... 512-472-4133 482 E
alison.poage@ssw.edu
POARCH, Mark .... 828-726-2214 360 F
mpoarch@cccti.edu
POAT, Erica .... 618-634-3375 159 A
ericap@shawneecc.edu
POATS, Lillian, B .... 713-313-7978 487 F
poats_lb@tsu.edu
POBAT, Peter .... 718-368-5109 320 A
ppobat@kbcc.cuny.edu
POBLENZ, Scott, B .... 978-468-7111 227 B
spoblenz@gcts.edu
POCAI, Rob .... 601-366-8880 271 E
rpocai@wbs.edu
POCHARD, Brad .... 864-294-3406 446 F
brad.pochard@furman.edu
POCHE, Paulette, M ..... 985-549-5638 208 E
ppoche@selu.edu
POCK, Arnyce .... 301-295-9945 548 D
Arnyce.pock@usuhs.edu
PODANY, Jeremy .... 970-491-5709.. 81 D
jeremy.podany@colostate.edu
PODELL, David .... 212-517-0520 332 A
dpodell@mmm.edu
PODESCHI, Amanda ...... 217-424-3506 153 A
apodeschi@millikin.edu
PODESTA, Guido .... 608-262-9833 539 D
gpodesta@wisc.edu
PODLIN, Michael .... 206-296-6100 526 F
podlinm@seattleu.edu
PODLONE, Kandice .... 510-780-4500.. 50 G
kpodlone@lifewest.edu
PODOLSKY, Daniel, K .. 214-648-2508 496 A
priscilla.alderman@utsouthwestern.edu
POE, JR., Donald .... 704-463-3041 367 F
don.poe@pfeiffer.edu
POE, Elmer .... 252-328-9066 369 E
poee@ecu.edu
POE, Scott .... 304-424-8212 533 E
scott.poe@wvup.edu
POE, Shawna .... 217-854-5506 140 F
shawna.poe@blackburn.edu
POEHLER, M.J .... 816-802-3393 276 F
mpoehler@kcai.edu
POEHLERT, Edward .... 760-757-2121.. 54 G
epoehlert@miracosta.edu
POELKER, Scott .... 843-574-6197 449 G
scott.poelker@tridenttech.edu
POELKING, Karen, L ..... 216-373-5234 388 A
kpoelking@ndc.edu
POELVOORDE, Tracy, L 309-779-7708 161 A
tracy.poelvoorde@trinitycollegeqc.edu
POELVOORDE, Tracy, L 309-779-7710 161 A
tracy.poelvoorde@trinitycollegeqc.edu
POERTNER, Gary .... 949-582-4840.. 67 D
gpoertner@soccd.edu
POETTKER, Tricia .... 617-537-6843 152 C
tapoettker@mckendree.edu
POFF, G. Elaine, N .... 954-262-7261 109 E
poff@nova.edu

POFF, Robert, C .... 812-941-2331 169 A
rcpoff@ius.edu
POGGENDORF,
Brenda, P .... 540-375-2270 512 B
poggendorf@roanoke.edu
POGGENDORF,
Richard, J .... 540-375-2043 512 B
rpoggendorf@roanoke.edu
POGONCHEFF, Elaine ... 517-483-1016 245 I
pogonce@lcc.edu
POGORELC, Anthony .... 650-289-3344.. 61 H
anthony.pogorelc@stpatricksseminary.org
POGORZELSKI, Elise ..... 304-296-8282 534 E
epogorzelski@wvjc.edu
POGROSZEWSKI,
Donna, J .... 585-292-3202 333 G
dpogroszewski@monroecc.edu
POGUE, Frank .... 610-399-2220 430 D
president@cheyney.edu
POGUE, Gregory .... 609-771-3078 301 E
pogueg@tcnj.edu
POGUE, Roslynn .... 318-342-5327 209 A
pogue@ulm.edu
POHAS, Joanie .... 310-338-3068.. 53 C
jpohas@lmu.edu
POHERO, Mary Jane .... 973-596-3106 304 D
mary.j.pohero@njit.edu
POHL, Charles, A .... 215-503-6988 436 F
charles.pohl@jefferson.edu
POHL, Don .... 314-286-3653 280 I
dpohl@ranken.edu
POHL, Henry, S .... 518-262-5919 314 I
pohlh@mail.amc.edu
POHL, Jonathan .... 860-832-1945.. 88 D
pohlj@ccsu.edu
POHL, Laurie .... 617-353-9814 224 E
lpohl@bu.edu
POHL, Sara .... 815-825-2086 149 E
sarapohl@kishwaukeecollege.edu
POHLGEERS, Linda .... 513-244-4824 387 A
linda.pohlgeers@msj.edu
POHLIG, Holly .... 407-646-2161 111 H
hpohlig@rollins.edu
POHLMAN, Nancy, A .... 815-740-3496 162 F
npohlman@stfrancis.edu
POHLSON, Scott .... 605-677-5759 453 F
scott.pohlson@usd.edu
POHOLSKY, Tim .... 816-604-3425 277 G
tim.poholsky@mcckc.edu
POIGER, Uta .... 617-373-5173 235 D
POINDEXTER, Jeanne .... 757-382-9900.. 96 H
POINDEXTER, Michael .. 916-558-2142.. 53 B
PoindeM@scc.losrios.edu
POINT, Matthew .... 215-965-4035 426 G
mpoint@moore.edu
POINTS, Dan .... 405-733-7359 401 L
dpoints@rose.edu
POINTS, Emily .... 309-694-8501 146 C
emily.points@icc.edu
POIRIER, Dawn .... 508-541-1809 225 G
dpoirier@dean.edu
POIRIER, J. Nicolas ..... 315-568-3197 334 F
npoirier@nycc.edu
POIRIER, Janet, L .... 603-641-7010 298 F
jpoirier@anselm.edu
POIRRIER, Gail, P .... 337-482-6808 208 F
poirrier@louisiana.edu
POISEL, Mark Allen ...... 706-737-1411 121 C
mpoisel@gru.edu
POISEL, Mark Allen ...... 212-346-1200 337 I
mpoisel@pace.edu
POISION, Rebecca .... 843-863-7517 444 B
rpoision@csuniv.edu
POISSON, Craig .... 413-748-3333 236 H
cpoisson@springfieldcollege.edu
POITER, Emilia .... 410-532-5184 217 F
epoiter@ndm.edu
POITRA, Peggy .... 218-879-0803 258 F
poitra@fdltcc.edu
POK, Shirley, M .... 209-667-3131.. 35 C
smpok@csustan.edu
POKORAK, Jeffrey .... 617-573-8000 237 B
jpokorak@suffolk.edu
POKORNAWSKI, Alex ... 701-777-2664 373 G
alexander.pokornawski@und.edu
POKORNY, Anita, R ...... 330-325-6760 387 F
app@neomed.edu
POKOT, Elena .... 262-472-1001 541 D
pokote@uww.edu
POKRAS, Martha .... 617-627-3389 237 C
martha.pokras@tufts.edu
POL, Aileen .... 708-209-3237 143 D
Aileen.Pol@cuchicago.edu
POL, Lou .... 402-554-2303 294 A
lpol@unomaha.edu
POLAK, Benjamin .... 203-432-4444.. 93 C
benjamin.polak@yale.edu
POLAK, Debra .... 707-468-3000.. 54 A
dpolak@mendocino.edu
POLAND, D'Ann .... 361-698-2209 473 F
dpoland@delmar.edu

POLAND, Russell .... 615-327-6171 458 F
rpoland@mmc.edu
POLANIECKI, Andrew .... 574-239-8315 167 C
apolaniecki@hcc-nd.edu
POLANSKY, Thomas ..... 323-259-2651.. 56 I
tpolansky@oxy.edu
POLASKI, Tamara, R ..... 515-294-5225 175 G
tra@iastate.edu
POLATAJKO, Mark, M .. 937-775-2002 396 A
mark.polatajko@wright.edu
POLCZYNSKI, Mimi ...... 618-545-3363 149 C
mpolczynski@kaskaskia.edu
POLD, Rein, A .... 814-393-2166 430 E
rpold@clarion.edu
POLDING, Carl .... 651-793-1777 259 E
carl.polding@metrostate.edu
POLDING, Carl .... 763-657-3750 259 E
carl.polding@metrostate.edu
POLDING, John .... 973-720-2887 309 I
poldingj@wpunj.edu
POLESHEK, Jeffrey, A ... 941-359-7635 111 F
jpoleshe@ringling.edu
POLETTI, Ed .... 215-972-2053 429 G
epoletti@pafa.edu
POLICASTRO, Mike .... 422-472-7141 462 D
mpolicastro@clevelandstatecc.edu
POLICASTRO,
Stephanie .... 212-517-0658 332 A
spolicastro@mmm.edu
POLING, Barbara .... 909-593-3511.. 73 B
bpoling@laverne.edu
POLISENO, Nick .... 212-226-7300 338 F
nickpoliseno@pbcny.edu
POLISHWALLA, Perzen . 701-483-2340 373 H
Perzen.Polishwalla@dickinsonstate.edu
POLISI, Joseph, W ...... 212-799-5000 329 I
POLITANO, John, P ...... 321-674-7239 103 R
jpolitan@fit.edu
POLITE-SOLOMON, Sue 229-430-4658 119 H
sue.solomon@asurams.edu
POLIZZI, Dianne .... 617-243-2133 227 K
dpolizzi@lasell.edu
POLK, Ali .... 831-476-9424.. 44 L
marketing@fivebranches.edu
POLK, Alisa, L .... 540-636-2900 506 H
finaid@christendom.edu
POLK, Coreylon .... 951-343-4374.. 30 D
cpolk@calbaptist.edu
POLK, JD .... 515-271-1515 177 H
james.polk@dmu.edu
POLK, Laura .... 301-934-7506 214 E
laurap@csmd.edu
POLK, Molly .... 262-551-5819 535 E
mpolk@carthage.edu
POLKABLA-BYERS, Joy . 330-941-2242 396 C
jlbyers@ysu.edu
POLL, Michael .... 970-248-1458.. 80 B
mpoll@coloradomesa.edu
POLLACK, Ann, M .... 310-794-0387.. 71 D
apollack@resadmin.ucla.edu
POLLACK, Emanuel .... 312-413-9461 161 F
epollack@uic.edu
POLLACK, Gary .... 509-335-4750 528 B
gary.pollack@wsu.edu
POLLACK, Glenn .... 914-323-5158 331 J
glenn.pollack@mville.edu
POLLACK, Martha, E ..... 734-764-9292 251 C
pollackm@umich.edu
POLLACK, Pamela .... 718-951-3118 318 F
pamela@brooklyn.cuny.edu
POLLAK, Dianne .... 802-224-3000 503 F
dianne.pollak@vsc.edu
POLLARD, Al .... 254-299-8669 478 C
apollard@mclennan.edu
POLLARD, III, Alton, B 202-806-0500.. 96 B
abpollard@howard.edu
POLLARD, Charles .... 479-524-7200.. 21 F
cpollard@jbu.edu
POLLARD, Cindy .... 940-898-3456 490 D
cpollard@twu.edu
POLLARD, Cindy .... 503-517-1018 411 A
cpollard@warnerpacific.edu
POLLARD, DeRionne, P 240-567-5264 217 B
president@montgomerycollege.edu
POLLARD, Diana .... 845-431-8403 324 D
pollard@sunydutchess.edu
POLLARD, James .... 781-239-4333 222 E
Jpollard@babson.edu
POLLARD, Jamie, B .... 515-294-0123 175 G
jbp@iastate.edu
POLLARD, Janet, L .... 361-593-2439 486 A
janet.pollard@tamuk.edu
POLLARD, Jennie .... 214-860-5833 472 F
jpollard@dcccd.edu
POLLARD, Leslie .... 256-726-7000.... 6 C
lpollard@oakwood.edu
POLLARD, Mary Lee ...... 518-464-8500 325 B
mpollard@excelsior.edu
POLLARD, Natalie, M ... 609-896-5340 306 A
pollardn@rider.edu

PORTER, Jennifer .... 617-735-9772 226 B
porterj@emmanuel.edu
PORTER, Jennifer .... 973-278-5400 316 D
jnp@berkeleycollege.edu
PORTER, Jennifer .... 973-278-5400 300 C
jnp@berkeleycollege.edu
PORTER, John, B .... 570-961-4772 425 D
porter@marywood.edu
PORTER, Jon, K .... 802-656-0123 503 C
jon.porter@uvm.edu
PORTER, Joseph .... 518-320-1344 343 B
joe.porter@suny.edu
PORTER, Joseph, B ...... 518-464-8500 325 B
jporter@excelsior.edu
PORTER, Kary .... 252-222-6224 361 A
porterk@carteret.edu
PORTER, Kim .... 325-235-7478 488 C
kim.porter@tstc.edu
PORTER, Lauren .... 512-476-2772 468 I
admissions@austingrad.edu
PORTER, Malorie .... 304-829-7064 529 H
mporter@bethanywv.edu
PORTER, Mario .... 210-341-1366 479 N
mporter@ost.edu
PORTER, Mark, J .... 401-863-3870 441 A
mark_porter@brown.edu
PORTER, Michael .... 651-962-4376 265 F
mporter@stthomas.edu
PORTER, Monica .... 313-583-6445 251 D
dmporte@umich.edu
PORTER, Nadine .... 240-567-5382 217 B
nadine.porter@montgomerycollege.edu
PORTER, Narda .... 276-328-0116 514 B
nnb3h@uvawise.edu
PORTER, Rebecca .... 701-858-3126 374 B
rebecca.porter@minotstateu.edu
PORTER, Rebecca, E ..... 317-274-0401 168 E
rporter@iupui.edu
PORTER, Sharon .... 864-587-4272 449 D
portersd@smcsc.edu
PORTER, Steve .... 620-665-3552 188 A
porters@hutchcc.edu
PORTER, Susie .... 801-581-8094 499 K
s.porter@utah.edu
PORTER, Thomas, R ..... 540-261-8563 512 J
tr.porter@svu.edu
PORTER, Timothy .... 702-895-2058 295 G
tim.porter@unlv.edu
PORTER, Tracy .... 863-297-3743 110 E
tporter@polk.edu
PORTER, Vincent .... 210-829-2770 492 B
porterv@uiwtx.edu
PORTER, Wilma, B .... 248-341-2182 248 E
wbporter@oaklandcc.edu
PORTERFIELD,
Daniel, R .... 717-291-3911 418 J
daniel.porterfield@fandm.edu
PORTERFIELD,
Deana, L .... 585-594-6100 339 F
presidentsoffice@roberts.edu
PORTERFIELD,
Deana, L .... 585-594-6100 337 A
presidentsoffice@roberts.edu
PORTERFIELD, Kent ...... 314-977-2226 281 M
kporter6@slu.edu
PORTERFIELD, Kim .... 512-245-9645 489 C
kp10@txstate.edu
PORTERFIELD, Rebecca 859-572-5551 199 A
porterfier1@nku.edu
PORTERVINT, Bernice ... 360-676-2772 524 D
bportervint@nwic.edu
PORTIER, Bonnie .... 301-447-5288 217 D
bportier@msmary.edu
PORTILLO, Cesar .... 909-537-5138.. 35 A
cportillo@csusb.edu
PORTIS-TURNER, Erica . 334-285-5177.... 4 K
erica.turner@istc.edu
PORTLOCK, Jeremy .... 785-594-8415 184 F
jeremy.portlock@bakerU.edu
PORTMAN, Tarrell .... 507-457-2570 262 D
tportman@winona.edu
PORTMANN, Brooke ...... 231-843-5866 252 H
bportmann@westshore.edu
PORTNOY, Robert, N ..... 402-472-7450 293 H
rportnoy1@unl.edu
PORTO, Enrico, A .... 304-367-4111 532 F
rick.porto@fairmontstate.edu
PORTUGAL, Alberto ...... 941-487-4360 115 B
portugal@ncf.edu
PORTWINE, Ronald, E .. 989-964-2064 249 G
report@svsu.edu
PORTWOOD, Amy .... 206-239-4500 520 K
alportwood@cityu.edu
PORTWOOD, Ryan .... 402-354-7848 291 P
ryan.portwood@methodistcollege.edu
PORTZ, Margaret, A ..... 610-758-5794 424 B
mak5@lehigh.edu
PORTZEL, Curt .... 310-506-4893.. 58 H
curt.portzel@pepperdine.edu
POSAMENTIER, Alfred ... 914-674-7447 332 E
aposamentier@mercy.edu
POSEJPAL, Gigi .... 312-369-7458 143 C
gposejpal@colum.edu
POSER, Susan .... 402-472-2161 293 H
sposer1@unl.edu
POSEY, Evan .... 770-484-1204 128 D
evan.posey@lutherrice.edu
POSEY, James, T .... 843-953-5708 445 B
poseyjt@cofc.edu
POSEY, Jamie .... 423-585-6894 464 C
jamie.posey@ws.edu
POSEY, Jeff .... 601-643-8411 266 J
jeff.posey@colin.edu
POSEY, Kathy .... 617-928-4003 234 D
kposey@mountida.edu
POSEY, Libby .... 601-857-3350 267 D
Olivia.Posey@hindscc.edu
POSEY, Monica .... 513-569-1511 379 K
monica.posey@cincinnatistate.edu
POSEY, Raymond .... 330-823-7362 394 A
poseyra@mountunion.edu
POSEY, Steven .... 505-473-6101 313 B
steven.posey@santafeuniversity.edu
POSHEK, Joe .... 714-432-5536.. 40 D
jposhek@occ.cccd.edu
POSILLICO, Joseph, J .. 973-618-3500 300 H
jposillico@caldwell.edu
POSING, Mary .... 815-802-8202 149 B
mposing@kcc.edu
POSKANZER, JR.,
Steven, G .... 507-222-4305 254 D
president@carleton.edu
POSLER, Brian .... 785-594-8312 184 F
brian.posler@bakeru.edu
POSLUSNY, Matthew .... 919-760-8514 359 B
mposlusny@meredith.edu
POSMAN, Jerald .... 718-270-5026 320 C
jposman@mec.cuny.edu
POSNER, Deborah .... 954-201-7482.. 99 G
dposner@broward.edu
POSNER, Kenneth .... 352-588-8992 111 L
kenneth.posner@saintleo.edu
POSNER, Marc .... 714-484-7006.. 56 E
mposner@cypresscollege.edu
POSNER, Mark .... 651-638-6383 254 A
m-posner@bethel.edu
POSNER, Sylvia .... 212-824-2211 327 C
sposner@huc.edu
POSS, Joe .... 509-313-6215 522 L
poss@gonzaga.edu
POSSEHL, DeAnn, L ..... 262-595-2454 540 C
deann.possehl@uwp.edu
POSSIN, Sandra .... 206-780-6214 525 F
sandra.possin@pinchot.edu
POST, Carole .... 212-431-2894 335 G
Carole.Post@nyls.edu
POST, Christine .... 304-424-8358 533 E
christine.post@wvup.edu
POST, John .... 479-788-7025.. 23 H
john.post@uafs.edu
POST, Julie .... 770-962-7580 127 C
jpost@gwinnetttech.edu
POST, Michael .... 301-447-5214 217 D
post@msmary.edu
POST, Nichole .... 607-729-1581 324 A
npost@davisny.edu
POST, Robert .... 610-361-5233 427 D
postr@neumann.edu
POST, Robert, C .... 203-432-1660.. 93 C
robert.post@yale.edu
POST, Scott .... 870-338-6474.. 24 F
POST, Tracee .... 806-651-2100 486 D
tpost@wtamu.edu
POST-LUNDQUIST,
Beth .... 518-580-5750 342 I
bpostlun@skidmore.edu
POSTEMA, Miles, J .... 231-591-3894 242 L
MilesPostema@ferris.edu
POSTER, Michael .... 612-436-7520 257 K
mposter@msbcollege.edu
POSTER, Michael, C ..... 563-333-6032 182 E
PosterMichaelC@sau.edu
POSTLETHWAITE,
Bonnie .... 816-235-1531 284 A
postlethwaiteb@umkc.edu
POSTLEWATE, Rusty ..... 410-455-3260 219 F
rpost@umbc.edu
POSTMA, Kurt .... 616-538-2330 243 C
kpostma@gbcol.edu
POSTMA, Laura .... 906-248-8420 240 J
lpostma@bmcc.edu
POSTON, Fred .... 517-884-7004 246 H
poston@msu.edu
POSTON, Kyle .... 619-574-6909.. 57 E
kposton@pacificcollege.edu
POSTON, Linda, K .... 845-675-4434 337 B
linda.poston@nyack.edu
POSTON, Michael, J ..... 336-316-2178 357 C
mposton@guilford.edu
POSTON, Muriel .... 909-621-8217.. 59 F
dean_faculty@pitzer.edu
POSTON, R. Stephen .... 704-233-8194 373 C
poston@wingate.edu
POSTUPACK,
Mary Frances .... 570-422-7920 430 F
mpostupack@esu.edu
POTASH, David .... 773-481-8175 142 D
dpotash@ccc.edu
POTEET, Tanya, J .... 614-236-6408 378 H
tpoteet@capital.edu
POTEETE-YOUNG,
Lanette .... 847-628-1097 149 A
lpoteete-young@judsonu.edu
POTEMPA, John .... 708-656-8000 153 G
john.potempa@morton.edu
POTEMPA, Kathleen, M 734-764-7185 251 C
potempa@umich.edu
POTERALA, Michael, R . 301-405-4942 219 D
poterala@umd.edu
POTH, Jean, C .... 978-556-3624 232 E
jpoth@necc.mass.edu
POTIER, Descatur .... 912-358-4154 131 A
potierd@savannahstate.edu
POTOCZAK, Mel .... 978-762-4000 232 D
mpotocza@northshore.edu
POTOKA, Lisa .... 913-758-6120 191 I
Lisa.Potoka@stmary.edu
POTRAFKA, Mark .... 573-341-4209 284 C
markp@mst.edu
POTRATZ, Mark .... 314-539-5178 281 H
mpotratz1@stlcc.edu
POTTEBAUM, Kevin ...... 712-274-5179 181 C
pottebaumk@morningside.edu
POTTEIGER, Jeffrey .... 616-331-7207 243 E
potteigj@gvsu.edu
POTTER, Adam .... 207-326-4771 211 G
adam.potter@mma.edu
POTTER, Alan .... 919-573-5350 368 H
POTTER, Aron .... 620-252-7005 186 C
potter.aron@coffeyville.edu
POTTER, Barbara .... 618-252-5400 159 F
barb.potter@sic.edu
POTTER, Billy .... 509-332-2706 521 F
billy.potter@sfcc.spokane.edu
POTTER, Cathryn, C ..... 848-932-7520 307 B
cathryn.potter@ssw.rutgers.edu
POTTER, Cheryl, J .... 704-406-4269 356 G
cpotter@gardner-webb.edu
POTTER, Cory .... 386-481-2334.. 99 F
potterc@cookman.edu
POTTER, Douglas, E ..... 704-847-5600 369 A
dpotter@ses.edu
POTTER, III, Earl, H ..... 320-308-2122 261 E
president@stcloudstate.edu
POTTER, Gia .... 606-218-5211 201 C
giapotter@upike.edu
POTTER, James .... 406-265-3727 288 A
potterj@msun.edu
POTTER, Jay .... 704-330-4409 361 D
jay.potter@cpcc.edu
POTTER, Jennifer, M .... 609-896-5009 306 A
jpotter@rider.edu
POTTER, Jonathan .... 848-932-8796 307 B
jonathan.potter@rutgers.edu
POTTER, Kay, C .... 205-853-1200.... 5 C
kpotter@jeffstateonline.com
POTTER, Keith .... 541-684-7439 407 I
kpotter@nwcu.edu
POTTER, Mike .... 425-739-8387 523 I
mike.potter@lwtech.edu
POTTER, Monifa .... 340-693-1151 559 B
mpotter@uvi.edu
POTTER, Rachel .... 540-887-7134 510 A
rpotter@mbc.edu
POTTER, Robert, A .... 401-254-3498 442 C
bobpotter@rwu.edu
POTTER, Sarah .... 207-786-6120 209 F
spotter@bates.edu
POTTER, Shawn .... 504-247-1237 207 F
spotter@tulane.edu
POTTER, Stephen, L ..... 336-841-9125 357 E
spotter@highpoint.edu
POTTER, Tammy .... 270-534-3278 197 E
tammy.potter@kctcs.edu
POTTER, Terri, L .... 603-535-2376 299 E
tpotter@plymouth.edu
POTTER, Terry .... 303-315-5830.. 86 G
terence.potter@ucdenver.edu
POTTER, William .... 231-591-2428 242 L
WilliamPotter@ferris.edu
POTTERVELD, Riess ...... 510-649-2410.. 46 E
president@gtu.edu
POTTORFF, JR.,
James, P .... 785-864-3276 191 G
jpottorff@ku.edu
POTTS, Amanda .... 419-267-1364 387 G
apotts@northweststate.edu
POTTS, Carla .... 413-755-4812 233 B
cjpotts@stcc.edu
POTTS, Cassie .... 706-233-7236 131 C
1150mgr@fheg.follett.com
POTTS, Colin .... 404-894-5551 125 D
colin.potts@cc.gatech.edu
POTTS, David, E .... 334-683-5102.... 5 D
dpotts@judson.edu
POTTS, Edward, J .... 215-871-6500 432 E
edpotts@com.edu
POTTS, Greg .... 215-951-2700 432 F
pottsg@philau.edu
POTTS, Greg .... 302-736-2529.. 94 E
greg.potts@wesley.edu
POTTS, Jason .... 617-928-4516 234 D
jpotts@mountida.edu
POTTS, Jonathan .... 412-397-5291 434 B
potts@rmu.edu
POTTS, Lawrence, C ..... 507-933-7529 256 A
cpotts@gustavus.edu
POTTS, Marcia .... 828-726-2471 360 F
mpotts@cccti.edu
POTTS, Nacole .... 828-884-8249 355 A
pottsna@brevard.edu
POTTS, Steven .... 310-506-4749.. 58 H
steve.potts@pepperdine.edu
POTTS, Teresa .... 912-443-5730 131 B
tpotts@savannahtech.edu
POTTS, Tim .... 662-915-7234 270 G
tapotts@olemiss.edu
POTVIN, David .... 601-968-5904 266 F
dpotvin@belhaven.edu
POTVIN, Martha .... 406-994-4371 287 G
mpotvin@montana.edu
POTVIN, Terrence .... 313-845-9760 243 I
tpotvin@hfcc.edu
POTVIN-GIORDANO,
Claudine .... 518-629-7451 328 D
c.potvingiordano@hvcc.edu
POU, Patricia .... 618-931-0600 160 B
patricia.pou@swic.edu
POUDRIER-AARONSON,
Lucinda .... 508-999-8145 228 H
lp.aaronson@umassd.edu
POUGET, Nicole .... 307-855-2332 545 a
npouget@cwc.edu
POULSEN, Chase .... 540-985-8490 509 D
crpoulsen@jchs.edu
POULTER, Patricia, S .... 470-578-6742 127 M
ppoulter@kennesaw.edu
POUNCIL, Matais .... 408-741-2136.. 76 F
matais.pouncil@westvalley.edu
POUNDS, Dennis, J ...... 304-462-4125 532 G
dennis.pounds@glenville.edu
POURCIAU, Lester .... 225-771-2680 207 A
lester_pourciau@subr.edu
POURCIAU, Lester, A ... 225-771-2680 206 K
lester_pourciau@sus.edu
POURE, Charles .... 480-726-4140.. 14 K
Charles.Poure@cgc.edu
POUREETEZADI, Sasan . 480-461-7840.. 15 A
sasan.poureetezadi@mesacc.edu
POURHAMIDI, Jaleh .... 702-968-1652 296 D
jpourhamidi@roseman.edu
POURIER, Arlis .... 605-455-6018 452 L
apourier@olc.edu
POURIER, Marilyn .... 605-455-6045 452 L
mpourier@olc.edu
POURIET-DE LA CRUZ,
Zacarias .... 787-480-2470 551 H
zpoueriet@sanjuanciudadpatria.com
POURZANJANI, Omid ... 714-895-8707.. 40 C
opourzanjani@gwc.cccd.edu
POUZAR, Sharree .... 513-721-7944 382 K
spouzar@gbs.edu
POVENTUD, Irem .... 787-841-2000 555 F
ipoventud@pucpr.edu
POWAZEK, Jack .... 310-825-7286.. 71 D
powazek@facnet.ucla.edu
POWEL, Wayne .... 814-472-3004 434 F
wpowel@francis.edu
POWELL, Adriane .... 309-556-1355 148 A
apowell@iwu.edu
POWELL, Alex .... 617-585-1103 234 H
alex.powell@necmusic.edu
POWELL, Andrew, L ..... 717-361-1000 418 B
powella@etown.edu
POWELL, Carl .... 734-487-1491 242 J
crpowell@emich.edu
POWELL, Charmaine ..... 502-447-1000 199 G
cpowell@spencerian.edu
POWELL, Chris .... 661-362-2208.. 53 F
cpowell@masters.edu
POWELL, Cody, J .... 513-529-7070 386 K
powellcj@miamioh.edu
POWELL, Curtis, N .... 518-276-6359 339 D
powelc2@rpi.edu
POWELL, Daniel .... 307-778-1157 546 F
dpowell@lccc.wy.edu
POWELL, Darrin .... 270-259-1540 195 K
darrin.powell@kctcs.edu
POWELL, David, M .... 269-964-6653 252 I
dave.powell@wmich.edu
POWELL, Deborah .... 301-447-5840 217 D
dpowell@msmary.edu

PRESCOD-CAESAR, Pamela ... 610-328-8397 436 A ppresco1@swarthmore.edu

PRESCOTT, Angel ... 785-738-9008 190 A aprescott@ncktc.edu

PRESCOTT, Herman ... 202-274-5072 .. 97 B tprescott@udc.edu

PRESCOTT, Jay, B ... 515-263-2890 178 H jprescott@grandview.edu

PRESCOTT, Loren, D ... 570-408-4000 440 B loren.prescott@wilkes.edu

PRESCOTT, Patricia, M . 516-671-0439 352 D pprescot@webb.edu

PRESCOTT, Roy ... 509-467-1727 523 E rprescott@interface.edu

PRESENT, Melissa ... 212-678-8820 329 H mepresent@jtsa.edu

PRESENT, Wendy ... 716-338-1070 329 E wendypresent@mail.sunyjcc.edu

PRESLEY, Alan ... 281-649-3446 475 B apresley@hbu.edu

PRESLEY, Brian ... 276-935-4349 504 L bpresley@asl.edu

PRESLEY, Dana ... 865-882-4567 463 F

PRESLEY, Doretha ... 601-977-4461 270 F dpresley@tougaloo.edu

PRESLEY, Jody ... 662-720-7299 269 D djpresleys@nemcc.edu

PRESNELL, Angela ... 317-788-3211 173 I presnella@uindy.edu

PRESNELL, Deena ... 509-313-6803 522 L presnell@gonzaga.edu

PRESNELL, Mark ... 847-491-3707 155 D mark.presnell@northwestern.edu

PRESNELL, Sam ... 828-766-1225 364 A spresnell@mayland.edu

PRESS, Andrew ... 714-533-3946 .. 36 D andrew@calums.edu

PRESS, Jim ... 231-995-1327 248 C jpress@nmc.edu

PRESSER, Art ... 800-290-4226 457 A apresser@hchs.edu

PRESSEY, Natalie ... 212-229-5660 334 C presseyn@newschool.edu

PRESSIMONE, J. Michael ... 314-889-1419 275 B mpressimone@fontbonne.edu

PRESSLEY, Dan ... 706-754-7791 129 B dpressley@northgatech.edu

PRESSLEY, Pamela ... 510-231-5000 .. 48 R

PRESSMAN, Avraham ... 570-346-1747 440 G

PRESSON, Mark, A ... 563-588-8000 178 E mpresson@emmaus.edu

PRESSWOOD, Kristy ... 386-506-3822 101 I presswk@DaytonaState.edu

PRESSWOOD, Theresa .. 281-283-2015 491 E presswood@uhcl.edu

PREST, Stacy ... 509-527-4294 527 H stacy.prest@wwcc.edu

PRESTA, James ... 847-970-4869 162 G jpresta@usml.edu

PRESTA, James ... 847-970-4869 162 G jpresta@udml.edu

PRESTAMO, Anne ... 305-348-5726 114 G anne.prestamo@fiu.edu

PRESTBY, Tony ... 310-434-4271 .. 65 B prestby_tony@smc.edu

PRESTFELDT, Carl, F ... 270-809-3472 198 I cprestfeldt@murraystate.edu

PRESTON, April ... 615-366-4404 461 B april.preston@tbr.edu

PRESTON, Daniel ... 503-883-2294 406 I dpreston@linfield.edu

PRESTON, Elizabeth ... 413-572-5201 230 F epreston@westfield.ma.edu

PRESTON, James ... 312-329-4140 153 C james.preston@moody.edu

PRESTON, James ... 559-925-3146 .. 76 C jamespreston@whccd.edu

PRESTON, Jeffrey, H ... 912-279-5751 123 B jpreston@ccga.edu

PRESTON, Jennifer ... 270-831-9804 196 C jennifer.preston@kctcs.edu

PRESTON, Joanne ... 541-552-7672 409 G prestonj@sou.edu

PRESTON, Jon ... 470-578-3545 127 M jprest20@kennesaw.edu

PRESTON, Karen ... 770-426-2688 128 C kpreston@life.edu

PRESTON, Keely ... 303-546-5283 .. 84 B kpreston@naropa.edu

PRESTON, Kenneth, G .. 330-972-8254 392 H kpreston@uakron.edu

PRESTON, Kenneth, G .. 330-972-7845 392 H kpreston@uakron.edu

PRESTON, Laura, C ... 443-412-2438 215 D lpreston@harford.edu

PRESTON, Lisa ... 212-229-5667 334 C lisa.preston@newschool.edu

PRESTON, Marisol ... 904-256-7663 106 Q mpresto1@ju.edu

PRESTON, Mindy ... 903-823-3198 484 D mindy.preston@texarkanacollege.edu

PRESTON, Robert ... 240-567-5327 217 B robert.preston@montgomerycollege.edu

PRESTON, Sarah ... 440-684-6073 394 G spreston@ursuline.edu

PRESTON, Thomas ... 302-857-7749 .. 93 E tpreston@desu.edu

PRESTON, Toni ... 937-708-5703 395 E kpreston@wilberforce.edu

PRESTON, Travis ... 661-255-1050 .. 31 B tpreston@calarts.edu

PRESTWICH, Aaron ... 303-404-5332 .. 82 J aaron.prestwich@frontrange.edu

PRETTI, Janet ... 541-888-1673 410 A jpretti@socc.edu

PRETTO, Felix ... 212-594-4000 349 J fpretto@tcicollege.edu

PRETTY, Keith, A ... 989-837-4203 248 D pretty@northwood.edu

PRETTY ON TOP, Dionne ... 406-638-3104 286 I prettyontop@lbhc.edu

PRETTYMAN, Ronald ... 812-237-4089 167 E ron.prettyman@indstate.edu

PRETZAT, Julie ... 315-312-2285 346 A julie.pretzat@oswego.edu

PREUS, Camille ... 541-278-5950 404 J cpreus@bluecc.edu

PREUSS, Gene ... 713-222-5308 491 F preussg@uhd.edu

PREUSS, Timothy ... 949-214-3286 .. 42 B timothy.preuss@cui.edu

PREUSZ, Mike ... 864-644-5048 449 B mpreusz@swu.edu

PREVAUX, Steven, D ... 813-974-1669 116 B prevaux@usf.edu

PREVETT, Daniel ... 912-583-3178 121 H dprevett@bpc.edu

PREVITA, Chris ... 617-739-1700 234 I cprevita@aii.edu

PREVOST, Blair ... 903-923-2364 473 I bprevost@etbu.edu

PREVOST, Emily ... 903-923-2074 473 I eprevost@etbu.edu

PREVOST, Suzanne, S .. 205-348-1040 .... 8 E suzanne.prevost@ua.edu

PREVOST-SCHULTZ, Justin ... 773-244-6263 154 G jprevost@northpark.edu

PREWETT, Nick ... 573-882-6200 283 H prewettn@missouri.edu

PREWITT, Michael ... 304-696-3765 532 H prewitta@marshall.edu

PREWITT, Steve ... 615-966-5804 458 C steve.prewitt@lipscomb.edu

PREWITT-FREILINO, Paul ... 508-286-3621 238 B ir@wheatoncollege.edu

PREZANT, Robert, S ... 973-655-5108 304 A prezantr@mail.montclair.edu

PRIBBENOW, Dean ... 608-663-2200 536 A DPribbenow@edgewood.edu

PRIBBENOW, Paul, C ... 612-330-1212 253 K president@augsburg.edu

PRIBULSKY, Christopher ... 814-262-3824 429 K cpribulsky@pennhighlands.edu

PRIBYL, Kim ... 319-399-8000 176 G kpribyl@coe.edu

PRICCI, Erica ... 570-955-1461 422 G priccie@lackawanna.edu

PRICE, Adrienne ... 909-274-5417 .. 54 J aprice@mtsac.edu

PRICE, Alan ... 805-965-0581 .. 64 N aprice3@sbcc.edu

PRICE, Alan Paul ... 262-335-5203 541 E paul.price@uwc.edu

PRICE, Angie, C ... 423-775-7269 455 F aprice6832@bryan.edu

PRICE, Bill ... 540-231-4025 507 D

PRICE, Bryan ... 540-458-8184 519 A bprice@wlu.edu

PRICE, Cecil, D ... 336-758-5218 372 G price@wfu.edu

PRICE, Chad, P ... 208-496-1260 137 F pricec@byui.edu

PRICE, Cynthia, J ... 206-281-2179 526 D cprice@spu.edu

PRICE, Danny ... 706-368-5644 121 E dprice@berry.edu

PRICE, David, E ... 706-778-8500 130 B dprice2@piedmont.edu

PRICE, Dawne ... 402-494-2311 291 M dprice@thenicc.edu

PRICE, Donna ... 931-221-7907 461 C priced@apsu.edu

PRICE, Douglas ... 918-595-7853 403 A douglas.price@tulsac.edu

PRICE, Elizabeth ... 254-647-3234 480 G eprice@rangercollege.edu

PRICE, Gary ... 541-259-5808 406 J priceg@linnbenton.edu

PRICE, Gordon ... 541-383-7592 404 K gprice@cocc.edu

PRICE, Greg ... 334-670-3507 .... 8 A wgprice@troy.edu

PRICE, Gregory, N ... 405-466-3275 398 E gnprice@langston.edu

PRICE, Irene, L ... 517-750-1200 250 F iprice@arbor.edu

PRICE, James ... 706-771-4096 121 B jprice@augustatech.edu

PRICE, James, B ... 610-436-3063 432 B jprice@wcupa.edu

PRICE, Jason ... 806-457-4200 474 E jprice@fpctx.edu

PRICE, Jennifer ... 518-262-5679 314 I pricej@mail.amc.edu

PRICE, Jennifer ... 717-358-2974 420 D jmprice@hacc.edu

PRICE, Jerry ... 714-997-6721 .. 38 B jprice@chapman.edu

PRICE, Jill ... 715-365-4531 543 G jmrjenovich@nicoletcollege.edu

PRICE, June, M ... 269-471-3211 239 D madrigal@andrews.edu

PRICE, Kendrick ... 252-493-7627 364 H kprice@email.pittcc.edu

PRICE, Kevin, L ... 208-496-1705 137 F priceke@byui.edu

PRICE, Leigh ... 912-478-5211 126 B llprice@georgiasouthern.edu

PRICE, Linda, A ... 301-784-5000 213 C lprice@allegany.edu

PRICE, Linda, L ... 812-877-8165 172 C price@rose-hulman.edu

PRICE, Lisa ... 618-437-5321 156 I price@rlc.edu

PRICE, JR., Major ... 419-755-9009 387 E mprice@ncstatecollege.edu

PRICE, Marla ... 717-755-2300 412 I maprice@aii.edu

PRICE, Megan ... 864-388-8019 447 E mprice@lander.edu

PRICE, Nicole, G ... 617-973-1101 237 B nprice@suffolk.edu

PRICE, Nikol ... 623-935-8087 .. 14 L nikol.price@estrellamountain.edu

PRICE, Pam ... 609-586-4800 303 D pricep@mccc.edu

PRICE, Philip ... 919-718-7214 361 C pprice@cccc.edu

PRICE, Robin ... 304-637-1243 529 I pricer@dewv.edu

PRICE, Ron ... 770-975-4000 122 H

PRICE, Ronald, N ... 708-216-9949 151 E rprice@lumc.edu

PRICE, Sarah ... 270-686-4501 197 A sarah.price@kctcs.edu

PRICE, Vincent ... 215-898-7227 437 I provost@upenn.edu

PRICE, Viviane ... 303-220-1200 .. 79 G viviane.price@cffp.edu

PRICE, W. Craig ... 504-282-4455 206 C cprice@nobts.edu

PRICE, William ... 432-552-2170 495 F price_w@utpb.edu

PRICE-PERRY, Cassandra, F ... 901-334-5821 459 B cfperry@memphisseminary.edu

PRICE-SEEGER, Marjorie ... 406-377-9406 286 F mpriceseeger@dawson.edu

PRICHARD, Patricia, A . 503-517-1806 411 C paprichard@westernseminary.edu

PRICHETT, Gordon ... 781-239-4428 222 E prichett@babson.edu

PRICHETT, Robert ... 404-756-4714 120 H rprichett@atlm.edu

PRICKEN, Stephanie ... 610-660-1379 434 G spricken@sju.edu

PRIDA, Jonas ... 802-773-5900 501 G jonas.prida@csj.edu

PRIDAL, Cathryn ... 816-501-3758 272 E cathryn.pridal@avila.edu

PRIDDY, Don ... 618-985-2828 148 G donpriddy@jalc.edu

PRIDDY, Don ... 618-985-3741 148 G donpriddy@jalc.edu

PRIDDY, Michele ... 615-297-7545 455 A priddym@aquinascollege.edu

PRIDE, Nicole ... 336-334-7940 370 B npride@ncat.edu

PRIDEAUX, Debra, K ... 785-628-4430 187 A dprideau@fhsu.edu

PRIDEAUX, Leslie, J ... 319-273-2355 176 A leslie.prideaux@uni.edu

PRIEB, Arnie ... 559-453-2128 .. 45 E apprieb@fresno.edu

PRIES, Lonnie ... 734-995-7310 241 F lonnie.pries@cuaa.edu

PRIEST, Barry ... 910-879-5579 360 C bpriest@bladencc.edu

PRIEST, Catherine ... 856-351-2624 308 B cpriest@salemcc.edu

PRIEST, Jeffrey, M ... 803-641-3755 450 C jeffp@usca.edu

PRIEST, Margaret ... 313-831-5200 242 K mpriest@etseminary.edu

PRIEST, Michelle ... 714-546-7600 .. 40 B

PRIETO, Adanid ... 787-766-1717 556 A a_prieto@suagm.edu

PRIETO, Beth ... 603-645-9724 298 H b.prieto@snhu.edu

PRIETO, Diana ... 970-491-5836 .. 81 D diana.prieto@colostate.edu

PRIETO, Diana ... 970-491-6947 .. 81 D diana.prieto@colostate.edu

PRIETO, Eduardo ... 803-323-2191 451 I prietoe@winthrop.edu

PRIGAL, Helena ... 212-431-2318 335 G Helena.Prigal@nyls.edu

PRIGG, Benson ... 256-726-7186 .... 6 C bprigg@oakwood.edu

PRIGGE, Amy ... 419-772-3961 388 I a-prigge@onu.edu

PRIGGIE, Richard, W ... 309-794-7213 139 K richardpriggie@augustana.edu

PRIHODA, Belinda ... 903-730-4890 476 L bprihoda@jarvis.edu

PRILL, Kristina, L ... 518-244-6001 340 A prillk@sage.edu

PRILLELTENSKY, Isaac .. 305-284-3505 118 A isaacp@miami.edu

PRIMAVERA, Louis, H .. 631-665-1600 350 C louis.primavera@touro.edu

PRIMERANO, Jessica ... 704-971-8500 355 J jprimerano@charlottelaw.edu

PRIMIANO, Leonard ... 610-902-8330 414 B leonard.primiano@cabrini.edu

PRIMICH, Tracy ... 573-341-4011 284 C primicht@mst.edu

PRIMO, John ... 405-733-7356 401 L jprimo@rose.edu

PRIMOFF, Mark ... 845-758-7412 315 G primoff@bard.edu

PRIMROSE, Bruce ... 909-599-5433 .. 50 H bprimrose@lifepacific.edu

PRIMUS, Joanna ... 303-360-4740 .. 81 I Joanna.Primus@CCAurora.edu

PRIMUS, Lester ... 860-906-5050 .. 89 A lprimus@ccc.commnet.edu

PRINCE, Bobby, A ... 901-678-1335 462 B baprince@memphis.edu

PRINCE, Christine, B ... 215-885-2360 425 C cprince@manor.edu

PRINCE, Iris ... 910-892-3178 357 D iprince@heritagebiblecollege.edu

PRINCE, James ... 916-278-6331 .. 34 E james.prince@csus.edu

PRINCE, James, E ... 269-337-7225 244 I James.Prince@kzoo.edu

PRINCE, Jeff ... 510-642-9494 .. 70 K jprince@berkeley.edu

PRINCE, Joan, M ... 414-229-3101 540 A jprince@uwm.edu

PRINCE, Judith ... 864-552-4243 451 A jprince@uscupstate.edu

PRINCE, Ken ... 812-866-7051 166 E princek@hanover.edu

PRINCE, Nate ... 661-362-2200 .. 53 F nprince@masters.edu

PRINCE, T. Greg ... 410-546-6938 220 E tgprince@salisbury.edu

PRINCESS-KELLY, Melody ... 901-369-0835 .. 96 H

PRINE, Shane ... 615-794-4254 460 A sprine@omorecollege.edu

PRINEAS, Matthew ... 240-684-2830 220 A matthew.prineas@umuc.edu

PRINGLE, Eboni ... 330-672-8700 384 H epringle@kent.edu

PRINGLE, Ernest ... 803-641-3345 450 C ernestp@usca.edu

PRINGLE, Nancy, E ... 607-274-3836 328 H npringle@ithaca.edu

PRINGLE, Randy ... 903-923-2233 473 I rpringle@etbu.edu

PRINZ, Lynn, L ... 812-941-2265 169 A mprinz@ius.edu

PRIOLEAU, Darwin ... 585-395-5806 345 A dpriolea@brockport.edu

PRIOLEAU, Florence ... 202-806-2250 .. 96 B florence.prioleau@howard.edu

PRIOLEAU, Florence ... 202-806-2650 .. 96 B florence.prioleau@howard.edu

PRIOLO, Bob ... 616-949-5300 241 G bob.priolo@cornerstone.edu

PRIOR, Roberta ... 203-285-2209 .. 89 B rprior@gwcc.commnet.edu

PRISCO, Anne .... 201-559-6022 302 I
priscoa@felician.edu
PRISELAC, Thomas .... 310-423-5711.. 37 K
PRITCHARD, Brett .... 256-215-4254.... 2 G
bpritchard@cacc.edu
PRITCHARD, Gary .... 562-860-2451.. 37 L
gpritchard@cerritos.edu
PRITCHARD, Lamar ...... 713-743-1253 491 D
flpritchard@uh.edu
PRITCHARD, Lisa .... 636-481-3160 276 E
lpritcha@jeffco.edu
PRITCHARD, Mandie .... 541-440-4600 410 E
mandie.pritchard@umpqua.edu
PRITCHARD, Michael .... 301-846-2417 214 I
mpritchard@frederick.edu
PRITCHARD, Rod .... 319-399-8605 176 G
rpritcha@coe.edu
PRITCHARD, Sarah, M . 847-491-7640 155 D
spritchard@northwestern.edu
PRITCHETT, Alondrea, J 334-229-4737.... 1 D
apritchett@alasu.edu
PRITCHETT, Beth .... 304-327-4139 532 D
bpritchett@bluefieldstate.edu
PRITCHETT, Donald .... 518-262-5521 314 I
pritchettd@mail.amc.edu
PRITCHETT, H. Franklin 678-839-6582 133 F
fpritche@westga.edu
PRITCHETT, Marie .... 586-445-7315 246 A
pritchettm@macomb.edu
PRITCHETT, Terry .... 325-649-8608 475 F
tpritchett@hputx.edu
PRITTING, Shannon ...... 315-792-7245 348 D
shannon.pritting@sunyit.edu
PRITTS, Barry .... 304-473-8040 534 G
pritts@wvwc.edu
PRITZ, Stephen, J .... 352-392-1374 115 D
spritz@ufl.edu
PRITZKER, Barry .... 518-580-5654 342 I
bpritzke@skidmore.edu
PRIVOTT, Ashley, E ...... 540-568-6234 509 C
privotae@jmu.edu
PROBST, Laura, K .... 218-299-4642 255 B
lprobst@cord.edu
PROBST, Robert .... 513-556-9808 393 B
robert.probst@uc.edu
PROBSTFELD, Carol, F . 941-752-5201 114 B
probstc@scf.edu
PROCARIO-FOLEY, Carl 914-633-2632 328 F
cprocariofoley@iona.edu
PROCELL, Derrick .... 985-448-7941 203 G
derrick.procell@fletcher.edu
PROCH, Margaret, P ..... 410-323-6211 214 G
Mproch@faiththeological.org
PROCHNOW, Allen .... 262-243-4303 241 F
allen.prochnow@cuw.edu
PROCHNOW, Allen, J ... 262-243-5700 535 I
allen.prochnow@cuw.edu
PROCTER, Everett .... 949-794-9090.. 68 F
eprocter@stanbridge.edu
PROCTER, Ken .... 478-445-4441 125 A
ken.procter@gcsu.edu
PROCTER, Sharon .... 313-664-1487 241 D
sprocter@collegeforcreativestudies.edu
PROCTOR, Avis .... 954-201-2202.. 99 G
aproctor@broward.edu
PROCTOR, Catherine ..... 732-247-5241 304 B
cproctor@nbts.edu
PROCTOR, Jon .... 303-797-5092.. 79 A
jon.proctor@arapahoe.edu
PROCTOR, Kelly .... 864-388-8398 447 E
kproctor@lander.edu
PROCTOR, Kristen .... 508-854-7552 232 F
kproctor@qcc.mass.edu
PROCTOR, Matt .... 417-626-1234 280 B
pres@occ.edu
PROCTOR, Michael, A .. 520-626-5531.. 18 E
mproctor@arizona.edu
PROCTOR, Richard, L .... 336-322-2243 364 G
Lee.Proctor@piedmontcc.edu
PROCTOR, William, L ... 904-819-6210 102 P
proctorw@flagler.edu
PROFETA, Patricia, C .... 772-462-7590 106 F
pprofeta@irsc.edu
PROFFITT, Beth .... 717-291-3871 418 J
beth.proffitt@fandm.edu
PROFFITT, Roger .... 620-227-9422 186 F
rproffitt@dc3.edu
PROFITT, Aaron .... 513-721-7944 382 K
aprofitt@gbs.edu
PROHASKA, Thomas, R 703-993-1918 507 K
tprohask@gmu.edu
PROHN, Deborah, W .... 716-888-2919 317 H
prohnd@canisius.edu
PROISY, Alize .... 252-222-6240 361 A
proisya@carteret.edu
PROITE, Rosanne .... 512-245-2931 489 C
rp45@txstate.edu
PROKOP, Jessica .... 413-755-4529 233 B
japrokop@stcc.edu
PROKOP, Paul .... 530-754-8568.. 71 A
pjprokop@ucdavis.edu
PROKOVICH, Jeffrey, D 724-458-3846 419 F
jdprokovich@gcc.edu
PROM, Cynthia .... 701-774-4259 375 C
cynthia.prom@willistonstate.edu
PROMADES,
Frederick, C .... 401-341-2117 442 D
promadef@salve.edu
PROMIN, Christine .... 704-216-3541 365 F
christine.promin@rccc.edu
PROPER, Sherry .... 808-689-2770 136 A
sproper@hawaii.edu
PROPST, Jennifer .... 828-448-6051 367 B
jpropst@wpcc.edu
PROPST, Joan, L .... 304-457-6201 529 C
propstjl@ab.edu
PROPST, Kent .... 660-248-6238 272 N
kpropst@centralmethodist.edu
PROPST, William, S ..... 310-794-6027.. 71 D
wpropst@finance.ucla.edu
PROSCIA, Domenic .... 718-429-6600 352 A
domenic.procsia@vaughn.edu
PROSPER, Yamilette ..... 787-891-0925 553 E
yprosper@aguadilla.inter.edu
PROSSER, Deborah .... 678-717-3466 133 A
deborah.prosser@ung.edu
PROSTANO, Laura .... 914-323-7124 331 J
laura.prostano@mville.edu
PROTAS, Elizabeth, J .... 409-772-3001 495 E
ejprotas@utmb.edu
PROTHERO, Charles, L . 570-945-8015 422 B
charlie.prothero@keystone.edu
PROTO, Bill .... 516-877-3680 314 F
proto@adelphi.edu
PROTO, Matthew .... 207-859-4802 210 A
matthew.proto@colby.edu
PROUDFIT, Ann .... 216-987-5892 381 A
ann.proudfit@tri-c.edu
PROUDFOOT,
Donald, W .... 903-510-2975 491 A
dpro@tjc.edu
PROUDFOOT,
Michael, A .... 520-621-8747.. 18 E
tproudfoot@email.arizona.edu
PROULX, David, R .... 717-291-3993 418 J
dave.proulx@fandm.edu
PROULX, Dennis .... 802-468-1249 503 G
dennis.proulx@castleton.edu
PROULX, Diane .... 402-399-2456 289 I
dproulx@csm.edu
PROUSE, Margaret, R ... 302-857-1065.. 94 A
mprouse@dtcc.edu
PROUT, Wilson .... 716-926-8910 327 F
wprout@hilbert.edu
PROUTY, Steve .... 941-752-5205 114 B
proutys@scf.edu
PROVAN, Amy .... 410-532-5379 217 F
aprovan@ndm.edu
PROVENCHER,
Catherine, A .... 603-862-1622 299 A
catherine.provencher@usnh.edu
PROVENCHER, Susan ... 603-668-6660 298 A
PROVENCIO-VASQUEZ,
Elias .... 915-747-8217 494 B
eprovenciovasquez@utep.edu
PROVENZA, Joseph, S . 904-819-6359 102 P
jprovenza@flagler.edu
PROVENZANO, Peter ..... 248-341-2102 248 E
pmproven@oaklandcc.edu
PROVINE, Rick, E .... 765-658-4435 165 G
provine@depauw.edu
PROVOST, David, J ...... 802-865-6400 501 F
djprovost@champlain.edu
PROVOST, Dawn .... 337-482-6391 208 F
dawn@louisiana.edu
PROVOST, Kathryn .... 802-485-2125 502 G
kathrynp@norwich.edu
PRUCE, Dora, J .... 216-397-4565 384 F
dpruce@jcu.edu
PRUCHNICKI, Jennifer .. 580-581-2209 397 A
jpruchni@cameron.edu
PRUCNAL, James, R ..... 256-549-8242.... 3 N
jprucnal@gadsdenstate.edu
PRUDE, Regina .... 615-256-1463 454 G
rprude@abcnash.edu
PRUDEN, Elizabeth .... 513-487-1232 392 F
elizabeth.pruden@myunion.edu
PRUDHOMME,
Harvey, J .... 503-370-6348 411 D
hprudhom@willamette.edu
PRUE, Stephen .... 785-832-6644 187 F
stephen.prue@bie.edu
PRUEFER, Peter .... 218-723-5924 255 A
ppruefer@css.edu
PRUETT, Diana .... 662-243-2675 267 C
dpruett@eastms.edu
PRUETT, Karen .... 910-521-6270 371 D
karen.pruett@uncp.edu
PRUETT, Robert, R .... 919-658-7760 369 B
rpruett@umo.edu
PRUETT, Tim .... 740-245-7358 394 D
tpruett@rio.edu
PRUITT, Aaron .... 541-684-7217 407 I
apruitt@nwcu.edu
PRUITT, Betty .... 205-391-2251.... 7 A
bpruitt@sheltonstate.edu
PRUITT, Beverly .... 305-284-2842 118 A
b.pruitt@miami.edu
PRUITT, Dennis, A .... 803-777-4172 450 B
dpruitt@sc.edu
PRUITT, Edith .... 256-726-7039.... 6 C
epruitt@oakwood.edu
PRUITT, George, A .... 609-984-1105 308 H
gpruitt@tesc.edu
PRUITT, Glenell .... 903-730-4890 476 L
gpruitt@jarvis.edu
PRUITT, Jason .... 470-239-3103 133 A
jason.pruitt@ung.edu
PRUITT, Karl .... 205-929-6348.... 5 E
kpruitt@lawsonstate.edu
PRUITT, Leah, L .... 864-587-4225 449 D
pruittl@smcsc.edu
PRUITT, Samory, T .... 205-348-8376.... 8 E
samory.pruitt@ua.edu
PRUITT, Steven .... 561-237-7834 108 E
spruitt@lynn.edu
PRUNTY, Bonnie, S ...... 607-274-3141 328 H
bprunty@ithaca.edu
PRUNTY, Kathleen, A ... 909-869-3380.. 32 F
kaprunty@cpp.edu
PRUS, Mark .... 607-753-2207 345 C
mark.prus@cortland.edu
PRUSANK, Diane .... 413-572-5374 230 F
dprusank@westfield.ma.edu
PRUSHA, Tammy .... 641-269-4481 178 I
prushatd@grinnell.edu
PRUSHA, Todd .... 319-398-5565 180 J
tprusha@kirkwood.edu
PRUSKOWSKI, Nancy ... 717-871-4086 431 E
nancy.pruskowski@millersville.edu
PRUSS, Julie, A .... 585-395-2361 345 A
jpruss@brockport.edu
PRUSSIN, Shari .... 212-217-4000 325 C
shari_prussin@fitnyc.edu
PRY, George .... 412-809-5100 433 D
pry.georgel@pti.edu
PRYJMAK, Myron .... 718-409-7311 348 C
mpryjmak@sunymaritime.edu
PRYLES, Kathryn .... 508-588-9100 232 A
PRYLO, Caelynn .... 518-743-2238 347 E
pryloc@sunyacc.edu
PRYOR, Benjamin .... 602-943-2311.. 18 K
Ben.Pryor@west.edu
PRYOR, Douglas .... 305-809-3184 104 A
douglas.pryor@fkcc.edu
PRYOR, Kim, A .... 336-342-4261 365 E
pryork@rockinghamcc.edu
PRYOR, LaShawne .... 302-857-6055.. 93 E
lpryor@desu.edu
PRYOR, Marcus .... 704-991-0278 366 D
mpryor7642@stanly.edu
PRYOR, Raymond, G .... 570-208-5828 422 D
rgpryor@kings.edu
PRYOR-HARRIS, Holli ... 312-567-3167 147 E
pryor@iit.edu
PRYSTOWSKY, Richard . 517-483-1156 245 I
prystowr@lcc.edu
PRZEKOP, Lisa .... 805-893-3641.. 72 D
lisa.przekop@sa.ucsb.edu
PRZEKURAT, Paris .... 405-422-1442 401 H
przekuratp@redlandscc.edu
PRZYBLYSKI, Jeannene 661-255-1050.. 31 B
jeannene@calarts.edu
PRZYBOROKI, Carol ..... 412-321-8383 414 A
office@bcs.edu
PRZYGOCKI, Ginny .... 989-686-9276 242 I
vlprzygo@delta.edu
PRZYGODA, Melitha, R 203-576-4588.. 92 B
mprzygod@bridgeport.edu
PRZYWARA, Ann Marie 518-580-5765 342 I
aprzywar@skidmore.edu
PRZYWARA, Richard, T 610-430-4156 432 B
rprzywara@wcufoundation.org
PSAILA, Marisa .... 585-475-4932 339 G
mxpdar@rit.edu
PTACEK, Kelly, K .... 402-280-1485 290 B
KellyPtacek@creighton.edu
PTACHIK, Robert, A ...... 646-664-9100 318 B
PUC, Gina .... 413-662-5416 230 C
g.puc@mcla.edu
PUCINE, Richard .... 315-792-5309 333 D
rpucine@mvcc.edu
PUCKETT, Caleb .... 620-431-2820 189 J
cpuckett@neosho.edu
PUCKETT, Christopher .. 303-315-6619.. 86 G
chris.puckett@ucdenver.edu
PUCKETT, Jack .... 252-492-2061 366 G
puckett@vgcc.edu
PUCKETT, Jackie, A ...... 864-488-4585 447 F
jpuckett@limestone.edu
PUCKETT, Jeffrey .... 616-395-7413 244 A
puckett@hope.edu
PUCKETT, Joan .... 812-888-4480 174 F
jpuckett@vinu.edu
PUCKETT-BOLER, Laura 864-503-5194 451 A
lpuckett-boler@uscupstate.edu
PUDDESTER,
Frederick, W .... 413-597-4421 238 E
frederick.w.puddester@williams.edu
PUENTES-GRIFFITH,
Raquel .... 209-954-5061.. 63 D
rpuentes-griffith@deltacollege.edu
PUETT, Debbie .... 828-395-1481 363 D
dpuett@isothermal.edu
PUFFENBARGER, Jess .. 270-534-3504 197 E
jess.puffenbarger@kctcs.edu
PUFHAL, Joy .... 207-780-5512 213 A
jpufhal@usm.maine.edu
PUGEL, Mary, E .... 336-758-3005 372 G
mpugel@wfu.edu
PUGH, Alicina .... 601-979-1325 267 H
alcinia.j.pugh@jsums.edu
PUGH, Benjamin, W ..... 318-670-9302 207 C
bpugh@susla.edu
PUGH, Bill .... 503-581-8600 405 F
bpugh@corban.edu
PUGH, Crystal .... 252-789-0293 363 H
cpugh@martincc.edu
PUGH, SR., Daniel, J ... 979-845-4728 485 C
djpughsr@vpsa.tamu.edu
PUGH, David .... 912-525-5000 130 H
dpugh@scad.edu
PUGH, Jason .... 601-928-6233 268 G
jason.pugh@mgccc.edu
PUGH, Kendra, L .... 804-524-5845 518 C
kpugh@vsu.edu
PUGH, Paul, F .... 610-519-4200 439 A
paul.pugh@villanova.edu
PUGH, Vicki .... 561-803-2012 109 G
viki_pugh@pba.edu
PUGLIESE, Beth .... 408-924-1116.. 36 B
beth.pugliese@sjsu.edu
PUGLIESE, Mike, A .... 918-663-9000 401 F
mikep@plattcollege.org
PUGLIESE, Stephen ...... 814-886-6459 427 B
spugliese@mtaloy.edu
PUGLIESI, Karen, L .... 928-523-9231.. 16 C
Karen.Pugliesi@nau.edu
PUGLISI, Emma .... 978-921-4242 234 B
emma.puglisi@montserrat.edu
PUGLISI, Michael, J ...... 276-944-6662 507 E
mpuglisi@ehc.edu
PUGNAIRE, Michele, P . 508-856-4250 229 B
michele.pugnaire@umassmed.edu
PUHALA, Kimberly .... 617-984-1727 235 H
kpuhala@quincycollege.edu
PUHL WINKLER, Jenn .. 701-777-0729 373 G
jennifer.puhlwinkler@und.edu
PUIG, Juan .... 787-815-0000 557 D
juan.puig@upr.edu
PULAKOS, Joan .... 208-885-6716 139 C
pulakos@uidaho.edu
PULCINI, Brad .... 740-755-7139 378 L
bpulcini@cotc.edu
PULEIO, Samuel, T .... 814-393-2280 430 E
spuleio@clarion.edu
PULIAFICO, Venus .... 216-368-4530 378 J
venus.puliafico@case.edu
PULIAFITO, Carmen, A . 323-442-1900.. 74 D
deanksom@usc.edu
PULICE, Jon .... 814-732-1763 430 G
jpulice@edinboro.edu
PULLEN, Richard, L .... 806-354-6024 467 E
rlpullen@actx.edu
PULLEN, Terri .... 513-862-7761 383 A
terri.pullen@email.gscollege.edu
PULLER, Beverly, J .... 219-785-5337 172 A
bpuller@pnc.edu
PULLEY, Brett .... 757-637-2018 508 C
brett.pulley@hamptonu.edu
PULLEY, Eric .... 618-985-3741 148 G
ericpulley@jalc.edu
PULLEY, Lawrence, B .... 757-221-2891 506 J
larry.pulley@mason.wm.edu
PULLIAM, Camden .... 816-414-3700 278 E
cpulliam@mbts.edu
PULLIAM, DeWayne .... 615-794-4254 460 A
dpulliam@omorecollege.edu
PULLIAM, Joni, L .... 315-792-3344 351 G
jpulliam@utica.edu
PULLIN, Daniel, W .... 405-325-0100 403 I
dpullin@ou.edu
PULLING, David .... 337-550-1390 205 B
dpulling@lsue.edu
PULLIZA, Carmen 787-743-7979 555M
cpulliza@suagm.edu
PULS, Jonathan .... 562-903-4807.. 29 F
jonathan.puls@biola.edu
PULS, Kevin .... 815-967-7329 157 C
kpuls@rockfordcareercollege.edu

PULTRO, Judith .... 239-985-3477 104 G
jpultro@fsw.edu
PULTZ, Stephen, F .... 619-260-4506.. 74 B
spultz@sandiego.edu
PULVER, Chad, A .... 219-866-6154 172 E
pulver@saintjoe.edu
PULVER, Pat .... 315-279-5662 329 K
ppulver@keuka.edu
PULVER, Shayne .... 615-226-3990 458 A
spulver@lincolntech.edu
PUMA, Lynn, M .... 716-878-5509 345 B
pumalm@buffalostate.edu
PUMERANTZ, Philip ..... 909-469-5200.. 76 I
ppumerantz@westernu.edu
PUMPHREY, Dennis ...... 970-351-2245.. 87 A
dennis.pumphrey@unco.edu
PUMROY, B.J .... 304-876-5155 532 I
bpumroy@shepherd.edu
PUNCHELLO-COBOS,
Catharine .... 609-984-1180 308 H
registrar@tesc.edu
PUNCHES, Kathy, M ..... 419-783-2590 381 G
kpunches@defiance.edu
PUNEKY, Warren .... 504-671-6100 203 F
wpunek@dcc.edu
PUNT, David .... 916-577-2200.. 77 F
dpunt@jessup.edu
PUPPALA, Kuldeep .... 973-313-6128 308 C
kuldeep.puppala@shu.edu
PURA, Robert, L .... 413-775-1410 231 E
pura@gcc.mass.edu
PURATICH, Kate .... 253-589-5846 521 B
kate.puratich@cptc.edu
PURCE, Thomas, J .... 610-436-3307 432 B
tpurce@wcupa.edu
PURCE, Thomas, L .... 360-867-6100 522 J
purcel@evergreen.edu
PURCELL, Anthony, B ... 205-934-2297.... 8 F
bpurcell@uab.edu
PURCELL, Brian .... 270-809-2154 198 I
rpurcell@murraystate.edu
PURCELL, Chris, A .... 405-325-4122 403 I
regentspurcell@ou.edu
PURCELL, Francesca ..... 781-239-3117 231 G
fpurcell@massbay.edu
PURCELL, Jeanine .... 716-880-2259 332 B
jp983@medaille.edu
PURCELL, Ladonna, M . 606-783-2323 198 H
l.purcell@moreheadstate.edu
PURCELL, Meredith .... 815-802-8512 149 B
mpurcell@kcc.edu
PURCELL, Ruth .... 724-287-8711 413 G
ruth.purcell@bc3.edu
PURCELL, Satch .... 949-794-9090.. 68 F
spurcell@stanbridge.edu
PURCELL, Stacy, R .... 757-446-6002 507 B
purcellsr@evms.edu
PURCELL, Terri .... 615-327-3927 457 G
purcell@guptoncollege.edu
PURCELL, William .... 412-392-3481 433 F
wpurcell@pointpark.edu
PURDOM, Kirk .... 859-233-8551 200 D
kpurdom@transy.edu
PURDUE-LYNCH,
Barbara .... 201-355-1122 302 I
lynchb@felician.edu
PURDY, Beth .... 502-863-8034 195 A
beth_purdy@georgetowncollege.edu
PURDY, G. Michael .... 212-854-1656 322 F
gmp63@columbia.edu
PURDY, Paulette .... 713-221-2746 491 F
purdyp@uhd.edu
PURDY, Ryan .... 308-535-3720 291 H
purdyr@mpcc.edu
PURECE, Sarita .... 415-257-0137.. 43 D
sarita.purece@dominican.edu
PURI, Anil .... 657-278-2592.. 33 E
apuri@fullerton.edu
PURIFOY, Tangela .... 251-578-1313.... 6 D
tpurifoy@rstc.edu
PURNELL, Rogeair .... 510-986-6941.. 59 B
rpurnell@peralta.edu
PUROHIT, Yasmin, S .... 412-397-5472 434 B
purohit@rmu.edu
PURRINGTON, Kristen .. 603-524-3207 296 L
kpurrington@ccsnh.edu
PURSER, Charles .... 252-335-0821 361 G
charles_purser@albemarle.edu
PURSLEY, Linda .... 617-349-8563 228 B
lpursley@lesley.edu
PURSOO, Eugene .... 718-270-5136 320 C
pursoo@mec.cuny.edu
PURSWANI, Pavan .... 410-337-6403 215 B
pavan.purswani@goucher.edu
PURVIANCE, Chris .... 509-313-5858 522 L
purviance@gonzaga.edu
PURVIS, Anne .... 678-359-5197 126 E
a_purvis@gordonstate.edu
PURVIS, Charlie .... 502-213-7295 196 E
charlie.purvis@kctcs.edu
PURVIS, Donnie .... 817-598-6284 497 A
dpurvis@wc.edu
PURVIS, Kathy .... 254-968-9070 485 A
kpurvis@tarleton.edu
PURVIS-ROBERTS,
Kathleen .... 909-621-8736.. 59 F
kpurvis@jsd.claremont.edu
PURWIN, Lori .... 908-737-4880 303 C
lpurwin@kean.edu
PURYEAR, Margaret ...... 303-352-3038.. 81 J
margaret.puryear@ccd.edu
PURYEAR,
Roberta (Robbi) .... 713-743-8780 491 C
rdpuryea@uh.edu
PUSECKER, Kathleen, L 302-831-8537.. 94 D
klp@udel.edu
PUSEY, Stephen, M ...... 615-248-1258 464 E
spusey@trevecca.edu
PUSHARD, Richard .... 207-941-7003 210 C
pushardr@husson.edu
PUSICH, Ruth .... 630-617-3080 144 G
ruthp@elmhurst.edu
PUSKA, Douglas, P ...... 978-762-4000 232 D
dpuska@northshore.edu
PUSTAY, Pamela, S ...... 330-471-8159 385 G
ppustay@malone.edu
PUSTZ, Charles .... 815-836-5050 150 F
pustzch@lewisu.edu
PUSZCZEWICZ, Tom ..... 517-264-7192 250 B
tpuszcze@sienaheights.edu
PUSZYNSKI, Jan, A ...... 605-394-2493 454 B
jan.puszynski@sdsmt.edu
PUTMAN, Jeffrey .... 718-270-2187 344 D
jeffrey.putman@downstate.edu
PUTMAN, Paul .... 518-736-3622 326 D
pputman@fmcc.suny.edu
PUTMAN, Stephen .... 256-765-4178.... 9 D
jsputman@una.edu
PUTNAM, Diana .... 518-736-3622 326 D
diana.putnam@fmcc.suny.edu
PUTNAM, Jessica, J ..... 641-422-4103 181 E
putnajes@niacc.edu
PUTNAM, Joshua .... 864-977-7669 448 A
joshua.putnam@ngu.edu
PUTNAM, Mark .... 281-756-3500 467 D
mputnam@alvincollege.edu
PUTNAM, Mark, L .... 641-628-5269 176 E
president@central.edu
PUTNAM, Robin .... 701-328-2960 373 F
robin.putnam@ndus.edu
PUTNAM, Timothy, J .... 641-422-4192 181 E
putnatim@niacc.edu
PUTNEY, Luanna .... 209-228-4417.. 71 E
lputney@ucmerced.edu
PUTO, Christopher .... 251-380-3865.... 7 F
cputo@shc.edu
PUTREVU, Sanjay .... 307-766-4194 546 K
sputrevu@uwyo.edu
PUTZKE, Robert .... 406-994-3220 287 G
rputzke@montana.edu
PYDO, Todd .... 715-682-1682 538 D
tpydo@northland.edu
PYE, Christopher .... 973-353-5679 307 C
cpye@rutgers.edu
PYER, Terri .... 831-755-6706.. 46 J
tpyer@hartnell.edu
PYFFEROEN, Michelle ... 507-285-7425 261 D
michelle.pyfferoen@rctc.edu
PYLE, Allison .... 972-708-7552 474 J
gial_alumni@gial.edu
PYLE, Brenda .... 770-962-7580 127 C
bpyle@gwinnetttech.edu
PYLE, Carla, S .... 260-399-7700 174 C
cpyle@sf.edu
PYLE, Elizabeth .... 413-538-2000 234 C
epyle@mtholyoke.edu
PYLE, John .... 507-457-1743 264 B
jpyle@smumn.edu
PYLE, Marsha, A .... 816-235-2010 284 A
pylem@umkc.edu
PYLE, Ray .... 925-229-6842.. 42 C
rpyle@4cd.edu
PYLE, Rowdy .... 816-604-6524 277 G
rowdy.pyle@mcckc.edu
PYLE, Sally .... 701-777-2219 373 G
sally.pyle@und.edu
PYLE, Thomas, C .... 724-847-5566 419 B
tcpyle@geneva.edu
PYLES, Gloria, D .... 803-536-8266 448 H
gpyles@scsu.edu
PYNCHON, Thomas ...... 315-229-5583 341 E
tpynchon@stlawu.edu
PYNES, Penelope, J ...... 336-334-5404 371 C
penelope_pynes@uncg.edu
PYNM, Paula .... 317-578-7353 163 K
PYO, George, F .... 814-472-3014 434 F
gpyo@francis.edu
PYRON, Susan .... 717-337-6542 419 C
spyron@gettysburg.edu

Q

QADER, Mirwais .... 608-246-6198 543 C
mqader@madisoncollege.edu
QAISSAUNEE, Laura, V . 732-224-2756 300 F
lqaissaunee@brookdalecc.edu
QATU, Mohamad .... 734-487-0354 242 J
QI, Feng .... 908-737-3737 303 C
fqi@kean.edu
QIN, Laura .... 860-215-9305.. 90 B
lqin@trcc.commnet.edu
QU, Jianmin .... 617-627-3237 237 C
jianmin.qu@tufts.edu
QU, Yanzhen .... 719-590-6852.. 81 H
yqu@coloradotech.edu
QUACH, Josephine .... 626-472-5121.. 43 F
jquach@esgvrop.org
QUACKENBUSH,
Kent, B .... 303-762-6923.. 82 C
kent.quackenbush@denverseminary.edu
QUACKENBUSH, Robert 509-359-2366 522 C
rquackenbush@ewu.edu
QUADE, Stephanie .... 414-288-1412 537 B
stephanie.quade@marquette.edu
QUAGLIANA, David ...... 423-614-8415 457 M
dquagliana@leeuniversity.edu
QUAID, Randi .... 760-547-1800.. 45 B
rquaid@fst.edu
QUAID-MALTAGLIATI,
Marian .... 805-922-6966.. 26 H
marianqm@hancockcollege.edu
QUAKENBUSH, Win ...... 910-893-1245 355 C
quakenbush@campbell.edu
QUALIA, Linda, R .... 972-881-5779 471 C
lqualia@collin.edu
QUALLS, Mike .... 479-979-1378.. 25 H
mqualls@ozarks.edu
QUAM, Jean, K .... 612-626-5177 265 C
jquam@umn.edu
QUAN, Gamward .... 909-447-2560.. 39 G
gquan@cst.edu
QUAN, Jeff .... 972-860-7371 472 E
JQuan@dcccd.edu
QUAN, Peter .... 323-343-2700.. 34 A
pquan@cslanet.calstatela.edu
QUANBECK, Kirsten, K . 949-824-5594.. 71 C
quanbeck@uci.edu
QUANSTROM, Mark .... 815-939-5011 155 G
mquanstr@olivet.edu
QUARBERG, Brad, R ..... 608-785-8572 539 G
bquarberg@uwlax.edu
QUARLES, Markel .... 661-654-3033.. 32 G
mquarles@csub.edu
QUARLES, Robert .... 404-756-4010 120 H
rquarles@atlm.edu
QUARLES, Robert .... 304-473-8163 534 G
quarles_r@wvwc.edu
QUARTEY, Kojo .... 734-384-4166 247 C
kquartey@monroeccc.edu
QUAST, Debra .... 805-565-6182.. 76 K
dquast@westmont.edu
QUATTRO, Mike .... 734-432-5341 246 B
mquattro@madonna.edu
QUATTROCCHI, John .... 518-743-2394 347 E
quattrocchij@sunyacc.edu
QUATTROCIOCCHI,
Stephen .... 858-513-9240.. 29 A
Stephen.Quattrociocchi@ashford.edu
QUAY, Sara .... 978-232-2200 226 C
squay@endicott.edu
QUAYE, Chandra .... 703-561-1600.. 96 H
chandra.quaye@strayer.edu
QUAYE, Sandra .... 608-899-4241 297 H
quayes@franklinpierce.edu
QUBBAJ, Ala .... 956-665-7899 494 C
qubbaj@utpa.edu
QUBEIN, Nido, R .... 336-841-9201 357 E
nqubein@highpoint.edu
QUDDUS, Munir .... 936-261-9200 484 F
muquddus@pvamu.edu
QUEEN, Harrell, W .... 706-245-7226 124 C
hqueen@ec.edu
QUEEN, Scott .... 636-949-4920 276 L
squeen@lindenwood.edu
QUEEN, Scott .... 336-506-4154 359 N
scott.queen@alamancecc.edu
QUEEN, Todd .... 225-578-9959 204 M
tqueen@lsu.edu
QUEEN-HUBERT, Jody .. 212-346-1950 337 I
jqueenhubert@pace.edu
QUEENAN, Rosemary ... 518-445-3394 314 H
rquee@albanylaw.edu
QUEENAN, Theresa ...... 410-651-6447 219 H
tqueenan@umes.edu
QUEENER, Sherry, F ..... 317-274-1577 168 E
queens@iupui.edu
QUEHL-ENGEL,
Catherine, M .... 319-895-4402 177 A
cquehl-engel@cornellcollege.edu
QUEIROZ, Hermano ...... 270-789-5202 194 D
hsqueiroz@campbellsville.edu
QUERO-MENDEZ, Doris 787-725-6500 551 A
dquero@albizu.edu
QUERRY, Michele .... 904-256-8000 106 Q
mquerry1@ju.edu
QUESADA, Edmond ...... 719-502-3352.. 84 J
edmond.quesada@ppcc.edu
QUESENBERRY, Madge 301-891-4000 221 C
madgej@wau.edu
QUEST, Karen .... 315-568-3060 334 F
kquest@nycc.edu
QUIATKOWSKI, Sandra 800-280-0307 163 I
sandra.quiatkowski@ace.edu
QUICK, Angela .... 865-981-8038 458 E
angela.quick@maryvillecollege.edu
QUICK, Debra .... 520-515-3640.. 13 B
quickd@cochise.edu
QUICK, Donna .... 803-786-3612 445 C
dquick@columbiasc.edu
QUICK, James, E .... 214-768-1115 482 J
jquick@smu.edu
QUICK, Matthew, D ...... 816-501-4127 281 B
matt.quick@rockhurst.edu
QUICK, Michael .... 213-740-2101.. 74 D
uscprovost@usc.edu
QUIETT, Corey .... 405-382-9501 402 C
c.quiett@sscok.edu
QUIGGLE, Gregg .... 312-329-4059 153 C
gregg.quiggle@moody.edu
QUIGLEY, Brian .... 603-358-2438 299 D
bquigley1@keene.edu
QUIGLEY, David .... 617-552-3260 224 B
david.quigley@bc.edu
QUIGLEY, James, M ..... 252-451-8227 364 E
jquigley@nashcc.edu
QUIGLEY, JR.,
Kenneth, K .... 617-333-2236 225 F
kquigley@curry.edu
QUIGLEY, Kevin, F .... 802-258-9245 502 B
kevin@marlboro.edu
QUIGLEY, Lori .... 518-244-2496 340 A
l.quigley@sage.edu
QUIGLEY, Mark, R .... 978-542-6078 230 E
mquigley@salemstate.edu
QUIGLEY, Peter .... 808-956-3869 136 B
quigleyp@hawaii.edu
QUIGLEY, Susan .... 773-380-6785 140 C
squigley@seabury.edu
QUIJANO, Xochil .... 303-797-5635.. 79 A
xochil.quijano@arapahoe.edu
QUIJANO SAX,
Jennifer .... 410-871-3376 217 A
jqsax@mcdaniel.edu
QUILES, Elisa .... 787-751-0178 555 K
ac_equiles@suagm.edu
QUILES, Elisa .... 787-257-7373 555 L
equiles@suagm.edu
QUILL, Robin .... 508-929-8013 230 G
rquill@worcester.edu
QUILLEN, Carol, E .... 704-894-2201 356 D
caquillen@davidson.edu
QUILLEN, David .... 630-466-7900 162 K
dquillen@waubonsee.edu
QUILLEN, Michael .... 859-256-3100 195 G
mike.quillen@kctcs.edu
QUILLEN, Michael, D ... 704-216-3475 365 F
michael.quillen@rccc.edu
QUIMBY, Kristyn .... 574-520-4154 168 F
krirhawk@iusb.edu
QUIMBY, Linda .... 603-899-4028 297 H
quimbyl@franklinpierce.edu
QUIMBY, T. Bart .... 907-786-1046.. 10 H
tbquimby@uaa.alaska.edu
QUINCY, Barbara, I .... 724-946-7928 439 D
quincybi@westminster.edu
QUINER, Michael, W ..... 509-527-4975 528 F
quinerm@whitman.edu
QUINET, Bart, P .... 615-322-7712 465 H
bart.p.quinet@vanderbilt.edu
QUININE, Donte .... 509-682-6865 528 C
dquinine@wvc.edu
QUINLAN, Brian .... 508-213-2112 235 C
brian.quinlan@nichols.edu
QUINLAN, Catherine ..... 213-821-2344.. 74 D
cquinlan@usc.edu
QUINLAN, Jeremiah ..... 203-432-9321.. 93 C
jeremiah.quinlan@yale.edu
QUINLAN, Joseph .... 201-761-7302 307 K
jquinlan@saintpeters.edu
QUINLAN, Maureen ...... 619-684-8779.. 56 B
mquinlan@newschoolarch.edu
QUINLAN BRAME,
Julie .... 414-382-6371 534 I
julie.quinlan@alverno.edu
QUINLEY, Melissa .... 828-398-7633 360 A
mquinley@abtech.edu
QUINLIVAN, Gary .... 724-537-4597 435 B
gary.quinlivan@email.stvincent.edu
QUINN, Aaron .... 740-245-7454 394 D
aquinn@rio.edu
QUINN, Anthony .... 734-384-4279 247 C
aquinn@monroeccc.edu

QUINN, Arthur .... 561-732-4424 112 C
aquinn@svdp.edu
QUINN, Bill .... 281-487-1170 486 F
bquinn@txchiro.edu
QUINN, Bonnie .... 781-768-7184 236 A
bonnie.quinn@regiscollege.edu
QUINN, Catherine .... 215-248-7137 415 D
quinnc@chc.edu
QUINN, Consuelo .... 706-821-8262 129 H
cquinn@paine.edu
QUINN, Cynthia, D ...... 808-956-8213 135 H
bor@hawaii.edu
QUINN, Donna, M .... 302-356-6819.. 94 G
donna.m.quinn@wilmu.edu
QUINN, Edward, M ...... 202-687-4134.. 95 E
quinne@georgetown.edu
QUINN, Erin .... 802-443-5253 502 E
quinn@middlebury.edu
QUINN, Frank .... 619-849-2338.. 59 K
frankquinn@pointloma.edu
QUINN, Gianna .... 215-641-5554 420 A
quinn.g@gmercyu.edu
QUINN, Gina .... 405-682-7502 399 K
gquinn@occc.edu
QUINN, Jack, F .... 716-851-1200 325 A
jquinn@ecc.edu
QUINN, Jeffery .... 845-675-4425 337 B
jeff.quinn@nyack.edu
QUINN, Joseph, G .... 718-817-3013 326 C
jgquinn@fordham.edu
QUINN, Kathy .... 314-529-9476 277 B
kquinn@maryville.edu
QUINN, Kevin .... 610-647-4400 421 B
uinn@immaculata.edu
QUINN, Kevin .... 610-647-4400 421 B
kquinn@immaculata.edu
QUINN, Kevin, C .... 315-443-8338 349 E
kcquinn@syr.edu
QUINN, SJ, Kevin, P .... 570-941-7500 438 F
presidentquinn@scranton.edu
QUINN, Kimbra .... 806-894-9611 482 F
kquinn@southplainscollege.edu
QUINN, Laurie .... 802-860-2729 501 F
lquinn@champlain.edu
QUINN, Leslie .... 913-469-8500 188 E
lquinn2@jccc.edu
QUINN, Linda .... 402-941-6280 291 I
quinn@midlandu.edu
QUINN, Margaret .... 609-652-4744 308 E
margaret.quinn@stockton.edu
QUINN, Marisa .... 615-297-7545 455 A
quinnm@aquinascollege.edu
QUINN, Michael .... 718-405-3334 322 A
michael.quinn@mountsaintvincent.edu
QUINN, Michael .... 206-296-5500 526 F
quinnm@seattleu.edu
QUINN, Michael, G .... 585-292-2151 333 G
mquinn@monroecc.edu
QUINN, Michael, J .... 434-947-8100 511 D
mjquinn@randolphcollege.edu
QUINN, Michael, P ...... 401-598-2945 441 D
mquinn@jwu.edu
QUINN, Michelle .... 970-351-2773.. 87 A
michelle.quinn@unco.edu
QUINN, Molly .... 319-226-2001 175 D
molly.quinn@allencollege.edu
QUINN, Penny .... 618-545-3010 149 C
Pquinn@kaskaskia.edu
QUINN, Randi .... 614-947-6543 382 H
randi.quinn@franklin.edu
QUINN, SSJ, Roseann .. 215-248-7031 415 D
quinnr@chc.edu
QUINN, Sandra .... 609-894-9311 306 B
squinn@bcc.edu
QUINN, Sarah, F .... 610-660-1230 434 G
squinn@sju.edu
QUINN, Shaman .... 307-754-6232 546 I
Shaman.Quinn@nwc.edu
QUINN, Sharon .... 410-455-2540 219 F
squinn@umbc.edu
QUINN, Stephen .... 973-618-3320 300 H
squinn@caldwell.edu
QUINN, Susan .... 707-524-1598.. 65 C
squinn@santarosa.edu
QUINN, Tania .... 914-654-5257 322 B
tquinn@cnr.edu
QUINN, Teresa .... 845-437-5370 351 H
tequinn@vassar.edu
QUINN, Thomas .... 989-275-5000 245 C
tom.quinn@kirtland.edu
QUINN, Wade .... 910-362-7062 360 G
wquinn@cfcc.edu
QUINN, Wayne .... 229-243-6994 121 D
wayne.quinn@bainbridge.edu
QUINN, William, P .... 302-356-6775.. 94 G
william.p.quinn@wilmu.edu
QUINNAN, Tim .... 817-272-6080 493 L
quinnan@uta.edu
QUINNETT, Jim .... 325-793-4611 478 D
jquinnett@mcm.edu
QUINONES, Carlos, A .. 787-753-0039 551 L
QUINONES, Irma .... 787-758-2525 558 C
irma.quinones1@upr.edu
QUINONES, Ivan, A ...... 717-780-2455 420 D
iaquinon@hacc.edu
QUINONES, Melinda ..... 610-282-1100 416 I
melinda.quinones@desales.edu
QUINONES, Ray .... 787-265-3866 558 B
ray.quinones@upr.edu
QUIÑONES, Roberto ...... 213-413-9500.. 68 A
robertoquinones@scusoma.edu
QUINONES, Rosa .... 787-257-0000 557 F
rosa.quinones1@upr.edu
QUINONEZ, Julie, R ..... 419-530-6213 394 E
julie.quinonez@utoledo.edu
QUINT, Christopher ...... 207-780-4200 213 A
cquint@usm.maine.edu
QUINT, Doug .... 620-242-0586 189 E
quintd@mcpherson.edu
QUINTAL, Jorge .... 336-334-5536 371 C
j_quinta@uncg.edu
QUINTAL, Rollande .... 508-849-3340 222 C
rquintal@annamaria.edu
QUINTANA, Javier .... 787-279-1912 553 H
jquintana@bayamon.inter.edu
QUINTANA, Pamela ...... 561-912-1211 102 N
pquintana@evergladesuniversity.edu
QUINTANA, Rosaura ..... 787-815-0000 557 D
rosaura.quintana@upr.edu
QUINTANILLA, Hector ... 817-531-4840 490 C
hquintanilla@txwes.edu
QUINTANILLA, Kelly ..... 361-825-2722 485 F
kelly.quintanilla@tamucc.edu
QUINTANS, Joel .... 817-272-2025 493 L
quintas@uta.edu
QUINTARA, Elena .... 312-662-4021 139 E
equintara@adler.edu
QUINTERO, Rebecca ..... 787-728-1515 559 A
rquintero@sagrado.edu
QUINTERO-JIMENEZ,
Noel .... 787-725-6500 551 A
nquintero@albizu.edu
QUINTYNE, Renee .... 845-398-4207 341 H
rquintyn@stac.edu
QUIRK, Donna .... 312-915-8723 151 E
dquirk@luc.edu
QUIRK-BAILEY, Sheila .. 847-925-6668 145 F
squirk@harpercollege.edu
QUIROGA,
Mercedes, A .... 954-201-6511.. 99 G
mquiroga@broward.edu
QUIROLGICO, Ray .... 626-396-2325.. 28 J
ray.quirolgico@artcenter.edu
QUIROS, Kristi .... 830-372-8060 487 C
kquiros@tlu.edu
QUIROZ, Gloria .... 773-878-3606 158 C
gquiroz@staugustine.edu
QUIS, Stephen .... 619-388-7752.. 62 H
squis@sdccd.edu
QUISENBERRY, Brian .... 205-226-4670.... 2 C
bqusenberry@bsc.edu
QUISENBERRY, JR.,
Henry, L .... 334-347-2623.... 3 H
cquisenberry@escc.edu
QUISTGARD, Fred .... 207-216-4406 211 F
fquistgard@yccc.edu
QUISTORF, Mark, W ..... 414-410-4016 535 C
mwquistorf@stritch.edu
QUIÑONES, Angel .... 787-258-1501 551 I
alquinones@columbiacentral.edu
QUIÑONES, Franco .... 787-751-1912 554 D
fquinone@juris.inte.edu
QUIÑONES, Loalis .... 787-285-2525 552 J
lquinones@hccpr.edu
QUIÑONES, Yolanda ...... 787-758-2525 558 C
yolanda.quinonez@upr.edu
QVARMSTROM, Jeanne . 432-837-8585 489 B
jqvarmstrom@sulross.edu

R

RAAB, David .... 646-565-6000 350 C
david.raab@touro.edu
RAAB, Jennifer, J .... 212-772-4242 319 E
jennifer.raab@hunter.cuny.edu
RAAB, Keith .... 541-881-5828 410 D
kraab@tvcc.cc
RAAB, Lettie, M .... 936-261-5900 484 F
lmraab@pvamu.edu
RAAB, Maryrose .... 315-792-7215 348 D
maryrose.raab@sunyit.edu
RAASCH, Christopher ... 734-995-7399 241 F
chris.raasch@cuaa.edu
RAATMA, Lucia .... 352-588-8572 111 L
lucia.raatma@saintleo.edu
RAATTAMA, Kristina ..... 305-348-2103 114 G
maija.raattama@fiu.edu
RABAGO, Cristine .... 650-543-3782.. 54 B
crabago@menlo.edu
RABALAIS, Lawrence 225-578-3231 204M
lrabal1@lsu.edu
RABALAIS, Nicole .... 615-248-1237 464 E
nrabalais@trevecca.edu
RABB, Ginia .... 901-369-0835.. 96 H
RABB, Harriet .... 212-327-8070 339 H
harriet.rabb@rockefeller.edu
RABBANY, Sina, Y .... 516-463-6672 328 A
sina.y.rabbany@hofstra.edu
RABBITT, Kara, M .... 973-720-2180 309 I
rabbittk@wpunj.edu
RABBITT, Rhonda, M ... 608-796-3384 542 H
rmrabbitt@viterbo.edu
RABE, Bonnie .... 203-596-4589.. 91 D
brabe@post.edu
RABEK, Jeffrey .... 409-772-6026 495 E
jrabek@utmb.edu
RABEL, P, J .... 402-465-2102 292 E
prabel@nebrwesleyan.edu
RABELO, Virginia .... 305-821-3333 104 C
vrabelo@fnu.edu
RABENOLD, Scott .... 865-974-9557 465 D
srabenol@utk.edu
RABER, II, Donald, R ... 864-833-8233 448 E
draber@presby.edu
RABIDEAU, Shelly, S ... 317-940-8423 164 L
srabidea@butler.edu
RABIL, Alison .... 919-684-3501 356 E
alison.rabil@duke.edu
RABIN, Sara .... 253-589-5535 521 B
sara.rabin@cptc.edu
RABINEAU, Kevin .... 269-965-3931 244 L
rabineauk@kellogg.edu
RABINOVICH, Sheryl .... 213-624-1200.. 44 I
srabinovich@fidm.edu
RABINOWITZ, Celia, E . 603-358-2736 299 D
Celia.Rabinowitz@keene.edu
RABINOWITZ, David, B 973-290-4084 301 F
drabinowitz@cse.edu
RABINOWITZ, Eli .... 718-377-0777 338 H
RABINOWITZ, Fred .... 909-748-8359.. 73 K
fred_rabinowitz@redlands.edu
RABINOWITZ, Stuart ..... 516-463-6800 328 A
president@hofstra.edu
RABITOY, Eric .... 626-914-8788.. 38 L
erabitoy@citruscollege.edu
RABITOY, Linda .... 909-667-4433.. 39 C
lrabitoy@claremontlincoln.org
RABLE, Michelle .... 419-824-3816 385 F
mrable@lourdes.edu
RABLE, Michelle, A ...... 419-824-3816 385 F
mrable@lourdes.edu
RABY, Domonic .... 601-877-6333 266 C
sm8053@bncollege.com
RABY, James, R .... 570-321-4137 425 B
raby@lycoming.edu
RABY, Sherry .... 252-249-1851 364 F
sraby@pamlicocc.edu
RABY, Susan .... 315-312-2260 346 A
susan.raby@oswego.edu
RABY-GENTRY, Tori ...... 931-393-1617 463 B
trabygentry@mscc.edu
RACANSKY, Pam .... 206-934-3600 525 K
pam.racansky@seattlecolleges.edu
RACCANELLO, Paul .... 415-485-3223.. 43 D
paul.raccanello@dominican.edu
RACE, Debbie .... 828-262-2050 369 D
racedw@appstate.edu
RACE, Mary Jo .... 412-624-4200 437 K
mar6@pitt.edu
RACEHORSE, Brenda ..... 785-749-8451 187 F
brenda.racehorse@bie.edu
RACETTE, Patrick .... 906-524-8301 245 B
patrick.racette@kbocc.edu
RACHAL, Bryan .... 256-765-4225.... 9 D
brachal@una.edu
RACHAL, Michael .... 504-865-2486 206 A
rachal@loyno.edu
RACHELL, Kelvin .... 803-536-7239 448 H
krachell@scsu.edu
RACHELL, Kelvin .... 804-524-5011 518 C
krachell@vsu.edu
RACHFORD, Jennifer .... 909-607-2201.. 60 A
jennifer.rachford@pomona.edu
RACHITA, David, A .... 281-283-2568 491 E
rachita@uhcl.edu
RACHOUH, Susan .... 201-216-3518 308 D
Susan.Rachouh@stevens.edu
RACICOT, Amelie .... 858-566-1200.. 43 A
aracicot@disd.edu
RACINA, Kris .... 907-474-2600.. 10 I
khracina@alaska.edu
RACINE, Anne .... 406-338-5441 286 C
RACINE, David .... 217-206-8417 161 G
draci2@uis.edu
RACINE, Gail, M .... 508-767-7283 222 D
gracine@assumption.edu
RACINE, Leo .... 508-678-2811 231 B
leo.racine@bristolcc.edu
RACIOPPI, Jerry .... 402-461-2503 289 D
jerryracioppi@cccneb.edu
RACKLEY, J. Mike .... 662-325-9311 269 A
mike.rackley@msstate.edu
RACKLEY, Richard, W ... 865-688-9422 456 J
info@fountainheadcollege.com
RACKLIFFE, Jerry, J ...... 404-413-3000 126 D
jracklif@gsu.edu
RACZYNSKI, James, M . 501-526-6600.. 24 B
RaczynskiJamesM@uams.edu
RACZYNSKI, Patricia, A 205-934-5121.... 8 F
trish@uab.edu
RADAKOVICH, Dan .... 864-656-1935 444 E
danrad1@clemson.edu
RADCLIFFE, Shelby .... 323-259-2961.. 56 I
radcliffe@oxy.edu
RADCLIFFE, Steve .... 513-244-4381 387 A
steve.radcliffe@msj.edu
RADDA, Hank .... 602-639-7500.. 14 A
RADEL, Marie .... 765-455-9468 168 B
meradel@iuk.edu
RADEL, Patti .... 585-594-6100 337 A
radelp@roberts.edu
RADEL, Patti .... 585-594-6100 339 F
radelp@roberts.edu
RADEMACHER, Eric ...... 513-556-3304 393 B
eric.rademacher@uc.edu
RADER, Brian .... 503-399-8074 404 L
brian.rader@chemeketa.edu
RADER, Claude, K .... 410-951-3858 220 C
drader@coppin.edu
RADER, Sherri .... 309-649-6255 160 F
sherri.rader@src.edu
RADFORD, Laurie .... 503-552-1617 407 F
lradford@ncnm.edu
RADFORD, Marilyn .... 270-384-8022 198 C
radfordm@lindsey.edu
RADFORD, Ron .... 256-395-2211.... 7 E
rradford@suscc.edu
RADFORD, Russell .... 877-366-0321 148 H
rradford@ellis.edu
RADHAKRISHNAN,
Rashmi .... 610-921-7225 411 E
rradhakrishnan@albright.edu
RADIK, Amy .... 518-736-3622 326 D
aradik@fmcc.suny.edu
RADIONOFF,
Kathleen, A .... 608-258-2309 543 C
kradionoff@madisoncollege.edu
RADISH, Ross .... 215-596-7573 438 E
r.radish@usciences.edu
RADKAR, Smruti .... 202-274-5000.. 97 B
RADKE, Cheryl .... 623-245-4600.. 18 C
cradke@uticuti.edu
RADLIFF, Mary .... 518-255-5211 346 E
radliffmd@cobleskill.edu
RADLOWSKI, Mark, E ... 315-792-5467 333 D
mradlowski@mvcc.edu
RADNEY, Ron .... 661-654-3271.. 32 G
rradney@csub.edu
RADSON, Darrell, J ...... 309-677-2255 140 H
radson@bradley.edu
RADT, Jennifer .... 513-732-8964 393 D
jennifer.radt@uc.edu
RADTKE, Elizabeth, L ... 651-523-2201 256 B
bradtke@hamline.edu
RADTKE, Scott, W .... 920-832-6574 536 R
scott.w.radtke@lawrence.edu
RADULESCU, Eugen 713-348-6725 480M
eugen@rice.edu
RADULSKI, Sandy .... 850-245-0466 114 C
sandy.radulski@flbog.edu
RADULSKI, Thomas, F . 304-457-6213 529 C
radulskift@ab.edu
RADVANSKY,
Sandy, M .... 740-284-5357 382 G
sradvansky@franciscan.edu
RADWAN, Ann .... 509-963-3612 520 E
intlprog@cwu.edu
RADYCKI, Diane .... 610-861-1627 426 H
dradycki@moravian.edu
RAE, Jon .... 813-988-5131 103 L
raej@floridacollege.edu
RAE, Lisa .... 802-258-3149 502 I
lisa.rae@worldlearning.org
RAE, Mike, E .... 570-326-3761 429 J
mrae@pct.edu
RAE, Nicol .... 406-994-5023 287 G
nicol.rae@montana.edu
RAE, Rosemarie .... 510-642-5737.. 70 K
timahu@berkeley.edu
RAEBER, Michael .... 706-542-0006 132 H
mraeber@uga.edu
RAEFORD, James, E ..... 540-828-5408 505 F
jraeford@bridgewater.edu
RAEL, Sylvia .... 970-248-1029.. 80 B
srael@coloradomesa.edu
RAFATTI, Colleen .... 863-784-7411 113 C
colleen.rafatti@southflorida.edu
RAFELD, Jessica .... 920-403-3071 538 K
jessica.rafeld@snc.edu
RAFFAELLE, Ryne .... 585-475-2055 339 G
ryne.raffaelle@rit.edu
RAFFAELLI, Bethany, M 920-924-6431 543 F
braffaelli@morainepark.edu

RAFFENSPERGER, Thomas .... 413-572-5233 230 F
traffensperger@westfield.ma.edu
RAFFETTO, William .... 281-998-6150 481 D
william.raffetto@sjcd.edu
RAFFETTO, William .... 281-998-6150 481 F
william.raffetto@sjcd.edu
RAFIEE, Farnoosh .... 606-326-2069 195 H
farnoosh.rafiee@kctcs.edu
RAFN, H. Jeffrey .... 920-498-5411 544 B
jeff.rafn@nwtc.edu
RAFOOL, Dawn, M .... 863-638-3818 118 L
dawn.rafool@warner.edu
RAFOTH, Mary Ann ...... 412-397-6020 434 B
rafoth@rmu.edu
RAGAIN, Charles .... 281-649-3314 475 B
cragain@hbu.edu
RAGAN, Jody .... 515-961-1517 182 I
jody.ragan@simpson.edu
RAGAN, Kathleen, E ..... 973-655-3450 304 A
ragank@mail.montclair.edu
RAGAN, Ronald, E .... 336-841-9193 357 E
rragan@highpoint.edu
RAGENOVICH, Cassie ... 509-527-2815 528 A
cassie.ragenovich@wallawalla.edu
RAGER, Michael .... 270-926-4040 194 K
mrager@daymarcollege.edu
RAGGO, Alan .... 812-888-5640 174 F
araggo@vinu.edu
RAGLAND, Ethel .... 630-829-6583 140 A
eragland@ben.edu
RAGLAND, Heather .... 901-272-5124 459 A
hragland@mca.edu
RAGLAND, Janet .... 903-233-3815 477 G
janetragland@letu.edu
RAGLAND, Lori .... 618-437-5321 156 I
ragland@rlc.edu
RAGLAND, Mary, A ...... 276-964-7286 517 A
mary.ragland@sw.edu
RAGLAND, Matthew ...... 334-244-3138.... 2 A
mragland@aum.edu
RAGNO, John .... 718-489-5364 340 E
jragno@sfc.edu
RAGNO, Kerry, S .... 757-822-1530 517 C
kragno@tcc.edu
RAGO, Jim .... 229-249-2672 134 I
jim.rago@wiregrass.edu
RAGSDALE, Chad .... 417-626-1234 280 B
ragsdale.chad@occ.edu
RAGSDALE, Jennifer ..... 201-761-6062 307 K
jragsdale@saintpeters.edu
RAGSDALE, Jill .... 507-284-9024 254 G
jill.ragsdale@mayo.edu
RAGSDALE, Lisa, B ...... 704-233-8710 373 C
lisa.ragsdale@wingate.edu
RAGSDALE, Lyn .... 713-348-4824 480 M
lyn.ragsdale@rice.edu
RAGSDALE, JR., Roy Lee .... 704-233-8118 373 C
lragsdale@wingate.edu
RAGUSA, Sal .... 510-436-1008.. 47 C
ragusa@hnu.edu
RAH, Yumee .... 213-381-0081.. 48 A
yumeerah@irus.edu
RAHE, April .... 816-531-5223 273 F
arahe@concorde.edu
RAHM, Clare .... 216-687-5541 380 D
c.rahm@csuohio.edu
RAHMAN, Pervez .... 773-907-4452 141 O
prahman@ccc.edu
RAHMANI, Loretta .... 909-593-3511.. 73 B
lrahmani@laverne.edu
RAHMANN, Jack .... 512-245-2124 489 C
jcr140@txstate.edu
RAHMATIAN, Marteza ... 657-278-1637.. 33 E
mrahmatian@fullerton.edu
RAHMLOW, Jeff .... 920-686-6166 539 A
Jeff.Rahmlow@sl.edu
RAHN, Adria .... 248-204-3030 245 J
bookstore@ltu.edu
RAHN, Daniel .... 501-686-5680.. 24 B
drahn@uams.edu
RAHN, Debra .... 618-235-2700 160 B
RAHN, Diane .... 419-251-1726 386 C
diane.rahn@mercycollege.edu
RAHN, Jason, M .... 651-641-8706 255 C
rahn@csp.edu
RAHN, Joel .... 512-313-3000 471 H
joel.rahn@concordia.edu
RAHNAMAY-AZAR, Amir .... 412-268-6011 414 J
aazar@cmu.edu
RAHNI, Michael .... 213-383-8999.. 26 E
RAHR, JR., Carl, H ...... 607-587-3535 347 D
rahrch@alfredstate.edu
RAI, Sanjay .... 240-567-5006 217 B
sanjay.rai@montgomerycollege.edu
RAIBLEY, Jon .... 503-517-1899 411 C
jraibley@westernseminary.edu
RAICH, Michael .... 218-322-2401 259 B
michael.raich@itascacc.edu
RAICH, Michael .... 218-262-6702 258 H
michaelraich@hibbing.edu
RAICHE, Carol .... 978-232-2068 226 C
craiche@endicott.edu
RAICHE, Cheryl .... 617-217-9224 223 A
craiche@baystate.edu
RAICHIK, Shimon .... 323-937-2079.. 77 J
RAIKES, Mark, H .... 574-372-5100 166 D
raikesmh@grace.edu
RAIKES-COLBERT, Deborah .... 845-575-3000 331 L
Deborah.Raikes-Colbert@marist.edu
RAILEY, Clayton .... 215-968-8043 413 F
clayton.railey@bucks.edu
RAILEY, George .... 805-922-6966.. 26 H
grailey@hancockcollege.edu
RAILEY, James, H .... 417-268-1000 272 D
raileyj@evangel.edu
RAILEY, Kevin, J .... 716-878-5601 345 B
raileykj@buffalostate.edu
RAILSBACK, Travis .... 205-348-4904.... 8 E
trailsback@sa.ua.edu
RAIMER, Ben, G .... 409-747-2789 495 E
bgraimer@utmb.edu
RAIMO, James .... 845-569-3227 333 I
james.raimo@msmc.edu
RAINE, Meredith .... 713-500-3050 495 A
meredith.raine@uth.tmc.edu
RAINE, Michael .... 505-454-3405 311 H
mraine@nmhu.edu
RAINER, Art .... 919-761-2100 368 K
arainer@sebts.edu
RAINER, Don .... 205-652-3576..... 9 G
drainer@uwa.edu
RAINER, Kairyn .... 617-585-1100 234 H
kairyn.rainer@necmusic.edu
RAINES, Amanda .... 940-552-6291 496 B
araines@vernoncollege.edu
RAINES, Deborah .... 703-284-1530 510 B
debbie.raines@marymount.edu
RAINES, Jess, N .... 740-374-8716 395 D
jraines@wscc.edu
RAINES, Patrick .... 615-460-6000 455 D
pat.raines@belmont.edu
RAINES, Ruby .... 940-565-2026 492 D
ruby.raines@unt.edu
RAINES, Stephany .... 912-525-5000 130 H
sraines@scad.edu
RAINES, Tammy .... 804-425-5797 506 G
traines@ccc-va.com
RAINEY, Jack, T .... 973-618-3230 300 H
jrainey@caldwell.edu
RAINEY, Jamie .... 325-481-9300 475 E
jrainey@howardcollege.edu
RAINEY, Kelli .... 704-378-1098 358 B
krainey@jcsu.edu
RAINFORD, William ...... 202-319-5454.. 95 A
rainford@cua.edu
RAINFORD, William ...... 202-319-5256.. 95 A
RAINONE, John, J .... 540-863-2827 515 B
rrainone@dslcc.edu
RAINS, Ben .... 501-812-2268.. 22 F
brains@pulaskitech.edu
RAINS, Debbie .... 361-582-2560 496 D
deborah.rains@victoriacollege.edu
RAINS, Jerry .... 863-667-5197 113 K
jdrains@seu.edu
RAINS, Thomas, J .... 414-410-4535 535 C
tjrains@stritch.edu
RAINS, Valerie .... 417-873-6965 274 E
vrains@drury.edu
RAINWATER, Jeanetta ... 918-781-7263 396 F
rainwaterj@bacone.edu
RAIOLA, Lisa .... 401-254-3302 442 C
lraiola@rwu.edu
RAISANEN, Gregg .... 320-762-4618 257 O
greggr@alextech.edu
RAISIAN, John .... 650-723-1198.. 68 G
raisian@hoover.stanford.edu
RAISL, Gary .... 858-646-3126.. 64 F
graisl@shpdiscovery.org
RAISOR, Jeremy .... 928-524-7462.. 16 E
jeremy.raisor@npc.edu
RAISOVICH, Andy .... 304-367-4682 532 F
andy.raisovich@fairmontstate.edu
RAISOVICH, Chris .... 317-788-2127 173 I
raisovichr@uindy.edu
RAISOVICH, Joanie .... 304-367-4131 532 F
Joanie.Raisovich@fairmontstate.edu
RAJA, Jay .... 704-687-5737 371 B
jraja@uncc.edu
RAJA, Tasleem .... 312-427-9580 144 D
tasleem@eastwest.edu
RAJALA, Sarah .... 515-294-9988 175 G
rajala@iastate.edu
RAJAM, Chandru .... 609-771-2797 301 E
rajam@tcnj.edu
RAJAN, Altaf .... 415-442-7859.. 46 A
arajan@ggu.edu
RAJAN, Ravi .... 914-251-6750 346 D
ravi.rajan@purchase.edu
RAJASEKARAN, Senthil, K .... 757-446-5630 507 B
rajasesk@evms.edu
RAJMAIRA, Christina .... 703-284-1615 510 B
christina.rajmaira@marymount.edu
RAJPUROHIT, Vikas ...... 817-515-1254 484 B
vikas.rajpurohit@tccd.edu
RAJPUT, Hussein .... 651-523-2204 256 B
hrajput01@hamline.edu
RAKER, Keith .... 336-249-8186 362 B
kdraker@davidsonccc.edu
RAKER, Russell .... 702-992-2356 295 E
russell.raker@nsc.edu
RAKES, Lee, L .... 540-464-7345 518 A
rakesel@vmi.edu
RAKES, Thomas, D .... 910-962-3174 372 A
rakest@uncw.edu
RAKESTRAW, Jennie ..... 803-323-2151 451 I
rakestrawj@winthrop.edu
RAKHSHA, Deborah, B . 801-581-3325 499 K
debbie.rakhsha@utah.edu
RAKITA, Gordon, F .... 904-620-2820 116 A
grakita@unf.edu
RAKOCZY, Michelle ...... 701-777-0754 373 G
michelle.rakoczy@und.edu
RAKOFF, Jill .... 860-701-5131.. 91 B
rakoff_j@mitchell.edu
RAKOW, Ernest, A .... 901-678-2399 462 B
erakow@memphis.edu
RALEIGH, Mary-Jeanne 910-521-6306 371 D
mary-jeanne.raleigh@uncp.edu
RALEIGH, Scott .... 602-639-7500.. 14 A
RALEY, Leonard, R .... 301-445-1941 219 C
raley@usmd.edu
RALL, John, P .... 270-809-3399 198 I
jrall@murraystate.edu
RALLIS, Jessica .... 203-576-4804.. 92 B
ubbookstore@bbasolutions.com
RALLS, Diana .... 209-228-4306.. 71 E
DRalls@UCMerced.edu
RALLS, Pam .... 314-837-6777 281 D
pralls@stlchristian.edu
RALLS, R. Scott .... 919-807-6951 359 M
ralls@nccommunitycolleges.edu
RALLS, Scott .... 703-323-3101 516 C
sralls@nvcc.edu
RALPH, Brian .... 704-337-2445 368 B
ralphb@queens.edu
RALPH, James .... 802-443-5320 502 E
ralph@middlebury.edu
RALPH, Ken .... 719-389-6945.. 79 M
ken.ralph@coloradocollege.edu
RALPH, Lynette .... 504-520-7304 209 E
Lralph@xula.edu
RALPH, Nicole, M .... 217-786-2342 151 C
nicole.ralph@llcc.edu
RALPH, Scott .... 317-955-6789 171 A
sralph@marian.edu
RALSTON, Craig .... 928-776-2311.. 18 L
craig.ralston@yc.edu
RALSTON, Nancy, M ..... 402-552-2557 289 H
ralston@clarksoncollege.edu
RALSTON, Pamela .... 805-546-3123.. 42 H
pamela_ralston@cuesta.edu
RALSTON, Ramona, M . 315-267-2154 346 C
ralstorm@potsdam.edu
RALSTON, Steven, M .... 606-783-2002 198 H
s.ralston@moreheadstate.edu
RALSTON, Tracy .... 203-596-4564.. 91 D
tralston@post.edu
RALSTON, Troy .... 804-727-6826 131 F
tralston@southuniversity.edu
RALTZ, Gene .... 714-542-8086.. 29 H
graltz@bristoluniversity.edu
RAM, Rosalind .... 808-675-3457 134 M
ramr@byuh.edu
RAMAEKERS, Eric .... 907-796-6255.. 11 A
esramaekers@uas.alaska.edu
RAMAGE, Emily .... 217-234-5403 150 B
eramage@lakeland.cc.il.us
RAMAGE, Sarah .... 323-259-2664.. 56 I
sramage@oxy.edu
RAMAGE, Thomas, R .... 217-351-2231 155 I
ramage@parkland.edu
RAMAGOS, Caroline ..... 601-928-6205 268 G
caroline.ramagos@mgccc.edu
RAMAKER, Dawn .... 641-585-8197 183 I
ramakerd@waldorf.edu
RAMAKER, Jason .... 641-585-8160 183 I
ramakerj@waldorf.edu
RAMAKRISHNAN, Jolly . 610-399-2032 430 D
jramakrishnan@cheyney.edu
RAMALHO, Erika, A ...... 814-871-5584 419 A
ramalho001@gannon.edu
RAMAN, Jaishankar ...... 219-464-6880 174 E
jaishankar.raman@valpo.edu
RAMAN, Saravana .... 714-300-0300.. 67 H
sraman@scitech.edu
RAMARUI, Robert .... 680-488-2471 550 C
roramarui@gmail.com
RAMASWAMI, Anand .... 609-894-9311 306 B
aramaswami@bcc.edu
RAMASWAMY, Nandini . 317-940-9032 164 L
nramaswa@butler.edu
RAMBEAU, Nadine .... 661-255-1050.. 31 B
nrambeau@calarts.edu
RAMBIKUR, Sara .... 512-892-2835 470 M
RAMBISH, Medea .... 630-466-7900 162 K
mrambish@waubonsee.edu
RAMBO, Amanda .... 212-355-1501 318 A
arambo@christies.edu
RAMBO, Andrea .... 805-378-1407.. 75 C
arambo@vcccd.edu
RAMBO, Bill .... 509-533-7038 521 E
Bill.Rambo@scc.spokane.edu
RAMBO, Helen, S .... 405-466-3260 398 E
hsrambo@langston.edu
RAMBO, Thomas, A .... 540-375-2310 512 B
rambo@roanoke.edu
RAMCHAND, Latha .... 713-743-4604 491 D
ramchand@uh.edu
RAMDATH, Danielle, D . 413-585-3017 236 G
dramdath@smith.edu
RAMDATH, Danielle, D . 413-585-3017 236 G
gradstdy@smith.edu
RAMDATH, Sanjay .... 718-289-5705 318 E
sanjay.ramdath@bcc.cuny.edu
RAMER, Nicholas .... 516-299-3034 330 G
nicholas.ramer@liu.edu
RAMER, Rod .... 509-434-5325 521 F
rod.ramer@ccs.spokane.edu
RAMER, Rod .... 509-434-5325 521 D
rramer@ccs.spokane.edu
RAMER, Rodney .... 509-434-5325 521 E
rod.ramer@ccs.spokane.edu
RAMES, Marysz .... 402-375-7200 292 D
marames1@wsc.edu
RAMESH, S, K .... 818-677-4501.. 34 D
s.ramesh@csun.edu
RAMET, Carlos .... 989-964-4042 249 G
ramet@svsu.edu
RAMEY, Alfred .... 201-200-2039 304 C
aramey@njcu.edu
RAMEY, Diana, M .... 254-710-2005 469 D
diana_ramey@baylor.edu
RAMEY, Iris .... 757-728-6836 508 C
iris.ramey@hamptonu.edu
RAMEY, Lane .... 816-501-4633 281 B
lane.ramey@rockhurst.edu
RAMEY, Rob .... 336-334-4822 363 A
grramey@gtcc.edu
RAMEY, Susan .... 814-641-0440 417 F
hcc@dbcollege.edu
RAMEY, Teresa .... 843-661-1182 446 E
tramey@fmarion.edu
RAMEZANE, Marsha ..... 650-574-6161.. 64 D
ramezane@smccd.edu
RAMEZANE, Marsha ..... 650-574-6413.. 64 D
ramezanem@smccd.edu
RAMI, Janet .... 225-771-3266 207 A
janet_rami@subr.edu
RAMIAN, Michael .... 219-866-6176 172 E
miker@saintjoe.edu
RAMICONE, Arthur, G ... 412-624-6577 437 K
aramicone@cfo.pitt.edu
RAMIREZ, Alberto .... 301-624-2636 214 I
aramirez@frederick.edu
RAMIREZ, Alfred .... 818-240-1000.. 45 I
aramirez@glendale.edu
RAMIREZ, Arnold .... 979-230-3235 469 G
arnold.ramirez@brazosport.edu
RAMIREZ, Arthur .... 831-459-2158.. 72 E
apr@soe.ucsc.edu
RAMIREZ, Aurelio .... 617-879-7847 230 B
aramirez@massart.edu
RAMIREZ, Cecilia .... 757-825-3525 517 B
ramirezc@tncc.edu
RAMIREZ, Daniel .... 956-872-6411 482 G
dramirez@southtexascollege.edu
RAMIREZ, David .... 610-328-8175 436 A
dramire1@swarthmore.edu
RAMIREZ, Desiree .... 404-756-8919 129 A
dramirez@msm.edu
RAMIREZ, Edward .... 614-837-4088 394 H
ramireze@valorcollege.com
RAMIREZ, Fausto .... 718-960-8593 319 C
fausto.ramirez@lehman.cuny.edu
RAMIREZ, Glenda .... 281-487-1170 486 F
gramirez@txchiro.edu
RAMIREZ, Irving .... 347-964-8600 316 J
iramirez@boricuacollege.edu
RAMIREZ, Janelle, R ..... 979-862-1723 485 C
janelle@tamu.edu
RAMIREZ, Jason .... 435-586-7700 499 L
RAMIREZ, Jason .... 262-551-5800 535 E
jramirez@carthage.edu
RAMIREZ, Jose .... 787-620-2040 550 D
jramirez@aupr.edu
RAMIREZ, Jose, L .... 915-831-2634 473 J
jramir20@epcc.edu

RAPOPORT, Nancy, B ... 702-895-3301 295 G
nancy.rapoport@unlv.edu
RAPOSA, Donna ... 781-239-2500 231 G
draposa@massbay.edu
RAPOSA, Kristina ... 781-292-2264 226 G
kristina.raposa@olin.edu
RAPOZA, Mark, F ... 401-865-2064 441 F
mrapoza@providence.edu
RAPP, Gary ... 316-295-5838 187 C
rappg@friends.edu
RAPP, John ... 713-798-4517 469 C
jrapp@bcm.edu
RAPP, Karen ... 323-260-8108.. 51 D
rappk@elac.edu
RAPP, Norman ... 615-329-8848 456 G
nrapp@fisk.edu
RAPP, Peter ... 503-494-8744 408 D
hutching@ohsu.edu
RAPP, Ryan ... 573-882-6435 283 G
rappr@umsystem.edu
RAPP, Timothy ... 301-295-4231 548 D
timothy.rapp@usuhs.edu
RAPP, Tracy ... 828-627-4509 363 C
tkrapp@haywood.edu
RAPP, Virginia ... 310-660-3773.. 43 G
vrapp@elcamino.edu
RAPP, William, E ... 717-245-4400 548 G
RAPPLEY, Carol ... 616-234-5722 251 G
RAPPLEY, Marsha, D ... 517-353-1730 246 H
rappley@msu.edu
RAQUEL, Lisa ... 707-654-1011.. 34 B
lraquel@csum.edu
RARIG, Jenny, M ... 610-359-5148 416 G
jrarig@dccc.edu
RARIG, Kris ... 757-825-2801 517 B
rarigk@tncc.edu
RASBAND, James, R ... 801-422-6383 497 J
james_rasband@byu.edu
RASBERRY, Charles, J .. 914-395-2522 342 C
crasberry@sarahlawrence.edu
RASBERRY, Todd ... 502-863-8044 195 A
Rasberry@georgetowncollege.edu
RASCH, J. Lee ... 608-785-9210 544 E
raschl@westerntc.edu
RASCH, Marvin ... 309-268-8423 145 H
marvin.rasch@heartland.edu
RASCH, Mike ... 218-751-8670 263 J
mikerasch@oakhills.edu
RASCH, Randolph ... 517-355-6527 246 H
randolph.rasch@hc.msu.edu
RASCON, Tricia ... 805-893-4275.. 72 D
tricia.rascon@sa.ucsb.edu
RASHED, D. Omar ... 864-622-6031 443 E
orashed@andersonuniversity.edu
RASHED, Jamal ... 513-244-4273 387 A
jamal.rashed@msj.edu
RASHEED, Waheed ... 510-356-4760.. 78 G
RASHID, Frank, D ... 313-927-1205 246 D
frashid@marygrove.edu
RASHID, John ... 218-726-8821 264 G
jrashid@d.umn.edu
RASIZER, Lee ... 303-360-4728.. 81 I
Lee.Rasizer@CCaurora.edu
RASK, Brenda ... 303-718-5907.. 78 J
brenda.rask@aims.edu
RASK, Brenda ... 970-339-6332.. 78 J
brenda.rask@aims.edu
RASK, Kevin ... 719-389-6446.. 79 M
kevin.rask@coloradocollege.edu
RASKIND, Wayne ... 313-577-2519 252 G
raskind@wayne.edu
RASKOVICH, Linda ... 218-262-7370 258 H
lindaraskovich@hibbing.edu
RASMUS, James ... 678-891-2546 125 G
james.rasmus@gpc.edu
RASMUSSEN, Brock ... 612-874-3749 257 D
brock_rasmussen@mcad.edu
RASMUSSEN, Bruce, D . 402-280-2487 290 B
bdrass@creighton.edu
RASMUSSEN, Carrie, M 209-667-3201.. 35 C
cmrasmussen@csustan.edu
RASMUSSEN, Cheryl ... 785-442-6021 187 I
crasmussen@highlandcc.edu
RASMUSSEN,
Connie, A ... 308-432-6366 292 B
crasmussen@csc.edu
RASMUSSEN, Darin ... 360-650-3555 528 D
darin.rasmussen@wwu.edu
RASMUSSEN, David, W 850-644-5488 115 A
dwrasmussen@admin.fsu.edu
RASMUSSEN,
George, A ... 361-593-3712 486 A
allen.rasmussen@tamuk.edu
RASMUSSEN, Jack, L ... 801-626-6273 500 C
jrasmussen@weber.edu
RASMUSSEN, Karla, R .. 757-455-3316 518 H
krasmussen@vwc.edu
RASMUSSEN, Linda ... 601-266-4050 271 B
linda.rasmussen@usm.edu
RASMUSSEN, Michele .. 773-702-7770 161 D
mrasmussen@uchicago.edu
RASMUSSEN, Misty ... 252-222-6190 361 A
rasmussenm@carteret.edu
RASMUSSEN, Phil ... 425-889-5271 524 G
phil.rasmussen@northwestu.edu
RASMUSSEN, Rob ... 815-479-7599 152 B
rrasmuss@mchenry.edu
RASMUSSEN, Robert, H 225-578-2154 204 L
rrasmus@lsu.edu
RASMUSSEN, Sarah ... 605-256-5048 453 H
sarah.rasmussen@dsu.edu
RASMUSSEN, Schauna . 608-243-4478 543 C
slrassmussen@madisoncollege.edu
RASMUSSEN, Scott ... 208-282-2507 138 C
rasmscot@isu.edu
RASMUSSON, Beth ... 605-626-2655 454 A
Beth.Rasmusson@northern.edu
RASNAKE, Martha, L ... 276-964-7389 517 A
martha.rasnake@sw.edu
RASNICK, Becky, D ... 501-450-5200.. 25 F
rebekahr@uca.edu
RASNICK, Natalie ... 417-690-2209 273 C
nrasnick@cofo.edu
RASNICK, JR.,
William, B ... 423-439-7900 461 D
rasnick@etsu.edu
RASOR, Mark ... 918-540-6213 398 L
mrasor@neo.edu
RASOR, Rob ... 502-231-5221 198 D
rrasor@myLBC.us
RASP, Allison, M ... 512-416-5888 481 B
allisonm@stedwards.edu
RASPILLER, Edward, E .. 804-594-1571 515 G
traspiller@jtcc.edu
RASS, Heike ... 215-972-2031 429 G
HRass@pafa.org
RASSOUL, Hamid ... 321-674-7573 103 R
rassoul@fit.edu
RAST, Lawrence, R ... 260-452-2101 165 E
lawrence.rast@ctsfw.edu
RASZEWSKI, Thomas ... 410-864-3621 218 C
traszewski@stmarys.edu
RATCHFORD, Robert ... 423-425-4074 465 E
robert-ratchford@utc.edu
RATCLIFF, Chris ... 870-460-1058.. 24 C
ratcliff@uamont.edu
RATCLIFF, Christine, L . 662-252-8000 270 C
cratcliff@rustcollege.edu
RATCLIFF, Lance ... 417-269-3667 274 A
lance.ratcliff@coxcollege.edu
RATCLIFF, Ozie ... 617-588-1358 223 D
oratcliff@bfit.edu
RATCLIFFE, R. Samuel .. 540-464-7560 518 A
ratcliffers@vmi.edu
RATERS, Michael, P ... 765-361-6289 175 B
ratersm@wabash.edu
RATH, Lorie ... 419-783-2307 381 G
lrath@defiance.edu
RATH, Phillip, S ... 812-888-5101 174 F
prath@vinu.edu
RATHBONE,
Thomas, M ... 607-436-3224 344 B
rathbotm@oneonta.edu
RATHBONE-WEBBER,
Gillian ... 410-516-6330 216 A
gillianrw@jhu.edu
RATHE, Dean ... 303-914-6303.. 85 C
dean.rathe@rrcc.edu
RATHEAL, Juli ... 432-552-2530 495 F
ratheal_j@utpb.edu
RATHERT, Greg ... 763-433-1864 257 P
gregory.rathert@anokaramsey.edu
RATHJE, James, A ... 507-354-8221 257 A
rathjeja@mlc-wels.edu
RATHJE, John ... 734-995-7419 241 F
john.rathje@cuaa.edu
RATHJE, John, M ... 501-569-3345.. 24 A
jmrathje@ualr.edu
RATHJEN, Arthur, H ... 920-424-1020 540 B
rathjena@uwosh.edu
RATHKE, Debra ... 567-661-7247 390 D
debra_rathke@owens.edu
RATIGAN, Jim ... 702-895-2380 295 G
james.ratigan@unlv.edu
RATLIFF, Jill, C ... 606-783-2256 198 H
ji.ratliff@moreheadstate.edu
RATLIFF, John ... 704-272-5325 366 A
jratliff@spcc.edu
RATLIFF, John, D ... 540-985-9814 509 D
jdratliff@jchs.edu
RATLIFF, Kelly ... 530-752-6368.. 71 A
kmratliff@ucdavis.edu
RATLIFF, Kerry ... 606-368-6064 192 H
kerryratliff@alc.edu
RATLIFF, Kevin, B ... 540-453-2264 514 H
ratliffk@brcc.edu
RATLIFF, Nicolle ... 816-802-3421 276 F
nratliff@kcai.edu
RATLIFF, Thomas ... 765-677-2116 169 C
thomas.ratliff@indwes.edu
RATLIFF, Thomas, R ... 304-462-4112 532 G
thomas.ratliff@glenville.edu
RATLIFF, Vickie ... 276-523-7467 516 A
vratliff@me.vccs.edu
RATLIFF-CRAIN, Jeffrey . 309-794-7331 139 K
jeffreyratliff-crain@augustana.edu
RATLIFFE, Jeannine ... 304-424-8262 533 E
jeannine.ratliffe@wvup.edu
RATLIFFE, Wally ... 800-962-7682 285 I
physicalplantdirector@wma.edu
RATNER, Mark, C ... 847-491-3276 155 D
weinberg-dean@northwestern.edu
RATTIGAN, Paulette ... 401-232-6320 441 B
prattiga@bryant.edu
RATTY, Michael ... 617-732-2130 233 E
michael.ratty@mcphs.edu
RAUB, Tammara ... 315-792-3011 351 G
tlraub@utica.edu
RAUBENHEIMER,
Dianne ... 919-760-8913 359 B
raubenhe@meredith.edu
RAUCH, Dena ... 319-398-5476 180 J
dena.rauch@kirkwood.edu
RAUCH, Jason ... 518-736-3622 326 D
jrauch@fmcc.suny.edu
RAUCH, Kenneth, E ... 260-422-5561 167 F
kerauch@Indianatech.edu
RAUDENBUSH, Reid, C 410-778-7855 221 D
rraudenbush2@washcoll.edu
RAUFMAN, Amy, E ... 216-421-7413 380 B
aeraufman@cia.edu
RAUHUT, Curt ... 478-387-4778 125 E
crauhut@gmc.edu
RAULUK, Ruth ... 412-392-3996 433 F
rrauluk@pointpark.edu
RAUSCH, David ... 423-425-5270 465 E
david-rausch@utc.edu
RAUSCH, Rebecca ... 317-738-8100 166 B
rrausch@franklincollege.edu
RAUSCH, Todd ... 712-274-6400 184 A
todd.rausch@witcc.edu
RAUSCHENBERGER,
Margaret ... 414-382-6276 534 I
margaret.rauschenberger@alverno.edu
RAUSCHER, Victor, F ... 518-445-3294 314 H
vraus@albanylaw.edu
RAUTZHAN, Peter ... 610-282-1100 416 I
peter.rautzhan@desales.edu
RAVAIOLI, Charlotte ... 570-945-8175 422 B
charlotte.ravaioli@keystone.edu
RAVE, Carole ... 360-676-2772 524 D
crave@nwic.edu
RAVELLI, James, B ... 503-943-7540 410 H
ravelli@up.edu
RAVELO, Mercedes ... 718-780-7942 317 A
mercedes.ravelo@brooklaw.edu
RAVENELLE, Robert, G . 508-767-7325 222 D
rravenel@assumption.edu
RAVER, C. Cybele ... 212-998-2274 336 C
cybele.raver@nyu.edu
RAVERT, Patricia ... 801-422-6547 497 J
patricia_ravert@byu.edu
RAVINDRAN,
Tharanee, M ... 256-824-6036.... 9 A
Tharanee.Ravindran@uah.edu
RAVISHANKER,
Ganesan ... 781-283-2095 237 F
gravisha@wellesley.edu
RAWICZ, Diane ... 707-654-1039.. 34 B
drawicz@csum.edu
RAWJEE, Roopa ... 508-531-6171 229 C
roopa.rawjee@bridgew.edu
RAWL, Carolyn, D ... 334-244-3934.... 2 A
crawl@aum.edu
RAWLEIGH, Camilla, B . 717-262-2010 440 D
camilla.rawleigh@wilson.edu
RAWLEY, Albert ... 434-791-5654 505 A
brawley@averett.edu
RAWLEY, Ben ... 901-381-3939 466 E
benrawley@visible.edu
RAWLINGS, Becky ... 360-383-3404 528 E
brawling@whatcom.ctc.edu
RAWLINGS, Michelle ... 859-233-8116 200 D
registrar@transy.edu
RAWLINGS, Scott ... 217-234-5519 150 B
srawlings39277@lakeland.cc.il.us
RAWLINS, Benjamin ... 502-863-8403 195 A
Ben_Rawlins@georgetowncollege.edu
RAWLINS, Brad ... 870-972-2468.. 19 F
brawlins@astate.edu
RAWLINS, Jim, H ... 541-346-3201 410 F
jrawlins@uoregon.edu
RAWLINS, Robert ... 212-616-7264 327 D
robert.rawlins@helenefuld.edu
RAWLINSON, Eddy ... 972-860-5210 472 D
ebrawlinson@dcccd.edu
RAWLINSON, Ina, R ... 919-735-5151 367 A
irrawlinson@waynecc.edu
RAWLS, Terry ... 828-262-6519 369 D
rawlsdt@appstate.edu
RAWSKI, Greg ... 812-488-2954 173 H
gr14@evansville.edu
RAWSKI, Jim ... 706-379-3111 134 J
jkrawski@yhc.edu
RAY, Aisha ... 312-893-7137 144 H
aray@erikson.edu
RAY, Ambria ... 606-218-5626 201 C
ambriaray@upike.edu
RAY, Anita ... 706-245-7226 124 C
aray@ec.edu
RAY, Anthony ... 708-656-8000 153 G
anthony.ray@morton.edu
RAY, Barry, D ... 864-231-2015 443 E
bray@andersonuniversity.edu
RAY, Brandon ... 360-442-2254 524 A
bray@lowercolumbia.edu
RAY, Cara ... 678-717-3877 133 A
cara.ray@ung.edu
RAY, JR., Charles, A ... 504-816-8010 206 C
cray@nobts.edu
RAY, Darby, K ... 207-786-8241 209 F
dray3@bates.edu
RAY, David ... 502-410-6200 194 N
dray@galencollege.edu
RAY, David ... 513-244-8182 379 I
david.ray@ccuniversity.edu
RAY, David, H ... 405-325-5291 403 I
dray@ou.edu
RAY, David, W ... 312-280-3500 147 C
dray@aii.edu
RAY, Edward, J ... 541-737-4133 408 F
pres.office@oregonstate.edu
RAY, Gary ... 940-898-3010 490 D
gray@twu.edu
RAY, Jacqueline ... 541-278-5916 404 J
jray@bluecc.edu
RAY, Jasmine ... 501-812-2241.. 22 F
jray@pulaskitech.edu
RAY, Jeffrey ... 828-227-7368 372 C
jeffray@wcu.edu
RAY, Jerry ... 912-583-3115 121 H
jray@bpc.edu
RAY, Jess, D ... 309-438-8586 147 I
jdray@ilstu.edu
RAY, Judy, K ... 336-841-9201 357 E
jray@highpoint.edu
RAY, Katerina, R ... 419-372-8575 377 I
krray@bgsu.edu
RAY, Kathlin, D ... 775-784-6500 295 H
kray@unr.edu
RAY, Ken ... 813-253-7054 106 C
kray6@hccfl.edu
RAY, Kiersten ... 607-735-1870 324 J
kray@elmira.edu
RAY, Leigh, A ... 931-372-3320 462 A
lray@tntech.edu
RAY, Mandy ... 978-542-7253 230 E
mandy.ray@salemstate.edu
RAY, Marsha, M ... 717-245-1029 417 B
rayma@dickinson.edu
RAY, Mary Beth ... 217-786-2472 151 C
marybeth.ray@llcc.edu
RAY, Monica ... 256-372-5555.... 1 A
monica.ray@aamu.edu
RAY, Nicholas, T ... 812-941-2411 169 A
nicray@ius.edu
RAY, Pamela ... 850-644-8643 115 A
pray2@fsu.edu
RAY, Phillip ... 979-458-6421 484 E
pray@tamus.edu
RAY, JR., R. Richard ... 616-395-7785 244 A
ray@hope.edu
RAY, Rhonda ... 503-760-3131 404 I
rhonda@birthingway.edu
RAY, Richard, A ... 423-652-4784 457 J
president@king.edu
RAY, Roxie, L ... 203-576-4292.. 92 B
roxieray@bridgeport.edu
RAY, Sally ... 270-659-6933 201 D
sally.ray@wku.edu
RAY, Sandy ... 850-484-1212 110 D
scesaretti@pensacolastate.edu
RAY, Scott ... 903-923-2148 473 I
sray@etbu.edu
RAY, Shanna ... 615-966-5833 458 C
shanna.ray@lipscomb.edu
RAY, Shenita, L ... 804-257-5667 518 E
slray@vuu.edu
RAY, Teresa ... 828-327-7000 361 B
tray@cvcc.edu
RAY, Vivyen ... 201-360-4073 303 A
vray@hccc.edu
RAY, William ... 503-352-2786 408 I
raywb@pacificu.edu
RAYBUCK, Diane, R ... 330-972-6427 392 H
drr9@uakron.edu
RAYBURN, T. Monroe .. 202-319-5765.. 95 A
rayburn@cua.edu
RAYCHAUDHURI,
Uttiyo ... 864-656-2457 444 E
Uttiyo@clemson.edu

REED, Dallas .... 973-278-5400 300 C
dfr@berkeleycollege.edu
REED, Dan .... 530-898-6451.. 33 A
dmreed@csuchico.edu
REED, Daniel .... 619-201-8727.. 62 D
daniel.reed@sdcc.edu
REED, Daniel .... 319-335-2132 175 H
daniel-reed@uiowa.edu
REED, Darcy .... 507-284-3796 254 G
darcy.reed@mayo.edu
REED, David, D .... 906-487-3043 247 A
ddreed@mtu.edu
REED, Debra .... 903-813-2445 468 G
dreed@austincollege.edu
REED, Dee .... 812-535-5212 172 F
dreed@smwc.edu
REED, Diane .... 757-594-7202 506 I
dreed@cnu.edu
REED, Donna .... 971-722-4497 409 C
donna.reed@pcc.edu
REED, Doug .... 870-245-5167.. 22 C
reedd@obu.edu
REED, Elizabeth .... 215-884-8942 440 E
elizabeth.reed@woninstitute.edu
REED, Eloise .... 903-923-3222 488 A
eloise.reed@tstc.edu
REED, Francesca .... 703-284-5906 510 B
francesca.reed@marymount.edu
REED, Gary .... 214-648-2631 496 A
gary.reed@utsouthwestern.edu
REED, George .... 719-255-4047.. 86 F
george.reed@uccs.edu
REED, Helen .... 970-351-2601.. 87 A
helen.reed@unco.edu
REED, James .... 979-830-4168 469 F
james.reed@blinn.edu
REED, Jeff .... 515-292-9694 175 E
jeff.reed@antiochschool.edu
REED, Jeffrey, G .... 920-923-8760 537 A
jreed@marianuniversity.edu
REED, Jennifer, R .... 636-227-2100 277 A
jennifer.reed@logan.edu
REED, Jeremy .... 262-472-1440 541 D
reedj@uww.edu
REED, Jerry .... 570-389-4040 430 B
jreed@bloomu.edu
REED, John .... 425-249-4800 527 D
john.reed@tlc.edu
REED, Jonathan .... 909-593-3511.. 73 B
jreed@laverne.edu
REED, Karen, A .... 419-755-4538 387 E
kreed@ncstatecollege.edu
REED, Kathy .... 310-338-4404.. 53 C
kathy.reed@lmu.edu
REED, Kathy, S .... 217-581-3227 144 E
ksreed@eiu.edu
REED, Kevin .... 310-206-1355.. 71 D
kreed@conet.ucla.edu
REED, Kevin .... 585-245-5571 345 D
reedk@geneseo.edu
REED, Kimberly .... 270-745-2434 201 D
kim.reed@wku.edu
REED, Kristen .... 217-245-3054 146 D
kristen.reed@mail.ic.edu
REED, LaTonya .... 870-574-4504.. 23 E
lreed@sautech.edu
REED, Lee .... 202-687-2435.. 95 E
athletics@georgetown.edu
REED, Lori .... 507-457-5005 262 D
lreed@winona.edu
REED, Mark .... 603-646-9410 297 G
mark.reed@dartmouth.edu
REED, Mark, C .... 610-660-1200 434 G
reed@sju.edu
REED, Mark, F .... 610-861-1360 426 H
reedm@moravian.edu
REED, Martin .... 209-228-2977.. 71 E
mreed9@ucmerced.edu
REED, Maryann .... 304-293-4611 533 D
maryann.reed@mail.wvu.edu
REED, Maryanne .... 304-293-5746 533 D
maryanne.reed@mail.wvu.edu
REED, Matthew .... 732-224-2265 300 F
REED, Meredith .... 504-398-2236 206 E
mreed@olhcc.edu
REED, Michael, E .... 717-245-1159 417 B
reedme@dickinson.edu
REED, Michael, J .... 570-326-3761 429 J
mjr18@pct.edu
REED, Michelle .... 985-549-2241 208 E
mreed@selu.edu
REED, Mike .... 618-282-6682 160 B
mike.reed@swic.edu
REED, Nancy .... 901-572-2662 455 C
nancy.reed@bchs.edu
REED, Natalie, K .... 630-515-6183 152 H
nreedx@midwestern.edu
REED, Pamela .... 806-874-3571 470 J
pamela.reed@clarendoncollege.edu
REED, Rahim .... 530-752-2071.. 71 A
rreed@ucdavis.edu
REED, Richard .... 216-687-4736 380 D
R.REED68@csuohio.edu
REED, Robert .... 443-334-2240 218 E
rreed1951@stevenson.edu
REED, Robert, A .... 504-865-3735 206 A
rareed@loyno.edu
REED, Rod .... 479-524-7134.. 21 F
rreed@jbu.edu
REED, Scott .... 541-737-2713 408 F
scott.reed@oregonstate.edu
REED, Sharon .... 614-251-4595 388 H
reeds@ohiodominican.edu
REED, Shelby .... 712-279-5239 176 B
shelby.reed@briarcliff.edu
REED, Shirley, A .... 956-872-8366 482 G
yolandao@southtexascollege.edu
REED, Stephanie .... 610-902-1061 414 B
stephanie.d.reed@cabrini.edu
REED, Stephen .... 715-425-3701 540 E
stephen.reed@uwrf.edu
REED, Steve, E .... 417-667-8181 273 H
sreed@cottey.edu
REED, Steven .... 615-460-6367 455 D
steven.reed@belmont.edu
REED, Stuart, C .... 205-329-7898.... 3 C
stu.reed@ecacolleges.com
REED, Sue .... 484-365-7929 424 E
sreed@lincoln.edu
REED, Tashena .... 513-241-4338 376 N
tashena.reed@antonellicollege.edu
REED, Teresa .... 256-782-5303.... 4 L
treed@jsu.edu
REED, Terri Harris .... 202-994-1000.. 95 D
treed@gwu.edu
REED, Thomas .... 804-524-5045 518 C
tereed@vsu.edu
REED, Tita .... 440-775-6200 388 B
tita.reed@oberlin.edu
REED, Tom .... 251-575-8283.... 1 C
treed@ascc.edu
REED, Tracy .... 989-775-4123 249 F
reed.tracy@sagchip.edu
REED, Van .... 337-550-1211 205 B
vreed@lsue.edu
REED, Wayne, E .... 404-413-9500 126 D
reedw@gsu.edu
REED, William, O .... 503-943-7191 410 H
reed@up.edu
REED DAVIS, Christine . 704-687-0345 371 B
crdavis@uncc.edu
REEDER, David, C .... 301-447-5207 217 D
reeder@msmary.edu
REEDER, Josh .... 909-621-8281.. 65 E
jreeder@scrippscollege.edu
REEDER, Lizzie .... 336-750-2000 372 D
REEDER, Lynne .... 910-962-3746 372 A
reederl@uncw.edu
REEDER, Mary .... 337-421-6902 204 F
mary.reeder@sowela.edu
REEDER, Pam .... 573-518-2204 278 F
preeder@mineralarea.edu
REEDER, Pamela, K ...... 660-831-4123 279 D
reedere@moval.edu
REEDER, Philip, P .... 412-396-4877 417 I
reederp@duq.edu
REEDSTROM,
Cynthia, P .... 651-631-5246 265 D
clreedstrom@unwsp.edu
REEDUS, Janice .... 815-280-6640 148 K
jreedus@jjc.edu
REEDY, William .... 802-224-3000 503 F
william.reedy@vsc.edu
REEGER, Jennifer .... 724-830-1069 435 E
jreeger@setonhill.edu
REEKS, Kevin, L .... 419-995-8081 384 E
reeks.k@rhodesstate.edu
REEL, Abby .... 309-672-5530 152 E
areel@methodistcol.edu
REEL, Sally, J .... 520-626-4030.. 18 E
sreel@email.arizona.edu
REEL, Stephanie .... 410-735-6700 216 A
sreel@jhu.edu
REEM, Marvin, P .... 864-242-5100 443 G
REEMER, Ronda, S .... 765-641-4010 164 B
rsreemer@anderson.edu
REEP, Jeff .... 937-766-7868 378 K
reepj@cedarville.edu
REES, David, G .... 802-440-4337 501 D
rees@bennington.edu
REES, Doug, C .... 626-395-5802.. 31 D
dcrees@caltech.edu
REES, Margaret .... 702-895-3890 295 G
peg.rees@unlv.edu
REES, Pamela, D .... 515-263-6098 178 H
prees@grandview.edu
REES, Richard .... 203-285-2170.. 89 B
rrees@gwcc.commnet.edu
REESE, Aaron, J .... 706-507-8735 123 D
reese_aaron@columbusstate.edu
REESE, JR., Benjamin ... 919-684-8222 356 E
ben.reese@duke.edu
REESE, Brian .... 717-337-6240 419 C
breese@gettysburg.edu
REESE, Brian, P .... 864-833-8242 448 E
bpreese@presby.edu
REESE, Camille .... 704-878-3264 364 C
creese@mitchellcc.edu
REESE, Carole, A .... 610-861-1555 426 H
reesec@moravian.edu
REESE, Cynthia .... 510-981-2851.. 58 J
creese@peralta.edu
REESE, David .... 503-725-2655 409 D
dcreese@pdx.edu
REESE, Debra, C .... 302-831-2164.. 94 D
dcreese@udel.edu
REESE, Donald, G .... 315-733-2300 351 E
dreese@uscny.edu
REESE, Kimberly .... 504-520-7575 209 E
kreese@xula.edu
REESE, Kimberly .... 336-750-3145 372 D
reesekf@wssu.edu
REESE, Michael .... 209-228-4430.. 71 E
mreese@UCMerced.edu
REESE, Mike .... 619-644-7163.. 46 H
mike.reese@gcccd.edu
REESE, Pamela .... 716-488-3020 329 D
pamelareese@jamestownbusinesscollege.edu
REESE, Robert .... 574-936-8898 164 A
gene.reese@ancilla.edu
REESE, Robert .... 610-902-8554 414 B
robert.reese@cabrini.edu
REESE, Robert, C .... 540-985-8374 509 D
rcreese@jchs.edu
REESE, Robert, S .... 843-953-2468 445 B
reeser@cofc.edu
REESE, Thomas, L .... 410-293-9320 549 B
treese@usna.edu
REESER, Michael, L ...... 254-867-3128 487 G
mike.reeser@systems.tstc.edu
REESER, Mike .... 254-867-4891 488 B
mike.reeser@systems.tstc.edu
REESER, Todd .... 706-565-3669 123 D
REESOR, Lori .... 701-777-2724 373 G
lori.reesor@und.edu
REETZ, David .... 630-844-5416 139 L
dreetz@aurora.edu
REEVE, Gilmore .... 225-578-5513 204 M
tgreeve@lsu.edu
REEVERS, Stephanie ..... 931-221-7572 461 C
reeverss@apsu.edu
REEVES, Brent, W .... 618-537-6938 152 C
breeves@mckendree.edu
REEVES, Bret .... 615-248-1464 464 E
breeves@trevecca.edu
REEVES, Brian .... 918-343-7538 401 I
breeves@rsu.edu
REEVES, Christina .... 732-987-2249 302 J
reevesc@georgian.edu
REEVES, Christopher .... 319-656-2447 182 G
REEVES, Daryka .... 205-247-8018.... 7 G
dreeves@stillman.edu
REEVES, Dayne .... 318-487-7157 202 L
marcel.reeves@lacollege.edu
REEVES, Earl, J .... 660-831-4108 279 D
REEVES, Gary, W .... 601-984-6000 270 H
greeves@umc.edu
REEVES, Herbert .... 334-670-3203.... 8 A
hreeves@troy.edu
REEVES, Jacqueline, A . 203-576-4496.. 92 B
purchase@bridgeport.edu
REEVES, James .... 310-377-5501.. 53 E
jreeves@marymountcalifornia.edu
REEVES, Jason .... 606-546-1209 200 E
jreeves@unionky.edu
REEVES, Jim .... 310-377-5501.. 53 E
jreeves@marymountcalifornia.edu
REEVES, Joey .... 912-478-8607 126 B
jreeves@georgiasouthern.edu
REEVES, Kay .... 325-674-2675 466 I
reevesk@acu.edu
REEVES, Kent .... 903-923-2226 473 I
klreeves@etbu.edu
REEVES, Lindsay .... 706-864-1625 133 A
lindsay.reeves@ung.edu
REEVES, Mamiko .... 989-837-4136 248 D
reevesm@northwood.edu
REEVES, Mark .... 678-839-5079 133 F
mreeves@westga.edu
REEVES, Mark .... 870-972-2108.. 19 F
mreeves@astate.edu
REEVES, Mark, T .... 864-644-5020 449 B
mreeves@swu.edu
REEVES, Michelle .... 706-880-8249 127 N
mreeves@lagrange.edu
REEVES, Rick .... 303-914-6400.. 85 C
rick.reeves@rrcc.edu
REEVES, Robert, F .... 215-885-2360 425 C
rreeves@manor.edu
REEVES, Rodney .... 417-328-1770 282 D
rreeves@sbuniv.edu
REEVES, Ronald .... 818-401-1022.. 41 F
rreeves@columbiacollege.edu
REEVES, Sparky .... 229-931-2150 131 E
sreeves@southgatech.edu
REEVES, Tracey .... 352-395-5507 112 H
tracey.reeves@sfcollege.edu
REFFETT, Lisa .... 573-592-5226 285 J
lisa.reffett@westminster-mo.edu
REGA, Elizabeth .... 909-469-5460.. 76 I
erega@westernu.edu
REGALADO, Juan .... 909-593-3511.. 73 B
jregalado@laverne.edu
REGALADO RODRIGUEZ,
Margery .... 831-479-6285.. 30 C
maregala@cabrillo.edu
REGALIA, Delphine .... 510-642-3881.. 70 K
dmregalia@berkeley.edu
REGAN, Anna .... 732-255-0400 304 E
aregan@ocean.edu
REGAN, Dan .... 802-635-1242 504 A
dan.regan@jsc.edu
REGAN, James .... 304-243-2314 534 H
jregan@wju.edu
REGAN, Joseph, P .... 312-341-2110 157 E
jregan@roosevelt.edu
REGAN, Kathleen .... 315-781-3700 327 G
regan@hws.edu
REGAN, Laurie .... 503-552-1507 407 F
lregan@ncnm.edu
REGAN, Sheila, A .... 910-272-3305 365 D
sregan@robeson.edu
REGAN, Teresa .... 425-889-5252 524 G
teresa.regan@northwestu.edu
REGEHR, Nanci .... 480-517-8314.. 15 D
nanci.regehr@riosalado.edu
REGENCIO, Eugenia ...... 973-596-3068 304 D
eugenia.regencio@njit.edu
REGER, Mark, A .... 864-488-8317 447 F
mreger@limestone.edu
REGGIO, Nancy .... 408-453-9900.. 46 L
nreggio@henley-putnam.edu
REGIER, Elaine .... 405-945-9104 400 F
elainrr@osuokc.edu
REGIER, Jeanette .... 816-322-0110 272 L
jeanette.regier@calvary.edu
REGIER, Philip, R .... 480-965-2457.. 11 J
phil.regier@asu.edu
REGINO, Rolando .... 760-245-4271.. 75 G
rolando.regino@vvc.edu
REGIS, Chris, C .... 214-768-1178 482 J
cregis@smu.edu
REGIST-TOMLINSON,
Tara .... 718-270-6938 320 C
trtomlinson@mec.cuny.edu
REGISTER, Bob .... 803-754-4100 445 D
REGISTER, Patrick .... 831-459-4404.. 72 E
jpregister@ucsc.edu
REGISTER, Tammy .... 307-382-1606 546 L
tregiste@wwcc.wy.edu
REGISTRE, Dee .... 904-470-8050 102 A
d.registre@ewc.edu
REGJO, Kathryn .... 970-945-8691.. 80 D
REGNER, Cecile .... 617-541-5383 233 A
CRegner@rcc.mass.edu
REGNERUS, Arlene .... 312-935-6233 157 A
aregnerus@robertmorris.edu
REGO, Dan .... 860-727-6907.. 90 F
drego@goodwin.edu
REGUEIRO, Maria, C .... 305-821-3333 104 C
mregueiro@fnu.edu
REGULSKA, Joanna .... 732-932-1777 306 F
regulska@gaiacenters.rutgers.edu
REHAK, Patricia .... 361-582-2533 496 D
patricia.rehak@victoriacollege.edu
REHBEIN, Edna .... 512-716-4422 489 C
er04@txstate.edu
REHBEIN, Matt .... 615-966-6043 458 C
matt.rehbein@lipscomb.edu
REHBERG, Kathy .... 850-718-2233 100 E
rehbergk@chipola.edu
REHG, SJ, William .... 314-977-3150 281 M
rehgsp@slu.edu
REHM, David, B .... 301-447-5218 217 D
rehm@msmary.edu
REHM, Julie, M .... 216-368-6070 378 J
julie.rehm@case.edu
REHM, Matthew .... 740-362-3136 386 D
mrehm@mtso.edu
REHM, Roger, E .... 989-774-1474 240 O
rehm1re@cmich.edu
REHMANN, Jill .... 718-940-5846 341 A
jrehmann@sjcny.edu
REICH, Amy, R .... 516-463-7580 328 A
amy.r.reich@hofstra.edu
REICH, Anna Marie .... 478-289-2039 124 B
areich@ega.edu
REICH, Lewis .... 901-722-3220 461 A
lreich@sco.edu
REICH, Mary .... 208-376-7731 137 D
mreich@boisebible.edu

REMBOLD, Scott .... 202-319-6909.. 95 A
rembold@cua.edu

REMBOLT, Michelle ...... 303-871-4478.. 86 H
mrembolt@du.edu

REMELTS, Glenn, A ...... 616-526-6299 240 L
remelt@calvin.edu

REMENDER,
Kathleen, A .... 810-762-9794 245 A
kremende@kettering.edu

REMER, Rosalind .... 215-895-1203 417 E
rosalind.remer@drexel.edu

REMHOF, Tamara .... 540-891-3013 515 E
tremhof@germanna.edu

REMIAS, Roberta .... 586-498-4170 246 A
remiasr@macomb.edu

REMICE, Melba .... 212-517-3929 343 A
m.remice@sothebysinstitute.com

REMIERES-MORIN,
Pamela .... 207-755-5224 210 L
premieres@cmcc.edu

REMILLARD, Theresa .... 413-755-4336 233 B
remillard@stcc.edu

REMINGTON, Brodie ..... 201-216-5214 308 D

REMINGTON, Debra ...... 440-375-7040 385 B
dremington@lec.edu

REMINGTON, Judith, V 847-491-8413 155 D
j-remington@northwestern.edu

REMLEY, Daniel, C .... 570-577-1195 413 E
dan.remley@bucknell.edu

REMMENGA, Brad .... 219-785-5749 172 A
bremmenga@pnc.edu

REMMERS, Dawn .... 903-813-2374 468 G
dremmers@austincollege.edu

REMOTTI, Melissa .... 805-437-8410.. 32 H
melissa.remotti@csuci.edu

REMSBURG, Barbara .... 801-587-0851 499 K
bremsburg@housing.utah.edu

REMSBURG, Robin, E ... 336-334-5016 371 C
reremsbu@uncg.edu

REMUND, Kathleen .... 651-255-6112 264 F
kremund@unitedseminary.edu

RENACIA,
Victorina M, Y .... 671-735-2978 549 G
vrenacia@uguam.uog.edu

RENAGHAN, Dorothy .... 617-287-5450 228 G
dorothy.renaghan@umb.edu

RENAUD, Angela .... 401-598-1400 441 D
arenaud@jwu.edu

RENAUD, Robert, E ...... 717-245-1072 417 B
renaudr@dickinson.edu

RENAULT, Heather .... 703-284-1500 510 B
heather.renault@marymount.edu

RENAULT, Tara, C .... 717-245-1390 417 B
renaultt@dickinson.edu

RENBARGER, Bridgette . 402-399-2646 289 I
brenbarger@csm.edu

RENBARGER,
Christopher .... 805-986-5826.. 75 D
crenbarger@vcccd.edu

RENCIS, Joseph .... 931-372-3172 462 A
jrencis@tntech.edu

RENDER, Philip .... 843-477-2171 446 I
philip.render@hgtc.edu

RENDON, James, E ...... 860-444-8285 548 H
James.E.Rendon@uscg.mil

RENDON, Michael .... 361-825-2414 485 F
michael.rendon@tamucc.edu

RENDON, Mindy, P ...... 785-670-1065 192 B
mindy.rendon@washburn.edu

RENDON, Rudolph, L ... 512-448-8445 481 B
rudolphr@stedwards.edu

RENEAR, Allen, H .... 217-333-3280 162 A
renear@illinois.edu

RENEAU, Clint-Michael 512-245-2278 489 C
cr49669@txstate.edu

RENER, Christine .... 616-331-3498 243 E
renerc@gvsu.edu

RENEY, Richard .... 978-762-4000 232 D
rreney@northshore.edu

RENFREW, Michelle ...... 907-474-5337.. 10 I
mmrenfrew@alaska.edu

RENFRO, Bryan .... 319-296-4427 179 B
bryan.renfro@hawkeyecollege.edu

RENFROE, Dennis .... 336-887-3000 358 E
drenfroe@laureluniversity.edu

RENGIIL, Yoichi, K .... 671-735-3707 549 G
yoichi@uguam.uog.edu

RENICK, James .... 601-979-2244 267 H
james.c.renick@jsums.edu

RENICK, Timothy, M .... 404-413-2580 126 D
trenick@gsu.edu

RENIFF, William, M ...... 440-826-2212 377 D
breniff@bw.edu

RENKEMA, Teresa .... 616-222-3000 245 D
trenkema@kuyper.edu

RENKEN, Tracy .... 202-884-9095.. 97 A
renkent@trinitydc.edu

RENN, Joanne, M .... 757-455-3303 518 H
jrenn@vwc.edu

RENN, Peter .... 708-209-3007 143 D
peter.renn@cuchicago.edu

RENNA, Kimberly .... 760-547-1800.. 45 B
krenna@fst.edu

RENNA, Matt .... 914-773-3813 337 I
mrenna@pace.edu

RENNER, Cynthia .... 215-489-2467 416 H
cynthia.renner@delval.edu

RENNER, Karen .... 404-876-1227 122 A
karen.renner@bccr.edu

RENNER, Lance .... 417-447-8202 280 C
rennerl@otc.edu

RENNERT, Chaim .... 718-438-5476 352 I

RENNIE, Christopher .... 810-989-5642 249 H
ccrennie@sc4.edu

RENNIE, Robert .... 203-392-5004.. 88 F
rennie@southernct.edu

RENNINGER, Laura .... 304-876-5461 532 I
lrenning@shepherd.edu

RENNIX, Louise .... 843-525-8318 449 E
lrennix@tcl.edu

RENO, Adam .... 301-846-2560 214 I
areno@frederick.edu

RENO, RET., Loren .... 937-766-7770 378 K
lreno@cedarville.edu

RENO-MUNRO, Jane .... 843-953-6378 445 B
munroj@cofc.edu

RENSBERGER,
Jeffrey, L .... 713-646-1853 482 H
jrensberger@stcl.edu

RENSHLER, E. Kevin ..... 419-434-4439 393 F
renshler@findlay.edu

RENSHLER, Kevin .... 252-399-6630 354 I
renshler@barton.edu

RENTHROPE, Jullin .... 504-286-5117 207 B
jrenthrope@suno.edu

RENTMEESTER, Matt, G 920-433-6657 534 K
matt.rentmeester@bellincollege.edu

RENTSCH, Janet, D .... 989-964-7120 249 G
jrentsch@svsu.edu

RENTSCH, Kathleen .... 508-854-2712 232 F
krentsch@qcc.mass.edu

RENTSCHLER, Gina .... 417-865-2815 274 L
rentschlerg@evangel.edu

RENTTO, Jessica .... 619-594-6018.. 35 E
jrentto@mail.sdsu.edu

RENTZ, Joyce, L .... 256-551-1712.... 4 J
joyce.rentz@drakestate.edu

RENTZ, Judy .... 916-577-2200.. 77 F
jrentz@jessup.edu

RENTZ, Linda, T .... 517-586-3010 241 B
lrentz@cleary.edu

RENVILLE, Allen .... 530-895-2239.. 30 B
renvilleal@butte.edu

RENWICK, Mairi .... 804-278-4222 513 F
mrenwick@upsem.edu

RENWICK, Michael, D .. 860-297-2055.. 92 A
michael.renwick@trincoll.edu

RENY, Denise .... 207-741-5568 211 D
dreny@smccme.edu

RENY, James .... 207-741-5888 211 D
jreny@smccme.edu

RENZ, Amy Button .... 785-532-5050 188 H
arenz@ksu.edu

RENZ, Christopher, M .. 510-883-2084.. 43 C
crenz@dspt.edu

RENZ, Dianna .... 307-382-1871 546 L
drenz@wwcc.wy.edu

RENZI, April .... 814-262-3833 429 K
arenzi@pennhighlands.edu

RENZULLI, Beth, W ...... 603-526-3717 296 I
brenzull@colby-sawyer.edu

REPAC, Richard, A .... 301-687-4335 220 D
rrepac@frostburg.edu

REPENNING, Thomas ... 301-934-7630 214 E
tomr@csmd.edu

REPETSKI, Michael .... 330-941-1457 396 C
michael.repetski@cis.ysu.edu

REPETTO, Martha .... 212-645-0030 335 D
mrepetto@sft.edu

REPETTO, Paul .... 212-431-2836 335 G
Paul.Repetto@nyls.edu

REPKO, Susan .... 410-532-3191 217 F
srepko@ndm.edu

REPP, A. Drew .... 260-399-7700 174 C
arepp@sf.edu

REPP, Ian .... 906-487-1885 247 A

REPP, Philip, C .... 765-285-1034 164 D
prepp@bsu.edu

REPPERT, Angela .... 610-398-5300 424 C
areppert@lincolntech.edu

REPPERT, David .... 610-796-8463 412 C
david.reppert@alvernia.edu

RERRICK, Charlotte .... 212-757-1190 315 C
crerrick@funeraleducation.org

RESENIC, Enid .... 814-938-1159 431 A
enid@iup.edu

RESHEF, Shai .... 626-264-8880.. 73 D

RESIDES, Diane, L .... 443-412-2142 215 D
dresides@harford.edu

RESIDORI, Amber .... 815-939-5135 155 G
alresidori@olivet.edu

RESINGER, Rodney .... 573-518-2110 278 F
rresinger@mineralarea.edu

RESNICK, Coleen .... 508-541-1655 225 G
cresnick@dean.edu

RESNICK, Donald .... 212-229-5600 334 C
resnickd@newschool.edu

RESNICK, Nancy, E .... 541-346-2987 410 F
nresnick@uoregon.edu

RESSEL, Dawn .... 406-243-5661 287 D
dawn.ressel@umontana.edu

RESSLER, Koreen .... 701-854-8001 375 F
koreenr@sbci.edu

RESSLER, Lawrence, E .. 903-923-2039 473 I
lressler@etbu.edu

RESTO, Angianette .... 787-884-3838 550 E
coord_mercadeo@atenascollege.edu

RESTO,
Maria de Lourdes ...... 787-250-1912 554 A
mresto@metro.inter.edu

RESTO, Maristella .... 787-257-0000 557 F
maristella.resto1@upr.edu

RESTO, Richelle .... 703-821-8570 513 A
rresto@stratford.edu

RESTO TORRES, Juan ... 787-765-4210 551 F
jresto@cempr.edu

RESTUCCIA, Katie .... 508-626-4575 230 A
krestuccia@framingham.edu

RETANA, Ruthie .... 562-908-3445.. 60 I
RRetana@riohondo.edu

RETASKET, Victoria .... 360-676-2772 524 D
vretasket@nwic.edu

RETCHIN, Sheldon, M .. 614-297-4477 389 A
retchin.1@osu.edu

RETELLE, Mary Louise .. 508-849-3333 222 C
mretelle@annamaria.edu

RETHERFORD, Kristine . 507-389-6315 260 A
kristine.retherford@mnsu.edu

RETHMAN, Shari .... 937-512-2881 391 D
shari.rethman@sinclair.edu

RETIF, Earl .... 504-865-5731 207 F
eretif@tulane.edu

RETKA, James .... 218-683-8643 260 F
james.retka@northlandcollege.edu

RETTERER, Tony .... 540-785-5440 514 C
tonyretterer@vbc.edu

RETTIG, Glenn .... 567-661-7457 390 D
glenn_rettig@owens.edu

RETTIG, James .... 410-293-6900 549 B
rettig@usna.edu

RETTIG, Perry .... 706-776-0110 130 B
prettig@piedmont.edu

RETTLER, Peter, J .... 262-335-5706 543 F
prettler@morainepark.edu

REUKAUF, Sue .... 608-822-2303 544 C
sreukauf@swtc.edu

REUSCHER, Karen .... 315-781-3722 327 G
reuscher@hws.edu

REUSS, Cindy .... 231-777-0575 247 G
cindy.reuss@muskegoncc.edu

REUSTLE, Maureen .... 732-255-0400 304 E
mreustle@ocean.edu

REUTER, William, D ..... 716-851-1700 325 A
reuter@ecc.edu

REUTTER, John .... 256-551-3119.... 4 J
john.reutter@drakestate.edu

REUTZEL, Ray .... 307-766-3145 546 K
ray.reutzel@uwyo.edu

REVELEY, III,
W. Taylor .... 757-221-1693 506 J
taylor@wm.edu

REVELEY, IV, W. Taylor 434-395-2001 509 H
reveleywt@longwood.edu

REVELS-BULLARD,
Angela .... 910-521-6279 371 D
angela.revels-bullard@uncp.edu

REVELT, Joseph, E .... 717-871-7871 431 E
joseph.revelt@millersville.edu

REVENAUGH, Ken .... 314-392-2356 278 G
revenaug@mobap.edu

REVENIS, Anthony .... 301-295-3068 548 D
anthony.revenis@usuhs.edu

REVIERE, Mallory .... 505-277-0111 313 H
mreviere@unm.edu

REVILLA, Elva .... 517-483-1413 245 I
revillae@lcc.edu

REVOLDT, Daryl .... 330-494-6170 391 J
drevoldt@starkstate.edu

REVZINA, Larisa .... 650-685-6616.. 46 I

REWERTS, Glen .... 815-939-5277 155 G
grewerts@olivet.edu

REWERTS, Wendy .... 828-398-2500 368 I

REX, Barbara .... 805-493-3175.. 31 H
rex@callutheran.edu

REX, Lisa Youngkin ..... 610-330-5060 423 A
rexl@lafayette.edu

REX, Scott .... 541-552-6745 409 G
rexs@sou.edu

REX-COOK, Beverly ...... 419-995-8177 384 E
rexcook.b@rhodesstate.edu

REXILIUS-TUTHILL,
Reiko .... 518-327-6319 338 B
rtuthill@paulsmiths.edu

REY, Jennifer .... 307-855-2113 545 a
jrey@cwc.edu

REYER, Otto .... 909-469-5350.. 76 I
oreyer@westernu.edu

REYES, Amy, S .... 570-321-4134 425 B
reyes@lycoming.edu

REYES, April .... 805-275-5394.. 29 J
areyes2@brooks.edu

REYES, Arturo .... 707-468-3071.. 54 A
areyes@mendocino.edu

REYES, Carlos .... 916-484-8428.. 52 I
reyesc@arc.losrios.edu

REYES, Edgardo .... 787-780-0070 550 G
ereyes@caribbean.edu

REYES, Ginger .... 805-437-8521.. 32 H
ginger.reyes@csuci.edu

REYES, Hector, M .... 787-894-2828 558 F
hector.reyes4@upr.edu

REYES, Irene .... 787-758-2525 558 C
irene.reyes1@upr.edu

REYES, Ivelisse .... 787-850-9332 558 A
ivelisse.reyes1@upr.edu

REYES, Jennifer .... 201-447-7456 300 B
jreyes@bergen.edu

REYES, Joseph .... 831-755-6950.. 46 J
jreyes@hartnell.edu

REYES, Loui .... 575-646-5746 312 A
louireye@nmsu.edu

REYES, Luz, C .... 787-884-3838 550 E
lreyes1@atenascollege.edu

REYES, Maria, A .... 480-726-4097.. 14 K
Maria.Reyes@cgc.edu

REYES, Mario, S .... 208-885-7146 139 C
mreyes@uidaho.edu

REYES, Monica, B .... 989-964-4168 249 G
mbreyes@svsu.edu

REYES, Nora .... 480-461-7151.. 15 A
nora.reyes@mesacc.edu

REYES, Ray .... 619-660-4206.. 46 G
ray.reyes@gcccd.edu

REYES, Raymond .... 509-313-5604 522 L
reyes@gu.gonzaga.edu

REYES, Robert, G .... 214-860-2090 472 F
rreyes@dcccd.edu

REYES, Rosana .... 570-740-0336 425 A
rreyes@luzerne.edu

REYES, Rudy .... 574-631-0694 174 A
rreyes@nd.edu

REYES, Saul .... 352-854-2322 100 P
reyess@cf.edu

REYES-GIL, Yanira .... 787-751-1912 554 D
yreyes@juris.inter.edu

REYMANN, Linda .... 443-352-4203 218 E
lreymann@stevenson.edu

REYNA, Angel .... 509-527-4299 527 H
angel.reyna@wwcc.edu

REYNA, Cynthia .... 870-864-7130.. 23 B
creyna@southark.edu

REYNA, Deirdre .... 956-764-5919 477 C
dreyna@laredo.edu

REYNA, Dorotea .... 415-575-6135.. 31 C
dreyna@ciis.edu

REYNA, Marilu, A .... 210-784-1101 486 B
mreyna@tamusa.tamus.edu

REYNA, Mario .... 956-872-6116 482 G
reyna@southtexascollege.edu

REYNA, Oscar .... 361-825-5934 485 F
oscar.reyna@tamucc.edu

REYNA, Patrick .... 210-297-9663 468 K
pgreyna@baptisthealthsystem.com

REYNA, Tony .... 713-942-5920 493 J
reynat@stthom.edu

REYNA, Yolanda .... 210-486-3333 467 A
yreyna@alamo.edu

REYNARD, Betty .... 409-984-6100 488 H
betty.reynard@lamarpa.edu

REYNDERS, John, C ..... 712-274-5100 181 C
reynders@morningside.edu

REYNOLD, Ellen .... 401-874-5155 442 E
ellen@uri.edu

REYNOLDS, Angela .... 479-968-0396.. 20 C
areynolds@atu.edu

REYNOLDS, Barry .... 276-638-8777 516 D
breynolds@patrickhenry.edu

REYNOLDS, Brad .... 706-865-2134 132 G
breynolds@truett.edu

REYNOLDS, Carolyn, H 276-523-2400 516 A
creynolds@me.vccs.edu

REYNOLDS, Cathy .... 404-527-4520 122 D
creynolds@carver.edu

REYNOLDS, Chris .... 309-677-2670 140 H
reynolds@fsmail.bradley.edu

REYNOLDS, Colleen ...... 309-268-8170 145 H
colleen.reynolds@heartland.edu

REYNOLDS, Curtis .... 352-392-1336 115 D
curtrey@ufl.edu

REYNOLDS, David .... 940-565-3990 492 D
David.Reynolds@unt.edu

RICE, Rachel .... 207-768-9447 212 H
rachel.rice@umpi.edu
RICE, Raymond, J .... 207-768-9518 212 H
raymond.rice@umpi.edu
RICE, Scott .... 217-333-0560 162 A
serice@uillinois.edu
RICE, Shelly .... 386-481-2580.. 99 F
rices@cookman.edu
RICE, Sherwin .... 910-879-5646 360 C
srice@bladencc.edu
RICE, Stephen .... 201-684-7407 305 F
srice@ramapo.edu
RICE, Susan, I .... 336-633-0282 365 A
sirice@randolph.edu
RICE, Tammy .... 949-582-4701.. 67 F
trice@saddleback.edu
RICE, Timothy, S .... 304-367-4917 532 F
Timothy.Rice@fairmontstate.edu
RICE, Vance .... 662-325-6731 269 A
rice@safdfairs.msstate.edu
RICE AYALA, Maggie .... 773-907-4041 141 O
mrice19@ccc.edu
RICE-CARROLL, Cynthia 760-757-2121.. 54 G
crice@miracosta.edu
RICE-CLAYBORN, Kathy 501-450-3134.. 25 F
kathyc@uca.edu
RICE-MASON, Jenifer .... 870-972-3964.. 19 F
jrmason@astate.edu
RICE-SADDLER, Lori ..... 404-880-8447 122 I
lrice@cau.edu
RICE-TUMA, Rachel ...... 800-567-2344 535 F
rrice@menominee.edu
RICH, Arthur .... 402-457-2681 291 E
aarich@mccneb.edu
RICH, Frank .... 432-335-6507 479 O
frich@odessa.edu
RICH, Jack, W .... 325-674-2013 466 I
richj@acu.edu
RICH, Jeffrey .... 952-885-5414 263 I
jbrich@nwhealth.edu
RICH, John .... 620-341-5274 186 H
jrich@emporia.edu
RICH, Kathy .... 781-280-3501 232 B
richk@middlesex.mass.edu
RICH, Kim .... 860-932-4141.. 90 A
krich@qvcc.commnet.edu
RICH, Laura .... 910-893-4364 355 C
richl@campbell.edu
RICH, Scott .... 620-278-4213 191 D
srich@sterling.edu
RICH, Sheri .... 979-830-4181 469 F
sheri.rich@blinn.edu
RICH, Steven .... 617-236-8800 226 F
srich@fisher.edu
RICH, Steven, W .... 217-581-6616 144 E
swrich@eiu.edu
RICH, Tammy .... 570-484-2128 431 C
trich@lhup.edu
RICH, Tammy, M .... 570-326-3761 429 J
tmr4@pct.edu
RICH, Timothy, A .... 651-631-5489 265 D
tarich@unwsp.edu
RICH-COATES, Robin .... 757-789-1748 515 D
rrich-coates@es.vccs.edu
RICHARD, Alison, A ..... 570-372-4111 435 I
arichard@susqu.edu
RICHARD, Arthur .... 252-940-6210 360 B
arthur.richard@beaufortccc.edu
RICHARD, Cindy .... 978-998-7762 226 C
cirichar@endicott.edu
RICHARD, Dan .... 904-620-2700 116 A
drichard@unf.edu
RICHARD, David .... 407-646-2232 111 H
dcrichard@rollins.edu
RICHARD, Deborah .... 407-708-2487 113 A
richardd@seminolestate.edu
RICHARD, Mark .... 256-840-4110.... 7 B
mrichard@snead.edu
RICHARD, Mark .... 205-665-6600.... 9 C
mrichard11@montevallo.edu
RICHARD, Renee .... 216-987-4865 381 A
renee.richard@tri-c.edu
RICHARD, Robert .... 337-482-6923 208 F
bookstore@louisiana.edu
RICHARD, Roseann ...... 707-654-1175.. 34 B
rrichard@csum.edu
RICHARD, Thomas .... 603-358-2326 299 D
trichard@keene.edu
RICHARD, Trish .... 409-772-8221 495 E
plrichar@utmb.edu
RICHARD, Valerie .... 704-403-3507 355 B
valerie.richard@carolinashealthcare.org
RICHARDELLO, Denise . 413-662-5201 230 C
denise.richardello@mcla.edu
RICHARDS, Belarmina .. 714-316-0366.. 70 D
belarmina.richards@trident.edu
RICHARDS, Char .... 262-524-6891 535 D
crichard@carrollu.edu
RICHARDS, Cheryl .... 980-224-8466 235 D
RICHARDS, Chris .... 715-346-3908 541 A
crichards@uwsp.edu
RICHARDS, Connie, L .. 229-333-5699 133 H
clrichards@valdosta.edu
RICHARDS, David .... 626-584-5458.. 45 F
richards@fuller.edu
RICHARDS, David, J ..... 517-321-0242 243 H
drichards@glcc.edu
RICHARDS, Debbie .... 304-424-8201 533 E
debbie.richards@wvup.edu
RICHARDS, Doug .... 573-651-5923 282 C
drichards@semo.edu
RICHARDS, Elizabeth .... 603-668-2211 298 H
e.richards1@snhu.edu
RICHARDS, Faith .... 605-455-6029 452 L
frichards@olc.edu
RICHARDS, Ginger .... 317-805-1783 530 G
vrichards@salemu.edu
RICHARDS, Gordon ...... 724-847-6718 419 B
grichard@geneva.edu
RICHARDS, Gwyn .... 812-855-2435 167 J
grichar@indiana.edu
RICHARDS, Harry, J ..... 603-862-3000 299 B
harry.richards@unh.edu
RICHARDS, James .... 314-516-4570 284 B
jamesrichards@umsl.edu
RICHARDS, Jeni .... 949-376-6000.. 49 K
jrichards@lcad.edu
RICHARDS, John .... 808-734-9518 136 C
john.richards@hawaii.edu
RICHARDS, Josh .... 816-936-8718 282 A
RICHARDS, Kathi, S ..... 937-778-7843 381 K
krichards@edisonohio.edu
RICHARDS, Kathy, A ..... 906-227-1237 248 B
kathrich@nmu.edu
RICHARDS, Katie, J ..... 701-788-4675 374 A
katie.judisch.2@mayvillestate.edu
RICHARDS, Kenneth ..... 505-583-1074 236 D
RICHARDS, Kent .... 218-733-5969 259 C
k.richards@lsc.edu
RICHARDS, Larry, J ...... 801-524-8101 498 J
lrichards@ldsbc.edu
RICHARDS, Lawrence ... 610-399-2405 430 D
police@cheyney.edu
RICHARDS, Leah .... 603-668-2211 298 H
l.richards1@snhu.edu
RICHARDS, Lee .... 614-235-4136 392 D
lrichards@TLSohio.edu
RICHARDS, Leon .... 808-734-9565 136 C
lr24@hawaii.edu
RICHARDS, Letha .... 662-621-4126 266 H
lrichards@coahomacc.edu
RICHARDS, Mark .... 510-642-5872.. 70 K
Mark_Richards@berkeley.edu
RICHARDS, Marty .... 704-216-3459 365 F
marty.richards@rccc.edu
RICHARDS, Marvin .... 216-987-4883 381 A
marvin.richards@tri-c.edu
RICHARDS, Maryanne ... 508-830-5039 230 D
mrichards@maritime.edu
RICHARDS, Matthew ..... 207-741-5927 211 D
mrichards@smccme.edu
RICHARDS, Michael, D . 702-651-5600 295 C
mike.richards@csn.edu
RICHARDS, Paul .... 801-524-8139 498 J
PRichards@ldsbc.edu
RICHARDS, Randy .... 561-803-2543 109 G
randy_richards@pba.edu
RICHARDS, Rhonda ...... 405-585-4602 399 I
rhonda.richards@okbu.edu
RICHARDS, Robin .... 650-306-3339.. 64 C
richardsr@smccd.edu
RICHARDS, Roger, C .... 850-263-3261.. 99 A
rcrichards@baptistcollege.edu
RICHARDS, Rosalie .... 386-822-7256 117 A
rrichar1@stetson.edu
RICHARDS, Sandra, K .. 850-263-3261.. 99 A
skrichards@baptistcollege.edu
RICHARDS, Sandra, K .. 800-328-2660.. 99 A
skrichards@baptistcollege.edu
RICHARDS, Sandra, K .. 850-263-3261.. 99 A
skrichards@baptistcollege.edu
RICHARDS, Scott .... 412-396-5140 417 I
richards@duq.edu
RICHARDS, Steve .... 320-762-4692 257 O
stever@alextech.edu
RICHARDS, Susan .... 307-754-6243 546 I
Susan.Richards@nwc.edu
RICHARDS, Terry .... 513-745-2984 396 B
richardst1@xavier.edu
RICHARDS, Tom, F .... 573-882-2612 283 G
richardstf@umsystem.edu
RICHARDS, Tracey .... 215-619-7330 426 E
trichards@mc3.edu
RICHARDSON, Ann .... 206-934-4567 525 K
ann.richardson@seattlecolleges.edu
RICHARDSON, Barbara . 520-586-1981.. 13 B
richardsonbarb@cochise.edu
RICHARDSON, Barbara . 520-384-4502.. 13 B
richardsonbarb@cochise.edu
RICHARDSON, Becky .... 229-391-2624 132 C
RICHARDSON,
Bernard, L .... 202-806-7280.. 96 B
brichardson@howard.edu
RICHARDSON,
Beverly, A .... 609-894-9311 306 B
brichardson@bcc.edu
RICHARDSON,
Bonita, L .... 412-237-4413 415 G
brichardson@ccac.edu
RICHARDSON, Brent ..... 847-628-2540 149 A
brichardson@judsonu.edu
RICHARDSON, Brian, A 804-371-3000 515 F
RICHARDSON, Brittany . 504-816-4797 202 F
brichardson@dillard.edu
RICHARDSON, Brittney . 215-885-2360 425 C
brichardson@manor.edu
RICHARDSON, Bruce .... 520-515-3602.. 13 B
richardsonb@cochise.edu
RICHARDSON, Camille . 252-940-6236 360 B
camille.richardson@beaufortccc.edu
RICHARDSON, Carol ..... 954-545-4500 113 B
studentlife@sfbc.edu
RICHARDSON, Carol ..... 858-642-8460.. 55 J
crichardson@nu.edu
RICHARDSON, Carole ... 319-208-5053 183 B
crichardson@scciowa.edu
RICHARDSON, JR.,
Charles .... 803-535-5207 444 D
crichardson@claflin.edu
RICHARDSON,
Charles, J .... 518-381-1210 342 E
richarcj@sunysccc.edu
RICHARDSON,
Christine .... 315-655-7147 317 J
cwrichardson@cazenovia.edu
RICHARDSON, Cinzia ... 973-720-2976 309 I
richardsonc@wpunj.edu
RICHARDSON, D. Scott 616-331-2215 243 E
richarsc@gvsu.edu
RICHARDSON, David .... 509-527-2511 528 A
david.richardson@wallawalla.edu
RICHARDSON, David, E 352-392-0780 115 D
der@ufl.edu
RICHARDSON, Denise .. 510-464-3224.. 59 B
drichardson@peralta.edu
RICHARDSON, Doug ..... 405-425-5260 399 J
book.store@oc.edu
RICHARDSON,
Elisabeth .... 606-546-1700 200 E
erichardson@unionky.edu
RICHARDSON, Greer ..... 215-951-1806 422 F
richards@lasalle.edu
RICHARDSON, Greg, C . 606-474-3250 195 F
greg@kcu.edu
RICHARDSON, Guy, L .. 601-923-1650 270 B
grichardson@rts.edu
RICHARDSON, Helena .. 302-622-8000.. 93 D
hrichardson@dcad.edu
RICHARDSON, Irene ..... 513-244-4432 387 A
irene.richardson@msj.edu
RICHARDSON, James ... 509-682-6400 528 C
jrichardson@wvc.edu
RICHARDSON,
James, A .... 225-578-6745 204 M
parich@lsu.edu
RICHARDSON, Jennifer . 518-454-2023 322 C
richardj@strose.edu
RICHARDSON, John ..... 706-771-4111 121 B
jrichard@augustatech.edu
RICHARDSON, John ..... 303-837-0825.. 79 C
jrichardson@aii.edu
RICHARDSON, CM,
John, T .... 312-362-8712 143 G
jrichard@depaul.edu
RICHARDSON, Karlene . 212-247-3434 331 G
krichardson@mandl.edu
RICHARDSON, Karry, D 573-629-3016 275 F
krichardson@hlg.edu
RICHARDSON, Kathleen 515-271-2295 177 K
kathleen.richardson@drake.edu
RICHARDSON,
Kathy Brittain .... 706-236-2216 121 E
krichardson@berry.edu
RICHARDSON, Krista .... 419-995-8312 384 E
richardson.k@rhodesstate.edu
RICHARDSON, Lilliard .. 317-274-2016 168 E
lillrichr@iupui.edu
RICHARDSON, Lisa, A .. 352-518-1301 110 B
richarl@phsc.edu
RICHARDSON, Logan ... 864-488-8277 447 F
lrichardson@limestone.edu
RICHARDSON, Lois ...... 678-407-5200 125 B
lrichardson@ggc.edu
RICHARDSON, Luns, C 803-934-3211 447 K
lcrichardson@morris.edu
RICHARDSON, Lynda .... 501-337-5000.. 20 H
lrichardson@coto.edu
RICHARDSON,
Lynne, D .... 540-654-1561 513 I
lrichar2@umw.edu
RICHARDSON, Maria .... 334-420-4499.... 7 I
mrichardson@trenholmstate.edu
RICHARDSON, Mark ..... 503-494-8220 408 D
somdeansoffice@ohsu.edu
RICHARDSON, Mary ..... 229-430-3588 119 I
mrichardson@albanytech.edu
RICHARDSON,
Matthew, O .... 801-422-2640 497 J
matt_richardson@byu.edu
RICHARDSON, Melanie . 505-438-8884 313 C
melanie@acupuncturecollege.edu
RICHARDSON, Melanie . 360-438-4367 525 H
mrichardson@stmartin.edu
RICHARDSON, Michael . 417-667-8181 273 H
mrichardson@cottey.edu
RICHARDSON, Michael . 607-274-3533 328 H
mrichardson@ithaca.edu
RICHARDSON,
Michael, W .... 406-496-4213 288 C
mrichardson@mtech.edu
RICHARDSON,
Ralph, C .... 913-541-1220 188 H
rcr@ksu.edu
RICHARDSON,
Raymond .... 806-720-7230 478 A
raymond.richardson@lcu.edu
RICHARDSON, Rebecca 707-545-3647.. 29 D
admissions@berginu.edu
RICHARDSON, Rick ...... 302-736-2461.. 94 E
rick.richardson@wesley.edu
RICHARDSON, Roger .... 607-274-1623 328 H
rrichard@ithaca.edu
RICHARDSON, Rusty .... 615-547-4401 456 C
rrichardson@cumberland.edu
RICHARDSON,
Sarah, D .... 402-280-2703 290 B
SarahRichardson@creighton.edu
RICHARDSON, Scott ..... 570-674-6247 426 D
srichard@misericordia.edu
RICHARDSON,
Silvana, F .... 608-796-3687 542 H
sfrichardson@viterbo.edu
RICHARDSON, Steven ... 562-860-2451.. 37 L
srichardson@cerritos.edu
RICHARDSON, Sydney .. 336-917-5588 368 F
RICHARDSON, Terry ..... 276-944-6231 507 E
trichard@ehc.edu
RICHARDSON, Thomas . 662-329-7142 269 B
tcrichardson@muw.edu
RICHARDSON,
Thomas, J .... 717-871-7084 431 E
tom.richardson@millersville.edu
RICHARDSON, Tracey ... 831-755-6752.. 46 J
trichardson@hartnell.edu
RICHARDSON, Tracy ..... 812-535-5154 172 F
trichard@smwc.edu
RICHARDSON, Trenace . 202-408-2400.. 96 H
RICHARDSON, Valerie .. 256-549-8228.... 3 N
vrichardson@gadsdenstate.edu
RICHARDSON, Valerie .. 334-291-4981.... 2 H
valerie.richardson@cv.edu
RICHARDSON, Virginia . 304-327-4402 532 D
jrichardson@bluefieldstate.edu
RICHARDSON,
W. Mark .... 510-204-0733.. 38 K
mrichardson@cdsp.edu
RICHARDSON, Wayne ... 954-545-4500 113 B
newsletter@sfbc.edu
RICHARDSON, William . 225-578-4161 204 M
brichardson@agcenter.lsu.edu
RICHARDSON-PHILLIPS,
Deborale .... 216-987-0204 381 A
deborale.richardson-phillips@tri-c.edu
RICHARDVILLE, Alane ... 863-638-7209 118 L
alane.richardville@warner.edu
RICHBURG, Andre .... 609-343-5086 299 G
arichbur@atlantic.edu
RICHBURG, Cindye, T .. 803-535-5575 444 D
crichburg@claflin.edu
RICHER, Jason, D .... 512-471-6231 493 M
oa.jrichter@austin.utexas.edu
RICHERSON, Melissa .... 805-546-3129.. 42 H
melissa_richerson@cuesta.edu
RICHERT, David, G .... 651-631-5376 265 D
dgrichert@unwsp.edu
RICHES, Jonathan, S .... 610-292-9852 433 J
jonathan.riches@reseminary.edu
RICHEY, Amber, L .... 937-255-6565 547 E
amber.richey@afit.edu
RICHEY, Angie .... 909-599-5433.. 50 H
arichey@lifepacific.edu
RICHEY, Anthony .... 334-244-3570.... 2 A
arichey@aum.edu
RICHEY, D. Michael ..... 859-257-3912 200 G
mrichey@email.uky.edu
RICHEY, James, H .... 321-433-7000 101 O
richeyj@easternflorida.edu
RICHEY, Lance, D .... 260-399-7700 174 C
lrichey@sf.edu

RICHEY, Melody, H ...... 901-843-3730 460 F
richey@rhodes.edu
RICHEY, Patrick .... 585-389-2020 334 B
prichey1@naz.edu
RICHEY, Suzanne .... 423-636-7303 464 F
srichey@tusculum.edu
RICHEY, Thomas .... 562-860-2451.. 37 L
trichey@cerritos.edu
RICHEY, Warren, A .... 901-843-3845 460 F
richeyw@rhodes.edu
RICHIE, Darren, A .... 303-963-3187.. 79 L
drichie@ccu.edu
RICHIE, Patricia, V .... 561-868-3540 109 H
richiep@palmbeachstate.edu
RICHISON, Anna, C ...... 260-982-5067 170 a
RICHMAN, Jack, M ...... 919-962-5650 371 A
jrichman@email.unc.edu
RICHMAN, John .... 701-671-2221 375 B
john.richman@ndscs.edu
RICHMAN, Steve .... 660-359-3948 279 L
srichman@mail.ncmissouri.edu
RICHMAN, William .... 301-322-0723 217 G
wrichman@pgcc.edu
RICHMOND, Jayne, E ... 401-874-5505 442 E
richmond@uri.edu
RICHMOND, Jennifer .... 412-304-0727 418 F
jrichmond@cci.edu
RICHMOND, Jillian .... 619-849-7082.. 59 K
jillianrichmondl@pointloma.edu
RICHMOND, Kerry .... 570-321-4202 425 B
richmond@lycoming.edu
RICHMOND, Lisa, T ..... 630-752-5101 163 G
lisa.richmond@wheaton.edu
RICHMOND, Margaret .. 603-358-2276 299 D
mrichmon@keene.edu
RICHMOND, Nicola .... 520-206-4414.. 17 A
ncrichmond@pima.edu
RICHMOND, Sally, S .... 540-458-8710 519 A
srichmond@wlu.edu
RICHMOND, Steve .... 606-783-5236 198 H
s.richmond@moreheadstate.edu
RICHMOND, Vicki .... 757-825-3810 517 B
richmondvc@tncc.edu
RICHTER, Deborah .... 563-244-7030 178 B
drichter@eicc.edu
RICHTER, Jennifer .... 865-974-1000 465 D
jrichter@utk.edu
RICHTER, Jerome, J ..... 701-355-8072 375 K
jjrichter@umary.edu
RICHTER, Mark, H .... 260-422-5561 167 F
mhrichter@indianatech.edu
RICHTER, Sara .... 580-349-1472 400 B
saraj@opsu.edu
RICHTER, Sheila, W ...... 814-824-2287 425 L
srichter@mercyhurst.edu
RICHTER, Suzanna, L ... 717-358-5843 418 J
suzanna.richter@fandm.edu
RICHTER, Thomas, P ..... 920-923-7640 537 A
tprichter32@marianuniversity.edu
RICHTER-NORGEL,
Ellen .... 651-690-8730 263 V
erichter-norgel@stkate.edu
RICHTERS, Stephen, P .. 318-342-1070 209 A
richters@ulm.edu
RICHTMAN, Meg .... 319-385-6212 180 A
meg.richtman@iw.edu
RICHWALSKY,
Michael, J .... 216-397-3022 384 F
mrichwalsky@jcu.edu
RICIOPPO, Eric .... 718-357-0500 341 F
ericioppo@stpaulsschoolofnursing.edu
RICK, Joseph .... 320-308-6158 261 F
jrick@sctcc.edu
RICK, Joseph .... 336-770-3284 372 B
rickj@uncsa.edu
RICK, Joseph .... 336-770-1312 372 B
rickj@uncsa.edu
RICK, Mary, A .... 517-750-1200 250 F
mrick@arbor.edu
RICKABAUGH, Timothy 419-783-2402 381 G
trickabaugh@defiance.edu
RICKARD, Jenny .... 253-879-3211 527 F
jrickard@pugetsound.edu
RICKARD, Larry .... 561-237-7118 108 E
lrickard@lynn.edu
RICKARD, Walter .... 518-828-4181 322 E
walter.rickard@sunycgcc.edu
RICKARDS, Brenden ...... 856-415-2297 306 C
brickards@rcgc.edu
RICKARDS, Laura .... 732-255-0400 304 E
lrickards@ocean.edu
RICKEL, Todd, A .... 330-972-2520 392 H
trickel@uakron.edu
RICKENBAKER, Becky ... 803-778-6602 443 I
rickenbakerbh@cctech.edu
RICKENBAKER, Michael 478-445-4467 125 A
michael.rickenbaker@gcsu.edu
RICKER, Curtis .... 912-478-0779 126 B
cricker@georgiasouthern.edu
RICKER, Deborah, D ..... 717-815-1510 440 H
dricker@ycp.edu
RICKER, Don .... 419-227-3141 394 B
dricker@unoh.edu
RICKER, Jean .... 781-292-2343 226 G
jean.ricker@olin.edu
RICKERT, Gail Ann .... 717-337-6579 419 C
grickert@gettysburg.edu
RICKERT, Paul .... 423-775-7185 455 F
paul.rickert@bryan.edu
RICKETT, Craig .... 509-533-3608 521 F
craig.rickett@ccs.spokane.edu
RICKETTS, Lloyd .... 609-771-2186 301 E
ricketts@tcnj.edu
RICKETTS, Mike .... 423-697-4433 462 C
mike.ricketts@chattanoogastate.edu
RICKETTS, Tracy .... 541-885-1118 408 E
tracy.ricketts@oit.edu
RICKEY, Jeffrey .... 315-229-5226 341 E
jrickey@stlawu.edu
RICKEY, Jeffrey .... 315-229-5286 341 E
jrickey@stlawu.edu
RICKFORD, Donald .... 202-274-5415.. 97 B
donald.rickford@udc.edu
RICKINGER, Rachel ...... 517-264-7172 250 B
rricking@sienaheights.edu
RICKLE, SJ, William ..... 304-243-2385 534 H
rickle@wju.edu
RICKMAN, Linda .... 239-489-9338 104 G
linda.rickman@fsw.edu
RICKNER, Donald .... 949-582-4968.. 67 F
drickner@saddleback.edu
RICKS, Suzy .... 208-535-5349 138 B
suzanne.ricks@my.eitc.edu
RICKS, Terri .... 225-216-8601 202 N
rickst@mybrcc.edu
RICKS, Venus .... 717-867-6165 423 I
ricks@lvc.edu
RICO, Antonio .... 915-779-8031 496 G
ccctrain@aol.com
RICO, Camilla .... 360-417-6442 525 A
crico@pencol.edu
RICO, Oscar .... 661-654-2394.. 32 G
orico@csub.edu
RICO-GUTIERREZ,
Luis, C .... 515-294-7427 175 G
lrico@iastate.edu
RICORDATI, Timothy .... 630-617-3089 144 G
timothy.ricordati@elmhurst.edu
RICOTTA, Helen .... 610-341-5934 418 A
0713mgr@follett.com
RIDD, Kaylee .... 801-649-5230 498 K
clinicaldeanassistant@midwifery.edu
RIDD-YOUNG, Kristi ..... 866-680-2756 498 K
president@midwifery.edu
RIDDELL, Jeffrey, R ...... 206-726-5020 521 G
jriddell@cornish.edu
RIDDELL, Richard .... 919-684-2641 356 E
richard.riddell@duke.edu
RIDDER, Cece .... 503-725-4457 409 D
ridder@pdx.edu
RIDDICK, Althea, L .... 252-335-8787 369 F
aariddick@ecsu.edu
RIDDICK, Rich .... 308-635-6067 294 C
riddickr@wncc.edu
RIDDICK, Vera, E .... 757-683-3689 510 I
vriddick@odu.edu
RIDDLE, Catherine .... 518-262-3593 314 I
riddlec@mail.amc.edu
RIDDLE, Christy .... 662-846-4336 267 A
criddle@deltastate.edu
RIDDLE, Heather .... 612-330-1177 253 K
riddle@augsburg.edu
RIDDLE, Jennifer .... 208-459-5688 137 J
jriddle@collegeofidaho.edu
RIDDLE, Joyce, E .... 304-462-6184 532 G
joyce.riddle@glenville.edu
RIDDLE, Kory .... 773-697-2031 144 B
kriddle@devry.edu
RIDDLE, Larry .... 770-426-2979 128 C
larry.riddle@life.edu
RIDDLE, Marianne .... 502-863-8020 195 A
marianne_riddle@georgetowncollege.edu
RIDDLE, Matthew .... 740-588-1252 396 E
mriddle@zanestate.edu
RIDDLE, Troy .... 312-427-2737 148 I
triddle@jmls.edu
RIDDLEMOSER, Roger .. 305-348-6849 114 G
roger.riddlemoser@fiu.edu
RIDEAUX, Larry .... 817-515-4507 484 B
larry.rideaux@tccd.edu
RIDENOUR, Nancy, A ... 505-272-6284 313 H
nridenour@salud.unm.edu
RIDEOUT, Kathy .... 585-275-8902 351 D
Kathy_Rideout@urmc.rochester.edu
RIDER, Jeff .... 870-759-4194.. 25 I
jrider@wbcoll.edu
RIDER, Jonathan .... 703-812-4757 509 E
jrider@leland.edu
RIDER, Robert .... 865-974-2201 465 D
brider@utk.edu
RIDGE, Terri .... 620-278-4220 191 D
tridge@sterling.edu
RIDGEDELL, Ken, W ..... 985-549-2121 208 E
kridgedell@selu.edu
RIDGES, J. Thomas ...... 704-847-5600 369 A
tridges@ses.edu
RIDGEWAY, Gloria .... 229-317-6919 123 H
gloria.ridgeway@darton.edu
RIDGWAY, Dan .... 216-649-8900 384 H
dridgway@kent.edu
RIDGWAY, Lori .... 307-855-2103 545 a
lridgway@cwc.edu
RIDGWAY, Susan, M ... 989-837-4219 248 D
ridgway@northwood.edu
RIDINGTON,
M. Thomas .... 610-341-4377 418 A
tridingt@eastern.edu
RIDLEY, Emmett, L .... 804-524-5068 518 C
eridley@vsu.edu
RIDLEY, Scott .... 806-742-1988 489 F
scott.ridley@ttu.edu
RIDLEY, Tim .... 661-654-2066.. 32 G
tridley@csub.edu
RIDLEY, JR., Wadell ..... 610-660-1223 434 G
wridley@sju.edu
RIDOUT, Thomas, M .... 563-562-3263 181 F
ridoutt@nicc.edu
RIDPATH, Tanya .... 540-375-2323 512 B
ridpath@roanoke.edu
RIECK, Ray .... 217-234-5224 150 B
rrieck@lakeland.cc.il.us
RIEDEL, Eric .... 612-338-7224 265 G
eric.riedel@waldenu.edu
RIEDEL, Herbert, H .... 334-222-6591.... 5 G
hriedel@lbwcc.edu
RIEDEL CARNEY,
Elizabeth .... 651-690-6836 263 V
eacarney@stkate.edu
RIEDER, Rick .... 660-626-2325 271 G
rrieder@atsu.edu
RIEDER, JR.,
Robert, W .... 256-824-6633.... 9 A
riederr@uah.edu
RIEDSTRA, Catherine .... 805-546-3130.. 42 H
cmachado@cuesta.edu
RIEDY, Joshua .... 701-777-4273 373 G
joshua.riedy@und.edu
RIEFKOHL, Jorge .... 787-780-0070 550 G
jriefkohl@caribbean.edu
RIEGER, Mark .... 302-831-2501.. 94 D
mrieger@udel.edu
RIEGLER, Alissa .... 563-588-6559 176 F
alissa.riegler@clarke.edu
RIEHL, Christine .... 503-338-2305 405 B
criehl@clatsopcc.edu
RIEHL, Gretchen, K ...... 972-860-7297 472 E
GRiehl@dcccd.edu
RIEHL, Shelle .... 503-517-1814 411 C
sriehl@westernseminary.edu
RIEHLE, Douglas .... 937-778-7979 381 K
driehle@edisonohio.edu
RIEHS, Steven .... 630-515-7702 144 A
sriehs@devry.edu
RIEKEMAN, Guy, F .... 770-426-2601 128 C
riekeman@life.edu
RIEKERT, Jennifer .... 914-594-4536 335 H
jennifer_riekert@nymc.edu
RIEKS, Stephen, J .... 716-673-4670 343 F
stephen.rieks@fredonia.edu
RIELLO, Heidi, A .... 413-662-5331 230 C
heidi.riello@mcla.edu
RIEMAN, Barbara, M .... 716-851-1421 325 A
rieman@ecc.edu
RIEMAN, Jeff .... 419-772-3100 388 I
j-rieman@onu.edu
RIEN, Nate .... 209-588-5182.. 78 B
rienn@yosemite.edu
RIEPMA, Edward .... 949-794-9090.. 68 F
eriepma@stanbridge.edu
RIERA, José-Luis .... 302-831-8939.. 94 D
jriera@udel.edu
RIES, Barry .... 507-389-1242 260 A
barry.ries@mnsu.edu
RIES, Heidi, R .... 937-255-3633 547 E
heidi.ries@afit.edu
RIES, Kenneth .... 320-629-5195 260 H
riesk@pinetech.edu
RIES, Thomas Karl .... 651-641-8211 255 C
ries@csp.edu
RIESBERG, Anthony ...... 507-389-7444 262 A
anthony.riesberg@southcentral.edu
RIESE, Sara .... 303-762-6995.. 82 C
sara.riese@denverseminary.edu
RIESGO, Andrea .... 760-366-5285.. 42 G
ariesgo@cmccd.edu
RIESINGER, Mick .... 701-483-2389 373 H
Michael.Riesinger@dickinsonstate.edu
RIESSLAND, Larry .... 308-865-8524 293 G
riesslandl@unk.edu
RIESTER, Jon .... 812-866-7021 166 E
riester@hanover.edu
RIESTER, Leslie .... 971-722-8288 409 C
lriester@pcc.edu
RIESTRA, Liza .... 787-841-2000 555 F
liza_riestra@pucpr.edu
RIESTRA, Miguel, A ...... 787-622-8000 556 H
mriestra@pupr.edu
RIETHLE, Theresa .... 413-565-1000 222 G
triethle@baypath.edu
RIFE, Oriana .... 419-517-8971 385 F
orife@lourdes.edu
RIFKIN, Benjamin .... 607-274-3113 328 H
brifkin@ithaca.edu
RIGALI, Mary .... 203-596-4504.. 91 D
mrigali@post.edu
RIGBY, Heather .... 248-689-8282 251 I
hrigby@walshcollege.edu
RIGG, Lesley .... 815-753-1883 154 I
lrigg@niu.edu
RIGGERT, Mark .... 402-557-7070 289 B
bubookstore@fheg.follett.com
RIGGINS, Darius .... 661-654-3277.. 32 G
driggins@csub.edu
RIGGINS, David, W .... 828-689-1219 359 A
driggins@mhu.edu
RIGGLE, Elise .... 419-755-4313 387 E
riggle.17@osu.edu
RIGGLE, Ron .... 217-786-2581 151 C
ron.riggle@llcc.edu
RIGGS, Alexia .... 325-649-8610 475 F
ariggs@hputx.edu
RIGGS, Allen .... 435-283-7125 500 D
allen.riggs@snow.edu
RIGGS, Becky .... 870-864-7146.. 23 B
briggs@southark.edu
RIGGS, Bonnie .... 423-697-4465 462 C
bonnie.riggs@chattanoogastate.edu
RIGGS, Channing .... 612-624-6868 265 C
riggs035@umn.edu
RIGGS, David .... 765-677-2808 169 C
david.riggs@indwes.edu
RIGGS, Jim .... 417-455-5466 274 B
jriggs@crowder.edu
RIGGS, Joyce .... 270-824-8581 196 F
joyce.riggs@kctcs.edu
RIGGS, Michelle .... 909-389-3391.. 62 B
mriggs@craftonhills.edu
RIGGS, Paul .... 570-408-4600 440 B
paul.riggs@wilkes.edu
RIGGS, Robert, F .... 214-887-5007 473 E
rriggs@dts.edu
RIGHI, Paul, A .... 617-228-3474 231 C
prighi@bhcc.mass.edu
RIGLER, Bill .... 303-546-3533.. 84 B
brigler@naropa.edu
RIGNEY, Doug .... 205-726-2032.... 6 F
drigney@samford.edu
RIGSBEE, Craig .... 530-895-2476.. 30 B
rigsbeecr@butte.edu
RIGSBEE, David .... 217-641-4533 148 J
drigsbee@jwcc.edu
RIHA, James .... 618-235-2700 160 B
james.riha@swic.edu
RIHACEK, Robin .... 708-210-5754 159 D
rrihacek@ssc.edu
RIHL-LEWINSKY,
Elizabeth .... 215-572-2956 412 F
rihll@arcadia.edu
RIIS, Janet .... 406-447-5423 286 D
jriis@carroll.edu
RIISE, Hege .... 361-570-4135 492 A
riiseh@uhv.edu
RIKAKIS, Thanassis ...... 540-231-6123 518 B
provost@vt.edu
RIKARD, Jennifer .... 619-594-5220.. 35 E
jrikard@mail.sdsu.edu
RIKEL, Randy .... 806-651-2092 486 D
rrikel@mail.wtamu.edu
RIKER, David, J .... 210-458-6143 494 D
DAVE.RIKER@UTSA.EDU
RILEY, Andrea .... 405-631-3399 398 A
ariley@heritage-education.com
RILEY, Bruce .... 608-785-8218 539 G
briley@uwlax.edu
RILEY, Carla .... 320-589-6066 265 A
rileycj@morris.umn.edu
RILEY, Chris .... 325-674-6802 466 I
cmr97t@acu.edu
RILEY, Connie .... 409-984-6200 488 H
connie.riley@lamarpa.edu
RILEY, Donna .... 619-660-4452.. 46 G
donna.riley@gcccd.edu
RILEY, Doreen, K .... 216-397-4345 384 F
driley@jcu.edu
RILEY, Edward .... 617-254-2610 236 B
rev.edward.riley@sjs.edu
RILEY, Elaine .... 254-526-1106 470 E
elaine.riley@ctcd.edu
RILEY, OSA, George, F 610-519-7715 439 A
george.riley@villanova.edu
RILEY, Jan .... 334-222-6591.... 5 G
lriley@lbwcc.edu
RILEY, Jeannette .... 508-999-8352 228 H
j1riley@umassd.edu

RILEY, Jill ... 931-540-2573 462 E
jriley9@columbiastate.edu
RILEY, Karen ... 303-871-7874 .. 86 H
kriley@du.edu
RILEY, Ken ... 432-685-4569 478 F
kriley@midland.edu
RILEY, Kimberly ... 816-604-4523 278 A
kim.riley@mcckc.edu
RILEY, Lisa ... 608-822-2440 544 C
lriley@swtc.edu
RILEY, Matt ... 406-243-5455 287 D
matt.riley@umontana.edu
RILEY, Michael ... 312-944-0882 150 D
mriley@chicago.chefs.edu
RILEY, P. Thomas ... 703-654-1040 513 I
priley@umw.edu
RILEY, Patrick ... 440-684-6022 394 G
priley@ursuline.edu
RILEY, Rebecca ... 936-273-7222 477 I
rebecca.riley@lonestar.edu
RILEY, Robert ... 781-768-7147 236 A
robert.riley@regiscollege.edu
RILEY, Robert, J ... 651-962-6032 265 F
rjriley@stthomas.edu
RILEY, Ron ... 253-833-9111 523 B
rriley@greenriver.edu
RILEY, Sabrina ... 402-486-2514 293 D
sariley@ucollege.edu
RILEY, Sarah ... 900-652-6176 .. 38 A
sarah.riley@chaffey.edu
RILEY, Sarah ... 305-899-3051 .. 99 B
sriley@barry.edu
RILEY, Scott, T ... 218-285-2205 261 A
scott.riley@rainyriver.edu
RILEY, Shawn ... 610-292-9852 433 J
RILEY, Stacy ... 262-564-3108 543 A
rileys@gtc.edu
RILEY, Susan ... 513-732-5324 393 D
rileysu@ucmail.uc.edu
RILEY, Tammy ... 409-984-6237 488 H
tammy.riley@lamarpa.edu
RILEY, Teri ... 330-941-4628 396 C
triley@ysu.edu
RILEY, Terisa ... 361-593-3612 486 A
terisa.riley@tamuk.edu
RILEY, Terisa, C ... 361-593-3612 486 A
terisa.riley@tamuk.edu
RILEY, Toni ... 312-567-5239 147 E
triley6@iit.edu
RILEY, Vicki ... 304-214-8800 531 G
vriley@wvncc.edu
RILEY, Whitney ... 513-529-1810 386 K
rileywc@miamioh.edu
RILEY HAUSER, Ellen ... 715-682-4591 544 F
ellen.hauser@witc.edu
RILING, Dean ... 918-836-6886 402 I
driling@mail.spartan.edu
RILL, Ann, M ... 540-785-5440 514 C
annmarierill@vbc.edu
RILL, Josef ... 941-752-5342 114 B
rillj@scf.edu
RILLEY, Karin ... 972-721-5363 491 B
krilley@udallas.edu
RILLING, David, S ... 864-488-4573 447 F
drilling@limestone.edu
RILLORTA, Rhoda ... 704-355-3243 355 G
rhoda.rillorta@carolinashealthcare.org
RIMA, Kyle ... 801-832-2008 501 C
krima@westminstercollege.edu
RIMAI, Monica ... 503-370-6728 411 D
mrimai@willamette.edu
RIMAL, Sanjana ... 973-353-5940 307 C
srimal@andromeda.rutgers.edu
RIMANDO, Rosie ... 206-934-6763 526 B
rosie.rimando@seattlecolleges.edu
RIMBY, Susan ... 570-484-2073 431 C
ser1116@lhup.edu
RIMER, Barbara, K ... 919-966-3215 371 A
brimer@unc.edu
RIMIRCH, Bruce ... 680-488-2471 550 C
brucer@palau.edu
RIMKIS, Robert, C ... 540-224-6973 509 D
RCRimkis@jchs.edu
RIMMER, Jessica ... 405-692-3275 398 I
jrimmer@macu.edu
RINARD, Pat ... 727-341-3064 112 A
rinard.pat@spcollege.edu
RINAS, Craig ... 972-825-4612 483 D
crinas@sagu.edu
RINAUDO, Brooke, H ... 318-797-5108 205 F
brooke.rinaudo@lsus.edu
RINCK, Jared ... 816-604-6740 277 G
jared.rinck@mcckc.edu
RINDE, Carla, M ... 610-409-3599 438 H
crinde@ursinus.edu
RINDERKNECHT,
Bethany ... 319-368-6467 181 D
brinderknecht@mtmercy.edu
RINDO, Michael, J ... 715-836-4742 539 E
rindomj@uwec.edu

RINE, Veronica ... 740-755-7600 378 L
vrine@cotc.edu
RINEHART, John ... 304-877-6428 529 G
registrar@abc.edu
RINEHART, Kathleen, A 773-298-3344 158 F
rinehart@sxu.edu
RINEHART, Kenton, W .. 845-575-3000 331 L
kent.rinehart@marist.edu
RINEHART, Lucy ... 773-325-7305 143 G
RINEHART, Lydia ... 806-457-4200 474 E
lrinehart@fpctx.edu
RINEHART, Robin, C ... 610-330-5070 423 A
rineharr@lafayette.edu
RINEHART, Shelley ... 281-998-6150 481 E
shelley.rinehart@sjcd.edu
RINEY, OSU, Judith, N 270-686-4288 193 G
judith.riney@brescia.edu
RING, Joshua ... 828-328-7927 358 G
joshua.ring@lr.edu
RING, Neal ... 864-242-5100 443 G
RING, Patricia ... 508-793-3459 225 C
pring@holycross.edu
RING, Ray ... 212-817-7394 319 B
rring@gc.cuny.edu
RINGA, Melanie ... 914-961-8313 341 I
finance@svots.edu
RINGENBERG, Ron ... 574-296-6212 163 M
rringenb@ambs.edu
RINGGOLD, Tonja ... 410-462-8001 213 G
tringgold@bccc.edu
RINGKAMP,
Patricia, M ... 570-577-3167 413 E
pat.ringkamp@bucknell.edu
RINGLE, John ... 217-206-6190 161 G
ringle.john@uis.edu
RINGLE, Martin, D ... 503-777-7254 409 E
martin.ringle@reed.edu
RINGLE, Suzanne ... 602-286-8110 .. 14 M
suzanne.ringle@gwmail.maricopa.edu
RINGLER, Neil, H ... 315-470-6606 347 B
neilringler@esf.edu
RINGO, Teresa ... 936-294-1061 489 A
reg_tat@shsu.edu
RINGOLD, Debra ... 503-370-6440 411 D
dringold@willamette.edu
RINGOLD, Gordon ... 831-459-4479 .. 72 E
ringold@ucsc.edu
RINGWOOD, Karen, K .. 203-597-9036 .. 92 B
klozada@bridgeport.edu
RINI, Anthony ... 617-373-4774 235 D
RINK, Darrell, C ... 479-788-7701 .. 23 H
chris.rink@uafs.edu
RINK, Jonathan ... 828-328-7249 358 G
jonathan.rink@lr.edu
RINK, Susan ... 734-481-2310 242 J
srink@emich.edu
RINKENBAUGH, Bill ... 316-322-3297 185 F
brinkenb@butlercc.edu
RINKENBAUGH,
Heather ... 316-323-6939 185 F
hrinkenb@butlercc.edu
RINKER, Craig ... 202-687-5867 .. 95 E
cmr235@georgetown.edu
RINKER, Jonathan, A ... 304-877-6428 529 G
jon.rinker@abc.edu
RINKER, Linda ... 616-554-5183 241 I
lrinker@davenport.edu
RINKOFF, Carol ... 626-529-8419 .. 57 F
crinkoff@pacificoaks.edu
RINN, Martha ... 830-372-8110 487 C
mrinn@tlu.edu
RINN, Susan ... 830-372-8001 487 C
srinn@tlu.edu
RINNE, Henry ... 904-256-7926 106 Q
hrinne@ju.edu
RINNE, Jason ... 660-831-4088 279 D
rinnej@moval.edu
RIO, Deborah ... 661-362-3298 .. 40 H
debbie.rio@canyons.edu
RIOLA, Allison ... 303-871-4201 .. 86 H
Allison.Riola@du.edu
RIOPEL, Becky ... 425-352-8545 520 D
briopel@cascadia.edu
RIORDAN, Charles ... 302-831-4007 .. 94 D
riordan@udel.edu
RIORDAN,
Christine, M ... 516-877-3838 314 F
cmr@adelphi.edu
RIORDAN, Jean ... 773-298-3135 158 F
riordan@sxu.edu
RIORDAN, Jennifer ... 717-564-4112 421 M
jriordan@kaplan.edu
RIORDAN, Kevin ... 708-596-2000 159 D
kriordan@ssc.edu
RIORDAN, Marsha ... 641-673-1045 184 B
riordanm@wmpenn.edu
RIORDAN, Matt ... 785-227-3380 185 A
riordanm@bethanylb.edu
RIORDAN, Phil ... 561-237-7749 108 E
priordan@lynn.edu

RIORDAN, Rob ... 619-929-9748 .. 47 B
rriordan@hightechhigh.org
RIORDON, Jermiah ... 413-775-1611 231 E
Riordonj@gcc.mass.edu
RIOS, Adlin ... 787-728-1545 559 A
adlinrios@sagrado.edu
RIOS, Alfonso ... 323-357-6209 .. 51 D
riosa@elac.edu
RIOS, Charlene ... 509-793-2020 520 B
charlener@bigbend.edu
RIOS, Crystie ... 541-485-1780 407 H
crystierios@newhop.edu
RIOS, Efrain ... 787-844-8181 558 D
efrain.rios@upr.edu
RIOS, Esther, A ... 671-735-5544 549 E
financialaid@guamcc.edu
RIOS, Francisca ... 956-665-2551 494 C
frios@utpa.edu
RIOS, Francisco ... 360-650-3319 528 D
francisco.rios@wwu.edu
RIOS, Lillian ... 787-758-2525 558 C
lillian.rios@upr.edu
RIOS, Lourdes ... 787-884-6000 552 K
lrios@icprjc.edu
RIOS, Patricia ... 312-369-7465 143 C
prios@colum.edu
RIOS, Shelia ... 352-854-2322 100 P
rioss@cf.edu
RIOS, Thomas, R ... 262-472-1172 541 D
riost@uww.edu
RIOS, Zilka ... 787-798-4050 556 F
zilka.rios@uccaribe.edu
RIOS GONZÁLEZ,
Palmira ... 787-751-0500 558 E
palmira.rios@upr.edu
RIOS-HUSAIN,
Silvia Patricia ... 704-922-6217 362 G
husain.silvia@gaston.edu
RIOS-KNAUF, Irene ... 203-575-8116 .. 89 F
irios-knauf@nv.edu
RIOTTO, Karen, M ... 585-395-5484 345 A
kriotto@brockport.edu
RIPICH, Danielle ... 207-602-2306 213 B
dripich@une.edu
RIPLEY, Anneliese ... 406-683-7309 287 E
anneliese.ripley@umwestern.edu
RIPLEY, Dave ... 701-477-7862 375 H
dripley@tm.edu
RIPLEY, Judith ... 207-795-5974 210 J
ripleyj@cmhc.org
RIPLEY, Kate ... 907-474-6218 .. 10 I
uaf-alumni@alaska.edu
RIPLEY, Melissa ... 423-636-7300 464 F
mripley@tusculum.edu
RIPPEN, Kelly ... 308-345-8107 291 H
rippenk@mpcc.edu
RIPPENTROP, Jan ... 773-256-0758 151 H
jrippentrop@lstc.edu
RIPPERDA, Jan ... 618-545-3041 149 C
jrippperda@kaskaskia.edu
RIPPETOE, Mark ... 866-323-0233 .. 60 E
studentlife@providencecc.edu
RIPPEY, Sharon, T ... 315-859-4672 327 A
srippey@hamilton.edu
RIPPINGER, Timothy ... 414-288-4771 537 B
timothy.rippinger@marquette.edu
RIPPKE, Greg ... 419-473-2700 381 F
grippke@daviscollege.edu
RIPPLE, David ... 614-292-3355 389 A
ripple.1@osu.edu
RIPPLE, Jacob ... 402-744-7271 292 G
jacob@northeast.edu
RIPTON, Elizabeth, R ... 585-292-2197 333 G
eripton@monroecc.edu
RIQUEZ, Elizabeth ... 646-312-1390 318 C
elizabeth.riquez@baruch.cuny.edu
RIS, Gary ... 631-451-4205 348 E
risg@sunysuffolk.edu
RISAN, Cynthia ... 503-594-3440 405 A
cynthiar@clackamas.edu
RISCHBIETER, Natalie ... 478-471-2732 128 H
natalie.rischbieter@mga.edu
RISDON, Michelle ... 530-541-4660 .. 50 A
risdon@ltcc.edu
RISELING, Susan ... 608-262-4527 539 D
riseling@wisc.edu
RISEMAN, Stacy ... 508-793-2741 225 C
sriseman@holycross.edu
RISHE, Karl ... 216-373-5177 388 A
krishe@ndc.edu
RISHLING, Ryan ... 702-651-5928 295 C
ryan.rishling@csn.edu
RISINGER, Jeff, A ... 501-686-7085 .. 24 B
jarisinger@uams.edu
RISNER, Sam ... 606-337-1457 194 F
srisner@ccbbc.edu
RISSE, Duane ... 303-352-3356 .. 81 J
duane.risse@ccd.edu
RISSE, Duane ... 303-360-4751 .. 81 I
Duane.Risse@CCAurora.edu

RISSEL, Timothy ... 610-921-7520 411 E
trissel@albright.edu
RISSER, Barbara, G ... 585-785-1201 325 E
barbara.risser@flcc.edu
RISSLER, Jennifer ... 415-749-4586 .. 62 I
jrissler@sfai.edu
RISSMEYER, Patricia ... 617-735-9722 226 B
rissmeye@emmanuel.edu
RISTAINO, John ... 401-341-2159 442 D
john.ristaino@salve.edu
RISTIG, David ... 805-765-9300 .. 64 G
RITACCO, Kevin ... 508-854-4200 232 F
kritacco@qcc.mass.edu
RITCHEY, Fred, L ... 903-233-4210 477 G
fredritchey@letu.edu
RITCHEY, Mary, K ... 706-886-6831 132 F
mritchey@tfc.edu
RITCHEY, Nathan ... 814-732-2440 430 G
nritchey@edinboro.edu
RITCHEY, Randy ... 918-293-4666 400 E
randy.ritchey@okstate.edu
RITCHEY, William, V ... 757-594-7047 506 I
bill.ritchey@cnu.edu
RITCHIE, David ... 765-998-5397 173 B
dvritchie@taylor.edu
RITCHIE, Gloria ... 412-809-5100 433 D
ritchie.gloria@pti.edu
RITCHIE, Jay ... 707-638-5802 .. 70 B
jay.ritchie@tu.edu
RITCHIE, Jeffrey ... 815-836-5129 150 F
ritchije@lewisu.edu
RITENBAUGH, III,
Robert, C ... 334-844-4190 .... 1 G
ritenrc@auburn.edu
RITER, Jayme, S ... 716-878-3041 345 B
riterjs@buffalostate.edu
RITER, Steve ... 915-747-7890 494 B
sriter@utep.edu
RITSCHDORFF, John ... 845-575-3000 331 L
john.ritschdorff@marist.edu
RITTENBERGER, Alexis . 724-503-1001 439 B
arittenberger@washjeff.edu
RITTER, Barbara ... 843-349-2640 444 G
britter@coastal.edu
RITTER, Donn ... 559-651-2500 .. 63 E
Donn.Ritter@sjvc.edu
RITTER, Eugene, W ... 336-322-2163 364 G
Gene.Ritter@piedmontcc.edu
RITTER, Gretchen ... 607-255-4146 323 C
gr72@cornell.edu
RITTER, Joseph ... 618-374-5155 156 C
joe.ritter@principia.edu
RITTER, Karen, R ... 336-633-0206 365 A
krritter@randolph.edu
RITTER, Kathy ... 904-620-2730 116 A
k.ritter@unf.edu
RITTER, Mark ... 864-503-5939 451 A
mritter@uscupstate.edu
RITTER, Michael ... 863-638-2968 119 A
ritterMJ@webber.edu
RITTER, Michael ... 618-664-7122 145 E
michael.ritter@greenville.edu
RITTER, Nancy ... 575-527-7650 312 D
naritter@nmsu.edu
RITTER, Pamela, S ... 423-439-4242 461 D
ritterp@etsu.edu
RITTER, Shane ... 815-939-5212 155 G
rsritter@olivet.edu
RITTER, Will ... 336-272-7102 357 B
will.ritter@greensboro.edu
RITTERBROWN,
Michael ... 818-240-1000 .. 45 I
michaelr@glendale.edu
RITTLE, Dennis, C ... 620-441-5234 186 E
dennis.rittle@cowley.edu
RITTLING, Mary, E ... 336-249-8186 362 B
merittli@davidsonccc.edu
RITTLING, Meg ... 716-829-7808 324 E
rittling@dyc.edu
RITTS, Bonnie, B ... 585-785-1281 325 E
bonnie.ritts@flcc.edu
RITZ, Cathy ... 661-362-3639 .. 40 H
cathy.ritz@canyons.edu
RITZ, Robert, L ... 434-592-4800 509 G
rlritz@liberty.edu
RITZ, Steven ... 831-459-2635 .. 72 E
sritz@scipp.ucsc.edu
RITZE, Nancy ... 718-289-5156 318 E
nancy.ritze@bcc.cuny.edu
RITZLINE, Pamela ... 330-490-7446 395 C
pritzline@walsh.edu
RITZMAN, Elizabeth ... 708-524-6520 144 C
eritzman@dom.edu
RITZMAN, Richard ... 901-678-2832 462 B
rritzman@memphis.edu
RIVALEAU, Susan, A ... 843-953-4973 445 B
rivaleaus@cofc.edu
RIVARA, Sara ... 503-491-7469 407 C
sara.rivara@mhcc.edu
RIVARD, Dawn ... 715-682-1812 538 D
drivard@northland.edu

ROBERSON, James, A .. 919-335-1020 366 H
jaroberson@waketech.edu
ROBERSON, Janet .... 434-791-5891 505 A
roberson@averett.edu
ROBERSON, Jessica ..... 919-497-3230 358 J
jroberson@louisburg.edu
ROBERSON, John .... 910-893-1278 355 C
robersonj@campbell.edu
ROBERSON, John, A .... 713-798-4676 469 C
jarobers@bcm.edu
ROBERSON, Judith .... 225-768-1700 206 F
ROBERSON, Kathleen ... 509-533-7042 521 E
kathleen.roberson@scc.spokane.edu
ROBERSON, Mark, A .... 951-552-8652.. 30 D
maroberson@calbaptist.edu
ROBERSON, Marla .... 864-646-1753 449 F
mrobers1@tctc.edu
ROBERSON, Miriam, C . 904-819-6204 102 P
robersonm@flagler.edu
ROBERSON, Richard, E 717-766-2511 426 B
rroberso@messiah.edu
ROBERSON, Rita, G ...... 304-236-7648 531 F
rita.roberson@southernwv.edu
ROBERSON, Valerie, R . 617-541-5301 233 A
vroberson@rcc.mass.edu
ROBERT, Bernadette ..... 310-954-4099.. 54 I
brobert@msmu.edu
ROBERT, Cortney .... 718-522-2300 340 E
crobert@sfc.edu
ROBERTS, Aaron .... 402-643-7233 289 J
aaron.roberts@cune.edu
ROBERTS, Adam .... 706-880-8004 127 N
aroberts@lagrange.edu
ROBERTS, Al .... 434-949-1019 516 H
al.roberts@southside.edu
ROBERTS, Alan, L .... 772-462-7235 106 F
aroberts@irsc.edu
ROBERTS, Alan, P .... 845-687-5050 350 I
robertsal@sunyulster.edu
ROBERTS, Alvin .... 443-352-4489 218 E
aroberts4@stevenson.edu
ROBERTS, Amber .... 616-331-3266 243 E
roberamb@gvsu.edu
ROBERTS, Amy .... 405-425-5910 399 J
amy.roberts@oc.edu
ROBERTS, Ann .... 847-735-5188 149 H
roberts@lakeforest.edu
ROBERTS, Barbara .... 360-676-2772 524 D
broberts@nwic.edu
ROBERTS, Betty .... 914-654-5501 322 B
broberts@cnr.edu
ROBERTS, Bob, E .... 304-293-3136 533 D
bob.roberts@mail.wvu.edu
ROBERTS, Brent .... 406-657-2320 287 H
broberts@msubillings.edu
ROBERTS, Carmen .... 406-771-4392 288 B
carmen.roberts@gfcmsu.edu
ROBERTS, Carolyn .... 313-927-1474 246 D
croberts@marygrove.edu
ROBERTS, Charles, H ... 859-846-5811 198 G
chroberts@midway.edu
ROBERTS, Chell .... 619-260-4627.. 74 B
croberts@sandiego.edu
ROBERTS, Cheryl .... 206-546-4551 526 G
cheryl.roberts@shoreline.edu
ROBERTS, Cheryl, A ..... 340-692-4192 559 B
crobert@live.uvi.edu
ROBERTS, Christine ...... 619-201-8760.. 62 D
christine.edwards@sdcc.edu
ROBERTS,
Christopher, B .... 334-844-2308.... 1 G
robercr@auburn.edu
ROBERTS, Colleen .... 540-831-5500 511 C
ctroberts@radford.edu
ROBERTS, Cynthia .... 219-785-5219 172 A
croberts@pnc.edu
ROBERTS, Daniel, M .... 804-524-6709 518 C
droberts@vsu.edu
ROBERTS, Dave .... 775-674-7100 295 F
droberts@tmcc.edu
ROBERTS, David, M ..... 213-740-4577.. 74 D
dave.roberts@usc.edu
ROBERTS, Dawn .... 515-244-4221 175 C
robertsd@aib.edu
ROBERTS, Dennis .... 530-938-5313.. 41 E
roberts@siskiyous.edu
ROBERTS, Doug .... 707-527-4421.. 65 C
droberts@santarosa.edu
ROBERTS, Dustin .... 870-584-4471.. 24 E
droberts@cccua.edu
ROBERTS, Frances (Tri) 859-246-4649 195 J
tri.roberts@kctcs.edu
ROBERTS, Gail .... 419-448-2013 383 C
groberts@heidelberg.edu
ROBERTS, Gary, A .... 501-450-3416.. 25 F
garyr@uca.edu
ROBERTS, Gary, O .... 607-871-2715 314 J
roberts@alfred.edu
ROBERTS, Gayla .... 903-675-6212 490 F
groberts@tvcc.edu
ROBERTS, Glenda, V .... 607-746-4545 347 G
robertgv@delhi.edu
ROBERTS, Gregory .... 219-866-6123 172 E
ROBERTS, Gregory, W .. 434-982-3200 514 A
groberts@Virginia.EDU
ROBERTS, Heather .... 916-660-7900.. 66 E
hroberts@sierracollege.edu
ROBERTS, Howard .... 704-669-4124 361 E
robertsh@clevelandcc.edu
ROBERTS, Howard, V ... 606-218-5019 201 C
howardroberts@upike.edu
ROBERTS, James .... 570-674-6758 426 D
jroberts@misericordia.edu
ROBERTS, James .... 843-863-8083 444 B
jroberts@csuniv.edu
ROBERTS, James, S ..... 919-684-3501 356 E
james.roberts@duke.edu
ROBERTS, Janet, E .... 248-341-2020 248 E
jerobert@oaklandcc.edu
ROBERTS, Jay .... 765-983-1269 165 H
roberja@earlham.edu
ROBERTS, Jayne .... 850-718-2209 100 E
robertsj@chipola.edu
ROBERTS, Jean .... 231-777-0519 247 G
jean.roberts@muskegoncc.edu
ROBERTS, Jeanne, M ... 813-253-6203 118 H
jroberts@ut.edu
ROBERTS, Jeri .... 207-509-7261 212 A
jroberts@unity.edu
ROBERTS, Jerilyn, C ..... 605-394-2251 454 B
jerilyn.roberts@sdsmt.edu
ROBERTS, Jim, O .... 910-893-1240 355 C
roberts@campbell.edu
ROBERTS, Jimmy .... 254-298-8340 484 C
jdr@templejc.edu
ROBERTS, John .... 903-593-8311 487 A
jroberts@texascollege.edu
ROBERTS, Jonathan ...... 912-344-2910 120 D
jonathan.roberts@armstrong.edu
ROBERTS, Jonathan ...... 501-279-4257.. 21 A
jroberts@harding.edu
ROBERTS, Juanita .... 334-727-8894.... 8 B
jroberts@tuskegee.edu
ROBERTS, Juli .... 909-593-3511.. 73 B
jroberts@laverne.edu
ROBERTS, Julia .... 910-642-7141 366 B
julia.roberts@sccnc.edu
ROBERTS, Kathleen .... 859-572-6630 199 A
robertsk10@nku.edu
ROBERTS, Kay Lynn ..... 580-745-2977 402 D
kroberts@se.edu
ROBERTS, Keith .... 909-748-8142.. 73 K
keith_roberts@redlands.edu
ROBERTS, Kelley .... 706-867-3280 133 A
kelley.roberts@ung.edu
ROBERTS, Kevin, D ...... 307-332-2930 547 C
kroberts@wyomingcatholiccollege.com
ROBERTS, Kevin, J .... 325-674-2675 466 I
robertsk@acu.edu
ROBERTS, Kevin, W ...... 518-564-5022 346 B
robertkw@plattsburgh.edu
ROBERTS, Kirk .... 903-463-8768 474 K
robertsk@grayson.edu
ROBERTS, Leonard .... 973-748-9000 300 E
leonard_roberts@bloomfield.edu
ROBERTS, Lila .... 678-466-4357 122 J
lilaroberts@clayton.edu
ROBERTS, Linda .... 423-585-2336 464 C
linda.roberts@ws.edu
ROBERTS, Lisa .... 618-374-5068 156 C
lisa.roberts@principia.edu
ROBERTS, Mark, A .... 770-720-5504 130 E
mar@reinhardt.edu
ROBERTS, Mary .... 478-445-5384 125 A
mary.roberts@gcsu.edu
ROBERTS, Matthew .... 423-652-4780 457 J
mroberts@king.edu
ROBERTS, Melvin .... 856-227-7200 301 A
mroberts@camdencc.edu
ROBERTS, Michael .... 907-773-4462 141 O
mroberts39@ccc.edu
ROBERTS, Michael, C ... 785-864-8040 191 G
mroberts@ku.edu
ROBERTS, Michael, H ... 843-349-2282 444 G
mroberts@coastal.edu
ROBERTS, Michelle, A .. 662-846-4000 267 A
mroberts@deltastate.edu
ROBERTS, Mike .... 319-398-7797 180 J
mrobert@kirkwood.edu
ROBERTS, Mitzi, C .... 901-572-2478 455 C
mitzi.roberts@bchs.edu
ROBERTS, Nancy .... 610-606-4640 415 A
nroberts@cedarcrest.edu
ROBERTS, Nathan .... 816-383-7100 279 E
nroberts4@missouriwestern.edu
ROBERTS, Pamela .... 360-385-4948 524 F
pam@nwboatschool.org
ROBERTS, Patrick, S ..... 330-569-5278 383 F
robertsps@hiram.edu
ROBERTS, Patty, J .... 318-869-5747 202 D
pjrobert@centenary.edu
ROBERTS, Paul .... 229-225-4098 132 C
proberts@southernregional.edu
ROBERTS, Paul .... 205-970-9221.... 7 D
proberts@sebc.edu
ROBERTS, Paul .... 405-585-4526 399 I
paul.roberts@okbu.edu
ROBERTS, Paul, G .... 773-508-8901 151 E
prober2@luc.edu
ROBERTS, Pauline .... 225-923-2524 201 E
ROBERTS, Perry .... 678-717-3851 133 A
perry.roberts@ung.edu
ROBERTS, Philip .... 508-531-1331 229 C
proberts@bridgew.edu
ROBERTS, Phyllis .... 276-964-7588 517 A
phyllis.roberts@sw.edu
ROBERTS, Rachel .... 870-245-5593.. 22 C
robertsr@obu.edu
ROBERTS, Rachel .... 617-585-1100 234 H
rachel.roberts@necmusic.edu
ROBERTS, Randal, R ..... 503-517-1860 411 C
rroberts@westernseminary.edu
ROBERTS, Randall .... 606-886-3863 195 I
randall.roberts@kctcs.edu
ROBERTS, Randy .... 620-235-4878 190 G
reroberts@pittstate.edu
ROBERTS, Richard .... 201-684-7616 305 F
rroberts@ramapo.edu
ROBERTS, Rick .... 904-620-2955 116 A
rtrobert@unf.edu
ROBERTS, Rick .... 830-372-8030 487 C
rroberts@tlu.edu
ROBERTS, Ricky .... 928-523-9998.. 16 C
Ricky.Roberts@nau.edu
ROBERTS, Robert, W .... 920-424-1415 540 B
robertw@uwosh.edu
ROBERTS, Robin .... 317-738-8759 166 B
rroberts@franklincollege.edu
ROBERTS, Roscoe, C .... 434-924-3586 514 A
rcr7d@virginia.edu
ROBERTS, Ruth .... 972-825-4656 483 D
rroberts@sagu.edu
ROBERTS, Sallyann .... 815-226-4083 157 D
sroberts@rockford.edu
ROBERTS, Sarah, E .... 615-353-3117 463 C
sarah.roberts@nscc.edu
ROBERTS, Scott .... 702-895-2816 295 G
scott.roberts@unlv.edu
ROBERTS, Shannon ...... 215-248-7111 415 D
roberts@chc.edu
ROBERTS, Stephanie ..... 304-326-1310 530 G
sroberts@salemu.edu
ROBERTS, Stephen .... 573-341-4687 284 C
stephen.roberts@mst.edu
ROBERTS, Susan .... 518-828-4181 322 E
roberts@sunycgcc.edu
ROBERTS, Tracy .... 270-809-3380 198 I
troberts@murraystate.edu
ROBERTS, Vanice .... 706-368-6943 121 E
vroberts@berry.edu
ROBERTS, Vonnie, W ... 405-466-2999 398 E
vwroberts@langston.edu
ROBERTS, Warren .... 972-524-3341 483 F
ROBERTS, Wayne .... 601-643-8351 266 J
wayne.roberts@colin.edu
ROBERTS, Wendy .... 256-551-5211.... 4 J
wendy.roberts@drakestate.edu
ROBERTS, William .... 201-692-2629 302 H
william_roberts@fdu.edu
ROBERTS, William, C ... 240-895-4387 218 B
wcroberts@smcm.edu
ROBERTS, William, R ... 906-487-2622 247 A
wrrobert@mtu.edu
ROBERTS-BRYAN,
Vanessa .... 325-793-4681 478 D
vroberts@mcm.edu
ROBERTS-CAMPS, Traci 209-946-2343.. 73 C
trobertscamps@pacific.edu
ROBERTS-CORB, Carol .. 562-985-4187.. 33 F
carol.roberts-corb@csulb.edu
ROBERTS-DEUTSCH,
Marcia .... 808-845-9110 136 E
robertsd@hawaii.edu
ROBERTS-JOHNSON,
Wendy-Anne .... 215-825-8200 426 C
wjohnson@phmc.org
ROBERTS-KIRCHOFF,
Elizabeth .... 313-993-1021 250 H
robkires@udmercy.edu
ROBERTS KRIEGER,
Robin .... 405-945-3228 400 F
robin.krieger@osuokc.edu
ROBERTS-LEONARD,
Terri, L .... 317-738-8119 166 B
troberts@franklincollege.edu
ROBERTSHAW, Amy ..... 719-549-2199.. 81 F
amy.robertshaw@csupueblo.edu
ROBERTSON, Alan .... 404-215-2675 128 L
arobertson@morehouse.edu
ROBERTSON, Ali .... 269-956-3931 244 L
robertsona@kellogg.edu
ROBERTSON, Beverly .... 828-689-1244 359 A
brobertson@mhu.edu
ROBERTSON, Brooke .... 706-821-8392 129 H
brobertson@paine.edu
ROBERTSON, Bruce ...... 920-403-3045 538 K
bruce.robertson@snc.edu
ROBERTSON, Carole ..... 920-565-1027 536 Q
robertsoncl@lakeland.edu
ROBERTSON, Chad .... 405-425-5161 399 J
chad.robertson@oc.edu
ROBERTSON, Charlene . 617-732-2786 233 E
charlene.robertson@mcphs.edu
ROBERTSON, Charles ... 318-487-7015 202 L
charles.robertson@lacollege.edu
ROBERTSON,
Christopher .... 205-929-1657.... 5 I
crobertson@miles.edu
ROBERTSON, Clay .... 904-256-1208 103 K
crobertson@fcsl.edu
ROBERTSON, Courtney . 941-907-2262 102 N
crobertson@evergladesuniversity.edu
ROBERTSON, Craig, L .. 618-537-6856 152 C
clrobertson@mckendree.edu
ROBERTSON, Craig, T .. 256-765-5006.... 9 D
ctrobertson@una.edu
ROBERTSON, Dalana ..... 615-322-5179 465 H
dalana.robertson@vanderbilt.edu
ROBERTSON, Dave .... 479-788-7799.. 23 H
dave.robertson@uafs.edu
ROBERTSON, Diana ...... 785-864-7224 191 G
drobertson@ku.edu
ROBERTSON, Don, E .... 270-809-6831 198 I
drobertson@murraystate.edu
ROBERTSON, Doug .... 504-456-3141 201 G
dougr@bluecliffcollege.com
ROBERTSON, Douglas .. 305-348-3681 114 G
douglas.robertson@fiu.edu
ROBERTSON,
Elizabeth, C .... 914-251-6039 346 D
elizabeth.robertson@purchase.edu
ROBERTSON, Gloria ...... 269-660-8021 249 C
robertsong@millercollege.edu
ROBERTSON, Ian .... 608-262-3482 539 D
irobertson@wisc.edu
ROBERTSON, Ian .... 828-298-3325 373 A
irobert@warren-wilson.edu
ROBERTSON, Iris .... 304-326-1274 530 G
iris.robertson@salemu.edu
ROBERTSON, J. D 435-652-7576 499M
jrobertson@dixie.edu
ROBERTSON, Janet .... 903-566-7325 494 E
jrobertson@uttyler.edu
ROBERTSON, Jeff .... 479-968-0498.. 20 C
jrobertson@atu.edu
ROBERTSON, Jennifer ... 407-582-3404 118 I
jrobertson@valenciacollege.edu
ROBERTSON, Jennifer ... 903-675-6215 490 F
jrobertson@tvcc.edu
ROBERTSON, Jill .... 303-273-3207.. 80 O
jirobert@is.mines.edu
ROBERTSON, Jim .... 845-574-4466 339 I
jrobert7@sunyrockland.edu
ROBERTSON, John .... 402-844-7011 292 G
johnr@northeast.edu
ROBERTSON, Jon, H .... 561-237-7701 108 E
jrobertson@lynn.edu
ROBERTSON, Jordon .... 612-343-4776 263 H
ROBERTSON,
Joseph, E .... 503-494-8252 408 D
president@ohsu.edu
ROBERTSON, Larry .... 405-682-7837 399 K
lrobertson@occc.edu
ROBERTSON,
Leonard, A .... 972-721-5236 491 B
lrobertson@udallas.edu
ROBERTSON,
M.G. (Pat) .... 757-352-4013 511 G
carodix@regent.edu
ROBERTSON,
Michael, N .... 901-722-3226 461 A
mike.robertson@sco.edu
ROBERTSON, Patricia ... 843-574-6057 449 G
patricia.robertson@tridenttech.edu
ROBERTSON, Quintin .... 215-248-7342 424 G
qrobertson@ltsp.edu
ROBERTSON, Richard ... 760-757-2121.. 54 G
drobertson@miracosta.edu
ROBERTSON,
Sharon, N .... 703-323-3087 516 C
srobertson@nvcc.edu
ROBERTSON, Stacey ..... 509-963-1858 520 E
srobertson@cwu.edu
ROBERTSON, Sue .... 630-889-6527 154 E
srobertson@nuhs.edu
ROBERTSON, Tim 202-685-2650 547M
timothy.robertson@ndu.edu
ROBERTSON, Trey .... 601-928-6264 268 G
trey.robertson@mgccc.edu

ROCHAT, Angela .... 970-247-7695.. 82 I
rochat_a@fortlewis.edu
ROCHE, Amarilis .... 787-848-1589 555 D
aroche@popac.edu
ROCHE, Daniel .... 973-655-4158 304 A
roched@mail.montclair.edu
ROCHE, GNSH,
Denise, A .... 716-829-7673 324 E
roche@dyc.edu
ROCHE, Isabel .... 802-440-4406 501 D
iroche@bennington.edu
ROCHE, James .... 413-545-6330 228 F
jroche@provost.umass.edu
ROCHE, Mary Beth .... 570-504-1589 422 G
rochem@lackawanna.edu
ROCHE, Missy .... 618-235-2700 160 B
melissa.roche@swic.edu
ROCHE, Patrick .... 315-268-3734 321 C
proche@clarkson.edu
ROCHE, Sara .... 610-341-5854 418 A
sroche@eastern.edu
ROCHE, Stephen, H ...... 407-303-8016.. 97 J
stephen.roche@adu.edu
ROCHEFORT, Mary .... 218-723-6505 255 A
mrochefo@css.edu
ROCHELEAU, James ..... 916-485-3276 392 F
james.rocheleau@myunion.edu
ROCHESTER, Sylvia ...... 410-462-8371 213 G
srochester@bccc.edu
ROCHETTE, Susan .... 802-447-6339 503 A
srochette@svc.edu
ROCHFORD, Rosemary . 315-464-5468 344 E
rochforr@upstate.edu
ROCHLITZ, Mendel .... 718-853-8500 350 B
ROCHON, Ronald, S ..... 812-465-1617 174 D
rochon@usi.edu
ROCHON, Sandra .... 978-762-4000 232 D
srochon@northshore.edu
ROCHON, Thomas, R ... 607-274-3111 328 H
president@ithaca.edu
ROCK, Arlene, M .... 413-782-1538 238 A
arlene.rock@wne.edu
ROCK, David .... 662-915-7063 270 G
rock@olemiss.edu
ROCK, Harry .... 413-748-3914 236 H
hrock@springfieldcollege.edu
ROCK, Jennifer .... 215-489-2917 416 H
Jennifer.Rock@delval.edu
ROCK, John .... 305-348-0570 114 G
John.Rock@fiu.edu
ROCK, Kimberly .... 413-528-7229 222 F
krock@simons-rock.edu
ROCK, Thomas .... 212-678-3083 349 I
tpr4@tc.columbia.edu
ROCKAFELLOW, Mollie . 815-740-3363 162 F
mrockafellow@stfrancis.edu
ROCKECHARLIE,
Barbara .... 704-372-0266 358 D
brockecharlie@kingscollegecharlotte.edu
ROCKETT, Jeri, M .... 651-962-6780 265 F
gmrockett@stthomas.edu
ROCKETT, Sandra .... 731-286-3238 462 F
rockett@dscc.edu
ROCKEY, Tim .... 210-486-0926 467 C
trockey@alamo.edu
ROCKHILL, Linda .... 718-779-1430 338 D
info@plazacollege.edu
ROCKHILL, Wendy .... 206-934-6921 526 A
wendy.rockhill@seattlecolleges.edu
ROCKHOLD, Robin .... 601-984-2810 270 H
rrockhold@umc.edu
ROCKLAND-MILLER,
Harry, S .... 413-545-2337 228 F
rockmill@uhs.umass.edu
ROCKLIN, Thomas, R ... 319-335-3557 175 H
thomas-rocklin@uiowa.edu
ROCKMAN, Adam .... 718-997-5500 320 E
adam.rockman@qc.cuny.edu
ROCKOW, Amanda, O .. 972-883-2106 494 A
arockow@utdallas.edu
ROCKWELL, Casey .... 501-337-5000.. 20 H
crockwell@coto.edu
ROCKWELL, Jason .... 405-945-3315 400 F
jrockwe@osuokc.edu
ROCKWELL, Kelly .... 716-851-1699 325 A
rockwell@ecc.edu
ROCKWELL, Susan .... 408-924-6047.. 36 B
susan.rockwell@sjsu.edu
RODARTE, Susana .... 915-831-2018 473 J
srodart7@epcc.edu
RODAS, Mary .... 516-364-0808 335 A
rodas@nycollege.edu
RODDEN, Greg, A .... 863-638-7215 118 L
greg.rodden@warner.edu
RODDEN, Jennifer .... 562-938-4695.. 51 A
jrodden@lbcc.edu
RODDINI, Martin .... 516-572-7331 334 A
martin.roddini@ncc.edu
RODDY, Jackie .... 615-226-3990 458 A
jroddy@lincolntech.edu
RODDY, Marilyn .... 865-694-6529 463 E
mlroddy@pstcc.edu
RODDY, Shirley .... 405-692-3262 398 I
sroddy@macu.edu
RODE, Joe .... 817-515-7741 484 B
joe.rode@tccd.edu
RODECKER, Daniel .... 518-580-5860 342 I
drodecke@skidmore.edu
RODENBORN,
Steven, M .... 512-637-5618 481 B
stevero@stedwards.edu
RODERICK, Amy, L .... 508-831-5577 238 G
alroderick@wpi.edu
RODERICK, Daniel .... 617-253-1392 233 C
RODERICK, Gerald, K ... 410-778-7810 221 D
jroderick2@washcoll.edu
RODERICK, Lori .... 309-794-7182 139 K
loriroderick@augustana.edu
RODGER, Doug .... 712-324-5061 182 A
drodger@nwicc.edu
RODGERS, Ardie .... 405-733-7434 401 L
arodgers@rose.edu
RODGERS, Barbara, J ... 574-807-7209 164 F
rodgerb@bethelcollege.edu
RODGERS, Beverly .... 785-242-5200 190 D
beverly.rodgers@ottawa.edu
RODGERS, JR., Bob ..... 404-835-6132 460 G
brodgers@richmont.edu
RODGERS, Chris, T ...... 402-280-2455 290 B
ChrisRodgers@creighton.edu
RODGERS, Christopher . 718-817-4755 326 C
chrodgers@fordham.edu
RODGERS, Corey .... 310-233-4091.. 51 F
rodgercd@lahc.edu
RODGERS, Denise .... 973-972-3645 306 F
denise.rutgers@rutgers.edu
RODGERS, Harold, E .... 574-807-7751 164 F
rodgerh@bethelcollege.edu
RODGERS, Kenneth, G . 919-530-5079 370 C
krodgers@nccu.edu
RODGERS, Larry .... 541-737-4582 408 F
larry.rodgers@oregonstate.edu
RODGERS, Mark, E .... 570-340-6001 425 D
mrodgers@marywood.edu
RODGERS, Mary, P .... 662-246-6263 268 F
mrodgers@msdelta.edu
RODGERS, Mike .... 270-686-4503 197 A
mike.rodgers@kctcs.edu
RODGERS, Mike .... 270-686-4481 197 A
mike.rodgers@kctcs.edu
RODGERS, Phillip .... 501-420-1249.. 19 B
phillip.rodgers@arkansasbaptist.edu
RODGERS, Ronald, F .... 603-862-0960 299 B
ron.rodgers@usnh.edu
RODGERS, Ronald, F .... 603-862-0960 299 A
ron.rodgers@usnh.edu
RODGERS, Ruby .... 270-534-3184 197 E
ruby.rodgers@kctcs.edu
RODGERS, Ruth .... 317-955-6321 171 A
rrodgers@marian.edu
RODGERS, Teresa, P .... 334-670-3221.... 8 A
trodgers@troy.edu
RODGERS, Terreta .... 404-225-4604 120 I
trodgers@atlantatech.edu
RODGERS, Victor .... 717-221-1361 420 D
vrodgers@hacc.edu
RODICIO, Lenore .... 305-237-3715 108 L
lrodicio@mdc.edu
RODKIN, Dan .... 352-395-4171 112 H
dan.rodkin@sfcollege.edu
RODLER, Trina .... 323-856-7699.. 27 H
trodler@afi.com
RODNE, Anne .... 561-912-1211 102 N
arodne@evergladesuniversity.edu
RODNING, Janet, M ...... 770-720-5954 130 E
jmr@reinhardt.edu
RODOCKER, Jason, L .... 540-458-8753 519 A
jrodocker@wlu.edu
RODOLF, Mark .... 405-974-3611 403 G
mrodolf@uco.edu
RODRGUEZ,
Nemaris, C .... 718-390-4351 340 G
rodrgun@stjohns.edu
RODRICK-SCHNAATH,
Heidi .... 215-248-6312 424 G
hrodrick-schnaath@ltsp.edu
RODRIGUE, Kelly, J ..... 985-448-4154 208 C
kelly.rodrigue@nicholls.edu
RODRIGUE, Morris .... 530-242-7525.. 66 C
mrodrigue@shastacollege.edu
RODRIGUES, Debra .... 561-912-1211 102 N
dveloso@evergladesuniversity.edu
RODRIGUES, Leon .... 651-201-1746 257 N
leon.rodrigues@so.mnscu.edu
RODRIGUES-DOOLABH,
Lisa .... 203-596-2104.. 89 F
lrodrigues-doolabh@nv.edu
RODRIGUEZ, Abel .... 787-834-9595 556 D
arodriguez@uaa.edu
RODRIGUEZ, Abiezer .... 787-834-9595 556 D
abrodriguez@uaa.edu
RODRIGUEZ, Adrian ..... 817-515-1007 484 B
adrian.rodriguez@tccd.edu
RODRIGUEZ, Aida, E .... 787-852-1430 552 J
arodriguez@hccpr.edu
RODRIGUEZ, Alba .... 352-365-3571 107 X
rodrigua@lssc.edu
RODRIGUEZ, Alfred ...... 210-999-7206 490 E
alfred.rodriguez@trinity.edu
RODRIGUEZ, Alma .... 805-289-6360.. 75 E
arodriguez@vcccd.edu
RODRIGUEZ, Andy .... 970-248-1337.. 80 B
arodrigu@coloradomesa.edu
RODRIGUEZ, Angel ...... 787-834-9595 556 D
anrodriguez@uaa.edu
RODRIGUEZ, Angel ...... 787-738-2161 557 G
angel.rodriguez40@upr.edu
RODRIGUEZ, Anita .... 402-449-2821 290 F
arodriguez@graceu.edu
RODRIGUEZ, Aristalia ... 212-772-4804 319 E
aristalia.rodriguez@hunter.cuny.edu
RODRIGUEZ, Arlene ..... 413-755-4218 233 B
arodriguez@stcc.edu
RODRIGUEZ, Armando . 787-279-1912 553 H
arodriguez@bayamon.inter.edu
RODRIGUEZ, Armando . 787-841-2000 555 F
armando_rodriguez@pucpr.edu
RODRIGUEZ, Art, D ...... 845-437-7300 351 H
arodriguez@vassar.edu
RODRIGUEZ, Barbara ... 305-821-3333 104 C
bjrodriguez@fnu.edu
RODRIGUEZ,
Barbara, J .... 305-821-3333 104 C
bjrodriguez@fnu.edu
RODRIGUEZ, Carlos ..... 787-777-0677 558 E
carlos.rodriguez80@upr.edu
RODRIGUEZ, Carlos ..... 787-765-4210 551 F
crodriguez@cempr.edu
RODRIGUEZ, Carmen .... 787-878-5475 553 F
clrodri@arecibo.inter.edu
RODRIGUEZ, Carmen ... 909-384-8592.. 62 C
marodrig@sbccd.cc.ca.us
RODRIGUEZ,
Carmen, J .... 787-480-2417 551 H
crodriguez03@sanjuanciudadpatria.com
RODRIGUEZ, Christina . 909-537-5250.. 35 A
chrodrig@csusb.edu
RODRIGUEZ, Claribel ... 787-621-2835 550 D
crodriguez@aupr.edu
RODRIGUEZ, Claribel ... 787-864-2222 553 J
claribel.rodriguez@guayama.inter.edu
RODRIGUEZ, Claribette 787-257-7373 555 L
clrodriguez@suagm.edu
RODRIGUEZ, Claudia ... 787-761-0640 557 A
asistenciaeconomica@utcpr.edu
RODRIGUEZ, Daisy .... 787-766-1717 556 A
drodriguez@mail.suagm.edu
RODRIGUEZ, Daniel, B . 312-503-3460 155 D
daniel.rodriguez@law.northwestern.edu
RODRIGUEZ, Daron ...... 312-279-3997.. 28 G
darodriguez@argosy.edu
RODRIGUEZ, Diana ...... 925-424-1406.. 37 O
drodriguez@laspositascollege.edu
RODRIGUEZ, Diana ...... 787-852-1430 552 J
drodriguez@hccpr.edu
RODRIGUEZ, Donna ..... 361-572-6480 496 D
donna.rodriguez@victoriacollege.edu
RODRIGUEZ, Ed .... 816-802-3436 276 F
erodriguez@kcai.edu
RODRIGUEZ, Edgar ...... 787-841-2000 555 F
edrodrios@pucpr.edu
RODRIGUEZ, Edgar ...... 203-582-3660.. 91 E
edgar.rodriguez@quinnipiac.edu
RODRIGUEZ, Edgar, D . 787-257-7373 555 L
ue_erodrigue@suagm.edu
RODRIGUEZ, Elisamuel 787-720-4476 556 G
decanatofinanzas@mizpa.edu
RODRIGUEZ, Elizabeth . 561-683-1400.. 97 G
erodriguez@anho.edu
RODRIGUEZ, Elizabeth . 573-882-8279 283 G
rodriguezea@umsystem.edu
RODRIGUEZ, Elsa .... 787-753-6335 552 K
e_rodriguez@icprjc.edu
RODRIGUEZ, Esaeas, J 260-422-5561 167 F
ejrodriguez@indianatech.edu
RODRIGUEZ, Francisco 787-250-8581 558 E
arquitecto.pr@gmail.com
RODRIGUEZ,
Francisco, C .... 213-891-2201.. 51 C
mazarild@email.laccd.edu
RODRIGUEZ, JR.,
Gerardo .... 956-872-3746 482 G
gerry@southtexascollege.edu
RODRIGUEZ, Ginger ..... 219-473-4305 165 A
grodriguez@ccsj.edu
RODRIGUEZ, Glorimar .. 787-780-5134 554 H
glrodriguez@nuc.edu
RODRIGUEZ, Guillermo 314-246-7881 285 G
rodriggu@webster.edu
RODRIGUEZ, Havidan ... 956-665-2100 494 C
president@utpa.edu
RODRIGUEZ, Havidan ... 956-665-2011 494 C
havidan@utpa.edu
RODRIGUEZ, Irma, I ..... 787-841-2000 555 F
irodriguez@pucpr.edu
RODRIGUEZ, Israel .... 787-780-0070 550 G
irodriguez@caribbean.edu
RODRIGUEZ, Jalibeth ... 787-841-2000 555 F
jalibeth_rodriguez@pucpr.edu
RODRIGUEZ, Janeth ..... 909-652-6541.. 38 A
janeth.rodriguez@chaffey.edu
RODRIGUEZ, Jordan ..... 208-459-5529 137 J
jrodriguez@collegeofidaho.edu
RODRIGUEZ, Jorge .... 787-257-7373 555 L
ac_jrodrigue@suagm.edu
RODRIGUEZ, Jorge .... 718-990-1485 340 G
rodriguj@stjohns.edu
RODRIGUEZ, Jose .... 305-237-2339 108 L
jrodri28@mdc.edu
RODRIGUEZ, Jose .... 787-279-1912 553 H
jarodriguez@bayamon.inter.edu
RODRIGUEZ, Jose .... 718-489-5315 340 E
jrodriguez@sfc.edu
RODRIGUEZ, Jose .... 214-860-8587 472 G
jcrodriguez@dcccd.edu
RODRIGUEZ,
Jose Ginel .... 787-269-4510 556 F
jose.ginel@uccaribe.edu
RODRIGUEZ,
Jose Ginel .... 787-798-6904 556 F
jose.ginel@uccaribe.edu
RODRIGUEZ, Josefina .. 787-257-0000 557 F
josefina.rodriguez@upr.edu
RODRIGUEZ, Juan .... 787-878-5475 553 F
jcrodrig@arecibo.inter.edu
RODRIGUEZ, Judith ...... 212-226-7300 338 F
judithrodriguez@pbcny.edu
RODRIGUEZ, Katrina .... 970-351-2796.. 87 A
katrina.rodriguez@unco.edu
RODRIGUEZ, Lee Ann .. 941-487-4649 115 B
lrodriguez@ncf.edu
RODRIGUEZ, Leslie ...... 847-233-7700 155 B
lrodriguez@nc.edu
RODRIGUEZ, Liliana ..... 303-871-3080.. 86 H
Liliana.Rodriguez@du.edu
RODRIGUEZ, Luis, R ..... 787-850-9324 558 A
luis.rodriguez40@upr.edu
RODRIGUEZ, Lynda ...... 305-348-0286 114 G
lynda.romaguera@fiu.edu
RODRIGUEZ, Maggie .... 832-252-4623 470 L
maggie.rodriguez@cbshouston.edu
RODRIGUEZ, Maria ...... 305-223-4561 111 J
rodriguez@sjvcs.edu
RODRIGUEZ, Maria ...... 787-852-1430 552 J
ma.rodriguez.r@hccpr.edu
RODRIGUEZ, Maria, I ... 787-738-2161 557 G
maria.rodriguez46@upr.edu
RODRIGUEZ,
Maria-Judith .... 413-542-2372 222 A
hr@amherst.edu
RODRIGUEZ, Marisela .. 956-764-5798 477 C
marisela.rodriguez@laredo.edu
RODRIGUEZ, Mark .... 216-987-5459 381 A
mark.rodriguez@tri-c.edu
RODRIGUEZ, Mary, J ... 419-755-4767 387 E
mrodriguez@ncstatecollege.edu
RODRIGUEZ, Mary Ann 503-883-2458 406 I
mrodrigu1@linfield.edu
RODRIGUEZ, Mayra ...... 787-743-7979 555 M
mrodrigu@suagm.edu
RODRIGUEZ, Melanie ... 787-720-4476 556 G
biblioteca@mizpa.edu
RODRIGUEZ, Melba ...... 773-442-4200 154 H
m-rodriguez44@neiu.edu
RODRIGUEZ, Miguel ..... 939-292-8915 558 F
miguel.rodriguez10@upr.edu
RODRIGUEZ, Millie ...... 330-941-1526 396 C
mjrodriguez02@ysu.edu
RODRIGUEZ, Moises ..... 210-924-4338 469 B
moises.rodriguez@bua.edu
RODRIGUEZ, Monica .... 510-215-3958.. 42 D
mrodriguez@contracosta.edu
RODRIGUEZ, Narce ...... 971-722-7249 409 C
nrodrigu@pcc.edu
RODRIGUEZ, Nilda .... 787-284-1912 554 B
nilrodri@ponce.inter.edu
RODRIGUEZ, Nilda .... 914-422-4213 337 I
nrodriguez@pace.edu
RODRIGUEZ, Nilda, E ... 787-852-1430 552 J
nrodriguez@hccpr.edu
RODRIGUEZ, Norma ..... 562-860-2451.. 37 L
nrodriguez@cerritos.edu
RODRIGUEZ, Olga .... 305-821-3333 104 C
ordriguez@fnu.edu
RODRIGUEZ, Oscar ...... 252-639-7342 369 B
orodriguez@umo.edu
RODRIGUEZ, Raquel ..... 559-934-2218.. 76 B
raquelrodriguez@whccd.edu
RODRIGUEZ, Raul .... 714-480-7450.. 60 F
rodriguez_raul@rsccd.edu

RODRIGUEZ, Rene 512-232-2780 493 M renerod@austin.utexas.edu

RODRIGUEZ, Reuban, B 804-828-8940 514 F rbrodriguez@vcu.edu

RODRIGUEZ, Ricardo 972-860-8325 472 E RicardoRodriguez@dcccd.edu

RODRIGUEZ, Richard 559-323-2100 63 C rrodriguez@sjcl.edu

RODRIGUEZ, Ron 209-667-3709 35 C rrodriguez36@csustan.edu

RODRIGUEZ, Ronald 985-448-4017 208 C ronald.rodriguez@nicholls.edu

RODRIGUEZ, Rosa 860-832-1652 88 D rosa.rodriguez@ccsu.edu

RODRIGUEZ, Rosalie, M 814-641-3125 421 L rodrigr@juniata.edu

RODRIGUEZ, Shari, M 574-284-4581 172 G srodriguez@saintmarys.edu

RODRIGUEZ, Sherri 818-947-2726 52 B rodrigsa@lavc.edu

RODRIGUEZ, Silvio 305-237-7445 108 L srodrig2@mdc.edu

RODRIGUEZ, Sonia 585-475-2395 339 G smrfa@rit.edu

RODRIGUEZ, Sonya, F 575-624-8066 311 K sonya@nmmi.edu

RODRIGUEZ, Stephanie 310-660-3601 43 G srodriguez@elcamino.edu

RODRIGUEZ, Steven 949-214-3003 42 B steven.rodriguez@cui.edu

RODRIGUEZ, Sylvia 925-424-1542 37 O srodriguez@laspositascollege.edu

RODRIGUEZ, Sylvia 925-424-1000 37 O

RODRIGUEZ, Sylvia, L 305-474-6871 112 B srodriguez@stu.edu

RODRIGUEZ, Teresa 787-620-2040 550 D trodriguez@aupr.edu

RODRIGUEZ, Teresita 310-434-4774 65 B rodriguez_teresita@smc.edu

RODRIGUEZ, Velia 559-730-3775 41 D veliar@cos.edu

RODRIGUEZ, Victor 361-593-5781 486 A tamukcso@tamuk.edu

RODRIGUEZ, Vince 714-241-6195 40 B vrodriguez@coastline.edu

RODRIGUEZ, Vincent 210-283-5096 492 B vincent@uiwtx.edu

RODRIGUEZ, Wanda 787-257-0000 557 F wanda.rodriguez@upr.edu

RODRIGUEZ, Widilia 787-815-0000 557 D widilia.rodriguez@upr.edu

RODRIGUEZ, Zulyn 787-764-0000 558 E zulyn.rodriguez@upr.edu

RODRIGUEZ-CANCEL, Jaime, L 787-723-4481 551 B jarodriguez@ceaprc.edu

RODRIGUEZ-CHARDAVOYNE, Esther 718-518-4308 319 D erodriguez@hostos.cuny.edu

RODRIGUEZ-DORESTANT, Simone 718-804-8805 320 C simone@mec.cuny.edu

RODRIGUEZ ESQUERDO, Pedro, J 787-764-0000 558 E pj.rodriguezesquerdo@upr.edu

RODRIGUEZ-FARRAR, Hanna 415-482-1927 43 D hrf@dominican.edu

RODRIGUEZ-GREGORY, Lisa 732-906-2550 303 F lgregory@middlesexcc.edu

RODRIGUEZ-GUILLEN, Linda 956-364-4427 487 H lindarodriguez-guillen@tstc.edu

RODRIGUEZ-HEFFNER, Ermelinda 831-656-3054 548 A erodriguez@nps.edu

RODRIGUEZ-LOPEZ, Miguel, A 787-723-4481 551 B centro@ceaprc.edu

RODRIGUEZ-MOLINA, Nilda, E 787-480-2351 551 H nilrodriguez@sanjuanciudadpatria.com

RODRIGUEZ-PAZ, Maria 787-620-2040 550 D mrodriguez_paz@aupr.edu

RODRIGUEZ-QUINONES, Jose 787-725-6500 551 A jrodriguezq@albizu.edu

RODRIGUEZ-VARGAS, Claribel 787-261-2835 550 D crodriguez@aupr.edu

RODRIGUEZ-VEGA, Shirley 312-996-5563 161 F srodri3@uic.edu

RODRIQUEZ, Camille 303-329-6355 81 B dean@cstcm.edu

RODRIQUEZ, Glendali 715-232-2421 541 B rodriquezg@uwstout.edu

RODRIQUEZ, Jason 503-883-2574 406 I jrodriqu@linfield.edu

RODRIQUEZ, Mike 505-984-6058 312 J

RODRIQUEZ, Nicky, M 219-942-1459 165 D nicky.rodriquez@ccr.edu

RODRUCK, Ryan 509-452-5100 524 J

RODRÍGUEZ, Deborah 787-894-2828 558 F deborah.rodriguez7@upr.edu

RODRÍGUEZ, Ibis 787-766-1717 556 A ibrodriguez@suagm.edu

RODRÍGUEZ, Israel 787-743-7979 555 M ut_irodriguez@suagm.edu

RODRÍGUEZ, Luis 787-850-9305 558 A luis.rodriguez39@upr.edu

RODRÍGUEZ, Yarelis 787-884-3838 550 E dir_registra@atenascollege.edu

RODRÍGUEZ-BONANO, Melysa 787-993-8852 557 E melysa.rodriguez@upr.edu

RODRÍGUEZ-ORTIZ, Marcia 787-993-8856 557 E marcia.rodriguez@upr.edu

RODRÍGUEZ-RIVERA, Rafael, E 787-751-1600 554 D rrodriguez@juris.inter.edu

RODRÍGUEZ-VALLÉS, Nora 787-993-8868 557 E nora.rodriguez1@upr.edu

RODUIN, Cheyenne, M 425-739-8657 523 I cheyenne.roduin@lwtech.edu

ROE, Aaron 309-649-6230 160 F aaron.roe@src.edu

ROE, Herb 605-221-3124 452 F hroe@kilian.edu

ROE, Michael 845-431-8018 324 D michael.roe@sunydutchess.edu

ROE, Micheal, D 206-281-2252 526 D mroe@spu.edu

ROE, Robert, M 989-774-3933 240 O roe1rm@cmich.edu

ROEBUCK, Randy 316-677-9437 192 C rroebuck@watc.edu

ROECKER, Pamela 617-735-9985 226 B roeckerp@emmanuel.edu

ROECKER-PHELPS, Carolyn 937-229-3334 393 E cphelps1@udayton.edu

ROEDEL, Glenn 215-780-1296 435 D groedel@salus.edu

ROEDER, Cathy 573-651-2235 282 C croeder@semo.edu

ROEDER, Jerry 413-782-1386 238 A gerard.roeder@wne.edu

ROEDER, Lynn, M 252-328-9297 369 E roederl@ecu.edu

ROEHL, Barb 406-377-9412 286 F broehl@dawson.edu

ROEHL, Bob 206-546-4514 526 G broehl@shoreline.edu

ROELFS, Melinda, A 620-235-4226 190 G maroelfs@pittstate.edu

ROELFSEMA, Cheryl, E 815-224-0419 147 J cheryl_roelfsema@ivcc.edu

ROELKE, Scott 651-423-8297 258 E scott.roelke@dctc.edu

ROELLKE, Christopher 845-437-5600 351 H chroellke@vassar.edu

ROELOFS, Lyle, D 859-985-3522 193 F roelofsl@berea.edu

ROEN, Duane 480-727-6513 11 J duane.roen@asu.edu

ROERIG, Sandra 318-675-7618 205 D sroeri@lsuhsc.edu

ROERIG, Sandra, C 318-675-7618 205 D sroeri@lsuhsc.edu

ROESCH, Adam 618-262-8641 147 B roescha@iecc.edu

ROESSLER, Billy 940-668-7731 479 K broessler@nctc.edu

ROESTI, Bobette 785-738-9060 190 A broesti@ncktc.edu

ROETHEMEYER, Robert, V 260-452-2146 165 E robert.roethemeyer@ctsfw.edu

ROETHER, Diane 940-668-4283 479 K droether@nctc.edu

ROETHLER, Don 701-224-5485 374 E donald.roethler@bismarckstate.edu

ROETTGER, Linda 219-464-5958 174 E linda.roettger@valpo.edu

ROETZEL, Mary 617-369-4292 236 E mroetzel@smfa.edu

ROEWER, Anita 815-455-8737 152 B aroewer@mchenry.edu

ROFFEL, Linda 845-434-5750 349 C lroffel@sunysullivan.edu

ROGALSKI, Kathryn 847-925-6221 145 F krogalsk@harpercollege.edu

ROGALSKY, Amy 405-974-5376 403 G arogalsky@uco.edu

ROGAN, Doreen 207-216-4320 211 F drogan@yccc.edu

ROGAN, Fred, R 205-726-2837 6 F cfrogan@samford.edu

ROGAN, Margaret 617-824-8590 226 A margaret_rogan@emerson.edu

ROGAN, Mary, T 718-960-8559 319 C mary.rogan@lehman.cuny.edu

ROGAN, Patricia, M 317-274-6862 168 E progan@iupui.edu

ROGAN, Richard 617-928-4515 234 D rrogan@mountida.edu

ROGAN, William, D 615-230-3595 464 B william.rogan@volstate.edu

ROGELSTAD, Todd 701-845-7209 374 D todd.rogelstad@vcsu.edu

ROGENTINE, Linda 218-723-6022 255 A lrogenti@css.edu

ROGER-GORDON, A. Patrick 212-346-1295 337 I arogergordon@pace.edu

ROGERS, Andria 970-339-6518 78 J andria.rogers@aims.edu

ROGERS, Ann 203-857-7270 89 H arogers@norwalk.edu

ROGERS, Beth 513-244-8442 379 I beth.rogers@ccuniversity.edu

ROGERS, Beth 513-244-8134 379 I beth.rogers@ccuniversity.edu

ROGERS, Blake 502-897-4720 199 D brogers@sbts.edu

ROGERS, Brian 503-494-8362 408 D cdrcadmin@ohsu.edu

ROGERS, Cheryl, L 903-510-3217 491 A crog@tjc.edu

ROGERS, Christina 212-659-7200 330 A crogers@tkc.edu

ROGERS, Cindy, A 972-860-8186 472 D car3810@dcccd.edu

ROGERS, Craig, L 270-789-5057 194 D crogers@campbellsville.edu

ROGERS, Dana 409-882-3372 488 G dana.rogers@lsco.edu

ROGERS, Dana, N 409-882-3397 488 G dana.rogers@lsco.edu

ROGERS, David, E 315-684-6044 347 A rogersde@morrisville.edu

ROGERS, Deborah 215-641-6506 426 E drogers@mc3.edu

ROGERS, Demetrius 503-517-1809 411 C drogers@westernseminary.edu

ROGERS, Donna 252-789-0290 363 H drogers@martincc.edu

ROGERS, Donnita 405-466-3262 398 E ddrogers@langston.edu

ROGERS, Edwin 808-675-3542 134 M rogerse@byuh.edu

ROGERS, Elizabeth, A 336-278-6350 356 F rogers@elon.edu

ROGERS, Fred, A 507-222-5411 254 D frogers@carleton.edu

ROGERS, Frederick 803-508-7272 443 C rogersf@atc.edu

ROGERS, Gail 423-746-5202 464 D grogers@twcnet.edu

ROGERS, Glen 414-382-6269 534 I glen.rogers@alverno.edu

ROGERS, Greg 623-845-4526 14 N greg.rogers@gccaz.edu

ROGERS, Greg 412-392-3924 433 F grogers@pointpark.edu

ROGERS, Harry, C 215-898-7091 437 I rogers@pobox.upenn.edu

ROGERS, Helen 808-932-7315 135 I hrogers@hawaii.edu

ROGERS, J. Orion 540-831-5958 511 C jorogers@radford.edu

ROGERS, James 212-517-0435 332 A jrogers@mmm.edu

ROGERS, James 212-327-8506 339 H jrogers@mail.rockefeller.edu

ROGERS, James 406-447-4536 286 D jarogers@carroll.edu

ROGERS, Janet 765-998-5330 173 B jnrogers@taylor.edu

ROGERS, Jason 615-460-6441 455 D jason.rogers@belmont.edu

ROGERS, Jason 615-460-6611 455 D jason.rogers@belmont.edu

ROGERS, Jaye, L 765-641-4442 164 B jlrogers2@anderson.edu

ROGERS, Jeffrey 704-406-4724 356 G jrogers3@gardner-webb.edu

ROGERS, Jenica, P 315-267-2482 346 C rogersjp@potsdam.edu

ROGERS, Jennifer 308-635-6551 294 C rogersj5@wncc.edu

ROGERS, Jessica 941-487-4900 115 B ncalum@ncf.edu

ROGERS, Jevita 719-255-3460 86 F jrogers3@uccs.edu

ROGERS, Jill 704-463-3406 367 F jill.rogers@pfeiffer.edu

ROGERS, Johnell 803-934-3256 447 K jrogers@morris.edu

ROGERS, Jolayne 816-322-0110 272 L jolayne.rogers@calvary.edu

ROGERS, Jolene, R 712-362-0431 179 G jrogers@iowalakes.edu

ROGERS, Jolynn 509-359-2383 522 C jrogers@ewu.edu

ROGERS, Joseph, T 610-527-0200 434 D jtrogers@rosemont.edu

ROGERS, Josh 928-536-6227 16 E joshua.rogers@npc.edu

ROGERS, Judith 340-692-4132 559 B jrogers@live.uvi.edu

ROGERS, Justin 716-926-8785 327 F jrogers@hilbert.edu

ROGERS, Kathleen, R 617-521-2276 236 F kathleen.rogers@simmons.edu

ROGERS, Katrina 805-898-2924 44 J krogers@fielding.edu

ROGERS, Kiri 267-502-4890 413 C kiri.rogers@brynathyn.edu

ROGERS, Lalita 318-670-9223 207 C lrogers@susla.edu

ROGERS, Lisa, C 615-898-5345 461 E lisa.rogers@mtsu.edu

ROGERS, Mark 478-274-7871 129 D mwrogers@oftc.edu

ROGERS, Mary 619-388-6591 62 E mrogers@sdccd.edu

ROGERS, Michael 229-430-4014 119 H michael.rogers@asurams.edu

ROGERS, Michael 202-274-5986 97 B michael.rogers@udc.edu

ROGERS, Michael, B 607-735-1891 324 J mrogers@elmira.edu

ROGERS, Michael, C 202-274-5314 97 B michael.rogers1@udc.edu

ROGERS, Michael, C 202-274-5000 97 B

ROGERS, Michelle 909-793-2121 73 K michelle_rogers@redlands.edu

ROGERS, Mike 209-946-2569 73 C mrogers@pacific.edu

ROGERS, Nancy, B 812-237-7900 167 E nancy.rogers@indstate.edu

ROGERS, Patricia 712-279-3149 182 F patricia.rogers@stlukescollege.edu

ROGERS, Patricia 781-891-2622 223 E progers@bentley.edu

ROGERS, Patricia 507-457-5010 262 D progers@winona.edu

ROGERS, Patrick 802-635-1417 504 A patrick.rogers@jsc.edu

ROGERS, Phil 208-459-5282 137 J progers@collegeofidaho.edu

ROGERS, Phyllis 254-295-4501 492 C progers@umhb.edu

ROGERS, Ralph, V 954-262-5796 109 E rvrogers@nova.edu

ROGERS, Randy 660-626-2395 271 G rrrogers@atsu.edu

ROGERS, Randy 336-386-3466 366 E rogersrj@surry.edu

ROGERS, Raymond, C 512-448-8532 481 B rrogers1@stedwards.edu

ROGERS, Richard, L 313-664-7474 241 D rrogers@collegeforcreativestudies.edu

ROGERS, Rodney, K 419-372-2915 377 I rrogers@bgsu.edu

ROGERS, Rus 316-284-5273 185 B rrogers@bethelks.edu

ROGERS, Russell 201-216-5688 308 D rrogers@stevens.edu

ROGERS, Sandra 801-422-1801 497 J sandra_rogers@byu.edu

ROGERS, Scott 828-726-2488 360 F srogers@cccti.edu

ROGERS, Scott 509-542-4834 521 C srogers@columbiabasin.edu

ROGERS, Scott, S 330-385-1070 390 A srogers@ovct.edu

ROGERS, Selwyn, O 409-772-5108 495 E sorogers@utmb.edu

ROGERS, Shannon 479-394-7622 22 H srogers@rmcc.edu

ROGERS, Sharon 609-894-9311 306 B srogers@bcc.edu

ROGERS, Stephanie 318-678-6000 203 A srogers@bpcc.edu

ROGERS, Susan 845-434-5750 349 C srogers@sullivan.suny.edu

ROGERS, Susan 972-883-4325 494 A susan.rogers@utdallas.edu

ROGERS, Tamara 617-496-3069 227 D tamara_rogers@harvard.edu

ROGERS, Tammy 706-880-8344 127 N trogers@lagrange.edu

ROGERS, Tamy .... 214-333-5158 471 L
tamyr@dbu.edu
ROGERS, Thomas .... 502-213-7310 196 E
thomas.rogers@kctcs.edu
ROGERS, Tim .... 503-399-7506 404 L
tim.rogers@chemeketa.edu
ROGERS, Timothy .... 315-866-0300 327 E
rogerstd@herkimer.edu
ROGERS, Toby .... 806-720-7627 478 A
toby.rogers@lcu.edu
ROGERS, Tracy .... 719-587-7990.. 78 I
tracy_rogers@adams.edu
ROGERS-ADKINSON,
Diana .... 573-651-2408 282 C
drogersadkinson@semo.edu
ROGERSON, Andrew .... 707-664-2028.. 36 C
andrew.rogerson@sonoma.edu
ROGERSON, Joanie .... 360-736-9391 520 F
jrogerson@centralia.edu
ROGERSON, Sarah .... 518-445-3246 314 H
sroge@albanylaw.edu
ROGGE, Ann .... 302-736-2445.. 94 E
ann.rogge@wesley.edu
ROGGENSTEIN, Gary .... 661-722-6300.. 27 P
groggenstein@avc.edu
ROGGIE, Edie .... 315-786-2327 329 G
eroggie@sunyjefferson.edu
ROGNRUD, Carol .... 240-567-7493 217 B
carol.rognrud@montgomerycollege.edu
ROGOTZKE, Kathy, M .... 641-422-4154 181 E
rogotkat@niacc.edu
ROGOVIN, Michael .... 914-594-4560 335 H
michael_rogovin@nymc.edu
ROGSTAD, Mark .... 509-574-4671 529 B
mrogstad@yvcc.edu
ROHAN, James, P .... 920-465-2075 539 F
rohanj@uwgb.edu
ROHANNA, Susan .... 610-902-8206 414 B
susan.rohanna@cabrini.edu
ROHDE, Ben .... 262-243-5700 535 I
benjamin.rohde@cuw.edu
ROHDE, Scott .... 860-685-2809.. 93 B
srohde@wesleyan.edu
ROHDER, Kelly .... 815-280-2915 148 K
krohder@jjc.edu
ROHDIN, Ben .... 973-353-5541 307 C
ben.rohdin@rutgers.edu
ROHENA, Ricardo .... 787-850-9328 558 A
ricardo.rohena@upr.edu
ROHLEDER, Ann .... 812-357-6610 173 A
arohleder@saintmeinrad.edu
ROHLEDER, John .... 651-779-3496 258 D
john.rohleder@century.edu
ROHLEDER-SOOK,
Wendy .... 785-628-4408 187 A
wmrohledersook@fhsu.edu
ROHLFS, Jen .... 206-934-6794 526 B
jen.rohlfs@seattlecolleges.edu
ROHLFS, Melissa .... 425-235-2356 525 G
mrohlfs@rtc.edu
ROHMAN, Lynda .... 207-404-5651 210 C
rohmanl@husson.edu
ROHN, Marisa .... 330-494-6170 391 J
mrohn@starkstate.edu
ROHNER, Christy .... 270-686-4243 193 G
christy.rohner@brescia.edu
ROHR, Ann .... 970-207-4550.. 83 P
AnnR@mckinleycollege.edu
ROHR, Ann .... 970-207-4500.. 87 D
AnnR@uscareerinstitute.edu
ROHR, Launa .... 574-535-7543 166 C
launar@goshen.edu
ROHR, Margie .... 973-290-4054 301 F
mrohr@cse.edu
ROHRBACH, Daniel, W . 937-255-6565 547 E
daniel.rohrbach@afit.edu
ROHRBACK, Jane, T .... 248-204-3160 245 J
jrohrback@ltu.edu
ROHRBAUGH,
Suzanne, Y .... 336-342-4261 365 E
rohrbaughs8858@rockinghamcc.edu
ROHRER, Douglas .... 270-901-3490 201 D
douglas.rohrer@wku.edu
ROHRER, Katherine .... 609-258-7800 305 C
krohrer@princeton.edu
ROIDT, Joseph, M .... 304-637-1277 529 I
roidtj@dewv.edu
ROIG, Katy .... 619-260-7404.. 74 B
kroig@sandiego.edu
ROJAS, Carlos .... 787-840-2575 555 E
crojas@psm.edu
ROJAS, Carmen, I .... 787-743-4041 551 I
crojas@columbiacentral.edu
ROJAS, Eddy, M .... 937-229-2306 393 E
erojas1@udayton.edu
ROJAS, Jason .... 860-297-4166.. 92 A
jason.rojas@trincoll.edu
ROJAS, Jesus .... 912-525-5000 130 H
jrojas@scad.edu
ROJAS, Pablo, E .... 787-891-0925 553 E
projas@aquadilla.inter.edu

ROJAS, Robyn, D .... 405-325-3337 403 I
rrojas@ou.edu
ROJAS, Rodney .... 213-613-2200.. 67 G
rodney_rojas@sciarc.edu
ROJAS ALVAREZ LOPEREN,
Clara .... 713-221-8179 491 F
rojasc@uhd.edu
ROJAS-HAYES, Silvia .... 215-324-0746 418 A
srojas@eastern.edu
ROJCEWICZ, Peter .... 626-571-8811.. 74 E
peterr@uwest.edu
ROKAS, Tracy .... 615-460-5405 455 D
tracy.rokas@belmont.edu
ROKICKY, Paul .... 216-987-5048 381 A
paul.rokicky@tri-c.edu
ROKOS, Jean, M .... 231-995-1248 248 C
jrokos@nmc.edu
ROKOWSKY, Eli .... 845-425-1370 337 E
ROKOWSKY, Israel .... 845-425-1370 337 E
ROKSANDIC, Stevo .... 614-234-1644 386 N
sroksandic@mchs.com
ROKUSEK, Jim .... 605-367-6109 454 D
jim.rokusek@southeasttech.edu
ROLAND, Cheryl .... 269-387-8412 252 I
cheryl.roland@wmich.edu
ROLAND, Christy .... 515-244-4221 175 C
rolandc@aib.edu
ROLAND, David, E .... 706-233-7329 131 C
droland@shorter.edu
ROLAND, Harriet, A .... 803-533-3790 448 H
rolandha@scsu.edu
ROLAND, Kirc, J .... 360-442-2471 524 A
kroland@lowercolumbia.edu
ROLAND, Meg .... 503-699-3336 407 A
mroland@marylhurst.edu
ROLDAN, Marggi .... 864-578-8770 448 G
mroldan@sherman.edu
ROLEN, Scott .... 541-917-4420 406 J
rolens@linnbenton.edu
ROLEY, V. Vance .... 808-956-8377 135 J
vroley@hawaii.edu
ROLFE, Cynthia .... 405-974-2688 403 G
crolfe@uco.edu
ROLFE, Rial, D .... 806-743-2905 490 A
rial.rolfe@ttuhsc.edu
ROLFES, Katherine .... 337-521-8906 204 E
katherine.rolfes@solacc.edu
ROLFS, Trevor .... 620-792-9378 184 I
rolfst@bartonccc.edu
ROLHEISER, Ronald .... 210-341-1366 479 N
rrolheiser@ost.edu
ROLL, Debbie .... 907-564-8220.. 10 D
droll@alaskapacific.edu
ROLLACK, Nikesha .... 919-278-2672 368 G
nrollack@shawu.edu
ROLLE, Jo-Ann .... 718-270-5110 320 C
jrolle@mec.cuny.edu
ROLLE, Kevin, A .... 256-372-5230.... 1 A
kevin.rolle@aamu.edu
ROLLENE, Jerry .... 479-524-7212.. 21 F
jrollene@jbu.edu
ROLLER, Robert .... 626-812-3085.. 29 B
rroller@apu.edu
ROLLER, Steven, A .... 617-228-2394 231 C
sroller@bhcc.mass.edu
ROLLESTON, George .... 440-826-2081 377 D
grollest@bw.edu
ROLLINGS, Cherie .... 763-424-0702 260 E
Cherie.Rollings@hennepintech.edu
ROLLINO, Richard .... 307-332-2930 547 C
rrollino@wyomingcatholiccollege.com
ROLLINS, Cheryl .... 443-885-4429 217 C
cheryl.rollins@morgan.edu
ROLLINS, Elizabeth, J .... 803-981-7122 451 K
erollins@yorktech.edu
ROLLINS, Judy .... 252-985-5111 367 E
jrollins@ncwc.edu
ROLLINS, Pam .... 334-420-4253.... 7 I
prollins@trenholmstate.edu
ROLLINS, Sandra .... 856-256-4276 306 D
rollinss@rowan.edu
ROLLINS, Stephen, J .... 907-786-1825.. 10 H
srollins@uaa.alaska.edu
ROLLISON, Jeffrey .... 610-647-4400 421 B
jrollison@immaculata.edu
ROLLMAN,
Catherine, A .... 804-752-7270 511 E
crollman@rmc.edu
ROLLO, Ann .... 315-364-3235 352 F
arollo@wells.edu
ROLLO, J. Michael .... 239-590-7910 114 F
jmrollo@fgcu.edu
ROLLS, Dickie .... 620-252-7575 186 C
dickier@coffeyville.edu
ROLON, Liberty .... 787-750-4100 557 F
liberty.rolon@upr.edu
ROLON, Reynaldo .... 787-279-1912 553 H
rrolon@bayamon.inter.edu
ROM, Cristine .... 216-421-7440 380 B
crom@cia.edu

ROM, Kjetil .... 541-881-5746 410 D
krom@tvcc.cc
ROMA, Jennifer .... 305-273-4499 100 K
jennifer.roman@cbt.edu
ROMA, Lawrence, J .... 607-777-2224 343 D
lroma@binghamton.edu
ROMAGNI, Joanne .... 423-425-1743 465 E
joanne-romagni@utc.edu
ROMAGNOLI, Janice .... 615-655-7274 317 J
jaromagnoli@cazenovia.edu
ROMAIN, Pete .... 212-517-0414 332 A
promain@mmm.edu
ROMALI, Reagan, F .... 773-907-4450 141 O
rromali@ccc.edu
ROMAN, Angela .... 231-591-2685 242 L
AngelaRoman@ferris.edu
ROMAN, Cynthia .... 248-942-3300 248 E
caroman@oaklandcc.edu
ROMAN, Juan, E .... 787-841-2000 555 F
jroman@pucpr.edu
ROMAN, Nilsa, M .... 787-891-0925 553 E
nroman@aguadilla.inter.edu
ROMAN, Vladimir .... 787-763-6425 553 D
vroman@inter.edu
ROMANCZUK, Jeffrey .... 704-886-6500.. 96 H
ROMANDINI, Russ .... 706-507-8898 123 D
romandini_russ@columbusstate.edu
ROMANDINI, Russ .... 513-618-1930 379 J
rromandini@ccms.edu
ROMANELLO, Mary .... 202-884-9677.. 97 A
romanellom@trinitydc.edu
ROMANO, C. Renee .... 217-333-1300 162 A
romano3@illinois.edu
ROMANO, Cenia, K .... 787-884-3838 550 E
vpacademico@atenascollege.edu
ROMANO, Christopher . 201-684-7309 305 F
cromano@ramapo.edu
ROMANO, Daniel, A .... 309-298-2517 163 A
da-romano@wiu.edu
ROMANO, Fred, D .... 630-515-6388 152 H
froman@midwestern.edu
ROMANO, Joan .... 401-254-3510 442 C
jromano@rwu.edu
ROMANO, Joyce, C .... 407-582-3401 118 I
jromano@valenciacollege.edu
ROMANO, Judith, J .... 864-294-3470 446 F
judith.romano@furman.edu
ROMANO, Michael .... 623-245-4600.. 18 C
mromano@uti.edu
ROMANO, Nicole .... 302-356-6846.. 94 G
nicole.romano@wilmu.edu
ROMANO, Pam .... 910-272-3531 365 D
promano@robeson.edu
ROMANO, Sandra .... 340-693-1238 559 B
sromano@live.uvi.edu
ROMANO, Susan, M .... 585-785-1277 325 E
susan.romano@flcc.edu
ROMANO, Wendy, W .... 215-871-6300 432 E
wendyr@pcom.edu
ROMANO, Xavier .... 541-962-3635 405 G
xromano@eou.edu
ROMANSKI, Beth, E .... 717-867-6336 423 I
romanski@lvc.edu
ROMANTIC,
Thomas, W .... 607-255-8574 323 C
twr2@cornell.edu
ROMARY, Marcy .... 252-328-6072 369 E
romarym@ecu.edu
ROMBOUTS,
Stephen, R .... 814-472-3009 434 F
srombouts@francis.edu
ROME, Alan, K .... 440-943-7600 391 A
cpl@dioceseofcleveland.org
ROME, Alan, K .... 440-943-7600 391 A
akrome@dioceseofcleveland.org
ROME, JoAnne .... 413-552-2259 231 F
jrome@hcc.edu
ROME, Kevin, D .... 573-681-5042 276 K
romek@lincolnu.edu
ROME, Michaela .... 212-229-8947 334 C
romem@newschool.edu
ROMELDA, Simmons .... 478-825-6219 124 E
simmonsr@fvsu.edu
ROMEO, Monica .... 716-286-8536 336 E
mromeo@niagara.edu
ROMER, Cheryl .... 831-479-6306.. 30 C
chromer@cabrillo.edu
ROMER, Christine, E .... 636-922-8362 281 C
cromer@stchas.edu
ROMER, Mark .... 941-405-1519 423 B
mromer@lecom.edu
ROMERAO-ALDAZ,
Patrick .... 617-928-4073 234 D
promeroaldaz@mountida.edu
ROMERO, Andy .... 505-747-2166 312 G
andy@nnmc.edu
ROMERO, Angel .... 787-765-1915 554 E
aromero@opto.inter.edu
ROMERO, Bianca .... 909-593-3511.. 73 B
bromero@laverne.edu

ROMERO, Carlos .... 505-277-4186 313 H
crom@unm.edu
ROMERO, Carol .... 305-821-3333 104 C
cromero@fnu.edu
ROMERO, Cecilia .... 505-747-5477 312 G
cromero@nnmc.edu
ROMERO, Christina .... 714-564-6091.. 60 G
romero_christina@sac.edu
ROMERO, Cynthia .... 757-446-7414 507 B
romerocc@evms.edu
ROMERO, Edward, W .... 903-886-5027 485 E
edward.romero@tamuc.edu
ROMERO, Georg .... 831-479-5771.. 30 C
geromero@cabrillo.edu
ROMERO, Herminio .... 787-622-8000 556 H
hromero@pupr.edu
ROMERO, Lizbeth .... 787-878-5475 553 F
lromero@arecibo.inter.edu
ROMERO, Manuel .... 212-220-1238 318 D
mromero@bmcc.cuny.edu
ROMERO, Narda .... 914-674-7841 332 E
nromero@mercy.edu
ROMERO, Peter .... 505-473-6328 313 B
peter.romero@santafeuniversity.edu
ROMERO, Ramona, E .... 609-258-2511 305 C
ramonar@princeton.edu
ROMERO, Rebecca .... 970-521-6649.. 84 H
rebecca.romero@njc.edu
ROMERO, Reyna .... 713-221-8460 491 F
Romeror@uhd.edu
ROMERO, Sally .... 970-943-2150.. 87 F
sromero@western.edu
ROMERO, Van, D .... 575-835-5646 311 I
vromero@nmt.edu
ROMERO, Victoria .... 909-621-8149.. 65 E
victoria.romero@scrippscollege.edu
ROMERO-LEGGOTT,
Valerie .... 505-272-2728 313 H
vromero@salud.unm.edu
ROMESBURG,
Rosemarie .... 304-367-4284 531 E
Rosemarie.Romesburg@pierpont.edu
ROMICH, Barbara .... 704-669-4163 361 E
romich@clevelandcc.edu
ROMIG, Kenneth, J .... 724-946-7141 439 D
romigkj@westminster.edu
ROMIG, Thomas, J .... 785-670-1662 192 B
thomas.romig@washburn.edu
ROMINGER, Anna .... 219-980-6636 168 C
arominge@iun.edu
ROMKEMA, Priscilla .... 605-642-6341 453 G
priscilla.romkema@bhsu.edu
ROMO, Nanette .... 520-515-5399.. 13 B
romon@cochise.edu
ROMO, Ricardo .... 210-458-4101 494 D
Ricardo.Romo@utsa.edu
ROMO, Wayne .... 210-436-3538 481 C
wromo@stmarytx.edu
ROMZEK, Barbara .... 202-885-6234.. 94 H
romzek@american.edu
RONCA, Paul, L .... 804-523-5239 515 F
pronca@reynolds.edu
RONCHETTI, Michele .... 815-836-5498 150 F
ronchemi@lewisu.edu
RONCOLATO, David .... 814-332-5318 411 F
droncola@allegheny.edu
RONDA, René, S .... 787-743-7979 555 M
rsronda@suagm.edu
RONDINELLI, Diane .... 904-826-0084.. 74 A
drondinelli@usa.edu
RONEVICH, Nancy, S .... 740-284-5232 382 G
nronevich@franciscan.edu
RONEY, Linda .... 214-333-5147 471 L
linda@dbu.edu
RONIS, Sheila, R .... 248-689-8282 251 I
sronis@walshcollege.edu
RONK, Chris .... 336-725-8344 368 A
ronkc@piedmontu.edu
RONKOSKI, Bob .... 636-922-8604 281 C
rronkoski@stchas.edu
RONNAU, John .... 956-665-2292 494 C
ronnaujp@utpa.edu
RONNING, Teresa .... 518-743-2261 347 E
ronningt@sunyacc.edu
RONNING LINDGREN,
Rachel .... 805-493-3690.. 31 H
rronning@callutheran.edu
RONVEAUX, Gail .... 951-343-5045.. 30 D
gronveaux@calbaptist.edu
ROOB, Sharon, L .... 920-565-1327 536 Q
roobsl@lakeland.edu
ROOCK, Mark .... 314-529-9673 277 B
mroock@maryville.edu
ROOD, Denine .... 262-691-5157 544 D
drood@wctc.edu
ROOD, Jessica .... 941-487-4150 115 B
jrood@ncf.edu
ROOD, Kathleen, C .... 617-262-5000 223 G
kathy.rood@the-bac.edu
ROOD, Robert .... 419-824-3730 385 F
rrood@lourdes.edu

ROSENBOOM, David ..... 661-255-1050.. 31 B david@calarts.edu
ROSENBURY, Laura, A . 352-273-0600 115 D rosenbury@law.ufl.edu
ROSENDAHL, Matt .... 218-726-8130 264 G lib@d.umn.edu
ROSENFELD, Sholom .... 718-774-5050 349 H ohaleitorah@aol.com
ROSENFELDT, Mary ...... 513-745-3022 396 B rosenfeldt@xavier.edu
ROSENGARDEN, Jeffrey 646-565-6000 350 C
ROSENGART, Sharon .... 973-720-3019 309 I rosengarts@wpunj.edu
ROSENGARTEN, Elaine . 419-559-2393 392 A erosengarten@terra.edu
ROSENGARTEN, Jayne .. 212-237-8624 319 F jrosengarten@jjay.cuny.edu
ROSENGARTEN, Jeffrey . 212-960-5239 353 P rosengar@yu.edu
ROSENGARTEN, Lewis .. 607-753-4808 345 C lewis.rosengarten@cortland.edu
ROSENGARTEN, Richard, A .... 773-702-8221 161 D raroseng@uchicago.edu
ROSENHECK, Sari .... 845-434-5750 349 C sarir@sullivan.suny.edu
ROSENHEIN, Jon .... 212-799-5000 329 I
ROSENKRANTZ, Laurie . 817-531-4420 490 C lerosenkrantz@txwes.edu
ROSENOW, Robert .... 714-872-5692.. 53 D rrosenow@ketchum.edu
ROSENRAUCH, Yair ...... 718-259-5300 316 K yrosen@bramsonort.edu
ROSENSAFT, Jean, B .... 212-824-2209 327 C jrosensaft@huc.edu
ROSENSTEIN, Arthur ..... 858-566-1200.. 43 A arthur@disd.edu
ROSENSTEIN, Gloria ..... 858-566-1200.. 43 A gloria@disd.edu
ROSENSTEIN, Ilena .... 860-768-4418.. 92 F rosenstei@hartford.edu
ROSENSTEIN, Ilene .... 213-740-7711.. 74 D irosenst@usc.edu
ROSENSTOCK, Jeffrey ... 718-997-4995 320 E jeffrey.rosenstock@qc.cuny.edu
ROSENSTOCK, Larry ..... 619-398-4902.. 47 B lrosenstock@hightechhigh.org
ROSENSTONE, Steven, J .... 651-201-1696 257 N steven.rosenstone@so.mnscu.edu
ROSENTHAL, Amy .... 817-202-6211 483 C arosenthal@swau.edu
ROSENTHAL, Elizabeth .. 773-907-6833 141 O erosenthal@ccc.edu
ROSENTHAL, Eric .... 847-925-6677 145 F erosenth@harpercollege.edu
ROSENTHAL, Jean-Laurent .... 626-395-4068.. 31 D rosentha@caltech.edu
ROSENTHAL, Jeffrey, E . 315-255-1743 317 I rosenthal@cayuga-cc.edu
ROSENTHAL, Julie .... 303-373-2008.. 85 I jroesenthal@rvu.edu
ROSENTHAL, Ken .... 818-677-2561.. 34 D ken.rosenthal@csun.edu
ROSENTHAL, Rachel ..... 916-608-6570.. 53 A rosentr@flc.losrios.edu
ROSENTHAL, Susan ...... 305-899-3050.. 99 B srosenthal@barry.edu
ROSENWALD, Nancy ..... 803-321-5229 447 L nancy.rosenwald@newberry.edu
ROSETH, Lisa .... 218-723-6016 255 A lroseth@css.edu
ROSETT, Terri .... 909-667-4445.. 39 C trosett@claremontlincoln.org
ROSEVEAR, Scott, G ..... 570-577-3647 413 E scott.rosevear@bucknell.edu
ROSEVEARE, Mark .... 864-592-4763 449 C rosevearem@sccsc.edu
ROSEWALL, Michael ..... 920-403-3272 538 K michael.rosewall@snc.edu
ROSIENE, Tracy .... 860-215-9287.. 90 B trosiene@trcc.commnet.edu
ROSINE, Gregory, J ...... 269-387-2071 252 I greg.rosine@wmich.edu
ROSINSKI-KAUS, Donna .... 732-255-0400 304 E drosinski-kaus@ocean.edu
ROSKY, Bruce .... 818-610-6543.. 51 H roskybr@piercecollege.edu
ROSMUS, Julie .... 802-773-5900 501 G julie.rosmus@csj.edu
ROSOFF, Nancy .... 215-572-2921 412 F rosoffn@arcadia.edu
ROSOVSKY, Leah .... 617-495-4193 227 D leah_rosovsky@harvard.edu
ROSOWSKY, David, V .. 802-656-1417 503 C david.rosowsky@uvm.edu
ROSPLOCK, Valerie, R .. 607-735-1174 324 J vrosplock@elmira.edu

ROSS, Amy .... 423-585-6972 464 C amy.ross@ws.edu
ROSS, Angela .... 304-710-3382 531 C rossa@mctc.edu
ROSS, Anissa .... 870-460-1036.. 24 C ross@uamont.edu
ROSS, Anthony, J .... 651-641-8815 255 C ross@csp.edu
ROSS, Beverly .... 334-420-4332.... 7 I bross@trenholmstate.edu
ROSS, Carla .... 510-869-6618.. 61 J cross@samuelmerritt.edu
ROSS, Charles .... 678-915-7206 127M cross39@kennesaw.edu
ROSS, Cheryl .... 858-822-2797.. 72 B caross@ucsd.edu
ROSS, Christine, C .... 434-223-6056 508 B cross@hsc.edu
ROSS, Corey .... 605-331-6811 454 E corey.ross@usiouxfalls.edu
ROSS, David .... 801-883-8336 498M dross@new.edu
ROSS, David .... 501-279-4930.. 21 A dross@harding.edu
ROSS, David, A .... 972-708-7340 474 J david_ross@gial.edu
ROSS, Dawn .... 508-626-4625 230 A dross@framingham.edu
ROSS, Donald, E .... 302-793-1101.. 94 C
ROSS, Donald, E .... 561-237-7782 108 E dross@lynn.edu
ROSS, Duffy .... 301-447-5366 217 D ross@msmary.edu
ROSS, Elizabeth .... 617-735-9701 226 B ross@emmanuel.edu
ROSS, Eric .... 660-263-4110 279 F ericr@macc.edu
ROSS, III, Frank .... 518-276-6201 339 D
ROSS, Gary, L .... 315-228-7401 321 H gross@colgate.edu
ROSS, George, E .... 989-774-3131 240 O president@cmich.edu
ROSS, Gerald .... 410-225-2399 216 F gross@mica.edu
ROSS, Gloria .... 662-254-3558 269 C gloria.ross@mvsu.edu
ROSS, James .... 434-961-5203 516 F jross@pvcc.edu
ROSS, James, A .... 734-384-4259 247 C jross@monroeccc.edu
ROSS, Jason .... 864-977-7026 448 A jason.ross@ngu.edu
ROSS, Jeffery .... 816-235-6212 284 A umkccontracts@umkc.edu
ROSS, Jennifer, A .... 260-422-5561 167 F jaross@indianatech.edu
ROSS, Jeremy, B .... 423-439-5353 461 D rossjb@etsu.edu
ROSS, JoAnn, L .... 304-766-4361 533 C jross15@wvstateu.edu
ROSS, Julia .... 410-455-3400 219 F jross@umbc.edu
ROSS, Julie, S .... 617-627-3360 237 C j.ross@tufts.edu
ROSS, Karen .... 734-432-5529 246 B kross@madonna.edu
ROSS, Kathleen .... 650-574-6532.. 64 D rossk@smccd.edu
ROSS, Keith .... 314-392-2301 278 G rossk@mobap.edu
ROSS, Ken .... 863-297-1096 110 E kross@polk.edu
ROSS, Kevin, M .... 561-237-7823 108 E kross@lynn.edu
ROSS, Laura .... 407-708-2058 113 A rossl@seminolestate.edu
ROSS, Lauren .... 937-512-2164 391 D lauren.ross@sinclair.edu
ROSS, Leigh, A .... 601-984-2620 270 H laross@umc.edu
ROSS, Linda .... 662-846-4666 267 A lross@deltastate.edu
ROSS, Mary .... 479-619-4259.. 22 B mross1@nwacc.edu
ROSS, Meg .... 662-562-3204 269 E mross@northwestms.edu
ROSS, Mindy .... 845-341-4541 337 G mindy.ross@sunyorange.edu
ROSS, Pam .... 706-385-1487 130 C pam.ross@point.edu
ROSS, Pam .... 864-231-2032 443 E pross@andersonuniversity.edu
ROSS, Patricia, A .... 801-585-7832 499 K p.ross@utah.edu
ROSS, Patricia, A .... 937-778-7887 381 K pross@edisonohio.edu
ROSS, Paul .... 307-382-1696 546 L pross@wwcc.wy.edu
ROSS, Peter, G .... 989-774-4456 240 O ross1pg@cmich.edu

ROSS, III, Phillip .... 410-704-4053 221 A pross@towson.edu
ROSS, Ramsey .... 850-729-5229 109 D ramseyr@nwfsc.edu
ROSS, Rebecca .... 610-436-2501 432 B rross2@wcupa.edu
ROSS, Reginald .... 973-720-2903 309 I rossr@wpunj.edu
ROSS, Richard, S .... 860-297-2258.. 92 A richard.ross@trincoll.edu
ROSS, Rick .... 360-417-6533 525 A rross@pencol.edu
ROSS, Robert .... 787-738-2161 557 G robert.ross@upr.edu
ROSS, Robin .... 828-327-7000 361 B rross@cvcc.edu
ROSS, Ronald .... 973-877-3078 302 F ross@essex.edu
ROSS, Ryan .... 303-556-3926.. 81 J ryan.ross@ccd.edu
ROSS, Sadie .... 518-587-2100 348 A sadie.ross@esc.edu
ROSS, Sandy .... 406-243-2572 287 D sandy.ross@umontana.edu
ROSS, Sarah .... 425-739-8287 523 I sarah.ross@lwtech.edu
ROSS, Scott .... 770-504-7595 132 B sross@sctech.edu
ROSS, Sonia .... 210-690-9000 474 L sross@hallmarkuniversity.edu
ROSS, Stephen, C .... 724-847-6541 419 B scross@geneva.edu
ROSS, Stuart, P .... 610-917-1493 438 G spross@valleyforge.edu
ROSS, Thelma .... 410-951-3000 220 C
ROSS, Thomas, W .... 919-962-4622 369 C tomross@northcarolina.edu
ROSS, Todd .... 626-815-6000.. 29 B tross@apu.edu
ROSS, Toni .... 901-321-3297 455 I tross@cbu.edu
ROSS, Tricia .... 212-799-5000 329 I
ROSS, Vikki, F .... 210-562-6200 495 B rossv@uthscsa.edu
ROSS-GARCIA, Tracy .... 210-486-2851 467 B tross20@alamo.edu
ROSS-JONES, Marvel, E .... 716-884-9120 317 C merossjones@bryantstratton.edu
ROSS-LEE, Barbara .... 516-686-3996 335 F brosslee@nyit.edu
ROSSBACH, Janet .... 646-660-6097 318 C janet.rossbach@baruch.cuny.edu
ROSSBACHER, Lisa .... 707-826-3311.. 35 D Lisa.Rossbacher@humboldt.edu
ROSSER, Keith, R .... 315-386-7082 347 F rosserk@canton.edu
ROSSER, Sue, V .... 415-338-1141.. 36 A srosser@sfsu.edu
ROSSER, Ulrike .... 614-825-6255 376 C urosser@aiam.edu
ROSSETTI, Elspeth .... 408-554-4861.. 65 A erossetti@scu.edu
ROSSETTI, Erin, S .... 802-626-6417 504 B erin.rossetti@lyndonstate.edu
ROSSI, Jaclyn, R .... 716-286-8761 336 E jrossi@niagara.edu
ROSSI, Jamal .... 585-274-1010 351 D jrossi@esm.rochester.edu
ROSSI, Jason .... 773-697-2215 144 B jrossi@devry.edu
ROSSI, John .... 315-312-5555 346 A john.rossi@oswego.edu
ROSSI, John, J .... 626-256-4673.. 39 B jrossi@coh.org
ROSSI, Laura .... 410-669-9200 216 F
ROSSI, Richard, E .... 402-280-2717 290 B rrossi@creighton.edu
ROSSI-LE, Laura .... 978-232-2055 226 C lrossile@endicott.edu
ROSSITER, Andrew .... 808-923-9741 135 J andrewro@hawaii.edu
ROSSKY, Peter .... 713-348-3350 480M peter.rossky@rice.edu
ROSSMAN, Rodger .... 252-335-0821 361 G rodger_rossman@albemarle.edu
ROSSMAN, Vicki .... 713-780-9777 467 G
ROSSMEIER, Joseph, G 301-322-0987 217 G rossmejg@pgcc.edu
ROSSON, Michael .... 718-368-5144 320 A mrosson@kbcc.cuny.edu
ROST, Gregory, S .... 215-898-7221 437 I gregrost@upenn.edu
ROSTAR, Jimmy .... 252-328-1275 369 E rostarj@ecu.edu
ROSYNSKY, Michelle .... 810-762-3431 251 E rosynsky@umflint.edu
ROSZELL, Nancy, J .... 937-255-3636 547 E nancy.roszell@afit.edu

ROSZKOWSKI, Michael, J .... 215-951-1428 422 F roszkows@lasalle.edu
ROT, Jeffrey .... 904-826-0084.. 74 A jrot@usa.edu
ROTENBERG, Mark, B .. 410-516-0480 216 A mrotenberg@jhu.edu
ROTER, Petra .... 920-424-4000 540 B roterp@uwosh.edu
ROTGER, Mariolga .... 787-850-9364 558 A mariolga.rotger@upr.edu
ROTH, Andrew, W .... 330-972-7340 392 H aroth1@uakron.edu
ROTH, Annette .... 763-488-2426 258 G annette.roth@hennepintech.edu
ROTH, Ben .... 217-786-2773 151 C ben.roth@llcc.edu
ROTH, Brenda .... 810-762-3488 251 E blroth@umflint.edu
ROTH, Brenda .... 503-375-7010 405 F broth@corban.edu
ROTH, Cindi .... 304-284-4040 533 D croth@mail.wvu.edu
ROTH, Don, F .... 530-754-5418.. 71 A droth@ucdavis.edu
ROTH, Frank, A .... 610-758-3572 424 B far4@lehigh.edu
ROTH, Gregg .... 518-736-3622 326 D gregg.roth@fmcc.suny.edu
ROTH, Henry .... 650-508-3721.. 56 H hroth@ndnu.edu
ROTH, Jason .... 702-968-1633 296 D jroth@roseman.edu
ROTH, Jodi .... 610-436-3379 432 B jroth@wcupa.edu
ROTH, John, C .... 718-940-5616 341 A jroth@sjcny.edu
ROTH, Karen .... 541-383-7412 404 K kroth1@cocc.edu
ROTH, Katie .... 847-735-6005 149 H roth@lakeforest.edu
ROTH, Laurie .... 610-861-1510 426 H rothl@moravian.edu
ROTH, Linda .... 301-696-3919 215 E roth@hood.edu
ROTH, Marjorie .... 585-389-2686 334 B mroth1@naz.edu
ROTH, Martha, T .... 773-702-6229 161 D mroth@uchicago.edu
ROTH, Martin .... 860-768-4243.. 92 F mroth@hartford.edu
ROTH, Megan .... 325-674-2885 466 I mkr15a@acu.edu
ROTH, Michael .... 707-527-6939.. 65 C mroth@santarosa.edu
ROTH, Michael, L .... 509-313-4204 522 L roth@athletics.gonzaga.edu
ROTH, Michael, S .... 860-685-3500.. 93 B mroth@wesleyan.edu
ROTH, OSB, Neal, G .... 360-491-4440 525 H theabbot@stmartin.edu
ROTH, Neil .... 304-473-8312 534 G roth@wvwc.edu
ROTH, Patty .... 231-995-1363 248 C proth@nmc.edu
ROTH, Paul, B .... 505-272-5849 313 H proth@salud.unm.edu
ROTH, Rebecca .... 706-880-8088 127 N rroth@lagrange.edu
ROTH, Sterling .... 404-413-1310 126 D roths@gsu.edu
ROTH, Tara, E .... 406-756-3912 286 G troth@fvcc.edu
ROTH, Ted .... 217-479-7027 151 J ted.roth@mac.edu
ROTH, Teresa .... 937-778-7983 381 K troth@edisonohio.edu
ROTH, JR., Toby .... 989-774-3871 240 O rothj1t@cmich.edu
ROTH, Tonya .... 715-394-8264 541 C troth1@uwsuper.edu
ROTHAMER, Russ .... 928-226-4224.. 13 D russ.rothamer@coconino.edu
ROTHAUS, Richard, M . 701-328-4136 373 F richard.rothaus@ndus.edu
ROTHBERG, Heidi .... 413-528-7201 222 F registrar@simons-rock.edu
ROTHBERG, Jacob .... 914-736-1500 337 D
ROTHBERG, Jayme, S .. 727-816-3284 110 B rothbej@phsc.edu
ROTHENBUHLER, Eric ... 314-246-7154 285 G erothenbuhler@webster.edu
ROTHENHOEFER, Lynn, S .... 610-527-0200 434 D lrothenhoefer@rosemont.edu
ROTHERY, Diane .... 318-869-5013 202 D drothery@centenary.edu
ROTHGEB, Helen .... 714-241-6150.. 40 B hrothgeb@coastline.edu
ROTHGERBER, Hank, J . 502-272-8045 193 E hrothgerber@bellarmine.edu

ROZEK, Charles, E .... 216-368-4390 378 J
cer2@case.edu
ROZEK, Richard, J .... 248-364-3562 248 K
rozek@oakland.edu
ROZELL, Laura .... 518-327-6291 338 B
lrozell@paulsmiths.edu
ROZELL, Liz .... 661-395-4231.. 49 E
mrozell@bakersfieldcollege.edu
ROZELL, Mark .... 703-993-4108 507 K
mrozell@gmu.edu
ROZEMA, Burton, J ...... 708-239-4760 160 L
burt.rozema@trnty.edu
ROZEMBAJGIER, John .. 614-885-5585 390 G
ROZEWSKI, Mark .... 203-392-5456.. 88 F
rozewskim@southernct.edu
ROZHON, Tamara .... 602-557-2433.. 18 H
tamara.rozhon@phoenix.edu
ROZIN, Miriam .... 503-399-8486 404 L
miriam.rozin@chemeketa.edu
ROZOWSKI, Casey .... 612-343-4430 263 H
cmrozows@northcentral.edu
RUANE, Beth .... 802-451-7577 502 B
bruane@marlboro.edu
RUANO, Norman .... 773-878-3894 158 C
nruano@iwe.staugustine.edu
RUBACK, Sally, A .... 920-929-2126 543 F
sruback@morainepark.edu
RUBAIN, Jennifer .... 718-982-2335 319 A
studentaffairs@csi.cuny.edu
RUBBELKE, Thomas, J . 651-641-8700 255 C
rubbelke@csp.edu
RUBEL, Barbara, G .... 617-627-3780 237 C
barbara.rubel@tufts.edu
RUBEL, Carol .... 617-587-5650 234 G
rubelc@neco.edu
RUBEL, Tom .... 641-683-5252 179 C
tom.rubel@indianhills.edu
RUBEMEYER, Susan ..... 636-922-8360 281 C
srubemeyer@stchas.edu
RUBENS, Dave .... 330-684-8906 393 A
drubens@uakron.edu
RUBENSTEIN, David ..... 856-256-4222 306 D
rubenstein@rowan.edu
RUBENSTEIN, David ..... 202-687-1972.. 95 E
dr94@georgetown.edu
RUBENZAHL, Ira, H ...... 413-755-4906 233 B
irubenzahl@stcc.edu
RUBERO, Maria, D .... 787-250-1912 554 A
mdrubero@metro.inter.edu
RUBIE, Jessica .... 979-845-2217 485 C
jrubie@tamu.edu
RUBIN, Beno .... 757-822-5077 517 C
brubin@tcc.edu
RUBIN, Beth .... 513-529-6069 386 K
rubinb@miamioh.edu
RUBIN, Carrie .... 773-697-2268 144 B
crubin@devry.edu
RUBIN, Gary, N .... 410-704-2358 221 A
grubin@towson.edu
RUBIN, Henry .... 646-565-6000 350 C
RUBIN, James .... 602-787-6546.. 15 B
james.rubin@paradisevalley.edu
RUBIN, Joshua .... 718-436-2122 349 G
RUBIN, Leona .... 573-884-1402 283 H
rubinl@missouri.edu
RUBIN, Lisa .... 770-426-2725 128 C
lrubin@life.edu
RUBIN, Rachel .... 860-486-2337.. 92 C
rachel.rubin@uconn.edu
RUBIN, Steve .... 719-219-9636.. 79 K
steverubindvm@att.net
RUBINO, David .... 814-824-2241 425 L
drubino@mercyhurst.edu
RUBINO, Joseph .... 410-293-1549 549 B
rubino@usna.edu
RUBINO, Karen, M .... 401-456-8849 442 A
krubino@ric.edu
RUBINO, Michael, H .... 508-767-7156 222 D
rubino@assumption.edu
RUBINSTEIN, Mark .... 603-513-1307 299 C
gsc.president@granite.edu
RUBIO, Dave .... 909-384-8640.. 62 C
drubio@sbccd.cc.ca.us
RUBIO, Olga, D .... 956-721-5296 477 C
drubio@laredo.edu
RUBIO, Paty .... 518-580-5705 342 I
prubio@skidmore.edu
RUBIO, Reuben, A .... 517-750-1200 250 F
rarubio@arbor.edu
RUBLE, Celeste .... 507-433-0666 261 C
celeste.ruble@riverland.edu
RUBLE, Joel .... 559-925-3127.. 76 C
joelruble@whccd.edu
RUBLE, Justin .... 304-260-4380 530 M
jruble@blueridgectc.edu
RUBLE, Michelle .... 301-934-4711 214 E
micheller@csmd.edu
RUBLE, Robert, W .... 607-735-1802 324 J
rruble@elmira.edu
RUBRITZ, Gerald .... 814-886-6460 427 B
grubritz@mtaloy.edu
RUCCIUS, Frederick ...... 215-955-8733 436 F
frederick.ruccius@jefferson.edu
RUCH, Terry .... 970-521-6652.. 84 H
terry.ruch@njc.edu
RUCHALA, Patsy, L ...... 775-784-6841 295 H
pruchala@unr.edu
RUCKER, Aithyni .... 704-971-8500 355 J
arucker@charlottelaw.edu
RUCKER, Cedric, B .... 540-654-1655 513 I
crucker@umw.edu
RUCKER, Marty, K .... 423-585-6983 464 C
marty.rucker@ws.edu
RUCKER, Nolan .... 800-950-8001.. 79 F
RUCKER, Paul .... 206-685-9223 527 G
uwalumni@uw.edu
RUCKER, Robert, E .... 662-685-4771 266 G
erucker@bmc.edu
RUCKER, Sherri, B .... 615-329-8555 456 G
srucker@fisk.edu
RUCKER, Sonia .... 573-651-2524 282 C
srucker@semo.edu
RUCKER-FRANKLIN,
Yvonne .... 870-633-4480.. 20 J
yrucker@eacc.edu
RUCKER-SHAMU,
Marian .... 301-860-3849 220 B
mshamu@bowiestate.edu
RUDA, Ryan .... 620-276-9597 187 D
ryan.ruda@gcccks.edu
RUDA, Ryan .... 620-276-9595 187 D
ryan.ruda@gcccks.edu
RUDASILL, Susann .... 850-644-1571 115 A
srudasill@fsu.edu
RUDATSIKIRA,
Emmanuel .... 269-471-6648 239 D
rudatsikira@andrews.edu
RUDAWITZ, Linda .... 503-517-1397 411 A
lrudawitz@warnerpacific.edu
RUDAWSKY, Donald, J . 954-262-5392 109 E
rudawsky@nova.edu
RUDD, M. David .... 901-678-2234 462 B
mdrudd@memphis.edu
RUDD, Martin .... 920-832-2610 541 E
martin.rudd@uwc.edu
RUDDELL, Larry .... 281-579-9977 266 F
lruddell@belhaven.edu
RUDDEN, David .... 847-214-7925 144 F
drudden@elgin.edu
RUDE, John .... 323-267-3724.. 51 D
rudejc@elac.edu
RUDEAU, William .... 609-771-2187 301 E
rudeau@tcnj.edu
RUDECOFF,
Christine, A .... 315-684-6055 347 A
rudecoc@morrisville.edu
RUDEN, Lynne .... 989-275-5000 245 C
lynne.ruden@kirtland.edu
RUDER, Ann .... 620-450-2179 190 H
annr@prattcc.edu
RUDGERS, Lisa, M .... 734-763-3526 251 C
rudgers@umich.edu
RUDIGER, Brenda .... 906-487-2400 247 A
brudiger@mtu.edu
RUDIGER, Jennifer .... 715-232-1151 541 B
rudigerj@uwstout.edu
RUDIN, Mark .... 208-426-5732 137 E
markrudin@boisestate.edu
RUDISILL, Frank .... 864-503-5511 451 A
frudisill@uscupstate.edu
RUDLEY, John, M .... 713-313-7044 487 F
rudleyjm@tsu.edu
RUDNEY, Gwen .... 320-589-6411 265 A
rudneygl@morris.umn.edu
RUDNICK, Joseph .... 310-825-1042.. 71 D
jrudnick@college.ucla.edu
RUDNICK, Virginia .... 607-962-9587 323 D
vrudnick@corning-cc.edu
RUDNICKI, Rosemary ... 512-448-8540 481 B
rosemars@stedwards.edu
RUDNITSKI, Rose .... 201-559-3551 302 I
rudnitskir@felician.edu
RUDOLPH, Alan, S .... 970-491-7194.. 81 D
alan.rudolph@colostate.edu
RUDOLPH, Margaret ..... 419-448-2111 383 C
mrudolph@heidelberg.edu
RUDOLPH, Mary Kay .... 707-524-1516.. 65 C
mrudolph@santarosa.edu
RUDOLPH, Meloni .... 303-556-8164.. 81 J
meloni.rudolph@ccd.edu
RUDOLPH, Noah .... 202-462-2101.. 96 C
rudolph@iwp.edu
RUDOWSKY, Catherine . 361-825-2643 485 F
catherine.rudowsky@tamucc.edu
RUDY, Joel .... 276-739-2512 517 D
jrudy@vhcc.edu
RUE, Penny .... 336-758-5943 372 G
rue@wfu.edu
RUEB, Jan, L .... 432-837-8178 489 B
jrueb@sulross.edu
RUEB, Shirley .... 316-942-4291 189 K
ruebs@newmanu.edu
RUEBEL, James, S .... 765-285-1024 164 D
jruebel@bsu.edu
RUEFF, Alicia .... 561-732-4424 112 C
arueff@svdp.edu
RUEFLE, Colleen .... 412-536-1069 422 E
colleen.ruefle@laroche.edu
RUEGG, Samuel (Tex) .. 817-515-4591 484 B
samuel.ruegg@tccd.edu
RUELAS, Abraham .... 510-485-7869.. 58 G
aruelas@patten.edu
RUELAS, Patricia .... 510-485-7865.. 58 G
pruelas@patten.edu
RUELLE, Joan .... 336-278-6572 356 F
jruelle@elon.edu
RUELLE, Maggie .... 903-510-2490 491 A
mrue@tjc.edu
RUESCH, Sherry .... 435-652-7551 499 M
ruesch@dixie.edu
RUESCHMANN, Eva ...... 413-559-5378 227 C
erueschmann@hampshire.edu
RUESS, Trish .... 740-587-5620 381 H
ruess@denison.edu
RUETTEN, Amy .... 417-667-8181 273 H
aruetten@cottey.edu
RUFF, Corey .... 325-674-2665 466 I
clr06a@acu.edu
RUFF, Joy, C .... 305-237-2090 108 L
jruff@mdc.edu
RUFF, Margaret .... 903-785-7661 480 B
mruff@parisjc.edu
RUFF, Rosemary, H ...... 479-575-3845.. 23 G
rruff@uark.edu
RUFFIN, Cynthia .... 919-572-1625 354 F
cruffin@apexsot.edu
RUFFIN, Finee .... 601-477-4082 268 A
finee.ruffin@jcjc.edu
RUFFIN, Gene .... 678-407-5000 125 B
gruffin@ggc.edu
RUFFIN, Kimberly, N .... 312-341-2281 157 E
kruffin@roosevelt.edu
RUFFIN, Shanda .... 803-780-1360 451 G
sruffin@voorhees.edu
RUFFING, Rebecca .... 315-866-0300 327 E
ruffingrj@herkimer.edu
RUFFINO, John, J .... 703-323-3023 516 C
jruffino@nvcc.edu
RUFFOLO, Anna .... 773-834-2571 160 J
RUFFRAGE, Jo .... 315-792-7172 348 D
ruffraj@sunyit.edu
RUFINO, Paul .... 856-415-2173 306 C
prufino@rcgc.edu
RUFO, Joseph .... 315-470-6622 347 B
jlrufo@esf.edu
RUGEMER, Ellen .... 410-857-2203 217 A
erugemer@mcdaniel.edu
RUGER, Theodore, W ... 215-898-7483 437 I
truger@law.upenn.edu
RUGG, Marilyn .... 315-228-7288 321 H
mrugg@colgate.edu
RUGG, William .... 406-265-3726 288 A
william.rugg@msun.edu
RUGGAR MARTIN, Jan . 323-469-3300.. 26 P
RUGGIERI, David .... 407-447-7300 105 E
druggieri@ftccollege.edu
RUGGIERO, Bruno .... 985-448-4262 208 C
bruno.ruggiero@nicholls.edu
RUGGIRELLO, Frank ...... 734-462-4400 250 A
fruggire@schoolcraft.edu
RUGGLES, Jennifer .... 216-368-1723 378 J
jor15@case.edu
RUGGLES, Shami .... 509-533-7085 521 E
Shami.Ruggles@ccs.spokane.edu
RUGGLES, Shami, R ..... 509-533-3567 521 D
shami.ruggles@ccs.spokane.edu
RUHL, Austin .... 406-586-3585 287 B
austin.ruhl@montanabiblecollege.edu
RUHL, Chris .... 317-921-4474 169 L
cruhl@ivytech.edu
RUHL, Taylor .... 619-644-7390.. 46 H
taylor.ruhl@gcccd.edu
RUHL-SMITH, Connie ... 605-626-7789 454 A
Connie.Ruhlsmith@northern.edu
RUHLAND, Gail .... 320-308-3081 261 E
GMRuhland@stcloudstate.edu
RUHLAND, Sheila .... 253-566-5100 527 C
sruhland@tacomacc.edu
RUHLANDT, Karin .... 315-443-3949 349 E
kruhland@syr.edu
RUIBAL, Pilar .... 787-751-0160 551 K
pruibal@cmpr.pr.gov
RUITER, Kathy .... 217-854-3231 140 F
RUIZ, Alberto .... 361-593-2837 486 A
alberto.ruiz@tamuk.edu
RUIZ, Alfredo .... 269-471-6979 239 D
jaruiz@andrews.edu
RUIZ, Andrew .... 806-894-9611 482 F
aruiz@southplainscollege.edu
RUIZ, Angel, J .... 787-863-2390 553 I
angel.ruiz@fajardo.inter.edu
RUIZ, Deborah .... 831-646-3097.. 54 H
druiz@mpc.edu
RUIZ, Ediltrudy .... 718-270-6131 320 C
eruiz@mec.cuny.edu
RUIZ, Ediltrudys .... 718-960-8421 319 C
ediltrudys.ruiz@lehman.cuny.edu
RUIZ, Encarnacion .... 209-228-4240.. 71 E
ERuiz@UCMerced.edu
RUIZ, Erick .... 503-251-2805 410 I
eruiz@uws.edu
RUIZ, Israel .... 617-253-4495 233 C
RUIZ, Joaquin .... 520-621-4090.. 18 E
jruiz@email.arizona.edu
RUIZ, OP, John Martin 202-495-3821.. 96 E
jruiz@dhs.edu
RUIZ, Jose .... 787-863-2390 553 I
jose.ruiz@fajardo.inter.edu
RUIZ, Kathleen .... 310-377-5501.. 53 E
kruiz@marymountcalifornia.edu
RUIZ, Kris .... 936-294-3492 489 A
kjk001@shsu.edu
RUIZ, Lucy .... 559-244-2637.. 68 J
lucy.ruiz@scccd.edu
RUIZ, Lucy .... 559-638-3641.. 69 C
lucy.ruiz@reedleycollege.edu
RUIZ, Luis, A .... 787-766-1717 556 A
um_lruiz@suagm.edu
RUIZ, Luis, E .... 787-250-1912 554 A
leruiz@metro.inter.edu
RUIZ, Magda .... 787-891-0925 553 E
mruiz@aguadilla.inter.edu
RUIZ, Melanie .... 425-564-2710 519 L
melanie.ruiz@bellevuecollege.edu
RUIZ, Miguel .... 713-221-8564 491 F
ruizm@uhd.edu
RUIZ, Rafael .... 787-257-0000 557 F
rafael.ruiz@upr.edu
RUIZ, Roseanna .... 909-537-7651.. 35 A
rruiz@csusb.edu
RUIZ, Sacha, M .... 787-891-0925 553 E
sruiz@aguadilla.inter.edu
RUIZ, Sina .... 903-875-7429 479 I
sina.ruiz@navarrocollege.edu
RUIZ, Zaida .... 787-786-3030 556 E
zrueiz@ucb.edu.pr
RUIZ-HUSTON, Ines ..... 209-946-2132.. 73 C
iruiz@pacific.edu
RUIZ-MATTEI, Enid .... 719-389-6699.. 79 M
enid.ruizmattei@coloradocollege.edu
RUKSNAITIS, Diane ...... 978-632-6600 232 C
d_ruksnaitis@mwcc.mass.edu
RULAND, Heather .... 508-373-9430 223 C
heather.ruland@becker.edu
RULAND, Judith, P .... 989-964-4145 249 G
jruland@svsu.edu
RULAND, Michael .... 409-880-8108 488 F
michael.ruland@lamar.edu
RULE, Anne .... 314-977-2495 281 M
ruleam@slu.edu
RULE, David .... 425-564-2301 519 L
dave.rule@bellevuecollege.edu
RULE, Scott .... 770-975-4000 122 H
RULLÁN, Agustín .... 787-265-3822 558 B
decano.ingenieria@upr.edu
RULLMAN, Loren, J ...... 734-763-1291 251 C
lrullman@umich.edu
RULLO, Michelle .... 718-779-1430 338 D
mrullo@plazacollege.edu
RUMER, Richard .... 215-204-5144 436 C
richard.rumer@temple.edu
RUMERY, Joyce, V .... 207-581-1655 212 C
rumery@maine.edu
RUMIANO, Sara .... 530-898-5134.. 33 A
srumiano@csuchico.edu
RUMLER, Robin .... 517-265-5161 238 H
rrumler@adrian.edu
RUMLEY, Timothy .... 616-538-2330 243 C
trumley@gbcol.edu
RUMMAGE, Spencer ..... 704-216-3738 365 F
spencer.rummage@rccc.edu
RUMMEL, J, D .... 402-280-1131 290 B
rummel@creighton.edu
RUMMEL, Tina .... 903-675-6376 490 F
trummel@tvcc.edu
RUMP, Rebecca .... 319-208-5065 183 B
brump@scciowa.edu
RUMPZA, Matthew, D .. 651-696-6551 256 L
mrumpza@macalester.edu
RUMSEY, Elizabeth .... 218-726-7471 264 G
erumsey@d.umn.edu
RUNAS, Arnulfo .... 626-300-5444.. 59 G
RUNBERG, Bruce, L ..... 919-962-7248 371 A
bruce_runberg@unc.edu
RUND, James, A .... 480-965-2200.. 11 J
james.rund@asu.edu
RUNDELL, Isabel .... 317-896-9324 173 G
RUNDELL, Jay, A .... 740-362-3121 386 D
jrundell@mtso.edu
RUNDELL, III, Merton .. 317-896-9324 173 G
RUNDSTROM, Amy, L .. 308-865-8501 293 G
rundstromal@unk.edu

RUTHERMAN, Kathy ..... 270-852-3143 198 A
krutherman@kwc.edu
RUTHKOSKY,
Kathleen, O .... 570-348-6203 425 D
ruthkosky@marywood.edu
RUTKOWSI, Leslie .... 315-470-6655 347 B
larutkow@esf.edu
RUTKOWSKI, Sandra .... 419-824-3762 385 F
srutkowski@lourdes.edu
RUTLEDGE, Brian .... 601-984-1010 270 H
brutledge@umc.edu
RUTLEDGE, Catherine ... 484-365-8087 424 E
crutledge@lincoln.edu
RUTLEDGE, James .... 662-846-4021 267 A
jrutledge@deltastate.edu
RUTLEDGE, Janet .... 410-455-1781 219 F
jrutledge@umbc.edu
RUTLEDGE, Melissa, B . 540-378-5120 512 B
rutledge@roanoke.edu
RUTLEDGE, Peter .... 706-542-7140 132 H
borut@uga.edu
RUTLEDGE, Susan .... 314-392-2355 278 G
rutledges@mobap.edu
RUTLEDGE, Todd .... 417-269-3873 274 A
trutle@coxcollege.edu
RUTLEDGE, Valerie .... 423-425-4249 465 E
valerie-rutledge@utc.edu
RUTSKY, Lisa .... 770-729-8400 120 F
RUTT, Charles, D .... 660-543-4370 283 F
rutt@ucmo.edu
RUTT, Richard .... 503-352-7377 408 I
ruttra@pacificu.edu
RUTTEN, Erich .... 651-962-6561 265 F
erutten@stthomas.edu
RUTTER, Evan .... 909-621-8153.. 39 F
evan.rutter@cmc.edu
RUTTER, Jeff .... 602-386-4191.. 11 F
jeff.rutter@arizonachristian.edu
RUTTER, Jeff .... 931-221-7213 461 C
rutterj@apsu.edu
RUTTER, John, P .... 919-299-4818 369 B
jrutter@umo.edu
RUTTER, Sandy .... 423-697-4475 462 C
sandy.rutter@chattanoogastate.edu
RUUD, William, N .... 319-273-2566 176 A
bill.ruud@uni.edu
RUVOLO, Louis .... 201-761-6475 307 K
lruvolo@saintpeters.edu
RUXTON, Brooke .... 815-753-1206 154 I
bruxton@niu.edu
RUYLE, Dianna .... 217-854-3231 140 F
dianna.ruyle@blackburn.edu
RUYS, Jasmine .... 661-362-3466.. 40 H
jasmine.ruys@canyons.edu
RUYS, Steve .... 818-364-7886.. 51 G
ruyssc@lamission.edu
RUZICH, Steve .... 708-596-2000 159 D
sruzich@ssc.edu
RUZICKA, James .... 402-461-7337 290 G
jruzicka@hastings.edu
RUZZANO, Ethan .... 303-360-4734.. 81 I
Ethan.Ruzzano@CCAurora.edu
RYALL, Patrick .... 503-768-7294 406 H
ryall@lclark.edu
RYALS, Kim .... 918-463-2931 397 I
kim.ryals@connorsstate.edu
RYALS, Reginald .... 540-423-9055 515 E
rryals@germanna.edu
RYAN, Andrew .... 718-862-8000 331 H
andrew.ryan@manhattan.edu
RYAN, Barry, T .... 619-477-6310.. 70 G
president@usuniversity.edu
RYAN, Bruce .... 607-844-8222 350 A
ryanb@tc3.edu
RYAN, Bryan, K .... 919-866-5146 366 H
bkryan@waketech.edu
RYAN, Caroll .... 714-882-7800.. 32 C
cryan@calsouthern.edu
RYAN, Casey .... 215-596-8570 438 E
c.ryan@usciences.edu
RYAN, Catherine .... 413-572-5218 230 F
cryan@westfield.ma.edu
RYAN, Christopher .... 508-830-5003 230 D
cryan@maritime.edu
RYAN, Curtis, W .... 801-832-2148 501 C
cryan@westminstercollege.edu
RYAN, Dennis .... 757-340-2121 506 E
registrarcvab@centura.edu
RYAN, Duane .... 575-562-2112 310 I
duane.ryan@enmu.edu
RYAN, Ed .... 408-554-5182.. 65 A
eryan@scu.edu
RYAN, Elaine .... 202-314-3300.. 96 A
RYAN, Gail, L .... 313-577-6595 252 G
gail.ryan@wayne.edu
RYAN, Greg .... 714-992-7092.. 56 F
gryan@fullcoll.edu
RYAN, Helen, G .... 502-272-8052 193 E
hryan@bellarmine.edu
RYAN, James .... 617-262-5000 223 G
James.Ryan@the-bac.edu
RYAN, James, E .... 617-495-3401 227 D
james_ryan@gse.harvard.edu
RYAN, James, G .... 336-217-5128 370 B
jgryan@ncat.edu
RYAN, Jenny .... 801-832-2502 501 C
sjryan@westminstercollege.edu
RYAN, CSC, John .... 570-208-5899 422 D
jjryan@kings.edu
RYAN, John, F .... 802-656-4418 503 C
jfryan@uvm.edu
RYAN, Kapono .... 808-735-4797 135 A
kryan@chaminade.edu
RYAN, Karen .... 386-822-7515 117 A
kryan@stetson.edu
RYAN, Kathleen .... 508-541-1515 225 G
kryan@dean.edu
RYAN, Kathleen .... 617-732-5042 233 E
Kathleen.Ryan@mcphs.edu
RYAN, Kathleen .... 614-823-1250 390 C
kryan@otterbein.edu
RYAN, Kent .... 386-246-4801 101 I
ryank@DaytonaState.edu
RYAN, Kevin .... 305-428-5700 109 A
kryan@aii.edu
RYAN, Kyle .... 781-899-5500 235 G
kryan@psjs.edu
RYAN, Larry .... 505-277-2847 313 H
larry@unm.edu
RYAN, Linda, S .... 515-271-2147 177 K
linda.ryan@drake.edu
RYAN, Mark, R .... 573-882-0314 283 H
ryanmr@missouri.edu
RYAN, Mary, A .... 651-962-6133 265 F
maryan@stthomas.edu
RYAN, Megan .... 315-279-5296 329 K
mryan1@keuka.edu
RYAN, Melissa .... 904-725-0525 100 Q
mryan@concorde.edu
RYAN, Michael .... 617-585-1187 234 H
michael.ryan@necmusic.edu
RYAN, Molly .... 661-255-1050.. 31 B
mryan@calarts.edu
RYAN, Pat .... 503-842-8222 410 C
ryan@tillamookbay.cc
RYAN, Patricia .... 858-513-9240.. 29 A
patricia.ryan@ashford.edu
RYAN, Patricia .... 540-674-3613 516 B
pryan@nr.edu
RYAN, Paula .... 641-628-5198 176 E
ryanp@central.edu
RYAN, Peter .... 662-325-3742 269 A
ryan@cvm.msstate.edu
RYAN, Robert .... 800-782-2422.. 32 A
robert.ryan@csun.edu
RYAN, Robin .... 858-795-5244.. 64 F
rryan@shpdiscovery.org
RYAN, Ron .... 954-262-8856 109 E
ronr@nova.edu
RYAN, Rosaleen .... 831-646-4035.. 54 H
rryan@mpc.edu
RYAN, Scott .... 817-272-3181 493 L
sdryan@uta.edu
RYAN, Sean, J .... 502-272-8376 193 E
sryan@bellarmine.edu
RYAN, Sharon .... 213-624-1200.. 44 I
sryan@fidm.edu
RYAN, Susan .... 386-822-7181 117 A
sryan@stetson.edu
RYAN, Suzanne .... 812-856-5572 167 J
sryan@indiana.edu
RYAN, Tiffiney .... 618-634-3242 159 A
tiffineyr@shawneecc.edu
RYAN, Tim .... 845-452-9600 323 E
t_ryan@culinary.edu
RYAN, Timothy, M .... 207-725-3247 209 H
tryan@bowdoin.edu
RYAN, Valerie .... 858-642-8513.. 55 J
vryan@nu.edu
RYAN BULONE, Mary ... 419-473-2700 381 F
mryan@davisccollege.edu
RYAN-HOFFMAN,
Maureen .... 732-987-2218 302 J
ryan-hoffman@georgian.edu
RYAN-SCHMOLL,
Amanda .... 952-358-8150 260 D
amanda.ryan-schmoll@normandale.edu
RYAN VAN ZEE,
Marynel .... 507-222-4300 254 D
mryanvanzee@carleton.edu
RYANT, Marion .... 229-430-4609 119 H
marion.ryant@asurams.edu
RYBERG, Bill .... 253-566-5336 527 C
bryberg@tacomacc.edu
RYBICKI, Bob .... 510-204-0725.. 38 K
brybicki@cdsp.edu
RYCHLEC, Tim .... 713-313-1810 487 F
rychlect@tsu.edu
RYCHLY, Carol .... 706-737-1422 121 C
crychly@gru.edu
RYCYNA, Mary .... 216-397-4921 384 F
mrycyna@jcu.edu
RYCZKOWSKI, Sandy ... 920-498-6829 544 B
sandra.ryczkowski@nwtc.edu
RYDELL, Laurie .... 541-956-7125 409 F
lrydell@roguecc.edu
RYDER, Ellen .... 508-793-2419 225 C
eryder@holycross.edu
RYDER, Jon .... 207-221-4081 213 B
jryder2@une.edu
RYDER, Lucas .... 772-546-5534 106 D
lucasryder@hsbc.edu
RYDER, Ulli .... 508-678-2811 231 B
RYDL, Chareny, L .... 979-845-3158 485 C
chareny@tamu.edu
RYE, Colleen .... 906-635-2626 245 H
crye@lssu.edu
RYE, Tara .... 402-449-2849 290 F
trye@graceu.edu
RYEA, Alan, E .... 802-656-3245 503 C
alan.ryea@uvm.edu
RYERSON, James .... 703-284-5910 510 B
james.ryerson@marymount.edu
RYKEN, Philip, G .... 630-752-5002 163 G
philip.ryken@wheaton.edu
RYMAN, Denny .... 631-420-2171 348 B
denny.ryman@farmingdale.edu
RYNNE, Jeanne .... 360-867-6115 522 J
rynnej@evergreen.edu
RYON, Diane .... 704-372-0266 358 D
dryon@kingscollegecharlotte.edu
RYSTROM, Andrea .... 651-779-3953 258 D
andrea.rystrom@century.edu
RZONCA, Chet, S .... 319-335-2527 175 H
chet-rzonca@uiowa.edu
RZONCA, Stephen .... 910-892-3178 357 D
srzonca@heritagebiblecollege.edu

S

SÁNCHEZ, José .... 787-764-0000 558 E
jose.sanchez18@upr.edu
SÁNCHEZ, Melba, G ..... 787-743-7979 555 M
msanchez@suagm.edu
SÁNCHEZ PINTOR,
Linda .... 787-725-8120 552 G
lsanchez0053@eap.edu
SAACKE, David .... 540-458-8400 519 A
dsaacke@wlu.edu
SAADI, Christine .... 610-796-8213 412 C
christine.saadi@alvernia.edu
SAAED, Jan .... 801-832-2232 501 C
jsaaed@westminstercollege.edu
SAARI, Mirranda .... 360-992-2671 521 A
msaari@clark.edu
SAARIAHO, Ginger, K ... 617-552-9168 224 B
ginger.saariaho@bc.edu
SAAVEDRA, Adrianna .... 520-494-5287.. 12 R
adriana.saavedra@centralaz.edu
SAAVEDRA, Mauricio .... 805-756-5406.. 32 E
msaavedr@calpoly.edu
SAAVEDRA, Michael ..... 505-454-3053 311 H
mjsaavedra@nmhu.edu
SAAVEDRA, Randy .... 575-835-5005 311 I
rsaavedra@admin.nmt.edu
SAAVEDRA, Rebecca ..... 409-772-2909 495 E
rsaavedr@utmb.edu
SABAN, Thomas .... 708-709-3568 156 A
tsaban@prairiestate.edu
SABATH, Michael .... 928-523-9011.. 16 C
SABATH BEIT-HALACHMI,
Rachel .... 513-221-1875 327 C
rsabath@huc.edu
SABATINE, Stephanie ... 906-635-6664 245 H
ssabatine@lssu.edu
SABATINI, JR.,
John, A .... 612-338-7224 265 G
john.sabatini@laureate.net
SABATINO, Charles, A .. 330-941-3589 396 C
casabatino@ysu.edu
SABATINO, Patricia .... 718-678-8817 332 E
psabatino@mercy.edu
SABATKA, Hauli .... 402-461-7433 290 G
hsabatka@hastings.edu
SABATTIS, Robert .... 610-330-5330 423 A
sabattir@lafayette.edu
SABBAGHI, Asghar .... 773-298-3944 158 F
sabbaghi@sxu.edu
SABBAR, Carol .... 262-551-5900 535 E
csabbar@carthage.edu
SABEY, Brenda .... 435-652-7841 499 M
sabey@dixie.edu
SABIBO, Marvin .... 888-897-3222.. 50 D
SABIN, Christopher, P . 910-938-6321 361 F
sabinc@coastalcarolina.edu
SABIN, Laurie .... 567-661-7282 390 D
laurie_sabin@owens.edu
SABIN, Melody .... 864-578-8770 448 G
msabin@sherman.edu
SABINE, Neil .... 765-973-8389 168 A
nsabine@iue.edu
SABINO, Diana .... 727-341-3352 112 A
sabino.diana@spcollege.edu
SABINO, Lyn .... 330-363-4227 377 C
lyn.sabino@aultman.com
SABINSON, Allen .... 215-895-1621 417 E
allen.c.sabinson@drexel.edu
SABIT, Farhad .... 510-659-6146.. 56 J
fsabit@ohlone.edu
SABITSANA, Andrea ...... 312-915-8722 151 E
asabits@luc.edu
SABLAN, Becky .... 670-237-6700 550 B
becky.sablan@marianas.edu
SABLAN-ZEBEDY, Ellia .. 207-834-7805 212 F
ellia.sablanzebedy@maine.edu
SABLE, Marjorie .... 573-882-0914 283 H
SableM@missouri.edu
SABLE, Ray .... 229-333-5875 133 H
rasable@valdosta.edu
SABLO, Kahan .... 814-732-2313 430 G
ksablo@edinboro.edu
SABOE, Mike .... 843-820-5090 449 G
mike.saboe@tridenttech.edu
SABOL, Ann .... 215-635-7300 419 D
asabol@gratz.edu
SABOLD, Steven .... 412-346-2122 433 B
ssabold@pia.edu
SABOLO, Martin .... 605-626-3007 454 A
Martin.Sabolo@northern.edu
SABOTA, Fred .... 727-864-8895 101 P
sabotafr@eckerd.edu
SABOU, Michelle, L ..... 864-977-7004 448 A
michelle.sabou@ngu.edu
SABOUNI, Ikhlas .... 936-261-9800 484 F
isabouni@pvamu.edu
SACAL-TRENT, Jessica .. 210-486-4111 466 K
jsacal-trent@alamo.edu
SACCENTI, Tom .... 864-294-2111 446 F
tom.saccenti@furman.edu
SACCO, Albert .... 806-742-3451 489 F
al.sacco-jr@ttu.edu
SACCO, John .... 617-322-3553 227 J
john_sacco@laboure.edu
SACCOCCIO, Louis, J .... 401-874-4486 442 E
ljslaw@uri.edu
SACHER, Lesley .... 850-644-8869 115 A
lsacher@admin.fsu.edu
SACHS, Elizabeth .... 212-772-4569 319 E
esachs@hunter.cuny.edu
SACHS, Michael .... 570-422-3798 430 F
msachs@esu.edu
SACHS, Steven, G .... 703-323-3387 516 C
ssachs@nvcc.edu
SACK, Bob .... 616-222-1421 241 G
bob.sack@cornerstone.edu
SACK, Chuck .... 610-558-5627 427 D
sackc@neumann.edu
SACKETT, Mike .... 562-947-8755.. 67 J
mikesackett@scuhs.edu
SACKMAN, Dwayne ...... 309-438-5451 147 I
dsackma@ilstu.edu
SACKS, Arlene .... 305-653-6713 392 F
arlene.sacks@myunion.edu
SACKS, Michael .... 404-727-1850 124 D
michael.sacks@emory.edu
SADAN, Avishai .... 213-740-3124.. 74 D
dentdean@usc.edu
SADAO, Amy .... 215-573-9973 437 I
asadao@ica.upenn.org
SADD, Tracy .... 717-361-1260 418 B
saddt@etown.edu
SADDIGH, Farah .... 310-233-4501.. 51 F
saddigf@lahc.edu
SADDLEMIRE, John ...... 401-232-6046 441 B
jsaddlemire@bryant.edu
SADDLEMIRE,
Melissa, A .... 570-961-4733 425 D
saddlemire@marywood.edu
SADDLER, Mike .... 620-431-2820 189 J
msaddler@neosho.edu
SADDLER, Ryan, C .... 563-333-5728 182 E
SaddlerRyanC@sau.edu
SADDORIS-TRAUGHBER,
Janiece, L .... 217-424-6253 153 A
jtraughber@millikin.edu
SADEGHIPOUR, Keya .... 215-204-5285 436 C
keya.sadeghipour@temple.edu
SADLEK, Gregory, M .... 216-687-3660 380 D
g.sadlek@csuohio.edu
SADLEK, Lance, A .... 563-333-6252 182 E
SadlekLanceA@sau.edu
SADLER, Kelley .... 253-566-5187 527 C
ksadler@tacomacc.edu
SADLER, Martin .... 404-687-4512 123 C
sadlerm@ctsnet.edu
SADLER, Paul, L .... 806-291-1163 496 K
sadlerp@wbu.edu
SADLER, Tommy .... 731-661-5218 464 G
tsadler@uu.edu
SADOWSKI, Jatha .... 573-882-4859 283 H
sadowskij@missouri.edu
SADOWSKI, Jeffrey .... 312-225-1166 162 H
jsadowski@vandercook.edu

SALOWITZ, Stewart, I ... 309-556-3206 148 A
salowitz@iwu.edu
SALOWITZ, Susan .... 860-343-5724.. 89 E
ssalowitz@mxcc.commnet.edu
SALSBURY, Greg .... 970-943-2114.. 87 F
gsalsbury@western.edu
SALSBURY, Lysa .... 208-885-9358 139 C
lsalsbur@uidaho.edu
SALTALAMACHIA,
Joseph .... 207-509-7205 212 A
jsalty@unity.edu
SALTER, Anne .... 404-364-8514 129 F
asalter@oglethorpe.edu
SALTER, Kareena .... 386-255-0295 119 D
SALTER, Sid .... 662-325-7454 269 A
ss51@msstate.edu
SALTER-SMITH,
Cassandra, L .... 716-839-8237 323 F
csalters@daemen.edu
SALTIEL, Henry .... 718-482-6120 320 B
hsaltiel@lagcc.cuny.edu
SALTON, Susan .... 607-431-4465 327 B
saltons@hartwick.edu
SALTONSTALL,
Thomas, L .... 617-228-3311 231 C
tlsaltonstall@bhcc.mass.edu
SALTSMAN, Terry .... 931-372-3387 462 A
tsaltsman@tntech.edu
SALTSMAN, Terry .... 931-372-3200 462 A
tsaltsman@tntech.edu
SALTZBERG, Alex .... 510-593-2995.. 65 D
asaltzberg@saybrook.edu
SALTZMAN, Robert .... 508-999-8025 228 H
rsaltzman@umassd.edu
SALVA, Miguel .... 787-894-2828 558 F
miguel.salva@upr.edu
SALVA, William, M .... 914-337-9300 323 A
william.salva@concordia-ny.edu
SALVADOR, Daniel .... 319-656-2447 182 G
SALVADOR, Susan .... 610-861-4558 427 F
ssalvador@northampton.edu
SALVAGE, Lynn .... 718-818-6470 341 G
SALVAGGIO, Brian .... 508-531-1276 229 C
SALVANTORIELLO,
Vincent .... 610-398-5300 424 C
vsalvantoriello@lincolntech.edu
SALVATO, Scott .... 516-323-3225 333 E
ssalvato@molloy.edu
SALVESEN, Guy .... 858-646-3114.. 64 F
gsalvesen@shpdiscovery.org
SALVINI, Tonia .... 785-830-2753 187 F
tsalvini@haskell.edu
SALVO, Robyn .... 732-571-3470 303 G
rsalvo@monmouth.edu
SALVUCCI, James .... 443-334-2215 218 E
jsalvucci@stevenson.edu
SALZMAN, Christine ..... 908-709-7485 309 A
SALZMANN, Nick .... 847-628-2492 149 A
nsalzmann@judsonu.edu
SALZMANN, Rana .... 773-256-3000 152 D
rsalzmann@meadville.edu
SAM, David .... 847-214-7374 144 F
dsam@elgin.edu
SAM, David, A .... 540-423-9039 515 E
dsam@germanna.edu
SAM, Mary .... 218-855-8159 258 C
msam@clcmn.edu
SAMAHA, Ahmed .... 803-641-3411 450 C
ahmeds@usca.edu
SAMALOT-RIVERA, OP,
Yamil, A .... 787-786-4508 552 C
ysamalot@cedoc.edu
SAMAN, Sarmad .... 508-678-2811 231 B
sarmad.saman@bristolcc.edu
SAMANGO, Melissa .... 610-526-6196 420 C
msamango@harcum.edu
SAMANIEGO, Sue .... 719-384-6821.. 84 I
sue.samaniego@ojc.edu
SAMANTA, Shivaji .... 540-857-6335 517 E
ssamanta@virginiawestern.edu
SAMARKOS, Christy ..... 619-594-5211.. 35 E
csamarko@mail.sdsu.edu
SAMBDMAN, Cory, W .. 563-333-6336 182 E
1312mgr@follett.com
SAMBERG, Wendy .... 203-285-2108.. 89 B
wsamberg@gwcc.commnet.edu
SAMBRANO, Richard .... 281-443-8900 487 D
SAMDAHL, JR.,
Donald, H .... 540-464-7228 518 A
samdahldh@vmi.edu
SAMDPERIL, Debra .... 617-369-3643 236 E
dsamdperil@smfa.edu
SAMEK, Linda .... 503-554-2871 406 A
lsamek@georgefox.edu
SAMENFINK,
William, H .... 978-232-2402 226 C
bsamenfi@endicott.edu
SAMET, Jan .... 301-696-3934 215 E
jsamet@hood.edu

SAMHAN, Tisha, L .... 318-795-4215 205 F
tisha.samhan@lsus.edu
SAMHAT, Nayef, H .... 864-597-4010 451 J
president@wofford.edu
SAMITORE, Wendy .... 509-527-4300 527 H
wendy.samitore@wwcc.edu
SAMMAKIA, Bahgat ...... 607-777-4818 343 D
bahgat@binghamton.edu
SAMMARCO, Ed .... 800-955-2527 187 E
esammarco@grantham.edu
SAMMARCO, Erica, C ... 716-888-2100 317 H
sammarce@canisius.edu
SAMMARTINO,
Kathleen .... 617-868-9600 228 B
SAMMIS, Robert, L .... 626-914-8550.. 38 L
rsammis@citruscollege.edu
SAMMONS, Gregory, S . 607-587-3911 347 D
sammongs@alfredstate.edu
SAMMONS, Kenneth, R 509-313-6951 522 L
ksammons@plant.gonzaga.edu
SAMOLEWICZ, Mark ..... 201-216-5218 308 D
msamolew@stevens.edu
SAMOLEWSKI,
Patrick, C .... 989-964-4221 249 G
pcs@svsu.edu
SAMORA, Tracy .... 719-549-2850.. 81 F
tracy.samora@csupueblo.edu
SAMP, Mike .... 307-766-5179 546 K
bowhntr@uwyo.edu
SAMPADIAN, Greg .... 510-436-1049.. 47 C
sampadian@hnu.edu
SAMPERTON, Amy .... 910-678-8236 362 E
samperta@faytechcc.edu
SAMPH, Thomas .... 203-596-4652.. 91 D
tsamph@post.edu
SAMPITE, Chris .... 318-869-5018 202 D
csampite@centenary.edu
SAMPLE, Bradford .... 740-477-7456 388 F
bsample@ohiochristian.edu
SAMPLE, Jay .... 909-667-4440.. 39 C
jsample@claremontlincoln.org
SAMPLE, Mark .... 704-991-0247 366 D
jsample7479@stanly.edu
SAMPLE, Michael .... 812-855-0850 167 I
mmsample@indiana.edu
SAMPLE, Mike .... 812-855-0850 167 J
mmsample@iu.edu
SAMPLE, Rick, A .... 301-369-2800 214 A
rsample@captechu.edu
SAMPLE, Steven, B .... 213-740-5400.. 74 D
SAMPLE, Valara .... 423-425-4304 465 E
valara-sample@utc.edu
SAMPLES, Donald, A .... 423-439-7457 461 D
samplesd@etsu.edu
SAMPLES, Robert, D ..... 314-516-5665 284 B
bob@umsl.edu
SAMPLEY, Curtis .... 334-387-3877.... 1 E
curtissampley@amridgeuniversity.edu
SAMPSON, Allison .... 213-621-2200.. 40 F
SAMPSON, Betty, J .... 509-865-8600 523 C
sampson_b@heritage.edu
SAMPSON, Christina .... 304-829-7401 529 H
csampson@bethanywv.edu
SAMPSON, Christopher 920-465-2527 539 F
sampsonc@uwgb.edu
SAMPSON, Connie, B ... 404-413-3230 126 D
csampson@gsu.edu
SAMPSON, David, G ..... 518-381-1370 342 E
sampsodg@sunysccc.edu
SAMPSON, Diana .... 206-546-4512 526 G
dsampson@shoreline.edu
SAMPSON, Jonathan .... 916-577-2200.. 77 F
jsampson@jessup.edu
SAMPSON, Mark .... 412-731-6000 433 K
msampson@rpts.edu
SAMPSON, Marsha .... 406-657-2085 287 H
msampson@msubillings.edu
SAMPSON, Marshall ...... 253-833-9111 523 B
SAMPSON, Michael .... 718-990-1305 340 G
sampsonm@stjohns.edu
SAMPSON, Robert .... 401-841-1323 548 B
SAMPSON, Sharon .... 412-731-6000 433 K
ssampson@rpts.edu
SAMPSON, Sonya .... 207-755-5246 210 L
ssampson@cmcc.edu
SAMPSON, Zora, J .... 608-342-1688 540 D
sampsonz@uwplatt.edu
SAMRA, Rajinder .... 925-424-1027.. 37 O
rsamra@laspositascollege.edu
SAMS, Catherine, T ...... 864-656-4233 444 E
willsam@clemson.edu
SAMS, Michelle .... 863-669-2823 110 E
msams@polk.edu
SAMS, Sean .... 614-837-4088 394 H
samss@valorcollege.com
SAMS, Susan .... 714-997-6829.. 38 B
sams@chapman.edu
SAMS, Tammy .... 707-546-4000.. 43 J
tsams@empirecollege.com
SAMS, Timothy .... 404-653-7858 128 L
tim.sams@morehouse.edu

SAMS, Wesley, S .... 843-953-5375 444 C
wsams@citadel.edu
SAMSA, Heather .... 706-886-6831 132 F
hsamsa@tfc.edu
SAMSON, Keri .... 563-589-3775 183 E
ksamson@dbq.edu
SAMSON, Kim, M .... 218-477-2133 260 B
samson@mnstate.edu
SAMTER, Wendy .... 401-232-6433 441 B
wsamter@bryant.edu
SAMUEL, Bryan .... 423-425-5670 465 E
bryan-samuel@utc.edu
SAMUEL, Jacinta .... 692-625-6724 550 A
jsamuel@cmi.edu
SAMUEL, Javiette, V ..... 502-597-5799 197 G
javiette.samuel@kysu.edu
SAMUEL, Jeanne .... 504-671-6219 203 F
jsamue@dcc.edu
SAMUEL, Prema .... 914-395-2305 342 C
psamuel@sarahlawrence.edu
SAMUEL LOFTUS,
Barbara .... 570-674-6195 426 D
bloftus@misericordia.edu
SAMUELS, A. Dexter ..... 615-327-6435 458 F
dsamuels@mmc.edu
SAMUELS, Darlette, C ... 731-426-7595 457 K
dsamuels@lanecollege.edu
SAMUELS, Deby, K .... 615-966-7133 458 C
deby.samuels@lipscomb.edu
SAMUELS, Elena .... 212-220-8061 318 D
esamuels@bmcc.cuny.edu
SAMUELS, Elias .... 517-787-0800 244 H
SamuelsEliasM@jccmi.edu
SAMUELS, Rick .... 217-732-3155 150 H
rsamuels@lincolncollege.edu
SAMUELS, Robert .... 401-874-2288 442 E
rsamuels@mail.uri.edu
SAMUELS, Rodney .... 914-654-5952 322 B
rsamuels@cnr.edu
SAMUELS, Sandra .... 973-353-5231 307 C
szsamuls@newark.rutgers.edu
SAMUELS, Vickie .... 828-398-2566 368 I
vsamuels@southcollegenc.edu
SAMUELSON, Erik .... 425-249-4759 527 D
erik.samuelson@tlc.edu
SAMUELSON, Pamela ... 570-372-4272 435 I
samuelson@susqu.edu
SAMUL, Margaret .... 203-582-8431.. 91 E
margaret.samul@quinnipiac.edu
SAN NICOLAS, Heidi, E 671-735-2481 549 G
heidi.sannicolas@guamcedders.org
SAN NICOLAS, Jennifer 760-384-6221.. 49 F
jsannico@cerrocoso.edu
SANAI, Fardin .... 518-956-8062 343 C
fsanai@albany.edu
SANANES, Amram .... 718-339-1090 353 J
amramsananes@mikdashmelech.org
SANANES, Josh .... 718-339-1090 353 J
rjsananes@mikdashmelech.org
SANBERG, Jennifer .... 309-457-2286 153 B
jsanberg@monmouthcollege.edu
SANBERG, Paul .... 813-974-5570 116 B
psanberg@health.usf.edu
SANBORN, Karen .... 734-432-5843 246 B
ksanborn@madonna.edu
SANBORN, Merlene .... 207-859-1102 211 I
sanbornm@thomas.edu
SANCHEZ, Alicia .... 316-978-3034 192 D
alicia.sanchez@wichita.edu
SANCHEZ, Ana Maria ... 863-292-3603 110 E
asanchez@polk.edu
SANCHEZ, Andrew .... 310-233-4340.. 51 F
sancheac@lahc.edu
SANCHEZ, Angel .... 559-278-3906.. 33 D
aansanchez@csufresno.edu
SANCHEZ, Bonifacio ..... 692-625-3394 550 A
bsanchez@cmi.edu
SANCHEZ, Brianne .... 206-934-4700 525 K
brianne.sanchez@seattlecolleges.edu
SANCHEZ, Cheryl .... 719-336-1516.. 83 N
cheryl.sanchez@lamarcc.edu
SANCHEZ, Cheryl, L ...... 830-591-7202 483 A
clsanchez547@swtjc.edu
SANCHEZ, Cristina .... 210-458-7203 494 D
cristina.sanchez@utsa.edu
SANCHEZ, Diane .... 210-829-5866 492 B
castaned@uiwtx.edu
SANCHEZ, Domingo ...... 505-747-2143 312 G
domingo_sanchez@nnmc.edu
SANCHEZ, Elda, E .... 361-593-3805 486 A
elda.sanchez@tamuk.edu
SANCHEZ, Frank .... 646-664-8759 318 B
frank.sanchez@cuny.edu
SANCHEZ, Gilbert .... 562-868-6488.. 49 H
SANCHEZ, Gregory .... 619-388-3354.. 62 F
gsanchez@sdccd.edu
SANCHEZ,
Hector Ruben .... 787-751-1912 554 D
hrsanchez@juris.inter.edu
SANCHEZ, Ines .... 787-850-9348 558 A
ines.sanchez@upr.edu

SANCHEZ, Ismael .... 212-694-1000 316 J
isanchez@boricuacollege.edu
SANCHEZ, Jacob .... 910-221-2224 357 A
jsanchez@gcd.edu
SANCHEZ, Jennifer .... 413-755-4480 233 B
jsanchez@stcc.edu
SANCHEZ, John .... 671-735-2444 549 G
soedean@triton.uog.edu
SANCHEZ, John .... 210-434-6711 479 P
jdsanchez@lake.ollusa.edu
SANCHEZ, Jorge, R .... 714-241-6338.. 40 B
jsanchez@coastline.edu
SANCHEZ, Jose .... 787-878-5475 553 F
jsanchez@arecibo.inter.edu
SANCHEZ, Joseph .... 817-735-2522 493 B
Joseph.Sanchez@unthsc.edu
SANCHEZ, Juan, M 512-471-2877 493M
jsanchez@austin.utexas.edu
SANCHEZ, Leopoldo, A 314-863-2772 273 G
sanchezl@csl.edu
SANCHEZ, Librada .... 973-720-2586 309 I
sanchezl@wpunj.edu
SANCHEZ, Lisa, M .... 626-396-2210.. 28 J
lisa.sanchez@artcenter.edu
SANCHEZ, Luis .... 520-494-5266.. 12 R
luis.sanchez@centralaz.edu
SANCHEZ, Luis, P .... 805-378-1403.. 75 C
lsanchez@vcccd.edu
SANCHEZ, Margaret ...... 415-239-3000.. 39 A
msanchez@ccsf.edu
SANCHEZ, Mark .... 831-755-6711.. 46 J
msanchez@hartnell.edu
SANCHEZ, Matthew ...... 214-860-8507 472 G
matthewsanchez@dcccd.edu
SANCHEZ, Noel .... 661-726-1911.. 70 I
noel.sanchez@uav.edu
SANCHEZ, Omar .... 305-821-3333 104 C
omarsnc@fnu.edu
SANCHEZ, Ophelia .... 305-442-9223 108 G
osanchez@mrc.edu
SANCHEZ, Pete .... 817-552-3700 477 B
pete.sanchez@tku.edu
SANCHEZ, Priscilla .... 979-230-3215 469 G
SANCHEZ, Rebecca .... 951-343-4368.. 30 D
rsanchez@calbaptist.edu
SANCHEZ, Roxanne .... 210-434-6711 479 P
rlsanchez@lake.ollusa.edu
SANCHEZ, Sandra .... 310-233-4041.. 51 F
sanches@lahc.edu
SANCHEZ, Stephanie .... 413-565-1000 222 G
ssanchez@baypath.edu
SANCHEZ, Steven 314-977-2611 281M
ssanche6@slu.edu
SANCHEZ, Suane .... 787-758-2525 558 C
suane.sanchez@upr.edu
SANCHEZ, Victor .... 312-341-2282 157 E
vsanchez03@roosevelt.edu
SANCHEZ, Vivian .... 619-684-8777.. 56 B
vsanchez@newschoolarch.edu
SANCHEZ-TIBBETTS,
Sherry .... 218-879-0898 258 F
sstibbetts@fdltcc.edu
SANCILIO, Leonard .... 585-245-5706 345 D
sancilio@geneseo.edu
SANCRANT, Lisa .... 419-251-1454 386 C
lisa.sancrant@mercycollege.edu
SAND, Sabra .... 360-992-2288 521 A
ssand@clark.edu
SANDBERG, Curtis .... 859-985-3208 193 F
curtis_sandberg@berea.edu
SANDBERG, Gary .... 614-236-7737 378 H
gsandberg@capital.edu
SANDBERG, Peter .... 507-786-3611 264 C
sandberg@stolaf.edu
SANDBERG, Robin .... 210-486-4134 466 K
rsandberg@alamo.edu
SANDBOTHE, Lindsay ... 312-461-0600 139 G
lsandbothe@aaart.edu
SANDBOTHE, Robin .... 913-667-5700 185 L
rsandbothe@cbts.edu
SANDBULTE, Deb .... 712-707-7224 182 C
debfs@nwciowa.edu
SANDE, Jeff, A .... 218-755-3988 258 B
jsande@bemidjistate.edu
SANDEEN, Beverly, A ... 916-568-3075.. 52 H
sandeen@losrios.edu
SANDEEN, Cathy .... 310-825-5551.. 71 D
csandeen@unex.ucla.edu
SANDEEN, Cathy .... 608-262-3786 541 E
cathy.sandeen@uwex.uwc.edu
SANDEFUR, Gary .... 405-744-5627 400 C
gary.sandefur@okstate.edu
SANDEL, Robert, H .... 540-857-7311 517 E
rsandel@virginiawestern.edu
SANDELL, Julie .... 617-358-5846 224 E
jsandell@bu.edu
SANDELL, Kamalika ...... 202-885-2123.. 94 H
ksandel@american.edu
SANDELL, Stanley, C .... 310-233-4181.. 51 F
sandelsc@lahc.edu

SANTORO, Stephanie .... 323-563-4856.. 38 C stephaniesantoro@cdrewu.edu
SANTOS, Annette, T ...... 671-735-2553 549 G atsantos@triton.uog.edu
SANTOS, Carlo .... 408-288-3761.. 63 O carlo.santos@sjeccd.org
SANTOS, Carmen, K ..... 671-735-5548 549 E carmen.kweksantos@guamcc.edu
SANTOS, Carol .... 508-999-8388 228 H csantos1@umassd.edu
SANTOS, Catherine .... 315-312-2500 346 A catherine.santos@oswego.edu
SANTOS, David, M .... 860-701-6787 548 H David.M.Santos@uscg.edu
SANTOS, Helena .... 617-243-2127 227 K hsantos@lasell.edu
SANTOS, Janet .... 314-362-9253 275 D JSantos@bjc.org
SANTOS, Joycette .... 787-841-4780 558 D joycette.santos@upr.edu
SANTOS, Mae .... 323-343-3555.. 34 A msantos@cslanet.calstatela.edu
SANTOS, Maria del, C .. 787-743-7979 555M ut_masantos@suagm.edu
SANTOS, Maricarmen ... 787-743-7979 555M m_santos@suagm.edu
SANTOS, Maritza .... 787-878-5475 553 F msantos@arecibo.inter.edu
SANTOS, Matthew .... 610-683-4113 431 B santos@kutztown.edu
SANTOS, Michelle .... 508-286-3857 238 B santos_michelle@wheatoncollege.edu
SANTOS, Paul .... 704-330-6689 361 D paul.santos@cpcc.edu
SANTOS, Ramon .... 305-223-4561 111 J santos@sjvcs.edu
SANTOS, Samuel .... 415-239-3762.. 39 A ssantos@ccsf.edu
SANTOS, Shelly .... 718-261-5800 316 K ssantos@bramsonort.edu
SANTOS, Susan .... 859-442-4165 196 A susan.santos@kctcs.edu
SANTOS, Victor .... 508-362-2131 231 D vsantos@capecod.edu
SANTOS, Victor .... 302-857-6001.. 93 E vsantos@desu.edu
SANTOS-COY, Katie ...... 714-449-7463.. 53 D ksantoscoy@ketchum.edu
SANTOS-GEORGE, Arlene .... 847-543-2310 142 G asgeorge@clcillinois.edu
SANTOS-PEREZ, Kennia, I .... 787-480-2355 551 H kisantos@sanjuanciudadpatria.com
SANTOSTEFANO, Donald .... 717-867-6341 423 I dsantost@lvc.edu
SANTOYO-MARIN, Patricia .... 309-794-8275 139 K patriciasantoyomarin@augustana.edu
SANTUCCI, Wayne .... 212-517-0544 332 A wsantucci@mmm.edu
SANYAL, Rajib, N .... 516-877-4661 314 F
SANYAL, Rajib, N .... 765-285-8192 164 D rnsanyal@bsu.edu
SANYAL, Sabyasachi .... 972-721-5156 491 B ssanyal@udallas.edu
SAPARILAS, John, W .... 919-866-5450 366 H jwsaparilas@waketech.edu
SAPERSTEIN, Shari .... 954-262-7201 109 E ssaperst@nova.edu
SAPHIRE, Diane, G .... 210-999-8483 490 E dsaphire@trinity.edu
SAPIENZA, Barb .... 314-977-7777 281M sapienzab@slu.edu
SAPIENZA, Christine .... 904-256-7626 106 Q csapien@ju.edu
SAPIENZA, Matthew ..... 646-746-4275 318 B matthew.sapienza@cuny.edu
SAPKOTA, Kayla .... 501-370-5252.. 22 E ksapkota@philander.edu
SAPP, Aimee .... 573-592-4368 286 A aimee.sapp@williamwoods.edu
SAPP, Buddy .... 912-871-1634 129 E bsapp@ogeecheetech.edu
SAPP, Fred .... 910-672-1204 370 A fsapp@uncfsu.edu
SAPP, Geneva .... 509-865-8631 523 C sapp_g@heritage.edu
SAPP, Judy .... 606-877-1421 197 B judy.sapp@kctcs.edu
SAPP, Sarah .... 662-562-3274 269 E ssapp@northwestms.edu
SAPPENFIELD, Elizabeth .... 317-738-8075 166 B esappenfield@franklincollege.edu
SAPPENFIELD, George, O .... 336-386-3280 366 E sappeng@surry.edu
SAPPINGTON, Eric .... 660-831-4168 279 D sappingtone@moval.edu
SAPPINGTON, Lee Ann 970-339-6223.. 78 J leeann.sappington@aims.edu
SARA, Ligaya .... 680-488-2471 550 C ligayas@palau.edu
SARA, Tejnder .... 334-727-8704.... 8 B tsara@tuskegee.edu
SARAC, Isa .... 703-591-7042 517 G isarac@viu.edu
SARAFIAN, Christopher 302-793-1101.. 94 C
SARAN, Rupa .... 714-432-5952.. 40 D rsaran@occ.cccd.edu
SARANI, Saeed .... 405-692-3246 398 I ssarani@macu.edu
SARANTAKOS, Paul ...... 217-351-2385 155 I psarantakos@parkland.edu
SARAT, Austin, D .... 413-542-2308 222 A adsarat@amherst.edu
SARATA, Andrew .... 708-974-5357 153 D sarataa@morainevalley.edu
SARAVANAPAVAN, Naomi .... 607-729-1581 324 A nsaravanapavan@davisny.edu
SARBER, John .... 765-455-9505 168 B jrsarber@iuk.edu
SARBER, Sarah .... 765-455-9204 168 B shawkins@iuk.edu
SARDINAS, Maria .... 617-739-1700 234 I msardinas@aii.edu
SARFF, Michelle .... 614-251-4758 388 H sarffm@ohiodominican.edu
SARGENT, Anneila, I ..... 626-395-6100.. 31 D afs@caltech.edu
SARGENT, Brent .... 802-879-2321 504 C bsargent@vtc.edu
SARGENT, Daniel .... 315-866-0300 327 E sargentda@herkimer.edu
SARGENT, Gary .... 254-295-4242 492 C gsargent@umhb.edu
SARGENT, Jeffrey .... 708-456-0300 161 C jeffsargent@triton.edu
SARGENT, Jenell .... 334-727-8011.... 8 B jsargent@mytu.tuskegee.edu
SARGENT, Joe, E .... 423-585-6836 464 C joe.sargent@ws.edu
SARGENT, Linda .... 618-842-3711 146 G sargentl@iecc.edu
SARGENT, Madeline ...... 215-568-9215 426 C msargent@phmc.org
SARGENT, Mark, L .... 805-565-6007.. 76 K msargent@westmont.edu
SARGENT, Peter, E .... 314-968-7006 285 G sargenpe@webster.edu
SARHAN, Mostafa .... 912-358-3388 131 A sarhanm@savannahstate.edu
SARIAN, Richard .... 216-421-7432 380 B rsarian@cia.edu
SARIDAKIS, Dianne, I ... 215-885-2360 425 C dsaridakis@manor.edu
SARIEGO, Ivan .... 787-751-0160 551 K isariego@cmpr.pr.gov
SARIN, Sanjiv .... 336-334-7920 370 B sarin@ncat.edu
SARIN, Sanjiv .... 336-285-2371 370 B sarin@ncat.edu
SARKAR, Ratna .... 713-348-4293 480M rgs1@rice.edu
SARKIS, Hashim .... 617-253-4401 233 C
SARKISIAN, Jodi .... 215-898-7221 437 I jodi@pobox.upenn.edu
SARLES, Harry .... 913-684-3097 548 F harry.sarles@us.army.mil
SARMA, Sanjay .... 617-715-4532 233 C
SARMIENTO, Reine .... 718-960-8429 319 C reine.sarmiento@lehman.cuny.edu
SARMIENTO, Steve .... 510-780-4500.. 50 G ssarmiento@lifewest.edu
SARNOVSKY, Joseph ..... 407-708-2430 113 A sarnovsj@seminolestate.edu
SARR, Papa .... 978-665-3599 229 D psarr@fitchburgstate.edu
SARRAFIAN, Armen .... 312-553-5922 141 N asarrafian@ccc.edu
SARRATORI, Peter .... 315-781-3647 327 G sarratori@hws.edu
SARRETT, David, C .... 804-828-7235 514 F dcsarrett@vcu.edu
SARRUBBO, Joseph, M 407-582-2586 118 I jsarrubbo@valenciacollege.edu
SARTAIN, Debra .... 303-837-0825.. 79 C dsartain@aii.edu
SARTAIN, Karen .... 423-636-7376 464 F ksartain@tusculum.edu
SARTARELLI, Jose, V ..... 910-962-3030 372 A sartarellij@uncw.edu
SARTINI, Chad .... 540-857-7731 517 E csartini@virginiawestern.edu
SARTOR, Curtis .... 847-628-1017 149 A csartor@judsonu.edu
SARTOR, Dan .... 708-239-4820 160 L dan.sartor@trnty.edu
SARTORI, Lillian .... 212-229-5300 334 C sartoril@newschool.edu
SARVELA, Paul .... 618-536-3465 159 G psarvela@siu.edu
SARVEY, Sharon .... 252-399-6401 354 I sisarvey@barton.edu
SARVIS, Randall, F .... 937-382-6661 395 F randy_sarvis@wilmington.edu
SASASKI, Hiroshi .... 626-571-8811.. 74 E hiroshis@uwest.edu
SASS, Pamela, D .... 718-270-1000 344 D
SASS, Sharon, A .... 561-868-3147 109 H sasss@palmbeachstate.edu
SASS, Terricita, E .... 203-392-9999.. 88 F sass@southernct.edu
SASSAMAN, Margo, J ... 717-871-7656 431 E margo.sassaman@millersville.edu
SASSEL, Rachel .... 619-688-0800.. 42 A rsassel@concorde.edu
SASSER, Jackson, N ..... 352-395-5164 112 H j.sasser@sfcollege.edu
SASSER, Jennifer .... 503-675-3964 407 A jsasser@marylhurst.edu
SASSER, Mackey .... 334-556-2416.... 4 A msasser@wallace.edu
SASSER, Tom .... 909-599-5433.. 50 H tsasser@lifepacific.edu
SASSMAN, Jen, L .... 319-352-8262 183 J jennifer.sassman@wartburg.edu
SASSO, Diana .... 412-396-6136 417 I sasso@duq.edu
SASSO, Gary, M .... 610-758-3221 424 B gms208@lehigh.edu
SASSSER, Craig-Ellis .... 662-720-7411 269 D cesasser@nemcc.edu
SASTRY, S. Shankar ...... 510-642-5771.. 70 K sastry@coe.berkeley.edu
SATCHWELL, Carol .... 315-655-7144 317 J csatchwell@cazenovia.edu
SATELE, Arleen .... 714-628-4717.. 60 H satele_arleen@sccollege.edu
SATHER, Steven, M ...... 609-258-6479 305 C sather@princeton.edu
SATKOWIAK, Ann, E ..... 865-539-7153 463 E asatkowiak@pstcc.edu
SATKOWSKI, John .... 313-845-9636 243 I jssatkowski@hfcc.edu
SATO, Deirdre .... 212-217-5380 325 C deirdre_sato@fitnyc.edu
SATO, Heidi .... 714-816-0366.. 70 D heidi.sato@trident.edu
SATO, Kay .... 516-299-2584 330 G kay.sato@liu.edu
SATO, Tami, A .... 714-449-7447.. 53 D tsato@ketchum.edu
SATO, Toshiko .... 949-480-4364.. 66 I tsato@soka.edu
SATRIANA, Dan .... 970-351-2399.. 87 A dan.satriana@unco.edu
SATTAR, Mo .... 413-565-1000 222 G msattar@baypath.edu
SATTERFIELD, Billy .... 281-283-2480 491 E satterfield@uhcl.edu
SATTERFIELD, Derick .... 336-342-4261 365 E satterfieldd@rockinghamcc.edu
SATTERFIELD, Jay .... 731-989-6058 456 K jsatterfield@fhu.edu
SATTERFIELD, Lacey, L . 770-720-5620 130 E LLS@reinhardt.edu
SATTERFIELD, Lisa .... 865-251-1800 460 J lsatterfield@southcollegetn.edu
SATTERLEE, Kevin .... 208-426-1233 137 E ksatterl@boisestate.edu
SATTERLEE, Richard ...... 718-862-7352 331 H richard.satterlee@manhattan.edu
SATTERLUND, Alysson, M .... 909-537-5185.. 35 A asatterlund@csusb.edu
SATTERLY, Eric .... 502-272-8098 193 E esatterly@bellarmine.edu
SATTERWHITE, Dawn .... 919-761-2209 368 K dsatterwhite@sebts.edu
SATTERWHITE, Kerry ..... 217-479-7079 151 J kerry.satterwhite@mac.edu
SATTERWHITE, Tanya, J .... 804-524-1497 518 C tsatterwhite@vsu.edu
SATTLER, Brian .... 409-880-8396 488 F brian.sattler@lamar.edu
SATTLER, Joan, L .... 309-677-3152 140 H jls@fsmail.bradley.edu
SATZ, Michael .... 208-364-4041 139 C msatz@uidaho.edu
SAUCHUK, Stacey, R .... 610-989-1203 438 I ssauchuk@vfmac.edu
SAUDER, Vinita .... 402-486-2500 293 D visauder@ucollege.edu
SAUDERS, Charlette, R . 574-372-5100 166 D saudercr@grace.edu
SAUER, Alan, R .... 860-297-2043.. 92 A alan.sauer@trincoll.edu
SAUER, Carrie .... 405-208-5873 400 A csauer@okcu.edu
SAUER, Greg .... 802-485-2170 502 G gsauer@norwich.edu
SAUER, James .... 610-341-5957 427 I jsauer@eastern.edu
SAUER, James, L .... 610-341-5957 418 A jsauer@eastern.edu
SAUER, Jenni .... 610-647-4400 421 B jsauer@immaculata.edu
SAUER, Marty, R .... 630-637-5801 154 F mrsauer@noctrl.edu
SAUER, Michael, L .... 702-895-1073 295 G michael.sauer@unlv.edu
SAUER, Mike .... 702-895-1073 295 G sauer@unlv.edu
SAUERBREI, Aaron .... 319-277-2490 179 B aaron.sauerbrei@hawkeyecollege.edu
SAUERMAN, Gretchen .. 321-674-7237 103 R gsauerman@fit.edu
SAUERS, Darlene .... 724-838-4210 435 E sauers@setonhill.edu
SAUERS, Gail .... 602-682-6800.. 12 A
SAUERWEIN, David, A .. 603-526-3758 296 I dsauerwein@colby-sawyer.edu
SAUK, John, J .... 502-852-5295 201 A john.sauk@louisville.edu
SAUL, Amy .... 610-861-1509 426 H saula@moravian.edu
SAUL, J. Beau .... 607-844-8222 350 A saulj@TC3.edu
SAUL, Sheryl .... 651-846-1384 261 G sheryl.saul@saintpaul.edu
SAULE, Mara, R .... 802-656-2020 503 C mara.saule@uvm.edu
SAULS, Jina, M .... 276-935-4349 504 L jsauls@asl.edu
SAULS, Steve .... 305-348-3505 114 G steve.sauls@fiu.edu
SAULSBERRY, Keith ...... 334-556-2470.... 4 A ksaulsberry@wallace.edu
SAUM, Rob .... 386-506-3484 101 I saumr@DaytonaState.edu
SAUNDERS, Aleister ...... 215-895-6772 417 E aleister.j.saunders@drexel.edu
SAUNDERS, Amber .... 318-371-3035 204 A ambersaunders@nwltc.edu
SAUNDERS, Brian .... 310-544-6487.. 61 I brian.saunders@usw.salvationarmy.org
SAUNDERS, C. Tom ..... 912-279-5757 123 B tsaunders@ccga.edu
SAUNDERS, Dustin .... 757-340-2121 506 E admdirectorcvab@centura.edu
SAUNDERS, Emily, M .... 336-841-9551 357 E esaunder@highpoint.edu
SAUNDERS, Gary .... 336-506-4152 359 N gary.saunders@alamancecc.edu
SAUNDERS, Gayle, M .... 217-875-7200 156 K gsaunder@richland.edu
SAUNDERS, Greer .... 804-819-4906 514 G gsaunders@vccs.edu
SAUNDERS, Joseph .... 304-766-3353 533 C saundejs@wvstateu.edu
SAUNDERS, Kara, C ..... 716-645-5725 343 E kcs23@buffalo.edu
SAUNDERS, Kari .... 314-744-5301 278 G saundersk@mobap.edu
SAUNDERS, Kathy .... 716-614-6201 336 D saunders@niagaracc.suny.edu
SAUNDERS, Keith .... 319-335-0553 175 H keith-saunders@uiowa.edu
SAUNDERS, Kenneth, K 516-572-7205 334 A kenneth.saunders@ncc.edu
SAUNDERS, Kevin .... 515-271-1984 177 K kevin.saunders@drake.edu
SAUNDERS, Kevin .... 831-582-3397.. 34 C kesaunders@csumb.edu
SAUNDERS, Laura .... 912-871-1600 129 E lsaunders@ogeecheetech.edu
SAUNDERS, Mark .... 405-878-5402 402 A msaunders@stgregorys.edu
SAUNDERS, Martha ...... 850-474-2035 116 E msaunders@uwf.edu
SAUNDERS, Mary, M .... 434-395-2063 509 H saundersmm@longwood.edu
SAUNDERS, Melinda, D 304-896-7364 531 F melinda.saunders@southernwv.edu
SAUNDERS, Richard ..... 435-865-8392 499 L rsaunders@suu.edu
SAUNDERS, Robert .... 334-241-5477.... 8 A rsaunders@troy.edu
SAUNDERS, Robert .... 334-983-6556.... 8 A rsaunders@troy.edu
SAUNDERS, Scott, D .... 716-673-3171 343 F scott.saunders@fredonia.edu
SAUNDERS, Sharon ...... 434-947-8114 511 D ssaunders@randolphcollege.edu
SAUNDERS, Sharon ...... 281-649-3206 475 B ssaunders@hbu.edu

SCHAEFFER, Angela, P . 413-597-2025 238 E
aps1@williams.edu
SCHAEFFER, Lisa .... 910-521-6175 371 D
lisa.schaeffer@uncp.edu
SCHAEFFER, Scot .... 563-387-1287 180 M
schasc01@luther.edu
SCHAEFFLER, Jan .... 203-332-5220.. 89 C
jschaeffler@hcc.commnet.edu
SCHAFER, Clark .... 316-942-4291 189 K
schaferc@newmanu.edu
SCHAFER, Jay .... 413-545-0284 228 F
jschafer@library.umass.edu
SCHAFER, Michael .... 419-772-2190 388 I
m-schafer@onu.edu
SCHAFER, William .... 304-293-5811 533 D
wschafer@mail.wvu.edu
SCHAFFER, Connie .... 567-661-7737 390 D
connie_schaffer@owens.edu
SCHAFFER, Doug .... 269-639-8442 245 E
dschaffer@lakemichigancollege.edu
SCHAFFER,
Frederick, P .... 646-664-9210 318 B
frederick.schaffer@cuny.edu
SCHAFFER, James, P .... 610-330-5000 423 A
schaffej@lafayette.edu
SCHAFFER, Jeff .... 732-987-2600 302 J
schafferj@georgian.edu
SCHAFFER, Joe .... 307-778-1102 546 F
jschaffer@lccc.wy.edu
SCHAFFER, Kerry .... 812-877-8172 172 C
schaffer@rose-hulman.edu
SCHAFFER, Lonnie .... 757-825-2952 517 B
schafferl@tncc.edu
SCHAFFER, Mindy, M ... 410-822-5400 214 D
mschaffer@chesapeake.edu
SCHAFFER, Sandy .... 931-393-1536 463 B
sschaffer@mscc.edu
SCHAFFER, William ...... 217-641-4314 148 J
bschaffer@jwcc.edu
SCHAFFHAUSER,
Anthony .... 218-736-1528 259 H
anthony.schaffhauserl@minnesota.edu
SCHAFFNER,
Barbara, H .... 614-823-1735 390 C
bschaffner@otterbein.edu
SCHAFFNER, Bradley .... 507-222-4267 254 D
bschaffner@carleton.edu
SCHAFRICK, James, A .. 203-773-8507.. 87 M
jschafrick@albertus.edu
SCHAKNOWSKI,
Jennifer .... 706-290-2167 121 E
jschaknowski@berry.edu
SCHALK, Lawrence, E ... 269-471-3484 239 D
schalk@andrews.edu
SCHALL, Jeffrey .... 603-752-1113 297 E
jschall@ccsnh.edu
SCHALL, Lawrence, M .. 404-364-8320 129 F
lschall@oglethorpe.edu
SCHALLER, Rhonda .... 718-636-5926 338 E
rshal20@pratt.edu
SCHALLOCK, Heather .... 715-365-4518 543 G
hschallock@nicoletcollege.edu
SCHAMANN, Matthew .. 716-926-8925 327 F
mschamann@hilbert.edu
SCHAMP, Rosemary ...... 856-374-4941 301 A
rschamp@camdencc.edu
SCHANCK, Donald, S ... 401-863-9570 441 A
donald_schanck@brown.edu
SCHANDEL,
Kimberly, A .... 508-767-7312 222 D
kschande@assumption.edu
SCHANK, Tyson .... 816-271-5909 279 E
tschank@missouriwestern.edu
SCHANTZ, Janet, D ...... 317-738-8009 166 B
jschantz@franklincollege.edu
SCHANTZ, Peter, K .... 740-368-3404 390 B
pkschant@owu.edu
SCHANZ, Jeff .... 518-276-6205 339 D
schanj@rpi.edu
SCHAPER, Angie, L .... 641-422-4327 181 E
schapang@niacc.edu
SCHAPER, Nikki .... 760-757-2121.. 54 G
nschaper@miracosta.edu
SCHAPER, Sue .... 208-459-5837 137 J
sschaper@collegeofidaho.edu
SCHAPIRO, Chaim .... 973-455-9031 305 E
chaimschap@aol.com
SCHAPIRO, Mendel ...... 323-937-3763.. 77 J
SCHAPIRO, Morton, O . 847-491-7456 155 D
nu-president@northwestern.edu
SCHAPIRO, Robert .... 404-712-8815 124 D
rschapi@emory.edu
SCHAPP, Rebecca, M ... 408-554-4528.. 65 A
rschapp@scu.edu
SCHAPPE, Mascheal ..... 314-529-9670 277 B
mschappe@maryville.edu
SCHAPPERT, David, G .. 570-961-4764 425 D
dschappert@marywood.edu
SCHARDT, Wendy, L ..... 308-865-8047 293 G
schardtwl@unk.edu
SCHARER, Gregory .... 937-775-2620 396 A
greg.scharer@wright.edu
SCHARER, Lloyd, S ...... 517-321-0242 243 H
lscharer@glcc.edu
SCHARF, Michael, P ..... 216-368-3283 378 J
michael.scharf@case.edu
SCHARFF, Virginia .... 505-277-2611 313 H
vscharff@unm.edu
SCHARLE, Joyce .... 215-646-7300 420 A
scharle.j@gmercyu.edu
SCHARLEMANN,
Linette, M .... 507-354-8221 257 A
scharllm@mlc-wels.edu
SCHARMAN, Janet, S ... 801-422-2387 497 J
Jan_Scharman@byu.edu
SCHARMER, Judy .... 575-624-8040 311 K
scharmer@nmmi.edu
SCHARN, Theresa .... 605-718-2402 454 F
theresa.scharn@wdt.edu
SCHARRE, Janice .... 215-780-1420 435 D
SCHARTMAN, Laura, A . 248-370-2387 248 K
schartma@oakland.edu
SCHATTMAN, Lisa .... 858-566-1200.. 43 A
lschattman@disd.edu
SCHATZ, Julianne .... 336-272-7102 357 B
julies@greensboro.edu
SCHATZBERG,
Jeffrey, W .... 520-621-2238.. 18 E
jschatzb@email.arizona.edu
SCHATZEL, Kim .... 734-487-2211 242 J
kschatze@emich.edu
SCHATZEL, Kim .... 734-487-3200 242 J
kschatze@emich.edu
SCHAUB, J. Michael ..... 202-687-3493.. 95 E
jms46@georgetown.edu
SCHAUB, Linda .... 517-750-1200 250 F
lindas@arbor.edu
SCHAUB, Mark .... 616-331-3898 243 E
schaubm@gvsu.edu
SCHAUB, Melissa .... 910-522-5800 371 D
melissa.schaub@uncp.edu
SCHAUBHUT, Diana ...... 504-398-2100 206 E
dschaubhut@olhcc.edu
SCHAUER, Anne, P ...... 513-529-3735 386 K
schauerap@miamioh.edu
SCHAUER, Ariane .... 310-377-5501.. 53 E
aschauer@marymountcalifornia.edu
SCHAUER, Rhonda .... 701-328-5445 373 F
rhonda.schauer@ndus.edu
SCHAUERMANN,
Brittany .... 813-935-5700 111 E
Brittany.Schauermann@remingtoncollege.edu
SCHAUFELBERGER,
John .... 206-685-4440 527 G
jesbcon@u.washington.edu
SCHAUMANN, Neils ...... 619-239-0391.. 36 E
nschaumann@cwsl.edu
SCHAURER, Susan .... 513-529-5040 386 K
susan.schaurer@miamioh.edu
SCHAUS, Jim .... 740-593-0982 389 H
schaus@ohio.edu
SCHEARS, Ben .... 620-441-5245 186 E
schears@cowley.edu
SCHECHTER, Aaron, M . 718-377-0777 338 H
SCHECHTER, Mendel ..... 718-377-0777 338 H
SCHECHTER, Steven ...... 718-951-5391 318 F
sschechter@brooklyn.cuny.edu
SCHECK, Stephen .... 503-838-8271 411 B
schecks@wou.edu
SCHECTER, David .... 661-654-6324.. 32 G
dschecter@csub.edu
SCHEDIN, Karen .... 603-897-8516 298 E
kschedin@rivier.edu
SCHEER, Cory .... 816-415-7872 285 K
scheerc@william.jewell.edu
SCHEER, Michael .... 409-266-2006 495 E
mischeer@utmb.edu
SCHEER, RuthAnn .... 319-895-4324 177 A
rscheer@cornellcollege.edu
SCHEER, Sage, A .... 303-753-6046.. 85 H
sage@rmcad.edu
SCHEER, Thomas .... 407-851-2525 102 I
thomas.scheer@zenith.org
SCHEERER, Teresa .... 215-785-0111 429 F
SCHEESSELE, Marc .... 314-977-4132 281 M
mscheess@slu.edu
SCHEETT, Rod .... 701-355-8181 375 K
scheett@umary.edu
SCHEETZ, Anita, A .... 406-768-6341 286 H
ascheetz@fpcc.edu
SCHEETZ, Charles .... 570-662-4854 431 D
cscheetz@mansfield.edu
SCHEFF, Deborah, M .... 314-977-2802 281 M
scheff@slu.edu
SCHEFF, Julie .... 510-666-8248.. 26 C
jscheff@aimc.edu
SCHEFFEL, Debora .... 303-963-3147.. 79 L
dscheffel@ccu.edu
SCHEFFEL, Kent .... 618-468-5000 150 E
kscheffe@lc.edu
SCHEHR, Terra .... 410-617-2271 216 D
tschehr@loyola.edu
SCHEIB, Roger .... 620-417-1240 191 A
roger.scheib@sccc.edu
SCHEIBMEIR,
Monica, S .... 785-670-1526 192 B
monica.scheibmeir@washburn.edu
SCHEID, Cheryl, R .... 901-448-4930 465 G
cscheid@uthsc.edu
SCHEIDT, Douglas .... 315-386-7202 347 F
scheidtd@canton.edu
SCHEIERN, Libby .... 618-374-5147 156 C
libby.scheiern@principia.edu
SCHEINBERG, Mark, E .. 860-727-6757.. 90 F
mscheinberg@goodwin.edu
SCHEINER, Steve .... 660-596-7208 282 H
sscheiner@sfccmo.edu
SCHEINES, Richard .... 412-268-2832 414 J
scheines@cmu.edu
SCHEINMAN, Steven, J 570-504-7000 415 E
sscheinman@tcmc.edu
SCHELCHER, Cindy .... 408-741-2165.. 76 F
cindy.schelcher@westvalley.edu
SCHELCHER, Cindy .... 408-741-2165.. 76 F
cindy.schelcher@wvm.edu
SCHELCHER, Cynthia .... 408-741-2165.. 76 D
cindy_schelcher@wvm.edu
SCHELIN, Kelly .... 510-215-3870.. 42 D
kschelin@contracosta.edu
SCHELINDER, Shawnda 320-629-5114 260 H
schelinders@pinetech.edu
SCHELL, Courtney .... 307-755-2122 547 D
cschell@wyotechstaff.edu
SCHELL, John .... 407-823-5711 115 C
rick.schell@ucf.edu
SCHELL, Karen .... 518-292-1719 340 A
schelk@sage.edu
SCHELL, Michael, J ...... 541-885-1452 408 E
michael.schell@oit.edu
SCHELL, Randa .... 830-591-2908 483 A
rschell@swtjc.edu
SCHELL, Shannon .... 507-453-2743 259 G
sschell@southeastmn.edu
SCHELLACK, Emil, F ..... 913-971-3299 189 F
cpolice@mnu.edu
SCHELLENBERGER,
Lauren .... 573-288-6429 274 C
lschellenberger@culver.edu
SCHELLER, William, L .. 814-871-7912 419 A
scheller002@gannon.edu
SCHELLING, Jeffrey .... 815-226-4107 157 D
Jschelling@rockford.edu
SCHEMENT, Jorge, R .... 848-932-2021 306 F
jr.schement@rutgers.edu
SCHEMENT, Jorge, R .... 848-932-2021 307 B
jr.schement@oldqueens.rutgers.edu
SCHEMPER, Lugene, L . 616-526-6121 240 M
lschempe@calvin.edu
SCHENCK, Merlin .... 706-886-6831 132 F
mschenck@tfc.edu
SCHENEWERK, Randal .. 573-875-7256 273 D
raschenewerk@ccis.edu
SCHENK, Edwin .... 612-343-4490 263 H
eschenk@northcentral.edu
SCHENK, Evelyn .... 989-275-5000 245 C
evelyn.schenk@kirtland.edu
SCHENK, Glenn .... 310-287-4275.. 52 C
schenkga@wlac.edu
SCHENK, Kimberely ...... 925-969-2036.. 42 E
schenk@dvc.edu
SCHENK, Mark .... 207-834-8646 212 F
mark.schenk@maine.edu
SCHENK, Matthew, R .... 757-446-6043 507 B
schenkmr@evms.edu
SCHENK, Rebecca, J .... 716-878-4312 345 B
schenkrj@buffalostate.edu
SCHENK, Stacy, L .... 814-886-6357 427 B
sschenk@mtaloy.edu
SCHENKEL, Beverly, S .. 660-562-1149 280 A
bevs@nwmissouri.edu
SCHENKER, Beth .... 312-922-9012 160 E
bschenker@spertus.edu
SCHEPEL, Bill .... 708-239-4805 160 L
bill.schepel@trnty.edu
SCHEPENS, Bennett ...... 845-675-4543 337 B
bennett.schepens@nyack.edu
SCHEPENS, Dona, P ..... 845-675-4618 337 B
dona.schepens@nyack.edu
SCHEPP, Robina, C ...... 212-346-1281 337 I
rschepp@pace.edu
SCHEPPARD, Carol, A .. 540-828-5608 505 F
cscheppa@bridgewater.edu
SCHER, Anne .... 510-869-6130.. 61 J
ascher@samuelmerritt.edu
SCHERBERGER, Tom ...... 727-864-7978 101 P
scherbte@eckerd.edu
SCHERCZINGER, Carol .. 704-216-3923 365 F
carol.scherczinger@rccc.edu
SCHERER, Amanda .... 612-330-1720 253 K
scherer@augsburg.edu
SCHERER, Jean .... 715-346-2123 541 A
jscherer@uwsp.edu
SCHERER, Melanie, L ... 410-777-2237 213 E
mlscherer@aacc.edu
SCHERER, Tim .... 989-275-5000 245 C
tim.scherer@kirtland.edu
SCHERGER, Celinda ...... 419-448-3313 392 B
schergercm@tiffin.edu
SCHERLING, Sarah .... 303-524-5198.. 79 L
sscherling@ccu.edu
SCHERR, Linda .... 609-586-4800 303 D
scherrl@mccc.edu
SCHERRENS,
Maurice, W .... 803-321-5102 447 L
mscherrens@newberry.edu
SCHERSTEN, Mark .... 517-264-7667 250 B
mschersten@sienaheights.edu
SCHERTZ, Mary, H .... 574-296-6218 163 M
mschertz@ambs.edu
SCHERTZ, Ronald, L ..... 401-825-2179 441 C
rschertz@ccri.edu
SCHERZER, Karen .... 812-357-6522 173 A
kscherzer@saintmeinrad.edu
SCHETTER, Sheila .... 920-693-1238 543 B
sheila.schetter@gotoltc.edu
SCHETTINI-LYNCH,
Anne Marie .... 914-633-2480 328 F
aschettinilynch@iona.edu
SCHETTLER, Martha, A .. 330-569-5205 383 F
shettlerma@hiram.edu
SCHEUERMANN, Aimee 317-940-8123 164 L
arust@butler.edu
SCHEUERMANN, Joe .... 504-671-5452 203 F
jscheu@dcc.edu
SCHEULEN, Kathy .... 573-897-5000 282 I
SCHEUTZOW, Janice ..... 585-389-2310 334 B
jscheut1@naz.edu
SCHEWE, Sharon, R ..... 651-641-8228 255 C
schewe@csp.edu
SCHEXNEIDER,
Martha, J .... 337-421-6925 204 F
jo.schexneider@sowela.edu
SCHEXNIDER-FIELDS,
Ingenue, S .... 504-520-6209 209 E
itschexn@xula.edu
SCHEY, Mary .... 608-243-4364 543 C
mschey@madisoncollege.edu
SCHEYETTE, Anna, M .... 803-777-7886 450 B
anna.scheyette@sc.edu
SCHIAVELLI, Mel, D ..... 703-323-4291 516 C
mschiavelli@nvcc.edu
SCHIAVONI, Emily .... 802-447-4013 503 A
eschiavoni@svc.edu
SCHIAZZA, Douglas, J . 413-597-3696 238 E
douglas.schiazza@williams.edu
SCHIBSTED, Leslie .... 619-594-7287.. 35 E
lschibsted@mail.sdsu.edu
SCHICK, Beth Ann .... 814-871-7659 419 A
shick001@gannon.edu
SCHICK, Edgar .... 301-696-3623 215 E
schick@hood.edu
SCHICK, Marvin .... 732-985-6533 305 D
SCHICK, Wendell .... 419-227-3141 394 B
wschick@unoh.edu
SCHICKLING, William .... 716-614-5931 336 D
bschickling@niagaracc.suny.edu
SCHIDLOW, Daniel .... 215-895-2000 417 E
daniel.schidlow@drexelmed.edu
SCHIEBER, Amy, K .... 660-944-2847 273 E
aschieber@conception.edu
SCHIEBER, Craig .... 206-239-4500 520 K
cschieber@cityu.edu
SCHIEBER, Gary, W .... 816-604-1320 277 F
gary.schieber@mcckc.edu
SCHIEBER, Jeanette ...... 660-944-2839 273 E
jschieber@conception.edu
SCHIEFEN, Kathleen ...... 585-345-6975 326 F
kmschiefen@genesee.edu
SCHIELE, Evelyn, R .... 847-543-2622 142 G
eschiele@clcillinois.edu
SCHIELE, Jerome, H ...... 301-860-3705 220 B
jschiele@bowiestate.edu
SCHIERBEEK, Hannah ... 616-222-3000 245 D
hschierbeek@kuyper.edu
SCHIERER, John .... 858-795-5138.. 64 F
jschierer@shpdiscovery.org
SCHIERS, LaMont .... 520-417-4007.. 13 B
schiersl@cochise.edu
SCHIFF, Emanuel .... 845-356-1980 338 I
SCHIFF, Susan .... 864-656-4668 444 E
sschiff@clemson.edu
SCHIFF-ABRAMS,
Lindsey .... 661-255-1050.. 31 B
SCHIFFER, Peter, E .... 217-333-0034 162 A
pschiffe@illinois.edu
SCHIFFGENS, Hope .... 412-536-1266 422 E
hope.schiffgens@laroche.edu

SCHMITZ, Donna .... 701-252-3467 375 J dschmitz@uj.edu
SCHMITZ, Nancy, A ...... 248-370-3352 248 K schmitz@oakland.edu
SCHMITZ, Polly .... 516-877-3156 314 F pschmitz@adelphi.edu
SCHMITZ, Stevie .... 406-657-1134 288 G schmitzs@rocky.edu
SCHMOKE, Kurt, L .... 410-837-4866 221 B president@ubalt.edu
SCHMOLL, Claire, B ...... 207-786-6100 209 F cschmoll@bates.edu
SCHMOLL, Kevin .... 618-650-3324 159 I kschmol@siue.edu
SCHMOLL, Robert .... 724-589-2102 436 E rschmoll@thiel.edu
SCHMOOCK, Allen .... 208-792-2215 138 E atschmoock@lcsc.edu
SCHMOTZER, Mark .... 516-299-3547 330 F mark.schmotzer@liu.edu
SCHMUCKER, Angie ...... 248-370-3698 248 K schmucke@oakland.edu
SCHMUTTE, Gregory, T . 413-205-3364 221 G gregory.schmutte@aic.edu
SCHMUTZ, Betsy .... 314-968-6960 285 G schmutz@webster.edu
SCHNABEL, Robert, B ... 812-856-1079 167 J deanl@informatics.indiana.edu
SCHNABEL, William ...... 907-474-6222.. 10 I weschnabel@alaska.edu
SCHNABL, JC .... 413-545-5542 228 F schnabl@admin.umass.edu
SCHNACKENBERG, Scott .... 212-678-3706 349 I sps19@tc.columbia.edu
SCHNAIDMAN, Yaakov . 570-346-1747 440 G
SCHNALL, David, J .... 212-340-7705 353 P dschnall@yu.edu
SCHNAPP, Derek .... 217-206-7823 161 G schnapp.derek@uis.edu
SCHNARR, Carmin, A ... 812-888-4332 174 F cschnarr@vinu.edu
SCHNATZ, Kristofer .... 219-980-6793 168 C kschnatz@iun.edu
SCHNEFKE, Emilee .... 314-421-0949 283 B eschnefke@siba.edu
SCHNEIDER, Amye .... 620-792-9302 184 I schneidera@bartonccc.edu
SCHNEIDER, Angela ...... 510-885-3000.. 33 C
SCHNEIDER, Brandt, L .. 806-743-2700 490 A brandt.schneider@ttuhsc.edu
SCHNEIDER, Carrie .... 651-423-8244 258 E carrie.schneider@dctc.edu
SCHNEIDER, Chad .... 740-389-4636 386 B schneiderc@mtc.edu
SCHNEIDER, Colleen .... 785-841-9640 190 F cschneider@pcitraining.edu
SCHNEIDER, Deb .... 415-749-4587.. 62 I dschneider@sfai.edu
SCHNEIDER, Debbie ...... 314-531-7925 281 M bksustlouis@bncollege.com
SCHNEIDER, Greg .... 913-288-7155 188 G gschneid@kckcc.edu
SCHNEIDER, Helen .... 410-617-2995 216 D hschneider@loyola.edu
SCHNEIDER, Howard .... 631-632-6265 344 C howard.schneider@stonybrook.edu
SCHNEIDER, Jed, S ...... 315-445-4500 330 B schneij@lemoyne.edu
SCHNEIDER, Jeffrey, A . 814-332-3355 411 F jschneider@allegheny.edu
SCHNEIDER, Joan .... 660-562-1250 280 A jschneider@nwmissouri.edu
SCHNEIDER, Joanne ..... 315-228-7362 321 H jschneider@colgate.edu
SCHNEIDER, Julia .... 816-271-4369 279 E schneide@missouriwestern.edu
SCHNEIDER, Karen .... 707-664-4004.. 36 C karen.schneider@sonoma.edu
SCHNEIDER, Kay .... 303-273-3087.. 80 O kschnei@mines.edu
SCHNEIDER, Kenneth, J .... 507-266-7095 254 F schneider.kenneth@mayo.edu
SCHNEIDER, Marc .... 770-426-2700 128 C marcs@life.edu
SCHNEIDER, Mary Ann . 216-381-1680 388 A mschneider@ndc.edu
SCHNEIDER, Mary Ann . 216-373-6534 388 A mschneider@ndc.edu
SCHNEIDER, Michael, P .... 620-242-0405 189 E schneidm@mcpherson.edu
SCHNEIDER, Richard, W .... 802-485-2065 502 G rschneider@norwich.edu
SCHNEIDER, Scott .... 417-255-7258 279 B scottshcneider@missouristate.edu
SCHNEIDER, Shelly, O .. 856-691-8600 301 H sschneider@cccnj.edu
SCHNEIDER, Steve .... 402-872-2393 292 C sschneider@peru.edu
SCHNEIDER, Tammi ...... 909-607-3217.. 39 E tammi.schneider@cgu.edu
SCHNEIDER, Terrance ... 678-407-5333 125 B tschneider@ggc.edu
SCHNEIDER, Tina .... 419-995-8326 384 E tschneider@lima.ohio-state.edu
SCHNEIDER, Todd .... 970-542-3218.. 84 A todd.schneider@morgancc.edu
SCHNEIDER, Tom .... 727-864-8409 101 P schneite@eckerd.edu
SCHNEIDER, Wayne, R . 785-827-5541 189 A kwaynes@kwu.edu
SCHNEIDER BINGHAM, Stacy Lee .... 845-437-5285 351 H stbingham@vassar.edu
SCHNEIDERMAN, Davis 847-735-5282 149 H dschneid@lakeforest.edu
SCHNEIDERMAN, Edward, S .... 718-933-6700 333 F eschneid@monroecollege.edu
SCHNEIKART-LUEBBE, Christine .... 316-978-3149 192 D christine.luebbe@wichita.edu
SCHNELL, Ann, B .... 585-785-1532 325 E ann.schnell@flcc.edu
SCHNELL, Carolyn, A ... 701-231-7189 374 C carolyn.schnell@ndsu.edu
SCHNELL, Lisa, J .... 802-656-9100 503 C lisa.schnell@uvm.edu
SCHNELL, William .... 610-353-7630 421 P
SCHNELLER, Beverly ..... 615-460-5630 455 D beverly.schneller@belmont.edu
SCHNELLER, Maribeth .. 215-895-6058 417 E maribeth.schneller@drexel.edu
SCHNEPF, Chester, H ... 203-285-2151.. 89 B cschnepf@gwcc.commnet.edu
SCHNETZLER, Greta ...... 415-476-5003.. 72 C gschnetzler@legal.ucsf.edu
SCHNIER, Kathleen .... 602-557-1228.. 18 H kathleen.schnier@phoenix.edu
SCHNIERLE, Caryn .... 312-567-5240 147 E cschnier@iit.edu
SCHNITKEY, Dawn, I ..... 517-750-1200 250 F danderso@arbor.edu
SCHNITZER, Carol, N ... 518-580-5849 342 I cschnitz@skidmore.edu
SCHNOOR, Barry .... 540-665-4543 512 E bschnoor@su.edu
SCHNOOR, Chuck .... 520-494-5303.. 12 R chuck.schnoor@centralaz.edu
SCHNOOR, Neal, H .... 308-865-8208 293 G schnoorn@unk.edu
SCHNUR, Fred .... 212-678-8008 329 H frschnur@jtsa.edu
SCHOBER, Michael .... 212-229-5727 334 C schober@newschool.edu
SCHOCHET, Ezra, B .... 323-937-3763.. 77 J eschochet@yoec.edu
SCHODOWSKI, Francis, G .... 717-867-6446 423 I schodows@lvc.edu
SCHOELER, Mary .... 608-757-7769 542 L mschoeler@blackhawk.edu
SCHOEN, David .... 716-286-8001 336 E schoen@niagara.edu
SCHOEN, Lauren .... 425-602-3105 519 J lschoen@bastyr.edu
SCHOEN, Randall .... 541-552-6258 409 G schoenr@sou.edu
SCHOEN, Susan .... 641-269-4580 178 I schoen@grinnell.edu
SCHOENBACHLER, Denise .... 815-753-1755 154 I denises@niu.edu
SCHOENBERG, Lynn ..... 386-822-7000 117 A
SCHOENBERGER, Alfred 718-384-5460 353 K
SCHOENECKE, Marvin ... 417-690-2204 273 C schoenecke@cofo.edu
SCHOENECKER, Mark ... 719-587-7696.. 78 I mwschoen@adams.edu
SCHOENEERGER, Susan .... 860-509-9519.. 90 G sschoeneerger@hartsem.edu
SCHOENFELD, Jennifer . 785-460-4684 186 D jennifer.schoenfeld@colbycc.edu
SCHOENFELD, Michael . 919-681-3788 356 E michael.schoenfeld@duke.edu
SCHOENFELD, Michael . 802-443-2272 502 E schoenfe@middlebury.edu
SCHOENFELD, Nancy .... 508-854-7426 232 F nschoenfeld@qcc.mass.edu
SCHOENFELDER, Louis . 605-995-2191 452 C loschoen@dwu.edu
SCHOENGOOD, Matthew, G .... 212-817-7400 319 B mschoengood@gc.cuny.edu
SCHOENHERR, Holly ..... 320-308-3203 261 E hjschoenherr@stcloudstate.edu
SCHOENIG, Demetra, C 574-631-7633 174 A dschoenig@nd.edu
SCHOENINGER, Patti .... 303-458-4347.. 85 G pschoeni@regis.edu
SCHOENLE, JR., Gerald, W .... 716-645-2230 343 E gws3@buffalo.edu
SCHOENWILL, Chad ..... 719-389-6941.. 79 M cschoenwill@coloradocollege.edu
SCHOEPHOERSTER, Richard, T .... 915-747-6444 494 B schoephoerster@utep.edu
SCHOFER, Marie .... 319-895-4159 177 A mschofer@cornellcollege.edu
SCHOFFMAN, Garth, D . 330-684-8938 393 A gds@uakron.edu
SCHOFIELD, Anna, M ... 614-222-3274 380 F aschofield@ccad.edu
SCHOFIELD, Audrey ...... 561-803-2145 109 G audrey_schofield@pba.edu
SCHOFIELD, John .... 410-293-1521 549 B pao@usna.edu
SCHOFIELD, Sherri .... 906-248-8424 240 J sschofield@bmcc.edu
SCHOFIELD, William ..... 559-244-5920.. 68 J wil.schofield@scccd.edu
SCHOH, Eric .... 507-457-5210 262 D eschoh@winona.edu
SCHOKKER, Andrea ...... 218-726-7104 264 G aschokke@d.umn.edu
SCHOKNECHT, Pat .... 407-646-2700 111 H pschoknecht@rollins.edu
SCHOL, Kristin .... 202-885-8675.. 97 E kschol@wesleyseminary.edu
SCHOLER, Steven, A ..... 402-280-2180 290 B StevenScholer@creighton.edu
SCHOLL, Bill .... 414-288-4796 537 B william.scholl@marquette.edu
SCHOLL, Heather .... 847-214-7177 144 F hscholl@elgin.edu
SCHOLL-FIEDLER, Anne 443-394-9257 218 E ascholl-fiedler@stevenson.edu
SCHOLLA, James .... 320-308-5028 261 F jscholla@sctcc.edu
SCHOLLES, Holly .... 503-760-3131 404 I holly@birthingway.edu
SCHOLLMEIER, John ..... 507-457-1436 264 B jschollm@smumn.edu
SCHOLTE, Hugh .... 509-793-2291 520 B
SCHOLTEN, Brian .... 607-274-3075 328 H bscholten@ithaca.edu
SCHOLZ, Ben .... 201-761-7109 307 K bscholz@saintpeters.edu
SCHOLZ, Claudia .... 404-270-5897 132 D cscholz@spelman.edu
SCHOLZ, Daniel, J .... 414-410-4010 535 C djscholz@stritch.edu
SCHOLZ, Joan, M .... 262-243-5700 535 I joan.scholz@cuw.edu
SCHOLZ, John, K .... 608-263-2303 539 D jkscholz@ls.wisc.edu
SCHOLZE, Roberta .... 217-351-2383 155 I rscholze@parkland.edu
SCHOMBURG, Jeff .... 210-431-5073 481 C jschomburg@stmarytx.edu
SCHONBERGER, Beth .... 215-635-7300 419 D bschonberger@gratz.edu
SCHONE, Jeffrey, L .... 507-354-8221 257 A schonejl@mlc-wels.edu
SCHONES, Savannath ... 580-774-3233 402 G savannah.schones@swosu.edu
SCHONFELD, Leah, S ... 843-953-6922 444 C leah.schonfeld@citadel.edu
SCHONGALLA-BOWMAN, Nancy, L .... 609-497-7890 305 B nancy.schongalla@ptsem.edu
SCHOOF, Aaron, D .... 773-244-5564 154 G aschoof@northpark.edu
SCHOOFF, Daniel, J ...... 608-363-2408 534 L schooffd@beloit.edu
SCHOOK, Lawrence ...... 217-265-5440 161 E schook@uillinois.edu
SCHOOLCRAFT, Tracy, A .... 717-477-1148 431 F tascho@ship.edu
SCHOOLMASTER, Andrew .... 817-257-7160 486 G a.schoolmaster@tcu.edu
SCHOON, Perry .... 309-438-2453 147 I pschoon@ilstu.edu
SCHOONARD, Eric .... 423-236-2290 460 K erics@southern.edu
SCHOONMAKER, Linda . 509-793-2002 520 B lindas@bigbend.edu
SCHOONMAKER, Martha .... 240-567-2007 217 B martha.schoonmaker@montgomerycollege.edu
SCHOONMAKER, Nancy 765-677-2605 169 C nancy.schoonmaker@indwes.edu
SCHOONMAKER, Stephen .... 501-337-5000.. 20 H sschoonmaker@coto.edu
SCHOONOVER, Sandra . 406-243-2611 287 D sandra.schoonover@umontana.edu
SCHOONVELD, Tim .... 616-395-7698 244 A schoonveld@hope.edu
SCHOOP, Michael .... 216-987-4034 381 A michael.schoop@tri-c.edu
SCHOOS, Ketwana .... 724-503-1001 439 B kschoos@washjeff.edu
SCHOPEN, Annamarie ... 847-214-7185 144 F aschopen@elgin.edu
SCHOPP, Mary, C .... 414-847-3215 537 F maryschopp@miad.edu
SCHOPP, Mary, E .... 312-942-7035 158 A me_schopp@rush.edu
SCHOPPERT, John .... 541-506-6080 405 C jschoppert@cgcc.edu
SCHORE, Robin .... 609-586-4800 303 D schorer@mccc.edu
SCHORNACK, Julie, A ... 714-449-7418.. 53 D jschornack@ketchum.edu
SCHORNACK, Kent, A ... 515-263-2986 178 H kschornack@grandview.edu
SCHORR, Timothy, B .... 608-796-3774 542 H tbschorr@viterbo.edu
SCHOTT, Brett, T .... 314-367-8700 281 G brett.schott@stlcop.edu
SCHOTT, Jonathan .... 585-271-3657 340 B admissions@stbernards.edu
SCHOTT, Linda, K .... 207-768-9525 212 H linda.schott@umpi.edu
SCHOTT, Richard, G ..... 716-839-8218 323 F rschott@daemen.edu
SCHOTTLAENDER, Brian E, C .... 858-534-3060.. 72 B becs@uscd.edu
SCHOU, Larry .... 605-677-5481 453 F larry.schou@usd.edu
SCHOUWE, Cecilia .... 657-278-3128.. 33 E cschowe@fullerton.edu
SCHOVANEC, Lawrence . 806-742-2184 489 F lawrence.schovanec@ttu.edu
SCHOWE, Dorothy, A .... 636-584-6507 274 J dot.schowe@eastcentral.edu
SCHRAD, Julie .... 563-884-5818 182 D julie.schrad@palmer.edu
SCHRADER, Cheryl, B .. 573-341-4116 284 C schrader@mst.edu
SCHRADER, Claudia, V . 718-289-5139 318 E claudia.schrader@bcc.cuny.edu
SCHRADER, Ed, L .... 770-534-6110 121 G eschrader@brenau.edu
SCHRADER, Kathleen .... 805-289-6430.. 75 E kschrader@vcccd.edu
SCHRADER, Marcus ...... 317-789-8240 165 F mschrader@crossroads.edu
SCHRADER, Thomas ..... 630-942-3890 142 F schrader@cod.edu
SCHRADER, Vicki .... 636-949-4908 276 L vschrader@lindenwood.edu
SCHRAGE, Charles .... 217-206-7395 161 G schrage.charles@uis.edu
SCHRAGE, Doug .... 907-474-7681.. 10 I drschrage@alaska.edu
SCHRAGE, Jim .... 661-362-3222.. 40 H jim.schrage@canyons.edu
SCHRAM, David .... 336-727-7102 357 B schramd@greensboro.edu
SCHRAM, Kandis .... 865-981-8290 458 E kandis.schram@maryvillecollege.edu
SCHRAMM, Beth .... 540-261-8596 512 J beth.schramm@svu.edu
SCHRAMM, Christine, M .... 937-229-2229 393 E cschramm1@udayton.edu
SCHRAMM, Dorothy .... 315-279-5862 329 K dschramm@keuka.edu
SCHRAMMEL, Debra, S 215-670-9270 428 A dsschrammel@peirce.edu
SCHRAMSKI, Holley, W 706-542-6860 132 H hscrams@uga.edu
SCHRAND, Rita .... 513-751-1206 376 A rita@aic-arts.edu
SCHRANZ, Michael .... 719-632-8116.. 83 H mschranz@intelliteccollege.edu
SCHRANZ, William .... 402-643-7246 289 J bill.schranz@cune.edu
SCHRAUTH, Jodi, S ...... 920-923-7615 537 A jsschrauth11@marianuniversity.edu
SCHRECK, Christopher, J .... 614-885-5585 390 G cschreck@pcj.edu
SCHRECK, Jayne, A ...... 309-457-2129 153 B jayne@monmouthcollege.edu
SCHRECK, Peter .... 484-384-2973 427 I pshreck@eastern.edu
SCHREFFLER, Paul .... 304-367-4920 531 E Paul.Schreffler@pierpont.edu

SCHREIBER, Amy ... 717-901-5145 420 I
aschreiber@harrisburgu.edu

SCHREIBER, Carl, W ... 540-338-1776 511 A

SCHREIBER, Cody ... 605-331-6632 454 E
cody.schreiber@usiouxfalls.edu

SCHREIBER, Jim ... 785-628-4279 187 A
jschreib@fhsu.edu

SCHREIBER, Meredith ... 503-399-2535 404 L
meredith.schreiber@chemeketa.edu

SCHREIBER, Nancy ... 512-428-1287 481 B
nschreib@stedwards.edu

SCHREIBER, Rachel ... 415-749-4583.. 62 I
rschreiber@sfai.edu

SCHREIBMAN, Andi ... 925-424-1585.. 37 O
aschreibman@laspositascollege.edu

SCHREIBMAN,
Marla, H ... 718-951-5065 318 F
marlag@brooklyn.cuny.edu

SCHREIER, Chad ... 406-657-1746 287 H
chad.schreier@msubillings.edu

SCHREIN, OSF,
Shannon ... 419-824-3819 385 F
sschrein@lourdes.edu

SCHREINER, Bruce ... 801-524-8162 498 J
Bruceas@ldsbc.edu

SCHREINER, Rebecca ... 618-537-6514 152 C
rlschreiner@mckendree.edu

SCHREINER, Steven ... 609-771-2529 301 E
schreine@tcnj.edu

SCHREINER, Tom ... 706-419-1255 123 F
tom.schreiner@covenant.edu

SCHRIEFER, John ... 304-647-6205 533 B
jschriefer@osteo.wvsom.edu

SCHRIER, Hugh ... 301-387-3098 215 A
hugh.schrier@garrettcollege.edu

SCHRINER, Brian ... 305-348-3181 114 G
Brian.Schriner@fiu.edu

SCHRIVER, Kevin ... 417-328-1725 282 D
kschriver@sbuniv.edu

SCHROCK, Lynford ... 740-857-1311 390 L
lschrock@rosedale.edu

SCHROCK, Missy, K ... 574-296-6223 163 M
mkschrock@ambs.edu

SCHRODER, Karen ... 610-796-8203 412 C
karen.schroder@alvernia.edu

SCHRODER, Michael ... 760-750-8727.. 35 B
mschrode@csusm.edu

SCHROEDER, Alisha ... 406-265-4191 288 A
alisha.schroeder@msun.edu

SCHROEDER, Brian ... 973-803-5000 305 A
brschroeder@pillar.edu

SCHROEDER, Brock ... 740-392-6868 387 B
brock.schroeder@mvnu.edu

SCHROEDER, Cynthia ... 636-949-4318 276 L
cschroeder@lindenwood.edu

SCHROEDER, David, E .. 973-803-5000 305 A
dschroeder@pillar.edu

SCHROEDER, Debbie ... 308-865-8950 293 G
schroederd@unk.edu

SCHROEDER, Debra ... 218-723-6595 255 A
dschroed@css.edu

SCHROEDER, Dennis, J 818-364-7650.. 51 G
Schroedj@lamission.edu

SCHROEDER,
Douglas, R ... 651-631-5160 265 D
drschroeder@unwsp.edu

SCHROEDER, Francie ... 512-863-1454 483 G
schroedf@southwestern.edu

SCHROEDER, Fritz ... 410-516-8631 216 A
fschroed@jhu.edu

SCHROEDER, Henning .. 612-625-2809 265 C
schro601@umn.edu

SCHROEDER, Jennifer ... 785-243-1435 186 A
jschroeder@cloud.edu

SCHROEDER, Lisa ... 409-880-2137 488 E
lwschroeder@lit.edu

SCHROEDER, Lori ... 309-341-7214 149 G
lkschroeder@knox.edu

SCHROEDER, Matt, J ... 419-530-2211 394 E
matt.schroeder@utoledo.edu

SCHROEDER, Nick ... 828-327-7000 361 B
nschroeder@cvcc.edu

SCHROEDER, Petra ... 608-262-1044 539 D
pschroeder@wisc.edu

SCHROEDER, Philip ... 719-587-7306.. 78 I
philip_schroeder@adams.edu

SCHROEDER, Ross ... 979-830-4118 469 F
ross.schroeder@blinn.edu

SCHROEDER, Sally ... 515-964-6291 177 B
ssschroeder@dmacc.edu

SCHROEDER, Sandra ... 620-343-4600 186 I
sschroeder@fhtc.edu

SCHROEDER, Stephanie 570-961-4161.. 16 L
Stephanie.Schroeder@PennFoster.edu

SCHROEDER, Stephanie 320-629-5126 260 H
schroeders@pinetech.edu

SCHROEDER,
Stephen, C ... 727-816-3403 110 B
schroes@phsc.edu

SCHROEDER, Steven ... 414-443-8601 542 I
steve.schroeder@wlc.edu

SCHROEDER, Tracy ... 617-353-1150 224 E
tas@bu.edu

SCHROEDER-BIEK,
Julie ... 574-284-4333 172 G
jsbiek@saintmarys.edu

SCHROEDER-GREEN,
Suzanna ... 440-646-8178 394 G
sschroeder@ursuline.edu

SCHROER, Tara ... 785-460-5487 186 D
tara.schroer@colbycc.edu

SCHROER, Timothy ... 507-786-3615 264 C
schroert@stolaf.edu

SCHROM, Patricia ... 701-671-2430 375 B
patricia.schrom@ndscs.edu

SCHROTE, James, D ... 202-994-0543.. 95 D
jschroth@gwu.edu

SCHROTH, Katie ... 715-346-3930 541 A
kschroth@uwsp.edu

SCHRUM, Jake, B ... 276-944-6107 507 E
jschrum@ehc.edu

SCHRUM, Mindi-Kim ... 505-566-3261 312 K
schrumm@sanjuancollege.edu

SCHUBERT, Donna ... 334-670-5830.... 8 A
schubert@troy.edu

SCHUBERT,
Marianne, A ... 336-758-5273 372 G
schubem@wfu.edu

SCHUBERT, Phil ... 325-674-2412 466 I
schubert@acu.edu

SCHUBERT, Susan ... 410-837-5993 221 B
sschubert@ubalt.edu

SCHUCH, Debra ... 717-299-7408 436 D
schuch@stevenscollege.edu

SCHUCHARDT, Bob ... 605-229-8406 453 A
bob.schuchardt@presentation.edu

SCHUCHARDT,
Maureen ... 605-229-8427 453 A
maureen.schuchardt@presentation.edu

SCHUCHERT, Michael ... 703-284-3810 510 B
michael.schuchert@marymount.edu

SCHUCK, Emily, G ... 740-376-4712 386 A
schucke@marietta.edu

SCHUCKEL, Harry ... 410-837-4743 221 B
hschuckel@ubalt.edu

SCHUELKE, Mark ... 231-591-5916 242 L
MarkSchuelke@ferris.edu

SCHUELKE, Nicholle ... 605-331-6765 454 E
nicholle.schuelke@usiouxfalls.edu

SCHUELLER, Kenneth ... 660-543-4721 283 F
schueller@ucmo.edu

SCHUENAMAN,
Bruce, R ... 361-593-3528 486 A
brs@tamuk.edu

SCHUEREN, Monika ... 516-686-7615 335 F
mschuere@nyit.edu

SCHUERMER, David, A . 270-824-8633 196 F
david.schuermer@kctcs.edu

SCHUESSLER, George ... 212-678-3302 349 I
gs56@tc.columbia.edu

SCHUESSLER, Jennifer .. 678-839-5640 133 F
jschuess@westga.edu

SCHUETTE, Jan ... 323-856-7741.. 27 H
schuette@afi.com

SCHUETTE, Stefani, M .. 636-949-4900 276 L
sschuette@lindenwood.edu

SCHUETZ, Bill ... 541-463-3355 406 F
schuetzb@lanecc.edu

SCHUETZ, Gina ... 618-545-3099 149 C
gschuetz@kaskaskia.edu

SCHUETZ, Ronald, L ... 317-738-8160 166 B
rschuetz@franklincollege.edu

SCHUH, Jane ... 701-231-8804 374 C
jane.schuh@ndsu.edu

SCHUH, Mary Paula ... 859-572-5122 199 A
schuh@nku.edu

SCHUHERT, Scott ... 607-778-5681 344 F
schuhertsm@sunybroome.edu

SCHUHMANN,
Richard, J ... 207-985-7976 210 H
schuhmann@landingschool.edu

SCHUILING, Kerri ... 906-227-2920 248 B
kschuili@nmu.edu

SCHULER, Carol, M ... 304-642-5576 529 I
schulerc@dewv.edu

SCHULER, Jill ... 502-447-1000 199 G
jschuler@spencerian.edu

SCHULER, Nathan ... 513-875-3344 379 G
nathan.schuler@chatfield.edu

SCHULER, Stephanie ... 304-647-6347 533 B
sschuler@osteo.wvsom.edu

SCHULL, Gail ... 208-732-6232 137 K
gschull@csi.edu

SCHULL,
Stephanie Grace ... 480-860-2700.. 13 Q
sschull@taliesin.edu

SCHULLER, Aimee ... 330-823-2683 394 A
schullal@mountunion.edu

SCHULMAN, Avrohom .. 908-354-6057 310 A

SCHULMAN, Jane ... 718-482-5302 320 B
janes@lagcc.cuny.edu

SCHULMAN, Sharon ... 609-626-3541 308 E
sharon.schulman@stockton.edu

SCHULT, Larry ... 231-591-2829 242 L
LarrySchult@ferris.edu

SCHULT, Richard ... 310-377-5501.. 53 E
mschult@marymountcalifornia.edu

SCHULT, Robert, W ... 909-621-8025.. 39 E
rwschult@cgu.edu

SCHULTE, Brandy ... 660-831-4108 279 D
schulteb@moval.edu

SCHULTE, Cynthia ... 641-844-5602 179 J
Cindy.Schulte@iavalley.edu

SCHULTE, David ... 314-529-9329 277 B
dschulte@maryville.edu

SCHULTE, Gerald ... 218-683-8557 260 F
gerald.schulte@northlandcollege.edu

SCHULTE, Mary ... 618-468-3300 150 E
mschulte@lc.edu

SCHULTE, Nancy ... 540-665-4530 512 E
nschulte@su.edu

SCHULTE, Priscilla ... 907-228-4548.. 11 A
priscilla.schulte@uas.alaska.edu

SCHULTE, R. Gregg ... 706-886-6831 132 F
gschulte@tfc.edu

SCHULTE, Tim ... 660-831-4148 279 D
schultet@moval.edu

SCHULTE, Vickie ... 618-437-5321 156 I
schultev@rlc.edu

SCHULTE-SHOBERG,
Kim ... 715-232-1285 541 B
schulteshobergk@uwstout.edu

SCHULTES, Brian ... 775-831-1314 296 F
bschultes@sierranevada.edu

SCHULTHEIS, Luke, D ... 804-827-8737 514 F
ldschultheis@vcu.edu

SCHULTHEIS, Stephen .. 678-466-4070 122 J
stephenschultheis@clayton.edu

SCHULTHEISS, Donna ... 216-687-9387 380 D
D.SCHULTHEISS@csuohio.edu

SCHULTINGKEMPER,
Kathy ... 910-323-5614 355 E
registrar@ccbs.edu

SCHULTIS, Ann ... 816-584-6704 280 F
ann.schultis@park.edu

SCHULTZ, Amber ... 320-308-3870 261 E
amschultz@stcloudstate.edu

SCHULTZ, Barb ... 563-425-5283 183 G
schultzb@uiu.edu

SCHULTZ, Barry ... 901-572-2500 455 C
barry.schultz@bchs.edu

SCHULTZ, Bruce ... 907-786-6108.. 10 H
brschultz@uaa.alaska.edu

SCHULTZ, David ... 940-565-3940 492 D
david.schultz@unt.edu

SCHULTZ, Eric ... 605-882-5284 452 G
eric.schultz@lakeareatech.edu

SCHULTZ, Jonathan ... 972-279-6511 467 F
JSchultz@amberton.edu

SCHULTZ, Joseph, P ... 607-777-2187 343 D
jschultz@binghamton.edu

SCHULTZ, Kelly ... 814-868-9900 418 C
schultzk@erieit.edu

SCHULTZ, Kevin, J ... 989-964-4049 249 G
kschultz@svsu.edu

SCHULTZ, Linda ... 860-768-4169.. 92 F
schultz@hartford.edu

SCHULTZ, Michael, J ... 618-650-4628 159 I
mschult@siue.edu

SCHULTZ, Robert ... 845-434-5750 349 C
rschultz@sullivan.suny.edu

SCHULTZ, Roger, D ... 434-592-4030 509 G
rschultz@liberty.edu

SCHULTZ, Roger, W ... 951-487-3002.. 55 A
rschultz@msjc.edu

SCHULTZ, William, A ... 414-955-4780 537 C
wschultz@mcw.edu

SCHULZ, Christa ... 360-416-7974 527 A
christa.schulz@skagit.edu

SCHULZ, Chuck ... 309-341-7205 149 G
cschulz@knox.edu

SCHULZ, Greg ... 714-992-7001.. 56 F
gschulz@fullcoll.edu

SCHULZ, Jack ... 701-483-1068 373 H
Jack.Schulz@dickinsonstate.edu

SCHULZ, Jerry ... 541-383-7275 404 K
jschulz@cocc.edu

SCHULZ, Karyn ... 410-837-4775 221 B
kschulz@ubalt.edu

SCHULZ, Kathy, L ... 201-216-5667 308 D
kathy.schulz@stevens.edu

SCHULZ, Kirk, H ... 785-532-6221 188 H
kirks@ksu.edu

SCHULZ, Michael ... 406-683-7492 287 E
mike.schulz@umwestern.edu

SCHULZ, Paul, A ... 914-337-9300 323 A
paul.schulz@concordia-ny.edu

SCHULZ, Phyllis ... 212-817-7460 319 B
pschulz@gc.cuny.edu

SCHULZ, Robert ... 619-594-5901.. 35 E
rschulz@mail.sdsu.edu

SCHULZ, Scott ... 623-845-3876.. 14 N
scott.schulz@gccaz.edu

SCHULZ, Scott ... 218-726-7171 264 G
sschulz1@d.umn.edu

SCHULZ, Scott ... 440-826-6970 377 D
saschulz@bw.edu

SCHULZ, Steve, D ... 641-422-4000 181 E
schulste@niacc.edu

SCHULZE, Edee ... 805-565-6028.. 76 K
eschulze@westmont.edu

SCHULZE, Lori, A ... 920-748-8310 538 I
schulzel@ripon.edu

SCHULZE, Louann, T ... 817-515-1280 484 B
louann.schulze@tccd.edu

SCHULZKE, Mario ... 406-243-2323 287 D
mario.schulzke@umontana.edu

SCHUM, Jennifer ... 919-530-6658 370 C
jschum@nccu.edu

SCHUMACHER, Bett ... 209-946-2314.. 73 C
bschumacher1@pacific.edu

SCHUMACHER, Betty, A 701-845-7412 374 D
betty.schumacher@vcsu.edu

SCHUMACHER,
Bryan, J ... 605-394-2215 454 B
bryan.schumacher@sdsmt.edu

SCHUMACHER,
Charlotte ... 806-291-3549 496 K
schumacherc@wbu.edu

SCHUMACHER,
Daniel, J ... 715-836-5858 539 E
schumadj@uwec.edu

SCHUMACHER, Frank ... 269-749-7668 249 A
fschumacher@olivetcollege.edu

SCHUMACHER, Gail ... 847-233-7700 155 B
gschumacher@nc.edu

SCHUMACHER, Janette . 484-664-3180 427 C
schumach@muhlenberg.edu

SCHUMACHER, Lauren .. 847-233-7700 155 B
lwschumacher@nc.edu

SCHUMACHER,
Lawrence ... 847-233-7700 155 B
lschumacher@nc.edu

SCHUMACHER, Lillian ... 419-448-3053 392 B
schumacherlb@tiffin.edu

SCHUMACHER,
Mary Jeanne ... 812-357-6501 173 A
mschumacher@saintmeinrad.edu

SCHUMACHER, Michele 540-831-5434 511 C
bov@radford.edu

SCHUMACHER, Ron ... 419-448-3584 392 B
schumacherrm@tiffin.edu

SCHUMACHER, Scott ... 979-830-4172 469 F
scott.schumacher@blinn.edu

SCHUMAKER, Ashley ... 304-766-3112 533 C
aschumaker@wvstateu.edu

SCHUMAKER, Terry, W . 641-422-4170 181 E
schumter@niacc.edu

SCHUMAN, Alan, M ... 410-386-8495 214 B
aschuman@carrollcc.edu

SCHUMAN, John ... 205-329-7945.... 3 C
john.schuman@ecacolleges.com

SCHUMAN, Shmuel ... 847-982-2500 146 A
schuman@htc.edu

SCHUMANN, James ... 651-523-2100 256 B
jschumann01@hamline.edu

SCHUMANN, Kenneth ... 503-352-2180 408 I
schumank@pacificu.edu

SCHUMANN, Patricia ... 518-244-2097 340 A
schump@sage.edu

SCHUMANN, Patricia, J 304-766-3020 533 C
pschumann@wvstateu.edu

SCHUMANN, Renae ... 281-649-3300 475 B
rschumann@hbu.edu

SCHUMANN, Sherry, L . 972-548-6803 471 C
sschumann@collin.edu

SCHUNK, Jill ... 812-855-5646 167 J
jschunk@iu.edu

SCHUPACK, Sara ... 773-481-8810 142 D
schupack1@ccc.edu

SCHUPPERT, Cindy ... 503-352-3191 408 I
schuppec@pacificu.edu

SCHUR, Jill ... 773-508-7392 151 E
jschur@luc.edu

SCHURMAN, Jane ... 610-957-5700 416 G
jschurman@dccc.edu

SCHURMAN, Susan, J .. 848-932-6965 307 B
schurman@dceo.rutgers.edu

SCHURMANN, Linda ... 605-886-6777 452 I
lschurmann@mtmc.edu

SCHUSTER, Danny ... 516-295-5700 354 A

SCHUSTER, Julian, Z ... 314-246-8242 285 G
julianschuster@webster.edu

SCHUSTER, Leslie ... 401-456-9723 442 A
lschuster@ric.edu

SCHUSTER,
Sheldon, M ... 909-607-0108.. 39 H
sheldon_schuster@kgi.edu

SCHUSTER, Stacy .... 609-771-3214 301 E
schuster@tcnj.edu
SCHUSTER-MATLOCK,
Tracy .... 563-333-6049 182 E
SchusterTracy@sau.edu
SCHUSTER WEBB,
Karen 937-769-1826 376M
kschusterwebb@antioch.edu
SCHUSTEREIT, Roger .... 806-874-3571 470 J
roger.schustereit@clarendoncollege.edu
SCHUTH, Kristen .... 585-345-6898 326 F
keschuth@genesee.edu
SCHUTT, Michelle .... 208-732-6863 137 K
mschutt@csi.edu
SCHUTT, Stephen, D ..... 847-735-5100 149 H
presiden@lakeforest.edu
SCHUTTA, Katharine ..... 312-629-6821 158 J
kschutta@saic.edu
SCHUTTE, Thomas, F .... 718-636-3647 338 E
tschutte@pratt.edu
SCHUTTEN, Mary .... 408-924-2915.. 36 B
mary.schutten@sjsu.edu
SCHUTTER, Amy .... 530-242-7628.. 66 C
aschutter@shastacollege.edu
SCHUTZ, Christine .... 208-459-5524 137 J
cschutz@collegeofidaho.edu
SCHUTZ, Greg .... 615-366-3933 461 B
greg.schutz@tbr.edu
SCHUTZLER, Lyndon ..... 831-646-4221.. 54 H
lschutzler@mpc.edu
SCHUTZMAN, Carissa ... 859-442-1706 196 A
carissa.schutzman@kctcs.edu
SCHUYLER, Lori, G 804-289-8781 513M
lschuyle@richmond.edu
SCHUYLER, Nancy .... 215-489-2946 416 H
nancy.schuyler@delval.edu
SCHWAB, Brandon .... 828-227-7495 372 C
beschwab@wcu.edu
SCHWAB, Kenneth, L .... 615-868-6503 459 E
kschwab@mtsa.edu
SCHWAB, Linda .... 615-383-4848 466 F
lschwab@watkins.edu
SCHWAB, Mary, S .... 540-828-5487 505 F
mschwab@bridgewater.edu
SCHWAB, Nancy .... 916-660-7900.. 66 E
nschwab@sierracollege.edu
SCHWAB, Richard .... 860-486-3813.. 92 C
richard.schwab@uconn.edu
SCHWAB, Steve, J .... 901-448-4796 465 G
sschwab@uthsc.edu
SCHWAB, Vicky .... 507-389-7219 262 A
vicky.schwab@southcentral.edu
SCHWAB, Victoria .... 952-358-8671 260 D
victoria.schwab@normandale.edu
SCHWABE, Jean, D .... 478-289-2464 124 B
jdschwabe@ega.edu
SCHWABROW, Lynsey .. 262-472-1801 541 D
schwabrl@uww.edu
SCHWAGER, Kathleen ... 860-773-1523.. 90 C
kschwager@txcc.commnet.edu
SCHWAIG, Kathy, S 470-578-6425 127M
kschwaig@kennesaw.edu
SCHWAIGER, Patsy .... 513-244-4371 387 A
patsy.schwaiger@msj.edu
SCHWALBACH, Eileen .... 414-256-1207 538 A
schwale@mtmary.edu
SCHWANKE, Shellie ...... 309-467-6316 145 A
sschwanke@eureka.edu
SCHWANTZ, Sara .... 217-732-3155 150 H
sschwantz@lincolncollege.edu
SCHWARTS, Brett 435-652-7593 499M
bschwartz@dixie.edu
SCHWARTZ, Adam .... 515-294-2770 175 G
director@ameslab.gov
SCHWARTZ, Alycia .... 570-961-7845 422 G
schwartza@lackawanna.edu
SCHWARTZ, Beth .... 419-448-2216 383 C
bschwartz@heidelberg.edu
SCHWARTZ, Celeste, M 215-641-6492 426 E
cschwartz@mc3.edu
SCHWARTZ, Corene ...... 909-652-6242.. 38 A
cory.schwartz@chaffey.edu
SCHWARTZ, David .... 845-783-9901 351 F
utamds@gmail.com
SCHWARTZ, David, J .... 248-370-3465 248 K
schwart3@oakland.edu
SCHWARTZ, Doreen ...... 847-635-1632 155 E
doreen@oakton.edu
SCHWARTZ, Eric .... 612-625-0669 265 C
eschwart@umn.edu
SCHWARTZ, Ernest .... 718-384-5460 353 K
SCHWARTZ, Gary .... 718-960-6093 319 C
gary.schwartz@lehman.cuny.edu
SCHWARTZ, Hayim .... 718-268-4700 339 B
SCHWARTZ, Janis .... 973-720-2175 309 I
schwartzj@wpunj.edu
SCHWARTZ, Jason .... 801-832-2262 501 C
jsj@westminstercollege.edu
SCHWARTZ, Jennifer ..... 317-955-6056 171 A
jschwartz@marian.edu
SCHWARTZ, Jessica 715-833-6256 542M
jschwartz31@cvtc.edu
SCHWARTZ, Joel, D ...... 757-221-2460 506 J
jxschw@wm.edu
SCHWARTZ, Joshua ...... 215-619-7419 426 E
jschwart1@mc3.edu
SCHWARTZ, Kenneth .... 504-865-5389 207 F
kschwartz@tulane.edu
SCHWARTZ, Lance, W .. 507-344-7427 253M
schwartz@blc.edu
SCHWARTZ, Laura .... 707-638-5824.. 70 B
laura.schwartz@tu.edu
SCHWARTZ, Mary, L ..... 301-295-3013 548 D
mary.schwartz.ctr@usuhs.edu
SCHWARTZ, Mary Beth . 803-327-8042 451 K
mbschwartz@yorktech.edu
SCHWARTZ, Matthew, J 812-888-5832 174 F
mschwartz@vinu.edu
SCHWARTZ, Melanie ..... 415-955-2100.. 26 I
mschwartz@alliant.edu
SCHWARTZ, Moses .... 845-782-1380 354 B
SCHWARTZ, Patti .... 412-392-3959 433 F
pschwartz@pointpark.edu
SCHWARTZ, Rachel .... 912-478-0049 126 B
rschwartz@georgiasouthern.edu
SCHWARTZ, Randi, D ... 914-594-4900 335 H
randi_schwartz@nymc.edu
SCHWARTZ, Robert .... 206-296-5831 526 F
schwartr@seattleu.edu
SCHWARTZ, Robert, W . 573-882-4378 283 H
schwartzrob@missouri.edu
SCHWARTZ, Sandor ...... 718-963-1212 329 J
kyrs@thejnet.com
SCHWARTZ, Shari, P .... 404-413-2273 126 D
spiotrowski@gsu.edu
SCHWARTZ, Shuly .... 212-678-8826 329 H
shschwartz@jtsa.edu
SCHWARTZ, Steven .... 212-938-5712 347 C
sschwartz@sunyopt.edu
SCHWARTZ, Steven, J .. 970-247-7196.. 82 I
schwartz_s@fortlewis.edu
SCHWARTZ, Teri .... 310-825-7891.. 71 D
tschwartz@tft.ucla.edu
SCHWARTZE, Derek ...... 573-681-5515 276 K
schwartzed@lincolnu.edu
SCHWARTZMAN,
Michael .... 215-596-8855 438 E
m.schwartman@usciences.edu
SCHWARZ, Felipe .... 978-837-5459 233 G
schwarzf@merrimack.edu
SCHWARZ, Marilyn .... 508-387-7231 398 J
mschwarz@mscok.edu
SCHWARZ, May, L .... 614-235-4136 392 D
mschwarz@TLSohio.edu
SCHWARZ, Steven .... 718-997-5903 320 E
steven.schwarz@qc.cuny.edu
SCHWARZ, Thomas, J .. 914-251-6010 346 D
thomas.schwarz@purchase.edu
SCHWARZ, Todd .... 208-732-6325 137 K
tschwarz@csi.edu
SCHWARZKOPF, David . 781-891-2783 223 E
dschwarzkopf@bentley.edu
SCHWARZMILLER, Paul 412-237-3034 415 G
pschwarzmiller@ccac.edu
SCHWEDER, Wendy ...... 803-641-3689 450 C
wendys@usca.edu
SCHWEIGERT, Rich .... 303-534-6290.. 81 C
rich.schweigert@colostate.edu
SCHWEITZER, Carrie ..... 972-860-4848 472 C
cschweitzer@dcccd.edu
SCHWEITZER,
Connie, J .... 989-964-4160 249 G
schw@svsu.edu
SCHWEITZER,
Glenna, L .... 734-763-9954 251 C
glenna@umich.edu
SCHWEITZER, Josh .... 612-359-6491 253 K
schweitj@augsburg.edu
SCHWEITZER, Laura ...... 518-631-9841 351 A
schweitzerl@uniongraduatecollege.edu
SCHWEITZER, Mike .... 210-999-8409 490 E
mschweit@trinity.edu
SCHWEITZER, Steven, J 800-287-8822 164 E
schwest@bethanyseminary.edu
SCHWENK, Monica .... 801-395-3781 498 O
schwenkm@owatc.edu
SCHWENK, Thomas, L .. 775-784-6001 295 H
tschwenk@medicine.nevada.edu
SCHWENN, Robin .... 608-249-6611 536 J
rschwenn@herzing.edu
SCHWENT, Margie .... 573-334-6825 282 B
mschwent@sehealth.org
SCHWERDTFEGER,
Patrick .... 951-487-3420.. 55 A
pschwerdtfeger@msjc.edu
SCHWERTNER, Melanie 325-574-6503 497 E
mschwertner@wtc.edu
SCHWIETERMAN, Jerry . 219-473-4239 165 A
jschwieterman@ccsj.edu
SCHWINABART,
Rhonda .... 301-387-3741 215 A
rhonda.schwinabart@garrettcollege.edu
SCHWINKE, Victoria ..... 573-897-5000 282 I
SCHWIRZBIN, Brian ...... 516-876-3242 345 E
schwirzbinb@oldwestbury.edu
SCIACCA, John .... 714-484-7000.. 56 E
jsciacca@cypresscollege.edu
SCIALABBA, Joseph, M 814-641-3114 421 L
scialaj@juniata.edu
SCIAME, Joseph, A .... 718-990-1941 340 G
sciamej@stjohns.edu
SCIAME-GIESECKE,
Susan .... 765-455-9221 168 B
sgieseck@iuk.edu
SCIANNA, Dominic .... 718-990-6185 340 G
sciannad@stjohns.edu
SCIBETTA, Nicholas ...... 631-632-6335 344 C
nicholas.scibetta@stonybrook.edu
SCICHILONE, Michelle .. 781-736-4464 224 F
mscich@brandeis.edu
SCIFO, Joe .... 309-794-7374 139 K
josephscifo@augustana.edu
SCIGLITANO, JR.,
Anthony, C .... 973-275-5847 308 C
anthony.sciglitano@shu.edu
SCIOLA, Michael .... 315-228-7380 321 H
msciola@colgate.edu
SCIOTTO, Page, C .... 401-598-2145 441 D
psciotto@jwu.edu
SCIPLE, Melinda .... 662-476-5040 267 C
msciple@eastms.edu
SCISM, Bruce, R .... 434-797-8400 515 C
bscism@dcc.vccs.edu
SCISM, Darby, C .... 812-237-5000 167 E
darby.scism@indstate.edu
SCIUTO, Jim .... 925-631-8043.. 61 G
jsciuto@stmarys-ca.edu
SCLAFANI, Michael .... 718-399-4211 338 E
msclafan@pratt.edu
SCLAFANI, Sandra .... 212-875-4675 315 F
ssclafani@bankstreet.edu
SCOATES, Christopher .. 248-645-3301 241 H
SCOBEE, Georgia .... 225-216-8608 202 N
scobeeg@mybrcc.edu
SCOBY, Jerry, L .... 231-591-2164 242 L
JerryScoby@ferris.edu
SCOBY, Rhonda .... 903-877-7077 495 C
rhonda.scoby@uthct.edu
SCOFIELD, Elizabeth, A . 215-951-1040 422 F
scofield@lasalle.edu
SCOFIELD, Jeff .... 206-296-5852 526 F
scofieldj@seattleu.edu
SCOGIN, James .... 903-223-3005 486 C
james.scogin@tamut.edu
SCOLA, Anthony .... 630-829-6319 140 A
ascola@ben.edu
SCOLARO, Diane .... 802-485-2358 502 G
dscolaro@norwich.edu
SCOLFORO, Karen .... 800-759-2727 415 B
karenscolforo@centralpenn.edu
SCOPAS, Constantine .... 212-686-9244 315 B
SCOPELLITI, Theresa .... 570-961-7840 422 G
scopellitit@lackawanna.edu
SCORDINO, Anthony ..... 914-606-6521 352 G
anthony.scordino@sunywcc.edu
SCORSE, Bill .... 417-873-7200 274 E
bscorse@drury.edu
SCOTKA, Mary .... 210-434-6711 479 P
mscotka@lake.ollusa.edu
SCOTT, A. Nicole .... 260-422-5561 167 F
anscott@indianatech.edu
SCOTT, Adrian .... 205-247-8145.... 7 G
ascott@stillman.edu
SCOTT, Adrian, L .... 205-247-8145.... 7 G
ascott@stillman.edu
SCOTT, Adrienne .... 717-757-1100 440 K
adrienne.scott@yti.edu
SCOTT, Alexander .... 973-290-4720 301 F
ascott@cse.edu
SCOTT, Amelia .... 508-999-8093 228 H
ascott4@umassd.edu
SCOTT, Amy .... 309-677-3538 140 H
alscott@fsmail.bradley.edu
SCOTT, Angela .... 305-899-3666.. 99 B
ascott@barry.edu
SCOTT, Anne .... 940-898-2586 490 D
ascott2@twu.edu
SCOTT, Annie .... 860-343-5767.. 89 E
ascott@mxcc.commnet.edu
SCOTT, Bart .... 530-938-5521.. 41 E
bscott6@siskiyous.edu
SCOTT, Billy .... 662-254-3319 269 C
bscott@mvsu.edu
SCOTT, Bob .... 580-349-1597 400 B
bobs@opsu.edu
SCOTT, Candice .... 830-792-7318 482 D
cscott@schreiner.edu
SCOTT, Carl .... 903-593-8311 487 A
cscott@texascollege.edu
SCOTT, Carolyn .... 352-435-6308 107 X
scottc@lssc.edu
SCOTT, Cecelia .... 252-940-6264 360 B
cecelia.scott@beaufortccc.edu
SCOTT, Charles .... 309-438-8851 147 I
cascott@ilstu.edu
SCOTT, Charles .... 423-425-4463 465 E
Charles-Scott@utc.edu
SCOTT, Cheryl .... 903-886-5035 485 E
cheryl.scott@tamuc.edu
SCOTT, Cheryl .... 971-722-7555 409 C
cscott@pcc.edu
SCOTT, Christopher ...... 713-755-4961 233 B
cdscott@stcc.edu
SCOTT, Christopher ...... 304-473-8007 534 G
scott.c@wvwc.edu
SCOTT, Christopher, D . 815-772-7218 153 E
cdscott@morrisontech.edu
SCOTT, Clifford .... 617-266-2030 234 G
scottc@neco.edu
SCOTT, Connie, L .... 314-434-2212 275 J
cscott@hickeycollege.edu
SCOTT, Constance, E .... 260-422-5561 167 F
cescott@indianatech.edu
SCOTT, Dave .... 970-245-8101.. 83 H
dscott@intelliteccollege.edu
SCOTT, Dave .... 360-416-7751 527 A
dave.scott@skagit.edu
SCOTT, David, L .... 850-474-3117 116 E
dscott@uwf.edu
SCOTT, Dawn, M .... 262-524-7297 535 D
dscott@carrollu.edu
SCOTT, Deborah, C .... 508-831-6075 238 G
dscott@wpi.edu
SCOTT, Delbert, L .... 913-722-0272 188 F
SCOTT, Deloria .... 270-707-3823 196 D
deloria.scott@kctcs.edu
SCOTT, Donna .... 512-404-4807 468 J
dscott@austinseminary.edu
SCOTT, Dwayne .... 901-333-5025 464 A
djscott@southwest.tn.edu
SCOTT, Ed .... 850-263-3261.. 99 A
eescott@baptistcollege.edu
SCOTT, Eileen .... 856-256-4139 306 D
scotte@rowan.edu
SCOTT, Elijah .... 706-295-6318 125 C
escott@highlands.edu
SCOTT, Eric .... 907-796-6389.. 11 A
eric.scott@uas.alaska.edu
SCOTT, Fionna .... 619-684-8800.. 56 B
fscott@newschoolarch.edu
SCOTT, Frances .... 732-987-2427 302 J
scottf@georgian.edu
SCOTT, Frank .... 615-966-1990 458 C
frank.scott@lipscomb.edu
SCOTT, Fred .... 979-230-3213 469 G
fred.scott@brazosport.edu
SCOTT, Gayanne .... 719-255-3388.. 86 F
gscott@uccs.edu
SCOTT, Greg .... 616-222-3000 245 D
gscott@kuyper.edu
SCOTT, Heather .... 605-626-2433 454 A
Heather.Scott@northern.edu
SCOTT, Heidi .... 618-468-5110 150 E
hscott@lc.edu
SCOTT, Henrietta .... 803-774-3339 443 I
scotth@cctech.edu
SCOTT, Jamal .... 630-466-7900 162 K
jscott@waubonsee.edu
SCOTT, James .... 305-899-3950.. 99 B
jscott@barry.edu
SCOTT, James, C .... 940-565-2791 492 D
james.scott@unt.edu
SCOTT, James, K .... 573-882-6008 283 H
scottj@missouri.edu
SCOTT, Janice, L .... 727-816-3424 110 B
cessnaj@phsc.edu
SCOTT, Jeff .... 216-373-5407 388 A
SCOTT, Jeffrey .... 404-894-7444 125 D
jeff.scott@business.gatech.edu
SCOTT, Jillian .... 212-355-1501 318 A
jscott@christies.edu
SCOTT, Jo Ann .... 662-252-8000 270 C
jscott2@rustcollege.edu
SCOTT, Joseph .... 937-878-7985 547 E
scottjoseph@aafes.com
SCOTT, Josha .... 210-486-7280 467 B
jscott@alamo.edu
SCOTT, Joylynn .... 423-236-2801 460 K
jmichals@southern.edu
SCOTT, Julie .... 229-333-2100 134 I
julie.scott@wiregrass.edu
SCOTT, Kathleen, E .... 937-255-3636 547 E
kathleen.scott@afit.edu
SCOTT, Kathleen, J .... 410-543-6070 220 E
kjscott@salisbury.edu
SCOTT, Kenneth .... 518-458-5359 322 C
scottk@strose.edu
SCOTT, Lana .... 580-477-7719 404 D
lana.scott@wosc.edu

SCOTT, Laura .... 707-864-7000.. 66 J
laura.scott@solano.edu
SCOTT, Linda .... 706-776-0116 130 B
lscott@piedmont.edu
SCOTT, Linda .... 804-524-5304 518 C
lscott@vsu.edu
SCOTT, Lisa, L .... 585-785-1454 325 E
lisa.scott@flcc.edu
SCOTT, Lisa, M .... 570-372-4415 435 I
scottl@susqu.edu
SCOTT, Louis, B .... 404-413-2400 126 D
lscott01@gsu.edu
SCOTT, Louise .... 563-425-5214 183 G
scottl@uiu.edu
SCOTT, Marcia .... 805-546-3119.. 42 H
mscott@cuesta.edu
SCOTT, CSA, Marie .... 920-923-7624 537 A
mscott@marianuniversity.edu
SCOTT, Mark .... 412-809-5100 433 D
scott.mark@pti.edu
SCOTT, Mark, J .... 901-321-4126 455 I
mscott5@cbu.edu
SCOTT, Martha Lou ...... 254-710-1761 469 D
martha_lou_scott@baylor.edu
SCOTT, Mary .... 617-984-1768 235 H
mscott@quincycollege.edu
SCOTT, Mary, K .... 949-214-3201.. 42 B
mary.scott@cui.edu
SCOTT, Megan .... 309-341-7948 149 G
mscott@knox.edu
SCOTT, Michael, H .... 817-257-7858 486 G
m.scott@tcu.edu
SCOTT, Michelle, T .... 240-567-5276 217 B
michelle.scott@montgomerycollege.edu
SCOTT, Monica, R .... 843-953-5579 445 B
scottmr@cofc.edu
SCOTT, Neil .... 334-386-7200.... 3 I
nscott@faulkner.edu
SCOTT, Nicole .... 609-894-9311 306 B
nscott@bcc.edu
SCOTT, Patricia, A .... 410-706-7347 219 E
pscott@umaryland.edu
SCOTT, Patty .... 541-888-7401 410 A
pscott@socc.edu
SCOTT, Phyllis .... 305-899-3900.. 99 B
pscott@barry.edu
SCOTT, Randa .... 512-313-3000 471 H
randa.scott@concordia.edu
SCOTT, Rebecca .... 707-256-7438.. 55 E
rscott@napavalley.edu
SCOTT, Renay, M .... 575-527-7510 312 D
daccpresident@dacc.nmsu.edu
SCOTT, Rhonda, J .... 423-236-2932 460 K
rjscott@southern.edu
SCOTT, Richard .... 269-965-3931 244 L
scottr@kellogg.edu
SCOTT, Richard .... 801-957-3334 500 E
richard.scott@slcc.edu
SCOTT, Richard, I .... 501-450-3198.. 25 F
ricks@uca.edu
SCOTT, Richard, M .... 352-365-3525 107 X
scottr@lssc.edu
SCOTT, Rob .... 770-426-2603 128 C
rob.scott@life.edu
SCOTT, Rob .... 785-827-5541 189 A
rob.scott@kwu.edu
SCOTT, Ronald, B .... 513-529-0143 386 K
scottrb@miamioh.edu
SCOTT, Sandra, E .... 803-533-3721 448 H
sscott17@scsu.edu
SCOTT, Sean .... 901-272-5139 459 A
sscott@mca.edu
SCOTT, Sharion .... 516-323-4110 333 E
sscott@molloy.edu
SCOTT, Sharon .... 802-635-1208 504 A
sharon.scott@jsc.edu
SCOTT, Sharron, R .... 802-635-1208 504 A
sharron.scott@jsc.edu
SCOTT, Sherrill, B .... 731-426-7522 457 K
sbscott@lanecollege.edu
SCOTT, Stephen, C .... 919-866-5141 366 H
scscott@waketech.edu
SCOTT, Steven, A .... 620-235-4100 190 G
sascott@pittstate.edu
SCOTT, Tawana .... 864-877-1598 448 A
tawana.scott@ngu.edu
SCOTT, Teresa, M .... 209-575-6530.. 78 A
scottt@yosemite.edu
SCOTT, Thomas .... 208-769-5906 138 G
ttscott@nic.edu
SCOTT, Thomas, R .... 864-656-7551 444 E
trscott@clemson.edu
SCOTT, Todd .... 323-953-4000.. 51 E
scottj@lacitycollege.edu
SCOTT, Vann .... 256-840-4188.... 7 B
vscott@snead.edu
SCOTT, Wayne .... 731-989-6790 456 K
wscott@fhu.edu
SCOTT, Wendy .... 601-925-7104 268 E
wbscott@mc.edu
SCOTT, William, J .... 260-399-7700 174 C
bscott@sf.edu
SCOTT, Winston .... 321-674-8470 103 R
wscott@fit.edu
SCOTT DUEX, Sandra ... 715-232-2131 541 B
duexs@uwstout.edu
SCOTT-JOHNSON,
Pamela .... 443-885-3509 217 C
pamela.scottjohnson@morgan.edu
SCOTT-KINNEY,
Wanda, A .... 803-705-4680 443 F
scottkinney@benedict.edu
SCOTT PAYNE, Moira ... 206-726-5181 521 G
mpayne@cornish.edu
SCOTT PRICE, Charles .. 318-371-3035 204 A
charlesprice@nwltc.edu
SCOTT-SCURRY,
Darlene .... 434-924-3200 514 A
ds7sb@virginia.edu
SCOTT-TRAMMELL,
Suzanne .... 205-934-4470.... 8 F
sstrammell@uab.edu
SCOTTI, Frank .... 714-879-3901.. 47 D
fscotti@hiu.edu
SCOTTO, TOR, Dominic 740-283-6276 382 G
dscotto@franciscan.edu
SCOUBES, Jim .... 530-283-0202.. 44 H
jscoubes@frc.edu
SCOUFOS, Lucretia .... 580-745-2278 402 D
lscoufos@se.edu
SCOVENS, Tarsha .... 215-751-8164 416 B
tscovens@ccp.edu
SCOVILLE, Jan .... 715-732-3888 544 B
jan.scoville@nwtc.edu
SCOZZARI, Ron .... 740-366-9294 378 L
rscozzar@cotc.edu
SCRAGG, Raymond .... 216-421-7312 380 B
rscragg@cia.edu
SCRANAGE, Kimberly ... 859-572-7852 199 A
scranagek1@nku.edu
SCRANTON, Alec .... 319-335-5672 175 H
alec-scranton@uiowa.edu
SCRAPER, Cassie .... 812-749-1225 171 I
cscraper@oak.edu
SCREEN, Tommy .... 504-864-7082 206 A
tscreen@loyno.edu
SCREMENTI, Lori .... 708-239-4842 160 L
lori.screment@trnty.edu
SCREWS, Doris .... 334-229-4250.... 1 D
dscrews@alasu.edu
SCREWS, Jacqueline, B 334-556-2485.... 4 A
jscrews@wallace.edu
SCRIBAILO, Robin .... 219-785-5255 172 A
rscribailo@pnc.edu
SCRIBBICK, Michelle .... 570-622-7622 425 I
michele.scribbick@mccann.edu
SCRIBNER, Andrea .... 518-736-3622 326 D
andrea.scribner@fmcc.suny.edu
SCRIBNER, Douglas ...... 575-527-7500 312 D
dscribner@nmsu.edu
SCRIMSHAW, Susan, C 518-244-2214 340 A
scrims@sage.edu
SCRIVENER,
Norma Jean .... 601-857-3850 267 D
njscrivener@hindscc.edu
SCROGGINS, Anita .... 205-970-9213.... 7 D
ascroggins@sebc.edu
SCROGGINS, Don .... 580-477-7751 404 D
don.scroggins@wosc.edu
SCROGGINS, Melinda ... 559-251-4215.. 30 E
financialaid@calchristiancollege.edu
SCROGGINS, Susan ...... 219-464-6395 174 E
susan.scroggins@valpo.edu
SCROGGINS,
William, T .... 909-274-4250.. 54 J
bscroggins@mtsac.edu
SCROGGS,
Catherine, C .... 573-882-6776 283 H
scroggsc@missouri.edu
SCRUGGS, Jeffrey .... 478-988-6800 122 F
jscruggs@centralgatech.edu
SCULCO, SC, Lois .... 724-838-4200 435 E
sculco@setonhill.edu
SCULL, Alex, K .... 864-833-8228 448 E
akscull@presby.edu
SCULLEY, Patrick .... 210-292-3272 548 D
patrick.sculley@usuhs.edu
SCULLY, Dale .... 712-749-2123 176 D
scullyd@bvu.edu
SCULLY, JR., Frank, E .. 215-646-7300 420 A
scully.f@gmercyu.edu
SCULLY, John .... 973-300-2357 308 F
jscully@sussex.edu
SCULLY, Joseph, F .... 856-256-4127 306 D
scullyj@rowan.edu
SCULLY, Pamela .... 201-360-4351 303 A
pscully@hccc.edu
SCURRY, Frank, P .... 336-315-8660 355 F
fscurry@carolinagrad.edu
SCUTELLA, Clifford, M .. 585-345-6832 326 F
cmscutella@genesee.edu
SCUTO, Donna, L .... 716-878-6700 345 B
scutodl@buffalostate.edu
SCUTTI, Diane .... 610-902-8415 414 B
diane.m.scutti@cabrini.edu
SEA, Karen .... 209-954-5151.. 63 D
ksea@deltacollege.edu
SEABERG, David, C .... 423-778-6956 465 G
dseaberg@uthsc.edu
SEABERG, Doug .... 570-372-4408 435 I
seaberg@susqu.edu
SEABERRY, Ben .... 408-270-6410.. 63 O
ben.seaberry@sjeccd.org
SEABERRY, Roosevelt ... 318-675-8125 205 D
rseabe@lsuhsc.edu
SEABOY, Donna .... 701-854-8013 375 F
donnas@sbci.edu
SEABROOK WRIGHT,
Gloria .... 803-934-3200 447 K
gwright@morris.edu
SEABROOKS, Joe .... 816-604-4205 278 A
joe.seabrooks@mcckc.edu
SEACOTT, Damon, M .... 517-750-1200 250 F
dseacott@arbor.edu
SEACRIST, Ronald .... 229-333-7816 133 H
SEACRIST, Ronald .... 806-742-3931 489 F
ronald.seacrist@ttu.edu
SEADLER, Alan, W .... 412-396-5168 417 I
seadlera@duq.edu
SEAGA, Andrew .... 305-237-7581 108 L
aseaga@mdc.edu
SEAGLE, Dennis .... 828-726-2705 360 F
dseagle@cccti.edu
SEAGO, Brenda .... 706-721-2856 121 C
bseago@gru.edu
SEAGRAVES, John, R .... 606-474-3272 195 F
johnseagraves@kcu.edu
SEAGRAVES, Ronda ...... 318-869-5087 202 D
rseagraves@centenary.edu
SEAGULL, Amon .... 954-262-2048 109 E
amons@nova.edu
SEAL, Jennifer .... 601-403-1146 270 A
jseal@prcc.edu
SEAL, John .... 510-649-2462.. 46 E
jseal@gtu.edu
SEAL, Robert .... 973-720-2104 309 I
sealr@wpunj.edu
SEAL, Robert, A .... 773-508-2657 151 E
rseal@luc.edu
SEAL, Sherry .... 706-754-7730 129 B
sseal@northgatech.edu
SEAL, Timothy .... 901-751-8453 459 C
tseal@mabts.edu
SEALE, Danette .... 865-471-3248 455 G
dseale@cn.edu
SEALE, Francis Marie ... 510-883-2068.. 43 C
sfmseale@dspt.edu
SEALE, Lisa .... 928-317-6438.. 12 B
lisa.seale@azwestern.edu
SEALINE, Alma .... 217-333-0610 162 A
asealine@illinois.edu
SEALS, Jennifer .... 605-718-2909 454 F
jennifer.seals@wdt.edu
SEALS, Lisa .... 760-355-6257.. 47 G
lisa.seals@imperial.edu
SEALS, Lisa .... 617-745-3869 225 H
lisa.seals@enc.edu
SEALS, Nireata .... 718-482-5900 320 B
nseals@lagcc.cuny.edu
SEALS, Victoria .... 770-962-7580 127 C
vseals@gwinnetttech.edu
SEALY, Mondell .... 718-262-2305 321 B
msealy@york.cuny.edu
SEAMAN, Amanda .... 417-873-6956 274 E
mseaman@drury.edu
SEAMAN, Chuck .... 615-248-1240 464 E
cseaman@trevecca.edu
SEAMAN, Cynthia .... 610-372-4721 433 H
cseaman@racc.edu
SEAMAN, Daniel, B .... 315-229-5601 341 E
dseaman@stlawu.edu
SEAMAN, David .... 315-443-5533 349 E
SEAMAN, Diane .... 937-328-6014 379 L
seamand@clarkstate.edu
SEAMAN, James .... 215-895-6012 417 E
jks35@drexel.edu
SEAMAN, Jennifer .... 415-503-6230.. 63 A
jseaman@sfcm.edu
SEAMAN, Meredith .... 402-449-2877 290 F
mseaman@graceu.edu
SEAMAN, Sara .... 501-760-4101.. 21 H
sseaman@npcc.edu
SEAMAN, Scott, H .... 740-593-2705 389 H
seaman@ohio.edu
SEAMAN, Shane .... 718-933-6700 333 F
sseaman@monroecollege.edu
SEAMEN, Erica .... 417-864-7220 275 A
eseamen@cci.edu
SEAMONS, Ron .... 540-261-4095 512 J
ron.seamons@svu.edu
SEAMS, Jennifer .... 304-645-6383 533 B
jseams@osteo.wvsom.edu
SEANE, Oupa .... 904-620-2475 116 A
oseane@unf.edu
SEAQUIST, Carl .... 717-815-2084 440 H
cseaquis@ycp.edu
SEARCH, Sally .... 850-201-8490 117 B
searchs@tcc.fl.edu
SEARCY, Douglas, N .... 540-654-1062 513 I
dsearcy@umw.edu
SEARCY, Douglas, N .... 252-399-6309 354 I
dsearcy@barton.edu
SEARCY, Scott .... 785-890-1511 190 C
scott.searcy@nwktc.edu
SEARFOSS, Alexis .... 727-873-4519 116 C
asearfoss@usfsp.edu
SEARING, Linda .... 585-389-2870 334 B
lsearin9@naz.edu
SEARLE, Mark, S .... 480-965-1224.. 11 J
mark.searle@asu.edu
SEARLE, Natalie .... 802-786-5148 503 H
natalie.searle@ccv.edu
SEARS, Andrew .... 816-960-2008 273 B
asears@cityvision.edu
SEARS, Andrew, L .... 814-865-3528 428 C
aus67@psu.edu
SEARS, Connie .... 562-938-4155.. 51 A
csears@lbcc.edu
SEARS, David .... 240-567-7492 217 B
david.sears@montgomerycollege.edu
SEARS, Douglas .... 617-358-4608 224 E
dsears@bu.edu
SEARS, Estella .... 512-492-3077 468 A
esears@aoma.edu
SEARS, James, R .... 313-577-4301 252 G
j.sears@wayne.edu
SEARS, John .... 303-220-1200.. 79 G
john.sears@cffp.edu
SEARS, John .... 401-874-5371 442 E
jsears@mail.uri.edu
SEARS, Laura .... 402-826-6773 290 C
laura.sears@doane.edu
SEARS, Melissa .... 859-442-1156 196 A
melissa.sears@kctcs.edu
SEARS, Norward .... 504-816-4711 202 F
nsears@dillard.edu
SEARS, Richard .... 678-839-5353 133 F
rsears@westga.edu
SEARS, Steve, R .... 956-326-2480 485 B
steve.sears@tamiu.edu
SEARS, Steven, A .... 401-865-2425 441 F
ssears@providence.edu
SEARS, Tad .... 218-723-6017 255 A
tsears@css.edu
SEARSON, Robert .... 216-987-3943 381 A
robert.searson@tri-c.edu
SEASTEDT, Erik .... 907-450-8222.. 10 G
eseastedt@alaska.edu
SEATON, Ann .... 845-758-6822 315 G
aseaton@bard.edu
SEATON, William, J .... 609-984-1120 308 H
bseaton@tesc.edu
SEAVER, Catherine .... 860-512-2623.. 89 D
cseaver@manchestercc.edu
SEAVER, Kent .... 972-273-3430 473 A
kseaver@dcccd.edu
SEAVERS, Norm .... 954-201-7813.. 99 G
nseavers@broward.edu
SEAWORTH, Timothy ...... 701-355-8150 375 K
seaworth@umary.edu
SEAY, Brooks .... 706-379-3111 134 J
cbseay@yhc.edu
SEAY, Gary .... 718-270-5031 320 C
garys@mec.cuny.edu
SEAY, Laodecea .... 334-214-4807.... 2 H
laodecea.seay@cv.edu
SEAY, Lonnie .... 530-242-7912.. 66 C
lseay@shastacollege.edu
SEBASTIAN, Chris .... 692-625-3291 550 A
csebastian@cmi.edu
SEBASTIAN, Denise .... 573-518-2249 278 F
denise@mineralarea.edu
SEBASTIAN, Donald, H . 973-596-8449 304 D
sebastian@njit.edu
SEBASTIAN,
J. Jayakiran .... 215-248-6306 424 G
jsebastian@ltsp.edu
SEBASTIAN,
J. Jayakiran .... 215-248-6306 424 G
Jsebastian@ltsp.edu
SEBASTIAN, John .... 504-865-2304 206 A
jtsebast@loyno.edu
SEBASTIAN, Juliann ...... 402-559-4000 293 I
julie.sebastian@unmc.edu
SEBASTIAN, Pam .... 660-831-4142 279 D
sebastianp@moval.edu
SEBASTIANI, Richard .... 713-221-8225 491 F
sebastianir@uhd.edu
SEBASTIEN, Anya .... 864-592-6207 449 C
sebastiena@sccsc.edu

SEBOLT, George, W ...... 412-291-6210 412 H
gsebolt@aii.edu
SEBOLT, Kevin, G .... 740-284-5192 382 G
ksebolt@franciscan.edu
SEBRANEK, Lori, A .... 608-243-4185 543 C
lsebranek@madisoncollege.edu
SECHLER, Elizabeth .... 304-876-5172 532 I
esechler@shepherd.edu
SECHLER, Mary Jo .... 620-431-2820 189 J
msechler@neosho.edu
SECHRIST, Ann .... 770-972-7580 127 C
asechrist@gwinnetttech.edu
SECHRIST, John .... 724-653-2184 417 D
jsechrist@dec.edu
SECHRIST, Shana .... 503-725-8310 409 D
shana.sechrist@pdx.edu
SECKA, Lamine .... 619-594-7903.. 35 E
lsecka@mail.sdsu.edu
SECKER, Eric .... 847-628-2084 149 A
webmaster@judsonu.edu
SECORD, Anne-Marie ... 858-541-7913.. 55 J
asecord@nu.edu
SECORD, Mark .... 361-354-2408 470 K
secordm@coastalbend.edu
SECORD, Paul .... 512-863-1211 483 G
secordp@southwestern.edu
SECREST, Kathy, L .... 330-471-8415 385 G
ksecrest@malone.edu
SECRIST, Tammi .... 304-336-8281 533 A
tsecrist@westliberty.edu
SEDA, Eric .... 718-357-0500 341 F
eseda@stpaulsschoolofnursing.edu
SEDA, Iris .... 787-264-1912 554 C
iris_seda_rodriguez@intersg.edu
SEDANO, George .... 510-594-5033.. 30 G
gsedano@cca.edu
SEDDIKI, Mohamed ...... 973-877-3080 302 F
seddiki@essex.edu
SEDDON, Tom, I .... 513-556-0831 393 B
seddontl@ucmail.uc.edu
SEDEN, John .... 415-749-4570.. 62 I
jseden@sfai.edu
SEDER, Diana .... 909-607-7785.. 39 F
diana.seder@cmc.edu
SEDILLO, Eileen .... 505-454-3430 311 H
sedillo_e@nmhu.edu
SEDILLO, Robert .... 928-226-4283.. 13 D
bobby.sedillo@coconino.edu
SEDLACEK, Bernard ...... 402-457-2529 291 E
bsedlacek@mccneb.edu
SEDLACEK, Beverly .... 402-354-7249 291 P
bev.sedlacek@methodistcollege.edu
SEDLACEK, Paige .... 607-778-5213 344 F
sedlacekpm@sunybroome.edu
SEDLAK, John .... 570-740-0234 425 A
jsedlak@luzerne.edu
SEDNA, Jennifer .... 707-546-4000.. 43 J
jsedna@cmpirecollege.com
SEDORE,
Christopher, M .... 315-443-3402 349 E
cmsedore@syr.edu
SEDRINE, Ben .... 904-363-6221 112 G
SEDUTTO, Dawn .... 603-668-2211 298 H
d.sedutto@snhu.edu
SEDYCIAS, Joao .... 607-436-2520 344 B
joao.sedycias@oneonta.edu
SEE, Catherine .... 434-947-8315 511 D
Csee@randolphcollege.edu
SEE, David .... 501-337-5000.. 20 H
dsee@coto.edu
SEE, Joan .... 212-812-4050 335 D
jsee@sft.edu
SEE, Jonathan .... 310-506-6256.. 58 H
Jonathan.See@pepperdine.edu
SEE, Leslie, C 304-260-4380 530M
lsee@blueridgectc.edu
SEEBER, Terry .... 740-374-8716 395 D
tseeber@wscc.edu
SEEBERGER, Debbie ..... 410-704-2360 221 A
dseeberger@towson.edu
SEEBO, Elane .... 806-291-3417 496 K
seeboe@wbu.edu
SEEGER, Daniel .... 828-298-3325 373 A
dseeger@warren-wilson.edu
SEEGER, Matthew .... 313-577-5342 252 G
matthew.seeger@wayne.edu
SEEGER, Rory .... 406-377-9410 286 F
rseeger@dawson.edu
SEEGMILLER, Jesse ...... 540-261-8454 512 J
jesse.seegmiller@svu.edu
SEEK, Linda .... 301-846-2457 214 I
lseek@frederick.edu
SEEKINS, Travis, P 325-670-1589 474M
seekins@hsutx.edu
SEEKLANDER, Marlene . 605-882-5284 452 G
seeklanm@lakeareatech.edu
SEELBACH, Brenda .... 540-636-2900 506 H
brendaseelbach@christendom.edu
SEELEY, Lisa .... 903-923-2175 473 I
lseeley@etbu.edu
SEELEY, Michael .... 321-674-8422 103 R
mseeley@fit.edu
SEELY, Bruce, E .... 906-487-2156 247 A
bseely@mtu.edu
SEEMAN, Steve, C .... 563-588-8000 178 E
financialaid@emmaus.edu
SEEMANN, Jeffrey .... 860-486-3619.. 92 C
jeff.seemann@uconn.edu
SEESE, Christine .... 410-225-2222 216 F
cseese@mica.edu
SEESTEDT-STANFORD,
Linda .... 540-887-4318 510 A
lstanford@mbc.edu
SEEVERS, JR., Gary ...... 417-862-9533 275 C
president@globaluniversity.edu
SEEVERS, Scott .... 402-643-7233 289 J
scott.seevers@cune.edu
SEFCIK, Jeffrey .... 325-942-2041 489 E
jeff.sefcik@angelo.edu
SEFFERS, Tracy .... 304-876-5463 532 I
tseffers@shepherd.edu
SEFFINGER, Michael ..... 909-469-5423.. 76 I
mseffinger@westernu.edu
SEFTON, Cindy .... 513-569-1699 379 K
cindy.sefton@cincinnatistate.edu
SEGAL, Gordon .... 691-320-2481 549 D
gsegal@comfsm.fm
SEGAL, Rick .... 612-455-3420 254 B
SEGAR, Robert, B .... 530-752-2172.. 71 A
rbsegar@ucdavis.edu
SEGAR, Thomas .... 304-876-5214 532 I
tsegar@shepherd.edu
SEGARRA, Alma .... 787-284-1912 554 B
asegarra@ponce.inter.edu
SEGARRA, Barbara .... 787-758-2525 558 C
barbara.segarra@upr.edu
SEGARRA, Carlos .... 787-264-1912 554 C
csegarra@intersg.edu
SEGARRA, Jose .... 787-878-5475 553 F
jsegarra@arecibo.inter.edu
SEGARS, Glenda .... 662-862-8383 267 F
grsegars@iccms.edu
SEGAT, Susana .... 617-879-7073 230 B
ssegat@massart.edu
SEGAVE, Robert .... 585-594-6357 339 F
segave_robert@roberts.edu
SEGAWA, Mike .... 253-879-2837 527 F
msegawa@pugetsound.edu
SEGERSON, Joan .... 401-739-5000 441 E
jsegerson@neit.edu
SEGGELKE, Linda .... 217-732-3168 150 G
lseggelke@lincolnchristian.edu
SEGGERMAN, Richard .. 319-352-8521 183 J
richard.seggerman@wartburg.edu
SEGGERMAN,
Richard, W .... 319-352-8276 183 J
richard.seggerman@wartburg.edu
SEGGOS, Rose .... 518-782-6783 342 H
rseggos@siena.edu
SEGOVIA, Ricardo .... 708-456-0300 161 C
rsegovia@triton.edu
SEGRAN, Sam .... 806-742-5151 489 F
sam.segran@ttu.edu
SEGROVES, Dawn, M .... 214-860-2064 472 F
dsegroves@dcccd.edu
SEGRUE, Gary .... 716-375-2525 340 C
gsegrue@sbu.edu
SEGUEL, Jaime .... 787-265-3807 558 B
decasac@uprm.edu
SEGUIN, Nancy .... 989-358-7212 239 C
seguinn@alpenacc.edu
SEGURA, Steve .... 916-570-5011.. 52 I
seguras@arc.losrios.edu
SEHEULT, Erin .... 909-558-4508.. 50 K
eseheult@llu.edu
SEHGAL, Varun .... 718-518-6641 319 D
vsehgal@hostos.cuny.edu
SEHL, JR., Patrick .... 316-295-5488 187 C
sehl@friends.edu
SEHLOFF, John, M 507-344-7342 253M
john@blc.edu
SEIBEL, Rosalie .... 701-662-1542 375 A
rosalie.seibel@lrsc.edu
SEIBERT, Diane .... 301-295-1080 548 D
diane.seibert@usuhs.edu
SEIBERT, Jon .... 620-431-2820 189 J
jseibert@neosho.edu
SEIBERT, Rhonda, K ..... 563-562-3263 181 F
seibertr@nicc.edu
SEIBERT, Susan .... 618-650-3708 159 I
sseiber@siue.edu
SEIBRING, Scott .... 309-556-3096 148 A
iwufaid@iwu.edu
SEIBRING, Steve, D ...... 309-556-3135 148 A
sseibrin@iwu.edu
SEIDEMANN, Jonathan . 410-484-7200 217 E
rjas@nirc.edu
SEIDEN, Peggy .... 610-328-8489 436 A
pseiden1@swarthmore.edu
SEIDENSTICKER,
Duane, P .... 414-847-3274 537 F
duaneseidensticker@miad.edu
SEIDLER, Nick .... 414-277-6922 537 G
SEIF, Gershon .... 874-982-2500 146 A
seif@htc.edu
SEIFARTH, Eric, M .... 803-536-7200 448 H
eseifart@scsu.edu
SEIFER, Jason .... 415-439-2350.. 27 F
SEIFERT, Alice .... 914-923-2616 337 I
aseifert@pace.edu
SEIFERT, Charles .... 518-783-2321 342 H
seifert@siena.edu
SEIGERMAN, David .... 845-434-5750 349 C
dseigerman@sunysullivan.edu
SEILER, David .... 512-863-1809 483 G
seilerd@southwestern.edu
SEILER, Kevin .... 303-352-3053.. 81 J
kevin.seiler@ccd.edu
SEILER, Susan .... 414-256-1230 538 A
mktg@mtmary.edu
SEILER, Tom .... 614-947-6103 382 H
tom.seiler@franklin.edu
SEIPEL, Joseph, H .... 804-828-2787 514 F
jseipel@vcu.edu
SEIPP, Dale .... 503-517-1024 411 A
dseipp@warnerpacific.edu
SEIRUP, Wendy .... 714-997-6712.. 38 B
wseirup@chapman.edu
SEITH, Mary Beth .... 330-325-6477 387 F
mseith@neomed.edu
SEITSEMA, Adriane .... 641-648-4611 179 K
adriane.seitsema@iavalley.edu
SEITZ, Brian .... 918-587-6789 403 F
Brian.Seitz@twsweld.com
SEITZ, Carl .... 586-498-4066 246 A
seitzc@macomb.edu
SEITZ, Greg .... 256-782-5279.... 4 L
gseitz@jsu.edu
SEITZ, Kathy .... 828-726-2269 360 F
kseitz@cccti.edu
SEITZ, Rebecca .... 573-592-4222 286 A
rebecca.seitz@williamwoods.edu
SEITZER, Joan, M .... 410-827-5808 214 D
jseitzer@chesapeake.edu
SEIVERS, Lana, C .... 615-898-2874 461 E
lana.seivers@mtsu.edu
SEIWERT, Lisa .... 773-896-2400 141 K
lseiwert@ctschicago.edu
SEIXAS, Karyn .... 626-395-6161.. 31 D
karyn@caltech.edu
SEJDINAJ, John, A .... 574-631-4130 174 A
sejdinaj.1@nd.edu
SEKELSKY, Mary Jo, S . 810-762-3434 251 E
maryjoss@umflint.edu
SEKHRI, Kiran .... 313-496-2811 252 A
ksekhri1@wcccd.edu
SEKOL, Jennifer .... 570-945-8117 422 B
jennifer.sekol@keystone.edu
SEKUL, Michelle .... 228-497-7647 268 G
michelle.sekul@mgccc.edu
SEKULICH, Brad .... 704-687-7747 371 B
sekulich@uncc.edu
SELANDER, Ralph .... 843-349-5296 446 I
ralph.selander@hgtc.edu
SELBER, Kimberly .... 956-665-8919 494 C
kp_selber@utpa.edu
SELBURG, Alyssa .... 309-672-5740 152 E
aselburg@methodistcol.edu
SELBY, David, K .... 317-788-3386 173 I
selbyd@uindy.edu
SELBY, Holly .... 410-337-6184 215 B
holly.selby@goucher.edu
SELBY, Rosemary .... 478-553-2055 129 C
rselby@oftc.edu
SELBY, Steve .... 714-992-7081.. 56 F
sselby@fullcoll.edu
SELBY, Tami .... 570-422-3080 430 F
tselby@esu.edu
SELBY, Terri, P .... 802-654-2462 502 H
tselby@smcvt.edu
SELDEN, Pete .... 870-733-6722.. 19 G
pjselden@midsouthcc.edu
SELF, George .... 520-335-1365.. 13 B
selfg@cochise.edu
SELF, Richard, B .... 336-322-2128 364 G
Richard.Self@piedmontcc.edu
SELF, Ronald 660-263-6408 272M
mrsself@att.net
SELF, Sheila 918-456-5511 398M
selfsj@nsuok.edu
SELF-DAVIS, LeAnn .... 731-989-6931 456 K
ldavis@fhu.edu
SELFRIDGE, Lauren .... 415-575-6171.. 31 C
lselfridge@ciis.edu
SELGO, Tim .... 616-331-8800 243 E
selgot@gvsu.edu
SELIG, C. Wood .... 757-683-3369 510 I
wselig@odu.edu
SELIGMAN, Joel .... 585-275-8356 351 D
seligman@rochester.edu
SELIGMAN, Joel .... 603-862-0653 299 B
joel.seligman@unh.edu
SELIGMAN, Richard, P . 626-395-6073.. 31 D
richard.seligman@caltech.edu
SELIGMANN, Wendy ...... 828-771-3033 373 A
wseligmann@warren-wilson.edu
SELIMO, Tony .... 973-300-2229 308 F
tselimo@sussex.edu
SELIN, Mark .... 920-403-3055 538 K
mark.selin@snc.edu
SELKIRK, Sara, E .... 816-654-7214 276 G
sselkirk@kcumb.edu
SELL, JR., Edgar, S ...... 410-857-2711 217 A
esell@mcdaniel.edu
SELL, Justin .... 605-688-5625 454 C
justin.sell@sdstate.edu
SELL, Kayla .... 414-443-3637 538 A
sellk@mtmary.edu
SELL, Phil .... 847-317-8031 161 B
psell@tiu.edu
SELLARS, John .... 641-784-5111 178 G
jsellars@graceland.edu
SELLARS, Telly .... 502-213-4294 196 E
telly.sellars@kctcs.edu
SELLARS, Telly .... 502-213-2181 196 E
telly.sellars@kctcs.edu
SELLECK, Mike .... 806-720-7775 478 A
michael.selleck@lcu.edu
SELLEN, Mary, K .... 757-594-7130 506 I
mary.sellen@cnu.edu
SELLERS, JR.,
Cleveland, L .... 803-780-1019 451 G
csellers@voorhees.edu
SELLERS, Emma .... 828-328-7288 358 G
emma.sellers@lr.edu
SELLERS, James, E .... 216-368-5872 378 J
jes3@case.edu
SELLERS, Jeff .... 937-708-5327 395 E
jsellers@wilberforce.edu
SELLERS, Jennifer .... 802-287-8072 501 I
sellersj@greenmtn.edu
SELLERS, Karen .... 401-841-6547 548 B
SELLERS, Lee .... 503-255-0332 407 D
lsellers@multnomah.edu
SELLERS, Martin .... 423-869-6815 458 B
martin.sellers@lmunet.edu
SELLERS, Patrick, J .... 704-894-2078 356 D
pasellers@davidson.edu
SELLERS, Randy .... 806-720-7161 478 A
randy.sellers@lcu.edu
SELLERS, Robert, M ...... 734-764-3982 251 C
rsellers@umich.edu
SELLERS, Terrie, O .... 912-443-5707 131 B
tsellers@savannahtech.edu
SELLERS, Timothy .... 315-279-5685 329 K
tsellers@keuka.edu
SELLERS, Tyler .... 903-923-2325 473 I
tsellers@etbu.edu
SELLHEIM, Linda .... 619-684-8862.. 56 B
lsellheim@newschoolarch.edu
SELLICK, Megan .... 570-208-5900 422 D
megansellick@kings.edu
SELLMANN, James, D .. 671-735-2805 549 G
jsellman@triton.uog.edu
SELLNER, Hildegard ...... 907-796-6226.. 11 A
hildegard.sellner@uas.alaska.edu
SELLS, Ben .... 765-998-5389 173 B
bnsells@taylor.edu
SELLS, Debra, K .... 615-898-5342 461 E
debra.sells@mtsu.edu
SELLS, Tamatha .... 864-941-8363 448 D
sells.t@ptc.edu
SELLS, Vicki, G .... 931-598-3220 460 I
vsells@sewanee.edu
SELMAN, Brenda, V ...... 573-884-9153 283 H
selmanb@missouri.edu
SELMER, Paula .... 518-244-2093 340 A
selmep@sage.edu
SELMO, Barbara .... 617-349-8267 228 B
bselmo@lesley.edu
SELMON, John .... 231-777-0265 247 G
john.selmon@muskegoncc.edu
SELMON, Michael, L .... 989-463-7176 239 B
selmon@alma.edu
SELNICK, Conrad .... 773-380-6787 140 C
cselnick@bexleyseabury.edu
SELORIO, Conrad .... 562-860-2451.. 37 L
cselorio@cerritos.edu
SELPH, Justin .... 941-351-5100 111 F
jselph@ringling.edu
SELTZER, Michael .... 813-935-5700 111 E
michael.seltzer@remingtoncollege.edu
SELVAGE, Samuel .... 937-722-9253 394 F
samuel.selvage@urbana.edu
SELVERA, Richard .... 713-222-5388 491 F
selverar@uhd.edu
SELWYN, Barbara .... 617-559-8610 227 E
bselwyn@hebrewcollege.edu
SELZER, Michael, M ..... 605-394-2436 454 B
michael.selzer@sdsmt.edu

SEXTON, Eric, L .... 316-978-3250 192 D
esexton@goshockers.edu
SEXTON, Gary .... 330-941-1778 396 C
sexton@wysu.org
SEXTON, Glenna, W ..... 970-247-7331.. 82 I
sexton_g@fortlewis.edu
SEXTON, John .... 212-998-2345 336 C
john.sexton@nyu.edu
SEXTON, Jon .... 641-269-3713 178 I
sextonj@grinnell.edu
SEXTON, Michele, D .... 620-235-4187 190 G
msexton@pittstate.edu
SEXTON, Mike, B .... 408-554-4700.. 65 A
mbsexton@scu.edu
SEXTON, Steve .... 615-248-7792 464 E
ssexton@trevecca.edu
SEXTON, Susan .... 651-690-6565 263 V
swsexton@stkate.edu
SEXTON, Susan, K .... 937-229-4333 393 E
ssexton1@udayton.edu
SEXTON, Thelma .... 478-757-3947 134 E
tsexton@wesleyancollege.edu
SEXTON-JOHNSON,
Sara .... 509-533-8486 521 D
ssexton-johnson@ccs.spokane.edu
SEYDEL, Tim .... 541-962-3740 405 G
tseydel@eou.edu
SEYERLE, Amy .... 626-529-8007.. 57 F
aseyerle@pacificoaks.edu
SEYMOUR, Avanti .... 617-449-7041 237 E
avanti.seymour@urbancollege.edu
SEYMOUR, Azanda .... 413-572-8802 230 F
aseymour@westfield.ma.edu
SEYMOUR, Dennis .... 815-939-5302 155 G
dseymour@olivet.edu
SEYMOUR, Heather, B .. 207-755-5100 210 L
SEYMOUR, Jodi, L .... 641-784-5112 178 G
seymour@graceland.edu
SEYMOUR, Michael .... 818-767-0888.. 77 G
michael.seymour@woodbury.edu
SEYMOUR, Michael ...... 218-733-7600 259 C
michael.seymour@lsc.edu
SEYMOUR, Sharon .... 217-479-7025 151 J
sharon.seymour@mac.edu
SEYMOUR, Susan .... 206-239-4500 520 K
sseymour@cityu.edu
SEYMOUR, William .... 423-478-6200 462 D
wseymour@clevelandstatecc.edu
SEYMOUR-ROUTE,
Paulette .... 508-856-5758 229 B
Paulette.SeymourRoute@umassmed.edu
SFRAGA, Mike .... 907-474-6533.. 10 I
msfraga@alaska.edu
SGANGA, Fred .... 631-444-8606 344 C
fred.sganga@stonybrook.edu
SGARLATA, Constance .. 410-857-2280 217 A
csgarlata@mcdaniel.edu
SGRO, Michael .... 607-753-2517 345 C
michael.sgro@cortland.edu
SHAABAN-MAGANA,
Lamea .... 205-348-5040.... 8 E
lshaaban@sa.ua.edu
SHAAK, Melissa, J .... 781-239-4398 222 E
shaak@babson.edu
SHABAHANG, Homa ..... 909-593-3511.. 73 B
hshabahang@laverne.edu
SHABAZZ, Amilcar .... 413-545-5703 228 F
shabazz@afroam.umass.edu
SHABAZZ, Ricky .... 909-384-8992.. 62 C
rshabazz@sbccd.cc.ca.us
SHABLIA, Nataliia .... 215-572-2887 412 F
shablian@arcadia.edu
SHABLIN, Steven, J ...... 248-370-3470 248 K
shablin@oakland.edu
SHABLOSKI, Regan .... 814-866-6641 423 B
rshabloski@lecom.edu
SHACHTER, Amy, M ..... 408-554-7041.. 65 A
ashachter@scu.edu
SHACKELFORD, Carol ... 601-635-2111 267 B
cshackelford@eccc.edu
SHACKELFORD, Harper . 910-678-8413 362 E
shackelh@faytechcc.edu
SHACKELFORD,
Peter, J .... 517-750-1200 250 F
pshackel@arbor.edu
SHACKLEFORD, Keith ... 949-451-5407.. 67 E
kshackleford@ivc.edu
SHACKLEFORD, JR.,
Robert, S .... 336-633-0287 365 A
rsshackleford@randolph.edu
SHADDY, Deborah .... 913-758-6143 191 I
shaddy15@stmary.edu
SHADE, Matthew, R ...... 717-736-4165 420 D
mrshade@hacc.edu
SHADE-DAVISON,
Stephanie .... 580-745-2267 402 D
sdavison@se.edu
SHADER, Gail .... 518-828-4181 322 E
gail.shader@sunycgcc.edu

SHADICK, Richard .... 212-346-1526 337 I
rshadick@pace.edu
SHADLE, Joseph .... 513-745-3570 396 B
shadlej@xavier.edu
SHADLE, Julie .... 848-932-2207 306 F
jshadle@winants.rutgers.edu
SHADOIAN, Holly, L ..... 401-456-8884 442 A
hshadoian@ric.edu
SHADY, Raymond .... 585-385-8098 340 F
rshady@sjfc.edu
SHAFER, Andrew .... 615-297-7545 455 A
shafera@aquinascollege.edu
SHAFER, Barb .... 406-657-2301 287 H
bshafer@msubillings.edu
SHAFER, Jack, L .... 610-499-4454 439 G
jlshafer@widener.edu
SHAFER, Jesse .... 215-951-5626 432 F
shaferj@philau.edu
SHAFER, John, R .... 317-738-8080 166 B
jshafer@franklincollege.edu
SHAFER, Kathrynne, G . 717-691-6003 426 B
kshafer@messiah.edu
SHAFER, Lisa .... 610-328-8009 436 A
lshafer1@swarthmore.edu
SHAFER, Lisa .... 530-541-4660.. 50 A
shaferl@ltcc.edu
SHAFER, Pamela .... 832-559-4217 477 I
pamela.n.shafer@lonestar.edu
SHAFER, Richard .... 214-768-1580 482 J
rashafer@smu.edu
SHAFER, Staci .... 618-985-3741 148 G
stacishafer@jalc.edu
SHAFER, Teresa .... 419-448-3309 392 B
tshafer@tiffin.edu
SHAFER, Trish .... 610-660-3101 434 G
tshafer@sju.edu
SHAFFER, Alan .... 740-392-6868 387 B
alan.shaffer@mvnu.edu
SHAFFER, Amy .... 912-443-5512 131 B
ashaffer@savannahtech.edu
SHAFFER, Barbara .... 315-312-3557 346 A
barbara.shaffer@oswego.edu
SHAFFER, Brian, W ...... 901-843-3976 460 F
shaffer@rhodes.edu
SHAFFER, Chris .... 334-670-3266.... 8 A
shafferc@troy.edu
SHAFFER, Chris .... 334-983-6556.... 8 A
shafferc@troy.edu
SHAFFER, Chris .... 503-494-6057 408 D
library@ohsu.edu
SHAFFER, Christopher .. 740-351-3207 391 C
cshaffer@shawnee.edu
SHAFFER, Dan, M .... 417-268-1000 272 D
shafferd@evangel.edu
SHAFFER, David .... 567-661-2625 390 D
david_shaffer5@owens.edu
SHAFFER, Deborah .... 740-593-1872 389 H
shafferd@ohio.edu
SHAFFER, Germaine ..... 606-487-3409 196 B
germaine.shaffer@kctcs.edu
SHAFFER, Jamie .... 615-794-4254 460 A
jshaffer@omorecollege.edu
SHAFFER, Janette .... 802-828-0124 503 H
janette.shaffer@ccv.edu
SHAFFER, Jason, S ...... 704-894-2188 356 D
jashaffer@davidson.edu
SHAFFER, Jon, L .... 618-453-1069 159 H
jonshaffer@siu.edu
SHAFFER, Kelli .... 254-968-9050 485 A
shaffer@tarleton.edu
SHAFFER, Kent .... 479-524-9500.. 21 F
SHAFFER, Patti .... 724-357-2621 431 A
pshaffer@iup.edu
SHAFFER, Ruth, E .... 309-692-4092 152 F
rshaffer@midstate.edu
SHAFFER, Steven, E ..... 716-878-6034 345 B
shaffese@buffalostate.edu
SHAFFER, Tammy .... 812-877-8003 172 C
shaffer@rose-hulman.edu
SHAFFER, Virginia .... 630-752-5623 163 G
virginia.shaffer@wheaton.edu
SHAFFER, W. Michael .. 706-721-4413 121 C
wshaffer@gru.edu
SHAFFER, Wade .... 806-651-2931 486 D
wshaffer@mail.wtamu.edu
SHAFFER, Wendy .... 978-556-3858 232 E
wshaffer@necc.mass.edu
SHAFFER LILIENTHAL,
Robin .... 641-844-5730 179 J
robin.lilienthal@iavalley.edu
SHAFFER LILIENTHAL,
Robin .... 641-844-5730 179 L
robin.lilienthal@iavalley.edu
SHAFFETT, John, E .... 850-263-3261.. 99 A
jeshaffett@baptistcollege.edu
SHAFFNER, Donna .... 315-792-3111 351 G
dlshaffner@utica.edu
SHAFTEL, Matthew, R ... 609-921-7100 306 A
mshaftel@rider.edu
SHAFTO, Carissa .... 502-410-6200 194 N
cshafto@galencollege.edu

SHAGER, Dorian .... 765-658-4270 165 G
dshager@depauw.edu
SHAH, Bindiya .... 434-528-5276 518 F
bshah@vul.edu
SHAH, Kashif .... 708-974-5348 153 D
shah@morainevalley.edu
SHAH, Manish .... 847-574-5174 150 A
mshah@lfgsm.edu
SHAH, Mubarak .... 407-823-5077 115 C
Mubarak.Shah@ucf.edu
SHAH-GORDON, Ruta ... 718-420-4254 352 C
rshahgor@wagner.edu
SHAHAN, J. Michael .... 409-882-3314 488 G
mike.shahan@lsco.edu
SHAHEED-SONUBI,
Taheera .... 716-851-1773 325 A
shaheed@ecc.edu
SHAHEEN, Lisa .... 212-229-8930 334 C
shaheenl@newschool.edu
SHAHID, Julia .... 903-813-2457 468 G
sshahid@austincollege.edu
SHAHIN, Hamdi .... 201-559-6076 302 I
shahinh@felician.edu
SHAHRABI, Kamal .... 631-420-2115 348 B
kamal.shahrabi@farmingdale.edu
SHAHROKHI, Hossein ... 713-221-8542 491 F
shahrokhi@uhd.edu
SHAIKH, Usama .... 516-876-4873 345 E
shaikhu@oldwestbury.edu
SHAILOR, Robert .... 360-596-5300 527 B
rshailor@spscc.edu
SHAIN, Sue .... 978-556-3710 232 E
sshain@necc.mass.edu
SHAIN, Yeruchim .... 732-431-1600 308 G
SHAKE, Miranda .... 217-709-0927 150 C
mshake@lakeviewcol.edu
SHAKIR, Salah .... 859-846-6248 198 G
sshakir@midway.edu
SHAKLEE, Ronald .... 330-941-4740 396 C
rshaklee@ysu.edu
SHALLBERG,
Mary Ann, H .... 281-283-2004 491 E
shallberg@uhcl.edu
SHALLEY, Heather .... 312-329-4272 153 C
heather.shalley@moody.edu
SHALLO, Michael, J .... 914-594-4574 335 H
michael_shallo@nymc.edu
SHAMAH, Irwin .... 347-394-1036 316 E
ishamah@ateret.net
SHAMASH, Yacov .... 631-632-8380 344 C
yacov.shamash@stonybrook.edu
SHAMBACH, Teresa ...... 330-369-3200 392 E
SHAMBAUGH,
Jeannine .... 330-363-5420 377 C
jeannine.shambaugh@aultman.com
SHAMBLIN, Michael ..... 318-487-7134 202 L
michael.shamblin@lacollege.edu
SHAMIM, Jina .... 415-476-8850.. 72 C
Jina.Shamim@ucsf.edu
SHAMOO, Yousif 713-348-5741 480M
shamoo@rice.edu
SHAMPENY, Renelle ..... 518-587-2100 348 A
renelle.shampeny@esc.edu
SHAMPINE,
Memorie, L .... 315-386-7042 347 F
shampinem@canton.edu
SHAMS, Arian .... 714-300-0300.. 67 H
ashams@scitech.edu
SHAMS, Nazila .... 714-300-0300.. 67 H
nshams@scitech.edu
SHAMS, Parviz .... 714-300-0300.. 67 H
pshams@scitech.edu
SHAMSUD-DIN, Ayasha 503-552-1608 407 F
ashamsud-din@ncnm.edu
SHANAFELT, Rebecca ... 727-816-3288 110 B
shanafr@phsc.edu
SHANAHAN, Catherine . 660-248-6221 272 N
cshanahan@centralmethodist.edu
SHANAHAN, Jenny .... 508-531-2764 229 C
jenny.shanahan@bridgew.edu
SHANAHAN, Megan ..... 906-353-4600 245 B
megan@kbocc.edu
SHANAHAN, Michael .... 805-652-5512.. 75 B
mshanahan@vcccd.edu
SHANAHAN, Thomas .... 919-962-0533 369 C
tcshanahan@northcarolina.edu
SHANBLATT, Stephanie . 215-968-8222 413 F
stephanie.shanblatt@bucks.edu
SHANDLEY, Thomas, C 704-894-2225 356 D
toshandley@davidson.edu
SHANE, Pam .... 740-284-5193 382 G
pshane@franciscan.edu
SHANER, Carl, L .... 570-326-3761 429 J
cshaner@pct.edu
SHANER, Megan, L ...... 919-209-2201 363 F
mlshaner@johnstoncc.edu
SHANGLE, Max, S .... 312-939-4975 145 G
mshangle@harrington.edu
SHANGRAW, Rick .... 480-965-7393.. 11 J
rick.shangraw@asu.edu

SHANK, Barbara .... 651-962-5801 263 V
bwshank@stthomas.edu
SHANK, Barbara, W ...... 651-962-5801 265 F
bwshank@stthomas.edu
SHANK, Harold .... 304-865-6003 530 F
harold.shank@ovu.edu
SHANK, Jeffrey, A .... 540-432-4206 507 A
jeff.shank@emu.edu
SHANK, Jennifer .... 931-372-3124 462 A
jshank@tntech.edu
SHANK, Larry, L .... 740-826-6109 387 C
lshank@muskingum.edu
SHANK, Leanne, M ...... 540-458-8940 519 A
lshank@wlu.edu
SHANK, Matthew, D ..... 703-284-1598 510 B
matthew.shank@marymount.edu
SHANK, Sherri .... 704-233-8025 373 C
s.shank@wingate.edu
SHANK, Theresa, M ..... 240-500-2000 215 C
tmshank@hagerstowncc.edu
SHANKEL, James, V ..... 412-578-6258 414 I
jvshankel@carlow.edu
SHANKLIN, Bart .... 309-298-1544 163 A
b-shanklin@wiu.edu
SHANKLIN, Carol .... 785-532-7927 188 H
shanklin@ksu.edu
SHANKLIN, Iris .... 404-756-4916 120 H
ishanklin@atlm.edu
SHANKMAN,
Kimberly, C .... 913-360-7413 184 K
kshankman@benedictine.edu
SHANKS, Carol .... 314-918-2538 274 K
cshanks@eden.edu
SHANKS, Martha .... 828-398-7112 360 A
mshanks@abtech.edu
SHANKWEILER, Jean .... 310-660-3119.. 43 G
jshankweiler@elcamino.edu
SHANLEY, OP, Brian, J 401-865-2153 441 F
nkelley@providence.edu
SHANLEY, Mark .... 870-543-5900.. 23 C
mshanley@seark.edu
SHANLEY, Mark .... 540-831-5433 511 C
mshanley@radford.edu
SHANLEY, Michael, V ... 978-665-3178 229 D
mshanley@fitchburgstate.edu
SHANMUGARATNAM,
Carol .... 781-283-2308 237 F
cshanmug@wellesley.edu
SHANNON, David .... 405-585-5249 399 I
david.shannon@okbu.edu
SHANNON, Denise .... 313-496-2744 252 A
dshanno1@wcccd.edu
SHANNON, Henry, D .... 909-652-6100.. 38 A
henry.shannon@chaffey.edu
SHANNON, Joe .... 903-693-2028 480 A
jshannon@panola.edu
SHANNON, John, F ...... 260-422-5561 167 F
dfshannon@indianatech.edu
SHANNON, John, T .... 973-655-4214 304 A
shannonj@mail.montclair.edu
SHANNON, Kelly .... 312-915-6159 151 E
kshann2@luc.edu
SHANNON, Linda, A ..... 718-990-6578 340 G
shannonl@stjohns.edu
SHANNON, Linita .... 252-335-3606 369 F
leshannon@ecsu.edu
SHANNON, Mike .... 513-244-8620 379 I
mike.shannon@ccuniversity.edu
SHANNON, Richard, P . 434-924-1082 514 A
rs3mt@virginia.edu
SHANNON, Scott, S ..... 315-470-6537 347 B
sshannon@esf.edu
SHANNON, Susan, K .... 717-766-2511 426 B
sshannon@messiah.edu
SHANNON, Tracey .... 334-876-9271.... 4 B
SHANNON, Vanessa ...... 617-228-2102 231 C
vshannon@bhcc.mass.edu
SHANNON, Vanessa ..... 707-778-3930.. 65 C
vshannon@santarosa.edu
SHANTON, David .... 646-660-6067 318 C
David.Shanton@baruch.cuny.edu
SHANTZ, Dale .... 989-275-5000 245 C
dale.shantz@kirkland.edu
SHAO, Alan, T .... 843-953-6651 445 B
shaoa@cofc.edu
SHAO, Lawrence .... 724-738-2093 432 A
lawrence.shao@sru.edu
SHAPARD, Christy .... 912-650-5675 131 F
cshapard@southuniversity.edu
SHAPE, Ronald .... 605-721-5214 452 J
rshape@national.edu
SHAPIRO, Adam .... 760-750-4195.. 35 B
ashapiro@csusm.edu
SHAPIRO, Alex .... 505-424-2309 310 L
ashapiro@iaia.edu
SHAPIRO, Alex A, G ..... 415-581-8842.. 71 B
shaprioa@uchastings.edu
SHAPIRO, Claire, R ...... 901-843-3750 460 F
shapiro@rhodes.edu
SHAPIRO, David, W ..... 717-867-6060 423 I
shapiro@lvc.edu

SHAPIRO, Jeff .... 973-877-3142 302 F
shapiro@essex.edu
SHAPIRO, Joe .... 619-594-5822.. 35 E
jshapiro@mail.sdsu.edu
SHAPIRO, Jon, A .... 920-924-3363 543 F
jshapiro@morainepark.edu
SHAPIRO, Jonathan ...... 641-472-1241 181 A
jshapiro@mum.edu
SHAPIRO, Joseph, I ..... 304-691-1700 532 H
shapiroj@marshall.edu
SHAPIRO, Larry, J .... 314-362-6827 285 E
shapirol@wustl.edu
SHAPIRO, Susan .... 718-940-5696 341 A
sshapiro@sjcny.edu
SHAPIRO, Tracie .... 502-863-8149 195 A
tracie_shapiro@georgetowncollege.edu
SHAPLEIGH, Shari .... 607-844-8222 350 A
shaples@tc3.edu
SHAPOVAL, Sandy .... 918-270-6459 401 C
sandy.shapoval@ptstulsa.edu
SHARAR, Bill .... 510-659-6524.. 56 J
wsharar@ohlone.edu
SHARBAUGH,
Catherine .... 610-896-1089 420 J
csharbau@haverford.edu
SHARBAUGH,
Sheila, M .... 302-356-3917.. 94 G
sheila.m.sharbaugh@wilmu.edu
SHARBAUGH, Tim .... 724-357-3011 431 A
timshar@iup.edu
SHARER, C. Gregory ...... 607-753-4721 345 C
greg.sharer@cortland.edu
SHARER, Jack .... 502-895-3411 198 E
jsharer@lpts.edu
SHARFMAN, Glenn .... 404-364-8318 129 F
gsharfman@oglethorpe.edu
SHARFMAN, Susie .... 404-364-8476 129 F
ssharfman@oglethorpe.edu
SHARIAT, Vahid .... 714-816-0366.. 70 D
vahid.shariat@trident.edu
SHARIK, Scott, A .... 419-358-3377 377 H
shariks@bluffton.edu
SHARIK, Terry .... 906-487-2454 247 A
SHARKEY, Eric .... 888-384-0849.. 26 O
esharkey@allied.edu
SHARKEY, Marguerite ... 617-266-1400 223 F
SHARKEY, Melissa .... 641-628-5180 176 E
sharkeym@central.edu
SHARKEY, Neil, A .... 814-865-6332 428 C
nas9@psu.edu
SHARMA, Madhav, P .... 570-389-4831 430 B
msharma@bloomu.edu
SHARMA, Pradeep .... 401-277-4945 442 B
psharma@risd.edu
SHARMA, Sanjay .... 802-656-3175 503 C
sanjay.sharma@uvm.edu
SHARMA, Sunny .... 561-391-1148 101 L
ssharma@dmac.edu
SHARMA, Venkat .... 607-436-2125 344 B
venkat.sharma@oneonta.edu
SHARMAN, Angel .... 307-268-2667 545 Z
asharman@caspercollege.edu
SHARON, Anthony, P ... 617-324-7130 233 C
SHARON, Daniel .... 914-632-5400 333 F
dsharon@monroecollege.edu
SHARP, Andrew .... 601-477-4198 268 A
andrew.sharp@jcjc.edu
SHARP, Antera .... 832-230-5555 479 J
antera@na.edu
SHARP, David .... 870-245-5181.. 22 C
sharpd@obu.edu
SHARP, Debbie .... 940-668-4213 479 K
dsharp@nctc.edu
SHARP, Diana .... 815-455-8996 152 B
dsharp@mchenry.edu
SHARP, George, T .... 954-545-4500 113 B
SHARP, Jennifer .... 630-434-7655 163 D
jsharp@westwood.edu
SHARP, Joe .... 561-803-2102 109 G
joe_sharp@pba.edu
SHARP, John .... 979-458-6000 484 E
chancellor@tamus.edu
SHARP, Jordon .... 435-652-7513 499 M
jsharp@dixie.edu
SHARP, Kelvin, W .... 806-716-2200 482 F
ksharp@southplainscollege.edu
SHARP, Linda .... 573-876-7277 283 A
lsharp@stephens.edu
SHARP, Marion .... 253-864-3212 525 C
msharpe@pierce.ctc.edu
SHARP, Melody .... 434-200-7025 505 L
melody.sharp@centrahealth.com
SHARP, Nick .... 417-690-2224 273 C
sharp@cofo.edu
SHARP, Randy .... 808-675-3400 134 M
sharpr@byuh.edu
SHARP, Sandra .... 203-576-5612.. 91 H
sandra.sharp@stvincentscollege.edu
SHARP, Shayna .... 208-535-5389 138 B
shayna.sharp@my.eitc.edu
SHARP, Valerie .... 417-865-2815 274 L
sharpv@evangel.edu
SHARPE, Allan .... 915-532-3737 497 D
asharpe@westerntech.edu
SHARPE, Aubrey, D ...... 903-510-2900 491 A
asha@tjc.edu
SHARPE, James .... 415-451-2867.. 63 B
jsharpe@sfts.edu
SHARPE, Jessica, G ..... 336-272-7102 357 B
jessica.sharpe@greensboro.edu
SHARPE, Karen .... 508-929-8786 230 G
Karen.Sharpe@worcester.edu
SHARPE, Lawrence .... 718-289-5313 318 E
lawrence.sharpe@bcc.cuny.edu
SHARPE, Rick .... 602-386-4104.. 11 F
rick.sharpe@arizonachristian.edu
SHARPE, Shane .... 205-348-5506.... 8 E
ssharpe@ua.edu
SHARPE, Stephen .... 903-233-3825 477 G
stephensharpe@letu.edu
SHARPE, Steve .... 903-233-3835 477 G
stevesharpe@letu.edu
SHARPHORN, Dan .... 512-499-4563 493 K
dsharphorn@utsystem.edu
SHARPLES, Russell .... 704-463-3401 367 F
russ.sharples@pfeiffer.edu
SHARPLES, Stacey .... 941-752-5000 114 B
SHARPNACK, Patricia ... 440-684-6032 394 G
psharpnack@ursuline.edu
SHARPS, Alonia, C .... 301-322-0170 217 G
sharpsac@pgcc.edu
SHARRAR, Jack .... 415-439-2412.. 27 F
jsharrar@act-sf.org
SHATTUCK, Larry .... 410-532-5551 217 F
lshattuck@ndm.edu
SHATTUCK, R. Cooper .. 205-348-8345.... 8 D
cshattuck@uasystem.ua.edu
SHAUB, Larry .... 610-796-8298 412 C
larry.shaub@alvernia.edu
SHAUGHNESSY, Angie .. 859-336-5082 199 B
ashaughnessy@sccky.edu
SHAUGHNESSY, Anne ... 617-824-8525 226 A
anne_shaughnessy@emerson.edu
SHAUGHNESSY,
Joseph .... 254-659-7821 475 A
jxs@hillcollege.edu
SHAUGHNESSY,
Joseph .... 781-768-7133 236 A
joseph.shaughnessy@regiscollege.edu
SHAUGHNESSY, Josette 915-831-6330 473 J
jshaugh2@epcc.edu
SHAUGHNESSY, Mark ... 631-656-2147 326 B
mark.shaughnessy@ftc.edu
SHAUGHNESSY,
Michael .... 724-503-1001 439 B
mshaughnessy@washjeff.edu
SHAUL, Lesa .... 205-652-3460.... 9 G
lcc@uwa.edu
SHAUNAK, Raj .... 662-243-1911 267 C
rshaunak@eastms.edu
SHAUNAK, Sudershan .. 760-757-2121.. 54 G
sshaunak@miracosta.edu
SHAVER, Debra, D .... 413-585-2523 236 G
dshaver@smith.edu
SHAVER, Joan, L .... 520-626-6152.. 18 E
jshaver@email.arizona.edu
SHAVER, Joseph, E .... 304-326-1481 530 G
jshaver@salemu.edu
SHAVERS, Tressa .... 301-423-3600.. 96 H
SHAW, Anne, C .... 910-938-6322 361 F
shawa@coastalcarolina.edu
SHAW, Barbara, L .... 209-946-2424.. 73 C
bshaw@pacific.edu
SHAW, Becky .... 413-585-4940 236 G
rshaw@smith.edu
SHAW, Brandy .... 713-525-2124 493 J
shawb1@stthom.edu
SHAW, Brian, D .... 804-828-1200 514 F
bdshaw@vcu.edu
SHAW, Brian, R .... 202-231-8698 547 N
brian.shaw@dodiis.mil
SHAW, Chester .... 708-974-5360 153 D
schawc6@morainevalley.edu
SHAW, Chip .... 806-743-1500 490 A
chip.shaw@ttuhsc.edu
SHAW, Dameon .... 662-254-3901 269 C
dameon.shaw@mvsu.edu
SHAW, Darlene, L .... 843-792-2228 447 G
shawd@musc.edu
SHAW, David .... 662-325-3570 269 A
dshaw@research.msstate.edu
SHAW, Howard .... 256-726-7312.... 6 C
hshaw@oakwood.edu
SHAW, James, A .... 606-783-2599 198 H
j.shaw@moreheadstate.edu
SHAW, Jane .... 650-723-1762.. 68 G
SHAW, Jen, D .... 352-392-1261 115 D
jends@dso.ufl.edu
SHAW, Jerone .... 662-621-4085 266 H
jshaw@coahomacc.edu
SHAW, Karen .... 765-455-9216 168 B
kshaw28@iuk.edu
SHAW, Karen, A .... 585-262-1501 333 G
kshaw@monroecc.edu
SHAW, Kathleen .... 804-828-6683 514 F
kshaw5@vcu.edu
SHAW, Katie, R .... 407-303-5548.. 97 J
katie.shaw@adu.edu
SHAW, Ken .... 817-202-6202 483 C
kshaw@swau.edu
SHAW, Kevin .... 909-469-5401.. 76 I
kshaw@westernu.edu
SHAW, Kristi .... 620-441-5206 186 E
kshaw@cowley.edu
SHAW, Linda .... 480-732-7307.. 14 K
Linda.Shaw@cgc.edu
SHAW, Linda .... 415-239-3303.. 39 A
lshaw@ccsf.edu
SHAW, Lori .... 620-331-2480 188 B
lshaw@indycc.edu
SHAW, Lorna, L .... 502-597-6443 197 G
lorna.shaw@kysu.edu
SHAW, Marc .... 646-664-3013 318 B
marc.shaw@cuny.edu
SHAW, Mary Ann .... 713-942-5036 493 J
shawme@sthom.edu
SHAW, Matthew .... 317-781-5763 173 I
shawm@uindy.edu
SHAW, Nancy .... 802-224-3000 503 F
nancy.shaw@vsc.edu
SHAW, Pankaj .... 614-292-1486 389 A
pshah@oh-tech.org
SHAW, Penelope .... 707-826-3942.. 35 D
pjs25@humboldt.edu
SHAW, Richard .... 806-291-1162 496 K
shawr@wbu.edu
SHAW, Rick .... 661-722-6300.. 27 P
rshaw@avc.edu
SHAW, Robert, S .... 570-348-6245 425 D
rsshaw@marywood.edu
SHAW, Russell .... 601-857-3961 267 D
RDShaw@hindscc.edu
SHAW, Stephen .... 937-769-1881 376 M
sshaw@antioch.edu
SHAW, Steve .... 937-769-1351 376 L
sshaw@antioch.edu
SHAW, Suzanne .... 417-836-5139 279 A
suzanneshaw@missouristate.edu
SHAW, Suzanne .... 706-385-1460 130 C
suzanne.shaw@point.edu
SHAW, Teresa .... 909-602-2505.. 60 A
teresa.shaw@pomona.edu
SHAW, Thomas .... 530-226-4773.. 66 G
tshaw@simpsonu.edu
SHAW, Timothy .... 972-883-5291 494 A
tim.shaw@utdallas.edu
SHAW, Tom .... 269-965-3931 244 L
shawt@kellogg.edu
SHAW, Wade, H .... 478-301-2459 128 G
shaw_wh@mercer.edu
SHAW-BURNETT,
Margaret, A .... 716-878-5907 345 B
shawma@buffalostate.edu
SHAW HORTON,
Sheilah .... 410-617-2842 216 D
sshorton@loyola.edu
SHAWCROFT, Sally .... 970-542-3151.. 84 A
sally.shawcroft@morgancc.edu
SHAWN, Donna, S .... 913-627-4171 188 G
dshawn@kckcc.edu
SHAWNEY, Lisa, L .... 603-513-1335 299 C
lisa.shawney@granite.edu
SHAWVER, Jeffrey .... 304-647-6325 533 B
jshawver@osteo.wvsom.edu
SHAWVER, Rebecca ...... 979-230-3313 469 G
rebecca.shawver@brazosport.edu
SHAWVER, William, G .. 513-529-9203 386 K
shawvewg@miamioh.edu
SHAY, Carla, E .... 231-843-5942 252 H
ceshay@westshore.edu
SHAY, Pamela .... 614-947-6135 382 H
pamela.shay@franklin.edu
SHAY, Patrick .... 612-436-7519 257 K
pshay@msbcollege.edu
SHAY, Robert .... 573-882-2606 283 H
shayr@missouri.edu
SHAY, Robert, S .... 303-492-7505.. 86 E
robert.shay@colorado.edu
SHAY, William .... 323-563-4840.. 38 C
williamshay@cdrewu.edu
SHCHEGOL, Alex .... 718-522-9073 315 E
ashchegol@asa.edu
SHCHEGOL, Alla .... 718-522-9073 315 E
allchik@asa.edu
SHEA, Catherine .... 303-492-7896.. 86 E
catherine.shea@colorado.edu
SHEA, Donna .... 617-353-5124 224 E
dshea@bu.edu
SHEA, James, P .... 701-355-8100 375 K
sjzander@umary.edu
SHEA, Jane .... 508-854-4358 232 F
jshea@qcc.mass.edu
SHEA, Kevin, J .... 617-552-3250 224 B
k.shea@bc.edu
SHEA, Rich, J .... 814-886-6474 427 B
rshea@mtaloy.edu
SHEAFF, Shannon .... 928-757-0817.. 15 K
ssheaff@mohave.edu
SHEAFFER, Andrea .... 510-649-2465.. 46 E
asheaffer@gtu.edu
SHEAFFER, Ellen .... 301-387-3003 215 A
ellen.sheaffer@garrettcollege.edu
SHEAFFER, Karen, M .... 570-321-4311 425 B
sheaffer@lycoming.edu
SHEAFFER, Vernon .... 913-758-6196 191 I
vernon.sheaffer@stmary.edu
SHEAHAN, John .... 217-351-2555 155 I
JSheahan@parkland.edu
SHEAHAN, Mary .... 701-483-2883 373 H
Mary.Sheahan@dickinsonstate.edu
SHEALEY, Monika .... 856-256-4751 306 D
shealey@rowan.edu
SHEAR, Skip .... 660-944-2853 273 E
sshear@conception.edu
SHEAR, Stephen .... 813-253-7014 106 C
sshear2@hccfl.edu
SHEARD, Reed .... 805-565-7171.. 76 K
rsheard@westmont.edu
SHEARED, Vanessa .... 916-278-6639.. 34 E
vsheared@saclink.csus.edu
SHEARER, Christine ...... 406-657-2177 287 H
c.shearercremean@msubillings.edu
SHEARER, Jonathan, L . 724-589-2700 436 E
jshearer@thiel.edu
SHEARER, Liz .... 410-704-2451 221 A
lshearer@towson.edu
SHEARER, Pam .... 601-318-6561 271 F
pshearer@wmcarey.edu
SHEARIN, Lisa .... 252-246-1310 367 D
lshearin@wilsoncc.edu
SHEARIN, Veronica .... 775-831-1314 296 F
vshearin@sierranevada.edu
SHEARIN, Wally, M ...... 336-506-4279 359 N
wally.shearin@alamancecc.edu
SHEARN, Robert .... 859-344-3683 200 C
shearnr@thomasmore.edu
SHEARON, James .... 910-892-3178 357 D
jshearon@heritagebiblecollege.edu
SHEARON, Randall .... 919-735-5151 367 A
shearon@waynecc.edu
SHEARRILL,
Charmagne .... 661-255-1050.. 31 B
cshearrill@calarts.edu
SHEBLE, Mary Ann .... 248-232-4512 248 E
masheble@oaklandcc.edu
SHEBLE, Mary Ann .... 248-942-3214 248 E
masheble@oaklandcc.edu
SHECKELLS, Sara .... 617-730-7072 235 B
sara.sheckells@newbury.edu
SHECKLER, Allyson .... 508-565-1724 237 A
asheckler@stonehill.edu
SHECTERLE, Ross, A ..... 414-425-8300 538 J
rector@shsst.edu
SHEDD, Cindy .... 618-374-5153 156 C
cindy.shedd@principia.edu
SHEDD, Jean, E .... 847-491-8546 155 D
j-shedd@northwestern.edu
SHEDD, Louis .... 205-391-2359.... 7 A
lshedd@sheltonstate.edu
SHEDD, Sally .... 757-455-3283 518 H
sshedd@vwc.edu
SHEDEK, Lindsay .... 319-399-8617 176 G
lshedek@coe.edu
SHEDRICK, Karen, R ..... 601-877-6111 266 C
karen@alcorn.edu
SHEDRON, Brandon ...... 314-264-1802 162 J
brandon.shedron@vatterott-college.edu
SHEEHAN, Diep .... 781-768-7078 236 A
diep.sheehan@regiscollege.edu
SHEEHAN, Eugene .... 970-351-2817.. 87 A
eugene.sheehan@unco.edu
SHEEHAN, Heather .... 701-224-5465 374 E
heather.sheehan@bismarckstate.edu
SHEEHAN, James, P ...... 413-545-1581 228 F
sheehan@admin.umass.edu
SHEEHAN, Jerry .... 406-994-2525 287 G
jsheehan@montana.edu
SHEEHAN, Laura .... 860-231-5297.. 93 A
lsheehan@usj.edu
SHEEHAN, Maria, C ...... 775-673-7025 295 F
msheehan@tmcc.edu
SHEEHAN, Rhonda .... 518-631-9835 351 A
sheehanr@uniongraduatecollege.edu
SHEEHAN, Robert, J ...... 410-546-4127 220 E
rjsheehan@salisbury.edu
SHEEHAN, Ryan .... 803-323-3023 451 I
sheehanr@winthrop.edu
SHEEHAN, Tim .... 801-957-2001 500 E
tim.scheehan@slcc.edu
SHEEHAN, Timothy .... 651-213-4166 256 C
tsheehan@hazelden.edu

SHEEHAN, JR.,
William, F .... 573-592-5327 285 J
bill.sheehan@westminster-mo.edu
SHEEHEY, John, D .... 802-654-2571 502 H
jsheehey@smcvt.edu
SHEEHY, Colette .... 434-924-3349 514 A
cc@virginia.edu
SHEEHY, Harry .... 603-646-2465 297 G
harry.sheehy@dartmouth.edu
SHEEKS, Gina .... 706-507-8730 123 D
sheeks_gina@columbusstate.edu
SHEELEY, Robert, G ...... 203-392-6050.. 88 F
sheeleyr1@southernct.edu
SHEERAN, Kate .... 415-503-6251.. 63 A
SHEERAN, Robert, M .... 513-745-2072 396 B
sheeran@xavier.edu
SHEERER, Marilyn .... 910-962-3389 372 A
sheererm@uncw.edu
SHEETS, Chad .... 651-423-8232 258 E
chad.sheets@dctc.edu
SHEETS, Christine .... 740-593-4094 389 H
sheetsch@ohio.edu
SHEETS, Helene .... 419-824-3965 385 F
hsheets@lourdes.edu
SHEETS, Julie .... 573-518-2206 278 F
jsheets@mineralarea.edu
SHEETZ, Ken .... 803-323-2275 451 I
sheetzk@winthrop.edu
SHEFF, Kimberly .... 207-509-7224 212 A
ksheff@unity.edu
SHEFFER, Ilene .... 574-520-4344 168 F
isheffer@iusb.edu
SHEFFIELD, Ann, D ...... 814-332-2357 411 F
asheffie@allegheny.edu
SHEFFIELD, Bethany, D 814-641-3101 421 L
sheffib@juniata.edu
SHEFFIELD,
Christopher, R .... 716-286-8425 336 E
crs@niagara.edu
SHEFFIELD, Linda .... 434-736-2002 516 H
linda.sheffield@southside.edu
SHEFFIELD, Roy, S .... 828-884-8312 355 A
scotts@brevard.edu
SHEFFIELD, Vonne .... 478-301-2500 128 G
sheffield_v@mercer.edu
SHEFFLETTE, Nancy, A .. 501-882-4581.. 19 E
nashefflette@asub.edu
SHEGAN, Christine .... 570-662-4900 431 D
cshegan@mansfield.edu
SHEHEANE, Dene .... 404-894-1238 125 D
dene.sheheane@dev.gatech.edu
SHEHEE, Amy .... 859-985-3002 193 F
sheheea@berea.edu
SHEIBLEY, Thomas, J ... 610-660-1030 434 G
tsheible@sju.edu
SHEID, Christopher ...... 307-382-1661 546 L
csheid@wwcc.wy.edu
SHEIKH, Ammad .... 410-532-5393 217 F
asheikh@ndm.edu
SHEILLEY, Holly .... 859-233-8300 200 D
hsheilley@transy.edu
SHEIN, David .... 845-758-7454 315 G
shein@bard.edu
SHEKLETON, James, F . 605-773-3455 453 E
jim.shekleton@sdbor.edu
SHELBURNE, Stephanie 818-785-2726.. 37 I
stephanie.shelburne@casalomacollege.edu
SHELBY, Jane .... 907-786-4708.. 10 H
njshelby@uaa.alaska.edu
SHELBY, Liz .... 541-552-6111 409 G
shelbyl@sou.edu
SHELDAHL, Tania .... 928-776-2128.. 18 L
tania.sheldahl@yc.edu
SHELDEN, Deborah, L .. 906-487-3112 247 A
dlassila@mtu.edu
SHELDON, Jane .... 308-865-8427 293 G
sheldonj@unk.edu
SHELDON, Marianne .... 510-430-3221.. 54 F
mshel@mills.edu
SHELDON, Michael .... 207-221-4591 213 B
msheldon@une.edu
SHELDON, Todd .... 402-363-5601 294 G
tlsheldon@york.edu
SHELEY, Joseph, F .... 209-667-3201.. 35 C
president@csustan.edu
SHELL, Cathy .... 828-898-8740 358 F
shell@lmc.edu
SHELL, Chandrea .... 423-461-8756 459 I
chshell@milligan.edu
SHELL, Christina .... 734-487-2382 242 J
cshell@emich.edu
SHELL, Martin .... 650-723-4186.. 68 G
mshell@stanford.edu
SHELL, Rick .... 907-786-1778.. 10 H
rshell@uaa.alaska.edu
SHELLABARGER,
Sheila, G .... 937-775-2685 396 A
sheila.shellabarger@wright.edu
SHELLBERG, David .... 208-562-3257 138 A
davidshellberg@cwidaho.cc
SHELLEDY, David, C ..... 210-567-8850 495 B
shelledyy@uthscsa.edu
SHELLEY, Chris, A .... 815-835-6298 158 I
chris.a.shelley@svcc.edu
SHELLEY, Daniel .... 585-475-6736 339 G
drsadm@rit.edu
SHELLEY, Ena, M .... 317-940-9752 164 L
eshelley@butler.edu
SHELLEY, Jeff .... 205-929-3416.... 5 E
jshelley@lawsonstate.edu
SHELLEY, MargE .... 913-469-8500 188 E
mshelley@jccc.edu
SHELLEY, Stephen .... 940-397-4110 478 G
stephen.shelley@mwsu.edu
SHELLY, Heather .... 715-682-1254 538 D
hshelly@northland.edu
SHELLY, Rubel .... 248-218-2019 249 D
rshelly@rc.edu
SHELPMAN, JR., David 561-912-2166 102 N
dshelpman@evergladesuniversity.edu
SHELTON, Alice .... 317-955-6022 171 A
ashelton@marian.edu
SHELTON, Amy .... 202-885-8657.. 97 E
ashelton@wesleyseminary.edu
SHELTON, Amy .... 614-794-4254 460 A
ashelton@omorecollege.edu
SHELTON, Brad .... 541-346-2090 410 F
shelton@uoregon.edu
SHELTON, Christie .... 256-782-5276.... 4 L
cshelton@jsu.edu
SHELTON, Courtney ...... 800-280-0307 163 I
courtney.shelton@ace.edu
SHELTON, Deena .... 903-233-4410 477 G
deenashelton@letu.edu
SHELTON, Donna .... 276-523-7478 516 A
dshelton@me.vccs.edu
SHELTON, Donna, M ..... 757-594-7155 506 I
dshelton@cnu.edu
SHELTON, Iverna .... 404-527-4520 122 D
ishelton@carver.edu
SHELTON, Janice .... 540-674-3611 516 B
jshelton@nr.edu
SHELTON, Jennifer .... 845-848-7500 324 B
jennifer.shelton@dc.edu
SHELTON, Julie .... 205-348-7917.... 8 E
jshelton@fa.ua.edu
SHELTON, JR.,
M. Dwight .... 540-231-8775 518 B
mdsjr@vt.edu
SHELTON, Maggie .... 270-901-1112 197 C
maggie.shelton@kctcs.edu
SHELTON, Melvin .... 229-430-2723 119 H
melvin.shelton@asurams.edu
SHELTON, Michelle ...... 610-499-4239 439 G
mmshelton@widener.edu
SHELTON, Myles .... 409-944-1200 474 G
mshelton@gc.edu
SHELTON, Nellie, R ...... 864-833-8213 448 E
nshelton@presby.edu
SHELTON, Robby .... 931-363-9890 458 D
rshelton@martinmethodist.edu
SHELTON, Robby, C ..... 931-363-9890 458 D
rshelton@martinmethodist.edu
SHELTON, Roosevelt, O 502-597-6415 197 G
roosevelt.shelton@kysu.edu
SHELTON, Tamara .... 765-641-4192 164 B
tsshelton@anderson.edu
SHELTON, Tasha .... 847-491-3024 155 D
t-shelton@northwestern.edu
SHELTON, Terri, L .... 336-256-0426 371 C
shelton@uncg.edu
SHELTON, Treva .... 812-866-7056 166 E
shelton@hanover.edu
SHELTON, Vickie .... 806-371-5017 467 E
vlshelton@actx.edu
SHELTON, W. Brian ...... 706-886-6831 132 F
bshelton@tfc.edu
SHELTON-CLARK, Anne 662-621-4220 266 H
ashelton-clark@coahomacc.edu
SHELTON-JOHNSON,
LaCoya .... 480-731-8103.. 14 J
lacoya.shelton-johnson@domail.maricopa.edu
SHEMMER, Rosalie .... 215-204-7981 436 C
rosalie.shemmer@temple.edu
SHEMTOV, Kasriel .... 248-414-6900 246 F
rabbi@theshul.net
SHEMWELL, Bridget ...... 870-762-3174.. 19 C
bshemwell@smail.anc.edu
SHEMWELL, James .... 870-762-3191.. 19 C
jshemwell@smail.anc.edu
SHEN, Chi .... 502-597-6083 197 G
chi.shen@kysu.edu
SHEN, Shiji .... 908-737-3470 303 C
sshen@kean.edu
SHEN, Sunny .... 516-739-1545 335 C
academic_dean@nyctcm.edu
SHENBERGER, Amy .... 940-565-2207 492 D
amy.shenberger@unt.edu
SHENDY, Joellen .... 240-684-2201 220 A
student-services@umuc.edu
SHENETTE, John .... 336-758-5000 372 G
shenetjj@wfu.edu
SHENK, Sara, W .... 574-295-3726 163 M
swshenk@ambs.edu
SHENNAN, Andrew .... 781-283-3583 237 F
ashennan@wellesley.edu
SHENNUM, Barry .... 602-944-3335.. 11 D
bshennum@aicag.edu
SHENOSKY, Joseph ...... 610-785-6271 434 E
jshenosky@scs.edu
SHENOSKY, Joseph, T .. 610-785-6520 434 E
jshenosky@scs.edu
SHENOY, Kallya .... 661-654-3425.. 32 G
kshenoy@csub.edu
SHENOY, Kallya .... 661-654-2155.. 32 G
kshenoy@csub.edu
SHENOY, Kallya .... 661-654-2115.. 32 G
kshenoy@csub.edu
SHEPARD, Bruce .... 360-650-3480 528 D
president@wwu.edu
SHEPARD, Charles .... 859-858-3511 193 A
charlie.shepard@asbury.edu
SHEPARD, Joseph .... 575-538-6238 314 E
shepardj@wnmu.edu
SHEPARD, Kathy, J .... 717-728-2261 415 B
kathyshepard@centralpenn.edu
SHEPARD, Kim .... 803-327-7402 444 F
kshepard@clintoncollege.edu
SHEPARD, Lorrie .... 303-492-6937.. 86 E
lorrie.shepard@colorado.edu
SHEPARD, Nancy .... 530-938-5881.. 41 E
shepard@siskiyous.edu
SHEPARD, Nicole .... 912-583-3298 121 H
nshepard@bpc.edu
SHEPARD, Nicole, G ..... 912-583-3298 121 H
nshepard@bpc.edu
SHEPARD, Robert .... 919-684-3633 356 E
robert.shepard@duke.edu
SHEPARD, Robin .... 209-381-6470.. 54 C
shepard.r@mccd.edu
SHEPARD, Wells .... 864-587-4254 449 D
shepardw@smcsc.edu
SHEPARD-SMITH,
Andrew .... 931-221-7881 461 C
shepardsmitha@apsu.edu
SHEPARDSON,
J. Andrew .... 781-891-2161 223 E
ashepardson@bentley.edu
SHEPELOV, Sergey .... 503-491-7411 407 C
sergey.shepelov@mhcc.edu
SHEPELSKY, Ernie .... 718-429-6600 352 A
ernie.shepelsky@vaughn.edu
SHEPHERD, Chad .... 314-367-8700 281 G
chad.shepherd@stlcop.edu
SHEPHERD, Gregory, J . 305-284-3420 118 A
shepherd@miami.edu
SHEPHERD, Janet .... 563-425-5788 183 G
shepherdj@uiu.edu
SHEPHERD, Jennifer ...... 260-982-5222 170 a
jkshepherd@manchester.edu
SHEPHERD, Karla, M .... 410-837-4760 221 B
kshepherd@ubalt.edu
SHEPHERD, Kristy .... 864-578-8770 448 G
kshepherd@sherman.edu
SHEPHERD, JR.,
Lewis, A .... 870-230-5081.. 21 B
shepherdl@hsu.edu
SHEPHERD,
Margaret, A .... 206-543-7604 527 G
mshep@uw.edu
SHEPHERD, Melissa, D 434-395-2951 509 H
shepherdmd@longwood.edu
SHEPHERD, Nancy .... 505-566-3264 312 K
shepherdn@sanjuancollege.edu
SHEPHERD, Paul .... 715-425-4444 540 E
paul.shepherd@uwrf.edu
SHEPHERD, Roger .... 334-387-3877.... 1 E
rogershephered@amridgeuniversity.edu
SHEPHERD, Sara .... 903-877-7967 495 C
sara.shepherd@uthct.edu
SHEPHERD, Tamara, A . 703-370-6600 511 B
SHEPLER, Kent .... 608-663-2000 536 S
kshepler@mediainstitute.edu
SHEPPARD, Ellen .... 704-355-5316 355 G
ellen.sheppard@carolinascollege.edu
SHEPPARD, Eric, J .... 757-728-6970 508 C
eric.sheppard@hamptonu.edu
SHEPPARD, James, A ... 620-229-6227 191 B
james.sheppard@sckans.edu
SHEPPARD, Kirsten ...... 865-273-8991 458 E
kirsten.sheppard@maryvillecollege.edu
SHEPPARD, Lyle .... 910-630-7225 359 C
lsheppard@methodist.edu
SHEPPARD, Matt .... 218-299-6519 259 H
matt.sheppard@minnesota.edu
SHEPPARD, Nancy .... 412-809-5100 433 D
sheppard.nancy@pti.edu
SHEPPARD, Phillip .... 508-588-9100 232 A
SHEPPARD, Ray .... 910-879-5542 360 C
rsheppard@bladencc.edu
SHEPPARD, Steve .... 210-436-3684 481 C
sheppard@stmarytx.edu
SHEPPARD, Tina .... 703-284-1608 510 B
tina.sheppard@marymount.edu
SHEPPARD, Varinya ...... 315-798-8125 340 D
vsheppard@secon.edu
SHEPPICK, Joyce .... 724-938-4430 430 C
sheppick@calu.edu
SHEPROW, Lauren .... 631-632-4896 344 C
lauren.sheprow@stonybrook.edu
SHEPTAK, Dale .... 440-375-7368 385 B
dsheptak@lec.edu
SHER, Ephraim, Y .... 845-434-5240 354 E
esher@fallsburgyeshiva.com
SHERADIN, Pamela .... 315-364-3260 352 F
psheradin@wells.edu
SHERBURNE, Gwen ...... 651-523-2804 256 B
gsherburne@hamline.edu
SHEREMAN, Sandra .... 562-985-5537.. 33 F
sandra.shereman@csulb.edu
SHEREN, Deborah .... 216-373-5347 388 A
dsheren@ndc.edu
SHERER, Michael .... 574-535-7406 166 C
msherer@goshen.edu
SHERF, Tom .... 215-702-4848 414 C
tsherf@cairn.edu
SHERFESEE, Kimberly ... 843-349-2138 444 G
ksherf@coastal.edu
SHERIDAN, Chris .... 216-368-2774 378 J
chris.sheridan@case.edu
SHERIDAN, John .... 620-341-5208 186 H
jsherida@emporia.edu
SHERIDAN, Mark .... 806-742-1832 489 F
mark.sheridan@ttu.edu
SHERIDAN, Nora .... 617-322-3506 227 J
nora_sheridan@laboure.edu
SHERIDAN, Pamela .... 610-436-3383 432 B
psheridan@wcupa.edu
SHERIDAN, TOR, Sean . 740-283-6216 382 G
ssheridan@franciscan.edu
SHERIDAN, Terence ...... 334-387-3877.... 1 E
terencesheridan@amridgeuniversity.edu
SHERIFF, Sarah, M .... 717-245-1787 417 B
sheriffs@dickinson.edu
SHERIFF-TAYLOR,
Patricia .... 601-979-2127 267 H
patricia.sherriff-taylor@jsums.edu
SHERINGHAM, Carole .. 802-447-6358 503 A
csheringham@svc.edu
SHERLIN, Joe, H .... 423-439-4210 461 D
sherlin@etsu.edu
SHERLIN, Merideth .... 701-231-9653 374 C
meredith.sherlin@ndsu.edu
SHERLOCK,
Christopher .... 410-287-6060 214 C
csherlock@cecil.edu
SHERLOCK, Jean .... 818-333-3558.. 56 A
SHERLOCK, Jerry .... 818-333-3558.. 56 A
SHERLOCK, Julia, B ...... 989-774-3068 240 O
julia.b.sherlock@cmich.edu
SHERLOCK, Richard, A . 724-946-7191 439 D
sherlora@westminster.edu
SHERMAN, Ann, M .... 415-405-3921.. 36 A
asherman@sfsu.edu
SHERMAN, Curt .... 402-643-7369 289 J
curt.sherman@cune.edu
SHERMAN, Daniel .... 713-500-3270 495 A
Daniel.Sherman@uth.tmc.edu
SHERMAN, Douglas, H . 401-739-5000 441 E
dsherman@neit.edu
SHERMAN, Eileen .... 414-382-6503 534 I
eileen.sherman@alverno.edu
SHERMAN, Elma, C .... 574-372-5100 166 D
elma.sherman@grace.edu
SHERMAN, Erin, L .... 210-486-4932 466 K
esherman6@alamo.edu
SHERMAN, Gary .... 240-895-2000 218 B
glsherman@smcm.edu
SHERMAN, George .... 718-631-6273 320 F
gsherman@qcc.cuny.edu
SHERMAN, George, M .. 978-232-2009 226 C
gsherman@endicott.edu
SHERMAN, Glen .... 973-720-2761 309 I
shermang@wpunj.edu
SHERMAN, Hugh .... 740-593-2000 389 H
shermanh@ohio.edu
SHERMAN, III, James .. 605-856-5880 453 B
james.sherman@sintegleska.edu
SHERMAN, Jeannine ...... 262-524-7242 535 D
shermanj@carrollu.edu
SHERMAN, Jennifer .... 719-549-3362.. 85 A
jennifer.sherman@pueblocc.edu
SHERMAN, Jill .... 502-456-6509 200 A
jsherman@sctd.edu
SHERMAN, Julee .... 660-248-6203 272 N
jsherman@centralmethodist.edu
SHERMAN, Michael .... 773-252-5135 156 J
michael.sherman@resu.edu
SHERMAN, Mike .... 330-972-7593 392 H
provost@uakron.edu

SHOEMAKE, Kellie .... 910-695-3714 365 H
shoemakek@sandhills.edu
SHOEMAKE, Monte .... 417-626-1234 280 B
shoemake.monte@occ.edu
SHOEMAKER, Ben .... 614-823-1534 390 C
bshoemaker@otterbein.edu
SHOEMAKER, Carol ...... 417-328-1531 282 D
cshoemaker@sbuniv.edu
SHOEMAKER, Chris ...... 276-326-4212 505 D
cshoemaker@bluefield.edu
SHOEMAKER, Cindy ..... 717-262-2006 440 D
cshoemaker@wilson.edu
SHOEMAKER, Jamie ..... 304-326-1540 530 G
jshoemaker@salemu.edu
SHOEMAKER, Jillian ...... 406-657-1104 288 G
jillian.shoemaker@rocky.edu
SHOEMAKER, Peter .... 202-319-5220.. 95 A
shoemaker@cua.edu
SHOEMAKER, Scott .... 619-849-2565.. 59 K
scottshoemaker@pointloma.edu
SHOEMAKER, Stowe ..... 702-895-3308 295 G
stowe.shoemaker@unlv.edu
SHOEMAKER, Troy .... 850-478-8496 110 C
SHOENBERGER, George 301-985-7873 220 A
cfo@umuc.edu
SHOENER, Gary .... 570-504-7949 422 G
shoenerg@lackawanna.edu
SHOENER, Pattie .... 504-282-4455 206 C
pshoener@nobts.edu
SHOFFNER, Dan .... 903-586-2518 476 K
dshoffner@jacksonville-college.edu
SHOGE, Ruth, C .... 410-778-7292 221 D
rshoge2@washcoll.edu
SHOGER, Diane, L .... 585-262-1504 333 G
dshoger@monroecc.edu
SHOJAI, Siamack .... 973-720-2964 309 I
shojais@wpunj.edu
SHOKRALLA, Diana .... 281-998-6150 481 G
diana.shkralla@sjcd.edu
SHOLLENBERGER,
Kevin .... 410-516-8382 216 A
ksholle1@jhu.edu
SHOLTEN, Bryan .... 303-963-3398.. 79 L
bsholten@ccu.edu
SHOMAKER, Kelli .... 979-830-4459 469 F
kelli.shomaker@blinn.edu
SHOMO, Thomas, H ..... 434-223-6262 508 B
tshomo@hsc.edu
SHONBRUN, Anne .... 718-270-4551 344 D
anne.shonbrun@downstate.edu
SHONK, Brian .... 870-612-2003.. 24 G
brian.shonk@uaccb.edu
SHONROCK,
Michael, D .... 636-949-4900 276 L
mshonrock@lindenwood.edu
SHONTZ, Gary, B .... 319-273-3576 176 A
gary.shontz@uni.edu
SHONTZ, Susan, F .... 814-641-3304 421 L
shontzs@juniata.edu
SHOOK, Douglas .... 213-740-4623.. 74 D
shook@esd.usc.edu
SHOOK, Douglas .... 213-740-7197.. 74 D
shook@usc.edu
SHOOK, Mark .... 706-880-8976 127 N
mshook@lagrange.edu
SHOOP, David .... 803-935-4294 131 F
dshoop@southuniversity.edu
SHOOT, Madge .... 217-234-5375 150 B
mbailey1292@lakeland.cc.il.us
SHOOTER, Rhonda .... 806-720-7125 478 A
rhonda.shooter@lcu.edu
SHOPE, Alicia .... 828-251-6600 370 E
ashope@unca.edu
SHOPE, Mary Ann .... 501-812-2251.. 22 F
mashope@pulaskitech.edu
SHOPE, Ronald, J .... 402-449-2872 290 F
rshope@graceu.edu
SHOR, Eric, M .... 304-457-6276 529 C
shorem@ab.edu
SHOR, Glen .... 617-324-0646 233 C
SHOR, Stuart, B .... 212-817-7604 319 B
sshor@gc.cuny.edu
SHORB, Deanna .... 641-269-4981 178 I
shorb@grinnell.edu
SHORE, Cliff .... 703-993-2580 507 K
cshore@gmu.edu
SHORE, Muriel .... 201-559-6030 302 I
shorem@felician.edu
SHOREIBAH, Al .... 414-297-6492 543 E
shoreiba@matc.edu
SHORES, Dennis .... 610-647-4400 421 B
dshores@immaculata.edu
SHORES, Robin, H .... 610-690-6879 436 A
rshores1@swarthmore.edu
SHORES, Sylvia .... 785-890-1521 190 C
sylvia.shores@nwktc.edu
SHOREY, David .... 978-468-7111 227 B
shorey@gcts.edu
SHORT, Al .... 303-722-5724.. 83 O
ashort@lincolntech.com
SHORT, Andrea .... 972-241-3371 472 A
ashort@dallas.edu
SHORT, Anthony, E ...... 419-372-7019 377 I
ashort@bgsu.edu
SHORT, Brent .... 352-588-8258 111 L
brent.short@saintleo.edu
SHORT, Colin, W .... 765-641-4101 164 B
cwshort@anderson.edu
SHORT, Curtis .... 317-931-2313 165 C
cshort@cts.edu
SHORT, David .... 276-328-0196 514 B
dps4v@uvawise.edu
SHORT, David .... 409-880-8060 488 E
David.Short@lamar.edu
SHORT, JR., David .... 409-880-8060 488 F
david.short@lamar.edu
SHORT, Donna .... 828-652-0631 364 B
donnas@mcdowelltech.edu
SHORT, Donna .... 828-652-0631 364 B
donnasho@mcdowelltech.edu
SHORT, Emily .... 615-230-3477 464 B
emily.short@volstate.edu
SHORT, Evelyn .... 360-417-6381 525 A
eshort@pencol.edu
SHORT, Evonn .... 210-690-9000 474 L
eshort@hallmarkuniversity.edu
SHORT, Genia .... 719-384-6890.. 84 I
genia.short@ojc.edu
SHORT, Joel, D .... 574-535-7784 166 C
joelds@goshen.edu
SHORT, John .... 301-687-4068 220 D
jtshort@frostburg.edu
SHORT, John .... 920-929-3602 541 E
john.short@uwc.edu
SHORT, Kyla .... 918-343-7865 401 I
kshort@rsu.edu
SHORT, Laura, M .... 740-392-6868 387 B
laura.short@mvnu.edu
SHORT, Paula, M .... 713-743-5227 491 D
pmshort@uh.edu
SHORT, Paula, M .... 713-743-5227 491 C
pmshort@uh.edu
SHORT, Rick .... 281-283-3300 491 E
short@uhcl.edu
SHORT, Rosanna .... 623-935-8941.. 14 L
rosanna.short@estrellamountain.edu
SHORT, Royce, B .... 864-242-5100 443 G
SHORT, Sheri .... 903-875-7576 479 I
sheri.short@navarrocollege.edu
SHORT, Trey .... 309-556-3017 148 A
tshort@iwu.edu
SHORT, William .... 407-646-2619 111 H
wshort@rollins.edu
SHORT-THOMPSON,
Cady .... 513-745-5660 393 C
shortcw@ucmail.uc.edu
SHORTBULL,
Thomas, H .... 605-455-6022 452 L
tshortb@olc.edu
SHORTER, Chavonne .... 404-270-5702 132 D
cshorter@spelman.edu
SHORTER, Dwayne, R ... 512-505-3024 475 G
drshorter@htu.edu
SHORTER, Paula .... 816-501-4115 281 B
paula.shorter@rockhurst.edu
SHORTER-GOODEN,
Kumea .... 301-405-6810 219 D
kshorter@umd.edu
SHORTS, Kathryn .... 541-962-3774 405 G
kshorts@eou.edu
SHORTT, Pamela .... 336-734-7224 362 F
pshortt@forsythtech.edu
SHORTT, Ronnie .... 276-328-2677 514 B
rls6k@uvawise.edu
SHORTY, Ursula .... 225-771-2790 207 A
ursula_shorty@subr.edu
SHOSTACK, Pauline ...... 315-498-2708 337 F
shostacp@sunyocc.edu
SHOSTELL, Joseph .... 218-281-8257 264 H
shostell@umn.edu
SHOSTROM, Brenda ...... 630-844-5135 139 L
bshostrom@aurora.edu
SHOTT, Brandy .... 704-233-8028 373 C
b.shott@wingate.edu
SHOTT, Diane, T .... 276-326-4201 505 D
dshott@bluefield.edu
SHOTWELL SMITH,
Mary .... 706-233-7278 131 C
msmith@shorter.edu
SHOUDY, Peter, D .... 610-499-1036 439 G
pdshoudy@widener.edu
SHOUN, Stan .... 314-286-4807 280 I
SHOUP, John .... 951-343-4205.. 30 D
jshoup@calbaptist.edu
SHOURESHI, Rahmat .... 516-686-7630 335 F
rshoures@nyit.edu
SHOUSE, Amy .... 540-338-2700 505 K
ashouse@cdu.edu
SHOVAN, Lisa .... 518-562-4130 321 D
lisa.shovan@clinton.edu
SHOVLAIN,
Raymond, J .... 563-333-6233 182 E
ShovlainRaymondJ@sau.edu
SHOWALTER, Jonathan . 740-857-1311 390 L
jshowalter@rosedale.edu
SHOWALTER, Matthew .. 740-857-1311 390 L
mshowalter@rosedale.edu
SHOWALTER,
Rodney, J .... 540-338-1776 511 A
ie@phc.edu
SHOWALTER,
Stephanie .... 215-836-2222 412 E
finaid@antonelli.edu
SHOWELL, Jeffrey, A .... 419-372-8603 377 I
jashowe@bgsu.edu
SHOWERS, Bill .... 412-809-5100 433 D
showers.william@pti.edu
SHOWERS, Dawn, R ..... 717-867-6071 423 I
dshowers@lvc.edu
SHOWERS, Nancy, C .... 248-341-2040 248 E
ncshower@oaklandcc.edu
SHOWERS, Shane .... 315-568-3125 334 F
sshowers@nycc.edu
SHOWS, Alicia .... 601-276-3706 270 E
showsa@smcc.edu
SHOWS, Deidre .... 601-318-6583 271 F
dede.shows@wmcarey.edu
SHOWS, John .... 228-897-4373 268 G
john.shows1@mgcc.edu
SHOWS-PEREZ, Cindy .. 337-482-6497 208 F
cperez@louisiana.edu
SHPER, Paul .... 802-322-1656 501 H
paul.shper@goddard.edu
SHPIRO, Heather .... 973-748-9000 300 E
heather_shpiro@bloomfield.edu
SHRADER, Daniel .... 714-432-5605.. 40 D
dshrader@occ.cccd.edu
SHRADER, Greg .... 817-598-6421 497 A
gshrader@wc.edu
SHRADER, Nick .... 912-344-3940 120 D
nick.shrader@armstrong.edu
SHRAYCK, Jessica .... 612-659-6527 259 F
jessica.shryack@minneapolis.edu
SHREFFLER, Christine ... 314-344-4440 278 C
cshreff@aol.com
SHREFLER, Christy, L ... 440-826-2231 377 D
chking@bw.edu
SHREVE, Barry, W .... 864-488-4589 447 F
bshreve@limestone.edu
SHREVE, Michael .... 912-525-5000 130 H
mshreve@scad.edu
SHREVE, Penny .... 760-252-2411.. 29 C
pshreve@barstow.edu
SHREVE, Teresa .... 205-348-7625.... 8 E
tshreve@bama.ua.edu
SHREVES, Michael .... 252-493-7289 364 H
mshreves@email.pittcc.edu
SHREVES, Shawn .... 432-335-6866 479 O
sshreves@odessa.edu
SHRIER, Douglas, M .... 540-868-7199 515 H
dshrier@lfcc.edu
SHRIMPTON, Nikki .... 315-472-5730 348 A
nikki.shrimpton@esc.edu
SHRINER, Michael, B ... 409-772-3501 495 E
mshriner@utmb.edu
SHRIVASTAV, Rahul ...... 706-583-0690 132 H
rahuls@uga.edu
SHRIVER, Michael .... 970-542-3174.. 84 A
michael.shriver@morgancc.edu
SHROCK, Joel, D .... 765-641-4441 164 B
jdshrock@anderson.edu
SHROFF, Meghana .... 612-874-3796 257 D
mshroff@mcad.edu
SHROKA, Julie .... 847-543-2847 142 G
julieshroka@clcillinois.edu
SHROM-RHOADS,
Kirstin .... 717-872-6840 431 E
kirstin.shrom-roads@millersville.edu
SHROPSHIRE, Douglas . 508-531-1281 229 C
dshropshire@bridgew.edu
SHROPSHIRE, Marty ..... 336-386-3453 366 E
shropshirem@surry.edu
SHROYER,
Margaret (Peg) .... 320-308-5030 261 F
pshroyer@sctcc.edu
SHRYOCK, Dawn .... 217-854-3231 140 F
dawn.shryock@blackburn.edu
SHTAMLER, Victoriya .... 718-522-9073 315 E
vshtamler@asa.edu
SHTROMBERG, Alisa ..... 425-739-8389 523 I
alisa.shtromberg@lwtech.edu
SHUBERT, David .... 316-942-4291 189 K
shubertd@newmanu.edu
SHUBERT, Lisa, A 507-344-7324 253M
lshubert@blc.edu
SHUCHAT, Rena .... 937-512-2919 391 D
rena.shuchat@sinclair.edu
SHUCK, Richard .... 765-658-4020 165 G
dickshuck@depauw.edu
SHUFFELTON, George ... 507-222-4300 254 D
gshuffel@carleton.edu
SHUFORD, Bettina .... 919-966-4045 371 A
bcshufor@email.unc.edu
SHUFORD, Eddie .... 828-652-0652 364 B
eddieshuford@mcdowelltech.edu
SHUGART, Marlene .... 405-682-1611 399 K
marlene.l.shugart@occc.edu
SHUGART, Michael .... 405-682-1611 399 K
mshugart@occc.edu
SHUGART, Sanford, C .. 407-582-3250 118 I
sshugart@valenciacollege.edu
SHUHY, Taryn .... 212-226-7300 338 F
tshuhy@pbcny.edu
SHUJAA, Mwalimu .... 504-286-5019 207 B
mshujaa@suno.edu
SHULER, Elton .... 803-793-5170 445 F
shulere@denmarktech.edu
SHULER, Peggy .... 803-321-5117 447 L
peggy.shuler@newberry.edu
SHULKEN, Mary, C .... 252-328-6481 369 E
schulkenma@ecu.edu
SHULL, Martha, S .... 870-512-7841.. 19 I
martha_shull@asun.edu
SHULL, Roger .... 806-894-9611 482 F
rshull@southplainscollege.edu
SHULL, Roxanna .... 260-459-4600 169 D
rshull@ibcfortwayne.edu
SHULMAN, Brian .... 973-275-2168 308 C
brian.shulman@shu.edu
SHULMAN, Connie .... 425-968-3402.. 65 D
cshulman@saybrook.edu
SHULMAN, David .... 954-201-7933.. 99 G
dshulman@broward.edu
SHULMAN, Jacob .... 732-367-1060 300 D
yshulman@bmg.edu
SHULOCK, Anne .... 415-749-4507.. 62 I
ashulock@sfai.edu
SHULTES, Kenneth, E ... 717-245-1272 417 B
shultes@dickinson.edu
SHULTIS, Terri .... 415-442-7079.. 46 A
tshultis@ggu.edu
SHULTZ, Dee .... 970-339-6434.. 78 J
dee.shultz@aims.edu
SHULTZ, John .... 913-758-6308 191 I
John.Shultz@stmary.edu
SHULTZ, John, C .... 419-289-5160 377 A
jshultz@ashland.edu
SHULTZ, Kari .... 423-236-2484 460 K
kshultz@southern.edu
SHULTZ, Michael .... 724-589-2167 436 E
mshultz@thiel.edu
SHULTZ, JR., Walter, J 570-326-3761 429 J
walter.shultz@pct.edu
SHUMAKE, Connie, C .. 502-852-3551 201 A
ccshum01@louisville.edu
SHUMAKER, Deb .... 989-275-5000 245 C
deb.shumaker@kirtland.edu
SHUMAKER, Nancy .... 507-285-7461 261 D
nancy.shumaker@rctc.edu
SHUMAKER, Ryan .... 619-660-4505.. 46 G
ryan.shumaker@gcccd.edu
SHUMAKER, Sandra ..... 309-677-3777 140 H
sshumaker@fsmail.bradley.edu
SHUMAN, Jenny .... 478-296-6117 129 D
jshuman@oftc.edu
SHUMAN, Kelli, R .... 605-394-1203 454 B
kelli.shuman@sdsmt.edu
SHUMAN, Michaeline ... 570-372-4146 435 I
shumanm@susqu.edu
SHUMAN, Scott .... 503-352-2236 408 I
scott.shuman@pacificu.edu
SHUMAN, Shari, A .... 904-620-2002 116 A
sshuman@unf.edu
SHUMAN, Victoria .... 304-793-6898 533 B
vshuman@osteo.wvsom.edu
SHUMATE, Connie .... 304-384-5366 532 E
cshumate@concord.edu
SHUMATE, David .... 480-245-7903.. 14 D
dave.shumate@faculty.ibcs.edu
SHUMATE, Jabar .... 405-325-7314 403 I
jabarshumate@ou.edu
SHUMATE, Walter .... 903-927-3249 497 G
wshumate@wileyc.edu
SHUMWAY, Nicolas 713-348-4810 480M
shumway@rice.edu
SHUNK, Jeremy .... 816-268-5424 279 K
jshunk@nts.edu
SHUNKWILER, Susan ... 313-845-9731 243 I
stshunkwiler@hfcc.edu
SHUPALA, Christine ..... 361-825-3383 485 F
christine.shupala@tamucc.edu
SHUPE, Gary .... 217-641-4505 148 J
gshupe@jwcc.edu
SHUPE, John .... 845-257-3335 344 A
shupej@newpaltz.edu
SHUPENUS, Sarah .... 217-424-6340 153 A
sshupenus@millikin.edu
SHUPP, Edward, K .... 610-758-4200 424 B
eks0@lehigh.edu

SILVERBLATT, Pamela, S 646-664-2977 318 B pamela.silverblatt@cuny.edu
SILVERI, Annmarie 313-993-1170 250 H silveran@udmercy.edu
SILVERI, Don 716-896-0700 352 B dsilveri@villa.edu
SILVERIA, John 617-573-8320 237 B jsilveria@suffolk.edu
SILVERII, Glenda 601-643-8440 266 J glenda.silverii@colin.edu
SILVERMAN, Edward 212-650-6480 318 G esilverman@ccny.cuny.edu
SILVERMAN, Lori 360-992-2077 521 A lsilverman@clark.edu
SILVERS, Cathy 859-344-3538 200 C silverc@thomasmore.edu
SILVERS, Liz 828-766-1273 364 A lsilvers@mayland.edu
SILVERSTEIN, Melinda 831-479-6338 30 C mesilver@cabrillo.edu
SILVERTHORN, Mike 989-463-7327 239 B silverthorn@alma.edu
SILVESTER, John 402-461-7477 290 G jsilvester@hastings.edu
SILVESTRI, Mary Ann 508-541-1602 225 G msilvestri@dean.edu
SILVESTRI, Sandro 313-845-9878 243 I sandro@hfcc.edu
SILVESTRINI, Maria 787-284-1912 554 B msilvest@ponce.inter.edu
SILVESTRO, Michael 973-684-6107 304 F msilvestro@pccc.edu
SILVEY, Greg 660-831-4183 279 D silveyg@moval.edu
SILVEY, Kelle 573-592-5195 285 J kelle.silvey@westminster-mo.edu
SILVIS, Kathryn 412-536-1297 422 E kathryn.silvis@laroche.edu
SILVYN, Jeffrey 520-206-4678 17 A jsilvyn@pima.edu
SILY, Michel 305-899-3781 99 B msily@barry.edu
SIMA, Andrea 909-274-5950 54 J asims@mtsac.edu
SIMALA, Jay 847-317-6507 161 B jsimala@tiu.edu
SIMAMA, Jabari 404-297-9522 126 A simamaj@gptc.edu
SIMAR, Gina, A 409-882-3311 488 G gina.simar@lsco.edu
SIMAS, Andrew 415-351-3537 62 I asimas@sfai.edu
SIMBURGER, Sherry 760-252-2411 29 C ssimburger@barstow.edu
SIMCOX, Mary Grace 717-544-4787 429 I mrsimcox@pacollege.edu
SIMEK, Kathy, M 503-943-7101 410 H simek@up.edu
SIMER, Lauren 864-250-8484 446 H lauren.simer@gvltec.edu
SIMERAL, RET., Robert 831-656-3276 548 A rlsimera@nps.edu
SIMERSON, Gordon 203-932-7290 92 G gsimerson@newhaven.edu
SIMES, Sharon 206-934-3615 525 K sharon.simes@seattlecolleges.edu
SIMFUKWE, David 904-470-8174 102 A dsimfukwe@ewc.edu
SIMHAI, Toofawn 701-662-1511 375 A toofawn.simhai@lrsc.edu
SIMIC, Laura 208-426-3236 137 E laurasimic@boisestate.edu
SIMILI, Sal 208-467-8365 138 H ssimili@nnu.edu
SIMINOE, Judith, P 320-308-2122 261 E jpsiminoe@stcloudstate.edu
SIMINOFF, Laura 215-204-8624 436 C lasiminoff@temple.edu
SIMIO, Frank 718-817-4975 326 C simio@fordham.edu
SIMION, Karen 691-320-2480 549 D ksimion@comfsm.fm
SIMKIN, Breanne 973-748-9000 300 E breanne_simkin@bloomfield.edu
SIMMA, April 812-535-5225 172 F asimma@smwc.edu
SIMMELINK, Scott, K 712-707-7170 182 C scotts@nwciowa.edu
SIMMERS, Susan 970-351-2109 87 A susan.simmers@unco.edu
SIMMONDS, Tom 914-674-7658 332 E tsimmonds1@mercy.edu
SIMMONS, Adeidre 580-559-5239 397 K asimmons@ecok.edu
SIMMONS, Alan, D 513-875-3344 379 G alan.simmons@chatfield.edu
SIMMONS, Alicia 256-782-8145 4 L asimmons@jsu.edu
SIMMONS, Annette 704-403-3517 355 B annette.simmons@carolinashealthcare.org
SIMMONS, Bette, M 973-328-5171 301 G bsimmons@ccm.edu
SIMMONS, Blair 510-869-1592 61 J bsimmons@samuelmerritt.edu
SIMMONS, Carletta 336-334-7600 370 B gcsimmons@ncat.edu
SIMMONS, Charlotte 405-974-2538 403 G cksimmons@uco.edu
SIMMONS, Christopher 919-668-6285 356 E chris.simmons@duke.edu
SIMMONS, D. Glenn 602-279-1011 496 K simmonsg@wbu.edu
SIMMONS, D. Kandy 408-481-9988 47 A
SIMMONS, David 770-975-4000 122 H
SIMMONS, Deborah 860-512-2674 89 D dsimmons@manchestercc.edu
SIMMONS, Doreen 408-733-1878 73 A doreen.simmons@uewm.edu
SIMMONS, Eddie 843-574-6268 449 G eddie.simmons@tridenttech.edu
SIMMONS, Elaine, R 620-792-9214 184 I simmonse@bartonccc.edu
SIMMONS, Elizabeth, H 517-353-6486 246 H esimmons@msu.edu
SIMMONS, Gail, M 516-463-5402 328 A gail.m.simmons@hofstra.edu
SIMMONS, Gerald 606-337-1164 194 F gp.simmons@ccbbc.edu
SIMMONS, Gregory 410-455-1452 219 F gsimmons@umbc.edu
SIMMONS, Guy 972-238-6263 473 B gsimmons@dcccd.edu
SIMMONS, Hezekiah, N 585-292-3320 333 G hsimmons@monroecc.edu
SIMMONS, Jacqueline 812-855-9730 167 J simmonja@iu.edu
SIMMONS, Jacqueline, A 812-855-9739 167 I simmonja@iu.edu
SIMMONS, Jay, K 515-961-1566 182 I jay.simmons@simpson.edu
SIMMONS, Jeff 405-425-5560 399 J jeffrey.simmons@oc.edu
SIMMONS, Jeffrey 301-447-6826 217 D simmons@msmary.edu
SIMMONS, Jennifer 914-594-4495 335 H jennifer_simmons@nymc.edu
SIMMONS, Jeremy 415-351-3510 62 I jsimmons@sfai.edu
SIMMONS, Kathryn, C 440-943-7600 391 A ksimmons@dioceseofcleveland.org
SIMMONS, Kathy 405-466-3228 398 E ksimmons@langston.edu
SIMMONS, Kelly, M 513-585-1317 379 H kelly.simmons@thechristhospital.com
SIMMONS, Kitty 951-785-2397 49 I ksimmons@lasierra.edu
SIMMONS, Laura, L 309-655-3450 158 D laura.l.simmons@osfhealthcare.org
SIMMONS, Lori 617-735-9825 226 B simmonslo@emmanuel.edu
SIMMONS, Martha 719-549-3303 85 A martha.simmons@pueblocc.edu
SIMMONS, Mary 407-888-8689 103 M msimmons@fcim.edu
SIMMONS, Max 405-682-1611 399 K msimmons@occc.edu
SIMMONS, Michael 724-738-3333 432 A michael.simmons@sru.edu
SIMMONS, Obadiah 318-274-4401 207 H
SIMMONS, Pamela 404-752-1761 129 A psimmons@msm.edu
SIMMONS, Patricia 507-284-7817 254 F simmons.patricia@mayo.edu
SIMMONS, Paul, M 651-962-6706 265 F pmsimmons@stthomas.edu
SIMMONS, Regina 704-463-3404 367 F regina.simmons@pfeiffer.edu
SIMMONS, Regina Ray 404-756-4047 120 H rsimmons@atlm.edu
SIMMONS, Richard, E 864-488-8344 447 F rsimmons@limestone.edu
SIMMONS, Rick 318-257-2912 208 A simmons@latech.edu
SIMMONS, Robert, A 816-235-1368 284 A simmonsr@umkc.edu
SIMMONS, Roy 304-205-6708 531 A roy.simmons@bridgevalley.edu
SIMMONS, Sam 866-931-4300 281 A sam.simmons@rockbridge.edu
SIMMONS, Sherry 773-244-6208 154 G srsimmons@northpark.edu
SIMMONS, Stefon 212-645-0030 335 D ssimmons@sft.edu
SIMMONS, Steven 803-508-7270 443 C simmonss@atc.edu
SIMMONS, Teisha 907-474-5441 10 I tmsimmons@alaska.edu
SIMMONS, Thomas 419-772-2450 388 I t-simmons@onu.edu
SIMMONS, Tiffany 651-730-5100 255 J tiffanysimmons@globeuniversity.edu
SIMMONS, Todd 480-517-8137 15 D todd.simmons@riosalado.edu
SIMMONS-HENRY, Linda 903-593-8311 487 A lhenry@texascollege.edu
SIMMONS-JOHNSON, Deborah 713-718-7332 475 C deborah.johnson@hccs.edu
SIMMONS-WALSTON, Valerie 770-531-3110 121 G vsimmons-walston@brenau.edu
SIMMS, Carl 559-442-8255 68 J carl.simms@scccd.edu
SIMMS, Kristy 601-815-5330 270 H ksimms@umc.edu
SIMMS, Marcie 740-351-3549 391 C msimms@shawnee.edu
SIMMS, Michele 713-942-5918 493 J simmsm@stthom.edu
SIMMS, Pat 501-337-5000 20 H pats@coto.edu
SIMMS, Rebecca 859-246-6761 195 J rebecca.simms@kctcs.edu
SIMMS, Sandra 303-384-2008 80 O ssims@mines.edu
SIMNING, Jennie 952-995-1533 258 G jennie.simning@hennepintech.edu
SIMOLO, Amy 315-568-3129 334 F asimolo@nycc.edu
SIMON, Alicia 313-664-1533 241 D asimon@collegeforcreativestudies.edu
SIMON, Barbara, J 563-588-7103 180 L barb.simon@loras.edu
SIMON, Bashe 212-463-0400 350 C simonb@touro.edu
SIMON, Caroline, J 509-777-3755 529 A csimon@whitworth.edu
SIMON, Darica 225-216-8171 202 N simond@mybrcc.edu
SIMON, David 920-565-2501 536 Q simondr@lakeland.edu
SIMON, Donald, E 718-933-6700 333 F dsimon@monroecollege.edu
SIMON, Elizabeth 845-675-4679 337 B elizabeth.simon@nyack.edu
SIMON, Janet 406-657-2278 287 H jsimon@msubillings.edu
SIMON, Jason, F 940-565-2085 492 D jason.simon@unt.edu
SIMON, Jennifer 406-496-4307 288 C jsimon@mtech.edu
SIMON, Jill, K 651-641-8211 255 C simon@csp.edu
SIMON, John, D 610-758-3156 424 B jds414@lehigh.edu
SIMON, John, D 434-924-3728 514 A jds2ts@virginia.edu
SIMON, Kathryn, C 859-233-8124 200 D ksimon@transy.edu
SIMON, Lou Anna, K 517-355-6560 246 H laksimon@msu.edu
SIMON, Marlene 310-954-4135 54 I msimon@msmc.la.edu
SIMON, Michael 936-639-1301 467 I msimon@angelina.edu
SIMON, Paul, M 203-837-8494 88 G simonp@wcsu.edu
SIMON, Robert 724-357-2217 431 A rjsimon@iup.edu
SIMON, Scott 419-824-3743 385 F ssimon@lourdes.edu
SIMON, Tina, L 419-372-2700 377 I tsimon@bgsu.edu
SIMONCELLI, Andrew 985-448-4131 208 C andrew.simoncelli@nicholls.edu
SIMONDS, Catherine, A 816-235-1375 284 A simondsca@umkc.edu
SIMONDS, Kurt 971-722-5573 409 C kurt.simonds@pcc.edu
SIMONDS, Linda, A 413-565-1000 222 G lsimonds@baypath.edu
SIMONE, Carmen, M 719-846-5541 86 A carmen.simone@trinidadstate.edu
SIMONE, Christine 334-833-4349 4 E csimone@huntingdon.edu
SIMONE, John 609-586-4800 303 D simonej@mccc.edu
SIMONE, Lucian 203-285-2223 89 B lsimone@gwcc.commnet.edu
SIMONE, Nick 516-323-4810 333 E nsimone@molloy.edu
SIMONEAU, Christopher (Chris), J 239-590-1067 114 F csimoneau@fgcu.edu
SIMONEAUX, Catherine 504-398-2167 206 E csimoneaux@olhcc.edu
SIMONEAUX, Wendy 225-578-8878 204 L wendys@lsu.edu
SIMONELLI, Ray 937-769-1845 376 M rsimonelli@antioch.edu
SIMONESCHI, Joseph, W 626-585-7338 58 F jwsimoneschi@pasadena.edu
SIMONETTI, Salvatore, J 585-292-2902 333 G ssimonetti@monroecc.edu
SIMONI, Mary 518-276-3315 339 D simonm@rpi.edu
SIMONIAN, Yasmen 801-626-7117 500 C ysimonian@weber.edu
SIMONS, Earl, G 718-262-3795 321 B esimons@york.cuny.edu
SIMONS, Ernest 252-493-7243 364 H esimons@email.pittcc.edu
SIMONS, Jill 870-972-3574 19 F jsimons@astate.edu
SIMONS, Kelly 281-998-2050 481 E kelly.simons@sjcd.edu
SIMONS, Ken 314-434-2212 275 J ksimons@hickeycollege.edu
SIMONS, Kenneth, B 414-955-4577 537 C ksimons@mcw.edu
SIMONS, Michael, A 718-990-6601 340 G simonsm@stjohns.edu
SIMONS, Sherri, J 308-432-6355 292 B ssimons@csc.edu
SIMONS, Shino 626-812-3053 29 B ssimons@apu.edu
SIMONSEN, Joe 406-771-4309 288 B joe.simonsen@gfcmsu.edu
SIMONSON, Brian 406-265-3525 288 A brian.simonson@msun.edu
SIMPER, Craig, J 435-797-1156 500 A craig.simper@usu.edu
SIMPKINS, Alice, M 706-396-8111 129 H asimpkins@paine.edu
SIMPKINS, Felix 708-709-3518 156 A fsimpkins@prairiestate.edu
SIMPKINS, Will 646-557-4709 319 F wsimpkins@jjay.cuny.edu
SIMPSON, Amanda 940-898-3456 490 D asimpson1@twu.edu
SIMPSON, Andy, L 651-631-5239 265 D alsimpson@unwsp.edu
SIMPSON, Angela 606-589-3025 197 D angela.simpson@kctcs.edu
SIMPSON, Anita 580-628-6237 399 E anita.simpson@noc.edu
SIMPSON, Anne 870-248-4000 20 E anne.simpson@blackrivertech.edu
SIMPSON, Atticus, J 828-448-3120 367 B asimpson@wpcc.edu
SIMPSON, Brendt 315-228-6208 321 H bsimpson@colgate.edu
SIMPSON, Brett 504-864-7787 206 A bsimpson@loyno.edu
SIMPSON, Caroline 304-724-3700 529 F csimpson@apus.edu
SIMPSON, Colleen 952-358-8146 260 D colleen.simpson@normandale.edu
SIMPSON, Cris, R 215-887-5511 439 E csimpson@wts.edu
SIMPSON, Cynthia 281-649-3232 475 B csimpson@hbu.edu
SIMPSON, Cynthia, F 718-990-6333 340 G simpsoc1@stjohns.edu
SIMPSON, Dennis 303-986-2320 80 N dennis@csha.net
SIMPSON, Donald, E 417-836-5521 279 A donsimpson@missouristate.edu
SIMPSON, Gina 303-986-2320 80 N gina@csha.net
SIMPSON, JR., Grant, W 512-448-8651 481 B grants@stedwards.edu
SIMPSON, Gregory 309-438-5669 147 I gsimpso@ilstu.edu
SIMPSON, Jack 423-461-8955 459 I jasimpson@milligan.edu
SIMPSON, Jacklyn, A 704-687-7501 371 B jasimpso@uncc.edu
SIMPSON, Jane 678-839-5306 133 F jsimpson@westga.edu
SIMPSON, Jeff 303-360-4722 81 I Jeff.Simpson@CCAurora.edu
SIMPSON, Jim 281-756-3789 467 D jsimpson@alvincollege.edu
SIMPSON, Joann 229-243-6940 121 D joann.simpson@bainbridge.edu
SIMPSON, Juliene 973-290-4207 301 F jsimpson@cse.edu
SIMPSON, Kevin 606-546-1714 200 E wsimpson@unionky.edu
SIMPSON, Kimberly 604-984-5009 270 H ksimpson@umc.edu
SIMPSON, Kurt 815-599-3501 146 B kurt.simpson@highland.edu
SIMPSON, Larry 662-562-3219 269 E jlsimpson@northwestms.edu

SIVLEY, Scott ... 310-577-3000.. 77 K
ssivley@yosan.edu
SIX, Jonathan ... 919-761-2100 368 K
jsix@sebts.edu
SIX, Margaret, J ... 304-336-8030 533 A
sixmj@westliberty.edu
SIXTA, Jeff ... 913-288-7613 188 G
jsixta@kckcc.edu
SIZEMORE, Amanda ... 636-922-8388 281 C
asizemore@stchas.edu
SIZEMORE, Debra ... 219-866-6149 172 E
debbie@saintjoe.edu
SIZEMORE, Dorethea ... 434-736-2051 516 H
dorethea.sizemore@southside.edu
SIZER, Judith ... 617-873-0171 225 A
Judith.Sizer@cambridgecollege.edu
SJOGREN, Michelle ... 859-442-1172 196 A
michelle.sjogren@kctcs.edu
SJOGREN, Roxie, L ... 785-227-3380 185 A
sjogrenr@bethanylb.edu
SJOQUIST, Corey ... 608-785-8939 539 G
csjoquist@uwlax.edu
SJORBERG, Connie ... 405-789-7661 402 F
connie.sjoberg@swcu.edu
SJUE, Jessie ... 575-624-7151 310 J
jessie.sjue@roswell.enmu.edu
SJUTS, Joseph, H ... 816-501-3700 272 E
joe.sjuts@avila.edu
SKACH, Peter ... 773-298-3548 158 F
skach@sxu.edu
SKADBERG, Ingrid ... 508-854-7545 232 F
iskadberg@qcc.mass.edu
SKAFTADOTTIR,
Margret ... 727-864-8363 101 P
skaftami@eckerd.edu
SKAGGS, Brandon ... 405-585-5250 399 I
brandon.skaggs@okbu.edu
SKAGGS, Derek, S ... 417-625-9378 278 I
skaggs-d@mssu.edu
SKAGGS, Steve ... 513-244-8456 379 I
steve.skaggs@ccuniversity.edu
SKALLERUD, Ron ... 715-365-4644 543 G
rskallerud@nicoletcollege.edu
SKALNIK, James ... 610-861-1435 426 H
skalnikj@moravian.edu
SKAMRA, Brian ... 920-748-8174 538 I
skamrab@ripon.edu
SKANTZ, Ingrid ... 423-236-2833 460 K
ilskantz@southern.edu
SKARDA, Mary Jo ... 641-782-1425 183 D
skarda@swcciowa.edu
SKARDON, Taylor ... 843-953-5012 444 C
tskardon@citadel.edu
SKARI, Lisa ... 206-878-3710 523 D
lskari@highline.edu
SKARRO, Scott ... 701-255-3285 375 I
sskaro@uttc.edu
SKARSTEN, Fawn ... 810-762-3327 251 E
skarsten@umflint.edu
SKARUPPA, Cindy ... 216-687-5353 380 D
C.SKARUPPA@csuohio.edu
SKARUPPA, Cindy ... 503-725-9854 409 D
skaruppa@pdx.edu
SKATES, Kathy ... 229-430-3524 119 I
kskates@albanytech.edu
SKAUG, Ben ... 415-380-1498.. 45 J
benskaug@ggbts.edu
SKEAN, Mark, E ... 701-788-4778 374 A
mark.skean@mayvillestate.edu
SKEDROS, James ... 617-850-1212 227 F
jskedros@hchc.edu
SKEENS, Randy ... 304-896-7366 531 F
randy.skeens@southernwv.edu
SKELLON, Hilary ... 720-890-8922.. 83 F
director@itea.edu
SKELLY, Dawn ... 612-659-6222 259 F
dawn.skelly@minneapolis.edu
SKELLY, Theresa ... 978-921-4242 234 B
theresa.skelly@montserrat.edu
SKELTON, Don ... 662-562-3354 269 E
SKELTON, Lonnie ... 714-867-5009.. 67 C
SKENANDORE, George . 920-498-5688 544 B
george.skenadore@nwtc.edu
SKENE, Kathy ... 801-524-8118 498 J
KSkene@ldsbc.edu
SKERRETT, Kahtleen, R . 804-289-8128 513 M
kskerrett@richmond.edu
SKERRETT-LLANOS,
Carmen ... 787-993-8870 557 E
carmen.skerrett@upr.edu
SKEVAKIS, Anthony ... 201-761-7364 307 K
askevakis@saintpeters.edu
SKIDMORE, Alan ... 304-766-3261 533 C
askidmore@wvstateu.edu
SKIDMORE, Charlene ... 515-271-2999 177 K
charlene.skidmore@drake.edu
SKIDMORE, Daniel, L ... 315-445-4759 330 B
skidmodl@lemoyne.edu
SKIDMORE, Heather ... 304-424-8210 533 E
heather.skidmore@wvup.edu

SKIDMORE, James, L ... 304-558-0265 530 L
skidmore@wvctcs.org
SKIDMORE, Sue ... 423-461-8729 459 I
shskidmore@milligan.edu
SKILES, Adam, L ... 260-359-4130 167 D
askiles@huntington.edu
SKILL, Thomas, D ... 937-229-3511 393 E
tskill1@udayton.edu
SKILLINGS, Laura ... 269-782-1312 250 D
lskillings@swmich.edu
SKILLINGS, Yvonne ... 404-270-5003 132 D
yskillings@spelman.edu
SKINDER, Michelle, M . 630-637-5754 154 F
mmskinder@noctrl.edu
SKINKLE, Lee ... 601-968-5942 266 F
lskinkle@belhaven.edu
SKINNER, Bruce ... 573-651-5103 282 C
bskinner@semo.edu
SKINNER, Celeste ... 310-265-6143.. 61 I
Celeste.Skinner@usw.salvationarmy.org
SKINNER, Dana ... 978-934-2310 229 A
dana_skinner@uml.edu
SKINNER, Daniel ... 973-748-9000 300 E
daniel_skinner@bloomfield.edu
SKINNER, David ... 847-317-7051 161 B
davids@tiu.edu
SKINNER, Dean ... 479-248-7236.. 20 K
dskinner@ecollege.edu
SKINNER, Deb ... 641-784-5108 178 G
dskinner@graceland.edu
SKINNER, Denese ... 806-651-2345 486 D
dskinner@wtamu.edu
SKINNER, Katherine ... 615-460-6407 455 D
kathryn.skinner@belmont.edu
SKINNER, Kendra ... 573-651-2274 282 C
ksskinner@semo.edu
SKINNER, Patricia, A ... 704-922-6475 362 G
skinner.pat@gaston.edu
SKINNER, Randall ... 928-428-8252.. 13 L
randall.skinner@eac.edu
SKINNER, Rick ... 580-774-3788 402 G
rick.skinner@swosu.edu
SKINNER, Robert ... 304-473-8557 534 G
skinner_b@wvwc.edu
SKINNER, Sally ... 208-459-5770 137 J
sskinner@collegeofidaho.edu
SKINNER, Thom ... 215-368-5000 412 K
tskinner@biblical.edu
SKINNER, Thomas ... 225-578-4713 204 M
tskinner@lsu.edu
SKIPP, Steven, I ... 904-819-6258 102 P
sskipp@flagler.edu
SKIPPER, Bob ... 270-745-4295 201 D
bob.skipper@wku.edu
SKIPPER, Curt ... 601-635-2111 267 B
cskipper@eccc.edu
SKIPPER, Eric ... 678-717-6219 133 A
eric.skipper@ung.edu
SKIPPER, Eric ... 678-717-3835 133 A
eric.skipper@ung.edu
SKIPPER, Eric ... 706-310-6219 133 A
eric.skipper@ung.edu
SKIPPER, Tawana ... 215-728-4478 427 H
tawana.skipper@jevs.org
SKIPPER, Wray ... 229-931-2354 131 E
wskipper@southgatech.edu
SKIPWORTH, Stan ... 909-621-8033.. 39 D
Stan_Skipworth@cuc.claremont.edu
SKIVIAT, David, M ... 740-283-6223 382 G
dskiviat@franciscan.edu
SKLANDER, Linda ... 262-524-7288 535 D
sklander@carrollu.edu
SKLAR, David ... 914-347-3910 352 G
David.Sklar@sunywcc.edu
SKLAR, Jay ... 314-434-4044 273 J
jay.sklar@covenantseminary.edu
SKLBA, Stephanie ... 262-564-2662 543 A
sklba@gtc.edu
SKLEDER, Anne ... 570-408-4200 440 B
anne.skleder@wilkes.edu
SKLUT, John ... 509-313-3715 522 L
sklut@gonzaga.edu
SKOFF, Robert, M ... 724-847-6581 419 B
rmskoff@geneva.edu
SKOGEN, Larry, C ... 701-328-2974 373 F
larry.skogen@ndus.edu
SKOGEN, Larry, C ... 701-224-5431 374 E
larry.skogen@bismarckstate.edu
SKOGLUND,
Elizabeth, A ... 410-543-6161 220 E
easkoglund@salisbury.edu
SKOLNIK, Richard, J ... 315-312-3168 346 A
richard.skolnik@oswego.edu
SKOLOS, Nancy ... 401-454-6280 442 B
nskolos@risd.edu
SKONER, Peter, R ... 814-472-3085 434 F
pskoner@francis.edu
SKORACZEWSKI, Paul .. 715-682-1841 538 D
pskoraczewski@northland.edu
SKORTZ, Brian ... 270-686-6416 193 G
brian.skortz@brescia.edu

SKOTNES, Andor ... 518-244-2021 340 A
skotna@sage.edu
SKOWYRA, Jamie ... 508-213-2131 235 C
jamie.skowyra@nichols.edu
SKRABACZ, Shari ... 314-968-6996 285 G
shariskrabacz98@webster.edu
SKRESLET, Stanley ... 804-355-0671 513 F
sskreslet@upsem.edu
SKRYD, Jackie ... 727-392-6809 112 A
skryd.jackie@spcollege.edu
SKUDZINSKAS, Al ... 610-399-2222 430 D
askudzinskas@cheyney.edu
SKUL, Jeanne ... 864-503-5960 451 A
SKURJA, Michael ... 801-375-5125 499 A
mskurja@rmuohp.edu
SKUTKA, Linda, L ... 240-895-4289 218 B
llskutka@smcm.edu
SKVARLA, Jiennifer ... 815-836-5201 150 F
skvarlje@lewisu.edu
SLAATS, Jacqueline ... 847-735-5285 149 H
slaats@lakeforest.edu
SLABACH, Donald ... 601-857-3751 267 D
Donald.Slabach@hindscc.edu
SLABACH, Frederick, G 817-531-4401 490 C
fslabach@txwes.edu
SLABAUGH, David ... 864-644-5558 449 B
dslabaugh@swu.edu
SLABAUGH, Katie ... 765-285-1545 164 D
kslabaugh@bsu.edu
SLABODEN, Carolyn ... 781-283-2216 237 F
cslaboden@wellesley.edu
SLACK, Craig ... 301-314-7164 219 D
cslack@umd.edu
SLACK, Elizabeth ... 304-357-4881 530 H
elizabethslack@ucwv.edu
SLACK, Gregory, C ... 315-268-6475 321 C
gslack@clarkson.edu
SLACK, Karen ... 320-762-4463 257 O
karens@alextech.edu
SLACK, Robert ... 626-914-8581.. 38 L
rslack@citruscollege.edu
SLADE, Patricia ... 973-877-3209 302 F
slade@essex.edu
SLADE, Priscilla ... 601-979-1781 267 H
priscilla.d.slade@jsums.edu
SLAFKOSKY, Mary, V ... 260-422-5561 167 F
mvslafkosky@indianatech.edu
SLAGELL, Jeff ... 662-846-4440 267 A
jslagell@deltastate.edu
SLAGER, Karen ... 815-802-8110 149 B
kslager@kcc.edu
SLAGLE, Judith, B ... 423-439-6076 461 D
slagle@etsu.edu
SLAICH, Lucy ... 410-704-2050 221 A
lslaich@towson.edu
SLANGER, Zvi Dov ... 410-486-0006 213 F
SLANN, Martin ... 903-566-7368 494 E
mslann@uttyler.edu
SLATER, Bernata ... 650-949-7364.. 45 A
slaterbernata@foothill.edu
SLATER, Jane Ann ... 210-434-6711 479 P
jslater@lake.ollusa.edu
SLATER, Janet ... 217-333-2350 162 A
slaterj@illinois.edu
SLATER, Peter ... 212-594-4000 349 J
pslater@tcicollege.edu
SLATER, Richard ... 312-850-7016 142 E
rslater4@ccc.edu
SLATER, Ryan ... 412-291-6313 412 H
SLATER, Troy ... 231-348-6610 248 A
tslater@ncmich.edu
SLATER-DUFFY, Carrie .. 715-682-1482 538 D
cslaterduffy@northland.edu
SLATON, Christa, D ... 575-646-3500 312 A
slatocd@nmsu.edu
SLATON, Gwendolyn ... 973-877-3233 302 F
slaton@essex.edu
SLATON, Nate ... 270-534-3244 197 E
nathaniel.slaton@kctcs.edu
SLATTERY, Daniel ... 410-704-2364 221 A
dslattery@towson.edu
SLATTERY, Katheryn ... 815-836-5275 150 F
slatteka@lewisu.edu
SLATTERY, Kimberly ... 610-436-0043 432 B
kslattery@wcupa.edu
SLATTERY, SCC,
Mary Catherine ... 973-957-0188 299 F
academicdean@acs350.org
SLAUGHTER, Arnie ... 859-572-5538 199 A
slaughtera@nku.edu
SLAUGHTER,
Barbara, R ... 713-798-6644 469 C
gayles@bcm.edu
SLAUGHTER, Beverly ... 321-433-5150 101 O
slaughterb@easternflorida.edu
SLAUGHTER,
Charlene, D ... 803-535-5077 444 D
cslaughter@claflin.edu
SLAUGHTER, Clinton ... 530-895-2366.. 30 B
slaughtercl@butte.edu

SLAUGHTER, Craig, A .. 765-658-4030 165 G
craigslaughter@depauw.edu
SLAUGHTER, Dane, S ... 864-622-6001 443 E
dslaughter@andersonuniversity.edu
SLAUGHTER,
Jacqueline ... 512-245-2273 489 C
js47@txstate.edu
SLAUGHTER, John ... 254-647-3234 480 G
jslaughter@rangercollege.edu
SLAUGHTER, Keith ... 404-614-6378 127 H
kslaughter@itc.edu
SLAUGHTER,
Matthew, J ... 603-646-2460 297 G
matthew.j.slaughter@dartmouth.edu
SLAUGHTER, Sabra, C .. 843-792-2228 447 G
slaughsc@musc.edu
SLAUGHTER, Shirley ... 510-981-2840.. 58 J
sslaughter@peralta.edu
SLAVIK, Kenneth ... 215-871-6527 432 E
kennethsl@pcom.edu
SLAVIN, Dennis ... 646-660-6504 318 C
Dennis.Slavin@baruch.cuny.edu
SLAVIN, Joan, L ... 714-850-4800.. 69 F
slavin@taftu.edu
SLAVIN, Matt ... 510-436-1335.. 47 C
slavin@hnu.edu
SLAVINSKAS, Brian ... 312-915-8787 151 E
bslavin@luc.edu
SLAVITT, Lesley ... 312-341-2351 157 E
lslavitt@roosevelt.edu
SLAWSON, Linda ... 903-785-7661 480 B
lslawson@parisjc.edu
SLAYMAKER, Valerie ... 651-213-4746 256 C
vslaymaker@hazelden.edu
SLAYTON, Deborah, L .. 217-420-6774 153 A
dslayton@millikin.edu
SLEDGE, Donald ... 205-929-6442.... 5 E
dsledge@lawsonstate.edu
SLEDGE, Janet ... 386-506-3899 101 I
sledgej@DaytonaState.edu
SLEEMAN, Geoffrey ... 313-664-7480 241 D
gsleeman@collegeforcreativestudies.edu
SLEEMAN, Kerri ... 906-487-2303 247 A
kasleema@mtu.edu
SLEESMAN, George ... 419-772-2521 388 I
g-sleesman@onu.edu
SLEETH, Cathy ... 509-359-6582 522 C
csleeth1@ewu.edu
SLEETH, Kate, M ... 626-256-4673.. 39 B
ksleeth@coh.org
SLEIGH-LAYMAN, Staci 509-963-2205 520 E
staci@cwu.edu
SLEIGHT, Garth ... 406-874-6212 287 A
sleightg@milescc.edu
SLEJKO, Christa ... 972-273-3010 473 A
cslejko@dcccd.edu
SLEKAR, Timothy ... 608-663-2293 536 A
tslekar@edgewood.edu
SLENSKI, Amanda ... 989-463-7245 239 B
slenskiar@alma.edu
SLEPITZA, Ron ... 816-501-3750 272 E
ron.slepitza@avila.edu
SLESARANSKY-POE,
Graciela ... 215-572-4692 412 F
slesarag@arcadia.edu
SLESNICK, Daniel, T ... 512-471-4363 493 M
slesnick@austin.utexas.edu
SLETTEN, Sheryl, L ... 605-336-6588 453 C
ssletten@sfseminary.edu
SLEVA, Michael ... 616-451-3511 241 I
msleva@davenport.edu
SLICK, Rebecca ... 641-782-1434 183 D
slick@swcciowa.edu
SLIDER, Joe ... 410-837-5688 221 B
jslider@ubalt.edu
SLIFE, Harry ... 315-792-3738 351 G
hfslife@utica.edu
SLIGH, Gary ... 352-323-3670 107 X
slighg@lssc.edu
SLIGO, Sarah ... 401-277-4863 442 B
ssligo@risd.edu
SLIMAN, David ... 601-266-6633 271 B
david.sliman@usm.edu
SLIMAN, George, S ... 412-578-8826 414 I
slimangs@carlow.edu
SLIMP, Mickey ... 903-877-1276 495 C
mickey.slimp@uthct.edu
SLINGER, Ron ... 303-914-6417.. 85 C
ron.slinger@rrcc.edu
SLINKARD, Tiffany ... 417-455-5636 274 B
TiffanySlinkard@crowder.edu
SLINKER, Bryan, K ... 509-335-9515 528 B
slinker@vetmed.wsu.edu
SLISZ, John, P ... 716-851-1851 325 A
slisz@ecc.edu
SLIZEWSKI, James ... 215-489-2220 416 H
james.slizewski@delval.edu
SLOAN, Barry ... 310-287-4278.. 52 C
sloanba@wlac.edu
SLOAN, Candice, Y ... 864-587-4282 449 D
sloanc@smcsc.edu

SMITH, Christine, J ...... 630-617-3150 144 G
chriss@elmhurst.edu
SMITH, Cindy .... 432-264-5034 475 E
csmith@howardcollege.edu
SMITH, Claire .... 210-999-8401 490 E
csmith9@trinity.edu
SMITH, Claire, L .... 410-777-7383 213 E
clsmith@aacc.edu
SMITH, Clarence, E ...... 662-252-8000 270 C
csmith@rustcollege.edu
SMITH, Cliff .... 913-627-4122 188 G
clsmith@kckcc.edu
SMITH, Cliff, L .... 864-379-8802 446 B
smith@erskine.edu
SMITH, Colleen, A .... 972-758-3880 471 C
csmith@collin.edu
SMITH, Connie .... 706-295-6972 125 F
csmith@gntc.edu
SMITH, Connor .... 214-333-5365 471 L
connors@dbu.edu
SMITH, Corey .... 662-246-6405 268 F
csmith@msdelta.edu
SMITH, Craig .... 406-768-5555 286 H
csmith@fpcc.edu
SMITH, Craig .... 413-236-2186 231 A
csmith@berkshirecc.edu
SMITH, Craig .... 413-236-2188 231 A
csmith@berkshirecc.edu
SMITH, Crystal .... 903-877-7718 495 C
crystal.smith@uthct.edu
SMITH, Curtis .... 405-425-5931 399 J
curtis.smith@oc.edu
SMITH, Cynthia .... 301-687-4328 220 D
colsmith@frostburg.edu
SMITH, Dale, T .... 914-831-0311 322 D
dsmith@cw.edu
SMITH, Dan .... 662-562-3305 269 E
dsmith@northwestms.edu
SMITH, Dan .... 812-855-6679 167 I
dansmith@indiana.edu
SMITH, Dana .... 760-944-4449.. 54 G
dsmith@miracosta.edu
SMITH, Daniel .... 562-860-2451.. 37 L
dsmith@cerritos.edu
SMITH, Daniel .... 864-242-5100 443 G
SMITH, Daniel, C .... 812-855-6679 167 J
dansmith@indiana.edu
SMITH, Daniel, C .... 252-334-2058 359 D
dan.smith@macuniversity.edu
SMITH, Daniel, J .... 706-355-5085 120 G
dsmith@athenstech.edu
SMITH, Daniel, P .... 802-728-1251 504 C
dsmith5@vtc.edu
SMITH, Darlene .... 301-687-4309 220 D
dcsmith@frostburg.edu
SMITH, Daryl .... 864-592-4600 449 C
smithd@sccsc.edu
SMITH, Daryl .... 716-829-7623 324 E
smithd@dyc.edu
SMITH, David .... 585-567-9321 328 C
david.smith@houghton.edu
SMITH, David .... 718-260-5345 320 D
dsmith@citytech.cuny.edu
SMITH, David .... 518-743-2313 347 E
smithd@sunyacc.edu
SMITH, David .... 765-677-2258 169 C
david.smith@indwes.edu
SMITH, David .... 970-675-3258.. 80 L
david.smith@cncc.edu
SMITH, David .... 620-331-4100 188 B
dsmith@indycc.edu
SMITH, David .... 561-912-2166 102 N
davsmith@evergladesuniversity.edu
SMITH, David .... 740-264-5591 381 J
dsmith@egcc.edu
SMITH, David, B .... 518-783-2432 342 H
dsmith@siena.edu
SMITH, David, J .... 315-443-2486 349 E
smithd@syr.edu
SMITH, David, M .... 310-506-5689.. 58 H
david.smith@pepperdine.edu
SMITH, Dayle, M .... 315-268-2300 321 C
dayle.smith@clarkson.edu
SMITH, DeAnna, M ...... 205-665-6012.... 9 C
dsmith23@montevallo.edu
SMITH, Debbie .... 281-669-4782 481 G
deborah.smith@sjcd.edu
SMITH, Deborah .... 409-212-5724 468 L
SMITH, Debra .... 252-536-7213 363 B
dsmith600@halifaxcc.edu
SMITH, Debra .... 252-536-7213 363 B
dsmith660@halifaxcc.edu
SMITH, Debra, M .... 330-665-1084 388 G
debbie@ocm.edu
SMITH, Delois .... 256-824-4600.... 9 A
delois.smith@uah.edu
SMITH, Denise .... 567-661-7250 390 D
denise_smith4@owens.edu
SMITH, Denise, D .... 757-683-4393 510 I
ddsmith@odu.edu
SMITH, Denise, M .... 603-862-3396 299 B
denise.smith@unh.edu
SMITH, Dennis .... 252-335-0821 361 G
dennis_smith@albemarle.edu
SMITH, Derek .... 215-489-2476 416 H
Derek.Smith@delval.edu
SMITH, Devin .... 402-643-7328 289 J
devin.smith@cune.edu
SMITH, Diana .... 303-762-6886.. 82 C
diana.smith@denverseminary.edu
SMITH, Dolores .... 951-639-5230.. 55 A
dolsmith@msjc.edu
SMITH, Don .... 229-931-2731 131 E
dsmith@southgatech.edu
SMITH, Donald .... 270-745-6256 201 D
donald.smith@wku.edu
SMITH, Donald .... 972-860-4808 472 C
dsmith@dcccd.edu
SMITH, Donald, E .... 848-445-1750 306 F
don.smith@rutgers.edu
SMITH, Donald, E .... 716-286-8348 336 E
des@niagara.edu
SMITH, Donald, R .... 318-342-1050 209 A
dosmith@ulm.edu
SMITH, Donna .... 601-925-3313 268 E
dsmith@mc.edu
SMITH, Donna .... 701-777-4171 373 G
donna.smith@und.edu
SMITH, Dorothy .... 504-816-4527 202 F
dsmith@dillard.edu
SMITH, Dorothy .... 213-763-5507.. 52 A
smithd@lattc.edu
SMITH, Doug .... 254-647-3234 480 G
dsmith@rangercollege.edu
SMITH, Doug .... 910-695-3811 365 H
smithd@sandhills.edu
SMITH, Douglas .... 408-270-6426.. 63 O
douglas.smith@sjeccd.org
SMITH, Douglas, F .... 610-796-8393 412 C
doug.smith@alvernia.edu
SMITH, Douglas, J .... 508-565-1341 237 A
dsmith@stonehill.edu
SMITH, Drew .... 870-230-5265.. 21 B
smithc@hsu.edu
SMITH, Dustin .... 479-788-7591.. 23 H
dustin.smith@uafs.edu
SMITH, Dustin .... 419-448-2260 383 C
dsmith@heidelberg.edu
SMITH, Dwayne .... 813-974-3151 116 B
mdsmith8@usf.edu
SMITH, Dwayne .... 314-340-3611 275 G
smithd@hssu.edu
SMITH, Dwight, L .... 973-328-5090 301 G
dsmith@ccm.edu
SMITH, Earl, L .... 713-743-1899 491 D
esmith@uh.edu
SMITH, Ed .... 615-550-3160 466 H
ed.smith@williamsoncc.edu
SMITH, Edith .... 229-732-5974 120 B
edithsmith@andrewcollege.edu
SMITH, Edmond, C ...... 276-964-7338 517 A
ed.smith@sw.edu
SMITH, Elizabeth .... 573-341-7783 284 C
elsmith@mst.edu
SMITH, Elizabeth .... 925-631-4278.. 61 G
jes5@stmarys-ca.edu
SMITH, Elizabeth .... 918-335-6870 400 I
esmith@okwu.edu
SMITH, Elmer, R .... 770-216-2960 127 E
ers@ict.edu
SMITH, Emmett .... 252-538-4317 363 B
esmith956@halifaxcc.edu
SMITH, Eric .... 315-464-5763 344 E
smither@upstate.edu
SMITH, Eric, J .... 570-577-2944 413 E
eric.smith@bucknell.edu
SMITH, Eric, L .... 906-227-1314 248 B
esmith@nmu.edu
SMITH, Ericka, M .... 336-334-7862 370 B
emsmith@ncat.edu
SMITH, Erin, T .... 724-946-7327 439 D
smithet@westminster.edu
SMITH, Erskine .... 309-298-1690 163 A
er-smith@wiu.edu
SMITH, Eva .... 425-640-1171 522 D
esmith@edcc.edu
SMITH, Everett .... 904-743-1122 107 C
esmith@jones.edu
SMITH, Farnum .... 916-577-2200.. 77 F
fsmith@jessup.edu
SMITH, Felicia .... 770-593-2257 127 A
gjcfs@gupton-jones.edu
SMITH, Frank .... 760-245-4271.. 75 G
frank.smith@vvc.edu
SMITH, JR., Frank, M .. 502-776-1443 199 C
fsmith@simmonscollegeky.edu
SMITH, Fred, R .... 740-376-4791 386 A
fred.smith@marietta.edu
SMITH, Frederick .... 201-200-3474 304 C
fsmith@njcu.edu
SMITH, Frederick, G ..... 518-562-4101 321 D
fred.smith@clinton.edu
SMITH, Frederick, M .... 517-264-7876 250 B
fsmith@sienaheights.edu
SMITH, Fritz .... 562-907-4951.. 77 E
fritz@whittier.edu
SMITH, G, T .... 304-637-1243 529 I
buck@dewv.edu
SMITH, G. Ben .... 704-637-4410 355 H
gbsmith@catawba.edu
SMITH, G. Mick .... 302-292-6100.. 96 H
SMITH, Gabie .... 336-278-6452 356 F
gsmith@elon.edu
SMITH, Gary .... 817-515-6400 484 B
gary.smithr@tccd.edu
SMITH, Gary, R .... 701-231-7494 374 C
gary.smith@ndsu.edu
SMITH, Geary .... 815-455-8788 152 B
gsmith@mchenry.edu
SMITH, Gene .... 919-735-5151 367 A
gsmith@waynecc.edu
SMITH, Gene .... 614-292-7572 389 A
smith.5407@osu.edu
SMITH, George .... 207-879-8955 210 D
SMITH, Gibson .... 802-862-9616 501 E
gsmith@burlington.edu
SMITH, Gina .... 515-271-7497 177 H
gina.smith@dmu.edu
SMITH, Gladys .... 313-927-1259 246 D
gsmith8938@marygrove.edu
SMITH, Glenn, C .... 503-280-8512 405 E
glsmith@cu-portland.edu
SMITH, Glenn, R .... 610-526-7935 413 D
gsmith@brynmawr.edu
SMITH, Grace .... 310-434-4454.. 65 B
smith_grace@smc.edu
SMITH, Grady .... 601-276-3704 270 E
gsmith@smcc.edu
SMITH, Greg, P .... 308-398-7300 289 D
gpsmith@cccneb.edu
SMITH, Gregory .... 662-720-7449 269 D
gsmith@nemcc.edu
SMITH, Gregory .... 714-449-7456.. 53 D
gsmith@ketchum.edu
SMITH, Gregory .... 605-626-2552 454 A
Gregory.Smith@northern.edu
SMITH, Gregory, L .... 920-465-2343 539 F
smithg@uwgb.edu
SMITH, Harlan .... 216-687-3909 380 D
h.smith@csuohio.edu
SMITH, Heather, C .... 508-531-1295 229 C
h2smith@bridgew.edu
SMITH, Helen .... 503-253-3443 408 B
hsmith@ocom.edu
SMITH, Herbert, C .... 410-857-2413 217 A
hsmith@mcdaniel.edu
SMITH, Hilary .... 212-355-1501 318 A
hsmith@christies.edu
SMITH, Holly .... 253-964-6408 525 C
hsmith@pierce.ctc.edu
SMITH, Howard, W .... 620-235-4518 190 G
smith@pittstate.edu
SMITH, Ian .... 765-983-1215 165 H
smithia@earlham.edu
SMITH, Idelia .... 413-552-2228 231 F
ismith@hcc.edu
SMITH, J, R .... 630-752-5061 163 G
jr.smith@wheaton.edu
SMITH, J Douglas .... 812-877-8211 172 C
j.d.smith@rose-hulman.edu
SMITH, J. Malcolm ...... 401-341-2206 442 D
malcolm.smith@salve.edu
SMITH, Jace .... 541-463-5561 406 F
smithj@lanecc.edu
SMITH, Jackie .... 256-233-8172.... 1 F
jackie.smith@athens.edu
SMITH, Jacqueline .... 334-876-9242.... 4 B
jacqueline.smith@wccs.edu
SMITH, Jacqueline .... 713-221-8541 491 F
smithja@uhd.edu
SMITH, Jake .... 612-343-4179 263 H
jsmith@northcentral.edu
SMITH, James .... 334-241-5436.... 8 A
jesmith@troy.edu
SMITH, James .... 740-392-6868 387 B
jsmith25@mvnu.edu
SMITH, James .... 718-489-5306 340 E
jsmith@sfc.edu
SMITH, James .... 909-384-8600.. 62 C
jsmith@sbccd.cc.ca.us
SMITH, James .... 937-376-6473 379 D
jsmith@centralstate.edu
SMITH, James .... 802-879-2337 504 C
jsmith@vtc.edu
SMITH, James .... 740-654-6711 389 H
smithj27@ohio.edu
SMITH, James, A .... 513-244-8621 379 I
jamie.smith@ccuniversity.edu
SMITH, James, M .... 605-626-2521 454 A
James.Smith@northern.edu
SMITH, Jane, L .... 630-942-2481 142 F
smithja@cod.edu
SMITH, Janet .... 423-869-6287 458 B
janet.smith@lmunet.edu
SMITH, Janet .... 601-643-8383 266 J
janet.smith@colin.edu
SMITH, Janet, F .... 931-540-2510 462 E
janet.smith@columbiastate.edu
SMITH, Janet, M .... 724-946-7143 439 D
smithjm@westminster.edu
SMITH, Jarret, L .... 540-828-5469 505 F
jlsmith@bridgewater.edu
SMITH, Jason .... 425-388-9142 522 I
SMITH, Jason .... 409-880-8188 488 E
jhsmith@lit.edu
SMITH, Jason .... 312-567-7112 147 E
jsmith31@iit.edu
SMITH, Jason .... 415-503-6281.. 63 A
jsmith@sfcm.edu
SMITH, Jason .... 269-782-1238 250 D
jsmith07@swmich.edu
SMITH, Jason .... 214-333-8877 471 L
jasons@dbu.edu
SMITH, Jason, S .... 832-842-9064 491 D
jsmith10@uh.edu
SMITH, Jason, S .... 832-842-9064 491 C
jsmith10@uh.edu
SMITH, Jean, L .... 610-989-1438 438 I
jsmith@vfmac.edu
SMITH, Jeannie .... 901-678-2261 462 B
jesmith@memphis.edu
SMITH, Jeff .... 585-395-2385 345 A
jsmith@brockport.edu
SMITH, Jeff .... 806-720-7482 478 A
jeff.smith@lcu.edu
SMITH, Jeff .... 423-461-8492 459 I
jbsmith@milligan.edu
SMITH, Jeff .... 970-339-6253.. 78 J
jeff.smith@aims.edu
SMITH, Jeff .... 941-487-4353 115 B
jsmith@ncf.edu
SMITH, Jeffrey, G .... 540-464-7212 518 A
smithjg@vmi.edu
SMITH, Jennifer, B .... 270-745-6824 201 D
Jennifer.smith@wku.edu
SMITH, Jenny .... 828-328-7252 358 G
jenny.smith@lr.edu
SMITH, Jeremy .... 601-276-3720 270 E
jsmith@smcc.edu
SMITH, Jeremy .... 716-829-7551 324 E
smithj@dyc.edu
SMITH, Jerry .... 928-344-7535.. 12 B
jerry.smith@azwestern.edu
SMITH, Jesse .... 661-255-1050.. 31 B
jsmith@calarts.edu
SMITH, Jesse, R .... 601-477-4100 268 A
jesse.smith@jcjc.edu
SMITH, Jessica .... 757-822-1949 517 C
jrsmith@tcc.edu
SMITH, Jessie, C .... 615-329-8731 456 G
jcsmith@fisk.edu
SMITH, Jill .... 818-677-2121.. 34 D
jill.smith@csun.edu
SMITH, Jim .... 907-786-1979.. 10 H
jgsmith3@uaa.alaska.edu
SMITH, Jim .... 918-293-5234 400 E
jim.smith10@okstate.edu
SMITH, Jimmy, D .... 606-546-1247 200 E
jdsmith@unionky.edu
SMITH, Jimmy, L .... 601-877-6170 266 C
jsmith@alcorn.edu
SMITH, Jo .... 615-353-3303 463 C
jo.smith@nscc.edu
SMITH, Joan .... 303-914-6410.. 85 C
joan.smith@rrcc.edu
SMITH, Joan, E .... 209-575-6508.. 78 A
smithj@yosemite.edu
SMITH, JoAnn .... 610-917-1456 438 G
jlsmith@valleyforge.edu
SMITH, Joanne, H .... 512-245-2152 489 C
js14@txstate.edu
SMITH, Joe .... 509-313-6801 522 L
smithj@gonzaga.edu
SMITH, Joe, L .... 321-433-7018 101 O
smithj@easternflorida.edu
SMITH, Joel .... 308-432-6345 292 B
jsmith@csc.edu
SMITH, Joel .... 503-226-4391 408 H
jsmith@pnca.edu
SMITH, Joel, M .... 607-746-4522 347 G
smithjm@delhi.edu
SMITH, Joel, M .... 607-746-4600 347 G
smithjm@delhi.edu
SMITH, John .... 251-460-6171.... 9 F
johns@southalabama.edu
SMITH, John .... 515-271-2969 177 K
john.smith@drake.edu
SMITH, John, W .... 309-298-1888 163 A
jw-smith@wiu.edu
SMITH, John, W .... 401-454-6501 442 B
jsmith@risd.edu

SMITH, JR., John, W ... 757-443-6200 547M john.smith@ndu.edu
SMITH, Joianne, L ... 847-635-1801 155 E joismith@oakton.edu
SMITH, Jolene ... 503-883-2408 406 I jsmith1@linfield.edu
SMITH, Jonathan, C ... 314-977-2242 281M smithj2@slu.edu
SMITH, Jordan ... 270-809-5706 198 I jsmith3@murraystate.edu
SMITH, Joseph, E ... 423-439-4317 461 D smithje@etsu.edu
SMITH, Joseph, T ... 410-706-7302 219 E jtsmith@umaryland.edu
SMITH, Josephine ... 412-809-5100 433 D smith.josephine@pti.edu
SMITH, Joshua ... 815-394-5058 157 D smith-joshua1@aramark.com
SMITH, Joy, S ... 864-656-0471 444 E joy@clemson.edu
SMITH, Joy, S ... 864-833-8275 448 E jssmith@presby.edu
SMITH, Joyya ... 912-478-8746 126 B joyyasmith@georgiasouthern.edu
SMITH, Judy ... 814-824-3650 425 L jsmith@mercyhurst.edu
SMITH, June ... 402-481-3967 289 C june.smith@bryanhealthcollege.edu
SMITH, Justin ... 503-534-4018 407 A jsmith@marylhurst.edu
SMITH, Justin ... 580-477-7915 404 D justin.smith@newmoodle.wosc.edu
SMITH, Kara ... 337-475-5148 208 B ksmith2@mcneese.edu
SMITH, Karen ... 815-455-8781 152 B ksmith@mchenry.edu
SMITH, Karin ... 267-502-2480 413 C karin.smith@brynathyn.edu
SMITH, Katherine ... 702-968-2010 296 D ksmith@roseman.edu
SMITH, Kathleen, E ... 562-902-3367.. 67 J kathleensmith@scuhs.edu
SMITH, Kathleen, M ... 502-852-5419 201 A kathleen@louisville.edu
SMITH, Kathryn, A ... 503-517-7462 409 E smithk@reed.edu
SMITH, Kathryn, G ... 707-476-4170.. 41 C kathy-smith@redwoods.edu
SMITH, Kathy ... 614-292-2991 389 A
SMITH, Kathy ... 614-234-2230 386 N ksmith@mccn.edu
SMITH, Kathy, S ... 336-888-6391 357 E ksmith@highpoint.edu
SMITH, Katie, J ... 651-631-5222 265 D kjsmith@unwsp.edu
SMITH, Katrina ... 806-291-3540 496 K smithk@wbu.edu
SMITH, Keith ... 973-328-5400 301 G ksmith@ccm.edu
SMITH, Keith ... 252-451-8264 364 E ksmith@nashcc.edu
SMITH, Kelli ... 607-777-2400 343 D kksmith@binghamton.edu
SMITH, Kelly, A ... 804-523-5449 515 F ksmith@reynolds.edu
SMITH, Kelly, E ... 585-594-6496 339 F smith_kellyE@roberts.edu
SMITH, Kelly, M ... 859-257-5290 200 G kelly.smith@uky.edu
SMITH, Ken, W ... 828-262-6432 369 D smithkw@appstate.edu
SMITH, Kendall ... 276-935-4349 504 L ksmith@asl.edu
SMITH, Kenneth ... 508-929-8121 230 G Kenneth.Smith@worcester.edu
SMITH, JR., Kent, J ... 405-466-3201 398 E president@langston.edu
SMITH, Kevin ... 312-553-5911 141 N ksmith230@ccc.edu
SMITH, Kevin, B ... 409-880-8400 488 F kevin.smith@lamar.edu
SMITH, Kevin, J ... 773-508-7605 151 E ksmit23@luc.edu
SMITH, Kevin, M ... 716-888-8501 317 H smithk@canisius.edu
SMITH, Khrystal ... 864-503-5125 451 A ksmith@uscupstate.edu
SMITH, Kraig ... 724-589-2027 436 E ksmith@thiel.edu
SMITH, Kris, M ... 703-993-8841 507 K ksmitr@gmu.edu
SMITH, Krista ... 229-928-1331 126 C krista.smith@gsw.edu
SMITH, Kristen ... 516-686-7751 335 F mksmith@nyit.edu
SMITH, Kristen, J ... 269-337-7090 244 I Kristen.Smith@kzoo.edu
SMITH, Krystal, D ... 304-462-4101 532 G krystal.smith@glenville.edu
SMITH, Kyle ... 325-235-7415 488 C kyle.smith@tstc.edu
SMITH, Kyle ... 979-230-3489 469 G kyle.smith@brazosport.edu
SMITH, Kyle, A ... 607-735-1775 324 J ksmith@elmira.edu
SMITH, Lane, M ... 205-726-2905.... 6 F
SMITH, Larry ... 310-954-4018.. 54 I lsmith@msmu.edu
SMITH, Laura ... 502-213-2136 196 E laura.smith@kctcs.edu
SMITH, Laura, L ... 361-570-4801 492 A smithl@uhv.edu
SMITH, Laurel, A ... 812-888-4176 174 F lasmith@vinu.edu
SMITH, Lauren ... 970-204-8113.. 82 J lauren.smith@frontrange.edu
SMITH, Laurens, H ... 435-797-2373 500 A lhsmith@cc.usu.edu
SMITH, Laurinda ... 636-227-2100 277 A laurinda.smith@logan.edu
SMITH, Lawrence ... 516-463-7202 328 A lawrence.smith@hofstra.edu
SMITH, Leanne ... 901-572-2440 455 C leanne.smith@bchs.edu
SMITH, Lee ... 205-934-2384.... 8 F lmsmith@uab.edu
SMITH, Leigh Ann ... 615-844-5241 466 G lasmith@welch.edu
SMITH, Leila ... 606-487-3504 196 B leila.smith@kctcs.edu
SMITH, Leslie ... 601-643-8340 266 J leslie.smith@colin.edu
SMITH, Leslie, M ... 812-888-4501 174 F lmsmith@vinu.edu
SMITH, Lewis ... 312-503-0501 155 D ljsmith@northwestern.edu
SMITH, Linda ... 706-864-1993 133 A linda.smith@ung.edu
SMITH, Linda ... 815-280-2660 148 K lsmith@jjc.edu
SMITH, Linda ... 650-543-3933.. 54 B lsmith@menlo.edu
SMITH, Linda ... 340-692-4023 559 B lsmith@live.uvi.edu
SMITH, Linda, D ... 919-209-2024 363 F ldsmith@johnstoncc.edu
SMITH, Lisa ... 352-854-2322 100 P smithl@cf.edu
SMITH, Lisa ... 307-754-6292 546 I Lisa.Smith@nwc.edu
SMITH, Lisa ... 406-874-6181 287 A smithl@milescc.edu
SMITH, Lisa ... 615-794-4254 460 A lsmith@omorecollege.edu
SMITH, Lois ... 704-991-0249 366 D smith0107@stanly.edu
SMITH, Lorenzo ... 916-278-6366.. 34 E lorenzo.smith@csus.edu
SMITH, Lorraine ... 559-244-2604.. 69 B lorraine.smith@fresnocitycollege.edu
SMITH, Lorraine ... 716-375-7873 340 C lsmith@sbu.edu
SMITH, LuAnn ... 801-863-8472 500 B smithlu@uvu.edu
SMITH, Luke ... 212-659-3615 330 A lsmith@tkc.edu
SMITH, Lura ... 978-656-3110 232 B smithlm@middlesex.mass.edu
SMITH, Lyle, S ... 719-365-1038.. 86 C scott.smith@UChealth.org
SMITH, Lynn ... 606-546-1206 200 E tlsmith@unionky.edu
SMITH, Mable, H ... 912-650-5678 131 F mhsmith@southuniversity.edu
SMITH, Mable, H ... 702-968-2075 296 D msmith@roseman.edu
SMITH, MacKenzie ... 530-752-2110.. 71 A macsmith@ucdavis.edu
SMITH, Malinda ... 607-274-3222 328 H mbsmith@ithaca.edu
SMITH, Marcie ... 334-844-5588.... 1 G smithmc@auburn.edu
SMITH, Marcus ... 575-769-4014 310 G marcus.smith@clovis.edu
SMITH, Margaret, D ... 931-540-2517 462 E margaret.smith@columbiastate.edu
SMITH, Marian ... 270-384-7351 198 C smithm@lindsey.edu
SMITH, Marian ... 410-225-2237 216 F mariansmith@mica.edu
SMITH, Marianne ... 626-914-8701.. 38 L msmith@citruscollege.edu
SMITH, Marianne ... 610-896-1298 420 J msmith@haverford.edu
SMITH, Maribel ... 305-628-6704 112 B maribel.smith@stu.edu
SMITH, Marie ... 928-350-2100.. 17 K msmith@prescott.edu
SMITH, Marilyn ... 763-433-1306 257 P marilyn.smith@anokaramsey.edu
SMITH, Marilyn ... 703-993-8728 507 K mtsmith@gmu.edu
SMITH, Mark ... 518-276-6266 339 D smithm@rpi.edu
SMITH, Mark ... 607-871-2494 314 J msmith@alfred.edu
SMITH, Mark ... 615-327-6336 458 F msmith@mmc.edu
SMITH, Mark, A ... 254-298-8341 484 C mark.a.smith@templejc.edu
SMITH, Mark, A ... 740-477-7713 388 F mark.smith@ohiochristian.edu
SMITH, Mark, L ... 219-785-5211 172 A mlsmith@pnc.edu
SMITH, Mark, W ... 314-935-6489 285 E msmith@wustl.edu
SMITH, Marla ... 317-955-6150 171 A msmith2@marian.edu
SMITH, Marla ... 605-995-7157 452 H marla.smith@mitchelltech.edu
SMITH, Marlaine ... 561-297-3207 114 E msmit230@fau.edu
SMITH, Martha, J ... 260-359-4040 167 D msmith@huntington.edu
SMITH, Martha, J ... 757-352-4070 511 G martsmi@regent.edu
SMITH, Martha, L ... 601-403-1269 270 A mbyrd@prcc.edu
SMITH, Martin, W ... 309-556-3710 148 A mwsmith@iwu.edu
SMITH, Marvin ... 563-288-6162 178 C msmith@eicc.edu
SMITH, Marvin ... 201-360-4054 303 A msmith@hccc.edu
SMITH, Marvin ... 304-766-3181 533 C smithm@wvstateu.edu
SMITH, Marvin, L ... 317-274-5924 168 E
SMITH, Mary, A ... 713-500-9236 495 A mary.a.smith@uth.tmc.edu
SMITH, Mary, C ... 478-289-2165 124 B mcsmith@ega.edu
SMITH, Matthew ... 717-815-6579 440 H cmsmith@ycp.edu
SMITH, Matthew, J ... 269-399-7700 174 C msmith@sf.edu
SMITH, Matthew, J ... 253-535-7550 524 I smithmf@plu.edu
SMITH, Maureen, A ... 617-322-3568 227 J maureen_smith@laboure.edu
SMITH, Melissa ... 415-439-2413.. 27 F mysmith@act-sf.org
SMITH, Micah ... 731-989-6005 456 K msmith@fhu.edu
SMITH, Michael ... 212-966-0300 334 D msmith@nyaa.edu
SMITH, Michael ... 812-488-2958 173 H ms337@evansville.edu
SMITH, Michael ... 806-720-7521 478 A michael.smith@lcu.edu
SMITH, Michael, A ... 434-223-6219 508 B msmith@hsc.edu
SMITH, Michael, D ... 617-495-1566 227 D mike_smith@harvard.edu
SMITH, Michael, J ... 973-278-5400 300 C mj@berkeleycollege.edu
SMITH, Michael, J ... 212-986-4343 316 D mj@berkeleycollege.edu
SMITH, Michael, R ... 919-966-4107 371 A msmith@sog.unc.edu
SMITH, Michael, W ... 202-687-4640.. 95 E smithm4@georgetown.edu
SMITH, Micheal, D ... 770-426-2039 128 C michael.smith@life.edu
SMITH, Michele, G ... 817-257-4739 469 H m.g.smith@tcu.edu
SMITH, Michelle ... 502-456-6509 200 A mbsmith@sctd.edu
SMITH, Mike ... 903-586-2518 476 K msmith@jacksonville-college.edu
SMITH, Mike ... 803-584-3446 450 F pmsmith@mailbox.sc.edu
SMITH, Miranda ... 479-619-4191.. 22 B msmith28@nwacc.edu
SMITH, Missy ... 303-963-3337.. 79 L masmith@ccu.edu
SMITH, Molly, E ... 360-438-4310 525 H msmith@stmartin.edu
SMITH, Monica ... 510-780-4500.. 50 G msmith@lifewest.edu
SMITH, Monica, M ... 610-660-1015 434 G msmith@sju.edu
SMITH, Morgan ... 603-428-2296 298 B msmith@nec.edu
SMITH, Myra, D ... 413-755-4414 233 B msmith@stcc.edu
SMITH, JR., Myron, J .. 423-636-7320 464 F jsmith@tusculum.edu
SMITH, N. Gregory ... 225-578-8492 205 E greg.smith@law.lsu.edu
SMITH, Nan, L ... 610-359-7355 416 G nsmith@dccc.edu
SMITH, Nancy ... 540-868-0638 515 H nsmith@lfcc.edu
SMITH, Nancy ... 719-255-4411.. 86 F nsmith2@uccs.edu
SMITH, Nancy ... 325-793-4667 478 D smith.nancy@mcm.edu
SMITH, Nancy, L ... 607-746-4665 347 G smithnl@delhi.edu
SMITH, Nate ... 804-527-1000.. 96 H
SMITH, Nichloas, A ... 508-767-7416 222 D na.smith@assumption.edu
SMITH, Nicole ... 540-362-6281 508 D csmith3@hollins.edu
SMITH, Noreen ... 212-343-1234 332 I nsmith@mcny.edu
SMITH, Norma, M ... 207-768-2788 211 C nsmith@nmcc.edu
SMITH, Norman ... 727-864-8897 101 P smithnr@eckerd.edu
SMITH, Norman ... 256-228-6001.... 6 A smithn@nacc.edu
SMITH, Ole, M ... 801-422-5500 497 J ole_smith@byu.edu
SMITH, Page, A ... 210-458-7470 494 D page.smith@utsa.edu
SMITH, Pam ... 727-341-3261 112 A smith.pam@spcollege.edu
SMITH, Pamela ... 518-694-7268 314 G pamela.smith@acphs.edu
SMITH, Pamela, A ... 918-631-2329 403M pamela-smith@utulsa.edu
SMITH, Pamela, J ... 215-368-5000 412 K psmith@biblical.edu
SMITH, Pat, A ... 559-323-2100.. 63 C psmith@sjcl.edu
SMITH, Patricia ... 909-537-5040.. 35 A psmith@csusb.edu
SMITH, Patricia ... 931-372-3331 462 A plsmith@tntech.edu
SMITH, Patricia, A ... 516-876-3092 345 E smithp@oldwestbury.edu
SMITH, Patricia, T ... 407-582-5411 118 I psmith50@valenciacollege.edu
SMITH, Paula ... 270-789-5211 194 D pjsmith@campbellsville.edu
SMITH, Paula ... 217-234-5252 150 B psmith12328@lakeland.cc.il.us
SMITH, Peggy ... 340-693-1446 559 B psmith@live.uvi.edu
SMITH, Penny, L ... 814-871-7748 419 A smith006@gannon.edu
SMITH, Penny, R ... 330-325-6300 387 F psmith4@neomed.edu
SMITH, Peter, L ... 563-589-3668 183 E plsmith@dbq.edu
SMITH, Philip, A ... 678-891-2445 125 G philip.smith@gpc.edu
SMITH, Quentin, R ... 806-356-4000 490 A quentin.smith@ttuhsc.edu
SMITH, Rachel, E ... 814-865-7641 428 C rem4@psu.edu
SMITH, Rae Marie ... 336-334-4822 363 A rmsmith@gtcc.edu
SMITH, Raechell ... 816-802-3574 276 F raechell@earthlink.net
SMITH, Randy ... 920-498-5505 544 B randall.smith@nwtc.edu
SMITH, Randy, L ... 405-585-5810 399 I randy.smith@okbu.edu
SMITH, Rashad ... 270-852-3120 198 A rsmith@kwc.edu
SMITH, Rebecca, F ... 614-823-1400 390 C rsmith@otterbein.edu
SMITH, Regina ... 323-953-4000.. 51 E
SMITH, Regina ... 212-757-1190 315 C rtsmith@funeraleducation.org
SMITH, Reginald ... 662-562-3271 269 E
SMITH, Renee, L ... 928-344-1723.. 12 B renee.smith@azwestern.edu
SMITH, Richard, A ... 540-375-2203 512 B rsmith@roanoke.edu
SMITH, Richard, S ... 718-409-7350 348 C rsmith@sunymaritime.edu
SMITH, Robert ... 601-979-2260 267 H robert.m.smith@jsums.edu
SMITH, Robert ... 612-728-5201 264 B rsmith@smunm.edu
SMITH, Robert ... 859-985-3330 193 F smithro@berea.edu
SMITH, Robert ... 912-344-2589 120 D robert.smith@armstrong.edu
SMITH, Robert ... 205-929-6470.... 5 E rsmith@lawsonstate.edu
SMITH, Robert ... 912-358-3202 131 A smithr@savannahstate.edu
SMITH, Robert ... 470-578-3609 127M rsmit@kennesaw.edu
SMITH, Robert ... 305-626-3168 104 B Robert.Smith@fmuniv.edu
SMITH, Robert ... 806-720-7111 478 A robert.smith@lcu.edu
SMITH, III, Robert ... 409-740-4403 485 C rsmith101839@tamu.edu

SMITH, Robert, M .... 731-881-7500 465 F
robert.smith@utm.edu
SMITH, Robert, R .... 520-621-7777.. 18 E
rrsmith@u.arizona.edu
SMITH, Robert, W .... 252-334-2018 359 D
bob.smith@macuniversity.edu
SMITH, Robin Ann .... 401-825-2096 441 C
rasmith@ccri.edu
SMITH, Roland, B 713-348-5688 480M
rbsmith@rice.edu
SMITH, Roland, K .... 512-463-1887 488 D
roland.smith@tsus.edu
SMITH, Ron .... 408-741-2126.. 76 D
ron_smith@wvm.edu
SMITH, Ronald .... 410-462-8302 213 G
rsmith@bccc.edu
SMITH, Ronette .... 515-244-4221 175 C
smithr@aib.edu
SMITH, Roxie .... 626-264-8880.. 73 D
SMITH, Rueben .... 626-585-7277.. 58 F
rcsmith@pasadena.edu
SMITH, Russell, L .... 502-597-6805 197 G
russell.smith@kysu.edu
SMITH, Ruth .... 757-825-2807 517 B
smithru@tncc.edu
SMITH, Ruth, S .... 407-582-1601 118 I
rsmith257@valenciacollege.edu
SMITH, Ryan .... 256-726-7398.... 6 C
resmith@oakwood.edu
SMITH, Ryan .... 916-649-8168.. 48 X
rsmith@kaplan.edu
SMITH, Ryan .... 309-438-2135 147 I
rlsmith@ilstu.edu
SMITH, Ryan, M .... 814-886-6373 427 B
rsmith@mtaloy.edu
SMITH, Sam .... 415-503-6265.. 63 A
ssmith@sfcm.edu
SMITH, Sam .... 615-966-6056 458 C
sam.smith@lipscomb.edu
SMITH, Sam, E .... 601-984-1065 270 H
sesmith@umc.edu
SMITH, Sandra, B .... 540-674-3600 516 B
ssmith@nr.edu
SMITH, Sandra, E .... 870-235-4041.. 23 D
sandrasmith@saumag.edu
SMITH, Sandy .... 760-366-5296.. 42 G
ssmith@cmccd.edu
SMITH, Sandy .... 540-231-6231 518 B
ssmith@vt.edu
SMITH, Sarah .... 276-376-4514 514 B
scs6p@uvawise.edu
SMITH, Sarah .... 615-230-3400 464 B
sarah.smith@volstate.edu
SMITH, Sarah, A .... 304-293-4963 533 D
sarah.smith@mail.wvu.edu
SMITH, Scott .... 719-365-1038.. 86 C
scott.smith@uchealth.org
SMITH, Scott, A .... 803-786-3672 445 C
scsmith@columbiasc.edu
SMITH, Scott, F .... 305-899-3085.. 99 B
sfsmith@barry.edu
SMITH, Sean .... 805-565-6061.. 76 K
sesmith@westmont.edu
SMITH, Sevealyn, V ...... 919-516-4160 368 E
svsmith@st-aug.edu
SMITH, Sharon .... 202-495-3830.. 96 E
secretary@dhs.edu
SMITH, Sharon .... 205-726-2247.... 6 F
ssmith12@samford.edu
SMITH, Sharon, E .... 616-632-2902 239 E
smithsha@aquinas.edu
SMITH, Sharon, P .... 828-652-0697 364 B
sharons@mcdowelltech.edu
SMITH, Sharon, P .... 724-836-9911 437 K
upgpres@pitt.edu
SMITH, SharonAnn .... 618-374-5199 156 C
sharonann.smith@principia.edu
SMITH, Shawn .... 217-732-3168 150 G
ssmith@lincolnchristian.edu
SMITH, Sheila .... 615-329-8710 456 G
shsmith@fisk.edu
SMITH, Sheila, K .... 253-535-7674 524 I
nurs@plu.edu
SMITH, Shelley .... 256-840-4128.... 7 B
ssmith@snead.edu
SMITH, Shirley .... 714-484-7455.. 56 E
ssmith@cypresscollege.edu
SMITH, Sommer .... 620-947-3121 191 E
smiths@tabor.edu
SMITH, Stan .... 702-895-3197 295 G
stan.smith@unlv.edu
SMITH, Stephanie .... 606-546-1259 200 E
sasmith@unionky.edu
SMITH, Stephanie .... 312-362-7552 143 G
ssmit185@depaul.edu
SMITH, Stephanie .... 304-696-2599 532 H
smiths@marshall.edu
SMITH, Stephanie, M ... 800-782-2422.. 32 A
smsmith@mail.cnuas.edu
SMITH, Stephen .... 206-546-4694 526 G
spsmith@shoreline.edu
SMITH, Stephen, C .... 415-338-3879.. 36 A
scsmith@sfsu.edu
SMITH, Stephen, E .... 918-465-1723 397 L
ssmith@eosc.edu
SMITH, Stephen, P .... 215-951-1153 422 F
smiths@lasalle.edu
SMITH, Steve .... 626-584-5393.. 45 F
stevensmith1@fuller.edu
SMITH, Steve .... 865-974-4127 465 D
SMITH, Steve .... 716-829-7600 324 E
smith@dyc.edu
SMITH, Steve .... 951-343-4360.. 30 D
ssmith@calbaptist.edu
SMITH, Steve .... 505-323-9282 496 K
smiths@wbu.edu
SMITH, Steve .... 432-264-5019 475 E
sismith@howardcollege.edu
SMITH, Steve .... 915-831-6472 473 J
ssmith54@epcc.edu
SMITH, Steve .... 512-837-2665 477 D
jbrooks@tca.edu
SMITH, Steve, A .... 801-422-6291 497 J
steve_smith@byu.edu
SMITH, Steven .... 707-826-3256.. 35 D
ss7006@humboldt.edu
SMITH, Steven .... 970-521-6657.. 84 H
steven.smith@njc.edu
SMITH, Steven .... 817-923-1921 483 E
swsmith@swbts.edu
SMITH, Steven .... 601-979-6944 267 H
steven.smith@jsums.edu
SMITH, Steven, F .... 989-774-7328 240 O
smith1sf@cmich.edu
SMITH, Steven, J .... 413-565-1000 222 G
ssmith@baypath.edu
SMITH, Steven, K .... 608-262-3956 539 D
sof@secfac.wisc.edu
SMITH, Steven, N .... 262-243-5700 535 I
steve.smith@cuw.edu
SMITH, Stuart, A .... 859-858-3511 193 A
stuart.smith@asbury.edu
SMITH, Sue .... 916-361-1660.. 37 A
ssmith@carrington.edu
SMITH, Susanne .... 614-947-6160 382 H
suzanne.smith@franklin.edu
SMITH, Suzanne .... 413-755-4221 233 B
smsmith@stcc.edu
SMITH, Sybil .... 425-352-8133 520 D
ssmith@cascadia.edu
SMITH, Tamalea .... 908-709-7093 309 A
tsmith@ucc.edu
SMITH, Tammy .... 716-338-1054 329 E
tammysmith@mail.sunyjcc.edu
SMITH, Tammy .... 540-674-3600 516 B
tsmith@nr.edu
SMITH, Teresa, L .... 714-879-3901.. 47 D
tlsmith@hiu.edu
SMITH, Teresa, L .... 504-278-6491 204 B
tsmith@nunez.edu
SMITH, Terri .... 661-763-7817.. 69 E
tsmith@taftcollege.edu
SMITH, Terri .... 336-249-8186 362 B
tlsmith@davidsonccc.edu
SMITH, Terry .... 732-247-5241 304 B
tsmith@nbts.edu
SMITH, Terry .... 713-646-1708 482 H
tsmith@stcl.edu
SMITH, Terry, S .... 512-505-3004 475 G
tssmith@htu.edu
SMITH, Therese, A .... 989-328-1284 247 D
terrys@montcalm.edu
SMITH, Thomas .... 314-392-2264 278 G
smitht@mobap.edu
SMITH, Thomas .... 970-351-2838.. 87 A
thomas.smith@unco.edu
SMITH, Thomas .... 951-827-5802.. 72 A
thomas.smith@ucr.edu
SMITH, Thomas .... 865-573-4517 457 H
TSmith@johnsonU.edu
SMITH, Thomas, J .... 616-234-3951 243 D
tsmith@grcc.edu
SMITH, Thomas, M 225-578-4843 204M
tmsmith@lsu.edu
SMITH, Thomas, P .... 570-941-7620 438 F
thomas.smith@scranton.edu
SMITH, Thomas, W .... 610-519-4651 439 A
thomas.w.smith@villanova.edu
SMITH, Tierra .... 813-253-7160 106 C
tsmith175@hccfl.edu
SMITH, Tim .... 773-838-7526 142 C
tsmith2@ccc.edu
SMITH, Tim .... 256-549-8317.... 3 N
tsmith@gadsdenstate.edu
SMITH, Timothy, L .... 864-231-2000 443 E
tlsmith@andersonuniversity.edu
SMITH, Tina .... 801-627-8304 498 O
smitht@owatc.edu
SMITH, Todd .... 815-455-8591 152 B
tsmith@mchenry.edu
SMITH, Todd .... 713-831-7225 493 J
tsmith1@stthom.edu
SMITH, Todd .... 801-818-8900 498 P
todd.smith@provocollege.edu
SMITH, Todd .... 541-463-5132 406 F
smitht@lanecc.edu
SMITH, Tom .... 479-575-3208.. 23 G
tecsmith@uark.edu
SMITH, Tomesa .... 256-352-8233.. 10 A
tomesa.smith@wallacestate.edu
SMITH, Tracina, A .... 260-422-5561 167 F
tasmith@indianatech.edu
SMITH, Tracy .... 601-403-1332 270 A
tsmith@prcc.edu
SMITH, Tracy, D .... 501-882-8806.. 19 E
tdsmith@asub.edu
SMITH, Travis .... 315-386-7300 347 F
smitht@canton.edu
SMITH, Trent .... 620-276-9510 187 D
trent.smith@gcccks.edu
SMITH, Treva .... 706-864-1902 133 A
treva.smith@ung.edu
SMITH, Tricia, G .... 410-548-3999 220 E
tgarveysmith@salisbury.edu
SMITH, Trina .... 912-344-2535 120 D
trina.smith@armstrong.edu
SMITH, Tyne .... 641-673-1703 184 B
smitht@wmpenn.edu
SMITH, Valerie, A .... 610-328-8314 436 A
vsmith1@swarthmore.edu
SMITH, Valerie, T .... 617-228-2032 231 C
vtsmith@bhcc.mass.edu
SMITH, Vayta .... 707-527-4508.. 65 C
vsmith@santarosa.edu
SMITH, Vergina .... 501-337-5000.. 20 H
vsmith@coto.edu
SMITH, Vernon .... 209-946-2503.. 73 C
vsmith1@pacific.edu
SMITH, Vicki .... 301-784-5000 213 C
vsmith@allegany.edu
SMITH, Vicki .... 412-731-6000 433 K
vsmith@rpts.edu
SMITH, Vicki .... 412-731-6000 433 K
bookstore@rpts.edu
SMITH, Vicky .... 815-455-8725 152 B
vsmith@mchenry.edu
SMITH, Victoria .... 315-279-5666 329 K
vsmith@keuka.edu
SMITH, Wanda .... 334-229-4223.... 1 D
wsmith@alasu.edu
SMITH, Wendall .... 610-896-1000 420 J
w1smith@haverford.edu
SMITH, Wendy .... 305-284-4101 118 A
wendy.smith@miami.edu
SMITH, Wendy, B .... 724-847-6104 419 B
wbsmith@geneva.edu
SMITH, Wendy, M .... 307-674-6446 546 H
wsmith@sheridan.edu
SMITH, Whitman .... 662-915-7226 270 G
whitman@olemiss.edu
SMITH, William .... 334-229-4200.... 1 D
Wesmith@alasu.edu
SMITH, William .... 731-426-7500 457 K
SMITH, William, C .... 508-767-7157 222 D
wc.smith@assumption.edu
SMITH, Willie .... 337-521-8909 204 E
willie.smith@solacc.edu
SMITH, Zana .... 859-442-1687 196 A
zana.smith@kctcs.edu
SMITH ABBOTT, Katy ... 802-443-5771 502 E
smithabb@middlebury.edu
SMITH-BATES,
Jacqui, S .... 206-281-2488 526 D
jacquisb@spu.edu
SMITH-BUTLER, Lisa ...... 843-377-2144 444 A
lsbutler@charlestonlaw.edu
SMITH-CAMPBELL,
Vesta .... 517-338-3042 241 B
vscampbell@cleary.edu
SMITH-COX, Cathy .... 276-964-7340 517 A
cathy.smith-cox@sw.edu
SMITH-EGGERT, Megan 312-935-4141 157 A
msmith@robertmorris.edu
SMITH-HOWELL, Deb ..... 402-554-3378 294 A
dsmith-howell@unomaha.edu
SMITH-HUPP, Karen ..... 301-934-7701 214 E
karens@csmd.edu
SMITH-IRONS, Nancy ... 312-935-6252 157 A
nsmithirons@robertmorris.edu
SMITH-KIAWU, Rena .... 718-997-5100 320 E
rena.smithkiawu@qc.cuny.edu
SMITH-MCQUEENIE,
Lisa .... 617-521-2120 236 F
lisa.smithmcqueenie@simmons.edu
SMITH MORGAN, Terry 334-683-5100.... 5 D
tmorgan1@judson.edu
SMITH-PATTERSON,
Trina .... 817-515-7059 484 B
trina.patterson@tccd.edu
SMITH QUIST, Bonnie .. 614-947-6068 382 H
bonnie.quist@frankli.edu
SMITH-ROBINSON,
Marilyn .... 404-225-4612 120 I
msmithro@atlantatech.edu
SMITH-RODRIGUEZ,
Sharlise .... 914-323-3134 331 J
sharlise.smith@mville.edu
SMITH-SIMMONS,
Margie .... 317-274-5434 168 E
smithsim@iu.edu
SMITH STALEY,
Charlesetta .... 317-917-3309 171 B
cstaley@martin.edu
SMITH-STEPHENS,
Shannon, L .... 606-783-2123 198 H
s.smithstephens@moreheadstate.edu
SMITH-TOURVILLE, Mel 801-649-5230 498 K
admissions@midwifery.edu
SMITH-WORTHINGTON,
Darlene .... 252-493-7429 364 H
dsmith@email.pittcc.edu
SMITHER, Robert .... 407-646-2280 111 H
rsmither@rollins.edu
SMITHERS, Marc .... 585-567-9227 328 C
marc.smithers@houghton.edu
SMITHSON, Amanda ..... 281-756-3500 467 D
asmithson@alvincollege.edu
SMITHSON, John, W .... 610-660-1216 434 G
smithson@sju.edu
SMITHSON, V. Scott ..... 219-785-5356 172 A
ssmithson@pnc.edu
SMITLEY, Debra, K .... 309-438-2373 147 I
dsmitle@ilstu.edu
SMITLEY, Gregory, A .... 260-359-4002 167 D
gsmitley@huntington.edu
SMITS, Karen .... 920-498-5615 544 B
karen.smits@nwtc.edu
SMITS, Sally, A .... 414-425-8300 538 J
ssmits@shsst.edu
SMOCK, Cathy .... 979-458-7120 484 E
cathy-smock@tamus.edu
SMOCK, Fredrick .... 410-888-9048 216 G
fsmock@muih.edu
SMOCK, Jordan .... 617-933-7491 233 A
jsmock@rcc.mass.edu
SMOCK, Leonard, A .... 804-827-5600 514 F
lsmock@vcu.edu
SMOKE, Gladden .... 864-592-4157 449 C
smokeg@sccsc.edu
SMOKOWSKI, Paul .... 785-864-4720 191 G
smokowski@ku.edu
SMOKOWSKI, Peter ...... 617-353-2148 224 E
psmokows@bu.edu
SMOLOVA, Alona .... 757-451-7764 510 H
asmolova@nsu.edu
SMOLOW, Bobbie .... 914-395-2476 342 C
bsmolow@sarahlawrence.edu
SMOLSKI, Lisa .... 401-456-2809 442 A
lsmolski@ric.edu
SMOLSKIS, Joseph .... 410-626-2514 218 A
joseph.smolskis@sjc.edu
SMOOT, Kathy .... 606-487-3091 196 B
kathy.smoot@kctcs.edu
SMOOT, Kyron .... 405-470-7942 402 F
kyron.smoot@swcu.edu
SMOOT, Lori .... 410-334-2898 221 E
lsmoot@worwic.edu
SMOROL, Bobbie, H ..... 315-792-3128 351 G
bsmorol@utica.edu
SMOTHERS, Garry .... 505-566-3284 312 K
smothersg@sanjuancollege.edu
SMOTHERS, SR.,
Roderick, L .... 501-370-5275.. 22 E
rsmothers@philander.edu
SMOTHERS, Traci .... 504-762-3004 203 F
tsmoth@dcc.edu
SMRHA, Judith .... 785-594-8337 184 F
judy.smrha@bakeru.edu
SMUDER, Kristin .... 813-253-7180 106 C
ksmuder@hccfl.edu
SMULSON, Erik .... 202-687-8496.. 95 E
ems62@georgetown.edu
SMURDON, Melissa, J . 317-940-8200 164 L
msmurdon@butler.edu
SMYRE HINES, Beverly . 706-771-4156 121 B
bsmyre@augustatech.edu
SMYRSKI, Rose, M .... 608-342-1282 540 D
smyrskir@uwplatt.edu
SMYTH, Conor .... 608-266-2991 542 K
conor.smyth@wtcsystem.edu
SMYTH, Nancy, J .... 716-645-1267 343 E
sw-dean@buffalo.edu
SMYTH-MCGAHA,
Bonnie .... 501-882-8826.. 19 E
bmsmyth@asub.edu
SNAPP, Diana .... 207-326-2243 211 G
diana.snapp@mma.edu
SNAPP, John 325-670-1507 474M
John.Snapp@hsutx.edu
SNARE, Charles .... 308-432-6203 292 B
csnare@csc.edu

SOLDINGER, Sarah ... 412-304-0722 418 F
ssoldinger@cci.edu
SOLDWISCH, Sandie ... 815-395-5088 158 B
SOLDZ, Stephen ... 617-277-3915 224 D
soldzs@bgsp.edu
SOLE, Mary, L ... 407-823-5496 115 C
mary.sole@ucf.edu
SOLECKI, Amanda ... 410-287-1003 214 C
asolecki@cecil.edu
SOLECKI, Jean ... 208-426-1979 137 E
jennifersolecki@boisestate.edu
SOLEIM, Heather, M ... 218-477-4060 260 B
heather.soleim@mnstate.edu
SOLEMSAAS, Rachel ... 775-673-7014 295 F
rsolemsaas@tmcc.edu
SOLER, Adrienne ... 802-831-1059 503 E
asoler@vermontlaw.edu
SOLERNOU, Sheila ... 203-285-2393.. 89 B
ssolernou@gwcc.commnet.edu
SOLHEIM, Derek, N ... 319-352-8330 183 J
derek.solheim@wartburg.edu
SOLHKHAH, Arbella ... 209-575-6664.. 78 C
solhkhaha@yosemite.edu
SOLIBAKKE, Karl ... 510-436-1250.. 47 C
solibakke@hnu.edu
SOLIMINI, Karen ... 603-577-6585 297 F
ksolimini@dwc.edu
SOLIS, Amy ... 701-627-4638 373 E
asolis@fortbertholdcc.edu
SOLIS, Carlos ... 512-245-2111 489 C
SOLIS, JR., Federico ... 956-794-4002 477 C
fsolis@laredo.edu
SOLIS, Ricardo ... 713-718-8173 475 C
ricardo.solis@hccs.edu
SOLIS, Robert ... 774-455-7711 228 E
rsolis@umassp.edu
SOLIS, Vincent, R ... 956-764-5950 477 C
vincent.solis@laredo.edu
SOLIZ, Sandra ... 713-525-3116 493 J
solizs@stthom.edu
SOLLARS, David ... 785-670-2045 192 B
david.sollars@washburn.edu
SOLLENBERGER,
Donna, K ... 409-772-6116 495 E
dksoll@utmb.edu
SOLLENBERGER,
Mitchel ... 313-593-5030 251 D
msollenb@umich.edu
SOLLER, Dan ... 301-447-7407 217 D
soller@msmary.edu
SOLLER, Kerry ... 614-251-4718 388 H
sollerk@ohiodominican.edu
SOLLIE, Donna, L ... 334-844-4396.... 1 G
sollidl@auburn.edu
SOLLOSI, Nancy, B ... 336-334-4822 363 A
nbsollosi@gtcc.edu
SOLMS, Daniel ... 260-356-6000 167 D
SOLNICK, Steven, L ... 828-298-3325 373 A
president@warren-wilson.edu
SOLO AQUINO,
Limaris ... 787-725-8120 552 G
lsolo@eap.edu
SOLOCHEK, Arlen ... 480-731-8232.. 14 J
arlen.solochek@domail.maricopa.edu
SOLODUCHA, Kathy, J . 816-501-4250 281 B
kathy.soloducha@rockhurst.edu
SOLOMAN, Tera ... 620-365-5116 184 C
soloman@allencc.edu
SOLOMON, Daniel, L ... 919-515-7277 370 D
solomon@ncsu.edu
SOLOMON, Debbie ... 425-235-2352 525 G
dsolomon@rtc.edu
SOLOMON, Ian, H ... 773-702-9781 161 D
iansolomon@uchicago.edu
SOLOMON, Ira ... 504-865-5422 207 F
isolomon@tulane.edu
SOLOMON, Jeffrey, S ... 508-831-5288 238 G
solomon@wpi.edu
SOLOMON, Jerome ... 408-498-5154.. 40 E
jsolomon@cogswell.edu
SOLOMON, Jill ... 617-277-3915 224 D
solomonj@bgsp.edu
SOLOMON, Kimberly ... 803-780-1266 451 G
ksolomon@voorhees.edu
SOLOMON, Mary Ellen . 412-396-1396 417 I
solomon3@duq.edu
SOLOMON, Mendel ... 973-267-9404 305 E
rabbisolo@aol.com
SOLOMON, Robert ... 912-754-2879 131 B
rsolomon@savannahtech.edu
SOLOMON, Ron ... 225-216-8267 202 N
solomonr@mybrcc.edu
SOLOMON, Samuel ... 401-454-6347 442 B
ssolomon@risd.edu
SOLOMON, Shoshana ... 973-267-9404 305 E
shoshanasolomon@rca.edu
SOLOMON, Sigrid, B ... 937-382-6661 395 F
sigrid_solomon@wilmington.edu
SOLOMON, Stephanie ... 803-754-4100 445 D
SOLOMON, Steven ... 850-201-6549 117 B
solomos@tcc.fl.edu
SOLOMON, William, G . 478-301-2771 128 G
solomon_wg@mercer.edu
SOLOMONS, Mary, L ... 518-580-5619 342 I
msolomon@skidmore.edu
SOLOMONT, Alan ... 617-627-3453 237 C
alan.solomont@tufts.edu
SOLOPERTO, Sheila ... 508-373-9502 223 C
sheila.soloperto@becker.edu
SOLORZANO, Fernando 562-985-4101.. 33 F
fernando.solorzano@csulb.edu
SOLORZANO, Jose ... 787-891-0925 553 E
jsolorza@aguadilla.inter.edu
SOLSKI, Ed ... 661-824-2977.. 55 I
esolski@ntps.edu
SOLT, Karen ... 630-942-2292 142 F
soltka@cod.edu
SOLT, Michael ... 562-985-5306.. 33 F
michael.solt@csulb.edu
SOLTANIAN, Rita ... 661-255-1050.. 31 B
SOLTIS, Kay, W ... 253-535-8725 524 I
soltiskw@plu.edu
SOLTMAN, Mary ... 360-596-5364 527 B
msoltman@spscc.edu
SOLTYS, Eugene ... 973-328-5096 301 G
esoltys@ccm.edu
SOLTZ, David, L ... 570-389-4526 430 B
dsoltz@bloomu.edu
SOLUM, Rachel ... 303-245-4804.. 84 B
rsolum@naropa.edu
SOLVASON, Nanette ... 650-940-7730.. 45 A
solvasonnanette@foothill.edu
SOLVERSON, Natalie ... 608-785-8006 539 G
nsolverson@uwlax.edu
SOM, Andrew ... 415-338-3145.. 36 A
asom@sfsu.edu
SOMAN, Sherril ... 616-331-3327 243 E
somans@gvsu.edu
SOMERA, R. Ray, D ... 671-735-5528 549 E
reneray.somera@guamcc.edu
SOMERLAD, Tracy ... 910-755-7422 360 E
somerladt@brunswickcc.edu
SOMERO, Audrey ... 757-826-1883 505 C
SOMERO, Marty ... 970-351-2502.. 87 A
marty.somero@unco.edu
SOMERS, Christine ... 570-674-6314 426 D
csomers@misericordia.edu
SOMERS, Cindy ... 303-797-5972.. 79 A
cindy.somers@arapahoe.edu
SOMERS, Kevin ... 870-743-3000.. 22 A
ksomers@northark.edu
SOMERS, Michael ... 508-531-1255 229 C
msomers@bridgew.edu
SOMERS, Micki ... 870-743-3000.. 22 A
msomers@northark.edu
SOMERS, Robert, J ... 410-455-2695 219 F
somers@umbc.edu
SOMERSET, Cheryl ... 864-587-4236 449 D
somersetc@smcsc.edu
SOMERSON, Rosanne ... 401-454-6764 442 B
president@risd.edu
SOMERVELL, Ronald ... 703-284-6941 510 B
ronald.somervell@marymount.edu
SOMERVILLE, Charles ... 304-696-2424 532 H
somervil@marshall.edu
SOMERVILLE,
Dionne, D ... 570-389-4062 430 B
dsomervi@bloomu.edu
SOMERVILLE, Mary ... 303-556-4587.. 86 G
mary.somerville@ucdenver.edu
SOMERVILLE, Tim ... 951-719-2994.. 60 D
doc@golfcollege.edu
SOMMA, Ann Marie ... 518-743-2273 347 E
sommam@sunyacc.edu
SOMMA, Lauren ... 951-781-2727.. 61 D
lsomma@sagecollege.edu
SOMMA, Victor ... 508-425-1216 232 F
vsomma@qcc.mass.edu
SOMMER, John ... 732-987-2416 302 J
sommerj@georgian.edu
SOMMER, Pete, F ... 757-822-1783 517 C
psommer@tcc.edu
SOMMER, Sally, W ... 419-358-3317 377 H
sommers@bluffton.edu
SOMMERER, Shaun ... 660-626-2395 271 G
ssommerer@atsu.edu
SOMMERFELD, Curtis ... 541-956-7016 409 F
curt@roguecc.edu
SOMMERFELDT,
Scott, D ... 801-422-2674 497 J
scott_sommerfeldt@byu.edu
SOMMERS, Janet, B ... 651-631-5201 265 D
jbsommers@unwsp.edu
SOMMERS, Kathleen, C 724-287-8711 413 G
SOMMERS, Mary ... 308-865-8520 293 G
sommersm@unk.edu
SOMMERS, Megan ... 252-940-6327 360 B
megan.sommers@beaufortccc.edu
SOMMERS, Rhoda, C ... 330-471-8538 385 G
rsommers@malone.edu
SOMMERS, William, E .. 717-477-1231 431 F
wesommers@ship.edu
SOMMERVILLE, Jan ... 616-395-7780 244 A
sommerville@hope.edu
SOMPOLSKI, Robert ... 847-635-1690 155 E
somplski@oakton.edu
SOMVICHIAN, Kamol ... 323-731-2383.. 57 H
ksomvichian@psuca.edu
SONDER, Henk, E ... 401-456-9577 442 A
hsonder@ric.edu
SONDEY, Joann ... 914-831-0288 322 D
jsondey@cw.edu
SONDEY, Stephen ... 201-684-7496 305 F
ssondey@ramapo.edu
SONES, Rodney ... 740-477-7786 388 F
rsones@ohiochristian.edu
SONES, Ron ... 903-233-3610 477 G
ronsones@letu.edu
SONEY, Ralph ... 336-334-4822 363 A
rgsoney@gtcc.edu
SONG, A. Li ... 516-364-0808 335 A
asong@nycollege.edu
SONG, Bok, H ... 636-327-4645 278 D
dbo@midwest.edu
SONG, Brian ... 714-525-0088.. 46 D
SONG, Connie ... 513-231-2223 377 B
csong@athenaeum.edu
SONG, Estee ... 714-683-1382.. 29 E
estee.song@buc.edu
SONG, Hee Sook ... 770-279-0507 124 F
joysong@gcuniv.edu
SONG, HeeSook ... 770-279-0507 124 F
joysong@gcuniv.edu
SONG, Jae, M ... 636-327-4645 278 D
vpson@midwest.edu
SONG, Jae, P ... 636-327-4645 278 D
jp@midwest.edu
SONG, James ... 636-327-4645 278 D
president@midwest.edu
SONG, John, M ... 213-385-2322.. 77 H
president@wmu.edu
SONG, Sarah ... 707-654-1074.. 34 B
sasong@csum.edu
SONG, Sumie ... 773-244-5571 154 G
ssong@northpark.edu
SONG, Young Joon ... 714-517-1945.. 29 E
president@buc.edu
SONGER, Nancy, B ... 215-895-2167 417 E
nancy.b.songer@drexel.edu
SONGSTER, Nora ... 707-546-4000.. 43 J
nsongster@empirecollege.com
SONGSTER, Roger ... 402-941-6127 291 I
songster@midlandu.edu
SONI, Bharat ... 931-372-3374 462 A
bsoni@tntech.edu
SONI, Jaya, K ... 512-505-3019 475 G
jksoni@htu.edu
SONI, Varun ... 213-740-6110.. 74 D
vasoni@usc.edu
SONIAT, Karen ... 225-578-8645 205 E
karen.soniat@law.lsu.edu
SONNEE, Anne ... 651-793-1805 259 E
anne.sonnee@metrostate.edu
SONNEMA, Roy ... 509-359-2227 522 C
rsonnema1@euw.edu
SONNENBERG, Jeff ... 602-557-1740.. 18 H
jeff.sonnenberg@phoenix.edu
SONNENBERGER,
David ... 630-829-6538 140 A
dsonnenberger@ben.edu
SONNENBLICK, Carol ... 718-552-1170 320 D
csonnenblick@citytech.cuny.edu
SONNENFELD, Gerald ... 401-874-4576 442 E
gsonnenfeld@uri.edu
SONNENSCHEIN, Nurit . 518-608-8307 325 B
nsonnens@excelsior.edu
SONNENSTEIN, Mark ... 718-933-6700 333 F
ssonnenstein@monroecollege.edu
SONNENSTRAHL,
Samuel ... 202-651-5060.. 95 C
samuel.sonnenstrahl@gallaudet.edu
SONNER, Mary ... 423-636-7345 464 F
msonner@tusculum.edu
SONNLEITNER,
Thomas, G ... 920-424-3030 540 B
sonnleit@uwosh.edu
SONNTAG, Dave ... 509-313-6192 522 L
sonntagd@gonzaga.edu
SONNTAG, Gabriela ... 909-748-8096.. 73 K
gabriela_sonntag@redlands.edu
SONODA, Kazuhiro ... 509-865-8581 523 C
sonoda_k@heritage.edu
SONQUIST, Eric, J ... 805-893-8585.. 72 D
eric.sonquist@ucsb.edu
SONRICKER, Nicholas .. 716-851-1282 325 A
sonrickern@ecc.edu
SONSTEBY, Jill ... 651-638-6254 254 A
jks44888@bethel.edu
SONTAG, Michael ... 513-244-4766 387 A
michael.sontag@msj.edu
SOODSMA, Heidi ... 920-693-1631 543 B
heidi.soodsma@gotoltc.edu
SOOHOO, Liane ... 206-239-2222 519 H
lsoohoo@aii.edu
SOOHOO-REFAEI,
Sandy ... 619-849-2783.. 59 K
sandysoohoorefaei@pointloma.edu
SOOKDEO, David ... 718-429-6600 352 A
david.sookdeo@vaughn.edu
SOONS, Peter, D ... 802-654-2374 502 H
psoons@smcvt.edu
SOOS, Lori ... 716-286-8390 336 E
lsoos@niagara.edu
SOPCHAK, Elaine ... 802-224-3001 503 F
elaine.sopchak@vsc.edu
SOPCICH, Joe ... 913-469-8500 188 E
jsopcich@jccc.edu
SOPCZYK, Debbie ... 518-464-8728 325 B
dsopczyk@excelsior.edu
SOPER, Sarah ... 765-973-8231 168 A
saeaton@iue.edu
SOPHEA, So ... 646-313-8000 321 A
sophea.so@guttman.cuny.edu
SOPHIEA, Karen ... 805-965-0581.. 64 N
sophiea@sbcc.edu
SOPKO, Bryn, M ... 503-943-8987 410 H
sopko@up.edu
SOPKO, Jennifer ... 312-949-7412 146 E
jsopko@ico.edu
SORA, Wendy ... 808-956-4399 135 J
wendys@hawaii.edu
SORBELLO, Barbara, C . 804-627-5300 505 E
barbara_sorbello@bshsi.org
SORBER, Ken ... 801-274-3280 501 B
ksorber@wgu.edu
SORBER, Todd ... 973-684-5656 304 F
tsorber@pccc.edu
SORCE, Tanya ... 973-290-4465 301 F
tsorce@cse.edu
SORDELET, Teresa, A ... 260-399-7700 174 C
tsordelet@sf.edu
SORELL, Rebecca ... 415-503-6287.. 63 A
rsorell@sfcm.edu
SORELLE, Patrick ... 920-498-5753 544 B
patrick.sorelle@nwtc.edu
SOREM, JR., James, R . 918-631-2288 403M
james-sorem@utulsa.edu
SOREN, Vicki ... 605-688-4989 454 C
vick.soren@sdstate.edu
SORENSEN, Carl, K ... 804-289-8166 513M
csorense@richmond.edu
SORENSEN, Dale ... 541-485-1780 407 H
dalesorensen@newhope.edu
SORENSEN, Elisabeth ... 425-739-8134 523 I
elisabeth.sorensen@lwtech.edu
SORENSEN, Gary ... 928-428-8247.. 13 L
gary.sorensen@eac.edu
SORENSEN, Niles, F ... 704-687-7201 371 B
nfsorens@uncc.edu
SORENSEN, Robin ... 704-378-1048 358 B
rsorensen@jcsu.edu
SORENSEN, Sarah ... 801-524-8149 498 J
ssorenson@ldsbc.edu
SORENSEN, Teresa ... 651-846-1479 261 G
teresa.sorensen@saintpaul.edu
SORENSEN, Zak ... 616-538-2330 243 C
zsorensen@gbcol.edu
SORENSON, Amanda ... 573-288-6420 274 C
asorenson@culver.edu
SORENSON, Amy ... 920-403-3165 538 K
amy.sorenson@snc.edu
SORENSON, David ... 605-274-5223 452 A
david.sorenson@augie.edu
SORENSON, Jennifer ... 612-332-3361 253 I
jsorenson@aii.edu
SORENSON, Nancee ... 813-253-7860 106 C
csorenson@hccfl.edu
SORENSON, Nancy ... 651-523-2103 256 B
nsorenson01@hamline.edu
SORENSON, Richard ... 847-947-5601 153 H
RSorenson@nl.edu
SORENSON, Sally ... 541-383-7216 404 K
ssorenson@cocc.edu
SORENSON, Tanya ... 253-589-6090 521 B
tanya.sorenson@cptc.edu
SOREY, Helaina ... 206-398-4627 526 F
soreyh@seattleu.edu
SOREY, Kellie, C ... 757-822-1065 517 C
ksorey@tcc.edu
SORG, Charlotte ... 843-574-6147 449 G
charlotte.sorg@tridenttech.edu
SORIA, Deborah ... 559-925-3316.. 76 C
deborahsoria@whccd.edu
SORIANO, Brenda ... 212-962-0002 334 E
bsoriano@nyci.edu
SORIERO, Julie ... 617-253-4499 233 C
SORK, Victoria ... 310-825-7755.. 71 D
vlsork@ucla.edu
SORRELL, Clyde, H ... 240-567-5271 217 B
rocky.sorrell@montgomerycollege.edu
SORRELL, Garry ... 660-596-7301 282 H
gsorrell@sfccmo.edu

SORRELL, Michael, J .... 214-379-5550 480 D president@pqc.edu
SORRELLS, Glenn .... 972-279-6511 467 F gsorrells@amberton.edu
SORRELS, Paul .... 830-279-3013 489 B psorrels@sulross.edu
SORRENTINO, Donna Marie .... 603-862-2930 299 B dms@unh.edu
SORRENTINO, Sebastian .... 860-768-4034.. 92 F sorrentin@hartford.edu
SORROW, Russell, L .... 770-484-1204 128 D russell.sorrow@lutherrice.edu
SORSHEK, Amanda .... 856-351-2910 308 B asorshek@salemcc.edu
SORTOR, Janet .... 207-629-4000 210 K jsortor@mccs.me.edu
SORTOR, Janet, M .... 207-741-5504 211 D jsortor@smccme.edu
SORTOR, Marci, J .... 507-786-3004 264 C sortor@stolaf.edu
SORVAAG, Scott .... 507-457-6612 264 B ssorvaag@smumn.edu
SOSA, Dona .... 212-343-1234 332 I dsosa@mcny.edu
SOSA, Horacio .... 856-256-4129 306 D sosa@rowan.edu
SOSA, Joe .... 619-684-8784.. 56 B jsosa@newschoolarch.edu
SOSA, Robert .... 210-829-6077 492 B sosa@uiwtx.edu
SOSA, Velma Leticia ..... 787-761-0640 557 A jefebiblioteca@utcpr.edu
SOSA, Victor .... 603-862-2001 299 B victor.sosa@unh.edu
SOSA-HEGARTY, Dina ... 903-886-5101 485 E dina.sosa@tamuc.edu
SOSA PIERONI, Alejandra .... 330-490-7101 395 C asosa@walsh.edu
SOSCIA, Peter .... 845-341-4180 337 G peter.soscia@sunyorange.edu
SOSEBEE, JR., Hugh, D .... 478-301-2302 128 G sosebee_hd@mercer.edu
SOSEVSKY, Chana .... 800-950-4824 350 C chana.sosevsky@touro.edu
SOSHOWSKI, Donna ..... 781-239-5264 222 E dsoshowski@babson.edu
SOSNOWSKI, Scott .... 815-455-8720 152 B ssosnowski@mchenry.edu
SOSSEN, Nina .... 413-545-4741 228 F nsossen@admin.umass.edu
SOSULSKI, Michael, J .. 269-337-7156 244 I Michael.Sosulski@kzoo.edu
SOTHERDEN, James, J . 717-691-6012 426 B jsotherd@messiah.edu
SOTHMANN, Mark, S ... 843-792-3031 447 G sothmann@musc.edu
SOTO, Amilcar .... 787-878-5475 553 F asoto@arecibo.inter.edu
SOTO, Arlene .... 541-756-6445 410 A asoto@socc.edu
SOTO, Bobby .... 214-333-6894 471 L bobby@dbu.edu
SOTO, Cecilia .... 602-286-8290.. 14 M cecilia.soto@gatewaycc.edu
SOTO, Edgar .... 520-206-3260.. 17 A esoto@pima.edu
SOTO, Emilia .... 787-269-4510 556 F emilia.soto@uccaribe.edu
SOTO, Emilia .... 787-740-6631 556 F emilia.soto@uccaribe.edu
SOTO, Jose .... 402-323-3412 293 A jsoto@southeast.edu
SOTO, Luis, A .... 787-864-2222 553 J luis.soto@guayama.inter.edu
SOTO, Megan .... 619-388-3475.. 62 F msoto@sdccd.edu
SOTO, Nelson .... 513-861-6400 392 F nelson.soto@myunion.edu
SOTO, Zulay .... 787-884-3838 550 E dir_asociada@atenascollege.edu
SOTO AQUINO, Limaris .... 787-725-8120 552 G lisotoa@eap.edu
SOTO-LÓPEZ, Heriberto 787-751-1912 554 D herisoto@juris.inter.edu
SOTTER, Trudy .... 724-964-8811 427 E tsotterfa@aol.com
SOTTILE, Christian .... 912-525-5000 130 H csottile@scad.edu
SOUCIER, JoEllen .... 713-718-8891 475 C joellen.soucier@hccs.edu
SOUCY, Erin .... 207-834-7830 212 F esoucy@maine.edu
SOUCY, Ken, R .... 937-229-2641 393 E ksoucy1@udayton.edu
SOUDAH, John, P .... 210-458-7531 494 D JOHN.SOUDAH@UTSA.EDU
SOUFLERIS, Dawn .... 585-475-2574 339 G dmsrhs@rit.edu
SOUL, Karen .... 318-869-5240 202 D ksoul@centenary.edu
SOULE, Lori .... 985-448-4402 208 C lori.soule@nicholls.edu
SOULES, Robert, C .... 518-388-6176 350 K soulesr@union.edu
SOURBEER, Dan .... 760-744-1150.. 58 D dsourbeer@palomar.edu
SOURBEER, Daniel .... 760-744-1150.. 58 D
SOUSA, Camellia .... 603-924-2787 298 C camellia@sharonarts.org
SOUSA, Jennifer .... 573-288-6343 274 C jsousa@culver.edu
SOUSA, Jorge, E .... 919-516-4012 368 E jesousa@st-aug.edu
SOUSA, Marsha .... 907-474-7931.. 10 I mcsousa@alaska.edu
SOUSA, Mitsy .... 305-442-9223 108 G msousa@mrc.edu
SOUSA-PEOPLES, Kim .. 336-334-5231 371 C ksp@uncg.edu
SOUTER, Sharon .... 254-295-4667 492 C ssouter@umhb.edu
SOUTH, Anne .... 410-225-2516 216 F asouth@mica.edu
SOUTH, Gregory .... 530-938-5375.. 41 E gsouth@siskiyous.edu
SOUTH, James, D .... 580-774-3771 402 G james.south@swosu.edu
SOUTH, III, John, T ..... 912-650-6200 131 F john.south@southuniversity.edu
SOUTH, Nick, G .... 828-398-2513 368 I nsouth@southcollegenc.edu
SOUTH, Stephen, A ...... 828-398-2500 368 I ssouth@southcollegetn.edu
SOUTH, Stephen, A ...... 865-251-1800 460 J ssouth@southcollegetn.edu
SOUTHALL, Ann .... 870-862-8131.. 23 B asouthall@southark.edu
SOUTHARD, Anne .... 850-729-6040 109 D southarda@nwfsc.edu
SOUTHARD, Sonya .... 270-686-4526 197 A sonya.southard@kctcs.edu
SOUTHERLAND, Johnnie .... 919-530-5321 370 C jsoutherland@nccu.edu
SOUTHERLAND, Nate .... 801-957-4542 500 E nate.southerland@slcc.edu
SOUTHERN, Debbie ...... 309-341-7225 149 G dsouther@knox.edu
SOUTHERN, Jeff .... 620-276-9631 187 D jeff.southern@gcccks.edu
SOUTHERN, Lori .... 254-299-8686 478 C lsouthern@mclennan.edu
SOUTHWELL, Michael ... 570-422-2871 430 F msouthwell@esu.edu
SOUTHWICK, Sally .... 765-983-1431 165 H southsa@earlham.edu
SOUTHWOOD, Lori .... 859-572-6383 199 A southwoodl1@nku.edu
SOUTHWORTH, Genna .. 541-956-7426 409 F gsouthworth@roguecc.edu
SOUTHWORTH, Linda ... 978-934-2373 229 A Linda_Southworth@uml.edu
SOUTHWORTH-FISHER, Barbara .... 727-816-3116 110 B fisherb@phsc.edu
SOUTTER, Cathey .... 214-768-4795 482 J csoutter@smu.edu
SOUVAINE, Diane .... 617-636-3536 237 C diane.souvaine@tufts.edu
SOUZA, Diana .... 231-348-6837 248 A dsouza@ncmich.edu
SOUZA, Nicole, L .... 212-346-1232 337 I nsouza@pace.edu
SOVA, Devin, A .... 336-318-7820 365 A dasova@randolph.edu
SOWELL, John, T .... 404-995-8484 270 B jsowell@rts.edu
SOWELL, Kathy .... 615-230-3476 464 B kathy.sowell@volstate.edu
SOWELL, Madison, U ... 540-261-4122 512 J madison.sowell@svu.edu
SOWELL, Stacey .... 919-546-8271 368 G ssowell@shawu.edu
SOWER, Michelle .... 530-541-4660.. 50 A sower@ltcc.edu
SOWERS, Donna, S .... 301-846-2466 214 I dsowers@frederick.edu
SOWERS, Karen .... 865-974-3176 465 D kmsowers@utk.edu
SOWINSKI, Tomasz ...... 212-472-1500 336 A tsowinski@nysid.edu
SOYER, Megan, M .... 817-257-5325 486 G m.m.soyer@tcu.edu
SOYRING, Mary .... 218-879-0811 258 F msoyring@fdltcc.edu
SOZZO, Anthony, M ..... 914-594-4491 335 H tony_sozzo@nymc.edu
SPACH, Robert, C .... 704-894-2420 356 D rospach@davidson.edu
SPACK, Martha .... 870-972-2056.. 19 F mspack@astate.edu
SPADE, Douglas, R ...... 713-798-7391 469 C dspade@bcm.edu
SPADEMAN, Robert ...... 216-523-7284 380 D r.spademan@csuohio.edu
SPAETH, Jason .... 320-629-5100 260 H spaethj@pinetech.edu
SPAETH, Nick .... 309-457-2311 153 B nspaeth@monmouthcollege.edu
SPAETH, Paul, J .... 716-375-2327 340 C pspaeth@sbu.edu
SPAETH-BAUM, Barbara .... 701-671-2483 375 B barbara.baum@ndscs.edu
SPAGNA, Michael, E .... 818-677-2590.. 34 D michael.spagna@csun.edu
SPAGNOLO, Jean Paul . 260-399-7700 174 C jspagnolo@sf.edu
SPAHR, Steven .... 301-687-4111 220 D sspahr@frostburg.edu
SPAID, Darla .... 814-732-1364 430 G dspaid@edinboro.edu
SPAIN, Ashley .... 309-692-4092 152 F arspain@midstate.edu
SPAIN, Joanie .... 505-473-6676 313 B joanie.spain@santafeuniversity.edu
SPAIN, Tammy .... 252-249-1851 364 F tspain@pamlicocc.edu
SPAIN, William, R .... 401-841-3499 548 B
SPAK, Gale, T .... 973-596-8540 304 D gale.spak@njit.edu
SPAKE, Deborah, F .... 330-672-6317 384 H dspake@kent.edu
SPAKE, Ellen .... 816-501-4597 281 B ellen.spake@rockhurst.edu
SPALDING, Carol .... 704-216-3450 365 F carol.spalding@rccc.edu
SPALDING, David, P .... 515-294-2422 175 G spalding@iastate.edu
SPALDING, Jane .... 206-296-6118 526 F spalding@seattleu.edu
SPALDING, Richard, E .. 413-597-2483 238 E richard.e.spalding@williams.edu
SPALDING, Sharon, S .. 540-887-7217 510 A sspalding@mbc.edu
SPALDING, Wendy .... 513-244-8492 379 I wendy.spalding@ccuniversity.edu
SPALLA, Tara .... 614-234-5950 386 N tspalla@mccn.edu
SPALTER, Mendel .... 323-937-3763.. 77 J mspalter@yoec.edu
SPALTER, Sholom .... 973-267-9404 305 E shspalter1@aol.com
SPANBAUER, John, K ... 716-286-8055 336 E jks@niagara.edu
SPANBAUER, Julie .... 312-427-2737 148 I 7spanbau@jmls.edu
SPANCAKE, Richard ...... 229-391-4890 119 F rspancake@abac.edu
SPANG, David .... 609-894-9311 306 B
SPANG, Kimberly .... 610-330-5021 423 A spangk@lafayette.edu
SPANG, Zane .... 406-477-6215 286 E zspang@cdkc.edu
SPANGENBERG, Eric ..... 949-824-8470.. 71 C ers@uci.edu
SPANGENBERG, Laurie . 906-786-5802 240 K laurie.spangenberg@baycollege.edu
SPANGLER, Anthony ..... 313-664-7462 241 D aspangler@collegeforcreativestudies.edu
SPANGLER, John, R ..... 717-334-6286 424 F jspangler@ltsg.edu
SPANGLER, Lee .... 406-994-4399 287 G spangler@montana.edu
SPANGLER, Michael ..... 702-651-4959 295 C michael.spangler@csn.edu
SPANGLER, Stephanie .. 203-432-4446.. 93 C stephanie.spangler@yale.edu
SPANGLER, Todd .... 315-655-7121 317 J tspangler@cazenovia.edu
SPANIOL, Lee .... 217-234-5263 150 B lspaniol@lakeland.cc.il.us
SPANJER, Pat .... 509-359-4557 522 C pspanjer@ewu.edu
SPANN, B. Steven .... 615-327-3927 457 G spann@guptoncollege.edu
SPANN, Chante .... 312-427-2737 148 I cspann@jmls.edu
SPANN, Sammy .... 419-530-5268 394 E sammy.spann@utoledo.edu
SPANN-PACK, Robin ...... 601-979-2015 267 H robin.m.spann-pack@jsums.edu
SPANO, David, B .... 704-687-0311 371 B dspano@uncc.edu
SPAR, Debora, L .... 212-854-2021 315 J dspar@barnard.edu
SPARACINO, Debra .... 864-656-2171 444 E registrar@clemson.edu
SPARGEN, Dan .... 402-399-2600 289 I dspargen@csm.edu
SPARKES, Mike .... 281-425-6327 477 F msparkes@lee.edu
SPARKMAN, Calvin .... 951-343-4356.. 30 D csparkman@calbaptist.edu
SPARKMAN, Margo .... 606-368-6039 192 H margosparkman@alc.edu
SPARKMAN, Susan .... 205-652-3587.... 9 G sgt@uwa.edu
SPARKS, Brad .... 618-235-2700 160 B bradley.sparks@swic.edu
SPARKS, Cheryl, T .... 432-264-5030 475 E csparks@howardcollege.edu
SPARKS, Doug .... 602-285-7254.. 15 C douglas.sparks@phoenixcollege.edu
SPARKS, George, E ...... 540-568-7073 509 C sparksge@jmu.edu
SPARKS, Jane .... 760-757-2121.. 54 G jsparks@miracosta.edu
SPARKS, Kenton .... 610-341-5929 418 A ksparks@eastern.edu
SPARKS, Kim .... 606-759-7141 196 G kim.sparks@kctcs.edu
SPARKS, Larry, D .... 662-915-7200 270 G lsparks@olemiss.edu
SPARKS, Maria .... 518-464-8768 325 B msparks@excelsior.edu
SPARKS, Mark .... 410-455-2872 219 F sparks@umbc.edu
SPARKS, Michele .... 859-233-8236 200 D msparks@transy.edu
SPARKS, Rick .... 509-793-2206 520 B ricks@bigbend.edu
SPARKS, Rick .... 540-231-7951 518 B rasparks@vt.edu
SPARKS, Sonny .... 662-472-9015 267 E ssparks@holmescc.edu
SPARKS, Steve .... 252-222-6087 361 A sparkss@carteret.edu
SPARKS, Terrell .... 801-878-1494 296 D tsparks@roseman.edu
SPARKS, William, O ..... 505-272-5849 313 H WSparks@salud.unm.edu
SPARNO, Annie .... 505-438-8884 313 C annie@acupuncturecollege.edu
SPARR, Cynthia .... 630-466-7900 162 K csparr@waubonsee.edu
SPARROW, Anita .... 860-512-3223.. 89 D asparrow@manchestercc.edu
SPARROW, Meghan ...... 304-357-4741 530 H meghansparrow@ucwv.edu
SPARROW, Rebecca, M 607-255-2723 323 C rms18@cornell.edu
SPARROW, Stephen ...... 907-474-7083.. 10 I sdsparrow@alaska.edu
SPARROW, Suzanne ..... 610-409-3600 438 H ssparrow@ursinus.edu
SPARY, Wayne .... 402-826-8228 290 C wayne.spary@doane.edu
SPATAFORE, Marisa ...... 408-864-8672.. 44 N spataforemarisa@deanza.edu
SPATARO, Keith .... 650-543-3853.. 54 B kspataro@menlo.edu
SPATARO-WILSON, Jennifer, A .... 540-665-5412 512 E jspataro@su.edu
SPATES, Gerald .... 336-334-7800 370 B gspates@ncat.edu
SPATH, Christine .... 303-784-8637.. 83 M cspath@jiu.edu
SPATIG, J. Robert .... 415-422-4019.. 74 C jrspatig@usfca.edu
SPATZ, Dan .... 541-506-6110 405 C dspatz@cgcc.edu
SPAULDING, Angela ..... 806-651-2730 486 D aspaulding@mail.wtamu.edu
SPAULDING, II, Henry, W .... 740-392-6868 387 B hspauldi@mvnu.edu
SPAULDING, Jeb .... 802-224-3000 503 F jeb.spaulding@vsc.edu
SPAULDING, Thad .... 303-556-3591.. 81 J thad.spaulding@ccd.edu
SPAVENTA, Marilynn .... 805-965-0581.. 64 N spaventa@sbcc.edu
SPAYER, Roger .... 847-925-6360 145 F rspayer@harpercollege.edu
SPAZIANI, Gina .... 978-656-3145 232 B spazianig@middlesex.mass.edu
SPEAKER, Cindy .... 315-364-3474 352 F cspeaker@wells.edu
SPEAKMAN, Thomas, W .... 989-774-1840 240 O speak1tw@cmich.edu
SPEAKS, Michael, A ..... 315-443-2255 349 E maspeaks@syr.edu
SPEAKS, Tiffany .... 202-885-3651.. 94 H tspeaks@american.edu

SPEAR, Diana 618-262-8641 147 B speard@iecc.edu
SPEAR, Pamela 603-526-3621 296 I pspear@colby-sawyer.edu
SPEAR, Robert 208-885-0243 139 C rspear@uidaho.edu
SPEAREN, Charlene 803-376-5780 443 D
SPEARING, Mike 205-348-5490 8 E mspearing@uasystem.ua.edu
SPEARMAN, Howard 815-921-4109 157 B h.spearman@rockvalleycollege.edu
SPEARMAN, Leonard, H 713-313-1198 487 F lespearman@tmslaw.tsu.edu
SPEARMAN, Tim 619-961-4221 69 J tspearman@tjsl.edu
SPEARS, Barbara Anne 256-215-4311 2 G bspears@cacc.edu
SPEARS, Curtis 479-788-7881 23 H curtis.spears@uafs.edu
SPEARS, Eric 478-445-0874 125 A eric.spears@gcsu.edu
SPEARS, Gary Lee 662-562-3227 269 E glspears@northwestms.edu
SPEARS, Gene 828-898-8744 358 F spears@lmc.edu
SPEARS, Jacqueline, A 409-882-3018 488 G jackie.spears@lsco.edu
SPEARS, James, W 304-462-6387 532 G james.spears@glenville.edu
SPEARS, Lanny 859-858-2298 192 O
SPEARS, Linda, C 615-963-5281 461 F lspears@tnstate.edu
SPEARS, Marty 501-279-4335 21 A mspears@harding.edu
SPEARS, Ron 806-894-9611 482 F rspears@southplainscollege.edu
SPEARS, Ronald 806-716-2341 482 F rspears@southplainscollege.edu
SPEARS, Sylvia 617-824-8500 226 A sylvia_spears@emerson.edu
SPEARS, Tim 802-443-5391 502 E spears@middlebury.edu
SPEARS-BOYD, Amy 931-540-2764 462 E aspears@columbiastate.edu
SPEAS, Philip, E 606-693-5000 197 F pspeas@kmbc.edu
SPEAS, Richard 218-683-8547 260 F richard.speas@northlandcollege.edu
SPEAS, Wanda 606-693-5000 197 F wspeas@kmbc.edu
SPECHLER, Julie 954-262-5348 109 E julies@nova.edu
SPECHT, Mark, A 610-566-1776 440 C mspecht@williamson.edu
SPECHT, Matthew, F 773-442-4600 154 H m-specht@neiu.edu
SPECHT, Nancy 585-275-5348 351 D nancy.specht@rochester.edu
SPECK, Anne 484-664-3165 427 C aspeck@muhlenberg.edu
SPECK, Christie 707-864-7000 66 J christie.speck@solano.edu
SPECTAR, Jem, M 814-269-2090 437 K spectar@pitt.edu
SPECTOR, Carol 617-824-8586 226 A carol_spector@emerson.edu
SPECTOR, Harvey 212-678-3042 349 I spector@tc.edu
SPECTOR, Phillip 410-516-8068 216 A pspector@jhu.edu
SPEECH, Angela 903-593-8311 487 A amarshall@texascollege.edu
SPEED, Bonnie 404-727-6289 124 D baspeed@emory.edu
SPEED, Coleen 318-274-3338 207 H speedc@gram.edu
SPEED, Cynthia 800-782-2422 32 A cspeed@mail.cnuas.edu
SPEEDIE, Marilyn, K 612-624-1900 265 C speed001@umn.edu
SPEEGLE, Diana 817-554-5950 478 E finaid@messengercollege.edu
SPEER, Brian 704-406-4269 356 G bspeer@gardner-webb.edu
SPEER, Brian 717-262-2607 440 D brian.speer@wilson.edu
SPEER, Jennifer 615-550-3170 466 H jennifer@earthlink.net
SPEER, Julie 716-614-6251 336 D speer@niagaracc.suny.edu
SPEHN, Steven 507-222-4271 254 D sspehn@carleton.edu
SPEIDEL, Daniel 603-897-8576 298 E dspeidel@rivier.edu
SPEIDEL, III, William 724-357-5661 431 A William.Speidel@iup.edu
SPEIGHT, Virginia 419-530-7262 394 E virginia.speight@utoledo.edu
SPEIR, Mary 540-828-5706 505 F mspeir@bridgewater.edu
SPEISER, Lynn 419-267-1312 387 G lspeiser@northweststate.edu
SPEISSER, Nancy 757-493-6946 131 F nspeisser@southuniversity.edu
SPELL, Donald, R 252-493-7211 364 H dspell@email.pittcc.edu
SPELL, Paul 601-477-4223 268 A paul.spell@jcjc.edu
SPELLMAN, Carlton 910-521-6326 371 D carlton.spellman@uncp.edu
SPELLMAN, Joseph 203-932-7134 92 G jspellman@newhaven.edu
SPELLMAN, Mary 909-621-8114 39 F mary.spellman@cmc.edu
SPELLMAN, Peter 617-266-1400 223 F
SPELLS, Doretha, J 757-727-5213 508 C doretha.spells@hamptonu.edu
SPELLS, Kaschia 252-246-1214 367 D kspells@wilsoncc.edu
SPELMAN, Amy 309-298-1914 163 A ae-spelman@wiu.edu
SPENCE, Bob, C 254-710-3731 469 D bob_spence@baylor.edu
SPENCE, Jeffery 215-572-2088 412 F spencej@arcadia.edu
SPENCE, Lisa 812-237-8439 167 E lisa.spence@indstate.edu
SPENCE, Mary 716-829-7736 324 E spencem@dyc.edu
SPENCE, Stan 817-461-8741 468 C sspence@arlingtonbaptistcollege.edu
SPENCE, Thomas 615-460-6417 455 D Thom.Spence@belmont.edu
SPENCE, Weymouth 301-891-4128 221 C wspence@wau.edu
SPENCER, A. Clayton 207-786-6100 209 F cspencer@bates.edu
SPENCER, Andrea, M 914-773-3870 337 I aspencer@pace.edu
SPENCER, Andrew, J 919-761-2234 368 K aspencer@sebts.edu
SPENCER, Barbara 269-749-7000 249 A bspencer@olivetcollege.edu
SPENCER, Brent 970-351-2396 87 A brent.spencer@unco.edu
SPENCER, Carol 508-999-8705 228 H cspencer@umassd.edu
SPENCER, Catherine 212-636-6522 326 C caspencer@fordham.edu
SPENCER, Christine 410-837-6134 221 B cspencer@ubalt.edu
SPENCER, Dan 254-298-8619 484 C dan.spencer@templejc.edu
SPENCER, Deborah 860-231-5390 93 A dspencer@usj.edu
SPENCER, DeLinda 254-647-3234 480 G dspencer@rangercollege.edu
SPENCER, Delmy 530-749-7994 78 F dspencer@yccd.edu
SPENCER, Erin 254-298-8590 484 C erin.spencer@templejc.edu
SPENCER, Estelle, H 413-205-3461 221 G estelle.spencer@aic.edu
SPENCER, Eugene 610-409-3789 438 H gspencer@ursinus.edu
SPENCER, James 312-329-4070 153 C james.spencer@moody.edu
SPENCER, Jed 801-626-6586 500 C jedspencer@weber.edu
SPENCER, Jeremy 508-626-4500 230 A jspencer1@framingham.edu
SPENCER, Joel 303-329-6355 81 B finaid@cstcm.edu
SPENCER, SJ, John 617-735-9780 226 B spencerj@emmanuel.edu
SPENCER, Judith 662-325-3713 269 A jspencer@hrm.msstate.edu
SPENCER, Keith, J 417-667-8181 273 H kspencer@cottey.edu
SPENCER, Krystal, F 812-888-4587 174 F kspencer@vinu.edu
SPENCER, Lisa 575-769-4115 310 G lisa.spencer@clovis.edu
SPENCER, Lori 901-761-9494 456 A lspencer@concorde.edu
SPENCER, Mark 812-488-2238 173 H ms628@evansville.edu
SPENCER, Mary 414-277-4517 537 G spencer@msoe.edu
SPENCER, Pamela 513-875-3344 379 G pam.spencer@chatfield.edu
SPENCER, Patrick 509-527-5398 528 F spencerp@whitman.edu
SPENCER, Richard 618-235-2700 160 B richard.spencer@swic.edu
SPENCER, Rick, E 630-637-5209 154 F respencer@noctrl.edu
SPENCER, Ruth 845-437-6820 351 H ruspencer@vassar.edu
SPENCER, Sandra, L 217-353-2637 155 I sspencer@parkland.edu
SPENCER, Scott 703-284-1520 510 B scott.spencer@marymount.edu
SPENCER, Scott, J 610-660-1018 434 G sspencer@sju.edu
SPENCER, Shanan 304-876-5053 532 I sspencer@shepherd.edu
SPENCER, Shannon 419-772-2036 388 I s-spencer@onu.edu
SPENCER, Shannon 419-372-6389 377 I spensha@bgsu.edu
SPENCER, Yvette 205-226-7720 2 C yspencer@bsc.edu
SPENGLER, Gregory, C 410-706-1264 219 E gspengler@umaryland.edu
SPENNER, Anne 816-235-1576 284 A spennerae@umkc.edu
SPERANZA, Dena, L 740-587-6526 381 H speranzad@denison.edu
SPERGER, Herb 610-785-6264 434 E hsperger@scs.edu
SPERLING, Chad 218-793-2436 260 F chad.sperling@northlandcollege.edu
SPERLING, Michael 845-905-4616 323 E m_sperli@culinary.edu
SPERLING, Susan, S 510-723-6641 37 N ssperling@chabotcollege.edu
SPEROS, Michael 916-278-6655 34 E msperos@saclink.csus.edu
SPERRAZZA, Alex 570-408-4465 440 B alexander.sperrazza@wilkes.edu
SPERRING, Tiffany 614-222-6183 380 F tsperring@ccad.edu
SPERRY, Sarah 412-396-5894 417 I sperrys@duq.edu
SPETKA, Rosemary, V 315-792-5495 333 D rspetka@mvcc.edu
SPEWOCK, Kelly 412-291-6244 412 H kspewock@aii.edu
SPEYER, Seth 202-885-5914 94 H speyer@american.edu
SPEZIA, Robert 313-883-8576 249 E spezia.robert@shms.edu
SPEZIALE, Michael 570-408-4679 440 B michael.speziale@wilkes.edu
SPEZIANI, Humberto, M 305-284-5450 118 A hmspez@miami.edu
SPEZIO, Kim, E 423-746-5205 464 D kespezio@twcnet.edu
SPEZZACATENA, Maricel 305-273-4499 100 K maricel@cbt.edu
SPICER, Christopher 360-650-6144 528 D kit.spicer@wwu.edu
SPICER, Donald, Z 301-445-2729 219 C dspicer@usmd.edu
SPICER, Erin 850-484-1706 110 D espicer@pensacolastate.edu
SPICER, Jacqueline 810-766-4273 239 G jacqueline.spicer@baker.edu
SPICER, Kim, A 479-979-1320 25 H kaspicer@ozarks.edu
SPICER, Michael 909-621-8142 60 A michael.spicer@pomona.edu
SPICER, Udella 229-217-4159 132 C uspicer@southernregional.edu
SPIECKER, Karl 719-549-2320 81 F karl.spiecker@csupueblo.edu
SPIEGEL, Allen, M 212-430-2801 353 P spiegel@aecom.yu.edu
SPIEGEL, Allen, M 212-960-3179 353 P aspiegel@aecom.yu.edu
SPIEGEL, Benjamin 732-367-1060 300 D
SPIEGEL, John 516-572-7118 334 A john.spiegel@ncc.edu
SPIEGEL, Mary, K 205-348-8666 8 E mary.spiegel@ua.edu
SPIEGEL, Sara 312-777-8616 147 C sspiegel@aii.edu
SPIEGELMAN, Kathy 617-373-2226 235 D
SPIELBAUER, Brian 660-248-6390 272 N bspielba@centralmethodist.edu
SPIELMAKER, Shallan 616-698-7111 241 I sspielmaker2@davenport.edu
SPIELMANN, Dan 920-465-2067 539 F spielmad@uwgb.edu
SPIELVOGEL, Jennifer 216-987-4767 381 A jennifer.spielvogel@tri-c.edu
SPIERS, Cynthia, E 419-995-8439 384 E spiers.c@rhodesstate.edu
SPIERS, William 850-201-8399 117 B spiersw@tcc.fl.edu
SPIES, Brent 314-889-4564 275 B bspies@fontbonne.edu
SPIES, Carolyn, I 973-748-9000 300 E carolyn_spies@bloomfield.edu
SPIES, Don 281-459-7629 481 F don.spies@sjcd.edu
SPIES, Gail 563-288-6004 178 C gspies@eicc.edu
SPIESMAN, John 440-375-7426 385 B jspiesman@lec.edu
SPIGELMYER, Kathleen 215-248-7025 415 D spigelmyerk@chc.edu
SPIKEREIT, Damien 417-626-1234 280 B spikereit.damien@occ.edu
SPILDE, Mary 541-463-5200 406 F spildem@lanecc.edu
SPILKER, Christopher 313-883-8651 249 E spilker.christopher@shms.edu
SPILKER, Eugene 636-227-2100 277 A gene.spilker@logan.edu
SPILLER, Elizabeth 540-231-6779 518 B espiller@vt.edu
SPILLER, James 585-395-2525 345 A jspiller@brockport.edu
SPILLER, Judith 603-862-2165 299 B judy.spiller@unh.edu
SPILLER, Marwin 309-694-5361 146 C marwin.spiller@icc.edu
SPILLMAN, Tom 951-487-3945 55 A tspillma@msjc.edu
SPILLUM, Carol 605-274-4090 452 A carol.spillum@augie.edu
SPILOVOY, Tanya 701-224-2498 373 F tanya.spilovoy@ndus.edu
SPINA, Anthony 716-829-7648 324 E spinaaw@dyc.edu
SPINA, Matthew, R 609-497-7870 305 B admissions@ptsem.edu
SPINA, Robert 409-880-8661 488 F robert.spina@lamar.edu
SPINARD, John 617-873-0689 225 A John.Spinard@cambridgecollege.edu
SPINATO, Donna 903-886-5860 485 E donna.spinato@tamuc.edu
SPINAZZA, Terri 208-426-2168 137 E tspinazz@boisestate.edu
SPINDLE, Blair 405-491-6608 402 E bspindle@snu.edu
SPINDLE, William 907-786-4622 10 H whspindle@uaa.alaska.edu
SPINELLI, Paul 727-341-3070 112 A spinelli.paul@spcollege.edu
SPINELLI, JR., Stephen 215-951-2727 432 F spinellis@philau.edu
SPINELLI-SEXTER, Eva 212-463-0400 350 C espinelli@touro.edu
SPINILLO, Anthony 570-340-6057 425 D spinillo@marywood.edu
SPINK, Nancy 907-450-8153 10 G nkspink@alaska.edu
SPINK-FORMANSKI, Christina 716-829-7775 324 E
SPINKS, Robert 337-475-5711 208 B rspinks@mcneese.edu
SPINNER, Arnold 212-463-0400 350 C arnold.spinner@touro.edu
SPINO, Catherine, D 330-494-6170 391 J cspino@starkstate.edu
SPINOSA, Hanna, S 413-542-5110 222 A hspinosa@amherst.edu
SPINOSA, Tony 202-685-3946 547 M spinosat@ndu.edu
SPINOSA DE VEGA, Leah 612-330-1650 253 K devega@augsburg.edu
SPIOTTI, Louis 585-475-2615 339 G lxs4798@rit.edu
SPIRES, Chris 803-641-3463 450 C chriss@usca.edu
SPIRES, Stuart 706-886-6831 132 F sspires@tfc.edu
SPIRES, Tracy, M 864-379-8773 446 B tspires@erskine.edu
SPIRIDON, Charles 203-837-8000 88 G spiridonc@wcsu.edu
SPISAK, Art, L 319-335-1681 175 H art-spisak@uiowa.edu
SPISAK-CAMERON, Jennifer 919-681-0417 356 E jennifer.cameron@dev.duke.edu
SPISSO, Johnese 206-744-5020 527 G jmspisso@uw.edu
SPITTAL, David, J 913-971-3392 189 F president@mnu.edu
SPITTAL, Ryan 815-939-5452 155 G rspittal@olivet.edu
SPITZ, Catherine 309-556-3120 148 A cspitz@iwu.edu
SPITZ, Cody 575-562-2178 310 I cody.spitz@enmu.edu
SPITZ, Laura, M 607-255-3014 323 C lauraspitz@cornell.edu
SPITZ, Simeon 405-878-5152 402 A frsimeon@stgregorys.edu
SPITZ, Tambi 703-416-1441 508 F tspitz@ipsciences.edu
SPITZER, Bruce 217-228-5432 156 D spitzbr@quincy.edu

STAGGS, Robert .... 606-218-5357 201 C
robertstaggs@upike.edu
STAGNARO, Leta .... 510-659-6220.. 56 J
lstagnaro@ohlone.edu
STAHL, Jason .... 989-686-9029 242 I
jfstahl@delta.edu
STAHL, Laurie Ann .... 716-829-7817 324 E
stahll@dyc.edu
STAHL, Stephen, D .... 440-826-2762 377 D
sstahl@bw.edu
STAHL, Timothy, W ...... 724-925-4073 439 F
stahlt@wccc.edu
STAHLE, Noel .... 641-673-1010 184 B
stahlen@wmpenn.edu
STAHLEY, Mem .... 321-433-7804 101 O
stahleym@easternflorida.edu
STAHURA, Kurt, A .... 716-286-8270 336 E
stahura@niagara.edu
STAIANO-COICO, Lisa ... 212-650-7285 318 G
president@ccny.cuny.edu
STAINE, Kristin .... 617-217-9228 223 A
kstaine@baystate.edu
STAINES, Gail .... 660-543-4140 283 F
staines@ucmo.edu
STAIRS, Donna .... 724-653-2216 417 D
dstairs@dec.edu
STAKENAS, Carol .... 617-369-3655 236 E
cstakenas@smfa.edu
STAKENAS, James, M .. 413-662-5245 230 C
j.stakenas@mcla.edu
STAKER, Julie .... 319-399-8500 176 G
jstaker@coe.edu
STAKES, Robert .... 915-747-5683 494 B
rlstakes@utep.edu
STAKES, Robert, L .... 915-747-5683 494 B
rlstakes@utep.edu
STALCUP, Susie .... 615-322-6673 465 H
susie.stalcup@vanderbilt.edu
STALDER, Michele .... 907-455-2850.. 10 I
mestalder@alaska.edu
STALEY, Marc .... 419-772-2462 388 I
m-staley@onu.edu
STALEY, Michael .... 407-708-2390 113 A
staleym@seminolestate.edu
STALEY, Priscilla, A ..... 214-860-2037 472 F
pstaley@dcccd.edu
STALEY, Sally .... 216-368-4306 378 J
sjs29@case.edu
STALKER, Michael .... 231-995-1058 248 C
mstalker@nmc.edu
STALLARD, Gary .... 936-633-5344 467 I
gstallard@angelina.edu
STALLARD, Michael ...... 570-586-2400 435 H
mstallard@summitu.edu
STALLER, Arlene, D ...... 713-500-3268 495 A
arlene.d.staller@uth.tmc.edu
STALLINGS, Tamya .... 870-512-7822.. 19 I
tamya_stallings@asun.edu
STALLINGS, Undria .... 404-215-7748 128 L
undria.stallings@morehouse.edu
STALLINGS,
Virginia (Lyn) .... 202-885-3724.. 94 H
vstalli@american.edu
STALLMAN, Jeanne .... 541-552-6221 409 G
stallman@sou.edu
STALLMAN, Scott, R ..... 217-287-7081 151 C
scott.stallman@llcc.edu
STALLMANN, Diane ...... 773-298-3089 158 F
stallmann@sxu.edu
STALNAKER, Samantha . 817-515-1795 484 B
samantha.stalnaker@tccd.edu
STALTER, Catherine ...... 217-351-2290 155 I
cstalter@parkland.edu
STALTER, Clifford .... 828-339-4250 366 C
c_stalter@southwesterncc.edu
STALVEY, John .... 907-786-1706.. 10 H
jstalvey@uaa.alaska.edu
STAM, Allan, C .... 434-924-0812 514 A
acs8tb@Virginia.EDU
STAM, Theodore, R ...... 207-798-4282 209 H
tstam@bowdoin.edu
STAMBAUGH, Barbara .. 740-587-8575 381 H
stambaughb@denison.edu
STAMM, Paul .... 563-876-3353 177 I
pstamm@dwci.edu
STAMM, Timothy .... 504-671-5482 203 F
tstamm@dcc.edu
STAMMEL, Andrew .... 607-436-2830 344 B
andrew.stammel@oneonta.edu
STAMP, Diane, L .... 540-568-6495 509 C
stampdl@jmu.edu
STAMP, Robert, L .... 203-392-6900.. 88 F
stampr1@southernct.edu
STAMPER, Andrea, L .... 606-474-3212 195 F
astamper@kcu.edu
STAMPER, R.J .... 954-262-2103 109 E
rstamper@nova.edu
STAMPER, Richard, E ... 812-877-8956 172 C
stamper@rose-hulman.edu
STAMPS, Clara, R .... 601-877-6130 266 C
cstamps@alcorn.edu
STAMPS,
Delores Bolden .... 601-977-7871 270 F
dbstamps@tougaloo.edu
STAMPS, Michael, T ..... 601-984-1363 270 H
mstamps@umc.edu
STANAITIS, Judi .... 610-558-5544 427 D
stanaitj@neumann.edu
STANBACK STROUD,
Regina .... 650-738-4110.. 64 E
stroudr@smccd.edu
STANBROUGH,
Beverly, J .... 248-522-3811 248 E
bjstanbr@oaklandcc.edu
STANBROUGH,
Beverly, J .... 248-246-2511 248 E
bjstanbr@oaklandcc.edu
STANCEL, George, M .... 713-500-9880 495 A
george.m.stancel@uth.tmc.edu
STANCIL, Jay .... 606-546-1292 200 E
jstancil@unionky.edu
STANCIU, Hope .... 330-490-7142 395 C
hstanciu@walsh.edu
STANDEN, Jeffrey .... 859-572-6406 199 A
standenj1@nku.edu
STANDERFER, Mary ...... 479-394-7622.. 22 H
mstanderfer@rmcc.edu
STANDERFORD, Chris .. 906-227-2092 248 B
cstander@nmu.edu
STANDIFIRD, Stephen .. 317-940-6307 164 L
sstandif@butler.edu
STANDISH, Leanna .... 425-602-3000 519 J
ljs@bastyr.edu
STANDISH, Trey .... 919-515-2191 370 D
STANDLEA, Donna .... 909-607-3305.. 39 E
donna.standlea@cgu.edu
STANDLEY, Jeanne .... 903-566-7351 494 E
jstandley@uttyler.edu
STANDLEY, Susan .... 309-794-7207 139 K
suestandley@augustana.edu
STANDRIDGE, JR., Joe . 940-898-3130 490 D
jstandridge@twu.edu
STANDRIDGE, Michelle 502-585-9911 199 E
mstandridge@spalding.edu
STANEK, Chris .... 541-552-7672 409 G
stanek@sou.edu
STANFIELD, Lori, J .... 785-539-3571 189 D
ljstanfield@mccks.edu
STANFIELD, Vicki .... 409-933-8213 471 B
vstanfield@com.edu
STANFIELD,
Vincent (Shelby) 512-475-7510 493M
s.stanfield@austin.utexas.edu
STANFIELD, Zelda .... 919-530-7887 370 C
zstanfield@nccu.edu
STANFILL, Sandy .... 731-968-5722 463 A
sstanfill@jscc.edu
STANFORD, Clark .... 312-996-1040 161 F
cmstan60@uic.edu
STANFORD, Erica .... 662-562-3206 269 E
STANFORD, Janice .... 912-344-2766 120 D
janice.stanford@armstrong.edu
STANFORD, Jeanne ...... 805-893-4411.. 72 D
jeanne.stanford@sa.ucsb.edu
STANFORD, Kathy .... 503-552-2009 407 F
kstanford@ncnm.edu
STANFORD, Linda .... 907-852-1838.. 10 F
linda.stanford@ilisagvik.edu
STANFORD, Roger .... 608-785-9106 544 E
stanfordr@westerntc.edu
STANFORD, Steve .... 601-925-3205 268 E
stanford@mc.edu
STANFORD, Steve .... 601-925-3247 268 E
stanford@mc.edu
STANG, Michael .... 815-753-6102 154 I
mstang@niu.edu
STANGE, Carl .... 507-457-5100 262 D
cstange@winona.edu
STANGE, Pat .... 402-460-2152 289 D
pstange@cccneb.edu
STANGE, Von .... 319-335-3000 175 H
von-stange@uiowa.edu
STANGEL, Jeanne, A ..... 920-465-2018 539 F
stangelj@uwgb.edu
STANGER, Christina ...... 410-455-2122 219 F
stanger@umbc.edu
STANGER, Winn .... 801-626-6876 500 C
wstanger@weber.edu
STANGL, Walt .... 562-903-4795.. 29 F
walt.stangl@biola.edu
STANGLE, James, R ...... 563-333-6060 182 E
StangleJamesR@sau.edu
STANGO, Linda .... 203-575-8016.. 89 F
lstango@nv.edu
STANICH, Chris .... 832-842-0545 491 C
cstanich@uh.edu
STANICH, Chris, M ...... 832-842-0545 491 D
cstanich@central.uh.edu
STANICIC, Rob .... 281-998-6150 481 D
rob.stanicic@sjcd.edu
STANIS, Karen .... 530-749-3851.. 78 F
kstanis@yccd.edu
STANISIC, Zoran .... 727-341-7135 112 A
stanisic.zoran@spcollege.edu
STANKEY, Michael .... 940-898-3350 490 D
mstankey1@twu.edu
STANKIEWICZ, Donna ... 973-684-5218 304 F
dstankiewicz@pccc.edu
STANKIEWICZ, Lisa ...... 215-567-7080 412 G
lstankiewicz@aii.edu
STANKOVIC, Toni .... 206-934-3605 525 K
toni.stankovic@seattlecolleges.edu
STANKOVICH, Joseph ... 518-580-5719 342 I
jstankovich@skidmore.edu
STANKOWSKI, Lisa .... 231-843-5802 252 H
lmstankowski@westshore.edu
STANLEY, Brian .... 478-471-2864 128 H
brian.stanley@mga.edu
STANLEY, Carol .... 706-355-5019 120 G
cstanley@athenstech.edu
STANLEY, Carol A, J .... 434-924-4122 514 A
cas4b@virginia.edu
STANLEY, Cheryl .... 413-572-5713 230 F
cstanley@westfield.ma.edu
STANLEY, Christine, A .. 979-458-2905 485 C
cstanley@tamu.edu
STANLEY, Cole .... 405-974-2590 403 G
cstanley2@uco.edu
STANLEY, David .... 724-838-4270 435 E
stanley@setonhill.edu
STANLEY, Deborah, F ... 315-312-2211 346 A
deborah.stanley@oswego.edu
STANLEY, Donna, G ..... 276-523-7493 516 A
dstanley@me.vccs.edu
STANLEY, Graydon .... 208-769-7863 138 G
gastanley@nic.edu
STANLEY, Harold, W .... 214-768-3219 482 J
hstanley@smu.edu
STANLEY, Jay .... 910-879-5503 360 C
jstanley@bladencc.edu
STANLEY, Jennifer .... 401-254-3123 442 C
jstanley@rwu.edu
STANLEY, Jenny .... 904-596-2528 117 G
jestanley@tbc.edu
STANLEY, Jeremiah ...... 904-596-2333 117 G
jstanley@tbc.edu
STANLEY, Joseph .... 617-521-2128 236 F
joseph.stanley@simmons.edu
STANLEY, Karen .... 910-521-6528 371 D
karen.stanley@uncp.edu
STANLEY, Kelly, M .... 970-247-7615.. 82 I
kmstanley@fortlewis.edu
STANLEY, Loreen .... 218-935-0417 266 A
loreen.stanley@wetcc.edu
STANLEY, Mark .... 712-325-3200 180 B
mstanley@iwcc.edu
STANLEY, Mark .... 712-325-3375 180 B
mstanley@iwcc.edu
STANLEY, Robert .... 630-829-6625 140 A
rstanley@ben.edu
STANLEY, Ryan .... 706-355-5114 120 G
rstanley@athenstech.edu
STANLEY, Samuel, L .... 631-632-6265 344 C
samuel.stanley@stonybrook.edu
STANLEY, Scott, A .... 603-513-1334 299 C
scott.stanley@granite.edu
STANLEY, Tuesday .... 724-925-4001 439 F
stanleyt@wccc.edu
STANLEY, Valarie, J ...... 203-432-0849.. 93 C
valarie.stanley@yale.edu
STANLEY-ANDERSON,
Clarenda .... 919-546-8529 368 G
csanderson@shawu.edu
STANLEY-MCAULAY,
Deborah .... 203-436-4072.. 93 C
deborah.stanley-mcaulay@yale.edu
STANOWSKI, Gary .... 573-875-7353 273 D
gstanowski@ccis.edu
STANSBERRY,
Donald, M .... 757-683-3442 510 I
dstansbe@odu.edu
STANSBERRY, Jason .... 970-207-4500.. 87 D
JasonS@uscareerinstitute.edu
STANSBERRY, Terri ...... 423-585-6813 464 C
terri.stansberry@ws.edu
STANSBURY, Calvin ...... 252-536-6381 363 B
cstansbury797@halifaxcc.edu
STANTON, Amanda .... 806-291-3414 496 K
stanton@wbu.edu
STANTON, Chad, K .... 330-287-0111 389 B
stanton.70@osu.edu
STANTON, Danielle .... 603-314-7820 298 H
d.stanton@snhu.edu
STANTON, Jeffrey, M .... 315-443-2879 349 E
jmstanto@syr.edu
STANTON, Joan .... 706-419-1117 123 F
joan.stanton@covenant.edu
STANTON, Lisa .... 541-956-7024 409 F
lstanton@roguecc.edu
STANTON, Mark .... 626-812-3087.. 29 B
mstanton@apu.edu
STANTON, Maureen, L . 530-752-2072.. 71 A
mlstanton@ucdavis.edu
STANTON, Michael, J ... 508-213-2285 235 C
michael.stanton@nichols.edu
STANTON, Paul .... 617-627-4239 237 C
paul.stanton@tufts.edu
STANTON, Paul, E .... 413-565-1000 222 G
pstanton@baypath.edu
STANTON, Sindy .... 661-824-2977.. 55 I
sstanton@ntps.edu
STANTON, Tim 715-833-6217 542M
tstanton@cvtc.edu
STANTON, Timothy, R .. 508-767-7205 222 D
tr.stanton@assumption.edu
STANTON GERROW,
Robin .... 915-747-5526 494 B
rrstantongerrow@utep.edu
STANZESKI,
Marialice, F .... 215-885-2360 425 C
mstanzeski@manor.edu
STAPLES, Mark .... 617-989-4592 237 G
staplesm@wit.edu
STAPLES, William, A ..... 281-283-2004 491 E
president@uhcl.edu
STAPLETON, Gregg .... 864-646-1796 449 F
gstaplet@tctc.edu
STAPLETON, Kemp .... 419-267-1308 387 G
kstapleton@northweststate.edu
STAPLETON, Marilyn ..... 518-243-4471 316 C
stapletonm@ellismedicine.org
STAPLETON, Sarah .... 931-598-3349 460 I
sstaplet@sewanee.edu
STAPLETON, Susan, R .. 269-387-8202 252 I
susan.stapleton@wmich.edu
STAPLETON, Tracy .... 601-979-2457 267 H
tracy.a.stapleton@jsums.edu
STARACE, Melissa, D .... 570-941-6252 438 F
melissa.starace@scranton.edu
STARASTA, Mike .... 217-732-3155 150 H
mstarasta@lincolncollege.edu
STARCEVICH, Joe .... 641-856-2224 179 C
joe.starcevich@indianhills.edu
STARCEVICH, Mick .... 319-398-5501 180 J
mstarce@kirkwood.edu
STARCHER, Kevin, M .... 304-637-1410 529 I
starcherk@dewv.edu
STARCK, Brenda .... 602-285-7503.. 15 C
brenda.starck@phoenixcollege.edu
STARCZEWSKI, Kirk ...... 518-587-2100 348 A
kirk.starczewski@esc.edu
STAREK, Renee .... 724-838-4276 435 E
rstarek@setonhill.edu
STARER, Paul .... 650-949-7227.. 45 A
starerpaul@foothill.edu
STARGARDTER,
Steven, A .... 619-651-2507.. 70 G
sstargardter@usuniversity.edu
STARGEL, Denton, L ..... 201-761-7425 307 K
dstargel@saintpeters.edu
STARICH, Gale, H .... 770-718-5304 121 G
gstarich@brenau.edu
STARK, Debbie .... 740-389-4636 386 B
starkd@mtc.edu
STARK, Debra .... 201-684-7221 305 F
dstark@ramapo.edu
STARK, Garry .... 208-769-7769 138 G
garry_stark@nic.edu
STARK, Gary .... 623-245-4600.. 18 C
gstark@uti.edu
STARK, Jared .... 402-363-5635 294 G
jastark@york.edu
STARK, Jason .... 304-205-6600 531 A
jason.stark@bridgevalley.edu
STARK, John, D .... 307-766-3930 546 K
jdstark@uwyo.edu
STARK, Louis, W .... 216-368-2020 378 J
lou.stark@case.edu
STARK, Mica .... 603-862-2450 299 B
mica.stark@unh.edu
STARK, Michael .... 903-886-5796 485 E
michael.stark@tamuc.edu
STARK, Michael, M ...... 608-246-6737 543 C
mmstark@madisoncollege.edu
STARK, Paul .... 419-448-2066 383 C
pstark@heidelberg.edu
STARK, Ronald, B .... 678-891-2515 125 G
ron.stark@gpc.edu
STARK, Scott .... 909-384-8958.. 62 C
sstark@sbccd.cc.ca.us
STARK, Wayne, F .... 434-381-6151 513 E
wstark@sbc.edu
STARK LANE, Nicole .... 661-255-1050.. 31 B
nstark@calarts.edu
STARKE, Antonio .... 904-470-8007 102 A
a.starke@ewc.edu
STARKE, Christhina ...... 800-962-7682 285 I
cstarke@wma.edu
STARKENBURG,
Rebekah, L .... 708-239-4597 160 L
becky.starkenburg@trnty.edu

STARKEY, Jeremy ... 304-424-8379 533 E
jeremy.starkey@wvup.edu
STARKEY, Kristy ... 714-556-3610.. 75 A
kstarkey@vanguard.edu
STARKEY, Laura, K ... 614-235-4136 392 D
lstarkey@TLSohio.edu
STARKEY, Michele ... 310-954-4086.. 54 I
mstarkey@msmu.edu
STARKEY, Paul, L ... 570-326-3761 429 J
pls1@pct.edu
STARKEY, Stan, R ... 865-882-4565 463 F
starkeys@roanestate.edu
STARKEY-WOODS, Lisa 607-431-4000 327 B
STARKMAN, Kenneth ... 714-992-7052.. 56 F
kstarkman@fullcoll.edu
STARKOVICH,
Steven, P ... 253-535-7126 524 I
starkovich@plu.edu
STARKS, Laura ... 512-471-5058 493 M
dean.starks@mccombs.utexas.edu
STARKS, Marilyn ... 662-621-4154 266 H
mstarks@coahomacc.edu
STARKS, Misha, K ... 312-939-0111 144 D
mthompson@eastwest.edu
STARKS, Sam, B ... 215-898-6993 437 I
sstarks@upenn.edu
STARKSON,
Mary Jo, H ... 507-344-7310 253 M
maryjo.starkson@blc.edu
STARLEY, Monica ... 478-445-4444 125 A
monica.starley@gcsu.edu
STARLING, Brent ... 336-887-3000 358 E
bstarling@laureluniversity.edu
STARLING, Buddy ... 334-670-3243.... 8 A
bstar@troy.edu
STARLING, Jennifer ... 423-279-7635 463 D
jgstarling@northeaststate.edu
STARLING, Sharron ... 206-726-5018 521 G
sstarling@cornish.edu
STARLING, William ... 910-592-8081 365 G
bstarlin@sampsoncc.edu
STARNER, Wendy, S ... 717-291-3993 418 J
wendy.starner@fandm.edu
STARNES, Richard ... 828-227-7646 372 C
starnes@wcu.edu
STARNES, Ronald ... 845-368-7212 342 A
ronald.starnes@use.salvationarmy.org
STARNES, Scott ... 434-592-4191 509 G
sastarnes@liberty.edu
STARR, Bettie, C ... 270-384-8030 198 C
starrb@lindsey.edu
STARR, Brian ... 806-720-7405 478 A
brian.starr@lcu.edu
STARR, Clara ... 415-241-2249.. 39 A
cstarr@ccsf.edu
STARR, Dolores ... 904-256-7016 106 Q
dstarr@ju.edu
STARR, Janice ... 406-265-3749 288 A
janice.starr@msun.edu
STARR, Jeannine ... 914-251-6014 346 D
jeannine.starr@purchase.edu
STARR, Kenneth, W ... 254-710-3555 469 D
ken_starr@baylor.edu
STARR, Pamela ... 619-594-1113.. 35 E
pjstarr@mail.sdsu.edu
STARR, Peter ... 202-885-2446.. 94 H
pstarr@american.edu
STARR, Sharon ... 704-406-4358 356 G
sstar@gardner-webb.edu
STARR, Trudy ... 309-796-5405 140 D
starrt@bhc.edu
STARR, Valorie ... 817-598-6252 497 A
vstarr@wc.edu
STARR FIEDLER,
Heather ... 412-392-3409 433 F
hstarr@pointpark.edu
STARRATT, Christopher 305-899-4757.. 99 B
cstarratt@barry.edu
STARRATT, Joseph ... 509-335-4558 528 B
jstarratt@wsu.edu
STARRETT, David ... 573-875-8700 273 D
dstarrett@ccis.edu
STARTUP, Kenneth, M .. 870-759-4128.. 25 I
kstartup@wbcoll.edu
STASA, Joan ... 419-530-2814 394 E
joan.stasa@utoledo.edu
STASAK, Eric ... 541-888-7402 410 A
eric.stasak@socc.edu
STASIAK, Joan, C ... 773-508-3143 151 E
jstasia@luc.edu
STASINSKAYA, Victoria . 214-648-1267 496 A
victoria.stasinskaya@utsouthwestern.edu
STASOLLA, Debbie ... 609-896-5228 306 A
dstasolla@rider.edu
STASSEN, Anne, K ... 215-972-2039 429 G
astassen@pafa.edu
STASSEN, Jodi ... 218-793-2539 260 F
jodistassen@northlandcollege.edu
STASSEN, Martha, L ... 413-545-5146 228 F
mstassen@acad.umass.edu
STASSIS, Bassel ... 973-684-6500 304 F
bstassis@pccc.edu
STATEN, Michael ... 270-384-8106 198 C
statenm@lindsey.edu
STATEN, Shannon, D ... 502-852-6636 201 A
sdstat01@louisville.edu
STATES, Hollyce ... 508-588-9100 232 A
STATMORE, Kelly ... 215-646-7300 420 A
statmore.k@gmercyu.edu
STATMORE, Michael ... 203-591-5056.. 91 D
mstatmore@post.edu
STATON, Ann ... 940-898-3326 490 D
astaton@twu.edu
STATON, Cecil ... 229-333-5952 133 H
cpstaton@valdosta.edu
STATON, Rae ... 419-358-3449 377 H
statonr@bluffton.edu
STATON, Trina, J ... 551-574-1312 179 F
staton@iowacentral.edu
STATON, Wendell ... 478-445-6341 125 A
wendell.staton@gcsu.edu
STATTON, Christine ... 559-730-3734.. 41 D
christines@cos.edu
STATZELL, Donna, S ... 952-995-1447 258 G
dstatzell@hennepintech.edu
STAUCHE, Ann ... 815-455-8710 152 B
astauche@mchenry.edu
STAUDERMAN,
Elizabeth ... 585-275-4124 351 D
elizabeth.stauderman@rochester.edu
STAUDINGER, Scott, J .. 701-355-8096 375 K
sjstaudinger@umary.edu
STAUDT, Cynthia ... 330-490-7044 395 C
cstaudt@walsh.edu
STAUDT, Denise ... 210-829-2761 492 B
staudt@uiwtx.edu
STAUDT, Loretta ... 202-319-5744.. 95 A
staudt@cua.edu
STAUDT, Nancy ... 314-935-6420 285 E
nstaudt@wustl.edu
STAUFFER, Denise ... 314-918-2565 274 K
dstauffer@eden.edu
STAUFFER, Donald ... 757-455-3384 518 H
dstauffer@vwc.edu
STAUFFER, George, B ... 848-932-5224 307 B
stauffer@masongross.rutgers.edu
STAUFFER, Gregory ... 801-321-7104 499 J
gstaufferr@ushe.edu
STAUFFER, Larry ... 208-885-6470 139 C
stauffer@uidaho.edu
STAUFFER, Lynn ... 707-664-2172.. 36 C
lynn.stauffer@sonoma.edu
STAUFFER, Patricia ... 978-478-3400 235 E
pstauffer@northpoint.edu
STAUFFER, Randy ... 818-767-0888.. 77 G
randy.stauffer@woodbury.edu
STAUFFER, II,
Ronald, E ... 570-577-3305 413 E
ron.stauffer@bucknell.edu
STAUGAARD, John ... 805-922-6966.. 26 H
jstaugaard@hancockcollege.edu
STAUNTON, Annette ... 419-448-3410 392 B
astaunto@tiffin.edu
STAUSS, Michelle ... 973-618-3555 300 H
mstauss@caldwell.edu
STAVE, Kim ... 503-255-0332 407 D
kstave@multnomah.edu
STAVENGA, Mink ... 619-482-6442.. 68 D
mstavenga@swccd.edu
STAVITSKY, Alan ... 775-784-6656 295 H
ags@unr.edu
STAVRIDIS, James ... 617-627-3050 237 C
james.stavridis@tufts.edu
STAYKOVA, Milena ... 540-985-8261 509 D
mpstaykova@jcsh.edu
STAYNER, Floyd ... 803-786-3007 445 C
fstayner@columbiasc.edu
STEAD, John ... 661-362-2626.. 53 F
jstead@masters.edu
STEADMAN, Barbara ... 843-383-8010 445 A
bsteadman@coker.edu
STEADMAN, Charles ... 972-721-5305 491 B
cstead@udallas.edu
STEADMAN, Jacqui ... 423-461-8686 459 I
jrsteadman@milligan.edu
STEADMAN, Jessica ... 937-695-0307 391 F
jsteadman@sscc.edu
STEADMAN, John ... 251-460-6140.... 9 F
jsteadman@southalabama.edu
STEADMAN, Mimi, H ... 716-839-8567 323 F
msteadma@daemen.edu
STEADMAN, Sheryl ... 801-832-2168 501 C
ssteadman@westminstercollege.edu
STEADMAN, II,
William, A ... 914-594-4607 335 H
gus_steadman@nymc.edu
STEAGALL, Jeffrey ... 801-626-6063 500 C
jeffsteagall@weber.edu
STEANE, Joanne, E ... 307-766-2130 546 K
jesteane@uwyo.edu
STEARNS, Andrew, L ... 515-964-0601 178 F
stearnsa@faith.edu
STEARNS, Gail ... 714-628-7289.. 38 B
stearns@chapman.edu
STEARNS, Jill ... 209-575-6067.. 78 C
stearnsj@mjc.edu
STEARNS, Keith ... 805-546-3228.. 42 H
keith_stearns@cuesta.edu
STEARNS, Marc ... 215-503-0155 436 F
marc.stearns@jefferson.edu
STEARNS, Mary, F ... 513-732-5278 393 D
mary.stearns@uc.edu
STEARNS, Roger ... 470-578-6206 127 M
rstearns@kennesaw.edu
STEARNS, Sandra ... 262-691-5368 544 D
sstearns@wctc.edu
STEARNS, Susan, M ... 515-263-2955 178 H
sstearns@grandview.edu
STEARNS, Thaine ... 707-664-2146.. 36 C
stearnst@sonoma.edu
STEARNS-SIMS,
Elizabeth ... 406-447-6903 287 F
e.stearnssims@umhelena.edu
STEBBINS, Barbara ... 207-228-8598 213 A
stebbins@usm.maine.edu
STEBBINS, Carla ... 515-271-1497 177 H
carla.stebbins@dmu.edu
STEBBINS, Chad ... 417-625-9736 278 I
stebbins-c@mssu.edu
STEBBINS, Gerald ... 304-829-7640 529 H
gstebbins@bethanywv.edu
STEBBINS, Tim ... 202-462-2101.. 96 C
tstebbins@iwp.edu
STEBBINS, Todd, H ... 608-246-6976 543 C
stebbins@madisoncollege.edu
STEBELTON, Jeanette ... 906-786-5802 240 K
stebeltj@baycollege.edu
STEC, Paul, T ... 518-783-2314 342 H
pstec@siena.edu
STECHSCHULTE,
Sharon, A ... 419-772-2030 388 I
s-stechschulte@onu.edu
STECK, Rachele, E ... 216-881-1700 389 G
rsteck@ohiotech.edu
STECKBAUER, Jill ... 715-422-5322 543 D
jill.steckbauer@mstc.edu
STECKER, Ann Page ... 603-526-3644 296 I
astecker@colby-sawyer.edu
STECKMAN, Rebecca ... 330-385-1070 390 A
STECKMANN, Chris ... 217-732-3155 150 H
csteckmann@lincolncollege.edu
STEED, Steve ... 254-968-9350 485 A
ssteed@tarleton.edu
STEEDLEY, Lorrie ... 863-638-7202 118 L
lorrie.steedley@warner.edu
STEEGE, David ... 262-551-5847 535 E
dsteege@carthage.edu
STEEGE, Judi ... 417-667-8181 273 H
jsteege@cottey.edu
STEEHLER, Jack, K ... 540-375-2540 512 B
jsteehler@roanoke.edu
STEEL, Ann, E ... 717-866-5775 418 E
asteel@evangelical.edu
STEEL, Diane, M ... 559-323-2100.. 63 C
dsteel@sjcl.edu
STEEL, Virginia ... 310-825-1201.. 71 D
vsteel@library.ucla.edu
STEELE, Anne, C ... 740-826-8115 387 C
asteele@muskingum.edu
STEELE, Brodie ... 661-362-5041.. 40 H
brodie.steele@canyons.edu
STEELE, Cherie ... 253-589-6010 521 B
cherie.steele@cptc.edu
STEELE, Claude, M ... 510-642-1961.. 70 K
annieyeh@berkeley.edu
STEELE, Clover ... 212-247-3434 331 G
csteele@mandl.edu
STEELE, David ... 408-924-3400.. 36 B
david.steele@sjsu.edu
STEELE, Diane ... 913-758-6102 191 I
steeled@stmary.edu
STEELE, Donna ... 731-989-6001 456 K
dsteele@fhu.edu
STEELE, E. Springs ... 610-660-1027 434 G
esteele@sju.edu
STEELE, Emily ... 859-371-9393 193 D
esteele@beckfield.edu
STEELE, Gail, T ... 340-693-1008 559 B
gsteele@uvi.edu
STEELE, Jessica ... 207-509-7293 212 A
jsteele@unity.edu
STEELE, Joanne ... 914-633-2691 328 F
jsteele@iona.edu
STEELE, Jonathan ... 727-791-5987 112 A
steele.jonathan@spcollege.edu
STEELE, Karen, B ... 718-631-6604 320 F
ksteele@qcc.cuny.edu
STEELE, Kemper ... 434-961-6585 516 F
ksteele@pvcc.edu
STEELE, Kevin ... 864-646-1858 449 F
ksteele@tctc.edu
STEELE, Kevin, L ... 913-971-3278 189 F
klsteele@mnu.edu
STEELE, Larry, W ... 540-283-6647 504 E
lsteele@national-college.edu
STEELE, Laura, L ... 714-879-3901.. 47 D
llsteele@hiu.edu
STEELE, Leslie ... 615-547-1268 456 C
lsteele@cumberland.edu
STEELE, Linda, M ... 614-947-6583 382 H
linda.steele@franklin.edu
STEELE, Lisa ... 615-966-5210 458 C
tenielle.buchanan@lipscomb.edu
STEELE, Michael ... 308-535-3723 291 H
steelem@mpcc.edu
STEELE, Misty ... 405-224-3140 403 L
msteele@usao.edu
STEELE, Mitzi, B ... 540-375-2249 512 B
steele@roanoke.edu
STEELE, Patricia, A ... 301-405-9127 219 D
pasteele@umd.edu
STEELE, Patrick, W ... 701-788-4794 374 A
Patrick.Steele@mayvillestate.edu
STEELE, Rachel ... 501-205-8873.. 20 G
rsteele@cbc.edu
STEELE, Richard ... 404-894-2803 125 D
rich.steele@gatech.edu
STEELE, Sarah, G ... 315-684-6038 347 A
steelesg@morrisville.edu
STEELE, Sarah, G ... 315-684-6829 347 A
steelesg@morrisville.edu
STEELE, Scott ... 859-985-3416 193 F
steeles@berea.edu
STEELE, Sharon ... 281-425-6389 477 F
ssteele@lee.edu
STEELE, Steven ... 970-223-2669.. 83 B
ssteele@ibmc.edu
STEELE, Todd ... 312-332-0707 160 K
todd.stelle@tfa.edu
STEELE, Valerie ... 212-217-4530 325 C
valerie_steele@fitnyc.edu
STEELE, Yolanda ... 706-385-1044 130 C
yolanda.steele@point.edu
STEELE-MARCELL, Lia ... 501-370-5217.. 22 E
lsteele@philander.edu
STEELE-MIDDLETON,
Amanda ... 937-775-5200 396 A
amanda.steele-middleton@wright.edu
STEELY, Jeffrey ... 254-710-2464 469 D
jeff_steely@baylor.edu
STEELY, Wayne ... 860-231-5257.. 93 A
wsteely@usj.edu
STEEN, Clayton ... 301-860-4363 220 B
csteen@bowiestate.edu
STEEN, Eric ... 206-934-6427 526 B
eric.steen@seattlecolleges.edu
STEEN, Franklin ... 646-565-6000 350 C
franklin.steen@touro.edu
STEEN, James ... 281-649-3208 475 B
jsteen@hbu.edu
STEEN, Kenneth, L ... 540-654-1159 513 I
ksteen@umw.edu
STEEN, Susan ... 256-824-2843.... 9 A
susan.steen@uah.edu
STEENHOEK, David ... 515-643-6680 181 B
dsteenhoek@mercydesmoines.org
STEENIS, Paul, R ... 309-341-7145 149 G
psteenis@knox.edu
STEENKEN, Betsy ... 304-327-4176 532 D
bsteenken@bluefieldstate.edu
STEENO, Sarah ... 816-444-0669 281 B
bookstore@rockhurst.edu
STEENSON, Greg ... 651-690-8825 263 V
gpsteenson@stkate.edu
STEENWYK, Thomas, L ... 616-526-6549 240 L
steeto@calvin.edu
STEEPLES, Don, W ... 785-864-3661 191 G
don@ku.edu
STEEVES, Myron, R ... 714-836-7500 161 B
msteeves@tiu.edu
STEFANCO, Carolyn, J .. 518-454-5120 322 C
stefancc@strose.edu
STEFANICK, Susan, A ... 609-896-5065 306 A
stefanic@rider.edu
STEFANOWICZ,
Michael ... 860-253-3102.. 88 H
mstefanowicz@asnuntuck.edu
STEFANSKI, Kimberly ... 303-404-5481.. 82 J
kimberly.stefanski@frontrange.edu
STEFANSKY, Chaim ... 718-259-2525 316 G
STEFANUCA, Pamela ... 410-225-2506 216 F
pstefanuca@mica.edu
STEFFAN, Dee ... 802-654-0505 503 H
steffand@ccv.edu
STEFFAN, Eileen ... 412-809-5100 433 D
steffan.eileen@pti.edu
STEFFANSON, Tyler ... 509-527-2615 528 A
tyler.steffanson@wallawalla.edu
STEFFEE, David, J ... 616-632-2895 239 E
steffdav@aquinas.edu
STEFFEN, Joseph ... 912-358-4057 131 A
steffenj@savannahstate.edu

STEFFEN, Lloyd, H .... 610-758-3877 424 B
lhs1@lehigh.edu
STEFFEN, Rebecca .... 269-927-8861 245 E
steffen@lakemichigancollege.edu
STEFFEN, Susan, S .... 630-617-3172 144 G
susanss@elmhurst.edu
STEFFEN, Wayne .... 559-453-2215.. 45 E
wsteffen@fresno.edu
STEFFENS, Kate .... 612-338-7224 265 G
kate.steffens@waldenu.edu
STEFFES, Gary .... 660-263-4110 279 F
garys@macc.edu
STEFFES, Thomas .... 765-983-1366 165 H
steffto@earlham.edu
STEGEMAN, Melanie ..... 918-540-6188 398 L
melanie.stegeman@neo.edu
STEGER, Alicia .... 516-572-9634 334 A
alicia.steger@ncc.edu
STEGMAN, Margaret ...... 816-604-4155 278 A
maggie.stegman@mcckc.edu
STEGMAN, Stephen, J .. 518-629-7158 328 D
s.stegman@hvcc.edu
STEGNER, Joe .... 208-334-2315 139 C
jstegner@uidaho.edu
STEHLE, Allen .... 207-947-4591 209 G
astehle@bealcollege.edu
STEHLE, Allen, T .... 207-947-4591 209 G
astehle@bealcollege.edu
STEHOUWER, Kristin ..... 989-837-4224 248 D
stehouwer@northwood.edu
STEIB, Summer 225-578-4807 204M
summers@lsu.edu
STEIBE-PASALICH,
Susan, C .... 574-631-7336 174 A
steibe-pasalich.1@nd.edu
STEIDEL, Michael .... 412-268-2082 414 J
ms44@andrew.cmu.edu
STEIDL, Douglas .... 330-672-2917 384 H
dsteidl@kent.edu
STEIN, Beki .... 610-796-8202 412 C
beki.stein@alvernia.edu
STEIN, Bob .... 207-621-3447 212 D
rstein@maine.edu
STEIN, Carla .... 303-678-3755.. 82 J
carla.stein@frontrange.edu
STEIN, Cliff .... 503-517-1878 411 C
cstein@westernseminary.edu
STEIN, Diane .... 818-364-7867.. 51 G
STEIN, Douglas .... 719-598-0200.. 81 H
dstein@coloradotech.edu
STEIN, Douglas .... 614-251-4786 388 H
steind@ohiodominican.edu
STEIN, Dov .... 248-414-6900 246 F
dstein@mji.edu
STEIN, Eva .... 717-757-1100 440 K
eva.stein@yti.edu
STEIN, Jeff .... 336-278-7304 356 F
jstein@elon.edu
STEIN, Jennifer .... 415-551-9313.. 30 G
jstein@cca.edu
STEIN, John .... 404-385-8772 125 D
john.stein@vpss.gatech.edu
STEIN, John .... 404-894-6367 125 D
john.stein@vpss.gatech.edu
STEIN, Joshua .... 907-852-1823.. 10 F
joshua.stein@ilisagvik.edu
STEIN, Karen P, Z .... 585-785-1298 325 E
karen.stein@flcc.edu
STEIN, Kathy .... 432-837-8770 489 B
kstein@sulross.edu
STEIN, Linda .... 610-917-1416 438 G
llstein@valleyforge.edu
STEIN, Lisa .... 308-432-6263 292 B
lstein@csc.edu
STEIN, Maria, K .... 617-373-2430 235 D
STEIN, Mark, A .... 507-354-8221 257 A
steinma@mlc-wels.edu
STEIN, Melanie .... 860-297-5244.. 92 A
melanie.stein@trincoll.edu
STEIN, N .... 732-364-1220 299 H
STEIN, Scott .... 802-447-6349 503 A
sstein@svc.edu
STEIN, Sonya .... 907-786-1517.. 10 H
sonya@uaa.alaska.edu
STEIN, Thomas, H .... 724-946-7105 439 D
steinth@westminster.edu
STEIN-SMITH, Kathy ..... 201-692-2653 302 H
stein@fdu.edu
STEINACKER, Kathy ...... 815-939-5359 155 G
ksteinac@olivet.edu
STEINBECK, Robin .... 951-571-6351.. 60 K
robin.steinbeck@mvc.edu
STEINBERG, Aaron .... 718-868-2300 316 B
STEINBERG, Bettie .... 516-562-1159 324 G
bsteinbe@lij.edu
STEINBERG, Bryan, E ... 302-356-6858.. 94 G
bryan.e.steinberg@wilmu.edu
STEINBERG, Don .... 802-258-3357 502 I
donald.steinberg@worldlearning.org
STEINBERG, James, B ... 315-443-5450 349 E
jbstein@syr.edu
STEINBERG, Kurt .... 617-879-7100 230 B
ksteinberg@massart.edu
STEINBERG, Laura, J .... 315-443-4341 349 E
ljs@syr.edu
STEINBERG, Scott .... 207-221-4208 213 B
ssteinberg@une.edu
STEINBERG, Stacey .... 414-847-3255 537 F
staceysteinberg@miad.edu
STEINBERGER, Eric, J ... 419-559-2228 392 A
esteinberger01@terra.edu
STEINBOCK, Valerie .... 928-541-7777.. 16 B
vsteinbock@ncu.edu
STEINER, David .... 440-646-8302 394 G
dsteiner@ursuline.edu
STEINER, Erika .... 860-723-0251.. 88 C
steinere@ct.edu
STEINER, Fred .... 313-845-9621 243 I
fred@hfcc.edu
STEINER, Frederick, R .. 512-471-1922 493M
fsteiner@austin.utexas.edu
STEINER, Glen, D .... 708-209-3328 143 D
glen.steiner@cuchicago.edu
STEINER, Gregory, G .... 276-944-6763 507 E
gsteiner@ehc.edu
STEINER, James, D ...... 563-589-3210 183 E
jsteiner@dbq.edu
STEINER, John .... 708-209-3625 143 D
John.Steiner@cuchicago.edu
STEINER, John .... 856-351-2638 308 B
jsteiner@salemcc.edu
STEINER, Joseph, F ...... 307-766-6556 546 K
joe.steiner@uwyo.edu
STEINER, Karl, V .... 410-455-5827 219 F
steinerk@umbc.edu
STEINER, Kate .... 912-344-2504 120 D
kate.steiner@armstrong.edu
STEINER, Kim .... 276-944-6112 507 E
ksteiner@ehc.edu
STEINER, Lori .... 316-942-4291 189 K
steinerl@newmanu.edu
STEINER, Mark .... 731-989-6099 456 K
msteiner@fhu.edu
STEINER, Michael .... 660-562-1197 280 A
msteiner@nwmissouri.edu
STEINER, Michael .... 330-287-7504 389 B
steiner.255@osu.edu
STEINER, Rita, L .... 410-617-2504 216 D
rsteiner@loyola.edu
STEINER, Ted .... 216-373-5387 388 A
tsteiner@ndc.edu
STEINER-LANG, Kathy ... 314-935-5910 285 E
ksteiner@wustl.edu
STEINERT, Brandon .... 620-792-9307 184 I
steinertb@bartonccc.edu
STEINERT, Roger, F ...... 949-824-5926.. 71 C
steinert@uci.edu
STEINFELD, Peter, K ..... 712-749-2205 176 D
steinfeld@bvu.edu
STEINFELD, Trudy, G .... 212-998-4735 336 C
trudy.steinfeld@nyu.edu
STEINHAGEN, Robert .... 206-316-2458 519 I
roberts@bgu.edu
STEINHARDT, Sydney ... 212-650-6460 318 G
ssteinhardt@ccny.cuny.edu
STEINHILBER, Steven ... 770-484-1204 128 D
steven.steinhilber@lutherrice.edu
STEINHOFF, Cynthia, K 410-777-2483 213 E
cksteinhoff@aacc.edu
STEINKE, Deana, B .... 304-877-6428 529 G
financialaid@abc.edu
STEINKE, Pamela .... 815-740-2272 162 F
psteinke@stfrancis.edu
STEINKE, Paul .... 206-876-6100 526 E
STEINKE, Robin .... 651-641-3211 256 J
rsteinke001@luthersem.edu
STEINKEOWAY, Louise . 407-628-5870 102 I
louise.steinke@zenith.org
STEINKIRCHNER,
Linda, M .... 585-385-5242 340 F
lsteinkirchner@sjfc.edu
STEINMAN, Joan .... 775-673-7060 295 F
jsteinman@tmcc.edu
STEINMAYER, Janet ...... 860-701-5027.. 91 B
steinmayer_j@mitchell.edu
STEINMETZ, JR.,
Edward, J .... 570-941-4289 438 F
edward.steinmetz@scranton.edu
STEINMETZ, Joseph, E . 614-292-5881 389 A
steinmetz.53@osu.edu
STEINMETZ, Paul .... 203-837-9805.. 88 G
steinmetzp@wcsu.edu
STEINMETZ, Rob, R ...... 717-736-4140 420 D
rrsteinm@hacc.edu
STEINNERD, Sarah .... 573-651-2588 282 C
ssteinnerd@semo.edu
STEINOUR, David .... 703-726-3602.. 95 D
steinour@gwu.edu
STEINRUCK,
Jessica, M .... 202-231-3344 547 N
jessica.steinruck@dodiis.mil
STEINWEDEL, Cheryl .... 419-227-3141 394 B
csteinwedel@unoh.edu
STEITZ, John, A .... 740-284-5177 382 G
jsteitz@franciscan.edu
STEJSKAL, Patricia .... 815-479-7530 152 B
pstejskal@mchenry.edu
STEKETEE, Gail .... 617-353-3760 224 E
steketee@bu.edu
STELLA, Hilda, V .... 787-284-1912 554 B
hstella@ponce.inter.edu
STELLA, Mark .... 304-384-5356 532 E
markstella@hotmail.com
STELLA, Steven .... 518-454-5139 322 C
stellas@strose.edu
STELLER, James, R .... 518-956-8045 343 C
jsteller@albany.edu
STELLER, Tom .... 612-455-3420 254 B
STELLO, Noelle .... 503-552-1544 407 F
nstello@ncnm.edu
STELTER, Caroline, W ... 804-758-6728 516 G
cstelter@rappahannock.edu
STELZER, Stuart, P .... 479-979-1381.. 25 H
sstelzer@ozarks.edu
STEM, Elaine .... 252-492-2061 366 G
steme@vgcc.edu
STEMBRIDGE, Allen, F .. 269-471-3622 239 D
stem@andrews.edu
STEMEN, Derek .... 419-358-3661 377 H
stemend@bluffton.edu
STEMKOSKI, Stephen ... 315-859-4301 327 A
sstemkos@hamilton.edu
STEMLEY, Edward .... 713-313-7777 487 F
stemleyec@tsu.edu
STEMMANN, Karsten .... 530-741-5564.. 78 F
kstemman@yccd.edu
STEMMER, John, K .... 502-272-8140 193 E
jstemmer@bellarmine.edu
STEMPEK, Thomas .... 563-884-5469 182 D
tom.stempek@palmer.edu
STEMPLE, JR.,
Frederick, E .... 757-822-7415 517 C
fstemple@tcc.edu
STEN, Andrea .... 503-493-6529 405 E
asten@cu-portland.edu
STENBERG, Josephine .. 808-845-9119 136 E
jstenber@hawaii.edu
STENBERG, Steve .... 503-517-1238 411 A
sstenberg@warnerpacific.edu
STENCIL, Debra .... 715-675-3331 544 A
stencil@ntc.edu
STENDARDI,
Deborah, M .... 585-475-5040 339 G
dmsgrl@rit.edu
STENDER, Julie 435-652-7703 499M
stender@dixie.edu
STENEHJEM, Keith, A ... 701-788-4711 374 A
Keith.Stenehjem@mayvillestate.edu
STENGEL, Mark .... 805-546-3159.. 42 H
mark_stengel@cuesta.edu
STENGER, JR.,
Harvey, G .... 607-777-2131 343 D
president@binghamton.edu
STENGER, Karen .... 440-826-2726 377 D
kstenger@bw.edu
STENGER, Tracy, L .... 716-673-3424 343 F
STENGLE, Anne, M .... 740-587-6287 381 H
stenglea@denison.edu
STENHOUSE, Andrew .... 714-556-3610.. 75 A
andrew.stenhouse@vanguard.edu
STENKO, Michael .... 860-465-4509.. 88 E
stenkom@easternct.edu
STENNES-SPIDAHL,
Nadia .... 319-363-1323 181 D
nstennes-spidahl@mtmercy.edu
STENNES-SPIDAHL,
Naomi, R .... 608-796-3481 542 H
nrstennesspidahl@viterbo.edu
STENNETT, Debbie .... 806-291-3500 496 K
stennettd@wbu.edu
STENSLAND, Traci, L .... 509-777-4306 529 A
tstensland@whitworth.edu
STENSON, Charlene ...... 701-845-7105 374 D
c.stenson@vcsu.edu
STENSON, Merry .... 602-429-4946.. 16 N
mstenson@ps.edu
STENZEL, Neal .... 918-495-6203 401 B
nstenzel@oru.edu
STEORTS, Ken .... 901-381-3939 466 E
ken@visible.edu
STEPEK, Agnes .... 847-735-5036 149 H
stepek@lakeforest.edu
STEPHAN, Andrew .... 330-494-6170 391 J
astephan@starkstate.edu
STEPHAN, Arline .... 215-641-6534 426 E
astephan@mc3.edu
STEPHAN, Josiah .... 954-545-4500 113 B
josiah.stephan@sfbc.edu
STEPHAN, Randy .... 212-998-1409 336 C
randy.stephan@nyu.edu
STEPHAN, W. Karl .... 989-837-4211 248 D
stephan@northwood.edu
STEPHAN, William, B ... 812-855-0850 167 I
wstephan@indiana.edu
STEPHAN, William, B ... 317-231-2114 167 J
wstephan@iu.edu
STEPHAN HAINS,
Theresa, R .... 716-878-6711 345 B
stephatr@buffalostate.edu
STEPHANSKI, Tracy ...... 302-622-8000.. 93 D
tstephanski@dcad.edu
STEPHEN, Carolyn .... 530-895-2311.. 30 B
stephenca@butte.edu
STEPHEN, Cathleen .... 610-607-6205 433 H
cstephen@racc.edu
STEPHEN, Jomysha ...... 212-854-2021 315 J
jstephen@barnard.edu
STEPHENOFF, Gail, C ... 614-292-5648 389 A
stephenoff.1@osu.edu
STEPHENS, Amy, M ...... 503-255-0332 407 D
astephens@multnomah.edu
STEPHENS, Andre .... 562-903-4752.. 29 F
andre.stephens@biola.edu
STEPHENS, Camille ...... 404-880-8020 122 I
cshipman@cau.edu
STEPHENS, Cathy .... 217-641-4515 148 J
cstephens@jwcc.edu
STEPHENS, Charlene .... 302-736-2505.. 94 E
charlene.stephens@wesley.edu
STEPHENS, Christina .... 207-326-2441 211 G
christina.stephens@mma.edu
STEPHENS, Crystal .... 661-726-1911.. 70 I
crystal.stephens@uav.edu
STEPHENS, David .... 877-442-0505.. 87 C
david.stephens@rockies.edu
STEPHENS, David, J ..... 931-363-9865 458 D
dstephens@martinmethodist.edu
STEPHENS, Denise .... 805-893-8989.. 72 D
denise.stephens@ucsb.edu
STEPHENS, Denise .... 805-893-3256.. 72 D
dstephens@library.ucsb.edu
STEPHENS, Diane, S ..... 818-677-5929.. 34 D
diane.stephens@csun.edu
STEPHENS, Edward .... 417-455-5596 274 B
EdwardStephens@crowder.edu
STEPHENS, Elisa .... 415-274-2200.. 25 L
STEPHENS, Fred, W ...... 407-303-5752.. 97 J
fred.stephens@adu.edu
STEPHENS, Gail, M ...... 731-881-3506 465 F
gstephe6@utm.edu
STEPHENS, JR.,
Harvard .... 773-256-0696 151 H
Harvard.Stephens@lstc.edu
STEPHENS, Hubert .... 575-624-8291 311 K
stephens@nmmi.edu
STEPHENS, Jay .... 208-426-4454 137 E
jaystephens@boisestate.edu
STEPHENS, Josh .... 806-720-7502 478 A
josh.stephens@lcu.edu
STEPHENS, Kevin, N ..... 309-655-2291 158 D
kevin.n.stephens@osfhealthcare.org
STEPHENS, Kristie .... 530-226-4727.. 66 G
kstephens@simpsonu.edu
STEPHENS, Lisa .... 760-379-5001.. 49 F
lisa.stephens@cerrocoso.edu
STEPHENS, Mark .... 931-372-3224 462 A
mstephens@tntech.edu
STEPHENS, Mark, R ...... 701-355-8123 375 K
STEPHENS, Mary .... 213-624-1200.. 44 I
mstephens@fidm.edu
STEPHENS, Mary, E .... 562-985-1658.. 33 F
mary.stephens@csulb.edu
STEPHENS, Matthew ..... 405-613-2536 402 F
matthew.stephens@swcu.edu
STEPHENS, Melinda, R . 724-847-5235 419 B
mstephen@geneva.edu
STEPHENS, Melinda, R . 724-847-6605 419 B
mstephen@geneva.edu
STEPHENS, Melissa ...... 203-837-8582.. 88 G
stephensm@wcsu.edu
STEPHENS, Myka, K ..... 717-290-8704 423 E
mkstephens@lancasterseminary.edu
STEPHENS, Nareiko ...... 334-872-2533..... 6 G
STEPHENS, Natasha, M 405-466-3445 398 E
nmstephens@langston.edu
STEPHENS, Paul .... 859-858-3511 193 A
paul.stephens@asbury.edu
STEPHENS, Ralph .... 361-593-3814 486 A
ralph.stephens@tamuk.edu
STEPHENS, Rick .... 607-871-2137 314 J
stephens@alfred.edu
STEPHENS, Robert .... 478-825-6092 124 E
stephensr@fvsu.edu
STEPHENS, Robert, E .... 816-654-7533 276 G
rstephens@kcumb.edu
STEPHENS, Robin .... 501-212-6608.. 20 G
rstephens@cbc.edu
STEPHENS, Rusty .... 252-246-1223 367 D
rstephens@wilsoncc.edu
STEPHENS, Sandra, S ... 901-722-3220 461 A
sandra@sco.edu

STEWART, David, C ... 304-293-5811 533 D
david.stewart@mail.wvu.edu
STEWART, David, R ... 651-638-6225 254 A
d-stewart@bethel.edu
STEWART, Dawn ... 614-823-3529 390 C
dstewart@otterbein.edu
STEWART, Dean ... 920-498-6995 544 B
dean.stewart@nwtc.edu
STEWART, Deborah ... 802-828-2800 503 H
das07200@ccv.vsc.edu
STEWART, Denise ... 251-809-1532 ... 5 B
STEWART, DeShaunta ... 773-907-4044 141 O
dstewart75@ccc.edu
STEWART, Diane ... 661-362-3503 .. 40 H
diane.stewart@canyons.edu
STEWART, Donette ... 864-503-5280 451 A
dstewart@uscupstate.edu
STEWART, Dorothy ... 313-993-1028 250 H
stewardm@udmercy.edu
STEWART, Doug ... 970-945-8691 .. 80 D
STEWART, Douglas ... 601-877-2419 266 C
stewartd@alcorn.edu
STEWART, Elizabeth, J .. 585-292-2536 333 G
estewart@monroecc.edu
STEWART, H.D ... 828-898-8756 358 F
stewarth@lmc.edu
STEWART, Jacqueline ... 606-368-6059 192 H
jacquelinestewart@alc.edu
STEWART, James ... 410-951-2639 220 C
jstewart@coppin.edu
STEWART, James ... 503-517-1898 411 C
jstewart@westernseminary.edu
STEWART, James ... 731-352-4093 455 E
stewartj@bethelu.edu
STEWART, Janeen, K ... 319-352-8331 183 J
janeen.stewart@wartburg.edu
STEWART, Janie ... 810-766-4209 239 H
janie.stewart@baker.edu
STEWART, Jeff ... 239-433-9119 104 G
jstewart10@fsw.edu
STEWART, Jellema ... 716-673-3398 343 F
jellema.stewart@fredonia.edu
STEWART, Jennifer ... 314-968-7105 285 G
jstewart15@webster.edu
STEWART, Jerry, D ... 515-294-6762 175 G
jdstewa@iastate.edu
STEWART, Jo Moore ... 404-270-5061 132 D
jstewart@spelman.edu
STEWART, Joan, H ... 315-859-4105 327 A
jstewart@hamilton.edu
STEWART, John, R ... 563-589-3642 183 E
jstewart@dbq.edu
STEWART, III, John, W 205-665-6001 ... 9 C
presidentsoffice@montevallo.edu
STEWART, Joseph, W ... 716-851-1977 325 A
stewart@ecc.edu
STEWART, Juarine ... 256-372-5750 ... 1 A
juarine.stewart@aamu.edu
STEWART, June ... 864-225-7653 446 D
junestewart@forrestcollege.edu
STEWART, Kara ... 830-372-8160 487 C
kstewart@tlu.edu
STEWART, Kate ... 850-201-6200 117 B
stewartk@tcc.fl.edu
STEWART, Larry ... 248-218-2023 249 D
lstewart@rc.edu
STEWART, Lea, P ... 848-932-7127 307 B
lstewart@rutgers.edu
STEWART, Leah ... 859-572-6437 199 A
stewartl1@nku.edu
STEWART, Lisa ... 850-599-3730 114 D
lisa.stewart@famu.edu
STEWART, Lisa ... 434-791-7186 505 A
lstewart@averett.edu
STEWART, Makena ... 704-290-5840 366 A
mstewart@spcc.edu
STEWART, Michael ... 478-471-2710 128 H
michael.stewart@mga.edu
STEWART, Michael ... 404-233-3949 460 G
mstewart@richmont.edu
STEWART, R. Wayne ... 580-349-1408 400 B
rwstewart@opsu.edu
STEWART, Renee ... 615-366-4416 461 B
renee.stewart@tbr.edu
STEWART, Rob ... 806-742-2184 489 F
rob.stewart@ttu.edu
STEWART, Robert ... 251-380-3030 ... 7 F
rstewart@shc.edu
STEWART, Robert ... 617-552-2671 224 B
bobstewart@theq.follett.com
STEWART, Rod, S ... 517-750-1200 250 F
rods@admin.arbor.edu
STEWART, Scott ... 616-222-1446 241 G
scott.stewart@cornerstone.edu
STEWART, Sheilynda ... 580-559-5668 397 K
sstewart@ecok.edu
STEWART, Sonja ... 931-221-7342 461 C
stewarts@apsu.edu
STEWART, Spencer ... 702-992-2040 295 E
spencer.stewart@nsc.edu
STEWART, Spencer ... 229-243-3017 121 D
sstewart@bainbridge.edu
STEWART,
Stephanie, M ... 920-433-6639 534 K
stephanie.stewart@bellincollege.edu
STEWART, Tammy ... 512-313-3000 471 H
tammy.stewart@concordia.edu
STEWART, Terri ... 607-274-3758 328 H
tastewart@ithaca.edu
STEWART, Thomas ... 510-485-7806 .. 58 G
tstewart@patten.edu
STEWART, Todd, I ... 937-255-2321 547 E
todd.stewart@afit.edu
STEWART, Todd, M ... 270-745-5276 201 D
todd.stewart@wku.edu
STEWART, Tommie, T ... 334-229-4232 ... 1 D
tstewart@alasu.edu
STEWART, Tommy ... 901-761-9494 456 A
tstewart@concorde.edu
STEWART, Tracy ... 907-564-8261 .. 10 D
tstewart@alaskapacific.edu
STEWART, Tracy ... 717-545-4747 422 C
STEWART, Trevor ... 530-895-2421 .. 30 B
stewarttr@butte.edu
STEWART, Vicki, L ... 717-815-1287 440 H
vstewart@ycp.edu
STEWART, Vincent, W .. 714-808-4829 .. 56 D
vstewart@nocccd.edu
STEWART, Walter, M ... 314-516-6377 284 B
siewertw@umsl.edu
STEWART, Wendy ... 760-757-2121 .. 54 G
wstewart@miracosta.edu
STEWART ALEXANDER,
Mary ... 203-837-8839 .. 88 G
alexanderm@wcsu.edu
STEWART FAHS,
Pamela ... 607-777-2311 343 D
psfahs@binghamton.edu
STEWART-JAMES, Joy ... 916-278-6461 .. 34 E
jsjames@csus.edu
STIBER, Greg, F ... 954-262-5381 109 E
stiber@nova.edu
STICE, J. Michael ... 405-325-4687 403 I
mstice@ou.edu
STICE, Mike ... 949-376-6000 .. 49 K
mstice@lcad.edu
STICH, Lisa ... 231-843-5923 252 H
lkstich@westshore.edu
STICHNOTE, Lynn ... 573-341-4075 284 C
lks@mst.edu
STICK, Jim ... 515-964-6429 177 B
jwstick@dmacc.edu
STICKEL, Marianne ... 415-458-3722 .. 43 D
mstickel@dominican.edu
STICKELMAIER, Laurie .. 608-363-2250 534 L
stickelmaierll@beloit.edu
STICKLER, Lin ... 970-945-8691 .. 80 D
STICKLEY, Ronald, G ... 540-665-4530 512 E
rstickle3@su.edu
STICKSEL, Lance ... 212-686-9244 315 B
STIEFEL, Joseph P, D ... 630-889-6604 154 E
jstiefel@nuhs.edu
STIEFFEL, Deborah ... 313-993-1496 250 H
deborah.stieffel@udmercy.edu
STIEGMEIER, Marie ... 703-416-1441 508 F
mstiegmeier@ipsciences.edu
STIENBARGER,
Mary Ann ... 765-983-1346 165 H
stienma@earlham.edu
STIER, Mark ... 941-487-4504 115 B
mstier@ncf.edu
STIFEL, David ... 860-932-4157 .. 90 A
dstifel@qvcc.commnet.edu
STIFF, Cindra, K ... 270-852-3113 198 A
cindrast@kwc.edu
STIFFIN, Rose Mary ... 305-626-3697 104 B
Rose.Stiffin@fmuniv.edu
STIFFLER, Daniel, J ... 314-367-8700 281 G
daniel.stiffler@stlcop.edu
STIFFLER, Faith ... 817-598-8874 497 A
STIFFLER, Gregory, S ... 989-837-4154 248 D
stiffler@northwood.edu
STIFFLER, Jamee ... 919-718-7526 361 C
jstiffler@cccc.edu
STIFTER, Michael, J ... 715-425-3827 540 E
michael.j.stifter@uwrf.edu
STILES, Alyce ... 413-775-1607 231 E
stilesa@gcc.mass.edu
STILES, Angela ... 561-683-1400 .. 97 G
astiles@anho.edu
STILES, Bill ... 610-796-3015 412 C
bill.stiles@alvernia.edu
STILES, Carl ... 207-941-7107 210 C
stilesc@husson.edu
STILES, Chip ... 978-837-5357 233 G
stilesc@merrimack.edu
STILES, Diane ... 605-882-5284 452 G
diane.stiles@lakeareatech.edu
STILES, John ... 513-732-5232 393 D
stilesjn@ucmail.uc.edu
STILES, Michael, D ... 712-279-3149 182 F
michael.stiles@stlukescollege.edu
STILES, Randall ... 641-269-4636 178 I
stilesr@grinnell.edu
STILES, Timothy ... 386-822-7315 117 A
tstiles@stetson.edu
STILL, George ... 434-797-8576 515 C
gstill@dcc.vccs.edu
STILL, Guy, M ... 856-225-2900 307 A
guystill@camden.rutgers.edu
STILL, Jill ... 936-468-5406 484 A
jstill@sfasu.edu
STILL, Kathy ... 276-376-0130 514 B
kls72d@uvawise.edu
STILL, Kennie, M ... 864-242-5100 443 G
STILL, Todd ... 254-710-3755 469 D
Todd_Still@baylor.edu
STILLE, Brand, R ... 864-597-4130 451 J
stillebr@wofford.edu
STILLE, Robyn, L ... 906-227-2661 248 B
rstille@nmu.edu
STILLE, Suzette ... 843-953-8148 445 B
stilles@cofc.edu
STILLERMAN, Harry ... 336-334-4822 363 A
hkstillerman@gtcc.edu
STILLEY, Dana ... 845-574-4224 339 I
dstilley@sunyrockland.edu
STILLEY, Kevin ... 214-818-1369 471 I
kstilley@criswell.edu
STILLMAN, Brian, C ... 208-467-8460 138 H
bcstillman@nnu.edu
STILLMAN, Bruce ... 516-367-8497 321 F
stillman@cshl.edu
STILLMAN, Cindy ... 760-773-7959 .. 41 A
cstillman@alumni.collegeofthedesert.edu
STILLMAN, John, P ... 801-581-3655 499 K
john.stillman@hsc.utah.edu
STILLMAN, Matt ... 541-552-8535 409 G
stillmam@sou.edu
STILLS, Karen ... 214-860-2033 472 F
kstills@dcccd.edu
STILWELL, Jackie ... 951-343-4239 .. 30 D
jstilwell@calbpatist.edu
STILWELL, Martha ... 269-965-3931 244 L
stilwellm@kellogg.edu
STIMAC, Robin ... 816-604-3071 277 J
robin.stimac@mcckc.edu
STIMELING, Kurt ... 603-897-8247 298 E
kstimeling@rivier.edu
STIMERS, Mitch ... 785-243-1435 186 A
mstimers@cloud.edu
STIMMEL, Glenn ... 323-442-1463 .. 74 D
stimmel@usc.edu
STIMPERT, Larry ... 765-658-4359 165 G
larrystimpert@depauw.edu
STIMPLE, Janet ... 216-687-3831 380 D
j.stimple@csuohio.edu
STINCHCOMB, Jan ... 410-225-2289 216 F
jstinchc@mica.edu
STINE, Cory ... 419-559-2355 392 A
cstine@terra.edu
STINE, Terry, E ... 208-376-7731 137 D
tstine@boisebible.edu
STINEMETZ, Charles, L 740-368-3101 390 B
clstinem@owu.edu
STINER, Margaret ... 440-826-8061 377 D
mstiner@bw.edu
STINES, Marsha ... 828-627-4529 363 C
mstines@haywood.edu
STINIS, Jane ... 407-831-9816 100 F
jstinis@citycollege.edu
STINIS, Jane ... 407-277-0311 102 N
jstinis@evergladesuniversity.edu
STINNER, Jerry ... 818-677-2004 .. 34 D
jerry.stinner@csun.edu
STINNETT, Gary, W ... 704-687-0644 371 B
gwstinne@uncc.edu
STINSON, Barbara, J ... 715-425-3141 540 E
barbara.stinson@uwrf.edu
STINSON, Becky ... 573-592-4237 286 A
becky.stinson@williamwoods.edu
STINSON, Charlie ... 256-761-6301 ... 7 H
cstinson@talladega.edu
STINSON, Claire ... 931-372-3311 462 A
cstinson@tntech.edu
STINSON, Greg ... 219-464-5212 174 E
greg.stinson@valpo.edu
STINSON, III, Harry, O . 502-597-6922 197 G
harry.stinson@kysu.edu
STINSON, Laura ... 760-630-1555 .. 49 C
lastinson@kaplan.edu
STINSON, Lori ... 208-792-2213 138 E
lstinson@lcsc.edu
STINSON, Matthew, P .. 724-946-7368 439 D
stinsomp@westminster.edu
STINSON, Niki ... 706-245-7226 124 C
nstinson@ec.edu
STINSON, Pam ... 580-628-6210 399 E
pam.stinson@noc.edu
STINSON, Randy ... 502-897-4897 199 D
rstinson@sbts.edu
STINSON, Willette ... 304-766-3239 533 C
wstinson@wvstateu.edu
STINTON, Martha ... 808-853-1040 135 F
marthastinton@pacrim.edu
STIPCAK, Sondra, L ... 570-321-4322 425 B
stipcak@lycoming.edu
STIPE, Richard ... 870-633-4480 .. 20 J
rstipe@eacc.edu
STIPEK, Deborah ... 650-725-9090 .. 68 G
STIPELMAN, Brian ... 631-244-1129 324 C
stipelmb@dowling.edu
STIRBER-GAMELIN,
Donna ... 717-545-4747 422 C
dstirber-gamelin@kti.edu
STIRDIVANT, Jeanette ... 818-240-1000 .. 45 I
jstirdivant@glendale.edu
STIREWALT, Jesse ... 218-879-0708 258 F
housing@fdltcc.edu
STIRLING, Diane, S ... 704-894-2462 356 D
distirling@davidson.edu
STIRLING, Wynn, C ... 801-422-4465 497 J
wynn_stirling@byu.edu
STIRTZ, Michele, D ... 402-552-2543 289 H
stirtz@clarksoncollege.edu
STISO, Joseph ... 978-632-6600 232 C
j_stiso@mwcc.mass.edu
STITELER, Chad ... 360-752-8313 520 A
cstiteler@btc.edu
STITES, Ann ... 815-967-7306 157 C
astites@rockfordcareercollege.edu
STITES, Dorothy, D ... 785-749-8456 187 F
dstites@haskell.edu
STITH, Kevin, U ... 740-368-3398 390 B
kustith@owu.edu
STITHEM, Diana ... 928-757-0801 .. 15 K
dstithem@mohave.edu
STITTS, Doria, K ... 336-750-2345 372 D
stittsd@wssu.edu
STIVEN, Janet, A ... 312-329-4123 153 C
janet.stiven@moody.edu
STIVERS, Laura ... 415-458-3734 .. 43 D
laura.stivers@dominican.edu
STIVERS,
Mary Elizabeth ... 515-263-2805 178 H
mestivers@grandview.edu
STOAKS, Lindsay ... 641-782-1338 183 D
stoaks@swcciowa.edu
STOB, Barbara ... 410-337-6011 215 B
bstob@goucher.edu
STOB, Michael ... 616-526-7114 240 L
stob@calvin.edu
STOBER, Dan ... 650-723-7162 .. 68 G
dan.stober@stanford.edu
STOBIE, Pete ... 816-654-7108 276 G
pstobie@kcumb.edu
STOBO, John, D ... 510-987-9071 .. 70 J
john.stobo@ucop.edu
STOCK, Jack, P ... 810-762-7873 245 A
jstock@kettering.edu
STOCK, Lawrence, E ... 724-287-8711 413 G
larry.stock@bc3.edu
STOCK, Lisa ... 612-330-1783 253 K
stock@augsburg.edu
STOCK, Lisa ... 641-648-4611 179 K
Lisa.Stock@iavalley.edu
STOCK, Renee ... 304-829-7572 529 H
rstock@bethanywv.edu
STOCK, Sue ... 773-442-4650 154 H
s-stock1@neiu.edu
STOCK, Susan ... 312-341-3548 157 E
sstock@roosevelt.edu
STOCK-KUPPERMAN,
Gretel, L ... 608-796-3272 542 H
glstock@viterbo.edu
STOCKARD, Holly ... 417-328-1806 282 D
hstockard@sbuniv.edu
STOCKE, Mike ... 253-964-6534 525 C
mstocke@pierce.ctc.edu
STOCKER, Jane Ellen ... 708-596-2000 159 D
jstocker@ssc.edu
STOCKER, Scott ... 650-723-2300 .. 68 G
STOCKERT, Brian ... 760-744-1150 .. 58 D
bstockert@palomar.edu
STOCKERT, Patricia, A .. 309-655-4124 158 D
patricia.a.stockert@osfhealthcare.org
STOCKING, Nancy ... 602-386-4138 .. 11 F
nancy.stocking@arizonachristian.edu
STOCKMAN, Deb ... 316-295-5377 187 C
deb_stockman@friends.edu
STOCKS, Chad ... 601-857-5261 267 D
clstocks@hindscc.edu
STOCKS, Janet ... 202-884-9380 .. 97 A
stocksj@trinitydc.edu
STOCKS, Morris ... 662-915-7111 270 G
chancllr@olemiss.edu
STOCKSLADER, Jon Jay 716-286-8189 336 E
js@niagara.edu
STOCKSTILL, Stephanie . 281-756-3531 467 D
sstockstill@alvincollege.edu
STOCKTON, Carl, A ... 281-283-3000 491 E
stockton@uhcl.edu

STOVALL, Alfred, J .... 662-252-8000 270 C
ajstovall@rustcollege.edu
STOVALL, Chris .... 940-397-4273 478 G
chris.stovall@mwsu.edu
STOVALL, George, A ..... 434-924-6431 514 A
gas5a@virginia.edu
STOVALL, Jerry .... 229-931-2562 131 E
jstovall@southgatech.edu
STOVALL, Michael .... 410-386-8206 214 B
mstovall@carrollcc.edu
STOVALL, Terri .... 817-923-1921 483 E
tstovall@swbts.edu
STOVALL, Tina .... 217-234-5250 150 B
tstovall@lakeland.cc.il.us
STOVALL, Trena .... 304-384-6292 532 E
tstovall@concord.edu
STOVALL, Vincent .... 703-284-1612 510 B
vstovall@marymount.edu
STOVER, Cheryln .... 425-602-3093 519 J
cstover@bastyr.edu
STOVER, Dennis, L .... 941-359-4200 116 D
STOVER, Janice .... 620-441-5247 186 E
janice.stover@cowley.edu
STOVER, Kathy, J .... 402-844-7268 292 G
kathy@northeast.edu
STOVER, Lois .... 703-284-1620 510 B
lois.stover@marymount.edu
STOVER, Mark .... 818-677-2271.. 34 D
mark.stover@csun.edu
STOVER, Mary .... 207-255-1223 212 G
mstover@maine.edu
STOVER, Paul, A .... 714-449-7461.. 53 D
pstover@ketchum.edu
STOVER, Ronalda, S ..... 803-778-6688 443 I
stoverrs@cctech.edu
STOVER, Stacey .... 734-462-4400 250 A
sstover@schoolcraft.edu
STOVER, Teri .... 903-223-3088 486 C
teri.stover@tamut.edu
STOVERINK, Al .... 870-972-2066.. 19 F
astoverink@astate.edu
STOW, George, B .... 215-951-1097 422 F
stow@lasalle.edu
STOWASSER, Melissa ... 843-574-6111 449 G
melissa.stowasser@tridenttech.edu
STOWE, Cindy .... 502-456-6504 200 B
cstowe@sullivan.edu
STOWE, Gwendolyn ...... 641-472-1110 181 A
admissions@mum.edu
STOWE, Lentz .... 252-940-6306 360 B
lentz.stowe@beaufortccc.edu
STOWE, Melissa .... 205-387-0511.... 2 B
mstowe@bscc.edu
STOWE, Ron, M .... 336-316-2907 357 C
stowerm@guilford.edu
STOWE, Susan .... 412-392-3931 433 F
sstowe@pointpark.edu
STOWELL, Dale .... 541-917-4214 406 J
stowelld@linnbenton.edu
STOWELL, Joseph, M ... 616-222-1428 241 G
joe.stowell@cornerstone.edu
STOWELL, Mike .... 616-538-2330 243 C
mstowell@gbcol.edu
STOWERS, Marian .... 269-337-7192 244 I
Marian.Stowers@kzoo.edu
STOWERS, Rebecca ...... 937-766-7872 378 K
stowersr@cedarville.edu
STOWIK, Stanley .... 401-232-6240 441 B
STOWMAN, Heidi .... 503-581-8600 405 F
hstowman@corban.edu
STRACHER, Janet .... 478-289-2109 124 B
jstrach@ega.edu
STRADA, Samuel .... 251-460-7189.... 9 F
sstrada@southalabama.edu
STRADA, Samuel, J .... 251-460-7189.... 9 F
sstrada@southalabama.edu
STRADER, Bob .... 325-674-2784 466 I
straderb@acu.edu
STRADER, Cynthia .... 979-230-3119 469 G
STRADER, Scott, C .... 727-864-8421 101 P
stradesc@eckerd.edu
STRAHL, Sonja .... 847-947-5032 153 H
Sonja.Strahl@nl.edu
STRAHN-KOLLER,
Brooke .... 319-398-4911 180 J
bstrahn@kirkwood.edu
STRAIT, LuAnn .... 605-882-5284 452 G
straitl@lakeareatech.edu
STRAIT, Micah .... 435-283-7145 500 D
micah.strait@snow.edu
STRAIT, Tia .... 417-625-9328 278 I
strait-t@mssu.edu
STRAITS, Jeffrey .... 202-885-8684.. 97 E
jstraits@wesleyseminary.edu
STRAKA, Richard .... 507-389-6621 260 A
richard.straka@mnsu.edu
STRAKA, Ronald .... 952-446-4127 255 E
strakar@crown.edu
STRAMPEL, William, D . 517-355-9616 246 H
strampe3@msu.edu
STRANDBERG, Kevin .... 309-556-3139 148 A
strandbe@iwu.edu
STRANEY, Donald, O .... 808-932-7348 135 I
dstraney@hawaii.edu
STRANG, Bryce, B .... 503-943-8009 410 H
strang@up.edu
STRANG, Steven .... 314-246-8025 285 G
stevenstrang87@webster.edu
STRANGE, Alan .... 219-864-2400 171 G
astrange@midamerica.edu
STRANGE, Kendra .... 864-587-4298 449 D
strangek@smcsc.edu
STRANGE, Richard .... 785-227-3311 185 A
STRANGE, Thomas .... 423-585-2668 464 C
thomas.strange@ws.edu
STRANIAK, Kimberly ..... 330-369-3200 392 E
kastraniak32@trumbull.edu
STRANO, Diana .... 603-897-8211 298 E
dstrano@rivier.edu
STRANO, Kimberly .... 845-257-3215 344 A
lavoiek@newpaltz.edu
STRASENBURGH,
David, R .... 585-395-2385 345 A
dstrasen@brockport.edu
STRASNER, Sam .... 479-498-6045.. 20 C
sstrasner@atu.edu
STRASSER, Nora .... 316-295-5818 187 C
strasser@friends.edu
STRATFORD-YOUNCE,
Carolyn .... 410-225-2263 216 F
cstratford@mica.edu
STRATMAN, Allan, M .... 217-333-2500 162 A
stratmn@illinois.edu
STRATMAN, Debbie .... 931-553-0071 459 G
debbie.stratman@miller-motte.com
STRATMAN, Jason .... 308-635-6740 294 C
stratman@wncc.edu
STRATMAN, Jason, L .... 308-635-6740 294 C
stratman@wncc.edu
STRATMAN, Victoria, D 626-395-5940.. 31 D
victoria.stratman@caltech.edu
STRATMANN,
Charles, M .... 904-632-3299 105 A
cstratma@fscj.edu
STRATTON, Chris .... 706-886-6831 132 F
cstratton@tfc.edu
STRATTON, Jonathan .... 772-546-5534 106 D
jonstratton@hsbc.edu
STRATTON, Michael ...... 518-454-5456 322 C
strattom@mail.strose.edu
STRAUB, Bernie .... 843-574-6994 449 G
bernie.straub@tridenttech.edu
STRAUB, Dahnja .... 707-546-4000.. 43 J
dstraub@empirecollege.com
STRAUB, Jeff, P .... 763-417-8250 254 E
STRAUB, Peter .... 609-652-4548 308 E
peter.straub@stockton.edu
STRAUB, Steve .... 920-735-5717 542 N
straub@fvtc.edu
STRAUCH, Allyson .... 217-544-6464 158 E
allyson.strauch@stjohnscollegespringfield.edu
STRAUCH, Pierre .... 203-287-3018.. 91 C
paier.admin@snet.net
STRAUCHLER, Orin .... 845-569-3547 333 I
orin.strauchler@msmc.edu
STRAUGHAN,
Robert, D .... 540-458-8609 519 A
straughanr@wlu.edu
STRAUGHN, Greg .... 325-674-2850 466 I
gbs00a@acu.edu
STRAUS, Laura .... 406-683-7537 287 E
laura.straus@umwestern.edu
STRAUSBAUGH, Greg ... 541-684-7357 407 I
gstrausbaugh@nwcu.edu
STRAUSBAUGH, Lisa .... 440-375-7379 385 B
lstrausbaugh@lec.edu
STRAUSBAUGH,
William, G .... 717-796-5375 426 B
strausba@messiah.edu
STRAUSE, Sandra .... 610-607-6210 433 H
sstrause@racc.edu
STRAUSS, Andrew, L .... 937-229-3795 393 E
astrauss1@udayton.edu
STRAUSS, Daniel .... 727-394-6217 154 E
dstrauss@nuhs.edu
STRAUSS, David, J .... 313-577-1010 252 G
davidstrauss@wayne.edu
STRAUSS, Douglas .... 608-785-9235 544 E
straussd@westerntc.edu
STRAUSS, Jason .... 510-841-9230.. 77 I
jstrauss@wi.edu
STRAUSS, Jerome .... 804-828-9788 514 F
sfstrauss@vcu.edu
STRAUSS, Jerome, F .... 804-828-9788 514 F
jfstrauss@vcu.edu
STRAUSS, Jon, C .... 914-323-5230 331 J
jon.strauss@mville.edu
STRAUSS, Kate .... 714-772-3330.. 27 M
admissions@anaheim.edu
STRAUSS, Ronald .... 919-962-4510 371 A
ron_strauss@unc.edu
STRAUSS-SOUKUP,
Juliane, K .... 402-280-3265 290 B
jksoukup@creighton.edu
STRAUTZ-SPRINGBORN,
Shelly .... 989-328-1243 247 D
shellys@montcalm.edu
STRAVERS, Meredith ..... 269-965-3931 244 L
straversm@kellogg.edu
STRAWDERMAN,
Andrea, A .... 252-334-2073 359 D
andrea.strawderman@macuniversity.edu
STRAWN, Roxanna .... 920-686-6150 539 A
Roxanna.Strawn@sl.edu
STRAWN, Scott .... 405-491-6306 402 E
sstrawn@snu.edu
STRAWSER, Jerry .... 979-845-4711 485 C
jstrawser@tamu.edu
STRAWSER, Joyce, A .... 973-761-9225 308 C
joyce.strawser@shu.edu
STRAYER, Colleen .... 419-530-2516 394 E
colleen.strayer@utoledo.edu
STRAYER, James, E .... 308-398-7355 289 D
jstrayer@cccneb.edu
STRAZDAS, Peter, J ...... 269-387-8584 252 I
peter.strazdas@wmich.edu
STREATER, Justin .... 405-382-9717 402 C
j.streater@sscok.edu
STREBE, Chet, A .... 715-675-3331 544 A
strebe@ntc.edu
STRECKER, Cheryl, G .... 785-532-5730 188 H
cstreck@ksu.edu
STRECKER, Deborah ...... 610-896-1129 420 J
dstrecke@haverford.edu
STRECKER, William .... 636-922-8607 281 C
wstrecker@stchas.edu
STREET, Aaron, J .... 870-235-5011.. 23 D
ajstreet@saumag.edu
STREET, Helen .... 662-252-8000 270 C
hstreet@rustcollege.edu
STREET, Kathleen, A ..... 909-869-2572.. 32 F
kastreet@cpp.edu
STREET, Kenneth .... 936-639-1301 467 I
kstreet@angelina.edu
STREET, Scott .... 409-984-6292 488 H
scott.street@lamarpa.edu
STREET, Scott, V .... 617-266-1400 223 F
STREET, Sheila .... 336-506-4186 359 N
sheila.street@alamancecc.edu
STREET, Zach .... 808-932-7446 135 I
zstreet@hawaii.edu
STREETER, Holly .... 319-425-5340 183 G
streeterh@uiu.edu
STREETER, Montrose .... 315-781-3900 327 G
streeter@hws.edu
STREETER, Paul .... 607-255-0155 323 C
ps33@cornell.edu
STREETMAN, Craig .... 423-652-4158 457 J
wcstreetman@king.edu
STREFF, Frederick, M ... 540-674-3637 516 B
fstreff@nr.edu
STREGE, Ron .... 715-346-3574 541 A
rstrege@uwsp.edu
STREHLE, Susan .... 607-777-2070 343 D
sstrehle@binghamton.edu
STREHLOW, Betty, J ..... 320-222-5203 261 B
betty.strehlow@ridgewater.edu
STREIB, Kimberly .... 217-479-7007 151 J
kimberly.streib@mac.edu
STREICH, Jodi .... 201-216-8724 308 D
jstreich@stevens.edu
STREIFFER, Rick .... 205-348-1288.... 8 E
rhstreiffer@cchs.ua.edu
STREIM, Nancy .... 212-678-7407 349 I
streim@tc.edu
STREIT, Carol, S .... 617-573-8000 237 B
cstreit@suffolk.edu
STREIT, Linda, A .... 678-547-6799 128 G
streit_la@mercer.edu
STREIT, Tina .... 320-363-5165 254 J
tstreit@csbsju.edu
STREMPEL, Eileen, L .... 513-556-2588 393 B
eileen.strempel@uc.edu
STRESE, Jeff .... 214-768-3589 482 J
jstrese@smu.edu
STRETCHER, Gary, D .... 409-984-6209 488 H
gary.stretcher@lamarpa.edu
STRETCHER, Nancy .... 409-984-6390 488 H
cammackn1@lamarpa.edu
STREUBERT, Helen .... 973-290-4474 301 F
hjstreubert@cse.edu
STREUFERT, Billie .... 605-274-4123 452 A
billie.streufert@augie.edu
STREY, Charles .... 641-628-5621 176 E
streyc@central.edu
STREY, Mary, M .... 641-628-5188 176 E
streym@central.edu
STRICHERZ, Shanda, L . 605-336-6588 453 C
shandas@sfseminary.edu
STRICKER, Edward, M .. 412-624-6880 437 K
edstrick@pitt.edu
STRICKER, Terri .... 816-322-0110 272 L
terri.stricker@calvary.edu
STRICKLAND, Brian ...... 251-580-2214.... 5 A
brian.strickland@faulknerstate.edu
STRICKLAND, Brooke .... 334-556-2418.... 4 A
bstrickland@wallace.edu
STRICKLAND, Carol ...... 620-341-5660 186 H
cstrickl@emporia.edu
STRICKLAND,
Carolyn, R .... 570-326-3761 429 J
cstrickl@pct.edu
STRICKLAND, Charles ... 252-862-1351 365 C
cwstrickland7072@roanokechowan.edu
STRICKLAND, Claire, I .. 207-581-1593 212 C
cpratt@maine.edu
STRICKLAND, Daniel ..... 205-665-6000.... 9 C
dstrickland@montevallo.edu
STRICKLAND,
Earnestine, J .... 512-505-3082 475 G
eestrickland@htu.edu
STRICKLAND, JR.,
Elliott .... 570-326-3761 429 J
estrickl@pct.edu
STRICKLAND, Fatisha ... 215-567-7080 412 G
fstrickland@aii.edu
STRICKLAND, Gary .... 912-279-5835 123 B
gstrickland@ccga.edu
STRICKLAND, Gary, E ... 605-336-6588 453 C
gstrickland@sfseminary.edu
STRICKLAND,
Haywood, L .... 903-927-3200 497 G
hstrickland@wileyc.edu
STRICKLAND, Henry, C 205-726-2704.... 6 F
hcstrick@samford.edu
STRICKLAND, Jason ..... 910-642-7141 366 B
Jason.Strickland@sccnc.edu
STRICKLAND, Jay .... 870-612-2020.. 24 G
jay.strickland@uaccb.edu
STRICKLAND, Jeff .... 706-355-5039 120 G
jstrickland@athenstech.edu
STRICKLAND, Joy .... 303-963-3012.. 79 L
jstrickland@ccu.edu
STRICKLAND, Ken .... 617-879-7365 230 B
kstrickland@massart.edu
STRICKLAND, Kristine ... 504-762-3188 203 F
kstric@dcc.edu
STRICKLAND, Les .... 480-423-6510.. 15 E
les.strickland@scottsdalecc.edu
STRICKLAND, Mark .... 727-394-6110 112 A
STRICKLAND,
Michael, D .... 615-460-6420 455 D
mike.strickland@belmont.edu
STRICKLAND, Michele .. 478-553-2097 129 C
mstrickland@oftc.edu
STRICKLAND, Ora .... 304-348-0231 114 G
ora.strickland@fiu.edu.edu
STRICKLAND, Randy ..... 502-585-9911 199 E
rstrickland@spalding.edu
STRICKLAND, Sherry .... 254-559-7707 488 C
sherry.strickland@tstc.edu
STRICKLAND, Sidney .... 215-327-8084 339 H
strickland@rockefeller.edu
STRICKLAND, Timothy .. 252-493-7330 364 H
tstrickland@email.pittcc.edu
STRICKLAND, Tonya ..... 864-644-5002 449 B
tstrickland@swu.edu
STRICKLAND, Valerie .... 770-962-7580 127 C
vstrickland@gwinnetttech.edu
STRICKLAND, Walter .... 919-761-2100 368 K
wstrickland@sebts.edu
STRICKLAND,
Wayne, G .... 503-255-0332 407 D
udub@multnomah.edu
STRICKLER, Andrew ...... 860-439-2200.. 90 D
andrew.strickler@conncoll.edu
STRICKLIN, Jan .... 503-352-2890 408 I
jstricklin@pacificu.edu
STRICKLIN, Linda .... 208-792-2388 138 E
lsstricklin@lcsc.edu
STRICKLIN, Scott .... 662-325-8082 269 A
sas24@msstate.edu
STRIDIRON, Dahlia .... 340-693-1136 559 B
dstridi@uvi.edu
STRIEF, Kristi, L .... 563-556-5110 181 F
striefk@nicc.edu
STRIGENS, Lora .... 414-288-1693 537 B
lora.strigens@marquette.edu
STRIGLE, Ashley .... 614-236-6714 378 H
astrigle@capital.edu
STRIKWERDA, Carl, J ... 717-361-1193 418 B
strikwerdac@etown.edu
STRIMKOVSKY, Lauri ..... 215-248-7168 415 D
strimkovsky@chc.edu
STRIMPLE, Karen .... 620-252-7555 186 C
karens@coffeyville.edu
STRINGER, Bobbi .... 817-552-3700 477 B
bobbi.stringer@tku.edu

STUMPF, Fran .... 573-897-5000 282 I
STUMPF, Jessica .... 651-450-3692 259 A
jstumpf@inverhills.edu
STUMPF, Michelle .... 814-262-6436 429 K
mstumpf@pennhighlands.edu
STUPAR, Eric, H .... 202-231-2767 547 N
eric.stupar@dodiis.mil
STURCH, Patty, J .... 740-264-5591 381 J
psturch@egcc.edu
STURDEVANT, Nancee .. 605-367-7464 454 D
nancee.sturdevant@southeasttech.edu
STURDEVANT, Peggy .... 641-784-5125 178 G
peggys@graceland.edu
STURDEVANT, Ruthie .... 573-681-5178 276 K
sturdevr@lincolnu.edu
STURDIVANT, Alvin ...... 206-296-6066 526 F
sturdial@seattleu.edu
STURDIVANT, Brian, C . 410-706-1678 219 E
bsturdivant@umaryland.edu
STURDY, Ryan .... 785-460-5548 186 D
ryan.sturdy@colbycc.edu
STURE, Linda .... 907-563-7575.. 10 C
STURE, Stein .... 303-492-5537.. 86 E
stein.sture@colorado.edu
STURGEON, Kathy, R .... 217-443-8805 143 F
ksturgeon@dacc.edu
STURGEON, Kimberley . 843-574-6195 449 G
kim.sturgeon@tridenttech.edu
STURGEON, Paul .... 270-706-8639 195 K
paul.sturgeon@kctcs.edu
STURGEON, Stacy .... 435-797-1266 500 A
stacy.sturgeon@usu.edu
STURGEON, Timothy, A 502-272-8131 193 E
tsturgeon@bellarmine.edu
STURGIS, Maureen .... 603-899-4165 297 H
sturgism@franklinpierce.edu
STURGIS, Paul .... 573-592-4463 286 A
paul.sturgis@williamwoods.edu
STURGIS, Thomas, C ... 601-877-6138 266 C
tsturgis@alcorn.edu
STURM, David .... 212-875-4645 315 F
dsturm@bankstreet.edu
STURM, James, P .... 716-926-8935 327 F
jsturm@hilbert.edu
STURM, Joel .... 212-410-8047 335 B
jsturm@nycpm.edu
STURM, Joey .... 337-482-6449 208 F
joey.sturm@louisiana.edu
STURM, Neal, M .... 973-443-8689 302 H
sturm@fdu.edu
STURM-SMITH, Melissa 515-271-2835 177 K
melissa.sturm-smith@drake.edu
STURRUP, Daniel, H ..... 207-581-1110 212 C
dsturrup@maine.edu
STURRUS, Teresa .... 231-777-0251 247 G
teresa.sturrus@muskegoncc.edu
STURRUS, W. Gregg ..... 330-941-3009 396 C
wgsturrus@ysu.edu
STURTEVANT, Valerie .... 617-730-7213 235 B
valerie.sturtevant@newbury.edu
STURTZ, Alan, J .... 860-913-2034.. 90 F
asturtz@goodwin.edu
STURTZ, Carma .... 641-628-5269 176 E
sturtzc@central.edu
STURZENBECKER,
Diane .... 716-488-3021 329 D
financialaid@jamestownbusinesscollege.edu
STUTES, Ann, B .... 806-291-1066 496 K
stutesa@wbu.edu
STUTES, Chris .... 337-521-8953 204 E
chris.stutes@solacc.edu
STUTEVILLE, Rebekkah .. 816-584-6597 280 F
rebekkah.stuteville@park.edu
STUTTS, Rosie .... 805-289-6313.. 75 E
rstutts@vcccd.edu
STUTZMAN, Dallas .... 620-327-8110 187 H
dallass@hesston.edu
STUTZMAN, Timothy .... 540-432-4197 507 A
timothy.stutzman@emu.edu
STYER, Daniel .... 916-558-2201.. 53 B
StyerD@scc.losrios.edu
STYLES, Elise .... 864-977-7018 448 A
elise.styles@ngu.edu
STYLES, Julie .... 864-977-1246 448 A
julie.styles@ngu.edu
STYRON, Kelli .... 254-968-9141 485 A
styron@tarleton.edu
STYRON, Ken .... 251-981-3771.... 3 A
ken.styron@columbiasouthern.edu
SU, Nancy .... 212-217-3640 325 C
nancy_su@fitnyc.edu
SU, Ren Jeng .... 503-725-8393 409 D
renjengs@pdx.edu
SU, Susan .... 516-739-1545 335 C
records@nyctcm.edu
SUAREZ, Angelica .... 619-482-6315.. 68 D
asuarez@swccd.edu
SUAREZ, Carmen, A ..... 208-885-4285 139 C
csuarez@uidaho.edu
SUAREZ, Doris, L .... 646-664-9109 318 B
doris.suarez@cuny.edu
SUAREZ, Enrique .... 787-850-9107 558 A
enrique.suarez@upr.edu
SUAREZ, Jeri, L .... 540-362-6000 508 D
jsuarez@hollins.edu
SUAREZ, Michelle .... 618-453-5855 159 H
msuarez@siu.edu
SUAREZ-ESPINAL,
Cynthia .... 718-289-5914 318 E
cynthia.suarez-espinal@bcc.cuny.edu
SUAREZ-HERRERO,
Ismael .... 787-863-2390 553 I
ismael.suarez@fajardo.inter.edu
SUAREZ-OROZCO,
Marcelo, M .... 310-825-8308.. 71 D
mms-o@gseis.ucla.edu
SUBBASWAMY,
Kumble, R .... 413-545-2211 228 F
chancellor@umass.edu
SUBBIONDO,
Joseph, L .... 415-575-6105.. 31 C
jsubbiondo@ciis.edu
SUBE, Bob .... 805-986-5821.. 75 D
bsube@vcccd.edu
SUBER, Jennifer .... 601-477-4040 268 A
jennifer.suber@jcjc.edu
SUBER, Megan .... 704-878-4395 364 C
msuber@mitchellcc.edu
SUBER, Tonia .... 941-487-4417 115 B
tsuber@ncf.edu
SUBLETT, Roger, H .... 513-861-6400 392 F
roger.sublett@myunion.edu
SUBLETTE, Gaylah .... 660-626-2860 271 G
gsublette@atsu.edu
SUBOTNICK, Stuart .... 718-625-2200 317 A
SUBRAMANI, Suresh .... 858-534-2230.. 72 B
evc@ucsd.edu
SUBRAMANIAN, Ashok . 712-749-2422 176 D
subramaniana@bvu.edu
SUBRAMANIAN,
Sandhya .... 440-775-8401 388 B
sandhya.subramanian@oberlin.edu
SUCHAN, Richard .... 716-847-8371 317 M
rsuchan@buffalodiocese.org
SUCHANIC, Angela, C .. 302-356-6924.. 94 G
angela.c.suchanic@wilmu.edu
SUCHON, Donnetta .... 281-425-6400 477 F
dsuchon@lee.edu
SUDAK, Sarah .... 615-898-5342 461 E
sarah.sudak@mtsu.edu
SUDDICK, Lori .... 920-498-5401 544 B
lori.suddick@nwtc.edu
SUDDITH, Judith, J ...... 540-843-0722 515 H
jsuddith@lfcc.edu
SUDEIKIS, Barbara .... 269-965-3931 244 L
sudeikisb@kellogg.edu
SUDERMAN, Bonnie ..... 661-722-6300.. 27 P
bsuderman@avc.edu
SUDHAKAR, Rama .... 212-237-8628 319 F
rsudhakar@jjay.cuny.edu
SUDHAKAR, Samuel ..... 909-537-5100.. 35 A
ssudhakar@csusb.edu
SUDKAMP, Thomas, A . 937-775-2097 396 A
thomas.sudkamp@wright.edu
SUDLER, Kimberly, R ... 302-857-7036.. 93 E
krsudler@desu.edu
SUDLOW, Jennifer .... 215-572-4483 412 F
sudlowj@arcadia.edu
SUDOL, Mary .... 845-434-5750 349 C
msudol@sullivan.suny.edu
SUDTELGTE, Beau .... 712-279-1633 176 B
beau.sudtelgte@briarcliff.edu
SUELFLOW, Sara, C ...... 651-696-6307 256 L
suelflow@macalester.edu
SUERTH, Matthew, P .... 815-224-0540 147 J
matt_suerth@ivcc.edu
SUESS, Jack, J .... 410-455-2582 219 F
jack@umbc.edu
SUESSER, John, P .... 724-346-2073 413 G
john.suesser@bc3.edu
SUFFEL, Charles .... 201-216-8031 308 D
csuffel@stevens.edu
SUGARMAN, Roger, P .. 859-257-7989 200 G
rpsuga0@email.uky.edu
SUGARMAN, Tammy, S 404-413-2700 126 D
tsugarman@gsu.edu
SUGG, Donald .... 870-743-3000.. 22 A
dsugg@northark.edu
SUGGS, Amber .... 618-634-3236 159 A
ambers@shawneecc.edu
SUGGS, Benny .... 919-515-3375 370 D
benny_suggs@ncsu.edu
SUGGS, Philana .... 205-929-6383.... 5 E
psuggs@lawsonstate.edu
SUGGS, Sheena .... 252-862-1316 365 C
srsuggs@roanokechowan.edu
SUGIHARA, Fumio .... 814-641-3113 421 L
sugihaf@juniata.edu
SUGIMOTO, Lara .... 808-845-9235 136 E
larahs@hawaii.edu
SUGRUE, Seana .... 239-280-2505.. 98 O
seana.sugrue@avemaria.edu
SUH, Duckin .... 262-554-2010 537 D
duckin_suh@yahoo.com
SUHAJDA, Kathleen ...... 312-935-6446 157 A
ksuhajda@robertmorris.edu
SUHAYDA, Rosemarie .. 312-942-6204 158 A
rosemarie_suhayda@rush.edu
SUHLER, Mitzi .... 620-278-4226 191 D
msuhler@sterling.edu
SUHR, Marin .... 402-461-7326 290 G
mnsuhr@hastings.edu
SUIB, Steven, L .... 860-486-4623.. 92 C
steven.suib@uconn.edu
SUIT, Teresa .... 256-233-8167.... 1 F
teresa.suit@athens.edu
SUITE, Denzil .... 206-543-4972 527 G
djsuite@uw.edu
SUJECKI, Gailmarie ...... 516-671-2277 352 D
gsujecki@webb.edu
SUK, Jeannine, D .... 716-880-2339 332 B
jeannine.e.suk@medaille.edu
SUKHATME, Uday .... 212-346-1956 337 I
provost@pace.edu
SUKKIL YOON, Mark .... 323-643-0301.. 27 G
SUKUMOTO, Erin .... 808-983-4115 135 D
esukumoto@tokai.edu
SULAIMAN-HARA,
Sadika .... 773-508-3335 151 E
ssulaimanhara@luc.edu
SULAIMAN HARA,
Sadika .... 415-485-9375.. 41 B
ssulaimanhara@marin.edu
SULESKI, Andrew .... 530-895-2353.. 30 B
suleskian@butte.edu
SULFRIDGE, Jay .... 606-337-1114 194 F
jsulfridge@ccbbc.edu
SULLEMUN, Racquel ..... 210-690-9000 474 L
rsullemun@hallmarkuniversity.edu
SULLENBERGER,
A. Gale .... 918-631-3184 403 M
gale-sullenberger@utulsa.edu
SULLINS, Dori .... 815-455-8559 152 B
dsullens@mchenry.edu
SULLINS, Richard, W .... 919-335-1200 366 H
rwsullins@waketech.edu
SULLINS, W. Robert ..... 813-974-4051 116 B
rsullins@usf.edu
SULLIVAN, A, R .... 502-451-0815 200 A
ars@sullivan.edu
SULLIVAN, A, R .... 502-451-0815 200 B
ars@sullivan.edu
SULLIVAN, Adelfa .... 702-992-2110 295 E
adelfa.sullivan@nsc.edu
SULLIVAN, Allison .... 864-231-2181 443 E
asullivan@andersonuniversity.edu
SULLIVAN, Anne, R ...... 212-854-4038 322 F
asullivan@columbia.edu
SULLIVAN, Annette, S .. 978-665-2717 229 D
asulli15@fitchburgstate.edu
SULLIVAN, Brendan ...... 508-565-1667 237 A
bjsullivan@stonehill.edu
SULLIVAN, Brian .... 513-558-1559 393 D
brian.sullivan@uc.edu
SULLIVAN, Brigitte .... 410-225-2209 216 F
bsullivan01@mica.edu
SULLIVAN, Bryce .... 615-460-6437 455 D
bryce.sullivan@belmont.edu
SULLIVAN, Cheryl .... 559-489-2232.. 69 B
cheryl.sullivan@fresnocitycollege.edu
SULLIVAN, Cheryl .... 231-995-1147 248 C
csullivan@nmc.edu
SULLIVAN,
Christopher, B .... 585-385-8001 340 F
csullivan@sjfc.edu
SULLIVAN, Crystal, C ... 937-229-3369 393 E
csulllivan1@udayton.edu
SULLIVAN, Dan .... 919-658-7748 369 B
dsullivan@umo.edu
SULLIVAN, Deb .... 563-336-3300 178 A
djsullivan@eicc.edu
SULLIVAN, Durelle .... 360-736-9391 520 F
dsullivan@centralia.edu
SULLIVAN, E. Thomas .. 802-656-7878 503 C
thomas.sullivan@uvm.edu
SULLIVAN, Eileen .... 508-457-1313 234 E
SULLIVAN, Eileen, G ..... 630-617-3050 144 G
esullivan@elmhurst.edu
SULLIVAN, Elizabeth .... 201-761-7106 307 K
esullivan2@saintpeters.edu
SULLIVAN, Erin .... 504-398-2190 206 E
esullivan@olhcc.edu
SULLIVAN, George, J ... 610-359-4151 416 G
gsulliva@dccc.edu
SULLIVAN, Gerald .... 706-867-2543 133 A
gerald.sullivan@ung.edu
SULLIVAN, Glenn, D ..... 502-451-0815 200 A
gds@sullivan.edu
SULLIVAN, Glenn, D ..... 502-451-0815 200 B
gds@sullivan.edu
SULLIVAN, Irby (Skip) .. 607-587-4010 347 D
sullivid@alfredstate.edu
SULLIVAN, Jack .... 973-328-5252 301 G
jsullivan@ccm.edu
SULLIVAN, James .... 423-775-7306 455 F
james@bryan.edu
SULLIVAN, James .... 570-340-6063 425 D
SULLIVAN, Jason .... 906-487-7272 242 M
jason.sullivan@finlandia.edu
SULLIVAN, Jay .... 252-940-6203 360 B
jay.sullivan@beaufortccc.edu
SULLIVAN, Jeff .... 715-874-4608 542 M
jsullivan25@cvtc.edu
SULLIVAN, Jem .... 202-495-3820.. 96 E
jrsullivan@dhs.edu
SULLIVAN, Joan, D ...... 781-768-7212 236 A
joan.sullivan@regiscollege.edu
SULLIVAN, John .... 727-864-8331 101 P
sullivjf@eckerd.edu
SULLIVAN, John, M ..... 508-286-3484 238 B
sullivan_john@wheatoncollege.edu
SULLIVAN, John, M ..... 513-562-8743 376 O
president@artacademy.edu
SULLIVAN, Joseph .... 805-965-0581.. 64 N
sullivanj@sbcc.edu
SULLIVAN, Joseph .... 508-910-6884 228 H
jsullivan15@umassd.edu
SULLIVAN, Julie, H .... 651-962-6500 265 F
jhsullivan@stthomas.edu
SULLIVAN, Kathleen ..... 845-848-7804 324 B
kathleen.sullivan@dc.edu
SULLIVAN, Kathleen ..... 207-893-7705 211 H
ksullivan@sjcme.edu
SULLIVAN, Keith .... 252-940-6302 360 B
keith.sullivan@beaufortccc.edu
SULLIVAN, Kenneth, A . 775-445-4246 296 A
ken.sullivan@wnc.edu
SULLIVAN, Kip .... 432-837-8134 489 B
sullivan@sulross.edu
SULLIVAN, Kristen .... 978-837-5301 233 G
sullivanke@merrimack.edu
SULLIVAN, Kristie .... 910-695-3907 365 H
sullivank@sandhills.edu
SULLIVAN, Kristin .... 817-272-2761 493 L
knsull@uta.edu
SULLIVAN, Laura .... 715-682-4591 544 F
laura.sullivan@witc.edu
SULLIVAN, Lawrence .... 212-237-8364 319 F
lsullivan@jjay.cuny.edu
SULLIVAN, Leah .... 440-646-8126 394 G
lsullivan@ursuline.edu
SULLIVAN, Leslie .... 269-749-7638 249 A
lsullivan@olivetcollege.edu
SULLIVAN, Liam .... 207-699-5037 210 I
lsullivan@meca.edu
SULLIVAN, Linda .... 310-434-3427.. 65 B
sullivan_linda@smc.edu
SULLIVAN, Lisa .... 334-475-5556 208 B
lsullivan@mcneese.edu
SULLIVAN, Maggie .... 401-456-8216 442 A
msullivan@ric.edu
SULLIVAN, Marcia .... 314-529-9340 277 B
marcia.sullivan@maryville.edu
SULLIVAN, Maria .... 508-565-1402 237 A
msullivan7@stonehill.edu
SULLIVAN, Marie .... 603-897-8246 298 E
mariesullivan@rivier.edu
SULLIVAN, Mark .... 614-825-6255 376 C
msullivan@aiam.edu
SULLIVAN, Martha .... 508-793-2276 225 C
sullivan@holycross.edu
SULLIVAN, Mary .... 401-874-5339 442 E
mcsullivan@uri.edu
SULLIVAN, Mary .... 570-740-0429 425 A
msullivan@luzerne.edu
SULLIVAN, Matthew ...... 502-231-5221 198 D
msullivan@myLBC.us
SULLIVAN, Melanie, P .. 502-272-8477 193 E
msullivan@bellarmine.edu
SULLIVAN, Melanie, R .. 401-865-2723 441 F
oir@providence.edu
SULLIVAN, Melissa .... 207-699-5043 210 I
msullivan@meca.edu
SULLIVAN, Michael .... 607-436-2825 344 B
michael.sullivan@oneonta.edu
SULLIVAN, Michael, D . 413-748-5555 236 H
msullivan@springfieldcollegel.edu
SULLIVAN, Monty .... 225-922-1643 202 M
msullivan@lctcs.edu
SULLIVAN, Nancy .... 781-292-2304 226 G
nancy.sullivan@olin.edu
SULLIVAN, Nancy .... 508-588-9100 232 A
SULLIVAN, Nancy .... 217-479-7033 151 J
nancy.sullivan@mac.edu
SULLIVAN, Patrick .... 610-499-4202 439 G
ptsullivan@widener.edu
SULLIVAN, Regina .... 865-471-4774 455 G
rsullivan@cn.edu

SULLIVAN, Renee 203-773-4474 87 M
rsullivan@albertus.edu
SULLIVAN, JR., Richard, F 617-333-2302 225 F
rsulliva@curry.edu
SULLIVAN, Rita 415-749-4576 62 I
rsullivan@sfai.edu
SULLIVAN, Rob 214-333-5671 471 L
roberts@dbu.edu
SULLIVAN, Robert, S 858-822-0830 72 B
rssullivan@ucsd.edu
SULLIVAN, Ruth, D 401-825-2488 441 C
ruthsullivan@ccri.edu
SULLIVAN, Samuel 706-821-8230 129 H
ssullivan@paine.edu
SULLIVAN, Sean 708-456-0300 161 C
ssulliva@triton.edu
SULLIVAN, Sean, M 202-319-5286 95 A
sullivansm@cua.edu
SULLIVAN, Serena 252-940-6326 360 B
serena.sullivan@beaufortccc.edu
SULLIVAN, Shawn, P 715-675-3331 544 A
sullivan@ntc.edu
SULLIVAN, Slade 325-674-2485 466 I
sullivans@acu.edu
SULLIVAN, Stephanie 770-426-2632 128 C
stephanie.sullivan@life.edu
SULLIVAN, Stephen 781-239-3152 231 G
ssullivan@massbay.edu
SULLIVAN, Stephen 325-649-8069 475 F
ssullivan@hputx.edu
SULLIVAN, Susan 812-749-1223 171 I
ssullivan@oak.edu
SULLIVAN, Suzanne 601-968-8746 266 F
ssullivan@belhaven.edu
SULLIVAN, Tara, B 318-797-5000 205 F
SULLIVAN, Teresa, A 434-924-3337 514 A
tas6n@virginia.edu
SULLIVAN, Terry 419-448-3019 392 B
tsullivan@tiffin.edu
SULLIVAN, Thomas 617-243-2059 227 K
tpsullivan@lasell.edu
SULLIVAN, Thomas 660-944-2860 273 E
thomas@conception.edu
SULLIVAN, Thomas, B 512-448-8727 481 B
toms@stedwards.edu
SULLIVAN, Timothy, J 508-929-8073 230 G
tsullivan@worcester.edu
SULLIVAN, Todd 928-523-3731 16 C
Todd.Sullivan@nau.edu
SULLIVAN, Tracy 708-235-2179 145 D
tsullivan@govst.edu
SULLIVAN, Wayne 315-792-3201 351 G
wasullivan@utica.edu
SULLIVAN, Wayne 662-862-8101 267 F
jwsullivan@iccms.edu
SULLIVAN, Wayne 505-277-2383 313 H
sullivan@unm.edu
SULLIVAN, William, E 765-494-9705 171 K
evpt@purdue.edu
SULLIVAN-CROWLEY, Lianne, C 609-258-2430 305 C
lsulliva@princeton.edu
SULLIVAN-TRAINOR, Deborah 651-638-6804 254 A
suldeb@bethel.edu
SULLIVANT, Stan 870-338-6474 24 F
SULLIVENT, Ernest, E 860-444-8352 548 H
ernest.e.sullivent@uscg.mil
SULLO, Fred 914-654-5555 322 B
fsullo@cnr.edu
SULLY, John, M 216-397-1965 384 F
jsully@jcu.edu
SULMASY, Glenn 401-232-6060 441 B
gsulmasy@bryant.edu
SULZBACH, J. Bonnie 443-412-2119 215 D
bsulzbach@harford.edu
SUMAS, Keith, P 404-413-0783 126 D
ksumas1@gsu.edu
SUMEREL, Michelle 662-620-5364 267 F
jmsumerel@iccms.edu
SUMICHRAST, Robert, T 540-231-6601 518 B
busdean@vt.edu
SUMLIN, Rene 334-683-2378 5 H
renesumlin@marionmilitary.edu
SUMMA, Louise, J 860-215-9298 90 B
lsumma@trcc.commnet.edu
SUMMARY, Sherry 618-985-3741 148 G
sherrysummary@jalc.edu
SUMME, Shawn 314-951-9895 281 H
ssumme@stlcc.edu
SUMMER, Gail 540-365-4206 507 H
gsummer@ferrum.edu
SUMMER, Mimi 937-433-3410 382 C
msummer@fortiscollege.edu
SUMMER, Rebekah 320-762-4612 257 O
rebekahs@alextech.edu
SUMMERLIN, Christopher, A 606-783-2060 198 H
c.summerlin@moreheadstate.edu
SUMMERLIN, Raymond, M 573-629-3265 275 F
Ray.Summerlin@hlg.edu
SUMMERLIN, Timothy 830-792-7345 482 D
tsummerlin@schreiner.edu
SUMMERS, Amanda 281-425-6533 477 F
asummers@lee.edu
SUMMERS, Brian 901-321-3370 455 I
bsummers@cbu.edu
SUMMERS, Chris 404-364-8355 129 F
csummers@oglethorpe.edu
SUMMERS, Christopher 850-201-6100 117 B
summersc@tcc.fl.edu
SUMMERS, II, Daniel 802-447-4696 503 A
dsummers@svc.edu
SUMMERS, Diane 713-646-1794 482 H
dsummers@stcl.edu
SUMMERS, Eric, J 985-549-3850 208 E
esummers@selu.edu
SUMMERS, Greg 715-346-4686 541 A
gsummers@uwsp.edu
SUMMERS, Janie, K 314-286-3665 280 I
jksummers@ranken.edu
SUMMERS, Jean 816-936-8729 282 A
jsummers@saintlukescollege.edu
SUMMERS, Jennifer 843-377-2410 444 A
jsummers@charlestonlaw.edu
SUMMERS, Jerry 903-923-2084 473 I
jsummers@etbu.edu
SUMMERS, Jim 740-362-3335 386 D
jsummers@mtso.edu
SUMMERS, LeRoy 336-517-2116 354 K
lsummers@bennett.edu
SUMMERS, Lori 201-200-3489 304 C
lsummers@njcu.edu
SUMMERS, Matthew, A 304-637-1373 529 I
summersm@dewv.edu
SUMMERS, Michael, D 757-822-7122 517 C
msummers@tcc.edu
SUMMERS, Michael, D 757-822-1066 517 C
msummers@tcc.edu
SUMMERS, Micheal 806-291-1165 496 K
summersm@wbu.edu
SUMMERS, Nathan 937-294-0592 391 B
nathan@saa.edu
SUMMERS, RaChele 828-327-7000 361 B
rsummers@cvcc.edu
SUMMERS, Ragan 904-470-8231 102 A
ragan.summers@ewc.edu
SUMMERS, Richard 601-984-1018 270 H
rsummers@umc.edu
SUMMERS, Robert 870-512-7710 19 I
robert_summers@asun.edu
SUMMERS, Susan 832-813-6592 477 I
susan.summers@lonestar.edu
SUMMERS, Tammi 262-564-2538 543 A
summerst@gtc.edu
SUMMERS, Tiffany 615-966-1791 458 C
tiffany.summers@lipscomb.edu
SUMMERS, Tony, E 972-238-6202 473 B
tesummers@dcccd.edu
SUMMERS, Wally 229-931-2040 131 E
wsummers@southgatech.edu
SUMMERSELL, Charley 518-587-2100 348 A
charley.summersell@esc.edu
SUMMERVILLE, Keith 515-271-2265 177 K
keith.summerville@drake.edu
SUMMIT, Jennifer 415-338-2206 36 A
jsummit@sfsu.edu
SUMNER, Dana 919-760-8341 359 B
sumnerd@meredith.edu
SUMNER, Henry, A 610-558-5513 427 D
hsumner@neumann.edu
SUMNER, Judith 303-546-3516 84 B
judith@naropa.edu
SUMNER, Lauren 804-862-6100 511 H
lwaymack@rbc.edu
SUMNER, Shelia 218-879-0715 258 F
ssumner@fdltcc.edu
SUMNER, Wesley, D 321-674-6218 103 R
wsumner@fit.edu
SUMNERS, Stephanie 417-447-2653 280 C
sumnerss@otc.edu
SUMPTER, Michael 208-426-1012 137 E
michaelsumpter@boisestate.edu
SUMPTION, Michael 530-226-4148 66 G
msumption@simpsonu.edu
SUMTER, LaQuata 229-434-8441 119 H
Laquata.Sumter@asurams.edu
SUN, James 518-464-8821 325 B
jSun@excelsior.edu
SUN, Weihong 313-993-3305 250 H
sunwe@udmercy.edu
SUN, Yan (Sunny) 410-888-9048 216 G
ssun@muih.edu
SUN, Yanling 973-655-4091 304 A
suny@mail.montclair.edu
SUNAHARA, Wayne 808-845-9272 136 E
waynens@hawaii.edu
SUNATA, Cem 805-756-6016 32 E
csunata@calpoly.edu
SUNBERG, Carl 816-268-5402 279 K
lkneely@nts.edu
SUND, Andrew, C 773-878-7502 158 C
asund@staugustine.edu
SUNDAY, Diana 209-588-5389 78 B
SUNDBERG, Lori 847-735-5034 149 H
lsundber@lakeforest.edu
SUNDBERG, Lori, H 847-735-5034 149 H
lsundber@lakeforest.edu
SUNDBERG, Lori, L 309-341-5214 140 I
lsundberg@sandburg.edu
SUNDBORG, SJ, Stephen, V 206-296-1891 526 F
sundborg@seattleu.edu
SUNDBY-THORP, Valerie 360-596-5451 527 B
vsundby-thorp@spscc.edu
SUNDERLAND, JR., Richard 304-724-3700 529 F
rsunderland@apus.edu
SUNDERMAN, Rick 614-947-6605 382 H
rick.sunderman@franklin.edu
SUNDERMANN, Brigitte 970-255-2600 80 B
bsunderm@coloradomesa.edu
SUNDGREN, Donald, E 434-982-5834 514 A
des5j@virginia.edu
SUNDQUIST, Mike 209-575-6081 78 C
sundquistm@yosemite.cc.ca.us
SUNDSEDT, Casey 847-628-1561 149 A
csundsedt@judsonu.edu
SUNDSMO, Alecia, D 717-245-1485 417 B
sundsmoa@dickinson.edu
SUNDSTEDT, Bernard 815-226-3371 157 D
bsunstedt@rockford.edu
SUNDSTROM, Sandra 507-786-3357 264 C
sundstro@stolaf.edu
SUNDY, Carolyn 606-589-3052 197 D
carolyn.sundy@kctcs.edu
SUNG, Donghyun 714-533-3946 36 D
davidit@calums.edu
SUNG, Mankyung 562-926-1023 60 B
psung@ptsa.edu
SUNI, Ellen, Y 816-235-1007 284 A
sunie@umkc.edu
SUNLEAF, Arthur, W 563-588-7137 180 L
arthur.sunleaf@loras.edu
SUNNYGARD, John 303-807-9956 86 G
john.sunnygard@ucdenver.edu
SUNQUIST, Scott, W 626-584-5265 45 F
sunquist@fuller.edu
SUNSER, James 585-345-6812 326 F
jmsunser@genesee.edu
SUNSHINE, Brian 254-526-7161 470 E
brian.sunshine@ctcd.edu
SUNSHINE, Lisbet 415-338-1120 36 A
lisbet@sfsu.edu
SUNSHINE, Phyllis 410-337-6046 215 B
psunshine@goucher.edu
SUOMI, Sue 864-977-2094 448 A
susan.suomi@ngu.edu
SUOREZ, Paula 760-384-6298 49 F
pasouroez@cerrocoso.edu
SUPAK, Brian 254-298-8609 484 C
brian.supak@templejc.edu
SUPERNAW, Robert, B 704-233-8015 373 C
supernaw@wingate.edu
SUPINSKI, Jessica 425-235-2352 525 G
jsupinski@rtc.edu
SUPLER, Robin 954-262-4349 109 E
rsupler@nsu.nova.edu
SUPOWITZ, Paul, A 412-624-2901 437 K
psupowit@pitt.edu
SUPPELSA, Robert, E 310-233-4051 51 F
suppelre@lahc.edu
SUPPLEE, JR., Jack 859-257-8288 200 G
supplee@uky.edu
SUPPLEE, Janice 937-766-8319 378 K
suppleej@cedarville.edu
SUPURGECI, Jonna 605-668-1515 452 I
jsupurgeci@mtmc.edu
SURANKSY, Shael, P 212-875-4595 315 F
ssuransky@bankstreet.edu
SURATY-CLARKE, Mercedes 713-743-1185 491 D
msclarke@uh.edu
SURBAUGH, Joyce 304-205-6600 531 A
joyce.surbaugh@bridgevalley.edu
SURBECK, III, Carlton, E 410-337-6100 215 B
carlton.surbeck@goucher.edu
SURBROOK, Will 619-388-6589 62 E
wsurbroo@sdccd.edu
SURDOVEL, Grace 570-408-3102 440 B
grace.surdovel@wilkes.edu
SURENDER, Sheelu, M 316-978-5337 192 D
sheelu.surender@wichita.edu
SURESH, Subra 412-268-2201 414 J
suresh@andrew.cmu.edu
SURETHING, Nicole, A 540-654-1053 513 I
nsurethi@umw.edu
SURGALA, David, J 570-577-3811 413 E
dsurgala@bucknell.edu
SURGENT, Karen 201-200-3041 304 C
ksurgent@njcu.edu
SURGEONER, James 610-607-6236 433 H
jsurgeoner@racc.edu
SURGES, Rebecca 414-258-4810 538 A
surgesr@mtmary.edu
SUROWIEC, Barbara 203-332-5049 89 C
bsurowiec@hcc.commnet.edu
SURPRENANT, Neil 518-327-6313 338 B
nsurprenant@paulsmiths.edu
SURRELL, Matt 662-472-9178 267 E
msurrell@holmescc.edu
SURRETT, Caron 828-884-8261 355 A
caron@brevard.edu
SURRETT, Charles, M 812-888-5886 174 F
csurrett@vinu.edu
SURRIDGE, Jack, F 773-244-5676 154 G
jsurridge@northpark.edu
SURRIDGE, Mary, K 773-244-6264 154 G
msurridge@northpark.edu
SURRRUSCO, Anet 203-576-5675 91 H
asurrusco@stvincentscollege.edu
SUSANA, Gil 619-961-4316 69 J
gsusana@tjsl.edu
SUSANKA, Thomas, J 805-525-4417 69 I
tsusanka@thomasaquinas.edu
SUSANTO, Yuliana 502-597-7014 197 G
yuliana.susanto@kysu.edu
SUSHINSKY, David, M 240-895-4282 218 B
dmsushinksy@smcm.edu
SUSICK, Timothy 724-938-4056 430 C
susick@calu.edu
SUSKI-LENCZEWSKI, Anna 860-832-1757 88 D
lenczewskia@mail.ccsu.edu
SUSMAN, Catherine, D 541-346-1255 410 F
susman@uoregon.edu
SUSMAN, Jeffrey, L 330-325-6122 387 F
jsusman@neomed.edu
SUSMANN, Phillip 802-485-2213 502 G
susmann@norwich.edu
SUSMARSKI, Aaron 814-860-5101 423 B
asusmarski@lecom.edu
SUSS, Stuart 718-368-5661 320 A
ssuss@kbcc.cuny.edu
SUSSENBACH, Michelle 618-664-7025 145 E
michelle.sussenbach@greenville.edu
SUSSKIND, Gary 718-953-5889 349 H
ohaleitorah@optonline.net
SUSSMAN, David 503-491-7258 407 C
david.sussman@mhcc.edu
SUSSMAN, Nan, M 718-982-2315 319 A
nan.sussman@csi.cuny.edu
SUSSWEIN, Gary, J 512-471-4945 493 M
susswein@austin.utexas.edu
SUSTAIRE, Karan 903-923-2296 473 I
ksustaire@etbu.edu
SUSTICH, Andrew 870-972-2025 19 F
sustich@astate.edu
SUTCH, Laurie 781-891-2103 223 E
lsutch@bentley.edu
SUTER, Cindy 419-448-2090 383 C
csuter@heidelberg.edu
SUTER, Vicki 541-552-8290 409 G
suterv@sou.edu
SUTERA, Paul, J 914-637-2710 328 F
psutera@iona.edu
SUTERA, Tom 360-538-4207 523 A
SUTHERLAND, David 218-879-0816 258 F
dsutherland@fdltcc.edu
SUTHERLAND, David 501-450-1254 21 C
sutherlandd@hendrix.edu
SUTHERLAND, Diane 864-231-2000 443 E
dsutherland@andersonuniversity.edu
SUTHERLAND, Jim 678-839-6410 133 F
sutherla@westga.edu
SUTHERLAND, Kathleen 973-408-3000 301 J
ksutherl@drew.edu
SUTHERLAND, Richard 989-358-7368 239 C
sutherlr@alpenacc.edu
SUTHERLAND, Ronald 765-998-5118 173 B
rnsutherl@taylor.edu
SUTHERLAND, Shari 319-363-1323 181 D
ssutherland@mtmercy.edu
SUTHERLAND, Timothy 219-980-6946 168 C
sutherla@iun.edu
SUTHERLAND, Tricia 712-274-6400 184 A
tricia.sutherland@witcc.edu
SUTHERLIN, Lea 314-340-3383 275 G
sutherlinl@hssu.edu
SUTKOWSKI, Ernest, H 914-831-0343 322 D
SUTKUS, Janel 412-268-8729 414 J
jsutkus@cmu.edu
SUTLIFF, Danielle 912-260-4419 131 D
dani.sutliff@sgsc.edu

SUTLIFF, Michael .... 714-432-0202.. 40 D
msutliff@occ.cccd.edu
SUTLIFF, Michael .... 714-432-5638.. 40 D
msutliff@occ.cccd.edu
SUTLIVE, Charles .... 404-962-3053 133 G
charles.sutlive@usg.edu
SUTPHEN, Debra .... 916-660-7502.. 66 E
dsutphen@sierracollege.edu
SUTPHIN, Mamie, M .... 336-734-7520 362 F
msutphin@forsythtech.edu
SUTTER, Crystal .... 217-228-5432 156 D
suttecr@quincy.edu
SUTTER, Frankie, K .... 910-592-8081 365 G
fsutter@sampsoncc.edu
SUTTER, Thaddeus .... 309-556-3059 148 A
tsutter@iwu.edu
SUTTERFIELD, Shirley ... 251-442-2414.... 9 B
ssutterfield@umobile.edu
SUTTLE, J. Lloyd .... 203-432-4453.. 93 C
j.suttle@yale.edu
SUTTON, Barbara .... 773-298-3504 158 F
sutton@sxu.edu
SUTTON, Barbara, B ..... 252-335-3224 369 F
bbsutton@ecsu.edu
SUTTON, Bob .... 847-866-3921 145 C
bob.sutton@garrett.edu
SUTTON, Cynthia .... 314-392-2291 278 G
suttonc@mobap.edu
SUTTON, Deborah .... 252-527-6223 363 G
dsutton@lenoircc.edu
SUTTON, Deborah, S .... 252-527-6223 363 G
dsutton@lenoircc.edu
SUTTON, Ellen .... 630-942-2353 142 F
suttone@cod.edu
SUTTON, Gentry .... 918-335-6285 400 I
gsutton@okwu.edu
SUTTON, Jama .... 865-774-5800 464 C
jama.sutton@ws.edu
SUTTON, John .... 812-749-1272 171 I
jsutton@oake.edu
SUTTON, Judith .... 304-485-5487 530 E
jsutton@msc.edu
SUTTON, Kay .... 309-690-6886 146 C
ksutton@icc.edu
SUTTON, Kenneth, W ... 410-778-7269 221 D
ksutton2@washcoll.edu
SUTTON, Lynn .... 336-758-5480 372 G
suttonls@wfu.edu
SUTTON, Melinda .... 662-915-7705 270 G
mjsutton@olemiss.edu
SUTTON, Michael .... 909-607-3562.. 39 F
mike.sutton@cms.claremont.edu
SUTTON, Nancy .... 217-351-2402 155 I
nsutton@parkland.edu
SUTTON, R. Anderson .. 808-956-8922 135 J
rasutton@hawaii.edu
SUTTON, Robert, E .... 509-452-5100 524 J
rsutton@pnwu.edu
SUTTON, Ronald .... 813-419-5100 252 J
suttonr@cooley.edu
SUTTON, Rosemary ...... 425-352-8255 520 D
rsutton@cascadia.edu
SUTTON, Stephanie ...... 440-365-5222 385 E
SUTTON-COLLIER,
Kayla .... 910-892-3178 357 D
ksutton@heritagebiblecollege.edu
SUTTON-HAYWOOD,
Marilyn .... 704-463-1360 367 F
marilyn.sutton-haywood@pfeiffer.edu
SUTTON-SMITH, Leslie . 973-408-3246 301 J
lsuttonsmith@drew.edu
SUTTON-WALLACE,
Pamela, M .... 434-924-9308 514 A
ps5gb@virginia.edu
SUTYAK, John .... 508-286-3987 238 B
sutyak_john@wheatoncollege.edu
SUTZKO, Christopher .... 570-208-5874 422 D
christophersutzko@kings.edu
SUVAK, Daniel, S .... 330-490-7183 395 C
dsuvak@walsh.edu
SUZO, Michael .... 419-783-2361 381 G
msuzo@defiance.edu
SUZOR, Michael, J .... 413-755-4044 233 B
msuzor@stcc.edu
SUZOW, Bo .... 213-738-6762.. 68 E
mis@swlaw.edu
SUZUKI, Joyce .... 707-664-4470.. 36 C
joyce.suzuki@sonoma.edu
SUZUKI, Takeo .... 479-788-7166.. 23 H
takeo.suzuki@uafs.edu
SVANDA, Gary .... 402-559-4432 293 I
gsvanda@unmc.edu
SVEC, Andrew .... 218-281-8438 264 H
asvec@umn.edu
SVEI, Yehuda .... 215-477-1000 436 B
talmudicalyeshiva@yahoo.com
SVENSSON, Nancy .... 510-841-1905.. 27 B
nsvensson@absw.edu
SVERID, Julie .... 517-338-3322 241 B
SVETE, Lee, J .... 574-631-5200 174 A
svete.1@nd.edu
SVETLIK, Brenda .... 361-570-4823 492 A
svetlikb@uhv.edu
SVILAR, Kendra, E .... 216-397-6630 384 F
ksvilar@jcu.edu
SVOBODA, Angela, M .. 512-448-8622 481 B
asvoboda@stedwards.edu
SVONAVEC, Stephen ..... 478-275-6769 128 H
stephen.svonavec@mga.edu
SWAFFORD, Denise ...... 239-489-9358 104 G
denise.swafford@fsw.edu
SWAFFORD, Denise ...... 541-956-7087 409 F
dswafford@roguecc.edu
SWAFFORD, Jeanna, C . 731-881-7629 465 F
jswafford@utm.edu
SWAFFORD, Russ .... 865-974-3242 465 D
bswaffor@utk.edu
SWAGER, Kendra .... 804-752-7374 511 E
kendraswager@rmc.edu
SWAGER, Sarah, L .... 509-963-1515 520 E
swagers@cwu.edu
SWAID, Samar .... 501-370-5335.. 22 E
sswaid@philander.edu
SWAIM, Kevin, C .... 765-361-6252 175 B
swaimk@wabash.edu
SWAIN, Ann .... 718-522-9073 315 E
aswain@asa.edu
SWAIN, Carole .... 925-631-4695.. 61 G
cswain@stmarys-ca.edu
SWAIN, Chalimar, L ..... 801-581-8876 499 K
c.swain@ic.utah.edu
SWAIN, Corliss .... 507-786-3277 264 C
swain@stolaf.edu
SWAIN, Cristal .... 970-351-1142.. 87 A
cristal.wain@unco.edu
SWAIN, Eddie .... 443-518-4974 215 F
eswain@howardcc.edu
SWAIN, Emily, L .... 304-367-4015 532 F
Emily.Swain@fairmontstate.edu
SWAIN, Eric .... 559-443-8523.. 69 B
eric.swain@fresnocitycollege.edu
SWAIN, Heather, C .... 517-355-2262 246 H
heather.swain@cabs.msu.edu
SWAIN, Jackie .... 406-275-4755 288 H
jackie_swain@skc.edu
SWAIN, Jeffrey, D .... 305-626-3674 104 B
Jeffrey.Swain@fmuniv.edu
SWAIN, Richard .... 610-436-2747 432 B
rswain@wcupa.edu
SWAIN, Robert .... 813-881-0007 112 E
rswain@sbtampa.com
SWAIN, Rodney .... 414-229-5895 540 A
rswain@uwm.edu
SWAIN, Stuart, G .... 207-255-1342 212 G
sswain@maine.edu
SWAIN, Valerie, T .... 443-412-2344 215 D
vswain@harford.edu
SWALGA, Dan .... 412-392-3911 433 F
dswalga@pointpark.edu
SWALLOW, John, R ...... 931-598-1101 460 I
jrswallo@sewanee.edu
SWALWELL, Joe .... 405-682-1611 399 K
jswalwell@occc.edu
SWAN, Beth Ann .... 215-503-8057 436 F
BethAnn.Swan@jefferson.edu
SWAN, Bobi .... 503-493-6526 405 E
bswan@cu-portland.edu
SWAN, Deba .... 254-526-1237 470 E
deborah.swan@ctcd.edu
SWAN, III, George, W .. 313-496-2344 252 A
gswan1@wcccd.edu
SWAN, John .... 916-577-2200.. 77 F
jswan@jessup.edu
SWAN, Kirsten .... 207-778-7347 212 E
kswan@maine.edu
SWAN, S. Tomeka .... 410-287-6060 214 C
tswan@cecil.edu
SWAN, Steve .... 360-650-3482 528 D
steve.swan@wwu.edu
SWAN, Terry, W .... 270-384-8148 198 C
swant@lindsey.edu
SWAN, William .... 718-636-3518 338 E
wswan@pratt.edu
SWANAGAN, Diana .... 706-233-7301 131 C
dswanagan@shorter.edu
SWANBERG, Jeff .... 815-967-7321 157 C
jswanberg@rockfordcareercollege.edu
SWANEY, Alica .... 864-225-7653 446 D
alicaswaney@forrestcollege.edu
SWANGER, Dustin .... 518-736-3622 326 D
dustin.swanger@fmcc.suny.edu
SWANGER, Rachel .... 310-393-0411.. 58 E
rachel_swanger@rand.org
SWANGER, Stefanie ...... 478-757-5257 134 E
sswanger@wesleyancollege.edu
SWANGER, Stefanie ...... 478-757-5218 134 E
sswanger@wesleyancollege.edu
SWANGER, Thomas ...... 760-750-4813.. 35 B
tswanger@csusm.edu
SWANK, Dennis, W ...... 570-577-3363 413 E
dennis.swank@bucknell.edu
SWANKER, Susanne ...... 413-205-3216 221 G
susanne.swanker@aic.edu
SWANN, Jason .... 618-437-5321 156 I
swannj@rlc.edu
SWANNACK, Patricia ..... 732-571-3546 303 G
pswannac@monmouth.edu
SWANQUIST, Leah .... 847-635-1780 155 E
lswanqui@oakton.edu
SWANSON, Adam .... 228-897-4377 268 G
adam.swanson@mgccc.edu
SWANSON, Alison .... 515-961-1696 182 I
alison.swanson@simpson.edu
SWANSON, Annette .... 567-661-7510 390 D
annette_swanson@owens.edu
SWANSON, Barry, K ...... 785-864-5978 191 G
bswanson@ku.edu
SWANSON, Becky .... 614-235-4136 392 D
bswanson@TLSohio.edu
SWANSON, Brian, R ...... 909-869-2261.. 32 F
bswanson@cpp.edu
SWANSON, Chris .... 402-552-3100 289 H
SWANSON, Chris .... 541-683-5141 406 B
cswanson@gutenberg.edu
SWANSON, Christopher 815-836-5393 150 F
swansoch@lewisu.edu
SWANSON, Cynthia .... 269-471-3288 239 D
swansonc@andrews.edu
SWANSON, Darren .... 320-363-5810 254 J
dswanson@csbsju.edu
SWANSON, Eleanor .... 732-571-7529 303 G
eswanson@monmouth.edu
SWANSON, Greg .... 262-472-6703 541 D
swansong@uww.edu
SWANSON, Gregory .... 704-461-5073 354 J
GregSwanson@bac.edu
SWANSON, James, E .... 574-372-5700 166 D
swansoje@grace.edu
SWANSON, Jeanne .... 760-795-6840.. 54 G
jswanson@miracosta.edu
SWANSON, Jim, M .... 719-389-6651.. 79 M
jswanson@coloradocollege.edu
SWANSON, JR., Joe ...... 404-752-1542 129 A
jswanson@msm.edu
SWANSON, Kai .... 309-794-7149 139 K
kaiswanson@augustana.edu
SWANSON, Kathrine ...... 816-604-1000 277 F
SWANSON, Kathrine ...... 215-641-6510 426 E
kswanson@mc3.edu
SWANSON, Kristen .... 206-296-5675 526 F
swansonk@seattleu.edu
SWANSON, Louis .... 970-491-6281.. 81 D
louis.swanson@colostate.edu
SWANSON,
Margaret, A .... 309-694-8584 146 C
margaret.swanson@icc.edu
SWANSON, Matt .... 702-808-8806 131 F
mswanson@southuniversity.edu
SWANSON, Robert .... 419-448-2125 383 C
rswanso1@heidelberg.edu
SWANSON, Robert, P ... 716-286-8538 336 E
rps@niagara.edu
SWANSON, Ronald .... 770-407-1001.. 28 G
raswanson@argosy.edu
SWANSON, Ryan, F .... 785-532-1373 188 H
rswanson@ksu.edu
SWANSON, Steven .... 415-575-6178.. 31 C
sswanson@ciis.edu
SWANSON, Steven, M .. 608-262-1414 539 D
swanson@pharmacy.wisc.edu
SWANSON-MADDEN,
Pamela .... 618-395-7777 146 F
swansonp@iecc.edu
SWANSON-ORR,
Tamara .... 503-845-3549 407 B
tamara.swanson@mtangel.edu
SWANT, Steven .... 404-894-4615 125 D
steve.swant@carnegie.gatech.edu
SWANTON, Deborah ...... 978-232-2430 226 C
dswanton@endicott.edu
SWANZEY, Thomas .... 201-692-2749 302 H
thomas_swanzey@fdu.edu
SWARBRICK, JR.,
John 'Jack', B .... 574-631-7546 174 A
swarbrick.1@nd.edu
SWARNES, Neal, R .... 417-667-8181 273 H
nswarnes@cottey.edu
SWARR, Amy .... 630-617-5370 144 G
amys@elmhurst.edu
SWARTHOUT, Jeanne ... 928-524-7420.. 16 E
jeanne.swarthout@npc.edu
SWARTOUT, Jennifer ..... 309-694-8984 146 C
jennifer.swartout@icc.edu
SWARTWOOD, Ronald .. 719-502-3053.. 84 J
ron.swartwood@ppcc.edu
SWARTZ, David, L .... 202-885-2612.. 94 H
dswartz@american.edu
SWARTZ, Mark .... 212-410-8457 335 B
mswartz@nycpm.edu
SWARTZ, Mary, K .... 757-683-5795 510 I
mswartz@odu.edu
SWARTZ, Stephen, E .... 978-665-4444 229 D
sswartz@fitchburgstate.edu
SWARTZ, Wendy .... 928-523-6081.. 16 C
Wendy.Swartz@nau.edu
SWARTZBAUGH, Keith .. 956-380-8140 481 A
kswartzbaugh@riogrande.edu
SWARTZENDRUBER,
Loren, E .... 540-432-4100 507 A
lorens@emu.edu
SWARTZENTRUBER,
Dale, E .... 740-368-3811 390 B
deswartz@owu.edu
SWARTZLANDER,
Barbara .... 207-602-2363 213 B
bswartzlander@une.edu
SWARTZWELDER,
Roger, L .... 205-329-7903.... 3 C
roger.swartzwelder@ecacolleges.com
SWATCHICK, Abby .... 610-568-1471 412 C
abby.swatchick@alvernia.edu
SWEANY, Lisa .... 912-344-2730 120 D
lisa.sweany@armstrong.edu
SWEARENGIN, Paul ...... 412-237-3050 415 G
pswearengin@ccac.edu
SWEARER, Randy .... 215-951-2705 432 F
swearerr@philau.edu
SWEARINGEN,
Catherine, W .... 253-535-7186 524 I
swearicw@plu.edu
SWEARINGEN, Jodie ..... 651-423-8216 258 E
jodie.swearingen@dctc.edu
SWEARINGIN, Bubba .... 940-325-2591 497 A
bswearingin@wc.edu
SWEATMAN, Robert, A . 217-245-3289 146 D
rsweatma@mail.ic.edu
SWEDICK, Nick .... 212-659-7200 330 A
nswedick@tkc.edu
SWEDLOW, Kathy .... 517-371-5140 252 J
swedlowk@cooley.edu
SWEEDLER, Alan, R ...... 619-594-1354.. 35 E
asweedler@mail.sdsu.edu
SWEELEY, Rebecca .... 209-228-4667.. 71 E
RSweeley@UCMerced.edu
SWEENER, Kathleen ...... 518-629-7320 328 D
k.sweener@hvcc.edu
SWEENEY, Beth .... 859-572-6371 199 A
sweeneyb@nku.edu
SWEENEY, Christina, C 302-857-1072.. 94 A
csweeney@dtcc.edu
SWEENEY, Donnie .... 256-331-5438.... 6 B
dsweeney@nwscc.edu
SWEENEY, Janet .... 770-479-9538 130 E
jkt@reinhardt.edu
SWEENEY, John, M .... 401-865-2299 441 F
john.sweeney@providence.edu
SWEENEY, Kathleen, J .. 978-656-3046 232 B
sweeneyk@middlesex.mass.edu
SWEENEY, Marc .... 937-766-7480 378 K
msweeney@cedarville.edu
SWEENEY, Michael .... 510-883-2083.. 43 C
msweeney@dspt.edu
SWEENEY, Michael, E ... 513-231-2223 377 B
msweeney@athenaeum.edu
SWEENEY, Michele .... 978-542-6582 230 E
msweeney@salemstate.edu
SWEENEY, Richard, T ... 973-596-3208 304 D
richard.sweeney@njit.edu
SWEENEY, Rick .... 978-867-4036 227 A
rick.sweeney@gordon.edu
SWEENEY, Robert, D .... 434-924-1008 514 A
rds2j@virginia.edu
SWEENEY, Robert, J ..... 937-775-3346 396 A
robert.sweeney@wright.edu
SWEENEY, Ronald .... 518-562-4122 321 D
ronald.sweeney@clinton.edu
SWEENEY, Sarah, R .... 414-410-4187 535 C
srsweeney@stritch.edu
SWEENEY, Stacy .... 617-217-9000 223 A
ssweeney@baystate.edu
SWEENEY, Stephen .... 303-715-3192.. 85 J
stephen.sweeney@archden.org
SWEENEY, Timothy .... 252-475-9250 361 G
timothy_sweeney@albemarle.edu
SWEENEY, Victoria .... 630-889-6572 154 E
vsweeney@nuhs.edu
SWEENEY, Yvette .... 816-604-4114 278 A
yvette.sweeney@mcckc.edu
SWEET, Brett .... 615-343-6735 465 H
brett.sweet@vanderbilt.edu
SWEET, Chris .... 503-594-3370 405 A
chris.sweet@clackamas.edu
SWEET, Cyndi .... 865-981-8095 458 E
cyndi.sweet@maryvillecollege.edu
SWEET, Darryl .... 415-565-4604.. 71 B
sweetd@uchastings.edu
SWEET, David, M .... 315-279-5682 329 K
dsweet@keuka.edu
SWEET, Don .... 252-328-9103 369 E
sweetd@ecu.edu

T

TAGGART, James 205-247-8927 7 G jtaggart@stillman.edu
TAGGART, James, R 801-627-8306 498 O taggartj@owatc.edu
TAGGART, Julie 614-222-4025 380 F jtaggart@ccad.edu
TAGGART, Thomas 904-256-1234 103 K ttaggart@fcsl.edu
TAGGART, William 404-215-2659 128 L william.taggart@morehouse.edu
TAGLIARENI, James 409-933-8989 471 B jtagliareni@com.edu
TAGLIATELA, Gayle, S 203-932-7455 92 G gtagliatela@newhaven.edu
TAGYE, Jim 515-643-6678 181 B jtagye@mercydesmoines.org
TAHA, Dianne 516-726-5837 548 I tahad@usmma.edu
TAHA, Sipel 760-630-1555 49 C staha@kaplan.edu
TAHERI, Reza 818-299-5500 75 K rTaheri@westcoastuniversity.edu
TAHIRI, Adrian 212-349-4330 326 G atahiri@globe.edu
TAHMASSEBI, Debbie 408-554-4455 65 A dtahmassebi@scu.edu
TAHTINEN, Dale, R 906-487-2318 247 A drtahtin@mtu.edu
TAI WANG, Yong 903-566-7043 494 E ywang@uttyler.edu
TAILLON, Gretchen 603-342-3003 297 E gtaillon@ccsnh.edu
TAILOR, Bhavna 973-661-0600 302 D
TAIT, Lane, H 830-792-7462 482 D ltait@schreiner.edu
TAIT, Melissa 847-214-7365 144 F mtait@elgin.edu
TAIT, Raymond 314-977-4817 281 M taitrc@slu.edu
TAITANO, Carlos 671-735-2600 549 G ctaitano@uguam.uog.edu
TAKACS, Audrey 586-445-7314 246 A takacsa@macomb.edu
TAKAHASHI, Jack 800-754-1009 537 E
TAKAHASHI, Tomoko 949-480-4047 66 I ttakahashi@soka.edu
TAKAMI, Andrew, B 812-590-9185 169 A atakami@purdue.edu
TAKAMURA, Jeanette, C 212-851-2288 322 F jct8@columbia.edu
TAKAO, Carol 415-502-3233 72 C Carol.Takao@ucsf.edu
TAKEDA-TINKER, Becky 800-462-7845 81 E
TAKEMOTO, Mary Ann 562-985-5146 33 F maryann.takemoto@csulb.edu
TAKES, Faith, A 518-786-0855 332 J faith.takes@mildred-elley.edu
TAKIGUCHI, Amy 808-735-4707 135 A ahigashi@chaminade.edu
TAKSAR, Stephen 603-535-2550 299 E sjtaksar@plymouth.edu
TALABER, Matthew 845-938-3415 549 A Matthew.Talaber@usma.edu
TALAVERA, Karla 661-255-1050 31 B talavera@calarts.edu
TALAVINIA, Phillip 419-358-3226 377 H talaviniap@bluffton.edu
TALBERT, Kelly 208-426-3844 137 E KellyTalbert@boisestate.edu
TALBOOM, Scott 928-226-4374 13 D scott.talboom@coconino.edu
TALBOT, A. Scott 435-652-7601 499 M talbot@dixie.edu
TALBOT, Ann 312-915-8902 151 E atalbot@luc.edu
TALBOT, Laura 956-872-5051 482 G ltalbot@southtexascollege.edu
TALBOT, William 212-594-4000 349 J btalbot@tcicollege.edu
TALBOTT, Jeffrey 909-748-8888 73 K jeffrey_talbott@redlands.edu
TALBOTT, John, E 805-893-2622 72 D john.talbott@ucsb.edu
TALBOTT, Linda 406-243-4215 287 D linda.talbott@umontana.edu
TALBOTT, Richard 251-445-9254 9 F rtalbott@southalabama.edu
TALBOTT, Robert 650-543-3714 54 B rtalbott@menlo.edu
TALBOTT, Sherry 540-828-5369 505 F stalbott@bridgewater.edu
TALDO, Tom 785-242-5200 190 D tom.taldo@ottawa.edu
TALENTINO, Andrea 802-485-2410 502 G atalenti@norwich.edu
TALENTINO, Karen, A 802-654-2216 502 H ktalentino@smcvt.edu
TALERICO, Katie 412-291-6247 412 H ktalerico@aii.edu
TALESH, Rameen, A 949-824-5590 71 C rtalesh@uci.edu
TALIAFERRO, Beth 702-434-6599 296 F btaliaferro@sierranevada.edu
TALIAFERRO, Kevin 813-529-2640 547 N kevin.c.taliaferro@centcom.mil
TALIENTO, Tamela, K 931-431-9700 459 N ttaliento@nci.edu
TALKINGTON, Barbara 206-592-4319 523 D btalkington@highline.edu
TALLANT, Pat, L 903-434-8102 479 L ptallant@ntcc.edu
TALLANT, Steven, H 361-593-3209 486 A steven.tallant@tamuk.edu
TALLARIDA, Ronald, J 856-256-5413 306 D tallarida@rowan.edu
TALLENT, Edward 617-333-2935 225 F etallent0811@curry.edu
TALLENT, Judy 606-679-8501 197 B judy.tallent@kctcs.edu
TALLERICO, Betty, L 724-458-3790 419 F bltallerico@gcc.edu
TALLEY, Ben 828-328-7244 358 G ben.talley@lr.edu
TALLEY, Braque 662-252-8000 270 C BraqueTalley@rustcollege.edu
TALLEY, Brent 870-777-5722 24 H brent.talley@uacch.edu
TALLEY, Chestley 903-730-4890 476 L ctalley@jarvis.edu
TALLEY, Frederico, J 240-895-2185 218 B fjtalley@smcm.edu
TALLEY, Kathryn 800-280-0307 163 I kathryn.talley@ace.edu
TALLEY-BECK, Justine 302-831-7033 94 D justinet@udel.edu
TALLMAN, Doug 402-486-2534 293 D dotallma@ucollege.edu
TALLMAN, Lawrence, J 304-457-6247 529 C tallmanlj@ab.edu
TALLON, Brooke 405-425-5104 399 J brooke.tallon@oc.edu
TALLON, William 920-424-1444 540 B tallon@uwosh.edu
TALMADGE, Rosemary 718-482-5059 320 B rtalmadge@lagcc.cuny.edu
TALMAN, Martha, A 970-247-7315 82 I matalman@fortlewis.edu
TALMO, Richard 760-744-1150 58 D rtalmo@palomar.edu
TAM, Stanley 607-871-2300 314 J tam@alfred.edu
TAM, Victor 650-949-7472 45 A tamvictor@foothill.edu
TAMADA, Mike 503-788-6613 409 E tamadam@reed.edu
TAMANAHA, David 808-984-3253 136 H davidt@hawaii.edu
TAMANDL, Salisha 480-994-9244 17 P salishat@swiha.edu
TAMASCO, Mary 973-353-5541 307 C tamasco@rutgers.edu
TAMAYO, Daniel 559-934-2432 76 B danieltamayo@whccd.edu
TAMBERT, John 703-284-5946 510 B john.tambert@marymount.edu
TAMBLE, Kim 952-888-4777 263 I ktamble@nwhealth.edu
TAMBOUE, Helene 803-705-4573 443 F tamboueh@benedict.edu
TAMEO, John 401-254-3859 442 C jtameo@rwu.edu
TAMERIUS, Travis 573-592-4241 286 A travis.tamerius@williamwoods.edu
TAMES, Kirk 512-499-4517 493 K ktames@utsystem.edu
TAMEZ, Meritza 713-226-5227 491 F tamezm@uhd.edu
TAMIM, Tanya 303-837-0825 79 C ttamim@aii.edu
TAMMARO, Susan 781-768-7390 236 A susan.tammaro@regiscollege.edu
TAMMEUS, Lisen 816-235-5613 284 A tammeusli@umkc.edu
TAMMONE, William 309-694-6921 146 C william.tammone@icc.edu
TAMTE-HORAN, Deborah 484-664-3190 427 C tamte-horan@muhlenberg.edu
TAN, Finian 909-396-6090 31 E
TAN, Jiang 518-255-5869 346 E tanj@cobleskill.edu
TAN, Lin-Ying 512-444-8082 487 B ltan@thsu.edu
TAN, Nestor 310-233-4053 51 F tanng@lahc.edu
TAN, Norbert, N 805-289-6160 75 E ntan@vcccd.edu
TAN, Sharon, M 651-255-6108 264 F stan@unitedseminary.edu
TANAKA, Elizabeth 254-295-4949 492 C etanaka@umhb.edu
TANAKA, Henry, Y 248-522-3911 248 E hytanaka@oaklandcc.edu
TANAKA, Jason, K 808-932-7394 135 I jasonkt@hawaii.edu
TANAKA, Kenneth 408-741-2092 76 D kenneth.tanaka@wvm.edu
TANAKA, Kenneth 408-855-5438 76 E kenneth.tanaka@wvm.edu
TANAKA, Lester 702-651-5639 295 C lester.tanaka@csn.edu
TANAKA, Paul, N 515-294-5352 175 G ptanaka@iastate.edu
TANAKA, Randy 731-352-4065 455 E tanakar@bethelu.edu
TANAKA, Winona, M 918-631-3054 403 M winona-tanaka@utulsa.edu
TANAKA, Yasuo 510-666-8248 26 C ytanaka@aimc.edu
TANAKEYOWMA, Lilia 714-564-6971 60 G tanakeyowma_lilia@sac.edu
TANASESCU, Mihaela 858-513-9240 29 A mihaela.tanasescu@ashford.edu
TANBARA, Sabrina 212-799-5000 329 I
TANCK, Buddy Jo 913-294-4178 187 B buddyt@fortscott.edu
TANDE, Korinne 402-471-2505 292 A ktande@nscs.edu
TANDON, Suteesh 563-336-3345 178 A standon@eicc.edu
TANG, Chris 212-998-2342 336 C chris.tang@nyu.edu
TANG, Len 626-584-5204 45 F lentang@fuller.edu
TANG, Meiling 707-638-5880 70 B meiling.tang@tu.edu
TANG, Philip 410-516-6087 216 A ptang@jhu.edu
TANGEMAN, Bruce 402-323-3408 293 A btangeman@southeast.edu
TANGREDI-HANNON, Alice 203-785-3222 93 C alice.tangredi-hannon@yale.edu
TANIGAWA, Shane 415-380-1388 45 J shanetanigawa@ggbts.edu
TANIS, Cheophat 239-732-1300 108 I
TANJI, Lorelei, A 949-824-5212 71 C ltanji@uci.edu
TANKERSLEY, Melody 330-672-2220 384 H mtankers@kent.edu
TANKING, Tony 913-360-7485 184 K ttanking@benedictine.edu
TANKSLEY, Wallace 614-222-6165 380 F wtanksley@ccad.edu
TANNENBAUM, Michael 607-431-4405 327 B tannenbaumm@hartwick.edu
TANNER, Beth, L 732-247-5241 304 B btanner@nbts.edu
TANNER, Cindy 912-287-5829 123 A ctanner@coastalpines.edu
TANNER, Douglas, R 229-333-5935 133 H dtanner@valdosta.edu
TANNER, Elizabeth 210-486-3933 467 A etanner@alamo.edu
TANNER, Jamie 912-260-4377 131 D jamie.tanner@sgsc.edu
TANNER, John, F 757-683-3520 510 I jtanner@odu.edu
TANNER, John, S 808-675-3700 134 M jstanner@byuh.edu
TANNER, Kim 765-983-1631 165 H tanneki@earlham.edu
TANNER, Margaret 479-788-7807 23 H margaret.tanner@uafs.edu
TANNER, Norma, J 251-460-6141 9 F ntanner@southalabama.edu
TANNER, Pamela 262-472-5227 541 D tannerp@uww.edu
TANNER, Paula 409-880-8185 488 E pltanner@lit.edu
TANNER, Paula 254-295-8671 492 C ptanner@umhb.edu
TANNER, Ray 803-777-4202 450 B rtanner@mailbox.sc.edu
TANNEY, Matt 309-298-1008 163 A m-tanney@wiu.edu
TANON, Alma 408-270-6432 63 P alma.tanon@evc.edu
TANOUYE, Allyson, M 808-956-7927 135 J atanouye@hawaii.edu
TANSEY, Barbara 252-940-6201 360 B barbara.tansey@beaufortccc.edu
TANSLEY, Robert 203-596-4502 91 D btansley@post.edu
TANTILLO, Astrida, O 312-413-7329 161 F tantillo@uic.edu
TANTILLO, Richard 315-859-4668 327 A rtantillo@hamilton.edu
TANTILLO, Richard, C 315-859-4412 327 A rtantill@hamilton.edu
TANYEL, Faruk 864-503-5587 451 A ftanyel@uscupstate.edu
TANZER, Ken 415-703-9592 30 G ktanzer@cca.edu
TAORMINA, Melanie 570-321-4036 425 B taormina@lycoming.edu
TAPEDO, Burgess 785-830-2774 187 F btapedo@bie.edu
TAPHORN, Rick, J 423-775-7411 455 F brtaphorn6113@bryan.edu
TAPIA, Damaris 773-442-4205 154 H d-tapia1@neiu.edu
TAPIA, Luis, A 787-894-2828 558 F luis.tapia@upr.edu
TAPIA URZUA, Andres 412-291-6423 412 H atapia-urzua@aii.edu
TAPIAS, Maria 641-269-3028 178 I tapias@grinnell.edu
TAPLEY, Robyn 321-674-8050 103 R rtapley@fit.edu
TAPP, Paul 903-923-2042 473 I ptapp@etbu.edu
TAPP, Rita 903-785-7661 480 B rtapp@parisjc.edu
TAPPAN, Charlene 860-512-2912 89 D ctappan@manchestercc.edu
TAPPE, Diane 563-387-1045 180 M tappdi01@luther.edu
TAPPER, Janet 503-251-5757 410 I jtapper@uws.edu
TAPSCOTT, Michael, R 202-994-1463 95 D tapscott@gwu.edu
TARANTAL, Stephen 215-717-6388 437 H starantal@uarts.edu
TARANTELLI, Thomas, L 518-276-6234 339 D tarant@rpi.edu
TARANTO, Amanda, J 315-684-6000 347 A
TARANTO, John, A 816-501-3630 272 E john.taranto@avila.edu
TARBELL, Donald, R 843-661-1119 446 E dtarbell@fmarion.edu
TARBELL, Levi 641-673-1024 184 B tarbelll@wmpenn.edu
TARBOX, James 619-594-4379 35 E jtarbox@mail.sdsu.edu
TARBOX, Norm 801-626-6003 500 C ntarbox@weber.edu
TARBOX, Sandra 717-477-1131 431 F sltarbox@ship.edu
TARBY, Jay 216-397-1703 384 F tarby@jcu.edu
TARBY, Wendy 315-498-2742 337 F tarbyw@sunyocc.edu
TARCA, Fred, E 203-582-3429 91 E fred.tarca@quinnipiac.edu
TARENCE, Elaine, P 334-387-3877 1 E elainetarence@amridgeuniversity.edu
TARGETT, Nancy, M 302-831-2111 94 D ntargett@udel.edu
TARGONSKI, Conrad, A 608-796-3804 542 H catargonski@viterbo.edu
TARHINI, Kassim, M 860-444-8334 548 H Kassim.m.tarhini@uscg.mil
TARIN, Lucille, M 570-577-3661 413 E lucille.tarin@bucknell.edu
TARMAN, Christopher 619-644-7000 46 H christopher.tarman@gcccd.edu
TARNOWSKI, Jeff 706-864-1547 133 A jeff.tarnowski@ung.edu
TARNOWSKI, Jeffrey 678-891-2558 125 G Jeffrey.Tarnowski@gpc.edu
TARNOWSKI, Susan 507-389-7228 262 A susan.tarnowski@southcentral.edu
TARO, Thomas 680-488-2746 550 C tarothomas@yahoo.com
TAROLI, Stacie 570-558-1818 418 I staroli@fortisinstitute.edu
TARPEY, Andrea 413-755-4847 233 B tarpey@stcc.edu
TARPEY, Gerard 914-923-2804 337 I gtarpey@pace.edu
TARPLEE, Marc 803-327-8017 451 K mtarplee@yorktech.edu
TARPLEY, Douglas 562-903-5529 29 F doug.tarpley@biola.edu
TARPLEY, Sue 706-236-2292 121 E starpley@berry.edu
TARQUINO, Beth, A 716-250-7500 317 B batarquino@bryantstratton.edu
TARRANT, Carole 540-857-6281 517 E ctarrant@virginiawestern.edu
TARRANT, David, S 208-467-8528 138 H dtarrant@nnu.edu
TARRANT, Fredrick, A 770-720-9221 130 E fkt@reinhardt.edu
TARRANT, Kaneesha 213-763-7078 52 A tarrankk@lattc.edu

TAYLOR, Malcolm 256-726-7356 6 C mgtaylor@oakwood.edu
TAYLOR, Marcia 918-781-7271 396 F taylorm@bacone.edu
TAYLOR, Marcie, J 765-641-4495 164 B mjtaylor@anderson.edu
TAYLOR, Margaret 870-575-8733 24 D taylorm@uapb.edu
TAYLOR, Marilyn 520-621-3876 18 E taylorm@email.arizona.edu
TAYLOR, Marilyn, J 215-898-3425 437 I mjtaylor@design.upenn.edu
TAYLOR, Mark 740-420-5919 388 F mtaylor@ohiochristian.edu
TAYLOR, Mark 601-477-4029 268 A mark.taylor@jcjc.edu
TAYLOR, Martha, M 334-844-4438 1 G taylomm@auburn.edu
TAYLOR, Mary, A 334-683-5100 5 D
TAYLOR, Matthew, A 601-979-3950 267 H matthew.a.taylor@jsums.edu
TAYLOR, Maurice 443-885-4075 217 C maurice.taylor@morgan.edu
TAYLOR, Melanie 562-903-4800 29 F melanie.taylor@biola.edu
TAYLOR, Melinda 714-992-7001 56 F mtaylor1@fullcoll.edu
TAYLOR, Melody 843-574-6225 449 G melody.taylor@tridenttech.edu
TAYLOR, Mervin, V 340-693-1560 559 B mtaylor2@live.uvi.edu
TAYLOR, Mia 617-449-7428 237 E taylor@urbancollege.edu
TAYLOR, Michael 617-449-7037 237 E michael.taylor@urbancollege.edu
TAYLOR, Michael 253-589-6085 521 B michael.taylor@cptc.edu
TAYLOR, Michael, A 812-877-8145 172 C michael.a.taylor@rose-hulman.edu
TAYLOR, Michelle 918-495-6581 401 B mtaylor@oru.edu
TAYLOR, Michelle 215-635-7300 419 D mtaylor@gratz.edu
TAYLOR, Michelle, O 801-863-6158 500 B taylormo@uvu.edu
TAYLOR, Nancy 860-515-3863 88 B nataylor@charteroak.edu
TAYLOR, Nancy, K 716-375-2317 340 C nktaylor@sbu.edu
TAYLOR, Orlando 213-615-2700 38 G
TAYLOR, Orlando 805-898-4038 44 J otaylor@fielding.edu
TAYLOR, Pat 417-328-1500 282 D ptaylor@sbuniv.edu
TAYLOR, Patricia 734-677-5003 251 J ptaylor@wccnet.edu
TAYLOR, Patty, L 920-565-1032 536 Q taylorpl@lakeland.edu
TAYLOR, OSB, Paul 724-805-2527 435 B paul.taylor@email.stvincent.edu
TAYLOR, Quinton 225-922-2391 202 M qtaylor@lctcs.edu
TAYLOR, R 503-399-6566 404 L r.taylor@chemeketa.edu
TAYLOR, Renee 312-413-2411 161 F rtaylor@uic.edu
TAYLOR, Richard 513-529-7135 386 K taylorrt@miamioh.edu
TAYLOR, Richard, A 214-887-5316 473 E rtaylor@dts.edu
TAYLOR, Rickie 417-447-4802 280 C taylorrd@otc.edu
TAYLOR, Robbie 910-410-1705 365 B rltaylor@richmondcc.edu
TAYLOR, Robbin, M 270-745-4586 201 D robbin.taylor@wku.edu
TAYLOR, Robert 530-938-5512 41 E rtaylor18@siskiyous.edu
TAYLOR, Robert 712-722-6077 177 J robert.taylor@dordt.edu
TAYLOR, Robert 850-561-2644 114 D robert.taylor@famu.edu
TAYLOR, Robert 806-874-3571 470 J
TAYLOR, Robert, F 860-701-6194 548 H Robert.F.Taylor@uscg.mil
TAYLOR, Robert, F 860-701-6194 548 H robert.f.taylor@uscg.mil
TAYLOR, Rogers, L 417-255-7233 279 B rogerstaylor@missouristate.edu
TAYLOR, Ron 209-384-6101 54 C ron.taylor@mccd.edu
TAYLOR, Ronald, K 304-462-4132 532 G ronald.taylor@glenville.edu
TAYLOR, Russell 828-898-8770 358 F taylorrg@lmc.edu
TAYLOR, Sandi 909-748-8428 73 K sandi_taylor@redlands.edu
TAYLOR, Sharon 562-985-4162 33 F sharon.taylor@csulb.edu
TAYLOR, Shawn 863-638-7655 118 L shawn.taylor@warner.edu
TAYLOR, Sherri 256-215-4273 2 G staylor@cacc.edu
TAYLOR, Sherry 417-447-8801 280 C taylorst@otc.edu
TAYLOR, Spence 864-455-7992 450 G staylor@ghs.org
TAYLOR, Stacey 617-732-2800 233 E stacey.taylor@mcphs.edu
TAYLOR, Stan 214-648-7518 496 A stan.taylor@utsouthwestern.edu
TAYLOR, Stephanie 412-291-6200 412 H staylor@aii.edu
TAYLOR, Stephanie 704-637-4470 355 H sataylor@catawba.edu
TAYLOR, Stephanie 423-614-8600 457 M staylor@leeuniversity.edu
TAYLOR, Stephanie, A 270-824-1743 196 F stephanie.taylor@kctcs.edu
TAYLOR, Steve 662-325-0939 269 A steve.taylor@msstate.edu
TAYLOR, Steve 252-789-0225 363 H staylor@martincc.edu
TAYLOR, Steve, P 262-243-5700 535 I steve.taylor@cuw.edu
TAYLOR, Steven, T 303-963-3138 79 L staylor@ccu.edu
TAYLOR, Suzanne 806-742-2121 489 F suzanne.taylor@ttu.edu
TAYLOR, T. A 214-638-0484 476 Y tataylor@kdstudio.com
TAYLOR, Tammy 903-927-3300 497 G ttaylor@wileyc.edu
TAYLOR, Tamra 801-524-8140 498 J ttaylor@ldsbc.edu
TAYLOR, Tawny 918-631-2315 403 M tawny-taylor@utulsa.edu
TAYLOR, Terri 931-372-3554 462 A ttaylor@tntech.edu
TAYLOR, Terry 206-546-4589 526 G ttaylor@shoreline.edu
TAYLOR, Theresa 719-365-5087 86 C Theresa.Taylor@uchealth.org
TAYLOR, Thomas 205-391-2617 7 A ttaylor@sheltonstate.edu
TAYLOR, Thomas 978-934-3933 229 A thomas_taylor@uml.edu
TAYLOR, Thomas, T 937-327-7012 395 I ttaylor@wittenberg.edu
TAYLOR, Timothy 803-376-5766 443 D
TAYLOR, Timothy, L 248-232-4500 248 E tltaylor@oaklandcc.edu
TAYLOR, Todd 503-280-8535 405 E totaylor@cu-portland.edu
TAYLOR, Tracy 605-668-1518 452 I tracy.taylor@mtmc.edu
TAYLOR, Traki 301-860-3230 220 B
TAYLOR, Valerie, A 570-941-6344 438 F valerie.taylor@scranton.edu
TAYLOR, Verna 337-269-0620 201 F vernat@bluecliffcollege.com
TAYLOR, Vernon 540-442-0395 55 J vtaylor@nu.edu
TAYLOR, Vicki 870-230-5148 21 B taylorv@hsu.edu
TAYLOR, Virginia 585-345-6886 326 F vmtaylor@genesee.edu
TAYLOR, Vorley 740-366-9443 378 L taylor.1051@osu.edu
TAYLOR, JR., Walter, F 614-235-4136 392 D wtaylor@TLSohio.edu
TAYLOR, William, F 804-706-5016 515 G ftaylor@jtcc.edu
TAYLOR, William, R 626-395-3727 31 D bill.taylor@caltech.edu
TAYLOR, Yolanda, D 918-631-2327 403 M yolanda-taylor@utulsa.edu
TAYLOR-ALLEYNE, Dian 215-572-2932 412 F taylor-alleyne@arcadia.edu
TAYLOR-ARCHER, Mordean 502-852-6153 201 A motayl01@louisville.edu
TAYLOR-BENNS, Kimberly 484-365-7218 424 E ktaylorbenns@lincoln.edu
TAYLOR-BURCH, Linda, J 856-225-6039 307 A ltburch@camden.rutgers.edu
TAYLOR-COLBERT, Alice 864-427-9409 450 I aclobert@mailbox.sc.edu
TAYLOR DUPREE, Lesa 318-678-6000 203 A ltaylordupre@bpcc.edu
TAYLOR-DUPREE, Lesa 318-678-6000 203 A ltaylordupre@bpcc.edu
TAYLOR HEARD, Janice 216-987-5556 381 A janice.taylor-heard@tri-c.edu
TAYLOR HEARD, Janice 216-987-5125 381 A janice.taylorheard@tri-c.edu
TAYLOR LOTTY, Monica 302-831-0530 94 D mmtaylor@udel.edu
TAYLOR-MINNIEFIELD, Cherilyn, Y 803-536-8698 448 H ctaylo37@scsu.edu
TAYLOR-SAWYER, Sandra 575-769-4138 310 G sandra.sawyer@clovis.edu
TAYLOR-THOMPKINS, Isis 313-927-1552 246 D itaylor@marygrove.edu
TAYLOR-WATKINS, Jody 219-866-6187 172 E jwatkins@saintjoe.edu
TEACHMAN, Debra, K 304-896-7412 531 F debra.teachman@southernwv.edu
TEACHMAN, Stephanie 425-640-1713 522 D stephanie.teachman@edcc.edu
TEAFF, Brad 254-442-5034 470 I brad.teaff@cisco.edu
TEAFF, Tracy 254-501-5821 485 D tracy.teaff@tamuct.edu
TEAGLE, Natalie 336-334-7314 370 B ntteagle@ncat.edu
TEAGUE, Barbara 606-546-4151 200 E bteague@unionky.edu
TEAGUE, Brad 501-450-3150 25 F bteague@uca.edu
TEAGUE, Chad 864-941-8479 448 D teague.c@ptc.edu
TEAGUE, Clay 478-757-3544 122 E cteague@centralgatech.edu
TEAGUE, Donna, O 812-488-2212 173 H dt52@evansville.edu
TEAGUE, Pam 501-205-8923 20 G pteague@cbc.edu
TEAGUE, Peter, W 717-560-8278 423 C pteague@lbc.edu
TEAGUE, Rebecca 951-487-3072 55 A rteague@msjc.edu
TEAGUE, Sharyn, J 910-221-2224 357 A steague@gcd.edu
TEAGUE, Tracie 805-969-3626 57 J tteague@pacifica.edu
TEAGUE, Willard 417-862-9533 275 C wteague@globaluniversity.edu
TEAHEN, Rebecca, M 231-995-1855 248 C rteahen@nmc.edu
TEAHEN, Roberta 231-591-3532 242 L RobertaTeahen@ferris.edu
TEAKELL, Joe 254-298-8459 484 C joe.teakell@templejc.edu
TEAL, Holly 970-248-1898 80 B hteal@coloradomesa.edu
TEAL, Lysa, D 401-456-8221 442 A lteal@ric.edu
TEAL, P, J 919-515-2191 370 D pj_teal@ncsu.edu
TEAL, Rick 864-592-4618 449 C tealr@sccsc.edu
TEAL, Rita 803-536-7000 448 H
TEAL, Rita, J 803-516-4586 448 H rfjteal@scsu.edu
TEALER, Eddie 972-273-3390 473 A etealer@dcccd.edu
TEAT, Jonathan 214-333-5128 471 L jonathan@dbu.edu
TEBAY, John 714-992-7035 56 F jtebay@fullcoll.edu
TEBBE, Robert 618-235-2700 160 B robert.tebbe@swic.edu
TEDDER, Tracey, D 863-680-4177 104 F ttedder@flsouthern.edu
TEDESCHI, Lisa, F 603-526-3451 296 I ltedeschi@colby-sawyer.edu
TEDESCO, Jonathan 440-375-7352 385 B jtedesco@lec.edu
TEDESCO, Joseph, W 713-743-4207 491 D jtedesco@uh.edu
TEDESCO, Kenneth 504-398-2217 206 E ktedesco@olhcc.edu
TEDESCO, Lisa, A 404-727-2669 124 D lisa.tedesco@emory.edu
TEDJESKE, David 610-519-6979 439 A david.tedjeske@villanova.edu
TEDRIS, Marina 630-743-0681 163 D mtedris@westwood.edu
TEEHAN, Dyan 617-928-4780 234 D dteehan@mountida.edu
TEEL, Katrin 207-947-4591 209 G kteel@bealcollege.edu
TEERINK, Susan, M 414-288-1583 537 B susan.teerink@marquette.edu
TEETER, Alison 585-389-2818 334 B ateeter7@naz.edu
TEETER, Deborah, J 785-864-4412 191 G irdjt@ku.edu
TEETERS, Rebecca 617-585-1311 234 H rebecca.teeters@necmusic.edu
TEETS, Andrew 814-871-5856 419 A teets001@gannon.edu
TEETSEL, Craig, M 260-399-7700 174 C cteetsel@sf.edu
TEFFT, Nicole 303-556-2400 83 Q
TEGART, Doris, A 502-272-8208 193 E dtegart@bellarmine.edu
TEGEGNE, Yahana 630-873-3486 148 H ytegegne@ellis.edu
TEGERSTRAND, Julene, M 208-467-8338 138 H jtegerstrand@nnu.edu
TEICHERT, Scott 801-626-7670 500 C ScottTeichert@weber.edu
TEICHMAN, Carl, F 309-556-3429 148 A cteich@iwu.edu
TEICHMAN, Shlomo 516-225-4700 338 L teichman@mlb.edu
TEICHMILLER, Cheryl, A 920-923-7618 537 A cteichmiller@marianuniversity.edu
TEIG, Kathy 563-588-6385 176 F kathy.teig@clarke.edu
TEIGMAN, Eli 718-268-4700 339 B
TEIS, Lawrence, B 512-245-2114 489 C lt10@txstate.edu
TEITELBAUM, Aharon 845-783-0994 351 F
TEITELBAUM, Jeremy 860-486-2713 92 C jeremy.teitelbaum@uconn.edu
TEITLBAUM, Zalman 718-963-9770 351 C ed@utsny.edu
TEJADA, Adan 925-631-4052 61 G at11@stmarys-ca.edu
TEKELY, Angela 610-647-4400 421 B atekely@immaculata.edu
TELATOVICH, Andrew 941-359-4200 116 D
TELBERG, Tamara 845-758-7433 315 G telberg@bard.edu
TELFORD, Emily 630-617-6137 144 G emily.telford@elmhurst.edu
TELFORD, Rebecca, P 937-778-7809 381 K btelford@edisonohio.edu
TELLEEN, Jane, A 651-523-2202 256 B jtelleen@hamline.edu
TELLEI, Patrick, U 680-488-1669 550 C tellei@palau.edu
TELLER, Harlan 815-753-2253 154 I hteller@niu.edu
TELLER, Ryan 402-486-2538 293 D ryteller@ucollege.edu
TELLES, Nick 505-428-1161 313 A nick.telles@sfcc.edu
TELLES-IRVIN, Patricia 847-491-5360 155 D tellesirvin@northwestern.edu
TELLEZ, J. Carlos 574-372-5100 166 D tellezjc@grace.edu
TELLEZ, Laura 915-831-6359 473 J ltellez8@epcc.edu
TELLI, Suzette 615-297-7545 455 A tellis@aquinascollege.edu
TELLO, Steven 978-934-4240 229 A Steven_Tello@uml.edu
TEMKIN, Aron 802-485-2624 502 G atemkin@norwich.edu
TEMORES-VALDEZ, Sandra 619-594-3641 35 E stemores@mail.sdsu.edu
TEMPERA, Jeffrey, L 631-451-4506 348 E temperj@sunysuffolk.edu
TEMPLE, Glena 608-796-3081 542 H ggtemple@viterbo.edu
TEMPLE, Glena, G 608-796-3393 542 H ggtemple@viterbo.edu
TEMPLE, H. Thomas 954-262-1556 109 E htemple@nova.edu
TEMPLE, Jack 334-387-3877 1 E jacktemple@amridgeuniversity.edu
TEMPLE, James 661-362-3535 40 H james.temple@canyons.edu
TEMPLE, Lori 702-895-3628 295 G lorit@unlv.edu
TEMPLE, Tisha 512-863-1538 483 G templet@southwestern.edu
TEMPLE, Vicki 318-678-6000 203 A vtemple@bpcc.edu
TEMPLE KNEUVEAN, Shelley 816-604-1253 277 F shelley.kneuvean@mcckc.edu
TEMPLETON, Debra 828-328-7335 358 G debra.templeton@lr.edu
TEMPLETON, Heidi 660-785-4016 283 E heidi@truman.edu
TEMPLETON, Jenna 412-365-1694 415 C jtempleton@chatham.edu
TEMPLETON, Leslie 501-450-1320 21 C templeton@hendrix.edu
TEMPLETON, William 907-786-4005 10 H anwgt@uaa.alaska.edu

TEMPLETON-CORNELL, Vicki, L ... 315-267-2190 346 C
templevl@postdam.edu
TEMPLIN, Carl, R ... 435-586-5401 499 L
templin@suu.edu
TEN NAPEL, Karmen ... 712-274-5191 181 C
tennapel@morningside.edu
TENA, Lydia ... 915-831-8818 473 J
lpere121@epcc.edu
TENBERGEN, Klaus ... 209-588-5142.. 78 B
tenbergenk@yosemite.edu
TENCHER, Donald, E ... 401-456-8007 442 A
dtencher@ric.edu
TENCZAR, JR., Robert, C ... 773-298-3326 158 F
tenczar@sxu.edu
TENDALL, Michael, W .. 309-794-7357 139 K
michaeltendall@augustana.edu
TENDALL, Stephen ... 563-333-6423 182 E
TendallStephen@sau.edu
TENENBAUM, Elchonon 707-638-5507.. 70 B
rabbi@tu.edu
TENER, Brent, B ... 615-343-1422 465 H
b.tener@vanderbilt.edu
TENG, Anthony ... 949-582-4895.. 67 F
TENG, Emma ... 617-253-8844 233 C
TENGLIN, Ingrid, K ... 773-244-5601 154 G
itenglin@northpark.edu
TENIENTE-MATSON, Cynthia ... 559-278-2083.. 33 D
cmatson@csufresno.edu
TENIENTE-MATSON, Cynthia ... 210-784-1600 486 B
cmatson@tamusa.tamus.edu
TENN, Jennifer ... 815-280-2217 148 K
jtenn@jjc.edu
TENNANT, Leslie, A ... 724-480-3552 416 A
leslie.tennant@ccbc.edu
TENNANT, Otto ... 270-789-5034 194 D
otennant@campbellsville.edu
TENNANT, Sanda ... 425-249-4751 527 D
sandy.tennant@tlc.edu
TENNENT, Timothy, C .. 859-858-2202 192 O
TENNER, Jack ... 713-743-5671 491 D
jdtenner@central.uh.edu
TENNER, Katangela ... 601-877-6147 266 C
ksampson@alcorn.edu
TENNEY, David ... 713-348-8036 480 M
dtenney@rice.edu
TENNEY, Randall ... 304-473-8099 534 G
tenney_r@wvwc.edu
TENNEY, Sheila ... 404-756-4012 120 H
stenney@atlm.edu
TENNILL, William ... 217-245-3338 146 D
bill.tennill@mail.ic.edu
TENNY, Elissa ... 312-899-5133 158 J
etenny@saic.edu
TENNYSON, Pat ... 423-869-6286 458 B
ptennyson@lmunet.edu
TENSEN, Jan ... 973-300-2153 308 F
jtensen@sussex.edu
TENSUAN, Theresa ... 610-896-1268 420 J
ttensuan@haverford.edu
TENUTA, Bob ... 815-455-8585 152 B
btenuta@mchenry.edu
TEODORESCU, Daniel ... 770-720-9130 130 E
dt1@reinhardt.edu
TEODOSIO, Alex, J ... 216-397-1905 384 F
ateodosio@jcu.edu
TEPATTI, Eileen, G ... 217-786-2885 151 C
eileen.tepatti@llcc.edu
TEPE, Chabha ... 563-884-5442 182 D
chabha.tepe@palmer.edu
TEPPER, Steven, J ... 480-965-8561.. 11 J
steven.tepper@asu.edu
TER HORST, Dan ... 760-480-8474.. 76 J
dterhorst@wscal.edu
TER MOLEN, Matthew .. 315-443-3579 349 E
termolen@syr.edu
TERAGAWACHI, Lori ... 808-984-3406 136 H
loritera@hawaii.edu
TEREBESSY, Hilarie ... 312-942-3013 158 A
hilarie_terebessy@rush.edu
TERELL, Beth ... 267-341-3208 420 K
bterell@holyfamily.edu
TERENZIO, Marion ... 518-255-5111 346 E
terenzma@cobleskill.edu
TERESA, Daniel ... 831-755-6840.. 46 J
dteresa@hartnell.edu
TERHAAR, Jody, L ... 320-363-5601 254 J
jterhaar@csbsju.edu
TERHUNE, James, S ... 207-859-4780 210 A
jterhune@colby.edu
TERKLA, David ... 617-287-6500 228 G
david.terkla@umb.edu
TERKLA, Dawn, G ... 617-627-3274 237 C
dawn.terkla@tufts.edu
TERMOTT, Kenneth ... 732-247-5241 304 B
ktermott@nbts.edu
TERMUHLEN, Paula ... 218-726-7572 264 G
ptermuhl@d.umn.edu
TERNAM, Tracey ... 303-937-4253.. 80 A
tternam@chu.edu
TERNES, Jerry ... 714-556-3610.. 75 A
jternes@vanguard.edu
TERNES, Roger ... 715-425-3246 540 E
roger.ternes@uwrf.edu
TERP, Cheryl ... 920-693-1134 543 B
cheryl.terp@gotoltc.edu
TERP, Douglas, C ... 207-859-4770 210 A
dcterp@colby.edu
TERP, Jeff ... 317-921-4225 169 L
jterp@ivytech.edu
TERPACK, Sallie, A ... 814-732-1024 430 G
terpack@edinboro.edu
TERPENNING, Linda ... 303-373-2008.. 85 I
lterpenning@rvu.edu
TERPENNING, Marlene, K ... 740-284-5179 382 G
mterpenning@franciscan.edu
TERPSTRA, Joylita ... 423-478-7707 460 C
jterpstra@ptseminary.edu
TERRANCE, Teah, M ... 585-385-8411 340 F
tterrance@sjfc.edu
TERRASI, Robert ... 340-693-1353 559 B
rterras@uvi.edu
TERRELL, Ashley ... 513-244-4979 387 A
ashley.terrell@msj.edu
TERRELL, Bill ... 915-532-3737 497 D
bterrell@westerntech.edu
TERRELL, Carleen ... 336-249-8186 362 B
carleen_terrell@davidsonccc.edu
TERRELL, Charles ... 304-434-8001 531 B
charles.terrell@easternwv.edu
TERRELL, Gaither, M ... 336-316-2143 357 C
gterrell@guilford.edu
TERRELL, Joyce ... 404-270-5717 132 D
jlterrell@spelman.edu
TERRELL, Mark ... 814-866-6641 423 B
mterrell@lecom.edu
TERRELL, Patricia ... 208-282-2315 138 C
terrpatr@isu.edu
TERRELL, Sherri, I ... 915-747-5302 494 B
siterrell@utep.edu
TERRELL-POWELL, Yvonne, L ... 206-546-4509 526 G
yterrell@shoreline.edu
TERRIO, Dan, M ... 509-527-4981 528 F
terrio@whitman.edu
TERRONEZ, Randy ... 515-244-4221 175 C
terronezr@aib.edu
TERRY, Bryan, J ... 336-334-5000 371 C
bjterry@uncg.edu
TERRY, Carol, S ... 401-454-6278 442 B
cterry@risd.edu
TERRY, Chihoko ... 910-410-1821 365 B
ckterry@richmondcc.edu
TERRY, Denise ... 574-372-5100 166 D
Denise.Terry@grace.edu
TERRY, Edward ... 828-726-2202 360 F
eterry@cccti.edu
TERRY, Heidi, L ... 330-325-6479 387 F
hterry@neomed.edu
TERRY, James, E ... 304-696-2486 532 H
terry@marshall.edu
TERRY, Justyn ... 724-266-3838 437 G
jterry@tsm.edu
TERRY, Laura, C ... 423-439-4210 461 D
terryl@etsu.edu
TERRY, LeRodrick ... 480-517-8105.. 15 D
Lerodrick.terry@riosalado.edu
TERRY, Martin, L ... 419-434-4521 393 F
terry@findlay.edu
TERRY, Mike ... 217-641-4529 148 J
mterry@jwcc.edu
TERRY, Missy, D ... 503-554-2101 406 A
terrym@georgefox.edu
TERRY, Neil, W ... 806-651-2530 486 D
nterry@mail.wtamu.edu
TERRY, Penelope ... 718-951-5924 318 F
pterry@brooklyn.cuny.edu
TERRY, Robert ... 602-386-4127.. 11 F
bob.terry@arizonachristian.edu
TERRY, Rondale ... 510-567-6174.. 69 D
rterry@sum.edu
TERRY, Scott ... 304-357-4363 530 H
scottterry@ucwv.edu
TERRY, Steven ... 804-330-0111 506 D
careercrim@centura.edu
TERRY, Susan ... 206-543-0535 527 G
nahe@uw.edu
TERRY, Teri ... 205-348-0609.... 8 E
teri.terry@ua.edu
TERRY, Tina ... 606-886-3863 195 I
tterry0025@kctcs.edu
TERRY, Troy, M ... 864-294-2213 446 F
troy.terry@furman.edu
TERRY, Willa ... 662-252-2491 270 C
wterry@rustcollege.edu
TERVALA, Debra ... 505-473-6292 313 B
debra.tervala@santafeuniversity.edu
TERWILLIGER, Linda ... 845-451-1342 323 E
l_terwil@culinary.edu
TESCHNER, Pam ... 503-375-7180 405 F
pteschner@corban.edu
TESFAGIORGIS, Gebre, H ... 515-294-1181 175 G
gebretes@iastate.edu
TESFAMARIAM, Biniam . 574-520-4104 168 F
biktesfa@iusb.edu
TESH, J. Michael ... 210-567-2590 495 B
tesh@uthscsa.edu
TESH, Vernon, L ... 979-862-4113 485 C
vltesh@tamu.edu
TESKE, Paul ... 303-315-2805.. 86 G
paul.teske@ucdenver.edu
TESKE, Yolanda, K ... 252-334-2029 359 D
yolanda.teske@macuniversity.edu
TESKEY, Michael, J ... 503-777-7593 409 E
michael.teskey@reed.edu
TESLUK, Paul, E ... 716-645-3221 343 E
ptesluk@buffalo.edu
TESORIERE, Joseph, P . 518-564-4601 346 B
tesorijp@plattsburgh.edu
TESS, Dan, E ... 570-484-2238 431 C
dtess@lhup.edu
TESS, Paul, A ... 507-354-8221 257 A
tesspa@mlc-wels.edu
TESSIER, Dorita ... 509-527-2646 528 A
dorita.tessier@wallawalla.edu
TESSIER, Michael, A ... 812-488-2956 173 H
mt28@evansville.edu
TESSIER-LAVIGNE, Marc ... 212-327-8080 339 H
marctl@rockefeller.edu
TESSLER, Faith ... 310-824-1586.. 25 K
TESSMAN, Brock ... 406-243-2541 287 D
brock.tessman@umontana.edu
TESSMANN, Cary, A ... 262-691-5214 544 D
ctessmann@wctc.edu
TESTA, Noelle ... 785-242-5200 190 D
noelle.testa@ottawa.edu
TESTA, Phil ... 607-778-5575 344 F
testapf@sunybroome.edu
TESTANI, Joe ... 585-275-2366 351 D
j.testani@rochester.edu
TESTI, Andrea ... 541-881-5761 410 D
atesti@tvcc.cc
TESTY, Kellye, Y ... 206-543-2586 527 G
lawdean@uw.edu
TETEN, Dixie ... 402-872-2226 292 C
dteten@peru.edu
TETERS, Charlene ... 505-424-2354 310 L
cteters@iaia.edu
TETI, Polly ... 215-242-7777 415 D
tetip@chc.edu
TETLOW, Tania ... 504-865-5261 207 F
ttetlow@tulane.edu
TETRAULT, Martha, R ... 413-597-2681 238 E
martha.r.tetrault@williams.edu
TETREAU, Jerry, C ... 480-245-7944.. 14 D
jerry.tetreau@ibcs.edu
TETREAU, Jerry, C ... 480-245-7969.. 14 D
jerry.tetreau@ibcs.edu
TETREAULT, Jules ... 203-392-5556.. 88 F
tetreaultj4@southernct.edu
TETREAULT, Patricia, L . 570-941-7767 438 F
patricia.tetreault@scranton.edu
TETRICK, Julie ... 801-818-8900 498 P
julia.tetrick@provocollege.edu
TETZLOFF, Jason ... 989-275-5000 245 C
jason.tetzloff@kirtland.edu
TETZLOFF, Lisa ... 920-465-2200 539 F
tetzlofl@uwgb.edu
TEURNER, Mary ... 660-596-7249 282 H
mteurner@sfccmo.edu
TEUTSCH, David ... 215-576-0800 433 I
dteutsch@rrc.edu
TEW, Mark ... 325-649-8002 475 F
mtew@hputx.edu
TEWKSBURY, Greg ... 810-762-3324 251 E
gtewks@umflint.edu
TEWS, Anne ... 269-927-8117 245 E
tews@lakemichigancollege.edu
TEXIDOR, Migdalia ... 787-250-1912 554 A
mtexidor@metro.inter.edu
TEXTOR, Laurie ... 920-424-1037 540 B
textorl@uwosh.edu
TEYMOURTASH, Janet, L ... 415-422-5898.. 74 C
janet@usfca.edu
TEZENO, Albert ... 225-216-8256 202 N
tezenoa@mybrcc.edu
TEZUKA, Hiroko ... 574-239-8341 167 C
htezuka@hcc-nd.edu
THACKER, Allison ... 713-348-4818 480 M
invest@rice.edu
THACKER, Karen, S ... 610-796-8306 412 C
karen.thacker@alvernia.edu
THACKER, Linda ... 314-529-9308 277 B
lthacker@maryville.edu
THADANI, Indra ... 510-464-3516.. 59 B
ithadani@peralta.edu
THADEN, Mark ... 540-654-2160 513 I
mthad2zw@umw.edu
THAMES, Brenda ... 209-575-6058.. 78 C
thamesb@mjc.edu
THAMES, James, H ... 214-887-5013 473 E
jthames@dts.edu
THAMES, Jamie ... 478-757-4024 134 E
jthames@wesleyancollege.edu
THAMES, Kathleen, A ... 337-482-6397 208 F
kat@louisiana.edu
THAO, Maisee ... 805-898-2927.. 44 J
mthao@fielding.edu
THAO, PaHnia ... 715-675-3331 544 A
ThaoP@ntc.edu
THARP, Brent ... 912-478-5444 126 B
btharp@georgiasouthern.edu
THARP, Carla ... 201-761-7360 307 K
ctharp@saintpeters.edu
THARP, Karen ... 931-598-1270 460 I
kmtharp@sewanee.edu
THARP, Katie ... 563-588-4990 180 L
katie.tharp@loras.edu
THARP, Michael ... 570-662-4831 431 D
mtharp@mansfield.edu
THARPE, Barbara ... 615-327-6827 458 F
btharpe@mmc.edu
THARPE, Brad ... 909-621-8519.. 59 F
Brad_Tharpe@pitzer.edu
THARRINGTON, Sally ... 434-949-1061 516 H
sally.tharrington@southside.edu
THATCHER, Derek ... 740-366-9453 378 L
dthatche@cotc.edu
THATCHER, Patricia ... 215-951-2730 432 F
thatcherp@philau.edu
THATCHER, Paula ... 503-352-1556 408 I
thatchep@pacificu.edu
THATCHER, Tom ... 513-244-8172 379 I
tom.thatcher@ccuniversity.edu
THAXTON, Deron ... 318-473-6574 205 A
dthaxton@lsua.edu
THAXTON, Deron ... 318-473-6409 205 A
dthaxton@lsua.edu
THAXTON, Gail ... 706-754-7701 129 B
gthaxton@northgatech.edu
THAXTON, Gail ... 706-355-5110 120 G
gthaxton@athenstech.edu
THAYER, Mary Ann ... 810-766-2057 239 H
maryann.thayer@baker.edu
THAYER, Scott ... 619-660-4301.. 46 G
scott.thayer@gcccd.edu
THAYER, Scott ... 304-829-7138 529 H
sthayer@bethanywv.edu
THAYER, Tammy ... 608-246-6451 543 C
tthayer2@madisoncollege.edu
THAYNE, Lewis, E ... 717-867-6211 423 I
thayne@lvc.edu
THE, James ... 817-202-6719 483 C
jthe@swau.edu
THEEUWES, Jim ... 251-580-2154.... 5 A
jim.theeuwes@faulknerstate.edu
THEIMER, Donna ... 970-824-1111.. 80 L
donna.theimer@cncc.edu
THEINERT, Amber ... 405-878-5171 402 A
adtheinert@stgregorys.edu
THEIS, Ann ... 567-661-7270 390 D
ann_theis@owens.edu
THEIS, Cindy ... 612-874-3777 257 D
ctheis@mcad.edu
THEIS, Lori, C ... 318-257-2238 208 A
ltheis@latech.edu
THEISEN, Darlene, A ... 814-871-7609 419 A
theisen001@gannon.edu
THEISEN, Jason ... 320-308-6012 261 F
jtheisen@sctcc.edu
THEISS, Danielle ... 913-758-6111 191 I
danielle.theiss@stmary.edu
THELANDER, Laura ... 651-641-3216 256 J
lthelander001@luthersem.edu
THELEN, Cindy ... 715-675-3331 544 A
Thelen@ntc.edu
THELEN, Craig ... 616-395-7833 244 A
thelen@hope.edu
THELEN, James, B ... 207-621-3452 212 B
university.counsel@maine.edu
THELLMAN, Wendy ... 678-717-3845 133 A
wendy.thellman@ung.edu
THEMISTOCLEOUS, Ann-Margaret, J ... 864-231-2185 443 E
athemistocleous@andersonuniversity.edu
THEOBALD, Brent ... 714-556-3610.. 75 A
brent.theobald@vanguard.edu
THEOBALD, Michael, J . 816-501-4061 281 B
mike.theobald@rockhurst.edu
THEOBALD, Neil, D ... 215-204-7405 436 C
president@temple.edu
THEOBALD, Paul ... 712-749-2277 176 D
theobaldp@bvu.edu

THEODORA, Dawn, S ... 805-756-5529.. 32 E theodora@calpoly.edu
THEODORE, Renelle ...... 570-586-2400 435 H rTheodore@summitu.edu
THEODORE, Steve .... 254-295-4500 492 C stheodore@umhb.edu
THEODOROPOULOS, Christine .... 805-756-1414.. 32 E ctheodor@calpoly.edu
THEODOSIOU, Constantine .... 718-862-7948 331 H constantine.theodosiou@manhattan.edu
THEODOULOU, Stella, Z .... 818-677-3317.. 34 D stella.theodoulou@csun.edu
THEONUGRAHA, Feliy .. 847-317-4062 161 B ftheonug@tiu.edu
THEORET, Julie .... 802-635-1333 504 A julie.theoret@jsc.edu
THERIAULT, Monique ... 206-726-5013 521 G mtheriault@cornish.edu
THERIEAU, Kelly, M ..... 802-258-3359 502 I kelly.therieau@worldlearning.org
THERIOT, Clifton .... 985-448-4621 208 C clifton.theriot@nicholls.edu
THERIOT, Lisa, M .... 214-860-2247 472 F ltheriot@dcccd.edu
THERMER, Clifford .... 860-913-2058.. 90 F cthermer@goodwin.edu
THEROUX, Robert, R .... 401-739-5000 441 E btheroux@neit.edu
THERRIEN, Michael ...... 603-271-6484 297 C mtherrien@ccsnh.edu
THESENVITZ, Michael, D .... 918-631-2583 403M michael-thesenvitz@utulsa.edu
THESING-RITTER, Jodi, M .... 715-836-2325 539 E thesinjm@uwec.edu
THEULE, Ryan .... 661-362-5930.. 40 H ryan.theule@canyons.edu
THEULEN, Michael .... 413-782-1377 238 A michael.theulen@wne.edu
THIBADEAU, Suzette ..... 920-424-0200 540 B thibadea@uwosh.edu
THIBEAULT, Alan .... 207-602-2253 213 B athibeault@une.edu
THIBEAULT, Dennis ...... 617-333-2158 225 F dthibeau@curry.edu
THIBEAULT, Nancy .... 937-512-2926 391 D nancy.thibeault@sinclair.edu
THIBEDEAU, Dawn .... 414-277-7126 537 G thibedeau@msoe.edu
THIBODEAU, Jim .... 402-457-2428 291 E jrthibodeau@mccneb.edu
THIBODEAU, John .... 262-564-3050 543 A thibodeauj@gtc.edu
THIBODEAU, Marianne . 207-255-1254 212 G mthibod@maine.edu
THIBODEAU, Wayne, J . 248-370-4240 248 K thibodea@oakland.edu
THIBODEAUX, Chad ..... 337-475-5524 208 B cthibodeaux@mcneese.edu
THIBODEAUX, Corrie ... 903-988-7517 477 A cthibodeaux@kilgore.edu
THIBOUTOT, Paul .... 507-222-4190 254 D pthibout@carleton.edu
THIE, Susan .... 605-331-6592 454 E susan.thie@usiouxfalls.edu
THIEHOFF, Jack, O .... 972-860-8365 472 E JThiehoff@dcccd.edu
THIEL, Becky .... 740-351-3017 391 C bthiel@shawnee.edu
THIEL, Chuck .... 810-762-5003 247 F chuck.thiel@mcc.edu
THIEL, OSF, Janet .... 610-358-4219 427 D thielj@neumann.edu
THIEL, John, E .... 203-254-4000.. 90 E jthiel@fairfield.edu
THIELE, Dianna .... 206-878-3710 523 D dthiele@highline.edu
THIELE, Dwain, L ...... 214-648-8711 496 A dwain.thiele@utsouthwestern.edu
THIELE, Nicholas ...... 573-276-4577 282 C njthiele@semo.edu
THIELEMANN, Heather .. 936-294-1345 489 A thielemann@shsu.edu
THIELEMIER, Brad .... 573-840-9077 283 D bthielemier@trcc.edu
THIEME, Sacha .... 812-855-9770 167 J sthieme@indiana.edu
THIEMENS, Mark, H ..... 858-534-6882.. 72 B mthiemens@ucsd.edu
THIERFELDER, William, K .... 704-461-6726 354 J billthierfelder@bac.edu
THIERSTEIN, Joel .... 513-244-4232 387 A president@msj.edu
THIES, Jeannie .... 636-949-4689 276 L jthies@lindenwood.edu
THIESEN, Lynn .... 707-476-4187.. 41 C lynn-thiesen@redwoods.edu
THIESFELDT, Steven, R . 507-354-8221 257 A thiesfsr@mlc-wels.edu
THIESSEN, Melissa .... 509-527-4675 527 H melissa.thiessen@wwcc.edu
THIGPEN, Buck .... 912-287-5813 123 A bthigpen@coastalpines.edu
THIGPEN, Paula, M ...... 410-864-3605 218 C pthigpen@stmarys.edu
THILL, Jesse .... 501-450-3130.. 25 F jthill@uca.edu
THILL, Robert .... 212-353-4348 323 B thill@cooper.edu
THILLMAN, Peter .... 920-693-1119 543 B peter.thillman@gotoltc.edu
THIMMESCH, Timothy .. 616-331-3845 243 E thimmest@gvsu.edu
THIROLF, Katherine ...... 734-477-8933 251 J kthirolf@wccnet.edu
THIRSK, William, T ...... 845-575-3000 331 L william.thirsk@marist.edu
THIS, Craig .... 937-775-4296 396 A craig.this@wright.edu
THISS, Ramona, H .... 540-985-9828 509 D rhthiss@jchs.edu
THISSEN, Sally, L .... 863-680-4127 104 F sthissen@flsouthern.edu
THISTLE, Dawn, M .... 508-767-7095 222 D dthistle@assumption.edu
THISTLETHWAITE, Polly 212-817-7060 319 B pthistlethwaite@gc.cuny.edu
THIVIERGE, Michelle .... 518-861-2536 331 K mthivierge@mariacollege.edu
THOBABEN, James .... 859-858-2369 192 O
THODE, Arnold .... 563-441-4131 178 D athode@eicc.edu
THOENNES, Karla .... 715-425-4555 540 E karla.thoennes@uwrf.edu
THOLEN, Robin .... 937-393-3431 391 F rtholen@sscc.edu
THOMAN, Richard, C ... 651-631-5100 265 D rcthoman@unwsp.edu
THOMAS, Adam .... 334-214-4880.... 2 H adam.thomas@cv.edu
THOMAS, Alan .... 615-898-2542 461 E alan.thomas@mtsu.edu
THOMAS, Alvetta, P ...... 404-225-4601 120 I athomas@atlantatech.edu
THOMAS, Amanda .... 410-617-5590 216 D athomas@loyola.edu
THOMAS, Amy .... 614-251-4690 388 H thomasa3@ohiodominican.edu
THOMAS, Andrine .... 212-616-7253 327 D andrine.thomas@helenefuld.edu
THOMAS, Angela .... 409-880-8878 488 F angela.thomas@lamar.edu
THOMAS, Anice .... 973-353-5805 307 C anice.thomas@rutgers.edu
THOMAS, Anita, J .... 317-788-6126 173 I ajthomas@uindy.edu
THOMAS, Anne .... 479-788-7033.. 23 H anne.thomas@uafs.edu
THOMAS, Anne, C .... 317-788-3543 173 I athomas@uindy.edu
THOMAS, Auden .... 518-580-5590 342 I athomas@skidmore.edu
THOMAS, Barbara .... 903-785-7661 480 B bthomas@parisjc.edu
THOMAS, Barbara, J ..... 415-422-6352.. 74 C thomasb@admin.usfca.edu
THOMAS, Becky .... 949-451-5484.. 67 E bthomas@ivc.edu
THOMAS, Bill .... 425-739-8164 523 I bill.thomas@lwtech.edu
THOMAS, Billy, R .... 501-296-1397.. 24 B BillyRThomas@uams.edu
THOMAS, Bonnie .... 443-334-2260 218 E blthomas@stevenson.edu
THOMAS, Brad .... 425-640-1884 522 D brad.thomas@edcc.edu
THOMAS, Brenna .... 503-493-6456 405 E bthomas@cu-portland.edu
THOMAS, Brent .... 828-898-8777 358 F thomasb@lmc.edu
THOMAS, Bridgett .... 217-732-3155 150 H bthomas@lincolncollege.edu
THOMAS, Carei .... 212-220-8085 318 D cthomas@bmcc.edu
THOMAS, Carl .... 541-885-1151 408 E carl.thomas@oit.edu
THOMAS, Carlos .... 225-771-6247 207 A carlos_thomas@subr.edu
THOMAS, Carol .... 626-914-8592.. 38 L cthomas@citruscollege.edu
THOMAS, Carol .... 614-287-2780 380 G cthoma13@cscc.edu
THOMAS, Carol .... 614-508-7233 383 L cthomas@hondros.edu
THOMAS, Carolyn .... 530-752-6068.. 71 A ccthomas@ucdavis.edu
THOMAS, Carolyn, D .... 504-520-7364 209 E cthomas@xula.edu
THOMAS, Carrie .... 603-526-3686 296 I cathomas@colby-sawyer.edu
THOMAS, Charles .... 248-341-2305 248 E ccthomas@oaklandcc.edu
THOMAS, JR., Charles, E .... 404-527-7711 127 H cthomas@itc.edu
THOMAS, Christine .... 916-691-7333.. 52 J thomasc@crc.losrios.edu
THOMAS, Christine, C .. 334-229-4327.... 1 D ccthomas@alasu.edu
THOMAS, Christine, L .. 715-346-4617 541 A cthomas@uwsp.edu
THOMAS, Christopher .. 337-475-5607 208 B thomas@mcneese.edu
THOMAS, Clancy .... 229-430-0548 119 H clancy.thomas@asurams.edu
THOMAS, Claudine .... 215-568-4012 426 G cthomas@moore.edu
THOMAS, Clyde, G .... 503-554-2013 406 A cthomas@georgefox.edu
THOMAS, Corlisse .... 201-216-3610 308 D corlisse.Thomas@stevens.edu
THOMAS, Daphne, J ..... 901-435-1539 457 N daphne_thomas@loc.edu
THOMAS, David .... 509-527-2194 528 A dave.thomas@wallawalla.edu
THOMAS, David, A .... 202-687-3883.. 95 E dat42@georgetown.edu
THOMAS, David, E .... 215-751-8000 416 B dthomas@ccp.edu
THOMAS, Debbie .... 860-906-5010.. 89 A dthomas@ccc.commnet.edu
THOMAS, Debera .... 928-523-2656.. 16 C Debera.Thomas@nau.edu
THOMAS, Deborah .... 502-776-1443 199 C dthomas@simmonscollegeky.edu
THOMAS, Deborah .... 402-559-5245 293 I thomasd@unmc.edu
THOMAS, Deborah .... 402-559-6301 293 I thomasd@unmc.edu
THOMAS, Dene Kay ...... 970-247-7100.. 82 I thomas_d@fortlewis.edu
THOMAS, Denee .... 361-570-4149 492 A thomasd@uhv.edu
THOMAS, Denita .... 601-635-2111 267 B dthomas@eccc.edu
THOMAS, Domani .... 718-368-5696 320 A dthomas@kbcc.cuny.edu
THOMAS, Donna .... 301-369-2800 214 A dgthomas@captechu.edu
THOMAS, Dorian .... 773-291-6384 142 B dthomas236@ccc.edu
THOMAS, Doug .... 978-665-4095 229 D dthoma27@fitchburgstate.edu
THOMAS, Downing .... 319-335-0370 175 H downing-thomas@uiowa.edu
THOMAS, III, E. Nathan .... 785-864-4932 191 G nathomas@ku.edu
THOMAS, Eddie, B .... 205-366-8848.... 7 G ebthomas@stillman.edu
THOMAS, Elizabeth .... 910-695-4971 365 H thomase@sandhills.edu
THOMAS, Fitzroy .... 301-891-4115 221 C fthomas@wau.edu
THOMAS, Flecia .... 815-479-7620 152 B fthomas@mchenry.edu
THOMAS, Fredel .... 605-995-2652 452 C frthomas@dwu.edu
THOMAS, Frederick, A .. 207-768-9580 212 H frederick.thomas@umpi.edu
THOMAS, Gayla .... 509-359-6874 522 C gthomas@ewu.edu
THOMAS, Glen .... 617-731-7107 235 F gthomas@pmc.edu
THOMAS, Gregory, A .... 708-709-3501 156 A gthomas2@prairiestate.edu
THOMAS, Helen .... 912-538-3126 132 A hthomas@southeasterntech.edu
THOMAS, Huw, F .... 617-636-6636 237 C huw.thomas@tufts.edu
THOMAS, Isaiah .... 610-957-6113 436 A ithomas1@swarthmore.edu
THOMAS, J. Matthew ... 770-534-6174 121 G mthomas@brenau.edu
THOMAS, Jack .... 309-298-1824 163 A j-thomas2@wiu.edu
THOMAS, James .... 269-387-8785 252 I jim.thomas@wmich.edu
THOMAS, James .... 910-296-1974 363 E jthomas@jamessprunt.edu
THOMAS, Jane .... 410-827-5802 214 D jthomas@chesapeake.edu
THOMAS, Janell, D .... 701-355-8244 375 K jdthomas@umary.edu
THOMAS, Janette, B ..... 607-587-4122 347 D thomasj@alfredstate.edu
THOMAS, Jeanne .... 954-763-9840.. 98 L library@atom.edu
THOMAS, Jeremy .... 979-209-7214 469 F jeremy.thomas@blinn.edu
THOMAS, Jerry, R .... 940-565-2231 492 D jerry.thomas@unt.edu
THOMAS, Jessica .... 361-593-2174 486 A jessica.thomas@tamuk.edu
THOMAS, Jim .... 209-468-4807.. 69 G jthomas@sjcoe.net
THOMAS, Jim .... 615-966-5828 458 C jim.thomas@lipscomb.edu
THOMAS, Joan .... 413-755-4817 233 B jthomas@stcc.edu
THOMAS, Joan .... 715-232-1181 541 B thomasj@uwstout.edu
THOMAS, Joe .... 541-888-7399 410 A jthomas@socc.edu
THOMAS, John .... 951-785-2064.. 49 I jthomas@lasierra.edu
THOMAS, John .... 661-255-1050.. 31 B
THOMAS, JR., John ..... 918-270-6455 401 C john.thomas@ptstulsa.edu
THOMAS, John, L .... 863-680-6215 104 F jthomas@flsouthern.edu
THOMAS, Joseph .... 317-788-6179 173 I jodthomas@uindy.edu
THOMAS, Joseph .... 212-752-1530 330 C joseph.thomas@limcollege.edu
THOMAS, Joseph .... 803-536-7033 448 H jthomas@scsu.edu
THOMAS, Joseph, M ..... 610-921-7643 411 E jthomas@albright.edu
THOMAS, Julia, M .... 585-385-8015 340 F jthomas@sjfc.edu
THOMAS, Julie .... 319-296-4275 179 B julie.thomas@hawkeyecollege.edu
THOMAS, Julie, B .... 252-823-5166 362 D thomasj@edgecombe.edu
THOMAS, K. B .... 318-487-7389 202 L kb.thomas@lacollege.edu
THOMAS, Kanet .... 310-506-4264.. 58 H kanet.thomas@pepperdine.edu
THOMAS, Karen .... 706-649-1854 123 E
THOMAS, Karla .... 773-298-3937 158 F kthomas@sxu.edu
THOMAS, Kathryn, S .... 706-355-5116 120 G kthomas@athenstech.edu
THOMAS, Kay .... 601-484-8689 268 B kthomas@meridiancc.edu
THOMAS, Kay, M .... 252-398-6226 356 B thomak@chowan.edu
THOMAS, Kelvin .... 973-803-5000 305 A kthomas@pillar.edu
THOMAS, Kenneth .... 334-229-4200.... 1 D kthomas@alasu.edu
THOMAS, Laurita, E ...... 734-647-5574 251 C laurita@umich.edu
THOMAS, LaVona .... 818-401-1031.. 41 F lthomas@columbiacollege.edu
THOMAS, Letrell .... 912-871-1624 129 E lthomas@ogeecheetech.edu
THOMAS, Linda .... 309-772-2177 140 I lthomas@sadnburg.edu
THOMAS, Linda .... 340-693-1324 559 B lthomas2@live.uvi.edu
THOMAS, Lisa .... 651-905-3490 264 E lthomas@browncollege.edu
THOMAS, Lyn .... 765-983-1211 165 H thomaly@earlham.edu
THOMAS, Marcia, R ..... 312-460-0600 139 G mthomas@aaart.edu
THOMAS, Maria .... 601-977-7769 270 F mthomas@tougaloo.edu
THOMAS, Marjorie .... 757-221-2510 506 J mthomas@wm.edu
THOMAS, Mark .... 863-638-2345 118 L mark.thomas@warner.edu
THOMAS, Mark .... 608-246-6301 543 C mthomasjr@madisoncollege.edu
THOMAS, Mary Beth ... 617-735-9766 226 B thomasmb@emmanuel.edu
THOMAS, Matthew, D ... 507-933-7510 256 A mthomas@gustavus.edu
THOMAS, Maurice .... 856-691-8600 301 H mthomas@cccnj.edu
THOMAS, Melissa .... 503-554-2214 406 A mthomas@georgefox.edu
THOMAS, Melissa, M ... 843-953-5635 445 B thomasmm1@cofc.edu
THOMAS, Michael .... 601-979-3060 267 H michael.thomas@jsums.edu
THOMAS, Michael .... 610-225-5073 418 A mthoma11@eastern.edu
THOMAS, Michael .... 618-985-3741 146 F thomasm@iecc.edu
THOMAS, Michael, A .... 706-880-8911 127 N mathomas@lagrange.edu
THOMAS, Michael, J .... 217-333-3631 162 A mthomas@illinois.edu

THOMPSON, Kirsten ..... 617-951-2350 234 F
kirsten.thompson@necb.edu
THOMPSON, Larry, R ... 941-359-7601 111 F
lthompson@ringling.edu
THOMPSON, Lenora, H 757-683-4401 510 I
lthompso@odu.edu
THOMPSON, Leroy .... 918-360-9694 396 F
thompsol@bacone.edu
THOMPSON, Lisa .... 425-640-1148 522 D
lthompson@edcc.edu
THOMPSON, Lonnie ..... 386-506-3824 101 I
thompsl@DaytonaState.edu
THOMPSON, Lori .... 304-473-8090 534 G
thompson_l@wvwc.edu
THOMPSON, Lynda .... 508-588-9100 232 A
THOMPSON, Lynn .... 386-481-2216.. 99 F
thompsol@cookman.edu
THOMPSON, Marc .... 706-821-8283 129 H
mthompson@paine.edu
THOMPSON, Marcy ...... 847-214-7486 144 F
mthompson@elgin.edu
THOMPSON, Maria .... 410-951-3838 220 C
THOMPSON, Mark .... 706-737-1418 121 C
mthompson@gru.edu
THOMPSON, Mark .... 641-683-5306 179 C
mark.thompson@indianhills.edu
THOMPSON, Mark .... 732-906-4252 303 F
MThompson@middlesexcc.edu
THOMPSON, Mark .... 315-228-7385 321 H
mdthompson@colgate.edu
THOMPSON, Mark, A .... 203-582-8914.. 91 E
mark.thompson@quinnipiac.edu
THOMPSON, Mary .... 626-585-7202.. 58 F
mhthompson@pasadena.edu
THOMPSON, Matt .... 641-683-5185 179 C
matt.thompson@indianhills.edu
THOMPSON,
Matthew, R .... 785-827-5541 189 A
matt.thompson@kwu.edu
THOMPSON, Maxine ..... 315-464-5234 344 E
thompsms@upstate.edu
THOMPSON, Michael .... 601-484-8700 268 B
mthompso@meridiancc.edu
THOMPSON, Michael .... 404-687-4530 123 C
thompsonm@ctsnet.edu
THOMPSON, Michael .... 850-599-3301 114 D
michael.thompson@famu.edu
THOMPSON, Michael .... 309-556-1041 148 A
mthomps4@iwu.edu
THOMPSON, Michelle ... 386-481-2330.. 99 F
thompsonmi@cookman.edu
THOMPSON, Mikah ...... 816-235-6910 284 A
thompsonmikah@umkc.edu
THOMPSON, Nancy ...... 620-343-4600 186 I
nthompson@fhtc.edu
THOMPSON, Nancy ...... 916-577-2200.. 77 F
nthompson@jessup.edu
THOMPSON, Nancy, R .. 315-859-4020 327 A
nthompso@hamilton.edu
THOMPSON, Naomi ...... 401-874-7077 442 E
Naomi@mail.uri.edu
THOMPSON, Natalie ..... 607-778-5477 344 F
thompsonm@sunybroome.edu
THOMPSON, Nigel .... 718-270-6136 320 C
nigel@mec.cuny.edu
THOMPSON, Pat .... 972-825-4670 483 D
pthompson@sagu.edu
THOMPSON, Patricia, A 607-735-1730 324 J
pthompson@elmira.edu
THOMPSON, III, Paul ... 312-553-5963 141 N
pthompson40@ccc.edu
THOMPSON, Peter .... 315-568-3123 334 F
pthompson@nycc.edu
THOMPSON, Phyllis ..... 803-705-4720 443 F
thompsop@benedict.edu
THOMPSON, Phyllis, A . 423-439-4125 461 D
thompsop@etsu.edu
THOMPSON,
Priscilla, C .... 301-322-0462 217 G
thompspc@pgcc.edu
THOMPSON,
Rachael, G .... 540-863-2837 515 B
rthompson@dslcc.edu
THOMPSON, Raymond . 252-985-5169 367 E
rthompson@ncwc.edu
THOMPSON, Rhonda .... 281-283-2021 491 E
thompsonr@uhcl.edu
THOMPSON,
Richard, P .... 989-964-4166 249 G
thompson@svsu.edu
THOMPSON, Robert ...... 229-243-3016 121 D
robert.thompson@bainbridge.edu
THOMPSON, Robert ...... 920-206-2377 536 T
rob.thompson@mbu.edu
THOMPSON, Robert, J .. 301-295-3013 548 D
robert.thompson@usuhs.edu
THOMPSON, Robin .... 909-607-3822.. 59 F
robin_thompson@pitzer.edu
THOMPSON, Roger, J ... 541-346-2542 410 F
rjt@uoregon.edu
THOMPSON, Ronald, C 864-294-2092 446 F
ron.thompson@furman.edu
THOMPSON, Ronelle .... 605-274-4921 452 A
ronelle.thompson@augie.edu
THOMPSON, Ryan .... 515-263-6149 178 H
rthompson@grandview.edu
THOMPSON, Sabrina .... 404-962-3000 133 G
sabrina.thompson@usg.edu
THOMPSON, Sara .... 303-492-5148.. 86 E
sara.thompson@colorado.edu
THOMPSON, Sarah .... 303-724-1679.. 86 G
sarah.thompson@ucdenver.edu
THOMPSON, Scott .... 530-242-7512.. 66 C
sthompson@shastacollege.edu
THOMPSON, Seth .... 607-844-8222 350 A
thompss@tc3.edu
THOMPSON, Sharling ... 803-705-4721 443 F
thompsons@benedict.edu
THOMPSON, Sharon ..... 215-751-8450 416 B
sthompson@ccp.edu
THOMPSON, Sharon ..... 910-755-7474 360 E
thompsons@brunswickcc.edu
THOMPSON, Sheila ...... 517-586-3013 241 B
sthompson@cleary.edu
THOMPSON, Sherwood 859-622-6587 194 L
sherwood.thompson@eku.edu
THOMPSON, Stacy .... 510-723-6627.. 37 N
sthompson@chabotcollege.edu
THOMPSON, Stephanie . 707-668-5663.. 42 K
THOMPSON, Steve .... 309-467-6377 145 A
sthompson@eureka.edu
THOMPSON, Stuart ...... 509-963-1004 520 E
Thompsst@cwu.edu
THOMPSON, Susan ...... 843-349-7818 446 I
susan.thompson@hgtc.edu
THOMPSON, Tahmeka .. 913-253-5026 190 K
tahmeka.thompson@spst.edu
THOMPSON, Teresa ...... 912-478-1863 126 B
thompson@georgiasouthern.edu
THOMPSON, Teresa ...... 520-621-6266.. 18 E
tlthompson@email.arizona.edu
THOMPSON, Terri .... 612-338-7224 265 G
terri.thompson@laureate.net
THOMPSON, Terry .... 304-327-4062 532 D
tthompson@bluefieldstate.edu
THOMPSON, Thomas ..... 928-428-8376.. 13 L
thomas.thompson@eac.edu
THOMPSON, Thomas ..... 229-430-1718 119 H
THOMPSON, Tola .... 850-599-3225 114 D
tola.thompson@famu.edu
THOMPSON, Tracey ...... 610-683-4112 431 B
thompson@kutztownufoundation.org
THOMPSON, Traci .... 719-219-9636.. 79 K
tthompson@cavt.edu
THOMPSON, Travis .... 501-279-4464.. 21 A
thompson@harding.edu
THOMPSON, Troy, J ..... 336-841-9404 357 E
tthompso@highpoint.edu
THOMPSON, Valerie ..... 601-877-6385 266 C
valerie@alcorn.edu
THOMPSON, Venesia .... 415-405-4061.. 36 A
venesia@sfsu.edu
THOMPSON, Vinton ...... 212-343-1234 332 I
vthompson@mcny.edu
THOMPSON, Virginia .... 918-781-7275 396 F
thompsonv@bacone.edu
THOMPSON, Walter ...... 603-880-8308 298 I
jthompson@thomasmorecollege.edu
THOMPSON, William ..... 856-374-4931 301 A
wthompson@camdencc.edu
THOMPSON, William ..... 859-572-5768 199 A
thompsonw4@nku.edu
THOMPSON, Zoe .... 804-330-0111 506 D
directorcrim@centura.edu
THOMPSON-BRADSHAW,
Adriane .... 419-772-2433 388 I
a-thompson@onu.edu
THOMPSON BROWN,
Kim .... 912-478-5224 126 B
kthompson@georgiasouthern.edu
THOMPSON-SELLERS,
Ingrid .... 678-891-2773 125 G
ingrid.thompson-sellers@gpc.edu
THOMPSON SMITH,
Amy .... 814-838-7673 418 G
athompson@fortisinstitute.edu
THOMPSON-STACY,
Cheryl .... 540-868-7101 515 H
cstacy@lfcc.edu
THOMPSON-TWEEDY,
Sara .... 845-434-5750 349 C
stweedy@sullivan.suny.edu
THOMPSON-WELLS,
Amy, C .... 270-384-8065 198 C
thompsoa@lindsey.edu
THOMS, Jacqueline ...... 410-626-2513 218 A
jacqueline.thoms@sjc.edu
THOMSEN, Cristina, M . 817-202-6732 483 C
thomsenc@swau.edu
THOMSEN, Marilyn .... 951-785-2000.. 49 I
mthomsen@lasierra.edu
THOMSEN, Pamela .... 218-855-8129 258 C
PThomsen@clcmn.edu
THOMSON, David, T ..... 870-230-5129.. 21 B
thomsond@hsu.edu
THOMSON, Gregg .... 925-631-4754.. 61 G
get1@stmarys-ca.edu
THOMSON, J. Michael . 216-987-3944 381 A
j.michael.thomson@tri-c.edu
THOMSON, III,
John, C .... 845-938-3103 549 A
8uscc@usma.edu
THOMSON, Kimberly .... 660-248-6680 272 N
kthomson@centralmethodist.edu
THOR, James, A .... 716-878-4312 345 B
thorja@buffalostate.edu
THOR, Nadine, L .... 810-762-7904 245 A
nthor@kettering.edu
THORDARSON, Karen ... 310-377-5501.. 53 E
kthodarson@marymountcalifornia.edu
THORE, Kim .... 336-272-7102 357 B
kim.thore@greensboro.edu
THORN, Andre .... 907-786-4080.. 10 H
eathorn@uaa.alaska.edu
THORN, George .... 908-737-5050 303 C
gthorn@kean.edu
THORN, Jackie .... 724-938-5064 430 C
thorn_j@calu.edu
THORN, Lawrence, B .... 318-342-5014 209 A
thorn@ulm.edu
THORN, Robert .... 724-938-4432 430 C
thorn@calu.edu
THORN, Sharon .... 610-399-2550 430 D
sthorn@cheyney.edu
THORN, Shirley, A .... 314-362-2129 275 D
Shirley.Thorn@bjc.org
THORN, Trevor .... 936-294-1584 489 A
trevor@shsu.edu
THORNBURG, David ..... 814-868-9900 418 C
davidt@erieit.edu
THORNBURG, Greg ...... 870-612-2014.. 24 G
greg.thornburg@uaccb.edu
THORNBURG, L. Steve . 704-669-4004 361 E
thornburg@clevelandcc.edu
THORNBURG, Marlon ... 620-252-7550 186 C
marlont@coffeyville.edu
THORNBURGH, Jordan . 707-965-6311.. 57 I
THORNBURY,
Gregory, A .... 212-659-7207 330 A
gthornbury@tkc.edu
THORNBURY, Kimberly 212-659-7209 330 A
kthornbury@tkc.edu
THORNDYKE, Luanne ... 508-856-3844 229 B
luanne.thorndyke@umassmed.edu
THORNE, Bradford, E .... 617-745-3894 225 H
bradford.e.thorne@enc.edu
THORNE, Debbie, M ..... 512-245-2322 489 C
dm29@txstate.edu
THORNE, Debbie, M ..... 512-245-1217 489 C
dm29@txstate.edu
THORNELL, John .... 256-765-5950.... 9 D
jthornell@una.edu
THORNELL, SND,
Susan .... 617-735-9824 226 B
thornsu@emmanuel.edu
THORNGREN, Jill .... 605-688-6181 454 C
jill.thorngren@sdstate.edu
THORNHILL, Kathy .... 707-826-4582.. 35 D
Kathy.Thornhill@humboldt.edu
THORNHILL, Mike, D .... 828-689-1298 359 A
mthornhill@mhu.edu
THORNHILL, Paula .... 318-342-3501 209 A
thornhill@ulm.edu
THORNHILL-HUDSON,
Valerie .... 617-879-2211 238 C
vhudson@wheelock.edu
THORNLEY, Mary .... 843-574-6241 449 G
mary.thornley@tridenttech.edu
THORNQUIST,
Cynthia, J .... 406-447-4389 286 D
cthornqu@carroll.edu
THORNS, Mamie, T ...... 989-964-4397 249 G
mtthorns@svsu.edu
THORNTHWAITE, Kevin 205-665-6351.... 9 C
kthornthwaite@montevallo.edu
THORNTON, Amy .... 608-785-9262 544 E
thorntona@westerntc.edu
THORNTON, Ann, D ...... 212-854-2247 322 F
adt2138@columbia.edu
THORNTON, Audrey ...... 315-279-5339 329 K
athornton1@keuka.edu
THORNTON, Barry, S .... 502-231-5221 198 D
bthornton@myLBC.us
THORNTON, Beth .... 706-213-2116 120 G
bthornton@athenstech.edu
THORNTON, Billy .... 601-925-3373 268 E
bthornto@mc.edu
THORNTON, Brian .... 334-229-6994.... 1 D
bthornton@alasu.edu
THORNTON, Brittany ..... 620-331-4100 188 B
bthornton@indycc.edu
THORNTON, Danielle .... 407-628-5870 102 I
danielle.thornton@zenith.org
THORNTON, Derek, K ... 240-895-4287 218 B
dkthornton@smcm.edu
THORNTON, Donna ...... 848-932-7061 306 F
dthornton@alumni.rutgers.edu
THORNTON, Evan .... 256-216-3310.... 1 F
evan.thornton@athens.edu
THORNTON, Glenda ...... 216-687-2475 380 D
g.thornton@csuohio.edu
THORNTON, James, L .. 336-334-5371 371 C
jlthorn3@uncg.edu
THORNTON, Jan .... 800-422-2418.. 99 C
jthornton@baymedical.org
THORNTON, Jessica ..... 985-448-7920 203 G
jessica.thornton@fletcher.edu
THORNTON, Julie .... 507-222-4075 254 D
jthornto@carleton.edu
THORNTON, Laura .... 770-537-5720 134 F
Laura.thornton@westgatech.edu
THORNTON, Linda .... 507-222-4171 254 D
lthornto@carleton.edu
THORNTON, Matha .... 434-947-8119 511 D
mthornton@randolphcollege.edu
THORNTON, Melanie .... 706-649-1845 123 E
mthornton@columbustech.edu
THORNTON, Paul .... 239-425-3274 114 F
pthornton@fgcu.edu
THORNTON, Ree'shema 415-338-2356.. 36 A
rthorn@sfsu.edu
THORNTON, Tom .... 617-369-3215 236 E
tthornton@smfa.edu
THORNTON, Willie .... 973-443-8929 302 H
wthornton@fdu.edu
THOROUGHMAN,
David .... 740-351-3888 391 C
dthoroughman@shawnee.edu
THORP,
Herbert Holden .... 314-935-3000 285 E
thorp@wustl.edu
THORP, Michael, F .... 765-361-6253 175 B
thorpm@wabash.edu
THORP, Stephen, M ..... 575-624-8442 311 K
thorp@nmmi.edu
THORPE, Abigail .... 718-933-6700 333 F
athorpe@monroecollege.edu
THORPE, Alayne .... 269-471-6581 239 D
alayne@andrews.edu
THORPE, Charles, E ..... 315-268-4430 321 C
cthorpe@clarkson.edu
THORPE, Derrick .... 336-744-0900 355 D
derrick.thorpe@carolina.edu
THORPE, Jennifer .... 573-875-7668 273 D
jcthorpe1@ccis.edu
THORPE, LaKeisha .... 610-625-7716 426 H
thorpel@moravian.edu
THORPE, Lauri, S .... 330-972-6367 392 H
lauri@uakron.edu
THORPE, Melissa .... 610-358-4588 427 D
thorpem@neumann.edu
THORPE, Queenston ..... 404-225-4420 120 I
qthorpe@atlantatech.edu
THORPE, Sima .... 509-313-6856 522 L
thorpe@gu.gonzaga.edu
THORPE, Stephen, W ... 610-499-4117 439 G
swthorpe@mail.widener.edu
THORPE-YOUNG,
Pamela .... 919-530-5402 370 C
pamela.young@nccu.edu
THORSETT, Stephen ...... 503-370-6209 411 D
president@willamette.edu
THORSON, Carola .... 218-281-6510 264 H
THORSON, Eric .... 218-262-7246 258 H
ericthorson@hibbing.edu
THORSON, Kip .... 507-372-3460 260 C
kip.thorson@mnwest.edu
THORSON, Phil .... 320-308-5396 261 E
pthorson@stcloudstate.edu
THORSON, Wendy .... 605-221-3100 452 F
wthorson@kilian.edu
THORSTAD, Todd, M .... 320-222-5572 261 B
todd.thorstad@ridgewater.edu
THORTON, Mike .... 325-574-6572 497 E
mthornton@wtc.edu
THOTA, Vykuntapathi .... 804-524-5024 518 C
vthota@vsu.edu
THRANE, Linda .... 713-348-6281 480 M
thrane@rice.edu
THRASH, Carrie .... 740-374-8716 395 D
cthrash@wscc.edu
THRASHER, Barbara, S . 434-947-8143 511 D
bthrasher@randolphcollege.edu
THRASHER, James, T .... 724-458-2200 419 F
jtthrasher@gcc.edu
THRASHER, John, E ..... 850-644-1085 115 A
jthrasher2@fsu.edu
THRASHER, Jordan, S .. 770-720-5634 130 E
jst@reinhardt.edu

THREET, Dwight .... 910-695-3831 365 H
threetd@sandhills.edu
THREINEN, Noni .... 562-902-3322.. 67 J
nonithreinen@scuhs.edu
THRO, William, E .... 859-257-2936 200 G
william.thro@uky.edu
THROCKMORTON, Julie 724-503-1001 439 B
jthrockmorton@washjeff.edu
THRONEBERRY, Angela 575-646-2431 312 A
athroneb@nmsu.edu
THROOP, Elizabeth, A .. 608-342-1151 540 D
throope@uwplatt.edu
THROWER, Merinda ...... 706-385-1106 130 C
merinda.thrower@point.edu
THROWER, Minda .... 816-501-4057 281 B
minda.thrower@rockhurst.edu
THRUMAN, Michelle ..... 815-588-3575 146 B
michelle.thruman@highland.edu
THRUSH, Claudia .... 570-389-4012 430 B
cthrush@bloomu.edu
THUESON, Mike, B .... 208-496-2311 137 F
THUHA, Permy, K .... 601-877-6118 266 C
pthuha@alcorn.edu
THUKRAL, Pim .... 202-687-6866.. 95 E
thukralp@georgetown.edu
THULIN, Andrew .... 805-756-2161.. 32 E
athulin@calpoly.edu
THULL, James .... 680-488-2470 550 C
jamest@palau.edu
THUM, Dennis, L .... 605-331-6777 454 E
dennis.thum@usiouxfalls.edu
THUM, Scott, W .... 260-422-5561 167 F
swthum@indianatech.edu
THUMMA, Scott .... 860-509-9571.. 90 G
sthumma@hartsem.edu
THURBER, John, P .... 609-984-1155 308 H
jthurber@tesc.edu
THURLER, Kimberly, M 617-627-3175 237 C
kim.thurler@tufts.edu
THURLOW, III, George . 805-893-4799.. 72 D
george.thurlow@ia.ucsb.edu
THURLOW, Hugh .... 303-753-6046.. 85 H
hthurlow@rmcad.edu
THURMAN, Constance .. 309-341-5251 140 I
cthurman@sandburg.edu
THURMAN, Kerri, L ...... 217-443-8850 143 F
kthurman@dacc.edu
THURMAN, Kevin .... 573-518-2261 278 F
kthurman@mineralarea.edu
THURMAN, Lynne, F .... 580-774-3267 402 G
THURMAN, Quint .... 575-492-2123 314 D
qthurman@usw.edu
THURMAN, Todd, A ..... 580-774-3068 402 G
todd.thurman@swosu.edu
THURSTON, Amy .... 610-917-1444 438 G
acthurston@valleyforge.edu
THURSTON, Cathryn, Q 202-231-4011 547 N
cathryn.thurston@dodiis.mil
THURSTON, Katie, S ..... 256-824-6042.... 9 A
katie.thurston@uah.edu
THURSTON, Maureen ... 720-279-8992.. 82 N
mthurston@csl.org
THURSTON, Steve .... 610-917-1476 438 G
sethurston@valleyforge.edu
THWEATT, Herbert .... 684-699-4834 549 C
h.thweatt@amsamoa.edu
THWEATT, Steven .... 303-492-7523.. 86 E
steven.thweatt@colorado.edu
THYEN, Gary, L .... 651-962-6107 265 F
glthyen@stthomas.edu
THYGERSON, John .... 256-824-2870.... 9 A
john.thygerson@uah.edu
THYREEN, Timothy, R .. 724-852-7777 439 C
thyreen@waynesburg.edu
TIAPO, Bernadette .... 815-740-3759 162 F
btiapo@stfrancis.edu
TIBBETTS, John .... 518-629-4552 328 D
j.tibbetts@hvcc.edu
TIBBS, Theresa .... 252-335-3229 369 F
trtibbs@ecsu.edu
TICCONI, Rhett .... 315-568-3256 334 F
rticconi@nycc.edu
TICE, Gene, E .... 270-684-9797 201 D
gene.tice@wku.edu
TICE, Jared .... 252-399-6372 354 I
jtice@barton.edu
TICE, Jessica .... 304-558-0699 532 C
jtice@hepc.wvnet.edu
TICE, Laura, L .... 850-263-3261.. 99 A
lltice@baptistcollege.edu
TICHENOR, Kristin, R ... 508-831-6720 238 G
tichenor@wpi.edu
TICK, Michael .... 859-257-1707 200 G
michael.tick@uky.edu
TIDWELL, Liz .... 801-818-8900 498 P
liz.tidwell@provocollege.edu
TIDWELL, Matthew .... 800-231-3803.. 12 G
TIDWELL, Matthew .... 800-354-1254.. 16 K
mtidwell@brightoncollege.edu
TIDWELL, Michael .... 734-487-4140 242 J
mtidwell@emich.edu

TIEDEMANN, Andrew .... 617-824-8540 226 A
andrew_tiedemann@emerson.edu
TIEDEMANN, John .... 732-571-3421 303 G
jtiedema@monmouth.edu
TIEDT, Penny .... 608-785-6501 539 G
ptiedt@uwlax.edu
TIEFENTHALER, Jill .... 719-389-6700.. 79 M
president@coloradocollege.edu
TIEMANN, Kathleen ...... 978-837-5599 233 G
tiemannk@merrimack.edu
TIEMEIER, Brian .... 314-434-4044 273 J
brian.tiemeier@covenantseminary.edu
TIEMEIER, Thomas, L ... 563-884-5653 182 D
tom.tiemeier@palmer.edu
TIEN, James, M .... 305-284-6035 118 A
jmtien@miami.edu
TIERCE, Joan .... 662-227-2312 267 E
jtierce@holmescc.edu
TIERCE, Meghan .... 559-730-3745.. 41 D
meghant@cos.edu
TIERNAN, Bernadette .... 973-720-2463 309 I
tiernanb@wpunj.edu
TIERNEY, Deborah, J .... 515-961-1699 182 I
deb.tierney@simpson.edu
TIERNEY, James .... 609-652-4381 308 E
james.tierney@stockton.edu
TIERNEY, Joan .... 815-280-2661 148 K
jtierney@jjc.edu
TIERNEY, John .... 202-462-2101.. 96 C
tierney@iwp.edu
TIERNEY, Kathleen .... 610-526-5364 413 D
ktierney01@brynmawr.edu
TIERNO, Mark, J .... 217-479-7025 151 J
mark.tierno@mac.edu
TIERNO, Scott .... 603-668-2211 298 H
s.tierno@snhu.edu
TIESZEN, Pamela .... 316-284-5349 185 B
ptieszen@bethelks.edu
TIETJE, Brian .... 805-756-1757.. 32 E
btietje@calpoly.edu
TIETJEN, Carl .... 585-275-5811 351 D
carl_tietjen@urmc.rochester.edu
TIETJEN, Rick .... 845-451-1380 323 E
r_tietje@culinary.edu
TIETZ, Leah Jo .... 406-444-6570 287 C
ltietz@montana.edu
TIFFANY, David, M .... 716-673-3321 343 F
david.tiffany@fredonia.edu
TIFFIN, Doug .... 972-708-7338 474 J
gial_dean-academic@gial.edu
TIFFIN, Lisa .... 585-594-6194 339 F
Tiffin_Lisa@roberts.edu
TIFFIN, Mary Sue .... 972-708-7552 474 J
marysue_tiffin@gial.edu
TIFFIN, Phyllis .... 817-598-6246 497 A
ptiffin@wc.edu
TIFFNEY, Bruce, H .... 805-893-3827.. 72 D
bruce.tiffney@ccs.ucsb.edu
TIFONE, Jay .... 215-895-3120 438 E
j.tifone@usciences.edu
TIGHE, Peter .... 718-262-2351 321 B
ptighe@york.cuny.edu
TIGNOR, Leslie .... 904-256-1137 103 K
ltignor@fcsl.edu
TIGUE, Brandon .... 828-227-2276 372 C
btigue@wcu.edu
TIJERINA, Shannon ...... 210-434-6711 479 P
sytijerina@lake.ollusa.edu
TIJERINA, Vanessa, J ... 765-641-4114 164 B
vjtijerina@anderson.edu
TIKALSKY, Paul, J .... 405-744-5140 400 C
paul.tikalsky@okstate.edu
TILDEN, Kevin .... 949-214-3127.. 42 B
kevin.tilden@cui.edu
TILDEN, Marsha, A .... 740-368-3163 390 B
matilden@owu.edu
TILGHMAN, Patricia, E . 410-651-6449 219 H
petilghman@umes.edu
TILL, Brian, D .... 414-288-6983 537 B
brian.till@marquette.edu
TILL, Ellen, P .... 850-474-2080 116 E
etill@uwf.edu
TILL, Kimberley, B .... 214-887-5061 473 E
ktill@dts.edu
TILL, Kimberly, B .... 214-887-5061 473 E
ktill@dts.edu
TILL, Stacey .... 636-227-2100 277 A
stacey.till@logan.edu
TILLAR, JR.,
Thomas, C .... 540-231-6285 518 B
ttillar@vt.edu
TILLARD, Bill .... 386-506-4433 101 I
tillarw@DaytonaState.edu
TILLBERG, Rebecca ...... 310-287-4361.. 52 C
tillberw@wlac.edu
TILLERY, Erica .... 239-513-1122 106 E
etillery@hodges.edu
TILLERY, Mariann, W ... 336-841-9286 357 E
mtillery@highpoint.edu

TILLERY TAYLOR,
Carmen .... 562-985-5587.. 33 F
carmen.taylor@csulb.edu
TILLETT, Kerry .... 609-771-3139 301 E
thompsok@tcnj.edu
TILLEY, Genoria .... 225-216-8292 202 N
tilleyg@mybrcc.edu
TILLEY, Jeff .... 979-830-4129 469 F
jeff.tilley@blinn.edu
TILLEY, Neil .... 828-689-1306 359 A
ntilley@mhu.edu
TILLINGHAST, David ..... 508-531-6140 229 C
dtillinghast@bridgew.edu
TILLIPMAN, David, A .... 310-338-7880.. 53 C
dtillipm@lmu.edu
TILLIS, Antonio, D .... 843-953-5507 445 B
TILLMAN, Harry, J .... 757-446-7073 507 B
tillmahj@evms.edu
TILLMAN, Henry, J .... 225-771-5497 206 K
henry_tillman@sus.edu
TILLMAN, Keith .... 815-280-2385 148 K
ktillman@jjc.edu
TILLMAN, Mark .... 334-670-3712.... 8 A
mdtillman@troy.edu
TILLMAN, Rosalyn, P ... 865-329-3101 463 E
rtillman@pstcc.edu
TILLMAN, Shalita .... 909-384-8659.. 62 C
scunningh@sbccd.cc.ca.us
TILLOTSON, James, R .. 515-964-0601 178 F
tillotsonj@faith.edu
TILLOTSON, Jeanette .... 607-778-5195 344 F
tillotsonjo@sunybroome.edu
TILSON, E. Vincent .... 704-233-8115 373 C
tilson@wingate.edu
TILSON, Linda .... 864-656-4542 444 E
nilson@clemson.edu
TILSTRA, Luanne .... 812-877-8741 172 C
tilstra@rose-hulman.edu
TILTON, Brent .... 715-232-2346 541 B
tiltonb@uwstout.edu
TILTON, Casey .... 360-442-2270 524 A
ctilton@lowercolumbia.edu
TILTON, James .... 401-863-2721 441 A
james_tilton@brown.edu
TILTON, Roger, L .... 803-754-4100 445 D
TIMBERLAKE, Gregory .. 419-755-4740 387 E
gtimberlake@ncstatecollege.edu
TIMBY, Tracy .... 215-968-8225 413 F
tracy.timby@bucks.edu
TIMKO, Michael, A .... 724-503-1001 439 B
mtimko@washjeff.edu
TIMLIN, Kevin, J .... 906-227-2428 248 B
ktimlin@nmu.edu
TIMLIN, Laynee, H .... 757-455-2137 518 H
etimlin@vwc.edu
TIMM, Robert .... 480-212-1704.. 17 M
TIMMANN, David .... 610-436-2984 432 B
dtimmann@wcupa.edu
TIMMER, Amy .... 517-371-5140 252 J
timmera@cooley.edu
TIMMER, JR., James .... 616-526-6037 240 L
jrt3@calvin.edu
TIMMERMAN, Candace . 402-375-7034 292 D
catimme1@wsc.edu
TIMMERMAN,
David, M .... 309-457-2325 153 B
dtimmerman@monmouthcollege.edu
TIMMINS, Alan, P .... 503-943-7507 410 H
timmins@up.edu
TIMMONS, Christopher 670-234-5498 550 B
TIMMONS, George .... 518-464-8830 325 B
gtimmons@excelsior.edu
TIMMONS, Joseph, F ... 918-631-2710 403 M
joseph-timmons@utulsa.edu
TIMMONS, Lora .... 312-935-6436 157 A
lotimmons@robertmorris.edu
TIMMONS, Tim .... 708-239-4787 160 L
tim.timmons@trnty.edu
TIMPONE, Peter .... 802-828-8554 503 D
peter.timpone@vcfa.edu
TIMPSON, Brigham .... 707-654-1788.. 34 B
btimpson@csum.edu
TIMS, Michael .... 410-888-9048 216 G
mtims@muih.edu
TIMS, Ray, L .... 919-532-5523 366 H
rltims@waketech.edu
TINCHER, Lee .... 800-280-0307 163 I
lee.tincher@ace.edu
TINCHER, Steven .... 317-921-4882 169 L
TINDALL, Amanda .... 502-213-2255 196 E
amanda.tindall@kctcs.edu
TINDALL, Carolyn .... 262-691-5566 544 D
ctindall@wctc.edu
TINDALL, David, W .... 206-281-2982 526 D
dtindall@spu.edu
TING, Helen .... 650-520-3451.. 58 B
hting@paloaltou.edu
TING, John .... 978-934-2215 229 A
John_Ting@uml.edu
TINGELSTAD, Erik .... 425-352-8162 520 D
etingelstad@cascadia.edu

TINGEY, Jeff .... 208-282-4064 138 C
tingjeff@isu.edu
TINGEY, Kent, M .... 208-282-3198 138 C
tingkent@isu.edu
TINGKANG, Monique ... 808-844-2398 136 E
monique4@hawaii.edu
TINGLE, Caroline, D ..... 386-312-4270 111 K
carolinetingle@sjrstate.edu
TINGLE-WILLIAMS,
Melinda .... 515-643-6604 181 B
mtingle-williams@mercydesmoines.org
TINGLEFF, Brian, P .... 515-643-6663 181 B
btingleff@mercydesmoines.org
TINGSON-GATUZ,
Connie .... 734-432-5883 246 B
ctingson-gatuz@madonna.edu
TINKEY, Danya .... 412-536-1029 422 E
dayna.tinkey@laroche.edu
TINKEY, Jim .... 412-536-1011 422 E
jim.tinkey@laroche.edu
TINKHAM, Brenda, S .... 252-398-6304 356 B
tinkhb@chowan.edu
TINKHAM, Shelley .... 413-572-5713 230 F
stinkham@westfield.ma.edu
TINLING, Walter .... 301-295-3083 548 D
walter.tinling@usuhs.edu
TINLING, Walter .... 301-295-6013 548 D
walter.tinling@usuhs.edu
TINNEY, Tina .... 985-893-7237 203 I
TINSLEY, Joseph .... 205-247-8885.... 7 G
jtinsley@stillman.edu
TINTERA, Judith, E .... 321-674-6303 103 R
jtintera@fit.edu
TINTLE, Nathan .... 712-722-6264 177 J
nathan.tintle@dordt.edu
TIO, Adrian .... 508-999-9295 228 H
atio@umassd.edu
TIPMORE, Barbara .... 270-686-4530 197 A
barbara.tipmore@kctcs.edu
TIPMORE, David .... 334-302-1013.... 5 H
dtipmore@marionmilitary.edu
TIPPIN, Mark .... 405-733-7343 401 L
mtippin@rose.edu
TIPPING, Christopher ... 215-489-4190 416 H
christopher.tipping@delval.edu
TIPPINS, Kira .... 559-442-4600.. 69 B
kira.tippins@fresnocitycollege.edu
TIPPS, Donna, F .... 256-765-4231.... 9 D
dftipps@una.edu
TIPPS, Jane .... 615-898-2670 461 E
jane.tipps@mtsu.edu
TIPS, Jean .... 817-735-5031 493 B
Jean.Tips@unthsc.edu
TIPTON, Alzada .... 630-617-3063 144 G
tiptona@elmhurst.edu
TIPTON, David, K .... 859-985-3728 193 F
tiptond@berea.edu
TIPTON, Joellen .... 936-294-1810 489 A
joellen@shsu.edu
TIPTON, Ryan .... 575-492-2137 314 D
rtipton@usw.edu
TIPTON-ROGERS,
Donna .... 828-835-4204 366 F
dtipton@tricounty.edu
TIRADO, Betty, M .... 607-436-2081 344 B
tiradoem@oneonta.edu
TIRELLA, Joseph .... 718-960-8013 319 C
joseph.tirella@lehman.cuny.edu
TIRONE, Shannon .... 330-941-3732 396 C
stirone@ysu.edu
TIRPAK, Anne, M .... 773-371-5417 141 C
atirpak@ctu.edu
TIRRELL, Matthew .... 773-834-2001 161 D
mtirrell@uchicago.edu
TISDALE, Bradley .... 601-923-1600 270 B
btisdale@rts.edu
TISDALE, Christy .... 207-786-6199 209 F
ctisdale@bates.edu
TISDALE, Henry, N .... 803-535-5412 444 D
tisdale@claflin.edu
TISDALE, James .... 843-208-8050 450 D
jtisdale@mailbox.sc.edu
TISDALE, Jilo .... 404-270-5305 132 D
jtisdale@spelman.edu
TISDALE, Travis .... 276-656-0311 516 D
ttisdale@patrickhenry.edu
TISDALE, Verlie, A .... 803-535-5433 444 D
vtisdale@claflin.edu
TISON, Jennifer, S .... 606-783-9507 198 H
j.tison@moreheadstate.edu
TITA, Charles .... 910-521-6352 371 D
charles.tita@uncp.edu
TITERA, Will .... 619-477-6310.. 70 G
wtitera@usuniversity.edu
TITHERADGE, Inge-Lise 626-584-5464.. 45 F
ititheradge@fuller.edu
TITLER, R. Barry .... 301-447-5357 217 D
titler@msmary.edu
TITSWORTH, Scott .... 740-593-4828 389 H
titswort@ohio.edu

TITTLE, Brandon .... 501-279-4442.. 21 A btittle@harding.edu
TITTLE, Katelyn .... 918-343-6816 401 I ktittle@rsu.edu
TITTMANN, Frederick .... 703-323-4220 516 C ftittmann@nvcc.edu
TITUS, Charlie .... 617-287-7895 228 G charlie.titus@umb.edu
TITUS, Elizabeth .... 575-646-1508 312 A etitus@nmsu.edu
TITUS, Garrett .... 701-627-4738 373 E gtitus@fortbertholdcc.edu
TITUS, Iyana .... 212-220-1236 318 D ititus@bmcc.cuny.edu
TITUS, Lisa .... 610-341-1955 418 A ltitus@eastern.edu
TITUS, Sherry .... 760-744-1150.. 58 D stitus@palomar.edu
TITUS, Steven, E .... 319-385-6204 180 A stitus@iw.edu
TITUS, Varkey, K .... 478-471-2724 128 H varkey.titus@mga.edu
TITUS, Winston .... 701-349-5774 375 G wtitus@trinitybiblecollege.edu
TIU, Carla .... 605-394-2649 454 B carla.tiu@sdsmt.edu
TIVEY, Margaret, K .... 508-289-3362 238 F mktivey@whoi.edu
TIWARI, Suresh .... 843-661-8101 446 C suresh.tiwari@fdtc.edu
TIYAMBE ZELEZA, Paul 203-582-8200.. 91 E paul.zeleza@quinnipiac.edu
TIZOL, Iris .... 787-258-1502 551 I itizol@columbiacentral.edu
TJADEN, Scott .... 651-846-2882.. 28 G stjaden@argosy.edu
TJEERDSMA, Mel .... 660-562-1212 280 A mtjeerdsma@nwmissouri.edu
TKACH, Christopher .... 832-813-6824 477 I christopher.t.tkach@lonestar.edu
TO, Dai, L .... 925-631-4362.. 61 G dlt4@stmarys-ca.edu
TO, Karen .... 719-389-6144.. 79 M kto@coloradocollege.edu
TOADER, Andreea .... 843-863-7826 444 B atoader@csuniv.edu
TOAY, Taun .... 845-758-7745 315 G toay@bard.edu
TOBAKOS, Leslie .... 248-645-3360 241 H ltobakos@cranbrook.edu
TOBEK, Alexandra, C .... 626-395-6594.. 31 D atobeck@caltech.edu
TOBEN, Bradley J, B .... 254-710-1911 469 D brad_toben@baylor.edu
TOBIA, Rajia, C .... 210-567-2400 495 B tobia@uthscsa.edu
TOBIAS, Barbara, A .... 330-325-6726 387 F btobias@neomed.edu
TOBIAS, David .... 508-565-1373 237 A dtobias@stonehill.edu
TOBIAS-JOHNSON, Jaynn .... 708-239-4759 160 L jaynn.tobias-johnson@trnty.edu
TOBIN, Ashlei .... 520-494-5345.. 12 R ashlei.tobin@centralaz.edu
TOBIN, Christopher .... 843-953-3694 445 B tobinc@cofc.edu
TOBIN, Donald .... 410-706-2041 219 E dtobin@law.umaryland.edu
TOBIN, Doreen .... 570-422-3463 430 F dtobin@esu.edu
TOBIN, Elizabeth, H .... 217-245-3010 146 D etobin@mail.ic.edu
TOBIN, Jim .... 516-773-5993 548 I jim.tobin@alumni.usmma.edu
TOBIN, John, M .... 617-373-7666 235 D
TOBIN, Kimberly .... 413-572-8241 230 F ktobin@westfield.ma.edu
TOBIN, Mary Ann .... 708-456-0300 161 C mtobin@triton.edu
TOBIN, JR., Walt .... 803-535-1201 448 C tobinw@octech.edu
TOBIN, William, M .... 765-658-4156 165 G wtobin@depauw.edu
TOBROCKE, Toby .... 518-587-2100 348 A toby.tobrocke@esc.edu
TODA, Frank .... 541-506-6103 405 C ftoda@cgcc.edu
TODARO, Carla .... 423-585-6956 464 C carla.todaro@ws.edu
TODARO, Julie .... 512-223-3071 468 H jtodaro@austincc.edu
TODD, Allysen .... 614-287-3820 380 G atodd12@cscc.edu
TODD, JR., Billy, R .... 214-887-5351 473 E btodd@dts.edu
TODD, Christine .... 440-934-3101 388 E ctodd@ohiobusinesscollege.edu
TODD, Christine .... 212-799-5000 329 I
TODD, Christopher .... 670-237-6797 550 B christopher.todd@marianas.edu
TODD, Diane, C .... 512-475-6203 493 M dtsprague@austin.utexas.edu
TODD, Dwayne .... 614-222-4015 380 F dtodd@ccad.edu
TODD, Greg .... 248-689-8282 251 I gtodd@walshcollege.edu
TODD, Harold .... 985-549-2222 208 E
TODD, James .... 209-575-6060.. 78 C toddj@mjc.edu
TODD, Jason, L .... 417-268-6005 272 F jtodd@gobbc.edu
TODD, Jimmie, L .... 806-291-1045 496 K toddj@wbu.edu
TODD, Mark .... 213-740-2101.. 74 D mtodd@usc.edu
TODD, Patricia, A .... 315-386-7333 347 F toddpa@canton.edu
TODD, Sarah .... 610-341-5384 418 A stodd@eastern.edu
TODD, Sarah, E .... 315-379-3975 347 F todds@canton.edu
TODD, Sharon, O .... 850-872-3891 105 Q stodd@gulfcoast.edu
TODD, Timothy .... 270-809-3744 198 I ttodd@murraystate.edu
TODD ROSKA, Kiely .... 651-255-6121 264 F ktoddroska@unitedseminary.edu
TODERO, Catherine, M . 402-280-2004 290 B CatherineTodero@creighton.edu
TODESCHI, Kevin .... 757-631-8101 504 O ktodeschi@atlanticuniv.edu
TODHUNTER, Jody .... 903-886-5072 485 E jody.todhunter@tamuc.edu
TODISH, Marian .... 616-632-2959 239 E todismar@aquinas.edu
TODOKI, Gayle .... 808-947-4788 137 C g.todoki@wmi.edu
TODT, David .... 641-472-7000 181 A dtodt@mum.edu
TOEBBEN, Martha, A .... 636-922-8243 281 C mtoebben@stchas.edu
TOENISKOETTER, Richard .... 812-464-1899 174 D rtoeniskoe@usi.edu
TOERING, Rose .... 605-221-3211 452 F rtoering@kilian.edu
TOEWS, Brian, G .... 215-702-4227 414 C provost@cairn.edu
TOGLIA, Joan .... 914-674-7813 332 E jtoglia@mercy.edu
TOKAR, Stephen, A .... 317-788-4905 173 I tokarsa@uindy.edu
TOKARSKY, Andra, M ... 412-578-8897 414 I tokarskyam@carlow.edu
TOKPAH, Christopher ... 610-359-5106 416 G
TOKUNAGA, Susan .... 808-984-3380 136 H suetoku@hawaii.edu
TOLAN, Beth .... 972-883-4037 494 A bnt031000@utdallas.edu
TOLAND, Vaughn .... 303-556-4498.. 83 Q tolandva@msudenver.edu
TOLAR, Allison .... 205-726-2762.... 6 F atolar@samford.edu
TOLBERT, Arnold, J .... 305-623-1440 104 B arnold.tolbert@fmuniv.edu
TOLBERT, Dawn, C .... 706-233-7215 131 C dtolbert@shorter.edu
TOLBERT, Jason .... 870-245-5410.. 22 C tolbertj@obu.edu
TOLBERT, Michael .... 848-932-4371 307 B mtolbert@rci.rutgers.edu
TOLBERT, Stephanie, B 919-497-3233 358 J stolbert@louisburg.edu
TOLBERT, Tom .... 802-258-3134 502 I tom.tolbert@worldlearning.org
TOLCHER, Edward, A .... 989-774-1441 240 O tolch1e@cmich.edu
TOLD, Thomas .... 303-373-2008.. 85 I ttold@rvu.edu
TOLEDO, Angelica .... 323-267-3746.. 51 D toledoa@elac.edu
TOLEDO, Armando .... 787-751-0160 551 K mtoledo@cmpr.pr.gov
TOLEDO, Diana .... 360-596-5206 527 B dtoledo@spscc.edu
TOLEDO, Rich .... 209-946-2211.. 73 C rtoledo@pacific.edu
TOLER, Paul .... 816-942-8400 272 E paul.toler@avila.edu
TOLER, Terry .... 405-491-6314 402 E ttoler@snu.edu
TOLER, Whiting .... 252-940-6334 360 B whiting.toler@beaufortccc.edu
TOLES, Mellanie .... 937-328-6002 379 L tolesm@clarkstate.edu
TOLFA, Jill .... 415-749-4530.. 62 I jtolfa@sfai.edu
TOLFREE, Timothy .... 910-938-6323 361 F tolfreet@coastalcarolina.edu
TOLIA, Sam .... 708-456-0300 161 C stolia@triton.edu
TOLISANO, Joseph .... 860-723-0125.. 88 C tolidanoj@ct.edu
TOLIVER, Felicia .... 270-706-8438 195 K felicia.toliver@kctcs.edu
TOLIVER-ROBERTS, Rita, J .... 215-670-9265 428 A rjtoliver@peirce.edu
TOLL, David, J .... 215-895-4982 417 E dtoll@drexel.edu
TOLL, Ronald, B .... 239-590-7035 114 F rtoll@fgcu.edu
TOLL, William .... 765-998-4931 173 B btoll@cse.taylor.edu
TOLLEFSON, Allen .... 530-752-5418.. 71 A jatollefson@ucdavis.edu
TOLLEFSON, Deborah ... 336-334-5702 371 C deborah_tollefson@uncc.edu
TOLLEFSON, Leah .... 218-879-0813 258 F leah@fdltcc.edu
TOLLESON, Jennifer .... 312-935-4244 148 B jtolleson@icsw.edu
TOLLESON, Joanne, P .. 770-781-6950 128 A jtolleso@laniertech.edu
TOLLEY, April .... 540-863-2808 515 B atolley@dslcc.edu
TOLLISON, Scott .... 662-329-7152 269 B cstollison@muw.edu
TOLLIVER, Joseph .... 315-229-5311 341 E jtolliver@stlawu.edu
TOLLIVER, Ona .... 903-565-5645 494 E otolliver@uttyler.edu
TOLSMA, Robert .... 303-315-3701.. 86 G robert.tolsma@ucdenver.edu
TOLSON, Chris .... 270-789-5013 194 D cytolson@campbellsville.edu
TOLSON, Stephanie .... 636-922-8512 281 C stolson@stchas.edu
TOM, Marlene, K .... 415-422-2350.. 74 C mktom@usfca.edu
TOM, Mike .... 808-235-7371 137 A miket@hawaii.edu
TOMAN, Janelle .... 605-773-3455 453 E janelle.toman@sdbor.edu
TOMANEK, Debra, J .... 520-621-7380.. 18 E dtomanek@email.arizona.edu
TOMANEK, Jody .... 308-535-3624 291 H tomanekj@mpcc.edu
TOMANENG, Rowena .... 408-864-8510.. 44 N tomanengrowena@deanza.edu
TOMANIO, David .... 561-297-3076 114 E
TOMAS, Don, L .... 828-339-4242 366 C d_tomas@southwesterncc.edu
TOMASELLO, Nicole .... 716-827-4352 350 H tomasellon@trocaire.edu
TOMASIK, Paula, J .... 304-336-8340 533 A ptomasik@westliberty.edu
TOMASZKIEWICZ, Ed .... 636-481-3501 276 E etomaszk@jeffco.edu
TOMASZKIEWICZ, Teri .. 630-844-5511 139 L ttomaszk@aurora.edu
TOMBARGE, Chuck .... 612-625-8510 265 C tombarge@umn.edu
TOMBARGE, John .... 540-458-8134 519 A tombargej@wlu.edu
TOMBERLIN, Lisa .... 229-468-2078 134 I lisa.tomberlin@wiregrass.edu
TOMBLIN, Joanne, J .... 304-896-7439 531 F joanne.tomblin@southernwv.edu
TOMBLIN, John, S .... 316-978-5234 192 D john.tomblin@wichita.edu
TOMBLIN-BYRD, Terri, L .... 304-710-3472 531 C tomblin@mctc.edu
TOMCZAK, Patricia .... 217-228-5432 156 D tomczpa@quincy.edu
TOMCZYK, Christie, L .. 304-243-2304 534 H ctomczyk@wju.edu
TOMEI, Lawrence, A .... 412-397-6229 434 B tomei@rmu.edu
TOMEK, Deb .... 402-552-3395 289 H tomekdeb@clarksoncollege.edu
TOMENENDAL, Robert, J .... 757-479-3706 514 D rtomenendal@vbts.edu
TOMESCU, Cosmin .... 212-592-2000 342 F ctomescu@sva.edu
TOMETSKO, Jim .... 814-824-2279 425 L jtometsko@mercyhurst.edu
TOMFOHRDE, Tammy ... 423-869-6465 458 B tammy.tomfohrde@lmunet.edu
TOMHAVE, Brad .... 253-879-3529 527 F btomhave@pugetsound.edu
TOMHAVE, Brian .... 909-599-5433.. 50 H btomhave@lifepacific.edu
TOMHAVE, Daniel, P .... 507-344-7451 253 M dtomhave@blc.edu
TOMKINS, Patrick .... 757-825-2799 517 B tomkinsp@tncc.edu
TOMKO, Amy, A .... 330-823-2674 394 A tomkoaa@mountunion.edu
TOMKOWIAK, John .... 847-578-3000 157 G John.Tomkowiak@rosalindfranklin.edu
TOMLIN, George .... 253-879-3522 527 F tomlin@pugetsound.edu
TOMLIN, Kathy, H .... 540-464-7323 518 A tomlinkh@vmi.edu
TOMLIN, Michael .... 719-587-7161.. 78 I miketomlin@adams.edu
TOMLIN, Ross .... 541-888-7417 410 A rtomlin@socc.edu
TOMLINSON, Bill .... 518-580-5177 342 I wtomlins@skidmore.edu
TOMLINSON, Elise .... 907-796-6300.. 11 A elise.tomlinson@uas.alaska.edu
TOMLINSON, Jan .... 740-364-9510 378 L jtomlins@cotc.edu
TOMLINSON, Jessica .... 207-699-5016 210 I jtomlinson@meca.edu
TOMLINSON, John, A .... 662-325-1008 269 A jtomlinson@pres.msstate.edu
TOMLINSON, Karen .... 706-864-1948 133 A karen.tomlinson@ung.edu
TOMLINSON, Keith .... 727-736-5082 112 I ktomlinson@schiller.edu
TOMLINSON, Meghan .. 641-844-5767 179 L meghan.tomlinson@iavalley.edu
TOMLINSON, Rob .... 573-840-9649 283 D rtomlinson@trcc.edu
TOMLINSON, Sasheika . 352-365-3526 107 X tomlins@lssc.edu
TOMLINSON, Tim .... 865-938-8186 456 B
TOMLINSON, Timothy .. 612-455-3420 254 B
TOMLINSON, Virginia ... 503-883-2575 406 I vtomlins@linfield.edu
TOMLINSON, Virginia ... 509-542-4881 521 C vtomlinson@columbiabasin.edu
TOMMASINO, Joseph ... 631-665-1600 350 C tpaphd@aol.com
TOMMEY, Dale .... 870-574-4512.. 23 E dtommey@sautech.edu
TOMPKINS, Anthony (Tony) .... 913-288-7150 188 G atompkins@kckcc.edu
TOMPKINS, OSB, John-Mary .... 724-805-2771 435 C johnmary.tompkins@stvincent.edu
TOMPKINS, OSB, John-Mary .... 724-805-2845 435 C johnmary.tompkins@stvincent.edu
TOMPKINS, Michael .... 845-758-7523 315 G tompkins@bard.edu
TOMPKINS, Perry .... 417-328-1488 282 D ptompkins@sbuniv.edu
TOMPKINS, Ricky .... 479-619-4325.. 22 B rtompkins1@nwacc.edu
TOMPKINS, Terrence .... 503-845-3569 407 B terry.tompkins@mtangel.edu
TOMPKINS, JR., Wendell .... 912-478-2586 126 B wtompkins@georgiasouthern.edu
TOMPOS, Betty .... 717-391-6947 436 D tomposb@stevenscollege.edu
TOMS, Lisa, C .... 870-235-4300.. 23 D lctoms@saumag.edu
TOMSIC, Frank .... 312-942-6832 158 A frank_tomsic@rush.edu
TOMSON, Kent .... 620-365-5116 184 C tomson@allencc.edu
TONAHILL, Kyle .... 360-779-9993 524 C ktonahill@ncad.edu
TONCHE, JR., Carlos .... 845-569-3249 333 I carlos.tonche@msmc.edu
TONCIC, JR., Andrew, A .... 724-458-2170 419 F aatoncic@gcc.edu
TONDER, Rick .... 701-777-4270 373 F rick.tonder@ndus.edu
TONE, Nicole .... 503-222-3225 405 H nicole.tone@zenith.org
TONELLI, Laura .... 978-921-4242 234 B laura.tonelli@montserrat.edu
TONELLI-BROWN, Judith .... 508-373-9719 223 C judith.tonellibrown@becker.edu
TONER, James, D .... 207-778-7494 212 E james.d.toner@maine.edu
TONEY, Eileen .... 269-782-1301 250 D etoney01@swmich.edu
TONEY, Glenn .... 706-245-7226 124 C gtoney@ec.edu
TONEY, Jeffrey .... 908-737-7030 303 C jetoney@kean.edu
TONEY, Patricia, A .... 508-854-4425 232 F ptoney@qcc.mass.edu
TONG, Vincent, P .... 203-285-2415.. 89 B vtong@gwcc.commnet.edu
TONI, Keith .... 508-678-2811 231 B keith.toni@bristolcc.edu
TONIONI, Renee .... 630-466-7900 162 K rtonioni@waubonsee.edu

TOWNER, Mark .... 978-232-2255 226 C
mtowner@endicott.edu
TOWNER, Valmadge, T . 662-621-4130 266 H
vtowner@coahomacc.edu
TOWNES, Emilie, M ...... 615-343-3966 465 H
emilie.m.townes@vanderbilt.edu
TOWNS, Gail .... 732-987-2266 302 J
townsg@georgian.edu
TOWNSEND, Alan .... 919-613-8004 356 E
alan.townsend@duke.edu
TOWNSEND, Bill .... 601-925-3257 268 E
btownsen@mc.edu
TOWNSEND,
Candace, V .... 337-475-5635 208 B
ctownsend@mcneese.edu
TOWNSEND, Carlethia .. 404-880-8566 122 I
ctownsend@cau.edu
TOWNSEND,
Elizabeth, R .... 336-322-2104 364 G
Elizabeth.Townsend@piedmontcc.edu
TOWNSEND, George ..... 913-667-5700 185 L
gtownsend@cbts.edu
TOWNSEND, Heidi .... 360-475-7160 524 H
htownsend@olympic.edu
TOWNSEND, Janis .... 972-721-4142 491 B
jtownsend@udallas.edu
TOWNSEND, JoAnn ...... 727-864-8223 101 P
townsej@eckerd.edu
TOWNSEND,
Joshua, W .... 410-334-2958 221 E
jtownsend@worwic.edu
TOWNSEND, Karen .... 617-369-3486 236 E
ktownsend@smfa.edu
TOWNSEND, Lori, A ..... 828-262-2190 369 D
townsendla@appstate.edu
TOWNSEND, Ralph .... 507-457-5017 262 D
rtownsend@winona.edu
TOWNSEND, Scott .... 701-349-5455 375 G
scott@trinitybiblecollege.edu
TOWNSLEY, Debra, M .. 919-508-2220 373 B
officeofthepresident@peace.edu
TOWNSLEY, R. Michael 260-422-5561 167 F
rmtownsley@indianatech.edu
TOWSLEY, Scott .... 507-574-4929 529 B
stowsley@yvcc.edu
TOY, Charles .... 517-371-5140 252 J
toyc@cooley.edu
TOY, Matthew .... 615-248-1380 464 E
mtoy@trevecca.edu
TOY, Tasha .... 706-368-6985 121 E
ttoy@berry.edu
TOYADA, Maria .... 617-573-8265 237 B
mtoyoda@suffolk.edu
TOYAMA, Gordon, K .... 503-370-6265 411 D
gtoyama@willamette.edu
TOYE-HALE, Bernadette 270-686-4506 197 A
bernie.hale@kctcs.edu
TRAAS, Michael .... 540-563-8000 512 F
mtraas@skyline.edu
TRACEY, CM,
Bernard, M .... 718-990-6570 340 G
traceyb@stjohns.edu
TRACEY, SC, Kathleen ... 718-405-3775 322 A
kathleen.tracey@mountsaintvincent.edu
TRACEY, Kevin, J .... 516-562-3467 324 G
TRACEY, Patrick .... 401-739-5000 441 E
ptracey@neit.edu
TRACHIAN, Barkev .... 336-725-8344 368 A
trachianb@piedmontu.edu
TRACHIER, Steven .... 817-531-4874 490 C
strachier@txwes.edu
TRACHTE, Kent, C .... 570-321-4101 425 B
trachte@lycoming.edu
TRACIA, Michele .... 617-582-4498 234 I
mtracia@aii.edu
TRACY, Carla, B .... 309-794-7266 139 K
carlatracy@augustana.edu
TRACY, David .... 508-588-9100 232 A
TRACY, II, Edward .... 313-993-1554 250 H
tracyeg@udmercy.edu
TRACY, Emily .... 315-733-2300 351 E
etracy@uscny.edu
TRACY, Geofrey, L .... 419-372-8262 377 I
gtracy@bgsu.edu
TRACY, Gloria .... 941-752-5323 114 B
tracyg@scf.edu
TRACY, James, W .... 785-864-7298 191 G
james.tracy@ku.edu
TRACY, Ken, A .... 513-244-8492 379 I
president@ccuniversity.edu
TRACY, Michael .... 229-931-2245 126 C
michael.tracy@gsw.edu
TRACY, Morgan, A .... 859-858-3511 193 A
morgan.tracy@asbury.edu
TRACY, Rhonda .... 859-256-3100 195 G
rhonda.tracy@kctcs.edu
TRACY, Sandra, G .... 901-843-3800 460 F
tracy@rhodes.edu
TRACY, Susan .... 641-472-7000 181 A
stracy@mum.edu

TRACY, Tim, S .... 859-257-5290 200 G
tim.tracy@uky.edu
TRACZYK, Joyce .... 763-433-1243 257 P
joyce.traczyk@anokaramsey.edu
TRAFECANTE, Michael .. 203-254-4000.. 90 E
mtrafecante@fairfield.edu
TRAGNI, Carolyn .... 845-451-1615 323 E
c_tragni@culinary.edu
TRAHAN, Shelia .... 409-984-6239 488 H
trahansc@lamarpa.edu
TRAIGER, Jeff .... 816-235-5660 284 A
traigerj@umkc.edu
TRAINA, Joyce .... 201-327-8877 302 E
jtraina@eastwick.edu
TRAINA, Louis .... 239-489-9215 104 G
ltraina@fsw.edu
TRAINA, Samuel .... 209-228-2857.. 71 E
STraina@UCMerced.edu
TRAINER, James, F ...... 610-519-7578 439 A
james.trainer@villanova.edu
TRAINER, Jason .... 701-777-3791 373 G
jason.trainer@und.edu
TRAINER, Jill .... 916-278-4655.. 34 E
jill.trainer@csus.edu
TRAINER, Karin .... 609-258-3170 305 C
ktrainer@princeton.edu
TRAINO, Joe .... 928-226-4285.. 13 D
joe.traino@coconino.edu
TRAINOR, David .... 617-552-3335 224 B
david.trainor.2@bc.edu
TRAINOR, Hope .... 563-425-5264 183 G
trainorh@uiu.edu
TRAINOR, Judith, L ...... 508-831-5423 238 G
jtrainor@wpi.edu
TRAINOR, Timothy .... 845-938-2000 549 A
8dean@usma.edu
TRAKTMAN, Paula .... 843-876-2405 447 G
traktman@musc.edu
TRAMDACK, Philip, J ... 724-738-2630 432 A
philip.tramdack@sru.edu
TRAME, Michael .... 217-351-2433 155 I
mtrame@parkland.edu
TRAME, Mike .... 217-351-2551 155 I
mtrame@parkland.edu
TRAMEL, Caitlin .... 646-745-8310 315 J
ctramel@barnard.edu
TRAMELLI, Marianne .... 212-678-3148 349 I
mt772@tc.columbia.edu
TRAMMEL, Sheila .... 318-257-2235 208 A
strammel@latech.edu
TRAMMELL, C. David ... 859-858-3511 193 A
david.trammell@asbury.edu
TRAMONTANO,
William, A .... 718-951-5864 318 F
tramontano@brooklyn.cuny.edu
TRAMONTE, Michael ..... 713-500-3158 495 A
michael.tramonte@uth.tmc.edu
TRAMPF, Judith, M ...... 262-472-4672 541 D
trampfj@uww.edu
TRAMUTA, Daniel, M ... 716-673-3253 343 F
daniel.tramuta@fredonia.edu
TRAMUTA, Daniel, M ... 716-673-3181 343 F
daniel.tramuta@fredonia.edu
TRAN, Bang .... 563-876-3353 177 I
btran@dwci.edu
TRAN, Christy .... 415-371-0002.. 57 B
TRAN, Deborah .... 415-565-4740.. 71 B
trand@uchastings.edu
TRAN, Hanh .... 818-778-5959.. 52 B
tranh@lavc.edu
TRAN, Lena .... 408-270-6434.. 63 P
lena.tran@evc.edu
TRAN, My Linh .... 773-907-4770 141 O
mtran@ccc.edu
TRAN, Nathanael .... 415-371-0002.. 57 B
TRANEL, Angela .... 817-552-3700 477 B
angela.tranel@tku.edu
TRANEL, Mark .... 314-516-5273 284 B
mtranel@umsl.edu
TRANG, Thuy .... 408-855-5081.. 76 E
thuy.trang@wvm.edu
TRANQUADA, Jim .... 323-259-2990.. 56 I
jtranqua@oxy.edu
TRANSUE, Mary .... 678-717-3410 133 A
mary.transue@ung.edu
TRANSUE, Mary .... 706-802-5457 125 C
mtransue@highlands.edu
TRANT, John, M .... 956-665-2404 494 C
trantjm@utpa.edu
TRANT, Meg .... 617-217-9118 223 A
mtrant@baystate.edu
TRANT, Rachel .... 508-626-4523 230 A
rtrant@framingham.edu
TRAPANICK,
Benjamin, J .... 508-626-4505 230 A
btrapanick@framingham.edu
TRAPASSO, Kristen, P .. 315-445-4265 330 B
trapaskp@lemoyne.edu
TRAPP, Daniel .... 313-883-8540 249 E
trapp.daniel@shms.edu

TRAPP, Lori .... 734-973-3529 251 J
lori@wccnet.edu
TRAQUAIR, Brianna ...... 651-641-8866 255 C
traquair@csp.edu
TRASK, Kristen .... 336-272-7102 357 B
kristen.trask@greensboro.edu
TRASK, III, Tallman ...... 919-684-6600 356 E
t3@duke.edu
TRASVINA, John, D ...... 415-422-6304.. 74 C
jdtrasvina@usfca.edu
TRAUB, Gilbert .... 718-409-7385 348 C
gtraub@sunymaritime.edu
TRAUBE, Eve .... 212-410-8006 335 B
etraube@nycpm.edu
TRAUGH, Cecelia .... 212-875-4668 315 F
ctraugh@bankstreet.edu
TRAUPMAN-CARR,
Carol .... 610-861-1348 426 H
traupman-carrc@moravian.edu
TRAUSCH, Diane, M ..... 312-261-3230 153 H
Diane.Trausch@nl.edu
TRAUTH, Denise, M ..... 512-245-2121 489 C
president@txstate.edu
TRAUTMAN, Karla .... 605-688-4792 454 C
karla.trautman@sdstate.edu
TRAUTMANN, Roger ..... 503-255-0332 407 D
rtrautmann@multnomah.edu
TRAUTWEILER,
Courtney .... 471-667-8181 273 H
ctrautweiler@cottey.edu
TRAVENICK, Ron .... 510-659-6107.. 56 J
rtravenick@ohlone.edu
TRAVER, William .... 518-458-5337 322 C
traverw@strose.edu
TRAVERS, Nan .... 518-587-2100 348 A
nan.travers@esc.edu
TRAVERS, Tony .... 510-593-2911.. 65 D
ttravers@saybrook.edu
TRAVERSE, Marshall ..... 425-558-0299 522 B
mtraverse@digipen.edu
TRAVERSI, Diane .... 415-485-9414.. 41 B
dtraversi@marin.edu
TRAVERSO, Celeste .... 787-620-2040 550 D
ctraverso@aupr.edu
TRAVERSO, Susan .... 717-361-1416 418 B
traversos@etown.edu
TRAVIS, Annie .... 662-252-8094 270 C
atravis@rustcollege.edu
TRAVIS, Antonio .... 404-756-4023 120 H
atravis@atlm.edu
TRAVIS, Artie, L .... 301-860-3391 220 B
atravis@bowiestate.edu
TRAVIS, Brantly, D .... 270-809-2155 198 I
btravis@murraystate.edu
TRAVIS, Brittany .... 718-779-1499 338 D
btravis@plazacollege.edu
TRAVIS, Cathy .... 920-403-3980 538 K
cathy.travis@snc.edu
TRAVIS, David .... 262-472-1710 541 D
travisd@uww.edu
TRAVIS, Deborah, J ...... 916-691-7321.. 52 J
travisd@crc.losrios.edu
TRAVIS, Delite .... 714-997-6681.. 38 B
dtravis@chapman.edu
TRAVIS, Frederick .... 641-472-7000 181 A
ftravis@mum.edu
TRAVIS, Jeremy .... 212-237-8600 319 F
jtravis@jjay.cuny.edu
TRAVIS, Scott .... 616-395-7251 244 A
remenschneider@hope.edu
TRAVIS-TEAGUE,
Dianne .... 805-969-3626.. 57 J
dtravis-teague@pacifica.edu
TRAVISANO,
Jacqueline, A .... 954-262-7555 109 E
jtravisano@nova.edu
TRAWEEK, Vicki .... 817-598-6218 497 A
vtraweek@wc.edu
TRAWICK, Rebecca .... 909-652-6493.. 38 A
rebecca.trawick@chaffey.edu
TRAWICK, Thomas .... 404-880-8812 122 I
ttrawick@cau.edu
TRAXLER, Matt .... 651-450-3000 259 A
mtraxle@inverhills.edu
TRAXLER, Matt .... 651-450-3885 259 A
mtraxle@inverhills.edu
TRAXLER, Pete .... 907-796-6139.. 11 A
pete.traxler@uas.alaska.edu
TRAXLER, Suzanne, A .. 608-342-1421 540 D
traxlers@uwplatt.edu
TRAYLOR, Angela .... 502-895-3411 198 E
atraylor@lpts.edu
TRAYLOR, Delores .... 256-761-6246.... 7 H
ddtraylor@talladega.edu
TRAYNHAM, Earle, C .... 904-620-2700 116 A
traynham@unf.edu
TRAYNOR, Carol, E ...... 407-582-1015 118 I
ctraynor@valenciacollege.edu
TRAYNOR, Kathy .... 715-682-1227 538 D
ktraynor@northland.edu

TRAYNOR, Scott .... 303-282-3427.. 85 J
father.traynor@archden.org
TRAYNUM, Elise .... 415-565-4715.. 71 B
traynume@uchastings.edu
TRAYSTMAN, Richard ... 303-724-8155.. 86 G
richard.traystman@ucdenver.edu
TREADAWAY,
Glenda, J .... 828-262-8038 369 D
treadawaygj@appstate.edu
TREADWAY, Carol .... 512-463-3280 488 D
carol.treadway@tsus.edu
TREADWELL, Andrew .... 772-462-4804 106 F
atreadwe@irsc.edu
TREADWELL, Jane, B .... 217-206-6597 161 G
treadwell.jane@uis.edu
TREADWELL, IV,
Lawrence .... 305-474-6860 112 B
ltreadwell@stu.edu
TREAKLE-MOORE,
Evelyn .... 202-806-7540.. 96 B
etreakle-moore@howard.edu
TREANOR, William, M .. 202-662-9032.. 95 E
wtreanor@georgetown.edu
TREAS, Misty .... 580-387-7151 398 J
mtreas@mscok.edu
TREAT, Cindy .... 817-461-8741 468 C
ctreat@arlingtonbaptistcollege.edu
TREAT, Rebekah .... 303-986-2320.. 80 N
careers@csha.net
TREAT, Tod .... 253-566-5022 527 C
ttreat@tacomacc.edu
TREBAR, Robert .... 440-375-7115 385 B
rtrebar@lec.edu
TREBER, Karen, A .... 301-687-4111 220 D
ktreber@frostburg.edu
TRECARTIN, Ralph, R ... 585-395-2119 345 A
rtrecart@brockport.edu
TREDE, Cara .... 712-325-3285 180 B
ctrede@iwcc.edu
TREDUP, Fred .... 702-895-3201 295 G
fred.tredup@unlv.edu
TREECE, Brian .... 419-434-4570 393 F
treeceb@findlay.edu
TREECE, T. Gerald .... 713-646-1776 482 H
gtreece@stcl.edu
TREFETHEN, Eva, M ..... 304-457-6342 529 C
trefethenem@ab.edu
TREFF, Shaya 732-370-3360 309M
TREFF, Yisroel Meir 732-370-3360 309M
TREFT, Paul .... 712-274-5221 181 C
treft@morningside.edu
TREICHEL, Jeff, D 512-232-5114 493M
jeff.treichel@austin.utexas.edu
TREJO, Alanna .... 805-437-2757.. 32 H
alanna.trejo@csuci.edu
TRELEVEN, Laurie .... 415-422-5368.. 74 C
ltreleven@usfca.edu
TRELISKY, Nina .... 973-720-2305 309 I
treliskyn@wpunj.edu
TRELOAR, Allison, H .... 757-822-1045 517 C
atreloar@tcc.edu
TRELOW, Cheryl, D ...... 660-543-4255 283 F
trelow@ucmo.edu
TRELSTAD-PORTER,
James .... 612-330-1686 253 K
porter@augsburg.edu
TREMAINE, Erica .... 620-278-4213 191 D
etremaine@sterling.edu
TREMAINE, Monique .... 937-529-2201 392 G
mtremaine@united.edu
TREMBLAY,
Christopher, W .... 269-387-4336 252 I
christopher.tremblay@wmich.edu
TREMBLAY, Pamela ...... 706-880-8313 127 N
ptremblay@lagrange.edu
TREMBLAY, Rocky .... 203-285-2185.. 89 B
rtremblay@gwcc.commnet.edu
TREMBLE, Gayle .... 912-443-5724 131 B
gtremble@savannahtech.edu
TREMBLEY, Michael ...... 336-309-5814 131 F
mtrembley@southuniversity.edu
TREMER, Tom .... 315-279-5672 329 K
tremer@keuka.edu
TREML, Colleen .... 216-397-1886 384 F
ctreml@jcu.edu
TREMONT, Rolando ...... 787-850-9387 558 A
rolando.tremont@upr.edu
TRENDT, Diana, J .... 608-342-1183 540 D
trendtd@uwplatt.edu
TRENIS, Neva, S .... 540-654-1688 513 I
ntrenis@umw.edu
TRENKLE, Lizza .... 254-659-7823 475 A
ltrenkle@hillcollege.edu
TRENOWETH, Arthur ..... 617-369-4049 236 E
atrenoweth@mfa.org
TRENT, Eunice .... 405-491-6602 402 E
etrent@snu.edu
TRENT, Malissa .... 423-354-2521 463 D
mbtrent@northeaststate.edu

TRENTACOSTE, Peter ..... 740-593-4090 389 H trentaco@ohio.edu
TRENTHEM, Richard ..... 901-843-3890 460 F trenthem@rhodes.edu
TREPAL, Michael, J ...... 212-410-8067 335 B mtrepal@nycpm.edu
TREPKOWSKI, Patti .... 616-234-4226 243 D ptrepkow@grcc.edu
TREPKOWSKI, Ronald, E .... 989-964-4285 249 G ret@svsu.edu
TRESCOTT, Sarah .... 330-244-4943 395 C strescott@walsh.edu
TRESELER, Kelly .... 781-768-7535 236 A kelly.treseler@regiscollege.edu
TRESER-OSGOOD, Nancy .... 909-621-8807.. 59 F Nancy_Treser-Osgood@pitzer.edu
TRESOLINI, Carol .... 919-962-3907 371 A carol_tresolini@unc.edu
TRESS, Samuel, D .... 410-837-5529 221 B stress@ubalt.edu
TRESSEL, James, P .... 330-941-3101 396 C jptressel@ysu.edu
TRETHEWEY, Angela ..... 530-898-4015.. 33 A atrethewey@csuchico.edu
TREUR, Rick .... 616-526-8442 240 L rickt@calvin.edu
TREVAN, Timothy, J ..... 818-677-2160.. 34 D timothy.j.trevan@csun.edu
TREVATHAN, Edwin ...... 254-710-3601 469 D Edwin_Trevathan@baylor.edu
TREVENA, Stan .... 209-667-3343.. 35 C strevena@csustan.edu
TREVINO, Crispin .... 361-593-4036 486 A crispin.trevino@tamuk.edu
TREVINO, JR., Esteban . 956-721-5140 477 C stevet@laredo.edu
TREVINO, Jennifer .... 817-735-2486 493 B Jennifer.Trevino@unthsc.edu
TREVINO, Jesus .... 605-677-5011 453 F jesus.trevino@usd.edu
TREVINO, Joe .... 425-739-8375 523 I joe.trevino@lwtech.edu
TREVINO, Mary, T .... 956-326-2275 485 B maryt@tamiu.edu
TREVINO, Melba .... 956-872-3113 482 G melbat@southtexascollege.edu
TREVINO, Miguel, A ..... 956-326-2283 485 B mtrevino@tamiu.edu
TREVINO, Monica .... 405-224-3140 403 L mtrevino@usao.edu
TREVINO, Nicole, G ...... 512-428-1037 481 B nicoleg@stedwards.edu
TREVINO, Rick .... 805-289-6155.. 75 E rtrevino@vcccd.edu
TREVIS, Michael .... 310-660-3101.. 43 G mtrevis@elcamino.edu
TREVISAN, Maurizio ..... 212-650-5275 318 G mtrevisan@ccny.cuny.edu
TREVISAN, Maurizio ..... 212-650-6638 318 G provost@ccny.cuny.edu
TREVISAN, Michael .... 509-335-4853 528 B trevisan@wsu.edu
TREVOR, Tyler .... 406-444-0307 287 C ttrevor@montana.edu
TREWERN, Jay, S .... 978-468-7111 227 B jtrewern@gcts.edu
TREXLER, Grant .... 805-756-1141.. 32 E gtrexler@calpoly.edu
TREXLER, William, H .... 814-886-6421 427 B wtrexler@mtaloy.edu
TRIANA, Caridad .... 305-442-6011 110 I
TRIANTIS, Alexander, J 301-405-2308 219 D atrianti@rhsmith.umd.edu
TRIBBEY, Ann .... 804-330-0111 506 D directoredcrim@centura.edu
TRIBBLE, Judy .... 812-535-5255 172 F jtribble@smwc.edu
TRIBE, Bill .... 503-552-1523 407 F btribe@ncnm.edu
TRIBLE, JR., Paul, S .... 757-594-7002 506 I ptrible@cnu.edu
TRIBLEY, Walter .... 831-646-4060.. 54 H wtribley@mpc.edu
TRICARICO, Kerri, J ..... 212-998-2913 336 C kerri.tricarico@nyu.edu
TRICE, Gwinetta, L .... 229-430-4739 119 H gwinetta.trice@asurams.edu
TRICE, Matt .... 229-430-6618 119 I mtrice@albanytech.edu
TRICHE, Casie .... 985-448-4077 208 C casie.triche@nicholls.edu
TRICHE, III, Charles, W .... 337-482-6396 208 F ctriche@louisiana.edu
TRICKEY, Rafe Edward .. 580-591-0203 397 G etrickey@cnc.cc.ok.us
TRICOLI, Robin, J .... 423-420-1225 456 M president@hiwassee.edu
TRIDENTE, Teresa .... 201-216-5176 308 D ttrident@stevens.edu
TRIER, Vicki .... 509-533-8090 521 E vicki.trier@scc.spokane.edu
TRIERWEILER, Charles, S .... 205-329-7907.... 3 C chuck.trierweiler@ecacolleges.com
TRIETLEY, JR., Richard, C .... 716-375-2513 340 C rtrietle@sbu.edu
TRIEZENBERG, Steven, J .... 616-234-5708 251 G
TRIFILO, Trish .... 806-291-3745 496 K trifilot@wbu.edu
TRIGALO, Ophir .... 312-567-3290 147 E trigalo@iit.edu
TRIGG, Debra .... 510-659-7376.. 56 J dtrigg@ohlone.edu
TRIGGER, Kelly .... 301-846-2518 214 I ktrigger@frederick.edu
TRILLI, Victor .... 316-942-4291 189 K trilliv@newmanu.edu
TRILOWSKY, Ulana .... 409-880-7030 488 F ulana.trilowsky@lamar.edu
TRIMBLE, Ashtin .... 309-796-5143 140 D trimblea@bhc.edu
TRIMBLE, Dave .... 212-785-0111 429 F
TRIMBLE, Ferris, E .... 323-241-5467.. 51 I trimblfe@lasc.edu
TRIMBLE, Karen .... 530-749-3804.. 78 D ktrimble@yccd.edu
TRIMBLE, LaDonna .... 661-722-6300.. 27 P ltrimble@avc.edu
TRIMBLE, Lisa .... 307-778-1603 546 F lisatrimble@lcccfoundation.edu
TRIMBLE, Marshall .... 480-423-6314.. 15 E marshall.trimble@scottsdalecc.edu
TRIMBLE, Michael, D .... 203-365-7557.. 91 G trimblem@sacredheart.edu
TRIMBOLI, James .... 716-614-6202 336 D trimboli@niagaracc.suny.edu
TRINIDAD, Vanessa .... 787-884-6000 552 K vtrinidad@icprjc.edu
TRINIDAD, Ysabel .... 805-437-8877.. 32 H ysabel.trinidad@csuci.edu
TRINKLEIN, Andrea .... 404-727-4144 124 D ajtrink@emory.edu
TRIONFI, Thomas, P .... 989-774-3166 240 O trion1tp@cmich.edu
TRIPATHI, Satish, K ..... 716-645-2901 343 E president@buffalo.edu
TRIPLETT, Beth .... 563-588-6468 176 F beth.triplett@clarke.edu
TRIPLETT, Clark .... 314-392-2221 278 G triplett@mobap.edu
TRIPLETT, Jill .... 404-270-5677 132 D jtriple1@spelman.edu
TRIPLETT, Teresa .... 910-642-7141 366 B Teresa.Triplett@sccnc.edu
TRIPODI, Michael, A .... 201-684-6975 305 F mtripodi@rmapo.edu
TRIPOVICH, Maria .... 409-944-1303 474 G mtripovi@gc.edu
TRIPP, Lexie .... 773-291-6313 142 B ltripp@ccc.edu
TRIPP, Susan .... 870-612-2053.. 24 G susan.tripp@uaccb.edu
TRIPP, Susan .... 315-866-0300 327 E trippsk@herkimer.edu
TRIPPETT, Brian .... 740-377-2520 392 C brian.trippett@tsbc.edu
TRIPPETT, William .... 608-263-7727 541 E william.trippett@uwc.edu
TRIPURANENI, Vinaya, L .... 909-593-3511.. 73 B vtripuraneni@laverne.edu
TRISEL, Donald, E .... 304-367-4642 532 F dtrisel@fairmontstate.edu
TRITLE, Candice .... 717-691-6024 426 B ctritle@messiah.edu
TRIVEDI, Sara .... 310-568-6105.. 53 C strivedi@lmu.edu
TRIVEDI, Tushar .... 201-761-6264 307 K ttrivedi@saintpeters.edu
TRIVUNOVICH, Nick ...... 813-974-4903 116 B ntrivuno@usf.edu
TRIZZINO-PECOR, June 212-965-8340 314 F trizzino@adelphi.edu
TRNCAK, Stephen .... 281-998-6348 481 D stephen.trncak@sjcd.edu
TROASTLE, Greta, J ...... 304-637-1331 529 I troastleg@dewv.edu
TROCHIM, Shawn .... 254-299-8811 478 C strochim@mclennan.edu
TROCHUCK, Mike .... 708-239-4836 160 L mike.trochuck@trnty.edu
TROELSTRA, Kate .... 678-466-4300 122 J katetroelstra@clayton.edu
TROGISCH, Colleen .... 845-431-8966 324 D trogisch@sunydutchess.edu
TROHA, James, A .... 814-641-3101 421 L trohaj@juniata.edu
TROIANO, Sandra .... 518-381-1422 342 E toiansm@sunysccc.edu
TROILO, David .... 212-938-5658 347 C dtroilo@sunyopt.edu
TROISI, Kenneth .... 678-603-0981 132 B ktroisi@sctech.edu
TROJAN, John .... 908-526-1200 305 G John.Trojan@raritanval.edu
TROLLINGER, Richard, W .... 859-238-5209 194 E richard.trollinger@centre.edu
TROMBELLA, Jerry .... 201-360-4771 303 A jtrombella@hccc.edu
TROMBLEY, Christina ... 920-465-2470 539 F tromblec@uwgb.edu
TROMBLEY, Jane, E ...... 212-817-7179 319 B jtrombley@gc.cuny.edu
TROMP, Marlene .... 602-543-4506.. 11 J marlene.tromp@asu.edu
TRONTO, Stacie .... 252-328-9025 369 E trontos@ecu.edu
TROPP, Judybeth .... 619-961-4319.. 69 J jtropp@tjsl.edu
TROSH, Sasha .... 803-981-7161 451 K strosh@yorktech.edu
TROST, Patricia, G .... 708-709-3637 156 A ptrost@prairiestate.edu
TROSTLE, Libby .... 410-386-8113 214 B ltrostle@carrollcc.edu
TROSVIG, Kelli .... 206-616-0114 527 G kelli@uw.edu
TROTMAN, Yvette .... 612-659-6325 259 F yvette.trotman@minneapolis.edu
TROTT, Garrett .... 503-375-7016 405 F gtrott@corban.edu
TROTT CLARK, Beth ...... 717-796-5066 426 B bclark@messiah.edu
TROTTA, Carianne .... 518-381-1176 342 E trottac@sunysccc.edu
TROTTA, Neil .... 617-236-8867 226 F ntrotta@fisher.edu
TROTTER, Cheryl .... 704-461-6714 354 J cheryltrotter@bac.edu
TROTTER, David .... 913-360-7656 184 K dtrotter@benedictine.edu
TROTTER, Dennis .... 215-248-7304 424 G dtrotter@ltsp.edu
TROTTER, Steve .... 360-867-6185 522 J trotters@evergreen.edu
TROTTIER, Sheila .... 701-477-7862 375 H strottier@tm.edu
TROTTIER, Tracey .... 413-755-4057 233 B tatrottier@stcc.edu
TROTTY, Willie, F .... 936-261-3500 484 F wftrotty@pvamu.edu
TROTTY, Willie, F .... 936-261-1550 484 F wftrotty@pvamu.edu
TROTZKE, Deanna .... 812-535-5299 172 F
TROUP, James .... 203-575-8220.. 89 F jtroup@nv.edu
TROUP, Pat .... 251-981-3771.... 3 A pat.troup@columbiasouthern.edu
TROUP, Patrick .... 612-659-6707 259 F patrick.troup@minneapolis.edu
TROUPE, Bonnie, L .... 508-565-1069 237 A btroupe@stonehill.edu
TROUSDELL, Roy .... 218-748-2413 259 D r.trousdell@mesabirange.edu
TROUT, Curtis, C .... 309-556-3195 148 A ctrout@iwu.edu
TROUT, Darice .... 847-925-6070 145 F dtrout@harpercollege.edu
TROUT, Margaret .... 503-370-6971 411 D mtrout@willamette.edu
TROUTH, Catherine .... 303-361-7365.. 81 I Catherine.Trouth@CCAurora.edu
TROUTMAN, Dara, L ...... 402-472-7143 293 F dtroutman@nebraska.edu
TROUTMAN, Donald ..... 570-321-4064 425 B troutman@lycoming.edu
TROUTMAN, Linda .... 850-478-8496 110 C ltroutman@pcci.edu
TROUTMAN, Marcus ..... 312-922-1884 151 I mtroutman@maccormac.edu
TROUTMAN, Matthew ... 301-696-3577 215 E troutman@hood.edu
TROUTMAN, Todd .... 810-762-0409 247 F todd.troutman@mcc.edu
TROUTT, Amy .... 618-545-3048 149 C atroutt@kaskaskia.edu
TROUTT, William, E ...... 901-843-3730 460 F trouttw@rhodes.edu
TROUTWINE, Jason .... 765-973-8444 168 A jtroutwi@iue.edu
TROVALL, Carl .... 512-313-3000 471 H carl.trovall@concordia.edu
TROVER, Clay .... 706-721-4854 121 C ctrover@gru.edu
TROW, Kirk .... 515-244-4221 175 C trowk@aib.edu
TROWBRIDGE, Christian, A .... 302-295-1151.. 94 G christian.a.trowbridge@wilmu.edu
TROWBRIDGE, Cory, D 316-322-0110 272 L cory.trowbridge@calvary.edu
TROY, Randy, D .... 260-399-7700 174 C rtroy@sf.edu
TROY, Robert .... 212-237-8118 319 F rtroy@jjay.cuny.edu
TROY, Shawn .... 989-386-6658 247 B stroy@midmich.edu
TROY SMYSER, Kathleen .... 717-396-7833 429 H ksmyser@pcad.edu
TROYER, Brian .... 414-229-4445 540 A troyerb@uwm.edu
TROYER, Cindy .... 903-566-7461 494 E ctroyer@uttyler.edu
TROYER, David .... 740-857-1311 390 L dtroyer@rosedale.edu
TROYER, Mark, J .... 859-858-3511 193 A mark.troyer@asbury.edu
TROYER, Melissa .... 402-437-2619 293 A mtroyer@southeast.edu
TRUBACZ, Joseph .... 727-873-4287 116 C trubacz@usfsp.edu
TRUBE, Julie .... 248-370-3915 248 K dichtel@oakland.edu
TRUCKENMILLER, Greg . 518-736-3622 326 D gtrucken@fmcc.suny.edu
TRUDEAU, Marc, V .... 805-482-2755.. 61 F rector@stjohnsem.edu
TRUDEAU, Mary, L .... 701-788-4754 374 A mary.trudeau@mayvillestate.edu
TRUDEAU, Sara, L .... 202-526-3799.. 96 F
TRUDEAU, Scott .... 248-204-3852 245 J strudeau@ltu.edu
TRUDEAU, Skip .... 765-998-5368 173 B sktrudeau@taylor.edu
TRUDEL, OP, Albert ...... 202-495-3836.. 96 E registrar@dhs.edu
TRUDEL, Jeannie .... 864-644-5486 449 B jtrudel@swu.edu
TRUDO, Glenn .... 740-695-9500 377 F gtrudo@belmontcollege.edu
TRUE, Christopher, J .... 240-895-4317 218 B cjtrue@smcm.edu
TRUE, Don .... 803-508-7491 443 C trued@atc.edu
TRUE, Elizabeth .... 207-326-2251 211 G elizabeth.true@mma.edu
TRUE, Robert, L .... 317-274-4860 168 E rtrue@iupui.edu
TRUEBLOOD-GAMBLE, Marjorie .... 541-552-6459 409 G truebloom@sou.edu
TRUELOVE, Bobbty .... 205-652-3601.... 9 G bjt@uwa.edu
TRUEMAN, Amy .... 607-844-8222 350 A truemaa@TC3.edu
TRUESDALE, Karen .... 678-891-2542 125 G karen.truesdale@gpc.edu
TRUESDELL, Cheryl, B .. 260-481-6506 168 D truesdel@ipfw.edu
TRUESDELL, Joanne ...... 503-594-3000 405 A joannet@clackamas.edu
TRUESDELL, Nancy, D .. 920-832-6596 536 R nancy.d.truesdell@lawrence.edu
TRUETT, William, M ..... 704-272-5363 366 A wtruett@spcc.edu
TRUFANT, Nicole .... 207-602-2157 213 B ntrufant@une.edu
TRUHLAR, Mary, R .... 631-632-8950 344 C mary.truhlar@stonybrookmedicine.edu
TRUILLO, Lawrence, T .. 607-778-5207 344 F truillolt@sunybroome.edu
TRUITT, Bettie .... 309-796-5001 140 D truittb@bhc.edu
TRUITT, Jennifer .... 217-228-5432 156 D truitje@quincy.edu
TRUITT, Terry, C .... 765-641-4354 164 B tctruitt@anderson.edu
TRUJILLO, Adrian .... 415-351-3515.. 62 I atrujillo@sfai.edu
TRUJILLO, Daniel, A ..... 718-990-6774 340 G trujilld@stjohns.edu
TRUJILLO, Fidel, J .... 505-454-3020 311 H fidel@nmhu.edu
TRUJILLO, George .... 301-985-7283 220 A george.trujillo@umuc.edu
TRUJILLO, Henrietta ..... 505-747-2134 312 G henri@nnmc.edu
TRUJILLO, Tamara .... 707-638-5317.. 70 B tamara.trujillo@tu.edu
TRULL, Gregory .... 503-588-2722 405 F gtrull@corban.edu
TRULOVE, Milyon .... 503-777-7510 409 E milyon.trulove@reed.edu

TRULSON, Gary .... 608-743-4526 542 L
gtrulson@blackhawk.edu
TRUMAN, Grace, H .... 561-868-3122 109 H
trumang@palmbeachstate.edu
TRUMAN, Kevin, Z .... 816-235-2399 284 A
trumank@umkc.edu
TRUMBLE, Jeremy .... 315-781-3806 327 G
trumble@hws.edu
TRUMBULL, William, N 843-953-7416 444 C
wtrumbul@citadel.edu
TRUMPICK, Susan, A ... 518-743-2248 347 E
trumpics@sunyacc.edu
TRUMPOWER, Peter ...... 330-494-6170 391 J
ptrumpower@starkstate.edu
TRUONG, Chris .... 714-564-6043.. 60 G
truong_chris@sac.edu
TRUONG, Lan .... 650-949-7823.. 45 A
truonglan@foothill.edu
TRUONG, Susan .... 510-981-2937.. 58 J
struong@peralta.edu
TRUSCH, Robert .... 413-755-4039 233 B
rbtrusch@stcc.edu
TRUSDELL, James .... 267-341-3329 420 K
jtrusdell@holyfamily.edu
TRUSHEIM, Dale .... 215-596-7291 438 E
d.trusheim@usciences.edu
TRUSS, B. Donta .... 478-827-7594 124 E
trussd@fvsu.edu
TRUSSELL, Jay .... 828-884-8340 355 A
trussellj@brevard.edu
TRUSTY, Denise .... 606-886-3863 195 I
denise.trusty@kctcs.edu
TRUSTY, Denise, M ...... 606-783-2000 198 H
dmtrusty@moreheadstate.edu
TRUSZ, Robert .... 740-351-3251 391 C
btrusz@shawnee.edu
TRUSZ, Robert .... 740-351-3610 391 C
btrusz@shawnee.edu
TRUSZKOWSKI, Alyssa . 215-965-4028 426 G
atruzkowski@moore.edu
TRUTNA, Kevin .... 530-283-0202.. 44 H
ktrutna@frc.edu
TRUXAL, Randy .... 903-463-8717 474 K
truxalr@grayson.edu
TRUXILLO, Betty, D ...... 225-923-2524 201 E
director@brsc.edu
TRYON, Sandy .... 515-964-6408 177 B
sbtryon@dmacc.edu
TRZASKA, Ken .... 217-641-4514 148 J
ktrzaska@jwcc.edu
TRZASKA, Ken, J .... 620-417-1010 191 A
ken.trzaska@sccc.edu
TRZEBIATOWSKI, Brian 773-481-8287 142 D
btrzebiatowski@ccc.edu
TRZECIAK, Jeffrey, G .... 314-935-5415 285 E
Jeffrey.Trzeciak@wustl.edu
TRZEPACZ, Angie .... 270-809-6861 198 I
atrzepacz@murraystate.edu
TSAFFARAS, Peter, H .... 617-984-1776 235 H
ptsaffaras@quincycollege.edu
TSAI, Maya, H .... 260-422-5561 167 F
mhtsai@indianatech.edu
TSAI, Patty .... 866-323-0233.. 60 E
registrar@providencecc.edu
TSANG, Edmund .... 269-276-3249 252 I
edmund.tsang@wmich.edu
TSARK, Gregory .... 321-674-7584 103 R
gtsark@fit.edu
TSATSOULIS, Costas ..... 940-565-3946 492 D
costas.tsatsoulis@unt.edu
TSATSOULIS, Costas ..... 940-565-4300 492 D
costas.tsatsoulis@unt.edu
TSCHEPIKOW, Kyle .... 706-542-9167 132 H
kyletsch@uga.edu
TSCHERTER, Andrea, G . 812-888-5794 174 F
atscherter@vinu.edu
TSCHETTER, Randall, C . 605-336-6588 453 C
rtschetter@sfseminary.edu
TSCHETTER, Sheryl .... 951-372-7017.. 61 A
sheryl.tschetter@norcocollege.edu
TSCHETTER, Wesley, G . 605-688-4920 454 C
wesley.tschetter@sdstate.edu
TSEGAI, Adiam .... 716-884-9120 317 C
aktsegai@bryantstratton.edu
TSEGAYE, Teferi, D .... 502-597-6310 197 G
teferi.tsegaye@kysu.edu
TSO, Jay .... 212-757-1190 315 C
jtso@funeraleducation.org
TSOLAKIS, Alcibiades ... 225-578-5863 204 M
atsolakis@lsu.edu
TSOUMAS, Linda, J .... 508-373-5709 233 E
linda.tsoumas@mcphs.edu
TSUKAYAMA, Robyn ..... 313-927-1725 246 D
rtsukaya@marygrove.edu
TSUQUIASHI-DADDESIO,
Eva .... 724-738-4863 432 A
eva.tsuquiashi@sru.edu
TSUTSUI, William, M .... 501-450-1351.. 21 C
tsutsui@hendrix.edu
TUBB, Joe .... 806-894-9611 482 F
jtubb@southplainscollege.edu
TUBBS, Jeffrey, L .... 704-406-4253 356 G
jtubbs@gardner-webb.edu
TUBBS, Richard, E .... 941-351-4742 111 F
rtubbs@ringling.edu
TUBBS, Teresa .... 910-272-3662 365 D
ttubbs@robeson.edu
TUBBS, Trenton .... 417-864-7220 275 A
ttubbs@cci.edu
TUBENS, Sylvia .... 787-738-2161 557 G
sylvia.tubens@upr.edu
TUBMAN, Jonathan, G . 202-885-3753.. 94 H
jtubman@american.edu
TUBMAN, Lynn .... 215-248-7046 415 D
tubmanl@chc.edu
TUCCI, Barbara .... 505-428-1264 313 A
barbara.tucci@sfcc.edu
TUCCI, Paul .... 518-587-2100 348 A
paul.tucci@esc.edu
TUCK, Amy .... 662-325-3221 269 A
at25@msstate.edu
TUCK, Inez .... 336-334-7751 370 B
ituck@ncat.edu
TUCK, Mark .... 618-468-3400 150 E
mtuck@lc.edu
TUCK, Martin .... 740-774-7200 389 H
tuck@ohio.edu
TUCKER, Adam .... 704-847-5600 369 A
atucker@ses.edu
TUCKER, Archie .... 256-372-8344.... 1 A
archie.tucker@aamu.edu
TUCKER, Arlene, C .... 337-550-1288 205 B
atucker@lsue.edu
TUCKER, Barbara .... 706-272-4420 123 G
btucker@daltonstate.edu
TUCKER, Barbara .... 608-822-2456 544 C
btucker@swtc.edu
TUCKER, Bill .... 601-276-3726 270 E
wtucker@smcc.edu
TUCKER, Brandon .... 734-677-5087 251 J
brtucker@wccnet.edu
TUCKER, Carol, M .... 713-221-8269 491 F
tuckerca@uhd.edu
TUCKER, Carolyn .... 360-416-7600 527 A
TUCKER, Cecelia, T .... 757-683-5210 510 I
ctucker@odu.edu
TUCKER, Cheryl .... 707-476-4293.. 41 C
cheryl-tucker@redwoods.edu
TUCKER, Cheryle, L ...... 618-650-3701 159 I
chtucke@siue.edu
TUCKER, David, C .... 812-888-4266 174 F
dtucker@vinu.edu
TUCKER, Dawn .... 919-718-7437 361 C
dmtucker@cccc.edu
TUCKER, Dayton .... 914-251-6915 346 D
dayton.tucker@purchase.edu
TUCKER, Diane, P .... 617-358-6887 224 E
dtucker@bu.edu
TUCKER, Eileen .... 610-660-1346 434 G
tucker@sju.edu
TUCKER, G.L. .... 218-846-3765 259 H
gl.tucker@minnesota.edu
TUCKER,
Gardiner (Tuck) .... 727-873-4882 116 C
gtucker@mail.usf.edu
TUCKER, Gary, R .... 517-750-1200 250 F
garyt@arbor.edu
TUCKER, Geraldine .... 512-223-7572 468 H
gtucker@austincc.edu
TUCKER, Gretchen, G ... 704-406-4491 356 G
gtucker1@gardner-webb.edu
TUCKER, Herman, V ...... 254-299-8660 478 C
htucker@mclennan.edu
TUCKER, Irene .... 775-445-4234 296 A
irene.tucker@wnc.edu
TUCKER, Jameel .... 610-526-6092 420 C
jtucker@harcum.edu
TUCKER, James .... 518-327-6286 338 B
jtucker@paulsmiths.edu
TUCKER, James, R .... 215-895-2800 417 E
jrt55@drexel.edu
TUCKER, Jean .... 251-460-6294.... 9 F
jtucker@southalabama.edu
TUCKER, Jim .... 785-749-8460 187 F
jtucker@haskell.edu
TUCKER, John, D .... 619-298-1829.. 68 C
jtucker@ssu.edu
TUCKER, Karen .... 630-752-5060 163 G
karen.tucker@wheaton.edu
TUCKER, Ken .... 205-652-3527.... 9 G
ktucker@uwa.edu
TUCKER, Kim .... 970-675-3335.. 80 L
kim.tucker@cncc.edu
TUCKER, Laura .... 703-416-1441 508 F
ltucker@ipsciences.edu
TUCKER, Mark .... 336-386-3217 366 E
tuckerm@surry.edu
TUCKER, Mary, E .... 520-621-9438.. 18 E
mtucker@email.arizona.edu
TUCKER, Melanie .... 701-483-2560 373 H
Melanie.Tucker@dickinsonstate.edu
TUCKER, Michael, A ..... 765-641-4295 164 B
matucker@anderson.edu
TUCKER, Murl .... 714-547-9625.. 30 F
mtucker@calcoast.edu
TUCKER, Nate .... 423-473-1190 457 M
ntucker@leeuniversity.edu
TUCKER, Ned .... 402-826-8601 290 C
ned.tucker@doane.edu
TUCKER, Patrick .... 860-832-1786.. 88 D
ptucker@ccsu.edu
TUCKER, Raymond, A ... 785-827-5541 189 A
rtucker@kwu.edu
TUCKER, Robert .... 325-670-1427 474 M
Robert.Tucker@hsutx.edu
TUCKER, Sandra .... 386-481-2106.. 99 F
tuckers@cookman.edu
TUCKER, Sarah .... 304-558-0265 532 C
tucker@wvctcs.org
TUCKER, Seth .... 315-498-2123 337 F
tuckers@sunyocc.edu
TUCKER,
Sharon (Nyota) .... 229-430-2799 119 H
nyota.tucker@asurams.edu
TUCKER, Sheryl .... 405-744-6368 400 C
sheryl.tucker@okstate.edu
TUCKER, Stacey .... 423-614-8637 457 M
stucker@leeuniversity.edu
TUCKER, Stacy .... 913-288-7239 188 G
stucker@kckcc.edu
TUCKER, Steven .... 205-348-8396.... 8 E
uadps01@bama.ua.edu
TUCKER, Tom, T .... 304-367-4110 532 F
tom.tucker@fairmontstate.edu
TUCKER, Tommy .... 870-307-7324.. 21 G
thomas.tucker@lyon.edu
TUCKER, William .... 510-587-6037.. 70 J
william.tucker@ucop.edu
TUCKER, William, T ...... 631-451-4760 348 E
tuckerw@sunysuffolk.edu
TUCKER-MCCLOUD,
Janice, L .... 740-826-8024 387 C
jtucker@muskingum.edu
TUDELA, Virginia, C ..... 671-735-5590 549 E
virginia.tudela@guamcc.edu
TUDOR, Donna, K .... 615-248-7703 464 E
dtudor@trevecca.edu
TUDOR, Gail .... 207-941-7039 210 C
tudorg@husson.edu
TUDOR, Lisa .... 239-489-9350 104 G
ltudor@fsw.edu
TUDRYN, Jonathan .... 413-755-4420 233 B
jtudryn@stcc.edu
TUEDIO, James, A .... 209-667-3531.. 35 C
jtuedio@csustan.edu
TUEL, Alexander .... 301-387-3028 215 A
alexander.tuel@garrettcollege.edu
TUELLER, Steven .... 808-675-3935 134 M
tuellers@byuh.edu
TUFANO, Joseph, J .... 718-990-5800 340 G
tufanoj@stjohns.edu
TUFANO, Tony .... 315-279-5251 329 K
atufano@keuka.edu
TUFAU-AFRIYIE,
Michelle .... 508-854-7568 232 F
mtufau@qcc.mass.edu
TUFEL, Peter .... 212-686-9244 315 B
TUGGLE, Joseph .... 601-477-4277 268 A
joseph.tuggle@jcjc.edu
TUIA, Jennifer .... 360-596-5369 527 B
jtuia@spscc.edu
TUITASI, Michael .... 310-434-4389.. 65 B
tuitasi_michael@smc.edu
TUITASI, Sifagatogo .... 684-699-9155 549 C
s.tuitasi@amsamoa.edu
TUITE, Kathleen .... 973-618-3534 300 H
ktuite@caldwell.edu
TUITT, Frank .... 303-871-2591.. 86 H
ftuitt@du.edu
TULAFONO, Grace .... 684-699-9155 549 C
g.tulafono@amsamoa.edu
TULAK, William .... 318-487-5443 203 D
williamtulak@cltc.edu
TULBERG, Gene .... 870-612-2037.. 24 G
gene.tulberg@uaccb.edu
TULL, Ashley .... 254-968-9080 485 A
tull@tarleton.edu
TULL, Wendell .... 415-575-6156.. 31 C
admissions@ciis.edu
TULLER, Jodi .... 413-528-7253 222 F
jtuller@simons-rock.edu
TULLEY, Nickolas, B ...... 240-895-4336 218 B
nbtulley@smcm.edu
TULLEY, Ronald .... 419-434-4445 393 F
rtulley@findlay.edu
TULLIER, Michelle .... 404-385-7344 125 D
michelle.tullier@gatech.edu
TULLIO, Ann .... 718-631-6215 320 F
atullio@qcc.cuny.edu
TULLOCH, Helen (Meg) 202-685-3948 547 M
tullochh@ndu.edu
TULLOS, Charlotte .... 225-578-3113 204 M
ctullos2@lsu.edu
TULLY, Greg, J .... 815-772-7218 153 E
gtully@morrisontech.edu
TULLY-DARTEZ,
Stephanie .... 870-862-8131.. 23 B
stully-dartez@southark.edu
TUMBLIN, Tom .... 859-858-2301 192 O
TUMELTY, Susanne, M . 718-960-1190 319 C
susanne.tumelty@lehman.cuny.edu
TUMEO, Mark, A .... 904-620-1350 116 A
m.tumeo@unf.edu
TUMEO, Michael, D .... 214-768-2808 482 J
mtumeo@smu.edu
TUMER, Lisa, L .... 540-568-7820 509 C
tumerll@jmu.edu
TUMLINSON, Karen, L .. 520-621-2516.. 18 E
kdenman@email.arizona.edu
TUMMINO, Pauline .... 718-990-6106 340 G
tumminop@stjohns.edu
TUMMOLO, Paul .... 212-353-4100 323 B
pault@cooper.edu
TUNCAP, Michael .... 253-833-9111 523 B
mtuncap@greenriver.edu
TUNE, Kathie .... 434-791-7106 505 A
ktune@averett.edu
TUNG, Lisa .... 617-879-7335 230 B
ltung@massart.edu
TUNG, Yuming .... 315-470-6861 347 B
ytung@esf.edu
TUNGSETH, Margaret .... 651-523-2203 256 B
mtungseth01@hamline.edu
TUNSTALL, Denise, S ... 804-523-5029 515 F
dtunstall@reynolds.edu
TUNSTILL, Hilda .... 931-393-1573 463 B
htunstill@mscc.edu
TUNSTILL, Jerry .... 931-393-1688 463 B
jtunstill@mscc.edu
TUOHEY, Christina .... 413-755-4475 233 B
cctuohey@stcc.edu
TUOMEY, Lianne, M ...... 802-656-2027 503 C
lianne.tuomey@uvm.edu
TUPALA, Kay .... 920-498-5482 544 B
kay.tupala@nwtc.edu
TUPPER, Barb .... 319-399-8000 176 G
btupper@coe.edu
TUPPER, Rick .... 605-274-4499 452 A
rick.tupper@augie.edu
TUPUOLA, Tafaimamao 684-699-9155 549 C
t.tupuola@amsamoa.edu
TURANO, Rosemary .... 617-964-1100 222 B
rturano@ants.edu
TURANSKY, June, S ...... 302-857-1126.. 94 A
june.turansky@dtcc.edu
TURAY, Abdul, M .... 502-597-6916 197 G
abdul.turay@kysu.edu
TURBEVILLE, Donna ...... 910-642-7141 366 B
Donna.Turbeville@sccnc.edu
TURBEVILLE, John .... 315-470-6660 347 B
jturbev@esf.edu
TURBIDE, Gerard .... 607-274-3124 328 H
gturbide@ithaca.edu
TURCIOS, Mirna .... 661-726-1911.. 70 I
mirna.turcios@uav.edu
TURCOTT, Scott .... 617-745-3000 225 H
scott.turcott@enc.edu
TURCOTTE, Colleen, D .. 401-825-2159 441 C
cdturcotte@ccri.edu
TURCOTTE, Jim .... 601-925-3809 268 E
turcotte@mc.edu
TUREK, John, G .... 714-879-3901.. 47 D
jgturek@hiu.edu
TUREK, Joseph .... 434-544-8651 509 I
turek@lynchburg.edu
TURELL, Susan .... 607-436-2125 344 B
susan.turell@onenta.edu
TUREN, Christopher ...... 310-965-0888.. 77 D
TURGEON, Paul .... 714-556-3610.. 75 A
paul.turgeon@vanguard.edu
TURGEON, Pennie .... 508-421-3813 225 B
pturgeon@clarku.edu
TURICO, Michael .... 602-538-9396.. 11 C
TURK, David, F .... 845-675-4422 337 B
david.turk@nyack.edu
TURK, Laura .... 540-831-5248 511 C
lturk@radford.edu
TURK, Mike .... 334-833-4322.... 4 E
mturk@huntingdon.edu
TURK FIECOAT,
Heather .... 775-784-1110 295 H
TURKS, Stacie .... 209-946-2225.. 73 C
sturks@pacific.edu
TURLETES, Christopher . 907-786-1110.. 10 H
cmturletes@uaa.alaska.edu
TURLEY, Alicestyne .... 859-985-3783 193 F
turlleya@berea.edu
TURLEY, Cricket .... 620-276-9574 187 D
cricket.turley@gcccks.edu
TURLEY, Mae .... 641-269-4631 178 I
turleym@grinnell.edu

TYNES, Craig .... 601-403-1155 270 A
ctynes@prcc.edu
TYNES, Sheryl, R .... 210-999-8201 490 E
stynes@trinity.edu
TYNON, Kathy .... 402-872-2365 292 C
ktynon@peru.edu
TYO, Keith, D .... 518-564-3930 346 B
tyokd@plattsburgh.edu
TYREE, Jonathan .... 434-947-8112 511 D
jtyree@randolphcollege.edu
TYREE, Tracy .... 203-392-5550.. 88 F
tyreet1@southernct.edu
TYRELL, Steve, J .... 518-891-2915 336 F
president@nccc.edu
TYRRELL, Elizabeth .... 408-270-6453.. 63 P
elizabeth.tyrrell@evc.edu
TYRRELL, Wil .... 914-323-7178 331 J
wil.tyrrell@mville.edu
TYSON, AJ .... 252-789-0232 363 H
atyson@martincc.edu
TYSON, April .... 901-572-2446 455 C
april.tyson@bchs.edu
TYSON, Chris .... 215-728-4424 427 H
chris.tyson@jevs.org
TYSON, Daquiri .... 229-732-5958 120 B
daquirityson@andrewcollege.edu
TYSON, James, B .... 870-575-8701.. 24 D
tysonj@uapb.edu
TYSON, Jennifer .... 859-246-6507 195 J
jennifer.tyson@kctcs.edu
TYSON, John, N .... 248-218-2011 249 D
jtyson@rc.edu
TYSON, Linda .... 252-399-6330 354 I
ltyson@barton.edu
TYSON, Shannon .... 570-484-3131 431 C
styson@lhup.edu
TYSON, Thayer .... 336-744-0900 355 D
tyrone@carolina.edu
TYSON, Thomas, N ...... 410-334-2913 221 E
ttyson@worwic.edu
TYSON, William, R .... 919-893-9101 361 C
btyson@cccc.edu
TYUS, Bing .... 863-297-1004 110 E
btyus@polk.edu
TZENG, Fei-Ing .... 408-260-0208.. 44 K
daom@fivebranches.edu
TZENG, Huey-Ming ...... 931-372-3651 462 A
htzeng@tntech.edu
TZENG, Walker .... 415-371-0002.. 57 B
TZIMBAL, Tootie .... 831-479-5730.. 30 C
totzimba@cabrillo.edu

U

UBAGO, Maria .... 323-343-2586.. 34 A
mubago@cslanet.calstatela.edu
UCCI, Anthony .... 508-678-2811 231 B
anthony.ucci@bristolcc.edu
UDALL, David .... 928-428-8295.. 13 L
david.udall@eac.edu
UDD, Kris, J .... 402-449-2811 290 F
registrar@graceu.edu
UDDIN, Rita .... 718-260-5610 320 D
ruddin@citytech.cuny.edu
UDE, Wayne .... 360-331-0307 524 E
UDEH, Igwe, E .... 504-286-5331 207 B
iudeh@suno.edu
UDELHOFEN,
Angela, M .... 608-342-1125 540 D
rulea@uwplatt.edu
UDELHOFEN, Denise .... 563-588-7742 180 L
bob.quinn@loras.edu
UDEN, Jayme .... 816-584-6595 280 F
jayme.uden@park.edu
UDEN, Michael .... 262-243-5700 535 I
michael.uden@cuw.edu
UDEOGALANYA,
Anthony .... 718-270-6213 320 C
anthonyu@mec.cuny.edu
UDERMANN, Brian .... 608-785-8181 539 G
budermann@uwlax.edu
UDIS-KESSLER,
Amanda .... 719-227-8177.. 79 M
audiskessler@coloradocollege.edu
UDOH, Emmanuel .... 502-456-6504 200 B
eudoh@sullivan.edu
UDOVIC, Edward, R ...... 312-362-8042 143 G
eudovic@depaul.edu
UDOVIC, CM,
Edward, R .... 312-362-8042 143 G
eudovic@depaul.edu
UDPA, Satish, S .... 517-355-5014 246 H
udpa@adminsv.msu.edu
UDUMA, Letitia .... 313-943-4058 252 A
luduma1@wcccd.edu
UDVARDY, Yolonda ...... 215-489-4966 416 H
yolonda.udvardy@delval.edu
UEDA, Rikklyn, S .... 619-239-0391.. 36 E
rueda@cwsl.edu
UEHARA, Edwina .... 206-685-2480 527 G
eddi@uw.edu
UEKI, Omdasu, T .... 680-488-2471 550 C
oueki@palau.edu
UERLING, Laura, J .... 508-565-1378 237 A
luerling@stonehill.edu
UESUGI, Koji .... 951-372-7082.. 61 A
koji.uesugi@norcocollege.edu
UETRECHT, Dan .... 573-341-6418 284 C
uetrecht@mst.edu
UFERT FAIRLESS,
Nancy, J .... 618-650-3187 159 I
nufert@siue.edu
UFFORD, Brian, K .... 207-778-7334 212 E
brian.ufford@maine.edu
UFFORD, Lori .... 541-506-6025 405 C
lufford@cgcc.edu
UFOMATA, Titilayo .... 315-781-3304 327 G
ufomata@hws.edu
UGALDE, Aileen, M ...... 305-284-2700 118 A
augalde@miami.edu
UGOCHUKWU,
Chioma, R .... 417-667-8181 273 H
cugochukwu@cottey.edu
UGOL, Sandra, H .... 205-329-7900.... 3 C
sandra.ugol@ecacolleges.com
UGORJI, Lauren, D ...... 973-596-5695 304 D
lauren.d.ugorji@njit.edu
UGRAS, Joseph, Y .... 215-951-5124 422 F
ugras@lasalle.edu
UHAL, Len .... 563-876-3353 177 I
luhal@dwci.edu
UHAZY, Les .... 661-722-6300.. 27 P
luhazy@avc.edu
UHDE, Alicia .... 701-224-5764 374 E
alicia.uhde@bismarckstate.edu
UHER, Bill .... 505-277-5598 313 H
wuher@salud.unm.edu
UHLENKAMP, James .... 641-784-5221 178 G
jim.uhlenkamp@graceland.edu
UHLER, Jill .... 803-508-7247 443 C
uhlerj@atc.edu
UHLINGER, Eleanor, S . 831-656-2342 548 A
euhlinger@nps.edu
UHLIR, James .... 715-232-2188 541 B
uhlirj@uwstout.edu
UHUAD, Betsy .... 207-780-4714 213 A
buhuad@usm.maine.edu
UKACHUKWU, Victoria . 973-618-3595 300 H
vukachukwu@caldwell.edu
UKPOLO, Fawn .... 504-398-2242 206 E
fukpolo@olhcc.edu
UKPOLO, Victor .... 504-286-5311 207 B
vukpolo@suno.edu
ULACIA, Jose .... 305-220-4120 108 F
Julacia@mattiacollege.edu
ULBRICH, Casandra ...... 586-445-7244 246 A
ulbrichc@macomb.edu
ULBRICHT,
Alexandra, K .... 330-569-5182 383 F
Ulbrichtak@hiram.edu
ULCH, Christine .... 609-894-9311 306 B
hulch@bcc.edu
ULIBARRI, Debbie .... 719-846-5533.. 86 A
debbie.ulibarri@trinidadstate.edu
ULIBARRI, Katherine ..... 505-224-4413 310 F
kulibarri8@cnm.edu
ULLEM, Ben .... 515-271-3985 177 K
ben.ullem@drake.edu
ULLMAN,
Christopher, C .... 847-259-1840 141 L
cullman@christianlifecollege.edu
ULLMAN, David, F .... 973-596-2915 304 D
david.ullman@njit.edu
ULLMAN, Julie .... 414-382-6053 534 I
julie.ullman@alverno.edu
ULLMANN, Brian .... 301-314-6650 219 D
ullmann@umd.edu
ULLOM, Craig, E .... 740-368-3135 390 B
ceullom@owu.edu
ULLRICH, Terry .... 504-568-5135 205 C
tullri@lsuhsc.edu
ULMAN, Cynthia .... 510-869-6511.. 61 J
culman@samuelmerritt.edu
ULMEN, Dan .... 406-265-3755 288 A
dulman@msun.edu
ULMER, Jeffrey .... 386-822-7738 117 A
julmer@stetson.edu
ULMER, L. Ward .... 612-338-7224 265 G
ward.ulmer@waldenu.edu
ULMER, Rholda, S .... 407-582-3861 118 I
rulmer@valenciacollege.edu
ULMER, Robert, R .... 702-895-0628 295 G
robert.ulmer@unlv.edu
ULMSCHNEIDER,
John, E .... 804-828-1105 514 F
jeulmsch@vcu.edu
ULRICH, Carlea .... 432-264-5027 475 E
culrich@howardcollege.edu
ULRICH, Dennis .... 513-569-1414 379 K
dennis.ulrich@cincinnatistate.edu
ULRICH, Gail, L .... 814-641-3194 421 L
ulrichg@juniata.edu
ULRICH, James .... 312-235-3523 159 B
j.ulrich@shimer.edu
ULRICH, James .... 312-235-3511 159 B
j.ulrich@shimer.edu
ULRICH, Paul .... 262-551-2112 535 E
pulrich@carthage.edu
ULRICH, Tina, J .... 231-995-1063 248 C
tulrich@nmc.edu
ULRICH, Trey, P .... 215-951-1671 422 F
ulrich@lasalle.edu
ULRICHSEN, Borre .... 510-885-4986.. 33 C
borre.ulrichsen@csueastbay.edu
ULSES, Randy .... 513-556-3511 393 B
ulsesrj@ucmail.uc.edu
ULSETH, Julie, A .... 810-762-9844 245 A
julseth@kettering.edu
ULSHAFER, Kevin, L ..... 478-757-5125 134 E
kulshafer@wesleyancollege.edu
ULZ, Mary Ann .... 847-566-6401 162 G
mulz@usml.edu
UMBAUGH, Rob .... 970-339-6237.. 78 J
rob.umbaugh@aims.edu
UMBLE, Diane .... 717-871-7318 431 E
diane.umble@millersville.edu
UMEHIRA, Ron .... 808-455-0228 136 G
umehira@hawaii.edu
UMFRESS, Jason, W ..... 912-279-5970 123 B
jumfress@ccga.edu
UMHOEFER, Gary, A ..... 920-403-3210 538 K
gary.umhoefer@snc.edu
UMHOLTZ, Lynn .... 316-322-3144 185 F
lumholtz@butlercc.edu
UMIDI, Joseph .... 757-352-4404 511 G
joseumi@regent.edu
UMMER,
Christopher, T .... 802-626-6477 504 B
christopher.ummer@lyndonstate.edu
UMPHRES, James .... 360-538-4085 523 A
UMSTATTD, Rustin .... 816-414-3700 278 E
rumstattd@mbts.edu
UNBEHAGEN, Leonard . 504-278-6438 204 B
lunbehagen@nunez.edu
UNDERCOFFER, Anita ... 909-652-6032.. 38 A
anita.undercoffer@chaffey.edu
UNDERCOFLER, James . 914-251-6707 346 D
james.undercofler@purchase.edu
UNDERDUE MURPH,
Yvette .... 218-477-2171 260 B
yvette.underduemurph@mnstate.edu
UNDERHILL, Terri .... 304-357-4980 530 H
terriunderhill@ucwv.edu
UNDERWOOD, Allen ..... 419-893-1986 383 C
aunderwo@heidelberg.edu
UNDERWOOD, Anita ..... 845-675-4476 337 B
anita.underwood@nyack.edu
UNDERWOOD, Ann ...... 806-651-2121 486 D
aunderwood@wtamu.edu
UNDERWOOD, Anthony 304-424-8209 533 E
anthony.underwood@wvup.edu
UNDERWOOD, Carrie ... 817-554-5950 478 E
cunderwood@messengercollege.edu
UNDERWOOD, Craig .... 610-861-1501 426 H
underwoodc@moravian.edu
UNDERWOOD, David .... 479-964-0540.. 20 C
dunderwood@atu.edu
UNDERWOOD, Dawn .... 812-237-3088 167 E
dawn.underwood@indstate.edu
UNDERWOOD,
Elizabeth .... 479-788-7008.. 23 H
elizabeth.underwood@uafs.edu
UNDERWOOD, Glenda .. 617-587-5662 234 G
underwoodg@neco.edu
UNDERWOOD, Kathryn . 252-335-3606 369 F
nkunderwood@ecsu.edu
UNDERWOOD,
Kathy, A .... 702-895-0283 295 G
kathyunderwood@unlv.edu
UNDERWOOD, Ken .... 865-573-4517 457 H
kunderwood@johnsonu.edu
UNDERWOOD, Lori, J .. 757-594-7052 506 I
underwoo@cnu.edu
UNDERWOOD, Mark ...... 830-591-7286 483 A
meunderwood@swtjc.edu
UNDERWOOD,
Michelle .... 503-255-0332 407 D
munderwood@multnomah.edu
UNDERWOOD, Rob ...... 212-228-1888 339 C
UNDERWOOD,
Robert, A .... 671-735-2990 549 G
raunderwood@triton.uog.edu
UNDERWOOD,
Robin, S .... 318-342-5420 209 A
runderwood@ulm.edu
UNDERWOOD, Ruth ..... 478-289-2134 124 B
runderwood@ega.edu
UNDERWOOD,
Timothy, J .... 304-462-4114 532 G
timothy.underwood@glenville.edu
UNDERWOOD, Von, E .. 580-581-2491 397 A
vonu@cameron.edu
UNDERWOOD,
William, D .... 478-301-2500 128 G
underwood_wd@mercer.edu
UNEBASAMI,
Michael, T .... 808-956-6280 136 B
mune@hawaii.edu
UNGAR, Jacob .... 845-362-3053 316 A
jacobu@bytsem.org
UNGAR, Samuel, D ...... 718-384-5460 353 K
UNGAR, Shaya .... 732-370-3360 309 M
UNGARO, John .... 843-574-6891 449 G
john.ungaro@tridenttech.edu
UNGER, Karen .... 845-758-7490 315 G
kunger@bard.edu
UNGER, Leigh .... 562-908-3415.. 60 I
LUnger@riohondo.edu
UNGER, Maggie .... 952-446-4323 255 E
ungerm@crown.edu
UNGER, Sue .... 630-889-6565 154 E
sunger@nuhs.edu
UNGERER, Dorothy .... 413-755-4438 233 B
daungerer@stcc.edu
UNIS, Corry .... 570-208-5848 422 D
corryunis@kings.edu
UNKE, James, M .... 507-354-8221 257 A
unkejm@mlc-wels.edu
UNNI, V, K .... 401-232-6227 441 B
vunni@bryant.edu
UNNIKRISHNAN,
Raman .... 657-278-3362.. 33 E
runnikrishnan@fullerton.edu
UNNITHAN, Shashi .... 970-204-8607.. 82 J
shashi.unnithan@frontrange.edu
UNRUH, David .... 310-825-1083.. 71 D
dunruh@summer.ucla.edu
UNRUH, David .... 215-895-2436 417 E
dlu23@drexel.edu
UNRUH, Greg .... 316-677-9507 192 C
gunruh@watc.edu
UNRUH, Nancy .... 620-276-9571 187 D
nancy.unruh@gcccks.edu
UNSWORTH, John .... 781-736-4540 224 F
unsworth@brandeis.edu
UNTERREINER, Colleen 406-756-3962 286 G
colleenu@fvcc.edu
UNVER, Amira .... 973-290-4233 301 F
aunver@cse.edu
UPCHURCH, Jim .... 815-939-5231 155 G
jupchurch@olivet.edu
UPCHURCH, Luke .... 704-922-8405 362 G
upchurch.luke@gaston.edu
UPCHURCH, Rick .... 601-968-5940 266 F
rupchurch@belhaven.edu
UPHAM, Steadman .... 918-631-3244 403 M
steadman-upham@utulsa.edu
UPNEJA, Arun .... 617-353-6744 224 E
aupneja@bu.edu
UPPALA, Guru .... 951-785-3531.. 49 I
guppala@lasierra.edu
UPSHAW, Jane .... 843-208-8242 450 D
jupshaw@uscb.edu
UPTON, Brian .... 417-865-2815 274 L
uptonb@evangel.edu
UPTON, Bryn .... 410-857-2416 217 A
bupton@mcdaniel.edu
UPTON, Yvette .... 912-344-2519 120 D
yvette.upton@armstrong.edu
UPWARD, Geoffrey, C .. 248-364-6240 248 K
upward@oakland.edu
URAN, Mike, T .... 320-308-2116 261 E
mturan@stcloudstate.edu
URBAITIS, Carol, S ...... 585-785-1212 325 E
carol.urbaitis@flcc.edu
URBAN, David .... 215-752-5800 414 C
durban@cairn.edu
URBAN, David, J .... 615-898-2764 461 E
david.urban@mtsu.edu
URBAN, Kenneth .... 231-843-5802 252 H
kurban@westshore.edu
URBAN, Kristi .... 979-830-4141 469 F
kristi.urban@blinn.edu
URBAN, Laura .... 320-762-4404 257 O
laurau@alextech.edu
URBAN, Matthew .... 608-329-8202 542 L
murban@blackhawk.edu
URBAN, Rhonda, P .... 309-692-4092 152 F
rpurban@midstate.edu
URBANCZYK, Aaron ...... 615-297-7545 455 A
urbanczyka@aquinascollege.edu
URBANEK, Andrew .... 518-454-5182 322 C
urbaneka@strose.edu
URBANEK, Lauren .... 617-585-1113 234 H
lauren.urbanek@necmusic.edu
URBANIAK, David .... 989-686-9083 242 I
drubani@delta.edu
URBANICK, John .... 231-591-2138 242 L
JohnUrbanick@ferris.edu
URBANO, George .... 863-297-1086 110 E
gurbano@polk.edu

URBANSKI, Thomas ..... 815-836-5015 150 F
urbansth@lewisu.edu
URBANSKI, Tom .... 218-879-0820 258 F
urbanski@fdltcc.edu
URBISH, Leona .... 361-825-5785 485 F
leona.urbish@tamucc.edu
URBONYA, Tim .... 608-263-9676 541 E
tim.urbonya@uwex.uwc.edu
URDAN, Joely, B .... 414-229-4278 540 A
jurdan@uwm.edu
URETZ, Alan .... 773-975-1295 537 D
dragongi@comcast.net
UREY, Denise .... 724-589-2009 436 E
durey@thiel.edu
URGO, Joseph .... 828-251-6470 370 E
jurgo@unca.edu
URIAGEREKA, Juan ...... 301-405-4252 219 D
juan@umd.edu
URIBE-JENNINGS,
Marcela .... 508-929-8543 230 G
muribejennings@worcester.edu
URICK, Cynthia .... 610-796-8428 412 C
cynthia.urick@alvernia.edu
URISH, Jonathan, E ...... 608-363-2663 534 L
urishj@beloit.edu
URNER-JONES,
Katharine .... 617-243-2223 227 K
kurnerjones@lasell.edu
URQUIDEZ,
Kasandra, K .... 520-621-3705.. 18 E
kasandra@email.arizona.edu
URRABAZO, Gloria .... 210-434-6711 479 P
gaurrabazo@lake.ollusa.edu
URREA, Edda .... 956-364-4522 487 H
edda.urrea@tstc.edu
URSENBACH, Angela .... 208-732-6575 137 K
angelaursenbach@csi.edu
URSO, David .... 540-453-2376 514 H
ursod@brcc.edu
URSUY, Andrea .... 989-686-9222 242 I
alnadols@delta.edu
URSUY, Andrea, L .... 989-686-9222 242 I
alnadols@delta.edu
URTECHO, Robert .... 559-730-3942.. 41 D
robertur@cos.edu
URTZ, Anastasia .... 315-498-2692 337 F
urtza@sunyocc.edu
URTZ, Mike .... 607-753-4953 345 C
mike.urtz@cortland.edu
USATCH, Jeri .... 518-255-5227 346 E
usatchj@cobleskill.edu
USCHER, Nancy, J .... 206-726-5000 521 G
nuscher@cornish.edu
USOFF, Catherine .... 508-793-7670 225 B
cusoff@clarku.edu
USSERY, Janyth .... 325-236-8209 488 C
janyth.ussery@tstc.edu
UTASH, Sheree .... 316-677-9536 192 C
sutash@watc.edu
UTASH, Sheree .... 316-677-9400 192 C
sutash@watc.edu
UTECH, Tracy .... 313-577-9278 252 G
tracy.utech@wayne.edu
UTHOFF, Jay, L .... 563-387-1012 180 M
uthoffja@luther.edu
UTLEY, Shawn .... 229-333-1294 134 I
shawn.utley@wiregrass.edu
UTSEY, James .... 870-574-4421.. 23 E
jutsey@sautech.edu
UTSMAN, Michael .... 704-945-7312 367 F
michael.utsman@pfeiffer.edu
UTT, Kevin .... 563-588-6555 176 F
kevin.utt@clarke.edu
UTTER, Alan .... 828-262-7459 369 D
utterac@appstate.edu
UTTERBACK, Jim, W ..... 405-382-9200 402 C
j.utterback@sscok.edu
UVA, Mariflor .... 978-762-4000 232 D
muva@northshore.edu
UVIN, Peter .... 909-621-8117.. 39 F
peter.uvin@cmc.edu
UWAKWEH,
Benjamin, O .... 336-334-7567 370 B
bouwakweh@ncat.edu
UYEHARA, Alan, M ...... 409-944-1285 474 G
auyehara@gc.edu
UYEHARA, Penny .... 808-455-0272 136 G
pennys@hawaii.edu
UYENO, Russell .... 808-845-9135 136 E
ruyeno@hawaii.edu
UYENO, Sandra .... 808-956-7038 136 B
uyeno@hawaii.edu
UZMAN, Akif .... 713-221-8015 491 F
uzmana@uhd.edu
UZNANSKI, Laurel .... 360-867-6361 522 J
uznanski@evergreen.edu
UZORUO, Petra .... 409-984-6151 488 H
petra.uzoruo@lamarpa.edu
UZZELL, Yolanda .... 714-628-7201.. 38 B
uzzell@chapman.edu

V

VÉLEZ, Silvio .... 787-257-7373 555 L
silvio1@suagm.edu
VÉLEZ RIVERA,
Marcos, A .... 787-725-8120 552 G
mvelez@eap.edu
VÁSQUEZ, Carmen .... 718-289-5151 318 E
carmen.vasquez@bcc.cuny.edu
VÁZQUEZ, Carlos, R .... 787-884-3838 550 E
gerente@atenascollege.edu
VÁZQUEZ, Efraín .... 787-850-9375 558 A
efrain.vazquez@upr.edu
VÁZQUEZ-ESPEJO,
Nelson .... 787-993-8957 557 E
nelson.vazquez1@upr.edu
VABRE, Bert .... 201-761-7834 307 K
bvabre@saintpeters.edu
VACCA, Sheryl, S .... 510-987-9090.. 70 J
sheryl.vacca@ucop.edu
VACCARI, Peter, I .... 914-968-6200 341 D
sjsr@archny.org
VACCARO, Anne .... 718-862-7409 331 H
anne.vaccaro@manhattan.edu
VACCARO, Paul .... 781-768-7354 236 A
paul.vaccaro@regiscollege.edu
VACCARO, Thomas .... 845-451-1618 323 E
t_vaccar@culinary.edu
VACCHIANO, Joanna .... 215-646-7300 420 A
vacchiano.j@gmercyu.edu
VACIK, Steve .... 606-759-7141 196 G
VADEN, David .... 716-250-7500 317 B
dvaden@bryantstratton.edu
VADEN-GOAD, Linda ..... 508-626-4582 230 A
lvadengoad@framingham.edu
VADER, Patricia .... 909-469-5318.. 76 I
pvader@westernu.edu
VADGAMA, Jadutt .... 323-563-9397.. 38 C
jayvadgama@cdrewu.edu
VAGLIENTI, Kendra .... 972-860-4332 472 C
kvaglienti@dcccd.edu
VAHEY, Karen .... 516-686-7742 335 F
Karen.Vahey@nyit.edu
VAHEY, Terry .... 408-924-7808.. 36 B
terry.vahey@sjsu.edu
VAHLBUSCH, Jefford, B 715-836-3621 539 E
vahlbujb@uwec.edu
VAHLE, Kirby, L .... 214-648-2400 496 A
kirby.vahle@utsouthwestern.edu
VAHSEN, Steven, S ...... 410-293-1568 549 B
vahsen@usna.edu
VAIDYA, Abhishek .... 510-628-8010.. 50 I
avaidya@lincolnuca.edu
VAIDYA, Ashish .... 320-308-4909 261 E
akvaidya@stcloudstate.edu
VAIL, Jody .... 207-974-4633 211 A
jvail@emcc.edu
VAIL, Mita, K .... 757-455-3217 518 H
mvail@vwc.edu
VAILAS, Arthur, C .... 208-282-3440 138 C
vailarth@isu.edu
VAILLANCOURT,
Allison, M .... 520-621-1684.. 18 E
vaillana@email.arizona.edu
VAIRO, Carl, A .... 610-565-1095 440 C
cvairo@williamson.edu
VAITHYLINGAM,
Mugunth .... 702-651-5900 295 C
mugunth.vaithylingam@csn.edu
VAKAMUDI, Ramesh .... 404-413-0721 126 D
fmdrkv@gsu.edu
VAKIL, David .... 951-571-6162.. 60 K
david.vakil@mvc.edu
VAKNIN, Lauren .... 619-660-4295.. 46 G
lauren.vaknin@gcccd.edu
VALASEK, Tricia .... 419-434-4429 393 F
valasek@findlay.edu
VALBUENA, Ruben .... 561-912-1211 102 N
rvalbuena@evergladesuniversity.edu
VALCIK, Nicolas .... 304-293-4245 533 D
nicolas.valcik@mail.wvu.edu
VALCKE, Cathy .... 765-455-9226 168 B
chightow@iuk.edu
VALCOURT, George .... 352-371-2833 101 M
director@dragonrises.edu
VALCOURT, George .... 352-371-2833 101 M
academicdean@dragonrises.edu
VALDÉS PIZZINI,
Manuel .... 787-265-3828 558 B
decano.arci@uprm.edu
VALDES, Didier .... 787-265-3809 558 B
egraduados.uprm@upr.edu
VALDES, Eduardo .... 409-772-8780 495 E
pvaldes@utmb.edu
VALDES, Jose, L .... 305-821-3333 104 C
jvaldes@fnu.edu
VALDES, Mario .... 262-243-5700 535 I
mario.valdes@cuw.edu
VALDES, Michael .... 734-487-2031 242 J
mvaldes@emich.edu
VALDES, Theresa .... 847-233-7700 155 B
tvaldes@nc.edu
VALDEZ, Al .... 951-785-2115.. 49 I
avaldez@lasierra.edu
VALDEZ, Alex .... 956-665-7021 494 C
alexv@utpa.edu
VALDEZ, Alfred, W .... 818-767-0888.. 77 G
alfredo.valdez@woodbury.edu
VALDEZ, Anna .... 707-527-4527.. 65 C
avaldez@santarosa.edu
VALDEZ, Benjamin, C .. 303-837-0825.. 79 C
valdezb@aii.edu
VALDEZ, Cristobal, O ... 307-855-2101 545 a
cvaldez@cwc.edu
VALDEZ, Jude .... 210-458-2401 494 D
jude.valdez@utsa.edu
VALDEZ, Patrick .... 718-405-3343 322 A
patrick.valdez@mountsaintvincent.edu
VALDISERRI, Rachel, R . 989-837-4140 248 D
valdiser@northwood.edu
VALDIVIA, Nicolas .... 562-985-8391.. 33 F
nick.valdivia@csulb.edu
VALE, SSJ, Carol Jean . 215-248-7021 415 D
cvale@chc.edu
VALE, Darla .... 513-244-4295 387 A
darla.vale@msj.edu
VALEK, Millicent, M ..... 979-230-3200 469 G
millicent.valek@brazosport.edu
VALENCIA, Dawn .... 951-222-8000.. 60 J
Dawn.Valencia@rcc.edu
VALENCIA, Dawn .... 951-222-8649.. 61 B
dawn.valencia@rcc.edu
VALENCIA, Jamie .... 904-332-0910 106 A
VALENCIA, Jose .... 718-522-9073 315 E
jvalencia@asa.edu
VALENCIA, Karen .... 214-860-3687 472 G
kvalencia@dcccd.edu
VALENCIA, Rebecca ...... 407-303-9203.. 97 J
rebecca.valencia@adu.edu
VALENCIA, Rose Mary .. 713-500-4472 495 A
Rose.Mary.Valencia@uth.tmc.edu
VALENCIA, Steven, J .... 580-327-8478 399 F
sjvalencia@nwosu.edu
VALENCIA, Susan .... 510-869-8628.. 61 J
svalencia@samuelmerritt.edu
VALENCIA-DAYE,
Carmelita, E .... 203-285-2172.. 89 B
cvalencia-daye@gwcc.commnet.edu
VALENTE, Aurelio .... 708-235-7594 145 D
avalente@govst.edu
VALENTE, Bianca .... 610-359-5292 416 G
bvalente@dccc.edu
VALENTE, Elizabeth .... 650-508-3515.. 56 H
evalentepigato@ndnu.edu
VALENTE, Jason .... 517-787-0800 244 H
valentejasonh@jccmi.edu
VALENTE, Laura .... 973-596-3470 304 D
laura.valente@njit.edu
VALENTE, Mario .... 760-757-2121.. 54 G
mvalente@miracosta.edu
VALENTI, Joseph .... 845-569-3216 333 I
jospeh.valenti@msmc.edu
VALENTIINE, Anne, P ... 317-921-4882 169 M
VALENTIN, Angel .... 787-786-3030 556 E
avalentin@ucb.edu.pr
VALENTIN, Annette .... 787-786-3030 556 E
anvalentin@ucb.edu.pr
VALENTIN,
Cruz Belinda .... 787-764-0000 558 E
cruz.valentin1@upr.edu
VALENTIN, Julio .... 407-708-2281 113 A
valentij@seminolestate.edu
VALENTIN, Luz, C .... 787-786-3030 556 E
lvalentin@ucb.edu.pr
VALENTIN, Maribel .... 787-728-1515 559 A
mvalentin@sagrado.edu
VALENTINE, Ann .... 319-887-3614 180 J
ann.valentine@kirkwood.edu
VALENTINE, Anne, P .... 317-921-4882 169 L
VALENTINE, Bryan .... 505-984-6096 312 J
bvalentine@sjc.edu
VALENTINE, Carey, G ... 248-204-3800 245 J
campfac@ltu.edu
VALENTINE, David .... 617-928-4710 234 D
dvalentine@mountida.edu
VALENTINE, Jared .... 503-517-1008 411 A
jvalentine@warnerpacific.edu
VALENTINE, Leanne .... 712-749-2164 176 D
valentinel@bvu.edu
VALENTINE, Maureen ... 724-503-1001 439 B
mvalentine@washjeff.edu
VALENTINE, Peggy .... 336-750-2570 372 D
valentinepe@wssu.edu
VALENTINE, Sidney ...... 863-784-7120 113 C
sid.valentine@southflorida.edu
VALENTINE, Sidney ...... 803-327-8017 451 K
svalentine@yorktech.edu
VALENTINI, James, J .... 212-854-2443 322 F
jjv1@columbia.edu
VALENTINO, Christina .. 401-874-2433 442 E
clvalentino@mail.uri.edu
VALENTINO, Teresa ...... 828-652-0657 364 B
teresavalentino@mcdowelltech.edu
VALENTO, Bernard .... 716-375-2128 340 C
bvalento@sbu.edu
VALENZA, John, A .... 713-486-4021 495 A
john.a.valenza@uth.tmc.edu
VALENZUELA,
Cesario, E .... 432-837-8076 489 B
cesariov@sulross.edu
VALENZUELA, Eileen ..... 925-473-7406.. 42 F
evalenzuela@losmedanos.edu
VALENZUELA, Ernesto .. 520-494-5459.. 12 R
ernesto.valenzuela@centralaz.edu
VALERA, Luis .... 702-895-2389 295 G
luis.valera@unlv.edu
VALERA, Marc .... 718-817-3842 326 C
valera@fordham.edu
VALERIANO, Oscar .... 323-265-8779.. 51 D
valerio@elac.edu
VALERIO, Brett .... 414-443-8785 542 I
brett.valerio@wlc.edu
VALERY, Susanne .... 805-922-6966.. 26 H
svalery@hancockcollege.edu
VALERY, Suzanne .... 805-922-6966.. 26 H
svalery@hancockcollege.edu
VALINES, Francisco ...... 305-348-2347 114 G
valinesf@fiu.edu
VALINTIS, Michelle .... 503-777-7705 409 E
mvalintis@reed.edu
VALIS, Ashley, R .... 410-706-5179 219 E
avalis@umaryland.edu
VALLANCE, Brenda, J ... 512-448-8550 481 B
brendav@stedwards.edu
VALLEJO, Isabel .... 408-273-2695.. 55 G
ivallejo@nhu.edu
VALLEJO, Jesus, G .... 832-824-4204 469 C
jvallejo@bcm.edu
VALLEJO, Maria, M .... 561-868-3400 109 H
vallejom@palmbeachstate.edu
VALLELLANES, Luz, N ... 787-786-3030 556 E
nereidav@ucb.edu.pr
VALLER, Thomas .... 970-945-8691.. 80 D
VALLEREUX, Alison .... 617-732-1655 226 B
vallereuxa@emmanuel.edu
VALLES, Arleen .... 575-835-5162 311 I
avalles@admin.nmt.edu
VALLEY, Timothy .... 414-277-7150 537 G
valley@msoe.edu
VALLI, Robert .... 516-299-4000 330 G
rob.valli@liu.edu
VALLOZZI, Jason .... 412-359-1000 437 F
tkucic@triangle-tech.edu
VALLS, Ophelia .... 305-442-9223 108 G
ovalls@mrc.edu
VALOSKY, Kenneth, G .. 610-519-4530 439 A
ken.valosky@villanova.edu
VALSARAJ, Kalliat, T .... 225-578-7696 204 M
valsaraj@lsu.edu
VALTOS, Jennifer .... 770-426-2762 128 C
jvaltos@life.edu
VALUCK, Angela .... 217-245-3002 146 D
angela.valuck@mail.ic.edu
VALUCKAS,
Christine, A .... 410-287-1027 214 C
cvaluckas@cecil.edu
VALVERDE, Shannon .... 508-541-1841 225 G
svalverde@dean.edu
VAN AKEN, Troy, D ..... 724-589-2100 436 E
tvanaken@thiel.edu
VAN ALLEN, George, H 615-353-3236 463 C
george.vanallen@nscc.edu
VAN ALLEN, Terry .... 810-766-3383 251 E
terryva@umflint.edu
VAN ALSBURG,
Teresa, D .... 304-457-6380 529 C
vanalsburgtd@ab.edu
VAN ALSTINE, Tim, M . 414-410-4839 535 C
tvanalstine@stritch.edu
VAN ARNAM, Sherrie ... 718-940-5754 341 A
svanarnam@sjcny.edu
VAN AUKEN, James ..... 757-631-8101 504 O
james.vanauken@atlanticuniv.edu
VAN AUKEN, Sharon .... 518-327-6242 338 B
svanauken100@paulsmiths.edu
VAN BERGEN, Mildred . 516-876-4076 348 A
mildred.vanbergen@esc.edu
VAN BERKOM, Debbie . 701-224-5431 374 E
debbie.vanberkom@bismarckstate.edu
VAN BLARCOM,
Ronald .... 949-214-3135.. 42 B
ron.vanblarcom@cui.edu
VAN BLOMMESTEIN,
Sharmain .... 315-267-2116 346 C
vanblos@potsdam.edu
VAN BOORST, James ... 518-956-8120 343 C
nwilson@albany.edu
VAN BROEKHOVEN,
Rollin .... 704-243-0737 460 B
rvanbroekhoven@futurelead.org

VAN BRUNT, Troy, G ... 956-721-5326 477 C
troyvb@laredo.edu
VAN BUREN, Jason ...... 610-409-3249 438 H
afeick@ursinus.edu
VAN CANNEYT,
Donna, S .... 901-678-2810 462 B
dvncnnyt@memphis.edu
VAN CLEAVE, Rachel .... 415-442-6601.. 46 A
rvancleave@ggu.edu
VAN CLEAVE, Robb ...... 541-506-6150 405 C
rvancleave@cgcc.edu
VAN CLEAVE,
Samuel, J .... 480-423-6003.. 15 E
samuel.vancleave@scottsdalecc.edu
VAN CLEAVE, William ... 504-865-5767 207 F
wvanclea@tulane.edu
VAN CLEEF, Robert .... 978-867-4610 227 A
robert.vancleef@gordon.edu
VAN CLEEF, Sarah, E ... 903-510-2033 491 A
svan@tjc.edu
VAN DAM, Dale .... 530-642-5615.. 53 A
vandamd@flc.losrios.edu
VAN DE CAR, Katharyn 702-651-4516 295 C
kathy.vandecar@csn.edu
VAN DE LOO, John ...... 715-365-4553 543 G
vandeloo@nicoletcollege.edu
VAN DE MOORTELL,
Raymond .... 617-254-2610 236 B
rev.raymond.vandemoortell@sjs.edu
VAN DE PUTTE,
André S, F .... 215-972-2047 429 G
avandeputte@pafa.edu
VAN DE VOORDE,
Peter .... 239-280-2500.. 98 O
peter.vandevoorde@avemaria.edu
VAN DEKKER, Angela ... 718-817-3800 326 C
avandekker@fordham.edu
VAN DEN ABBEELE,
Georges .... 949-824-5133.. 71 C
gvandena@uci.edu
VAN DEN HEEVER,
Nicolaas .... 949-783-4800.. 75 K
nvandenheever@westcoastuniversity.edu
VAN DEN HEUVEL,
Nicole .... 713-348-4055 480 M
nvdh@rice.edu
VAN DEN HUL,
Richard, D .... 360-650-3182 528 D
rich.vandenhul@wwu.edu
VAN DENEND,
Michael, J .... 616-526-6142 240 L
vanden@calvin.edu
VAN DER AA, Jan .... 901-448-2500 465 G
jvandera@uthsc.edu
VAN DER BURG, Anna . 860-685-2810.. 93 B
avanderburg@wesleyan.edu
VAN DER GIESSEN,
Hans .... 203-576-4668.. 92 B
hvdg@bridgeport.edu
VAN DER KAAY,
Christopher .... 863-784-7413 113 C
christopher.vanderkaay@southflorida.edu
VAN DER KARR, Carol . 607-753-2206 345 C
carol.vanderkarr@cortland.edu
VAN DER KLEY, Jan ..... 269-387-2365 252 I
jan.vanderkley@wmich.edu
VAN DER MERWE,
Derek .... 931-221-6206 461 C
vandermerwed@apsu.edu
VAN DER POL, Willem . 657-278-3133.. 33 E
wvanderpol@fullerton.edu
VAN DER SCHYF,
Cornelis .... 208-282-3134 138 C
vandcorn@isu.edu
VAN DER SCHYF,
Cornelis .... 208-282-2490 138 C
vandcorn@isu.edu
VAN DER VEER,
Mary Caroline .... 518-587-2100 348 A
marycaroline.powers@esc.edu
VAN DER VELDEN,
Andre .... 530-283-0202.. 44 H
avandervelden@frc.edu
VAN DER WALL,
Melissa .... 201-684-7540 305 F
mvanderw@ramapo.edu
VAN DER WALL,
Melissa .... 201-684-7457 305 F
mvanderw@ramapo.edu
VAN DEREN, Jessica .... 802-728-1244 504 C
jvanderen@vtc.edu
VAN DERVEER,
Rachael, E .... 724-847-6596 419 B
revander@geneva.edu
VAN DEVEN, Randy ...... 903-468-8181 485 E
randy.vandeven@tamuc.edu
VAN DONSELAAR,
Brian .... 712-722-6299 177 J
brian.vandonselaar@dordt.edu

VAN DUSEN, Michael .... 561-912-2166 102 N
mvandusen@evergladesuniversity.edu
VAN DUYNE, Patrick .... 815-280-6696 148 K
pvanduyn@jjc.edu
VAN DUZER, Jeffrey, B 206-281-2508 526 D
vandj@spu.edu
VAN DYK, Leanne .... 404-687-4514 123 C
vandykl@ctsnet.edu
VAN DYK, Vanessa ...... 406-496-4322 288 C
vvandyk@mtech.edu
VAN DYKE, Jon .... 217-234-5378 150 B
jvandyke@lakeland.cc.il.us
VAN DYKE, Karin .... 906-487-7344 242 M
karin.vandyke@finlandia.edu
VAN DYKE, Patricia ...... 716-829-7802 324 E
vandykep@dyc.edu
VAN DYKEN, Douglas .. 616-395-7810 244 A
vandyken@hope.edu
VAN DYNE, Karen .... 617-619-1900 227 G
karen.vandyne@hult.edu
VAN ECK, Thomas, A ... 616-526-8553 240 L
tveck@calvin.edu
VAN ESS, Jami .... 928-226-4209.. 13 D
jami.vaness@coconino.edu
VAN-ESS, Michelle .... 212-217-4132 325 C
michelle_vaness@fitnyc.edu
VAN FLEET, Julie, L ..... 309-341-5213 140 I
jlvanfleet@sandburg.edu
VAN FOSSEN,
Dell Jean .... 951-785-2088.. 49 I
dvanfoss@lasierra.edu
VAN FOSSEN, Drew ...... 920-403-4427 538 K
drew.vanfossen@snc.edu
VAN GALEN, Dean, A ... 715-425-3201 540 E
dean.vangalen@uwrf.edu
VAN GILDER, Holly ...... 330-490-7146 395 C
hvangilder@walsh.edu
VAN GILS-PIERCE,
Adriane .... 508-793-7587 225 B
avangils@clarku.edu
VAN GINHOVEN,
Lee, H .... 269-927-8611 245 E
vanginhoven@lakemichigancollege.edu
VAN GORDON, Beth ..... 219-981-4282 168 C
vgordon@iun.edu
VAN GORDON,
Elizabeth .... 574-520-4463 168 F
vgordon@iusb.edu
VAN GORDON,
Elizabeth .... 317-274-3022 169 A
vgordon@iu.edu
VAN GRONINGEN,
Willis .... 708-239-4880 160 L
bill.vangroningen@trnty.edu
VAN GRUENSVEN,
Sheryl .... 920-465-2326 539 F
vangrues@uwgb.edu
VAN GUILDER, Sean .... 352-588-8268 111 L
sean.vanguilder@saintleo.edu
VAN GUNDY, Douglas . 304-473-8243 534 G
vangundy@wvwc.edu
VAN HAMERSVELD,
Pete .... 310-243-3825.. 33 B
pvanhamersveld@csudh.edu
VAN HARPEN,
Robin, L .... 414-229-4461 540 A
rvanharp@uwm.edu
VAN HEERDEN, Elna .... 858-513-9240.. 29 A
Elna.VanHeerden@ashford.edu
VAN HEMERT, John, L . 540-674-3660 516 B
jvanhemert@nr.edu
VAN HOECK, Michele ... 707-654-1097.. 34 B
mvanhoeck@csum.edu
VAN HOESEN, Matthew 816-584-6432 280 F
matthew.vanhoesen@park.edu
VAN HOLLAND,
Phyllis, L .... 360-417-6291 525 A
pvanholland@pencol.edu
VAN HOOK, Dianne, G 661-362-3400.. 40 H
dianne.vanhook@canyons.edu
VAN HOOK, Jayson ..... 423-614-8695 457 M
jvanhook@leeuniversity.edu
VAN HORN, Brian, W .. 270-809-4159 198 I
bvanhorn@murraystate.edu
VAN HORN, Donald, L . 304-696-6433 532 H
vanhorn@marshall.edu
VAN HORN, Drew .... 828-328-7108 358 G
drew.vanhorn@lr.edu
VAN HORN, Leigh .... 713-221-8991 491 F
vanhornl@uhd.edu
VAN HORN, Stuart ...... 559-934-2131.. 76 A
stuartvanhorn@whccd.edu
VAN HORN, Wayne ...... 601-925-3297 268 E
wvanhorn@mc.edu
VAN HOUTEN, Carol .... 201-360-4722 303 A
cvanhouten@hccc.edu
VAN HOUTEN, Michael 517-629-0567 239 A
mvanhouten@albion.edu
VAN HOUTEN, Pete ..... 307-268-3088 545 Z
pvanhouten@caspercollege.edu

VAN KERCKVOORDE,
Colette .... 413-528-7232 222 F
colette@simons-rock.edu
VAN KEUREN,
Karen, A .... 585-785-1206 325 E
karen.vankeuren@flcc.edu
VAN KIRK, Shannon .... 775-673-7000 295 F
svankirk@tmcc.edu
VAN KLEY, Eric .... 641-628-5310 176 E
vankleye@central.edu
VAN KLEY, Sandy .... 712-707-7145 182 C
svankley@nwciowa.edu
VAN KLOMPENBERG,
Brian .... 312-862-3217.. 70 D
Brian.Vanklompenberg@kirkland.com
VAN KOOTEN, Rick ...... 812-855-3931 167 J
rvankoot@indiana.edu
VAN KOOY, Samantha . 856-415-2276 306 C
svankooy@rcgc.edu
VAN LANINGHAM,
Kathy, M .... 479-575-5910.. 23 G
kvl@uark.edu
VAN LEAR, Eryn .... 804-355-8135 505 B
evanlear@btsr.edu
VAN LEIDEN, Melissa .. 785-594-8306 184 F
melissa.vanleiden@bakeru.edu
VAN LIERE, Lori .... 419-866-0261 391 L
Lori.VanLiere@sctoday.edu
VAN LIEW, Fred .... 303-937-4035.. 80 A
fvanliew@chu.edu
VAN LOO, Scott, D ...... 419-289-5088 377 A
svanloo@ashland.edu
VAN METER, Eric .... 605-995-2919 452 C
ervanmet@dwu.edu
VAN NESS, Forrest, L ... 314-516-6680 284 B
vannessf@umsl.edu
VAN NIEKERK, Andre ... 818-767-0888.. 77 G
andre.vanniekerk@woodbury.edu
VAN NOORT, Kimberly . 817-272-0777 493 L
vannoort@uta.edu
VAN NORMAN, Karen .. 973-761-9076 308 C
karen.vannorman@shu.edu
VAN OMMEREN, Ryan .. 805-493-3211.. 31 H
rvommere@callutheran.edu
VAN OORT, Harlan .... 712-707-7190 182 C
hvanoort@nwciowa.edu
VAN OOT, Amy .... 860-701-5019.. 91 B
vanoot_a@mitchell.edu
VAN ORMAN, Kit .... 315-364-3317 352 F
kit@wells.edu
VAN ORMAN, Sarah, A 608-262-1885 539 D
svanorman@uhs.wisc.edu
VAN ORSDEL, Lee .... 616-331-2621 243 E
vanorsdl@gvsu.edu
VAN OSTERN, Kristyn ... 603-230-3509 296 J
kvanostern@ccsnh.edu
VAN PELT, Donna .... 515-294-1280 175 G
dvanpelt@foundation.iastate.edu
VAN RIJN, Paul .... 215-885-2360 425 C
pvanrijn@manor.edu
VAN SCHARREL,
Mark, H .... 773-256-0676 151 H
mvanscha@lstc.edu
VAN SCOTT, Michael .... 252-328-9479 369 E
vanscottm@ecu.edu
VAN SLYKE, Craig .... 928-523-7345.. 16 C
Craig.Vanslyke@nau.edu
VAN SOELEN, Timothy . 712-722-6228 177 J
timothy.vansoelen@dcrdt.edu
VAN STRATEN, Amy ..... 920-831-4355 542 N
vanstrat@fvtc.edu
VAN TASSEL, Kristin ..... 785-227-3380 185 A
vantasselk@bethanylb.edu
VAN TASSELL, TOR,
Malachi .... 814-472-3001 434 F
mvantassell@francis.edu
VAN TIL, Seth, J .... 724-458-3887 419 F
sjvantil@gcc.edu
VAN TRAN, Lac .... 312-942-3400 158 A
lac_tran@rush.edu
VAN TUYL, Jonah .... 928-350-4406.. 17 K
jvantuyl@prescott.edu
VAN UUM, Elizabeth .... 314-516-5774 284 B
vanuum@umsl.edu
VAN VLECK, Thomas .... 660-626-2138 271 G
tvanvleck@atsu.edu
VAN VLERAH, Abagail .. 516-299-2255 330 G
abby.vanvlerah@liu.edu
VAN VOLKENBURGH,
Linda, C .... 513-861-6400 392 F
linda.van@myunion.edu
VAN VOORHIS,
Amanda .... 508-999-9114 228 H
avanvoorhis@umassd.edu
VAN VOORHIS, Sue, N 612-625-8098 265 C
vanvo002@umn.edu
VAN WAGNER, Molly ... 715-425-3195 540 E
molly.van-wagner@uwrf.edu

VAN WAGNER,
Thomas .... 202-231-4193 547 N
thomas.vanwagner@dodiis.mil
VAN WAGONER,
Randall, J .... 315-792-5333 333 D
rvanwagoner@mvcc.edu
VAN WIE, Lisa .... 518-629-8143 328 D
l.vanwie@hvcc.edu
VAN WINKLE, Ken .... 575-439-3640 312 B
kvanwink@nmsu.edu
VAN WINKLE, Robynne 541-440-4668 410 E
robynne.vanwinkle@umpqua.edu
VAN WYK, Natalie .... 610-361-5418 427 D
vanwykn@neumann.edu
VAN ZANDT, David ...... 212-229-5656 334 C
vanzandt@newschool.edu
VAN ZANDT,
Patricia, R .... 423-439-4337 461 D
vanzandt@etsu.edu
VAN ZEE, Ryan .... 605-995-2902 452 C
ryvanzee@dwu.edu
VAN ZEE, Trudy .... 410-516-8056 216 A
tvanzee@jhu.edu
VAN ZINDEREN, Gary .. 701-252-3467 375 J
gvanzind@uj.edu
VAN ZYL, Henry .... 609-292-4000 308 H
phvanzyl@tesc.edu
VANANDEN, Ian .... 301-447-5310 217 D
vananden@msmary.edu
VANARSDALL, Cathy ..... 765-361-6421 175 B
vanarsdc@wabash.edu
VANASSE, Dennis .... 508-849-3372 222 C
dvanasse@annamaria.edu
VANASSE, Nancy .... 508-999-8133 228 H
nvasasse@umassd.edu
VANAUSDLE, Steven, L 509-527-4274 527 H
steven.vanausdle@wwcc.edu
VANBERGEIJK, Ernst .... 631-348-3117 335 F
evanberg@nyit.edu
VANBOOVEN, Gerry ...... 818-299-5526.. 75 K
gvanbooven@westcoastuniversity.edu
VANBROCKLIN,
Michael .... 903-233-4332 477 G
mikevanbrocklin@letu.edu
VANCE, Carl .... 503-768-7801 406 H
cvance@lclark.edu
VANCE, Elaine .... 202-651-5288.. 95 C
janet.vance@gallaudet.edu
VANCE, Gina, M .... 724-946-7110 439 D
vancegm@westminster.edu
VANCE, Maria .... 707-965-7000.. 57 I
mvance@puc.edu
VANCE, Mickey .... 601-635-6338 267 B
mvance@eccc.edu
VANCE, Otis .... 207-333-7743 210 J
vanceot@cmhc.org
VANCE, Richard, N .... 765-658-4233 165 G
richardvance@depauw.edu
VANCE, Sheilah .... 610-399-2430 430 D
svance@cheyney.edu
VANCE, W.C .... 419-289-4142 377 A
wvance@ashland.edu
VANCKO, Candace, S ... 607-746-4090 347 G
vanckocs@delhi.edu
VANCLEAVE, Donna ...... 804-819-4695 514 G
dvancleave@vccs.edu
VANCOTT,
Mary Grooms .... 707-826-3146.. 35 D
vancott@humboldt.edu
VANDAL, Courtney .... 701-228-5613 374 F
courtney.vandal@dakotacollege.edu
VANDAL, Magdeleine ... 410-386-8386 214 B
mvandal@carrollcc.edu
VANDALL,
Christopher, P .... 608-258-2448 543 C
cvandall@madisoncollege.edu
VANDE YACHT, Daniel . 715-425-3342 540 E
daniel.vandeyacht@uwrf.edu
VANDE ZANDE,
Carleen .... 920-424-3190 540 B
vandezac@uwosh.edu
VANDEL, Laurie .... 406-496-4119 288 C
lvandel@mtech.edu
VANDELL, Deborah, L .. 949-824-8026.. 71 C
dvandell@uci.edu
VANDEMAN, Nancy .... 740-753-7009 383 G
vandemann@hocking.edu
VANDENAKKER, John ... 313-883-8750 249 E
vandenakker.john@shms.edu
VANDENAVOND, Steve . 906-227-6767 248 B
svanden@nmu.edu
VANDENBARK, Cyndi ... 970-521-6763.. 84 H
cyndi.vandenbark@njc.edu
VANDENBERG, Mary, L 616-957-6021 240 M
mvberg96@calvinseminary.edu
VANDENBERG, Matt ..... 989-463-7081 239 B
vandenbergmp@alma.edu
VANDENBERG, Rex .... 805-922-6966.. 26 H
rVandenberg@hancockcollege.edu

VASQUEZ, Amanda .... 915-747-5544 494 B
avasquez6@utep.edu
VASQUEZ, Andrew .... 830-372-8017 487 C
avasquez@tlu.edu
VASQUEZ, Andy .... 830-372-6811 487 C
avasquez@tlu.edu
VASQUEZ, Becky .... 386-226-6948 102 B
vasquezb@erau.edu
VASQUEZ, Graciela .... 562-860-2451.. 37 L
gvasquez@cerritos.edu
VASQUEZ, James .... 718-260-5244 320 D
jvazquez@citytech.cuny.edu
VASQUEZ, Jeffrey .... 206-934-3643 525 K
jeffrey.vasquez@seattlecolleges.edu
VASQUEZ, Lisa, R .... 972-758-3894 471 C
lvasquez@collin.edu
VASQUEZ, Patricia .... 617-745-3851 225 H
patty.vasquez@enc.edu
VASQUEZ, Rojelio .... 559-442-8222.. 69 B
rojelio.vasquez@fresnocitycollege.edu
VASQUEZ, Sandy .... 915-747-7873 494 B
svasquez@utep.edu
VASQUEZ, Sharon .... 860-768-4505.. 92 F
svasquez@hartford.edu
VASQUEZ DE VELASCO,
Guillermo, P .... 765-285-5863 164 D
guillermo@bsu.edu
VASQUEZ-LEVY, David .. 510-849-8223.. 57 G
president@psr.edu
VASS, Robert .... 203-576-4228.. 92 B
rvass@bridgeport.edu
VASSALLO, Donna .... 609-343-4972 299 G
dvassall@atlantic.edu
VASSAR, John, S .... 318-797-5326 205 F
john.s.vassar@lsus.edu
VASSAR, Pam .... 913-469-8500 188 E
pvassar@jccc.edu
VASUDEVAN,
Palligarnai, T .... 603-862-3290 299 B
vasu@unh.edu
VATANDOOST, Cyrus .... 615-514-2787 459 O
cyrus@nossi.edu
VATANDOOST, Nossi .... 615-514-2787 459 O
nossi@nossi.edu
VATER, Ruth .... 608-363-2606 534 L
vaterr@beloit.edu
VATISTAS, Vatistas .... 262-551-6001 535 E
vvatistas@carthage.edu
VAUGHAN, Anthony ...... 212-678-8816 329 H
anvaughan@jtsa.edu
VAUGHAN, Bruce, F ..... 757-455-3309 518 H
bvaughan@vwc.edu
VAUGHAN, Cathy, A ..... 270-824-1705 196 F
cathy.vaughan@kctcs.edu
VAUGHAN, Cheryl .... 804-763-6300.. 96 H
cheryl.vaughan@strayer.edu
VAUGHAN, Chris .... 309-794-7292 139 K
chrisvaughan@augustana.edu
VAUGHAN, Dixie .... 740-374-8716 395 D
dvaughan@wscc.edu
VAUGHAN, Greg .... 562-903-4752.. 29 F
greg.vaughan@biola.edu
VAUGHAN, Icer .... 316-942-4291 189 K
vaughani@newmanu.edu
VAUGHAN, Jesse .... 804-524-5877 518 C
jvaughan@vsu.edu
VAUGHAN, Joseph .... 909-621-8613.. 46 K
joseph_vaughan@hmc.edu
VAUGHAN, II, Juan, E . 252-862-1375 365 C
wpvann6919@roanokechowan.edu
VAUGHAN, Karen .... 908-526-1200 305 G
Karen.Vaughan@raritanval.edu
VAUGHAN, Larry, F ...... 615-547-1222 456 C
lvaughan@cumberland.edu
VAUGHAN, Leslie .... 617-989-4510 237 G
vaughanl@wit.edu
VAUGHAN, JR.,
Robert, A .... 678-466-4100 122 J
robertvaughan@clayton.edu
VAUGHAN, Sally, J ...... 585-385-8196 340 F
svaughan@sjfc.edu
VAUGHAN, Terri .... 515-271-2871 177 K
terri.vaughan@drake.edu
VAUGHN, Deborah, S .. 662-915-1687 270 G
dvaughn@olemiss.edu
VAUGHN, Erin .... 601-979-2326 267 H
erin.c.vaughn@jsums.edu
VAUGHN, Katherine ...... 870-743-3000.. 22 A
kvaughn@northark.edu
VAUGHN, Kellie .... 270-789-5001 194 D
kpvaughn@campbellsville.edu
VAUGHN, Lori .... 413-565-1000 222 G
lvaughn@baypath.edu
VAUGHN, Patti .... 617-262-5000 223 G
Patti.Vaughn@the-bac.edu
VAUGHN, Ray .... 256-824-6100.... 9 A
ray.vaughn@uah.edu
VAUGHN, Robert .... 323-856-7661.. 27 H
rvaughn@afi.com
VAUGHN, Ronald, L ..... 813-253-6201 118 H
president@ut.edu
VAUGHN, Sandra, C .... 662-252-8000 270 C
svaughn@rustcollege.edu
VAUGHN, Suzanne, A .. 661-395-4301.. 49 E
svaughn@bakersfieldcollege.edu
VAUGHN, Woodrow ..... 256-726-7306.... 6 C
wvaughn@oakwood.edu
VAUGHT, Wayne .... 816-235-2815 284 A
vaughtw@umkc.edu
VAUPEL, Christian .... 516-877-3258 314 F
cpvaupel@adelphi.edu
VAUX-MICHEL, Teresa .. 570-561-1818 435 A
teresa.vauxmichel@stots.edu
VAVASOUR, JoEllen, L . 914-654-5541 322 B
jvavasour@cnr.edu
VAVOLIZZA, Ann .... 845-848-4001 324 B
ann.vavolizza@dc.edu
VAVREK, Milan, C .... 304-462-6111 532 G
milan.vavrek@glenville.edu
VAVRICKA, Janda .... 414-277-2234 537 G
vavricka@msoe.edu
VAWTER, Cheryl, D ...... 509-777-4518 529 A
cvawter@whitworth.edu
VAYDA, Michael, E .... 479-575-2034.. 23 G
mvayda@uark.edu
VAZ, Maria, J .... 248-204-2400 245 J
provost@ltu.edu
VAZQUEZ, Adela .... 787-620-2040 550 D
avazquez@aupr.edu
VAZQUEZ, Airlyn .... 787-882-2065 556 C
biblioteca@unitecpr.net
VAZQUEZ, Carlos .... 787-738-2161 557 G
carlos.vazquez5@upr.edu
VAZQUEZ, Carmen, M . 619-260-4588.. 74 B
carmenvazquez@sandiego.edu
VAZQUEZ, David .... 239-590-1123 114 F
dvazquez@fgcu.edu
VAZQUEZ, Drianfel, E ... 787-844-8181 558 D
drianfel.vazquez@upr.edu
VAZQUEZ, Elizabeth ..... 561-586-0121 105 R
evazquez@hci.edu
VAZQUEZ, Felice .... 908-737-7000 303 C
fvazquez@kean.edu
VAZQUEZ, Frank .... 888-384-0849.. 26 O
fvazquez@allied.edu
VAZQUEZ, Heber .... 787-834-9595 556 D
heberv@uaa.edu
VAZQUEZ, Hector .... 787-765-3560 552 E
hvazquez@edpuniversity.edu
VAZQUEZ, Jaime .... 787-780-0070 550 G
jvazquez@caribbean.edu
VAZQUEZ, Maria .... 787-864-2222 553 J
maria.vazquez@guayama.inter.edu
VAZQUEZ, Maria .... 787-725-8120 552 G
mvazquez0060@eap.edu
VAZQUEZ, Marie .... 402-457-2430 291 E
mvazquez@mccneb.edu
VAZQUEZ, Obed .... 925-969-2423.. 42 E
ovazquez@dvc.edu
VAZQUEZ, Rosabel .... 787-620-2040 550 D
rvazquez@aupr.edu
VAZQUEZ, Silvio .... 805-565-6200.. 76 K
svazquez@westmont.edu
VAZQUEZ, Vilmaris ...... 787-878-5475 553 F
vvazquez@arecibo.inter.edu
VAZQUEZ-BARQUET,
Ernesto .... 787-754-8000 556 H
evazquez@pupr.edu
VAZQUEZ-CALLE,
Fernando .... 787-738-2161 557 G
fernando.vazquezcalle@upr.edu
VAZQUEZ-LONG, Mitzi . 216-687-3968 380 D
M.VAZQUEZLONG@csuohio.edu
VAZQUEZ-MARTINEZ,
Ernesto .... 787-622-8000 556 H
Evazquezjr@pupr.edu
VAZQUEZ MEDINA,
Edwin .... 787-890-2681 557 C
edwin.vazquez7@upr.edu
VAZQUEZ-SKILLINGS,
Rebecca, D .... 614-823-1354 390 C
rvazquez-skillings@otterbein.edu
VAZQUEZ-VERA, Efrain . 787-850-0000 557 B
rectoria.uprh@upr.edu
VAZQUEZCALLE,
Fernando .... 787-738-2161 557 G
fernando.vazquezcalle@upr.edu
VEACH, Grace .... 863-667-5061 113 K
gveach@seu.edu
VEALE, Keith .... 740-392-6868 387 B
keith.veale@mvnu.edu
VEAZ, Maria, G .... 787-257-7373 555 L
m_veaz@suagm.edu
VEAZEY, Barbara .... 270-534-3082 197 E
barbara.veazey@kctcs.edu
VEAZEY, David, A .... 253-535-8145 524 I
veazeyda@plu.edu
VECCHIO, Maria .... 201-559-6017 302 I
vecchiom@felician.edu
VECCHIO, Paul .... 607-871-2193 314 J
vecchio@alfred.edu
VECCHIONE, Tom .... 209-946-2365.. 73 C
VECHINI, Jose, A .... 787-864-2222 553 J
jose.vechini@guayama.inter.edu
VEDDER, Lori .... 810-762-3444 251 E
lvedder@umflint.edu
VEDRO, Angela, M .... 724-480-3440 416 A
angela.vedro@ccbc.edu
VEDVICK, Kathryn, A .... 206-934-6415 526 B
kathy.vedvick@seattlecolleges.edu
VEECH, Guthrie .... 314-837-6777 281 D
gveech@stlchristian.edu
VEENEMAN, Larry .... 404-250-8520 141 D
lveeneman@chamberlain.edu
VEENSTRA, Tim .... 517-586-3014 241 B
tveenstra@cleary.edu
VEER, Chelly .... 701-766-1302 373 D
chelly.veer@littlehoop.edu
VEESER, Margaret, I ..... 901-321-3324 455 I
pveeser@cbu.edu
VEGA, Aixa .... 787-834-9595 556 D
avega@uaa.edu
VEGA, Annette .... 787-878-5475 553 F
avega@arecibo.inter.edu
VEGA, Barbara .... 432-837-8810 489 B
bvega@sulross.edu
VEGA, Daisy .... 787-882-2065 556 C
recursoshumanos@unitecpr.net
VEGA, Erlinda .... 787-264-1912 554 C
linvega@intersg.edu
VEGA, Evelyn .... 787-250-1912 554 A
evega@metro.inter.edu
VEGA, Francesca .... 818-677-2123.. 34 D
francesca.vega@csun.edu
VEGA, Fredrick .... 787-250-1912 554 A
fredrickvega@metro.inter.edu
VEGA, Javier .... 212-592-2000 342 F
jvega@sva.edu
VEGA, Juan .... 787-844-8181 558 D
juan.vegavega@upr.edu
VEGA, Kennethia, J ...... 714-564-6975.. 60 G
vega_kennethia@sac.edu
VEGA, Lourdes .... 787-738-2161 557 G
lourdes.vega@upr.edu
VEGA, Manfredo .... 787-620-2040 550 D
mvega@aupr.edu
VEGA, Matt .... 731-989-6310 456 K
mvega@fhu.edu
VEGA, Patricia .... 773-878-7837 158 C
pvega@staugustine.edu
VEGA, Zaida .... 787-766-1717 556 A
zvega@suagm.edu
VEGA-GONZALEZ,
Melvin .... 787-480-2396 551 H
melvega@sanjuanciudadpatria.com
VEGA-GUTIERREZ,
Guadalupe .... 787-993-8958 557 E
guadalupe.vega@upr.edu
VEGA-LA SERNA,
Jennifer .... 559-730-3823.. 41 D
jenniferl@cos.edu
VEGA-SANTIAGO,
Angel, O .... 787-250-0000 557 B
angel.vega7@upr.edu
VEGHTS, Darlene .... 412-924-1350 433 E
dveghts@pts.edu
VEHR, Gregory, J .... 513-556-3028 393 B
greg.vehr@uc.edu
VEHRKENS, Kenneth, T 201-692-2671 302 H
vehrkens@fdu.edu
VEILLEUX, John .... 817-531-4269 490 C
jveilleux@txwes.edu
VEIT, Kathy .... 650-723-2300.. 68 G
VEIT, Kenneth, J .... 215-871-6770 432 E
kenv@pcom.edu
VEITCH, Jonathan .... 323-259-2691.. 56 I
VEITH, Gene, E .... 540-338-1776 511 A
provost@phc.edu
VEKER KING, Elizabeth 906-524-8111 245 B
elizabeth.king@kbocc.edu
VELA, Alicia, L .... 512-448-8515 481 B
aliciav@stedwards.edu
VELA, JR., Cesar, E ...... 956-721-5370 477 C
cvela@laredo.edu
VELA, Eddie .... 530-898-6262.. 33 A
evela@csuchico.edu
VELA, Jason .... 307-674-6446 546 H
jvela@sheridan.edu
VELA, Robert .... 210-486-0961 466 J
rvela63@alamo.edu
VELA, Robert, H .... 210-486-0959 467 C
rvela63@alamo.edu
VELAR-PRIETO, Jorge ... 787-993-8869 557 E
jorge.velar@upr.edu
VELASCO, Amy .... 805-756-2982.. 32 E
aevelasc@calpoly.edu
VELASCO, Debbie .... 612-767-7064 253 F
debbie.velasco@alfredadler.edu
VELASCO, Steven, C ...... 805-893-2434.. 72 D
steven.velasco@ucsb.edu
VELASCO, Ulises .... 707-468-3110.. 54 A
uvelasco@mendocino.edu
VELASQUEZ, Lorrie .... 719-846-5534.. 86 A
lorrie.velasquez@trinidadstate.edu
VELASQUEZ, Tom .... 661-654-2211.. 32 G
tvelasquez2@csub.edu
VELAZQUEZ, Acmin .... 787-844-2750 558 D
acmin.velazquez@upr.edu
VELAZQUEZ,
Carmen, G .... 787-253-7373 555 L
ue_evelazquez@suagm.edu
VELAZQUEZ, Ginger ...... 217-333-9634 162 A
gmayol@uillinois.edu
VELAZQUEZ, Isander .... 787-753-6335 552 K
ivelazquez@icprjc.edu
VELAZQUEZ, Zoraida .... 787-841-2000 555 F
zvelazquez@pucpr.edu
VELDERMAN, Joe .... 708-239-4837 160 L
joe.velderman@trnty.edu
VELENCHIK, Ann .... 781-283-3583 237 F
avelenchik@wellesley.edu
VELEZ, Angel .... 787-250-1912 554 A
avelez@metro.inter.edu
VELEZ, Ashley .... 787-841-2000 555 F
avelez@pucpr.edu
VELEZ, Carlos .... 319-399-8000 176 G
cvelez@coe.edu
VELEZ, Daniel, C .... 716-878-3506 345 B
velezdc@buffalostate.edu
VELEZ, Ginny .... 787-840-8108 558 D
ginny.velez@upr.edu
VELEZ, Marcelina .... 787-786-3030 556 E
mvelez@ucbedupr.onmicrosoft.com
VELEZ, Roland .... 718-518-4406 319 D
rvelez@hostos.cuny.edu
VELEZ, Rosa .... 787-758-2525 558 C
rosa.velez2@upr.edu
VELEZ, Sarah, M .... 716-878-3136 345 B
yacklysm@buffalostate.edu
VELEZ, Wanda .... 845-675-4792 337 B
wanda.velez@nyack.edu
VELEZ, Wilda .... 787-848-1520 555 D
wvelez1@popac.edu
VELEZ AROCHO,
Jorge, I .... 787-841-2000 555 F
jivelezarocho@pucpr.edu
VELEZ LUCE, Melissa ... 773-244-5273 154 G
mvelezluce@northpark.edu
VELEZ-ROLON, Olga, L . 787-250-0000 557 B
olga.velez1@upr.edu
VELEZ-YELIN, Johanna . 856-256-5440 306 D
velez-yelin@rowan.edu
VELGUTH, Peter .... 989-386-6622 247 B
pvelguth@midmich.edu
VELIE, Julia, L .... 603-366-5257 296 L
jvelie@ccsnh.edu
VELIKY, Dawn .... 252-536-7227 363 B
rveliky004@halifaxcc.edu
VELKOFF, Townsend ...... 570-321-4258 425 B
velkoff@lycoming.edu
VELLACCIO, Frank .... 508-793-3010 225 C
fvellacc@holycross.edu
VELLUZZI, Nicholas ...... 509-527-3685 527 H
nicholas.velluzzi@wwcc.edu
VELORIA, Ruth .... 602-557-1544.. 18 H
ruth.veloria@phoenix.edu
VELOVICI, Silvio .... 714-533-3946.. 36 D
VELTRI, Sandra .... 303-404-5497.. 82 J
sandy.veltri@frontrange.edu
VELTRI, Valerie, L .... 412-531-4433 416 F
info@deantech.edu
VELVEL, Lawrence, R ..... 978-681-0800 233 D
velvel@mslaw.edu
VENABLE, James, E ...... 901-722-3260 461 A
jvenable@sco.edu
VENABLE, Julie .... 951-487-3040.. 55 A
jvenable@msjc.edu
VENABLE, Margaret ...... 706-272-4436 123 G
mvenable@daltonstate.edu
VENABLE, Margaret ...... 678-359-5018 126 E
mvenable@gordonstate.edu
VENABLE-RIDLEY,
Carlos 402-494-2311 291M
cvenableridley@thenicc.edu
VENDITTI, Ferdinand .... 518-262-5376 314 I
venditf@mail.amc.edu
VENDITTI, Leona .... 515-289-9200 179 E
lvenditti@inste.edu
VENDITTI, Nicholas ...... 515-289-9200 179 E
nvenditti@inste.edu
VENEGAS, Valerie, A .... 714-895-5117.. 40 C
vvenegas@gwc.cccd.edu
VENEKLASE, Dave .... 616-698-7111 241 I
dveneklase@davenport.edu
VENEMA, Cornelius ...... 219-864-2400 171 G
cvenema@midamerica.edu
VENEZIA, Shannon .... 740-374-8716 395 D
svenezia@wscc.edu
VENKAT, Rama .... 702-895-1094 295 G
rama.venkat@unlv.edu

VIGIL, Cynthia ... 509-533-3405 521 F cynthia.vigil@sfcc.spokane.edu

VIGIL, Georgette ... 928-523-3937.. 16 C Georgette.Vigil@nau.edu

VIGIL, James ... 304-876-5219 532 I jvigil@shepherd.edu

VIGIL, Renee ... 719-587-7526.. 78 I reneevigil@adams.edu

VIGILANTE-WEBB, Danielle ... 717-867-6224 423 I vigilant@lvc.edu

VIGNA, Natan ... 951-785-2100.. 49 I nvigna@lasierra.edu

VIGNERON, David ... 978-232-2376 226 C dvignero@endicott.edu

VIGNES, Beau ... 251-981-3771.... 3 A beau.vignes@columbiasouthern.edu

VIGO VERESTIN, Milka . 787-763-6700 552 H milkavigo@gmail.com

VIJITHA-KUMARA, Kanaka ... 309-467-6434 145 A kumara@eureka.edu

VIKANDER, David ... 507-537-6281 262 B David.Vikander@smsu.edu

VILA, Cherly, T ... 692-625-3394 550 A cvila@cmi.edu

VILA, Dendy ... 787-765-3560 552 E dmvila@edpuniversity.edu

VILA, Joaquin ... 505-747-2194 312 G joaquinv@nnmc.edu

VILABOY, Teresa ... 619-388-7485.. 62 H tvilaboy@sdccd.edu

VILACRUZ, Geraldo, G .. 608-246-6442 543 C gvilacruz@madisoncollege.edu

VILE, John, R ... 615-898-2152 461 E john.vile@mtsu.edu

VILEGI PAYNE, Deborah ... 570-740-0232 425 A dvilegi@luzerne.edu

VILELLE, Luke ... 540-362-6592 508 D lvilelle@hollins.edu

VILES, Vickery ... 541-383-7258 404 K vviles@cocc.edu

VILIC, Boris ... 609-896-5033 306 A bvilic@rider.edu

VILKINA, Galina ... 212-616-7270 327 D galina.vilkina@helenefuld.edu

VILLA, Christopher, M . 559-442-4600.. 69 B chris.villa@fresnocitycollege.edu

VILLA, James, C ... 608-262-4464 539 C jvilla@uwsa.edu

VILLA, William ... 808-739-4695 135 A william.villa@chaminade.edu

VILLAGOMEZ, Maria ... 718-960-8144 319 C 1270mgr@fheg.follett.com

VILLAGRANA, Ana, L .... 530-661-5711.. 78 E avillagr@yccd.edu

VILLAIZAN, Sonia ... 787-878-5475 553 F svillaiz@arecibo.inter.edu

VILLALOBOS, Alex ... 559-934-2373.. 76 B alexjvillalobos@whccd.edu

VILLALOBOS, Bobbi ... 310-233-4028.. 51 F villalb@lahc.edu

VILLAMARIA, Paul ... 303-282-3318.. 85 J paul.villamaria@archden.org

VILLAMIL-TORRES, Margarita, E ... 787-250-0000 557 B margarita.villamil@upr.edu

VILLANTI, Athony ... 315-792-3053 351 G avillanti@utica.edu

VILLANUEVA, Brianna ... 617-364-3510 224 A bvillanueva@boston.edu

VILLANUEVA, Christina 210-431-6789 481 C cvillanueva@stmarytx.edu

VILLANUEVA, Daniel, G 818-364-7772.. 51 G villand@lamission.edu

VILLANUEVA, Donna-Mae ... 818-719-6444.. 51 H villandm@piercecollege.edu

VILLANUEVA, Gil ... 804-289-8640 513 M gvillanu@richmond.edu

VILLANUEVA, Ismael .... 787-890-2681 557 C ismael.villanueva@upr.edu

VILLANUEVA, Lynda ... 979-230-3422 469 G lynda.villanueva@brazosport.edu

VILLANUEVA, Rebecca .. 432-264-5190 475 E rvillanueva@howardcollege.edu

VILLANUEVA, Sumaya .. 212-484-1346 319 F svillanueva@jjay.cuny.edu

VILLAR, Dianne ... 610-527-0200 434 D dvillar@rosemont.edu

VILLAR, Jeremy ... 323-953-4000.. 51 E villarjv@lacitycollege.edu

VILLAREAL, Henry ... 650-574-6590.. 64 D henry.villareal@smccd.edu

VILLARREAL, Abe ... 575-538-6336 314 E news@wnmu.edu

VILLARREAL, Carlos ... 713-743-5688 491 D cvillarr@central.uh.edu

VILLARREAL, Dante ... 616-331-7370 243 E villarda@gvsu.edu

VILLARREAL, Elisabeth . 210-829-2736 492 B villaret@uiwtx.edu

VILLARREAL, James ... 210-431-4312 481 C jvillarreal12@stmarytx.edu

VILLARREAL, Luis ... 713-313-1089 487 F luis.villarreal@tsu.edu

VILLARREAL, Oscar ... 956-665-2770 494 C oscar@utpa.edu

VILLARREAL, Oscar ... 559-925-3347.. 76 C oscarvillarreal@whccd.edu

VILLARREAL, Pete ... 530-749-3879.. 78 F pvillarre@yccd.edu

VILLARREAL, Rick ... 940-565-2662 492 D rickv@unt.edu

VILLARREAL, Velda ... 210-485-0735 466 J vvillarreal@alamo.edu

VILLARROEL, Gratzia ... 920-403-3887 538 K gratzia.villarroel@snc.edu

VILLARRUEL, Antonia ... 215-898-8281 437 I nursingdean@nursing.upenn.edu

VILLAVICENCIO, Libby .. 740-753-6088 383 G villavicenciol@hocking.edu

VILLEGAS, Kevin, J ... 717-766-2511 426 B kvillega@messiah.edu

VILLEGAS, Lucille ... 310-954-4010.. 54 I lvillegas@msmu.edu

VILLEGAS-VIDAL, Ludi .. 818-364-7643.. 51 G villegl@lamission.edu

VILLELLA, John ... 610-436-3111 432 B jvillella@wcupa.edu

VILLELLA, Theresa ... 814-732-1297 430 G tvillella@edinboro.edu

VILLENEUVE, Martha .... 603-897-8260 298 E mvilleneuve@rivier.edu

VILLINES, Trish ... 870-743-3000.. 22 A tvillines@northark.edu

VILLOLDO, Sergio ... 787-754-8000 556 H svilloldo@pupr.edu

VINBERG, Dawn ... 206-546-6955 526 G dvinberg@shoreline.edu

VINCENT, Alisha ... 605-995-2937 452 C alvincen@dwu.edu

VINCENT, Andrew ... 502-897-4785 199 D avincent@sbts.edu

VINCENT, Angela ... 814-732-2921 430 G vincent@edinboro.edu

VINCENT, Danny, E ... 740-826-8110 387 C dvincent@muskingum.edu

VINCENT, Deborah, S ... 708-239-4793 160 L deborah.vincent@trnty.edu

VINCENT, Endas, W ... 225-771-3670 206 K endas_vincent@sus.edu

VINCENT, Gregory, J .... 512-471-3212 493 M gvincent@mail.utexas.edu

VINCENT, Kitt ... 909-593-3511.. 73 B kvincent@laverne.edu

VINCENT, Michael ... 928-523-8632.. 16 C Michael.Vincent@nau.edu

VINCENT, Nelson, C ... 513-556-2323 393 B nelson.vincent@uc.edu

VINCENT, Rebecca ... 478-289-2361 124 B rvincent@ega.edu

VINCENT, Sara ... 860-512-3100.. 89 D svincent@manchestercc.edu

VINCENT, William, K .... 951-639-5201.. 55 A bvincent@msjc.edu

VINCZE, John ... 203-285-2310.. 89 B jvincze@gwcc.commnet.edu

VINE, Scott ... 717-291-3843 418 J scott.vine@fandm.edu

VINES, Erin, E ... 661-722-6300.. 27 P evines@avc.edu

VINES, Robert ... 239-590-7044 114 F rvines@fgcu.edu

VINEYARD, Christy, L .. 340-693-1316 559 B cvineya@uvi.edu

VINEYARD, Ed ... 580-548-2207 399 E edwin.vineyard@noc.edu

VINEYARD, Judy ... 618-985-3741 148 G judyvineyard@jalc.edu

VINEYARD, Julie ... 785-242-2067 189 J jvineyard@neosho.edu

VINGER, Christopher .... 212-472-1500 336 A cvinger@nysid.edu

VINIAR, Barbara, A ... 410-827-5802 214 D bviniar@chesapeake.edu

VINING, Isaac ... 404-225-4750 120 I ivining@atlantatech.edu

VINK, Cher ... 715-468-2815 544 F cher.vink@witc.edu

VINOVRSKI, Bernie ... 559-278-2061.. 33 D bernard_vinovrski@csufresno.edu

VINSON, Ben ... 202-994-6130.. 95 D bvinson3@gwu.edu

VINSON, Charles ... 205-226-4918.... 2 C cvinson@bsc.edu

VINSON, Larry, J ... 402-552-6108 289 H vinson@clarksoncollege.edu

VINSON, Richard ... 336-721-2619 368 F richard.vinson@salem.edu

VINSON, Terence ... 318-670-9426 207 C tvinson@susla.edu

VINSON, Wendy ... 706-245-7226 124 C wvinson@ec.edu

VINSON, William ... 608-249-6611 536 J wvinson@msn.herzing.edu

VINTON, Donna, E ... 319-273-3343 176 A donna.vinton@uni.edu

VINYARD, Lisa ... 636-481-3101 276 E lvinyard@jeffco.edu

VINZANT, Becky ... 601-266-5000 271 B rebecca.vinzant@usm.edu

VINZANT, Douglas ... 601-266-5005 271 B douglas.vinzant@usm.edu

VINZANT, Jeffrey, P ... 334-244-3576.... 2 A jvinzant@aum.edu

VIOLA, Anthony ... 617-730-7255 235 B anthony.viola@newbury.edu

VIOLA, Joe ... 541-383-7776 404 K jviola@cocc.edu

VIOLA, Judah ... 312-261-3527 153 H judah.viola@nl.edu

VIOLANTI, Karen ... 410-857-2750 217 A kviolanti@mcdaniel.edu

VIOLET, Matt ... 510-845-6232.. 68 I mviolet@sksm.edu

VIOLETT, Ed ... 225-768-1700 206 F

VIOLETTE, Mike ... 706-771-4037 121 B mviolette@augustatech.edu

VIOLLT, Kathleen ... 312-935-6444 157 A kviollt@robertmorris.edu

VIOLLT, Michael, P ... 312-935-6600 157 A mviollt@robertmorris.edu

VIRASAWMI, Errol ... 516-364-0808 335 A errol@nycollege.edu

VIRAY, Sydnee ... 802-656-3874 503 C sydnee.viray@uvm.edu

VIRELLO, Mark ... 617-322-3502 227 J mark_virello@laboure.edu

VIRES, Charles ... 731-989-6171 456 K cvires@fhu.edu

VIRGIN, Richard, P ... 402-280-2741 290 B RichardVirgin@creighton.edu

VIRJEE, Framroze, M .... 562-951-4500.. 32 D fvirjee@calstate.edu

VIRK, Surinder ... 718-997-5760 320 E surinder.virk@qc.cuny.edu

VIRKLER, Lyndon ... 802-225-3258 502 F lyndon.virkler@neci.edu

VIRTS, Paul, H ... 651-631-5096 265 D phvirts@unwsp.edu

VIRTUE, Alicia ... 707-524-1664.. 65 C avirtue@santarosa.edu

VISCHER, Robert ... 651-962-4838 265 F rkvischer@stthomas.edu

VISCOME, Susan ... 315-312-2378 346 A susan.viscome@oswego.edu

VISCONAGE, Elizabeth, L ... 410-864-4261 218 C bvisconage@stmarys.edu

VISCUSI, Nicolette ... 518-262-6008 314 I

VISCUSI, Peter ... 304-384-5241 532 E pviscusi@concord.edu

VISCUSI, Raymond ... 610-359-5070 416 G rviscusi@dccc.edu

VISEL, OSB, Jeana ... 812-357-6721 173 A jvisel@saintmeinrad.edu

VISENTIN, Peter ... 203-837-8680.. 88 G visentinp@wcsu.edu

VISIN, David ... 319-335-5026 175 H david-visin@uiowa.edu

VISKER, Thomas ... 574-807-7259 164 F viskert@bethelcollege.edu

VISKOZKI, Lynette ... 318-869-5137 202 D lviskozki@centenary.edu

VISOT, Cynthia, S ... 813-974-1678 116 B cvisot@usf.edu

VISSEPO, Cesar ... 787-764-0000 558 E cesar.vissepo@upr.edu

VISSER, Erik ... 707-864-7000.. 66 J erik.visser@solano.edu

VISSER, Jen ... 319-895-4167 177 A jvisser@cornellcollege.edu

VISSER, Sarah ... 616-526-6453 240 L sav36@calvin.edu

VISTOCCO, Valerie ... 315-781-3309 327 G vistocco@hws.edu

VISUANO, Denise ... 503-838-8349 411 B visuanod@wou.edu

VITA, Claudine ... 610-526-6012 420 C cvita@harcum.edu

VITA, Paul ... 314-977-2500 281 M vitap@slu.edu

VITALE, Bob ... 319-385-6270 180 A bob.vitale@iw.edu

VITALE, Eve ... 810-762-9525 245 A evitale@kettering.edu

VITALE, Fran ... 480-423-6133.. 15 E fran.vitale@scottsdalecc.edu

VITALE, Frank ... 410-888-9048 216 G fvitale@muih.edu

VITALE, Joseph ... 973-328-5060 301 G jvitale@ccm.edu

VITALE, JR., Joseph ... 440-775-5573 388 B jvitale@oberlin.edu

VITALE, Michael ... 913-288-7689 188 G mvitale@kckcc.edu

VITALE, Tim ... 435-797-1351 500 A tim.vitale@usu.edu

VITALI, John ... 215-596-8862 438 E j.vitali@usciences.edu

VITALOS, Mark ... 610-606-4642 415 A mavitalo@cedarcrest.edu

VITANGCOL REGOSO, Aimee ... 269-471-3375 239 D aimeev@andrews.edu

VITANGELI, Kory, M ... 317-788-3485 173 I kvitangeli@uindy.edu

VITATOE, David, A ... 216-397-1984 384 F dvitatoe@jcu.edu

VITATOE, Steven, P ... 216-397-4277 384 F svitatoe@jcu.edu

VITELLI, Chris ... 209-384-6185.. 54 C chris.vitelli@mccd.edu

VITELLI, Kelly ... 814-732-1965 430 G kvitelli@edinboro.edu

VITELLI, Mary ... 407-628-6303 111 H mvitelli@rollins.edu

VITO, Christine ... 704-886-6500.. 96 H

VITO, Melissa ... 520-621-0963.. 18 E mmvito@email.arizona.edu

VITOLA, Anthony ... 203-332-5034.. 89 C avitola@hcc.commnet.edu

VITTER, Jeffrey, S ... 785-864-4904 191 G jsv@ku.edu

VITTETOE, Stanley ... 727-791-2475 112 A vittetoe.stan@spcollege.edu

VITTI, Anthony ... 203-576-4735.. 92 B anthonyv@bridgeport.edu

VITTITOE, Sheryl, S ... 772-462-4705 106 F svittito@irsc.edu

VITTO, Cindy ... 856-256-3553 306 D vitto@rowan.edu

VITTONE, Jason ... 573-592-4387 286 A jason.vittone@williamwoods.edu

VITUCCI, S. Stephen ... 254-501-5827 485 D vitucci@tamuct.edu

VITUCCI, Tom ... 954-262-7304 109 E tomv@nova.edu

VIVE, Mia ... 210-567-2648 495 B vivei@uthscsa.edu

VIVEIROS, Derek ... 508-678-2811 231 B derek.viveiros@bristolcc.edu

VIVERETTE, Maggie, J .. 229-333-5463 133 H mviveret@valdosta.edu

VIVERITO, Diane ... 708-974-5334 153 D viverito@morainevalley.edu

VIVIAN, Daniel ... 716-645-4540 343 E dtvivian@buffalo.edu

VIVIANO, Paul ... 619-543-6654.. 72 B pviviano@ucsd.edu

VIVIANO-BRODERICK, Tamara ... 352-854-2322 100 P vivianot@cf.edu

VIVONA, Joseph, F ... 301-445-1923 219 C jvivona@usmd.edu

VIZZACCHERO, Janice, P ... 201-761-6010 307 K jvizzacchero@saintpeters.edu

VIZZINI, Anthony ... 316-978-3010 192 D tony.vizzini@wichita.edu

VIZZINI, Gail ... 631-451-4236 348 E vizzig@sunysuffolk.edu

VLACH, Erin ... 614-222-4000 380 F evlach@ccad.edu

VLAHOS, John ... 408-741-4606.. 76 F john.vlahos@westvalley.edu

VLAHOV, David ... 415-476-1805.. 72 C david.vlahov@nursing.ucsf.edu

VLASTOS, Elizabeth ... 610-372-1722 412 J elizabeth.vlastos@berks.edu

VO, Thoa Hoang ... 972-860-4604 472 C tVo@dcccd.edu

VO, Thomas ... 561-868-3389 109 H vot@palmbeachstate.edu

VO-KUMAMOTO, Tram . 510-981-2933.. 58 J tvokumamoto@peralta.edu

VOELCKER, Aaron ... 714-628-4990.. 60 H voelcker_aaron@sccollege.edu

VOELZ, Zach, R ... 920-565-1022 536 Q voelzZR@lakeland.edu

VOETTERL RIECKER, Robin ... 315-866-0300 327 E voetterra@herkimer.edu

VOGAN, Jessica ... 970-943-2891.. 87 F jvogan@western.edu

VOGAN, Randall ... 314-516-5478 284 B vogan@umsl.edu

VOGEL, Allan .... 507-537-6253 262 B
Allan.Vogel@smsu.edu
VOGEL, Daniel, T .... 240-500-2000 215 C
dtvogel@hagerstowncc.edu
VOGEL, Erik .... 507-537-6147 262 B
Erik.Vogel@smsu.edu
VOGEL, Joanne, E .... 214-768-2821 482 J
jvogel@smu.edu
VOGEL, Justin .... 859-344-3307 200 C
vogelc@thomasmore.edu
VOGEL, Kristin, D .... 920-403-3290 538 K
kristin.vogel@snc.edu
VOGEL, Kristin, M .... 651-641-8839 255 C
vogel@csp.edu
VOGEL, Petra .... 802-586-7711 503 B
pvogel@sterlingcollege.edu
VOGEL, Rich .... 352-588-8361 111 L
rich.vogel@saintleo.edu
VOGEL, Richard .... 631-420-2189 348 B
richard.vogel@farmingdale.edu
VOGEL, Robert .... 785-227-3380 185 A
president@bethanylb.edu
VOGEL, Robert .... 412-536-1032 422 E
bob.vogel@laroche.edu
VOGEL, Ron .... 323-343-3800.. 34 A
ron.vogel@calstatela.edu
VOGEL, Terri .... 660-562-1151 280 A
tvogel@nwmissouri.edu
VOGELEY, Timothy .... 559-297-4500.. 47 H
VOGELMANN,
Thomas, C .... 802-656-0137 503 C
thomas.vogelmann@uvm.edu
VOGEN, Shawn .... 708-216-5642 151 E
svogen@lumc.edu
VOGGEL, Gerhard .... 315-267-4875 346 C
voggelgo@potsdam.edu
VOGHEL-OCHS, Sydney 203-575-8297.. 89 F
svoghel-ochs@nv.edu
VOGL, Joseph, A .... 989-964-4051 249 G
javogl@svsu.edu
VOGL-BAUER, Sally ...... 608-757-6320 542 L
svoglbauer@blackhawk.edu
VOGT, Anthony, J .... 860-444-8286 548 H
anthony.j.vogt@uscg.mil
VOGT, Gail .... 619-574-6909.. 57 E
gvogt@pacificcollege.edu
VOGT, Mark, A .... 502-410-6200 194 N
mvogt@galencollege.edu
VOGT, Marlene .... 815-479-7559 152 B
mvogt@mchenry.edu
VOGT, Randy .... 559-244-5940.. 68 J
randy.vogt@scccd.edu
VOGT, Tracy .... 734-384-4230 247 C
tvogt@monroeccc.edu
VOGTMAN, Jena .... 715-394-6677 544 F
jena.vogtman@witc.edu
VOHRA, Promod .... 815-753-2256 154 I
pvohra@niu.edu
VOIGHT, Patrick .... 218-935-0417 266 A
patrick.voight@wetcc.edu
VOIGT, Darry .... 307-268-2596 545 Z
dvoigt@caspercollege.edu
VOIGT, Francis .... 802-225-3207 502 F
francis.voigt@neci.edu
VOIGT, Lea .... 615-794-4254 460 A
lvoigt@omorecollege.edu
VOIGT, Leda .... 253-833-9111 523 B
lvoigt@greenriver.edu
VOIGT, Lydia .... 504-865-2277 206 A
VOIGT, Shannon .... 757-490-1241 504 D
svoigt@auto.edu
VOIGTS, Adam, J .... 515-263-2821 178 H
avoigts@grandview.edu
VOIGTS, Sheryl .... 859-858-3511 193 A
sheryl.voigts@asbury.edu
VOISIN, Anthony, A ...... 989-774-3346 240 O
voisi1a@cmich.edu
VOISINE, Scott, A .... 207-834-8644 212 F
voisine@maine.edu
VOISS, SJ, Jim .... 509-313-6191 522 L
voiss@gonzaga.edu
VOKES, Bill .... 724-838-4282 435 E
vokes@setonhill.edu
VOLANT, Adam, C .... 540-464-7221 518 A
volantac@vmiaa.org
VOLCY, Ty .... 714-484-7309.. 56 E
tvolcy@cypresscollege.edu
VOLDEN, Lora .... 907-786-6190.. 10 H
llvolden@uaa.alaska.edu
VOLES, Lorraine, A .... 202-994-8810.. 95 D
lvoles@gwu.edu
VOLETY, Aswani .... 910-962-7232 372 A
voletya@uncw.edu
VOLITIS, Matt .... 802-387-6786 502 A
mattvolitis@landmark.edu
VOLK, Mark .... 570-961-7850 422 G
volkm@lackawanna.edu
VOLK, Michael, S .... 616-554-5695 241 I
mvolk@davenport.edu
VOLKERS, Erica .... 505-224-3699 310 F
evolkers@cnm.edu
VOLKERT, Jo .... 415-338-7264.. 36 A
jvolkert@sfsu.edu
VOLL, William .... 914-923-2772 337 I
wvoll@pace.edu
VOLLENDORF, Lisa .... 408-924-4300.. 36 B
lisa.vollendorf@sjsu.edu
VOLLER, Julie .... 602-285-7558.. 15 C
julie.voller@phoenixcollege.edu
VOLLRATH, David, A .... 574-520-4260 168 F
vollrath@iusb.edu
VOLNICK, Stacy .... 561-297-0143 114 E
svolnick@fau.edu
VOLPE, David .... 337-521-8951 204 E
david.volpe@solacc.edu
VOLPE, Greg .... 609-894-9311 306 B
gvolpe@bcc.edu
VOLPI, Karla .... 520-383-8401.. 18 A
kvolpi@tocc.edu
VOLPI, Kirsten .... 303-273-3240.. 80 O
kvolpi@mines.edu
VOLPI, Robert, P .... 413-597-2121 238 E
robert.p.volpi@williams.edu
VOLTAS, Cathy .... 401-341-2904 442 D
cathy.voltas@salve.edu
VOLTURO, Tom .... 918-343-7861 401 I
tvolturo@rsu.edu
VOLTZ, Deborah, L .... 205-934-8320.... 8 F
voltz@uab.edu
VOLTZ, Larry, E .... 202-274-6195.. 97 B
lvoltz@udc.edu
VOLZ, David .... 617-850-1294 227 F
dvolz@hchc.edu
VON, Mary .... 503-352-7299 408 I
maryvon@pacificu.edu
VON ARB, David .... 515-643-6708 181 B
dvonarb@mercydesmoines.org
VON ARX, SJ,
Jeffrey, P .... 203-254-4000.. 90 E
president@fairfield.edu
VON DAUM THOLL,
Susan .... 617-264-7659 226 B
tholl@emmanuel.edu
VON DER MEHDEN,
Kass .... 707-546-4000.. 43 J
kvondermehden@empirecollege.com
VON EYE, Rochelle .... 605-995-2625 452 C
rovoneye@dwu.edu
VON KLAN, Gwen .... 760-872-2000.. 42 J
gvonklan@deepsprings.edu
VON KLEIST, Eric .... 800-895-7411 504 L
VON MUNKWITZ-SMITH,
Jeffrey .... 617-353-8353 224 E
jvon@bu.edu
VON RUDEN, Matthew . 206-934-2647 526 A
matthew.vonruden@seattlecolleges.edu
VON SCHLIEDER, Lynn . 202-546-4734 526 G
lvonschl@shoreline.edu
VONDER HEIDE, Dan ... 773-508-6093 151 E
dvonder@luc.edu
VONDRAK, Jane, M ...... 216-368-2000 378 J
jane.vondrak@case.edu
VONDRAK, Ronnette ..... 515-271-1447 177 H
Ronnettee.Vondrak@dmu.edu
VONDRASEK, Tammy ... 507-453-2639 259 G
tvondrasek@southeastmn.edu
VONHAHMANN,
Jennifer .... 315-568-3270 334 F
jvonhahmann@nycc.edu
VONHANDORF, Teri ...... 859-442-4173 196 A
teri.vonhandorf@kctcs.edu
VONVILLE, Gerry .... 304-384-5266 532 E
lgvonville@concord.edu
VOORHEES, Bill .... 918-293-5394 400 E
bill.voorhees@okstate.edu
VOORHEES, Herschel .... 940-565-4911 492 D
herschel.voorhees@unt.edu
VOORHEES, Lorraine, I . 714-449-7445.. 53 D
lvoorhees@ketchum.edu
VOORHEES, Rhondie .... 406-243-5225 287 D
rhondie.voorhees@umontana.edu
VOOS, Angela .... 641-269-3000 178 I
voos@grinnell.edu
VOOS, Gerard .... 828-232-5040 370 E
gvoos@unca.edu
VORDERBRUEGGE,
Anne .... 703-284-3323 510 B
Anne.Vorderbruegge@marymount.edu
VORDRIEDE-PATTON,
Sarah, R .... 563-333-6112 182 E
VordtriedeSarah@sau.edu
VORFELD, Patti .... 603-899-4108 297 H
vorfeldr@franklinpierce.edu
VORMWALD, Sean .... 315-498-2847 337 F
vormwals@sunyocc.edu
VOROUS, Teresa .... 863-297-1089 110 E
tvorous@polk.edu
VORP, Donald, M .... 609-497-7935 305 B
don.vorp@ptsem.edu
VORP, Laurie, A .... 716-338-1090 329 E
laurievorp@mail.sunyjcc.edu
VORTHERMS, Kristie ..... 605-367-5688 454 D
kristie.vortherms@southeasttech.edu
VOS, Dale, R .... 810-989-5671 249 H
dvos@sc4.edu
VOS, Donald .... 914-337-9300 323 A
donald.vos@concordia-ny.edu
VOS, Lois .... 503-255-0332 407 D
lvos@multnomah.edu
VOSATKA, Carol .... 518-255-5380 346 E
vosatc@cobleskill.edu
VOSBURGH, Grant .... 931-363-9815 458 D
gvosburgh@martinmethodist.edu
VOSBURGH, Tracy .... 607-255-9929 323 C
tv33@cornall.edu
VOSEVICH, Kathi .... 706-233-7276 131 C
kvosevich@shorter.edu
VOSEVICH, Mary, S ...... 859-257-5929 200 G
mary.vosevich@uky.edu
VOSKANIAN, Vince .... 818-333-3558.. 56 A
VOSKUIL, Dave .... 276-944-6133 507 E
dvoskuil@ehc.edu
VOSPER, Susan .... 206-398-4317 526 F
vospers@seattleu.edu
VOSS, Ingrid .... 559-251-4215.. 30 E
izv@fpu.edu
VOSS, Lori .... 507-223-7252 260 C
lori.voss@mnwest.edu
VOSS, Todd, S .... 864-644-5011 449 B
tvoss@swu.edu
VOSS, Trish .... 406-390-0084 194 M
trish.voss@frontier.edu
VOTRUBA, Nell .... 402-844-7051 292 G
nell@northeast.edu
VOTTERO, Timothy, J ... 605-394-2347 454 B
tim.vottero@sdsmt.edu
VOUDRY, Kathy .... 407-708-2148 113 A
voudryk@seminolestate.edu
VOURNELIS, April, J .... 203-576-4914.. 92 B
vourneli@bridgeport.edu
VOUTSINAS, Mickie ...... 305-899-3087.. 99 B
mvoutsinas@barry.edu
VOVES, Mary .... 509-359-4210 522 C
mvoves@ewu.edu
VOVES, Renee .... 319-352-8491 183 J
renee.voves@wartburg.edu
VOWELS, Kelly, J .... 913-360-7418 184 K
kvowels@benedictine.edu
VOWELS, Robert .... 313-993-1700 250 H
robert.vowels@udmercy.edu
VOYLES, Brad .... 706-419-1107 123 F
voyles@covenant.edu
VOYLES, Russell .... 704-669-4243 361 E
voylesr068@clevelandcc.edu
VOYTEK, Robert .... 928-226-4208.. 13 D
bob.voytek@coconino.edu
VOYTOVICH, Steven, A . 570-561-1818 435 A
steven.voytovich@stots.edu
VRACHNOS,
Anastasia, T .... 609-258-2560 305 C
atv@princeton.edu
VRANOS, Kathleen .... 413-775-1471 231 E
vranosk@gcc.mass.edu
VRATTOS, Constance .... 617-349-8836 228 B
cvrattos@lesley.edu
VRIESMAN, Douglas ..... 616-538-2330 243 C
dvriesman@gbcol.edu
VRIEZE, Scott .... 715-246-6561 544 F
scott.vrieze@witc.edu
VROMAN, Mona, O ...... 315-267-2120 346 C
vromanmo@potsdam.edu
VU, Nancy .... 619-961-4325.. 69 J
nancyv@tjsl.edu
VU, Tommy .... 425-564-5710 519 L
tommy.vu@bellevuecollege.edu
VUCELICH, Tom .... 412-809-5100 433 D
vucelich.tom@pti.edu
VUCHINICH, Donna ...... 808-956-3711 135 H
donna.vuchinich@uhfoundation.org
VUE, Charles, C .... 715-836-3367 539 E
vuecc@uwec.edu
VUE, Ger .... 651-846-1406 261 G
ger.vue@saintpaul.edu
VUJNOVICH, Denise, T . 608-785-9190 544 E
vujnovichd@westerntc.edu
VUKELICH, Carol .... 302-831-2394.. 94 D
vukelich@udel.edu
VUKIC, Kelsey .... 626-529-8453.. 57 F
kvukic@pacificoaks.edu
VUKSTA, Rebecca .... 864-294-2448 446 F
rebecca.vuksta@furman.edu
VULAJ, Julie .... 248-204-2313 245 J
jvulaj@ltu.edu
VULLO, Russell .... 478-301-2902 128 G
vullo_ra@mercer.edu
VULLO, Stephanie .... 718-780-0605 317 A
stephanie.vullo@brooklaw.edu
VULOVICH, Daisy .... 941-363-7200 114 B
vulovid@scf.edu
VUONO, Vincent .... 610-989-1232 438 I
vvuono@vfmac.edu
VUORI, Kristiina .... 858-646-3100.. 64 F
kvuori@shpdiscovery.org
VURDIEN, Rajen .... 626-585-7201.. 58 F
rvurdien@pasadena.edu
VUTHIPADADON,
Somchan .... 402-280-1164 290 B
yingv@creighton.edu
VYE, Christopher .... 651-962-4666 265 F
cvye@stthomas.edu
VYHMEISTER, Ken .... 509-527-2202 528 A
ken.vyhmeister@wallawalla.edu
VYSKOCIL, Cindy .... 714-438-4707.. 40 A
cvyskocil@mail.cccd.edu
VYSKOCIL, Michelle ...... 989-275-5000 245 C
michelle.vyskocil@kirtland.edu

W

WABLER, Timothy, J .... 937-229-2165 393 E
TWabler1@udayton.edu
WACH, Howard .... 718-482-5478 320 B
hwach@lagcc.cuny.edu
WACHOWSKI, Robert .... 773-325-7762 143 G
bwachows@depaul.edu
WACHS, Joy, E .... 423-439-7881 461 D
wachs@etsu.edu
WACHS, Saul .... 215-635-7300 419 D
swachs@gratz.edu
WACHSMUTH,
Wayne, R .... 847-259-1840 141 L
wwachsmuth@christianlifecollege.edu
WACHTEL, Jeffrey, H .... 650-725-0589.. 68 G
jwachtel@stanford.edu
WACHTEL, Lynn, A .... 401-456-8520 442 A
lwachtel@ric.edu
WACHTER, Renee .... 715-394-8221 541 C
rwachter@uwsuper.edu
WACK, Mary, F .... 509-335-8044 528 B
mwack@wsu.edu
WACKER, Cary, E .... 903-813-2042 468 G
cwacker@austincollege.edu
WACKER, Robbyn .... 970-351-2305.. 87 A
robbyn.wacker@unco.edu
WACTAWSKI-WENDE,
Jean .... 716-829-3434 343 E
jww@buffalo.edu
WADA, Frank, Y .... 310-825-4321.. 71 D
WADA-MCKEE, Nancy ... 323-343-6076.. 34 A
n.wadamckee@calstatela.edu
WADDELL, Barbara .... 419-372-5312 377 I
bwaddel@bgsu.edu
WADDELL, Edwin, B ..... 336-734-7326 362 F
ewaddell@forsythtech.edu
WADDELL, Jenetta .... 662-685-4771 266 G
jwaddell@bmc.edu
WADDELL, Sandy .... 816-501-4689 281 B
sandy.waddell@rockhurst.edu
WADDLE, Chris .... 308-398-7325 289 D
cwaddle@cccneb.edu
WADDLE, Tonya .... 252-492-2061 366 G
waddlet@vgcc.edu
WADDY, Jeff .... 708-596-2000 159 D
jwaddy@ssc.edu
WADE, Aletha, R .... 301-369-2800 214 A
arwade@captechu.edu
WADE, Alton .... 901-321-4102 455 I
awade2@cbu.edu
WADE, Andrea, C .... 585-292-2170 333 G
awade13@monroecc.edu
WADE, Anthony .... 972-860-8224 472 D
awade@dcccd.edu
WADE, Bernadette .... 914-674-7473 332 E
bwade@mercy.edu
WADE, Chandra .... 773-947-6300 152 A
cwade@mccormick.edu
WADE, Connie, H .... 678-359-5053 126 E
connie_w@gordonstate.edu
WADE, Courtney .... 413-597-4139 238 E
courtney.wade@williams.edu
WADE, Damon, R .... 318-274-7701 207 H
waded@gram.edu
WADE, David .... 606-337-1103 194 F
dwade@ccbbc.edu
WADE, Douglas .... 661-654-2251.. 32 G
dwade3@csub.edu
WADE, Gourdine .... 334-229-6810.... 1 D
gwade@alasu.edu
WADE, H. Keith .... 863-638-2940 119 A
wadehk@webber.edu
WADE, James, E .... 256-782-5649.... 4 L
jwade@jsu.edu
WADE, Jennifer, G .... 901-843-3850 460 F
goodloe@rhodes.edu
WADE, Jerrel .... 281-998-6150 481 F
jerrel.wade@sjcd.edu
WADE, John .... 859-622-1405 194 L
john.wade@eku.edu
WADE, John .... 847-635-2602 155 E
jwade@oakton.edu
WADE, Kaleb .... 214-638-0484 476 Y
kalebwade@kdstudio.com

WADE, Katharine .... 352-854-2322 100 P wadek@cf.edu
WADE, Keith .... 706-865-2134 132 G kwade@truett.edu
WADE, Lara .... 813-974-9060 116 B larawade@usf.edu
WADE, Marcia .... 310-434-4010.. 65 B wade_marcia@smc.edu
WADE, Margaret .... 432-685-4615 478 F mwade@midland.edu
WADE, Melanie .... 570-408-4400 440 B melanie.mickelson@wilkes.edu
WADE, Melissa .... 954-969-9771 103 P melissaw@steinerleisure.com
WADE, Noreen .... 516-572-3559 334 A noreen.wade@ncc.edu
WADE, Scott .... 509-963-2160 520 E wades@cwu.edu
WADE, Susan .... 785-594-8382 184 F susan.wade@bakeru.edu
WADE, Veronica .... 206-934-5216 526 B veronica.wade@seattlecolleges.edu
WADE, Virginia .... 310-377-5501.. 53 E vwade@marymountcalifornia.edu
WADIAN, Becky .... 563-425-5270 183 G wadianb@uiu.edu
WADKINS, Jesse, E ...... 479-248-7236.. 20 K jwadkins@ecollege.edu
WADLEIGH, Jackie .... 817-552-3700 477 B jackie.wadleigh@tku.edu
WADSWORTH, Michael 517-629-0224 239 A mwadsworth@albion.edu
WAECHTER, James .... 727-341-3267 112 A jwaechter@spcollege.edu
WAECHTER, Julie .... 719-587-7165.. 78 I jmwaecht@adams.edu
WAELCHLI, Paul .... 319-895-4260 177 A pwaelchli@cornellcollege.edu
WAFA, Marwan, A .... 812-372-8266 168 E mawafa@iupuc.edu
WAGEMAN, Magxina .... 773-481-8830 142 D mwageman@ccc.edu
WAGEMESTER, Doug .... 319-398-4909 180 J dwageme@kirkwood.edu
WAGENER, Mark .... 973-278-5400 316 D maw@berkeleycollege.edu
WAGENER, Mark .... 973-278-5400 300 C maw@berkeleycollege.edu
WAGENER, William, C .. 304-336-8177 533 A wagenerw@westliberty.edu
WAGENSONNER, Eric ... 510-485-7832.. 58 G ewagensonner@patten.edu
WAGER, Lisa .... 212-217-4700 325 C lisa_wager@fitnyc.edu
WAGERS, Karen, C .... 859-280-1236 198 B kwagers@lextheo.edu
WAGES, Charlene .... 843-661-1146 446 E cwages@fmarion.edu
WAGES, Sam .... 210-805-5836 492 B wages@uiwtx.edu
WAGGENER, Anna .... 251-981-3771.... 3 A anna.waggener@columbiasouthern.edu
WAGGONER, Bill .... 970-339-6290.. 78 J bill.waggoner@aims.edu
WAGGONER, David .... 410-837-6877 221 B dwaggoner@ubalt.edu
WAGGONER, Earl .... 714-256-1311.. 45 J earlwaggoner@ggbts.edu
WAGGONER, George .... 603-206-8081 297 A gwaggoner@ccsnh.edu
WAGGONER, Julia .... 715-682-1302 538 D jwaggoner@northland.edu
WAGGONER, Reneau .... 502-213-2620 196 E reneau.waggoner@kctcs.edu
WAGGONER, Todd .... 417-862-9533 275 C twaggoner@globaluniversity.edu
WAGGONER, Wes, K .... 214-768-2110 482 J wwaggoner@smu.edu
WAGNER, Alex .... 617-236-8879 226 F awagner@fisher.edu
WAGNER, Amy .... 859-344-3309 200 C wagnera@thomasmore.edu
WAGNER, Andrew .... 989-775-4123 249 F wagner.andrew@sagchip.edu
WAGNER, Anne Marie .. 513-244-4810 387 A anne.marie.wagner@msj.edu
WAGNER, Anthony, E ... 706-721-2901 121 C awagner@gru.edu
WAGNER, Ashley .... 619-684-8825.. 56 B awagner@newschoolarch.edu
WAGNER, Claire, M ...... 513-529-7592 386 K wagnercm@miamioh.edu
WAGNER, Clark .... 920-498-6859 544 B clark.wagner@nwtc.edu
WAGNER, Craig .... 641-472-1177 181 A Wagner-Craig@aramark.com
WAGNER, Daniel .... 419-755-4817 387 E dwagner@ncstatecollge.edu
WAGNER, Danielle .... 610-558-5502 427 D wagnerd@neumann.edu
WAGNER, Dave .... 615-966-5683 458 C dave.wagner@lipscomb.edu
WAGNER, Deanna .... 614-236-6904 378 H dwagner1453@capital.edu
WAGNER, Donald, I ...... 901-678-4265 462 B diwagner@memphis.edu
WAGNER, Donna .... 575-646-2810 312 A dlwagner@nmsu.edu
WAGNER, James, M ..... 214-648-2168 496 A james.wagner@utsouthwestern.edu
WAGNER, James, W ..... 404-727-6013 124 D james.wagner@emory.edu
WAGNER, Jane .... 617-682-1511 226 D jwagner@eds.edu
WAGNER, Janet, M ...... 609-652-4534 308 E janet.wagner@stockton.edu
WAGNER, Jean .... 503-491-6113 407 C jean.wagner@mhcc.edu
WAGNER, Jeanne, A ..... 717-901-5117 420 I jwagner@harrisburgu.edu
WAGNER, Jeff .... 320-308-2286 261 E JSWagner@stcloudstate.edu
WAGNER, JoAnn .... 937-529-2201 392 G jwagner@united.edu
WAGNER, Jodi .... 509-527-2772 528 A jodi.wagner@wallawalla.edu
WAGNER, Joseph .... 413-592-3189 225 D wagnerj@elms.edu
WAGNER, Ken .... 808-675-3760 134 M wagnerk@byuh.edu
WAGNER, Kevin, J .... 740-826-6129 387 C kevinw@muskingum.edu
WAGNER, Kimberly ...... 260-481-6103 168 D wagnerk@ipfw.edu
WAGNER, Lana .... 325-649-8076 475 F lwagner@hputx.edu
WAGNER, Laura .... 219-866-6116 172 E lwagner@saintjoe.edu
WAGNER, Linda, L .... 814-871-7423 419 A wagner001@gannon.edu
WAGNER, Marci, K .... 724-450-4089 419 F mkwagner@gcc.edu
WAGNER, Marilyn, D ... 940-565-3487 492 D mwagner@unt.edu
WAGNER, Mark .... 888-777-7675 522 K mwagner@faithseminary.edu
WAGNER, Mary .... 803-777-7700 450 B mary.wagner@sc.edu
WAGNER, Mervin .... 816-322-0110 272 L merv.wagner@calvary.edu
WAGNER, Mervin .... 816-322-0110 272 L mervin.wagner@calvary.edu
WAGNER, Michael, F ... 603-646-0459 297 G michael.f.wagner@dartmouth.edu
WAGNER, Michelle .... 262-243-5700 535 I michelle.wagner@cuw.edu
WAGNER, Mike .... 309-556-3561 148 A mwagner@iwu.edu
WAGNER, Patrick, W .... 704-406-4250 356 G pwagner@gardner-webb.edu
WAGNER, Rich .... 612-374-5800 255 G rwagner@dunwoody.edu
WAGNER, Richard, A .... 413-796-2306 238 A richard.wagner@wne.edu
WAGNER, Richard, T .... 240-895-3421 218 B rtwagner@smcm.edu
WAGNER, Robert, A ..... 971-722-4696 409 C robert.wagner3@pcc.edu
WAGNER, Robin .... 717-337-7000 419 C rowagner@gettysburg.edu
WAGNER, Roger, W ..... 760-245-4271.. 75 G roger.wagner@vvc.edu
WAGNER, Sandra .... 620-672-5641 190 H pamd@prattcc.edu
WAGNER, Steve .... 218-733-5934 259 C s.wagner@lsc.edu
WAGNER, Susan .... 520-795-0787.. 11 I registrar@asaom.edu
WAGNER, Tammy .... 540-868-7182 515 H twagner@lfcc.edu
WAGNER, Teresa, J ..... 315-464-4252 344 E wagnert@upstate.edu
WAGNER, Tina .... 651-690-8890 263 V tmwagner@stkate.edu
WAGNER, Tracy, A .... 941-359-7511 111 F twagner@ringling.edu
WAGNER-FOSSEN, Dena .... 406-771-4312 288 B dfossen@gfcmsu.edu
WAGNER-LIND, Wendy . 954-308-2620.. 98 I wwagner@aii.edu
WAGNITZ, Jeff .... 206-878-3711 523 D jwagnitz@highline.edu
WAGNON, Bill .... 601-635-6242 267 B bwagnon@eccc.edu
WAGNON, Shelley .... 313-993-1588 250 H wagnonsm@udmercy.edu
WAGONER, Jessica ...... 657-278-2570.. 33 E jwagoner@fullerton.edu
WAGONER, Natalie, M . 260-399-7700 174 C nwagoner@sf.edu
WAGONER, Zandra, L ... 909-593-3511.. 73 B zwagoner@laverne.edu
WAGSTAFF, Grayson ..... 202-319-5417.. 95 A wagstaff@cua.edu
WAGSTAFF, Robert .... 617-951-2350 234 F robert.wagstaff@necb.edu
WAGSTAFFE, Paul .... 916-686-8816.. 32 B
WAGUESPACK, Cathy ... 504-398-2111 206 E cwaguespack@olhcc.edu
WAHL, Chris .... 201-360-4030 303 A cwahl@hccc.edu
WAHL, David .... 925-473-7415.. 42 F dwahl@losmedanos.edu
WAHL, Doug, J .... 715-232-2501 541 B wahld@uwstout.edu
WAHL, Katherine .... 585-271-3657 340 B kwahl@stbernards.edu
WAHL, Lynette .... 651-523-3000 256 B lwahl@hamline.edu
WAHL, Robert .... 860-255-3472.. 90 C rwahl@txcc.commnet.edu
WAHLBERG, David, C .. 218-477-2175 260 B david.wahlberg@mnstate.edu
WAHLERS, Mark, E .... 503-280-8578 405 E mwahlers@cu-portland.edu
WAHLFELDT, Tracy, D .. 217-443-8772 143 F twahlfeldt@dacc.edu
WAHLSTROM, David, A 617-989-4552 237 G wahlstromd@wit.edu
WAHR, David .... 567-661-7401 390 D david_wahr@owens.edu
WAHR, Linda .... 312-329-2213 153 C linda.wahr@moody.edu
WAHRHAFTIG, Matt ...... 937-382-6661 395 F matt_wahrhaftig@wilmington.edu
WAID, Monica, K .... 941-359-7511 111 F mwaid@ringling.edu
WAID, Patti, W .... 209-228-4483.. 71 E pwaid@UCMerced.edu
WAIDE, Rory .... 806-720-7313 478 A rory.waide@lcu.edu
WAINES, Bridgette .... 904-680-7780 103 K bwaines@fcsl.edu
WAINWRIGHT, Lisa ...... 312-629-1236 158 J lwainwright@saic.edu
WAINWRIGHT, Peter, C 530-752-6764.. 71 A pcwainwright@ucdavis.edu
WAINWRIGHT, Philip ... 404-727-7504 124 D pwainwr@emory.edu
WAINWRIGHT, William, S .... 985-732-6640 203 I
WAIS, Marc, L .... 212-998-4401 336 C marc.wais@nyu.edu
WAIT, Mark .... 615-322-7660 465 H mark.wait@vanderbilt.edu
WAITE, Boyd, A .... 410-293-1582 549 B waite@usna.edu
WAITE, Dan .... 949-214-3472.. 42 B dan.waite@cui.edu
WAITE, Joann .... 509-313-5870 522 L waite@gonzaga.edu
WAITE, Kristi .... 952-806-3910 263 L
WAITE, Michelle .... 402-472-2116 293 H mwaite1@unl.edu
WAITE, William .... 973-300-2100 308 F wwaite@sussex.edu
WAITE, Zauyah .... 412-365-2794 415 C zwaite@chatham.edu
WAITE-FRANZEN, Ellen, J .... 603-646-2643 297 G ellen.waite-franzen@dartmouth.edu
WAITERS, Destinee .... 713-718-7514 475 C destinee.waiters@hccs.edu
WAITERS, Destinee .... 940-898-3250 490 D dwaiters@twu.edu
WAITERS, Ernest .... 301-860-4040 220 B ewaiters@bowiestate.edu
WAITES, Cheryl, E .... 313-577-4400 252 G deanssw@wayne.edu
WAITLEY, Erin .... 970-521-6662.. 84 H erin.waitley@njc.edu
WAITS, David .... 405-744-2325 400 C david.waits@okstate.edu
WAITS, Lisa .... 707-638-5270.. 70 B lisa.waits@tu.edu
WAITZ, Ian, A .... 617-253-0218 233 C
WAJDA, Phillip, J .... 518-388-8394 350 K wajdap@union.edu
WAJERT, Susan .... 419-251-1314 386 C susan.wajert@mercycollege.edu
WAKEFIELD, Donna ...... 513-751-1206 376 A donna@aic-arts.edu
WAKEFIELD, Jill .... 206-934-3872 525 J jill.wakefield@seattlecolleges.edu
WAKEFIELD, Larry .... 229-430-4609 119 H larry.wakefield@asurams.edu
WAKEFIELD, Sandra ..... 563-355-3500 180 F swakefield@kaplan.edu
WAKELEE, Dan .... 805-437-8542.. 32 H dan.wakelee@csuci.edu
WAKELING, William, M 617-373-5001 235 D
WAKEMAN, Joe .... 740-753-6098 383 G wakemanj@hocking.edu
WAKEMAN, Matt .... 213-738-6719.. 68 E finaid@swlaw.edu
WAKEMAN, Rebecca ..... 740-477-7549 388 F rwakeman@ohiochristian.edu
WAKSDAHL, Robert, B . 715-394-8017 541 C rwaksdah@uwsuper.edu
WALBERT, Mark .... 309-438-7018 147 I mswalber@ilstu.edu
WALBERT, Tim .... 501-812-2366.. 22 F twalbert@pulaskitech.edu
WALBORN, Ronald .... 845-770-5716 337 B ronald.walborn@nyack.edu
WALBORN, Wanda, F ... 845-675-4457 337 B wanda.walborn@nyack.edu
WALCERZ, Douglas ...... 973-877-3483 302 F dwalcerz@essex.edu
WALCHER, Sheldon ...... 630-942-3628 142 F walchers@cod.edu
WALCHESKI, Michael .... 651-603-6184 255 C walcheski@csp.edu
WALCHLE, John .... 740-392-6868 387 B john.walchle@mvnu.edu
WALCK, Barbara .... 716-614-5902 336 D bwalck@niagaracc.suny.edu
WALCROFT, Marie, B .... 215-699-5700 423 F mwalcroft@LSB.edu
WALCZAK, Mary .... 507-786-3498 264 C walczak@stolaf.edu
WALD, Cara .... 651-638-6400 254 A c-wald@bethel.edu
WALD, Donna .... 972-438-6932 480 C
WALD, Frederica, N ...... 212-346-1200 337 I fwald@pace.edu
WALDECK, Steve .... 661-362-2767.. 53 F swaldeck@masters.edu
WALDEN, Carol .... 662-246-6318 268 F cwalden@msdelta.edu
WALDEN, Dan .... 323-953-4000.. 51 E waldendw@lacitycollege.edu
WALDEN, David .... 315-859-4340 327 A
WALDEN, Valerie .... 361-570-4815 492 A waldenv@uhv.edu
WALDHOF, Kenneth ...... 718-862-7362 331 H kenneth.waldhof@manhattan.edu
WALDMANN, Carol ...... 217-581-3714 144 E cawaldmann@eiu.edu
WALDMANN, Robert, G 718-429-6600 352 A robert.waldmann@vaughn.edu
WALDNER, Joanne, L ... 978-232-2013 226 C jwaldner@endicott.edu
WALDNER, Louann .... 559-688-3027.. 41 D louannw@cos.edu
WALDO, Hilary .... 404-872-3593 121 A hwaldo@johnmarshall.edu
WALDREP, Dwain .... 205-970-9231.... 7 D dwaldrep@sebc.edu
WALDRON, David, E .... 512-448-8453 481 B dwaldron@stedwards.edu
WALDRON, Gregory, T . 401-865-2290 441 F gregory.waldron@providence.edu
WALDRON, Kathleen .... 973-720-2222 309 I waldronk@wpunj.edu
WALDRON, Kevin .... 215-646-7300 420 A waldron.k@gmercyu.edu
WALDRON, Sara .... 973-408-3390 301 J swaldron@drew.edu
WALDRON, Steve .... 888-947-2684 187 E swaldron1@grantham.edu
WALDROP, Heath .... 870-862-8131.. 23 B hwaldrop@southark.edu
WALDROP, Jean .... 501-279-4349.. 21 A jwaldrop@harding.edu
WALDROP, Tony, G ...... 251-460-6111.... 9 F twaldrop@southalabama.edu
WALDROP, Tracy .... 256-331-5330.... 6 B tracy@nwscc.edu
WALDROUP, LeAnn ...... 706-379-5237 134 J klwaldroup@yhc.edu
WALDROUP, Linda, L ... 812-888-4333 174 F lwaldroup@vinu.edu
WALDRUP, J. Charles .. 336-334-7592 370 B cwaldrup@ncat.edu
WALDSTEIN, Edith, J .... 319-352-8272 183 J edith.waldstein@wartburg.edu
WALDSTEIN, Steve .... 712-324-5061 182 A swaldstein@nwicc.edu
WALDVOGEL, Marlene .. 517-264-7190 250 B mwaldvogel@sienaheights.edu
WALDVOGEL, Todd, S .. 817-257-7955 486 G todd.waldvogel@tcu.edu
WALEK, Chuck .... 972-708-7574 474 J chuck_walek@gial.edu
WALENGA, Gail, A .... 513-529-7506 386 K walengga@miamioh.edu
WALENTA, Michael .... 616-331-6775 243 E walentam@gvsu.edu
WALES, Beth .... 518-861-2506 331 K bwales@mariacollege.edu

WALLACE, Bryan .... 303-784-8016.. 83 M
bwallace@jiu.edu
WALLACE, Chad, E ...... 765-641-4374 164 B
cewallace@anderson.edu
WALLACE, Christina ...... 718-780-0305 317 A
christina.wallace@brooklaw.edu
WALLACE, Cindy .... 704-406-4103 356 G
cwallace@gardner-webb.edu
WALLACE, Cindy, A ...... 828-262-2060 369 D
wallaceca@appstate.edu
WALLACE, Dave .... 972-800-4616.. 69 D
dwallace@sum.edu
WALLACE, David .... 562-985-5381.. 33 F
david.wallace@csulb.edu
WALLACE, David .... 270-534-3859 197 E
david.wallace@kctcs.edu
WALLACE, David .... 573-882-6601 283 H
wallaced@missouri.edu
WALLACE, Debbie .... 870-543-5996.. 23 C
dwallace@seark.edu
WALLACE, Deborah .... 818-677-2305.. 34 D
deborah.wallace@csun.edu
WALLACE, Debra, S ...... 919-866-5920 366 H
dswallace@waketech.edu
WALLACE, Denise .... 504-816-4546 202 F
dwallace@dillard.edu
WALLACE, Don .... 509-527-2147 528 A
don.wallace@wallawalla.edu
WALLACE, Donald .... 760-921-5499.. 58 C
donald.wallace@paloverde.edu
WALLACE, Douglas, J ... 864-833-8312 448 E
dwallace@presby.edu
WALLACE, Effie .... 540-261-8492 512 J
effie.wallace@svu.edu
WALLACE, Elaine .... 954-262-1407 109 E
ewallace@nova.edu
WALLACE, Gillian .... 650-508-3718.. 56 H
gwallace@ndnu.edu
WALLACE, JR.,
Glenn, E .... 912-525-5000 130 H
gwallace@scad.edu
WALLACE, Greg .... 641-269-3800 178 I
wallace@grinnell.edu
WALLACE, JR., James .. 219-980-6601 168 C
jamewall@iun.edu
WALLACE, James, A ..... 405-466-6765 398 E
jawallace@langston.edu
WALLACE, Jamey .... 206-834-4100 519 J
jwallace@bastyr.edu
WALLACE, Jason .... 303-282-3422.. 85 J
father.wallace@archden.org
WALLACE, Jeff .... 765-998-5395 173 B
jfwallace@taylor.edu
WALLACE, Joel .... 817-202-6333 483 C
jwallace@swau.edu
WALLACE, Jon, R .... 626-812-3075.. 29 B
jwallace@apu.edu
WALLACE, Joshua .... 254-647-1414 480 G
jwallace@rangercollege.edu
WALLACE, Joyce .... 214-333-5229 471 L
joycew@dbu.edu
WALLACE, Kim .... 303-404-5671.. 82 J
kim.wallace@frontrange.edu
WALLACE, Kim .... 303-404-5316.. 83 N
kim.wallace@frontrange.edu
WALLACE, Kimberly ...... 239-590-1087 114 F
kwilliam@fgcu.edu
WALLACE, Kristen .... 325-235-7482 488 C
kristen.wallace@tstc.edu
WALLACE, Laura, J .... 434-592-7330 509 G
jwallac@liberty.edu
WALLACE, Leigh .... 229-217-4143 132 C
lwallace@southernregional.edu
WALLACE, Linda .... 765-455-9288 168 B
lwallace@iuk.edu
WALLACE, Lynn .... 215-702-4337 414 C
lwallace@cairn.edu
WALLACE, Lynn, C .... 304-724-3700 529 F
WALLACE, Margaret ...... 610-526-6001 420 C
mwallace@harcum.edu
WALLACE, Mary Beth ... 941-359-4200 116 D
WALLACE, Mike, J .... 408-554-4981.. 65 A
mjwallace@scu.edu
WALLACE, Paula .... 912-525-5000 130 H
pwallace@scad.edu
WALLACE, Paula, J .... 434-947-8126 511 D
pwallace@randolphcollege.edu
WALLACE, Randy .... 512-499-4527 493 K
rwallace@utsystem.edu
WALLACE, Ray .... 812-941-2200 169 A
raywall@ius.edu
WALLACE, Renee, L ...... 512-471-9266 493 M
rlwallace@austin.utexas.edu
WALLACE, Sam, G .... 318-257-2769 208 A
wallace@latech.edu
WALLACE, Sherrie .... 330-823-2286 394 A
wallacsj@mountunion.edu
WALLACE, Susan .... 312-893-7120 144 H
swallace@erikson.edu
WALLACE, Tami .... 615-230-3573 464 B
tami.wallace@volstate.edu
WALLACE, Teresa .... 307-268-2621 545 Z
twallace@caspercollege.edu
WALLACE, Terry .... 501-370-5224.. 22 E
twallace@philander.edu
WALLACE, Thomas .... 661-654-2161.. 32 G
twallace4@csub.edu
WALLACE, Tiffany .... 662-254-3440 269 C
trwallace@mvsu.edu
WALLACE, Tim .... 864-587-4267 449 D
wallacet@smcsc.edu
WALLACE, Tom .... 615-898-2271 461 E
tom.wallace@mtsu.edu
WALLANDER,
Marcia, M .... 412-578-8772 414 I
mmwallander@carlow.edu
WALLEN, Esther .... 773-252-5133 156 J
esther.wallen@resu.edu
WALLENFELSZ, Nicole .. 843-863-8054 444 B
WALLER, Art .... 801-774-9900 496 I
awaller@vistacollege.edu
WALLER, Christine .... 315-792-7100 348 D
cwaller@sunycnse.com
WALLER, Cynthia, G ..... 615-353-3645 463 C
cynthia.waller@nscc.edu
WALLER, Frank .... 301-860-3813 220 B
fwaller@bowiestate.edu
WALLER, J.J .... 912-525-5000 130 H
jwaller@scad.edu
WALLER, Janet .... 256-824-6282.... 9 A
janet.waller@uah.edu
WALLER, Jennifer .... 662-645-3555 267 A
jwaller@deltastate.edu
WALLER, Karen .... 325-235-7341 488 C
karen.waller@tstc.edu
WALLER, Lorie .... 919-735-5151 367 A
loriew@waynecc.edu
WALLER, Melinda .... 941-907-2262 102 N
mwaller@evergladesuniversity.edu
WALLER, Peter .... 970-945-8691.. 80 D
WALLER, Steve .... 610-372-4721 433 H
swaller@racc.edu
WALLER, Steven .... 225-578-5388 204 M
swaller@lsu.edu
WALLER, Steven .... 402-472-2201 293 H
swaller1@unl.edu
WALLER, Wanda, M ..... 318-670-6466 207 C
wmwaller@susla.edu
WALLERSTEIN,
Mitchel, B .... 646-312-3310 318 C
president@baruch.cuny.edu
WALLESER, Diane .... 614-287-2727 380 G
dwallese@cscc.edu
WALLET, Robert, M ...... 717-361-1524 418 B
walletrm@etown.edu
WALLEY, Anna-Jean ..... 559-251-4215.. 30 E
bookkeeper@calchristiancollege.edu
WALLEY, Jennifer .... 559-251-4215.. 30 E
jwalley@calchristiancollege.edu
WALLEY, Trent .... 559-251-4215.. 30 E
admissions@calchristiancollege.edu
WALLEY, Wendell, L ..... 559-251-4215.. 30 E
wwalley@calchristiancollege.edu
WALLIN, Celeste .... 212-616-7273 327 D
celeste.wallin@helenefuld.edu
WALLIN, Jon .... 540-261-8535 512 J
jon.wallin@svu.edu
WALLIN, William .... 303-329-6355.. 81 B
registrar@cstcm.edu
WALLING, Brenda .... 580-559-5350 397 K
bwalling@ecok.edu
WALLING, Lisa .... 931-526-3660 456 H
lisaq.walling@fortisinstitute.edu
WALLING, Ray .... 785-594-8389 184 F
ray.walling@bakeru.edu
WALLINGA, Michael ..... 712-707-7108 182 C
mwalling@nwciowa.edu
WALLIS, Madeline .... 978-762-4000 232 D
mwallis@northshore.edu
WALLIS, Matthew .... 817-257-5808 486 G
matthew.wallis@tcu.edu
WALLIS, Sarah .... 937-769-1862 376 M
swallis@antioch.edu
WALLIS, Sherry, L .... 660-263-3900 272 M
sherrywallis@cccb.edu
WALLMAN, Marc .... 701-231-8640 374 C
marc.wallman@ndsu.edu
WALLNER, Steve .... 262-595-2451 540 C
steve.wallner@uwp.edu
WALLS, Arnita .... 651-641-3599 256 J
WALLS, Elizabeth, M .... 402-465-2337 292 E
ewalls@nebrwesleyan.edu
WALLS, George, H .... 301-369-2800 214 A
ghwalls@captechu.edu
WALLS, Maryanna .... 301-962-5111 221 F
mwalls@yeshiva.edu
WALLS, Randy, C .... 417-268-1000 272 D
wallsr@evangel.edu
WALLS, Skip .... 972-686-7878 480 I
WALLS-MCKAY,
Maureen, J .... 434-395-2409 509 H
wallsmckaymj@longwood.edu
WALLY, William .... 680-488-6223 550 C
willyw@palau.edu
WALN, Ursula .... 505-224-4000 310 F
uwaln@cnm.edu
WALPIN, Ned .... 505-984-6000 312 J
WALPOLE, Tommy .... 318-342-5419 209 A
walpole@ulm.edu
WALSH, Bernadette .... 215-646-7300 420 A
walsh.b@gmercyu.edu
WALSH, Brendan .... 845-451-1616 323 E
b_walsh@culinary.edu
WALSH, Carolyn .... 304-829-7516 529 H
cwalsh@bethanywv.edu
WALSH, Clifton .... 915-747-6636 494 B
cwalsh@utep.edu
WALSH, CSSP, Daniel ... 412-396-4827 417 I
walshd@duq.edu
WALSH, Debra .... 715-852-1353 542 M
dwalsh7@cvtc.edu
WALSH, Frannie .... 480-994-9244.. 17 P
franniew@swiha.edu
WALSH, James, V .... 831-656-3658 548 A
jvwalsh@nps.edu
WALSH, Jeffrey .... 813-226-4901 111 L
jeffrey.walsh@saintleo.edu
WALSH, Jennifer .... 626-815-6000.. 29 B
jwalsh@apu.edu
WALSH, John .... 520-417-4081.. 13 B
walshd@cochise.edu
WALSH, John .... 978-632-6600 232 C
j_walsh@mwcc.mass.edu
WALSH, John, T .... 909-748-8368.. 73 K
john_walsh@redlands.edu
WALSH, Joseph, T .... 847-491-3485 155 D
vp-research@northwestern.edu
WALSH, Julie .... 845-257-2632 344 A
walshj@newpaltz.edu
WALSH, Kimberly, A .... 563-588-7417 180 L
kimberly.walsh@loras.edu
WALSH, Lenore, J .... 516-876-4974 345 E
walshle@oldwestbury.edu
WALSH, Margaret .... 614-251-4605 388 H
walshm@ohiodominican.edu
WALSH, Margurete .... 215-951-1013 422 F
walshm@lasalle.edu
WALSH, Mariellen .... 570-945-8162 422 B
mariellen.walsh@keystone.edu
WALSH, Mark .... 813-974-2660 116 B
mwalsh@usf.edu
WALSH, Mary, T .... 504-314-2537 207 F
mary@tulane.edu
WALSH, Mary Lee .... 434-961-6540 516 F
mwalsh@pvcc.edu
WALSH, Melissa .... 610-526-6197 420 C
mwalsh@harcum.edu
WALSH, Michael .... 414-297-6246 543 E
walshm@matc.edu
WALSH, Michael, D ...... 540-568-5681 509 C
walshmd@jmu.edu
WALSH, Michele .... 781-891-2070 223 E
mwalsh1@bentley.edu
WALSH, Patricia .... 773-995-3862 141 J
pwalsh@csu.edu
WALSH, Patricia, J .... 913-971-3453 189 F
pwalsh@mnu.edu
WALSH, Peter, J .... 512-448-8441 481 B
peterjw@stedwards.edu
WALSH, Rosalie, K .... 406-447-5440 286 D
rwalsh@carroll.edu
WALSH, Susan .... 209-384-6105.. 54 C
walsh.s@mccd.edu
WALSH, Susan .... 209-384-6082.. 54 C
walsh.s@mccd.edu
WALSH, Susan .... 541-552-6114 409 G
walsh@sou.edu
WALSH, Tammy, S .... 941-359-7505 111 F
twalsh@ringling.edu
WALSH, Teresa .... 732-255-0400 304 E
twalsh@ocean.edu
WALSH, Timothy .... 919-684-5055 356 E
tim.walsh@duke.edu
WALSH, Timothy, J .... 716-878-4201 345 B
walshtj@buffalostate.edu
WALSHOK, Mary, L .... 858-534-3411.. 72 B
mwalshok@ucsd.edu
WALSKI, Don .... 507-457-5555 262 D
dwalski@winona.edu
WALSTEAD, Brenda .... 360-992-2474 521 A
bwalstead@clark.edu
WALSTER, Jane .... 360-992-2447 521 A
jwalster@clark.edu
WALSTON, Angie .... 252-399-6313 354 I
amwalston@barton.edu
WALSTROM, Katherine .. 941-487-4493 115 B
walstrom@ncf.edu
WALTER, B. Kaye .... 201-447-7237 300 B
president@bergen.edu
WALTER, Blakely .... 630-942-2353 142 F
walterb@cod.edu
WALTER, Jim .... 706-355-5120 120 G
jwalter@athenstech.edu
WALTER, John, M .... 661-362-2239.. 53 F
jwalter@masters.edu
WALTER, Kelly .... 617-353-3530 224 E
kwalter@bu.edu
WALTER, Kristy .... 617-243-2147 227 K
kwalter@lasell.edu
WALTER, Lisa, A .... 715-232-2266 541 B
walterl@uwstout.edu
WALTER, Rachel .... 419-434-4570 393 F
walterr@findlay.edu
WALTER, Robyn, C .... 636-584-6617 274 J
robyn.walter@eastcentral.edu
WALTER, Scott .... 773-325-8023 143 G
swalte11@depaul.edu
WALTER, Shulem .... 718-855-4092 338 M
swalter@rcosy.org
WALTER, Toni .... 660-596-7222 282 H
awalter@sfccmo.edu
WALTER, Willis .... 386-481-2087.. 99 F
walterw@cookman.edu
WALTER-MACK, Kathy ... 816-604-1587 277 F
kathy.walter-mack@mcckc.edu
WALTERREIT, Jay .... 989-358-7215 239 C
walterrj@alpenacc.edu
WALTERS, Almar .... 614-236-6011 378 H
awalters@capital.edu
WALTERS, Carmen .... 228-497-7700 268 G
carmen.walters@mgccc.edu
WALTERS, Carolyn .... 812-855-3403 167 J
cwalters@indiana.edu
WALTERS, Charity .... 406-683-7471 287 E
charity.walters@umwestern.edu
WALTERS, Dana .... 216-987-4620 381 A
dana.walters@tri-c.edu
WALTERS, Dave .... 270-789-5007 194 D
dlwalters@campbellsville.edu
WALTERS, David .... 828-669-8012 359 K
dwalters@montreat.edu
WALTERS, Evon .... 269-660-8021 249 C
walterse@millercollege.edu
WALTERS, George .... 760-252-2411.. 29 C
gwalters@barstow.edu
WALTERS, Greg .... 208-885-3478 139 C
gregwalters@uidaho.edu
WALTERS, Isaac .... 267-256-0200.. 96 H
WALTERS, Jayme .... 270-685-3131 193 G
Jayme.walters@brescia.edu
WALTERS, Jennifer .... 419-783-2563 381 G
jwalters@defiance.edu
WALTERS, Jennifer, L ... 413-585-2797 236 G
jwalters@smith.edu
WALTERS, Jim .... 951-343-4323.. 30 D
jmwalters@calbaptist.edu
WALTERS, Joanna .... 785-242-5200 190 D
joanna.walters@ottawa.edu
WALTERS, Jodi .... 304-462-6416 532 G
jodi.walters@glenville.edu
WALTERS, June .... 870-762-3102.. 19 C
jwalters@smail.anc.edu
WALTERS, Kenneth .... 412-268-1151 414 J
walters1@andrew.cmu.edu
WALTERS, Kent, L .... 904-264-2172 111 G
kwalters@iws.edu
WALTERS, Laurel .... 314-275-3560 156 C
laurel.walters@principia.edu
WALTERS, Linda .... 570-740-0462 425 A
lwalters@luzerne.edu
WALTERS, Mark .... 608-262-3666 539 D
mwalters@ohr.wisc.edu
WALTERS, Paula .... 423-236-2657 460 K
pkwalters@southern.edu
WALTERS, Ricki .... 507-433-0534 261 C
rwalters@riverland.edu
WALTERS, Rita .... 410-669-9200 216 F
WALTERS, Robby .... 828-395-1602 363 D
rwalters@isothermal.edu
WALTERS, Roland .... 540-365-4267 507 H
rwalters@ferrum.edu
WALTERS, Tamara .... 814-824-2000 425 L
WALTERS, Tamyra .... 269-749-7197 249 A
twalters@olivetcollege.edu
WALTERS, Tigh .... 512-472-2472 482 E
tigh.walters@ssw.edu
WALTERS, Timothy, L ... 509-359-2777 522 C
twalters@ewu.edu
WALTERS, Tracey .... 601-928-6337 268 G
tracey.walters@mgccc.edu
WALTERS, Tyler .... 540-231-5595 518 B
tyler.walters@vt.edu
WALTERS, William .... 718-862-7166 331 H
william.walters@manhattan.edu
WALTERS, William, D ... 336-334-5824 371 C
bill_walters@uncg.edu
WALTERS-BOWER,
Sharon .... 434-544-8100 509 I
WALTERSCHEID,
Dianne .... 940-668-4274 479 K
dwalterscheid@nctc.edu
WALTHER, Barb .... 734-995-7499 241 F
barb.walther@cuaa.edu

WARE, Steven, J .... 218-751-8670 263 J
stevenware@oakhills.edu
WARE, Thomas .... 662-476-5087 267 C
tware@eastms.edu
WARE JOSEPH, Caran .. 303-765-3111.. 83 C
cwarejoseph@iliff.edu
WARFIELD, Aimee, S .... 518-381-1207 342 E
warfieas@sunysccc.edu
WARFIELD, Martha, B .. 269-387-6313 252 I
martha.warfield@wmich.edu
WARFIELD, Tasha .... 517-787-0800 244 H
WarfielTashaC@jccmi.edu
WARFORD, Jill .... 620-223-2700 187 B
jillw@fortscott.edu
WARFORD, Lindsey ...... 212-229-5600 334 C
warfordl@newschool.edu
WARFORD, Pam .... 281-425-6361 477 F
pwarford@lee.edu
WARGO, Lisa .... 318-678-6000 203 A
lwargo@bpcc.edu
WARGO, Melissa .... 828-227-7100 372 C
wargo@wcu.edu
WARK, Maureen .... 978-921-4242 234 B
maureen.wark@montserrat.edu
WARKENTIN, Don .... 559-925-3217.. 76 C
donwarkentin@whccd.edu
WARMA, Karl .... 217-228-5432 156 D
warmaka@quincy.edu
WARMACK, Dwaun .... 314-340-3380 275 G
president@hssu.edu
WARMAN, Cassie .... 503-352-3096 408 I
warman@pacificu.edu
WARMANN, Cheryl .... 847-635-1719 155 E
cwarmann@oakton.edu
WARMOTH, Kristin .... 701-858-3822 374 B
kris.warmoth@minotstateu.edu
WARN, Dara .... 480-947-6644.. 16 L
WARNAS, Jennifer .... 801-524-1965 498 J
jwarnas@ldsbc.edu
WARNE, Janie .... 573-334-9181 277 C
janie@metrobusinesscollege.edu
WARNER, Amy, C .... 317-274-7400 168 E
awarner@iupui.edu
WARNER, Andre .... 484-365-7345 424 E
akwarner@lincoln.edu
WARNER, Charles .... 610-436-2117 432 B
cwarner@wcupa.edu
WARNER, Charles .... 740-351-3468 391 C
cwarner@shawnee.edu
WARNER, Chris .... 214-771-4572 485 E
chris.warner@tamuc.edu
WARNER, Dave .... 509-452-5100 524 J
WARNER, David .... 240-500-2000 215 C
cdwarner@hagerstowncc.edu
WARNER, Donald, D .... 406-874-6201 287 A
warnerd@milescc.edu
WARNER, Isiah, M 225-578-7230 204M
iwarner@lsu.edu
WARNER, JR.,
J. Curtis .... 617-266-1400 223 F
WARNER, Janice .... 732-987-2662 302 J
warnerj@georgian.edu
WARNER, John .... 214-645-5476 496 A
john.warner@utsouthwestern.edu
WARNER, Karen, R .... 330-471-8120 385 G
kwarner@malone.edu
WARNER, Kathy .... 410-888-9048 216 G
kwarner@muih.edu
WARNER, Kee .... 719-255-3203.. 86 F
kwarner@uccs.edu
WARNER, Linda .... 913-288-7194 188 G
lwarner@kckcc.edu
WARNER, Mark .... 507-538-0554 254 F
warner.mark@mayo.edu
WARNER, Mark, J .... 540-568-3685 509 C
warnermj@jmu.edu
WARNER, Mark, S .... 319-335-3127 175 H
mark-warner@uiowa.edu
WARNER, Martin, O ..... 610-328-8299 436 A
mwarner1@swarthmore.edu
WARNER, Meredith .... 480-461-7178.. 15 A
meredith.warner@mesacc.edu
WARNER, Rebecca .... 541-737-0732 408 F
rwarner@oregonstate.edu
WARNER, Ryan .... 740-351-3127 391 C
rwalker@shawnee.edu
WARNER, Sandra .... 913-469-8500 188 E
swarner@jccc.edu
WARNER, Susan .... 516-686-7647 335 F
swarner@nyit.edu
WARNER, Susan, T ...... 440-826-2476 377 D
swarner@bw.edu
WARNER, Thomas, R ... 504-278-6468 204 B
twarner@nunez.edu
WARNER, Timothy, R ... 650-723-4567.. 68 G
trw@stanford.edu
WARNICK, Lorin, D ...... 607-253-3030 323 C
ldw3@cornell.edu
WARNICK, Mark .... 870-236-6901.. 20 I
mwarnick@crc.edu
WARNKE, Kelly .... 419-448-2517 383 C
kwarnke@heidelberg.edu
WARNOCK, Brenda .... 928-317-7601.. 12 B
brenda.warnock@azwestern.edu
WARPNESS, Wm. Guy .. 307-755-2120 547 D
gwarpness@wyotechstaff.edu
WARR, Fred .... 208-459-5006 137 J
fwarr@collegeofidaho.edu
WARREN, Aileen .... 402-559-8992 293 I
aileen.warren@unmc.edu
WARREN, Anika, K .... 215-895-6652 417 E
anika.k.warren@drexel.edu
WARREN, Becky .... 870-612-2048.. 24 G
becky.warren@uaccb.edu
WARREN, Beverly .... 619-594-2569.. 35 E
bwarren@mail.sdsu.edu
WARREN, Beverly, J ..... 330-672-2210 384 H
beverlywarren@kent.edu
WARREN, Carol .... 901-572-2640 455 C
carol.warren@bchs.edu
WARREN, Carolyn .... 662-562-3205 269 E
cwarren@northwestms.edu
WARREN, Charlotte, J .. 217-786-2273 151 C
charlotte.warren@llcc.edu
WARREN, Chris .... 601-643-8306 266 J
chris.warren@colin.edu
WARREN, Cleve, E .... 904-632-3218 105 A
clwarren@fscj.edu
WARREN, David .... 717-464-7050 423 D
WARREN, Debra, P .... 260-422-5561 167 F
dpwarren@indianatech.edu
WARREN, Diana .... 812-535-5284 172 F
dwarren@smwc.edu
WARREN, Doris, C .... 281-649-3013 475 B
dcwarren@hbu.edu
WARREN, E.J .... 405-682-7569 399 K
ejwarren@occc.edu
WARREN, Earl .... 256-782-5306.... 4 L
ewarren@jsu.edu
WARREN, Greg .... 918-465-1756 397 L
gwarren@eosc.edu
WARREN, Helen .... 507-786-3009 264 C
warren1@stolaf.edu
WARREN, JR., James ... 212-410-8063 335 B
jwarren@nycpm.edu
WARREN, Jason, D ...... 270-707-3801 196 D
jason.warren@kctcs.edu
WARREN, Joan .... 636-481-3110 276 E
jwarren@jeffco.edu
WARREN, Joan, D .... 212-779-5000 329 I
WARREN, John, S .... 850-474-2415 116 E
jwarren@uwf.edu
WARREN, Kim .... 913-253-5050 190 K
kim.warren@spst.edu
WARREN, Leslie, A .... 906-227-2117 248 B
lwarren@nmu.edu
WARREN, Pamela .... 920-923-7614 537 A
pwarren@marianuniversity.edu
WARREN, Patricia .... 503-338-2306 405 B
pwarren@clatsopcc.edu
WARREN, Richard, A .... 610-660-1282 434 G
warren@sju.edu
WARREN, Robert .... 401-739-5000 441 E
bwarren@neit.edu
WARREN, Russell .... 410-532-5321 217 F
rwarren@ndm.edu
WARREN, Sara .... 410-225-2264 216 F
swarren@mica.edu
WARREN, Shannon .... 304-645-6382 533 B
swarren@osteo.wvsom.edu
WARREN, Sydney .... 270-686-6415 193 G
sydney.warren@brescia.edu
WARREN, Teresa .... 479-936-5171.. 22 B
twarren4@nwacc.edu
WARREN, Todd .... 251-380-3095.... 7 F
twarren@shc.edu
WARREN, William, J .... 801-581-6773 499 K
william.warren@utah.edu
WARREN-MARLATT,
Rebeccah .... 909-389-3355.. 62 B
rmarla@craftonhills.edu
WARRICK, JR.,
Douglas, R .... 803-641-3406 450 C
randyw@usca.edu
WARRINGTON, Adam ... 802-654-0505 503 H
adam.warrington@ccv.edu
WARRINGTON, Myrna .. 800-567-2344 535 F
mwarrington@menominee.edu
WARRINGTON, Richard 800-567-2344 535 F
richwarrington@menominee.edu
WARRINGTON,
Sarah, G .... 802-656-2925 503 C
sarah.warrington@uvm.edu
WARRINGTON, Traci .... 401-341-2477 442 D
traci.warrington@salve.edu
WARSHAWSKI, Evelyn .. 661-362-5305.. 40 H
evy.warshawski@canyons.edu
WARSHEL, Chad .... 315-568-3297 334 F
cwarshel@nycc.edu
WARTERS, Alissa .... 843-661-1616 446 E
twarters@fmarion.edu
WARTHMAN, Susan ...... 401-739-5000 441 E
swarthman@neit.edu
WARTMAN, Bruce .... 215-728-4422 427 H
bruce.wartman@jevs.org
WARTMAN, Jed .... 207-859-4261 210 A
jed.wartman@colby.edu
WARWICK, Ann .... 212-938-5600 347 C
awarwick@sunyopt.edu
WARWICK, Jay .... 334-953-1303 547 F
jay.warwick@us.af.mil
WARWICK, John, J .... 618-453-4321 159 H
warwick@siu.edu
WARYCK, Susan, H ...... 740-826-8086 387 C
shoglund@muskingum.edu
WASAN, Darsh, T .... 312-567-3001 147 E
wasan@iit.edu
WASCHULL, Stefanie ..... 352-395-5175 112 H
stefanie.waschull@sfcollege.edu
WASDEN, Mitch .... 573-884-8738 283 G
wasdenm@health.missouri.edu
WASDIN, Angela .... 912-260-4428 131 D
angela.wasdin@sgsc.edu
WASESCHA, Anna .... 860-343-5703.. 89 E
awasescha@mxcc.commnet.edu
WASHAM, Ronnie .... 606-337-1722 194 F
rwasham@ccbbc.edu
WASHBURN, Jackie ...... 269-660-8021 249 C
washburnj@millercollege.edu
WASHBURN, Tayloe ..... 206-467-5481 235 D
WASHINGTON,
A. Eugene .... 919-684-2255 356 E
eugene.washington@duke.edu
WASHINGTON,
A. Eugene .... 310-825-5687.. 71 D
ewashington@mednet.ucla.edu
WASHINGTON, Andre ... 859-442-4176 196 A
andre.washington@kctcs.edu
WASHINGTON,
August, J .... 615-343-9750 465 H
august.j.washington@vanderbilt.edu
WASHINGTON,
Brandon .... 239-745-4367 114 F
bwashington@fgcu.edu
WASHINGTON, Carla .... 919-516-4118 368 E
cawashington@st-aug.edu
WASHINGTON, Chad .... 803-376-5700 443 D
WASHINGTON, Cheryl .. 334-874-5700.... 3 B
cwashington@ccal.edu
WASHINGTON,
Christopher, L .... 614-947-6129 382 H
christopher.washington@franklin.edu
WASHINGTON, Crystal . 773-838-7535 142 C
cwashington59@ccc.edu
WASHINGTON, Dana .... 815-802-8962 149 B
dwashington@kcc.edu
WASHINGTON,
Dennis, C .... 804-342-5203 518 E
dcwashington@vuu.edu
WASHINGTON,
DeSandra .... 910-678-0037 362 E
washingd@faytechcc.edu
WASHINGTON, Earlie ... 269-387-2638 252 I
earlie.washington@wmich.edu
WASHINGTON,
Eddie, L .... 734-763-8391 251 C
washine@umich.edu
WASHINGTON, Eric ...... 718-960-8181 319 C
eric.washington@lehman.cuny.edu
WASHINGTON, Erin ...... 864-587-4249 449 D
washingtone@smcsc.edu
WASHINGTON, Fred, E . 936-261-2140 484 F
fewashington@pvamu.edu
WASHINGTON,
Geovette .... 412-624-4141 437 K
gew@pitt.edu
WASHINGTON, Gregory 612-338-7224 265 G
gregory.washington@waldenu.edu
WASHINGTON, Gregory 949-824-6002.. 71 C
gregory.washington@uci.edu
WASHINGTON, Ingrid ... 859-442-1148 196 A
ingrid.washington@kctcs.edu
WASHINGTON, J. Leon 610-758-3100 424 B
jnw207@lehigh.edu
WASHINGTON,
James Bernard .... 252-536-7220 363 B
jwashington660@halifaxcc.edu
WASHINGTON, Jennifer 860-515-3820.. 88 B
jwashington@charteroak.edu
WASHINGTON, Jewel ... 301-405-5648 219 D
jmwashin@umd.edu
WASHINGTON, Kaye ..... 318-670-9450 207 C
kwashington@susla.edu
WASHINGTON,
Kheysia, H .... 318-670-9417 207 C
kwashington@susla.edu
WASHINGTON,
L. Marshall .... 304-929-5472 531 D
lmwashington@newriver.edu
WASHINGTON, Leila .... 410-951-3660 220 C
lwashington@coppin.edu
WASHINGTON, Mary .... 229-317-6761 123 H
mary.washington@darton.edu
WASHINGTON,
Maurice .... 404-653-7857 128 L
maurice.washington@morehouse.edu
WASHINGTON, Michael 901-435-1601 457 N
michael_washington@loc.edu
WASHINGTON, Pamela . 405-974-3773 403 G
pwashington@uco.edu
WASHINGTON, Sharon . 510-430-2096.. 54 F
swashington@mills.edu
WASHINGTON, Shawn .. 832-230-5555 479 J
swashington@na.edu
WASHINGTON, Ted, M . 615-353-3228 463 C
ted.washington@nscc.edu
WASHINGTON,
Troy, W .... 937-229-2554 393 E
TWashington1@udayton.edu
WASHINGTON, William 651-638-6300 254 A
w-washington@bethel.edu
WASHINGTON, Willie ... 803-705-4734 443 F
washingtonw@benedict.edu
WASHINGTON-LACEY,
Bonita .... 765-983-1515 165 H
washibo@earlham.edu
WASHINGTON-SCOTT,
Robin .... 410-462-8380 213 G
rwashington-scott@bccc.edu
WASHINGTON WHITE,
Kendal, H .... 520-621-7057.. 18 E
kwashing@email.arizona.edu
WASHINGTON-WOODS,
Paula .... 870-235-4145.. 23 D
pwwoods@saumag.edu
WASHKEVICH, Stephen 978-632-6600 232 C
s_washkevich@mwcc.mass.edu
WASHKO, Mary Jo .... 804-523-5345 515 F
mwashko@reynolds.edu
WASHOUSKY,
Richard, C .... 716-851-1500 325 A
washousky@ecc.edu
WASHUT, Kyle .... 307-332-2930 547 C
kwashut@wyomingcatholiccollege.com
WASIELEWSKI, Dan ...... 641-472-1156 181 A
dwasielewski@mum.edu
WASIELEWSKI, Laura .... 603-656-6051 298 F
lwasielewski@anselm.edu
WASILENKO,
William, J .... 757-446-8480 507 B
wasilewj@evms.edu
WASILESKI, Suzanne .... 603-342-3010 297 E
swasileski@ccsnh.edu
WASILEWSKI, Frank, M 415-422-2402.. 74 C
fmwasilewski@usfca.edu
WASKIE, Kenneth, G .... 607-777-2184 343 D
kwaskie@binghamton.edu
WASKIEWICZ, Rhonda .. 207-992-4913 210 C
waskiewiczr@husson.edu
WASKOSKY, Julia .... 815-802-8510 149 B
jwaskosky@kcc.edu
WASMUND, Ann, P .... 920-433-6665 534 K
ann.wasmund@bellincollege.edu
WASSBERG, Catherine .. 651-523-2616 256 B
cwassberg01@hamline.edu
WASSENAAR, Dave .... 714-484-7345.. 56 E
dwassenaar@cypresscollege.edu
WASSENMILLER, Angie . 402-643-3651 289 J
Angela.Wassenmiller@cune.edu
WASSERMAN, David ...... 718-631-6697 320 F
dwasserman@qcc.cuny.edu
WASSERMAN, Ed .... 510-642-3383.. 70 K
ed.wasserman@berkeley.edu
WASSERMAN, Harriet .... 206-934-4344 526 A
harriet.wasserman@seattlecolleges.edu
WASSERMAN, Keith ...... 856-691-8600 301 H
kwasserman@cccnj.edu
WASSERMAN, Matthew . 303-315-2067.. 86 G
matt.wasserman@ucdenver.edu
WASSON, Dale .... 817-272-5401 493 L
wasson@uta.edu
WASSON, Thomas .... 601-857-3367 267 D
thwasson@hindscc.edu
WASSUM, Keith, N .... 704-687-5747 371 B
knwassum@uncc.edu
WASTAWY, Sohair .... 321-674-7111 103 R
wastawy@fit.edu
WASTVEDT, Ross .... 515-263-6036 178 H
rwastvedt@grandview.edu
WASUKANIS, John, T .... 561-868-3480 109 H
wasukanj@palmbeachstate.edu
WATANABE, Mie .... 808-956-6423 135 H
mie@hawaii.edu
WATERCUTTER, Beckie .. 419-772-2038 388 I
r-watercutter@onu.edu
WATERFIELD, James, R 757-683-5070 510 I
rwater@odu.edu
WATERMAN, Ben .... 630-620-2155 154 J
bwaterman@seminary.edu

WAWRZASZEK, Susan, V .... 508-286-8225 238 B
wawrzaszek_susan@wheatoncollege.edu
WAWRZUSIN, Andrea ... 513-745-3009 396 B
wawrzusin@xavier.edu
WAXLER, Lawrence ...... 207-780-4413 213 A
larryw@usm.maine.edu
WAXMAN, Deborah ...... 215-576-0800 433 I
dwaxman@rrc.edu
WAY, Joshua .... 845-675-4416 337 B
joshua.way@nyack.edu
WAY, Kimera, K .... 715-836-5180 539 E
waykk@uwec.edu
WAY, Philip .... 724-738-2170 432 A
philip.way@sru.edu
WAY, Sara, A .... 305-684-6030 347 A
waysa@morrisville.edu
WAY, Sara, A .... 315-684-6030 347 A
waysa@morrisville.edu
WAY BOLT, Mary .... 410-287-1025 214 C
mbolt@cecil.edu
WAYE, Holly Anne .... 315-568-3055 334 F
hwaye@nycc.edu
WAYE, Kathy .... 315-279-5602 329 K
kwaye@keuka.edu
WAYLAND, Marilina, L . 787-250-1912 554 A
mwayland@metro.inter.edu
WAYMAN, Abby .... 217-222-8020 156 D
WAYMAN, Susan .... 508-213-2230 235 C
susan.wayman@nichols.edu
WAYMAN-GORDON, Ellen .... 201-200-3026 304 C
ewaymangordo@njcu.edu
WAYNE, Erika .... 407-708-2136 113 A
waynee@seminolestate.edu
WAYNE, William .... 315-568-3025 334 F
bwayne@nycc.edu
WAYNE, William, R ...... 405-325-4611 403 I
wwayne@ou.edu
WAYT, Missy .... 304-865-6003 530 F
missy.wayt@ovu.edu
WEAKLEY, Jerry .... 785-594-8332 184 F
jerry.weakley@bakeru.edu
WEARDEN, Stanley .... 312-369-7495 143 C
swearden@colum.edu
WEARN, Mary .... 478-471-2730 128 H
mary.wearn@mga.edu
WEASENFORTH, Donald, L .... 972-881-5794 471 C
dweasenforth@collin.edu
WEAST, Wade .... 336-770-3251 372 B
weastw@uncsa.edu
WEATHERALL, Maureen 310-338-1949.. 53 C
maureen.weatherall@lmu.edu
WEATHERBY, Beth .... 406-683-7151 287 E
beth.weatherby@umwestern.edu
WEATHERFORD, Dani ... 765-658-4540 165 G
daniweatherford@depauw.edu
WEATHERFORD, Melinda .... 360-442-2662 524 A
mweatherford@lowercolumbia.edu
WEATHERFORD, Tess ... 870-368-2006.. 22 D
tess.weatherford@ozarka.edu
WEATHERINGTON, Elsie, S .... 804-524-5040 518 C
eweatherington@vsu.edu
WEATHERLY, Alice .... 870-543-5900.. 23 C
aweatherly@seark.edu
WEATHERMAN, Donald, V .... 870-307-7201.. 21 G
president@lyon.edu
WEATHERMAN, Tammy 559-934-2117.. 76 A
tammyweatherman@whccd.edu
WEATHERS, Diane .... 718-289-5770 318 E
diane.weathers@bcc.cuny.edu
WEATHERS, Jon, M ...... 601-266-4466 271 B
jon.m.weathers@usm.edu
WEATHERS, Madonna, B .... 606-783-2070 198 H
m.weathers@moreheadstate.edu
WEATHERS, Melonie ..... 336-386-3207 366 E
weathersm@surry.edu
WEATHERSBEE, Byron .. 254-295-4150 492 C
bweathersbee@umhb.edu
WEATHERSPOON, David .... 847-543-2138 142 G
dweatherspoon@clcillinois.edu
WEATHERWAX, Alan ...... 978-837-5234 233 G
weatherwaxa@merrimack.edu
WEAVER, Allen .... 815-802-8304 149 B
aweaver@kcc.edu
WEAVER, Beckie .... 501-279-4640.. 21 A
bweaver@harding.edu
WEAVER, Bradley, K ..... 765-361-6308 175 B
weaverb@wabash.edu
WEAVER, Candace .... 601-477-4075 268 A
candace.weaver@jcjc.edu
WEAVER, Carol .... 304-457-6331 529 C
weaverc@ab.edu
WEAVER, Carolyn .... 515-271-1426 177 H
carolyn.weaver@dmu.edu
WEAVER, Dan .... 970-351-2032.. 87 A
dan.weaver@unco.edu
WEAVER, Danielle .... 716-839-8200 323 F
dweaver2@daemen.edu
WEAVER, David .... 907-786-7212.. 10 H
dweaver@uaa.alaska.edu
WEAVER, Deirdre .... 310-434-4791.. 65 B
weaver_deirdre@smc.edu
WEAVER, Donna .... 530-895-2568.. 30 B
weaverdo@butte.edu
WEAVER, Ernestine .... 860-723-0000.. 88 C
weavere@ct.edu
WEAVER, Gina .... 585-345-6808 326 F
gmweaver@genesee.edu
WEAVER, Greg .... 417-864-7220 275 A
gweaver@cci.edu
WEAVER, Harry .... 415-380-1376.. 45 J
harryweaver@ggbts.edu
WEAVER, James, S .... 740-376-4611 386 A
jim.weaver@marietta.edu
WEAVER, Jeff .... 501-760-4113.. 21 H
jweaver3@npcc.edu
WEAVER, Jim .... 541-383-7212 404 K
jweaver@cocc.edu
WEAVER, John .... 325-674-2476 466 I
jbw11a@acu.edu
WEAVER, Joseph .... 229-245-3737 133 H
jgweaver@valdosta.edu
WEAVER, JR., Joseph, B .... 405-744-2690 400 C
joe.weaver@okstate.edu
WEAVER, Julie .... 231-439-6306 248 A
jweaver@ncmich.edu
WEAVER, Karyn .... 870-733-6722.. 19 G
kweaver@midsouthcc.edu
WEAVER, Kathleen .... 909-593-3511.. 73 B
kweaver@laverne.edu
WEAVER, Kenneth .... 620-341-5367 186 H
kweaver@emporia.edu
WEAVER, Laura .... 219-785-5742 172 A
lweaver@pnc.edu
WEAVER, Laura .... 510-659-6518.. 56 J
lweaver@ohlone.edu
WEAVER, Marianne .... 541-962-3524 405 G
mweaver@eou.edu
WEAVER, Melanie .... 419-772-2272 388 I
m-weaver@onu.edu
WEAVER, Mischelle ...... 309-341-5456 140 I
WEAVER, Nancy .... 870-512-7833.. 19 I
nancy_weaver@asun.edu
WEAVER, Neal .... 985-448-4134 208 C
neal.weaver@nicholls.edu
WEAVER, Paula .... 518-736-3622 326 D
pweaver@fmcc.suny.edu
WEAVER, Rhonda .... 704-403-1756 355 B
rhonda.weaver@carolinashealthcare.org
WEAVER, Sam .... 501-370-5317.. 22 E
sweaver@philander.edu
WEAVER, Sandie .... 562-903-4760.. 29 F
sandie.weaver@biola.edu
WEAVER, Sean .... 505-545-3380 311 H
slweaver@nmhu.edu
WEAVER, Sean, F .... 412-396-2560 417 I
weavers2@duq.edu
WEAVER, Steven .... 479-979-1000.. 25 H
WEAVER, Tammy .... 479-968-0272.. 20 C
tweaver@atu.edu
WEAVER, Terri, E .... 312-996-7808 161 F
teweaver@uic.edu
WEAVER, Theresa .... 906-635-2733 245 H
tweaver@lssu.edu
WEAVER, Vickie, L .... 609-896-5029 306 A
weaver@rider.edu
WEAVER, Vincent .... 256-372-4276.... 1 A
vincent.weaver@aamu.edu
WEAVER, Wendy .... 414-443-3608 538 A
weaverw@mtmary.edu
WEAVER-GRIGGS, Linda .... 803-327-8024 451 K
lwgriggs@yorktech.edu
WEAVER HART, Ann ..... 520-621-5511.. 18 E
president@email.arizona.edu
WEAVIL, Vicki .... 336-770-3266 372 B
weavilv@uncsa.edu
WEBB, Anda, L .... 434-924-0999 514 A
al6b@virginia.edu
WEBB, Arla, J .... 443-518-4690 215 F
awebb@howardcc.edu
WEBB, Barbara .... 989-686-9228 242 I
brwebb@delta.edu
WEBB, Brent, W .... 801-422-6201 497 J
webb@byu.edu
WEBB, Burton, J .... 208-467-8419 138 H
bwebb@nnu.edu
WEBB, Carol .... 281-487-1170 486 F
cwebb@txchiro.edu
WEBB, Charlie .... 806-720-7156 478 A
charles.webb@lcu.edu
WEBB, Cheryl, A .... 803-327-7402 444 F
cwebb@clintoncollege.edu
WEBB, Dan .... 423-425-4729 465 E
dan-webb@utc.edu
WEBB, Dann .... 478-218-3321 122 E
dwebb@centralgatech.edu
WEBB, Dann .... 478-988-6800 122 F
dwebb@centralgatech.edu
WEBB, Dixie .... 931-221-6346 461 C
webbd@apsu.edu
WEBB, Donna .... 229-391-5001 119 F
dwebb@abac.edu
WEBB, Donnetta .... 916-558-2408.. 53 B
webbd@scc.losrios.edu
WEBB, Duncan .... 312-461-0600 139 G
dwebb@aaart.edu
WEBB, Elnora, T .... 510-464-3236.. 59 B
ewebb@peralta.edu
WEBB, Eric .... 620-450-2188 190 H
ericw@prattcc.edu
WEBB, Eric .... 307-766-3059 546 K
ewebb1@uwyo.edu
WEBB, Eric, C .... 484-365-7451 424 E
ewebb@lincoln.edu
WEBB, II, Ernest, R ...... 915-831-5051 473 J
ewebb1@epcc.edu
WEBB, Gwen .... 919-546-8223 368 G
gwebb@shawu.edu
WEBB, James, D .... 806-651-1240 486 D
jwebb@mail.wtamu.edu
WEBB, Jay, K .... 434-544-8218 509 I
webb@lynchburg.edu
WEBB, Jeanie .... 405-733-7300 401 L
jwebb@rose.edu
WEBB, Jen .... 715-675-2775 183 G
webbj@uiu.edu
WEBB, Jennifer .... 254-295-4526 492 C
jwebb@umhb.edu
WEBB, Jerrad .... 620-276-9521 187 D
jerrad.webb@gcccks.edu
WEBB, Jodi .... 419-372-9348 377 I
jwebb@bgsu.edu
WEBB, Joshua, M .... 989-964-4359 249 G
jmwebb@svsu.edu
WEBB, Karen .... 805-756-2661.. 32 E
kwebb@calpoly.edu
WEBB, Katheryn .... 812-749-1392 171 I
kwebb@oak.edu
WEBB, Kathleen, M ...... 937-229-4263 393 E
kwebb1@udayton.edu
WEBB, Kathryn, J .... 404-527-5785 127 H
kwebb@itc.edu
WEBB, Keith .... 404-270-5279 132 D
kwebb5@spelman.edu
WEBB, Ken .... 619-680-4430.. 30 H
ken.webb@cc-sd.edu
WEBB, Kenneth .... 903-785-7661 480 B
kwebb@parisjc.edu
WEBB, Kyle .... 901-843-3760 460 F
webb@rhodes.edu
WEBB, Lee .... 870-512-7849.. 19 I
lee_webb@asun.edu
WEBB, Leslie .... 208-426-4208 137 E
lesliewebb@boisestate.edu
WEBB, Lynda .... 432-685-6884 478 F
lwebb@midland.edu
WEBB, Mark, F .... 931-598-1284 460 I
mwebb@sewanee.edu
WEBB, Melessia, D .... 423-354-5106 463 D
mdwebb@northeaststate.edu
WEBB, Michael .... 815-921-2151 157 B
m.webb@rockvalleycollege.edu
WEBB, Michelle .... 207-453-5020 211 B
mwebb@kvcc.me.edu
WEBB, Pat .... 214-860-8789 472 G
pwebb@dcccd.edu
WEBB, R. Brian .... 254-710-8797 469 D
brian_webb@baylor.edu
WEBB, Randy .... 870-733-6750.. 19 G
rwebb@midsouthcc.edu
WEBB, Reggie .... 540-828-8014 505 F
rwebb@bridgewater.edu
WEBB, Reginal .... 863-298-6828 110 E
rwebb@polk.edu
WEBB, Sandy .... 641-782-1422 183 D
webb@swcciowa.edu
WEBB, Terrance, S .... 608-246-6270 543 C
tswebb@madisoncollege.edu
WEBB, Tom .... 937-775-5680 396 A
thomas.webb@wright.edu
WEBB, Travis .... 414-805-8622 537 C
pwebb@mcw.edu
WEBB, Troycia .... 229-430-3396 119 I
WEBB, Vicki .... 870-307-7227.. 21 G
vicki.webb@lyon.edu
WEBB, Walter, W .... 815-939-5333 155 G
wwebb@olivet.edu
WEBB, JR., William, C . 810-762-3324 251 E
bwebb@umflint.edu
WEBB-CURTIS, Susan ... 423-472-7141 462 D
susanwebb-curtis@clevelandstatecc.edu
WEBB SHARPE, Lisa .... 517-483-1106 245 I
sharpel@lcc.edu
WEBBER, Adrienne, C .. 803-536-8638 448 H
awebber@scsu.edu
WEBBER, Andrew .... 480-965-5906.. 11 J
andrew.webber@asu.edu
WEBBER, Diane .... 202-685-7375 547 M
diane.webber@ndu.edu
WEBBER, Henry, S .... 314-935-7877 285 E
hwebber@wustl.edu
WEBBER, Kimberly .... 918-595-7809 403 A
kimberly.webber@tulsacc.edu
WEBBER, Leah .... 617-928-4513 234 D
lwebber@mountida.edu
WEBBER, Louise .... 909-621-8265.. 39 E
louise.webber@cgu.edu
WEBBER, Meg .... 803-323-2220 451 I
webberm@winthrop.edu
WEBBER, Michael, J .... 415-422-2648.. 74 C
webberm@usfca.edu
WEBBER, Robert .... 802-831-1209 503 E
rwebber@vermontlaw.edu
WEBBER, Rochelle .... 716-851-1169 325 A
webberr@ecc.edu
WEBBER, Wendi .... 617-364-3510 224 A
wwebber@boston.edu
WEBBER MCLEAN, Kalynda .... 818-610-6567.. 51 H
mcleankw@piercecollege.edu
WEBER, A. Scott .... 716-645-6029 343 E
sweber@buffalo.edu
WEBER, Brad .... 620-252-7076 186 C
bradw@coffeyville.edu
WEBER, Bruce, W .... 302-831-1211.. 94 D
bweber@udel.edu
WEBER, Chris .... 301-447-5114 217 D
cweber@msmary.edu
WEBER, Chris .... 231-995-1039 248 C
cweber@nmc.edu
WEBER, Daniel, R .... 773-442-4000 154 H
d-weber3@neiu.edu
WEBER, Dave .... 352-365-3530 107 X
weberd@lssc.edu
WEBER, Dawn .... 419-289-4142 377 A
dweber1@ashland.edu
WEBER, Debra .... 262-695-7842 544 D
dweber28@wctc.edu
WEBER, Eric .... 801-957-4136 500 E
eric.weber@slcc.edu
WEBER, Girard, W .... 847-543-2201 142 G
jweber@clcillinois.edu
WEBER, J. Christopher . 570-577-1795 413 E
weber@bucknell.edu
WEBER, Jacqueline, J ... 573-592-5307 285 J
jackie.weber@westminster-mo.edu
WEBER, Janet .... 419-473-2700 381 F
jweber@daviscollege.edu
WEBER, Jennifer .... 701-224-2540 373 F
jennifer.weber@ndus.edu
WEBER, Jim, P .... 330-972-5908 392 H
jpw@uakron.edu
WEBER, Jodi .... 903-434-8114 479 L
jweber@ntcc.edu
WEBER, Joe .... 440-375-7000 385 B
jweber@lec.edu
WEBER, Joe .... 931-221-7618 461 C
weberj@apsu.edu
WEBER, John .... 219-785-5368 172 A
jweber@pnc.edu
WEBER, Jolanta, A .... 509-313-6504 522 L
weberj@gonzaga.edu
WEBER, Julie .... 575-646-3202 312 A
jeweber@nmsu.edu
WEBER, Kevin .... 502-585-9911 199 E
kweber@spalding.edu
WEBER, Krista .... 608-822-2315 544 C
kweber@swtc.edu
WEBER, Laurie .... 701-858-3375 374 B
laurie.weber@minotstateu.edu
WEBER, Lou Anne .... 864-503-5197 451 A
lweber@uscupstate.edu
WEBER, Margaret .... 740-284-5244 382 G
mweber@franciscan.edu
WEBER, Mark .... 920-498-5663 544 B
mark.weber@nwtc.edu
WEBER, Marsha, L .... 218-477-2076 260 B
marsha.weber@mnstate.edu
WEBER, Mary .... 831-646-4048.. 54 H
mweber@mpc.edu
WEBER, Melissa .... 320-589-6414 265 A
weberm@morris.umn.edu
WEBER, Merlin, D .... 530-226-4501.. 66 G
mweber@simpsonu.edu
WEBER, Nancy .... 843-525-8226 449 E
nweber@tcl.edu
WEBER, Peter, M .... 401-863-7799 441 A
peter_weber@brown.edu
WEBER, Phil .... 740-857-1311 390 L
pweber@rosedale.edu
WEBER, Randy .... 913-469-8500 188 E
rweber@jccc.edu

WEINTROP, Joseph ...... 646-312-3092 318 C
Joseph.Weintrop@baruch.cuny.edu
WEIPPERT, Linda .... 620-229-6175 191 B
linda.weippert@sckans.edu
WEIR, Amy .... 765-361-6078 175 B
weira@wabash.edu
WEIR, Ashley, M .... 304-462-6133 532 G
ashley.weir@glenville.edu
WEIR, Dennis .... 434-961-5447 516 F
dweir@pvcc.edu
WEIR, George .... 361-593-2831 486 A
george.weir@tamuk.edu
WEIR, James .... 304-232-0361 530 K
jweir@wvbc.edu
WEIR, Karissa, L .... 704-406-4732 356 G
kweir@gardner-webb.edu
WEIR, Laura .... 239-433-6941 104 G
lweir2@fsw.edu
WEIR, Lljuna .... 601-877-6700 266 C
weir@alcorn.edu
WEIR, Robert .... 303-860-5600.. 86 D
bob.weir@cu.edu
WEIR, Robert .... 617-287-5240 228 G
bob.weir@umb.edu
WEIR, Roseanne, N ...... 315-786-2408 329 G
rweir@sunyjefferson.edu
WEIR, Walter, G .... 402-472-2862 293 F
wweir@nebraska.edu
WEIRICK, Chad .... 740-755-7327 378 L
cweirick@cotc.edu
WEIS, Bob, M .... 863-638-2920 119 A
weisrm@webber.edu
WEIS, Charlene .... 701-255-3285 375 I
cweis@uttc.edu
WEIS, Dallas .... 509-527-2608 528 A
dallas.weis@wallawalla.edu
WEIS, Ed .... 914-674-7632 332 E
eweis@mercy.edu
WEIS, Mary .... 630-844-3866 139 L
mweis@aurora.edu
WEIS, Richard .... 859-280-1256 198 B
rweis@lextheo.edu
WEIS, Tim .... 217-228-5432 156 D
weisti@quincy.edu
WEISBERG, Bradley ...... 408-741-4012.. 76 F
bradley.weisberg@westvalley.edu
WEISBORD, Beryl .... 410-484-7200 217 E
WEISBROD, Angela ...... 507-457-1493 264 B
aweisbro@smumn.edu
WEISEN, Jan, G .... 617-745-3705 225 H
jan.weisen@enc.edu
WEISEN, Sheryl .... 317-745-3703 225 H
sheryl.weisen@enc.edu
WEISENBURGER, Earl ... 605-626-2529 454 A
Earl.Weisenburger@northern.edu
WEISENBURGER, Leigh 207-786-6000 209 F
lweisenb@bates.edu
WEISENBURGER, Perk .. 231-591-2863 242 L
PerkWeisenburger@ferris.edu
WEISENSTEIN, Greg, R . 610-436-2471 432 B
gweisenstein@wcupa.edu
WEISER, Bridget, R .... 785-827-5541 189 A
bridget@kwu.edu
WEISER, Hazel .... 212-431-2854 335 G
Hazel.Weiser@nyls.edu
WEISER, Kent, L .... 620-341-5350 186 H
kweiser@emporia.edu
WEISER, Philip, J .... 303-492-3084.. 86 E
phil.weiser@colorado.edu
WEISER, Sharon .... 660-357-6300 279 L
sweiser@mail.ncmissouri.edu
WEISER, Tedd .... 352-588-8234 111 L
tedd.weiser@saintleo.edu
WEISGERBER,
James (Chip) .... 423-869-7758 458 B
james.weisgerber@lmunet.edu
WEISGRAM, Molly .... 605-773-3455 453 E
molly.weisgram@sdbor.edu
WEISHAAR, Mary .... 618-650-3785 159 I
mweisha@siue.edu
WEISHAR, Peter .... 850-644-5244 115 A
pweishar@fsu.edu
WEISKOPFF,
Jacqueline .... 973-290-4393 301 F
jeiskopff@cse.edu
WEISMAN, Iris .... 937-769-1890 376 L
iweisman@antioch.edu
WEISMAN, Sarah .... 607-962-9385 323 D
sweismal@corning-cc.edu
WEISMAN, Susan, E ..... 718-489-5379 340 E
sweisman@sfc.edu
WEISNER, Andrew .... 828-328-7248 358 G
andrew.weisner@lr.edu
WEISNER, Silvestro ...... 202-994-5300.. 95 D
sweisner@gwu.edu
WEISPFENNING, John .. 714-628-4930.. 60 H
weispfenning_john@sccollege.edu
WEISS, Charles .... 508-793-2735 225 C
cweiss@holycross.edu
WEISS, David .... 210-567-3709 495 B
weissd@uthscsa.edu
WEISS, H .... 732-364-1220 299 H
WEISS, Ira, R .... 919-515-5560 370 D
ira_weiss@ncsu.edu
WEISS, Janet, A .... 734-764-4401 251 C
janetw@umich.edu
WEISS, Jeffery, I .... 718-990-6357 340 G
weissj@stjohns.edu
WEISS, Johanna .... 804-594-1500 515 G
jweiss@jtcc.edu
WEISS, Karen .... 618-252-5400 159 F
karen.weiss@sic.edu
WEISS, Kay .... 909-384-8535.. 62 C
kweiss@sbccd.cc.ca.us
WEISS, Nicolas .... 303-245-4664.. 84 B
nweiss@naropa.edu
WEISS, Rod, P .... 858-499-0202.. 40 G
rweiss@coleman.edu
WEISS, Shelley .... 513-244-8183 379 I
shelley.weiss@ccuniversity.edu
WEISS, Stephanie .... 612-330-1476 253 K
weisss@augsburg.edu
WEISS, Valerie .... 313-664-7852 241 D
vweiss@collegeforcreativestudies.edu
WEISS-COOK, Laura ...... 785-320-4541 189 C
lauraweiss-cook@matc.net
WEISSENBURGER,
David .... 254-968-9464 485 A
weissenburger@tarleton.edu
WEISSENFLUH, Anji ...... 541-962-3236 405 G
aweissen@eou.edu
WEISSMAN, Julie .... 314-246-4256 285 G
julieweissman22@webster.edu
WEISSMAN, Neil, B ...... 717-245-1321 417 B
weissmne@dickinson.edu
WEITER, Stephen .... 315-470-6715 347 B
spweiter@esf.edu
WEITHERS, Deborah ..... 269-471-6684 239 D
rdw@andrews.edu
WEITZ, Anna, D .... 610-607-6210 433 H
aweitz@racc.edu
WEITZ, Eric .... 212-650-8166 318 G
eweitz@ccny.cuny.edu
WEITZE, Jann .... 417-667-8181 273 H
jweitzel@cottey.edu
WEITZER, Joseph .... 262-695-7824 544 D
jweitzer@wctc.edu
WEITZMAN, Lauren ...... 801-581-6826 499 K
lweitzman@sa.utah.edu
WEIZER, Paul, I .... 978-665-3272 229 D
pweizer@fitchburgstate.edu
WEKESA, Kennedy .... 334-229-4316.... 1 D
wekesai@alasu.edu
WELAGE, Lynda, S .... 505-272-0906 313 H
LSWelage@salude.unm.edu
WELBORN, Ruth, B .... 512-245-3300 489 C
rw01@txstate.edu
WELBURN, Janice .... 414-288-7214 537 B
janice.welburn@marquette.edu
WELBURN, William .... 414-288-8028 537 B
william.welburn@marquette.edu
WELCH, Alexis .... 252-527-6223 363 G
awelch@lenoircc.edu
WELCH, April .... 312-567-3196 147 E
welcha@iit.edu
WELCH, Ba-Shen, T ..... 205-929-1574.... 5 I
bwelch@miles.edu
WELCH, Becky .... 253-680-7100 519 K
bwelch@bates.ctc.edu
WELCH, Brian .... 574-936-8898 164 A
brian.welch@ancilla.edu
WELCH, Charles, L .... 501-660-1000.. 19 D
president@asusystem.edu
WELCH, Dan .... 814-866-8151 423 B
dwelch@lecom.edu
WELCH, Denise .... 903-693-1121 480 A
dwelch@panola.edu
WELCH, Dirk .... 940-397-4972 478 G
dirk.welch@mwsu.edu
WELCH, Edwin .... 765-998-5523 173 B
edwelch@taylor.edu
WELCH, Edwin, H .... 304-357-4713 530 H
edwinwelch@ucwv.edu
WELCH, Frances, C ...... 943-953-5613 445 B
welchf@cofc.edu
WELCH, George .... 619-684-8826.. 56 B
gwelch@newschoolarch.edu
WELCH, James .... 405-224-3140 403 L
jwelch@usao.edu
WELCH, Jennifer .... 251-344-1203.... 3 J
WELCH, Jennifer, C ...... 315-464-4570 344 E
welchj@upstate.edu
WELCH, John .... 412-924-1401 433 E
jwelch@pts.edu
WELCH, Julia .... 707-638-5425.. 70 B
julia.perhac@tu.edu
WELCH, Kathleen .... 831-479-5076.. 30 C
kawelch@cabrillo.edu
WELCH, Lena .... 615-248-1393 464 E
lwelch@trevecca.edu
WELCH, Leo .... 970-351-2515.. 87 A
leo.welch@unco.edu
WELCH, Lynne .... 908-709-7167 309 A
welch@ucc.edu
WELCH, Marc .... 765-361-6480 175 B
welchm@wabash.edu
WELCH, Marjorie .... 712-325-3202 180 B
mwelch@iwcc.edu
WELCH, Matt .... 254-968-9002 485 A
welch@tarleton.edu
WELCH, Michael .... 847-578-3238 157 G
Michael.Welch@rosalindfranklin.edu
WELCH, Mike .... 269-927-1000 245 E
WELCH, Nick .... 740-588-1224 396 E
nwelch@zanestate.edu
WELCH, Olga, M .... 412-396-1360 417 I
welcho@duq.edu
WELCH, Patricia .... 443-885-3385 217 C
pwelch@morgan.edu
WELCH, Paul .... 415-955-2100.. 26 I
pwelch@alliant.edu
WELCH, Paul .... 508-626-4640 230 A
pwelch@framingham.edu
WELCH, Regina, E .... 804-627-5350 505 E
regina_welch2@bshsi.org
WELCH, Renee .... 970-351-2127.. 87 A
renee.welch@unco.edu
WELCH, Ronald, W .... 843-953-6499 444 C
rwelch1@citadel.edu
WELCH, Sally .... 313-927-1319 246 D
swelch@marygrove.edu
WELCH, Sandra, T .... 210-458-4706 494 D
sandra.welch@utsa.edu
WELCH, Sharon .... 773-256-3000 152 D
swelch@meadville.edu
WELCH, Sherri, L .... 856-691-8600 301 H
swelch@cccnj.edu
WELCH, Susan .... 814-865-7691 428 C
sxw11@psu.edu
WELCH, Susan, T .... 518-564-5062 346 B
welchst@plattsburgh.edu
WELCH, Terry .... 828-227-7100 372 C
welcht@wcu.edu
WELCH, Thomas .... 843-661-1136 446 E
rwelch@fmarion.edu
WELCH, Val .... 208-376-7731 137 D
vwelch@boisebible.edu
WELD, Jeff .... 802-468-1241 503 G
jeff.weld@castleton.edu
WELDEN, David .... 770-962-7580 127 C
dwelden@gwinnetttech.edu
WELDEN, Jonathan .... 901-272-5121 459 A
jweldon@mca.edu
WELDEN, Soraya .... 601-484-8628 268 B
swelden@meridiancc.edu
WELDON, James .... 803-780-1119 451 G
jweldon@voorhees.edu
WELDON, Leslie .... 618-634-3337 159 A
lesliew@shawneecc.edu
WELDON, Rich .... 803-508-7382 443 C
weldonr@atc.edu
WELDON, Sherrie .... 561-237-7788 108 E
sweldon@lynn.edu
WELDON, Stephanie, J . 603-206-8111 297 A
sjweldon@ccsnh.edu
WELDON, Wray .... 972-883-6994 494 A
wray.weldon@utdallas.edu
WELDY, Eric .... 815-753-1573 154 I
eweldy@niu.edu
WELKER, Dan .... 928-428-8300.. 13 L
dan.welker@eac.edu
WELKER, Joan, C .... 570-484-2181 431 C
jwelker@lhup.edu
WELKER, Josh .... 217-641-4110 148 J
jwelker2@jwcc.edu
WELKER, Kristen .... 605-668-1577 452 I
kristen.welker@mtmc.edu
WELKER, Mark, A .... 309-341-7255 149 G
mawelker@knox.edu
WELKER, Sharon, L ...... 919-866-5611 366 H
sfwelker@waketech.edu
WELKEY, Sharon .... 210-832-2115 492 B
welkey@uiwtx.edu
WELLBORN, Linda .... 417-865-2815 274 L
wellbornl@evangel.edu
WELLENZOHN,
Nancy, A .... 716-888-8234 317 H
wellenzn@canisius.edu
WELLER, Eddie .... 281-998-6150 481 F
eddie.weller@sjcd.edu
WELLER, Eddie .... 281-998-6150 481 E
eddie.weller@sjcd.edu
WELLER, Eddie .... 281-998-6150 481 G
eddie.weller@sjcd.edu
WELLER, Julie .... 231-777-0461 247 G
julie.weller@muskegoncc.edu
WELLER, Lisa .... 610-225-5007 418 A
lweller2@eastern.edu
WELLER-DENGEL,
Pamela .... 507-389-6061 260 A
pamela.weller-dengel@mnsu.edu
WELLES, Julia .... 816-802-3302 276 F
jwelles@kcai.edu
WELLHAUSEN, Chad ..... 712-542-5117 180 B
cwellhausen@iwcc.edu
WELLINGS, Keith .... 304-724-3700 529 F
kwellings@apus.edu
WELLINGTON, Eric .... 610-359-5394 416 G
ewellington@dccc.edu
WELLINGTON, Katie ...... 580-559-5651 397 K
katmwel@ecok.edu
WELLINGTON-BAKER,
Kristi .... 509-527-4263 527 H
kristi.wellington-baker@wwcc.edu
WELLMAN, Barbara .... 217-228-5432 156 D
wellmba@quincy.edu
WELLMAN, Chris .... 941-752-5443 114 B
wellmac@scf.edu
WELLMAN, Debra .... 407-646-2175 111 H
dwellman@rollins.edu
WELLMAN, Ronald, D ... 336-758-5616 372 G
wellmanr@wfu.edu
WELLNER, Justin .... 805-756-7003.. 32 E
jwellner@calpoly.edu
WELLOCK, Barbara .... 530-221-4275.. 66 B
bwellock12@shasta.edu
WELLS, Allison .... 225-768-1700 206 F
WELLS, Barbara .... 901-333-4259 464 A
bwells@southwest.tn.edu
WELLS, Barbara .... 865-981-8278 458 E
barbara.wells@maryvillecollege.edu
WELLS, Beth .... 503-845-3243 407 B
beth.wells@mtangel.edu
WELLS, Billy .... 706-864-1630 133 A
billy.wells@ung.edu
WELLS, Bonnie .... 860-439-5001.. 90 D
bonnie.wells@conncoll.edu
WELLS, Brian, J .... 502-776-1443 199 C
bwells@simmonscollegeky.edu
WELLS, C. Gene .... 812-488-2664 173 H
gw5@evansville.edu
WELLS, C. Richard .... 605-342-0317 452 E
WELLS, Carol .... 909-384-8925.. 62 C
cwells@sbccd.cc.ca.us
WELLS, Carole .... 610-683-4212 431 B
wells@kutztown.edu
WELLS, Christopher, J . 765-658-4270 165 G
christopherwells@depauw.edu
WELLS, Dan .... 713-743-2619 491 D
dwells2@uh.edu
WELLS, Douglas .... 605-394-1763 454 B
douglas.wells@sdsmt.edu
WELLS, Elaine .... 212-938-5690 347 C
ewells@sunyopt.edu
WELLS, Geordy .... 901-381-3939 466 E
geordy@visible.edu
WELLS, JR., Henry, D .. 919-572-1625 354 F
hdwells@apexsot.edu
WELLS, Jeff .... 843-953-2232 444 C
jeff.wells@citadel.edu
WELLS, Jennifer .... 270-901-1004 197 C
jennifer.wells@kctcs.edu
WELLS, Jeremy .... 706-591-3012.. 74 A
jwells@usa.edu
WELLS, Jesse .... 607-778-5296 344 F
wellsje@sunybroome.edu
WELLS, Johann .... 334-291-4954.... 2 H
johann.wells@cv.edu
WELLS, John, T .... 804-684-7103 506 J
wells@vims.edu
WELLS, John, W .... 828-689-1250 359 A
jwells@mhu.edu
WELLS, Jovita .... 202-274-6260.. 97 B
jwells@udc.edu
WELLS, Kathy .... 307-855-2031 545 a
kwells@cwc.edu
WELLS, Keith, P .... 303-762-6963.. 82 C
keith.wells@denverseminary.edu
WELLS, Kyle 435-652-7887 499M
kwells@dixie.edu
WELLS, Lisa .... 540-887-7330 510 A
lwells@mbc.edu
WELLS, Marilyn .... 507-389-1334 260 A
marilyn.wells@mnsu.edu
WELLS, Matt .... 937-393-3431 391 F
mwells@sscc.edu
WELLS, Melissa .... 619-239-0391.. 36 E
mwells@cwsl.edu
WELLS, Michael .... 910-893-1275 355 C
wellsm@campbell.edu
WELLS, Nancy, L .... 716-645-4666 343 E
nwells@buffalo.edu
WELLS, Nick .... 620-227-9269 186 F
nwells@dc3.edu
WELLS, Peter, D .... 508-767-7350 222 D
pd.wells@assumption.edu
WELLS, R. Hal .... 612-874-3634 257 D
hal_wells@mcad.edu
WELLS, Robert .... 434-592-3406 509 G
rlwells3@liberty.edu
WELLS, JR., Robert, J .. 864-656-0244 444 E
rjwells@clemson.edu
WELLS, Ronald .... 865-273-8882 458 E
ronald.wells@maryvillecollege.edu

WESTCOTT, III, S. Wickes .... 864-656-0161 444 E westc@clemson.edu
WESTDYKE, Anne, E ..... 512-492-3147 481 B anneew@stedwards.edu
WESTEEN, Kelly .... 479-788-7106.. 23 H kelly.westeen@uafs.edu
WESTENBROEK, Steve .. 402-399-2465 289 I swestenbroek@csm.edu
WESTENDORF, Thomas, J .... 937-229-4141 393 E twestendorf1@udayton.edu
WESTER, Ken .... 479-968-0218.. 20 C kwester@atu.edu
WESTERBERG PRAGER, Susan .... 213-738-6710.. 68 E deansoffice@swlaw.edu
WESTERFIELD, Barbara, M .... 601-984-1080 270 H bwesterfield@umc.edu
WESTERFIELD, Mary Ann .... 856-691-8600 301 H mwesterfield@cccnj.edu
WESTERFIELD, Michael, W .... 573-592-4383 286 A michael.westerfield@williamwoods.edu
WESTERHOUSE, Joni, L 314-286-0120 285 E westerhousej@wustl.edu
WESTERMAN, III, W. Scott .... 517-355-8314 246 H wsw@msu.edu
WESTERMEYER, Lawrence, W .... 314-516-4010 284 B larry_westermeyer@umsl.edu
WESTERMEYER, Susan, M .... 317-940-9135 164 L swesterm@butler.edu
WESTERN, Lindajean, H .... 330-569-5174 383 F westernlh@hiram.edu
WESTERVELT, Robert, K 503-554-2136 406 A rwestervelt@georgefox.edu
WESTFALL, Andrew .... 410-337-6500 215 B andrew.westfall@goucher.edu
WESTFALL, Michael ...... 509-359-7099 522 C mwestfall@ewu.edu
WESTFALL, Sarah, B ..... 269-337-7209 244 I Sarah.Westfall@kzoo.edu
WESTGARD, Joyce .... 360-438-4333 525 H jwestgard@stmartin.edu
WESTHOFF, James .... 207-992-4909 210 C westhoffj@husson.edu
WESTHOFF, Randall ...... 218-755-2016 258 B rwesthoff@bemidjistate.edu
WESTLAKE, Christopher, J .... 850-872-3212 105 Q cwestlake@gulfcoast.edu
WESTLAKE, Rachel .... 925-969-2003.. 42 E rwestlake@dvc.edu
WESTLEY, Elizabeth, K .. 757-594-7345 506 I elizabeth.westley@cnu.edu
WESTLEY, Lindsey .... 708-456-0300 161 C lwestley@triton.edu
WESTLUND, Julie, A ..... 218-726-7985 264 G jwestlun@d.umn.edu
WESTMAN, Craig .... 856-225-6510 307 A craig.westman@rutgers.edu
WESTMAN, Dennis .... 580-371-7121 398 J dwestman@mscok.edu
WESTMAN, Hans .... 412-291-6409 412 H hwestman@aii.edu
WESTMORELAND, T. Andrew .... 205-726-2727.... 6 F tawestmo@samford.edu
WESTON, JR., Donald, E .... 609-258-3407 305 C donw@princeton.edu
WESTON, John, H .... 507-284-2073 254 F weston.john@mayo.edu
WESTON, Penelope .... 661-255-1050.. 31 B
WESTON, Wayne .... 605-455-6083 452 L wweston@olc.edu
WESTOVER, Kristin .... 276-656-0315 516 D kwestover@patrickhenry.edu
WESTPHAL, Arthur, P ... 507-344-7375 253M awest@blc.edu
WESTPHAL, Donald, M . 507-344-7320 253M dwestpha@blc.edu
WESTPHAL, Kenneth, C 507-933-7499 256 A kwestpha@gustavus.edu
WESTPHAL, Kristianne, R .... 507-933-7495 256 A kristi@gustavus.edu
WESTPHAL, Lee .... 402-557-5235 289 B lee.westphal@bellevue.edu
WESTPHAL, Lorraine, M .... 757-594-7608 506 I lwestpha@cnu.edu
WESTPHAL, Matt .... 918-540-6249 398 L mwestphal@neo.edu
WESTRA, Jeff .... 608-249-6611 536 J careers@msn.herzing.edu
WESTRA, Kayla .... 507-372-3435 260 C kayla.westra@mnwest.edu
WESTRICK, Karyn, J ..... 419-434-4758 393 F westrick@findlay.edu
WESTWATER, Julia .... 508-289-3379 238 F jwestwater@whoi.edu
WETHERBEE-METCALF, Pamela .... 410-617-2330 216 D pwetherbeemetcalf@loyola.edu
WETHERELL, Bill .... 386-506-3813 101 I wetherb@DaytonaState.edu
WETHERELL, Dale, R .... 401-825-2109 441 C drwetherell@ccri.edu
WETHERILL, Elsbeth ..... 510-204-0700.. 38 K ewetherill@cdsp.edu
WETHERILL, G. Richard 580-559-5455 397 K rwethrll@ecok.edu
WETHERINGTON, Lee ... 252-527-6223 363 G lwetherington@lenoircc.edu
WETHERINGTON, Nicole .... 310-453-8300.. 43 I nicole@emperors.edu
WETMORE, Angela .... 620-862-5252 184 H angela.wetmore@barclaycollege.edu
WETMORE, Ashley .... 620-227-9376 186 F awetmore@dc3.edu
WETMORE, David .... 620-227-9201 186 F dwetmore@dc3.edu
WETMORE, Dawn .... 567-661-7338 390 D dawn_wetmore@owens.edu
WETSELL, Linda, S .... 814-332-4790 411 F lwetsell@allegheny.edu
WETSTEIN, Kenneth .... 419-783-2463 381 G kwetstein@defiance.edu
WETSTEIN, Matt .... 209-954-5047.. 63 D mwetstein@deltacollege.edu
WETTER, Kevin .... 808-356-5261 135 C kvetter@hpu.edu
WETTERGREN, Steve ..... 815-740-5080 162 F swettergren@stfrancis.edu
WETTSTEIN, Deena .... 608-757-7716 542 L dwettstein@blackhawk.edu
WETZEL, Derrick .... 610-282-1100 416 I derrick.wetzel@desales.edu
WETZEL, Kathryn .... 972-860-4751 472 C kwetzel@dcccd.edu
WETZEL, Mary, E .... 717-728-2260 415 B marywetzel@centralpenn.edu
WETZEL, Mike .... 717-358-4759 418 J mike.wetzel@fandm.edu
WETZEL, Robert .... 215-637-7700 420 K rwetzel@holyfamily.edu
WETZEL, Shelby .... 307-754-6110 546 I Shelby.Wetzel@nwc.edu
WETZEL, Suzanne, M ... 734-384-4206 247 C swetzel@monroeccc.edu
WETZEL HARDER, Wendy .... 949-480-4081.. 66 I wwharder@soka.edu
WETZSTEIN, James .... 219-464-5096 174 E james.wetzstein@valpo.edu
WEVODAU, Clint, D ...... 570-577-7439 413 E clint.wevodau@bucknell.edu
WEXLER, Joan, G .... 718-780-7900 317 A joan.wexler@brooklaw.edu
WEXLER, Jonathan, D .. 518-276-6143 339 D
WEXLER, Judie .... 415-575-6104.. 31 C jwexler@ciis.edu
WEXLER, Robert .... 310-476-9777.. 27 J
WEY, Lora .... 309-438-2592 147 I lwey@ilstu.edu
WEYAND, Andy .... 330-490-7320 395 C aweyand@walsh.edu
WEYAND, Joel .... 402-826-8242 290 C joel.weyand@doane.edu
WEYANDT, Anne .... 651-690-7701 263 V afweyandt@stkate.edu
WEYERS, Lori, A .... 715-675-3331 544 A weyers@ntc.edu
WEYGANT, Susan .... 914-923-2397 337 I sweygant@pace.edu
WEYHENMEYER, James, A .... 404-413-3516 126 D jweyhenmeyer@gsu.edu
WEYHING, Kathy .... 859-336-5082 199 B kathyweyhing@sccky.edu
WEYL, Ronnie .... 908-526-1200 305 G Ronnie.Weyl@raritanval.edu
WEZNER, Kelley, C .... 270-809-3340 198 I kwezner@murraystate.edu
WHALEN, Alice .... 636-584-6532 274 J alice.whalen@eastcentral.edu
WHALEN, David .... 845-451-1406 323 E d_whalen@culinary.edu
WHALEN, David .... 517-607-2321 243 J dwhalen@hillsdale.edu
WHALEN, Jeff .... 209-588-5126.. 78 B whalenj@yosemite.edu
WHALEN, Lynn .... 217-786-2219 151 C lynn.whalen@llcc.edu
WHALEN, Melissa .... 913-253-5091 190 K melissa.whalen@spst.edu
WHALEN, Michael .... 860-685-2895.. 93 B mwhalen@wesleyan.edu
WHALEN, Michael .... 419-251-1824 386 C michael.whalen@mercycollege.edu
WHALEN, Patricia .... 814-824-3070 425 L pwhalen@mercyhurst.edu
WHALEN, Scott, M .... 315-255-1743 317 I scott.whalen@cayuga-cc.edu
WHALEN, Shawn .... 415-338-1948.. 36 A swhalen@sfsu.edu
WHALEN, Steve .... 718-997-5054 320 E steven.whalen@qc.cuny.edu
WHALEN, Thomas .... 212-229-5456 334 C whalent@newschool.edu
WHALEN, Tina .... 513-558-7485 393 B tina.whalen@uc.edu
WHALEN, Toni .... 502-213-2118 196 E toni.whalen@kctcs.edu
WHALEN-SMITH, Heather, C .... 315-655-7132 317 J hcwhalensmith@cazenovia.edu
WHALEY, Chris .... 865-882-4501 463 F whaleycl@roanestate.edu
WHALEY, David .... 270-809-6849 198 I dwhaley2@murraystate.edu
WHALEY, David, J .... 802-485-2300 502 G davew@norwich.edu
WHALEY, Frances, A .... 815-224-0387 147 J frances_whaley@ivcc.edu
WHALEY, Melanie, A .... 814-871-7470 419 A whaley003@gannon.edu
WHALEY, Michael .... 636-949-4561 276 L mwhaley@lindenwood.edu
WHALEY, Michael, J ..... 860-685-3160.. 93 B mwhaley@wesleyan.edu
WHALEY, Mitchell, H ... 765-285-5818 164 D mwhaley@bsu.edu
WHALEY, Sheree .... 530-242-7667.. 66 C swhaley@shastacollege.edu
WHALEY, Stephanie, E . 859-846-5408 198 G swhaley@midway.edu
WHALEY, Vernon .... 434-582-2562 509 G vwhaley@liberty.edu
WHAM, Ben .... 843-953-5088 444 C ben.wham@citadel.edu
WHANG, Kyu-Jung .... 607-255-4394 323 C kw253@cornell.edu
WHAPHAM, Ted .... 972-721-4068 491 B twhapham@udallas.edu
WHARTON, Barbara ...... 740-593-1059 389 H whartonb@ohio.edu
WHARTON, Beverly, A .. 712-279-5400 176 B beverly.wharton@briarcliff.edu
WHARTON, Bill .... 636-227-2100 277 A bill.wharton@logan.edu
WHARTON, Kristin .... 704-233-8366 373 C kwharton@wingate.edu
WHARTON, Martha, L .. 410-617-2988 216 D mwharton1@loyola.edu
WHARTON, Randy .... 740-588-1379 396 E rwharton@zanestate.edu
WHATELY, Lorrie .... 253-752-2020 522 K admissions@faithseminary.edu
WHATLEY, Melissa .... 657-278-2380.. 33 E mkwhatley@fullerton.edu
WHATLEY, Sherri .... 903-566-7247 494 E swhatley@uttyler.edu
WHEAT, Casie .... 650-949-7200.. 45 A wheatcasie@fhda.edu
WHEAT, Gary .... 417-626-1234 280 B gwheat@occ.edu
WHEATLEY, Diane .... 757-789-1754 515 D dwheatley@es.vccs.edu
WHEATLEY, Michelle, M .... 509-313-4238 522 L wheatleym@gonzaga.edu
WHEATLY, Stephen .... 805-493-3828.. 31 H wheatly@callutheran.edu
WHEATON, David, M .... 651-696-6211 256 L wheaton@macalester.edu
WHEATON, Timothy, W 207-859-4904 210 A tim.wheaton@colby.edu
WHEATON, Tom .... 605-642-6446 453 G tom.wheaton@bhsu.edu
WHEELAND, Craig .... 610-519-4520 439 A craig.wheeland@villanova.edu
WHEELAND, Todd .... 815-455-8564 152 B twheeland@mchenry.edu
WHEELDON, Tim, T ...... 515-263-6152 178 H twheeldon@grandview.edu
WHEELER, Alfred .... 864-646-1425 449 F awheele4@tctc.edu
WHEELER, Amy .... 603-206-8131 297 A awheeler@ccsnh.edu
WHEELER, Brad .... 812-856-5595 167 J bwheeler@indiana.edu
WHEELER, Brad, C .... 812-855-3478 167 I bwheeler@indiana.edu
WHEELER, Cassandra, L .... 956-326-4473 485 B cwheeler@tamiu.edu
WHEELER, Cecilia, B .... 919-528-4737 366 G wheelerc@vgcc.edu
WHEELER, David .... 912-344-2919 120 D david.wheeler@armstrong.edu
WHEELER, Erin .... 518-631-9850 351 A wheelere@uniongraduatecollege.edu
WHEELER, Frank, E ...... 402-363-5646 294 G fwheeler@york.edu
WHEELER, H. William ... 434-592-3003 509 G hwwheeler@liberty.edu
WHEELER, Ike .... 870-512-7865.. 19 I ike_wheeler@asun.edu
WHEELER, Jeff .... 803-754-4100 445 D
WHEELER, Jessica .... 213-613-2200.. 67 G jessica_wheeler@sciarc.edu
WHEELER, John .... 253-752-2020 522 K registrar@faithseminary.edu
WHEELER, John, D .... 216-368-5555 378 J john.wheeler@case.edu
WHEELER, Kara .... 620-331-4100 188 B kwheeler@indycc.edu
WHEELER, Laurie .... 707-965-7200.. 57 I lwheeler@puc.edu
WHEELER, Linda .... 706-272-4547 123 G lwheeler@daltonstate.edu
WHEELER, Lisa .... 318-678-6000 203 A lwheeler@bpcc.edu
WHEELER, Lisa .... 952-358-8286 260 D lisa.wheeler@normandale.edu
WHEELER, Mark .... 714-564-6319.. 60 G wheeler_mark@sac.edu
WHEELER, Mark .... 208-426-1140 137 E mwheeler@boisestate.edu
WHEELER, Mark .... 208-467-8772 138 H mwheeler@nnu.edu
WHEELER, Mary .... 254-526-1200 470 E mary.wheeler@ctcd.edu
WHEELER, Michelle ...... 907-564-8210.. 10 D mwheeler@alaskapacific.edu
WHEELER, Michelle ...... 248-476-1122 246 G mwheeler@mispp.edu
WHEELER, Nolan .... 360-442-2201 524 A nwheeler@lowercolumbia.edu
WHEELER, Paul .... 541-383-7588 404 K pwheeler@cocc.edu
WHEELER, Quentin, D .. 315-470-6681 347 B qwheeler@esf.edu
WHEELER, Sharon .... 434-582-3036 509 G swheeler@liberty.edu
WHEELER, Sherrell .... 575-439-3668 312 B swheeler@nmsu.edu
WHEELER, Susan .... 309-694-8855 146 C swheeler@icc.edu
WHEELER, Susan, L ...... 540-568-3727 509 C wheel2sl@jmu.edu
WHEELER, Thomas .... 816-604-5240 277 H thomas.wheeler@mcckc.edu
WHEELER, Tim .... 425-739-8252 523 I tim.wheeler@lwtech.edu
WHEELER, Walter .... 252-789-0259 363 H wwheeler@martincc.edu
WHEELING, Barbara ..... 406-657-1651 287 H barbara.wheeling@msubillings.edu
WHEELIS, Tina .... 870-368-2008.. 22 D twheelis@ozarka.edu
WHEELOCK, Pam .... 612-624-3557 265 C wheelock@umn.edu
WHEELOCK, William ..... 330-941-3165 396 C wwheelock@ysu.edu
WHELAN, JR., Donald, J .... 817-257-7785 486 G d.whelan@tcu.edu
WHELAN, Janet .... 410-837-4779 221 B jwhelan@ubalt.edu
WHELAN, John .... 812-855-2239 167 J whelanj@iu.edu
WHELAN, John .... 812-855-3027 167 I whelanj@indiana.edu
WHELAN, Lara .... 706-238-5876 121 E lwhelan@berry.edu
WHELAN, Matthew .... 631-632-6833 344 C matthew.whelan@stonybrook.edu
WHELAN, Michaele ...... 617-824-8570 226 A michaele_whelan@emerson.edu
WHELAN, Robert .... 718-289-5162 318 E robert.whelan@bcc.cuny.edu
WHELIHAN, Tom .... 218-846-3778 259 H tom.whelihan@minnesota.edu
WHERRY, Cassandra, J 641-269-3424 178 I wherry@grinnell.edu
WHETSTINE, Courtney .. 541-383-7700 404 K cwhetstine@cocc.edu
WHETSTONE, Joseph .... 540-261-8487 512 J joseph.whetstone@svu.edu
WHETSTONE, Kimarie ... 803-323-2551 451 I whetstone@winthrop.edu

WHITE, Stephen, F .... 615-898-5454 461 E
stephen.white@mtsu.edu
WHITE, Stephone .... 336-334-7600 370 B
oswhite@ncat.edu
WHITE, Steven .... 316-978-3782 192 D
steven.white@wichita.edu
WHITE, Susan, E .... 912-583-3169 121 H
swhite@bpc.edu
WHITE, Susan, K .... 913-627-4125 188 G
swhite@kckcc.edu
WHITE, Tamara .... 303-360-4703.. 81 I
Tamara.White@CCAurora.edu
WHITE, Tamisia .... 212-870-1229 336 B
finaid@nyts.edu
WHITE, Tammy, S .... 205-652-3651.... 9 G
thw@uwa.edu
WHITE, Thelma .... 270-706-8409 195 K
thelma.white@kctcs.edu
WHITE, Theodore .... 816-235-1330 284 A
whitetc@umkc.edu
WHITE, Thomas, R .... 508-929-8023 230 G
twhite@worcester.edu
WHITE, Timothy, L .... 352-846-0850 115 D
tlwhite@ufl.edu
WHITE, Timothy, P .... 562-951-4700.. 32 D
twhite@calstate.edu
WHITE, Tracy .... 608-356-8351 541 E
tracy.white@uwc.edu
WHITE, W. Scott .... 704-406-4259 356 G
swhite@gardner-webb.edu
WHITE, Wayman .... 252-335-0821 361 G
waywhite@albemarle.edu
WHITE, Wendy, S .... 215-746-5240 437 I
wendy.white@ogc.upenn.edu
WHITE, William .... 303-457-2757.. 82 H
william.white@zenith.org
WHITE, William, A .... 407-582-1185 118 I
bwhite@valenciacollege.edu
WHITE BULL, David ..... 605-455-6076 452 L
dwhitebull@olc.edu
WHITE CASTENADA,
April .... 626-395-8167.. 31 D
april@caltech.edu
WHITECAVAGE,
Michele .... 714-449-7404.. 53 D
mwhitecavage@ketchum.edu
WHITED, Frances, P ..... 330-287-1216 389 B
whited.16@osu.edu
WHITED, Jimmy, R .... 540-375-2308 512 B
WHITEFIELD, Joe .... 615-904-8375 461 E
joe.whitefield@mtsu.edu
WHITEFORD, Aaron ...... 503-768-7944 406 H
ahw@lclark.edu
WHITEFORD, Marion .... 802-442-5427 503 A
WHITEHAIR, Bruce .... 814-332-2451 411 F
bwhitehair@allegheny.edu
WHITEHEAD, Alan .... 540-261-8421 512 J
alan.whitehead@svu.edu
WHITEHEAD, Debbie .... 503-255-0332 407 D
debbiew@multnomah.edu
WHITEHEAD, Doug 435-652-7500 499M
dkw@dixie.edu
WHITEHEAD, Gwen .... 409-882-3926 488 G
gwen.whitehead@lsco.edu
WHITEHEAD, Heidi, M . 812-888-4313 174 F
hwhitehead@vinu.edu
WHITEHEAD, Jeffrey, R 412-648-2299 437 K
jrwst43@pitt.edu
WHITEHEAD, JR.,
Joe, B .... 336-334-7965 370 B
jbwhiteh@ncat.edu
WHITEHEAD, Johnny 713-348-6000 480M
johnny.whitehead@rice.edu
WHITEHEAD, Joyce, E .. 630-889-6610 154 E
jwhitehead@nuhs.edu
WHITEHEAD, Kim .... 662-241-6850 269 B
kmwhitehead@muw.edu
WHITEHEAD,
Kimberly, D .... 410-651-3553 219 H
kdwhitehead@umes.edu
WHITEHEAD, Launa ...... 540-261-8575 512 J
launa.whitehead@svu.edu
WHITEHEAD,
Richard, G .... 540-261-4095 512 J
richard.whitehead@svu.edu
WHITEHEAD, Susan ...... 617-984-1721 235 H
swhitehead@quincycollege.edu
WHITEHEAD, Teresa ..... 575-769-4066 310 G
teresa.whitehead@clovis.edu
WHITEHOUSE, Deborah 859-622-1523 194 L
deborah.whitehouse@eku.edu
WHITEHOUSE, Jennifer . 985-867-2240 206 J
jwhitehouse@sjasc.edu
WHITEHURST, Alan .... 540-261-8598 512 J
alan.whitehurst@svu.edu
WHITEHURST,
Marcus, A .... 814-865-5906 428 C
maw163@psu.edu

WHITEHURST-MCLEAN,
Makitta .... 252-335-3355 369 F
mmmclean@ecsu.edu
WHITELAW, Kenneth .... 603-513-1375 299 C
kenneth.whitelaw@granite.edu
WHITELAW, Lydia .... 610-896-1177 420 J
lwhitela@haverford.edu
WHITELEY, Janell .... 360-475-7504 524 H
jwhiteley@olympic.edu
WHITELY, Patricia, A .... 305-284-4922 118 A
pwhitely@miami.edu
WHITEMAN, Betty .... 386-822-8869 117 A
bwhiteman@stetson.edu
WHITEMAN, Charles, H 814-863-0448 428 C
chw17@psu.edu
WHITEMAN, Michael .... 704-330-6706 361 D
mike.whiteman@cpcc.edu
WHITEMAN,
Raymond, E .... 574-807-7139 164 F
ray.whiteman@bethelcollege.edu
WHITEMORE, Alan, T ... 617-989-4307 237 G
whitemorea@wit.edu
WHITESIDE, Harold, D . 615-898-2900 461 E
harold.whiteside@mtsu.edu
WHITEY, Jeff .... 541-888-7634 410 A
jwhitey@socc.edu
WHITFIELD, Aleczander 704-378-3501 358 B
awhitfield@jcsu.edu
WHITFIELD, Christina ... 859-256-3100 195 G
christina.whitfield@kctcs.edu
WHITFIELD, Deidra .... 205-970-9210.... 7 D
deidra.whitfield@sebc.edu
WHITFIELD, Gary .... 209-588-5112.. 78 B
whitfieldg@yosemite.edu
WHITFIELD, Henry .... 478-934-3167 128 H
henry.whitfield@mga.edu
WHITFIELD, Jacques .... 530-741-6976.. 78 D
jwhitfie@yccd.edu
WHITFIELD, Jacques .... 530-741-6976.. 78 F
jwhitfie@yccd.edu
WHITFIELD, Keith .... 919-761-2127 368 K
kwhitfield@sebts.edu
WHITFIELD, Keith .... 919-660-0330 356 E
keith.whitfield@duke.edu
WHITFIELD, Meredith ... 828-227-7059 372 C
mcwhitfield@wcu.edu
WHITFIELD, Rick .... 910-962-3383 372 A
whitfieldr@uncw.edu
WHITFIELD, Rick, N ..... 910-962-3383 372 A
whitfieldr@uncw.edu
WHITFILL, Jill .... 731-352-4083 455 E
whitfillj@bethelu.edu
WHITFORD, Betty Lou .. 334-844-4448.... 1 G
blw0017@auburn.edu
WHITFORD, Daryl 808-675-3730 134M
whitford@byuh.edu
WHITFORD, Jewel, L .... 406-395-4875 288 I
jewelwhitford@hotmail.com
WHITHAM, John, H ...... 610-526-1308 412 D
john.whitham@theamericancollege.edu
WHITHAUS, Becky .... 573-897-5000 282 I
WHITING, Alison 808-675-3552 134M
whitinga@byuh.edu
WHITING, J. Scott .... 334-874-5700.... 3 B
swhiting@ccal.edu
WHITING, Mary .... 870-460-1026.. 24 C
whitingm@uamont.edu
WHITING, Sarah, M 713-348-4044 480M
sarah.whiting@rice.edu
WHITING, Shari, K .... 315-859-4313 327 A
swhiting@hamilton.edu
WHITIS, Andrew .... 419-434-4767 393 F
whitis@findlay.edu
WHITIS, Harold .... 210-485-0605 466 J
hwhitis2@alamo.edu
WHITIS, Matt .... 815-939-5350 155 G
mwhitis@olivet.edu
WHITLATCH, Frank .... 707-826-5101.. 35 D
frank@humboldt.edu
WHITLATCH,
Michael, D .... 712-749-2172 176 D
whitlatch@bvu.edu
WHITLEDGE, Terry .... 907-474-7229.. 10 I
terry@ims.uaf.edu
WHITLEY, Darrell, S ..... 252-985-5105 367 E
dwhitley@ncwc.edu
WHITLEY, Freddy .... 252-823-5166 362 D
whitleyf@edgecombe.edu
WHITLEY, Rebecca .... 575-492-2546 311 J
rwhitley@nmjc.edu
WHITLING, Jacqueline .. 570-484-3045 431 C
jwhitlin@lhup.edu
WHITLOCK, David, W ... 405-585-5801 399 I
david.whitlock@okbu.edu
WHITLOCK, Eugene ...... 650-358-6883.. 64 B
whitlocke@smccd.edu
WHITLOCK, John, L ..... 727-816-3325 110 B
whitloj@phsc.edu
WHITLOCK, Kevin .... 320-308-2038 261 E
kcwhitlock@stcloudstate.edu

WHITLOCK, Monica ...... 509-777-4216 529 A
mwhitlock@whitworth.edu
WHITLOCK, Stephen ..... 678-839-6426 133 F
swhitlock@westga.edu
WHITLOCK, Tonya, F .... 678-664-0532 134 F
tonya.whitlock@westgatech.edu
WHITMAN, Carl, E .... 240-567-3146 217 B
carl.whitman@montgomerycollege.edu
WHITMAN, David .... 651-604-4118 257 C
WHITMAN, Deirdre .... 914-674-7316 332 E
dwhitman@mercy.edu
WHITMAN, Joshua, H .. 314-935-5288 285 E
whitman@wustl.edu
WHITMAN, Mary Ann ... 701-349-5403 375 G
mwhitman@trinitybiblecollege.edu
WHITMAN, Melissa .... 252-249-1851 364 F
mwhitman@pamlicocc.edu
WHITMAN, Paul .... 803-321-5600 447 L
paul.whitman@newberry.edu
WHITMAN, R. Douglas . 313-577-1625 252 G
dwhitman@wayne.edu
WHITMAN, Rebecca, R . 616-234-4010 243 D
rwhitman@grcc.edu
WHITMAN, JR.,
William .... 202-238-2338.. 96 B
william.whitman@howard.edu
WHITMAN, William, D . 989-386-6696 247 B
wwhitman@midmich.edu
WHITMER, Ann .... 517-629-0440 239 A
awhitmer@albion.edu
WHITMIRE, Teresa .... 479-619-4175.. 22 B
twhitmire@nwacc.edu
WHITMORE, Joe .... 256-782-5777.... 4 L
whitmore@jsu.edu
WHITMORE,
Kimberly, N .... 515-574-1138 179 F
whitmore@iowacentral.edu
WHITMORE, Michele .... 802-635-1452 504 A
michele.whitmore@jsc.edu
WHITMORE, Petia .... 781-239-4543 222 E
pwhitmore1@babson.edu
WHITMORE, Vincent ..... 410-462-8594 213 G
vwhitmore@bccc.edu
WHITNEY, Candice .... 408-848-4754.. 45 G
cwhitney@gavilan.edu
WHITNEY, Cynthia .... 605-229-8381 453 A
cynthia.whitney@presentation.edu
WHITNEY, Gleaves .... 616-331-2770 243 E
whitneyg@gvsu.edu
WHITNEY, Glenda .... 573-897-5000 282 I
WHITNEY, Heather .... 518-743-2342 347 E
charpentierh@sunyacc.edu
WHITNEY, Heidi .... 802-468-6072 503 G
heidi.whitney@castleton.edu
WHITNEY, J.J .... 501-450-1263.. 21 C
whitney@hendrix.edu
WHITNEY, Jarrid .... 626-395-6341.. 31 D
jwhitney@caltech.edu
WHITNEY, Joan, G .... 610-519-4050 439 A
joan.whitney@villanova.edu
WHITNEY, Karen .... 928-541-7777.. 16 B
kwhitney@ncu.edu
WHITNEY, Karen, M ..... 814-393-2220 430 E
president@clarion.edu
WHITNEY, Laura .... 860-768-5691.. 92 F
lwhitney@hartford.edu
WHITNEY, Marian, D .... 315-684-6010 347 A
whitnemd@morrisville.edu
WHITNEY, Patricia .... 603-645-9609 298 H
p.whitney@snhu.edu
WHITNEY, Patrick, F .... 312-595-4900 147 E
whitney@id.iit.edu
WHITNEY, Paul .... 401-874-5224 442 E
pwhitney@uri.edu
WHITNEY, Richard .... 641-269-3300 178 I
whitney@grinnell.edu
WHITNEY, Roger .... 650-723-2300.. 68 G
WHITSON, Brian .... 757-221-7876 506 J
bwwhit@wm.edu
WHITSON, Janet .... 512-313-3000 471 H
janet.whitson@concordia.edu
WHITSON, Jennifer .... 507-786-3000 264 C
whitson@stolaf.edu
WHITSON, Tony .... 901-435-1733 457 N
tony_whitson@loc.edu
WHITT, Cynthia, L .... 423-869-6394 458 B
cindy.whitt@lmunet.edu
WHITT, David, T .... 205-726-2386.... 6 F
dtwhitt@samford.edu
WHITT, Edith, L .... 828-689-1151 359 A
ewhitt@mhu.edu
WHITT, Elizabeth .... 209-228-2317.. 71 E
ewhitt@ucmerced.edu
WHITT, Ellen .... 317-955-6597 171 A
ewhitt@marian.edu
WHITT, Julie .... 817-257-6571 486 G
j.whitt@tcu.edu
WHITT, Susan .... 910-521-6212 371 D
susan.whitt@uncp.edu
WHITTAKER, A. Dale .... 407-823-2303 115 C
Dale.Whittaker@ucf.edu

WHITTAKER, Bethany ... 269-782-1484 250 D
bwhittaker@swmich.edu
WHITTAKER, Jeremy ..... 901-755-9399 225 A
Jeremy.Whittaker@cambridgecollege.edu
WHITTAKER, Jim .... 541-278-5811 404 J
jwhittaker@bluecc.edu
WHITTAKER, Joanne ..... 808-734-9520 136 C
joannewh@hawaii.edu
WHITTAKER, Kristine 435-672-7753 499M
whittaker@dixie.edu
WHITTAKER, Nancy, H . 205-348-4534.... 8 E
nwhittaker@fa.ua.edu
WHITTAKER-DAVIS,
Sharon .... 205-366-8838.... 7 G
swhittaker@stillman.edu
WHITTED, Tenial .... 708-596-2000 159 D
WHITTEMORE, Steve ..... 508-626-4923 230 A
swhittemore@framingham.edu
WHITTEN, James .... 207-844-2103 211 D
jwhitten@smccme.edu
WHITTEN, Mandy .... 864-503-5420 451 A
mwhitten@uscupstaet.edu
WHITTEN, Pamela .... 706-583-0506 132 H
pwhitten@uga.edu
WHITTEN, Patrice .... 850-484-1714 110 D
pswhitten@pensacolastate.edu
WHITTEN, Steve .... 719-598-0200.. 81 H
swhitten@coloradotech.edu
WHITTENBURG, Nashia 912-344-2514 120 D
nashia.whittenburg@armstrong.edu
WHITTENBURG, Scott ... 406-243-6670 287 D
scott.whittenburg@umontana.edu
WHITTENTON, Kathy .... 870-307-7505.. 21 G
kathy.whittenton@lyon.edu
WHITTEY, Chris .... 216-421-7455 380 B
cwhittey@cia.edu
WHITTINGHAM,
Michelle .... 831-459-1453.. 72 E
michelle@ucsc.edu
WHITTINGHAM, Rachel 501-205-8876.. 20 G
rwhittingham@cbc.edu
WHITTINGTON, Connie 318-869-5101 202 D
cwhitt@centenary.edu
WHITTINGTON, Donna . 225-743-8500 204 C
dwhittington@rpcc.edu
WHITTINGTON,
Elizabeth .... 713-623-2040 468 F
ewhittington@aii.edu
WHITTINGTON,
Gerald, O .... 336-278-5434 356 F
whitting@elon.edu
WHITTINGTON,
Kimberlee .... 281-425-6457 477 F
kwhittin@lee.edu
WHITTINGTON, Lee ...... 828-766-1196 364 A
lwhittington@mayland.edu
WHITTINGTON, Ray ...... 312-362-6781 143 G
rwhittin@depaul.edu
WHITTLESEY,
Valerie, D 470-578-6023 127M
vwhittle@kennesaw.edu
WHITTUM, Terry .... 617-536-6340 224 C
twhittum@bostonconservatory.edu
WHITWELL, Jeff .... 615-898-2700 461 E
jeff.whitwell@mtsu.edu
WHITWORTH, Amy .... 210-486-4287 466 K
awhitworth@alamo.edu
WHITWORTH, Bruce ..... 559-278-2795.. 33 D
bwhitwor@csufresno.edu
WHITWORTH, Jerry ...... 940-898-2202 490 D
jwhitworth@twu.edu
WHITWORTH, Ling, Y .. 434-395-2319 509 H
whitworthly@longwood.edu
WHOLEBEN, Belinda ..... 815-226-4065 157 D
bwholeben@rockford.edu
WHORLEY, William .... 517-607-2454 243 J
wwhorley@hillsdale.edu
WHORTON, Susan .... 864-656-6256 444 E
whorton@clemson.edu
WHTYE, William .... 262-564-3228 543 A
whytew@gtc.edu
WHYNOTT, Anne .... 262-564-2758 543 A
whynotta@gtc.edu
WHYTE, Novia, P .... 516-463-6928 328 A
novia.p.whyte@hofstra.edu
WHYTE, William .... 262-564-3228 543 A
whytew@gtc.edu
WIBBELS, Alan .... 954-771-0376 107 V
awibbels@knoxseminary.edu
WIBBENMEYER, Kana ... 773-508-3489 151 E
kwibben@luc.edu
WIBLE, Doug .... 949-214-3029.. 42 B
doug.wible@cui.edu
WICHERN, Adam .... 718-405-3776 322 A
adam.wichern@mountsaintvincent.edu
WICHERT, Jerome, L .... 580-774-3786 402 G
jerome.wichert@swosu.edu
WICHROSKI, Pamela, J 207-786-6207 209 F
pwichros@bates.edu

WICHSER, John 301-696-3545 215 E wichser@hood.edu
WICK, Martha 641-683-5231 179 C martha.wick@indianhills.edu
WICK, Michael, R 715-836-2033 539 E wickmr@uwec.edu
WICKE, Thomas 303-975-5010 87 H twicke@westwood.edu
WICKEHAM, Daniel 414-955-8826 537 C dwickeha@mcw.edu
WICKER, Jeff 803-321-5676 447 L jeffrey.wicker@newberry.edu
WICKER-MCCREE, Ingrid, L 919-530-7057 370 C iwicker@nccu.edu
WICKERING, Deborah 616-632-2075 239 E wickedeb@aquinas.edu
WICKERSHAM, Walter 617-358-0300 224 E wnw@bu.edu
WICKERT, Jonathan, A 515-294-0070 175 G wickert@iastate.edu
WICKETT, Brenda, K 515-961-1611 182 I brenda.wickett@simpson.edu
WICKIZER, Della, H 434-395-2075 509 H wickizerdh@longwood.edu
WICKLAND, Mary 409-984-6125 488 H mary.wickland@lamarpa.edu
WICKLESS, Megan 402-552-6119 289 H wicklessmegan@clarksoncollege.edu
WICKLIFFE, Cari, S 314-977-2350 281 M wicklics@slu.edu
WICKLIFFE-CAMPBELL, Carol 631-451-4169 348 E wicklic@sunysuffolk.edu
WICKLINE, Jason 217-424-6217 153 A jwickline@millikin.edu
WICKLUND, Greg, A 817-202-6743 483 C wicklund@swau.edu
WICKS, Donna 810-762-7853 245 A dwicks@kettering.edu
WICKS, Michelle, D 304-205-6705 531 A michelle.wicks@bridgevalley.edu
WICKSTROM, Brian 318-342-5361 209 A wickstrom@ulm.edu
WICKSTROM, Sherry 763-576-4874 258 A swickstrom@anokatech.edu
WIDDOWS, Daniella 434-223-6311 508 B dwiddows@hsc.edu
WIDELL, Mike 405-945-3284 400 F mike@okstate.edu
WIDEMAN, Ben 920-686-6141 539 A Ben.Wideman@sl.edu
WIDEMAN, Gene 918-595-7262 403 A gene.wideman@tulsacc.edu
WIDENER, J, J 620-417-1202 191 A jj.widener@sccc.edu
WIDENHOFER, Stephen, B 217-424-6300 153 A swidenhofer@millikin.edu
WIDENMANN, Sally 541-917-4534 406 J widenms@linnbenton.edu
WIDGER, Mari Jo 308-345-8106 291 H widgerm@mpcc.edu
WIDING, II, Robert, E 216-368-1156 378 J
WIDMER, Robert, D 309-268-8100 145 H rob.widmer@heartland.edu
WIDNER, Kenneth 662-329-7021 269 B kwidner@muw.edu
WIDNER, Melissa 229-420-4070 119 H melisa.widner@asurams.edu
WIDNEY, Kaye 304-367-4303 532 F kwidney@fairmontstate.edu
WIEBE, Harold, D 740-368-3656 390 B hdwiebe@owu.edu
WIEBE, Nancy 620-792-9367 184 I wieben@barrtonccc.edu
WIECHMAN, Jeffery, P 507-354-8221 257 A wiechmjp@mlc-wels.edu
WIECKI, Lisa 864-388-8035 447 E lwiecki@lander.edu
WIECKOWSKI, Ellen, G 412-397-6901 434 B wieckowski@rmu.edu
WIED, Christine 979-830-4224 469 F cwied@blinn.edu
WIEDOW, Gale 605-256-5177 453 H gale.wiedow@dsu.edu
WIEGAND, Joe 706-865-2134 132 G jwiegand@truett.edu
WIEGAND, Mark 502-272-8368 193 E mwiegand@bellarmine.edu
WIEGAND, Randall, V 671-735-2905 549 G wiegandr@triton.uog.edu
WIEGANDT, Scott, P 502-272-8496 193 E swiegandt@bellarmine.edu
WIEGEL, Lisa 563-288-6003 178 C lwiegel@eicc.edu
WIEGENSTEIN, Steve, C 573-875-8700 273 D scwiegenstein@ccis.edu
WIELAND, John 502-213-3653 196 E john.wieland@kctcs.edu
WIELAND, William 605-626-2497 454 A William.Wieland@northern.edu
WIELEBINSKI, Daria 570-422-3282 430 F dwielebinski@esu.edu
WIELENGA, Jay 712-707-7111 182 C jayw@nwciowa.edu
WIELGUS, Jeanne 707-826-4206 35 D jw7001@humboldt.edu
WIELHORSKI, Karen 281-283-3930 491 E wielhorski@uhcl.edu
WIELINSKI, Peter 218-631-7810 259 H peter.wielinski@minnesota.edu
WIENCEK, John, M 208-885-6448 139 C provost@uidaho.edu
WIENER, William, R 336-334-5375 371 C wrwiener@uncg.edu
WIERBICKI ABRAHAMS, Jill 617-928-4633 234 D jwabrahams@mountida.edu
WIERDA, Bruce 231-777-0657 247 G bruce.wierda@muskegoncc.edu
WIERS, Alison 336-334-4822 363 A ajwiers@gtcc.edu
WIERTEL, Anthony 716-926-8818 327 F twiertel@hilbert.edu
WIERZBICKI, Andrzej 251-460-6280 9 F awierzbicki@southalabama.edu
WIESCAMP, Cheryl 970-247-7364 82 I wiescamp_c@fortlewis.edu
WIESE, Barry 636-227-2100 277 A barry.wiese@logan.edu
WIESE, Joelle, D 202-687-7150 95 E jdw237@georgetown.edu
WIESE, Vicki 605-995-3023 452 H vicki.wiese@mitchelltech.edu
WIESEHAN, Terry 765-973-8221 168 A twieseha@iue.edu
WIESEMANN, Lois 801-957-4255 500 E lois.wiesemann@slcc.edu
WIESENBERG, Mark 801-863-8740 500 B mwiesenberg@uvu.edu
WIESENTHAL, Steve 773-834-3529 161 D swiesenthal@uchicago.edu
WIESEPAPE, Craig 979-830-4195 469 F craig.wiesepape@blinn.edu
WIESNER, Bob 803-641-3522 450 C bobw@usca.edu
WIESNER, Don 316-942-4291 189 K wiesnerd@newmanu.edu
WIEWEL, Wim 503-725-4411 409 D president@pdx.edu
WIFFIN, Bridget 802-485-2824 502 G bwiffin@norwich.edu
WIGBOLDY, Kyle 616-222-3000 245 D kwigboldy@kuyper.edu
WIGFALL, Arthur 212-463-0400 350 C arthur.wigfall@touro.edu
WIGGINS, Amy, F 252-862-1225 365 C afwiggins7415@roanokechowan.edu
WIGGINS, Annette 715-634-4790 536 P awiggins@lco.edu
WIGGINS, Charles 828-395-1306 363 D cpwiggins@isothermal.edu
WIGGINS, David, J 952-446-4112 255 E wigginsj@crown.edu
WIGGINS, Devon 903-510-2385 491 A dwig@tjc.edu
WIGGINS, Donnell 937-722-9239 394 F admissions@urbana.edu
WIGGINS, Jack 409-839-2014 488 E jowiggins@lit.edu
WIGGINS, Jill 417-836-5636 279 A jillwiggins@missouristate.edu
WIGGINS, Lavaugn 334-874-5700 3 B lwiggins@ccal.edu
WIGGINS, Michael 870-743-3000 22 A mwiggins@northark.edu
WIGGINS, Nimmi, K 859-257-6547 200 G nwiggin@uky.edu
WIGGINS, Rick 513-556-2891 393 B rick.wiggins@uc.edu
WIGGINS, Rob 503-517-1876 411 C rwiggins@westernseminary.edu
WIGGINS, Roy 781-891-3166 223 E rwiggins@bentley.edu
WIGGINS, Sarah 954-201-6455 99 G swiggins@broward.edu
WIGGINS, Shelia 252-527-6223 363 G swiggins@lenoircc.edu
WIGGINS, Symphoni 706-396-7594 129 H swiggins@paine.edu
WIGGINS, Timothy 630-515-3136 144 A twiggins@devrygroup.com
WIGGINS, Urban 225-771-4150 207 A urban_wiggins@subr.edu
WIGGINTON, Van 281-542-2082 481 D van.wigginton@sjcd.edu
WIGGINTON, Van 281-542-2050 481 E van.wigginton@sjcd.edu
WIGHT, Charles, A 801-626-6001 500 C president@weber.edu
WIGHT, Laura 406-771-4318 288 B laura.wight@gfcmsu.edu
WIGHT, Randall 870-245-5107 22 C wight@obu.edu
WIGHTKIN, Steven, P 312-942-5947 158 A steven_wightkin@rush.edu
WIGHTMAN, Beth, A 818-677-2969 34 D beth.wightman@csun.edu
WIGHTMAN, Todd 208-535-5440 138 B todd.wightman@my.eitc.edu
WIGINTON, Chad 580-477-7918 404 D chad.wiginton@wosc.edu
WIGINTON, Melissa 512-404-4862 468 J mwiginton@austinseminary.edu
WIGNALL, Eric 574-936-8898 164 A eric.wignall@ancilla.edu
WIGNALL, Scott 309-467-6302 145 A swignall@eureka.edu
WIGNALL, Scott, D 724-946-7135 439 D wignalsd@westminster.edu
WIGNER, Dee 620-276-9577 187 D dee.wigner@gcccks.edu
WIGNES, David, R 608-785-9140 544 E wignesd@westerntc.edu
WIGTIL, Brad 254-710-2222 469 D Brad_Wigtil@baylor.edu
WIHBEY, Jean 561-207-5400 109 H wihbeyj@palmbeachstate.edu
WIILKINSON, Joann, F 314-516-5301 284 B wilkinsonj@umsl.edu
WIKE, Lauren, C 910-630-7167 359 C lwike@methodist.edu
WIKOFF, Elizabeth 636-949-4975 276 L ewikoff@lindenwood.edu
WILBANKS, Cynthia, H 734-763-5554 251 C wilbanks@umich.edu
WILBANKS, Jennifer 660-596-7229 282 H jwilbanks@sfccmo.edu
WILBANKS, Jennifer 803-276-9000 448 D wilbanks.j@ptc.edu
WILBANKS, Laura 734-481-2318 242 J laura.wilbanks@emich.edu
WILBER, Renita 800-567-2344 535 F rwilber@menominee.edu
WILBERG, Ed 763-433-1685 258 A ed.wilberg@anokaramsey.edu
WILBERG, Ed 763-433-1685 257 P ed.wilberg@anokaramsey.edu
WILBORN, Colin 254-295-8642 492 C cwilborn@umhb.edu
WILBUR, Denise 484-365-7436 424 E dwilbur@lincoln.edu
WILBUR, Gregg 518-736-3622 326 D gregg.wilbur@fmcc.suny.edu
WILBUR, Janice 508-849-3406 222 C jwilbur@annamaria.edu
WILBUR, Kathleen, M 989-774-7161 240 O wilbu1km@cmich.edu
WILBUR, Peter, B 401-254-3365 442 C pwilbur@rwu.edu
WILBUR, Roy, A 215-965-8561 426 G rwilbur@moore.edu
WILBUR, Shelley 941-487-4100 115 B mwilbur@ncf.edu
WILBURN, Eric 903-923-2099 473 I ewilburn@etbu.edu
WILBURN, Howard, L 336-725-8344 368 A piedmontu@piedmontu.edu
WILBURN, James, R 310-506-7490 58 H james.wilburn@pepperdine.edu
WILBURN, Jonathan 859-442-1163 196 A jonathan.wilburn@kctcs.edu
WILCH, Peter, J 415-422-6423 74 C pwilch@usfca.edu
WILCOTS, Barbara 303-871-2706 86 H bwilcots@du.edu
WILCOX, Anthony 978-665-3482 229 D awilcox@fitchburgstate.edu
WILCOX, Bonnie 417-873-7811 274 E bwilcox@drury.edu
WILCOX, Cordelia, A 919-658-7494 369 B cwilcox@umo.edu
WILCOX, Dan 910-362-7676 360 G dwilcox@cfcc.edu
WILCOX, Dean 336-770-3243 372 B wilcoxd@uncsa.edu
WILCOX, Denise 909-469-5393 76 I dwilcox@westernu.edu
WILCOX, Dorothy 518-255-5624 346 E wilcoxds@cobleskill.edu
WILCOX, Heather 303-797-5674 79 A heather.wilcox@arapahoe.edu
WILCOX, Jerry 203-837-8242 88 G wilcoxj@wcsu.edu
WILCOX, Kathleen, J 937-328-6060 379 L wilcoxk@clarkstate.edu
WILCOX, Kenneth 718-522-9073 315 E coachwilcox@asa.edu
WILCOX, Kevin 518-956-8120 343 C kwilcox@albany.edu
WILCOX, Kim 970-351-2496 87 A kim.wilcox@unco.edu
WILCOX, Kim, A 951-827-5201 72 A chancellor@ucr.edu
WILCOX, Nancy 228-896-3809 268 G nancy.wilcox@mgccc.edu
WILCOX, Ralph 813-974-8347 116 B rcwilcox@usf.edu
WILCOX, Reed, N 540-261-4100 512 J reed.wilcox@svu.edu
WILCOX, Robbin 419-267-1460 387 G rwilcox@northweststate.edu
WILCOX, Robert, M 803-777-6857 450 B wilcoxrm@law.sc.edu
WILCOX, Sharon 414-382-6127 534 I sharon.wilcox@alverno.edu
WILCOX, Stan 850-644-2525 115 A swilcox2@fsu.edu
WILCOX, Tamera 785-309-3183 190 L tamera.wilcox@salinatech.edu
WILCOXEN, Andrica 913-288-7652 188 G awilcoxen@kckcc.edu
WILCOXEN, Jan 260-459-4501 169 D jwilcoxen@ibcfortwayne.edu
WILCOXSON, Douglas, A 517-750-1200 250 F dwilcoxs@arbor.edu
WILCZEK, Amity 760-572-2000 42 J awilczek@deepsprings.edu
WILD, Bradford 617-989-4361 237 G wildb@wit.edu
WILD, Larry 847-628-2036 149 A lwild@judsonu.edu
WILD, Lorie 206-281-2608 526 D wildl@spu.edu
WILD, Lynn, A 585-475-6543 339 G lynn.wild@rit.edu
WILD, Robert, M 314-935-8081 285 E rob.wild@wustl.edu
WILDA, Christine 774-455-7549 228 E cwilda@umassp.edu
WILDE, Elin 262-646-6507 538 B ewilde@nashotah.edu
WILDE, Jerry 765-973-8554 168 A jwilde@iue.edu
WILDECK, Steve, C 608-265-3040 541 E steve.wildeck@uwex.uwc.edu
WILDENTHAL, B. Hobson 972-883-2271 494 A wildenbh@utdallas.edu
WILDER, Aliza 860-486-4038 92 C aliza.wilder@uconn.edu
WILDER, Carmen, C 704-216-6009 358 I cwilder@livingstone.edu
WILDER, Carrie 229-931-2351 131 E cwilder@southgatech.edu
WILDER, Dana 860-486-6527 92 C dana.wilder@uconn.edu
WILDER, Diane 610-896-1209 420 J dwilder@haverford.edu
WILDER, Jim 419-434-4220 395 H jwilder@winebrenner.edu
WILDER, John 229-931-2068 131 E jwilder@southgatech.edu
WILDER, Keith 719-549-3082 85 A keith.wilder@pueblocc.edu
WILDER, Kristie 423-236-2206 460 K kwilder@southern.edu
WILDER, Linda 860-515-3862 88 B lwilder@charteroak.edu
WILDER, Martin, A 540-654-1301 513 I mwilder@umw.edu
WILDER, Michael 630-752-5818 163 G michael.wilder@wheaton.edu
WILDER, Paul, J 812-888-5131 174 F pwilder@vinu.edu
WILDER, Richard, D 352-294-3220 115 D rwilder@ufl.edu
WILDER, Stanley 225-578-2217 204 M wilder@lsu.edu
WILDER, Sterly 919-684-5114 356 E sterly.wilder@daa.duke.edu
WILDER, W. Mark 662-915-7265 270 G acwilder@olemiss.edu
WILDER-BYRD, Ellen, M 803-323-2236 451 I wilderbyrde@winthrop.edu
WILDERMUTH, Amy 801-581-8763 499 K amy.wildermuth@utah.edu
WILDES, David 850-201-8177 117 B wildesd@tcc.fl.edu
WILDES, SJ, Kevin, W 504-865-3847 206 A wildesk@loyno.edu
WILDEY, Diane 518-743-2337 347 E daltod@sunyacc.edu
WILDING, Michael 661-362-3498 40 H michael.wilding@canyons.edu

WILDING-FARRELL, Jody .... 281-649-3070 475 B jwilding@hbu.edu
WILDMAN, Patricia .... 256-228-6001.... 6 A wildmanp@nacc.edu
WILDNER-BASSETT, Mary, E .... 520-621-9294.. 18 E wildnerb@email.arizona.edu
WILEBSKI, Jason .... 563-355-3500 180 F jwilebski@kaplan.edu
WILENSKY, Heather ...... 410-857-2289 217 A hwilensky@mcdaniel.edu
WILES, Jan .... 618-842-3711 146 G wilesj@iecc.edu
WILES, Mari, E .... 252-398-6268 356 B wilesm@chowan.edu
WILES, Patrick, J .... 716-851-1901 325 A wiles@ecc.edu
WILEY, Byron, A .... 864-656-3553 444 E bwiley@clemson.edu
WILEY, Casey .... 864-455-8204 450 G wileyc@greenvillemed.sc.edu
WILEY, Ellen .... 717-544-5038 429 I ewiley@pacollege.edu
WILEY, Fran, K .... 864-941-8351 448 D wiley.f@ptc.edu
WILEY, Jeanelle .... 314-968-7123 285 G jeanellewiley10@webster.edu
WILEY, Jeffrey .... 315-786-2200 329 G jwiley@sunyjefferson.edu
WILEY, Joe .... 731-989-6001 456 K jwiley@fhu.edu
WILEY, Karen .... 815-455-8547 152 B kwiley@mchenry.edu
WILEY, Karen .... 903-923-2018 473 I kwiley@etbu.edu
WILEY, Kevin .... 312-915-6699 151 E kwiley5@luc.edu
WILEY, Louise .... 903-983-8242 477 A lwiley@kilgore.edu
WILEY, LuSharon .... 850-474-2161 116 E lwiley@uwf.edu
WILEY, Marilyn .... 940-565-3097 492 D marilyn.wiley@unt.edu
WILEY, Nina .... 937-328-7936 379 L wileyn@clarkstate.edu
WILEY, Paul, G .... 931-598-1731 460 I pwiley@sewanee.edu
WILEY, Stacey .... 585-245-5721 345 D wileys@geneseo.edu
WILEY-HARRIS, Courtney .... 212-870-1253 336 B cwiley@nyts.edu
WILF, Carol .... 870-762-3121.. 19 C cwilf@smail.anc.edu
WILFAHRT, Dannette, C .... 651-631-5190 265 D dcwilfahrt@unwsp.edu
WILGENBUSCH, Sandy . 563-876-3353 177 I wilgenbu@dwci.edu
WILHELM, Jane .... 608-663-2203 536 A jwilhelm@edgewood.edu
WILHELM, John, L ...... 402-280-2762 290 B JohnWilhelm@creighton.edu
WILHELM, Laura .... 773-256-0741 151 H lwilhelm@lstc.edu
WILHELM, Robert, W .... 704-687-8428 371 B rgwilhel@uncc.edu
WILHELMI, Lisa .... 254-299-8640 478 C lwilhelmi@mclennan.edu
WILHELMS, Angela ...... 541-346-5561 410 F wilhelms@uoregon.edu
WILHELMSON, Paul ...... 608-796-3040 542 H pjwilhelmson@viterbo.edu
WILHITE, David .... 502-863-8016 195 A david_wilhite@georgetowncollege.edu
WILHITE, Lee .... 562-903-4079.. 29 F lee.wilhite@biola.edu
WILHITE, Saige .... 318-869-5115 202 D awilhite@centenary.edu
WILHITE, Stephen, C .... 610-499-4101 439 G scwilhite@widener.edu
WILHOUR, Reo .... 217-351-2558 155 I rwilhour@parkland.edu
WILJANEN, Mark .... 502-456-6504 200 B mwiljanen@sullivan.edu
WILK, Thomas .... 586-445-7135 246 A wilkt@macomb.edu
WILKE, Dennis, F .... 412-521-6200 434 C dennis.wilke@rosedaletech.org
WILKE, Ekkehard, T ...... 312-939-0111 144 D wil3t@eastwest.edu
WILKE, Janet, S .... 308-865-8595 293 G wilkej@unk.edu
WILKE, Larry .... 325-235-7355 488 C larry.wilke@tstc.edu
WILKE, Stephen, K ...... 620-229-6277 191 B steve.wilke@sckans.edu
WILKEN, Danielle .... 860-727-6714.. 90 F dwilken@goodwin.edu
WILKEN, Danielle, S .... 860-727-6780.. 90 F dwilken@goodwin.edu
WILKENS, Richard, T .... 631-244-3395 324 C provost@dowling.edu
WILKERSON, Aimee, J . 270-824-8696 196 F aimee.wilkerson@kctcs.edu
WILKERSON, Ame .... 912-260-4407 131 D ame.wilkerson@sgsc.edu
WILKERSON, Charles ... 931-372-3634 462 A cwilkerson@tntech.edu
WILKERSON, Jeffrey .... 563-387-1005 180 M wilkerje@luther.edu
WILKERSON, Jon .... 303-937-4273.. 80 A jwilkerson@chu.edu
WILKERSON, Karen, D . 816-235-2757 284 A wilkersonkd@umkc.edu
WILKERSON, Lindsey, S .... 318-342-1530 209 A lwilkerson@ulm.edu
WILKERSON, Lois .... 714-241-6160.. 40 B lwilkerson@coastline.edu
WILKERSON, Mathew, C .... 540-654-1048 513 I mwilkers@umw.edu
WILKERSON, Sharon, A .... 979-436-0111 485 C swilkerson44@tamu.edu
WILKERSON, Tanya ...... 443-885-3170 217 C tanya.wilkerson@morgan.edu
WILKERSON, Terry ...... 618-437-5321 156 I wilkersont@rlc.edu
WILKERSON, William ... 256-824-2339.... 9 A william.wilkerson@uah.edu
WILKERSON, Zeda .... 870-368-2028.. 22 D zwilkerson@ozarka.edu
WILKES, Barrie, J .... 989-774-3334 240 O wilke1bj@cmich.edu
WILKES, C. Gene .... 817-274-4284 469 E gwilkes@bhcarroll.edu
WILKES, Deborah .... 706-886-6831 132 F dwilkes@tfc.edu
WILKES, Eileen .... 850-872-3801 105 Q ewilkes@gulfcoast.edu
WILKES, Jeremy .... 901-572-2670 455 C jeremy.wilkes@bchs.edu
WILKES, Yvette .... 505-454-3197 311 H ydwilkes@nmhu.edu
WILKEY, Jill, J .... 701-231-8466 374 C jill.wilkey@ndsu.edu
WILKIE, Marilyn, L ...... 212-517-0453 332 A mwilkie@mmm.edu
WILKIN, John .... 419-448-2227 383 C jwilkin@heidelberg.edu
WILKIN, John, P .... 217-333-0790 162 A jpwilkin@illinois.edu
WILKIN, Noel, E .... 662-915-1198 270 G
WILKIN, Noel, E .... 662-915-1071 270 G nwilkin@olemiss.edu
WILKINS, Ashli .... 334-556-2226.... 4 A awilkins@wallace.edu
WILKINS, Brian, J .... 716-839-8395 323 F bwilkins@daemen.edu
WILKINS, Courtney ...... 970-521-6655.. 84 H courtney.wilkins@njc.edu
WILKINS, Deborah, T ... 270-745-5398 201 D deborah.wilkins@wku.edu
WILKINS, Derrick .... 252-335-3324 369 F dlwilkins@ecsu.edu
WILKINS, Harry .... 304-724-3700 529 F hwilkins@apus.edu
WILKINS, Harry, T .... 614-508-7277 383 L hwilkins@hondros.edu
WILKINS, Ken .... 702-968-5568 296 D kwilkins@roseman.edu
WILKINS, Linda .... 317-632-5553 170 Z lwilkins@lincolntech.com
WILKINS, Lorinda .... 575-624-7345 310 J lorinda.wilkins@roswell.enmu.edu
WILKINS, Mardell .... 775-753-2265 295 D mardell.wilkins@gbcnv.edu
WILKINS, Patricia, A .... 512-505-3081 475 G pawilkins@htu.edu
WILKINS, Pyeper .... 214-378-1538 472 B PWilkins@dcccd.edu
WILKINSON, Christine, K .... 480-965-7782.. 11 J c.wilkinson@asu.edu
WILKINSON, Elizabeth .. 602-827-2556.. 16 C Elizabeth.Wilkinson@nau.edu
WILKINSON, Jay .... 515-961-1288 182 I jay.wilkinson@simpson.edu
WILKINSON, John .... 704-878-3202 364 C jwilkinson@mitchellcc.edu
WILKINSON, Joni .... 601-276-3708 270 E jwilkinson@smcc.edu
WILKINSON, Julie .... 941-782-5678 423 B jwilkinson@lecom.edu
WILKINSON, Linda .... 312-341-3659 157 E lpwilkinson@roosevelt.edu
WILKINSON, Lonnie ...... 225-771-3015 207 A lonnie_wilkinson@subr.edu
WILKINSON, Melissa .... 309-647-4645 160 F
WILKINSON, Michael ... 361-485-4409 492 A wilkinsonmr@uhv.edu
WILKINSON, Mike .... 817-923-1921 483 E mwilkinson@swbts.edu
WILKINSON, Mike .... 405-692-3132 398 I mwilkinson@macu.edu
WILKINSON, Missy .... 309-649-6305 160 F missy.wilkinson@src.edu
WILKINSON, Patrick, J . 920-424-2147 540 B wilkinso@uwosh.edu
WILKINSON, Robert ...... 260-481-6375 168 D wilkinrb@ipfw.edu
WILKINSON, Timothy, J .... 509-777-4585 529 A twilkinson@whitworth.edu
WILKINSON, Todd .... 252-399-6552 354 I twilkinson@barton.edu
WILKINSON, W. David . 601-974-1172 268 D wilkiwd@millsaps.edu
WILKINSON, William, J 215-204-4775 436 C william.wilkinson@temple.edu
WILKOSKI, Donna, M ... 215-698-8203 413 F wilkoski@bucks.edu
WILKOW, Beth .... 516-299-2589 330 F beth.wilkow@liu.edu
WILKS, Barbara .... 704-378-1042 358 B bwilks@jcsu.edu
WILKS, David .... 302-736-2508.. 94 E
WILKS, Karrin .... 212-220-8321 318 D kwilks@bmcc.cuny.edu
WILKS, Kerry .... 316-978-3095 192 D kerry.wilks@wichita.edu
WILKS, Preston .... 509-793-2194 520 B prestonw@bigbend.edu
WILKS, Ronald, W .... 317-788-3517 173 I wilks@uindy.edu
WILL, Eleanor .... 828-771-2082 373 A ewill@warren-wilson.edu
WILL, John .... 715-468-2815 544 F john.will@witc.edu
WILL, Kris .... 303-986-2320.. 80 N kris@csha.net
WILL, Lee .... 480-245-7937.. 14 D lee.will@ibcs.edu
WILLAMON, Nancy, R .. 217-351-2533 155 I nwillamon@parkland.edu
WILLAN, Dawn, E .... 843-953-5997 445 B willande@cofc.edu
WILLAN, Emily .... 303-556-2413.. 81 J emily.willan@ccd.edu
WILLAN, William .... 740-593-2551 389 H willanw@ohio.edu
WILLARD, Joseph .... 215-991-3586 422 F willard@lasalle.edu
WILLARD, Paul, S .... 727-376-6911 117 H paul.willard@trintycollege.edu
WILLBANKS, Stephanie 802-831-1277 503 E swillbanks@vermontlaw.edu
WILLBORG, Erik .... 406-657-1032 288 G erik.willborg@rocky.edu
WILLCOX, Abby .... 239-489-9059 104 G awillcox@fsw.edu
WILLCOX, Jan, M .... 540-231-0920 507 D
WILLCOX, Wayne .... 912-344-2689 120 D wayne.willcox@armstrong.edu
WILLE, Diane, E .... 812-941-2300 169 A dwille@ius.edu
WILLEKENS, Rene, G .... 623-935-8069.. 14 L rene.willekens@estrellamountain.edu
WILLEMAN-BUCKELEW, Diana, L .... 540-224-4491 509 D dlwilleman@jchs.edu
WILLEMS, Greg .... 785-532-6266 188 H gregw@found.ksu.edu
WILLEMSEN, David, W . 972-825-4630 483 D dwillemsen@sagu.edu
WILLENBERG, Lisa ...... 501-977-2025.. 25 A willenberg@uaccm.edu
WILLENBORG, Andy, B 563-589-0217 183 K awillenborg@wartburgseminary.edu
WILLENBRINK, Bob ...... 816-271-4575 279 E rwillenbrink@missouriwestern.edu
WILLENSKY, Violet, J ... 908-526-1200 305 G Violet.Willensky@raritanval.edu
WILLER, Anthony .... 701-483-2215 373 H Anthony.Willer@dickinsonstate.edu
WILLETT, Dana .... 931-221-7779 461 C willettd@apsu.edu
WILLETT, Terrence ...... 831-477-5656.. 30 C terrence@cabrillo.edu
WILLEY, Sharon .... 408-924-7096.. 36 B sharon.willey@sjsu.edu
WILLEY, Sue, C .... 317-788-3412 173 I swilley@uindy.edu
WILLGING, Gregory, A . 563-556-5110 181 F willging@nicc.edu
WILLGING, Pete .... 815-599-3421 146 B pete.willging@highland.edu
WILLHITE, Rosanna ...... 859-858-3511 193 A rosanna.willhite@asbury.edu
WILLIAMS, Adam .... 757-352-4894 511 G awilliams@regent.edu
WILLIAMS, Adelia .... 212-346-1555 337 I awilliams@pace.edu
WILLIAMS, Alex .... 402-363-5689 294 G aawilliams@york.edu
WILLIAMS, Alfred .... 860-932-4172.. 90 A awilliams@qvcc.commnet.edu
WILLIAMS, Alfred .... 508-588-9100 232 A
WILLIAMS, Alison .... 603-623-0313 298 C alisonwilliams@nhia.edu
WILLIAMS, Alison, P .... 740-587-6469 381 H williamsa@denison.edu
WILLIAMS, Allison .... 617-277-3915 224 D williamsa@bgsp.edu
WILLIAMS, Alvin .... 208-769-3348 138 G al_williams@nic.edu
WILLIAMS, Amanda ...... 913-288-7218 188 G awilliams@kckcc.edu
WILLIAMS, Amber, S .... 402-472-0671 293 H amber.williams@unl.edu
WILLIAMS, Amy, H ...... 704-637-4414 355 H ahwillia@catawba.edu
WILLIAMS, Andre .... 252-331-4881 361 G andre_williams@albemarle.edu
WILLIAMS, Andy .... 847-543-2210 142 G wwilliams@clcillinois.edu
WILLIAMS, Angela .... 303-797-5715.. 79 A angela.williams@arapahoe.edu
WILLIAMS, Angela .... 803-738-7691 447 H williamsa@midlandstech.edu
WILLIAMS, Angela, L ... 410-651-8420 219 H alwilliams@umes.edu
WILLIAMS, Angela, S ... 479-575-2806.. 23 G angelaw@uark.edu
WILLIAMS, Ann, L .... 570-961-4725 425 D awilliams@marywood.edu
WILLIAMS, Annette ...... 540-453-2332 514 H williamsa@brcc.edu
WILLIAMS, Annie .... 501-370-8506.. 22 E amwilliams@philander.edu
WILLIAMS, Annie .... 719-549-2116.. 81 F annie.williams@csupueblo.edu
WILLIAMS, Anthony ...... 323-357-4994.. 38 C Anthonywilliams@cdrewu.edu
WILLIAMS, Anthony ...... 312-980-9255 158 H awilliams@iadtchicago.edu
WILLIAMS, Anthony ...... 425-388-9282 522 I anwilliams@everettcc.edu
WILLIAMS, Anthony ...... 212-343-1234 332 I awilliams@mcny.edu
WILLIAMS, Anthony, T . 325-674-5288 466 I williamsa@acu.edu
WILLIAMS, Antonio ...... 410-706-7032 219 E awilliams@police.umaryland.edu
WILLIAMS, Archie .... 478-825-6832 124 E williamsa01@fvsu.edu
WILLIAMS, Arley .... 307-766-4839 546 K arley.williams@uwyo.edu
WILLIAMS, Audrey .... 352-365-3510 107 X williama@lssc.edu
WILLIAMS, Audrey .... 903-875-7414 479 I audrey.williams@navarrocollege.edu
WILLIAMS, Audrey, J ... 865-539-7198 463 E ajwilliams@pstcc.edu
WILLIAMS, Barry .... 570-208-5932 422 D barrywilliams@kings.edu
WILLIAMS, Bert .... 478-387-4782 125 E bwilliams@gmc.edu
WILLIAMS, Betty, B ...... 843-383-8055 445 A bwilliams@coker.edu
WILLIAMS, BJ .... 907-834-1649.. 11 B bjwilliams@pwscc.edu
WILLIAMS, Bobby .... 936-294-4205 489 A ath_brw@shsu.edu
WILLIAMS, Brad .... 954-262-7282 109 E bradwill@nsu.nova.edu
WILLIAMS, Brad .... 405-945-3204 400 F bradford.williams@osuokc.edu
WILLIAMS, Bradley, E .. 530-226-4172.. 66 G bwilliams@simpsonu.edu
WILLIAMS, Brandon ...... 859-622-5094 194 L brandon.williams@eku.edu
WILLIAMS, Brandy .... 662-329-7293 269 B bmwilliams@muw.edu
WILLIAMS, Brenda, K ... 256-372-5254.... 1 A brenda.williams@aamu.edu
WILLIAMS, Brian .... 503-223-2245 406 G bwilliams@portland.chefs.edu
WILLIAMS, Brian, G ...... 216-397-4252 384 F bwilliams@jcu.edu
WILLIAMS, Brockton ..... 615-343-4411 465 H brock.williams@vanderbilt.edu
WILLIAMS, Byron .... 513-244-8462 379 I byron.williams@ccuniversity.edu
WILLIAMS, Calvin .... 607-962-9233 323 D williams@corning-cc.edu
WILLIAMS, Calvin, H .... 717-815-1226 440 H cwilliam@ycp.edu

WILLIAMS, Lucille, W .. 803-934-3258 447 K
lwilliams@morris.edu
WILLIAMS, Lyn .... 610-606-4666 415 A
lcwillia@cedarcrest.edu
WILLIAMS, Lynn .... 803-641-3352 450 C
lynnw@usca.edu
WILLIAMS, Lynne .... 218-726-6141 264 G
lwilliam@d.umn.edu
WILLIAMS, Lyrae .... 719-389-6699.. 79 M
lyrae.williams@coloradocollege.edu
WILLIAMS, Mandy .... 303-963-3365.. 79 L
aewilliams@ccu.edu
WILLIAMS, Marcellette . 617-287-7050 228 E
mwilliams@umassp.edu
WILLIAMS,
Marchetta, L .... 803-938-3721 450 H
mlwillia@uscsumter.edu
WILLIAMS, Margaret ..... 701-777-5963 373 G
margaret.williams@und.edu
WILLIAMS, Mark .... 661-763-7871.. 69 E
mwilliams@taftcollege.edu
WILLIAMS, Martha .... 601-484-8614 268 B
mwilliam@meridiancc.edu
WILLIAMS, Martinique .. 336-334-7555 370 B
mcwilli2@ncat.edu
WILLIAMS, Mary Beth .. 717-262-2006 440 D
marybeth.williams@wilson.edu
WILLIAMS, Matt .... 919-536-7201 362 C
williamsm@durhamtech.edu
WILLIAMS, Max, E .... 423-585-6861 464 C
max.williams@ws.edu
WILLIAMS, Melanie, K . 269-337-7220 244 I
williams@kzoo.edu
WILLIAMS, Melissa ...... 254-295-4020 492 C
mford@umhb.edu
WILLIAMS, Melvenia .... 803-535-5412 444 D
mwilliams@claflin.edu
WILLIAMS, Melvin .... 386-481-2900.. 99 F
wiliamsm@cookman.edu
WILLIAMS, Melvin, G ... 202-994-7818.. 95 D
vadm1@gwu.edu
WILLIAMS, Michael ...... 510-642-5316.. 70 K
athletic.director@berkeley.edu
WILLIAMS, Michael ...... 207-768-2707 211 C
mwilliams@nmcc.edu
WILLIAMS, Michael ...... 817-735-2509 493 B
WILLIAMS, Michael ...... 609-984-1130 308 H
mwilliams@tesc.edu
WILLIAMS, Michael, D . 334-386-7103.... 3 I
mwilliams@faulkner.edu
WILLIAMS, Michelle ..... 570-961-7833 422 G
williamsm@lackawanna.edu
WILLIAMS, Michelle, D 978-468-7111 227 B
mwilliams@gcts.edu
WILLIAMS, Michelle, L . 314-286-4863 280 I
mlwilliams@ranken.edu
WILLIAMS, Mike .... 704-461-6200 354 J
MikeWIlliams@bac.edu
WILLIAMS, Miraim .... 612-436-7541 257 K
mwilliams@msbcollege.edu
WILLIAMS, Molly .... 802-258-9259 502 B
mollyw@marlboro.edu
WILLIAMS, Monica .... 313-993-1028 250 H
leonarmj@udmercy.edu
WILLIAMS, Murray .... 404-225-4545 120 I
mwilliams@atlantatech.edu
WILLIAMS, Myles .... 803-778-6643 443 I
williamsmh@cctech.edu
WILLIAMS, Nancy .... 515-244-4221 175 C
nancyw@aib.edu
WILLIAMS, Nate .... 254-295-4696 492 C
nwilliams@umhb.edu
WILLIAMS, Nichelle ...... 661-722-6300.. 27 P
nwilliams@avc.edu
WILLIAMS, Nicole .... 508-999-9208 228 H
nwilliams2@umassd.edu
WILLIAMS, Nicole .... 910-755-7391 360 E
williamsn@brunswickcc.edu
WILLIAMS, Nikisha .... 212-752-1530 330 C
nikisha.williams@limcollege.edu
WILLIAMS, Oleida .... 443-394-3339.. 96 H
WILLIAMS, Owen .... 218-281-8395 264 H
owilliam@umn.edu
WILLIAMS, Patricia, A .. 515-263-2912 178 H
pwilliams@grandview.edu
WILLIAMS, Patricia, R .. 585-292-3026 333 G
pwilliams@monroecc.edu
WILLIAMS, Patti .... 912-583-3156 121 H
pwilliams@bpc.edu
WILLIAMS, Paul .... 229-391-4900 119 F
pwwilliams@abac.edu
WILLIAMS, Paul .... 678-839-6380 133 F
paulw@westga.edu
WILLIAMS, Paul .... 804-330-0111 506 D
p.williams@centura.edu
WILLIAMS, Paulita, N ... 336-322-2170 364 G
Tasha.Williams@piedmontcc.edu
WILLIAMS, Peter .... 317-940-9700 164 L
williams@butler.edu
WILLIAMS, Philip, C .... 337-475-5556 208 B
pwilliams@mcneese.edu
WILLIAMS, Philip, M ..... 315-733-2300 351 E
pwilliams@uscny.edu
WILLIAMS, Phillip, L .... 706-542-0939 132 H
pwilliam@uga.edu
WILLIAMS, Ramona, A . 423-439-4219 461 D
ramona@etsu.edu
WILLIAMS, Randy .... 336-278-7243 356 F
rwilliams32@elon.edu
WILLIAMS, Rayanne ..... 619-594-1686.. 35 E
william7@mail.sdsu.edu
WILLIAMS, Rayshaun ... 920-686-6237 539 A
Rayshaun.Williams@sl.edu
WILLIAMS, Reina .... 773-481-8400 142 D
williams341@ccc.edu
WILLIAMS, Rich .... 775-674-7979 295 F
rwilliams@tmcc.edu
WILLIAMS, Richard .... 229-430-4754 119 H
richard.williams@asurams.edu
WILLIAMS, Richard .... 724-805-2084 435 B
richard.williams@stvincent.edu
WILLIAMS, Richard, B .. 435-652-7502 499 M
president@dixie.edu
WILLIAMS, Rick .... 870-743-3000.. 22 A
rickw@northark.edu
WILLIAMS, Rick .... 336-316-2134 357 C
williamsrl@guilford.edu
WILLIAMS, Rick, E .... 909-558-4510.. 50 K
rwilliams@llu.edu
WILLIAMS, Rob .... 870-236-6901.. 20 I
rwilliams@crc.edu
WILLIAMS, Robert .... 310-825-8011.. 71 D
bwilliams@asucla.ucla.edu
WILLIAMS, Robert .... 662-252-8000 270 C
rwilliams5@rustcollege.edu
WILLIAMS, Robin .... 661-362-3240.. 40 H
robin.williams@canyons.edu
WILLIAMS, Ron .... 478-471-2490 128 H
ron.williams@mga.edu
WILLIAMS, Ron .... 915-747-7390 494 B
rwilliams@utep.edu
WILLIAMS, Ronald .... 309-298-1066 163 A
rc-williams@wiu.edu
WILLIAMS, Ronda, L .... 304-462-6430 532 G
ronda.williams@glenville.edu
WILLIAMS, Ronnie, D ... 501-450-3416.. 25 F
ronniew@uca.edu
WILLIAMS, Rosemary ... 718-270-5104 320 C
rosemary@mec.cuny.edu
WILLIAMS, Ryan .... 845-569-3105 333 I
ryan.williams@msmc.edu
WILLIAMS, Ryan, A ...... 309-624-9268 158 D
ryan.a.williams@osfhealthcare.org
WILLIAMS, Sabrina .... 252-335-3969 369 F
srwilliams@ecsu.edu
WILLIAMS, Sanchia ...... 954-492-5353 100 G
sawilliams@citycollege.edu
WILLIAMS, Sara .... 402-399-2467 289 I
swilliams@csm.edu
WILLIAMS, Saundra ...... 919-807-6976 359 M
swilliams@nccommunitycolleges.edu
WILLIAMS, Scott .... 270-686-4508 197 A
scott.willliams@kctcs.edu
WILLIAMS, Scott, E ...... 276-944-6242 507 E
swilliams@ehc.edu
WILLIAMS, Scott, K ...... 315-733-2300 351 E
swilliams@uscny.edu
WILLIAMS, Scott, T ...... 706-542-3375 132 H
scottw@uga.edu
WILLIAMS, Selase, W ... 617-349-8518 228 B
williams@lesley.edu
WILLIAMS, Shane .... 601-484-8620 268 B
swilliam@meridiancc.edu
WILLIAMS, Shannon ..... 803-793-5109 445 F
williamss@denmarktech.edu
WILLIAMS, Shaun .... 817-515-5154 484 B
shaun.williams@tccd.edu
WILLIAMS, Shelitha ...... 585-262-1665 333 G
swilliams@monroecc.edu
WILLIAMS, Sheree .... 502-213-2156 196 E
sheree.williams@kctcs.edu
WILLIAMS, Sherry .... 828-327-7000 361 B
swilliams@cvcc.edu
WILLIAMS, Shirley, J ... 610-796-8340 412 C
shirley.williams@alvernia.edu
WILLIAMS, Sonya .... 405-682-1611 399 K
swilliams@occc.edu
WILLIAMS, Sophia .... 414-297-6288 543 E
wills12@matc.edu
WILLIAMS, Stacie .... 803-641-3321 450 C
staciew@usca.edu
WILLIAMS, Stelfanie ..... 252-492-2061 366 G
swilliams@vgcc.edu
WILLIAMS, Stephanie ... 270-852-3107 198 A
clemasters@kwc.edu
WILLIAMS, Stephen ...... 414-277-7114 537 G
williams@msoe.edu
WILLIAMS, Stephen, R . 419-755-4811 387 E
swilliam@ncstatecollege.edu
WILLIAMS, Steve .... 256-840-4174.... 7 B
swilliams@snead.edu
WILLIAMS, Steve .... 903-886-5189 485 E
steve.williams@tamuc.edu
WILLIAMS, Steve .... 903-693-2023 480 A
swilliams@panola.edu
WILLIAMS, Sue .... 360-992-2619 521 A
swilliams@clark.edu
WILLIAMS, Susan .... 304-255-0793 532 E
swilliams@concord.edu
WILLIAMS, Susan .... 626-650-2306.. 46 C
WILLIAMS, Susan .... 828-448-3178 367 B
swilliams@wpcc.edu
WILLIAMS, Susan, D .... 828-694-1824 360 D
susanw@blueridge.edu
WILLIAMS, Susan, D .... 203-576-4651.. 92 B
swilliams@bridgeport.edu
WILLIAMS, Susan, L .... 302-831-8436.. 94 D
susanlyn@udel.edu
WILLIAMS, Suzanne ..... 213-477-2861.. 54 I
swilliams@msmu.edu
WILLIAMS, Sylvia, R .... 843-953-5333 444 C
swilli22@citadel.edu
WILLIAMS, T. H. Lee .... 405-325-6670 403 I
lwilliams@ou.edu
WILLIAMS, Tamara .... 704-330-4119 361 D
tamara.williams@cpcc.edu
WILLIAMS, Tamara, R .. 253-531-7203 524 I
williatr@plu.edu
WILLIAMS, Tara, A .... 336-633-0279 365 A
tawil@randolph.edu
WILLIAMS, Tasha .... 312-850-7120 142 E
tholmes@ccc.edu
WILLIAMS, Teresa .... 815-599-3445 146 B
teresa.williams@highland.edu
WILLIAMS, Teresa .... 615-966-1788 458 C
teresa.williams@lipscomb.edu
WILLIAMS, Teresa, G ... 704-233-8210 373 C
tgwilliams@wingate.edu
WILLIAMS, Terrence ..... 610-409-3719 438 H
twilliams@ursinus.edu
WILLIAMS, Terria, C ..... 803-535-5720 444 D
twilliams@claflin.edu
WILLIAMS, Terry .... 601-484-8615 268 B
twilliam@meridiancc.edu
WILLIAMS, Teyanna ...... 818-240-1000.. 45 I
twilliams@glendale.edu
WILLIAMS,
Theodore, D .... 304-829-7465 529 H
twilliams@bethanywv.edu
WILLIAMS, Thomas .... 630-512-8867 141 D
twilliams@devrygroup.com
WILLIAMS, Tiffany, S ... 816-235-5599 284 A
williamsti@umkc.edu
WILLIAMS, Tim .... 502-895-3411 198 E
twilliams@lpts.edu
WILLIAMS, Tim .... 765-973-8320 168 A
timwill@iue.edu
WILLIAMS, Todd, J .... 215-702-4861 414 C
president@cairn.edu
WILLIAMS, Tom .... 318-678-6000 203 A
twilliams@bpcc.edu
WILLIAMS, Tommy .... 979-458-6040 484 E
twilliams@tamus.edu
WILLIAMS, Tonjua, L .... 727-341-3344 112 A
williams.tonjua@spcollege.edu
WILLIAMS, Tonya .... 706-396-7591 129 H
tjwilliams@paine.edu
WILLIAMS, Traci, N ...... 423-746-5213 464 D
twilliams@twcnet.edu
WILLIAMS, Tracy .... 651-523-2651 256 B
twilliams05@hamline.edu
WILLIAMS, Tracy, S ..... 229-430-4654 119 H
tracy.williams@asurams.edu
WILLIAMS, Travis .... 707-826-5038.. 35 D
tjw17@humboldt.edu
WILLIAMS, Treby .... 609-258-7097 305 C
trebyw@princeton.edu
WILLIAMS, Trudy .... 412-392-8085 433 F
twilliams@pointpark.edu
WILLIAMS, Trysta .... 785-320-4565 189 C
trystawilliams@matc.net
WILLIAMS, Tyler, R ...... 208-496-1301 137 F
williamst@byui.edu
WILLIAMS, Valerie .... 229-430-3867 119 I
vwilliams@albanytech.edu
WILLIAMS, Vaughn, A .. 470-578-6284 127 M
vwilliam@kennesaw.edu
WILLIAMS, Vernon, A ... 317-274-4417 168 E
veawill@iupui.edu
WILLIAMS, Vicki .... 501-492-0570.. 19 B
vicki.williams@arkansasbaptist.edu
WILLIAMS, Vicki .... 662-846-4011 267 A
vwilliams@deltastate.edu
WILLIAMS, Vickie .... 907-796-6363.. 11 A
vickie.williams@uas.alaska.edu
WILLIAMS, Vickie .... 334-214-4803.... 2 H
vickie.williams@cv.edu
WILLIAMS, Victoria .... 870-972-2054.. 19 F
vrwilliams@astate.edu
WILLIAMS, Victoria .... 610-796-5511 412 C
victoria.williams@alvernia.edu
WILLIAMS, Virginia, M . 530-221-4275.. 66 B
vwilliams@shasta.edu
WILLIAMS, Walter .... 518-587-2100 348 A
walter.williams@esc.edu
WILLIAMS, Wendell ...... 832-813-6841 477 I
wendell.williams@lonestar.edu
WILLIAMS, Wendy, E ... 843-953-5506 445 B
williamsw@cofc.edu
WILLIAMS, Willie .... 402-449-2924 290 F
wwilliams4931@graceu.edu
WILLIAMS, Winifred ..... 312-915-6175 151 E
wwilliams5@luc.edu
WILLIAMS-BETHEA,
Melanie .... 212-678-3702 349 I
mwilliams@tc.edu
WILLIAMS-GAUDIOSO,
Amy .... 610-359-5341 416 G
awilliam@dccc.edu
WILLIAMS-GOLDSTEIN,
Brittany, A .... 201-684-7609 305 F
bwilla1@ramapo.edu
WILLIAMS-HARMON,
Arlitha .... 559-791-2374.. 49 G
arlitha.williams@portervillecollege.edu
WILLIAMS-KIRKSEY,
Shirley .... 404-880-8667 122 I
skirksey@cau.edu
WILLIAMS KNIGHT,
Emily .... 312-752-2104 149 D
emily.knight@kendall.edu
WILLIAMS LESSANE,
Patricia .... 843-953-7234 445 B
lessanepw@cofc.edu
WILLIAMS LOSTON,
Adena .... 210-486-2900 466 J
aloston@alamo.edu
WILLIAMS LOSTON,
Adena .... 210-486-2900 467 B
aloston@alamo.edu
WILLIAMS-PEREZ,
Kendra .... 319-226-2040 175 D
Kendra.Williams-Perez@AllenCollege.edu
WILLIAMS RUSHIN,
Palisa .... 859-246-6522 195 J
palisa.rushin@kctcs.edu
WILLIAMS-SOWERS,
Kelly .... 334-291-4921.... 2 H
kelly.williams@cv.edu
WILLIAMS-THOMAS,
Tafflyn .... 503-552-1625 407 F
twiliams-thomas@ncnm.edu
WILLIAMSON, Angela ... 417-690-2208 273 C
awilliamson@cofo.edu
WILLIAMSON, Betty ...... 860-215-9260.. 90 B
bwilliamson@trcc.commnet.edu
WILLIAMSON, Bob .... 360-992-2123 521 A
bwilliamson@clark.edu
WILLIAMSON, Carla ..... 919-658-7749 369 B
cwilliamson@umo.edu
WILLIAMSON, Carol ..... 641-628-7667 176 E
williamsonc@central.edu
WILLIAMSON, Cathy .... 641-673-1700 184 B
williamsonc@wmpenn.edu
WILLIAMSON, Celia ...... 940-565-4961 492 D
celia@unt.edu
WILLIAMSON, David ..... 601-266-1000 271 B
david.williamson@usm.edu
WILLIAMSON, Dean ..... 936-261-2188 484 F
cdwilliamson@pvamu.edu
WILLIAMSON, Debbie ... 843-863-7050 444 B
dwilliam@csuniv.edu
WILLIAMSON, Emily ..... 406-657-2188 287 H
emily.williamson@msubillings.edu
WILLIAMSON, George .. 619-849-2610.. 59 K
georgewilliamson@pointloma.edu
WILLIAMSON, Handy .... 573-882-9061 283 H
williamsonha@missouri.edu
WILLIAMSON,
Harold, A .... 573-882-5606 283 G
williamsonh@health.missouri.edu
WILLIAMSON, JR.,
Harold, A .... 573-882-5606 283 H
williamsonh@health.missouri.edu
WILLIAMSON, Heather .. 866-931-4300 281 A
heather.williamson@rockbridge.edu
WILLIAMSON, Hilda ..... 757-727-5251 508 C
hilda.williamson@hamptonu.edu
WILLIAMSON,
James, E .... 706-542-5813 132 H
jwilliamson@police.uga.edu
WILLIAMSON,
James, R .... 858-784-8469.. 66 A
gradprgm@scripps.edu
WILLIAMSON, Jane, K .. 901-334-5812 459 B
jwilliamson@memphisseminary.edu
WILLIAMSON, Jeff .... 507-372-3408 260 C
jeff.williamson@mnwest.edu
WILLIAMSON, Jenna ..... 701-483-2091 373 H
Jenna.Williamson@dickinsonstate.edu

WILLIAMSON, Jennifer . 610-921-7700 411 E jwilliamson@albright.edu
WILLIAMSON, Joann .... 803-641-3473 450 C joannw@usca.edu
WILLIAMSON, Jon .... 214-648-1500 496 A jon.williamson@utsouthwestern.edu
WILLIAMSON, Kathleen 757-683-3047 510 I kcwillia@odu.edu
WILLIAMSON, Kathy ..... 252-246-1263 367 D kwilliamson@wilsoncc.edu
WILLIAMSON, Keith ...... 940-397-4231 478 G keith.williamson@mwsu.edu
WILLIAMSON, Keith, M 804-524-5285 518 C kwilliamson@vsu.edu
WILLIAMSON, Kimberly 252-493-7217 364 H kwilliamson@email.pittcc.edu
WILLIAMSON, Laurel .... 281-998-6182 481 E laurel.williamson@sjcd.edu
WILLIAMSON, Laurel .... 281-998-6182 481 F laurel.williamson@sjcd.edu
WILLIAMSON, Laurel .... 281-998-6182 481 D laurel.williamson@sjcd.edu
WILLIAMSON, Laurel .... 281-484-1900 481 G laurel.williamson@sjcd.edu
WILLIAMSON, Lisa .... 715-682-1678 538 D lwilliamson@northland.edu
WILLIAMSON, Marty ..... 661-654-2111.. 32 G mwilliamson@csub.edu
WILLIAMSON, Michael . 843-383-8300 445 A mwilliamson@coker.edu
WILLIAMSON, Nancy .... 516-572-7406 334 A nancy.williamson@ncc.edu
WILLIAMSON, Patricia, A .... 815-224-0440 147 J patty_williamson@ivcc.edu
WILLIAMSON, Randall, H .... 202-231-3351 547 N randall.williamson@dodiis.mil
WILLIAMSON, Rhea ...... 707-826-4189.. 35 D Rhea.Williamson@humboldt.edu
WILLIAMSON, Sean ...... 706-245-7226 124 C swilliamson@ec.edu
WILLIAMSON, Shane .... 636-949-4728 276 L swilliamson@lindenwood.edu
WILLIAMSON, Sharon .. 806-742-4250 489 F sharon.williamson@ttu.edu
WILLIAMSON, Stan .... 205-652-3652.... 9 G swilliamson@uwa.edu
WILLIAMSON, Steve ..... 319-385-6332 180 A swilliams@iw.edu
WILLIAMSON, Sue .... 206-878-3710 523 D swilliamson@highline.edu
WILLIAMSON, Suzanne 717-720-4070 431 A swilliamson@passhe.edu
WILLIAMSON, Tommy .. 336-721-2824 368 F tommy.williamson@salem.edu
WILLIARD, Stacey .... 724-266-3838 437 G swilliard@tsm.edu
WILLIE, John .... 215-335-0800 424 D jwillie@lincolntech.edu
WILLIE, Vernon .... 505-566-3306 312 K williev@sanjuancollege.edu
WILLIFORD, Andrea, G . 478-757-5131 134 E awilliford@wesleyancollege.edu
WILLIFORD, Brent .... 979-830-4146 469 F brent.williford@blinn.edu
WILLIFORD, Darryl .... 301-860-4186 220 B dwilliford@bowiestate.edu
WILLIFORD, David .... 615-844-5205 466 G dwilliford@welch.edu
WILLIFORD, Don .... 325-670-1491 474M willifrd@hsutx.edu
WILLIFORD, G. Craig ... 503-255-0332 407 D cwilliford@multnomah.edu
WILLIFORD, Joey .... 662-720-7564 269 D jewilliford@nemcc.edu
WILLIFORD, Lynn, E .... 919-962-1339 371 A lynn_williford@unc.edu
WILLIFORD, Pamela, K 325-670-1347 474M pwillifo@hsutx.edu
WILLIHNGANZ, Shirley, C .... 502-852-6153 201 A scwill01@louisville.edu
WILLING, Cindy .... 517-607-4315 243 J cwilling@hillsdale.edu
WILLINGER, Katie .... 920-693-1247 543 B katie.willinger@gotoltc.edu
WILLINGHAM, Paul ...... 281-283-2222 491 E willingham@uhcl.edu
WILLINGHAM, Ralph .... 817-598-6248 497 A rwillingham@wc.edu
WILLINGHAM-HINTON, Shelley, M .... 919-516-4190 368 E swhinton@st-aug.edu
WILLIS, Amy .... 229-391-5007 119 F apwillis@abac.edu
WILLIS, Brian .... 828-398-7929 360 A bwillis@abtech.edu
WILLIS, Carla .... 908-737-3340 303 C cawillis@kean.edu
WILLIS, Christine .... 617-369-3581 236 E cwillis@smfa.edu
WILLIS, Christopher ..... 412-536-1194 422 E christopher.willis@laroche.edu
WILLIS, Cliff, K .... 814-332-2860 411 F cwillis@allegheny.edu
WILLIS, Connie .... 510-723-6618.. 37 N cwillis@chabotcollege.edu
WILLIS, Darley .... 716-851-1118 325 A willis@ecc.edu
WILLIS, David .... 931-372-3214 462 A dwillis@tntech.edu
WILLIS, Dennis .... 602-492-9223.. 12 E dwillis@collin.edu
WILLIS, Douglas, G ...... 972-377-1793 471 C dwillis@collin.edu
WILLIS, Edward, M ...... 757-823-8141 510 H emwillis@nsu.edu
WILLIS, Eric, R .... 319-352-8470 183 J rick.willis@wartburg.edu
WILLIS, Franklin, K ...... 918-781-6284 396 F willisf@bacone.edu
WILLIS, Gerry .... 401-341-2200 442 D willisg@salve.edu
WILLIS, Gregory .... 323-663-2167.. 73 E
WILLIS, Harvey .... 973-328-5232 301 G hwillis@ccm.edu
WILLIS, Howard .... 707-256-7225.. 55 E hwillis@napavalley.edu
WILLIS, James, A .... 585-395-2129 345 A jwillis@brockport.edu
WILLIS, Jane .... 803-321-5278 447 L jane.willis@newberry.edu
WILLIS, Jeannett .... 479-979-1378.. 25 H jwillis@ozarks.edu
WILLIS, Jeff .... 270-384-8097 198 C willisj@lindsey.edu
WILLIS, Jeff .... 337-550-1287 205 B jwillis@lsue.edu
WILLIS, Joy .... 601-857-3224 267 D Joy.Willis@hindscc.edu
WILLIS, Kara .... 740-245-7221 394 D kwillis@rio.edu
WILLIS, Kathy .... 618-468-5700 150 E kwillis@lc.edu
WILLIS, Kimberley .... 585-245-5566 345 D willis@geneseo.edu
WILLIS, Lesia .... 718-522-9073 315 E lwillis@asa.edu
WILLIS, Lisa .... 312-850-7066 142 E lwillis01@ccc.edu
WILLIS, Lori, A .... 541-383-7572 404 K lwillis@cocc.edu
WILLIS, Matesina .... 684-699-9155 549 C m.willis@amsamoa.edu
WILLIS, Michaela .... 402-872-2221 292 C mwillis@peru.edu
WILLIS, Paul .... 229-391-5001 119 F
WILLIS, Sherilyn .... 760-862-1333.. 41 A swillis@collegeofthedesert.edu
WILLIS, Susan .... 918-343-7663 401 I swillis@rsu.edu
WILLIS, Tamie, L .... 405-425-5320 399 J tamie.willis@oc.edu
WILLITS, Mary Lou .... 802-287-8316 501 I willitsml@greenmtn.edu
WILLKIE, Dan .... 619-388-7527.. 62 H dwillkie@sdccd.edu
WILLLIAMS, Susan, H .. 936-468-2201 484 A shwilliams@sfasu.edu
WILLLIAMS, Yohuru ..... 203-254-4000.. 90 E ywilliams@fairfield.edu
WILLMARTH, Ephraim .. 315-858-0945 328 B ejwillmarth@hts.edu
WILLMON, Nixon .... 256-228-6001.... 6 A willmonn@nacc.edu
WILLOME, Donna .... 585-389-2501 334 B dwillom0@naz.edu
WILLOQUET-MARICONDI, Paula .... 802-651-5924 501 F pwilloquetmaricondi@champlain.edu
WILLOUGHBY, Dan ...... 714-992-7036.. 56 F dwilloughby@fullcoll.edu
WILLOUGHBY, G. Case 724-287-8711 413 G gordon.willoughby@bc3.edu
WILLOUGHBY, Karen, P .... 412-536-1201 422 E karen.willoughby@laroche.edu
WILLOUGHBY, Lorraine 701-858-3314 374 B lori.willoughby@minotstateu.edu
WILLOUGHBY, Monty, L .... 913-684-2905 548 F monty.willoughby@leavenworth.army.mil
WILLOUGHBY, Thomas 303-871-3383.. 86 H twilloug@du.edu
WILLRICH, Penny, L ..... 602-682-6833.. 12 A pwillrich@azsummitlaw.edu
WILLS, Barbara .... 850-201-8590 117 B willsba@tcc.fl.edu
WILLS, Deri .... 803-641-3787 450 C deriw@usca.edu
WILLS, G. Benjamin ..... 702-968-1611 296 D bwills@roseman.edu
WILLS, Greg .... 502-897-4112 199 D gwills@sbts.edu
WILLS, Joe .... 530-898-4143.. 33 A jwills@csuchico.edu
WILLS, Mike .... 573-592-1191 286 A mike.wills@williamwoods.edu
WILLS, Mike .... 417-836-7635 279 A mikewills@missouristate.edu
WILLS, Penelope .... 928-776-2122.. 18 L penny.wills@yc.edu
WILLS, Scott, D .... 419-772-2705 388 I s-wills@onu.edu
WILLS, Sheri .... 401-454-6183 442 B finearts@risd.edu
WILLS, Tim .... 618-437-5321 156 I wills@rlc.edu
WILLSON, Robert, R ..... 692-625-3394 550 A rrwillson@cmi.edu
WILLY, Randy .... 877-366-0321 148 H rwilly@ellis.edu
WILLYARD, Paul .... 918-595-2067 403 A paula.willyard@tulsacc.edu
WILMER, Elizabeth .... 540-857-7313 517 E ewilmer@virginiawestern.edu
WILMES, David .... 703-284-5960 510 B david.wilmes@marymount.edu
WILMES, Gerald .... 660-562-1350 280 A gwilmes@nwmissouri.edu
WILMESHERR, Jon .... 828-766-1360 364 A jwilmesherr@mayland.edu
WILMOT, Lynne .... 507-222-5500 254 D lwilmot@carleton.edu
WILMOT, Tracey .... 914-633-2067 328 F twilmot@iona.edu
WILMOTH, Dirk, E .... 276-944-6814 507 E dwilmoth@ehc.edu
WILMOTH, Jamie .... 865-882-4270 463 F wilmoth@roanestate.edu
WILMOTT, Teresa .... 909-607-0317.. 39 E teresa.wilmott@cgu.edu
WILMOUTH, Robert ...... 406-657-1015 288 G bob.wilmouth@rocky.edu
WILMOWSKY, Joseph ... 718-774-3430 317 L
WILMS, Amy .... 909-793-2121.. 73 K amy_wilms@redlands.edu
WILSEY, Mary, M .... 585-785-1360 325 E mary.wilsey@flcc.edu
WILSHUSEN, Peter, R ... 570-577-1951 413 E peter.wilshusen@bucknell.edu
WILSKE, Don .... 517-483-1765 245 I wilsked@lcc.edu
WILSON, Alan .... 706-385-1059 130 C alan.wilson@point.edu
WILSON, Alan, G .... 660-263-3900 272M alanwilson@cccb.edu
WILSON, Alla .... 215-572-4691 412 F wilsona@arcadia.edu
WILSON, Ally .... 828-298-3325 373 A awilson@warren-wilson.edu
WILSON, Amanda .... 317-921-4949 169 L amanda.wilson@ivytech.edu
WILSON, Amy, R .... 740-245-7382 394 D awilson@rio.edu
WILSON, Andrew, A ..... 731-881-7626 465 F awilso93@utm.edu
WILSON, Andrew, G ..... 412-578-2095 414 I wilsonag@carlow.edu
WILSON, Angela .... 618-252-5400 159 F angela.wilson@sic.edu
WILSON, Angela .... 940-565-2550 492 D angela.wilson@unt.edu
WILSON, Angulus .... 559-453-2094.. 45 E angulus.wilson@fresno.edu
WILSON, Arthur, L .... 260-359-4031 167 D alwilson@huntington.edu
WILSON, Barbara .... 217-333-1350 162 A bjwilson@illinois.edu
WILSON, Barbara .... 719-389-6791.. 79M bwilson@coloradocollege.edu
WILSON, Barbara .... 770-534-6203 121 G bwilson@brenau.edu
WILSON, Barbara, J ..... 217-333-6290 162 A bjwilson@illinois.edu
WILSON, Barbara-Jan ... 860-685-2547.. 93 B bjwilson@wesleyan.edu
WILSON, Becky .... 806-742-3681 489 F becky.wilson@ttu.edu
WILSON, Bob .... 714-556-3610.. 75 A bwilson@vanguard.edu
WILSON, Bradley .... 724-738-2003 432 A bradley.wilson@sru.edu
WILSON, Bruce .... 904-680-7720 103 K bwilson@fcsl.edu
WILSON, Bryan, P .... 210-458-5919 494 D BRYAN.WILSON@UTSA.EDU
WILSON, Bryan, W .... 828-652-0635 364 B bryanwi@mcdowelltech.edu
WILSON, Carla .... 816-235-1052 284 A wilsonca@umkc.edu
WILSON, Carlton, E ...... 919-530-6794 370 C cwilson@nccu.edu
WILSON, Carmen .... 608-758-6565 541 E carmen.wilson@uwc.edu
WILSON, Carol, J .... 815-740-3840 162 F cwilson@stfrancis.edu
WILSON, Cathy .... 616-234-3971 243 D cwilson@grcc.edu
WILSON, Cecil, B .... 304-293-2021 533 D cbwilson@mail.wvu.edu
WILSON, Charlene .... 909-558-4040.. 50 K cwilson@llu.edu
WILSON, Charles .... 704-922-6428 362 G wilson.charles@gaston.edu
WILSON, JR., Charles, E .... 757-683-3925 510 I cwilson@odu.edu
WILSON, Cheryl, L .... 817-257-7834 486 G c.l.wilson@tcu.edu
WILSON, Chris .... 518-454-5436 322 C wilsonc@strose.edu
WILSON, Christen .... 610-902-1070 414 B christen.r.wilson@cabrini.edu
WILSON, Christine .... 785-243-1435 186 A cwilson@cloud.edu
WILSON, Chuck, A .... 301-314-8249 219 D chuckw@umd.edu
WILSON, Cleveland ...... 803-535-1419 448 C wilsonc@octech.edu
WILSON, Clive .... 937-298-3399 385 A clive.wilson@kc.edu
WILSON, JR., Clyde ..... 386-481-2483.. 99 F wilsonc@cookman.edu
WILSON, Corey, L .... 317-791-2556 173 I clwilson@uindy.edu
WILSON, Cynthia .... 251-928-8133.... 9 F cwilson@southalabama.edu
WILSON, Cynthia, A ..... 847-866-3936 145 C cynthia.wilson@garrett.edu
WILSON, Cynthia, L ..... 713-348-5048 480M clwilson@rice.edu
WILSON, D. Joanne ..... 608-342-1262 540 D wilsonj@uwplatt.edu
WILSON, Dani .... 714-992-7040.. 56 F dwilson@fullcoll.edu
WILSON, Daniel, B .... 740-826-8165 387 C dwilson@muskingum.edu
WILSON, Darin .... 678-407-5000 125 B
WILSON, David .... 636-949-4737 276 L dwilson@lindenwood.edu
WILSON, David .... 432-837-0107 489 B dwilson@sulross.edu
WILSON, David .... 443-885-3200 217 C david.wilson@morgan.edu
WILSON, David .... 615-966-6219 458 C david.wilson@lipscomb.edu
WILSON, David, C .... 314-968-7160 285 G wilson@webster.edu
WILSON, David, E .... 215-895-6038 417 E david.e.wilson@drexel.edu
WILSON, David, P .... 814-472-3211 434 F dwilson@francis.edu
WILSON, Deborah .... 509-574-6872 529 B dwilson@yvcc.edu
WILSON, Debra, J .... 906-248-8442 240 J dwilson@bmcc.edu
WILSON, Debra, J .... 208-732-6245 137 K dwilson@csi.edu
WILSON, Delwin, C ...... 207-725-3706 209 H dwilson@bowdoin.edu
WILSON, Denise .... 704-290-5247 366 A dwilson@spcc.edu
WILSON, JR., Donald, D .... 770-720-5953 130 E ddw@reinhardt.edu
WILSON, Donna .... 570-484-2576 431 C dwilson@lhup.edu
WILSON, Doug .... 251-442-2406.... 9 B dwilson@umobile.edu
WILSON, Douglas .... 205-726-4266.... 6 F dwilson@samford.edu
WILSON, Douglas .... 208-882-1566 138 F dougwils@christkirk.com
WILSON, Dwayne .... 731-989-6094 456 K dwilson@fhu.edu
WILSON, D'Andre .... 202-722-8111.. 96 H
WILSON, Elaine .... 606-679-8501 197 B elaine.wilson@kctcs.edu
WILSON, Eleanor .... 302-857-6001.. 93 E ewilson@desu.edu
WILSON, Elighie .... 708-709-3758 156 A ewilson@prairiestate.edu
WILSON, Elizabeth, K ... 404-471-6000 119 G ewilson@agnesscott.edu
WILSON, III, Ernest, J . 213-740-9891.. 74 D ernestw@usc.edu
WILSON, Evelyn .... 978-542-7321 230 E evelyn.wilson@salemstate.edu
WILSON, Fleetwood, L . 206-934-3789 525 K fleetwood.wilson@seattlecolleges.edu

WILSON, Floarine, A 502-597-6277 197 G floarine.wilson@kysu.edu
WILSON, Fred 714-816-0366 70 D fred.wilson@trident.edu
WILSON, Gary 816-604-6732 277 G gary.wilson@mcckc.edu
WILSON, Gena 229-931-2000 126 C gena.wilson@gsw.edu
WILSON, Glen 303-410-2446 85 E gwilson@redstone.edu
WILSON, Gordon, N 801-581-3079 499 K gordon.wilson@aux.utah.edu
WILSON, Heather 502-456-6509 200 A hwilson@sctd.edu
WILSON, Heather 605-394-2411 454 B heather.wilson@sdsmt.edu
WILSON, Holly 318-473-6581 205 A hwilson@lsua.edu
WILSON, Howard 712-722-6000 177 J howard.wilson@dordt.edu
WILSON, Huie, G 850-263-3261 99 A hgwilson@baptistcollege.edu
WILSON, J. David 270-809-2310 198 I jwilson@murraystate.edu
WILSON, Jacqueline 334-683-2309 5 H jwilson@marionmilitary.edu
WILSON, Jamelle 804-289-8428 513 M jwilson9@richmond.edu
WILSON, James 336-316-2132 357 C jwilson@guilford.edu
WILSON, JR., James, D 302-295-1194 94 G jim.d.wilson@wilmu.edu
WILSON, JR., James, J 936-261-2175 484 F jjwilson@pvamu.edu
WILSON, JR., James, J 936-261-5256 484 F jjwilson@pvamu.edu
WILSON, James, R 740-826-8113 387 C jrwilson@muskingum.edu
WILSON, Jan 316-295-5824 187 C jan_wilson@friends.edu
WILSON, JD 901-381-3939 466 E jd@visible.edu
WILSON, Jeff 615-966-7617 458 C jeff.wilson@lipscomb.edu
WILSON, Jeffrey, G 512-505-3030 475 G jwilson@htu.edu
WILSON, Jerry 719-255-3594 86 F jwilson@uccs.edu
WILSON, Jim 641-844-5550 179 J jim.wilson@iavalley.edu
WILSON, Jo 252-577-6223 363 G djwilson45@lenoircc.edu
WILSON, Jocelyn, M 516-671-2215 352 D jwilson@webb.edu
WILSON, John 212-217-4200 325 C john_wilsonn@fitnyc.edu
WILSON, John 504-816-4723 202 F jwilson@dillard.edu
WILSON, John 706-867-2844 133 A john.wilson@ung.edu
WILSON, John 843-863-7102 444 B jewilson@csuniv.edu
WILSON, John, R 804-278-4330 513 F jwilson@upsem.edu
WILSON, JR., John, S 404-215-2645 128 L
WILSON, Jonathan 501-205-8889 20 G jwilson@cbc.edu
WILSON, Jonathan 601-984-1010 270 H jwilson5@umc.edu
WILSON, Josh 870-368-2007 22 D josh.wilson@ozarka.edu
WILSON, Josh 706-272-2473 123 G jwilson@daltonstate.edu
WILSON, Joshua 641-472-1190 181 A alumni@mum.edu
WILSON, Judge 859-985-3131 193 F judge_wilson@berea.edu
WILSON, Julie 307-778-1218 546 F jwilson@lccc.wy.edu
WILSON, Kathi 865-981-8211 458 E kathi.wilson@maryvillecollege.edu
WILSON, Kathryn 585-395-2137 345 A kwilson@brockport.edu
WILSON, Kathy, A 863-638-2930 119 A wilsonka@webber.edu
WILSON, Keisha 704-330-1455 358 B kwilson@jcsu.edu
WILSON, Kelly 417-625-9363 278 I wilson-k@mssu.edu
WILSON, Kelly 740-264-5591 381 J kwilson@egcc.edu
WILSON, Kenneth 912-358-4166 131 A wilsonk@savannahstate.edu
WILSON, Kenny 636-481-3356 276 E kwilso20@jeffco.edu
WILSON, Kevin 570-945-8376 422 B kevin.wilson@keystone.edu
WILSON, Kim, L 402-472-9212 293 H kwilson4@unl.edu
WILSON, Kimberly, P 859-257-4751 200 G kwilson@email.uky.edu
WILSON, Kimberly, X 540-224-4313 509 D kxwilson@jchs.edu
WILSON, Kyla 773-907-4443 141 O kwilson@ccc.edu
WILSON, LaDrina 563-441-4016 178 D lnwilson@eicc.edu
WILSON, Larry, L 972-860-7218 472 E LarryWilson@dcccd.edu
WILSON, Laura, J 410-778-7849 221 D lwilson3@washcoll.edu
WILSON, Laura, L 650-723-9633 68 G laura.wilson@stanford.edu
WILSON, Laurie 402-935-9400 291 L lwilson@nechristian.edu
WILSON, Leon, C 334-229-5176 1 D lwilson@alasu.edu
WILSON, Leslie, K 319-273-6240 176 A Leslie.Wilson@uni.edu
WILSON, Lisa 478-825-6253 124 E wilsonl@fvsu.edu
WILSON, Lisa 505-566-3217 312 K wilsonl@sanjuancollege.edu
WILSON, Lizabeth, A 206-543-1760 527 G betsyw@uw.edu
WILSON, Lori, J 570-577-3334 413 E lwilson@bucknell.edu
WILSON, Lucy, P 478-301-2460 128 G wilson_l@mercer.edu
WILSON, Lynn 863-669-2898 110 E lwilson@polk.edu
WILSON, Lynn, Y 715-836-5521 539 E wilsonly@uwec.edu
WILSON, M. Roy 313-577-2230 252 G president@wayne.edu
WILSON, Maleta 504-865-3262 206 A mawilson@loyno.edu
WILSON, Marcus 806-743-6443 490 A marcus.wilson@ttuhsc.edu
WILSON, Mardell 314-977-8500 281 M wilsonma@slu.edu
WILSON, Margaret 660-626-2354 271 G mwilson@atsu.edu
WILSON, Mark 605-995-3024 452 H mark.wilson@mitchelltech.edu
WILSON, Mark 931-372-3961 462 A mwilson@tntech.edu
WILSON, Mark 423-472-7141 462 D mwilson@clevelandstatecc.edu
WILSON, Mark, R 215-887-5511 439 E mwilson@wts.edu
WILSON, Martha 207-221-4985 213 B mwilson13@une.edu
WILSON, Mary 931-598-1381 460 I mewilson@sewanee.edu
WILSON, MaryRose 301-846-2436 214 I mwilson@frederick.edu
WILSON, Matthew 734-462-4400 250 A mwilson@schoolcraft.edu
WILSON, Matthew, J 330-972-6197 392 H mjwilson@uakron.edu
WILSON, Megan 307-754-6031 546 I Megan.Wilson@nwc.edu
WILSON, Melanie 865-974-2521 465 D
WILSON, Michael, D 714-556-3610 75 A mdwilson@vanguard.edu
WILSON, Michael, P 610-861-1365 426 H wilsonm@moravian.edu
WILSON, Michele 304-424-8355 533 E michele.wilson@wvup.edu
WILSON, Michelle 870-633-4480 20 J rwilson@eacc.edu
WILSON, Mike 864-294-3464 446 F mike.wilsont@furman.edu
WILSON, Mindy 518-743-2252 347 E wilsonm@sunyacc.edu
WILSON, Natalie, L 412-578-6171 414 I wilsonnl@carlow.edu
WILSON, Neyle 843-349-5201 446 I neyle.wilson@hgtc.edu
WILSON, Pam 940-898-3503 490 D pwilson@twu.edu
WILSON, Pamala, P 270-831-9649 196 C pamala.wilson@kctcs.edu
WILSON, Pamela 803-780-1049 451 G pamelaw@voorhees.edu
WILSON, Pat 941-359-4200 116 D
WILSON, Pat 256-306-2743 2 F pwilson@calhoun.edu
WILSON, Patricia 205-366-8151 7 G mpwilson@stillman.edu
WILSON, Patrick 615-366-3917 461 B patrick.wilson@tbr.edu
WILSON, Peggy, M 865-694-6403 463 E pwilson@pstcc.edu
WILSON, Perry, T 843-661-1486 446 E pwilson@fmarion.edu
WILSON, Phillip 479-394-7622 22 H pwilson@rmcc.edu
WILSON, Qiana 478-445-2037 125 A qiana.wilson@gcsu.edu
WILSON, Richard, F 309-556-3151 148 A president@iwu.edu
WILSON, Robert, H 512-471-8947 493 M dean.r.wilson@austin.utexas.edu
WILSON, Roger 425-889-5336 524 G roger.wilson@northwestu.edu
WILSON, Ronalyn 518-736-3622 326 D rwilson@fmcc.suny.edu
WILSON, Roosevelt 719-549-2210 81 F roosevelt.wilson@csupueblo.edu
WILSON, Rowena, G 757-823-8668 510 H rgwilson@nsu.edu
WILSON, Sandra 313-664-7471 241 D sandra@collegeforcreativestudies.edu
WILSON, Scott 651-846-1694 261 G scott.wilson@saintpaul.edu
WILSON, Scott, L 641-269-3500 178 I wilsons@grinnell.edu
WILSON, Shain 205-853-1200 5 C swilson@jeffstateonline.com
WILSON, Shawn 989-964-7090 249 G swilson@svsu.edu
WILSON, Sheila 252-399-6309 354 I spwilson@barton.edu
WILSON, Sherry 828-726-2306 360 F swilson@cccti.edu
WILSON, Sherwood, G 540-231-4416 518 B sgwilson@vt.edu
WILSON, Shirley 213-624-1200 44 I swilson@fidm.edu
WILSON, Sonali, B 216-687-3543 380 D s.b.wilson@csuohio.edu
WILSON, Stacey 704-403-1639 355 B stacey.wilson@carolinashealthcare.org
WILSON, Stanley 954-262-1266 109 E swilson@nova.edu
WILSON, Stephan, M 405-744-9805 400 C stephan.m.wilson@okstate.edu
WILSON, Stephanie Gray 614-236-6894 378 H honors@capital.edu
WILSON, Stephen 478-445-5331 125 A steve.wilson@gcsu.edu
WILSON, Stephen 804-862-6172 511 H swilson@rbc.edu
WILSON, Steven, H 817-515-4506 484 B steven.wilson@tccd.edu
WILSON, Susan 219-785-5236 172 A swilson@pnc.edu
WILSON, Susan 952-446-4120 255 E wilsons@crown.edu
WILSON, Susan 816-235-6704 284 A wilsonsb2@umkc.edu
WILSON, Susan, A 802-322-1641 501 H susan.wilson@goddard.edu
WILSON, Sylvia 573-681-6107 276 K wilsons@lincolnu.edu
WILSON, Ted 608-796-3000 542 H
WILSON, Ted, H 270-707-3865 196 D ted.wilson@kctcs.edu
WILSON, Terez 901-321-3254 455 I twilso22@cbu.edu
WILSON, Terry 515-244-4221 175 C
WILSON, Thalia 901-333-5112 464 A twilson@southwest.tn.edu
WILSON, Tiffany 803-778-6668 443 I wilsontd@cctech.edu
WILSON, Timothy, B 805-565-6038 76 K twilson@westmont.edu
WILSON, Tommy 706-649-1894 123 E twilson@columbustech.edu
WILSON, Tony 336-725-8344 368 A wilsont@piedmontu.edu
WILSON, Tracy 651-403-4118 261 G tracy.wilson@saintpaul.edu
WILSON, Tressey, D 936-361-1700 484 F tdwilson@pvamu.edu
WILSON, Valeri 619-660-4221 46 G valeri.wilson@gcccd.edu
WILSON, Valerie 870-574-4514 23 E vwilson@sautech.edu
WILSON, Valerie 740-477-7530 388 F vwilson@ohiochristian.edu
WILSON, Valvia 601-977-7844 270 F vwilson@tougaloo.edu
WILSON, Vicki 859-246-6316 195 J vicki.wilson@kctcs.edu
WILSON, Vicki 724-852-3375 439 C vwilson@waynesburg.edu
WILSON, Victor, K 706-542-3564 132 H wilsonv@uga.edu
WILSON, W. Bruce 909-869-3065 32 F wbwilson@cpp.edu
WILSON, W. Chandler 503-255-0332 407 D chandlerwilson@multnomah.edu
WILSON, Warren 605-642-6930 453 G warren.wilson@bhsu.edu
WILSON, Wendy 229-317-6925 123 H wendy.wilson@darton.edu
WILSON, Wendy 713-221-8568 491 F wilsonwe@uhd.edu
WILSON, William 423-354-2541 463 D wrwilson@northeaststate.edu
WILSON, William 216-687-4686 380 D william.wilson@csuohio.edu
WILSON, William, M 918-495-6175 401 B president@oru.edu
WILSON, Yolanda 803-327-8021 451 K ywilson@yorktech.edu
WILSON, Yvette 212-280-1396 351 B ywilson@uts.columbia.edu
WILSON, Zaphon 919-516-4280 368 E zrwilson@st-aug.edu
WILSON-FENNELL, Nicole 734-462-4400 250 A nwilson@schoolcraft.edu
WILSON-OYELARAN, Eileen, B 269-337-7220 244 I wilsonoy@kzoo.edu
WILSON-PORTER, Cyndi 210-829-2706 492 B porter@uiwtx.edu
WILSON-SPARROW, Sarah 518-381-1314 342 E
WILSON-STALLINGS, Samaria 617-682-1508 226 D swilson@eds.edu
WILSON-TAYLOR, Sharon 312-369-7221 143 C swilson-taylor@colum.edu
WILT, Darrell 717-815-1288 440 H dwilt1@ycp.edu
WILT, Jason 269-783-2159 250 D jwilt@swmich.edu
WILT, Richard, W 610-799-1164 424 A rwilt@lccc.edu
WILT, Valerie 386-481-2004 99 F Collmanv@cookman.edu
WILTENMUTH, III, John, P 540-654-1047 513 I jwiltenm@umw.edu
WILTGEN, JR., Jim 501-450-1222 21 C wiltgen@hendrix.edu
WILTON, John 510-642-3100 70 K vcaf@berkeley.edu
WILTROUT, Deborah 239-590-1089 114 F dwiltrout@fgcu.edu
WILTSCHEK, Walt 260-982-5243 170 a wjwiltschek@manchester.edu
WILTSE, Mary Alane 518-828-4181 322 E wiltse@sunycgcc.edu
WILTSHIRE, Rolly 718-289-5186 318 E rolly.wiltshire@bcc.cuny.edu
WILTZ, Ofelia 305-220-4120 108 F owiltz@mattiacollege.edu
WILTZIUS, Pierre 805-893-5024 72 D mlpsdean@ltsc.ucsb.edu
WIMBERLEY, Bernadette, H 302-225-6312 94 B wimberlb@gbc.edu
WIMBERLEY, Carrie 478-471-2712 128 H carrie.wimberley@mga.edu
WIMBERLY, Frances 706-396-7596 129 H fwimberly@paine.edu
WIMBERLY, Yvette 501-420-1207 19 B yvette.wimberly@arkansasbaptist.edu
WIMBISH, Jennifer, L 972-860-8251 472 D jwimbish@dcccd.edu
WIMBLEY, Eric, L 269-337-5739 244 I Eric.Wimbley@kzoo.edu
WIMBUSH, James 812-856-5700 167 I jwimbush@indiana.edu
WIMBUSH, James 812-855-2739 167 J jwimbush@indiana.edu
WIMBUSH, James 812-855-2739 167 J jwimbush@iu.edu
WIMER, Valinda 386-822-8850 117 A vwimer@stetson.edu
WIMS, Daniel, K 256-372-5275 1 A daniel.wims@aamu.edu
WIMS, Lois, A 508-929-8038 230 G lwims@worcester.edu
WINANS, Bill 940-668-3353 479 K bwinans@nctc.edu
WINBORNE, Malverne 734-487-2086 242 J mwinborne@emich.edu
WINCHELL, Barbara 845-569-3298 333 I barbara.winchell@msmc.edu
WINCHESTER, Andrea 731-425-2644 463 A awinchester@jscc.edu
WINCHESTER, Gina, S 270-809-5086 198 I gwinchester@murraystate.edu
WINCHESTER, Linda 207-454-1033 211 E lwinchester@wccc.me.edu
WINCHESTER, Paul 316-295-5836 187 C winchp@friends.edu
WINCHESTER, Samuel 919-573-5350 368 H
WINCHESTER, Sara 732-255-0400 304 E swinchester@ocean.edu

WISHING, III, Lee, S ... 724-458-3332 419 F
lswishing@gcc.edu
WISHON, Angela .... 214-648-0455 496 A
angela.wishon@utsouthwestern.edu
WISHON, Gordon, D .... 480-965-9334.. 11 J
gordon.wishon@asu.edu
WISHON, Phillip, M ..... 540-568-6572 509 C
wishonpm@jmu.edu
WISLOCK, Robert .... 570-389-4529 430 B
rwislock@bloomu.edu
WISNER, Arthur, S .... 410-857-2218 217 A
awisner@mcdaniel.edu
WISNER, David .... 716-896-0700 352 B
dmwisner@villa.edu
WISNER, Marie .... 651-638-6543 254 A
m-wisner@bethel.edu
WISNER, Paul .... 714-892-7711.. 40 C
pwisner@gwc.cccd.edu
WISNER-CARLSON,
Joan .... 410-435-0100 217 F
jwisnercarlson@ndm.edu
WISNESKI, Thomas, E .. 610-566-1776 440 C
twisneski@williamson.edu
WISNEWSKI, Michael ... 401-341-2201 442 D
michael.wisnewski@salve.edu
WISNIEWSKA, Sophia ... 727-873-4466 116 B
wiesniewska@mail.usf.edu
WISNIEWSKA,
Sophia, T .... 727-873-4151 116 C
wisniewska@usfsp.edu
WISNIEWSKI, Amy .... 308-635-6363 294 C
wisniews@wncc.edu
WISNIEWSKI, Helena .... 907-786-4833.. 10 H
hswisniewski@uaa.alaska.edu
WISNIEWSKI, Michael .. 215-871-6170 432 E
WISNIEWSKI, Mike .... 312-942-2558 158 A
Michael_A_Wisniewski@rush.edu
WISNIOWICZ, Lisa .... 630-844-6852 139 L
lwisni@aurora.edu
WISSINGER, Kristin ...... 724-222-5330 428 B
kwissinger@penncommercial.edu
WISSMAN, Alex .... 858-499-0202.. 40 G
awissman@coleman.edu
WISSMILLER, Andrew ... 310-206-6771.. 71 D
awissmiller@ais.ucla.edu
WISSMILLER, Becky ...... 563-425-5248 183 G
wissmillerb@uiu.edu
WISTROM, Carl, H .... 773-244-4961 154 G
cwistrom@northpark.edu
WISWALL, Derry .... 660-248-6296 272 N
dwiswall@centralmethodist.edu
WITCHER, Pamela, M ... 508-531-1295 229 C
pamela.witcher@bridgew.edu
WITCHNER, Anne .... 412-268-4886 414 J
awow@andrew.cmu.edu
WITCOMBE, Giulia, V ... 434-381-6334 513 E
jys@sbc.edu
WITEK, Paul, J .... 570-561-1818 435 A
paul.witek@stots.edu
WITH, Elizabeth .... 940-565-4909 492 D
elizabeth.with@unt.edu
WITHEM, Ron .... 402-472-7132 293 F
rwithem@nebraska.edu
WITHERELL, Meghan .... 530-938-5500.. 41 E
witherellm@siskiyous.edu
WITHERELL, Michael, S 805-893-8270.. 72 D
witherell@research.ucsb.edu
WITHERELL, Paula .... 716-839-8472 323 F
paula.witherell@daemen.edu
WITHERINGTON,
Jennifer .... 912-688-6966 129 E
jlwitherington@ogeecheetech.edu
WITHERITE, Richard, L . 606-337-1015 194 F
rwitherite@ccbbc.edu
WITHEROW, Laurie, B .. 615-898-2111 461 E
laurie.witherow@mtsu.edu
WITHERS, Allen, B .... 304-929-5011 531 D
awithers@newriver.edu
WITHERS, Ben, C .... 859-257-8450 200 G
bwithers@uky.edu
WITHERS, Dale .... 707-965-7150.. 57 I
dwithers@puc.edu
WITHERS, Gary .... 503-493-6207 405 E
gwithers@cu-portland.edu
WITHERS, Jennifer .... 701-483-2999 373 H
jennifer.withers@dickinsonstate.edu
WITHERS, Stacie .... 816-995-2832 280 J
stacie.withers@researchcollege.edu
WITHERSPOON,
Alanna, S .... 312-850-7031 142 E
awitherspoon5@ccc.edu
WITHERSPOON,
Everette, L .... 336-750-2131 372 D
witherspoone@wssu.edu
WITHERSPOON, Karen .. 212-650-6400 318 G
kwitherspoon@ccny.cuny.edu
WITHERSPOON,
Patricia .... 915-747-7018 494 B
withersp@utep.edu

WITHERUP, Philip .... 570-321-4220 425 B
witherup@lycoming.edu
WITHROW, Amy, S .... 717-221-1303 420 D
aswithro@hacc.edu
WITHROW, Lisa .... 740-362-3343 386 D
lwithrow@mtso.edu
WITHUS, George .... 701-858-4444 374 B
george.withus@minotstateu.edu
WITKOVSKY, Lowell, D 814-641-3360 421 L
witkovl@juniata.edu
WITKOWSKI, Barbara ... 609-894-9311 306 B
bwitkowski@bcc.edu
WITMER, Kenneth, D .... 610-436-2321 432 B
kwitmer@wcupa.edu
WITMER, Timothy, Z .... 215-572-3831 439 E
twitmer@wts.edu
WITRYK, Ted .... 269-337-7391 244 I
Ted.Witryk@kzoo.edu
WITSON, Mike .... 740-588-1237 396 E
mwitson@zanestate.edu
WITT, JR., Al .... 704-334-6882 355 I
awitt@charlottechristian.edu
WITT, Allen .... 813-259-6151 106 C
awitt3@hccfl.edu
WITT, Anne .... 704-334-6882 355 I
abwitt@charlottechristian.edu
WITT, Betsy, A .... 864-488-8288 447 F
bwitt@limestone.edu
WITT, Don, E .... 859-257-3458 200 G
dwitt@email.uky.edu
WITT, Jack .... 567-661-7314 390 D
fjwitt@owens.edu
WITT, Karla .... 605-455-6001 452 L
kwitt@olc.edu
WITT, Linda .... 615-327-6724 458 F
lwitt@mmc.edu
WITT, Marie, D .... 215-898-1199 437 I
witt@upenn.edu
WITT, Robert, E .... 205-348-9731.... 8 D
witt@uasystem.ua.edu
WITT, Tiffanie .... 270-824-8575 196 F
tiffanie.witt@kctcs.edu
WITTE, Bob .... 417-626-1234 280 B
witte.bob@occ.edu
WITTE, Dennis, E .... 708-209-3205 143 D
dennis.witte@cuchicago.edu
WITTE, John .... 616-526-6547 240 L
jwitte@calvin.edu
WITTE, Kevin .... 360-992-2356 521 A
kwitte@clark.edu
WITTE, Lois, J .... 417-667-8181 273 H
lwitte@cottey.edu
WITTE, III, Paul, R .... 616-526-7920 240 L
prw3@calvin.edu
WITTE, Peter, T .... 816-235-2731 284 A
wittep@umkc.edu
WITTE, Sandra .... 559-278-2448.. 33 D
WITTE, Sarah .... 541-962-3511 405 G
switte@eou.edu
WITTENBERG, Diane ..... 626-396-2326.. 28 J
diane.wittenberg@artcenter.edu
WITTENMYER, Kathryn .. 415-503-6223.. 63 A
klw@sfcm.edu
WITTER, Kevin, G .... 540-857-7341 517 E
kwitter@virginiawestern.edu
WITTER, Pamela .... 716-827-4344 350 H
witterp@trocaire.edu
WITTER, Terry .... 903-877-7704 495 C
terry.witter@uthct.edu
WITTGENFELD, Tania .... 773-291-6359 142 B
twittgenfeld@ccc.edu
WITTHOFT, Andrea .... 618-437-5321 156 I
witthoft@rlc.edu
WITTIG, Stephanie .... 215-461-1139 426 E
swittig@mc3.edu
WITTIG, William .... 313-993-1532 250 H
wittigw@udmercy.edu
WITTLER, Kim .... 301-369-2800 214 A
kwittler@captechu.edu
WITTLER, Michele, A .... 920-748-8119 538 I
wittlerm@ripon.edu
WITTMAN, William .... 301-295-3185 548 D
william.wittman@usuhs.edu
WITTMER, Michael .... 636-227-2100 277 A
michael.wittmer@logan.edu
WITTNER, Charity .... 251-442-2507.... 9 B
cwittner@umobile.edu
WITTROCK, David, A .... 701-231-7033 374 C
david.wittrock@ndsu.edu
WITTROCK, Monica .... 920-403-3146 538 K
monica.wittrock@snc.edu
WITTY, Janeen .... 803-705-4761 443 F
wittyj@benedict.edu
WITZ, MaryJo, A .... 585-292-2188 333 G
mwitz@monroecc.edu
WITZEL, Stephanie .... 707-668-5663.. 42 K
WIXON, Tom .... 559-934-2132.. 76 A
tomwixon@whccd.edu
WIXSOM, Richard .... 413-236-3003 231 A
rwixsom@berkshirecc.edu

WIXSON, Karen .... 336-334-3403 371 C
kkwixson@uncg.edu
WNUK, Beth .... 414-443-3631 538 A
wnukb@mtmary.edu
WOBBE, Michelle .... 314-918-2599 274 K
mwobbe@eden.edu
WOBBY, Lauren .... 802-485-2040 502 G
laurenw@norwich.edu
WOBIG, Jayne .... 507-457-1438 264 B
jwobig@smumn.edu
WOBSCHALL, Rachel, A 651-962-6992 265 F
rawobschall@stthomas.edu
WODKA, Chris .... 520-494-5230.. 12 R
chris.wodka@centralaz.edu
WOEBKENBERG, Eric .... 610-499-4090 439 G
eewoebkenberg@widener.edu
WOELKERS, Joseph, F .. 903-877-7750 495 C
joseph.woelkers@uthct.edu
WOELL, John .... 517-629-0222 239 A
jwoell@albion.edu
WOERDEHOFF,
Valorie, A .... 563-588-7565 180 L
woerdehoff.valorie@loras.edu
WOERHEIDE, Walter, J . 610-526-1398 412 D
walt.woerheide@theamericancollege.edu
WOGAN, Maureen .... 773-298-3010 158 F
wogan@sxu.edu
WOGAN, Thomas .... 773-995-3576 141 J
twogan@csu.edu
WOGEN, Brian, M .... 641-422-4177 181 E
wogenbri@niacc.edu
WOHL, David .... 803-323-2323 451 I
wohld@winthrop.edu
WOHL, James .... 860-486-5143.. 92 C
jim.wohl@uconn.edu
WOHLER, Tina .... 620-278-4218 191 D
twohler@sterling.edu
WOHLERS, Anton .... 580-581-6775 397 A
awohlers@cameron.edu
WOHLERT, Amy .... 505-277-1092 313 H
awohlert@unm.edu
WOHLETZ, Dale .... 318-357-5581 208 D
wohletz@nsula.edu
WOHLMAN, Jason, L .... 530-752-9793.. 71 A
jlwohlman@ucdavis.edu
WOHLMAN, Katie .... 828-328-7699 358 G
katie.wohlman@lr.edu
WOHLPART, A. James .. 319-273-2517 176 A
jim.wohlpart@uni.edu
WOHLSTEIN, Melissa ... 540-831-5407 511 C
mwohlstein@radford.edu
WOIKE, David .... 734-487-0076 242 J
dwoike@emich.edu
WOITOWITZ, Chris .... 417-455-5712 274 B
cwoitowitz@crowder.edu
WOIWODE, Kristin .... 309-672-5530 152 E
kwoiwode@methodistcol.edu
WOJAK, Angie .... 212-592-2000 342 F
awojak@sva.edu
WOJCIECHOWSKA,
Bogusia .... 617-228-2025 231 C
bwojciechowska@bhcc.mass.edu
WOJCIECHOWSKI, Keli . 708-524-6827 144 C
kallen@dom.edu
WOJCIK, Alketa .... 760-757-2121.. 54 G
awojcik@miracosta.edu
WOJKE, Katie .... 360-491-4700 525 H
kwojke@stmartin.edu
WOJNAS, Sherry .... 315-798-8144 340 D
WOJNOWSKI, Mark, E .. 716-286-9718 336 E
mew@niagara.edu
WOJTAL, Steve .... 440-775-8410 388 B
swojtal@oberlin.edu
WOJTALEWICZ,
Jeanette .... 402-398-5527 289 G
WOJTAS, Susan, A .... 508-849-3298 222 C
swojtas@annamaria.edu
WOJTOWICZ, Robert ..... 757-683-4885 510 I
rwojtowi@odu.edu
WOLANIN, Monique ..... 860-932-4174.. 90 A
mwolanin@qvcc.commnet.edu
WOLANSKYJ,
Alexandra, A .... 507-284-3627 254 G
wolanskyj.alexandra@mayo.edu
WOLAVER, Rob .... 254-867-3366 488 B
rob.wolaver@tstc.edu
WOLBERT, Jodi .... 603-513-1302 299 C
jodi.wolbert@granite.edu
WOLCH, Jennifer .... 510-642-0831.. 70 K
wolch@berkeley.edu
WOLCOTT, Richard, D .. 716-851-1615 325 A
wolcott@ecc.edu
WOLCOWITZ, Jeffrey .... 216-368-2928 378 J
jeffrey.wolcowitz@case.edu
WOLD, Lisa .... 503-255-0332 407 D
lwold@multnomah.edu
WOLD, Mark, C .... 608-363-2359 534 L
woldm@beloit.edu
WOLD, Paul, G 507-344-7346 253M
pwold@blc.edu

WOLD-MCCORMICK,
Kristi .... 303-492-6970.. 86 E
kristi.woldmccormick@colorado.edu
WOLDU, Feseha .... 202-865-4806.. 96 B
feseha.woldu@howard.edu
WOLEVER, Jack .... 805-893-4581.. 72 D
jack.wolever@dcs.ucsb.edu
WOLF, Andrea .... 617-521-2488 236 F
andrea.wolf@simmons.edu
WOLF, Andreas .... 650-574-6461.. 64 D
wolf@smccd.edu
WOLF, Bill .... 865-573-4517 457 H
bwolf@johnsonu.edu
WOLF, Elyse .... 603-577-6209 297 F
ewolf@dwc.edu
WOLF, George .... 517-264-7177 250 B
gwolf@sienaheights.edu
WOLF, Greg .... 508-856-4296 229 B
greg.wolf@umassmed.edu
WOLF, Howard, E .... 650-724-5992.. 68 G
howardwolf@stanford.edu
WOLF, Jay, D .... 812-888-4172 174 F
jwolf@vinu.edu
WOLF, Jeffery, M .... 812-488-2183 173 H
jw268@evansville.edu
WOLF, Jonathan .... 814-619-3183 414 E
jwolf@crbc.net
WOLF, Kelly, B .... 541-346-3165 410 F
kbwolf@uoregon.edu
WOLF, Kenneth .... 973-720-2432 309 I
wolfk@wpunj.edu
WOLF, Laurie .... 515-964-6437 177 B
lawolf@dmacc.edu
WOLF, Linda .... 614-251-4715 388 H
wolfl2@ohiodominican.edu
WOLF, Nick .... 619-849-2384.. 59 K
nickwolf@pointloma.edu
WOLF, Rachel, B .... 972-860-7358 472 E
RWolf@dcccd.edu
WOLF, Rebecca, E .... 501-882-8867.. 19 E
rewolf@asub.edu
WOLF, JR., Thomas ..... 269-387-5473 252 I
tom.wolf@wmich.edu
WOLF JOHNSON,
Cynthia .... 704-687-7226 371 B
cwolfjo@uncc.edu
WOLFE, Andrew .... 315-792-7234 348 D
andrew.wolfe@sunyit.edu
WOLFE, Ben .... 509-533-8861 521 E
ben.wolfe@scc.spokane.edu
WOLFE, Bill .... 318-797-5279 205 F
bill.wolfe@lsus.edu
WOLFE, Clarissa .... 509-574-4651 529 B
cwolfe@yvcc.edu
WOLFE, Elizabeth .... 304-696-6007 532 H
mccormi8@marshall.edu
WOLFE, Erin, M .... 570-372-4314 435 I
wolfeerin@susqu.edu
WOLFE, Gregory .... 508-565-1357 237 A
gwolfe@stonehill.edu
WOLFE, James, E .... 812-464-1782 174 D
jwolfe2@usi.edu
WOLFE, Joel .... 205-970-9253.... 7 D
jwolfe@sebc.edu
WOLFE, Johanna .... 713-221-8909 491 F
wolfej@uhd.edu
WOLFE, John, S .... 812-877-8590 172 C
john.s.wolfe@rose-hulman.edu
WOLFE, Ken .... 727-864-8835 101 P
wolfefk@eckerd.edu
WOLFE, Michael .... 419-267-1322 387 G
mwolfe@northweststate.edu
WOLFE, Peggy, L .... 337-475-5820 208 B
pwolfe@mcneese.edu
WOLFE, Thomas, V ...... 303-765-3102.. 83 C
tvwolfe@iliff.edu
WOLFE, Tim, A .... 757-221-3980 506 J
tawolfe@wm.edu
WOLFE, Tim, M .... 573-882-2011 283 G
wolfet@umsystem.edu
WOLFE, Tina .... 618-533-4111 149 C
twolfe@kaskaskia.edu
WOLFE, Todd .... 818-677-3700.. 34 D
todd.wolfe@csun.edu
WOLFE, Vicki .... 205-970-9245.... 7 D
vwolfe@sebc.edu
WOLFE-LEE, Chyerl .... 360-650-3774 528 D
chyerl.wolfe-lee@wwu.edu
WOLFE-STEPRO,
Charlene .... 603-206-8072 297 A
cwolfe@ccsnh.edu
WOLFER, Diane, G .... 859-371-9393 193 D
dwolfer@beckfield.edu
WOLFERSBERGER,
Mark 808-675-3628 134M
mark.wolfersberger@byuh.edu
WOLFERT, Kelly .... 920-693-1171 543 B
ltc.bookstore@gotoltc.edu
WOLFF, David .... 605-642-6504 453 G

WOODBURN, Steven .... 606-326-2077 195 H
steve.woodburn@kctcs.edu
WOODDELL, Joseph ..... 214-818-1336 471 I
jwooddell@criswell.edu
WOODDELL, Kathleen ... 540-338-2700 505 K
kwooddell@cdu.edu
WOODEN, K. Mark .... 602-639-7500.. 14 A
WOODEN, Ontario, S ... 919-530-5235 370 C
owooden@nccu.edu
WOODEN, Ontario, S ... 919-530-5069 370 C
owooden@nccu.edu
WOODESHICK, Alisha ... 859-371-9393 193 D
awoodeshick@beckfield.edu
WOODFAULK, Ashley ... 773-947-6276 152 A
awoodfau@lstc.edu
WOODFIELD, Richard ... 419-995-8222 384 E
woodfield.r@rhodesstate.edu
WOODFIELD, Richard ... 740-588-1260 396 E
rwoodfield@zanestate.edu
WOODFORD, Steve .... 865-251-1800 460 J
swoodford@southcollegetn.edu
WOODFORK,
Joshua, C .... 518-580-5700 342 I
jwoodfor@skidmore.edu
WOODHAM, Margo ...... 478-471-2800 128 H
margo.woodham@mga.edu
WOODHOUSE,
Bryan, M .... 608-246-6337 543 C
woodhouse@madisoncollege.edu
WOODHOUSE,
Michelle, W .... 757-822-2242 517 C
mwoodhouse@tcc.edu
WOODLE, Tom .... 843-349-2357 444 G
twoodle@coastal.edu
WOODLEE,
Stephanie, A .... 325-674-2413 466 I
stephanie.woodlee@acu.edu
WOODLEY, Michael, P . 701-252-3467 375 J
woodley@uj.edu
WOODLEY, Sandra, K ... 225-342-6950 207 G
ulspresident@la.gov
WOODMAN, Richard .... 207-985-7976 210 H
woodman@landingschool.edu
WOODMANSEE, Holly ... 253-680-7123 519 K
hwoodmansee@bates.ctc.edu
WOODMANSEE, Ken ..... 901-843-3874 460 F
woodmanseek@rhodes.edu
WOODRICK, Rebecca ... 601-266-6618 271 B
rebecca.woodrick@usm.edu
WOODRING, Donna ..... 606-693-5000 197 F
dwoodring@kmbc.edu
WOODROW, Adam .... 520-335-8424.. 13 B
woodrowa@cochise.edu
WOODROW, Adam .... 413-782-1583 238 A
adam.woodrow@wne.edu
WOODRUFF, Aaron .... 309-438-8631 147 I
apwoodr@ilstu.edu
WOODRUFF, JR.,
Edward, W .... 727-614-7285 112 A
woodruff.edward@spcollege.edu
WOODRUFF,
Kenneth, A .... 843-953-6859 444 C
ken.woodruff@citadel.edu
WOODRUFF, Kristin ...... 785-442-6016 187 I
kwoodruff@highlandcc.edu
WOODRUFF, Martha ..... 903-983-8287 477 A
mwoodruff@kilgore.edu
WOODRUFF, Steven, W 336-342-4261 365 E
woodruffs@rockinghamcc.edu
WOODRUFF, Tina .... 215-871-6870 432 E
tinawo@pcom.edu
WOODS, Amy, K .... 845-575-3000 331 L
amy.k.coppola@marist.edu
WOODS, Betsy .... 937-294-0592 391 B
betsy@saa.edu
WOODS, Billy .... 336-838-6496 367 C
billy.woods@wilkescc.edu
WOODS, Brandy .... 618-634-3417 159 A
brandyw@shawneecc.edu
WOODS, Brett .... 828-339-4241 366 C
b_woods@southwesterncc.edu
WOODS, Brian .... 954-776-4476 107 F
brianw@keiseruniversity.edu
WOODS, Byron .... 559-730-3908.. 41 D
byronw@cos.edu
WOODS, Carolyn .... 717-264-4141 440 D
carolyn.woods@wilson.edu
WOODS, Dannie .... 601-925-3830 268 E
drwoods@mc.edu
WOODS, Dean .... 864-231-2000 443 E
DWoods@andersonuniversity.edu
WOODS, Deborah .... 765-361-6092 175 B
woodsde@wabash.edu
WOODS, Debra .... 714-449-7434.. 53 D
danderson@ketchum.edu
WOODS, Debra, D .... 724-925-4083 439 F
woodsde@wccc.edu
WOODS, Donovan .... 405-945-6705 400 F
dwoods@osugiving.com
WOODS, Ed .... 503-589-7746 404 L
ed.woods@chemeketa.edu
WOODS, Ed .... 214-870-3772 480 D
ewoods@pqc.edu
WOODS, Elizabeth .... 508-854-4294 232 F
ewoods@qcc.mass.edu
WOODS, Gilda, Q .... 540-365-4298 507 H
gwoods@ferrum.edu
WOODS, James, M ...... 630-515-6173 152 H
jwoods@midwestern.edu
WOODS, Jami .... 336-386-3266 366 E
woodsj@surry.edu
WOODS, Jason .... 563-588-7829 180 L
jason.woods@loras.edu
WOODS, Jeffrey .... 479-968-0274.. 20 C
jwoods@atu.edu
WOODS, John .... 205-552-1284.... 3 C
john.woods@ecacolleges.com
WOODS, John, J .... 601-857-3387 267 D
jjwoods@hindscc.edu
WOODS, Kimberly, J .... 830-792-7282 482 D
kjwoods@schreiner.edu
WOODS, Kristin, J .... 804-289-8026 513 M
kwoods@richmond.edu
WOODS, Kristy, F .... 202-865-7470.. 96 B
kristy.woods@howard.edu
WOODS, Lauren .... 312-567-5167 147 E
lwoods1@iit.edu
WOODS, Linda .... 619-388-7434.. 62 H
lwoods@sdccd.edu
WOODS, Marty .... 864-587-4044 449 D
woodsm@smcsc.edu
WOODS, Mary Lou .... 909-621-8000.. 60 A
marylou.woods@pomona.edu
WOODS, Maura, A .... 718-990-1985 340 G
woodsm@stjohns.edu
WOODS, Phillip .... 423-478-7993 460 C
pwoods@ptseminary.edu
WOODS, Rebekah .... 517-787-0800 244 H
woodsrebekahs@jccmi.edu
WOODS, Richard, G ...... 765-361-6188 175 B
woodsr@wabash.edu
WOODS, Rochelle .... 657-278-2738.. 33 E
rwoods@fullerton.edu
WOODS, Roderick .... 803-327-7402 444 F
rwoods@clintoncollege.edu
WOODS, Serrita .... 815-395-5089 158 B
WOODS, Sharmon .... 520-325-0123.. 17 Q
WOODS, Sharon .... 864-503-5354 451 A
swoods@uscupstate.edu
WOODS, Shelton .... 208-426-1368 137 E
swoods@boisestate.edu
WOODS, Susan .... 781-280-3200 232 B
woodss@middlesex.mass.edu
WOODS, Timothy .... 559-226-0720.. 68 J
tim.woods@fresnocitycollege.edu
WOODS, Timothy .... 559-489-2352.. 69 B
tim.woods@fresnocitycollege.edu
WOODS, Tracie, J .... 225-771-4680 206 K
traice_woods@sus.edu
WOODS, Tracy .... 478-289-2035 124 B
twoods@ega.edu
WOODS, Tricia .... 417-864-7220 275 A
twoods@cci.edu
WOODSIDE,
Christina, S .... 704-847-5600 369 A
cwoodside@ses.edu
WOODSON, Corliss, B . 804-523-5877 515 F
cwoodson@reynolds.edu
WOODSON, Heather ..... 704-922-6310 362 G
woodson.heather@gaston.edu
WOODSON, Kendra, B . 864-833-8220 448 E
kbwoodson@presby.edu
WOODSON, Lenee .... 973-290-4227 301 F
lwoodson@cse.edu
WOODSON, Lovisa .... 215-635-7300 419 D
lwoodson@gratz.edu
WOODSON, Sandra ...... 916-577-2200.. 77 F
swoodson@jessup.edu
WOODSON,
Terrance, S .... 214-887-5371 473 E
twoodson@dts.edu
WOODSON, William ...... 937-708-5711 395 E
wwoodson@wilberforce.edu
WOODSON,
William Randy .... 919-515-2191 370 D
randy_woodson@ncsu.edu
WOODSON DAY,
Beverly .... 210-458-4536 494 D
BEVERLY.WOODSONDAY@UTSA.EDU
WOODWARD, Angus ...... 225-768-1704 206 F
angus.woodward@ololcollege.edu
WOODWARD, Beth .... 503-534-4023 407 A
bwoodward@marylhurst.edu
WOODWARD, Bill .... 434-791-7103 505 A
woodward@averett.edu
WOODWARD, Clifford .. 973-290-4345 301 F
cwoodward@cse.edu
WOODWARD, David, B 920-748-8101 538 I
woodwardd@ripon.edu
WOODWARD,
Elisabeth, M .... 610-660-1242 434 G
ewoodwar@sju.edu
WOODWARD,
Gregory, S .... 262-551-5858 535 E
president@carthage.edu
WOODWARD, Holleigh . 828-669-8012 359 K
holleigh.woodward@montreat.edu
WOODWARD, John ...... 253-879-3375 527 F
woodward@pugetsound.edu
WOODWARD, Jonathan 228-896-2519 268 G
jonathan.woodward@mgccc.edu
WOODWARD, Kimberly 903-927-3254 497 G
kwoodward@wileyc.edu
WOODWARD, LouAnn .. 601-984-1010 270 H
lawoodward@umc.edu
WOODWARD, Scott ...... 206-543-2212 527 G
huskyad@uw.edu
WOODWARD, Scott ...... 210-341-1366 479 N
rsw@ost.edu
WOODWARD, Travis ..... 432-552-2806 495 F
woodward_t@utpb.edu
WOODWARD, Wade ..... 864-596-9072 445 E
wade.woodward@converse.edu
WOODWARD, Wendy .... 630-752-5656 163 G
wendy.woodward@wheaton.edu
WOODWORTH, Jody ..... 402-354-7000 291 P
jody.woodworth@methodistcollege.edu
WOODWORTH, Judith .. 215-965-4059 426 G
jwoodworth@moore.edu
WOODWORTH-NEY,
Laura .... 208-282-2171 138 C
woodlaur@isu.edu
WOODY, Craig .... 303-871-3588.. 86 H
cwoody@du.edu
WOODY, Jaime .... 512-863-1624 483 G
woodyj@southwestern.edu
WOODY, Jeannine, H ... 336-249-8186 362 B
jwoody@davidsonccc.edu
WOODY, Keith, W .... 425-602-3045 519 J
kwoody@bastyr.edu
WOODY, Pam .... 865-882-4501 463 F
woodypm@roanestate.edu
WOODY, Tammie .... 585-785-1274 325 E
tammie.woody@flcc.edu
WOODYARD, Steve .... 714-241-6240.. 40 B
WOOLARD, Emily .... 252-940-6204 360 B
emily.woolard@beaufortccc.edu
WOOLARD, Larry .... 217-732-3168 150 G
lwoolard@lincolnchristian.edu
WOOLBERT, Stephanie . 617-277-3915 224 D
woolberts@bgsp.edu
WOOLCOCK, Karen .... 787-766-1912 553 D
woolcock@inter.edu
WOOLCOTT, Thecla .... 913-385-7700 192 F
twoolcott@wrightcc.edu
WOOLDRIDGE,
Deborah, G .... 419-372-7851 377 I
dgwoold@bgsu.edu
WOOLDRIDGE, Heath .... 870-612-2039.. 24 G
heath.wooldridge@uaccb.edu
WOOLDRIDGE, James .. 951-222-8420.. 61 B
jim.wooldridge@rcc.edu
WOOLDRIDGE, Peter .... 919-536-7200 362 C
wooldridgep@durhamtech.edu
WOOLEVER, James .... 650-543-3757.. 54 B
jwoolever@menlo.edu
WOOLEY, Christine, A .. 240-895-4441 218 B
cawooley@smcm.edu
WOOLEY, Travis .... 407-303-9440.. 97 J
travis.wooley@adu.edu
WOOLF, Neil .... 509-359-6584 522 C
nwoolf@ewu.edu
WOOLF, Sarah .... 617-731-7083 235 F
woolfsar@pmc.edu
WOOLFOLK, Alan .... 904-819-6248 102 P
awoolfolk@flagler.edu
WOOLFOLK, Jerald .... 315-312-3214 346 A
jerald.woolfolk@oswego.edu
WOOLFORD, Ann .... 540-891-3051 515 E
awoolford@germanna.edu
WOOLIVER, Matt .... 918-293-4888 400 E
matt.wooliver@okstate.edu
WOOLLEN, Elizabeth, G 405-325-5141 403 I
lwoollen@ou.edu
WOOLLEY, Craig .... 937-775-4008 396 A
craig.woolley@wright.edu
WOOLLEY, Mark .... 718-409-7200 348 C
mwoolley@sunymaritime.edu
WOOLLEY, Peter .... 973-443-8084 302 H
woolley@fdu.edu
WOOLLEY, Rose, M ...... 412-578-6274 414 I
rmwoolley@carlow.edu
WOOLLISCROFT,
James, O .... 734-764-8175 251 C
woolli@umich.edu
WOOLMAN, Janet, R .... 337-475-5125 208 B
jwoolman@mcneese.edu
WOOLRIDGE, Cindy, B . 910-938-6145 361 F
burkhartc@coastalcarolina.edu
WOOLSEY, Andrew .... 949-480-4112.. 66 I
awoolsey@soka.edu
WOOLSEY, Clint .... 812-749-1440 171 I
cwoolsey@oak.edu
WOOLSEY, Roger, W .... 603-646-2215 297 G
roger.w.woolsey@dartmouth.edu
WOOLSTON, Paul (PJ) . 317-955-6307 171 A
pwoolston@marian.edu
WOOLSTON, William .... 410-287-1605 214 C
bwoolston@cecil.edu
WOOLWINE, Lora .... 304-384-5224 532 E
lwoolwine@concord.edu
WOON, Tommy .... 303-245-4613.. 84 B
twoon@naropa.edu
WOOSLEY, Wendy .... 417-864-7220 275 A
wwoosley@cci.edu
WOOST, Michael, G ..... 440-943-7600 391 A
mgwoost@yahoo.com
WOOSTER, Ginger .... 979-230-3210 469 G
ginger.wooster@brazosport.edu
WOOSTER, Phyllis, L .... 973-655-4212 304 A
woosterp@mail.montclair.edu
WOOSTER, Timothy, T .. 617-745-3707 225 H
timothy.t.wooster@enc.edu
WOOTEN, Bradley .... 847-635-1912 155 E
bwooten@oakton.edu
WOOTEN, Cornelius ..... 724-357-2202 431 A
Cornelius.Wooten@iup.edu
WOOTEN, Dean, A .... 757-352-4062 511 G
deanwoo@regent.edu
WOOTEN, Dolores .... 662-560-1105 269 E
dbwooten@northwestms.edu
WOOTEN, Jennifer, L ... 912-583-3208 121 H
jwooten@bpc.edu
WOOTEN, Manat .... 413-662-5332 230 C
m.wooten@mcla.edu
WOOTEN, Maria .... 901-751-8453 459 C
mwooten@mabts.edu
WOOTEN, Pam .... 662-562-3349 269 E
pwooten@northwestms.edu
WOOTEN, Randall .... 832-447-1331 487 G
randall.wooten@marshall.tstc.edu
WOOTEN, Rodney .... 304-865-6113 530 F
rodney.wooten@ovu.edu
WOOTEN, Sheila .... 973-748-9000 300 E
sheila_wooten@bloomfield.edu
WOOTEN, Susan .... 828-726-2233 360 F
swooten@cccti.edu
WOOTEN, Susan, B ...... 864-231-2151 443 E
swooten@andersonuniversity.edu
WOOTON, Chris .... 502-895-3411 198 E
cwooton@lpts.edu
WOOTTON, Katie .... 304-424-8203 533 E
katie.wootton@wvup.edu
WOOTTON, Tim .... 562-938-4072.. 51 A
twootton@lbcc.edu
WORD, John .... 559-791-2254.. 49 G
jword@portervillecollege.edu
WORDELL, Kathleen, A . 508-678-2811 231 B
kathleen.wordell@bristolcc.edu
WORDEN, Jeannie, M .. 715-675-3331 544 A
worden@ntc.edu
WORDEN, Jennifer .... 208-459-5307 137 J
jworden@collegeofidaho.edu
WORDEN, Jodi .... 509-527-4561 527 H
jodi.worden@wwcc.edu
WORDEN, Michael .... 845-341-4901 337 G
michael.worden@sunyorange.edu
WORDEN, Randy .... 559-453-7154.. 45 E
randy.worden@fresno.edu
WORDEN, Richard, B ... 315-568-3095 334 F
rworden@nycc.edu
WORDEN, Sylvia .... 714-432-5026.. 40 D
sworden@occ.cccd.edu
WORK, Christine .... 845-341-4763 337 G
christine.work@sunyorange.edu
WORK, Denise .... 402-552-2796 289 H
workdenise@clarksoncollege.edu
WORK, Galen, J .... 848-445-1747 307 C
gwork@rutgers.edu
WORK, Patricia .... 202-495-3835.. 96 E
assistant@dhs.edu
WORKMAN, Andrew, A 401-254-3030 442 C
aworkman@rwu.edu
WORKMAN, Christine ... 410-857-2267 217 A
cworkman@mcdaniel.edu
WORKMAN, Cindy, R ... 402-280-2969 290 B
cworkman@creighton.edu
WORKMAN, Greg .... 336-887-3000 358 E
gworkman@laureluniversity.edu
WORKMAN, Nikki .... 740-389-4636 386 B
workman@mtc.edu
WORKMAN, Sue, B .... 216-368-2000 378 J
WORKMAN, Tamara ..... 618-453-2903 159 H
tworkman@siu.edu
WORKU, Adu .... 707-965-6242.. 57 I
aworku@puc.edu
WORLAND, Brooke, A .. 317-738-8167 166 B
bworland@franklincollege.edu
WORLAND, Joe .... 641-784-5110 178 G
joew1@graceland.edu

WROBBEL, Karen .... 847-317-7178 161 B kwrobbel@tiu.edu
WROBEL, Deborah, R ... 443-412-2240 215 D dwrobel@harford.edu
WROBLEWSKI, Kathleen .... 413-565-1000 222 G kwroblew@baypath.edu
WRUCK, Craig .... 707-826-5101.. 35 D craig.wruck@humboldt.edu
WRUCK, Peter .... 507-389-7462 262 A peter.wruck@southcentral.edu
WU, Adam .... 909-593-3511.. 73 B awu@laverne.edu
WU, David .... 703-993-8776 507 K davidwu@gmu.edu
WU, Diana .... 510-642-4181.. 70 K dwu@unex.berkeley.edu
WU, Felix .... 518-442-3535 343 C fwu@albany.edu
WU, Frank, H .... 415-565-4700.. 71 B wuf@uchastings.edu
WU, Hannah .... 808-932-7381 135 I hannahwu@hawaii.edu
WU, Helen .... 262-554-3278 537 D helen_wu@yahoo.com
WU, Hong .... 804-523-5324 515 F hwu@reynolds.edu
WU, John .... 640-466-7900 162 K jwu@waubonsee.edu
WU, Jonathan .... 626-289-9004.. 26 G jwu@amu.edu
WU, Qianzhi .... 512-454-1188 468 A qwu@aoma.edu
WU, Richard .... 559-934-2231.. 76 A richardwu@whccd.edu
WU, Shao-Wei .... 845-848-7822 324 B shao-wei.wu@dc.edu
WU, Sonia .... 941-487-5000 115 B swu@ncf.edu
WU, Steven .... 626-571-5110.. 50 J stevenwu@les.edu
WU, Yenbo .... 415-338-1293.. 36 A ywu@sfsu.edu
WUBAH, Daniel .... 540-458-8418 519 A dwubah@wlu.edu
WUBBEN, Kris .... 608-822-2706 544 C kwubben@swtc.edu
WUCHENICH, Christopher, L .... 803-777-8400 450 B clw@mailbox.sc.edu
WUENSCHEL, Carol, M . 301-696-3556 215 E wuenschel@hood.edu
WUERTZ, John, A .... 319-352-8318 183 J john.wuertz@wartburg.edu
WUEST, Beth, E .... 512-245-8113 489 C bw09@txstate.edu
WULF, Lincoln .... 719-502-3178.. 84 J lincoln.wulf@ppcc.edu
WULFERT, Edelgard ...... 518-442-4654 343 C ewulfert@albany.edu
WULFF, Deborah .... 805-546-3122.. 42 H deborah_wulff@cuesta.edu
WULFF, Debra .... 908-835-2309 309 G dwulff@warren.edu
WUNDERLICH, Kathryn . 607-844-8222 350 A wunderk@tc3.edu
WUNDERLICH, Mark, E 518-388-8031 350 K wunderlm@union.edu
WUNDERLICH, Warren, P .... 507-933-7507 256 A wwunderl@gustavus.edu
WUNDERLY, Nancy .... 610-683-4060 431 B wunderly@kutztown.edu
WUNKER, Charles .... 863-638-2916 119 A wunkerc@webber.edu
WUNNAVA, Kalpana ..... 408-481-9988.. 47 A
WUNSCH, Mark .... 540-636-2900 506 H mwunsch@christendom.edu
WUNSCH, Michael .... 732-263-5355 303 G mwunsch@monmouth.edu
WUORI, Misti, L .... 701-788-4631 374 A Misti.Wuori@mayvillestate.edu
WURM, Sharon .... 775-673-7074 295 F swurm@tmcc.edu
WURMFELD, Claire .... 802-447-6310 503 A cwurmfeld@svc.edu
WURSTER, Paul, E .... 585-292-2814 333 G pwurster@monroecc.edu
WURTZ, Joseph .... 913-360-7500 184 K jwurtz@benedictine.edu
WURTZ, Keith .... 909-389-3206.. 62 B kwurtz@craftonhills.edu
WURTZEL, Barbara .... 413-755-4816 233 B bwurtzel@stcc.edu
WURTZEL, Julie, A .... 563-562-3263 181 F wurtzelj@nicc.edu
WURZER, Christine ...... 916-608-6645.. 53 A wurzerc@flc.losrios.edu
WUSTMAN, Brent .... 803-641-3293 450 C wustman-brent@aramark.com
WUTHRICH, Chris .... 208-426-1484 137 E chriswuthrich@boisestate.edu
WUTHRICH, Philip .... 979-532-6305 497 F philipw@wcjc.edu
WUTOH, Anthony .... 202-806-6530.. 96 B awutoh@howard.edu
WUTOH, Anthony, K ..... 202-806-2550.. 96 B awutoh@howard.edu
WUTOH, Rita .... 301-860-4170 220 B rwutoh@bowiestate.edu
WYAND, Diane, A .... 518-564-2130 346 B wyandda@plattsburgh.edu
WYANDOTTE, Annette, M .... 812-941-2208 169 A awyandot@ius.edu
WYATT, Adrian .... 903-730-4890 476 L awatts@jarvis.edu
WYATT, Ben .... 859-280-1246 198 B bwyatt@lextheo.edu
WYATT, Bill, J .... 540-568-4908 509 C wyattwj@jmu.edu
WYATT, Charles, W ...... 864-488-4603 447 F cwyatt@limestone.edu
WYATT, Clarence, R ..... 309-457-2127 153 B cwyatt@monmouthcollege.edu
WYATT, Danny .... 808-696-0714 136 G dwyatt@hawaii.edu
WYATT, Gary .... 620-341-5254 186 H gwyatt@emporia.edu
WYATT, Harry, E .... 804-828-9647 514 F hewyatt@vcu.edu
WYATT, Jan .... 603-668-6660 298 A
WYATT, Jimmy .... 865-471-7164 455 G jwyatt@cn.edu
WYATT, Joy, D .... 440-826-2180 377 D jwyatt@bw.edu
WYATT, Mark, A .... 951-343-4474.. 30 D mwyatt@calbaptist.edu
WYATT, Molly .... 252-985-5194 367 E mwyatt@ncwc.edu
WYATT, Robert, L .... 843-383-8010 445 A rwyatt@coker.edu
WYATT, Scott, L .... 435-586-7700 499 L
WYATT, Shay .... 801-832-2344 501 C swyatt@westminstercollege.edu
WYATT, Terri .... 804-257-5726 518 E vuu@bkstr.com
WYATT, Tracey .... 402-363-5675 294 G tlwyatt@york.edu
WYATT, Tracey, L .... 402-363-5675 294 G tlwyatt@york.edu
WYBAN, Bruce .... 310-434-4376.. 65 B wyban_bruce@smc.edu
WYBLE, Shannon .... 410-778-7200 221 D swyble2@washcoll.edu
WYBOURNE, Martin, N 603-646-4091 297 G martin.n.wybourne@dartmouth.edu
WYCH, Kyle .... 830-372-8066 487 C kwych@tlu.edu
WYCHE, Lynn .... 850-973-9404 109 C wychel@nfcc.edu
WYCHE, Sandy .... 972-860-4282 472 C swyche@dcccd.edu
WYCKOFF, Blaine, M .... 330-325-6191 387 F bwyckoff@neomed.edu
WYCKOFF, Harold .... 910-678-8287 362 E wyckoffh@faytechcc.edu
WYCKOFF, Steven .... 718-960-8720 319 C steven.wyckoff@lehman.cuny.edu
WYCO, Jeff .... 304-205-6611 531 A jeff.wyco@bridgevalley.edu
WYCOFF-HORN, Marcie 608-785-8127 539 G mwycoff-horn@uwlax.edu
WYDEN, Leon .... 419-448-3272 392 B wydenl@tiffin.edu
WYDER, Bruce .... 330-494-6170 391 J bwyder@starkstate.edu
WYETT, Megan .... 315-792-7530 348 D megan.wyett@sunyit.edu
WYKE, Rebecca .... 207-621-3403 212 D wyke@maine.edu
WYKES, Paul .... 508-793-7385 225 B pwykes@clarku.edu
WYKOFF, Dan .... 706-410-1129 123 F dan.wykoff@covenant.edu
WYKOFF, Randolph, F .. 423-439-4243 461 D wykoff@etsu.edu
WYLD, Jean, A .... 413-748-3959 236 H jwyld@springfieldcollege.edu
WYLIE, Amy .... 859-344-4069 200 C wyliea@thomasmore.edu
WYLIE, Brian .... 978-232-2440 226 C bwylie@endicott.edu
WYLIE, Kathrine .... 707-962-2662.. 41 C katherine-wylie@redwoods.edu
WYLIE, Michael .... 513-569-1492 379 K michael.wylie@cincinnatistate.edu
WYLIE, Richard, E .... 978-232-2001 226 C rwylie@endicott.edu
WYLIE, Rick .... 770-454-9270.. 96 H
WYMAN, J. Vernon ...... 401-874-2501 442 E jvern@uri.edu
WYMER, Cindy .... 423-461-8415 459 I clwymer@milligan.edu
WYMER, Greg .... 605-688-4482 454 C greg.wymer@sdstate.edu
WYND, Christine, A ..... 614-234-5800 386 N cwynd@mccn.edu
WYNDER, Robin .... 301-687-4050 220 D rwynder@frostburg.edu
WYNEGAR, Robert .... 775-445-4431 296 A robert.wynegar@wnc.edu
WYNES, David, L .... 404-727-3889 124 D david.wynes@emory.edu
WYNES, Tim .... 651-423-8213 258 E tim.wyes@dctc.edu
WYNES, Timothy .... 651-450-3641 259 A twynes@inverhills.edu
WYNN, Amanda .... 757-352-4148 511 G amanwyn@regent.edu
WYNN, Bobby, C .... 910-672-1232 370 A bwynn@uncfsu.edu
WYNN, Curt, J .... 757-822-1460 517 C cjwynn@tcc.edu
WYNN, Denise, Y .... 919-530-7331 370 C dwynn3@nccu.edu
WYNN, Deryl .... 913-288-7180 188 G dwynn@kckcc.edu
WYNN, Hal .... 334-386-7285.... 3 I hwynn@faulkner.edu
WYNN, Keren .... 229-333-2103 134 I keren.wynn@wiregrass.edu
WYNN, Renell .... 703-993-9511 507 K rwynn3@gmu.edu
WYNN, Sandra .... 304-327-4213 532 D swynn@bluefieldstate.edu
WYNN, Steve .... 617-746-1990 227 G steve.wynn@hult.edu
WYNNE, Joe .... 713-221-2799 491 F wynnejo@uhd.edu
WYNNE, Joshua .... 701-777-2516 373 G joshua.wynne@med.und.edu
WYNNE, Joshua .... 701-777-2514 373 G joshua.wynne@med.und.edu
WYNTER, Cadence .... 949-582-4958.. 67 F cwynter@saddleback.edu
WYONT, Kimberly .... 704-922-6482 362 G wyont.kimberly@gaston.edu
WYPISZYNSKI, Gregory 920-424-0007 540 B wypiszyn@uwosh.edu
WYRICK, Cheryl .... 909-869-2400.. 32 F crwyrick@cpp.edu
WYRICK, Chris .... 479-575-6800.. 23 G cwyrick1@uark.edu
WYRICK, Kathleen .... 907-564-8265.. 10 D kwyrick@alaskapacific.edu
WYSE, Joe .... 530-242-7510.. 66 C jwyse@shastacollege.edu
WYSOCKI, Barbara .... 630-515-6321 152 H bwysoc@midwestern.edu
WYSOCKI, Joseph, T ..... 815-740-2274 162 F jwysocki@stfrancis.edu
WYSOCKI, Sheree .... 727-873-4195 116 C wysocki@usfsp.edu
WYSOGLAD, Anne .... 773-481-8634 142 D awysoglad@ccc.edu
WYSONG, James .... 813-253-7236 106 C rwysong@hccfl.edu
WYSTEPEK, Christopher .... 413-782-1794 238 A christopher.wystepek@wne.edu

X

XANTHOS, Christopher . 619-594-6018.. 35 E cxanthos@mail.sdsu.edu
XAVIER, Bob .... 617-912-9148 224 C bxavier@bostonconservatory.edu
XIANG, Yun .... 503-915-6118 223 C yun.xiang@becker.edu
XIE, Jin Hua .... 262-554-2010 537 D drj-xie@yahoo.com
XIE, Ping .... 718-405-3733 322 A ping.xie@mountsaintvincent.edu
XIMENEZ, David .... 817-515-5354 484 B david.ximenez@tccd.edu
XIMINES, Sheryl, H ...... 919-516-4343 368 E sximines@st-aug.edu
XIONG, Joua .... 414-326-2334 535 H joua.xiong@ccon.edu
XIONG-CHAN, Mai Nhia .... 651-523-2440 256 B mxiongchan01@hamline.edu
XIPPOLITOS, Lee .... 631-444-3549 344 C lee.xippolitos@stonybrook.edu
XIRINACHS, Susan .... 207-947-4591 209 G sxirinachs@bealcollege.edu
XU, Jackie .... 202-274-5545.. 97 B jxu@udc.edu
XU, Shuli .... 508-373-5640 233 E shuli.xu@mcphs.edu
XU, Wenying .... 904-256-7030 106 Q wxu@ju.edu

Y

YACAVONE, Mark .... 607-753-4711 345 C mark.yacavone@cortland.edu
YACKEE, Grace, B .... 734-384-4221 247 C gyackee@monroeccc.edu
YACYNYCH, Holly .... 610-799-1718 424 A hyacynych@lccc.edu
YADEGAR, Mahvash ..... 310-662-2101.. 55 J myadegar@nu.edu
YAEAGER, Mona .... 312-944-0882 150 D ryaeger@chicago.chefs.edu
YAEGER, Evelyn .... 810-762-9782 245 A eyaeger@kettering.edu
YAEGER, John, W .... 202-685-0080 547 M yaegerj@ndu.edu
YAEGER, Lisa .... 802-485-2075 502 G lyaeger@norwich.edu
YAGER, David .... 831-459-4940.. 72 E yager@ucsc.edu
YAGIL, Oren .... 717-736-4102 420 D oyagil@hacc.edu
YAGNITINSKY, Roman .. 800-955-2527 187 E ryagnitinsky@grantham.edu
YAHNG, Charles .... 314-529-9312 277 B cyahng@maryville.edu
YAHNKE, Eric .... 503-838-8459 411 B yahnkee@wou.edu
YAHR, Scott .... 907-745-3201.. 10 B syahr@akbible.edu
YAHYAZADEH, Bizhan .. 802-485-2145 502 G bizhan@norwich.edu
YAKLICH, Richard .... 305-430-1167 104 B Richard.Yaklich@fmuniv.edu
YAKOVLEV, Ilya .... 262-595-2010 540 C yakovlev@uwp.edu
YAKOWICZ, William ..... 201-612-5253 300 B wyakowicz@bergen.edu
YAKSHE, Patti, L .... 412-281-2600 433 A
YALE, Amanda, A .... 724-738-2011 432 A amanda.yale@sru.edu
YALE, Janet .... 402-557-7095 289 B janet.yale@bellevue.edu
YALOWITZ, Daniel .... 802-258-3178 502 I daniel.yalowitz@sit.edu
YAM, Marylou .... 410-532-5300 217 F
YAMADA, Emiko .... 650-508-3749.. 56 H eyamada@ndnu.edu
YAMADA, Frank, M .... 773-947-6301 152 A fyamada@mccormick.edu
YAMAGATA-NOJI, Audrey .... 909-274-4505.. 54 J ayamagat@mtsac.edu
YAMAGUCHI, Steve ...... 626-584-5370.. 45 F steveyamaguchi@fuller.edu
YAMAKAWA, Lynn .... 310-233-4387.. 51 F yamakalm@lahc.edu
YAMAMOTO, Catherine . 402-472-7749 293 H cyamamoto1@unl.edu
YAMAMOTO, Cindy .... 808-984-3288 136 H cindy@hawaii.edu
YAMAMOTO, Howard .... 707-654-1275.. 34 B HYamamoto@csum.edu
YAMAMOTO, June, Y .... 909-389-3216.. 62 B jyamamoto@craftonhills.edu
YAMAMOTO, Kayoko ..... 831-476-9424.. 44 L studentaccounts@fivebranches.edu
YAMAMOTO, Lance .... 808-956-5148 136 B lance@hawaii.edu
YAMAMOTO, Louise ...... 808-734-9513 136 C yamamotl@hawaii.edu
YAMAMURA, Whitney ... 916-691-7326.. 52 J yamamuw@crc.losrios.edu
YAMANE, Noreen, R ...... 808-934-2504 136 D noreeny@hawaii.edu
YAMASE, Universe .... 691-320-2480 549 D uyamase@comfsm.fm
YAMAUCHI, Kent .... 626-585-7995.. 58 F ktyamauchi@pasadena.edu
YAMBA, A. Zachary .... 973-877-3022 302 F yamba@essex.edu
YAMBA, Mohamed .... 724-938-4240 430 C yamba@calu.edu
YAMEEN, Deanna .... 508-588-9100 232 A
YAMIL AVILA, Julio .... 787-725-8120 552 G jyamil@eap.edu
YAMILKOSKI, Vince, J . 770-534-6134 121 G vyamilkoski@brenau.edu
YAMPOLSKY, Chana ..... 212-964-2830 332 G cpy145@aol.com
YAMRICK, Emmalyn ...... 212-774-0740 332 A eyamrick@mmm.edu
YAMIN, Isabel .... 787-728-1515 559 A iyamin@sagrado.edu
YAN, Ruth .... 319-226-2080 175 D Ruth.Yan@AllenCollege.edu
YANCEY, Deborah .... 540-857-7986 517 E dyancey@virginiawestern.edu

YANCEY, Jennifer, L ..... 361-582-2519 496 D jennifer.yancey@victoriacollege.edu
YANCHAK, Frank .... 614-947-6723 382 H frank.yanchak@franklin.edu
YANCHAK, Frank .... 937-484-1353 394 F fyanchak@urbana.edu
YANCKELLO, Robert ..... 407-823-2711 115 C bob.yanckello@ucf.edu
YANCY, Chad .... 205-929-3497.... 5 E cyancy@lawsonstate.edu
YANDA, Wayne .... 619-482-6414.. 68 D wyanda@swccd.edu
YANES, Kenneth .... 212-484-1339 319 F kyanes@jjay.cuny.edu
YANEZ, Mercedes .... 310-233-4127.. 51 F yanezm@lahc.edu
YANG, Alice .... 831-459-2328.. 72 E ayang@ucsc.edu
YANG, Chuayi .... 715-425-3531 540 E chuayi.yang@uwrf.edu
YANG, Don .... 770-279-0507 124 F dyang@gcuniv.edu
YANG, Faxian .... 908-526-1200 305 G Faxian.Yang@raritanval.edu
YANG, Henry, T .... 805-893-2231.. 72 D henry.yang@ucsb.edu
YANG, Hong .... 401-232-6885 441 B hyang@bryant.edu
YANG, Honggang .... 954-262-3016 109 E yangh@nsu.nova.edu
YANG, Neng .... 503-838-8590 411 B yangn@wou.edu
YANG, Nicole .... 920-693-1120 543 B nicole.yang@gotoltc.edu
YANG, Olivia .... 509-335-5571 528 B olivia.yang@wsu.edu
YANG, Olivia .... 509-335-5524 528 B olivia.yang@wsu.edu
YANG, Paul .... 626-448-0023.. 48 C
YANG, Philip .... 408-532-5567.. 56 C
YANG, Richard .... 916-558-2376.. 53 B YangR@scc.losrios.edu
YANG, Sixian .... 719-549-2110.. 81 F sixian.yang@csupueblo.edu
YANG, Steve .... 651-450-3330 259 A syang@inverhills.edu
YANG, Thy .... 320-308-4287 261 E tyang3@stcloudstate.edu
YANG, Xiaoyun .... 336-770-1457 372 B yangx@uncsa.edu
YANG, Zhanjun .... 954-776-4476 107 F zyang@keiseruniversity.edu
YANISH, Paula .... 970-339-6537.. 78 J paula.yanish@aims.edu
YANKELEWITZ, Yoel ..... 718-846-1940 353 L yyankelewitz@gmail.com
YANKELITIS, Wendy ..... 570-348-6201 425 D yankelitis@marywood.edu
YANKEY, Terry, L .... 606-474-3222 195 F tly@kcu.edu
YANNI, Stephen .... 906-248-8478 240 J syanni@bmcc.edu
YANNICK, Lisa .... 610-436-3075 432 B lyannick@wcupa.edu
YANNIELLO, Michael, C .... 516-876-3146 345 E yanniellom@oldwestbury.edu
YANNUZZI, Raymond ... 856-227-7200 301 A ryannuzzi@camdencc.edu
YAO, Chunmei .... 910-775-4375 371 D
YAO, Min .... 858-534-3396.. 72 B myao@ucsd.edu
YAQUB, Samia .... 530-895-2484.. 30 B yaqubsa@butte.edu
YARABECK, John .... 936-294-1785 489 A slo_jxy@shsu.edu
YARBROUGH, David ..... 707-546-4000.. 43 J dyarbrough@empirecollege.com
YARBROUGH, David ..... 337-482-1015 208 F yarbrough@louisiana.edu
YARBROUGH, Denise ... 585-275-4321 351 D dyarbrough@admin.rochester.edu
YARBROUGH, Ernest .... 216-687-2048 380 D e.b.yarbrough@csuohio.edu
YARBROUGH, Joannie .. 706-295-6328 125 C jyarbrou@highlands.edu
YARBROUGH, John ...... 706-865-2134 132 G jyarbrough@truett.edu
YARBROUGH, Kenny .... 615-230-3443 464 B kenny.yarbrough@volstate.edu
YARBROUGH, Laura ..... 870-762-1020.. 19 C
YARBROUGH, Laura ..... 870-762-3105.. 19 C lyarbrough@smail.anc.edu
YARBROUGH, Laura, L . 336-249-8186 362 B llyarbro@davidsoncc.edu
YARBROUGH, Mark, M 214-887-5011 473 E myarbrough@dts.edu
YARBROUGH, Nancy, J 731-881-7800 465 F nyarbrough@utm.edu
YARBROUGH, Scott ...... 843-863-7563 444 B syarbrou@csuniv.edu
YARDLEY, Katherine, W 207-778-7154 212 E kyardley@maine.edu
YARDLEY, Owen .... 402-472-8809 293 H oyardley2@unl.edu
YARGICI, Rosemary ...... 254-526-1302 470 E ctc.international@ctcd.edu
YARKIN, Cherisa .... 206-934-6903 526 A cherisa.yarkin@seattlecolleges.edu
YARLOTT, JR., David .... 406-638-3107 286 I davidyarlott@lbhc.edu
YARNELL, Ellen .... 503-552-1528 407 F eyarnell@ncnm.edu
YARNELL, Thomas, V ... 614-823-1502 390 C tyarnell@otterbein.edu
YAROSLASKI, Paul .... 620-227-9324 186 F dolphins@dc3.edu
YARRISH, James .... 215-895-1114 438 E j.yarris@usciences.edu
YARRISH, Julie .... 310-434-3762.. 65 B yarrish_julie@smc.edu
YARRISH, Karen .... 570-945-8516 422 B karen.yarrish@keystone.edu
YARSIAH, James .... 803-780-1264 451 G jyarsiah@voorhees.edu
YARWORTH, Joseph ..... 610-921-6758 411 E jyarworth@albright.edu
YASBIN, Ronald .... 314-516-5504 284 B yasbinr@umsl.edu
YASINSAC, Alec .... 251-460-6390.... 9 F yasinsac@southalabama.edu
YASSKY, David .... 914-422-4407 337 I dyassky@pace.edu
YASUDA, Cathy .... 541-881-5585 410 D cyasuda@tvcc.cc
YASUDA, Jon .... 626-584-5491.. 45 F jyasuda@fuller.edu
YASUHARA, June .... 808-739-4603 135 A jyasuhar@chaminade.edu
YASUKOCHI, Dennis ..... 206-934-5660 525 K dennis.yasukochi@seattlecolleges.edu
YATER, Ann .... 317-917-5915 169 L aniebrug@ivytech.edu
YATES, Brian .... 434-592-4108 509 G bcyates@liberty.edu
YATES, Cheryl .... 812-749-1416 171 I cyates@oak.edu
YATES, Dorothy, C .... 307-766-5320 546 K dyates4@uwyo.edu
YATES, Frances .... 765-973-8470 168 A fyates@iue.edu
YATES, Jacob .... 606-337-4524 194 F registrar@ccbbc.edu
YATES, Kristin .... 402-472-5242 293 F kyates@nebraska.edu
YATES, Latoro .... 718-262-2188 321 B lyates@york.cuny.edu
YATES, Liz .... 610-861-1503 426 H yatese@moravian.edu
YATES, Mark .... 903-923-2339 473 I myates@etbu.edu
YATES, Marvin, L .... 985-549-5250 208 E myates@selu.edu
YATES, Sandra .... 202-274-7050.. 97 B syates@udc.edu
YATES, Travis, W .... 662-915-7274 270 G twyates@olemiss.edu
YATES, Vivian, M .... 216-987-4468 381 A vivian.yates@tri-c.edu
YATOOMA, Chris .... 916-660-7600.. 66 E cyatooma@sierracollege.edu
YATS, Kirk, M .... 989-774-3674 240 O yats1km@cmich.edu
YAU, Lishan .... 864-294-3609 446 F lishan.yau@furman.edu
YAU, Tow, Y .... 513-556-0648 393 B tow.yau@uc.edu
YAUN, John .... 909-537-5000.. 35 A
YAUN, John .... 304-696-3152 532 H yaun@marshall.edu
YAUNEY, Alan, J .... 518-381-1256 342 E yauneyaj@sunysccc.edu
YAVNEH, Naomi .... 504-865-7330 206 A yavneh@loyno.edu
YAW, Edward, J .... 973-328-5031 301 G eyaw@ccm.edu
YAZDANI, Linda .... 303-914-6536.. 85 C linda.yazdani@rrcc.edu
YAZDI, Aliakbar, R .... 205-853-1200.... 5 C ayazdi@jeffstateonline.com
YBANEZ, Elsa .... 210-436-3725 481 C eybanez@stmarytx.edu
YBARRA, Kathy .... 206-296-2810 526 F ybarrak@seattleu.edu
YBARRA, Nancy .... 925-473-7405.. 42 F nybarra@losmedanos.edu
YBARRA, Tomas .... 509-574-4640 529 B tybarra@yvcc.edu
YE, Eugene .... 630-942-3821 142 F yee8@cod.edu
YEAGER, Andrew .... 716-880-2336 332 B ayeager@medaille.edu
YEAGER, Cody .... 541-888-7312 410 A cody.yeager@socc.edu
YEAGER, David .... 812-866-7075 166 E yeagerd@hanover.edu
YEAGER, Ed .... 480-732-7177.. 14 K Ed.Yeager@cgc.edu
YEAGER, Eric .... 432-335-6412 479 O eyeager@odessa.edu
YEAGER, Phyllis .... 859-442-1150 196 A phyllis.yeager@kctcs.edu
YEAGER, Randy .... 504-816-4131 202 F ryeager@dillard.edu
YEAGER, Robert, E .... 812-749-1210 171 I ryeager@oak.edu
YEAGLEY, JR., William . 989-774-3081 240 O yeagl1b@cmich.edu
YEAKLEY, Randy .... 325-649-8804 475 F ryeakley@hputx.edu
YEAROUT, Danielle .... 785-594-4597 184 F danielle.yearout@bakeru.edu
YEAROUT, Teresa, A ..... 276-964-7266 517 A teresa.yearout@sw.edu
YEARWOOD, George, A 919-508-2035 373 B ryearwood@peace.edu
YEARWOOD, Jody .... 478-387-4846 125 E jyearwood@gmc.edu
YEARWOOD, Jody .... 478-387-4233 125 E jyearwood@gmc.edu
YEARWOOD, Robinette . 802-447-4678 503 A ryearwood@svc.edu
YEATER, Michael .... 409-882-3342 488 G mike.yeater@lsco.edu
YEATMAN, Arla .... 828-669-8012 359 K ayeatman@montreat.edu
YEATS, John Mark .... 816-414-3731 278 E jmyeats@mbts.edu
YEATTS, Debra .... 910-630-7385 359 C dyeatts@methodist.edu
YEATTS, Dewey .... 240-567-7356 217 B dewey.yeatts@montgomerycollege.edu
YEBEI, Philemon .... 765-455-9291 168 B pyebei@iuk.edu
YEBOAH, Barima .... 718-405-3414 322 A barima.yeboah@mountsaintvincent.edu
YEBOAH, Yaw .... 850-410-6258 115 A yyeboah@eng.fsu.edu
YECKE, Cheri .... 501-279-4335.. 21 A checke@harding.edu
YEE, Alice .... 818-364-7866.. 51 G YeeAM@lamission.edu
YEE, David .... 415-239-3669.. 39 A dyee@ccsf.edu
YEE, Diane .... 212-229-5900 334 C yeed@newschool.edu
YEE, Sandra, G .... 313-577-4059 252 G sandra.yee@wayne.edu
YEH, Robert .... 315-792-7116 348 D robert.yeh@sunyit.edu
YEHL, Robert, F .... 870-230-5014.. 21 B yehlb@hsu.edu
YEHUDAH, Shoshana ... 646-565-6000 350 C shulys@touro.edu
YEIGH, Bjong, W .... 425-352-5221 527 G yeigh@uwb.edu
YEISER, Jimmie .... 870-460-1033.. 24 C yeiserj@uamont.edu
YEISER, Linda .... 870-460-1028.. 24 C yeiser@uamont.edu
YEKOVICH, Robert .... 713-348-4837 480M yekovr@rice.edu
YELKUR, Rama .... 989-964-4064 249 G ryelkur@svsu.edu
YELLE, Dave .... 413-565-1000 222 G dyelle@baypath.edu
YELLE, Richard, W .... 203-576-4222.. 92 B ryelle@bridgeport.edu
YELLEN, David, N .... 312-915-7838 151 E dyellen@luc.edu
YELLMAN, Kim .... 301-934-2251 214 E kyellman@csmd.edu
YELNOSKY, Michael, J . 401-254-4509 442 C myelnosky@law.rwu.edu
YELNOSKY, Robert, E ... 814-641-3707 421 L yelnosr@juniata.edu
YELTON, Kristen .... 636-481-3296 276 E kyelton@jeffco.edu
YELVINGTON, Philip, R 901-321-3396 455 I pyelving@cbu.edu
YEN, Charlie .... 310-434-3002.. 65 B yen_charlie@smc.edu
YEN, David .... 607-436-3458 344 B david.yen@oneonta.edu
YEN, Jion .... 815-838-5640 150 F yenji@lewisu.edu
YEN, Johanna, C .... 954-763-9840.. 98 L atom@atom.edu
YEN, S.C. Max .... 260-481-6839 168 D yens@ipfw.edu
YENCHA, Matthew .... 610-606-4666 415 A myencha@cedarcrest.edu
YENCHA, Tom .... 304-424-8309 533 E tom.yencha@wvup.edu
YENCHO, Thomas .... 610-409-3491 438 H tyencho@ursinus.edu
YENTES, Matt .... 863-638-2963 119 A yentesms@webber.edu
YEO, Frances .... 850-484-1795 110 D fyeo@pensacolastate.edu
YEO, Frederick, L .... 920-424-3322 540 B yeof@uwosh.edu
YEOM, Kyong, S .... 636-327-4645 278 D finance@midwest.edu
YEOM, Kyong, S .... 636-327-4645 278 D iss@midwest.edu
YEOM, Kyong, S .... 636-327-4645 278 D yeom900@gmail.com
YEOMANS, Jennifer ...... 603-888-1311 298 E jyeomans@rivier.edu
YEONOPOLUS, Jim .... 254-526-1781 470 E jim.yeonopolus@ctcd.edu
YEP, Katie .... 651-846-1372 261 G katie.yep@saintpaul.edu
YEPES, Hernan .... 203-332-5017.. 89 C hyepes@housatonic.edu
YEPES, Maria, E .... 323-265-8957.. 51 D yepesme@elac.edu
YEPES, Maria Elena ...... 323-265-8957.. 51 D yepesme@elac.edu
YERDON, Wayne .... 419-559-2341 392 A wyerdon@terra.edu
YERGEN, Norman .... 951-785-2307.. 49 I nyergen@lasierra.edu
YERGER, Mark, E .... 570-577-1795 413 E mark.yerger@bucknell.edu
YERIAN, Diane .... 540-568-8090 509 C yeriandg@jmu.edu
YERK, Melanie .... 941-907-2262 102 N myerk@evergladesuniversity.edu
YESTRAMSKI, Joanne .... 978-934-2206 229 A Joanne_Yestramski@uml.edu
YETMAN, Barbara, H ..... 215-968-8045 413 F yetmanb@bucks.edu
YETMAR, Theresa .... 785-594-8316 184 F theresa.yetmar@bakeru.edu
YEVICH, Nicolette .... 660-248-6255 272 N nyevich@centralmethodist.edu
YEW, Phillip .... 213-487-0110.. 43 E chinese@dula.edu
YIANILOS, Chris .... 571-858-3005 518 B chrisyianilos@vt.edu
YIANOUKOS, Steven, J 315-268-6622 321 C stevey@clarkson.edu
YIGZAW, Erika .... 503-244-0726 404 G erikayigzaw@achs.edu
YIH, T. C .... 239-590-7021 114 F tcyih@fgcu.edu
YILIBUW, Dolores .... 859-280-1224 198 B dyilibuw@lextheo.edu
YIM, Mee So .... 919-658-7763 369 B myim@umo.edu
YIN, Carol .... 706-880-8339 127 N cyin@lagrange.edu
YIN, Kong .... 713-221-8975 491 F YinK@uhd.edu
YING, Amber .... 800-280-0307 163 I amber-nicole.ying@ace.edu
YING, Robin L, P .... 757-822-1970 517 C rying@tcc.edu
YINGLING, Julie, R .... 419-434-4550 393 F yinglingj@findlay.edu
YINGLING, Kevin, W .... 304-696-3170 532 H yingling@marshall.edu
YIP, Koyuki .... 610-526-6004 420 C kyip@harcum.edu
YIP, Leanna .... 718-997-5590 320 E leanna.yip@qc.cuny.edu
YITZCHAK, Hertzel .... 847-982-2500 146 A yitzchak@htc.edu
YLINEN, Jeff .... 612-374-5800 255 G jylinen@dunwoody.edu
YOACHIM, Ann .... 423-425-4111 465 E ann-yoachim@utc.edu
YOACHIM, Maureen ...... 610-740-3725 415 A bookstore@cedarcrest.edu
YOAKUM, Cole .... 248-218-2042 249 D cyoakum@rc.edu
YOAKUM, Katrina, M ... 785-864-3261 191 G kyoakum@ku.edu
YOANNONE, Carol .... 412-237-4421 415 G cyoannone@ccac.edu
YOCHUM, Denise .... 253-964-6776 525 C dyochum@pierce.ctc.edu
YOCKEY, Denton, J ...... 904-276-6839 111 K dentonyockey@sjrstate.edu
YOCKEY, Glenn .... 830-372-8040 487 C gyockey@tlu.edu
YOCOM, Amber .... 419-267-1317 387 G ayocom@northweststate.edu
YOCOM, Jim .... 574-520-4806 168 F jyocom@iusb.edu

YOCUM, Carrie, A .... 574-372-5100 166 D yocumca@grace.edu
YODER, Brent .... 620-327-8207 187 H brent.yoder@hesston.edu
YODER, Dan .... 541-440-4600 410 E dan.yoder@umpqua.edu
YODER, Donna, K .... 814-886-6368 427 B dyoder@mtaloy.edu
YODER, James, A .... 508-289-2252 238 F jyoder@whoi.edu
YODER, John .... 903-877-7443 495 C john.yoder@uthct.edu
YODER, Joseph, S .... 570-326-3761 429 J jyoder@pct.edu
YODER, Julie .... 301-387-3101 215 A julie.yoder@garrettcollege.edu
YODER, Kathleen .... 574-535-7501 166 C kathleeny@goshen.edu
YODER, Kathy .... 330-287-1224 389 B yoder.332@osu.edu
YODER, Mari .... 419-267-1268 387 G myoder@northweststate.edu
YODER, Mindy, J .... 260-399-7700 174 C myoder@sf.edu
YODER, Norris .... 828-328-7145 358 G norris.yoder@lr.edu
YODER, Robert, E .... 574-535-7244 166 C robertey@goshen.edu
YODER, Twila, K .... 540-432-4100 507 A yodertk@emu.edu
YOHANNES, Paulos .... 678-891-2876 125 G paulos.yohannes@gpc.edu
YOHE, Roger .... 480-461-7325.. 15 A roger.yohe@mesacc.edu
YOHN, Richard, V .... 303-963-3485.. 79 L ryohn@ccu.edu
YOHNK, Dean .... 715-234-8176 541 E dean.yohnk@uwc.edu
YOHO, Robert .... 515-271-1464 177 H robert.yoho@dmu.edu
YOHO, Vicki, G .... 419-289-5031 377 A vyoho@ashland.edu
YOIA, Dominic .... 203-582-5224.. 91 E dominic.yoia@quinnipiac.edu
YOKITIS, Maria .... 904-256-8000 106 Q mpelleg@ju.edu
YOKLIC, Deborah .... 520-206-4650.. 17 A dyoklic@pima.edu
YOKOYAMA, Janis, K ... 213-738-6714.. 68 E deansoffice@swlaw.edu
YOKUM, Dru .... 410-296-5350 219 A
YOLITZ, Brian, D .... 651-201-1777 257 N brian.yolitz@so.mnscu.edu
YONAN, Jonathan .... 610-225-5704 418 A jyonan@eastern.edu
YONEMITSU, Lori .... 206-546-4552 526 G lyonemitsu@shoreline.edu
YONG, Henry, C .... 408-270-6471.. 63 P henry.yong@evc.edu
YONG, Yanyan .... 540-834-1048 515 E yyong@germanna.edu
YONKE, Eric .... 715-346-3693 541 A eyonke@uwsp.edu
YONKERS, Molly, L ...... 507-933-7588 256 A myunkers@gustavus.edu
YONTZ, Jennifer .... 231-591-3817 242 L JenniferYontz@ferris.edu
YOOK, JungMo .... 714-525-0088.. 46 D gmu@gm.edu
YOON, Mary .... 213-384-2318.. 52 G
YOON, Michelle .... 562-926-1023.. 60 B mhyoon@ptsa.edu
YOPP, Jan .... 919-966-4364 371 A jan_yopp@unc.edu
YORK, Barry .... 412-731-6000 433 K byork@rpts.edu
YORK, Brenda .... 406-994-2824 287 G byork@montana.edu
YORK, Corey .... 914-251-6080 346 D corey.york@purchase.edu
YORK, David .... 512-492-3032 468 A dyork@aoma.edu
YORK, Kathy, E .... 540-985-8356 509 D KECochenour@jchs.edu
YORK, Patrick .... 660-944-2920 273 E pyork@conception.edu
YORK, Stan .... 912-681-5667 129 E syork@ogeecheetech.edu
YORK, Tammy .... 805-922-6966.. 26 H tyork@hancockcollege.edu
YORK-LANGSTON, Aaron .... 903-875-7328 479 I aaron.york@navarrocollege.edu
YORK-LEMELIN, Lisa .... 207-453-5128 211 B lyork@kvcc.me.edu
YORKER, Beatrice .... 323-343-4600.. 34 A byorker@calstatela.edu
YORKIN, Sheila .... 801-832-2685 501 C syorkin@westminstercollege.edu
YORKOWITZ, Johnathan .... 325-670-1026 474 M johnathan.yorkowitz@hsutx.edu
YORTSOS, Yannis, C .... 213-740-0617.. 74 D yortsos@usc.edu
YOSHIDA, James, M .... 808-934-2508 136 D jamesyos@hawaii.edu
YOSHIMI, Garrett .... 808-956-3501 135 H gyoshimi@hawaii.edu
YOSHIMORI-YAMAMOTO, Denise .... 808-956-0864 136 B dfyoshim@hawaii.edu
YOSHIMURA, Marlys .... 408-453-9900.. 46 L myoshimura@henley-putnam.edu
YOSHIMURA, Nancy ..... 949-480-4045.. 66 I nyoshimura@soka.edu
YOSHIMURA, Takuya .... 808-983-4105 135 D tyoshimura@tokai.edu
YOSHINA, Eileen .... 360-596-5383 527 B eyoshina@spscc.edu
YOSHINO, Lori .... 909-621-8856.. 59 F lori_yoshino@pitzer.edu
YOSHIOKA, Marianne ... 413-585-7977 236 G myoshioka@smith.edu
YOUATT, June, P .... 517-355-1524 246 H youatt@msu.edu
YOUGH, Kelly .... 845-569-3184 333 I kelly.yough@msmc.edu
YOUHOUSE, John .... 610-558-5518 427 D youhousej@neumann.edu
YOUKEY, Jerry, R .... 864-455-7992 450 G jyoukeymd@ghs.org
YOUKEY, Jerry, R .... 864-455-7880 450 B youkey@mailbox.sc.edu
YOUMANS, Jacob .... 512-313-3000 471 H jacob.youmans@concordia.edu
YOUMANS, Karen .... 405-208-5680 400 A kdyoumans@okcu.edu
YOUNG, Aaron .... 505-984-6140 312 J aaron.young@sjc.edu
YOUNG, Al .... 205-929-3424.... 5 E ayoung@lawsonstate.edu
YOUNG, Alissa .... 270-707-3717 196 D alissa.young@kctcs.edu
YOUNG, Allene .... 510-981-2908.. 58 J ayoung@peralta.edu
YOUNG, Amber .... 256-824-6604.... 9 A Amber.Young@uah.edu
YOUNG, Andrew .... 812-888-4323 174 F ayoung@vinu.edu
YOUNG, Ann, S .... 859-238-5480 194 E ann.young@centre.edu
YOUNG, Barbara .... 626-966-4576.. 27 I
YOUNG, Barbara .... 662-562-3202 269 E ba_young@northwestms.edu
YOUNG, Benjamin .... 317-916-7918 169 L byoung@ivytech.edu
YOUNG, Beth .... 815-825-2086 149 E beth.young@kishwaukeecollege.edu
YOUNG, Betty .... 478-553-2090 129 C byoung@oftc.edu
YOUNG, Betty .... 740-753-3591 383 G
YOUNG, Betty, K .... 713-718-7628 475 C betty.young@hccs.edu
YOUNG, Bradley, J .... 310-233-4066.. 51 F youngbj@lahc.edu
YOUNG, Brandon .... 217-540-3512 150 B byoung17159@lakeland.cc.il.us
YOUNG, Brandon, L .... 386-226-7245 102 B youngbr@erau.edu
YOUNG, Brenda .... 907-277-1000.. 10 E brenda.young@chartercollege.edu
YOUNG, Brian .... 719-389-6870.. 79 M bay@coloradocollege.edu
YOUNG, C. Bryan .... 785-864-4225 191 G cbyoung@ku.edu
YOUNG, Cathy .... 617-912-9139 224 C cyoung@bostonconservatory.edu
YOUNG, Charles .... 203-596-4604.. 91 D cyoung@post.edu
YOUNG, Charles .... 336-334-4822 363 A hcyoung@gtcc.edu
YOUNG, Cheryl .... 409-933-8232 471 B cyoung@com.edu
YOUNG, Cheryl, D .... 513-529-8600 386 K youngcd@miamioh.edu
YOUNG, Christopher .... 219-980-6563 168 C cjy@iun.edu
YOUNG, Colletta .... 541-956-7296 409 F cyoung@roguecc.edu
YOUNG, Connie .... 217-709-0931 150 C cyoung@lakeviewcol.edu
YOUNG, Corey, D .... 601-877-4063 266 C cyoung1@alcorn.edu
YOUNG, Dana .... 541-881-5580 410 D dyoung@tvcc.cc
YOUNG, Danene .... 937-708-5710 395 E dyoung@wilberforce.edu
YOUNG, Danielle .... 440-775-8692 388 B danielle.young@oberlin.edu
YOUNG, Darlene, P ...... 812-941-2306 169 A dyoung01@ius.edu
YOUNG, David .... 405-974-2490 403 G dyoung28@uco.edu
YOUNG, David, L .... 434-582-2071 509 G dlyoung@liberty.edu
YOUNG, Denise .... 706-867-3281 133 A denise.young@ung.edu
YOUNG, Djuana .... 832-842-9058 491 D dyoun2@central.uh.edu
YOUNG, Donald, B .... 808-956-7703 135 J young@hawaii.edu
YOUNG, Donna .... 480-423-6300.. 15 E donna.young@scottsdalecc.edu
YOUNG, Eldon .... 714-484-7177.. 56 E eyoung@cypresscollege.edu
YOUNG, Elizabeth .... 262-551-2145 535 E eyoung@carthage.edu
YOUNG, Evelyn .... 661-654-2241.. 32 G eyoung3@csub.edu
YOUNG, Floyd .... 413-205-3502 221 G floyd.young@aic.edu
YOUNG, Frank .... 801-863-7202 500 B frank.young@uvu.edu
YOUNG, Gail, B .... 773-298-3301 158 F young@sxu.edu
YOUNG, Garland .... 423-461-8720 459 I rgyoung@milligan.edu
YOUNG, Gerald .... 507-222-4057 254 D gyoung@carleton.edu
YOUNG, Grace .... 978-556-3449 232 E gyoung@necc.mass.edu
YOUNG, Gretchen .... 508-286-8200 238 B young_gretchen@wheatoncollege.edu
YOUNG, Gwyn .... 601-643-8318 266 J gwyn.young@colin.edu
YOUNG, Heather, M ..... 916-734-4745.. 71 A heather.young@ucdmc.ucdavis.edu
YOUNG, Henry .... 401-739-5000 441 E hyoung@neit.edu
YOUNG, Hester .... 843-863-8020 444 B hyoung@csuniv.edu
YOUNG, J.R .... 412-536-1100 422 E JR.young@laroche.edu
YOUNG, Jackie .... 502-585-9911 199 E jyoung04@spalding.edu
YOUNG, Jeff .... 931-372-3311 462 A jyoung@tntech.edu
YOUNG, Jill .... 570-389-4950 430 B jyoung@bloomu.edu
YOUNG, Joanna .... 517-353-0722 246 H jcyoung@msu.edu
YOUNG, John .... 315-781-3748 327 G jyoung@hws.edu
YOUNG, John .... 973-328-5026 301 G jyoung@ccm.edu
YOUNG, John .... 303-360-4707.. 81 I John.Young@CCAurora.edu
YOUNG, John .... 937-327-7800 395 I jyoung@wittenberg.edu
YOUNG, John, O .... 248-370-2946 248 K joyoung@oakland.edu
YOUNG, Johnny .... 757-683-3442 510 I jwyoung@odu.edu
YOUNG, Jon .... 910-672-1460 370 A jyoung@uncfsu.edu
YOUNG, Joseph .... 619-388-7672.. 62 H jyoung@sdccd.edu
YOUNG, Julian, M .... 843-661-1228 446 E jyoung@fmarion.edu
YOUNG, Kalbert, K .... 808-956-8903 135 H kalbert@hawaii.edu
YOUNG, Karmalee .... 406-874-6305 287 A youngk@milescc.edu
YOUNG, Katie .... 501-683-7302.. 24 A kcyoung@ualr.edu
YOUNG, Kay .... 817-598-6303 497 A kyoung@wc.edu
YOUNG, Kay, F .... 508-213-2114 235 C kay.young@nichols.edu
YOUNG, Ken .... 516-323-4501 333 E kyoung@molloy.edu
YOUNG, Kerry, A .... 315-786-2279 329 G kyoung@sunyjefferson.edu
YOUNG, Kimberly .... 760-252-2411.. 29 C kyoung@barstow.edu
YOUNG, Kirk .... 716-338-1060 329 E kirkyoung@mail.sunyjcc.edu
YOUNG, Kristen .... 702-895-0143 295 G kristen.young@unlv.edu
YOUNG, Kristine .... 775-881-7509 296 F kyoung@sierranevada.edu
YOUNG, Kristine, M ..... 845-341-4701 337 G president@sunyorange.edu
YOUNG, Lakisha .... 312-341-3530 157 E lyoung@roosevelt.edu
YOUNG, Laura .... 501-450-3126.. 25 F lyoung@uca.edu
YOUNG, Laura, R .... 336-334-4374 371 C lryoung2@uncg.edu
YOUNG, Lavern .... 312-949-7430 146 E lyoung@ico.edu
YOUNG, Lee .... 620-235-4109 190 G lyoung@pittstate.edu
YOUNG, Lenna .... 864-250-8185 446 H lenna.young@gvltec.edu
YOUNG, Lily, Y .... 848-932-4636 307 B
YOUNG, Linda, C .... 334-556-2234.... 4 A lyoung@wallace.edu
YOUNG, Linda, K .... 715-836-5287 539 E younglk@uwec.edu
YOUNG, Linda, L .... 440-826-2127 377 D lyoung@bw.edu
YOUNG, Lorraine .... 909-748-8289.. 73 K lorraine_young@redlands.edu
YOUNG, Luria .... 225-771-2290 207 A luria_young@subr.edu
YOUNG, Luria .... 225-771-2291 207 A luria_young@subr.edu
YOUNG, Marie .... 814-472-3022 434 F myoung@francis.edu
YOUNG, Mark, S .... 303-762-6902.. 82 C president@denverseminary.edu
YOUNG, Mary, E .... 903-823-3369 484 D maryellen.young@texarkanacollege.edu
YOUNG, MaryAnne .... 941-487-4801 115 B myoung@ncf.edu
YOUNG, MaryAnne .... 413-538-2756 234 C mayoung@mtholyoke.edu
YOUNG, Meghan .... 301-369-2800 214 A myoung@captechu.edu
YOUNG, Michael .... 212-674-2600.. 56 A
YOUNG, Michael .... 508-531-1295 229 C myoung@bridgew.edu
YOUNG, Michael, E ...... 270-809-6831 198 I myoung@murraystate.edu
YOUNG, Michael, K ...... 979-845-2217 485 C president@tamu.edu
YOUNG, Michael, W .... 212-327-8000 339 H michael.young@rockefeller.edu
YOUNG, Michaela, J .... 315-386-7204 347 F youngm@canton.edu
YOUNG, Michelle, L ..... 315-268-4465 321 C myoung@clarkson.edu
YOUNG, Misty .... 573-681-5580 276 K youngm@lincolnu.edu
YOUNG, Monica .... 336-334-4822 363 A mwyoung@gtcc.edu
YOUNG, Myriam .... 219-980-6548 168 C myyoung@iun.edu
YOUNG, Nancy .... 410-455-2393 219 F nyoung@umbc.edu
YOUNG, Nancy .... 816-960-2008 273 B
YOUNG, Nate .... 602-331-7500.. 12 C nlyoung@aii.edu
YOUNG, Nicole .... 731-989-6768 456 K nyoung@fhu.edu
YOUNG, Norman .... 860-768-7819.. 92 F young@hartford.edu
YOUNG, Patricia .... 707-864-7124.. 66 J patricia.young@solano.edu
YOUNG, Patricia .... 925-969-4229.. 42 E tyoung@dvc.edu
YOUNG, Patty, R .... 804-257-5605 518 E pryoung@vuu.edu
YOUNG, Paul, R .... 307-674-6446 546 H pyoung@sheridan.edu
YOUNG, Peter, C .... 240-684-5268 220 A pete.young@umuc.edu
YOUNG, Randy .... 660-359-3948 279 L ryoung@mail.ncmissouri.edu
YOUNG, Raymond .... 609-984-1141 308 H ryoung@tesc.edu
YOUNG, Rena .... 270-707-3732 196 D rena.young@kctcs.edu
YOUNG, Rhett .... 740-283-6441 382 G ryoung@franciscan.edu
YOUNG, Richard .... 207-581-1700 212 C ryoung@maine.edu
YOUNG, Robert .... 501-370-5365.. 22 E ryoung@philander.edu
YOUNG, Robert .... 540-453-2500 514 H youngb@brcc.edu
YOUNG, Robert .... 423-236-2805 460 K ryoung@southern.edu
YOUNG, Roger .... 567-242-5906 384 E young.r@rhodesstate.edu
YOUNG, Ronald .... 269-782-1272 250 D hyoung@swmich.edu
YOUNG, Sandra .... 610-989-1456 438 I syoung@vfmac.edu
YOUNG, Sarah, M .... 716-878-4631 345 B youngsm@buffalostate.edu
YOUNG, Scott .... 816-235-1154 284 A youngsc@umkc.edu
YOUNG, Sean, B .... 262-243-5700 535 I sean.young@cuw.edu
YOUNG, Shantreese ..... 251-344-1203.... 3 J syoung@fortiscollege.edu
YOUNG, Shauna .... 562-907-4986.. 77 E syoung2@whittier.edu

ZAPPIA, Charles ... 619-388-2801 .. 62 G
czappia@sdccd.edu
ZAPPIA, Gerard ... 585-389-2570 334 B
gzappia4@naz.edu
ZAPROROZHETZ,
Laurene, E ... 937-255-5894 547 E
laurene.zaporozhetz@afit.edu
ZARAGOZA, Federico ... 210-485-0015 466 J
fzaragoza@alamo.edu
ZARCHI, Shloime ... 718-434-0784 317 L
ZAREMBA, Terah ... 269-965-3931 244 L
zarembat@kellogg.edu
ZARET, David ... 812-855-5021 167 I
zaret@iu.edu
ZARET, David ... 812-855-5021 167 J
ovpia@iu.edu
ZARFAS, Ellen ... 503-375-7006 405 F
ezarfas@corban.edu
ZARGES, Bradford ... 617-745-3638 225 H
bradford.zarges@enc.edu
ZARKOWSKI, Pamela ... 313-993-1585 250 H
zarkowp1@udmercy.edu
ZARLING, Mark, G ... 507-354-8221 257 A
zarlinmg@mlc-wels.edu
ZARRILLO, Deirdre ... 518-292-1704 340 A
zarrid@sage.edu
ZARRINNAM, Ali, R ... 608-246-6446 543 C
azarrinnam@madisoncollege.edu
ZART, Leilani ... 319-352-8565 183 J
leilani.zart@wartburg.edu
ZARTNER, Ken ... 432-335-6606 479 O
kzartner@odessa.edu
ZARVATANY, Donna ... 610-789-6700 433 G
dzarvatany@prismcareerinstitute.edu
ZASTOUPIL, Brenda ... 701-224-2541 373 F
brenda.zastoupil@ndus.edu
ZATAR, Wael ... 304-696-6043 532 H
zatar@marshall.edu
ZATZ, Marjorie ... 209-228-4723 .. 71 E
mzatz@ucmerced.edu
ZAUFT, Richard ... 617-349-8001 228 B
richard.zauft@lesley.edu
ZAUHAR, Frances, M ... 570-348-6233 425 D
zauhar@marywood.edu
ZAVADA, Michael ... 432-552-2220 495 F
ZAVADA, Robert ... 570-674-8018 426 D
rzavada@misericordia.edu
ZAVALA, Joseph ... 858-642-8024 .. 55 J
jzavala@nu.edu
ZAVALA-COLÓN,
Maria de los Angeles 787-993-8877 557 E
maria.zavala1@upr.edu
ZAVALA-QUIÑONES,
Javier ... 787-993-8854 557 E
javier.zavala@upr.edu
ZAVARICH, Joyce ... 610-519-4080 439 A
joyce.zavarich@villanova.edu
ZAWAIDEH, Ashraf ... 818-767-0888 .. 77 G
ashraf.zawaideh@woodbury.edu
ZAWALICH, Barbara ... 508-849-3401 222 C
bzawalich@annamaria.edu
ZAWIA, Nasser, H ... 401-874-5909 442 E
nzawia@uri.edu
ZAWISTOWSKI, Lee ... 845-569-3229 333 I
lee.zawistowski@msmc.edu
ZAWODNY, Laurel, E ... 419-372-2211 377 I
lzawodn@bgsu.edu
ZAYAITZ, Anne, E ... 610-683-4305 431 B
zayaitz@kutztown.edu
ZAYAS, Brendaliz ... 787-258-1501 551 I
bzayas@columbiacentral.edu
ZAYAS, David ... 787-841-2000 555 F
dzayaz@pucpr.edu
ZAYAS, Luis, H ... 512-471-1937 493 M
lzayas@austin.utexas.edu
ZAYAS, Myriam ... 787-841-2000 555 F
mzayas@pucpr.edu
ZAYAS, Niza ... 787-786-3030 556 E
nzayas@ucb.edu.pr
ZAYAS-HERNÁNDEZ,
Haydee, M ... 787-480-2370 551 H
hzayas@sanjuanciudadpatria.com
ZAZUETA, Fedro, S ... 352-392-0371 115 D
fsz@ufl.edu
ZAZZALI, Robert ... 856-256-4110 306 D
zazzali@rowan.edu
ZBIKOWSKI, Lawrence . 773-702-8500 161 D
larry@uchicago.edu
ZDANCEWICZ, Heather . 703-370-6600 511 B
ZDZIARSKI, Gene ... 312-362-8854 143 G
ezdziars@depaul.edu
ZEALAND, Matthew, J .. 434-582-2000 509 G
mjzealan@liberty.edu
ZEBALLOS, Jorge ... 269-965-3931 244 L
zeballosj@kellogg.edu
ZEBEDIS, Frank, J ... 803-323-3333 451 I
zebedisf@winthrop.edu
ZEBROWSKI,
Michael, J ... 414-288-7172 537 B
michael.zebrowski@marquette.edu

ZECCA, Frank ... 956-665-5078 494 C
zecca@utpa.edu
ZECH, Susan ... 212-686-9244 315 B
ZECKOVICH, Kim ... 906-932-4231 243 B
kimz@gogebic.edu
ZEEK, Raymond ... 203-285-2210 .. 89 B
rzeek@gwcc.commnet.edu
ZEFF, Ira, A ... 402-465-2360 292 E
izeff@nebrwesleyan.edu
ZEFF, Jane ... 973-720-2379 309 I
zeffj@wpunj.edu
ZEGARSKI, Len ... 619-684-8788 .. 56 B
lzegarski@newschoolarch.edu
ZEGER, Brian ... 212-799-5000 329 I
ZEGLEN, Marie ... 352-392-0456 115 D
zeglenm@ufl.edu
ZEH, David ... 775-784-1110 295 H
zehd@unr.edu
ZEHEL, Renee, G ... 570-961-4715 425 D
rzehel@marywood.edu
ZEHNDER, Sarah ... 785-227-3380 185 A
zehndersb@bethanylb.edu
ZEHR, David ... 603-535-2235 299 E
zehr@plymouth.edu
ZEHREN, Carolyn, F ... 218-477-2085 260 B
zehren@mnstate.edu
ZEICH, Heidi, E ... 202-319-5615 .. 95 A
zeich@cua.edu
ZEICHNER, Veronica ... 201-360-4043 303 A
vzeichner@hccc.edu
ZEIDENSTEIN, Darrow .. 713-348-6090 480 M
darrowz@rice.edu
ZEIFANG, Kathleen ... 202-884-9705 .. 97 A
zeifangk@trinitydc.edu
ZEIGER, Erin ... 360-442-2131 524 A
mbrown@lowercolumbia.edu
ZEIGLER, Letherio ... 615-329-8585 456 G
lzeigler@fisk.edu
ZEIGLER, Michael ... 803-535-5340 444 D
mike.zeigler@claflin.edu
ZEIGLER, Michael, C ... 717-867-6060 423 I
zeigler@lvc.edu
ZEIGLER, Sara ... 859-622-2222 194 L
sara.zeigler@eku.edu
ZEILBERGER,
Yeruchom ... 203-325-4351 .. 88 A
ZEILE, Carol ... 989-463-7227 239 B
zeile@alma.edu
ZEILENGA, Jeffrey ... 573-882-5397 283 H
zeilingaj@missouri.edu
ZEIMANTZ, Erich ... 414-256-0169 538 A
zeimante@mtmary.edu
ZEIMET, Dan, L ... 563-333-6202 182 E
ZeimetDanielL@sau.edu
ZEIRD, Susan ... 706-233-7466 131 C
szeird@shorter.edu
ZEISER, Richard, A ... 860-768-4181 .. 92 F
zeiser@hartford.edu
ZEISS, P. Anthony ... 704-330-6566 361 D
tony.zeiss@cpcc.edu
ZEISS, Timothy ... 732-224-2887 300 F
tzeiss@brookdalecc.edu
ZEITHAML, Carl, P ... 434-924-3176 514 A
cpz6n@virginia.edu
ZELASKO, Sandra ... 360-538-4000 523 A
szelasko@ghc.edu
ZELDNER, Cynthia ... 860-512-3214 .. 89 D
czeldner@manchestercc.edu
ZELECHOWSKI,
Deborah ... 773-697-2200 144 B
dzelechowski@devry.edu
ZELENAK, Angeline ... 248-204-2216 245 J
azelenak@ltu.edu
ZELENAK, Christine ... 609-896-5395 306 A
czelenak@rider.edu
ZELENSKI, Paul ... 517-371-5140 252 J
zelensp@cooley.edu
ZELENZ, Margot ... 715-682-1495 538 D
mzelenz@northland.edu
ZELESNIK, Kelly ... 440-365-5222 385 E
ZELEZNY, Lynnette ... 559-278-2636 .. 33 D
lynnette@csufresno.edu
ZELINSKI, Bob ... 352-854-2322 100 P
zelinskb@cf.edu
ZELINSKI, Debbie ... 312-329-4231 153 C
debbie.zelinski@moody.edu
ZELL, Jennifer ... 845-687-5049 350 I
zellj@sunyulster.edu
ZELLAR, Nel ... 507-433-0832 261 C
nel.zellar@riverland.edu
ZELLER, John, H ... 215-898-5169 437 I
jzeller@upenn.edu
ZELLER, Lisa, L ... 303-963-3210 .. 79 L
lzeller@ccu.edu
ZELLERS, Andrew ... 270-831-9627 196 C
andrew.zellers@kctcs.edu
ZELLERS, Jeff, W ... 740-826-8011 387 C
jzellers@muskingum.edu
ZELLMER, Jill, A ... 617-627-3298 237 C
jill.zellmer@tufts.edu

ZELLNER, Alan ... 570-662-4071 431 D
ezellner@mansfield.edu
ZELTWANGER, Todd ... 574-936-8898 164 A
todd.zeltwanger@ancilla.edu
ZEMAN, Janet ... 845-569-3159 333 I
janet.zeman@msmc.edu
ZEMAN, Mary Beth ... 973-720-2971 309 I
zemanm@wpunj.edu
ZEMAN, Scott ... 401-341-2222 442 D
scott.zeman@salve.edu
ZEMBAR, Mary Jo ... 937-327-7921 395 I
mzembar@wittenberg.edu
ZEMBRODT, Belle ... 859-572-5634 199 A
zembrodt@nku.edu
ZEMKE, Mary Ann ... 541-885-1105 408 E
maryann.zemke@oit.edu
ZEMP, William ... 603-644-3179 298 H
w.zemp@snhu.edu
ZENCHECK, Jack ... 718-430-8889 353 P
zencheck@yu.edu
ZENDMAN, Ellen ... 914-606-6733 352 G
ellen.zendman@sunywcc.edu
ZENELIS, John, G ... 703-993-2223 507 K
jzenelis@gmu.edu
ZENG, Zheng ... 512-454-1188 468 A
info@aoma.edu
ZENGER, Sheahon ... 785-864-3143 191 G
kuathletics@ku.edu
ZENK, Leslie ... 704-687-5766 371 B
lzenk@uncc.edu
ZENO, Mark ... 419-448-2058 383 C
mzeno@heidelberg.edu
ZENTENO, Liz ... 432-685-4507 478 F
lzenteno@midland.edu
ZENTMEYER, James, R . 248-370-3570 248 K
zentmeye@oakland.edu
ZENZ, David ... 517-607-2576 243 J
dzenz@hillsdale.edu
ZEPEDA, Andrea ... 918-335-6833 400 I
azepeda@okwu.edu
ZEPPOS, Nicholas ... 615-322-1813 465 H
nick.zeppos@vanderbilt.edu
ZERANGUE, David ... 985-448-4090 208 C
david.zerangue@nicholls.edu
ZERBE, Bryan ... 415-565-4623 .. 71 B
zerbeb@uchastings.edu
ZERBE, Jack ... 336-316-2351 357 C
jzerbe@guilford.edu
ZERBE, Linda ... 610-282-1100 416 I
linda.zerbe@desales.edu
ZERBIAN, Lindsey ... 815-802-8513 149 B
lzerbian@kcc.edu
ZERBONIA, Liza ... 563-355-3500 180 F
lzerbonia@kaplan.edu
ZERILLO, Barbara ... 617-236-8800 226 F
bzerillo@fisher.edu
ZERMENO, Christina ... 714-997-6517 .. 38 B
curiel@chapman.edu
ZERNICKE, Ronald, F ... 734-764-5210 251 C
zernicke@umich.edu
ZERTUCHE, Bernie ... 210-486-4879 466 K
zertuche@alamo.edu
ZERZAN, Phil ... 503-725-4782 409 D
pzerzan@pdx.edu
ZESWITZ, John ... 717-560-8278 423 C
jzeswitz@lbc.edu
ZETARSKI, Jennifer ... 802-225-3230 502 F
jennifer.zetarski@neci.edu
ZETTERGREN, David, G 901-678-2121 462 B
dzttrgrn@memphis.edu
ZETTLER, Chuck, H ... 561-868-4055 109 H
zettlerc@palmbeachstate.edu
ZEWE, Beth ... 814-732-1420 430 G
zewe@edinboro.edu
ZHAI, Lijuan ... 559-489-2224 .. 69 B
lijuan.zhai@fresnocitycollege.edu
ZHAI, Meihua ... 706-452-3183 132 H
mzhai@uga.edu
ZHAN, Lin ... 901-678-2020 462 B
lzhan@memphis.edu
ZHANG, Cheryl ... 212-226-7300 338 F
czhang@pbcny.edu
ZHANG, Chunsheng ... 256-765-4898 .... 9 D
czhang@una.edu
ZHANG, James ... 810-762-7949 245 A
jzhang@kettering.edu
ZHANG, Jane ... 510-763-7787 .. 26 A
jane@acchs.edu
ZHANG, Jiajie, W ... 713-500-3922 495 A
jiajie.zhang@uth.tmc.edu
ZHANG, Li ... 530-754-8924 .. 71 A
lizhang@ucdavis.edu
ZHANG, Ling ... 408-260-0208 .. 44 L
sjadmin@fivebranches.edu
ZHANG, Ming ... 360-650-4454 528 D
ming.zhang@wwu.edu
ZHANG, Minghua ... 631-632-8781 344 C
minghua.zhang@stonybrook.edu
ZHANG, Robert ... 412-365-1292 415 C
rzhang@chatham.edu

ZHANG, Sha Li ... 406-243-6800 287 D
shali.zhang@umontana.edu
ZHANG, Shouhong ... 605-688-6312 454 C
shouhong.zhang@sdstate.edu
ZHANG, Tong-Ai ... 361-570-4323 492 A
zhangt@uhv.edu
ZHANG, William, B ... 336-285-3048 370 B
wbzhang@ncat.edu
ZHANG, Xiao, Y ... 716-673-4806 343 F
xiao.zhang@fredonia.edu
ZHAO, Jielu ... 831-242-5801 547 H
jielu.zhao.civ@mail.mil
ZHAO, Joanna ... 831-476-9424 .. 44 L
dean@fivebranches.edu
ZHAO, Joanna ... 408-260-0208 .. 44 K
dean@fivebranches.edu
ZHAO, Lianna ... 949-451-5238 .. 67 E
lzhao@ivc.edu
ZHAO, Yiping ... 516-739-1545 335 C
clinicmanager@nyctcm.edu
ZHENG, Jilian ... 402-559-5656 293 I
jzheng@unmc.edu
ZHENG, John ... 662-254-3452 269 C
zheng@mvsu.edu
ZHONG, Baisong ... 713-780-9777 467 G
info@acaom.edu
ZHOU, Chenn ... 219-989-2665 171 L
czhou@purduecal.edu
ZHOU, Claire ... 914-337-9300 323 A
claire.zhou@concordia-ny.edu
ZHOU, Kai ... 518-782-6888 342 H
kzhou@siena.edu
ZHOU, Wei ... 619-660-4221 .. 46 G
wei.zhou@gcccd.edu
ZHOU, Wei ... 301-985-7705 220 A
institutional-planning@umuc.edu
ZHOU, Wei ... 724-938-4074 430 C
zhou@calu.edu
ZHOU, Ying ... 252-737-1912 369 E
zhouy14@ecu.edu
ZHU, Jianping ... 216-687-3588 380 D
J.ZHU94@csuohio.edu
ZHUANG, Miao ... 361-593-4480 486 A
miao.zhuang@tamuk.edu
ZIADY, Eric ... 302-831-4006 .. 94 D
eziady@udel.edu
ZIADY, Nicola ... 513-556-3015 393 B
nicola.ziady@uc.edu
ZIAJKA, Alan, L ... 415-422-2846 .. 74 C
ziajka@usfca.edu
ZIAVRAS, Sotirios, G ... 973-596-3462 304 D
sotirios.g.ziavras@njit.edu
ZIBELL, Tammy ... 509-533-8135 521 E
tammy.zibell@scc.spokane.edu
ZIBLUK, Patricia, M ... 203-392-6800 .. 88 F
ziblukp1@southernct.edu
ZIC, Anthony ... 516-759-2040 352 D
azic@webb.edu
ZICCARDI, C. Anthony . 973-313-6053 308 C
anthony.ziccardi@shu.edu
ZICHER, Marie-Ange ... 708-456-0300 161 C
mzicher@triton.edu
ZIEBARTH, Timothy, J .. 574-372-5100 166 D
ziebartj@grace.edu
ZIEBARTH, Timothy, J .. 574-372-5100 166 D
tjziebarth@grace.edu
ZIEGENGEIST, Roy, P ... 860-701-6509 548 H
Roy.P.Ziegengeist1@uscg.mil
ZIEGLER, Chris ... 734-432-5662 246 B
cziegler@madonna.edu
ZIEGLER, Jennifer ... 219-464-5271 174 E
jennifer.ziegler@valpo.edu
ZIEGLER, John ... 724-738-9000 432 A
john.ziegler@sru.edu
ZIEGLER, William ... 607-777-3583 343 D
ziegler@binghamton.edu
ZIELASKOWSKI, Cindy . 518-743-2275 347 E
zielaskowskic@sunyacc.edu
ZIELINSKI, David ... 760-355-6470 .. 47 G
david.zielinski@imperial.edu
ZIELINSKI, Georgene ... 610-372-4721 433 H
gzielinski@racc.edu
ZIEMBA, Christine ... 661-255-1050 .. 31 B
ZIEMBA, David ... 508-362-2131 231 D
dziemba@capecod.edu
ZIEMIANSKI, Michael ... 812-357-6501 173 A
mziemianski@saintmeinrad.edu
ZIEMNICK, Tom ... 540-338-1776 511 A
ZIENCIK, Catherine ... 919-497-3306 358 J
cziencik@louisburg.edu
ZIENIEWICZ,
Stephen, P ... 206-598-6364 527 G
stephenz@uw.edu
ZIENTARSKI,
Nicholas, A ... 914-367-8216 341 D
nzientarski@dunwoodie.org
ZIER, Joni, I ... 423-236-2895 460 K
jzier@southern.edu
ZIERDT, Ginger ... 507-389-6214 260 A
ginger.zierdt@mns.edu

Accreditation Index of Institutions by Regional, National, Professional and Specialized Agencies

Degree levels are shown by the following symbols: (C) diploma/certificate; (A) associate; (B) baccalaureate; (M) master's; (S) beyond master's but less than doctorate; (FP) first professional; (D) doctorate.

AA: Commission on Accreditation of Allied Health Education Programs: anesthesiologist assistant (M)

AAB: Aviation Accreditation Board International: aviation (A,B,M)

AAFCS: American Association of Family and Consumer Sciences: family and consumer science (B)

ABHES: Accrediting Bureau of Health Education Schools: allied health (C,A,B)

ACAE: Accreditation Commission for Audiology Education: audiology (D)

ACBSP: Accreditation Council for Business Schools and Programs: business administration, management, accounting and related business fields (A,B,M,D)

ACCSC: Accrediting Commission of Career Schools and Colleges: occupational, trade, and technical education (C,A,B,M)

ACFEI: American Culinary Federation, Inc.: culinary arts and culinary management (C,A,B)

ACICS: Accrediting Council for Independent Colleges and Schools: business and business related programs (C,A,B,M)

- South Hills School of Business and Technology ... PA ... 435
- Atlantic University College ... PR ... 550
- Dewey University ... PR ... 551
- EDIC College ... PR ... 552
- Humacao Community College ... PR ... 552
- Instituto de Banca y Comercio ... PR ... 553
- Trinity College of Puerto Rico ... PR ... 556
- Universal Technology College of Puerto Rico ... PR ... 556
- Forrest College ... SC ... 446
- Daymar Institute ... TN ... 456
- Kaplan College ... TN ... 457
- Miller-Motte Technical College ... TN ... 459
- National College ... TN ... 459
- Career Point College ... TX ... 470
- International Business College ... TX ... 475
- Kaplan College ... TX ... 476
- Le Cordon Bleu College of Culinary Arts in Austin ... TX ... 477
- North American University ... TX ... 479
- Sanford-Brown College ... TX ... 482
- Texas Health and Science University ... TX ... 487
- Texas School of Business ... TX ... 487
- Vet Tech Institute of Houston ... TX ... 496
- Broadview University ... UT ... 498
- Eagle Gate College ... UT ... 498
- Neumont University ... UT ... 498
- Provo College ... UT ... 498
- American National University ... VA ... 504
- Bon Secours Memorial College of Nursing ... VA ... 505
- Columbia College ... VA ... 506
- Everest College ... VA ... 507
- Fortis College ... VA ... 507
- Global Health College ... VA ... 508
- iGlobal University ... VA ... 508
- Miller-Motte Technical College ... VA ... 510
- Sentara College of Health Sciences ... VA ... 512
- Stratford University ... VA ... 513
- University of North America ... VA ... 513
- Virginia International University ... VA ... 517
- Everest College ... WA ... 522
- ITT Technical Institute ... WA ... 523
- Pinchot University ... WA ... 525
- Mountain State College ... WV ... 530
- Valley College - Beckley Campus ... WV ... 530
- West Virginia Business College ... WV ... 530
- West Virginia Junior College ... WV ... 534
- Madison Media Institute-College of Media Arts ... WI ... 536
- Wright Graduate University for the Realization of Human Potential ... WI ... 545

ACUP: Accreditation Commission for Acupuncture and Oriental Medicine: acupuncture (C,M,D)

- #Arizona School of Acupuncture and Oriental Medicine ... AZ ... 11
- Han University of Traditional Medicine ... AZ ... 14
- Phoenix Institute of Herbal Medicine and Acupuncture ... AZ ... 16
- Academy of Chinese Culture and Health Sciences ... CA ... 26
- Acupuncture and Integrative Medicine College-Berkeley ... CA ... 26
- Alhambra Medical University ... CA ... 26
- California Institute of Integral Studies ... CA ... 31
- Dongguk University ... CA ... 43
- Emperor's College of Traditional Oriental Medicine ... CA ... 43
- Five Branches University, Graduate School of Traditional Chinese Medicine . CA ... 44
- @Nine Star University of Health Sciences ... CA ... 56
- Pacific College of Oriental Medicine ... CA ... 57
- South Baylo University ... CA ... 67
- Southern California University of Health Sciences ... CA ... 67
- Southern California University School of Oriental Medicine & Acupuncture ... CA ... 68
- @Stanton University ... CA ... 68
- University of East-West Medicine ... CA ... 73
- Yo San University of Traditional Chinese Medicine ... CA ... 77
- Colorado School of Traditional Chinese Medicine ... CO ... 81
- Institute of Taoist Education and Acupuncture ... CO ... 83
- University of Bridgeport ... CT ... 92
- Academy for Five Element Acupuncture ... FL ... 97
- Acupuncture & Massage College ... FL ... 97
- Atlantic Institute of Oriental Medicine ... FL ... 98
- Dragon Rises College of Oriental Medicine ... FL ... 101
- East West College of Natural Medicine ... FL ... 101
- Florida College of Integrative Medicine ... FL ... 103
- Institute of Clinical Acupuncture and Oriental Medicine ... HI ... 135
- World Medicine Institute ... HI ... 137
- National University of Health Sciences ... IL ... 154
- Maryland University of Integrative Health . MD .. 216
- New England School of Acupuncture ... MA .. 235
- American Academy of Acupuncture and Oriental Medicine ... MN .. 253
- Northwestern Health Sciences University . MN .. 263
- Southwest Acupuncture College ... NM .. 313
- New York Chiropractic College ... NY ... 334
- New York College of Health Professions .. NY ... 335
- New York College of Traditional Chinese Medicine ... NY ... 335
- Tri-State College of Acupuncture ... NY ... 350
- Daoist Traditions College of Chinese Medical Arts ... NC .. 356
- American Institute of Alternative Medicine OH .. 376
- National College of Natural Medicine ... OR .. 407
- Oregon College of Oriental Medicine ... OR .. 408
- Won Institute of Graduate Studies ... PA ... 440
- American College of Acupuncture and Oriental Medicine ... TX ... 467
- AOMA Graduate School of Integrative Medicine ... TX ... 468
- Texas Health and Science University ... TX ... 487
- @Kings Park University ... VA ... 509
- Virginia University of Oriental Medicine ... VA ... 518
- Bastyr University ... WA .. 519
- Seattle Institute of Oriental Medicine ... WA .. 526
- Midwest College of Oriental Medicine ... WI ... 537

ADNUR: Accreditation Commission for Education in Nursing: nursing (A)

- Alabama Southern Community College ... AL ... 1
- Bevill State Community College ... AL ... 2
- Bishop State Community College ... AL ... 2
- Calhoun Community College ... AL ... 2
- Central Alabama Community College ... AL ... 2
- Chattahoochee Valley Community College AL ... 2
- Gadsden State Community College ... AL ... 3
- George C. Wallace Community College - Dothan ... AL ... 4
- George Corley Wallace State Community College - Selma ... AL ... 4
- James H. Faulkner State Community College ... AL ... 5
- Jefferson Davis Community College ... AL ... 5
- Jefferson State Community College ... AL ... 5
- Lawson State Community College ... AL ... 5
- Lurleen B. Wallace Community College ... AL ... 5
- Northeast Alabama Community College ... AL ... 6
- Northwest - Shoals Community College ... AL ... 6
- Shelton State Community College ... AL ... 7
- Snead State Community College ... AL ... 7
- Southern Union State Community College AL ... 7
- Troy University ... AL ... 8
- University of Mobile ... AL ... 9
- University of West Alabama, The ... AL ... 9
- Wallace State Community College - Hanceville ... AL ... 10
- University of Alaska Anchorage ... AK ... 10
- Arizona Western College ... AZ ... 12
- Central Arizona College ... AZ ... 12
- Chandler-Gilbert Community College ... AZ ... 14
- Estrella Mountain Community College ... AZ ... 14
- Gateway Community College ... AZ ... 14
- Glendale Community College ... AZ ... 14
- Mesa Community College ... AZ ... 15
- Mohave Community College ... AZ ... 15
- Northland Pioneer College ... AZ ... 16
- Paradise Valley Community College ... AZ ... 15
- Phoenix College ... AZ ... 15
- Pima Community College ... AZ ... 17
- Scottsdale Community College ... AZ ... 15
- Yavapai College ... AZ ... 18
- Arkansas Northeastern College ... AR ... 19
- Arkansas State University-Jonesboro ... AR ... 19
- East Arkansas Community College ... AR ... 20
- National Park Community College ... AR ... 21
- North Arkansas College ... AR ... 22
- Phillips Community College of the University of Arkansas ... AR ... 24
- Southeast Arkansas College ... AR ... 23
- Southern Arkansas University ... AR ... 23
- University of Arkansas at Little Rock ... AR ... 24
- University of Arkansas Community College at Batesville ... AR ... 24
- Cerritos College ... CA ... 37
- Chaffey College ... CA ... 38
- College of Marin ... CA ... 41
- College of the Canyons ... CA ... 40
- Cypress College ... CA ... 56
- Evergreen Valley College ... CA ... 63
- Golden West College ... CA ... 40
- Grossmont College ... CA ... 46
- Long Beach City College ... CA ... 51
- Los Angeles Harbor College ... CA ... 51
- Los Angeles Valley College ... CA ... 52
- Monterey Peninsula College ... CA ... 54
- Moorpark College ... CA ... 75
- Ohlone College ... CA ... 56
- Pacific Union College ... CA ... 57
- Palomar College ... CA ... 58
- Riverside City College ... CA ... 61
- Saddleback College ... CA ... 67
- San Bernardino Valley College ... CA ... 62
- San Diego City College ... CA ... 62
- San Joaquin Delta College ... CA ... 63
- Santa Ana College ... CA ... 60
- Santa Barbara City College ... CA ... 64
- Santa Monica College ... CA ... 65
- Southwestern College ... CA ... 68
- Ventura College ... CA ... 75
- Aims Community College ... CO ... 78
- Arapahoe Community College ... CO ... 79
- Colorado Mesa University ... CO ... 80
- Colorado Mountain College ... CO ... 80
- Colorado Northwestern Community College ... CO ... 80
- Denver School of Nursing ... CO ... 82
- Front Range Community College ... CO ... 82
- Lamar Community College ... CO ... 83
- Morgan Community College ... CO ... 84
- Northeastern Junior College ... CO ... 84
- Otero Junior College ... CO ... 84
- Pikes Peak Community College ... CO ... 84
- Pueblo Community College ... CO ... 85
- Capital Community College ... CT ... 89
- Gateway Community College ... CT ... 89
- Goodwin College ... CT ... 90
- Naugatuck Valley Community College ... CT ... 89
- Northwestern Connecticut Community-Technical College ... CT ... 89
- Norwalk Community College ... CT ... 89
- St. Vincent's College ... CT ... 91
- Three Rivers Community College ... CT ... 90
- Delaware Technical Community College, Terry Campus ... DE ... 94
- University of the District of Columbia ... DC ... 97
- Adventist University of Health Sciences ... FL ... 97
- Broward College ... FL ... 99
- Chipola College ... FL ... 100
- College of Central Florida ... FL ... 100
- Daytona State College ... FL ... 101
- Florida Gateway College ... FL ... 103
- Florida SouthWestern State College ... FL ... 104
- Florida State College at Jacksonville ... FL ... 105
- Gulf Coast State College ... FL ... 105
- Hillsborough Community College ... FL ... 106
- Indian River State College ... FL ... 106
- Keiser University ... FL ... 107
- Lake-Sumter State College ... FL ... 107
- Miami Dade College ... FL ... 108
- Northwest Florida State College ... FL ... 109
- Palm Beach State College ... FL ... 109
- Pasco-Hernando State College ... FL ... 110
- Pensacola State College ... FL ... 110
- Polk State College ... FL ... 110
- St. Johns River State College ... FL ... 111
- St. Petersburg College ... FL ... 112
- Santa Fe College ... FL ... 112
- Seminole State College of Florida ... FL ... 113
- South Florida State College ... FL ... 113
- State College of Florida, Manatee-Sarasota ... FL ... 114
- Tallahassee Community College ... FL ... 117
- Valencia College ... FL ... 118
- Abraham Baldwin Agricultural College ... GA .. 119
- Athens Technical College ... GA .. 120
- Bainbridge State College ... GA .. 121
- College of Coastal Georgia ... GA .. 123
- Columbus Technical College ... GA .. 123
- Dalton State College ... GA .. 123
- Darton State College ... GA .. 123
- Georgia Highlands College ... GA .. 125
- Georgia Northwestern Technical College . GA .. 125
- Georgia Perimeter College ... GA .. 125
- Gordon State College ... GA .. 126
- Gwinnett Technical College ... GA .. 127
- Middle Georgia State University ... GA .. 128
- South Georgia State College ... GA .. 131
- Southern Regional Technical College ... GA .. 132
- University of North Georgia ... GA .. 133
- West Georgia Technical College ... GA .. 134
- Kapiolani Community College ... HI ... 136
- University of Hawaii Hawaii Community College ... HI ... 136
- University of Hawaii Kauai Community College ... HI ... 136
- University of Hawaii Maui College ... HI ... 136
- Brigham Young University-Idaho ... ID ... 137
- College of Southern Idaho ... ID ... 137
- College of Western Idaho ... ID ... 138
- Idaho State University ... ID ... 138
- North Idaho College ... ID ... 138
- Black Hawk College ... IL ... 140
- Carl Sandburg College ... IL ... 140
- City Colleges of Chicago Harry S Truman College ... IL ... 141
- City Colleges of Chicago Richard J. Daley College ... IL ... 142
- College of DuPage ... IL ... 142
- College of Lake County ... IL ... 142
- Danville Area Community College ... IL ... 143
- Elgin Community College ... IL ... 144
- Harper College ... IL ... 145
- Heartland Community College ... IL ... 145
- Illinois Central College ... IL ... 146
- Illinois Eastern Community Colleges Frontier Community College ... IL ... 146
- Illinois Eastern Community Colleges Lincoln Trail College ... IL ... 146
- Illinois Eastern Community Colleges Olney Central College ... IL ... 147
- Illinois Eastern Community Colleges Wabash Valley College ... IL ... 147
- Illinois Valley Community College ... IL ... 147
- Joliet Junior College ... IL ... 148
- Kaskaskia College ... IL ... 149
- Lake Land College ... IL ... 150
- Lewis and Clark Community College ... IL ... 150
- Lincoln Land Community College ... IL ... 151
- Moraine Valley Community College ... IL ... 153
- Morton College ... IL ... 153
- Oakton Community College ... IL ... 155
- Parkland College ... IL ... 155
- Prairie State College ... IL ... 156
- Richland Community College ... IL ... 156
- Robert Morris University - Illinois ... IL ... 157
- Southwestern Illinois College ... IL ... 160
- Trinity College of Nursing & Health Sciences ... IL ... 161
- Triton College ... IL ... 161
- Waubonsee Community College ... IL ... 162
- Bethel College ... IN ... 164
- Ivy Tech Community College of Indiana-Central Indiana ... IN ... 169
- University of Indianapolis ... IN ... 173
- University of Saint Francis ... IN ... 174
- Vincennes University ... IN ... 174
- Des Moines Area Community College ... IA ... 177
- Mercy College of Health Sciences ... IA ... 181
- North Iowa Area Community College ... IA ... 181
- St. Luke's College ... IA ... 182
- Barton County Community College ... KS ... 184
- Butler Community College ... KS ... 185
- Cloud County Community College ... KS ... 186
- Colby Community College ... KS ... 186
- Dodge City Community College ... KS ... 186
- Fort Scott Community College ... KS ... 187
- Garden City Community College ... KS ... 187
- Hesston College ... KS ... 187
- Hutchinson Community College ... KS ... 188
- Johnson County Community College ... KS ... 188
- Kansas City Kansas Community College . KS ... 188
- Labette Community College ... KS ... 189
- Manhattan Area Technical College ... KS ... 189
- Neosho County Community College ... KS ... 189
- North Central Kansas Technical College .. KS ... 190
- Seward County Community College/Area Technical School ... KS ... 191
- Ashland Community and Technical College ... KY ... 195
- Bluegrass Community and Technical College ... KY ... 195
- Eastern Kentucky University ... KY ... 194
- Elizabethtown Community and Technical College ... KY ... 195
- Henderson Community College ... KY ... 196
- Hopkinsville Community College ... KY ... 196
- Jefferson Community and Technical College ... KY ... 196
- Kentucky State University ... KY ... 197
- Madisonville Community College ... KY ... 196
- Midway University ... KY ... 198
- Morehead State University ... KY ... 198
- St. Catharine College ... KY ... 199
- Somerset Community College ... KY ... 197
- Southeast Kentucky Community and Technical College ... KY ... 197
- West Kentucky Community and Technical College ... KY ... 197
- Western Kentucky University ... KY ... 201
- Baton Rouge Community College ... LA ... 202
- Bossier Parish Community College ... LA ... 203
- Delgado Community College ... LA ... 203
- Louisiana Delta Community College ... LA ... 203
- Louisiana State University at Alexandria .. LA ... 205
- Louisiana State University at Eunice ... LA ... 205
- Louisiana Tech University ... LA ... 208
- McNeese State University ... LA ... 208
- Northwestern State University ... LA ... 208
- Our Lady of the Lake College ... LA ... 206
- Southern University at Shreveport-Louisiana ... LA ... 207
- Central Maine Community College ... ME .. 210
- Eastern Maine Community College ... ME .. 211
- Kennebec Valley Community College ... ME .. 211
- Maine College of Health Professions ... ME .. 210
- Northern Maine Community College ... ME .. 211

ANEST: Council on Accreditation of Nurse Anesthesia Educational Programs: nurse anesthesia (C,M,D)

ARCPA: Accreditation Review Commission on Education for the Physician Assistant: physician assisting programs (C,A,B,M)

Institution	State	Page
Alderson Broaddus University	WV	529
#University of Charleston	WV	530
West Liberty University	WV	533
Carroll University	WI	535
#Concordia University Wisconsin	WI	535
Marquette University	WI	537
University of Wisconsin-La Crosse	WI	539
University of Wisconsin-Madison	WI	539

ART: National Association of Schools of Art and Design: art and design (C,A,B,M,D)

Institution	State	Page
Alabama State University	AL	1
Auburn University	AL	1
Jacksonville State University	AL	4
University of Alabama at Birmingham	AL	8
University of Alabama in Huntsville	AL	9
University of Alabama, The	AL	8
University of Montevallo	AL	9
University of North Alabama	AL	9
University of Alaska Anchorage	AK	10
Arizona State University	AZ	11
University of Arizona	AZ	18
Arkansas State University-Jonesboro	AR	19
University of Arkansas at Little Rock	AR	24
University of Arkansas at Pine Bluff	AR	24
University of Central Arkansas	AR	25
Academy of Art University	CA	25
American Film Institute Conservatory	CA	27
Art Center College of Design	CA	28
Azusa Pacific University	CA	29
Biola University	CA	29
California College of the Arts	CA	30
California Institute of the Arts	CA	31
California Polytechnic State University-San Luis Obispo	CA	32
California State Polytechnic University-Pomona	CA	32
California State University-Chico	CA	33
California State University-Fullerton	CA	33
California State University-Long Beach	CA	33
California State University-Los Angeles	CA	34
California State University-Northridge	CA	34
California State University-Sacramento	CA	34
California State University-San Bernardino	CA	35
California State University-Stanislaus	CA	35
Columbia College Hollywood	CA	41
Dominican University of California	CA	43
FIDM/Fashion Institute of Design and Merchandising-Los Angeles	CA	44
Humboldt State University	CA	35
Laguna College of Art & Design	CA	49
Los Angeles Academy of Figurative Art	CA	51
Loyola Marymount University	CA	53
New York Film Academy, Los Angeles	CA	56
Otis College of Art and Design	CA	57
San Diego State University	CA	35
San Francisco Art Institute	CA	62
San Francisco State University	CA	36
San Jose State University	CA	36
Sonoma State University	CA	36
University of the Pacific	CA	73
Woodbury University	CA	77
Metropolitan State University of Denver	CO	83
Rocky Mountain College of Art & Design	CO	85
University of Denver	CO	86
University of Northern Colorado	CO	87
University of Bridgeport	CT	92
University of Connecticut	CT	92
University of Hartford	CT	92
University of New Haven	CT	92
Delaware College of Art and Design	DE	93
George Washington University	DC	95
Howard University	DC	96
Florida International University	FL	114
Florida State University	FL	115
Miami Dade College	FL	108
Ringling College of Art and Design	FL	111
University of Florida	FL	115
University of South Florida	FL	116
Augusta University	GA	121
Columbus State University	GA	123
Georgia Institute of Technology	GA	125
Georgia Southern University	GA	126
Georgia State University	GA	126
Kennesaw State University	GA	127
University of Georgia	GA	132
University of West Georgia	GA	133
Valdosta State University	GA	133
Boise State University	ID	137
University of Idaho	ID	139
Bradley University	IL	140
College of DuPage	IL	142
Eastern Illinois University	IL	144
Illinois State University	IL	147
Northeastern Illinois University	IL	154
Northern Illinois University	IL	154
School of the Art Institute of Chicago	IL	158
Southern Illinois University Carbondale	IL	159
University of Illinois at Urbana-Champaign	IL	162
Western Illinois University	IL	163
Ball State University	IN	164
Indiana State University	IN	167
Indiana University Bloomington	IN	167
Indiana University-Purdue University Fort Wayne	IN	168
Ivy Tech Community College of Indiana-Central Indiana	IN	169
Purdue University Main Campus	IN	171
Saint Mary's College	IN	172
University of Indianapolis	IN	173
University of Notre Dame	IN	174
University of Saint Francis	IN	174
University of Southern Indiana	IN	174
Vincennes University	IN	174
Drake University	IA	177
Iowa State University	IA	175
Emporia State University	KS	186
Kansas State University	KS	188
University of Kansas Main Campus	KS	191
Washburn University	KS	192
Wichita State University	KS	192
Morehead State University	KY	198
Murray State University	KY	198
University of Kentucky	KY	200
Western Kentucky University	KY	201
Louisiana State University and Agricultural and Mechanical College	LA	204
Louisiana Tech University	LA	208
McNeese State University	LA	208
Nicholls State University	LA	208
Northwestern State University	LA	208
Southeastern Louisiana University	LA	208
University of Louisiana at Lafayette	LA	208
University of New Orleans	LA	205
Maine College of Art	ME	210
University of Maine	ME	212
University of Southern Maine	ME	213
Community College of Baltimore County, The	MD	214
Maryland Institute College of Art	MD	216
Bridgewater State University	MA	229
Endicott College	MA	226
Framingham State University	MA	230
Lesley University	MA	228
Massachusetts College of Art and Design	MA	230
Montserrat College of Art	MA	234
Mount Ida College	MA	234
Salem State University	MA	230
School of the Museum of Fine Arts, Boston	MA	236
Suffolk University	MA	237
University of Massachusetts Dartmouth	MA	228
University of Massachusetts Lowell	MA	229
Wentworth Institute of Technology	MA	237
Central Michigan University	MI	240
College for Creative Studies	MI	241
Cranbrook Academy of Art	MI	241
Ferris State University	MI	242
Grand Rapids Community College	MI	243
Grand Valley State University	MI	243
Hope College	MI	244
Lawrence Technological University	MI	245
Siena Heights University	MI	250
University of Michigan-Ann Arbor	MI	251
Western Michigan University	MI	252
Minneapolis College of Art and Design	MN	257
Minnesota State University Moorhead	MN	260
Minnesota State University, Mankato	MN	260
Normandale Community College	MN	260
St. Cloud State University	MN	261
St. Olaf College	MN	264
University of Minnesota Duluth	MN	264
Belhaven University	MS	266
Delta State University	MS	267
Jackson State University	MS	267
Mississippi State University	MS	269
Mississippi University for Women	MS	269
Mississippi Valley State University	MS	269
University of Mississippi	MS	270
University of Southern Mississippi	MS	271
East Central College	MO	274
Kansas City Art Institute	MO	276
Maryville University of Saint Louis	MO	277
Saint Louis University	MO	281
University of Central Missouri	MO	283
Washington University in St. Louis	MO	285
Montana State University	MT	287
Montana State University - Billings	MT	287
University of Montana - Missoula	MT	287
University of Nebraska at Omaha	NE	294
University of Nebraska - Lincoln	NE	293
Wayne State College	NE	292
University of Nevada, Las Vegas	NV	295
New Hampshire Institute of Art	NH	298
Plymouth State University	NH	299
Kean University	NJ	303
Montclair State University	NJ	304
New Jersey City University	NJ	304
New Jersey Institute of Technology	NJ	304
Rowan University	NJ	306
William Paterson University of New Jersey	NJ	309
Institute of American Indian Arts	NM	310
Alfred University	NY	314
College of Saint Rose, The	NY	322
Cooper Union	NY	323
Fashion Institute of Technology	NY	325
Hartwick College	NY	327
New School, The	NY	334
New York Academy of Art	NY	334
New York School of Interior Design	NY	336
Pratt Institute	NY	338
Purchase College, State University of New York	NY	346
Roberts Wesleyan College	NY	339
Rochester Institute of Technology	NY	339
Sage Colleges, The	NY	340
St. John's University	NY	340
School of Visual Arts	NY	342
Skidmore College	NY	342
Sotheby's Institute of Art	NY	343
State University of New York at Fredonia	NY	343
State University of New York at New Paltz	NY	344
State University of New York College at Buffalo	NY	345
State University of New York College at Oswego	NY	346
Syracuse University Main Campus	NY	349
Appalachian State University	NC	369
East Carolina University	NC	369
Fayetteville State University	NC	370
North Carolina State University	NC	370
University of North Carolina at Pembroke	NC	371
Western Carolina University	NC	372
North Dakota State University Main Campus	ND	374
University of North Dakota	ND	373
Art Academy of Cincinnati	OH	376
Bowling Green State University	OH	377
Central State University	OH	379
Cleveland Institute of Art	OH	380
Columbus College of Art & Design	OH	380
Kent State University Main Campus	OH	384
Lorain County Community College	OH	385
Miami University	OH	386
Ohio State University Main Campus, The	OH	389
Sinclair Community College	OH	391
University of Akron, Main Campus, The	OH	392
University of Cincinnati-Blue Ash College	OH	393
University of Cincinnati Main Campus	OH	393
University of Dayton	OH	393
University of Toledo	OH	394
Youngstown State University	OH	396
University of Central Oklahoma	OK	403
Oregon College of Art and Craft	OR	408
Pacific Northwest College of Art	OR	408
University of Oregon	OR	410
Arcadia University	PA	412
Bloomsburg University of Pennsylvania	PA	430
Bucks County Community College	PA	413
California University of Pennsylvania	PA	430
Clarion University of Pennsylvania	PA	430
Drexel University	PA	417
Edinboro University	PA	430
Harrisburg Area Community College	PA	420
Indiana University of Pennsylvania	PA	431
Kutztown University of Pennsylvania	PA	431
La Roche College	PA	422
Marywood University	PA	425
Messiah College	PA	426
Millersville University of Pennsylvania	PA	431
Moore College of Art and Design	PA	426
Penn State University Park	PA	428
Pennsylvania Academy of the Fine Arts	PA	429
Pennsylvania College of Art & Design	PA	429
Philadelphia University	PA	432
Slippery Rock University of Pennsylvania	PA	432
Temple University	PA	436
University of the Arts, The	PA	437
West Chester University of Pennsylvania	PA	432
Escuela de Artes Plasticas de Puerto Rico	PR	552
Rhode Island College	RI	442
Rhode Island School of Design	RI	442
Salve Regina University	RI	442
Anderson University	SC	443
Benedict College	SC	443
Clemson University	SC	444
Coastal Carolina University	SC	444
Coker College	SC	445
Columbia College	SC	445
Converse College	SC	445
Francis Marion University	SC	446
Lander University	SC	447
South Carolina State University	SC	448
University of South Carolina Columbia	SC	450
University of South Carolina Upstate	SC	451
Winthrop University	SC	451
Northern State University	SD	454
University of South Dakota, The	SD	453
Austin Peay State University	TN	461
Belmont University	TN	455
Carson-Newman University	TN	455
East Tennessee State University	TN	461
Memphis College of Art	TN	459
Middle Tennessee State University	TN	461
Tennessee State University	TN	461
Tennessee Technological University	TN	462
Union University	TN	464
University of Memphis, The	TN	462
University of Tennessee at Chattanooga	TN	465
University of Tennessee, Knoxville	TN	465
Watkins College of Art, Design & Film	TN	466
Brookhaven College	TX	472
Del Mar College	TX	473
Midwestern State University	TX	478
Sam Houston State University	TX	489
Southern Methodist University	TX	482
Stephen F. Austin State University	TX	484
Texas A & M University - Commerce	TX	485
Texas Christian University	TX	486
Texas Tech University	TX	489
University of North Texas	TX	492
University of Texas at Arlington, The	TX	493
University of Texas at Austin	TX	493
University of Texas at San Antonio	TX	494
University of Texas of the Permian Basin	TX	495
Brigham Young University	UT	497
Southern Utah University	UT	499
Utah State University	UT	500
Weber State University	UT	500
Champlain College	VT	501
George Mason University	VA	507
James Madison University	VA	509
Old Dominion University	VA	510
Virginia Commonwealth University	VA	514
Virginia Polytechnic Institute and State University	VA	518
Virginia State University	VA	518
Cornish College of the Arts	WA	521
Western Washington University	WA	528
West Virginia University	WV	533
Milwaukee Institute of Art & Design	WI	537
University of Wisconsin-Green Bay	WI	539
University of Wisconsin-Madison	WI	539
University of Wisconsin-Stevens Point	WI	541
University of Wisconsin-Stout	WI	541
University of Wisconsin-Whitewater	WI	541
Casper College	WY	545
Northwest College	WY	546

AUD: American Speech-Language-Hearing Association: audiology (D)

Institution	State	Page
Auburn University	AL	1
University of South Alabama	AL	9
Arizona State University	AZ	11
University of Arizona	AZ	18
University of Arkansas for Medical Sciences	AR	24
San Diego State University	CA	35
University of California-San Diego	CA	72
@University of the Pacific	CA	73
University of Colorado Boulder	CO	86
University of Northern Colorado	CO	87
University of Connecticut	CT	92
Gallaudet University	DC	95
Nova Southeastern University	FL	109
University of Florida	FL	115
University of South Florida	FL	116
Idaho State University	ID	138
Illinois State University	IL	147
Northern Illinois University	IL	154
Northwestern University	IL	155
Rush University	IL	158
University of Illinois at Urbana-Champaign	IL	162
#Ball State University	IN	164
Indiana University Bloomington	IN	167
Purdue University Main Campus	IN	171
University of Iowa	IA	175
University of Kansas Main Campus	KS	191
Wichita State University	KS	192
University of Louisville	KY	201
Louisiana State University Health Sciences Center-New Orleans	LA	205
Louisiana Tech University	LA	208
Towson University	MD	221
University of Maryland College Park	MD	219
Northeastern University	MA	235
University of Massachusetts	MA	228
Central Michigan University	MI	240
Wayne State University	MI	252
Western Michigan University	MI	252
University of Minnesota-Twin Cities	MN	265
University of Southern Mississippi	MS	271
Missouri State University	MO	279

Washington University in St. Louis ... MO .. 285
University of Nebraska - Lincoln ... NE ... 293
Montclair State University ... NJ ... 304
Adelphi University ... NY ... 314
City University of New York Brooklyn College ... NY ... 318
City University of New York Hunter College ... NY ... 319
Hofstra University ... NY ... 328
St. John's University ... NY ... 340
Syracuse University Main Campus ... NY ... 349
University at Buffalo-SUNY ... NY ... 343
East Carolina University ... NC .. 369
University of North Carolina at Chapel Hill NC .. 371
Kent State University Main Campus ... OH .. 384
Ohio State University Main Campus, The . OH .. 389
Ohio University Main Campus ... OH .. 389
University of Akron, Main Campus, The ... OH .. 392
University of Cincinnati Main Campus ... OH .. 393
@Pacific University ... OR .. 408
Bloomsburg University of Pennsylvania ... PA ... 430
Salus University ... PA ... 435
University of Pittsburgh ... PA ... 437
#University of Puerto Rico-Medical Sciences Campus ... PR ... 558
University of South Dakota, The ... SD ... 453
#East Tennessee State University ... TN ... 461
University of Memphis, The ... TN ... 462
University of Tennessee, Knoxville ... TN ... 465
Vanderbilt University ... TN ... 465
Lamar University ... TX ... 488
Texas Tech University Health Sciences Center ... TX ... 490
University of North Texas ... TX ... 492
University of Texas at Austin ... TX ... 493
University of Texas at Dallas, The ... TX ... 494
University of Utah, The ... UT ... 499
Utah State University ... UT ... 500
James Madison University ... VA ... 509
University of Washington ... WA .. 527
West Virginia University ... WV .. 533
University of Wisconsin-Madison ... WI ... 539
University of Wisconsin-Stevens Point ... WI ... 541

BBT: Commission on Accreditation of Allied Health Education Programs: blood bank technology (C,M)

Rush University ... IL ... 158
Johns Hopkins University ... MD .. 216
University of Texas Medical Branch, The . TX ... 495

BI: Association for Biblical Higher Education: bible college education (C,A,B,M,FP,D)

Heritage Christian University ... AL ... 4
Huntsville Bible College ... AL ... 4
@Legacy Christian University ... AL ... 5
Selma University ... AL ... 6
Southeastern Bible College ... AL ... 7
Alaska Bible College ... AK ... 10
Ecclesia College ... AR ... 20
American Evangelical University ... CA ... 27
Bethesda University of California ... CA ... 29
@Eternity Bible College ... CA ... 44
Grace Mission University ... CA ... 46
Hope International University ... CA ... 47
Horizon University ... CA ... 47
International Reformed University and Seminary ... CA ... 48
Life Pacific College ... CA ... 50
@Methodist Theological Seminary in America ... CA ... 54
Olivet University ... CA ... 57
Presbyterian Theological Seminary in America ... CA ... 60
SUM Bible College and Theological Seminary ... CA ... 69
William Jessup University ... CA ... 77
World Mission University ... CA ... 77
Nazarene Bible College ... CO ... 84
Hobe Sound Bible College ... FL ... 106
Robert E. Webber Institute for Worship Studies, The ... FL ... 111
South Florida Bible College ... FL ... 113
Trinity College of Florida ... FL ... 117
Beulah Heights University ... GA .. 121
Carver College ... GA .. 122
Luther Rice College and Seminary ... GA .. 128
Pacific Rim Christian University ... HI ... 135
Boise Bible College ... ID ... 137
Lincoln Christian University ... IL ... 150
Moody Bible Institute ... IL ... 153
Crossroads Bible College ... IN ... 165
@Faith Bible Seminary ... IN ... 165
@Union Bible College ... IN ... 173
Emmaus Bible College ... IA ... 178
Faith Baptist Bible College and Seminary IA ... 178
Barclay College ... KS ... 184
@Kansas Christian College ... KS ... 188
Manhattan Christian College ... KS ... 189
Clear Creek Baptist Bible College ... KY ... 194
Kentucky Mountain Bible College ... KY ... 197
Louisville Bible College ... KY ... 198
Simmons College of Kentucky ... KY ... 199
Northpoint Bible College ... MA .. 235
Grace Bible College ... MI ... 243
Great Lakes Christian College ... MI ... 243
Kuyper College ... MI ... 245
@Bethany Global University ... MN .. 253
Bethlehem College and Seminary ... MN .. 254
Oak Hills Christian College ... MN .. 263
Southeastern Baptist College ... MS .. 270
Baptist Bible College ... MO .. 272
@Brookes Bible College ... MO .. 272
Calvary Bible College and Theological Seminary ... MO .. 272
Central Christian College of the Bible ... MO .. 272
@Heartland Christian College ... MO .. 275
Midwest University ... MO .. 278
Ozark Christian College ... MO .. 280
Saint Louis Christian College ... MO .. 281
Montana Bible College ... MT ... 287
@Yellowstone Christian College ... MT ... 289
Grace University ... NE ... 290
Nebraska Christian College ... NE ... 291
@Summit Christian College ... NE ... 293
Pillar College ... NJ ... 305
Davis College ... NY ... 324
Carolina Christian College ... NC .. 355
Carolina College of Biblical Studies ... NC .. 355
Grace College of Divinity ... NC .. 357
Laurel University ... NC .. 358
@Native American Bible College ... NC .. 359
Trinity Bible College ... ND .. 375
Allegheny Wesleyan College ... OH .. 376
Cincinnati Christian University ... OH .. 379
God's Bible School and College ... OH .. 382
Ohio Christian University ... OH .. 388
Rosedale Bible College ... OH .. 390
Tri-State Bible College ... OH .. 392
@Valor Christian College ... OH .. 394
Family of Faith College ... OK .. 397
Multnomah University ... OR .. 407
New Hope Christian College ... OR .. 407
@Pacific Bible College ... OR .. 408
Cairn University ... PA ... 414
Lancaster Bible College ... PA ... 423
Summit University of Pennsylvania ... PA ... 435
Universidad Pentecostal Mizpa ... PR ... 556
Universidad Teologica Del Caribe ... PR ... 557
Columbia International University ... SC ... 445
American Baptist College ... TN ... 454
Johnson University ... TN ... 457
Mid-South Christian College ... TN ... 459
Welch College ... TN ... 466
Williamson College ... TN ... 466
Arlington Baptist College ... TX ... 468
Baptist University of the Americas ... TX ... 469
B.H. Carroll Theological Institute ... TX ... 469
College of Biblical Studies-Houston ... TX ... 470
Dallas Christian College ... TX ... 472
King's University, The ... TX ... 477
Rio Grande Bible Institute ... TX ... 481
Bethel College ... VA ... 505
Washington University of Virginia ... VA ... 519
@Wave Leadership College ... VA ... 519
Appalachian Bible College ... WV .. 529

BUS: AACSB-The Association to Advance Collegiate Schools of Business: business and management (B,M,D)

Auburn University ... AL ... 1
Auburn University at Montgomery ... AL ... 2
Jacksonville State University ... AL ... 4
Samford University ... AL ... 6
Tuskegee University ... AL ... 8
University of Alabama at Birmingham ... AL ... 8
University of Alabama in Huntsville ... AL ... 8
University of Alabama, The ... AL ... 8
University of Montevallo ... AL ... 9
University of South Alabama ... AL ... 9
University of Alaska Anchorage ... AK ... 10
University of Alaska Fairbanks ... AK ... 10
Arizona State University ... AZ ... 11
Northern Arizona University ... AZ ... 16
University of Arizona ... AZ ... 18
Arkansas State University-Jonesboro ... AR ... 19
Arkansas Tech University ... AR ... 20
Henderson State University ... AR ... 21
Ouachita Baptist University ... AR ... 22
Southern Arkansas University ... AR ... 23
University of Arkansas at Fort Smith ... AR ... 23
University of Arkansas at Little Rock ... AR ... 24
University of Arkansas Main Campus ... AR ... 23
University of Central Arkansas ... AR ... 25
California Polytechnic State University-San Luis Obispo ... CA ... 32
California State Polytechnic University-Pomona ... CA ... 32
California State University-Bakersfield ... CA ... 32
California State University-Chico ... CA ... 33
California State University-East Bay ... CA ... 33
California State University-Fresno ... CA ... 33
California State University-Fullerton ... CA ... 33
California State University-Long Beach ... CA ... 33
California State University-Los Angeles ... CA ... 34
California State University-Northridge ... CA ... 34
California State University-Sacramento ... CA ... 34
California State University-San Bernardino CA ... 35
California State University-Stanislaus ... CA ... 35
Chapman University ... CA ... 38
Claremont Graduate University ... CA ... 39
Loyola Marymount University ... CA ... 53
Menlo College ... CA ... 54
Naval Postgraduate School ... CA ... 548
Pepperdine University ... CA ... 58
Saint Mary's College of California ... CA ... 61
San Diego State University ... CA ... 35
San Francisco State University ... CA ... 36
San Jose State University ... CA ... 36
Santa Clara University ... CA ... 65
Sonoma State University ... CA ... 36
Stanford University ... CA ... 68
University of California-Berkeley ... CA ... 70
University of California-Davis ... CA ... 71
University of California-Irvine ... CA ... 71
University of California-Los Angeles ... CA ... 71
University of California-Riverside ... CA ... 72
University of California-San Diego ... CA ... 72
University of San Diego ... CA ... 74
University of San Francisco ... CA ... 74
University of Southern California ... CA ... 74
University of the Pacific ... CA ... 73
Woodbury University ... CA ... 77
Colorado State University ... CO ... 81
Colorado State University-Pueblo ... CO ... 81
Fort Lewis College ... CO ... 82
United States Air Force Academy ... CO .. 548
University of Colorado Boulder ... CO ... 86
University of Colorado Colorado Springs .. CO ... 86
University of Colorado Denver|Anschutz Medical Campus ... CO ... 86
University of Denver ... CO ... 86
University of Northern Colorado ... CO ... 87
Central Connecticut State University ... CT ... 88
Fairfield University ... CT ... 90
Quinnipiac University ... CT ... 91
Sacred Heart University ... CT ... 91
United States Coast Guard Academy ... CT ... 548
University of Connecticut ... CT ... 92
University of Hartford ... CT ... 92
University of New Haven ... CT ... 92
Yale University ... CT ... 93
Delaware State University ... DE ... 93
University of Delaware ... DE ... 94
American University ... DC ... 94
George Washington University ... DC ... 95
Georgetown University ... DC ... 95
Howard University ... DC ... 96
Barry University ... FL ... 99
Florida Atlantic University ... FL ... 114
Florida Gulf Coast University ... FL ... 114
Florida International University ... FL ... 114
Florida Southern College ... FL ... 104
Florida State University ... FL ... 115
Jacksonville University ... FL ... 106
Rollins College ... FL ... 111
Stetson University ... FL ... 117
University of Central Florida ... FL ... 115
University of Florida ... FL ... 115
University of Miami ... FL ... 118
University of North Florida ... FL ... 116
University of South Florida ... FL ... 116
University of South Florida St. Petersburg FL ... 116
University of Tampa ... FL ... 118
University of West Florida ... FL ... 116
Augusta University ... GA .. 121
Berry College ... GA .. 121
Clark Atlanta University ... GA .. 122
Clayton State University ... GA .. 122
Columbus State University ... GA .. 123
Dalton State College ... GA .. 123
Emory University ... GA .. 124
Georgia College & State University ... GA .. 125
Georgia Institute of Technology ... GA .. 125
Georgia Southern University ... GA .. 126
Georgia Southwestern State University ... GA .. 126
Georgia State University ... GA .. 126
Kennesaw State University ... GA .. 127
Mercer University ... GA .. 128
Morehouse College ... GA .. 128
Savannah State University ... GA .. 131
University of Georgia ... GA .. 132
University of North Georgia ... GA .. 133
University of West Georgia ... GA .. 133
Valdosta State University ... GA .. 133
University of Hawaii at Hilo ... HI ... 135
University of Hawaii at Manoa ... HI ... 135
Boise State University ... ID ... 137
Idaho State University ... ID ... 138
University of Idaho ... ID ... 139
Bradley University ... IL ... 140
DePaul University ... IL ... 143
Dominican University ... IL ... 144
Eastern Illinois University ... IL ... 144
Illinois Institute of Technology ... IL ... 147
Illinois State University ... IL ... 147
Loyola University Chicago ... IL ... 151
Northern Illinois University ... IL ... 154
Northwestern University ... IL ... 155
Saint Xavier University ... IL ... 158
Southern Illinois University Carbondale ... IL ... 159
Southern Illinois University Edwardsville ... IL ... 159
University of Chicago ... IL ... 161
University of Illinois at Chicago ... IL ... 161
University of Illinois at Springfield ... IL ... 161
University of Illinois at Urbana-Champaign IL ... 162
Western Illinois University ... IL ... 163
Ball State University ... IN ... 164
Butler University ... IN ... 164
Indiana State University ... IN ... 167
Indiana University Bloomington ... IN ... 167
Indiana University Kokomo ... IN ... 168
Indiana University Northwest ... IN ... 168
Indiana University-Purdue University Fort Wayne ... IN ... 168
Indiana University South Bend ... IN ... 168
Indiana University Southeast ... IN ... 169
Purdue University Calumet ... IN ... 171
Purdue University Main Campus ... IN ... 171
University of Evansville ... IN ... 173
University of Notre Dame ... IN ... 174
University of Southern Indiana ... IN ... 174
Valparaiso University ... IN ... 174
Iowa State University ... IA ... 175
University of Iowa ... IA ... 175
University of Northern Iowa ... IA ... 176
Emporia State University ... KS ... 186
Kansas State University ... KS ... 188
Pittsburg State University ... KS ... 190
University of Kansas Main Campus ... KS ... 191
Washburn University ... KS ... 192
Wichita State University ... KS ... 192
Bellarmine University ... KY ... 193
Eastern Kentucky University ... KY ... 194
Morehead State University ... KY ... 198
Murray State University ... KY ... 198
Northern Kentucky University ... KY ... 199
University of Kentucky ... KY ... 200
University of Louisville ... KY ... 201
Western Kentucky University ... KY ... 201
Grambling State University ... LA ... 207
Louisiana State University and Agricultural and Mechanical College ... LA ... 204
Louisiana State University in Shreveport .. LA ... 205
Louisiana Tech University ... LA ... 208
Loyola University New Orleans ... LA ... 206
McNeese State University ... LA ... 208
Nicholls State University ... LA ... 208
Northwestern State University ... LA ... 208
Southeastern Louisiana University ... LA ... 208
Southern University and A&M College ... LA ... 207
Southern University at New Orleans ... LA ... 207
Tulane University ... LA ... 207
University of Louisiana at Lafayette ... LA ... 208
University of Louisiana at Monroe ... LA ... 209
University of New Orleans ... LA ... 205
University of Maine ... ME .. 212
University of Southern Maine ... ME .. 213
Frostburg State University ... MD .. 220
Loyola University Maryland ... MD .. 216
Morgan State University ... MD .. 217
Salisbury University ... MD .. 220
Towson University ... MD .. 221
University of Baltimore ... MD .. 221
University of Maryland College Park ... MD .. 219
University of Maryland Eastern Shore ... MD .. 219
Babson College ... MA .. 222
Bentley University ... MA .. 223
Boston College ... MA .. 224
Boston University ... MA .. 224
Brandeis University ... MA .. 224
Clark University ... MA .. 225
Harvard University ... MA .. 227
Massachusetts Institute of Technology ... MA .. 233
Northeastern University ... MA .. 235
Simmons College ... MA .. 236
Stonehill College ... MA .. 237
Suffolk University ... MA .. 237
University of Massachusetts ... MA .. 228
University of Massachusetts Boston ... MA .. 228
University of Massachusetts Dartmouth ... MA .. 228
University of Massachusetts Lowell ... MA .. 229

Western New England University ... MA .. 238
Worcester Polytechnic Institute ... MA .. 238
Central Michigan University ... MI ... 240
Eastern Michigan University ... MI ... 242
Grand Valley State University ... MI ... 243
Michigan State University ... MI ... 246
Michigan Technological University ... MI ... 247
Northern Michigan University ... MI ... 248
Oakland University ... MI ... 248
Saginaw Valley State University ... MI ... 249
University of Detroit Mercy ... MI ... 250
University of Michigan-Ann Arbor ... MI ... 251
University of Michigan-Dearborn ... MI ... 251
University of Michigan-Flint ... MI ... 251
Wayne State University ... MI ... 252
Western Michigan University ... MI ... 252
Minnesota State University Moorhead ... MN .. 260
Minnesota State University, Mankato ... MN .. 260
St. Cloud State University ... MN .. 261
University of Minnesota Duluth ... MN .. 264
University of Minnesota-Twin Cities ... MN .. 265
University of Saint Thomas ... MN .. 265
Winona State University ... MN .. 262
Jackson State University ... MS .. 267
Millsaps College ... MS .. 268
Mississippi State University ... MS .. 269
University of Mississippi ... MS .. 270
University of Southern Mississippi ... MS .. 271
Drury University ... MO .. 274
Missouri State University ... MO .. 279
Missouri University of Science & Technology ... MO .. 284
Missouri Western State University ... MO .. 279
Rockhurst University ... MO .. 281
Saint Louis University ... MO .. 281
Southeast Missouri State University ... MO .. 282
Truman State University ... MO .. 283
University of Central Missouri ... MO .. 283
University of Missouri - Columbia ... MO .. 283
University of Missouri - Kansas City ... MO .. 284
University of Missouri - Saint Louis ... MO .. 284
Washington University in St. Louis ... MO .. 285
Montana State University ... MT .. 287
Montana State University - Billings ... MT .. 287
University of Montana - Missoula ... MT .. 287
Creighton University ... NE ... 290
University of Nebraska at Kearney ... NE ... 293
University of Nebraska at Omaha ... NE ... 294
University of Nebraska - Lincoln ... NE ... 293
University of Nevada, Las Vegas ... NV ... 295
University of Nevada, Reno ... NV ... 295
Dartmouth College ... NH .. 297
University of New Hampshire ... NH .. 299
College of New Jersey, The ... NJ ... 301
Fairleigh Dickinson University ... NJ ... 302
Monmouth University ... NJ ... 303
Montclair State University ... NJ ... 304
New Jersey Institute of Technology ... NJ ... 304
Ramapo College of New Jersey ... NJ ... 305
Rider University ... NJ ... 306
Rowan University ... NJ ... 306
Rutgers the State University of New Jersey Camden Campus ... NJ ... 307
Rutgers the State University of New Jersey Newark Campus ... NJ ... 307
Seton Hall University ... NJ ... 308
Stevens Institute of Technology ... NJ ... 308
William Paterson University of New Jersey ... NJ ... 309
New Mexico State University Main Campus ... NM .. 312
University of New Mexico Main Campus .. NM .. 313
Adelphi University ... NY ... 314
Alfred University ... NY ... 314
Baruch College/City University of New York ... NY ... 318
Canisius College ... NY ... 317
Clarkson University ... NY ... 321
Columbia University in the City of New York ... NY ... 322
Cornell University ... NY ... 323
Fordham University ... NY ... 326
Hofstra University ... NY ... 328
Iona College ... NY ... 328
Ithaca College ... NY ... 328
Le Moyne College ... NY ... 330
LIU Post ... NY ... 330
Manhattan College ... NY ... 331
Marist College ... NY ... 331
New York Institute of Technology ... NY ... 335
New York University ... NY ... 336
Niagara University ... NY ... 336
Pace University ... NY ... 337
Rensselaer Polytechnic Institute ... NY ... 339
Rochester Institute of Technology ... NY ... 339
St. Bonaventure University ... NY ... 340
St. John Fisher College ... NY ... 340
St. John's University ... NY ... 340
Siena College ... NY ... 342
State University of New York at Binghamton ... NY ... 343
State University of New York at New Paltz NY ... 344
State University of New York at Oneonta . NY ... 344
State University of New York College at Geneseo ... NY ... 345
State University of New York College at Oswego ... NY ... 346
State University of New York College at Plattsburgh ... NY ... 346
State University of New York, The College at Brockport ... NY ... 345
SUNY Polytechnic Institute ... NY ... 348
Syracuse University Main Campus ... NY ... 349
Union Graduate College ... NY ... 351
University at Albany, SUNY ... NY ... 343
University at Buffalo-SUNY ... NY ... 343
University of Rochester ... NY ... 351
Yeshiva University ... NY ... 353
Appalachian State University ... NC .. 369
Duke University ... NC .. 356
East Carolina University ... NC .. 369
Elizabeth City State University ... NC .. 369
Elon University ... NC .. 356
Fayetteville State University ... NC .. 370
Meredith College ... NC .. 359
North Carolina Agricultural and Technical State University ... NC .. 370
North Carolina Central University ... NC .. 370
North Carolina State University ... NC .. 370
Queens University of Charlotte ... NC .. 368
University of North Carolina at Asheville .. NC .. 370
University of North Carolina at Chapel Hill NC .. 371
University of North Carolina at Charlotte .. NC .. 371
University of North Carolina at Greensboro ... NC .. 371
University of North Carolina at Pembroke NC .. 371
University of North Carolina Wilmington ... NC .. 372
Wake Forest University ... NC .. 372
Western Carolina University ... NC .. 372
Winston-Salem State University ... NC .. 372
North Dakota State University Main Campus ... ND .. 374
University of North Dakota ... ND .. 373
Bowling Green State University ... OH .. 377
Case Western Reserve University ... OH .. 378
Cleveland State University ... OH .. 380
John Carroll University ... OH .. 384
Kent State University Main Campus ... OH .. 384
Miami University ... OH .. 386
Ohio Northern University ... OH .. 388
Ohio State University Main Campus, The . OH .. 389
Ohio University Main Campus ... OH .. 389
University of Akron, Main Campus, The ... OH .. 392
University of Cincinnati Main Campus ... OH .. 393
University of Dayton ... OH .. 393
University of Toledo ... OH .. 394
Wright State University Main Campus ... OH .. 396
Xavier University ... OH .. 396
Youngstown State University ... OH .. 396
Oklahoma City University ... OK .. 400
Oklahoma State University ... OK .. 400
Southeastern Oklahoma State University . OK .. 402
University of Oklahoma Norman Campus . OK .. 403
University of Tulsa ... OK .. 403
Oregon State University ... OR .. 408
Portland State University ... OR .. 409
University of Oregon ... OR .. 410
University of Portland ... OR .. 410
Willamette University ... OR .. 411
Bloomsburg University of Pennsylvania ... PA ... 430
Bucknell University ... PA ... 413
Carnegie Mellon University ... PA ... 414
Clarion University of Pennsylvania ... PA ... 430
Drexel University ... PA ... 417
Duquesne University ... PA ... 417
Indiana University of Pennsylvania ... PA ... 431
King's College ... PA ... 422
Kutztown University of Pennsylvania ... PA ... 431
La Salle University ... PA ... 422
Lehigh University ... PA ... 424
Penn State University Park ... PA ... 428
Robert Morris University ... PA ... 434
Saint Joseph's University ... PA ... 434
Shippensburg University of Pennsylvania . PA ... 431
Susquehanna University ... PA ... 435
Temple University ... PA ... 436
University of Pennsylvania ... PA ... 437
University of Pittsburgh ... PA ... 437
University of Scranton, The ... PA ... 438
Villanova University ... PA ... 439
West Chester University of Pennsylvania . PA ... 432
Widener University ... PA ... 439
Universidad Del Turabo ... PR ... 555
University of Puerto Rico-Rio Piedras Campus ... PR ... 558
Bryant University ... RI ... 441
Providence College ... RI ... 441
Roger Williams University ... RI ... 442
University of Rhode Island ... RI ... 442
Citadel, The Military College of South Carolina, The ... SC ... 444
Clemson University ... SC ... 444
Coastal Carolina University ... SC ... 444
College of Charleston ... SC ... 445
Francis Marion University ... SC ... 446
Lander University ... SC ... 447
South Carolina State University ... SC ... 448
University of South Carolina Aiken ... SC ... 450
University of South Carolina Columbia ... SC ... 450
University of South Carolina Upstate ... SC ... 451
Winthrop University ... SC ... 451
Black Hills State University ... SD ... 453
University of South Dakota, The ... SD ... 453
Belmont University ... TN ... 455
East Tennessee State University ... TN ... 461
Middle Tennessee State University ... TN ... 461
Tennessee State University ... TN ... 461
Tennessee Technological University ... TN ... 462
Union University ... TN ... 464
University of Memphis, The ... TN ... 462
University of Tennessee at Chattanooga .. TN ... 465
University of Tennessee at Martin ... TN ... 465
University of Tennessee, Knoxville ... TN ... 465
Vanderbilt University ... TN ... 465
Abilene Christian University ... TX ... 466
Baylor University ... TX ... 469
Lamar University ... TX ... 488
Midwestern State University ... TX ... 478
Prairie View A & M University ... TX ... 484
Rice University ... TX ... 480
St. Mary's University ... TX ... 481
Sam Houston State University ... TX ... 489
Southern Methodist University ... TX ... 482
Stephen F. Austin State University ... TX ... 484
Texas A & M International University ... TX ... 485
Texas A & M University ... TX ... 485
Texas A & M University - Commerce ... TX ... 485
Texas A & M University - Corpus Christi .. TX ... 485
Texas Christian University ... TX ... 486
Texas Southern University ... TX ... 487
Texas State University ... TX ... 489
Texas Tech University ... TX ... 489
Texas Wesleyan University ... TX ... 490
Trinity University ... TX ... 490
University of Dallas ... TX ... 491
University of Houston ... TX ... 491
University of Houston - Clear Lake ... TX ... 491
University of Houston - Downtown ... TX ... 491
University of Houston - Victoria ... TX ... 492
University of North Texas ... TX ... 492
University of St. Thomas ... TX ... 493
University of Texas at Arlington, The ... TX ... 493
University of Texas at Austin ... TX ... 493
University of Texas at Dallas, The ... TX ... 494
University of Texas at El Paso ... TX ... 494
University of Texas at San Antonio ... TX ... 494
University of Texas at Tyler ... TX ... 494
University of Texas of the Permian Basin . TX ... 495
University of Texas Rio Grande Valley ... TX ... 494
West Texas A & M University ... TX ... 486
Brigham Young University ... UT ... 497
Southern Utah University ... UT ... 499
University of Utah, The ... UT ... 499
Utah State University ... UT ... 500
Utah Valley University ... UT ... 500
Weber State University ... UT ... 500
University of Vermont ... VT ... 503
Christopher Newport University ... VA ... 506
College of William & Mary ... VA ... 506
George Mason University ... VA ... 507
James Madison University ... VA ... 509
Longwood University ... VA ... 509
Norfolk State University ... VA ... 510
Old Dominion University ... VA ... 510
Radford University ... VA ... 511
Shenandoah University ... VA ... 512
University of Richmond ... VA ... 513
University of Virginia ... VA ... 514
Virginia Commonwealth University ... VA ... 514
Virginia Military Institute ... VA ... 518
Virginia Polytechnic Institute and State University ... VA ... 518
Virginia State University ... VA ... 518
Washington and Lee University ... VA ... 519
Central Washington University ... WA .. 520
Eastern Washington University ... WA .. 522
Gonzaga University ... WA .. 522
Pacific Lutheran University ... WA .. 524
Seattle Pacific University ... WA .. 526
Seattle University ... WA .. 526
University of Washington ... WA .. 527
Washington State University ... WA .. 528
Western Washington University ... WA .. 528
Marshall University ... WV .. 532
West Virginia University ... WV .. 533
Marquette University ... WI ... 537
University of Wisconsin-Eau Claire ... WI ... 539
University of Wisconsin-La Crosse ... WI ... 539
University of Wisconsin-Madison ... WI ... 539
University of Wisconsin-Milwaukee ... WI ... 540
University of Wisconsin-Oshkosh ... WI ... 540
University of Wisconsin-Parkside ... WI ... 540
University of Wisconsin-River Falls ... WI ... 540
University of Wisconsin-Whitewater ... WI ... 541
University of Wyoming ... WY .. 546

BUSA: AACSB-The Association to Advance Collegiate Schools of Business: accounting (B,M,D)

Auburn University ... AL ... 1
Auburn University at Montgomery ... AL ... 2
University of Alabama at Birmingham ... AL ... 8
University of Alabama, The ... AL ... 8
University of South Alabama ... AL ... 9
University of Alaska Fairbanks ... AK ... 10
Arizona State University ... AZ ... 11
University of Arizona ... AZ ... 18
University of Arkansas Main Campus ... AR ... 23
California State University-Fullerton ... CA ... 33
San Diego State University ... CA ... 35
Santa Clara University ... CA ... 65
University of San Diego ... CA ... 74
University of Southern California ... CA ... 74
University of Colorado Denver|Anschutz Medical Campus ... CO ... 86
University of Denver ... CO ... 86
University of Northern Colorado ... CO ... 87
University of Connecticut ... CT ... 92
University of Delaware ... DE ... 94
George Washington University ... DC ... 95
Howard University ... DC ... 96
Florida International University ... FL ... 114
Florida State University ... FL ... 115
Stetson University ... FL ... 117
University of Central Florida ... FL ... 115
University of Florida ... FL ... 115
University of Miami ... FL ... 118
University of North Florida ... FL ... 116
University of South Florida ... FL ... 116
University of South Florida St. Petersburg FL ... 116
Georgia Southern University ... GA ... 126
Georgia State University ... GA ... 126
Kennesaw State University ... GA ... 127
University of Georgia ... GA ... 132
University of West Georgia ... GA ... 133
Boise State University ... ID ... 137
Idaho State University ... ID ... 138
University of Idaho ... ID ... 139
Bradley University ... IL ... 140
DePaul University ... IL ... 143
Eastern Illinois University ... IL ... 144
Illinois State University ... IL ... 147
Loyola University Chicago ... IL ... 151
Northern Illinois University ... IL ... 154
Southern Illinois University Carbondale ... IL ... 159
Southern Illinois University Edwardsville .. IL ... 159
University of Illinois at Chicago ... IL ... 161
University of Illinois at Urbana-Champaign IL ... 162
Western Illinois University ... IL ... 163
Ball State University ... IN ... 164
Indiana University Bloomington ... IN ... 167
University of Notre Dame ... IN ... 174
University of Southern Indiana ... IN ... 174
Iowa State University ... IA ... 175
University of Iowa ... IA ... 175
Kansas State University ... KS ... 188
University of Kansas Main Campus ... KS ... 191
Wichita State University ... KS ... 192
University of Kentucky ... KY ... 200
University of Louisville ... KY ... 201
Western Kentucky University ... KY ... 201
Louisiana Tech University ... LA ... 208
Nicholls State University ... LA ... 208
Southeastern Louisiana University ... LA ... 208
University of Louisiana at Lafayette ... LA ... 208
University of Louisiana at Monroe ... LA ... 209
University of New Orleans ... LA ... 205
Loyola University Maryland ... MD ... 216
Morgan State University ... MD ... 217
Salisbury University ... MD ... 220
Towson University ... MD ... 221
Bentley University ... MA ... 223
Suffolk University ... MA ... 237
University of Massachusetts ... MA ... 228
Central Michigan University ... MI ... 240
Grand Valley State University ... MI ... 243
Michigan State University ... MI ... 246
Oakland University ... MI ... 248
Western Michigan University ... MI ... 252
Mississippi State University ... MS ... 269
University of Mississippi ... MS ... 270
University of Southern Mississippi ... MS ... 271
Missouri State University ... MO ... 279
Truman State University ... MO ... 283
University of Central Missouri ... MO ... 283
University of Missouri - Columbia ... MO .. 283

CA: National Accrediting Agency for Clinical Laboratory Sciences: clinical assistant (C)

CAATE: Commission on Accreditation of Athletic Training Education: athletic training (B,M)

CACREP: Council for Accreditation of Counseling & Related Educational Programs: addiction counseling, career counseling, marriage, couple and family counseling, mental health counseling, school counseling, student affairs and college counseling (M) and counselor education and supervision (D)

CAEP: Council for the Accreditation of Educator Preparation: teacher education (B,M,D)

CAHIIM: Commission on Accreditation for Health Informatics and Information Management Education: health information management and health informatics (A,B,M)

CARTE: Commission on Accreditation of Recreational Therapy Education: recreational therapy (B,M)

CEA: Commission on English Language Program Accreditation: english language (C)

Michigan Technological University ... MI ... 247
Saginaw Valley State University ... MI ... 249
University of Michigan-Dearborn ... MI ... 251
University of Michigan-Flint ... MI ... 251
Western Michigan University ... MI ... 252
University of Minnesota Duluth ... MN .. 264
Missouri State University ... MO .. 279
Missouri University of Science & Technology ... MO .. 284
University of Central Missouri ... MO .. 283
College of Southern Nevada ... NV ... 295
University of Nevada, Reno ... NV ... 295
Rutgers the State University of New Jersey New Brunswick Campus ... NJ ... 307
University of Northern New Jersey ... NJ ... 309
Columbia University in the City of New York ... NY ... 322
University at Buffalo-SUNY ... NY ... 343
East Carolina University ... NC .. 369
University of North Carolina Wilmington ... NC .. 372
Ashland University ... OH .. 377
Cleveland State University ... OH .. 380
University of Findlay, The ... OH .. 393
Wright State University Main Campus ... OH .. 396
Xavier University ... OH .. 396
Oregon State University ... OR .. 408
Portland State University ... OR .. 409
University of Oregon ... OR .. 410
Willamette University ... OR .. 411
Drexel University ... PA ... 417
Duquesne University ... PA ... 417
Penn State University Park ... PA ... 428
University of Pennsylvania ... PA ... 437
University of Pittsburgh ... PA ... 437
Wilkes University ... PA ... 440
University of South Carolina Columbia ... SC ... 450
Lincoln Memorial University ... TN ... 458
Lone Star College System ... TX ... 477
San Antonio College ... TX ... 467
Stephen F. Austin State University ... TX ... 484
Texas A & M University ... TX ... 485
Texas State University ... TX ... 489
University of Houston ... TX ... 491
University of North Texas ... TX ... 492
University of Texas at Arlington, The ... TX ... 493
University of Texas at Austin ... TX ... 493
University of Utah, The ... UT ... 499
Utah State University ... UT ... 500
Utah Valley University ... UT ... 500
Weber State University ... UT ... 500
Saint Michael's College ... VT ... 502
American National University ... VA ... 504
George Mason University ... VA ... 507
Virginia Commonwealth University ... VA ... 514
Virginia Polytechnic Institute and State University ... VA ... 518
Gonzaga University ... WA ... 522
University of Washington ... WA ... 527
Washington State University ... WA ... 528
University of Wisconsin-Milwaukee ... WI ... 540

CGTECH: National Accrediting Agency for Clinical Laboratory Sciences: cytogenetic technologist (B)

University of Connecticut ... CT ... 92
Kennesaw State University ... GA .. 127
Northern Michigan University ... MI ... 248
University of Texas M.D. Anderson Cancer Center, The ... TX ... 495

CHIRO: Council on Chiropractic Education: chiropractic education (FP,D)

Life Chiropractic College West ... CA ... 50
Southern California University of Health Sciences ... CA ... 67
University of Bridgeport ... CT ... 92
Life University ... GA .. 128
National University of Health Sciences ... IL ... 154
Palmer College of Chiropractic ... IA ... 182
Cleveland University - Kansas City ... KS ... 185
Northwestern Health Sciences University . MN .. 263
Logan University ... MO .. 277
D'Youville College ... NY ... 324
New York Chiropractic College ... NY ... 334
University of Western States ... OR .. 410
Sherman College of Chiropractic ... SC ... 448
Parker University ... TX ... 480
Texas Chiropractic College ... TX ... 486

CIDA: Council for Interior Design Accreditation: interior design (B,M)

Auburn University ... AL ... 1
Samford University ... AL ... 6
University of Alabama, The ... AL ... 8
University of North Alabama ... AL ... 9
Virginia College ... AL ... 3
Arizona State University ... AZ ... 11
Art Institute of Phoenix, The ... AZ ... 12
Southwest University of Visual Arts ... AZ ... 17
Harding University Main Campus ... AR ... 21
University of Arkansas Main Campus ... AR ... 23
University of Central Arkansas ... AR ... 25
#Academy of Art University ... CA ... 25
California College of the Arts ... CA ... 30
California State Polytechnic University-Pomona ... CA ... 32
California State University-Fresno ... CA ... 33
California State University-Northridge ... CA ... 34
California State University-Sacramento ... CA ... 34
Design Institute of San Diego ... CA ... 43
Interior Designers Institute ... CA ... 47
#San Diego State University ... CA ... 35
Woodbury University ... CA ... 77
Art Institute of Colorado, The ... CO ... 79
Colorado State University ... CO ... 81
Rocky Mountain College of Art & Design . CO ... 85
George Washington University ... DC ... 95
Art Institute of Fort Lauderdale, The ... FL ... 98
Florida International University ... FL ... 114
Florida State University ... FL ... 115
Miami International University of Art & Design ... FL ... 109
Ringling College of Art and Design ... FL ... 111
Sanford-Brown College Tampa ... FL ... 112
University of Florida ... FL ... 115
Art Institute of Atlanta, The ... GA .. 120
Brenau University ... GA .. 121
Georgia Southern University ... GA .. 126
Savannah College of Art and Design ... GA .. 130
University of Georgia ... GA .. 132
Chaminade University of Honolulu ... HI ... 135
University of Idaho ... ID ... 139
Columbia College Chicago ... IL ... 143
Harrington College of Design ... IL ... 145
Illinois Institute of Art, The ... IL ... 147
Illinois State University ... IL ... 147
Southern Illinois University Carbondale ... IL ... 159
Ball State University ... IN ... 164
Indiana State University ... IN ... 167
Indiana University Bloomington ... IN ... 167
Indiana University-Purdue University Indianapolis ... IN ... 168
Purdue University Main Campus ... IN ... 171
Iowa State University ... IA ... 175
Kansas State University ... KS ... 188
Sullivan College of Technology and Design ... KY ... 200
University of Kentucky ... KY ... 200
#University of Louisville ... KY ... 201
Louisiana State University and Agricultural and Mechanical College ... LA ... 204
Louisiana Tech University ... LA ... 208
University of Louisiana at Lafayette ... LA ... 208
Boston Architectural College ... MA .. 223
Endicott College ... MA .. 226
Mount Ida College ... MA .. 234
Suffolk University ... MA .. 237
Wentworth Institute of Technology ... MA .. 237
Central Michigan University ... MI ... 240
College for Creative Studies ... MI ... 241
Eastern Michigan University ... MI ... 242
Ferris State University ... MI ... 242
Lawrence Technological University ... MI ... 245
Michigan State University ... MI ... 246
Western Michigan University ... MI ... 252
Dunwoody College of Technology ... MN .. 255
University of Minnesota-Twin Cities ... MN .. 265
Mississippi College ... MS .. 268
Mississippi State University ... MS .. 269
University of Southern Mississippi ... MS .. 271
Maryville University of Saint Louis ... MO .. 277
University of Central Missouri ... MO .. 283
University of Missouri - Columbia ... MO .. 283
University of Nebraska at Kearney ... NE ... 293
University of Nebraska - Lincoln ... NE ... 293
University of Nevada, Las Vegas ... NV ... 295
Kean University ... NJ ... 303
New Jersey Institute of Technology ... NJ ... 304
Cornell University ... NY ... 323
Fashion Institute of Technology ... NY ... 325
New York Institute of Technology ... NY ... 335
New York School of Interior Design ... NY ... 336
Pratt Institute ... NY ... 338
Rochester Institute of Technology ... NY ... 339
School of Visual Arts ... NY ... 342
#State University of New York College at Buffalo ... NY ... 345
Syracuse University Main Campus ... NY ... 349
Villa Maria College of Buffalo ... NY ... 352
Appalachian State University ... NC .. 369
East Carolina University ... NC .. 369
High Point University ... NC .. 357
Meredith College ... NC .. 359
University of North Carolina at Greensboro ... NC .. 371
Western Carolina University ... NC .. 372
North Dakota State University Main Campus ... ND .. 374
Columbus College of Art & Design ... OH .. 380
Kent State University Main Campus ... OH .. 384
Miami University ... OH .. 386
Ohio State University Main Campus, The . OH .. 389
Ohio University Main Campus ... OH .. 389
University of Akron, Main Campus, The ... OH .. 392
University of Cincinnati Main Campus ... OH .. 393
Oklahoma Christian University ... OK .. 399
Oklahoma State University ... OK .. 400
University of Central Oklahoma ... OK .. 403
University of Oklahoma Norman Campus . OK .. 403
Art Institute of Portland, The ... OR .. 404
Marylhurst University ... OR .. 407
University of Oregon ... OR .. 410
Art Institute of Philadelphia ... PA ... 412
Art Institute of Pittsburgh ... PA ... 412
Chatham University ... PA ... 415
Drexel University ... PA ... 417
La Roche College ... PA ... 422
Moore College of Art and Design ... PA ... 426
Philadelphia University ... PA ... 432
Converse College ... SC ... 445
Winthrop University ... SC ... 451
South Dakota State University ... SD ... 454
Middle Tennessee State University ... TN ... 461
O'More College of Design ... TN ... 460
University of Memphis, The ... TN ... 462
University of Tennessee at Chattanooga .. TN ... 465
University of Tennessee, Knoxville ... TN ... 465
Watkins College of Art, Design & Film ... TN ... 466
Abilene Christian University ... TX ... 466
Art Institute of Houston, The ... TX ... 468
Baylor University ... TX ... 469
Sam Houston State University ... TX ... 489
Stephen F. Austin State University ... TX ... 484
Texas Christian University ... TX ... 486
Texas State University ... TX ... 489
Texas Tech University ... TX ... 489
University of North Texas ... TX ... 492
University of Texas at Arlington, The ... TX ... 493
University of Texas at Austin ... TX ... 493
University of Texas at San Antonio ... TX ... 494
University of the Incarnate Word ... TX ... 492
Utah State University ... UT ... 500
Weber State University ... UT ... 500
Marymount University ... VA ... 510
Radford University ... VA ... 511
Virginia Commonwealth University ... VA ... 514
Virginia Polytechnic Institute and State University ... VA ... 518
Art Institute of Seattle, The ... WA .. 519
Bellevue College ... WA .. 519
Washington State University ... WA .. 528
University of Charleston ... WV ... 530
Mount Mary University ... WI ... 538
University of Wisconsin-Madison ... WI ... 539
University of Wisconsin-Stevens Point ... WI ... 541
University of Wisconsin-Stout ... WI ... 541

CLPSY: American Psychological Association: clinical psychology (D)

Auburn University ... AL ... 1
University of Alabama at Birmingham ... AL ... 8
University of Alabama, The ... AL ... 8
University of Alaska Anchorage ... AK ... 10
University of Alaska Fairbanks ... AK ... 10
Arizona State University ... AZ ... 11
University of Arizona ... AZ ... 18
University of Arkansas Main Campus ... AR ... 23
Alliant International University-San Diego . CA ... 26
Argosy University, Orange County ... CA ... 28
Azusa Pacific University ... CA ... 29
Biola University ... CA ... 29
California Lutheran University ... CA ... 31
Fielding Graduate University ... CA ... 44
Fuller Theological Seminary ... CA ... 45
John F. Kennedy University ... CA ... 48
Loma Linda University ... CA ... 50
Palo Alto University ... CA ... 58
Pepperdine University ... CA ... 58
San Diego State University ... CA ... 35
University of California-Berkeley ... CA ... 70
University of California-Los Angeles ... CA ... 71
University of California-San Diego ... CA ... 72
University of La Verne ... CA ... 73
University of Southern California ... CA ... 74
Wright Institute, The ... CA ... 77
University of Colorado Boulder ... CO ... 86
University of Colorado Colorado Springs .. CO ... 86
University of Colorado Denver|Anschutz Medical Campus ... CO ... 86
University of Denver ... CO ... 86
University of Connecticut ... CT ... 92
University of Hartford ... CT ... 92
Yale University ... CT ... 93
University of Delaware ... DE ... 94
American University ... DC ... 94
Catholic University of America, The ... DC ... 95
Gallaudet University ... DC ... 95
George Washington University ... DC ... 95
Howard University ... DC ... 96
Florida Institute of Technology ... FL ... 103
Florida State University ... FL ... 115
Nova Southeastern University ... FL ... 109
University of Central Florida ... FL ... 115
University of Florida ... FL ... 115
University of Miami ... FL ... 118
University of South Florida ... FL ... 116
Emory University ... GA .. 124
Georgia Southern University ... GA .. 126
Georgia State University ... GA .. 126
University of Georgia ... GA .. 132
University of Hawaii at Manoa ... HI ... 135
Idaho State University ... ID ... 138
Adler University ... IL ... 139
DePaul University ... IL ... 143
Illinois Institute of Technology ... IL ... 147
Loyola University Chicago ... IL ... 151
Midwestern University ... IL ... 152
Northern Illinois University ... IL ... 154
Northwestern University ... IL ... 155
Roosevelt University ... IL ... 157
Rosalind Franklin University of Medicine & Science ... IL ... 157
Southern Illinois University Carbondale ... IL ... 159
University of Illinois at Chicago ... IL ... 161
University of Illinois at Urbana-Champaign IL ... 162
Wheaton College ... IL ... 163
Indiana State University ... IN ... 167
Indiana University Bloomington ... IN ... 167
Indiana University-Purdue University Indianapolis ... IN ... 168
Purdue University Main Campus ... IN ... 171
University of Indianapolis ... IN ... 173
University of Iowa ... IA ... 175
University of Kansas Main Campus ... KS ... 191
Wichita State University ... KS ... 192
Spalding University ... KY ... 199
University of Kentucky ... KY ... 200
University of Louisville ... KY ... 201
#Louisiana State University and Agricultural and Mechanical College ... LA ... 204
University of Maine ... ME .. 212
Loyola University Maryland ... MD .. 216
Uniformed Services University of the Health Sciences ... MD .. 548
University of Maryland Baltimore County .. MD .. 219
University of Maryland College Park ... MD .. 219
Boston University ... MA .. 224
Clark University ... MA .. 225
Harvard University ... MA .. 227
Suffolk University ... MA .. 237
University of Massachusetts ... MA .. 228
University of Massachusetts Boston ... MA .. 228
William James College ... MA .. 238
Central Michigan University ... MI ... 240
Eastern Michigan University ... MI ... 242
Michigan State University ... MI ... 246
University of Detroit Mercy ... MI ... 250
University of Michigan-Ann Arbor ... MI ... 251
Wayne State University ... MI ... 252
Western Michigan University ... MI ... 252
University of Minnesota-Twin Cities ... MN .. 265
Jackson State University ... MS .. 267
University of Mississippi ... MS .. 270
University of Southern Mississippi ... MS .. 271
Saint Louis University ... MO .. 281
University of Missouri - Columbia ... MO .. 283
University of Missouri - Kansas City ... MO .. 284
University of Missouri - Saint Louis ... MO .. 284
Washington University in St. Louis ... MO .. 285
University of Montana - Missoula ... MT .. 287
University of Nebraska - Lincoln ... NE ... 293
University of Nevada, Las Vegas ... NV ... 295
University of Nevada, Reno ... NV ... 295
Fairleigh Dickinson University ... NJ ... 302
Rutgers the State University of New Jersey New Brunswick Campus ... NJ ... 307
University of New Mexico Main Campus .. NM .. 313
Adelphi University ... NY ... 314
City University of New York John Jay College of Criminal Justice ... NY ... 319
City University of New York Queens College ... NY ... 320
City University of New York The City College ... NY ... 318
Fordham University ... NY ... 326
Hofstra University ... NY ... 328
New School, The ... NY ... 334
St. John's University ... NY ... 340
State University of New York at Binghamton ... NY ... 343
Stony Brook University ... NY ... 344

Syracuse University Main Campus .... NY ... 349
Teachers College, Columbia University .... NY ... 349
University at Albany, SUNY .... NY ... 343
University at Buffalo-SUNY .... NY ... 343
University of Rochester .... NY ... 351
Yeshiva University .... NY ... 353
Duke University .... NC .. 356
East Carolina University .... NC .. 369
University of North Carolina at Chapel Hill NC .. 371
University of North Carolina at Charlotte .. NC .. 371
University of North Carolina at Greensboro .... NC .. 371
University of North Dakota .... ND .. 373
Bowling Green State University .... OH .. 377
Case Western Reserve University .... OH .. 378
Kent State University Main Campus .... OH .. 384
Miami University .... OH .. 386
Ohio State University Main Campus, The . OH .. 389
Ohio University Main Campus .... OH .. 389
University of Cincinnati Main Campus ...... OH .. 393
University of Toledo .... OH .. 394
Wright State University Main Campus ...... OH .. 396
Xavier University .... OH .. 396
Oklahoma State University .... OK .. 400
University of Tulsa .... OK .. 403
George Fox University .... OR .. 406
Pacific University .... OR .. 408
University of Oregon .... OR .. 410
Chestnut Hill College .... PA ... 415
Drexel University .... PA ... 417
Duquesne University .... PA ... 417
Immaculata University .... PA ... 421
Indiana University of Pennsylvania .... PA ... 431
La Salle University .... PA ... 422
Marywood University .... PA ... 425
Penn State University Park .... PA ... 428
Philadelphia College of Osteopathic Medicine .... PA ... 432
Temple University .... PA ... 436
University of Pennsylvania .... PA ... 437
University of Pittsburgh .... PA ... 437
Widener University .... PA ... 439
Carlos Albizu University .... PR ... 551
Ponce School of Medicine & Health Sciences .... PR ... 555
University of Rhode Island .... RI ... 442
University of South Carolina Columbia ..... SC ... 450
University of South Dakota, The .... SD ... 453
East Tennessee State University .... TN ... 461
University of Memphis, The .... TN ... 462
University of Tennessee, Knoxville .... TN ... 465
Vanderbilt University .... TN ... 465
Baylor University .... TX ... 469
Sam Houston State University .... TX ... 489
Southern Methodist University .... TX ... 482
Texas A & M University .... TX ... 485
Texas Tech University .... TX ... 489
University of Houston .... TX ... 491
University of North Texas .... TX ... 492
University of Texas at Austin .... TX ... 493
University of Texas Southwestern Medical Center .... TX ... 496
Brigham Young University .... UT ... 497
University of Utah, The .... UT ... 499
University of Vermont .... VT ... 503
Eastern Virginia Medical School .... VA ... 507
George Mason University .... VA ... 507
Norfolk State University .... VA ... 510
Old Dominion University .... VA ... 510
Regent University .... VA ... 511
University of Virginia .... VA ... 514
Virginia Commonwealth University .... VA ... 514
Virginia Polytechnic Institute and State University .... VA ... 518
Seattle Pacific University .... WA .. 526
University of Washington .... WA .. 527
Washington State University .... WA .. 528
Marshall University .... WV .. 532
West Virginia University .... WV .. 533
Marquette University .... WI ... 537
University of Wisconsin-Madison .... WI ... 539
University of Wisconsin-Milwaukee .... WI ... 540
Wisconsin School of Professional Psychology .... WI ... 542
University of Wyoming .... WY .. 546

CNCE: Accrediting Council for Continuing Education and Training: continuing education (C,A)

Southwest Institute of Healing Arts .... AZ 17
Asher College .... CA 28
Intercoast College .... CA 47
Los Angeles ORT College .... CA 52
United Education Institute .... CA 70
Hawaii Medical College .... HI 135
Chicago ORT Technical Institute .... IL 141
National Institute of Massotherapy .... OH .. 387
Mech-Tech College .... PR .. 554
Interface College .... WA .. 523
Brensten Education .... WI ... 535

COARC: Commission on Accreditation for Respiratory Care: respiratory care (A,B,M)

George C. Wallace Community College - Dothan .... AL 4
#Shelton State Community College .... AL 7
University of Alabama at Birmingham .... AL 8
University of South Alabama .... AL 9
#Virginia College .... AL 3
Wallace State Community College - Hanceville .... AL 10
#Cochise College .... AZ 13
Gateway Community College .... AZ 14
Pima Community College .... AZ 17
Pima Medical Institute-Tucson .... AZ 17
#Arkansas State University-Mid-South .... AR 19
#Arkansas State University-Mountain Home AR 19
#Black River Technical College .... AR 20
#National Park Community College .... AR 21
NorthWest Arkansas Community College . AR 22
Pulaski Technical College .... AR 22
South Arkansas Community College .... AR 23
Southeast Arkansas College .... AR 23
University of Arkansas for Medical Sciences .... AR 24
American Career College-Ontario .... CA 27
American River College .... CA 52
Antelope Valley College .... CA 27
Butte College .... CA 30
California College San Diego .... CA 30
Concorde Career College .... CA 41
Concorde Career College .... CA 42
Crafton Hills College .... CA 62
East Los Angeles College .... CA 51
El Camino College .... CA 43
Foothill College .... CA 45
Fresno City College .... CA 69
Grossmont College .... CA 46
#Hartnell College .... CA 46
Kaplan College .... CA 49
Loma Linda University .... CA 50
Los Angeles Valley College .... CA 52
Modesto Junior College .... CA 78
Mt. San Antonio College .... CA 54
Napa Valley College .... CA 55
Ohlone College .... CA 56
Orange Coast College .... CA 40
#Platt College .... CA 59
San Joaquin Valley College, Inc. - Visalia CA 63
Skyline College .... CA 64
Victor Valley College .... CA 75
Concorde Career College .... CO 82
Pueblo Community College .... CO 85
#Goodwin College .... CT 90
Manchester Community College .... CT 89
Naugatuck Valley Community College ...... CT 89
Norwalk Community College .... CT 89
University of Hartford .... CT 92
University of the District of Columbia .... DC 97
Broward College .... FL 99
Concorde Career Institute .... FL ... 100
#Concorde Career Institute .... FL ... 100
Concorde Career Institute .... FL ... 101
Daytona State College .... FL ... 101
Florida Agricultural and Mechanical University .... FL ... 114
#Florida National University Hialeah Campus .... FL ... 104
Florida SouthWestern State College .... FL ... 104
Florida State College at Jacksonville .... FL ... 105
Gulf Coast State College .... FL ... 105
Hillsborough Community College .... FL ... 106
Indian River State College .... FL ... 106
Keiser University .... FL ... 107
Miami Dade College .... FL ... 108
#Nova Southeastern University .... FL ... 109
Palm Beach State College .... FL ... 109
Polk State College .... FL ... 110
St. Johns River State College .... FL ... 111
St. Petersburg College .... FL ... 112
Santa Fe College .... FL ... 112
Seminole State College of Florida .... FL ... 113
Tallahassee Community College .... FL ... 117
Valencia College .... FL ... 118
Armstrong State University .... GA .. 120
Augusta Technical College .... GA .. 121
Augusta University .... GA .. 121
Coastal Pines Technical College .... GA .. 123
Columbus Technical College .... GA .. 123
Dalton State College .... GA .. 123
Darton State College .... GA .. 123
Georgia Northwestern Technical College . GA .. 125
Georgia State University .... GA .. 126
Gwinnett Technical College .... GA .. 127
Middle Georgia State University .... GA .. 128
Oconee Fall Line Technical College-South Campus .... GA .. 129
Southern Crescent Technical College .... GA .. 132
#Southern Regional Technical College .... GA .. 132
Kapiolani Community College .... HI 136
Boise State University .... ID 137
Idaho State University .... ID 138
#Blessing-Rieman College of Nursing .... IL 140
College of DuPage .... IL 142
Illinois Central College .... IL 146
Kankakee Community College .... IL 149
Kaskaskia College .... IL 149
Lincoln Land Community College .... IL 151
Malcolm X College, One of the City Colleges of Chicago .... IL 142
Moraine Valley Community College .... IL 153
Parkland College .... IL 155
Rock Valley College .... IL 157
Rush University .... IL 158
St. Augustine College .... IL 158
Southwestern Illinois College .... IL 160
Trinity College of Nursing & Health Sciences .... IL 161
Ivy Tech Community College of Indiana-Central Indiana .... IN 169
University of Southern Indiana .... IN 174
Des Moines Area Community College ...... IA 177
Hawkeye Community College .... IA 179
Kirkwood Community College .... IA 180
Northeast Iowa Community College .... IA 181
St. Luke's College .... IA 182
Southeastern Community College .... IA 183
#Hutchinson Community College .... KS ... 188
Johnson County Community College .... KS ... 188
Kansas City Kansas Community College . KS ... 188
Labette Community College .... KS ... 189
Newman University .... KS ... 189
Northwest Kansas Technical College .... KS ... 190
Seward County Community College/Area Technical School .... KS ... 191
Washburn University .... KS ... 192
Bellarmine University .... KY ... 193
Big Sandy Community and Technical College .... KY ... 195
Bluegrass Community and Technical College .... KY ... 195
Elizabethtown Community and Technical College .... KY ... 195
Jefferson Community and Technical College .... KY ... 196
Madisonville Community College .... KY ... 196
Northern Kentucky University .... KY ... 199
Somerset Community College .... KY ... 197
Southcentral Kentucky Community and Technical College .... KY ... 197
Southeast Kentucky Community and Technical College .... KY ... 197
#Spencerian College .... KY ... 199
Bossier Parish Community College .... LA ... 203
Delgado Community College .... LA ... 203
L.E. Fletcher Technical Community College .... LA ... 203
#Louisiana State University at Eunice .... LA ... 205
Louisiana State University Health Sciences Center at Shreveport .... LA ... 205
Louisiana State University Health Sciences Center-New Orleans .... LA ... 205
Our Lady of the Lake College .... LA ... 206
Southern University at Shreveport-Louisiana .... LA ... 207
Kennebec Valley Community College .... ME .. 211
Southern Maine Community College .... ME .. 211
Allegany College of Maryland .... MD .. 213
#Baltimore City Community College .... MD .. 213
Community College of Baltimore County, The .... MD .. 214
Frederick Community College .... MD .. 214
#Prince George's Community College .... MD .. 217
Salisbury University .... MD .. 220
Berkshire Community College .... MA .. 231
Massasoit Community College .... MA .. 232
North Shore Community College .... MA .. 232
Northern Essex Community College .... MA .. 232
Quinsigamond Community College .... MA .. 232
Springfield Technical Community College MA .. 233
Delta College .... MI ... 242
Ferris State University .... MI ... 242
Henry Ford College .... MI ... 243
Jackson College .... MI ... 244
Kalamazoo Valley Community College ..... MI ... 244
Macomb Community College .... MI ... 246
Monroe County Community College .... MI ... 247
Mott Community College .... MI ... 247
Muskegon Community College .... MI ... 247
Oakland Community College .... MI ... 248
Lake Superior College .... MN .. 259
Northland Community and Technical College .... MN .. 260
St. Catherine University .... MN .. 263
Saint Paul College-A Community & Technical College .... MN .. 261
University of Minnesota-Twin Cities .... MN .. 265
#Coahoma Community College .... MS .. 266
Copiah-Lincoln Community College .... MS .. 266
Hinds Community College .... MS .. 267
Itawamba Community College .... MS .. 267
Meridian Community College .... MS .. 268
Northeast Mississippi Community College MS .. 269
Northwest Mississippi Community College MS .. 269
Pearl River Community College .... MS .. 270
Concorde Career College .... MO .. 273
Missouri Southern State University .... MO .. 278
Missouri State University - West Plains .... MO .. 279
Ozarks Technical Community College ...... MO .. 280
University of Missouri - Columbia .... MO .. 283
Great Falls College Montana State University .... MT .. 288
University of Montana - Missoula .... MT .. 287
Metropolitan Community College .... NE ... 291
Midland University .... NE ... 291
Nebraska Methodist College .... NE ... 291
Southeast Community College .... NE ... 293
College of Southern Nevada .... NV ... 295
River Valley Community College .... NH .. 297
Bergen Community College .... NJ ... 300
Brookdale Community College .... NJ ... 300
County College of Morris .... NJ ... 301
Central New Mexico Community College . NM .. 310
Eastern New Mexico University-Roswell ... NM .. 310
New Mexico State University Dona Ana Community College .... NM .. 312
#San Juan College .... NM .. 312
Santa Fe Community College .... NM .. 313
City University of New York Borough of Manhattan Community College .... NY ... 318
Erie Community College .... NY ... 325
Genesee Community College .... NY ... 326
Hudson Valley Community College .... NY ... 328
#Mandl School .... NY ... 331
Mohawk Valley Community College .... NY ... 333
Molloy College .... NY ... 333
Nassau Community College .... NY ... 334
State University of New York Upstate Medical University .... NY ... 344
Stony Brook University .... NY ... 344
#Sullivan County Community College .... NY ... 349
Westchester Community College .... NY ... 352
Carteret Community College .... NC .. 361
Catawba Valley Community College .... NC .. 361
Central Piedmont Community College .... NC .. 361
Durham Technical Community College ...... NC .. 362
Edgecombe Community College .... NC .. 362
Fayetteville Technical Community College NC .. 362
Forsyth Technical Community College ..... NC .. 362
Pitt Community College .... NC .. 364
Robeson Community College .... NC .. 365
Rockingham Community College .... NC .. 365
Sandhills Community College .... NC .. 365
Southwestern Community College .... NC .. 366
Stanly Community College .... NC .. 366
Wilkes Community College .... NC .. 367
North Dakota State University Main Campus .... ND .. 374
University of Mary .... ND .. 375
Cincinnati State Technical and Community College .... OH .. 379
Columbus State Community College .... OH .. 380
Cuyahoga Community College .... OH .. 381
Eastern Gateway Community College - Jefferson County Campus .... OH .. 381
James A. Rhodes State College .... OH .. 384
Kettering College .... OH .. 385
Lakeland Community College .... OH .. 385
North Central State College .... OH .. 387
Ohio State University Main Campus, The . OH .. 389
Shawnee State University .... OH .. 391
Sinclair Community College .... OH .. 391
Stark State College .... OH .. 391
University of Akron, Main Campus, The ... OH .. 392
University of Cincinnati-Clermont College . OH .. 393
University of Rio Grande .... OH .. 394
University of Toledo .... OH .. 394
Washington State Community College ..... OH .. 395
Youngstown State University .... OH .. 396
Northern Oklahoma College .... OK .. 399
Rose State College .... OK .. 401
Tulsa Community College .... OK .. 403
Concorde Career College .... OR .. 405
Lane Community College .... OR .. 406
Mt. Hood Community College .... OR .. 407
Oregon Institute of Technology .... OR .. 408
#Carlow University .... PA ... 414
Community College of Allegheny County . PA ... 415
Community College of Philadelphia .... PA ... 416
Delaware County Community College ...... PA ... 416
Gannon University .... PA ... 419
Gwynedd Mercy University .... PA ... 420
Harrisburg Area Community College .... PA ... 420
Indiana University of Pennsylvania .... PA ... 431
Kaplan Career Institute .... PA ... 421

COARCP: Commission on Accreditation for Respiratory Care: polysomnography (C)

COE: Council on Occupational Education: occupational, trade, and technical education (C,A)

COMTA: Commission on Massage Therapy Accreditation: massage therapy, bodywork, aesthetics/esthetics and skin care (C,A)

CONST: American Council for Construction Education: construction education (A,B)

COPSY: American Psychological Association: counseling psychology (D)

CORE: Council of Rehabilitation Education: rehabilitation counseling and rehabilitation services (B,M)

CS: ABET, Inc.: computer science (B)

CSHSE: Council for Standards in Human Services Education: human services (A,B,M)

University of Alaska Anchorage ... AK ... 10
California State University-Fullerton ... CA ... 33
Community College of Denver ... CO ... 81
Metropolitan State University of Denver ... CO ... 83
Delaware Technical Community College, Terry Campus ... DE ... 94
University of Delaware ... DE ... 94
Hillsborough Community College ... FL ... 106
Darton State College ... GA ... 123
University of North Georgia ... GA ... 133
College of DuPage ... IL ... 142
Elgin Community College ... IL ... 144
Ivy Tech Community College of Indiana-Central Indiana ... IN ... 169
Allegany College of Maryland ... MD ... 213
Anne Arundel Community College ... MD ... 213
Community College of Baltimore County, The ... MD ... 214
Stevenson University ... MD ... 218
Fitchburg State University ... MA ... 229
Northern Essex Community College ... MA ... 232
Baker College of Flint ... MI ... 239
Metropolitan Community College ... NE ... 291
Southeast Community College ... NE ... 293
Great Basin College ... NV ... 295
Clinton Community College ... NY ... 321
New York City College of Technology/City University of New York ... NY ... 320
Montgomery Community College ... NC ... 364
Pitt Community College ... NC ... 364
Vance-Granville Community College ... NC ... 366
Columbus State Community College ... OH ... 380
James A. Rhodes State College ... OH ... 384
Sinclair Community College ... OH ... 391
University of Oregon ... OR ... 410
Clarion University of Pennsylvania ... PA ... 430
Harrisburg Area Community College ... PA ... 420
Lehigh Carbon Community College ... PA ... 424
Montgomery County Community College ... PA ... 426
Pennsylvania College of Technology ... PA ... 429
University of Scranton, The ... PA ... 438
Florence - Darlington Technical College ... SC ... 446
Trident Technical College ... SC ... 449
Wharton County Junior College ... TX ... 497
Madison Area Technical College ... WI ... 543
University of Wisconsin-Oshkosh ... WI ... 540

CVT: Commission on Accreditation of Allied Health Education Programs: cardiovascular technology (C,A,B)

Grossmont College ... CA ... 46
Loma Linda University ... CA ... 50
Orange Coast College ... CA ... 40
Florida SouthWestern State College ... FL ... 104
Florida State College at Jacksonville ... FL ... 105
Polk State College ... FL ... 110
Sanford-Brown College Tampa ... FL ... 112
Sanford-Brown Institute ... FL ... 112
Santa Fe College ... FL ... 112
Valencia College ... FL ... 118
Augusta Technical College ... GA ... 121
Central Georgia Technical College ... GA ... 122
Darton State College ... GA ... 123
Gwinnett Technical College ... GA ... 127
Sanford-Brown College ... GA ... 130
Spencerian College ... KY ... 199
Louisiana State University Health Sciences Center-New Orleans ... LA ... 205
Howard Community College ... MD ... 215
Grand Valley State University ... MI ... 243
Kirtland Community College ... MI ... 245
Northland Community and Technical College ... MN ... 260
Saint Cloud Technical and Community College ... MN ... 261
Bryan College of Health Sciences ... NE ... 289
Eastwick College ... NJ ... 302
City University of New York Hunter College ... NY ... 319
Molloy College ... NY ... 333
Central Piedmont Community College ... NC ... 361
Forsyth Technical Community College ... NC ... 362
Mercy College of Ohio ... OH ... 386
Tulsa Community College ... OK ... 403
Harrisburg Area Community College ... PA ... 420
Pennsylvania College of Health Sciences ... PA ... 429
Clemson University ... SC ... 444
Piedmont Technical College ... SC ... 448
Southeast Technical Institute ... SD ... 454
Northeast State Community College ... TN ... 463
El Centro College ... TX ... 472
Sanford-Brown College ... TX ... 482
Sentara College of Health Sciences ... VA ... 512
Spokane Community College ... WA ... 521
Milwaukee Area Technical College ... WI ... 543

CYTO: Commission on Accreditation of Allied Health Education Programs: cytotechnology (C,B,M)

University of Arkansas for Medical Sciences ... AR ... 24
Loma Linda University ... CA ... 50
University of California-Los Angeles ... CA ... 71
Indiana University-Purdue University Indianapolis ... IN ... 168
University of Mississippi Medical Center ... MS ... 270
Saint Louis University ... MO ... 281
University of Nebraska Medical Center ... NE ... 293
Albany College of Pharmacy and Health Sciences ... NY ... 314
Central Piedmont Community College ... NC ... 361
University of North Dakota ... ND ... 373
Thomas Jefferson University ... PA ... 436
University of Puerto Rico-Medical Sciences Campus ... PR ... 558
University of Rhode Island ... RI ... 442
University of Tennessee Health Science Center ... TN ... 465
University of Texas M.D. Anderson Cancer Center, The ... TX ... 495
University of Utah, The ... UT ... 499
University of Vermont ... VT ... 503
Old Dominion University ... VA ... 510
Marshall University ... WV ... 532
University of Wisconsin-Madison ... WI ... 539

DA: American Dental Association: dental assisting (C,A)

Calhoun Community College ... AL ... 2
Fortis College ... AL ... 3
James H. Faulkner State Community College ... AL ... 5
Lawson State Community College ... AL ... 5
Trenholm State Technical College ... AL ... 7
Wallace State Community College - Hanceville ... AL ... 10
University of Alaska Anchorage ... AK ... 10
Phoenix College ... AZ ... 15
Pima Community College ... AZ ... 17
Rio Salado College ... AZ ... 15
Arkansas Northeastern College ... AR ... 19
Pulaski Technical College ... AR ... 22
Cerritos College ... CA ... 37
Chaffey College ... CA ... 38
Citrus College ... CA ... 38
City College of San Francisco ... CA ... 39
College of Alameda ... CA ... 59
College of Marin ... CA ... 41
College of San Mateo ... CA ... 64
College of the Redwoods Community College District ... CA ... 41
Cypress College ... CA ... 56
Diablo Valley College ... CA ... 42
Foothill College ... CA ... 45
Moreno Valley College ... CA ... 60
Orange Coast College ... CA ... 40
Palomar College ... CA ... 58
Pasadena City College ... CA ... 58
Sacramento City College ... CA ... 53
San Diego Mesa College ... CA ... 62
San Jose City College ... CA ... 64
Santa Rosa Junior College ... CA ... 65
Front Range Community College ... CO ... 82
IBMC College ... CO ... 83
Pikes Peak Community College ... CO ... 84
Pueblo Community College ... CO ... 85
Goodwin College ... CT ... 90
Lincoln College of New England ... CT ... 91
Tunxis Community College ... CT ... 90
Broward College ... FL ... 99
College of Central Florida ... FL ... 100
Daytona State College ... FL ... 101
Eastern Florida State College ... FL ... 101
Florida State College at Jacksonville ... FL ... 105
Gulf Coast State College ... FL ... 105
Hillsborough Community College ... FL ... 106
Indian River State College ... FL ... 106
Lincoln Tech Fern Park Orlando Campus ... FL ... 108
Northwest Florida State College ... FL ... 109
Palm Beach State College ... FL ... 109
Santa Fe College ... FL ... 112
South Florida State College ... FL ... 113
Tallahassee Community College ... FL ... 117
Albany Technical College ... GA ... 119
Athens Technical College ... GA ... 120
Atlanta Technical College ... GA ... 120
Augusta Technical College ... GA ... 121
Columbus Technical College ... GA ... 123
Georgia Northwestern Technical College ... GA ... 125
Gwinnett Technical College ... GA ... 127
Lanier Technical College ... GA ... 128
Ogeechee Technical College ... GA ... 129
Savannah Technical College ... GA ... 131
Southern Crescent Technical College ... GA ... 132
Wiregrass Georgia Technical College ... GA ... 134
University of Hawaii Maui College ... HI ... 136
College of Western Idaho ... ID ... 138
Elgin Community College ... IL ... 144
Illinois Valley Community College ... IL ... 147
John A. Logan College ... IL ... 148
Kaskaskia College ... IL ... 149
Lewis and Clark Community College ... IL ... 150
Indiana University Northwest ... IN ... 168
Indiana University-Purdue University Fort Wayne ... IN ... 168
Indiana University-Purdue University Indianapolis ... IN ... 168
University of Southern Indiana ... IN ... 174
Des Moines Area Community College ... IA ... 177
Hawkeye Community College ... IA ... 179
Indian Hills Community College ... IA ... 179
Iowa Western Community College ... IA ... 180
Kirkwood Community College ... IA ... 180
Marshalltown Community College ... IA ... 179
Northeast Iowa Community College ... IA ... 181
Scott Community College ... IA ... 178
Vatterott College-Des Moines ... IA ... 183
Western Iowa Tech Community College ... IA ... 184
Flint Hills Technical College ... KS ... 186
Labette Community College ... KS ... 189
Salina Area Technical College ... KS ... 190
Wichita Area Technical College ... KS ... 192
West Kentucky Community and Technical College ... KY ... 197
University of Maine at Augusta ... ME ... 212
Hagerstown Community College ... MD ... 215
Massasoit Community College ... MA ... 232
Middlesex Community College ... MA ... 232
Mount Wachusett Community College ... MA ... 232
Northern Essex Community College ... MA ... 232
Quinsigamond Community College ... MA ... 232
Springfield Technical Community College ... MA ... 233
Delta College ... MI ... 242
Grand Rapids Community College ... MI ... 243
Lake Michigan College ... MI ... 245
Mott Community College ... MI ... 247
Northwestern Michigan College ... MI ... 248
Washtenaw Community College ... MI ... 251
Wayne County Community College District ... MI ... 252
Central Lakes College ... MN ... 258
Century College ... MN ... 258
Dakota County Technical College ... MN ... 258
Hennepin Technical College ... MN ... 258
Hibbing Community College, A Technical and Community College ... MN ... 258
Minneapolis Community and Technical College ... MN ... 259
Minnesota State Community and Technical College ... MN ... 259
Minnesota West Community and Technical College ... MN ... 260
Northwest Technical College ... MN ... 260
Rochester Community and Technical College ... MN ... 261
Saint Cloud Technical and Community College ... MN ... 261
South Central College ... MN ... 262
Hinds Community College ... MS ... 267
Meridian Community College ... MS ... 268
Pearl River Community College ... MS ... 270
Metropolitan Community College - Penn Valley ... MO ... 278
Missouri College ... MO ... 278
Ozarks Technical Community College ... MO ... 280
State Technical College of Missouri ... MO ... 282
Great Falls College Montana State University ... MT ... 288
Salish Kootenai College ... MT ... 288
Central Community College ... NE ... 289
Metropolitan Community College ... NE ... 291
Mid-Plains Community College ... NE ... 291
Southeast Community College ... NE ... 293
College of Southern Nevada ... NV ... 295
Truckee Meadows Community College ... NV ... 295
NHTI-Concord's Community College ... NH ... 297
Camden County College ... NJ ... 301
Central New Mexico Community College ... NM ... 310
Luna Community College ... NM ... 311
New Mexico State University Dona Ana Community College ... NM ... 312
Santa Fe Community College ... NM ... 313
Monroe Community College ... NY ... 333
University at Buffalo-SUNY ... NY ... 343
Alamance Community College ... NC ... 359
Asheville - Buncombe Technical Community College ... NC ... 360
Cape Fear Community College ... NC ... 360
Central Carolina Community College ... NC ... 361
Central Piedmont Community College ... NC ... 361
Coastal Carolina Community College ... NC ... 361
Fayetteville Technical Community College ... NC ... 362
Forsyth Technical Community College ... NC ... 362
Guilford Technical Community College ... NC ... 363
Martin Community College ... NC ... 363
Montgomery Community College ... NC ... 364
Rowan-Cabarrus Community College ... NC ... 365
University of North Carolina at Chapel Hill ... NC ... 371
Wake Technical Community College ... NC ... 366
Wayne Community College ... NC ... 367
Western Piedmont Community College ... NC ... 367
Wilkes Community College ... NC ... 367
North Dakota State College of Science ... ND ... 375
Eastern Gateway Community College - Jefferson County Campus ... OH ... 381
Fortis College ... OH ... 382
Rose State College ... OK ... 401
Blue Mountain Community College ... OR ... 404
Central Oregon Community College ... OR ... 404
Chemeketa Community College ... OR ... 404
Lane Community College ... OR ... 406
Linn-Benton Community College ... OR ... 406
Portland Community College ... OR ... 409
Bradford School ... PA ... 413
Harcum College ... PA ... 420
Harrisburg Area Community College ... PA ... 420
Luzerne County Community College ... PA ... 425
Manor College ... PA ... 425
Westmoreland County Community College ... PA ... 439
University of Puerto Rico-Medical Sciences Campus ... PR ... 558
Community College of Rhode Island ... RI ... 441
Aiken Technical College ... SC ... 443
Florence - Darlington Technical College ... SC ... 446
Greenville Technical College ... SC ... 446
Horry-Georgetown Technical College ... SC ... 446
Midlands Technical College ... SC ... 447
Spartanburg Community College ... SC ... 449
Tri-County Technical College ... SC ... 449
Trident Technical College ... SC ... 449
York Technical College ... SC ... 451
Lake Area Technical Institute ... SD ... 452
Chattanooga State Community College ... TN ... 462
Concorde Career College ... TN ... 456
Kaplan College ... TN ... 457
Northeast State Community College ... TN ... 463
Volunteer State Community College ... TN ... 464
Del Mar College ... TX ... 473
El Paso Community College ... TX ... 473
Grayson College ... TX ... 474
Houston Community College ... TX ... 475
San Antonio College ... TX ... 467
Germanna Community College ... VA ... 515
J. Sargeant Reynolds Community College ... VA ... 515
Northern Virginia Community College ... VA ... 516
Bates Technical College ... WA ... 519
Bellingham Technical College ... WA ... 520
Clover Park Technical College ... WA ... 521
Lake Washington Institute of Technology ... WA ... 523
Renton Technical College ... WA ... 525
South Puget Sound Community College ... WA ... 527
Spokane Community College ... WA ... 521
Blackhawk Technical College ... WI ... 542
Fox Valley Technical College ... WI ... 542
Gateway Technical College ... WI ... 543
Northeast Wisconsin Technical College ... WI ... 544
Western Technical College ... WI ... 544

DANCE: National Association of Schools of Dance: dance (C,A,B,M,D)

University of Alabama, The ... AL ... 8
University of Arizona ... AZ ... 18
California Institute of the Arts ... CA ... 31
California State University-Fullerton ... CA ... 33
California State University-Long Beach ... CA ... 33
Chapman University ... CA ... 38
Loyola Marymount University ... CA ... 53
San Jose State University ... CA ... 36
University of California-Santa Barbara ... CA ... 72
University of Hartford ... CT ... 92
Florida State University ... FL ... 115
Jacksonville University ... FL ... 106
Miami Dade College ... FL ... 108
University of Florida ... FL ... 115
University of South Florida ... FL ... 116
Brenau University ... GA ... 121
University of Georgia ... GA ... 132
University of Illinois at Urbana-Champaign ... IL ... 162
Ball State University ... IN ... 164
Butler University ... IN ... 164
University of Iowa ... IA ... 175
Wichita State University ... KS ... 192
Western Kentucky University ... KY ... 201
Towson University ... MD ... 221
University of Maryland Baltimore County ... MD ... 219
Hope College ... MI ... 244
Oakland University ... MI ... 248
University of Michigan-Ann Arbor ... MI ... 251
Wayne State University ... MI ... 252

Western Michigan University ... MI ... 252
St. Olaf College ... MN .. 264
University of Minnesota-Twin Cities ... MN .. 265
Belhaven University ... MS .. 266
University of Southern Mississippi ... MS .. 271
University of Missouri - Kansas City ... MO .. 284
University of Nebraska - Lincoln ... NE .. 293
Montclair State University ... NJ ... 304
Rutgers the State University of New Jersey New Brunswick Campus ... NJ ... 307
University of New Mexico Main Campus .. NM .. 313
Barnard College ... NY ... 315
Fordham University ... NY ... 326
State University of New York, The College at Brockport ... NY ... 345
Appalachian State University ... NC .. 369
University of North Carolina at Greensboro ... NC .. 371
Kent State University Main Campus ... OH .. 384
Ohio State University Main Campus, The . OH .. 389
Ohio University Main Campus ... OH .. 389
University of Akron, Main Campus, The ... OH .. 392
University of Cincinnati Main Campus ... OH .. 393
Mercyhurst University ... PA ... 425
Point Park University ... PA ... 433
Slippery Rock University of Pennsylvania . PA ... 432
Temple University ... PA ... 436
Columbia College ... SC ... 445
University of South Carolina Columbia ... SC ... 450
Winthrop University ... SC ... 451
Southern Methodist University ... TX ... 482
Texas Christian University ... TX ... 486
Texas Tech University ... TX ... 489
Texas Woman's University ... TX ... 490
University of Texas at Austin ... TX ... 493
Brigham Young University ... UT ... 497
Southern Utah University ... UT ... 499
University of Utah, The ... UT ... 499
James Madison University ... VA ... 509
Virginia Commonwealth University ... VA ... 514
University of Wisconsin-Madison ... WI ... 539
University of Wisconsin-Milwaukee ... WI ... 540
University of Wisconsin-Stevens Point ... WI ... 541
Casper College ... WY .. 545

DEAC: Distance Education Accrediting Commission: home study schools (A,B,M,D)

Columbia Southern University ... AL ... 3
Acacia University ... AZ ... 11
Brighton College ... AZ ... 12
Dunlap-Stone University ... AZ ... 13
Harrison Middleton University ... AZ ... 14
National Paralegal College ... AZ ... 16
Paralegal Institute at Brighton College, The ... AZ ... 16
Penn Foster College ... AZ ... 16
Sessions College for Professional Design AZ ... 17
Sonoran Desert Institute ... AZ ... 17
Abraham Lincoln University ... CA ... 25
Allied American University ... CA ... 26
American Graduate University ... CA ... 27
Anaheim University ... CA ... 27
Apollos University ... CA ... 28
APT College ... CA ... 28
California Coast University ... CA ... 30
California Intercontinental University ... CA ... 31
California National University for Advanced Studies ... CA ... 32
California Southern University ... CA ... 32
Grace Communion Seminary ... CA ... 46
Henley-Putnam University ... CA ... 46
Southwestern Law School ... CA ... 68
Taft Law School ... CA ... 69
University of Philosophical Research ... CA ... 73
University of St. Augustine for Health Sciences ... CA ... 74
University of the People ... CA ... 73
Westcliff University ... CA ... 76
American Sentinel University ... CO ... 78
Aspen University ... CO ... 79
Holmes Institute of Consciousness Studies ... CO ... 82
McKinley College ... CO ... 83
U.S. Career Institute ... CO ... 87
William Howard Taft University ... CO ... 87
William Loveland College ... CO ... 87
Ashworth College ... GA .. 120
Babel University Professional School of Translation ... HI ... 134
Ellis University ... IL ... 148
Antioch School of Church Planting and Leadership Development ... IA ... 175
Inste Bible College ... IA ... 179
Shiloh University ... IA ... 182
Grantham University ... KS ... 187
NationsUniversity ... LA ... 206
Southwest University ... LA ... 207
American Business & Technology University ... MO .. 271
City Vision University ... MO .. 273
Global University ... MO .. 275
Rockbridge Seminary ... MO .. 281
EC-Council University ... NM .. 310
Lakewood College ... OH .. 385
American College of Healthcare Sciences OR .. 404
Huntington College of Health Sciences ... TN ... 457
New Charter University ... UT ... 498
Atlantic University ... VA .. 504
Catholic Distance University ... VA ... 505
University of Fairfax ... VA ... 513
University of Management & Technology . VA ... 513
Northwest Institute of Literary Arts ... WA .. 524
Martinsburg College ... WV .. 530

DENT: American Dental Association: dentistry (FP,D)

University of Alabama at Birmingham ... AL ... 8
University of Arkansas at Little Rock ... AR ... 24
Loma Linda University ... CA ... 50
University of California-Los Angeles ... CA ... 71
University of California-San Francisco ... CA ... 72
University of Southern California ... CA ... 74
University of the Pacific ... CA ... 73
Western University of Health Sciences ... CA ... 76
United States Air Force Academy ... CO .. 548
University of Colorado Denver|Anschutz Medical Campus ... CO ... 86
Howard University ... DC ... 96
Jacksonville University ... FL ... 106
Nova Southeastern University ... FL ... 109
University of Florida ... FL ... 115
University of Miami ... FL ... 118
Augusta University ... GA .. 121
Emory University ... GA .. 124
Idaho State University ... ID ... 138
Loyola University Chicago ... IL ... 151
Midwestern University ... IL ... 152
Southern Illinois University Edwardsville ... IL ... 159
University of Illinois at Chicago ... IL ... 161
Indiana University-Purdue University Indianapolis ... IN ... 168
University of Iowa ... IA ... 175
Wichita State University ... KS ... 192
University of Kentucky ... KY ... 200
University of Louisville ... KY ... 201
Louisiana State University Health Sciences Center at Shreveport ... LA ... 205
Louisiana State University Health Sciences Center-New Orleans ... LA ... 205
University of New England ... ME .. 213
University of Maryland Baltimore ... MD .. 219
Boston University ... MA .. 224
Harvard University ... MA .. 227
Tufts University ... MA .. 237
University of Detroit Mercy ... MI ... 250
University of Michigan-Ann Arbor ... MI ... 251
University of Minnesota-Twin Cities ... MN .. 265
University of Mississippi Medical Center ... MS .. 270
A. T. Still University of Health Sciences ... MO .. 271
Saint Louis University ... MO .. 281
University of Missouri - Kansas City ... MO .. 284
Creighton University ... NE .. 290
University of Nebraska Medical Center ... NE .. 293
Roseman University of Health Sciences ... NV .. 296
University of Nevada, Las Vegas ... NV .. 295
University of New Mexico Main Campus .. NM .. 313
Columbia University in the City of New York ... NY ... 322
Icahn School of Medicine at Mount Sinai . NY ... 328
New York Medical College ... NY ... 335
New York University ... NY ... 336
State University of New York Upstate Medical University ... NY ... 344
Stony Brook University ... NY ... 344
University at Buffalo-SUNY ... NY ... 343
University of Rochester ... NY ... 351
Yeshiva University ... NY ... 353
East Carolina University ... NC .. 369
University of North Carolina at Chapel Hill NC .. 371
Wake Forest University ... NC .. 372
Case Western Reserve University ... OH .. 378
Ohio State University Main Campus, The . OH .. 389
University of Cincinnati Main Campus ... OH .. 393
University of Toledo ... OH .. 394
Oregon Health & Science University ... OR .. 408
Drexel University ... PA ... 417
Seton Hill University ... PA ... 435
Temple University ... PA ... 436
Thomas Jefferson University ... PA ... 436
University of Pennsylvania ... PA ... 437
University of Pittsburgh ... PA ... 437
University of Puerto Rico-Medical Sciences Campus ... PR ... 558
Medical University of South Carolina ... SC ... 447
Meharry Medical College ... TN ... 458
University of Tennessee Health Science Center ... TN ... 465
University of Tennessee, Knoxville ... TN ... 465
Vanderbilt University ... TN ... 465
Texas A & M University ... TX ... 485
University of Texas Health Science Center at Houston (UTHealth), The ... TX ... 495
University of Texas Health Science Center at San Antonio ... TX ... 495
University of Texas M.D. Anderson Cancer Center, The ... TX ... 495
University of Texas Medical Branch, The . TX ... 495
University of Utah, The ... UT ... 499
University of Vermont ... VT ... 503
University of Virginia ... VA ... 514
Virginia Commonwealth University ... VA ... 514
University of Washington ... WA .. 527
West Virginia University ... WV .. 533
Marquette University ... WI ... 537
Medical College of Wisconsin ... WI ... 537

DH: American Dental Association: dental hygiene (C,A,B,M)

Wallace State Community College - Hanceville ... AL ... 10
University of Alaska Anchorage ... AK ... 10
University of Alaska Fairbanks ... AK ... 10
Mesa Community College ... AZ ... 15
Mohave Community College ... AZ ... 15
Northern Arizona University ... AZ ... 16
Phoenix College ... AZ ... 15
Pima Community College ... AZ ... 17
Rio Salado College ... AZ ... 15
University of Arkansas at Fort Smith ... AR ... 23
University of Arkansas for Medical Sciences ... AR ... 24
Cabrillo College ... CA ... 30
Carrington College - Sacramento ... CA ... 37
Cerritos College ... CA ... 37
Chabot College ... CA ... 37
Concorde Career College ... CA ... 41
Concorde Career College ... CA ... 42
Cypress College ... CA ... 56
Diablo Valley College ... CA ... 42
Foothill College ... CA ... 45
Fresno City College ... CA ... 69
Loma Linda University ... CA ... 50
Moreno Valley College ... CA ... 60
Oxnard College ... CA ... 75
Pasadena City College ... CA ... 58
Sacramento City College ... CA ... 53
San Joaquin Valley College, Inc. - Visalia CA ... 63
Santa Rosa Junior College ... CA ... 65
Shasta College ... CA ... 66
Southwestern College ... CA ... 68
Taft College ... CA ... 69
University of Southern California ... CA ... 74
University of the Pacific ... CA ... 73
West Los Angeles College ... CA ... 52
Colorado Northwestern Community College ... CO ... 80
Community College of Denver ... CO ... 81
Concorde Career College ... CO ... 82
Pueblo Community College ... CO ... 85
Goodwin College ... CT ... 90
Lincoln College of New England ... CT ... 91
Tunxis Community College ... CT ... 90
University of Bridgeport ... CT ... 92
University of New Haven ... CT ... 92
Howard University ... DC ... 96
Broward College ... FL ... 99
Daytona State College ... FL ... 101
Eastern Florida State College ... FL ... 101
Florida SouthWestern State College ... FL ... 104
Florida State College at Jacksonville ... FL ... 105
Gulf Coast State College ... FL ... 105
Hillsborough Community College ... FL ... 106
Indian River State College ... FL ... 106
Miami Dade College ... FL ... 108
Palm Beach State College ... FL ... 109
Pasco-Hernando State College ... FL ... 110
Pensacola State College ... FL ... 110
St. Petersburg College ... FL ... 112
Sanford-Brown Institute ... FL ... 112
Santa Fe College ... FL ... 112
South Florida State College ... FL ... 113
State College of Florida, Manatee-Sarasota ... FL ... 114
Tallahassee Community College ... FL ... 117
Valencia College ... FL ... 118
Athens Technical College ... GA .. 120
Atlanta Technical College ... GA .. 120
Augusta University ... GA .. 121
Central Georgia Technical College ... GA .. 122
Clayton State University ... GA .. 122
Columbus Technical College ... GA .. 123
Darton State College ... GA .. 123
Georgia Highlands College ... GA .. 125
Georgia Perimeter College ... GA .. 125
Lanier Technical College ... GA .. 128
Savannah Technical College ... GA .. 131
Southeastern Technical College ... GA .. 132
West Georgia Technical College ... GA .. 134
Wiregrass Georgia Technical College ... GA .. 134
University of Hawaii at Manoa ... HI ... 135
University of Hawaii Maui College ... HI ... 136
College of Southern Idaho ... ID ... 137
Idaho State University ... ID ... 138
Carl Sandburg College ... IL ... 140
City Colleges of Chicago Kennedy-King College ... IL ... 142
College of DuPage ... IL ... 142
College of Lake County ... IL ... 142
Harper College ... IL ... 145
Illinois Central College ... IL ... 146
John A. Logan College ... IL ... 148
Lake Land College ... IL ... 150
Lewis and Clark Community College ... IL ... 150
Parkland College ... IL ... 155
Prairie State College ... IL ... 156
Rock Valley College ... IL ... 157
Southern Illinois University Carbondale ... IL ... 159
Indiana University Northwest ... IN ... 168
Indiana University-Purdue University Fort Wayne ... IN ... 168
Indiana University-Purdue University Indianapolis ... IN ... 168
Indiana University South Bend ... IN ... 168
University of Southern Indiana ... IN ... 174
Des Moines Area Community College ... IA ... 177
Hawkeye Community College ... IA ... 179
Iowa Central Community College ... IA ... 179
Iowa Western Community College ... IA ... 180
Kirkwood Community College ... IA ... 180
Flint Hills Technical College ... KS ... 186
Johnson County Community College ... KS ... 188
Manhattan Area Technical College ... KS ... 189
Wichita State University ... KS ... 192
Big Sandy Community and Technical College ... KY ... 195
Bluegrass Community and Technical College ... KY ... 195
Henderson Community College ... KY ... 196
University of Louisville ... KY ... 201
Western Kentucky University ... KY ... 201
Louisiana State University Health Sciences Center-New Orleans ... LA ... 205
Southern University at Shreveport-Louisiana ... LA ... 207
University of Louisiana at Monroe ... LA ... 209
University of Maine at Augusta ... ME .. 212
University of New England ... ME .. 213
Allegany College of Maryland ... MD .. 213
Baltimore City Community College ... MD .. 213
Community College of Baltimore County, The ... MD .. 214
Hagerstown Community College ... MD .. 215
Howard Community College ... MD .. 215
University of Maryland Baltimore ... MD .. 219
Bristol Community College ... MA .. 231
Cape Cod Community College ... MA .. 231
MCPHS University ... MA .. 233
Middlesex Community College ... MA .. 232
Mount Ida College ... MA .. 234
Mount Wachusett Community College ... MA .. 232
Quinsigamond Community College ... MA .. 232
Springfield Technical Community College MA .. 233
Delta College ... MI ... 242
Ferris State University ... MI ... 242
Grand Rapids Community College ... MI ... 243
Kalamazoo Valley Community College ... MI ... 244
Kellogg Community College ... MI ... 244
Lansing Community College ... MI ... 245
Mott Community College ... MI ... 247
Oakland Community College ... MI ... 248
University of Detroit Mercy ... MI ... 250
University of Michigan-Ann Arbor ... MI ... 251
Wayne County Community College District ... MI ... 252
Century College ... MN .. 258
Lake Superior College ... MN .. 259
Minnesota State University Moorhead ... MN .. 260
Minnesota State University, Mankato ... MN .. 260
Normandale Community College ... MN .. 260
Rochester Community and Technical College ... MN .. 261
Saint Cloud Technical and Community College ... MN .. 261
University of Minnesota-Twin Cities ... MN .. 265
Meridian Community College ... MS .. 268
Mississippi Delta Community College ... MS .. 268
Northeast Mississippi Community College MS .. 269
Pearl River Community College ... MS .. 270
University of Mississippi Medical Center ... MS .. 270
Concorde Career College ... MO .. 273
Missouri College ... MO .. 278
Missouri Southern State University ... MO .. 278
North Central Missouri College ... MO .. 279

DIETC: Academy of Nutrition and Dietetics: coordinated dietetics programs (B,M)

DIETD: Academy of Nutrition and Dietetics: didactic dietetics programs (B,M)

DIETI: Academy of Nutrition and Dietetics: dietetic post-baccalaureate internships

DIETT: Academy of Nutrition and Dietetics: dietetic technician (A)

DMOLS: National Accrediting Agency for Clinical Laboratory Sciences: diagnostic molecular scientist (C,B,M)

DMS: Commission on Accreditation of Allied Health Education Programs: diagnostic medical sonography (C,A,B,M)

DNUR: Accreditation Commission for Education in Nursing: nursing (C)

DT: American Dental Association: dental laboratory technology (C,A)

EH: New England Association of Schools and Colleges, Commission on Institutions of Higher Education

EMT: Commission on Accreditation of Allied Health Education Programs: emergency medical technician-paramedic (C,A,B)

Institution	State	Page
University of Alaska Anchorage	AK	10
University of Alaska Fairbanks	AK	10
Central Arizona College	AZ	12
Glendale Community College	AZ	14
Mohave Community College	AZ	15
Paradise Valley Community College	AZ	15
Pima Community College	AZ	17
Yavapai College	AZ	18
Arkansas Northeastern College	AR	19
Arkansas State University-Beebe	AR	19
Arkansas State University-Mountain Home	AR	19
Arkansas Tech University	AR	20
Black River Technical College	AR	20
East Arkansas Community College	AR	20
National Park Community College	AR	21
North Arkansas College	AR	22
NorthWest Arkansas Community College	AR	22
South Arkansas Community College	AR	23
Southeast Arkansas College	AR	23
University of Arkansas at Monticello	AR	24
University of Arkansas Community College at Batesville	AR	24
University of Arkansas Community College at Hope	AR	24
University of Arkansas for Medical Sciences	AR	24
American River College	CA	52
Bakersfield College	CA	49
Butte College	CA	30
California State University-Sacramento	CA	34
City College of San Francisco	CA	39
College of the Redwoods Community College District	CA	41
Crafton Hills College	CA	62
Cuesta College	CA	42
Foothill College	CA	45
Fresno City College	CA	69
Imperial Valley College	CA	47
Moreno Valley College	CA	60
Mt. San Antonio College	CA	54
Napa Valley College	CA	55
Palomar College	CA	58
Point Loma Nazarene University	CA	59
Saddleback College	CA	67
Santa Rosa Junior College	CA	65
Southwestern College	CA	68
University of Antelope Valley	CA	70
University of California-Los Angeles	CA	71
Ventura College	CA	75
Victor Valley College	CA	75
Aims Community College	CO	78
Arapahoe Community College	CO	79
Colorado Mountain College	CO	80
Community College of Aurora	CO	81
Pikes Peak Community College	CO	84
Pueblo Community College	CO	85
Capital Community College	CT	89
Goodwin College	CT	90
Delaware Technical Community College, Terry Campus	DE	94
Broward College	FL	99
City College	FL	100
College of Central Florida	FL	100
Daytona State College	FL	101
Eastern Florida State College	FL	101
Florida Gateway College	FL	103
Florida SouthWestern State College	FL	104
Florida State College at Jacksonville	FL	105
Gulf Coast State College	FL	105
Hillsborough Community College	FL	106
Indian River State College	FL	106
Miami Dade College	FL	108
Northwest Florida State College	FL	109
Palm Beach State College	FL	109
Pasco-Hernando State College	FL	110
Pensacola State College	FL	110
Polk State College	FL	110
St. Petersburg College	FL	112
Santa Fe College	FL	112
Seminole State College of Florida	FL	113
South Florida State College	FL	113
Tallahassee Community College	FL	117
Valencia College	FL	118
Athens Technical College	GA	120
Atlanta Technical College	GA	120
Central Georgia Technical College	GA	122
Darton State College	GA	123
Georgia Northwestern Technical College	GA	125
Georgia Piedmont Technical College	GA	126
Gwinnett Technical College	GA	127
Lanier Technical College	GA	128
Southeastern Technical College	GA	132
Southern Crescent Technical College	GA	132
Southern Regional Technical College	GA	132
Kapiolani Community College	HI	136
Brigham Young University-Idaho	ID	137
College of Southern Idaho	ID	137
Idaho State University	ID	138
Black Hawk College	IL	140
Illinois Central College	IL	146
Loyola University Chicago	IL	151
Malcolm X College, One of the City Colleges of Chicago	IL	142
Parkland College	IL	155
Southwestern Illinois College	IL	160
Waubonsee Community College	IL	162
Indiana University-Purdue University Indianapolis	IN	168
Vincennes University	IN	174
Clinton Community College	IA	178
Indian Hills Community College	IA	179
Iowa Central Community College	IA	179
Iowa Western Community College	IA	180
Kirkwood Community College	IA	180
Mercy College of Health Sciences	IA	181
Muscatine Community College	IA	178
Scott Community College	IA	178
Southeastern Community College	IA	183
University of Iowa	IA	175
Western Iowa Tech Community College	IA	184
Barton County Community College	KS	184
Coffeyville Community College	KS	186
Cowley County Community College	KS	186
Garden City Community College	KS	187
Hutchinson Community College	KS	188
Johnson County Community College	KS	188
Kansas City Kansas Community College	KS	188
Ashland Community and Technical College	KY	195
Eastern Kentucky University	KY	194
Owensboro Community and Technical College	KY	197
Bossier Parish Community College	LA	203
Delgado Community College	LA	203
South Louisiana Community College	LA	204
Eastern Maine Community College	ME	211
Kennebec Valley Community College	ME	211
Northern Maine Community College	ME	211
Southern Maine Community College	ME	211
Anne Arundel Community College	MD	213
Cecil College	MD	214
Chesapeake College	MD	214
College of Southern Maryland	MD	214
Community College of Baltimore County, The	MD	214
Garrett College	MD	215
Hagerstown Community College	MD	215
Howard Community College	MD	215
Prince George's Community College	MD	217
University of Maryland Baltimore County	MD	219
Wor-Wic Community College	MD	221
Springfield College	MA	236
Kalamazoo Valley Community College	MI	244
Lansing Community College	MI	245
Macomb Community College	MI	246
Wayne County Community College District	MI	252
Century College	MN	258
Inver Hills Community College	MN	259
Mesabi Range College	MN	259
Northland Community and Technical College	MN	260
Ridgewater College	MN	261
Saint Cloud Technical and Community College	MN	261
South Central College	MN	262
East Central Community College	MS	267
East Mississippi Community College	MS	267
Hinds Community College	MS	267
Holmes Community College	MS	267
Itawamba Community College	MS	267
Jones County Junior College	MS	268
Meridian Community College	MS	268
Mississippi Gulf Coast Community College	MS	268
Northwest Mississippi Community College	MS	269
Crowder College	MO	274
East Central College	MO	274
Metropolitan Community College - Penn Valley	MO	278
Mineral Area College	MO	278
Missouri Southern State University	MO	278
Ozarks Technical Community College	MO	280
Flathead Valley Community College	MT	286
Great Falls College Montana State University	MT	288
Montana State University - Billings	MT	287
Central Community College	NE	289
Creighton University	NE	290
Metropolitan Community College	NE	291
Mid-Plains Community College	NE	291
Northeast Community College	NE	292
College of Southern Nevada	NV	295
Truckee Meadows Community College	NV	295
NHTI-Concord's Community College	NH	297
Ocean County College	NJ	304
Central New Mexico Community College	NM	310
Eastern New Mexico University-Roswell	NM	310
New Mexico State University Dona Ana Community College	NM	312
San Juan College	NM	312
University of New Mexico Main Campus	NM	313
City University of New York Borough of Manhattan Community College	NY	318
Dutchess Community College	NY	324
Erie Community College	NY	325
Herkimer County Community College	NY	327
Hudson Valley Community College	NY	328
Monroe Community College	NY	333
St. John's University	NY	340
State University of New York College of Agriculture and Technology at Coble skill	NY	346
Asheville - Buncombe Technical Community College	NC	360
Blue Ridge Community College	NC	360
Catawba Valley Community College	NC	361
Durham Technical Community College	NC	362
Gaston College	NC	362
Guilford Technical Community College	NC	363
Lenoir Community College	NC	363
Piedmont Community College	NC	364
Southwestern Community College	NC	366
Western Carolina University	NC	372
Bismarck State College	ND	374
North Dakota State College of Science	ND	375
Central Ohio Technical College	OH	378
Columbus State Community College	OH	380
Cuyahoga Community College	OH	381
Fortis College	OH	382
Lorain County Community College	OH	385
Mercy College of Ohio	OH	386
Owens Community College	OH	390
Shawnee State University	OH	391
Sinclair Community College	OH	391
University of Cincinnati-Blue Ash College	OH	393
Youngstown State University	OH	396
Oklahoma City Community College	OK	399
Oklahoma State University - Oklahoma City	OK	400
Redlands Community College	OK	401
Rogers State University	OK	401
Central Oregon Community College	OR	404
Chemeketa Community College	OR	404
Lane Community College	OR	406
National College of Technical Instruction-College of Emergency Services	OR	407
Oregon Health & Science University	OR	408
Portland Community College	OR	409
Rogue Community College	OR	409
Southwestern Oregon Community College	OR	410
Umpqua Community College	OR	410
Community College of Allegheny County	PA	415
Delaware County Community College	PA	416
Fortis Institute	PA	418
Harrisburg Area Community College	PA	420
Luzerne County Community College	PA	425
Pennsylvania College of Health Sciences	PA	429
Pennsylvania College of Technology	PA	429
University of Pittsburgh	PA	437
Roger Williams University	RI	442
Greenville Technical College	SC	446
Horry-Georgetown Technical College	SC	446
Trident Technical College	SC	449
Lake Area Technical Institute	SD	452
Chattanooga State Community College	TN	462
Columbia State Community College	TN	462
Dyersburg State Community College	TN	462
Jackson State Community College	TN	463
Northeast State Community College	TN	463
Roane State Community College	TN	463
Southwest Tennessee Community College	TN	464
Tennessee Technological University	TN	462
Volunteer State Community College	TN	464
Walters State Community College	TN	464
Amarillo College	TX	467
Austin Community College District	TX	468
Blinn College	TX	469
Brazosport College	TX	469
Brookhaven College	TX	472
Central Texas College	TX	470
College of the Mainland	TX	471
Collin County Community College District	TX	471
El Paso Community College	TX	473
Galveston College	TX	474
Grayson College	TX	474
Hill College	TX	475
Houston Community College	TX	475
Howard College	TX	475
Lamar Institute of Technology	TX	488
Lone Star College System	TX	477
Midland College	TX	478
Navarro College	TX	479
North Central Texas College	TX	479
Odessa College	TX	479
Panola College	TX	480
Paris Junior College	TX	480
San Antonio College	TX	467
San Jacinto College Central	TX	481
San Jacinto College North	TX	481
South Plains College	TX	482
South Texas College	TX	482
Tarrant County College District	TX	484
Temple College	TX	484
Texas State Technical College Waco	TX	488
Texas State Technical College West Texas	TX	488
Trinity Valley Community College	TX	490
Tyler Junior College	TX	491
University of Texas Health Science Center at San Antonio	TX	495
University of Texas Southwestern Medical Center	TX	496
Weatherford College	TX	497
Wharton County Junior College	TX	497
Dixie State University	UT	499
University of Utah, The	UT	499
Utah Valley University	UT	500
Weber State University	UT	500
American National University	VA	504
Central Virginia Community College	VA	515
J. Sargeant Reynolds Community College	VA	515
Jefferson College of Health Sciences	VA	509
Lord Fairfax Community College	VA	515
Northern Virginia Community College	VA	516
Patrick Henry Community College	VA	516
Piedmont Virginia Community College	VA	516
Southside Virginia Community College	VA	516
Southwest Virginia Community College	VA	517
Tidewater Community College	VA	517
Virginia Commonwealth University	VA	514
Central Washington University	WA	520
Columbia Basin College	WA	521
Tacoma Community College	WA	527
University of Washington	WA	527
Blue Ridge Community and Technical College	WV	530
New River Community and Technical College	WV	531
Pierpont Community & Technical College	WV	531
Fox Valley Technical College	WI	542
Lakeshore Technical College	WI	543
Madison Area Technical College	WI	543
Mid-State Technical College	WI	543
Moraine Park Technical College	WI	543
Northcentral Technical College	WI	544
Northeast Wisconsin Technical College	WI	544
Waukesha County Technical College	WI	544
Western Technical College	WI	544
Casper College	WY	545
Laramie County Community College	WY	546

ENG: ABET, Inc.: engineering (B,M)

Institution	State	Page
Alabama Agricultural and Mechanical University	AL	1
Auburn University	AL	1
Tuskegee University	AL	8
University of Alabama at Birmingham	AL	8
University of Alabama in Huntsville	AL	9
University of Alabama, The	AL	8
University of South Alabama	AL	9
University of Alaska Anchorage	AK	10
University of Alaska Fairbanks	AK	10
Arizona State University	AZ	11
Northern Arizona University	AZ	16
University of Arizona	AZ	18
Arkansas State University-Jonesboro	AR	19
Arkansas Tech University	AR	20
Harding University Main Campus	AR	21
John Brown University	AR	21
University of Arkansas at Little Rock	AR	24
University of Arkansas Main Campus	AR	23
California Baptist University	CA	30
California Institute of Technology	CA	31
California Polytechnic State University-San Luis Obispo	CA	32
California State Polytechnic University-Pomona	CA	32
California State University-Chico	CA	33
California State University-East Bay	CA	33
California State University-Fresno	CA	33
California State University-Fullerton	CA	33
California State University-Long Beach	CA	33
California State University-Los Angeles	CA	34
California State University Maritime Academy	CA	34
California State University-Northridge	CA	34
California State University-Sacramento	CA	34
California State University-San Bernardino	CA	35
Harvey Mudd College	CA	46
Humboldt State University	CA	35
Loyola Marymount University	CA	53
National Test Pilot School	CA	55
Naval Postgraduate School	CA	548
San Diego State University	CA	35

ENGR: ABET, Inc.: applied science (A,B,M)

Institution	State	Page
University of California-Los Angeles	CA	71
Colorado State University	CO	81
Trinidad State Junior College	CO	86
University of Florida	FL	115
University of South Florida	FL	116
Kennesaw State University	GA	127
Idaho State University	ID	138
University of Illinois at Chicago	IL	161
Purdue University Calumet	IN	171
Purdue University Main Campus	IN	171
Purdue University North Central Campus	IN	172
University of Iowa	IA	175
Murray State University	KY	198
Nicholls State University	LA	208
Southeastern Louisiana University	LA	208
Tulane University	LA	207
Johns Hopkins University	MD	216
Morgan State University	MD	217
Uniformed Services University of the Health Sciences	MD	548
University of Massachusetts Lowell	MA	229
Kettering University	MI	245
Oakland University	MI	248
University of Michigan-Ann Arbor	MI	251
Wayne State University	MI	252
St. Cloud State University	MN	261
University of Minnesota-Twin Cities	MN	265
University of Central Missouri	MO	283
Montana Tech of The University of Montana	MT	288
University of Nevada, Las Vegas	NV	295
City University of New York Hunter College	NY	319
Air Force Institute of Technology	OH	547
University of Akron, Main Campus, The	OH	392
University of Cincinnati Main Campus	OH	393
University of Findlay, The	OH	393
University of Toledo	OH	394
Oregon Institute of Technology	OR	408
Oregon State University	OR	408
Indiana University of Pennsylvania	PA	431
Millersville University of Pennsylvania	PA	431
Universidad Politecnica De Puerto Rico	PR	556
Clemson University	SC	444
Chattanooga State Community College	TN	462
East Tennessee State University	TN	461
Texas A & M University - Corpus Christi	TX	485
University of Houston - Clear Lake	TX	491
University of Texas Health Science Center at Houston (UTHealth), The	TX	495
University of Utah, The	UT	499
Utah State University	UT	500
James Madison University	VA	509
Fairmont State University	WV	532
Marshall University	WV	532
West Virginia University	WV	533

ENGT: ABET, Inc.: engineering technology (A,B)

Institution	State	Page
Alabama Agricultural and Mechanical University	AL	1
Arizona State University	AZ	11
University of Arkansas at Little Rock	AR	24
California State Polytechnic University-Pomona	CA	32
California State University Maritime Academy	CA	34
Colorado State University-Pueblo	CO	81
Metropolitan State University of Denver	CO	83
Central Connecticut State University	CT	88
Naugatuck Valley Community College	CT	89
Three Rivers Community College	CT	90
University of Hartford	CT	92
Florida Agricultural and Mechanical University	FL	114
Augusta Technical College	GA	121
Fort Valley State University	GA	124
Georgia Piedmont Technical College	GA	126
Georgia Southern University	GA	126
Kennesaw State University	GA	127
Savannah State University	GA	131
Savannah Technical College	GA	131
Idaho State University	ID	138
Bradley University	IL	140
DeVry University - Chicago Campus	IL	144
Morrison Institute of Technology	IL	153
Northern Illinois University	IL	154
Southern Illinois University Carbondale	IL	159
Indiana State University	IN	167
Indiana University-Purdue University Fort Wayne	IN	168
Indiana University-Purdue University Indianapolis	IN	168
Purdue University Calumet	IN	171
Purdue University Main Campus	IN	171
Purdue University North Central Campus	IN	172
University of Northern Iowa	IA	176
Butler Community College	KS	185
Pittsburg State University	KS	190
Murray State University	KY	198
Northern Kentucky University	KY	199
Delgado Community College	LA	203
Grambling State University	LA	207
Louisiana Tech University	LA	208
McNeese State University	LA	208
Northwestern State University	LA	208
Southern University and A&M College	LA	207
Central Maine Community College	ME	210
Maine Maritime Academy	ME	211
University of Maine	ME	212
Capitol Technology University	MD	214
Northeastern University	MA	235
Springfield Technical Community College	MA	233
University of Massachusetts Lowell	MA	229
Wentworth Institute of Technology	MA	237
Baker College of Flint	MI	239
Eastern Michigan University	MI	242
Ferris State University	MI	242
Lake Superior State University	MI	245
Michigan Technological University	MI	247
Northern Michigan University	MI	248
Wayne State University	MI	252
Western Michigan University	MI	252
Minnesota State University, Mankato	MN	260
University of Southern Mississippi	MS	271
Missouri Southern State University	MO	278
Missouri Western State University	MO	279
Southeast Missouri State University	MO	282
State Technical College of Missouri	MO	282
Montana State University	MT	287
Montana State University - Northern	MT	288
College of Southern Nevada	NV	295
Nashua Community College	NH	297
NHTI-Concord's Community College	NH	297
University of New Hampshire	NH	299
County College of Morris	NJ	301
Essex County College	NJ	302
Fairleigh Dickinson University	NJ	302
Middlesex County College	NJ	303
New Jersey Institute of Technology	NJ	304
Passaic County Community College	NJ	304
Rowan College at Burlington County	NJ	306
Thomas Edison State College	NJ	308
New Mexico State University Main Campus	NM	312
Northern New Mexico College	NM	312
Alfred State College	NY	347
City University of New York Bronx Community College	NY	318
City University of New York Queensborough Community College	NY	320
College of Staten Island CUNY	NY	319
Erie Community College	NY	325
Excelsior College	NY	325
Farmingdale State College	NY	348
Hudson Valley Community College	NY	328
Mohawk Valley Community College	NY	333
Monroe Community College	NY	333
Nassau Community College	NY	334
New York City College of Technology/City University of New York	NY	320
New York Institute of Technology	NY	335
Onondaga Community College	NY	337
Paul Smith's College	NY	338
Rochester Institute of Technology	NY	339
State University of New York College at Buffalo	NY	345
State University of New York College of Agriculture and Technology at Morrisville	NY	347
State University of New York College of Environmental Science and Forestry	NY	347
SUNY Broome Community College	NY	344
SUNY Canton-College of Technology	NY	347
SUNY Polytechnic Institute	NY	348
Technical Career Institutes	NY	349
Vaughn College of Aeronautics and Technology	NY	352
Central Piedmont Community College	NC	361
Forsyth Technical Community College	NC	362
Gaston College	NC	362
University of North Carolina at Charlotte	NC	371
Western Carolina University	NC	372
Bismarck State College	ND	374
Cincinnati State Technical and Community College	OH	379
Cleveland State University	OH	380
Columbus State Community College	OH	380
Cuyahoga Community College	OH	381
James A. Rhodes State College	OH	384
Lakeland Community College	OH	385
Lorain County Community College	OH	385
Miami University	OH	386
Sinclair Community College	OH	391
Stark State College	OH	391
University of Akron, Main Campus, The	OH	392
University of Cincinnati Main Campus	OH	393
University of Dayton	OH	393
University of Toledo	OH	394
Youngstown State University	OH	396
Zane State College	OH	396
Oklahoma State University	OK	400
Oklahoma State University Institute of Technology-Okmulgee	OK	400
Southwestern Oklahoma State University	OK	402
Oregon Institute of Technology	OR	408
Bloomsburg University of Pennsylvania	PA	430
California University of Pennsylvania	PA	430
Drexel University	PA	417
Pennsylvania College of Technology	PA	429
Point Park University	PA	433
Temple University	PA	436
University of Puerto Rico-Aguadilla	PR	557
University of Puerto Rico at Arecibo	PR	557
University of Puerto Rico at Bayamon	PR	557
University of Puerto Rico at Ponce	PR	558
University of Puerto Rico-Humacao	PR	558
New England Institute of Technology	RI	441
Denmark Technical College	SC	445
Greenville Technical College	SC	446
Midlands Technical College	SC	447
Orangeburg-Calhoun Technical College	SC	448
Piedmont Technical College	SC	448
South Carolina State University	SC	448
Spartanburg Community College	SC	449
University of South Carolina Upstate	SC	451
York Technical College	SC	451
Austin Peay State University	TN	461
Belmont University	TN	455
Chattanooga State Community College	TN	462
East Tennessee State University	TN	461
Middle Tennessee State University	TN	461
Southwest Tennessee Community College	TN	464
University of Memphis, The	TN	462
University of Tennessee at Chattanooga	TN	465
Houston Community College	TX	475
LeTourneau University	TX	477
Prairie View A & M University	TX	484
Texas A & M University	TX	485
Texas A & M University - Corpus Christi	TX	485
Texas Southern University	TX	487
Texas Tech University	TX	489
University of Houston	TX	491
University of Houston - Downtown	TX	491
University of North Texas	TX	492
Brigham Young University	UT	497
Southern Utah University	UT	499
Weber State University	UT	500
Vermont Technical College	VT	504
James Madison University	VA	509
Old Dominion University	VA	510
Virginia State University	VA	518
Central Washington University	WA	520
Eastern Washington University	WA	522
Western Washington University	WA	528
Bluefield State College	WV	532
BridgeValley Community & Technical College	WV	531
Fairmont State University	WV	532
Milwaukee School of Engineering	WI	537
Northeast Wisconsin Technical College	WI	544
University of Wisconsin-Stout	WI	541
Waukesha County Technical College	WI	544

EXSC: Commission on Accreditation of Allied Health Education Programs: exercise science (C,B,M)

Institution	State	Page
Metropolitan State University of Denver	CO	83
Central Connecticut State University	CT	88
Southern Connecticut State University	CT	88
University of North Florida	FL	116
Georgia State University	GA	126
Valdosta State University	GA	133
Southern Illinois University Edwardsville	IL	159
Indiana Wesleyan University	IN	169
University of Indianapolis	IN	173
Murray State University	KY	198
University of Louisville	KY	201
University of Louisiana at Monroe	LA	209
University of Southern Maine	ME	213
Salisbury University	MD	220
Lasell College	MA	227
Springfield College	MA	236
Westfield State University	MA	230
St. Catherine University	MN	263
Missouri Baptist University	MO	278
State University of New York, The College at Brockport	NY	345
University of North Carolina at Charlotte	NC	371
North Dakota State University Main Campus	ND	374
University of Mary	ND	375
Bowling Green State University	OH	377
Kent State University Main Campus	OH	384
Ohio Northern University	OH	388
Wright State University Main Campus	OH	396
University of Central Oklahoma	OK	403
Bloomsburg University of Pennsylvania	PA	430
East Stroudsburg University of Pennsylvania	PA	430
Eastern University	PA	418
Grove City College	PA	419
Indiana University of Pennsylvania	PA	431
Saint Francis University	PA	434
Slippery Rock University of Pennsylvania	PA	432
West Chester University of Pennsylvania	PA	432
South Dakota State University	SD	454
Lyndon State College	VT	504
George Mason University	VA	507
Liberty University	VA	509
Longwood University	VA	509
Lynchburg College	VA	509
Old Dominion University	VA	510
University of Wisconsin-Oshkosh	WI	540

FEPAC: American Academy of Forensic Sciences: forensic science (B,M)

Institution	State	Page
University of Alabama at Birmingham	AL	8
California State University-Los Angeles	CA	34
University of New Haven	CT	92
George Washington University	DC	95
Florida International University	FL	114
University of Tampa	FL	118
Albany State University	GA	119
Loyola University Chicago	IL	151
University of Illinois at Chicago	IL	161
Indiana University-Purdue University Indianapolis	IN	168
Eastern Kentucky University	KY	194
Towson University	MD	221
Boston University	MA	224
Madonna University	MI	246
Michigan State University	MI	246
University of Mississippi	MS	270
City University of New York John Jay College of Criminal Justice	NY	319
State University of New York College at Buffalo	NY	345
Ohio University Main Campus	OH	389
Arcadia University	PA	412
Cedar Crest College	PA	415
Duquesne University	PA	417
Penn State University Park	PA	428
West Chester University of Pennsylvania	PA	432
Sam Houston State University	TX	489
Texas A & M University	TX	485
University of North Texas	TX	492
University of North Texas Health Science Center at Fort Worth	TX	493
Virginia Commonwealth University	VA	514
Marshall University	WV	532
West Virginia University	WV	533

FUSER: American Board of Funeral Service Education: funeral service education (C,A,B)

Institution	State	Page
Bishop State Community College	AL	2
Jefferson State Community College	AL	5
Mesa Community College	AZ	15
Arkansas State University-Mountain Home	AR	19
University of Arkansas Community College at Hope	AR	24
American River College	CA	52
Cypress College	CA	56
Arapahoe Community College	CO	79
Lincoln College of New England	CT	91
University of the District of Columbia	DC	97
Florida State College at Jacksonville	FL	105
Miami Dade College	FL	108
St. Petersburg College	FL	112
Gupton Jones College of Funeral Service	GA	127
Ogeechee Technical College	GA	129
Carl Sandburg College	IL	140
Malcolm X College, One of the City Colleges of Chicago	IL	142
Southern Illinois University Carbondale	IL	159
Worsham College of Mortuary Science	IL	163
Ivy Tech Community College of Indiana-Central Indiana	IN	169
Mid-America College of Funeral Service	IN	171
Vincennes University	IN	174
Des Moines Area Community College	IA	177
Kansas City Kansas Community College	KS	188
Southeast Kentucky Community and Technical College	KY	197
Delgado Community College	LA	203
Community College of Baltimore County, The	MD	214
FINE Mortuary College	MA	226
Mount Ida College	MA	234
Wayne State University	MI	252
University of Minnesota-Twin Cities	MN	265
East Mississippi Community College	MS	267

Holmes Community College ... MS .. 267
Mississippi Gulf Coast Community College ... MS .. 268
Northwest Mississippi Community College MS .. 269
Mercer County Community College ... NJ ... 303
American Academy McAllister Institute of Funeral Service ... NY ... 315
Hudson Valley Community College ... NY .. 328
Nassau Community College ... NY ... 334
SUNY Canton-College of Technology ... NY ... 347
Fayetteville Technical Community College NC .. 362
Cincinnati College of Mortuary Science ... OH .. 379
University of Central Oklahoma ... OK .. 403
Mt. Hood Community College ... OR .. 407
Northampton Community College ... PA ... 427
Pittsburgh Institute of Mortuary Science ... PA ... 433
Piedmont Technical College ... SC ... 448
John A. Gupton College ... TN ... 457
Amarillo College ... TX ... 467
Commonwealth Institute of Funeral Service ... TX ... 471
Dallas Institute of Funeral Service ... TX ... 473
San Antonio College ... TX ... 467
Salt Lake Community College ... UT ... 500
#John Tyler Community College ... VA ... 515
Tidewater Community College ... VA ... 517
Lake Washington Institute of Technology . WA .. 523
#Milwaukee Area Technical College ... WI ... 543

HSA: Commission on Accreditation of Healthcare Management Education: healthcare management (B,M)

University of Alabama at Birmingham ... AL ... 8
University of Arkansas for Medical Sciences ... AR ... 24
California State University-Long Beach ... CA ... 33
San Diego State University ... CA ... 35
University of California-Los Angeles ... CA ... 71
University of Southern California ... CA ... 74
University of Colorado Denver|Anschutz Medical Campus ... CO ... 86
George Washington University ... DC ... 95
Georgetown University ... DC ... 95
Florida International University ... FL ... 114
University of Central Florida ... FL ... 115
University of Florida ... FL ... 115
University of Miami ... FL ... 118
University of North Florida ... FL ... 116
University of South Florida ... FL ... 116
Armstrong State University ... GA ... 120
Georgia State University ... GA ... 126
Governors State University ... IL ... 145
Rush University ... IL ... 158
University of Illinois at Chicago ... IL ... 161
Indiana University-Purdue University Indianapolis ... IN ... 168
University of Iowa ... IA ... 175
University of Kansas Main Campus ... KS ... 191
University of Kentucky ... KY ... 200
Tulane University ... LA ... 207
University of Southern Maine ... ME .. 213
Johns Hopkins University ... MD .. 216
Boston University ... MA .. 224
Simmons College ... MA .. 236
University of Michigan-Ann Arbor ... MI ... 251
University of Minnesota-Twin Cities ... MN .. 265
University of Saint Thomas ... MN .. 265
Saint Louis University ... MO .. 281
University of Missouri - Columbia ... MO .. 283
Seton Hall University ... NJ ... 308
Baruch College/City University of New York ... NY ... 318
Columbia University in the City of New York ... NY ... 322
Cornell University ... NY ... 323
New York University ... NY ... 336
Union Graduate College ... NY ... 351
University of North Carolina at Chapel Hill NC .. 371
University of North Carolina at Charlotte .. NC .. 371
Ohio State University Main Campus, The . OH .. 389
Xavier University ... OH .. 396
Portland State University ... OR .. 409
Penn State University Park ... PA ... 428
Temple University ... PA ... 436
University of Pittsburgh ... PA ... 437
University of Scranton, The ... PA ... 438
Widener University ... PA ... 439
University of Puerto Rico-Medical Sciences Campus ... PR ... 558
Medical University of South Carolina ... SC ... 447
University of South Carolina Columbia ... SC ... 450
University of Memphis, The ... TN ... 462
Baylor University ... TX ... 469
Texas A & M University ... TX ... 485
Texas State University ... TX ... 489
Texas Woman's University ... TX ... 490
Trinity University ... TX ... 490
University of North Texas Health Science Center at Fort Worth ... TX ... 493
University of the Incarnate Word ... TX ... 492
University of Utah, The ... UT ... 499
Weber State University ... UT ... 500
George Mason University ... VA ... 507
Marymount University ... VA ... 510
Virginia Commonwealth University ... VA ... 514
University of Washington ... WA .. 527
Washington State University ... WA .. 528

HT: National Accrediting Agency for Clinical Laboratory Sciences: histologic technology (C,A,B)

Phoenix College ... AZ ... 15
Mt. San Antonio College ... CA ... 54
Goodwin College ... CT ... 90
Barry University ... FL ... 99
Florida State College at Jacksonville ... FL ... 105
Miami Dade College ... FL ... 108
Darton State College ... GA .. 123
Elgin Community College ... IL ... 144
Indiana University-Purdue University Indianapolis ... IN ... 168
Harford Community College ... MD .. 215
Lansing Community College ... MI ... 245
North Hennepin Community College ... MN .. 260
State University of New York College of Agriculture and Technology at Coble skill ... NY ... 346
Carolinas College of Health Sciences ... NC .. 355
University of North Dakota ... ND .. 373
Lakeland Community College ... OH .. 385
Drexel University ... PA ... 417
Harcum College ... PA ... 420
University of Pittsburgh ... PA ... 437
Community College of Rhode Island ... RI ... 441
Medical University of South Carolina ... SC ... 447
University of Tennessee Health Science Center ... TN ... 465
Houston Community College ... TX ... 475
St. Philip's College ... TX ... 467
Tarleton State University ... TX ... 485
University of Texas Health Science Center at San Antonio ... TX ... 495
University of Texas M.D. Anderson Cancer Center, The ... TX ... 495
Clover Park Technical College ... WA .. 521
West Virginia University ... WV .. 533

IACBE: International Assembly for Collegiate Business Education: business programs in institutions that grant bachelor/graduate degrees (A,B,M,D)

Stillman College ... AL ... 7
Alaska Pacific University ... AK ... 10
University of the Ozarks ... AR ... 25
Ashford University ... CA ... 29
Azusa Pacific University ... CA ... 29
California State University Maritime Academy ... CA ... 34
Humboldt State University ... CA ... 35
John F. Kennedy University ... CA ... 48
National University ... CA ... 55
Pacific Union College ... CA ... 57
Albertus Magnus College ... CT ... 87
Goldey-Beacom College ... DE ... 94
Wilmington University ... DE ... 94
Edward Waters College ... FL ... 102
Florida Institute of Technology ... FL ... 103
Hodges University ... FL ... 106
Lynn University ... FL ... 108
Nova Southeastern University ... FL ... 109
Palm Beach Atlantic University ... FL ... 109
Saint Leo University ... FL ... 111
Webber International University ... FL ... 119
Thomas University ... GA ... 132
University of Guam ... GU .. 549
Chaminade University of Honolulu ... HI ... 135
Lewis-Clark State College ... ID ... 138
Lincoln College ... IL ... 150
McKendree University ... IL ... 152
National-Louis University ... IL ... 153
North Park University ... IL ... 154
Robert Morris University - Illinois ... IL ... 157
Rockford University ... IL ... 157
Bethel College ... IN ... 164
Grace College and Seminary ... IN ... 166
Marian University ... IN ... 171
Oakland City University ... IN ... 171
Purdue University Calumet ... IN ... 171
Saint Joseph's College ... IN ... 172
Maharishi University of Management ... IA ... 181
Northwestern College ... IA ... 182
University of Saint Mary ... KS ... 191
Campbellsville University ... KY ... 194
Kentucky Wesleyan College ... KY ... 198
Lindsey Wilson College ... KY ... 198
Spalding University ... KY ... 199
Sullivan University ... KY ... 200
Our Lady of Holy Cross College ... LA ... 206
Husson University ... ME .. 210
University of Maine at Fort Kent ... ME .. 212
Capitol Technology University ... MD .. 214
Mount St. Mary's University ... MD .. 217
University of Maryland College Park ... MD .. 219
American International College ... MA .. 221
College of Our Lady of the Elms ... MA .. 225
Fitchburg State University ... MA .. 229
Massachusetts Maritime Academy ... MA .. 230
Nichols College ... MA .. 235
Springfield College ... MA .. 236
Wentworth Institute of Technology ... MA .. 237
Andrews University ... MI ... 239
Baker College of Flint ... MI ... 239
Davenport University ... MI ... 241
Lawrence Technological University ... MI ... 245
Bemidji State University ... MN .. 258
Saint Mary's University of Minnesota ... MN .. 264
Belhaven University ... MS .. 266
Avila University ... MO .. 272
Culver-Stockton College ... MO .. 274
Harris-Stowe State University ... MO .. 275
Carroll College ... MT .. 286
University of Montana Western, The ... MT .. 287
Bellevue University ... NE .. 289
Clarkson College ... NE .. 289
College of Saint Mary ... NE .. 289
Concordia University ... NE .. 289
Wayne State College ... NE .. 292
Roseman University of Health Sciences ... NV .. 296
Franklin Pierce University ... NH .. 297
Centenary College ... NJ ... 301
Felician College ... NJ ... 302
Saint Peter's University ... NJ ... 307
Cazenovia College ... NY ... 317
Daemen College ... NY ... 323
Dominican College of Blauvelt ... NY ... 324
Dowling College ... NY ... 324
D'Youville College ... NY ... 324
Excelsior College ... NY ... 325
Keuka College ... NY ... 329
Manhattanville College ... NY ... 331
Medaille College ... NY ... 332
Mount Saint Mary College ... NY ... 333
Nazareth College of Rochester ... NY ... 334
Roberts Wesleyan College ... NY ... 339
Sage Colleges, The ... NY ... 340
St. Thomas Aquinas College ... NY ... 341
State University of New York College at Potsdam ... NY ... 346
State University of New York Empire State College ... NY ... 348
Vaughn College of Aeronautics and Technology ... NY ... 352
Montreat College ... NC .. 359
Dickinson State University ... ND .. 373
Minot State University ... ND .. 374
University of Jamestown ... ND .. 375
University of Mary ... ND .. 375
Defiance College, The ... OH .. 381
Franklin University ... OH .. 382
Lake Erie College ... OH .. 385
Lourdes University ... OH .. 385
University of Rio Grande ... OH .. 394
#Urbana University ... OH .. 394
Ursuline College ... OH .. 394
Bacone College ... OK .. 396
Oklahoma Wesleyan University ... OK .. 400
Southwestern Oklahoma State University . OK .. 402
Central Oregon Community College ... OR .. 404
Eastern Oregon University ... OR .. 405
Marylhurst University ... OR .. 407
Northwest Christian University ... OR .. 407
Oregon Institute of Technology ... OR .. 408
Cairn University ... PA ... 414
Chatham University ... PA ... 415
Gwynedd Mercy University ... PA ... 420
Keystone College ... PA ... 422
Mercyhurst University ... PA ... 425
Misericordia University ... PA ... 426
Point Park University ... PA ... 433
Saint Francis University ... PA ... 434
Seton Hill University ... PA ... 435
Inter American University of Puerto Rico San German Campus ... PR ... 554
Universidad Politecnica De Puerto Rico ... PR ... 556
Salve Regina University ... RI ... 442
Charleston Southern University ... SC ... 444
National American University ... SD ... 452
Presentation College ... SD ... 453
University of Sioux Falls ... SD ... 454
Bryan College ... TN ... 455
Southern Adventist University ... TN ... 460
Concordia University Texas ... TX ... 471
Howard Payne University ... TX ... 475
LeTourneau University ... TX ... 477
Southwestern Adventist University ... TX ... 483
Hampton University ... VA ... 508
Davis & Elkins College ... WV .. 529
Ohio Valley University ... WV .. 530
Shepherd University ... WV .. 532
West Liberty University ... WV .. 533
Concordia University Wisconsin ... WI ... 535
Herzing University ... WI ... 536
Marian University ... WI ... 537

IFSAC: International Fire Service Accreditation Congress Degree Assembly: fire and emergency related degree (A,B)

Central Arizona College ... AZ ... 12
Yavapai College ... AZ ... 18
NorthWest Arkansas Community College . AR ... 22
Oxnard College ... CA ... 75
Aims Community College ... CO ... 78
Southern Illinois University Carbondale ... IL ... 159
Johnson County Community College ... KS ... 188
Ashland Community and Technical College ... KY ... 195
Bluegrass Community and Technical College ... KY ... 195
Eastern Kentucky University ... KY ... 194
Elizabethtown Community and Technical College ... KY ... 195
Gateway Community and Technical College ... KY ... 196
Hazard Community and Technical College KY ... 196
Jefferson Community and Technical College ... KY ... 196
Madisonville Community College ... KY ... 196
Maysville Community and Technical College ... KY ... 196
Owensboro Community and Technical College ... KY ... 197
Somerset Community College ... KY ... 197
Southcentral Kentucky Community and Technical College ... KY ... 197
West Kentucky Community and Technical College ... KY ... 197
Lake Superior State University ... MI ... 245
Lansing Community College ... MI ... 245
Hennepin Technical College ... MN .. 258
Ozarks Technical Community College ... MO .. 280
New Mexico State University Dona Ana Community College ... NM .. 312
Catawba Valley Community College ... NC .. 361
Gaston College ... NC .. 362
Cincinnati State Technical and Community College ... OH .. 379
Lakeland Community College ... OH .. 385
University of Akron, Main Campus, The ... OH .. 392
Chemeketa Community College ... OR .. 404
Portland Community College ... OR .. 409
Holy Family University ... PA ... 420
Montgomery County Community College . PA ... 426
Blinn College ... TX ... 469
Utah Valley University ... UT ... 500
South Puget Sound Community College .. WA .. 527
University of Wisconsin-Oshkosh ... WI ... 540

IPSY: American Psychological Association: pre-doctoral internships in professional psychology

University of Alabama at Birmingham ... AL ... 8
Arizona State University ... AZ ... 11
University of Arizona ... AZ ... 18
University of Arkansas for Medical Sciences ... AR ... 24
California State University-Long Beach ... CA ... 33
California State University-Northridge ... CA ... 34
Loma Linda University ... CA ... 50
San Jose State University ... CA ... 36
Stanford University ... CA ... 68
University of California-Berkeley ... CA ... 70
University of California-Davis ... CA ... 71
University of California-Irvine ... CA ... 71
University of California-Los Angeles ... CA ... 71
University of California-Riverside ... CA ... 72
University of California-San Diego ... CA ... 72
University of California-San Francisco ... CA ... 72
University of California-Santa Barbara ... CA ... 72
University of California-Santa Cruz ... CA ... 72
University of San Diego ... CA ... 74
University of San Francisco ... CA ... 74
University of Southern California ... CA ... 74
University of the Pacific ... CA ... 73
Colorado State University ... CO ... 81
University of Colorado Boulder ... CO ... 86
University of Colorado Denver|Anschutz Medical Campus ... CO ... 86
University of Denver ... CO ... 86
University of Northern Colorado ... CO ... 87

University of Connecticut ... CT ... 92
Yale University ... CT ... 93
University of Delaware ... DE ... 94
American University ... DC ... 94
Catholic University of America, The ... DC ... 95
Howard University ... DC ... 96
Florida International University ... FL ... 114
Florida State University ... FL ... 115
Nova Southeastern University ... FL ... 109
University of Central Florida ... FL ... 115
University of Florida ... FL ... 115
University of Miami ... FL ... 118
University of South Florida ... FL ... 116
Augusta University ... GA ... 121
Emory University ... GA ... 124
Georgia Institute of Technology ... GA ... 125
Georgia State University ... GA ... 126
University of Hawaii at Manoa ... HI ... 135
University of Idaho ... ID ... 139
Adler University ... IL ... 139
Illinois State University ... IL ... 147
Northern Illinois University ... IL ... 154
Northwestern University ... IL ... 155
Rush University ... IL ... 158
Southern Illinois University Carbondale ... IL ... 159
University of Chicago ... IL ... 161
University of Illinois at Chicago ... IL ... 161
University of Illinois at Urbana-Champaign IL ... 162
Ball State University ... IN ... 164
Butler University ... IN ... 164
Indiana University Bloomington ... IN ... 167
Indiana University-Purdue University Indianapolis ... IN ... 168
Purdue University Main Campus ... IN ... 171
University of Notre Dame ... IN ... 174
Iowa State University ... IA ... 175
University of Iowa ... IA ... 175
Kansas State University ... KS ... 188
University of Kansas Main Campus ... KS ... 191
Wichita State University ... KS ... 192
University of Kentucky ... KY ... 200
University of Louisville ... KY ... 201
Louisiana State University and Agricultural and Mechanical College ... LA ... 204
Louisiana State University Health Sciences Center-New Orleans ... LA ... 205
Tulane University ... LA ... 207
University of Maine ... ME ... 212
Johns Hopkins University ... MD ... 216
Towson University ... MD ... 221
University of Maryland Baltimore ... MD ... 219
University of Maryland Baltimore County ... MD ... 219
University of Maryland College Park ... MD ... 219
Boston University ... MA ... 224
Harvard University ... MA ... 227
Suffolk University ... MA ... 237
Tufts University ... MA ... 237
University of Massachusetts ... MA ... 228
University of Massachusetts Medical School ... MA ... 229
William James College ... MA ... 238
Grand Valley State University ... MI ... 243
Michigan State University ... MI ... 246
University of Michigan-Ann Arbor ... MI ... 251
Western Michigan University ... MI ... 252
University of Minnesota-Twin Cities ... MN ... 265
University of Saint Thomas ... MN ... 265
University of Mississippi Medical Center ... MS ... 270
University of Missouri - Columbia ... MO ... 283
University of Missouri - Kansas City ... MO ... 284
University of Missouri - Saint Louis ... MO ... 284
Montana State University ... MT ... 287
University of Nebraska - Lincoln ... NE ... 293
Dartmouth College ... NH ... 297
University of New Hampshire ... NH ... 299
University of New Mexico Main Campus ... NM ... 313
Albany Medical College ... NY ... 314
Columbia University in the City of New York ... NY ... 322
Icahn School of Medicine at Mount Sinai ... NY ... 328
New York University ... NY ... 336
Pace University ... NY ... 337
State University of New York Upstate Medical University ... NY ... 344
Stony Brook University ... NY ... 344
University at Albany, SUNY ... NY ... 343
University at Buffalo-SUNY ... NY ... 343
University of Rochester ... NY ... 351
Yeshiva University ... NY ... 353
Appalachian State University ... NC ... 369
Duke University ... NC ... 356
University of North Carolina at Chapel Hill NC ... 371
University of North Carolina at Charlotte ... NC ... 371
University of North Dakota ... ND ... 373
Bowling Green State University ... OH ... 377
Miami University ... OH ... 386
Ohio State University Main Campus, The ... OH ... 389
University of Akron, Main Campus, The ... OH ... 392
Wright State University Main Campus ... OH ... 396
Oregon Health & Science University ... OR ... 408
Oregon State University ... OR ... 408
Pacific University ... OR ... 408
University of Oregon ... OR ... 410
Immaculata University ... PA ... 421
Penn State University Park ... PA ... 428
Philadelphia College of Osteopathic Medicine ... PA ... 432
Temple University ... PA ... 436
University of Pennsylvania ... PA ... 437
University of Pittsburgh ... PA ... 437
Widener University ... PA ... 439
Brown University ... RI ... 441
Clemson University ... SC ... 444
Medical University of South Carolina ... SC ... 447
University of South Carolina Columbia ... SC ... 450
University of Memphis, The ... TN ... 462
University of Tennessee Health Science Center ... TN ... 465
University of Tennessee, Knoxville ... TN ... 465
Vanderbilt University ... TN ... 465
Baylor College of Medicine ... TX ... 469
Texas A & M University ... TX ... 485
Texas State University ... TX ... 489
Texas Tech University ... TX ... 489
Texas Woman's University ... TX ... 490
University of Houston ... TX ... 491
University of Texas at Austin ... TX ... 493
University of Texas at Dallas, The ... TX ... 494
University of Texas Health Science Center at San Antonio ... TX ... 495
University of Texas Southwestern Medical Center ... TX ... 496
Brigham Young University ... UT ... 497
University of Utah, The ... UT ... 499
Utah State University ... UT ... 500
University of Vermont ... VT ... 503
College of William & Mary ... VA ... 506
Eastern Virginia Medical School ... VA ... 507
George Mason University ... VA ... 507
James Madison University ... VA ... 509
University of Virginia ... VA ... 514
Virginia Commonwealth University ... VA ... 514
Virginia Polytechnic Institute and State University ... VA ... 518
Central Washington University ... WA ... 520
University of Washington ... WA ... 527
Washington State University ... WA ... 528
West Virginia University ... WV ... 533
University of Wisconsin-Madison ... WI ... 539

JOUR: Accrediting Council on Education for Journalism and Mass Communications: journalism and mass communications (B,M)

Auburn University ... AL ... 1
Jacksonville State University ... AL ... 4
University of Alabama, The ... AL ... 8
University of North Alabama ... AL ... 9
#University of Alaska Anchorage ... AK ... 10
University of Alaska Fairbanks ... AK ... 10
Arizona State University ... AZ ... 11
University of Arizona ... AZ ... 18
Arkansas State University-Jonesboro ... AR ... 19
University of Arkansas Main Campus ... AR ... 23
California State University-Chico ... CA ... 33
California State University-Fullerton ... CA ... 33
California State University-Long Beach ... CA ... 33
California State University-Northridge ... CA ... 34
San Diego State University ... CA ... 35
San Francisco State University ... CA ... 36
#San Jose State University ... CA ... 36
University of California-Berkeley ... CA ... 70
University of Southern California ... CA ... 74
Colorado State University ... CO ... 81
University of Colorado Boulder ... CO ... 86
University of Connecticut ... CT ... 92
American University ... DC ... 94
Howard University ... DC ... 96
Florida Agricultural and Mechanical University ... FL ... 114
Florida International University ... FL ... 114
University of Florida ... FL ... 115
University of South Florida St. Petersburg FL ... 116
Savannah State University ... GA ... 131
University of Georgia ... GA ... 132
University of Idaho ... ID ... 139
Eastern Illinois University ... IL ... 144
Northwestern University ... IL ... 155
Southern Illinois University Carbondale ... IL ... 159
Southern Illinois University Edwardsville ... IL ... 159
University of Illinois at Urbana-Champaign IL ... 162
Ball State University ... IN ... 164
Indiana University Bloomington ... IN ... 167
University of Southern Indiana ... IN ... 174
Drake University ... IA ... 177
Iowa State University ... IA ... 175
University of Iowa ... IA ... 175
Kansas State University ... KS ... 188
University of Kansas Main Campus ... KS ... 191
Murray State University ... KY ... 198
University of Kentucky ... KY ... 200
Western Kentucky University ... KY ... 201
Grambling State University ... LA ... 207
Louisiana State University and Agricultural and Mechanical College ... LA ... 204
Loyola University New Orleans ... LA ... 206
Nicholls State University ... LA ... 208
Southern University and A&M College ... LA ... 207
University of Louisiana at Lafayette ... LA ... 208
University of Maryland College Park ... MD ... 219
Central Michigan University ... MI ... 240
Michigan State University ... MI ... 246
St. Cloud State University ... MN ... 261
University of Minnesota-Twin Cities ... MN ... 265
University of Mississippi ... MS ... 270
University of Southern Mississippi ... MS ... 271
Southeast Missouri State University ... MO ... 282
University of Missouri - Columbia ... MO ... 283
University of Montana - Missoula ... MT ... 287
University of Nebraska - Lincoln ... NE ... 293
University of Nevada, Reno ... NV ... 295
University of New Mexico Main Campus ... NM ... 313
City University of New York Graduate Center ... NY ... 319
Columbia University in the City of New York ... NY ... 322
Hofstra University ... NY ... 328
Iona College ... NY ... 328
New York University ... NY ... 336
State University of New York College at Buffalo ... NY ... 345
Stony Brook University ... NY ... 344
Syracuse University Main Campus ... NY ... 349
Elon University ... NC ... 356
North Carolina Agricultural and Technical State University ... NC ... 370
University of North Carolina at Chapel Hill NC ... 371
Bowling Green State University ... OH ... 377
Kent State University Main Campus ... OH ... 384
Ohio University Main Campus ... OH ... 389
Oklahoma State University ... OK ... 400
University of Oklahoma Norman Campus ... OK ... 403
University of Oregon ... OR ... 410
Penn State University Park ... PA ... 428
Shippensburg University of Pennsylvania ... PA ... 431
Temple University ... PA ... 436
University of Puerto Rico at Arecibo ... PR ... 557
University of Puerto Rico-Rio Piedras Campus ... PR ... 558
University of South Carolina Columbia ... SC ... 450
Winthrop University ... SC ... 451
South Dakota State University ... SD ... 454
#University of South Dakota, The ... SD ... 453
Middle Tennessee State University ... TN ... 461
University of Memphis, The ... TN ... 462
University of Tennessee at Chattanooga ... TN ... 465
University of Tennessee at Martin ... TN ... 465
University of Tennessee, Knoxville ... TN ... 465
Abilene Christian University ... TX ... 466
Baylor University ... TX ... 469
Texas Christian University ... TX ... 486
Texas State University ... TX ... 489
University of North Texas ... TX ... 492
University of Texas at Austin ... TX ... 493
Brigham Young University ... UT ... 497
Hampton University ... VA ... 508
Norfolk State University ... VA ... 510
Virginia Commonwealth University ... VA ... 514
Washington and Lee University ... VA ... 519
University of Washington ... WA ... 527
Marshall University ... WV ... 532
West Virginia University ... WV ... 533
Marquette University ... WI ... 537
#University of Wisconsin-Eau Claire ... WI ... 539
University of Wisconsin-Oshkosh ... WI ... 540

KIN: Commission on Accreditation of Allied Health Education Programs: kinesiotherapy (B)

University of Southern Mississippi ... MS ... 271
Shaw University ... NC ... 368
Norfolk State University ... VA ... 510

LAW: American Bar Association: law (FP,D)

Faulkner University ... AL ... 3
Samford University ... AL ... 6
University of Alabama, The ... AL ... 8
Arizona State University ... AZ ... 11
Arizona Summit Law School ... AZ ... 12
University of Arizona ... AZ ... 18
University of Arkansas at Little Rock ... AR ... 24
University of Arkansas Main Campus ... AR ... 23
California Western School of Law ... CA ... 36
Chapman University ... CA ... 38
Golden Gate University ... CA ... 46
Loyola Marymount University ... CA ... 53
Pepperdine University ... CA ... 58
Santa Clara University ... CA ... 65
Southwestern Law School ... CA ... 68
Stanford University ... CA ... 68
Thomas Jefferson School of Law ... CA ... 69
University of California-Berkeley ... CA ... 70
University of California-Davis ... CA ... 71
University of California-Hastings College of the Law ... CA ... 71
University of California-Irvine ... CA ... 71
University of California-Los Angeles ... CA ... 71
#University of La Verne ... CA ... 73
University of San Diego ... CA ... 74
University of San Francisco ... CA ... 74
University of Southern California ... CA ... 74
University of the Pacific ... CA ... 73
Whittier College ... CA ... 77
University of Colorado Boulder ... CO ... 86
University of Denver ... CO ... 86
Quinnipiac University ... CT ... 91
University of Connecticut ... CT ... 92
Yale University ... CT ... 93
American University ... DC ... 94
Catholic University of America, The ... DC ... 95
George Washington University ... DC ... 95
Georgetown University ... DC ... 95
Howard University ... DC ... 96
University of the District of Columbia ... DC ... 97
Ave Maria School of Law ... FL ... 98
Barry University ... FL ... 99
Florida Agricultural and Mechanical University ... FL ... 114
Florida Coastal School of Law ... FL ... 103
Florida International University ... FL ... 114
Florida State University ... FL ... 115
Nova Southeastern University ... FL ... 109
St. Thomas University ... FL ... 112
Stetson University ... FL ... 117
University of Florida ... FL ... 115
University of Miami ... FL ... 118
Atlanta's John Marshall Law School ... GA ... 121
Emory University ... GA ... 124
Georgia State University ... GA ... 126
Mercer University ... GA ... 128
University of Georgia ... GA ... 132
University of Hawaii at Manoa ... HI ... 135
University of Idaho ... ID ... 139
DePaul University ... IL ... 143
John Marshall Law School ... IL ... 148
Loyola University Chicago ... IL ... 151
Northern Illinois University ... IL ... 154
Northwestern University ... IL ... 155
Southern Illinois University Carbondale ... IL ... 159
University of Chicago ... IL ... 161
University of Illinois at Urbana-Champaign IL ... 162
Indiana University Bloomington ... IN ... 167
Indiana University-Purdue University Indianapolis ... IN ... 168
University of Notre Dame ... IN ... 174
Valparaiso University ... IN ... 174
Drake University ... IA ... 177
University of Iowa ... IA ... 175
University of Kansas Main Campus ... KS ... 191
Washburn University ... KS ... 192
Northern Kentucky University ... KY ... 199
University of Kentucky ... KY ... 200
University of Louisville ... KY ... 201
Louisiana State University Paul M. Hebert Law Center ... LA ... 205
Loyola University New Orleans ... LA ... 206
Southern University Law Center ... LA ... 207
Tulane University ... LA ... 207
University of Southern Maine ... ME ... 213
University of Baltimore ... MD ... 221
University of Maryland Baltimore ... MD ... 219
Boston College ... MA ... 224
Boston University ... MA ... 224
Harvard University ... MA ... 227
New England Law | Boston ... MA ... 234
Northeastern University ... MA ... 235
Suffolk University ... MA ... 237
#University of Massachusetts Dartmouth ... MA ... 228
Western New England University ... MA ... 238
Michigan State University ... MI ... 246
University of Michigan-Ann Arbor ... MI ... 251
Wayne State University ... MI ... 252
Western Michigan University Cooley Law School ... MI ... 252
Hamline University ... MN ... 256
University of Minnesota-Twin Cities ... MN ... 265
University of Saint Thomas ... MN ... 265
William Mitchell College of Law ... MN ... 266
Mississippi College ... MS ... 268
University of Mississippi ... MS ... 270
Saint Louis University ... MO ... 281
University of Missouri - Columbia ... MO ... 283
University of Missouri - Kansas City ... MO ... 284

LIB: American Library Association: librarianship (M)

LSAR: American Society of Landscape Architects: landscape architecture (B,M)

M: Middle States Commission on Higher Education

MAAB: Accrediting Bureau of Health Education Schools: medical assisting (C,A)

MAC: Commission on Accreditation of Allied Health Education Programs: medical assisting (C,A)

National College ... TN ... 459
South College ... TN ... 460
Cisco College ... TX ... 470
College of the Mainland ... TX ... 471
El Centro College ... TX ... 472
El Paso Community College ... TX ... 473
Hallmark University ... TX ... 474
Houston Community College ... TX ... 475
Kaplan College ... TX ... 476
Lone Star College System ... TX ... 477
McLennan Community College ... TX ... 478
Northeast Texas Community College ... TX ... 479
Richland College ... TX ... 473
San Antonio College ... TX ... 467
San Jacinto College North ... TX ... 481
Texas School of Business ... TX ... 487
Texas State Technical College Harlingen . TX ... 487
Texas State Technical College Waco ... TX ... 488
#LDS Business College ... UT ... 498
Ogden-Weber Applied Technology College ... UT ... 498
Salt Lake Community College ... UT ... 500
Stevens-Henager College ... UT ... 499
American National University ... VA ... 504
Miller-Motte Technical College ... VA ... 510
Clark College ... WA .. 521
Clover Park Technical College ... WA .. 521
Columbia Basin College ... WA .. 521
Everest College ... WA .. 522
Everett Community College ... WA .. 522
Highline College ... WA .. 523
Lake Washington Institute of Technology . WA .. 523
Lower Columbia College ... WA .. 524
#North Seattle College ... WA .. 525
Olympic College ... WA .. 524
Renton Technical College ... WA .. 525
Skagit Valley College ... WA .. 527
South Puget Sound Community College .. WA .. 527
Spokane Community College ... WA .. 521
Walla Walla Community College ... WA .. 527
Wenatchee Valley College ... WA .. 528
Whatcom Community College ... WA .. 528
Yakima Valley Community College ... WA .. 529
Huntington Junior College ... WV .. 530
Mountwest Community and Technical College ... WV .. 531
West Virginia Northern Community College ... WV .. 531
#Blackhawk Technical College ... WI ... 542
Chippewa Valley Technical College ... WI ... 542
Concordia University Wisconsin ... WI ... 535
Fox Valley Technical College ... WI ... 542
Lac Courte Oreilles Ojibwa Community College ... WI ... 536
Madison Area Technical College ... WI ... 543
Mid-State Technical College ... WI ... 543
Milwaukee Area Technical College ... WI ... 543
Moraine Park Technical College ... WI ... 543
Nicolet Area Technical College ... WI ... 543
Northcentral Technical College ... WI ... 544
Northeast Wisconsin Technical College ... WI ... 544
Southwest Wisconsin Technical College .. WI ... 544
Waukesha County Technical College ... WI ... 544
Western Technical College ... WI ... 544
Wisconsin Indianhead Technical College . WI ... 544

MACTE: Montessori Accreditation Council for Teacher Education: Montessori teacher education (C)

South Mountain Community College ... AZ ... 15
Saint Mary's College of California ... CA ... 61
Barry University ... FL ... 99
Kennesaw State University ... GA .. 127
Chaminade University of Honolulu ... HI ... 135
Xavier University ... OH ... 396
Oklahoma City University ... OK .. 400
Chestnut Hill College ... PA ... 415
Lander University ... SC ... 447
Westminster College ... UT ... 501
University of Wisconsin-River Falls ... WI ... 540

MEAC: Midwifery Education Accreditation Council: midwifery education (C,A,B,M,D)

National College of Midwifery ... NM .. 311
Birthingway College of Midwifery ... OR .. 404
Midwives College of Utah ... UT ... 498
Bastyr University ... WA .. 519
Southwest Wisconsin Technical College .. WI ... 544

MED: Liaison Committee on Medical Education: medicine (FP,D)

University of Alabama at Birmingham ... AL ... 8
University of South Alabama ... AL ... 9
University of Arizona ... AZ ... 18
University of Arkansas for Medical Sciences ... AR ... 24
#California Northstate University College of Pharmacy ... CA ... 32
Loma Linda University ... CA ... 50
Stanford University ... CA ... 68
University of California-Davis ... CA ... 71
University of California-Irvine ... CA ... 71
University of California-Los Angeles ... CA ... 71
#University of California-Riverside ... CA ... 72
University of California-San Diego ... CA ... 72
University of California-San Francisco ... CA ... 72
University of Southern California ... CA ... 74
University of Colorado Denver|Anschutz Medical Campus ... CO ... 86
#Quinnipiac University ... CT ... 91
Yale University ... CT ... 93
George Washington University ... DC ... 95
Georgetown University ... DC ... 95
Howard University ... DC ... 96
Florida Atlantic University ... FL ... 114
Florida International University ... FL ... 114
Florida State University ... FL ... 115
University of Central Florida ... FL ... 115
University of Florida ... FL ... 115
University of Miami ... FL ... 118
University of South Florida ... FL ... 116
Augusta University ... GA .. 121
Emory University ... GA .. 124
Mercer University ... GA .. 128
Morehouse School of Medicine ... GA .. 129
University of Hawaii at Manoa ... HI ... 135
Loyola University Chicago ... IL ... 151
Northwestern University ... IL ... 155
Rosalind Franklin University of Medicine & Science ... IL ... 157
Rush University ... IL ... 158
Southern Illinois University Carbondale ... IL ... 159
University of Chicago ... IL ... 161
University of Illinois at Chicago ... IL ... 161
Indiana University-Purdue University Indianapolis ... IN ... 168
University of Iowa ... IA ... 175
University of Kentucky ... KY ... 200
#University of Louisville ... KY ... 201
Louisiana State University Health Sciences Center at Shreveport ... LA ... 205
Louisiana State University Health Sciences Center-New Orleans ... LA ... 205
Tulane University ... LA ... 207
Johns Hopkins University ... MD .. 216
Uniformed Services University of the Health Sciences ... MD .. 548
University of Maryland Baltimore ... MD .. 219
Boston University ... MA .. 224
Harvard University ... MA .. 227
Tufts University ... MA .. 237
University of Massachusetts Medical School ... MA .. 229
#Central Michigan University ... MI ... 240
Michigan State University ... MI ... 246
Oakland University ... MI ... 248
University of Michigan-Ann Arbor ... MI ... 251
Wayne State University ... MI ... 252
Mayo Medical School ... MN .. 254
University of Minnesota-Twin Cities ... MN .. 265
University of Mississippi Medical Center ... MS .. 270
Saint Louis University ... MO .. 281
University of Missouri - Columbia ... MO .. 283
University of Missouri - Kansas City ... MO .. 284
Washington University in St. Louis ... MO .. 285
Creighton University ... NE ... 290
University of Nebraska Medical Center ... NE ... 293
University of Nevada, Reno ... NV ... 295
Dartmouth College ... NH ... 297
#Rowan University ... NJ ... 306
University of New Mexico Main Campus .. NM .. 313
Albany Medical College ... NY ... 314
#City University of New York The City College ... NY ... 318
Columbia University in the City of New York ... NY ... 322
Hofstra University ... NY ... 328
Icahn School of Medicine at Mount Sinai . NY ... 328
New York Medical College ... NY ... 335
New York University ... NY ... 336
State University of New York Upstate Medical University ... NY ... 344
Stony Brook University ... NY ... 344
SUNY Downstate Medical Center ... NY ... 344
University at Buffalo-SUNY ... NY ... 343
University of Rochester ... NY ... 351
Yeshiva University ... NY ... 353
Duke University ... NC .. 356
East Carolina University ... NC .. 369
University of North Carolina at Chapel Hill NC .. 371
Wake Forest University ... NC .. 372
University of North Dakota ... ND .. 373
Case Western Reserve University ... OH .. 378
Northeast Ohio Medical University ... OH .. 387
Ohio State University Main Campus, The . OH .. 389
University of Cincinnati Main Campus ... OH .. 393
University of Toledo ... OH .. 394
Wright State University Main Campus ... OH .. 396
Oregon Health & Science University ... OR .. 408
Commonwealth Medical College, The ... PA ... 415
Drexel University ... PA ... 417
Temple University ... PA ... 436
Thomas Jefferson University ... PA ... 436
University of Pennsylvania ... PA ... 437
University of Pittsburgh ... PA ... 437
Ponce School of Medicine & Health Sciences ... PR ... 555
San Juan Bautista School of Medicine ... PR ... 555
Universidad Central Del Caribe ... PR ... 556
University of Puerto Rico-Medical Sciences Campus ... PR ... 558
Brown University ... RI ... 441
Medical University of South Carolina ... SC ... 447
University of South Carolina Columbia ... SC ... 450
#University of South Carolina School of Medicine Greenville ... SC ... 450
University of South Dakota, The ... SD ... 453
East Tennessee State University ... TN ... 461
Meharry Medical College ... TN ... 458
University of Tennessee Health Science Center ... TN ... 465
Vanderbilt University ... TN ... 465
#Baylor College of Medicine ... TX ... 469
Texas A & M University ... TX ... 485
Texas Tech University ... TX ... 489
Texas Tech University Health Sciences Center ... TX ... 490
#University of Texas at Austin ... TX ... 493
University of Texas Health Science Center at Houston (UTHealth), The ... TX ... 495
University of Texas Health Science Center at San Antonio ... TX ... 495
University of Texas Medical Branch, The . TX ... 495
University of Texas Southwestern Medical Center ... TX ... 496
University of Utah, The ... UT ... 499
University of Vermont ... VT ... 503
Eastern Virginia Medical School ... VA ... 507
University of Virginia ... VA ... 514
Virginia Commonwealth University ... VA ... 514
Virginia Tech Carilion School of Medicine VA ... 518
University of Washington ... WA .. 527
Marshall University ... WV .. 532
West Virginia University ... WV .. 533
Medical College of Wisconsin ... WI ... 537
University of Wisconsin-Madison ... WI ... 539

MFCD: American Association for Marriage and Family Therapy: marriage and family therapy (M,D)

Auburn University ... AL ... 1
Northcentral University ... AZ ... 16
Alliant International University-San Diego . CA ... 26
Chapman University ... CA ... 38
#Hope International University ... CA ... 47
Loma Linda University ... CA ... 50
San Diego State University ... CA ... 35
University of San Diego ... CA ... 74
Colorado State University ... CO ... 81
Regis University ... CO ... 85
Central Connecticut State University ... CT ... 88
Fairfield University ... CT ... 90
Southern Connecticut State University ... CT ... 88
University of Connecticut ... CT ... 92
University of Saint Joseph ... CT ... 93
Florida State University ... FL ... 115
Nova Southeastern University ... FL ... 109
Mercer University ... GA .. 128
University of Georgia ... GA .. 132
Valdosta State University ... GA .. 133
Northern Illinois University ... IL ... 154
Northwestern University ... IL ... 155
Christian Theological Seminary ... IN ... 165
Indiana Wesleyan University ... IN ... 169
Purdue University Calumet ... IN ... 171
Friends University ... KS ... 187
Kansas State University ... KS ... 188
Louisville Presbyterian Theological Seminary ... KY ... 198
#University of Kentucky ... KY ... 200
University of Louisville ... KY ... 201
University of Louisiana at Monroe ... LA ... 209
University of Maryland College Park ... MD .. 219
University of Massachusetts Boston ... MA .. 228
Michigan State University ... MI ... 246
Bethel University ... MN .. 254
Capella University ... MN .. 254
St. Cloud State University ... MN .. 261
Saint Mary's University of Minnesota ... MN .. 264
University of Minnesota-Twin Cities ... MN .. 265
Reformed Theological Seminary ... MS .. 270
University of Southern Mississippi ... MS .. 271
Saint Louis University ... MO .. 281
University of Nebraska - Lincoln ... NE ... 293
University of Nevada, Las Vegas ... NV ... 295
University of New Hampshire ... NH .. 299
Seton Hall University ... NJ ... 308
Iona College ... NY ... 328
Syracuse University Main Campus ... NY ... 349
University of Rochester ... NY ... 351
Appalachian State University ... NC .. 369
East Carolina University ... NC .. 369
Pfeiffer University ... NC .. 367
North Dakota State University Main Campus ... ND .. 374
#Ohio State University Main Campus, The . OH .. 389
University of Akron, Main Campus, The ... OH .. 392
Oklahoma State University ... OK .. 400
Lewis and Clark College ... OR .. 406
University of Oregon ... OR .. 410
Drexel University ... PA ... 417
Evangelical Theological Seminary ... PA ... 418
La Salle University ... PA ... 422
#Seton Hill University ... PA ... 435
Thomas Jefferson University ... PA ... 436
University of Rhode Island ... RI ... 442
Converse College ... SC ... 445
Abilene Christian University ... TX ... 466
Our Lady of the Lake University ... TX ... 479
St. Mary's University ... TX ... 481
Texas Tech University ... TX ... 489
University of Houston - Clear Lake ... TX ... 491
Brigham Young University ... UT ... 497
Utah State University ... UT ... 500
Virginia Polytechnic Institute and State University ... VA ... 518
Pacific Lutheran University ... WA .. 524
Seattle Pacific University ... WA .. 526
Seattle University ... WA .. 526
#Edgewood College ... WI ... 536
University of Wisconsin-Stout ... WI ... 541

MIDWF: Accreditation Commission for Midwifery Education: nurse midwifery (C,M,D)

California State University-Fullerton ... CA ... 33
San Diego State University ... CA ... 35
University of California-San Francisco ... CA ... 72
University of Colorado Denver|Anschutz Medical Campus ... CO ... 86
Yale University ... CT ... 93
Georgetown University ... DC ... 95
University of Florida ... FL ... 115
Emory University ... GA .. 124
University of Illinois at Chicago ... IL ... 161
University of Indianapolis ... IN ... 173
Frontier Nursing University ... KY ... 194
University of Michigan-Ann Arbor ... MI ... 251
Wayne State University ... MI ... 252
@Bethel University ... MN .. 254
University of Minnesota-Twin Cities ... MN .. 265
University of New Mexico Main Campus .. NM .. 313
Columbia University in the City of New York ... NY ... 322
New York University ... NY ... 336
Stony Brook University ... NY ... 344
SUNY Downstate Medical Center ... NY ... 344
East Carolina University ... NC .. 369
Case Western Reserve University ... OH .. 378
Ohio State University Main Campus, The . OH .. 389
University of Cincinnati Main Campus ... OH .. 393
Oregon Health & Science University ... OR .. 408
Philadelphia University ... PA ... 432
University of Pennsylvania ... PA ... 437
University of Puerto Rico-Medical Sciences Campus ... PR ... 558
Vanderbilt University ... TN ... 465
Baylor University ... TX ... 469
Texas Tech University ... TX ... 489
University of Utah, The ... UT ... 499
Shenandoah University ... VA ... 512
Seattle University ... WA .. 526
University of Washington ... WA .. 527
Marquette University ... WI ... 537

MIL: Commission on Accreditation of Allied Health Education Programs: medical illustrator (M)

Augusta University ... GA .. 121
University of Illinois at Chicago ... IL ... 161
Johns Hopkins University ... MD .. 216

MLTAB: Accrediting Bureau of Health Education Schools: medical laboratory technician (C,A)

Spencerian College ... KY ... 199

MLTAD: National Accrediting Agency for Clinical Laboratory Sciences: medical laboratory technician (C,A)

Calhoun Community College ... AL ... 2

MT: National Accrediting Agency for Clinical Laboratory Sciences: medical technology/laboratory scientist (C,B)

MUS: National Association of Schools of Music: music (C,A,B,M,D)

NAIT: The Association of Technology, Management, and Applied Engineering: technology, applied technology, engineering technology and technology-related programs (A,B,M)

NATUR: Council on Naturopathic Medical Education: naturopathic medical education (FP,D)

NDT: Commission on Accreditation of Allied Health Education Programs: neurodiagnostic technology (C,A)

NH: Higher Learning Commission, North Central Association

NMT: Joint Review Committee on Education Programs in Nuclear Medicine Technology: nuclear medicine technology (C,A,B)

NRPA: National Recreation and Park Association: recreation, park resources, and leisure studies (B)

NUR: Accreditation Commission for Education in Nursing: nursing (B, M,D)

NURSE: Commission on Collegiate Nursing Education: nursing (B,M,D)

NW: Northwest Commission on Colleges and Universities

NY: New York State Board of Regents

OPD: Commission on Opticianry Accreditation: opticianry (A)

OPE: Commission on Accreditation of Allied Health Education Programs: orthotics and prosthetics (C,B,M)

OPLT: Commission on Opticianry Accreditation: opthalmic laboratory technician (C)

OPT: American Optometric Association: optometry (FP,D)

OPTR: American Optometric Association: optometric residency programs

OPTT: American Optometric Association: optometric technician (C,A)

OSTEO: American Osteopathic Association, Office of Osteopathic Education: osteopathic medicine (FP,D)

OT: American Occupational Therapy Association: occupational therapy (M,D)

OTA: American Occupational Therapy Association: occupational therapy assistant (C,A)

Institution	State	Page
Cossatot Community College of the University of Arkansas	AR	24
Pulaski Technical College	AR	22
South Arkansas Community College	AR	23
Grossmont College	CA	46
Sacramento City College	CA	53
Santa Ana College	CA	60
Stanbridge College	CA	68
Pueblo Community College	CO	85
Goodwin College	CT	90
Housatonic Community College	CT	89
#Lincoln College of New England	CT	91
Manchester Community College	CT	89
Adventist University of Health Sciences	FL	97
Concorde Career Institute	FL	100
Daytona State College	FL	101
Florida State College at Jacksonville	FL	105
Keiser University	FL	107
Polk State College	FL	110
State College of Florida, Manatee-Sarasota	FL	114
Augusta Technical College	GA	121
Chattahoochee Technical College	GA	122
Darton State College	GA	123
Georgia Northwestern Technical College	GA	125
Middle Georgia State University	GA	128
Kapiolani Community College	HI	136
City Colleges of Chicago Wilbur Wright College	IL	142
Illinois Central College	IL	146
John A. Logan College	IL	148
Kaskaskia College	IL	149
Lewis and Clark Community College	IL	150
Lincoln Land Community College	IL	151
McHenry County College	IL	152
Parkland College	IL	155
Rend Lake College	IL	156
Shawnee Community College	IL	159
South Suburban College of Cook County	IL	159
Southeastern Illinois College	IL	159
University of Southern Indiana	IN	174
Hawkeye Community College	IA	179
Indian Hills Community College	IA	179
Kirkwood Community College	IA	180
Brown Mackie College-Salina	KS	185
Neosho County Community College	KS	189
Newman University	KS	189
Washburn University	KS	192
Jefferson Community and Technical College	KY	196
Madisonville Community College	KY	196
Bossier Parish Community College	LA	203
Delgado Community College	LA	203
University of Louisiana at Monroe	LA	209
Kennebec Valley Community College	ME	211
Allegany College of Maryland	MD	213
Community College of Baltimore County, The	MD	214
Bristol Community College	MA	231
North Shore Community College	MA	232
Quinsigamond Community College	MA	232
Springfield Technical Community College	MA	233
Grand Rapids Community College	MI	243
Macomb Community College	MI	246
Mott Community College	MI	247
Anoka Technical College	MN	258
Northland Community and Technical College	MN	260
St. Catherine University	MN	263
Holmes Community College	MS	267
Itawamba Community College	MS	267
Pearl River Community College	MS	270
Crowder College	MO	274
East Central College	MO	274
Jefferson College	MO	276
Metropolitan Community College - Penn Valley	MO	278
Moberly Area Community College	MO	279
North Central Missouri College	MO	279
Ozarks Technical Community College	MO	280
St. Charles Community College	MO	281
State Fair Community College	MO	282
Three Rivers Community College	MO	283
University of Missouri - Kansas City	MO	284
Central Community College	NE	289
River Valley Community College	NH	297
Eastwick College	NJ	302
Eastern New Mexico University-Roswell	NM	310
San Juan College	NM	312
#Western New Mexico University	NM	314
Erie Community College	NY	325
Jamestown Community College	NY	329
La Guardia Community College/City University of New York	NY	320
Maria College of Albany	NY	331
Mercy College	NY	332
Orange County Community College	NY	337
Rockland Community College	NY	339
Touro College	NY	350
Cabarrus College of Health Sciences	NC	355
Cape Fear Community College	NC	360
Central Piedmont Community College	NC	361
Durham Technical Community College	NC	362
Pitt Community College	NC	364
South College-Asheville	NC	368
North Dakota State College of Science	ND	375
Cincinnati State Technical and Community College	OH	379
Cuyahoga Community College	OH	381
James A. Rhodes State College	OH	384
Lorain County Community College	OH	385
Marion Technical College	OH	386
North Central State College	OH	387
Owens Community College	OH	390
Shawnee State University	OH	391
Sinclair Community College	OH	391
Stark State College	OH	391
Zane State College	OH	396
Murray State College	OK	398
Oklahoma City Community College	OK	399
Southwestern Oklahoma State University	OK	402
Tulsa Community College	OK	403
Linn-Benton Community College	OR	406
Central Penn College	PA	415
Community College of Allegheny County	PA	415
Harcum College	PA	420
Kaplan Career Institute - ICM Campus	PA	422
Lehigh Carbon Community College	PA	424
Mercyhurst University	PA	425
Pennsylvania College of Technology	PA	429
Philadelphia University	PA	432
Inter American University of Puerto Rico Ponce Campus	PR	554
Community College of Rhode Island	RI	441
New England Institute of Technology	RI	441
Greenville Technical College	SC	446
Trident Technical College	SC	449
Lake Area Technical Institute	SD	452
Concorde Career College	TN	456
Nashville State Community College	TN	463
Roane State Community College	TN	463
Amarillo College	TX	467
Austin Community College District	TX	468
Del Mar College	TX	473
Houston Community College	TX	475
Laredo Community College	TX	477
Lone Star College System	TX	477
Navarro College	TX	479
Panola College	TX	480
St. Philip's College	TX	467
South Texas College	TX	482
Trinity University	TX	490
Weatherford College	TX	497
Salt Lake Community College	UT	500
Jefferson College of Health Sciences	VA	509
Northern Virginia Community College	VA	516
Southwest Virginia Community College	VA	517
Tidewater Community College	VA	517
Virginia Highlands Community College	VA	517
Bates Technical College	WA	519
Green River Community College	WA	523
#Lake Washington Institute of Technology	WA	523
Spokane Falls Community College	WA	521
University of Charleston	WV	530
Fox Valley Technical College	WI	542
Madison Area Technical College	WI	543
Milwaukee Area Technical College	WI	543
Western Technical College	WI	544
Wisconsin Indianhead Technical College	WI	544
Casper College	WY	545

PA: National Accrediting Agency for Clinical Laboratory Sciences: pathologist's assistant (C,M)

Institution	State	Page
Quinnipiac University	CT	91
Rosalind Franklin University of Medicine & Science	IL	157
Indiana University-Purdue University Indianapolis	IN	168
University of Maryland Baltimore	MD	219
Wayne State University	MI	252
Duke University	NC	356
Drexel University	PA	417
West Virginia University	WV	533

PAST: Association for Clinical Pastoral Education: clinical pastoral education

Institution	State	Page
University of Alabama at Birmingham	AL	8
Jefferson Regional Medical Center School of Nursing	AR	21
Loma Linda University	CA	50
University of California-Davis	CA	71
University of California-Los Angeles	CA	71
University of California-San Francisco	CA	72
Denver Seminary	CO	82
University of Colorado Denver|Anschutz Medical Campus	CO	86
Yale University	CT	93
Georgetown University	DC	95
Emory University	GA	124
Rush University	IL	158
University of Illinois at Chicago	IL	161
Indiana University-Purdue University Indianapolis	IN	168
St. Luke's College	IA	182
University of Iowa	IA	175
University of Kentucky	KY	200
Dartmouth College	NH	297
Albany Medical College	NY	314
Jewish Theological Seminary of America	NY	329
New York Medical College	NY	335
State University of New York Upstate Medical University	NY	344
University of Rochester	NY	351
Duke University	NC	356
University of North Carolina at Chapel Hill	NC	371
Kettering College	OH	385
Thomas Jefferson University	PA	436
University of Pennsylvania	PA	437
University of Tennessee, Knoxville	TN	465
Baylor University	TX	469
Oblate School of Theology	TX	479
University of Texas M.D. Anderson Cancer Center, The	TX	495
University of Texas Southwestern Medical Center	TX	496
Eastern Mennonite University	VA	507
University of Virginia	VA	514
Virginia Commonwealth University	VA	514
University of Washington	WA	527
West Virginia University	WV	533

PCSAS: Psychological Clinical Science Accreditation System: psychological clinical science (D)

Institution	State	Page
Arizona State University	AZ	11
University of Arizona	AZ	18
University of California-Berkeley	CA	70
University of California-Los Angeles	CA	71
University of Southern California	CA	74
University of Delaware	DE	94
University of South Florida	FL	116
Emory University	GA	124
University of Georgia	GA	132
Northwestern University	IL	155
University of Illinois at Urbana-Champaign	IL	162
Indiana University Bloomington	IN	167
University of Iowa	IA	175
University of Kentucky	KY	200
Harvard University	MA	227
University of Minnesota-Twin Cities	MN	265
University of Missouri - Columbia	MO	283
Washington University in St. Louis	MO	285
Stony Brook University	NY	344
Duke University	NC	356
Ohio State University Main Campus, The	OH	389
University of Oregon	OR	410
University of Pennsylvania	PA	437
University of Pittsburgh	PA	437
University of Virginia	VA	514
Virginia Polytechnic Institute and State University	VA	518
University of Wisconsin-Madison	WI	539

PDPSY: American Psychological Association: post-doctoral residency in professional psychology

Institution	State	Page
Stanford University	CA	68
University of California-San Diego	CA	72
University of Southern California	CA	74
Johns Hopkins University	MD	216
University of Michigan-Ann Arbor	MI	251
University of Rochester	NY	351
Brown University	RI	441
University of Washington	WA	527
Medical College of Wisconsin	WI	537

PERF: Commission on Accreditation of Allied Health Education Programs: perfusionist (C,B,M)

Institution	State	Page
University of Arizona	AZ	18
Quinnipiac University	CT	91
Barry University	FL	99
Rush University	IL	158
University of Iowa	IA	175
University of Nebraska Medical Center	NE	293
State University of New York Upstate Medical University	NY	344
University of Pittsburgh	PA	437
Medical University of South Carolina	SC	447
Vanderbilt University	TN	465
Milwaukee School of Engineering	WI	537

PH: Council on Education for Public Health: public health (B,M,D)

Institution	State	Page
University of Alabama at Birmingham	AL	8
University of Alaska Anchorage	AK	10
University of Arizona	AZ	18
University of Arkansas for Medical Sciences	AR	24
California State University-Fresno	CA	33
California State University-Fullerton	CA	33
California State University-Long Beach	CA	33
California State University-Northridge	CA	34
Charles R. Drew University of Medicine & Science	CA	38
Claremont Graduate University	CA	39
Loma Linda University	CA	50
National University	CA	55
San Diego State University	CA	35
San Francisco State University	CA	36
San Jose State University	CA	36
Touro University California	CA	70
University of California-Berkeley	CA	70
University of California-Davis	CA	71
University of California-Irvine	CA	71
University of California-Los Angeles	CA	71
University of San Francisco	CA	74
University of Southern California	CA	74
Colorado State University	CO	81
University of Colorado Denver|Anschutz Medical Campus	CO	86
University of Northern Colorado	CO	87
Southern Connecticut State University	CT	88
Yale University	CT	93
George Washington University	DC	95
Florida Agricultural and Mechanical University	FL	114
Florida International University	FL	114
Florida State University	FL	115
Nova Southeastern University	FL	109
University of Florida	FL	115
University of Miami	FL	118
University of North Florida	FL	116
University of South Florida	FL	116
University of West Florida	FL	116
Armstrong State University	GA	120
Augusta University	GA	121
Emory University	GA	124
Georgia Southern University	GA	126
Georgia State University	GA	126
Mercer University	GA	128
Morehouse School of Medicine	GA	129
University of Georgia	GA	132
University of Hawaii at Manoa	HI	135
Idaho State University	ID	138
Benedictine University	IL	140
DePaul University	IL	143
Northern Illinois University	IL	154
Northwestern University	IL	155
Southern Illinois University Carbondale	IL	159
University of Illinois at Chicago	IL	161
University of Illinois at Urbana-Champaign	IL	162
Indiana University Bloomington	IN	167
Indiana University-Purdue University Indianapolis	IN	168
Des Moines University	IA	177
University of Iowa	IA	175
Kansas State University	KS	188
University of Kansas Main Campus	KS	191
Eastern Kentucky University	KY	194
University of Kentucky	KY	200
University of Louisville	KY	201
Western Kentucky University	KY	201
Louisiana State University Health Sciences Center-New Orleans	LA	205
Tulane University	LA	207
University of New England	ME	213
Johns Hopkins University	MD	216
Morgan State University	MD	217
Uniformed Services University of the Health Sciences	MD	548
University of Maryland Baltimore	MD	219
University of Maryland College Park	MD	219
Boston University	MA	224
Harvard University	MA	227
Northeastern University	MA	235
Tufts University	MA	237
University of Massachusetts	MA	228
University of Michigan-Ann Arbor	MI	251
Wayne State University	MI	252
University of Minnesota-Twin Cities	MN	265
Jackson State University	MS	267
University of Southern Mississippi	MS	271
A. T. Still University of Health Sciences	MO	271
Missouri State University	MO	279
Saint Louis University	MO	281
University of Missouri - Columbia	MO	283
Washington University in St. Louis	MO	285
University of Montana - Missoula	MT	287
University of Nebraska Medical Center	NE	293

University of Nevada, Las Vegas ... NV ... 295
University of Nevada, Reno ... NV ... 295
Dartmouth College ... NH .. 297
University of New Hampshire ... NH .. 299
Montclair State University ... NJ ... 304
New Jersey Institute of Technology ... NJ ... 304
Rutgers the State University of New Jersey New Brunswick Campus ... NJ ... 307
New Mexico State University Main Campus ... NM .. 312
University of New Mexico Main Campus .. NM .. 313
City University of New York Brooklyn College ... NY ... 318
City University of New York Graduate Center ... NY ... 319
City University of New York Herbert H. Lehman College ... NY ... 319
City University of New York Hunter College ... NY ... 319
Columbia University in the City of New York ... NY ... 322
Icahn School of Medicine at Mount Sinai . NY ... 328
New York Medical College ... NY ... 335
New York University ... NY ... 336
State University of New York Upstate Medical University ... NY ... 344
Stony Brook University ... NY ... 344
SUNY Downstate Medical Center ... NY ... 344
Syracuse University Main Campus ... NY ... 349
University at Albany, SUNY ... NY ... 343
University at Buffalo-SUNY ... NY ... 343
University of Rochester ... NY ... 351
East Carolina University ... NC .. 369
University of North Carolina at Chapel Hill NC .. 371
University of North Carolina at Charlotte .. NC .. 371
University of North Carolina at Greensboro ... NC .. 371
Bowling Green State University ... OH .. 377
Case Western Reserve University ... OH .. 378
Cleveland State University ... OH .. 380
Northeast Ohio Medical University ... OH .. 387
Ohio State University Main Campus, The . OH .. 389
Ohio University Main Campus ... OH .. 389
University of Akron, Main Campus, The ... OH .. 392
University of Cincinnati Main Campus ... OH .. 393
University of Toledo ... OH .. 394
Wright State University Main Campus ... OH .. 396
Youngstown State University ... OH .. 396
Oregon Health & Science University ... OR .. 408
Oregon State University ... OR .. 408
Portland State University ... OR .. 409
Arcadia University ... PA ... 412
Drexel University ... PA ... 417
East Stroudsburg University of Pennsylvania ... PA ... 430
Temple University ... PA ... 436
Thomas Jefferson University ... PA ... 436
University of Pennsylvania ... PA ... 437
University of Pittsburgh ... PA ... 437
#West Chester University of Pennsylvania . PA ... 432
Ponce School of Medicine & Health Sciences ... PR ... 555
University of Puerto Rico-Medical Sciences Campus ... PR ... 558
Brown University ... RI ... 441
University of South Carolina Columbia ... SC ... 450
East Tennessee State University ... TN ... 461
Meharry Medical College ... TN ... 458
Tennessee State University ... TN ... 461
University of Memphis, The ... TN ... 462
University of Tennessee, Knoxville ... TN ... 465
Vanderbilt University ... TN ... 465
Baylor University ... TX ... 469
Texas A & M University ... TX ... 485
University of North Texas Health Science Center at Fort Worth ... TX ... 493
University of Texas at El Paso ... TX ... 494
University of Texas Health Science Center at Houston (UTHealth), The ... TX ... 495
University of Texas Medical Branch, The . TX ... 495
Brigham Young University ... UT ... 497
University of Utah, The ... UT ... 499
Westminster College ... UT ... 501
Eastern Virginia Medical School ... VA ... 507
George Mason University ... VA ... 507
Old Dominion University ... VA ... 510
University of Virginia ... VA ... 514
Virginia Commonwealth University ... VA ... 514
Virginia Polytechnic Institute and State University ... VA ... 518
University of Washington ... WA .. 527
West Virginia University ... WV .. 533
Medical College of Wisconsin ... WI ... 537
University of Wisconsin-La Crosse ... WI ... 539
University of Wisconsin-Madison ... WI ... 539

PHAR: Accreditation Council for Pharmaceutical Education: pharmacy (FP,D)

Auburn University ... AL ... 1
Samford University ... AL ... 6
University of Arizona ... AZ ... 18
Harding University Main Campus ... AR ... 21
University of Arkansas for Medical Sciences ... AR ... 24
@California Health Sciences University ... CA ... 31
California Northstate University College of Pharmacy ... CA ... 32
@Chapman University ... CA ... 38
@Keck Graduate Institute ... CA ... 39
Loma Linda University ... CA ... 50
Touro University California ... CA ... 70
University of California-San Diego ... CA ... 72
University of California-San Francisco ... CA ... 72
University of Southern California ... CA ... 74
University of the Pacific ... CA ... 73
@West Coast University ... CA ... 75
Western University of Health Sciences ... CA ... 76
Regis University ... CO ... 85
University of Colorado Denver|Anschutz Medical Campus ... CO ... 86
University of Connecticut ... CT ... 92
University of Saint Joseph ... CT ... 93
Howard University ... DC ... 96
Florida Agricultural and Mechanical University ... FL ... 114
Nova Southeastern University ... FL ... 109
Palm Beach Atlantic University ... FL ... 109
University of Florida ... FL ... 115
University of South Florida ... FL ... 116
Mercer University ... GA .. 128
South University ... GA .. 131
University of Georgia ... GA .. 132
University of Hawaii at Hilo ... HI ... 135
Idaho State University ... ID ... 138
Chicago State University ... IL ... 141
Midwestern University ... IL ... 152
Roosevelt University ... IL ... 157
Rosalind Franklin University of Medicine & Science ... IL ... 157
Southern Illinois University Edwardsville ... IL ... 159
University of Illinois at Chicago ... IL ... 161
Butler University ... IN ... 164
@Manchester University ... IN ... 170
Purdue University Main Campus ... IN ... 171
Drake University ... IA ... 177
University of Iowa ... IA ... 175
University of Kansas Main Campus ... KS ... 191
Sullivan University ... KY ... 200
University of Kentucky ... KY ... 200
University of Louisiana at Monroe ... LA ... 209
Xavier University of Louisiana ... LA ... 209
Husson University ... ME .. 210
University of New England ... ME .. 213
Notre Dame of Maryland University ... MD .. 217
University of Maryland Baltimore ... MD .. 219
University of Maryland Eastern Shore ... MD .. 219
MCPHS University ... MA .. 233
Northeastern University ... MA .. 235
Western New England University ... MA .. 238
Ferris State University ... MI ... 242
University of Michigan-Ann Arbor ... MI ... 251
Wayne State University ... MI ... 252
University of Minnesota-Twin Cities ... MN .. 265
University of Mississippi ... MS .. 270
University of Mississippi Medical Center ... MS .. 270
St. Louis College of Pharmacy ... MO .. 281
University of Missouri - Kansas City ... MO .. 284
University of Montana - Missoula ... MT .. 287
Creighton University ... NE ... 290
University of Nebraska Medical Center ... NE ... 293
Roseman University of Health Sciences ... NV ... 296
@Fairleigh Dickinson University ... NJ ... 302
Rutgers the State University of New Jersey New Brunswick Campus ... NJ ... 307
University of New Mexico Main Campus .. NM .. 313
Albany College of Pharmacy and Health Sciences ... NY ... 314
D'Youville College ... NY ... 324
St. John Fisher College ... NY ... 340
St. John's University ... NY ... 340
Touro College ... NY ... 350
University at Buffalo-SUNY ... NY ... 343
Campbell University ... NC .. 355
University of North Carolina at Chapel Hill NC .. 371
Wingate University ... NC .. 373
North Dakota State University Main Campus ... ND .. 374
@Cedarville University ... OH .. 378
Northeast Ohio Medical University ... OH .. 387
Ohio Northern University ... OH .. 388
Ohio State University Main Campus, The . OH .. 389
University of Cincinnati Main Campus ... OH .. 393
University of Findlay, The ... OH .. 393
University of Toledo ... OH .. 394
Southwestern Oklahoma State University . OK .. 402
Oregon State University ... OR .. 408
Pacific University ... OR .. 408
Duquesne University ... PA ... 417
Lake Erie College of Osteopathic Medicine ... PA ... 423
Temple University ... PA ... 436
Thomas Jefferson University ... PA ... 436
University of Pittsburgh ... PA ... 437
University of the Sciences in Philadelphia PA ... 438
Wilkes University ... PA ... 440
University of Puerto Rico-Medical Sciences Campus ... PR ... 558
University of Rhode Island ... RI ... 442
Medical University of South Carolina ... SC ... 447
Presbyterian College ... SC ... 448
University of South Carolina Columbia ... SC ... 450
South Dakota State University ... SD ... 454
Belmont University ... TN ... 455
East Tennessee State University ... TN ... 461
Lipscomb University ... TN ... 458
South College ... TN ... 460
Union University ... TN ... 464
University of Tennessee Health Science Center ... TN ... 465
Texas A & M University - Kingsville ... TX ... 486
Texas Southern University ... TX ... 487
Texas Tech University Health Sciences Center ... TX ... 490
University of Houston ... TX ... 491
@University of North Texas Health Science Center at Fort Worth ... TX ... 493
University of Texas at Austin ... TX ... 493
@University of Texas at Tyler ... TX ... 494
University of the Incarnate Word ... TX ... 492
University of Utah, The ... UT ... 499
Appalachian College of Pharmacy ... VA ... 504
Hampton University ... VA ... 508
Shenandoah University ... VA ... 512
Virginia Commonwealth University ... VA ... 514
University of Washington ... WA .. 527
Washington State University ... WA .. 528
@Marshall University ... WV .. 532
University of Charleston ... WV .. 530
West Virginia University ... WV .. 533
Concordia University Wisconsin ... WI ... 535
University of Wisconsin-Madison ... WI ... 539
University of Wyoming ... WY .. 546

PHLEB: National Accrediting Agency for Clinical Laboratory Sciences: phlebotomist (C)

Phillips Community College of the University of Arkansas ... AR ... 24
South Arkansas Community College ... AR ... 23
Southeast Arkansas College ... AR ... 23
Otero Junior College ... CO ... 84
Dalton State College ... GA .. 123
Kapiolani Community College ... HI ... 136
College of Lake County ... IL ... 142
Kankakee Community College ... IL ... 149
Moraine Valley Community College ... IL ... 153
South Suburban College of Cook County . IL ... 159
Bossier Parish Community College ... LA ... 203
Delgado Community College ... LA ... 203
L.E. Fletcher Technical Community College ... LA ... 203
Southern University at Shreveport-Louisiana ... LA ... 207
Mid Michigan Community College ... MI ... 247
St. Catherine University ... MN .. 263
University of Southern Mississippi ... MS .. 271
Miles Community College ... MT .. 287
Western Nebraska Community College ... NE ... 294
Orange County Community College ... NY ... 337
Trocaire College ... NY ... 350
Asheville - Buncombe Technical Community College ... NC .. 360
Brunswick Community College ... NC .. 360
Cape Fear Community College ... NC .. 360
Carolinas College of Health Sciences ... NC .. 355
Halifax Community College ... NC .. 363
Nash Community College ... NC .. 364
Rockingham Community College ... NC .. 365
Southeastern Community College ... NC .. 366
Southwestern Community College ... NC .. 366
Wake Technical Community College ... NC .. 366
Bismarck State College ... ND .. 374
Turtle Mountain Community College ... ND .. 375
Columbus State Community College ... OH .. 380
Edison State Community College ... OH .. 381
Lorain County Community College ... OH .. 385
Seminole State College ... OK .. 402
Tulsa Community College ... OK .. 403
Community College of Beaver County ... PA ... 416
Community College of Philadelphia ... PA ... 416
Montgomery County Community College . PA ... 426
Southwest Tennessee Community College ... TN ... 464
Austin Community College District ... TX ... 468
Weatherford College ... TX ... 497
Mid-State Technical College ... WI ... 543
Milwaukee Area Technical College ... WI ... 543
Northcentral Technical College ... WI ... 544

PLNG: Planning Accreditation Board: certified planning (B,M)

Alabama Agricultural and Mechanical University ... AL ... 1
Arizona State University ... AZ ... 11
University of Arizona ... AZ ... 18
California Polytechnic State University-San Luis Obispo ... CA ... 32
California State Polytechnic University-Pomona ... CA ... 32
San Jose State University ... CA ... 36
University of California-Berkeley ... CA ... 70
University of California-Irvine ... CA ... 71
University of California-Los Angeles ... CA ... 71
University of Southern California ... CA ... 74
University of Colorado Denver|Anschutz Medical Campus ... CO ... 86
Florida Atlantic University ... FL ... 114
Florida State University ... FL ... 115
University of Florida ... FL ... 115
Georgia Institute of Technology ... GA .. 125
University of Hawaii at Manoa ... HI ... 135
University of Illinois at Chicago ... IL ... 161
University of Illinois at Urbana-Champaign IL ... 162
Ball State University ... IN ... 164
Iowa State University ... IA ... 175
University of Iowa ... IA ... 175
Kansas State University ... KS ... 188
University of Kansas Main Campus ... KS ... 191
University of Louisville ... KY ... 201
University of New Orleans ... LA ... 205
Morgan State University ... MD .. 217
University of Maryland College Park ... MD .. 219
Harvard University ... MA .. 227
Massachusetts Institute of Technology ... MA .. 233
Tufts University ... MA .. 237
University of Massachusetts ... MA .. 228
Eastern Michigan University ... MI ... 242
Michigan State University ... MI ... 246
University of Michigan-Ann Arbor ... MI ... 251
Wayne State University ... MI ... 252
University of Minnesota-Twin Cities ... MN .. 265
Jackson State University ... MS .. 267
Missouri State University ... MO .. 279
University of Nebraska - Lincoln ... NE ... 293
Rutgers the State University of New Jersey New Brunswick Campus ... NJ ... 307
University of New Mexico Main Campus .. NM .. 313
City University of New York Hunter College ... NY ... 319
Columbia University in the City of New York ... NY ... 322
Cornell University ... NY ... 323
New York University ... NY ... 336
Pratt Institute ... NY ... 338
University at Albany, SUNY ... NY ... 343
University at Buffalo-SUNY ... NY ... 343
East Carolina University ... NC .. 369
University of North Carolina at Chapel Hill NC .. 371
Cleveland State University ... OH .. 380
Ohio State University Main Campus, The . OH .. 389
University of Cincinnati Main Campus ... OH .. 393
University of Oklahoma Norman Campus . OK .. 403
Portland State University ... OR .. 409
University of Oregon ... OR .. 410
Indiana University of Pennsylvania ... PA ... 431
Temple University ... PA ... 436
University of Pennsylvania ... PA ... 437
University of Puerto Rico-Rio Piedras Campus ... PR ... 558
Clemson University ... SC ... 444
University of Memphis, The ... TN ... 462
Texas A & M University ... TX ... 485
Texas Southern University ... TX ... 487
University of Texas at Arlington, The ... TX ... 493
University of Texas at Austin ... TX ... 493
University of Utah, The ... UT ... 499
University of Virginia ... VA ... 514
Virginia Commonwealth University ... VA ... 514
Virginia Polytechnic Institute and State University ... VA ... 518
Eastern Washington University ... WA .. 522
University of Washington ... WA .. 527
University of Wisconsin-Madison ... WI ... 539
University of Wisconsin-Milwaukee ... WI ... 540

PNUR: Accreditation Commission for Education in Nursing: practical nursing (C)

Bevill State Community College ... AL ... 2

POD: American Podiatric Medical Association: podiatry (FP,D)

POLYT: Commission on Accreditation of Allied Health Education Programs: polysomnographic technologist education (C,A)

PSPSY: American Psychological Association: combined professional-scientific psychology (D)

PTA: American Physical Therapy Association: physical therapy (M,D)

PTAA: American Physical Therapy Association: physical therapy assistant (A)

RABN: Association of Advanced Rabbinical and Talmudic Schools: rabbinical and Talmudic education (B,M,D)

RAD: Joint Review Committee on Education in Radiologic Technology: radiography (C,A,B)

RADDOS: Joint Review Committee on Education in Radiologic Technology: medical dosimetry (C, B,M)

RADMAG: Joint Review Committee on Education in Radiologic Technology: magnetic resonance (C,B)

RTT: Joint Review Committee on Education in Radiologic Technology: radiation therapist/technologist (C, A,B)

SC: Southern Association of Colleges and Schools, Commission on Colleges

SCPSY: American Psychological Association: school psychology (D)

SP: American Speech-Language-Hearing Association: speech-language pathology (M)

SPAA: Network of Schools of Public Policy, Affairs and Administration: public affairs and administration (M)

SURGA: Commission on Accreditation of Allied Health Education Programs: surgical assistant (C,A)

SURGT: Commission on Accreditation of Allied Health Education Programs: surgical technology (C,A)

SURTEC: Accrediting Bureau of Health Education Schools: surgical technologist (C,A)

SW: Council on Social Work Education: social work (B,M)

TEAC: Teacher Education Accreditation Council: teacher education (B,M,D)

TED: National Council for Accreditation of Teacher Education: teacher education (B,M,S,D)

Marian University ... WI ... 537
Marquette University ... WI ... 537
University of Wisconsin-Stout ... WI ... 541
University of Wisconsin-Whitewater ... WI ... 541
Viterbo University ... WI ... 542
University of Wyoming ... WY .. 546

THEA: National Association of Schools of Theatre: theatre (C,A,B, M,D)

Alabama State University ... AL ... 1
Auburn University ... AL ... 1
Jacksonville State University ... AL ... 4
Samford University ... AL ... 6
University of Alabama at Birmingham ... AL ... 8
University of Alabama, The ... AL ... 8
University of Arizona ... AZ ... 18
Arkansas State University-Jonesboro ... AR ... 19
University of Arkansas at Little Rock ... AR ... 24
University of Central Arkansas ... AR ... 25
AMDA College and Conservatory of the Performing Arts ... CA ... 26
California State University-Chico ... CA ... 33
California State University-Dominguez Hills ... CA ... 33
California State University-Fresno ... CA ... 33
California State University-Fullerton ... CA ... 33
California State University-Long Beach ... CA ... 33
California State University-Northridge ... CA ... 34
California State University-San Bernardino CA ... 35
California State University-Stanislaus ... CA ... 35
Chapman University ... CA ... 38
Dell'Arte International School of Physical Theatre ... CA ... 42
Loyola Marymount University ... CA ... 53
San Diego State University ... CA ... 35
San Francisco State University ... CA ... 36
San Jose State University ... CA ... 36
Theatre of Arts ... CA ... 69
University of California-Los Angeles ... CA ... 71
Vanguard University of Southern California ... CA ... 75
Metropolitan State University of Denver ... CO ... 83
University of Northern Colorado ... CO ... 87
University of Hartford ... CT ... 92
Howard University ... DC ... 96
Florida International University ... FL ... 114
Florida State University ... FL ... 115
Miami Dade College ... FL ... 108
University of Florida ... FL ... 115
University of South Florida ... FL ... 116
Columbus State University ... GA .. 123
Georgia Southern University ... GA .. 126
Kennesaw State University ... GA .. 127
University of Georgia ... GA .. 132
University of West Georgia ... GA .. 133
Valdosta State University ... GA .. 133
Boise State University ... ID ... 137
Idaho State University ... ID ... 138
Bradley University ... IL ... 140
Eastern Illinois University ... IL ... 144
Illinois State University ... IL ... 147
Loyola University Chicago ... IL ... 151
Northern Illinois University ... IL ... 154
Southern Illinois University Carbondale ... IL ... 159
Southern Illinois University Edwardsville ... IL ... 159
University of Illinois at Urbana-Champaign IL ... 162
Western Illinois University ... IL ... 163
Ball State University ... IN ... 164
Butler University ... IN ... 164
Indiana University Bloomington ... IN ... 167
Indiana University-Purdue University Fort Wayne ... IN ... 168
Purdue University Main Campus ... IN ... 171
Vincennes University ... IN ... 174
University of Iowa ... IA ... 175
University of Northern Iowa ... IA ... 176
Kansas State University ... KS .. 188
Morehead State University ... KY ... 198
Murray State University ... KY ... 198
University of Kentucky ... KY ... 200
University of Louisville ... KY ... 201
Western Kentucky University ... KY ... 201
Grambling State University ... LA ... 207
Louisiana State University and Agricultural and Mechanical College ... LA ... 204
Northwestern State University ... LA ... 208
University of New Orleans ... LA ... 205
Community College of Baltimore County, The ... MD .. 214
Towson University ... MD .. 221
College of the Holy Cross ... MA .. 225
Salem State University ... MA .. 230
Hope College ... MI ... 244
Oakland University ... MI ... 248
Wayne State University ... MI ... 252
Western Michigan University ... MI ... 252
Normandale Community College ... MN .. 260
St. Cloud State University ... MN .. 261
St. Olaf College ... MN .. 264
University of Minnesota-Twin Cities ... MN .. 265
Winona State University ... MN .. 262
Belhaven University ... MS .. 266
University of Mississippi ... MS .. 270
University of Southern Mississippi ... MS .. 271
Missouri State University ... MO .. 279
Southeast Missouri State University ... MO .. 282
University of Central Missouri ... MO .. 283
University of Missouri - Kansas City ... MO .. 284
University of Montana - Missoula ... MT .. 287
University of Nebraska - Lincoln ... NE .. 293
Kean University ... NJ ... 303
Montclair State University ... NJ ... 304
Rowan University ... NJ ... 306
University of New Mexico Main Campus .. NM .. 313
AMDA College and Conservatory of the Performing Arts ... NY ... 315
American Academy of Dramatic Arts ... NY ... 315
Ithaca College ... NY ... 328
New York Conservatory for Dramatic Arts, The ... NY ... 335
State University of New York at Fredonia . NY ... 343
State University of New York at New Paltz NY ... 344
State University of New York at Oneonta . NY ... 344
State University of New York College at Buffalo ... NY ... 345
State University of New York College at Oswego ... NY ... 346
State University of New York College at Potsdam ... NY ... 346
State University of New York, The College at Brockport ... NY ... 345
Appalachian State University ... NC .. 369
East Carolina University ... NC .. 369
Mars Hill University ... NC .. 359
North Carolina Agricultural and Technical State University ... NC .. 370
North Carolina Central University ... NC .. 370
University of North Carolina at Greensboro ... NC .. 371
Western Carolina University ... NC .. 372
North Dakota State University Main Campus ... ND .. 374
University of North Dakota ... ND .. 373
Bowling Green State University ... OH .. 377
Kent State University Main Campus ... OH .. 384
Miami University ... OH .. 386
Ohio State University Main Campus, The . OH .. 389
Ohio University Main Campus ... OH .. 389
Otterbein University ... OH .. 390
Sinclair Community College ... OH .. 391
University of Cincinnati Main Campus ... OH .. 393
Youngstown State University ... OH .. 396
Oklahoma State University ... OK .. 400
University of Oklahoma Norman Campus . OK .. 403
Portland State University ... OR .. 409
University of Portland ... OR .. 410
Bloomsburg University of Pennsylvania ... PA ... 430
California University of Pennsylvania ... PA ... 430
Indiana University of Pennsylvania ... PA ... 431
Lehigh University ... PA ... 424
Messiah College ... PA ... 426
Penn State University Park ... PA ... 428
Slippery Rock University of Pennsylvania . PA ... 432
Temple University ... PA ... 436
University of Pittsburgh ... PA ... 437
West Chester University of Pennsylvania . PA ... 432
Coastal Carolina University ... SC ... 444
College of Charleston ... SC ... 445
Francis Marion University ... SC ... 446
University of South Carolina Columbia ... SC ... 450
Winthrop University ... SC ... 451
University of South Dakota, The ... SD ... 453
Belmont University ... TN ... 455
East Tennessee State University ... TN ... 461
Middle Tennessee State University ... TN ... 461
University of Memphis, The ... TN ... 462
University of Tennessee at Chattanooga .. TN ... 465
University of Tennessee, Knoxville ... TN ... 465
Baylor University ... TX ... 469
Del Mar College ... TX ... 473
KD Conservatory College of Film and Dramatic Arts ... TX ... 476
Midwestern State University ... TX ... 478
Southern Methodist University ... TX ... 482
Stephen F. Austin State University ... TX ... 484
Texas Tech University ... TX ... 489
University of Texas Rio Grande Valley ... TX ... 494
University of the Incarnate Word ... TX ... 492
West Texas A & M University ... TX ... 486
Brigham Young University ... UT ... 497
Snow College ... UT ... 500
Christopher Newport University ... VA ... 506
James Madison University ... VA ... 509
Longwood University ... VA ... 509
Old Dominion University ... VA ... 510
Radford University ... VA ... 511
Virginia Commonwealth University ... VA ... 514
Virginia Polytechnic Institute and State University ... VA ... 518
Davis & Elkins College ... WV .. 529
West Virginia University ... WV .. 533
Marquette University ... WI ... 537
University of Wisconsin-Madison ... WI ... 539
University of Wisconsin-Stevens Point ... WI ... 541
University of Wisconsin-Whitewater ... WI ... 541
Casper College ... WY .. 545

THEOL: Association of Theological Schools: theology (M,FP,D)

@Faulkner University ... AL ... 3
Samford University ... AL ... 6
Phoenix Seminary ... AZ ... 16
American Baptist Seminary of the West ... CA ... 27
Azusa Pacific University ... CA ... 29
Biola University ... CA ... 29
California Lutheran University ... CA ... 31
China Evangelical Seminary North America ... CA ... 38
@Christian Witness Theological Seminary ... CA ... 38
Church Divinity School of the Pacific ... CA ... 38
Claremont School of Theology ... CA ... 39
Dominican School of Philosophy and Theology ... CA ... 43
Franciscan School of Theology ... CA ... 45
Fresno Pacific University ... CA ... 45
Fuller Theological Seminary ... CA ... 45
Golden Gate Baptist Theological Seminary ... CA ... 45
@Grace Mission University ... CA ... 46
Graduate Theological Union ... CA ... 46
International Theological Seminary ... CA ... 48
La Sierra University ... CA ... 49
Logos Evangelical Seminary ... CA ... 50
Loyola Marymount University ... CA ... 53
Pacific School of Religion ... CA ... 57
Saint John's Seminary ... CA ... 61
Saint Patrick's Seminary & University ... CA ... 61
San Francisco Theological Seminary ... CA ... 63
Santa Clara University ... CA ... 65
Shepherd University School of Theology .. CA ... 66
Starr King School for the Ministry ... CA ... 68
Westminster Theological Seminary in California ... CA ... 76
World Mission University ... CA ... 77
@Augustine Institute ... CO ... 79
Denver Seminary ... CO ... 82
Iliff School of Theology ... CO ... 83
St. John Vianney Theological Seminary ... CO ... 85
Hartford Seminary ... CT ... 90
Yale University ... CT ... 93
Catholic University of America, The ... DC ... 95
Howard University ... DC ... 96
Pontifical Faculty of the Immaculate Conception at the Dominican House of S tudies ... DC ... 96
Wesley Theological Seminary ... DC ... 97
Barry University ... FL ... 99
Knox Theological Seminary ... FL ... 107
St. Vincent De Paul Regional Seminary ... FL ... 112
Columbia Theological Seminary ... GA .. 123
Emory University ... GA .. 124
@Georgia Christian University ... GA .. 124
Interdenominational Theological Center ... GA .. 127
Mercer University ... GA .. 128
Bexley Seabury ... IL ... 140
Catholic Theological Union ... IL ... 141
Chicago Theological Seminary ... IL ... 141
Garrett-Evangelical Theological Seminary IL ... 145
Lincoln Christian University ... IL ... 150
Lutheran School of Theology at Chicago .. IL ... 151
McCormick Theological Seminary ... IL ... 152
Meadville Lombard Theological School ... IL ... 152
Moody Bible Institute ... IL ... 153
North Park University ... IL ... 154
Northern Seminary ... IL ... 154
Trinity International University ... IL ... 161
University of Chicago ... IL ... 161
University of Saint Mary of the Lake-Mundelein Seminary ... IL ... 162
Anabaptist Mennonite Biblical Seminary ... IN ... 163
Anderson University ... IN ... 164
Bethany Theological Seminary ... IN ... 164
Christian Theological Seminary ... IN ... 165
Concordia Theological Seminary ... IN ... 165
Earlham College and Earlham School of Religion ... IN ... 165
Grace College and Seminary ... IN ... 166
Indiana Wesleyan University ... IN ... 169
Mid-America Reformed Seminary ... IN ... 171
Oakland City University ... IN ... 171
Saint Meinrad School of Theology ... IN ... 173
University of Notre Dame ... IN ... 174
University of Dubuque ... IA ... 183
Wartburg Theological Seminary ... IA ... 183
Central Baptist Theological Seminary ... KS ... 185
Saint Paul School of Theology ... KS ... 190
Asbury Theological Seminary ... KY ... 192
Baptist Seminary of Kentucky ... KY ... 193
Lexington Theological Seminary ... KY ... 198
Louisville Presbyterian Theological Seminary ... KY ... 198
Southern Baptist Theological Seminary, The ... KY ... 199
New Orleans Baptist Theological Seminary ... LA ... 206
Notre Dame Seminary, Graduate School of Theology ... LA ... 206
Mount St. Mary's University ... MD .. 217
Saint Mary's Seminary and University ... MD .. 218
Andover Newton Theological School ... MA .. 222
Boston College ... MA .. 224
Boston University ... MA .. 224
Episcopal Divinity School ... MA .. 226
Gordon-Conwell Theological Seminary ... MA .. 227
Harvard University ... MA .. 227
Hellenic College-Holy Cross Greek Orthodox School of Theology ... MA .. 227
Pope St. John XXIII National Seminary ... MA .. 235
Saint John's Seminary ... MA .. 236
Andrews University ... MI ... 239
Calvin Theological Seminary ... MI ... 240
Cornerstone University ... MI ... 241
Ecumenical Theological Seminary ... MI ... 242
Puritan Reformed Theological Seminary .. MI ... 249
Sacred Heart Major Seminary ... MI ... 249
SS. Cyril and Methodius Seminary ... MI ... 250
Western Theological Seminary ... MI ... 253
Bethel University ... MN .. 254
Luther Seminary ... MN .. 256
Saint John's University ... MN .. 264
United Theological Seminary of the Twin Cities ... MN .. 264
University of Saint Thomas ... MN .. 265
Reformed Theological Seminary ... MS .. 270
Wesley Biblical Seminary ... MS .. 271
Aquinas Institute of Theology ... MO .. 272
Assemblies of God Theological Seminary MO .. 272
Concordia Seminary ... MO .. 273
Covenant Theological Seminary ... MO .. 273
Eden Theological Seminary ... MO .. 274
Kenrick-Glennon Seminary-Kenrick School of Theology ... MO .. 276
Midwestern Baptist Theological Seminary MO .. 278
Nazarene Theological Seminary ... MO .. 279
Urshan Graduate School of Theology ... MO .. 284
Drew University ... NJ ... 301
New Brunswick Theological Seminary ... NJ ... 304
Princeton Theological Seminary ... NJ ... 305
Seton Hall University ... NJ ... 308
Christ the King Seminary ... NY ... 317
Colgate Rochester Crozer Divinity School NY ... 321
General Theological Seminary ... NY ... 326
New York Theological Seminary ... NY ... 336
Northeastern Seminary ... NY ... 337
Nyack College ... NY ... 337
Saint Bernard's School of Theology & Ministry ... NY ... 340
Saint Joseph's Seminary ... NY ... 341
Saint Vladimir's Orthodox Theological Seminary ... NY ... 341
Union Theological Seminary ... NY ... 351
Campbell University ... NC ... 355
Carolina Graduate School of Divinity ... NC ... 355
Duke University ... NC .. 356
Gardner-Webb University ... NC ... 356
Hood Theological Seminary ... NC ... 357
Lenoir-Rhyne University ... NC ... 358
Shaw University ... NC ... 368
@Shepherds Theological Seminary ... NC ... 368
Southeastern Baptist Theological Seminary ... NC .. 368
Wake Forest University ... NC ... 372
Ashland University ... OH ... 377
Athenaeum of Ohio ... OH ... 377
Bexley Seabury ... OH .. 377
Cincinnati Christian University ... OH ... 379
Methodist Theological School in Ohio ... OH ... 386
Payne Theological Seminary ... OH ... 390
Pontifical College Josephinum ... OH .. 390
Saint Mary Seminary and Graduate School of Theology ... OH .. 391
Trinity Lutheran Seminary ... OH .. 392
United Theological Seminary ... OH .. 392
Winebrenner Theological Seminary ... OH .. 395
Oral Roberts University ... OK .. 401
Phillips Theological Seminary ... OK .. 401
George Fox University ... OR .. 406
Mount Angel Seminary ... OR .. 407
Multnomah University ... OR .. 407
Western Seminary ... OR .. 411
Biblical Theological Seminary ... PA ... 412
Byzantine Catholic Seminary of SS. Cyril and Methodius ... PA ... 414
Evangelical Theological Seminary ... PA ... 418
Lancaster Theological Seminary ... PA ... 423

TRACS: Transnational Association of Christian Colleges and Schools: christian studies education (C,A,B, M,D)

VET: American Veterinary Medical Association: veterinary medicine (FP,D)

WC: Western Association of Schools and Colleges, Accrediting Commission for Senior Colleges and Universities

WJ: Western Association of Schools and Colleges, Accrediting Commission for Community and Junior Colleges

Index of FICE Numbers

001354 .... Iliff School of Theology .... CO 83
001355 .... Lamar Community College .... CO 83
001358 .... Colorado Mesa University .... CO 80
001359 .... Colorado Northwestern Cmty College .... CO 80
001360 .... Metropolitan State Univ Denver .... CO 83
001361 .... Northeastern Junior College .... CO 84
001362 .... Otero Junior College .... CO 84
001363 .... Regis University .... CO 85
001365 .... Colorado State University-Pueblo .... CO 81
001368 .... Trinidad State Junior College .... CO 86
001369 .... United States Air Force Academy .... CO 548
001370 .... University of Colorado Boulder .... CO 86
001371 .... University of Denver .... CO 86
001372 .... Western State Colorado University .... CO 87
001374 .... Albertus Magnus College .... CT 87
001378 .... Central Connecticut State Univ .... CT 88
001379 .... Connecticut College .... CT 90
001380 .... Western Connecticut State Univ .... CT 88
001385 .... Fairfield University .... CT 90
001387 .... Hartford Seminary .... CT 90
001389 .... Holy Apostles College and Seminary .... CT 90
001392 .... Manchester Community College .... CT 89
001393 .... Mitchell College .... CT 91
001397 .... University of New Haven .... CT 92
001398 .... Northwestern CT Cmty-Tech College .... CT 89
001399 .... Norwalk Community College .... CT 89
001401 .... Post University .... CT 91
001402 .... Quinnipiac University .... CT 91
001403 .... Sacred Heart University .... CT 91
001406 .... Southern Connecticut State Univ .... CT 88
001409 .... University of Saint Joseph .... CT 93
001414 .... Trinity College .... CT 92
001415 .... United States Coast Guard Academy .... CT 548
001416 .... University of Bridgeport .... CT 92
001417 .... University of Connecticut .... CT 92
001422 .... University of Hartford .... CT 92
001424 .... Wesleyan University .... CT 93
001425 .... Eastern Connecticut State Univ .... CT 88
001426 .... Yale University .... CT 93
001428 .... Delaware State University .... DE 93
001429 .... Goldey-Beacom College .... DE 94
001431 .... University of Delaware .... DE 94
001433 .... Wesley College .... DE 94
001434 .... American University .... DC 94
001436 .... Capitol Technology University .... MD 214
001437 .... The Catholic University of America .... DC 95
001441 .... Univ of the District of Columbia .... DC 97
001443 .... Gallaudet University .... DC 95
001444 .... George Washington University .... DC 95
001445 .... Georgetown University .... DC 95
001448 .... Howard University .... DC 96
001459 .... Strayer University .... DC 96
001460 .... Trinity Washington University .... DC 97
001464 .... Wesley Theological Seminary .... DC 97
001466 .... Barry University .... FL 99
001467 .... Bethune Cookman University .... FL 99
001468 .... St. Thomas University .... FL 112
001469 .... Florida Institute of Technology .... FL 103
001470 .... Eastern Florida State College .... FL 101
001471 .... College of Central Florida .... FL 100
001472 .... Chipola College .... FL 100
001475 .... Daytona State College .... FL 101
001477 .... Florida SouthWestern State College .... FL 104
001478 .... Edward Waters College .... FL 102
001479 .... Embry-Riddle Aeronautical Univ .... FL 102
001480 .... Florida A and M University .... FL 114
001481 .... Florida Atlantic University .... FL 114
001482 .... Florida College .... FL 103
001484 .... Florida State College Jacksonville .... FL 105
001485 .... Florida Keys Community College .... FL 104
001486 .... Florida Memorial University .... FL 104
001487 .... Eckerd College .... FL 101
001488 .... Florida Southern College .... FL 104
001489 .... Florida State University .... FL 115
001490 .... Gulf Coast State College .... FL 105
001493 .... Indian River State College .... FL 106
001495 .... Jacksonville University .... FL 106
001497 .... Jones College .... FL 107
001499 .... Everest Univ-North Orlando Campus .... FL 102
001500 .... Broward College .... FL 99
001501 .... Florida Gateway College .... FL 103
001502 .... Lake-Sumter State College .... FL 107
001504 .... State Col of FL, Manatee-Sarasota .... FL 114
001505 .... Lynn University .... FL 108
001506 .... Miami Dade College .... FL 108
001507 .... New College of Florida .... FL 115
001508 .... North Florida Community College .... FL 109
001509 .... Nova Southeastern University .... FL 109
001510 .... Northwest Florida State College .... FL 109
001512 .... Palm Beach State College .... FL 109
001513 .... Pensacola State College .... FL 110
001514 .... Polk State College .... FL 110
001515 .... Rollins College .... FL 111
001519 .... Santa Fe College .... FL 112
001520 .... Seminole State College of Florida .... FL 113
001521 .... Southeastern University .... FL 113
001522 .... South Florida State College .... FL 113
001523 .... St. Johns River State College .... FL 111
001526 .... Saint Leo University .... FL 111
001528 .... St. Petersburg College .... FL 112
001531 .... Stetson University .... FL 117
001533 .... Tallahassee Community College .... FL 117
001535 .... University of Florida .... FL 115
001536 .... University of Miami .... FL 118
001537 .... University of South Florida .... FL 116
001538 .... University of Tampa .... FL 118
001540 .... Webber International University .... FL 119
001541 .... Abraham Baldwin Agricultural Coll .... GA 119
001542 .... Agnes Scott College .... GA 119
001543 .... Darton State College .... GA 123
001544 .... Albany State University .... GA 119
001545 .... Andrew College .... GA 120
001546 .... Armstrong State University .... GA 120
001547 .... Point University .... GA 130
001554 .... Berry College .... GA 121
001555 .... Thomas University .... GA 132
001556 .... Brenau University .... GA 121
001557 .... Brewton-Parker College .... GA 121
001558 .... College of Coastal Georgia .... GA 123
001559 .... Clark Atlanta University .... GA 122
001560 .... Columbia Theological Seminary .... GA 123
001561 .... Columbus State University .... GA 123
001562 .... Georgia Perimeter College .... GA 125
001563 .... Emmanuel College .... GA 124
001564 .... Emory University .... GA 124
001566 .... Fort Valley State University .... GA 124
001568 .... Interdenominational Theol Center .... GA 127
001569 .... Georgia Institute of Technology .... GA 125
001571 .... Georgia Military College .... GA 125
001572 .... Georgia Southern University .... GA 126
001573 .... Georgia Southwestern State Univ .... GA 126
001574 .... Georgia State University .... GA 126
001575 .... Gordon State College .... GA 126
001577 .... Kennesaw State University .... GA 127
001578 .... LaGrange College .... GA 127
001579 .... Augusta University .... GA 121
001580 .... Mercer University .... GA 128
001582 .... Morehouse College .... GA 128
001585 .... University of North Georgia .... GA 133
001586 .... Oglethorpe University .... GA 129
001587 .... Paine College .... GA 129
001588 .... Piedmont College .... GA 130
001589 .... Reinhardt University .... GA 130
001590 .... Savannah State University .... GA 131
001591 .... Shorter University .... GA 131
001592 .... South Georgia State College .... GA 131
001594 .... Spelman College .... GA 132
001596 .... Toccoa Falls College .... GA 132
001597 .... Truett McConnell College .... GA 132
001598 .... University of Georgia .... GA 132
001599 .... Valdosta State University .... GA 133
001600 .... Wesleyan College .... GA 134
001601 .... University of West Georgia .... GA 133
001602 .... Georgia College & State University .... GA 125
001604 .... Young Harris College .... GA 134
001605 .... Chaminade University of Honolulu .... HI 135
001606 .... Brigham Young University Hawaii .... HI 134
001610 .... University of Hawaii at Manoa .... HI 135
001611 .... University of Hawaii at Hilo .... HI 135
001612 .... Univ of Hawaii Honolulu Cmty Col .... HI 136
001613 .... Kapiolani Community College .... HI 136
001614 .... Univ of Hawaii Kauai Cmty College .... HI 136
001615 .... Univ of Hawaii Maui College .... HI 136
001616 .... Boise State University .... ID 137
001617 .... The College of Idaho .... ID 137
001619 .... College of Southern Idaho .... ID 137
001620 .... Idaho State University .... ID 138
001621 .... Lewis-Clark State College .... ID 138
001623 .... North Idaho College .... ID 138
001624 .... Northwest Nazarene University .... ID 138
001625 .... Brigham Young University-Idaho .... ID 137
001626 .... University of Idaho .... ID 139
001628 .... American Academy of Art .... IL 139
001632 .... Aquinas Institute of Theology .... MO 272
001633 .... Augustana College .... IL 139
001634 .... Aurora University .... IL 139
001636 .... Southwestern Illinois College .... IL 160
001637 .... Bethany Theological Seminary .... IN 164
001638 .... Black Hawk College .... IL 140
001639 .... Blackburn College .... IL 140
001640 .... Prairie State College .... IL 156
001641 .... Bradley University .... IL 140
001643 .... Spoon River College .... IL 160
001647 .... City Colleges of Chicago .... IL 141
001648 .... City Cols of Chicago Harry Truman .... IL 141
001649 .... City Cols of Chicago RJ Daley Col .... IL 142
001650 .... Malcolm X College .... IL 142
001652 .... City Cols of Chicago Washington Col .... IL 141
001654 .... City Cols of Chicago Kennedy-King .... IL 142
001655 .... City Cols of Chicago W Wright Col .... IL 142
001657 .... Midwestern University .... IL 152
001659 .... Rosalind Franklin U of Med/Science .... IL 157
001661 .... Chicago Theological Seminary .... IL 141
001663 .... Spertus Inst for Jewish Lrng & Ldrs .... IL 160
001664 .... University of St. Francis .... IL 162
001665 .... Columbia College Chicago .... IL 143
001666 .... Concordia University Chicago .... IL 143
001669 .... Danville Area Community College .... IL 143
001671 .... DePaul University .... IL 143
001672 .... DeVry University - Home Office .... IL 144
001674 .... Eastern Illinois University .... IL 144
001675 .... Elgin Community College .... IL 144
001676 .... Elmhurst College .... IL 144
001678 .... Eureka College .... IL 145
001681 .... Highland Community College .... IL 146
001682 .... Garrett-Evangelical Theol Seminary .... IL 145
001684 .... Greenville College .... IL 145
001685 .... Hebrew Theological College .... IL 146
001688 .... Illinois College .... IL 146
001689 .... Illinois College of Optometry .... IL 146
001691 .... Illinois Institute of Technology .... IL 147
001692 .... Illinois State University .... IL 147
001693 .... Northeastern Illinois University .... IL 154
001694 .... Chicago State University .... IL 141
001696 .... Illinois Wesleyan University .... IL 148
001698 .... John Marshall Law School .... IL 148
001699 .... Joliet Junior College .... IL 148
001700 .... Judson University .... IL 149
001701 .... Kaskaskia College .... IL 149
001703 .... Kendall College .... IL 149
001704 .... Knox College .... IL 149
001705 .... Illinois Valley Community College .... IL 147
001706 .... Lake Forest College .... IL 149
001707 .... Lewis University .... IL 150
001708 .... Lincoln Christian University .... IL 150
001709 .... Lincoln College .... IL 150
001710 .... Loyola University Chicago .... IL 151
001712 .... Lutheran School of Theology Chicago .... IL 151
001716 .... MacCormac College .... IL 151
001717 .... MacMurray College .... IL 151
001721 .... McCormick Theological Seminary .... IL 152
001722 .... McKendree University .... IL 152
001723 .... Meadville Lombard Theol School .... IL 152
001724 .... Millikin University .... IL 153
001725 .... Monmouth College .... IL 153
001727 .... Moody Bible Institute .... IL 153
001728 .... Morton College .... IL 153
001732 .... National Univ of Health Sciences .... IL 154
001733 .... National-Louis University .... IL 153
001734 .... North Central College .... IL 154
001735 .... North Park University .... IL 154
001736 .... Northern Seminary .... IL 154
001737 .... Northern Illinois University .... IL 154
001739 .... Northwestern University .... IL 155
001741 .... Olivet Nazarene University .... IL 155
001742 .... Illinois Eastern CC Olney Central .... IL 147
001744 .... Principia College .... IL 156
001745 .... Quincy University .... IL 156
001746 .... Robert Morris University - Illinois .... IL 157
001747 .... Rock Valley College .... IL 157
001748 .... Rockford University .... IL 157
001749 .... Roosevelt University .... IL 157
001750 .... Dominican University .... IL 144
001752 .... Sauk Valley Community College .... IL 158
001753 .... School of the Art Institute Chicago .... IL 158
001754 .... Bexley Seabury .... IL 140
001756 .... Shimer College .... IL 159
001757 .... Southeastern Illinois College .... IL 159
001758 .... Southern Illinois Univ Carbondale .... IL 159
001759 .... Southern Illinois Univ Edwardsville .... IL 159
001765 .... Univ of Saint Mary Lake-Mundelein .... IL 162
001767 .... Benedictine University .... IL 140
001768 .... Saint Xavier University .... IL 158
001769 .... South Suburban Col of Cook County .... IL 159
001771 .... Trinity Christian College .... IL 160
001772 .... Trinity International University .... IL 161
001773 .... Triton College .... IL 161
001774 .... University of Chicago .... IL 161
001775 .... Univ of Illinois Urbana-Champaign .... IL 162
001776 .... University of Illinois at Chicago .... IL 161
001778 .... VanderCook College of Music .... IL 162
001779 .... Illinois Eastern CC Wabash Valley .... IL 147
001780 .... Western Illinois University .... IL 163
001781 .... Wheaton College .... IL 163
001783 .... Worsham College of Mortuary Science .... IL 163
001784 .... Ancilla College .... IN 164
001785 .... Anderson University .... IN 164
001786 .... Ball State University .... IN 164
001787 .... Bethel College .... IN 164
001788 .... Butler University .... IN 164
001789 .... Christian Theological Seminary .... IN 165
001792 .... DePauw University .... IN 165
001793 .... Earlham Col/Earlham Sch of Rel .... IN 165
001795 .... University of Evansville .... IN 173
001798 .... Franklin College of Indiana .... IN 166
001799 .... Goshen College .... IN 166
001800 .... Grace College and Seminary .... IN 166
001801 .... Hanover College .... IN 166
001803 .... Huntington University .... IN 167
001804 .... University of Indianapolis .... IN 173
001805 .... Indiana Tech .... IN 167
001807 .... Indiana State University .... IN 167
001808 .... University of Southern Indiana .... IN 174
001809 .... Indiana University Bloomington .... IN 167
001811 .... Indiana University East .... IN 168
001813 .... Indiana Univ-Purdue Un Indianapolis .... IN 168
001814 .... Indiana University Kokomo .... IN 168
001815 .... Indiana University Northwest .... IN 168
001816 .... Indiana University South Bend .... IN 168
001817 .... Indiana University Southeast .... IN 169
001820 .... Manchester University .... IN 170
001821 .... Marian University .... IN 171
001822 .... Indiana Wesleyan University .... IN 169
001823 .... Anabaptist Mennonite Biblical Sem .... IN 163
001824 .... Oakland City University .... IN 171
001825 .... Purdue University Main Campus .... IN 171

004646 .... Minnesota School of Business .... MN 257
004650 .... Chesapeake College .... MD 214
004661 .... Hampshire College .... MA 227
004666 .... Salter College .... MA 236
004667 .... Sch of the Museum Fine Arts, Boston .... MA 236
004673 .... Baker College of Flint .... MI 239
004688 .... Univ of Mississippi Medical Center .... MS 270
004697 .... San Mateo County CC District Office .... CA 64
004703 .... Logan University .... MO 277
004707 .... Covenant Theological Seminary .... MO 273
004711 .... State Technical College of Missouri .... MO 282
004713 .... Three Rivers Community College .... MO 283
004729 .... Mount Washington College .... NH 298
004731 .... Daniel Webster College .... NH 297
004736 .... Bergen Community College .... NJ 300
004740 .... Mercer County Community College .... NJ 303
004741 .... Rutgers State Univ - Camden .... NJ 307
004742 .... Central New Mexico Cmty College .... NM 310
004743 .... Clovis Community College .... NM 310
004759 .... CUNY York College .... NY 321
004765 .... CUNY Graduate Center .... NY 319
004776 .... Central Yeshiva Tomchei Tmimim .... NY 317
004788 .... Herkimer County Community College .... NY 327
004798 .... Mirrer Yeshiva Central Institute .... NY 333
004799 .... Monroe College .... NY 333
004804 .... New York Institute of Technology .... NY 335
004835 .... Caldwell Cmty College & Tech Inst .... NC 360
004838 .... Guilford Technical Community Col .... NC 363
004844 .... Wake Technical Community College .... NC 366
004845 .... Wilson Community College .... NC 367
004852 .... Clark State Community College .... OH 379
004853 .... Bradford School .... OH 378
004855 .... Davis College .... OH 381
004861 .... University of Northwestern Ohio .... OH 394
004866 .... Stautzenberger College .... OH 391
004868 .... Univ of Cincinnati-Blue Ash College .... OH 393
004878 .... Clackamas Community College .... OR 405
004882 .... Oregon Health & Science University .... OR 408
004889 .... Cambria-Rowe Business College .... PA 414
004890 .... Central Penn College .... PA 415
004893 .... DuBois Business College .... PA 417
004898 .... McCann School of Business & Tech .... PA 425
004902 .... Penn Commercial Business/Tech Sch .... PA 428
004910 .... Kaplan Career Institute .... PA 421
004920 .... Trident Technical College .... SC 449
004923 .... Clinton College .... SC 444
004924 .... Forrest College .... SC 446
004925 .... Horry-Georgetown Technical College .... SC 446
004926 .... Tri-County Technical College .... SC 449
004927 .... University of South Carolina Union .... SC 450
004934 .... Daymar Institute .... TN 456
004937 .... Jackson State Community College .... TN 463
004938 .... South College .... TN 460
004949 .... Baylor College of Medicine .... TX 469
004951 .... University of Texas HSC at Houston .... TX 495
004952 .... The Univ of Texas Medical Branch .... TX 495
004972 .... Galveston College .... TX 474
004977 .... South Texas College of Law/Houston .... TX 482
004988 .... Central Virginia Community College .... VA 515
004992 .... Miller-Motte Technical College .... VA 510
004996 .... Dabney S. Lancaster Community Col .... VA 515
004999 .... Bellingham Technical College .... WA 520
005000 .... Pierce College District .... WA 525
005001 .... Edmonds Community College .... WA 522
005006 .... Walla Walla Community College .... WA 527
005007 .... West Virginia Junior College .... WV 534
005008 .... Mountain State College .... WV 530
005015 .... University of Wisconsin-Parkside .... WI 540
005019 .... Univ Adventista de las Antillas .... PR 556
005022 .... Universidad Central de Bayamon .... PR 556
005026 .... Inter Amer Univ of PR Arecibo .... PR 553
005027 .... Inter Amer Univ of PR Barranquitas .... PR 553
005028 .... Inter Amer Univ of PR Bayamon .... PR 553
005029 .... Inter Amer Univ of PR Ponce .... PR 554
005204 .... Beal College .... ME 209
005208 .... The College of Westchester .... NY 322
005220 .... Salt Lake Community College .... UT 500
005223 .... New River Community College .... VA 516
005245 .... Univ of Arkansas Cmty Col/Morrilton .... AR 25
005252 .... Ridgewater College .... MN 261
005254 .... Lanier Technical College .... GA 128
005256 .... Wiregrass Georgia Tech College .... GA 134
005257 .... GA Northwestern Technical College .... GA 125
005258 .... Univ of Hawaii Cmty College .... HI 136
005260 .... J.F. Drake State Cmty & Tech Col .... AL 4
005263 .... Minnesota West Cmty & Tech College .... MN 260
005264 .... Flint Hills Technical College .... KS 186
005265 .... North Central Kansas Tech College .... KS 190
005267 .... Northwest Kansas Technical College .... KS 190
005271 .... Southcentral KY Cmty & Tech Col .... KY 197
005273 .... Gateway Cmty & Technical College .... KY 196
005276 .... Central Maine Community College .... ME 210
005277 .... Eastern Maine Community College .... ME 211
005291 .... White Mountains Community College .... NH 297
005294 .... Waukesha County Technical College .... WI 544
005301 .... NE Wisconsin Technical College .... WI 544
005304 .... Chippewa Valley Technical College .... WI 542
005306 .... Bates Technical College .... WA 519
005309 .... Lake Area Technical Institute .... SD 452
005310 .... Pittsburgh Institute of Aeronautics .... PA 433
005313 .... North Central State College .... OH 387
005316 .... Coastal Carolina Community College .... NC 361
005317 .... Forsyth Technical Community College .... NC 362
005318 .... Catawba Valley Community College .... NC 361
005320 .... Cape Fear Community College .... NC 360
005363 .... Denmark Technical College .... SC 445
005372 .... South Puget Sound Community College .... WA 527
005373 .... Lake Washington Inst of Technology .... WA 523
005378 .... Northeast State Community College .... TN 463
005380 .... Mid-State Technical College .... WI 543
005384 .... Nicolet Area Technical College .... WI 543
005387 .... Northcentral Technical College .... WI 544
005389 .... Gateway Technical College .... WI 543
005390 .... Blackhawk Technical College .... WI 542
005447 .... Randolph Community College .... NC 365
005448 .... Durham Technical Community College .... NC 362
005449 .... Central Carolina Community College .... NC 361
005461 .... Salem Community College .... NJ 308
005463 .... Alamance Community College .... NC 359
005464 .... Richmond Community College .... NC 365
005467 .... Sowela Technical Community College .... LA 204
005480 .... Central LA TCC Huey P Long Campus .... LA 203
005489 .... Central LA Tech Community College .... LA 203
005498 .... Wichita Area Technical College .... KS 192
005499 .... Salina Area Technical College .... KS 190
005500 .... Manhattan Area Technical College .... KS 189
005511 .... Coastal Pines Technical College .... GA 123
005525 .... Southern Maine Community College .... ME 211
005526 .... S Central LA Tech Col Young Mem Cam .... LA 204
005533 .... St Paul Col A Cmty & Tech College .... MN 261
005534 .... Saint Cloud Technical & Cmty Coll .... MN 261
005535 .... Pine Tech & Cmty College .... MN 260
005537 .... South Central College .... MN 262
005541 .... Minnesota State Cmty & Tech College .... MN 259
005544 .... Alexandria Technical & Cmty Col .... MN 257
005599 .... Augusta Technical College .... GA 121
005600 .... Athens Technical College .... GA 120
005601 .... Albany Technical College .... GA 119
005615 .... Southern Regional Technical College .... GA 132
005617 .... South Georgia Technical College .... GA 131
005618 .... Savannah Technical College .... GA 131
005619 .... North Georgia Technical College .... GA 129
005621 .... Southern Crescent Technical College .... GA 132
005622 .... Georgia Piedmont Technical College .... GA 126
005624 .... Columbus Technical College .... GA 123
005691 .... Shelton State Community College .... AL 7
005692 .... Reid State Technical College .... AL 6
005697 .... Northwest-Shoals Community College .... AL 6
005699 .... George Wallace St Cmty Col-Selma .... AL 4
005707 .... Southeast Arkansas College .... AR 23
005732 .... Univ of Arkansas CC at Hope .... AR 24
005733 .... Bevill State Community College .... AL 2
005734 .... Trenholm State Technical College .... AL 7
005752 .... Clover Park Technical College .... WA 521
005753 .... Owens Community College .... OH 390
005754 .... Rowan-Cabarrus Community College .... NC 365
005757 .... Lake Superior College .... MN 259
005759 .... Northwest Technical College .... MN 260
005760 .... Northern Maine Community College .... ME 211
005761 .... L.E. Fletcher Technical Cmty Coll .... LA 203
005763 .... Central Georgia Technical College .... GA 122
006165 .... Los Angeles County Col of Nursing .... CA 52
006191 .... St. Vincent's College .... CT 91
006214 .... Blessing-Rieman College of Nursing .... IL 140
006225 .... Trinity Col Nursing/Hlth Sci .... IL 161
006228 .... Methodist College .... IL 152
006240 .... St Francis Med Ctr Col of Nursing .... IL 158
006250 .... Resurrection University .... IL 156
006273 .... Mercy College of Health Sciences .... IA 181
006305 .... Maine College of Health Professions .... ME 210
006324 .... Laboure College .... MA 227
006385 .... Chamberlain Col of Nursing-Addison .... IL 141
006389 .... Goldfarb School of Nursing .... MO 275
006392 .... Research College of Nursing .... MO 280
006399 .... Bryan College of Health Sciences .... NE 289
006404 .... Nebraska Methodist College .... NE 291
006438 .... Phillip Beth Israel Sch of Nursing .... NY 338
006443 .... Cochran School of Nursing .... NY 321
006445 .... Pomeroy Col of Nurs @ Crouse Hosp .... NY 316
006448 .... The Belanger School of Nursing .... NY 316
006461 .... St. Elizabeth College of Nursing .... NY 340
006467 .... St. Joseph's College of Nursing .... NY 341
006477 .... Cabarrus College of Health Sciences .... NC 355
006487 .... Aultman College Nursing/Health Sci .... OH 377
006489 .... Christ Col of Nursing & Health Sci .... OH 379
006494 .... Good Samaritan Col Nursing/Hlth Sci .... OH 383
006606 .... Baptist Hlth Sys Sch Hlth Profess .... TX 468
006622 .... Jefferson Col of Health Sciences .... VA 509
006639 .... Bellin College, Inc. .... WI 534
006640 .... Columbia College of Nursing .... WI 535
006656 .... College of DuPage .... IL 142
006661 .... Angelina College .... TX 467
006720 .... College of Alameda .... CA 59
006724 .... KY Community & Technical Col System .... KY 195
006725 .... Univ of Tennessee Health Sci Center .... TN 465
006731 .... Casa Loma College-Van Nuys .... CA 37
006750 .... Valencia College .... FL 118
006751 .... Univ of Hawaii Community Colleges .... HI 136
006753 .... Illinois Central College .... IL 146
006755 .... Brown Mackie College-Salina .... KS 185
006756 .... Northshore Technical Community Col .... LA 203
006760 .... University of Maine at Augusta .... ME 212
006768 .... Mid Michigan Community College .... MI 247
006771 .... College for Creative Studies .... MI 241
006775 .... Rainy River Community College .... MN 261
006777 .... Flathead Valley Community College .... MT 286
006782 .... Genesee Community College .... NY 326
006785 .... Schenectady County Cmty College .... NY 342
006787 .... Clinton Community College .... NY 321
006788 .... Tompkins Cortland Community College .... NY 350
006789 .... Columbia-Greene Community College .... NY 322
006791 .... Purchase College, SUNY .... NY 346
006799 .... Craven Community College .... NC 362
006804 .... Lakeland Community College .... OH 385
006807 .... Community College of Beaver County .... PA 416
006810 .... Lehigh Carbon Community College .... PA 424
006811 .... Luzerne County Community College .... PA 425
006815 .... Orangeburg-Calhoun Technical Col .... SC 448
006819 .... Blue Ridge Community College .... VA 514
006823 .... Evangelical Seminary of Puerto Rico .... PR 552
006835 .... Dyersburg State Community College .... TN 462
006836 .... Motlow State Community College .... TN 463
006858 .... Unity College .... ME 212
006863 .... Ventura County Cmty College Dist .... CA 75
006865 .... Camden County College .... NJ 301
006867 .... Columbus State Community College .... OH 380
006871 .... Thomas Nelson Community College .... VA 517
006895 .... University of Nebraska Medical Ctr .... NE 293
006901 .... Rowan College at Gloucester County .... NJ 306
006911 .... Montgomery College .... MD 217
006931 .... Waubonsee Community College .... IL 162
006938 .... Linn-Benton Community College .... OR 406
006941 .... Dallas Christian College .... TX 472
006942 .... Mid-America Christian University .... OK 398
006949 .... Kalamazoo Valley Community College .... MI 244
006951 .... Univ of South Carolina Upstate .... SC 451
006960 .... Maysville Cmty & Technical College .... KY 196
006961 .... Jefferson Cmty & Tech Col .... KY 196
006962 .... Hazard Community & Technical Coll .... KY 196
006964 .... Rutgers State Univ - New Brunswick .... NJ 307
006973 .... Canada College .... CA 64
006975 .... Lincoln University .... CA 50
006977 .... Great Basin College .... NV 295
006982 .... Naugatuck Valley Community College .... CT 89
006991 .... Rancho Santiago Cmty Col District .... CA 60
006994 .... Kern Community College District .... CA 49
007006 .... Grossmont-Cuyamaca C C District .... CA 46
007012 .... Samuel Merritt University .... CA 61
007022 .... CUNY Herbert H. Lehman College .... NY 319
007026 .... Icahn Sch of Medicine at Mt Sinai .... NY 328
007031 .... Pamlico Community College .... NC 364
007032 .... MidAmerica Nazarene University .... KS 189
007035 .... Kettering College .... OH 385
007047 .... Los Angeles Southwest College .... CA 51
007085 .... Mount Vernon Nazarene University .... OH 387
007091 .... Everest Institute .... PA 418
007096 .... College of the Mainland .... TX 471
007099 .... Virginia Highlands Community Col .... VA 517
007107 .... Essex County College .... NJ 302
007108 .... Univ of Puerto Rico-Rio Piedras .... PR 558
007109 .... SUNY College at Old Westbury .... NY 345
007110 .... Delaware County Community College .... PA 416
007111 .... North Country Community College .... NY 336
007113 .... Arizona Christian University .... AZ 11
007115 .... Moorpark College .... CA 75
007118 .... Parkland College .... IL 155
007119 .... Rend Lake College .... IL 156
007120 .... Des Moines Area Community College .... IA 177
007121 .... Faith Baptist Bible Col & Seminary .... IA 178
007164 .... Bryan University .... CA 30
007170 .... Lincoln Land Community College .... IL 151
007171 .... Kirtland Community College .... MI 245
007178 .... Western Seminary .... OR 411
007191 .... Northampton Community College .... PA 427
007206 .... University of Puerto Rico at Cayey .... PR 557
007228 .... Univ of Puerto Rico at Arecibo .... PR 557
007260 .... Southwest Virginia Community Col .... VA 517
007263 .... Holy Cross College .... IN 167
007264 .... Mesivta Torah Vodaath Seminary .... NY 332
007265 .... Carl Sandburg College .... IL 140
007266 .... Pima Community College .... AZ 17
007273 .... Baruch College/CUNY .... NY 318
007275 .... Eastern Gateway CC - Jefferson Co. .... OH 381
007276 .... Saint Meinrad School of Theology .... IN 173
007279 .... Hawaii Pacific University .... HI 135
007283 .... Central Arizona College .... AZ 12
007287 .... Brazosport College .... TX 469
007289 .... Central Wyoming College .... WY 545
007291 .... St. Luke's College .... IA 182
007296 .... Coleman University .... CA 40
007297 .... Redstone College .... CO 85
007304 .... The Culinary Institute of America .... NY 323
007316 .... Western Iowa Tech Community College .... IA 184
007329 .... ITT Technical Institute .... IN 169
007350 .... Anoka Technical College .... MN 258
007351 .... Sanford-Brown Col-Mendota Heights .... MN 264
007358 .... Univ of NE-NE Col of Tech Agricult .... NE 294
007362 .... MedTech College .... IN 171
007375 .... Island Drafting and Technical Inst .... NY 328
007394 .... Berkeley College .... NY 316
007401 .... Mandl School .... NY 331
007405 .... Wood Tobe-Coburn School .... NY 352
007430 .... Antonelli Institute .... PA 412
007436 .... Kaplan Career Inst - ICM Campus .... PA 422
007437 .... Pittsburgh Technical Institute .... PA 433
007439 .... Fountainhead College of Technology .... TN 456

009992 .... Oak Hills Christian College .... MN 263
009994 .... Passaic County Community College .... NJ 304
010010 .... American Samoa Community College .... AS 549
010014 .... Garrett College .... MD 215
010017 .... Payne Theological Seminary .... OH 390
010019 .... University Texas SW Medical Center .... TX 496
010020 .... Lewis and Clark Community College .... IL 150
010027 .... James A. Rhodes State College .... OH 384
010043 .... Bon Secours Memorial Col of Nursing .... VA 505
010051 .... La Guardia Community College/CUNY .... NY 320
010056 .... Aiken Technical College .... SC 443
010060 .... Vernon College .... TX 496
010074 .... St Patrick's Seminary & University .... CA 61
010097 .... CUNY Medgar Evers College .... NY 320
010098 .... Neumont University .... UT 498
010106 .... Seattle Colleges .... WA 525
010111 .... Cerro Coso Community College .... CA 49
010115 .... University of Texas at San Antonio .... TX 494
010130 .... Wade College .... TX 496
010142 .... Touro College .... NY 350
010148 .... Colorado Technical University .... CO 81
010149 .... Pepperdine University .... CA 58
010153 .... Helene Fuld College of Nursing .... NY 327
010170 .... Western Dakota Technical Institute .... SD 454
010176 .... Westmoreland County Community Col .... PA 439
010182 .... Rogue Community College .... OR 409
010195 .... Art Institute of Fort Lauderdale .... FL 98
010198 .... ECPI University .... VA 507
010248 .... The Art Institutes International MN .... MN 253
010256 .... Benedictine College .... KS 184
010264 .... South College-Asheville .... NC 368
010266 .... Hillsdale Free Will Baptist College .... OK 398
010279 .... Hickey College .... MO 275
010286 .... SUNY Empire State College .... NY 348
010316 .... Lincoln College of Technology .... IL 151
010338 .... Eastern Virginia Medical School .... VA 507
010340 .... Los Medanos College .... CA 42
010343 .... College of Micronesia-FSM .... FM 549
010345 .... Cincinnati State Tech & Cmty Col .... OH 379
010362 .... College of Southern Nevada .... NV 295
010363 .... Western Nevada College .... NV 296
010364 .... Whatcom Community College .... WA 528
010365 .... Charles Drew Univ of Med & Science .... CA 38
010374 .... Metropolitan State University .... MN 259
010378 .... Rabbinical College of Long Island .... NY 338
010387 .... El Paso Community College .... TX 473
010388 .... Reading Area Community College .... PA 433
010391 .... Oklahoma City Community College .... OK 399
010395 .... University of San Diego .... CA 74
010402 .... Dakota County Technical College .... MN 258
010405 .... Pinnacle Career Institute .... MO 280
010410 .... TESST College of Technology .... MD 219
010434 .... Renton Technical College .... WA 525
010438 .... Haskell Indian Nations University .... KS 187
010439 .... Southwest Tennessee Community Coll .... TN 464
010441 .... Pardee RAND Grad Sch of Policy Stds .... CA 58
010453 .... Washington State Community College .... OH 395
010460 .... American Baptist College .... TN 454
010474 .... Marymount California University .... CA 53
010487 .... West Georgia Technical College .... GA 134
010489 .... American National University .... IN 163
010491 .... Hennepin Technical College .... MN 258
010501 .... Lakeview College of Nursing .... IL 150
010503 .... Wichita Technical Institute .... KS 192
010509 .... Hallmark University .... TX 474
010529 .... Memphis Theological Seminary .... TN 459
010530 .... Quinebaug Valley Community College .... CT 90
010546 .... Century College .... MN 258
010549 .... Kehilath Yakov Rabbinical Seminary .... NY 329
010554 .... Concordia College Alabama .... AL 3
010567 .... Colegio Universitario de San Juan .... PR 551
010573 .... West Virginia Junior College .... WV 534
010618 .... Mid-America College of Funeral Svc .... IN 171
010633 .... Houston Community College .... TX 475
010652 .... Pasco-Hernando State College .... FL 110
010674 .... Texas Tech University Health Sci Ct .... TX 490
010684 .... Erie Community College .... NY 325
010687 .... The Ohio State University AT Inst .... OH 389
010724 .... Carlos Albizu University .... PR 551
010727 .... DeVry University - Chicago Campus .... IL 144
010736 .... Marion Technical College .... OH 386
010761 .... Dallas Institute of Funeral Service .... TX 473
010771 .... Gupton Jones Coll of Funeral Svc .... GA 127
010784 .... Cmty Colleges of Spokane Dist 17 .... WA 521
010805 .... University of Cincinnati-Clermont .... OH 393
010813 .... Amer Acad McAllister Inst Funeral .... NY 315
010814 .... Pittsburgh Inst of Mortuary Science .... PA 433
010818 .... The University of Akron-Wayne Col .... OH 393
010819 .... Conservatory of Music Puerto Rico .... PR 551
010854 .... Thomas Jefferson School of Law .... CA 69
010861 .... West Virginia Business College .... WV 530
010879 .... Richland Community College .... IL 156
010880 .... Chatfield College .... OH 379
010881 .... Stark State College .... OH 391
010906 .... Cincinnati Col of Mortuary Science .... OH 379
010913 .... Madison Media Inst-Col Media Arts .... WI 536
010923 .... Union Institute & University .... OH 392
010943 .... Rabbinical College Beth Shraga .... NY 338
010975 .... Univ of Puerto Rico at Bayamon .... PR 557
010997 .... East Georgia State College .... GA 124
010998 .... Pennsylvania Institute of Tech .... PA 429
011009 .... Palau Community College .... PW 550
011031 .... Technical Career Institutes .... NY 349
011046 .... Central Ohio Technical College .... OH 378
011074 .... Bainbridge State College .... GA 121
011112 .... FIDM/Fashion Inst Design & Merch-LA .... CA 44
011113 .... Maharishi University of Management .... IA 181
011117 .... Alliant International Univ-SanDiego .... CA 26
011127 .... Bay Medical Center .... FL 99
011133 .... Eastern Idaho Technical College .... ID 138
011145 .... Lone Star College System .... TX 477
011150 .... Asnuntuck Community College .... CT 88
011161 .... Texas A&M University-Corpus Christi .... TX 485
011163 .... University of Texas at Tyler .... TX 494
011165 .... Uintah Basin Applied Tech Coll .... UT 499
011166 .... Broadview University .... UT 498
011167 .... Community College of Vermont .... VT 503
011189 .... United Talmudical Seminary .... NY 351
011192 .... Beth Hamedrash Shaarei Yosher Inst .... NY 316
011194 .... Stanly Community College .... NC 366
011197 .... Mayland Community College .... NC 364
011210 .... Bunker Hill Community College .... MA 231
011220 .... Univ of Hawaii Windward Cmty Col .... HI 137
011245 .... West Virginia School of Osteo Med .... WV 533
011385 .... College of the Atlantic .... ME 210
011460 .... National University .... CA 55
011462 .... University of Alaska Anchorage .... AK 10
011572 .... Colorado School of Trades .... CO 81
011626 .... Westwood College-South Bay .... CA 77
011644 .... Univ of Maryland University College .... MD 220
011647 .... SBI Campus-Affil of Sanford-Brown .... NY 342
011649 .... Loyola Marymount University .... CA 53
011667 .... Northeast Community College .... NE 292
011670 .... Yeshiva of Nitra Rabbinical College .... NY 353
011672 .... Mendocino College .... CA 54
011673 .... Maine College of Art .... ME 210
011678 .... SUNY Polytechnic Institute .... NY 348
011689 .... The Refrigeration School .... AZ 17
011711 .... University of Houston - Clear Lake .... TX 491
011719 .... Universidad Del Turabo .... PR 555
011721 .... University of Houston System .... TX 491
011727 .... DE Tech Cmty College, Terry Campus .... DE 94
011732 .... Mayo Medical School .... MN 254
011745 .... Ohio Technical College .... OH 389
011792 .... Franciscan School of Theology .... CA 45
011810 .... Taylor Business Institute .... IL 160
011820 .... San Diego Miramar College .... CA 62
011821 .... Yeshivath Zichron Moshe .... NY 354
011824 .... Wisconsin Indianhead Tech College .... WI 544
011862 .... Northland Pioneer College .... AZ 16
011864 .... Mohave Community College .... AZ 15
011922 .... Beth Hatalmud Rabbinical College .... NY 316
011930 .... Roxbury Community College .... MA 233
011934 .... Vermont Law School .... VT 503
011940 .... ICPR Junior College .... PR 552
011941 .... American University of Puerto Rico .... PR 550
011984 .... Ohr Hameir Theological Seminary .... NY 337
011989 .... Talmudical Academy of New Jersey .... NJ 308
012011 .... Talmudical Seminary Oholei Torah .... NY 349
012015 .... Austin Community College District .... TX 468
012031 .... San Diego Christian College .... CA 62
012050 .... Rosedale Technical Institute .... PA 434
012059 .... Trinity Bible College .... ND 375
012064 .... Hamilton Technical College .... IA 179
012088 .... Sullivan Col of Technology & Design .... KY 200
012105 .... National Park Community College .... AR 21
012120 .... Assemblies of God Theol Seminary .... MO 272
012123 .... University of Puerto Rico-Aguadilla .... PR 557
012154 .... California Inst of Integral Studies .... CA 31
012165 .... Atlanta Metropolitan State College .... GA 120
012182 .... Chattahoochee Valley Community Coll .... AL 2
012183 .... Burlington College .... VT 501
012203 .... Memorial School of Nursing .... NY 332
012260 .... East Arkansas Community College .... AR 20
012261 .... North Arkansas College .... AR 22
012277 .... New York Chiropractic College .... NY 334
012300 .... Palmer College of Chiropractic .... IA 182
012309 .... University of Western States .... OR 410
012315 .... Cornish College of the Arts .... WA 521
012328 .... Northwestern Health Sciences Univ .... MN 263
012358 .... Plaza College .... NY 338
012362 .... Northwestern College .... IL 155
012364 .... St. Paul's School of Nursing .... NY 341
012393 .... Thomas Jefferson University .... PA 436
012452 .... Evergreen Valley College .... CA 63
012500 .... Ranken Technical College .... MO 280
012523 .... Talmudical Yeshiva of Philadelphia .... PA 436
012525 .... Caribbean University .... PR 550
012550 .... Los Angeles Mission College .... CA 51
012561 .... Five Towns College .... NY 326
012574 .... Ringling College of Art and Design .... FL 111
012580 .... Saint Louis Christian College .... MO 281
012584 .... The Illinois Institute of Art .... IL 147
012586 .... Metropolitan Community College .... NE 291
012627 .... Western Mich Univ Cooley Law School .... MI 252
012670 .... Bel-Rea Inst of Animal Technology .... CO 79
012693 .... Pellissippi State Community College .... TN 463
012744 .... Southside Reg Med Ctr Prof Schs .... VA 512
012750 .... Edison State Community College .... OH 381
012803 .... PFIC at Dominican House of Studies .... DC 96
012813 .... John Wood Community College .... IL 148
012842 .... Oxnard College .... CA 75
012860 .... Arkansas Northeastern College .... AR 19
012870 .... Southern State Community College .... OH 391
012891 .... Antonelli College .... OH 376
012896 .... Virginia Marti Col of Art & Design .... OH 395
012907 .... Lake Tahoe Community College .... CA 50
012912 .... MTI College .... CA 55
012954 .... Hudson County Community College .... NJ 303
012976 .... Nebraska Christian College .... NE 291
013007 .... Nazarene Bible College .... CO 84
013022 .... City University of Seattle .... WA 520
013026 .... Machzikei Hadath Rabbinical College .... NY 331
013027 .... Yeshivath Viznitz .... NY 354
013029 .... Boricua College .... NY 316
013039 .... South University .... GA 131
013103 .... California Western School of Law .... CA 36
013132 .... International Col of Broadcasting .... OH 383
013134 .... Yeshiva Beth Moshe .... PA 440
013208 .... Baptist Bible College .... MO 272
013231 .... University of Houston - Victoria .... TX 492
013263 .... South Hills School of Bus & Tech .... PA 435
014659 .... Oglala Lakota College .... SD 452
015361 .... Guam Community College .... GU 549
020503 .... Academy College .... MN 253
020520 .... Kaplan College .... OH 384
020522 .... Black River Technical College .... AR 20
020530 .... Liberty University .... VA 509
020537 .... Eastwick College .... NJ 302
020543 .... Trumbull Business College .... OH 392
020552 .... Harrington College of Design .... IL 145
020554 .... Bossier Parish Community College .... LA 203
020555 .... Delta Sch of Business & Technology .... LA 202
020603 .... MIAT College of Technology .... MI 246
020609 .... Brown College of Court Reporting .... GA 122
020630 .... Montserrat College of Art .... MA 234
020635 .... Coastline Community College .... CA 40
020637 .... Sherman College of Chiropractic .... SC 448
020653 .... Prescott College .... AZ 17
020662 .... The New School .... NY 334
020681 .... Adler University .... IL 139
020682 .... Cox College .... MO 274
020683 .... Douglas Education Center .... PA 417
020690 .... New York School of Interior Design .... NY 336
020693 .... Vatterott College-Quincy .... IL 162
020705 .... Concordia University .... CA 42
020732 .... Telshe Yeshiva-Chicago .... IL 160
020735 .... Univ of Arkansas CC at Batesville .... AR 24
020739 .... Wor-Wic Community College .... MD 221
020744 .... Illinois Eastern CC Frontier CC .... IL 146
020746 .... South Arkansas Community College .... AR 23
020748 .... Life University .... GA 128
020753 .... Pulaski Technical College .... AR 22
020757 .... Briarcliffe College .... NY 316
020758 .... Southern Calif Inst of Architecture .... CA 67
020771 .... Milwaukee Institute of Art & Design .... WI 537
020774 .... North Lake College .... TX 473
020780 .... Sacred Heart Sem & School of Theol .... WI 538
020789 .... The Art Institute of Colorado .... CO 79
020814 .... Arlington Baptist College .... TX 468
020836 .... TESST College of Technology .... MD 218
020839 .... Northern New Mexico College .... NM 312
020870 .... Ozarka College .... AR 22
020876 .... Concordia Theological Seminary .... IN 165
020896 .... Concorde Career Institute .... FL 100
020902 .... Triangle Tech, Erie .... PA 437
020907 .... Cleveland University - Kansas City .... KS 185
020917 .... Kaplan College .... CA 49
020923 .... Eastwick College .... NJ 302
020925 .... Laurel Technical Institute .... PA 423
020937 .... Long Island Business Institute .... NY 330
020961 .... Fielding Graduate University .... CA 44
020983 .... Western Technical College .... TX 497
020988 .... University of Phoenix .... AZ 18
020992 .... American Conservatory Theater .... CA 27
020995 .... Central Community College .... NE 289
021000 .... Universidad Politecnica De PR .... PR 556
021002 .... Brookhaven College .... TX 472
021049 .... Sumner College .... OR 410
021064 .... O'More College of Design .... TN 460
021067 .... Trinity Lutheran College .... WA 527
021068 .... Bramson ORT College .... NY 316
021073 .... Pennsylvania Academy of Fine Arts .... PA 429
021077 .... Truckee Meadows Community College .... NV 295
021078 .... University of Hawaii - West Oahu .... HI 136
021102 .... Columbia College Hollywood .... CA 41
021108 .... California College San Diego .... CA 30
021111 .... Rich Mountain Community College .... AR 22
021113 .... Cuyamaca College .... CA 46
021116 .... Danville Reg Med Ctr Sch Hlth Prof .... VA 506
021122 .... Great Lakes Institute of Technology .... PA 419
021136 .... American InterContinental Univ .... IL 139
021142 .... Johnson College .... PA 421
021160 .... Sanford-Brown College .... GA 130
021163 .... Pueblo Community College .... CO 85
021171 .... The Art Institute of Houston .... TX 468
021175 .... Naropa University .... CO 84
021191 .... Mission College .... CA 76
021206 .... Saybrook University .... CA 65
021207 .... San Joaquin Valley Col Inc-Visalia .... CA 63
021211 .... Midwest Institute .... MO 278
021274 .... YTI Career Institute .... PA 440
021286 .... AIC College of Design .... OH 376
021290 .... Triangle Tech, Greensburg .... PA 437
021366 .... Wisconsin Lutheran College .... WI 542
021383 .... Palo Alto University .... CA 58

Code	Institution	State	Page
030018	Welch College	TN	466
030021	Kentucky Mountain Bible College	KY	197
030025	J.F. Ingram State Technical College	AL	4
030026	Central LA Tech Col Oakdale Campus	LA	203
030063	IBMC College	CO	83
030070	Frontier Nursing University	KY	194
030073	Oregon College of Art and Craft	OR	408
030079	Gallipolis Career College	OH	382
030086	Florida College of Natural Health	FL	103
030106	Virginia College	AL	3
030108	Fortis Institute	PA	418
030113	California State Univ-San Marcos	CA	35
030115	Fortis Institute	PA	418
030116	Fortis Institute	PA	418
030149	Platt College	CO	84
030160	Univ of Puerto Rico-Carolina	PR	557
030219	EDIC College	PR	552
030224	College of the Marshall Islands	MH	550
030226	Le Cordon Bleu Col Cul Arts Prtlnd	OR	406
030255	Mech-Tech College	PR	554
030256	Dell'Arte Intl Sch Phys Theatre	CA	42
030265	Remington College-Dallas Campus	TX	480
030277	Pacific Col of Oriental Medicine	CA	57
030282	Trinity College of Florida	FL	117
030290	Chattahoochee Technical College	GA	122
030297	Universal Technology College of PR	PR	556
030299	Consolidated School of Business	PA	416
030300	Ogeechee Technical College	GA	129
030314	Sanford-Brown College Tampa	FL	112
030323	School of Automotive Machinists	TX	482
030330	Northern Marianas College	MP	550
030345	Owensboro Cmty & Technical College	KY	197
030357	Las Positas College	CA	37
030358	Heritage Institute-Jacksonville	FL	106
030375	Hodges University	FL	106
030399	Fremont College	CA	45
030430	United States Naval Academy	MD	549
030431	Thomas More College of Liberal Arts	NH	298
030432	Kaplan College	NV	294
030439	NewSchool of Arch & Design	CA	56
030519	Adler Graduate School	MN	253
030612	Midwest Col of Oriental Medicine	WI	537
030627	Platt College	CA	59
030633	NW Arkansas Community College	AR	22
030662	Bryan University	KS	185
030663	Bryan University	MO	272
030665	Southeastern Technical College	GA	132
030666	Bay Mills Community College	MI	240
030669	IntelliTec College	CO	83
030675	Institute of Technology	CA	47
030691	Allen College	IA	175
030695	Sage College	CA	61
030709	SE MO Hosp Coll Nurs & Health Sci	MO	282
030716	College of Business and Technology	FL	100
030718	ITT Technical Institute	WA	523
030719	Mount Carmel College of Nursing	OH	386
030722	Chandler-Gilbert Community College	AZ	14
030725	World Medicine Institute	HI	137
030727	Westwood College-Los Angeles Campus	CA	77
030737	Paralegal Inst at Brighton College	AZ	16
030761	Southwestern College	NM	313
030763	Beulah Heights University	GA	121
030775	Rabbi Jacob Joseph School	NJ	305
030790	ETI Technical College of Niles	OH	382
030791	North Central Institute	TN	459
030792	Westwood College-DuPage	IL	163
030799	City College	FL	100
030819	YTI Career Institute	PA	440
030830	Ozarks Technical Community College	MO	280
030837	Galen College of Nursing	KY	194
030838	Heartland Community College	IL	145
030844	Valley College - Beckley Campus	WV	530
030888	Watkins College of Art/Design/Film	TN	466
030893	Heritage Bible College	NC	357
030908	Lake Erie College of Osteo Medicine	PA	423
030913	Regent University	VA	511
030926	Messenger College	TX	478
030927	Skyline College	VA	512
030955	ASA College	NY	315
030964	Leech Lake Tribal College	MN	256
030970	Mercy College of Ohio	OH	386
030980	St. John's College	IL	158
030982	Yo San Univ of Trad Chinese Med	CA	77
031004	Coconino Community College	AZ	13
031007	Carroll Community College	MD	214
031009	Luther Rice College and Seminary	GA	128
031013	Granite State College	NH	299
031015	Bidwell Training Center	PA	413
031019	Trinity Baptist College	FL	117
031033	JNA Institute of Culinary Arts	PA	421
031034	South Texas College	TX	482
031042	Carolinas Col of Health Sciences	NC	355
031060	Missouri State Univ-West Plains	MO	279
031062	Our Lady of the Lake College	LA	206
031065	Sentara College of Health Sciences	VA	512
031070	SW Col of Naturopathic Med/Hlth Sci	AZ	17
031085	Everglades University	FL	102
031090	Living Arts Col @ Sch of Commun Art	NC	358
031091	MCC Computer Technology Institute	PA	426
031095	Dongguk University	CA	43
031108	Bakke Graduate University	WA	519
031121	Dewey University	PR	551
031136	Southern Calif Institute of Tech	CA	67
031147	The Praxis Institute	FL	110
031150	Arizona College	AZ	11
031151	Heritage College	OK	398
031155	Adventist University of Health Sci	FL	97
031158	Kaplan College	TX	476
031159	Trinity College of Puerto Rico	PR	556
031163	Ohio College of Massotherapy	OH	388
031166	E San Gabriel Vly Reg Occ Pgm Tech	CA	43
031169	Baptist Theol Seminary Richmond	VA	505
031203	CollegeAmerica-Flagstaff	AZ	13
031207	NY Conservatory for Dramatic Arts	NY	335
031226	Eastern International College	NJ	302
031229	York County Community College	ME	211
031239	Southeastern College	FL	113
031251	College of Menominee Nation	WI	535
031264	Centura College	VA	506
031268	Pacifica Graduate Institute	CA	57
031271	Yeshivas Novominsk	NY	354
031275	Advanced Technology Institute	VA	504
031281	The Col of Health Care Professions	TX	470
031287	Mount Sierra College	CA	55
031291	Fond du Lac Tribal & Cmty College	MN	258
031292	Rabbinical College Ohr Shimon Yisr	NY	338
031305	Urban College of Boston	MA	237
031313	Five Brn Univ Grad Sch Trad Chn Med	CA	44
031473	Yeshiva D'Monsey Rabbinical College	NY	353
031533	Amer Col Acupuncture & Oriental Med	TX	467
031555	Oconee Fall Line Tech Col-North	GA	129
031563	Estrella Mountain Community College	AZ	14
031564	AOMA Grad Sch Integrative Medicine	TX	468
031576	Colegio de Cinema Artes y Televis	PR	551
031633	Pacific States University	CA	57
031643	Creative Center	NE	290
031703	Texas A & M University - Texarkana	TX	486
031713	Univ of St Augustine for Health Sci	CA	74
031733	Atlanta's John Marshall Law School	GA	121
031773	San Juan Bautista Sch of Medicine	PR	555
031795	Texas Health and Science University	TX	487
031804	Pennsylvania Highlands Cmty Col	PA	429
031823	New Hampshire Institute of Art	NH	298
031893	National Defense University	DC	547
031943	Boston Grad Sch of Psychoanalysis	MA	224
031983	Universidad Pentecostal Mizpa	PR	556
031993	Christian Life College	IL	141
032063	Mesalands Community College	NM	311
032103	Le Cordon Bleu Col of Culinary Arts	CA	50
032163	Unification Theological Seminary	NY	350
032183	University of the Potomac	DC	97
032253	American Univ of Health Sciences	CA	27
032353	MA School of Law at Andover	MA	233
032383	Florida College of Integrative Med	FL	103
032423	CNI College	CA	39
032483	Boston Baptist College	MA	224
032503	CBD College	CA	37
032553	Florida Gulf Coast University	FL	114
032563	Yeshiva Gedolah Rabbinical College	FL	119
032603	California State Univ-Monterey Bay	CA	34
032613	Metropolitan Cmty Col-Blue River	MO	277
032643	South Florida Bible College	FL	113
032663	Bethesda University of California	CA	29
032673	Capella University	MN	254
032723	Kaplan College	TX	476
032783	Charter College-Canyon Country	CA	38
032793	Myotherapy Institute	NE	291
032803	Seattle Inst of Oriental Medicine	WA	526
032843	Michigan Jewish Institute	MI	246
032883	Academy of Chinese Culture & Health	CA	26
032893	Colorado Heights University	CO	80
032943	Blue Cliff College	LA	201
032993	Pacific College	CA	57
033083	Bristol University	CA	29
033104	Rabbi Isaac Elchanan Theol Seminary	NY	338
033164	FINE Mortuary College	MA	226
033173	The American College Financial Svcs	PA	412
033213	The Scripps Research Institute	CA	66
033233	Little Priest Tribal College	NE	291
033274	Acupnct & Integrat Med Col-Berkeley	CA	26
033323	Southern California Seminary	CA	67
033394	Western Governors University	UT	501
033433	South Orange County Cmty Col Dist	CA	67
033434	North Dakota Univ System Office	ND	373
033436	Iowa Valley Cmty College District	IA	179
033437	Colorado State Univ System Office	CO	81
033438	SD State Board of Regents Sys Ofc	SD	453
033440	WV Higher Educ Policy Commission	WV	532
033441	Nebraska State College System	NE	292
033442	The Texas State University System	TX	488
033443	Board of Regents, State of Iowa	IA	175
033444	University of Louisiana System Ofc	LA	207
033445	NC Community College System	NC	359
033463	Acad for Nurs & Health Occupations	FL	97
033473	Intl Baptist College & Seminary	AZ	14
033484	Mattia College	FL	108
033554	Richmont Graduate University	TN	460
033673	Professional Golfers Career College	CA	60
033674	Community Care College	OK	397
033723	Northwest Vista College	TX	466
033733	Beacon College	FL	99
033743	Florida Coastal School of Law	FL	103
033903	Lincoln Tech Fern Park Orlando Camp	FL	108
033965	Texas State Tech Col Marshall	TX	488
034003	Quest College	TX	480
034033	Epic Bible College & Graduate Sch	CA	43
034095	Chester Career College	VA	506
034145	Acupuncture & Massage College	FL	97
034165	Dallas Nursing Institute	TX	473
034194	Northeastern Seminary	NY	337
034224	College of Biblical Studies-Houston	TX	470
034225	Blue Cliff College	LA	201
034226	Blue Cliff College	LA	201
034253	Rosedale Bible College	OH	390
034263	The Col of Health Care Professions	TX	470
034275	University of Antelope Valley	CA	70
034283	Klamath Community College	OR	406
034296	Atlantic Inst of Oriental Medicine	FL	98
034297	East West College of Natural Med	FL	101
034343	Fortis College	FL	105
034383	Pacific Islands University	GU	549
034403	Baptist College of Health Sciences	TN	455
034433	New York Coll of Trad Chinese Med	NY	335
034563	Cld Sprg Hrbr Lab/Watson Sc Bio Sci	NY	321
034567	Crossroads Bible College	IN	165
034573	Allegheny Wesleyan College	OH	376
034613	Ilisagvik College	AK	10
034633	UT Col Dental Hygiene Careers Unltd	UT	499
034664	The Seattle Sch of Theology & Psych	WA	526
034684	National Institute of Massotherapy	OH	387
034754	Tri-State Bible College	OH	392
034784	Phoenix Seminary	AZ	16
034803	Fortis College	LA	202
034835	Cascadia College	WA	520
034963	Yeshiva Shaarei Torah of Rockland	NY	353
035043	National Grad Sch of Quality Mgmt	MA	234
035103	Erikson Institute	IL	144
035134	Apex School of Theology	NC	354
035135	Williamson College	TN	466
035163	The King's University	TX	477
035243	Academy Five Element Acupuncture	FL	97
035283	Midwest University	MO	278
035324	Advanced Training Associates	CA	26
035343	Jones International University	CO	83
035344	American Inst Alternative Medicine	OH	376
035393	American Public University System	WV	529
035423	Concorde Career Institute	TX	471
035424	Copper Mountain College	CA	42
035443	Atenas College	PR	550
035453	University of the Rockies	CO	87
035493	Ultimate Medical Acad-Clearwater	FL	117
035533	Southeastern College	FL	113
035593	Appalachian School of Law	VA	504
035703	Carolina Christian College	NC	355
035705	Northpoint Bible College	MA	235
035793	Texas County Technical College	MO	283
035844	Colorado School of Healing Arts	CO	80
035924	City of Hope	CA	39
035933	Southwest Institute of Healing Arts	AZ	17
036115	Southern Evangelical Seminary	NC	369
036175	Phoenix Inst of Herbal Med/Acup	AZ	16
036183	Institute of Technical Arts	FL	106
036273	Lamar Institute of Technology	TX	488
036353	Carver College	GA	122
036393	West Coast Ultrasound Institute	CA	75
036543	Career Training Solutions	VA	505
036633	Hood Theological Seminary	NC	357
036653	Christendom College	VA	506
036654	Christie's Education, New York	NY	318
036663	Pillar College	NJ	305
036683	Birthingway College of Midwifery	OR	404
036763	Family of Faith College	OK	397
036863	Colorado Sch of Trad Chinese Med	CO	81
036894	Faith Evangelical Col & Seminary	WA	522
036914	Ave Maria School of Law	FL	98
036954	The Salvation Army Ofr Trng Crestmt	CA	61
036955	Arizona Sch of Acup/Oriental Med	AZ	11
036957	Santiago Canyon College	CA	60
036963	University of the West	CA	74
036964	Saber College	FL	111
036983	West Coast University	CA	75
037093	Edward Via Col of Osteo Med	VA	507
037133	Beis Medrash Heichal Dovid	NY	316
037233	Culinary Institute LeNotre	TX	471
037243	DigiPen Institute of Technology	WA	522
037303	Baton Rouge Community College	LA	202
037333	Baptist University of the Americas	TX	469
037353	Inst Clin Acupuncture/Oriental Med	HI	135
037384	SS. Cyril and Methodius Seminary	MI	250
037473	Bexley Seabury	OH	377
037524	SUM Bible Col & Theol Seminary	CA	69
037573	Advance Science Institute	FL	97
037603	Hawaii Tokai International College	HI	135
037723	Saginaw Chippewa Tribal College	MI	249
037844	Tohono O'odham Community College	AZ	18
037863	Advanced College	CA	26
037894	River Parishes Community College	LA	204
038023	U.T.A. Mesivta of Kiryas Joel	NY	351
038044	Medtech College	GA	128
038103	Silicon Valley University	CA	66
038133	Northcentral University	AZ	16
038144	Soka University of America	CA	66
038214	Universal College of Healing Arts	NE	293
038224	Maple Springs Baptist Bible College	MD	216
038273	Charlotte Christian Col & Theol Sem	NC	355
038303	SAE Institute Nashville	TN	460

Index of Universities, Colleges and Schools